Concise Dictionary
of
American Biography

CONCISE
DICTIONARY
OF AMERICAN
BIOGRAPHY

CHARLES SCRIBNER'S SONS, *New York*

Preface

The *Dictionary of American Biography*—the distinguished parent of the present book—is a multivolume standard reference work to be found today in every general library here and abroad. Sponsored by the American Council of Learned Societies and edited under its supervision, the *Dictionary* contains 14,870 biographies of Americans who have made memorable contributions to our national life. Each of these biographies is a "book in little"— each is the work of a specialist, written with authority and scrupulous scholarship. No living person is included. In order to maintain the standards of scholarship and objectivity instituted by the original projectors of the work, an interval of at least ten years is allowed to elapse between the death of any potential subject and his consideration for inclusion by the Editorial Committee.

This plan and philosophy of the parent work should be borne in mind by users of the *Concise Dictionary of American Biography*. It makes no attempt to exceed the scope of its original, whose coverage at present does not extend to any subject whose death took place later than December 31, 1940.

The *Concise Dictionary* provides the essential facts of each biography in the larger work for ready reference by students, research workers, journalists, and indeed anyone who wishes to inform himself quickly about the dates of birth and death, ancestry, education, thought and accomplishments of notable Americans—minor figures and major alike. Every biography contained in the parent work has been summarized; none has been omitted. As in the original work, the order of the entries is alphabetical by the last name of the subject. Entries from the supplementary volumes have been introduced at their appropriate positions in a single alphabet and noted so as to facilitate further reference to the multi-volume *Dictionary*. As the arrangement of articles is alphabetical, and as most users of the *Concise Dictionary* will refer to it for information about a person whose last name at least they already know, an Index was considered unnecessary.

A maximum of 1,300 pages in clear, well-spaced type was set as a reasonable physical limit for the *Concise Dictionary of American Biography*. The number of words allotted to each subject by the original editors of the large *Dictionary* determined the length of each concise entry. The scale of reduction to be employed was fixed at approximately 1–14. It was understood from the start, however, that no strictly mathematical rule of reduction could be applied and the scale has been varied liberally in the interest of clarity. Often a comparatively unimportant subject required rather full treatment because his single achievement, to be comprehensible, had to be explained in detail. On the other hand, outstanding men and women whose contribution to society was general rather than specific could often be dealt with in three or four lines. Inventors and technicians, for example, tended to fall in the first category; naval officers, proceeding in the course of exemplary service careers from one command to another without any obvious high point of drama, are typical of the second, as are many clergymen and educators.

Generally speaking, the *Concise Dictionary of American Biography* contains three types of entries:

1. *Minimal,* giving (a) the places and dates of the subject's birth and death, (b) his occupation, (c) a reference to his genealogy *if he were related to any person or persons also cited in the work,* (d) his education *if it played a significant role in his career,* (e) the date of his arrival in the United States *if he were an immigrant,* and (f) a brief statement of his outstanding achievements.
2. *Median,* in which all the information provided in a minimal entry is given, plus critical comment on the subject's achievements and a brief appraisal of his character and influence. If an author, the titles and dates of publication of his principal works are cited; if a soldier, the campaigns and battles in which he distinguished himself; if a jurist, his leading opinions.
3. *Extended entries,* in which the content, style and spirit of the original biographies have been preserved as fully as possible.

In the shorter entries, the facts of the subject's career have been the principal concern; the editors have tried to present those facts and characteristics upon which the original biographers appeared to lay most stress. They have attempted no interpretations or additions of their own.

In composing many of the minimal entries considerations of space dictated the use of an elliptical style, much like that used in similar entries in the *Concise Dictionary of National Biography*—the linking of dissociated facts in a sequence separated by semi-colons. Consideration of space also forbade any extended explanation in shorter articles of the historical processes with which the subjects were concerned. Participation in a treaty negotiation, for example, is merely stated; the reader must look elsewhere for a full account of the details and significance of the treaty in question.

Some of the articles have been amended to include new information which recent scholarship has brought to light. The editors presently engaged in preparing the monumental editions of the papers of Benjamin Franklin and Alexander Hamilton, for example, were generous with advice. The extended article on Thomas Jefferson was revised by the author of the original biography, Mr. Dumas Malone. In a few instances, where the original biography contained serious errors, an entirely new treatment has been provided. All errata presently cited at the head of Volume I of the parent work have been included in the *Concise* versions.

The Associates whose names are listed facing the title-page were chosen by the members of the Advisory Editorial Board and were responsible for the first stage in the task of condensation. Each Associate provided a preliminary or "raw" draft of a specific section of the work, which the editors then checked against the original biographies in the parent set, and amended, amplified or cut down as each individual

biographical note seemed to require. Each condensed biography was then brought into loose conformation with a general style (except in the case of extended entries in which the original style was, at least in part, preserved) and the amended versions were once again checked for accuracy against the original text of the large *Dictionary*.

The editors are grateful to the members of the Advisory Editorial Board for invaluable preliminary advice and continuing interest, and to the Associates for their courage and energy in producing the preliminary draft. Special thanks is owed to Mr. Edward T. James, the present editor of the parent *Dictionary* and its Supplements; to Messrs. Harold C. Syrett and Jacob E. Cooke, editors of the Alexander Hamilton papers; to Mr. Leonard W. Labaree and the staff of the Benjamin Franklin papers. Important corrections in the article on John Howard Payne were kindly furnished by Miss Grace Overmyer. Mr. Curtis C. Davis supplied correct summaries of the lives of Lewis Littlepage and William A. Caruthers. The Misses Edythe Greissman and Antoinette Boysen supervised the physical preparation of the entire manuscript and read a great part of the proofs. We are grateful to them, and also to their assistants in reading the proofs, Mrs. Thelma Grube and Messrs. Thomas Berger and Bruce Wendell.

Important Note to Users

Genealogical data given immediately after the statement of a subject's occupation or profession indicate his relation to a person or persons represented elsewhere in the work. The use of italics or the "q.v." symbol was avoided in this connection in order to free the pages of the *Concise Dictionary* from unnecessary clutter. Where an important genealogical reference is made to a foreigner, he is identified as a rule at the point of citation. A specific reference to an individual within the body of an article usually indicates that the person cited is also the subject of a biography elsewhere in the work. Dates cited in full in parentheses after a proper name serve to distinguish that person from another individual of exactly similar name.

Details of a subject's education have been given where it was an important element in his career, and also whenever it possessed an interest in itself as reflecting the preferences or prejudices of the region from which he came.

Designation of the political parties to which statesmen and members of Congress belonged is based in most instances on precise statements in the original text. In a few cases, an inference has been drawn from the subject's political associations, especially in the period between the years 1815 and 1836.

The dates of Congressional and legislative terms have been conformed to the period of actual service; i.e., from the beginning of the first session attended by the subject after his election to the end of the last session attended before his retirement. However, where it is clear from the original text that a member of Congress entered at an unconventional time, or was appointed to serve out an unexpired term, the original statement has been followed exactly.

Service in state legislatures has not been described in detail unless it had peculiar significance in the subject's subsequent career. Service in colonial legislatures is, as a rule, specifically described.

Abbreviations and other directive symbols used in the *Concise Dictionary of American Biography* are, for the most part, conventional. Among those frequently employed are:

ante, before

b., born

c., circa or about, indicating uncertainty

d., died

fl., flourished, or was active. Used where precise dates of birth and death are lacking.

post, after, in the sense of subsequent to

o.s., in dates, indicates a date based on the Julian calendar, which continued in official use in England until 1752. Where two dates are given, separated by a slant line, the first date stands for the legal or Julian year; the second for the unofficial, or historical, year, based on the reformed Gregorian calendar.

n.s., in dates, indicates a date based on the Gregorian calendar, adopted on the Continent of Europe (except for Russia, Greece and Great Britain) in 1582, and designed to correct the errors of the Julian calendar.

Supp. 1, indicates the first supplementary volume in the multi-volume *Dictionary.*

Supp. 2, indicates the second supplementary volume.

Most of the designations of geographical areas and states of the Union should present no difficulty. The following, however, are specially cited:

B.W.I., British West Indies

D.W.I., Danish West Indies

L.I., Long Island (New York)

N.B., New Brunswick

N.S., Nova Scotia

P.E.I., Prince Edward Island

P.I., Philippine Islands

S.I., Staten Island (New York)

V.I., Virgin Islands.

Concise Dictionary
of
American Biography

CONCISE DICTIONARY
OF
AMERICAN BIOGRAPHY

ABBE, CLEVELAND (*b. New York, N.Y., 1838; d. 1916*), astronomer, meteorologist. Issued pioneer weather forecasts based on telegraphic reports, 1869; with U.S. Weather Service, 1871–1916.

ABBETT, LEON (*b. Philadelphia, Pa., 1836; d. Jersey City, N.J., 1894*), lawyer. As Democratic governor of New Jersey, 1883–86, imposed equitable taxes on railroad and other corporations.

ABBEY, EDWIN AUSTIN (*b. Philadelphia, Pa., 1852; d. London, England, 1911*), illustrator, mural painter. Studied at Pennsylvania Academy; joined staff of illustrators, *Harper's Weekly*, 1871, resigning in 1874 to free-lance. Concentrating on faithful recreation of 17th and 18th century modes and manners in pen and water-color, he developed a charming, original style. Commissioned to sketch in England in 1878, he remained there save for brief visits to America. His best work is found in *Selections from the Poetry of Robert Herrick* (1882), Goldsmith's *She Stoops to Conquer* (1886), *Old Songs* (1889); as muralist, he won fame for designs in the Boston Public Library and the Pennsylvania state capitol.

ABBEY, HENRY (*b. Rondout, N.Y., 1842; d. Tenafly, N.J., 1911*), minor poet.

ABBEY, HENRY EUGENE (*b. Akron, O., 1846; d. 1896*), theatrical and operatic manager. Presented finest European talents in "road" tours of smaller American cities.

ABBOT, BENJAMIN (*b. Andover, Mass., 1762; d. Exeter, N.H., 1849*), educator. Graduated Harvard, 1788. Principal of Phillips Exeter Academy, a position he held with great influence, 1788–1838.

ABBOT, EZRA (*b. Jackson, Maine, 1819; d. 1884*), Biblical scholar, librarian, teacher, editor. In his generation, the greatest American critic of the New Testament text.

ABBOT, FRANCIS ELLINGWOOD (*b. Boston, Mass., 1836; d. 1903*), Unitarian clergyman, philosopher. Rejected contemporary Unitarianism for what he termed "Free Religion." His subtle criticism of the then dominant idealism in philosophy was premature and without immediate influence.

ABBOT, GORHAM DUMMER (*b. Brunswick, Maine, 1807; d. South Natick, Mass., 1874*), Presbyterian clergyman, educator. Active in higher education for women; established Spingler Institute in New York City; influenced Matthew Vassar to devote his wealth to education.

ABBOT, HENRY LARCOM (*b. Beverly, Mass., 1831; d. 1927*), army engineer. Graduated West Point, 1854. Assisted Capt. A. A. Humphreys's investigation of channel improvement along lower Mississippi and with him advocated use of levees in flood control. After serving in Civil War, developed the army's Engineer School of Application making it a research center for problems of military engineering. Promoted to brigadier-general upon retirement in 1895. Acted as consulting engineer to French and American Panama Canal companies; the decision to build a lock-canal rather than a sea-level canal was based on his report. Professor of hydraulic engineering, George Washington University, 1905–10.

ABBOT, JOEL (*b. Westford, Mass., 1793; d. Hong Kong, China, 1855*), naval officer. Distinguished service, War of 1812; commanded frigate in Perry's Japanese expedition, 1852–54.

ABBOT, WILLIS JOHN (*b. New Haven, Conn., 1863; d. Brookline, Mass., 1934*), journalist, author. Editor, *Christian Science Monitor*, 1921–27; promoted *Monitor* peace plan; actively interested in international adjudication and peace organizations.
[*Supp. 1*]

ABBOTT, AUSTIN (*b. Boston, Mass., 1831; d. New York, N.Y., 1896*), lawyer. Brother of Benjamin V. Abbott, Edward Abbott and Lyman Abbott. Author of *Trial Evidence* (1880); counsel for defense in *Tilton vs. Beecher*. Dean of Law School, New York University, 1891–96.

ABBOTT, BENJAMIN (*b. 1732; d. Salem, N.J., 1796*), religious enthusiast. Methodist circuit preacher in southern New Jersey.

ABBOTT, BENJAMIN VAUGHAN (*b. Boston, Mass., 1830; d. Brooklyn, N.Y., 1890*), lawyer, author. Collaborated with brother Austin Abbott in writing treatises, digests, reports and briefs. Son of Jacob Abbott.

ABBOTT, CHARLES CONRAD (*b. Trenton, N.J., 1843; d. Bristol, Pa., 1919*), naturalist, archaeologist. Wrote semi-popular accounts of nature study along the Delaware. Student of American Indian culture.

ABBOTT, EDWARD (*b. Farmington, Maine, 1841; d. 1908*), Congregational and Episcopal clergyman, author. Editor *Literary World*, 1878–88, 1895–1903; rector, St. James Episcopal Church, North Cambridge, Mass. Brother of Austin, Benjamin V., and Lyman Abbott.

ABBOTT, EMMA (*b. Chicago, Ill., 1850; d. Salt Lake City, Utah, 1891*), dramatic soprano. Formed Abbott English Opera Co. popularizing opera in America, 1878–91.

ABBOTT, FRANK (*b. Shapleigh, Maine, 1836; d. 1897*), dentist. Invented operative instruments for almost every phase of dental work. Dean, New York College of Dentistry, 1869–97.

ABBOTT, FRANK FROST (*b. Redding, Conn., 1860; d. Montreux, Switzerland, 1924*), classical scholar. Professor of Latin, University of Chicago, 1891–1908; Princeton, 1908–1924. Specialist in Roman social and political life.

ABBOTT, GRACE (*b. Grand Island, Nebr., 1878; d. Chicago, Ill., 1939*), social worker, administrator of the first Child Labor Act; chief, federal Children's Bureau, 1921–34. [*Supp. 2*]

ABBOTT, HORACE (*b. Sudbury, Mass., 1806; d. Baltimore, Md., 1887*), iron manufacturer. Produced armor plates for the original *Monitor* and vessels of her class. Leader in Baltimore business and financial circles.

ABBOTT, JACOB (*b. Hallowell, Maine, 1803; d. Farmington, Maine, 1879*), Congregational clergyman, educator, writer of children's books. Author of the famous *Rollo* series which combined simple stories with instruction in ethics, religion, science and history. Brother of Gorham D. and John S. C. Abbot(t); father of Austin, Benjamin V., and Lyman Abbott.

ABBOTT, JOHN STEVENS CABOT (*b. Brunswick, Maine, 1805; d. Fair Haven, Conn., 1877*), Congregational clergyman. Brother of Gorham D. Abbot and Jacob Abbott; author of a popular eulogistic *History of Napoleon Bonaparte* (1855).

ABBOTT, JOSEPH CARTER (*b. Concord, N.H., 1825; d. Wilmington, N.C., 1881*), journalist, politician. Active Republican leader in reconstruction of North Carolina, 1866–71.

ABBOTT, LYMAN (*b. Roxbury, Mass., 1835; d. 1922*), Congregational clergyman, author. Son of Jacob Abbott; brother of Austin and Benjamin V. Abbott. During Civil War held pastorate at Terre Haute, Indiana; resigned at end of war to join commission of laymen and ministers dedicated to aid Southern reconstruction. Appointed editor, *The Illustrated Christian Weekly*, 1870; left in 1876 to become associated with Henry Ward Beecher in editorship of *Christian Union*; at Beecher's removal became editor-in-chief and so continued after paper was renamed *Outlook*, 1893. Succeeded Beecher as pastor of Plymouth Congregational Church, Brooklyn, N.Y., 1890–99. Supported important reform movements and made *Outlook* a powerful exponent of progressive Christianity. Influential works: *The Life and Literature of the Ancient Hebrews* (1901), *Theology of an Evolutionist* (1897).

ABBOTT, ROBERT SENGSTACKE (*b. St. Simon's Island, Ga., 1868; d. Chicago, Ill., 1940*), newspaper editor. Founder (1905) and publisher of the *Chicago Defender*. [*Supp. 2*]

ABBOTT, SAMUEL WARREN (*b. Woburn, Mass., 1837; d. 1904*), physician, statistician. M.D., Harvard, 1862. Civil War surgeon; pioneer leader of public health movement in America; early student of demography.

ABBOTT, WILLIAM HAWKINS (*b. Middlebury, Conn., 1819; d. 1901*), petroleum producer and refiner. Constructed first oil refinery at Titusville, Pa., 1861; promoted business and civic development of that city.

ABEEL, DAVID (*b. New Brunswick, N.J., 1804; d. Albany N.Y., 1846*), missionary of Dutch Reformed Church in Far East *post* 1830.

ABEL, JOHN JACOB (*b. near Cleveland, O., 1857; d. Baltimore, Md., 1938*), pharmacologist and biological chemist. Director of laboratory for endocrine research at Johns Hopkins medical school. [*Supp. 2*]

ABELL, ARUNAH SHEPHERDSON (*b. East Providence, R.I., 1806; d. Baltimore, Md., 1888*), journalist. With W. M. Swain and A. H. Simmons, began Philadelphia "penny paper," the *Public Ledger*, 1836. This successful venture resulted in the same partners' foundation of a second paper under Abell's sole management, the *Baltimore Sun*, 1837. Moving to Baltimore, he built the *Sun* into an accurate, impartial and independent journal. He was a pioneer in modern impersonal journalism; in the classification and systematic gathering of local news; and in the development of speedy general news service using pony express, carrier pigeons and Morse's recently invented telegraph.

ABERCROMBY, JAMES (*b. Glassaugh, Banffshire, Scotland, 1706; d. 1781*), British general. Given full command of British forces in America, spring 1758; met bloody and total defeat at Ticonderoga; recalled to England, fall 1758.

ABERNETHY, GEORGE (*b. New York, N.Y., 1807; d. Portland, Oreg., 1877*), merchant, churchman, administrator. Pioneer businessman in Oregon; associate of Rev. Jason Lee; provisional governor, 1845 and 1847.

ABERT, JOHN JAMES (*b. Shepherdstown(?), Va., 1788; d. Washington, D.C., 1863*), topographical engineer. Attended West Point, 1808–11. Practiced law in Washington, D.C., and Ohio. After serving as a volunteer in the War of 1812, he was appointed major in the Topographical Engineers. Assisted Ferdinand Rudolph Hassler in making geodetic surveys along the Atlantic Coast and topographical surveys in eastern United States; was chief of the Topographical Bureau from 1834 to 1861, and responsible for the extensive surveys of the West made during this period.
[Supp. 1]

ABORN, MILTON (*b. Marysville, Calif., 1864; d. New York, N.Y., 1933*), operatic impresario.
[Supp. 1]

ABRAMS, ALBERT (*b. San Francisco, Calif., 1863; d. 1924*), physician. Founder of "E.R.A." system of universal diagnosis and treatment of disease, based on changes of electrical potential in the skin.

ACCAU (ACCAULT), MICHEL. [See Aco, Michel, fl. 1680–1702.]

ACHESON, EDWARD GOODRICH (*b. Washington, Pa., 1856; d. New York, N.Y., 1931*), inventor, pioneer of electrothermal industry. After only a few years' schooling, he became a timekeeper at a blast furnace; in 1873 patented a rock-boring machine to be used in coal mines; in 1880 worked as a draftsman for Thomas A. Edison at Menlo Park; thereafter, spent several years in Europe helping to install lighting plants. On returning to America he set up his own laboratory and sold rights for an anti-induction telephone wire. His interest in abrasives led to the development of an electric furnace, a procedure for making artificial graphite, and the discovery of carborundum. Founded at least five companies dependent on the electrothermal process. [Supp. 1]

ACKER, CHARLES ERNEST (*b. Bourbon, Ind., 1868; d. Ossining, N.Y., 1920*), inventor, manufacturer. Perfected process for producing caustic soda and chlorine by electrolysis of molten salt; held over forty electrochemical patents.

ACO, MICHEL (*fl. 1680–1702*), French explorer. Sent by La Salle to explore upper Mississippi, 1680. Business partner of La Salle's associates, Tonty and La Forest, 1693.

ACRELIUS, ISRAEL (*b. Öster-Åker, Sweden, 1714; d. 1800*), Lutheran clergyman, author. Pastor at Christina (Wilmington, Del.), 1749–56; wrote *History of New Sweden* (1759), describing region under Swedish, Dutch and English rule.

ADAIR, JAMES (*b. Ireland, c. 1709; d. c. 1783*), Indian trader, author. His *History of the American Indians* (1775) is an eye-witness record of aboriginal manners, customs and languages.

ADAIR, JOHN (*b. Chester Co., S.C., 1757; d. Mercer Co., Ky., 1840*), soldier, politician, Indian fighter. Nine times elected to Kentucky legislature; governor of Kentucky, 1820–24; representative in Congress, 1831–33. Partisan of the common people and "relief" leader.

ADAMS, ABIGAIL (*b. Weymouth, Mass., 1744; d. Quincy, Mass., 1818*), wife of Pres. John Adams. Wrote distinguished letters containing vivid pictures of the times.

ADAMS, ABIJAH (*b. Boston, Mass., c. 1754; d. Boston, 1816*), journalist. Edited Boston *Independent Chronicle*, chief supporter of Jeffersonian principles in New England, 1800–16.

ADAMS, ALVA (*b. Iowa Co., Wis., 1850; d. 1922*), businessman. Democratic governor of Colorado, 1886–88, 1896–98. Developed the state's school and prison systems; re-elected 1904 but was disqualified.

ADAMS, ALVIN (*b. Andover, Vt., 1804; d. 1877*), pioneer in express business. Founded Adams Express Co., 1840.

ADAMS, ANDREW (*b. Stratford, Conn., 1736; d. 1797*), Revolutionary patriot, Connecticut legislator and jurist.

ADAMS, ANDY (*b. Whitley Co., Ind., 1859; d. Colorado Springs, Colo., 1935*), cowboy, author. Gained knowledge for his *Log of a Cowboy* (1903) "from the hurricane deck of a Texas horse."
[Supp. 1]

ADAMS, BROOKS (*b. Quincy, Mass., 1848; d. Boston, Mass., 1927*), historian. Brother of Charles Francis Adams (1835–1915) and Henry B. Adams. His first work, *The Emancipation of Massachusetts* (1887), attracted attention by its vigorous assault upon the traditional approach to early New England history. Studying trade-routes and their influence upon history, he next published *Law of Civilization and Decay* (1895) attempting to prove that human societies were differentiated because of unequal natural endowment of energy. In subsequent volumes he extended this "law" into modern times hoping to forecast the direction of social movement. Although his books were based on sound research they are permeated by strong prejudices which dominate and sometimes distort their conclusions.

ADAMS, CHARLES (*b. Pomerania, Germany, 1845?; d. Denver, Colo., 1895*), soldier, diplomat. Indian fighter; agent to the Utes, 1872–74; minister to Bolivia, 1880–82; post-office inspector, 1882–85.

ADAMS, CHARLES BAKER (*b. Dorchester, Mass., 1814; d. St. Thomas, V.I., 1853*), naturalist. His *Contributions to Conchology* (1849–52) and *Catalogue of Shells collected at Panama* (1852) are still standard manuals.

ADAMS, CHARLES FOLLEN (*b. Dorchester, Mass., 1842; d. 1918*), poet. *Leedle Yawcob Strauss, and Other Poems* (1877) represents his skill and originality in German dialect verse.

ADAMS, CHARLES FRANCIS (*b. Boston, Mass., 1807; d. Boston, 1886*), diplomat, son of John Quincy Adams. Graduated Harvard, 1825; practiced law. Elected to Massachusetts legislature as a Whig, 1840; served three years in the House and two in the state senate. Elected to Congress as a Republican, 1858, he gained recognition for his moderate views. Appointed minister to England, 1861. For seven years he stayed at that post utilizing all his personal and intellectual powers in the *Trent* affair, the *Alabama* case and other matters involving the neutrality of England and the rivalry between Union and Confederate representatives seeking European recognition. In an England that tended to favor the Confederacy he enhanced the Northern position without resorting to humiliating compromises or war. As biographer and editor of the works of his grandfather, Pres. John Adams, he worked with care and discretion.

ADAMS, CHARLES FRANCIS (*b. Boston, Mass., 1835; d. Washington, D.C., 1915*), railroad expert, civic leader, historian. Son of the preceding; brother of Brooks Adams and Henry B. Adams. Graduated Harvard, 1856; practiced law. Served as cavalry officer during Civil War; mustered out as brevet brigadier-general, 1865. Exposed criminal actions of railroad speculators in *Chapters of Erie* (1871); headed Massachusetts Board of Railroad Commissioners, 1872; made chairman of the government directors of Union Pacific Railroad, 1878, he became president of that road in 1884. His participation in Quincy city government resulted in important educational reforms there and in his subsequent appointment to a park commission for Boston and vicinity. He was author of a number of papers and several books on topics in New England history and a biography of his father.

ADAMS, CHARLES KENDALL (*b. Derby, Vt., 1835; d. Redlands, Calif., 1902*), historian. President of Cornell University, 1885–92, and of University of Wisconsin, 1892–1901; author *Democracy and Monarchy in France.*

ADAMS, CHARLES R. (*b. Charlestown, Mass., 1834; d. West Harwich, Mass., 1900*), opera singer. Greatest American tenor of his time; teacher of Hiltz, Melba and Eames.

ADAMS, CYRUS CORNELIUS (*b. Naperville, Ill., 1849; d. New York, N.Y., 1928*), geographical writer, editor. Helped establish study of geography as an American university subject. [*Supp.* 1]

ADAMS, DANIEL (*b. Townsend, Mass., 1773; d. Keene, N.H., 1864*), physician, educator. Author of two once widely used school texts, *The Scholar's Arithmetic* (1801) and *The Understanding Reader* (c. 1803).

ADAMS, DANIEL WEISSIGER (*b. Frankfort, Ky., 1820; d. New Orleans, La., 1872*), lawyer, Confederate brigadier-general. Brother of William Wirt Adams.

ADAMS, DUDLEY W. (*b. Winchendon, Mass., 1831; d. 1897*), horticulturist. Established Iron Clad Nursery at Waukon, Iowa, 1856; promoter of National Grange; was elected its Master, 1873. Framed proposals for railroad-freight legislation which were introduced into Congress, 1873–74; although no federal legislation was secured at that time, his suggestions for fixed rates and the abolition of discriminatory practices were later incorporated into national and state regulations governing railroads. Moved to Florida in 1875, planted extensive orange and other fruit orchards and did much to develop horticultural industry there.

ADAMS, EBENEZER (*b. New Ipswich, N.H., 1765; d. 1841*), educator. Graduated Dartmouth, 1791. Professor at Dartmouth, 1809–33; a factor in the celebrated "Dartmouth College Case."

ADAMS, EDWARD DEAN (*b. Boston, Mass., 1846; d. 1931*), banker, industrialist. Leader in utilizing Niagara Falls for electrical power production; reorganizer and director of many railroads; art connoisseur.
[*Supp.* 1]

ADAMS, EDWIN (*b. Medford, Mass., 1834; d. 1877*), actor. Considered one of America's best light comedians, he supported Edwin Booth, and had his greatest success in the role of "Enoch Arden," 1869.

ADAMS, ELIPHALET (*b. Dedham, Mass., 1677; d. New London, Conn., 1753*), clergyman. Pastor at New London, 1708/09–52; trustee of Yale College, 1720–38.

ADAMS, EPHRAIM DOUGLASS (*b. Decorah, Iowa, 1865; d. 1930*), historian, teacher. Author of *Great Britain and the American Civil War* (1925); directed assembling of materials for the Hoover War Library.
[*Supp.* 1]

ADAMS, FREDERICK UPHAM (*b. Boston, Mass., 1859; d. Larchmont, N.Y., 1921*), inventor, author. Improved electric lighting and railway equipment.

ADAMS, GEORGE BURTON (*b. Fairfield, Vt., 1851; d. 1925*), historian. Professor of history at Yale, 1888–1925; authoritative writer on medieval subjects and on English constitutional history.

ADAMS, HANNAH (*b. Medfield, Mass., 1755; d. Boston, Mass., 1831*), compiler of historical information. Probably the first professional female writer in America.

ADAMS, HENRY BROOKS (*b. Boston, Mass., 1838; d. Washington, D.C., 1918*), historian. Great-grandson of John Adams, grandson of John Quincy Adams, son of Charles Francis Adams (1807–1886); brother of Brooks Adams and Charles Francis Adams (1835–1915). Graduated Harvard, 1858. Studied civil law at Berlin and Dresden, 1859–60, but made little progress. In Washington, D.C., as secretary to father, 1860–61; despite wish to serve in Union army, he went with father to London and continued to act as secretary during father's eventful term as United States minister to Court of St. James, 1861–68. On return to America, was at once fascinated and repelled by the crudeness and strength of American life, and its contrasts with the cultivated society of Europe. Accepted appointment as assistant professor of history at Harvard, 1870. His instinct for perfection made him rate his academic work as a failure, but he introduced the seminar system of study and trained some brilliant students. Married Marian Hooper, 1872. In 1877, left Harvard and made his home in Washington, D.C., regarding his "function in life to be stable-companion to statesmen." His fastidious response to the knavery of political life at that time was expressed in an anonymous novel, *Democracy* (1880). Abandoning hopes of a political career, he became a scholarly and disillusioned observer, withdrawn among a small circle of intimates such as John Hay, statesman, Clarence King, geologist and traveler, and John LaFarge, artist. After the death of his wife in 1885, he traveled in the Orient and returned to continue his research into the beginnings of our national government, producing his *History of the United States* (1889–91), a masterly study of the administrations of Jefferson and Madison. After further travel to the South Seas, Mexico, the Far West and Europe, the direction of his interests shifted from early American history to the study of the resolution of spiritual and material forces in medieval Europe and the exposition of a personal philosophy of history in *Mont-St.-Michel and Chartres* (1904; 1913), in the enigmatic *Education of Henry Adams* (1907; 1918) and *A Letter to American Teachers of History* (1910). Among his other books are *Documents Relating to New England Federalism* (1877), *The Life of Albert Gallatin* (1879), *Esther* (1884).

ADAMS, HENRY CARTER (*b. Davenport, Iowa, 1851; d. 1921*), economist, statistician. Early opponent of *laissez-faire* economics; student of American financial and administrative problems.

ADAMS, HENRY CULLEN (*b. Oneida Co., N.Y., 1850; d. 1906*), congressman from Wisconsin, 1902–06. Supported dual statehood for New Mexico, Arizona; active in passage of the Meat Inspection Law,

the National Food and Drug Act and the Adams Act, providing agricultural research funds.

ADAMS, HERBERT BAXTER (*b. Shutesbury, Mass., 1850; d. 1901*), historian. Instrumental in development of the study of political science and history at Johns Hopkins University; active with Moses C. Tyler and Charles K. Adams in organization of American Historical Association, 1884.

ADAMS, ISAAC (*b. Rochester, N. H., 1802; d. 1883*), inventor. Devised "Adams Power Press" in 1827, a machine widely used in book printing prior to introduction of modern cylinder press.

ADAMS, JAMES HOPKINS (*b. Richmond Co., S.C., 1812; d. 1861*), politician, planter. Strong advocate of States' Rights. During governorship of South Carolina, 1854–58, proposed reopening of African slave trade.

ADAMS, JASPER (*b. East Medway, Mass., 1793; d. 1841*), Episcopal clergyman. President of Charleston College, Charleston, S.C., 1824–26, 1828–36; first president of Hobart College, 1826–28.

ADAMS, JOHN (*b. Braintree, Mass., 1735; d. Quincy, Mass., 1826*), president of the United States. Graduated Harvard, 1755. Taught school at Worcester, Mass.; studied law and was admitted to Boston bar, 1758. Married Abigail Smith, 1764. Was early identified with the cause of American independence by his association with Gridley and Otis in their presentation of Boston's memorial against the closing of the courts and by his legal opposition to Stamp Act and other British measures for taxation of the colonies. Elected to General Court as representative of Boston, 1770, he served a one-year term. His condemnation of the Boston Port Act brought him back to public life, and he was chosen in 1774 to act as one of the delegates representing Massachusetts in the first Continental Congress. In the second Congress, 1775–77, he was active in persuading the hesitant Congress to declare its independence from English rule, seconding Richard Henry Lee's motion for independence, foreign alliances and confederacy, and working on the Declaration of Independence itself although his contributions to the text of that document were negligible. When the Declaration was brought before the Congress he was, as Jefferson wrote, "its ablest advocate and defender against the multifarious assaults it encountered."

He served on a number of congressional committees and on the newly created Board of War. From 1778 to 1788 he acted in diplomatic capacities in France, Holland and England; with John Jay and Benjamin Franklin he settled the provisional articles of the Treaty of Peace with Great Britain. After serving three years as first envoy to the Court of St. James, he returned to America in 1788.

When Washington was unanimously chosen president under the new Constitution, Adams received enough of the scattered votes to be made vice-president. Re-elected in 1792, he aided Hamilton's financial measures but was never fully able to gain his complete confidence. Hamilton intervened in the election of 1796 hoping to keep Adams in the vice-presidency; the plan failed in that Adams was chosen president, but it drew enough votes to mortify him and make Jefferson his vice-president. His administration faced two serious problems: abroad, relations with the revolutionary government of France had deteriorated to a dangerous degree; at home he was surrounded by antagonistic Jeffersonians and a cabinet who looked to Hamilton and not to the president as the party leader. John Marshall, C. C. Pinckney and Elbridge Gerry were commissioned to renew diplomatic relations with France, but they were rebuffed. Adams, prepared for this failure, had to face the possibilities of war with the French Republic. Congress, under Hamilton's influence, passed the Alien and Sedition Acts, 1798, and planned a large provisional army with Washington at its head to defend America against French invasion; a navy department was also created. Gerry, who stayed on in France after his fellow commissioners departed, landed at Boston in the fall of 1798 with news of a French desire to renew negotiations. Adams did not exclude the possibility of a peaceful solution if American envoys were accorded proper treatment; however, Hamilton was urging war with France, an attack on Spanish America and the creation of a large standing army. On his own initiative, Adams appointed W. Vans Murray as minister to the French Republic and proposed the choice of a special peace commission. Congress was outraged, but his bold act was acclaimed by the popular press, and neither Hamilton nor Congress could thwart it. Adams's disloyal cabinet, believing Bourbon restoration was at hand, opposed the president's policy and frustrated it at first. Adams, however, completed instructions for the mission and authorized its departure by Nov. 1, 1799. (Peace was concluded on Sept. 30, 1800, at Morfontaine.) He had surprised and angered his advisers and antagonized Hamilton, but he had prevented a war with France and honorably preserved the neutrality of the United States. The price was his own political career. Federalist leaders regarded him as a traitor to the party and did their best thenceforward to discredit him. Adams ousted Hamilton's friends Pickering and McHenry from his cabinet and replaced them with Samuel Dexter and John Marshall, yet the unsuspected Wolcott remained to act as informer to the opposition. Facing the election of 1800 without party backing and with the added disadvantage of Hamilton's recently published attack, *Letter Concerning the Public Conduct and Character of John Adams,* he lost the presidency to Thomas Jefferson. In closing his controversial presidential career he created a large number of life appointments to federal posts and by so doing increased the enmity of Jefferson.

He then retired to Quincy where he was completely isolated from national affairs except for his interest in the *Chesapeake* incident and in the career of his son, John Quincy Adams. If party success were the only criterion in judgment of a man of politics, John Adams would be ranked as a failure, for the Federalists lost their influence as a party during his time in office. But he was never a partisan. Loyalty to his country and devotion to the office of the presidency were not to be sacrificed in the choice of a politically expedient solution. Disinterested, careful of his independence and jealous of others, he stood alone, and so largely lost the benefit he might have gained from consultation and mutual action.

ADAMS, JOHN (*b. Canterbury, Conn., 1772; d. 1863*), educator. Fourth principal of Phillips Academy, Andover, Mass., 1810–32.

ADAMS, JOHN (*b. Nashville, Tenn., 1825; d. 1864*), Confederate soldier. Graduated West Point, 1846. Served in 1st Dragoons, 1846–60, rising to captain. As Confederate brigadier-general, killed at battle of Franklin.

ADAMS, JOHN COLEMAN (*b. Malden, Mass., 1849; d. Hartford, Conn., 1922*), Universalist clergyman.

ADAMS, JOHN QUINCY (*b. Braintree, Mass., 1767; d. Washington, D.C., 1848*), president of the United States. Eldest son of John (1735–1826) and Abigail (Smith) Adams. Attended several European universities and academies; acted as secretary to Francis Dana, American minister to Russia, 1781–83, and as secretary to John Adams during peace negotiations, 1783. Returned to America and graduated Harvard, 1787. Entered legal profession, 1790. Commissioned by Washington as minister to the Netherlands, 1794; married Louisa Catherine Johnson, 1797; served as minister to Berlin. Resumed Boston law practice, 1801. Elected to U.S. Senate, 1803. Believing that the current bill for the possession of Louisiana was a violation of the Constitution, he introduced several resolutions aimed at its correction. His report on Senator John Smith, his attitude on the impeachment of Judge Pickering, his apparent support of the administration in the *Chesapeake* affair and his votes in favor of the Embargo of 1807 were all in opposition to the Federalist party's views. A special senatorial election was called, and he was forced to resign in 1808. The Federalist tendency to placate the English forced him at times into the Republican camp, but he remained an independent, suspected by both parties. Appointed minister to Russia by Madison, 1809, he was nominated and confirmed to Supreme Court of U.S., 1811, but declined and remained at St. Petersburg where he was able to conclude favorable trade agreements. Russia, invaded by Napoleon, joined forces with Great Britain against France; meanwhile America had declared war on the English. Finding his allies in opposing camps, the Tsar offered to mediate between the two countries. Adams, James A. Bayard and Albert Gallatin were dispatched to represent American interests, 1813. This first peace mission proved to be premature. A second one, including the aforementioned along with Jonathan Russell and Henry Clay, was successful at Ghent, 1814, owing mainly to Adams and Gallatin who managed to work in concert. Clay and Adams differed on important issues, particularly over Clay's wish to prolong the war.

Appointed secretary of state by Monroe in 1817, Adams's previous experience was invaluable, but his blunt, direct methods made him unpopular in the cabinet, and he was soon to learn that the "era of good feeling" was more apparent than real. Many men were contending for the presidency; Clay was in opposition; and the revolting Spanish colonies in America brought many serious problems before the new secretary of state. The Floridas, still Spanish possessions, were a refuge for hostile Indians and malefactors who raided bordering states at will. When Andrew Jackson campaigned against these raiders and pursued them into Spanish territory, Adams defended the trespass on the grounds that Americans were obliged to act in self-defense since Spain had proved incapable of policing her territories; thus Jackson's conduct was justified, and British and Spanish protests were silenced. In 1819 Adams completed the treaty whereby the United States obtained the Floridas; to accomplish this it was necessary to give up claims on Texas. He also reached an agreement with Great Britain postponing the Oregon question by permitting a ten-year joint occupation of that territory.

In 1822 Monroe formally recognized the independence of the Spanish colonies in America. Adams urged the president to formulate his opposition to the forceful interference of European powers in South America into an American policy. The president's message embodying this principle is known as the Monroe Doctrine, with credit for it equally divided between him and Adams.

The presidential election of 1824 gave none of the four candidates a majority of the votes. Jackson received 99; Adams, 84; Crawford, 41; and Clay, 37. Disliking Jackson, Clay gave his support to Adams who later made him his secretary of state after Adams's choice as president by the House of Representatives. The defeated Jackson claimed mistakenly that Adams and Clay had entered into a corrupt bargain in order to bring themselves into power. In his inaugural address, President Adams outlined a broad plan for internal improvements. Northern strict constructionists were astonished to learn that he proposed extension of federal powers; Southerners feared that slavery might be abolished in the course of the "improvements"; therefore, a congressional opposition formed at the very beginning of the administration, and Adams's program met with bitter opposition.

Defeated by Jackson in his bid for re-election in 1828, he retired to his farm and books. Elected to Congress in 1831 as an independent, he represented his district in eight successive Congresses, for a period of almost 17 fruitful years. After 1835 he was consistently opposed to slavery and its extension into recently acquired territories. Adams made the then (1836) revolutionary suggestion that in case of "civil, servile or foreign" war in the South, slavery might be abolished by military authority; that is, the president or commander could rightly order universal emancipation. He debated and acted with complete independence. Even as chairman of the Committee on Foreign Affairs he figured prominently in questions of slavery; his position in the case of slaves who gained their freedom by capturing the vessel *Creole* caused the resignation of all of the southern committee members. In the case of a revolt of slaves on another ship, the *Amistad*, Adams appeared before the Supreme Court, 1841, and argued in behalf of their freedom.

Interested in science, he prepared a report on the standardization of weights and measures, urged the government to establish an astronomical observatory and was chairman of the committee responsible for the proper usage of the funds made available for the construction of the Smithsonian Institution. The best summary of his remarkable congressional years is to be found in his *Address of John Quincy Adams to his Constituents of the Twelfth Congressional District* (1842) which embodied his conception of what the South and the slave power had done or wished to do, and how far their policy had been aided by a sacrifice of principle by the North.

A student of political institutions often deeply engrossed by immediate problems, a man who voted and spoke without the party discipline that made others more prudent or silent, his individual course appeared to be an erratic one but it was guided by his unquestioned patriotism, his belief in natural law and rights and his passion for freedom of all men, including slaves. His *Memoirs* (ed. C. F. Adams, 1874–77) and *Life in a New England Town* (ed. C. F. Adams, Jr., 1903) are sources of important autobiographical and historical material.

ADAMS, JOSEPH ALEXANDER (*b. New Germantown, N.J., 1803; d. New Jersey, 1880*), wood engraver. Protegé of Alexander Anderson; his principal work, the sixteen hundred illustrations for Harper's *Illuminated Bible* (1843).

ADAMS, NEHEMIAH (*b. Salem, Mass., 1806; d. 1878*), Congregational clergyman. During the Unitarian controversy he published many pamphlets and books in defense of orthodoxy.

ADAMS, ROBERT (*b. Philadelphia, Pa., 1846; d. 1906*), lawyer, legislator. Republican congressman from Pennsylvania, 1893–1906; drafted, introduced and forced passage of resolution declaring war against Spain, 1898.

ADAMS, SAMUEL (*b. Boston, Mass., 1722; d. Boston, 1803*), Revolutionary statesman. Graduated Harvard, 1740; studied law; failed in various business enterprises. Acted as tax collector to the Town of Boston, 1756–64. Married Elizabeth Checkley, 1749 (d. 1757); Elizabeth Wells, 1764.

Although unable to manage his own affairs he showed an early talent for local politics, founding a political club and contributing articles to its newspaper, the *Independent Advertiser*. Associated with a popular party hostile to the wealthy minority who held political power in Massachusetts, he personally disliked the outstanding member of this "aristocracy," Thomas Hutchinson, lieutenant-governor, member of the Council and chief justice. In 1764 the Sugar and Stamp Acts brought Adams and his party into prominence; they denounced the conservative Hutchinson and accused him of sympathizing with oppressive British measures. Elected to the Massachusetts House of Representatives, 1765, Adams acted with colleagues in the Caucus Club and the Sons of Liberty to secure a majority of radicals in the House and excluded five conservative members from the Council, including Hutchinson. Re-elected in 1766 and gaining radical party leadership, he opposed Governor Bernard and Lieutenant-Governor Hutchinson, fought enforcement of the Townshend Acts by various Commissioners of Customs, drafted the famous "Circular Letter" to the assemblies of other provinces and that for the "Convention" of the patriot party held in Boston in 1768, and stirred up a popular hatred for British garrison troops which climaxed in the Boston Massacre of 1770. Effective as a polemical writer, he wrote many letters to prominent persons in England and America, contributed articles to the *Boston Gazette* and other journals and drafted most of the official papers of the House. He formulated basic premises as early as 1765 from which could be deduced the conclusions reached in the Declaration of Independence; e.g., that taxation without representation was unconstitutional and that colonial legislatures were "subordinate" but not "subject" to Parliament. His political theories gave him an intercolonial reputation and were influential in the later establishment of state legislatures limited by a "fixed" constitution. After repeal of the Townshend duties, 1770, hostility against Great Britain tended to subside, but Adams worked to renew it by writing some forty bitter articles to Boston newspapers protesting the removal of the General Court from Boston to Cambridge, criticizing the independent tenure of judges and the fact that Governor Hutchinson received his salary from the Crown and not from the General Court. Not content with mere verbal action, he moved Boston Town Meeting to appoint in 1772 a committee of correspondence which would state the rights and grievances of the Colonies "to the several towns and to the world." This action may be regarded as the origin of revolutionary government in Massachusetts. As a member of the committee, he drafted a declaration of rights stressing America's legislative independence of Parliament; the alarmed Governor Hutchinson prepared a carefully worded reply that temporarily checked formation of correspondence committees. Adams countered by publishing some of Hutchinson's private letters which set forth views hostile to the radical faction. Realizing that the arrival of tea ships, cleared under North's Tea Act, might be used to precipitate a crisis, Adams drafted a resolution adopted by Boston Town Meeting declaring all who aided in the landing or selling of tea shipped by the East India Company to be enemies of America and moved, during a mass meeting at Faneuil Hall, that the tea "shall be returned to the place from which it came at all events." On Dec. 16, 1773, the day on which a lately arrived tea cargo had to be entered or confiscated, learning that Hutchinson had refused clearance for the return of the tea ships, he gave the signal which sent the "Mohawks" down to the wharf where they threw the tea into the harbor.

With the enactment of the Coercive Acts Adams took a lead in organizing resistance, strongly supporting the creation of an intercolonial congress. Appointed delegate to the first Continental Congress, 1774, he was instrumental in organizing the convention that adopted the famous "Suffolk Resolves" virtually placing Massachusetts in a state of rebellion. Elected to the second Congress, 1775, he favored immediate independence, supported the resolution for the formation of independent state governments, proposed a confederation of such colonies as were ready for independence and voted for and signed the Declaration of Independence. Essentially a revolutionary agitator, he possessed little talent as a constructive statesman. His influence and popularity declined after the final breach with Great Britain. He served in Congress until 1781, when he returned to Boston. He was defeated in a bid for Congress, 1788; was elected lieutenant-governor of Massachusetts, 1789–93, and subsequently governor, 1794–97.

ADAMS, THOMAS SEWALL (*b. Baltimore, Md., 1873; d. 1933*), economist, professor at University of Wisconsin, Cornell and Yale. Expert on taxation.

[*Supp. 1*]

ADAMS, WILLIAM (*b. Colchester, Conn., 1807; d. 1880*), Presbyterian clergyman. Graduated from Yale, 1827. A founder of Union Theological Seminary, 1836, and its president, 1874–80.

ADAMS, WILLIAM LYSANDER (*b. Painesville, O., 1821; d. Hood River, Oreg., 1906*), Campbellite preacher, physician. Editor, the *Oregon City Argus*; one of the founders of the Republican party in Oregon.

ADAMS, WILLIAM TAYLOR (*b. Bellingham, Mass., 1822; d. Boston, Mass., 1897*), writer of juvenile stories under the name "Oliver Optic." His first attempt at writing a book for boys, *The Boat Club* (1855), was a great popular success; he wrote five more volumes in *The Boat Club* series and other series, including *Great Western, Lake Shore, Onward and Upward, Yacht Club, Riverdale Story Books* and *Woodville Stories*. Extended travels through Europe, Asia and Africa furnished material for the *Young American Abroad* and *All Over the World* series; the Civil War forms the background of *Army and Navy* and *Blue and Gray* series. In all, he wrote 126 books and about a thousand short tales for periodicals which he edited.

ADAMS, WILLIAM WIRT (*b. Frankfort, Ky., 1819; d. Jackson, Miss., 1888*), Confederate soldier, brother of Daniel W. Adams. Raised and commanded the 1st Mississippi Cavalry; promoted brigadier-general, 1863.

ADDAMS, JANE (*b. Cedarville, Ill., 1860; d. 1935*), social reformer, founder of Hull-House settlement in Chicago. Graduated from Rockford College; went on to Woman's Medical College in Philadelphia, where her health broke in 1882. During invalidism in Europe, studied settlement work. Opened Hull-House in a needy Chicago section in 1889. Her tact in handling people, affection for children and impulse to help attracted love and disarmed criticism. By 1905 she had financed and built the finest plant devoted to working-class recreation and education in the United States. Her supreme practical achievement was to recruit and hold many able women who acknowledged her leadership. Artists and educators also brought to Hull-House a cultural program which included a music school, a labor museum and the Hull-House Players. She brought her work to public attention by her many books, of which *Twenty Years at Hull-House* (1910) was outstanding. From 1915 to 1934 she opposed war as the supreme social evil.

[*Supp.* 1]

ADDICKS, JOHN EDWARD O'SULLIVAN (*b. Philadelphia, Pa., 1841; d. New York, N.Y., 1919*), promoter. Promoted and speculated in securities of gas companies on east coast; organized Gas Trust in Chicago; was unsuccessful in a unique seventeen-year fight to become U.S. senator from Delaware.

ADEE, ALVEY AUGUSTUS (*b. Astoria, Oreg., 1842; d. 1924*), diplomat. Held various foreign and domestic posts in state department, 1869–1924; expert drafter of diplomatic messages, treaties and other state papers.

ADGATE, ANDREW (*d. Philadelphia, Pa., 1793*), musician. An early promoter of musical education in Philadelphia.

ADLER, CYRUS (*b. Van Buren, Ark., 1863; d. Philadelphia, Pa., 1940*), orientalist, educational administrator, Jewish leader. A graduate of the University of Pennsylvania and Johns Hopkins, Adler became president of Dropsie College in 1908, after teaching and administrative posts at Johns Hopkins, the U.S. National Museum, and the Smithsonian Institution. A leader of American Judaism, Adler opposed Zionism but cooperated with Zionist leaders after the Balfour Declaration. He became president of the Jewish Theological Seminary in 1924, of the American Jewish Committee in 1929. He founded the American Jewish Historical Society, 1888, and edited the *Jewish Quarterly Review*, 1910–40. [*Supp.* 2]

ADLER, FELIX (*b. Alzey, Germany, 1851; d. 1933*), religious leader, educator. Came to America as a child; A.B., Columbia (N.Y.), 1870; Ph.D., Heidelberg, 1873. In 1876 he founded the Society for Ethical Culture, a movement which became the central activity of his life. His philosophical position is found in two of his books, *An Ethical Philosophy of Life* (1918) and *The Reconstruction of the Spiritual Ideal* (1924). His appeal lay in a combination of moral insight, intellectual range, and a dedication to the ethical motive as a way of deepening and extending beneficent relations between the individual and the group. [*Supp.* 1]

ADLER, GEORGE J. (*b. Leipzig, Germany, 1821; d. New York, N.Y., 1868*), philologist. Professor of modern languages at New York University, 1846–53. Compiled *Dictionary of the German and English Languages* (1849).

ADLER, SAMUEL (*b. Worms, Germany, 1809; d. 1891*), rabbi of Emanu-El Temple, New York City, *post* 1857. Prominent in the foundation of Reform Judaism. Father of Felix Adler.

ADLUM, JOHN (*b. York, Pa., 1759; d. Georgetown, D.C., 1836*), pioneer in viticulture. Cultivated, studied and improved American grapes, popularizing the Catawba variety.

ADRAIN, ROBERT (*b. Carrickfergus, Ireland, 1775; d. 1843*), mathematician. Taught at Pennsylvania, Rutgers and Columbia universities, 1809–34; did original work on the exponential law of error.

AFFLECK, THOMAS (*b. Dumfries, Scotland, 1812; d. 1868*), agricultural writer. Came to America, 1832. Advanced agriculture in the South through his writings and the example of his successful undertakings in Mississippi and Texas. An early advocate of diversified farming.

AGASSIZ, ALEXANDER (*b. Neuchâtel, Switzerland, 1835; d. 1910*), zoologist, oceanographer, mine operator, son of Jean Louis Agassiz. Came to America, 1849; studied mining, engineering, chemistry and natural history at Harvard; received A.B., 1855, B.S. in engineering, 1857. Superintendent at copper mines, Calumet, Mich., 1867–69; greatly improved output and working conditions. Began issuing the most important work of his scientific career, *Revision of the Echini*, in 1872. Curator of Harvard University Museum, 1874. Developing a new interest in marine biology, he began a series of cruises exploring the Gulf Stream, West Indies, Bahamas, Hawaiian Islands and the Pacific aboard the government-owned *Blake* and *Albatross*, and private vessels, 1877–1904; published extensive reports on expeditions. Although he did little classroom teaching, his generosity toward young scientists and his interest in their work gave him an influence which transcended classroom instruction.

AGASSIZ, ELIZABETH CABOT CARY (*b. Boston, Mass., 1822; d. Arlington Heights, Mass., 1907*), educator. Author of a life of her husband, Jean Louis Agassiz; one of the founders of Radcliffe College.

AGASSIZ, JEAN LOUIS RODOLPHE (*b. Motier-en-Vuly, Switzerland, 1807; d. Cambridge, Mass., 1873*), naturalist. Studied medicine, 1824–30, at Universities of Zurich and Heidelberg, and at University of Munich with the embryologist Döllinger. In 1829, published *The Fishes of Brazil,* one of the most important accounts of a local fish-fauna presented to that time. Met the master comparative anatomist Cuvier in Paris, 1831; continued his researches on fossil fish by utilizing the collections available at the Jardin des Plantes. Influenced by Cuvier's attempts to found a classification of animals on a structural basis, he wrote *Recherches sur les Poissons fossiles* (1833–44), a pioneer work on the fish-fauna of the primitive seas. Through the intervention of the distinguished explorer Humboldt, he had obtained a post as professor of natural history at Neuchâtel, 1832. His teaching years were not devoid of zoological research; he gained European fame through the publication of: *History of the Fresh Water Fishes of Central Europe* (1839–42), *Études critiques sur les Mollusques fossiles* (1840–45), *Nomenclator Zoologicus* (1842–46) and *Monograph on the Fossil Fishes of the Old Red or Devonian of the British Isles and Russia* (1844–45). Learning of de Charpentier and Venetz's recently expounded theory of local glacial action, he extended it to include large portions of Europe and explained present geological formations and land contours in terms of the glacial movements of an earlier epoch, the Ice Age. After eight years of studying existing glaciers he wrote *Études sur les Glaciers* (1840) to be followed by *Système Glaciare* (1846) and *Nouvelles études et expériences sur les Glaciers actuels* (1847). Visiting America in 1846, Agassiz stayed and made several trips on Coast Survey steamers as a guest of the government in 1847; he accepted the chair of natural history at Harvard University, 1848. He led group exploring the northern and eastern shores of Lake Superior, 1848, and a ten weeks' exploration of the Florida Reefs, 1851. Began *c.* 1856 assembling material for his ten-volume *Contributions to the Natural History of the United States;* four of the projected ten volumes were published. The first volume, containing the *Essay on Classification* (1857), was considered to be his greatest contribution to natural history during his life in America. In the *Essay* he developed Cuvier's ideas, attempting to relate embryonic changes to the succession of geological ages; it was his extension of Cuvier's work plus his own idealism that led him to oppose the Darwinian theory of evolution by natural selection. Abroad in summer of 1859, he returned to Cambridge, raised funds through public and private appropriations, and began construction of a museum of comparative zoology. Made extensive exploration of Brazil, 1865; studied glacial phenomena in Rocky Mountains, 1868. In 1869 he lectured at Cornell, participated in Coast Survey dredging operations near Cuba and presented an exhaustive memoir on the life and work of Humboldt. Strain of this heavy work schedule caused an attack of apoplexy which prevented his return to the Museum until November 1870. Aboard the Coast Survey vessel *Hassler,* on her 1871 trip to California, he was unable to do any effective deep-sea dredging, as he had planned, but he saw new evidence for his glacier theory around the Magellan Straits and the Chiloë Islands. Shortly prior to his death he founded the Anderson School of Natural History, a summer school where teachers could study science by directly observing the natural life available in their immediate surroundings. In October 1873 he gave his final course of lectures at the Museum and then wrote what was to be his last article, "Evolution and Permanence of Type," a justification of his attitude toward current trends in biology.

His influence on American thought was twofold: first, his prestige, enthusiasm and teaching methods greatly accelerated the serious study of natural history; and secondly, his criticisms of current educational practices, especially rote memorization and classical studies, resulted in a new emphasis on advanced and original work as factors in mental training.

AGATE, ALFRED T. (*b. Sparta, N.Y., 1812; d. Washington, D.C., 1846*), miniature painter, illustrator. Botanical artist on the Wilkes Exploring Expedition, 1838–42.

AGATE, FREDERICK STYLES (*b. Sparta, N.Y., 1803; d. Sparta, 1844*), painter, brother of Alfred T. Agate. Historical and portrait painter; a founder of the National Academy of Design.

AGGREY, JAMES EMMAN KWEGYIR (*b. Anamabu, West Africa, 1875; d. New York, N.Y., 1927*), African educator. [*Supp. 1*]

AGNEW, CORNELIUS REA (*b. New York, N.Y., 1830; d. 1888*), ophthalmologist. Graduated Columbia College, 1849; M.D., College of Physicians and Surgeons, New York, 1852; studied abroad, 1855. Surgeon-general of New York state militia, 1858; medical director of the New York State Hospital for Volunteers, 1861; an organizer of the U.S. Sanitary Commission. With Drs. Van Buren and Gibbs prepared plans for Judiciary Square Hospital at Washington, model for the pavilion system of hospitals. Active in foundation of Columbia School of Mines, in an ophthalmic clinic at College of Physicians and Surgeons and in both the Brooklyn and Manhattan Eye and Ear

Hospitals. Professor of eye and ear diseases at College of Physicians and Surgeons, 1869–88.

AGNEW, DAVID HAYES (*b. Lancaster Co., Pa., 1818; d. 1892*), surgeon, teacher of anatomy and surgery. Graduated medical department, University of Pennsylvania, 1838. Bought, 1852, and revived Philadelphia School of Anatomy where he acquired reputation of being an extremely able lecturer and demonstrator. Served during Civil War as surgeon in government hospitals and became an expert in gun-shot wounds. In 1870 he was appointed professor of clinical surgery, and in the following year professor of surgery, at University of Pennsylvania, retiring as professor emeritus in 1889. Noted as a consultant and author of *Treatise on the Principles and Practice of Surgery* (1878, 1881, 1883).

AGNEW, ELIZA (*b. New York, N.Y., 1807; d. Oodooville, Ceylon, 1883*), missionary to Ceylon, 1840–83, for American Board of Commissioners for Foreign Missions; pioneer in education of Ceylonese women.

AGNUS, FELIX (*b. Lyons, France, 1839; d. 1925*), Union soldier, newspaperman. Came to America, 1860; won Civil War brevet of brigadier-general. Managed and published *Baltimore American*, 1869–1920.

AGRAMONTE Y SIMONI, ARISTIDES (*b. Camaguey, Cuba, 1868; d. New Orleans, La., 1931*), pathologist, expert in tropical medicine. Took a conspicuous part in the work of the Reed Yellow Fever Board. [*Supp. 1*]

AIKEN, CHARLES AUGUSTUS (*b. Manchester, Vt., 1827; d. Princeton, N.J., 1892*), educator. Professor of Latin at Dartmouth, 1859–66, and Princeton, 1866–69; president of Union College, Schenectady, N.Y., 1869–71; professor, Christian ethics and apologetics at Princeton, 1871–92.

AIKEN, DAVID WYATT (*b. Winnsboro, S.C., 1828; d. 1887*), Confederate soldier, agricultural editor. Congressman, Democrat, from South Carolina, 1876–86; spokesman for militant agrarian interests.

AIKEN, GEORGE L. (*b. Boston, Mass., 1830; d. Jersey City, N.J., 1876*), actor and playwright. Wrote the original successful dramatization of Harriet Beecher Stowe's novel *Uncle Tom's Cabin* (1852).

AIKEN, WILLIAM (*b. Charleston, S.C., 1806; d. Flat Rock, N.C., 1887*), planter, statesman, philanthropist. Governor of South Carolina, 1844–46; representative in Congress, 1851–57; influenced important legislation through his position on leading committees and his acceptability to all Democratic factions.

AIKENS, ANDREW JACKSON (*b. Barnard, Vt., 1830; d. 1909*), editor, publisher. A founder of the Chicago and New York Newspaper Unions, ancestors of the present Western Newspaper Union.

AIME, VALCOUR (*b. St. Charles, La., 1798; d. St. James Parish, La., 1867*), sugar planter. Sugar was refined for first time in the United States at his refinery in St. James Parish. In 1829, Aime applied steam power to his machinery; he accepted new and superior processes as they appeared and was the leading advocate of the Rillieux apparatus. He experimented with cane planted at varying distances, early adopted fertilizers, used peas and clover on his land and urged Southern planters to diversify their crops to the point of complete self-sufficiency. Successful in overcoming losses suffered in Civil War, in later years he donated large sums of money to religious and educational institutions.

AINSLIE, HEW (*b. Bargeny Mains, Ayrshire, Scotland, 1792; d. Louisville, Ky., 1878*), poet. Came to America, 1822. Published *Scottish Songs, Ballads, and Poems* (1855).

AINSLIE, PETER (*b. Dunnsville, Va., 1867; d. Baltimore, Md., 1934*), Disciples of Christ minister; advocate of Christian unity. [*Supp. 1*]

AINSWORTH, FREDERICK CRAYTON (*b. Woodstock, Vt., 1852; d. Washington, D.C., 1934*), army officer. Chief of Record and Pension Office, War Department, 1892–1904; adjutant general until 1912. [*Supp. 1*]

AITKEN, ROBERT (*b. Dalkeith, Scotland, 1734; d. 1802*), printer, publisher, engraver. Issued at Philadelphia *Aitken's General American Register* (1773); published the *Pennsylvania Magazine* (1775–76) to which Thomas Paine, Francis Hopkinson and John Witherspoon were contributors. When the outbreak of the Revolution stopped the importation of English-printed Bibles, he undertook his greatest publishing enterprise, the first complete English Bible printed in America (1782). This venture was a financial failure despite congressional authorization and the support of religious organizations.

AKELEY, CARL ETHAN (*b. Clarendon, N.Y., 1864; d. Africa, 1926*), taxidermist, inventor, naturalist, explorer. Developed techniques for construction of habitat groups; collected specimens and made groups for Field Museum and the American Museum of Natural History; invented the Akeley Cement Gun and a motion-picture camera.

AKERMAN, AMOS TAPPAN (*b. Portsmouth, N.H., 1821; d. Cartersville, Ga., 1880*), lawyer, public official. Conservative Republican in postwar Georgia; member of Georgia state constitutional convention, 1868; U.S. attorney general, 1870–71.

AKERS, BENJAMIN PAUL (*b. Saccarappa, Maine, 1825; d. Philadelphia, Pa., 1861*), neo-classic sculptor. His best-known works: "Una and the Lion," "St. Elizabeth of Hungary" and the "Dead Pearl Diver."

AKERS, ELIZABETH CHASE (*b. Strong, Maine, 1832; d. Tuckahoe, N.Y., 1911*), writer. Wife of Benjamin P. Akers; author of "Rock Me to Sleep" (1860) and other minor verse.

AKO, MICHEL. [See Aco, Michel, *fl.* 1680–1702.]

ALARCÓN, HERNANDO DE (*fl.* 1540), Spanish explorer. When Coronado departed on his overland expedition in search of the Seven Cities of Cíbola, Alarcón was sent along the Mexican coast to provide sea support. He entered the Gulf of California and proceeded up the Colorado River attempting to establish contact with Coronado; failing, he returned to the Gulf. A second attempt took him up the Colorado to a point not far from the beginning of the Grand Canyon. A substantial achievement of Alarcón's expedition was a map of the Gulf of California drawn (1541) by his pilot. On this map the Gulf was shown to be a true one and not a passage; therefore California was not an island as had been suspected.

ALBEE, EDWARD FRANKLIN (*b. Machias, Maine, 1857; d. Palm Beach, Fla., 1930*), theatre manager and builder. Along with B. F. Keith, founded a vaudeville circuit and raised standards of popular entertainment.
[*Supp.* 1]

ALBEE, ERNEST (*b. Langdon, N.H., 1865; d. 1927*), philosopher. Instructor and professor of philosophy, Cornell University, 1892–1927; author of *The History of English Utilitarianism* (1902).

ALBRIGHT, JACOB (*b. Pottstown, Pa., 1759; d. 1808*), Methodist religious leader. Traveled through Pennsylvania, Maryland and Virginia, 1796–1808, preaching to German settlers.

ALBRO, LEWIS COLT (*b. Pittsfield, Mass., 1876; d. 1924*), architect. One of the best modern American domestic designers.

ALCORN, JAMES LUSK (*b. near Golconda, Ill., 1816; d. 1894*), lawyer. Raised in Kentucky. Served as Whig member of Mississippi senate, 1848–56; as representative, 1846, 1856, 1865; was author and foremost champion of the legislation establishing the levee system along the Mississippi River. Delegate to Mississippi secession convention, 1861. After the Civil War he entered the Republican party hoping to utilize the Negro vote in the best interests of the state. Elected governor of Mississippi, 1869; resigned two years later to enter U.S. Senate. As a senator, 1871–77, he urged the removal of the political disabilities of his people, resisted all efforts to enforce social equality by legislation, denounced the federal cotton tax and defended separate schools for both races in Mississippi.

ALCOTT, AMOS BRONSON (*b. near Wolcott, Conn., 1799; d. 1888*), educator, author, mystic. Held various teaching positions, 1823–33; although an able teacher he was unsuccessful because of his advanced educational and religious views. Opened a school in Boston, 1834; rightly suspected of encouraging independent thinking in religious matters, he lost pupils and the school failed. Moved to Concord, Mass., 1840; founded Fruitlands, a short-lived Utopian community, 1844–45. Appointed superintendent of Concord schools, 1859, he introduced some of his best educational innovations which included singing, calisthenics, and study of physiology, also a parent-teachers club. A writer of both verse and prose, he is best remembered for his association with Hawthorne, Emerson and Thoreau and for the extreme form of transcendental idealism which he cultivated and used as a guide for his own actions.

ALCOTT, LOUISA MAY (*b. Germantown, Pa., 1832; d. Boston, Mass., 1888*), author, daughter of Amos Bronson Alcott and Abigail (May) Alcott. She showed an early talent for literature, writing poems, plays and short stories; by 1860 her work began to be published in the *Atlantic Monthly*. Served as a hospital nurse during the Civil War. Visited Europe, 1865, and then returned to America where she became editor of a children's magazine, *Merry's Museum*, 1867. Her novel *Little Women* (1868, 1869), based on her own family life, brought great personal success, established her as a writer of books for children and enabled her to make her family financially independent. Among her other works are *Hospital Sketches* (1863), *An Old Fashioned Girl* (1870) and *Little Men* (1871).

ALCOTT, WILLIAM ANDRUS (*b. Wolcott, Conn., 1798; d. Newton, Mass., 1859*), educator, physician, pioneer in physical education. A cousin of Amos Bronson Alcott; wrote numerous works on educational reform and healthful living.

ALDEN, CYNTHIA MAY WESTOVER (*b. Afton, Iowa, 1862; d. 1931*), philanthropic promoter; founder and president of the International Sunshine Society.
[*Supp.* 1]

ALDEN, EBENEZER (*b. Randolph, Mass., 1788; d. Randolph, 1881*), medical historian, bibliophile and genealogist. Author of a history of the Massachusetts Medical Society (1838).

ALDEN, HENRY MILLS (*b. Mt. Tabor, Vt., 1836; d. New York, N.Y., 1919*), editor, author. Under his editorship, 1869–1919, *Harper's Magazine* became the most widely circulated American periodical of its type.

ALDEN, ICHABOD (*b. Duxbury, Mass., 1739; d. Cherry Valley, N.Y., 1778*). Revolutionary soldier. Appointed to command at Cherry Valley, he disregarded advance warnings and was killed in the Nov. 11, 1778 massacre by Tories and Indians under Walter Butler and Brant.

ALDEN, ISABELLA MACDONALD (*b. Rochester, N.Y., 1841; d. Palo Alto, Calif., 1930*), author. Editor and writer for Sunday-school periodicals; author of the "Pansy" books for young people. [*Supp.* 1]

ALDEN, JAMES (*b. Portland, Maine, 1810; d. San Francisco, Calif., 1877*), naval officer. Served in Wilkes Exploring Expedition, 1838–42. As captain of U.S.S. *Brooklyn* at Mobile Bay, his hesitation drew forth Farragut's famous "Damn the torpedoes!" remark.

ALDEN, JOHN (*b.* c. *1599; d. Duxbury, Mass., 1687*), one of the *Mayflower* Pilgrims; signer of *Mayflower* Compact. Removed from Plymouth to Duxbury, *c.* 1627. He held various public offices including: surveyor of highways; member of local committee for raising a force against the Indians; deputy from Duxbury, *c.* 1641 to 1649; member of local council of war, 1675; member of colony's council of war in 1646, 1653, 1658 and 1667; treasurer, 1656–58; governor's assistant, Jan. 1, 1632/33 through 1640–41, and again in 1650–86. He was "deputy governor" in 1664–65, also in 1677 following King Philip's War. Married Priscilla Mullens (or Molines). The famous story used by Longfellow in the *Courtship of Miles Standish* is without foundation.

ALDEN, JOHN FERRIS (*b. Cohoes, N.Y., 1852; d. 1917*), civil engineer. Directed Rochester Bridge & Iron Works, 1885–1901; built many railroad bridges in United States and Canada.

ALDEN, JOSEPH (*b. Cairo, N. Y., 1807; d. 1885*), educator. Taught at Williams College, 1835–52; at Lafayette College, 1852–57. President of Jefferson College, 1857–62; principal of State Normal School, Albany, 1867–82.

ALDEN, RAYMOND MACDONALD (*b. New Hartford, N.Y., 1873; d. Philadelphia, Pa., 1924*), philologist. Edited variorum edition of *The Sonnets of Shakespeare* (1916).

ALDEN, TIMOTHY (*b. Yarmouth, Mass., 1771; d. Pittsburgh, Pa., 1839*), Congregational clergyman, college president, antiquarian. Graduated Harvard, 1794; founded Allegheny College, 1817. Author of *A Collection of American Epitaphs* (1814).

ALDEN, WILLIAM LIVINGSTON (*b. Williamstown, Mass., 1837; d. Buffalo, N.Y., 1908*), journalist. Introduced the sport of canoeing to America.

ALDERMAN, EDWIN ANDERSON (*b. Wilmington, N.C., 1861; d. 1931*), educator and orator. Leader in the field of popular education; outstanding president of University of Virginia, 1904–31. [*Supp.* 1]

ALDRICH, CHESTER HOLMES (*b. Providence, R.I., 1871; d. Rome, Italy, 1940*), architect. Partner in Delano & Aldrich; director, American Academy in Rome, 1935–40. [*Supp.* 2]

ALDRICH, EDGAR (*b. Pittsburg, N.H., 1848; d. 1921*), jurist. U.S. district judge of New Hampshire, 1891–1921; appointed Master in the litigation involving Mary Baker Eddy, 1907.

ALDRICH, LOUIS (*b. Ohio, 1843; d. Kennebunkport, Maine, 1901*), actor. Versatile in support of E. Forrest, E. Booth and C. Cushman; had greatest success as Joe Saunders in Bartley Campbell's *My Partner,* 1879–85.

ALDRICH, NELSON WILMARTH (*b. Foster, R.I., 1841; d. 1915*), statesman, financier. Achieved early success in business; married Abby Chapman, 1866. Elected to Congress, 1878, 1880; made an independent campaign for the Rhode Island seat left vacant by death of Gen. Burnside and entered the U.S. Senate, 1881. Soon became identified with a small group of Republican senatorial leaders who, like himself, could act independently without fear of losing their constituencies. A protectionist and spokesman for business, he challenged the Mills Bill and brought forward a counter-proposal, 1888; in 1890 he was concerned with the Silver Purchase Act, the Anti-Trust Act, the Force Act, and the McKinley Tariff. In 1892, a time of great Democratic victories, he and a few other successful Republican senators obtained control of their party's power in the upper house. Four years later, when the Republican party regained strength, the coterie—called the "Big Four" and composed of Aldrich, Allison of Iowa, Platt of Connecticut and Spooner of Wisconsin—acting with almost complete unanimity dominated the Senate until Platt's death in 1905. Aldrich's association with the Dingley Tariff of 1897 gave him a popular reputation as the protectionist senator *par excellence;* however, his true aims were the maintenance of the *status quo,* the unification of his party and the preparation of important legislation necessary to resolve impending monetary problems. The following year, the "Four" struggled hard to prevent war with Spain, reluctantly accepted McKinley's reversal of policy and then gave obligatory support to the war. Theodore Roosevelt's accession to the presidency did not alter the influence of the "Four" who supported his program in Congress and advised him on matters regarding Cuba. In 1902 Aldrich and his group met with Roosevelt and determined the official position of the party in the approaching elections; yet, within two years, Roosevelt's defiance of the Senate transformed Aldrich into the leader of the opposition. The Aldrich-Roosevelt political duel centered about Roosevelt's attempts to control foreign policy without seeking the Senate's advice and his approval of the Hepburn Rate Bill (1906), a bill giving extensive railway rate-fixing powers to the Interstate Commerce Commission.

In 1908, after contributing to Taft's nomination, Aldrich went abroad to make a thorough study of modern banking as chairman of the National Monetary Commission, which had been established by the Aldrich-Vreeland Act, an emergency measure made necessary by the panic of 1907. He returned to America determined to introduce important and extensive changes in the existing banking system; instead he faced another tariff battle in Congress. Certain Western Republicans, including La Follette, formed a *bloc* whose aim was not a reduction of the tariff but a rearrangement of rates which would favor their sectional interests. Eastern senators opposed these insurgents; their differences were forcibly resolved in the Payne-Aldrich Tariff, 1909. His dominant position challenged and rendered untenable by the Republican insurgents, Aldrich ended his senatorial career in 1911. The Aldrich Plan, a scheme for banking reform, was the principal interest of his remaining years. Possessed of great skill as a parliamentarian, Aldrich was a superb judge of human nature in individual instances but defective in assessing mass psychology.

ALDRICH, RICHARD (*b. Providence, R.I., 1863; d. Rome, Italy, 1937*), principal music critic of the *New York Times*, 1902–23. [*Supp.* 2]

ALDRICH, THOMAS BAILEY (*b. Portsmouth, N.H., 1836; d. 1907*), poet, writer of fiction, editor. Held numerous editorial positions in New York, 1856–61; war correspondent, 1861–62; moved to Boston, 1865, as editor of *Every Saturday;* made acquaintance of Longfellow, Lowell, Holmes, Hawthorne and Whittier. Editor of the *Atlantic Monthly*, 1881–90. His best prose work is *The Story of a Bad Boy* (1870). His short stories, notably *Marjorie Daw* (1873), are superior to his longer fiction. Aldrich's poetry is marked by technical skill and polish but is minor in range.

ALDRIDGE, IRA FREDERICK (*b. New York, N.Y.?, 1807; d. Lodz, Poland, 1867*), tragedian. A Negro, and a protegé of Edmund Kean, he was considered one of the ablest interpreters of Shakespeare of his day both in England and on the Continent.

ALEMANY, JOSÉ SADOC (*b. Vich, Spain, 1814; d. Spain, 1888*), Roman Catholic clergyman, Dominican missionary. Came to America, 1841; consecrated bishop of Monterey, 1850. Was exemplary bishop and archbishop of San Francisco, 1853–84.

ALEXANDER, ABRAHAM (*b. 1717; d. 1786*), Revolutionary patriot. As member of the Committee for Safety, Mecklenburg Co., N.C., he presided over the meeting at Charlotte, May 31, 1775, whose resolutions called for creation of a county government independent of England.

ALEXANDER, ARCHIBALD (*b. Lexington, Va., 1772; d. 1851*), Presbyterian clergyman, educator, author. First professor at theological seminary in Princeton; held chair of theology, 1812–51.

ALEXANDER, BARTON STONE (*b. Nicholas Co., Ky., 1819; d. 1878*), Union soldier, engineer. Graduated West Point, 1842; a principal agent in planning and constructing defenses of Washington City, 1861–65.

ALEXANDER, DE ALVA STANWOOD (*b. Richmond, Maine, 1845; d. 1925*), Republican representative from New York, historian. Author of *Political History of the State of New York* (1906, 1909, 1923).

ALEXANDER, EDWARD PORTER (*b. Washington, Ga., 1835; d. 1910*), Confederate artillerist, author, railroad executive. Graduated West Point, 1857. As army engineer, aided in development of the breech-loading rifle and the "wig-wag" signaling system. At Georgia's secession he resigned his commission and served in Confederate signal service and ordnance. Appointed November 1862 to command of a battalion of artillery in Longstreet's corps, he participated in battles of Fredericksburg, Chancellorsville, and Gettysburg. Accompanied Longstreet to Georgia, then to Knoxville and the Tennessee mountains; made brigadier-general, 1864, and served with Lee's army until surrender, 1865. After the war Alexander held important positions in the railroad industry. His comprehensive and important *Military Memoirs of a Confederate* appeared in 1907.

ALEXANDER, FRANCIS (*b. Killingly, Conn., 1800; d. Florence, Italy ?, c. 1881*), painter, lithographer. A popular portraitist in Boston, 1832–1860.

ALEXANDER, GROSS (*b. Scottsville, Ky., 1852; d. Long Beach, Calif., 1915*), Methodist clergyman. Professor of Greek, Vanderbilt University, 1884–1902; editor of Methodist publications.

ALEXANDER, HARTLEY BURR (*b. Lincoln, Nebr., 1873; d. Claremont, Calif., 1939*), philosopher, anthropologist; special interest in mythology of the American Indian. Taught at University of Nebraska and Scripps College. [*Supp.* 2]

ALEXANDER, JAMES (*b. Scotland, 1691; d. Albany, N.Y., 1756*), lawyer, politician, statesman. Fled to America in consequence of involvement with the Rebellion of 1715; studied and practiced law. Made member of the New York Council, 1721, and in 1723, of the New Jersey Council; attorney-general of New Jersey, 1723–27. An active opponent of Gov. Cosby's arbitrary rule, he was dismissed from Council of New York, 1732, and in 1735 removed from Council of New Jersey. His greatest prominence was attained in 1735 when he, with William Smith, volunteered to serve as counsel to the printer and publisher John Peter Zenger. In course of Zenger's trial, both were declared in contempt and stricken from the roll of attorneys. Reinstated as a member of the bar, Alexander was recalled to both Councils on Cosby's death, and from 1736–56 was active in both capacities. He died at Albany while opposing legislation he considered oppressive to the people of the colony.

ALEXANDER, JOHN HENRY (*b. Annapolis, Md., 1812; d. 1867*), geologist, coal-mining executive. Author of *A Universal Dictionary of Weights and Measures, Ancient and Modern* (1850).

ALEXANDER, JOHN WHITE (*b. Allegheny, Pa., 1856; d. 1915*), painter. Began his career as an illustrator for *Harper's*, 1874; studied in France, Germany and Italy. Primarily a portraitist, his output was distinguished and prodigious. He also painted landscapes and was chosen to paint the murals around the grand staircase of the Carnegie Institute, Pittsburgh. He gave long and devoted service as an officer in art societies both at home and abroad.

ALEXANDER, JOSEPH ADDISON (*b. Philadelphia, Pa., 1809; d. 1860*), educator, linguist, author. Son of Archibald Alexander (1772–1851). Instructor and professor of Biblical language and literature, Princeton Seminary, 1834–60; editor of *Biblical Repertory* and author of several Biblical commentaries.

ALEXANDER, SAMUEL DAVIES (*b. Princeton, N.J., 1819; d. New York, N.Y., 1894*), Presbyterian clergyman, author. Son of Archibald Alexander (1772–1851). Graduated Princeton Seminary, 1847; pastor of Fifteenth Street Church of New York, 1856–89.

ALEXANDER, STEPHEN (*b. Schenectady, N.Y., 1806; d. 1883*), astronomer. Associated with Joseph Henry, 1830–32; professor of astronomy at Princeton, 1834–77, and author of astronomical works.

ALEXANDER, WILLIAM (*b. New York, N.Y., 1726; d. 1783*), Revolutionary soldier, better known as Lord Stirling; son of James Alexander (1691–1756). Wealthy and socially prominent, he was surveyor-general of New Jersey, member of the Council and assistant to the governor. Active in the popular cause, on the outbreak of the Revolution he was commissioned brigadier-general with chief command of New York City and directed building of defensive fortifications. Commended for brave leadership during battle of Long Island, Aug. 27, 1776, he participated in battle of Trenton and was promoted to major-general early in 1777. He led a division at Brandywine and held his last important battle command at Monmouth. His talent for organization and his energetic yet prudent character made him highly esteemed in the Continental army.

ALEXANDER, WILLIAM DEWITT (*b. Honolulu, Hawaii, 1833; d. Honolulu, 1913*), historian, geographer. Graduated Yale University, 1855. One of Hawaii's ablest scholars, he wrote *Brief History of the Hawaiian People* (1891) and a history of the revolution of 1893.

ALFONCE (ALFONSE), JEAN. [See ALLEFONSCE, JEAN, c. 1482–1557.]

ALGER, CYRUS (*b. Bridgewater, Mass., 1781; d. 1856*), iron-master, inventor. Established an iron foundry in South Boston, 1809; achieved financial success through government ammunition contracts during War of 1812 and through bold real-estate speculation, especially in development of South Boston. By 1827 his was the largest and best-equipped iron works in the United States. Widely known as an inventor, he designed the first cylinder stoves in 1822, held several patents for cast-iron articles and produced the first rifled gun in 1834. He perfected a process for strengthening cast-iron, improved reverberatory furnaces and turned out the first perfect brass cannon ever made for the American government. Active in Boston politics, he was a member of the common council, 1822, and served as alderman, 1824, 1827.

ALGER, HORATIO (*b. Revere, Mass., 1832; d. Natick, Mass., 1899*), successful writer of boys' stories. Graduated Harvard Divinity School, 1860. Accepted post as minister but resigned in 1866 and moved to New York to establish a literary career. Through his charitable interest in the Newsboys' Lodging House, he obtained a detailed knowledge of the life of street urchins and then sentimentalized and idealized that life in his very popular novels, *Ragged Dick* (1867), *Luck and Pluck* (1869), *Tattered Tom* (1871) and many others. His books, preaching the philosophy that virtue is always rewarded with wealth, have left a deeper mark on the American character than the works of many a greater mind.

ALGER, RUSSELL ALEXANDER (*b. Ohio, 1836; d. 1907*), lumber dealer, Union soldier. Elected Republican governor of Michigan, 1884; chosen commander of Grand Army of the Republic, 1889. Served as secretary of war, March 1897 to July 1899, and resigned at McKinley's request after a tenure marked by mismanagement.

ALGER, WILLIAM ROUNSEVILLE (*b. Freetown, Mass., 1822; d. 1905*), Unitarian clergyman. Graduated Harvard Divinity School, 1847. Wrote *Critical History of the Doctrine of a Future Life* (1864) and other works.

ALISON, FRANCIS (*b. Leck, Ireland, 1705; d. Philadelphia, Pa., 1779*), Presbyterian clergyman, educator. Emigrated to America, 1735. Taught at Philadelphia Latin Academy, 1752–79; regarded by contemporaries as America's greatest classical scholar.

ALLAIRE, JAMES PETER (*b. New Rochelle, N.Y., 1785; d. 1858*), master mechanic, engine builder. Founded first steam-engine works in New York City, 1816; leading manufacturer of steam-boat engines.

ALLAN, JOHN (*b. Edinburgh Castle, Scotland, 1746/7; d. Lubec Mills, Maine, 1805*), Revolutionary soldier. Member of provincial Assembly, Nova Scotia, 1770–76. Forced to leave Nova Scotia because of his opposition to British government, he settled in Machias, Maine. In 1777, the Continental Congress appointed him agent to the Eastern Indians whose friendship he secured for the American cause.

ALLEFONSCE, JEAN (*b. Saintonge, France, c. 1482; d. c. 1557*), French navigator, chief pilot of Roberval's expedition, 1542. In search of a western passage to Cathay, he may have ascended the St. Lawrence River to the Saguenay.

ALLEN, ALEXANDER VIETS GRISWOLD (*b. Otis, Mass., 1841; d. Cambridge, Mass., 1908*), Episcopal clergyman. His *Continuity of Christian Thought* (1884) emphasized the contributions of the Greek theologians.

ALLEN, ANDREW (*b. Philadelphia, Pa., 1740; d. London, England, 1825*), lawyer, Pennsylvania official, Loyalist. Son of William Allen (1704–1780).

ALLEN, ANTHONY BENEZET (*b. Hampshire Co., Mass., 1802; d. Flushing, N.Y., 1892*), farmer, writer, manufacturer and dealer in farm machinery. Founded the *American Agriculturist*, 1842; made and popularized improved mowers, plows and reapers.

ALLEN, CHARLES (*b. Greenfield, Mass., 1827; d. Boston, Mass., 1913*), jurist. Attorney-general of Massachusetts, 1867–72; associate justice of supreme court, Massachusetts, 1882–98.

ALLEN, DAVID OLIVER (*b. Barre, Mass., 1799; d. Lowell, Mass., 1863*), Congregational missionary to India, 1827–53; worked on translation of the Scriptures into the Marathi language.

ALLEN, ELISHA HUNT (*b. 1804; d. Washington, D.C., 1883*), Whig representative from Maine, diplomat. American consul at Honolulu; held important cabinet posts in the Hawaiian government, 1857–76.

ALLEN, ELIZABETH CHASE AKERS. [See Akers, Elizabeth Chase, 1832–1911.]

ALLEN, ETHAN (*b. Litchfield, Conn., 1737/8; d. Burlington, Vt., 1789*), Revolutionary soldier, author. Residing, 1769, in New Hampshire Grants (present state of Vermont), he became involved in the dispute between New York and New Hampshire for its control and commanded Green Mountain Boys, 1770–75. Aided in capture of Fort Ticonderoga, 1775, and was imprisoned by British when taken during the 1775 expedition against Canada. Upon his release, 1778, he was active in local affairs in Vermont and unsuccessfully presented its claim for separate status to Continental Congress. Together with his brothers Ira and Levi Allen, he was implicated in a 1780–83 attempt to negotiate a separate treaty with Britain, favorable to Vermont. Allen was author of a narrative of his captivity (1779), several pamphlets on Vermont's claims, and a defense of free-thinking in religion.

ALLEN, FREDERIC DE FOREST (*b. Oberlin, O., 1844; d. 1897*), classical scholar. Professor of classical philology, Harvard, 1880–97; director of American School of Classical Studies at Athens, 1885–86; author of *Remnants of Early Latin* (1880).

ALLEN, GEORGE (*b. Milton, Vt., 1808; d. Philadelphia, Pa., 1876*), educator, Episcopal clergyman, author. Professor of languages, Delaware College, 1837–45; professor of Latin and Greek, University of Pennsylvania, 1845–76.

ALLEN, HARRISON (*b. Philadelphia, Pa., 1841; d. 1897*), anatomist, physician. A pioneer American laryngologist, his most original contributions were made to the study of comparative anatomy. He held professorships at University of Pennsylvania medical school *post* 1865.

ALLEN, HENRY TUREMAN (*b. Sharpsburg, Ky., 1859; d. Buena Vista Spring, Pa., 1930*), soldier. Organized and led Philippine Constabulary; tactful and brilliant commander of American occupation forces in Germany, 1919–23. [*Supp. 1*]

ALLEN, HENRY WATKINS (*b. Prince Edward Co., Va., 1820; d. Mexico City, Mexico, 1866*), Confederate soldier, lawyer, sugar planter. Raised in Missouri, he volunteered for Texas army, 1842, settling thereafter in Mississippi and Louisiana as a lawyer and planter. As colonel of the 4th Louisiana, he distinguished himself at Shiloh and in defense of Vicksburg, and was incapacitated for field duty by wounds received at Baton Rouge. Elected governor of Louisiana, 1864, he established a system of state stores, factories and foundries and restored the state's fallen industry and commerce. After Lee's surrender he saved Louisiana from invasion by negotiating surrender of the strong Confederate forces west of the Mississippi. Allen was the single great administrator produced by the Confederacy.

ALLEN, HORATIO (*b. Schenectady, N.Y., 1802; d. near South Orange, N.J., 1899*), civil engineer, inventor. Graduated Columbia College, 1823. While resident engineer to Delaware and Hudson canal company, 1828, he was sent to England to purchase the first steam locomotives to be used in America (Honesdale, Pa., 1829). As chief engineer, South Carolina Railroad Co., he directed construction of "Best Friend," the first locomotive built for sale in the United States. Appointed assistant principal engineer of the Croton Aqueduct, 1838, he was also consulting engineer to New York & Erie Railroad Co. and a proprietor of Stillman, Allen & Co., specializing in building marine engines. He retired in 1870 but was consulted in planning of Brooklyn Bridge and Panama Railroad.

ALLEN, IRA (*b. Cornwall, Conn., 1751; d. Philadelphia, Pa., 1814*), political leader, brother of Ethan Allen. Delegate to Windsor Convention and aided in drafting constitution of Vermont, 1777; served as secretary of the Council of Safety, member of Governor's Council, first state treasurer and as representative in negotiations for Vermont's independence. Hoping to force the Continental Congress to recognize Vermont, he joined his brothers in moves to effect separate peace with Britain, 1780–83.

ALLEN, JAMES LANE (*b. near Lexington, Ky., 1849; d. 1925*), novelist, short-story writer. Popularized Blue Grass region of Kentucky in *Flute and Violin* (1891), *A Kentucky Cardinal* (1894), *Aftermath* (1895) and other works.

ALLEN, JEREMIAH MERVIN (*b. Enfield, Conn., 1833; d. Hartford, Conn., 1903*), engineer, pioneer in steam-boiler insurance. Managed, 1867–1903, first company organized to inspect steam-boilers and insure their owners against explosion damage.

ALLEN, JOEL ASAPH (*b. near Springfield, Mass., 1838; d. 1921*), zoologist, author. Curator of birds, Harvard Museum of Comparative Zoology, 1867–85;

headed department of birds and mammals, American Museum of Natural History, 1885–1921.

ALLEN, JOHN (*b. Broome Co., N.Y., 1810; d. Plainfield, N.J., 1892*), dentist. Invented a superior artificial denture, the "continuous gum" type, patented 1851.

ALLEN, JOHN F. (*b. England, 1829; d. New York, N.Y., 1900*), engineer, inventor. Came to America as a boy. Aided in development of the Porter-Allen engine, a pioneer high-speed steam engine, and of pneumatic riveting devices.

ALLEN, JOHN JAMES (*b. Woodstock, Va., 1797; d. Botetourt Co., Va., 1871*), jurist. Judge of Virginia court of appeals, 1840–65.

ALLEN, JOSEPH HENRY (*b. Northboro, Mass., 1820; d. Cambridge, Mass., 1898*), Unitarian clergyman. Author with J.B. Greenough of several popular Latin manuals.

ALLEN, LEWIS FALLEY (*b. Westfield, Mass., 1800; d. Buffalo, N.Y., 1890*), stock breeder, farm writer. Founder and editor of *American Shorthorn Herdbook.*

ALLEN, NATHAN (*b. Princeton, Mass., 1813; d. Lowell, Mass., 1889*), physician. Attempted to establish a general law of propagation applicable to all organic life.

ALLEN, NATHAN H. (*b. Marion, Mass., 1848; d. 1925*), musician, composer. Organist at First Church, Hartford, Conn., 1883–1906; composer of songs, cantatas and organ works.

ALLEN, PAUL (*b. Providence, R.I., 1775; d. Baltimore, Md., 1826*), editor, poet. Published *Original Poems, Serious and Entertaining* (1801); editor (with Nicholas Biddle) of the *History of the Expedition under the Command of Captains Lewis and Clark* (1814).

ALLEN, PHILIP (*b. Providence, R.I., 1785; d. 1865*), textile manufacturer. Governor of Rhode Island, 1851–53, he gained control of state Democratic party machinery after struggle with Thomas Dorr. He served as U.S. senator, 1853–59.

ALLEN, RICHARD (*b. Philadelphia, Pa., 1760; d. 1831*), founder and first bishop, 1816, of African Methodist Episcopal Church.

ALLEN, RICHARD LAMB (*b. Westfield, Mass., 1803; d. Stockholm, Sweden, 1869*), agriculturist, editor, manufacturer. Brother of Anthony B. and Lewis F. Allen. Co-founder of *American Agriculturist,* 1842; manufacturer of agricultural implements and author of agricultural handbooks.

ALLEN, ROBERT (*b. Ohio, 1812; d. Geneva, Switzerland, 1886*), Union soldier. Graduated West Point, 1836; able and honest chief quartermaster for the armies in the West, 1861–65.

ALLEN, THOMAS (*b. Pittsfield, Mass., 1813; d. Washington, D.C., 1882*), railroad builder. A prime mover in the National Railroad Convention at St. Louis, Mo., 1849, and in initiation of policy of state loans to railroads. President, Pacific Railroad, 1851–54. As partner in Allen, Copp and Nisbet, financed early railroads in Missouri and Illinois.

ALLEN, THOMAS M. (*b. Shenandoah [now Warren] Co., Va., 1797; d. 1871*). Pioneer minister of Disciples of Christ in Kentucky and Missouri.

ALLEN, TIMOTHY FIELD (*b. Westminster, Vt., 1837; d. New York, N.Y., 1902*), physician, botanist. His practice and writings contributed largely to establishment of homeopathic medicine; dean of New York Homeopathic Medical College, 1882–93.

ALLEN, WILLIAM (*b. Philadelphia, Pa., 1704; d. 1780*), merchant, jurist. Chief justice of Pennsylvania, 1750–74; benefactor of educational and civic enterprises in Pennsylvania; founder of Allentown. Retired to England on failure of his plan for reconciliation, 1774.

ALLEN, WILLIAM (*b. Pittsfield, Mass., 1784; d. 1868*), Congregationalist clergyman, educator, author. Compiled *American Biographical and Historical Dictionary* (1809), earliest of its kind; president of Bowdoin College, 1819–31, 1833–38.

ALLEN, WILLIAM (*b. Edenton, N.C., 1803; d. near Chillicothe, O., 1879*), Ohio lawyer. An ardent expansionist Democrat, he served in Congress from Ohio, 1833–35, 1837–49; was Democratic governor of Ohio, 1874–76.

ALLEN, WILLIAM FRANCIS (*b. Northboro, Mass., 1830; d. 1889*), classical scholar. Professor of ancient languages and history, University of Wisconsin, 1867–89; author of *Short History of the Roman People* (1890) and co-author with his brother Joseph H. Allen of the "Allen and Greenough" Latin text series.

ALLEN, WILLIAM FREDERICK (*b. Bordentown, N.J., 1846; d. 1915*), railroad expert. His most important work was in adoption of standard time for railways. Acting as secretary and treasurer of the General Time Convention and the later American Railway Association, 1875–1915, he devised a plan for reduction of the fifty existing time standards to four time zones which was officially recognized on Nov. 18, 1883.

ALLEN, WILLIAM HENRY (*b. Providence, R.I., 1784; d. 1813*), naval officer. Served on frigates *Chesapeake* and *United States,* 1807–12; received command of sloop-of-war *Argus,* 1813; killed in action with H.M.S. *Pelican.*

ALLEN, WILLIAM HENRY (*b. Manchester, Maine, 1808; d. 1882*), educator. Graduated Bowdoin, 1833; professor, Dickinson College, 1836–46; president of Girard College, 1849–62, 1867–82, and of Pennsylvania Agricultural College, 1865–67.

ALLEN, WILLIAM JOSHUA (*b. Wilson Co., Tenn., 1829; d. Hot Springs, Ark., 1901*), jurist, lawyer. Removed to Illinois, 1830; active in movement to separate southern Illinois from the Union in 1862. U.S. district judge for southern Illinois, 1887–1901.

ALLEN, WILLIAM VINCENT (*b. Midway, O., 1847; d. Madison, Nebr., 1924*), lawyer. Acclaimed "the intellectual giant of Populism," he served as U.S. senator from Nebraska, 1893–1901.

ALLEN, YOUNG JOHN (*b. Burke Co., Ga., 1836; d. Shanghai, China, 1907*), Methodist missionary to China, 1859–1907.

ALLEN, ZACHARIAH (*b. Providence, R.I., 1795; d. Providence, 1882*), inventor, author, reformer. Invented centrifugal ball governor for steam engines, 1834, and many other devices, including leather-belt power transmission and central heating by hot air. Promoted free education for working people and wrote numerous popular scientific works.

ALLERTON, ISAAC (*b. England, c. 1586; d. New Haven, Conn., 1658/9*), Pilgrim father, trader. Arrived in Plymouth on the *Mayflower*, 1620; served as assistant to Gov. Bradford, 1621–24, and in 1625 was requested to negotiate with merchant-financiers who no longer wished to support the colony. In successive trips to England, he reached a settlement, 1626, for repayment of the original expense of equipping the colony; borrowed money to purchase much-needed supplies; arranged for the emigration of the remainder of the Leyden congregation, 1629; interested a new group of English merchants in the venture, and secured the Patent of 1630 which at last gave the Pilgrims a title to their lands and property. He then purchased a large consignment of trading goods without the colony's authorization, doubled their indebtedness, and lost his position as agent, 1631. After he left Plymouth, his private trading ventures with Virginia, the West Indies, and Manhattan made him a wealthy man.

ALLERTON, SAMUEL WATERS (*b. Amenia Union, N.Y., 1828; d. South Pasadena, Calif., 1914*), capitalist. Engaged in small livestock ventures, 1852–59. In 1860 he moved to Chicago, Ill., and made his formal and profitable entrance into the business world by cornering the pork market. Considered one of the founders of modern Chicago, he was the chief factor in organizing the First National Bank of Chicago, 1863; began the movement for the successful establishment of a union stockyard, 1865–66; and brought about the adoption of the street-railway cable car, 1880–82. Founder and president of the Allerton Packing Co., he invested his rapidly growing fortune in the stockyards of Pittsburgh, Baltimore, and Jersey City, and in large tracts of Western farm lands.

ALLIBONE, SAMUEL AUSTIN (*b. Philadelphia, Pa., 1816; d. Lucerne, Switzerland, 1889*), lexicographer, librarian. Author of *A Critical Dictionary of English Literature* (1858, 1871); cataloguer of the Lenox Library, New York City.

ALLINE, HENRY (*b. Newport, R.I., 1748; d. North Hampton, N.H., 1784*), revivalist. Migrated to Nova Scotia, 1760. A self-taught itinerant preacher, he has been called "the Whitefield of Nova Scotia."

ALLINSON, ANNE CROSBY EMERY (*b. Ellsworth, Maine, 1871; d. Hancock Point, Maine, 1932*), educator and writer. Classicist; dean of women at Wisconsin and Brown Universities. [*Supp. 1*]

ALLINSON, FRANCIS GREENLEAF (*b. Burlington, N.J., 1856; d. Hancock Point, Maine, 1931*), classicist. Professor of Greek at Brown University; translator of Menander. [*Supp. 1*]

ALLIS, EDWARD PHELPS (*b. Cazenovia, N.Y., 1824; d. 1889*), manufacturer. Established the Reliance Iron Works in Milwaukee, Wis., 1861, later the Allis Co., manufacturers of heavy machinery and steam engines.

ALLISON, NATHANIEL (*b. Webster Co., Mo., 1876; d. La Jolla, Calif., 1932*), orthopedic surgeon, professor of surgery. Devised standard splints and dressings for army, 1917. [*Supp. 1*]

ALLISON, RICHARD (*b. Orange Co., N.Y., 1757; d. Cincinnati, O., 1816*), army medical officer. Head of army medical service in the 1790's; leading practitioner of Cincinnati, O., post 1805. [*Supp. 1*]

ALLISON, WILLIAM BOYD (*b. Perry Township, O., 1829; d. 1908*), Republican political leader. Removed to Dubuque, Iowa, c. 1857, and entered practice of law there. Congressman from Iowa, 1862–70, when his views on the currency issue and the wool and iron tariff schedules marked him as a moderationist who could balance both party and sectional loyalties. His entanglement with J. G. Blaine in railroad construction jobbery did him no permanent political harm. Capable of uniting opposing groups, he served in the U.S. Senate, 1872–1908, holding the chairmanships of Appropriations, 1881–1908, and of the caucus, 1897–1908. His associate Nelson Aldrich described his special ability in calling him "a master of the arts of conciliation and construction." As a senior senator he declined cabinet offers and worked to strengthen his own political influence as a party harmonizer and manipulator.

ALLOEZ (ALLOUES), CLAUDE JEAN. [See ALLOUEZ, CLAUDE JEAN, 1622–1689.]

ALLOUEZ, CLAUDE JEAN (*b. Saint-Didier, Haute Loire, France, 1622; d. near the present Niles, Mich., 1689*), Jesuit missionary. Ordained priest, 1655; in 1658 went to Canada. Appointed vicar general, 1663, for all traders and natives of the Northwest, he visited tribes in that territory, regulated the relations of traders with natives and opened new missions. He traveled extensively amongst the Indians of the Lakes Superior and Nipigon regions, 1665–67. On other Western journeys he visited Green Bay, Lake Winnebago and the site of present Oshkosh; he founded a mission at De Pere (Wis.) in 1671. Upon Marquette's death in 1675, Allouez was ordered to continue his work among the Illinois; except for one trip to Green Bay, he spent the remainder of his life in Illinois country.

ALLSTON, ROBERT FRANCIS WITHERS (*b. All Saints' Parish, S.C., 1801; d. 1864*), South Carolina planter. Graduated West Point, 1821. Served as state senator, 1833–56, and as governor, 1856–58; outstanding as a scientific agriculturist.

ALLSTON, WASHINGTON (*b. South Carolina, 1779; d. Cambridge, Mass., 1843*), artist, author. Studied painting under Benjamin West, Royal Academy, London, 1801–03; went on an artistic tour of the Continent, 1803–08, and while in Italy established friendships with Coleridge and Washington Irving. After a short return trip to America, 1808–10, he settled in England where he produced his greatest painting, "Dead Man Revived by Touching the Bones of the Prophet Elisha." His career interrupted by illness, he issued a volume of verse, *The Sylphs of the Seasons* (1813), painted Coleridge's portrait and resumed artistic productivity with "Uriel in the Sun" and "Jacob's Ladder." In 1818 financial reverses forced a return to America, where his artistic career terminated abruptly despite the efforts of friends who commissioned a vast "Belshazzar's Feast," still uncompleted at his death.

ALLYN, ROBERT (*b. Ledyard, Conn., 1817; d. 1894*), educator. Held numerous educational posts including presidency of Wesleyan Female Academy, McKendree College and Southern Illinois State University.

ALMY, JOHN JAY (*b. Newport, R.I., 1815; d. Washington, D.C., 1895*), naval officer. During Civil War, commanded cruiser blockading Confederate ports; retired in 1877 after performing longest service at sea of any officer since founding of the navy.

ALOES (ALOUES), CLAUDE JEAN. [See ALLOUEZ, CLAUDE JEAN, 1622–1689.]

ALPHONCE (ALPHONSE), JEAN. [See ALLEFONSCE, JEAN, c. 1482–c. 1557.]

ALPHONSA, MOTHER (*b. Lenox, Mass., 1851; d. 1926*), philanthropist, religious superior. Born Rose Hawthorne, youngest daughter of Nathaniel Hawthorne; married G. P. Lathrop, 1871; converted to the Roman Catholic faith, 1891. Inheriting rich literary and cultural traditions from her parents, she published some verse, several short sketches and *Memories of Hawthorne* (1897). *Post* 1896, she devoted her life to the care of cancer patients, founding the order

of nuns known as the Servants of Relief for Incurable Cancer.

ALSOP, GEORGE (*b. England, 1638*). Author of *A Character of the Province of Mary-Land* (London, 1666), an enthusiastic and exaggerated account of that colony.

ALSOP, RICHARD (*b. Middletown, Conn., 1761; d. Flatbush, N.Y., 1815*), satirist, poet. One of the "Hartford Wits," best known for his anti-Republican political satires *The Echo* (1791–1805; 1807) and *The Political Greenhouse* (1799).

ALSTON, JOSEPH (*b. All Saints' Parish, S.C., c. 1779; d. 1816*), lawyer, planter, legislator. Married Theodosia Burr, 1801, and was involved in the Burr Conspiracy, 1806. Governor of South Carolina, 1812–14.

ALSTON, THEODOSIA (BURR). [See BURR, THEODOSIA, 1783–1813.]

ALTER, DAVID (*b. Westmoreland Co., Pa., 1807; d. 1881*), physician, physicist. Among his many minor inventions and discoveries were a successful electric clock, a method of purifying bromine and a model electric locomotive. Of greater importance were his deflecting-needle electric telegraph, 1836, and his method of obtaining coal-oil from coal. His most important work was done in connection with spectrum analysis. Independently and almost simultaneously he and Angstrom published what has come to be known as Kirchhoff's Second Law. Alter's discovery, appearing in an American journal, did not receive full recognition, but there is no evidence for those who charge Kirchhoff with theft of Alter's ideas.

ALTGELD, JOHN PETER (*b. Nieder Selters, Germany, 1847; d. 1902*), lawyer, political leader, reformer. Brought to United States in infancy. Elected to superior court, Cook Co. (Chicago), Ill., 1886, resigned as chief justice, 1891; elected Democratic governor of Illinois, 1892. In 1893, after studying the appeals of four men under conviction of complicity in the murders during the Chicago Haymarket Riot of 1886, he issued pardons on the grounds of a miscarriage of justice in the original trial. He protested federal military intervention in the Pullman strike of 1894, and in 1896, accepting the doctrine of free silver, influenced acceptance by the Democrats of a 16:1 plank in the national election platform. He was renominated, 1896, but lost the election to John R. Tanner.

ALTHAM, JOHN (*b. 1589; d. St. Mary's, Md., 1640*), Jesuit missionary. Joined initial group of Maryland settlers, 1633; explored Potomac River with Calvert and conducted missions to Indians.

ALTMAN, BENJAMIN (*b. New York, N.Y., 1840; d. New York, 1913*), merchant, philanthropist, art patron. Founder of B. Altman & Co., New York City department store.

ALTSHELER, JOSEPH ALEXANDER (*b. Three Springs, Ky., 1862; d. 1919*), editor, author. Using American history as his theme, he wrote six popular series of novels for boys (1897–1919).

ALVARADO, JUAN BAUTISTA (*b. Monterey, Calif., 1809; d. 1882*), governor of Mexican California. Assumed governorship, 1836, in a move for local control; organized his department into districts and subdistricts, overcame personal jealousies of rivals and made unsuccessful attempts to resuscitate the secularized missions and to establish a superior court. Illness forced him to surrender his office to Gen. Manuel Micheltorena, 1841.

ALVEY, RICHARD HENRY (*b. St. Mary's Co., Md., 1826; d. Hagerstown, Md., 1906*), jurist. Sponsored "Alvey Resolution" favoring secession, 1861; held important judicial posts in Maryland and District of Columbia, 1867–1904.

ALVORD, BENJAMIN (*b. Rutland, Vt., 1813; d. 1884*), Union soldier. Graduated West Point, 1833; during Civil War commanded in Oregon Territory and successfully opposed secessionist sympathies there.

ALVORD, CLARENCE WALWORTH (*b. Greenfield, Mass., 1868; d. 1929*), historian. Instructor and professor of history, University of Illinois, 1901–20; influential in development of Mississippi Valley Historical Association; general editor, *Illinois Historical Collections;* author of *Mississippi Valley in British Politics* (1917).

ALVORD, CORYDON ALEXIS (*b. Winchester, Conn., 1813; d. 1874*), printer. A specialist in antiquarian printing jobs; superintendent for the Tweed-controlled New York Printing Co.

ALVORD, HENRY ELIJAH (*b. Greenfield, Mass., 1844; d. 1904*), educator, specialist in dairy husbandry. Pioneer leader in establishment of coöperative creamery system; held numerous agricultural teaching posts in land-grant colleges.

AMADAS, PHILIP (*fl. 1584–85*), English navigator. Commanded ships in Raleigh's expeditions to America, 1584, 1585.

AMATEIS, LOUIS (*b. Turin, Italy, 1855; d. 1913*), sculptor. Best-known works are bronze doors made for west entrance of Capitol, Washington, D.C., and numerous monuments in Texas.

AMBLER, JAMES MARKHAM MARSHALL (*b. Markham, Va., 1848; d. Siberia, 1881*), military surgeon, explorer. Surgeon aboard the *Jeannette* during its disastrous voyage to Arctic regions, 1879–81.

AMENT, WILLIAM SCOTT (*b. Owosso, Mich., 1851; d. China, 1909*), Congregational clergyman. Missionary to China, 1877–85, 1888–1909; exhibited great courage in aiding Christian converts during Boxer Rebellion.

AMES, ADELBERT (*b. Rockland, Maine, 1835; d. 1933*), Union soldier. Graduated West Point, 1861. After brilliant Civil War service, was Reconstruction senator and governor of Mississippi. He was compelled to resign as governor, 1876. [*Supp. 1*]

AMES, CHARLES GORDON (*b. Dorchester, Mass., 1828; d. Boston, Mass., 1912*), Baptist and Unitarian clergyman, editor.

AMES, EDWARD RAYMOND (*b. Adams Co., O., 1806; d. Baltimore, Md., 1897*), Methodist bishop.

AMES, EZRA (*b. Framingham, Mass., 1768; d. Albany, N.Y., 1836*), portrait painter. Painted miniatures and oils of celebrated New Yorkers during residence at Albany, N.Y., 1795–1836.

AMES, FISHER (*b. Dedham, Mass., 1758; d. Dedham, 1808*), statesman, publicist. Graduated Harvard, 1774. Congressman from Massachusetts, 1789–97; highest-minded of Federalists, he was unselfish in belief that the ideals of the Roman republic could be realized in the United States by the rule of an aristocracy of talent. An outstanding parliamentary orator, his greatest speech was made, 1796, in defense of Jay's Treaty. Always suspicious of democracy, the events of the French Revolution inspired him with a passionate fear of Jacobinism which colored all his later thinking and writing. Son of Nathaniel Ames (1708–1764).

AMES, FREDERICK LOTHROP (*b. North Easton, Mass., 1835; d. 1893*), philanthropist, capitalist. Son of Oliver Ames (1807–77); active in his family's manifold business concerns.

AMES, HERMAN VANDENBURG (*b. Lancaster, Mass., 1865; d. Philadelphia, Pa., 1935*), historian, dean of graduate school, University of Pennsylvania. Inspired and directed preservation of state archives. [*Supp. 1*]

AMES, JAMES BARR (*b. Boston, Mass., 1846; d. 1910*), educator, legal writer. Successfully furthered C. C. Langdell's system of teaching law by the study of reported cases; professor at Harvard Law School *post* 1877; dean, *post* 1895.

AMES, JAMES TYLER (*b. Lowell, Mass., 1810; d. 1883*), mechanic, manufacturer. From 1847 to 1874 he headed the Ames Manufacturing Co., one of America's largest producers of tools, textile machinery, and munitions.

AMES, JOSEPH ALEXANDER (*b. Roxbury, Mass., 1816; d. New York, N.Y., 1872*), portrait painter.

AMES, MARY CLEMMER. [See CLEMMER, MARY, 1831–1884.]

AMES, NATHAN PEABODY (*b. Chelmsford, Mass., 1803; d. 1847*), metal-worker, manufacturer. With brother James Tyler Ames, he developed a family cutlery business into the Ames Manufacturing Co. at

Chicopee, Mass., a principal factor in the industrial development of western Massachusetts.

AMES, NATHANIEL (*b. Bridgewater, Mass., 1708; d. Dedham, Mass., 1764*), almanac-maker, physician. Founder and editor, 1725–64, of an almanac which was a household word in New England.

AMES, OAKES (*b. Easton, Mass., 1804; d. North Easton, Mass., 1873*), manufacturer, capitalist, politician. In 1844 became partner with brother Oliver (1807–77) in Oliver Ames and Sons, the family shovel-making business; great prosperity came with agricultural development of the West and the Civil War. From 1862–73 Oakes Ames served as Republican congressman from Massachusetts. Both he and his brother were drawn, 1865, into the Crédit Mobilier scheme for building the Union Pacific Railroad; fearing legislative investigation of the scheme, early in 1868 he distributed shares of stock in the Crédit Mobilier to fellow-congressmen in the hope of influencing them in the company's favor. Revelation of this during the presidential campaign of 1872 brought Ames a censure by resolution of the House of Representatives.

AMES, OLIVER (*b. West Bridgewater, Mass., 1779; d. North Easton, Mass., 1863*), pioneer manufacturer. Father of Oliver (1807–77) and Oakes Ames; founder of the Ames shovel factories.

AMES, OLIVER (*b. Plymouth, Mass., 1807; d. North Easton, Mass., 1877*), manufacturer, railroad promoter. Brother of Oakes Ames whom he joined in building the Easton Branch Railroad and then in the financing and building of the Union Pacific Railroad. Served as president of the Union Pacific, 1866–71. On his brother's death in 1873, he successfully reorganized the family business, Oliver Ames and Sons, and restored its prosperity.

AMES, OLIVER (*b. North Easton, Mass., 1831; d. 1895*), capitalist, philanthropist. Son of Oakes Ames. Became dominant figure in Oliver Ames and Sons on the death of his uncle (Oliver Ames, 1807–77) with whom he had worked to restore the firm. A fortunate and far-seeing financier, he was director of many banks, railroads and land companies. Served ably as Republican governor of Massachusetts, 1886–90, and retired to give his time to business, travel, cultural interests and charities.

AMES, SAMUEL (*b. Providence, R.I., 1806; d. Providence, 1865*), jurist.

AMES, WINTHROP (*b. North Easton, Mass., 1870; d. Boston, Mass., 1937*), theatrical manager and producer. Noted for impeccable taste and high standards; active in the New York theatre, 1908–29. [*Supp. 2*]

AMHERST, JEFFERY (*b. Riverhead, Kent, England, 1717; d. 1797*), British soldier. After serving in several important continental campaigns, he was ordered to America in 1758. The French stronghold of Louisburg, Cape Breton Island, fell to his army and a supporting fleet under Boscawen on July 27. This was the first British victory in the Seven Years' War, and towns in several New England states were named Amherst in his honor. As commander-in-chief in North America, Amherst was to support Wolfe in the Quebec campaign of 1759, but was delayed by the need to capture Ticonderoga and Crown Point on his way northward from winter quarters in Albany. After Wolfe's sole success at Quebec, Amherst directed the capture of Montreal in 1760, and made Canada a part of the British empire. Amherst had been appointed governor of Virginia, but did not reside there and was superseded. Returning to England in the winter of 1763–64, he served thereafter as a military adviser to the cabinet until 1778 when he was made commander-in-chief of British forces in England. He was made Baron Amherst in 1776, and in 1796 given the rank of field marshal.

AMIDON, CHARLES FREMONT (*b. Chautauqua Co., N.Y., 1856; d. Tucson, Ariz., 1937*), jurist. U.S. district judge for North Dakota, 1896–1928, whose progressive opinions had national influence.

[*Supp. 2*]

AMMEN, DANIEL (*b. Ohio, 1819; d. near Washington, D.C., 1898*), naval officer. A distinguished ship commander in Civil War; retired as rear-admiral, 1878.

AMMEN, JACOB (*b. Fincastle, Va., 1807; d. Lockland, O., 1894*), Union soldier. Brother of Daniel Ammen; capable administrator of the East Tennessee district, 1864–65.

AMMONS, ELIAS MILTON (*b. Macon Co., N.C., 1860; d. 1925*), ranchman. Went with family to Colorado, 1871; entered cattle business, 1886, and throughout life retained an interest in all forms of agriculture. Held several state offices as a Republican; in 1896 became a "Silver Republican" and accepted Democratic nominations in 1904 and 1906, winning election in 1912 as governor. During the great strike in the Colorado coal fields, 1913–14, he was accused of favoring the mine-owners. In 1915, after expiration of his term in office, he returned to business and civic enterprises.

AMORY, THOMAS (*b. Limerick, Ireland, 1682; d. Boston, Mass., 1728*), merchant. Settled in Boston, 1720; developed an extensive trade both inland and abroad.

ANAGNOS, MICHAEL (*b. Papingo, Greece, 1837; d. 1906*), Greek patriot, American educator of the blind. Director of Perkins Institution for blind, 1876–1906; founded first kindergarten for blind children.

ANDERSON, ALEXANDER (*b. New York, N.Y., 1775; d. Jersey City, N.J., 1870*), engraver. A self-taught engraver at 12 years of age, he entered medical studies, 1789, but continued engraving on type metal and made illustrations for *The Pilgrim's Progress, Tom*

Thumb's Folio, Dilworth's Spelling Book and *Webster's Spelling Book*. In 1794, after seeing some Bewick illustrations, he undertook wood engraving, becoming America's first worker in that medium and a most prolific one to the end of his life. A faithful student of Bewick's method, he redrew and engraved 300 illustrations for the first American edition of Bewick's *General History of Quadrupeds* (1804).

ANDERSON, DAVID LAWRENCE (*b. Summerhill, S.C., 1850; d. China, 1911*), Methodist missionary, educator. Founder and first president of Soochow University, 1901–10.

ANDERSON, ELIZABETH MILBANK (*b. New York, N.Y., 1850; d. 1921*), philanthropist. Contributed liberally to Barnard College, Children's Aid Society of New York and to many social welfare agencies; established Milbank Memorial Fund.

ANDERSON, GALUSHA (*b. Clarendon, N.Y., 1832; d. 1918*), Baptist clergyman. Active abolitionist; president of (old) University of Chicago, 1878–85, and of Denison University, 1887–90.

ANDERSON, GEORGE THOMAS (*b. Georgia, 1824; d. Anniston, Ala., 1901*), Confederate brigadier-general. Served principally with R. E. Lee's army; distinguished at Antietam and Gettysburg.

ANDERSON, HENRY TOMPKINS (*b. Caroline Co., Va., 1812; d. Washington, D.C., 1872*), Disciples of Christ clergyman, scholar, translator of New Testament (1864).

ANDERSON, JAMES PATTON (*b. Franklin Co., Tenn., 1822; d. 1872*), Confederate soldier. Colonel, 1st Florida Regiment; commissioned brigadier, 1862, and major-general, 1864.

ANDERSON, JOHN ALEXANDER (*b. Washington Co., Pa., 1834; d. Liverpool, England, 1892*), Presbyterian clergyman. President of Kansas State Agricultural College, 1873–78; member of Congress from Kansas, 1878–91; appointed consul-general to Cairo, Egypt, 1891.

ANDERSON, JOSEPH (*b. White Marsh, Pa., 1757; d. 1837*), jurist. U.S. senator from Tennessee, 1797–1815; comptroller of U.S. Treasury, 1815–1836.

ANDERSON, JOSEPH REID (*b. near Fincastle, Va., 1813; d. Isles of Shoals, N.H., 1892*), Confederate soldier, manufacturer. Graduated West Point, 1836; resigned from army, 1837. In 1843 he leased the Tredegar Iron Co., Richmond, Va.; in 1848 he became its owner and developed it into a leading producer of locomotives, munitions, and naval machinery. A secessionist, he supplied cannon and ammunition to the Southern states, entered the Confederate army and was commissioned brigadier-general, 1861. The Tredegar Works became the sole Confederate source of heavy guns, 1861–63, the laboratory for Confederate ordnance experiment, and an active producer of projectiles, iron-clad plates, railroad rolling-stock, and furnace machinery.

ANDERSON, MARTIN BREWER (*b. Brunswick, Maine, 1815; d. Lake Helen, Fla., 1890*), educator. President of University of Rochester, 1853–88; an editor of *Johnson's Cyclopaedia;* president of American Baptist Missionary Union.

ANDERSON, MARY (*b. Sacramento, Calif., 1859; d. Worcestershire, England, 1940*), actress. Acclaimed for her beauty, and talent in classical roles; retired to England in 1889. [*Supp. 2*]

ANDERSON, PAUL YEWELL (*b. Knox Co., Tenn., 1893; d. Washington, D.C., 1938*), journalist. Pulitzer Prize-winning Washington correspondent for the *St. Louis Post-Dispatch.* [*Supp. 2*]

ANDERSON, RICHARD CLOUGH (*b. Hanover Co., Va., 1750; d. near Louisville, Ky., 1826*), Revolutionary soldier. As surveyor-general of Virginia western lands, settled in Kentucky *post* 1783.

ANDERSON, RICHARD CLOUGH (*b. Louisville, Ky., 1788; d. Turbaco, Colombia, 1826*), statesman, diplomat. Son of the preceding; appointed minister plenipotentiary to Colombia, 1823.

ANDERSON, RICHARD HERON (*b. Statesburg, S.C., 1821; d. 1879*), Confederate soldier. Graduated West Point, 1842; served on Western frontier and saw action during Mexican War. Commissioned brigadier-general, Confederate army, 1861, he assisted Bragg at Pensacola and was sent to Virginia to command a brigade in Longstreet's division. Commissioned major-general, 1862, and given a divisional command, he participated in second battle of Bull Run, and was wounded at Antietam. He served under Lee's direct command during battle of Chancellorsville, 1863, and played a vital role at Gettysburg. Replacing the badly wounded Longstreet as corps commander in the Wilderness, 1864, he captured Spotsylvania; after Longstreet's return to duty, Anderson accepted divisional commands during the remainder of the war.

ANDERSON, ROBERT (*b. near Louisville, Ky., 1805; d. Nice, France, 1871*), Union soldier. Son of Richard C. Anderson (1750–1826). Graduated West Point, 1825; served in Scott's campaign against City of Mexico, 1847; promoted major, 1857. When secession became imminent, he was sent to command forts in Charleston Harbor, S.C. On Dec. 20, 1860, South Carolina passed an ordinance of secession; six days later Anderson spiked the guns at Fort Moultrie and moved the garrison to Fort Sumter which he surrendered after siege on Apr. 13, 1861. Promoted brigadier-general, May 1861, he helped save Kentucky for the Union.

ANDERSON, WILLIAM (*b. Accomac Co., Va., 1762; d. Chester, Pa., 1829*), soldier, legislator. Served in U.S. House of Representatives as a member from

Pennsylvania, 1808–18, supporting Jefferson's policies; judge, Delaware Co. court, Pennsylvania, 1826–29.

ANDRÉ, LOUIS (*b. St. Remy, France, 1623 or 1631; d. Quebec, Canada, 1715*), Jesuit missionary, Indian linguist. Preached to Indians in northern Wisconsin and Canada.

ANDREIS, ANDREW JAMES FELIX BARTHOLO-MEW DE (*b. Piedmont, Italy, 1778; d. St. Louis, Mo., 1820*), Vincentian priest. Volunteered, 1815, to assist Bishop Louis Du Bourg on American mission; worked in Kentucky and Missouri.

ANDREW, ABRAM PIATT (*b. La Porte, Ind., 1873; d. Gloucester, Mass., 1936*), economist. Professor of economics, Harvard, 1903–09; government adviser on banking reform ("Aldrich Plan"); Republican representative from Massachusetts, 1921–36. [*Supp. 2*]

ANDREW, JAMES OSGOOD (*b. Wilkes Co., Ga., 1794; d. Mobile, Ala., 1871*). Elected bishop by General Conference of Methodist Church, 1832. Although he renounced all rights and control over slaves owned by his wife, the General Conference ruled in 1844 that he should forego his episcopal office until his connection with slave ownership should cease. Southern delegates challenged this ruling, and a "Plan of Separation" and division of the church was drawn up, making the Methodist church in the South independent and self-governing. Bishop Andrew then served as a bishop of the Methodist Episcopal Church, South, until his retirement in 1866.

ANDREW, JOHN ALBION (*b. Windham, Maine, 1818; d. Boston, Mass., 1867*), governor of Massachusetts. Graduated Bowdoin, 1837; admitted to bar, 1840. Achieved Republican leadership upon election to state legislature, 1857. After John Brown's raid he solicited funds for him and his family and became so widely identified with the incident that he was cited to appear before a senatorial committee investigating it and was chosen chairman of the state delegation to the 1860 Republican National Convention. A leader of anti-slavery opinion in Massachusetts, he was elected governor, 1860. He sent state militia to aid in defense of Washington; mobilized all the resources of his state in support of the Union; joined other Northern governors at the 1862 Altoona conference; urged organization of separate corps and regiments for Negro soldiers. Reëlected governor, 1864, he retired, 1866, the embodiment of the patriotic spirit of his state.

ANDREW, SAMUEL (*b. Cambridge, Mass., 1656; d. Milford, Conn., 1738*), Congregational clergyman, one of the founders of Yale College, and from 1707 to 1719 its acting rector.

ANDREWS, ALEXANDER BOYD (*b. near Franklinton, N.C., 1841; d. 1915*), railroad promoter. Conspicuous among the men who rebuilt the South in the half-century following the Civil War.

ANDREWS, CHARLES (*b. New York Mills, N.Y., 1827; d. Syracuse, N. Y., 1918*), jurist. Judge, New York court of appeals, 1870–1897; chief justice, 1881–82; 1892–97.

ANDREWS, CHARLES BARTLETT (*b. N. Sunderland, Mass., 1836; d. 1902*), jurist. Governor of Connecticut, 1879–81; outstanding judge of the superior court, *post* 1881.

ANDREWS, CHAUNCEY HUMMASON (*b. Vienna, O., 1823; d. 1893*), mine operator, railroad builder, manufacturer. Developed coal industry and short-line railroads in Ohio and western Pennsylvania.

ANDREWS, CHRISTOPHER COLUMBUS (*b. Hillsboro, N.H., 1829; d. St. Paul, Minn., 1922*), lawyer, author. Emigrated to Kansas, 1854; to Minnesota, 1857. Served with distinction as Union soldier. U.S. minister to Norway and Sweden, 1869–77; consul-general to Brazil, 1882–85; pioneer forest conservationist.

ANDREWS, EDWARD GAYER (*b. New Hartford, N.Y., 1825; d. Brooklyn, N.Y., 1907*), Methodist bishop. Principal of Cazenovia Seminary, 1855–64; reorganized Methodist churches in Europe and India.

ANDREWS, ELISHA BENJAMIN (*b. Hinsdale, N.H., 1844; d. Interlachen, Fla., 1917*), college president. Graduated Brown University, 1870; studied at Newton Theological Institution, 1872–74; president and professor of philosophy, Denison University, 1875–79; professor of history, Brown, 1883–88; president of Brown, 1889–98. The modern period in Brown's history begins with Andrews's accession. He greatly increased student enrollment and the size of the faculty; founded the Women's College; created important new departments; and provided strong, personal leadership in meeting administrative problems. Resigned, 1897, because his right to express his views on the silver question was challenged by the corporation; withdrew resignation after influential educators and alumni petitioned the university. Served as vigorous and effective chancellor, University of Nebraska, 1900–08.

ANDREWS, GARNETT (*b. Georgia, 1837; d. Chattanooga, Tenn., 1903*), lawyer, Confederate soldier. Organized a regiment of foreigners drawn from ranks of federal prisoners, the "Galvanized Yankees."

ANDREWS, GEORGE LEONARD (*b. Bridgewater, Mass., 1828; d. Brookline, Mass., 1899*), Union soldier. In command of territorial district about Baton Rouge; organized and trained Negro troops, 1862–65. Professor of modern languages, West Point, 1871–92.

ANDREWS, GEORGE PIERCE (*b. Bridgton, Maine, 1835; d. 1902*), jurist. Prosecutor in the Gordon case (a slaver arrested for piracy), 1862; New York supreme court justice, 1883–1902.

ANDREWS, ISRAEL DeWOLF (*b. Campobello, New Brunswick, or Eastport, Maine, c. 1813–1820; d. Bos-*

ton, Mass., 1871), consul, lobbyist. Chief promoter of the Canadian-American trade reciprocity treaty of 1854. [Supp. 1]

ANDREWS, ISRAEL WARD (b. Danbury, Conn., 1815; d. Hartford, Conn., 1888), educator. President of Marietta College, Ohio, 1855–85.

ANDREWS, JOHN (b. Cecil Co., Md., 1746; d. 1813), Episcopal clergyman, educator.

ANDREWS, JOSEPH (b. Massachusetts, c. 1805; d. Boston or Hingham, Mass., 1873), engraver. One of America's best line-engravers; excelled in portrait work.

ANDREWS, LORIN (b. Ashland, O., 1819; d. Gambier, O., 1861), educator. President of Kenyon College, 1853–61.

ANDREWS, LORRIN (b. East Windsor [now Vernon], Conn., 1795; d. Honolulu, Hawaii, 1868), missionary, educator. As missionary to Hawaii, 1828–41, he established a teacher training school and the first newspaper; held important offices in Hawaiian government, 1845–59.

ANDREWS, SAMUEL JAMES (b. Danbury, Conn., 1817; d. 1906), clergyman, author. An early supporter and pastor of the Catholic Apostolic Church; younger brother of William W. Andrews.

ANDREWS, SHERLOCK JAMES (b. Wallingford, Conn., 1801; d. 1880), lawyer, jurist, Whig congressman from Ohio, 1840–42. Prominent in early development of Cleveland, O. A member of the Ohio constitutional convention, 1850–51, he supported Negro rights at a critical time.

ANDREWS, SIDNEY (b. Sheffield, Mass., 1835; d. 1880), journalist. Traveled through Carolina and Georgia as a special correspondent for Northern newspapers, 1864–69.

ANDREWS, STEPHEN PEARL (b. Templeton, Mass., 1812; d. New York, N.Y., 1886), abolitionist, reformer, eccentric philosopher. Spelling reform and short-hand enthusiast; established "Universology," a deductive science of the universe.

ANDREWS, WILLIAM LORING (b. New York, N.Y., 1837; d. 1920), bibliophile. A founder of the Grolier Club and the Society of Iconophiles, New York City.

ANDREWS, WILLIAM WATSON (b. Windham, Conn., 1810; d. 1897), clergyman. Traveling evangelist of the Catholic Apostolic Church (Irvingites); brother of Samuel J. Andrews.

ANDROS, SIR EDMUND (b. London, England, 1637; d. London, 1714), soldier, colonial governor. Governor of New York, 1674–81; recalled to England; knighted, c. 1681. James II, wishing to consolidate the individualistic New England colonies into one royal province, formed the Dominion of New Eng-

land with Andros as governor, 1686. The new government, administered by royal appointees, conflicted with the claims and interests of the colonists; at the instigation of Increase and Cotton Mather they rose in revolt against Andros in 1689, imprisoning him along with other Dominion officials. His reputation undamaged by his New England experience, he was appointed governor of Virginia, 1692, and retired to England in 1697.

ANGEL, BENJAMIN FRANKLIN (b. Burlington, N.Y., 1815; d. Geneseo, N.Y., 1894), lawyer, diplomat. Held diplomatic posts in Hawaii, China, Norway, and Sweden.

ANGELA, MOTHER (b. near Brownsville, Pa., 1824; d. 1887), educator. Name in religion of Eliza Maria Gillespie. Served almost 30 years as superior of the Sisters of the Holy Cross in the United States; supervised Civil War nursing work of her nuns; founded St. Mary's, Notre Dame, Ind.

ANGELL, GEORGE THORNDIKE (b. Southbridge, Mass., 1823; d. Boston, Mass., 1909), reformer. With Mrs. William Appleton founded Massachusetts Society for the Prevention of Cruelty to Animals.

ANGELL, ISRAEL (b. Providence, R.I., 1740; d. Smithfield, R.I., 1832), Revolutionary soldier. Served at siege of Boston and at battles of Brandywine, Red Bank, Monmouth, and, notably, Springfield, N.J.

ANGELL, JAMES BURRILL (b. near Scituate, R.I., 1829; d. Ann Arbor, Mich., 1916), journalist, college president, diplomat. Graduated Brown University, 1849; studied in Europe, 1851–52; returned to take chair of modern languages at Brown, 1853. In 1858 he began contributing leading articles to the *Providence Journal* giving particular attention to European and international politics; resigned his chair at Brown, 1860, in order to assume editorship of the newspaper. Under his direction the *Journal* endorsed Lincoln as the Republican candidate, at first dismissed Southern threats of secession, and consistently supported the government during the Civil War. After unsuccessfully attempting to purchase the paper from its owner, Henry B. Anthony, Angell accepted presidency of the University of Vermont, 1866. The university, chartered by the legislature in 1791, received no state support and was in poor financial condition. The new president was forced to speak before public meetings in several New England states soliciting contributions for the school. As a result of this canvass, $100,000 was raised, new buildings were constructed on the campus, and the people of the state were brought to regard the university as an integral and necessary part of public education. The University of Michigan in 1871 was one of the largest American educational institutions of that time. Its curriculum was liberal and its faculty relatively large and well selected, yet, due to the state's policy of financial support, its equipment and salary scale were inadequate. Angell, elected to the presidency of Michigan, proposed for the state "the higher positive office of promoting by all means the intellectual and moral growth of the citizens." His achievements as president, 1871–1909, were of a dual nature: first, his personal influence as a teacher and administrator who interested himself in his students; second, his organizational and educational innovations —broadening of curriculum to include those who had not had classical preparation; establishment of first permanent system of admission requirements for medical schools, 1874; creation of first professorship in the science and art of teaching, 1879; and institution of comprehensive examinations as part of the requirements for a bachelor's degree, 1877. He supplemented the duties of president by undertaking occasional but important national diplomatic missions. In 1880, as minister to China, he concluded a treaty whereby the United States might "regulate, limit or suspend" but not "absolutely prohibit" the entry and residence of Chinese laborers; at the same time a commercial treaty governing opium trade was signed. He was minister to Turkey during the Spanish-American War, 1897–98. Angell was a regent of the Smithsonian Institution, one of the founders of the American Historical Association, 1884, and its president, 1893–94.

ANGELL, JOSEPH KINNICUTT (*b. Providence, R.I., 1794; d. Boston, Mass., 1857*), lawyer. Author of several authoritative legal treatises, including *The Law of Private Corporations Aggregate* (1832).

ANGELL, WILLIAM GORHAM (*b. Providence, R.I., 1811; d. 1870*), inventor. Improved screw-making machinery; president, American Screw Co.

ANNEKE, MATHILDE FRANZISKA. [See GIESLER-ANNEKE, MATHILDE FRANZISKA, 1817–1884.]

ANSHUTZ, THOMAS POLLOCK (*b. Newport, Ky., 1851; d. Fort Washington, Pa., 1912*), painter, teacher at Pennsylvania Academy of Fine Arts; among other eminent painters, his pupils included Robert Henri, John Sloan, George Luks and William Glackens.

ANSON, ADRIAN CONSTANTINE (*b. Marshalltown, Iowa, 1852; d. 1922*), baseball player. Batted an average of .331 over 22 seasons, 1876–97, as first baseman, captain and manager of the Chicago club, National League.

ANTES, HENRY (*b. Freinsheim, Germany, 1701; d. Frederick, Pa., 1755*), religious leader. Came to America, *c.* 1720; associated with Moravians, 1741–55.

ANTHON, CHARLES (*b. New York, N.Y., 1797; d. New York, N.Y., 1867*), classical scholar. Graduated Columbia College, 1815. Chosen adjunct professor of Greek and Latin, Columbia, 1820; in 1830 made Jay Professor of Greek language and literature and put in charge of Columbia Grammar School. During the middle of the 19th century his influence upon the study of classics in the United States was probably greater than that of any other one man. He was one

of those who introduced the results of foreign (mainly German) scholarship into the United States. His *Horatii Poemata* (1830) was the first American critical and exegetical edition of a classical author. For thirty years he edited annually at least one volume of a classical text for school and college use.

ANTHON, CHARLES EDWARD (*b. New York, N.Y., 1823; d. Bremen, Germany, 1883*), educator, numismatist. Son of John Anthon.

ANTHON, JOHN (*b. Detroit, Mich., 1784; d. 1863*), lawyer. Brother of Charles Anthon. Assisted in founding New York Law Institute; elected its president, 1852–63.

ANTHONY, ANDREW VARICK STOUT (*b. New York, N.Y., 1835; d. West Newton, Mass., 1906*), wood engraver. Superintended production of fine illustrated editions for Ticknor and Fields and successor firms, 1866–89.

ANTHONY, GEORGE TOBEY (*b. near Mayfield, N.Y., 1824; d. 1896*), businessman, Union soldier. Removed to Leavenworth, Kans., 1865; influenced agricultural methods as editor of *Kansas Farmer;* effective and honest Republican governor of Kansas, 1876–80.

ANTHONY, HENRY BOWEN (*b. Coventry, R.I., 1815; d. 1884*), journalist, politician. Proprietor, *Providence Journal;* governor of Rhode Island, 1849, 1850; U.S. senator, conservative Republican, 1858–84.

ANTHONY, JOHN GOULD (*b. Providence, R.I., 1804; d. 1877*), zoologist. Collected and studied fresh water mollusks; scientific associate of Louis Agassiz.

ANTHONY, SISTER (*b. Limerick, Ireland, 1814; d. 1897*), nurse. Born Mary O'Connell; educated by Ursulines, Charlestown, Mass.; entered American Sisters of Charity, 1835. Worked in hospitals, Cincinnati, O., 1837–80. With other members of her community, she won special commendation for field and hospital work during the Civil War.

ANTHONY, SUSAN BROWNELL (*b. Adams, Mass., 1820; d. Rochester, N.Y., 1906*), reformer. Prevented from speaking at a temperance meeting because of her sex, she and others formed in 1852 the Woman's State Temperance Society of New York. Convinced that women could work effectively for social betterment only if they had rights and privileges held by men, she spent her life in lecture tours and campaigns through various states in the interest of woman suffrage. She supported Negro suffrage for male and female, took a radical abolitionist stand prior to the Civil War and was instrumental in formation of the National Woman Suffrage Association. In 1892, after merger of the organization with a rival group, she was elected president of the combined societies and served until 1900.

ANTHONY, WILLIAM ARNOLD (*b. Coventry, R.I., 1835; d. New York, N.Y., 1908*), physicist, pioneer in teaching of electrical engineering. Contributed to development of gas-filled lamp. [*Supp.* 1]

ANTOINE, PÈRE (*b. Sedella, Spain, 1748; d. New Orleans, La., 1829*), Capuchin friar. Parish priest in New Orleans, 1785–90; 1795–1805; 1819–29. A complex and controversial figure.

ANZA, JUAN BAUTISTA DE (*b. Sonora, Mexico, 1735*), Spanish explorer. Hoping to anticipate possible occupation by the Russians or the English, Spain planned to occupy the Pacific Coast of North America as far as the bay of Monterey and beyond. Anza, with a group of soldiers, set forth from his presidio of Tubac to establish an overland supply route from Sonora to Monterey, 1774. He proved the practicability of such a route and was rewarded with the rank of lieutenant-colonel. On his second California expedition, 1775, he explored the land about San Francisco Bay, ascended the San Joaquin River for a short distance and chose a site for the San Francisco presidio. He served as governor of New Mexico, 1777–88.

APES, WILLIAM (*b. near Colrain, Mass., 1798*), Pequot Indian, missionary and author.

APPENZELLER, HENRY GERHARD (*b. Suderton, Pa., 1858; d. near Kunsan, Korea, 1902*), Methodist missionary. Established a Methodist printing house in Korea, edited *Korean Review,* and established Pai Chai School for boys in Seoul.

APPLE, THOMAS GILMORE (*b. Easton, Pa., 1829; d. 1898*), theologian, educator. President of Mercersburg College, 1865–71; president, Franklin and Marshall College, 1877; identified with the so-called "Mercersburg Theology" system.

APPLEBY, JOHN FRANCIS (*b. Westmoreland, N.Y., 1840; d. 1917*), inventor. Removed to Wisconsin as a child. At eighteen he conceived the idea of a machine that would bind reaped sheaves of grain; lack of funds prevented its development. In 1867, he displayed his first complete binder at Mazomanie, Wis.; in 1878 he was granted patents for a perfected twine binder. Manufacture of the "Appleby Knotter" on a large scale was begun by Gammon and Deering in 1878. Other manufacturers of harvesters procured rights, and it remains today the most popular binding machine.

APPLEGATE, JESSE (*b. Kentucky, 1811; d. 1888*), surveyor, legislator, publicist. Joined the 1843 emigration to Oregon and settled in Willamette Valley; was leader of party which opened southern road into Oregon in 1845. A member of the legislative committee of the Provisional Government, he secured the adherence to it of the managers of the British Hudson's Bay Co., thus politically unifying the Oregon settlement for the first time. Active in state constitutional convention, 1857, he was also influential in securing Lincoln's election and maintaining the national cause during the Civil War. In 1849 he settled on a large ranch in the Umpqua Valley and raised beef cattle. Author of *A Day with the Cow Column in 1843.*

APPLETON, DANIEL (*b. Haverhill, Mass., 1785; d. New York, N.Y., 1849*), publisher. With his son, William Henry Appleton, founded the firm of D. Appleton & Co.

APPLETON, JAMES (*b. Ipswich, Mass., 1785; d. 1862*), reformer, one of the first (1832) to propose state prohibition as a remedy for intemperance.

APPLETON, JESSE (*b. New Ipswich, N.H., 1772; d. Brunswick, Maine, 1819*), theologian, educator. President of Bowdoin College, 1807–19.

APPLETON, JOHN (*b. New Ipswich, N.H., 1804; d. 1891*), legal reformer and theorist. Associate justice, 1852–62, chief justice, 1862–83, of Maine supreme judicial court; author of *The Rules of Evidence* (1860).

APPLETON, JOHN (*b. Beverly, Mass., 1815; d. Portland, Maine, 1864*), lawyer, Maine congressman, diplomat. Assistant secretary of state, 1857–60; minister to Russia, 1860–61.

APPLETON, NATHAN (*b. New Ipswich, N.H., 1779; d. Boston, Mass., 1861*), manufacturer, banker. Brother of Samuel Appleton. Invested in Francis Lowell's power mill for making cotton cloth at Waltham, Mass., 1813; there, with his associates, established the principles of the American textile industry—power machinery with cheap female labor, and a separate selling organization. Successful at Waltham, they founded the industrial city of Lowell and built manufacturing centers at Manchester, N.H., and Lawrence, Mass. Elected to Congress, 1830, Appleton assisted in framing and defending the protective tariff of 1832 and supported Biddle and Clay against Jackson in the Bank of the U.S. controversy. He was an organizer of the Boston Athenaeum and its treasurer, 1816–27.

APPLETON, NATHANIEL WALKER (*b. Boston, Mass., 1755; d. 1795*), physician. Incorporator of the Massachusetts Medical Society, 1781, and its recording secretary for the first ten years of its existence.

APPLETON, SAMUEL (*b. New Ipswich, N.H., 1766; d. Boston, Mass., 1853*), merchant. Brother of Nathan Appleton; trader and investor in New England real estate and industry; retired at sixty to devote his income to philanthropy.

APPLETON, THOMAS GOLD (*b. Boston, Mass., 1812; d. 1884*), essayist, poet, and artist; a witty member of the literary coterie which made Boston famous in the middle of the 19th century.

APPLETON, WILLIAM HENRY (*b. Haverhill, Mass., 1814; d. New York, N.Y., 1899*), publisher. Joined father, Daniel Appleton, in firm of D. Appleton & Co., 1838.

APPLETON, WILLIAM WORTHEN (*b. Brooklyn, N.Y., 1845; d. New York N.Y., 1924*), publisher. Son of William H. Appleton.

APTHORP, WILLIAM FOSTER (*b. Boston, Mass., 1848; d. Vevey, Switzerland, 1913*), music critic. Music editor, *Atlantic Monthly,* and dramatic and music critic for several Boston newspapers.

ARBUCKLE, JOHN (*b. Pittsburgh, Pa., 1839; d. Brooklyn, N.Y., 1912*), merchant. Leading coffee importer and ship owner; inventor of machinery used in food packaging and ship salvage.

ARCHBOLD, JOHN DUSTIN (*b. Leesburg, O., 1848; d. 1916*), capitalist. Speculator in Pennsylvania oil fields, 1866. When the South Improvement Co., whose membership included John D. Rockefeller, blocked the advance of Pennsylvania oil producers by obtaining railroad freight rebates, Archbold united the leading men of the Titusville region and defeated this strong Cleveland group. He then joined the Cleveland combination in working out a national organization to control the oil industry; from 1882 until his death he was dominant in Standard Oil Co. policy, acted as spokesman for the company, and improved the product and its distribution. In 1911, at the dissolution of the original company, he became president of Standard Oil of New Jersey.

ARCHDALE, JOHN (*b. England, c. 1642; d. England, c. 1717*), colonial governor. Agent for Gorges claims in Maine, 1664–65; governor of Carolina, 1694; passed colony's first recorded liquor law.

ARCHER, BRANCH TANNER (*b. Virginia, 1790; d. 1856*), political leader in Texas. A commissioner to the United States, 1836; member of first Texas Congress; secretary of war in cabinet of President Lamar.

ARCHER, FREDERIC (*b. Oxford, England, 1838; d. Pittsburgh, Pa., 1901*), organist. One of the first players to popularize the organ recital in America; director of music, Carnegie Institute, Pittsburgh, Pa., 1895–1901.

ARCHER, JAMES J. (*b. Stafford, Md., 1817; d. 1864*), Confederate soldier. Commissioned brigadier-general, 1862; fought in Seven Days Battles, Cedar Mountain, Second Manassas, Antietam, Fredericksburg, Chancellorsville.

ARCHER, JOHN (*b. Churchville, Md., 1741; d. Harford Co., Md., 1810*), physician, medical teacher. Received first medical degree (B.M., Philadelphia College of Medicine, 1768) ever earned in this country.

ARCHER, SAMUEL (*b. near Columbus, N.J., 1771; d. Philadelphia, Pa., 1839*), merchant, philanthropist. Engaged in importing from India and China, and from Europe; first merchant to export American cotton goods to Asia on a large scale; an original manager of Philadelphia Saving Fund Society, 1816.

ARCHER, STEVENSON (*b. Harford Co., Md., 1786; d. Harford Co., 1848*), jurist. Judge, Maryland court of appeals, 1824–48.

ARCHER, WILLIAM SEGAR (*b. Amelia Co., Va., 1789; d. Amelia Co., 1855*). Congressman, Whig, from Virginia, 1820–35; U.S. senator from Virginia, 1841–47; advocated annexation of Texas.

ARDEN, EDWIN HUNTER PENDLETON (*b. St. Louis, Mo., 1864; d. 1918*), actor, manager, playwright. Starred in a series of his own plays, 1883–92; noted for his appearance with Maude Adams in Rostand's *L'Aiglon,* 1900.

ARENTS, ALBERT (*b. Clausthal, Germany, 1840; d. Alameda, Calif., 1914*), metallurgist. Emigrated to America, 1865; his siphon lead-well was a revolutionary step in lead-silver smelting.

ARGALL, PHILIP (*b. Newtownards, Ireland, 1854; d. 1922*), engineer, metallurgist. Came to United States in 1887; applied new cyanide process for gold extraction in Colorado mines, 1895; consulting engineer to British and American mining firms.

ARGALL, SIR SAMUEL (*fl. 1609–1624*), adventurer, deputy governor of Virginia. Pioneered direct trans-Atlantic route from England to Virginia, 1609. Accompanied Lord Delaware to Virginia, 1610; went to Cape Cod to secure fish for starving Virginia colonists. Subsequent trading trips northward resulted in his appointment to expel encroaching French in the Mt. Desert area, 1613; he later forced the Dutch settlement on the Hudson to declare allegiance to England. Deputy governor of Virginia, 1617–19. At end of his administration most of the public property was wasted and the colony was poverty-stricken.

ARMISTEAD, GEORGE (*b. New Market, Va., 1780; d. Baltimore, Md., 1818*), soldier. Commanded at Fort McHenry during famous defense against British attack in 1814.

ARMISTEAD, LEWIS ADDISON (*b. Newbern, N.C., 1817; d. Gettysburg, Pa., 1863*), Confederate soldier. Distinguished in war with Mexico. Appointed brigadier-general, 1862; killed leading a brigade in Pickett's charge.

ARMOUR, PHILIP DANFORTH (*b. Stockbridge, N.Y., 1832; d. Chicago, Ill., 1901*), meat packer. Entered meat packing trade with John Plankinton, Milwaukee, Wis., 1863; first great success in business a speculation in pork, 1865. Added a pork packing plant to brother's grain business, 1868. By 1875, the expanding Armour interests were concentrated in Chicago, Ill. One of the earliest Chicago packers, Armour introduced economies by improving slaughtering techniques and finding use for waste; he adopted modern refrigeration methods, purchased his own railroad cars, and established eastern distribution centers. About 1880, he began preparation of canned meats on a large scale and the shipment of his products abroad. Much of his wealth was expended for philanthropic purposes.

ARMSBY, HENRY PRENTISS (*b. Northbridge, Mass., 1853; d. 1921*), agricultural chemist. Professor of agricultural chemistry, University of Wisconsin, 1879–86; organized Pennsylvania Agricultural Station and served as its director, 1887–1907; dean of Pennsylvania School of Agriculture, 1890–1902; after 1907 did research at Pennsylvania Institute of Animal Nutrition. His influential treatise *A Manual of Cattle Feeding* (1880) was the first of his classic researches into the fundamental physiological laws governing animal nutrition. He developed a respiration calorimeter for farm animals, demonstrated the validity of the principle of conservation of energy in cattle, and studied the efficiency of different types and ages of animals as converters of "waste" into animal food.

ARMSTRONG, DAVID MAITLAND (*b. near Newburgh, N.Y., 1836; d. New York, N.Y., 1918*), painter, worker in stained glass. Painted frescoes for Chicago World's Fair, 1893; made stained-glass windows, Columbia University Chapel.

ARMSTRONG, FRANK C. (*b. Choctaw Agency, Indian Territory, 1835; d. Bar Harbor, Maine, 1909*), Confederate soldier. Held numerous cavalry commands in the Western campaigns; commissioned brigadier-general, 1863.

ARMSTRONG, GEORGE BUCHANAN (*b. County Armagh, Ireland, 1822; d. Chicago, Ill., 1871*). Came to America in 1830. Suggested sorting of mail on trains, 1864; instituted and developed the railway mail service.

ARMSTRONG, GEORGE DOD (*b. Mendham, N.J., 1813; d. Norfolk, Va., 1899*), Presbyterian clergyman and controversial writer. Author of *The Christian Doctrine of Slavery* (1857).

ARMSTRONG, GEORGE WASHINGTON (*b. Boston, Mass., 1836; d. 1901*). Founded Armstrong Transfer Co., a transfer, news, and restaurant service on New England railways.

ARMSTRONG, JOHN (*b. Brookborough Parish, Ireland, 1717; d. Carlisle, Pa., 1795*), Pennsylvania soldier, politician. Captured Indian headquarters at Kittanning, Pa., 1756; held several commands during Revolution; commissioned major-general, 1777.

ARMSTRONG, JOHN (*b. New Jersey, 1755; d. Armstrong's Station, Ind., 1816*), soldier, explorer. After serving as an officer in the Revolution he undertook duties on the Ohio frontier, becoming one of the best-known woodsmen, explorers, and military characters of the early West. Commandant at Fort Pitt, 1785–86. In 1790, acting under secret government orders, he explored Spanish territory, proceeding up the Missouri some distance above St. Louis; intertribal Indian wars ended this one-man forerunner of the Lewis and Clark expedition. Resigning from army, 1793, he served as treasurer of Northwest Territory and held local offices.

ARMSTRONG, JOHN (*b. Carlisle, Pa., 1758; d. Red Hook, N.Y., 1843*), soldier, diplomat. Son of John Armstrong (1717–95). Served as officer during Revolution; composed the notorious "Newburgh Letters" (1783) suggesting that the army should take matters into their own hands if Congress failed to meet their demands for arrears of pay. Originally a Federalist, his marriage to Alida Livingston in 1789 brought him Republican political preferment; he served as U.S. senator from New York, 1800–02, 1803–04, resigning to become minister to France. Little glory could be won by an American minister at Napoleon's court during Armstrong's residence there, 1804–10, but it is to his credit that he objected to the subservient attitude of the American administration. Anxious to retire in triumph, he accepted the 1810 note in which the French sought to convince the Americans that Napoleon had revoked the Berlin and Milan decrees. This note, with its apparent yielding to the United States, was accepted without any probing into the true meaning of the new French policy; thus Armstrong must accept part of the responsibility for the break with England and the War of 1812. Appointed secretary of war by President Madison in 1813, his one notable achievement—the advancement of Generals Andrew Jackson, Jacob Brown, and Winfield Scott—is overshadowed by many mistakes and failures which culminated in losses on the northern frontier and the capture of Washington by the British, 1814. He resigned from his secretaryship and political life in 1814 and retired to a life as a gentleman farmer.

ARMSTRONG, PAUL (*b. Kidder, Mo., 1869; d. New York, N.Y., 1915*), playwright. A writer of melodramas; author of *Alias Jimmy Valentine* (1909).

ARMSTRONG, ROBERT (*b. Abingdon, Va., 1792; d. 1854*), soldier. Brigadier-general during second Seminole War; unsuccessful Tennessee gubernatorial candidate, 1837.

ARMSTRONG, SAMUEL CHAPMAN (*b. Maui, Hawaii, 1839; d. 1893*), educator. Attended Williams College, 1861. Volunteered for Civil War and was commissioned colonel of 9th Regiment, U.S. Negro troops, 1864; at end of war received brevet rank of brigadier-general. Because of his conspicuous success in working with Negro soldiers he was appointed an agent of the Freedmen's Bureau, in charge of a camp of emancipated slaves near Hampton, Va. Realizing the need of industrial education for the freedman, he brought about the founding of Hampton Normal and Industrial Institute, 1868.

ARMSTRONG, SAMUEL TURELL (*b. Dorchester, Mass., 1784; d. 1850*), publisher, banker, Massachusetts Whig politician.

ARNOLD, AZA (*b. Smithfield, R.I., 1788; d. Washington, D.C., 1865*), inventor. Made valuable improvement in cotton-roving machines, increasing both quantity and quality of product.

ARNOLD, BENEDICT (*b. Norwich, Conn., 1741; d. London, England, 1801*), Revolutionary patriot and traitor. Arnold joined colonial troops in French and Indian War, 1755; saw service on Lakes George and Champlain. Moved to New Haven, 1762; became a prosperous trader, and captain in the Connecticut militia. At outbreak of the Revolution he formed a plan to obtain military supplies for the Committee of Safety of Massachusetts by capturing Fort Ticonderoga; while en route to Ticonderoga he met Ethan Allen heading a similar expedition. After some difficulties the rival leaders agreed to issue joint commands; on May 10, 1775, they captured the fort. Arnold then sailed to the northern end of Lake Champlain and captured the fort at St. Johns. He returned to Connecticut when further conflict regarding jurisdiction resulted in his being "investigated" and superseded. Gen. Washington, approving Arnold's project of an attack on Canada, sent Schuyler to capture Montreal while Arnold was ordered to Quebec by a new way across Maine. With forces decimated by disease, fatigue, and starvation, Arnold joined Montgomery (who replaced Schuyler) in an unsuccessful attack on Quebec, Dec. 31, 1775. Arnold, though badly wounded in the assault, blockaded the city until spring when British reinforcements arrived. Foreseeing a contest for the Lakes, he hastily assembled a "fleet" and met Carleton's British war vessels on Champlain, Oct. 11, 1776; the American "fleet" was defeated, but Arnold's fierce resistance upset British plans to capture Ticonderoga. He returned to New England to learn that Congress had failed to give him a deserved promotion to major-general; angry at the slight, he was dissuaded from resigning by Washington's personal plea. When the British attacked Connecticut in 1777, he defeated their superior force and was promoted to major-general, but not retroactively. Later that year his enemies in Congress attempted to investigate his conduct in Canada; he offered his resignation and once more Washington intervened, this time stating that Arnold's services were needed to halt Burgoyne's southern advance from Canada. Arnold raised the siege of crucial Fort Stanwix, rejoined the main army under Gates, and with him defeated Burgoyne at Saratoga Sept.–Oct., 1777. Named commander at Philadelphia, June, 1778, and marrying into Philadelphia society, he began his betrayal of the American cause. His motives were fourfold: Anger at repeated slights of Congress; need for ready money to maintain his social position; resentment at the Pennsylvania authorities; indignation of a Protestant at an alliance with the Catholic French. He regularly sent important military information to Sir Henry Clinton, 1779–80, and, when assigned to command of the strategic post at West Point, offered to surrender the garrison to him. The price of betrayal was set, and Arnold met the British spy André to arrange the surrender in September, 1780; shortly thereafter André was captured, and Arnold fled to the British. He led marauding expeditions into Virginia and Connecticut, and in 1781 sailed with his family to an unhappy life in England where he received no further rewards for his past services to the Crown.

ARNOLD, GEORGE (*b. New York, N.Y., 1834; d. Monmouth Co., N.J., 1865*), poet. Associated with the New York "Bohemian" group which met at Pfaff's beer cellar; author of light verse and short stories.

ARNOLD, HAROLD DeFOREST (*b. Woodstock, Conn., 1883; d. Summit, N.J., 1933*), scientist. Joined the Western Electric Co. in 1911 when industrial research was in its infancy. Developed a mercury arc amplifier and directed improvements in the 3-electrode vacuum tube which led to transcontinental telephony in 1914 and intercontinental radio telephony in 1915. As director of research at Western Electric Co. and later at the Bell Telephone Laboratories, he inaugurated physical and chemical investigations which have been applied in radio, motion pictures, transoceanic cables and high fidelity phonographs as well as the telephone. [*Supp. 1*]

ARNOLD, ISAAC NEWTON (*b. Hartwick, N.Y., 1815; d. 1884*), lawyer, historian. Congressman, Republican, from Illinois, 1860–64; introduced important legislation prohibiting slavery. A founder of the Chicago Historical Society.

ARNOLD, JONATHAN (*b. Providence, R.I., 1741; d. St. Johnsbury, Vt., 1793*), Revolutionary patriot. Drafted 1776 law repealing Rhode Island oath of allegiance to England; leading founder of St. Johnsbury, Vt.

ARNOLD, LAUREN BRIGGS (*b. Fairfield, N.Y., 1814; d. 1888*), dairy husbandman. Spent his life in the discovery and teaching of better methods of dairy practice; especially noted for his improvements in manufacture of cheese.

ARNOLD, LEWIS GOLDING (*b. New Jersey, 1817; d. 1871*), Union general. Graduated West Point, 1837. Organized defense of strategic Fort Jefferson in the Dry Tortugas, 1861.

ARNOLD, RICHARD (*b. Providence, R.I., 1828; d. Governor's Island, N.Y., 1882*), Union soldier, artillerist. Graduated West Point, 1850.

ARNOLD, RICHARD DENNIS (*b. Savannah, Ga., 1808; d. Savannah, 1876*), physician, politician. A founder of the American Medical Association, 1846.

ARNOLD, SAMUEL (*c. 1838–1906*). [See BOOTH, JOHN WILKES.]

ARNOLD, SAMUEL GREENE (*b. Providence, R.I., 1821; d. Middletown, R.I., 1880*), historian. Author of *History of Rhode Island and Providence Plantation* (1859).

ARRINGTON, ALFRED W. (*b. Iredell Co., N.C., 1810; d. Chicago, Ill., 1867*), lawyer, poet. Practiced law in Arkansas, Texas, and Illinois. Author of novels, newspaper sketches, and *Poems* (1869).

ARTHUR, CHESTER ALAN (*b. Fairfield, Vt., 1830; d. New York, N.Y., 1886*), president of the United States. Graduated Union College, 1848; practiced law in New York City. Closely associated with New York's Republican governor, Edwin D. Morgan, he served as quartermaster-general of the State of New York, 1861–62. In 1871 President Grant recognized his active participation in Republican party affairs by making him collector of the Port of New York. Trained in the school of practical politics, he viewed the Custom House as a branch of Senator Roscoe Conkling's political machine; even though his administration was an honest one, the Custom House was overstaffed with clerks and laborers who recognized their obligations on election days. In 1876, on the election of President Hayes, reforms were ordered in the operation of the New York Custom House; Arthur opposed them and was ousted. Considered a martyr to party devotion, he was nominated vice-president at the 1880 Republican convention in order to pacify Grant's supporters; when the incoming President Garfield was assassinated in 1881, Arthur assumed the presidency. He surprised political friends and enemies by conducting his administration with independence and integrity. He supported a proposed reform of the civil service and attempted a revision of the tariff, but his efforts were not enough to stem the popular trend toward the Democratic party. The professional Republican politicians were alienated by his nonpartisan zeal for effective administration, and he was refused renomination in 1884.

ARTHUR, PETER M. (*b. Scotland, 1831; d. Winnipeg, Canada, 1903*), labor leader. Arrived in America, 1842. Associated with the Brotherhood of Locomotive Engineers, 1863–1903, he made it into one of the strongest and most conservative of labor unions.

ARTHUR, TIMOTHY SHAY (*b. near Newburgh, N.Y., 1809; d. Philadelphia, Pa., 1885*), editor, author. After serving as a watchmaker's apprentice and clerk, he chose a career in writing and held editorial positions on five Baltimore journals. He soon found a steady market in *Godey's Lady's Book* and other magazines for his moralistic stories. His first important book was a group of temperance tales (1842), but his greatest success was achieved in 1854 with *Ten Nights in a Barroom,* a temperance novel whose contemporary sale was second only to that of *Uncle Tom's Cabin.*

ARTHUR, WILLIAM (*b. near Ballymena, Ireland, 1797; d. Newtonville, N.Y., 1875*), Baptist clergyman, antiquarian. Held pastorates in Vermont and New York; father of Chester A. Arthur.

ASBOTH, ALEXANDER SANDOR (*b. Keszthely, Hungary, 1811; d. Buenos Aires, Argentina, 1868*), Union soldier. Came to the United States with Kossuth. Won brevet as major-general of volunteers, 1865; died soon after appointment as U.S. minister to Uruguay and Argentina.

ASBURY, FRANCIS (*b. near Birmingham, England, 1745; d. Virginia, 1816*), pioneer Methodist preacher and bishop. Converted to Methodism through the influence of his emotional and devout mother, he and Richard Wright volunteered to go as missionaries to America, 1771. In America he joined Richard Boardman on his preaching circuit but soon left him and preached in the villages of Westchester Co., N.Y.; appointed superintendent of Methodists in America, Oct. 1772, he was relieved of the post, June 1773. He quarreled with his successor, Thomas Rankin, and was ordered to return to England in 1775. At this critical moment he determined to stay on, await the eventual departure of Rankin and obtain a unique place in an independent American Methodist organization. During the Revolution the Methodists were suspected of Loyalist sympathies, but Asbury, although he refused to take the Maryland oath of allegiance, became convinced of eventual American victory and became a citizen of Delaware. Controversy involving the Northern and Southern Methodist ministers was resolved by him at a conference that was a complete victory for the Northern party and a personal triumph for Asbury. By 1782 Asbury was the virtual head of the Methodist organization in America. When Wesley sent Thomas Coke in 1784 to act jointly with him in superintending the Methodist societies, Asbury insisted that the appointment be made by a regular conference; chosen as joint superintendent, he assumed the title of bishop and gained practical control of the Methodist organization. Although in theory a servant of the Methodist conference, he was an autocratic ruler who appointed preachers as he chose and accepted but subdued the associate bishop elected to aid him. He traveled widely through all of the colonies and was the planner of those far-flung preaching campaigns which made the circuit-rider a familiar frontier figure. As an organizer and administrator, Francis Asbury holds a primacy in the annals of his sect.

ASCH, MORRIS JOSEPH (*b. Philadelphia, Pa., 1833; d. 1902*), laryngologist, soldier. Saw extensive medical service during Civil War and in the West; practiced thereafter in New York City. Deviser of "Asch operation" for deviation of nasal septum.

ASHBURNER, CHARLES ALBERT (*b. Philadelphia, Pa., 1854; d. 1889*), geologist. Surveyed Pennsylvania iron and oil districts, organized and headed survey of the anthracite field, 1880–86.

ASHBY, TURNER (*b. near Markham, Va., 1828; d. near Harrisonburg, Va., 1862*), Confederate soldier. Distinguished in the Valley campaign, 1862.

ASHE, JOHN (*b. Grovely, N.C. ?, c. 1720; d. Sampson Co., N.C., 1781*), soldier, politician. His defeat at Briar Creek in 1778 resulted in the British capture of Georgia.

ASHE, JOHN BAPTISTA (*b. Rocky Point, N.C., 1748; d. Halifax, N.C., 1802*). Member of Continental Congress, 1787–88; U.S. representative from North Carolina, 1789–93; governor, 1802.

ASHE, SAMUEL (*b. near Beaufort, N.C., 1725; d. Rocky Point, N.C., 1813*), jurist, Revolutionary patriot. Presiding judge of the first North Carolina supreme court; governor of North Carolina, 1795–98.

ASHE, THOMAS SAMUEL (*b. Orange Co., N.C., 1812; d. 1887*), legislator. Served in Confederate Congress; elected to U.S. Congress, 1872; state supreme court judge, 1878–87.

ASHE, WILLIAM SHEPPERD (*b. Rocky Point, N.C., 1814; d. Rocky Point, 1862*), planter, lawyer. Grandson of Samuel Ashe. Congressman, Democrat, from North Carolina, 1849–52; president, Wilmington & Weldon Railroad; directed Confederate government transportation, New Orleans to Richmond.

ASHER, JOSEPH MAYOR (*b. Manchester, England, 1872; d. New York, N.Y., 1909*), rabbi. Professor of homiletics, Jewish Theological Seminary of America, 1902–09; served several New York congregations as eloquent preacher.

ASHFORD, BAILEY KELLY (*b. Washington, D.C., 1873; d. San Juan, P.R., 1934*), physician, research worker in tropical medicine. His discovery that the hookworm was the cause of tropical anemia and his successful campaign against the disease in Puerto Rico led to a later world-wide campaign by the Rockefeller Institute. [*Supp. 1*]

ASHHURST, JOHN (*b. Philadelphia, Pa., 1839; d. 1900*), surgeon, author. Professor of surgery, University of Pennsylvania; author of *Principles and Practise of Surgery* (1871) and editor of *International Encyclopedia of Surgery* (1881–86).

ASHLEY, JAMES MITCHELL (*b. Allegheny Co., Pa., 1824; d. 1896*), congressman. Originally a Democrat, his intense antagonism to slavery swept him into the Republican camp in 1854. While U.S. representative from Ohio, 1859–69, he sponsored the first bill to introduce minority representation in the territorial governments, prepared the first measure for the reconstruction of the Southern states presented to Congress, and with Lot M. Morrill drew up the 1862 bill to abolish slavery in the District of Columbia. He considered his greatest achievement to be his successful introduction of the first proposition to abolish slavery by a constitutional amendment. Andrew Johnson's impeachment was initiated by him, and the president's acquittal brought Ashley's defeat in 1868. Appointed governor of Montana in 1869, he later served as president of the Toledo, Ann Arbor and Northern Michigan Railroad.

ASHLEY, WILLIAM HENRY (*b. Powhatan Co., Va., c. 1778; d. Cooper Co., Mo., 1838*), fur trader, explorer, congressman. Settled in Missouri between 1803 and 1805 and engaged in the manufacture of gunpowder and the mining of saltpeter and lead; elected lieutenant-governor of Missouri, 1820. In 1822–23 he and Andrew Henry turned to fur trading and dispatched expeditions up the Missouri to the Yellowstone and across South Pass into the Green River valley. A year later Ashley abandoned the fixed trading method of operation, substituting for it an annual rendezvous of trappers and traders conducted at any convenient and accessible place. The first of these was held at the confluence of Henry's Fork and the Green River. Between 1824 and 1826, Ashley and his men covered a great range of territory in present-day Nebraska, Colorado, Wyoming and Utah as they carried supplies to the "mountain men" at the rendezvous and brought the furs back to St. Louis. He was congressman from Missouri on an anti-Jackson ticket, 1831–37, and championed Western interests.

ASHMEAD, ISAAC (*b. Germantown, Pa., 1790; d. 1870*), printer. Introduced composition roller, and hydraulic press for smooth-pressing wet sheets; printer to the American Sunday School Union.

ASHMEAD, WILLIAM HARRIS (*b. Philadelphia, Pa., 1855; d. 1908*), entomologist. Author of important papers on taxonomy of insect pests.

ASHMORE, WILLIAM (*b. Putnam, O., 1824; d. Wallaston, Mass., 1909*), Baptist missionary to China, 1850–1903.

ASHMUN, GEORGE (*b. Blandford, Mass., 1804; d. Springfield, Mass., 1870*), lawyer, legislator. Congressman, Whig, from Massachusetts, 1845–51; opposed Mexican War. Served as chairman of the 1860 Republican Convention at Chicago and was an adviser to President Lincoln.

ASHMUN, JEHUDI (*b. Champlain, N.Y., 1794; d. New Haven, Conn., 1828*), colonial agent. Graduated University of Vermont, 1816; entered Congregational ministry. While editor of the *Theological Repertory* he became interested in the work of the American Colonization Society and was appointed a special U.S. government representative to Liberia in 1822. With 37 new colonists he sailed to Africa and found the settlement in a desperate situation; most of the settlers were ill, supplies were exhausted and a large native force threatened to attack. Assuming leadership, he built defenses and repulsed the enemy. In May 1823, he was superseded by a new agent who soon returned to America. Shortly thereafter, Ashmun was fully authorized as agent and headed the enterprise until 1828.

ASPINWALL, WILLIAM (*b. Brookline, Mass., 1743; d. 1823*), physician. Military surgeon in the Revolution; opened inoculation hospital for smallpox in 1783, second of its kind in America.

ASPINWALL, WILLIAM HENRY (*b. New York, N.Y., 1807; d. 1875*), merchant. Succeeded his uncles in the management of the great G.G. and S. Howland trading firm, 1837. In 1850 he resigned active leadership in Howland and Aspinwall, entered the Pacific Railroad & Panama Steamship Co. and directed the building of a railroad across the isthmus of Panama. The railroad in conjunction with his Pacific Mail Steamship Co. gave the Aspinwall interests a monopoly on the best passenger and trade route to California during the gold-rush years. After the Civil War he retired from active business and interested himself in the social, civic and artistic life of New York City.

ASTOR, JOHN JACOB (*b. Waldorf, Germany, 1763; d. New York, N.Y., 1848*), fur trader, capitalist. While en route to America in 1784 he met a fellow immigrant who had successfully traded for furs with the Indians, and decided to enter this business; by 1786 he was established in his own shop on Water St., New York City, and made frequent trips into Canada in connection with his fur trading ventures. By 1800 he had amassed a fortune of $250,000, was acknowledged the leading factor in the trade, and began to make large purchases of New York real-estate. The Louisiana Purchase opened new trading vistas to him. In 1808 he consolidated his holdings in the American Fur Co. and made plans to circumvent the St. Louis control of the fur trade in the Far West by planting a central depot at the mouth of the Columbia River through which furs collected in the interior would be shipped most efficiently to Chinese markets. The vessels would then load merchandise for European trading, complete the European circuit and reload with items for American markets. Astoria was founded as the exchange center in 1811, and a vessel carrying men and supplies was dispatched to the Oregon territory. A series of disasters and the coming of the War of 1812 ended this enterprise; in 1813 the British took possession of Astor's establishment at the mouth of the Columbia. Astoria was a victim of the war, but its owner was repaid by lending money at a ruinous rate of interest to the U.S. government. At the signing of peace he attempted once again to monopolize fur trading in the trans-Mississippi region; but Western opposition was strong, and the returns of his bold campaigns were diminished by losses to the Indians and a decline in fur value. In 1834 he sold all his fur interests and retired to the administration of his twenty-million dollar fortune. Founded Astor Library, New York City.

ASTOR, JOHN JACOB (*b. New York, N.Y., 1822; d. New York, 1890*), capitalist. Son of William Backhouse Astor; administered the family estate and expanded facilities of the Astor Library.

ASTOR, JOHN JACOB (*b. Rhinebeck, N.Y., 1864; d. 1912*), capitalist, inventor. Great-grandson of John Jacob Astor (1763–1848). Managed family estate; died in *Titanic* disaster.

ASTOR, WILLIAM BACKHOUSE (*b. New York, N.Y., 1792; d. New York, 1875*), capitalist. Son of John Jacob Astor (1763–1848). Continued his father's policy of investing in New York real-estate.

ASTOR, WILLIAM WALDORF (*b. New York, N.Y., 1848; d. Brighton, England, 1919*), capitalist. Son of John Jacob Astor (1822–90). Moved to England, 1890, becoming a British subject in 1899 and raised to peerage as Viscount Astor, 1917.

ATCHISON, DAVID RICE (*b. Frogtown, Ky., 1807; d. Gower, Mo., 1886*), lawyer, senator. Removed to Missouri, 1830; U.S. senator, Democrat, from Missouri, 1843–55. He was chairman of the important Committee on Indian Affairs, promoted land-grant legislation to aid Missouri railroads and was elected president *pro tempore* of the Senate 16 times. Associated with the pro-slavery faction, and an opponent of Thomas H. Benton, he worked for the repeal of the Missouri Compromise and influenced passage of the Kansas-Nebraska bill. After failing of election in 1855 he lapsed into obscurity.

ATHERTON, CHARLES GORDON (*b. Amherst, N.H., 1804; d. 1853*), lawyer, politician. Democratic congressman from New Hampshire, 1836–43; U.S. senator, 1843–49. Introduced 1838 "gag resolutions" forbidding introduction of memorials on slavery.

ATHERTON, GEORGE WASHINGTON (*b. Boxford, Mass., 1837; d. 1906*), college president. Championed land-grant colleges; became president of Pennsylvania State College, 1882, and can be considered its real founder.

ATHERTON, JOSHUA (*b. Harvard, Mass., 1737; d. Amherst, N.H., 1809*), lawyer, Loyalist during the Revolution, early anti-slavery leader.

ATKINS, JEARUM (*b. Vermont; fl. 1840–80*), inventor. Devised automatic mechanism to rake severed grain from reaper platform, 1852.

ATKINSON, EDWARD (*b. Brookline, Mass., 1827; d. 1905*), industrialist, economist. Helped establish and later headed the Boston Manufacturers Mutual Insurance Co.; improved industrial architecture by insisting on safe construction of factories.

ATKINSON, GEORGE FRANCIS (*b. Raisinville, Mich., 1854; d. Tacoma, Wash., 1918*), botanist. First president of the American Botanical Society; an outstanding mycologist and the author of *Studies of American Fungi* (1900).

ATKINSON, GEORGE HENRY (*b. Newburyport, Mass., 1819; d. 1889*), Congregational clergyman, educator, community builder. As missionary in Oregon, he fostered public education there and became an enthusiastic propagandist for settling and farming the Pacific Northwest.

ATKINSON, GEORGE WESLEY (*b. Kanawha Co., Va., 1845; d. 1925*), author, lecturer, jurist. Republican governor of West Virginia, 1896; judge of U.S. Court of Claims, 1905–16.

ATKINSON, HENRY (*b. North Carolina, 1782; d. Jefferson Barracks, Mo., 1842*), soldier. Entered the regular army, 1808; promoted colonel, 1815; assigned command of the 1819 "Yellowstone Expedition," an unsuccessful project aimed at warning Indians and British fur traders by sending American soldiers to the mouth of the Yellowstone River. In 1825 he commanded another expedition to the upper Missouri, reached the Yellowstone mouth, held treaty councils with a number of Indian tribes and on his return to St. Louis selected the site for the historic post Jefferson Barracks. He was in general command of troops in the Black Hawk war, 1832, and supervised the removal of the Winnebagos from Wisconsin, 1840.

ATKINSON, JOHN (*b. Deerfield, N.Y., 1835; d. Haverstraw, N.Y., 1897*), Methodist clergyman. Author of several important histories of American Methodism and of the hymn "Shall We Meet Beyond the River?"

ATKINSON, THOMAS (*b. Dinwiddie Co., Va., 1807; d. Wilmington, N.C., 1881*), Episcopal bishop of North Carolina, 1853–81; aided establishment of University of the South; supported the Confederate cause.

ATKINSON, WILLIAM BIDDLE (*b. Haverford, Pa., 1832; d. 1909*), obstetrician. Author of a valuable reference work on American medical biography, *The Physicians and Surgeons of the United States* (1878).

ATKINSON, WILLIAM YATES (*b. Oakland, Ga., 1854; d. Newnan, Ga., 1899*), lawyer. Governor of Georgia, 1894–98.

ATKINSON, WILMER (*b. Bucks Co., Pa., 1840; d. 1920*), journalist. Founded and edited the *Farm Journal*, 1877–1917.

ATLEE, JOHN LIGHT (*b. Lancaster, Pa., 1799; d. Lancaster, 1885*), physician. Expert in obstetrical surgery.

ATLEE, WASHINGTON LEMUEL (*b. Lancaster, Pa., 1808; d. 1878*), surgeon. Brother of John L. Atlee, and with him an early proponent of ovariotomy.

ATTERBURY, WILLIAM WALLACE (*b. New Albany, Ind., 1866; d. 1935*), railroad president. Converted Pennsylvania R.R. line from New York to Washington to electric operation; director-general of transportation, American Expeditionary Forces in World War I. [*Supp. 1*]

ATTUCKS, CRISPUS (*b. c. 1723; d. Boston, Mass., 1770*), leader of the mob which precipitated the so-called "Boston Massacre"; lost his life in the affray.

ATWATER, CALEB (*b. North Adams, Mass., 1778; d. Circleville, O., 1867*), pioneer, author. Settled in Ohio, 1815, where he practiced law; elected to Ohio legislature, 1821; supported the construction of highways and canals and the provision of popular education. He was one of three commissioners appointed by President Jackson to treat with the Indians at Prairie du Chien, 1829; in 1838 he published *A History of the State of Ohio, Natural and Civil.* Atwater was a social and intellectual pioneer of the Middle West, and perhaps the first advocate of forest conservation; he was one of the first to predict the success of the railway, the first historian of his state and the founder of its school system.

ATWATER, LYMAN HOTCHKISS (*b. New Haven, Conn., 1813; d. Princeton, N.J., 1883*), Congregational clergyman, educator. Professor of philosophy, Princeton, 1854–83; prolific writer in defense of old-school Calvinism.

ATWATER, WILBUR OLIN (*b. Johnsburg, N.Y., 1844; d. 1907*), pioneer in agricultural chemistry. Studied chemistry at Yale University and at Leipzig and Berlin; professor of chemistry, Wesleyan University, Middletown, Conn., 1873–1907. Aided in establishment of the first state agricultural station in the United States (Middletown, Conn., 1875). Through Atwater's efforts Congress made funds available to every state for at least one such station, 1887. As a chemist, he discovered that free atmospheric nitrogen is assimilated by leguminous plants, 1881. With E. B. Rosa he built the Atwater-Rosa calorimeter, 1892–97; he thereafter demonstrated that the law of conservation of energy is valid for human beings and prepared an elaborate table giving the calorific value of various foodstuffs.

ATWOOD, CHARLES B. (*b. Charlestown, Mass., 1849; d. 1895*), architect. Designed the twin Vanderbilt houses, Fifth Avenue, New York City; served as designer-in-chief of the Chicago World's Fair, 1893.

ATWOOD, DAVID (*b. Bedford, N.H., 1815; d. Madison, Wis., 1889*), editor, politician. Founded the politically influential *Wisconsin State Journal*, 1852.

ATWOOD, LEWIS JOHN (*b. Goshen, Conn., 1827; d. Waterbury, Conn., 1909*), inventor, manufacturer. With Hiram W. Hayden he invented sheet-brass lampburners for use with petroleum, 1855; also devised a scrap-metal press.

ATZERODT, GEORGE A. (*c. 1832–1865*). [See BOOTH, JOHN WILKES.]

AUCHMUTY, RICHARD TYLDEN (*b. New York, N.Y., 1831; d. Lenox, Mass., 1893*), architect. Founded New York Trade School in 1881, one of the earliest institutions to combine theoretical instruction and shop practice.

AUCHMUTY, ROBERT (*b. Scotland; d. Roxbury, Mass., 1750*), colonial jurist. Judge of admiralty, Massachusetts, 1733–41.

AUCHMUTY, ROBERT (*b. Boston, Mass.; d. England, 1788*), colonial jurist. Son of the preceding; served with John Adams as counsel to Capt. Preston in the "Boston Massacre" case, 1770; removed to England, 1776.

AUCHMUTY, SAMUEL (*b. Boston, Mass., 1722; d. New York, N.Y., 1777*), Anglican minister, Loyalist. Brother of Robert Auchmuty (d. 1788); rector of Trinity Church, New York City, 1764–77.

AUDSLEY, GEORGE ASHDOWN (*b. Elgin, Scotland, 1838; d. 1925*), architect, organ designer. Practiced in America, 1892–1925; author of many books on ornament, in particular *The Ornamental Arts of Japan* (1884).

AUDUBON, JOHN JAMES (*b. Les Cayes, Santo Domingo, 1785; d. New York, N.Y., 1851*), artist, ornithologist. Natural son of Jean Audubon, a French sea captain, trader and planter, and a Creole mistress, John James Audubon was taken to France in 1789 and formally adopted by his father and his father's legal wife. At the age of fifteen, he began a collection of original drawings of French birds; in 1802–03, he studied drawing in Paris under David. Early in 1804 he took up residence in America on an estate his father owned near Philadelphia; there, he made the first "banding" experiment ever made on the young of an American wild bird. In 1805 he went back to France; in the following year, having formed a partnership with Ferdinand Rozier, he returned to America and opened (with Rozier) a general store in Louisville, Ky. He married Lucy Bakewell in 1808.

Audubon roamed the country in eager pursuit of rare birds to study and sketch while his partner "kept store"; in the spring of 1810 the store was moved down the Ohio to Henderson, Ky., but it was not a success at either location. A series of other business enterprises ended in 1819 with Audubon's bankruptcy.

While he was attempting to support his family by portrait sketching, and as a tutor and drawing master, he determined to publish his bird drawings. At Philadelphia, where he had gone seeking a publisher, he was advised to offer his work in Europe where interest in the subject would be greater and where skilled engravers could be found. Accordingly he sailed in 1826, and was successful in finding subscribers for his work in Liverpool, Edinburgh and London; he was also fortunate in securing the services of Robert Havell, Jr., as engraver for the project. The *Birds of America* in large folio size began to appear in 1827 and was published in parts, the final part appearing in 1838. The *Ornithological Biography*, a text commentary on the hand-colored plates in the *Birds*, was published between 1831 and 1839; in this he had the help of William MacGillivray, who also assisted in the methodical catalogue entitled *Synopsis of the Birds of North America* (1839).

Audubon returned to the United States in 1831 with a European reputation as naturalist and artist.

He continued his explorations and sketching in Texas, Florida and Labrador until 1834 when he went back to Edinburgh. He came home once again, 1839, and began preparation of an octavo edition of the *Birds* (New York and Philadelphia, 1840–44). He also undertook with John Bachman a work on the *Viviparous Quadrupeds of North America* (plates, 1842–45; text, 1846–54).

Despite criticism of his work, both as art and as science, Audubon remains at the head of early American ornithologists. His only rival, Alexander Wilson, produced work which was more original and more steadily scientific, but it lacked the scope, magnificence and general usefulness of the *Birds of America*.

AUGUR, CHRISTOPHER COLUMBUS (*b. Kendall, N.Y., 1821; d. Georgetown, D.C., 1898*), Union soldier. Graduated West Point, 1843. Served in Mexican War; in Oregon, 1852–56; and with distinction in several theaters of the Civil War. Promoted brigadier-general, regular army, 1869, he retired in 1885.

AUGUR, HEZEKIAH (*b. New Haven, Conn., 1791; d. 1858*), sculptor. Overcame paternal objections and financial difficulties to become an interesting precursor in American sculpture.

AUGUSTUS, JOHN (*b. 1785; d. Boston, Mass., 1859*), philanthropist. From 1841 to 1859, served without pay as a pioneer probation officer and friend to the unfortunate of Boston.

AUSTELL, ALFRED (*b. near Dandridge, Tenn., 1814; d. Atlanta, Ga., 1881*), financier. Removed to Campbellton, Ga., 1836; in 1858, foreseeing future importance of Atlanta, he settled there as a merchant. At the end of the Civil War he organized the Atlanta National Bank, the first Southern bank to be chartered under the Act of 1863, and made it an outstanding factor in the economic development of Georgia and the rebuilding of the South. He was also active and successful in railroad enterprises and in cotton brokerage.

AUSTEN, PETER TOWNSEND (*b. Clifton, N.Y., 1852; d. 1907*), chemist. Professor of chemistry, Rutgers, 1878–91; thereafter a consultant and inventor of dyeing and bleaching processes.

AUSTIN, BENJAMIN (*b. Boston, Mass., 1752; d. 1820*), political leader. A successful merchant, he succeeded Samuel Adams as leader of the more radical Boston Republicans (Democrats) during the troubled years 1789–96. Author of *Constitutional Republicanism, in Opposition to Fallacious Federalism* (1803).

AUSTIN, DAVID (*b. New Haven, Conn., 1759; d. Bozrah, Conn., 1831*), Congregational clergyman. Widely known in his day for his preachings and writings on the millennium.

AUSTIN, HENRY (*b. Mt. Carmel, Conn., 1804; d. New Haven, Conn., 1891*), architect. Trained in office of Ithiel Town; designed many private and public buildings in New Haven, including a library for Yale (1842).

AUSTIN, JAMES TRECOTHICK (*b. Boston, Mass., 1784; d. Boston, 1870*), lawyer. Son of Jonathan L. Austin. Attorney-general of Massachusetts, 1832–43; a foe of abolitionism.

AUSTIN, JANE GOODWIN (*b. Worcester, Mass., 1831; d. 1894*), author. Her novels of early New England were based on careful research and include *Standish of Standish* (1889), and *Betty Alden* (1891).

AUSTIN, JONATHAN LORING (*b. Boston, Mass., 1748; d. Boston, 1826*), brother and partner of Benjamin Austin; served as confidential messenger and secretary for the American commissioners to France, 1777–79.

AUSTIN, MARY (*b. Carlinville, Ill., 1868; d. Santa Fé, N. Mex., 1934*), author, feminist. Her best work is nature-writing in the tradition of John Muir and Thoreau. Among her more important books are: *The Land of Little Rain* (1903) and *A Woman of Genius* (1912). [*Supp. 1*]

AUSTIN, MOSES (*b. Durham, Conn., 1761; d. 1821*), merchant. First interested in lead mining during the Revolution, he worked a mine in southwestern Virginia between 1789 and 1798, moving in the latter year to Missouri; there he reopened the old Mine à Burton and founded the town of Potosi. His fortune lost in the collapse of the Bank of St. Louis and the depression of 1819, he applied in December 1820 to the Spanish authorities for a permit to settle 300 families in Texas. The permit was granted in January 1821; but Austin died before making the move, and his son Stephen F. Austin carried out the proposed colonization.

AUSTIN, SAMUEL (*b. New Haven, Conn., 1760; d. 1830*), Congregational clergyman. Pastor of the First Church in Worcester, Mass., 1790–1815; a firm opponent of Unitarianism. President of the University of Vermont, 1815–21.

AUSTIN, STEPHEN FULLER (*b. Wythe Co., Va., 1793; d. Texas, 1836*), founder of Texas. Son of Moses Austin, he was successively a storekeeper, manager of the family lead mines in Missouri, adjutant of the militia and a member of the Missouri territorial legislature, 1814–20, before the collapse of the family fortunes (*see* Moses Austin). He moved to Arkansas and then to Louisiana, where he studied law and assisted on the staff of the *Louisiana Advertiser*. This training, added to an intimate understanding of frontier life, fitted him to be founder and ruler of a wilderness commonwealth.

Sceptical at first of his father's scheme for settling 300 families in Texas, he soon dedicated himself to the task. He visited Texas in 1821, and in January 1822 planted the first legal settlement of Anglo-Americans there on a fertile, well-watered site bordering the Gulf of Mexico. A question of right arising, Austin secured ratification by the new independent Mexican government of the grant made to his father by the dispossessed Spanish authorities.

Until 1828, Austin acted as executive, lawmaker, chief judge and military commander within his grant. Even after organization of a constitutional local government, his influence continued great and he directed the colony in effect until 1832. Under laws passed in 1825 by the Mexican federal government he was able to extend his grant, and was the most successful of all the *empresarios*, as those who contracted to settle colonists were called. During the early years, his labors were enormous. He fixed and administered the land system, pushed back the Indians, mapped the province and charted its rivers and bays, brought in many new immigrants, fostered the commerce of the colony and provided for the establishment of schools. He was largely responsible for enactment of liberal laws with respect to colonization, debt and criminal process; he was also responsible for a law permitting continued introduction of slaves in the form of indentured servants.

Austin, loyal to Mexico, counseled aloofness from the party struggles which were racking the republic. He felt that Texas would develop best as a state of Mexico, and favored complete independence over any annexation by the United States. In April 1833, however, relations between the settlers and the Mexican government reached a critical stage; although Austin considered it inexpedient, a convention was held and a petition written requesting separation of Texas from the state of Coahuila and the creation of an independent state government. Sent to Mexico City to secure approval of this, Austin was jailed on the charge that he was plotting to annex Texas to the United States. Released without trial in July 1835, he returned to Texas and was soon engaged in the Texas Revolution, serving first as commander of the volunteer army and then as a commissioner to the United States in an effort to secure aid and sympathy. Partially successful in this mission, he and his colleagues came home in June 1836; in September, Sam Houston defeated him in the election for the presidency of the Republic of Texas. He served as secretary of state under Houston until December when he died.

AUSTIN, WILLIAM (*b. Lunenburg, Mass., 1778; d. Charlestown, Mass., 1841*), author. His short story "Peter Rugg, the Missing Man" (1824) is perhaps the most original and imaginative American tale before Hawthorne and Poe.

AVERELL, WILLIAM WOODS (*b. Cameron, N.Y., 1832; d. Bath, N.Y., 1900*), Union soldier. Graduated West Point, 1855. An outstanding cavalryman; commanded the 2nd cavalry division in action at Kelly's Ford, 1863.

AVERY, BENJAMIN PARKE (*b. New York, N.Y., 1828; d. Peking, China, 1875*), journalist, diplomat. Editor of San Francisco *Bulletin*, 1863–73; appointed minister to China, 1874.

AVERY, ISAAC WHEELER (*b. St. Augustine, Fla., 1837; d. 1897*), Confederate soldier. Active in the politics and journalism of the Reconstruction era in Georgia.

AVERY, JOHN (*b. Conway, Mass., 1837; d. North Bridgeton, Maine, 1887*), linguist. His scholarly interests were concerned chiefly with the languages and literature of India.

AVERY, SAMUEL PUTNAM (*b. New York, N.Y., 1822; d. 1904*), art connoisseur, philanthropist. An art dealer whose advice was valued by the principal American collectors of his time.

AVERY, WILLIAM WAIGSTILL (*b. Burke Co., N.C., 1816; d. Morganton, N.C., 1864*), lawyer, member of Confederate Provisional Congress.

AWL, WILLIAM MACLAY (*b. Harrisburg, Pa., 1799; d. 1876*), alienist. Promoted bill founding first Ohio "State Hospital" for the insane, appointed its superintendent, 1838; helped establish Ohio State Medical Society.

AXTELL, SAMUEL BEACH (*b. Franklin Co., O., 1819; d. Morristown, N.J., 1891*), lawyer, politician, jurist. Governor of Utah, 1874, and of New Mexico, 1875–78; chief justice, supreme court of New Mexico, 1882–85.

AYALA, JUAN MANUEL DE (*fl. 1775*), Spanish navigator. Explored and charted San Francisco Bay, 1775.

AYCOCK, CHARLES BRANTLEY (*b. Wayne Co., N.C., 1859; d. 1912*), governor of North Carolina, 1901–05, Democrat. Led successful campaigns for improvement of public educational work.

AYER, EDWARD EVERETT (*b. Kenosha, Wis., 1841; d. Pasadena, Calif., 1927*), railway lumberman, bibliophile, collector. A founder of the Field Museum of Natural History, Chicago, and its president, 1893–98; trustee of Newberry Library, 1892–1911.

AYER, FRANCIS WAYLAND (*b. Lee, Mass., 1848; d. 1923*), advertising agent. Started advertising firm of N. W. Ayer & Son in Philadelphia, Pa., 1869; published the well-known *American Newspaper Annual and Directory*. Ayer introduced the "open-contract" plan whereby the agent made strict accounting of his use of client's money; he also developed use of trademarks, slogans, pictorial displays and all the usual devices of present-day advertising. An honorable man, he did much to raise ethical standards of American advertising.

AYER, JAMES COOK (*b. Ledyard, Conn., 1818; d. Winchendon, Mass., 1878*), physician. Proprietor of "Cherry Pectoral" and other patent medicines; promoter of textile and mining enterprises.

AYLLON, LUCAS VASQUEZ DE (*b. Toledo, Spain, c. 1475; d. 1526*), Spanish explorer. A judge of the supreme court of Hispaniola (Santo Domingo), he fitted out an expedition in 1520 to search for a fabled land of great wealth supposed to lie to the north and west. In June 1521, his captains reached the mouth of a large river on the coast of what is now the Carolinas; the Indians whom they met called the land "Chicora." Soon after the return of the expedition, Ayllon went to Spain and was granted the new-found region under terms by Charles V. Ayllon himself did not make a voyage there until 1526, but ships sent by him took possession of the land in the name of the Spanish King and cruised for some 250 leagues along the coast. In June or July 1526, Ayllon sailed from Santo Domingo with five or six hundred settlers and landed at what is thought to have been the mouth of the Cape Fear river; he then sailed in an uncertain direction to another river mouth (the Peedee, the Santee and the James have all been suggested) where he founded a colony called San Miguel de Gualdape. Many of the colonists sickened and died; Ayllon died in October. The survivors abandoned the colony and returned to Santo Domingo.

AYLWIN, JOHN CUSHING (*b. Quebec, Canada, c. 1780; d. 1813*), naval officer. Sailing master of U.S.S. *Constitution;* killed in action with the *Java.*

AYRES, ANNE (*b. London, England, 1816; d. New York, N.Y., 1896*), original member of the Sisterhood of the Holy Communion, was the first woman in the United States to become a Protestant nun.

AYRES, BROWN (*b. Memphis, Tenn., 1856; d. 1919*), engineer, educator. President of University of Tennessee, 1904–19; responsible for its expansion and reorganization.

AYRES, ROMEYN BECK (*b. Montgomery Co., N.Y., 1825; d. Fort Hamilton, N. Y., 1888*), Union soldier. Graduated West Point, 1847. Chief of artillery and infantry commander in Army of the Potomac.

AZARIAS, BROTHER (*b. near Killenaule, Ireland, 1847; d. 1893*), educator, author. Born Patrick Mullany; entered Brothers of the Christian Schools, 1862. Author of a remarkable *Essay Contributing to a Philosophy of Literature* (1874) and other books.

BABBITT, BENJAMIN TALBOT (*b. Westmoreland, N.Y., 1809; d. 1889*), inventor, manufacturer of baking-powder and "Babbitt's Best Soap"; held numerous chemical and mechanical patents.

BABBITT, IRVING (*b. Dayton, O., 1865; d. Cambridge, Mass., 1933*), teacher and author, neo-humanist. After graduating from Harvard in 1889 he returned in 1894 to begin a brilliant teaching career there and at many other universities as guest lecturer. His six major books treat the problem of modern culture in the light of the humanism established in ancient Greece, China and the Renaissance: *Literature and the American College* (1908), *The New Laokoon* (1910), *The Masters of Modern French Criticism* (1912), *Rousseau and Romanticism* (1919), *Democracy and Leadership* (1924) and *On Being Creative* (1932). The problem as he saw it was to re-establish critical standards which had been undermined by romanticism and naturalism. [*Supp.* 1]

BABBITT, ISAAC (*b. Taunton, Mass., 1799; d. Somerville, Mass., 1862*). Invented a superior journal-box and its alloy lining; a widely used bearing-metal was named for him.

BABCOCK, GEORGE HERMAN (*b. near Otsego, N.Y., 1832; d. 1893*), engineer, inventor. With his father in 1854, Babcock invented the first polychromatic printing-press and a commercially successful job printing-press. While employed at Hope Iron Works, Providence, R.I., he and Stephen Wilcox invented and brought out the Babcock and Wilcox steam-engine, an early automatic cut-off engine of excellent design. The two inventors formed a partnership and secured a patent in 1867 for a water-tube high-pressure boiler; in 1868 they moved to New York to manufacture the boiler; in 1881 the highly successful firm was incorporated with Babcock as president.

BABCOCK, JAMES FRANCIS (*b. Boston, Mass., 1844; d. 1897*), chemist. Massachusetts state assayer of alcoholic beverages, 1875–85; as Boston inspector of milk he rigidly enforced laws against adulteration.

BABCOCK, JAMES WOOD (*b. Chester, S.C., 1856; d. 1922*), psychiatrist. Investigated or stimulated the investigation of many important problems in psychiatry and the care of the insane; published (1908) the first comprehensive American account of pellagra.

BABCOCK, JOSEPH WEEKS (*b. Swanton, Vt., 1850; d. Washington, D.C., 1909*). Representative in Congress from Wisconsin, 1892–1906; chairman of Republican Congressional Campaign Committee, 1894–1904.

BABCOCK, MALTBIE DAVENPORT (*b. Syracuse, N.Y., 1858; d. Naples, Italy, 1901*), Presbyterian clergyman, author. Pastor, Brown Memorial Church, Baltimore, 1887–99, and Brick Presbyterian Church, New York City, 1899–1901.

BABCOCK, ORVILLE E. (*b. Franklin, Vt., 1835; d. Mosquito Inlet, Fla., 1884*), engineer, soldier. Graduated West Point, 1861. Private secretary to President Grant who defended him when accused of complicity in the "Whisky Ring" frauds, 1869–75.

BABCOCK, STEPHEN MOULTON (*b. Bridgewater, N.Y., 1843; d. Madison, Wis., 1931*), agricultural chemist. Made many valuable contributions to agri-

culture; best known for invention of the milk-fat test which bears his name. [*Supp.* 1]

BABCOCK, WASHINGTON IRVING (*b. Stonington, Conn., 1858; d. New York, N.Y., 1917*), naval architect. Introduced the mould system of ship construction and designed the first large ships specially built for traffic on the Great Lakes.

BACHE, ALEXANDER DALLAS (*b. Philadelphia, Pa., 1806; d. 1867*), physicist. Great-grandson of Benjamin Franklin. Professor of natural philosophy and chemistry, University of Pennsylvania, 1828–1836. In 1836 he was appointed first president of Girard College; because of delay in opening Girard he spent three years in reorganizing the Philadelphia public schools and then resumed his professorship. On Dec. 12, 1843 he was made superintendent of the U.S. Coast Survey, a position he held until his death. Throughout his career he kept up his interest in scientific research, especially in terrestrial magnetism; he founded the first magnetic observatory in America and made magnetic work an important part of the regular operations of the Coast Survey. He was a regent of the Smithsonian Institution and the first president of the National Academy of Sciences.

BACHE, BENJAMIN FRANKLIN (*b. Philadelphia, Pa., 1769; d. Philadelphia, 1798*), journalist. Grandson of Benjamin Franklin; founder of the Philadelphia *General Advertiser*, better known as the *Aurora*, a journal supporting the Democratic-Republican party. The paper contained extended accounts of European and domestic affairs but was notorious for virulent abuse of public figures; Washington was accused of overdrawing his salary, and forged letters attributed to him were reprinted by the *Aurora* in 1796. Bache made public the text of the secret Jay treaty in 1795; opened his columns to the French minister Adet in 1796 and published a particularly abusive "valedictory" at Washington's retirement in 1797. In June 1798, Bache was arrested under the Sedition Act for libeling President Adams.

BACHE, FRANKLIN (*b. Philadelphia, Pa., 1792; d. 1864*), teacher, chemist, physician. Son of Benjamin Franklin Bache; made important early contributions to development of chemical theory.

BACHE, RICHARD (*b. Settle, England, 1737; d. 1811*), merchant. Emigrated to New York City in 1765. Successful trader and issuer of private insurance policies; succeeded his father-in-law, Benjamin Franklin, as postmaster-general.

BACHE, THEOPHYLACT (*b. Settle, England, 1734/35; d. New York, N.Y., 1807*), merchant, Loyalist. Brother and partner of Richard Bache; emigrated to New York City in 1751; president of New York Chamber of Commerce, 1773.

BACHELDER, JOHN (*b. Weare, N.H., 1817; d. Houghton, Mich., 1906*), inventor, manufacturer. Improved the Howe sewing machine by developing the continuous feed, the vertical needle and the horizontal table.

BACHER, OTTO HENRY (*b. Cleveland, O., 1856; d. Bronxville, N.Y., 1909*), etcher. Worked with Duveneck and Whistler in Venice; a leading pen-and-ink illustrator in the 1890's.

BACHMAN, JOHN (*b. Rhinebeck, N.Y., 1790; d. Columbia, S.C., 1874*), naturalist, Lutheran clergyman. Best known for collaboration with J. J. Audubon upon *The Viviparous Quadrupeds of North America.*

BACKUS, AZEL (*b. Norwich, Conn., 1765; d. Clinton, N.Y., 1816*), Congregational clergyman; first president of Hamilton College, 1812–16.

BACKUS, ISAAC (*b. Norwich, Conn., 1724; d. Middleborough, Mass., 1806*), Separatist and Baptist minister, historian. A Norwich Separatist from Congregationalism in 1746, he served as a New Light minister, 1748–56; converted to Baptist principles, he organized a Baptist church at Middleborough, Mass., in 1756 and served it as pastor until his death. A tireless itinerant preacher, his influence was wide and always on the side of independence and democratic control of each local church; he was a champion of religion against civil control—the greatest since Roger Williams. His *History of New England, with Particular Reference to the Denomination of Christians Called Baptists* (1777–96) is a primary source for students of colonial religious problems.

BACKUS, TRUMAN JAY (*b. Milan, N.Y., 1842; d. Brooklyn, N.Y., 1908*), educator. President, Packer Collegiate Institute, Brooklyn, 1883–1908.

BACON, ALICE MABEL (*b. New Haven, Conn., 1858; d. 1918*), writer, teacher, lecturer. Taught at Hampton Institute, 1883–88, 1889–99, and at schools in Japan.

BACON, AUGUSTUS OCTAVIUS (*b. Bryan Co., Ga., 1839; d. Washington, D.C., 1914*), lawyer. U.S. senator, Democrat, from Georgia, 1894–1914; introduced resolution opposing acquisition of the Philippines.

BACON, BENJAMIN WISNER (*b. Litchfield, Conn., 1860; d. 1932*), clergyman, teacher, writer. Known for his free and suggestive application of higher criticism to the origin and nature of the four Gospels.
[*Supp. 1*]

BACON, DAVID (*b. Woodstock, Conn., 1771; d. Hartford, Conn., 1817*), Congregational clergyman. Missionary to Indians in Lake Erie and Mackinac Islands region; founded Tallmadge, Ohio, 1807.

BACON, DELIA SALTER (*b. Tallmadge, O., 1811; d. 1859*), author. In *Philosophy of the Plays of Shakspere Unfolded* (1857), she maintained that the plays were really the work of Raleigh, Spenser and Sir Francis Bacon.

BACON, EDWARD PAYSON (*b. Reading, N.Y., 1834; d. Daytona, Fla., 1916*). Organized E. P. Bacon & Co., a leading grain trading firm in Chicago and Milwaukee, and was influential in formulating the Interstate Commerce Law of 1906.

BACON, EDWIN MUNROE (*b. Providence, R.I., 1844; d. Cambridge, Mass., 1916*), journalist. Editor, *Boston Globe*, 1873–78; *Daily Advertiser*, 1883–86; *Boston Post*, 1886–91. Author of books descriptive of Boston and New England.

BACON, FRANK (*b. Marysville, Calif., 1864; d. Chicago, Ill., 1922*), actor, playwright. With Winchell Smith, wrote the long-run play *Lightnin'* (1918).

BACON, HENRY (*b. Watseka, Ill., 1866; d. 1924*), architect. Trained in office of McKim, Mead and White, he worked in partnership (1887 to 1902) with James Brite; thereafter on his own. A devoted adherent of the theory of Greek architecture, he became interested in monumental work and the design of pedestals and architectural settings for statues and worked jointly on many occasions with Saint-Gaudens and D. C. French. In 1923 he was awarded the gold medal of the American Institute of Architects for his greatest achievement, the Lincoln Memorial in Washington, D.C.

BACON, JOHN (*b. Canterbury, Conn., 1738; d. Stockbridge, Mass., 1820*), Congregational clergyman, legislator. A leading Jeffersonian Democrat of western Massachusetts.

BACON, LEONARD (*b. Detroit, Mich., 1802; d. New Haven, Conn., 1881*), Congregational clergyman. Son of Rev. David Bacon. Graduated Yale, 1820, and Andover Theological Seminary; minister to the First Church of New Haven, Conn., 1825–66; acting professor of revealed theology, 1866–71, and lecturer on church polity and American church history, 1871–81, Yale Divinity School. As a speaker and as editor of the *Christian Spectator* and the *New Englander*, he influenced Congregationalism by arousing pride in its traditions and its polity; he was also author of *The Genesis of the New England Churches* (1874), a history of Congregationalism. An early leader in the antislavery cause, he had no sympathy with extreme abolitionists; he organized a society for the improvement of New Haven Negroes and was a founder and chief editor of the free-soil paper, the *Independent.*

BACON, LEONARD WOOLSEY (*b. New Haven, Conn., 1830; d. 1907*), Congregational clergyman. Son of Rev. Leonard Bacon. Author of a number of forceful polemical works.

BACON, NATHANIEL (*b. Suffolk, England, 1647; d. Gloucester Co., Va., 1676*), colonial leader. An emigrant to Virginia, with powerful relatives in England, he settled at Curl's Neck on James River. Leader of an unauthorized, popular expedition against the Indians in 1676, he dispersed the enemy and then forced Governor Berkeley to call a new Assembly at which he meant to introduce changes in the law of the colony. After arrest by Berkeley, pardon and release, he led his followers to Jamestown and extorted from the governor a formal commission to march against the Indians. Thereafter, on news that the governor had proclaimed him a rebel, he turned his force against Jamestown, burnt it and compelled all citizens within his power to swear fealty to himself. Just as he was about to introduce an alleged program of reforms he died and the rebellion collapsed.

BACON, ROBERT (*b. Jamaica Plain, Mass., 1860; d. 1919*), banker, diplomat, soldier. Partner in J. P. Morgan & Co.; assistant secretary of state, 1905–09; an advocate of American entry into the first World War, in which he served with distinction.

BACON, THOMAS (*b. Isle of Man, England, c. 1700; d. Frederick, Md., 1768*), clergyman of the Church of England in Maryland, 1744/5–68; editor, *Laws of Maryland at Large* (1765), an important work.

BADÈ, WILLIAM FREDERIC (*b. Carver, Minn., 1871; d. Berkeley, Calif., 1936*), archeologist. Excavated Tell en-Nasbeh, Palestine; professor of Semitic languages and Old Testament literature, Pacific School of Religion, 1902–36. [*Supp. 2*]

BADEAU, ADAM (*b. New York, N.Y., 1831; d. Ridgewood, N.J., 1895*), author, soldier, diplomat. Closely associated in military and civilian life with the subject, he wrote *Military History of Ulysses S. Grant* (1868, 1881) and helped Grant write his *Memoirs*.

BADGER, CHARLES JOHNSTON (*b. Rockville, Md., 1853; d. Blue Ridge Summit, Md., 1932*), naval officer. Head of the General Board of the Navy, 1917–21. [*Supp. 1*]

BADGER, GEORGE EDMUND (*b. New Bern, N.C., 1795; d. 1866*), jurist, secretary of the navy. U.S. senator, Whig, from North Carolina, 1846–55; as a lawyer he ranked before the U.S. Supreme Court with Webster, Crittenden, Berrien and Cushing.

BADGER, JOSEPH (*b. Charlestown, Mass., 1708; d. Boston, Mass., 1765*), artist. The principal portrait painter in Boston from about 1748 to 1760.

BADGER, JOSEPH (*b. Wilbraham, Mass., 1757; d. Perrysburg, O., 1846*), Congregational clergyman. Founded first church in the Western Reserve at Austinburg, O.; served as missionary in Ohio, 1800–35.

BADGER, OSCAR CHARLES (*b. Mansfield, Conn., 1823; d. 1899*), naval officer. An authority on ordnance, he served with distinction along the Atlantic Coast during the Civil War.

BADIN, STEPHEN THEODORE (*b. Orleans, France, 1768; d. Cincinnati, O., 1853*), missionary. Fled from the revolutionary fury in France to Baltimore, Md., 1792, where he continued studies for the priesthood; was ordained by Bishop Carroll in 1793, the first Roman Catholic priest ordained in the United States. Assigned to Kentucky, he rode horseback all along the frontier, visiting isolated communities and setting up log chapels; by 1800 he was vicar-general for Kentucky. Retiring to France in 1819, he returned to America in 1828. He served briefly as pastor of a parish at Monroe, Mich., and then as a missionary to the Potawatomi Indians in western Michigan. About 1832 he acquired either by grant or purchase the land on which the University of Notre Dame is presently located.

BAER, GEORGE FREDERICK (*b. near Lavansville, Pa., 1842; d. 1914*), lawyer. After success in bringing several damage suits against the Philadelphia & Reading Railway Co., he was employed by that company as counsel, 1870. A director of the Reading, he opposed company plans to invade the railway territory of his friend J. P. Morgan and resigned; Morgan gained control of the Reading, reorganized it, and made Baer president. In 1902, year of the great anthracite coal strike, he became the leader of forces resisting the strike and gained nation-wide fame by publication of a letter in which he implied that God had given the propertied interests control over laboring men.

BAER, WILLIAM STEVENSON (*b. Baltimore, Md., 1872; d. Baltimore, 1931*), orthopedic surgeon. Rediscoverer of cure for osteomyelitis; operated to restore motion in fused joints by introduction of animal membranes. [*Supp. 1*]

BAERMANN, CARL (*b. Munich, Germany, 1839; d. Newton, Mass., 1913*), teacher of music, pianist. Student of Liszt; settled in Boston, Mass., 1881, where he taught a number of distinguished students.

BAETJER, FREDERICK HENRY (*b. Baltimore, Md., 1874; d. Catonsville, Md., 1933*), physician, pioneer roentgenologist. Advanced the use of the X-ray by great personal sacrifice. [*Supp. 1*]

BAGBY, ARTHUR PENDLETON (*b. Louisa Co., Va., 1794; d. Mobile, Ala., 1858*). Removed to Alabama, 1818. Governor of Alabama, Democrat, 1837–41; U.S. senator, 1841–48; opposed Tyler's nomination for presidency, rewarded with U.S. ministry to Russia, 1848–49.

BAGBY, GEORGE WILLIAM (*b. Buckingham Co., Va., 1828; d. Richmond, Va., 1883*), editor, popular lecturer and humorist; his representative work to be found in *The Old Virginia Gentleman, etc.* (1910).

BAILEY, ANN (*b. Liverpool, England, 1742; d. Gallia Co., O., 1825*), pioneer. Came to America, 1761. Served as a scout and messenger on the Virginian border, 1774–92.

BAILEY, ANNA WARNER (*b. Groton, Conn., 1758; d. 1851*), heroine at battle of Groton Heights, 1781;

contributed her flannel petticoat for cartridge wadding, Groton, Conn., 1813.

BAILEY, EBENEZER (*b. 1795; d. Lynn, Mass., 1839*), educator. Principal of first high school for girls in Massachusetts, 1826.

BAILEY, FRANCIS (*b. Lancaster, Co., Pa., c. 1735; d. 1815*), printer, journalist. Published *Lancaster Almanac;* edited *The Freeman's Journal, post* 1781. Official printer for Congress and the State of Pennsylvania.

BAILEY, FRANK HARVEY (*b. Cranesville, Pa., 1851; d. Arizona, 1921*), engineer, naval officer. Designed the *Columbia* and *Minneapolis,* two of the fastest large vessels of their day, 1890–1900.

BAILEY, GAMALIEL (*b. Mount Holly, N.J., 1807, d. 1859*), physician, journalist, anti-slavery agitator. In 1837 he became sole editor and proprietor of the *Cincinnati Philanthropist,* the first anti-slavery newspaper in the West, which he issued in spite of mob opposition; he also founded a daily, the *Herald.* In 1847 he moved to Washington, D.C., as editor-in-chief of the *National Era,* sponsored by the American and Foreign Anti-Slavery Society. For the next 12 years he exerted a wide moral and political influence; although the *Era* had many distinguished contributors (John G. Whittier, Theodore Parker and Harriet Beecher Stowe, for example), Bailey's wise and fair direction was responsible for its success.

BAILEY, JACOB (*b. Rowley, Mass., 1731; d. Annapolis, Nova Scotia, 1818*), pioneer missionary of the Church of England in Maine, 1760–79; Loyalist.

BAILEY, JACOB WHITMAN (*b. Ward, now Auburn, Mass., 1811; d. 1857*), botanist, chemist, geologist. Graduated West Point, 1832, where he taught chemistry, mineralogy and geology, 1834–57. Distinguished for research among minor algae, and a pioneer American microscopist.

BAILEY, JAMES ANTHONY (*b. Detroit, Mich., 1847; d. Mount Vernon, N.Y., 1906*), showman. A founder of Cooper & Bailey circus, 1872; united with P. T. Barnum, 1881, as Barnum & Bailey show.

BAILEY, JAMES MONTGOMERY (*b. Albany, N.Y., 1841; d. Danbury, Conn., 1894*), journalist, the "Danbury News Man."

BAILEY, JOSEPH (*b. Pennsville, O., 1825; d. near Nevada, Mo., 1867*), Union soldier, engineer. Rendered outstanding service in the Red River campaign, 1864, by devising means for the fleet to return downstream in low water.

BAILEY, JOSEPH WELDON (*b. Crystal Springs, Miss., 1863; d. Sherman, Texas, 1929*), lawyer. U.S. senator from Texas, Democrat, 1901–13. Helped pass Hepburn Rate Bill, 1906; center of so-called "Bailey Controversy," 1907. [*Supp.* 1]

BAILEY, LYDIA R. (*b. 1779; d. Philadelphia, Pa., 1869*), printer. Worked successfully in Philadelphia, 1808–61.

BAILEY, RUFUS WILLIAM (*b. North Yarmouth, Maine, 1793; d. Texas, 1863*), Congregational clergyman. After a long career of teaching and preaching in South Carolina, North Carolina and Virginia, served as president of Austin College, Texas, 1858–63.

BAILEY, SOLON IRVING (*b. Lisbon, N.H., 1854; d. 1931*), astronomer. Pioneer in the photography and discovery of distant galaxies; first detected small variations in stars close packed in the globular clusters.
[*Supp.* 1]

BAILEY, THEODORUS (*b. Chateaugay, N.Y., 1805; d. Washington, D.C., 1877*), naval officer. Second in command under Farragut in the attack on New Orleans, 1862; retired 1866 as rear-admiral.

BAILLY, JOSEPH ALEXIS (*b. Paris, France, 1825; d. Philadelphia, Pa., 1883*), sculptor. Came to America, *post* 1848. Attained considerable reputation in Philadelphia.

BAIN, GEORGE LUKE SCOBIE (*b. Stirling, Scotland, 1836; d. 1891*), merchant-miller. Pioneered in developing the direct exportation of flour from St. Louis, Mo., to foreign countries.

BAINBRIDGE, WILLIAM (*b. Princeton, N.J., 1774; d. Philadelphia, Pa., 1833*), naval officer. Commanded merchant vessels in the European trade, 1793–98. When French aggressions and the depredations of the Barbary States awoke the American navy to new life, he received command of the 14-gun *Retaliation* with rank of lieutenant commandant. Cruising in the West Indies, fall of 1798, he was captured by two French frigates but saved his consorts, the *Montezuma* and *Norfolk,* by convincing the French commander of their superior firepower; after imprisonment in Guadaloupe, he returned to America, was promoted to master commandant and given command of the *Norfolk.* Bainbridge's account of the indignities suffered by Americans at Guadaloupe was partly responsible for the prompt passing by Congress of the Retaliation Act. After numerous successes in the West Indies he was ordered to cruise off Havana, and rendered excellent service in convoying and blockading enemy privateers; on May 2, 1800, he was promoted to captain, the highest naval rank at that time. In the same month he was given command of the 24-gun *George Washington* and ordered to bear America's tribute to the powerful Dey of Algiers; he performed this humiliating task in a diplomatic manner. Given command of the frigate *Philadelphia,* with orders to join Preble's squadron operating against the Barbary States, he proceeded to Tripoli, inadvertently grounded his ship in the harbor and was imprisoned with his crew, October 1803. Released from imprisonment, 1805, he returned to America. For the next seven years he saw some merchant service and held several naval commands; in February 1812, he joined Commodore Charles Stewart in protesting the government's proposal to lay up all naval vessels lest they be captured by the powerful British fleet. Succeeding Isaac Hull in command of the *Constitution*, he sailed for the South Atlantic where he attacked and captured a British frigate; he returned to Boston, February 1813. During the rest of the war, he oversaw construction of the 74-gun *Independence*, thereafter taking her to the Mediterranean where he succeeded Commodore Decatur in command. His last service afloat was aboard the *Columbus* in 1820.

BAIRD, ABSALOM (*b. Washington, Pa., 1824; d. near Relay, Md., 1905*), Union soldier. Graduated West Point, 1849. Outstanding division commander at Chickamauga; accompanied Sherman on march through Georgia; brevetted major-general, 1864.

BAIRD, CHARLES WASHINGTON (*b. Princeton, N.J., 1828; d. Rye, N.Y., 1887*), Presbyterian clergyman, historian. Author of *The Chronicle of a Border Town: A History of Rye, 1660–1870* (1871), and *The History of the Huguenot Emigration to America,* (1885).

BAIRD, HENRY CAREY (*b. Bridesburg, Pa., 1825; d. Wayne, Pa., 1912*), publisher, economic writer. Established Henry Carey Baird & Co. in 1849, the first publishing company in America to specialize in books on technical and industrial subjects. He is best known as an expositor and popularizer of the teachings of the "Pennsylvania School" of "national economists" of which his uncle Henry Carey and grandfather Mathew Carey were founders.

BAIRD, HENRY MARTYN (*b. Philadelphia, Pa., 1832; d. Yonkers, N.Y., 1906*), Presbyterian clergyman, historian. Professor of Greek, New York University, 1860–1902; like his brother Charles W. Baird, wrote extensively on the history of the Huguenots.

BAIRD, MATTHEW (*b. near Londonderry, Ireland, 1817; d. 1877*), locomotive builder. Came to America, 1821. Purchased interest in Baldwin's locomotive works at Philadelphia, Pa., 1854; became sole proprietor in 1866.

BAIRD, ROBERT (*b. near Pittsburgh, Pa., 1798; d. 1863*), Presbyterian clergyman. Father of Charles W. and Henry M. Baird. Influenced passage of legislation establishing public school system in New Jersey.

BAIRD, SAMUEL JOHN (*b. Newark, O., 1817; d. West Clifton Forge, Va., 1893*), Presbyterian clergyman, author. Edited *Collection of the Acts, Deliverances and Testimonies . . . of the Presbyterian Church . . .* (1854), a codification of the decisions of the General Assembly.

BAIRD, SPENCER FULLERTON (*b. Reading, Pa., 1823; d. Wood's Hole, Mass., 1887*), zoologist. Graduated Dickinson College, 1840; appointed professor of natural history there, 1846. At Dickinson he inaugu-

rated the method of field study of botany and zoology so successfully used by Agassiz and expanded the fish and reptile collections of the college museum; became also professor of chemistry, 1848. Two years later he went to the Smithsonian Institution, Washington, as assistant secretary to the director, Joseph Henry; upon Henry's death, 1878, he was elected to the secretaryship. He developed a huge network of agencies, both private and governmental, to gather material for the Smithsonian collections; in 1879 Congress authorized a building to house these collections. For nearly twenty years Baird was a prolific writer on ornithology and zoology, publishing *Catalogue of North American Birds* (1858); *Review of American Birds* (1864–66); *A History of North American Birds* (1874), with T. M. Brewer and R. Ridgway; *North American Reptiles* (1853), with C. Girard; and *Catalogue of North American Mammals* (1857). It was as an accurate observer and reporter, not as a theorist, that he influenced ornithology and founded the "Baird School," so ably represented by E. Coues, J. A. Allen, R. Ridgway, J. Cassin and T. M. Brewer. The third stage in Baird's career dates from the foundation of the U.S. Commission of Fish and Fisheries, 1871, when President Grant requested him to head the new organization. The work of the Commission comprised all forms of ichthyological knowledge and fish-protection. Thorough studies of the life histories of American fish were instituted; the deep waters of the Atlantic and Pacific were explored; numerous fish hatcheries increased the abundance of local fishes and introduced foreign species. The principal headquarters for investigation were at Wood's Hole, Mass., now one of the world's great marine laboratories.

BAKER, BENJAMIN A. (*b. New York, N.Y., 1818; d. New York, 1890*), playwright, actor, manager. Introduced local conditions as background of melodrama; *A Glance at New York in 1848* and *New York As It Is* (1848) portrayed "Mose, the Bowery Boy."

BAKER, BENJAMIN FRANKLIN (*b. Wenham, Mass., 1811; d. 1889*), musician, teacher, composer. Established Boston Music School, 1857–68; published songs, vocal quartets, cantatas and musical theory textbooks.

BAKER, DANIEL (*b. Midway, Ga., 1791; d. Austin, Texas, 1857*), Presbyterian clergyman, educator. While missionary to Texas in 1840, participated in organization of the first presbytery there; was president of Austin College, 1853–57.

BAKER, EDWARD DICKINSON (*b. London, England, 1811; d. 1861*), lawyer. Came to America as a child. Practiced in Springfield, Ill., *post* 1835, and was Lincoln's successful opponent for Whig congressional nomination, 1844. Served as Illinois congressman, 1845–47, 1849–51; as U.S. senator, Republican, from Oregon, 1860–61; killed in action with Union army at Ball's Bluff, Va.

BAKER, FRANK (*b. Pulaski, N.Y., 1841; d. Washington, D.C., 1918*), anatomist, historian of medicine. Professor of anatomy, Georgetown University, 1883–1918.

BAKER, GEORGE AUGUSTUS (*b. New York, N.Y., 1821; d. 1880*), portrait painter, miniaturist.

BAKER, GEORGE FISHER (*b. 1840; d. 1931*), banker, philanthropist. Director of many corporations; principal association with the First National Bank of New York. [*Supp.* 1]

BAKER, GEORGE PIERCE (*b. Providence, R.I., 1866; d. New York, N.Y., 1935*), instructor in playwriting. Graduated Harvard, 1887; became an instructor there the following year. Experimented in 1905 with a course in practical playwriting, something never done before in American colleges; founded the famous course "English 47" in 1906 at Harvard. The "47 Workshop" followed which included non-student workers and an audience who wrote criticisms after each performance. Students included Eugene O'Neill, Sidney Howard and George Abbott. Baker moved the Workshop to Yale in 1925 where he remained until retirement in 1933. He secured academic respect for the theatre arts, influenced both amateur and professional stages and raised the standard of playwriting in America. [*Supp.* 1]

BAKER, HARVEY HUMPHREY (*b. Brookline, Mass., 1869; d. Brookline, 1915*), first judge of the juvenile court of Boston, appointed 1906.

BAKER, JAMES (*b. Belleville, Ill., 1818; d. Little Snake River valley, Wyo., 1898*), trapper, guide, pioneer settler. Chief of scouts for Gen. W. S. Harney, 1855–58.

BAKER, JAMES HEATON (*b. Monroe, O., 1829; d. 1913*), politician, soldier, journalist. Secretary of state, Ohio, 1855–57, and Minnesota territory, 1859–61; federal commissioner of pensions, 1871–75; surveyor general of Minnesota, 1875–79.

BAKER, JAMES HUTCHINS (*b. near Harmony, Maine, 1848; d. Denver, Colo., 1925*), educator. Principal of Denver High School, 1874–91; president of University of Colorado, 1892–1914.

BAKER, JEHU (*b. Fayette Co., Ky., 1822; d. 1903*), lawyer, editor, radical Republican congressman from Illinois. [*Supp.* 1]

BAKER, LA FAYETTE CURRY (*b. Stafford, N.Y., 1826; d. Philadelphia, Pa., 1868*), detective, Civil War chief of U.S. Secret Service. Planned and directed expedition that captured John Wilkes Booth and D. C. Herold.

BAKER, LAURENCE SIMMONS (*b. Coles Hill, N.C., 1830; d. Suffolk, Va., 1907*), Confederate soldier. Cavalry officer actively engaged in all operations of Lee's army, 1862–63; held commands in North and South Carolina, 1864–65.

BAKER, LORENZO DOW (*b. Wellfleet, Mass., 1840; d. 1908*), sea captain, planter, merchant. First importer of Jamaican bananas; managing director, Jamaica division, United Fruit Co., 1897–1908.

BAKER, MARCUS (*b. Kalamazoo, Mich., 1849; d. Washington, D.C., 1903*), geographer. *Post* 1886, a member of the U.S. Geological Survey, he directed the topographic work of the northeastern division; was a founder of the National Geographic Society.

BAKER, NEWTON DIEHL (*b. Martinsburg, W. Va., 1871; d. Shaker Heights, O., 1937*), lawyer, mayor of Cleveland, secretary of war. Graduated Johns Hopkins, 1892; obtained law degree from Washington and Lee, 1894. Practiced law briefly in Martinsburg, served for a year as secretary to Postmaster-General William L. Wilson, then joined a Cleveland, Ohio, law firm. Married Elizabeth Leopold, 1902. Baker soon attracted the attention of Tom Loftin Johnson, reform mayor of Cleveland. As assistant director of the city's law department, then as city solicitor, Baker wholeheartedly supported Johnson's program of sound municipal government. Active in tax-reform plans, he played a major role in obtaining a 3-cent fare on the city transport lines. Johnson was defeated in 1909, but Baker was returned as city solicitor. Elected mayor in 1911 and re-elected in 1913, Baker obtained a new "home rule" charter for the city, built a municipal power plant and provided many other basic services.

A supporter of Woodrow Wilson in 1912, Baker became Wilson's secretary of war in March 1916, playing a rather static role during his first year in office. After April 1917, however, he showed good sense and vigor in administering the wartime conscription act, reorganizing the War Department and supporting General Pershing. Baker was criticized by professional soldiers, by publicists like Oswald Garrison Villard, and by members of both political parties for his conduct of his duties. He was hampered by many factors beyond his control, but if he was not a great secretary of war he did satisfy his president and became one of Wilson's most trusted confidants.

After the war Baker returned to Cleveland and the practice of law. As counsel for many large companies he became increasingly conservative, breaking with President Franklin D. Roosevelt over the constitutionality of the Tennessee Valley Authority. The year before his death he was mentioned as a vice-presidential candidate on a coalition ticket of Republicans and conservative Democrats. [*Supp.* 2]

BAKER, OSMON CLEANDER (*b. Marlow, N.H., 1812; d. Concord, N.H., 1871*), Methodist bishop. Organizer of Newbury Seminary; professor of homiletics, Methodist General Biblical Institute; authority on Methodist law and discipline.

BAKER, PETER CARPENTER (*b. North Hempstead, N.Y., 1822; d. 1889*), printer, publisher. Founder of the New York Typothetae, a printing trade organization; partner in Baker, Voorhis and Co., law book publishers.

BAKER, REMEMBER (*b. Woodbury, Conn., 1737; d. St. Johns, Canada, 1775*), soldier. Settled in what is now Vermont, 1764; commanded a company of Green Mountain Boys; associate of Ethan Allen.

BAKER, WILLIAM MUMFORD (*b. Washington, D.C., 1825; d. Boston, Mass., 1883*), Presbyterian clergyman. Held pastorates in Arkansas and Texas, 1850–65; author of *Inside: A Chronicle of Secession* (1866) under pseudonym of George F. Harrington.

BALBACH, EDWARD (*b. Karlsruhe, Germany, 1839; d. 1910*), metallurgist. Emigrated to New Jersey, 1850; with father, introduced European processes of smelting silver-lead ores.

BALCH, GEORGE BEALL (*b. Shelbyville, Tenn., 1821; d. Raleigh, N.C., 1908*), naval officer. Held responsible commands in Mexican and Civil Wars; promoted rear-admiral, 1878; superintendent of U.S. Naval Academy, 1879–81.

BALCH, THOMAS WILLING (*b. Wiesbaden, Germany, 1866; d. Atlantic City, N.J., 1927*), lawyer. A man of wealth, he practiced law in Philadelphia and published numerous books on special interests, notably genealogy and international arbitration.

BALDWIN, ABRAHAM (*b. North Guilford, Conn., 1754; d. Washington, D.C., 1807*), statesman. Graduated Yale, 1772; served as chaplain during Revolutionary war; removed to Georgia, 1784. Author of Georgia charter providing for a complete state educational system, he was also titular president of the projected state university and organizer of Franklin College, now University of Georgia. Ablest Georgia delegate to the Federal Convention, 1787, he served as congressman, (Democrat) Republican, 1789–99, and as U.S. senator, 1799–1807.

BALDWIN, ELIHU WHITTLESEY (*b. Durham, N.Y., 1789; d. 1840*), Presbyterian clergyman, educator. First president of Wabash College, Crawfordsville, Ind., 1836–40.

BALDWIN, EVELYN BRIGGS (*b. Springfield, Mo., 1862; d. Washington, D.C., 1933*), Arctic explorer. Made unsuccessful dash to the North Pole in 1902. [*Supp. 1*]

BALDWIN, FRANK STEPHEN (*b. New Hartford, Conn., 1838; d. 1925*), inventor. In 1874, designed one of the first adding machines ever to be sold in the United States; in 1902, invented a calculator which, in association with J. R. Monroe, he successfully marketed as the Monroe Calculating Machine.

BALDWIN, HENRY (*b. New Haven, Conn., 1780; d. Philadelphia, Pa., 1844*), jurist. Half-brother of Abraham Baldwin. Graduated Yale, 1797, studied law with Alexander J. Dallas and practiced in western

Pennsylvania. Appointed by Andrew Jackson an associate justice of the U.S. Supreme Court, 1830.

BALDWIN, HENRY PERRINE (*b. Lahaina, Maui, Hawaii, 1842; d. Makawao, 1911*), sugar planter, capitalist. Influential in Hawaiian affairs, 1887–1904. [*Supp. 1*]

BALDWIN, HENRY PORTER (*b. Coventry, R.I., 1814; d. 1892*), businessman, politician. Settled in Detroit, Mich., 1838. President of Detroit National Bank, 1863–87; Republican governor of Michigan, 1869–73.

BALDWIN, JAMES MARK (*b. Columbia, S.C., 1861; d. Paris, France, 1934*), psychologist. Co-founder and editor, *Psychological Review*, 1894–1909; his most valuable work was in child and social psychology. [*Supp. 1*]

BALDWIN, JOHN (*b. North Branford, Conn., 1799; d. Baldwin, La., 1884*), grindstone manufacturer. Founder of Baldwin-Wallace College, Berea, O., 1845; Baker University, Kansas, 1859; Baldwin Public School, Louisiana, 1867.

BALDWIN, JOHN BROWN (*b. Staunton, Va., 1820; d. 1873*), lawyer, politician. Devised a code of procedural rules still in use in Virginia House of Delegates.

BALDWIN, JOHN DENISON (*b. North Stonington, Conn., 1809; d. Worcester, Mass., 1883*), journalist. Owner and editor of the *Worcester Spy*, 1859–83.

BALDWIN, JOSEPH (*b. Newcastle, Pa., 1827; d. 1899*), educator. Founder of normal school system in Missouri; first professor of pedagogy at University of Texas, 1891.

BALDWIN, JOSEPH GLOVER (*b. near Winchester, Va., 1815; d. 1864*), jurist, author. Removed to Southwest, 1836, after self-education in law; practiced in both Mississippi and Alabama. In 1853 he published *The Flush Times of Alabama and Mississippi*, a lively and satiric interpretative study of backwoods society, and in 1855 a serious volume of essays on American political figures entitled *Party Leaders*. He settled in California in 1854, becoming an associate justice of the state supreme court in 1858 and returning to private practice in 1862.

BALDWIN, LOAMMI (*b. North Woburn, Mass., 1744/5; d. North Woburn, 1807*), civil engineer, soldier. Leading projector and chief engineer of the Middlesex Canal, a means of connecting the Charles and Merrimac rivers; this work, authorized by the Massachusetts legislature in 1793, was not completed until 1803. While surveying for the canal, he found an apple tree with superior fruit, cut scions for grafting, and produced the "Baldwin," the standard winter apple of eastern America.

BALDWIN, LOAMMI (*b. North Woburn, Mass., 1780; d. 1838*), civil engineer, lawyer. Son of the preceding. Constructed Fort Strong, Boston Harbor, 1814; in 1819 was made engineer of improvements in Boston. Between 1817 and 1820 he was engaged on public works in Virginia; in 1821 he began work as engineer of the Union Canal (extending from Reading to Middletown, Pa.), one of the outstanding projects of the time. After a year in Europe, 1824–25, he determined the correct proportions for the Bunker Hill Monument and surveyed the route for a proposed canal to link Boston Harbor with the Hudson River and the Erie Canal. He also designed and built large naval dry docks at Charlestown, Mass., and Norfolk, Va.

BALDWIN, MATTHIAS WILLIAM (*b. Elizabethtown, N.J., 1795; d. Frankford, Pa., 1866*), manufacturer, philanthropist. In partnership with David Mason, 1825–27, he manufactured hydraulic presses, textile printing machinery and stationary steam engines. *Post* 1831, he built for Phila. and Germantown RR. "Old Ironsides," one of the first American locomotives to be actually employed in transportation. Subsequent to 1841, he manufactured only locomotives at his Philadelphia shops, and at the time of his death (since 1854 in partnership with Matthew Baird) the Baldwin Locomotive Works had turned out more than 1500. Baldwin's charities were extensive.

BALDWIN, ROGER SHERMAN (*b. New Haven, Conn., 1793; d. 1863*), lawyer. Son of Simeon Baldwin, grandson of Roger Sherman. U.S. senator, Whig, from Connecticut, 1847–51; defense counsel in *Amistad* case (decided 1841).

BALDWIN, SIMEON (*b. Norwich, Conn., 1761; d. 1851*), jurist. Representative in Congress, Federalist, from Connecticut, 1803–05; judge, supreme court of errors, Connecticut, 1806–18.

BALDWIN, SIMEON EBEN (*b. New Haven, Conn., 1840; d. 1927*), jurist. Son of Roger S. Baldwin. Graduated Yale, 1861; admitted to the bar, 1863. A founder and president of the American Bar Association, professor in the Yale Law School, 1869-1919, and chief justice of the Connecticut supreme court, retiring in 1910. Never a professional politician, he early became identified with Connecticut political life; he served as governor (Democrat), 1910–14, but was defeated in a bid for the U.S. Senate, 1915. He was named to various state commissions of legal reform and was a U.S. delegate to International Prison Congresses, 1899 and 1905. He was a member of many historical, philosophical, scientific and artistic societies.

BALDWIN, THERON (*b. Goshen, Conn., 1801; d. Orange, N.J., 1870*), Congregational clergyman, pioneer missionary in Illinois.

BALDWIN, WILLIAM (*b. Newlin, Pa., 1779; d. Franklin, Mo., 1819*), physician. Botanist on Maj.

Stephen Long's expedition to the Rocky Mountains, 1819.

BALDWIN, WILLIAM HENRY (*b. Boston, Mass., 1863; d. 1905*), railroad executive. Served with Union Pacific, 1886–91; vice-president, Pere Marquette, 1891–94; vice-president, Southern, 1894–96; president, Long Island Railroad, 1896–1905.

BALESTIER, CHARLES WOLCOTT (*b. Rochester, N.Y., 1861; d. Dresden, Germany, 1891*), author. American publisher and friend of Rudyard Kipling; collaborated with him in *The Naulahka* (1892).

BALL, ALBERT (*b. Boylston, Mass., 1835; d. Claremont, N.H., 1927*), engineer, inventor. Chief mechanical engineer, Sullivan Machine Co., 1868–1914; designer of the diamond-core drill and other mining and quarrying tools.

BALL, EPHRAIM (*b. Lake Township, O., 1812; d. 1872*), manufacturer, inventor. Formed a company to manufacture threshers, 1840; designed the very popular "Blue Plough" and manufactured the "Hussey Reaper." A series of experiments resulted in Ball's principal contribution to the development of agricultural machinery, the "Ohio Mower," patented in 1857; this was the first of the two-wheeled flexible or hinged bar mowers to gain a wide reputation.

BALL, THOMAS (*b. Charlestown, Mass., 1819; d. Montclair, N.J., 1911*), sculptor. A self-trained painter and engraver, his greatest work, an equestrian statue of Washington, was erected in the Boston Public Garden in 1869. His most significant pieces include: "St. John the Evangelist," 1875 (Forest Hills Cemetery); "Emancipation," showing Lincoln and a kneeling slave, 1875 (Washington, D.C.); and statues of Webster (Central Park, New York City), Josiah Quincy (Boston City Hall) and Charles Sumner (Public Garden, Boston).

BALLARD, BLAND WILLIAMS (*b. near Fredericksburg, Va., 1759; d. Shelby Co., Ky., 1853*), pioneer. Settled in Kentucky, 1780, and was active in frontier Indian wars until 1795; served five terms in Kentucky legislature.

BALLINGER, RICHARD ACHILLES (*b. Boonesboro, Iowa, 1858; d. Seattle, Wash., 1922*), lawyer. Graduated Williams, 1884. Removed to Washington Territory *post* 1886; served as reform mayor of Seattle, 1904–06. Appointed by President Taft to succeed J. R. Garfield as secretary of the interior, 1909, Ballinger was accused of failure to support the policies of public-land conservation instituted by the preceding president, Theodore Roosevelt. The controversy that followed was damaging to the Taft administration, and Ballinger resigned his post in 1911.

BALLOU, ADIN (*b. Cumberland, R.I., 1803; d. 1890*), Universalist clergyman, reformer. Editor of the *Independent Messenger*, 1831–39; founder of the utopian Hopedale Community at Milford, Mass., 1841–68.

BALLOU, HOSEA (*b. Richmond, N.H., 1771; d. Boston, Mass., 1852*), Universalist clergyman. Missionary and leader in the Universalist Church; editor of *Universalist Magazine*, 1819–28, and *Universalist Expositor*, 1830–44.

BALLOU, HOSEA (*b. Guilford, Vt., 1796; d. 1861*), Universalist clergyman. Grandnephew of the preceding. Author of *Ancient History of Universalism* (1829); first president of Tufts College, 1854–61.

BALLOU, MATURIN MURRAY (*b. Boston, Mass., 1820; d. Cairo, Egypt, 1895*), journalist, traveler, author. Son of Hosea Ballou (1771–1852). Edited, 1851–59, *Gleason's Pictorial*, later called *Ballou's Pictorial*, an early American illustrated paper; editor, *Boston Daily Globe*, 1872–74.

BALTIMORE, CHARLES CALVERT, Third Lord. [See Calvert, Charles, 1629–1715.]

BALTIMORE, GEORGE CALVERT, First Lord. [See Calvert, George, c. 1580–1632.]

BANCROFT, AARON (*b. Reading, Mass., 1755; d. Worcester, Mass., 1839*), clergyman, author. Father of George Bancroft; a founder and first president of the American Unitarian Association, 1825–36.

BANCROFT, CECIL FRANKLIN PATCH (*b. New Ipswich, N.H., 1839; d. Andover, Mass., 1901*), educator. Graduated Dartmouth, 1860; Andover Theological Seminary, 1867. Appointed principal of Phillips Academy, Andover, Mass., in 1873, he found the Academy at a critical moment in its history. During the 28 years of his administration he transformed Andover both materially and scholastically; he replaced the three-year program with a four-year one, increased the endowments and strengthened the faculty.

BANCROFT, EDGAR ADDISON (*b. Galesburg, Ill., 1857; d. Karuizawa, Japan, 1925*), lawyer, orator, diplomat. Counsel to several railroads, and to the International Harvester Co., 1907–20; ambassador to Japan, 1924–25.

BANCROFT, EDWARD (*b. Westfield, Mass., 1744; d. Margate, England, 1821*), writer, inventor. Acted as a double spy for both England and America, 1776–83.

BANCROFT, GEORGE (*b. Worcester, Mass., 1800; d. Washington, D.C., 1891*), historian, diplomat. Son of Aaron Bancroft. Graduated Harvard, 1817; took doctorate at University of Göttingen, 1820. After a tour on the Continent he returned to Harvard where he taught for one year as a tutor in Greek; his foreign social and educational views irritated both the students and the authorities. Two more unsuccessful ventures followed: the publication of a volume of poems in 1823, and an attempt to establish a superior boys' school, based on European models, at Round Hill, Northampton, Mass. After quitting the school in 1831, he began preparation of his famous *History of the United States*. The first volume was published in 1834; the second, with a second edition of the first, appeared in 1837; the third in 1840. At this point, Bancroft had completed his survey of the period of colonization. The success of the work was gratifying and immediate, although some perceptive critics noted a marked political bias in favor of Jacksonian democracy. The Democrats had few intellectual supporters in Whiggish New England, hence Bancroft rose rapidly in his party's councils; as a delegate to the National Democratic Convention in 1844 he played an important part in the nomination of James K. Polk for the presidency and was rewarded with the secretaryship of the navy in Polk's cabinet. During a short term of 18 months, he established the Naval Academy at Annapolis, aided the work of the Naval Observatory and was a faithful supporter of his chief's policies. In 1846 he went to London as U.S. minister to Great Britain; in addition to fulfilling the demands of his post he undertook extensive researches into French and English documentary sources and amassed material for the continuation of his great historical project.

On his return to America in 1849 he devoted himself primarily to his historical work, issuing six volumes between 1852 and 1866 in which the story of the American Revolution was told. At first considering President Lincoln quite inadequate for the tasks confronting him in the Civil War, Bancroft early recognized Lincoln's quality and gave him support with voice and pen. He was close to President Andrew Johnson and received from him an appointment as U.S. minister to Berlin in 1867; there, until 1874, he showed himself an able diplomat, moved in the best social and academic circles and engaged in the research for the tenth and final volume of the *History*, which was published in 1874. In 1876 he brought out a "thoroughly revised" edition of the entire work in six volumes; in 1882, a *History of the Formation of the Constitution of the United States;* and in 1883–85 a final revision of the *History* in which he corrected errors and toned down the floridity of his earlier style.

Bancroft wrote always with the strong bias of an ardent believer in democratic government, and his style of expression is tinged with the enthusiasm of the old-style patriotic orator, yet his title "Father of American History" is a just one.

BANCROFT, HUBERT HOWE (*b. Granville, O., 1832; d. 1918*), historian. Went to California in 1852; prospered as a merchant and publisher in San Francisco. Out of an interest in collecting books on Pacific Coast history, evolved the project of a vast history of the coast and Rocky Mountain region, extending also to Alaska, and to Mexico and Central America. With H. L. Oak as assistant, Bancroft organized a force of archivists, copyists and reporters who sought out source data wherever it was to be found; in many instances, surviving pioneers were interviewed and their recollections noted. After organization and editing, five volumes on the native races of the area, 28 volumes of history, and six volumes of "essays" were published between 1875 and 1890.

BANDELIER, ADOLPH FRANCIS ALPHONSE (*b. Berne, Switzerland, 1840; d. Seville, Spain, 1914*), historian, explorer, anthropologist. Came to America, 1848; educated at home (Highland, Ill.) and at the University of Berne where he studied geology. His earliest scholarly contributions dealt with the society of the ancient Mexicans (1877–79); in 1880 he was engaged by the Archaeological Institute of America to conduct researches in New Mexico where he was active until 1889. After publication of studies on the Indians and history of the Southwest, he worked from 1892 to 1902 on archaeological and archival research in Peru and Bolivia. His devotion to original sources resulted in the discrediting of the romantic school of American aboriginal history.

BANGS, FRANCIS NEHEMIAH (*b. New York, N.Y., 1828; d. Ocala, Fla., 1885*), lawyer. Active in removal of corrupt New York judges after "Tweed Ring" exposure, 1871.

BANGS, FRANK C. (*b. Alexandria, Va., 1833; d. 1908*), actor. Supported Forrest, Hackett, Booth and others, 1851–72.

BANGS, JOHN KENDRICK (*b. Yonkers, N.Y., 1862; d. 1922*), humorist, editor, lecturer. Best known for *Three Weeks in Politics* (1894) and *A Houseboat on the Styx* (1895).

BANGS, NATHAN (*b. Stratford, Conn., 1778; d. 1862*), Methodist clergyman. Editor of the Methodist Book Concern, New York; founder of the Methodist Missionary Society; acting president of Wesleyan University, 1841—43.

BANISTER, JOHN (*b. Twigworth, England, 1650; d. Virginia, 1692*), botanist. Author of catalogues of Virginia plants in John Ray's *Historia Plantarum* and of unfinished "Natural History of Virginia."

BANISTER, JOHN (*b. Bristol Parish, Va., 1734; d. 1788*), Revolutionary patriot. Member of Virginia Convention, 1776, Virginia House of Burgesses, 1777; a delegate to the Continental Congress, 1778–79; a framer and signer of the Articles of Confederation.

BANISTER, ZILPAH POLLY GRANT (*b. Norfolk, Conn., 1794; d. 1874*), educator. Associate of Mary Lyon in schools at Derry, N.H., and Ipswich, Mass.

BANKHEAD, JOHN HOLLIS (*b. Moscow, Ala., 1842; d. 1920*). U.S. senator from Alabama, Democrat, 1907–20; promoted federal aid for improvement of roads, 1916.

BANKHEAD, WILLIAM BROCKMAN (*b. Moscow, Ala., 1874; d. Bethesda, Md., 1940*), Democratic congressman from Alabama, 1916–40. Speaker of the House of Representatives, 1936–40; son and brother of Senators John H. Bankhead I and II; father of Tallulah. [*Supp. 2*]

BANKS, CHARLES EDWARD (*b. Portland, Maine, 1854; d. Hartford, Conn., 1931*), public health official, historian, and genealogist. Wrote important studies of Plymouth Colony settlers and New England towns. [*Supp. 1*]

BANKS, NATHANIEL PRENTISS (*b. Waltham, Mass., 1816; d. Waltham, 1894*), Union soldier, Massachusetts legislator. Congressman, Democrat and "Know-Nothing," from Massachusetts, 1853–57; his election as speaker of the House, 1856, was hailed as an anti-slavery victory. He sought and won the governorship of Massachusetts as a Republican, 1858–60. Commissioned major-general of volunteers in 1861, he began a military career marked by courage if not always by the greatest tactical skill; he fought in Shenandoah Valley, 1862, received thanks of Congress for his 1863 capture of Port Hudson and headed the disastrous 1864 Red River Expedition. Returned to Congress as a Republican, 1865–73; as a Democrat, 1875–77; again as a Republican, 1878–79 and 1889–90.

BANNER, PETER (*fl. Boston, Mass., 1794–1828*), architect. Designed Eben Crafts House, Roxbury, Mass., and Park Street Church, Boston.

BANNISTER, NATHANIEL HARRINGTON (*b. 1813; d. 1847*), playwright, actor. Popular actor in South and West; author of *Putnam* (1844) and other melodramas; one of the most prolific of early American dramatists.

BANVARD, JOHN (*b. New York, N.Y., 1815; d. Watertown, S. Dak., 1891*), painter, writer. Painted (*post* 1840) and exhibited a huge, crude panorama of the Mississippi River.

BANVARD, JOSEPH (*b. New York, N.Y., 1810; d. Neponset, Mass., 1887*), author, Baptist clergyman. Held several New England pastorates; wrote a number of moralizing works on American history.

BAPST, JOHN (*b. La Roche, Switzerland, 1815; d. Mount Hope, Md., 1887*), Jesuit priest, educator. Missionary in Maine, 1848–59; first rector of Boston College, 1860–69.

BARAGA, FREDERIC (*b. near Döbernig, Austria, 1797; d. Marquette, Mich., 1868*), Roman Catholic priest. Missionary to Indians of Lake Superior region; wrote important grammar (1850) and dictionary (1853) of the Chippewa language; consecrated bishop of Sault Ste. Marie, 1853, and of Marquette, 1865.

BARANOV, ALEXANDER ANDREEVICH (*b. 1746; d. 1819*), fur-trader. Directed affairs of the Russian American Company in Alaska, 1790–1818.

BARBER, AMZI LORENZO (*b. Saxton's River, Vt., 1843; d. 1909*), capitalist. First to exploit the so-called pitch lake on the Island of Trinidad, using its asphalt for street paving.

BARBER, DONN (*b. Washington, D.C., 1871; d. 1925*), architect. Trained in office of Carrère and Hastings and at the Beaux Arts in Paris; his buildings include the Connecticut Supreme Court and State Library in Hartford, Conn., and the Department of Justice building, Washington, D.C.

BARBER, EDWIN ATLEE (*b. Baltimore, Md., 1851; d. 1916*), archeologist. A leading authority on ceramic art in all its branches.

BARBER, FRANCIS (*b. Princeton, N.J., 1751; d. Newburgh, N.Y., 1783*), soldier. After distinguished service, 1776–81, was sent by Washington to quell mutiny of New Jersey and Pennsylvania troops in the latter year.

BARBER, JOHN WARNER (*b. East Windsor, Conn., 1798; d. New Haven, Conn., 1885*), engraver, historian. With Henry Howe, produced a series of illustrated books on antiquities and local history of the states of the Union.

BARBER, OHIO COLUMBUS (*b. Middlebury, O., 1841; d. Akron, O., 1920*), manufacturer. Founded the Diamond Match Co., 1881; active in industrial development of the Akron area.

BARBOUR, CLARENCE AUGUSTUS (*b. Hartford, Conn., 1867; d. Providence, R.I., 1937*), Baptist clergyman; president, Colgate Rochester Divinity School, 1928–29; president, Brown University, 1929–37. [*Supp. 2*]

BARBOUR, JAMES (*b. Barboursville, Va., 1775; d. Barboursville, 1842*), statesman. Governor of Virginia, 1812–15; U.S. senator, 1815–25; secretary of war, 1825–28. Originally a Jeffersonian Democrat, he became a strong supporter of John Q. Adams and eventually a Whig.

BARBOUR, JOHN STRODE, JR. (*b. Culpeper Co., Va., 1820; d. 1892*), lawyer, financier. President of Orange and Alexandria Railroad, 1852–85. Revived Democratic party in Virginia, 1883–89, breaking control of William Mahone.

BARBOUR, OLIVER LORENZO (*b. Cambridge, N.Y., 1811; d. Saratoga Springs, N.Y., 1889*), lawyer. Nephew and confidential clerk of Reuben H. Walworth; a prolific writer on chancery and equity practice; editor of reports on N.Y. supreme court decisions, 1848–78.

BARBOUR, PHILIP PENDLETON (*b. Barboursville, Va., 1783; d. Orange Co., Va., 1841*), lawyer, statesman. Brother of James Barbour. Congressman from Virginia, Democrat, 1814–25; 1827–30. President, Virginia constitutional convention, 1829–30; counsel for the state in the case of *Cohens vs. Virginia;*

federal judge, 1830–36; Supreme Court justice, 1836–41. An uncompromising advocate of state rights.

BARCLAY, THOMAS (*b. New York, N.Y., 1753; d. New York, 1830*), Loyalist.

BARD, JOHN (*b. Burlington, N.J., 1716; d. Hyde Park, N.Y., 1799*), physician. Apprenticed in medicine to John Kearsly in Philadelphia and practiced there until 1746. At his friend Benjamin Franklin's urging, he moved then to New York where he built up a large practice; in 1759 he instituted a quarantine system for the port of New York, and as early as 1750 had participated in the first recorded dissection of a body for the purpose of instructing medical students. He was chosen first president of the Medical Society of the State of New York, 1788.

BARD, SAMUEL (*b. Philadelphia, Pa., 1742; d. Hyde Park, N.Y., 1821*), physician. Son of John Bard. Graduated King's College (Columbia), 1760; studied medicine at London and took the M.D. degree at Edinburgh, 1765. Practiced in New York with his father, specializing in obstetrics on which he later (1807) wrote a textbook. A Loyalist during the Revolution, Bard practiced during the British occupation of New York but lost no credit thereby with the Americans. Owing in part to his efforts, New York Hospital was opened, 1791. In 1792, when the medical school in New York (in which he had taught theory and practice of medicine *post* 1768) was united with Columbia College, he became dean; in 1811 he was elected president of the original College of Physicians and Surgeons.

BARD, WILLIAM (*b. Philadelphia, Pa., 1778; d. Staten Island, N.Y., 1853*). Son of Samuel Bard; founded New York Life Insurance and Trust Co. (chartered 1830), the first firm to make life insurance a specialty.

BARDEEN, CHARLES WILLIAM (*b. Groton, Mass., 1847; d. Syracuse, N.Y., 1924*), publisher. Editor of the *School Bulletin*, 1874–1924.

BARKER, ALBERT SMITH (*b. Hanson, Mass., 1843; d. 1916*), naval officer. Graduated U.S. Naval Academy, 1863; promoted rear-admiral, 1905, after holding many important commands.

BARKER, BENJAMIN FORDYCE (*b. Wilton, Maine, 1818; d. 1891*), physician. Graduated Bowdoin, 1837; M.D., Bowdoin, 1841; studied also at Paris. Came to New York in 1849 at suggestion of Willard Parker to take chair of obstetrics at New York Medical College; in 1861 obtained charter for the Bellevue Hospital Medical School, which he served as professor of obstetrics and gynecology until 1891. He is said to have introduced the use of the hypodermic syringe into American medicine.

BARKER, GEORGE FREDERICK (*b. Charlestown, Mass., 1835; d. 1910*), chemist, physicist. Graduated Yale, 1858. Professor of physics, University of Pennsylvania, 1873–1900; was also distinguished as a consultant, an editor of scientific periodicals and an early writer on radioactivity.

BARKER, JACOB (*b. Swan Island, Maine, 1779; d. Philadelphia, Pa., 1871*), merchant, lawyer, financier. Barker's eventful career was marked by alternate successes and reverses on a grand scale; he is credited with providing financial support for the government in 1812–15.

BARKER, JAMES NELSON (*b. Philadelphia, Pa., 1784; d. Washington, D.C., 1858*), dramatist. His *The Indian Princess* (produced 1808) was the first acted play by an American on an Indian theme, the first to deal with Pocahontas and the first to be acted in England after its American production. He served as comptroller of the treasury, 1838–41, and thereafter in various treasury posts.

BARKER, JAMES WILLIAM (*b. White Plains, N.Y., 1815; d. Rahway, N.J., 1869*), merchant. Active in New York and national politics; Know-Nothing party candidate for mayor of New York City, 1854.

BARKER, JEREMIAH (*b. Scituate, Mass., 1752; d. Gorham, Maine, 1835*), physician, medical theorist.

BARKER, JOSIAH (*b. Marshfield, Mass., 1763; d. Charlestown, Mass., 1847*), ship-builder. Built the men-of-war *Virginia*, *Vermont* and *Cumberland*; master carpenter on the *Independence*; rebuilt U.S.S. *Constitution*, 1834.

BARKER, WHARTON (*b. Philadelphia, Pa., 1846; d. 1921*), financier, publicist. Active in Philadelphia banking firms; presidential candidate of "middle of the road" Populists, 1900.

BARKSDALE, WILLIAM (*b. Rutherford Co., Tenn., 1821; d. Gettysburg, Pa., 1863*), Confederate soldier. Congressman, Democrat, from Mississippi, 1853–61; appointed brigadier-general, 1862; killed in action.

BARLOW, FRANCIS CHANNING (*b. Brooklyn, N.Y., 1834; d. New York, N.Y., 1896*), Union soldier. Held brigade commands at Antietam and Gettysburg; promoted major-general, 1865. After the war practiced law and was effective as a reforming public official.

BARLOW, JOEL (*b. Redding, Conn., 1754; d. near Cracow, Poland, 1812*), poet, statesman. Graduated Yale, 1778. Versatile, ambitious, he early projected an epic on glories of America, served as chaplain of 4th Massachusetts brigade, helped edit a periodical, engaged in business and joined with the "Hartford Wits" in writing the *Anarchiad* (1786–87). The first version of his epic appeared in 1787; entitled *The Vision of Columbus*, its stately, inflated couplets brought him immediate recognition. Admitted to the bar in 1786, he associated himself with the Scioto Company, a land-speculation, and went to France in 1788 as the company's agent. His own inexperience

and the dishonesty of several of his associates caused the firm to fail; from 1790 to 1792 he lived in London, supporting himself by his pen and becoming identified with the most advanced radical thinkers of the time. His political prose works belong to this period: *A Letter to the National Convention of France* (1792), *Advice to the Privileged Orders* (1792); and also the verse philippic *The Conspiracy of Kings* (1792). Proscribed by the British government, he went to Paris; by 1794, through speculation in French bonds, he was a rich man.

Returning to America in 1805, after a decade of activity abroad during which he served as American consul to Algiers, he settled on an estate named "Kalorama" near Washington, D.C. He published *The Columbiad* in 1807, a reworking of the epic theme of the *Vision of Columbus;* he also projected a great national institution for research and study of the arts and sciences. Appointed minister to France in 1811 by President Madison, he hoped to persuade Napoleon to give American commerce more generous treatment; after a year of diplomatic evasion he was informed that Napoleon would discuss terms of a treaty with him at Vilna, Poland. The French defeat in Russia ended all hopes of the conference and Barlow left Vilna for Paris. Taken seriously ill between Warsaw and Cracow, he died at the village of Zarnowiec. His epic efforts are rarely read; he is remembered best for a humorous poem, *Hasty Pudding*, written in 1793 and published in 1796.

BARLOW, JOHN WHITNEY (*b. Perry, N.Y., 1838; d. Jerusalem, 1914*), army engineer. Graduated West Point, 1861. Commanded engineer detachment on first government exploration of Yellowstone region, 1871, and on the Muscle Shoals project, 1886–90.

BARLOW, SAMUEL LATHAM MITCHILL (*b. Granville, Mass., 1826; d. Glen Cove, N.Y., 1889*), lawyer, bibliophile. Successful specialist in large corporation practice.

BARNABEE, HENRY CLAY (*b. Portsmouth, N.H., 1833; d. 1917*), actor, singer. Comedian, associated with light-opera in Boston; starred in DeKoven's *Robin Hood* as the "Sheriff of Nottingham."

BARNARD, CHARLES (*b. Boston, Mass., 1838; d. Pasadena, Calif., 1920*), writer on gardening; minor playwright.

BARNARD, CHARLES FRANCIS (*b. Boston, Mass., 1808; d. Somerville, Mass., 1884*), Unitarian clergyman, philanthropist. Founder of Warren Street Chapel, Boston; devoted himself to care and education of waifs.

BARNARD, DANIEL DEWEY (*b. Sheffield, Mass., 1796; d. Albany, N.Y., 1861*), lawyer. Congressman, Whig, from New York, 1827–29; 1839–45. Served as U.S. minister to Prussia, 1850–53.

BARNARD, EDWARD EMERSON (*b. Nashville, Tenn., 1857; d. 1923*), astronomer. Pioneer in astronomical photography.

BARNARD, FREDERICK AUGUSTUS PORTER (*b. Sheffield, Mass., 1809; d. New York, N.Y., 1889*), college president. Graduated Yale, 1828. Active in education in Alabama and Mississippi, 1837–61; president of Columbia University, 1864–89. Encouraged elective system of studies and from 1879 to his death urged the admission of women to the university on equal basis with men. Barnard College, a result of his efforts, was opened six months after his death.

BARNARD, GEORGE GREY (*b. Bellefonte, Pa., 1863; d. New York, N.Y., 1938*), sculptor. Studied at the Chicago Art Institute and the École des Beaux Arts in Paris. Exhibiting at the Beaux Arts Salon in 1894, he won quick acclaim. Chief among his many important commissions were sculptures for the State Capitol, Harrisburg, Pa. His collection of Gothic and Romanesque sculpture formed the nucleus of the Metropolitan Museum's collection at "The Cloisters" in New York's Fort Tryon Park. Barnard usually carved his monumental realistic figures directly in stone, in contrast with many of his contemporaries who thought and worked only in clay. [*Supp. 2*]

BARNARD, HENRY (*b. Hartford, Conn., 1811; d. Hartford, 1900*), educator. Shares with Horace Mann the credit for stimulating and directing the movement for free public education. Graduated Yale, 1830. As secretary of Connecticut board of commissioners for education, 1838–42, he woke the state from its apathy but was legislated out of office. From 1843 until 1849, he revolutionized the public schools of Rhode Island. Returning to Connecticut in 1849 as superintendent of common schools, and also as principal of the normal school, he continued his work until 1855 when he resigned to undertake publication at his own expense of the *American Journal of Education* (1855–82), an encyclopedic survey of educational literature. His example in Connecticut and Rhode Island, and the information which he made available to those in charge of schools, have had a lasting effect on the American public school system.

BARNARD, JOHN (*b. Boston, Mass., 1681; d. Marblehead, Mass., 1770*), Congregational clergyman. Graduated Harvard, 1700. A mathematician and scholar, he was largely responsible for the prosperity of Marblehead where he served as minister, 1716–70.

BARNARD, JOHN GROSS (*b. Sheffield, Mass., 1815; d. 1882*), Union soldier. Brother of F. A. P. Barnard; graduated West Point, 1833. Fortifications expert; engineer on major river and harbor improvements; chief engineer on defenses of Washington, D.C., in the Civil War; chief engineer on the staffs of Generals McClellan and Grant.

BARNES, ALBERT (*b. Rome, N.Y., 1798; d. Philadelphia, Pa., 1870*), Presbyterian clergyman. A prominent figure in the division between the Old and New schools of American Presbyterianism, 1837.

BARNES, CHARLES REID (*b. Madison, Ind., 1858; d. Chicago, Ill., 1910*), botanist. Taught at universities of Wisconsin and Chicago, 1887–1910; with J. M. Coulter and others, prepared textbooks stressing experimental and morphological method of botanical instruction.

BARNES, CHARLOTTE MARY SANFORD (*b. New York, N.Y., 1818; d. 1863*), actress. Author of *Octavia Bragaldi* (produced 1837), a romantic tragedy on the Beauchamp murder case in Kentucky, and other plays.

BARNES, JAMES (*b. Boston, Mass., 1801; d. Springfield, Mass., 1869*), Union soldier, engineer. Graduated West Point, 1829. Resigned commission, 1836, and became engineer and superintendent in railroad construction. Appointed colonel of 18th Massachusetts, 1861; held brigade and divisional commands; received brevet as major-general, 1864.

BARNES, JOSEPH K. (*b. Philadelphia, Pa., 1817; d. Washington, D.C., 1883*), military surgeon. Served in Seminole, Mexican and Civil Wars; appointed surgeon-general of the army, 1864. Attended both Lincoln and Garfield on their deathbeds.

BARNES, MARY DOWNING SHELDON (*b. Oswego, N.Y., 1850; d. London, England, 1898*), educator. Daughter of Edward A. Sheldon. Graduated University of Michigan, 1874; taught at Wellesley and Leland Stanford.

BARNETT, GEORGE ERNEST (*b. Cambridge, Md., 1873; d. Baltimore, Md., 1938*), economist. Johns Hopkins University faculty, 1901–38; specialist in labor economics. [*Supp. 2*]

BARNEY, JOSHUA (*b. Baltimore Co., Md., 1759; d. Pittsburgh, Pa., 1818*), naval officer. Distinguished as navy and privateer captain, 1775–1815. In action between the *Hyder-Ally* and the British *General Monk*, 1782, he fought brilliantly; his management of his flotilla in defense of Washington, D.C., 1814, and his conduct at the battle of Bladensburg were outstanding events of the War of 1812.

BARNUM, FRANCES COURTENAY BAYLOR [See BAYLOR, FRANCES COURTENAY, 1848–1920.]

BARNUM, HENRY A. (*b. Jamesville, N.Y., 1833; d. New York, N.Y., 1892*), Union soldier. Commissioned colonel, 1862, after gallant action at Malvern Hill; brigadier-general, 1865.

BARNUM, PHINEAS TAYLOR (*b. Bethel, Conn., 1810; d. Bridgeport, Conn., 1891*), showman. Celebrated for his practical exposition of the philosophy of humbug, Barnum made his first trial of public credulity in 1835 with Joice Heth, an ancient crone alleged to have been George Washington's nurse. His American Museum in New York was opened in 1842; along with legitimate curios and a menagerie, it featured a succession of ingenious and humorous shows including the woolly horse, the Feejee mermaid, the bearded lady, the "Egress," General Tom Thumb the dwarf, and many others. Barnum's genius for advertising and his acute measurement of how much the public would take brought him fame and fortune. On sheer nerve, he promoted Jenny Lind's concert tour in America (1850) into a financial and personal triumph. His last speculation, a circus billed as "the Greatest Show on Earth," opened in Brooklyn, N.Y., 1871. Ten years later, Barnum joined forces with the keenest of his competitors and the circus was thereafter presented as Barnum and Bailey's. For years, one of its main attractions was the elephant Jumbo who was described by the master of publicity as "the only mastodon left on earth."

BARNUM, ZENUS (*b. near Wilkes-Barre, Pa., 1810; d. Baltimore, Md., 1865*), hotel-keeper, capitalist. Proprietor of Barnum's Hotel, Baltimore; a pioneer in the telegraph and railroad industries.

BARNWELL, JOHN (*b. Ireland, c. 1671; d. 1724*), colonial agent. Emigrated to South Carolina, 1701; became a colonial official and led punitive expedition against the Tuscarora Indians, 1711–12.

BARNWELL, ROBERT WOODWARD (*b. near Beaufort, S.C., 1801; d. Columbia, S.C., 1882*), educator, statesman. Graduated Harvard, 1821. While congressman from South Carolina, 1829–33, signed the ordinance of nullification; was president of South Carolina College, 1835–41. During a six-month term in the U.S. Senate, 1850, as Calhoun's successor, he was an active but moderate defender of the Southern view; in 1861 he was temporary chairman of the Southern Congress in Montgomery and a signer of the Confederate constitution. Confederate senator from South Carolina, 1861–65, he served as chairman of the faculty, University of South Carolina, 1865–73.

BARR, AMELIA EDITH HUDDLESTON (*b. Ulverston, England, 1831; d. 1919*), author. Came to America, 1853; resided New York City *post* 1868. Among her eighty books, *A Bow of Orange Ribbon* (1886) is notable.

BARR, CHARLES (*b. Gourock, Scotland, 1864; d. Southampton, England, 1911*), sea captain. From 1884, when he came to America, until his death he was an outstanding skipper of racing yachts.

BARRADALL, EDWARD (*b. England, 1704; d. Williamsburg, Va., 1743*), lawyer. Attorney-general of Virginia, 1737–43; wrote *Cases Adjudged in the General Court of Virginia from April 1733 to October 1741*, a valuable source.

BARRELL, JOSEPH (*b. New Providence, N.J., 1869; d. 1919*), geologist, engineer. Professor of geology, Yale, 1903–19. His investigations of magmatic stoping, in connection with a Montana mine, resulted in a classic paper in the literature covering igneous in-

trusions. Regional geology, evolution, genesis of the earth, and especially isostasy (the problem of the stability of the earth's crust under changing conditions of erosion and sedimentation) were all subjects of papers published by Barrell. Of equal importance and magnitude were his writings on rhythms in geological processes and measurements of geological time.

BARRETT, ALBERT MOORE (*b. Austin, Ill., 1871; d. Ann Arbor, Mich., 1936*), psychiatrist, neuropathologist. First director, Michigan State Psychopathic Hospital, 1906–36; professor of psychiatry, University of Michigan, 1907–36. [*Supp. 2*]

BARRETT, BENJAMIN FISKE (*b. Dresden, Maine, 1808; d. Philadelphia, Pa., 1892*), preacher and writer of the New Church. Held ministries in New York City, Cincinnati and Philadelphia; a founder of the Swedenborg Publishing Association.

BARRETT, CHARLES SIMON (*b. Pike Co., Ga., 1866; d. Union City, Ga., 1935*), president of the Farmers' Union, 1906–28. [*Supp. 1*]

BARRETT, GEORGE HORTON (*b. Exeter, England, 1794; d. New York, N.Y., 1860*), actor, theatre manager.

BARRETT, JOHN (*b. Grafton, Vt., 1866; d. Bellows Falls, Vt., 1938*), diplomat, publicist. Director-general of the Pan-American Union, 1907–20. [*Supp. 2*]

BARRETT, KATE WALLER (*b. Clifton, Va., 1858; d. Alexandria, Va., 1925*), philanthropic worker. Identified with the National Florence Crittenton Mission for wayward girls; vice-president and general superintendent in 1897; president, 1909–25.

BARRETT, LAWRENCE (*b. Paterson, N.J., 1838; d. New York, N.Y., 1891*), actor. After touring in supporting roles, 1853–57, he played briefly in New York with Edwin Booth who was henceforward to be his friend and frequent professional associate; during 1858–60 he played with several Boston companies. Save for war service, 1861–62, all his study and energies were devoted to the stage; he was a player and a manager in New York, Philadelphia, New Orleans, Cincinnati and San Francisco. He is remembered today especially for his roles in support of Booth, and in particular "Cassius" in *Julius Caesar*. His energy, capacity for study and diligence won him high place among actors of the 19th century.

BARRINGER, DANIEL MOREAU (*b. near Concord, N.C., 1806; d. White Sulphur Springs, W. Va., 1873*), lawyer, diplomat. Congressman, Whig, from North Carolina, 1843–49; minister to Spain, 1849–53.

BARRINGER, RUFUS (*b. near Concord, N.C., 1821; d. 1895*), lawyer, Confederate soldier. An able cavalry officer; appointed brigadier-general, 1864. Brother of Daniel M. Barringer.

BARRON, CLARENCE WALKER (*b. Boston, Mass., 1855; d. 1928*), financial editor. Founder of *Barron's*, president of Dow, Jones & Co. [*Supp. 1*]

BARRON, JAMES (*b. 1768; d. Norfolk, Va., 1851*), naval officer. Commissioned lieutenant, U.S. Navy, 1798; captain, 1799. Commanded the *Essex* and the *President*, and was active in Mediterranean operations until 1805. In 1807, as commodore aboard the ill-prepared *Chesapeake* he bore the brunt of blame for her disgrace in an engagement with *H.M.S. Leopard* and was sentenced by court-martial to suspension without pay for five years. Restored to duty in 1813, he was refused active service at sea; convinced that he was victim of a plot by fellow-officers he challenged and killed Stephen Decatur in a duel, 1820.

BARRON, SAMUEL (*b. Hampton, Va., 1809; d. 1888*), Confederate naval officer. Captain in the Confederate States Navy; took a leading part in distribution of ordnance, organization of coastal defense and procurement of commerce raiders abroad.

BARROW, WASHINGTON (*b. Davidson Co., Tenn., 1817; d. St. Louis, Mo., 1866*). Whig politician; editor of Nashville *Republican Banner, post* 1844.

BARROWS, JOHN HENRY (*b. near Medina, Mich., 1847; d. 1902*), Congregational clergyman. Supervised "Parliament of Religions" at World's Columbian Exposition, 1893; president, Oberlin College, 1898–1902.

BARROWS, SAMUEL JUNE (*b. New York, N.Y., 1845; d. 1909*), Unitarian clergyman, prison reformer. Secured passage of New York's first probation law; largely instrumental in enactment of the federal parole law; editor, the *Christian Register*, 1880–96.

BARRY, JOHN (*b. Tacumshane, Ireland, 1745; d. 1803*), naval officer. Settled in Philadelphia, Pa., 1760. The *Lexington*, under his command in 1776, was the first regularly commissioned American cruiser to capture a British war-ship; he later commanded the *Effingham*, the *Raleigh* and, in 1781–82, the *Alliance*. He was named senior captain in 1794 and given command of the *United States;* four years later he took charge of all naval forces in West Indian waters. After escorting the American envoys to France in 1799, he commanded the Guadaloupe station, 1799–1801. He died at the head of the navy.

BARRY, JOHN STEWART (*b. Amherst, N.H., 1802; d. Constantine, Mich., 1870*), governor of Michigan, Democrat, 1842–46, 1849–51. Stabilized state finances after collapse of the 1835–41 boom in finance and internal improvements.

BARRY, PATRICK (*b. near Belfast, Ireland, 1816; d. Rochester, N.Y., 1890*), horticulturist. Pioneer fruit-grower in western New York; wrote (1851) *The Fruit Garden* (later called *Barry's Fruit Garden*).

BARRY, WILLIAM FARQUHAR (*b. New York, N.Y., 1818; d. Fort McHenry, Md., 1879*), Union soldier. Graduated West Point, 1838. Chief of artillery, Army of the Potomac; also on Grant's and Sherman's staffs in the same capacity.

BARRY, WILLIAM TAYLOR (*b. Lunenburg, Va., 1785; d. Liverpool, England, 1835*), lawyer, statesman. From early boyhood a resident of Lexington, Ky., Barry became a leader in the Democratic party in that state. Elected lieutenant-governor in 1821, he supported the "relief" measures instituted to rescue the people from the effects of bank failures and general depression that had followed the prosperity and speculative optimism of the years 1815–19. His support of Andrew Jackson in 1828 won him appointment as postmaster-general; in 1834–35, he denounced a congressional investigation of his department as a piece of partisan spite and resigned. Jackson immediately appointed him minister to Spain, but he died on his way to his post.

BARRY, WILLIAM TAYLOR SULLIVAN (*b. Columbus, Miss., 1821; d. Columbus, 1868*), Confederate statesman and soldier. A leader in the disunionist wing of the Democratic party in Mississippi; member of the Confederate Congress, 1861–62; colonel, 35th Mississippi infantry, 1862–65.

BARRYMORE, GEORGIANA EMMA DREW (*b. 1856; d. Santa Barbara, Calif., 1893*), actress. Daughter of John Drew (1827–1862) and Louisa Lane Drew. Distinguished in light, witty roles; mother of Ethel, Lionel and John Barrymore.

BARRYMORE, MAURICE (*b. Fort Agra, India, 1847; d. 1905*), actor. Born Herbert Blythe, he chose Barrymore as a professional name when he went on the stage in 1872; came to America three years later. Notable in supporting roles with such actors as Jefferson, Fanny Davenport, Modjeska and Mrs. Fiske, his many attempts to star by himself were unsuccessful. He married Georgiana Drew, 1876.

BARSOTTI, CHARLES (*b. Bagni di San Giuliano, Italy, 1850; d. Coytesville, N.J., 1927*), publisher. Came to America, 1872. Founded *Il Progresso* (New York, 1880), first Italian daily newspaper in the United States.

BARSTOW, WILLIAM AUGUSTUS (*b. Connecticut, 1813; d. 1865*), politician. Settled in Wisconsin, 1839; Democratic governor of Wisconsin, 1853–56; later engaged in banking, milling and railroad development.

BARTH, CARL GEORG LANGE (*b. Christiana [Oslo], Norway, 1860; d. Philadelphia, Pa., 1939*), mechanical engineer. Pioneer (with Frederick W. Taylor) of scientific management for industry.

[*Supp. 2*]

BARTHOLDT, RICHARD (*b. Schleiz, Germany, 1855; d. St. Louis, Mo., 1932*). Came to America, 1872. Editor of *St. Louis Tribune;* congressman, Republican, from Missouri, 1892–1915. Took a leading part in all peace movements before the outbreak of World War I. [*Supp. 1*]

BARTHOLOMEW, EDWARD SHEFFIELD (*b. Colchester, Conn., 1822; d. Naples, Italy, 1858*), sculptor in neo-classic style.

BARTHOLOW, ROBERTS (*b. New Windsor, Md., 1831; d. Philadelphia, Pa., 1904*), physician. Army surgeon, 1855–64; thereafter taught and practiced in Cincinnati, O., and Philadelphia. A voluminous writer on medical subjects.

BARTLET, WILLIAM (*b. Newburyport, Mass., 1748; d. Newburyport, 1841*), merchant. Generous benefactor of Andover Theological Seminary.

BARTLETT, ELISHA (*b. Smithfield, R.I., 1804; d. Smithfield, 1855*), physician. Taught medicine, 1832–55, at Berkshire Medical Institution, Transylvania University, Maryland, New York University, Louisville, and College of Physicians and Surgeons (New York). Author of *The Fevers in the United States* (1842) and a classic *Essay on the Philosophy of Medicine* (1844).

BARTLETT, HOMER NEWTON (*b. Olive, N.Y., 1845; d. Hoboken, N.J., 1920*), musical composer. Organist at several New York churches, 1862–1912; wrote 269 compositions including "Grand Polka de Concert" (1867).

BARTLETT, ICHABOD (*b. Salisbury, N.H., 1786; d. Portsmouth, N.H., 1853*), lawyer, politician. One of counsel in Dartmouth College Case, 1817; a leader of the New Hampshire bar; congressman, National Republican, from New Hampshire, 1822–29.

BARTLETT, JOHN (*b. Plymouth, Mass., 1820; d. Cambridge, Mass., 1905*), editor, publisher. Partner in Little, Brown & Co.; edited *Familiar Quotations* (first ed., 1855).

BARTLETT, JOHN RUSSELL (*b. Providence, R.I., 1805; d. Providence, 1886*), bibliographer, author. A New York bookseller, 1836–50, and active in New-York Historical Society; served as U.S. commissioner to run boundary line between Texas and Mexico, 1850–53; secretary of state of Rhode Island, 1855–72. Was associated with John Carter Brown in building his Americana library at Providence, 1856–86. Author of *Dictionary of Americanisms* (1848); *Personal Narrative of Explorations . . . with United States and Mexican Boundary Commission* (1854). Edited *Records of the Colony of Rhode Island: 1636–1792* and the *John Carter Brown Catalogue* (1865–82), a pioneer descriptive bibliography.

BARTLETT, JOHN SHERREN (*b. Dorsetshire, England, 1790; d. 1863*), physician, journalist. Established the *Albion* (New York, 1822–48), a newspaper for British residents of the United States.

BARTLETT, JOSEPH (*b. Plymouth, Mass., 1762; d. 1827*), lawyer, politician, eccentric. Graduated Harvard, 1782. Practiced law in Massachusetts, Maine and New Hampshire. Author of a remarkable volume of original aphorisms (Portsmouth, N.H., 1810).

BARTLETT, JOSIAH (*b. Amesbury, Mass., 1729; d. Kingston, N.H., 1795*), physician. Signer of the Declaration of Independence from New Hampshire; member of Continental Congress, 1774; 1775–76; 1778–79; chief justice, New Hampshire court of common pleas, 1779–82. Justice, state superior court, 1782–88; chief justice, 1788–90. President (governor) of New Hampshire, 1790–92; first governor, 1793–94.

BARTLETT, PAUL WAYLAND (*b. New Haven, Conn., 1865; d. Paris, France, 1925*), sculptor. Studied in Paris. Won early recognition for studies of animals; his later work featured romantic portrait statues of heroic size and concept, also allegorical subjects. Best known for the bronze Columbus and the Michelangelo in the Library of Congress, the sculptures on the pediment of the House wing of the Capitol, Washington, D.C., and the bronze equestrian Lafayette in the court of the Louvre, Paris.

BARTLETT, SAMUEL COLCORD (*b. Salisbury, N.H., 1817; d. Hanover, N.H., 1898*), Congregational clergyman. Professor of Biblical literature, Chicago Theological Seminary, 1858–77; president, Dartmouth College, 1877–92.

BARTLETT, WILLIAM HOLMES CHAMBERS (*b. Lancaster Co., Pa., 1804; d. Yonkers, N.Y., 1893*), mathematician. Best known for his *Elements of Analytical Mechanics* (1853), the first work of its kind published in the United States. [*Supp. 1*]

BARTLEY, MORDECAI (*b. Fayette Co., Pa., 1783; d. Mansfield, O., 1870*), farmer, merchant. Settled in Ohio, 1809. As congressman, National Republican, from Ohio, 1823–31, was first to propose use of land grants in that state for support of public schools. Served as Whig governor, 1844–46.

BARTOL, CYRUS AUGUSTUS (*b. Freeport, Maine, 1813; d. Boston, Mass., 1900*), Unitarian clergyman. Pastor, West Church, Boston, 1837–89; pastor emeritus until death. A follower of Ralph Waldo Emerson.

BARTON, BENJAMIN SMITH (*b. Lancaster, Pa., 1766; d. Philadelphia, Pa., 1815*), physician, naturalist. Studied at Edinburgh, London, and Göttingen (M.D., 1789); practiced in Philadelphia, and taught at University of Pennsylvania, 1791–1815. Author of *Collections for an Essay Towards a Materia Medica of the United States* (1798, 1804) and *Elements of Botany* (1803), the first textbook on botany written by an American.

BARTON, CLARA (*b. Oxford, Mass., 1821; d. Glen Echo, near Washington, D.C., 1912*), organizer of the American Red Cross. As a successful school-teacher, 1836–54, she displayed her basic characteristics of quick, practical response to an immediate need, delight in difficulties, aggressive independence and extraordinary nervous energy. While working in the Patent Office, Washington, D.C., 1861, she met the tragic lack of supplies for the Civil War wounded by organizing a distributing agency for contributions to the soldiers' welfare and by personally delivering what was needed at the very point of action; she later acted as superintendent of nurses with the Army of the James, and for four years after the war superintended a search for missing soldiers. Abroad for her health in 1869–70, she distributed relief in Strassburg, Paris, Lyons and other cities in association with the International Red Cross of Geneva (consequent on the Franco-Prussian war); she returned to America, 1873. In 1877, approved by the authorities at Geneva, she revived an earlier effort to associate the United States with the International Red Cross; in 1881 the National Society of the Red Cross was organized and incorporated, with Clara Barton as president; in 1882, the U.S. Senate approved adoption of the Geneva Convention as a result of her continuous effort and pressure.

From 1882 to 1904, Clara Barton directed the activities of the American Red Cross; the founder's refusal to delegate responsibility, however, and her proneness to arbitrary action resulted in a loss of public confidence. In 1900 the society was reincorporated with a new charter, but continuing dissensions over the founder's policies ended in 1904 with an investigation by a special committee. No report was ever presented by the committee but Clara Barton resigned in June 1904, and the society was completely reorganized.

BARTON, DAVID (*b. near Greenville, Tenn., 1783; d. near Boonville, Mo., 1837*), statesman. First U.S. senator from Missouri, 1821–31; foe of Thomas Hart Benton, and center of violent political battles.

[*Supp. 1*]

BARTON, JAMES LEVI (*b. Charlotte, Vt., 1855; d. Brookline, Mass., 1936*), Congregational clergyman. Missionary at Harpoot, Turkey, 1885–94; foreign secretary of American Board of Commissioners for Foreign Missions, 1894–1927. [*Supp. 2*]

BARTON, JOHN RHEA (*b. Lancaster, Pa., 1794; d. Philadelphia, Pa., 1871*), surgeon. Nephew of Benjamin S. Barton. Pioneer in orthopedic procedures; deviser of "Barton's bandage" for jaw fractures.

BARTON, ROBERT THOMAS (*b. Winchester, Va., 1842; d. 1917*), lawyer. Authority on Chancery practice; editor, *Virginia Colonial Decisions . . . General Court of Virginia, 1728–1741* (1909).

BARTON, SETH MAXWELL (*b. Fredericksburg, Va., 1829; d. Washington, D.C., 1900*), Confederate soldier. Graduated West Point, 1849. Acted as Jackson's chief engineer, 1861–62; relieved of brigade command on charges, 1864, but restored that same year.

BARTON, THOMAS PENNANT (*b. Philadelphia, Pa., 1803; d. 1869*), bibliophile. Son of Benjamin S. Barton; son-in-law of Edward Livingston. His notable collection of rare books went to Boston Public Library.

BARTON, WILLIAM (*b. Warren, R.I., 1748; d. Providence, R.I., 1831*), Revolutionary soldier. Made daring capture of British General Prescott at Rhode Island, July 1777.

BARTON, WILLIAM ELEAZAR (*b. Sublette, Ill., 1861; d. Brooklyn, N.Y., 1930*), Congregationalist clergyman of wide influence; author of many books about Abraham Lincoln. [*Supp. 1*]

BARTON, WILLIAM PAUL CRILLON (*b. Philadelphia, Pa., 1786; d. Philadelphia, 1856*), botanist, surgeon. Nephew of Benjamin S. Barton whom he succeeded as professor of botany, University of Pennsylvania, 1815. Appointed U.S. Navy surgeon, 1809; first chief of Navy Bureau of Medicine and Surgery, 1842–44. Author of *Vegetable Materia Medica of the United States* (1817–19) and other works.

BARTRAM, JOHN (*b. Marple, Pa., 1699; d. 1777*), first native American botanist. His early interest in plants was encouraged probably by James Logan (1674–1751); in 1728 he laid out a botanic garden on land he had bought at Kingsessing on the Schuylkill and began what were probably the first hybridizing experiments in America. He began a correspondence and exchange of specimens with Peter Collinson, the English plantsman, *c.* 1733; through Collinson, Bartram's American plants were distributed abroad and he became internationally celebrated. Linnaeus called him the greatest "natural botanist" then in the world. Bartram made many journeys at his own expense to the frontiers in order to gather seeds and bulbs for transplanting; in 1738 to western Virginia and the Blue Ridge, in 1755 through the Catskills, in 1760 to the Carolinas. In 1765, as Royal Botanist, he journeyed from Charleston, S.C., to St. Augustine, Fla., and explored the St. John's River by canoe; on this trip he observed all forms of life, examined mineral resources and prepared a map of the river.

Bartram's ideas were anticipatory of modern thinking, particularly in geology. His suggestion of a great survey trip westward, made to Benjamin Franklin, bears strong resemblance to Jefferson's later instructions given to Lewis and Clark. His botanic garden, enlarged by his son William, still survives as part of Philadelphia's park system.

He was author of *Observations on the Inhabitants, Climate, Soil, etc. . . . made by John Bartram in his travels from Pensilvania to Lake Ontario* (1751); his explorations in Georgia and Florida are in Stork's

Description of East Florida, with a Journal by John Bartram (London, 1769).

BARTRAM, WILLIAM (*b. Kingsessing, now Philadelphia, Pa., 1739; d. Kingsessing, 1823*), traveler and naturalist. Son of John Bartram, whom he accompanied on Florida journey, 1765–66. On behalf of British botanist John Fothergill, William Bartram explored southeastern part of what is now United States, 1773–77, sending his patron colored botanical drawings, journals, seeds and specimens. Subsequent to his father's death in 1777, he became a partner in the family botanic garden with his brother John. His *Travels through North and South Carolina, Georgia, East and West Florida, the Cherokee Country, etc.* (Philadelphia, 1791) is the chief cause of his fame; a literary as well as a scientific triumph, it was translated into several languages and influenced among others Chateaubriand, Coleridge and Wordsworth. Most of the plates in Benjamin S. Barton's *Elements of Botany* (1803) were engraved after drawings by Bartram. Alexander Wilson was inspired by him to produce his *American Ornithology.*

BARUCH, SIMON (*b. Schwersen, Germany, 1840; d. 1921*), physician. Emigrated as a youth and received professional training in Charleston, S.C., and at Medical College of Virginia; served 1862–65 as surgeon, Confederate Army. Practiced in Camden, S.C., 1865–81, and then removed to New York City where he became known as a leading exponent of hydrotherapy and a public-health advocate.

BARUS, CARL (*b. Cincinnati, O., 1856; d. Providence, R.I., 1935*), physicist. Professor, and Dean of Graduate School, Brown University. Made important contributions to geophysics. Inventor of the displacement interferometer. [*Supp. 1*]

BARZYŃSKI, VINCENT (*b. Sulislawice, Poland, 1838; d. Chicago, Ill., 1899*), Roman Catholic priest. Served in Texas, 1866–74. Thereafter, as pastor of St. Stanislaus Kostka Church, Chicago, he was a notable force in improving the spiritual and material condition of Polish immigrants.

BASCOM, HENRY BIDLEMAN (*b. Hancock, N.Y., 1796; d. Louisville, Ky., 1850*), Methodist clergyman. Removed as a child to Maysville, Ky., later to Brown Co., Ohio. Circuit rider *post* 1813; chaplain to Congress, 1823. President, Transylvania University, 1842–49; elected bishop, Methodist Episcopal Church South, 1850.

BASCOM, JOHN (*b. Genoa, N.Y., 1827; d. Williamstown, Mass., 1911*), philosopher, educator. Graduated Williams College, 1849; influenced by teaching of Laurens Hickok while attending Auburn Seminary. Taught at Williams, 1852–74, 1891–1903; president, University of Wisconsin, 1874–87.

BASHFORD, COLES (*b. New York State, 1816; d. Prescott, Ariz., 1878*), politician. Controversial Republican governor of Wisconsin, 1856; active in early territorial government of Arizona.

BASHFORD, JAMES WHITFORD (*b. Fayette, Wis., 1849; d. Pasadena, Calif., 1919*), Methodist clergyman. President, Ohio Wesleyan University, 1889–1904; missionary bishop, China area, 1904–15.

BASKERVILLE, CHARLES (*b. Deer Brook, Miss., 1870; d. New York, N.Y., 1922*), chemist. Director, chemical laboratories, College of the City of New York, 1904–22; an effective teacher and able industrial consultant.

BASS, EDWARD (*b. Dorchester, Mass., 1726; d. Newburyport, Mass., 1803*), Episcopal clergyman. Graduated Harvard, 1744; ordained in London, 1752. Rector, St. Paul's, Newburyport, 1752–1803; consecrated first bishop of Massachusetts, 1797.

BASS, SAM (*b. near Mitchell, Ind., 1851; d. Round Rock, Texas, 1878*), bandit, train-robber, killed in an attempt to rob the Round Rock bank.

BASS, WILLIAM CAPERS (*b. Augusta, Ga., 1831; d. Macon, Ga., 1894*), Methodist clergyman. President, Methodist Wesleyan Female College, Macon, 1874–94.

BASSE, JEREMIAH (*d. Burlington, N.J., 1725*), colonial official. Commissioned governor of East and West Jersey, 1697; favored anti-proprietary party, and was superseded, 1699. Secretary of the royal government of New Jersey, 1702–14.

BASSETT, JAMES (*b. Mundus, Canada, 1834; d. Los Angeles, Calif., 1906*), Presbyterian clergyman. Missionary to Persia, 1871–84; thereafter in pastoral work in United States.

BASSETT, JOHN SPENCER (*b. Tarboro, N.C., 1867; d. Washington, D.C., 1928*), historian. Graduated Trinity (Duke), 1888; Ph. D., Johns Hopkins, 1894. Taught at Duke, 1894–1906; professor, Smith College, 1906–28. Author, among others, of *Regulators of North Carolina* (1895); *The Federalist System* (1906); *Life of Andrew Jackson* (1911). Editor of a number of valuable primary historical sources.

BASSETT, RICHARD (*b. Cecil Co., Md., 1745; d. Bohemia Manor, Md., 1815*), statesman. U.S. senator, Federalist, from Delaware, 1789–93; governor of Delaware, 1799–1801.

BASSETT, WILLIAM HASTINGS (*b. New Bedford, Mass., 1868; d. Cheshire, Conn., 1934*), metallurgical engineer. Pioneer in the microscopic examination of copper alloys and the manufacture of brass goods of standard quality. [*Supp. 1*]

BATCHELDER, JOHN PUTNAM (*b. Wilton, N.H., 1784; d. New York, N.Y., 1868*), surgeon. Innovator in operating techniques for eye and facial surgery; an inventor and improver of surgical instruments.

BATCHELDER, SAMUEL (*b. Jaffrey, N. H., 1784; d. Cambridge, Mass., 1879*), cotton maufacturer. Invented, among other mill devices, a dynamometer for measuring power of belt-driven machinery.

BATCHELLER, GEORGE SHERMAN (*b. Batchellerville, N.Y., 1837; d. Paris, France, 1908*), Union soldier, statesman, lawyer. U.S. judge, International Tribunal in Egypt, 1876–85, 1898–1908.

BATCHELOR, GEORGE (*b. Southbury, Conn., 1836; d. 1923*), Unitarian clergyman. Editor, *Christian Register,* 1898–1911.

BATE, WILLIAM BRIMAGE (*b. Bledsoe's Lick, Tenn., 1826; d. Washington, D.C., 1905*), politician. Served in Mexican War; rose from private to major-general in Confederate Army, and distinguished himself at Shiloh, Murfreesboro, Chattanooga and in the Atlanta and Tennessee campaigns. Active in opposition to Brownlow's postwar government. Served as Democratic governor of Tennessee, 1882–86; as U.S. senator, 1886–1905.

BATEMAN, KATE JOSEPHINE (*b. 1843; d. London, England, 1917*), actress. Appeared 1846–54 as child prodigy with sister Ellen; as mature player won success in *Leah the Forsaken* (1863) and in support of Henry Irving at the Lyceum, London.

BATEMAN, NEWTON (*b. Fairton, N.J., 1822; d. Galesburg, Ill., 1897*), educator. Removed to Illinois, 1833; was a leader in building up common schools, serving as superintendent of public instruction, 1859–63, 1865–75. A friend of Abraham Lincoln. President, Knox College, 1874–92; emeritus, 1892–97.

BATEMAN, SIDNEY FRANCES COWELL (*b. New York, N.Y.?, 1823; d. London, England, 1881*), actress, playwright, manager. Mother of Kate and Ellen Bateman. Managed Lyceum Theatre, London, 1871–78; Sadler's Wells, 1878–81.

BATES, ARLO (*b. East Machias, Maine, 1850; d. Boston, Mass., 1918*), educator, author. Graduated Bowdoin, 1876. Editor, *Boston Sunday Courier,* 1880–93; author during this time of fiction and verse. Professor of English, Massachusetts Institute of Technology, *post* 1893.

BATES, BARNABAS (*b. Edmonton, England, 1785; d. Boston, Mass., 1853*), clergyman. Came to America as a child. *Post* 1839, agitated for postal reform and a reduction of rates.

BATES, DANIEL MOORE (*b. Laurel, Del., 1821; d. Richmond, Va., 1879*), jurist. Chancellor of Delaware, 1865–73. Editor, *Reports of Cases . . . Court of Chancery of Delaware* (1876, 1878).

BATES, EDWARD (*b. Goochland Co., Va., 1793; d. St. Louis, Mo., 1869*), statesman. Brother of Frederick Bates, at whose suggestion he removed to St. Louis, 1814, and began practice of law, 1816. Congressman, Whig, from Missouri, 1827–29, he thereafter held local office until his speech at the 1847 River and Harbor Improvement Convention, Chicago, made him nationally prominent. He opposed repeal of the Missouri Compromise and the admission of Kansas under the Lecompton Constitution, thus drawing closer to the nascent Republican party although he presided over the Whig National Convention at Baltimore, 1856. Border state leaders favored him as Republican nominee for the presidency in 1860. His choice as Lincoln's attorney-general made him the first cabinet officer to be chosen from west of the Mississippi; he served 1861–64, resigning over abuses he attributed to Seward, Chase and Stanton. Thereafter he fought the policies of the Radical Republicans in Missouri and elsewhere as a conspiracy against all government by law.

BATES, FREDERICK (*b. Goochland Co., Va., 1777; d. near Chesterfield, Mo., 1825*), lawyer. Brother of Edward Bates. Removed to Detroit, Mich., 1797, where he prospered as a merchant until 1805. Appointed secretary of Louisiana Territory, 1806, and served until 1812 when he became secretary of Missouri Territory. He was elected governor of the state of Missouri, 1824.

BATES, GEORGE HANDY (*b. Dover, Del., 1845; d. 1916*), lawyer. Son of Daniel M. Bates. Influential in Democratic politics; author of a report on Samoan affairs, 1886, and one of U.S. commissioners at conference on Samoa, Berlin, 1889.

BATES, JAMES (*b. Greene, Maine, 1789; d. 1882*), physician, surgeon, congressman.

BATES, JOHN COALTER (*b. St. Charles Co., Mo., 1842; d. San Diego, Calif., 1919*), soldier. Son of Edward Bates. Remained in the army after Civil War service. Prominent in assault on El Caney, 1898, and in the Philippine insurrection. Commissioned lieutenant-general on becoming chief of staff, 1906.

BATES, JOSHUA (*b. Weymouth, Mass., 1788; d. 1864*), financier, philanthropist. Removed to England, 1816, as general agent for Boston merchant William Gray; became partner in great banking firm of Baring Brothers, 1828, and eventually senior partner. Largest contributor to founding of the Boston Public Library.

BATES, KATHERINE LEE (*b. Falmouth, Mass., 1859; d. 1929*), educator, poet, author of "America the Beautiful." [*Supp. 1*]

BATES, ONWARD (*b. St. Charles Co., Mo., 1850; d. Augusta, Ga., 1936*), civil engineer, specialist in railroad bridges. [*Supp. 2*]

BATES, SAMUEL PENNIMAN (*b. Mendon, Mass., 1827; d. 1902*), educator. Graduated Brown University, 1851; active in Pennsylvania public school work.

BATES, WALTER (*b. Darien, Conn., 1760; d. 1842*), Loyalist. Removed in 1783 to Nova Scotia, where he served for many years as sheriff of King's Co. Author of *Kingston and the Loyalists . . . of 1783* (1889) and *The Mysterious Stranger* (1816).

BATTERSON, JAMES GOODWIN (*b. Wintonbury, Conn., 1823; d. Hartford, Conn., 1901*), businessman. After successful operation of New England Granite Works, he founded the Travelers Insurance Co., 1863.

BATTEY, ROBERT (*b. Augusta, Ga., 1828; d. Rome, Ga., 1895*), physician, surgeon. Studied privately and at University of Pennsylvania; M.D., Jefferson Medical College, Phila., 1857. Served in Confederate medical corps as field surgeon and hospital director, 1861–65; practiced thereafter in Rome, Ga. Celebrated since 1858 for his work with hernias and fistulas, he opened up an important field of surgery in 1872 with "Battey's Operation" for the removal of human ovaries by abdominal, and later by vaginal, section.

BATTLE, BURRELL BUNN (*b. Hinds Co., Miss., 1838; d. Little Rock, Ark., 1917*), jurist. Began practice of law at Lewisville, Ark., 1858. After service in Confederate Army, 1861–65, was a leader in opposition to Governors Clayton and Hadley. Justice, Arkansas supreme court, 1885–1911.

BATTLE, CULLEN ANDREWS (*b. Powelton, Ga., 1829; d. Greensboro, N.C., 1905*), politician. Removed to Eufaula, Ala., as a child; admitted to Alabama bar, 1852. An uncompromising secessionist, he served with distinction in the Confederate Army, 1861–65; after the war he returned to practice in Tuskegee, Ala., removing to Newbern, N.C. in 1880.

BATTLE, KEMP PLUMMER (*b. Franklin Co., N.C., 1831; d. 1919*), educator. Son of William H. Battle. President, University of North Carolina, 1876–91; professor of history, 1891–1907; emeritus thereafter. Author of *History of the University of North Carolina* (1907, 1912).

BATTLE, WILLIAM HORN (*b. Edgecombe Co., N.C., 1802; d. Chapel Hill, N.C., 1879*), lawyer, jurist. Professor of law, University of North Carolina, 1845–68; justice, state supreme court, 1852–68; revised North Carolina statutes, 1833–37, and again in 1873.

BATTS, ROBERT LYNN (*b. Bastrop, Texas, 1864; d. Austin, Texas, 1935*), lawyer, judge. Outstanding in fostering the growth of the University of Texas. [Supp. 1]

BAUER, LOUIS AGRICOLA (*b. Cincinnati, O., 1865; d. 1932*), physicist and magnetician. Conducted world magnetic survey; studied magnetic effect directly attributable to solar activity. [Supp. 1]

BAUGHER, HENRY LOUIS (*b. Abbottstown, Pa., 1804; d. Gettysburg, Pa., 1868*), Lutheran clergyman. Professor of Greek and rhetoric, Gettysburg College, 1831–50; president, 1850–68.

BAUM, LYMAN FRANK (*b. Chittenango, N.Y., 1856; d. Hollywood, Calif., 1919*), author. Followed success of *The Wonderful Wizard of Oz* (1900, with artist W. W. Denslow) with thirteen further *Oz* stories and numerous works for children issued over such pen-names as "Schuyler Staunton," "Floyd Akers" and "Edith Van Dyne."

BAUSMAN, BENJAMIN (*b. near Lancaster, Pa., 1824; d. Reading, Pa., 1909*), clergyman of the German Reformed Church. Pastor, St. Paul's, Reading, Pa., 1863–1909.

BAXLEY, HENRY WILLIS (*b. Baltimore, Md., 1803; d. 1876*), physician, surgeon. Graduated in medicine, University of Maryland, 1824. Co-founded (1839) the Baltimore College of Dental Surgery, the first to be organized formally either here or abroad; endowed the chair of pathology, Johns Hopkins Medical School.

BAXTER, ELISHA (*b. Rutherford Co., N.C., 1827; d. Batesville, Ark., 1899*), lawyer. Removed to Arkansas, 1852. An opponent of secession; raised and commanded Arkansas Unionist troops in Civil War. During Reconstruction period, Baxter headed reform elements in Republican party in Arkansas, contesting governorship with Joseph Brooks, 1873–74.

BAXTER, HENRY (*b. Sidney Plains, N.Y., 1821; d. Jonesville, Mich., 1873*), Union soldier. Entered Civil War as captain of Michigan volunteers; after service in Army of the Potomac, 1861–65, was mustered out as brevet major-general.

BAXTER, JOHN (*b. Rutherford Co., N.C., 1819; d. 1886*), lawyer. Brother of Elisha Baxter. Removed to Knoxville, Tenn., 1857, after success at North Carolina bar. A leading Tennessee Unionist, he became a political follower of William G. Brownlow *post* 1872 and was appointed U.S. circuit judge, 1877.

BAXTER, WILLIAM (*b. Leeds, England, 1820; d. New Castle, Pa., 1880*), clergyman of the Christian (Disciples) Church. Emigrated to America as a child. His book *Pea Ridge and Prairie Grove* (1864) is an authentic record of his experiences as a Union sympathizer in Arkansas, 1860–63.

BAYARD, JAMES ASH(E)TON (*b. Philadelphia, Pa., 1767; d. Wilmington, Del., 1815*), statesman, diplomat. Graduated Princeton, 1784. Studied law with Joseph Reed and Jared Ingersoll; admitted to bar at New Castle and Philadelphia, 1787; began practice at Wilmington, Del., 1787. Married Ann, daughter of Richard Bassett, Chief Justice of Delaware, 1795. Congressman, Federalist, from Delaware, 1797–1803; U.S. senator, 1805-13. As congressman, Bayard played a decisive role in the choice of Thomas Jefferson for president of the United States over Aaron Burr by the House of Representatives,

1800–01. Sane and moderate in his views, he exerted himself to prevent war, 1809–12, advising Federalist support for all acts which would improve the nation's defensive strength. Served with John Q. Adams and Albert Gallatin as United States representative at Ghent, 1813–14, and was chosen to serve as member of commission to negotiate commercial treaty with Great Britain, 1814–15. His health failing, he sailed from England, June 1815, and died at his home six days after arrival in the United States.

BAYARD, JAMES ASHETON (*b. Wilmington, Del., 1799; d. Wilmington, 1880*), lawyer. Son of James A. Bayard (1767–1815). Graduated Union College, 1818; admitted to Delaware bar, 1822; counsel in many important cases. U.S. senator, Democrat, from Delaware, 1851–64, 1867–69. A conservative Unionist from a border state, Bayard became a Republican *post* 1857 but returned to the Democratic party after Lincoln's death. Even as a Republican, he opposed most anti-slavery measures as invasions of property rights; he resigned from the Senate, 1864, in protest against the test oath for office-holders.

BAYARD, JOHN BUBENHEIM (*b. Bohemia Manor, Md., 1738; d. New Brunswick, N.J., 1807*), merchant, Revolutionary patriot. Uncle of James A. Bayard (1767–1815). Active in protests against British rule, 1766–76; major and colonel, Philadelphia Associators, and commended for gallantry at Princeton; speaker, Pennsylvania Assembly, 1777–78. A leader among the Federalists.

BAYARD, NICHOLAS (*b. Alphen, Holland, 1644; d. New York, N.Y., 1707*), colonial official. Brought to New Amsterdam, 1647; nephew of Peter Stuyvesant. Clerk to the Dutch secretary of the province, he succeeded him in office after 1664 and was later appointed surveyor of customs. Imprisoned under the English Governor Andros, he was favored by Governor Dongan, serving as a councillor and as mayor of New York, 1685–87; he was imprisoned again during Jacob Leisler's usurpation and had further difficulties wth Governor Bellomont, 1697–1701.

BAYARD, RICHARD HENRY (*b. Wilmington, Del., 1796; d. Philadelphia, Pa., 1868*), lawyer. Son of James A. Bayard (1767–1815). Mayor of Wilmington, 1832–35; U.S. senator, Democrat, from Delaware, 1836–39, 1840–45.

BAYARD, SAMUEL (*b. Philadelphia, Pa., 1767; d. Princeton, N.J., 1840*), jurist. Son of John B. Bayard. Agent for American claims before British admiralty courts, 1795–99; *post* 1806, served as presiding judge, court of common pleas, Somerset Co., N.J., and was identified with New Jersey civic and educational affairs.

BAYARD, THOMAS FRANCIS (*b. Wilmington, Del., 1828; d. Dedham, Mass., 1898*), statesman. Son of James A. Bayard (1799–1880). Admitted to the bar 1851, he practiced with great success in his native city. As U.S. senator, Democrat, from Delaware, 1869–85, he opposed expansion of federal power and class legislation of every kind; he felt that lawmaking should be restricted to necessary measures only and that administration should be honest and frugal above all else. He received considerable support for the presidential nomination in 1880 and again in 1884, and was appointed secretary of state by Grover Cleveland in 1885. His policies were consistently on the side of peace and arbitration, but the three major diplomatic issues of his term were unsolved when he left office: the North Atlantic Fisheries question; the Bering Sea sealing dispute; the adjustment of conflicting interests in Samoa. Appointed ambassador to Great Britain, 1893, he served until 1897, refusing to be stampeded into unfriendly speech or action during the Venezuela dispute of 1895–96. He was throughout his life a man of high ideals and exalted patriotism.

BAYARD, WILLIAM (*b. New York, N.Y., 1761; d. New York, 1826*), merchant. Partner in LeRoy, Bayard & Co., 1786–1826, a leading commercial house and shipping concern.

BAYLES, JAMES COPPER (*b. New York, N.Y., 1845; d. 1913*), editor of the *Iron Age*, 1869–89; distinguished as a writer on engineering subjects.

BAYLEY, JAMES ROOSEVELT (*b. Rye, N.Y., 1814; d. Newark, N.J., 1877*), Roman Catholic clergyman. Grandson of Richard Bayley; nephew of Elizabeth A. B. Seton. Ordained in the Episcopal ministry, 1835, he resigned in 1841 on appearance of Newman's *Tract XC* and became a Catholic in Rome, April 1842. After study at St. Sulpice in Paris, he was ordained by Archbishop Hughes of New York in 1844; he served as the archbishop's secretary, 1848–53. Consecrated first bishop of Newark, N.J., 1853, he was promoted to the archiepiscopal see of Baltimore, 1872. An able administrator, he was also author of *A Brief Sketch of the Early History of the Catholic Church on the Island of New York* (1853, 1874) and *Memoirs of the Rt. Rev. Simon Bruté* (1855, 1876).

BAYLEY, RICHARD (*b. Fairfield, Conn., 1745; d. New York, N.Y., 1801*), physician. Studied with John Charlton in New York and with William Hunter in London. His pathological studies during a fatal croup epidemic, 1774, helped him cut the mortality of the disease almost in half. In 1792 he became professor of anatomy, and later in surgery, on the medical faculty of Columbia College, New York City. As a practicing physician and as health physician to the port of New York, he did heroic service during the yellow fever epidemics *post* 1795. He was author of *An Account of the Epidemic Fever . . . of 1795* (1796) and *Letters from the Health Office Submitted to the New York Common Council;* he also helped in the early formulation of both the federal and state quarantine laws.

BAYLIES, FRANCIS (*b. Taunton, Mass., 1783; d. 1852*), lawyer. As acting minister to Buenos Aires, 1832, broke off treaty talks in dispute over Falkland Islands fisheries.

BAYLOR, FRANCES COURTENAY (*b. Fort Smith, Ark., 1848; d. Winchester, Va., 1920*), novelist and miscellaneous writer. Author, among others, of *Juan and Juanita* (1888).

BAYLOR, GEORGE (*b. Caroline Co., Va., 1752; d. Bridgetown, Barbados, 1784*), aide-de-camp to Washington in Revolutionary War; his dragoon detachment slaughtered in British surprise at Old Tappan, 1778.

BAYLOR, ROBERT EMMET BLEDSOE (*b. Kentucky, 1793 ?; d. Washington Co., Texas, 1873*), jurist, Baptist preacher. Removed to Alabama, 1820; to Texas, 1839, where he served as a judge until the Civil War. Co-founder of Baylor University.

BAYLY, THOMAS HENRY (*b. near Accomac, Va., 1810; d. 1856*), lawyer, planter. Congressman, Democrat, from Virginia, 1844–56; influential in carrying through the compromises of 1850.

BAYMA, JOSEPH (*b. Ciriè, Italy, 1816; d. Santa Clara, Calif., 1892*), Jesuit priest, mathematician, physicist. Ordained, 1847; was professor of philosophy at Stonyhurst College, England, 1858–69. Assigned to California, he served as president (1869–72) and as professor of higher mathematics (1872–80) at St. Ignatius College, San Francisco. His chief scientific work was his innovating *Elements of Molecular Mechanics* (1866).

BAYNHAM, WILLIAM (*b. South Carolina ?, 1749; d. Virginia ?, 1814*), physician, surgeon. Credited with performance of the first successful operation for extra-uterine pregnancy, he practiced *post* 1785 in Essex, Va.

BEACH, ALFRED ELY (*b. Springfield, Mass., 1826; d. 1896*), inventor, editor. Son of Moses Y. Beach. Partner in *Scientific American*, 1846–96; also editor. Inventor of pneumatic carrier systems, an improved tunneling shield, and a typewriter (1847).

BEACH, FREDERICK CONVERSE (*b. Brooklyn, N.Y., 1848; d. 1918*), patent solicitor. Succeeded his father, Alfred E. Beach, as a director of the Scientific American Co.

BEACH, HARLAN PAGE (*b. Essex Co., N.J., 1854; d. Winter Park, Fla., 1933*), missionary to China. Professor of missions at Yale University, 1906–21. [*Supp. 1*]

BEACH, MOSES SPERRY (*b. Springfield, Mass., 1822; d. Peekskill, N.Y., 1892*), journalist. Son of Moses Y. Beach. Proprietor of the *New York Sun*, 1848–68.

BEACH, MOSES YALE (*b. Wallingford, Conn., 1800; d. Wallingford, 1868*), journalist, inventor. Worked at his trade as a cabinet-maker and experimented unsuccessfully with mechanical devices until his invention of a rag-cutting machine for use in paper-mills secured him an interest in a mill at Saugerties, N.Y., 1829. This enterprise failing, he became manager of the mechanical department of the *New York Sun;* he bought out the founder, Benjamin H. Day, in 1838. On his retirement in 1848, the *Sun* was considered the leading penny newspaper; its circulation was about 50,000 and it claimed the largest cash advertising patronage in the nation. Beach was also a founder of the New York Associated Press and is credited with inventing the syndicated news article (1841).

BEACH, WILLIAM AUGUSTUS (*b. Saratoga Springs, N.Y., 1809; d. 1884*), lawyer. After successful practice at Saratoga and Troy, N.Y., 1833–70, Beach moved to New York City as attorney for Vanderbilt interests. He appeared in many leading cases, 1870–84, including the Barnard impeachment and the Beecher-Tilton trial.

BEACH, WOOSTER (*b. Trumbull, Conn., 1794; d. 1868*), physician. Author of *The American Practice of Medicine* (1833) and other unconventional medical works; founder of the *Eclectic Medical Journal*, 1836; president, National Eclectic Medical Association, 1855.

BEADLE, ERASTUS FLAVEL (*b. Otsego Co., N.Y., 1821; d. Cooperstown, N.Y., 1894*), printer, originator of the "dime novel." [*Supp. 1*]

BEADLE, WILLIAM HENRY HARRISON (*b. Parke Co., Ind., 1838; d. San Francisco, Calif., 1915*), educator. As surveyor-general and, later, superintendent of public instruction, Dakota Territory (1869–89), Beadle fought for the principle that school lands should never be sold for less than ten dollars an acre; this principle was written into the constitutions of several Western states.

BEAL, WILLIAM JAMES (*b. Adrian, Mich., 1833; d. Amherst, Mass., 1924*), teacher, pioneer in the "new botany." Pupil of Agassiz and Asa Gray, he taught at Michigan Agricultural College, 1871–1910. His efforts resulted in establishment of the state Forestry Commission, 1887.

BEALE, EDWARD FITZGERALD (*b. District of Columbia, 1822; d. Washington, D.C., 1893*), explorer. As young naval officer, served under Stockton in California, 1846, and with Kit Carson distinguished himself as messenger from Gen. Kearny after battle of San Pasqual. Thereafter as dispatch bearer traveled to Washington, February-June 1847, and in July-September 1848 made another transcontinental journey carrying first official news of California gold. In all, before resignation from service, 1851, he made six journeys from ocean to ocean. Subsequently he acted as Indian agent for California and Nevada, and with G. H. Heap made survey,

1853, for a railroad route from Missouri frontier through southern Colorado and Utah to Los Angeles. He also made several Western road surveys, 1857–59.

BEALE, RICHARD LEE TURBERVILLE (*b. Westmoreland Co., Va., 1819; d. Hague, Va., 1893*), lawyer, politician. Served in Confederate cavalry, 1861–65.

BEALL, JOHN YATES (*b. Jefferson Co., Va., 1835; d. Governors Island, N.Y., 1865*), Confederate soldier. Arrested, December 1864, for sabotage and other activities on Canadian border; executed as spy.

BEALL, SAMUEL WOOTTON (*b. Montgomery Co., Md., 1807; d. Helena, Mont., 1868*), public official, politician. Active in fight for Wisconsin's statehood, 1840–48. Led exploration to Pike's Peak, 1859; helped found city of Denver, Colo.

BEAMAN, CHARLES COTESWORTH (*b. Houlton, Maine, 1840; d. New York, N.Y., 1900*), lawyer. Graduated Harvard, 1861. Acted for United States in controversy with England over Alabama Claims, 1871–76; partner in Evarts, Southmayd and Choate.

BEAN, TARLETON HOFFMAN (*b. Bainbridge, Pa., 1846; d. 1916*), ichthyologist. Fish culturist and authority on fresh-water fish in America; initiated national movement for preservation of native fish.

BEARD, GEORGE MILLER (*b. Montville, Conn., 1839; d. 1883*), physician. Graduated Yale, 1862; College of Physicians and Surgeons, New York, 1866. Pioneer in neurology in America; known internationally for research on electro-therapeutics.

BEARD, JAMES CARTER (*b. Cincinnati, O., 1837; d. New Orleans, La., 1913*), illustrator. Son of James H. Beard. Celebrated for drawings and articles on plant and animal life.

BEARD, JAMES HENRY (*b. Buffalo, N.Y., 1812; d. Flushing, N.Y., 1893*), artist. Itinerant portrait painter, 1830–45; settled in New York City, 1846; specialized in painting domestic animals.

BEARD, RICHARD (*b. Sumner Co., Tenn., 1799; d. 1880*), Cumberland Presbyterian clergyman. President, Cumberland College, Kentucky, 1843-54; professor of theology, Cumberland University, Tennessee, *post* 1854.

BEARD, THOMAS FRANCIS (*b. Cincinnati, O., 1842; d. 1905*), illustrator, cartoonist. Son of James H. Beard.

BEARD, WILLIAM HOLBROOK (*b. Painesville, O., 1824; d. New York, N.Y., 1900*), artist. Brother of James H. Beard. Known especially for humorous story-pictures of animals in human roles.

BEARDSHEAR, WILLIAM MILLER (*b. Ohio, 1850; d. Iowa, 1902*), United Brethren clergyman. President, Western College, Toledo, Iowa, 1881–89; Iowa State College of Agriculture, 1891–1902.

BEARDSLEY, EBEN EDWARDS (*b. Stepney, Conn., 1808; d. New Haven, Conn., 1891*), Episcopal clergyman. Rector, St. Thomas's Church, New Haven, 1848–91. Author of lives of Samuel Johnson, D.D., and Bishop Samuel Seabury, and *History of the Episcopal Church in Connecticut* (1865, 1868).

BEARDSLEY, SAMUEL (*b. Hoosick, N.Y., 1790; d. Utica, N.Y., 1860*), jurist, congressman. Attorney-General of New York, 1836–39; justice, New York supreme court, 1844–47; chief justice, 1847.

BEASLEY, FREDERICK (*b. near Edenton, N.C., 1777; d. Elizabethtown, N.J., 1845*), Episcopal clergyman. Professor of philosophy, University of Pennsylvania, 1813–28. Author of *A Search of Truth* (1822), defending Locke.

BEASLEY, MERCER (*b. Philadelphia, Pa., 1815; d. Trenton, N.J., 1897*), jurist. Son of Frederick Beasley. Distinguished chief justice, New Jersey, 1864–97.

BEATTIE, FRANCIS ROBERT (*b. Guelph, Canada, 1848; d. Louisville, Ky., 1906*), Presbyterian clergyman. Professor of theology, Presbyterian Seminary, Louisville, Ky., 1893–1906. Author of *Apologetics* (1903).

BEATTY, ADAM (*b. Hagerstown, Md., 1777; d. Mason Co., Ky., 1858*), lawyer, agricultural writer. Author of *Essays on Practical Agriculture* (1844).

BEATTY, CHARLES CLINTON (*b. Co. Antrim, Ireland, c. 1715; d. Barbados, 1772*), Presbyterian clergyman. Came to America, 1729. Attended the Log College under William Tennant; was popular preacher and frontier missionary in Pennsylvania, Virginia and North Carolina.

BEATTY, JOHN (*b. Neshaminy, Pa., 1749; d. near Princeton, N.J., 1826*), Revolutionary soldier, politician, physician. Son of Charles C. Beatty. Secretary of state of New Jersey, 1795–1805.

BEATTY, JOHN (*b. near Sandusky, O., 1828; d. 1914*), soldier, legislator, banker. Partner with brother in private bank, Cardington, O.; rose to brigade command in Union Army; congressman, Republican, from Ohio, 1868–73. Organized Citizens Savings Bank, Columbus, O., and served as president, 1873–1903.

BEATTY, WILLIAM HENRY (*b. Monclova, O., 1838; d. San Francisco, Calif., 1914*), jurist. Removed to California, 1853; district judge in Nevada, 1864–75; justice, supreme court of Nevada, 1875–80; chief justice of California, 1888–1914.

BEATY, AMOS LEONIDAS (*b. Red River Co., Texas, 1870; d. New York, N.Y., 1939*), lawyer, oil executive. President of Texas Co., 1920–26, and American Petroleum Institute. [*Supp. 2*]

BEAUCHAMP, WILLIAM (*b. Kent Co., Del., 1772; d. Paoli, Ind., 1824*), Methodist clergyman. Itinerant preacher, 1794–1815; editor, *Western Christian Monitor,* 1816; served thereafter in Illinois, Missouri and Indiana.

BEAUCHAMP, WILLIAM MARTIN (*b. Coldenham, N.Y., 1830; d. 1925*), Episcopal clergyman, historian. Authority on history of the Iroquois; archeologist, New York State Museum.

BEAUMONT, JOHN COLT (*b. Wilkes-Barre, Pa., 1821; d. Durham, N.H., 1882*), naval officer. Served in Mexican War; commanded USS *Miantonomoh,* first monitor to cross the Atlantic, 1866.

BEAUMONT, WILLIAM *b. Lebanon, Conn., 1785; d. St. Louis, Mo., 1853*), surgeon. Son of a Connecticut farmer, Beaumont is believed to have had only a common school education. Apprenticed, 1810, to Dr. Benjamin Chandler in St. Albans, Vt., he was licensed to practice medicine in Vermont, June 1812, and was commissioned surgeon's mate to the 6th infantry at Plattsburg, N.Y., in the same year. Resigning from the army in 1815, he began private practice at Plattsburg; he enlisted again in 1820 and was sent as post surgeon to Fort Mackinac.

Alexis St. Martin, a young Canadian laborer, was accidentally shot in the stomach on June 6, 1822. Beaumont found him with an open wound "more than the size of the palm of a man's hand" and parts of the lung and punctured stomach protruding from it. Although he thought it impossible the man could survive, Beaumont had St. Martin placed in the military hospital, where he dressed the wound daily for about a year. The stomach adhered to the intercostal muscles and did not drop back into the abdominal cavity. Ultimately a flap of skin covered the opening in the organ, but it could be pushed back so as to expose the interior of the stomach. After a year St. Martin was judged a pauper and ordered returned to Lower Canada, though Beaumont pleaded the trip would kill him. His pleas unheeded, he took the patient into his own home to care for him.

About 1825 Beaumont formed the idea of using his patient for pioneer studies in the processes of digestion. Not long after his experiments had begun, St. Martin ran away. Beaumont published his preliminary findings in which he showed that gastric juice, when removed from the stomach and placed in bottles, digests food the same way but more slowly than under natural conditions. His observations were sufficient to overthrow many prevalent theories on digestion.

While stationed at other army posts, Beaumont continued to search for St. Martin, finally locating him in Lower Canada where he had married. The man and his family were transported to Fort Crawford at Beaumont's expense in August 1829, and the experiments were continued for two years. Patient and family then went back to Canada, agreeing to return when requested. St. Martin kept his promise,

and Beaumont worked with him again from November 1832 to March 1834; in 1833, he published his *Experiments and Observations on the Gastric Juice and the Physiology of Digestion,* the greatest contribution ever made to the knowledge of gastric digestion and the physiology of the stomach. Beaumont had conferred with many chemists in his endeavor to secure a precise analysis of the gastric juice; Prof. Robley Dunglison of the University of Virginia found that it contained free hydrochloric acid and a second digestive factor which later research proved to be pepsin. The 238 experiments detailed in the book established the relative digestibility of many articles of diet. Beaumont's discoveries began a new era in the study of the stomach and its functions.

St. Martin returned to Canada in 1834, and Beaumont was unsuccessful in attempts to bring him back. In 1838, after disagreements with the newly appointed surgeon-general, Beaumont resigned from the army and entered private practice in St. Louis.

BEAUPRÉ, ARTHUR MATTHIAS (*b. Oswego Township, Ill., 1853; d. Chicago, Ill., 1919*), lawyer, diplomat. Consul and minister to Colombia, 1899–1903; handled details of Hay-Herrán Treaty. Minister also to the Argentine, Netherlands and Cuba.

BEAUREGARD, PIERRE GUSTAVE TOUTANT (*b. near New Orleans, La., 1818; d. New Orleans, 1893*), Confederate soldier. Graduated West Point, 1838. Engineer officer on Scott's staff in Mexican War; chief engineer for draining operations, New Orleans, 1858–61. As Confederate brigadier, commanded forces around Charleston, S.C., 1861. Although junior to Joseph E. Johnston, issued orders for first battle of Bull Run and was promoted to full general. Succeeded A. S. Johnston in command at Shiloh, 1862; soon thereafter his illness caused his replacement in Western theatre by Braxton Bragg. Defended South Carolina and Georgia coasts, 1863–64; soundly defeated Butler at Drewry's Bluff, May 1864, and foiled Union drive on Richmond. After administrative command in West, he returned to fight in Carolina campaign under J. E. Johnston. Postwar he held various civil positions including managership of Louisiana Lottery. As a commander he was courageous and skilled in fortification but weak in strategy and method.

BEAVER, JAMES ADDAMS (*b. Millerstown, Pa., 1837; d. 1914*), Union soldier, lawyer. Governor of Pennsylvania, Republican, 1887–91; judge, Pennsylvania superior court, 1895–1914.

BECK, CARL (*b. Neckargemünd, Germany, 1856; d. Pelham, N.Y., 1911*), surgeon. Graduated, M.D. Jena, 1879. Came to America, 1881; pioneer in application of X-ray to medicine and surgery.

BECK, CHARLES (*b. Heidelberg, Germany, 1798; d. Cambridge, Mass., 1866*), classical scholar. Ph.D.

Tübingen, 1823; came to America, 1824. Professor of Latin, Harvard, 1832–50; helped introduce German scholarship into the United States.

BECK, JAMES MONTGOMERY (*b. Philadelphia, Pa., 1861; d. Washington, D.C., 1936*), corporation lawyer. Admitted to Philadelphia bar, 1884; assistant U.S. attorney-general, 1900–03. A leading Republican critic of Woodrow Wilson's war policies, Beck welcomed Harding's election as a triumph for conservatism. Appointed solicitor-general, 1921, he resigned in 1925; served as congressman from Pennsylvania, 1927–34. Author of *The Constitution of the United States* (1922) and *The Vanishing Rights of the States* (1926). [*Supp. 2*]

BECK, JOHANN HEINRICH (*b. Cleveland, O., 1856; d. Cleveland, 1924*), conductor, composer. Director, Cleveland "Pop" Orchestra, 1901–12.

BECK, JOHN BRODHEAD (*b. Schenectady, N.Y., 1794; d. Rhinebeck, N.Y., 1851*), physician. M.D., 1817, College of Physicians and Surgeons, New York. Collaborated with brother Theodric R. Beck in treatise on Medical Jurisprudence.

BECK, LEWIS CALEB (*b. Schenectady, N.Y., 1798; d. Albany, N.Y., 1853*), physician, naturalist, chemist. Brother of John B. Beck and Theodric R. Beck. Professor of chemistry, Albany Medical College and Rutgers. Author of works on botany, chemistry and food adulteration.

BECK, MARTIN (*b. Liptó Szent Miklos, Hungary, 1867; d. New York, N.Y., 1940*), vaudeville impresario (Orpheum Vaudeville Circuit, Palace Theatre) and theatrical manager. [*Supp. 2*]

BECK, THEODRIC ROMEYN (*b. Schenectady, N.Y., 1791; d. Utica, N.Y., 1855*), physician, philanthropist. Author of *Elements of Medical Jurisprudence* (1823), first authoritative book on subject published in the United States. Brother of John B. and Lewis C. Beck.

BECKER, GEORGE FERDINAND (*b. New York, N.Y., 1847; d. Washington, D.C., 1919*), geologist, mathematician, physicist. Graduated Harvard, 1868; Ph.D., Heidelberg, 1869; Berlin Academy of Mines, 1871. Taught mining and metallurgy, University of California, Berkeley, 1874–79. Served on King survey of 40th Parallel. His *Geology of the Comstock Lode* (1882) marked a new era in geological investigations in America. Becker also studied quicksilver deposits of Pacific Coast and made investigations abroad. His valuable contributions were in abstruse chemico-physical problems and methods of solving them. Carnegie Geophysical Laboratory was largely an outgrowth of his work.

BECKNELL, WILLIAM (*b. Amherst Co., Va., c. 1796; d. 1865*), explorer, trader, pioneer in Santa Fe trade. Took pack train via upper Arkansas to Santa Fe and Taos, 1821; took wagon train via Cimarron to San Miguel, 1822, establishing new route. Removed to Texas, 1834.

BECKWITH, CLARENCE AUGUSTINE (*b. Charlemont, Mass., 1849; d. Bangor, Maine, 1931*), Congregational clergyman, educator. Professor of theology, Bangor Seminary, 1893–1905; Chicago Seminary, 1905–26. [*Supp. 1*]

BECKWITH, JAMES CARROLL (*b. Hannibal, Mo., 1852; d. New York, N.Y., 1917*), painter. Studied Chicago Academy, 1868–71; New York National Academy, 1871–73; and in Paris with Yvon and Duran; a friend of J. S. Sargent. Returned to America, 1878, and was successful as portrait painter and in genre work. Breaking with the conservatives, Beckwith and other young artists formed the Society of American Artists and also organized Art Students League, at which he was an influential teacher.

BECKWOURTH, JAMES P. (*b. Virginia, 1798; d. c. 1867*). His roving exploits as hunter and squawman are described in T. D. Bonner's *Life and Adventures of J. P. Beckwourth* (1856).

BEDFORD, GUNNING (*b. 1742; d. 1797*), Revolutionary soldier, politician. Cousin of Gunning Bedford (1747–1812). Governor of Delaware, 1796–97.

BEDFORD, GUNNING (*b. Philadelphia, Pa., 1747; d. Wilmington, Del., 1812*), Revolutionary statesman. Champion of rights of small states in Federal Convention, 1787; federal judge, 1789–1812.

BEDINGER, GEORGE MICHAEL (*b. York Co., Pa., 1756; d. near Blue Licks, Ky., 1843*), Revolutionary soldier. Early Kentucky settler and opponent of slavery.

BEE, BARNARD ELLIOTT (*b. Charleston, S.C., 1824; d. Bull Run, Va., 1861*), Confederate soldier. Raised in Texas; graduated West Point, 1845; meritorious service in Mexican War and on frontier. As Confederate brigadier, commanded key point at first battle of Bull Run, where he was killed. His reference to T. J. Jackson's brigade "standing like a stone wall" was origin of Jackson's nickname "Stonewall."

BEE, HAMILTON PRIOLEAU (*b. Charleston, S.C., 1822; d. San Antonio, Texas, 1897*), Confederate soldier. Brother of Barnard E. Bee. Commanded at Brownsville, Texas, and expedited importation of munitions across Mexican border.

BEECHER, CATHARINE ESTHER (*b. East Hampton, N.Y., 1800; d. 1878*), educator, reformer. Daughter of Lyman Beecher.

BEECHER, CHARLES (*b. Litchfield, Conn., 1815; d. Georgetown, Mass., 1900*), Congregational clergyman. Son of Lyman Beecher. Pastor, First Congregational Church, Georgetown, Mass., 1857–81, and held other pastorates. Shared family propensity for reform.

BEECHER, CHARLES EMERSON (*b. Dunkirk, N.Y., 1856; d. New Haven, Conn., 1904*), paleontologist. Curator, Yale geological collections, 1888–1904.

BEECHER, EDWARD (*b. East Hampton, N.Y., 1803; d. Brooklyn, N.Y., 1895*), Congregational clergyman. President, Illinois College, 1830–44; held pastorates in Boston, Galesburg, Ill., and Brooklyn, N.Y.; active in anti-slavery work. Son of Lyman Beecher.

BEECHER, HENRY WARD (*b. Litchfield, Conn., 1813; d. Brooklyn, N.Y., 1887*), clergyman, publicist. Son of Lyman Beecher and Roxana (Foote) Beecher. Graduated Amherst, 1834; studied at Lane Theological Seminary, Cincinnati. Licensed to preach, 1837, but was refused ordination by Old School Presbytery in Indiana to which a local church had called him. Married Eunice White Bullard, 1837. Ordained by Cincinnati New School Presbytery, 1838, he was for eight years pastor of Second Presbyterian Church, Indianapolis. Unconventional in dress and manner, he believed that a sermon was effective only when it altered the moral character of the listeners; he strove deliberately for emotional response. His direct, pithy style, touches of humor and flights of imagination made him a popular preacher; the same qualities in his writing won him a wide audience in periodicals. In 1847, his growing fame brought him to the pastorate of Plymouth Church, Brooklyn, N.Y. (Congregationalist). Few American clergymen have attained the influence and public position which soon became his. His theatrical techniques of expression, his bold and often wise pronouncements on public questions such as slavery and municipal reform, his very genuine sympathy with and understanding of human difficulties, all combined to fascinate his generation. Believing that slavery was fundamentally wrong, he held that the Constitution forbade interference with it in the slave states; left to itself it would wither. Meanwhile, all means should be employed to prevent its spread to the new Territories. He campaigned for Frémont in 1856, and for Lincoln, and was a strong supporter of the Civil War.

After the war, he supported President Johnson's policy of re-admitting the seceded states and withdrawing military government from them. Not a brilliant or original thinker, his genius lay in the practical use of other men's ideas and their propagation by means of his overflowing energy and oratorical talents. Freedom was a passion with him, and he had singularly little prejudice. His latter years were disturbed by accusations of sexual immorality made, 1872, by a member of his church. A subsequent civil suit for damages brought about a sensational trial at which the jury failed to agree. His popularity, though diminished, was not destroyed;

a council of Congregational churches examined the evidence and exonerated him. He continued his work on the lecture platform and at Plymouth Church until his death.

BEECHER, LYMAN (*b. New Haven, Conn., 1775; d. Brooklyn, N.Y., 1863*), Presbyterian clergyman. Father of Catharine E., Charles, Edward, Henry Ward, Thomas K. Beecher and Harriet Beecher Stowe. Graduated Yale, 1797; ordained 1799. Pastor, Presbyterian Church, East Hampton, N.Y., 1799–1810; Litchfield, Conn., 1810–26; Hanover Street Church, Boston, 1826–32, where he conducted a continuous revival which resulted in a growth in intolerance. First president, Lane Theological Seminary, Cincinnati, 1832–50, and center of much theological controversy and opposition from conservative Presbyterians.

BEECHER, THOMAS KINNICUT (*b. Litchfield, Conn., 1824; d. Elmira, N.Y., 1900*), Congregational clergyman. Pastor, Congregational Church, Elmira, N.Y., 1854–1900. Pioneer in church social work activity. Son of Lyman Beecher.

BEER, GEORGE LOUIS (*b. Staten Island, N.Y., 1872; d. 1920*), historian. Graduated Columbia, 1892. Retiring from business, 1903, he began research along economic lines which resulted in the three major works: *British Colonial Policy, 1754–65* (1907); *The Origins of the British Colonial System, 1578–1660* (1908); and *The Old Colonial System: Part I* (1912). These did much to correct long prevalent errors in American thinking on the subject. Beer served with ability as chief of the colonial division, American delegation to Paris Peace Conference, helping to draft mandates for administration of former German colonies.

BEER, THOMAS (*b. Council Bluffs, Iowa, 1889; d. New York, N.Y., 1940*), writer. Author, among others, of *Stephen Crane* (1923) and *The Mauve Decade* (1926). [*Supp. 2*]

BEER, WILLIAM (*b. Plymouth, England, 1849; d. New Orleans, La., 1927*), librarian, Howard Memorial Library, New Orleans, 1891–1927; was a prominent figure in social and literary life of that city.

BEERS, ETHEL LYNN (*b. Goshen, N.Y., 1827; d. New York, N.Y., 1879*), poet. Published *All Quiet Along the Potomac, and Other Poems* (1879); the title-poem first appeared, 1861, as "The Picket Guard."

BEERS, HENRY AUGUSTIN (*b. Buffalo, N.Y., 1847; d. 1926*), author, educator. Graduated Yale, 1869; taught English literature there, 1871–1916; professor emeritus, 1916–26. Author of studies on romanticism.

BEHAN, WILLIAM JAMES (*b. New Orleans, La., 1840; d. New Orleans, 1928*), sugar planter, political leader. Mayor, New Orleans, 1882–84; later turned Republican in protest against Democratic plan to cut sugar tariff.

BEHREND, BERNARD ARTHUR (*b. Villeneuve, Switzerland, 1875; d. 1932*), electrical engineer. Designer of turbo-electric machinery. [*Supp.* 1]

BEHRENDS, ADOLPHUS JULIUS FREDERICK (*b. Nymwegen, Holland, 1839; d. Brooklyn, N.Y., 1900*), clergyman. Brought to America as a child. Originally a Baptist, he won reputation as pastor of Central Congregational Church, Brooklyn, 1883–1900.

BEHRENS, HENRY (*b. Munstadt, Germany, 1815; d. 1895*), Jesuit priest. Superior of Buffalo (N.Y.) Mission, 1872–78, 1886–92. Established St. Ignatius College (now John Carroll University), Cleveland, O., 1886.

BEISSEL, JOHANN CONRAD (*b. Eberbach, Germany, 1690; d. 1768*), hymn-writer, founder of Solitary Brethren of the Community of Seventh Day Baptists at Ephrata, Lancaster Co., Pa., 1732.

BELASCO, DAVID (*b. San Francisco, Calif., 1853; d. 1931*), actor, dramatist, producer. As a boy, recited ballads in public for pennies and wrote plays based on dime novels. After acting and directing in San Francisco, 1871–79, went to New York as hack dramatist and stage manager. Achieved financial independence in 1895 with *The Heart of Maryland*. *Madame Butterfly* (1900) and other successes followed. His ability to create illusion of reality and atmosphere and his painstaking perfectionism set a new standard of technical excellence in the American theatre. [*Supp.* 1]

BELCHER, JONATHAN (*b. Cambridge, Mass., 1681/2; d. Elizabethtown, N.J., 1757*), merchant. Graduated Harvard, 1699; traveled extensively in Europe; returning to Boston, he became successful in trade. Elected to Massachusetts Council, 1718, he was re-elected seven times. Appointed governor of Massachusetts and New Hampshire, 1729/30, he failed in efforts to please both colonial and royal interests, and was dismissed from both governorships in 1741. After rehabilitating himself with the government in England, he was appointed governor of New Jersey, 1746, where he was active in founding the College of New Jersey (Princeton).

BELCOURT, GEORGE ANTOINE (*b. Bay du Febvre, Canada, 1803; d. Shediac, New Brunswick, 1874*), Roman Catholic priest. Pioneer missionary in western Canada and North Dakota; student of the Saulteux (Chippewa) language.

BELDEN, JOSIAH (*b. Cromwell, Conn., 1815; d. New York, N.Y., 1892*), California pioneer, member of Bartleson-Bidwell party from Independence, Mo., to the Pacific, 1841. Later rancher, storekeeper, first mayor of San José.

BELKNAP, GEORGE EUGENE (*b. Newport, N.H., 1832; d. Key West, Fla., 1903*), naval officer.

BELKNAP, JEREMY (*b. Boston, Mass., 1744; d. Boston, 1798*), Congregational clergyman, historian. Graduated Harvard, 1762; pastor at Dover, N.H., 1766–86; at Federal Street Church, Boston, 1787 until his death. Author of outstanding three-volume *History of New Hampshire* (1784, 1791, 1792); *The Foresters* (1792); *American Biography* (1794, 1798); and other works. In 1790–91 he helped form an antiquarian society which in 1794 became the Massachusetts Historical Society, first of its kind in the United States.

BELKNAP, WILLIAM WORTH (*b. Newburgh, N.Y., 1829; d. Washington, D.C., 1890*), lawyer, Union soldier. Secretary of war, 1869–76; resigned in face of charges of malfeasance in office.

BELL, ALEXANDER GRAHAM (*b. Edinburgh, Scotland, 1847; d. Cape Breton, Nova Scotia, 1922*), inventor of telephone, leader in education of the deaf. Son of Alexander Melville Bell, scientist and author in the field of vocal physiology and elocution, and grandson of Alexander Bell, a professor of elocution in London. Alexander Graham Bell went to London *c.* 1868 as professional assistant to his father, who had taken over the grandfather's work there; he assumed complete charge while his father was on a lecture tour in America in 1868 and worked with him until the family moved to Canada in 1870. While in London he took courses in anatomy and physiology at University College. His work for the deaf began in this period. His father had invented "Visible Speech," a system of symbols indicating the position of the vocal organs in speaking; the younger Bell adapted this system for use in teaching the deaf to talk.

After the family came to Canada, Bell went to Boston in 1871 to train the teachers at a special day school for the deaf, the first of its kind anywhere, which had been started by the Boston School Board and began a private class for teachers of the deaf, 1872. Appointed professor of vocal physiology and the mechanics of speech at Boston University, 1873, he instituted a similar class there, started a series of conventions for teachers of speech to the deaf and took private pupils as well.

Bell did his first original scientific study in 1865 on the resonance pitches of the mouth cavities during utterance of vowel sounds. Amid his other activities, 1873–76, he was experimenting with a phonautograph, a multiple telegraph and an electric speaking telegraph or telephone. He conceived the theory of the telephone in 1874; a year later, encouraged by Prof. Joseph Henry and while experimenting on the multiple telegraph, he finally hit upon the practical solution to the problem of reproducing the human voice electrically. Experiments to improve quality continued; in 1876 the first complete intelligible sentence was transmitted. The following year a conversation between Boston and New York was conducted. Patents were issued to Bell in 1876 and 1877, but many claimants contested his rights. After extensive litigation, the U.S. Supreme Court upheld all of Bell's claims. The first organization for commercial development of the invention, the Bell Telephone Co., was formed in 1877. That same year Bell married Mabel G. Hubbard, who had been deaf from early childhood. After traveling with her in Europe to introduce the telephone to England and France, he returned to Washington, D.C., in 1878, where he continued inventive activity in fields related to the telephone. He became a citizen of the United States in 1882. At the Volta Laboratory which he financed, he and two associates worked on numerous projects including Bell's photophone, the induction balance and the audiometer; they also invented and patented several improvements on Edison's phonograph. Bell was president of the National Geographic Society, 1896–1904, and did much to forward the success of the Society and its magazine.

Aviation was Bell's primary interest after 1897. He encouraged the work of Samuel P. Langley, invented the tetrahedral kite, and in 1907 founded the Aerial Experiment Association, under whose auspices the first public flight of a heavier-than-air machine was made in 1908.

BELL, ALEXANDER MELVILLE (*b. Edinburgh, Scotland, 1819; d. 1905*), educator. Father of Alexander G. Bell. Author of *Visible Speech* (1867).

BELL, CHARLES HENRY (*b. Chester, N.H., 1823; d. Exeter, N.H., 1893*), lawyer, politician. Author of *The Bench and Bar of New Hampshire* (1894) and other works on history of that state.

BELL, CLARK (*b. Whitesville, N.Y., 1832; d. New York, N.Y., 1918*), lawyer, expert in medical jurisprudence.

BELL, FREDERIC SOMERS (*b. Webster City, Iowa, 1859; d. Winona, Minn., 1938*), lumberman. President, Weyerhaeuser Timber Co., 1928–34.

[*Supp. 2*]

BELL, HENRY HAYWOOD (*b. North Carolina, 1808; d. near Osaka, Japan, 1868*), naval officer. Served as chief of staff to Farragut, 1862; commanded West Gulf Squadron, 1863; in Asiatic waters, 1865 and after.

BELL, ISAAC (*b. New York, N.Y. 1846; d. 1889*), cotton merchant, politician. Established one of first brokerage firms to unite operations in the cotton region with Northern speculative market.

BELL, JACOB (*b. Middlesex, now Darien, Conn., 1792; d. 1852*), ship-builder. His New York shipyard built sailing packets for the Collins Line, the *Trade Wind* and other well-known clipper ships, and the first ocean steamships launched in New York (1840).

BELL, JAMES FRANKLIN (*b. near Shelbyville, Ky., 1856; d. 1919*), army officer. Graduated West Point, 1878. Served in West, 1878–98, and with special distinction in the Philippine insurrection; promoted major-general, 1907; chief of staff of the army, 1906–11. [*Supp. 1*]

BELL, JAMES MADISON (*b. Gallipolis, O., 1826; d. 1902*), Negro poet, lecturer. Friend of John Brown; worked against slavery; resident *post* 1865 in Toledo, O. Author of *Poetical Works* (1901).

BELL, JAMES STROUD (*b. Philadelphia, Pa., 1847; d. 1915*), merchant miller. Reorganizer, 1888, and president of the Washburn-Crosby Co., 1889–1915; innovator in promoting cereal sales by packaging and advertising.

BELL, JOHN (*b. near Nashville, Tenn., 1797; d. Stewart Co., Tenn., 1869*), Southern statesman. Graduated Cumberland College, 1814; began practice of law at Franklin, Tenn., later removing to Nashville, where he led the bar. As congressman, Democrat, 1827–41, Bell was at first a supporter of Jackson but became ultimately the leader of the Whig party in Tennessee and accepted cabinet post of secretary of war from President W. H. Harrison, 1841. In opposition to President Tyler, he resigned in the same year.

After six years' retirement, Bell was elected to the U.S. Senate in 1847, continuing to serve until 1859. During this period of increasing bitterness between North and South, Bell distinguished himself as one of the most consistently conservative and nationally minded Southerners. Although a slave owner, he never became an apostle of slavery, and was opposed to extremism on either side. As a member of the lower house he had supported John Quincy Adams in defense of the right of petition, opposing those who sought to prevent reception or consideration of anti-slavery petitions. In the Senate, when controversy arose over the question of slavery in the territories the United States had acquired from Mexico, Bell affirmed the constitutionality of congressional prohibition of slavery in the territories, although he did not agree with the policy. He supported President Taylor's plan of admitting the territories to statehood even if the exclusion of slavery should result. In 1854 he broke with other Southerners and opposed reopening the bitter controversy over slavery by passage of the Kansas-Nebraska Act; four years later he defied instructions from the Tennessee legislature to support the admission of Kansas under the Lecompton constitution, believing it wrong to force slavery upon an unwilling people. Bitterly denounced in the South for his moderate attitude, he gained respect in the North.

By 1858 the Whig party was dead. Bell supported the short-lived Native Americans and also considered uniting former Southern Whigs with moderate Republicans. But by this time moderation was not popular. In 1860 a group of moderates, most of them former Whigs, supported Bell for president and Edward Everett for vice-president on the ticket of the Constitutional Union Party. Bell received the electoral votes of Tennessee, Kentucky, and Virginia. His campaign had been a plea for preservation of the Union. He and his followers opposed secession, and he sought to promote compromise even after Lincoln's administration began. Yet when Fort Sumter was fired upon and Lincoln called for troops, Bell advised Tennessee to enter into "alliance" with the seceded states if the federal government attempted their coercion. This ended his career. He spent his remaining years lamenting the war and what it had brought both to the South and to the nation.

BELL, LOUIS (b. New Hampshire, 1864; d. 1923), physicist, engineer. Graduated Dartmouth, 1884; began serious work in physics and chemistry at Johns Hopkins, his most important work there being determination of wave-length of D_1 line in spectrum of sodium. Appointed chief engineer in power transmission department of General Electric, 1893, he became authority on polyphase transmission. After 1895, as consulting engineer in Boston, did "diagnostic work on sick electric railways." Co-author of The Electric Railway (1892); author, Power Transmission for Electric Railroads (1896), The Art of Illumination (1902), and The Telescope (1922). Over forty patents testify to his originality.

BELL, LUTHER VOSE (b. Francestown, N.H., 1806; d. Budd's Ferry, Md., 1862), physician, politician. Son of Samuel Bell. Superintendent, McLean Hospital for Insane, Charlestown, Mass., 1836–56. Described a form of insanity (1848) thereafter known as Bell's Disease or Bell's Mania.

BELL, PETER HANSBOROUGH (b. near Fredericksburg, Va., 1808; d. Warren Co., N.C., 1898), soldier. Fought at San Jacinto and as Texas Ranger in Mexican War; governor of Texas, 1849–52; congressman, Democrat, from Texas, 1853–57.

BELL, ROBERT (b. Glasgow, Scotland, c. 1732; d. Richmond, Va., 1784), bookseller. Came to America c. 1766; famous for wit and drollery. Published at Philadelphia the first edition of Paine's Common Sense (1776), the first American edition of Blackstone's Commentaries and other notable works.

BELL, SAMUEL (b. Londonderry, N.H., 1770; d. Chester, N.H., 1850), lawyer. Graduated Dartmouth, 1793. (Democrat) Republican governor of New Hampshire, 1819–23; U.S. senator, 1823–35. The rise of Jacksonian democracy caused his retirement from Congress.

BELLAMY, EDWARD (b. Chicopee Falls, Mass., 1850; d. Chicopee Falls, 1898), author, utopian socialist. Studied law; with brother Charles founded Springfield Daily News, 1880; contributed to magazines. Becoming more seriously concerned with so-

cial questions, devoted himself exclusively to them. Author of The Duke of Stockbridge (1879, newspaper publication; 1900, book form); Looking Backward (1888), a famous utopian romance; Equality (1897) and other books.

BELLAMY, ELIZABETH WHITFIELD CROOM (b. near Quincy, Fla., 1837; d. Mobile, Ala., 1900), teacher, author of romantic novels of life in the South.

BELLAMY, JOSEPH (b. Cheshire, Conn., 1719; d. Bethlehem, Conn., 1790), theologian. Graduated Yale, 1735. Follower of Jonathan Edwards; wrote on New Light theology; pastor at Bethlehem, Conn., 1738–90.

BELLEW, FRANK HENRY TEMPLE (b. Cawnpore, India, 1828; d. 1888), illustrator. Came to America, 1850. Worked for leading magazines as comic artist and caricaturist.

BELLINGHAM, RICHARD (b. Boston, England, c. 1592; d. 1672), lawyer. Came to Boston, New England, 1634. Held various posts, 1635–65; was governor of Massachusetts, 1641, 1654, 1665–72. Espoused popular cause against Winthrop.

BELLOMONT, Earl of. [See COOTE, RICHARD, 1636–1701.]

BELLOWS, ALBERT FITCH (b. Milford, Mass., 1829; d. 1883), landscape painter, etcher. A painstaking depicter of rural scenes.

BELLOWS, GEORGE WESLEY (b. Columbus, O., 1882; d. New York, N.Y., 1925), painter, lithographer, illustrator. Studied under Robert Henri and was influenced by theories of Jay Hambidge and by example of Goya and Daumier; interested especially in everyday subjects and city street life. Taught at Art Students League, New York City, and Art Institute, Chicago. By 1915 he expanded his interests to include country subjects and the horrors of war; his pictures of events in World War I are among his best. Post 1916 he gave particular attention to lithography and undertook book illustration. Bellows's works in all types were stamped with his own personality and rank with the best art of his period.

BELLOWS, HENRY WHITNEY (b. Boston, Mass., 1814; d. New York, N.Y., 1882), Unitarian clergyman. Graduated Harvard, 1832; Harvard Divinity School, 1837. Pastor, First Unitarian Church (later, Church of All Souls), New York City, 1839–82. Founder and president, U.S. Sanitary Commission in the Civil War; editor, Christian Examiner, 1866–77.

BELMONT, ALVA ERTSKIN SMITH VANDERBILT (b. Mobile, Ala., 1853; d. Paris, France, 1933), social leader, suffragette. [Supp. 1]

BELMONT, AUGUST (b. Alzei, Germany, 1816; d. New York, N.Y., 1890), capitalist. Trained in Rothschild's office, Frankfurt, he managed branch offices of the firm and profited by the panic of 1837 to begin banking business in New York, establishing what became August Belmont and Co., and acting as agent for the Rothschilds. Soon a leading banker, he became a U.S. citizen, married a daughter of Matthew C. Perry and was active in the Democratic party. Served as minister to Netherlands, 1853–57. In the Civil War, he aided Union cause by his influence in European political and financial circles.

BELO, ALFRED HORATIO (*b. Salem, N.C., 1839; d. 1901*), Confederate soldier, journalist. A publisher of *Galveston News*, 1866–1901; established *Dallas News*, 1885; an incorporator of Associated Press.

BEMAN, NATHAN SIDNEY SMITH (*b. New Lebanon, N.Y., 1785; d. 1871*), Presbyterian clergyman. Pastor, First Presbyterian Church, Troy, N.Y., 1823–63. Head of New School movement; author of *Letters to Rev. John Hughes* (1851). President, Rensselaer Polytechnic Institute, 1845–65.

BEMENT, CALEB N. (*b. New York, 1790; d. Poughkeepsie, N.Y., 1868*), agriculturalist, inventor, publicist. Author of *American Poulterer's Companion* (1844); a strong influence in his time towards improvement of American agriculture.

BEMENT, CLARENCE SWEET (*b. Mishawaka, Ind., 1843; d. 1923*), machine-tool manufacturer, collector of books, coins and minerals.

BEMIS, GEORGE (*b. Waltham, Mass., 1816; d. Nice, France, 1878*), lawyer. Graduated Harvard, 1835; Harvard Law School, 1839. Practiced criminal law in Boston; acted in Webster-Parkman case and in Alabama Claims cases.

BEMIS, HAROLD EDWARD (*b. Cawker City, Kans., 1883; d. 1931*), veterinarian, soldier, educator. As head of department at Iowa State College, 1909–27, made substantial contributions to study of veterinary surgery. [*Supp. 1*]

BENAVIDES, ALONZO DE (*fl. 1600–64*), Franciscan friar. Arrived in New Mexico, 1622, to work among Apaches; set up missions at Picuries, Taos, Acoma and other places, converting more than 16,000 tribesmen. His *Memorial* to the king of Spain (presented 1630, revised 1634) gives history of the missions and description of physical aspects of the country. Assigned to Goa, India, 1634, he became Archbishop of that place.

BENBRIDGE, HENRY (*b. Philadelphia, Pa., 1744; d. 1812*), portrait painter. Possibly trained by Wallaston; studied in Italy; encouraged by Benjamin West. Returned to America, 1770; practiced in Philadelphia, Charleston, S.C., and Norfolk, Va.

BENEDICT, DAVID (*b. Norwalk, Conn., 1779; d. 1874*), Baptist clergyman, historian. Author of pioneer studies in history of his church.

BENEDICT, ERASTUS CORNELIUS (*b. Branford, Conn., 1800; d. New York, N.Y., 1880*), lawyer. Specialist in admiralty cases; a prime factor, 1840–80, in New York's educational progress and in founding College of the City of New York.

BENEDICT, STANLEY ROSSITER (*b. Cincinnati, O., 1884; d. Elmsford, N.Y., 1936*), biological chemist. Graduated University of Cincinnati, 1906; Ph.D. Yale, 1908. Professor of chemistry, Cornell University Medical College, 1931–36. Married Ruth Fulton, 1913, who, as Ruth Benedict, became a well-known anthropologist. Benedict's major contributions were in the area of analytical biochemistry; he originated Benedict's solution, a universally used reagent for testing sugar in the urine, and with associates made many fruitful studies in quantitative blood chemistry and metabolism. [*Supp. 2*]

BENEZET, ANTHONY (*b. San Quentin, France, 1713; d. Philadelphia, Pa., 1784*), philanthropist, teacher. Became Quaker convert, and removed to Philadelphia, 1731. Author of *A Caution and Warning to Great Britain and Her Colonies on the Calamitous State of the Enslaved Negroes* (1766) and *Historical Account of Guinea* (1771).

BENHAM, HENRY WASHINGTON (*b. Quebec, Canada, 1813; d. 1884*), engineer, soldier. Graduated West Point, 1837. Served as engineer in Mexican and Civil Wars; in charge of New York and Boston harbor defenses, 1865–82.

BENJAMIN, ASHER (*b. Greenfield, Mass., 1773; d. Springfield, Mass., 1845*), architect. Designed many houses and churches in Windsor, Vt., Boston, Springfield, Mass., and other places in New England. His importance lies primarily in his writings on architecture, which include *The Country Builder's Assistant* (1797), *The American Builder's Companion* (1806), *The Rudiments of Architecture* (1814) and *The Practical House Carpenter* (1830). Through these tasteful books, late colonial details and designs won wide influence among builders.

BENJAMIN, GEORGE HILLARD (*b. New York, N.Y., 1852; d. 1927*), lawyer, engineer, patent expert, inventor. Son of Park Benjamin (1809–64).

BENJAMIN, JUDAH PHILIP (*b. St. Thomas, B.W.I., 1811; d. Paris, France, 1884*), lawyer, statesman. Son of Philip Benjamin, an English Jew, and Rebecca de Mendes of a Portuguese Jewish family. Taken to Charleston, S.C., as a child; studied at Fayetteville Academy, North Carolina; briefly at Yale. *Post* 1828 worked in New Orleans and studied law; with Thomas Slidell, issued a *Digest of the Reported Decisions of the Superior Court of the Late Territory of Orleans and of the Supreme Court of Louisiana* (1834). Became nationally known through participation in case of brig *Creole*; acquired sugar plantation. Failure of a friend whom he had endorsed cost him his plantation and threw him back upon law practice.

Served as Whig in state legislature; as U.S. senator from Louisiana, 1852–61. Sharing the general Southern belief that the upsetting of sectional balance in Compromise of 1850 demanded some foreign expansion for redress, he began to favor a "Southern party." In 1856 he declared himself a Democrat, supported Buchanan and was returned to Senate as Democrat, 1858. One of the earliest Southern senators to advocate secession, he resigned his seat, 1861. Three weeks later Jefferson Davis appointed him attorney-general of the Confederacy. In September 1861 he was made head of Confederate War Department, whose position, not generally known in South, was already critical because of poor credit, inadequate supplies. Blamed for the loss of Roanoke Island, 1862, though it appears now there was little ground for holding him responsible, he was widely attacked but Davis stood behind him; on resignation of R. M. T. Hunter as secretary of state, Davis appointed Benjamin to the post while investigation of the Roanoke Island affair was still under way. Bitter attacks continued, the appointment being described as "reckless defiance of popular sentiment." Benjamin, however, maintained his calm, was mainstay of the over-sensitive Davis. More realistic in viewing the Confederacy's desperate position than many Southerners, he began to develop a plan for using slaves as soldiers on assumption they would then receive their freedom. This possibility terrified more conventional Southerners. The Confederate Congress defeated the recommendation and provided for slave soldiers but not for emancipation.

When the Northern armies in 1865 finally shattered all hopes, Benjamin calmly made his last recommendations in connection with the terms of J. E. Johnston's surrender, then escaped via the West Indies to England, 1866. There, he built a new career at the English bar. His standing in the legal world received unique recognition when he was admitted to the bar after five months as a student. He joined the northern circuit, which included Liverpool, where his professional skill was already known. His *Treatise on the Law of Sale of Personal Property* (1868) showed remarkable familiarity with English and Civil law and immediately became a standard work. Rapidly establishing himself as without a superior in appeal cases, he was in such demand he finally declined to appear before any court other than the House of Lords or the Judicial Committee of the Privy Council without a special fee. Between 1872 and 1882 he appeared in no less than 136 reported cases before these tribunals, all involving questions of great legal significance or affecting large financial interests. His capacity for logical analysis, remarkable facility with language and his profound legal knowledge combined to make him preëminent in many fields of law.

BENJAMIN, NATHAN (*b. Catskill, N.Y., 1811; d. Constantinople, Turkey, 1855*), Congregational clergyman. Missionary to Greece and Armenia, 1836–52.

BENJAMIN, PARK (*b. Demerara, British Guiana, 1809; d. New York, N.Y., 1864*), editor. Came to Norwich, Conn., as a child. Graduated Trinity College, Hartford, 1829. Restless and temperamental, he abandoned law practice for journalism *post* 1834 and was associated among others with the *New England Magazine*, Horace Greeley's *New Yorker*, the *New World* and the New York *Evening Signal*. Benjamin was known for the caustic quality of his critical writing and as the author of much minor verse.

BENJAMIN, PARK (*b. New York, N.Y., 1849; d. 1922*), author, patent lawyer. Son of Park Benjamin (1809–64). Graduated Annapolis, 1867; admitted to bar, 1870. Wrote extensively on scientific subjects.

BENJAMIN, SAMUEL GREENE WHEELER (*b. Argos, Greece, 1837; d. Burlington, Vt., 1914*), author, painter, diplomat. Son of Nathan Benjamin. Graduated Williams, 1859; first American minister to Persia, 1883–85.

BENNER, PHILIP (*b. Chester Co., Pa., 1762; d. Bellefonte, Pa., 1832*), merchant, leading ironmaster in Centre Co., Pa., for forty years.

BENNET, SANFORD FILLMORE (*b. Eden, N.Y., 1836; d. 1898*), physician. Author of songs and hymns, including "The Sweet By and By." Practiced medicine in Illinois and Wisconsin, *post* 1865.

BENNETT, CALEB PREW (*b. Kennett Township, Pa., 1758; d. Wilmington, Del., 1836*), Revolutionary soldier. Moved to Delaware as a child. First Democratic governor of Delaware, 1833–36.

BENNETT, CHARLES EDWIN (*b. Providence, R.I., 1858; d. 1921*), classical scholar. Graduated Brown, 1878; additional studies, Harvard, Leipzig, Berlin, Heidelberg. Professor of Latin, Cornell, 1892–1921. Author among many other books of *A Latin Grammar* (1895) and scholarly texts of the Latin classics.

BENNETT, DE ROBIGNE MORTIMER (*b. near Otsego Lake, N.Y., 1818; d. New York, N.Y., 1882*), freethinker. Published the *Truthseeker*, *post* 1873.

BENNETT, EDMUND HATCH (*b. Manchester, Vt., 1824; d. 1898*), jurist, legal writer. Dean, Boston University Law School, 1876–98.

BENNETT, EMERSON (*b. Monson, Mass., 1822; d. Philadelphia, Pa., 1905*), author. A busy contributor of fiction to popular journals and newspapers. Among his romantic melodramas are *The League of the Miami* (1845), *The Bandits of the Osage* (1847), *Mike Fink* (1848) and *The Prairie Flower* (1849), all of which are in the dime-novel class.

BENNETT, FLOYD (*b. near Warrensburg, N.Y., 1890; d. Quebec, Canada, 1928*), aviator. Navy pilot; friend and associate of Adm. R. E. Byrd on polar explorations *post* 1925.

BENNETT, JAMES GORDON (*b. Keith, Scotland, 1795; d. New York, N.Y., 1872*), editor, publisher.

Attended a Catholic seminary at Aberdeen for a few years; emigrated 1819 to Halifax, N.S., thence to Portland, Maine, and Boston, Mass., where he worked as a copyboy and as clerk in a bookstore. After a year of various employments in New York (1822) and some months in South Carolina on the staff of the *Charleston Courier,* he settled in New York and became by 1826 a regular contributor to several newspapers including the *New York Courier.* His attacks on sharpers and speculators won him a local reputation and aroused considerable resentment. He was on the staff of the *New York Enquirer* during 1827–28, reporting from both New York and Washington, and winning national attention for a series of bold, personal sketches of leading men in the capital. At his suggestion, J. W. Webb, proprietor of the *Courier,* purchased the *Enquirer,* the first issue of the combined papers appearing in May 1829. That fall, Bennett became associate editor of the *Courier and Enquirer* and made it a forceful organ of Jacksonian democracy. On Webb's sudden espousal of the Whig cause in 1832, Bennett resigned.

Resolving to begin operations on his own, and with the recent success of the penny *New York Sun* as an encouraging example, Bennett began publication of the penny *New York Herald* in May 1835. He had little capital and no party support, yet the *Herald* was an immediate success because of its comprehensive and piquant coverage of local news, its reports on the stock and money markets, and its highly independent editorials on all manner of subjects. Viciously attacked by other journals for the *Herald's* flippancy and sensationalism, Bennett saw the circulation rise in proportion to the attacks, and by 1842 the *Herald* occupied its own building with facilities for printing some fifty thousand copies daily. To his political feuds with Van Buren and Seward, he now added personal disputes with Daniel O'Connell, the Irish liberator, and Archbishop Hughes of New York.

After 1844, Bennett's life was comparatively uneventful, being identified with the steady rise of the *Herald* to preëminence as a news-gathering sheet through the efforts of an unrivaled corps of European and American correspondents. The *Herald* was the first paper to make lavish use of the telegraph. For the most part, it supported the Democrats in politics and Bennett was accused of favoring the Southern point of view in the great controversies of the 1850's. In 1856, however, Bennett supported Frémont, reverting in 1860 to Douglas. After some hesitation, Bennett supported Lincoln in 1864. Although he retired in 1867, he continued to direct the policies of the paper and to write for it. At the time of his retirement, the *Herald* had a daily circulation of ninety thousand, its advertising revenue was surpassed only by the London *Times,* and its annual profits approached $400,000.

BENNETT, JAMES GORDON (*b. New York, N.Y., 1841; d. Beaulieu, France, 1918*), editor, capitalist. Son of James Gordon Bennett (1795–1872); educated mainly in Europe; served as lieutenant, U.S. Navy, during Civil War. As managing editor and director of the *New York Herald,* 1867–1918, he was explosive, erratic and domineering, although up to 1877 he showed a capacity for gathering men of ability about him. Stanley's famous search for Dr. Livingstone, 1870–71, was inspired by him. After 1877 he was a virtual expatriate in France, managing his newspaper properties by cable and refusing to delegate adequate authority to his home staff. By the 1890's the *Herald's* once-commanding position was slowly being lost. He was widely known as a sportsman. The James Gordon Bennett trophies for automobile driving, balloon racing and aviation were donated by him.

BENNETT, NATHANIEL (*b. Clinton, N.Y., 1818; d. San Francisco, Calif., 1886*), lawyer, jurist. Emigrated to California, 1849; practiced law in San Francisco. Reported early decisions of California supreme court (1852); became leader of state bar.

BENNING, HENRY LEWIS (*b. Columbia Co., Ga., 1814; d. Columbus, Ga., 1875*), jurist, statesman, Confederate soldier. An ardent secessionist, he favored withdrawal from Union in 1850 crisis; as justice of Georgia supreme court, 1853–59, delivered opinion that a state supreme court is not bound by U.S. Supreme Court on constitutional questions, the two being "coordinate and co-equal." Had distinguished record in Civil War.

BENSON, EGBERT (*b. New York, N.Y., 1746; d. Jamaica, N.Y., 1833*), Revolutionary leader, New York legislator and jurist. A Federalist, he was considered second only to Alexander Hamilton in legal learning.

BENSON, EUGENE (*b. Hyde Park, N.Y., 1839; d. Venice, Italy, 1908*), painter.

BENSON, WILLIAM SHEPHERD (*b. Bibb Co., Ga., 1855; d. Washington, D.C., 1932*), naval officer. From 1877, on graduation from Annapolis, until World War I, Admiral Benson served in many capacities ashore and afloat. Made chief of Naval Operations in 1915, he organized this new office and prepared the navy for war. Postwar Chairman of the U.S. Shipping Board, he served as a member of the Board until 1928. [*Supp.* 1]

BENT, CHARLES (*b. Charleston, Va., now W. Va., 1799; d. Taos, N. Mex., 1847*), frontier trader. Raised in Ohio and Missouri and trained in fur trade; with brother William, and Ceran St. Vrain built stockade on upper Arkansas, 1824. In 1828 they began building the famous trading post, Bent's Fort, 80 miles north by east of Taos, completing it in 1832. Charles led trade caravans from American frontier to Santa Fe in 1829, 1832 and 1833. Appointed civil governor of New Mexico, 1846, after American conquest he was killed in 1847 uprising at Taos.

BENT, JOSIAH (*b. Milton, Mass., 1771; d. 1836*), manufacturer of first "water-crackers" produced in this country.

BENT, SILAS (*b. South St. Louis, Mo., 1820; d. Shelter Island, N.Y., 1887*), naval officer, oceanographer. Brother of Charles and William Bent. Carried out surveys in Japanese waters on Perry expedition, 1852–54, including study of Kuro Siwo current in Pacific.

BENT, WILLIAM (*b. St. Louis, Mo., 1809; d. Boggsville, Colo., 1869*), frontiersman, trader, first permanent white settler in Colorado. Brother of Charles and Silas Bent. Directed building of Bent's Fort, 1828–32; managed it for many years. *Post* 1849 built trading post, later known as Fort Lyon; settled, 1859, near mouth of the Purgatoire as rancher.

BENTLEY, WILLIAM (*b. Boston, Mass., 1759; d. Salem, Mass., 1819*), Unitarian clergyman, author. Graduated Harvard, 1777. Pastor, East Church, Salem, 1783–1819. A pioneer in Unitarianism when New England was still Calvinistic, he was, unlike most of the clergy, a Jeffersonian Republican, and his church became a center of liberalism. He was noted for his regular contributions to the *Salem Register;* his diary of the years 1784–1819 (published 1905–14) gives a unique picture of a New England seaport in early years of the new nation.

BENTLEY, WILSON ALWYN (*b. Jericho, Vt., 1865; d. Jericho, 1931*), meteorologist. Photographer of snow crystals. [*Supp. 1*]

BENTON, ALLEN RICHARDSON (*b. Ira, N.Y., 1822; d. Lincoln, Nebr., 1914*), educator. Organized University of Nebraska, 1871.

BENTON, JAMES GILCHRIST (*b. Lebanon, N.H., 1820; d. Springfield, Mass., 1881*), ordnance expert. Graduated West Point, 1842. Commanded Springfield Armory, 1866–81; invented numerous improvements for Springfield rifle.

BENTON, JOEL (*b. Amenia, N.Y., 1832; d. Poughkeepsie, N.Y., 1911*), journalist.

BENTON, JOSIAH HENRY (*b. Addison, Vt., 1843; d. Boston, Mass., 1917*), railroad lawyer.

BENTON, THOMAS HART (*b. Hillsboro, N.C., 1782; d. Washington, D.C., 1858*), statesman. In early youth, supervised widowed mother's large farm near Nashville, Tenn.; admitted to bar, 1811; served in War of 1812. Removed to St. Louis, Mo., 1815, where he edited the *Missouri Enquirer* and enjoyed a lucrative law practice. Elected to the U.S. Senate in 1820,

in 1821 he began a career of 30 years in that body and became involved in his life-long interest, defense of sound money. He favored settlers, opposed land speculation, promoted navigation of the Mississippi and was in all things a champion of the West. Estranged from Jackson as a result of an incident during the War of 1812, he renewed friendship, worked for him in campaign of 1828 and became administration spokesman in the Senate. His views on slavery changed materially at this time. Opposed in 1820 to all slavery restriction in Missouri, by 1828 he favored gradual abolition. Slavery was hindering settlement, and to a Westerner and expansionist this was a serious indictment.

Senate floor leader in the fight against the National Bank, his speeches won a popular support which enabled Jackson to veto re-charter in 1836. As champion of hard money, Benton caused ratio between gold and silver to be changed from 15 to 1 to 16 to 1, returned gold to circulation. The stipulation that public lands be paid for in hard money, sponsored by Benton and carried through by Jackson, also supported this movement. Such profound changes in the nation's financial structure hastened the panic of 1837, but Benton unfairly attributed the panic to the Bank's activities. The fight for specie divided the Democratic party into the "Hard" and "Soft" factions and won Benton the nickname "Old Bullion."

Holding strong views on distribution of public lands, Benton took a democratic position, favoring lower cash prices and the grant of free homesteads of 160 acres based on five years' settlement and improvement.

A Van Buren supporter in 1840, Benton took sides with Tyler against the Whigs. He was opposed to the acquisition of Texas, also to the extremist position on the Oregon question, preferring compromise to war. However, he upheld the government in the subsequent war with Mexico.

Essentially moderate, he remained so on the slavery question, difficult though this was. Opposing both extension and abolition, he wished only for peace and the maintenance of the Union. In 1847 he refused to follow instructions from the Missouri legislature on the Calhoun Resolutions, believing them subversive of the Union. During the debate on the Compromise of 1850 he opposed too generous concessions to secessionists; sensing that they would be unsatisfied with anything but complete control, he felt the compromise was a sham. His attitude offended his constituents. Although he had championed essential Western interests, such as the pony express, the telegraph, and the railroad, they could not forgive him, and in 1850 Missouri elected a Whig. Benton then sought election to the House where he fought vainly against the Missouri Compromise repeal. In a brief period of retirement before his death, he wrote *Thirty Years' View* (1854–56), one of the outstanding political au-

69

tobiographies, and completed an *Abridgement of the Debates of Congress from 1789 to 1856* (1857–61).

BENTON, THOMAS HART (*b. Williamson Co., Tenn., 1816; d. St. Louis, Mo., 1879*), educator. Nephew of Thomas H. Benton (1782–1858). Secured legislation which was basis for public school system of Iowa; was Iowa superintendent of public instruction, 1848–54.

BERG, JOSEPH FREDERIC (*b. Antigua, B.W.I., 1812; d. 1871*), Dutch Reformed clergyman. Withdrew from German Reformed Church to Dutch, 1852; held pastorates in Pennsylvania.

BERGER, DANIEL (*b. near Reading, Pa., 1832; d. 1920*), United Brethren clergyman.

BERGER, VICTOR LOUIS (*b. Nieder-Rehbach, Austria, 1860; d. 1929*), socialist, journalist. Came to America, 1878; settled in Milwaukee, Wis. Founded the *Wisconsin Vorwärts*, 1892, and devoted himself to socialist journalism and politics. With Debs and Seymour Stedman, founded the Socialist Democratic party which, with the Socialist Labor party, became the Socialist party in 1901. Served as congressman from Wisconsin, 1911–13, first Socialist elected to Congress. Indicted, 1918, under Espionage Act after publication of articles opposing entry of the United States in World War I; re-elected to Congress, 1918 and 1919, but was denied seat because of anti-war position. When the Supreme Court reversed the lower court's decision, he returned to Congress, 1923, and remained until 1928. Berger's career is largely the story of socialist political development in America. [*Supp. 1*]

BERGH, CHRISTIAN (*b. near Rhinebeck, N.Y., 1763; d. New York, N.Y., 1843*), shipbuilder. Father of Henry Bergh. Built frigate *President* and many sailing packets.

BERGH, HENRY (*b. New York, N.Y., 1811; d. New York, 1888*), founder, 1866, and first president of American Society for the Prevention of Cruelty to Animals.

BERGMANN, CARL (*b. Ebersbach, Germany, 1821; d. New York, N.Y., 1876*), orchestral conductor. Came to America, 1849. Conducted New York Philharmonic Society, 1858–76; introduced many works by romantic school to the United States.

BERKELEY, JOHN (*b. England; d. Virginia, 1622*), English ironmaster. Came to America, 1621. Built first ironworks in British America near Richmond, Va., 1622.

BERKELEY, NORBORNE. [See BOTETOURT, NORBORNE BERKELEY, BARON DE, *c.* 1718–1770].

BERKELEY, Sir WILLIAM (*b. Somersetshire, England, 1606; d. England, 1677*), colonial governor. Courtier and playwright, in 1642 he assumed governorship of Virginia and helped quiet faction-torn colony. Encouraged diversification of crops; promoted exploration to find easiest route through mountains; led defense against Indians, 1644. Deposed by Commonwealth *post* 1648, he returned to office at Restoration. Thereafter he gave colonists little voice even in local affairs. His course of executions and confiscations after Bacon's rebellion, 1676, brought investigation by England, resulting in appointment of successor to whom Berkeley at first refused to yield.

BERKENMEYER, WILHELM CHRISTOPH (*b. Bodenteich, Germany, 1686; d. Athens, N.Y., 1751*), Lutheran clergyman. Came to New York, 1725. For many years only regularly ordained Lutheran minister in Upper New York State.

BERKMAN, ALEXANDER (*b. Vilna, Russia, 1870; d. Nice, France, 1936*), anarchist, author. Emigrated to America, 1887; imprisoned 14 years for attempt to assassinate Henry Frick; deported, 1919, with Emma Goldman. [*Supp. 2*]

BERKOWITZ, HENRY (*b. Pittsburgh, Pa., 1857; d. 1924*), rabbi. Graduated University of Cincinnati, 1881, and Hebrew Union College. One of first four rabbis ordained in the United States (1883). After early pastorates in South and West, became rabbi of Rodeph Scholem Synagogue, Philadelphia, 1892–1922. Founded Jewish Chautauqua Society, 1893.

BERLINER, EMILE (*b. Hanover, Germany, 1851; d. Washington, D.C., 1929*), inventor. Educated in Germany; came to Washington, D.C., 1870. Discovered that variations in battery current through a telegraph key could be produced by variations in contact pressure; this led to his invention of the microphone, 1877. In 1887, he invented the "Gramophone," which recorded and reproduced sounds on a disc rather than on a cylinder, the basis of the modern phonographic industry. Under his direction, 1919, his son Henry devised a working helicopter. [*Supp. 1*]

BERMUDEZ, EDOUARD EDMOND (*b. New Orleans, La., 1832; d. New Orleans, 1892*), lawyer, Confederate soldier. Judge, Louisiana supreme court, 1880–92.

BERNARD, BAYLE. [See BERNARD, WILLIAM BAYLE, 1807–1875.]

BERNARD, Sir FRANCIS (*b. England, 1712; d. Aylesbury, England, 1779*), barrister, colonial governor. Appointed governor of New Jersey, 1758; governor of Massachusetts, 1760. He ruled for nine turbulent years, which included period of Sugar Act, Writs of Assistance, Stamp Act, quartering of troops in Boston. More understanding of colonial viewpoint than many, he tried to have sugar duty lowered, thought Stamp Act inexpedient. Later, he strongly opposed political desires of colonists; letters from him to officials in England were published, 1769, in Boston and caused removal from post in that year.

BERNARD, JOHN (*b. Portsmouth, England, 1756; d. England, 1828*), actor, theatrical manager. Came to America, 1797; managed companies in Boston and Albany; excelled as comedian.

BERNARD, SIMON (*b. Dôle, France, 1779; d. France, 1839*), French military engineer. After Napoleon's fall, acted as virtual chief of engineers, U.S. Army, in planning coast defenses. Returned to France, 1830.

BERNARD, WILLIAM BAYLE (*b. Boston, Mass., 1807; d. England, 1875*), dramatist. Son of John Bernard. Removed to England, 1819, where he became successful minor playwright and editor of father's *Retrospections of the Stage* (1830) and other works.

BERNAYS, AUGUSTUS CHARLES (*b. Highland, Ill., 1854; d. 1907*), surgeon. M.D. Heidelberg, 1876; studied also in Berlin and Vienna. Taught and practiced in St. Louis, Mo.; pioneer in antiseptic and aseptic surgery.

BERNET, JOHN JOSEPH (*b. Brant, N.Y., 1868; d. Cleveland, O., 1935*), railroad executive. President of New York, Chicago and St. Louis; the Erie; the Chesapeake and Ohio and other railroads. [*Supp. 1*]

BERNSTEIN, HERMAN (*b. Neustadt-Scherwindt, Russia, 1876; d. Sheffield, Mass., 1935*), journalist, diplomat. Emigrated to America, 1893. Translator of Chekhov, Gorki, Andreyev, and other Russian writers, his "scoop" story of the *Potemkin* revolt (1905) caused a sensation. Until the outbreak of World War I he reported from Europe the inner workings of the Russian government for the *New York Times;* his interviews with famous Europeans were widely read. Returning to Russia in 1917, he came upon and published the famous "Willy-Nicky" correspondence and exposed the forged *Protocols of the Wise Men of Zion.* Founded *The Day,* 1914; edited the *Jewish Tribune,* 1925–29; served as an interpreter of Jewish life and ideals. Minister to Albania, 1930–33.

[*Supp. 1*]

BERRIEN, JOHN MACPHERSON (*b. New Jersey, 1781; d. Savannah, Ga., 1856*), jurist, politician. Raised in Georgia, graduated Princeton, 1796. Studied law in Savannah, Ga.; admitted to bar there, 1799; judge of eastern circuit, 1810–21. U.S. senator, Democrat, 1824–29. Became Jackson's attorney-general, 1829; resigned over Eaton affair, 1831. Returned to Senate as Whig, served 1841–52 and became a leader of his party, supporting Whigs on Bank question, protective tariffs, compromise of slavery issue. *Post* 1850, changed position and opposed Clay's compromise, admission of California, abolition of slave trade in District of Columbia. Convinced the Whigs would not protect Southern interests, he withdrew from party, 1850. Later joined Know-Nothing party.

BERRY, HIRAM GREGORY (*b. Thomaston, Maine, 1824; d. Chancellorsville, Va., 1863*), businessman, Union soldier. Colonel of Maine militia, rose to major-general, distinguishing himself at Fair Oaks and Fredericksburg.

BERRY, JAMES HENDERSON (*b. Jackson Co., Ala., 1841; d. 1913*), lawyer, Confederate soldier. Democratic governor of Arkansas, 1882–84; U.S. senator, 1885–1907.

BERRY, NATHANIEL SPRINGER (*b. Bath, Maine, 1796; d. Bristol, N.H., 1894*), businessman, politician. Extreme abolitionist; Republican governor of New Hampshire, 1861–63; ranked high among Civil War governors.

BERTRAM, JOHN (*b. Isle of Jersey, England, 1796; d. 1882*), sea-captain, merchant. Came to America, 1807. Identified with trade out of Salem, *post* 1812, especially to Zanzibar; made fortune in Pacific trade *post* 1848.

BERWIND, EDWARD JULIUS (*b. Philadelphia, Pa., 1848; d. New York, N.Y., 1936*), business executive and capitalist. President, 1886–1930, Berwind-White Coal Co., reputedly the world's largest owner of coal-mining properties. [*Supp. 2*]

BESSEY, CHARLES EDWIN (*b. Wayne Co., O., 1845; d. 1915*), botanist. Graduated Michigan Agricultural College, 1869; studied under Asa Gray. Professor of agriculture and botany, dean and chancellor, University of Nebraska, 1884–1915.

BETHUNE, GEORGE WASHINGTON (*b. New York, N.Y., 1805; d. Florence, Italy, 1862*), Dutch Reformed clergyman, author. Distinguished pastor, Utica, Brooklyn, and New York, N.Y.; also Philadelphia, Pa. Edited first American edition of Walton's *Angler.*

BETTENDORF, WILLIAM PETER (*b. Mendota, Ill., 1857; d. 1910*), manufacturer. Invented Bettendorf Metal Wheel for wagons, and machinery for its manufacture; also widely used railroad car equipment.

BETTS, SAMUEL ROSSITER (*b. Richmond, Mass., 1786; d. 1868*), jurist. Admitted to bar, 1809; appointed, 1823, circuit judge, supreme court of New York; served, 1826–67, as federal judge, New York southern district; outstanding in admiralty law.

BEVERIDGE, ALBERT JEREMIAH (*b. Highland Co., O., 1862; d. 1927*), politician, historian, orator. Raised on an Illinois farm. Graduated DePauw (then Asbury College), 1885; practiced law in Indianapolis, Ind. An outstanding Republican campaigner, he served as U.S. senator from Indiana, 1899–1911. He was one of the "insurgents" who formed the Progressive party, 1912. Supporting Theodore Roosevelt, he favored prevention of trust abuses, opposed injurious child labor, desired non-partisan tariff commission. A distinguished writer of history, his principal work is *The Life of John Marshall* (1916, 1919). His biography of Lincoln remained unfinished at his death.

BEVERLEY, ROBERT (*b. Middlesex Co., Va., c. 1673; d. Beverly Park, Va., 1722*), colonial official, planter, historian. Educated in England; held important posts in provincial government. Author of *History and Present State of Virginia* (1705, revised 1722).

BEWLEY, ANTHONY (*b. Tennessee, 1804; d. Fort Worth, Texas, 1860*), Methodist clergyman, missionary to Arkansas and Texas. Murdered by mob for his antislavery views.

BIARD, PIERRE (*b. Grenoble, France, c. 1567; d. Avignon, France, 1622*), Jesuit missionary. Entered Society of Jesus, 1583; came to Canada, 1611; kidnapped from settlement in present Maine by Samuel Argall, 1613. Author of a *Relation* of his experiences (1616).

BIBB, GEORGE MORTIMER (*b. Prince Edward Co., Va., 1776; d. Georgetown, D.C., 1859*), lawyer. "War Hawk" senator from Kentucky, 1811–14; Democratic senator, 1829–35; Kentucky jurist, 1835–44; U.S. secretary of treasury, 1844–45.

BIBB, WILLIAM WYATT (*b. Amelia Co., Ga., 1781; d. Autauga Co., Ala., 1820*), physician, politician. Removed to Georgia, 1801; congressman, Democrat, 1805–13; U.S. senator, 1813–16. Governor of Alabama territory (and later state), 1817–20.

BICKEL, LUKE WASHINGTON (*b. Cincinnati, O., 1866; d. 1917*), sea captain. Baptist missionary to islands in Inland Sea of Japan.

BICKERDYKE, MARY ANN BALL (*b. Knox Co., O., 1817; d. Bunker Hill, Kans., 1901*), nurse. Known as "Mother Bickerdyke," aided sick and wounded in Civil War; agent, U.S. Sanitary Commission.

BICKETT, THOMAS WALTER (*b. Monroe, N.C., 1869; d. 1921*), lawyer, politician. Attorney-general, North Carolina, 1908–16; as Democratic governor, 1916–20, pressed measures for tax reform, increased teacher salaries, broader agricultural education.

BICKMORE, ALBERT SMITH (*b. Tenant's Harbor, Maine, 1839; d. Nonquitt, Mass., 1914*), educator, naturalist. Dominant factor in founding American Museum of Natural History, New York City; was its superintendent, 1869–84, and its curator of public instruction, 1884–1904.

BIDDLE, CLEMENT (*b. Philadelphia, Pa., 1740; d. Philadelphia, 1814*), Revolutionary soldier, merchant. An aide and friend of Greene and Washington.

BIDDLE, HORACE P. (*b. Fairfield Co., O., 1811; d. 1900*), Indiana jurist.

BIDDLE, JAMES (*b. Philadelphia, Pa., 1783; d. Philadelphia, 1848*), naval officer. Became midshipman, 1800; thereafter served in campaigns against Tripoli; obtained first independent command, 1810, sloop-of-war *Syren*. In War of 1812, as first lieutenant of *Wasp*, led boarding party which took HMS *Frolic;* commanding sloop-of-war *Hornet,* took British brig *Penguin*. Afterward Biddle held many important commands at sea; negotiated first treaty between United States and China, 1846.

BIDDLE, NICHOLAS (*b. Philadelphia, Pa., 1750; d. off Charleston, S.C., 1778*), naval officer. Trained in merchant service; entered British Navy, 1772; shipped as coxswain on Royal Geographical Society polar expedition, 1773, in company with Horatio Nelson. Resigned commission on return from Arctic; offered services to Congress. Commanded brig *Andrea Doria*, 1775–76, making numerous captures of British vessels in North Atlantic. In command of the *Randolph*, after a successful West Indian cruise, he engaged HMS *Yarmouth* off Charleston, S.C., March 1778, in which action his ship blew up.

BIDDLE, NICHOLAS (*b. Philadelphia, Pa., 1786; d. Philadelphia, 1844*), scholar, statesman, financier. Brother of James Biddle; nephew of Nicholas Biddle (1750–1778). Studied at University of Pennsylvania; graduated College of New Jersey (Princeton), 1801. Traveled over much of Europe, 1804–07, serving as secretary to John Armstrong in U.S. mission to France, and as secretary of legation at London under James Monroe.

Returning from abroad, Biddle was admitted to the bar, 1809; in the same year he became a member of the "Tuesday Club" established by Joseph Dennie to encourage contributions to the *Port Folio* magazine. Primarily a man of letters, 1809–14, Biddle served in the Pennsylvania legislature, 1810–11.

Requested in 1810 by William Clark to write a narrative of his Louisiana expedition with Meriwether Lewis, Biddle worked (1810–12) at weaving notes, journals and Clark's oral statements into a cohesive narrative. It was published in 1814 as *History of the Expedition of Captains Lewis and Clark* after being seen through the press by journalist Paul Allen. Meanwhile Biddle had become increasingly active in editorial management of the *Port Folio;* when Dennie died in 1812, Biddle became editor of what was then the leading literary periodical in America.

Drawn from scholarly life by pressures of the War of 1812, Biddle aided in getting loans for the War Department, entered state senate, 1814, and initiated measures for protection of Philadelphia. Invited by President Monroe to become one of the five government directors of the (second) Bank of the United States, he threw himself into the study of banking and soon became one of the best informed and most efficient members of the board. He served as president of the Bank, 1823–39, engaging in a celebrated controversy with President Jackson (1828–33) over the Bank's right to a national charter.

After his resignation, he retired to "Andalusia," his country place on the Delaware. There he entertained distinguished guests, maintained his interest in literature, architecture and education, and wrote numerous papers and addresses on economic and literary subjects.

BIDLACK, BENJAMIN ALDEN (*b. Paris, N.Y., 1804; d. 1849*), lawyer, diplomat. Negotiated Treaty of 1846 (ratified 1848) between the United States and New Granada, giving right-of-way across Isthmus of Panama.

BIDWELL, BARNABAS (*b. Tyringham, Mass., 1763; d. 1833*), lawyer. Graduated Yale, 1785. Prominent in Massachusetts politics, 1791–1810; absconded to Canada after shortage in accounts. Author of a tragedy, *The Mercenary Match* (1785).

BIDWELL, JOHN (*b. Chautauqua Co., N.Y., 1819; d. California, 1900*), pioneer, politician. Raised in Ohio; removed to Missouri frontier, 1839. Left Independence, Mo., 1841, with the Bartleson party, the first emigrant train to make the journey to California from Missouri. Naturalized a Californian, 1844, at outbreak of 1844 revolt against Micheltorena he and Sutter were imprisoned, but soon made peace with the rebels. On July 4, 1846, Bidwell was one of those who drew up the resolution of independence from Mexico. Made a second lieutenant of the California battalion after accompanying Frémont to Monterey, he became magistrate of San Luis Rey district, and served as major in reconquest of Los Angeles. Prospected on Feather River, first to find gold there. Acquired Rancho Chico, north of Sacramento, 1849, and developed it for the rest of his life, becoming most noted agriculturalist in state.

BIDWELL, MARSHALL SPRING (*b. Stockbridge, Mass., 1799; d. New York, N.Y., 1872*), lawyer, Canadian politician. Son of Barnabas Bidwell. Forced to leave Canada for political reasons, 1837, he practiced law with great success in New York.

BIDWELL, WALTER HILLIARD (*b. Farmington, Conn., 1798; d. Saratoga Springs, N.Y., 1881*), editor, publisher. Graduated Yale, 1827; Yale Divinity School, 1833. *Post* 1841 edited numerous religious publications, including *Eclectic Magazine* which he owned, 1846–81.

BIEN, JULIUS (*b. Naumburg, Germany, 1826; d. 1909*), lithographer, map engraver. Studied graphic arts at Cassel and Frankfurt. Came to America, 1849; started lithographic business in New York City. Observing low standard of maps produced here, after interview with Secretary of War Jefferson Davis, he undertook engraving of maps for Pacific Railroad surveys, *post* 1855, one of which became standard map of the West for over 25 years. There-after he engraved and printed maps for most major government geographical and geological publications. During his career he did more than any other person to create and establish scientific standards for American cartography.

BIENVILLE, JEAN BAPTISTE LE MOYNE, Sieur de (*b. Longueuil, Canada, 1680; d. France, 1767*), pioneer, explorer, founder of Mobile and New Orleans. Brother of Pierre Le Moyne, Sieur d'Iberville, with whom he served in naval battles in North Atlantic and Hudson Bay, 1695–98. He accompanied Iberville on an expedition to rediscover the mouth of the Mississippi and to form a French colony there, landing off what is now Biloxi, Miss., late in 1698, and making the first settlement on the coast at Old Biloxi. In 1699, Bienville explored the lower reaches of the Mississippi; in 1700 he explored the Red River as far as Natchitoches; in 1701 he succeeded to full command over the colony. Resolving in 1702 to move to a better site, he built Fort Louis on Mobile Bay which was removed in 1710 to the present site of Mobile, Ala. He was dismissed as governor of Louisiana after the colony was granted to Crozat's company in 1712 and served as second in command during Cadillac's administration, 1713–16. When John Law's colonization company took over Louisiana in 1717, Bienville was restored to command of the province; realizing the importance of changing its base to the Mississippi, he had New Orleans laid out in 1718 although it did not become the capital until 1722. Lack of support by the controlling Company of the Indies and increasing difficulties with the Natchez Indians brought about Bienville's recall to France in 1725. Despite a notable defense of his administration, he was deprived of all his offices and lived quietly in Paris until 1732 when he was reinstated as governor, returning to the colony in 1733. After a decade of struggle against the Indians which resulted in an indecisive peace, he offered his resignation and left Louisiana in May 1743, never to return. His maintenance of Louisiana for so many years with such meagre resources is proof of his abilities.

BIERCE, AMBROSE GWINETT (*b. Meigs Co., O., 1842; d. Mexico, 1914 ?*), journalist, author. Pseudonym, "Dod Grile." Raised on farm; had no formal education. Served with Indiana infantry in Civil War; severely wounded at Kenesaw Mountain. Settling in San Francisco *post* 1866, he won recognition for caustic wit in contributions to weekly journals, especially the *Argonaut* and the *News Letter* of which he became editor. His first fiction was published in the *Overland Monthly*, 1871. Worked in England as a journalist, 1872–76; returning to San Francisco, he wrote for the *Wasp* and the *Argonaut* and conducted a column in Hearst's *Examiner*, 1887–96. In 1897 he became Washington correspondent of the *New York American*. Disillusioned, and no longer effective in his creative work, he disappeared into Mexico, 1913. He was author of *The Fiend's Delight* (1872), *Nuggets and Dust* (1872), *Cobwebs from an Empty Skull* (1874), *Tales of Soldiers and Civilians* (1891), *The Monk and the Hangman's Daughter* (1892, with G. A. Danziger), *Can Such Things Be?* (1893), and *The Devil's Dictionary* (1906). He had a masterly touch with unusual and abnormal fictional plots and a fine compression of style.

BIERSTADT, ALBERT (*b. Solingen, Germany, 1830; d. 1902*), landscape painter. Came to America in infancy; raised in New Bedford, Mass. Studied at Düsseldorf and Rome, 1853–57. Returning home, he joined Gen. Lander's 1858 surveying expedition for an overland wagon route and made sketches of Far West which were basis for heroic canvases painted later, including "Laramie Peak," "In the Rocky Mountains" and many others.

BIGELOW, ERASTUS BRIGHAM (*b. West Boylston, Mass., 1814; d. Boston, Mass., 1879*), inventor, economist. Invented a power loom, 1837, for production of coach lace, and formed the Clinton Co., 1838, to build and operate the looms. He is remembered principally as the inventor and perfecter of power looms for producing carpets.

BIGELOW, FRANK HAGAR (*b. Concord, Mass., 1851; d. Vienna, Austria, 1924*), meteorologist, Episcopal clergyman. Demonstrated, 1896–1901, that centers of extra-tropical cyclones occur on line of separation between warm and cold air masses.

BIGELOW, HENRY JACOB (*b. Boston, Mass., 1818; d. 1890*), surgeon. Son of Jacob Bigelow. Graduated Harvard, 1837; studied medicine with father, at medical schools of Dartmouth and Harvard, and in Paris, France. Received M.D., Harvard, 1841; practiced in Boston after 1844. Was associated with discovery of surgical anaesthesia, 1846, when, probably through his influence, ether was administered by W. T. G. Morton in an operation at Massachusetts General Hospital. For almost forty years the dominating figure in New England surgery, Bigelow also taught and made important surgical contributions. He improved an instrument for crushing bladder stones and perfected an evacuator to remove the fragments, designating the operation "litholapaxy." His *Manual of Orthopedic Surgery* (1844) directed attention to a field previously neglected in America.

BIGELOW, JACOB (*b. Sudbury, Mass., 1787; d. Boston, Mass., 1879*), botanist, physician. Graduated Harvard, 1806; M.D., University of Pennsylvania, 1810, where he studied under Dr. B. S. Barton. Practiced in Boston as successor to James Jackson; lectured on botany. Professor of materia medica, Harvard Medical School, 1815–55. Bigelow's *Florula Bostoniensis* (1814) was standard work in New England botany until Gray's *Manual* appeared, 1848. His principal work was *American Medical Botany* (1817, 1818, 1820), and he had an important share in editing the first *American Pharmacopaeia* (1820). His *Discourse on Self-limited Diseases* (1835) was said by Holmes to have exerted more influence on medical practice in America than any other work that had ever been published in this country.

BIGELOW, JOHN (*b. Bristol, N.Y., 1817; d. 1911*), editor, diplomat, author. Graduated Union College, 1835. Admitted to New York bar, 1838. Shared in owning and editing New York *Evening Post*, 1848–61; was outspoken against slavery and for free trade. Appointed consul-general at Paris, 1861, minister to France, 1865, his diplomatic work during Civil War ranks second in importance only to that of Charles Francis Adams at London. Editor of Franklin's *Autobiography* (1868) and *The Complete Works of Benjamin Franklin* (1887–88); author of lives of Franklin, Samuel J. Tilden and others.

BIGELOW, MELVILLE MADISON (*b. near Eaton Rapids, Mich., 1846; d. Boston, Mass., 1921*), educator, legal writer. University of Michigan, A.B. 1866, LL.B. 1868; Harvard, Ph.D. 1879. Admitted to Tennessee bar, 1868. Interested in historical development of law, he went to Boston, 1870, to undertake research and remained there to practice and as faculty member and dean of Boston University Law School, 1872–1921. Among his many scholarly works were *The Law of Estoppel and its Application in Practice* (1872) which established his reputation, *Elements of the Law of Torts* (1878) which became a standard textbook, and *The Law of Fraud on its Civil Side* (1888–90).

BIGELOW, WILLIAM STURGIS (*b. 1850; d. 1926*), physician, orientalist. Son of Henry J. Bigelow. Authority on Japanese language, religion, philosophy; made collections of Japanese art now in Boston Art Museum.

BIGGERS, EARL DERR (*b. Warren, O., 1884; d. Pasadena, Calif., 1933*), novelist, dramatist. Creator of the fictional detective "Charlie Chan." [*Supp.* 1]

BIGGS, ASA (*b. Williamston, N.C., 1811; d. Norfolk, Va., 1878*), jurist, politician. Joint codifier of North Carolina laws, 1851–55; district judge, 1858–65.

BIGGS, HERMANN MICHAEL (*b. Trumansburg, N.Y., 1859; d. 1923*), pioneer in preventive medicine. Professor, Bellevue Medical College, New York, *post* 1886; health official in New York City and State, 1892–1923. Introduced use of diphtheria antitoxin in United States, 1894, and was active in fight against tuberculosis.

BIGLER, JOHN (*b. near Carlisle, Pa., 1805; d. 1871*), lawyer, pioneer. Removed to Illinois; then overland to California, 1849. His wife was the first white woman to make a home in Sacramento. Elected to first state legislature, San Jose, 1849; elected Democratic governor, 1851; re-elected 1853. Effective minister to Chile, 1857–61. On return to California he practiced law and was active in Democratic politics.

BIGLER, WILLIAM (*b. Shermansburg, Pa., 1814; d. 1880*), printer, lumberman, railroad promoter. Democratic governor of Pennsylvania, 1851–54; U.S. senator, 1856–62.

BILLINGS, CHARLES ETHAN (*b. Wethersfield, Vt., 1835; d. 1920*), manufacturer, tool-maker. Developed (*post* 1862) treatment process for drop-forgings that made possible machine production of pistol frames and other articles previously fabricated by hand.

BILLINGS, FRANK (*b. Highland, Wis., 1854; d. Chicago, Ill., 1932*), physician. Demonstrated the causal relation of focal infections to systematic disease; associated with development of Chicago medical schools and societies. [*Supp. 1*]

BILLINGS, FREDERICK (*b. Royalton, Vt., 1823; d. 1890*), lawyer, railroad executive, philanthropist. Graduated University of Vermont, 1844. Removed to California, 1849, and opened a law office which developed into the leading San Francisco law firm of its time. An original partner in the Northern Pacific Railroad, Billings organized its land department and conducted it with great success, keeping prices low and advertising extensively. After reorganizing the road subsequent to the panic of 1873, he became its president in 1879 and financed completion of its trackage from Dakota to the Columbia. Forced out by Henry Villard in 1881, he became an active promoter of the Nicaraguan canal project and a benefactor of the University of Vermont, Amherst College, and other institutions. The town of Billings, Mont., is named for him.

BILLINGS, JOHN SHAW (*b. Switzerland Co., Ind., 1838; d. 1913*), librarian, surgeon. Graduated Miami University, 1857; M.D., Medical College of Ohio, 1860. Union medical officer, 1862–64; with surgeon-general's office, 1864–94. Published, with Dr. Robert Fletcher, an *Index Catalogue* (1880–95) of the library of the surgeon-general's department, a most important contribution to American medicine. Billings planned Johns Hopkins Hospital and was a pioneer in preventive medicine. His last seventeen years were spent in New York. Called there to consolidate the Astor, Lenox and Tilden libraries into New York Public Library, he was really its creator.

BILLINGS, JOSH. [See Shaw, Henry Wheeler, 1818–1885.]

BILLINGS, WILLIAM (*b. Boston, Mass., 1746; d. 1800*), early singing-master, composer. A tanner by trade, he was a choir singer, interested in music and weary of the then poor state of church music. With more enthusiasm than knowledge, he wrote hymn tunes, became a singing teacher, trained choirs at several Boston churches. He introduced the pitch-pipe in churches; impressed by counterpoint, he composed in this manner, and his efforts met with success despite their crudeness. Author of *The New England Psalm-Singer* (1770), *The Singing Master's Assistant or Key to Practical Music* (1778), *The Suffolk Harmony* (1786) and other books.

BILLY THE KID (*b. New York, N.Y., 1859; d. Fort Sumner, N. Mex., 1881*), desperado. True name, William H. Bonney.

BIMELER, JOSEPH MICHAEL (*b. Germany, c. 1778; d. Tuscarawas Co., O., 1853*), founder of communal Society of Zoar in Ohio. Came to America, 1817.

BINGHAM, AMELIA (*b. Hicksville, O., 1869; d. New York, N.Y., 1927*), actress. One of the most popular of American road attractions; had great success in Clyde Fitch's *The Climbers* (1901).

BINGHAM, ANNE WILLING (*b. Philadelphia, Pa., 1764; d. Bermuda, 1801*), society leader, *saloniste*. Beautiful and witty wife of William Bingham; reigned over the "Republican Court" in Philadelphia, 1789–99.

BINGHAM, CALEB (*b. Salisbury, Conn., 1757; d. Boston, Mass., 1817*), bookseller, pioneer writer of text-books. Graduated Dartmouth, 1782. Prominent advocate of free public schools; edited *The Columbian Orator* (1797).

BINGHAM, GEORGE CALEB (*b. Augusta Co., Va., 1811; d. Kansas City, Mo., 1879*), portrait and genre painter. Began early to copy engravings and to paint; by 1834 had made art his vocation. Studied briefly at Pennsylvania Academy of Fine Arts, lived in Washington, D.C., 1840–44, and in Europe 1856–58, but spent most of his life in Missouri where his family had settled in 1819. His first genre painting to receive much attention was "Jolly Flatboatmen," selected by American Art Union for annual engraving, 1846. Interested in politics, he held state offices; many of his pictures are on political subjects ("Canvassing for a Vote," "Stump Speaking"). His genre work has preserved with realism and humor characteristic scenes from old-time Missouri life.

BINGHAM, HARRY (*b. Concord, Vt., 1821; d. 1900*), New Hampshire lawyer and Democratic legislator.

BINGHAM, HIRAM (*b. Bennington, Vt., 1789; d. New Haven, Conn., 1869*), Congregational clergyman. Sandwich Islands missionary, 1820–40; devised alphabet for language; with associates translated Bible into Hawaiian.

BINGHAM, HIRAM (*b. Honolulu, Hawaii, 1831; d. Baltimore, Md., 1908*), Congregational clergyman.

Son of Hiram Bingham (1789–1869). Missionary to Micronesia.

BINGHAM, JOHN ARMOR (*b. Mercer, Pa., 1815; d. Cadiz, O., 1900*), lawyer, Ohio politician. As congressman, Whig and Republican, 1855–73 (except for 38th Congress), played a leading rôle in trial of Lincoln's assassins, also in impeachment trial of President Johnson.

BINGHAM, ROBERT WORTH (*b. Orange Co., N.C., 1871; d. Baltimore, Md., 1937*), lawyer, newspaper proprietor, diplomat. LL.B., University of Louisville, 1897. In 1918 acquired control of the Louisville *Courier-Journal* and *Louisville Times*. An independent Democrat, interested especially in agricultural progress, his newspapers in 1932 supported Roosevelt, who appointed Bingham ambassador to the Court of St. James, a post he held until his death. [*Supp. 2*]

BINGHAM, WILLIAM (*b. Philadelphia, Pa., 1752; d. 1804*), trader, privateer owner. Founder and director, Bank of North America, 1781; successful land speculator and turnpike promoter; U.S. senator from Pennsylvania, 1795–1801.

BINGHAM, WILLIAM (*b. North Carolina, 1835; d. Orange Co., N.C., 1873*), educator.

BINKLEY, ROBERT CEDRIC (*b. Mannheim, Pa., 1897; d. Cleveland, O., 1940*), historian. Librarian, Hoover Library, Stanford University, 1922–27; authority on the reproduction and preservation of research materials. [*Supp. 2*]

BINNEY, AMOS (*b. Boston, Mass., 1803; d. 1847*), zoologist. Graduated Brown, 1821; M.D., Harvard, 1826. Won an international reputation for his *Terrestrial Air-Breathing Mollusks,* published posthumously (1851).

BINNEY, HORACE (*b. Philadelphia, Pa., 1780; d. Philadelphia, 1875*), lawyer. Graduated Harvard, 1797. Studied law in office of Jared Ingersoll; admitted to bar, 1800. By 1809, when he issued the first volume of his *Reports of Cases Adjudged in the Supreme Court of Pennsylvania* (six volumes in all, covering cases to 1814), he was in successful practice as an expert in marine cases and had represented the United States Bank before the Supreme Court. He occupied a leading position at the bar, 1816–37, when he retired virtually from court work and confined himself to giving opinions particularly on land titles. An anti-Jackson man, he served a single term in Congress, 1833–35. Sincere, devoted to principle, he gave notable service to his city and state; subsequent to his retirement from practice in 1850 he gave much time to writing on constitutional questions. His reputation rests on two great cases in which he appeared: *Lyle vs. Richards,* 1823; and the Girard trust case of 1844 (*Vidal et al. vs. Philadelphia et al.*)

BINNS, JOHN (*b. Dublin, Ireland, 1772; d. 1860*), journalist, politician, author. Associate of William Godwin and English radicals; emigrated to Pennsylvania, 1801. Published the outspoken, radical *Democratic Press* (Philadelphia, 1807–29).

BINNS, JOHN ALEXANDER (*b. Loudoun Co., Va., c. 1761; d. 1813*), Virginia farmer, soil conservationist. Applied gypsum to his crops as fertilizer, 1784; increased yields encouraged further experiments on clover, grass, grains. His ideas on agricultural improvements were published in *A Treatise on Practical Farming* (1803). The "Loudoun System" of planting and plowing thus became widely known and practiced in Maryland and Virginia.

BIRCH, THOMAS (*b. England, 1779; d. 1851*), pioneer landscape and marine painter. Son of William R. Birch. Came to America, 1794. Celebrated for paintings of sea battles in War of 1812; also painted views of historic buildings around Philadelphia.

BIRCH, WILLIAM RUSSELL (*b. Warwickshire, England, 1755; d. 1834*), painter, engraver. Came to America, 1794. Won high reputation for miniatures on enamel.

BIRD, ARTHUR (*b. Cambridge, Mass., 1856; d. 1923*), composer. Spent most of life abroad, principally in Berlin. Prolific composer in almost all forms; winner of Paderewski prize, 1901.

BIRD, FREDERIC MAYER (*b. Philadelphia, Pa., 1838; d. South Bethlehem, Pa., 1908*), Lutheran and Episcopal clergyman, hymnologist, editor. Son of Robert M. Bird.

BIRD, ROBERT MONTGOMERY (*b. New Castle, Del., 1806; d. Philadelphia, Pa., 1854*), physician, playwright, novelist. His romantic tragedies *The Gladiator* (produced New York, 1831), *Oralloossa* (produced Philadelphia, 1832), the domestic tragedy *The Broker of Bogota* (produced New York, 1834), and other plays were written for Edwin Forrest, with whom Bird had a disagreement over money owed him. Turning to the novel, Bird published *Calavar* (1834); *The Infidel* (1835); *The Hawks of Hawk Hollow* (1835); his best work, *Nick of the Woods* (1837), and several minor works.

BIRD WOMAN. [See SACAGAWEA, *c. 1787–1812.*]

BIRGE, HENRY WARNER (*b. Hartford, Conn., 1825; d. New York, N.Y., 1888*), Union soldier, merchant. Brigade and division commander in New Orleans and Port Hudson campaigns, and later in Red River campaign.

BIRKBECK, MORRIS (*b. Settle, England, 1764; d. Fox River, Ill., 1825*), pioneer, publicist. Emigrated to Illinois, 1817; an associate of George Flower. Author of *Notes on a Journey in America* (1817) and *Letters from Illinois* (1818).

BIRNEY, DAVID BELL (*b. Huntsville, Ala., 1825; d. Philadelphia, Pa., 1864*), Union soldier. Son of James G. Birney. Fought with Army of the Potomac; commanded 10th Army Corps under Grant.

BIRNEY, JAMES (*b. Danville, Ky., 1817; d. Bay City, Mich., 1888*), lawyer, diplomat. Son of James G. Birney. Established Bay City *Chronicle*, 1871. U.S. minister to The Hague, 1876–82.

BIRNEY, JAMES GILLESPIE (*b. Danville, Ky., 1792; d. Eagleswood, N.J., 1857*), anti-slavery leader. Graduated Princeton, 1810; admitted to bar, 1814; practiced in Danville. Removed to Alabama, 1818. *Post* 1826, was interested in African colonization movement and restriction of slavery and domestic slave trade. Returned in 1832 to Danville and grew more aggressive in anti-slavery activities; issued first number of the *Philanthropist* in Ohio, 1836, removing the publication to New York in 1837. In it he attacked Democrats and Whigs, and urged necessity of political action on abolitionists as against the policies urged by W. L. Garrison. Birney was anti-slavery presidential candidate in 1840 and 1844 (Liberty party). He occupied a peculiar position in the American anti-slavery movement, passing as he did from belief in amelioration and gradual emancipation to abolition by constitutional and peaceful means.

BIRNEY, WILLIAM (*b. Madison Co., Ala., 1819; d. Washington, D.C., 1907*), Union soldier, lawyer. Son and biographer of James G. Birney.

BISHOP, ABRAHAM (*b. New Haven, Conn., 1763; d. New Haven, 1844*), Jeffersonian politician. Delivered noteworthy addresses against conservatives and Federalists; collector of the port of New Haven, 1803–29.

BISHOP, CHARLES REED (*b. Glens Falls, N.Y., 1822; d. California, 1915*), banker in Hawaii, philanthropist. Benefactor of Hawaiian schools. [*Supp. 1*]

BISHOP, JOEL PRENTISS (*b. Volney, N.Y., 1814; d. Cambridge, Mass., 1901*), lawyer. Wrote treatises on legal subjects, including *Commentaries on Marriage, Divorce and Separation* (1852) and *Criminal Law* (1856–58) which became classics.

BISHOP, NATHAN (*b. Vernon, N.Y., 1808; d. Saratoga Springs, N.Y., 1880*), educator, philanthropist.

BISHOP, ROBERT HAMILTON (*b. Whitburn, Scotland, 1777; d. Pleasant Hill, O., 1855*), pioneer Presbyterian minister in Kentucky and Ohio. Came to America, 1802; president, Miami University, 1824–41; anti-slavery advocate. [*Supp. 1*]

BISHOP, ROBERT ROBERTS (*b. Medfield, Mass., 1834; d. Newton, Mass., 1909*), lawyer. Associate justice, Massachusetts Superior Court, 1888–1909.

BISHOP, SETH SCOTT (*b. Fond du Lac, Wis., 1852; d. 1923*), Chicago laryngologist. Author of *Diseases of the Ear, Nose and Throat* (1897), and *The Ear and Its Diseases* (1906).

BISHOP, WILLIAM DARIUS (*b. Bloomfield, N.J., 1827; d. 1904*), railway official. President, New York and New Haven Railroad, 1866–79.

BISPHAM, DAVID SCULL (*b. Philadelphia, Pa., 1857; d. 1921*), baritone. Sang opera at Covent Garden and Metropolitan; helped establish high standards in American song recitals. Wrote *A Quaker Singer's Recollections* (1920).

BISSELL, EDWIN CONE (*b. Schoharie, N.Y., 1832; d. Chicago, Ill., 1894*), Congregational clergyman, Hebrew scholar. Author of *The Pentateuch, Its Origin and Structure* (1885).

BISSELL, GEORGE EDWIN (*b. New Preston, Conn., 1839; d. Mt. Vernon, N.Y., 1920*), sculptor.

BISSELL, GEORGE HENRY (*b. Hanover, N.H., 1821; d. 1884*), promoter of petroleum industry. Graduated Dartmouth, 1845. After work in journalism and education in the South, he began law practice with J. G. Eveleth in New York, 1853. On a visit to Dartmouth, he became interested in petroleum samples from Oil Creek region of Pennsylvania. After investigation, he and Eveleth leased lands, organized The Pennsylvania Rock Oil Co., 1854, first U.S. oil company. Boring for oil in manner of artesian wells, an important innovation, was first suggested by Bissell.

BISSELL, WILLIAM HENRY (*b. Yates Co., N.Y., 1811; d. 1860*), physician, lawyer. Removed to Illinois, 1834. Congressman, Democrat and Independent, 1848–54; Republican governor, 1856–60.

BISSELL, WILSON SHANNON (*b. Oneida Co., N.Y., 1847; d. Buffalo, N.Y., 1903*), lawyer. Associated in law firm with Grover Cleveland; postmaster-general, 1893–94.

BITTER, KARL THEODORE FRANCIS (*b. Vienna, Austria, 1867; d. New York, N.Y., 1915*), sculptor. Trained as a decorative modeler in Vienna. Came to New York in 1889 and found work with firm of architectural modelers; became protégé of architect Richard M. Hunt; won competition for one of bronze gates of Trinity Church, 1891. His exterior and interior decorations were in great demand, but *post* 1900 he refused "commercial" orders and limited himself to work of a more idealistic character. His enormous production included civic monuments, historical figures, portraits and memorials.

BIXBY, HORACE EZRA (*b. Geneseo, N.Y., 1826; d. Maplewood, Mo., 1912*), Mississippi pilot. Mark Twain's instructor and partner on the river.

BIXBY, JAMES THOMPSON (*b. Barre, Mass., 1843; d. Yonkers, N.Y., 1921*), Unitarian clergyman. Leader in Liberal Ministers' Association.

BJERREGAARD, CARL HENRIK ANDREAS (*b. Fredericia, Denmark, 1845; d. 1922*), mystical philosopher, librarian. Worked at Astor Library and its successor, New York Public Library, 1879–1922.

BLACK, EUGENE ROBERT (*b. Atlanta, Ga., 1873; d. Atlanta, 1934*), banker. Governor of Federal Reserve Board in the critical period, 1933–34.

[*Supp. 1*]

BLACK, FRANK SWETT (*b. Limington, Maine, 1853; d. 1913*), lawyer, Republican governor of New York, 1897–99.

BLACK, GREENE VARDIMAN (*b. near Winchester, Ill., 1836; d. 1915*), dentist. Began practice in Winchester, 1857. Taught at dental colleges in Missouri, Iowa and Chicago, 1870–91; from 1891 until his death he was a professor at Northwestern University Dental School, becoming dean in 1897. His first important publication of original research appeared in 1869 and dealt with the causes of the loss of workability by cohesive gold when stored. Other important papers by him presented new views on diseases of the peridental membrane, the extension of cavities in order to prevent further decay, the falsity of the theory that the density of a tooth had anything to do with its proneness to decay, and the preparation of stable amalgam alloys. His several books included *Dental Anatomy* (1891), a standard text in its field.

BLACK, JAMES (*b. Lewisburg, Pa., 1823; d. 1893*), lawyer. Founder of the National Prohibition Party. Active in temperance movement from 1840 to death; first Prohibition candidate for presidency, 1872.

BLACK, JEREMIAH SULLIVAN (*b. near Stony Creek, Pa., 1810; d. York, Pa., 1883*), lawyer, statesman. Educated at local schools; studied law with Chauncey Forward in Somerset, Pa.; admitted to bar, 1830. Gained experience as deputy attorney-general for his county; was active in politics as a Jacksonian Democrat. Judge of court of common pleas, 16th district, 1842–51; justice of supreme court of Pennsylvania, 1851–57. Appointed U.S. attorney-general by President Buchanan, 1857, he served until December, 1860. Temperamental, stubborn, absent-minded, Black held strong opinions on many issues. His most important service as attorney-general concerned California land titles; with assistance of Edwin M. Stanton and others, he uncovered a system of fraud in district court decisions. Resolute in enforcing the law, even when unpopular, he defended Buchanan's administration policy, attacked Stephen Douglas' "squatter sovereignty," and upheld Kansas Lecompton Constitution.

In secession crisis, he argued that while the Executive might not coerce a seceding state, he was duty bound to enforce the laws and protect federal property. Buchanan failed to take the advice which Black urged on him until it was too late. On resignation of Lewis Cass as secretary of state, Black took his post in December, 1860, and served in the difficult days preceding Lincoln's inauguration. Physically ill and in financial difficulties, Black restored his fortunes as an expert in litigation over California land titles. He opposed secession, gave tacit approval to the prosecution of the Civil War, but was a sharp critic of the administration's arbitrary actions, confiscation policy and disregard of civil rights. He later counseled President Andrew Johnson, defended Samuel J. Tilden before the Electoral Commission, championed unpopular causes. He helped revise the Pennsylvania constitution, 1873.

BLACK, JOHN CHARLES (*b. Lexington, Miss., 1839; d. 1915*), lawyer, Union soldier. Raised in Illinois where he practiced law; active Democrat; member, and for nine years president, U.S. Civil Service Commission, 1903–13.

BLACK, WILLIAM MURRAY (*b. Lancaster, Pa., 1855; d. 1933*), army officer and engineer. Graduated West Point, 1877; Chief of Army Engineers, 1916–19. [*Supp. 1*]

BLACK HAWK (*b. Sauk village on Rock River, Ill., 1767; d. Iowa, 1838*), Sauk war chief, protagonist of the "Black Hawk War." Resentful of Americans and disavowing Sauk cession of ancestral lands by treaty of 1804, Black Hawk helped British in War of 1812 and was a leader under Tecumseh. In late spring, 1832, in an effort to repossess Sauk lands in Illinois from white settlers, he was opposed by troops under Gen. Henry Atkinson and by Illinois volunteers and defeated at battle of Bad Axe. Taken east, he met President Jackson and was returned to Iowa after brief confinement. His autobiography (published 1833) has become an American classic.

BLACKBURN, GIDEON (*b. Augusta Co., Va., 1772; d. 1838*), Presbyterian clergyman, educator. Missionary to Cherokee Indians.

BLACKBURN, JOSEPH (*fl. 1753–63 in Boston, Mass., and Portsmouth, N.H.*), colonial portrait painter.

BLACKBURN, JOSEPH CLAY STYLES (*b. Woodford Co., Ky., 1838; d. 1918*), lawyer, Confederate soldier. Congressman, Democrat, from Kentucky, 1875–85; U.S. senator, 1885–97 and 1901–07. Active in unearthing scandals of Grant administration.

BLACKBURN, LUKE PRYOR (*b. Fayette Co., Ky., 1816; d. Frankfort, Ky., 1887*), physician, Democratic governor of Kentucky, 1879–83. Fought yellow-fever epidemics in several states; induced federal government to aid in control of the disease.

BLACKBURN, WILLIAM MAXWELL (*b. Carlisle, Ind., 1828; d. Pierre, S. Dak., 1898*), Presbyterian clergyman. Professor of Biblical history, Northwest Seminary, Chicago, Ill., 1868–81; president, Pierre University (later Huron College), 1885–98.

BLACKFORD, CHARLES MINOR (*b. Fredericksburg, Va., 1833; d. Lynchburg, Va., 1903*), lawyer, Confederate soldier.

BLACKSTONE, WILLIAM (*b. near Salisbury, England, 1595; d. near present Pawtucket, R.I., 1675*), New England colonist. Came to Massachusetts, *c.* 1623, first settler in what is now Boston; moved after disagreements with Puritans, 1634.

BLACKWELL, ANTOINETTE LOUISA BROWN (*b. Henrietta, N.Y., 1825; d. 1921*), reformer, Congregational pastor. Eloquent speaker and writer, active for abolition, woman's rights, prohibition.

BLACKWELL, ELIZABETH (*b. Bristol, England, 1821; d. Hastings, England, 1910*), first woman medical doctor of modern times. Came to America, 1832. Taught school; began reading medicine in 1845. Admitted after great difficulties to Geneva Medical School of Western New York, she received much-publicized M.D., 1849. Studied and practiced in Paris and London; opened with sister Emily a private dispensary in New York which later (1857) became incorporated into New York Infirmary and College for Women. Active during Civil War in organizing field nurses, in 1869 she settled permanently in England.

BLACKWELL, HENRY BROWN (*b. Bristol, England, 1825; d. Dorchester, Mass., 1909*), editor. Brother of Elizabeth Blackwell. Early advocate of woman suffrage, other liberal movements. Married to Lucy Stone.

BLACKWELL, LUCY STONE. [See STONE, LUCY.]

BLADEN, WILLIAM (*b. Hemsworth, England, 1673; d. Maryland, 1718*), publisher. Came to Maryland, 1690. Active in public affairs, he held many official posts; as clerk of Assembly, supervised printing of colony laws *post* 1700.

BLAIKIE, WILLIAM (*b. New York, N.Y., 1843; d. 1904*), lawyer, athlete, promoter of physical training. Published popular *How to Get Strong and How to Stay So,* 1879.

BLAINE, JAMES GILLESPIE (*b. West Brownsville, Pa., 1830; d. Washington, D.C., 1893*), statesman. Graduated Washington College, Pa. Began to teach in Kentucky, but not liking the South, took a teaching position at the Pennsylvania Institute for the Blind, Philadelphia, 1852–54, studying law while in that city. Married Harriet Stanwood, 1850. Her family were settled in Augusta, Maine, and Blaine entered journalism there, 1854, purchasing an interest in the *Kennebec Journal.* He was identified with Maine thereafter.

In his first year of editorship he abandoned his formal Whig allegiance and was instrumental in giving the name "Republican" currency in the East. A delegate to the first Republican convention, 1856, he was one of that party's founders, and expected it to carry on Whig measures as well as to oppose slavery. An orator of thrilling power, with talent for interpreting election returns and for remembering names and faces, he became chairman of the Maine Republican committee, 1859, holding the post until 1881 and becoming accepted party dictator in the state. Elected to the Maine legislature, 1858, and twice re-elected, he was speaker in his last two terms. Entering Congress in 1863, he served in the House until 1876; as speaker, 1869–75. He was U.S. senator, 1876–81.

Firm in support of Lincoln, he was less radical and vindictive in the Reconstruction period than many of his fellow Republicans. Favoring Negro suffrage, he helped pass an amendment to Thaddeus Stevens's military government bill which insisted on what Radicals called "universal suffrage and universal amnesty" as basis for reconstruction. This was a notable victory for a young congressman. Coming through this period with the reputation of a level-headed liberal who could nevertheless be trusted even by the Grand Army, he built up popularity in the West. Associated with James A. Garfield and W. B. Allison, he made one lasting enemy, Roscoe Conkling of New York. Conkling became a leading Grant supporter, or "Stalwart," Blaine head of the opposition within the party, the "Half-Breeds." His chance for presidential nomination in 1876 seemed good, but charges brought against him by a Democratic committee investigating railroad graft were imperfectly refuted by Blaine, the "Stalwarts" opposed him and the nomination went to Rutherford B. Hayes. Blaine worked to build up his position in preparation for the 1880 campaign, meanwhile supporting Hayes's administration against attacks by Conkling. Garfield, however, was nominated. As before, Blaine took it with good grace, worked with Garfield in the campaign and became his secretary of state, resigning in 1881 after Garfield was shot. Finally in 1884, though the Republicans were still divided, Blaine was nominated for the presidency on the first ballot. Defection of "Mugwump" Republicans because of the railroad graft affair, apprehension over his foreign policy and the Burchard incident in New York lost him key states. Grover Cleveland won the election.

Still the most powerful Republican, Blaine was expected to be renominated in 1888, but refused a candidacy and was influential in the nomination of Benjamin Harrison. He became secretary of state under Harrison, serving 1889–92.

Blaine's permanent influence was through his foreign policy. Known as a politician, he was generally expected to emphasize political aspects of the office, but shattered this expectation by his genuine interest in building a constructive policy which would be adjusted to changing conditions. Despite shortcomings, common to his generation, of lack of training in international law or diplomatic history, he was a forerunner of American world interests and much in advance of his time.

Active in formulating an Isthmian canal policy and in securing treaties for protection of migratory animal life, his most constructive work had to do with South America. Since the Civil War, relations between Latin America and Great Britain had been growing more intimate at the expense of the United States; this had important economic aspects. Dissatisfied with the negative aspects of the Monroe Doctrine, Blaine in his first period as secretary of state evolved a policy which would unite the American nations into a real system, use good offices of the United States to maintain peace, have joint conferences to plan measures of mutual advantage. His whole policy of Pan-Americanism was dropped when he resigned in 1881, but he continued to urge his views in magazine articles and through friends in Congress and implemented them in his later term of office. In October 1889, when the Pan-American Congress met in Washington, Blaine was influential in drawing up recommendations and laid foundation of the Bureau of American Republics at Washington. He also worked to promote reciprocity treaties and increase trade with Latin American countries, and is conspicuous as the only outstanding public figure between Seward and Hay who was genuinely interested in foreign affairs.

BLAINE, JOHN JAMES (*b. near Castle Rock, Wis., 1875; d. Wisconsin, 1934*), lawyer, politician. Progressive Republican governor of Wisconsin, 1921–27; U.S. senator, 1927–32. [*Supp. 1*]

BLAIR, AUSTIN (*b. Caroline, N.Y., 1818; d. 1894*), lawyer. Removed to Michigan, 1841. Energetic Republican governor of that state, 1860–65.

BLAIR, FRANCIS PRESTON (*b. Abingdon, Va., 1791; d. 1876*), journalist, politician. Graduated Transylvania University, 1811. Served briefly in War of 1812. Returning to Kentucky home, he actively fought "Old Court" party as assistant on *Argus of Western America.* Soon joined Jacksonians; wrote in favor of lower tariff, cheap land, direct election of president; opposed Bank of the United States. Jackson called him to Washington where he established administration organ, the *Globe,* 1830, continuing as editor until 1845. In these years Blair exerted much power, was member of Jackson's Kitchen Cabinet. He later turned to Republicans, supported Lincoln in 1860 and backed Lincoln's reconstruction program but was driven back to Democratic party by extremists.

BLAIR, FRANCIS PRESTON (*b. Lexington, Ky., 1821; d. St. Louis, Mo., 1875*), Union soldier, statesman. Son of Francis P. Blair (1791–1876). Graduated Princeton, 1841. Admitted to bar, and practiced in St. Louis, Mo., *post* 1842. Fought in Mexican War. Organized Free-Soil party in Missouri, opposed slave

interests on moral and economic grounds. As congressman, Free-Soil, 1856–58, Republican, 1860–62, was a leader in saving Missouri for Union and rose to major-general in active Civil War service. Recalled to Congress, 1864, he backed Lincoln's policy on reconstruction, was later involved in Missouri controversy between Radical Republicans and moderates like himself. Reverting to Democratic party, he cooperated with Liberal Republicans, was elected to Missouri legislature and was chosen U.S. senator by that body, 1871–73.

BLAIR, HENRY WILLIAM (*b. Campton, N.H., 1834; d. 1920*), lawyer, Union soldier. Congressman, Republican, from New Hampshire, 1875–79; U.S. senator, 1879–91. Proponent of federal aid to public schools, woman suffrage, labor legislation.

BLAIR, JAMES (*b. Scotland, 1655; d. Virginia, 1743*), founder and first president, William and Mary College. Came to Virginia as missionary, 1685. Appointed Bishop of London's commissary, 1689, he urged establishment of a college which was chartered 1693. Blair was named president. Minister at Jamestown, later Williamsburg, he managed, despite opposition, indifference and a disastrous fire, to see the college well established before he died.

BLAIR, JOHN (*b. probably Virginia, 1687; d. 1771*), acting governor of Virginia, 1758 and 1768. Nephew of James Blair.

BLAIR, JOHN (*b. Williamsburg, Va., 1732; d. Williamsburg, 1800*), jurist. Son of John Blair (1687–1771). Patriot, Virginia judge, delegate to constitutional convention. Associate justice, U.S. Supreme Court, 1789–96.

BLAIR, JOHN INSLEY (*b. near Belvidere, N.J., 1802; d. 1899*), capitalist, philanthropist. Began as storekeeper and miller; expanding interests to mining, he participated, 1846, in founding Lackawanna Coal and Iron Co. and was one of largest stockholders in Delaware, Lackawanna and Western Railroad. Interested in development of western railroads, he joined in getting charter of Union Pacific, was at one time president of 16 roads, and laid out sites for over 80 towns in the West. Benefactor of Princeton, Blair Academy, Presbyterian Church.

BLAIR, MONTGOMERY (*b. Franklin Co., Ky., 1813; d. 1883*), lawyer, statesman. Son of Francis P. Blair (1791–1876). Graduated West Point, 1835; resigned commission, 1836, to study law. Settled in St. Louis, 1837. Protégé of Thomas Hart Benton; practiced law, served as mayor and judge. Moving to Maryland, 1853, practiced chiefly before U.S. Supreme Court. A border man, he believed slavery question could be settled peaceably; was counsel for Dred Scott. A Democrat turned moderate Republican, he was postmaster-general under Lincoln, organized army postal system, introduced compulsory payment of postage, other improvements. Forced by

Radicals to resign, 1864, he continued loyal to Lincoln and his reconstruction plan, but eventually drifted back to Democrats, supporting Seymour in 1868 and acting as Samuel J. Tilden's counsel before Electoral Commission.

BLAIR, SAMUEL (*b. Ulster, Ireland, 1712; d. Chester Co., Pa., 1751*), Presbyterian clergyman.

BLAKE, ELI WHITNEY (*b. Westborough, Mass., 1795; d. New Haven, Conn., 1886*), inventor, manufacturer. Best known for stone crushing machine, patented 1858.

BLAKE, FRANCIS (*b. Needham, Mass., 1850; d. 1913*), inventor, physicist. Patented telephone transmitter, 1878, the mechanical features of which made practical the fundamental principles of Berliner microphone.

BLAKE, HOMER CRANE (*b. Dutchess Co., N.Y., 1822; d. 1880*), naval officer.

BLAKE, JOHN LAURIS (*b. Northwood, N.H., 1788; d. Orange, N.J., 1857*), Episcopal clergyman, author of popular encyclopedias.

BLAKE, LILLIE DEVEREUX (*b. Raleigh, N.C., 1835; d. New York, N.Y., 1913*), author, reformer. Championed woman suffrage, economic reforms for women. Wrote stories, novels, including *Fettered for Life* (1874).

BLAKE, LYMAN REED (*b. South Abington, Mass., 1835; d. 1883*), inventor. Conceived idea of a machine which could sew soles of shoes to uppers. First designed a shoe that could be sewed, essentially the present-day shoe, then made and patented (1858) a machine which would sew it. Sold patent to Gordon McKay; later worked with him to promote and improve machine which came into almost universal use.

BLAKE, MARY ELIZABETH McGRATH (*b. Dungarven, Ireland, 1840; d. Boston, Mass., 1907*), author of *Poems* (1882) and numerous other ephemeral works.

BLAKE, WILLIAM PHIPPS (*b. New York, N.Y., 1825; d. 1910*), geologist, mining engineer, teacher.

BLAKE, WILLIAM RUFUS (*b. Halifax, N.S., 1805; d. Boston, Mass., 1863*), actor. Popular comedian, made American debut in New York, 1824; managed theatres in New York, Philadelphia, Boston; a member of Burton's, Laura Keene's and Wallack's stock companies.

BLAKELOCK, RALPH ALBERT (*b. New York, N.Y., 1847; d. New York State, 1919*), landscape painter. Self-taught but influenced by rich colors and enamel-like technique of A. P. Ryder. Suffering a mental breakdown, c. 1899, he was elected to National Academy, 1913, while in an asylum. His works, essentially romantic mood pictures, recall 18th century Dutch and English landscapes influenced by Rembrandt.

BLAKELY, JOHNSTON (*b. Seaford, Ireland, 1781; d. at sea, 1814*), naval officer. Came to America as a child. Became midshipman in navy, 1800; served in Mediterranean. Commanding brig *Enterprise*, 1811–13, and sloop-of-war *Wasp*, 1814, won several engagements with British. After engagement with British brig *Atalanta* in September 1814, east of Madeira, the *Wasp* is known to have sailed farther south, but nothing more was ever heard from her.

BLAKESLEE, ERASTUS (*b. Plymouth, Conn., 1838; d. Brookline, Mass., 1908*), Congregational clergyman. Organized Bible Study Union, Boston, 1892, which published lessons for all grades, widely used in Protestant churches.

BLALOCK, NELSON GALES (*b. Mitchell Co., N.C., 1836; d. Walla Walla, Wash., 1913*), physician, agriculturist.

BLANC, ANTOINE (*b. Sury, France, 1792; d. New Orleans, La., 1860*), Roman Catholic clergyman. Came to America, 1817. Consecrated bishop of New Orleans, 1835; raised to archbishop, 1851.

BLANCHARD, JONATHAN (*b. Rockingham, Vt., 1811; d. 1892*), Presbyterian clergyman. Graduated Middlebury, 1832. President, Knox College, Galesburg, Ill., 1845–57; Wheaton College, Ill., 1860–82, and emeritus to 1892.

BLANCHARD, NEWTON CRAIN (*b. Rapides Parish, La., 1849; d. 1922*), lawyer. Congressman, Democrat, from Louisiana, 1881–93; U.S. senator, 1893–97; governor of Louisiana, 1904–08.

BLANCHARD, THOMAS (*b. Sutton, Mass., 1788; d. 1864*), inventor. While working on problem of turning gun-stocks at the Springfield Arsenal, he developed the whole principle of turning irregular forms from a pattern. His machine, declared by Congress to stand among the chief American inventions, consisted of a friction wheel touching the pattern and a cutting wheel secured to the same shaft. Many machine tools and woodworking machines depend on this principle. Continuing to invent, he patented a steam carriage (1825) and designed and built stern-wheel steamboats for use on shallow rivers.

BLANCHET, FRANÇOIS NORBERT (*b. Quebec Prov., Canada, 1795; d. Portland, Oreg., 1883*), Catholic missionary. Ordained in Quebec, 1819. Worked as missionary to Indians in New Brunswick and at parish in Montreal. Responding to need for priests among trappers, traders and Iroquois of Oregon region, he went west and was highly successful, establishing missions in Walla Walla, Vancouver, Astoria and elsewhere in northwest. Made bishop, 1843, and in 1846 archbishop of newly established see of Oregon City, he traveled in Europe and South America to collect money and enlist priests and nuns for service in Oregon. Despite many difficulties, he built up his see, removing it to Portland, 1862.

BLAND, RICHARD (*b. Virginia, 1710; d. 1776*), statesman. Son of Virginia planter, educated at William and Mary. Member of House of Burgesses, 1742–75. Became champion of public rights as early as 1753; opposed clergy, helped draw up 1764 resolution respecting taxation imposed on Virginia from outside. Author of *An Inquiry into the Rights of the British Colonies* (1766), earliest published defense of colonial attitude on taxation. Hopeful for peace, he opposed Patrick Henry's plan for arming of colony, 1775. Member of revolutionary conventions of March 1775, July 1775, May 1776 and the first two Continental Congresses. Learned and able, he preserved many valuable historical documents and records.

BLAND, RICHARD PARKS (*b. near Hartford, Ky., 1835; d. 1899*), lawyer, congressional leader of "Free Silver" movement. Congressman, Democrat, from Missouri, 1872–95, 1897–99. As chairman of Committee on Mines and Mining, 1875–77, led fight for free silver coinage; became a national figure with passage of Bland-Allison Act over Hayes's veto, 1878. Opposed Sherman Silver Purchase Act, led Free Silver wing of Democratic party. Urged advantages of Free Silver to "producing classes" in general, not only agrarian group. Strongly opposed monopolies, protective tariff, imperialism.

BLAND, THEODORICK (*b. Prince George Co., Va., 1742; d. 1790*), planter, physician, Revolutionary soldier.

BLAND, THOMAS (*b. Newark, England, 1809; d. 1885*), naturalist. Settled in New York, 1852. Became authority on North American mollusks. Co-author, Part I, "Land and Fresh-Water Shells of North America" in *Smithsonian Collections* (1869).

BLANKENBURG, RUDOLPH (*b. Barntrup, Germany, 1843; d. 1918*), merchant. Reform mayor of Philadelphia, 1911–15. Author of the phrase "the powers that prey."

BLASDEL, HENRY GOODE (*b. Dearborn Co., Ind., 1825; d. 1900*), merchant, miner. Governor of Nevada, Republican, 1864–70.

BLASHFIELD, EDWIN HOWLAND (*b. New York, N.Y., 1848; d. South Dennis, Mass., 1936*), mural painter. Left engineering school to study figure painting with Léon Bonnat in Paris. Success of mural commission for Chicago World's Fair, 1893, led to many major assignments, including murals for the Library of Congress and the state capitols of Minnesota, Iowa, South Dakota and Wisconsin as well as many private commissions. Blashfield was a founder of the Municipal Art Society, New York City, and president of the National Academy of Design, 1920–26. [*Supp. 2*]

BLATCH, HARRIOT EATON STANTON (*b. Seneca Falls, N.Y., 1856; d. Greenwich, Conn., 1940*), social reformer. Daughter of Henry Brewster and Elizabeth Cady Stanton. Founder, 1907, Equality League of Self-Supporting Women; writer on woman suffrage and peace. [*Supp. 2*]

BLATCHFORD, RICHARD MILFORD (*b. Stratford, Conn., 1798; d. Newport, R.I., 1875*), lawyer. Counsel, post 1826, for Bank of the United States, also for Bank of England in the United States. Commissioner of New York Central Park, 1859–70.

BLATCHFORD, SAMUEL (*b. New York, N.Y., 1820; d. Newport, R.I., 1893*), lawyer, jurist. Son of Richard M. Blatchford. Specialist in maritime and patent law. Associate justice, U.S. Supreme Court, 1882–93.

BLAUSTEIN, DAVID (*b. Lida, Russian Poland, 1866; d. 1912*), rabbi, educator. Came to America, 1886. Graduated Harvard, 1893. First of trained Jewish social workers. Superintendent, Educational Alliance, New York, which set example for Jewish settlements elsewhere.

BLAVATSKY, HELENA PETROVNA HAHN (*b. Ekaterinoslav, Russia, 1831; d. London, England, 1891*), founder of Theosophical movement. Resided in New York, N.Y., 1873–78.

BLECKLEY, LOGAN EDWIN (*b. Rabun Co., Ga., 1827; d. 1907*), jurist. Associate justice, Georgia supreme court, 1875–80; chief justice, 1887–94. Decisions widely quoted because of witty style, faculty for simple statement of complex matters.

BLEDSOE, ALBERT TAYLOR (*b. Kentucky, 1809; d. Alexandria, Va., 1877*), Confederate official, lawyer, educator. Edited *Southern Review*, 1867–77, representing attitude of unreconstructed Southerners on Civil War, industrialism, evolution, democracy.

BLEECKER, ANN ELIZA (*b. New York, N.Y., 1752; d. Tomhanick, N.Y., 1783*), poet. Her lyrics and prose were published in *Posthumous Works* (New York, 1793).

BLENK, JAMES HUBERT (*b. Neustadt, Bavaria, 1856; d. New Orleans, La., 1917*), Roman Catholic clergyman. Came to America in infancy. A Marist, he became bishop of Puerto Rico, 1899, and archbishop of New Orleans, 1906.

BLENNERHASSETT, HARMAN (*b. Hampshire, England, 1765; d. Isle of Guernsey, England, 1831*), associate of Aaron Burr. Educated at Trinity College, Dublin; admitted to Irish bar, 1790. Came to America, 1796; settled on island in Ohio River, establishing elaborate home there. Met Aaron Burr, 1805. His apparent means and enthusiasm attracted Burr; the island became a center for Burr's separatist activities in the West. Blennerhassett helped make first payment on Bastrop Purchase. Suspicious Virginia militia raided and looted the island, Dec. 11, 1806. Blennerhassett had left the night before; joined Burr at mouth of Cumberland. Later arrested and brought to trial, Blennerhassett went free when Burr failed to be convicted.

BLEYER, WILLARD GROSVENOR (*b. Milwaukee, Wis., 1873; d. 1935*), professor of journalism, University of Wisconsin, 1905–35. Author of pioneer textbooks in the field; standardized teaching of journalism on a national scale. [*Supp. 1*]

BLINN, HOLBROOK (*b. San Francisco, Calif., 1872; d. Croton, N.Y., 1928*), actor. Popular in England and America. Organized Princess Theatre, New York, 1913.

BLISS, AARON THOMAS (*b. Peterboro, N.Y., 1837; d. 1906*), lumberman. Removed to Saginaw, Mich., 1865. Republican governor of Michigan, 1900–04; progressive and able.

BLISS, CORNELIUS NEWTON (*b. Fall River, Mass., 1833; d. 1911*), textile merchant, politician. Conservative Republican, active in New York City and national politics; U.S. secretary of interior, 1896–98.

BLISS, DANIEL (*b. Georgia, Vt., 1823; d. 1916*), Congregational clergyman, missionary. Founder, first president, Syrian Protestant College (now American University), Beirut, 1866–1902.

BLISS, EDWIN ELISHA (*b. Putney, Vt., 1817; d. 1892*), Congregational clergyman. Missionary to Armenia and Turkey, 1843–92.

BLISS, EDWIN MUNSELL (*b. Erzerum, Turkey, 1848; d. Washington, D.C., 1919*), Congregational clergyman. Bible Society agent in Levant. Edited *Encyclopædia of Missions*, 1889–91.

BLISS, ELIPHALET WILLIAMS (*b. Fly Creek, N.Y., 1836; d. Brooklyn, N.Y., 1903*), manufacturer. Founded E. W. Bliss Co., 1867, whose machine shops made tools and dies for sheet metal work, torpedoes, shells for navy.

BLISS, FREDERICK JONES (*b. Suq al-Gharb, Syria, 1859; d. White Plains, N.Y., 1937*), archeologist. Son of Daniel Bliss. Graduated Amherst, 1880. Active, 1891–1901, in Palestinian excavations, excelling at chronological determinations. [*Supp. 2*]

BLISS, GEORGE (*b. Northampton, Mass., 1816; d. 1896*), merchant, banker. Settled in New York, N.Y., 1844. Made fortune in dry goods by foreseeing Civil War price rise. Partner of Levi P. Morton in banking firm.

BLISS, GEORGE (*b. Springfield, Mass., 1830; d. Wakefield, R.I., 1897*), lawyer. Graduated Harvard, 1851; admitted to New York bar, 1857. A skilled legislative draftsman, he drew up, among many other laws, the 1873 charter of New York City and its first Tenement House Act. In 1882, he was special prosecutor in the "Star Route" cases.

BLISS, HOWARD SWEETSER (*b. Suq al-Gharb, Syria, 1860; d. Saranac Lake, N.Y., 1920*), Congregational clergyman, missionary educator. President, Syrian Protestant College, succeeding father, Daniel Bliss, in 1903.

BLISS, JONATHAN (*b. Springfield, Mass., 1742; d. Frederickton, Canada, 1822*), jurist. Graduated Harvard, 1763. As member of General Court *post* 1768, he was a consistent Tory and removed to England, 1775. Returning in 1785 to New Brunswick, he served as attorney-general and chief justice.

BLISS, PHILEMON (*b. North Canton, Conn., 1814; d. St. Paul, Minn., 1889*), Ohio congressman, Missouri jurist. Dean, University of Missouri school of law, 1872–89.

BLISS, PHILIP PAUL (*b. Clearfield Co., Pa., 1838; d. Ashtabula, O., 1876*), singing evangelist. Co-author with Ira Sankey of *Gospel Songs* (1874) containing "Hold the Fort" and other popular hymns.

BLISS, PORTER CORNELIUS (*b. Cattaraugus Reservation, N.Y., 1838; d. New York, N.Y., 1885*), traveler, explorer, journalist. Expert on Latin America; an editor of *New York Herald*.

BLISS, TASKER HOWARD (*b. Lewisburg, Pa., 1853; d. 1930*), soldier, scholar, diplomat. Graduated West Point, 1876. Assigned to the artillery, he was recalled to West Point to teach under Maj.-Gen. J. M. Schofield, then superintendent. When Gen. Schofield succeeded Gen. Sheridan as commanding general of the army in 1888, he chose Bliss as his aide. When war broke out in 1898, Bliss was made a major and took part in the Puerto Rican campaign. Was chief of Cuban customs houses during the occupation and later negotiated the Cuban reciprocity treaty. Was made brigadier-general by President McKinley and became founding president of the new Army War College. In 1905 he was sent to the Philippines to command the Department of Luzon, then Mindanao, and finally the Philippine Division. Returning to Washington, 1909, he became assistant chief of staff; was acting chief of staff soon after World War I broke out, and chief of staff, September 1917. In October, Bliss went to Europe as military aide under Edward M. House to effect better coordination of the Allied effort, and on his return presented an exhaustive report urging the importance of prompt and unified action. He returned to Europe as military representative on the Supreme War Council, where in President Wilson's absence, Bliss had a statesman's role. His letters to Newton D. Baker reveal how the Allied leaders early sought to circumvent the President's Fourteen Points and his plans for a League of Nations. He was for a unified field command and supported Gen. Pershing's insistence that American troops should not be infiltrated into Allied armies. He was for unconditional surrender of the German army and, farsightedly, for the support of the German Republic to insure its endurance. Chosen delegate to the Peace Conference, he opposed granting a mandate over Shantung to Japan. He was relieved as chief of staff in 1918. In his declining years his great interest was in advocating the entry of the United States into the World Court, and peace through reduction of armaments. [*Supp. 1*]

BLISS, WILLIAM DWIGHT PORTER (*b. Constantinople, Turkey, 1856; d. New York, N.Y., 1926*), Congregationalist, later Episcopal clergyman. Son of Edwin E. Bliss. Organized first Christian Socialist Society in United States, 1889.

BLITZ, ANTONIO (*b. ? England, 1810; d. Philadelphia, Pa., 1877*), magician. Varied talents included sleight-of-hand and ventriloquism.

BLOCK, ADRIAEN (*fl. 1610–24*), Dutch mariner, explorer. First detailed map of southern New England coast (1616) drawn as far as Cape Ann from his data. Block Island named for him.

BLODGET, LORIN (*b. near Jamestown, N.Y., 1823; d. 1901*), statistician, climatologist, publicist. Associated with Smithsonian Institution; wrote *Climatology of the United States* (1857), first important American work on subject.

BLODGET, SAMUEL (*b. Woburn, Mass., 1724; d. Derryfield, Mass., 1807*), merchant, manufacturer. Planned and built, 1794–1807, canal around Amoskeag Falls on Merrimac.

BLODGET, SAMUEL (*b. Goffstown, N.H., 1757; d. Baltimore, Md., 1814*), merchant, economist, architect. Son of Samuel Blodget (1724–1807). Made fortune in East India trade. Moved to Philadelphia, 1789; became a director of Insurance Company of North America. Designed building for first Bank of the United States, Philadelphia. Began buying Washington, D.C., real estate, 1792; was active in promoting city's development. Submitted plan in competition for U.S. Capitol design, suggested founding a national university at Washington.

BLODGETT, BENJAMIN COLMAN (*b. Boston, Mass., 1838; d. Seattle, Wash., 1925*), pianist, organist, music-teacher, composer. Director, Smith College School of Music, 1880–1903.

BLODGETT, HENRY WILLIAMS (*b. Amherst, Mass., 1821; d. 1905*), lawyer. Raised in Illinois. U.S. district judge in Illinois, 1869–92.

BLOEDE, GERTRUDE (*b. Dresden, Germany, 1845; d. Baldwin, N.Y., 1905*), poet. Came to America as a child. Published several volumes of verse under pseudonym of Stuart Sterne.

BLOOD, BENJAMIN PAUL (*b. Amsterdam, N.Y., 1832; d. 1919*), philosopher, mystic, poet.

BLOODGOOD, JOSEPH COLT (*b. Milwaukee, Wis., 1867; d. 1935*), surgeon, surgical pathologist. Professor of surgery, Johns Hopkins, 1895–1935; a leading authority on cancer. [*Supp. 1*]

BLOODWORTH, TIMOTHY (*b. New Hanover Co., N.C., 1736; d. Washington, N.C., 1814*), politician, radical anti-federalist. U.S. senator from North Carolina, 1795–1807.

BLOOMER, AMELIA JENKS (*b. Homer, N.Y., 1818; d. Council Bluffs, Iowa, 1894*), reformer. Attended first meeting on women's rights, Seneca Falls, N.Y., 1848, but only as spectator, her earliest reform activity being in the temperance movement. Founded the *Lily*, 1849, one of first papers published by a woman, and wrote on unjust marriage laws, suffrage, education. She is thus one of the pioneers in the women's rights movement, but through publicity and ridicule her name is associated primarily with dress reform and the "Bloomer costume."

BLOOMFIELD, JOSEPH (*b. Woodbridge, N.J., 1753; d. Burlington, N.J., 1823*), lawyer, Revolutionary soldier. (Democrat) Republican governor of New Jersey, 1801, 1803–12.

BLOOMFIELD-ZEISLER, FANNIE. [See Zeisler, Fannie Bloomfield, 1863–1927.]

BLOOMFIELD, MAURICE (*b. Bielitz, Austria, 1855; d. San Francisco, Calif., 1928*), Orientalist, philologist. Came to America as a child. Educated at Furman, Yale, Johns Hopkins. Chief work was the editing, translating, interpreting of sacred texts of the Vedas.

BLOOMFIELD, MEYER (*b. Bucharest, Roumania, 1878; d. New York, N.Y., 1938*), social worker, lawyer. Came to New York as a child. Graduated College of City of New York, 1899; Harvard, 1901. Pioneer in vocational guidance and personnel management. [*Supp. 2*]

BLOOMGARDEN, SOLOMON (*b. Wertzblowo, Lithuania, 1870; d. 1927*), writer. Came to America, 1890. Wrote extensively under pen-name "Yehoash," mainly in Yiddish; translated Jewish Bible into Yiddish.

BLOUNT, JAMES HENDERSON (*b. Jones Co., Ga., 1837; d. Macon, Ga., 1903*), lawyer, congressman, diplomatic envoy. Special commissioner to Hawaii, 1893. His criticism of American involvement in revolution against Liliuokalani determined policy against annexation.

BLOUNT, THOMAS (*b. Edgecombe Co., N.C., 1759; d. Washington, D.C., 1812*), Revolutionary soldier, merchant, (Democrat) Republican politician. Congressman from North Carolina, 1793–99, 1805–09, 1811–12.

BLOUNT, WILLIAM (*b. Edgecombe Co., N.C., 1749; d. Knoxville, Tenn., 1800*), politician. Brother of Thomas Blount; half-brother of Willie Blount. After Revolutionary War service, was four times in North Carolina House of Commons, twice in state Senate; he was later a delegate to Congress, 1782–

83, 1786–87, and a member of the federal constitutional convention, 1787. Considered plain, honest and sincere by contemporaries, he became governor of Tennessee territory, 1790, and concurrently superintendent of Indian Affairs, Southern Department. Popular and sympathetic with settlers, he was elected U.S. senator in 1796 when the territory became a state. In financial difficulties over speculations in land, he became involved in a scheme to transfer control of Spanish Florida and Louisiana to Great Britain and was expelled from the Senate, 1797; his impeachment was later dismissed. Returning to Tennessee, he served in the state senate as speaker until death.

BLOUNT, WILLIE (b. North Carolina, 1768; d. Montgomery Co., Tenn., 1835), planter, jurist. Halfbrother of Thomas and William Blount. (Democrat) Republican governor of Tennessee, 1809–15.

BLOW, HENRY TAYLOR (b. Virginia, 1817; d. 1875), capitalist, diplomat. Removed to St. Louis, Mo., c. 1830. A pioneer in lead and lead-products business, he was instrumental in developing lead mines of southwestern Missouri and transforming St. Louis into a commercial center. Opposing extension of slavery, he became a Free-Soiler and helped organize Republican party in state. Elected to Congress, 1862 and 1864, he served on joint committee on Reconstruction. Appointed minister to Brazil, 1869–71, he helped bring closer relations with that country.

BLOW, SUSAN ELIZABETH (b. St. Louis, Mo., 1843; d. New York, N.Y., 1916). Daughter of Henry T. Blow. Trained by follower of Froebel. Opened first American public kindergarten, St. Louis, 1873; also training school, 1874.

BLOWERS, SAMPSON SALTER (b. Boston, Mass., 1742; d. Halifax, N.S., 1842), jurist. Graduated Harvard, 1763. Loyalist, settled in Nova Scotia after Revolution; chief justice there, 1797–1833.

BLOXHAM, WILLIAM DUNNINGTON (b. Tallahassee, Fla., 1835; d. Tallahassee, 1911), planter, public servant. Governor of Florida, 1881–85, 1897–1901; a conservative Democrat, his highly successful administrations improved the state's financial condition.

BLUE, VICTOR (b. Richmond Co., N.C., 1865; d. 1928), naval officer. Graduated Annapolis, 1887. Established presence of Cervera's squadron in Santiago harbor, June, 1898.

BLUEMNER, OSCAR FLORIANS (b. Hanover, Germany, 1867; d. South Braintree, Mass., 1938), architect, experimental painter. Came to America, 1892. Sought to establish analogies between music and painting. [Supp. 2]

BLUM, ROBERT FREDERICK (b. Cincinnati, O., 1857; d. New York, N.Y., 1903), painter. Apprentice in lithographic firm; fellow-student with Kenyon Cox in Cincinnati and Philadelphia; went to New York,

1878, and worked as illustrator in style of Fortuny. In 1889 he made a long-deferred trip to Japan; his two-year stay produced much outstanding work. Moved to Greenwich Village soon after returning, a pioneer in migration of artists there. Distinguished in many mediums.

BLUNT, EDMUND MARCH (b. Portsmouth, N.H., 1770; d. Sing Sing, N.Y., 1862), hydrographer. Publisher and bookseller in Newburyport, Mass. Published American Coast Pilot (ed. Furlong), 1796; also brought out New Practical Navigator (1799) and Bowditch's New American Practical Navigator (1801). These, with preparation of charts, made Blunt's shop the center of American nautical publications. Removing to New York, post 1805, Blunt continued his business; among his later publications was Stranger's Guide to the City of New York (1817).

BLUNT, GEORGE WILLIAM (b. Newburyport, Mass., 1802; d. New York, N.Y., 1878), hydrographer. Son of Edmund M. Blunt. Associated with father and brother Edmund in making charts and nautical instruments. Editor, among other works, of The Young Sea Officer's Sheet Anchor (1843).

BLUNT, JAMES GILLPATRICK (b. Trenton, Maine, 1826; d. Washington, D.C., 1881), physician, Union soldier. Kansas associate of John Brown.

BLY, NELLIE. [See SEAMAN, ELIZABETH COCHRANE, 1867–1922.]

BLYTHE, HERBERT. [See BARRYMORE, MAURICE, 1847–1905.]

BOARDMAN, THOMAS DANFORTH (b. Litchfield, Conn., 1784; d. Hartford, Conn., 1873), pewterer. Last pure representative of ancient tradition in pewtermaking; pioneered in manufacture of britannia-ware, block tin.

BOAS, EMIL LEOPOLD (b. Goerlitz, Germany, 1854; d. Greenwich, Conn., 1912). General manager, later sole American director, Hamburg-American line, 1892–1912.

BÔCHER, MAXIME (b. Boston, Mass., 1867; d. 1918), mathematician. Graduated Harvard, 1888; Ph.D., Göttingen, 1891. Successful teacher at Harvard, 1891–1918.

BOCOCK, THOMAS STANLEY (b. Buckingham Co., Va., 1815; d. near Appomattox Court House, Va., 1891), lawyer. Congressman, Democrat, from Virginia, 1847–61. Speaker, Confederate House of Representatives, in both First and Second Congresses.

BODANZKY, ARTUR (b. Vienna, Austria, 1877; d. 1939), opera and orchestra conductor. Came to America, 1915. With Metropolitan Opera, 1915–39; Society of the Friends of Music, 1920–31. [Supp. 2]

BOEHLER, PETER (b. Frankfurt-am-Main, Germany, 1712; d. England, 1775), bishop in Moravian

Church. Started mission in Savannah, 1738; helped found Moravian settlement, Bethlehem, Pa. Later vice-superintendent, American Province.

BOEHM, HENRY (*b. Lancaster Co., Pa., 1775; d. 1875*), Methodist itinerant preacher. Son of Martin Boehm. Preached in English and German, superintended translation of Methodist doctrine into German. Traveled circuits in many states, 1800–64.

BOEHM, JOHN PHILIP (*b. Hochstadt, Germany, 1683; d. Hellertown, Pa., 1749*), German Reformed clergyman. Came to America, 1720. Founder of German Reformed Church in Pennsylvania.

BOEHM, MARTIN (*b. Conestoga Township, Pa., 1725; d. 1812*), Mennonite bishop, United Brethren bishop. Expelled by Mennonites for lack of orthodoxy, helped found United Brethren in Christ; also affiliated with Methodists.

BOELEN, JACOB (*b. Netherlands, c. 1654; d. New York, N.Y., 1729*), silversmith. Came to America as a child. Ranks among best silverworkers in early New York.

BOGARDUS, EVERARDUS (*b. Woerden, Netherlands, 1607; d. off Welsh coast, 1647*), second minister of New Netherland, 1633–47. Involved in much controversy with colonial officials.

BOGARDUS, JAMES (*b. Catskill, N.Y., 1800; d. New York, N.Y., 1874*), inventor. Apprenticed early to watchmaker; specialized in engraving and die-sinking. Patented "ring flyer," 1830, used in cotton-spinning machinery for over fifty years. Other inventions include eccentric sugar-grinding mill, gas meter, engraving machine for watch dials, a rice-grinder, a dynamometer and many others. Probably his greatest contribution was introduction of cast-iron in building construction, used for his own factory building, erected 1850. Later he erected many other iron buildings including Public Ledger Building in Philadelphia, Birch Building in Chicago, Baltimore *Sun* offices.

BOGART, JOHN (*b. Albany, N.Y., 1836; d. 1920*), engineer. Graduated Rutgers, 1853. Worked for New York Central Railroad, served as engineer in Civil War. Showing great versatility, he was best known for work in park planning and improvement in New York and other cities, and for work on hydro-electric development in United States and Canada. He had great influence in decision as to system adopted at Niagara and was chief engineer of 60,000 horsepower plant project in Tennessee River near Chattanooga. Also prepared plans for first subway system in New York and for tunnels under the Hudson to Jersey City and Hoboken.

BOGGS, CHARLES STUART (*b. New Brunswick, N.J., 1811; d. 1888*), naval officer. Served conspicuously in Mexican and Civil Wars; commanded *Varuna*, first vessel to pass Confederate guns below New Orleans, 1862. Became rear admiral, 1870.

BOGGS, LILLBURN W. (*b. Lexington, Ky., 1792; d. Napa Valley, Calif., 1860*), storekeeper, merchant. Removed to St. Louis, Mo., 1816. Democratic governor of Missouri, 1836–40. Removed to California, 1846, where he served as *alcalde* of northern part until start of state government.

BOGUE, VIRGIL GAY (*b. Norfolk, N.Y., 1846; d. at sea, 1916*), civil engineer. Worked chiefly with railroads, first in South America, later for various railways in West; expert on railroad economics.

BOGY, LEWIS VITAL (*b. Sainte Genevieve, Mo., 1813; d. 1877*), lawyer. Leader in reconstruction of Democratic party in Missouri after Civil War; U.S. senator, 1872–77.

BOHM, MAX (*b. Cleveland, O., 1861; d. Provincetown, Mass., 1923*), painter. Studied at Cleveland Art School and in Paris. His early marines and later subject pieces were essentially romantic and idealistic.

BOHUNE, LAWRENCE (*d. West Indies, 1621*), first physician general of London Co. in Virginia, appointed 1620. Transported 300 colonists.

BOIES, HENRY MARTYN (*b. Lee, Mass., 1837; d. 1903*), capitalist. President of powder manufacturing firm in Scranton, Pa.; later of Dickson Manufacturing Co., which gained international position in manufacture of engines, machinery.

BOIES, HORACE (*b. Erie Co., N.Y., 1827; d. 1923*), lawyer. Settled in Waterloo, Iowa, 1867. Democratic governor of Iowa, 1889–93.

BOISE, REUBEN PATRICK (*b. Blandford, Mass., 1819; d. 1907*), jurist. Removed to Portland, Oreg., 1850. Active in formulating Oregon's constitution, 1857; judge, Oregon supreme and district courts.

BOISSEVAIN, INEZ MILHOLLAND (*b. New York, N.Y., 1886; d. 1916*), reformer. Graduated Vassar, 1909. Worked for women's rights in fields of education, working conditions, suffrage. Active in National Woman's Party campaign, 1916.

BOK, EDWARD WILLIAM (*b. den Helder, Netherlands, 1863; d. Lake Wales, Fla., 1930*), editor, author, philanthropist, peace advocate. Emigrated to New York, 1870; until 1889 tried his hand at stenography, the stock market, editorial work, advertising, and supplying his own newspaper syndicate with a "woman's page." Became editor of the *Ladies' Home Journal*, 1889. His innovations not only outsold its competitors but effected many reforms including passage of conservation laws and the Food and Drug Acts of 1906. Author of 1921 Pulitzer prize autobiography, *The Americanization of Edward Bok* (1920). A generous and civic-minded benefactor of the arts and education. [*Supp.* 1]

BOKER, GEORGE HENRY (*b. Philadelphia, Pa., 1823; d. Philadelphia, 1890*), poet, playwright, diplomat. Graduated College of New Jersey (Princeton),

1842. His blank verse tragedy *Calaynos* (1848) was produced first in London, 1849, and not until 1851 in Philadelphia. After writing five more plays, several of which were produced, he brought out his dramatic masterpiece, *Francesca da Rimini* (produced New York, 1855; revived 1882, 1901), but grew dissatisfied with what he considered lack of recognition. He published his lyric poems, notably his sonnets, together with his verse plays in *Plays and Poems* (1856). During the Civil War, in addition to writing and publishing *Poems of the War* (1864) he was active in founding and managing the Union League in Philadelphia, first in the country; after the war he continued to publish poetry and to give effective, quiet encouragement to other writers, particularly to William G. Simms and Paul H. Hayne. His diplomatic service was as minister to Turkey, 1871–75, and to Russia, 1875–78.

BOLDT, GEORGE C. (*b. Island of Rugen, 1851; d. 1916*), hotelman. Came to America, 1864. Projected and managed New York's Waldorf-Astoria hotel and Philadelphia's Bellevue-Stratford. Raised standards of American hotel-keeping.

BOLL, JACOB (*b. Bremgarten, Switzerland, 1828; d. Texas, 1880*), geologist, naturalist. Collected and worked in Texas *post* 1869; discovered many new fossil species.

BOLLAN, WILLIAM (*b. England, c. 1710; d. c. 1782*), lawyer. Colonial agent of Massachusetts, 1745–62.

BOLLER, ALFRED PANCOAST (*b. Philadelphia, Pa., 1840; d. 1912*), civil engineer. Graduated Rensselaer Polytechnic, 1861. Expert on foundations and bridges, particularly draw-spans.

BOLLES, FRANK (*b. Winchester, Mass., 1856; d. 1894*), nature writer. Secretary of Harvard University, 1887–94; built his office into one of wide influence. Founded Harvard Coöperative Society.

BOLLMAN, JUSTUS ERICH (*b. Hoya, Hanover, 1769; d. Jamaica, 1821*), physician. Aided in escape of Lafayette from Olmütz; came to America, 1796. As agent of Aaron Burr, delivered Burr's cipher letter to Gen. Wilkinson, 1806. Refused pardon offered if he gave testimony on Burr's plans.

BOLTON, HENRY CARRINGTON (*b. New York, N.Y., 1843; d. Washington, D.C., 1903*), chemist, bibliographer of chemistry.

BOLTON, SARAH KNOWLES (*b. Farmington, Conn., 1841; d. 1916*), author, reformer. Active in temperance movement; interested also in education for women.

BOLTON, SARAH TITTLE BARRETT (*b. Newport, Ky., 1814; d. 1893*), poet. Author of the popular "Paddle Your Own Canoe."

BOLTWOOD, BERTRAM BORDEN (*b. Amherst, Mass., 1870; d. Maine, 1927*), chemist, physicist. Graduated Yale, 1892. Studied in Munich and Leipzig, then taught at Yale; received Ph.D. there, 1897. Professor of radio-chemistry, Yale, 1910–27. Devoted much time to building of Sloane Physics Laboratory, later to construction of Sterling Chemical Laboratory. Made many basic contributions to knowledge of radioactivity, including the proof that radium is a disintegration product of uranium; the discovery of ionium; the experimental work on which the science of isotopy is based; and a method of calculating age of uranium minerals, used in geology. Also did first investigation in this country of radioactivity of natural waters.

BOLTZIUS, JOHANN MARTIN (*b. Germany, 1703; d. 1765*), Lutheran clergyman. Came to America, 1734, as pastor of Salzburger emigrants; helped establish and was spiritual and business leader of colony at Ebenezer, Ga., 1734–65.

BOMBERGER, JOHN HENRY AUGUSTUS (*b. Lancaster, Pa., 1817; d. 1890*), German Reformed clergyman. A founder and first president (1869–90) of Ursinus College.

BOMFORD, GEORGE (*b. New York, N.Y., 1782; d. Boston, Mass., 1848*), soldier. Greatest ordnance expert of his time; chief of U.S. army ordnance, *post* 1832. Invented Columbiad howitzer.

BONAPARTE, CHARLES JOSEPH (*b. Baltimore, Md., 1851; d. near Baltimore, 1921*), lawyer, municipal and civil service reformer. Grandson of Jerome Bonaparte and Elizabeth P. Bonaparte. Graduated Harvard, 1872; Harvard Law School, 1874. Practicing in Baltimore, he helped found Baltimore Reform League and National Civil Service Reform League; interest in civil service reform brought him in contact with Theodore Roosevelt. He served as U.S. secretary of the navy, 1905–06, and as attorney-general, 1906–09; strongly anti-trust, his most notable achievement was dissolution of the American Tobacco Co.

BONAPARTE, ELIZABETH PATTERSON (*b. Baltimore, Md., 1785; d. Baltimore, 1879*), wife of Jerome Bonaparte, brother of Emperor Napoleon I; married in Baltimore, 1803. Napoleon refused to recognize the marriage. Jerome returned to France in 1805 to negotiate a reconciliation but was unsuccessful and the marriage was declared null by French council of state. Elizabeth received 60,000 francs annually on condition she stay in America, renounce Bonaparte name. She later secured an American divorce and went to Europe where she received much attention in society. Her son's legitimacy was recognized by Napoleon III, but right to succession disallowed.

BONAPARTE, JEROME NAPOLEON (*b. Baltimore, Md., 1830; d. Pride's Crossing, Mass., 1893*), soldier. Grandson of Jerome Bonaparte and Elizabeth P. Bonaparte. Graduated West Point, 1852; resigned from U.S. Army and served with French Army from Crimean War until 1870.

BONARD, LOUIS (*b. Rouen, France, 1809; d. New York, N.Y., 1871*), businessman, inventor. Left all his property to American Society for Prevention of Cruelty to Animals.

BOND, ELIZABETH POWELL (*b. Dutchess Co., N.Y., 1841; d. 1926*), educator, author. Dean of Swarthmore College, 1890–1906.

BOND, GEORGE PHILLIPS (*b. Dorchester, Mass., 1825; d. 1865*), astronomer. Son of William C. Bond. Director, Harvard College Observatory, 1859–65. Credited with discovery of Hyperion; founder of photographic astronomy.

BOND, HUGH LENNOX (*b. Baltimore, Md., 1828; d. 1893*), jurist. Maryland criminal court judge, 1860–67; judge of fourth U.S. circuit court, 1870–93. Broke Ku Klux reign of terror in South Carolina; gave decision which made Hayes president.

BOND, SHADRACH (*b. Baltimore Co., Md., c. 1773; d. Kaskaskia, Ill., 1832*). Held several offices in Illinois territory; first delegate to Congress, 1812–14; first governor of state of Illinois, 1818–22.

BOND, THOMAS (*b. Calvert Co., Md., 1712; d. 1784*), physician. Studied first with Dr. Alexander Hamilton in Annapolis, completed medical education in Europe. Began practicing in Philadelphia about 1734. Interested in hygiene and epidemiology, he was also a skilled surgeon and a leader in founding the Pennsylvania Hospital. Conceived of by Bond, promoted by Benjamin Franklin, the hospital opened in 1752, Bond and others giving services free. Bond there began (1766) first course of clinical lectures given in United States.

BOND, WILLIAM CRANCH (*b. Falmouth, Maine, 1789; d. 1859*), clockmaker, instrument-maker, astronomer. Gathered data in Europe for proposed Harvard College Observatory; its first director, 1839–59.

BONER, JOHN HENRY (*b. Salem, N.C., 1845; d. Washington, D.C., 1903*), editor, poet.

BONFILS, FREDERICK GILMER (*b. Lincoln Co., Mo., 1860; d. Denver, Colo., 1933*) and **HARRY HEYE TAMMEN** (*b. Baltimore, Md., 1856; d. Denver, Colo., 1924*), newspaper publishers. Bonfils, having made money operating a lottery in Kansas City, was persuaded to invest $12,500 in the Denver *Evening Post* by Tammen, a former bartender and dabbler in journalism. Naming the paper the *Denver Post*, the partners, by unconventional methods, screaming headlines, attacks on public officials and by support of progressive causes, pushed the week-day circulation to 150,000. The *Post* became hated and feared. Their sensational operations became a

national issue in the Teapot Dome scandal when the *Post's* attacks were associated with a suit against Harry F. Sinclair. [*Supp.* 1]

BONHAM, MILLEDGE LUKE (*b. Red Bank, S.C., 1813; d. 1890*), lawyer, Confederate soldier. Graduated South Carolina College, 1834. Served in Seminole War, and with distinction in Mexican War. Congressman, Democrat, 1857–60; Confederate brigadier; governor of South Carolina, 1862–65.

BONNER, JOHN (*b. ? London, England, c. 1643; d. Boston, Mass., 1725/26*), mariner, map-maker. Came to Boston c. 1670. Shipowner, skilled pilot, shipbuilder. Published a celebrated map of Boston (1722).

BONNER, ROBERT (*b. near Londonderry, Ireland, 1824; d. 1899*), newspaper editor, turfman. Came to America, 1839; learned printing trade. Published *New York Ledger, post* 1851, which by advertising and lavish spending for "family" fiction reached almost half-million circulation.

BONNEVILLE, BENJAMIN LOUIS EULALIE DE (*b. near Paris, France, 1796; d. Fort Smith, Ark., 1878*), soldier. Came to America as a child. Graduated West Point, 1815; served in various capacities until 1866. He is remembered for his fur-hunting expedition of 1832–35, a controversial episode in which Washington Irving was his partisan.

BONNEY, CHARLES CARROLL (*b. Hamilton, N.Y., 1831; d. Chicago, Ill., 1903*), lawyer, educationist, reformer. Advocated international court of justice, legal and constitutional reforms. Prominent in planning 1893 World's Fair congresses.

BONNEY, WILLIAM H. (*1859–1881*). [See BILLY THE KID.]

BONSTELLE, JESSIE (*b. Greece, N.Y., 1872; d. 1932*), actress, producer, stock company manager. Leader in the community theatre movement; discovered many well-known players. [*Supp.* 1]

BONWILL, WILLIAM GIBSON ARLINGTON (*b. Camden, Del., 1833; d. 1899*), dentist. Inventor of electro-magnetic mallet (patented 1873), the automatic engine-mallet and many other dental instruments and processes. He was the first to devise an anatomical articulator.

BONZANO, ADOLPHUS (*b. Ehingen, Germany, 1830; d. 1913*), engineer, inventor. Came to America, 1850. A leader in American bridge construction, 1865–98. Chief among his many inventions is the rail joint which bears his name.

BOONE, DANIEL (*b. near Reading, Pa., 1734; d. Missouri, 1820*), pioneer, Indian fighter. Of Quaker stock; became a hunter of game and furs at twelve years of age. Started off with his family for North Carolina, 1750; spent about a year in Shenandoah valley before settling at Buffalo Lick on north fork of the Yadkin, 1751. Daniel accompanied a North Carolina contingent as a teamster in Braddock's campaign, 1755, thereby meeting John Finley, a hunter, who told him stories of the Kentucky wilderness. Returning to his father's farm, he married Rebeccah Bryan, 1756. In 1765, after visiting Florida, he proposed to settle in Pensacola; his wife objected to the plan and Boone gave it up.

Still interested in Kentucky, he journeyed to a point in present Floyd Co., 1767, returning home in the spring of 1768. With Finley and several others he went westward again in 1769, traversed Cumberland Gap and set up a camp at Station Camp Creek; he returned home, 1771. As agent for Col. Richard Henderson of the Transylvania Co., he led out the first division of settlers to Kentucky in March, 1775. In April he reached the place which was to become Boonesborough and began erection of a fort. That fall, he journeyed back to North Carolina and returned with his own family and twenty recruits for the settlement.

Hunting, surveying and Indian fighting occupied him for the next two years. Captured by the Shawnees, 1778, he escaped and in September of that year helped in the defense of Boonesborough. After a trip east, he returned in October 1779, with a new party of settlers. The repudiation of Henderson's land titles by Virginia sent him east again in the spring of 1780 with $20,000 collected from settlers for purchase of land warrants; on the way he was robbed of the entire amount, and on his return moved to Boone's Station. He was made lieutenant-colonel of Fayette Co. when Kentucky was divided into three counties; later he served in other offices and in the legislature. Although he had taken up many tracts of land, all had been improperly entered; in 1785, the first of a series of ejectment suits by which he was to lose all his holdings was begun. In 1786, he moved to Maysville.

Boone left Kentucky in the fall of 1788 for Point Pleasant, at the mouth of the Great Kanawha in what is now West Virginia. He was appointed lieutenant-colonel of Kanawha Co., 1789, and in 1791 was chosen its legislative delegate. Some time in 1798 or 1799, deprived of his last Kentucky holding, he moved to what is now Missouri, obtaining a grant of land at the mouth of Femme Osage Creek. He was appointed magistrate of this district, 1800, holding the post until the territory was ceded to the United States, 1804. Once again his land title was voided by the U.S. land commissioners, but was confirmed by Congress after many delays in February 1814. His wife died, 1813; his remaining years were spent mostly at the home of his son Nathan, where he died.

Modern criticism has dealt harshly with the Boone legend. He first came into general notice through his so-called autobiography in John Filson, *The Discovery, Settlement, and Present State of Kentucke*

(1784), which was known in Europe through its reprinting in later editions of Gilbert Imlay's *Topographical Description of the Western Territory of North America*. The stanzas devoted to Boone in the eighth canto of Byron's *Don Juan* gave him world-wide celebrity and he gradually became the one, overshadowing, frontier heroic figure. He was acclaimed as the discoverer of Kentucky, its first explorer, its first settler, even "the First White Man of the West," although none of these distinctions were his by right. His true titles to fame were in his character; he had the frontier virtues of courage, endurance, a mastery of woodcraft and expertness with a rifle. Although almost illiterate, he had strong native intelligence; his counsel was eagerly sought. Modest, loyal and honest, he never harbored resentment, even when wronged.

BOORMAN, JAMES (*b. Kent, England, 1783; d. 1866*), New York merchant. Came to America, 1795. Originator of Hudson River Railroad; a founder of Bank of Commerce.

BOOTH, AGNES (*b. Sydney, Australia, 1846; d. 1910*), actress. Born Marian Agnes Rookes. Wife of Junius Brutus Booth the younger.

BOOTH, BALLINGTON (*b. Brighouse, England, 1857; d. Blue Point, N.Y., 1940*). Founder, 1896, of Volunteers of America, a religious and social-welfare organization. Son of William Booth, who founded the Salvation Army. [*Supp. 2*]

BOOTH, EDWIN THOMAS (*b. near Bel Air, Md., 1833; d. New York, N.Y., 1893*), actor. Son of Junius Brutus Booth. At an early age began to accompany his talented, erratic father on theatrical tours. Made debut in a minor role in *Richard III*, Boston, 1849. Played occasional juvenile parts in support of father but had no success in longer roles. Between 1852 and 1856, trouped with varying success in California, Australia, Hawaii; first took public's fancy as stock-company leading man in Sacramento, 1856. Now an accomplished actor, his style modeled on his father's and the tradition of Edmund Kean, but with a sustained power and intellectual quality which were all his own, he went East, played in Baltimore and the South, and made triumphant appearances in Boston and New York, 1857, rising almost at once to the top of his profession. He married Mary Devlin, an actress, 1860. After engagements in London, Liverpool and Manchester, he was seen at the New York Winter Garden, 1862–63, retiring temporarily from the stage when his wife died in February 1863. He then undertook management of the Winter Garden, also purchasing a theatre in Philadelphia with John S. Clarke. In 1864–65 he played *Hamlet* for a famous run of a hundred nights in New York. After his brother John Wilkes Booth assassinated President Lincoln, he went into brief retirement although he had been entirely loyal to the

Union. When he returned to the stage in 1866 his audience showed itself equally loyal to him. Managing the Winter Garden, he put on a series of the most lavishly staged performances in America, terminated by a disastrous fire, March 1867, which destroyed scenery, costumes and library. Almost immediately he started plans for Booth's Theatre, which opened February 1869. The seasons of 1869–74 at the new theatre marked an epoch in the history of the American stage. Booth performed in Shakespearean and other roles supported by many leading stars of the day. The theatre failed financially during the panic of 1873–74 and Booth went into bankruptcy. He carried on gallantly for almost twenty years, touring with great success in America, in the British Isles and on the continent. He remained to the end one of the greatest actors of his time, in spite of gradually declining powers. His last performance was in *Hamlet* at Brooklyn, N.Y., 1891.

BOOTH, JAMES CURTIS (*b. Philadelphia, Pa., 1810; d. 1888*), chemist. An outstanding teacher and expert in analysis. Melter and refiner at Philadelphia mint, 1849–88.

BOOTH, JOHN WILKES (*b. near Bel Air, Md., 1838; d. 1865*), actor, assassin of President Lincoln. Son of Junius Brutus Booth; brother of Edwin Booth. Made his début at St. Charles Theatre, Baltimore, 1855. Acted in Philadelphia, 1857–58; played leading Shakespearean roles in a Richmond stock company, 1859; later toured with notable success in South, Southwest and North. His acting was marked more by inspiration and daring innovation than by finish. His charm and handsome appearance also gained him popularity. In 1863 illness brought temporary retirement from the stage, although he gave two notable performances in 1864–65. Unlike the rest of his family, he sympathized with the South, regarding slavery as a God-given blessing and becoming gradually more fanatical in his views. In 1859 he had been a member of a Virginia militia company which took part in the arrest and execution of John Brown. As early as the fall of 1864 he formed a plan to abduct Lincoln, hoping to end the war or at least secure an exchange of Southern prisoners; to this end, he gathered a band of associates which included Samuel Arnold, Michael O'Laughlin, John H. Surratt, David Herold, George Atzerodt and Lewis Powell (Payne). He and his accomplices lay in wait for Lincoln on the outskirts of Washington, March 20, 1865, but the president failed to appear. Soon afterward Richmond was captured, Lee surrendered, and the plot came to naught.

It was probably after Lincoln's speech on April 11, advocating limited Negro suffrage, that Booth decided upon assassination. The details were not arranged until April 14, when Booth learned that Lincoln was to attend Laura Keene's performance of *Our Amer-*

ican Cousin at Ford's Theatre that night. Atzerodt, deputed to murder Vice-president Andrew Johnson, did nothing, but Payne seriously wounded Secretary of State W. H. Seward. Booth, after shooting Lincoln, fell as he leaped from the theatre box to the stage and broke his leg, but managed to flee on his horse. Herold, who had accompanied Payne, joined Booth in Maryland. The two went to the home of Dr. Samuel Mudd, who set Booth's leg. Thus delayed, they hid in the woods nearly a week before they could cross the Potomac to Virginia. Then they proceeded to the house of Richard H. Garrett, in whose barn they were apprehended on April 26. It has never been established whether Booth shot himself or was killed by Boston Corbett, a fanatical soldier who disobeyed orders and fired. Although it was quite certain from his behavior and from the objects found on the body that the man thus slain was indeed Booth, and although the body was identified by several persons including a doctor and a dentist, a legend arose that Booth escaped alive. He was reported seen in many places in America and abroad. Booth's various accomplices were tried before a military commission in one of the most irregular trials in history; all received severe sentences.

BOOTH, JUNIUS BRUTUS (*b. London, England, 1796; d. en route to Cincinnati, O., 1852*), actor. Brilliant, erratic father of John W. and Edwin Booth. Came to America, 1821. Foremost tragedian of his day in America.

BOOTH, MARY LOUISE (*b. Yaphank, N.Y., 1831; d. 1889*), author, translator. Edited *Harper's Bazar*, 1867–89. Author of *History of the City of New York* (1859) and other works.

BOOTH, NEWTON (*b. Salem, Ind., 1825; d. Sacramento, Calif., 1892*), lawyer, merchant, Republican governor of California, 1871–75. As U.S. senator, 1875–81, was active for adoption of the silver certificate, settlement of land titles.

BOOTH-TUCKER, EMMA MOSS (*b. Gateshead, England, 1860; d. near Dean Lake, Mo., 1903*), Consul of Salvation Army. Worked in India; in America, 1896–1903.

BOOTT, KIRK (*b. Boston, Mass., 1790; d. Lowell, Mass., 1837*), manufacturer. Active in establishment of mill village which became Lowell. A pioneer of industrial feudalism, his management of Lowell determined character of many American industrial communities.

BORAH, WILLIAM EDGAR (*b. Jasper Township, Ill., 1865; d. Washington, D.C., 1940*), U.S. senator from Idaho. Son of a stern Presbyterian minister who intended him for the ministry, he attended the University of Kansas, 1885–87, was called to the Kansas bar and moved West in 1890 to practice law in Boise, Idaho. Soon active in politics, he became chairman of the Republican State Central Committee in 1892, and ran unsuccessfully for Congress on a Silver Republican ticket in 1896. In 1895 he married Mary O'Connell, daughter of Idaho's governor. Running successfully as a Roosevelt supporter in 1906, he was sent, January 1907, to the U.S. Senate, where he served without interruption until his death. Though he had been a corporation lawyer and had won national prominence as prosecutor of the I.W.W. leader William Dudley Haywood, Borah sponsored bills to create the Department of Labor and the Children's Bureau, led the fight in the Senate for the income tax and uncompromisingly opposed the trusts. A Jeffersonian Democrat in his political philosophy, Borah stressed equality of opportunity; his interest in social reform, however, was tempered by a dislike of federal centralization and a devotion to state rights. He was a political maverick, inconsistent in his voting record. Opposing most of the progressive legislation of the Wilson administration, Borah was the leader of the bitter-end irreconcilables opposing the League of Nations. In favor of international action so long as political decisions and military sanctions were not required, he helped bring about the Washington disarmament conference of 1921 and the (Kellogg-Briand) Pact of Paris. He hoped to achieve world peace by extending the rule of law, and favored an international court with compulsory jurisdiction but no sanctions other than those of public opinion. As chairman of the Senate Committee on Foreign Relations (from 1924), Borah was the most powerful force in foreign affairs in the country.

Borah enthusiastically supported Herbert Hoover in 1928 but soon resumed his familiar role of the Great Opposer. He felt Hoover was not doing enough to relieve the depression and later supported much New Deal legislation, though not the NRA or the Supreme Court bill. A magnificent orator, a constitutionalist with a concept of society often irrelevant to 20th-century America, Borah had few equals in his ability to rouse the country on public questions and was often mentioned as a possible presidential candidate. [Supp. 2]

BORDEN, GAIL (b. Norwich, N.Y., 1801; d. Borden, Texas, 1874), surveyor, inventor. Raised as farm boy in Kentucky and Indiana, learned surveying from his father. Taught in backwoods schools of Indiana territory, also in Mississippi where he was U.S. deputy surveyor. Farmed and raised stock at Stephen Austin's colony in Texas; superintended official surveys; laid out city of Galveston and was agent for Galveston City Co., 1839-51. Concerned with pioneers' hardships, he began work on idea for preparing concentrated food. After failure with a "meat biscuit," he patented a process for evaporating milk, 1856; during Civil War its use spread rapidly as soldiers introduced it to the civilian population.

BORDEN, LIZZIE ANDREW (b. Fall River, Mass., 1860; d. 1927), alleged murderess in a case widely publicized. [Supp. 1]

BORDEN, RICHARD (b. Freetown, Mass., 1795; d. 1874), manufacturer, executive. Helped form Fall River Iron Works; was treasurer and agent, 1821-74. Prominent also in cotton milling, railroad building, steamship transportation.

BORDEN, SIMEON (b. Fall River, Mass., 1798; d. 1856), skilled mechanic, civil engineer. An outstanding surveyor, he constructed base bar for Massachusetts town survey, 1830, the most accurate instrument of its kind at that time in the United States.

BORDLEY, JOHN BEALE (b. Annapolis, Md., 1727; d. 1804), lawyer, agriculturalist. Farmed on large scale on island at mouth of Wye River, post 1770. Experimented with crop rotation, grew wheat in place of tobacco, also hemp, flax, other products. Brought about formation of Philadelphia Society for Promoting Agriculture, 1785. Results of his farm operations and experiments were published as Essays and Notes on Husbandry and Rural Affairs (1799, 1801).

BORÉ, JEAN ÉTIENNE (b. Louisiana, 1741; d. near New Orleans, La., 1820), sugar planter. Generally credited with having established the sugar industry in Louisiana, 1795.

BOREMAN, ARTHUR INGRAM (b. Waynesburg, Pa., 1823; d. 1896), lawyer. Active in preventing secession of western Virginia. Governor of West Virginia, 1863-68; U.S. senator, Republican, 1869-75.

BORGLUM, SOLON HANNIBAL (b. Ogden, Utah, 1868; d. 1922), sculptor. Brother of Gutzon Borglum. Particularly effective in studies of animals and in depicting American frontier life.

BORIE, ADOLPH EDWARD (b. Philadelphia, Pa., 1809; d. Philadelphia, 1880), merchant, financier.

BORIE, ADOLPHE (b. Philadelphia, Pa., 1877; d. 1934), portrait painter. [Supp. 1]

BORING, WILLIAM ALCIPHRON (b. Carlinville, Ill., 1859; d. New York, N.Y., 1937), architect. First dean, 1931-34, School of Architecture, Columbia University. [Supp. 2]

BORLAND, SOLON (b. near Suffolk, Va., 1808; d. in or near Houston, Texas, 1864), physician, diplomat. U.S. senator from Arkansas, 1848-53; minister to Nicaragua, 1853. Brigadier-general in Confederate Army.

BOSS, LEWIS (b. Providence, R.I., 1846; d. 1912), astronomer. Authority on star positions; published The Preliminary General Catalogue of 6188 Stars for the Epoch 1900 (Carnegie Institution, 1910).

BOSTON, CHARLES ANDERSON (*b. Baltimore, Md., 1863; d. New York, N.Y., 1935*), lawyer and legal scholar. Active in movements for reform of judicial and professional ethics. [*Supp. 1*]

BOSWORTH, EDWARD INCREASE (*b. Elgin, Ill., 1861; d. 1927*), Congregational clergyman, educator. Long associated with Oberlin College and Theological Seminary.

BOSWORTH, FRANCKE HUNTINGTON (*b. Marietta, O., 1843; d. 1925*), laryngologist. Graduated Yale, 1862. After service in Civil War, settled in New York; graduated M.D. from Bellevue Hospital and Medical College, 1868, and taught there *post* 1873. Published *Handbook upon Diseases of the Throat and Nose* (1879) and a celebrated *Manual of the Diseases of the Throat and Nose* (1881). Most extensive work was *A Treatise on Diseases of the Nose and Throat* (1889, 1892). His contributions to the subject, together with those of J. Solis-Cohen and Sir Morrell MacKenzie, may be said to have created science of laryngology; he was also important in developing science of rhinology.

BOTELER, ALEXANDER ROBINSON (*b. Virginia, 1815; d. Shepherdstown, W. Va., 1892*), U.S. and Confederate congressman. Served as aide on staffs of T. J. Jackson and J. E. B. Stuart.

BOTETOURT, NORBORNE BERKELEY, Baron de (*b. England, c. 1718; d. Williamsburg, Va., 1770*), colonial governor of Virginia, 1768–70. Able, well-intentioned, he was powerless to halt the drift toward rebellion.

BOTSFORD, GEORGE WILLIS (*b. West Union, Iowa, 1862; d. New York, N.Y., 1917*), historian. Taught ancient history at Harvard, and at Columbia University, 1902–17.

BOTTA, ANNE CHARLOTTE LYNCH (*b. Bennington, Vt., 1815; d. New York, N.Y., 1891*), educator, author. Presided at her New York home, *post* 1845, over first important salon in history of American letters; friend of Poe, Greeley, Margaret Fuller and many others.

BOTTA, VINCENZO (*b. Cavallermaggiore, Italy, 1818; d. New York, N.Y., 1894*), scholar. Husband of Anne C. L. Botta. Came to America, 1853. Taught Italian at New York University; author of a study on Dante and other works.

BOTTINEAU, PIERRE (*b. Minnesota, c. 1817; d. 1895*), Chippewa half-breed, called "Kit Carson of the Northwest." Guide to many expeditions, 1850–70, including I. I. Stevens's railroad survey, 1853, the Fisk expedition, 1862, and Gen. Sibley's Sioux campaign, 1863.

BOTTOME, MARGARET McDONALD (*b. New York, N.Y., 1827; d. 1906*), writer. Organizer (1886) of International Order of the King's Daughters and Sons.

BOTTS, CHARLES TYLER (*b. Virginia, 1809; d. Oakland, Calif., 1884*), lawyer, editor. Brother of John M. Botts. Established popular agricultural journal, the *Southern Planter,* 1841. Removed to California, 1848.

BOTTS, JOHN MINOR (*b. Dumfries, Va., 1802; d. 1869*), lawyer, author. Virginia legislator, Whig, 1833–39; congressman, 1839–43, 1847–49. Vocal and aggressive foe of the Democrats, he opposed annexation of Texas, the Mexican War and President Tyler's bank and tariff vetoes. Played vital part in passage of 1850 Compromise. Convinced that Democrats were engaged in a conspiracy to provoke secession by any means, he struggled to hold Virginia in Union. At outbreak of Civil War, he withdrew to his farm near Richmond; imprisoned by Confederates, 1862, he later settled in Culpeper Co. He led conservative wing of Virginia Unionists *post* 1865, but accepted radical position and lost influence.

BOUCHER, HORACE EDWARD (*b. Italy, 1873; d. 1935*), ship modeler and naval architect. [*Supp. 1*]

BOUCHER, JONATHAN (*b. Blencogo, England, 1737/8; d. England, 1804*), Loyalist, Anglican clergyman. Tutor, schoolmaster and rector in Virginia and Maryland, 1759–75; preached against colonial resistance. Author of *A View of the Causes and Consequences of the American Revolution* (1797).

BOUCICAULT, DION (*b. Dublin, Ireland, 1820; d. New York, N.Y., 1890*), dramatist, actor. Acted in provincial theatres in England, and in London; wrote and adapted many plays for English stage, including the well-known *London Assurance* (produced 1841). Came to America, 1853. Toured as actor; wrote topical melodramas; opened theatre in Washington, 1858; directed New York's Winter Garden, 1859. In this same year he wrote *The Octoroon,* a play about slavery which was a great success; in 1860, his *The Colleen Bawn* was first of a long series of Irish dramas, including *Arrah-na-Pogue* (1864) and *The Shaughraun* (1874). In London 1862–72, he then returned to America. Boucicault wrote or adapted in all 132 plays. He inaugurated the "long run" system, and did much to keep American drama lively in the mid-19th century.

BOUCK, WILLIAM C. (*b. Schoharie Co., N.Y., 1786; d. Schoharie Co., 1859*), farmer, politician. New York canal commissioner, 1821–40; superintended part of Erie Canal construction. Democratic governor of New York, 1843–44.

BOUDINOT, ELIAS (*b. Philadelphia, Pa., 1740; d. Burlington, N.J., 1821*), lawyer, Revolutionary statesman. Close associate of Washington. Commissary-general of prisoners; member of Continental Congress, 1777–84, and president of Congress, 1782; secretary of foreign affairs, 1783–84. Federalist congressman from New Jersey, 1789–95. Director of U.S. Mint, 1795–1805.

BOUDINOT, ELIAS (*b. Georgia, c. 1803; d. Indian Territory, 1839*), Indian editor. Edited *Cherokee Phoenix*, 1824–35. Murdered for his part in agreeing to removal of Cherokees to West.

BOUDINOT, ELIAS CORNELIUS (*b. near present Rome, Ga., 1835; d. Indian Territory, 1890*), lawyer. Son of Elias Boudinot (1803–1839). Cherokee delegate from Indian Territory to Confederate Congress. After Civil War, helped restore peaceful relations between Cherokees and United States.

BOULIGNY, DOMINIQUE (*b. New Orleans, La., c. 1771; d. New Orleans, 1833*), legislator. Prominent in Louisiana politics in early 19th century. U.S. senator from Louisiana, 1824–29.

BOUNETHEAU, HENRY BRINTNELL (*b. Charleston, S.C., 1797; d. Charleston, 1877*), miniature painter. Primarily a businessman; worked in manner of Charles Fraser.

BOUQUET, HENRY (*b. Rolle, Switzerland, 1719; d. Pensacola, Fla., 1765*), soldier. Entered service of Holland as cadet, 1736; rose to lieutenant-colonel. Accepted lieutenant-colonelcy of first battalion, Royal American Regiment of British army, 1755; went to America 1756. Promoted colonel, 1758, he served as second under Gen. John Forbes in expedition against Fort Duquesne. Gaining much experience along frontier, he adapted discipline of European armies to exigencies of wilderness warfare and was far in advance of military practice of the day. In Pontiac's conspiracy he proved worth of his methods at Edgehill and Bushy Run, 1763. In 1764 he brought about surrender of all prisoners in Indian hands and concluded a general peace.

BOUQUILLON, THOMAS JOSEPH (*b. Warneton, Belgium, 1840; d. Brussels, Belgium, 1902*), Roman Catholic clergyman, theologian. Studied at Menin, Roulers, Bruges, Gregorian University at Rome. Ordained, Rome, 1865; D.D., 1867. Professor of moral theology, Bruges, 1867–77; professor of theology, University of Lille, 1877–85. Accepted chair of moral theology at new Catholic University, Washington, D.C., 1889; taught there until his death. Bouquillon's chief contribution to Catholic thought lay in his effort to restore to moral theology the scientific and historical prestige with which St. Thomas and other early thinkers had invested it; his major work on this subject is *Theologia Moralis Fundamentalis* (3rd edition, Bruges, 1903). Influential in development of Catholic University, he was also active in Catholic controversy on education, 1891–92.

BOURGMONT, ÉTIENNE VENYARD, Sieur de (*b. France, c. 1680; d. c. 1730*), French adventurer. Explored extensively up Missouri River *ante* 1717; built Fort Orléans, 1723. Undertook expedition, 1724,

penetrating to western border of what became Kansas.

BOURKE, JOHN GREGORY (*b. Philadelphia, Pa., 1846; d. 1896*), soldier, ethnologist. Served in Civil War; graduated West Point, 1869, and was assigned to frontier duty with 3rd Cavalry. Author of valuable first-hand studies of plains and Southwest Indian tribes.

BOURNE, BENJAMIN (*b. Bristol, R.I., 1755; d. 1808*), Revolutionary soldier, jurist. Active for ratification of Constitution in Rhode Island; served in first four U.S. congresses; judge, U.S. district court in Rhode Island, *post* 1801.

BOURNE, EDWARD GAYLORD (*b. Strykersville, N.Y., 1860; d. New Haven, Conn., 1908*), historian. Graduated Yale, 1883; Ph.D., 1892. Professor of history at Yale, *post* 1895. Author of *Essays in Historical Criticism* (1901), *Spain in America* (1904) and other works.

BOURNE, GEORGE (*b. Westbury, England, 1780; d. New York, N.Y., 1845*), Presbyterian and Dutch Reformed clergyman, abolitionist, journalist. Fanatical opponent of slavery, woman's rights and the Catholic Church. Author of *Lorette* (1834) and other works.

BOURNE, JONATHAN (*b. New Bedford, Mass., 1855; d. Washington, D.C., 1940*), U.S. senator, Republican, from Oregon, 1906–12. The first senator to be elected by direct primary. [*Supp. 2*]

BOURNE, NEHEMIAH (*b. London, England, c. 1611; d. England, 1691*), ship builder, British rear admiral. Built ships in Boston, 1638–c.1642, including Gov. Winthrop's *Trial*, first vessel of any size laid down at Boston. Prominent in the navy of the Commonwealth, 1650–60.

BOURNE, RANDOLPH SILLIMAN (*b. Bloomfield, N.J., 1886; d. New York, N.Y., 1918*), essayist. Graduated Columbia, 1913. Author of *Youth and Life* (1913); *The Gary Schools* (1916); *Education and Living* (1917); and *The History of a Literary Radical* (1920).

BOUTELL, HENRY SHERMAN (*b. Boston, Mass., 1856; d. San Remo, Italy, 1926*), lawyer, diplomat. Prominent Chicago attorney; congressman, Republican, from Illinois, 1897–1911; envoy to Switzerland, 1911–13. Taught international and constitutional law at Georgetown University, 1914–23.

BOUTELLE, CHARLES ADDISON (*b. Damariscotta, Maine, 1839; d. 1901*), journalist. Served in U.S. navy in Civil War. Editor, *Whig and Courier*, Bangor, Maine, *post* 1870; congressman, Republican, from Maine, 1882–1901. Championed modern strong navy.

BOUTON, JOHN BELL (*b. Concord, N.H., 1830; d. 1902*), author. Son of Nathaniel Bouton. Editor,

Cleveland Plain-Dealer, 1851–57; later with *Journal of Commerce, Appleton's Annual Cyclopedia.*

BOUTON, NATHANIEL (*b. Norwalk, Conn., 1799; d. Concord, N.H., 1878*), Congregational clergyman. State historian of New Hampshire, whose documentary history he edited and published, 1867–77.

BOUTWELL, GEORGE SEWALL (*b. Brookline, Mass., 1818, d. 1905*), politician, lawyer. Free-soil and Democratic governor of Massachusetts, 1851–52; an organizer of Republican party in that state. Congressman, radical Republican, 1863–69; a leader in movement to impeach President Johnson. Secretary of treasury, 1869–73; U.S. senator from Massachusetts, 1873–77.

BOUVET, MARIE MARGUERITE (*b. New Orleans, La., 1865; d. Reading, Pa., 1915*), linguist, writer of books for young people.

BOUVIER, JOHN (*b. Condognan, France, 1787; d. 1851*), judge, legal writer. Came to America, *c.* 1801. Practiced in Philadelphia *post* 1823. Author of a celebrated *Law Dictionary* (first edition, 1839).

BOWDEN, JOHN (*b. Ireland, 1751; d. Ballston Spa, N.Y., 1817*), Anglican clergyman. Studied at Princeton; graduated King's College (Columbia), N.Y., 1772; ordained 1774. Held rectorates in Connecticut; first principal of Episcopal Academy at Cheshire, 1796–1802. Professor of philosophy, logic, at Columbia, 1802–17.

BOWDITCH, CHARLES PICKERING (*b. 1842; d. 1921*), archaeologist. Graduated Harvard, 1863. Grandson of Nathaniel Bowditch. Scholar of Maya hieroglyphics, published *Numeration, Calendar Systems and Astronomical Knowledge of the Mayas* (1910). Harvard's Peabody Museum received his collections and valuable library.

BOWDITCH, HENRY INGERSOLL (*b. Salem, Mass., 1808; d. 1892*), physician, abolitionist. Son of Nathaniel Bowditch. Graduated Harvard, 1828; M.D., Harvard Medical School, 1832. After two years' study in Paris, returned to Boston to practice. Became follower of W. L. Garrison, assisted runaway slaves, actively fostered anti-slavery cause in North. Associated with Massachusetts General Hospital, 1838–92; professor, Harvard Medical School, 1859–67. Contributions to medicine include studies of tuberculosis, popularizing of procedure for removal of pleural effusions, and, most important, his influence in stimulating public health movement in Massachusetts and the nation. Published *Public Hygiene in America* (1877).

BOWDITCH, HENRY PICKERING (*b. Boston, Mass., 1840; d. 1911*), physiologist. Grandson of Nathaniel Bowditch. Graduated Harvard, 1861; served in Civil War; studied comparative anatomy at Lawrence Scientific School; M.D., Harvard Medical School, 1868. Studied in Paris, and at Leipzig under Carl Ludwig, 1869–71. Established at Harvard Medical School, 1871, first physiological laboratory in United States, remaining there as professor until retirement, 1906, and serving as Dean, Medical School, 1883–93. Versatile, inventive, he also did important studies of growth rates in school children. Foremost American physiologist after Beaumont, Bowditch made findings which are classical on the *Treppe* or "All or None" principle of cardiac muscle behavior (Leipzig, 1871), and on the indefatigability of nerve fiber (1885).

BOWDITCH, NATHANIEL (*b. Salem, Mass., 1773; d. Boston, Mass., 1838*), astronomer, mathematician. Son of a shipmaster and cooper, he left school to help his father, 1783, became a clerk or apprentice in a ship-chandlery at twelve years of age, and continued there until his first sea voyage, 1795. During these years he read voraciously, and with his retentive memory acquired information on many subjects; he constructed an almanac, studied French and Euclid, learned Latin in order to read Newton. Between 1795 and 1803 he made five voyages, the last as master and supercargo. At the suggestion of a publisher in Newburyport, he checked accuracy of a popular English work, *The Practical Navigator* by J. H. Moore, and made revisions published in an American edition (1799), with his brother William collaborating. More revisions and additions were made, so many that the third edition, printed 1801, was issued in 1802, titled *The New American Practical Navigator.* Ten editions were published in Bowditch's lifetime; many more have appeared since. Bowditch was elected a Fellow of the American Academy of Arts and Sciences, 1799; in 1802 he received an honorary Master of Arts degree from Harvard. Appointed president of the Essex Fire and Marine Insurance Co., 1804, he held office until 1823 when he became actuary of the Massachusetts Hospital Life Insurance Co. in Boston.

Bowditch did most of his scientific work during his years in Salem. In addition to the work already mentioned, he made a chart of the harbors of Salem, Beverly and Manchester (published 1806, second edition, 1834), and also proposed and solved a dozen problems in Adrain's *Analyst* (1808, 1814). Far more important, however, were papers published in the American Academy's *Memoirs* (1804–20), and the preparation of the translation, with much of the commentary, of the first four volumes of Laplace's *Mécanique céleste.* This translation was done before 1818, but was not published until 1829–39. So elaborate were the notes, in elucidation and in attempting to bring the subjects up-to-date, that the translated work was more than double the size of the original. It has been described as making "an epoch in American science by bringing the great work of Laplace down to the reach of the best American students of his time." Not a genius or discoverer, but rather an exceptionally able critic, Bowditch accomplished much scientific work and won a prominent place among early American intellectuals even though most of his time was devoted to other affairs.

BOWDOIN, JAMES (*b. Boston, Mass., 1726; d. Boston, 1790*), Revolutionary statesman, merchant. Married, 1748, Elizabeth Erving, daughter of another prosperous Boston merchant. He met serious losses in the Revolutionary period, but remained wealthy because of large holdings in Boston real estate and Maine lands.

Bowdoin's political career began in 1753 with his election to the General Court. Serving three terms in the lower house, he was chosen a member of the Council, 1757. This body had generally favored the British viewpoint; Bowdoin's influence was important in aligning it with colonial interests. He stressed particularly the economic aspects of the dispute with England. In 1774 Gen. Gage negatived Bowdoin's election to the Council. The General Court elected him delegate to the Continental Congress, but failure of his own health and his wife's forced him to decline. John Hancock took his place. In August 1775 the Provincial Congress appointed him first member of its executive council; he resigned in 1777 for reasons of health. Elected to the state constitutional convention, 1779, he was chosen president of the convention, and chairman of the subcommittee which drafted the instrument. John Adams wrote most of the final document, but Bowdoin exercised much influence.

After Hancock retired as governor, 1785, it was apparent that serious economic and social troubles threatened the new commonwealth of Massachusetts. Bowdoin ran for the office against the candidate of the "popular" interest, Thomas Cushing, and won after the election was thrown into the legislature, which was dominated by commercial and property interests. He was re-elected in 1786. During his administration occurred the crisis of 1786–87 known as "Shays's Rebellion." Although greater statesmanship might have averted insurrection, Bowdoin's handling of the actual crisis was prompt and vigorous, and helped to stabilize both the state and ultimately the new nation by insistence on the paramount importance of law and order. He had previously shown vision in urging increased federal powers to permit control of commerce which he believed essential to economic stabilization, thus taking an early part in the movement for a Federal Constitution. Although Bowdoin's suppression of the insurgent debtors by force was widely approved outside Massachusetts, there his prestige suffered; many citizens believed that needed reforms had been too slow in forthcoming. Bowdoin retired from the governorship in April 1787. His last public service came in January 1788 when he was a delegate to the Massachusetts convention to pass on adoption of the Federal Constitution.

Bowdoin was also interested in science and literature. First president of the American Academy of Arts and Sciences, he was especially interested in physics and astronomy and wrote many papers for the Academy's *Transactions*. His chief memorial, appropriately, is the college named for him which was chartered in Maine four years after his death.

BOWDOIN, JAMES (*b. Boston, Mass., 1752; d. Naushon Island, Mass., 1811*), merchant, diplomat. Son of James Bowdoin (1726–1790). Appointed minister to Spain by Jefferson, he participated (1804–08) in unsuccessful negotiations regarding Florida. Benefactor, Bowdoin College.

BOWEN, ABEL (*b. Greenbush, N.Y., 1790; d. 1850*), wood engraver, publisher. Removed to Boston, Mass., 1811. Designer-engraver of *The Naval Monument* (1816), *Picture of Boston* (1828) and other works.

BOWEN, FRANCIS (*b. Charlestown, Mass., 1811; d. 1890*), philosopher. Graduated Harvard, 1833. Taught philosophy and political economy at Harvard, *post* 1835; editor, *North American Review*, 1843–53. Author of *Modern Philosophy from Descartes to Schopenhauer and Hartmann* (1877) and many other works.

BOWEN, GEORGE (*b. Middlebury, Vt., 1816; d. Bombay, India, 1888*), missionary. Preached in Bombay, 1848–88; *post* 1873 was a Methodist. Edited *Bombay Guardian*, 1854–88.

BOWEN, HENRY CHANDLER (*b. Woodstock, Conn., 1813; d. Brooklyn, N.Y., 1896*), merchant. A founder, and later publisher and proprietor, of Congregationalist *Independent*. Associate of Henry W. Beecher and Theodore Tilton.

BOWEN, HERBERT WOLCOTT (*b. Brooklyn, N.Y., 1856; d. 1927*), lawyer, diplomat. Son of Henry C. Bowen. Graduated Yale, 1878. Consul-general in Spain, Persia; minister to Venezuela in crisis of 1902. Dismissed from diplomatic service, 1905, after difficulties with Theodore Roosevelt.

BOWEN, THOMAS MEADE (*b. near Burlington, Iowa, 1835; d. Pueblo, Colo., 1906*), miner, lawyer, politician. U.S. senator, Republican, from Colorado, 1883–89.

BOWERS, ELIZABETH CROCKER (*b. Ridgefield, Conn., 1830; d. Washington, D. C., 1895*), actress. Played in leading roles in America and England, 1846–94, and in support of Edwin Booth, Lawrence Barrett and many others.

BOWERS, LLOYD WHEATON (*b. Springfield, Mass., 1859; d. 1910*), lawyer. General counsel, Chicago and North Western Railroad; played conspicuous part in litigation over government control of railroads. Effective U.S. solicitor-general, 1909–10.

BOWERS, THEODORE SHELTON (*b. Hummelstown, Pa., 1832; d. Garrison, N.Y., 1866*), Union soldier. Faithful aide to Gen. U.S. Grant, 1862–66.

BOWIE, JAMES (*b. Logan Co., Ky., 1796; d. Texas, 1836*), Texas soldier. Spent most of childhood in Catahoula Parish, La. Little is known of his earliest exploits. About 1828, he went to Texas, settling in San Antonio, acquiring land and becoming a Mexican citizen in 1830. As tension grew between Americans and the Mexican government, Bowie was usually on side of resistance and was a captain in the fight at Nacogdoches, 1832. He played a leading part when hostilities broke out in 1835; as colonel of the revolutionary forces, he was important in campaign which cleared Texas of the Mexican army. When Santa Anna returned in 1836, Bowie was among the Americans who made the famous stand at the Alamo, where all were killed. Bowie was reputedly inventor of the "bowie knife."

BOWIE, ODEN (*b. Prince Georges Co., Md., 1826; d. Prince Georges Co., 1894*), businessman, turf patron. President, Baltimore and Potomac Railroad, 1860–94. Democratic governor of Maryland, 1867–72; *de facto*, 1869–72.

BOWIE, RICHARD JOHNS (*b. Georgetown, D.C., 1807; d. Montgomery Co., Md., 1881*), lawyer, politician. Congressman, Whig, from Maryland, 1849–53. Outstanding chief justice, Maryland court of appeals, 1861–81.

BOWIE, ROBERT (*b. near Nottingham, Md., 1750; d. Nottingham, 1818*), Revolutionary soldier, politician. Democratic-Republican governor of Maryland, 1803–07; 1811–12.

BOWIE, WILLIAM (*b. Anne Arundel Co., Md., 1872; d. Washington, D.C., 1940*), geodesist. Chief, Division of Geodesy, U.S. Coast and Geodetic Survey, 1909–36. [*Supp. 2*]

BOWKER, RICHARD ROGERS (*b. Salem, Mass., 1848; d. Stockbridge, Mass., 1933*), editor, publisher, bibliographer, author, library promoter. Graduated from City College of New York, 1868. Held posts on several New York papers. In 1879, purchased *Publishers' Weekly*, which he edited from 1884 until his death, and took over issuance of the *American Catalog* listing all books in print in the United States. With Leypoldt and Dewey, founded the *Library Journal* and arranged the organization meeting of the American Library Association. He was an able business executive in many fields. An independent Republican, he attacked bossism, drafted the original national civil-service-reform plank, drew up a postal code, and at almost 85 was attracted to the New Deal. [*Supp. 1*]

BOWLER, METCALF (*b. London, England, 1726; d. 1789*), Rhode Island patriot, businessman. Came to America, *c.* 1743. Prospered in trade at Newport, R.I. but was virtually ruined by the Revolution.

BOWLES, SAMUEL (*b. Hartford, Conn., 1797; d. Springfield, Mass., 1851*), printer, newspaper editor. Formed partnership with John Francis, 1819, in publishing *Hartford Times*. This having failed, he moved to Springfield, Mass. 1824, to establish a new weekly there. First issue of *Springfield Republican* appeared Sept. 8, 1824. It grew steadily owing to editorial independence and outstanding local coverage. The daily *Republican* first appeared March 27, 1844. Bowles's chief contribution was in establishing firmly the paper which his son made nationally famous.

BOWLES, SAMUEL (*b. Springfield, Mass., 1826; d. Springfield, 1878*), editor. Son of Samuel Bowles (1797–1851). Joined *Springfield Republican*, 1843, as general helper. Within a year he assumed most of the extra work incident to issue of a daily edition. His health broke down in the winter of 1844–45. After recuperating in Louisiana, he continued his work on the daily with such energy that it was soon established on a permanent basis. In 1848 the paper absorbed the *Springfield Gazette*, and established its supremacy in western Massachusetts. Telegraphic news was rapidly developed; many new features were instituted; pithy and pungent editorials began to displace the longer articles on the editorial page.

In 1851 when his father died the younger Bowles was able to take complete control of the paper. Its political course had not yet developed firmly. In 1848 it stated "Our motto is NO COMPROMISE, NO MORE SLAVE TERRITORY." But it wavered in 1850 and supported Clay's compromise plan. Early in 1851 Bowles announced that the paper was still Whig although the Whig party was clearly on the wane. In the early fifties, still conservative on slavery, the paper attacked the Abolitionists, supported the fugitive slave act, but with the Kansas-Nebraska struggle a new aggressive policy developed. Bowles declared the Kansas-Nebraska bill "a huge stride backward." By 1854 he had repudiated the Whigs. Scorning the pretensions of the Native American party, he kept urging establishment of a new party of freedom. One of the earliest editors to advocate nomination of Frémont, Bowles worked indefatigably for his election. With its espousal of the Republican party, the *Springfield Republican* entered the flood-tide of its success. Its circulation rose rapidly; it was hailed by the *New York Tribune* as "the best and ablest country journal ever published on this continent." Well edited, offering leadership in its editorial views, it had circulation and influence throughout all the free states and territories.

At this time Bowles, although he had previously refused a position on the *New York Tribune* as well as editorship of a projected new daily in Philadelphia, resigned editorship of the *Republican* and assumed that of a new Boston newspaper, the *Traveller*. It was to be Republican, independent, and progressive, and take the lead among Boston papers. Its backers, however, were not united, nor was it as strong financially as it had appeared. Thwarted in all his efforts,

Bowles resigned after four months, returning to the *Republican* in which he had retained controlling ownership. Throughout the pre-Civil War years he increased the power of the paper, primarily through the weekly edition which dealt in national rather than local news. Bowles drove himself and his staff incessantly, producing a paper with high standards both in news and editorials. He denounced the execution of John Brown, supported Lincoln, but did not agree with radicals who urged harsh measures against all rebels. Criticizing Lincoln for wartime infringements on civil rights, he supported his renomination and his reconstruction policies.

The political and financial corruption of the seventies found in Bowles a strong assailant. He denounced James Fisk, provoking a libel suit which was not pressed. He also exposed D. D. Field, the counsel for Fisk, Gould, and Tweed. Shocked by the Crédit Mobilier and other scandals, he joined in the Liberal Republican movement of 1872, working for nomination of Charles Francis Adams. Disappointed at Greeley's nomination, he supported him nevertheless.

Bowles's last twenty years were marked by ill health. The *Republican's* prosperity had made possible an enlarged staff, and he was able to take frequent vacations, but when at work he continued at his usual intense pace. Erratic, impulsive, devoted to the *Republican* above all else, he was at times ruthless, alienating others by his tactless actions. Dissatisfied with the methods of his younger brother, Benjamin Franklin Bowles, long in charge of the paper's counting room, he dismissed him by letter in 1875.

A pioneer in establishment of independent journalism, Bowles gave the nation its first demonstration of what a provincial newspaper might accomplish. For a quarter-century he was a real leader of American opinion.

BOWLES, SAMUEL (*b. Springfield, Mass., 1851; d. 1915*), editor. Son of Samuel Bowles (1826–1878). Early trained by his father to take charge of the *Springfield Republican,* he undertook business management of the newspaper, 1875. His father's illness threw more responsibility on him; at the elder Bowles's death he assumed full charge. Editor, publisher, and treasurer for nearly forty years, he maintained the *Republican's* high standards and continued its editorial independence, supporting Cleveland, opposing Bryan and waging war on jingoism and imperialism.

BOWLES, WILLIAM AUGUSTUS (*b. Frederick Co., Md., 1763; d. Havana, Cuba, 1805*), adventurer. Incited Creek Indians against Spain in three Florida filibustering expeditions, 1788, 1791–92, 1799.

BOWMAN, JOHN BRYAN (*b. Mercer Co., Ky., 1824; d. 1891*), founder of Kentucky University, of which he was regent, 1865–74.

BOWMAN, THOMAS (*b. Berwick, Pa., 1817; d. 1914*), Methodist clergyman, educator. Graduated

Dickinson College, 1837. President, Asbury (later De Pauw) University, 1858–72; elected bishop, 1872.

BOWNE, BORDEN PARKER (*b. Leonardville, N.J., 1847; d. 1910*), Methodist clergyman, philosopher. Headed department of philosophy, Boston University, 1876–1910; was also dean of the graduate school there. Opposed mechanistic determinism, developed philosophy of Personalism.

BOWNE, JOHN (*b. Matlock, England, 1627/8; d. Flushing, N.Y., 1695*), Quaker leader. Came to America, 1649; settled in Flushing, 1653. His banishment for conducting meetings at his house brought establishment, 1663, of religious liberty in New Netherland.

BOYCE, JAMES PETIGRU (*b. Charleston, S.C., 1827; d. Pau, France, 1888*), Baptist minister, educator. Active in founding Southern Baptist Theological Seminary, Greenville, S.C., 1859.

BOYD, BELLE (*b. Martinsburg, Va., 1844; d. Kilbourne, Wis., 1900*), Confederate spy, actress. Published account of activities in *Belle Boyd in Camp and Prison* (London, 1865); lectured on her exploits.

BOYD, DAVID FRENCH (*b. Wytheville, Va., 1834; d. Baton Rouge, La., 1899*), educator, Confederate soldier. Graduated University of Virginia, 1856. Important in development of Louisiana State University and its president, 1865–80. Dismissed for political reasons, he was recalled in 1884 but soon resigned.

BOYD, JOHN PARKER (*b. Newburyport, Mass., 1764; d. 1830*), soldier. After service at end of Revolution, was in India, 1789–1808, as a mercenary. Re-entering U.S. Army, he fought at Tippecanoe; made poor showing as brigadier-general, War of 1812.

BOYD, LYNN (*b. Nashville, Tenn., 1800; d. 1859*), lawyer. Raised in Christian Co., Ky. Congressman, Democrat, from Kentucky, 1835–37; 1839–55. Speaker of the House, 1851–55. Led fight in House for passage of 1850 Compromise.

BOYD, RICHARD HENRY (*b. Noxubee Co., Miss., 1843; d. 1922*), Baptist clergyman. Leader among Negro Baptists in Texas. Organized National Baptist Publishing Board, 1897.

BOYD, THOMAS ALEXANDER (*b. Defiance, O., 1898; d. 1935*), novelist and biographer. [*Supp.* 1]

BOYD, THOMAS DUCKETT (*b. Wytheville, Va., 1854; d. 1932*), Southern educator; influential president of Louisiana State University, 1896–1927.
[*Supp.* 1]

BOYD, WILLIAM KENNETH (*b. Curryville, Mo., 1879; d. Durham, N.C., 1938*), historian. Graduated Trinity College (Duke), 1897; Ph.D., Columbia, 1906. Taught at Duke, *post* 1906. Specialist in social and economic history of the South. [*Supp.* 2]

BOYDEN, ROLAND WILLIAM (*b. Beverly, Mass., 1863; d. Beverly, 1931*), lawyer, statesman. Advocated "ability to pay" policy in dealing with German reparations; member of Reparations Commissions, and Permanent Court of Arbitration *post* first World War. [*Supp.* 1]

BOYDEN, SETH (*b. Foxborough, Mass., 1788; d. Hilton, N.J., 1870*), inventor, manufacturer. Brother of Uriah A. Boyden. His many inventions include the first American "patent" leather process and a process for making malleable cast-iron (patented 1831). He made the first application of cut-off governing to stationary steam-engines and developed the Wetherill grate for making oxide of zinc.

BOYDEN, URIAH ATHERTON (*b. Foxborough, Mass., 1804; d. Boston, Mass., 1879*), engineer, inventor. Worked for brother, Seth Boyden, and afterwards in railroad and mill construction. Self-taught, he became engineer for Amoskeag Manufacturing Co. and designed hydraulic works at Manchester, N.H.; he also designed highly efficient turbine water-wheel, 1844, for Appleton mills at Lowell, Mass., improving on design of Fourneyron. The Boyden water-wheel was soon adopted in many mills and power-plants.

BOYÉ, MARTIN HANS (*b. Copenhagen, Denmark, 1812; d. Coopersburg, Pa., 1909*), research chemist, physicist, geologist. Came to America, 1836. M.D., University of Pennsylvania, 1844. Associated in research with James C. Booth and others. Refined cottonseed oil, 1845.

BOYESEN, HJALMAR HJORTH (b. *Frederiksvärn, Norway, 1848; d. 1895*), author, educator. Came to America, 1869. A protegé of W.D. Howells, his novel *Gunnar* (1874) established him. Taught German at Cornell, 1874–80; at Columbia, 1881–95. A prolific writer of fiction and literary criticism.

BOYLE, JEREMIAH TILFORD (*b. Kentucky, 1818; d. 1871*), lawyer, Union soldier. Son of John Boyle. Controversial military commander of Kentucky, 1862–64; took severe measures against non-combatants suspected of favoring Confederacy.

BOYLE, JOHN (*b. near Tazewell, Va., 1774; d. near Danville, Ky., 1835*), judge. Congressman, Democratic-Republican, from Kentucky, 1803–09. Conservative, highly regarded chief justice, Kentucky court of appeals, 1810–26; later U.S. district judge for Kentucky.

BOYLE, JOHN J. (*b. New York, N.Y., 1851; d. New York, 1917*), sculptor. Studied with Thomas Eakins at Pennsylvania Academy and at Beaux Arts, Paris. Celebrated for heroic groups, massive in design, and for masculine vigor in portraits such as his Franklin (Phila.) and John Barry (Washington, D.C.).

BOYLE, THOMAS (*b. Marblehead, Mass., 1776 ?; d. at sea, 1825 ?*), merchant mariner. Outstanding privateer captain of War of 1812. In *Comet* and *Chasseur*, took some eighty prizes; instituted a burlesque one-ship blockade of the British Isles, 1814.

BOYLSTON, ZABDIEL (*b. Muddy River, now Brookline, Mass., 1679; d. Brookline, 1766*), physician, first to introduce practice of smallpox inoculation in America. On outbreak of smallpox in Boston, 1721, Cotton Mather, having learned of inoculation of slaves in Africa, urged the practice on Boston physicians. Boylston began inoculating in June. He and Mather were attacked physically and in the press; feeling became so intense that they wrote several pamphlets defending the practice and themselves. By the following February, Boylston had inoculated 241 persons, of whom only six died. His results were published in his *Historical Account of the Smallpox* (London, 1726), a masterly clinical presentation and the first of its kind from an American physician.

BOYNTON, CHARLES BRANDON (*b. West Stockbridge, Mass., 1806; d. Cincinnati, O., 1883*), Presbyterian and Congregational clergyman. Served long pastorates at Vine Street Church, Cincinnati. Author of *A Journey Through Kansas* (1855) and other works on world politics and naval affairs.

BOYNTON, EDWARD CARLISLE (*b. Windsor, Vt., 1824; d. Newburgh, N.Y., 1893*), soldier. Graduated West Point, 1846. Author of *History of West Point.*

BOZEMAN, JOHN M. (*b. Georgia, 1835; d. at Yellowstone crossing, Mont., 1867*), trail-maker. Opened Bozeman Trail to Virginia City, Mont., 1863–65.

BOZEMAN, NATHAN (*b. Butler Co., Ala., 1825; d. 1905*), surgeon. Improved on J. Marion Sims's method for treating vesico-vaginal fistula; introduced operation of kolpokleisis, 1859. Practiced in New York City *post* 1865.

BOZMAN, JOHN LEEDS (*b. Oxford Neck, Md., 1757; d. 1823*), lawyer. Author of *History of Maryland, from its First Settlement . . . to the Restoration* (published 1837).

BRACE, CHARLES LORING (*b. Litchfield, Conn., 1826; d. Campfer, Switzerland, 1890*), philanthropist. Influential in founding Children's Aid Society, 1853. Pioneer in modern philanthropic methods based on self-help. Author of *The Dangerous Classes of New York* (1872) and other works.

BRACE, CHARLES LORING (*b. Hastings-on-Hudson, N.Y., 1855; d. Santa Barbara, Calif., 1938*), social welfare worker. Son of Charles L. Brace (1826–1890). Secretary, Children's Aid Society, 1890–1928.
[*Supp.* 2]

BRACE, DEWITT BRISTOL (*b. Wilson, N.Y., 1859; d. 1905*), physicist. Graduated Boston University, 1881; Ph.D., Berlin, 1885. Headed physics department, University of Nebraska, 1888–1905. Optics specialist concerned with velocity of propagation of light; constructed Brace spectrophotometer and other devices.

BRACE, JOHN PIERCE (*b. Litchfield, Conn., 1793; d. Litchfield, 1872*), educator, author. Graduated Williams, 1812. Principal, Hartford Female Seminary, 1832–47. Editor, *Hartford Courant*, 1849–63.

BRACHVOGEL, UDO (*b. Herrengrebin, German Poland, 1835; d. New York, N.Y., 1913*), author. Came to America, 1866. Editor of several German-language journals; his *Gedichte* (Leipzig and New York, 1912), is a collection of his best poems and translations.

BRACKENRIDGE, HENRY MARIE (*b. Pittsburgh, Pa., 1786; d. near Pittsburgh, 1871*), lawyer, author. Son of Hugh H. Brackenridge. Varied career included law practice in Baltimore and elsewhere, service in Maryland legislature, extensive travel in the West and Southwest and residence as an official in Florida, 1821–32. His pamphlet *South America, A Letter . . . to James Monroe* (1817) urged recognition of South American nations and a policy like that later defined in Monroe Doctrine; he became secretary of commission sent to study situation in South America. Among his books are: *Views of Louisiana* (1814); *History of the Late War* (1816); *Voyage to South America* (1819); *Recollections of Persons and Places in the West* (1834); and *History of the Insurrection in Western Pennsylvania* (1859).

BRACKENRIDGE, HUGH HENRY (*b. near Campbeltown, Scotland, 1748; d. Carlisle, Pa., 1816*), jurist, author. Came to York Co., Pa., as small child. Graduated Princeton, 1771 (M.A., 1774). Taught school; studied divinity; wrote in support of Revolution and served as chaplain. After studying law with Samuel Chase in Annapolis, Brackenridge removed to Pittsburgh, Pa., 1781; there, he practiced, helped establish first newspaper (*Pittsburgh Gazette*, 1786), engaged in politics. An active Democratic-Republican, he served *post* 1799 as judge of the Pennsylvania supreme court. His picaresque novel *Modern Chivalry* (in parts, 1792–1815), a satire on democratic excesses, is important in American literature and the first literary work of the West. Among his other works are: *The Rising Glory of America* (with Philip Freneau, 1772); *The Battle of Bunker's Hill* (1776); *The Death of General Montgomery* (1777); *Six Political Discourses* (1788); and *Law Miscellanies* (1814).

BRACKENRIDGE, WILLIAM D. (*b. Ayr, Scotland, 1810; d. Baltimore, Md., 1893*), botanist. Came to America, *c.* 1837. Served on Wilkes's exploring expedition in Pacific, 1838–42; wrote the report on ferns (1854; Vol. XVI of the expedition's reports).

BRACKETT, ANNA CALLENDER (*b. Boston, Mass., 1836; d. 1911*), educator. First woman to head a normal school in United States (St. Louis, Mo.), *c.* 1862; conducted girl's school in New York City, 1870–95.

BRACKETT, EDWARD AUGUSTUS (*b. Vassalboro, Maine, 1818; d. 1908*), sculptor, pisciculturist. Chairman, Massachusetts Fish Commission; inventor of the hatching-trap presently in use.

BRADBURY, JAMES WARE (*b. Parsonsfield, Maine, 1802; d. 1901*), lawyer, leader among Maine Democrats. U.S. senator, 1846–52. Union supporter, he led split when Democratic state convention denounced Civil War, 1861.

BRADBURY, THEOPHILUS (*b. Newbury, Mass., 1739; d. Newburyport, Mass., 1803*), lawyer. Justice, supreme judicial court of Massachusetts, 1797–1803.

BRADBURY, WILLIAM BATCHELDER (*b. York, Maine, 1816; d. Montclair, N.J., 1868*), music teacher, piano manufacturer. Pupil of Lowell Mason; compiled over fifty singing books for church choirs.

BRADDOCK, EDWARD (*b. Scotland, 1695; d. near Great Meadows, Pa., 1755*), British general. Ensign, Coldstream Guards, 1710; rose to major-general, 1754. Chosen to command all British forces in North America in campaign against French on the Ohio, Braddock landed in Virginia, February 1755. His task made more difficult by inadequate preparation in England, inter-colonial jealousies, and his own disdain of provincial troops and their methods, he began operations against Fort Duquesne (present site of Pittsburgh, Pa.) by cutting a road westward from the frontier settlements in Pennsylvania, the first road across the Alleghanies. Ambushed by French and Indians as he was nearing Fort Duquesne, July 9, 1755, Braddock lost over half his army and was himself mortally wounded, dying four days later.

BRADFORD, ALDEN (*b. Duxbury, Mass., 1765; d. 1843*), politician, editor. His *Massachusetts State Papers* (1815) and *Life of Jonathan Mayhew* (1838) are still of value for the original historical documents they contain.

BRADFORD, ALEXANDER WARFIELD (*b. Albany, N.Y., 1815; d. New York, N.Y., 1867*), lawyer. Able New York City surrogate, 1848–58. Highly successful in private practice, expert in civil and canon law.

BRADFORD, AMORY HOWE (*b. Granby, N.Y., 1846; d. 1911*), Congregational minister, author. Pastor, Montclair, N.J., 1870–1911.

BRADFORD, ANDREW (*b. Pennsylvania, 1686; d. Philadelphia, Pa., 1742*), pioneer printer. Son of William Bradford (1663–1752). Issued *American Weekly Mercury*, 1719, first newspaper in Pennsylvania, third in United States; also published *American Magazine*, 1741.

BRADFORD, AUGUSTUS WILLIAMSON (*b. Bel Air, Md., 1806; d. Baltimore, Md., 1881*), lawyer. Practiced in Bel Air and Baltimore; settled permanently in Baltimore, 1838. Prominent in Whig party. Elected Unionist governor of Maryland, 1861, he strongly but unsuccessfully urged Lincoln to prevent interference by federal army in 1863 election at which he was re-elected. The state convention of 1864, which adopted constitution abolishing slavery in Maryland, was called by him.

BRADFORD, EDWARD GREEN (*b. Bohemia Manor, Md., 1819; d. Wilmington, Del., 1884*), jurist. U.S. district attorney for Delaware, 1861–66; federal district judge for Delaware, *post* 1871.

BRADFORD, EDWARD HICKLING (*b. Roxbury, Mass., 1848; d. 1926*), orthopedic surgeon. Graduated Harvard, 1869; M.D., Harvard, 1873. Associated with Boston Children's Hospital; professor and dean at Harvard Medical School. Founded first school for handicapped children in America, Boston, 1893.

BRADFORD, GAMALIEL (*b. Boston, Mass., 1831; d. Boston, 1911*), banker, publicist. Advocate of civil service and other reforms.

BRADFORD, GAMALIEL (*b. Boston, Mass., 1863; d. Wellesley Hills, Mass., 1932*), biographer, critic. Exponent of "psychographic" method of biography in *Lee the American* (1912), *A Naturalist of Souls* (1917), and others. [*Supp. 1*]

BRADFORD, JOHN (*b. Prince William Co., Va., 1749; d. Lexington, Ky., 1830*), pioneer printer of Kentucky. Brought out first number of *Kentucke Gazette* (spelling changed, March 1789) on Aug. 11, 1787; also issued *Kentucke Almanac,* pioneer pamphlet of the West, 1788. Published acts of first Kentucky legislature, 1792; this was the first book printed there.

BRADFORD, JOSEPH (*b. near Nashville, Tenn., 1843; d. 1886*), actor, journalist, poet, playwright. Christened William Randolph Hunter.

BRADFORD, THOMAS (*b. Philadelphia, Pa., 1745; d. Philadelphia, 1838*), printer and publisher. Son of William Bradford (1721/2–1791). Started *Merchants' Daily Advertiser,* Philadelphia, 1797. Financial and book pages of modern newspaper go back to innovations made by him.

BRADFORD, WILLIAM (*b. Austerfield, England, 1589/90; d. Plymouth, Mass., 1657*), Pilgrim Father. As a boy, he began to read the Bible and to attend sermons of noted nonconformist, Rev. Richard Clyfton, at Babworth. Soon he joined the group which met at William Brewster's house in Scrooby, which became a separatist church in 1606; he accompanied the group to Holland, 1609. Bradford became a tradesman and citizen of Leyden; in this period (1609–20) he must have acquired the wide theological and general knowledge to which his writings attest. He was much influenced by the liberal spirit of John Robinson and William Brewster.

Bradford took a responsible part in the preparations for moving to the New World. From the sailing of the *Speedwell* from Delfshaven (*c.* Aug 1, 1620), his life is inseparable from the history of the Pilgrim colony. He signed the *Mayflower* Compact; shared all the experiences of the landing and the settlement at Plymouth; was ill the first winter, but recovered. In April 1621, on the death of John Carver, he was elected governor of the colony.

By the time Bradford took office, the great sickness had taken 13 of the 24 heads of families, all but four of their wives, and all but six of the unattached men. The *Mayflower* had returned to England, provisions were low and no harvest would come for four months. In like circumstances other colonies had perished. But a combination of good fortune (which Bradford attributed to the guiding hand of God), his own leadership and the aid of men like Brewster, Winslow and Standish on whom he leaned, helped Plymouth to survive.

Bradford was re-elected governor thirty times between 1622 and 1656. His difficulties in the early days were augmented by the presence of persons engaged as servants or attached to the colony by the London merchants who had financed the venture. Some pulled their weight, but others started factions, cheated the Pilgrims and armed the Indians. Bradford dealt with them ably, as a Christian and as a consummate politician. When the original "merchant adventurers" or stockholders were bought out in 1627 by Bradford and the leading Pilgrims, it was decided that all in the colony should share in the land, houses, tools and cattle acquired. This placed the colony on a sound economic basis, and assimilated the outsiders to Pilgrim ideals. When the "Warwick patent" in 1630 made Bradford proprietor of jurisdiction and soil, he at once shared his right with the "Old Comers." In all his business management, he kept in mind that the colony would not prosper unless its members had a stake in its prosperity.

In his first 15 years in office, Bradford had more plenary authority than any other English colonial governor between 1619 and 1685. Until 1636, when laws were drafted placing the government on a quasi-constitutional basis, he was principal judge and treasurer. Even after this he acted with great independence. Democracy has been read into the Pilgrim government by later historians; it is not found in the records, but Bradford's ability and discretion, both in internal matters and in relations with other colonies, maintained him in office with only one recorded incident of discontent with his rule.

Bradford began writing his *History of Plimmoth Plantation* about 1630, completing it in 1651. Probably intended to be handed down in his family, it was not printed in full until 1856, although historians had used the manuscript earlier. The work of an educated man, well versed in the Geneva version of the Bible, it tells a worthy story well, but is equally valuable for what it reflects of the simplicity and sincerity of the author's character. It has been largely responsible for giving the Pilgrims and their colony the prominent place they occupy in American history and popular tradition.

BRADFORD, WILLIAM (*b. Barnwell, England, 1663; d. New York, N.Y., 1752*), pioneer printer of the English middle colonies. Set up press in Pennsylvania, 1685. Harassed and disappointed, he went back to England, 1689. Persuaded to return by promise of greater encouragement, he became involved in the turbulence over the schism led by George Keith. His press was seized and he was arrested, but freed after jury disagreed. Made official printer to the Crown in New York, 1693, he removed there and served until retirement, 1742. Among his imprints are many public documents, including "Votes" of the assembly and collections of New York laws. Bradford printed the first New York paper currency, 1709; the first American Book of Common Prayer, 1710; the first history of New York, 1727. He also issued New York's first newspaper, *New-York Gazette*, 1725.

BRADFORD, WILLIAM (*b. New York, N.Y., 1721/2; d. Philadelphia, Pa., 1791*), "patriot-printer of 1776." Grandson of William Bradford (1663–1752); nephew of Andrew Bradford, who was his master in the trade. Began business in Philadelphia, 1742, at "The Sign of the Bible." Issued first number of *Weekly Advertiser*, 1742; widely circulated, it continued almost uninterrupted until 1793. Published *American Magazine and Monthly Chronicle*, 1757–58; also *American Magazine, or General Repository*, 1769. Opponent of the Stamp Act and early advocate of a continental congress; made printer to Congress, 1775. He fought with the Pennsylvania militia and was severely wounded at Princeton; his health and fortune suffered severely thereby.

BRADFORD, WILLIAM (*b. Philadelphia, Pa., 1755; d. 1795*), Revolutionary soldier, jurist. Son of William Bradford (1721/2–1791). U.S. attorney-general, 1794–95.

BRADFORD, WILLIAM (*b. Fairhaven, Mass., 1823; d. 1892*), marine painter. His careful, realistic views of ships and coastline from New England to the Arctic were popular here and abroad.

BRADISH, LUTHER (*b. Cummington, Mass., 1783; d. Newport, R.I., 1863*), diplomat, lawyer, statesman. U.S. agent to government of Turkey, 1820; traveled in Europe until 1826. Thereafter active as a Whig in New York State politics, and in philanthropic work.

BRADLEY, CHARLES HENRY, (*b. Johnson, Vt., 1860; d. 1922*). Headed Farm and Trades School, Boston, 1888–1922. His innovations and improvements gave it a national reputation.

BRADLEY, CHARLES WILLIAM (*b. New Haven, Conn., 1807; d. New Haven, 1865*), Episcopal clergyman, diplomat, Sinologist. U.S. consul in China and Malaya, 1849–60; bequeathed library to American Oriental Society.

BRADLEY, DENIS MARY (*b. Ireland, 1846; d. 1903*), Roman Catholic clergyman. Came to America as a child. Consecrated first bishop of Manchester, N.H., 1884, and served until death.

BRADLEY, FRANK HOWE (*b. New Haven, Conn., 1838; d. near Nacoochee, Ga., 1879*), geologist. Participated in state surveys of Illinois, Indiana, Idaho. Taught at University of Tennessee, 1869–75.

BRADLEY, FREDERICK WORTHEN (*b. Nevada Co., Calif., 1863; d. Alta, Calif., 1933*), mining engineer. [*Supp. 1*]

BRADLEY, JOHN EDWIN (*b. Lee, Mass., 1839; d. Randolph, Mass., 1912*), educator. Outstanding as principal, Albany, N.Y. Free Academy, 1868–86. President, Illinois College, 1892–1900. Superintendent of schools, Minneapolis, Minn., and Randolph, Mass.

BRADLEY, JOSEPH P. (*b. Berne, N.Y., 1813; d. 1892*), lawyer, Supreme Court justice. Graduated Rutgers, 1836. Admitted to New Jersey bar, 1839; specialized in patent, commercial, corporation cases. Originally a Whig, he became strong Unionist after attack on Fort Sumter. Named to U.S. Supreme Court, 1870. Influenced by John Marshall and strongly conservative, Bradley wrote many notable opinions: his concurring opinion in *Knox vs. Lee* invokes obviously for first time in a Supreme Court decision the doctrine that the national government possesses certain inherent powers; his dissent in Slaughter House Cases anticipates later interpretations of the Fourteenth Amendment. Bradley also contributed in drawing line between "exclusive" power of Congress over interstate commerce and the taxing powers of the states and made important rulings in *Boyd vs. U.S., ex parte Siebold* and *Hans vs. Louisiana*.

BRADLEY, LYDIA MOSS (*b. Vevay, Ind., 1816; d. 1908*), philanthropist. Successful business woman, benefactor of many institutions in Peoria, Ill.; founded Bradley Polytechnic Institute.

BRADLEY, MILTON (*b. Vienna, Maine, 1836; d. 1911*), pioneer American game manufacturer. Promoted interest in kindergartens in America; published children's books and manufactured kindergarten materials.

BRADLEY, STEPHEN ROW (*b. Wallingford, Conn., 1754; d. 1830*), Revolutionary soldier, jurist. Judge of Vermont supreme court; U.S. senator, (Democrat) Republican, 1791–94 and 1801–13.

BRADLEY, WILLIAM CZAR (*b. Westminster, Vt., 1782; d. 1867*), lawyer. Son of Stephen R. Bradley. Congressman, Democrat, from Vermont, 1813–15, 1823–27. Leader of Jacksonian Democrats in Vermont, he was later a Free-Soiler and a Republican.

BRADLEY, WILLIAM O'CONNELL (*b. near Lancaster, Ky., 1847; d. Washington, D.C., 1914*), lawyer. A Republican leader in Kentucky and governor of the state, 1896–1900; U.S. senator, 1908–14.

BRADSTREET, ANNE (*b. Northampton ?, England, c. 1612; d. N. Andover, Mass., 1672*), poet. Came to Massachusetts Bay, 1630, with Winthrop's party, which included her husband, Simon Bradstreet, and her father, Thomas Dudley. Settling at Ipswich, the Bradstreets moved to North Andover about 1644. Author of *The Tenth Muse* (London, 1650), the first book of poems by an Englishwoman in America.

BRADSTREET, JOHN (*b. Nova Scotia ?, c. 1711; d. New York, 1774*), soldier. Served with British and colonial forces, 1735–74; distinguished at capture of Fort Frontenac, 1758.

BRADSTREET, SIMON (*b. England, 1603; d. Salem, Mass., 1697*), colonial statesman. Came to Massachusetts, 1630; held many public offices, including secretary of the colony, assistant; was governor, 1679–86, 1689–92. Commissioner, New England Confederation, 1644–77.

BRADWELL, JAMES BOLESWORTH (*b. Loughborough, England, 1828; d. Chicago, Ill., 1907*), lawyer, jurist. Practiced in Chicago, 1855–1903; expert on probate law. Prepared *Illinois Appellate Court Reports*.

BRADWELL, MYRA (*b. Manchester, Vt., 1831; d. Chicago, Ill., 1894*), lawyer, editor. Wife of James B. Bradwell. Established *Chicago Legal News*, 1868. Fought for legislation allowing women free choice of profession; active in Suffrage movement.

BRADY, ALICE (*b. New York, N.Y., 1892; d. Hollywood, Calif., 1939*), stage and screen actress. Daughter of actor-producer William A. Brady. [*Supp. 2*]

BRADY, ANTHONY NICHOLAS (*b. Lille, France, 1843; d. 1913*), businessman. Came to America as a child. Raised in Troy, N.Y. Prospered as tea-store owner and general contractor, later as promoter of public utilities and municipal traction lines.

BRADY, CYRUS TOWNSEND (*b. Allegheny, Pa., 1861; d. Yonkers, N.Y., 1920*), Episcopal clergyman, novelist.

BRADY, JAMES TOPHAM (*b. New York, N.Y., 1815; d. New York, 1869*), lawyer. Leader at New York bar, *post* 1840.

BRADY, JOHN GREEN (*b. New York, N.Y., 1848; d. Sitka, Alaska, 1918*), governor of Alaska, 1897–1906. Did much to inform the American public of Alaska's resources and needs. [*Supp. 1*]

BRADY, MATHEW B. (*b. Warren Co., N.Y., c. 1823; d. New York, N.Y., 1896*), photographer. Already celebrated as a daguerreotypist *post* 1842, he turned to the photographic process, 1855. Famous for his *Gallery of Illustrious Americans* (1850) and for his monumental photographic coverage of the Civil War.

BRAGG, BRAXTON (*b. Warrenton, N.C., 1817; d. Galveston, Texas, 1876*), Confederate soldier. Graduated West Point, 1837. Distinguished in Mexican War; brevetted lieutenant-colonel for extraordinary work at Buena Vista. Resigned from army, 1856; settled in Louisiana as planter; as commissioner of

public works, he designed state drainage and levee systems. Commissioned Confederate brigadier-general, 1861, he was effective in command of right wing on first day of Shiloh. Promoted full general, he relieved Beauregard in command of Army of Tennessee, June 1862. At Perryville and Stone River his withdrawals after initial success caused dissatisfaction, but he retained command by favor of Jefferson Davis. Victorious at Chickamauga, September 1863, he laid siege to Federals in Chattanooga but they attacked in November and forced Bragg to retreat into Georgia. He surrendered command to J. E. Johnston in December, and served in Richmond during 1864, nominally commander-in-chief. After the war he practiced as a civil engineer in Alabama and Texas.

BRAGG, EDWARD STUYVESANT (*b. Unadilla, N.Y., 1827; d. Fond du Lac, Wis., 1912*), Union soldier, lawyer. Removed to Wisconsin, 1850, settling at Fond du Lac. Commissioned captain in 6th Wisconsin Infantry, he rose by the end of the Civil War to brigadier-general on merit alone. Congressman, Democrat, from Wisconsin, 1877–83, 1885–87; author of epigram in defense of Grover Cleveland, "We love him for the enemies he has made." A leading "Gold Democrat," *post* 1896.

BRAGG, THOMAS (*b. Warrenton, N.C., 1810; d. 1872*), lawyer, Confederate statesman. Brother of Braxton Bragg. Democratic governor of North Carolina, 1855–59; U.S. senator, 1859–61. Confederate attorney-general, 1861–March 1862.

BRAINARD, DANIEL (*b. Oneida Co., N.Y., 1812; d. Chicago, Ill., 1866*), surgeon, pioneer in medical education. Settled in Chicago, 1836. Dominating figure at Rush Medical College from its founding, 1843, to his death. Author of a classic essay on treatment of fractures (1854) and other works.

BRAINARD, JOHN GARDINER CALKINS (*b. New London, Conn., 1796; d. New London, 1828*), poet. Author of *Occasional Pieces of Poetry* (1825) and *Fugitive Tales* (1830). Praised by Whittier, damned by Poe.

BRAINERD, DAVID (*b. Haddam, Conn., 1718; d. Northampton, Mass., 1747*), missionary to the Indians in western Massachusetts, New York and New Jersey. Author of a celebrated spiritual journal, published 1746 and 1749.

BRAINERD, ERASTUS (*b. Middletown, Conn., 1855; d. Seattle, Wash., 1922*), editor. Served on newspapers in several eastern cities; removed to Seattle, 1890; edited *Seattle Post-Intelligencer*, 1904–11. Publicized Seattle as starting point for Yukon gold-rushers, 1897.

BRAINERD, EZRA (*b. St. Albans, Vt., 1844; d. 1924*), botanist, geologist, educator. Worked many years on hybridism in violets. President, Middlebury College, 1885–1906.

BRAINERD, JOHN (*b. Haddam, Conn., 1720; d. Deerfield, N.J., 1781*), missionary to the Indians. Brother of David Brainerd, whose work he continued.

BRAINERD, LAWRENCE (*b. East Hartford, Conn., 1794; d. 1870*), merchant, farmer, banker in Vermont. Active in steamboat and railroad development. U.S. senator, Free-Soiler, from Vermont, 1854.

BRAINERD, THOMAS (*b. Leyden, N.Y., 1804; d. Scranton, Pa., 1866*), Presbyterian clergyman, editor. Associate of Lyman Beecher in Cincinnati, O.; later pastor (1837–66) at Third Church, Philadelphia. Author of *Life of John Brainerd* (1865).

BRAMLETTE, THOMAS E. (*b. Cumberland Co., Ky., 1817; d. Louisville, Ky., 1875*), lawyer, jurist. Union Democrat, governor of Kentucky, 1863–67; gradually became bitter critic of Lincoln.

BRANCH, JOHN (*b. Halifax, N.C., 1782; d. Enfield, N.C., 1863*), planter, politician. Democratic governor of North Carolina, 1817–20; strongly advocated state aid to education, abolition of imprisonment for debt, internal improvements. U.S. senator, 1823–29; secretary of navy, 1829–31, forced to resign because of involvement in Eaton affair. Elected to Congress, 1831, he retired after one term; his last public service was as governor of Florida, 1843–45.

BRANCH, LAWRENCE O'BRYAN (*b. Enfield, N.C., 1820; d. Sharpsburg, Md., 1862*), lawyer, Confederate soldier. Nephew of John Branch. Congressman, Democrat, from North Carolina, 1855–61. Killed in action.

BRANDEGEE, FRANK BOSWORTH (*b. New London, Conn., 1864; d. Washington, D.C., 1924*), lawyer, politician. Congressman, Republican, from Connecticut, 1902–05; U.S. senator, 1905–24. Opposed League of Nations, income tax, child-labor legislation, direct election of senators. Delighted in obstruction.

BRANDEGEE, TOWNSHEND STITH (*b. Berlin, Conn., 1843; d. Berkeley, Calif., 1925*), botanist. A pioneer collector in the West and authority on plants of California region. Author of *Plantae Mexicanae Purpusianae* (1909–24).

BRANDON, GERARD CHITTOCQUE (*b. near Natchez, Miss., 1788; d. near Fort Adams, Miss., 1850*), lawyer, planter. Governor of Mississippi, 1827–32, the first native Mississippian to hold the office.

BRANN, WILLIAM COWPER (*b. Humboldt, Ill., 1855; d. Waco, Texas, 1898*), journalist, editor of the successful Waco *Iconoclast*. His career of bitter invective and wide-ranging antipathies climaxed in his death in a gun battle. [*Supp.* 1]

BRANNAN, JOHN MILTON (*b. near Washington, D.C., 1819; d. New York, N.Y., 1892*), Union soldier. Graduated West Point, 1841. Artillery specialist, distinguished in Mexican and Civil Wars; brevetted major-general, 1865.

BRANNAN, SAMUEL (*b. Saco, Maine, 1819; d. Escondido, Calif., 1889*), California pioneer. Moved to Ohio, 1833; learned printing, visited most of states as journeyman printer. Became Mormon, 1842; published papers in New York for Mormon church. Led Mormon group from New York to California by sea, arriving July 1846, first Anglo-American settlers to arrive after California's capture by United States. Brannan was soon a leader in San Francisco. He is said to have been the first to bring news of the gold strike at Sutter's to the town. He also issued the first number of the *California Star*, San Francisco's first newspaper, January 1847; served on first city council and helped organize Society of California Pioneers. The San Francisco Committee of Vigilance of 1851 was formed in his office. Investing in real estate, he became one of wealthiest men in California, but later lost fortune.

BRANNER, JOHN CASPER (*b. New Market, Tenn., 1850; d. Stanford, Calif., 1922*), geologist. Surveyed in Brazil, compiled geological map of that country. Professor at Leland Stanford, 1891–1916; president, 1913–16.

BRANNON, HENRY (*b. Winchester, Va., 1837; d. 1914*), jurist. Justice, supreme court of appeals of West Virginia, 1888–1912. Had preponderant share in shaping law of state in its early days.

BRANT, JOSEPH (*b. 1742; d. 1807*), Mohawk chief. Indian name, Thayendanegea. Accompanied Sir William Johnson in campaign of 1755; in school at Lebanon, Conn., 1761–63; fought against Pontiac. Worked to bring Iroquois to aid of British in Revolution. Commissioned captain, he visited England, where he was "lionized" in society; returning to America he commanded Indian partisans, terrorizing Mohawk Valley region, directing Cherry Valley massacre, 1778. After the war, Brant induced Gov. Haldimand of Canada to assign land to Mohawks. In England, 1785, he procured funds to indemnify Iroquois for losses and for purchase of new lands. Later he opposed attempts of speculators to take Mohawk lands.

BRANTLEY, THEODORE (*b. Wilson Co., Tenn., 1851; d. 1922*), jurist. Chief justice, Montana supreme court, 1898–1922. His decisions on water rights and other local issues brought about a reformed constitution and a new state system of law.

BRASHEAR, JOHN ALFRED (*b. Brownsville, Pa., 1840; d. Pittsburgh, Pa., 1920*), maker of astronomical lenses and precision instruments.

BRASLAU, SOPHIE (*b. New York, N.Y., 1892; d. New York, 1935*), operatic contralto; with Metropolitan Opera Co., 1913–1920. [*Supp.* 1]

BRATTLE, THOMAS (*b. Boston, Mass., 1658; d. Boston, 1713*), merchant. Organized Brattle Street Church, 1698. As treasurer, Harvard College, 1693–1713, almost tripled its resources.

BRATTLE, WILLIAM (*b. Boston, Mass., 1662; d. 1716/7*), Congregational clergyman, educator. Brother of Thomas Brattle. Pastor of the church in Cambridge, Mass., *post* 1696; Harvard tutor.

BRATTON, JOHN (*b. Winnsboro, S.C., 1831; d. Winnsboro, 1898*), physician, Confederate soldier.

BRAWLEY, WILLIAM HIRAM (*b. Chester, S.C., 1841; d. Charleston, S.C., 1916*), jurist, Confederate soldier. Congressman, Democrat, from South Carolina, 1890–94; opponent of Free Silver. U.S. district judge for South Carolina, *post* 1894.

BRAXTON, CARTER (*b. Newington, Va., 1736; d. Richmond, Va., 1797*), Revolutionary statesman. Member, House of Burgesses, 1761–75; served in Revolutionary conventions, 1774–76, and in Continental Congress, 1776. Signer of the Declaration of Independence. Served as Virginia legislator, 1776–97.

BRAY, THOMAS (*b. Marton, England, 1656; d. London, England, 1729/30*), Anglican clergyman. As bishop of London's commissary for Maryland, was largely responsible for establishment of Church of England in that colony, 1696–1702. To support dissemination of books among colonial clergy and, later, clergy at home, he founded Society for Promoting Christian Knowledge (1699) and strongly promoted Society for the Propagation of the Gospel (1701). His interest in the colonies continued until his death.

BRAYMAN, MASON (*b. Buffalo, N.Y., 1813; d. Kansas City, Mo., 1895*), lawyer, editor, Union soldier. Practiced law in Illinois, *post* 1842; rose to major-general in Civil War; led wandering life thereafter as journalist. Appointed territorial governor of Idaho, 1876, he served a single controversial term.

BRAYTON, CHARLES RAY (*b. Apponaug, R.I., 1840; d. Providence, R.I., 1910*), politician, Union soldier. Agent for Republican senators H. B. Anthony and N. W. Aldrich in corrupt management of state politics, *c.* 1870–1906.

BRAZER, JOHN (*b. Worcester, Mass., 1789; d. Salem, Mass., 1846*), Unitarian clergyman. Graduated Harvard, 1813; professor of Latin there, 1817–20. Pastor, North Church, Salem, 1820–46. His thought is an anticipation of Transcendentalism and Emerson's later doctrines.

BREARLY, DAVID (*b. Spring Grove, N.J., 1745; d. 1790*), jurist. As chief justice of New Jersey supreme court, gave opinion in *Holmes vs. Walton* (1780) in which was asserted the principle of judicial power over unconstitutional legislation.

BREASTED, JAMES HENRY (*b. Rockford, Ill., 1865; d. New York, N.Y., 1935*), Egyptologist, archeologist, and historian. Graduated A.M., Yale, 1892; Ph.D., 1894, University of Berlin. At University of Chicago became first teacher of Egyptology in America. Published *A History of Egypt* (1905), a collation and translation of *Ancient Records of Egypt* (1906–07), and, in collaboration, many excellent textbooks. Presented a new chapter in the history of human thought in *Development of Religion and Thought in Ancient Egypt* (1912). Founded Oriental Institute, University of Chicago, 1919. [*Supp.* 1]

BREAUX, JOSEPH ARSENNE (*b. Iberville Parish, La., 1838; d. 1926*), jurist. Reformed Louisiana public school laws and practice, 1888; chief justice, state supreme court, 1904–14.

BRECK, GEORGE WILLIAM (*b. Washington, D.C., 1863; d. Flushing, N.Y., 1920*), mural painter. Director, American Academy of Fine Arts, Rome, 1904–09.

BRECK, JAMES LLOYD (*b. near Philadelphia, Pa., 1818; d. Benicia, Calif., 1876*), Episcopal clergyman. Missionary in Wisconsin and Minnesota, 1841–67; founder of Seabury Divinity School, Faribault, Minn.

BRECK, SAMUEL (*b. Boston, Mass., 1771; d. 1862*), merchant. Removed to Philadelphia, 1792, and took a leading social and political position there. Wrote *Recollections* (published 1877), a valuable source volume.

BRECKENRIDGE, JAMES (*b. Botetourt Co., Va., 1763; d. Botetourt Co., 1833*), Revolutionary soldier, lawyer. Congressman, Federalist, from Virginia, 1809–17; a leader of his party in that state. Brother of John Breckinridge (1760–1806).

BRECKINRIDGE, DESHA (*b. Lexington, Ky., 1867; d. Lexington, 1935*), editor, publisher, civic leader, horseman. Under his management the *Lexington Herald* earned a national reputation. [*Supp.* 1]

BRECKINRIDGE, JOHN (*b. near Staunton, Va., 1760; d. near Lexington, Ky., 1806*), lawyer, statesman. Brother of James Breckenridge. Moved to Kentucky, 1792. Served as state attorney-general, 1795–96; in state legislature, 1797–1801 (speaker, in second term); in U.S. Senate, 1801–05. Appointed U.S. attorney-general, 1805. An outstanding Democratic-Republican spokesman for the new West, he assisted Jefferson on the Kentucky Resolutions, 1798, reformed Kentucky penal code, and was influential in formulation of the state's second constitution.

BRECKINRIDGE, JOHN (*b. near Lexington, Ky., 1797; d. near Lexington, 1841*), Presbyterian clergyman. Son of John Breckinridge (1760–1806). Graduated Princeton, 1818; Princeton Seminary, 1820–21; ordained 1823. An aggressive champion of the Old School theology, he engaged Rev. John Hughes in public debate, 1833 and 1835–36, on the issue of Protestantism *vs.* Catholicism.

BRECKINRIDGE, JOHN CABELL (*b. near Lexington, Ky., 1821; d. Lexington, 1875*), statesman, soldier. Grandson of John Breckinridge (1760–1806). Graduated Centre College, 1839; continued studies at

College of New Jersey and Transylvania College. Practiced law at Lexington beginning 1845; served briefly in war with Mexico. Entered state legislature, 1849; won election as congressman, 1851, Democrat, from one of Henry Clay's strongest Whig districts, and was re-elected, 1853. Established as one of the most popular men in his section, he was nominated for vice-presidency, 1856; served ably with Buchanan. When Southern delegates quit Democratic convention at Charleston, 1860, and held own convention at Baltimore, Breckinridge was nominated by them for the presidency on a platform reaffirming extreme Southern view on slavery; during campaign that followed he defended self against charge of encouraging disunion, received 72 electoral votes at the election but did not carry his own state. As vice-president during rest of term, he advocated Crittenden Compromise; in his view, the Constitution did not give the federal government power to coerce any state. He returned to Kentucky after Lincoln's inauguration; when that state abandoned its first position of neutrality and welcomed Union troops he fled to escape arrest and joined army of the Confederacy.

Despite lack of experience, he served ably at battles of Shiloh, Vicksburg, Baton Rouge, Port Hudson and Murfreesboro, rising to divisional command and the rank of major-general. In May 1863, attached to Gen. J. E. Johnston's army, he was present at battle of Jackson, Miss.; later, he commanded a division of the Army of Tennessee at Chickamauga and Missionary Ridge. Called by Lee to the Shenandoah valley, he then commanded a division at Cold Harbor and participated in the raids on Washington, D.C., July 1864; he was appointed Confederate secretary of war, Feb. 1865.

After Lee's surrender he fled the country, remaining abroad and in Canada until permitted to return to Lexington, 1869, where he resumed his law practice and took a prominent part in the development of railroads in his state.

BRECKINRIDGE, ROBERT JEFFERSON (*b. near Lexington, Ky., 1800; d. Danville, Ky., 1871*), lawyer, Presbyterian clergyman. Son of John Breckinridge (1760–1806). Chiefly responsible for the "Act and Testimony" of 1834 which led to split of "Old" and "New" Schools in Presbyterianism; reformer of state public schools, 1847–51; professor at Danville Theological Seminary, 1851–69; bitter opponent of slavery, Catholicism, Universalism.

BRECKINRIDGE, WILLIAM CAMPBELL PRESTON (*b. Baltimore, Md., 1837; d. Lexington, Ky., 1904*), lawyer, editor. Son of Robert J. Breckinridge. Served with Confederate forces, 1862–65. Editor, *Lexington Observer and Reporter*, 1866–68; chief editorial writer, *Lexington Morning Herald*, 1897–1904.

BREED, EBENEZER (*b. Lynn, Mass., 1766; d. Lynn, 1839*), wholesale shoe merchant. Instrumental in passage of tariff act, 1789, which protected domestic shoe manufacturers.

BREEN, PATRICK (*b. Ireland, date unknown; d. San Juan Bautista, Calif., 1868*), diarist of the ill-fated Donner party of California emigrants (1846).

BREESE, KIDDER RANDOLPH (*b. Philadelphia, Pa., 1831; d. 1881*), naval officer. Fleet-captain under Adm. D. D. Porter, 1864–65; commandant of midshipmen, U.S. Naval Academy, 1873.

BREESE, SIDNEY (*b. Whitesboro, N.Y., 1800; d. 1878*), jurist, politician. Graduated Union College, 1818. Removed to Kaskaskia, Ill.; was admitted to bar, 1820; became active Democratic politician; served as U.S. senator from Illinois, 1843–49. Elected justice of state supreme court, 1857, he served with great ability until his death. His most famous decision was in the case of *Munn vs. Illinois* (1876) when he upheld the doctrine of the regulative power of the state over corporations in whose business the public interest is involved.

BRENNAN, ALFRED LAURENS (*b. Louisville, Ky., 1853; d. Brooklyn, N.Y., 1921*), illustrator. One of the finest pen-and-ink artists of his time.

BRENNER, VICTOR DAVID (*b. Shavli, Russia, 1871; d. New York, N.Y., 1924*), sculptor, medalist. Designer of the Lincoln cent (1909).

BRENT, CHARLES HENRY (*b. Newcastle, Ontario, Canada, 1862; d. Lausanne, Switzerland, 1929*), Protestant Episcopal clergyman. Graduated Trinity College, Toronto, 1884; was ordained priest in 1887. In 1901 elected first Episcopal missionary bishop to the Philippines, he began a life-long battle against the opium trade. When the United States entered World War I, he went to France as a chaplain of the Young Men's Christian Association and was soon made chaplain at general headquarters by General Pershing. His greatest work was done after the war in the field of Christian unity. [*Supp. 1*]

BRENT, MARGARET (*b. Gloucester, England, 1600; d. 1670/71*), America's first feminist. Migrated to St. Mary's, Md., with sister and two brothers, 1638. Family relationships and political affiliations secured to them large land grants and high offices. The first woman of Maryland to hold land in her own right, she aided Gov. Calvert in suppressing the Claiborne Rebellion, 1646. In 1648, she appealed to Assembly for two votes in their proceedings, one for herself as landowner and the other as attorney for Lord Baltimore. On denial of her plea, in resentment she moved to Virginia, 1650.

BRENTANO, LORENZ (*b. Mannheim, Germany, 1813; d. Chicago, Ill., 1891*), statesman, journalist. Emigrated to America, 1850. Developed *Illinois Staatszeitung* into influential Chicago daily and leading German Republican paper in Northwest.

BRERETON, JOHN. [See BRIERTON, JOHN, fl. 1572–1619.]

BRETT, GEORGE PLATT (*b. London, England, 1858; d. Fairfield, Conn., 1936*), publisher. Came to America, 1869. President, Macmillan Co. (1896–1931). [*Supp. 2*]

BRETT, WILLIAM HOWARD (*b. Braceville, O., 1846; d. 1918*), librarian. Built Cleveland Public Library into great city-wide system, 1884–1918. Organized (1894) and headed Library School of Western Reserve University.

BREVOORT, JAMES RENWICK (*b. Yonkers, N.Y., 1832; d. Yonkers, 1918*), landscape painter.

BREWER, CHARLES (*b. Boston, Mass., 1804; d. Jamaica Plain, Mass., 1885*), sea captain, merchant. Headed prosperous Honolulu trading firm, C. Brewer & Co.

BREWER, DAVID JOSIAH (*b. Smyrna, Asia Minor, 1837; d. Washington, D.C., 1910*), jurist. Graduated Yale, 1856; read law with uncle, David Dudley Field, and graduated Albany Law School, 1858. Resided Leavenworth, Kans., 1858–90, serving as justice of state supreme court, 1870–84. Named federal justice for 8th circuit, 1884, he was appointed in 1889 to the U.S. Supreme Court by President Harrison, serving until death. A moderate conservative, he resisted the drift toward federal centralization of power and was stern in defense of personal liberty and property rights. In 1895–97 he was president of commission appointed by Congress to investigate Venezuela-British Guiana boundary dispute.

BREWER, MARK SPENCER (*b. Oakland Co., Mich., 1837; d. Washington, D.C., 1901*). Congressman, Republican, from Michigan, 1876–80; 1887–91; member of Civil Service Commission, 1898–1901.

BREWER, THOMAS MAYO (*b. Boston, Mass., 1814; d. 1880*), ornithologist, oölogist. Author of *North American Oölogy* (1857), and of biographies in Baird, Brewer and Ridgway's *History of North American Birds* (1875).

BREWER, WILLIAM HENRY (*b. Poughkeepsie, N.Y., 1828; d. 1910*), botanist, geologist, agriculturist. Assisted J. D. Whitney in geological survey of California, 1860–64; established first American agricultural experiment station. Professor of agriculture, Sheffield Scientific School, Yale, 1864–1903.

BREWSTER, BENJAMIN HARRIS (*b. Salem Co., N.J., 1816; d. Philadelphia, Pa., 1888*), attorney-general of the United States. Prosecuted Star Route frauds in Post Office Department, 1881–84.

BREWSTER, FREDERICK CARROLL (*b. Philadelphia, Pa., 1825; d. Salisbury, N.C., 1898*), lawyer, jurist. Brother of Benjamin H. Brewster. A leader of the Pennsylvania bar.

BREWSTER, JAMES (*b. Preston, Conn., 1788; d. New Haven, Conn., 1866*), carriage-builder, railway-promoter, philanthropist. Developed the "Brewster wagon" and set a new standard for American vehicles of all types.

BREWSTER, OSMYN (*b. Worthington, Mass., 1797; d. 1889*), printer. Partner in Crocker & Brewster, publishers of religious books, 1825–76.

BREWSTER, WILLIAM (*b. England, 1567; d. Plymouth, Mass., 1644*), Pilgrim Father, Elder of the church at Plymouth. Spent his childhood in Scrooby, Nottinghamshire, where his father was bailiff and postmaster; attended Peterhouse, Cambridge, for a brief period where he first acquired Separatist ideas. A trusted aid in the foreign service, 1583–89, he returned to Scrooby and assumed father's positions, 1589. Became leading member of Puritan group at Scrooby, emigrating with them to Holland, 1608, and moving with them to Leyden, 1609, where he became Elder and teacher of the new church and a printer of Puritan books. Served as principal agent in 1617 negotiations with Virginia Company over a land grant and permission to colonize; thereafter took a minor part in settling details of emigration. Sailed aboard *Mayflower*, 1620. Although not "called" as a minister, he was the real religious leader in Plymouth colony and was second only to Bradford in administrative decisions.

BREWSTER, WILLIAM (*b. Wakefield, Mass., 1851; d. 1919*), ornithologist. His collection of North American birds (now in Museum of Comparative Zoology, Cambridge, Mass.) was the finest of its time.

BRICE, CALVIN STEWART (*b. Denmark, O., 1845; d. New York, N.Y., 1898*), railroad builder, lawyer. Graduated Miami University, 1863; rose to rank of lieutenant-colonel in Civil War. Gained distinction as corporation lawyer. In 1870 became projector and manager of railroad enterprises, outlining plan for a road to link Toledo and Ohio coal fields. President of Lake Erie and Western RR. *post* 1887; active in many other American railroads, as well as a project for exclusive right of way between Canton and Hankow in China. National Democratic chairman, 1889; U.S. senator from Ohio, 1891–96.

BRICKELL, ROBERT COMAN (*b. Tuscumbia, Ala., 1824; d. Huntsville, Ala., 1900*), jurist. Chief justice, Alabama supreme court, 1874–84.

BRIDGER, JAMES (*b. Richmond, Va., 1804; d. near Kansas City, Mo., 1881*), fur trader, frontiersman, scout. Removed with family to St. Louis, Mo., about 1812; orphaned at age 13; in 1822 joined Ashley's fur-trapping venture to the sources of Missouri River. Connected with northwest fur companies, 1822–42; first white man to visit Great Salt Lake, 1824. Established Fort Bridger, a way-station in southwestern Wyoming, 1843; was a friend of notable figures in westward movement. Driven out by Mormons, 1853, he returned as guide to Gen. A. S. Johnston's Utah invasion, 1857–58. Served also as guide to Raynolds Yellowstone expedition, 1859–60, Berthoud's engineering party, 1861, and Powder River expeditions, 1865–66; retired 1868.

BRIDGERS, ROBERT RUFUS (*b. Edgecombe Co., N.C., 1819; d. Columbia, S.C., 1888*), Confederate congressman, industrialist. President, Wilmington & Weldon and Columbia & Augusta railroads, 1865–88.

BRIDGES, CALVIN BLACKMAN (*b. Schuyler Falls, N.Y., 1889; d. Los Angeles, Calif., 1938*), geneticist. Graduated Columbia University, B.S., 1912, Ph.D., 1916, where he worked, 1910–28, with the zoologist Thomas Hunt Morgan. With Morgan, A. H. Sturtevant, and H. J. Muller, Bridges did pioneering studies of the genetics of the fruit fly *Drosophila*. Bridges's researches were especially concerned with proving the chromosome theory of heredity, and culminated in the formulation of the theory of "genic balance." Moving with Morgan to the California Institute of Technology in 1928, Bridges's later work was notable for investigations of the giant chromosomes in larval salivary glands, affording a new approach to the study of gene mutations. [*Supp. 2*]

BRIDGES, ROBERT (*d. 1656*), magistrate of Lynn, Mass. Instrumental in establishment of Saugus Iron Works, 1643, first in the colonies.

BRIDGES, ROBERT (*b. Philadelphia, Pa., 1806; d. 1882*), physician, botanist. Professor of chemistry, Philadelphia College of Pharmacy, 1842–79.

BRIDGMAN, ELIJAH COLEMAN (*b. Belchertown, Mass., 1801; d. China, 1861*). Missionary to China for the American Board, 1830–61. Edited *Chinese Repository*, 1832–47. Published *Chinese Chrestomathy*, (1841), a practical manual of the Cantonese dialect.

BRIDGMAN, FREDERIC ARTHUR (*b. Tuskegee, Ala., 1847; d. Rouen, France, 1927*), painter. Pupil of Gérôme; painted oriental and archeological subjects.

BRIDGMAN, HERBERT LAWRENCE (*b. Amherst, Mass., 1844; d. 1924*), newspaper publisher, explorer.

BRIDGMAN, LAURA DEWEY (*b. Hanover, N.H., 1829; d. Boston, Mass., 1889*), pupil of S. G. Howe at Perkins Institution, 1837; the first blind deaf-mute to be systematically educated.

BRIERTON, JOHN (*b. Norwich, England, 1572; d. post 1619*). Author of *A Briefe and True Relation of the Discoverie of the North Part of Virginia* (1602), the earliest English work about New England.

BRIGGS, CHARLES AUGUSTUS (*b. New York, N.Y., 1841; d. New York, 1913*), Presbyterian, later Episcopal, clergyman. Professor at Union Theological Seminary, 1874–1913. Tried for heresy, 1892, because of views on Biblical criticism. Edited *International Critical Commentary, International Theological Library*.

BRIGGS, CHARLES FREDERICK (*b. Nantucket, Mass., 1804; d. Brooklyn, N.Y., 1877*), journalist. Founded *Broadway Journal*, 1844; an editor, *Putnam's Magazine*, the *New York Times*, and *The Independent*; author of *The Adventures of Harry Franco* (1839) and other books.

BRIGGS, CLARE A. (*b. Reedsburg, Wis., 1875; d. New York, N.Y., 1930*), graphic humorist whose versatile output included "Mr. and Mrs." and "When a Feller Needs a Friend." [*Supp. 1*]

BRIGGS, GEORGE NIXON (*b. Adams, Mass., 1796; d. 1861*), lawyer, statesman. Congressman, Whig, from Massachusetts, 1831–43; governor of Massachusetts, 1844–51; a consistent opponent of slavery.

BRIGGS, LeBARON RUSSELL (*b. Salem, Mass., 1855; d. Milwaukee, Wis., 1934*), educator. Professor and dean, Harvard University, 1878–1925; president, Radcliffe College, 1903–23. Author of *School, College, and Character* (1901), and *Routine and Ideals* (1904). [*Supp. 1*]

BRIGHAM, ALBERT PERRY (*b. Perry, N.Y., 1855; d. 1932*), geographer, university professor. Made notable contributions to the geographic interpretation of history; active in Association of American Geographers. [*Supp. 1*]

BRIGHAM, AMARIAH (*b. New Marlboro, Mass., 1798; d. 1849*), physician. Founded *American Journal of Insanity*, 1844; wrote on mental health.

BRIGHAM, JOSEPH HENRY (*b. Lodi, O., 1838; d. 1904*), agriculturist. Master, National Grange, for four terms from 1889.

BRIGHAM, MARY ANN (*b. Westboro, Mass., 1829; d. 1889*), educator. Associate principal, Brooklyn Heights Seminary, 1863–89; chosen first president of Mount Holyoke College, but died before taking office.

BRIGHT, EDWARD (*b. Kington, England, 1808; d. 1894*). Emigrated as a child to Utica, N.Y. Editor of the *Examiner*, leading Baptist newspaper, *post* 1855.

BRIGHT, JAMES WILSON (*b. Aaronsburg, Pa., 1852; d. 1926*), philologist. Professor of English, Johns Hopkins, 1893–1925. Editor, *Modern Language Notes*, 1886–1915; editor-in-chief, 1916–25.

BRIGHT, JESSE DAVID (*b. Norwich, N.Y., 1812; d. Baltimore, Md., 1875*), politician. Led pro-slavery wing of Indiana Democratic party; U.S. senator from Indiana, 1845–62. Expelled from Senate, 1862, for treason.

BRIGHT EYES (*b. Omaha Reservation, Nebr., 1854; d. near Bancroft, Nebr., 1903*), advocate of Indian rights. Named Susette La Flesche; made protest tour in East, 1879, against arbitrary removals of tribes.

BRIGHTLY, FREDERICK CHARLES (*b. Bungay, England, 1812; d. Germantown, Pa., 1888*), lawyer. Emigrated to America, 1831; author of valuable digests of early laws.

BRILL, NATHAN EDWIN (*b. New York, N.Y., 1859; d. New York, 1925*), physician. Attending physician, Mt. Sinai Hospital, 1893–1923; outstanding diagnostician and clinician.

BRINCKLÉ, WILLIAM DRAPER (*b. St. Jones' Neck, Del., 1798; d. Groveville, N.J., 1862*), physician, pomologist.

BRINKERHOFF, JACOB (*b. Niles, N.Y., 1810; d. 1880*), jurist, legislator. Congressman, Democrat, from Ohio, 1843–47; became Free Soiler and Republican. Justice, Ohio supreme court, 1856–71. Claimed authorship of Wilmot Proviso.

BRINKERHOFF, ROELIFF (*b. Cayuga Co., N.Y., 1828; d. Mansfield, O., 1911*), lawyer, penologist.

BRINTON, DANIEL GARRISON (*b. Thornbury, Pa., 1837; d. 1899*), pioneer anthropologist. Graduated Yale, 1858; M.D., Jefferson Medical College, 1861; served as military surgeon, 1862–65. Editor, *Medical and Surgical Reporter*, 1874–87, retiring to give full time to anthropology. Never a field worker, his researches were of great and lasting value. Of particular merit were *Notes on the Floridian Peninsula* (1859) and *The American Race* (1891). His *Library of Aboriginal American Literature* (v.d.), an editing and translation of texts, included the Maya Chronicles (1882).

BRINTON, JOHN HILL (*b. Philadelphia, Pa., 1832; d. Philadelphia, 1907*), surgeon. Lecturer in and professor of surgery, Jefferson Medical College, 1855–1906; helped prepare *Medical and Surgical History of the War of the Rebellion* (1870–88), in which he had served with distinction.

BRISBANE, ALBERT (*b. Batavia, N.Y., 1809; d. Richmond, Va., 1890*), Utopian social reformer. Educated privately; studied in Paris with Cousin and Guizot, and in Berlin with Hegel. Strongly influenced by Fourier's theory of association, Brisbane spent two years in study with Fourier and returned to America, 1834, to propagate the doctrine. Was encouraged by Horace Greeley, but public interest was not caught for long. Author of *Social Destiny of Man* (1840), *Association* (1843) and *General Introduction to Social Sciences* (1876).

BRISBANE, ARTHUR (*b. Buffalo, N.Y., 1864; d. New York, N.Y., 1936*), newspaper editor and writer. Son of the social reformer Albert Brisbane, after European schooling he became a reporter on the New York *Sun*, 1885. In 1890 he joined Joseph Pulitzer's New York *World;* six years later, as editor of the *Sunday World,* he engaged in a sensational circulation battle with the *Journal* of William Randolph Hearst. Brisbane joined Hearst in 1897 and provided the sensational appeal to mass tastes, the jingoistic propaganda, the surface learning and adjustable conscience that the ambitious publisher wanted in his editor. Brisbane remained with Hearst until his death, editing the *Journal* and other papers, and writing a widely syndicated column, "Today." [*Supp. 2*]

BRISTED, CHARLES ASTOR (*b. New York, N.Y., 1820; d. 1874*), author. Great-grandson of John Jacob Astor. Graduated Yale, 1839; graduated Trinity College, Cambridge, 1845. Wrote studies in philology and somewhat acid sketches of American society.

BRISTED, JOHN (*b. Sherborne, England, 1778; d. Bristol, R.I., 1855*), Episcopal clergyman. Came to America as lawyer, 1806; ordained *c.* 1828. Father of C. A. Bristed.

BRISTOL, JOHN BUNYAN (*b. Hillsdale, N.Y., 1826; d. New York, N.Y., 1909*), landscape painter.

BRISTOL, MARK LAMBERT (*b. Glassboro, N.J., 1868; d. Washington, D.C., 1939*), naval officer and diplomat. High commissioner to Turkey, 1919–27. [*Supp. 2*]

BRISTOL, WILLIAM HENRY (*b. Waterbury, Conn., 1859; d. New Haven, Conn., 1930*), mechanical engineer, university professor, inventor and pioneer manufacturer of recording instruments. Graduated M.E. from Stevens Institute of Technology, 1884; returned two years later to teach until 1907. While at Stevens he patented a steel fastener for joining leather belts, and with his brother Franklin B. Bristol organized the Bristol Co. in 1889 to manufacture them. Perfected devices for measuring pressure and temperature which were accepted throughout industry as the standard of accuracy. Invented the Bristolphone for synchronized recording of sound and action. [*Supp. 1*]

BRISTOW, BENJAMIN HELM (*b. Elkton, Ky., 1832; d. New York, N.Y., 1896*), lawyer, statesman. Graduated Jefferson College, Pennsylvania, 1851; admitted to bar 1853; fought in Civil War as ardent Unionist. Served in Kentucky senate, 1863–65; fought for ratification of 13th Amendment and Lincoln's re-election. U.S. attorney for Kentucky, 1866–70. Appointed solicitor-general, 1870, and secretary of treasury, 1874; in latter office broke up Whiskey Ring. Resignation forced by President Grant, 1876, on ground that Bristow was scheming for presidential nomination. Removed to New York City, 1878, where he became a leader of the bar.

BRISTOW, GEORGE FREDERICK (*b. Brooklyn, N.Y., 1825; d. 1898*), composer, violinist, teacher.

BRITTON, NATHANIEL LORD (*b. New Dorp, S.I., N.Y., 1859; d. 1934*), botanist and author. Organized and directed the New York Botanical Garden, 1896–1929. [*Supp. 1*]

BROADHEAD, GARLAND CARR (*b. near Charlottesville, Va., 1827; d. 1912*), geologist, engineer. Differentiated coal measures of Missouri and Kansas; established Ozarkian Series.

BROADHEAD, JAMES OVERTON (*b. near Char-lottesville, Va., 1819; d. 1898*), outstanding Missouri lawyer. Brother of Garland C. Broadhead. Special commissioner to France, 1885, on Spoliation Claims.

BROADUS, JOHN ALBERT (*b. western Virginia, 1827; d. 1895*), Baptist clergyman. Professor, Southern Baptist Seminary, Greenville, S.C., 1858; later its president at Louisville, Ky., 1889–95.

BROCKETT, LINUS PIERPONT (*b. Canton, Conn., 1820; d. Brooklyn, N.Y., 1893*), author, physician.

BROCKMEYER, HENRY C. [See BROKMEYER, HENRY C., 1828–1906.]

BROCKWAY, ZEBULON REED (*b. Lyme, Conn., 1827; d. 1920*), penologist. Superintendent, House of Correction, Detroit, 1861–72; superintendent, Elmira State Reformatory, 1876–1900.

BRODERICK, DAVID COLBRETH (*b. Washington, D.C., 1820; d. California, 1859*), politician. Moved to New York City, 1834; father's death in 1837 left him to support mother and younger brother. Active in Tammany politics, 1840–48, he owned a saloon and prospered. Moved to California, 1849, and engaged again in politics; by 1854 was a power in the local Democratic party and president of the state senate. Chosen U.S. senator in 1857, he traded off the seat to William M. Gwin in return for a promise of federal patronage which was not honored. Hostile to the pro-slavery elements in his party, he lost his life in a duel with David S. Terry, one of the pro-slavery leaders.

BRODHEAD, DANIEL (*b. Albany, N.Y., 1736; d. Milford, Pa., 1809*), soldier. Moved to Reading, Pa., 1773; commanded Pennsylvania troops in Revolution; subdued Indians along Allegheny River, 1779 and 1781.

BRODHEAD, JOHN ROMEYN (*b. Philadelphia, Pa., 1814; d. New York, N.Y., 1873*), historian, archivist. Author of classic *History of the State of New York* (1853, 1871).

BROKMEYER, HENRY C. (*b. near Minden, Prussia, 1828; d. 1906*), philosopher. Came to America, 1844. Translated Hegel's *Larger Logic,* and initiated the "St. Louis Movement" of German (Hegelian) idealism.

BROMFIELD, JOHN (*b. Newburyport, Mass., 1779; d. Boston, Mass., 1849*), philanthropist, China merchant. Benefactor to Boston charities and institutions.

BROMLEY, ISAAC HILL (*b. Norwich, Conn., 1833; d. Norwich, 1898*), journalist. Editorial staff, *New York Tribune*, 1873–82; 1891–98.

BRONDEL, JOHN BAPTIST (*b. Bruges, Belgium, 1842; d. Helena, Mont., 1903*), Roman Catholic clergyman. Missionary in the Northwest *post* 1864; bishop of Vancouver, 1879–84, and of Helena, Mont., thereafter.

BRONSON, HENRY (*b. Waterbury, Conn., 1804; d. New Haven, Conn., 1893*), physician, historian. Professor, Yale Medical School, 1842–60; author of *History of Waterbury* (1858).

BRONSON, WALTER COCHRANE (*b. Roxbury, Mass., 1862; d. Oxford, England, 1928*), educator, anthropologist, editor. Professor of English literature, Brown University, 1905–27.

BROOKE, FRANCIS TALIAFERRO (*b. Smithfield, Va., 1763; d. 1851*), Revolutionary soldier. Judge, Virginia supreme court of appeals, 1811–51.

BROOKE, JOHN MERCER (*b. near Tampa, Fla., 1826; d. Lexington, Ky., 1906*), naval officer, scientist. Midshipman, U.S. Navy, 1841; graduated Annapolis, 1847; with Coast Survey, 1849–50. At Naval Observatory, 1851–53; invented deep-sea sounding apparatus, which made possible mapping topography of ocean bottom; explored North Pacific and prepared charts, 1854; surveyed Japanese east coast, 1858–60. Entered Confederate States navy, 1861. Planned reconstruction of *Merrimack;* developed "Brooke" gun; was chief of Bureau of Ordnance and Hydrography. Professor of physics and astronomy, Virginia Military Institute, 1866–99.

BROOKE, JOHN RUTTER (*b. Montgomery Co., Pa., 1838; d. Philadelphia, Pa., 1926*), Union soldier. Distinguished at Gettysburg. As major-general, commanded 1st Corps, 1898.

BROOKER, CHARLES FREDERICK (*b. Litchfield, Conn., 1847; d. Daytona, Fla., 1926*), manufacturer, financier. Formed American Brass Co., 1899; was its president, 1900–20.

BROOKINGS, ROBERT SOMERS (*b. Cecil Co., Md., 1850; d. Washington, D.C., 1932*), business executive, philanthropist, educator. With little more than elementary school education, became virtual head of the Cupples woodenware company, St. Louis, at 22. Built Cupples Station, 1895, a railroad terminal which revolutionized the distribution of goods in St. Louis and served as a model for other cities. Retired from business in 1896 and devoted himself to higher education. Developed Washington University, St. Louis, especially the medical school. From his 1917 experience as chairman of the price-fixing committee came his interest in public affairs which resulted in the establishment of the Brookings Institution, 1928. [*Supp.* 1]

BROOKS, ALFRED HULSE (*b. Ann Arbor, Mich., 1871; d. 1924*), geologist, geographer. Headed Alaskan division, U.S. Geological Survey, 1902–24; author of *Geography and Geology of Alaska* (1906).

BROOKS, BYRON ALDEN (*b. Theresa, N.Y., 1845; d. Brooklyn, N.Y., 1911*), teacher, inventor. Improved typewriter, 1878, by putting both capital and small letters on same striking lever, with a key to shift position.

BROOKS, CHARLES (*b. Medford, Mass., 1795; d. Medford, 1872*), Unitarian clergyman. Wrote *Family*

Prayer Book, 1821. Influential in normal-school movement, 1835–39.

BROOKS, CHARLES TIMOTHY (*b. Salem, Mass., 1813; d. Newport, R.I., 1883*), Unitarian clergyman, poet. Pastor, Unitarian Church, Newport, 1837–71. Able translator of German literature.

BROOKS, ELBRIDGE STREETER (*b. Lowell, Mass., 1846; d. Somerville, Mass., 1902*). Editor, D. Lothrop & Co., 1887–1902; author of historical sketches for children.

BROOKS, ERASTUS (*b. Portland, Maine, 1815; d. Staten Island, N.Y., 1886*), journalist, politician. Editor, *New York Express,* 1844–77; active in Know-Nothing party. Brother of James Brooks.

BROOKS, GEORGE WASHINGTON (*b. Elizabeth City, N.C., 1821; d. 1882*), lawyer. Southern Unionist; U.S. judge, district of North Carolina, 1865–82.

BROOKS, JAMES (*b. Portland, Maine, 1810; d. 1873*), journalist. Brother of Erastus Brooks. Noted correspondent in Washington; publisher, *New York Express,* 1836–73. Received Crédit Mobilier bribe, 1868, while a government director of the Union Pacific.

BROOKS, JAMES GORDON (*b. Red Hook, N.Y., 1801; d. Albany, N.Y., 1841*), editor, poet. Author, with wife, of *The Rivals of Este* (1829).

BROOKS, JOHN (*b. Medford, Mass., 1752; d. Medford, 1825*), physician, Revolutionary soldier. On "Newburgh Address" committee, 1783. Federalist governor of Massachusetts, 1816–22.

BROOKS, JOHN GRAHAM (*b. Acworth, N.H., 1846; d. Cambridge, Mass., 1938*), sociologist and reformer. Left the Unitarian ministry, 1891, to devote his career to analyzing and writing about labor-employer relationships.   [Supp. 2]

BROOKS, MARIA GOWEN (*b. Medford, Mass., c. 1794; d. Cuba, 1845*), poet. Pen-name, "Maria del Occidente." Works include *Zóphiël* (1833), prose tale *Idomen* (1843).

BROOKS, NOAH (*b. Castine, Maine, 1830; d. Pasadena, Calif., 1903*), journalist. Close friend of Lincoln. Editor, *New York Tribune,* 1871–76, *New York Times,* 1876–84, and other newspapers in both East and West; author of *The Boy Emigrants* (1876).

BROOKS, PETER CHARDON (*b. North Yarmouth, Maine, 1767; d. Boston, Mass., 1849*), Boston merchant and insurance broker, 1789–1803. Reputed the wealthiest man in New England.

BROOKS, PHILLIPS (*b. Boston, Mass., 1835; d. Boston, 1893*), Episcopal clergyman. Graduated Harvard, 1855; entered seminary at Alexandria, Va., and was ordained, 1859. His sermon at Independence Hall, Philadelphia, 1865, over Lincoln's body received nationwide attention; also his sermon at 1865 Harvard

commemoration of Civil War dead. Wrote "O Little Town of Bethlehem" for Sunday-school, 1868. Rector of Trinity Church, Boston, 1869–91; delivered *Lectures on Preaching,* Yale Divinity School, 1877; bishop of Massachusetts, 1891–93. Outstanding as pulpit orator and pastor; a "broad" churchman.

BROOKS, PRESTON SMITH (*b. Edgefield, S.C., 1819; d. Washington, D.C., 1857*). Attacked Charles Sumner of Massachusetts, 1856, for slur on uncle, Sen. A. P. Butler of South Carolina. Congressman, Democrat, from South Carolina, 1853–57.

BROOKS, RICHARD EDWIN (*b. Braintree, Mass., 1865; d. Washington, D.C., 1919*), sculptor and portrait medalist.

BROOKS, THOMAS BENTON (*b. Monroe, N.Y., 1836; d. 1900*), geologist, mining engineer. Attended Union College School of Engineering, 1856–58; rose to brevet-colonel in Civil War. General manager of Iron Cliff mine in Marquette District, Mich., *post* 1865; directed economic division, state geological survey of Upper Peninsula, 1869–73. His report was a full manual of every phase of mining and smelting iron ores of Lake Superior region.

BROOKS, WILLIAM KEITH (*b. Cleveland, O., 1848; d. 1908*), zoologist. Founded Chesapeake Zoological Laboratory, 1878. Taught morphology and biology, Johns Hopkins, 1876–1908. Author of *Law of Heredity* (1883), *Foundations of Zoology* (1899).

BROOKS, WILLIAM ROBERT (*b. Maidstone, England, 1844; d. Geneva, N.Y., 1921*), astronomer. Came to America, 1857. A pioneer in application of photography to celestial observation; discoverer of twenty-seven comets; professor of astronomy, Hobart College.

BROOKS, WILLIAM THOMAS HARBAUGH (*b. New Lisbon, O., 1821; d. Huntsville, Ala., 1870*), Union soldier. Graduated West Point, 1841. Served in Mexican War and on frontier; rose to division commander in Civil War.

BROPHY, TRUMAN WILLIAM (*b. Goodings Grove, Ill., 1848; d. 1928*), oral surgeon. Originated successful operation to correct cleft palate and harelip. Wrote *Oral Surgery* (1915) and *Cleft Lip and Palate* (1923).

BROSS, WILLIAM (*b. Sussex Co., N.J., 1813; d. Chicago, Ill., 1890*), journalist. Established Chicago *Democratic Press,* 1852; combined it with the *Tribune,* 1857; thereafter the *Tribune* prospered with the rise of Chicago.

BROUGH, CHARLES HILLMAN (*b. Clinton, Miss., 1876; d. Washington, D.C., 1935*), educator, lecturer, public servant. Governor of Arkansas, 1916–18.

[Supp. 1]

BROUGH, JOHN (*b. Marietta, O., 1811; d. 1865*). Editor, *Cincinnati Enquirer;* successful railroad executive. Republican governor of Ohio, 1864–65.

BROUGHAM, JOHN (*b. Dublin, Ireland, 1810; d. New York, N.Y., 1880*), actor, playwright. Began American career in New York, N.Y., 1842. Excelled in comic writing and impersonations.

BROUN, HEYWOOD CAMPBELL (*b. Brooklyn, N.Y., 1888; d. New York, N.Y., 1939*), newspaper columnist, author, organizer of the American Newspaper Guild, 1933. Attended Harvard, 1906–10. Reporter, sports writer, drama and literary critic, and war correspondent for the *New York Tribune*, 1912–21. Joined the New York *World*, 1921, as a columnist; disagreements resulting from his views on the Sacco-Vanzetti case led to his dismissal in 1928. While a columnist for the New York *Telegram* and *World-Telegram*, 1928–July 1939, Broun published his own literary and humourous weekly and presided over the union he had helped to organize. His syndicated column, often in disagreement with the policies of the newspapers in which it appeared and expressive of his own views and personality, set a new pattern in American journalism. [*Supp. 2*]

BROWARD, NAPOLEON BONAPARTE (*b. Duval Co., Fla., 1857; d. 1910*). Governor of Florida, Democrat, 1905–10; promoted drainage of Everglades.

BROWER, JACOB VRADENBERG (*b. York, Mich., 1844; d. 1905*), explorer, archeologist. Located aboriginal mounds at Mille Lac, Minn., also the site of Quivira in Kansas.

BROWERE, JOHN HENRI ISAAC (*b. New York, N.Y., 1792; d. New York, 1834*), sculptor. Created series of life masks of great Americans, perfected by a process now unknown.

BROWN, AARON VENABLE (*b. Brunswick Co., Va., 1795; d. 1859*), lawyer. Democratic Congressman from Tennessee, 1839–45; a champion of Oregon occupation and Texas annexation. Governor of Tennessee, 1845–47; postmaster-general in Buchanan cabinet (1857–59).

BROWN, ADDISON (*b. West Newbury, Mass., 1830; d. New York, N.Y., 1913*), lawyer. Federal judge, southern district of New York, 1881–1901. Co-author of *Illustrated Flora of the Northern United States* (1896–98).

BROWN, ALBERT GALLATIN (*b. Chester District, S.C., 1813; d. near Terry, Miss., 1880*), lawyer, politician. Moved to Mississippi, 1823. Congressman, Democrat, 1839–41; 1848–61. Able governor of Mississippi, 1844–48. Confederate senator, 1862–65.

BROWN, ALEXANDER (*b. Co. Antrim, Ireland, 1764; d. Baltimore, Md., 1834*), one of the foremost mercantile figures of his time. Came to America, 1800, and opened a linen shop in Baltimore. The business expanded into world-wide trading and shipping activities; branches were managed by sons (Brown Brothers & Co., in New York and Philadelphia; Brown, Shipley & Co., Liverpool, etc.). Extensive commercial ties abroad encouraged the change of a mercantile business into a merchant banking house; its greatest period of growth was between 1824 and 1834. Brown and his sons were among the founders of the Baltimore and Ohio Railroad and were active in many other civic and commercial movements.

BROWN, ALEXANDER (*b. Glenmore, Va., 1843; d. 1906*), historian. Active in revision of old concepts of Virginia's colonial history; author of *The Genesis of the United States* (1890) and other carefully researched works.

BROWN, ALEXANDER EPHRAIM (*b. Cleveland, O., 1852; d. Cleveland, 1911*), engineer, manufacturer. Inventor of the Brown hoisting and conveying machine (1879) for handling coal and ores.

BROWN, ANTOINETTE. [See BLACKWELL, ANTOINETTE LOUISA BROWN, 1825–1921.]

BROWN, BEDFORD (*b. Caswell Co., N.C., 1792; d. 1870*), North Carolina legislator. U.S. senator, 1829–40; supporter of Andrew Jackson's policies.

BROWN, BENJAMIN GRATZ (*b. Lexington, Ky., 1826; d. 1885*), lawyer, statesman. Graduated Yale, 1847; admitted to Kentucky bar; moved to St. Louis, Mo., 1849. Served in lower branch of Missouri legislature, 1852–59; his 1857 speech against a joint resolution which declared abolition of slavery impracticable is regarded as start of Free-Soil movement in Missouri. Defeated in 1857 as Free-Soil Democrat candidate for governorship, he was active in formation of Republican party in the state, was a delegate to the 1860 Chicago convention, and cooperated with his cousin Frank P. Blair, Jr., and with Gen. Lyon in opposing the Missouri secessionists. As U.S. senator, 1863–67, he spoke for universal suffrage, for government ownership and operation of telegraph lines, and for the merit system in civil service; as Liberal Republican governor of Missouri, 1871–73, he opposed radical reconstruction policy. In 1872, he ran for vice-president of the United States on the Liberal Republican ticket headed by Horace Greeley; after his defeat he resumed his law practice.

BROWN, CHARLES BROCKDEN (*b. Philadelphia, Pa., 1771; d. Philadelphia, 1810*), novelist, journalist, the first American to make authorship his principal profession. A romantic revolutionary and a writer of sombre intensity, he was strongly influenced by the work of William Godwin. Author of *Alcuin: A Dialogue* (1798), *Wieland* (1798), *Arthur Mervyn* (1799, 1800), *Ormond* (1799), *Edgar Huntly* (1799), *Clara Howard* (1801), *Jane Talbot* (1801) and various pamphlets and translations. He also edited *The Monthly Magazine and American Review* (N.Y., 1799–1800), *The Literary Magazine and American Register* (Phila., 1803–07), and *The American Register or General Repository, etc.* (Phila., 1807–11).

BROWN, CHARLES RUFUS (*b. East Kingston, N.H., 1849; d. Stoneham, Mass., 1914*), Baptist clergyman. Taught Old Testament studies at Newton Theological Institution, 1883–1914.

BROWN, CHARLOTTE EMERSON (*b. Andover, Mass., 1838; d. East Orange, N.J., 1895*). An organizer, and first president (1890), of the General Federation of Women's Clubs.

BROWN, DAVID PAUL (*b. Philadelphia, Pa., 1795; d. Philadelphia, 1872*), lawyer, orator. Author of *Sertorius*, a tragedy (produced 1830), a vehicle for Junius Brutus Booth, and other plays.

BROWN, EBENEZER (*b. probably Chesterfield, Mass., 1795; d. Baltimore, Md., 1889*), Methodist clergyman. Served in New Orleans, 1819, as first missionary sent out by Methodist Board; in 1829, manufactured first detachable collars at Troy, N.Y.

BROWN, ELMER ELLSWORTH (*b. Kiantone, N.Y., 1861; d. 1934*), chancellor of New York University. During his term, 1911–1933, the university became one of the largest in the United States. [*Supp. 1*]

BROWN, ERNEST WILLIAM (*b. Hull, England, 1866; d. New Haven, Conn., 1938*), mathematician, student of celestial mechanics. Attended Cambridge University, B.A., 1887, M.A., 1891. Came to America to teach at Haverford College, 1891–1907; professor of mathematics at Yale, 1907–32. Brown's interest in the moon's motion led to his *An Introductory Treatise on the Lunar Theory* (1896). He then constructed a new lunar theory, based on researches of George William Hill. Brown's monumental *Tables of the Motion of the Moon* (1919) immediately established the superiority of his theory. His explanation of the observed fluctuations of the moon as being due to irregular changes in the earth's rate of rotation was fully confirmed in 1939. He also contributed to planetary theory.
[*Supp. 2*]

BROWN, ETHAN ALLEN (*b. Darien, Conn., 1766; d. Indianapolis, Ind., 1852*), politician. Established a law practice at Cincinnati, O., 1804. Democratic governor of Ohio, 1818–22; U.S. senator, 1822–25. Promoted canals and internal improvements.

BROWN, FAYETTE (*b. North Bloomfield, O., 1823; d. Cleveland, O., 1910*), banker, iron manufacturer. Patented improvements in blast furnace design and charging hoists; a pioneer in water transport of ore on Great Lakes; promoted loading inventions of son, Alexander Ephraim Brown.

BROWN, FRANCIS (*b. Chester, N.H., 1784; d. Hanover, N.H., 1820*). President of Dartmouth College, 1815–20; Congregational clergyman.

BROWN, FRANCIS (*b. Hanover, N.H., 1849; d. New York, N.Y., 1916*), professor of theology. Son of Samuel Gilman Brown. Graduated Dartmouth, 1870; Union Theological Seminary, 1877; was a disciple of Charles A. Briggs and his successor in 1890 as professor of Old Testament languages at Union. Editor of *Hebrew and English Lexicon of the Old Testament* (completed 1906); president of Union Seminary, 1908–16.

BROWN, FREDERIC TILDEN (*b. New York, N.Y., 1853; d. Bethel, Maine, 1910*), surgeon. Developed improved instruments for use in his genito-urinary specialty.

BROWN, GEORGE (*b. Ballymena, Ireland, 1787; d. Baltimore, Md., 1859*), banker. Son of Alexander Brown (1764–1834). A projector and first treasurer of the Baltimore and Ohio railroad.

BROWN, GEORGE (*b. Wilton, N.H., 1823; d. Barre, Mass., 1892*), physician. Improved techniques for instruction of feeble-minded at Elm Hill School, Barre, Mass., 1850–92.

BROWN, GEORGE PLINY (*b. Lenox township, O., 1836; d. Bloomington, Ill., 1910*), educator. President, Indiana State Normal School, Terre Haute, 1879–86; editor, *School and Home Education*, 1888–1910.

BROWN, GEORGE WILLIAM (*b. Baltimore, Md., 1812; d. 1890*), lawyer. As Baltimore mayor, 1859–61, broke grip of Know-Nothing party on city; imprisoned for short period at start of Civil War on suspicion of Southern sympathies, he served as judge, supreme bench of Baltimore, 1872–88.

BROWN, GOOLD (*b. Providence, R.I., 1791; d. Lynn, Mass., 1857*), grammarian. Author of *Institutes of English Grammar* (1823), for many years a popular text.

BROWN, HENRY BILLINGS (*b. South Lee, Mass., 1836; d. Bronxville, N.Y., 1913*), jurist. Authority on admiralty law; associate justice, U.S. Supreme Court, 1890–1906.

BROWN, HENRY CORDIS (*b. near St. Clairsville, O., 1820; d. San Diego, Calif., 1906*), capitalist. Prospered in Denver, Colo., real estate, 1860–93; builder of Brown Palace Hotel, Denver, 1889.

BROWN, HENRY KIRKE (*b. Leyden, Mass., 1814; d. Newburgh, N.Y., 1886*), sculptor. Teacher of J. Q. A. Ward; executed equestrian Washington statue, Union Square, New York City, and other works.

BROWN, ISAAC VAN ARSDALE (*b. Pluckemin, N.J., 1784; d. 1861*), Presbyterian clergyman. Founded Lawrenceville School, 1810; served as its principal until 1833.

BROWN, JACOB JENNINGS (*b. Bucks Co., Pa., 1775; d. 1828*), soldier. After teaching school, and surveying in Ohio, promoted a settlement at Brownsville, N.Y., near Watertown, 1799, and prospered in farming and land operations. Active in the militia *post* 1809, he successfully defended Sackett's Harbor, 1813. In 1814, appointed major-general commanding in western New York, he began an invasion of Canada which was successful at the ably fought battles of Chippewa and Niagara (or Lundy's Lane) but met ultimate failure for lack of naval support. He commanded the army of the United States, 1821–28.

BROWN, JAMES (*b. near Staunton, Va., 1766; d. Philadelphia, Pa., 1835*), lawyer. U.S. senator, Democrat, from Louisiana, 1813–17 and 1819–23; U.S. minister to France, 1823–29.

BROWN, JAMES (*b. Ireland, 1791; d. New York, N.Y., 1877*), banker. Son of Alexander Brown. Founded Brown Brothers and Co., New York branch of his father's Baltimore firm.

BROWN, JAMES (*b. Acton, Mass., 1800; d. 1855*), bookseller, publisher. With C. C. Little, founded Boston publishing firm of Little, Brown & Co., 1837.

BROWN, JAMES SALISBURY (*b. Pawtucket, R.I., 1802; d. Pawtucket, 1879*), inventor, head of the Brown Machine Works. Introduced many improvements in cotton machinery; devised a variety of special tools.

BROWN, JOHN (*b. Providence, R.I., 1736; d. Providence, 1803*), merchant. Brother of Nicholas (1729–1791), Joseph, and Moses (1738–1836) Brown. At first their partner, he withdrew *c.* 1770 from the family business to trade on his own account. Headed raiding party against British vessel *Gaspee*, 1772; employed his ships and trade connections in service of Congress during Revolutionary War. Brown and Francis, his firm, sent out the first Providence vessel to engage in the East India and China trade, 1787. He served for twenty years as treasurer of Brown University (Rhode Island College).

BROWN, JOHN (*b. Haverhill, Mass., 1744; d. near Stone Arabia, N.Y., 1780*), lawyer, soldier. Gathered Canadian intelligence for Gen. Schuyler, 1775; with Ethan Allen attacked Montreal; with Montgomery and Arnold before Quebec, Dec. 1775. Captured Fort George, N.Y., 1777; killed in expedition against Tories and Mohawks.

BROWN, JOHN (*b. Staunton, Va., 1757; d. Frankfort, Ky., 1837*), statesman. Removed to Kentucky, 1782; first U.S. senator from that state, 1792–1805; an outstanding spokesman for the West.

BROWN, JOHN (*b. Torrington, Conn., 1800; d. Charlestown, W. Va., 1859*), "Brown of Osawatomie." Child of a roving father and a mentally unstable maternal stock; spent boyhood in Hudson, O.; was by turns a drover, a tanner, a land speculator, and a dealer in sheep. Brown's career before 1855 was a record of bankruptcies, law-suits and drifting from place to place. Always an abolitionist, the idea that slaves must be freed by force became obsessive in his mind about the time of the free-soil *vs.* slave-interest fight for Kansas, 1855. From a free-soil settlement they had established on the Osawatomie there, he and his sons led a murderous guerrilla attack on

a pro-slave settlement in reprisal for the sack of Lawrence, Kans., during May 1856. Driven from Kansas, Brown returned East to become the idol of the abolition party; he was encouraged by Gerrit Smith and others in a plan to establish a free state for escaped slaves and free Negroes in the mountains of Maryland and Virginia, wherefrom active hostility against slave-owners could be directed. After a brief 1858 skirmish on the Kansas-Missouri border, Brown fixed on Harper's Ferry, Va., as a base for future operations; in midsummer, 1859, his 21-man "army" assembled at a farm nearby; on the night of Oct. 16 he raided Harper's Ferry, seizing on the U.S. armory there and securing the bridges. Local militia and a company of U.S. marines under Col. R. E. Lee penned Brown and his followers in the engine-house of the armory; following his refusal to surrender, the soldiers took the place by storm. After a trial for treason he was sentenced to death. He was hanged on Dec. 2, 1859.

BROWN, JOHN A. (*b. Ireland, 1788; d. 1872*), banker. Son of Alexander Brown. Established Philadelphia branch of father's firm, 1818; it was later Brown and Bowen, and finally Brown Brothers & Co.

BROWN, JOHN APPLETON (*b. West Newbury, Mass., 1844; d. New York, N.Y., 1902*), landscape painter.

BROWN, JOHN CALVIN (*b. Giles Co., Tenn., 1827; d. Red Boiling Springs, Tenn., 1889*), lawyer, Confederate soldier. Democratic governor of Tennessee, 1870–74; supervised construction of Texas & Pacific railroad *post* 1876. Brother of Neill S. Brown.

BROWN, JOHN CARTER (*b. Providence, R.I., 1797; d. 1874*), book collector. Assembled the great library which bears his name, now at Brown University. Son of Nicholas Brown (1769–1841).

BROWN, JOHN GEORGE (*b. Durham, England, 1831; d. New York, N.Y., 1913*), painter. Came to America *c.* 1853; specialized in popular renderings of American town and country types; was a president of the National Academy.

BROWN, JOHN MIFFLIN (*b. Odessa, Del., 1817; d. Washington, D.C., 1893*), bishop of the African Methodist Episcopal Church, 1868–93; principal of Union Seminary, Ohio; founder of Paul Quinn College, Waco, Texas.

BROWN, JOHN NEWTON (*b. New London, Conn., 1803; d. 1868*), Baptist clergyman. Pastor, scholar and editor; an author of the *New Hampshire Confession of Faith* (1833).

BROWN, JOHN PORTER (*b. Chillicothe, O., 1814; d. Constantinople, Turkey, 1872*), diplomat, Orientalist. Served in various capacities at the American legation, Constantinople, 1832–72.

BROWN, JOHN YOUNG (*b. Elizabethtown, Ky., 1835; d. 1904*), lawyer. Democratic governor of Kentucky, 1891–95.

BROWN, JOSEPH (*b. Providence, R.I., 1733; d. 1785*), merchant, scientist. Brother of Nicholas (1729–1791), Moses (1738–1836), and John Brown (1736–1803); withdrew from family firm to conduct experiments in electricity and mechanics.

BROWN, JOSEPH EMERSON (*b. Pickens District, S.C., 1821; d. 1894*), lawyer, statesman. Practiced law in Canton, Ga.; active in Democratic politics. Able, controversial governor of Georgia, 1857–65; active as a Republican, 1866–71; re-entered Democratic party, and served as U.S. senator, 1880–91. President of Western & Atlantic railroad.

BROWN, JOSEPH ROGERS (*b. Warren, R.I., 1810; d. Isles of Shoals, N.H., 1876*), inventor, manufacturer. Designer and builder of high-precision machine-tools; head of Brown & Sharpe Manufacturing Co.

BROWN, LAWRASON (*b. Baltimore, Md., 1871; d. Saranac Lake, N.Y., 1937*), physician. Resident and consulting physician, Trudeau Sanitarium, 1900–37; a national leader in the control of tuberculosis. [Supp. 2]

BROWN, MATHER (*b. Boston, Mass., 1761; d. London, England, 1831*), painter. Pupil of Gilbert Stuart and Benjamin West. Miniaturist in Boston until 1780 when he went abroad; thereafter painted portraits and historical subjects in London, 1784–1809, in the English provincial towns until 1824, and in London again until death.

BROWN, MORRIS (*b. Charleston, S.C., 1770; d. 1849*), bishop of the African Methodist Episcopal Church, 1828–49. Was responsible for a wide extension of the denomination during his episcopacy.

BROWN, MOSES (*b. Providence, R.I., 1738; d. Providence, 1836*), manufacturer and philanthropist. Brother of Nicholas Brown (1729–1791), John Brown (1736–1803) and Joseph Brown (1733–1785). Member of firm of Nicholas Brown & Co., 1763–73. After the Revolutionary War, he was among first cotton manufacturers in the United States, and induced Samuel Slater to set up Arkwright machines here.

BROWN, MOSES (*b. Newbury, Mass., 1742; d. Newburyport, Mass., 1827*), merchant. A benefactor and founding donor of Andover Theological Seminary.

BROWN, NEILL SMITH (*b. Giles Co., Tenn., 1810; d. Nashville, Tenn., 1886*), lawyer, politician. Brother of John Calvin Brown. Whig governor of Tennessee, 1847–49; U.S. minister to Russia, 1850–53.

BROWN, NICHOLAS (*b. Providence, R.I., 1729; d. 1791*), merchant. Brother of John Brown (1736–1803), Joseph Brown (1733–1785) and Moses Brown (1738–1836); senior partner in trading firm established by their father and known after 1762 as Nicholas Brown & Co. Before the Revolutionary War the firm's vessels ventured to all West Indian and European ports, while the brothers interested themselves in development of local industries such as whale oil, iron manufacture and distilling. Brown and his brother Joseph were responsible for the location of Rhode Island College at Providence, 1767; in 1804, after further family benefactions, it became known as Brown University.

BROWN, NICHOLAS (*b. Providence, R.I., 1769; d. Providence, 1841*), merchant, philanthropist. Son of Nicholas Brown (1729–1791), father of John Carter Brown. Carried on firm established by father and uncles, extending its interests to the Far East, to cotton manufacture and to western land speculation; a benefactor of Brown University.

BROWN, OBADIAH (*b. Providence, R.I., 1771; d. 1822*), merchant. Son of Moses Brown (1738–1836); joined his father as a partner in cotton manufacture, 1792.

BROWN, OLYMPIA (*b. Prairie Ronde, Mich., 1835; d. Baltimore, Md., 1926*), feminist. Ordained minister in Universalist Church, 1863, the first woman to be ordained in America to a regularly constituted religious body; after 1866, an ardent campaigner for woman suffrage.

BROWN, PHOEBE HINSDALE (*b. Canaan, N.Y., 1783; d. Monson, Mass. (?), 1861*), hymn writer.

BROWN, SAMUEL (*b. Rockbridge Co., Va., 1769; d. near Huntsville, Ala., 1830*), physician. Brother of James Brown (1766–1835) and John Brown (1757–1837).

BROWN, SAMUEL GILMAN (*b. Hanover, N.H., 1813; d. Utica, N.Y., 1885*), educator. Professor of oratory, philosophy, political economy at Dartmouth, 1840–67; president, Hamilton College, 1867–81.

BROWN, SAMUEL ROBBINS (*b. East Windsor, Conn., 1810; d. Monson, Mass., 1880*), missionary to China and Japan for Dutch Reformed Church.

BROWN, SIMON (*b. Newburyport, Mass., 1802; d. near Concord, Mass., 1873*), editor of the *New England Farmer, post* 1858.

BROWN, SOLYMAN (*b. Litchfield, Conn., 1790; d. Dodge Center, Minn., 1876*), a pioneer in the American dental profession. Graduated Yale, 1812; with Eleazar Parmly organized first dental association, in New York, N.Y., 1834; served also as a Swedenborgian minister.

BROWN, SYLVANUS (*b. Valley Falls, R.I., 1747; d. Pawtucket, R.I., 1824*), inventor, millwright. Built the first American power spinning machine from Samuel Slater's description of the parts, 1790.

BROWN, WILLIAM (*b. Haddingtonshire, Scotland, 1752; d. Alexandria, Va., 1792*), physician. While in service with Revolutionary army, wrote the first pharmacopeia to be published in the United States (1778).

BROWN, WILLIAM CARLOS (*b. Norway, N.Y., 1853; d. Pasadena, Calif., 1924*), railroad executive. Raised in Iowa. Rose from engine fireman to general manager of Chicago, Burlington & Quincy Railroad; president of New York Central, 1909–14.

BROWN, WILLIAM GARROTT (*b. Marion, Ala., 1868; d. New Canaan, Conn., 1913*), author of *The Lower South in American History* (1902) and lives of Andrew Jackson, Stephen Douglas and Oliver Ellsworth.

BROWN, WILLIAM HENRY (*b. Little Britain Township, Pa., 1836; d. Belfast, Ireland, 1910*), civil engineer. Self-taught, Brown was chief engineer of the Pennsylvania Railroad, 1881–1906, and responsible for a vast amount of bridge and terminal construction.

BROWN, WILLIAM HILL (*b. Boston, Mass., 1765; d. Murfreesboro, N.C., 1793*), author of *The Power of Sympathy* (1789), considered the first American novel. [*Supp. 1*]

BROWN, WILLIAM HUGHEY (*b. North Huntington Township, Pa., 1815; d. Philadelphia, Pa., 1875*), coal operator. First mine operator to ship coal in towed flatboats, 1858; supplied coal for Union warships on Mississippi in Civil War.

BROWN, WILLIAM WELLS (*b. Lexington, Ky., c. 1816; d. Chelsea, Mass., 1884*), Negro reformer. Escaped from slavery, 1834; was celebrated in his own time as a lecturer and historian of his race.

BROWNE, BENJAMIN FREDERICK (*b. Salem, Mass., 1793; d. Salem, 1873*), druggist. His narrative of a privateer cruise, 1812–15, was edited by Nathaniel Hawthorne as "Papers of an Old Dartmoor Prisoner" in *U.S. Magazine* (serially, through 1846) and republished with additions in 1926 as *The Yarn of a Yankee Privateer.*

BROWNE, CHARLES FARRAR (*b. Waterford, Maine, 1834; d. Southampton, England, 1867*), "Artemus Ward," humorist. His reporting of the adventures and opinions of a traveling showman in the Cleveland *Plain Dealer*, 1858, was continued in the New York periodical *Vanity Fair* and published in book-form as *Artemus Ward: His Book* (1862). Speaking in the person of his character, Browne toured the entire country as a "moral lecturer" with great success; his hilarious comments coupled with a mock-lugubrious delivery won him the admiration of Abraham Lincoln and the young Mark Twain. Returning from the West, Browne appeared in 1864 with a new "lecture," a comic panorama of life in Utah with the title "Artemus Ward among the Mormons." A triumphant visit to England, 1866–67, crowned his career. He died of tuberculosis.

BROWNE, DANIEL JAY (*b. Fremont, N.H., 1804; no data on death*), agricultural and scientific writer.

BROWNE, FRANCIS FISHER (*b. South Halifax, Vt., 1843; d. Santa Barbara, Calif., 1913*), editor of the *Dial* (Chicago), 1880–1913, a journal of critical opinion.

BROWNE, IRVING (*b. Marshall, N.Y., 1835; d. Buffalo, N.Y., 1899*), legal writer. Editor, *Albany Law Journal*, 1879–93; author of numerous textbooks and legal compilations.

BROWNE, JOHN (*d. Wannamoisett, R.I., 1662*), a liberal and influential magistrate of Plymouth Colony, 1635–54.

BROWNE, JOHN ROSS (*b. Dublin, Ireland, 1821; d. Oakland, Calif., 1875*), author. Came to America, 1832 or 1833; was raised in Kentucky. Traveled extensively for more than a quarter-century; was official reporter for California constitutional convention, 1849. Wrote, and illustrated, among others: *Etchings of a Whaling Cruise* (1846); *Crusoe's Island* (1864); and *Adventures in the Apache Country* (1869).

BROWNE, JUNIUS HENRI (*b. Seneca Falls, N.Y., 1833; d. New York, N.Y., 1902*), journalist. War correspondent, *New York Tribune*, 1861–63; wrote *Four Years in Secessia* (1865).

BROWNE, THOMAS (*no data on birth; d. St. Vincent, British West Indies, 1825*), Tory partisan commander in Georgia, 1776–82.

BROWNE, WILLIAM (*b. Salem, Mass., 1737; d. London, England, 1802*), Loyalist. Graduated Harvard, 1755. A man of property, a colonial judge, and a *mandamus* Councillor in 1774, he removed to London, 1776, after the fall of Boston. He served with great ability as governor of Bermuda, 1781–88.

BROWNE, WILLIAM HAND (*b. Baltimore, Md., 1828; d. Baltimore, 1912*), educator, author. Associated with Johns Hopkins University as librarian and professor, 1879–1912; editor, *Archives of Maryland.*

BROWNELL, HENRY HOWARD (*b. Providence, R.I., 1820; d. East Hartford, Conn., 1872*), author of *Lyrics of a Day* (1864), a notable collection of narrative poems on Civil War engagements.

BROWNELL, THOMAS CHURCH (*b. Westport, Mass., 1779; d. Hartford, Conn., 1865*), Episcopal clergyman. Consecrated bishop of Connecticut, 1819; first president of Trinity College, Hartford, 1823–31.

BROWNELL, WILLIAM CRARY (*b. New York, N.Y., 1851; d. New York, 1928*), critic. Graduated Amherst, 1871. Editor, Charles Scribner's Sons, 1888–1928; author of *French Traits* (1889); *Victorian Prose Masters* (1901); *American Prose Masters* (1909).

BROWNING, JOHN MOSES (*b. Ogden, Utah, 1855; d. near Liège, Belgium, 1926*), inventor. Designer of guns, notably the automatic pistol, the heavy machine-gun and the light automatic rifle used by the U.S. Army in the first World War.

BROWNING, ORVILLE HICKMAN (*b. Harrison Co., Ky., 1806; d. 1881*), lawyer, statesman. Settled in Quincy, Ill., 1831; active as a Whig in politics until 1856, thereafter a Republican until after the Civil War. Appointed to the U.S. Senate for sessions of 1861–62, he at first supported Lincoln's policy but opposed Emancipation Proclamation. Secretary of interior in Andrew Johnson's cabinet, he stood by the President in the impeachment crisis and left office in 1869. Elected on Democratic ticket to Illinois constitutional convention, 1869–70. Thereafter practiced as a railroad lawyer.

BROWNLEE, WILLIAM CRAIG (*b. Lanarkshire, Scotland, 1784; d. 1860*), Presbyterian clergyman. Came to America, c. 1808; served churches in New Jersey, Pennsylvania and New York; a stout orthodox Calvinist and anti-Catholic.

BROWNLOW, WILLIAM GANNAWAY (*b. Wythe Co., Va., 1805; d. Knoxville, Tenn., 1877*), Methodist clergyman, journalist, politician. Taken to Tennessee as a child; served as itinerant minister, 1826–36. Edited several newspapers, 1838–49; edited *Knoxville Whig*, 1849–61, and made it an uncompromising voice against secession. After brief imprisonment by Confederates, he was driven out of Tennessee, 1862, returning the next year with the Union Army. As governor of Tennessee, 1865–69, he stood for disfranchisement of all who had fought against the Union in the Civil War.

BROWNSON, ORESTES AUGUSTUS (*b. Stockbridge, Vt., 1803; d. Detroit, Mich., 1876*), philosopher, author. After long identification with New England liberal movements, and pastorates as a Universalist and Unitarian minister, he became a Catholic, 1844. His trenchant, profoundly thought-out views on society and politics were expressed in his *Boston Quarterly Review* (1838–42) and *Brownson's Quarterly Review* (1844–65; and *post* 1872). His books include: *The Convert* (1857) and *The American Republic* (1865).

BROWNSON, WILLARD HERBERT (*b. Lyons, N.Y., 1845; d. Washington, D.C., 1935*), naval officer. [*Supp. 1*]

BRUCE, ANDREW ALEXANDER (*b. Nunda Drug, Madras Presidency, India, 1866; d. 1934*), professor of law at universities of Wisconsin, North Dakota and Minnesota, and at Northwestern University. [*Supp. 1*]

BRUCE, ARCHIBALD (*b. New York, N.Y., 1777; d. New York, 1818*), physician, mineralogist. Graduated Columbia, A.B., 1797; M.D., Edinburgh, 1800. Discoverer of brucite; founded the *American Mineralogical Journal* (1810).

BRUCE, BLANCHE K. (*b. Farmville, Va., 1841; d. Washington, D.C., 1898*), politician, planter. A Negro, Bruce served as U.S. senator from Mississippi, 1875–81.

BRUCE, GEORGE (*b. Edinburgh, Scotland, 1781; d. New York, N.Y., 1866*), typefounder. Came to America, c. 1796. With brother David introduced stereotype process, c. 1812; invented a type-casting machine.

BRUCE, PHILIP ALEXANDER (*b. Staunton Hill, Va., 1856; d. Charlottesville, Va., 1933*), historian. Chronicler of colonial Virginia; historian of the University of Virginia. [*Supp. 1*]

BRUCE, ROBERT (*b. Scone, Scotland, 1778; d. Pittsburgh, Pa., 1846*), Presbyterian clergyman, educator. Came to America, 1806; settled in Pittsburgh, 1808; served as pastor of First United Presbyterian church, 1808–46. Principal, Western University of Pennsylvania, 1822–43.

BRÜHL, GUSTAV (*b. Herdorf, Germany, 1826; d. Cincinnati, O., 1903*), physician, author. Came to America, 1848; practiced and taught medicine in Cincinnati; wrote archeological studies and poetry.

BRULÉ, ÉTIENNE (*b. Champigny, France, c. 1592; d. 1632*), explorer. Came to New France, 1608, with Champlain; probably the first white man to see the Great Lakes, all of which he explored with exception of Lake Michigan.

BRUMBY, RICHARD TRAPIER (*b. Sumter District, S.C., 1804; d. 1875*), educator. Graduated South Carolina College, 1824. Professor of chemistry, University of Alabama, 1834–49; prepared (1838) first systematic report of Alabama mineral resources.

BRUMIDI, CONSTANTINO (*b. Rome, Italy, 1805; d. Washington, D.C., 1880*), painter. Came to America, 1852. Designed and painted the frescoes in the U.S. Capitol.

BRUNNER, ARNOLD WILLIAM (*b. New York, N.Y., 1857; d. 1925*), architect, city planner. Graduated Massachusetts Institute of Technology, 1879; worked in office of George B. Post. Principal works are in New York City, Harrisburg, Pa., and Cleveland, O.

BRUNTON, DAVID WILLIAM (*b. Ayr, Canada, 1849; d. 1927*), mining engineer, inventor. Manager of mines at Leadville and Aspen, Colo., where he developed his specialty of driving long tunnels; became technical adviser to Anaconda interests. Inventor of a mechanical ore-sampler and of the Brunton pocket-transit.

BRUSH, CHARLES FRANCIS (*b. Cuyahoga Co., O., 1849; d. Cleveland, O., 1929*), inventor. Graduated University of Michigan, 1869, as a mining engineer; perfected a dynamo that came into wide use. Announced invention of the Brush arc light, 1878.

Other inventions related to electroplating, storage batteries, and dynamos. After his Brush Electric Co. was taken over by the General Electric Co., Brush improved on Carl Linde's process for extracting oxygen from liquid air; became founder and first president of the Linde Air Products Co. [*Supp.* 1]

BRUSH, EDWARD NATHANIEL (*b. Glenwood, N.Y., 1852; d. 1933*), psychiatrist. Associated editorially with *American Journal of Psychiatry,* 1878–84; 1897–1931. [*Supp.* 1]

BRUSH, GEORGE JARVIS (*b. Brooklyn, N.Y., 1831; d. 1912*), mineralogist. Professor of mineralogy, Sheffield Scientific School, 1855–72; director, Sheffield, 1872–98. Author of *Manual of Determinative Mineralogy* (1874).

BRUTÉ DE RÉMUR, SIMON WILLIAM GABRIEL (*b. Rennes, France, 1779; d. Vincennes, Ind., 1839*), Roman Catholic clergyman. Graduated from medical school at Paris with highest prize; entered Seminary of St. Sulpice; on ordination, 1808, joined Sulpicians. Volunteered to accompany Bishop Flaget of Kentucky back to America; taught in St. Mary's Seminary, Baltimore, St. Mary's College, Emittsburg, and was then appointed rector of Baltimore seminary. His health failing, he returned to Emittsburg and taught there, 1818–1834. Named first bishop of Vincennes, 1834.

BRYAN, GEORGE (*b. Dublin, Ireland, 1731; d. Philadelphia, Pa., 1791*), jurist, politician. Pennsylvania assemblyman, 1764–65, 1779; instrumental in drafting 1779 act for gradual abolition of slavery; judge, Pennsylvania supreme court, 1780–91; opposed Federal Constitution.

BRYAN, MARY EDWARDS (*b. near Tallahassee, Fla., 1842; d. 1913*), journalist, author. Associate editor, *Sunny South,* 1874–84; wrote *Manch* (1880), *Wild Work* (1881) and many other melodramatic tales.

BRYAN, THOMAS BARBOUR (*b. Alexandria, Va., 1828; d. Washington, D.C., 1906*), lawyer. Influenced choice of Chicago as site of 1893 World's Fair; vice-president of Fair.

BRYAN, WILLIAM JENNINGS (*b. Salem, Ill., 1860; d. Dayton, Tenn., 1925*), political leader. Graduated Illinois College, 1881; read law at Union College of Law, Chicago, and in Lyman Trumbull's office; practiced law in Jacksonville, Ill., 1883–87. Married Mary Baird, 1884. Moved to Lincoln, Nebr., where after successful but not brilliant law career he entered politics. Elected to Congress as Democrat, 1890, in normally Republican district; re-elected, 1892. He sat on Ways and Means Committee in Congress; spoke fluently on tariff; voted against repeal of silver purchase law of 1890 and attacked President Cleveland for urging unconditional repeal. His candidacy for U.S. Senate, 1894, was unsuccessful. He

then worked as editor-in-chief of *Omaha World-Herald* and as a Chautauqua lecturer; was vigorous speaker for free silver.

In 1896, Bryan received Democratic presidential nomination on fifth ballot, after his famous "Cross of Gold" speech stampeded the Chicago convention: "You shall not press down upon the brow of labor this cross of thorns, you shall not crucify mankind upon a cross of gold." In face of abusive treatment, he carried his ideas to the country as no other candidate since Henry Clay. Bryan campaigned with vigor and skill, stressing the social and sectional struggle between Wall Street and the "toiling masses," and the silver issue; he lost to McKinley by 600,000 votes in a total vote of 13,600,000, with electoral vote 271 to 176. After the Spanish-American War, he resumed leadership of Democratic party and accepted presidential nomination in 1900 on condition that silver plank be retained but that "expansion" would be "paramount issue." Defeated on issue of expansion by greater margin than in 1896 (electoral vote 292 to 155), he wrote for a weekly newspaper, the *Commoner;* the paper was bitterly denounced by opponents as demagogic, setting poor against rich. Eastern Democrats displaced Bryan with Alton B. Parker in 1904 convention, in belief that business would support a conservative against Theodore Roosevelt, but Parker's poor showing re-established Bryan's position as party leader.

His third and last nomination came in 1908 on first ballot, but he received only 162 of 483 electoral votes. In the 1912 convention he helped nominate Woodrow Wilson. As secretary of state from Wilson's inauguration until June, 1915, when deep pacifist convictions forced his resignation, he used influence unselfishly to carry administration reform measures through Congress. He approved the administration's Mexican policy, was in accord with decision not to continue government support to Six-Power loan to China and opposed "dollar diplomacy" in Latin America. In his own view, his notable service was negotiation of arbitration treaties with thirty foreign states. After resignation, he refused to criticize Wilson and campaigned for him in 1916. At his last political appearance in the 1924 Democratic convention, Bryan supported W. G. McAdoo against Alfred E. Smith. Hostile to modern evolutionary theory of man, he acted for prosecution in 1925 trial of J. T. Scopes for breaking a Tennessee statute by teaching Darwinism.

BRYANT, GRIDLEY (*b. Scituate, Mass., 1789; d. Scituate, 1867*), civil engineer, inventor. Devised portable derrick, 1823; engineer of Quincy Railroad for transportation of granite, 1826, introducing iron-plated rails and the eight-wheeled car.

BRYANT, JOHN HOWARD (*b. Cummington, Mass., 1807; d. Princeton, Ill., 1902*). Pioneer settler (1832) in Bureau Co., Ill.; brother of William Cullen Bryant.

BRYANT, JOSEPH DECATUR (*b. East Troy, Wis., 1845; d. 1914*), surgeon. Graduated Bellevue Hospital Medical College, 1868. Performed operation for sarcoma on Grover Cleveland's jaw, 1893; author of *Manual of Operative Surgery* (1884); editor, *American Practice of Surgery* (1906–11).

BRYANT, RALPH CLEMENT (*b. Princeton, Ill., 1877; d. New Haven, Conn., 1939*), forester and educator. Organized and directed, 1906–39, the educational program in logging and lumbering at Yale School of Forestry. [*Supp.* 2]

BRYANT, WILLIAM CULLEN (*b. Cummington, Mass., 1794; d. New York, N.Y., 1878*), poet, editor. His father was a physician and surgeon, fond of music and poetry; his early education was had in district schools, and from Rev. Thomas Snell and Rev. Moses Hallock. Precocious and a voracious reader, Bryant was encouraged to write verses by his father who also provided sound criticism. The natural beauty of his boyhood surroundings inspired in him an intense and lifelong love of nature. After a year (1810–11) at Williams College, he read law, 1811–14; was admitted to the bar, August 1815, and practiced until 1825. Removing to New York City in that year, he became assistant editor of the *Evening Post*, 1826. Succeeding William Coleman as editor in 1829, he held the post until his own death.

An anti-Jefferson satire *The Embargo* (1808) had appeared from his pen, but his first great poem "Thanatopsis" was not written until 1811 and remained unpublished until 1817 when an abbreviated version was printed in the September issue of the *North American Review*. Meanwhile a reading of Wordsworth's *Lyrical Ballads* dimmed the earlier influences of Pope, Kirke White, Blair and Cowper; Bryant understood that his impulse to be a poet could best be realized in expression of the natural beauty which he felt so immediately and strongly. His poetic fame was unchallenged after he published *Poems* (1821), a small volume but important, containing an improved version of "Thanatopsis" and lyrics of genius such as "Green River," "To a Waterfowl," and "The Yellow Violet." In 1824–25, the period of his greatest productivity, he wrote "Rizpah," "Autumn Woods," and "Forest Hymn" which rank among his finest poems.

Regarding journalism at first as a secondary interest, he hoped to live off it while devoting the major part of his time to pure literature. The *Evening Post's* rapid decline between 1830–36, when he left its actual management in the hands of assistants, taught him a sharp lesson; he labored day and night to restore the paper and from that time gave it his first concern. By 1840, he had become one of the leading Democratic editors in the nation; he supported Jackson and Van Buren, opposed high tariffs, advocated a complete separation between government and banking, and began to take an advanced position against slav-

ery. As a poet, he suffered from the heavy demands his work made on his time, yet he published new work in *Poems* (1832), *The Fountain, and Other Poems* (1842), and *The White-Footed Doe* (1844).

Bryant and the *Evening Post* broke sharply with the Democratic party in 1848, supporting Van Buren's Free-Soil candidacy; in 1850, he opposed Clay's Compromise, urging the free states not to yield on a single principle; by 1853, the *Post* reached a radical antislavery position. In the campaign of 1856, Bryant enthusiastically threw his influence behind Frémont and during the four years following made his paper one of the most vigorous of "Black Republican" organs. He introduced Abraham Lincoln at Cooper Union in 1860 and supported him in 1864, although assailing his policies of moderation in dealing with the South and his hesitation in proclaiming full emancipation of slaves. After the Civil War, Bryant broke away from the Radical Republicans and supported Andrew Johnson's policies. Although estranged from the Grant administration by its low moral tone, its tariff policy and its treatment of the South, he remained a Republican and kept the *Evening Post* Republican.

Untired in civic, social and charitable endeavors, Bryant's last important literary enterprise was a translation of all Homer's works in blank verse (published 1870–71–72). Acknowledged great as a poet of nature, he lacked warmth of emotion in human concerns and intellectual depth; within his restricted range, however, he produced a small body of imperishable poetry.

BRYCE, LLOYD STEPHENS (*b. Flushing, N.Y., 1851; d. 1917*), politician, author. Editor, *North American Review*, 1889–96.

BUCHANAN, FRANKLIN (*b. Baltimore, Md., 1800; d. Talbot Co., Md., 1874*), naval officer. Became midshipman, 1815; promoted commander, 1841; in 1845, having submitted plan for new Naval School at Annapolis, he was appointed its first superintendent. Commanded sloop *Germantown* throughout Mexican War; commanded steam frigate *Susquehanna*, flagship of Perry's Japan squadron; promoted captain, 1855. Joined Confederate States Navy as captain, 1861. Commanded Chesapeake Bay Squadron, 1862, with flag on reconstructed *Merrimack*; surprised Union squadron in Hampton Roads, destroying *Congress* and *Cumberland*. Became admiral and ranking officer; commanded in battle of Mobile Bay, 1864.

BUCHANAN, JAMES (*b. near Mercersburg, Pa., 1791; d. near Lancaster, Pa., 1868*), president of the United States. He was descended from North-Ireland Scottish Presbyterians; his father, a successful storekeeper, came to America, 1783. James graduated Dickinson College, 1809; read law at Lancaster, Pa., and was admitted to the bar, 1812. Oratorical power and sound legal knowledge brought him professional success. Elected as a Federalist to state House of Representatives, 1814, he was re-elected, 1815; retiring from politics, the death of his intended wife brought him back into the arena. He was elected to U.S. Congress as a Federalist, 1820; re-elected as a Democrat, 1824.

During J. Q. Adams's administration, Buchanan made his first public statement on slavery in a debate on the Panama Mission: it was a moral and political evil; it was irremediable; it was a duty to help people of the South in the event of slave insurrections. For services in Jackson campaign of 1828, Buchanan was appointed chairman of committee on judiciary; in 1831, he accepted the ministry to Russia. On return to the United States, he was elected to the U.S. Senate to fill an unfinished term; he was elected for a full term in 1837, and again in 1843. As senator from Pennsylvania, he opposed slavery in the abstract but recognized duty of government to protect it where it existed; he denounced abolitionists but upheld right of petition. A "favorite son" possibility for presidency in 1844, he supported James K. Polk after nomination and helped carry Pennsylvania for him. Appointed secretary of state in Polk's cabinet, Buchanan served the full term, contributing powerful aid in the settlement of the Oregon question with Great Britain and in the delicate negotiations over annexation of Texas, 1845. His delaying tactics until a revolutionary change in Mexico gave a new prospect of settlement coincided with a military skirmish on the Texas border and lent justification to Polk's message to Congress declaring that a state of war existed by Mexico's own acts. Meanwhile he had ended the dispute over Oregon by a treaty based on a compromise of territorial claims, and was responsible for Polk's restatement of the Monroe Doctrine against British ambitions in California and Central America.

After four years' retirement, Buchanan campaigned for Franklin Pierce, 1852, but was passed over for W. L. Marcy in choice of secretary of state; he accepted ministry to Great Britain. He joined in drawing up the Ostend Manifesto on the status of Cuba, 1854. Returning home in April 1856, he was more than ever a presidential possibility; by his absence he had escaped involvement in the bitter fight over the Kansas-Nebraska bill and received nomination on the 17th ballot. His platform proclaimed the finality of the Compromise of 1850 and endorsed principle of non-interference by Congress with slavery in territories. At the election, he received 1,-800,000 votes; Frémont, the Republican candidate, received 1,300,000; Fillmore, the Whig-"Know-Nothing" candidate, about 900,000. His inaugural address declared for strict construction of the Constitution; as for slavery in the territories, he declared the question one for judicial decision and referred to the Dred Scott case (then pending) as destined to offer a solution to which all good citizens should submit. He divided representation in his cabinet equally between slave-holding and free states.

Reasonably successful in foreign policy, his strict-constructionist views kept him from asserting any leadership in recovery from the financial panic of 1857. Accepting, as he did, the Dred Scott decision as final word on status of slavery in Kansas-Nebraska, he split the Democratic party by recommending early in 1858 the pro-slavery Lecompton constitution for Kansas. In the crisis that followed, and in the desperate months between Lincoln's election and the end of his term, Buchanan denied the right of any state to secede but confessed his helplessness in the face of actual secession; while his administration fell to pieces through resignations, he did his best to use his own personal influence for reconciliation. Early in 1861, he adopted a stiffer policy toward South Carolina and instituted legislation to broaden the president's powers. He took his part in Lincoln's inauguration and then retired to "Wheatland," his estate near Lancaster, Pa. He supported the administration throughout the Civil War as a Union Democrat.

Northern criticism that his lack of vigor encouraged secession and the formation of the Confederacy is unjustified. Primarily a constitutional lawyer, secure in the belief that legal solutions and compromises were all-sufficient, he was fitted neither by nature nor training to "ride the whirlwind" of his time.

BUCHANAN, JOHN (*b. Prince Georges Co., Md., 1772; d. 1844*), jurist. Chief justice, Maryland court of appeals, 1824–44; made important decisions in *Chesapeake & Ohio Canal Co. vs. Baltimore & Ohio*, and in *Calvert vs. Davis*.

BUCHANAN, JOSEPH (*b. Washington Co., Va., 1785; d. Louisville, Ky., 1829*), educator, inventor. Lecturer in medicine, Transylvania University; called "the earliest native physiological psychologist"; journalist in Kentucky; projector and builder of a steam-driven wagon, 1824–25.

BUCHANAN, JOSEPH RAY (*b. Hannibal, Mo., 1851; d. Montclair, N.J., 1924*), labor agitator. Active in western trade-union affairs, 1880–88, and in Knights of Labor; an organizer of the Populist party; in later life, labor editor of American Press Association and *New York Evening Journal*.

BUCHANAN, JOSEPH RODES (*b. Frankfort, Ky., 1814; d. San José, Calif., 1899*), physician, eccentric. Author of treatises on healing sciences of his own devisal, "Sarcognomy" and "Psychometry."

BUCHANAN, ROBERT CHRISTIE (*b. Baltimore, Md., 1811; d. Washington, D.C., 1878*), Union soldier. Graduated West Point, 1830. Distinguished in Black Hawk, Seminole, Mexican and Civil wars; major-general by brevet, 1865; commanded Department of Louisiana, 1868.

BUCHANAN, THOMAS (*b. Glasgow, Scotland, 1744; d. New York, N.Y., 1815*), merchant. Came to America, 1763; a partner in W. & T. Buchanan; vice-president, N.Y. Chamber of Commerce, 1780–83.

119

BUCHANAN, WILLIAM INSCO (*b. Covington, O., 1852; d. 1909*), businessman, diplomat. Promoter of "Corn Palaces," Sioux City, Iowa; chief of agriculture department, Chicago World's Fair, 1893. Served on many missions to Central and South America.

BUCHER, JOHN CONRAD (*b. Neunkirch, Switzerland, 1730; d. Annville, Pa., 1780*), soldier, German Reformed clergyman. Came to America, *post* 1755; officer in French & Indian war and Pontiac uprising. Ordained, 1767, he served frontier congregations and was first to preach in German beyond Alleghenies.

BUCHTEL, JOHN RICHARDS (*b. Green Township, O., 1820; d. Akron, O., 1892*), businessman, philanthropist. Helped develop mineral resources of Hocking Valley; benefactor, Akron University.

BUCK, ALBERT HENRY (*b. New York, N.Y., 1842; d. 1922*), otologist, medical historian. Son of Gurdon Buck. College of Physicians and Surgeons, New York, M.D. 1867. Author of *Diagnosis and Treatment of Ear Diseases* (1880); also, *Growth of Medicine* (1917) and *Dawn of Modern Medicine* (1920). Co-editor, *American Practice of Surgery* (1906–11).

BUCK, DANIEL (*b. Hebron, Conn., 1753; d. Vermont, 1816*), lawyer, legislator. A first settler of Norwich, Vt., *c.* 1784, where he afterwards practiced; congressman, Federalist, from Vermont, 1795–97.

BUCK, DUDLEY (*b. Hartford, Conn., 1839; d. Orange, N.J., 1909*), composer, organist. Studied music in his birthplace, and at Leipzig, Dresden and Paris. After 1862, organist at churches in Hartford, Chicago, Boston and Brooklyn, N.Y. One of the first American composers to possess solid musicianship; American organ music practically begins with his compositions for Protestant church services. Of his larger works, the most important are concert cantatas which include "Paul Revere's Ride," "The Centennial Meditation of Columbia" (1876) and "The Light of Asia" (1889).

BUCK, GURDON (*b. New York, N.Y., 1807; d. New York, 1877*), surgeon. College of Physicians and Surgeons, New York, M.D. 1830; studied for two years in Paris, Berlin and Vienna; settled to practice in New York, 1837. A great surgeon of the pre-Lister period, his chief contributions were in management of fractures (Buck's Extension) and in plastic surgery.

BUCK, LEFFERT LEFFERTS (*b. Canton, N.Y., 1837; d. 1909*), civil engineer. Graduated Rensselaer Polytechnic Institute, 1868. One of the great bridge builders of his time, remembered principally for his work in bridging Niagara Falls and for the Williamsburg Bridge, New York City.

BUCK, PHILO MELVIN (*b. Corning, N.Y., 1846; d. 1924*), Methodist clergyman. Missionary to India, 1870–76; 1879–1914.

BUCKALEW, CHARLES ROLLIN (*b. Columbia Co., Pa., 1821; d. Bloomsburg, Pa., 1899*), lawyer, legislator. U.S. senator, Democrat, from Pennsylvania, 1863–69; a proponent of penal code reform and proportional representation; opposed Republican policies after Civil War.

BUCKHOUT, ISAAC CRAIG (*b. Eastchester, N.Y., 1830; d. White Plains, N.Y., 1874*), civil engineer. Designed and built old Grand Central station, the Fourth Avenue cut and other constructions for the New York & Harlem Railroad.

BUCKINGHAM, JOSEPH TINKER (*b. Windham, Conn., 1779; d. Cambridge, Mass., 1861*), editor. An able and imaginative journalist, publisher of the *Polyanthos* (1806–07; 1812–14), the *New England Galaxy* (1817–28), the *Boston Courier* (1824–48), the *New England Magazine* (1831–34) and others. Author of two useful books of reminiscent history, *Specimens of Newspaper Literature* (1850) and *Personal Memoirs* (1852).

BUCKINGHAM, WILLIAM ALFRED (*b. Lebanon, Conn., 1804; d. 1875*), businessman, legislator. Governor of Connecticut, Republican, 1858–66; a constant and able supporter of Lincoln in the Civil War. U.S. senator from Connecticut, 1869–75.

BUCKLAND, CYRUS (*b. East Hartford, Conn., 1799; d. Springfield, Mass., 1891*), inventor. Pattern-maker and designer of machine-tools, Springfield Armory, 1828–57; his inventions include a gunstock process (1846) and a rifling machine (1855).

BUCKLAND, RALPH POMEROY (*b. Leyden, Mass., 1812; d. Fremont, O., 1892*), lawyer, soldier. Commended by Sherman for work as brigade commander at Shiloh; brevet major-general, 1866.

BUCKLER, THOMAS HEPBURN (*b. near Baltimore, Md., 1812; d. 1901*), physician. Prominent Baltimore practitioner, active in study of cholera and other epidemic diseases and in modern treatment of tuberculosis. Practiced in Paris, France, 1866–90.

BUCKLEY, JAMES MONROE (*b. Rahway, N.J., 1836; d. 1920*), Methodist clergyman. Editor, *Christian Advocate*, 1880–1912.

BUCKLEY, SAMUEL BOTSFORD (*b. Torrey, N.Y., 1809; d. Austin, Texas, 1883*), botanist, field naturalist. Associated with geological surveys in Texas; collected specimens of plants, etc., in Alabama, Tennessee and the Carolinas; discovered a zeuglodon skeleton, Alabama, 1842.

BUCKMINSTER, JOSEPH STEVENS (*b. Portsmouth, N.H., 1784; d. Boston, Mass., 1812*), Unitarian clergyman. Graduated Harvard, 1800; ordained and installed at Brattle Street Church, Boston, 1805. Brilliant preacher and scholar; a founder of Boston Athenaeum.

BUCKNELL, WILLIAM (*b. near Marcus Hook, Pa., 1811; d. 1890*), businessman, philanthropist. Acquiring wealth in realty speculation and public utilities, he became large contributor to Baptist missions and to University of Lewisburg, renamed Bucknell in 1887.

BUCKNER, SIMON BOLIVAR (*b. near Munfordville, Ky., 1823; d. near Munfordville, 1914*), Confederate soldier. Graduated West Point, 1844. After gallant service in Mexican War and on frontiers, resigned from army, 1855; entered business in Chicago, Ill., where he prospered. Settled in Louisville, Ky., 1858; brought Kentucky militia to high efficiency by 1861. Identified with early effort to keep the state neutral in Civil War, Buckner joined Confederate forces as brigadier-general when state legislature abandoned neutrality. Surrendered Fort Donelson to Grant, 1862; on exchange was promoted major-general and, in 1864, lieutenant-general, serving capably until end of war. In business, New Orleans, 1866–68; permitted to return to Kentucky in the latter year, he became editor of *Louisville Courier*. Successful in effort to recover some of his sequestrated property, he entered politics; he was Democratic governor of Kentucky, 1887–91.

BUDD, JOSEPH LANCASTER (*b. near Peekskill, N.Y., 1835; d. Phoenix, Ariz., 1904*), horticulturist. Removed to Iowa in the 1860's; was a successful nurseryman and orchardist, and professor of horticulture and forestry, Iowa Agricultural College, 1876–96. He adapted standard practices to the climate of the Northwest, introducing hardier varieties of trees and extending successful fruit-growing much further north than had been thought possible.

BUEHLER, HUBER GRAY (*b. Gettysburg, Pa., 1864; d. Lakeville, Conn., 1924*), educator. Headmaster, Hotchkiss School, Lakeville, 1904–24.

BUEL, JESSE (*b. Coventry, Conn., 1778; d. Danbury, Conn., 1839*), agriculturist. Printer and newspaper publisher, New York State, 1797–1820; founder of Albany, N.Y., *Argus*. From 1821 to 1839, experimented in scientific agriculture on a farm west of Albany; as a member of New York Assembly, 1823–35, Buel devoted all energies to improvement of agriculture and rural life, pressing for establishment of a state agricultural school. His writings and influence had effect long after his own time.

BUELL, ABEL (*b. Killingworth, Conn., 1741/42; d. New Haven, Conn., 1822*), silversmith, typefounder, engraver. A most ingenious, if morally unstable, craftsman, Buell designed and cast printing types in 1769, probably the first ever made by an American; his map of the United States (published March 1784) was the first map of the new nation to be engraved by one of its own citizens. For some years, he engaged in various activities in New Haven, setting up a cotton mill (1795), operating a line of packet boats, etc. In 1799, he removed to Hartford, thereafter to Stockbridge, Mass., and returned at last to New Haven where he died in the Alms House.

BUELL, DON CARLOS (*b. near Marietta, O., 1818; d. Rockport, Ky., 1898*), Union soldier. Graduated West Point, 1841; served with credit in Mexican War and thereafter in adjutant-general's office. Appointed brigadier-general, 1861, he helped organize Army of the Potomac; in November 1861, commanding Army of the Ohio, he attempted to liberate eastern Tennessee. Buell's aid to Grant at Shiloh was decisive in that battle. Promoted major-general, March 1862, he was discharged in 1864 after a lengthy investigation of his conduct after battle of Perryville, October 1862.

BUFFALO BILL. [See CODY, WILLIAM FREDERICK, 1846–1917.]

BUFFUM, ARNOLD (*b. Smithfield, R.I., 1782; d. Perth Amboy, N.J., 1859*), anti-slavery lecturer. A Quaker and a maker of hats, Buffum was president of New England Anti-Slavery Society, 1832, and its lecturing agent in Pennsylvania, Ohio and Indiana; his daughter was Elizabeth Chace.

BUFORD, ABRAHAM (*b. Culpeper Co., Va., 1749; d. near Georgetown, Ky., 1833*), Revolutionary soldier. Defeated by Tarleton, 1780, in the no-quarter engagement at the Waxhaws.

BUFORD, ABRAHAM (*b. Woodford Co., Ky., 1820; d. Danville, Ind., 1884*), Confederate soldier. Graduated West Point, 1841; served in Mexican War and on the frontiers as cavalry officer. Resigned from army, 1854, and bred horses and cattle in Kentucky. Appointed brigadier-general by Confederates, 1862; served under Bragg, Loring and Forrest. Resumed stock-breeding after Civil War.

BUFORD, JOHN (*b. Woodford Co., Ky., 1826; d. Washington, D.C., 1863*), Union soldier. Graduated West Point, 1848; served with cavalry in Texas, New Mexico, Nebraska and in the Mormon expedition, 1857–58. After minor service in Washington, 1861, Buford was appointed brigadier-general, July 1862; he was severely wounded at Lewis Ford in August, returning to duty as chief of cavalry, Army of the Potomac in September. Early in 1863, he took command of the reserve cavalry and distinguished himself in covering Hooker's retreat after Chancellorsville; he commanded a division with great credit at Gettysburg. On leave of absence because of failing health, he was commissioned major-general in December 1863, just before his death.

BUFORD, NAPOLEON BONAPARTE (*b. Woodford Co., Ky., 1807; d. Chicago, Ill., 1883*), Union soldier. Half-brother of John Buford; graduated West Point, 1827; resigned from army, 1835, and settled in Rock Island, Ill., 1842 as a businessman, railroad promoter and banker. Colonel of 27th Illinois volunteers, 1861, he fought in the Western campaigns; he was promoted brigadier-general, April 1862, and did his best work as commander of the East Arkansas District, 1863–65. Mustering out as brevet major-general, he returned to business in Colorado and Chicago, Ill.

BULFINCH, CHARLES (*b. Boston, Mass., 1763; d. Boston, 1844*), architect. Son of a wealthy and cultivated Boston family; graduated Harvard, 1781; interest in architecture stimulated by European tour, 1785–87; Jefferson's classical tendency also influenced him. Designed churches in Boston, Taunton and Pittsfield, Mass.; classical interest seen in his Beacon monument (1789) and triumphal arch for Washington's Boston reception (1789); designed State House at Hartford, Conn., begun in 1792. His public work of this first period was crowned by Massachusetts State House on Beacon Hill, completed 1800. He exerted also at this time important influence upon New England domestic architecture introducing delicate detail in the Adam style, oval parlors and the use for the first time in New England of curved staircases. Franklin Crescent, Boston, the first attempt in America to erect a row of houses in a coherent design, was begun by him in 1793.

Elected to board of selectmen of Boston, 1791, he served, with one interval, for 26 years. Financial depression in 1795 left him bankrupt; his architectural talents, hitherto generously exercised for others, now became the basis for a professional practice. The years of his chairmanship of the board of selectmen, 1799–1817, were those of the great development of old Boston, for which his dual capacity as official and architect was in great part responsible. He turned the neglected Common into a park and fronted it on three sides with buildings of uniform character; he laid out the lands on Boston Neck, in South Boston, and on site of the Mill Pond; he designed India Wharf, the Almshouse, two schools, the enlargement of Faneuil Hall, the Boylston Market, and the Court House. During this period he did public buildings elsewhere in Massachusetts: the State Prison at Charlestown, the Massachusetts General Hospital, banks, churches, and private homes; of the churches the most notable were the Cathedral of the Holy Cross and the New South Church, both in Boston, and Christ Church in Lancaster.

At resignation of Latrobe, architect of the Capitol, in 1817, President Monroe offered the post to Bulfinch, who removed to Washington, D.C. with his family. Called on to complete the wings and construct the central part along lines already established by earlier architects, his own chief contribution was the detailed form of the western front. Returning to Boston, 1830, he lived in retirement until death. He exercised a wide influence on New England architecture where his version of the Adam style became characteristic of the early Republican period, remaining dominant until advent c. 1820 of the Greek revival.

BULFINCH, THOMAS (*b. Newton, Mass., 1796; d. Boston, Mass., 1867*), author. Son of Charles Bulfinch;

graduated Harvard, 1814. Unsuccessful in business, he took a clerkship in the Merchants' Bank, Boston, which he held from 1837 to his death; he devoted his leisure to study of literature and natural history, and to writing. Among his books, the best-known are two highly successful attempts to retell classic and other myths in popular form: *The Age of Fable* (1855) and *The Age of Chivalry* (1858).

BULKELEY, MORGAN GARDNER (*b. East Haddam, Conn., 1837; d. 1922*), businessman, politician. President, Aetna Life Insurance Co., 1879–1922; a director of many other corporations. Mayor, Hartford, Conn., 1880–88; governor of Connecticut, Republican, 1888–92; U.S. senator from Connecticut, 1905–11.

BULKELEY, PETER (*b. Odell, England, 1582/3; d. Concord, Mass., 1658/9*), Puritan clergyman. Emigrated to Massachusetts, 1636; a founder and the first minister of Concord.

BULKLEY, JOHN WILLIAMS (*b. Fairfield, Conn., 1802; d. 1888*), educator. Superintendent of schools, Brooklyn, N.Y.; first president of New York state teachers' association (1845) and a founder of the National Teachers' Association (now National Education Association).

BULKLEY, LUCIUS DUNCAN (*b. New York, N.Y., 1845; d. 1928*), physician, dermatologist. Founded New York Skin and Cancer Hospital, 1882; advocated non-surgical treatment of cancer; author of *Manual of Diseases of the Skin* (1882).

BULL, EPHRAIM WALES (*b. Boston, Mass., 1806; d. 1895*), horticulturist. Developed the "Concord" grape, first exhibited 1853.

BULL, WILLIAM (*b. South Carolina, 1683; d. 1755*), lieutenant-governor of South Carolina, 1738–55. During his administration, constitutional reforms included governor's exclusion from Council's legislative sessions, Commons House control of money bills.

BULL, WILLIAM (*b. Ashley Hall, S.C., 1710; d. London, England, 1791*), colonial governor of South Carolina. Son of William Bull (1683–1755). Studied medicine at Leyden; was first native-born American to receive M.D. degree, but devoted himself to agriculture and politics. Member of Commons House, 1736–49; speaker in 1740–42 and 1744–49. Appointed to the Council, 1748, he served ably until he became lieutenant-governor, 1759; acting as governor for some eight years between 1760 and 1775, he tried to stem revolutionary sentiment *post* 1764, but by 1774 power had passed to the Provincial Congress. Bull retained respect of people, and his estates were exempted from confiscation; he left colony with British troops, 1782, and spent remaining years in London.

BULL, WILLIAM TILLINGHAST (*b. Newport, R.I., 1849; d. New York, N.Y., 1909*), surgeon. Graduated Harvard, 1869; M.D., College of Physicians and

Surgeons, New York, 1872; made clinical studies in Europe. Professor of surgery, College of Physicians and Surgeons, 1889–1904. Specialized in surgery of abdomen, contributing procedures for treatment of gunshot wounds of abdomen; wrote on hernia for medical textbooks; published noteworthy paper on cancer of the breast (1894). Influenced by work of Lister, he was one of first American surgeons to adopt antisepsis.

BULLARD, HENRY ADAMS (*b. Pepperell, Mass., 1788; d. New Orleans, La., 1851*), jurist. Judge, Louisiana supreme court, 1834–46; congressman from Louisiana, Whig, 1830–34, 1850–51. Founder, Louisiana Historical Society, 1836.

BULLARD, WILLIAM HANNUM GRUBB (*b. Media, Pa., 1866; d. 1927*), naval officer. Graduated U.S. Naval Academy, 1886. Reorganized electrical engineering department at Naval Academy, 1907–11; superintendent of naval radio service, 1912–16; commanded battleship *Arkansas*, 1916–18; director of communications, Navy Department, 1919–21; promoted rear-admiral, 1919. Has been called "the father of American radio." Prevented foreign acquisition of patent rights in Alexanderson alternator and counseled formation of what developed into Radio Corporation of America.

BULLITT, ALEXANDER SCOTT (*b. Dumfries, Va., 1762; d. Jefferson Co., Ky., 1816*), planter, Kentucky legislator. Lieutenant-governor of Kentucky, 1800–04.

BULLITT, HENRY MASSIE (*b. Shelby County, Ky., 1817; d. Louisville, Ky., 1880*), physician, teacher. Founded Kentucky School of Medicine, 1850, and Louisville Medical College, 1868.

BULLOCH, ARCHIBALD (*b. Charleston, S.C. 1729/30; d. 1777*), lawyer, planter. First president of the Provincial Congress of Georgia, 1775–77; an active patriot.

BULLOCH, JAMES DUNWODY (*b. near Savannah, Ga., 1823; d. 1901*), naval officer, Confederate agent. Appointed midshipman, U.S. Navy, 1839; commanded various vessels in mail service to Gulf of Mexico, *post* 1851. Retiring from navy, he entered private mail shipping service, becoming identified with New York interests. At start of Civil War, he was named Confederate navy agent to buy or build war vessels in England; all Confederate cruisers except the *Georgia* were equipped and sent out under his instructions. *Post* March 1863, he moved his operations to Paris, France. He settled in Liverpool, England, at end of war, engaging in cotton business there.

BULLOCK, RUFUS BROWN (*b. Bethlehem, N.Y., 1834; d. Atlanta, Ga., 1907*), businessman, politician. Governor of Georgia, Republican, 1868–71; indicted and tried for embezzlement of public funds, 1876, but acquitted.

BULLOCK, WILLIAM A. (*b. Greenville, N.Y., 1813; d. 1867*), inventor, manufacturer. His Bullock Press (1865) was the first to print from a continuous roll of paper, first to cut the sheet either before or after printing, first to print both sides of the sheet.

BUMSTEAD, FREEMAN JOSIAH (*b. Boston, Mass., 1826; d. 1879*), surgeon. Graduated Williams College, 1847; M.D., Harvard, 1851. One of first reputable practitioners to specialize in venereal diseases; author of classic *Pathology and Treatment of Venereal Diseases* (1861).

BUMSTEAD, HENRY ANDREWS (*b. Pekin, Ill., 1870; d. 1920*). Professor of physics and director of Sloane Laboratory, Yale, 1906–20. Investigated properties of delta rays emitted by metals under influence of alpha rays, 1911–20.

BUMSTEAD, HORACE (*b. Boston, Mass., 1841; d. 1919*), Congregational minister, educator. Brother of Freeman J. Bumstead. As president of Atlanta University, 1888–1907, advocated broad, liberal arts education for Negro leaders.

BUNCE, OLIVER BELL (*b. New York, N.Y., 1828; d. New York, 1890*), publisher. Literary manager, D. Appleton & Co.; editor, *Appleton's Journal*; a specialist in devising successful subscription sets and illustrated "gift" books.

BUNCE, WILLIAM GEDNEY (*b. Hartford, Conn., 1840; d. Hartford, 1916*), painter. An impressionist who did his principal work in Venice.

BUNDY, JONAS MILLS (*b. Colebrook, N.H., 1835; d. Paris, France, 1891*), journalist. Founder and editor, *New York Evening Mail;* later edited *Mail and Express.* Prepared appeal to public against Tweed Ring, 1871; wrote campaign biography of James A. Garfield (1880).

BUNNER, HENRY CUYLER (*b. Oswego, N.Y., 1855; d. Nutley, N.J., 1896*), author. Staff writer and editor, *Puck*, 1877–96; suggested famous cartoon (1884) satirizing James G. Blaine as the "Tattooed Man"; contributed verse, parodies, editorials. His short fiction is distinguished by skillful construction and word economy; French influences are obvious. His works include: *Airs from Arcady* (1884); *The Midge* (1886); *The Story of a New York House* (1887); *Zadoc Pine* (1891); and *Made in France* (1893).

BURBANK, LUTHER (*b. Lancaster, Mass., 1849; d. Santa Rosa, Calif., 1926*), plant breeder. Educated in district school and at local academy; influenced by Darwin's *Variation of Animals and Plants under Domestication* and other works by Darwin. Became a market gardener, *c.* 1870; removed to Santa Rosa, Calif., 1875, where he conducted plant breeding experiments for fifty years. Produced many better varieties of cultivated plants; implications of his work for scientific research were lost, however, as he kept no systematic collection of data observed. Burbank's

123

genius lay in his sensitive recognition and careful selection of desirable variations; his most intensive work was done with plums, berries and lilies.

BURBRIDGE, STEPHEN GANO (*b. Scott Co., Ky., 1831; d. Brooklyn, N.Y., 1894*), Union soldier. Commanded District of Kentucky, 1864–65; was ruthless in suppression of guerrilla warfare.

BURCHARD, SAMUEL DICKINSON (*b. Steuben, N.Y., 1812; d. Saratoga, N.Y., 1891*), Presbyterian clergyman. Memorable as author of the "Rum, Romanism and Rebellion" catchword in the presidential campaign of 1884; pastor, Houston Street Church, New York, 1839–79; president, Rutgers Female Academy.

BURDEN, HENRY (*b. Dunblane, Scotland, 1791; d. Woodside, N.Y., 1871*), ironmaster. Emigrated to Albany, N.Y., 1819. Inventor of machines for making horseshoes (1835), hook-head railroad spikes (1836, 1840), and for rolling iron into cylindrical bars (1840). Established firm of H. Burden & Sons, 1848.

BURDETTE, ROBERT JONES (*b. Greensboro, Pa., 1844; d. 1914*), humorist, lyceum lecturer, Baptist clergyman. Won reputation as columnist on Burlington, Iowa, *Hawk-Eye*, 1874 et seq.; author of *The Rise and Fall of the Moustache* (1877); became pastor, Temple Baptist Church, Los Angeles, Calif., 1903.

BURDICK, FRANCIS MARION (*b. De Ruyter, N.Y., 1845; d. De Ruyter, 1920*), legal writer. Graduated Hamilton College, 1869; LL.B., Hamilton, 1872. Practiced law in Utica, N.Y.; reform mayor of Utica, 1882. Professor of law at Hamilton; at Cornell University, 1887–91; Dwight Professor of Law, Columbia University, 1891–1916. His works include: *Cases on Torts* (1891); *The Law of Sales of Personal Property* (1897); *The Law of Partnership* (1899); *The Law of Torts* (1905).

BURGESS, ALEXANDER (*b. Providence, R.I., 1819; d. St. Albans, Vt., 1901*), Episcopal clergyman. First bishop of Quincy, Ill., elected and consecrated, 1878; especially skilled in canon law.

BURGESS, EDWARD (*b. West Sandwich, Mass., 1848; d. Boston, Mass., 1891*), yacht designer, entomologist. Among yachts designed by him were *Puritan*, *Mayflower* and *Volunteer*, successful contenders for America's Cup, 1885–87.

BURGESS, GEORGE (*b. Providence, R.I., 1809; d. 1866*), Episcopal clergyman. Brother of Alexander Burgess. Bishop of Maine, elected and consecrated, 1847.

BURGESS, GEORGE KIMBALL (*b. Newton, Mass., 1874; d. 1932*), physicist. Director of the National Bureau of Standards, 1923–32; known for his work in the standardization of light and temperature scales. [*Supp.* 1]

BURGESS, JOHN WILLIAM (*b. Giles Co., Tenn., 1844; d. Brookline, Mass., 1931*), university professor and dean, author. The son of slaveowners who upheld the Union, he served with Union Army, 1862–64. Graduated Amherst College, 1867; studied in Germany, 1871–73. At Columbia College, New York City, he organized a faculty and school of political science, 1880, the first in the United States devoted to the systematic study of politics and public law. Founded the *Political Science Quarterly*. His influence was strong in the development of Columbia as a true university. In his many books he developed a unique theory of nationalism and the state. [*Supp.* 1]

BURGESS, NEIL (*b. Boston, Mass., 1851 (?); d. 1910*), actor. Specialized in burlesque portrayals of elderly women; most popular performance in *The County Fair*.

BURGEVINE, HENRY ANDREA (*b. New Bern or Chapel Hill, N.C., 1836; d. China, 1865*), adventurer. Took command of mercenary "Ever Victorious Army" in China, 1862; after dismissal, sided with Taiping rebels and was charged with treason.

BURGIS, WILLIAM (*fl. New York and Boston, 1718–31*), artist, engraver. His surviving works are of great antiquarian interest and include: "South Prospect of . . . New York" (1718); "South East View of . . . Boston" (1723/24); "Prospect of the Colledges in Cambridge in New England" (1726); and "View of the New Dutch Church (New York)" (1731 or 1732).

BURK, FREDERIC LISTER (*b. Blenheim, Canada, 1862; d. 1924*), educator. Graduated University of California, 1883; Ph.D., Clark University, 1898. President, State Normal School, San Francisco; proponent of a "motivated individual instruction" theory.

BURK, JOHN DALY (*b. Ireland, c. 1775; d. Petersburg, Va., 1808*), author. Came to America, 1796. His works include *History of Virginia* (in four volumes, 1804, 1805, 1816), and the plays *Bunker Hill* (produced 1797) and *Female Patriotism* (produced 1798).

BURKE, AEDANUS (*b. Galway, Ireland, 1743; d. Charleston, S.C., 1802*), Revolutionary soldier, congressman, jurist. Appointed associate judge in South Carolina, 1778; representative in legislature, 1781–82 and 1784–89; pamphleteered for leniency in treatment of Loyalists after Revolution; attacked idea of an American aristocracy in *Considerations on the Order of the Cincinnati* (1783). Voted against adoption of Federal Constitution; attacked eligibility of president to succeed himself; in first Congress opposed excise tax and establishment of United States Bank, but favored assumption of state debt and paying Continental obligations at par; firm proponent of slavery. Served on commission to revise and digest South Carolina law, 1785–89; elected chancellor of court of equity, 1799.

BURKE, CHARLES ST. THOMAS (*b. 1822; d. New York, 1854*), actor, dramatist. Specialized in comic parts, with the companies of Joseph Jefferson II, and W. E. Burton.

BURKE, JOHN G. [See BOURKE, JOHN GREGORY, 1846–1896.]

BURKE, JOHN JOSEPH (*b. New York, N.Y., 1875; d. Washington, D.C., 1936*), Roman Catholic clergyman, Paulist. Editor, the *Catholic World*, 1904–22; secretary, National Catholic Welfare Conference, 1919–36. [*Supp.* 2]

BURKE, STEVENSON (*b. near Ogdensburg, N.Y., 1826; d. Cleveland, O., 1904*), lawyer, railroad promoter. Admitted to Ohio bar, 1848. President, Cleveland & Mahoning Valley Railway, 1880–1904.

BURKE, THOMAS (*b. Co. Galway, Ireland, c. 1747; d. Orange Co., N.C., 1783*), Revolutionary statesman. Settled in Virginia after emigration, practicing medicine and then law; removed to North Carolina, 1771, and represented Orange Co. in all provincial congresses except the first. Was aligned with radical group in framing a state government; advocated annual elections, sovereignty of the people, separation of church and state, and ratification by the people in the 1776 sessions at Halifax. Served in Continental Congress, 1776–81; governor of North Carolina, 1781–spring of 1782.

BURKE, THOMAS (*b. Clinton Co., N.Y., 1849; d. New York, N.Y., 1925*), lawyer. Admitted to Michigan bar, 1873; removed to Seattle, Wash., 1875, where he became that city's foremost citizen.

BURLEIGH, CHARLES CALISTUS (*b. Plainfield, Conn., 1810; d. Northampton, Mass., 1878*), abolitionist, associate of Samuel J. May and William Lloyd Garrison.

BURLEIGH, GEORGE SHEPARD (*b. Plainfield, Conn., 1821; d. 1903*), poet, reformer. Brother of Charles C. Burleigh.

BURLEIGH, WILLIAM HENRY (*b. Woodstock, Conn., 1812; d. Brooklyn, N.Y., 1871*), journalist, reformer. Brother of Charles C. and George S. Burleigh. Editor, *Christian Freeman*, 1843; *Prohibitionist*, 1849–55. Author of *Poems* (1841); *The Rum Fiend* (1871).

BURLESON, ALBERT SIDNEY (*b. San Marcos, Texas, 1863; d. Austin, Texas, 1937*), Democratic congressman, 1899–1913; postmaster-general, 1913–21. A conservative Texas politician, criticized by both business and labor interests. [*Supp.* 2]

BURLESON, EDWARD (*b. Buncombe Co., N.C., 1798; d. Austin, Texas, 1851*), soldier, frontier leader. Commander at siege of San Antonio, 1835; fought at San Jacinto. Elected to first Texas senate, 1836; as Republic of Texas vice-president, 1841.

BURLESON, HUGH LATIMER (*b. Northfield, Minn., 1865; d. 1933*), Episcopal clergyman. Missionary bishop of South Dakota, 1916–31; an expert on Indian problems. [*Supp.* 1]

BURLESON, RUFUS CLARENCE (*b. Morgan Co., Ala., 1823; d. 1901*), Baptist clergyman, educator. President, Baylor University, 1851–61; established Waco University, 1861. President of both schools when consolidated, 1886–97.

BURLIN, NATALIE CURTIS (*b. New York, N.Y., 1875; d. Paris, France, 1921*), student of Indian and Negro music. Published *The Indians' Book* (1907); *Hampton Series Negro Folk-Songs* (1918–19).

BURLINGAME, ANSON (*b. New Berlin, N.Y., 1820; d. St. Petersburg, Russia, 1870*), diplomat. Congressman, Free-Soil and Republican, from Massachusetts, 1855–60; minister to China, 1861–67. Head of the first diplomatic mission sent by China to foreign powers, 1867–70, which resulted in the Burlingame Treaty with the United States (July 1868) and an equivalent declaration from Great Britain acknowledging sovereignty of China.

BURLINGAME, EDWARD LIVERMORE (*b. Boston, Mass., 1848; d. 1922*), editor. Son of Anson Burlingame, and served as his secretary in China and on his special mission, 1867–70. Literary adviser, Charles Scribner's Sons, *post* 1879; editor, *Scribner's Magazine*, 1886–1914.

BURNAM, JOHN MILLER (*b. Irvine, Ky., 1864; d. Pomona, Calif., 1921*), educator. Graduated Yale, A.B. 1884, Ph.D. 1886. Professor of Latin, University of Cincinnati; specialist in palaeography.

BURNAP, GEORGE WASHINGTON (*b. Merrimac, N.H., 1802; d. Baltimore, Md., 1859*), Unitarian clergyman. Pastor, First Independent Church, Baltimore, 1828–59.

BURNET, DAVID GOUVERNEUR (*b. Newark, N.J., 1788; d. Galveston, Texas, 1870*), politician. Joined Miranda revolts in Venezuela, 1806 and 1808; in business in Ohio and Louisiana; lived for a time among Comanches on upper Colorado River. Settled in Texas, 1831; active in events which led up to Texas rebellion against Mexico; served in convention which issued Texas Declaration of Independence. President of Republic of Texas, 1836, he was succeeded in October of that year by Sam Houston whom he bitterly opposed thereafter. Son of William Burnet (1730–1791).

BURNET, JACOB (*b. Newark, N.J., 1770; d. Cincinnati, O., 1853*), lawyer, politician. Brother of David G. Burnet. Settled in Cincinnati, 1796; played leading part in organization of Ohio, in passing Land Act of 1820, and in financing internal improvements. Judge of Ohio supreme court, 1821–28; U.S. senator, Federalist, from Ohio, 1828–31.

BURNET, WILLIAM (*b. The Hague, Holland, 1688; d. Boston, Mass., 1729*), colonial governor. Son of Gilbert Burnet, Bishop of Salisbury; godson of King

William III of England. Appointed governor of New York and New Jersey, 1720, where his statesmanlike Indian policy won him enmity of traders and Provincial Assembly. Reassigned as governor of Massachusetts, 1728.

BURNET, WILLIAM (*b. near Newark, N.J., 1730; d. Newark, 1791*), physician. Father of David G. and Jacob Burnet. Graduated College of New Jersey (Princeton), 1749. Active in opposition to English rule; chairman, Essex Co. committee of safety, 1775–76; member of Continental Congress, 1776–77 and 1780; physician and surgeon-general, Eastern District military hospitals.

BURNETT, CHARLES HENRY (*b. Philadelphia, Pa., 1842; d. Bryn Mawr, Pa., 1902*), otologist. Deviser of operations for relief of chronic catarrhal otitis; an outstanding investigator of the physiology of hearing.

BURNETT, FRANCES ELIZA HODGSON (*b. Manchester, England, 1849; d. 1924*), author. Raised in poverty, she came with her family to America, 1865, settling near Knoxville, Tenn. Her plays and her forty or more novels were very popular in their day, although marked by sentimentality and an excess of romantic imagination. She is remembered chiefly for *Little Lord Fauntleroy* (1886), *Sara Crewe* (1888), and *Little Saint Elizabeth* (1890), "fairy tales of real life" as they have been called.

BURNETT, HENRY LAWRENCE (*b. Youngstown, O., 1838; d. New York, N.Y., 1916*), lawyer, Union soldier. Prominent in military trials, 1863–65; prepared evidence in trials of Lincoln's assassins. Practiced law in Cincinnati and New York, serving as federal district-attorney, southern district of New York, 1898–1906.

BURNETT, JOSEPH (*b. Southborough, Mass., 1820; d. 1894*), manufacturing chemist. Founded St. Mark's School, 1865.

BURNETT, PETER HARDEMAN (*b. Nashville, Tenn., 1807; d. San Francisco, Calif., 1895*), pioneer. Went to Oregon in 1843; settled on farm near mouth of Willamette, later near present site of Hillsboro, Oreg. Served on Oregon legislative committee, 1844; as judge of supreme court, 1845; elected to legislature, 1848. Led company to California goldfields, 1848; appointed judge of superior court of California, August 1849; elected governor of California, November 1849, serving until January 1851. Founder and president of Pacific Bank, San Francisco.

BURNETT, SWAN MOSES (*b. New Market, Tenn., 1847; d. Washington, D.C., 1906*), physician. Husband of Frances Hodgson Burnett. Specialist in ophthalmology and otology.

BURNHAM, CLARA LOUISE ROOT (*b. Newtown, Mass., 1854; d. Casco Bay, Maine, 1927*), author of popular novels.

BURNHAM, DANIEL HUDSON (*b. Henderson, N.Y., 1846; d. Heidelberg, Germany, 1912*), architect. As a child, moved to Chicago, Ill.; studied architecture there and entered office of Carter, Drake and Wight, 1872. In successful partnership with John W. Root, 1873–91, employed new structural concepts and materials in skyscrapers such as the Chicago Montauk and Monadnock Buildings. Burnham and Root were made supervisors in planning the 1893 World's Columbian Exposition at Chicago (Root, consulting architect; Burnham, chief of construction); owing to Root's death in 1891 the task of coordinating efforts of principal artists and architects in erecting and decorating the great series of related buildings fell on Burnham. Success of the enterprise was attributed to Burnham's energy, taste and ability to organize. Forming a new partnership, he undertook many important commissions; in 1901 he accepted chairmanship of a commission for development of Washington, D.C. The 1902 report of this commission (which included Charles F. McKim, Augustus Saint-Gaudens and Frederick L. Olmsted, Jr.) marks the beginning of the modern city-planning movement in the United States. Burnham also made city plans for Cleveland, O., San Francisco, Calif., Manila, P.I., and his native Chicago which owes the development of its lake front to the Burnham Plan. He was chairman of the National Commission of Fine Arts and a founder of the American Academy in Rome.

BURNHAM, SHERBURNE WESLEY (*b. Thetford, Vt., 1838; d. 1921*), senior astronomer, Yerkes Observatory, 1897–1914; published *General Catalogue of Double Stars* (1906).

BURNS, ANTHONY (*b. Stafford Co., Va., 1834; d. St. Catherine's, Canada, 1862*), fled north from slavery, 1854, was arrested in Boston and was center of a great public commotion there when returned as a fugitive slave. His freedom was later purchased, and he served as minister of a Baptist church.

BURNS, OTWAY (*b. Onslow Co., N.C., 1775?; d. Portsmouth, N.C., 1850*), privateersman, shipbuilder. As captain of the *Snap-Dragon*, 1812–14, preyed on British commerce from Greenland to Brazil; in a single 1813 cruise, he accounted for goods worth over two-and-a-half million dollars.

BURNS, WILLIAM JOHN (*b. Baltimore, Md., 1861; d. Sarasota, Fla., 1932*), detective, founder of the detective agency bearing his name. [*Supp. 1*]

BURNSIDE, AMBROSE EVERETT (*b. Liberty, Ind., 1824; d. Bristol, R.I., 1881*), Union soldier. Graduated West Point, 1847; resigned commission, 1853; engaged unsuccessfully in business in Rhode Island. Appointed major-general of state militia. Organized and led 1st Rhode Island regiment, 1861; fought successful campaign on North Carolina coast, January to April 1862, and was commissioned major-general of volunteers; twice offered command of Army of the

Potomac, which he refused. At Antietam, September 1862, poor reconnaissance by Burnside resulted in ineffective use of his corps; appointed commander of the Army of the Potomac over his own protest, he met defeat with heavy loss at Fredericksburg, December 1862. Assigned to command Department of the Ohio, March 1863, his strategic retreat to Knoxville, Tenn., helped Grant defeat Bragg at Chattanooga, November 1863. In command of 9th Corps, January to July 1864, Burnside was held responsible for loss at Petersburg crater; he resigned commission towards end of the war. Held corporate positions subsequently; was governor of Rhode Island, 1866–68, and U.S. senator from Rhode Island, 1875–81.

BURR, AARON (*b. Fairfield, Conn., 1715/16; d. Princeton, N.J., 1757*), Presbyterian clergyman. Pastor, First Church, Newark, N.J.; president, College of New Jersey (Princeton), 1748–57.

BURR, AARON (*b. Newark, N.J., 1756; d. Port Richmond, N.Y., 1836*), Revolutionary soldier, lawyer, vice-president of the United States. Son of Aaron Burr (1715/16–1757) and Esther Edwards, daughter of Jonathan Edwards (1703–1758). Reared by a maternal uncle, Timothy Edwards, and tutored for a time by Tapping Reeve, young Burr graduated with distinction from the College of New Jersey, 1772. Hesitant over choice of a career, he began study of theology; he left off in 1774 to study law. After serving with credit on the American invasion of Canada, 1775–76, he joined Washington's staff in New York with rank of major; mutual antagonism caused Burr's transfer to Gen. Israel Putnam's staff with whom he did good service at Long Island and during evacuation of New York. Appointed lieutenant-colonel in the Continental Line, July 1777, ill health brought on by over-exertion forced him to resign from army, March 1779. After further study of law, he was licensed in New York early in 1782 as attorney. He married Mrs. Theodosia (Bartow) Prevost, in July 1782; despite disparity in their ages and her invalidism, he was devoted to her and to their daughter, Theodosia Burr. Successful in practice of law in New York, 1783–89, he tried to increase income by extensive speculations; his generosity and self-indulgence, however, made of him an incurable spendthrift. At first balked in attempts to enter politics because Alexander Hamilton, his rival, led one New York faction, and George Clinton, leader of the opposing faction, did not seek his support, he made himself of sufficient value to Clinton to be named state attorney-general by him in 1789. After participating in a questionable sale of state lands, Burr was transferred to the U.S. Senate in which he represented New York, 1791–97. Unaccepted by either major party group, and having won the enmity of Hamilton by opposing his financial policies, Burr failed of re-election to the Senate; he was chosen a state assemblyman, however, in April 1797. His connection with a bill to aid the Holland Land Co., in which he had a financial interest, and another to secure a charter for the Manhattan Company caused his defeat in 1799. By means of the political machine which he had built up, the Democratic-Republican party won control of the New York legislature in 1800 and Burr was able to secure indorsement of himself for the vice-presidency; he then secured a pledge from Democratic-Republican members of Congress to support him equally with Thomas Jefferson at the election. Owing to this agreement, he tied for the presidency but immediately disclaimed any competition for the highest office and served as vice-president under Jefferson. In office, he alienated the Democratic-Republicans and was supplanted as their candidate in 1804 by George Clinton; defeated this same year by Morgan Lewis in a contest for the governorship of New York, he ended a 15-year period of patience with Hamilton's private and public invective against him by challenging Hamilton to a duel. His enemy's death, after their meeting at Weehawken, N.J., July 11, 1804, caused Burr to flee southward to escape indictment.

For some time hopeful of exploiting current difficulties with Spain to his own advantage, Burr conferred with a fellow-schemer, James Wilkinson, at Philadelphia; he also approached Robert Merry, British minister, requesting financial and naval aid in bringing about the separation of the western states from the Union but it is supposed that he never intended to act on this treasonable proposal. Meanwhile he presided with great impartiality and dignity over the impeachment of Supreme Court Justice Samuel Chase, his last act as retiring vice-president.

Burr persisted in his separatist schemes with Wilkinson and others; on a journey in 1805 from Pittsburgh to New Orleans he received marked attentions everywhere and there was great speculation as to what he intended. Speculation soon turned to suspicion, and a diplomatic settlement of differences between Spain and the United States having ended the chance of a legitimate reason for seizure or invasion of any of the Spanish colonies, Burr and his associates were left with only the chance of some provocative border incident setting the frontier aflame. Burr's second trip westward in August 1806 led to his arraignment twice in Kentucky before a federal grand jury and a third arraignment early in 1807 in Mississippi Territory, all of which resulted in acquittal. Fearing that his associate Wilkinson (who had betrayed him) would seize him for trial by court-martial, Burr fled toward Mobile but was apprehended near the border and brought back for trial before Chief Justice Marshall in the Virginia circuit court. This famous trial began formally on May 22, 1807, and ended in September with the jury's finding that Burr was innocent of treason as defined by the Chief Justice. A second charge of misdemeanor for organizing an invasion of Spanish territory was also dismissed.

Burr sailed abroad in June 1808. He proposed to

Great Britain a scheme for revolutionizing Mexico; in 1810, he attempted to persuade Napoleon to aid in freeing the Spanish colonies and Louisiana, going so far as an offer to act as head of a conspiracy to embroil the United States in war with the English. Unsuccessful in these and other plans, he returned to the United States in May 1812 and re-entered legal practice in New York. Serenely spendthrift to the end of his long life, in July 1833 he married the wealthy widow of Stephen Jumel who sued him for divorce a year later.

BURR, ALFRED EDMUND (*b. 1815; d. Hartford, Conn., 1900*). Editor, Hartford *Daily Times*, 1841–1900; influenced state Democratic platforms; a pioneer in tariff-reform policy.

BURR, ENOCH FITCH (*b. Greens Farms, Conn., 1818; d. Hamburg, Conn., 1907*), Congregational minister. Sought scientific proofs of religion, writing *Parish Astronomy* (1867), *Pater Mundi* (1870), *Doctrine of Evolution* (1873).

BURR, GEORGE LINCOLN (*b. Oramel, N.Y., 1857; d. Ithaca, N.Y., 1938*), historian and librarian. Teacher of medieval history, 1881–1922, librarian, 1888–1938, at Cornell University. [*Supp. 2*]

BURR, THEODOSIA (*b. Albany, N.Y., 1783; d. 1813*), daughter of Aaron Burr. Married Joseph Alston, 1801. Father's confidante and agent during exile; lost at sea.

BURR, WILLIAM HUBERT (*b. Waterford, Conn., 1851; d. 1934*), engineer. Professor of engineering, Columbia University, 1893–1916; served on Isthmian Canal Commissions. [*Supp. 1*]

BURRAGE, HENRY SWEETSER (*b. Fitchburg, Mass., 1837; d. 1926*), editor, historian. Edited *Zion's Advocate*, Portland, Maine, 1873–1905. Became Maine state historian, 1907. Writings include *History of Baptists of Maine* (1904).

BURRAGE, WALTER LINCOLN (*b. Boston, Mass., 1860; d. Brookline, Mass., 1935*), physician, gynecologist. Historian of the Massachusetts Medical Society. [*Supp. 1*]

BURRALL, WILLIAM PORTER (*b. Canaan, Conn., 1806; d. Hartford, Conn., 1874*), lawyer, railroad executive. President, Housatonic Railroad, 1839–54; Hartford and New Haven, 1867–72.

BURRELL, DAVID JAMES (*b. Mount Pleasant, Pa., 1844; d. New York, N.Y., 1926*), clergyman. Pastor of Presbyterian and Dutch Reformed churches; active advocate of temperance.

BURRILL, ALEXANDER MANSFIELD (*b. New York, N.Y., 1807; d. 1869*), lawyer, author. Works include *Practice of Supreme Court of New York in Personal Actions* (1840), *New Law Dictionary* (1850–51).

BURRILL, JAMES (*b. Providence, R.I., 1772; d. Washington, D.C., 1820*), lawyer, politician. Rhode Island attorney-general, 1797–1813; state assemblyman, 1813–16 (speaker, 1814–16); U.S. senator, Federalist, from Rhode Island, 1817–20.

BURRILL, THOMAS JONATHAN (*b. near Pittsfield, Mass., 1839; d. 1916*), botanist, horticulturist. Removed to Illinois, 1848; graduated Illinois State Normal School, 1865. Professor of natural history, University of Illinois; also vice-president of that institution, and acting president, 1891–94, 1902. A leading figure in Illinois Horticultural Society and the Society of American Bacteriologists, Burrill was among the first of modern microscopists and a pioneer in study of bacterial diseases of plants.

BURRINGTON, GEORGE (*b. England, c. 1680; d. London, England, 1759*). As colonial governor of North Carolina, 1723–25, 1731–34, he undertook extensive public works, largely self-financed; development of Cape Fear section was owing to him.

BURRITT, ELIHU (*b. New Britain, Conn., 1810; d. New Britain, 1879*), "The Learned Blacksmith," linguist, reformer. Formed League of Universal Brotherhood, 1846; organized world peace congresses, beginning at Brussels, 1848.

BURROUGHS, BRYSON (*b. Hyde Park, Mass., 1869; d. 1934*), artist. Curator of paintings, Metropolitan Museum of Art, New York City, 1906–34. [*Supp. 1*]

BURROUGHS, JOHN (*b. near Roxbury, N.Y., 1837; d. 1921*), author. Mainly self-taught, Burroughs was a school-teacher, 1854–63, delighting in nature-study and modeling his thought and style on Emerson. From 1863 to 1873, he lived in Washington, D.C., working as a treasury department clerk and cultivating the friendship of Walt Whitman. Subsequent to 1873, he resided mainly near Esopus, N.Y., writing on the average of a book every two years for the remainder of his long life. Distinguished in his own time as a sage and prophet, and much in the company of Theodore Roosevelt and other enthusiasts for nature, his importance today lies in his establishment of the American "nature essay" as a literary type and in the vividness and felicity of his style. His works include: *Notes on Walt Whitman as Poet and Person* (1867; 1871); *Wake-Robin* (1871); *Winter Sunshine* (1875); *Locusts and Wild Honey* (1879); *Fresh Fields* (1885); *Leaf and Tendril* (1908); *The Breath of Life* (1915).

BURROUGHS, JOHN CURTIS (*b. Stamford, N.Y., 1817; d. Chicago, Ill., 1892*), Baptist clergyman. First president of (old) University of Chicago, 1857–73.

BURROUGHS, WILLIAM SEWARD (*b. Auburn, N.Y., 1855; d. Citronelle, Ala., 1898*), inventor. Patented in 1892 a practical adding machine that recorded both the separate items and the final result. [*Supp. 1*]

BURROWES, EDWARD THOMAS (*b. Sherbrooke, Canada, 1852; d. 1918*), window-shade and screen manufacturer; holder of forty patents on such devices. Removed to Portland, Maine, as a youth and resided there all his life.

BURROWES, THOMAS HENRY (*b. Strasburg, Pa., 1805; d. 1871*), lawyer, politician. Influential in organizing Pennsylvania public school system, 1836–38.

BURROWS, JULIUS CAESAR (*b. Northeast, Pa., 1837; d. Kalamazoo, Mich., 1915*), lawyer. Removed to Ohio as a boy, and later to Michigan. Congressman, Republican, from Michigan, 1873–74, 1879–83, 1885–94; U.S. senator from Michigan, 1894–1911. Member of Monetary Commission, 1909–12.

BURROWS, WILLIAM (*b. Kinderton, Pa., 1785; d. 1813*), naval officer. Killed commanding U.S.S. *Enterprise* in victory over H.M.S. *Boxer*, 1813.

BURSON, WILLIAM WORTH (*b. Utica, Pa., 1832; d. Rockford, Ill., 1913*), inventor, manufacturer. Patented twine and wire grain binders (1860, 1861 and later patents); also developed automatic knitting machinery.

BURT, JOHN (*b. Wales, N.Y., 1814; d. Detroit, Mich., 1886*), inventor, capitalist. Son of William A. Burt. Removed to Michigan, 1824; worked with father as surveyor of Michigan upper peninsula, 1841–51. Thereafter, located and operated mines in that region, developed and built railroads and canals. His patents included improvements in iron manufacture and a new type of canal lock.

BURT, MARY ELIZABETH (*b. Lake Geneva, Wis., 1850; d. Coytesville, N.J., 1918*), educator. Editor of numerous readers and texts for schools.

BURT, WILLIAM AUSTIN (*b. Petersham, Mass., 1792; d. 1858*), surveyor, inventor. Developed mechanical skill at early age; taught himself surveying, mathematics, mechanics while helping father on farm; worked as millwright, 1813–31. Settled near Detroit, Mich., 1824, and held many civic posts; appointed surveyor of Macomb Co., 1831, and U.S. Deputy Surveyor, 1833. Ran surveys of Michigan upper peninsula and also the course of the 5th Principal Meridian in Iowa. Discoverer of iron deposits in Marquette Co., Mich., 1844. Invented a writing-machine, the "Typographer," 1829; a solar compass to offset magnetic attraction, 1836; the equatorial sextant, 1856. He was also a prime mover in construction of Sault Ste. Marie canal.

BURTON, ASA (*b. Stonington, Conn., 1752; d. Thetford, Vt., 1836*), Congregational clergyman, teacher of theology and pastor at Thetford *post* 1779.

BURTON, CLARENCE MONROE (*b. Sierra Co., Calif., 1853; d. 1932*), historian, lawyer, founder and donor of the Burton Historical Collection of the Detroit Public Library. [*Supp. 1*]

BURTON, ERNEST DE WITT (*b. Granville, O., 1856; d. 1925*), Baptist clergyman. Professor of New Testament literature, University of Chicago, 1892–1923; president, University of Chicago, 1923–25. Author of *Harmony of the Gospels* (1894).

BURTON, FREDERICK RUSSELL (*b. Jonesville, Mich., 1861; d. Lake Hopatcong, N.J., 1909*), composer, author of *American Primitive Music* (1909).

BURTON, HUTCHINS GORDON (*b. Virginia, or Granville Co., N.C., c. 1774; d. 1836*), lawyer. Congressman from North Carolina, 1819–24; governor of North Carolina, 1824–27.

BURTON, MARION LE ROY (*b. Brooklyn, Iowa, 1874; d. 1925*), Congregational clergyman. President of Smith College, 1910–17; of University of Minnesota, 1917–20; of University of Michigan, 1920–25; raised large endowments for each.

BURTON, NATHANIEL JUDSON (*b. Trumbull, Conn., 1824; d. 1887*), Congregational clergyman.

BURTON, RICHARD EUGENE (*b. Hartford, Conn., 1861; d. Winter Park, Fla., 1940*), poet, literary critic, lecturer. Chairman, department of English, University of Minnesota, 1898–1902; 1906–25. [*Supp. 2*]

BURTON, THEODORE ELIJAH (*b. Jefferson, O., 1851; d. 1929*), U.S. senator and representative from Ohio. A Republican, he was the foe of "pork-barrel" legislation and was singularly independent in his legislative record. [*Supp. 1*]

BURTON, WARREN (*b. Wilton, N.H., 1800; d. 1866*), Unitarian and Swedenborgian clergyman. Proponent of social reform through education; an early advocate of parent-teacher associations. Author of *The District School as it Was* (1833) and *Helps to Education* (1863).

BURTON, WILLIAM (*b. Sussex Co., Del., 1789; d. 1866*), physician. Democratic governor of Delaware, 1859–63; a loyal Unionist, he opposed federal encroachments on Delaware rights.

BURTON, WILLIAM EVANS (*b. London, England, 1804; d. New York, N.Y., 1860*), actor. Came to America, 1834, and was successful in comic roles; managed Burton's Theatre, Chambers St., New York City, 1848–56, with outstanding success.

BUSCH, ADOLPHUS (*b. Mainz on the Rhine, 1839; d. near Langenschwalbach, Germany, 1913*), brewer, industrialist. Came to America, 1857. A founder of Anheuser-Busch; pioneer in mechanical refrigeration and diesel engine building; donor to many charities. [*Supp. 1*]

BUSH, GEORGE (*b. Norwich, Vt., 1796; d. 1859*), Presbyterian and Swedenborgian clergyman. Professor of Hebrew, New York University, 1831–47.

BUSH, LINCOLN (*b. Cook Co., Ill., 1860; d. East Orange, N.J., 1940*), civil engineer, specializing in railroad and bridge work. [*Supp. 2*]

BUSH-BROWN, HENRY KIRKE (*b. Ogdensburg, N.Y., 1857; d. 1935*), sculptor. [*Supp. 1*]

BUSHNELL, ASA SMITH (*b. Rome, N.Y., 1834; d. Columbus, O., 1904*), businessman, politician. Removed to Ohio as a child; prospered after Civil War in the manufacture of harvesters. Republican governor of Ohio, 1895–99.

BUSHNELL, DAVID (*b. Saybrook, Conn., c. 1742; d. Warrenton, Ga., 1824*), inventor, "father of the submarine." Graduated Yale, 1775; in the same year completed a man-propelled submarine which carried outside a wooden magazine of powder and a clock mechanism for igniting it at any chosen time. "Bushnell's Turtle," as it was called, was equipped with vertical and horizontal screws; a foot-operated valve in the keel let in water for submerging, two hand-operated pumps ejected it for ascending. After unsuccessful attempts to destroy British ships with the device, 1776–77, Bushnell yielded to ridicule and gave up further experimentation.

BUSHNELL, GEORGE ENSIGN (*b. Worcester, Mass., 1853; d. 1924*), tuberculosis specialist. Headed U.S. Army tuberculosis hospital, Fort Bayard, N. Mex., 1904–17; introduced rapid methods for detection of disease; author of *Epidemiology of Tuberculosis* (1920).

BUSHNELL, HORACE (*b. Bantam, Conn., 1802; d. Hartford, Conn., 1876*), Congregational clergyman, theologian. Graduated Yale, 1827; studied law there while acting as tutor in Yale College, 1828–31. While awaiting admission to bar, participation in a spiritual revival influenced him to enter Yale Divinity School. Reacting against Nathaniel W. Taylor's defense of the Calvinist system of theology, his intuitive, imaginative mind found inspiration in S. T. Coleridge's *Aids to Reflection,* a book which had a greater influence on him than any except the Bible. Ordained pastor of North Church, Hartford, Conn., 1833, at a time when Old and New Schools of New England theology were in fierce debate, he sided with neither, attempting in his own words: "to comprehend, if possible, the truth contended for in both." Broken in health, 1845, he spent a year in European travel. In 1849, he sustained a mystical experience whose meaning he explained in his *God in Christ;* orthodox reviewers were severe with the book, and he answered their objections and redefined his views in *Christ in Theology* (1851). Increasing bronchial trouble dictated a move to California, 1856; while there he was offered presidency of what later became University of California, but declined the post.

Returning to Hartford, he published *Sermons for the New Life* (1858). Although he resigned his pastorate in 1861 for reasons of health, the vigor of his mind was unimpaired; his works in retirement include: *Christian Nurture* (1861); *Work and Play* (1864); *Christ and his Salvation* (1864); and *The Vicarious*

Sacrifice (1866) which is the most permanently significant of his books and contains his concept of the atoning work of Christ, commonly known as the "moral influence" theory of the Atonement. These were followed by *Moral Uses of Dark Things* (1868); *Women's Suffrage* (1869); *Sermons on Living Subjects* (1872); and a restatement, somewhat modified, of his views on the Atonement in *Forgiveness and Law* (1874). He applied his principle of seeing truth on both sides to national questions also, opposing both the fugitive slave law and abolitionism.

The distinctive character of Bushnell's contribution to theology may be stated thus: Theologians of the 19th century were no longer comfortable with Jonathan Edwards's reshaping of Calvinist thought and its conception of human nature; yet, although they disagreed in many respects, they were as one in seeing theology as an intellectual system to be established by precise processes of logic. Bushnell, like a poet, apprehended truth by intuition; he appealed to life rather than to logic. He broke with prevailing theological views, first, in suggesting that churches turn toward giving the young an early and clearly defined doctrine of Christian growth rather than focus on conversion of adults; second, in his view of the Trinity; third, in his interpretation of the meaning of the Cross and his repudiation of the penal and governmental theories of the Atonement; fourth, in declaring that no sharp line should be drawn between natural and supernatural, reason and revelation, sacred and profane, and denying that human nature and nature itself were involved in the fall of Adam. The key to his thought, according to his best biographer, lies in his conception of God as immanent in His works.

BUSSEY, CYRUS (*b. Hubbard, O., 1833; d. Washington, D.C., 1915*), Union soldier. Commanded Iowa troops in Missouri campaigns, 1861; served in West and Southwest, 1861–65.

BUTLER, ANDREW PICKENS (*b. Ninety Six District, S.C., 1796; d. Edgefield, S.C., 1857*), lawyer. A leader of the Calhoun faction; U.S. senator, Democrat, from South Carolina, 1846–57. Charles Sumner's attack on Butler in the Senate, May 1856, led to Sumner's beating by Preston Brooks.

BUTLER, BENJAMIN FRANKLIN (*b. Columbia Co., N.Y., 1795; d. Paris, France, 1858*), lawyer, politician. Admitted to New York bar, 1817; from 1817–21 in office of Martin Van Buren; district attorney, Albany Co., N.Y., 1821–24. One of commission to revise New York Statutes, 1825. U.S. attorney-general, 1833–37, acting also as secretary of war from October 1836 to March 1837; U.S. attorney for southern district of New York, 1838–41 and 1845–48. Thereafter he devoted himself entirely to the law as a leader of the New York bar. Originally a Jackson Democrat, he supported Van Buren on the Free-Soil ticket in 1848 and joined the Republican party at its inception.

BUTLER, BENJAMIN FRANKLIN (*b. Deerfield, N.H., 1818; d. Washington, D.C., 1893*), Union soldier, politician. Graduated Waterbury (now Colby) College, 1838. Admitted to Massachusetts bar, 1840, he built up an extensive and lucrative practice. Believing strongly in the Union and in his own ability, he served 1861–65 in various commands, sometimes brilliantly and always controversially. He originated the term "contraband" for slaves fleeing from their owners to the Union lines; his administration of New Orleans, 1862, won him the violent hatred of the South and the imputation of corruption in office. Originally a Democrat, at the war's end Butler was identified with the radical wing of the Republicans; as a member of Congress, 1866–75, he was prominent in the impeachment of Andrew Johnson and an advocate of harsh Reconstruction policies. Detested by all Massachusetts conservatives, he was twice defeated in campaigns for governor of that state; in 1878, he returned to Congress as an independent Greenbacker. In 1882, running as a Democrat, he was elected governor of Massachusetts, failing of re-election in 1883. His last political activity was in securing nomination for the presidency, 1884, by the Anti-Monopoly and Greenback parties; he polled a very small vote.

BUTLER, CHARLES (*b. Kinderhook Landing, Columbia Co., N.Y., 1802; d. New York, N.Y., 1897*), lawyer, philanthropist. Brother of Benjamin F. Butler (1795–1858). Acquired extensive holdings in Chicago property and was active in development of Midwestern railroads; in 1843 and 1846, prevented repudiation of state bonds by Indiana and Michigan. A founder, 1836, of Union Theological Seminary, New York.

BUTLER, EZRA (*b. Lancaster, Mass., 1763; d. 1838*), Baptist clergyman. Settled in Waterbury, Vt., after the Revolutionary War, in which he served. An able public servant, and Democratic governor of Vermont, 1826–27.

BUTLER, HOWARD CROSBY (*b. Croton Falls, N.Y., 1872; d. Neuilly, France, 1922*), archeologist. Professor of art and archeology, Princeton, 1901–22; excavator of ancient Sardis. Author of *Archaeology and Other Arts* (1903) and *Sardis* (1922).

BUTLER, JOHN (*b. New London, Conn., 1728; d. Niagara, Canada, 1796*), Loyalist, Indian agent. Commanded Indian forces on British drive down Mohawk Valley, 1777; recruited and commanded Butler's Rangers in Tory raid on Wyoming Valley, 1778; defeated by Gen. John Sullivan at Newtown (Elmira), N.Y., 1779.

BUTLER, JOHN WESLEY (*b. Shelburn Falls, Mass., 1851; d. Mexico City, Mexico, 1918*), Methodist clergyman. Missionary in Mexico, 1874–1918.

BUTLER, MARION (*b. Sampson Co., N.C., 1863; d. Takoma Park, Md., 1938*), farm leader. President, Southern Alliance, 1894; national chairman, Populist party, 1896–1904. [*Supp. 2*]

BUTLER, MATTHEW CALBRAITH (*b. Greenville, S.C., 1836; d. Columbia, S.C., 1909*), Confederate soldier, politician. Nephew of Andrew Pickens Butler. Served with distinction in Confederate Army, 1861–65, rising to major-general; U.S. senator, Democrat, from South Carolina, 1877–94.

BUTLER, PIERCE (*b. Carlow Co., Ireland, 1744; d. Philadelphia, Pa., 1822*), planter, politician. Settled in Prince William's Parish, S.C., *post* 1771; in state legislature, 1778–82, 1784–89, where he championed democratic reforms. Worked for strong central government in federal convention, 1787. U.S. senator, Federalist, from South Carolina, 1789–96, 1802–06.

BUTLER, PIERCE (*b. near Northfield, Minn., 1866; d. Washington, D.C., 1939*), lawyer, justice of the U.S. Supreme Court. Son of Irish immigrants, he graduated from Carleton College, 1887, was admitted to the Minnesota bar, 1888, and began practice in St. Paul. Forceful, tenacious, with an extraordinary command of facts, he became an expert in railroad rate cases, and senior partner in one of the great law firms of the Northwest. Appointed as a Democrat to the Supreme Court in 1922, his views were authoritarian and conservative. Totally opposed to the New Deal, Butler dissented in 73 cases (more than half his total dissents) in his last three terms. [*Supp. 2*]

BUTLER, PIERCE MASON (*b. Mount Willing, S.C., 1798; d. Churubusco, Mexico, 1847*), politician, soldier. Brother of Andrew Pickens Butler. Governor of South Carolina, 1836–38; agent to the Cherokees, 1838–46; killed in action as colonel of Palmetto Regiment.

BUTLER, RICHARD (*b. Dublin, Ireland, 1743; d. 1791*), Revolutionary soldier, Indian agent. Served in all theaters of the war *post* 1776 and was brevetted brigadier-general, 1783. Appointed Indian Commissioner by Congress, he negotiated important treaties with Iroquois, Delaware, Chippewa and Shawnee tribes, 1784–86. He was killed in the rout of Gen. Arthur St. Clair's expedition against the Ohio tribes, 1791.

BUTLER, SIMEON (*b. West Hartford, Conn., 1770; d. Northampton, Mass., 1847*), bookseller and publisher in Northampton, *post* 1790.

BUTLER, SMEDLEY DARLINGTON (*b. West Chester, Pa., 1881; d. Philadelphia, Pa., 1940*), Marine Corps officer. "Old Gimlet Eye"; a picturesque and controversial soldier. [*Supp. 2*]

BUTLER, THOMAS BELDEN (*b. Wethersfield, Conn., 1806; d. Hartford, Conn., 1873*), physician, jurist. Justice of state superior court, 1855–61; of supreme court of errors, 1861–73.

BUTLER, WALTER N. (*b. near Johnstown, N.Y., date unknown; d. 1781*), Loyalist, soldier. Son of John Butler. Led Tory and Indian attack on Cherry

Valley, N.Y., November 1778; killed at West Canada Creek on retreat after raid on Mohawk Valley.

BUTLER, WILLIAM (*b. Prince William Co., Va., 1759; d. Edgefield District, S.C., 1821*), Revolutionary soldier. Father of Andrew P. Butler and Pierce M. Butler. Congressman, (Democrat) Republican, from South Carolina, 1800–13.

BUTLER, WILLIAM (*b. Dublin, Ireland, 1818; d. Old Orchard, Maine, 1899*), Methodist clergyman. Came to America, 1850. Father of John Wesley Butler. Headed Methodist mission in India, 1856–64; in Mexico, 1873–79.

BUTLER, WILLIAM ALLEN (*b. Albany, N.Y., 1825; d. Yonkers, N.Y., 1902*), lawyer, author. Son of Benjamin F. Butler (1795–1858); authority on admiralty law. His best-known work is the sparkling satirical poem *Nothing to Wear* (1857).

BUTLER, WILLIAM ORLANDO (*b. Jessamine Co., Ky., 1791; d. Carrollton, Ky., 1880*), soldier, lawyer, farmer, statesman. Served with great distinction in War of 1812 and Mexican War. Congressman, Democrat, from Kentucky, 1839–43; Democratic vice-presidential candidate, 1848; a staunch Union Democrat during Civil War.

BUTLER, ZEBULON (*b. Ipswich, Mass., 1731; d. Wilkesbarre, Pa., 1795*), soldier. Reared in Lyme, Conn.; led Connecticut settlers along Susquehanna in the so-called Pennamite wars with Pennsylvania, 1769–75. Unsuccessfully defended Wyoming Valley against Tory-Indian raid, 1778.

BUTTERFIELD, DANIEL (*b. Utica, N.Y., 1831; d. Cold Spring, N.Y., 1901*), Union soldier. Son of John Butterfield; graduated Union College, 1849; employed in father's express business. Entered Civil War as colonel, 12th New York Regiment, and served with great distinction, 1861–65; during the war he was chief of staff to Generals Hooker and Meade, was several times wounded, and was honored at the end by a brevet of major-general of regulars. On retirement from the army in 1870, he returned to business in which he had a varied and successful career.

BUTTERFIELD, JOHN (*b. Berne, N.Y., 1801; d. Utica, N.Y., 1869*), expressman, financier. Active in western New York stage lines, steamboat operation and railroad promotion, he was an organizer of the American Express Co., 1850. In 1857, he and associates undertook the first transcontinental stage line and Butterfield as president of the Overland Mail Co. planned and established the service.

BUTTERFIELD, KENYON LEECH (*b. Lapeer, Mich., 1868; d. 1935*), college president, rural sociologist. Leader in the country-life movement; president, Massachusetts Agricultural College, 1906–24; Michigan State College, 1924–28. [*Supp. 1*]

BUTTERICK, EBENEZER (*b. Sterling, Mass., 1826; d. 1903*), inventor (with wife) of standardized paper clothes patterns, first marketed commercially in 1863.

BUTTERWORTH, BENJAMIN (*b. Hamilton Township, O., 1837; d. Thomasville, Ga., 1898*), lawyer, politician. Congressman, Republican, from Ohio, 1879–83, 1885–90; special counsel in South Carolina election cases, 1882–83; U.S. commissioner of patents, 1883–85, 1897–98.

BUTTERWORTH, HEZEKIAH (*b. Warren, R.I., 1839; d. 1905*), journalist. Prolific contributor to *Youth's Companion*, 1870–94.

BUTTRICK, WALLACE (*b. Potsdam, N.Y., 1853; d. Baltimore, Md., 1926*), Baptist clergyman. As secretary (1903–17), president (1917–23) and chairman (1923–26) of the Rockefeller General Education Board, he promoted progress in education, particularly in the South; he was also active in promotion of education for the professions.

BUTTS, ISAAC (*b. Dutchess Co., N.Y., 1816; d. 1874*), publisher and editor of the *Daily Advertiser*, Rochester, N.Y., and later of the Rochester *Daily Union*.

BUTTZ, HENRY ANSON (*b. Middle Smithfield, Pa., 1835; d. 1920*), Methodist clergyman. Notable president of Drew Theological Seminary, 1880–1912; emeritus, 1912–20. Learned in Greek and New Testament exegesis.

BYERLY, WILLIAM ELWOOD (*b. Philadelphia, Pa., 1849; d. Swarthmore, Pa., 1935*), mathematician. Author of textbooks on the calculus; a prime factor in growth of Radcliffe College. [*Supp. 1*]

BYFORD, WILLIAM HEATH (*b. Eaton, O., 1817; d. Chicago, Ill., 1890*), gynecologist. Professor of gynecology, Rush Medical College, 1879–90; a pioneer in his field. Author of *Treatise on the Theory and Practice of Obstetrics* (1870) and other works.

BYINGTON, CYRUS (*b. Stockbridge, Mass., 1793; d. 1868*), Congregational clergyman. Missionary to Choctaw Indians *post* 1820; author of a grammar and dictionary of the Choctaw language.

BYLES, MATHER (*b. Boston, Mass., 1706/7; d. Boston, 1788*), Congregational clergyman. Graduated Harvard, 1725; ordained minister of Hollis Street Church, Boston, 1732. Dismissed from his pulpit for Tory sympathies, 1776. Cheerful and witty, he was a correspondent of Pope and Isaac Watts; he was author of *Poems on Several Occasions* (1744) and numerous theological works of an orthodox Calvinist character.

BYNUM, WILLIAM PRESTON (*b. Stokes Co., N.C., 1820; d. Charlotte, N.C., 1909*), jurist, Confederate soldier.

BYRD, WILLIAM (*b. London, England, 1652; d. 1704*), planter, merchant, Indian trader. Came to

Virginia when young; by uncle's will inherited lands at present site of Richmond, 1671. Served in House of Burgesses, 1677–82; became member of the Council of State, 1683. Took up residence at Westover, 1691. In 1703 he became president of the Council. Byrd's wealth was based on tobacco planting and export; the importation of Negro slaves and all manner of manufactured articles; fur trading with the Indians; land speculation.

BYRD, WILLIAM (*b. Virginia, 1674; d. Westover, Va., 1744*), planter, colonial official, author. Son of William Byrd (1652–1704). Schooled abroad, 1684–92; studied at Middle Temple, London. Elected to House of Burgesses, 1692, on return to Virginia; in England, 1697–1704; entered Council of State, 1709. Resisted Governor Spotswood's attempts to remove supreme judicial power from Council. Lived in ease and state at Westover *post* 1720, managing with a rather lax hand the properties left him by his father. His witty, graceful writings remained unpublished until 1841; they include *The History of the Dividing Line, A Journey to the Land of Eden,* and the *Progress to the Mines.* His letters and diaries have also been published and are valuable historical sources.

BYRNE, ANDREW (*b. Navan, Ireland, 1802; d. Little Rock, Ark., 1862*), Roman Catholic clergyman. Came to America, 1820; ordained, 1827; served as pastor of churches in Charleston, S.C., and New York, N.Y. Appointed first bishop of Little Rock, 1844.

BYRNE, DONN. [See DONN-BYRNE, BRIAN OSWALD, 1889–1928.]

BYRNE, JOHN (*b. Kilkeel, Ireland, 1825; d. Montreux, Switzerland, 1902*), physician, surgeon. M.D. Edinburgh, 1846. Came to America, 1848, and practiced in Brooklyn, N.Y. Adapted electric cautery-knife to surgery of malignant disease of uterus, *c.* 1870.

BYRNES, THOMAS (*b. Ireland, 1842; d. 1910*), policeman, "Inspector Byrnes." Brought to America in infancy; joined New York City police force, 1863. Won fame in solving Manhattan Savings Bank case, 1878; reorganized New York detective bureau, 1880, making it highly efficient.

BYRNS, JOSEPH WELLINGTON (*b. Robertson Co., Tenn., 1869; d. Washington, D.C., 1936*). Congressman, Democrat, from Tennessee, 1909–36 (majority leader, 1932–35; speaker, 1935–36). [*Supp. 2*]

CABELL, JAMES LAWRENCE (*b. Nelson Co., Va., 1813; d. Albemarle Co., Va., 1889*), physician. M.D. University of Maryland, 1834. Professor of anatomy, surgery and physiology, University of Virginia, 1837–89; author of *Testimony of Modern Science to the Unity of Mankind* (1858).

CABELL, JOSEPH CARRINGTON (*b. Amherst, now Nelson, Co., Va., 1778; d. 1856*), principal coadjutor

of Thomas Jefferson in founding University of Virginia. Brother of William H. Cabell. Identified by choice with Virginia affairs although fitted for national eminence. Pioneer of James River and Kanawha Canal project.

CABELL, NATHANIEL FRANCIS (*b. "Warminster," Nelson Co., Va., 1807; d. 1891*), author. Wrote voluminously on topics of religion, genealogy, and agricultural history of Virginia; editor, *The Lee Papers* (1858–60).

CABELL, SAMUEL JORDAN (*b. Amherst, now Nelson Co., Va., 1756; d. Nelson Co., 1818*), Revolutionary soldier. Son of William Cabell. Commissioned major for bravery at Saratoga, 1777; served under Washington, 1778–79, and under General Lincoln in southern campaign. Congressman, Democratic-Republican, from Virginia, 1795–1803.

CABELL, WILLIAM (*b. Virginia, 1729/30; d. Nelson Co., Va., 1798*), Revolutionary patriot. Member of committee of safety, and of committee which prepared Declaration of Rights and a form of government for Virginia. Served in both houses of state legislature; voted against ratification of Federal Constitution.

CABELL, WILLIAM H. (*b. near Cartersville, Va., 1772; d. Richmond, Va., 1853*), lawyer. Brother of Joseph C. Cabell. Elected governor of Virginia, 1805; served three terms. Judge of state court of appeals, 1811–51 (president of the court, 1842–51).

CABELL, WILLIAM LEWIS (*b. Danville, Va., 1827; d. 1911*), Confederate soldier, lawyer. Graduated West Point, 1850. Resigned from army, 1861, and was thereafter on staffs of Confederate generals Beauregard and J. E. Johnston; served with distinction in Trans-Mississippi department, 1862–64. Studied law after the war and removed to Dallas, Texas, 1872; mayor of Dallas, 1874–76 and 1882.

CABET, ÉTIENNE (*b. Dijon, France, 1788; d. St. Louis, Mo., 1856*), reformer, communist. Set forth a social doctrine in his *Voyage en Icarie* (1839) which he hoped to realize in a utopian settlement on the Red River in Texas. Failing there, his followers leased the old Mormon settlement at Nauvoo, Ill., where he presided, 1849–55.

CABLE, GEORGE WASHINGTON (*b. New Orleans, La., 1844; d. St. Petersburg, Fla., 1925*), author. Began to write after service, 1863–65, with Confederate cavalry; became a reporter for New Orleans *Picayune,* 1869, but soon took position as clerk with a firm of cotton factors. Fascinated by stories on which he chanced in a survey of old city records, he set them down in a series of sketches which were immediately successful on publication in *Scribner's Monthly,* 1873–76. They appeared in book form as *Old Creole Days* (1879). Subsequent publication of *The Grandissimes* (1880) and *Madame Delphine* (1881) established him as a writer of sensitivity and mood who had added a new "region" to American fiction; with Bret Harte, he was a pioneer in "local color" work. Although he continued to write until his death, his later books lacked the quality of his earlier ones; he became active in movements for reform of prisons, election laws, and the condition of the Negro, and aroused the resentment of Southerners. After 1885, he made his home in Northampton, Mass. His later books include: *Dr. Sevier* (1885); *The Silent South* (1885); *The Negro Question* (1888); *John March, Southerner* (1894); *The Cavalier* (1901).

CABOT, ARTHUR TRACY (*b. Boston, Mass., 1852; d. 1912*), surgeon. Graduated Harvard, A.B., 1872; M.D., 1876. In London, 1877, to study surgical pathology, he heard Lister's inaugural address and was thereafter an apostle of the antiseptic system; returning to Boston, he built up a general practice, specializing in surgery *post* 1886. He served as instructor, Harvard Medical School, 1878–80 and 1885–96, and was active in public health promotion; his extensive writings appeared mainly in the *Boston Medical and Surgical Journal*.

CABOT, EDWARD CLARKE (*b. Boston, Mass., 1818; d. Brookline, Mass., 1901*), architect. Designer of Boston Athenaeum (1845), Boston Theater (1852–53) and Johns Hopkins University hospital (completed 1889). These and his many excellent country houses were distinguished for delicacy and restraint.

CABOT, GEORGE (*b. Salem, Mass., 1752; d. Boston, Mass., 1823*), merchant, politician. Escaped dismissal from Harvard, 1768; went to sea; was skipper of a schooner within two years. Gave up active seafaring, *c.* 1777, and entered family shipping and trading firm. In partnership with Joseph Lee, 1785–95, he earned a "reasonable and sufficient" fortune in shipping and trading. Temperament and interest made him favor a strong, central government. He was early identified with the Federalist point of view and was a trusted follower and adviser of Alexander Hamilton. As U.S. senator from Massachusetts, 1791–96, he favored the Jay Treaty and close alliance with Great Britain. On retirement from public life, he expanded his business interests and indulged a growing pessimism over the course of the nation; he opposed Jefferson and his policies, but as president of the Hartford Convention (1814) worked with Harrison G. Otis to prevent radical action by that body.

CABOT, RICHARD CLARKE (*b. Brookline, Mass., 1868; d. Cambridge, Mass., 1939*), physician, medical reformer, social worker. Graduated, 1892, from Harvard Medical School, he taught there, 1899–1933, and was on the staff of Massachusetts General Hospital from 1898 to 1921, from 1912 as chief of staff. Convinced of the importance of social and psychic factors in the diagnosis and treatment of disease (especially in the case of clinic patients), Cabot inaugurated, 1905, a medical social service unit at Massachusetts General, a pioneer form of medical social work. A

distinguished teacher and practitioner, he was also a productive writer—on medical subjects, social work, and social ethics. He occupied the chair of social ethics at Harvard College from 1920 to 1934.

[*Supp.* 2]

CABRILLO, JUAN RODRIGUEZ (*d. San Miguel Island, Calif., 1543*), explorer of the coast of California, 1542.

CABRINI, FRANCIS XAVIER (*b. Sant' Angelo Lodigiano, Lombardy, Italy, 1850; d. Chicago, Ill., 1917*), foundress of a religious community and first citizen of the United States to be canonized a saint of the Church. Taught school and supervised an orphanage before becoming prioress (1877) of her foundation, the Institute of the Missionary Sisters of the Sacred Heart. After founding orphanages and schools, she was sent by Pope Leo XIII to the United States to help Italian immigrants, living in slums, who were losing the Catholic faith. Disappointments she faced on her arrival in 1889 did not discourage her from establishing 70 hospitals and educational institutions throughout the Western Hemisphere and western Europe. Pronounced venerable in 1933, Mother Cabrini was canonized in 1946. [*Supp.* 1]

CADILLAC, ANTOINE DE LA MOTHE (*b. Gascony, France, c. 1656; d. Castle Sarrazin, Gascony, 1730*), founder of Detroit. Came to Canada, 1683; lived at Port Royal and for a brief time on his grant in what is now Maine. Through friendship of Count Frontenac, he received command of post at Mackinac, 1694, but was relieved of it in 1697. In 1699, he went to France with a scheme for protecting the French fur trade from English raids by erecting a post on Detroit River; receiving a grant of Detroit and a trade monopoly, he led a body of colonists there in 1701. Zealous, enthusiastic, covetous and highhanded, Cadillac after many difficulties was recalled in 1711 and appointed governor of the new colony of Louisiana where he arrived in 1713. He was soon at odds with the colonists and was superseded, 1716, returning to France.

CADMAN, SAMUEL PARKES (*b. Wellington, England, 1864; d. Plattsburg, N.Y., 1936*), clergyman. Originally a Methodist, he became pastor of Brooklyn's Central Congregational Church, 1900–36. One of the first "radio pastors." [*Supp.* 2]

CADWALADER, JOHN (*b. Philadelphia, Pa., 1742; d. 1786*), Revolutionary soldier. Appointed brigadier-general of Pennsylvania militia, 1776; fought at Trenton, Princeton, Brandywine, Germantown, and Monmouth. His duel with General Conway caused the collapse of the so-called "Conway Cabal" against Washington.

CADWALADER, JOHN (*b. Philadelphia, Pa., 1805; d. Philadelphia, 1879*), jurist. Graduated University of Pennsylvania, 1821; admitted to the bar, 1825. Counsel to Bank of the United States, *post* 1830;

acted in behalf of the United States in the "Cloth Cases" of 1839; was associated with Daniel Webster in the Girard Will Case. Judge of U.S. district court, eastern district of Pennsylvania, 1858–79.

CADWALADER, LAMBERT (*b. Trenton, N.J., 1743; d. "Greenwood," near Trenton, 1823*). Brother of John Cadwalader (1742–1786); Revolutionary patriot and soldier.

CADWALADER, THOMAS (*b. Philadelphia, Pa., 1707 or 1708; d. Trenton, N.J., 1799*), physician. Father of John (1742–1786) and Lambert Cadwalader. Studied medicine with physician uncle and in England and France; had large practice in Philadelphia. Lived in Trenton, N.J., 1738–50, returning to Philadelphia. Active in civic and cultural affairs and in early stages of resistance to English rule. Performed in 1742 one of the earliest recorded autopsies in America.

CADY, DANIEL (*b. Chatham, N.Y., 1773; d. Johnstown, N.Y., 1859*), jurist. Specialist in equity and real property law; father of Elizabeth Cady Stanton.

CADY, SARAH LOUISE ENSIGN (*b. Northampton, Mass., 1829; d. New York, N.Y., 1912*), educator. Principal and proprietor, West End Institute, New Haven, Conn., 1870–99.

CAFFERY, DONELSON (*b. near Franklin, La., 1835; d. New Orleans, La., 1906*), sugar-planter, statesman. U.S. senator, Democrat, from Louisiana, 1892–1901; opposed free silver, the sugar bounty and the war with Spain.

CAFFIN, CHARLES HENRY (*b. Sittingbourne, Kent, England, 1854; d. 1918*), author. Came to America, 1892; art critic and writer of popular books on art.

CAIN, RICHARD HARVEY (*b. Greenbrier Co., Va., 1825; d. 1887*), Methodist clergyman, politician. Licensed to preach at Hannibal, Mo., 1844, he allied himself with the African Methodist Episcopal church and held pastorates in Iowa, New York and South Carolina. As member of Congress from South Carolina during Reconstruction, he strove for clean politics; elected bishop, 1880, his last years were spent in Louisiana and Texas.

CAIN, WILLIAM (*b. Hillsboro, N.C., 1847; d. 1930*), mathematician. Professor, and head of department of engineering, University of North Carolina, 1888–1920; a pioneer in writing American civil engineering textbooks. [*Supp. 1*]

CAINES, GEORGE (*b. 1771; d. Catskill, N.Y., 1825*), lawyer. First official reporter of legal decisions, appointed by the New York supreme court, 1804; editor, *Caines' Cases in Error* (1805–07) and other works.

CAJORI, FLORIAN (*b. Switzerland, 1859; d. 1930*), historian of mathematics and professor, University of California, 1918–29. Author of many authoritative works, including *A History of Mathematical Notations* (1928–29). [*Supp. 1*]

CALDWELL, ALEXANDER (*b. Drake's Ferry, Pa., d. Leavenworth, Kans., 1917*), businessman, politician. Contractor for delivery of army stores to posts west of the Missouri, 1861; promoter of Kansas railroads, *post* 1870. Denied seat in U.S. Senate, 1871, on charge that bribery dictated his appointment.

CALDWELL, CHARLES (*b. Caswell Co., N.C., 1772; d. 1853*), physician. Pioneer medical educator in Mississippi valley; founded and directed medical school, Transylvania (Lexington, Ky.), 1819–37; professor, Louisville Medical Institute, 1837–49.

CALDWELL, CHARLES HENRY BROMEDGE (*b. Hingham, Mass., 1823; d. 1877*), naval officer. In command of *Itasca*, April 1862, helped open passage to New Orleans for Farragut's fleet.

CALDWELL, DAVID (*b. Lancaster Co., Pa., 1725; d. North Carolina, 1824*), Presbyterian clergyman. Prominent in patriotic affairs during the Revolution; pastor at Alamance, N.C., 1768–1820.

CALDWELL, EUGENE WILSON (*b. Savannah, Mo., 1870; d. 1918*), Roentgenologist. Inventor of many improvements in X-ray apparatus; died of injuries suffered in experimentation.

CALDWELL, HENRY CLAY (*b. Marshall Co., Va., 1832; d. Los Angeles, Calif., 1915*), jurist. Raised in Iowa; appointed U.S. judge for war-ravaged Arkansas district, 1864, he served until 1890 with scrupulous impartiality; presiding justice, 8th Federal District, 1890–1903.

CALDWELL, JAMES (*b. Charlotte Co., Va., 1734; d. Elizabeth, N.J., 1781*), Presbyterian clergyman, patriot. Graduated Princeton, 1759; settled as pastor, Elizabeth, N.J.; known as the "Soldier Parson" in Revolutionary War.

CALDWELL, JOSEPH (*b. Lamington, N.J., 1773; d. 1835*), mathematician, educator. Graduated Princeton, 1791. Professor of mathematics, University of North Carolina, 1796–1804 and 1812–17; its president, 1804–12 and 1817–35; a force for internal improvements and public education in North Carolina.

CALEF, ROBERT (*b. probably England, 1648; d. Roxbury, Mass., 1719*), merchant. His book *More Wonders of the Invisible World* (written 1697, printed in London, 1700) was a powerful arraignment of the Salem witchcraft trials of 1692 and a blow at domination of New England thought by the Mather dynasty.

CALHOUN, JOHN (*b. Boston, Mass., 1806; d. St. Joseph, Mo., 1859*), politician. Settled in Springfield, Ill., 1830; helped Abraham Lincoln study surveying. Served thrice as mayor of Springfield; appointed surveyor of Kansas and Nebraska, 1854, he became involved in the alleged frauds connected with the Lecompton constitutional convention, 1857.

CALHOUN, JOHN CALDWELL (*b. Abbeville District, S.C., 1782; d. Washington, D.C., 1850*), statesman, political philosopher. Descended from Scotch-Irish pioneers who entered Pennsylvania *c.* 1733. Subsequent to Braddock's defeat (1755), the family moved south and settled in the South Carolina uplands near the Savannah River. Calhoun's father, Patrick, was for many years a member of the South Carolina legislature; his death in 1796 thrust family burdens on the son and interrupted his formal education until 1800. He then resumed school and graduated from Yale, 1804. After law studies at Tapping Reeve's school, Litchfield, Conn., and in office of Henry W. DeSaussure, Charleston, S.C., he began practice in Abbeville, S.C. Finding legal work uncongenial, he was fortunate in a marriage (1811) with Floride Bouneau whose means added to his own left him financially independent.

Active from youth in politics, he was elected to the South Carolina legislature in 1808 and had a share in the revision of representation in that body whereby control of the lower house was given the upland districts and preponderance in the state senate to the lowlands. This device of mutual checks or "concurrent majorities" he was later to propose for relief of sectional differences on the national scale. Elected congressman, (Democrat) Republican, in 1810, he served as acting chairman, committee on foreign affairs; his report, presented June 3, 1812, recommending war on Great Britain, was written by Monroe but won popular notice for Calhoun. During the War of 1812, he was tireless in support of the war and the administration; thereafter, he distrusted efficacy of the Treaty of Ghent and was zealous in promoting national strength, urging an effective navy, an adequate standing army, a road-building policy, a system of internal revenue, a national bank, and the encouragement of native manufactures. At this period he favored a protective tariff. Appointed secretary of war in Monroe's cabinet (1817–25), he improved army organization and established the offices of surgeon-general, commissary-general, and quartermaster-general.

Elected vice-president by a large majority in 1824, he presided over the Senate with meticulous abstinence from the partisanship of the period; obviously shaping his course for the presidency, he allied himself with Andrew Jackson and was elected for a second term as vice-president in 1828. Soon alienated from Jackson, Calhoun found himself in an equal quandary over protectionism. Opposition to protection was rising in the South, but his Northern supporters favored it. Basing his decision on the national interest, he had voted against the Woollens Bill (1827); he had expressed himself in confidence as opposed to any policy which would put the geographical interests in hostile array, or would "make two of one nation." Now in 1828,

fearing that the insistence of Congress on the so-called "tariff of abominations" would force the South to a desperate reaction, he composed the "South Carolina Exposition" for issue by the state legislature; as his authorship remained a secret until 1831, its bold warning that pursuance of a protectionist program would result in the counter-stroke which was to become famous as "nullification" committed him to nothing at the time. His efforts to achieve intersectional accord failing, and with President Jackson approving the systematically protective tariff of 1832, Calhoun published that August a letter to Governor Hamilton in which he gave logic and substance to the doctrine of nullification. Premising that sovereignty is in the people and that both central and state governments under the American federal system are only organs of popular power, he declared that in the event of an exceeding of power by the central government against the will of the people of any state, the people could hold a convention and declare the act of Congress null; they could also require the state government to prohibit enforcement of the obnoxious act within the limits of the state. He developed all phases of this doctrine extensively and was careful to distinguish the right of nullification from the right of secession.

President Jackson's forceful reaction to nullification having ended in a face-saving compromise, a new alignment of political forces took place and Whig was opposed to Democrat; Calhoun at first held himself aloof from both but his dislike of Jackson and Jackson's favorites inclined him to act as a Whig auxiliary. Under Van Buren, he shifted to the Democratic side. Early in 1833, he had resigned the vice-presidency and now sat in Congress as senator from South Carolina where his able attention to public business increased his following in the South and won back for him the respect of many Northerners.

The rise of the abolition movement made it impossible for Calhoun to return to his earlier nationalistic position. Menaced by destruction of their capital (as represented by their slaves) and a potential social chaos, Southerners looked for a strategy of defense; Calhoun came to be regarded as the main source of plans, arguments and inspiration. Although he had shown only lukewarm acquiescence in the slave-system earlier in his career, the agitation of Garrison and others altered his mind; in 1833 he said that slavery might give the South greater reason than the tariff to cherish state-rights and by 1837 he was found asserting that slavery was a positive good. He deprecated controversy over disputes between the sections which he considered unessential, but on vital issues he was aggressive in defense of "Southern Rights." Active under President Tyler in whose cabinet he served for a time as secretary of state, he retired to private life at the outset of President Polk's term; he returned to the Senate as war threatened with Mexico, war which he vehemently opposed.

Wilmot's proposal to prohibit slavery in all areas to

be acquired by the war involved Calhoun in furious controversy. He urged that all territories were an estate owned by the states of the Union in common; that the federal government administered them only as a trustee; that any citizen of any state had full right to emigrate to any territory, carrying with him whatever property he owned and was entitled to federal protection of his property until the territory should become a state. No slaveholder, therefore, could be debarred from transport and continued use of his slaves. In effect, Congress was estopped from restricting the spread of slaveholding. As a permanent expression of his philosophy of government, he wrote his *Disquisition on Government* and his *Discourse on the Constitution and Government of the United States;* these appeared in published form after his death.

The doctrines contained in these treatises were studied with respect at home and abroad, especially his plea for adequate checks against encroachments of government and the spoliation of minorities in promotion of majority interests, and his restatement of the right of the people to challenge any assumptions of undelegated authority. As a device to perpetuate the Union and secure at the same time the tranquillity of the South, he advocated amendment of the Constitution to allow election of two chief executives, each to represent one of the great sections of the country.

Convinced as he was that the South was doomed under the existing state of party government, Calhoun summoned a meeting in January 1849 of Southern statesmen to consider an address which he had written for their signature and issue to their constituents. It reviewed the history of the slavery issue, prophetically foretold the evils that were to come, and called for unity in holding Southern Rights paramount to party allegiance. Only a minority signed it. He then endeavored to promote a convention of the slaveholding states. Before the end of the year, California's application for statehood under a constitution excluding slavery reopened legislative battle. Ill and old, Calhoun tottered to his place in the Senate chamber to preach resistance by the South to the point of independence if that should prove essential for her social security.

He gave his adverse opinion of Henry Clay's Omnibus Bill which proposed to settle the many issues on a give-and-take basis in his last formal speech. This was read by Senator Mason on March 4, 1850, while its author sat voiceless in his chair. Virtually his last spoken words were, "The South, the poor South."

CALHOUN, WILLIAM BARRON (*b. Boston, Mass., 1795; d. Springfield, Mass., 1865*), lawyer, politician, educator. Graduated Yale, 1814; admitted to Massachusetts bar, 1818. Held numerous public offices with credit; had a lifelong interest in teacher-training.

CALHOUN, WILLIAM JAMES (*b. Pittsburgh, Pa., 1848; d. Chicago, Ill., 1916*), diplomat. Practiced law, Danville, Ill., 1875–98; thereafter in Chicago. His re-

ports on condition of Cuba, 1897, reconciled McKinley to intervention; he served as minister to China, 1909–13.

CALIFORNIA JOE (*b. near Stanford, Ky., 1829; d. Camp Robinson, Neb., 1876*), army scout. Born Moses Embree Miller, he went west in 1849, served in the Civil War, and after the war as a guide and scout on the plains; he was associated with General Custer's commands, *post* 1868, and won fame in the writings of Custer and his wife.

CALKINS, MARY WHITON (*b. Hartford, Conn., 1863; d. 1930*), the first American woman to attain eminence in the field of philosophy. Pupil of Josiah Royce, she taught psychology and philosophy at Wellesley College, 1890–1929. [*Supp. 1*]

CALKINS, NORMAN ALLISON (*b. Gainesville, N.Y., 1822; d. New York, N.Y., 1895*), educator. Author of *Primary Object Lessons for a Graduated Course of Development* (1861), a Pestalozzian treatise which had great influence in primary school teaching.

CALKINS, PHINEAS WOLCOTT (*b. Painted Post, now Corning, N.Y., 1831; d. 1924*), Congregational clergyman. Held many eastern and midwestern pastorates; at death, pastor emeritus of Montvale Church, Woburn, Mass.

CALKINS, WOLCOTT. [See CALKINS, PHINEAS WOLCOTT]

CALL, RICHARD KEITH (*b. Prince George Co., Va., 1791; d. 1862*), lawyer, politician. Moved to Kentucky as a boy; schooled in Tennessee. Served under Andrew Jackson in War of 1812 and Creek campaigns; resigned army commission, 1821, and set up law practice in Pensacola, Fla. Territorial delegate from Florida, 1823–25. Built third railroad in U.S. (Tallahassee-St. Marks), 1832–34. Democratic governor of Florida, 1836–39; Whig governor of Florida, 1841–44. Strove to hold Florida in the Union, but went with his state on secession.

CALLAHAN, PATRICK HENRY (*b. Cleveland, O., 1865; d. Louisville, Ky., 1940*), paint manufacturer, proponent of industrial partnership, crusading Catholic layman. Instituted, 1915, profit-sharing in his Louisville Varnish Co. [*Supp. 2*]

CALLAWAY, MORGAN (*b. Cuthbert, Ga., 1862; d. Austin, Texas, 1936*), philologist. Author of authoritative studies of Old English syntax; professor of English, University of Texas, 1890–1936. [*Supp. 2*]

CALLAWAY, SAMUEL RODGER (*b. Toronto, Canada, 1850; d. 1904*), railroad executive. His reorganization of Toledo, St. Louis & Kansas City line, 1887–95, led to presidency of New York Central, 1898–1901; he was first president of American Locomotive Co., 1901–04.

CALLENDER, GUY STEVENS (*b. Hartsgrove, O., 1865; d. 1915*), historian, economist. Professor of political economy, Sheffield Scientific School, Yale, 1903–15. Author of masterly *Selections from the Economic History of the United States* (1909).

CALLENDER, JAMES THOMSON (*b. Scotland, 1758; d. Richmond, Va., 1803*), political writer. Came to America, *post* 1793, and was patronized by Thomas Jefferson. Author of scurrilous *History of the United States for 1796* (1797), *The Prospect Before Us* (1800–01), and other tracts.

CALLENDER, JOHN (*b. Boston, Mass., 1706; d. Newport, R.I., 1748*), Baptist clergyman. Pastor at Newport, 1731–48; author of valuable *Historical Discourse on the Civil and Religious Affairs of the Colony of Rhode Island* (1739).

CALVERLEY, CHARLES (*b. Albany, N.Y., 1833; d. Essex Fells, N.J., 1914*), sculptor. Pupil of Erastus D. Palmer; specialized in portrait busts and medallions.

CALVERT, CHARLES (*b. England, 1637; d. 1715*), third Lord Baltimore, son of Cecilius Calvert. Governor of Maryland, 1661–75; proprietor, 1675–1715.

CALVERT, CHARLES BENEDICT (*b. Riverdale, Md., 1808; d. Riverdale, 1864*), agriculturist. Prime mover in founding Maryland Agricultural College; as a congressman, 1861–64, active in establishing federal Bureau (now Department) of Agriculture, 1862.

CALVERT, GEORGE (*b. Kipling, Yorkshire, England, c. 1580; d. 1632*), first Lord Baltimore, projector of Maryland. Educated at Oxford; served Sir Robert Cecil as secretary, 1606–12; knighted, 1617; secretary of state and Privy Councillor, 1619–25; created Baron Baltimore, 1625. In 1624, announced his conversion to Catholic faith and resigned offices but was retained as a Privy Councillor. Had become in 1620 proprietor by purchase of part of Newfoundland; this was erected by royal grant into province of Avalon, 1623, but the colony did not thrive. Calvert petitioned for a grant in warmer climate, 1629; in 1632, Charles I granted him territory in what is now Virginia. Opposition by Virginia settlers and the Virginia Company caused substitution of lands between 40th degree, north latitude, and Potomac River, extending westward to longitude of that river's first source. Calvert died before charter of Maryland passed the Great Seal; it was issued to his son Cecilius, first proprietor of Maryland.

CALVERT, GEORGE HENRY (*b. Riverdale, Md., 1803; d. Newport, R.I., 1889*), author. Brother of Charles B. Calvert; settled in Newport, 1843, after extensive travel abroad. Author of minor verse, studies of Goethe and the English Romantic poets, and an essay on manners, *The Gentleman* (1863).

CALVERT, LEONARD (*b. England, 1606; d. Maryland, 1647*), colonial governor. Son of George Calvert; brother of Cecilius Calvert, second Lord Baltimore. Came to Maryland with first colonists aboard the *Ark* and the *Dove*, March 1634, and set up a government at St. Mary's City. Formally commissioned gov-

ernor, 1637, he served until his death in that capacity. His support of laws passed by the Assembly over his brother's veto led to the right of initiative in legislation passing to that body.

CALVERTON, VICTOR FRANCIS (*b. Baltimore, Md., 1900; d. New York, N.Y., 1940*), originally named George Goetz. Applied Marxist critical principles to the social sciences and literature. [*Supp. 2*]

CALVIN, SAMUEL (*b. Wigtonshire, Scotland, 1840; d. 1911*), geologist. Emigrated to America, 1851; raised in Buchanan Co., Iowa. Professor of natural history, Iowa State *post* 1874; state geologist, 1892–1904 and 1906–11. Did valuable work on fossils of upper Mississippi valley.

CAMBRELENG, CHURCHILL CALDOM (*b. Washington, N.C., 1786; d. West Neck, L.I., N.Y., 1862*), politician. Successful in business in New York City, 1802–21; congressman, Democrat, from New York, 1821–39, and administration leader in the House for both Jackson and Van Buren. Minister to Russia, 1840–41. Took prominent part in New York "Barnburner" movement, 1847–48.

CAMDEN, JOHNSON NEWLON (*b. Collins Settlement, Va., 1828; d. 1908*), businessman. Pioneered in oil on the Little Kanawha, 1860; entered refinery business, Parkersburg, W. Va., 1869; promoted railroads in area and became a Standard Oil Co. director. U.S. senator, Democrat, from West Virginia, 1881–87; 1893–95.

CAMERON, ANDREW CARR (*b. Berwick-on-Tweed, England, 1836; d. 1892*), labor leader, editor. Emigrated to America, *c.* 1851; was printer on Chicago *Courant* (later *Times*), and active in typographical union. Edited *Workingman's Advocate*, 1864–80; helped organize National Labor Union, devoted to formation of an independent labor party.

CAMERON, ARCHIBALD (*b. Lochaber, Scotland, c. 1771; d. Kentucky, 1836*), Presbyterian clergyman. Raised by an elder brother in Nelson Co., Ky. Ordained, 1796, he was leading exponent of orthodox Calvinism in Nelson, Shelby and Jefferson counties.

CAMERON, JAMES DONALD (*b. Middletown, Pa., 1833; d. 1918*), businessman, politician. Son of Simon Cameron, whom he aided in family enterprises and in control of Republican party in Pennsylvania, succeeding to the leadership after father's retirement. President, Northern Central Railroad, 1863–74; secretary of war, 1876–77; U.S. senator from Pennsylvania, 1877–97.

CAMERON, ROBERT ALEXANDER (*b. Brooklyn, N.Y., 1828; d. Canon City, Colo., 1894*), Union soldier, colonizer. Joined with Nathan C. Meeker in post-Civil War Union Colony movement for planting farm colonies in West. Active in founding Greeley, Colo., and Colorado Springs.

CAMERON, SIMON (*b. Lancaster Co., Pa., 1799; d. 1889*), businessman, politician. Managed newspapers, 1821–26. Ownership of Harrisburg, Pa., *Republican* gave him influence in state and national politics; lucrative appointment as state printer provided means for his branching out into canal building and the creation of a network of local railroads which he later united in the Northern Central. He also engaged in banking, iron making and insurance. Soon wealthy, he was a staunch supporter of protective tariffs. Originally a Democrat, he maneuvered his election to the U.S. Senate in 1845 by means which won him enmity of James Buchanan and regular party men; he failed of election in 1849 and again in 1855. Becoming a Republican he was returned to the Senate in 1857; thereafter he strengthened his position as dictator of Pennsylvania politics. Support of Lincoln in 1860 won him post of secretary of war; his corrupt conduct of office caused his removal, 1862, by appointment as minister to Russia. Returning home, 1863, he ran unsuccessfully for the Senate; in 1867 he was elected and served as senator until 1877 when he forced the subservient Pennsylvania legislature to accept his son, James Donald Cameron, as his successor. His iron control of his state was based on patronage and shrewd manipulation of men.

CAMERON, WILLIAM EVELYN (*b. Petersburg, Va., 1842; d. 1927*), newspaper editor. Joined "Readjuster" faction of Virginia Democrats, 1879; served as governor of the state, 1882–86. Editor, *Norfolk Virginian* (1908–15) and *Virginian-Pilot* (1915–19).

CAMM, JOHN (*b. Hornsea, England, 1718; d. 1778*), Anglican clergyman. Appointed minister, Newport Parish, Va., 1745; professor of divinity, College of William and Mary, 1749. Leader of clergy in assailing Two Penny Acts, 1755 and 1758. President, William and Mary, 1771–77.

CAMMERHOFF, JOHN CHRISTOPHER FREDERICK (*b. Hillersleben, Germany, 1721; d. Pennsylvania, 1751*), Moravian missionary to Pennsylvania and New York settlers, and to the Iroquois, 1746–51.

CAMP, DAVID NELSON (*b. Durham, Conn., 1820; d. 1916*), educator. Professor and principal, Connecticut Normal School, 1849–66; associate of Henry Barnard; principal, New Britain (Conn.) Seminary.

CAMP, HIRAM (*b. Plymouth, Conn., 1811; d. New Haven, Conn., 1893*), clock manufacturer, philanthropist. President, New Haven Clock Co., 1853–92. A founder of Mount Hermon School and Northfield Seminary.

CAMP, JOHN LAFAYETTE (*b. near Birmingham, Ala., 1828; d. San Antonio, Texas, 1891*), lawyer, planter. Moved to Gilmer, Texas, 1849; served with distinction in Civil War as colonel, 14th Texas Cavalry. Active in local politics; helped prepare Texas constitution of 1876; served on state bench, 1878–84.

CAMP, JOHN LAFAYETTE (*b. Gilmer, Texas, 1855; d. San Antonio, Texas, 1918*), jurist. Son of the preceding. State district judge, 1897–1914; federal attorney, western Texas district, 1914–18. Instrumental in preserving the Alamo.

CAMP, WALTER CHAUNCEY (*b. New Britain, Conn., 1859; d. New York, N.Y., 1925*), promoter of American football. Graduated Yale, 1880; attended Yale Medical School. Associated 1883–1925 with New Haven Clock Co.; *post* 1888, became athletic director and head advisory football coach at Yale. Many of the rules of the game as now played were suggested by Camp; he developed its strategy, and raised its level of sportsmanship. He originated the All-American selections, 1889, and the "Daily Dozen" exercises for keeping physically fit.

CAMPANIUS, JOHN (*b. Stockholm, Sweden, 1601; d. Sweden, 1683*), Lutheran clergyman, missionary. Accompanied Governor Printz to Swedish colony on Delaware; chaplain to settlers at Fort Christina (now Wilmington, Del.), 1643–48. His efforts to convert the Delaware Indians to Christianity were reasonably successful; he studied their folkways and language and translated Luther's *Shorter Catechism* into Delaware (printed 1696). His grandson, Thomas Campanius "Homiensis," incorporated John's account of his voyage to America in his *Description of the Province of New Sweden*.

CAMPAU, JOSEPH (*b. Detroit, Mich., 1769; d. Detroit, 1863*), trader. Invested profits from Indian trading in purchase of real estate which growth of Detroit made increasingly valuable; was considered Michigan's wealthiest citizen.

CAMPBELL, ALEXANDER (*b. Co. Antrim, Ireland, 1788; d. Bethany, W. Va., 1866*), one of the founders of the Disciples of Christ. Emigrated to America, 1809. Succeeded his father as pastor of an independent church at Brush Run, Pa., 1813; affiliated with Baptists; lectured and wrote in the *Christian Baptist*, 1823 and after, with hope of promulgating his own opinions, but was forced into a separate denomination. Author of an English translation of the Bible (1827) and other works; founder of Bethany College, 1840.

CAMPBELL, ALLAN (*b. Albany, N.Y., 1815; d. New York, N.Y., 1894*), civil engineer. Helped construct railroads in Georgia, New York and the Republic of Chile; chief engineer, and later president of the Harlem Railroad. Active in New York civic work.

CAMPBELL, ANDREW (*b. near Trenton, N.J., 1821; d. 1890*), inventor, manufacturer. As foreman in shop of A. B. Taylor & Co., developed paper-feed mechanisms and automatic features for printing-presses, 1853–58. Invented and manufactured the Campbell Country Press, 1861–66; a two-revolution picture press, 1867; and others.

CAMPBELL, BARTLEY (*b. Pittsburgh, Pa., 1843; d. Middletown, N.Y., 1888*), playwright. Shares with

Augustin Daly and Bronson Howard the honor of establishing in America the profession of the playwright on a firm basis. Author of *The Virginian* (produced 1873); *My Partner* (his best, produced 1879); and *The White Slave* (produced 1882) which contains the immortal line "Rags are royal raiment when worn for virtue's sake."

CAMPBELL, CHARLES (*b. Petersburg, Va., 1807; d. 1876*), historian. Author of *An Introduction to the History of the Colony and Ancient Dominion of Virginia* (1847; new edition, 1860), a work which established him as a local historian; he was also editor of the *Bland Papers* (1840–43).

CAMPBELL, FRANCIS JOSEPH (*b. Winchester, Tenn., 1832; d. 1914*), educator of the blind. Sightless from the age of four, he became a teacher of music at Perkins Institution, Boston, and co-founder of Royal Academy of Music for the Blind, London.

CAMPBELL, GEORGE WASHINGTON (*b. Tongue, Scotland, 1769; d. Nashville, Tenn., 1848*), lawyer, diplomat. Brought to North Carolina as a child; graduated Princeton, 1794. Removed to Knoxville, Tenn. and practiced law. Congressman, Democratic-Republican, 1803–09; elected U.S. senator, 1811; entered cabinet as secretary of treasury, 1814, but soon resigned and returned to Senate. Minister to Russia, 1818–20, after which he retired to private life.

CAMPBELL, GEORGE WASHINGTON (*b. Cherry Valley, N.Y., 1817; d. 1898*), horticulturist. Celebrated as a grape-breeder; developer of the "Campbell Early."

CAMPBELL, HENRY FRASER (*b. Augusta, Ga., 1824; d. 1891*), physician. Graduated M.D., University of Georgia, 1842. Held various professorates at Medical College of Georgia, 1854–66, 1868–91; made original studies on nature of autonomic nervous system. A pioneer in preventive medicine.

CAMPBELL, JAMES (*b. Southwark, Pa., 1812; d. 1893*), lawyer, Pennsylvania jurist. As U.S. postmaster-general, 1853–57, tried earnestly to improve the efficiency of the department.

CAMPBELL, JAMES HEPBURN (*b. Williamsport, Pa., 1820; d. near Wayne, Pa., 1895*), lawyer. Congressman, Whig, from Pennsylvania, 1845–56; elected as Republican, 1858–62; chairman of special committee on Pacific Railroad; ardent protectionist.

CAMPBELL, JAMES VALENTINE (*b. Buffalo, N.Y., 1823; d. 1890*), jurist. Moved as a child to Detroit, Mich. Justice, Michigan supreme court, 1858–90; law professor, University of Michigan, 1859–85.

CAMPBELL, JOHN. [See LOUDOUN, JOHN CAMPBELL, FOURTH EARL OF, 1705–1782.]

CAMPBELL, JOHN (*b. Scotland, 1653; d. Boston, Mass., 1727/8*), journalist. Postmaster at Boston, 1702–18; published *Boston News-Letter*, 1704–22, the first established and continuously published American newspaper.

CAMPBELL, JOHN ARCHIBALD (*b. Washington, Ga., 1811; d. 1889*), jurist. Graduated Franklin College (University of Georgia), 1825; attended West Point; studied law, and was admitted to practice by special act of Georgia legislature, 1829. Removed first to Montgomery, then to Mobile, Ala. Rose rapidly in profession; served as delegate to Nashville Convention, 1850. Appointed justice of U.S. Supreme Court, 1853. Of great ability and integrity, he cared little for public opinion; he opposed monopolies and upheld strict construction of the Constitution; he was denounced in his own section for severity to Latin American filibusters and by abolitionists for his opinion in the Dred Scott case. Opposed to secession, he was suspected by Confederates for his part in Seward's scheme to relieve Fort Sumter; yet he resigned his judicial position, followed his state, and served as assistant secretary of war in Confederate government, 1862–65. On post-war return to practice in New Orleans, he appeared in many important actions, including the "Slaughterhouse Cases" and *New York and New Hampshire vs. Louisiana.*

CAMPBELL, JOHN WILSON (*b. Augusta Co., Va., 1782; d. Ohio, 1833*), jurist. Congressman, Democrat, from Ohio, 1817–27; U.S. district judge, 1829–33.

CAMPBELL, JOSIAH A. PATTERSON (*b. Waxhaw Settlement, S.C., 1830; d. 1917*), jurist. Practiced law in Mississippi, *post* 1847; served in Confederate Army, 1862–65. Justice of Mississippi supreme court, 1876–94.

CAMPBELL, LEWIS DAVIS (*b. Franklin, O., 1811; d. 1882*), editor, diplomat, lawyer. Congressman, Whig, from Ohio, 1848–58. Appointed minister to Mexico, 1866, he failed badly in an attempt to mediate in the Maximilian-Juarez conflict and was superseded.

CAMPBELL, MARIUS ROBINSON (*b. Garden Grove, Iowa, 1858; d. Pinellas Park, Fla., 1940*), geologist and physiographer. With U.S. Geological Survey, 1888–1932; made geologic studies of national coal resources. [*Supp. 2*]

CAMPBELL, PRINCE LUCIEN (*b. Newmarket, Mo., 1861; d. 1925*), president of University of Oregon, 1902–25.

CAMPBELL, ROBERT (*b. Aughlane, Ireland, 1804; d. St. Louis, Mo., 1879*), fur trapper, capitalist. Came to America, *c.* 1824; went out with Ashley's second fur expedition, 1825, thereafter personally engaging in northern region fur trade until 1835. Partner in Sublette & Campbell, 1832–42. Prospered as merchant and banker in St. Louis.

CAMPBELL, THOMAS (*b. Ireland, 1763; d. Bethany, W. Va., 1854*), clergyman. Came to America,

1807. With his son, Alexander Campbell, a founder of the Disciples of Christ.

CAMPBELL, THOMAS JOSEPH (*b. New York, N.Y., 1848; d. Monroe, N.Y., 1925*), Jesuit priest. Ordained 1880. President, St. John's College (Fordham), 1885–88 and 1896–1900. Editor, *America*, 1910–14; author of *The Jesuits: 1534–1921* (1921), and many other works.

CAMPBELL, LORD WILLIAM (*d. Southampton, England, 1778*), colonial governor of South Carolina. Arrived at Charleston, June 1775. After ineffectual efforts to rally Tories and Indians in support of royal cause, fled to H.M.S. *Tamar;* served as volunteer in British attack on Charleston, 1776.

CAMPBELL, WILLIAM (*b. Augusta Co., Va., 1745; d. Rocky Mills, Va., 1781*), Revolutionary soldier. Settled near Abingdon, Va.; brother-in-law of Patrick Henry. Active in Indian border wars; colonel of Virginia militia, and distinguished at battles of King's Mountain, 1780, and Guilford, 1781.

CAMPBELL, WILLIAM (*b. Gateshead-on-Tyne, England, 1876; d. New York, N.Y., 1936*), metallurgist. Teacher of geology and metallurgy, Columbia University, 1903–36. [*Supp. 2*]

CAMPBELL, WILLIAM BOWEN (*b. Sumner Co., Tenn., 1807; d. 1867*), lawyer, politician. Congressman, Whig, from Tennessee, 1837–43; Unionist, 1865–67. Elected governor of Tennessee, 1851, after distinguished service in Mexican War. Strong anti-secessionist.

CAMPBELL, WILLIAM HENRY (*b. Baltimore, Md., 1808; d. New Brunswick, N.J., 1890*), Reformed Church clergyman. President, Rutgers College, 1863–82.

CAMPBELL, WILLIAM W. (*b. Cherry Valley, N.Y., 1806; d. 1881*), jurist, historian. Congressman, "Know-Nothing" from New York, 1845–47; justice of superior court, New York City, 1849–55; justice of state supreme court, 1857–65. Author of *Annals of Tryon County* (1831).

CAMPBELL, WILLIAM WALLACE (*b. Hancock Co., O., 1862; d. San Francisco, Calif., 1938*), astronomer. Graduated University of Michigan, 1886. From 1890 to 1923 he was at Lick Observatory, Mount Hamilton, Calif., becoming director in 1901. His work with the Mills spectrograph, which he designed, helped lay the foundations for the new science of astrophysics. His interest in spectrographic measurement of stellar radial velocities to determine the sun's motion through the stars led to the publication (1928) of a definitive catalogue by Campbell and Joseph H. Moore. He was president of the University of California, 1923–30. [*Supp. 2*]

CANAGA, ALFRED BRUCE (*b. Scio, O., 1850; d. Boston, Mass., 1906*), naval engineer. Chief designer of propulsion and other machinery for U.S. Navy under Admiral George W. Melville.

CANBY, EDWARD RICHARD SPRIGG (*b. Kentucky, 1817; d. California, 1873*), Union soldier. Graduated West Point, 1839; served in Florida War and was twice brevetted for gallantry in Mexican War. Commanded Department of New Mexico during Civil War, frustrating Confederate plan to seize California, 1861–62; served thereafter in Washington, New York, and as commander of Division of West Mississippi. Captured Mobile, Ala., April 1865; in May received surrender of last Confederate armies in field. Appointed brigadier-general, regular army, 1866, he served with great ability in the South and was assigned to command on Pacific coast, 1870. He was killed on a peace mission to the Modoc tribe in northern California.

CANDEE, LEVERETT (*b. Oxford, Conn., 1795; d. 1863*), pioneer rubber manufacturer under Goodyear patent, 1842; made overshoes at Hamden, Conn.

CANDLER, ALLEN DANIEL (*b. Lumpkin Co., Ga., 1834; d. 1910*), educator, businessman. After Confederate war service, taught in Georgia schools. Moved to Gainesville, Ga., 1870, and entered contracting business; president of Gainesville, Jefferson & Southern Railroad, 1879–92. Congressman, Democrat, 1882–90; governor of Georgia, 1898–1902.

CANDLER, ASA GRIGGS (*b. near Villa Rica, Ga., 1851; d. 1929*), manufacturer, philanthropist. Trained as a pharmacist; bought Coca-Cola formula, 1887. Developed the enterprise and sold it, 1919, for $25 million; prospered also in Atlanta, Ga., real estate. Generous in gifts for public improvements in that city, he was also a principal benefactor of Emory University.

CANFIELD, JAMES HULME (*b. Delaware, O., 1847; d. New York, N.Y., 1909*), educator. Graduated Williams, 1868; practiced law at St. Joseph, Mich., 1872–77. Professor, University of Kansas, 1877–91; chancellor, University of Nebraska, 1891–95; president, Ohio State University, 1895–99; librarian, Columbia University, 1899–1909. An able and tactful administrator.

CANFIELD, RICHARD A. (*b. New Bedford, Mass., 1855; d. 1914*), gambler, art collector. Proprietor of gambling houses in Providence and Newport, R.I., New York City, and elsewhere; collector of furniture, ceramics, and the work of J. A. M. Whistler.

CANNON, CHARLES JAMES (*b. New York, N.Y., 1800; d. 1860*), author of minor periodical verse and fiction, and of several plays; *The Oath of Office* (produced 1850, published 1854) is his best drama.

CANNON, GEORGE QUAYLE (*b. Liverpool, England, 1827; d. 1901*), Mormon leader. Migrated to Nauvoo, Ill., 1842; to Salt Lake valley, 1847. Missionary in California and in Hawaii; private secretary to

Brigham Young. Utah delegate to Congress, 1872–82. Chosen an Apostle in Church of Latter-day Saints, 1859.

CANNON, HARRIET STARR (*b. Charleston, S.C., 1823; d. Peekskill, N.Y., 1896*), a foundress and first Mother Superior of the Episcopal Sisterhood of St. Mary, 1865–96.

CANNON, JAMES GRAHAM (*b. Delhi, N.Y., 1858; d. 1916*), banker. Associated *c.* 1876–1914 with Fourth National Bank, New York City; president, 1910–14. Authority on credit analysis and clearing-house practice.

CANNON, JOSEPH GURNEY (*b. New Garden, N.C., 1836; d. 1926*), politician. Raised in Indiana, "Uncle Joe" Cannon studied law and began practice at Shelbyville, Ill., 1858; later he removed to Danville, his home for the rest of his life. Congressman, Republican, from Illinois, 1873–91; 1893–1913; 1915–23. Coarse, unprogressive, yet by reason of his long membership in the House of Representatives rising to important committee posts, he served as speaker, 1903–11; his arbitrary, partisan control of procedure in that post became known as "Cannonism."

CANNON, NEWTON (*b. Guilford Co., N.C., 1781; d. 1841*), planter, politician. Removed with parents to frontier settlement of Cumberland, Tenn., 1790. Congressman from Tennessee, 1814–23 (save for one term); first Whig governor of Tennessee, 1835–39.

CANNON, WILLIAM (*b. near Bridgeville, Del., 1809; d. 1865*), vigorous supporter of the federal government as Union Party governor of Delaware, 1863–65.

CANONCHET (*d. Stonington, Conn., 1676*), chief sachem of the Narragansetts, defeated in the "Great Swamp Fight" near present South Kingston, R.I., 1675.

CANONGE, LOUIS PLACIDE (*b. New Orleans, La., 1822; d. 1893*), journalist. Contributor to *L'Abeille* and other French journals; author of a number of plays produced in French at New Orleans, 1840–56; excelled as a writer of *feuilletons*.

CANONICUS (*b. c. 1565; d. 1647*), Narragansett chief. Granted Rhode Island to Roger Williams.

CAPEN, ELMER HEWITT (*b. Stoughton, Mass., 1838; d. 1905*), Universalist clergyman. Ordained 1865, he held pastorates in Gloucester, Mass., St. Paul, Minn., and Providence, R.I. President, Tufts College, *post* 1875.

CAPEN, NAHUM (*b. Canton, Mass., 1804; d. 1886*), miscellaneous writer. As postmaster of Boston, Mass., 1857–61, he is said to have introduced street letter-boxes.

CAPEN, SAMUEL BILLINGS (*b. Boston, Mass., 1842; d. Shanghai, China, 1914*), merchant. Active in civic affairs, and in Congregational church work;

president, American Board of Commissioners for Foreign Missions, 1899–1914; trustee of Wellesley College.

CAPERS, ELLISON (*b. Charleston, S.C., 1837; d. Columbia, S.C., 1908*), Confederate soldier, Episcopal clergyman. Entered ministry after rising to rank of brigadier-general in Civil War; held pastorates in Alabama and South Carolina; consecrated assistant bishop of South Carolina, 1893.

CAPERS, WILLIAM (*b. St. Thomas' Parish, S.C., 1790; d. near Anderson Court House, S.C., 1855*), Methodist clergyman. Bishop, Methodist Church South, 1846–55. Father of Ellison Capers. Ordained elder in South Carolina Conference, 1812, he became the most popular Methodist preacher in the South; he worked extensively among Creek Indians and plantation Negroes.

CAPPS, WASHINGTON LEE (*b. Portsmouth, Va., 1864; d. Washington, D.C., 1935*), naval officer. Chief of U.S. Navy Bureau of Construction, 1903–10; devised skeleton mast and the "all big gun" ship.
[*Supp.* 1]

CAPRON, HORACE (*b. Attleboro, Mass., 1804; d. Washington, D.C., 1885*), agriculturist. Began large-scale, scientific farming while in charge of a cotton factory in Laurel, Md. Removed to Illinois, 1854, and continued farming until appointment as U.S. commissioner of agriculture, 1867. Revolutionized Japanese farming methods while adviser in development of Hokkaido island, 1871–75.

CAPTAIN JACK (*b. c. 1837; d. Fort Klamath, Oreg., 1873*). Indian name, Kientpoos; led hostiles in Modoc War, 1872–73. Taken after stubborn defense of the lava beds south of Tule Lake, Calif., Jack was hanged for murder of peace commissioners Gen. E. R. S. Canby and Rev. Eleazer Thomas.

CARAWAY, THADDEUS HORATIUS (*b. Spring Hill, Mo., 1871; d. Little Rock, Ark., 1931*), U.S. senator from Arkansas, 1920–31; liberal Democrat and reformer. [*Supp.* 1]

CARBUTT, JOHN (*b. Sheffield, England, 1832; d. Philadelphia, Pa., 1905*), photographic innovator. Emigrated to America, 1853, and settled in Chicago. Successfully used gelatine in preparation of dry plates as early as 1868, producing a plate which did not require development for months after the image was taken; marketed the first American gelatine dry plates, 1879; made notable contributions to color photography.

CÁRDENAS, GARCÍA LÓPEZ de (*fl. 1540*), explorer. Discovered the Grand Canyon of the Colorado while a member of the Coronado expedition, 1540–42.

CARDOZO, BENJAMIN NATHAN (*b. New York, N.Y., 1870; d. Port Chester, N.Y., 1938*), lawyer, jurist, justice of the U.S. Supreme Court. Graduated from Columbia University, B.A., 1889; M.A., 1890, and was admitted to the New York bar in 1891. For the next 22 years he practiced law, principally as counsel for other lawyers, at times as referee in complex commercial cases. In 1913 he was elected to the supreme court of New York, but within six weeks he received a temporary appointment to the court of appeals. In 1917 he was elected to the latter court for a 14-year term; in 1926 he was chosen chief judge. As he had been a lawyers' lawyer, so Cardozo became a judges' judge. His legal mastery, conveyed with great felicity, gave unusual distinction to the New York Reports. His philosophic temper of mind was reflected not only in his legal opinions but also in four volumes of essays written during this period: *The Nature of the Judicial Process* (1921), *The Growth of the Law* (1924), *The Paradoxes of Legal Science* (1928), and *Law and Literature* (1931).

In 1932 President Hoover, upon the resignation of Justice Oliver Wendell Holmes, appointed Cardozo to the U.S. Supreme Court. With great rapidity Cardozo made the adjustment from preoccupation with the comparatively restricted problems of private litigation to the exacting demands of legal statesmanship. He regarded his role as that of "historian and prophet all in one," and like his master Holmes he made of the judicial process a blend of continuity and creativeness, a compound of wisdom from the past and insight into the future. His few short years on the Supreme Bench coincided with one of the most tempestuous periods in the Court's history—the years of its invalidation of much of the New Deal legislation and the consequent proposal of President Roosevelt for reconstruction of the Court. Cardozo faced courageously the application of the Constitution to a rapidly changing world. With Justices Stone and Brandeis he joined in a series of dissents which charted the course for a later broader interpretation of federal powers. Shy and sensitive, immensely learned yet natively humble, Cardozo transcended the heated controversies of his day to take place as one of the dozen or so truly great judges in the Court's history. [*Supp. 2*]

CARDOZO, JACOB NEWTON (*b. Savannah, Ga., 1786; d. Savannah, 1873*), economist. Edited *Southern Patriot*, Charleston, S.C., 1817–45; drew up first petition from the South on behalf of free-trade, *c.* 1827. Author of *Notes on Political Economy* (1826), advancing doctrine later developed by Henry C. Carey and the American National School.

CAREY, HENRY CHARLES (*b. Philadelphia, Pa., 1793; d. 1879*), economist. Son of Mathew Carey. His numerous works, influential here and abroad, took issue with the English classical school of economists and interpreted in an optimistic spirit the rapid expansion of American economic life during his time. A stout believer in *laissez-faire*, about 1844 he was "converted" to protectionism. He and his followers constitute what has been called the American National School of political economy. The evolution of his thought may be traced in: *Essay on the Rate of Wages* (1835); *Principles of Political Economy* (1837, 1838, 1840); *Past, Present and Future* (1848); *Harmony of Interests* (1851); *The Principles of Social Science* (1858, 1859) and *The Unity of Law* (1872).

CAREY, JOSEPH MAULL (*b. Milton, Del., 1845; d. 1924*), lawyer. Served as justice of supreme court of Wyoming, 1872–76, and thrice as territorial delegate to Congress; introduced bill for Wyoming admission as state, 1890. First U.S. senator from Wyoming, Republican, 1890–96; Democratic governor, 1911–15.

CAREY, MATHEW (*b. Dublin, Ireland, 1760; d. Philadelphia, Pa., 1839*), publisher, economist. Father of Henry C. Carey who developed his economic ideas. Came to America, 1784, after involvement in Irish revolutionary activity; set up as a publisher-bookseller in Philadelphia with aid from Lafayette. Published the *Pennsylvania Herald* (starting January 1785); also the eclectic periodical *The American Museum*, 1787–92, in which much valuable material was reprinted. His book-publishing activities prospered and his firm became a leader in the period 1795–1835. *Post* 1815 he became an active exponent of protectionism in support of which he wrote many tracts and essays. Among his books are *The Olive Branch* (1814), and *Vindiciae Hibernicae* (1819) which defended the Irish character.

CARLETON, HENRY (*b. Virginia, c. 1785; d. 1863*), Louisiana jurist. Translator (with Louis M. Lislet) of *Las Siete Partidas* (1820), the principal Spanish law code long enforced in Louisiana.

CARLETON, HENRY GUY (*b. Fort Union, N. Mex., 1856; d. Atlantic City, N.J., 1910*), playwright. Author of *The Gilded Fool* (1892), *Butterflies* (1894), and other plays.

CARLETON, WILL (*b. near Hudson, Mich., 1845; d. Brooklyn, N.Y., 1912*), poet. Author of many ballads of simple life, notably "Betsy and I Are Out" (1871), "Over the Hill to the Poor House" and others which appeared in his book *Farm Ballads* (1873). He was author also of *Farm Legends* (1875), *Farm Festivals* (1881) and *City Ballads* (1885), and was one of the first poets to give public readings from his own works.

CARLILE, JOHN SNYDER (*b. Winchester, Va., 1817; d. Clarksburg, W. Va., 1878*), lawyer. Drafted Unionist address to people of western Virginia, 1861; mismanaged bill erecting new state of West Virginia.

CARLISLE, JAMES MANDEVILLE (*b. Alexandria, Va., 1814; d. Washington, D.C., 1877*), lawyer. Specialist in international cases; served as counsel for Spain, Great Britain, Colombia and Costa Rica.

CARLISLE, JOHN GRIFFIN (*b. Campbell, now Kenton, Co., Ky., 1835; d. 1910*), lawyer, statesman.

Admitted to the bar, 1858, began practice in Covington, Ky.; was neutral during Civil War. Served in state legislature, and was elected lieutenant-governor, 1871. Congressman, Democrat, 1877–90 (outstanding speaker of the House, 1883–90), he resigned to accept appointment as U.S. senator. Active in tariff reform movement and rebuilding of U.S. merchant marine, he left Senate to be secretary of treasury, 1893–96; his support of "sound money" principles then, and in campaign of 1896, brought him virtual banishment from Kentucky. He removed to New York City where he resumed legal practice.

CARLL, JOHN FRANKLIN (*b. Bushwick, L.I., N.Y., 1828; d. Waldron, Ark., 1904*), civil engineer, geologist. His work with Pennsylvania Geological Survey, 1874–85, was basic in establishing geology of petroleum along scientific lines.

CARMACK, EDWARD WARD (*b. Sumner Co., Tenn., 1858; d. Nashville, Tenn., 1908*), editor, prohibitionist. As editor of *Columbia Herald, Nashville American* and *Memphis Commercial Appeal,* and also as congressman and U.S. senator from Tennessee, an influential and militant crusader for good government and prohibition of the liquor traffic.

CARMICHAEL, WILLIAM (*b. Queen Annes Co., Md.; d. Madrid, Spain, 1795*), diplomat. Secretary to Franklin, Silas Deane and Arthur Lee during their commission to enlist France in aid of the revolting colonies; individually responsible for Lafayette's coming to America. Secretary to John Jay during Spanish mission, 1780–82, thereafter acting as *chargé d'affaires* at Madrid, 1782–92, and as commissioner with William Short to secure a treaty with Spain, 1792–94. An outstanding public servant.

CARNAHAN, JAMES (*b. Cumberland Co., Pa., 1775; d. 1859*), Presbyterian clergyman. President of Princeton University, 1823–54.

CARNEGIE, ANDREW (*b. Dunfermline, Scotland, 1835; d. Shadowbrook, Mass., 1919*), manufacturer, self-styled "distributor of wealth for the improvement of mankind." Son of a handloom weaver active in Chartist and anti-Corn Law agitation; grandson of Thomas Morrison, a well-informed and irrepressible Scottish agitator for social and political reform. Early inspired by an uncle with a romantic love of Scottish history and poetry, Carnegie came with his family to Allegheny, Pa., in 1848 where he went to work as bobbin boy in a cotton factory. His spare time was spent in self-education by reading; at the age of sixteen he was contributing letters to the *New York Tribune.* Employed as messenger in a Pittsburgh telegraph office, he taught himself to distinguish the letters by sound and became an operator; Thomas A. Scott of the Pennsylvania Railroad employed him as personal telegrapher and private secretary. While with the railroad, 1853–65, he introduced use of Pullman sleeping cars, acquiring one-eighth interest in the

Woodruff Co., original holder of the Pullman patents; he was also active in the transportation of troops during the Civil War and organized the military telegraph department.

Resigning from the railroad in 1865, he turned all his energies to the iron industry which had received a great impetus during the war; his Keystone Bridge Co. succeeded largely through his own gifts as a salesman. By 1873, after success in oil operations and in the sale of railroad securities abroad, he committed all his profits to what was then a new American industry—steel. His declared policy of "putting all his eggs in one basket, and then watching the basket," was brilliantly successful. By 1889, American steel production had passed Great Britain's and stood first in the world. Carnegie believed his success was due to organization. He once suggested as his epitaph: "Here lies the man who was able to surround himself with men far cleverer than himself," for his associates included Capt. "Bill" Jones, Henry Clay Frick, and Charles M. Schwab. His company, until shortly before its absorption in U.S. Steel (1901), was never a corporation; it was a limited partnership, every share being held by working associates. Carnegie always held a majority interest, and the remainder was distributed on the basis of each man's record, thus driving his associates to put forth their best efforts. He was a successful innovator, insisting upon up-to-date machinery, for which he made immense outlays during times of depression, when costs were low; his competitors meanwhile would face returning prosperity with outdated equipment, thus giving him a competitive advantage.

Throughout his later life Carnegie maintained many friendships in the literary and political world; with Matthew Arnold, Herbert Spencer—"the man to whom I owe most," William E. Gladstone, James Bryce, James G. Blaine, Theodore Roosevelt, Mark Twain and Elihu Root. His volume *Triumphant Democracy* (1886) contained a glowing account of American progress. From 1883 to 1919 his closest friend was the scholar John Morley.

In possession of a vast fortune through his daring and efficient operations, he set forth in an article entitled "Wealth" (*North American Review,* 1889) his concept of stewardship, or the responsibility of rich men to regard surplus wealth as held in trust for the public benefit. Since the accumulator of great wealth was *prima facie* an exceptional person, it was his duty to employ the talents which had made the fortune in its distribution for the "improvement of mankind." By 1900 he was ready to put his theory into practice, and in 1901 sold the Carnegie Co. to the newly formed U.S. Steel Corporation for $250 million. Thereafter, through the Carnegie Corporation of New York and other agencies he disposed of some $350 million in many public benefactions which included support of scientific research, erection of public library buildings, the advancement of teaching, the furthering of international peace, and the reward of heroic acts.

CARNEY, THOMAS (*b. Delaware Co., O., 1824; d. 1888*), businessman. Prospered in wholesale trade in Cincinnati, O.; removed to Leavenworth, Kans., 1858 or 1859. Republican governor of Kansas, 1862–64.

CARNOCHAN, JOHN MURRAY (*b. Savannah, Ga., 1817; d. 1887*), surgeon. Graduated College of Physicians and Surgeons, New York, 1836; did graduate work in Paris and London. A brilliant pioneer in many fields; author of *Contributions to Operative Surgery* (first series 1858, second series 1877–78).

CARONDELET, FRANCISCO LUIS HECTOR, Baron de (*b. Noyelles, Flanders, c. 1748; d. Quito, Ecuador, 1807*), Spanish governor of Louisiana and West Florida, 1791–97. Devoted to public works, he built a canal to link New Orleans with the Gulf via Lake Pontchartrain, reformed the police, instituted a street-lighting system. His attempts to extend Spanish rule over all the Mississippi valley, to protect Louisiana commerce and to hold off encroaching American frontiersmen were unfortunate and embarrassed his home government; his domestic policy alienated the Creoles.

CAROTHERS, WALLACE HUME (*b. Burlington, Iowa, 1896; d. Philadelphia, Pa., 1937*), chemist, inventor of nylon. Graduated from Tarkio (Mo.) College, B.S., 1920, and the University of Illinois, M.S., 1921; Ph.D., 1924. After teaching at Illinois and Harvard he joined E. I. du Pont de Nemours Co. in 1928 to direct a new fundamental research program in organic chemistry. He initiated investigations of vinylacetylene, which led to the commercial development of the synthetic rubber, "neoprene." From 1929 to 1937 Carothers and his associates made comprehensive studies of the synthesis of polymers of high molecular weight. These researches provided a general theory of polymerization processes, culminating in 1939 in the commercial production of nylon fiber, and laying the basis for other synthetic fibers. [*Supp. 2*]

CARPENTER, CYRUS CLAY (*b. Harford, Pa., 1829; d. 1898*), Republican governor of Iowa, 1871–75. The "Granger Law" regulating railroads in Iowa was passed during his administration.

CARPENTER, EDMUND JANES (*b. North Attleboro, Mass., 1845; d. Milton, Mass., 1924*), journalist. On staff of Boston *Globe, Advertiser* and *Transcript;* author of *A Woman of Shawmut* (1891).

CARPENTER, FRANCIS BICKNELL (*b. Homer, N.Y., 1830; d. New York, N.Y., 1900*), portrait painter. The painting of Lincoln reading the Emancipation Proclamation to his cabinet which hangs in the Capitol is his; he was author of *Six Months at the White House* (1866), a first-hand study of the president.

CARPENTER, FRANK GEORGE (*b. Mansfield, O., 1855; d. Nanking, China, 1924*), author of syndicated letters, books, and several series of geographical *Readers,* the fruit of 36 years of travel.

CARPENTER, FRANKLIN REUBEN (*b. Parkersburg, W. Va., 1848; d. Denver, Colo., 1910*), mining engineer. Expert in processes for smelting and treating metals.

CARPENTER, GEORGE RICE (*b. Eskimo River, Labrador, 1863; d. 1909*), educator, author. Professor of rhetoric, Columbia University, 1893–1909; author of a number of literary textbooks and lives of Whittier and Whitman.

CARPENTER, MATTHEW HALE (*b. Moretown, Vt., 1824; d. 1881*), lawyer. Removed to Wisconsin, 1848; U.S. senator, Republican, from Wisconsin, 1869–75 and 1879–81. Counsel for W. W. Belknap at impeachment trial and for Samuel J. Tilden before electoral commission.

CARPENTER, STEPHEN CULLEN (*b. Ireland; d. Washington, D.C., c. 1820*), journalist. Came to America, *c.* 1802, and established Federalist *Courier* at Charleston, S.C., 1803. Moved to New York and edited anti-French *Peoples' Friend,* 1806–07; edited *Mirror of Taste and Dramatic Censor* at Philadelphia, 1810–11. Author of *Memoirs of Jefferson* (1809).

CARPENTER, STEPHEN HASKINS (*b. Little Falls, N.Y., 1831; d. Geneva, N.Y., 1878*), educator. Professor of English, University of Wisconsin, 1868–78; author of *Introduction to the Study of the Anglo-Saxon Language* (1875).

CARR, BENJAMIN (*b. England, 1769; d. Philadelphia, Pa., 1831*), musician. Came to Philadelphia, 1793; established first music store there and became famous as singer, organist and promoter of music. His works include a "Federal Overture" (1796), an opera *The Archers* (produced in New York, 1796), a volume of *Masses, Vespers and Litanies* (1805), and others.

CARR, DABNEY (*b. Virginia, 1773; d. Richmond, Va., 1837*), jurist. Justice of Virginia supreme court of appeals, 1824–37.

CARR, DABNEY SMITH (*b. Albemarle Co., Va., 1802; d. Charlottesville, Va., 1854*), diplomat, journalist. Founded pro-Jackson *Baltimore Republican and Commercial Advertiser,* 1827. Naval officer of Baltimore, Md. port, 1829–43; minister to Turkey, 1843–50.

CARR, ELIAS (*b. near Tarboro, N.C., 1839; d. near Tarboro, 1900*), agriculturist. President, state Farmers' Alliance, 1891; Democratic governor of North Carolina, 1893–97. An able administrator and proponent of public education.

CARR, EUGENE ASA (*b. Concord, N.Y., 1830; d. Washington, D.C., 1910*), Union soldier. Graduated West Point, 1850. Won Medal of Honor for gallantry as division commander, Pea Ridge, 1862. Highly reputed as Indian fighter on the frontier, 1868–91.

CARR, JOSEPH BRADFORD (*b. Albany, N.Y., 1828; d. Troy, N.Y., 1895*), Union brigadier-general, Republican politician, businessman.

CARR, MATTHEW. [See CARR, THOMAS MATTHEW, 1750–1820.]

CARR, THOMAS MATTHEW (*b. probably Galway, Ireland, 1750; d. Philadelphia, Pa., 1820*), Augustinian friar. Came to America, 1796; founded the first establishment of his order in the United States, St. Augustine's Church, Philadelphia, 1796.

CARRÈRE, JOHN MERVEN (*b. Rio de Janeiro, Brazil, 1858; d. New York, N.Y., 1911*), architect. Graduated École des Beaux Arts, Paris, 1882; entered office of McKim, Mead and White; formed partnership with Thomas Hastings. Earliest commissions of firm executed in modified Spanish Renaissance style, mainly at St. Augustine, Fla., 1887–90. Carrère and Hastings designed many public and commercial buildings as well as elaborate country houses in French Renaissance style; their chief works were the U.S. Senate and House Office Buildings, Washington, D.C. (1905 and 1906), the New Theater, New York City (1906–09), and the New York Public Library, completed in 1911.

CARRICK, SAMUEL (*b. York Co., Pa., 1760; d. Knoxville, Tenn., 1809*), Presbyterian clergyman. A missionary on the Tennessee frontier, he organized the first Presbyterian church in Knoxville, c. 1792; in 1794 he became president of Blount College (later the University of Tennessee).

CARRINGTON, HENRY BEEBEE (*b. Wallingford, Conn., 1824; d. 1912*), lawyer, soldier. Graduated Yale, 1845; entered practice of law, Columbus, O., 1848; was locally prominent in organization of Republican party. As adjutant-general of Ohio militia, he put nine regiments in field, 1861, and helped save West Virginia for the Union. Active throughout Civil War in raising and training troops, he continued in army as colonel, 18th Infantry; in service against Indians, 1865–69, he built Fort Phil Kearny, served in the Red Cloud campaign, and protected the builders of the Union Pacific Railroad against Indian raids. He was author of *Battles of the American Revolution* (1876) and revised his wife's book *Ab-sa-ra-ka, Home of the Crows* (1868, and subsequent editions).

CARRINGTON, PAUL (*b. Cumberland Co., Va., 1733; d. "Mulberry Hill," Charlotte Co., Va., 1818*), jurist. Active in the Revolution, he served as chief justice of the Virginia general court, 1780–89, and as justice of the court of appeals, 1789–1807.

CARROLL, CHARLES (*b. Annapolis, Md., 1737; d. Baltimore, Md., 1832*), Revolutionary leader, signer of the Declaration of Independence. Son of Charles Carroll and Elizabeth Brooke; educated locally by the Society of Jesus and in their colleges at St. Omer, Flanders, Rheims and Paris. Returned to Maryland, 1765, after further study of law in London; began development of Carrollton Manor, Frederick Co., and lived life of landed proprietor. Entered political life as opponent of Daniel Dulany, 1773; the controversy in the *Maryland Gazette* established Carroll as a popular leader. He served on Committees of Correspondence and Safety and accompanied Benjamin Franklin and Samuel Chase on their ill-fated journey to Canada, 1776, seeking union between Canada and the revolting colonies. Member of Continental Congress, 1776–78; U.S. senator, Federalist, from Maryland, 1789–92. Active in trade and land development, he was an original director of the Baltimore & Ohio Railroad.

CARROLL, DANIEL (*b. Upper Marlboro, Md., 1730; d. Rock Creek, Md., 1796*), commissioner of the District of Columbia, 1791–95. Cousin of Charles Carroll; brother of John Carroll; U.S. senator, Federalist, from Maryland, in the first Congress.

CARROLL, HOWARD (*b. Albany, N.Y., 1854; d. New York, N.Y., 1916*), journalist, businessman. Inspector-general, New York State troops, 1898.

CARROLL, JAMES (*b. Woolwich, England, 1854; d. 1907*), investigator of yellow fever. Emigrated to Canada, 1869. Enlisted in U.S. Army, 1874; served nine years in infantry and as hospital steward, 1883–98. Studied medicine at University of the City of New York, 1886–87, and at University of Maryland, 1889–91; received M.D. degree from Maryland and also studied bacteriology and pathology at Johns Hopkins. Made assistant to Walter Reed at Army Medical Museum, 1895; appointed acting assistant surgeon, 1898, and to the Yellow Fever Commission, 1900. Believing with Reed that Dr. Carlos Finlay's theory of yellow fever transmission was most promising, Carroll underwent experiment of applying an infected mosquito to his arm; the resulting attack of fever proved the theory and caused Carroll a permanent heart lesion. Carroll also demonstrated that the virus of yellow fever was ultra-microscopic. In 1902, he succeeded Reed as Professor of Bacteriology and Pathology at Columbian University, Washington, D.C., and at the Army Medical School.

CARROLL, JOHN (*b. Upper Marlboro, Md., 1735; d. Baltimore, Md., 1815*), first Roman Catholic bishop in the United States, first archbishop of Baltimore. Brother of Daniel Carroll, cousin of Charles Carroll. Educated at St. Omer's College in French Flanders; entered Society of Jesus, 1753, and studied at Watten, Bruges and Liège; ordained at Liège, 1767 or 1769. On suppression of the Society, 1773, went to England and then returned home; lived privately in mother's house at Rock Creek, Md., serving spiritual needs of neighboring Catholic families. Accompanied Charles Carroll, Franklin and Chase on fruitless 1776 mission to Canada. Joined in 1784 clergy petition to Rome to provide frame of government for Church in America; in 1784–85 was named Superior of American missions by Pope Pius VI, and in 1790 was consecrated first bishop of American hierarchy. Became archbishop, 1808. Outstanding as administrator under difficult circumstances. Founder of Georgetown University, 1789, he established St. Mary's diocesan seminary, Baltimore, and Mt. St. Mary's College, Emmitsburg, Md., and was associated with organization of Sisters of Charity by Mother Elizabeth Seton.

CARROLL, JOHN LEE (*b. "Homewood" near Baltimore, Md., 1830; d. Washington, D.C., 1911*), lawyer. Great-grandson of Charles Carroll; Democratic governor of Maryland, 1875–79.

CARROLL, SAMUEL SPRIGG (*b. Washington, D.C., 1832; d. Montgomery Co., Md., 1893*), Union soldier. Graduated West Point, 1856. Served throughout Civil War as brigade and division commander; three times wounded, retired as major-general, 1869.

CARROLL, WILLIAM (*b. near Pittsburgh, Pa., 1788; d. 1844*), soldier, politician. Removed to Nashville, Tenn., c. 1810; served in Creek War; succeeded Andrew Jackson as major-general, Tennessee militia, and supported him in battle of New Orleans. Democratic governor of Tennessee, 1821–27 and 1829–35.

CARRUTH, FRED HAYDEN (*b. Wabasha Co., Minn., 1862; d. 1932*), humorist, author. Editor, *Woman's Home Companion*, 1905–17. [*Supp.* 1]

CARRYL, GUY WETMORE (*b. New York, N.Y., 1873; d. New York, 1904*), author. Resided in Paris, 1896–1902; wrote mildly cynical verse, and among other prose a collection of short stories *Zut and Other Parisians* (1903).

CARSON, CHRISTOPHER (*b. Madison Co. Ky., 1809; d. Fort Lyon, Colo., 1868*), "Kit" Carson, trapper, guide, Indian agent, soldier. Removed with family to Boone's Lick district of Missouri, 1811. Ran away from apprenticeship to a saddler, 1826, and joined a Santa Fe expedition as "cavvy boy." Engaged in trapping party out of Taos, August 1829, he crossed Mohave Desert to California, and returned to Taos, 1831; from this he emerged an experienced trapper and Indian fighter. In the fall of 1831, he joined Thomas Fitzpatrick in a trapping venture to the north; thereafter until 1841 he trapped in the northern regions (present-day Utah, Montana, Idaho, Wyoming). Returning from a trip to St. Louis, Mo., early in 1842, he met John Charles Frémont and served as guide on Frémont's first expedition, June–October 1842; he shared honors as guide with Thomas Fitzpatrick on Frémont's second expedition, 1843–44. Present on the third expedition, he shared in the conquest of California, 1846–47, and accompanied Edward Fitzgerald Beale eastward in March, bearing dispatches to Washington.

Settling down in Taos after refusal of the Senate to confirm a commission granted him in the regular army, Carson served as agent for the Utes, 1853–61. During this time he dictated the narrative of his life

and adventures which appeared in 1858, edited by DeWitt C. Peters. He resigned as agent at outbreak of the Civil War and organized and led the 1st New Mexican Volunteer Infantry; he took part in the battle of Valverde, 1862, and in successful campaigns against the Mescalero Apaches and the Navajos, the Kiowas and the Comanches. He received a brevet of brigadier-general, March 1865. Commanding at Fort Garland, Colo., 1866–67, his health began to fail; after a fruitless journey East in hope of medical relief, he returned to his new home in Boggsville, Colo., in April 1868. He died about six weeks later.

Plain-spoken, modest and unlettered, Carson's integrity was remarked on by all with whom he had contact.

CARSON, HAMPTON LAWRENCE (*b. Philadelphia, Pa., 1852; d. 1929*), lawyer, historian. Authority on constitutional law; book collector and benefactor of Philadelphia libraries. [*Supp.* 1]

CARSON, JOHN RENSHAW (*b. Pittsburgh, Pa., 1886; d. New Hope, Pa., 1940*), electrical engineer. Graduated Princeton University, B.S., 1907; E.E., 1909; M.S., 1912. In 1914 he joined the American Telephone and Telegraph Co. Carson's mathematical analysis of the vacuum thermionic amplifier (triode) led to his greatest invention—the single-sideband carrier-suppressed method of high-frequency transmission. Another major contribution was in using operational calculus to advance the theory of transient oscillations in transmission lines and networks. From 1934 he was with the Bell Telephone Laboratories as transmission theory engineer and research mathematician. About 50 scientific papers and 25 U.S. patents evidence Carson's profundity and creativeness.

[*Supp.* 2]

CARSON, JOSEPH (*b. Philadelphia, Pa., 1808; d. 1876*), physician. Professor of materia medica and pharmacy, University of Pennsylvania, 1850–76; author of *Illustrations of Medical Botany* (1847), *History of the Medical Department of the University of Pennsylvania* (1869) and other works.

CARTER, CAROLINE LOUISE DUDLEY (*b. Lexington, Ky.?, 1862; d. Santa Monica, Calif., 1937*), actress. Starred, as Mrs. Leslie Carter, in *The Heart of Maryland* and many other plays. [*Supp.* 2]

CARTER, ELIAS (*b. Ward, Mass., 1781; d. Worcester, Mass., 1864*), architect. Worked in Greek Revival style, adapting it to New England use; best examples of his skill to be found in houses at Worcester *post* 1828.

CARTER, FRANKLIN (*b. Waterbury, Conn., 1837; d. Williamstown, Mass., 1919*), educator. President, Williams College, 1881–1901, in which time he modernized the curriculum, improved the faculty and built up the endowment.

CARTER, HENRY ALPHEUS PEIRCE (*b. Honolulu, Hawaii, 1837; d. New York, N.Y., 1891*), merchant, diplomat. Negotiated Hawaii-United States sugar reciprocity treaty, 1876; Hawaiian minister to the United States, 1883–91.

CARTER, HENRY ROSE (*b. Caroline Co., Va., 1852; d. Washington, D.C., 1925*), epidemiologist, sanitarian. Graduated University of Virginia, 1873, as civil engineer; University of Maryland, 1879, as M.D.

Entering the Marine Hospital Service, he interested himself in yellow fever research and problems of marine quarantine; represented federal government in fight against yellow fever epidemics in Southern states, 1893, and 1897–98. Author of classical papers on yellow fever. In 1913 he conducted the first campaign for malaria control conducted in the United States; in 1915, he was commissioned assistant surgeon-general of the U.S. Public Health Service.

CARTER, JAMES COOLIDGE (*b. Lancaster, Mass., 1827; d. New York, N.Y., 1905*), lawyer. Graduated Harvard, 1850. Admitted to New York bar, 1853; associated with Charles O'Conor in Jumel Will case and Tweed Ring cases, and with many other important cases in New York. Prominent in movements for municipal reform and leader of the fight against codification of the common law as proposed by David Dudley Field. In the last years of his practice he engaged chiefly in cases involving constitutional questions.

CARTER, JAMES GORDON (*b. Leominster, Mass., 1795; d. Chicago, Ill., 1849*), educator. Graduated Harvard, 1820. As teacher, legislator, and author of textbooks, he was in forefront of reform and improvement of New England common schools, 1821–40.

CARTER, JESSE BENEDICT (*b. New York, N.Y., 1872; d. Cervignano, Italy, 1917*), classical scholar. Graduated Princeton, 1893; Ph.D., University of Halle, 1898. Authority on Roman religion. Director, American School of Classical Studies in Rome, 1907–11; director, Classical School, American Academy in Rome, 1911–13, and of the Academy, 1913–17.

CARTER, JOHN (*b. Virginia, 1737; d. 1781*), pioneer. One of first settlers (*c.* 1770) in western North Carolina; chairman of the commissioners of the Watauga Association; at his death, one of the largest landholders west of the Allegheny mountains.

CARTER, JOHN (*b. Philadelphia, Pa., 1745; d. Providence, R.I., 1814*), printer. Editor-publisher of the *Providence Gazette*, 1768–1814. Great-grandfather of John Carter Brown.

CARTER, LANDON (*b. Virginia, 1760; d. Tennessee, 1800*), pioneer. Son of John Carter (1737–81). Supported the movement to erect northeast Tennessee into the independent state of Franklin; held public offices under the government of Franklin, of the Southwest Territory, and of Tennessee.

CARTER, MRS. LESLIE. [See CARTER, CAROLINE LOUISE DUDLEY, 1862–1937.]

CARTER, ROBERT (*b. Lancaster Co., Va., 1663; d. Lancaster Co., 1732*), colonial official and landholder, popularly known as "King" Carter. A prominent member of the Virginia Assembly, he was speaker in 1696 and 1699; from 1699 to 1732, a member of the Council, he was president, 1726–32. Agent for the Fairfax family, proprietors of the "Northern Neck," 1702–11 and 1722–32. At his death, one of the wealthiest men in the colonies.

CARTER, ROBERT (*b. Albany, N.Y., 1819; d. Cambridge, Mass., 1879*), author. Co-editor with James Russell Lowell of the *Pioneer* (1843); editor, among others, of the Boston *Commonwealth* and the Rochester, N.Y., *Democrat*.

CARTER, SAMUEL POWHATAN (*b. Elizabethton, Tenn., 1819; d. Washington, D.C., 1891*), naval and army officer, the only American who has ever been both rear-admiral and major-general. Graduated Annapolis, 1846. Organized first Union troops from Tennessee and served as brigade and division commander, 1861–65. Returned to naval duty, 1866; served at sea, and as commandant of midshipmen, Annapolis, 1870–73.

CARTER, THOMAS HENRY (*b. Scioto Co. O., 1854; d. 1911*), lawyer. Studied law at Burlington, Iowa; removed, 1882, to Helena, Mont. Elected territorial delegate, Republican, from Montana, 1888; first congressman, 1889; U.S. senator, 1895, and again in 1905. A strong partisan of Western interests.

CARTER, WILLIAM SAMUEL (*b. Austin, Texas, 1859; d. Baltimore, Md., 1923*), trade-union official. Editor, Brotherhood of Locomotive Firemen and Enginemen's magazine, 1894–1904; secretary-treasurer of the union, 1904–09; president, 1909–22.

CARTERET, PHILIP (*b. Isle of Jersey, England, 1639; d. East Jersey, 1682*), colonial official. Came to what is today Elizabethport, N.J., 1665, as first governor of New Jersey; summoned first session of New Jersey legislature, 1668. After brief period of Dutch reconquest of New Netherland, Carteret became governor of East Jersey portion of the province but his authority was challenged by Sir Edmund Andros *post* 1680. He resigned the office, 1682.

CARTWRIGHT, PETER (*b. Amherst Co., Va., 1785; d. 1872*), Methodist clergyman. Raised in Logan Co., Ky., where his father located in 1793. Converted to Methodism, 1801, and given an exhorter's license, 1802; became a traveling preacher, 1803. His early itineraries took him through Kentucky, Tennessee, Indiana and Ohio; he became one of the most celebrated frontier preachers and was ordained elder in 1808. In 1824, because of his hatred of slavery, he had himself transferred to the Sangamon Circuit in Illinois and made his home at Pleasant Hills. Until his death he was a leader in Western religious activities. Twice a member of the Illinois legislature, he was defeated for Congress by Abraham Lincoln in 1846.

CARTY, JOHN JOSEPH (*b. Cambridge, Mass., 1861; d. Baltimore, Md., 1932*), electrical engineer. Entered service of the Bell Telephone company in 1879. His early years were notable for his invention of the "common battery" which made the commercial development of telephony in metropolitan areas practical; for development of a high-resistance-bridging signal bell for substations which permitted a widespread extension of telephone service; and for his discovery that the principal cause of cross interference between telephone circuits was electrostatic, not electromagnetic unbalance. As chief engineer of the American Telephone and Telegraph Co., he supervised experimentation which led to modern long-distance telephony overland and transoceanic radio-telephony. [*Supp. 1*]

CARUS, PAUL (*b. Ilsenburg, Germany, 1852; d. 1919*), rationalist philosopher, identified with the *Open Court* publications, Chicago, Ill., *post* 1887.

CARUSO, ENRICO (*b. Naples, Italy, 1873; d. Naples, 1921*), grand opera tenor. Debut, November 1894, at Teatro Nuovo, Naples; won international reputation, 1898, in premiere of *Fedora* at Teatro Lirico, Milan. Opened his first season at Metropolitan Opera, New York, November 1903, in *Rigoletto;* thereafter, until failure of his health in 1920, he was the idol of American operagoers. Generous, kindly and unspoiled by success, he sang on every occasion as if it were the high point of his career.

CARUTHERS, WILLIAM ALEXANDER (*b. Lexington, Va., 1802; d. Marietta, Ga., 1846*), physician. Author of *The Kentuckian in New York* (1834), *The Cavaliers of Virginia* (1834–35), and *The Knights of the Horse-Shoe* (1845).

CARVER, JOHN (*b. Nottinghamshire or Derbyshire, England, c. 1576; d. Plymouth, Mass., 1621*), first governor of Plymouth. Emigrated to Holland, 1609; joined Pilgrims at Leyden, *c.* 1610–11. Active in Pilgrim projects for American settlement, he organized those sailing direct from England, hired the *Mayflower* and sailed aboard her, 1620. Aside from his March 1621 treaty with Massasoit, we know nothing of his activities or policies as governor.

CARVER, JONATHAN (*b. Weymouth, Mass., 1710; d. 1780*), traveler. At instance of Maj. Robert Rogers, Carver set out westward in 1766 along the Great Lakes from Mackinac. He crossed to the Mississippi by the Green Bay-Fox-Wisconsin route, ascended the river, reached Lake Superior by the Chippewa and St. Croix rivers, and returned in the fall of 1767 to Mackinac. Disappointed in hope of publishing his narrative of travel in America, he sailed for England, 1769, residing there for the remainder of his life. His book *Travels in Interior Parts of America* (London, 1778) ran through many editions.

CARY, ALICE (*b. near Cincinnati, O., 1820; d. New York, N.Y., 1871*), poet. Author (with sister Phoebe) of *Poems* (1849); author also of *Clovernook Papers* (1852) and other works. First president of the first American woman's club.

CARY, ANNIE LOUISE (*b. Wayne, Maine, 1842; d. New York, N.Y., 1921*), contralto singer. Operatic debut at Copenhagen, 1867–68; returned to America, 1870. Until retirement, 1882, one of the most celebrated contraltos in opera, appearing in London and St. Petersburg as well as New York.

CARY, ARCHIBALD (*b. Virginia, 1721; d. Ampthill, Va., 1787*), planter, industrialist. *Post* 1750, extended his father's manufacturing projects at Ampthill, operating a furnace and foundry and a flour mill. Representative of Chesterfield Co. in Virginia Assembly from 1756; a member of all Virginia Revolutionary conventions.

CARY, EDWARD (*b. Albany, N.Y., 1840; d. New York, N.Y., 1917*), editorial writer, *New York Times*, 1871–1917.

CARY, ELISABETH LUTHER (*b. Brooklyn, N.Y., 1867; d. Brooklyn, 1936*), art critic of the *New York Times*, 1908–36, the newspaper's first full-time specialist in this field. [*Supp. 2*]

CARY, LOTT (*b. Charles City Co., Va., c. 1780; d. Liberia, 1828*), Baptist clergyman. Purchased freedom from slavery for self and family, *c.* 1813, and received license to preach. Removed to Freetown, Liberia, 1821, as pastor of first Baptist church there; he and associates settled at Cape Montserado. Chosen vice-agent of the colony, 1826, he was killed while helping defend the colony against the Deys.

CARY, PHOEBE (*b. near Cincinnati, O., 1824; d. New York, N.Y., 1871*), poet. Sister of Alice Cary; author of the hymn "One Sweetly Solemn Thought."

CASANOWICZ, IMMANUEL MOSES (*b. Zhaludok, Russia, 1853; d. Washington, D.C., 1927*), orientalist, archeologist. Came to America, *c.* 1882; Ph.D., Johns Hopkins, 1892. Associated with U.S. National Museum *post* 1906.

CASE, JEROME INCREASE (*b. Williamstown, N.Y., 1818; d. 1891*), manufacturer and designer of improved farm machinery. Founded the J. I. Case Co. of Racine, Wis.; prominent in local politics and banking.

CASE, LEONARD (*b. Westmoreland Co., Pa., 1786; d. Cleveland, O., 1864*), lawyer, land agent. Emigrated with family to Warren, O., 1800; as clerk of local court began study of law and was admitted to bar, 1814. From 1816 to his death, identified with the growth of Cleveland, O., as real estate trader, lawyer and public official. Served as agent for the Connecticut Land Co., 1827–55.

CASE, LEONARD (*b. Cleveland, O., 1820; d. Cleveland, 1880*), philanthropist. Succeeding to the large fortune of his father (Leonard Case, 1786–1864), he was a benefactor of the Cleveland Library, the Western Reserve Historical Society and other civic and charitable activities. In 1877, he gave a large part of his property to found the Case School of Applied Science.

CASE, WILLIAM SCOVILLE (*b. Tariffville, Conn., 1863; d. 1921*), lawyer, jurist. Graduated Yale, 1885; admitted to Connecticut bar, 1887. Judge of the common pleas, Hartford Co., 1897–1901; of the superior court, 1901–19; of the supreme court of errors thereafter.

CASEY, JOSEPH (*b. Washington Co., Md., 1814; d. 1879*), jurist. Congressman, Whig, from Pennsylvania, 1848–51; editor of "Casey's Reports," 1856–61. Appointed justice of U.S. Court of Claims, 1861, and chief justice, 1863, he resigned in 1870.

CASEY, SILAS (*b. East Greenwich, R.I., 1807; d. Brooklyn, N.Y., 1882*), Union soldier. Graduated West Point, 1826. Served on Midwestern frontier and in Seminole War; served under Scott in Mexico, 1847, and was wounded in storming of Chapultepec. Author of "Casey's Tactics" (1862), long standard. Distinguished in early campaigns of Civil War; *post* 1862, commanded part of the defenses of Washington, D.C., as major-general of volunteers. Retired from active service, 1868.

CASEY, THOMAS LINCOLN (*b. Sackett's Harbor, N.Y., 1831; d. Washington, D.C., 1896*), army engineer. Specialist in fortifications; completed construction in 1884 of the Washington Monument. [*Supp. 1*]

CASILEAR, JOHN WILLIAM (*b. New York, N.Y., 1811; d. Saratoga, N.Y., 1893*), engraver, painter. Apprentice of Peter Maverick, he became a banknote engraver and a partner in American Bank Note Co. *Post* 1854, he gave most of his time to landscape painting.

CASS, GEORGE WASHINGTON (*b. near Dresden, O., 1810; d. 1888*), engineer. Nephew of Lewis Cass. Graduated West Point, 1832; assigned to duty with Topographical Engineers. Assisted in construction of Cumberland Road, 1832–36. Resigning commission, he entered business, organizing first steamboat line on Monongahela River; thereafter was president of Adams Express Co., the Pittsburgh, Fort Wayne and Chicago Railroad and Northern Pacific Railroad.

CASS, LEWIS (*b. Exeter, N.H., 1782; d. Detroit, Mich., 1866*), soldier, statesman. Moving west in 1799, he established a law practice at Marietta, O., 1802, but soon removed to Zanesville. Elected to Ohio legislature, 1806, he opposed Aaron Burr's schemes and won Jefferson's favorable notice. During War of 1812 as colonel of the 2nd Ohio, he won distinction at Malden and at the battle of the Thames; he was appointed governor of Michigan Territory, 1813. His term (1813–31) was marked by helpful, firm and constructive service; he was particularly

effective in dealing with the Indians. Following service as secretary of war in Andrew Jackson's cabinet (1831–36), he was appointed minister to France; he resigned after a dispute with Daniel Webster which increased his national prestige. As U.S. senator, Democrat, from Michigan, 1845–48, he favored a strong attitude toward England on the Oregon question, approved the war with Mexico, and opposed the Wilmot Proviso. His views on the containment of slavery anticipated Douglas's later doctrine of "squatter sovereignty."

Nominated for the presidency, 1848, he was defeated because Van Buren divided the Democratic vote; in 1851 he was re-elected to the Senate. His career reached its high point 1857–60, when as secretary of state in Buchanan's cabinet he scored diplomatic victories in disputes with Great Britain and Paraguay. Pre-eminently a nationalist and a Union man, he resigned in December 1860 as a protest against the decision not to reinforce the forts in Charleston harbor. In his last public appearance, 1862, he urged enlistment in the Federal army; during his retirement he resumed the scholarly and literary interests which had always served him for relaxation.

CASSATT, ALEXANDER JOHNSTON (*b. Pittsburgh, Pa., 1839; d. 1906*), civil engineer, railroad executive. Graduated Rensselaer Polytechnic Institute, 1859. Entered engineering department of the Pennsylvania Railroad, 1861; pioneered in introduction of the air-brake, and was made general superintendent, 1870. In 1873 he became general manager of lines east of Pittsburgh and was concerned in the general expansion of the system that then took place; chosen first vice-president in 1880, he retired from active duty, 1882. Recalled to take the presidency of the Pennsylvania, 1899, he served until his death. As president, he improved the operating condition of the road and nearly doubled its earnings. His "community of interest" solution of the rebate problem was an acceptable stop-gap until the passage of the Hepburn Act. Another of his outstanding achievements was the construction of the Pennsylvania Terminal in New York.

CASSATT, MARY (*b. Allegheny City, Pa., 1845; d. Mesnil-Théribus, France, 1926*), artist. Sister of Alexander Johnston Cassatt. After 1874 a permanent resident of France, she became an artistic disciple of Degas; she exhibited with the Impressionists, 1879–86, and gave her first independent exhibit at Paris, 1893. Original and successful in her work with pastels and in oils, she is regarded as the most distinguished etcher, excepting Whistler, that America has produced.

CASSIDY, WILLIAM (*b. Albany, N.Y., 1815; d. Albany, 1873*), journalist. Editor of the Albany *Atlas*, and *post* 1856 of the combined *Atlas* and *Argus;* a vehement supporter of the Democratic party.

CASSIN, JOHN (*b. near present-day Media, Pa., 1813; d. 1869*), ornithologist. As manager of Bowen's engraving and lithographing plant in Philadelphia, he produced illustrations for many government scientific publications; in his spare time, he arranged and identified the great collection of birds belonging to the Academy of Natural Sciences. In addition to contributions to government exploration reports, he wrote many papers for the Academy *Proceedings* and also *Illustrations of the Birds of California, Texas, Oregon, British and Russian America* (1856), in supplement to Audubon.

CASSODAY, JOHN BOLIVAR (*b. Fairfield, N.Y., 1830; d. 1907*), jurist. Chief justice, supreme court of Wisconsin, 1895–1907. [*Supp. 1*]

CASTLE, VERNON BLYTHE (*b. Norwich, England, 1887; d. Fort Worth, Texas, 1918*), dancer. Born Vernon Blythe; assumed the name "Castle," 1907. With his wife Irene (Foote) Castle, he revolutionized popular dancing in the years 1912–14, creating the one-step, turkey-trot and many other dances. After gallant service in Royal Flying Corps, 1916–18, he crashed while instructing aviation cadets.

CASWELL, ALEXIS (*b. Taunton, Mass., 1799; d. 1877*), president of Brown University, 1868–72, after 35 years of service there as professor of mathematics, natural philosophy and astronomy.

CASWELL, RICHARD (*b. Cecil Co., Md., 1729; d. Fayetteville, N.C., 1789*), Revolutionary soldier, politician. Major-general, North Carolina militia; governor of North Carolina, 1776–80 and 1785–87.

CATALDO, JOSEPH MARIA (*b. Terracina, Sicily, 1837; d. St. Andrew's Mission, Pendleton, Oreg., 1928*), Jesuit missionary in the Pacific Northwest, 1866–1928; founder of Gonzaga University, Spokane, Wash., 1887. [*Supp. 1*]

CATESBY, MARK (*b. Sudbury, England, c. 1679; d. London, England, 1749*), naturalist and traveler. In Virginia, 1712–19; in South Carolina, Georgia, Florida, 1722–25/6. Wrote and illustrated *The Natural History of Carolina, Florida, and the Bahama Islands* (1731, 1743 and 1748).

CATHCART, JAMES LEANDER (*b. Mt. Murragh, Ireland, 1767; d. Washington, D.C., 1843*), consul. Brought to America as a child; served at sea during the Revolution. Taken prisoner by Algerines, 1785, he rose high in service of the Dey. Associated with William Eaton in Tripoli adventure; later consul at Madeira and Cadiz.

CATHCART, WILLIAM (*b. Londonderry Co., Ireland, 1826; d. 1908*), Baptist clergyman. Came to America, 1853; pastor of Second Baptist Church, Philadelphia, Pa. Best known as editor of the *Baptist Encyclopedia* (1883).

CATHERWOOD, MARY HARTWELL (*b. Luray, O., 1847; d. Chicago, Ill., 1902*), novelist. Author of, among others, *The Romance of Dollard* (1889); *The Story of Tonty* (1890); *Old Kaskaskia* (1893); *Mackinac and Lake Stories* (1899).

CATLIN, GEORGE (*b. Wilkesbarre, Pa., 1796; d. 1872*), artist. Practiced law in western Pennsylvania until 1823, when he set up in Philadelphia as a portraitist. He worked mainly in Washington, D.C., 1824–29, but visited Albany, N.Y., 1828, where he painted portraits of DeWitt Clinton and other New York notables. On seeing at Philadelphia a delegation of Indians from the Far West, he resolved "to use my art and so much of the labors of my future life as might be required in rescuing from oblivion the looks and customs of the vanishing races of native man in America." From 1829 to 1838 he painted some 600 portraits of distinguished Indians, accompanied by pictures of villages, games, religious ceremonies and occupations; he exhibited this collection here and abroad, 1837–52. His published works include: *Letters and Notes on . . . North American Indians* (1841); *Catlin's North American Indian Portfolio* (1845); *Life Among the Indians* (1867).

CATON, JOHN DEAN (*b. Monroe, N.Y., 1812; d. Chicago, Ill., 1895*), jurist. Settled in Chicago, 1833, opening first law office there. Chief justice, Illinois supreme court, 1855–64.

CATRON, JOHN (*b. Pennsylvania, c. 1786; d. 1865*), jurist. Raised in Virginia and Kentucky, he moved to Tennessee, 1812. Admitted to the bar, 1815, he was proficient in land law and successful; from 1824 to 1834 he served as a judge of the supreme court of errors and appeals, from 1831 to 1834 chief justice. Appointed by Andrew Jackson to the U.S. Supreme Court, 1837, he was regarded as particularly strong in dealing with cases involving the common law and equity jurisprudence. He was a strong Unionist during the Civil War.

CATTELL, ALEXANDER GILMORE (*b. Salem, N.J., 1816; d. 1894*), banker, politician. Moved to Philadelphia, 1846; president of Corn Exchange Bank, 1858–71. U.S. senator, Republican, from Pennsylvania, 1866–72.

CATTELL, WILLIAM CASSADAY (*b. Salem, N.J., 1827; d. 1898*), Presbyterian clergyman. President, Lafayette College, Easton, Pa., 1863–83.

CAWEIN, MADISON JULIUS (*b. Louisville, Ky., 1865; d. 1914*), poet. Author of 36 volumes of verse expressing a romantic idealism and a love of nature.

CAYVAN, GEORGIA (*b. Bath, Maine, 1858; d. Flushing, N.Y., 1906*), actress. Made professional debut at Boston, Mass., 1879; leading lady of the Lyceum Theatre Stock Company, New York, 1888–94.

CAZENOVE, THÉOPHILE (*b. Amsterdam, Holland, 1740; d. Paris, France, 1811*), financier. Arrived in America, 1790, as agent for Dutch speculators in U.S. state and federal securities; persuaded them to buy wild lands in western New York and Pennsylvania commonly called the "Holland Purchase" which he developed until 1799. Cazenovia, N.Y., is named for him.

CÉLORON DE BLAINVILLE, PIERRE JOSEPH DE (*b. Montreal, Canada, 1693; d. 1759*), explorer. Commanded at Michilimackinac, 1734–42; at Detroit, Niagara, and Crown Point, 1742–47. In June 1749, he headed an expedition down the Ohio to expel English traders from the region and assert French claims there.

CERMAK, ANTON JOSEPH (*b. Kladno, Czechoslovakia, 1873; d. Miami, Fla., 1933*), Democratic mayor of Chicago, killed by an assassin's bullet aimed at President-elect F. D. Roosevelt. [*Supp. 1*]

CERRÉ, JEAN GABRIEL (*b. Montreal, Canada, 1734; d. St. Louis, Mo., 1805*), merchant, fur trader. Established at Kaskaskia, Ill., by 1755; he became one of the wealthiest men in the Illinois country. Removed to St. Louis *ante* 1780.

CESNOLA, LUIGI PALMA DI (*b. Rivarolo, Italy, 1832; d. 1904*), soldier, archeologist. Came to America, 1860. Appointed U.S. consul at Cyprus after distinguished service in Civil War. Between 1865 and 1876, at his own expense, he pioneered in excavating ancient sites on the island, digging up 35,573 objects. From 1879 until his death he was director of the Metropolitan Museum of Art, New York City.

CHACE, ELIZABETH BUFFUM (*b. Providence, R.I., 1806; d. Central Falls, R.I., 1899*), anti-slavery and woman-suffrage advocate. Daughter of Arnold Buffum.

CHADBOURNE, PAUL ANSEL (*b. North Berwick, Maine, 1823; d. New York, N.Y., 1883*), educator. President, Massachusetts Agricultural College, 1866 and 1882–83; University of Wisconsin, 1867–70; Williams College, 1872–81.

CHADWICK, FRENCH ENSOR (*b. Morgantown, W. Va., 1844; d. New York, N.Y., 1919*), naval officer. Graduated U.S. Naval Academy (Newport), 1864. Active in naval intelligence, *post* 1882; commanded U.S.S. *New York* in Spanish-American War; president, Naval War College, 1900–03; retired as rear-admiral, 1903.

CHADWICK, GEORGE WHITEFIELD (*b. Lowell, Mass., 1854; d. 1931*), composer. Studied at New England Conservatory of Music, 1872–75, and in Germany, 1877–80. Taught at, and was later director, New England Conservatory, 1882–1931. Belongs as a composer to the so-called New England group which reflected the influence of the classic-romantic German composers of the 19th century. His major works include the *Rip Van Winkle Overture, Melpomene*, and *Ecce Jam Noctis*. [*Supp. 1*]

CHADWICK, HENRY (*b. Exeter, England, 1824; d. 1908*), sportsman. Came to America, 1837. A newspaperman on New York and Brooklyn dailies, he became the first important sports writer in America, 1856–86. The rules of baseball are largely his work, and he was editor of *Spalding's Official Baseball Guide*.

CHADWICK, JAMES READ (*b. Boston, Mass., 1844; d. 1905*), physician. Graduated Harvard, 1865; Harvard Medical School, 1871. For many years a gynecologist and professor of that subject at Harvard. Established Boston Medical Library, 1875.

CHADWICK, JOHN WHITE (*b. Marblehead, Mass., 1840; d. Brooklyn, N.Y., 1904*), Unitarian clergyman. Wrote extensively in favor of Darwinism; pastor in Brooklyn, N.Y.

CHAFFEE, ADNA ROMANZA (*b. Orwell, O., 1842; d. Los Angeles, Calif., 1914*), soldier. Commissioned from the ranks during Civil War; served in southwest Indian campaigns, 1867–92, with 6th and 9th Cavalry. As brigadier-general, 1898, he was outstanding at battle of El Caney; he later commanded the American contingent in the Boxer uprising. Promoted major-general, 1901, he commanded in the Philippines; as lieutenant-general, he was chief of staff of the army, 1904–06, retiring in the latter year.

CHAFFEE, JEROME B. (*b. near Lockport, N.Y., 1825; d. Westchester Co., N.Y., 1886*), banker, political leader. Raised in Adrian, Mich. Migrated to Pike's Peak region, 1860, and prospered in mining operations. A founder and president of First National Bank, Denver, Colo., 1865–80; a proponent of Colorado statehood, and first U.S. senator from Colorado, Republican, 1877–79.

CHAFIN, EUGENE WILDER (*b. East Troy, Wis., 1852; d. Long Beach, Calif., 1920*), lawyer, temperance leader. Prohibition party candidate for president, 1908 and 1912.

CHAILLÉ-LONG, CHARLES (*b. Princess Anne, Md., 1842; d. 1917*), explorer, lawyer. Explored upper Nile basin, 1874, as staff officer of Egyptian army. Practiced international law in Paris. Served as U.S. consul in Egypt and Korea.

CHALKLEY, THOMAS (*b. Southwark, England, 1675; d. Tortola, V.I., 1741*), Quaker minister, merchant mariner. Author of a celebrated journal, first published in *A Collection of the Works of Thos. Chalkley* (Philadelphia, 1749). Resident in or near Philadelphia, Pa., *post* 1701, he made numerous journeys "in the ministry."

CHALMERS, JAMES RONALD (*b. Halifax Co., Va., 1831; d. Memphis, Tenn., 1898*), lawyer. Left law practice in Mississippi to serve in Confederate forces; at end of Civil War commanded first division of Forrest's cavalry. An aggressive figure in Mississippi politics, 1876–86, he served as congressman, Democrat and Independent, 1877–81 and 1884–85.

CHALMERS, WILLIAM JAMES (*b. Chicago, Ill., 1852; d. Chicago, 1938*), industrialist. Executive officer of Fraser & Chalmers Co., and Allis-Chalmers Co., manufacturers of power machinery. [*Supp. 2*]

CHAMBERLAIN, ALEXANDER FRANCIS (*b. Kenninghall, England, 1865; d. Worcester, Mass., 1914*), anthropologist. Graduated University of Toronto, 1886; Clark University, Ph.D., 1892. A teacher of anthropology at Clark University, 1893–1914; editor, *Journal of American Folk-Lore.*

CHAMBERLAIN, DANIEL HENRY (*b. West Brookfield, Mass., 1835; d. Charlottesville, Va., 1907*), lawyer. After Civil War service, settled in South Carolina, 1866–77; Republican governor of that state, 1874–76. Thereafter, practiced law in New York.

CHAMBERLAIN, GEORGE EARLE (*b. near Natchez, Miss., 1854; d. 1928*), lawyer. Settled in Oregon, 1876. Democratic governor of Oregon, 1902–09; U.S. senator, 1909–21; sharp critic of War Department, 1917, as chairman of Senate Military Affairs committee.

CHAMBERLAIN, HENRY RICHARDSON (*b. Peoria, Ill., 1859; d. London, 1911*), editor and foreign correspondent. Brilliant representative of *New York Sun* in London, 1892–1911.

CHAMBERLAIN, JACOB (*b. Sharon, Conn., 1835; d. 1908*), Dutch Reformed minister. Raised in Hudson, O.; missionary to India, 1860–1908.

CHAMBERLAIN, JOSHUA LAWRENCE (*b. Brewer, Maine, 1828; d. Portland, Maine, 1914*), educator. Graduated Bowdoin, 1852. Teacher of modern languages *et al.*, Bowdoin, 1856–62; president of Bowdoin, 1871–83. Received the Medal of Honor for gallantry at Gettysburg; promoted brigadier-general on the field at Petersburg; mustered out, 1866, as brevet major-general of volunteers. Republican governor of Maine, 1866–70.

CHAMBERLAIN, MELLEN (*b. Pembroke, N.H., 1821; d. 1900*), lawyer, jurist, historian. Graduated Dartmouth, 1844; Harvard Law School, 1848. Practiced law in Boston, Mass.; served in state legislature. Associate justice and chief justice, Boston municipal court, 1866–78. Librarian, Boston Public Library, 1878–90. Author of numerous studies of early U.S. history.

CHAMBERLAIN, NATHAN HENRY (*b. Sandwich, Mass., c. 1828; d. Sandwich, 1901*), Episcopal clergyman. Ordained to Unitarian ministry, 1857; to Episcopal priesthood, 1864. Served as rector of churches in Connecticut, New York, Wisconsin and Massachusetts, 1864–89.

CHAMBERLAIN, WILLIAM ISAAC (*b. Sharon, Conn., 1837; d. 1920*), agriculturist. Brother of Jacob Chamberlain. Raised in Hudson, O., where he applied scientific management to farming; elected Ohio secretary of agriculture, 1880–86. President, Iowa Agricultural College, 1886–90. Author of *Tile Drainage* (1891).

CHAMBERLIN, THOMAS CHROWDER (*b. Mattoon, Ill., 1843; d. 1928*), geologist. Graduated Beloit College, 1866, and attended graduate school of University of Michigan. Taught at Beloit, Columbian University and University of Chicago; assistant state geologist of Wisconsin, 1873–76, and chief, 1877–82. Founder and editor, *Journal of Geology*, 1893–1922. Regarded as the ranking geologist of America, he made a threefold contribution to science: through research in glacial phenomena, through investigations of geological climates, and in cosmic geology.

CHAMBERS, CHARLES JULIUS. [See CHAMBERS, JAMES JULIUS, 1850–1920.]

CHAMBERS, EZEKIEL FORMAN (*b. Chestertown, Md., 1788; d. 1867*), jurist. U.S. senator, Whig, from Maryland, 1826–34; district judge and judge of state court of appeals, 1834–50.

CHAMBERS, GEORGE (*b. Chambersburg, Pa., 1786; d. Chambersburg, 1866*), lawyer. Graduated Princeton, 1804. Admitted to bar, 1807, he became expert in Pennsylvania land law. The largest landowner in Franklin Co., he devoted much time to promotion of education and agriculture there.

CHAMBERS, JAMES JULIUS (*b. Bellefontaine, O., 1850; d. 1920*), journalist. Explored headwaters of Mississippi River, 1872. On staff of *New York Herald*, 1873–89; organized Paris *Herald*, 1887. Managing editor, *New York World*, 1889–91; a free-lance writer thereafter.

CHAMBERS, JOHN (*b. Bromley Bridge, N.J., 1780; d. Paris, Ky., 1852*), lawyer, politician. Removed to Washington, Ky., 1794; admitted to practice law, 1800. Congressman, Whig, from Kentucky, 1828–29 and 1835–39. Governor, Iowa Territory, 1841–45; notably successful in handling Indian affairs.

CHAMBERS, JULIUS [See CHAMBERS, JAMES JULIUS, 1850–1920.]

CHAMBERS, ROBERT WILLIAM (*b. Brooklyn, N.Y., 1865; d. New York, N.Y., 1933*), novelist and illustrator. Produced 72 books of which *Cardigan* (1901) is best remembered. [*Supp. 1*]

CHAMBERS, TALBOT WILSON (*b. Carlisle, Pa., 1819; d. 1896*), Dutch Reformed clergyman, theologian. Pastor at Somerville, N.J., 1840–49; a minister of Collegiate Reformed Church, New York City, 1849–96; strongly conservative.

CHAMPLAIN, SAMUEL DE (*b. Brouage, France, c. 1567; d. Quebec, Canada, 1635*), explorer, founder of Canada. Son of a naval captain; as a young man saw service in French army and navy. Commanding ship

St. Julien on an enforced voyage to New Spain, 1599–1601, he had an unusual opportunity to visit Spanish possessions in the West Indies, Mexico, Central America and northern South America. His elaborate report to Henry IV of France on his observations won him a pension, a patent of nobility, and the King's encouragement to attempt foundation of a permanent colony in North America. In 1603 he made a preliminary voyage thither in company with a fur-trading expedition, exploring the St. Lawrence River as far as Lachine Rapids and publishing his observations of the country and its inhabitants on his return. Under patronage of the Sieur de Monts (who disapproved of a settlement on the St. Lawrence and directed the choice of a warmer region), Champlain sailed in 1604 and founded a colony on Douchet Island at the mouth of the St. Croix in present-day New Brunswick. As this site proved unhealthy, he removed the colony to Port Royal, Nova Scotia, in 1605, where it remained until 1607. During this time, he was the mainstay of the colony; he also made three exploring expeditions along the coast of New England, discovering and naming Mount Desert and reaching as far as Vineyard Sound to the southward.

Having persuaded the King to permit foundation of a colony on the St. Lawrence, Champlain founded and settled Quebec in 1608. While aiding Huron Indians in a war against their enemies the Iroquois in 1609, he entered on the lake which still bears his name and, by subduing the Iroquois with firearms, won their lasting enmity for France.

After a visit home in 1610 and the arrangement of a new charter for the colony (1611) under patronage of the Prince de Condé, he determined to explore westward in hope of finding a route to the western sea. He ascended the Ottawa River in 1613 as far as Morrison Island, and in 1615 went with some Hurons to their home on Georgian Bay; he was the first to describe, map and name Lake Huron. Joining in another war party against the Iroquois that autumn he crossed the east end of Lake Ontario and recognized it as source of the St. Lawrence; severely wounded in a fight with Iroquois in what is now Madison Co., N.Y., he returned home with the Hurons and spent the winter with them. He returned to France in 1616.

Thenceforward he devoted himself to the development of his colony; he spent the years 1620–24 in Canada. In 1625, he won Richelieu's interest in the colony which resulted in the formation (1627) of the Company of One Hundred Associates, a means for recruitment and equipping of new colonists. Taken prisoner during a 1629 raid on Quebec by English freebooters, Champlain remained out of New France until 1633. He then returned as governor and did not quit Canada for the remainder of his life. Jean Nicolet made his explorations of 1634–35 at Champlain's direction.

Champlain was author of: the description of his voyage of 1603 entitled *Des Sauvages; Les Voyages du Sieur de Champlain* (Paris, 1613) which included his map of 1612; *Voyages et Descouvertes faites en la Nouvelle France* (Paris, 1619); *Les Voyages de la Nouvelle France Occidentale dicte Canada . . . 1603 jusques en l'an 1629* (Paris, 1632) which included a map of the St. Lawrence and its sources.

CHAMPLIN, JOHN DENISON (*b. 1834; d. 1915*), editor of encyclopedias and reference works, including *Cyclopedia of Painters and Paintings* (1886–87).

CHAMPLIN, JOHN WAYNE (*b. Kingston, N.Y., 1831; d. Grand Rapids, Mich., 1901*), jurist. Removed to Michigan, 1854; studied law and began practice, 1855. Elected to numerous offices in Grand Rapids, including mayor, 1867. Justice of state supreme court, 1884–90; chief justice, 1890–91.

CHAMPLIN, STEPHEN (*b. South Kingston, R.I., 1789; d. 1870*), naval officer. Cousin of Oliver H. Perry and Matthew C. Perry. Served in lake campaigns, War of 1812, including battle of Lake Erie where he commanded the *Scorpion;* he later wrote a narrative of the battle.

CHAMPNEY, BENJAMIN (*b. New Ipswich, N.H., 1817; d. 1907*), painter. Assisted Vanderlyn on "Landing of Columbus" in the Capitol, Washington, D.C.; a follower of the "Hudson River" school of landscapists.

CHAMPNEY, JAMES WELLS (*b. Boston, Mass., 1843; d. 1903*), painter, illustrator. Did successful pastel portraits *post* 1885; was one of the first American painters to apply French Impressionist theory of "values."

CHANCHE, JOHN MARY JOSEPH (*b. Baltimore, Md., 1795; d. Frederick City, Md., 1852*), Roman Catholic clergyman, Sulpician. Consecrated first bishop of Natchez, Miss., 1841.

CHANDLER, CHARLES FREDERICK (*b. Lancaster, Mass., 1836; d. 1925*), industrial chemist. Studied at Lawrence Scientific School, Harvard, and at Berlin and Göttingen where he received the doctorate. Returning to America, he taught chemistry, geology and mineralogy at Columbia University; in 1864 he was a co-founder of the Columbia School of Mines, of which he was later dean. He succeeded Charles A. Joy as head of the chemistry department at Columbia and remained in that post until 1910. His brilliant work as a teacher was only a small part of his total achievement. He was a leading authority on water supplies, sanitation, oil refining and assaying. He gave outstanding service to New York City on its Board of Health, 1866–83, exposing food adulteration and abating nuisances. His valuable contributions to applied chemistry, in the words of a 1920 honors citation, placed the entire world in his debt.

CHANDLER, ELIZABETH MARGARET (*b. Centre, Del., 1807; d. Lenawee Co., Mich., 1834*), author.

Contributor of verse and prose to the *Genius of Universal Emancipation;* author of *Essays, Philanthropic and Moral* (1836) and *Poetical Works* (edited by Benjamin Lundy, 1836), both published posthumously.

CHANDLER, JOHN (*b. Epping, N.H., 1762; d. 1841*), soldier. After service in Revolution, settled in then district of Maine, 1784. A zealous militiaman, he was commissioned brigadier-general in War of 1812 and served in northern campaigns. Chosen U.S. senator, Democrat, from state of Maine, 1820–29.

CHANDLER, JOHN SCUDDER (*b. Madura, India, 1849; d. Madura, 1934*), Congregationalist missionary; editor of the *Tamil Lexicon;* aided in revising the Old and New Testaments in Tamil. [*Supp.* 1]

CHANDLER, JOSEPH RIPLEY (*b. Kingston, Mass., 1792; d. Philadelphia, Pa., 1880*), journalist. Editor, *Gazette of the United States* and *North American,* 1822–47; editor, *Graham's Magazine,* 1843–49. Congressman, Whig, from Pennsylvania, 1849–55. U.S. minister to Naples, 1858–61. A strong foe of religious intolerance and a prison reformer.

CHANDLER, JULIAN ALVIN CARROLL (*b. Caroline Co., Va., 1872; d. 1934*), educator, president of the College of William and Mary, 1919–34.

[*Supp.* 1]

CHANDLER, PELEG WHITMAN (*b. New Gloucester, Maine, 1816; d. 1889*), lawyer. Prominent in Boston civic life, 1840–65, and considered the best jury pleader of his time in Massachusetts.

CHANDLER, SETH CARLO (*b. Boston, Mass., 1846; d. Wellesley, Mass., 1913*), astronomer. Constructor of the almucantar; editor of the *Astronomical Journal;* worked for many years on demonstration of the variation of latitude.

CHANDLER, THOMAS BRADBURY (*b. Woodstock, Conn., 1726; d. Elizabethtown, N.J., 1790*), Anglican clergyman. Graduated Yale, 1745; ordained, 1751. Rector, St. John's, Elizabethtown, N.J. A leading advocate for an American episcopacy, he was a Loyalist in the Revolution; he spent the years 1775–85 in England, but returned to his parish in the latter year. He was author of several pamphlets on the episcopal question, and possibly the author of the Tory tract *What Think Ye Of The Congress Now* (1775).

CHANDLER, WILLIAM EATON (*b. Concord, N.H., 1835; d. Concord, 1917*), lawyer, politician, journalist. Active in state politics, he held office in Navy and Treasury departments under Lincoln and Johnson and was a prominent Republican party strategist, *post* 1867. As secretary of the navy, 1882–85, he established program of steel warship construction but was severely criticized for its early failure in details. He was U.S. senator from New Hampshire, 1887–1901.

CHANDLER, ZACHARIAH (*b. Bedford, N.H., 1813; d. 1879*), politician. Removed to Detroit, Mich., 1833, and grew rich in trade, banking and land speculation. At first a Whig, he was a signer of the call for the meeting at Jackson, Mich., 1854, which launched the Republican party. He served as U.S. senator from Michigan, 1857–75, and again in 1879; allied with the radical Republican and anti-slavery element of his party, he pressed for the fullest prosecution of the war against the seceding states and regarded the Reconstruction acts as too lax. His use of federal patronage to sustain his political power and his partisan, despotic control of the Republican machine in Michigan made him for years the undisputed boss of the state. Defeated, 1874, for re-election to the Senate, he was made secretary of the interior in 1875 and reorganized the department by wholesale dismissals for alleged dishonesty or incompetence, leaving office in March, 1877.

CHANEY, LON (*b. Colorado Springs, Colo., 1883; d. 1930*), screen actor, "the man of a thousand faces." Distinguished by his great skill as a pantomimist and make-up artist. [*Supp.* 1]

CHANFRAU, FRANCIS S. (*b. New York, N.Y., 1824; d. 1884*), actor. Achieved fame in 1848 as "Mose" in *A Glance at New York;* starred in *Kit, the Arkansas Traveller* for twelve seasons *post* 1872.

CHANFRAU, HENRIETTA BAKER (*b. Philadelphia, Pa., 1837; d. Burlington, N.J., 1909*), actress. Wife of Francis S. Chanfrau. Active in the theater, 1854–84; "discoverer" of Mary Anderson.

CHANG AND ENG (*b. Meklong, Siam, 1811; d. 1874*), "the Siamese Twins." Made extensive tours of United States and Europe; settled as farmers in North Carolina.

CHANNING, EDWARD (*b. Dorchester, Mass., 1856; d. 1931*), historian. Son of William E. Channing (1818–1901); nephew of Margaret Fuller. Stimulated at Harvard by the teaching of Henry Adams, Channing took his doctorate in 1880 and began his career as teacher of American history there in 1883. His essay of that year, "Town and County Government in the English Colonies," won a prize, was printed in the *Johns Hopkins Studies* series, and was the first paper delivered at the first meeting of the American Historical Association. Disliked for his personality but respected for his scholarly integrity and for the worth of what he taught, he continued to teach until 1929. Very early in his career, he had determined to write a history of the United States which should be all his own, relating what had happened, why, and what it meant, with emphasis on deflating popular myths and on the social, economic and intellectual factors. Working on a strict research regimen, he concentrated on this task, publishing the first volume (*The Planting of a New Nation in the New World: 1000–1660*) in 1905. Succeeding volumes appeared at approximately four-year intervals. *The War for Southern Independence* (1925) was the sixth volume; much of volume seven was ready for publication when he died. He was author also of several popular textbooks.

[*Supp.* 1]

CHANNING, EDWARD TYRRELL (*b. Newport, R.I., 1790; d. Cambridge, Mass., 1856*), brother of Walter and William E. Channing (1780–1842). Boylston professor of rhetoric at Harvard, 1819–51.

CHANNING, WALTER (*b. Newport, R.I., 1786; d. 1876*), physician. Brother of Edward T. and William E. Channing (1780–1842). Dean of Harvard Medical School, 1819–47; pioneered with ether in childbirth cases.

CHANNING, WILLIAM ELLERY (*b. Newport, R.I., 1780; d. 1842*), Unitarian clergyman, was descended from the best New England stock. As a student at Harvard he was described as serious and over-thoughtful and inclined to introspection, but acutely sensitive to conditions around him. After graduation, 1798, he spent a year-and-a-half as tutor in a Richmond, Va., family. During this period he acquired habits of overwork and ascetic discipline which undermined his health. Upon his return to Newport Channing turned to theology. He continued his studies while serving *post* 1802 as a "Regent" or proctor at Harvard. Ordained and installed as minister of the Federal Street Church, Boston, in 1803, he retained this pastorate until his death. He married his cousin, Ruth Gibbs, in 1814. Channing was by nature a Broad Churchman who accepted Christianity as a way of life and was eager only to persuade others to walk in it. He had no new doctrines to propose. His real contribution to theology is expressed in the inscription on his statue in the Boston Public Gardens, "He breathed into theology a humane spirit." Searching the Christian scriptures for support of the Calvinism in which he had been reared, he found there no justification for belief in a "jealous" God, a mankind conceived in iniquity, the vicarious sacrifice of an innocent victim as atonement for "sin" in which man's will had no part, or election by grace. Instead, he preached a gospel of the goodness of God, the essential virtue and perfectability of man, and the freedom of the will with its consequent responsibility for action. Channing's sermons and writings brought to a focus the unrest and dissatisfaction with orthodox Calvinist doctrine which had been gathering within the sects in New England. However, he had no desire to form a new denomination. He hesitated to adopt the name Unitarian for fear that the formation of a new group with a distinctive name would soon produce a "Unitarian orthodoxy" as rigid as the old, but when he recognized that the movement had gone beyond his control, he devoted himself to it and became its leader. In 1819 he preached a sermon defining the position of the Unitarian party and defending the right of its members to Christian fellowship. In 1820 he organized the Berry Street Conference of liberal ministers out of which developed, in 1825, the American Unitarian Association. "Channing Unitarianism" came to be and has remained the recognized term for that form of religious liberalism which, while unwavering in its assertion of the right of the human reason as a part of the essential dignity of human nature, still clung fondly to the supernatural element of the Christian tradition. Channing made clear in his epoch-making sermon, "The Moral Argument against Calvinism," that his objection to contemporary Trinitarian orthodoxy was not so much to its doctrine about the nature of the God-head, as to its view of the nature of man. The concept of the essential depravity of human nature was abhorrent to him. His conception of Christ linked him with Arians like John Milton.

As a preacher Channing was noted for the arresting quality of his voice and the charm of his manner. His style was unadorned by illustration, but there are few of his sermons which do not have their moments of real eloquence. In 1822 poor health caused him to take a prolonged vacation in Europe; after his return a large part of his ministerial work was assumed by Rev. Ezra Stiles Gannett, and Channing devoted much of his energy to writing. His essays on Milton, Fénelon, and Napoleon had wide circulation. In *Self-Culture* (1838) Channing made a plea for adult education and advocated the policy of setting apart the funds derived from the sale of public lands to support public education. The influence of Channing on American literature was very direct. Emerson, Bryant, Longfellow, Lowell, and Holmes were all closely associated with the Unitarian movement, and acknowledged their indebtedness to Channing. In his *Remarks on American Literature* (1830), Channing urged American writers to find inspiration in what is characteristic of their own land rather than to imitate English models.

Politics was always of interest to Channing. His early associations were with the Federalists, but the trend of his own thought allied him with Jefferson rather than with Hamilton. He was conscious of the tremendous revolutionary forces which were at work in society. Distinguishing between the "inner" and the "outer" revolution, his aim was to make the outer revolution peaceful and beneficial by the timely release of the moral forces which he believed to be stored up in the individual soul. Channing held slavery to be an unspeakable evil; but he considered war to be also an evil, and civil war the most dreadful of all wars to contemplate. He was attacked by both southerners and northerners for his views on the slavery question, but his addresses (e.g., *Slavery*, 1835) did much to prepare people to understand and follow Abraham Lincoln. He was also a pioneer in the modern movement against war, and the Massachusetts Peace Society was organized in his study. In his discussion of temperance, the condition of laborers, and public education, Channing was clearly in advance of his time; his views were surprisingly anticipatory of the thought of present-day social workers.

CHANNING, WILLIAM ELLERY (*b. Boston, Mass., 1818; d. 1901*), poet. Son of Walter Channing; friend of Thoreau, Emerson, Hawthorne. Wrote the first biography of Thoreau (1873).

CHANNING, WILLIAM FRANCIS (*b. Boston, Mass., 1820; d. 1901*), inventor. Son of William E. Channing (1780–1842). With Moses G. Farmer invented magnetic-electric fire-alarm telegraph from which the modern fire-alarm system has evolved.

CHANNING, WILLIAM HENRY (*b. Boston, Mass., 1810; d. London, Eng., 1884*), Unitarian clergyman, reformer. Nephew of William E. Channing (1780–1842) whose biography he wrote in 1848.

CHANUTE, OCTAVE (*b. Paris, France, 1832; d. 1910*), civil engineer, aerial navigator. Came to America as a child; educated in New York City. Successful in engineering career with Western railroads and as private consultant, his major contribution was in aerial navigation. Studying the work of Otto and Gustav Lilienthal, Chanute made in 1896–97 probably the first scientific gliding experiments in America; he designed the Chanute biplane upon which the Wrights largely modelled their first glider. He wrote extensively on aerial navigation and on the engineering problems of flight.

CHAPELLE, PLACIDE LOUIS (*b. Runes, France, 1842; d. New Orleans, La., 1905*), Catholic Archbishop of New Orleans, 1898–1905; apostolic delegate to Cuba, Porto Rico and the Philippines.

CHAPIN, AARON LUCIUS (*b. Hartford, Conn., 1817; d. 1892*), Congregational clergyman. First president of Beloit College, Wisconsin, 1850–86.

CHAPIN, ALONZO BOWEN (*b. Somers, Conn., 1808; d. Hartford, Conn., 1858*), Episcopal clergyman. Wrote extensively on Biblical and local history; outstanding work a *View of the Organization and Order of the Primitive Church* (1842).

CHAPIN, CALVIN (*b. Chicopee, Mass., 1763; d. 1851*), Congregational clergyman. A founder of the American Board of Foreign Missions and a pioneer in the temperance cause. Pastor, Wethersfield, Conn., 1794–1851.

CHAPIN, CHESTER WILLIAM (*b. Ludlow, Mass., 1798; d. Springfield, Mass., 1883*), railroad promoter. Active in development of transportation in the Connecticut Valley; president of Boston and Albany Railroad, 1854–77.

CHAPIN, EDWIN HUBBELL (*b. Union Village, N.Y., 1814; d. 1880*), Universalist clergyman. Eloquent preacher and voluminous writer. The Church of the Divine Paternity, New York, N.Y., was his principal pastorate.

CHAPIN, ROY DIKEMAN (*b. Lansing, Mich., 1880; d. Detroit, Mich., 1936*), automobile manufacturer. Worked for the Olds Motor Works, 1901–06. Determined to head his own company, Chapin and Howard E. Coffin secured financial backing for a car designed by Coffin, and achieved financial independence in 1910 with the acquisition of the Hudson Motor Car Co. As president, 1910–23, Chapin introduced the popular-priced Essex, popularized the closed car, and reorganized Hudson's finances; resumed presidency of the firm in 1933. He devoted much time and effort to the cause of good roads. An energetic individualist and convincing speaker, he served as U. S. secretary of commerce from July 1932 to March 1933. [*Supp. 2*]

CHAPLIN, JEREMIAH (*b. Rowley, Mass., 1776; d. Hamilton, N.Y., 1841*), Baptist clergyman. As president (1817–33) of Waterville College, Maine, laid foundations for later success of Colby College.

CHAPMAN, ALVAN WENTWORTH (*b. Southampton, Mass., 1809; d. Apalachicola, Fla., 1899*), physician, botanist. Leader in Southern botany for fifty years; author of pioneering manual, *Flora of the Southern States* (1860).

CHAPMAN, HENRY CADWALADER (*b. Philadelphia, Pa., 1845; d. Bar Harbor, Maine, 1909*), physician, biologist.

CHAPMAN, JOHN (*b. Massachusetts, c. 1775; d. Allen Co., Ind., 1847*), popularly known as "Johnny Appleseed." Carried apple seed and seeds of vegetables and herbs from Pennsylvania to be planted in the Middle West; after 1810 apparently made Ashland Co., Ohio, his center of activity. Was considered a great medicine man by the Indians. During War of 1812 earned gratitude of frontier settlers by warning them of impending Indian attacks. His legendary life has inspired numerous literary works.

CHAPMAN, JOHN GADSBY (*b. Alexandria, Va., 1808; d. 1889*), painter. Studied at Pennsylvania Academy of Fine Arts, and at Rome and Florence. Taught and practiced wood-engraving, painted portraits, illustrated publications. *The American Drawing Book* (1847) by Chapman is said to be the finest drawing book ever published. His "Baptism of Pocahontas" is in the rotunda of the Capitol, Washington, D.C. An artist of great ability, his work has quality, charm and skill. After 1848 he resided principally in Rome.

CHAPMAN, JOHN JAY (*b. New York, N.Y., 1862; d. Poughkeepsie, N.Y., 1933*), essayist, poet. [*Supp. 1*]

CHAPMAN, JOHN WILBUR (*b. Richmond, Ind., 1859; d. 1918*), Presbyterian evangelist.

CHAPMAN, MARIA WESTON (*b. Weymouth, Mass., 1806; d. 1885*), reformer. Active in abolitionist societies, she aided W. L. Garrison in anti-slavery agitation. Edited and wrote for the *Non-Resistant,* the *Liberator,* and the *Liberty Bell.*

CHAPMAN, NATHANIEL (*b. Summer Hill, Va., 1780; d. 1853*), physician. Pupil of Benjamin Rush; M.D., University of Pennsylvania, 1801; practiced and taught in Philadelphia. Founded Medical Institute of Philadelphia; was first president of American Medical Association, 1848.

CHAPMAN, REUBEN (*b. Virginia, 1802; d. Alabama, 1882*), lawyer. Congressman, Democrat, from Alabama, 1835–47; governor of Alabama, 1847–51.

CHAPMAN, VICTOR EMMANUEL (*b. New York, N.Y., 1890; d. near Douaumont, France, 1916*), first pilot of Lafayette Escadrille to be killed in action. Son of John Jay Chapman.

CHAPPELL, ABSALOM HARRIS (*b. Hancock Co., Ga., 1801; d. Columbus, Ga., 1878*), lawyer. Georgia legislator and congressman. A state-rights Whig.

CHARLES, WILLIAM (*b. Edinburgh, Scotland, 1776; d. Philadelphia, Pa., 1820*), etcher, engraver. Noted for his etched caricatures in the manner of Gillray and Rowlandson, on events of the War of 1812.

CHARLESS, JOSEPH (*b. Westmeath, Ireland, 1772; d. 1834*). Founded *Missouri Gazette* (St. Louis), in 1808; this pioneer newspaper of the West exerted wide influence in support of Henry Clay and his policies.

CHARLEVOIX, PIERRE FRANÇOIS XAVIER de (*b. St. Quentin, France, 1682; d. La Flèche, France, 1761*), Jesuit priest, explorer, historian. Taught at Quebec, 1705–09. Returned to New France in 1720 to ascertain the boundaries of Acadia and to find a new route to the West. He traveled up the St. Lawrence and through the Great Lakes, visited the Illinois settlements, and finally reached New Orleans and Biloxi early in 1722. The record of his journey, *Journal historique,* was appended to his *Histoire de la Nouvelle France* (1744) and also published separately. It is important because of his accurate observations and because he was the only traveler in the first part of the eighteenth century to describe interior America. He published several other historical studies.

CHARLTON, THOMAS USHER PULASKI (*b. Camden, S.C., 1779; d. Savannah, Ga., 1835*), jurist, author. Held various public offices in Georgia; is noted as compiler of the first volume of Georgia court decisions (1824).

CHASE, GEORGE (*b. Portland, Maine, 1849; d. 1924*), law professor. Graduated Yale, 1870; Columbia Law School, 1873. Founder and dean of New York Law School *post* 1891.

CHASE, IRAH (*b. Stratton, Vt., 1793; d. 1864*), Baptist clergyman. Professor at Newton Theological Institution, 1825–45, where he stressed scientific study of the Scriptures.

CHASE, PHILANDER (*b. Cornish, N.H., 1775; d. 1852*), Episcopal clergyman. Graduated Dartmouth, 1796; ordained, 1799. Served as pastor in New York, New Orleans, La., and Hartford, Conn., before undertaking missionary activity in Ohio, 1817. Consecrated bishop of Ohio at Philadelphia, 1819. Anxious to provide a local seminary for the West, he founded it with aid from Lord Kenyon and other Englishmen, whence its name Kenyon College. He resigned his bishopric, 1831, and removed to Michigan; in 1835, the newly organized diocese of Illinois elected him to its episcopate. Champion of the "low church" position, he was chosen presiding bishop of the Church in 1843.

CHASE, PLINY EARLE (*b. Worcester, Mass., 1820; d. 1886*), scientist. Brother of Thomas Chase. Professor of natural sciences, Haverford College, 1871–75; of philosophy, 1875–86.

CHASE, SALMON PORTLAND (*b. Cornish, N.H., 1808; d. New York, N.Y., 1873*), statesman. Nephew of Philander Chase, bishop of Ohio, who guided him after his father's death in 1817, and with whom he lived near Columbus, O. He attended Cincinnati College and was graduated from Dartmouth, 1826. He then conducted a school for boys in Washington, D.C., and read law under the nominal supervision of William Wirt. Admitted to the bar in 1829, he soon settled in Cincinnati and became occupied, in addition to legal duties, with anti-slavery activities and various literary ventures. He compiled the *Statutes of Ohio* (1833–35), a standard work which proved most serviceable to lawyers. Despite scornful opposition Chase defended escaped slaves and was called "the attorney-general for runaway negroes." In politics Chase subordinated party interests to the central issue of slavery. Originally a Whig, he joined the Liberty Party in 1840 and became one of its outstanding leaders. He was active in the Free Soil movement of 1848. In 1849 the Free Soilers and the Democrats in the Ohio legislature elected Chase to the U.S. Senate.

By this time he had come to realize the weakness of a party founded on a purely anti-slavery basis and was considering the possibility of capturing the Democratic party for the anti-slavery cause. The keynote of Chase's senatorial policy was the writing of slavery restrictions into national law wherever possible and paving the way for a new Democratic party that would be free from pro-slavery "domination." He opposed the compromise measures of 1850, and in 1854 issued his "Appeal of the Independent Democrats," denouncing Douglas' Nebraska bill as a "criminal betrayal of precious rights." With the fall of the Whigs and the rise of the Republican party,

Chase cast his lot with the new party; in 1855 he was nominated by the Republicans for governor of Ohio and elected. He was re-elected in 1859. In 1856 Chase had been an avowed aspirant for the Republican presidential nomination, but his position was weaker than Frémont's; in 1860 he was again prominently mentioned for the presidency. When at the Chicago convention he polled only 49 votes on the first ballot, his friends threw their votes to Lincoln. Chosen U.S. senator again in 1860, Chase resigned to become Lincoln's Secretary of the Treasury.

As director of the country's finances, 1861–64, Chase shouldered a variety of heavy responsibilities. The state of public credit was poor and Chase was fortunate to have the assistance of Jay Cooke in marketing federal bonds. Chase opposed at first the bill for immense issues of paper money with a legal tender feature, but later gave his reluctant approval. Perhaps his most constructive piece of statesmanship was the origination of the national banking system, established by law in 1863. As a Cabinet member Chase helped formulate policy on the major questions of the war; in general he supported measures which were directed toward its vigorous prosecution. Relations between the President and Chase were strained, however. Chase felt that Lincoln lacked force and that his administration was lax. In 1862 a group of radical senators expressed a lack of confidence in the President and tried to force a reconstruction of the Cabinet in which Chase would be the major power and Seward would be made to resign. Although this move failed, both Seward and Chase submitted their resignations, which Lincoln refused to accept. In 1864 the confidential "Pomeroy Circular" criticized Lincoln and urged Chase's nomination for president. When this paper was made public, Chase again offered to resign and Lincoln once more refused. Later in the year, after a difference of opinion over an appointment, Chase again presented his resignation and Lincoln accepted it.

In the summer of 1864 there was a movement to revive Chase's candidacy and to induce Lincoln to withdraw; the movement was unsuccessful and Chase campaigned for Lincoln. In October Chase was appointed chief justice of the U.S. Supreme Court. Though he advocated Negro suffrage and favored the radical policy of Reconstruction, he became disillusioned with the corruption and excesses of the postwar years. When faced with the question of reopening the federal courts in the South, Chase delayed until he was convinced that military authority did not extend to the courts. A painful duty for Chase was that of presiding over the trial of Jefferson Davis for treason. Chase favored the quashing of the grand jury indictment. The case was appealed to the Supreme Court, but proceedings were terminated with the issuance of President Johnson's universal pardon in December, 1868. Presiding over the Senate in the impeachment trial of President Johnson, Chase insisted that the Senate was a court which must follow proper procedures and he asserted his prerogatives as presiding judge. He was heavily criticized for this and accused of being a partisan of the President. Chase's presidential ambitions were again manifested in 1868 when, after being ignored in the Republican convention, he became the subject of a determined but unsuccessful boom among Democrats. In the meantime, the Supreme Court was called upon to decide a series of perplexing cases, many dealing with questions of Reconstruction, in which Chase acted with scrupulous impartiality.

Although ambition colored the more prominent phases of his career and often blinded his judgment, it did not prompt unworthy bargains or blunt his moral courage. His work as chief justice was characterized by a practical emphasis on main principles rather than by brilliance or depth of legal learning.

CHASE, SAMUEL (*b. Somerset Co., Md., 1741; d. 1811*), lawyer, Revolutionary leader, justice of the United States Supreme Court. A delegate to the Maryland Assembly (1764–84), Chase was also an active member of the Continental Congress until 1778 when he was attacked by Hamilton for questionable business dealings. He influenced Maryland opinion in favor of independence, and signed the Declaration in August 1776. *Post* 1788, he served as chief judge of the Baltimore criminal court and of the general court of Maryland. An opponent of the Constitution, he later became a Federalist and in 1796 a member of the U.S. Supreme Court where his performance ranks as the most notable previous to Marshall. His high-handedness led to impeachment proceedings in 1804–05 which, despite Jefferson's pressure, ended in Chase's acquittal.

CHASE, THOMAS (*b. Worcester, Mass., 1827; d. Providence, R.I., 1892*), classical scholar. Graduated Harvard, 1848. Taught at Harvard and at Haverford College; served as president of Haverford, 1875–86.

CHASE, WILLIAM MERRITT (*b. Williamsburg, Ind., 1849; d. 1916*), artist. After studying and painting in Indianapolis, New York and St. Louis, he went to Munich in 1872 and worked under F. Wagner and Karl von Piloty. Returning to New York in 1878, he became a successful teacher and, as president of the Society of American Artists, a leader among younger painters dissatisfied with the conventions governing the National Academy. No American painter taught such large numbers of students while at the same time producing so much original work. He excelled in still-life.

CHATARD, FRANCIS SILAS (*b. Baltimore, Md., 1834; d. Indianapolis, Ind., 1918*), physician, Roman Catholic bishop of Vincennes, 1878–98; of Indianapolis, 1898–1918. Rector, American College at Rome, 1868–78.

CHAUMONOT, PIERRE JOSEPH MARIE (*b. Burgundy, France, 1611; d. Quebec, Canada, 1693*), Jesuit missionary. Worked among Indian tribes in New France, 1639–92, chiefly among the fugitive Christian Hurons.

CHAUNCEY, ISAAC (*b. Black Rock, Conn., 1772; d. Washington, D.C., 1840*), naval officer. Organized and commanded U.S. naval forces on Lakes Ontario and Erie, 1812–15; later held important administrative posts in navy.

CHAUNCY, CHARLES (*b. Yardley-bury, England, 1592; d. Cambridge, Mass., 1671/2*), nonconformist clergyman, second president of Harvard College (1654–71/2). Came to New England, 1638; served churches in Plymouth and Scituate, Mass., before appointment to Harvard.

CHAUNCY, CHARLES (*b. Boston, Mass., 1705; d. Boston, 1787*), clergyman. Great-grandson of Charles Chauncy, (1592–1671/2). Graduated Harvard, 1721; minister of the First Church in Boston, 1727–87. Acknowledged leader of the liberals of his generation, the most influential clergyman of his time in Boston and, with the exception of Jonathan Edwards, in all New England. His numerous writings were concerned primarily with three controversies: Revivalism, Episcopacy, and the Benevolence of God, in which he opposed the emotionalism of Edwards and Whitefield, the institution of an American episcopacy, and excessive rigorism.

CHAUVENET, WILLIAM (*b. Milford, Pa., 1820; d. St. Paul, Minn., 1870*), mathematician, astronomer. Graduated Yale, 1840. Appointed professor of mathematics in the navy, he became head of the Philadelphia school for midshipmen, 1842, and was largely responsible for establishing the U.S. Naval Academy on a firm, scientific basis. He was author, among other works, of classic treatises on trigonometry and astronomy which had international reputation. He served as chancellor of Washington University, St. Louis, Mo., 1862–69.

CHAVIS, JOHN (*b. c. 1763; d. 1838*), Presbyterian missionary, educator. Born either in the West Indies or near Oxford, N.C., Chavis was a full-blooded Negro. Educated under President Witherspoon of the College of New Jersey and at Washington Academy (now Washington and Lee University), he established a classical school at which many prominent North Carolinians were prepared for college, 1810–32.

CHEATHAM, BENJAMIN FRANKLIN (*b. Nashville, Tenn., 1820; d. 1886*), Confederate major-general. Engaged in dispute with Hood over conduct of Spring Hill battle in Tennessee campaign, 1864.

CHECKLEY, JOHN (*b. Boston, Mass., 1680; d. 1754*), Anglican clergyman, bookseller, controversial writer.

CHEESMAN, FORMAN (*b. New York, N.Y., 1763; d. 1821*), shipbuilder, naval architect. Instrumental in promoting growth of New York shipbuilding industry, 1800–20.

CHEETHAM, JAMES (*b. Manchester [?], England, 1772; d. New York, N.Y., 1810*), journalist. Came to America, *post* 1798; edited the Republican newspaper *The American Citizen*. A bitter political enemy of Aaron Burr, Cheetham was author of a *Life of Thomas Paine* (1809).

CHEEVER, EZEKIEL (*b. London, England, 1614/15; d. Boston, Mass., 1708*), educator, classicist. Came to New England, 1637. Taught at New Haven, Conn., Ipswich and Charlestown, Mass. Outstanding as Master of Boston Latin School, 1670–1708; author of renowned *Accidence, a Short Introduction to the Latin Tongue*.

CHEEVER, GEORGE BARRELL (*b. Hallowell, Maine, 1807; d. Englewood, N.J., 1890*), Congregational clergyman, reformer.

CHEEVER, HENRY THEODORE (*b. Hallowell, Maine, 1814; d. Worcester, Mass., 1897*), Congregational clergyman, liberal theologian. Brother of George B. Cheever.

CHENEY, BENJAMIN PIERCE (*b. Hillsborough, N.H., 1815; d. 1895*), pioneer in New England express business. Founded the United States & Canada Express Co. which he later merged with the American Express Co. Active in promotion of western railroads, and in banking.

CHENEY, CHARLES EDWARD (*b. Canandaigua, N.Y., 1836; d. 1916*), clergyman. After controversy with his bishop, 1869–72, over excessive evangelicalism in his Chicago parish, he helped organize the Reformed Episcopal Church (1873); he served the new body as bishop, and continued as pastor of Christ Church, Chicago, until his death.

CHENEY, EDNAH DOW LITTLEHALE (*b. Boston, Mass., 1824; d. 1904*), author, reformer. Wife of Seth W. Cheney. Supported anti-slavery cause, Freedman's Society, and woman's suffrage.

CHENEY, JOHN (*b. South Manchester, Conn., 1801; d. South Manchester, 1885*), engraver. Brother of Seth W. and Ward Cheney. His small engravings, published in annuals and similar books, are unexcelled in their kind.

CHENEY, JOHN VANCE (*b. Groveland, N.Y., 1848; d. San Diego, Calif., 1922*), author. Librarian of Free Public Library, San Francisco, 1887–94; of Newberry Library, Chicago, 1894–1909.

CHENEY, OREN BURBANK (*b. Holderness, N.H., 1816; d. 1903*), Baptist clergyman. Graduated Dartmouth, 1839. Helped found Bates College, Maine, and was its first president, 1864–94; emeritus to 1903.

CHENEY, PERSON COLBY (*b. Holderness, N.H., 1828; d. 1901*), paper manufacturer. Republican governor of New Hampshire, 1875–77.

CHENEY, SETH WELLS (*b. South Manchester, Conn., 1810; d. 1856*), crayon artist, engraver. Brother of John and Ward Cheney. Successful as a crayon portrait artist in Boston, Mass., 1841–53.

CHENEY, WARD (*b. South Manchester, Conn., 1813; d. 1876*), pioneer silk manufacturer. Brother of John and Seth W. Cheney. President, Cheney Brothers Silk Mfg. Co., 1854–76, and noted for business acumen and concern for employees.

CHESEBROUGH, CAROLINE (*b. Canandaigua, N.Y., 1825; d. Piermont, N.Y., 1873*), novelist.

CHESHIRE, JOSEPH BLOUNT (*b. Tarborough, N.C., 1850; d. Charlotte, N.C., 1932*), Episcopal clergyman. Bishop of North Carolina, 1893–1932.
[*Supp. 1*]

CHESNUT, JAMES (*b. Camden, S.C., 1815; d. Saarsfield, S.C., 1885*), lawyer, planter, Confederate soldier. Graduated Princeton, 1835; practiced law in Camden, S.C. Democrat and secessionist member of South Carolina General Assembly *post* 1840; president of senate, 1856–58. Elected to U.S. Senate, 1858, he vigorously defended slavery. Resigning in 1860, he helped draft ordinance of secession in South Carolina convention. In the Provisional Congress of the Confederate States he aided in drafting the permanent constitution. After service as aide to General Beauregard and on President Davis' staff, 1861–64, he became brigadier-general in command of reserve forces in South Carolina. He took an active part in opposing reconstruction of South Carolina.

CHESTER, COLBY MITCHELL (*b. New London, Conn., 1844; d. Rye, N.Y., 1932*), naval officer. Graduated Annapolis, 1863. The "Chester Claims" to trade concessions in Turkey, 1922, received wide publicity in connection with agitation against "dollar diplomacy." [*Supp. 1*]

CHESTER, GEORGE RANDOLPH (*b. Ohio, 1869; d. New York, N.Y., 1924*), author of *Get-Rich-Quick Wallingford* (1908) and other novels and stories.

CHESTER, JOSEPH LEMUEL (*b. Norwich, Conn, 1821; d. England, 1882*), genealogist, journalist.

CHETLAIN, AUGUSTUS LOUIS (*b. St. Louis, Mo., 1824; d. 1914*), Union soldier, banker. Organized and was president of Home National Bank, Chicago.

CHEVER, JAMES W. (*b. Salem, Mass. 1791; d. Salem, 1857*), privateersman. Captain of the successful privateer *America*, 1813–15. Later commanded Salem merchant ships.

CHEVERUS, JOHN LOUIS ANN MAGDALEN LEFEBRE de (*b. Mayenne, France, 1768; d. Bordeaux, France, 1836*), Roman Catholic clergyman. Ordained in Paris, 1790. On refusing oath to support civil constitution of clergy was deprived of his parish and imprisoned; escaped from Cordeliers prison to London, 1792; came to Boston, 1796. Ministered to Maine Penobscots and to scattered New England congregations, earning respect and warm liking of Protestants. Assisted in founding the Boston Athenaeum, to which he left his library. Consecrated bishop of Boston with all New England as his diocese, 1810, he served until 1823 when he returned to France as bishop of Montauban. Became Archbishop of Bordeaux, 1826, and was elevated to the cardinalate, 1836.

CHEVES, LANGDON (*b. Abbeville District, S.C., 1776; d. Columbia, S.C., 1857*), lawyer, financier. Admitted to bar, 1797; practiced successfully in Charleston, S.C. Held several state offices. As congressman, Democratic-Republican, 1810–15, he was an effective debater and prominent in the group which precipitated War of 1812. As president of the United States Bank, 1819–22, he restored the Bank to sound financial condition. Returning to South Carolina, 1829, though a strong believer in secession, he opposed separate state action. The unpopularity of his views caused him to withdraw from public life.

CHEW, BENJAMIN (*b. West River, Md., 1722; d. 1810*), lawyer. Chief justice of Pennsylvania supreme court, 1774–76; judge and president of high court of errors and appeals, 1791–1808.

CHICKERING, JONAS (*b. Mason Village, N.H., 1798; d. 1853*), piano manufacturer. Founded firm of Stewart & Chickering in Boston, Mass., 1823, and soon assumed full control; in 1837 he built the first grand piano with full iron frame made in a single casting, and in 1843 patented a new deflection of the strings. Chickering invented the first practical method of over-stringing grand pianos in 1845. He has been called the "father of American pianoforte-making."

CHIERA, EDWARD (*b. Rome, Italy, 1885; d. 1933*), Orientalist. Came to America, 1907. Professor of Assyriology, University of Chicago. Editor of the Assyrian Dictionary, 1927–33; author of works on Sumerian texts. [*Supp. 1*]

CHILD, DAVID LEE (*b. West Boylston, Mass., 1794; d. Wayland, Mass., 1874*), lawyer, journalist, anti-slavery reformer.

CHILD, FRANCIS JAMES (*b. Boston, Mass., 1825; d. Cambridge, Mass., 1896*), philologist. Graduated Harvard, 1846; studied at Göttingen and Berlin. Returning to Harvard, he was Boylston professor of rhetoric and oratory, 1851–76; professor of English, 1876–96. The most notable philologists of the succeeding generation were trained in his classroom, and his total influence on the culture of the nation was great. His chief works include *Poetical Works of Edmund Spenser* (1855), the best text and fullest biography of Spenser available at the time; "Observations on the Language of Chaucer" (1863) which began a new era of Chaucerian scholarship; "Observations on the Language of Gower's 'Confessio Amantis'" (1873); and the monumental *English and Scottish Popular Ballads* (1883–98).

CHILD, FRANK SAMUEL (*b. Exeter, N. Y., 1854; d. Fairfield, Conn., 1922*), Congregational clergyman. Pastor at Fairfield, 1888–1922; author of *The Colonial Parson of New England* (1896) and other works on colonial history.

CHILD, LYDIA MARIA FRANCIS (*b. Medford, Mass., 1802; d. 1880*), abolitionist. Author of the novels *Hobomok* (1824) and *The Rebels* (1825); wrote many other works representative of her diverse interests.

CHILD, RICHARD WASHBURN (*b. Worcester, Mass., 1881; d. New York, N.Y., 1935*), author, diplomat. [*Supp. 1*]

CHILD, ROBERT (*b. Northfleet, England, c. 1613; d. Ireland, 1654*), physician, Remonstrant. Among those who petitioned the General Court, 1646, for the rights of freemen to be established in Massachusetts. [*Supp. 1*]

CHILDE, JOHN (*b. West Boylston, Mass., 1802; d. Springfield, Mass., 1858*), pioneer civil engineer. Graduated West Point, 1827. Solved many engineering problems in establishment of new railroad lines.

CHILDS, CEPHAS GRIER (*b. Plumstead Township, Pa., 1793; d. 1871*), engraver, editor, publisher. Pioneered in establishing lithography on a commercial basis in this country. Edited several Philadelphia commercial periodicals.

CHILDS, GEORGE WILLIAM (*b. Baltimore, Md., 1829; d. Philadelphia, Pa., 1894*), publisher. Successful in the book trade, and as proprietor of the Philadelphia *Public Ledger*, 1864–94.

CHILDS, THOMAS (*b. Pittsfield, Mass., 1796; d. Fort Brooke, Fla., 1853*), soldier. Served with distinction in War of 1812, the second Seminole War and the Mexican War.

CHILTON, WILLIAM PARIS (*b. near Elizabethtown, Ky., 1810; d. Montgomery, Ala., 1871*), jurist. Chief justice of Alabama Supreme Court 1852–56; influential member of both regular Confederate Congresses.

CHINI, EUSEBIO FRANCISCO. [See KINO, EUSEBIO FRANCISCO, 1645–1711.]

CHIPMAN, DANIEL (*b. Salisbury, Conn., 1765; d. 1850*), lawyer. Active in Vermont politics; influential in five constitutional conventions. Author of *The Life of Hon. Nathaniel Chipman* (1846), his brother.

CHIPMAN, NATHANIEL (*b. Salisbury, Conn., 1752; d. Tinmouth, Vt., 1843*), jurist. Graduated Yale, 1777; practiced law in Tinmouth, Vt. In 1787 became assistant justice of the supreme court of Vermont; served as chief justice of the court at three different times. Was prominent in Bennington constitutional convention (1791) and helped to negotiate for admittance of Vermont to the Union. Served as federal judge in the district of Vermont, 1791–93; as U.S. Senator, 1798–1804. As member of a committee to revise the state code, he was largely responsible for the statutes of 1797.

CHIPMAN, WARD (*b. Marblehead, Mass., 1754; d. New Brunswick, Canada, 1824*), loyalist. Served with British forces in the Revolution; removed to New Brunswick, 1784, where he practiced law and served as solicitor-general and as a judge of the supreme court.

CHISHOLM, HUGH JOSEPH (*b. Niagara Falls, Canada, 1847; d. 1912*), paper manufacturer. Organized Maine paper manufacturing firms; was a founder of International Paper Co., 1898.

CHISOLM, ALEXANDER ROBERT (*b. Beaufort, S.C., 1834; d. 1910*), Confederate soldier, financier. Removed to New York City, 1869; was stock broker and founder of *Financial and Mining Record*.

CHISOLM, JOHN JULIAN (*b. Charleston, S.C., 1830; d. Petersburg, Va., 1903*), surgeon, oculist. Author of Confederate *Manual of Military Surgery* (1861); University of Maryland professor, 1869–93; specialist in ophthalmology.

CHISUM, JOHN SIMPSON (*b. Hardeman Co., Tenn., 1824; d. Eureka Springs, Ark., 1884*). One of the first (1866) Texas cattlemen to shift his operations to the ranges of New Mexico. Despite frequent Indian raids and the depredations of white "rustlers," Chisum prospered; he established himself at South Spring, N. Mex., 1873. Probably the largest individual cattle owner in the United States, for many years he was known as the "cattle king of America." His part, if any, in the famous Lincoln County War of 1878–79 is a matter of dispute. He later became a leader in the movement to end lawlessness in New Mexico.

CHITTENDEN, HIRAM MARTIN (*b. Yorkshire, N.Y., 1858; d. Seattle, Wash., 1917*), military engineer, historian. Graduated West Point, 1884. Engineering service in Yellowstone National Park awakened his interest in western history and topography and a desire to preserve the Park area. Despite an arduous professional life he was author of important historical studies which include *The Yellowstone National Park* (1895); *The American Fur Trade of the Far West* (1902); and *The History of Early Steamboat Navigation on the Missouri River* (1903).

CHITTENDEN, MARTIN (*b. Salisbury, Conn., 1763; d. Williston, Vt., 1840*). Son of Thomas Chittenden. Federalist governor of Vermont, 1813–15.

CHITTENDEN, SIMEON BALDWIN (*b. Guilford, Conn., 1814; d. Brooklyn, N.Y., 1889*), merchant. Student of economics and theorist on currency problems.

CHITTENDEN, THOMAS (*b. East Guilford, Conn., 1730; d. 1797*), politician. In 1774 received a grant of land in Williston, Vt. Was prominent in the conventions which culminated in formation of the State of Vermont; in 1777 helped draw up declaration for the new state and, with others, unsuccessfully petitioned the Continental Congress for recognition; was president of the Council of Safety. Helped Ira Allen draw up Vermont constitution. In 1778 became first Vermont governor, an office he held, except for the year 1789–90, until 1797. Participated with Ethan Allen and others in secret negotiations with General Haldimand, commander of British forces in Canada, 1780–83.

CHIVERS, THOMAS HOLLEY (*b. near Washington, Ga., 1809; d. Decatur, Ga., 1858*), poet. Friend and rival of Edgar Allan Poe. His visionary and prolific output includes: *The Lost Pleiad and Other Poems* and *Eonchs of Ruby* (1850).

CHOATE, JOSEPH HODGES (*b. Salem, Mass., 1832; d. New York, N.Y., 1917*), lawyer, diplomat. Graduated Harvard, 1852; Harvard Law School, 1854. Became a partner in Butler, Evarts and Southmayd, New York law firm; handled a wide variety of cases in his long and successful career. Probably his most important arguments were in the Income Tax cases before the United States Supreme Court, 1895. Choate was a leader in cultural and humanitarian activities, an active Republican, a prominent "club man," and a celebrated after-dinner speaker. As ambassador to Great Britain, 1899–1905, he was noted for his success in settling Alaskan boundary question and in abrogating Clayton-Bulwer treaty; also for good will he gained for the United States. He was prominent at the Second Hague Conference of 1907 where he served as head of the American delegation.

CHOATE, RUFUS (*b. Hog Island, Mass., 1799; d. Halifax, Canada, 1859*), lawyer, statesman. Graduated Dartmouth, 1819; admitted to bar, 1822; began his law practice in Danvers, Mass. With Daniel Webster, Everett, and Cushing organized Whig party in Massachusetts, and served out Webster's term in U.S. Senate, 1841–45. In 1850, he defended Webster's position on the Compromise, and in 1855 denounced the Republican party as "sectional" and "anti-Union." Choate's fame rests on his oratorical skill and on his eminent leadership of the bar. Few American lawyers have ever been more talked about; as a cross-examiner and an advocate he has had no superior.

CHOPIN, KATE O'FLAHERTY (*b. St. Louis, Mo., 1851; d. 1904*), author. Noted for interpretations of the Creoles in *Bayou Folk* (1894), *The Awakening* (1899), and other books.

CHORPENNING, GEORGE (*b. Somerset, Pa., 1820; d. 1894*), pioneer western mail man. Operated mail service from Utah to the Pacific coast, 1851–60, under conditions of great hardship.

CHOUART, MEDART. [See GROSSEILLIERS, MEDART CHOUART, SIEUR DES, 1621?–1698?]

CHOUTEAU, AUGUSTE. [See CHOUTEAU, RENÉ AUGUSTE, 1749–1829.]

CHOUTEAU, AUGUSTE PIERRE (*b. St. Louis, Mo., 1786; d. near Fort Gibson, I.T., 1838*), fur trader, frontier soldier. Son of Jean Pierre Chouteau.

CHOUTEAU, JEAN PIERRE (*b. New Orleans, La., 1758; d. St. Louis, Mo., 1849*), fur trader. U.S. Agent for the Osages; co-founder of Saint Louis Missouri Fur Co., 1809, with Manuel Lisa, William Clark *et al.*

CHOUTEAU, PIERRE (*b. St. Louis, Mo., 1789; d. St. Louis, 1865*), merchant, fur trader, financier. Son of Jean Pierre Chouteau.

CHOUTEAU, RENÉ AUGUSTE (*b. New Orleans, La., 1749; d. St. Louis, Mo., 1829*), trader, assistant to Pierre Laclede in founding of St. Louis. Commanded party beginning construction of St. Louis, early in 1764; derived fortune from trading, especially with Osage Indians; served as territorial justice, colonel of St. Louis militia, chairman of board of trustees of town of St. Louis. Negotiated several Indian treaties as federal commissioner. Described as "a man of incorruptible integrity," he became St. Louis' wealthiest citizen and largest landholder.

CHOVET, ABRAHAM (*b. London, England, 1704; d. Philadelphia, Pa., 1790*), surgeon, anatomist. Came to Philadelphia, *ante* 1774, where he practiced successfully and taught anatomy.

CHRISTIAN, WILLIAM (*b. Staunton, Va., c. 1743; d. near Jeffersonville, Ind., 1786*), soldier, politician. Member of Virginia Committee of Safety; led punitive expeditions against the Cherokee and other Indian tribes.

CHRISTIANCY, ISAAC PECKHAM (*b. Johnstown, N.Y., 1812; d. Monroe, Mich., 1890*), lawyer. Removed to Michigan, 1836. Judge of state supreme court, 1858–74; U.S. senator, Republican, 1874–79.

CHRISTY, DAVID (*b. 1802*), anti-slavery writer, geologist. As agent of American Colonization Society in Ohio, advocated Negro emigration to Liberia; author of the important study *Cotton Is King* (1855).

CHRISTY, EDWIN P. (*b. Philadelphia, Pa., 1815; d. New York, N.Y., 1862*), minstrel. Originated the Christy Minstrels at Buffalo, N.Y., 1842; perfected "blackface" or modern Negro minstrelsy.

CHRYSLER, WALTER PERCY (*b. Wamego, Kans., 1875; d. Great Neck, N.Y., 1940*), automobile manufacturer. After high school graduation, became a railroad mechanic and by 1912 was works manager of the American Locomotive Co. That same year, he joined the Buick Motor Co. as works manager at $6,000 a year. His practical talents applied to a rapidly expanding industry were spectacularly successful; he became president of Buick in 1916 at $500,000 a year. Leaving Buick in 1920 he reorganized and became president of the Maxwell Motor Car Co., producing in 1924 the popular car bearing his name. In 1925 Maxwell became the Chrysler Corporation, purchasing Dodge Brothers in 1928. By 1935, when Chrysler retired, his company was second in the industry. [*Supp. 2*]

CHURCH, ALONZO (*b. near Brattleboro, Vt., 1793; d. near Athens, Ga., 1862*), educator. Graduated Middlebury College, 1816; effective president of University of Georgia, 1829–59.

CHURCH, BENJAMIN (*b. Plymouth, Mass., 1639; d. near Little Compton, R.I., 1718*), soldier. As captain of a Plymouth company, fought in King Philip's War; was wounded at the "Great Swamp Fight," 1675, and ambushed Philip near Mount Hope (Bristol, R.I.), 1676. Thereafter, he served occasionally as magistrate and selectman; also, during King William's and Queen Anne's wars, as major and colonel in five raids against the French and Indians in Maine and Nova Scotia. Retired from active service in 1704.

CHURCH, BENJAMIN (*b. Newport, R.I., 1734; d. at sea, 1778?*), physician, traitor, author. Grandson of Benjamin Church (1639–1718). Graduated Harvard, 1754. High in the councils of the patriots and an associate of John Adams and Joseph Warren, Church was a paid informant of the British authorities in Boston. Appointed director and chief physician of the American army hospital at Cambridge, Mass., 1775, he was detected in cipher correspondence with the enemy and was court-martialed in October of that year.

CHURCH, FREDERICK EDWIN (*b. Hartford, Conn., 1826; d. New York, N.Y., 1900*), landscape painter. A pupil of Thomas Cole. Chief among his works, "The Heart of the Andes" (1859, exhibited) and "Niagara Falls" (1857).

CHURCH, FREDERICK STUART (*b. Grand Rapids, Mich., 1842; d. 1924*), painter, illustrator.

CHURCH, GEORGE EARL (*b. New Bedford, Mass., 1835; d. London, England, 1910*), civil engineer, explorer, writer. Authority on Latin American geography and history.

CHURCH, IRVING PORTER (*b. Ansonia, Conn., 1851; d. Ithaca, N.Y., 1931*), educator. Professor of civil engineering, Cornell University, 1876–1916; author of textbooks on engineering. [*Supp. 1*]

CHURCH, JOHN ADAMS (*b. Rochester, N.Y., 1843; d. 1917*), metallurgist. Graduated Columbia, School of Mines, 1867. Improved smelter techniques; introduced American mining methods in China.

CHURCH, PHARCELLUS (*b. Seneca, N.Y., 1801; d. 1886*), Baptist clergyman. Held pastorates in Rochester, N.Y., Boston, Mass., and Brooklyn, N.Y. Wrote theological works and was active in religious journalism.

CHURCH, WILLIAM CONANT (*b. Rochester, N.Y., 1836; d. 1917*), editor. Son of Pharcellus Church. Co-founder and editor of *Army and Navy Journal* (1863) and *Galaxy Magazine* (1866).

CHURCHILL, THOMAS JAMES (*b. Jefferson Co., Ky., 1824; d. 1905*), planter, lawyer, Confederate soldier. Removed to Arkansas, 1848. Directed defense of Arkansas Post, 1862; elected Democratic governor of Arkansas, 1880.

CHURCHILL, WILLIAM (*b. Brooklyn, N.Y., 1859; d. 1920*), philologist, ethnologist. Graduated Yale, 1882. Began study of Polynesian languages as consul-general to Samoa, 1896–99. Author of *Polynesian Wanderings* (1910).

CHURCHMAN, WILLIAM HENRY (*b. Baltimore, Md., 1818; d. 1882*), educator of the blind. A superior administrator, he did his best work at Indiana Institution for the Education of the Blind.

CILLEY, JOSEPH (*b. Nottingham, N.H., 1734; d. Nottingham, 1799*), Revolutionary soldier, judge, politician. As major-general of militia, quashed New Hampshire rebellion of 1786.

CIST, CHARLES (*b. St. Petersburg, Russia, 1738; d. Bethlehem, Pa., 1805*), printer, publisher. Born Charles Thiel; changed name on emigration to Philadelphia, Pa., 1769. Published Paine's *The American Crisis* (1776) and other important works. Helped organize Lehigh Coal Mine Company, 1792.

CIST, CHARLES (*b. Philadelphia, Pa., 1792; d. College Hill, O., 1868*), merchant, editor. Son of Charles Cist (1738–1805). Published statistical and historical studies of Cincinnati and Ohio.

CIST, HENRY MARTYN (*b. Cincinnati, O., 1839; d. Rome, Italy, 1902*), Union soldier, lawyer, military historian. Son of Charles Cist (1792–1868). Author of *The Army of the Cumberland* (1882).

CIST, JACOB (*b. Philadelphia, Pa., 1782; d. Wilkes-Barre, Pa., 1825*), naturalist, anthracite coal pioneer, inventor. Son of Charles Cist (1738–1805). Postmaster of Wilkes-Barre; did geological and botanical studies in that area; tried unsuccessfully to promote use of anthracite coal.

CLAFLIN, HORACE BRIGHAM (*b. Milford, Mass., 1811; d. 1885*), merchant. Pioneer in manufacturing own goods for jobbing to retailers; founder of H. B. Claflin and Co., New York, N.Y., 1843.

CLAFLIN, JOHN (*b. Brooklyn, N.Y., 1850; d. Morristown, N.J., 1938*), merchant. Son of Horace B. Claflin. Headed H. B. Claflin Co., 1885–1914. [Supp. 2]

CLAFLIN, TENNESSEE (*1845–1923*). [*See* WOODHULL, VICTORIA, 1838–1927.]

CLAFLIN, WILLIAM (*b. Milford, Mass., 1818; d. 1905*), shoe manufacturer. Republican governor of Massachusetts, 1869–71.

CLAGETT, WYSEMAN (*b. Bristol, England, 1721; d. Litchfield, N.H., 1784*), lawyer. Served as King's Attorney for New Hampshire, 1765–69; during the Revolution was active in provincial congresses and the Committee of Public Safety and was influential in drafting the New Hampshire constitution. Solicitor-general of New Hampshire, 1781–84.

CLAGHORN, GEORGE (*b. Chilmark, Mass., 1748; d. Seekonk, R.I., 1824*), Revolutionary soldier, shipbuilder. Built first American whaler to double Cape Horn; was naval constructor of frigate *Constitution*.

CLAIBORNE, JOHN FRANCIS HAMTRAMCK (*b. near Natchez, Miss., 1807; d. 1884*), congressman, historian. Edited Democratic newspapers in Mississippi and Louisiana. Author of *Life and Times of Sam Dale* (1860), a life of John A. Quitman, and an unfinished history of Mississippi.

CLAIBORNE, NATHANIEL HERBERT (*b. Sussex Co., Va., 1777; d. Franklin Co., Va., 1859*), politician. Congressman, Democrat, from Virginia, 1825–37; an opponent of governmental waste.

CLAIBORNE, WILLIAM (*b. Westmoreland Co., England, c. 1587; d. c. 1677*), colonist. Appointed surveyor for colony of Virginia, 1621; became secretary of state and a member of the Council. Opposed Lord Baltimore's claims to land within the boundaries of the 1609 Virginia Company grant, and established himself as trader on Kent Island in Chesapeake Bay, 1631. Unsuccessfully resisted Lord Baltimore's claim to Kent Island. Exploiting anti-Catholic feelings in Maryland, Claiborne incited insurrection and held province from October 1644 to December 1646, and was member of a Parliamentary commission for government of Chesapeake Bay plantations, 1652–57.

CLAIBORNE, WILLIAM CHARLES COLES (*b. Sussex Co., Va., 1775; d. 1817*), lawyer, statesman. Member of Tennessee constitutional convention and judge of state supreme court. Congressman, Democratic-Republican, from Tennessee, 1797–1801; governor of Mississippi Territory, 1801–03, and of Louisiana, 1804–16. Unfamiliar with local customs and sentiment, Claiborne encountered much opposition despite his evident honesty and kindness; he also had difficulty with Andrew Jackson during defense of New Orleans in War of 1812. Elected to the U.S. Senate, January, 1817, he died before taking office.

CLAP, THOMAS (*b. Scituate, Mass., 1703; d. 1767*), Congregational clergyman. Graduated Harvard, 1722. A rigid Calvinist and a stern disciplinarian, he was elected president of Yale in 1739 and served until his resignation in 1766.

CLAPP, ASA (*b. Mansfield, Mass., 1762; d. Portland, Maine, 1848*), shipmaster, merchant.

CLAPP, CHARLES HORACE (*b. Boston, Mass., 1883; d. 1935*), geologist. President, Montana State University, 1921–35. [*Supp. 1*]

CLAPP, GEORGE ALFRED. [See DOCKSTADER, LEW, 1856–1924.]

CLAPP, WILLIAM WARLAND (*b. Boston, Mass., 1826; d. Boston, 1891*), journalist, author. Edited *Boston Journal;* published *A Record of the Boston Stage* (1853); wrote and adapted plays.

CLARK, ABRAHAM (*b. near Elizabethtown, N.J., 1726; d. near Elizabethtown, 1794*), surveyor, lawyer, farmer, signer of the Declaration of Independence. Member of New Jersey provincial congress, 1775, and of Continental Congress, 1776, he was thrice rechosen as a New Jersey representative with interim service in the state legislature. Democratic in theory and practice, he served with ability as U.S. congressman, 1791–94.

CLARK, ALVAN (*b. Ashfield, Mass., 1804; d. 1887*), portrait painter, astronomer, renowned maker of astronomical lenses.

CLARK, ALVAN GRAHAM (*b. Fall River, Mass., 1832; d. 1897*), maker of astronomical lenses, astronomer. Son of Alvan Clark. Discovered Sirius companion; produced 40-inch lenses of Yerkes telescope.

CLARK, ARTHUR HAMILTON (*b. Boston, Mass., 1841; d. Newburyport, Mass., 1922*), master mariner, historian. Sailed on every ocean. Lloyd's New York agent, 1895–1920. Author of *The Clipper Ship Era* (1910) and other authoritative works.

CLARK, CHAMP (*b. near Lawrenceburg, Ky., 1850; d. 1921*), lawyer, politician. Graduated Bethany College, 1873. Practiced law in Kansas and Missouri; edited local Democratic newspapers; sat in Missouri legislature, 1889–91. Congressman, Democrat, from Missouri, 1893–1921 (except for 1895–97); speaker of the House, 1911–19. In 1912 lost Democratic presidential nomination to Woodrow Wilson after 14th ballot. Opposed Selective Draft Act of 1917; was minority leader in 1919–21 term.

CLARK, CHARLES (*b. Cincinnati, O., 1810; d. 1877*), planter, Confederate brigadier-general. Removed to Mississippi, c. 1831. Crippled in battle, 1862, he was elected governor of Mississippi and served until May, 1865.

CLARK, CHARLES EDGAR (*b. Bradford, Vt., 1843; d. 1922*), naval officer. Commanded U.S.S. *Oregon* on its dash around Cape Horn, 1898.

CLARK, CHARLES HEBER (*b. Berlin, Md., 1847; d. Conshohocken, Pa., 1915*), journalist, humorist. Under pseudonym "Max Adeler," wrote *Out of the Hurly Burly* (1874) and other books.

CLARK, CHARLES HOPKINS (*b. Hartford, Conn., 1848; d. Hartford, 1926*), editor. Long associated with the *Hartford Courant;* editor, 1900–26.

CLARK, DANIEL (*b. Sligo, Ireland, 1766; d. 1813*), merchant. Came to New Orleans, 1786; prospered in river and sea trade; as consul at New Orleans was associated with James Wilkinson in his intrigues. Elected delegate to Congress from Orleans Territory, 1806, he served one term. He was author of *Proofs of the Corruption of Gen. James Wilkinson* (1809).

CLARK, DANIEL (*b. Stratham, N.H., 1809; d. 1891*), politician, jurist. U.S. senator, Republican, from New Hampshire, 1857–66; vigorously opposed slavery and secession. Federal judge, district of New Hampshire, 1866–91.

CLARK, FRANCIS EDWARD (*b. Aylmer, Canada, 1851; d. 1927*), Congregational clergyman. As pastor in Portland, Maine, organized the Christian Endeavor Society, 1881.

CLARK, GEORGE ROGERS (*b. near Charlottesville, Va., 1752; d. near Louisville, Ky., 1818*), soldier. Trained as a surveyor; in 1773 explored down the Ohio River; in 1774 took part in Dunmore's War and surveyed for the Ohio Company along the Kentucky River. Active in opposition to speculators who wished to make Kentucky a proprietary colony. Commanded Kentucky militia at opening of Revolution. Made plan in 1778 to attack and take over the Illinois country; by August his little army of 175 men had captured Kaskaskia, Cahokia and Vincennes. Clark then stopped a British counter-offensive which had reached Vincennes, and made the English force surrender. During 1779 and 1780 he consolidated his gains and prevented the English from recapturing the Illinois country, the Falls of the Ohio (Louisville), Pittsburgh and Fort Cumberland. He also marched to the relief of St. Louis and Cahokia, and defeated a force of British and Indians at Piqua. The war in the West continued after Cornwallis's surrender, and Clark, as Virginia brigadier-general, won another encounter with the Shawnees at Chillicothe in November 1782. Clark's military dominance over the Northwest country was a prime factor in confirming its cession to the United States in the 1783 treaty of Paris.

After the war Clark served on the Board of Commissioners to supervise land allotment in the Illinois grant to his former soldiers, and on a commission concluding a treaty with the Indians. In 1786 during an unsuccessful expedition against the Wabash tribes, Clark seized goods brought to Vincennes by Spanish traders. This act was utilized by James Wilkinson, former Continental brigadier-general, to discredit Clark who stood in Wilkinson's path toward preferment in Kentucky. Clark lost the support of Virginia and the national government. He was prevented (1793) by Washington from enlisting in an expedition on behalf of France for the conquest of Louisiana. On the failure of another (1798) military project on behalf of the French, he returned to Louisville, and in 1803 went to live at Clarksville on the Indiana side of the Ohio River where he spent his time supervising land apportionment and running a grist mill. After a stroke of paralysis and the loss of one leg, he returned to live with his sister at Locust Grove near Louisville. His own account of the conquest of the Northwest is to be found in a *Memoir* which he wrote in 1791.

CLARK, GEORGE WHITEFIELD (*b. South Orange, N.J., 1831; d. 1911*), Baptist clergyman. Author of *Clark's People's Commentary* on the New Testament.

CLARK, GREENLEAF (*b. Plaistow, N.H., 1835; d. Lamanda Park, Calif., 1904*), railroad lawyer, practicing in St. Paul, Minn., 1858–88.

CLARK, HENRY JAMES (*b. Easton, Mass., 1826; d. 1873*), zoologist, botanist. Pupil of Asa Gray and Agassiz; excelled in histological research. Author of *Mind in Nature* (1865), and an associate with Agassiz in *Contributions to the Natural History of the United States* (1857–62).

CLARK, HORACE FRANCIS (*b. Southbury, Conn., 1815; d. 1873*), lawyer, banker. *Post* 1857, became a heavy investor in railroads and was associated with the ventures of his father-in-law, Commodore Vanderbilt.

CLARK, JAMES (*b. Bedford Co., Va., 1779; d. 1839*), lawyer, jurist. Removed to Kentucky when a boy. Judge, circuit court of Kentucky, 1817–24; active in Whig party, he was governor of Kentucky, 1836–39.

CLARK, JOHN (*b. Edgecombe Co., N.C., 1766; d. St. Andrew's Bay, Fla., 1832*), soldier. Son of Elijah Clarke. Governor of Georgia, 1819–23; leader of frontier people against the Troup faction of wealthy planters.

CLARK, JOHN BATES (*b. Providence, R.I., 1847; d. New York, N.Y., 1938*), economist. Attended Brown University and Amherst College, graduating from Amherst, 1872. He had planned to enter the ministry; instead he did advanced work in economics in Germany, then taught economics at Carleton, Smith and Amherst colleges before joining, 1895, the faculty of Columbia University, where he remained until his retirement in 1923.

Clark's first book, *The Philosophy of Wealth* (1886), reflected his concern with ethical values and contained in germinal form the principles of his formal economic analysis. These principles were definitively outlined in his most important book, *The Distribution of Wealth* (1899), which confirmed his position as the premier original economic theorist of America. Clark's "marginal utility" theory was founded on the following premises: 1) a sharp distinction between economic statics and economic dynamics, the first being used as a means to the eventual goal of dynamic analysis; 2) the universal applicability of the marginal analysis to both labor and capital; 3) a distinction between capital and capital goods, capital being a fund perpetuated and made mobile by replacement of capital goods, (labor being a somewhat similar mobile fund); 4) the identification of normal wages with the marginal product of labor and normal interest with the marginal product of capital; 5) the identification of profits and losses which depart from this norm as dynamic phenomena, profit being a reward for productive improvements; 6) the basing of all these results on free and fair competition, an organic social process which, in an effort to offer the buyer more, must improve production, thus keeping the economy fluid and serving as the most powerful driving force for progress.

Other books by Clark include *The Control of Trusts* (1901), *Essentials of Economic Theory* (1907), *Social Justice Without Socialism* (1914) and *A Tender of Peace* (1935). Though a symbol of conservatism in his later years, the logic and incisiveness of his economic writings exerted a wide influence. [Supp. 2]

CLARK, JONAS (*b. Newton, Mass., 1730 o.s.; d. Lexington, Mass., 1805*), Congregational clergyman, patriot. Pastor at Lexington, 1755–1805; advisor of Samuel Adams and John Hancock.

CLARK, JONAS GILMAN (*b. Hubbardston, Mass., 1815; d. Worcester, Mass., 1900*), merchant. Founder of Clark University, Worcester, Mass., 1887.

CLARK, JOSEPH SYLVESTER (*b. South Plymouth, Mass., 1800; d. 1861*), Congregational clergyman. Author of *A Historical Sketch of the Congregational Churches of Massachusetts* (1858).

CLARK, LEWIS GAYLORD (*b. Otisco, N.Y., 1808; d. Piermont, N.Y., 1873*). Twin brother of Willis G. Clark. Editor of the *Knickerbocker Magazine*, 1834–61; author of *Knick-Knacks from an Editor's Table* (1852).

CLARK, MYRON HOLLEY (*b. Naples, N.Y., 1806; d. 1892*), politician, businessman. Governor of New York, 1854–58; elected by a coalition of Whigs, Free-soilers and Prohibitionists which is said to have originated the Republican party in New York.

CLARK, SHELDON (*b. Oxford, Conn., 1785; d. Oxford, 1840*), farmer. A notable benefactor to Yale; founded Clark Professorship of Philosophy there.

CLARK, THOMAS MARCH (*b. Newburyport, Mass., 1812; d. Newport, R.I., 1903*), Episcopal clergyman.

Graduated Yale, 1831; ordained in Episcopal Church, 1836; consecrated Bishop of Rhode Island, 1854.

CLARK, WALTER (*b. Halifax Co., N.C., 1846; d. 1924*), Confederate soldier, jurist. Judge, North Carolina superior court, 1885–88; supreme court, 1889–1924. Served as chief justice, 1902–24.

CLARK, WALTER LEIGHTON (*b. Philadelphia, Pa., 1859; d. Stockbridge, Mass., 1935*), mechanical engineer, art patron. Founder, Grand Central Galleries, New York City. [Supp. 1]

CLARK, WILLIAM (*b. Caroline Co., Va., 1770; d. St. Louis, Mo., 1838*), explorer, Indian agent. Brother of George Rogers Clark. Moved with his family to Louisville, Ky., 1785; participated in military expeditions against marauding Indians. After St. Clair's defeat, 1791, Clark enlisted for regular service and was commissioned as lieutenant of infantry, 1792. He served under General Wayne, commanded a supply party to the Chickasaw Indians, was stationed at Vincennes and Cincinnati, participated in the battle of Fallen Timbers and was sent on a truce mission to the Spanish forces at Natchez. He resigned from the army in 1796 and traveled widely on behalf of his brother George Rogers Clark, whose Revolutionary accounts Virginia refused to settle. In 1803 he accepted offer of Meriwether Lewis to join in an expedition to explore the continent and find a route to the Pacific Ocean. The expedition set out on May 14, 1804, up the Missouri River; wintered among the Mandans in North Dakota, and in 1805 ascended the upper Missouri, crossed the continental divide, and followed the Columbia to its mouth. Retracing their route overland, they discovered other mountain passes and returned to St. Louis, September 23, 1806. Clark contributed to the success of the expedition his frontier experience, his map-drawing skill and his ability to sketch birds, fish, and other animals.

Appointed brigadier-general of the militia for Louisiana (later Missouri) Territory and superintendent of Indian affairs at St. Louis, Clark made his home there for the rest of his life. As governor of Missouri Territory he was in charge of Indian defense during the War of 1812; after the war he successfully reconciled the Western Indians, appointed agents and factors and, together with Governor Lewis Cass, negotiated Indian treaty of Prairie du Chien, 1825.

CLARK, WILLIAM ANDREWS (*b. Fayette Co., Pa., 1839; d. 1925*), merchant, mine operator. Removed to Iowa, 1856; worked in Colorado and Montana gold mines; operated mining-town stores. *Post* 1872, invested profits in mining claims at Butte, Mont., and built stamp mills and smelters. Represented mining interests in Montana politics and feuded with his fellow Democrat Marcus Daly. A refined but coldly practical man, he built up one of the West's greatest mining businesses and served as U.S. senator from Montana, 1901–07.

CLARK, WILLIAM BULLOCK (*b. Brattleboro, Vt., 1860; d. North Haven, Maine, 1917*), geologist. Graduated Amherst, 1884; Ph.D., Munich, 1887. Taught geology, Johns Hopkins, 1887–1917; Maryland State Geologist, 1896–1917.

CLARK, WILLIAM SMITH (*b. Ashfield, Mass., 1826; d. 1886*), Union soldier, scientist. President, Massachusetts Agricultural College, 1867–79.

CLARK, WILLIAM THOMAS (*b. Norwalk, Conn., 1831; d. 1905*), Union soldier, lawyer. Practiced law, Davenport, Iowa, 1856–61; served in Western theatre of Civil War; congressman, Republican, from Texas, 1869–72.

CLARK, WILLIS GAYLORD (*b. Otisco, N.Y., 1808; d. Philadelphia, Pa., 1841*), poet, editor. Twin brother of Lewis G. Clark. His literary remains and poems were edited by his brother.

CLARKE, Sir CASPAR PURDON (*b. Richmond, Ireland, 1846; d. 1911*), architect, archeologist, art connoisseur. Director, Victoria and Albert Museum, London; Metropolitan Museum of Art, New York, 1905–10.

CLARKE, ELIJAH (*b. Edgecombe Co., N.C., 1733; d. Wilkes Co., Ga., 1799*), Revolutionary soldier. A troublesome factor on the Georgia frontier, 1787–94, involved in intrigues with the Indians, the French and the English.

CLARKE, FRANCIS DEVEREUX (*b. Raleigh, N.C., 1849; d. Flint, Mich., 1913*), educator of the deaf. Director, Arkansas Institute for the Deaf, Little Rock; State School for the Deaf, Flint, Mich., 1892–1913.

CLARKE, FRANK WIGGLESWORTH (*b. Boston, Mass., 1847; d. 1931*), geological chemist. Student of Wolcott Gibbs. Chairman of the International Committee on Atomic Weights, 1900–22; author of *The Data of Geochemistry* (1908, rev. 1924).
[*Supp. 1*]

CLARKE, GEORGE (*b. near Bath, England, 1676; d. Cheshire, England, 1760*), colonial official. Secretary of the Province of New York, 1703–43; lieutenant-governor, 1736–43.

CLARKE, HELEN ARCHIBALD (*b. Philadelphia, Pa., 1860; d. Boston, Mass., 1926*), author, editor, musician. Founder and editor of *Poet Lore*.

CLARKE, JAMES FREEMAN (*b. Hanover, N.H., 1810; d. 1888*), Unitarian clergyman. Graduated Harvard, 1829; Harvard Divinity School, 1833. As minister in Louisville, Ky., 1833–40, edited the *Western Messenger*. Pastor at Boston, Mass., of the Church of the Disciples, 1841–50, 1854 until death. He was active in behalf of temperance, woman suffrage and abolition of slavery. A Transcendentalist, his most notable characteristics were balance and wisdom.

CLARKE, JAMES PAUL (*b. Yazoo City, Miss., 1854; d. Little Rock, Ark., 1916*), lawyer. Governor of Arkansas, 1893–95; U.S. senator, Democrat, from Arkansas, 1903–16.

CLARKE, JOHN (*b. Westhorpe, England, 1609; d. Newport, R.I., 1676*), Baptist clergyman, statesman. Came to Boston, 1637, but emigrated to Rhode Island where in 1639 with William Coddington he founded Newport. Largely instrumental in securing royal charter for Rhode Island, 1663.

CLARKE, JOHN MASON (*b. Canandaigua, N.Y., 1857; d. 1925*), paleontologist. Graduated Amherst, 1877. New York State paleontologist, 1898–1925; built up New York State Museum, Albany.

CLARKE, JOHN SLEEPER (*b. Baltimore, Md., 1833; d. 1899*), distinguished comedian and manager here and in England, 1851–87. Married a daughter of Junius Brutus Booth.

CLARKE, JONAS. [See CLARK, JONAS, 1730–1805.]

CLARKE, JOSEPH IGNATIUS CONSTANTINE (*b. Kingstown, Ireland, 1846; d. 1925*), journalist. Came to America, 1868, after involvement in Irish revolutionary activities; won high reputation as editor and writer on *New York Herald* and *Morning Journal*. Publicity director, Standard Oil Co., 1906–13.

CLARKE, MARY BAYARD DEVEREUX (*b. Raleigh, N.C., 1827; d. New Bern, N.C., 1886*), author.

CLARKE, MARY FRANCIS (*b. Dublin, Ireland, 1803; d. 1887*), foundress, and first superior, of Sisters of Charity of the Blessed Virgin Mary at Philadelphia, 1833.

CLARKE, McDONALD (*b. Bath, Maine, 1798; d. Blackwell's Island, N.Y., 1842*), the "Mad Poet." A New York character, 1819–41; friend of Fitz-Greene Halleck and other writers.

CLARKE, REBECCA SOPHIA (*b. Norridgewock, Maine, 1833; d. Norridgewock, 1906*), writer of children's books under pseudonym "Sophie May." Wrote *Little Prudy* and *Dotty Dimple* stories.

CLARKE, RICHARD (*b. Boston, Mass., 1711; d. London, England, 1795*), Boston merchant, Loyalist.

CLARKE, ROBERT (*b. Annan, Scotland, 1829; d. Glendale, O., 1899*), publisher, bookseller. Operated leading Western book publishing firm in Cincinnati, O.; specialized in bibliographies of American history and archeology.

CLARKE, THOMAS BENEDICT (*b. New York, N.Y., 1848; d. New York, 1931*), art collector.
[*Supp. 1*]

CLARKE, THOMAS SHIELDS (*b. Pittsburgh, Pa., 1860; d. New York, N.Y., 1920*), sculptor, painter. Studied at Art Students' League and in Paris under Boulanger, Gérôme and others. Among his best works in sculpture are four caryatids on New York City Appellate Court Building.

CLARKE, WALTER (*b. Newport, R.I., c. 1638; d. Newport, 1714*), colonial official. Deputy governor of Rhode Island, 1679–86 and 1700–14; governor, 1676–77, 1686 and 1696–98; opposed Gov. Andros.

CLARKE, WILLIAM NEWTON (*b. Cazenovia, N.Y., 1841; d. Deland, Fla., 1912*), Baptist clergyman, educator. Author of *An Outline of Christian Theology* (1898).

CLARKSON, COKER FIFIELD (*b. Frankfort, Maine, 1811; d. Des Moines, Iowa, 1890*), editor. Settled in Iowa, 1855; editor, *Iowa State Register*, 1870–90; a pioneer in Iowa agricultural education.

CLARKSON, JOHN GIBSON (*b. Cambridge, Mass., 1861; d. Waltham, Mass., 1909*), baseball player. Pitcher for Chicago, Boston and Cleveland; with Mike Kelly, part of the $10,000 Battery.

CLARKSON, MATTHEW (*b. New York, N.Y., 1758; d. New York, 1825*), Revolutionary soldier. A leading citizen of his city; supported many public improvement societies.

CLAUSEN, CLAUS LAURITZ (*b. Aerö, Denmark; 1820; d. Paulsbo, Wash., 1892*), pioneer Lutheran clergyman. Pastor in Wisconsin, Iowa and Minnesota, 1843–85; founder of St. Ansgar, Iowa.

CLAXTON, KATE (*b. Somerville, N.J., 1848; d. New York, N.Y., 1924*), actress. Made debut in Chicago, 1869; famous as Louise in *The Two Orphans*.

CLAY, ALBERT TOBIAS (*b. Hanover, Pa., 1866; d. 1925*), Lutheran clergyman, Orientalist. Taught Assyriology at University of Pennsylvania and at Yale; noted editor of cuneiform texts.

CLAY, CASSIUS MARCELLUS (*b. Madison Co., Ky., 1810; d. 1903*), abolitionist. Son of Green Clay. Graduated Yale, 1832. Entered Kentucky politics as an advocate of internal improvements. Inspired by William Lloyd Garrison, he published the *True American*, an abolitionist paper, in Lexington, 1845. Evicted from there, he issued the paper from Cincinnati and from Louisville, where he called it the *Examiner*. Fought with distinction in the Mexican War. In 1849 built up emancipation party in Kentucky; supported Frémont and Lincoln; fought briefly in Civil War. U.S. minister to Russia, 1861–62 and 1863–69.

CLAY, CLEMENT CLAIBORNE (*b. near Huntsville, Ala., 1816; d. 1882*), lawyer. Son of Clement Comer Clay. U.S. senator, Democrat, from Alabama, 1853–61; sought unsuccessfully to conduct informal peace negotiations with the North, Canada, 1864.

CLAY, CLEMENT COMER (*b. Halifax Co., Va., 1789; d. Huntsville, Ala., 1866*), lawyer. Removed to Huntsville, 1811. Held numerous offices in Alabama; congressman, Democrat, 1829–35; governor, 1836–37; U.S. senator, 1837–41.

CLAY, EDWARD WILLIAMS (*b. Philadelphia, Pa., 1799; d. New York, N.Y., 1857*), etcher, engraver, caricaturist. Author of *Life in Philadelphia* (1828–29).

CLAY, GREEN (*b. Powhatan Co., Va., 1757; d. Kentucky, 1826*), soldier. Father of Cassius M. Clay. Removed to Kentucky c. 1777; worked as surveyor and prospered in land purchases. Served as Virginia and Kentucky legislator; as major-general, Kentucky militia, raised siege of Fort Meigs, 1813.

CLAY, HENRY (*b. Hanover Co., Va., 1777; d. Washington, D.C., 1852*), statesman. Had three years of formal schooling in a log school. When he was fourteen his family moved to Richmond where Henry worked in a retail store, in the office of the clerk of the High Court of Chancery, and as amanuensis for Chancellor George Wythe. Clay began study of law in the office of Attorney-General Robert Brooke in 1796 and within one year secured license to practice. He moved to Lexington, Kentucky, 1797, where he gained an excellent reputation as a criminal lawyer. Entered politics in 1798, when he denounced the sedition law in a speech at Lexington. Served in Kentucky legislature, 1803–06, and showed himself typically Western in his point of view. Conservative where sanctity of law and established usages were concerned, he opposed the repeal of the charter of the Kentucky Insurance Company on the ground of the inviolability of contracts, and limited the exclusion from Kentucky courts of English precedents to the period after July 4, 1776. He agreed to defend Aaron Burr and, before leaving for Washington to fill out John Adair's term in the U.S. Senate, received Burr's written statement of innocence. After being persuaded by Jefferson of Burr's guilt, he never again spoke to Burr. During 1806–07 Senate sessions Clay supported internal improvements. After serving as speaker of the Kentucky legislature, 1807–09, he returned to the Senate where he introduced resolutions praising Jefferson's embargo measures. Speaking in favor of home manufactures in 1810, he laid the foundations for his "American system." He opposed the chartering of the United States Bank as being dangerous to democratic institutions and unconstitutional (a doctrine which he later abandoned) and upheld the Perdido River as eastern boundary of the Louisiana Purchase.

Desiring to be "an immediate representative of the people," he left the U.S. Senate for the House, was elected speaker (1811) and became spokesman for the "war hawks," pushing Madison into war with Britain in 1812. In the 1814 peace negotiations at Ghent, he strongly opposed Adams' recommendations to exchange the right of free navigation on the Mississippi for the Newfoundland fisheries. He re-entered the House after his return from Ghent and served there until 1821 (as speaker until 1820). Declining offers of diplomatic posts and of the secretaryship of war, Clay nursed an ambition for the presidency which haunted him to his dying days and made his life an unending series of disappointments. He became a persistent critic of national administrations and an advocate of internal improvements, rechartering of the Bank, protection of American industries, and strong national defense. The Bank was re-chartered and the protective principle was incorporated in the tariff of 1816, but Clay's program of internal improvements was not carried out during his lifetime. He incurred the enmity of Andrew Jackson in 1819 when he attacked him for his invasion of Florida.

In the debates on the Missouri Compromise Clay saw the struggle as one for continuance of the Union of equal states, not for the extension or restriction of slavery. Looking on the danger of any extension of federal power as settled by the Compromise, Clay returned to Kentucky to look after his private affairs. Reentering the Congress, 1823, he was again House speaker. In 1824 he secured passage of the highest protective tariff enacted up to then. As a candidate in the disputed presidential election of 1824 he failed to receive enough support to be voted upon by the House. Instructed by the Kentucky legislature to cast his vote for Jackson, Clay ignored these instructions and voted for Adams, effecting Adams' election. When Adams appointed Clay secretary of state, Clay was accused of a "corrupt bargain," a charge which was to follow him throughout his career. Clay's four years as secretary of state proved uneventful and uninteresting. The 1828 victory of Jackson disheartened Clay who resented seeing a military chieftain in the White House. Re-elected to the U.S. Senate in 1831, a bitter adversary of Jackson, Clay found his bills for bank recharter and distribution of land sale proceeds vetoed by the President. Defeated as anti-Jackson candidate in the presidential election of 1832, Clay, with the aid of Calhoun, solved the South Carolina nullification crisis by securing passage for his compromise tariff bill of 1833. The next year he was instrumental in having the Senate censure Jackson for his removal of bank deposits, although in 1837 the Senate expunged the censure resolutions from the record. After Van Buren's election and the panic of 1837 Clay opposed Van Buren's subtreasury system and in so doing parted company with Calhoun. Thanks to maneuvers of Thurlow Weed, the 1840 Whig convention threw the presidential nomination to W. H. Harrison with John Tyler as running-mate. Though enraged over Weed's trickery, Clay campaigned for the Whig ticket. He rejected the secretaryship of state for himself, and in the Senate proposed as the new administration's program the repeal of the sub-treasury system, the re-chartering of the United States Bank, the distribution among the states of proceeds from public land sales and the passage

of a new tariff. When Tyler succeeded to the presidency after Harrison's death, Clay found his program rejected except for the repeal of the subtreasury system. Deeply disappointed, Clay resigned from the Senate in 1842, only to find himself nominated by several states as Whig presidential candidate for the 1844 elections. Both he and Van Buren, who expected to be the Democratic nominee, agreed to oppose the immediate annexation of Texas, but, as the Democrats were determined on expansion, Van Buren lost the nomination to Polk. Clay, who had been nominated by acclamation, then declared that slavery was not an issue in the Texas question and endorsed Texan annexation "without dishonor, without war, with the common consent of the Union, and upon just and fair terms." This maneuver lost him New York and thereby the election. He supported the war with Mexico after it was declared.

Popular enthusiasm shown him in eastern cities prompted Clay in 1848 again to announce his candidacy. But this time the Whigs, feeling that Clay could not be elected, deserted him; General Zachary Taylor was nominated and elected. Deeply worried by the rising sectional struggle, Clay returned to the Senate in 1849 and introduced his resolutions for gradual emancipation. He sought to restrain radicals of both North and South, warned the South against secession, and supported the Compromise of 1850. He spent his last years in this effort and died, in 1852, in the service of his country. He was buried in Lexington cemetery amid national mourning. No man in American public life has had more ardent supporters or more bitter enemies than Clay. Kentucky absorbed his strong Unionism, but refused to adopt his plan of emancipation. Frequently tempted to seek the pleasures of private life, he could never resist the importunities of his friends and his love of debate. Enthusiasm and warmth characterized his speaking, getting the best of his reason at times and leading him into untenable positions. He lacked the profound knowledge of Webster and the philosophical powers of Calhoun, but he excelled in his understanding of human nature, in his ability to appeal to the common reason, and in his absolute fearlessness in stating his convictions.

CLAY, JOSEPH (*b. Yorkshire, England, 1741; d. 1804*), merchant, Revolutionary officer, member of the Continental Congress. Nephew of James Habersham. Emigrated to Georgia, 1760. Prospered as Savannah, Ga., merchant and planter; a "father" of the University of Georgia.

CLAY, JOSEPH (*b. Savannah, Ga., 1764; d. Boston, Mass., 1811*), Baptist clergyman, lawyer, jurist. Son of Joseph Clay (1741–1804). Influential member of Georgia constitutional convention of 1795; pastor, First Baptist Church, Boston, 1807–09.

CLAY, MATTHEW (*b. Halifax Co., Va., 1754; d. Halifax Court House, Va., 1815*), Revolutionary soldier, planter. Congressman, (Democrat) Republican, from Virginia, 1795–1813; 1815.

CLAYPOLE, EDWARD WALLER (*b. Ross, England, 1835; d. Long Beach, Calif., 1901*), geologist, educator. Came to America, 1872. Taught at Antioch and Buchtel Colleges, Ohio; worked briefly on Geological Survey of Pennsylvania. Discovered fish remains in Pennsylvania Silurian rocks.

CLAYTON, AUGUSTIN SMITH (*b. Fredericksburg, Va., 1783; d. 1839*), lawyer. Removed as an infant to Georgia; practiced law in Athens. As Georgia circuit judge, in *Worcester vs. Georgia*, Clayton overruled Worcester's contention that Georgia lacked authority to extend its jurisdiction over the Cherokee nation. When the Supreme Court declared Georgia's position unconstitutional, Clayton voiced his objections. In 1831 he entered Congress as a Democrat and became a firm advocate of state sovereignty. The only avowed nullifier among first-rank Georgia politicians, he was an equally radical anti-Bank man. He retired from Congress in 1835.

CLAYTON, HENRY DE LAMAR (*b. Barbour Co., Ala., 1857; d. Eufaula, Ala., 1929*), lawyer. Congressman, Democrat, from Alabama, 1896–1914; U.S. district judge, 1914–29; largely responsible for the amendment to the Sherman anti-trust law which bears his name. [Supp. 1]

CLAYTON, JOHN (*b. Fulham, England, c. 1685; d. 1773*), botanist. Came to Virginia, 1705, and was clerk of Gloster Co. until his death. Collected Virginia plants; his researches were presented in Gronovius's *Flora Virginica* (1739, 1743, 1762).

CLAYTON, JOHN MIDDLETON (*b. Dagsborough, Del., 1796; d. Dover, Del., 1856*), farmer, lawyer, statesman. Studied at Yale and Litchfield law school; practiced law in Dover, Del., *post* 1819. A loyal Adams supporter, he entered the U.S. Senate as Delaware Whig in 1828, supported Jackson on nullification, but opposed him on the tariff and bank issues. Re-elected in 1834, Clayton resigned in 1836, became chief justice of Delaware. He returned to the Senate, 1845; in 1848 he supported Zachary Taylor and was appointed secretary of state. He opened up trade relations with the Orient, and with England concluded Clayton-Bulwer Treaty which provided for a neutralized international canal across Central America. Resigning office in 1850, he returned once more to the Senate, 1852.

CLAYTON, JOSHUA (*b. Cecil Co., Md., 1744; d. Bohemia Manor, Del., 1798*), physician, Revolutionary soldier. President-governor of Delaware, 1789–96; U.S. senator, 1798.

CLAYTON, POWELL (*b. Bethel Co., Pa., 1833; d. Washington, D.C., 1914*), Union soldier, planter, politician. Republican boss of Arkansas after 1868; carpet-bag governor of Arkansas, 1868–71; served also in Senate and as ambassador to Mexico.

CLAYTON, THOMAS (*b. Massey's Cross Roads, Md., 1777; d. New Castle, Del., 1854*), jurist. Delaware secretary of state, attorney-general and chief justice; a moderate, independent Whig, he served as U.S. senator, 1824–28 and 1837–47.

CLEAVELAND, MOSES (*b. Canterbury, Conn., 1754; d. Canterbury, 1806*), lawyer, Revolutionary soldier. As a director of Connecticut Land Co., supervised settlement of Cleveland, O., in Western Reserve, 1796.

CLEAVELAND, PARKER (*b. Byfield, Mass., 1780; d. Brunswick, Maine, 1858*), scientist. Graduated Harvard, 1799. Tutored mathematics and natural philosophy at Harvard, and taught at Bowdoin College, 1805–58. Wrote first American work on mineralogy and geology (1816).

CLEBURNE, PATRICK RONAYNE (*b. Cork Co., Ireland, 1828; d. Franklin, Tenn., 1864*), Confederate soldier, lawyer. Came to America, 1849, and settled in Arkansas. Commended for valor at Shiloh, Chickamauga, Missionary Ridge; rose to rank of major-general. Died in battle.

CLEMENS, JEREMIAH (*b. Huntsville, Ala., 1814; d. Huntsville, 1865*), soldier, author. Served against Cherokees, and in war for Texas independence and Mexican War. Author of *Bernard Lile* (1856), *The Rivals* (1860) and other historical novels. U.S. senator, Democrat, from Alabama, 1849–56; a strong Unionist.

CLEMENS, SAMUEL LANGHORNE (*b. Florida, Mo., 1835; d. Redding, Conn., 1910*), humorist, novelist, better known by his pseudonym "Mark Twain." Resided in Hannibal, Mo., a small town on the Mississippi River, 1839–53. On death of his father, 1847, young Clemens was apprenticed to a printer; he became expert at the trade, read widely and began to write for his brother's newspaper, published in Hannibal, and for other papers elsewhere. In 1853–54, he worked his way as a journeyman printer to St. Louis, New York, Philadelphia and back to Keokuk, Iowa, where he was employed by his brother who had left Hannibal. From Keokuk, after an abortive plan to make his fortune in South America, he set out in 1857 for New Orleans, on the way apprenticing himself to a river pilot. His four years as a pilot on the Mississippi were his "university"; they gave him an epic theme, broadened his experience of human nature, and supplied him with abundant colorful material for his later work.

When the Civil War closed the river, and after a brief experience of military life, Clemens took a post in Nevada as secretary to his brother Orion, who had been appointed secretary to the territorial governor. Turning at first to prospecting and mining, Clemens became in 1862 a reporter in Virginia City using the pseudonym "Mark Twain." So he began his true career. Having no particular literary principles, he readily adapted himself to frontier journalism in all its boisterous and burlesque phases. His ambition broadened with the arrival in Virginia City of the humorist Artemus Ward (Charles Farrar Browne), who gave him encouragement. He left for California in 1864, worked as a reporter, met Bret Harte, and in 1865 wrote the story of the "Jumping Frog" which was promptly reprinted in newspapers the country over. A local celebrity, he made a journalistic trip to the Sandwich Islands and came east on the first leg of a similar tour around the world, commissioned by a California newspaper. Characteristically changing his plans, he stopped in New York to deliver a triumphant lecture at Cooper Union and to publish his first book (*The Celebrated Jumping Frog of Calaveras County, and Other Sketches, 1867*). He then sailed to the Holy Land with a party of excursionists aboard the *Quaker City*, a trip which he described in a book which made him a national figure, *The Innocents Abroad* (1869). Through an acquaintance made on this voyage, he met and married Olivia Langdon in 1870, a marriage whose effect on the writer's art has been the subject of controversy.

Now with his roots permanently in the East, he met a popular taste for knowledge of the Old South and the Far West with works which exploited all his knowledge of, and feeling for, these two subjects. *Roughing It* (1872) was a classic account of his days in Nevada; *The Gilded Age* (1873, written in collaboration with Charles Dudley Warner) satirized contemporary life but drew on the author's recollections of his own boyhood. His turning away from satire in his next important work, *The Adventures of Tom Sawyer* (1876), has occasioned much debate among critics, but it is fair to consider that the impulse to satirize was only a part of Clemens's mental constitution. His theological, political, economic and social opinions were rough-and-ready, not grounded in any set of principles and therefore susceptible to influence by the more intricate conditions of the settled society of the East. His immense delight in life in general, his comic energy, were the determinants of what he wrote at the height of his powers (1869–89). This very robustness of his art made him an uneven writer who poured out the pages as they came and had later to decide, or have it decided for him, to what degree they required editing. The *Sketches, New and Old* (1875) and similar collections are plainly inferior to *Roughing It, The Gilded Age, Tom Sawyer, A Tramp Abroad* (1880), and *The Adventures of Huckleberry Finn* (1885), nor are these themselves of equal merit. Without much question, he touched his peak in *Huckleberry Finn* and in the first part of *Life on the Mississippi* (1883); in these works, he dealt with the river and with his own youth, two subjects about which he was pre-

eminently well informed and which employed his superior talent for humorous autobiography. His style was largely governed by his ear; as a lecturer, he had learned to fit rhythm, diction, tempo and pauses to listeners rather than readers; this in turn accounts for certain defects of taste in his work.

Despite his success, Clemens refused to confine himself to exploitation of his Mississippi experiences. *The Prince and the Pauper* (1882) takes place in Elizabethan England; *A Connecticut Yankee in King Arthur's Court* (1889) drew comedy from the presence of a modern utilitarian American in the ancient world of chivalry.

After his marriage and his settlement at Hartford, Conn., in the early seventies, Clemens had written constantly, traveled as a lecturer in Europe and through much of the United States, dabbled with the stage, invested heavily and without success in a mechanical type-setter and other speculative ventures, and had become his own publisher by putting money into the firm of Charles L. Webster & Co., which prospered for a time but failed disastrously in 1894. During the nineties, his physical strength waned and his literary output was less steady and unified. The works of this period include *The American Claimant* (1892), two sequels to *Tom Sawyer*, and *The Tragedy of Pudd'nhead Wilson* (1894); all these inclined too much to melodrama. The *Personal Recollections of Joan of Arc* (1896) expressed the quintessence of that tenderness which was as much a part of him as his earlier boisterousness and his later bitterness.

Personal tragedies now began to color his view of life. Following his bankruptcy in 1894, he set off on a lecture tour around the world whereby he was able to pay off his debts by 1898; his contact with the older, static societies of Asia, however, served to deepen his pessimism. This attitude is shown in the record of his lecture tour, *Following the Equator* (1897). His extension of this mood will be found in three works written in 1898: *The Man That Corrupted Hadleyburg* (1900); *What Is Man?* (privately printed, 1906); and *The Mysterious Stranger* (not published until 1916). They are in dialectic on about a level with Ingersoll's "village atheist" posturing, but are significant in showing how a representative American responded to his observations in a way diametrically opposite to the standard optimism of the period.

After the dark year of 1898 Clemens apparently grew in resignation, pitying rather than despising mankind. He remained a restless traveler, commented freely on contemporary matters and was an untiring public lecturer. In 1907 he wrote *Christian Science*, an attack upon what he deemed a menacing new cult, and in 1904, *Is Shakespeare Dead?*, an unimportant addition to the Baconian controversy. His wife died in 1904. During his last days he received many honors, but he cherished most the Oxford degree of Doctor of Literature, conferred in 1907. He died at his house "Stormfield" in Redding, Conn. While during his life Clemens could never correct the popular impression of him as chiefly a fun-maker, the posthumous publication of his later works and of his autobiography revealed his inner life of rage and contempt, of dissent and disillusion, of despair and pity.

CLEMENT, EDWARD HENRY (*b. Chelsea, Mass., 1843; d. Concord, Mass., 1920*), journalist. Associate editor Boston *Transcript*, 1875–81; editor, 1881–1906.

CLEMENTS, JUDSON CLAUDIUS (*b. Walker Co., Ga., 1846; d. 1917*), lawyer. Congressman, Democrat, from Georgia, 1881–91; an able and respected member of Interstate Commerce Commission, 1892–1917.

CLEMENTS, WILLIAM LAWRENCE (*b. Ann Arbor, Mich., 1861; d. Bay City, Mich., 1934*), industrialist, book collector. Gave Clements Library of Americana to the University of Michigan. [*Supp. 1*]

CLEMMER, MARY (*b. Utica, N.Y., 1839; d. Washington, D.C., 1884*), author. Her best work took the form of Washington letters to newspapers and columns on topics of public interest.

CLEMSON, THOMAS GREEN (*b. Philadelphia, Pa., 1807; d. 1888*), mining engineer, founder of Clemson College, South Carolina. Son-in-law of John C. Calhoun.

CLERC, LAURENT (*b. La Balme, France, 1785; d. 1869*), educator of the deaf. Pupil of Abbé Sicard. With Thomas H. Gallaudet, opened first American school for the deaf at Hartford, Conn., 1817.

CLEVELAND, AARON (*b. Cambridge, Mass., 1715; d. Philadelphia, Pa., 1757*), Congregational, later Episcopal, clergyman. Graduated Harvard, 1735. Pastor to several churches in New England. After ordination by Bishop of London, 1754, returned to America as missionary of Society for the Propagation of the Gospel.

CLEVELAND, BENJAMIN (*b. Prince William Co., Va., 1738; d. South Carolina, 1806*), Revolutionary soldier, frontier judge. Commanded North Carolina partisan troops.

CLEVELAND, CHAUNCEY FITCH (*b. Hampton, Conn., 1799; d. Hampton, 1887*), lawyer. Reforming Democratic governor of Connecticut, 1842–43; a war Republican, he later returned to the Democratic party.

CLEVELAND, GROVER. [See CLEVELAND, STEPHEN GROVER, 1837–1908.]

CLEVELAND, HORACE WILLIAM SHALER (*b. Lancaster, Mass., 1814; d. Hinsdale, Ill., 1900*), landscape architect. Son of Richard J. Cleveland. Worked mainly in Midwest. Among his best-known works are the Minneapolis and Omaha park systems; Natural Bridge, Va., grounds; Sleepy Hollow Cemetery, Concord, Mass.

CLEVELAND, RICHARD JEFFRY (*b. Salem, Mass., 1773; d. Danvers, Mass., 1860*), merchant navigator. Went to sea at 18; was captain at 24. The account of his extraordinary career and his feats of navigation in small sailing vessels will be found in his *Narrative of Voyages and Commercial Enterprises* (1842), a classic work on the sea.

CLEVELAND, STEPHEN GROVER (*b. Caldwell, N.J., 1837; d. Princeton, N.J., 1908*), president of the United States. Mainly self-educated, owing to early death of his father, a Presbyterian clergyman, and his consequent responsibility to care for his brothers and mother. Resident near Buffalo, N.Y., he studied law, was admitted to the bar, 1859, and became known as a careful, dependable legal workman. A Democrat by conviction, he entered politics and served as assistant district attorney and sheriff of Erie Co., N.Y. He was elected reform mayor of Buffalo in 1881, and was nominated and elected governor of New York in 1882. Stubborn honesty and independence of political control distinguished his term in office and won him the lasting enmity of Tammany Hall, the powerful New York City Democratic organization.

In 1884, since many Republicans distrusted their candidate, James G. Blaine, and would be willing to support an "unbossed" Democrat, Cleveland was nominated for the presidency. Elected after a campaign of unusual virulence and bitterness, the first Democrat to be president since the Civil War, he showed himself adamant against graft, extravagance and excessive tariff protection although he was forced to temper with expediency his own instinct for reform of the civil service. Renominated, he lost the election of 1888 to Benjamin Harrison and retired to private law practice. Popular revolt against Republican tariff policies and some adroit campaigning by his friends brought Cleveland the Democratic nomination and election in 1892.

His taking office in 1893 was coincident with a great financial panic. Firmly opposed in principle to currency inflation, he forced Congress to repeal the Sherman Silver Purchase Act, thereby alienating southern and western Democrats but stabilizing the nation's money position. The treasury surplus existing at the end of his first term had dwindled away during Harrison's administration, and Cleveland was forced to use desperate but successful means of maintaining a gold balance. Labor strife accompanied the depression of business, and he employed federal troops to repress violence. He also opposed nascent American imperialistic tendencies, refusing to permit aid to rebel movements in Hawaii and Cuba; but in a boundary dispute between England's colony of

Guiana and Venezuela, he vigorously supported the Monroe Doctrine and persuaded England to arbitrate. His painstaking, highly individual style of action was too just and fair for the bulk of his party, and in 1896 the Democrats repudiated his policies by nominating William J. Bryan. Cleveland retired to private life in Princeton, N.J., serving in important business capacities and occupying a commanding elder statesman position until his death.

CLEVENGER, SHOBAL VAIL (*b. near Middletown, O., 1812; d. at sea, 1843*), sculptor. Self-taught; worked in Cincinnati, O. His work consists almost entirely of portrait busts.

CLEVENGER, SHOBAL VAIL (*b. Florence, Italy, 1843; d. 1920*), psychiatrist. Son of Shobal V. Clevenger (1812–1843). An engineer, he turned to medicine. Author of *Comparative Physiology and Psychology* (1884) and *Spinal Concussion* (1889), a neurological classic which gave him an international reputation.

CLEWELL, JOHN HENRY (*b. Salem, N.C., 1855; d. 1922*), Moravian clergyman. Principal and president, Winston-Salem Academy and College, 1888–1909; president, Moravian Seminary and College for Women, Bethlehem, Pa., 1909–22.

CLEWS, HENRY (*b. Staffordshire, England, 1834; d. 1923*), financier. During Civil War his firm, later Henry Clews & Co., ranked second to Jay Cooke & Co. in amount of government bonds sold.

CLIFFORD, JOHN HENRY (*b. Providence, R.I., 1809; d. New Bedford, Mass., 1876*), lawyer. Served as attorney-general and governor of Massachusetts; president, Boston & Providence Railroad, 1867–76.

CLIFFORD, NATHAN (*b. Rumney, N.H., 1803; d. 1881*), jurist. A Jackson Democrat, he served as speaker in the Maine Assembly, as state attorney-general, and as congressman from Maine, 1838–43. In 1846 President Polk appointed him U.S. attorney-general; in addition to his legal duties he was entrusted with diplomatic negotiations with Mexico. He retired to the practice of law in Portland, Maine, after his recall in 1849. In 1858 he was appointed to the U.S. Supreme Court. During his 23 years of service he wrote the Court's opinion in 398 cases and penned 8 concurring and 49 dissenting opinions. His specialties were commercial and maritime law, Mexican land grants, procedure and practice. His opinions tended to draw sharp dividing lines between federal and state authority. As senior associate justice he presided over the Hayes-Tilden Electoral Commission, 1877.

CLIFFTON, WILLIAM (*b. Philadelphia, Pa., 1772; d. Philadelphia, 1799*), poet. Author of *The Group* (1796), a satiric attack on Gallatin, and other satires; his collected poems were published at New York in 1800.

CLIFTON, JOSEPHINE (*b. New York, N.Y., 1813; d. New Orleans, La., 1847*), actress. First American to star in England, 1834. N. P. Willis's *Bianca Visconti* was written for her, 1837.

CLINCH, CHARLES POWELL (*b. New York, N.Y., 1797; d. New York, 1880*), author. An associate and friend of F. G. Halleck and the "Knickerbocker" group.

CLINGMAN, THOMAS LANIER (*b. Huntersville, N.C., 1812; d. 1897*), politician, Confederate soldier. Congressman from mountain region of North Carolina, first Whig, later Democrat, 1843–45, 1847–58; U.S. senator, 1858–61. Left Whig party, 1852, over the slavery issue.

CLINTON, DeWITT (*b. Little Britain, N.Y., 1769; d. Albany, N.Y., 1828*), statesman, philanthropist, man of letters. Son of James Clinton. Graduated Columbia, 1786. Studied law, and in 1787 published letters signed "A Countryman" in the *New York Journal* opposing the proposed U.S. Constitution. He served as secretary to his uncle George Clinton, anti-Federalist New York governor, and as secretary of the board of regents and of the board of fortification. With the fall of his party in 1795 he lost his offices and turned for the time to the study of natural science. In 1797 he was elected to the state assembly, in 1798 to the state senate, and in 1801 to the governor's council of appointment. There he claimed the council members' right to propose candidates for office, rather than simply to ratify or reject the governor's nominations, and proceeded to supplant Federalist appointees with Republicans.

Appointed in 1802 to the U.S. Senate, he opposed the seizure of New Orleans, and introduced the Twelfth Amendment. In October 1803 he resigned to accept the mayoralty of New York City which he held from 1803 to 1815 with exception of two annual terms (1807–08 and 1810–11). No mayor has done more for the City. He was chief organizer of the Public School Society, 1805, the chief patron of the City's Orphan Asylum and of the City Hospital. He inspected markets and docks, quelled mobs, strengthened the City's fortifications, resisted British attempts to impress sailors in New York harbor and to blockade the Narrows, and was last mayor to preside in the mayor's court; he also served as state senator, 1806–11, and lieutenant-governor, 1811–13. The state's most powerful political leader, he broke with Gov. Morgan Lewis whom he had supported in 1804, and in 1807 supplanted him with Daniel D. Tompkins. His independence of Democratic-Republican party control won him favor with the Federalists who considered him as a possible candidate for the presidency in 1812, although they did not formally nominate him. As he had already been nominated by the Republicans of the New York legislature, his position seemed equivocal, and he was defeated by an electoral vote of 128 to 89. His consorting with Federalists cost him the confidence of his own party; he was not renominated for lieutenant-governor, and in 1815 was removed from his office of mayor.

Clinton now devoted himself to the promotion of a project for a state canal which would join the Great Lakes with the Hudson. On April 17, 1816, the legislature accepted his plan, and he was appointed to the canal commission. When he was elected governor of New York the next year, he continued active prosecution of the canal project. Believing in constructive leadership and active government, he gained the support of many Federalists during his term but at the same time built up a strong opposition among disgruntled Tammany politicians. He won the reelection for governor by only a slight margin, and did not seek a third term in 1822. When he retired he was the strongest man in New York's public life, but the weakest in partisan support. He returned to the governorship two years later, however, aided rather than hindered by the precipitate action of his enemies the "Albany Regency" who, in April 1824, had removed him from his office as canal commissioner. As governor, he took a prominent part in the celebration over completion of the Erie and Champlain canals in 1825. He had been responsible for making New York rather than New Orleans the port of the Northwest.

Clinton's achievements exceed those of the politician and statesman. He was the foremost spokesman for public education in New York and the leading promoter of Lancasterian schools in the whole country. A naturalist of real ability, he discovered a native American wheat and a new variety of fish; he published papers on pigeons, swallows, rice and other topics, as well as his *Introductory Discourse* (1814), an able summary and review of scientific knowledge in America. He was active in many scientific and literary societies. In 1806 he succeeded in removing the political disabilities of Roman Catholics in New York, and was admired as a man of liberal ideas and administrative competence. He was always inept at intrigue, rather overbearing in manner, and indifferent to his political supporters. Personally unpopular, he was disliked by Republicans for his aristocratic tastes and by Federalists for his democratic principles.

CLINTON, GEORGE (*b. England, c. 1686; d. England, 1761*), colonial official. Father of Sir Henry Clinton. In 1708 entered the British Navy in which he rose to the rank of admiral of the white squadron and, in 1757, to the position of senior flag officer. From 1741 to 1753 he served as governor of New York, proving to be a weak executive, dominated successively by Chief Justice De Lancey and Senior Councillor Cadwallader Colden, and losing control of appropriations and appointment of officers to the Assembly. His administration permanently weakened royal government in New York and increased popular control.

CLINTON, GEORGE (*b. Little Britain, N.Y., 1739; d. Washington, D.C., 1812*), Revolutionary soldier, statesman. Served as New York delegate to Second Continental Congress and brigadier-general in Continental Army. In 1777 was elected New York governor, a post which he held for six successive terms. A believer in state rights, he vigorously opposed adoption of the Constitution and wrote the famous "Cato" letters in the *New York Journal*, 1787. In 1789 and 1793 he met increasing hostility from Federalists, and in 1795 declined to stand for reelection. The Republican victory of 1800 brought Clinton back as governor, and in 1804 and 1808 he was elected vice-president of the United States.

CLINTON, GEORGE WYLIE (*b. Lancaster Co., N.C., 1859; d. 1921*), bishop of the A.M.E. Zion Church, post 1896. Edited *Afro-American Spokesman* and *Star of Zion*.

CLINTON, JAMES (*b. Ulster Co., N.Y., 1733; d. Little Britain, N.Y., 1812*), Revolutionary soldier. Brother of George Clinton (1739–1812); father of DeWitt Clinton. Defended Hudson highlands, 1777; with Gen. John Sullivan, destroyed power of Indians in upper New York state, 1779; commanded a brigade at Yorktown.

CLOPTON, DAVID (*b. Putnam Co., Ga., 1820; d. Montgomery, Ala., 1892*), jurist. Removed to Alabama, 1844; served in U.S. and Confederate Congresses, 1859–65; judge, Alabama supreme court, 1884–92.

CLOPTON, JOHN (*b. New Kent Co., Va., 1756; d. 1816*), Revolutionary soldier. Congressman, Democratic-Republican, 1795–1816, excepting the Sixth Congress when he was defeated by John Marshall.

CLOSSON, WILLIAM BAXTER (*b. Thetford, Vt., 1848; d. 1926*), painter, wood engraver.

CLOUD, NOAH BARTLETT (*b. Edgefield, S.C., 1809; d. Montgomery, Ala., 1875*), planter, politician. Removed to Alabama, 1846. Edited at Montgomery the *American Cotton Planter*, 1853–61; his work of primary importance in agricultural progress of the state.

CLOUGH, JOHN EVERETT (*b. near Frewsburg, N.Y., 1836; d. Rochester, N.Y., 1910*), Baptist clergyman. Ordained 1864, Burlington, Iowa, he worked in India as a missionary until 1905.

CLOUGH, WILLIAM PITT (*b. Freetown, N.Y., 1845; d. 1916*), lawyer. Removed to Minnesota, 1867. A close associate of James J. Hill, he was a vice-president of Northern Securities Co. and the Northern Pacific Railway.

CLYMAN, JAMES (*b. Fauquier Co., Va., 1792; d. Napa, Calif., 1881*), trapper, pioneer settler. Served as mounted ranger in War of 1812; in 1823 went to St. Louis and joined Ashley's second expedition to ascend the Missouri. Journeyed to Green River with Smith-Fitzpatrick party, 1824; thus was one of first whites to cross South Pass from the east. After further adventures in the West opened store at Danville, Ill.; served in Black Hawk war; fought Indians on Wisconsin frontier. In 1844 traveled to Oregon and California. After return to Independence, Mo., 1846, he guided an 1848 immigrant party to California; there he married and established his own ranch. His diaries and reminiscences, edited as *James Clyman, American Frontiersman* (1928), are a rich source of early Western history.

CLYMER, GEORGE (*b. Philadelphia, Pa., 1739; d. Philadelphia, 1813*), merchant, signer of Declaration of Independence and of the U.S. Constitution. As a member of Pennsylvania Council of Safety, Continental treasurer and congressman (1776–77, 1780–82), he served ably on many commissions and on the boards of war and of the treasury. His services were of particular value in financial matters. As a member of the U.S. Congress, 1789–91, he supported Washington but favored a pro-French and Jeffersonian economic policy.

CLYMER, GEORGE E. (*b. Bucks Co., Pa., 1754; d. London, England, 1834*), inventor. A carpenter and joiner, he devised a unique plow especially adapted to Pennsylvania soils, and a superior pump which was used in the construction of piers for the first permanent Schuylkill River bridge. His most important invention (1817), the "Columbian" hand-printing press, the first real American invention in printing, was the result of 16 years' effort. Its price, however, prevented its ready sale in America. In 1817 Clymer took it to England where it was widely used as well as in other countries of Europe.

COAKLEY, CORNELIUS GODFREY (*b. Brooklyn, N.Y., 1862; d. New York, N.Y., 1934*), laryngologist. [*Supp.* 1]

COALTER, JOHN. [See COLTER, JOHN, c. 1775–1813.]

COAN, TITUS (*b. Killingworth, Conn., 1801; d. 1882*), Presbyterian clergyman. Missionary to Hawaii, 1834–82.

COATES, FLORENCE EARLE (*b. Philadelphia, Pa., 1850; d. Philadelphia, 1927*), poet.

COATES, GEORGE HENRY (*b. Windsor, Vt., 1849; d. 1921*), inventor, manufacturer. At Worcester, Mass., developed large hair-clipper manufacturing plant. Patented (1892) a flexible shaft for transmission of power to drilling and grinding machinery.

COATES, SAMUEL (*b. Philadelphia, Pa., 1748; d. Philadelphia, 1830*), merchant, philanthropist. Active benefactor of Pennsylvania Hospital, overseer of Philadelphia Quaker schools and a director of First United States Bank.

COBB, ANDREW JACKSON (*b. Athens, Ga., 1857; d. 1925*), jurist, law teacher. Son of Howell Cobb. Taught at University of Georgia; was dean of Atlanta Law School. Served as associate justice of Georgia supreme court, 1896–1908. Gave decision in first U.S. "right of privacy" case.

COBB, DAVID (*b. Attleborough, Mass., 1748; d. Boston, Mass., 1830*), Revolutionary officer, judge, politician.

COBB, ELIJAH (*b. Brewster, Mass., 1768; d. Brewster, 1848*), sea captain. His colorful and typical career is to be found in his autobiography, *Elijah Cobb, a Cape Cod Skipper* (ed., 1925, by R. D. Paine).

COBB, FRANK IRVING (*b. Shawnee Co., Kans., 1869; d. 1923*), journalist. Raised in Michigan. Editorial writer, Detroit *Evening News*, 1899–1903; adviser to Joseph Pulitzer on New York *World*, 1904–11, editor-in-chief, 1911–23.

COBB, HOWELL (*b. Jefferson Co., Ga., 1815; d. New York, N.Y., 1868*), lawyer, politician. Belonged to planter-class family with long record of public service. Graduated University of Georgia, 1834; admitted to bar, 1836. Congressman, Democrat, from Georgia, 1843–51, 1855–57. Supported annexation of Texas, the Mexican War; opposed Calhoun's call for a Southern party, 1849. In 1850 led Union Democrats to victory in Georgia, but drew upon himself the relentless hatred of Southern Rights people. His greatest victory came with his 1851 election as governor on a Unionist ticket. Read out of Georgia Democratic party, he was not re-elected, returning to Congress. Efficient as secretary of the treasury, 1857–60. After Lincoln's election, advocated immediate secession and was chairman of Montgomery convention to organize Southern Confederacy. After war service as Confederate major-general, returned to law practice and opposed reconstruction policies.

COBB, JONATHAN HOLMES (*b. Sharon, Mass., 1799; d. 1882*), lawyer. Practiced in Dedham, Mass.; promoted silk manufacture in Massachusetts and established, 1837, one of earliest silk mills in the United States.

COBB, LYMAN (*b. Lenox, Mass., 1800; d. Colesburg, Pa., 1864*), educator. Wrote spelling, reading, and arithmetic textbooks. A Pestalozzian, he was author of *Evil Tendencies of Corporal Punishment* (1847).

COBB, NATHAN AUGUSTUS (*b. Spencer, Mass., 1859; d. Baltimore, Md., 1932*), nematologist, agronomist. [*Supp.* 1]

COBB, SYLVANUS (*b. Norway, Maine, 1798; d. Boston, Mass., 1866*), Universalist clergyman. Chief missionary of Universalism in Maine; published *The Christian Freeman*, 1839–62.

COBB, SYLVANUS (*b. Waterville, Maine, 1823; d. Hyde Park, Mass., 1887*), author of melodramatic popular fiction, mainly for Bonner's *New York Ledger*.

COBB, THOMAS READE ROOTES (*b. Jefferson Co., Ga., 1823; d. Fredericksburg, Va., 1862*), lawyer, Confederate soldier. Brother of Howell Cobb. Codified Georgia laws (1851); was ardent promoter of secession; a brigadier-general, he died in battle.

COBB, WILLIAM HENRY (*b. Marion, Mass., 1846; d. Boston, Mass., 1923*), Congregational clergyman, librarian. Old Testament scholar of international standing, authority on history of Congregationalism and an editor of *Journal of Biblical Literature*.

COBBETT, WILLIAM (*b. Farnham, England, 1763; d. 1835*), journalist, pseudonym "Peter Porcupine." Living in the United States as a political refugee from 1792 to 1800 and from 1817 to 1819, he was a founder of American party journalism. His anti-Jacobin pamphlets include *Observations on the Emigration of Dr. Priestley* (1794), *A Bone to Gnaw for the Democrats* (1795) and *The Life and Adventures of Peter Porcupine* (1796). In his *Political Censor,* and his newspaper *Porcupine's Gazette* (1797–1800), he upheld the Federalists and lambasted the Democrats with savage sarcasm. In 1799 he was fined for libel of Dr. Benjamin Rush, and in 1800 left for England. Returning in 1817, he settled at New Hyde Park, L.I., and devoted himself to agriculture and authorship until his return home in 1819. The major phases of his career belong to English history, in which he figures as one of the great radical pamphleteers.

COBURN, ABNER (*b. Canaan, Maine, 1803; d. 1885*), businessman, philanthropist. A land and lumber dealer, he was president of Maine Central Railroad, and served as Republican governor of Maine, 1863–66 with a non-partisan efficiency that cost him renomination.

COBURN, FOSTER DWIGHT (*b. Cold Springs, Wis., 1846; d. 1924*), agricultural editor, administrator. Removed to Kansas, 1867. Edited *Livestock Indicator;* served as secretary of Kansas State Board of Agriculture. Author of *Swine in America* (1909).

COCHRAN, ALEXANDER SMITH (*b. Yonkers, N.Y., 1874; d. Saranac Lake, N.Y., 1929*), manufacturer, philanthropist. Liberal president of Alexander Smith Carpet Co.; benefactor of many institutions including the Metropolitan Museum of Art and Yale University.

COCHRAN, JOHN (*b. Sadsbury, Pa., 1730; d. Palatine, N.Y., 1807*), physician. Practiced in New Jersey; during the Revolution served with great distinction as surgeon and director-general of Continental Army hospitals, 1777–83.

COCHRANE, ELIZABETH. [See SEAMAN, ELIZABETH COCHRANE, 1867–1922.]

COCHRANE, HENRY CLAY (*b. Chester, Pa., 1842; d. 1913*), marine corps officer, 1861–1905. Commended for service in Egypt, the Philippines and China.

COCHRANE, JOHN (*b. Palatine, N.Y., 1813; d. 1898*), lawyer, politician. Grandson of John Cochran. As congressman from New York, Democrat, 1857–61, he upheld Southern viewpoint, but in 1861 joined Union Army. Nominated for vice-president, 1864, he withdrew before election. In 1872 supported Horace Greeley.

COCKE, JOHN HARTWELL (*b. Surry Co., Va., 1780; d. 1866*), planter, publicist. Promoter of new agricultural methods in Virginia; opponent of slavery. With Jefferson and J. C. Cabell, aided founding University of Virginia.

COCKE, PHILIP ST. GEORGE (*b. Fluvanna Co., Va., 1809; d. Powhatan Co., Va., 1861*), soldier, planter. Son of John H. Cocke. Graduated West Point, 1832. Benefactor of Virginia Military Institute; brigadier-general in Confederate Army.

COCKE, WILLIAM (*b. Amelia Co., Va., 1748; d. 1828*), soldier, legislator, Indian agent. Removed *c.* 1774 to the Holston Valley frontier; a leader in Separatist "State of Franklin" movement; U.S. senator from Tennessee, 1796–97, 1799–1805.

COCKERILL, JOHN ALBERT (*b. Adams Co., O., 1845; d. Cairo, Egypt, 1896*), journalist. Managing editor, *Cincinnati Enquirer* and *Baltimore Gazette;* aid to Joseph Pulitzer on *St. Louis Post-Dispatch* and *New York World;* died as a special correspondent for *New York Herald*.

COCKRAN, WILLIAM BOURKE (*b. Co. Sligo, Ireland, 1854; d. 1923*), lawyer, orator. Came to America, *c.* 1871. A force in New York Democratic politics, although constantly in opposition; served in Congress, 1887–89, 1891–95, 1905–09, 1921–23.

COCKRELL, FRANCIS MARION (*b. near Columbus, Mo., 1834; d. 1915*), Confederate soldier, lawyer. U.S. senator, Democrat, from Missouri, 1875–1905.

CODDINGTON, WILLIAM (*b. Boston, England, 1601; d. Newport, R.I., 1678*), governor of Aquidneck. Came to Massachusetts, 1630. Protested treatment of Anne Hutchinson, 1637; withdrew, 1638, to Aquidneck (R.I.) and in 1639 founded Newport. Reluctantly agreed to unification of Aquidneck with Providence Plantations.

CODMAN, JOHN (*b. Dorchester, Mass., 1814; d. Boston, Mass., 1900*), sea captain. Active in merchant service, 1834–65.

CODY, WILLIAM FREDERICK (*b. Scott Co., Iowa, 1846; d. Denver, Colo., 1917*), scout, showman, better known as "Buffalo Bill." As a youth worked as "cavvy boy," as mounted messenger for Russell, Majors & Waddell, as Pony Express rider and, during Civil War, as scout and trooper. Furnished buffalo meat for food contractors to Kansas Pacific Railroad, which gave him his nickname. Was chief scout of 5th Cavalry. Played leading role, 1872–76, in Col. E. Z. C. Judson's play, *Scouts of the Prairies*. During Sioux War of 1876, returned to 5th Cavalry. In partnership with Maj. Frank North, took up cattle ranching near North Platte, Nebr. In 1883 started his "Wild West" exhibition in which he toured all over the world. *Post* 1894, he settled on a ranch in the Big Horn Basin in Wyoming.

COE, GEORGE SIMMONS (*b. Newport, R.I., 1817; d. Englewood, N.J., 1896*), banker. President of American Exchange Bank, 1860–94, and, in 1881, of American Bankers Association; helped establish New York Clearing House.

COE, ISRAEL (*b. Goshen, Conn., 1794; d. Waterbury, Conn., 1891*), brass manufacturer. A pioneer in brass rolling industry.

COERNE, LOUIS ADOLPHE (*b. Newark, N.J., 1870; d. Boston, Mass., 1922*), composer, teacher of music. His best work is the opera *Zenobia*.

COFER, MARTIN HARDIN (*b. Elizabethtown, Ky., 1832; d. Frankfort, Ky., 1881*), Confederate soldier, jurist. Judge, Kentucky circuit court, 1870–74; justice, state court of appeals, 1874–81; chief justice, 1881.

COFFEY, JAMES VINCENT (*b. New York, N.Y., 1846; d. 1919*), jurist. Practiced in California, *post* 1869. Judge of probate, San Francisco Co., for 36 years *post* 1882.

COFFIN, CHARLES ALBERT (*b. Somerset Co., Maine, 1844; d. 1926*), industrialist. Originally in shoe and leather business, became one of Lynn Syndicate which established Thomson-Houston Co. at Lynn, Mass. In 1892, became president of General Electric Co., which was formed through merger of Thomson-Houston Co. with the Edison General Electric Co. of New York; was chairman of board of directors, *post* 1913. Coffin's leadership led to company's phenomenal growth.

COFFIN, CHARLES CARLETON (*b. Boscawen, N.H., 1823; d. Brookline, Mass., 1896*), Civil War correspondent, author. His books for boys, especially *The Boys of '76* (1876), were deservedly popular.

COFFIN, CHARLES FISHER (*b. North Carolina, 1823; d. Chicago, Ill., 1916*), banker, Quaker minister. Raised in Indiana and was a successful banker there. As clerk of Indiana Yearly Meeting of Friends, 1857–85, was one of America's leading Quakers.

COFFIN, HOWARD EARLE (*b. near West Milton, O., 1873; d. Sea Island, Ga., 1937*), chief engineer and vice president, Hudson Motor Co., 1910–30.

Contributed to technical standardization in automobile and aircraft industries. [*Supp. 2*]

COFFIN, Sir ISAAC (*b. Boston, Mass., 1759; d. 1839*), British admiral, Loyalist, philanthropist. Entered Royal Navy, 1773; promoted full admiral, 1814. Brother of John Coffin.

COFFIN, JAMES HENRY (*b. Martha's Vineyard, Mass., 1806; d. 1873*), mathematician, meteorologist. Graduated Amherst, 1828. After several teaching posts, served as professor of mathematics, Lafayette College, 1846 to his death. Author of *Winds of the Globe* (1875).

COFFIN, JOHN (*b. Boston, Mass., 1756; d. New Brunswick, Canada, 1838*), Loyalist. Fought through the Revolution with Tory units; removed after the war to New Brunswick. Brother of Sir Isaac Coffin.

COFFIN, LEVI (*b. New Garden, N.C., 1789; d. 1877*), leader in operations of the "Underground Railroad," 1826–46; his home in Newport, Ind., was a station on the route to freedom.

COFFIN, LORENZO S. (*b. near Alton, N.H., 1823; d. 1915*), philanthropist. Was responsible for Congressional legislation requiring self-couplers and air-brakes on freight trains; founded railroad workers' Temperance Association.

COFFIN, WILLIAM ANDERSON (*b. Allegheny, Pa., 1855; d. 1925*), painter, art critic. Distinguished for landscapes; wrote art criticism for the *Nation,* the New York *Evening Post* and the *Sun.*

COFFMAN, LOTUS DELTA (*b. near Salem, Ind., 1875; d. Minneapolis, Minn., 1938*), educator. Dean of college of education, 1915–20, and president, 1920–38, of University of Minnesota. [*Supp. 2*]

COGDELL, JOHN STEVENS (*b. Charleston, or Georgetown, S.C., 1778; d. Charleston, 1847*), sculptor, painter, lawyer.

COGGESHALL, GEORGE (*b. Milford, Conn., 1784; d. Milford, 1861*), privateer, merchant mariner and captain. Author of several volumes of voyages, and *History of the American Privateers* (1856).

COGGESHALL, WILLIAM TURNER (*b. Lewistown, Pa., 1824; d. near Quito, Ecuador, 1867*), journalist. His outstanding work was *Poets and Poetry of the West* (1860). He was American minister to Ecuador, 1866–67.

COGHLAN, ROSE (*b. Peterborough, England, 1851; d. Harrison, N.Y., 1932*), actress. Noted for her success in artificial high comedy in Wallack's Company, 1877–88. [*Supp. 1*]

COGSWELL, JOSEPH GREEN (*b. Ipswich, Mass., 1786; d. Cambridge, Mass., 1871*), teacher, librarian. Graduated Harvard, 1806; studied law under Fisher Ames and Judge Prescott; engaged in mercantile ventures in southern Europe. With Edward Everett and George Ticknor, studied at Göttingen, 1817; met and later corresponded with Goethe; traveled widely in Europe. In 1820 became librarian and professor of mineralogy and geology at Harvard; in 1823 with George Bancroft established Round Hill School at Northampton, Mass. Became John Jacob Astor's adviser in establishment of the Astor Public Library in New York; from 1848 to 1861 served as its superintendent and compiled its printed catalogues.

COGSWELL, WILLIAM BROWNE (*b. Oswego, N.Y., 1834; d. 1921*), mining engineer. Introduced Solvay Process of manufacturing soda to America.

COHEN, JACOB DA SILVA SOLIS (*b. New York, N.Y., 1838; d. 1927*), physician. Expert in use of laryngoscope; wrote book on inhalation (1867) and *Diseases of the Throat* (1872).

COHEN, JOHN SANFORD (*b. Augusta, Ga., 1870; d. 1935*), journalist. Outstanding editor of the *Atlanta Journal*, 1900–35; prominent in Democratic politics. [*Supp. 1*]

COHEN, MENDES (*b. Baltimore, Md., 1831; d. Baltimore, 1915*), engineer. Associated with Baltimore & Ohio, Hudson River, Ohio & Mississippi and other railroads as engineer or president. Active in many civic and historical societies.

COIT, HENRY AUGUSTUS (*b. Wilmington, Del., 1830; d. Concord, N.H., 1895*), Episcopal clergyman. First rector of St. Paul's School, Concord, N.H., 1856–95; ranked with Arnold, Fellenberg and Muhlenberg as a master pedagogue.

COIT, HENRY LEBER (*b. Peapack, N.J., 1854; d. Newark, N.J., 1917*), physician. Led campaign, *post* 1889, for the introduction of "certified milk" to reduce infant mortality; promoted establishment of Newark's Babies' Hospital.

COIT, THOMAS WINTHROP (*b. New London, Conn., 1803; d. 1885*), Episcopal clergyman, educator. Author of *Puritanism, or a Churchman's Defense* (1845).

COKE, RICHARD (*b. Williamsburg, Va., 1829; d. Waco, Texas, 1897*), lawyer, Confederate soldier. Removed to Texas, 1850; Democratic governor of Texas, 1874–76; U.S. senator, 1876–94.

COKE, THOMAS (*b. Brecon, Wales, 1747; d. England, 1814*), Methodist bishop. An Anglican curate, he joined John Wesley, 1777, and assisted him as correspondent, becoming in 1782 president of Irish Methodist conference. In 1784 Wesley appointed him first superintendent of the Methodist Church in America. Coke preached in Delaware, Maryland, Pennsylvania and Virginia and presided over the 1784 general conference of the American Methodist Church, where Francis Asbury's views prevailed. From 1784 to 1803 Coke made nine voyages to America, exercising only nominal control over American Methodism. As president of the Methodist missionary committee *post* 1804, Coke was conspicuously successful.

COKER, DAVID ROBERT (*b. Hartsville, S.C., 1870; d. Hartsville, 1938*), agriculturist, philanthropist. Son of James L. Coker. Breeder of improved strains of short-staple cotton. [*Supp. 2*]

COKER, JAMES LIDE (*b. near Society Hill, S.C., 1837; d. Hartsville, S.C., 1918*), manufacturer. A versatile businessman, he engaged in farming, banking, retailing, railroad building; founded Coker College for women, Hartsville, S.C.

COLBURN, DANA POND (*b. West Dedham, Mass., 1823; d. Bristol, R.I., 1859*), educator. A Pestalozzian, he employed rational rather than memory methods; taught at Rhode Island normal schools.

COLBURN, IRVING WIGHTMAN (*b. Fitchburg, Mass., 1861; d. 1917*), manufacturer. Inventor of machines and process for drawing continuous sheets of glass (patented 1908) which were exploited commercially by Libbey-Owens Co.

COLBURN, WARREN (*b. Dedham, Mass., 1793; d. Lowell, Mass., 1833*), teacher. His mathematics textbooks on the inductive method (1821–25) broke new ground.

COLBURN, ZERAH (*b. Cabot, Vt., 1804; d. Norwich, Vt., 1839*), mathematical prodigy. Author of an autobiography (1833).

COLBY, FRANK MOORE (*b. Washington, D.C., 1865; d. 1925*), author. Editor, *New International Year Book*, 1898–1925; contributed to many encyclopedias and periodicals. Author of brief pungent essays as in *Constrained Attitudes* (1910).

COLBY, GARDNER (*b. Bowdoinham, Maine, 1810; d. Newton, Mass., 1879*), merchant, philanthropist. Prospered in Civil War clothing contracts. President, Wisconsin Central Railroad. Helped finance school at Waterville, Maine, later Colby College.

COLBY, LUTHER (*b. Amesbury, Mass., 1814; d. 1894*), spiritualist. Editor, the *Banner of Light*, 1857–94.

COLDEN, CADWALLADER (*b. Ireland, 1688 n.s.; d. Long Island, N.Y., 1776*), Loyalist, philosopher, scientist. Came to New York, 1718; was made colony's surveyor-general, 1720; in 1721 was appointed to Governor's Council; lieutenant-governor of the colony, 1761–76. Published contributions to history, applied mathematics, botany, physics, medicine and philosophy, and corresponded with eminent scientists of his day. Among his books are *The History of the Five Indian Nations* (1727) and *An Explication of the First Causes of Action in Matter* (1745, revised 1751). An honest and able public servant, he refused to go along with popular agitation subsequent to the Stamp Act and grew progressively unpopular although he managed to keep a fair balance between radicals and conservatives until 1774.

COLDEN, CADWALLADER DAVID (*b. Flushing, N.Y., 1769; d. Jersey City, N.J., 1834*), lawyer. Grandson of Cadwallader Colden. Federalist mayor of New York, 1818–20; congressman from New York, 1821–23. Actively interested in navigation, internal improvements and reform.

COLDEN, JANE (*b. probably New York, N.Y., 1724; d. 1766*), first woman botanist in New World. Daughter of Cadwallader Colden, she cooperated in Colden's study of the New York flora according to Linnaeus's system.

COLE, CHESTER CICERO (*b. Oxford, N.Y., 1824; d. 1913*), jurist, teacher of law. Graduated Harvard Law School, 1848. Settled in Des Moines, Iowa, 1856; judge, Iowa supreme court, 1864–76; taught law at Drake University.

COLE, FRANK NELSON (*b. Ashland, Mass., 1861; d. 1926*), mathematician. Graduated Harvard, 1882; Ph.D., 1886. Taught at Harvard, Michigan, Columbia; editor, American Mathematical Society Bulletin, 1897–1925.

COLE, GEORGE WATSON (*b. Warren, Conn., 1850; d. California, 1939*), bibliographer. First librarian, 1920–24, Henry E. Huntington Library and Art Gallery, San Marino, Calif. [*Supp. 2*]

COLE, JOSEPH FOXCROFT (*b. Jay, Me., 1837; d. Winchester, Mass., 1892*), painter. A commercial lithographer, he studied art in France; painted serious, low-toned landscapes in French manner; brought French art to New England's attention.

COLE, THOMAS (*b. Bolton-le-Moor, England, 1801; d. Catskill, N.Y., 1848*), artist, pioneer of the "Hudson River School." Came to America, 1819. Worked as block-engraver in his father's wall-paper factory at Steubenville, O., 1820–22; *post* 1824, worked in New York, N.Y. and at Catskill. Became celebrated for his romantic landscapes, which were praised by John Trumbull, William Dunlap and William Cullen Bryant. Visited Europe, 1829–32; after return to New York painted "The Course of Empire," the most remarkable of his works, and "The Voyage of Life."

COLE, TIMOTHY (*b. London, England, 1852; d. 1931*), wood-engraver. Founded the "New School" of American reproductive wood-engraving. [*Supp. 1*]

COLEMAN, CHARLES CARYL (*b. Buffalo, N.Y., 1840; d. Capri, Italy, 1928*), painter. Worked with William Hunt and Elihu Vedder in Rome; the subjects of his mature work were landscapes.

COLEMAN, LEIGHTON (*b. Philadelphia, Pa., 1837; d. 1907*), Episcopal bishop of Delaware, 1888–1907.

COLEMAN, LYMAN (*b. Middlefield, Mass., 1796; d. Easton, Pa., 1882*), Congregational clergyman,

educator. Graduated Yale, 1817. Professor of classics at Amherst and Princeton, and at Lafayette College, 1861–82.

COLEMAN, WILLIAM (*b. Boston, Mass., 1766; d. New York, N.Y., 1829*), Federalist journalist. Editor, New York *Evening Post*, 1801–29; associate and supporter of Alexander Hamilton.

COLEMAN, WILLIAM TELL (*b. near Cynthiana, Ky., 1824; d. San Francisco, Calif., 1893*), merchant. Emigrated to California, 1849; operated stores at Placerville, Sacramento and San Francisco; a leader in Vigilantes, 1851 and 1856.

COLES, EDWARD (*b. Albemarle Co., Va., 1786; d. Philadelphia, Pa., 1868*), abolitionist. Secretary to James Madison, 1809–15. Settled in Illinois, 1819, where he emancipated his slaves; Democratic governor of Illinois, 1822–26.

COLFAX, SCHUYLER (*b. New York, N.Y., 1823; d. Mankato, Minn., 1885*), politician. Removed to Indiana, 1836; edited principal Whig newspaper in northern Indiana; took active part in forming Republican party in that state. Congressman from Indiana, 1855–69; speaker of the House, 1863–69; vice-president of the United States, 1869–73. His implication in Crédit Mobilier scandal and others ruined him politically.

COLGATE, JAMES BOORMAN (*b. New York, N.Y., 1818; d. 1904*), stockbroker. Son of William Colgate. Benefactor of Colgate University.

COLGATE, WILLIAM (*b. Hollingbourn, England, 1783; d. New York, N.Y., 1857*), manufacturer. Came to America, 1795. Worked as a tallow chandler; in 1806 started his own firm for the manufacture of soap which became outstanding. A Baptist, he was a generous benefactor of the schools which later became Colgate University.

COLLAMER, JACOB (*b. Troy, N.Y., 1791; d. Woodstock, Vt., 1865*), lawyer, Vermont legislator and jurist. Congressman, Whig, from Vermont, 1843–49; U.S. postmaster-general, 1849–50; U.S. senator, Republican, from Vermont, 1864–65.

COLLENS, THOMAS WHARTON (*b. New Orleans, La., 1812; d. 1879*), jurist, writer. Held various posts in Louisiana judiciary, 1842–73. Wrote several tragedies locally produced.

COLLES, CHRISTOPHER (*b. Ireland, 1739; d. New York, 1816*), engineer, inventor, promoter of internal improvements. Came to America, *post* 1765. One of the first Americans to design a steam engine and probably the first (1785) to propose a canal connecting the Great Lakes with the Hudson River. Surveyed roads of New York and Pennsylvania; engaged in business, but always returned to invention of useful devices, to astronomical calculations, and to schemes for canals and roads. Held position in custom service. Author of *A Survey of the Roads of the United States* (1789).

COLLIER, BARRON GIFT (*b. Memphis, Tenn., 1873; d. New York, N.Y., 1939*), advertising promoter, developer of Florida lower West Coast properties. [*Supp. 2*]

COLLIER, HENRY WATKINS (*b. Lunenburg Co., Va., 1801; d. Bailey Springs, Ala., 1855*), lawyer. Practiced in Alabama; chief justice of state supreme court, 1837–49; Democratic governor of Alabama, 1849–53. A middle-of-the-road conservative in national affairs.

COLLIER, HIRAM PRICE (*b. Davenport, Iowa, 1860; d. Fünen Island, Denmark, 1913*), author. Unitarian minister in Massachusetts, 1882–91. Wrote numerous books of which *Mr. Picket Pin and His Friends* (1894) and *England and the English* (1909) are best known.

COLLIER, PETER (*b. Chittenango, N.Y., 1835; d. Ann Arbor, Mich., 1896*), agricultural chemist. Graduated Yale, 1861, Ph.D., 1866; M.D., University of Vermont, 1870. Chief chemist, U.S. Department of Agriculture, 1877–83. Author of *Sorghum, Its Culture and Manufacture* (1884). Director, N.Y. Agricultural Station, Geneva, N.Y., 1887–95.

COLLIER, PETER FENELON (*b. Co. Carlow, Ireland, 1849; d. 1909*), publisher. Came to America, 1866. Founder of P. F. Collier & Co.; in 1888 founded *Once a Week*, replaced in 1896 by *Collier's Weekly*.

COLLIER, PRICE. [See COLLIER, HIRAM PRICE, 1860–1913.]

COLLINS, EDWARD KNIGHT (*b. Truro, Mass., 1802; d. New York, N.Y., 1878*), shipowner. Operator of packet lines to Vera Cruz and New Orleans, in 1836 he started the "Dramatic Line" from New York to England. Impressed with the success of the subsidized British Cunard mail steamers, Collins in 1847 obtained a contract with the U.S. postmaster-general specifying the construction and subsidized operation of five mail-carrying steamships. The steamers of the "Collins Line" exceeded the speed of the Cunard liners, attracted the cream of the passenger trade and forced reduction of British freight rates. Disaster came with the sinking of the *Arctic*, 1854, the disappearance of the *Pacific*, 1856, and the cancellation of the congressional subsidy. In 1858 Collins had to dissolve his company.

COLLINS, FRANK SHIPLEY (*b. Boston, Mass., 1848; d. New Haven, Conn., 1920*), botanist. Earned his living as a factory manager. Became authority on American algae; author of *The Green Algae of North America* (1909).

COLLINS, GUY N (*b. Mertensia, N.Y., 1872; d. Lanham, Md., 1938*), plant explorer, geneticist. With U.S. Department of Agriculture, 1901–38; used biometrics to plan and evaluate experiments, especially studies of maize. [*Supp. 2*]

COLLINS, JOHN (*b. Newport, R.I., 1717; d. 1795*), Revolutionary patriot. Governor of Rhode Island, 1786–90.

COLLINS, JOHN ANDERSON (*b. Manchester, Vt., c. 1810; d. c. 1879*), abolitionist, social reformer. General agent, Massachusetts Anti-Slavery Society; founded unsuccessful Fourieristic community at Skaneateles, N.Y. Last heard of in California, 1879.

COLLINS, NAPOLEON (*b. Pennsylvania, 1814; d. Callao, Peru, 1875*), naval officer. Captured Confederate raider *Florida*, 1864, at Bahia, Brazil; a rear admiral after 1874, he commanded South Pacific Squadron.

COLLINS, PATRICK ANDREW (*b. Ballinafauna, Ireland, 1844; d. Virginia Hot Springs, 1905*), politician. Came to America as a child; raised in Massachusetts and Ohio; returned to Boston, 1859. Graduated Harvard Law School, 1871. A Democrat, he served in Massachusetts general court, in Congress, 1883–89, and as mayor of Boston, 1901–05.

COLLYER, ROBERT (*b. Keighley, England, 1823; d. 1912*), clergyman. Came to America, 1850. At first a Methodist lay-preacher, he served as a Unitarian pastor in Chicago, Ill., 1859–79, and as pastor of the Church of the Messiah, New York City *post* 1879.

COLMAN, BENJAMIN (*b. Boston, Mass., 1673; d. 1747*), clergyman. Graduated Harvard, 1692. Minister of Boston's Brattle Street Church, 1699–1747; a fellow and overseer of Harvard, he endorsed the Great Awakening.

COLMAN, HENRY (*b. Boston, Mass., 1785; d. Islington, England, 1849*), Unitarian minister, agricultural writer. Pastor of Independent Congregational Church, Salem, Mass., 1825–31; made agricultural surveys in Massachusetts, 1837–38; published report on European agriculture (1844).

COLMAN, JOHN (*b. London, England, 1670; d. c. 1753*), merchant. Brother of Benjamin Colman. Came to Boston, Mass., as an infant. Active in local currency and banking disputes, 1714–39.

COLMAN, LUCY NEWHALL (*b. Sturbridge, Mass., 1817; d. Syracuse, N.Y., 1906*), abolitionist, anti-slavery lecturer.

COLMAN, NORMAN JAY (*b. near Richfield Springs, N.Y., 1827; d. 1911*), agricultural journalist, lawyer. Practiced in Indiana; removing to Missouri, he published *Colman's Rural World*, 1865–1911. First U.S. secretary of agriculture (February 1889), he had previously while commissioner written the Hatch Bill which originated agricultural experiment stations.

COLMAN, SAMUEL (*b. Portland, Maine, 1832; d. New York, N.Y., 1920*), landscape painter. Pupil of A. B. Durand.

COLQUITT, ALFRED HOLT (*b. Walton Co., Ga., 1824; d. 1894*), statesman, Confederate soldier. Son of Walter T. Colquitt. An extreme pro-Southern Democrat, he served in the Georgia legislature and as congressman, 1853–55. Subsequent to his war service, he fought the Reconstruction policies of Congress and served ably if arbitrarily as Democratic governor of Georgia, 1876–82; U.S. senator, 1883–94.

COLQUITT, WALTER TERRY (*b. Halifax Co., Va., 1799; d. 1855*), lawyer, statesman. Raised in Georgia. Congressman, state-rights Whig, 1838–43; U.S. senator, Democrat, 1843–48.

COLSTON, RALEIGH EDWARD (*b. Paris, France, 1825; d. Richmond, Va., 1896*), Confederate soldier. Graduated Virginia Military Institute, 1846, and taught there. After effective Civil War service, was colonel in Egyptian army, 1873–79.

COLT, LeBARON BRADFORD (*b. Dedham, Mass., 1846; d. 1924*), jurist. Graduated Yale, 1868. Began practice of law in Chicago; removed, 1875, to Bristol, R.I. Federal judge, 1881–1913; U.S. senator, Republican, from Rhode Island, 1913–24.

COLT, SAMUEL (*b. Hartford, Conn., 1814; d. 1862*), inventor, manufacturer. Between 1831 and 1833 applied for patent and constructed models of the first practical multi-shot pistol and rifle of the revolving barrel type, for which he received his first U.S. patent in 1836. Unsuccessful in persuading armed forces to adopt them, he lost his rights to them *post* 1842. At outbreak of Mexican War, on receipt of order for a thousand of his pistols from the government, he recaptured his patents and began to manufacture firearms. In 1848 after a year at Whitneyville, Conn., he established the business at Hartford, Conn.

COLTER, JOHN (*b. in or near Staunton, Va., c. 1775; d. near Dundee, Mo., 1813*), trapper, explorer. Served ably on expedition of Lewis and Clark, 1803–06; then joined Manuel Lisa's trapping party and explored the Yellowstone region, 1807. Trapped along upper Missouri and Yellowstone, 1808–10.

COLTON, CALVIN (*b. Longmeadow, Mass., 1789; d. Savannah, Ga., 1857*), clergyman, journalist, politician. Official biographer of Henry Clay and editor of his works.

COLTON, ELIZABETH AVERY (*b. Indian Territory, 1872; d. 1924*), educator. Prominent in raising standards of Southern colleges for women; head of English department, Meredith College, Raleigh, N.C.

COLTON, GARDNER QUINCY (*b. Georgia, Vt., 1814; d. Rotterdam, Holland, 1898*), anaesthetist. Brother of Walter Colton. Introduced nitrous oxide as anaesthetic for dental practice, 1844–63.

COLTON, GEORGE RADCLIFFE (*b. Galesburg, Ill., 1865; d. 1916*), customs expert. A Nebraska banker, he organized Philippine customs service and was governor of Porto Rico from 1909 to 1913.

COLTON, WALTER (*b. Rutland Co., Vt., 1797; d. Philadelphia, Pa., 1851*), Congregational clergyman, journalist. A navy chaplain, 1831–51; played a notable part in conquest of California, 1846–49; author of several books including the valuable *Three Years in California* (1850).

COLVER, NATHANIEL (*b. Orwell, Vt., 1794; d. 1870*), Baptist clergyman. An abolitionist, his principal pastorate was at Tremont Temple, Boston, Mass., 1839–52; he was a founder of Chicago University Divinity School.

COLVER, WILLIAM BYRON (*b. Wellington, O., 1870; d. 1926*), editor, chairman of Federal Trade Commission. Vigorous champion of public causes, he wrote for *Cleveland Plain Dealer* and *Press* and supported reforms of Tom L. Johnson; general editorial director, Scripps-Howard, 1919–24.

COLVIN, STEPHEN SHELDON (*b. Phenix, R.I., 1869; d. 1923*), educational psychologist, author. Graduated Brown, 1891; studied in Europe and under G. Stanley Hall; taught at Brown, Illinois, Columbia; wrote *The Learning Process* (1911) and other works.

COLVOCORESSES, GEORGE MUSALAS (*b. Chios, Greece, 1816; d. Bridgeport, Conn., 1872*), naval officer. Author of *Four Years in a Government Exploring Expedition* (1852).

COLWELL, STEPHEN (*b. Brooke Co., Va., 1800; d. Philadelphia, Pa., 1871*), political economist, lawyer. A protectionist, of the school of Henry C. Carey, he also stressed the social implication of the Christian doctrine.

COMAN, CHARLOTTE BUELL (*b. Waterville, N.Y,. 1833; d. Yonkers, N.Y., 1924*), artist. Studied with James R. Brevoort, and in Europe. Painted landscapes after the manner of Corot and Daubigny.

COMBS, LESLIE (*b. Clarke Co., Ky., 1793; d. Lexington, Ky., 1881*), soldier, Kentucky legislator and lawyer, Unionist.

COMBS, MOSES NEWELL (*b. Morris Co., N.J., 1753; d. Newark, N.J., 1834*), manufacturer, philanthropist. Known as "Father of Newark industries," he prospered in shoe and leather business. Founded one of the first night schools at Newark, 1794.

COMER, BRAXTON BRAGG (*b. Barbour Co., Ala., 1848; d. 1927*), businessman. As governor of Alabama, 1907–11, he secured state railroad code, prohibition and child-labor laws; obtained unprecedentedly large appropriations for colleges and schools.

COMFORT, WILL LEVINGTON (*b. Kalamazoo, Mich., 1878; d. Los Angeles, Calif., 1932*), war correspondent, novelist, occultist. [*Supp.* 1]

COMSTOCK, ANTHONY (*b. New Canaan, Conn., 1844; d. 1915*), reformer. *Post* 1871, supported by the Y.M.C.A., he began a crusade, which ended only with his death, against publishers and sellers of obscene literature. He forced the adoption of postal legislation preventing mail shipment of obscene materials; was secretary of Society for Suppression of Vice and a special agent of the Post Office Department. Incorruptible and zealous, he was unable to distinguish between good art and bad and frequently attacked works of artistic and literary value.

COMSTOCK, ELIZABETH L. (*b. Maidenhead, England, 1815; d. Union Springs, N.Y., 1891*), Quaker minister. Settled in Rollin, Mich., 1858; advocated abolition, temperance and prison reform; during Civil War ministered to wounded and imprisoned soldiers.

COMSTOCK, GEORGE CARY (*b. Madison, Wis., 1855; d. Beloit, Wis., 1934*), astronomer. Director, Washburn Observatory, 1899–1922. Demonstrated that many stars are apparently faint because they are intrinsically of low luminosity, not because they are far away. [*Supp.* 1]

COMSTOCK, GEORGE FRANKLIN (*b. near Williamstown, N.Y., 1811; d. Syracuse, N.Y., 1892*), jurist. Justice, New York court of appeals, 1855–61; a profound equity lawyer; initiated organization of Syracuse University.

COMSTOCK, HENRY TOMPKINS PAIGE (*b. Trenton, Canada, 1820; d. near Bozeman, Mont., 1870*), trapper, prospector. Claimant of ground where Comstock Lode, named for him, was found.

COMSTOCK, JOHN HENRY (*b. Janesville, Wis., 1849; d. Ithaca, N.Y., 1931*), entomologist. Professor of entomology, Cornell University, 1882–1914; his original studies in *Wings of Insects* (1918) formed the basis of the greatest advance of the period in entomology. [*Supp.* 1]

CONANT, ALBAN JASPER (*b. Chelsea, Vt., 1821; d. New York, N.Y., 1915*), artist, archaeologist. Settled in St. Louis, Mo., 1857; promoted artistic interests; wrote pioneer studies, *The Archaeology of Missouri* (1876) and *Footprints of Vanished Races in the Mississippi Valley* (1879).

CONANT, CHARLES ARTHUR (*b. Winchester, Mass., 1861; d. Havana, Cuba, 1915*), journalist. Washington correspondent, specializing in finance, 1889–1901; later a banker, and financial expert in Philippines, Nicaragua and elsewhere.

CONANT, HANNAH O'BRIEN CHAPLIN (*b. Danvers, Mass., 1809; d. 1865*), writer. Wife of Thomas J. Conant, whom she assisted in his theological work.

CONANT, HEZEKIAH (*b. Dudley, Mass., 1827; d. 1902*), inventor, manufacturer. Invented "gas check" for breech-loading firearms, 1856; devised and patented many improvements in the manufacture of thread.

CONANT, ROGER (*b. East Budleigh, England, c. 1592; d. Beverly, Mass., 1679*). Settled at Nantasket, 1624; upon request of settlers served as governor on Cape Ann, 1625, and at new settlement at Salem, 1626.

CONANT, THOMAS JEFFERSON (*b. Brandon, Vt., 1802; d. Brooklyn, N.Y., 1891*), Baptist clergyman, philologist. Member of American Bible Revision Committee; author of a simple, forceful translation of the Bible, and other works.

CONATY, THOMAS JAMES (*b. Kilnalec, Ireland, 1847; d. Los Angeles, Calif., 1915*), Roman Catholic clergyman, educator. Graduated Holy Cross College, 1869; ordained 1872. Pastor at Worcester, Mass.; was rector of Catholic University, 1897–1903, and president of National Catholic Education Association, 1899–1903. Bishop of Monterey and Los Angeles, *post* 1903.

CONBOY, SARA AGNES McLAUGHLIN (*b. Boston, Mass., 1870; d. 1928*), labor leader. Secretary-treasurer, United Textile Workers; first woman to wield influence in A.F. of L. councils; effective in securing labor legislation and as conciliator.

CONDIT, JOHN (*b. New Jersey, 1755; d. Orange, N.J., 1834*), surgeon. Congressman, Democratic-Republican, from New Jersey, 1799–1803, 1819–20; U.S. senator, 1803–17.

CONDON, THOMAS (*b. near Fermoy, Ireland, 1822; d. 1907*), Congregational clergyman, geologist. Came to America as a boy; served as missionary in Oregon, 1853–73; taught geology at Pacific University and University of Oregon, 1873–1905; a pioneer in local paleontology.

CONE, MOSES HERMAN (*b. Jonesboro, Tenn., 1857; d. 1908*), cotton merchant, denim manufacturer at Greensboro, N.C.

CONE, ORELLO (*b. Lincklaen, N.Y., 1835; d. 1905*), New Testament scholar. His *Gospel Criticism and Historical Christianity* (1891) was ablest American work on higher criticism; taught at St. Lawrence University, Canton, N.Y.

CONE, SPENCER HOUGHTON (*b. Princeton, N.J., 1785; d. New York, N.Y., 1855*), Baptist clergyman. Was actor, journalist, soldier. An outstanding preacher, he was a founder and head of the American and Foreign Bible Society, 1837–50, and president of American Bible Union.

CONEY, JABEZ (*b. Dedham, Mass., 1804; d. 1872*), millwright, engineer. At South Boston, 1848, built machinery for U.S.S. *Saranac*, the first steam vessel in the navy.

CONEY, JOHN (*b. Boston, Mass., 1655; d. 1722*), silversmith. A fine craftsman, he engraved plates for first Massachusetts paper money; Apollos Rivoire (father of Paul Revere) was his apprentice.

CONGDON, CHARLES TABER (*b. New Bedford, Mass., 1821; d. New York, N.Y., 1891*), journalist. As *New York Tribune* staff member, 1857–82, known as "Greeley's right hand"; author of *Tribune Essays* (1869) and *Reminiscences of a Journalist* (1880).

CONGER, EDWIN HURD (*b. near Galesburg, Ill., 1843; d. 1907*), Union soldier, diplomat. A successful Iowa businessman, he served in several diplomatic posts, distinguishing himself as minister to China, 1898–1904, during Boxer troubles.

CONKLIN, JENNIE MARIA DRINKWATER. [See DRINKWATER, JENNIE MARIA, 1841–1900.]

CONKLING, ALFRED (*b. Amagansett, N.Y., 1789; d. Utica, N.Y., 1874*), lawyer, jurist. Father of Roscoe Conkling. Federal judge, northern New York district, 1825–52; U.S. minister to Mexico, 1852; author of several legal treatises.

CONKLING, ROSCOE (*b. Albany, N.Y., 1829; d. New York, N.Y., 1888*), politician, lawyer. Son of Alfred Conkling. Admitted to the bar, 1850. Skilled in "spread-eagle" oratory, he rose rapidly in Whig party councils and was mayor of Utica, N.Y., 1858. Except for the years 1863–65, he served as congressman, 1859–67, becoming a "War Republican" and an advocate of vigorous repression in Reconstruction of the South. Ambitious and able, he was elected U.S. senator from New York, 1867; from then, until his resignation from the Senate in 1881, he was Republican leader in his state and an aspirant to the presidency. A friend and supporter of Grant, Conkling was a bitter enemy of Presidents Hayes and Garfield, and of James G. Blaine. He opposed civil service reform and gave up politics after an unsuccessful fight against Garfield's appointments to federal jobs which he considered political perquisites of the New York organization.

CONNELLY, CORNELIA (*b. Philadelphia, Pa., 1809; d. 1879*), foundress of the Society of the Holy Child Jesus, 1846.

CONNELLY, HENRY (*b. Nelson Co., Ky., 1800; d. Santa Fe, N. Mex., 1866*), physician, pioneer trader. As governor of New Mexico, 1861–66, he was largely responsible for New Mexico's stand against the Confederacy.

CONNELLY, PIERCE FRANCIS (*b. Grand Coteau, La., 1841*), sculptor. Son of Cornelia Connelly. Worked abroad; exhibited in America with great success in 1876.

CONNER, CHARLOTTE MARY SANFORD BARNES [See BARNES, CHARLOTTE MARY SANFORD, 1818–63.]

CONNER, DAVID (*b. Harrisburg, Pa., 1792; d. Philadelphia, Pa., 1856*), naval officer. Won two Congressional medals for service on the *Hornet*, 1811–17; during Mexican War commanded naval forces in Caribbean and Gulf.

CONNER, JAMES (*b. Charleston, S.C., 1829; d. Richmond, Va., 1883*), lawyer, Confederate soldier. South Carolina attorney-general, 1876–77; established legality of Wade Hampton government.

CONNEY, JOHN. [See CONEY, JOHN, 1655–1722.]

CONNOLLY, JOHN (*b. York Co., Pa., c. 1743; d. Montreal, Canada, 1813*), Loyalist, agent of Lord Dunmore. After incomplete apprenticeship to a physician, served as medical officer in frontier Indian campaigns, 1762–64. Supported Dunmore in claiming for Virginia territory around Fort Pitt. Commissioned commandant at the fort by Dunmore, 1773, he halted the Pennsylvania trade with the Indians. In 1775, after winning Indian support for England, he planned with Dunmore to recapture Fort Pitt and use it as a base for a joint operation to divide the colonies. Was imprisoned, 1776–80, exchanged and recaptured at Yorktown. As lieutenant-governor of Detroit, he intrigued, 1788, to win Kentucky allegiance to Britain. [*Supp. 1*]

CONNOLLY, JOHN (*b. Slane, Ireland, 1750; d. 1825*), Dominican priest. Consecrated second bishop of New York, 1814. Successfully overcame dangers of racial antagonism and lay trusteeism; established orphan asylum.

CONNOR, HENRY GROVES (*b. Wilmington, N.C., 1852; d. 1924*), jurist. Author of Connor Act, 1884; as federal district judge, 1909–24, broke post-bellum prejudice of North Carolina against federal courts.

CONNOR, PATRICK EDWARD (*b. Co. Kerry, Ireland, 1820; d. 1891*), pioneer, soldier, Indian fighter. Came to America as a child. Fought in Seminole and Mexican wars; removed to California, 1849. Commanded in district of Utah, 1861–64; and on Powder River campaign, 1865. Thereafter, he engaged in business and was a leader of the anti-Mormons in Utah.

CONOVER, OBADIAH MILTON (*b. Dayton, O., 1825; d. London, England, 1884*), educator, lawyer. Taught classic languages and literature at University of Wisconsin; was reporter of Wisconsin supreme court, 1864–84, and state librarian.

CONRAD, CHARLES MAGILL (*b. Winchester, Va., 1804; d. New Orleans, La., 1878*), lawyer, statesman. A Whig, he served briefly in Louisiana legislature, as congressman and U.S. senator, as secretary of war, 1850–53, and prominently in Confederate Congress.

CONRAD, HOLMES (*b. Winchester, Va., 1840; d. Winchester, 1916*), lawyer. Influential Democratic legislator and leader of Virginia bar; U.S. solicitor-general, 1895–97; outstanding in appeals before U.S. Supreme Court.

CONRAD, ROBERT TAYLOR (*b. Philadelphia, Pa., 1810; d. Philadelphia, 1858*), dramatist, jurist. His first play, *Conrad, King of Naples,* was produced successfully in Philadelphia, 1832; his best-known work was produced first in 1835 as *Aylmere,* but was later rewritten and under the title *Jack Cade* was part of the repertory of Forrest, John McCullough and others. Conrad was a distinguished figure in Philadelphia journalism; he served also as a judge of the city criminal court and as Know-Nothing mayor of Philadelphia, 1854–56. His poems and the text of *Jack Cade* were published as *Aylmere, or the Bondman of Kent; and Other Poems* (1852).

CONRIED, HEINRICH (*b. Bielitz, Austria, 1855; d. Meran, Austria, 1909*), actor, impresario. Came to America, *c.* 1877, to manage the German stock companies at the Thalia and Irving Place theatres, New York. His excellent productions of drama and operetta won him wide recognition. As manager of the Metropolitan Opera, 1903–08, he gave an outstanding production of Wagner's *Parsifal,* 1903.

CONSIDÉRANT, VICTOR PROSPER (*b. Salins, France, 1808; d. Paris, France, 1893*), social philosopher, Fourierist. Founder of Utopian community of Reunion, near Dallas, Texas, 1855.

CONVERSE, CHARLES CROZAT (*b. Warren, Mass., 1832; d. Highwood, N.J., 1918*), composer, lawyer. Studied music at Leipzig; wrote songs, orchestral pieces, cantatas, and popular hymns including "What a Friend we have in Jesus."

CONVERSE, EDMUND COGSWELL (*b. Boston, Mass., 1849; d. Pasadena, Calif., 1921*), inventor, capitalist, philanthropist. Patented lock-joint for gas and water pipes, 1882; organized National Tube Company, 1899. President, Liberty National Bank and Bankers' Trust Co., New York.

CONVERSE, FREDERICK SHEPHERD (*b. Newton, Mass., 1871; d. Westwood, Mass., 1940*), composer of the first American opera performed at New York City's Metropolitan Opera House (*The Pipe of Desire,* 1910) and many other works. [*Supp. 2*]

CONVERSE, JAMES BOOTH (*b. Philadelphia, Pa., 1844; d. 1914*), Presbyterian clergyman. Missionary and pastor in Kentucky and east Tennessee; author of *The Bible and Land* (1889), inspired by Henry George's *Progress and Poverty.*

CONVERSE, JOHN HEMAN (*b. Burlington, Vt., 1840; d. 1910*), locomotive builder. From 1870 to 1909, associated with Baldwin Locomotive Works; on its incorporation, 1909, was elected president.

CONWAY, ELIAS NELSON (*b. Greene Co., Tenn., 1812; d. 1892*), politician. Brother of James S. Conway. Went to Arkansas, 1833; served as auditor and administrator of public lands. As Democratic governor, 1852–60, stabilized state's financial affairs.

CONWAY, FREDERICK BARTLETT (*b. Clifton, England, 1819; d. Manchester, Mass., 1874*), actor. Made American debut, 1850; co-starring with his wife, he played in stock in Brooklyn, N.Y., Philadelphia, Boston and Cincinnati.

CONWAY, JAMES SEVIER (*b. Greene Co., Tenn., 1798; d. Lafayette Co., Ark., 1855*), politician, planter. Brother of Elias N. Conway. Removed to Arkansas, 1820. As first governor of State of Arkansas, 1836–40, he secured the chartering of the ill-fated State Bank and Real Estate Bank.

CONWAY, MARTIN FRANKLIN (*b. Harford Co., Md., 1827; d. Washington, D.C., 1882*), lawyer, printer. Removed to Kansas, 1854. Was an active free-stater; served as president of Leavenworth constitutional convention, 1858, and as congressman, Republican, from Kansas, 1861–63.

CONWAY, MONCURE DANIEL (*b. near Falmouth, Va., 1832; d. Paris, France, 1907*), preacher. Author of *Life of Thomas Paine* (1892) and editor of Paine's works. He also produced a number of other works on slavery, liberal theology, and an autobiography (1904).

CONWAY, THOMAS (*b. Ireland, 1735; d. c. 1800*), Revolutionary soldier. Raised in France, he reached rank of colonel in the French army, 1772. On recommendation of Silas Deane, he was appointed brigadier-general in the Continental army, arriving in America, April 1777. Washington's opposition to his promotion to major-general was overborne by Congress which commissioned him on December 14, 1777, and appointed him inspector-general of the army. Entering into correspondence with Horatio Gates and others, he criticized Washington and contributed to a movement in Congress to oust the commander-in-chief. Although the movement has gone down in history as the "Conway Cabal," Conway was not the prime mover in the conspiracy but merely the one who was caught. Attached to an abortive expedition against Canada, January 1778, Conway began to intrigue for a separate command; instead, he was ordered back to Peekskill to serve under General McDougall. His resignation from the army was accepted, April 28, 1778. Subsequently, after coming close to death in a duel with General Cadwalader over his conduct, he wrote Washington a full apology for the injury he had done him and returned to France.

CONWELL, HENRY (*b. Moneymore, Ireland, c. 1745; d. Philadelphia, Pa., 1842*), Roman Catholic clergyman. Consecrated bishop of Philadelphia, 1820; was involved in struggle over lay trusteeism, 1821–26.

CONWELL, RUSSELL HERMAN (*b. South Worthington, Mass., 1843; d. 1925*), Union soldier, Baptist clergyman. Pastor of Philadelphia's Grace Baptist Church, *post* 1880; founded Temple University; author of famous *Acres of Diamonds* lecture.

CONYNGHAM, GUSTAVUS (*b. Co. Donegal, Ireland, c. 1744; d. Philadelphia, Pa., 1819*), naval officer, privateer. Successful as captain of the cutter *Revenge*, 1777–78; made daring escape from Mill Prison, Plymouth, 1779.

COODE, JOHN (*d. 1709*), adventurer. As captain of militia of a "Protestant Association," Coode seized control of the government of Maryland, 1689.

COOK, ALBERT STANBURROUGH (*b. Montville, N.J., 1853; d. 1927*), scholar. Graduated Rutgers, 1872; studied at Göttingen and Leipzig, London and Jena (Ph.D., 1882). Organized English department at Johns Hopkins; taught at California and at Yale, 1889–1921; specialist in Old and Middle English.

COOK, CLARENCE CHATHAM (*b. Dorchester, Mass., 1828; d. 1900*), art critic, journalist. His *New York Tribune* art column (1863–69) was feared by American artists. Editor, *The Studio*, 1884–92; author of *The House Beautiful* (1878).

COOK, FLAVIUS JOSEPHUS (*b. Ticonderoga, N.Y., 1838; d. 1901*), lecturer. Gave Boston Monday lectures at Tremont Temple on relation of science to religion, *post* 1874.

COOK, FREDERICK ALBERT (*b. Hortonville, N.Y., 1865; d. New Rochelle, N.Y., 1940*), physician and polar explorer. Surgeon and ethnologist on the 1891–92 Greenland expedition of Robert E. Peary. After several later exploratory expeditions, Cook, accompanied by two young Eskimos, claimed to have reached the North Pole, April 1908. Almost simultaneously with Cook's announcement, Peary claimed to be the first to have reached the Pole, and challenged Cook's claim. The controversy raged for years. Cook failed to convince official and scientific opinion that he was telling the truth. [*Supp. 2*]

COOK, GEORGE CRAM (*b. Davenport, Iowa, 1873; d. Greece, 1924*), founder and director of Provincetown Players; established Macdougal Street (New York) playhouse, 1915, for encouragement of American dramatic talent.

COOK, GEORGE HAMMELL (*b. Hanover, N.J., 1818; d. 1889*), geologist, educator. As professor of chemistry at Rutgers, 1853–89, promoted establishment of agricultural college and experiment station; was state geologist, 1864–89. Author of many lucid and practical reports, and of *Geology of New Jersey* (1872).

COOK, ISAAC (*b. Long Branch, N.J., 1810; d. Eureka Springs, Ark., 1886*), politician, wine merchant. Prospered in Chicago, *post* 1834; president, American Wine Co., St. Louis., Mo., 1859–86.

COOK, JAMES MERRILL (*b. Ballston Spa, N.Y., 1807; d. 1868*), capitalist, New York Whig politician. As superintendent of State Banking Department, 1856–61, stabilized state finances.

COOK, JOHN WILLISTON (*b. near Oneida, N.Y., 1844; d. 1922*), educator. Removed to Illinois, 1851. Taught at Illinois State Normal University; edited *Illinois Schoolmaster* and *Illinois School Journal*; president of National Education Association, 1904.

COOK, JOSEPH. [See COOK, FLAVIUS JOSEPHUS, 1838–1901.]

COOK, MARTHA ELIZABETH DUNCAN WALKER (*b. Northumberland, Pa., 1806; d. Hoboken, N.J., 1874*), author, editor, translator. Sister of Robert J. Walker.

COOK, PHILIP (*b. Twiggs Co., Georgia, 1817; d. Georgia, 1894*), lawyer, Confederate soldier. Congressman, Democrat, 1873–83; secretary of state of Georgia, 1890–94.

COOK, ROBERT JOHNSON (*b. near Cookstown, Pa., 1849; d. Belle Vernon, Pa., 1922*), publisher, rowing coach at Yale. Originator of Bob Cook stroke.

COOK, RUSSELL S. (*b. New Marlboro, Mass., 1811; d. Pleasant Valley, N.Y., 1864*), Congregational clergyman. Corresponding secretary, American Tract Society, 1839–56; popularized "colportage."

COOK, TENNESSEE CELESTE CLAFLIN, Lady (*1845–1923*). [See WOODHULL, VICTORIA, 1838–1927.]

COOK, WALTER (*b. Buffalo, N.Y., 1846; d. New York, N.Y., 1916*), architect. Graduated Harvard, 1869; studied at Paris and Munich. *Post* 1877, headed several firms, ultimately Cook & Welch. Designed DeVinne Press Building, New York Life Insurance Building, Andrew Carnegie's residence, and the Choir School, St. John the Divine Cathedral, all in New York City.

COOK, ZEBEDEE (*b. Newburyport, Mass., 1786; d. South Framingham, Mass., 1858*), insurance man, horticulturist. A founder of Massachusetts Horticultural Society.

COOKE, EBENEZER (*b. c. 1670; d. c. 1732*), poet. His *Sot-weed Factor* (1708) and *Sotweed Redivivus* (1730) give a satirical picture of Maryland in the early 18th century. [*Supp. 1*]

COOKE, ELISHA (*b. Boston, Mass., 1637; d. 1715*), physician. Took leading part in overthrow and imprisonment of Andros and Dudley, 1689; agent of Massachusetts in London, 1690–92; an opponent of clericalism and royal prerogative.

COOKE, ELISHA (*b. Boston, Mass., 1678; d. Boston, 1737*), physician, statesman. Son of Elisha Cooke

(1637–1715), whose ideas of popular government he inherited. Served for 18 years in Massachusetts General Court and on the Council; opposed Governors Shute and Belcher.

COOKE, GEORGE WiLLIS (*b. Comstock, Mich., 1848; d. Revere, Mass., 1923*), Unitarian clergyman, lecturer. A liberal in theology and a socialist, he was author of a life of Emerson (1881) and *Unitarianism in America* (1902).

COOKE, HENRY DAVID (*b. Sandusky, O., 1825; d. 1881*), journalist, banker. Brother of Jay Cooke, for whom he lobbied at Washington, D.C.

COOKE, JAY (*b. Sandusky, O., 1821; d. 1905*), banker, financier. In 1839 entered banking firm in Philadelphia; from 1861 to 1873 was head of Jay Cooke & Co., one of the country's best-known banking houses. After success in negotiating a government loan in 1861, Cooke was appointed treasury agent in 1862 and succeeded by extensive advertisement in distributing a $500,000,000 government loan, a feat which he repeated in 1865. After the Civil War he entered general banking with branches in New York and London. The failure of his project to finance a northern railroad route from Duluth to Tacoma and the consequent collapse of his firm precipitated the panic of 1873.

COOKE, JOHN ESTEN (*b. Bermuda, 1783; d. 1853*), physician. Came to Virginia, 1791; M.D., University of Pennsylvania, 1805. Author of *Treatise on Pathology*, etc. (1828), said to have been earliest American systematic textbook on medicine; taught at Transylvania University and Louisville, Ky., Medical Institute.

COOKE, JOHN ESTEN (*b. Winchester, Va., 1830; d. 1886*), novelist, Confederate soldier. Son of John R. Cooke. Author of *Leather Stocking and Silk* (1854), *The Virginia Comedians* (1854), *Surry of Eagle's Nest* (1866), *Mohun* (1869) and other works.

COOKE, JOHN ROGERS (*b. Bermuda, 1788; d. 1854*), lawyer. Brother of John E. Cooke (1783–1853) and Philip St. George Cooke. A leading lawyer of western Virginia *post* 1812, he removed to Richmond, 1840. He was particularly distinguished as a delegate to the Virginia constitutional convention, 1829–30.

COOKE, JOSIAH PARSONS (*b. Boston, Mass., 1827; d. Newport, R.I., 1894*), chemist, teacher. Graduated Harvard, 1848; Erving Professor there *post* 1850; pioneered in the classification of elements by their atomic weights (1854). Author of *Elements of Chemical Physics* (1860), *The New Chemistry* (1874) and other works.

COOKE, PHILIP PENDLETON (*b. Martinsburg, Va., now W. Va., 1816; d. 1850*), poet, lawyer. Son

of John R. Cooke. His romantic poems were published in *Froissart Ballads* (1847).

COOKE, PHILIP ST. GEORGE (*b. Leesburg, Va., 1809; d. 1895*), soldier. Brother of John E. (1783–1853) and John R. Cooke. Graduated West Point, 1827. Served in the frontier West and in far western phase of Mexican War; was Union brigadier-general in Civil War; retired, 1873. Author of *Cavalry Tactics* (1861) and *The Conquest of New Mexico and California* (1878).

COOKE, ROSE TERRY (*b. near Hartford, Conn., 1827; d. Pittsfield, Mass., 1892*), story-writer, poet.

COOLBRITH, INA DONNA (*b. Nauvoo, Ill., 1841; d. Berkeley, Calif., 1928*), poet. Niece of Joseph Smith. Removed to California, 1851; was co-editor of Bret Harte's *Overland Monthly*, 1868, and later a librarian in Oakland and San Francisco.

COOLEY, EDWIN GILBERT (*b. Strawberry Point, Iowa, 1857; d. Chicago, Ill., 1923*), educator. Superintendent of Chicago schools, 1900–09; accomplished many reforms. [*Supp.* 1]

COOLEY, LYMAN EDGAR (*b. Canandaigua, N.Y., 1850; d. 1917*), civil engineer. Graduated Rensselaer Polytechnic, 1874. First chief engineer of Chicago Sanitary and Ship Canal, and associated with the work of the Chicago Sanitary District, 1885–1916. With James B. Angell and John E. Russell established feasibility of a Great Lakes-Atlantic ship canal. Was prolific writer on engineering subjects.

COOLEY, THOMAS McINTYRE (*b. near Attica, N.Y., 1824; d. Ann Arbor, Mich., 1898*), jurist. Removed to Michigan, 1843; admitted to the bar, 1846; practiced in Michigan and Ohio. Became official reporter of Michigan supreme court, 1858; edited *Michigan Reports*, 1858–64. Justice, Michigan supreme court, 1864–85; professor of law at University of Michigan, 1859–84; professor of American history and constitutional law, 1885–98. He wrote *A Treatise on . . . Constitutional Limitations* (1868); *The General Principles of Constitutional Law* (1880); an authoritative *Treatise on the Law of Torts* (1879) and other works. As chairman of the Interstate Commerce Commission, 1887–91, he made it into an effective judicial tribunal.

COOLIDGE, ARCHIBALD CARY (*b. Boston, Mass., 1866; d. 1928*), historian. Taught at Harvard; was director of Harvard Library *post* 1910 and the first editor of *Foreign Affairs*.

COOLIDGE, CALVIN (*b. Plymouth Notch, Vt., 1872; d. Northampton, Mass., 1933*), president of the United States. Son of parents who operated a general store and post office, he grew up with the traits of his ancestors and those of the community: frugality, taciturnity, industry, piety and honesty. Prepared for college in Vermont private schools, he entered Amherst in the class of 1895 and graduated *cum laude.* After studying law for 20 months, he was admitted to the bar and opened his own office in Northampton, Mass., in 1898. In 1905 he was married to Grace Anna Goodhue.

After filling various local offices Coolidge was elected to the Massachusetts House of Representatives, 1906, served two terms as mayor of Northampton, and went to the Massachusetts Senate in 1911. He became lieutenant-governor of the state in 1915. By party loyalty, industry and an ingrained conservatism, Coolidge impressed the leaders of his Republican party. Pushed by Frank Waterman Stearns, he was elected governor of Massachusetts in 1918 and made a national reputation by settling the controversial Boston police strike in 1919. His statement that "There is no right to strike against the public safety by anybody, anywhere, any time" sounded a popular chord, and he was re-elected.

At the 1920 Republican National Convention in Chicago he was nominated for vice-president in a revolt against boss dictation and, when elected, profited by being the antithesis of President Harding. His advent to the presidency on August 4, 1923, saved the Republican party the full obloquy of the exposure of corrupt oil leases and other scandals under the late president.

In the campaign of 1924 Coolidge's appearance of thrift, caution, and honesty, industry, self-reliance and homely sagacity won him nomination on the first ballot. Few lamented his total want of leadership, or perceived that his democracy was combined with an extraordinary deference to big business. The electoral vote in 1924 was for Coolidge, 379; for John W. Davis, 139; and for Robert M. La Follette, 13.

The four following years were those of a national inertia which Coolidge administered. He opposed subsidizing the farmers, action to punish business excesses, government operation of Muscle Shoals, measures to assist the League of Nations or World Court in international stabilization, and reduction of tariffs. His few recommendations to Congress were generally ignored. As speculation pushed the stock market higher, his statements encouraged it. In foreign affairs Coolidge left the direction of policy primarily to Secretaries Hughes and Kellogg.

Although his popularity remained high and he probably could have been re-elected in 1928, Coolidge knew that the country needed bolder leadership and he decided to retire. His last four years after leaving the White House were spent mainly in writing his *Autobiography* and articles preaching individualism, economy and *laissez faire.* [*Supp.* 1]

COOLIDGE, CHARLES ALLERTON (*b. Boston, Mass., 1858; d. Locust Valley, N.Y., 1936*), architect. Worked for Henry Hobson Richardson, 1883–86, subsequently forming with various partners his own firm, which became in 1924, Coolidge, Shepley, Bulfinch & Abbott. The firm specialized in designs for college, public and commercial buildings, among them the Ames Building, Boston; the Chicago Public Library, and Art Institute; various buildings for the Rockefeller Institute, New York City, and for the University of Chicago, Stanford and Harvard universities. [*Supp.* 2]

COOLIDGE, THOMAS JEFFERSON (*b. Boston, Mass., 1831; d. 1920*), merchant, financier, diplomat. Active in cotton-spinning industry, banking, railroad management; served as minister to France, 1892–96.

COOMBE, THOMAS (*b. Philadelphia, Pa., 1747; d. London, England, 1822*), Anglican clergyman, Loyalist, poet. Left America in 1779. A forceful preacher, his *The Peasant of Auburn* (London, 1783) recounted the unhappy fate of emigrants to the Ohio.

COONTZ, ROBERT EDWARD (*b. Hannibal, Mo., 1864; d. Bremerton, Wash., 1935*), naval officer. Graduated Annapolis, 1885. Chief of Naval Operations, 1919–23. [*Supp.* 1]

COOPER, EDWARD (*b. New York, N.Y., 1824; d. New York, 1905*), manufacturer, metallurgist. Son of Peter Cooper. Invented regenerative hot-blast stove for blast furnaces; helped break "Tweed Ring"; was mayor of New York, 1879–81.

COOPER, ELIAS SAMUEL (*b. near Somerville, O., 1820; d. San Francisco, Calif., 1862*), surgeon. Brother of Jacob Cooper. Founded first medical college on Pacific coast, 1858; pioneered with alcoholic wound dressings and use of metallic sutures for fractures.

COOPER, EZEKIEL (*b. Caroline Co., Md., 1763; d. 1847*), Methodist clergyman. Agent of Methodist Book Concern, 1789–1808; vigorously opposed slavery.

COOPER, HENRY ERNEST (*b. New Albany, Ind., 1857; d. Long Beach, Calif., 1929*), lawyer. Helped organize Hawaii revolution, 1893; promoted American annexation of Hawaii and was first secretary of the Territory.

COOPER, HUGH LINCOLN (*b. Sheldon, Minn., 1865; d. Stamford, Conn., 1937*), hydroelectric engineer. Designer of pioneer low-head hydroelectric plants; consultant on many foreign power projects. [*Supp.* 2]

COOPER, JACOB (*b. near Somerville, O., 1830; d. 1904*), Presbyterian clergyman, educator. Studied at Yale, Berlin, Halle, Edinburgh; taught Greek at Centre College, Ky., and Greek and moral philosophy at Rutgers, 1866–1904.

COOPER, JAMES (*b. Frederick Co., Md., 1810; d. Camp Chase, O., 1863*), lawyer, Union soldier, Pennsylvania legislator. U.S. senator, Whig, 1849–55.

COOPER, JAMES FENIMORE (*b. Burlington, N.J., 1789; d. Cooperstown, N.Y., 1851*), novelist. Grew up at Otsego Hall, Cooperstown, N.Y., the residence of his father William Cooper who held land in that area for development. Cooper's youth was spent in a manorial house located at the edge of the frontier wilderness; thus the elements of the pioneer and the gentleman were provided to serve as a theme of struggle throughout Cooper's life. Educated in the Albany household of an Episcopal rector of Federalist, anti-New England sentiments, he attended Yale for three years, then shipped before the mast, 1806. Commissioned a navy midshipman, 1807, he served on Lake Ontario, Lake Champlain and on the Atlantic. Married to Susan A. De Lancey in 1811, he resigned from the navy; he and his wife settled down to country life at Mamaroneck, N.Y., and subsequently at Cooperstown and Scarsdale, N.Y. In 1822 he went to New York City to pursue his literary interests. He had published his first novel *Precaution* in 1820, but the book, conventional in manner and content, was not a success. With *The Spy* (1821), Cooper turned to an American setting and the period of the American Revolution, producing a story of romantic adventure and suspenseful excitement. The book also revealed his social attitudes, a curious mixture of democratic profession and aristocratic condescension. The vigor of Cooper's narrative and his characteristic formula of flight and pursuit made *The Spy* a success. In 1823 *The Pioneers* appeared, introducing the great character of Natty Bumppo (Leather-Stocking), and also *The Pilot* which set the mode for later sea stories. *The Spy, The Pioneers* and *The Pilot* respectively drew on the three regions of memory with which Cooper was most familiar: the New York past, the northern frontier, the high seas.

Having won a reputation as an author, Cooper founded the Bread and Cheese Club in New York City, served on the welcoming committee for Lafayette in 1824 and received an honorary Master of Arts degree from Columbia College. In 1825 he published *Lionel Lincoln,* a story dealing with the Boston of Bunker Hill days. In *The Last of the Mohicans* (1826), Cooper revived the character of Natty Bumppo and portrayed him as a youthful, competent scout during the French and Indian War. In *The Prairie* (1827), the same character appears in a setting beyond the Mississippi as an old trapper of wide benevolence, a type of the wisdom attained through having lived in the boundless wilderness. In these books the forest is the symbol of whatever is spacious and elevated in life, the breeding ground of heroism. Cooper's Indian characters were meant to be figures of romance rather than portraits and were shown as chivalrous, noble and uncorrupted by civilization.

From 1826 to 1833 Cooper lived in Europe, chiefly in Paris. He traveled to England, Switzerland, Italy, Munich and Dresden. During these years he wrote several romances: *The Red Rover* (1828); *The Wept of Wish-ton-Wish* (1829); *The Water-Witch* (1831); *The Bravo* (1831); *The Heidenmauer* (1832); *The*

Headsman (1833); and the satiric *Notions of the Americans* (1828). While his work abroad displayed much bumptious, ardent patriotism and endorsed republican principles, his European experiences also stiffened some of his early aristocratic prejudices. He experienced a profound shock on his return to America. He missed the simplicity, the decorum, the private and public virtue, the enlightened patriotism which he had romantically declared to be natural to Americans. He now discovered that the ideal wilderness of his fantasy did not exist. In his efforts to preach reform and a return to the old virtues, he grew intemperate and shrill, as in *A Letter to his Countrymen* (1834). In *The Monikins* (1835), *Sketches of Switzerland* (1836), *Gleanings in Europe: France* (1837), *Gleanings in Europe: England* (1837), *Gleanings in Europe: Italy* (1838), he savagely poured out his judgments on Europe, to which he had preferred his mythical America, and also on that actual America which was so unlike his dream. He sought to state his thesis of democratic decline directly in *The American Democrat* (1838) and to illustrate it in the novels *Homeward Bound* (1838) and *Home as Found* (1838). Often justified in his accusations of American vulgarity, stupidity, dishonesty and cruelty, he made his protagonists show a patriotism so confused with snobbishness as to be beyond sympathy or respect. The American public punished him by neglecting his works, and newspapers attacked him violently and libelously. Cooper, however, emerged victorious in a series of libel suits against the offending papers, produced a scholarly *History of the Navy of the United States of America* (1839), and brought out *The Pathfinder* (1840) and *The Deerslayer* (1841). These novels show a marked gain in portraiture and round out the full character of Leather-Stocking, completing the outline of the most truly epical figure in American fiction. The real triumph of Cooper's craft lies in the variety of inventive devices by which he fills the existence of his heroes with enough actions, desires, fears, victories, defeats, sentiments, and thoughts to make the barren frontier seem a splendid stage.

From 1840 to 1846 other books appeared in rapid succession. *Mercedes of Castile* (1840) went back to Columbus's first voyage; *The Two Admirals* (1842) concerned itself with the British navy before the Revolution; *The Wing-and-Wing* (1842) told of a French privateer; *Ned Myers* (1843) was the biography of an actual sailor who had sailed with Cooper long before; *Lives of Distinguished American Naval Officers* (1846) carried on the naval history theme; *Afloat and Ashore* (two parts, 1844) dealt with the evils of impressment and with life in early New York. *Le Mouchoir* (1843) described fashionable contemporary Manhattan. The *Littlepage Manuscripts* trilogy (*Satanstoe,* 1845; *The Chainbearer,* 1845; *The Redskins,* 1846) attempted a cyclic scheme similar to that of the Leather-Stocking books.

Satanstoe must still be considered one of America's most distinguished historical novels in its vivid recreation of the life of the New York gentry in the mid-18th century.

After 1846 Cooper grew more bigoted in his opinions and in his anti-New England bias. He carried his animosities into the plots of his latest novels— *The Crater* (1848), *The Oak Openings* (1848), *The Sea Lions* (1849), *The Ways of the Hour* (1850)— and lost all touch with the magical, mythical wilderness which he himself had created.

COOPER, JAMES GRAHAM (*b. New York, N.Y., 1830; d. Hayward, Calif., 1902*), physician, naturalist. Made pioneer contributions to the botany, zoology, and geology of California and Washington.

COOPER, JOSEPH ALEXANDER (*b. Whitley Co., Ky., 1823; d. Stafford Co., Kans., 1910*), soldier. An East Tennessee Unionist farmer, he served brilliantly during Civil War; was breveted major-general.

COOPER, MARK ANTHONY (*b. Hancock Co., Ga., 1800; d. Etowah, Ga., 1885*), businessman, politician. Engaged in cotton-milling, banking, railroading, iron-manufacturing, coal-mining; was Whig, later Calhoun-Democratic congressman, 1839–43.

COOPER, MYLES (*b. Cumberland Co., England, 1737; d. England, 1785*), Episcopal clergyman, Loyalist. Able president of King's College (Columbia), New York City, 1763–75. An ardent propagandist for the royal cause, he returned to England in May 1775.

COOPER, OSWALD BRUCE (*b. Mount Gilead, O., 1879; d. Chicago, Ill., 1940*), letterer and typographic designer. [*Supp. 2*]

COOPER, PETER (*b. New York, N.Y., 1791; d. 1883*), manufacturer, inventor, philanthropist. Worked with his father as hatter, brewer, store-keeper, and brick-maker; was apprenticed to a New York coach-maker. He then began a cloth-shearing business of his own, and in 1813 opened a retail grocery store. Next he bought a glue factory and soon won a monopoly for his superior American-made glue and isinglass. In 1828 he and two partners erected the Canton Iron Works at Baltimore, Md.; here in 1829–30 Cooper built "Tom Thumb," the first steam locomotive built in America. In 1836 he sold the Canton Works for stock of the Baltimore & Ohio Railroad. He then acquired a wire manufactory in Trenton, N.J.; blast furnaces in Phillipsburg, Pa.; a rolling mill in New York; foundries at Ringwood, N.J., and Durham, Pa.; and iron mines in New Jersey. In 1854 he rolled the first structural iron for fireproof buildings. Cooper served as president of the New York, Newfoundland & London Telegraph Co. (Atlantic cable), and of the North American Telegraph Co. He invented a washing machine, a machine for mortising hubs, and others for propelling ferry-boats, for utilizing the tide for power and for moving canal

barges by an endless chain. Cooper served as New York City alderman, advocated paid police and fire departments, sanitary water conditions, and public schools. He was a presidential candidate on the Greenback ticket in 1876. His greatest monument is the Cooper Union (or Cooper Institute) of New York City, a free educational institution uniquely combining general scientific education with practical training, which he founded, 1857–59.

COOPER, SAMUEL (*b. Boston, Mass., 1725; d. 1783*), clergyman, Revolutionary patriot, pastor of Boston's Brattle Square Church, 1743–83.

COOPER, SAMUEL (*b. Hackensack, N.J., 1798; d. Alexandria, Va., 1876*), Confederate soldier. Served many years as staff officer in Washington D.C. In 1861 went with the South and was appointed adjutant- and inspector-general of Confederate Army in which his long experience in administration was highly valued.

COOPER, SARAH BROWN INGERSOLL (*b. Cazenovia, N.Y., 1836; d. 1896*), philanthropist, founder of kindergartens. Removed to San Francisco, 1869; was president of Woman's Congress and, in 1892, of International Kindergarten Union.

COOPER, SUSAN FENIMORE (*b. Westchester Co., N.Y., 1813; d. 1894*), author, daughter of James Fenimore Cooper. Was her father's amanuensis; wrote *Rural Hours* (1850) and prefaces to Household Edition (1876–84) of Cooper's works.

COOPER, THEODORE (*b. Cooper's Plain, N.Y., 1839; d. 1919*), civil engineer, bridge-builder. Graduated Rensselaer Polytechnic, 1858. Served as navy engineer, 1861–1872; introduced wheel-load instead of uniform load analysis for railway bridges.

COOPER, THOMAS (*b. Westminster, England, 1759; d. Columbia, S.C., 1839*), agitator, scientist, educator. Studied at Oxford; took up medicine in London and Manchester. Entered a firm of calico-printers, was a barrister and dabbled in philosophy and chemistry. Joseph Priestley nominated him for the Royal Society, but Cooper's materialist philosophy, his Unitarian theology and his revolutionary political thought rendered him unacceptable. He agitated for abolition of the slave-trade and repeal of the Corporation and Test Acts, and was attacked by Burke for instituting a correspondence between the Manchester Constitutional Society and the French Jacobins, 1792. Disgusted with the Terror in France and the conservative reaction in England, he went with Priestley to the United States in 1794. He practiced law and medicine in Pennsylvania, and by 1800 emerged as a Jeffersonian pamphleteer, attacking the Sedition Law under which he himself was imprisoned and fined. As a Pennsylvania county commissioner, 1801–04, and state judge, 1804–11, he became identified with the conservative faction in opposition to the more radical democrats who attacked the judiciary. Removed from office, he turned to science and teaching. He was professor of chemistry at Carlisle (now Dickinson) College, 1811–15, and professor of applied chemistry and mineralogy at the University of Pennsylvania, 1815–19. He was honored by membership in the American Philosophical Society and by Jefferson's unsuccessful attempts to appoint him at the University of Virginia. In January 1820 he went to South Carolina College; shortly thereafter he was elected its president and taught chemistry, mineralogy and political economy until 1834. He helped found the state's first medical school and first insane asylum. Embroiled in controversy with the Presbyterian clergy over his biblical criticism and materialist doctrines, he strengthened his position through his defense of the extreme state-rights party, of slavery and of the Southern view on the tariff question. The academic philosopher of state rights, he favored nullification and, valuing union too little because he loved liberty too well, became one of the first advocates of secession. After his retirement from the college in 1834, he edited the South Carolina statutes, supported the Second Bank against Jackson, and conspired with Nicholas Biddle to bring about the latter's nomination for the presidency in 1840. Cooper's chief influence came through his masterly use of the pen in political controversies. Always a passionate hater of tyranny, he wrote a pioneer American textbook, the *Lectures on the Elements of Political Economy* (1826). His modernist theological views will be found in his *Tracts* (1789). His legal scholarship is documented by his *Institutes of Justinian* (1812) and his South Carolina *Statutes at Large* (1836–39). His most interesting theoretical writings on science are his descriptions of Priestley's experiments, his *Introductory Lecture* on chemistry (1812), and his *Discourse on the Connexion between Chemistry and Medicine* (1818). These writings serve as a valuable index to the state of American scientific knowledge in Cooper's day and reveal his own persistent faith in salvation by enlightenment.

COOPER, THOMAS ABTHORPE (*b. Harrow-on-the-Hill, England, 1776; d. Bristol, Pa., 1849*), actor, theatrical manager. Raised by William Godwin; trained and coached by Thomas Holcroft. Came to America, 1796; by 1800 he was recognized as the unrivaled tragic actor of America and rapidly made a fortune. *Post* 1815, he devoted himself entirely to starring engagements here and abroad; he last appeared on the New York stage in 1835 after a decade of waning popularity and financial reverses. Thereafter he held several minor government posts. He is best known for his powerful portrayals of Macbeth, Hamlet, and Othello.

COOPER, WILLIAM (*b. Byberry, Pa., 1754; d. Albany, N.Y., 1809*), jurist, landowner. Father of James Fenimore Cooper. Founded and settled Cooperstown, N.Y.

COOPER, WILLIAM JOHN (*b. Sacramento, Calif., 1882; d. Kearney, Nebr., 1935*), educator. U.S. commissioner of education, 1929–33. [*Supp. 1*]

COOPER-POUCHER, MATILDA S. (*b. Blauveltville, N.Y., 1839; d. Oswego, N.Y., 1900*), educator. Devoted herself to the successful work of the Oswego State Normal School; served there as critic, teacher, placement director, and preceptress.

COOTE, RICHARD (*b. 1636; d. New York, N.Y., 1701*), Earl of Bellomont, colonial governor. A supporter of William of Orange, he received extensive land grants in Ireland, and was member of Parliament, 1688–95. In 1697 he was appointed governor of New York, Massachusetts, and New Hampshire. By restraining the dealings of New York merchants with pirates, he aroused the hostility of merchants; since he seemed to appease the "Leisler democrats," the landed proprietors opposed his efforts to secure a more orderly conduct of colonial affairs.

COPE, CALEB (*b. Greensburg, Pa., 1797; d. Philadelphia, Pa., 1888*), merchant, financier. Active in numerous Philadelphia business and charitable enterprises.

COPE, EDWARD DRINKER (*b. Philadelphia, Pa., 1840; d. Philadelphia, 1897*), zoologist, paleontologist. Student of S. F. Baird and Joseph Leidy; authority on extinct vertebrates of the far West; owner and editor of *American Naturalist*.

COPE, THOMAS PYM (*b. Lancaster, Pa., 1768; d. 1854*), merchant, philanthropist. Established first regular packet line between Philadelphia and Liverpool, 1821; promoted canal and railroad construction; served in state legislature.

COPE, WALTER (*b. Philadelphia, Pa., 1860; d. 1902*), architect. Designed notable buildings chiefly in adaptation of English Collegiate Gothic for Bryn Mawr, University of Pennsylvania, Princeton, and Washington University at St. Louis.

COPELAND, CHARLES W. (*b. Coventry, Conn., 1815; d. 1895*), naval engineer. Designed machinery of the *Fulton*, the first steam war-vessel built (1836) under navy supervision; also designed record-breaking trans-Atlantic merchant steamers.

COPELAND, ROYAL SAMUEL (*b. near Dexter, Mich., 1868; d. Washington, D.C., 1938*), physician, teacher and medical writer. M.D., University of Michigan, 1889. Removed to New York, 1908. New York City public health commissioner, 1918–22; U.S. senator from New York, Democrat, 1922–38.

[*Supp. 2*]

COPLEY, JOHN SINGLETON (*b. Boston, Mass., 1738 [?]; d. London, England, 1815*), painter. Grew up in the Boston home of his step-father, Peter Pelham, a teacher, portraitist and engraver. Copley later lamented the limited opportunities for artistic training in Boston, but benefited greatly from his association with craftsmen at his step-father's home and workshop. He started as a professional portrait painter before he was of age; he worked in oil, but also was a pioneer American pastellist. The exhibition in England of Copley's "The Boy with the Squirrel" in 1766 led to his election as a Fellow of the Society of Artists of Great Britain. Benjamin West urged Copley to come to England for study, but Copley was kept in Boston by his success; the foremost personages of New England came to his painting-room as sitters. Married in 1769 to Susannah Clarke, he established himself in a house on Beacon Hill. He took little or no part in town and church affairs. In 1771 he went to New York for several months of portrait painting and also visited Philadelphia.

With the rise of the revolutionary spirit in Boston, Copley's family connections being Loyalist and his English friends urging him to come to London, he left Boston in June 1774. He traveled and made studies in France, Italy, Germany and the Low Countries, returning to London where he was reunited with his family who had left Boston in May 1775, as refugees from the Revolution. Copley's technique was so well established, his habits of industry so well confirmed and the reputation that had preceded him from America was so extraordinary, that he could hardly fail to make a place for himself among British artists. Yet the pictures of his maturity did not always reach the standard of the best works of his youth. He began now to paint historical pieces, best-known among which are "A Youth Rescued from a Shark" and "The Death of Lord Chatham." These and many others were characterized by Copley's painstaking efforts to obtain good personal likenesses and correct historical accessories. He continued to paint portraits, among them those of several members of the royal family and numerous British and American celebrities. Between 1776 and 1815 he sent 43 paintings to exhibitions of the Royal Academy, of which he was elected an associate member in 1776 and a full member in 1783. Copley's industry injured his health and he became nervous from overwork. Personally liberal and sympathetic to the American cause, he was prevented by his professional labor from ever returning to the United States. During the last years of his life, Copley was beset by financial difficulties and was assisted by his son who is celebrated in English history as Lord Lyndhurst.

COPLEY, LIONEL (*d. 1693*). Colonial governor of Maryland, commissioned 1691. Died in office.

COPLEY, THOMAS (*b. Madrid, Spain, 1595; d. c. 1652*), Jesuit missionary. Active in settlement of Maryland, 1637–45, where he was for a time superior of the mission. Arrested and carried to England, he returned to Maryland after two years' imprisonment and died there.

COPPÉE, HENRY (*b. Savannah, Ga., 1821; d. Bethlehem, Pa., 1895*), soldier, educator. Graduated West Point, 1845; taught literature and history at West Point and University of Pennsylvania. President of Lehigh University, 1866–75, 1893–95.

COPPENS, CHARLES (*b. Turnhout, Belgium, 1835; d. Chicago, Ill., 1920*), Roman Catholic priest, educator. Entered Society of Jesus at St. Louis, Mo., 1853; ordained, 1865. Taught at Jesuit colleges in Midwest and was author of widely used textbooks and devotional works.

COPPET, EDWARD J. de. [See DE COPPET, EDWARD J., 1855–1916.]

COPWAY, GEORGE (*b. Ontario, Canada, 1818; d. near Pontiac, Mich. (?), c. 1863*), Chippewa chief, Methodist missionary. Author of *Life, History and Travels of Kah-Ge-Ga-Gah-Bowh* (1847, an autobiography) and other works.

COQUILLETT, DANIEL WILLIAM (*b. Pleasant Valley, Ill., 1856; d. 1911*), entomologist. Helped acclimatize Australian ladybird beetle which saved California citrus culture; experimented with use of hydrocyanic-acid gas against scale insects.

CORAM, THOMAS (*b. Lyme Regis, England, 1668; d. 1751*), merchant, shipbuilder, colony promoter. Strengthened Anglican church in Massachusetts where he lived at Taunton, 1697–1703; promoted settlement schemes between Kennebec and St. Lawrence and in Nova Scotia.

CORBETT, HENRY WINSLOW (*b. Westboro, Mass., 1827; d. 1903*), merchant, banker, railroad promoter, politician. Settled in Oregon, 1851, and became leading businessman of Portland. U.S. senator, Republican, from Oregon, 1867–73.

CORBETT, JAMES JOHN (*b. San Francisco, Calif., 1866; d. Bayside, N.Y., 1933*), pugilist, "Gentleman Jim." Defeated John L. Sullivan for world's heavyweight title, 1892; lost championship to Robert Fitzsimmons, 1897. [*Supp. 1*]

CORBIN, AUSTIN (*b. Newport, N.H., 1827; d. near Newport, 1896*), capitalist, railroad executive. Began banking career in Iowa; removed to New York, 1865, where he reorganized Long Island Railroad and the Philadelphia & Reading.

CORBIN, DANIEL CHASE (*b. Newport, N.H., 1832; d. 1918*), financier. Brother and associate of Austin Corbin. Built railroads in Pacific Northwest and developed Spokane, Wash., as transportation and distributing center.

CORBIN, HENRY CLARK (*b. near Batavia, O., 1842; d. New York, N.Y., 1909*), soldier. Adjutant-general of the army during Spanish-American War. [*Supp. 1*]

CORBIN, MARGARET (*b. Franklin Co., Pa., 1751; d. Westchester Co., N.Y., 1800*), Revolutionary heroine.

CORBY, WILLIAM (*b. Detroit, Mich., 1833; d. 1897*), Roman Catholic clergyman. Chaplain of New York's Irish Brigade, 1861–65; earned title of "second founder" of Notre Dame University as president, 1866–72, 1877–81. Served as U.S. Provincial and Assistant General of his order, the Congregation of the Holy Cross.

CORCORAN, JAMES ANDREW (*b. Charleston, S.C., 1820; d. Philadelphia, Pa., 1889*), Roman Catholic clergyman, theologian, editor. Secretary of Baltimore Councils of 1855, 1858, 1866, and theologian for preparatory commission for Vatican Council; drew up "Spalding formula" on Papal Infallibility.

CORCORAN, WILLIAM WILSON (*b. Georgetown, D.C., 1798; d. 1888*), banker, philanthropist. Began his career as dry-goods merchant, entered banking, and in 1840 opened the successful banking firm of Corcoran & Riggs. The Corcoran Gallery of Art, begun in 1859, was inaugurated in Washington, D.C., 1872; Corcoran's personal collection was its nucleus, and he endowed it. His other philanthropic activities include the founding of the Louise Home for needy "gentlewomen," and donations to universities, churches and religious institutions.

COREY, WILLIAM ELLIS (*b. Braddock, Pa., 1866; d. 1934*), steel manufacturer. Developed a process for toughening armor plate to resist projectiles; president, U.S. Steel Corp., 1903–11. [*Supp. 1*]

CORLISS, GEORGE HENRY (*b. Easton, N.Y., 1817; d. 1888*), inventor, manufacturer. His invention of separate rotary valves for steam and exhaust ports and a governor which by a system of levers controlled the valves and the admission of steam to the engine cylinder was made 1846–51. It revolutionized the construction and operation of steam engines. He became president of Corliss Engine Co. in Providence, R.I., 1856. Patents for a gear-cutting machine, an improved boiler and a pumping engine were also granted him. He is ranked equally with Watt in the development of the steam engine.

CORNBURY, EDWARD HYDE, Viscount (*b. England, 1661; d. 1723*), colonial governor of New York and New Jersey, 1702–08. His administration suffered from his arrogance, vanity and financial dishonesty.

CORNELL, ALONZO B. (*b. Ithaca, N.Y., 1832; d. Ithaca, 1904*), politician. Son of Ezra Cornell. Official of Western Union Co.; as Republican governor of New York, 1879–83, modernized state government.

CORNELL, EZEKIEL (*b. Scituate, R.I., 1733; d. Milford, Mass., 1800*), Revolutionary soldier. Commanded Rhode Island State Brigade; distinguished himself at battle of Rhode Island, August 29, 1778.

CORNELL, EZRA (*b. Westchester Co., N.Y., 1807; d. Ithaca, N.Y., 1874*), capitalist. Began life as a carpenter and millwright. After devising a satisfactory means for insulating telegraph wires on poles, he aided S. F. B. Morse in erecting the Baltimore-Washington line. Thereafter he financed and built other lines and soon became the chief figure in the new industry. In 1855 he joined in the founding of the Western Union Telegraph Co., of which he became a director and was for years the largest stockholder. In association with Andrew D. White he brought about the establishment of Cornell University.

CORNING, ERASTUS (*b. Norwich, Conn., 1794; d. 1872*), businessman, capitalist. Removed to Albany, N.Y., 1814, and began career as iron manufacturer; associated *post* 1837 with John F. Winslow, he built the business into one of the most extensive in the country. As president of the Utica & Schenectady Railroad, 1833–53, Corning was a prime mover in the consolidation of New York lines and was elected first president of the New York Central, a post he held until 1864. He served also as mayor of Albany, state senator, Democratic congressman, and as a regent and vice-chancellor of the University of New York.

CORNOYER, PAUL (*b. St. Louis, Mo., 1864; d. East Gloucester, Mass., 1923*), painter, teacher of art.

CORNSTALK (*c. 1720–1777*), Shawnee Indian chief. Fought English settlers on Ohio-Virginia frontier during French and Indian War, Pontiac's War, Lord Dunmore's War; was loyal to the Americans after the treaty of Camp Charlotte. His murder at the fort at the mouth of the Kanawha brought down the enmity of the Shawnees on the whites for nearly a score of years.

CORNWALLIS, KINAHAN (*b. London, Eng., 1839; d. New York, N.Y., 1917*), lawyer, editor, writer.

CORONADO, FRANCISCO VÁZQUEZ (*b. Salamanca, Spain, 1510; d. Mexico, 1554*), explorer. Came to Mexico, 1535. As governor of Nueva Galicia, 1538, he aided Fray Marcos de Nizza, and was named commander of an expedition to check on the friar's alleged explorations. Departing in February 1540, in July he reached and conquered the Zuni pueblos. Members of the expedition explored much unknown territory: the mouth of the Gila River, part of the California peninsula, the Moqui pueblos, the Grand Canyon. After wintering near Isleta, in April 1541 Coronado set out for the fabled Gran Quivira in eastern Kansas. He traversed the "Llanos del Cíbola," the Texas Panhandle and Oklahoma. At Quivira he found only an Indian settlement and, disappointed, returned to Mexico. His journey ranks as one of history's epochal explorations. Removed as governor of Nueva Galicia in 1544, Coronado served until death as a regidor in Mexico City.

CORRIGAN, MICHAEL AUGUSTINE (*b. Newark, N.J., 1839; d. New York, N.Y., 1902*), Roman Catholic clergyman. Bishop of Newark, 1873–80; coadjutor bishop of New York, 1880–85. Succeeded Cardinal McCloskey as archbishop, 1885. A conservative, a strict canonist, and an able administrator.

CORROTHERS, JAMES DAVID (*b. Calvin, Mich., 1869; d. West Chester, Pa., 1917*), clergyman, poet. Author of verse and prose sketches of Negro life.

CORSE, JOHN MURRAY (*b. Pittsburgh, Pa., 1835; d. Winchester, Mass., 1893*), Union soldier. Raised in Iowa. Won fame through his gallant defense of Allatoona Pass, October, 1864; was postmaster of Boston's "model post office."

CORSON, HIRAM (*b. Philadelphia, Pa., 1828; d. Ithaca, N.Y., 1911*), educator. Taught literature at Cornell, 1870–1903. Author of *Aims of Literary Study* (1895) and other works.

CORSON, JULIET (*b. Roxbury, Mass., 1842; d. New York, N.Y., 1897*), pioneer teacher of cooking.

CORSON, ROBERT RODGERS (*b. New Hope, Pa., 1831; d. Philadelphia, Pa., 1904*), coal merchant, humanitarian. Active in Civil War relief work and in many reform causes.

CORTAMBERT, LOUIS RICHARD (*b. Paris, France, 1808; d. New York, N.Y., 1881*), author, journalist, disciple of Thoreau.

CORTELYOU, GEORGE BRUCE (*b. New York, N.Y., 1862; d. Huntington, N.Y., 1940*), public utility executive. Became stenographer to President Cleveland in 1895, then secretary to Presidents McKinley and Theodore Roosevelt. In 1903 Roosevelt appointed him secretary of the newly created Department of Commerce and Labor. Impressing the president with his administrative ability and political sagacity, Cortelyou managed Roosevelt's 1904 campaign and subsequently was appointed postmaster-general, effecting a major reorganization of his department. In 1907 he became secretary of the treasury, acting effectively to meet the financial panic of that year and framing legislation for a central banking system. From 1909 to 1935 Cortelyou was president of what became the Consolidated Edison Co., New York City, greatly expanding the company's business. [*Supp. 2*]

CORTHELL, ELMER LAWRENCE (*b. South Abington, Mass., 1840; d. 1916*), civil engineer. Specialist in railroad, bridge and harbor work.

CORWIN, EDWARD TANJORE (*b. New York, N.Y., 1834; d. 1914*), clergyman, historian. Published many works on Reformed Dutch Church in America; edited *Ecclesiastical Records of the State of New York* (1901–16).

CORWIN, THOMAS (*b. Bourbon Co., Ky., 1794; d. Washington, D.C., 1865*), lawyer. Raised in Ohio, which state he represented as congressman, Whig, 1831–40, and U.S. senator, 1845–50; he was also secretary of the treasury under Fillmore, and minister to Mexico, 1861–64. He reached the high point of his career as U.S. senator when he denounced the Mexican War as unjust and predicted that a Civil War would be one of its effects.

CORY, CHARLES BARNEY (*b. Boston, Mass., 1857; d. 1921*), ornithologist. Curator, Chicago's Field Museum; published *Birds of the Americas* (1918–19), a synopsis and synonymy.

COSBY, WILLIAM (*b. c. 1690; d. 1735/6*). Unenlightened royal governor of New York and New Jersey, 1731–1735/6.

COSTANSÓ, MIGUEL (*fl. 1769–1811*), Spanish cosmographer, army engineer. His accounts of an expedition to settle Alta California, 1769, are major contributions to California history.

COSTER, F. DONALD. [See MUSICA, PHILIP MARIANO FAUSTO, 1884–1938.]

COSTIGAN, EDWARD PRENTISS (*b. near Beulahville, Va., 1874; d. Denver, Colo., 1939*), lawyer. Brother of George P. Costigan. A Republican turned Progressive, he was a tariff commissioner, 1916–28; then served in U.S. Senate from Colorado as a Democrat, 1930–36. [*Supp. 2*]

COSTIGAN, GEORGE PURCELL (*b. Chicago, Ill., 1870; d. 1934*), professor of law, Northwestern University, 1909–22; University of California, 1922–34. Insisted in his teaching on the recognition of human values and social responsibilities by lawyers; was author of a number of casebooks and critical articles on legal problems. [*Supp. 1*]

COTTON, JOHN (*b. Derby, England, 1584; d. Boston, Mass., 1652*), Puritan clergyman, author. Studied at Trinity College, Cambridge; won fellowship to Emmanuel College where he became head lecturer and dean; was ordained, 1610, and in 1612 was chosen vicar of St. Botolph's Church at Boston, Lincolnshire. By about 1615 he began abandoning practices of the Church of England for the Puritan form of worship. His nonconformism was tolerated by his bishop, although Cotton did not entirely escape opposition. In 1632, however, summoned to appear before the Court of High Commission, he fled to London; in May 1633, resigned his charge. Having been a friend of John Winthrop, he went to America and landed at Boston in September 1633. He became teacher of the Boston church and quickly rose to a dominant position in the religious and political affairs of the colony. In the Antinomian controversy he at first took the side of Anne Hutchinson, but, finding himself alone among the colony's leaders, he went over to the side of the persecutors. However honest his opinions may have been, from 1638 on he became narrower and more bitter in his views. In two controversies with Roger Williams he rejected Williams's view that a definite renunciation of the Church of England should be the prerequisite for membership in the church in New England, and insisted in opposition to Williams that the authority of magistrates should extend over religious as well as secular affairs. An indefatigable worker, he spent as much as six hours a day in praying and preaching and wrote voluminously. His catechism *Milk for Babes* (1646) was a standard textbook for New England children. He wrote many controversial pamphlets, works on prayer, church music, and on the theory and methods of Congregationalism as practiced in New England. To the latter belong his *The Way of the Churches of Christ in New England* (1645), *The Keyes of the Kingdom of Heaven* (1644), and *The Way of the Congregational Churches Cleared* (1648). Undoubtedly one of the ablest and most influential men of his day in Massachusetts, through a perhaps unconscious desire to retain his prestige and influence he gradually became more and more reactionary. A non-conformist himself in England, he came in later life, like most of the Massachusetts leaders, to uphold staunchly the power of the civil magistrate over the conscience of citizens and was willing to grant the civil authorities power of life and death to bring about conformity. Like Winthrop, he had no faith in the common man and advocated a strong government by the few.

COTTON, JOSEPH POTTER (*b. Newport, R.I., 1875; d. Baltimore, Md., 1931*), lawyer. Assistant secretary of state, 1929–31. [*Supp.* 1]

COTTRELL, CALVERT BYRON (*b. Westerly, R.I., 1821; d. Westerly, 1893*), inventor, manufacturer. Greatly improved the printing press; invented a rotary color press, and a shifting tympan for a web perfecting press.

COUCH, DARIUS NASH (*b. Southeast, N.Y., 1822; d. Norwalk, Conn., 1897*), Union general. Graduated West Point, 1846. An able division commander, 1861–65, although handicapped by disease contracted during the Mexican War.

COUDERT, FREDERIC RENÉ (*b. New York, N.Y., 1832; d. 1903*), lawyer. Graduated Columbia, 1850; made his greatest mark in international law; was long interested in politics as an independent Democrat and served on many international commissions.

COUES, ELLIOTT (*b. Portsmouth, N.H., 1842; d. 1899*), physician, ornithologist. Made outstanding contributions to the knowledge of American birds; author of *Key to North American Birds* (1872), *Birds of the Northwest* (1874) and *Birds of the Colorado Valley* (1878). Edited early source materials for the history of the West.

COULDOCK, CHARLES WALTER (*b. London, England, 1815; d. New York, N.Y., 1898*), actor. Came to America in 1849; remained a public favorite until his death.

COULTER, JOHN MERLE (*b. Ningpo, China, 1851; d. 1928*), botanist. Pupil of Asa Gray. Taught at University of Chicago, 1896–1925; founded and edited *Botanical Gazette*. A morphologist, he trained many of America's leading botanists.

COUNCILMAN, WILLIAM THOMAS (*b. Pikesville, Md., 1854; d. York Village, Maine, 1933*), pathologist. Associate, and resident pathologist, John Hopkins University, 1887–92; professor of pathology, Harvard, 1892–1921. [*Supp.* 1]

COUPER, JAMES HAMILTON (*b. 1794; d. Georgia, 1866*), planter. Studied methods of water control in Holland; based the operations of his Georgia coastal plantations on scientific diking and drainage. He substituted sugar cane for long staple cotton, erected a sugar mill, but in 1838 gave up sugar growing for rice. He introduced olive trees and Bermuda grass, and pioneered in the crushing of cottonseed for oil. By 1834 he operated two cottonseed oil mills. His fame as a scientific farmer, experimenter, geologist and conchologist attracted many noted visitors from Europe. The Civil War brought ruin to his plantations and broke his health and fortune.

COURTNEY, CHARLES EDWARD (*b. Union Springs, N.Y., 1849; d. 1920*), single sculler, rowing coach at Cornell, 1883–1916.

COUZENS, JAMES (*b. Chatham, Canada, 1872; d. Detroit, Mich., 1936*), automobile manufacturer. Removed to Detroit, 1890. In 1903 put up $2,500 of the original capital in the Ford Motor Co.; in 1919 sold out for more than $29,000,000. Meanwhile he had served as Ford's business manager and virtual partner. Leaving Ford in 1915, "nauseated" just with "making money," Couzens became police commissioner, then mayor, 1918–22, of Detroit, effecting an unprecedented public improvements program. Appointed to the U.S. Senate from Michigan in 1922 and re-elected in 1924 and 1930, Couzens, a Republican, was an unorthodox and controversial political figure. He opposed the Harding and Coolidge tax programs, criticized Hoover's ineffectual depression policies, and became a warm supporter of President Roosevelt's New Deal. [*Supp.* 2]

COVODE, JOHN (*b. Westmoreland Co., Pa., 1808; d. Harrisburg, Pa., 1871*), manufacturer. Known as "Honest John"; served in the Pennsylvania legislature and as congressman, Whig (later Republican), 1854–63, 1867–71. Was chairman of Covode Investigation, 1860; introduced House impeachment resolution against President Johnson.

COWAN, EDGAR (*b. Greensburg, Pa., 1815; d. 1885*), lawyer. U.S. senator, Republican, from Pennsylvania, 1861–67; opposed many Civil War measures; supported Johnson during impeachment proceedings.

COWELL, SIDNEY FRANCES. [See BATEMAN, SIDNEY FRANCES COWELL, 1823–81.]

COWEN, JOHN KISSIG (*b. Holmes Co., O., 1844; d. 1904*), corporation lawyer. *Post* 1876, was general counsel for Baltimore & Ohio Railroad and later its receiver and president.

COWLES, EDWIN (*b. Austinburg, O., 1825; d. 1890*), journalist. Owner and editor of the *Cleveland Leader* and a founder of the Republican party; later aided sons in development of new methods of electric smelting.

COWLES, HENRY CHANDLER (*b. Kensington, Conn., 1869; d. Chicago, Ill., 1939*), botanist, geographer, pioneer ecologist. Graduated Oberlin College, 1893; Ph.D., University of Chicago, 1898. Taught at Chicago until 1934; was one of a group of geologists and botanists investigating the new field of ecology. Two classic papers by Cowles, one on the Lake Michigan sand dunes (1899), the other on the physiographic ecology of the Chicago area (1901), did much to advance the change in emphasis from the purely descriptive, static study of vegetation to the study of the processes involved in its development and stabilization. Co-author of the important *Textbook of Botany for Colleges and Universities* (1910–11). [*Supp. 2*]

COWLEY, CHARLES (*b. Eastington, England, 1832; d. Lowell, Mass., 1908*), lawyer. Came to America as a child. Championed labor legislation in Massachusetts. Author of many books on local history.

COX, GEORGE BARNSDALE (*b. Cincinnati, O., 1853; d. 1916*), Ohio politician. Helped build Republican machine in Ohio and dominated it from 1888 to 1910; thereafter devoted himself to business.

COX, HANNAH PEIRCE (*b. Chester Co., Pa., 1797; d. Chester Co., 1876*), Quaker anti-slavery worker.

COX, HENRY HAMILTON (*b. Ireland, c. 1769; d. Ireland, 1821*), farmer, poet, religionist. In Pennsylvania from 1799 to 1817; became a Quaker; author of *Metrical Sketches* (1817).

COX, JACOB DOLSON (*b. Montreal, Canada, 1828; d. Maine, 1900*), lawyer, Union general. Graduated Oberlin, 1851. Began his career as high school principal; known for his anti-slavery sentiments, he helped organize Ohio Republican party and served in state senate. Rose to major-general during Civil War. As Republican governor of Ohio, 1866–68, Cox advocated forcible segregation of Negroes and lost favor with his party. As secretary of interior, 1869–70, Cox was staunch defender of civil service reform and resigned in protest over Grant's policies. Cox now was identified with the Liberal Republicans,

served briefly in Congress, and was dean of Cincinnati Law School, 1881–97. His books on military history are highly regarded.

COX, KENYON (*b. Warren, O., 1856; d. 1919*), painter, art critic. Son of Jacob D. Cox. Studied at Pennsylvania Academy of Fine Arts, and at Duran's and Gérôme's *ateliers* in Paris. Returning to America, he found no buyer for his classic nudes, but fared better with portraits, and was instrumental in ushering in a new era of mural decoration. His murals graced the 1893 Chicago Exposition and others can be seen at the New York Appellate Court, the Library of Congress, the Iowa and Minnesota state capitols, and the Wilkes-Barre, Pa., court house. An able teacher, lecturer and writer, he stood for the authority of tradition in an age of license.

COX, LEMUEL (*b. Boston, Mass., 1736; d. Charlestown, Mass., 1806*), mechanic, bridge-builder. Supervised construction of Boston-Charlestown bridge across Charles River, 1785–86, and other massive works in Massachusetts, Maine and Ireland.

COX, PALMER (*b. Granby, Canada, 1840; d. Granby, 1924*), author, illustrator. Created the "Brownie" stories for *St. Nicholas Magazine;* over a million copies of his books for children were sold, from *The Brownies, Their Book* (1887) to *The Brownies' Many More Nights* (1913).

COX, ROWLAND (*b. Philadelphia, Pa., 1842; d. Plainfield, N.J., 1900*), patent lawyer. Acquired national reputation as expert in trade-mark and copyright law; wrote *Manual of Trade Mark Cases* (1881).

COX, SAMUEL HANSON (*b. Rahway, N.J., 1793; d. Bronxville, N.Y., 1880*), Presbyterian clergyman, educator. A New School Presbyterian leader, a founder of New York University, and a director of Union Theological Seminary.

COX, SAMUEL SULLIVAN (*b. Zanesville, O., 1824; d. 1889*), lawyer, politician. Known as "Sunset" Cox. Graduated Brown, 1846. After brief practice of law and journalism in Cincinnati and Columbus, entered Congress as a Democrat from Ohio, 1857; thereafter, except for 1864–68, he was almost continuously a member of the lower house, representing a New York district *post* 1868. A liberal, independent thinker, Cox worked for adjustment of sectional differences and the speedy restoration of peace and union *post* 1861; he aided in settling the *Trent* case and was consistently opposed to centralizing tendencies in government and infringement of personal rights. He favored complete amnesty for Confederates, tariff reform, reform of the civil service and of census procedures; he was also active in securing legislation for development of the West.

COX, WILLIAM RUFFIN (*b. Scotland Neck, N.C., 1832; d. 1919*), Confederate soldier, politician. In legal practice at Raleigh, N.C., after a distinguished

Civil War record; congressman, Democrat, from North Carolina, 1880–86.

COXE, ARTHUR CLEVELAND (*b. Mendham, N.J., 1818; d. 1896*), Episcopal bishop. Son of Samuel Hanson Cox. Consecrated bishop of western New York, 1865; wrote *Christian Ballads* (1840). Rejected contemporary scientific tendencies in his *Holy Writ and Modern Thought* (1892).

COXE, DANIEL (*b. London, England, 1673; d. Trenton, N.J., 1739*), landowner, politician. Came to America, 1702; was commander of forces in West Jersey and in 1706 was appointed to Governor's Council and made associate judge of West Jersey supreme court. Removed from Council 1713, he was elected to assembly in 1714, and in 1716 was chosen speaker. Upon urging of Governor Hunter, Coxe was expelled and fled first to Pennsylvania and then to London where he published *A Description of the English Province of Carolana* (1722) which sets forth what is believed to be the first printed plan for a confederation of North American colonies. Returning to New Jersey, he was candidate for the assembly in 1725 and supreme court judge, 1734–39.

COXE, ECKLEY BRINTON (*b. Philadelphia, Pa., 1839; d. 1895*), mining engineer. Grandson of Tench Coxe. Developed Wilkes-Barre, Pa., anthracite deposits; greatly improved mining techniques.

COXE, JOHN REDMAN (*b. Trenton, N.J., 1773; d. 1864*), physician. Grandson of John Redman. Studied in London, Edinburgh, Paris and under Benjamin Rush in Philadelphia. He practiced in Philadelphia, was physician to the Pennsylvania Hospital, taught chemistry, materia medica, and pharmacy at the University of Pennsylvania. He was an early advocate of vaccination, an expert pharmacist, and is said to have introduced the Jalap plant into the United States. He edited the *Medical Museum* (1805–11) and the *American Dispensatory* (1808); he published a *Medical Dictionary* (1808) and several books on the history of medicine. His library contained the "best collection of the Fathers of Medicine and of Theology" in America.

COXE, RICHARD SMITH (*b. Burlington, N.J., 1792; d. Washington, D.C., 1865*), lawyer. Son of William Coxe. A specialist in real property law, he was prominent as counsel before the Supreme Court.

COXE, TENCH (*b. Philadelphia, Pa., 1755; d. Philadelphia, 1824*), merchant, political economist. Brother of William Coxe. A neutralist during the Revolution, he was a member of the Annapolis Convention and the Continental Congress of 1788. A Federalist from 1788 to 1797, he served as assistant secretary of the treasury and commissioner of the revenue. Dismissed by Adams, he turned Republican and served as purveyor of public supplies, 1803–12. A nationalist in his economic views, he advocated development of native manufactures, a revenue tariff, unrestricted interstate commerce, confinement of import and coast-wise trade to American vessels. His promotion of cotton culture in the South earned him the title of father of America's cotton industry.

COXE, WILLIAM (*b. Philadelphia, Pa., 1762; d. near Burlington, N.J., 1831*), pomologist. Grandson of Daniel Coxe; brother of Tench Coxe. Outstanding authority on fruit trees; helped introduce Seckel pear into England; served in New Jersey legislature and as Federalist Congressman.

COXETTER, LOUIS MITCHELL (*b. Nova Scotia, Canada, 1818; d. Charleston, S.C., 1873*), mariner. The Confederacy's most celebrated privateersman and most successful blockade-runner.

COZZENS, FREDERICK SWARTWOUT (*b. Brooklyn, N.Y., 1818; d. 1869*), humorist, wine merchant. Author of *Prismatics* (1853, under pseudonym of Richard Haywarde); *The Sparrowgrass Papers* (1856); *Acadia; or a Month with the Bluenoses* (1859); *The Sayings of Dr. Bushwhacker* (1867).

CRABTREE, LOTTA (*b. New York, N.Y., 1847; d. 1924*), actress. Began her career in California mining camps, 1855; her free, infectious humor made her outstanding in American burlesque and extravaganza until her retirement, 1891.

CRADDOCK, CHARLES EGBERT. [See MURFREE, MARY NOAILLES, 1850–1922.]

CRAFTS, JAMES MASON (*b. Boston, Mass., 1839; d. 1917*), chemist, teacher, administrator. Graduated from Lawrence Scientific School, 1858; studied also at Freiberg, Heidelberg and Paris. Bunsen and Wurtz were among his teachers. In 1868 he became professor of chemistry at Cornell; in 1871 at Massachusetts Institute of Technology. From 1874 until 1891 he did research at the École des Mines in Paris, and there with Charles Friedel discovered the "Friedel-Crafts reaction." Returning to Cambridge, he taught at and served as president of the Massachusetts Institute of Technology and devoted himself to a study of catalysis and accurate thermometry. He was a Chevalier of the Legion of Honor and a recipient of the Rumford Medal.

CRAFTS, WILLIAM (*b. Charleston, S.C., 1787; d. Lebanon Springs, N.Y., 1826*), lawyer, South Carolina legislator. Author of local satires and descriptive poems.

CRAIG, AUSTIN (*b. Peapack, N.J., 1824; d. 1881*), clergyman, educator. A staunch foe of denominationalism, he was one of America's best New Testament Greek scholars, an adviser of Horace Mann in the work at Antioch College, and president of the Christian Biblical Institute (Stanfordville, N.Y.) 1869–81.

CRAIG, DANIEL H. (*b. Rumney, N.H., c. 1814; d. Asbury Park, N.J., 1895*), journalist. Used carrier pigeons to report advance shipping news for the

Boston Daily Mail and *New York Herald;* was president of Associated Press, 1861–66.

CRAIG, THOMAS (*b. Pittston, Pa., 1855; d. 1900*), mathematician. Taught at Johns Hopkins University; edited *American Journal of Mathematics* (1894–99); was eminent geometer.

CRAIGHEAD, EDWIN BOONE (*b. Ham's Prairie, Mo., 1861; d. 1920*), educator. Was college president in South Carolina, Missouri, Louisiana (Tulane) and Montana; in Montana fought business influence on education.

CRAIGIE, ANDREW (*b. Boston, Mass., 1743; d. Cambridge, Mass., 1819*), apothecary, financier, speculator. Apothecary-general, Continental Army, 1777–83.

CRAIK, JAMES (*b. Arbigland, Scotland, 1730; d. near Alexandria, Va., 1814*), chief physician and surgeon of the Continental Army. Emigrated, 1750; served with Braddock's expedition, 1755; was George Washington's friend and personal physician.

CRAMER, MICHAEL JOHN (*b. near Schaffhausen, Switzerland, 1835; d. Carlisle, Pa., 1898*), Methodist clergyman, educator. Came to America as a child. Brother-in-law of Ulysses S. Grant, who named him U.S. minister to Denmark and Switzerland.

CRAMP, CHARLES HENRY (*b. Philadelphia, Pa., 1828; d. 1913*), shipbuilder. Son of William Cramp. President of William Cramp and Sons Shipbuilding Co., 1879–1903; one of the leading naval architects of his day. He built the record-breaking liners *St. Louis* and *St. Paul,* and the battleships *Maine, New York, Indiana* and *Massachusetts;* installed the first American triple-expansion engine in the yacht *Peerless* and the first American three-screw propulsion system in the cruiser *Columbia.*

CRAMP, WILLIAM (*b. Philadelphia, Pa., 1807; d. Atlantic City, N.J., 1879*), shipbuilder. Founded William Cramp Shipbuilding Co. at Philadelphia, 1830. Successfully adapted his yard to the change from wood to iron to steel as shipbuilding materials.

CRANCH, CHRISTOPHER PEARSE (*b. Alexandria, D.C., 1813; d. 1892*), painter, critic, poet, Unitarian minister. Son of William Cranch; friend of R. W. Emerson and George W. Curtis.

CRANCH, WILLIAM (*b. Weymouth, Mass., 1769; d. Washington, D.C., 1855*), jurist. Nephew of Pres. John Adams. Chief justice of U.S. circuit court of District of Columbia, 1805–55; reporter of U.S. Supreme Court, 1802–17.

CRANDALL, CHARLES HENRY (*b. Greenwich, N.Y., 1858; d. Stamford, Conn., 1923*), poet. Wrote patriotic verse for magazines.

CRANDALL, PRUDENCE (*b. Hopkinton, R.I., 1803; d. Elk Falls, Kans., 1890*), educator, reformer. Fought a losing battle to establish schools for Negroes in Connecticut, 1833–34.

CRANE, ANNE MONCURE (*b. Baltimore, Md., 1838; d. Stuttgart, Germany, 1872*), author. Her novels include *Emily Chester* (1864), *Opportunity* (1867), *Reginald Archer* (1871) and were condemned as immoral in their day.

CRANE, CHARLES RICHARD (*b. Chicago, Ill., 1858; d. Palm Springs, Calif., 1939*), businessman, philanthropist. Left his family's plumbing supply business in 1914 to devote himself to world travel, the cultivation of international friendships, and public service. A supporter of Woodrow Wilson, Crane was a member of a special diplomatic mission to Russia in 1917, served on the Inter-Allied Commission on Mandates in Turkey, 1919, and was minister to China, 1920–21, where he was active in famine relief. His philanthropies were many and included support for the American colleges in Istanbul, and the establishment in 1925 of the Institute of Current World Affairs. [*Supp. 2*]

CRANE, FRANK (*b. Urbana, Ill., 1861; d. Nice, France, 1928*), Methodist and Congregational clergyman. Author of syndicated, inspirational, newspaper essays, 1909–28.

CRANE, HAROLD HART (*b. Garretsville, O., 1899; d. 1932*), poet. Incompatible parents subjected him to tensions which marked his whole life. He began principal work *The Bridge* (1930) in 1923; this poem was to be a mystical synthesis of America, a refutation of the disillusion of Eliot's *Waste Land.* Its structure is characterized by free association of images and symphonic organization of rhythms. Despairing of his work and of himself, he drowned himself off the Florida coast. [*Supp. 1*]

CRANE, JOHN (*b. Braintree, Mass., 1744; d. 1805*), Revolutionary soldier. Associated with Boston's Sons of Liberty; took part in the tea party; brevetted brigadier-general, 1783, for outstanding service as an artillery officer.

CRANE, JONATHAN TOWNLEY (*b. Connecticut Farms, N.J., 1819; d. Port Jervis, N.Y., 1880*), Methodist clergyman. Father of Stephen Crane.

CRANE, STEPHEN (*b. Newark, N.J., 1871; d. Badenweiler, Germany, 1900*), writer, novelist. Son of Jonathan Townley Crane. Trained in newspaper work on Jersey and New York papers; first successful with *Red Badge of Courage* (1895). Became a newspaper syndicate writer, traveling in the West and Mexico, and covering Cuban filibustering and the Graeco-Turkish War; removed to England, 1898, where he was friend to Joseph Conrad, H. G. Wells, and other writers. War correspondent in Spanish-American War. Died of tuberculosis. Crane's work set fresh standards for American writing in its intensity and its use of startling yet inevitable descriptive phrasing. His books include: *Maggie, A Girl of the Streets* (1892); *The Red Badge of Courage* (1895); *The Black Riders and Other Lines* (1895); *The Little Regiment* (1896); *George's Mother* (1896); *The Third Violet* (1897); *The Open Boat* (1898); *Active Service* (1899); *War Is Kind* (1899); *The Monster* (1899); *Wounds in the Rain* (1900); *Whilomville Stories* (1900) and others.

CRANE, THOMAS FREDERICK (*b. New York, N.Y., 1844; d. 1927*), lawyer, teacher, scholar. Taught modern languages at Cornell University, 1868–1909, and served twice as acting president; pioneer in study of medieval literature and of folk-lore.

CRANE, WILLIAM HENRY (*b. Leicester, Mass., 1845; d. Hollywood, Calif., 1928*), actor, comedian. Played in partnership with Stuart Robson; his greatest hit was *David Harum*, 1900–03.

CRANE, WILLIAM MONTGOMERY (*b. Elizabeth, N.J., 1784; d. 1846*), naval officer. Served at Tripoli and during War of 1812; commanded Mediterranean Squadron, 1827–29; chief of Bureau of Ordnance and Hydrography, 1842–46.

CRANE, WINTHROP MURRAY (*b. Dalton, Mass., 1853; d. Dalton, 1920*), paper manufacturer. Devised (*c. 1879*) production process for silk-threaded paper used for U.S. notes. Served on Republican National Committee; was elected lieutenant-governor of Massachusetts in 1896; governor, 1900–02. His personal arbitration of Boston teamsters' strike, 1902, served as model for Roosevelt's action in anthracite strike. As U.S. senator, 1904–12, he was judged the Senate's most influential member. Lost his fight to persuade 1920 Republican National Convention to favor America's entrance in the League of Nations.

CRANSTON, EARL (*b. Athens, O., 1840; d. New Richmond, O., 1932*), Methodist clergyman and bishop. Influential in bringing about reunion of that church's northern and southern branches. [*Supp. 1*]

CRANSTON, JOHN (*b. London, England, 1625; d. Rhode Island, 1680*), physician. Emigrated to Rhode Island, *c. 1637*. Served as major during King Philip's War; was commissioner from Newport in Rhode Island General Assembly, and governor of the colony, 1678–80.

CRANSTON, SAMUEL (*b. Newport, R.I., 1659; d. 1727*). Son of John Cranston. Colonial governor of Rhode Island, 1698–1727. Prevented loss of Rhode Island charter rights, settled boundary disputes with Massachusetts and Connecticut.

CRAPSEY, ADELAIDE (*b. New York, N.Y., 1878; d. Saranac Lake, N.Y., 1914*), poet. Daughter of Algernon S. Crapsey. Graduated Vassar, 1901. Her book *Verse* (1915) sponsored an original verse form, the cinquain.

CRAPSEY, ALGERNON SIDNEY (*b. Fairmount, O., 1847; d. 1927*), Episcopal clergyman, author. Widely known as preacher, pastor and missioner, he was deposed after trial for heresy, 1906.

CRARY, ISAAC EDWIN (*b. Preston, Conn., 1804; d. Marshall, Mich., 1854*), lawyer, educator. First congressman from Michigan, 1837–41.

CRATTY, MABEL (*b. Bellaire, O., 1868; d. New York, N.Y., 1928*), social worker. General secretary of Y.W.C.A. National Board, 1906–28.

CRAVATH, ERASTUS MILO (*b. Homer, N.Y., 1833; d. 1900*), Congregational clergyman, first president of Fisk University. Served as chaplain during Civil War; helped establish Atlanta and Fisk universities.

CRAVATH, PAUL DRENNAN (*b. Berlin Heights, O., 1861; d. Locust Valley, N.Y., 1940*), corporation lawyer. Son of Erastus M. Cravath. [*Supp. 2*]

CRAVEN, BRAXTON (*b. Randolph Co., N.C., 1822; d. 1882*), first president of Trinity College (now Duke University).

CRAVEN, JOHN JOSEPH (*b. Newark, N.J., 1822; d. Patchogue, N.Y., 1893*), inventor, physician. Invented cable insulation for under-water use; as military surgeon attended Jefferson Davis during imprisonment at Fortress Monroe.

CRAVEN, THOMAS TINGEY (*b. District of Columbia, 1808; d. Boston, Mass., 1887*), naval officer. Initiated Annapolis practice cruise; served with Farragut in Mississippi River campaign; retired, 1869, as rear-admiral.

CRAVEN, TUNIS AUGUSTUS MACDONOUGH (*b. Portsmouth, N.H., 1813; d. off Mobile, Ala., 1864*), naval officer. Brother of Thomas T. Craven. A leading surveyor and hydrographer of the navy; commanded ironclad *Tecumseh*, 1863–64 and went down with her in Mobile Bay.

CRAWFORD, FRANCIS MARION (*b. Bagni di Lucca, Italy, 1854; d. Sorrento, Italy, 1909*), novelist, historian. Son of Thomas Crawford. Among his more than forty novels, the *Saracinesca* trilogy on Rome in the 19th century is outstanding.

CRAWFORD, GEORGE WALKER (*b. near Augusta, Ga., 1798; d. 1872*). As Whig governor of Georgia from 1843 to 1847, excelled as administrator; was secretary of war, 1849–50.

CRAWFORD, JAMES PYLE WICKERSHAM (*b. Lancaster, Pa., 1882; d. Philadelphia, Pa., 1939*), professor of Romanic languages, University of Pennsylvania, 1914–39. Author of *Spanish Drama Before Lope de Vega* (1922); first editor, *Hispanic Review* (1933–39). [*Supp. 2*]

CRAWFORD, JOHN (*b. North Ireland, 1746; d. Baltimore, Md., 1813*), physician. Worked in Barbados and Demerara; in Baltimore after 1796, he developed a theory of infection through parasitic organisms.

CRAWFORD, JOHN MARTIN (*b. Herrick, Pa., 1845; d. Cincinnati, O., 1916*), physician. Translated Finnish epic *Kalevala* and Esthonian epic *Kalevipoeg;* served as consul-general in Russia and translated *Industries of Russia* (1893).

CRAWFORD, JOHN WALLACE (CAPTAIN JACK) (*b. Co. Donegal, Ireland, 1847; d. Brooklyn, N.Y., 1917*), "the poet scout." Came to America as a boy. After service in Union army, 1862–65, went West; succeeded Buffalo Bill Cody as chief of scouts, Sioux campaign, 1876, and served in later Apache wars. Author of sincere but banal verse.

CRAWFORD, MARTIN JENKINS (*b. Jasper Co., Ga., 1820; d. Columbus, Ga., 1883*), lawyer. Congressman, Democrat, from Georgia, 1855–61; later a judge of Georgia district and supreme courts.

CRAWFORD, SAMUEL JOHNSON (*b. near Bedford, Ind., 1835; d. 1913*), lawyer, Union soldier. Republican governor of Kansas, 1864–68.

CRAWFORD, THOMAS (*b. New York, N.Y., c. 1813; d. London, England, 1857*), sculptor. Worked as wood-carver and marble cutter in New York; in Rome studied under Thorwaldsen. Charles Sumner raised subscription in Boston to buy Crawford's "Orpheus" for the Athenaeum. This, like his other works, was idealistically conceived and allegorically or mythologically portrayed. In 1849 Crawford won the Richmond, Va., competition for an equestrian monument to Washington. He was entrusted with the designing of the marble pediment and bronze doors of the Capitol's Senate wing and with the "Armed Liberty" capping the dome. His art was based largely on the imitation of classic forms.

CRAWFORD, WILLIAM (*b. Frederick Co., Va., 1732; d. near modern Crawfordsville, O., 1782*), Revolutionary soldier. Served on Indian frontier in Braddock's campaign, Forbes's expedition, Pontiac War, Dunmore's War and Revolutionary War.

CRAWFORD, WILLIAM HARRIS (*b. Nelson Co., Va., 1772; d. Georgia, 1834*), statesman. A Columbia Co., Ga., plantation owner and circuit court judge, he entered the state legislature in 1803 and allied with the Jackson-Troup faction. As U.S. senator, Democratic-Republican, 1807–13, he advocated conservative financial policies. In 1813 he served as minister to France, in 1815 as secretary of war, and as secretary of the treasury, 1816–25. In 1816, urged to run against Monroe as the Democratic-Republican nominee for the presidency, he demurred; from 1820 to 1824 Crawford's friends sought again to prepare the ground for Crawford's nomination, this time with his active cooperation. Stricken with paralysis in 1823, friends sought unsuccessfully to nominate him by congressional caucus and failed. An able administrator and financier, Crawford has suffered in reputation by his use as a foil for biographers of Clay, Calhoun and other of his political rivals.

CRAZY HORSE (*b. c. 1849; d. near Camp Robinson, Nebr., 1877*), Chief of Oglala Sioux. Fought under Red Cloud in Wyoming, 1865–68; married to a Cheyenne woman, he led Southern Sioux and Northern Cheyennes in their forays off the reservations. Forced General Crook to withdraw from the upper Rosebud, 1876; fought Custer at the Little Big Horn; was driven by Crook to withdraw to the Wolf Mountains where he was attacked by Colonel Miles and forced to retire. Desertions of his supporters and lack of supplies led him to surrender at the Red Cloud Agency, May 6, 1877. He was fatally wounded when he sought to resist confinement.

CREAMER, DAVID (*b. Baltimore, Md., 1812; d. Baltimore, 1887*), hymnologist. Wrote *Methodist Hymnology* (1848), a comprehensive study of John and Charles Wesley's poetical works.

CREATH, JACOB (*b. near Cumberland, Nova Scotia, 1777; d. 1854*), clergyman. Raised in North Carolina; migrated to Kentucky, 1803. As Kentucky evangelist, became leading Campbellite and was excluded from Baptist church; organized Kentucky churches of the Disciples of Christ.

CREATH, JACOB (*b. Mecklenburg County, Va., 1799; d. 1886*), clergyman. Nephew of the preceding. An intense polemicist, established Campbellite churches in Kentucky and Missouri; wrote *A Blow at the Root of Episcopalianism* (1848).

CREELMAN, JAMES (*b. Montreal, Canada, 1859; d. Berlin, Germany, 1915*), journalist, war correspondent.

CREESY, JOSIAH PERKINS (*b. Marblehead, Mass., 1814; d. Salem, Mass., 1871*), sea captain, master of the *Flying Cloud.* Set speed records on New York to San Francisco run, 1851 and 1854.

CREIGHTON, EDWARD (*b. Belmont or Licking Co., O., 1820; d. 1874*), pioneer telegraph builder, banker, philanthropist. Helped build transcontinental telegraph to Salt Lake City; provided initial capital to found Creighton University, Omaha, Nebr.

CREIGHTON, JAMES EDWIN (*b. Pictou, Nova Scotia, 1861; d. 1924*), philosopher. Protégé of Jacob G. Schurman. Taught at Cornell, 1889–1924; edited *Philosophical Review*, 1902–24.

CREIGHTON, JOHN ANDREW (*b. Licking Co., O., 1831; d. 1907*), philanthropist. Brother and associate of Edward Creighton.

CREIGHTON, WILLIAM (*b. Berkeley Co., Va., 1778; d. 1851*), lawyer. Removed to Chillicothe, O., 1799. Was Ohio's first secretary of state, 1803–08; served as U.S. district attorney, and as congressman, (Democrat) Republican, 1813–17; 1827–33. He was later identified with the Whig party.

CRERAR, JOHN (b. New York, N.Y., 1827; d. Chicago, Ill., 1889), financier, philanthropist. An incorporator and director of Pullman Co.; left his estate for philanthropic purposes, including the John Crerar Library, Chicago.

CRESAP, MICHAEL (b. Allegany Co., Md., 1742; d. New York, N.Y., 1775), border leader, trader, Revolutionary soldier. Son of Thomas Cresap. Accused of brutality to Indians and death of Logan, 1774.

CRESAP, THOMAS (b. Skipton, England, c. 1702; d. c. 1790), trader, pioneer. Came to America, c. 1717. In his stockaded house on the Appalachian border of Maryland, Cresap acted as intermediary between the colony government, the Iroquois and the Cherokees.

CRESPI, JUAN (b. Mallorca, Spain, 1721; d. Carmel, Calif., 1782), Franciscan missionary, explorer. His diaries record major Pacific Coast expeditions 1769–74, the discovery of San Francisco Bay, the sea route to Alaska.

CRESSON, ELLIOTT (b. Philadelphia, Pa., 1796; d. 1854), Quaker merchant, philanthropist.

CRESSON, EZRA TOWNSEND (b. Byberry, Pa., 1838; d. 1926), entomologist. Helped found first American entomological society, 1859; specialized in the order Hymenoptera.

CRESWELL, JOHN ANGEL JAMES (b. Port Deposit, Md., 1828; d. Elkton, Md., 1891), lawyer, politician. Made sweeping and constructive reforms in Post Office Department as postmaster-general, 1869–74.

CRÉTIN, JOSEPH (b. Montluel, France, 1799; d. St. Paul, Minn., 1857), first Roman Catholic bishop of St. Paul, Minn. A missionary at Dubuque, Iowa, and Prairie du Chien, 1839–50; consecrated bishop, 1851.

CRÈVECOEUR, J. HECTOR ST. JOHN. [See CRÈVECOEUR, MICHEL-GUILLAUME JEAN DE, 1735–1813.]

CRÈVECOEUR, MICHEL-GUILLAUME JEAN de (b. near Caen, France, 1735; d. Sarcelles, France, 1813), essayist. Served in Canada under Montcalm; went to New York, 1759; traveled in Pennsylvania, New York and the Carolinas. Lived on a farm in Orange Co., N.Y., from 1769 to 1780. During these years he composed the later published Letters from an American Farmer (1782) and most of the Sketches of Eighteenth Century America (1925). Crèvecoeur went to France in 1780; returning to America in 1783, he served as French consul in New York until 1790. As a writer, Crèvecoeur is brilliant, excelling in his description of American frontier life as well as in his understanding of new economic and social

forces. He was author also of Voyages dans la Haute Pensylvanie etc. (Paris, 1801).

CRIMMINS, JOHN DANIEL (b. New York, N.Y., 1844; d. 1917), contractor, capitalist. Built large part of New York's elevated railroad and subway system.

CRISP, CHARLES FREDERICK (b. Sheffield, England, 1845; d. 1896), lawyer, Confederate soldier. Raised in Georgia. Congressman, Democrat, 1883–96; speaker of the House post 1891. A leading advocate of Interstate Commerce Act and of free silver. Ranked among the ablest Georgians of his time.

CRITTENDEN, GEORGE BIBB (b. Russellville, Ky., 1812; d. Danville, Ky., 1880), soldier. Son of John J. Crittenden. Graduated West Point, 1832. Served in Black Hawk War, with Texans in 1843, and in Mexican War; joined Confederate Army in 1861, and after censure for conduct as brigadier-general served without rank.

CRITTENDEN, JOHN JORDAN (b. near Versailles, Ky., 1787; d. Frankfort, Ky., 1863), lawyer, statesman. Practised law with success and held various Ky. state offices, 1809–35; filled out a term in U.S. Senate, 1817–19; became a friend and supporter of Henry Clay. Elected to the U.S. Senate as a Whig, 1835, he remained a national figure until his death. He served as U.S. senator, 1835–41, 1842–48, 1854–61; as U.S. attorney-general, 1841 and 1849–53; as congressman, 1861–63. He was for a brief time governor of Kentucky. An advocate of conservative policies, he urged a congressional policy of non-intervention in the territories over slavery. The greatest effort of his life was made during his last three years when he sought to save the Union by the Crittenden propositions and other measures for peace. During the Civil War, he consistently opposed radical policies of both the North and the South.

CRITTENDEN, THOMAS LEONIDAS (b. Russellville, Ky., 1819; d. Annandale, N.Y., 1893), lawyer, soldier. Son of John J. Crittenden. Served with Union Army, 1861–64, rising to major-general. Re-entered Army, 1867, and served until retirement, 1881.

CRITTENDEN, THOMAS THEODORE (b. near Shelbyville, Ky., 1832; d. Kansas City, Mo., 1909), lawyer. Nephew of John J. Crittenden. Removed to Missouri, 1857, and as Democratic governor, 1881–85, broke up Jesse James gang.

CRITTENTON, CHARLES NELSON (b. Henderson, N.Y., 1833; d. San Francisco, Calif., 1909), philanthropist. A successful New York businessman, he founded the Florence Crittenton Missions to save unfortunate women.

CROCKER, ALVAH (b. Leominster, Mass., 1801; d. 1874), manufacturer, politician, railroad builder. Built up one of New England's largest paper-manufacturing concerns. Helped establish Fitchburg Mutual Fire Insurance Co.; organized the Turners

Falls Co. which developed water-power of that Massachusetts community. Promoted construction of the Fitchburg Railroad (Boston-Fitchburg, 1843–45), of the Vermont & Massachusetts (Fitchburg-Brattleboro, Vt., 1845–49) and of the Troy & Greenfield Railroad which included the Hoosac Tunnel. He served also in Massachusetts General Court and as Republican congressman, 1872–74.

CROCKER, CHARLES (*b. Troy, N.Y., 1822; d. Monterey, Calif., 1888*), merchant, railroad builder, capitalist. Established forge in Marshall Co., Ind., near a bed of iron he discovered in 1845; took up gold mining in California in 1850; opened a store in Sacramento, 1852, and by 1854 was one of the town's wealthiest men. Served in city council and state legislature. With Leland Stanford, C. P. Huntington, and Mark Hopkins, built Central Pacific Railroad across the Sierra Nevada Mountains, 1863–69. Crocker supervised the actual construction of the line and was president of the Contract and Finance Co. In 1871 he was elected president of the Southern Pacific Railroad of California; in 1884 he consolidated the Central and Southern Pacific. He was interested financially in many real estate, irrigation and industrial projects in California, and in banking.

CROCKER, FRANCIS BACON (*b. New York, N.Y., 1861; d. 1921*), electrical engineer. Graduated Columbia School of Mines, 1882. In partnership with Charles G. Curtis and, after 1886, with Schuyler S. Wheeler, designed the commercial electric motor of standard specification. As "father of American electrical standards," Crocker helped formulate the National Electric Code, introduced "henry" as name for the international unit of inductance, and at the 1906 International Electrotechnical Commission in London insured international standardization of electrical manufacturing. In 1917 he and Peter Cooper Hewitt developed the first American helicopter capable of flight.

CROCKER, HANNAH MATHER (*b. Boston, Mass., 1752; d. Boston, 1829*), writer. Granddaughter of Cotton Mather. An early advocate of woman's rights, she also championed Masonry and warned sailors against intemperance and vice.

CROCKER, URIEL (*b. Marblehead, Mass., 1796; d. 1887*), printer, Boston publisher.

CROCKETT, DAVID (*b. near present Rogersville, Tenn., 1786; d. Texas, 1836*), frontiersman. After a wandering youth, married Polly Findlay *c.* 1804 and settled down on a rented tract in his home county. Though he was a mighty hunter, he was a poor farmer and did not prosper; he soon moved with his family to Lincoln Co. near the Alabama line. He served with distinction as a scout under Andrew Jackson in the Creek War of 1813–14. After his wife's death in 1815 he married again; settling in Giles Co., he was appointed justice of the peace,

elected colonel of the militia, and in 1821 to the Tennessee legislature. Moving further west near the junction of the Obion with the Mississippi, he devoted himself to bear-hunting. He was again elected to the legislature in 1823. Taking seriously a jocular proposal, he ran for Congress and was elected on an anti-Jackson ticket; he served 1827–31 and 1833–35. In April 1834 he commenced his celebrated "tour of the North," visiting Baltimore, Philadelphia, New York, and Boston. His opposition to Jackson brought political defeat in 1835, and Crockett joined the movement for Texan independence. He met his death during the heroic defense of the Alamo. Happily innocent of learning and with little understanding of public questions, Crockett was a man of sterling independence, good nature and exceptional self-confidence. He excelled as a brave soldier, an able scout, and an expert rifleman. His authorship of the autobiographical writings issued in his name is doubtful.

CROGHAN, GEORGE (*b. Ireland; d. Passyunk, Pa., 1782*), Indian trader and agent, land speculator. Emigrated to Pennsylvania, 1741. His home near Carlisle, Pa., was base for trading operations throughout the upper Ohio country. As representative of Pennsylvania, Croghan was the leading English agent at Indian treaty councils; by arousing the fears of the French for their claims on the Ohio, he drew upon himself and the English settlers the French attack on Pickawillany in 1752. Croghan assisted Washington, Braddock, Forbes and Bouquet in their Indian campaigns and negotiated with the Northwest tribes. Sent to open the Illinois country, he was taken prisoner, freed, and made a treaty with Pontiac. In 1768 he helped negotiate treaty of Fort Stanwix. After 1772 he turned to land speculation and was a charter member of the Grand Ohio Co. The Revolution reduced him to poverty.

CROGHAN, GEORGE (*b. near Louisville, Ky., 1791; d. New Orleans, La., 1849*), soldier. Nephew of George R. Clark and William Clark. Distinguished himself at Tippecanoe, Fort Defiance, Fort Meigs, and in particular at Fort Stephenson (Ohio), August 1813.

CROIX, TEODORO DE (*b. 1730; d. Madrid, Spain, 1792*), Spanish soldier. As commandant general of Provincias Internas of Mexico, 1776–83, he was a highly efficient administrator of Texas, New Mexico and California.

CROKER, RICHARD (*b. Cloghnakilty, Ireland, 1841; d. 1922*), New York City politician, "Boss Croker." Reared in New York City, he worked as a machinist, was a leader of the "Fourth Avenue Tunnel Gang" and a prize fighter. In 1868, as a member of Tammany's "Young Democracy," he participated in the struggle to oust Boss Tweed. He became Tammany leader in 1886 and dominated city politics until 1894. He regained his hold from 1897 to 1901.

He then moved to England, and later Ireland, where he devoted himself to his racing stables.

CROLY, DAVID GOODMAN (*b. Cloghnakilty, Ireland, 1829; d. 1889*), journalist. Came to America as a child and was raised in New York City. His book *Miscegenation* (1864) is the first use of the title word which he coined; he was an ardent Positivist.

CROLY, HERBERT DAVID (*b. New York, N.Y., 1869; d. Santa Barbara, Calif., 1930*), editor, author. Son of David G. and Jane C. Croly. Wrote *The Promise of American Life* (1909), a manifesto of liberalism; edited *The New Republic*, 1914–30.

[*Supp. 1*]

CROLY, JANE CUNNINGHAM (*b. Market Harborough, England, 1829; d. New York, N.Y., 1901*), journalist. Wife of David G. Croly. Founded Sorosis and the Women's Press Club; wrote *History of the Woman's Club Movement in America* (1898).

CROMPTON, GEORGE (*b. Holcombe, England, 1829; d. 1886*), inventor, manufacturer. Came to America, 1839. Son of William Crompton. Trained in Colt's pistol factory at Hartford and in his father's plant at Taunton, Mass., he began loom manufacture at Worcester, Mass. He improved practically every part of the loom, added 60% to its producing capacity, and invented many new textile fabrics. Crompton served on Worcester's board of aldermen and on the common council. He was a founder of the Hartford Steam Boiler Inspection & Insurance Co. and a founder and director of the Crompton Carpet Co.

CROMPTON, WILLIAM (*b. Preston, England, 1806; d. Windsor, Conn., 1891*), textile machinery inventor, manufacturer. Came to America, 1836. Employed by Crocker & Richmond at Taunton, Mass., he invented a loom for easily exchangeable fancy patterns. In England from 1837 to 1839, he returned to Taunton and introduced his loom at the Middlesex Mills, Lowell, Mass., 1840. This was probably the first instance of fancy woolens being woven by power.

CROMWELL, GLADYS LOUISE HUSTED (*b. Brooklyn, N.Y., 1885; d. France, 1919*), poet. Author of *Gates of Utterance* (1915), *Poems* (1920); in 1918 did Red Cross work at Châlons-sur-Marne.

CROOK, GEORGE (*b. near Dayton, O., 1829; d. Chicago, Ill., 1890*), soldier. After graduation from West Point in 1852, served on Northwestern frontier. During Civil War rose from rank of major to major-general; was distinguished for service with cavalry at South Mountain, Antietam, Chickamauga, Winchester, Fisher's Hill, Cedar Creek and Appomattox. Pacified the Indians of the Boise district, and the Apaches of northern Arizona. Took a prominent part in the Sioux War of 1876. Returned to Arizona, 1882, and until 1885 sought to pacify the Chiricahua Apaches. After 1888 he served as commander of the Division of the Missouri. A splendid frontier soldier, he understood the Indians well and advocated for them the granting of full citizenship privileges.

CROOKS, GEORGE RICHARD (*b. Philadelphia, Pa., 1822; d. 1897*), Methodist Episcopal clergyman, educator. Taught historical theology at Drew Seminary; edited *The Methodist*, 1860–75; wrote school texts and theological works.

CROOKS, RAMSAY (*b. Greenock, Scotland, 1787; d. New York, N.Y., 1859*), fur-trader. Emigrated to Canada, 1803, and entered fur trade. In 1807 established trading post near Calhoun, Nebr.; in 1810 became partner in Astor's Pacific Fur Co. Discouraged by hardships and poor prospects of the venture at Astoria, he returned to St. Louis in 1813. Appointed general manager of Astor's American Fur Co., 1817, he promoted the establishment of the company's Western Department and in 1834 became president of the Northern Department. A superb manager, he left much interesting historical information in his letters. He also served as president of the Mohawk & Hudson Railroad Co. and as trustee of New York's Astor Library.

CROPSEY, JASPAR FRANCIS (*b. Rossville, N.Y., 1823; d. 1900*), painter. Architect for the Sixth Avenue elevated railroad stations, New York; famous for autumn landscapes.

CROSBY, ERNEST HOWARD (*b. New York, N.Y., 1856; d. 1907*), author, social reformer. Son of Howard Crosby. Championed the single tax, antimilitarism, industrial arbitration, vegetarianism, settlement work.

CROSBY, FANNY (*b. Southeast, N.Y., 1820; d. Bridgeport, Conn., 1915*), hymn-writer. Taught at New York Institution for the Blind; wrote about 6,000 hymns.

CROSBY, HOWARD (*b. New York, N.Y., 1826; d. New York, 1891*), Presbyterian clergyman, reformer. A Greek scholar, he was pastor, 1863–91, at New York's Fourth Avenue Presbyterian church; founded Society for the Prevention of Crime.

CROSBY, JOHN SCHUYLER (*b. Albany, N.Y., 1839; d. Newport, R.I., 1914*), Union soldier, public official. Brevetted lieutenant-colonel, 1865, resigned from army, 1870. Served as U.S. consul in Florence, Italy, 1876–82, and as territorial governor of Montana, 1882–84.

CROSBY, PEIRCE (*b. Delaware Co., Pa., 1824; d. Washington, D.C., 1899*), naval officer. Distinguished himself under Farragut at New Orleans, 1862, in command of U.S.S. *Pinola*.

CROSBY, WILLIAM OTIS (*b. Decatur, O., 1850; d. 1925*), geologist. Consulting engineer for construction of dams in Idaho, Texas, Mexico and at Keokuk, Iowa.

CROSS, ARTHUR LYON (*b. Portland, Maine, 1873; d. Ann Arbor, Mich., 1940*), historian. Instructor and professor at University of Michigan, 1899–1940; specialist in Anglo-American legal history. [*Supp. 2*]

CROSS, EDWARD (*b. Virginia, 1798; d. Little Rock, Ark., 1887*), Arkansas jurist and Democratic congressman.

CROSWELL, EDWIN (*b. Catskill, N.Y., 1797; d. Princeton, N.J., 1871*), journalist, politician. As editor of the Albany *Argus*, was mouthpiece of the Democratic "Albany Regency."

CROSWELL, HARRY (*b. West Hartford, Conn., 1778; d. New Haven, Conn., 1858*). Controversial Federalist editor of the Hudson, N.Y., *Balance* and *The Wasp*. Post 1814, an Episcopal clergyman.

CROTHERS, SAMUEL McCHORD (*b. Oswego, Ill., 1857; d. Cambridge, Mass., 1927*), Presbyterian and Unitarian clergyman, essayist.

CROUNSE, LORENZO (*b. Sharon, N.Y., 1834; d. Omaha, Nebr., 1909*), jurist. Removed to Nebraska, 1864; served in many state and national offices and in Congress; an independent Republican, his opposition to railroad interests won him the governorship, 1892–94.

CROUTER, ALBERT LOUIS EDGERTON (*b. near Belleville, Canada, 1846; d. 1925*), educator. Superintendent of celebrated Pennsylvania Institution for the Deaf, 1884–1925.

CROWDER, ENOCH HERBERT (*b. Edinburg, Mo., 1859; d. Washington, D.C., 1932*), army officer, diplomat, lawyer. Graduated West Point, 1881; assigned to frontier duty in Texas. Detailed to teach military science at the University of Missouri where he received LL.B. degree, 1886. Served as judge-advocate in the Philippines during Spanish-American War and as military observer in Russo-Japanese War. Supervised Cuban elections in 1908, heading advisory law commission which drafted most of the organic laws of the Republic. Appointed judge-advocate-general of the army in 1911. Chief credit for the draft law of 1917 belongs to Crowder who was promoted to major-general in that year. His term as ambassador to Cuba, 1923–27, and previous service as special representative in Cuba, won him acclaim in both Havana and Washington. [*Supp. 1*]

CROWELL, LUTHER CHILDS (*b. West Dennis, Mass., 1840; d. West Dennis, 1903*), inventor. In 1862 he obtained a patent for an aerial machine; in 1867 for a machine to make paper bags. He devised the square-bottomed bag and the side-seam bag and the machines for manufacturing them, and in 1873 a sheet-delivery and folding mechanism for printing presses. With R. Hoe and Co., 1879–1903, he perfected the double supplement press, double and quadruple presses, and combined pamphlet-printing

and wire-binding machines. He obtained over 280 U.S. patents for printing machinery alone. At the time of his death he was working on a wrapping and mailing machine.

CROWNE, JOHN (*b. Shropshire (?), England, 1640; d. London, England, 1712*), Restoration dramatist. Son of William Crowne. First Harvard College playwright; attended Harvard for three years *post* 1657 but did not graduate. Author of *Sir Courtly Nice, The Destruction of Jerusalem* and other plays. Returned to England, 1661.

CROWNE, WILLIAM (*b. England, c. 1617; d. Boston, Mass., 1683*), adventurer, land speculator. Lost his property on Penobscot River through cession of Nova Scotia to France, 1667; resided in America, 1657–61; 1667–83.

CROWNINSHIELD, BENJAMIN WILLIAMS (*b. Salem, Mass., 1772; d. Boston, Mass., 1851*), merchant, politician. President of Merchants Bank of Salem; served in state and national legislatures; secretary of the navy, 1814–18.

CROWNINSHIELD, FREDERIC (*b. Boston, Mass., 1845; d. Capri, Italy, 1918*), painter, writer. Director of American Academy in Rome, 1900–11.

CROWNINSHIELD, GEORGE (*b. Salem, Mass., 1766; d. Salem, 1817*), sea-captain, merchant, pioneer yachtsman. Built first American yacht, the *Jefferson*, and the first sea-going yacht of her class, *Cleopatra's Barge*.

CROWNINSHIELD, JACOB (*b. Salem, Mass., 1770; d. Washington, D.C., 1808*), sea-captain, merchant, congressman. Ablest member of this celebrated Salem family; secretary of the navy, 1805–09.

CROZER, JOHN PRICE (*b. West Dale, Pa., 1793; d. 1866*), manufacturer, philanthropist. Crozer Theological Seminary at Chester, Pa., is named for him.

CROZET, CLAUDE (*b. Villefranche, France, 1790; d. 1864*), soldier, engineer. An artillery officer in the French army, 1807–15, the second restoration of the Bourbons prompted him to emigrate to America where he taught engineering at West Point, 1816–23. Here, as later at the Virginia Military Institute, Crozet introduced the study of descriptive geometry. From 1823 to 1832 he served as Virginia state engineer and planned an inland communication system which gave Virginia one of the best road systems of that time. He also located and built a railroad through the Blue Ridge. As president of the Board of Visitors to the Virginia Military Institute, 1839–45, Crozet modeled its curriculum after that of West Point.

CRUGER, HENRY (*b. New York, N.Y., 1739; d. New York, 1827*), merchant. Resided in England, 1757–90. As Edmund Burke's fellow member in Parliament for Bristol, Cruger served 1774–80 and 1784–90; in the Commons he was an outspoken friend to America. On his return to New York he was elected to the state senate.

CRUGER, JOHN (*b. New York, N.Y., 1710; d. New York, 1791*), mayor of New York, 1756–65. Speaker of the last New York colonial assembly, first president of New York Chamber of Commerce, 1768. Prominent in resistance to British policies before 1776.

CRUMP, WILLIAM WOOD (*b. Henrico Co., Va., 1819; d. Richmond, Va., 1897*), jurist. A strong secessionist, he served as assistant secretary of the treasury of the Confederacy; excelled as advocate before a jury.

CRUNDEN, FREDERICK MORGAN (*b. Gravesend, England, 1847; d. St. Louis, Mo., 1911*), educator, librarian. Came to America as a child. Chief promoter of the St. Louis Public Library.

CUBERO, PEDRO RODRÍGUEZ (*b. Calatayud, Spain, 1645; d. Mexico, 1704*), Spanish governor of New Mexico, 1697–1703.

CUDAHY, MICHAEL (*b. Callan, Ireland, 1841; d. 1910*), meat-packer. Came to America, 1849. Revolutionized industry through introduction of summer curing of meat under refrigeration.

CUFFE, PAUL (*b. Cuttyhunk, Elizabeth Islands, Mass., 1759; d. 1817*), Negro seaman. Prospered as shipowner; founded the Friendly Society to facilitate emigration of American Negroes to Sierra Leone.

CULBERSON, CHARLES ALLEN (*b. Dadeville, Ala., 1855; d. Washington, D.C., 1925*), lawyer, statesman. Son of David B. Culberson. A Democrat, he was Texas attorney-general, 1890–94; governor, 1894–98; and U.S. senator, 1899–1923.

CULBERSON, DAVID BROWNING (*b. Troup Co., Ga., 1830; d. Jefferson, Texas, 1900*), lawyer, Confederate soldier, statesman. Removed to Dadeville, Ala., 1851, to Upshur Co., Tex., 1856, and to Jefferson, Tex., 1860. A Democrat, he served in Congress, 1875–1897. The ablest constitutional lawyer in the House, he was a conservative, interested in judicial reforms and the limitation of tariffs.

CULLINAN, JOSEPH STEPHEN (*b. Sharon, Pa., 1860; d. Palo Alto, Calif., 1937*), corporation executive. Creator and head of three major oil companies: Texas, Magnolia, and American Republics.
[*Supp. 2*]

CULLIS, CHARLES (*b. Boston, Mass., 1833; d. 1892*), homeopathic physician, leader in faith-cure movement.

CULLOM, SHELBY MOORE (*b. Kentucky, 1829; d. 1914*), lawyer, statesman. Grew up in Illinois; admitted to the bar in Springfield, 1855. Republican after 1858, he served in state legislature, in Congress, as governor of Illinois, 1876–83, and as U.S. senator, 1883–1913. A champion of state regulation of rail-

roads in Illinois, he was instrumental as senator in the establishment of the Interstate Commerce Commission and became chairman of the Senate's Interstate Commerce Committee. After 1901 he was chairman of the Committee on Foreign Relations and in 1906 helped secure passage of the Hepburn Act. Independent in his thinking but colorless, his seniority rights gave him a prominent place within the Republican party.

CULLUM, GEORGE WASHINGTON (*b. New York, N.Y., 1809; d. 1892*), author, soldier. Graduated West Point, 1833. Author of *Biographical Register of Officers and Graduates* of West Point (1850, 1868, 1891).

CULPEPER, THOMAS, Lord (*b. England, 1635; d. London, England, 1689*). Royal governor of Virginia, commissioned 1675 but served by deputy until 1680. At first conciliatory and popular, he turned dictatorial and was removed from office in 1683 for having left the colony without royal permission.

CUMING, Sir ALEXANDER (*b. c. 1690; d. London, England, 1775*). Eccentric Scottish baronet who persuaded Cherokee Indians to accept British sovereignty, 1730. Died a debtor and a poor brother of Charterhouse.

CUMING, FORTESCUE (*b. Strabane, Ireland, 1762; d. Vermilionville, La., 1828*), traveler. Author of *Sketches of a Tour to the Western Country* (Pittsburgh, 1810).

CUMMING, ALFRED (*b. Augusta, Ga., 1802; d. near Augusta, 1873*), territorial governor of Utah. Appointed by Buchanan in 1857 to replace Brigham Young; resigned upon Lincoln's inauguration.

CUMMINGS, AMOS JAY (*b. Conkling, N.Y., 1841; d. 1902*), journalist. On staffs of New York *Tribune* and *Sun;* founded and edited evening *Sun.* In Congress as Tammany regular, 1886–88, 1890–94, 1896–1902.

CUMMINGS, CHARLES AMOS (*b. Boston, Mass., 1833; d. 1905*), architect. Author of *History of Architecture in Italy* (1901).

CUMMINGS, EDWARD (*b. 1861; d. 1926*), Unitarian minister, student and worker in social ethics. Minister and pastor of Boston's South Congregational Society; promoter of the World Peace Foundation.

CUMMINGS, JOHN (*b. Woburn, Mass., 1785; d. 1867*), tanner. A pioneer in the modernization of the leather industry.

CUMMINGS, JOSEPH (*b. Falmouth, Maine, 1817; d. 1890*), Methodist clergyman. President of Genesee College, 1854–57; Wesleyan University, 1857–75; Northwestern University, 1881–1890.

CUMMINGS, THOMAS SEIR (*b. Bath, England, 1804; d. Hackensack, N.J., 1894*), painter. An expert miniaturist; helped found National Academy of Design, 1825; taught at University of the City of New York.

CUMMINS, ALBERT BAIRD (*b. Carmichaels, Pa., 1850; d. 1926*), lawyer, statesman. Gained reputation in Iowa for his legal victory over the barbed-wire trust; as Republican governor of Iowa, 1901–08, brought Progressivism to the state, broke political domination of the railroads and witnessed adoption of a new primary law. As U.S. senator, 1909–26, Cummins became chairman of the Committee on Interstate Commerce and played an important role in passage of the Transportation Act of 1920. He urged, however, compulsory consolidation and arbitration, provisions which were not adopted.

CUMMINS, GEORGE DAVID (*b. near Smyrna, Del., 1822; d. Lutherville, Md., 1876*), clergyman, founder of the Reformed Episcopal Church, 1873.

CUMMINS, MARIA SUSANNA (*b. Salem, Mass., 1827; d. Dorchester, Mass., 1866*). Author of moralistic stories and novels; *The Lamplighter* (1854) had an extraordinary success.

CUNLIFFE-OWEN, PHILIP FREDERICK (*b. London, England, 1855; d. New York, N.Y., 1926*), editor, publicist. An outstanding international interpreter of foreign affairs on the *New York Tribune*, and later in syndicated articles signed "Marquise de Fontenoy."

CUNNINGHAM, ANN PAMELA (*b. Laurens Co., S.C., 1816; d. Laurens Co., 1875*), founder and first Regent of Mount Vernon Ladies' Association which preserved Washington's home for posterity.

CUPPLES, SAMUEL (*b. Harrisburg, Pa., 1831; d. St. Louis, Mo., 1912*), merchant, manufacturer, philanthropist.

CURRAN, JOHN JOSEPH (*b. Hawley, Pa., 1859; d. Wilkes-Barre, Pa., 1936*), Roman Catholic clergyman. Son of a coal miner, he began work as a child in the Pennsylvania coal fields. Graduated, 1882, from St. Vincent College, Latrobe, Pa.; ordained 1887. Serving parishes in Wilkes-Barre from 1895 until his death, Curran actively supported the mine workers and their union. He acted as intermediary in a number of labor disputes, notably the anthracite strikes of 1900 and 1902. A supporter of both Presidents Roosevelt, Curran was characterized by his friend T. R. as "the kind of priest needed in a democracy."
[*Supp.* 2]

CURRIER, CHARLES WARREN (*b. St. Thomas, Virgin Islands, 1857; d. Maryland, 1918*), Roman Catholic clergyman. Active in pastoral work, and for a brief time bishop of Matanzas, Cuba, he was an outstanding Hispanist and enthusiastic promoter of Pan-Americanism.

CURRIER, MOODY (*b. Boscawen, N.H., 1806; d. 1898*), financier, politician. A Manchester, N.H.,

banker, he served as state senator, and as governor of New Hampshire, 1885–87.

CURRIER, NATHANIEL (*b. Roxbury, Mass., 1813; d. New York, N.Y., 1888*), lithographic printer, publisher. Apprentice in shops of W. S. and John Pendleton, in 1835 he issued his first popular lithograph, drawn by J. H. Bufford, "The Ruins of the Merchants' Exchange." This was the beginning of the series best known as Currier & Ives prints which for nearly seventy years gave a lively picture of manners and history of the American people. J. Merritt Ives became Currier's partner in 1850. Great fires, disasters, the California gold rush, the development of railroads and commerce from the clipper ship to the steamship, political changes, sports and the making of the West were the subjects which were portrayed in color by the staff artists of this notable firm.

CURRY, GEORGE LAW (*b. Philadelphia, Pa., 1820; d. 1878*), territorial governor of Oregon, 1854–59. Edited *Oregon Spectator*; founded *Oregon Free Press*, 1848. Remembered for his vigorous defense of the settlers against the Indians, 1855.

CURRY, JABEZ LAMAR MONROE (*b. Lincoln Co., Ga., 1825; d. 1903*), statesman, author, educator. Inspired by Horace Mann's zeal for universal education and John C. Calhoun's theory of politics. After a widely diversified career in law, politics, war and diplomacy, Curry made an outstanding contribution to educational progress in the South as agent of the Peabody Fund after 1881, as agent of the Slater Fund after 1890 and as supervising director of the Southern Education Board.

CURTIN, ANDREW GREGG (*b. Bellefonte, Pa., 1815?; d. 1894*), lawyer, politician. Admitted to the bar, 1839. Campaigned for Harrison in 1840, for Clay in 1844, for Taylor in 1848 and for Scott in 1852. Appointed secretary of Pennsylvania and ex-officio superintendent of common schools, 1854. As Republican governor, 1861–67, Curtin secured Pennsylvania's support for the Union, established the Pennsylvania Reserve Corps and devoted himself to the welfare of the state's soldiers. In 1869 Grant appointed him minister to Russia. Supporting Greeley in 1872, Curtin lost the favor of the Republican party and joined the Democrats. From 1881 to 1887 he served as a Democratic congressman.

CURTIN, JEREMIAH (*b. Detroit, Mich., 1835; d. 1906*), linguist, student of comparative mythology. Contributed primarily to Celtic, Slavonic, Mongolian and American Indian ethnology; translated Sienkievicz, Tolstoy, Zagoskin and others.

CURTIS, ALFRED ALLEN (*b. Pocomoke, Md., 1831; d. Baltimore, Md., 1908*), Roman Catholic clergyman. Bishop of Wilmington, Del., 1886–96.

CURTIS, BENJAMIN ROBBINS (*b. Watertown, Mass., 1809; d. Newport, R.I., 1874*), jurist. Graduated Harvard, 1829; attended Harvard Law School. Practiced in Northfield, Mass., and Boston. Appointed to the U.S. Supreme Court, 1851, Curtis dissented in the Dred Scott decision (1857), holding that residence in a free state enabled an ex-slave to vindicate his freedom in slave state courts. Curtis also objected to the Court's ruling on the merits of the case after having denied that a slave is a citizen, and resigned from the Court. Thereafter, as a recognized leader of the bar, Curtis argued many cases before the United States and the Massachusetts supreme courts, and was President Johnson's chief counsel during the impeachment proceedings.

CURTIS, CHARLES (*b. North Topeka, Kans., 1860; d. Washington, D.C., 1936*), lawyer. Congressman, Republican, from Kansas, 1892–1907; U.S. senator, 1907–1929; vice-president of the United States, 1929–33. [*Supp. 2*]

CURTIS, CYRUS HERMANN KOTZSCHMAR (*b. Portland, Maine, 1850; d. Wyncote, Pa., 1933*), publisher. Founder and business head of the Curtis Publishing Co.; publisher of the *Ladies' Home Journal* and *Saturday Evening Post*. [*Supp. 1*]

CURTIS, EDWARD LEWIS (*b. Ann Arbor, Mich., 1853; d. 1911*), Presbyterian clergyman, educator. Graduated Yale, 1874, and Union Theological Seminary. Taught Hebrew at McCormick Theological Seminary and at Yale; published *Critical and Exegetical Commentary on the Books of Chronicles* (1910).

CURTIS, EDWIN UPTON (*b. Roxbury, Mass., 1861; d. 1922*), lawyer. Carried out major reforms of Boston city government as mayor, 1894–95. As police commissioner, 1918–22, reorganized department after 1919 strike.

CURTIS, GEORGE (*b. Worcester, Mass., 1796; d. Jacksonville, Fla., 1856*), banker. Served in Rhode Island legislature; as president of Continental Bank, New York, drew up "Constitution" of New York Clearing House, 1854.

CURTIS, GEORGE TICKNOR (*b. Watertown, Mass., 1812; d. New York, N.Y., 1894*), lawyer. Brother of Benjamin R. Curtis. A celebrated patent attorney and of counsel for plaintiff in Dred Scott case, his reputation rests chiefly on his *Constitutional History of the United States* (1889, 1896).

CURTIS, GEORGE WILLIAM (*b. Providence, R.I., 1824; d. Staten Island, N.Y., 1892*), author, orator. Son of George Curtis. As a young man, spent two years at Brook Farm; traveled for four years in Europe and Near East. Returning to New York, was associated with the *Tribune*, with *Putnam's Magazine*, and served as editor of *Harper's Weekly*, 1863–92. Idealist and Puritan, Curtis employed his talents as speaker and writer in numerous movements for reform, beginning with the antislavery campaigns *post*

1855, and including municipal reform, women's rights and enfranchisement, and civil service. He was author, among other books, of *Potiphar Papers* (1853), *Prue and I* (1857) and numerous published orations.

CURTIS, JOHN GREEN (*b. New York, N.Y., 1844; d. 1913*), physiologist. Son of George Curtis; half-brother of George W. Curtis. As professor at College of Physicians and Surgeons, New York, 1883–1909, he made his laboratory there a research center of note; he also contributed to the scholarly study of the history of his specialty.

CURTIS, MOSES ASHLEY (*b. Stockbridge, Mass., 1808; d. Hillsboro, N.C., 1872*), botanist, Episcopal minister. Graduated Williams, 1827. Made valuable contributions to knowledge of fungi; collected unusually complete mycological herbaria.

CURTIS, NEWTON MARTIN (*b. De Peyster, N.Y., 1835; d. Ogdensburg, N.Y., 1910*), Union soldier, New York legislator and congressman.

CURTIS, OLIN ALFRED (*b. Frankfort, Maine, 1850; d. 1918*), Methodist clergyman. Taught at Boston University and Drew Theological Seminary, 1889–1914; the most influential Methodist theologian of his time.

CURTIS, SAMUEL RYAN (*b. near Champlain, N.Y., 1805; d. Council Bluffs, Iowa, 1866*), soldier, lawyer, engineer. Graduated West Point, 1831. Active in railroad construction and river improvement projects; as Union brigadier, defeated Confederates at Pea Ridge, Ark., 1862.

CURTIS, WILLIAM ELEROY (*b. Akron, O., 1850; d. Philadelphia, Pa., 1911*), journalist, traveler, publicist. First director of present Pan-American Union, 1889–93.

CURTISS, GLENN HAMMOND (*b. Hammondsport, N.Y., 1878; d. Buffalo, N.Y., 1930*), aviator, inventor. Interest in bicycle and motorcycle racing led to venture in motorcycle manufacture. With Thomas Scott Baldwin, Curtiss built the first army dirigible in 1905. Became director of Alexander Graham Bell's Aerial Experiment Association; developed the *June Bug*, an airplane which won the *Scientific American* trophy in 1908; invented the hydroplane and flying boat, 1911–12. In World War I, the Curtiss Aeroplane and Motor Co. manufactured 5000 "Jennies," a mass-produced plane. A Navy Curtiss flying boat made the first Atlantic crossing by air in 1919. In the development of aviation Curtiss's place is alongside the Wright brothers and Langley. [*Supp. 1*]

CURTISS, SAMUEL IVES (*b. Union, Conn., 1844; d. 1904*), theologian. Professor at Chicago Theological Seminary; disciple of Franz Delitzsch; author of *Primitive Semitic Religion Today* (1902).

CURWEN, SAMUEL (*b. Salem, Mass., 1715; d. Salem, 1802*), Loyalist. In England, 1775–84; described fellow-exiles in his journal and letters.

CURWOOD, JAMES OLIVER (*b. Owosso, Mich., 1878; d. Owosso, 1927*), author of popular novels of out-of-doors adventure.

CUSHING, CALEB (*b. Salisbury Township, Mass., 1800; d. Newburyport, Mass., 1879*), statesman. Grew up in Newburyport. Graduated Harvard, 1817. Studied at the Harvard Law School, tutored mathematics at Harvard, and in 1821 began law practice in Newburyport. He also contributed to the *North American Review,* edited the Newburyport newspaper and delivered many public addresses. As a supporter of John Quincy Adams, he entered the Massachusetts General Court in 1824, and in 1826 became a state senator, but lost election to Congress, 1826. After several bitter contests he was elected to the House of Representatives on the Whig ticket and served, 1835–43.

Conservative by temperament yet morally opposed to slavery, Cushing agreed with Everett, Webster and other Massachusetts Whigs that the North had no constitutional right to interfere in Southern affairs. He believed the preservation of the Union to be more important than the abolition of slavery, but upheld the rights of his constituents to petition Congress against slavery. Cushing criticized Van Buren's administration and voted against all Democratic measures, but on President Harrison's death in 1841 he became estranged from the Whig party. Antagonized by Clay's dictatorial dominance, Cushing sided with Tyler against the Clay Whigs, and until the Civil War voted consistently for Democratic principles and candidates. He left Congress in 1843.

Accepting the post of commissioner to China, he concluded the commercial Treaty of Wang Hiya in 1844, which opened five Chinese ports to American merchants, settled disputed tariff and trade regulations and established the principle of exterritoriality for U.S. citizens in China. After a trip through Wisconsin and Minnesota, he was elected again to the Massachusetts General Court and there advocated military expansion, favored the annexation of Oregon and Texas and supported President Polk's policy on the Mexican war issue. In 1847 he raised a regiment, and as brigadier-general entered Mexico City. Defeated in the gubernatorial elections, 1847 and 1848, in 1851 he became mayor of Newburyport, and in 1852 served as associate justice of the Massachusetts supreme judiciary court. Having been instrumental in Franklin Pierce's election in 1852, Cushing was appointed U.S. attorney-general. An influential cabinet member, he spoke out against abolitionism and in foreign affairs became the spokesman of "Young America" and the apostle of "manifest destiny." In 1857 he returned to the Massachusetts legislature. Though he remained a foe of slavery, he condemned Garrison's abolitionists and John Brown's raid. He came, however, by 1860 to see a separation of the states as the only practicable solution to the con-

troversy, and prophesied civil war and the dictatorship of some "man on horseback."

As permanent chairman of the Democratic Convention in Charleston and Baltimore (Apr.–June, 1860), Cushing vainly labored for compromise. He then chaired the seceding rival convention which nominated Breckinridge. Unable to prevent passage of the secession ordinance in Charleston (December 1860), he returned to Washington and offered his services to Lincoln. He became a Republican and was legal consultant to both Seward and Lincoln. After the war he conducted a law practice in Washington, was chairman of a commission which revised and codified the United States statutes and was one of the chief American negotiators of the *Alabama* claims. He was a major architect of the 1871 Treaty of Washington which provided for an international tribunal of arbitration. When President Grant nominated Cushing in 1873 to be chief justice of the Supreme Court, Cushing's enemies revived old slanders, and he failed to be confirmed for purely partisan reasons.

From 1873 to 1877 Cushing served as minister to Spain where he proved to be one of America's most popular and able diplomats. He spent his last years among his books in Newburyport. Cushing was an extraordinarily erudite scholar in the most diverse fields. His genius was acquisitive and critical rather than creative but found an outlet in his many historical and biographical contributions to the *Encyclopedia Americana,* the *American Annual Register,* and the *North American Review.* He wrote a *History of Newburyport* (1826), a *Review Historical and Political of the Late Revolution in France* (1833) and *Reminiscences of Spain* (1833). He spoke French, Spanish, Italian, German and Manchu, and could read easily all European tongues. He was a favorite speaker on the lyceum stage and an excellent lawyer who impressed judges with the intellectual quality of his arguments. In politics, his intellectuality made him appear aloof from the people. Having little personal magnetism and small power to arouse enthusiasm, he suffered from the practical ineffectiveness of his belief in reason as the best means of bringing men to his point of view.

CUSHING, FRANK HAMILTON (*b. North East, Pa., 1857; d. 1900*), ethnologist. Associated for many years with Smithsonian Institution, Bureau of American Ethnology; author of *Zuni Creation Myths* (1896).

CUSHING, HARVEY WILLIAMS (*b. Cleveland, O., 1869; d. New Haven, Conn., 1939*), neurological surgeon. His father, grandfather, and great-grandfather were physicians. After graduating from Yale, 1891, Cushing received A.M. and M.D. degrees *cum laude* from Harvard Medical School, 1895. His ability to draw anatomical structures with remarkable fidelity early focused attention on his capabilities.

Attracted to surgery by an instinctive ability to handle delicate tissues, he interned at the Massachusetts General Hospital, then became a resident at the Johns Hopkins Hospital. Here he learned his slow, meticulous technique under William Stewart Halsted and became increasingly interested in cerebral surgery. At Hopkins too began Cushing's long association with Dr. William Osler.

Cushing spent the year 1900–01 abroad, meeting many important scientists, and doing work on problems of intracranial pressure and cerebral circulation in European laboratories. Upon his return to Baltimore, Cushing began a general surgical practice and continued teaching at the Johns Hopkins Hospital. The earliest of his brain tumor operations were disappointing, but his original and increasingly skillful operative procedures resulted in dramatic reductions in mortality, a record he continued to better throughout his career and which was equaled by no other neuro-surgeon of his time. A successful operation for brain tumor on General Leonard Wood in 1910 enhanced Cushing's reputation, as did his monograph (1912) on the pituitary body, a field in which he had become increasingly interested.

In 1912 Cushing became surgeon-in-chief of the Peter Bent Brigham Hospital in Boston and professor of surgery at Harvard Medical School, positions he held until his retirement in 1932. During World War I he served abroad for several years with medical units he had organized. As a result of his many operations he contributed (1918) a classic paper on wartime injuries of the brain. Though the war undermined his health, Cushing returned to a period of intense activity, training young men from all over the world, writing the Pulitzer Prize-winning biography *The Life of Sir William Osler* (1925), and publishing some of his most important monographs. Among them was his description of pituitary basophilism (Cushing's disease), one of his most original contributions to clinical medicine.

In 1933 Cushing became professor of neurology at Yale and later director of studies in the history of medicine. Long interested in medical history and in book collecting, his extensive collection became the nucleus of the historical medical library at Yale.
[Supp. 2]

CUSHING, JOHN PERKINS (*b. Boston, Mass., 1787; d. Watertown, Mass., 1862*), merchant, philanthropist. Nephew of Thomas H. Perkins. Made his fortune in China, 1803–30, where he was the most highly respected foreign merchant.

CUSHING, JOSIAH NELSON (*b. North Attleboro, Mass., 1840; d. 1905*), Baptist missionary in Burma. Developed Judson College in Rangoon, translated the Shan Bible and prepared a Shan Bible Dictionary.

CUSHING, LUTHER STEARNS (*b. Lunenberg, Mass., 1803; d. Boston, Mass., 1856*), jurist. Served in Massachusetts General Court; was reporter of state supreme court; author of a celebrated *Manual of Parliamentary Procedure* (1844).

CUSHING, THOMAS (*b. Boston, Mass., 1725; d. Boston, 1788*), merchant, politician. Speaker of Massachusetts General Court, 1766–74; member of First and Second Continental Congresses; served as Massachusetts lieutenant-governor, 1780–88.

CUSHING, WILLIAM (*b. Scituate, Mass., 1732; d. Scituate, 1810*), jurist. Graduated Harvard, 1751. Served as register of deeds and probate judge in Lincoln Co., 1760–71; a judge of Massachusetts superior court after 1772, he refused in conformity with instructions from the General Court to accept a royal salary. Cushing was senior associate judge of the new court as reorganized by the revolutionary council, and chief justice, 1777–89. He was vice-president of the state convention which ratified the Constitution, and first associate justice appointed to the U.S. Supreme Court. During Jay's absence Cushing administered the oath at Washington's second inauguration. In 1796 he declined appointment as chief justice. He devoted himself chiefly to his duties in the federal circuit courts.

CUSHING, WILLIAM BARKER (*b. Delafield, Wis., 1842; d. Washington, D.C., 1874*), naval officer. During Civil War he carried out brilliant and daring missions, among them the torpedoing of the Confederate ram *Albemarle*.

CUSHMAN, CHARLOTTE SAUNDERS (*b. Boston, Mass., 1816; d. Boston, 1876*), actress. Debut as a singer, Boston, 1835. In New York and Philadelphia, 1837–44, she displayed as actress a "rude, strong, uncultivated talent." Engagements in London disciplined and polished her acting without robbing it of its passionate power to move audiences. She toured the United States, 1849–52, acclaimed as the leading actress of our stage. Resident in London and on the continent until 1870, she returned at intervals to play American engagements. Tall, deep-voiced, almost masculine in many respects, inheritor of the great acting tradition of Garrick and Kean, she won fame and fortune by the intelligence of her interpretations.

CUSHMAN, GEORGE HEWITT (*b. Windham, Conn., 1814; d. Jersey City Heights, N.J., 1876*), miniature painter, engraver. Pupil of Washington Allston, Seth and John Cheney. Second only to Malbone among American miniature painters.

CUSHMAN, JOSHUA (*b. Halifax, Mass., 1761; d. Augusta, Maine, 1834*), Congregational clergyman. Congressman, Democrat, from Massachusetts and Maine, 1819–25.

CUSHMAN, PAULINE (*b. New Orleans, La., 1833; d. San Francisco, Calif., 1893*), Union spy, actress.

CUSHMAN, ROBERT (*b. Canterbury, England, c. 1579; d. England, 1625*), an organizer of the Pilgrim emigration to America. With John Carver, made financial arrangements with English merchants which the Pilgrims accepted at Leyden, 1620.

CUSHMAN, SUSAN WEBB (*b. Boston, Mass., 1822; d. Liverpool, England, 1859*), actress. Younger sister of Charlotte Cushman with whose companies she acted until 1848.

CUSHNY, ARTHUR ROBERTSON (*b. Fochabers, Scotland, 1866; d. near Edinburgh, 1926*), physician. Educated in Scotland and on the Continent, he taught pharmacology at the University of Michigan from 1893 until 1905 when he accepted the chair of pharmacology at University College, London. In 1918 he succeeded Sir Thomas Fraser at Edinburgh. Cushny's contributions to pharmacology were outstanding. His *Text-Book of Pharmacology and Therapeutics* (1899) has held the field in English almost without a rival; he was author among other works of *The Action and Uses in Medicine of Digitalis and Its Allies* (1925) and *The Biological Relation of Optically Isometric Substances* (1926).

CUSTER, GEORGE ARMSTRONG (*b. New Rumley, O., 1839; d. Little Big Horn, 1876*), soldier. Graduated West Point, 1861; rose by merit to major-general of volunteers in Civil War. Appointed lieutenant-colonel, 7th Cavalry (regular army), 1866, Custer saw hard service against hostile plains Indians, 1867–70 and 1873–75. His frank testimony about frauds in the Indian Bureau brought him disfavor of President Grant and removal from independent command in the 1876 expedition to round up hostile Sioux and Cheyennes; he was however restored to command of his regiment and permitted to serve in the expedition under Gen. Terry. Encountering a great body of Indians encamped on the Little Big Horn River in presentday southern Montana, Custer attacked them and was defeated, dying with his entire immediate command in a battle which is still the subject of violent controversy. He was author of memoirs of his Civil War service and of *My Life on the Plains* (1874).

CUSTIS, GEORGE WASHINGTON PARKE (*b. 1781; d. Arlington, Va., 1857*), playwright. Son of John P. Custis, George Washington's stepson; father-in-law of Robert E. Lee. Wrote and produced several plays; the most successful, *Pocahontas, or the Settlers of Virginia*, was produced at Philadelphia, 1830.

CUTBUSH, JAMES (*b. Philadelphia, Pa., 1788; d. West Point, N.Y., 1823*), chemist. Author of a *Philosophy of Experimental Chemistry* (1813), one of the first chemical textbooks published by a native American; professor of chemistry, West Point, 1820–23.

CUTLER, CARROLL (*b. Windham, N.H., 1829; d. 1894*), Congregational clergyman, educator. Graduated Yale, 1854. President, Western Reserve College (later University), 1871–88.

CUTLER, JAMES GOOLD (*b. Albany, N.Y., 1848; d. Rochester, N.Y., 1927*), architect, inventor, banker. Devised, patented (1883) and manufactured the mail chute used in modern office buildings.

CUTLER, LIZZIE PETIT (*b. Milton, Va., 1831; d. Richmond, Va., 1902*). Author of *Light and Darkness, a Story of Fashionable Life* (1855) and other fiction.

CUTLER, MANASSEH (*b. Killingly, Conn., 1742; d. Hamilton, Mass., 1823*), Congregational clergyman, botanist, Ohio colonizer. Graduated Yale, 1765; studied law and divinity; was ordained 1771 as pastor of church in Ipswich Hamlet, later Hamilton, Mass.; served as chaplain in Revolution. A versatile man, Cutler practiced medicine and undertook various scientific investigations; he prepared the first systematic account of New England flora. He is best known for his part in founding the Ohio Company, securing for it from Congress in 1787 the right to take up a million and a half acres of land around the junction of the Ohio and Muskingum rivers at cost of about eight cents an acre. He visited the Ohio settlements in 1788–89.

CUTLER, TIMOTHY (*b. Charlestown, Mass., 1684; d. Boston, Mass., 1765*), Congregational and Episcopal clergyman. Graduated Harvard, 1701. Rector of Yale College, 1719–22. After taking Episcopal orders in England, 1723, he served as rector of Christ Church, Boston, Mass., until his death.

CUTLER, CHARLES AMMI (*b. Boston, Mass., 1837; d. Walpole, N.H., 1903*), librarian. Graduated Harvard, 1855. Assisted in Harvard library, 1860–68; librarian of the Boston Athenaeum, 1868–93. Compiled the *Catalogue* of the Athenaeum library (1874–82) and published *Rules for a Printed Dictionary Catalogue* (1875).

CUTLER, EPHRAIM (*b. Woburn, Mass., 1832; d. West Falmouth, Mass., 1917*), physician, inventor of medical and surgical appliances.

CUTLER, GEORGE WASHINGTON (*b. Quebec, Canada, 1801; d. Washington, D.C., 1865*), lawyer, poet.

CUTTING, BRONSON MURRAY (*b. Oakdale, N.Y., 1888; d. Atlanta, Mo., 1935*), U.S. senator from New Mexico, 1927–35. Liberal Republican; vigorous critic of President Hoover's administration; supported the New Deal. [*Supp. 1*]

CUTTING, JAMES AMBROSE (*b. Hanover, N.H., 1814; d. Worcester, Mass., 1867*), inventor. Patented the "ambrotype" (1854), an improvement of the collodion process of photography designed to insure greater permanency of picture.

CUTTING, ROBERT FULTON (*b. New York, N.Y., 1852; d. 1934*), financier, New York civic leader, philanthropist. [*Supp. 1*]

CUYLER, THEODORE (*b. Poughkeepsie, N.Y., 1819; d. Philadelphia, Pa., 1876*), lawyer. Won fame for his brilliant advocacy in Christiana treason case, 1851. He later became general counsel for the Pennsylvania Railroad.

CUYLER, THEODORE LEDYARD (*b. Aurora, N.Y., 1822; d. 1909*), Presbyterian clergyman, writer. Principal pastorate at Lafayette Avenue Church, Brooklyn, N.Y., *post* 1860. Conservative and a noted preacher.

DABLON, CLAUDE (*b. Dieppe, France, 1619 or 1618; d. Quebec, Canada, 1697*), Jesuit missionary. Served among Iroquois, 1655–58; associate of Allouez and Marquette on Ottawa mission and in Wisconsin; superior of Canadian missions, 1671–80 and 1686–93.

DABNEY, RICHARD (*b. Louisa Co., Va., 1787; d. Louisa Co., 1825*), poet. His *Poems* (1812, 1815) include miscellaneous lyrics and translations and reveal more intellectual vigor than metrical talent.

DABNEY, ROBERT LEWIS (*b. Louisa Co., Va., 1820; d. Victoria, Texas, 1898*), Presbyterian theologian, teacher, author. A powerful defender of religious orthodoxy and the Confederate cause; taught at (Va.) Union Theological Seminary, 1853–83, and at University of Texas.

DABNEY, THOMAS SMITH GREGORY (*b. King and Queen Co., Va., 1798; d. 1885*), planter. Removed to Hinds Co., Miss., 1835. Embodiment of Southern patrician character in reverses of post-Civil War years.

DABNEY, VIRGINIUS (*b. Gloucester Co., Va., 1835; d. New York, N.Y., 1894*), teacher, author. Son of Thomas S. G. Dabney. A whimsical, shrewd, and wise critic of post-Civil War America, he wrote *The Story of Don Miff* (1886).

DABOLL, NATHAN (*b. Groton, Conn., 1750; d. 1818*), teacher of navigation, mathematician. Edited the *New England Almanack; post* 1773 was author of several textbooks.

DABROWSKI, JOSEPH (*b. Zoltance, Poland, 1842; d. Detroit, Mich., 1903*), Roman Catholic priest. Came to America, 1869. Pastor in Wisconsin, 1870–83; founded Saints Cyril and Methodius Seminary in Detroit, 1884, for training Polish priests in America.

DA COSTA, JACOB MENDEZ (*b. St. Thomas, V.I., 1833; d. Villanova, Pa., 1900*), physician. A skillful and honored teacher and clinician, Da Costa taught at Jefferson Medical College, Philadelphia, 1872–91. His *Medical Diagnosis* (1864) influenced teaching and clinical methods.

DA COSTA, JOHN CHALMERS (*b. Washington, D.C., 1863; d. Philadelphia, Pa., 1933*), surgeon. Graduated University of Pennsylvania, 1882; M.D., Jefferson Medical College, 1885. Interned at Philadelphia General Hospital and served as assistant physician in Pennsylvania Hospital for the Insane. Starting as assistant demonstrator of anatomy at Jefferson Medical College, he advanced in 1907 to Gross professor of surgery, a position he filled until his death. Known as a great teacher, he made a unique contribution to the literature of surgery with his textbook, *A Manual of Modern Surgery, General and Operative* (1894). Encyclopedic in scope and detail, it was the most used text in surgery for forty years. [*Supp. 1*]

DAEGER, ALBERT THOMAS (*b. North Vernon, Ind., 1872; d. Santa Fe, N.Mex., 1932*), Franciscan missionary to the Indians and Mexicans of New Mexico; archbishop of Santa Fe, 1919–32. [*Supp. 1*]

DAFT, LEO (*b. Birmingham, England, 1843; d. 1922*), electrical engineer, inventor. Came to America, 1866. His firm supplied apparatus for New York Power Company's first distributing stations and (for the Massachusetts Electric Power Co.) built the first (1884) complete central station for the generation and distribution of electricity for power purposes on a commercial scale. Daft began electric-railroad experiments in 1883; in 1885 he built in Baltimore the first commercially operated electric railroad in the United States. He also invented a process now generally used for vulcanizing rubber onto metal.

DAGG, JOHN LEADLEY (*b. near Middleburg, Va., 1794; d. Hayneville, Ala., 1884*), Baptist clergyman, educator. President, Mercer University, 1844–1856.

DAGGETT, DAVID (*b. Attleboro, Mass., 1764; d. New Haven, Conn., 1851*), lawyer, politician, jurist. Best known for his opinion in the case of Prudence Crandall (1833) that free Negroes were not citizens of the United States.

DAGGETT, ELLSWORTH (*b. Canandaigua, N.Y., 1845; d. 1923*), mining engineer. Graduated Sheffield Scientific School (Yale), 1864. The first U.S. surveyor-general of Utah, Daggett was among the earliest American hydrometallurgists and an effective advocate of state irrigation projects.

DAGGETT, NAPHTALI (*b. Attleboro, Mass., 1727; d. New Haven, Conn., 1780*), Congregational clergyman. First incumbent of first professorship in Yale College, and its acting president, 1766–77.

DAHL, THEODOR HALVORSON (*b. Baastad, Norway, 1845; d. Minneapolis, Minn., 1923*), Lutheran clergyman. A successful home missionary among Norwegians in America; active in forming the United Norwegian Lutheran Church of America.

DAHLGREN, JOHN ADOLPHUS BERNARD (*b. Philadelphia, Pa., 1809; d. Washington, D.C., 1870*), naval officer, inventor. After service at sea and with the Coast Survey, Dahlgren was assigned to ordnance duty in Washington, 1847, and became chief,

Bureau of Ordnance, 1862. His innovations revolutionized naval armament. Two guns of his design, cast-iron and smoothbore, distinguished by great thickness at the breech rapidly diminishing from trunnions to muzzle, were called "Dahlgrens." He commanded at the Washington Navy Yard, 1861–63. Promoted rear admiral, 1863, he succeeded DuPont in command of the South Atlantic Blockading Squadron, 1863–65.

DAHLGREN, SARAH MADELEINE VINTON (*b. Gallipolis, O., 1825; d. Washington, D.C., 1898*), author. Married John A. B. Dahlgren, 1865.

DAKIN, JAMES HARRISON (*b. Hudson, N.Y., 1806; d. Baton Rouge, La., 1852*), architect. Pupil of Alexander Jackson Davis. Practiced in Louisiana, *post* 1835, where he designed among other buildings St. Patrick's Church, New Orleans, and the Louisiana Capitol. [*Supp. 1*]

DALCHO, FREDERICK (*b. London, England, 1770; d. Charleston, S.C., 1836*), physician, Episcopal clergyman. Author of *Ahiman Rezon* (1807), a handbook for Freemasons.

DALE, RICHARD (*b. Norfolk Co., Va., 1756; d. Philadelphia, Pa., 1826*), naval officer. Served with distinction in the American Revolution; was first lieutenant of *Bon Homme Richard* in fight with *Serapis,* 1779. A merchant captain, 1783–94, he returned to the navy but retired in 1802 after a number of disputes over rank.

DALE, SAMUEL (*b. Rockbridge Co., Va., 1772; d. Lauderdale Co., Miss., 1841*), pioneer, soldier. Removed as a boy to frontier Georgia. A scout and trader, he became a guide for immigrants to Mississippi *c.* 1810 and an Indian fighter; he was later a legislator in both Alabama and Mississippi.

DALE, Sir THOMAS (*d. India, 1619*), soldier, colonizer, naval commander. Marshal of Virginia, 1611–16. Although the colonists disliked his stern measures, he left Virginia tranquil and prosperous.

DALL, CAROLINE WELLS HEALEY (*b. Boston, Mass., 1822; d. Washington, D.C., 1912*), reformer, woman's rights publicist.

DALL, WILLIAM HEALEY (*b. Boston, Mass., 1845; d. 1927*), naturalist. A specialist in mollusks, he served with the Geological Survey, 1884–1923, and was author, among other books, of *Alaska and Its Resources* (1870).

DALLAS, ALEXANDER JAMES (*b. Jamaica, W.I., 1759; d. Philadelphia, Pa., 1817*), lawyer, statesman. Emigrated to the United States, 1783; became a lawyer in Philadelphia. Appointed secretary of Pennsylvania, 1791; commissioned U.S. attorney for Eastern District of Pennsylvania, 1801. A moderate (Democrat) Republican with a record of ability and skill, Dallas became secretary of the treasury, 1814.

His measures restored public confidence, provided revenue for the bankrupt treasury. His recommendations in regard to a protective tariff were the basis of American policy for the next 30 years. Dallas resigned the secretaryship in 1816 and returned to practice of law.

DALLAS, GEORGE MIFFLIN (*b. Philadelphia, Pa., 1792; d. Philadelphia, 1864*), lawyer, statesman, diplomat. Son of Alexander J. Dallas. Graduated Princeton, 1810. Secretary to Albert Gallatin on mission to Russia, 1813. After holding several local offices in Pennsylvania, he served as U.S. senator, Democrat, 1831–33, and as minister to Russia, 1837–39. He was vice-president of the United States, 1845–49. As minister to Great Britain, 1856–61, Dallas secured a convention clarifying Central American problems under the Clayton-Bulwer treaty and obtained a final disavowal of the long-disputed right of search.

D'ALOES, CLAUDE JEAN. [See ALLOUEZ, CLAUDE JEAN, 1622–1689.]

DALTON, JOHN CALL (*b. Chelmsford, Mass., 1825; d. 1889*), physiologist. Graduated Harvard, 1844; Harvard Medical, 1847. First American physician to devote life to experimental physiology.

DALTON, ROBERT (*b. ? Cass Co., Mo., 1867; d. Coffeyville, Kans., 1892*), desperado. With his brothers Grattan and Emmett, began as a horse-thief in Kansas *ante* 1890; later robbed trains in California and Oklahoma.

DALY, ARNOLD. [See DALY, PETER CHRISTOPHER ARNOLD, 1875–1927.]

DALY, AUGUSTIN. [See DALY, JOHN AUGUSTIN, 1838–1899.]

DALY, CHARLES PATRICK (*b. New York, N.Y., 1816; d. Sag Harbor, N.Y., 1899*), jurist. Outstanding judge of common pleas, New York City, 1844–85; chief justice, 1858–85. A Democrat, he was legal adviser to Lincoln and W. H. Seward on many occasions.

DALY, JOHN AUGUSTIN (*b. Plymouth, N.C., 1838; d. Paris, France, 1899*), playwright, producer. Author of *Under the Gaslight* (1867) and author and adapter of many other dramas; proprietor of Daly's Theater, New York, whose company and productions were celebrated for taste, 1869–99.

DALY, MARCUS (*b. Ireland, 1841; d. 1900*), miner, capitalist. Came to America, 1856. Organized Anaconda Copper Mining Co. His feud with William A. Clark dominated Montana society and politics from 1888 to 1900.

DALY, PETER CHRISTOPHER ARNOLD (*b. Brooklyn, N.Y., 1875; d. New York, N.Y., 1927*), actor. His productions of G. B. Shaw's plays in New

York, 1903–05, marked an important step forward in the American theater.

DALZELL, JOHN (*b. New York, N.Y., 1845; d. Altadena, Calif., 1927*), lawyer, parliamentarian. Congressman, Republican, from Pennsylvania, 1886–1912; dominant in Rules Committee of the House.

DALZELL, ROBERT M. (*b. near Belfast, Ireland, 1793; d. Rochester, N.Y., 1873*), millwright, inventor. Introduced and perfected the elevator system for storing grain and meal which is now used in all large ports.

DAMROSCH, FRANK HEINO (*b. Breslau, Silesia, 1859; d. New York, N.Y., 1937*), music educator. Son of Leopold Damrosch. Founder (with James Loeb) of Institute of Musical Art, 1905, later the undergraduate section of the Juilliard School.

[*Supp. 2*]

DAMROSCH, LEOPOLD (*b. Posen, Poland, 1832; d. New York, N.Y., 1885*), conductor, composer, violinist. Came to America, 1871, as conductor of New York Arion Society. Active in many fields, he raised the standard of musical taste and appreciation in America.

DANA, CHARLES ANDERSON (*b. Hinsdale, N.H., 1819; d. Dosoris Island, Glen Cove, N.Y., 1897*), newspaper editor. Matriculated Harvard, 1839; left in junior year because of failing eyesight. Spent five years at Brook Farm and became "the best all-round man" there. Joined staff of *New York Tribune* and stood second in the office to Greeley alone when he resigned, 1862, to serve in the War Department. As reporter and observer, he gave valuable aid to Grant and Sherman. After an unsuccessful newspaper venture in Chicago, Dana became owner-editor of *New York Sun*, 1868. A perverse, cynical and often reactionary leader of public opinion, he achieved high distinction as a news editor, especially emphasizing the human interest story and cleverness of style and reporting technique.

DANA, CHARLES LOOMIS (*b. Woodstock, Vt., 1852; d. Harmon, N.Y., 1935*), neurologist. Brother of John C. Dana. M.D., Columbian University, 1876; College of Physicians and Surgeons, 1877. His clinical descriptions of combined scleroses of the spinal chord and observations on alcoholism are of outstanding importance. [*Supp. 1*]

DANA, EDWARD SALISBURY (*b. New Haven, Conn., 1849; d. 1935*), mineralogist. Son of James D. Dana. Graduated Yale, 1870; Ph.D., 1876. His revision (1892) of his father's *System of Mineralogy* (1837) has been with its appendices the standard reference in the field. [*Supp. 1*]

DANA, FRANCIS (*b. Charlestown, Mass., 1743; d. Cambridge, Mass., 1811*), diplomat, jurist. Son of Richard Dana; nephew of Edmund Trowbridge. Graduated Harvard, 1762; admitted to the bar, 1767.

At first in favor of reconciliation with Great Britain, *post* 1776 he took a leading part in the Revolution and was secretary of legation with John Adams in Paris, 1780. He spent 1781–83 in Russia vainly attempting to obtain recognition of the United States and a treaty. He was associate justice of Massachusetts supreme court, 1785–1806; from 1791 to 1806 he was chief justice of that body. A true Federalist, he supported the Alien and Sedition Bills and regarded Jeffersonians as a national menace.

DANA, JAMES (*b. Cambridge, Mass., 1735; d. New Haven, Conn., 1812*), Congregational clergyman. Leading character in the "Wallingford Controversy," 1758; pastor, First Church, New Haven, 1789–1805.

DANA, JAMES DWIGHT (*b. Utica., N.Y., 1813; d. 1895*), geologist, zoologist. Attended Yale, 1830–33; left to become instructor in the navy. Served as geologist and mineralogist with the U.S. South Seas Expedition under Capt. Wilkes, 1838–42. Editor of the *American Journal of Science*. Professor of natural history at Yale, *post* 1849; professor of geology, 1864–90. Despite poor health, Dana was a tireless writer; in addition to his reports from the Wilkes expedition, he wrote standard texts including *Manual of Geology* (1862) and *Textbook of Geology* (1864). Influential as teacher and scholar, Dana was America's foremost geologist throughout his active life.

DANA, JAMES FREEMAN (*b. Amherst, N.H., 1793; d. 1827*), chemist. Graduated Harvard, 1813. Brother of Samuel L. Dana. Taught chemistry at Harvard, Dartmouth, and the College of Physicians and Surgeons, New York.

DANA, JOHN COTTON (*b. Woodstock, Vt., 1856; d. New York, N.Y., 1929*), librarian, museum director, author, printer. Graduated Dartmouth, 1878. For reasons of health abandoned practice of law; after trials at engineering and newspaper work, became librarian in 1889 of the Denver (Colo.) Public Library which flourished under his administration. In 1898 he became librarian of the City Library, Springfield, Mass., and in 1902 of the Public Library, Newark, N.J. He greatly increased the circulation of the Newark library, making it the most effective institution of its kind in the United States. As director of the Newark Museum he made it as popular in its sphere as the library. Author of a standard textbook, *Library Primer* (1896), his pungent style is best represented in *Libraries: Addresses and Essays* (1916).

DANA, NAPOLEON JACKSON TECUMSEH (*b. Eastport, Maine, 1822; d. Portsmouth, N.H., 1905*), soldier, business executive. Graduated West Point, 1842. Served in Mexican War and was Union major-general of volunteers.

DANA, RICHARD (*b. Cambridge, Mass., 1700; d. Boston, Mass., 1772*), lawyer. Graduated Harvard, 1718. A leader at the bar, Dana was an original member of the Sons of Liberty and one of committee which investigated Boston Massacre, 1770.

DANA, RICHARD HENRY (*b. Cambridge, Mass., 1787; d. Boston, Mass., 1879*), poet, essayist. Son of Francis Dana. Educated at Harvard; received degree as of class of 1808; admitted to bar, 1811, but soon abandoned law for literature. Many years associated with *North American Review.* Author of periodical *The Idle Man* (1821); *The Buccaneer and Other Poems* (1827); *Poems and Prose Writings* (1833, 1850).

DANA, RICHARD HENRY (*b. Cambridge, Mass., 1815; d. Rome, Italy, 1882*), author, lawyer. Son of Richard H. Dana (1787–1879). Graduated Harvard, 1837, having interrupted his course to sail around Cape Horn to California as a common sailor. His *Two Years Before the Mast* (1840), written from notes made during this voyage, is a lively, unconventional account of sea life from the viewpoint of the forecastle which has attained classic stature. His manual, *The Seaman's Friend* (1841), became a standard work on maritime law. A founder of the Free-Soil party, Dana was deeply involved in the anti-slavery movement. In 1867–68, with William M. Evarts, he was counsel for the United States in the trial of Jefferson Davis. He died before completing a projected study of international law.

DANA, SAMUEL LUTHER (*b. Amherst, N.H., 1795; d. Lowell, Mass., 1868*), chemist. Brother of James F. Dana. Introduced improvements in bleaching and calico-printing. Author of *A Muck Manual for Farmers* (1842), an early work on soil chemistry.

DANA, SAMUEL WHITTELSEY (*b. Wallingford, Conn., 1760; d. 1830*), lawyer, statesman. Son of James Dana. Congressman, Federalist, from Connecticut, 1797–1810; U.S. senator, 1810–21.

DANCEL, CHRISTIAN (*b. Cassel, Germany, 1847; d. Brooklyn, N.Y., 1898*), inventor of machines for sewing shoes. His work made the widely used Goodyear Welt System a success.

DANE, NATHAN (*b. Ipswich, Mass., 1752; d. Beverly, Mass., 1835*), lawyer, statesman. Graduated Harvard, 1778; admitted to the bar, 1782. Served in the General Court of Massachusetts, 1782–85. Elected to the Continental Congress, he helped draft the Ordinance for the Northwest Territory and introduced the article prohibiting slavery in the Territory. An opponent of the Federal Constitution, he retired from Congress, 1788, serving thereafter in the Massachusetts Senate, 1790 and 1793–98. His *General Abridgment and Digest of American Law* (1823) was the first comprehensive compendium of law prepared and printed on this continent.

DANENHOWER, JOHN WILSON (*b. Chicago, Ill., 1849; d. Annapolis, Md., 1887*), Arctic explorer. Graduated Annapolis, 1870. Author of *Lieutenant Danenhower's Narrative of the Jeannette* (1882).

DANFORTH, CHARLES (*b. Norton, Mass., 1797; d. Paterson, N.J., 1876*), inventor, manufacturer. Invented and developed the cap spinner, an improvement in spinning frames; headed the Danforth locomotive building works, 1852–71.

DANFORTH, MOSELEY ISAAC (*b. Hartford, Conn., 1800; d. 1862*), engraver, painter.

DANFORTH, THOMAS (*b. Framlingham, England, 1623; d. 1699*), deputy-governor of Massachusetts, 1679–86. An early supporter and treasurer of Harvard College and a leader of the anti-prerogative party.

DANFORTH, THOMAS (*b. Taunton, Mass., 1703; d. c. 1786*), pewterer. Ancestor of the two largest pewtering families in America, the Danforths and the Boardmans.

DANIEL, JOHN MONCURE (*b. Stafford Co., Va., 1825; d. Richmond, Va., 1865*), journalist, diplomat. Editor of the *Richmond Examiner,* 1847–53 and 1861–65. An ardent secessionist.

DANIEL, JOHN WARWICK (*b. Lynchburg, Va., 1842; d. 1910*), lawyer, Confederate soldier. U.S. senator, Democrat, from Virginia, 1885–1910.

DANIEL, PETER VIVIAN (*b. Stafford Co., Va., 1784; d. Richmond, Va., 1860*), jurist. Associate justice, U.S. Supreme Court, 1841–60.

DANIELS, FRANK ALBERT (*b. Dayton, O., 1856; d. West Palm Beach, Fla., 1935*), musical comedy star. Made his reputation in Hoyt's *The Rag Baby* (1884) and Victor Herbert's first hit, *The Wizard of the Nile* (1895). [*Supp. 1*]

DANIELS, FRED HARRIS (*b. Hanover Center, N.H., 1853; d. 1913*), engineer, metallurgist. Inventor of devices for manufacturing steel rods and wire which made possible faster, less costly production.

DANNREUTHER, GUSTAV (*b. Cincinnati, O., 1853; d. 1923*), violinist, conductor, teacher. Founded Beethoven (later Dannreuther) String Quartet, 1884.

DA PONTE, LORENZO (*b. Ceneda, Italy, 1749; d. New York, N.Y., 1838*), poet, librettist, expositor of Italian culture in America. After an adventurous youth, Da Ponte was appointed "Poet to the Italian Theater" in Vienna and as librettist in collaboration with Mozart produced *Le Nozze di Figaro* (1786), *Don Giovanni* (1787) and *Cosí Fan Tutte* (1790). Da Ponte left Vienna for London and in 1805 emigrated to America, where he succeeded as a teacher of Italian after numerous business reverses. Appointed professor of Italian literature in Columbia College in 1825, he imported Italian books, encouraged the study of Dante and furthered Italian opera in America.

DARBY, JOHN (*b. North Adams, Mass., 1804; d. New York, N.Y., 1877*), educator. Graduated Williams, 1831. Author of *A Botany of the Southern States* (1841), an authoritative manual for the flora of that area, and other textbooks.

DARBY, WILLIAM (*b. Lancaster County, Pa., 1775; d. 1854*), geographer. Darby's surveys and researches were basis for John Melish's map of the United States (1818). Author of *A Tour from . . . New York to Detroit* (1819), and author or editor of many other geographical and statistical studies, 1816–41.

DARE, VIRGINIA (*b. Roanoke, Va., 1587*), the first English child born in America.

DARGAN, EDMUND STROTHER (*b. Montgomery Co., N.C., 1805; d. Mobile, Ala., 1879*), jurist, congressman. Judge, supreme court of Alabama, 1847–52; chief justice, 1849–52.

DARGAN, EDWIN PRESTON (*b. Barboursville, Va., 1879; d. Chicago, Ill., 1940*), educator. Professor of French literature, University of Chicago, 1911–40; Balzac scholar. [*Supp. 2*]

DARKE, WILLIAM (*b. Pennsylvania, 1736; d. 1801*), soldier. Raised near present Shepherdstown, W. Va. Served ably in Revolution; commanded left wing in St. Clair's defeat, 1791.

DARLEY, FELIX OCTAVIUS CARR (*b. Philadelphia, Pa., 1822; d. 1888*), illustrator. Early work appeared in periodicals. Facility in caricature shown in work for Carey & Hart's "Library of American Humorous Works" (1840's); displayed more serious ability in *Scenes in Indian Life* (1843) and in illustrations for Judd's *Margaret* and for works by Irving and Cooper. Prolific and versatile and always a careful craftsman, Darley had an essentially American genius and was at his best in depicting American scenes and characters.

DARLING, FLORA ADAMS (*b. Lancaster, N.H., 1840; d. New York, N.Y., 1910*). Co-foundress, Daughters of the American Revolution, 1890; foundress of two similar patriotic organizations.

DARLING, HENRY (*b. Reading, Pa., 1823; d. Clinton, N.Y., 1891*), Presbyterian clergyman. Pastor at Albany, N.Y., Hudson, N.Y., Philadelphia, Pa.; president, Hamilton College, 1881–91.

DARLING, SAMUEL TAYLOR (*b. Harrison, N.J., 1872; d. near Beirut, Syria, 1925*), pathologist, authority on tropical medicine. Graduated M.D., Baltimore College of Physicians, 1903. Joined Isthmian Canal Commission, 1906, and served as chief of laboratories at the Panama Canal Zone until 1915. Appointed, 1915, to the staff of the International Health Board, he studied the cause of anemia common in Southeast Asia. After a period of teaching he became director of the field laboratory for malaria research under the International Health Board. Darling's study of sanitation helped make possible the construction of the Panama Canal. He also contributed significantly to the knowledge and control of hookworm disease.

DARLINGTON, WILLIAM (*b. Dilworthtown, Pa., 1782; d. 1863*), physician, botanist. Wrote *Florula Cestrica* (1826) and memoirs of William Baldwin, John Bartram and Humphrey Marshall.

DARROW, CLARENCE SEWARD (*b. near Kinsman, O., 1857; d. Chicago, Ill., 1938*), lawyer, social reformer. Attended Allegheny College and law school of University of Michigan; was admitted to bar in Ohio, 1878. Reared in traditions of 19th century rationalism and self-educated in liberal social doctrines of his time, Darrow embodied a variety of intellectual influences; these included skepticism in religion and philosophy, determinism in psychology, a firm faith in evolutionary doctrine, and an attitude in politics which drew on elements of progressive Democracy, socialism and anarchism. After nine years' practice in Ohio small towns, he removed to Chicago, Ill., 1887, where his professional rise was rapid. Among his better-known partners were John P. Altgeld (1897–1902) and Edgar Lee Masters (1903–1911). Successful in civil practice, he lost his first major criminal case (the appeal of the murderer of Carter H. Harrison, 1894) but soon won wide repute in handling labor cases. Among his principal defense efforts in this field were the cases of Eugene V. Debs (argued 1895), of William D. Haywood (1906–1907), and of the McNamara brothers (1911). Gradually entering the third phase of his career, criminal law, Darrow was counsel in a number of lesser cases but achieved national publicity in the Loeb-Leopold murder case (1924), the Scopes trial in Tennessee (1925), and the Massie trial (Honolulu, Hawaii, 1932). Basing his jury appeals on his view that men are the victims of social and physiological forces which they cannot control, he was successful in making atrocious crimes appear comprehensible; he was also adept at jury selection, was painstaking in pre-trial investigations, and in the hope of securing public understanding and sympathy for his clients deliberately tried his cases in the newspaper headlines. Cherishing as he did the independent rural society into which he was born, he never could adapt himself to monopolistic and bureaucratic industrial capitalism; out of this basic dilemma arose the many contradictions in thought which appeared in his writings and speeches. [*Supp. 2*]

DART, HENRY PLAUCHÉ (*b. Fort St. Philip, La., 1858; d. New Orleans, La., 1934*), lawyer. An outstanding trial advocate; promoted study of Louisiana colonial history. [*Supp. 1*]

DAVEIS, CHARLES STEWART (*b. Portland, Maine, 1788; d. Portland, 1865*), lawyer. Graduated

Bowdoin, 1807. Active in settlement of dispute with Great Britain over Maine's northeastern boundary, 1827–42.

DAVEISS, JOSEPH HAMILTON (*b. Bedford Co., Va., 1774; d. Tippecanoe, 1811*), lawyer. As federal district attorney for Kentucky, charged Aaron Burr, 1806, with leading a conspiracy in the Western states but failed to get indictment. Killed in battle with Indians. Brother-in-law of John Marshall.

DAVENPORT, EDWARD LOOMIS (*b. Boston, Mass., 1815; d. Canton, Pa., 1877*), actor. Made his debut at Providence, R.I., with Junius Brutus Booth in *New Way to Pay Old Debts,* c. 1837; first decade in theatre was spent in stock companies playing every variety of character. Went to England, 1847, as leading man for Anna Cora Mowatt. Davenport developed as a Shakespearean actor during six years in England, and in 1849 married Fanny Vining, a popular English actress. Returning to America, 1854, Davenport took place among America's leading actors, acclaimed for the intelligence of his impersonations.

DAVENPORT, FANNY LILY GYPSY (*b. London, England, 1850; d. South Duxbury, Mass., 1898*), actress. Daughter of Edward L. Davenport. Played with parents, in stock, and as leading lady in Augustin Daly's company; later headed her own company. Famous in Sardou's *Fédora* and *Tosca.*

DAVENPORT, GEORGE (*b. Lincolnshire, England, 1783; d. 1845*), soldier, fur trader. Came to America, 1804. One of the founders of Davenport, Iowa, which is named for him.

DAVENPORT, HERBERT JOSEPH (*b. Wilmington, Vt., 1861; d. New York, N.Y., 1931*), economist. Distinguished teacher at University of Missouri and Cornell; author of *Value and Distribution* (1908) and *The Economics of Enterprise* (1913).

[*Supp. 1*]

DAVENPORT, HOMER CALVIN (*b. Silverton, Oreg., 1867; d. 1912*), cartoonist. An advocate of municipal reform, his depictions of Mark Hanna's dollar-marked clothes and the "Trust" figure were permanent contributions to cartoon symbolism.

DAVENPORT, IRA ERASTUS (*b. 1839; d. Mayville, N.Y., 1911*), medium. With his brother William H. H. Davenport, he performed a spiritualist act which was successful here and in Europe, c. 1860–77.

DAVENPORT, JAMES (*b. Stamford, Conn., 1716; d. 1757*), clergyman. Graduated Yale, 1732. Influenced by George Whitefield, he had a stormy career as itinerant preacher and revivalist.

DAVENPORT, JOHN (*b. Coventry, England, 1597; d. Boston, Mass., 1669/70*), clergyman. Attended Oxford. Active in ministry in London *post* 1619, he interested himself in procuring the Massachusetts Company charter, 1629; by 1632 he was definitely a non-conformist. In Holland *post* 1633, he returned briefly to England in 1637 and sailed in June of that year in company with Theophilus Eaton for America. After about nine months in Boston, he and Eaton together with their company of emigrants settled an independent colony at present New Haven, Conn.; Eaton was governor and Davenport pastor. In 1661, Davenport sheltered the regicides Whalley and Goffe; he stoutly opposed the "Half Way Covenant," and in 1662 opposed the absorption of New Haven Colony by Connecticut. Against the will of his congregation, he accepted a call to Boston's First Church in 1667.

DAVENPORT, THOMAS (*b. Williamstown, Vt., 1802; d. Salisbury, Vt., 1851*), blacksmith, inventor of the electric motor. After experiments with electro-magnets *post* 1831, in 1834 he built a little machine composed of four opposed electro-magnets connected through a commutator to an electric battery. This device unquestionably embodied the principles of the modern electric motor. After many difficulties, Davenport's motor was patented in 1837. He tried to establish a market for his machine, but never succeeded, although he enlarged and improved it.

DAVENPORT, WILLIAM H. (1841–1877). [See DAVENPORT, IRA ERASTUS, 1839–1911].

DAVEY, JOHN (*b. Somersetshire, England, 1846; d. 1923*), "the father of tree surgery in America." Came to America, c. 1872; settled eventually in Kent, O.

D'AVEZAC, AUGUSTE GENEVIEVE VALENTIN (*b. Santo Domingo, 1780; d. New York, N.Y., 1851*), lawyer. Raised in New Orleans, La. Brother-in-law of Edward Livingston. Held diplomatic posts in the Netherlands and Naples.

DAVID, JOHN BAPTIST MARY (*b. Couëron, France, 1761; d. 1841*), Roman Catholic clergyman, Sulpician, missionary, theologian. Came to America, 1792. Assistant to Bishop Flaget in Bardstown, Ky., 1811–32, David succeeded him, resigning the bishopric, 1833. He founded the Sisters of Charity of Nazareth.

DAVIDGE, JOHN BEALE (*b. Annapolis, Md., 1768; d. Baltimore, Md., 1829*), anatomist, surgeon. Known for his work on yellow fever, Davidge developed several operative techniques; his method of amputation became known as the "American" method.

DAVIDGE, WILLIAM PLEATER (*b. London, England, 1814; d. Wyoming, 1888*), actor. Came to America, 1850. "Dick Deadeye" in the first American production of *H.M.S. Pinafore;* member of Daly's company (1869–77) and others.

DAVIDSON, GEORGE (*b. Nottingham, England, 1825; d. 1911*), geodesist, geographer. Came to America as a child. Headed 1850 survey of the Pacific Coast for purposes of navigation. A noted astronomer, he operated first (1879) observatory in California; he also advised on building Lick Observatory.

DAVIDSON, ISRAEL (*b. Yanova, Russia, 1870; d. Great Neck, N.Y., 1939*), Hebrew scholar. Came to America, 1888. Graduated College of City of New York, 1895; Ph.D., Columbia, 1902. Author of *Thesaurus of Mediaeval Hebrew Poetry* (1924–33). [*Supp. 2*]

DAVIDSON, JAMES WOOD (*b. Newberry Co., S.C., 1829; d. 1905*), author, journalist, Confederate soldier. Edited *Living Writers of the South* (1869).

DAVIDSON, JOHN WYNN (*b. Fairfax Co., Va., 1823; d. St. Paul, Minn., 1881*), soldier. Graduated West Point, 1845. Served against Indians in the Southwest and as Union major-general; distinguished in Arkansas and Missouri campaigns, 1863–65.

DAVIDSON, LUCRETIA MARIA (*b. 1808; d. 1825*) and **MARGARET MILLER** (*b. 1823; d. 1838*), poets. Born in Plattsburg, N.Y., both sisters wrote precociously and died of tuberculosis. The sentimental tragedy of their lives held vast appeal to their contemporaries.

DAVIDSON, ROBERT (*b. Elkton, Md., 1750; d. 1812*), Presbyterian clergyman. Professor in Dickinson College and pastor in Carlisle, Pa., *post* 1784.

DAVIDSON, THOMAS (*b. Aberdeenshire, Scotland, 1840; d. 1900*), philosopher, teacher, wandering scholar. Came to the United States, c. 1867. A follower first of W. T. Harris, later of Rosmini.

DAVIDSON, WILLIAM LEE (*b. Lancaster Co., Pa., 1746; d. 1781*), Revolutionary soldier. Served with the North Carolina line and militia; was killed at Cowan's Ford on the Catawba. Davidson College is named for him.

DAVIE, WILLIAM RICHARDSON (*b. Egremont, England, 1756; d. Lancaster Co., S.C., 1820*), lawyer, Revolutionary soldier. Came to America as a child. Federalist governor of North Carolina; "father" of the University of North Carolina.

DAVIES, ARTHUR BOWEN (*b. Utica, N.Y., 1862; d. Florence, Italy, 1928*), painter. Studied with a local painter in Ithaca, N.Y., at Chicago Art Institute and at Art Students' League, New York; encouraged by the dealer William Macbeth and by Benjamin Altman. Early works are small idylls, recalling the quality of Watteau; around 1900, he changed style, producing larger canvases of cooler color and with abstract figures symbolical of poetic ideas. In his third manner, the figure compositions in his mythologies and abstractions are dense and elaborate and tend to assume form of a frieze. He also experimented in cubism, and did many admirable lithographs and etchings.

DAVIES, HENRY EUGENE (*b. New York, N.Y., 1836; d. Middleboro, Mass., 1894*), lawyer, Union soldier. Served 1861–65; called "a cavalryman by instinct," he rose to major-general of volunteers.

DAVIES, JOHN VIPOND (*b. Swansea, Wales, 1862; d. Flushing, N.Y., 1939*), civil engineer. Came to America, 1889. With his partner, Charles M. Jacobs, he pioneered in sub-aqueous and pneumatic foundation work. [*Supp. 2*]

DAVIES, SAMUEL (*b. New Castle Co., Del., 1723; d. Princeton, N.J., 1761*), Presbyterian clergyman. President, College of New Jersey (Princeton), 1759–61.

DAVIESS, JOSEPH HAMILTON [See DAVEISS, JOSEPH HAMILTON, 1774–1811.]

DAVIESS, MARIA THOMPSON (*b. Harrodsburg, Ky., 1872; d. New York, N.Y., 1924*), painter. Author of sentimental romances, of which the best-known was *The Melting of Molly* (1912).

DAVIS, ALEXANDER JACKSON (*b. New York, N.Y., 1803; d. West Orange, N.J., 1892*), architect. Began as draftsman, producing excellent architectural views in lithography and line; was probably apprenticed to J.C. Brady. Employed as draftsman by Ithiel Town, he was associated with him (save for a brief hiatus), 1829–43; thereafter he practiced by himself for more than twenty years. Davis collaborated in design of the North Carolina State Capitol and designed the original buildings of Virginia Military Institute; he produced also a great variety of superior work throughout the then United States. His designs were distinguished by versatility and romantic imagination.

DAVIS, ANDREW JACKSON (*b. Blooming Grove, N.Y., 1826; d. 1910*), spiritualist.

DAVIS, ANDREW McFARLAND (*b. Worcester, Mass., 1833; d. 1920*), lawyer, antiquarian. Brother of John C. B. Davis. Author of many important papers and monographs on the history of currency and banking in the colony of Massachusetts.

DAVIS, ARTHUR POWELL (*b. near Decatur, Ill., 1861; d. 1933*), hydraulic and irrigation engineer. Nephew of John W. and William B. Powell. Topographer in U.S. Geological Survey, 1882–96. Appointed hydrographer, 1896, he supervised all stream measurements in the United States, and made rainfall and stream studies for the proposed Nicaraguan and Panama Canal routes. On organization of the Reclamation Service, Davis was appointed supervising engineer (1903), and from 1914 to 1923 was director. The Reclamation Service under his direction built more than 100 dams, including Shoshone and Arrowrock dams and the Gunnison Tunnel. [*Supp. 1*]

DAVIS, CHARLES HAROLD (*b. Amesbury, Mass., 1856; d. Mystic, Conn., 1933*), artist. Created an individual style; was temperamentally akin to Ryder and Blakelock. [*Supp. 1*]

DAVIS, CHARLES HENRY (*b. Boston, Mass., 1807; d. Washington, D.C., 1877*), naval officer. Active in scientific work connected with the navy, 1842–56, he also distinguished himself in active administration, planning duties and command at sea, 1861–65.

DAVIS, CHARLES HENRY (*b. Cambridge, Mass., 1845; d. 1921*), naval officer. Son of Charles H. Davis (1807–1877).

DAVIS, CHARLES HENRY STANLEY (*b. Goshen, Conn., 1840; d. Meriden, Conn., 1917*), physician, philologist, Orientalist.

DAVIS, CUSHMAN KELLOGG (*b. Henderson, N.Y., 1838; d. 1900*), lawyer. Republican governor of Minnesota, 1873–75; U.S. senator, 1887–1900.

DAVIS, DAVID (*b. Cecil Co., Md., 1815; d. Bloomington, Ill., 1886*), jurist. A graduate of Yale Law School, 1835, Davis set up practice in Bloomington, Ill. From 1848 to 1862 he was judge of 8th judicial circuit, Illinois. During this time he formed a friendship with Abraham Lincoln, and at the Chicago convention in 1860 led the Lincoln forces. Appointed, 1862, to the U.S. Supreme Court, he delivered opinion in the Milligan case, 1866, antagonizing the radical Republicans. Nominated, 1872, for the presidency by the Labor Reform Convention, he withdrew when the Liberal Republicans did not endorse him. Elected U.S. senator from Illinois, 1877, he resigned from the Supreme Court and upset the expected composition of the Electoral Commission created to decide between Hayes and Tilden. He owed his place to the Democrats but generally supported the Republicans before retiring in 1883.

DAVIS, EDMUND JACKSON (*b. St. Augustine, Fla., 1827; d. Austin, Texas, 1883*), lawyer. Raised in Texas. A Unionist and a bitter radical reconstructionist. Republican governor of Texas, 1869–73.

DAVIS, EDWIN HAMILTON (*b. Hillsboro, O., 1811; d. 1888*), physician, archeologist. Collaborated with E. G. Squier in a survey of a hundred Indian mounds and a study, *Ancient Monuments of the Mississippi Valley* (1847), the first work issued by the Smithsonian Institution. The book is still valuable in itself and as a record of mounds since sacrificed to farming and building.

DAVIS, GARRET (*b. Mount Sterling, Ky., 1801; d. 1872*), lawyer. Congressman, Whig, from Kentucky, 1839–47. In turn a Know-Nothing and a radical Unionist, he was U.S. senator, 1861–72. Abandoning his radical views, 1864, he was thereafter a strong critic of Lincoln and the Republicans and ran as a Democrat, 1867.

DAVIS, GEORGE (*b. Porter's Neck, N.C., 1820; d. Wilmington, N.C., 1896*), lawyer. Attorney-general of the Confederacy, 1864–65. Later became counsel to the Atlantic Coast Line in its formative period.

DAVIS, GEORGE BRECKENRIDGE (*b. Ware, Mass., 1847; d. Washington, D.C., 1914*), soldier. Graduated West Point, 1871. Author of several works on military law; supervised publication of *War of the Rebellion: Official Records.*

DAVIS, GEORGE WHITEFIELD (*b. Thompson, Conn., 1839; d. 1918*), soldier, engineer. Governor of Canal Zone, 1904–05, and a member of the Isthmian Canal Commission.

DAVIS, HENRY (*b. East Hampton, N.Y., 1771; d. Clinton, N.Y., 1852*), clergyman. President, Middlebury College, 1809–17; Hamilton College, 1817–32.

DAVIS, HENRY GASSAWAY (*b. Woodstock, Md., 1823; d. Washington, D.C., 1916*), merchant, lumberman, railroad builder. U.S. senator, Democrat, from West Virginia, 1871–83.

DAVIS, HENRY GASSETT (*b. Trenton, Maine, 1807; d. Everett, Mass., 1896*), pioneer orthopedic surgeon. Graduated Yale, M.D., 1839; practiced in Worcester and Millbury, Mass., and later in New York, N.Y., where he founded so-called "traction" school of orthopedic surgery, c. 1856, his work providing the basis for the modern approach to problems of deformity. He influenced among others Lewis A. Sayre, Charles Fayette Taylor and Edward Hickling Bradford. His most important book, *Conservative Surgery* (1867) was first notable textbook in American orthopedics.

DAVIS, HENRY WINTER (*b. Annapolis, Md., 1817; d. Baltimore, Md., 1865*), lawyer, politician, statesman. Congressman, Know-Nothing, from Maryland, 1855–61; Republican, 1863–64. His vote for the Republican candidate for speaker of the House in 1860 broke a deadlock and made him a national figure; that same year he supported the successful Bell and Everett party in Maryland. Though an ardent Unionist, Davis strenuously opposed Lincoln and his program, especially protesting violations of *habeas corpus* and the plan for a moderate Southern reconstruction. Defeated in the congressional elections of 1864, Davis led the attack on Andrew Johnson in the "lame duck" session. He was author of the "Wade-Davis Manifesto" (1864).

DAVIS, HORACE (*b. Worcester, Mass., 1831; d. San Francisco, Calif., 1916*), flour manufacturer. Son of John Davis (1787–1854). Removed to California, c. 1849. President, University of California, 1888–90.

DAVIS, JEFF (*b. Little River Co., Ark., 1862; d. 1913*), lawyer. Democratic governor of Arkansas,

1901–07; U.S. senator, 1907–13. Excelled in ability to appeal to popular passions and prejudices.

DAVIS, JEFFERSON (*b. Christian, now Todd, Co., Ky., 1808; d. New Orleans, La., 1889*), president of the Confederate States of America. Tenth child of Samuel and Jane (Cook) Davis, originally of Georgia, who removed again to Wilkinson Co., Mississippi, while Jefferson was still very young. His eldest brother, Joseph Emory Davis, prospered in Mississippi and was Jefferson's patron. Sensitive and imaginative, Jefferson Davis studied at St. Thomas's College, Kentucky, at local schools, and at Transylvania University. Nominated to West Point, he graduated in 1828 and performed his early service at Wisconsin and Illinois frontier posts. Stationed at Fort Crawford, Wis., 1833, under Col. Zachary Taylor, Davis fell in love with Taylor's daughter Sarah and married her against her father's wishes, resigning from the army, 1835. Three months after his marriage, his wife died.

From 1835 to 1845, Davis was a planter at "Brierfield" in Mississippi, hard-working and intensely interested in his plantation. Guided by his brother Joseph, who was his neighbor, he became an extensive reader, especially in politics and history. He became devoted to his environment and its social system, and by his marriage to Varina Howell in 1845 associated himself conclusively with the local slave-holding aristocracy. Himself gentle and patriarchal in his relations with his slaves, he resented the Abolitionist attack which emerged at this time, and opposed it with state-rights arguments. A temperamental influence in this decade was his deep-seated love of the army and military life, for which he never lost his zeal. Indeed, in the darkest hours of the Confederacy, Davis believed himself the equal of the greatest generals. Yet his military self-esteem rested on one brief year of service in 1846 and one gallant action in 1847. Elected to Congress as a Democrat in 1845, Davis resigned to command a volunteer regiment in the Mexican War. At the battle of Buena Vista his regiment made a gallant stand which probably turned defeat into victory.

In 1847 Davis withdrew from the army and was chosen U.S. senator from Mississippi. He supported Polk and the policy of seizing Mexican territory, fought proposals to organize the Oregon territory without slavery, and was one of the ten senators who opposed to the last the admission of California. The debate over California aroused secession sentiment in the South. Extreme state-rights men like R. B. Rhett and W. L. Yancey wished their states to secede whether or not other states followed suit. Another faction, the cooperationists, or party of "Southern nationalism," having concluded that it was impossible to effect immediate group secession, wanted to arrest the movement until the whole South could act together. A third party, headed by Sen. Henry S.

Foote, who had opposed his colleague Davis's stand on California, regarded the compromise measures of 1850 as the opening of a satisfactory new chapter in the history of the Union. By September 1851 it was evident that Foote, nominated for governor of Mississippi on a "Union" anti-secession ticket, would carry the election against the secessionist John A. Quitman. Mississippi Democrats, apparently wishing to retreat from an extreme secession position, persuaded Davis to resign from the Senate and replace Quitman as candidate and party leader of the state. Defeated by Foote, Davis returned to his life as a planter.

Becoming secretary of war in the cabinet of Franklin Pierce, 1853, he entered the happiest phase of his career. His policies were governed by a desire to enlarge the territory and develop the economy of the South. He frequently opposed the secretary of state, William L. Marcy, who favored the northern wing of his party. Davis urged a transcontinental railway routed close to the Mexican border and terminating in southern California. The monumental railroad surveys of the West were made under his supervision. To make a southern route possible, he induced Pierce and Marcy to acquire the Gadsden Purchase.

Davis returned to the Senate in 1857. In the internal wrangles of the Democratic party from the Dred Scott decision in 1857 to the Charleston convention in 1860, Davis and Stephen Douglas championed opposing forces. Ostensibly Douglas defended "popular sovereignty" while Davis held that neither Congress nor local law could interfere with slavery in a territory. His reluctance to support immediate secession in 1860, however, suggests that he may have wished to win "dominion status" for the South. Following Lincoln's election Davis was passive until the president declared there should be no more slave states. This decision, denying the possibility of Southern expansion, determined Davis's choice. When Mississippi seceded he withdrew from the Senate.

Davis expected war and hoped to become chief commander of the Southern armies. To his disappointment he was chosen provisional president of the Confederacy, inaugurated at Montgomery, Ala., Feb. 18, 1861. A tired man in very delicate health, Davis was unable to control events. He kept a close hand on the management of the army, yet uncompromising in both animosities and friendships he was not wise in choosing men to trust. His efforts to win support in Europe were failures.

When it became apparent that Davis's loyalty was to the South as a whole, an anti-Davis party formed around the idea of state sovereignty. Davis angered this opposition in a number of ways, notably by proposing and enacting a general conscription law. As economic conditions became increasingly difficult with the fall in value of Confederate money and the tightening of the federal blockade, the opposition grew stronger, and the complaints against the president's so-called egotism and vanity louder. General elections in 1863 returned to Congress a majority hostile to Davis. It had been agreed that the government should not own slaves, but should rent them from their owners and use them as laborers only. One white man from every plantation of fifteen or more slaves was exempted to serve as overseer. This law produced envy in men of small property, who also resented the system of hiring substitutes for army service. Davis's annual message in 1864, urging outright government purchase of 40,000 slaves to be freed when the government was through with them, was looked on as one more step toward a despotism. His proposal was probably designed to see if the South would endorse arming slaves to re-enforce the sadly diminished army. Eventually a bill was passed permitting a levy of 300,000 men "irrespective of color," but omitting any mention of emancipation.

Through the winter of 1864–65, Davis seems to have had no doubt of eventual victory. He re-enforced the army by a general order revoking all exemptions, stripping the plantations of overseers and recalling all furloughed or hospitalized soldiers "except those unable to travel." His efforts to rally the people of the South behind the army only aroused further suspicions that he was planning a *coup d'etat*. He never understood the seriousness of Sherman's march to the sea.

Various attempts at reconciliation were made. In January 1865, Francis P. Blair proposed to Davis a reunion of the states, the abandonment of slavery and an expedition against Maximilian of Mexico in which Davis should play a leading part. Consequent to this, Davis appointed commissioners to confer with Northern authorities on terms of peace, and the South might have won reconciliation on good terms at the Hampton Roads Conference (Feb. 3, 1865) had not Davis refused to accept any terms short of Confederate independence.

On April 3, 1865, Davis left falling Richmond for Danville, Va., where he issued a final proclamation asking for resistance to the last and promising the recovery of Richmond. Following Lee's surrender, he turned southward and at Charlotte, N.C., on April 24 held his last council with his cabinet. On May 10 he was captured by Federal cavalry at Irwinville, Ga., and imprisoned two years in Fortress Monroe. Though put in irons at first, he was later accorded better treatment. He was never brought to trial. His last years were valiant though sad. *The Rise and Fall of the Confederate Government* (1881) is his own account of the great events in which he played a part.

DAVIS, JEFFERSON COLUMBUS (*b. Clark Co., Ind., 1828; d. Chicago, Ill., 1879*), Union soldier. A distinguished and able military man, he failed of

further promotion after killing his commanding officer in a Louisville hotel, 1862.

DAVIS, JEROME DEAN (*b. Groton, N.Y., 1838; d. 1910*), Congregational clergyman. Missionary to Japan, 1871–1910; helped found Kobe College and later the Doshisha University, Kyoto.

DAVIS, JOHN (*b. Plymouth, Mass., 1761; d. Boston, Mass., 1847*), jurist. Graduated Harvard, 1781. Judge, district court of Massachusetts, 1801–41; president, Massachusetts Historical Society, 1818–35.

DAVIS, JOHN (*b. c. 1780; d. c. 1838*), operatic and theatrical manager. Came to New Orleans from San Domingo. Built the Théâtre d'Orléans, 1813, 1819; as manager, made New Orleans the first American city to have an annual opera season.

DAVIS, JOHN (*b. Northboro, Mass., 1787; d. Worcester, Mass., 1854*), lawyer, statesman. Graduated Yale, 1812. Congressman, National Republican, from Massachusetts, 1824–32; governor of Massachusetts, 1833–34, and (as a Whig), 1840–41; U.S. senator, Whig, 1835–40, 1845–53. Nicknamed "Honest John"; conservative protectionist.

DAVIS, JOHN CHANDLER BANCROFT (*b. Worcester, Mass., 1822; d. Washington, D.C., 1907*), lawyer, diplomatist. Son of John Davis (1787–1854); nephew of George Bancroft. As assistant secretary of state, Davis prepared (1871–72) the American case against Great Britain arising from Confederate cruiser action in Civil War.

DAVIS, JOHN LEE (*b. Carlisle, Ind., 1825; d. Washington, D.C., 1889*), naval officer. Son of John W. Davis, he was among the younger ship commanders of note in the Civil War. Retired as rear admiral, 1887.

DAVIS, JOHN WESLEY (*b. New Holland, Pa., 1799; d. Carlisle, Ind., 1859*), physician, politician. Removed to Carlisle, Ind., 1823. Congressman, Democrat, from Indiana; speaker of the House, 1845–47. Governor of Oregon Territory, 1853–54.

DAVIS, JOSEPH ROBERT (*b. Woodville, Miss., 1825; d. 1896*), lawyer, Confederate soldier. Nephew of Jefferson Davis.

DAVIS, KATHARINE BEMENT (*b. Buffalo, N.Y., 1860; d. Pacific Grove, Calif., 1935*), prison reformer. First chairman of New York City Prison Parole Commission, 1915–18. [*Supp. 1*]

DAVIS, MARY EVELYN MOORE (*b. Talladega, Ala., 1852; d. New Orleans, La., 1909*), author.

DAVIS, MATTHEW LIVINGSTON (*b. probably New York, N.Y., 1773; d. Manhattanville, N.Y., 1850*), politician, journalist. Friend, henchman and unwise biographer of Aaron Burr.

DAVIS, NATHAN SMITH (*b. Greene, N.Y., 1817; d. 1904*), physician, "father of the American Medical

Association." Practiced and taught in Chicago, Ill., 1849–1904.

DAVIS, NOAH (*b. Haverhill, N.H., 1818; d. New York, N.Y., 1902*), jurist. N.Y. supreme court justice, 1857–68, 1872–86; tried and sentenced William M. Tweed, 1873.

DAVIS, NOAH KNOWLES (*b. Philadelphia, Pa., 1830; d. Charlottesville, Va., 1910*), teacher, author. An effective teacher, he was associated with various Baptist colleges, 1852–72, and professor of moral philosophy at University of Virginia, 1873–1906.

DAVIS, OSCAR KING (*b. Baldwinsville, N.Y., 1866; d. Bronxville, N.Y., 1932*), journalist, Washington and foreign correspondent. [*Supp.* 1]

DAVIS, PAULINA KELLOGG WRIGHT (*b. Bloomfield, N.Y., 1813; d. Providence, R.I., 1876*), editor, suffragist. Established *Una*, 1853, the first distinctively woman's rights paper published in this country.

DAVIS, PHINEAS (*b. Grafton Co., N.H., 1800; d. Maryland, 1835*), inventor. Built prize-winning locomotive "York" for the Baltimore & Ohio Railroad, 1831. Produced in 1832 with Israel Gardner the first of the "Grasshopper" type engines used on the road.

DAVIS, RAYMOND CAZALLIS (*b. Cushing, Maine, 1836; d. Ann Arbor, Mich., 1919*), mariner, librarian. Librarian, University of Michigan, 1877–1905.

DAVIS, REBECCA BLAINE HARDING (*b. Washington, Pa., 1831; d. Mount Kisco, N.Y., 1910*), novelist. Mother of Richard Harding Davis. Her early stories (e.g. *Margaret Howth*, 1862) were pioneer works in American realism.

DAVIS, REUBEN (*b. near Winchester, Tenn., 1813; d. Huntsville, Ala., 1890*), lawyer. Congressman, Democrat, from Mississippi, 1857–61; member of Confederate Congress, 1861–64. A strong critic of Confederate war policy.

DAVIS, RICHARD HARDING (*b. Philadelphia, Pa., 1864; d. Mount Kisco, N.Y., 1916*), journalist, author. Son of Rebecca Harding Davis. Began career as newspaperman, 1886; won fame as reporter, feature writer, traveling correspondent. Covered revolt in Cuba, Greco-Turk war, Spanish-American, Boer, Russo-Japanese wars, and opening phases of World War I. His infallible news-sense and eye for picturesque detail were joined with a taste for sensation and over-drama. "Popular" appeal in the bad sense marked his skillfully told fiction and dramas. Among his books were: *Gallegher, and Other Stories* (1891); *Van Bibber and Others* (1892); *Soldiers of Fortune* (1897); *Cuba in War Time* (1897).

DAVIS, VARINA ANNE JEFFERSON (*b. Richmond, Va., 1864; d. Narragansett Pier, R.I., 1898*), daughter of Jefferson Davis and Varina Howell Davis, author.

DAVIS, VARINA HOWELL (*b. near Natchez, Miss., 1826; d. New York, N.Y., 1906*), wife of Jefferson Davis.

DAVIS, WILLIAM AUGUSTINE (*b. Barren Co., Ky., 1809; d. St. Joseph, Mo., 1875*), postmaster. Invented railway post-office and railway mail-car, 1862.

DAVIS, WILLIAM MORRIS (*b. Philadelphia, Pa., 1850; d. Pasadena, Calif., 1934*), geographer, geologist. Graduated, 1870, Lawrence Scientific School, Harvard, as mining engineer. After various expeditions at home and abroad, became in 1876 assistant in geology at Harvard, rising to the Sturgis-Hooper professorship of geology in 1898. Evolved the concept of "the cycle of erosion." *Post* 1898, he traveled widely studying landforms and developed his major contribution, the science of geomorphology. Author of the classic *Die erklärende Beschreibung der Landformen* (1912) and *The Coral Reef Problem* (1928); also prepared studies in meteorology and oceanography. Considered himself a geographer and is largely responsible for having made geography a science in America. [*Supp.* 1]

DAVIS, WILLIAM THOMAS (*b. Plymouth, Mass., 1822; d. Plymouth, 1907*), lawyer, author. Authority on history of his native town; edited Plymouth records.

DAVIS, WINNIE. [See DAVIS, VARINA ANNE JEFFERSON, 1864–1898.]

DAVISON, GREGORY CALDWELL (*b. Jefferson City, Mo., 1871; d. Lyme, Conn., 1935*), naval officer. Graduated Annapolis, 1892. Inventor of the balanced turbine torpedo, the first non-recoil gun for airplanes, and the Y-gun depth charge projector. [*Supp.* 1]

DAVISON, HENRY POMEROY (*b. Troy, Pa., 1867; d. 1922*), banker. Devised plan of Bankers' Trust Co.; partner in J. P. Morgan and Co.; distinguished as head of Red Cross War Council, 1917–19.

DAWES, HENRY LAURENS (*b. Cummington, Mass., 1816; d. Pittsfield, Mass., 1903*), lawyer, legislator. Massachusetts congressman, Republican, 1857–75, and U.S. senator, 1875–92. Had great influence in House, becoming chairman Appropriations Committee, 1869, and of Ways and Means, 1871; was a consistent protectionist. At suggestion of Cleveland Abbe, he initiated weather bulletin plan which became U.S. Weather Bureau. As chairman, Senate Indian Affairs committee, he improved condition of Indians and was author of liberating Dawes Act, 1887.

DAWES, RUFUS CUTLER (*b. Marietta, O., 1867; d. Evanston, Ill., 1940*), businessman, public utilities operator. Assistant to brother Charles G. Dawes on "Dawes Plan"; president, Chicago World's Fair, 1933–34. [*Supp.* 2]

DAWES, WILLIAM (*b. Boston, Mass., 1745; d. Boston, 1799*). With Paul Revere, a warner on night of 18th of April, 1775.

DAWKINS, HENRY (*fl. New York and Philadelphia, 1753–1780*), one of the earliest copper-plate engravers in America. Arrested on suspicion of counterfeiting, 1776.

DAWSON, FRANCIS WARRINGTON (*b. London, England, 1840; d. Charleston, S.C., 1889*), journalist. Came to America, 1861, as volunteer in Confederate Navy. Purchased *Charleston News*, 1867, later merged with the *Courier*, and served as editor. A moderate liberal, he urged economic measures for rebuilding the *post-bellum* South.

DAWSON, HENRY BARTON (*b. Lincolnshire, England, 1821; d. Tarrytown, N.Y., 1889*), editor. Came to America, 1834. Author of numerous historical works and editor of the *Historical Magazine*, 1866–76. His "revisionist" tendencies and trenchant style provoked controversy.

DAWSON, JOHN (*b. Virginia, 1762; d. 1814*), statesman. Graduated Harvard, 1782. Member of Virginia House of Delegates. An ardent Jeffersonian, he served in Congress, 1797–1814.

DAWSON, THOMAS CLELAND (*b. Hudson, Wis., 1865; d. 1912*), lawyer, diplomat. The "foremost Latin-American diplomat of the government," he served with distinction in many Latin-American countries, 1897–1911.

DAWSON, WILLIAM CROSBY (*b. Greene Co., Ga., 1798; d. Greensboro, Ga., 1856*), lawyer. As U.S. senator, Whig, from Georgia, 1849–55, he led in adoption of "Georgia Platform" and in support of Clay's 1850 compromise measures.

DAY, BENJAMIN HENRY (*b. West Springfield, Mass., 1810; d. New York, N.Y., 1889*), printer. Came to New York City, 1830, and in 1833 began publication of the New York *Sun*, a penny daily. Its success was immediate; by 1835 it boasted the highest circulation in the world. Day sold the *Sun* to Moses Yale Beach in 1838. Not a great journalist, he proved that newspapers at a popular price could be successful.

DAY, CLARENCE SHEPARD (*b. New York, N.Y., 1874; d. 1935*), author. Grandson of Benj. H. Day. Graduated Yale, 1896. Wrote *This Simian World* (1920); *God and My Father* (1932); *Life with Father* (1935). [*Supp.* 1]

DAY, DAVID ALEXANDER (*b. Adams Co., Pa., 1851; d. at sea, 1897*). Lutheran missionary in Liberia, 1874–97.

DAY, DAVID TALBOT (*b. East Rockport, O., 1859; d. Washington, D.C., 1925*), chemist, geologist. Chief, Mineral Resources Division, U.S. Geological Survey, 1886–1907; inaugurated study of oil-shales.

DAY, FRANK MILES (*b. Philadelphia, Pa., 1861; d. Philadelphia, 1918*), architect. Studied at University of Pennsylvania, and in London. His outstanding work was in collegiate buildings, notably at Princeton, Wellesley and University of Colorado.

DAY, HENRY NOBLE (*b. New Preston, Conn., 1808; d. New Haven, Conn., 1890*), Congregational clergyman, educator.

DAY, HOLMAN FRANCIS (*b. Vassalboro, Maine, 1865; d. Mill Valley, Calif., 1935*), journalist, novelist. [*Supp.* 1]

DAY, HORACE H. (*b. Great Barrington, Mass., 1813; d. Manchester, N.H., 1878*), manufacturer. In 1839, opened a small factory to manufacture rubber fabrics. His interests soon conflicted with those of Charles Goodyear, who had patented (1844) the process of vulcanization. After a series of complicated law suits in which Daniel Webster and Rufus Choate were of counsel, Day was enjoined permanently from further rubber manufacture in 1852.

DAY, JAMES GAMBLE (*b. Jefferson Co., O., 1832; d. Des Moines, Iowa, 1898*), jurist. Judge, supreme court of Iowa, 1870–84. Overruled a popular prohibition amendment to Iowa constitution as unconstitutional, 1882, and was refused re-election.

DAY, JAMES ROSCOE (*b. Whitneyville, Maine, 1845; d. Atlantic City, N.J., 1923*), Methodist clergyman, educator. A colorful and popular preacher, Day was chancellor of Syracuse University, 1904–22.

DAY, JEREMIAH (*b. New Preston, Conn., 1773; d. 1867*), Congregational clergyman, educator. Graduated Yale, 1795. Tutor and professor at Yale; president, 1817–47. Conservative and unselfish, he exerted great influence by force of character.

DAY, LUTHER (*b. Granville, N.Y., 1813; d. Ravenna, O., 1885*), Ohio jurist.

DAY, STEPHEN (*b. England, c. 1594; d. Cambridge, Mass., 1668*), first printer in British America. Locksmith by trade, Day emigrated to New England, 1638, under contract to work two years for Rev. Jesse Glover. Glover, who brought with him a printing press, a font of type and paper, died on the voyage to Boston. His widow settled in Cambridge, where the press was set up. At least 22 imprints, including the *Bay Psalm Book* (1640), were made by the Cambridge Press before 1649, when Samuel Green became the printer. Day's relationship to the press is in doubt. It is presumed that he set it up and managed it for Mrs. Glover.

DAY, WILLIAM RUFUS (*b. Ravenna, Ohio, 1849; d. Mackinac Island, Mich., 1923*), lawyer, jurist. Son of Luther Day. Graduated University of Michigan, 1870; admitted to the bar, 1872. Practicing in Ohio, he became acquainted with William McKinley, who as president appointed Day secretary of state, 1898. Day served with the U.S. commission to make peace with Spain, and in 1903 was appointed associate justice of the U.S. Supreme Court, where he served until 1922. A learned and liberal judge, he was celebrated for the clarity and concision of his opinions.

DAYTON, ELIAS (*b. Elizabeth-Town, N.J., 1737; d. Elizabeth, N.J., 1807*), storekeeper, Revolutionary brigadier-general.

DAYTON, JONATHAN (*b. Elizabeth-Town, N.J., 1760; d. Elizabeth, N.J., 1824*), Revolutionary soldier, lawyer, politician. Son of Elias Dayton. Congressman, Federalist, from New Jersey, 1791–99; U.S. senator, 1799–1805. Indicted, 1807, for complicity in Aaron Burr's schemes, but released on *nolle prosequi*. Dayton, Ohio, is named for him.

DAYTON, WILLIAM LEWIS (*b. Baskingridge, N.J., 1807; d. 1864*), lawyer, politician, diplomat. Great-grandson of Elias Dayton. Graduated Princeton, 1825. U.S. senator, Whig, from New Jersey, 1842–51; Republican nominee for vice-president, 1856. As U.S. minister to France, 1861–64, he successfully opposed Confederate attempts to secure French aid and recognition.

DEADY, MATTHEW PAUL (*b. near Easton, Md., 1824; d. Portland, Oreg., 1893*), jurist. Emigrated to Oregon, 1849; practiced law; presided over constitutional convention of Oregon (1857). U.S. district judge for Oregon, 1859–93.

DEAN, AMOS (*b. Barnard, Vt., 1803; d. Albany, N.Y., 1868*), lawyer, educator.

DEAN, BASHFORD (*b. New York, 1867; d. Battle Creek, Mich., 1928*), zoologist, ichthyologist, armor expert. Curator of arms and armor, Metropolitan Museum of Art, 1906–27.

DEAN, JULIA (*b. Pleasant Valley, N.Y., 1830; d. 1868*), one of America's most beloved actresses, at her peak, 1846–55.

DEAN, SIDNEY (*b. Glastonbury, Conn., 1818; d. Brookline, Mass., 1901*), Methodist clergyman, congressman, journalist.

DEANE, CHARLES (*b. Biddeford, Maine, 1813; d. 1889*), Boston merchant, historian. After retiring from business in 1864, Deane devoted himself to tireless, very able research in American colonial history. Among his works, his discovery and editing of Bradford's *History of Plymouth Plantation* (1856) is considered most important.

DEANE, SAMUEL (*b. Dedham, Mass., 1733; d. Portland, Maine, 1814*), Congregational clergyman, agricultural writer. Author of *The New England*

Farmer or Georgical Dictionary (1790), an encyclopedic work, the first of its kind in this country.

DEANE, SILAS (*b. Groton, Conn., 1737; d. at sea near Deal, England, 1789*), member of the Continental Congress, diplomat. Graduated Yale, 1758. Admitted to the bar, 1761, he began successful practice in Wethersfield, Conn. He married twice; both alliances improved his economic and social situation. Deane was an early leader of the Revolutionary movement in Connecticut. He became a member of the General Assembly, 1772, and in May 1773 was secretary of the newly appointed legislative committee of correspondence. He was a delegate to the first and second Continental Congresses, but, for some reason, the Connecticut Assembly did not reappoint him for 1776.

Unwilling to lose his services, Congress in March 1776 sent him to France as a representative of two separate committees. One, the commercial committee, authorized five merchants (of whom Deane was one) to buy colonial produce with money furnished by Congress; to ship commodities so purchased abroad; to sell them there, and invest the proceeds in supplies needed by the colonies. The other, the "Committee of Secret Correspondence," instructed Deane to buy clothing, arms, munitions and artillery. He was also to discover if an American ambassador would be received in France, and if the French government would form treaties of alliance and commerce with the colonies.

Deane's mission was successful. With the aid of Beaumarchais, he secured eight shiploads of military supplies which were of material help in the Saratoga campaign of 1777. He also commissioned and sent to America many European military officers, some of whom, especially Lafayette, De Kalb, Steuben and Pulaski, were valuable to the American cause. Unfortunately he also sent many soldiers of fortune who proved an embarrassment to Congress and a liability to the country.

In September 1776, Congress appointed a commission of three—Deane, Benjamin Franklin and Arthur Lee—to strengthen its connection with France. In February 1778, the commissioners signed two treaties with the French government, one of commerce, the other providing for an offensive and defensive alliance. Soon thereafter, Congress ordered Deane home. The reason for his recall lay in Arthur Lee's insinuations that Deane was charging Congress for supplies which had been intended as free gifts to the Americans by the French government. Because he did not have proper vouchers to cover his financial transactions, Deane was unable to effect a settlement with Congress. After two years, he returned to Europe, hoping to speed up the auditing of his accounts. Embittered and ill, Deane lost confidence in the American cause. In 1781 he wrote friends in America advising them to abandon the war and seek reconciliation with England. These letters, intercepted and printed by a New York Loyalist press, further blackened Deane's reputation in his homeland. After the war Deane lived as a bankrupt exile in Ghent, and later in England.

Deane's services to America were substantial and his personal losses heavy. In 1842 Congress made partial restitution to his heirs, voting them the sum of $37,000.

DE ANGELIS, THOMAS JEFFERSON (*b. San Francisco, Calif., 1859; d. 1933*), actor, light-opera comedian. The song "Tammany" from *Fantana* was his greatest personal hit and was always associated with him. [*Supp. 1*]

DEARBORN, HENRY (*b. Hampton, N.H., 1751; d. Roxbury, Mass., 1829*) physician, soldier. Served with distinction in the Revolution, eventually joining Washington's staff. Represented the District of Maine in Congress, 1793–97, and served as secretary of war, 1801–09. Given command of the northeast area from the Niagara River to the New England coast in 1812, it was soon apparent that the military ability he had once shown himself to possess had disappeared with age and disuse. His failure to implement his own plans for invasion of Canada directly contributed to Hull's defeat at Detroit. After another American defeat at Queenston, mismanagement of a proposed attack at Kingston, and the near-capture of Sackett's Harbor, Dearborn was removed in July 1813.

DEARBORN, HENRY ALEXANDER SCAMMELL (*b. Exeter, N.H., 1783; d. Portland, Maine, 1851*), lawyer, politician, author. Son of Henry Dearborn. Collector of the port of Boston, 1812–29.

DEARING, JOHN LINCOLN (*b. Webster, Maine, 1858; d. 1916*), Baptist clergyman. Missionary to Japan, 1889–1916.

DEARTH, HENRY GOLDEN (*b. Bristol, R.I., 1864; d. 1918*), landscape and genre painter, distinguished for unusual skill with color.

DEAS, ZACHARIAH CANTEY (*b. ? Charleston, S.C., 1819; d. 1882*), cotton broker, Confederate soldier. Nephew of James Chesnut, Jr.

DEAVER, JOHN BLAIR (*b. Lancaster Co., Pa., 1855; d. Wyncote, Pa., 1931*), surgeon. M.D., University of Pennsylvania, 1878. A tireless and brilliant operator; one of the first to adopt and develop appendectomy and to insist on prompt surgical interference. [*Supp. 1*]

DE BARDELEBEN, HENRY FAIRCHILD (*b. Alabama, 1840; d. 1910*), industrialist. Ward of Daniel Pratt whose daughter, Ellen, he later married, De Bardeleben managed Pratt's Red Mountain Iron & Coal Co. and the development of the Helena mines. When Pratt died, 1873, De Bardeleben inherited his

fortune. He helped organize the Eureka Coal Co. and other coal and iron companies, founded the town of Bessemer and had extensive holdings of mineral lands. In 1891 he sold his properties to the Tennessee Coal, Iron and Railroad Co. Three years later he lost most of his fortune in an attempt to gain control of that company. De Bardeleben's enterprises were the basis for modern Birmingham, Ala., and its industrial district.

DE BARENNE, JOANNES GREGORIUS DUSSER. [See Dusser De Barenne, Joannes Gregorius, 1885–1940.]

DE BERDT, DENNYS (*b. London, England, c. 1694; d. 1770*), merchant, colonial agent in London for Massachusetts and Delaware. Both colonies acknowledged his services in securing repeal of the Stamp Act.

DE BOW, JAMES DUNWOODY BROWNSON (*b. Charleston, S.C., 1820; d. Elizabeth, N.J., 1867*), editor, statistician. Graduated College of Charleston, 1843. Was admitted to the bar but practiced journalism, becoming editor of the *Southern Quarterly Review*. In 1846 he founded at New Orleans the *Commercial Review of the South and Southwest* which in three years gained the largest circulation of any magazine published in the South. It occupied a place in its area like that of *Hunt's Merchants' Magazine* in the country at large. De Bow advocated instruction in economics at the University of Louisiana and occupied its chair of political economy. He was also superintendent of the seventh U.S. census. De Bow retained some measure of nationalism in his thinking but drifted with the secessionist tide and became increasingly a violent Southern partisan. During the Civil War, he was chief Confederate agent for the purchase and sale of cotton.

DE BRAHM, WILLIAM GERARD (*b. probably Holland, 1717; d. Philadelphia, Pa., c. 1799*), surveyor general of the Southern District of North America, 1764–83. Founded Bethany settlement, Georgia, 1751; drew first map of Georgia and South Carolina; with Bernard Romans charted the Florida coast and made inland surveys.

DEBS, EUGENE VICTOR (*b. Terre Haute, Ind., 1855; d. Elmhurst, Ill., 1926*), Socialist advocate. Helped organize a lodge of the Brotherhood of Locomotive Firemen, 1875; by 1880 was a national officer of the Brotherhood and editor of its magazine. An advocate of "industrial" organization, in 1893 he promoted and was president of the American Railway Union, later prominent in strikes against the Great Northern Railroad and the Pullman Co. Debs became a Socialist, 1895; in 1900, 1904, 1908, 1912 and 1920 he was Socialist nominee for president of the United States. He was imprisoned, 1919–21, for publicly denouncing the prosecution of persons charged with sedition. Never an intellectual leader of his party, Debs's character and moral earnestness made him an effective standard-bearer.

DE CAMP, JOSEPH RODEFER (*b. Cincinnati, O., 1858; d. Bocagrande, Fla., 1923*), painter. Student of Frank Duveneck; a sound, capable portrait-painter and an efficient teacher.

DECATUR, STEPHEN (*b. Newport, R.I., 1752; d. near Frankford, Pa., 1808*), privateer, naval officer.

DECATUR, STEPHEN (*b. Sinepuxent, Md., 1779; d. Bladensburg, Md., 1820*), naval officer. Son of Stephen Decatur (1752–1808). Commissioned midshipman, 1798, he advanced rapidly and in 1803 assumed his first command. Active throughout the Tripolitan War, Decatur became famous for heroic actions. His capture and burning of frigate *Philadelphia*, 1804, was called "the most bold and daring act of the age." Returning to America, 1805, he was in 1808 given command of naval forces on the southeastern coast. In that same year he was a member of the court-martial that suspended Capt. James Barron after the *Chesapeake-Leopard* incident. During the War of 1812, commanding the *United States* on an independent cruise, he defeated *H.M.S. Macedonian* off Madeira, Oct. 25, 1812, in a celebrated action but was blockaded with his prize in New London, Conn., soon after his return. Attempting to run the British blockade of New York with the *President* early in 1815, he surrendered after a heavy action with *H.M.S. Endymion* and *Pomone* off Long Island. During the summer of 1815, as commodore commanding a squadron of nine ships, he dictated a treaty with Algiers, ending tribute and requiring full payment for injuries suffered by Americans; he then exacted payment for similar wartime depredations on American commerce from Tunis and Tripoli. Replying to a toast after his return, he spoke the oft-quoted: "Our country . . . may she always be in the right; but our country, right or wrong." Serving thereafter as a Navy Commissioner, Decatur was killed in a duel by Capt. James Barron.

DE COPPET, EDWARD J. (*b. 1855; d. 1916*), New York banker, stock-broker, patron of music. Founded the Flonzaley Quartet, 1904.

DE COSTA, BENJAMIN FRANKLIN (*b. Charlestown, Mass., 1831; d. 1904*), clergyman, historian. Wrote chiefly on early American discovery and exploration.

DEEMER, HORACE EMERSON (*b. Bourbon, Ind., 1858; d. 1917*), jurist. Judge, Iowa supreme court, 1894–1917, the longest continuous tenure in that court.

DEEMS, CHARLES FORCE (*b. Baltimore, Md., 1820; d. New York, N.Y., 1893*), clergyman, teacher. Headed Church of the Strangers, New York City; founded American Institute of Christian Philosophy, 1881.

DEERE, JOHN (*b. Rutland, Vt., 1804; d. 1886*), manufacturer. Left Vermont in 1837 and settled eventually at Grand Detour, Ill., where he opened a blacksmith shop. Contact with farmers revealed that plows brought from the East were unsatisfactory for working prairie soil. Deere after considerable experiment began to develop improved plows which became popular. About 1846 Deere established a new company in Moline, Ill. Convinced that better plows could be produced with a higher grade of steel plate, he imported steel from England to test his theory. After a successful trial he began negotiations in Pittsburgh for steel of equal quality and so brought about the first rolling of plow steel in the United States (*c.* 1847).

DEERFOOT (*b. Cattaraugus Reservation, Erie Co., N.Y., 1828; d. Erie Co., 1897*), professional name of Lewis Bennett, a Seneca Indian. A remarkable distance runner, trained under the old Indian system; ran in England, 1861–63.

DEERING, NATHANIEL (*b. Portland, Maine, 1791; d. near Portland, 1881*), author, editor, dramatist.

DEERING, WILLIAM (*b. South Paris, Maine, 1826; d. Cocoanut Grove, Fla., 1913*), manufacturer. After experience as dry-goods merchant, he entered partnership with Elijah H. Gammon who had purchased rights to manufacture the hand-binding harvester developed by the Marsh brothers. The firm also undertook production of the Gordon wire binder and in 1879, when Deering had become sole owner, began making a twine binder after John F. Appleby's design. Under Deering's tireless management, the business grew steadily. In 1902 it merged with the International Harvester Co.

DE FONTAINE, FELIX GREGORY (*b. Boston, Mass., 1834; d. Columbia, S.C., 1896*), journalist, author. Confederate war correspondent, 1861–65; later worked on N.Y. *Telegram* and *Herald*.

DE FOREST, DAVID CURTIS (*b. Huntington, Conn., 1774; d. 1825*), merchant. Established the first permanent American commercial house in Buenos Aires. Acted as Argentine consul general to the United States, 1818–1822.

DE FOREST, ERASTUS LYMAN (*b. Watertown, Conn., 1834; d. 1888*), mathematician. Graduated Yale, 1854; Sheffield Scientific School, 1856. Known for his studies in the theory of probability and errors, unrecognized by contemporaries but now considered outstanding.

DE FOREST, JOHN KINNE HYDE (*b. Westbrook, Conn., 1844; d. Tokyo, Japan, 1911*), Congregational clergyman, missionary to Japan, 1874–1911.

DE FOREST, JOHN WILLIAM (*b. Humphreysville, Conn., 1826; d. New Haven, Conn., 1906*), author. Published in 1851 a solid *History of the Indians of*

Connecticut, and in the decade thereafter several minor novels and reminiscences of travel. Service in the Civil War, 1861–65, won him rank of major; he continued to serve until 1868 as captain in command of a Freedman's Bureau district at Greenville, S.C. His war experiences gave him material for his best work which is outstanding for its vigorous realism and satiric reading of character. Among his novels are: *Miss Ravenel's Conversion from Secession to Loyalty* (1867); *Kate Beaumont* (1872); *Honest John Vane* (1875); *The Bloody Chasm* (1881).

DE FOREST, ROBERT WEEKS (*b. New York, N.Y., 1848; d. 1931*), lawyer, businessman, philanthropist. Patron of art; champion of conservation; leader in the movement that led to the founding of a national association to fight tuberculosis. [*Supp. 1*]

DE GRAFFENRIED, CHRISTOPHER. [See GRAFFENRIED, CHRISTOPHER, BARON DE, 1661–1743.]

DE HAAS, JACOB. [See HAAS, JACOB JUDAH AARON DE, 1872–1937.]

DE HAAS, JOHN PHILIP (*b. Holland, c. 1735; d. Philadelphia, Pa., 1786*), Revolutionary soldier. Brought to Lancaster Co., Pa., as a child. Served in French and Indian War frontier campaigns. After rising to brigadier-general in Continental service, he resigned in 1777.

DE HAVEN, EDWIN JESSE (*b. Philadelphia, Pa., 1816; d. Philadelphia, 1865*), naval officer. In 1850–51 De Haven commanded an Arctic expedition to search for Sir John Franklin and acquire scientific information. Discovered and named Grinnell Land.

DEINDÖRFER, JOHANNES (*b. near Nürnberg, Bavaria, 1828; d. Waverly, Iowa, 1907*), Lutheran clergyman. Came to America, 1851. After differing with the Missouri Synod, he removed from Michigan to Iowa and helped found the German Lutheran Synod at St. Sebald, 1854.

DEITZLER, GEORGE WASHINGTON (*b. Pine Grove, Pa., 1826; d. Arizona, 1884*), anti-slavery leader in Kansas. Solicited arms for the free-state cause in Boston; fought in Wakarusa War, 1855; served in free-state Kansas territorial legislature, 1857–58, and with distinction in Civil War.

DE KAY, GEORGE COLMAN (*b. in or near New York, N.Y., 1802; d. Washington, D.C., 1849*), mariner. Won engagements at sea while serving the Argentine Republic in its war with Brazil, 1826–1827. Brother of James E. De Kay.

DE KAY, JAMES ELLSWORTH (*b. Lisbon, Portugal, 1792; d. Oyster Bay, N.Y., 1851*), naturalist, physician. An intimate of the Knickerbocker writers in New York. Author of the *Zoology of New York* (1842–44). Brother of George C. De Kay.

DE KOVEN, HENRY LOUIS REGINALD (*b. Middletown, Conn., 1859; d. 1920*), composer. His romantic comic opera *Robin Hood* was first heard in Chicago, Ill., 1890. In the years that followed De Koven wrote many light opera scores and served as music-critic for newspapers in Chicago and New York. His best-known song "O Promise Me" was interpolated in the *Robin Hood* score.

DE KOVEN, JAMES (*b. Middletown, Conn., 1831; d. Racine, Wis., 1879*), Episcopal clergyman. A representative of high-church views and a defender of ritualism, he was active as clergyman and teacher in Wisconsin *post* 1855.

DE LACY, WALTER WASHINGTON (*b. Petersburg, Va., 1819; d. 1892*), soldier, engineer. Employed in constructing the "Mullan Road," 1858, and various Western railroads. De Lacy made the first map of Montana (1864–65) which was for many years the best.

DELAFIELD, EDWARD (*b. New York, N.Y., 1794; d. 1875*), ophthalmologist, surgeon. Son of John Delafield. A founder of New York Eye Infirmary, 1820, and American Ophthalmological Society, 1864; president, College of Physicians and Surgeons, New York, 1858–75.

DELAFIELD, FRANCIS (*b. 1841; d. Noroton, Conn., 1915*), pathologist, physician. Son of Edward Delafield. A graduate of Yale, he received the M.D. degree in 1863 from College of Physicians and Surgeons, New York. He continued medical studies in Europe where he was influenced by Rudolf Virchow. *Post* 1876, he taught at his *alma mater* and in 1886 helped found and served as president of the Association of American Physicians. His textbook, *A Handbook of Post Mortem Examinations and of Morbid Anatomy* (1872), was unusually successful. Delafield made contributions of the first importance to pathology, especially of nephritis and of the diseases of the colon.

DELAFIELD, JOHN (*b. England, 1748; d. Long Island, N.Y., 1824*), merchant. Emigrated to New York City, 1783, and prospered in trade, later engaging in insurance.

DELAFIELD, JOHN (*b. New York, N.Y., 1786; d. Geneva, N.Y., 1853*), banker, farmer. Son of John Delafield (1748–1824). Entered banking in London after experience in merchant shipping, 1803–08. Returning to America, 1820, he throve as a banker and a civic leader. Losses in 1838 led to his retirement to Seneca Co., N.Y., where he established a model farm.

DELAFIELD, RICHARD (*b. New York, N.Y., 1798; d. 1873*), military engineer. Son of John Delafield (1748–1824). Graduated West Point, 1818, and served twice as its superintendent. Commanded the Corps of Engineers, 1864–66, until his retirement as major-general.

DE LAMAR, JOSEPH RAPHAEL (*b. Amsterdam, Holland, 1843; d. New York, N.Y., 1918*), capitalist.

DELAMATER, CORNELIUS HENRY (*b. Rhine-beck, N.Y., 1821; d. 1889*), mechanical engineer. As a young man, Delamater and his cousin Peter Hogg acquired the Phoenix Foundry in New York City. In 1839 Delamater met John Ericsson, after whose designs the foundry built the first iron boats and the first steam fire-engines used here. During the Civil War, Delamater's foundry built, according to Ericsson's plans, the famous iron-clad *Monitor*. During its battle with the *Merrimac*, the *Monitor*'s engines were operated by Delamater's workmen. The firm was noted also for its gunboats, propellers and air compressors and for building (1881) the first successful submarine torpedo-boat designed by John P. Holland.

DE LANCEY, JAMES (*b. New York, N.Y., 1703; d. 1760*), New York colonial political leader. After study in England, he returned to America in 1725 and was admitted to the bar. Appointed to supreme court of New York, 1731, he became chief justice in 1733 by favor of Gov. William Cosby. During the prosecution of John Peter Zenger, De Lancey's decision to disbar James Alexander and William Smith, leaders of the legal profession, made him unpopular. Granted in 1744 a commission as chief justice for good behavior, De Lancey used his new immunity to control both Council and Assembly and block the governor's leadership in the colony. In 1753 he became lieutenant-governor of New York and managed to retain both his high offices until his death. The classic division of New York politics into the "De Lancey Party" of Episcopalians and the Presbyterian "Livingston Party" survived him.

DE LANCEY, JAMES (*b. New York, 1732; d. Bath, England, 1800*), politician. Son of James De Lancey (1703–1760), he was educated in England and acquired sporting tastes. The "Father of the New York Turf," De Lancey was probably the first to import thoroughbreds to New York. Becoming head of the powerful De Lancey family upon his father's death, he displayed gifts for dexterous management equaling his father's, and won several political contests. As a member of New York's last provincial Assembly, he voted against approval of the proceedings of the First Continental Congress. Shortly thereafter he retired to England.

DE LANCEY, JAMES (*b. New York, 1746; d. Nova Scotia, Canada, 1804*), Loyalist. Cousin of James De Lancey (1732–1800). Leader of a troop, known as "De Lancey's Horse," in the irregular partisan warfare about New York, 1777–82.

DE LANCEY, OLIVER (*b. 1718; d. Beverley, England, 1785*), merchant, colonial politician, Loyalist soldier. Brother of James De Lancey (1703–1760).

DE LANCEY, WILLIAM HEATHCOTE (*b. Mamaroneck, N.Y., 1797; d. Geneva, N.Y., 1865*), Episcopal clergyman. Grandson of James De Lancey (1703–1760). Graduated Yale, 1817; ordained, 1822.

Provost of University of Pennsylvania, 1828–33. First bishop of the diocese of western New York, consecrated 1839.

DE LANGLADE, CHARLES MICHEL (*b. Mackinac, Canada, 1729; d. Green Bay, Wis., c. 1801*), soldier. Son of Augustin Mouet de Langlade and an Ottawa Indian woman, he was educated by Jesuits, wrote a good hand and was received as a gentleman. As a cadet in the French colonial troops, he drove the English from Pickawillany, 1752; during the French and Indian War, he led the Indian auxiliaries and was credited with defeating Braddock. He also served on the lakes in 1757 and in the Quebec campaign, 1759. After surrendering the Mackinac post to the English, he became a British subject and served the Crown faithfully during the Revolution.

DELANO, AMASSA (*b. Duxbury, Mass., 1763; d. Boston, Mass., 1823*), ship-captain. Author of *Narrative of Voyages and Travels in the Northern and Southern Hemispheres . . .* (1817).

DELANO, COLUMBUS (*b. Shoreham, Vt., 1809; d. 1896*), lawyer, politician. Raised in Ohio. Congressman from Ohio, Whig, 1845–47; Republican, 1865–69. As secretary of the interior, 1870–75, Delano was criticized for frauds in the Bureau of Indian Affairs.

DELANO, JANE ARMINDA (*d. Townsend, N.Y., 1862; d. France, 1919*), teacher, nurse. As chairman of the National Committee of Red Cross nurses, directed the recruitment of nurses during World War I.

DELANY, MARTIN ROBINSON (*b. Charlestown, W. Va., 1812; d. Xenia, Ohio, 1885*), physician, journalist, Negro leader.

DELANY, PATRICK BERNARD (*b. Killavilla, Ireland, 1845; d. South Orange, N.J., 1924*), electrical engineer. Came to America as a child; raised in Hartford, Conn. His inventions for telegraphic systems include the anti-Page relay, anti-induction cables, a synchronous multiplex telegraph; he also invented devices for submarine detection.

DELAVAN, EDWARD CORNELIUS (*b. Westchester Co., N.Y., 1793; d. Schenectady, N.Y., 1871*), reformer, publisher. Helped organize New York State Temperance Society, 1829.

DE LA WARR, THOMAS WEST, Baron (*b. Hampshire ?, England, 1577; d. 1618*), first governor and captain general of the Virginia colony. Author of *The Relation of . . . the Lord De-la-Warre . . . of the Colonie, planted in Virginea* (London, 1611).

DE LEON, DANIEL (*b. Curaçao, 1852; d. New York, N.Y., 1914*), Socialist advocate. Settled in New York City, c. 1874; taught school and studied law, receiving LL.B. from Columbia, 1878. In 1890 joined Socialist Labor party; in 1891 became its national lecturer and in 1892 editor of its weekly, *The People.*

He was Socialist candidate for governor of New York in 1891 and 1902. Dominant in the party and a complete *doctrinaire*, De Leon criticized the leadership and organization of existing trade-unions and caused a major split in the Socialist movement. In 1905, he helped to found the I.W.W. De Leon's propagandist writings were admired by Lenin.

DE LEON, THOMAS COOPER (*b. Columbia, S.C., 1839; d. Mobile, Ala., 1914*), author, Confederate soldier. Managing editor and, later, editor of the *Mobile Register;* author of Civil War reminiscences, parodies and local-color novels.

DELÉRY, FRANÇOIS CHARLES (*b. St. Charles Parish, La., 1815; d. Bay St. Louis, La., 1880*), physician, writer. Best known for his works on yellow fever; also wrote on educational, philosophical and political subjects.

DELLENBAUGH, FREDERICK SAMUEL (*b. McConnelsville, O., 1853; d. New York, N.Y., 1935*), artist, author, explorer. His *A Canyon Voyage* (1908) is the story of Maj. John Wesley Powell's 1871 Colorado River expedition. [*Supp. 1*]

DEL MAR, ALEXANDER (*b. New York, N.Y., 1836; d. Little Falls, N.J., 1926*), mining engineer, economist. Author of *A History of the Precious Metals from the Earliest Times to the Present* (1880) and other works on money and coinage.

DELMAS, DELPHIN MICHAEL (*b. France, 1844; d. Santa Monica, Calif., 1928*), lawyer. Came to San José, Calif., as a child. An accomplished advocate, he achieved notoriety while defending Harry K. Thaw at his 1907 trial for murder of Stanford White.

DELMONICO, LORENZO (*b. Marengo, Switzerland, 1813; d. 1881*), restaurateur. Came to New York City, 1832; established with two uncles a restaurant which provided food cooked and served in the best European manner of the day. Within twenty years, he set new standards for American dining and made New York famous the world over as a center of good living. Through his example and success, he was largely responsible for the growth of the restaurant as an institution in American cities.

DE LONG, GEORGE WASHINGTON (*b. New York, N.Y., 1844; d. Lena Delta, Siberia, 1881*), Arctic explorer. Graduated U.S. Naval Academy, 1865. Led *Jeannette* expedition, 1879–81. His journal, *The Voyage of the Jeannette*, was published, 1883.

DE MÉZIÈRES Y CLUGNY, ATHANASE (*b. Paris, France, c. 1715; d. San Antonio, Texas, 1779*), soldier, explorer. Came to Louisiana, *c.* 1733; was a soldier at Natchitoches, 1743, and also engaged in planting and trading. On surrender of Louisiana to Spain, he entered Spanish service and for ten years ruled the Red River valley, supervising Indian trade and winning to Spanish allegiance the tribes of Lou-

isiana, Texas, Arkansas and Oklahoma. His diaries and reports in *Athanase de Mézières and the Louisiana-Texas Frontier: 1768–80* (ed. H. E. Bolton, 1914) give us our first definite information about a large part of northern Texas.

DE MILLE, HENRY CHURCHILL (*b. Washington, N.C., 1853; d. Pompton, N.J., 1893*), playwright. Father of William C. and Cecil B. De Mille. Wrote society drama vehicles for skilled actors, often in association with David Belasco.

DEMING, HENRY CHAMPION (*b. Colchester, Conn., 1815; d. Hartford, Conn., 1872*), lawyer, Union soldier, politician. Gifted as an orator.

DEMING, PHILANDER (*b. Carlisle, N.Y., 1829; d. Albany, N.Y., 1915*), lawyer. A pioneer law stenographer and verbatim court reporter, Deming was author of *Adirondack Stories* (1880) and other books.

DEMING, WILLIAM. [See DENNING, WILLIAM, 1736–1830.]

DEMME, CHARLES RUDOLPH (*b. Mühlhausen, Germany, 1795; d. 1863*), Lutheran clergyman. Came to Philadelphia, 1818; served at St. Michael's and Zion's Church there, 1822–59, and *emeritus* to 1863. A famous preacher in German and a notable scholar.

DEMPSTER, JOHN (*b. Florida, N.Y., 1794; d. 1863*), Methodist clergyman. Encouraged establishment (1845) of Wesley Theological Institute (which became the Theological School of Boston University); was a founder of Garrett Biblical Institute, 1854–55.

DEMUTH, CHARLES (*b. Lancaster, Pa., 1883; d. Lancaster, 1935*), artist. Studied at Pennsylvania Academy with Anschutz and W. M. Chase, also in Paris. Illustrator of Henry James's *The Turn of the Screw* and Zola's *Nana;* painter of still life, semiabstract in character. [*Supp. 1*]

DENBY, CHARLES (*b. Mount Joy, Va., 1830; d. Jamestown, N.Y., 1904*), lawyer, Union soldier, diplomat. Graduated Virginia Military Institute, 1850. Removed to Indiana, 1853. Honored by China for services as U.S. minister there, 1885–98.

DENBY, EDWIN (*b. Evansville, Ind., 1870; d. Detroit, Mich., 1929*), lawyer. Son of Charles Denby. As secretary of the navy, 1921–24, was implicated in Teapot Dome scandal. Though not impeached, widespread criticism led to his resignation from office.

DENNIE, JOSEPH (*b. Boston, Mass., 1768; d. Philadelphia, Pa., 1812*), essayist, editor. Graduated Harvard, 1790. Admitted to the bar, 1794, he soon abandoned practice. After failure of a weekly paper he started in Boston, Dennie settled in Walpole, N.H., where he became center of a group of wits and contributed to the *Farmer's Weekly Museum* a series of essays entitled generally "The Lay Preacher"; in 1796 he became editor of the *Museum*. The strong Federalist bias with which he wrote won him appointment as secretary to Secretary of State Pickering and a staff post on Fenno's Federalist *Gazette of the United States.* He made the necessary remove to Philadelphia, 1799, but his bright prospects soon evaporated. As editor of *The Port Folio,* 1801–11, he was constantly in financial difficulties but he made that magazine a distinguished literary journal and should rank with Freneau and Charles Brockden Brown as a pioneer American man of letters.

DENNING, WILLIAM (*b. 1736; d. Cumberland Co., Pa., 1830*), cannon maker for the Revolutionary army; said to have made first successful attempt to employ wrought iron in cannon-founding.

DENNIS, ALFRED LEWIS PINNEO (*b. Beirut, Syria, 1874; d. Worcester, Mass., 1930*), historian. Son of James S. Dennis. Specialist in international relations; author of *Adventures in American Diplomacy, 1896–1906* (1928). [*Supp. 1*]

DENNIS, FREDERIC SHEPARD (*b. Newark, N.J., 1850; d. New York, N.Y., 1934*), surgeon. Brother of James S. Dennis. M.D., Bellevue Hospital Medical School, 1874; studied at Edinburgh. Introduced Listerian technique of surgery in the United States.
[*Supp. 1*]

DENNIS, GRAHAM BARCLAY (*b. London, England, 1855; d. 1923*), capitalist. Came to America as a boy. Settled in Spokane, Wash., 1885, and was a leader in mining and other development in the Northwest area.

DENNIS, JAMES SHEPARD (*b. Newark, N.J., 1842; d. Montclair, N.J., 1914*), Presbyterian clergyman, missionary to Syria. Author of *Christian Missions and Social Progress* (1897, 1899, 1906), an exhaustive study of social effect of Protestant missions on non-Christian peoples.

DENNISON, AARON LUFKIN (*b. Freeport, Maine, 1812; d. England, 1895*), pioneer watch manufacturer. Designed and made the first machine-made, factory-produced watches utilizing a system of interchangeable parts, *c.* 1850 at Roxbury, Mass. His Boston Watch Co., bankrupt in 1857, was continued by others as the American Waltham Watch Co.

DENNISON, WALTER (*b. Saline, Mich., 1869; d. 1917*), educator, scholar. Graduated University of Michigan, 1893; Ph.D., 1897. A distinguished classicist; taught at Oberlin, University of Michigan, Swarthmore.

DENNISON, WILLIAM (*b. Cincinnati, O., 1815; d. Columbus, O., 1882*), lawyer, businessman. Republican governor of Ohio, 1859–61; took prompt, effective action for the Union at start of Civil War.

DENT, FREDERICK TRACY (*b. St. Louis Co., Mo., 1821; d. 1892*), soldier. Graduated West Point, 1843. Brother-in-law of Ulysses S. Grant, whom he served

as aide in Civil War and as military secretary during presidency. He retired as colonel, 1st Artillery, 1883.

DENVER, JAMES WILLIAM (*b. Winchester, Va., 1817; d. Washington, D.C., 1892*), lawyer, soldier. Raised in Ohio; removed to California, 1850. Congressman, Democrat, from California, 1855-57; prominent as chairman of Special Committee on Pacific Railroads. In 1857 he became Commissioner of Indian Affairs and in 1858 governor of the Territory of Kansas. The city of Denver, Colo., was named for him. A brigadier-general of volunteers, 1861–63, he served in Kansas and with the Army of the Tennessee. He stayed politically active in the post-War years. Remarkably energetic and farsighted, his fearlessness in discharging public office was fully appreciated in the West.

DE PAUW, WASHINGTON CHARLES (*b. Salem, Ind., 1822; d. 1887*), manufacturer, banker, philanthropist. Principal benefactor of De Pauw University, named for him in 1884.

DEPEW, CHAUNCEY MITCHELL (*b. Peekskill, N.Y., 1834; d. New York, N.Y., 1928*), lawyer, railway president, wit. Graduated Yale, 1856; admitted to the bar, 1858; began practice in Peekskill. Republican member of New York legislature, 1862–63; New York secretary of state, 1863–65. Appointed first U.S. minister to Japan, 1866, Depew resigned to become attorney and legislative contact man for Commodore Cornelius Vanderbilt's railroads. Rising steadily in the Vanderbilt system, he was president of the New York Central, 1885–98. Elected U.S. senator, Republican, from New York in 1899, he served until 1911. A charming man and an accomplished raconteur, he was widely influential in his day.

DE PEYSTER, ABRAHAM (*b. New Amsterdam, 1657; d. New York, 1728*), colonial merchant. Held almost every office in the city and province of New York between 1685 and 1722.

DE PEYSTER, JOHN WATTS (*b. New York, N.Y., 1821; d. 1907*), author, soldier.

DE QUILLE, DAN. [See Wright, William, 1829–1898.]

DERBIGNY, PIERRE AUGUSTE CHARLES BOURGUIGNON (*b. Laon, France, 1767; d. Gretna, La., 1829*), jurist. Emigrated from France to West Indies, 1793, thence ultimately to Louisiana. Judge of Louisiana's first supreme court, 1813–20; helped revise state Civil Code; as governor, 1828-29, worked to resolve differences between French and English factions.

DERBY, ELIAS HASKET (*b. Salem, Mass., 1739; d. Salem, 1799*), merchant. Son of Richard Derby. Profits of Revolutionary War privateers and many successful trading voyages made him one of New England's wealthiest merchants. Embarking on extensive, pioneering, foreign ventures, he sent ships to Russia and the Orient, 1784–86; he later profited by demand for neutral vessels during Napoleonic wars. Astute in seeking out new commercial fields, he was wise also in his choice of superior masters and supercargoes. Although his business was destroyed by the Embargo, the trade he had begun with the Baltic, China and the East Indies was the foundation of American commerce in those parts of the world.

DERBY, ELIAS HASKET (*b. Salem, Mass., 1766; d. Londonderry, N.H., 1826*), merchant. Son of Elias Hasket Derby (1739–1799). Established Derby firm as dominant American commercial house on Isle of France (Mauritius).

DERBY, ELIAS HASKET (*b. Salem, Mass., 1803; d. Boston, Mass., 1880*), lawyer. Son of Elias H. Derby (1766–1826). Won distinction in railroad cases; served as president, Old Colony Railroad.

DERBY, GEORGE HORATIO (*b. Dedham, Mass., 1823; d. New York, N.Y., 1861*), army officer, humorist. Graduated West Point, 1846; served with Topographical Engineers, and with distinction in the Mexican War. Sent to California, 1849, he remained on the Pacific coast until 1856 and there won general fame as a practical joker and wit. Originally published in local newspapers and magazines, his satires and burlesques were gathered into two collections: *Phoenixiana* (1856) and *The Squibob Papers* (1865). The first of these was immensely popular; the latter contains work which he did after his return to the East. His writings are important as representing one of the earliest developments of so-called "Western" humor and had marked influence on later writers of whom Mark Twain is most noteworthy.

DERBY, RICHARD (*b. Salem, Mass., 1712; d. 1783*), merchant, shipowner, Revolutionary patriot. Father of Elias Hasket Derby (1739–1799). Traded successfully to Spain and the West Indies.

DERCUM, FRANCIS XAVIER (*b. Philadelphia, Pa., 1856; d. Philadelphia, 1931*), physician, teacher, writer. M.D., University of Pennsylvania, 1877. Specialist in neurology; produced (1892) the first original contribution on adiposis dolorosa, or Dercum's disease. [*Supp.* 1]

DERN, GEORGE HENRY (*b. near Scribner, Nebr., 1872; d. Washington, D.C., 1936*), mine operator in Utah. Democratic governor of Utah, 1924–32, notable for tax revision program. U.S. secretary of war, 1933–36. [*Supp.* 2]

DE ROSSET, MOSES JOHN (*b. Wilmington, N.C., 1838; d. New York, N.Y., 1881*), physician, Confederate Army surgeon. Specialist in diseases of the eye and ear.

DE SAUSSURE, HENRY WILLIAM (*b. Pocotaligo, S.C., 1763; d. Charleston, S.C., 1839*), lawyer. Studied law in Philadelphia with Jared Ingersoll. Returning to South Carolina, he served in the General Assembly at various times between 1790 and 1808, favoring a program of gradual concessions to the poorly represented up-country settlers. During his term as director of the U.S. Mint (1795), he brought about our first coinage of gold. He performed notable service in organizing the South Carolina system of equity as chancellor *post* 1808.

DE SCHWEINITZ, EDMUND ALEXANDER. [See SCHWEINITZ, EDMUND ALEXANDER DE, 1825–1887.]

DE SCHWEINITZ, GEORGE EDMUND. [See SCHWEINITZ, GEORGE EDMUND DE, 1858–1938.]

DESHA, JOSEPH (*b. Monroe Co., Pa., 1768; d. Georgetown, Ky., 1842*), soldier, politician. Raised in frontier Kentucky and Tennessee; settled in Mason Co., Ky., 1792; served in Indian campaigns under Wayne, 1794–95. Congressman, Democratic-Republican from Kentucky, 1807–19; an extreme "War Hawk." Governor of Kentucky, 1824–28.

DE SMET, PIERRE-JEAN (*b. Termonde, Belgium, 1801; d. St. Louis, Mo., 1873*), Jesuit missionary. Came to America, 1821, entering Jesuit novitiate at Whitemarsh, near Baltimore, Md.; made further studies and was ordained in 1827 at Florissant, Mo. Began work as missionary to Potawatomies near present Council Bluffs, Iowa. Between 1840 and 1846, he worked in Oregon country, the Rockies, and generally in the Pacific Northwest, setting up mission stations and affecting almost every tribe in the Columbia valley and its neighborhood; during the same period he traveled to the east and to Europe on behalf of the missions. By 1850, he was known and respected by the plains tribes as well and served many times thereafter as a peacemaker in their conflicts with one another and with the whites. His most famous exploit in diplomacy came in 1868 when he was successful in effecting a truce with Sitting Bull's hostile band in the Bighorn valley.

DE SOTO, HERNANDO (*b. Barcarrota, Spain, c. 1500; d. 1542*), explorer, soldier, discoverer of the Mississippi River. Accompanied Pedrarias Dávila to Central America, 1519. Participated in conquest of Peru; after sack of Cuzco, returned to Spain with a fortune. In 1537, Charles V commissioned him to conquer Florida; he was also made governor of Cuba. After landing in Florida, May 1539, he marched north, entering successively Georgia, the Carolinas, Tennessee, Alabama, Mississippi, Arkansas, Oklahoma and Texas; detachments of his party may have entered Missouri and Louisiana. With brief interludes, the march was made in constant warfare with the native peoples. He made the first conscious discovery of the Mississippi River in April 1541. A year later, endeavoring to cross the Mississippi on his way homeward, De Soto died after naming Luis de Moscoso his successor. His body was consigned to the river.

DETMOLD, CHRISTIAN EDWARD (*b. Hanover, Germany, 1810; d. New York, N.Y., 1887*), civil engineer. Came to America, 1826. Active in railway surveys; supervising engineer and architect, New York Crystal Palace, 1852–53.

DE TROBRIAND, RÉGIS DENIS DE KEREDERN (*b. near Tours, France, 1816; d. Bayport, N.Y., 1897*), soldier. Came to America, 1841. A volunteer in Union Army, 1861–65, he rose to major-general and continued in regular army, 1866–79. Author of *Four Years with the Army of the Potomac* (published in French, 1867–68).

DEUTSCH, GOTTHARD (*b. Kanitz, Austria, 1859; d. 1921*), educator, Jewish scholar. Pupil of Graetz, Weiss and Jellinek; Ph.D., Vienna, 1881. Professor of history and philosophy of religion, Hebrew Union College, Cincinnati, O., 1891–1921.

DE VARGAS ZAPATA Y LUJAN PONCE DE LEON, DIEGO (*b. Madrid, Spain, c. 1650; d. New Mexico, 1704*), soldier, administrator. Spanish governor of New Mexico, 1688–97; 1703–04; reconquered the province for Spain, 1692–93.

DEVENS, CHARLES (*b. Charlestown, Mass., 1820; d. Boston, Mass., 1891*), Union soldier, jurist. Graduated Harvard, 1838; admitted to bar, 1840; served in Massachusetts legislature and as U.S. marshal. Won brevet as major-general in Civil War. Justice, state superior court, 1867–73; state supreme court, 1873–77. After service as U.S. attorney-general, 1877–81, he resumed his place on the state supreme court bench and served until his death.

DE VERE, MAXIMILIAN SCHELE. [See SCHELE DE VERE, MAXIMILIAN, 1820–1898.]

DEVEREUX, JOHN HENRY (*b. Marblehead, Mass., 1832; d. Cleveland, O., 1886*), civil engineer. Manager and president of several Midwestern railroads, including Lake Shore and Michigan Southern and the "Big Four."

DEVIN, THOMAS CASIMER (*b. New York, N.Y., 1822; d. New York, 1878*), Union soldier. Brigade and division commander of cavalry, Civil War; on frontier service, 8th and 3rd Cavalry, 1866–78.

DE VINNE, THEODORE LOW (*b. Stamford, Conn., 1828; d. 1914*), printer, historian of printing. Author of *The Invention of Printing* (1876), *Historic Printing Types* (1886), and other works.

DEVOY, JOHN (*b. Kill, Ireland, 1842; d. Atlantic City, N.J., 1928*), journalist, Fenian leader. After involvement in Irish revolutionary movement, 1861–66, and five years' imprisonment, Devoy came to America in 1871 and worked for the *New York Herald* and other papers. Founder and editor of the *Irish Nation*, 1881–85; of the *Gaelic American*, 1903–28; exponent of physical force in Irish revolt. Author of *Recollections of an Irish Rebel* (1929).

DE VRIES, DAVID PIETERSEN (*b. La Rochelle, France, c. 1592; place and date of death uncertain*), merchant skipper, colonizer of New Netherland. About 1630, entered into partnership with directors of the West India Co. to plant a colony on the Delaware. Thereafter De Vries made three voyages to America (1632–33, 1634–36, 1638–44). He established a small settlement on Staten Island and a colony near Tappan, which he called Vriessendael. Both were destroyed in the Indian war of 1643. His account of his voyages, *Korte Historiael etc.* (1655), is a valuable source for the history of New Netherland.

DEW, THOMAS RODERICK (*b. King and Queen Co., Va., 1802; d. Paris, France, 1846*), economist. Graduated William and Mary, 1820; traveled in Europe. Appointed professor of political law at William and Mary, 1827. His *Lectures on the Restrictive System* (1829) upheld the free-trade argument and foretold that disunion would follow if protection were pressed by the industrial North. His *Review of the Debate . . .* (1832), better known after its incorporation in the volume of essays entitled *The Pro-Slavery Argument* (1852), was widely influential; De Bow said that this pro-slavery essay won for Dew "the lasting gratitude of the whole South." Dew became president of William and Mary in 1836 and substantially increased its enrollment and prosperity.

DEWEES, WILLIAM POTTS (*b. near Pottstown, Pa., 1768; d. Philadelphia, Pa., 1841*), obstetrician. Author of *A Compendious System of Midwifery* (1852), America's first authoritative work on the subject.

DEWEY, CHESTER (*b. Sheffield, Mass., 1784; d. Rochester, N.Y., 1867*), Congregational clergyman, scientist. Graduated Williams, 1806. A born teacher and versatile scientific investigator; first professor of chemistry and natural sciences at the University of Rochester, 1850–61.

DEWEY, GEORGE (*b. Montpelier, Vt., 1837; d. Washington, D.C., 1917*), naval officer. Graduated Annapolis, 1858; served under Farragut during the Civil War. Promoted captain, 1884, he became chief of the Bureau of Equipment, 1889, and president of the Board of Inspection and Survey, 1895. In these posts he became acquainted with the modern battleships, cruisers and torpedo-boats of the "New Navy." Taking command of the Asiatic Squadron early in 1898, he made most careful preparations for any event, and upon receiving news of war with Spain, executed the capture of Manila. His victory made the United States a principal power in the East and demonstrated the quality of the new types of ships. Given rank as Admiral of the Navy, he returned home to great ovations in New York and elsewhere; he served as president of the Navy General Board *post* 1900.

DEWEY, MELVIL (*b. Adams Center, N.Y., 1851; d. Florida, 1931*), librarian. Graduated Amherst, 1874. After experience as assistant in Amherst library, published *A Classification and Subject Index for Cataloguing and Arranging . . . a Library* (1876). This decimal system of classification, although not original in its essential features, came into wide use because of its workability and because of the missionary zeal of its author's pupils. Secretary of the American Library Association, 1876–90, editor of the *Library Journal*, 1876–80, and organizer of the Library Bureau, Dewey started the first library school in the United States in 1887 while librarian of Columbia College, New York City (1883–88). Removing the school to Albany, N.Y., 1889, he served as director, New York State Library, December 1888–1905. Abounding in energy and self-confidence, he was tactless and indiscreet. [*Supp.* 1]

DEWEY, ORVILLE (*b. Sheffield, Mass., 1794; d. Sheffield, 1882*), clergyman, author. Graduated Williams, 1814. Fourth president of the American Unitarian Association, 1845–47. Interested in social questions, he opposed both slavery and abolitionism.

DEWEY, RICHARD SMITH (*b. Forestville, N.Y., 1845; d. La Cañada, Calif., 1933*), psychiatrist. M.D., University of Michigan, 1869. Served as surgeon in German army during Franco-Prussian War. Assistant physician, Elgin (Ill.) State Hospital, 1872–79; superintendent at Kankakee, 1879–93, where he introduced the "cottage plan," an innovation which replaced the massive, traditional, mental hospital building with comparatively small detached cottages. From 1895 to 1920 he directed the Milwaukee Sanitarium, a private institution at Wauwatosa, Wis. [*Supp.* 1]

DEWING, FRANCIS (*fl. Boston, Mass., 1716–1722*), the first important engraver on copper in America. Engraved Capt. John Bonner's "The Town of Boston," 1722.

DEWING, MARIA RICHARDS OAKEY (*b. New York, N.Y., 1845; d. New York, 1927*), painter. Best known for flower painting, in which she was rivaled only by La Farge in America and Fantin-Latour in France. Married Thomas W. Dewing, 1881.

DEWING, THOMAS WILMER (*b. Boston, Mass., 1851; d. New York, N.Y., 1938*), figure and portrait painter. Trained as a lithographer; studied in Paris under Lefebvre. His lyrical, idealistic work is best represented in the Freer and Gellatly Collections, Washington, D.C. [*Supp.* 2]

DeWITT, SIMEON (*b. Wawarsing, N.Y., 1756; d. Ithaca, N.Y., 1834*), surveyor-general of New York, 1784–1834; surveyor and military mapmaker in Revolutionary War.

DE WOLF, JAMES (*b. Bristol Co., R.I., 1764; d. New York, N.Y., 1837*), slave-trader, manufacturer. U.S. senator from Rhode Island, 1821–25. Ardent advocate of high tariffs.

DEXTER, FRANKLIN (*b. Charlestown, Mass., 1793; d. Beverly, Mass., 1857*), lawyer. Son of Samuel Dexter (1761–1816).

DEXTER, FRANKLIN BOWDITCH (*b. Fairhaven, Mass., 1842; d. New Haven, Conn., 1920*), antiquarian, historian. Graduated Yale, 1861. His many publications dealt with the history of Yale, its graduates, and the colony and city of New Haven.

DEXTER, HENRY (*b. Nelson, N.Y., 1806; d. Boston, Mass., 1876*), sculptor. A blacksmith by trade, self-taught as a sculptor, Dexter made portrait-busts of Longfellow, Agassiz, Charles Dickens and many other contemporaries. They were distinguished chiefly for verisimilitude.

DEXTER, HENRY (*b. West Cambridge, Mass., 1813; d. New York, N.Y., 1910*), businessman. Consolidated newspaper dealers into the American News Co., of which he was president for many years.

DEXTER, HENRY MARTYN (*b. Plympton, Mass., 1821; d. New Bedford, Mass., 1890*), Congregational clergyman. Editor, *The Congregationalist*, 1851–90.

DEXTER, SAMUEL (*b. Dedham, Mass., 1726; d. Mendon, Mass., 1810*), merchant, Revolutionary patriot.

DEXTER, SAMUEL (*b. Boston, Mass., 1761; d. Athens, N.Y., 1816*), lawyer. Son of Samuel Dexter (1726–1810). Graduated Harvard, 1781. A Federalist congressman from Massachusetts, 1793–95, and U.S. senator, 1799–1800, he served as secretary of war in 1800 and secretary of the treasury from January 1801 to January 1802. He later attained high eminence at the Massachusetts bar.

DEXTER, TIMOTHY (*b. Malden, Mass., 1747; d. Newburyport, Mass., 1806*), merchant, speculator, eccentric. Author of *A Pickle for the Knowing Ones* (1802).

DEXTER, WIRT (*b. Dexter, Mich., 1832; d. Chicago, Ill., 1890*), lawyer. Grandson of Samuel Dexter (1761–1816). A recognized leader of the Chicago bar.

DE YOUNG, MICHEL HARRY (*b. St. Louis, Mo., 1849; d. 1925*), editor, publisher. Removed to California as a child. With his brother Charles, founded and edited the *Daily Dramatic Chronicle*, 1865, later titled the *San Francisco Chronicle*.

DIAZ, ABBY MORTON (*b. Plymouth, Mass., 1821; d. 1904*). Author of *The William Henry Letters* (1870) and other stories for children.

DIBBLE, ROY FLOYD (*b. Portland, N.Y., 1887; d. New York, N.Y., 1929*), teacher. Author of *Strenuous Americans* (1923) and other works.

DIBRELL, GEORGE GIBBS (*b. Sparta, Tenn., 1822; d. Sparta, 1888*), merchant, planter, industrialist. Organized and led 8th Tennessee Cavalry (Confederate); saw much service under Gen. N. B. Forrest, and succeeded to command of his "Old Brigade" in 1863.

DICK, ELISHA CULLEN (*b. near Marcus Hook, Pa., 1762; d. Alexandria, Va., 1825*), physician. Studied with Benjamin Rush and William Shippen, and at University of Pennsylvania. Called in consultation by Dr. James Craik at George Washington's last illness.

DICK, ROBERT PAINE (*b. Greensboro, N.C., 1823; d. 1898*), jurist. Helped organize Republican party in North Carolina, *post* 1866. Justice, North Carolina supreme court, 1868–72; thereafter federal district judge.

DICKERSON, EDWARD NICOLL (*b. Paterson, N.J., 1824; d. near Far Rockaway, N.Y., 1889*), lawyer. Son of Philemon Dickerson. Studied at Princeton, where he met Joseph Henry and was influenced by Henry to study science and mechanics. Admitted to the bar, 1845, his scientific knowledge was basis for his rise to recognition as leading patent lawyer in the United States. Among the important cases in which he acted were *Colt* vs. *Massachusetts Arms Co.* (establishing validity of Samuel Colt's firearms patent) and *Goodyear* vs. *Day* (involving validity of Charles Goodyear's patent for rubber vulcanization). He was later concerned with suits involving electrical patents of Thomas A. Edison, rights of the Western Union Co., and of the American Bell Telephone Co.

DICKERSON, MAHLON (*b. Hanover Neck, N.J., 1770; d. Succasunna, N.J., 1853*), lawyer, manufacturer, statesman. Graduated College of New Jersey (Princeton), 1789; licensed as attorney, 1793. Left legal profession to manage family iron works at Succasunna, 1810. An ultra-protectionist for the remainder of his career, he held numerous public offices; among these were governor of New Jersey, 1815–17; U.S. senator, Democrat, from New Jersey, 1817–33; secretary of the navy, 1834–38.

DICKERSON, PHILEMON (*b. Succasunna, N.J., 1788; d. Paterson, N.J., 1862*), jurist. Brother of Mahlon Dickerson. Graduated University of Pennsylvania, 1808; licensed as attorney, 1813. Congressman, Democrat, from New Jersey, 1833–36, 1839–41; governor of New Jersey, 1836–37; U.S. district judge, 1842–62.

DICKEY, THEOPHILUS LYLE (*b. Paris, Ky., 1811; d. Atlantic City, N.J., 1885*), Illinois jurist, Union soldier.

DICKIE, GEORGE WILLIAM (*b. Arbroath, Scotland, 1844; d. 1918*), engineer, ship-builder. Came to San Francisco, Calif., 1869; as manager of Union Iron Works, 1883–1905, he was responsible for constructing some eleven vessels of the "new" steel navy, including the *Oregon* and *Olympia*.

DICKINS, JOHN (*b. London, England, 1747; d. Philadelphia, Pa., 1798*), Methodist clergyman. Intimate friend and counselor of Francis Asbury. Ordained deacon, 1784; made elder, 1786. His most important contribution to Methodism was in education. He helped in founding of Cokesbury College and, from 1789 to his death, managed the Methodist Book Concern, establishing it as a permanent institution.

DICKINSON, ANNA ELIZABETH (*b. Philadelphia, Pa., 1842; d. Goshen, N.Y., 1932*), orator, actress, playwright. An eccentric egoist, acclaimed as a heroine by the Abolitionists, she made wildly emotional platform pleas for harsh treatment of the South. [*Supp. 1*]

DICKINSON, ANSON (*b. Milton, Conn., 1779; d. Milton, 1852*), portrait painter in miniature and oils. Influenced by Edward Malbone. Chiefly distinguished as a colorist.

DICKINSON, CHARLES MONROE (*b. near Lowville, N.Y., 1842; d. Binghamton, N.Y., 1924*), lawyer, newspaperman, diplomat. In consular service, 1897–1908, in Bulgaria, Turkey and Middle East.

DICKINSON, DANIEL STEVENS (*b. Goshen, Conn., 1800; d. New York, N.Y., 1866*), lawyer, politician. A leading conservative Democrat, he was U.S. senator from New York, 1844–51.

DICKINSON, DONALD McDONALD (*b Port Ontario, N.Y., 1846; d. Trenton, Mich., 1917*), lawyer. Raised in Michigan. Graduated University of Michigan Law School and admitted to the bar, 1867. Became a leading lawyer in the Middle West; presented the Homestead Cases (155 *U.S.* 356 ff) before the U.S. Supreme Court. A liberal and active Democrat, he led his party in Michigan *post* 1884.

DICKINSON, EMILY ELIZABETH (*b. Amherst, Mass., 1830; d. Amherst, 1886*), poet. Her father, Edward Dickinson, was dominant and austere; neither Emily nor her sister, Lavinia, married. Educated at Amherst Academy and Mount Holyoke Female Seminary, Emily was early noted for her wit and love of drollery; until her middle twenties she participated freely in village amusements. Thereafter she became increasingly impatient of formal social occasions.

Details of an abortive love affair *c.* 1854 are unclear. For the rest of her life she lived quietly in Amherst, drifting into a habit of seclusion and finding her satisfactions in nature and "the little toil of love" of household routine. Her preoccupation with poetry by her own statement began in 1861–62 and contributed to the desire for "polar privacy," which was deepened by her father's death and mother's invalidism (1874).

Though her outer life seems uneventful, Emily Dickinson's poems reveal an intense inner life and a lively mind capable of deep understanding, metaphysical speculation and imaginative sympathy. Only two of her poems were printed during her lifetime. One was sent to the *Springfield Republican* (Feb. 14, 1866) by her sister-in-law. Emily's friend Helen Hunt Jackson was responsible for the inclusion of the other, without signature, in G. P. Lathrop's *A Masque of Poets* (1878). By a fortunate decision of her sister Lavinia, Emily Dickinson's poems were preserved and published after her death in three series: *Poems* (1890), *Poems* (1891), *Poems* (1896). *The Single Hound* (1914) contains messages in swift, spontaneous verse that Emily Dickinson was in the habit of sending across the lawn to her sister-in-law; *Further Poems* (1929) includes a series of love poems reflecting her frustrated attachment. Since that time, several additional collections have been published in which "corrections" by the original editors of her work have been noted critically and a truer text established.

DICKINSON, JACOB McGAVOCK (*b. Columbus, Miss., 1851; d. 1928*), lawyer. Practiced in Nashville, Tenn., 1874–99; thereafter in Chicago, Ill. Counsel to several railroads; secretary of war, 1909–11.

DICKINSON, JOHN (*b. Talbot Co., Md., 1732; d. Wilmington, Del., 1808*), statesman. Educated at home and in London at the Middle Temple. Returned to Philadelphia, 1757, and entered practice. Elected to the Assembly of the Lower Counties (Delaware), 1760, and became speaker. Chosen representative from Philadelphia to Pennsylvania legislature, 1762, Dickinson led conservative opposition to Franklin and, in the debate of 1764, opposed a change in the proprietary system.

In 1765 he published *The Late Regulations Respecting the British Colonies*, a pamphlet designed to show the injury that would be done to British mercantile interests by enforcement of the Sugar and Stamp acts. Appointed a Pennsylvania delegate to the Stamp Act Congress in 1765, he opposed all violent resistance to the obnoxious law.

In 1767 he began publishing anonymously in the *Pennsylvania Chronicle* the series of essays later known in pamphlet form as *Letters from a Farmer in Pennsylvania to the Inhabitants of the British Colonies* (1768), in which he suggested force as an ultimate remedy, but held that conciliation was possible. In April 1768, at a meeting in Philadelphia, Dickinson urged adoption of the Non-Importation and Non-Exportation agreement. Re-elected a member of the legislature, he drafted their 1771 "Petition to the King" which was unanimously adopted. He still opposed resort to force, however, and in 1774, sanctioned only expressions of sympathy to

Boston because she had destroyed hope of conciliation. Nonetheless Dickinson became chairman of the Philadelphia Committee of Correspondence and at the conference of July 1774, wrote three papers representative of conservative sentiment before the Declaration of Independence which were unanimously adopted. They included a series of resolutions stating the principles upon which the colonies based their claim to redress; instructions to Congressional delegates to be chosen by the Assembly; and a treatise on Great Britain's constitutional power to tax the colonies.

A member of the Continental Congress in 1774, Dickinson drafted the congressional "Petition to the King" and the "Address to the people of Canada." He was chairman of a Committee of Safety and Defense, 1775–76. At the second Continental Congress, 1775, Dickinson, still seeking a peaceful settlement, wrote the second "Petition to the King," which angered New England members. He also drafted much, if not all, of the "Declaration of the Causes of taking up Arms." In the Assembly, 1775, he drafted resolutions instructing delegates to the Congress of 1776 to seek means of redressing grievances but to avoid measures anticipating separation.

Many Americans felt that separation was the only solution in early 1776, but Dickinson clung to conciliation and voted against the Declaration of Independence as a matter of principle. He was, however, one of the two congressmen who actually volunteered for armed service. In 1781, he was chosen president of the Supreme Executive Council of Delaware and, thereafter, elected to the same office in Pennsylvania. He was a delegate from Delaware to the Federal Constitutional Convention, 1787, and took an active part in its proceedings.

DICKINSON, JOHN WOODBRIDGE (*b. Chester, Mass., 1825; d. 1901*), educator. Secretary of the Board of Education of Massachusetts, 1877–93.

DICKINSON, JONATHAN (*b. Hatfield, Mass., 1688; d. 1747*), Presbyterian clergyman, first president of the College of New Jersey (Princeton), 1747. Graduated Yale, 1706. Ordained pastor at Elizabeth Town, N.J., 1709, and served there until death.

DICKINSON, PHILEMON (*b. Talbot Co., Md. ?, 1739; d. 1809*), lawyer, Revolutionary soldier. Brother of John Dickinson. Major-general and commander-in-chief of New Jersey militia. U.S. senator from New Jersey, 1790–93.

DICKINSON, PRESTON (*b. New York, N.Y., 1889; d. Irun, Spain, 1930*), painter. Influenced by Cézanne and the art of China. [*Supp. 1*]

DICKMAN, JOSEPH THEODORE (*b. Dayton, O., 1857; d. Washington, D.C., 1927*), soldier. Graduated West Point, 1881. An original member of Army General Staff, 1903–06. Among the ablest American generals in France in the first World War.

DICKSON, DAVID (b. Hancock Co., Ga., 1809; d. Hancock Co., 1885), farmer, agricultural writer. An extraordinarily successful farmer, Dickson introduced original agricultural methods in the South, including (1846) the use of Peruvian guano as fertilizer.

DICKSON, ROBERT (b. Dumfries, Scotland, c. 1765; d. Drummond Island, Mich., 1823), fur-trader. Aided British in capture of Michilimackinac and Detroit, War of 1812.

DICKSON, SAMUEL HENRY (b. Charleston, S.C., 1798; d. Philadelphia, Pa., 1872), physician. Founded Medical College of South Carolina, 1833; professor at New York University, 1847–50, and at Jefferson Medical College, 1858–72.

DICKSON, THOMAS (b. Leeds, England, 1824; d. 1884), foundryman, machinist, capitalist. Came to America as a child. President of Delaware and Hudson Canal Co., post 1869; developer of coal and other industries at Scranton, Pa.

DIDIER, EUGENE LEMOINE (b. Baltimore, Md., 1838; d. Baltimore, 1913). Author of The Life and Poems of Edgar Allan Poe (1877), Poe Cult (1909) and other works.

DIELMAN, FREDERICK (b. Hanover, Germany, 1847; d. Ridgefield, Conn., 1935), painter, illustrator, etcher. Among his best-known works are two overmantels in mosaic, "Law" and "History" in the Library of Congress. [Supp. 1]

DIETRICHSON, JOHANNES WILHELM CHRISTIAN (b. Fredrikstad, Norway, 1815; d. Norway, 1883), Lutheran clergyman. Came to America, 1844. Organized Norwegian Lutheran congregations in Wisconsin, giving them constitutions which became the basis of future development. Author of a volume of travels in the United States (1846). Returned to Norway, 1850.

DIKE, SAMUEL WARREN (b. Thompson, Conn., 1839; d. Auburndale, Mass., 1913), Congregational clergyman, sociologist. Early a student of American family conditions, Dike founded and conducted the National Divorce Reform League, 1881–1913.

DILL, JAMES BROOKS (b. Spencerport, N.Y., 1854; d. 1910), corporation lawyer, jurist. Graduated Yale, 1876; New York University Law School, 1878. Drafted the 1889 New Jersey statute which legalized the holding company and allowed incorporation for almost any purpose. The consequent rush of business to New Jersey inspired Dill to organize the Corporation Trust Co. there—a corporation to organize other corporations. His publications on corporation law were invaluable guides for the business world since Dill had largely created the law he expounded.

DILLARD, JAMES HARDY (b. Nansemond Co., Va., 1856; d. Charlottesville, Va., 1940), educator.

First president and director, 1907–31, Negro Rural School Fund (Jeanes Fund); worked to advance race relations. [Supp. 2]

DILLER, JOSEPH SILAS (b. near Plainfield, Pa., 1850; d. 1928), geologist. With U.S. Geological Survey, 1883–1923. Specialist in vulcanology. [Supp. 1]

DILLINGER, JOHN (b. Indianapolis, Ind., 1902; d. Chicago, Ill., 1934), bandit. "Public Enemy Number One"; killed by federal officers. [Supp. 1]

DILLINGHAM, CHARLES BANCROFT (b. Hartford, Conn., 1868; d. 1934), theatrical producer of 200 plays; famous for his lavish, tuneful and clean musical comedies and revues. [Supp. 1]

DILLINGHAM, WILLIAM PAUL (b. Waterbury, Vt., 1843; d. Montpelier, Vt., 1923), lawyer, politician. Republican governor of Vermont, 1888–90; U.S. senator, 1900–23. Advocated quota principle of immigration restriction and incorporated his views in the "Dillingham Bill," 1921.

DILLON, JOHN FORREST (b. Montgomery Co., N.Y., 1831; d. 1914), jurist. Removed to Iowa as a child. Studied medicine and law; admitted to bar, 1852. Iowa supreme court justice, 1862–68; federal circuit judge, 1869–79. Professor of law, Columbia, 1879–82; he engaged thereafter in corporation practice. His reputation rests upon contributions to legal scholarship, especially his monumental Municipal Corporations (1872), which created that subject as a separate field of law.

DILLON, SIDNEY (b. Northampton, N.Y., 1812; d. New York, N.Y., 1892), railroad-builder, financier. Having worked as foreman on several railroad projects, Dillon contracted to build a section of what is now the Boston & Albany Railroad, completing it in 1840. Thereafter, he built thousands of miles of railroad in America and was principal contractor for the Union Pacific Railroad, 1865–69. He served as director of that road, and as its president, 1874–84, 1890–92.

DIMAN, JEREMIAH LEWIS (b. Bristol, R.I., 1831; d. 1881), Congregational clergyman, educator. Graduated Brown, 1851; Andover Theological Seminary, 1856. Gave up brilliant career in ministry to become professor of history and political economy at Brown University, 1864–81.

DIMITRY, ALEXANDER (b. New Orleans, La., 1805; d. New Orleans, 1883), educator, public official. First state superintendent of education in Louisiana, 1847–50.

DIMITRY, CHARLES PATTON (b. Washington, D.C., 1837; d. New Orleans, La., 1910), journalist, author. Son of Alexander Dimitry.

DINGLEY, NELSON (b. Durham, Maine, 1832; d. 1899), publisher. Graduated Dartmouth, 1855. Editor-publisher, Lewiston Evening Journal. Republican governor of Maine, 1874–76; congressman, 1881–99. Prepared the protectionist tariff adopted in 1897, commonly known as the Dingley Act.

DINSMOOR, ROBERT (*b. Windham, N.H., 1757; d. 1836*), poet. The "Rustic Bard," and friend of John G. Whittier. His verses were published in 1828 and again in 1898.

DINWIDDIE, ALBERT BLEDSOE (*b. Lexington, Ky., 1871; d. 1935*), educator and administrator. Nephew of Albert T. Bledsoe. Graduated University of Virginia, 1889; Ph.D., 1892. President of Tulane University, 1918–35. [*Supp. 1*]

DINWIDDIE, EDWIN COURTLAND (*b. Springfield, O., 1867; d. Washington, D.C., 1935*), Evangelical Lutheran clergyman, lecturer, reformer. Played a significant part in securing the adoption of the 18th Amendment and the "Volstead Act." [*Supp. 1*]

DINWIDDIE, ROBERT (*b. near Glasgow, Scotland, 1693; d. Bristol, England, 1770*), colonial administrator. Appointed collector of customs for Bermuda, 1727; surveyor-general for the Southern Part of America, 1738. An active and honest public servant, he was named lieutenant-governor of Virginia, 1751. By provoking a quarrel with the House of Burgesses over land-patent fees, he lost its cooperation at a critical time. In 1754 Dinwiddie sent troops to prevent French settlement in the Ohio region, but after a defeat near present Pittsburgh in which George Washington played a part, the Assembly would not support his measures, nor did neighboring governors help him. Braddock's attempt in 1755 also failed, and until 1757 Dinwiddie had to hold the frontier with companies of rangers, one regiment, and erratic aid from friendly Indians. As an early advocate of intercolonial cooperation and the man who precipitated the struggle leading to the downfall of New France, Dinwiddie is a major figure in American history.

DISBROW, WILLIAM STEPHEN (*b. Newark, N.J., 1861; d. 1922*), physician, collector. Especially interested in natural sciences, medical history and numismatics, his collections of books and specimens were distributed among many museums including the Smithsonian and the Newark Museum.

DISSTON, HENRY (*b. Tewkesbury, England, 1819; d. 1878*), saw and tool manufacturer. By technological innovations at his factories in and near Philadelphia, Pa., Disston won world markets for his products.

DISTURNELL, JOHN (*b. Lansingburg, N.Y., 1801; d. New York, N.Y., 1877*), publisher and compiler of maps, guidebooks, gazetteers and resort directories.

DITRICHSTEIN, LEO (*b. Tamesvar, Hungary, 1865; d. Auersperg, Jugoslavia, 1928*), actor, dramatist. Made American debut, New York, 1890; thereafter, having gained facility in English, was successful as actor and as adapter of foreign plays.

DITSON, GEORGE LEIGHTON (*b. Westford, Mass., 1812; d. New York, N.Y., 1895*), author, theosophist.

DITSON, OLIVER (*b. Boston, Mass., 1811; d. Boston, 1888*), music publisher.

DITTEMORE, JOHN VALENTINE (*b. Indianapolis, Ind., 1876; d. New York, N.Y., 1937*), business executive, Christian Science leader. Expelled, 1919, from the Church's board of directors, he led for a time a rival movement. [*Supp. 2*]

DIVEN, ALEXANDER SAMUEL (*b. Catherine, now Watkins, N.Y., 1809; d. 1896*), lawyer, Union soldier, railroad promoter. Financed and oversaw construction of the New York & Erie, 1844–50; was active in promoting and constructing several other railroads including Missouri Pacific. Leading citizen of Elmira, N.Y.

DIX, DOROTHEA LYNDE (*b. Hampden, Maine, 1802; d. Trenton, N.J., 1887*), humanitarian. At ten years of age, she left an unhappy home to live with grandmother in Boston; at fourteen, was teaching school in Worcester, Mass. Soon thereafter she established in Boston a school for young girls which she conducted until 1835. Her school stressed the natural sciences and moral character; among her pupils were the children of Rev. William Ellery Channing, to whose congregation she belonged. During this period she also wrote a number of now-forgotten books. When ill-health forced her to abandon the school, she resided for a while in England, returning to Boston in 1838 still an invalid.

In 1841 she undertook a Sunday-school class in the East Cambridge (Mass.) House of Correction. Visiting the jail, she found insane persons in an unheated room, treatment which was not unusual at a time when the insane were regarded as fallen to a brute condition. Having obtained relief for these persons, Miss Dix spent two years investigating the shocking condition of the insane in jails, poorhouses and similar institutions throughout Massachusetts. Influential men, chosen by her and supplied with the facts she had unearthed, presented a memorial of protest to the state legislature and, over objections and disbelief, a bill was carried for the enlargement of the Worcester insane asylum.

Well aware that the principal reform would come through state asylums staffed by intelligent, trained personnel, she made her work national in scope. She followed the same procedure in each state: thorough, independent research; wise choice of spokesmen; influence of the press. She never appeared in public; her gentle manner and quiet dignity turned aside hostile comment. Three main factors supported her in public work which was at that time considered unfeminine: her independence of spirit; emotionally intense compassion; the profound influence of Dr. Channing who insisted that every human being was capable of endless spiritual development.

Between 1841 and 1845, three hospitals for the insane were enlarged or reorganized at Worcester, Mass., Providence, R.I., and Utica, N.Y.; three new hospitals were founded at Trenton, N.J., Harrisburg, Pa., and Toronto, Canada. Between 1845 and 1852, eleven state legislatures were induced to vote for erection of state hospitals. Her great effort for a federal land grant whose taxes would be set aside for the care of the insane was defeated by presidential veto in 1854.

Between 1854 and 1857, she traveled in England and on the Continent investigating care of the insane and effecting reforms. She was active not only in her own field but in many other humanitarian projects. Throughout the Civil War, she served as "Superintendent of Women Nurses," selecting and assigning nurses for hospitals. It was a frustrating task and deserves more credit than it is usually accorded. From the war's end until her death, she was constantly at work, investigating, advising and supporting her hospitals and creating new ones.

DIX, JOHN ADAMS (*b. Boscowen, N.H., 1798; d. New York, N.Y., 1879*), soldier, lawyer, statesman. Dix's father, a man of marked individuality and versatile talents, gave his boy a good elementary education and then sent him to the College of Montreal for tuition in French and contact with a different civilization. Recalled at the outbreak of the War of 1812, he obtained an army commission and participated in the battle of Lundy's Lane. After his father was killed in the campaign of 1813, having to contribute to the support of his family, he remained in the army, rising to the rank of major. Seeking a larger field for his talents, however, he studied law and was admitted to the bar in 1824.

In 1826 he married the adopted daughter of John J. Morgan, a New York landowner who offered Dix the position of managing agent at Cooperstown. There Dix settled in 1828, practiced law, became county Democratic leader, and was appointed adjutant-general of the state in 1830. From then on his political career prospered. He made an especial mark as secretary of state, 1833–39, working to improve the training of teachers in the public schools and taking the first step toward organizing a geological survey of New York State.

Dix was elected to the United States Senate in 1845 for the five unexpired years of Silas Wright's term. Here he displayed a special interest in international affairs and also the free-soil sentiments that ultimately put him at odds with the Democratic party. He might have become a leader of the Democracy in the fifties had not the pro-slavery wing of the party interfered, preventing his appointment as U.S. secretary of state and as minister to France.

After a decade's concentration on private affairs, he was appointed by Buchanan to straighten out affairs in the New York City post-office. In January 1861, he became secretary of the treasury on demand of the alarmed business and money interests of the East. His chief service to the Union was this brief term at the Treasury Department. His dispatch of January 29, 1861, to a treasury official in New Orleans which ended: "If anyone attempts to haul down the American flag, shoot him on the spot!" was a clarion call to the North. When he turned over his reorganized department in excellent condition to Salmon P. Chase in March, he was made a major-general and did excellent if unspectacular service, notably as commander of the departments of Maryland and of the East.

After the War he served as minister to France, 1866–69. In 1872, though still a Democrat, he was nominated for governor of New York by the Republicans. Elected, he discharged the routine duties of his office capably until 1874.

DIX, JOHN HOMER (*b. Boston, Mass., 1811; d. Boston, 1884*), ophthalmologist. Performed one of the first operations in America for congenital strabismus, 1840. A leader in his specialty, he is also credited with introducing, 1856–57, the apartment house into the United States.

DIX, MORGAN (*b. New York, N.Y., 1827; d. New York, 1908*), Episcopal clergyman. Son of John A. Dix. Graduated Columbia, 1848; General Theological Seminary, 1852. Assigned to Trinity Parish, New York City, in 1855, he was its rector, 1862–1908.

DIXON, JAMES (*b. Enfield, Conn., 1814; d. Hartford, Conn., 1873*), lawyer, politician. Congressman, Whig, from Connecticut, 1845–49; U.S. senator, Republican, 1856–69. An ardent supporter of Andrew Johnson, he ran for the Senate as a Democrat, 1868, and failed of re-election.

DIXON, JOSEPH (*b. Marblehead, Mass., 1799; d. 1869*), inventor, manufacturer. After long years of experiment, developed and patented graphite crucibles for use in pottery and steel industries (1850, 1858).

DIXON, LUTHER SWIFT (*b. Underhill, Vt., 1825; d. Milwaukee, Wis., 1891*), jurist. Removed to Wisconsin, 1850; commenced practice of law; held minor offices. Chief justice, state supreme court, 1859–74, he appeared thereafter in important railroad cases.

DIXON, ROLAND BURRAGE (*b. Worcester, Mass., 1875; d. 1934*), anthropologist, teacher. Graduated Harvard, 1897, Ph.D., 1900. Author of more than eighty works; especially noted for work on ethnography of California. [*Supp. 1*]

DIXON, WILLIAM (*b. Ohio Co., W. Va., 1850; d. Oklahoma, 1913*), frontiersman, known as "Billy" Dixon. Left home as a boy to become a muleskinner and buffalo hunter; fought at second battle of Adobe

Walls, 1874; as army scout, won Congressional Medal for bravery.

DIXWELL, JOHN (*b. near Rugby, England, c. 1607; d. New Haven, Conn., 1688/9*), regicide. A signer of Charles I's death warrant, Dixwell fled, *post* 1660, to Germany; he is first mentioned as in America, 1664/5. Soon after, he settled at New Haven under name of James Davids.

DOAK, SAMUEL (*b. Augusta Co., Va., 1749; d. Bethel, Tenn., 1830*), Presbyterian clergyman, educator. Graduated Princeton, 1775. Began ministry on Tennessee frontier, founding Salem Church near Jonesboro and what was later Washington College; in 1818, he opened Tusculum Academy.

DOANE, GEORGE WASHINGTON (*b. Trenton, N.J., 1799; d. 1859*), Episcopal clergyman. Graduated Union, 1818; one of the first students at General Theological Seminary (N.Y.), he was ordained, 1823. Consecrated bishop of New Jersey, 1832, he served also as rector of St. Mary's Church, Burlington, N.J. Leader of the High Church party in his time, he was author of a number of well-known hymns.

DOANE, THOMAS (*b. Orleans, Mass., 1821; d. West Townsend, Vt., 1897*), mechanical engineer. Did his principal work for Boston & Maine and other New England railroads; chief engineer, Hoosac Tunnel construction *post* 1863.

DOANE, WILLIAM CROSWELL (*b. Boston, Mass., 1832; d. 1913*), Episcopal clergyman. Son of George W. Doane. Consecrated bishop of Albany, N.Y., 1869.

DOBBIN, JAMES COCHRAN (*b. Fayetteville, N.C., 1814; d. Fayetteville, 1857*), lawyer. As secretary of the navy, 1853–57, he remade that service and greatly increased its technical efficiency. He recommended a radical increase in number of steam vessels, forced an act for reform of personnel procedures through Congress, and generally restored morale.

DOBBS, ARTHUR (*b. Co. Antrim, Ireland, 1689; d. 1765*), colonial governor of North Carolina, 1754–65. An opponent of popular government, his administration was in constant difficulties over questions of Crown and governmental prerogative.

DOCK, CHRISTOPHER (*No reliable information available as to birth; d. Montgomery Co., Pa., 1771*), Mennonite schoolmaster. Came to Pennsylvania between 1710 and 1714; taught at Skippack and Salford, Pa. Author of the earliest treatise on schoolkeeping in America yet discovered, his *Schulordnung* (written, 1750; published, 1770).

DOCKSTADER, LEW (*b. Hartford, Conn., 1856; d. New York, N.Y., 1924*), minstrel. Original name, George Alfred Clapp; one of the most popular comedians of his time.

DOD, ALBERT BALDWIN (*b. Mendham, N.J., 1805; d. Princeton, N.J., 1845*), Presbyterian clergyman. Son of Daniel Dod. Professor of mathematics, Princeton University, 1830–45.

DOD, DANIEL (*b. Virginia, 1778; d. 1823*), inventor, engine-builder. Raised in Mendham, N.J. Nephew of Thaddeus Dod. Trained as a watch and instrument maker, he received (1811 and 1812) U.S. patents for steam-engines to be used in steamboats as well as mills. In partnership with Aaron Ogden, Dod built a ferryboat which went in service in 1813. He continued to build machinery for boats, including the engines for the S. S. *Savannah*, the first steam-vessel to cross the Atlantic, despite his bankruptcy, 1819. His death resulted from a boiler explosion on the East River, N.Y.

DOD, THADDEUS (*b. Newark, N.J., 1740; d. Ten Mile Creek, Pa., 1793*), Presbyterian clergyman, educator. Graduated Princeton, 1773; ordained, 1777, for work on western frontier. As pastor at Ten Mile Creek, Washington Co., Pa., Dod opened first classical school west of the Alleghenies, 1782; he was later a trustee of Washington Academy, and its first principal, 1789–90.

DODD, FRANK HOWARD (*b. Bloomfield, N.J., 1844; d. 1916*), publisher. *Post* 1870, senior partner of Dodd, Mead & Co.

DODD, LEE WILSON (*b. Franklin, Pa., 1879; d. 1933*), author. Son of Samuel C. T. Dodd. His satiric wit best displayed in *The Great Enlightenment* (1928). [*Supp. 1*]

DODD, SAMUEL CALVIN TATE (*b. Franklin, Pa., 1836; d. 1907*), lawyer. Originally an "antirebate" lawyer in Pennsylvania oil regions, he became an attorney for Standard Oil, 1881, and organized the Standard Oil Trust, 1882.

DODD, WILLIAM EDWARD (*b. near Clayton, N.C., 1869; d. Round Hill, Va., 1940*), historian. Graduated Virginia Polytechnic Institute, 1895; Ph.D., Leipzig, 1900. Professor at University of Chicago, 1908–33, specializing in history of the South; ambassador to Germany, 1933–37. [*Supp. 2*]

DODDRIDGE, JOSEPH (*b. near Bedford, Pa., 1769; d. 1826*), Methodist and Episcopal clergyman, physician, author. Brother of Philip Doddridge. Author of *Notes on the Settlement and Indian Wars of the Western Parts of Virginia and Pennsylvania* (1824).

DODDRIDGE, PHILIP (*b. near Bedford, Pa., 1773; d. Washington, D.C., 1832*), lawyer, politician. Removed to what is now Wellsburg, W. Va., c. 1790. As a member of the Virginia House of Delegates, an aggressive protagonist of the West against the "tidewater" interests, he was congressman from his section, 1829–32.

DODGE, AUGUSTUS CAESAR (*b. Ste. Genevieve, Mo., 1812; d. Burlington, Iowa, 1883*), politician, diplomat. Son of Henry Dodge. Removed to Wisconsin, 1827, and to Iowa, 1838. Territorial delegate from Iowa, 1840–46; U.S. senator, Democrat, 1848–54; minister to Spain, 1855–59.

DODGE, DAVID LOW (*b. Brooklyn, Conn., 1774; d. 1852*), dry-goods merchant. Founded New York Peace Society, 1815, said to have been the first organization of its kind.

DODGE, EBENEZER (*b. Salem, Mass., 1819; d. 1890*), Baptist clergyman. President of Madison (now Colgate) University, *post* 1868.

DODGE, GRACE HOADLEY (*b. New York, N.Y., 1856; d. New York, 1914*), philanthropist, social worker. Granddaughter of William Earl Dodge. Among her many interests, her work in support of Teachers College (New York) and the Young Women's Christian Association was outstanding.

DODGE, GRENVILLE MELLEN (*b. Danvers, Mass., 1831; d. 1916*), civil engineer. Employed as a railroad surveyor, Illinois and Iowa; settled as a contractor and merchant in Council Bluffs, *circa* 1854. Rose to major-general of volunteers in Civil War, performing outstanding service as builder of bridges and railroads. Chief engineer, Union Pacific Railroad, 1866–70. Thereafter active as projector, builder, financier and director of many railroads in the Southwest and West, he was called "ablest railroad lobbyist of his time."

DODGE, HENRY (*b. Vincennes, Ind., 1782; d. 1867*), soldier, pioneer. Raised in Ste. Genevieve district of present Missouri, where his father farmed and mined lead; served as sheriff of district and in War of 1812. Removed to region of present Dodgeville, Wis., *c.* 1827; commanded mounted volunteers in Winnebago War, 1827, and Black Hawk War, 1832; appointed colonel, 1st U.S. Dragoons, 1833. Territorial governor of Wisconsin, 1836–41, 1845–48; territorial delegate, Democrat, 1841–45; U.S. senator, state of Wisconsin, 1848–57.

DODGE, JACOB RICHARDS (*b. New Boston, N.H., 1823; d. Nashua, N.H., 1902*), agricultural journalist. Editor and statistician, U.S. Department of Agriculture, 1862–93.

DODGE, MARY ABIGAIL (*b. Hamilton, Mass., 1833; d. 1896*), journalist. Writer of caustic, clever miscellanies under pseudonym of "Gail Hamilton."

DODGE, MARY ELIZABETH MAPES (*b. New York, N.Y., 1831; d. Onteora, N.Y., 1905*), editor, author. Especially remembered for her children's classic *Hans Brinker; or, the Silver Skates* (1865), and for her very able editorship of *St. Nicholas Magazine*, 1873–1905.

DODGE, THEODORE AYRAULT (*b. Pittsfield, Mass., 1842; d. near Nanteuil-le-Haudouin, France, 1909*), Union soldier, businessman, military historian.

Author of careful studies of Alexander, Gustavus Adolphus, Napoleon and others.

DODGE, WILLIAM DE LEFTWICH (*Liberty, Va., 1867; d. 1935*), artist. Studied at Munich and with Gérôme in Paris. The 24 large murals in the Flag Room of the New York State Capitol are representative of his work. [*Supp. 1*]

DODGE, WILLIAM EARL (*b. Hartford, Conn., 1805; d. 1883*), merchant. Son of David L. Dodge. Left wholesale dry-goods business, 1833, to join in Phelps, Dodge & Co., developers of copper and iron properties; maintained lifelong interest in philanthropies and in various reform movements, notably temperance.

DODS, JOHN BOVEE (*b. New York, N.Y., 1795; d. Brooklyn, N.Y., 1872*), spiritualist.

DOE, CHARLES (*b. Derry, N.H., 1830; d. Rollinsford, N.H., 1896*), jurist. Graduated Dartmouth, 1849. Justice, New Hampshire supreme judicial court, 1859–74; chief justice, state supreme court, 1876–96. Made radical and effective reforms in state legal procedure.

DOHENY, EDWARD LAURENCE (*b. near Fond du Lac, Wis., 1856; d. Beverly Hills, Calif., 1935*), oil producer. Developed fields in California and Mexico; with Albert B. Fall, secretary of the interior under President Harding, was tried for conspiracy and bribery in leasing government oil lands.

[*Supp. 1*]

DOHERTY, HENRY LATHAM (*b. Columbus, O., 1870; d. Philadelphia, Pa., 1939*), public utility engineer, executive. Began work at twelve in Columbus Gas Co. A remarkable example of self-education, he rose to chief engineer, then became general manager of gas and electric properties in some thirty cities. By 1905 he headed his own firm, providing engineering and financial services to utilities. In 1910 he formed Cities Service, a holding company which acquired, reorganized and refinanced dozens of operating companies, and extended into gas and petroleum production. A brilliant and unorthodox engineer, he translated complex new technologies into goods and services by high-pressure financial methods which were sharply curbed by New Deal legislation. [*Supp. 2*]

DOLAN, THOMAS (*b. Montgomery Co., Pa., 1834; d. 1914*), capitalist. Successful with Keystone Knitting Mills, he became a major figure in development of public utilities in Philadelphia and elsewhere; he was center of a 1905 Philadelphia gas company scandal.

DOLD, JACOB (*b. Tuttlingen, Germany, 1825; d. Buffalo, N.Y., 1909*), meat-packer. Came to Buffalo, 1844; began own business, 1848, achieving great expansion after Civil War.

DOLE, CHARLES FLETCHER (*b. Brewer, Maine, 1845; d. 1927*), Congregational clergyman. Pastor, First Church, Jamaica Plain, Mass., 1876–1916.

DOLE, NATHAN HASKELL (*b. Chelsea, Mass., 1852; d. Yonkers, N.Y., 1935*), author, editor. Brother of Charles F. Dole. Among the earlier translators who introduced American readers to Russian literature. [*Supp.* 1]

DOLE, SANFORD BALLARD (*b. Honolulu, Hawaii, 1844; d. Honolulu, 1926*), lawyer, jurist. Son of an American missionary, Dole was educated in the United States, returning to Hawaii to practice law and engage in public affairs. Elected to the legislature as a reform candidate, 1884 and 1886, he was a leader in the revolution of 1887 whereby King Kalakaua was forced to grant a new constitution under which the monarch was reduced in status. Also in 1887, Dole was appointed a justice of the supreme court and held that office until 1893 when he became head of the revolutionary Provisional Government which had overthrown the monarchy. Balked of immediate annexation to the United States by President Cleveland's opposition, Dole accepted presidency of the Republic of Hawaii, 1894, and served until 1900 when he became first governor of the Territory of Hawaii. Resigning in 1903, he was made judge of the U.S. district court for Hawaii.

DOLLAR, ROBERT (*b. Falkirk, Scotland, 1844; d. San Rafael, Calif., 1932*), ship owner. Emigrated to Canada, 1858; removed to Michigan, 1882, and to California, 1888. Founded steamship companies bearing his name; began first round-the-world passenger service. [*Supp.* 1]

DOLLIVER, JONATHAN PRENTISS (*b. near Kingwood, Va., 1858; d. 1910*), statesman. Removed to Iowa, *c.* 1878; won local fame as orator in Republican campaign, 1884. As congressman, 1889–1900, Dolliver was a useful member of the conservative Republican group; however, as U.S. senator, 1901–10, he grew increasingly "insurgent" and aligned himself with La Follette and the liberals.

DOLPH, JOSEPH NORTON (*b. Dolphsburg, N.Y., 1835; d. 1897*), lawyer. Settling in Portland, Oreg., after the Civil War, he represented Northwest railroad interests and served as U.S. senator, Republican, from Oregon, 1882–94.

DOMBROWSKI, JOSEPH. [See DABROWSKI, JOSEPH, 1842–1903.]

DONAHOE, PATRICK (*b. Munnery, Ireland, 1811; d. Boston, Mass., 1901*), editor, publisher. Emigrated to Boston as a child; learned printer's trade; began publication of the Boston *Pilot* with H. L. Devereaux, 1836. Notable for his philanthropies.

DONAHUE, PETER (*b. Glasgow, Scotland, 1822; d. San Francisco, Calif., 1885*), capitalist. Emigrated to America as a child; settled in California, 1849. Founded Union Iron Works, San Francisco, *c.* 1850; was pioneer also in California public utility development.

DONALDSON, HENRY HERBERT (*b. Yonkers, N.Y., 1857; d. West Philadelphia, Pa., 1938*), neurologist. Graduated Yale, 1879; Ph.D., Johns Hopkins, 1885. Joining the faculty of Clark University in 1889, Donaldson published (1891) a classic anatomical study of the brain of Laura Bridgman (a woman whose hearing had been lost and sight impaired through infection in infancy), which led to his remarkable monograph, *The Growth of the Brain* (1895). Donaldson was professor of neurology, University of Chicago, 1892–1906; he then joined the Wistar Institute in Philadelphia. Here he developed the important "Wistar Strain" of the albino rat on which he carried out his studies of the growth and development of the nervous system. [*Supp.* 2]

DONCK, ADRIAEN VAN DER. [See VAN DER DONCK, ADRIAEN, 1620–1655.]

DONELSON, ANDREW JACKSON (*b. near Nashville, Tenn., 1799; d. Memphis, Tenn., 1871*), soldier, lawyer, diplomat. Raised in the home of Andrew Jackson; graduated West Point; served as aide to Jackson in Seminole War. Resigning from army, he studied law and was admitted to the bar, 1823. Served as Jackson's confidential secretary, 1824–28, and as his private secretary in Washington, 1828–36. Handled U.S. relations with Republic of Texas; served as minister to Prussia, 1846–49.

DONGAN, THOMAS (*b. Castletown, Ireland, 1634; d. London, England, 1715*), soldier, colonial administrator. Governor of New York (commissioned, 1682), 1683–88. One of the best of all the colonial governors, Dongan did his utmost to check the growing power of France in North America; during his term, a representative assembly was called and the so-called "Dongan Charter" of liberties was formulated.

DONIPHAN, ALEXANDER WILLIAM (*b. near Maysville, Ky., 1808; d. Richmond, Mo., 1887*), lawyer, soldier, statesman. Removed to Missouri, 1830, and was successful in practice of law. As colonel, 1st Missouri Mounted Volunteers, he led a remarkable western campaign during the Mexican War which is still considered one of the most brilliant long marches ever made. He favored Missouri neutrality in the Civil War although he opposed secession.

DONLEVY, HARRIET FARLEY. [See FARLEY, HARRIET, 1817–1907.]

DONN-BYRNE, BRIAN OSWALD (*b. New York, N.Y., 1889; d. Co. Cork, Ireland, 1928*), author. Among his colorful stories, distinguished for their word-music, are: *Stranger's Banquet* (1919); *Messer Marco Polo* (1921); and *Blind Raftery* (1924).

DONNELL, JAMES C. (*b. Ireland, 1854; d. Findlay, O., 1927*), oil producer. Came to America as a child. Active *post* 1872 in Pennsylvania and Ohio oil fields; later associated with Standard Oil.

DONNELL, ROBERT (*b. Guilford Co., N.C., 1784; d. Athens, Ala., 1855*), Cumberland Presbyterian clergyman; a notable camp-meeting preacher.

DONNELLY, CHARLES FRANCIS (*b. Athlone, Ireland, 1836; d. Boston, Mass., 1909*), lawyer. Emigrated to Canada as an infant; to Providence, R.I., 1848. Graduated Harvard Law School, 1859. In practice in Boston, he served for many years as counsel for the Catholic Church in New England, particularly in constitutional matters. He was active also in child welfare and public charities.

DONNELLY, ELEANOR CECILIA (*b. Philadelphia, Pa., 1838; d. West Chester, Pa., 1917*), author. Sister of Ignatius Donnelly.

DONNELLY, IGNATIUS (*b. Philadelphia, Pa., 1831; d. 1901*), politician, reformer. Projected a town (Nininger, Minn.), on whose site he turned farmer after panic of 1857 killed the scheme. As congressman, Republican, 1863–69, he was active in promoting railroad land-grants; after his defeat for re-election, he left the Republican party and was successively Liberal Republican, Granger and Greenbacker in his opinions. He was later active in formation of the Populist party. Among his books, each written to advance some unusual theory, are: *Atlantis* (1882); *The Great Cryptogram* (1888); and *Caesar's Column* (1891).

DONOGHUE, JOHN (*b. Chicago, Ill., 1853; d. near New Haven, Conn., 1903*), sculptor. Studied in Chicago, and in Paris under Jouffroy. Showed promise but never reached first rank and is remembered chiefly for his "Young Sophokles."

DONOVAN, JOHN JOSEPH (*b. Rumney, N.H., 1858; d. Bellingham, Wash., 1937*), pioneer railroad builder, lumberman, and community leader in the Pacific Northwest. [*Supp. 2*]

D'OOGE, MARTIN LUTHER (*b. Zonnemaire, Netherlands, 1839; d. Ann Arbor, Mich., 1915*), Greek scholar. Came to America as a child. Graduated University of Michigan, 1862; Ph.D., Leipzig, 1872. Taught Greek at Michigan, 1867–1912; author of *The Acropolis of Athens* (1908) and other works.

DOOLITTLE, AMOS (*b. Cheshire, Conn., 1754; d. New Haven, Conn., 1832*), engraver. Produced prints of battles at Lexington and Concord after Ralph Earle, 1775, and a great variety of maps, book-illustrations, portraits.

DOOLITTLE, CHARLES LEANDER (*b. Ontario, Ind., 1843; d. 1919*), astronomer. Graduated University of Michigan, 1874; taught at Lehigh and at University of Pennsylvania; director, Flower Observatory, 1896–1912.

DOOLITTLE, ERIC (*b. Ontario, Ind., 1869; d. 1920*), astronomer. Son of Charles L. Doolittle.

DOOLITTLE, JAMES ROOD (*b. Washington Co., N.Y., 1815; d. 1897*), lawyer, statesman. After rising to prominence as a leader of the "barnburner" faction of Democrats in New York, Doolittle removed to Racine, Wis., 1851. Served as U.S. senator, Republican, 1857–69. A friend and adviser of Abraham Lincoln, he sacrificed his political career in support of Andrew Johnson's policies.

DORCHESTER, DANIEL (*b. Duxbury, Mass., 1827; d. 1907*), Methodist clergyman, legislator. An able pastor and preacher, interested in temperance and other reforms, he supervised U.S. Indian Schools, 1889–93. Author of *History of Christianity in the United States* (1888) and other works.

DOREMUS, ROBERT OGDEN (*b. New York, N.Y., 1824; d. 1906*), chemist, inventor, educator. M.D., New York University, 1851. A versatile, inspiring teacher of science at several New York institutions, in particular at College of the City of New York, 1852–1903.

DOREMUS, SARAH PLATT HAINES (*b. New York, N.Y., 1802; d. 1877*), social worker. Active with J. Marion Sims in establishing the Woman's Hospital (1855); long identified with charitable enterprises in New York.

DORGAN, THOMAS ALOYSIUS (*b. San Francisco., Calif., 1877; d. Great Neck, N.Y., 1929*), cartoonist. Famous as "Tad" for his political satire, his "Indoor Sports" and other series, and his gift for coinage of original slang.

DORION, MARIE (*b. Iowa Nation, c. 1791; d. near present Salem, Oreg., 1850*), wife and trail companion of Pierre Dorion, interpreter of the Astoria land expedition, 1811–12.

DORNIN, THOMAS ALOYSIUS (*b. Ireland, 1800; d. Savannah, Ga., 1874*), naval officer. Retired as commodore, 1862.

DORR, JULIA CAROLINE RIPLEY (*b. Charleston, S.C., 1825; d. Rutland, Vt., 1913*), poet, novelist.

DORR, THOMAS WILSON (*b. Providence, R.I., 1805; d. 1854*), politician, reformer. Graduated Harvard, 1823; studied law under James Kent. As member of state legislature, led fight for reform of Rhode Island's archaic suffrage laws, 1834–40; took leading part in agitation in 1840–42 of "People's Party" for a constitution. Tried for treason, he was committed to prison, 1844–45. Restored to civil rights, 1851.

DORRELL, WILLIAM (*b. Yorkshire, England, 1752; d. Leyden, Mass., 1846*), founder of the Dorrellites, a fanatical sect which flourished in Franklin Co., Mass., *post* 1794.

DORSCH, EDUARD (*b. Würzburg, Bavaria, 1822; d. Monroe, Mich., 1887*), physician, poet.

DORSET, MARION (*b. Columbia, Tenn., 1872; d. Washington, D.C., 1935*), chemist. Graduated University of Tennessee, 1893; M.D., Columbian University, 1896. Known for his work with the Bureau of Animal Husbandry; he was a pioneer investigator of the chemistry of the tubercle bacillus and developed an effective method of controlling and preventing hog cholera. [*Supp. 1*]

DORSEY, ANNA HANSON McKENNEY (*b. Georgetown, D.C., 1815; d. Washington, D.C., 1896*), author.

DORSEY, GEORGE AMOS (*b. Hebron, O., 1868; d. New York, N.Y., 1931*), anthropologist, teacher. Author of *Why We Behave Like Human Beings* (1925). [*Supp. 1*]

DORSEY, JAMES OWEN (*b. Baltimore, Md., 1848; d. 1895*), ethnologist. Expert in linguistics and sociology of Indian tribes of the plains; author of many valuable specialized studies.

DORSEY, JOHN SYNG (*b. Philadelphia, Pa., 1783; d. Philadelphia, 1818*), surgeon. Nephew of Philip Syng Physick, whose student he was; M.D., University of Pennsylvania, 1802. Author of *The Elements of Surgery* (1813), he was associated with the Pennsylvania Hospital as surgeon and taught at University of Pennsylvania.

DORSEY, SARAH ANNE ELLIS (*b. near Natchez, Miss., 1829; d. New Orleans, La., 1879*), author.

DORSEY, STEPHEN WALLACE (*b. Benson, Vt., 1842; d. Los Angeles, Calif., 1916*), businessman, promoter. While active in fraudulent railroad promotions in Arkansas, he served as U.S. senator, Republican, from that state, 1873–76; he was indicted with T. W. Brady in "Star Route" scandal, 1881.

DORSHEIMER, WILLIAM EDWARD (*b. Lyons, N.Y., 1832; d. Savannah, Ga., 1888*), lawyer, politician, journalist. Prominent in New York Democratic politics, 1874–88; author of Grover Cleveland's campaign biography, 1884.

DOS PASSOS, JOHN RANDOLPH (*b. Philadelphia, Pa., 1844; d. New York, N.Y., 1917*), lawyer. Left thriving criminal practice to specialize in problems of finance and exchange. Author of a standard *Treatise on the Law of Stockbrokers and Stock Exchanges* (1882) and other works.

DOTY, ELIHU (*b. Berne, N.Y., 1809; d. Amoy, China, 1864*), Dutch Reformed clergyman. Missionary to Borneo and China; author of works on the Amoy dialect.

DOTY, JAMES DUANE (*b. Salem, N.Y., 1799; d. Salt Lake City, Utah, 1865*), politician, lawyer, speculator. Removed to Detroit, 1819, and became a judge in northern Michigan, 1823. Was later the stormy petrel of early Wisconsin politics, serving as delegate to Congress and as governor, and continuously involved in both capacities with promoting his own private interests.

DOUBLEDAY, ABNER (*b. Ballston Spa, N.Y., 1819; d. Mendham, N.J., 1893*), soldier, traditional inventor of baseball. Graduated West Point, 1842. Served in Mexican War, and as division commander in Civil War. Distinguished himself particularly at Gettysburg by holding Confederates in check on first day of battle.

DOUBLEDAY, FRANK NELSON (*b. Brooklyn, N.Y., 1862; d. Coconut Grove, Fla., 1934*), publisher. Founded Doubleday & McClure, 1897; Doubleday, Page & Co., 1900. [*Supp. 1*]

DOUBLEDAY, NELTJE DE GRAFF (*b. Chicago, Ill., 1865; d. China, 1918*), naturalist. Wife of Frank N. Doubleday.

DOUGHERTY, RAYMOND PHILIP (*b. Lebanon, Pa., 1877; d. 1933*), United Brethren clergyman, missionary educator, Assyriologist. Author of *The Sealand of Ancient Arabia* (1932). [*Supp. 1*]

DOUGHTY, THOMAS (*b. Philadelphia, Pa., 1793; d. New York, N.Y., 1856*), painter. Rated for a time the foremost landscape painter of the Hudson River school, Doughty was among the first American landscapists to attain general recognition.

DOUGHTY, WILLIAM HENRY (*b. Augusta, Ga., 1836; d. Augusta, 1905*), physician, Confederate Army surgeon. An efficient general practitioner, he was also a student of climatology and its relation to medicine.

DOUGLAS, AMANDA MINNIE (*b. New York, N.Y., 1831; d. Newark, N.J., 1916*). Author of the Kathie Series, the Little Girl Series and other books for children which reflect her love of domestic life.

DOUGLAS, BENJAMIN (*b. Northford, Conn., 1816; d. Middletown, Conn., 1894*), pump manufacturer. Co-inventor of revolving cistern stand pump.

DOUGLAS, HENRY KYD (*b. Shepherdstown, W. Va., 1838; d. 1903*), lawyer, Confederate soldier. Douglas's brigade of Lee's army was the last unit to surrender at Appomattox.

DOUGLAS, JAMES (*b. Quebec, Canada, 1837; d. 1918*), metallurgist, mining engineer, industrialist. Headed the Copper Queen Consolidated Mining Co. (Arizona).

DOUGLAS, STEPHEN ARNOLD (*b. Brandon, Vt., 1813; d. Chicago, Ill., 1861*), Democratic leader, statesman. Lost father in infancy. Apprenticed to cabinetmaker's trade, he later began study of law. Hopeful of early admission to bar, he journeyed west, 1833, and after many wanderings, settled as school-master in Winchester, Ill. Licensed to practice law at Jacksonville, Ill., 1834, within a year he was elected state's attorney for the first judicial district.

As a politician Douglas owed much to the Demo-cratic political machine in Illinois, which he helped to fashion. Having noted the methods of New York's "Albany Regency," he urged party organization and discipline. He was elected to the legislature and soon thereafter became register of the land office at Springfield. Nominated for Congress in 1837, Doug-las lost the election by only 35 votes. Rising higher in party councils, he served as chairman of the Democratic state committee in 1840 and after con-ducting a successful campaign was named secretary of state. On reorganization of the state supreme court, he received one of the five new judgeships. Elected to Congress in 1843, during his first term he made so favorable an impression as a party orator that he was asked to take an active part in the 1844 presi-dential campaign for Polk in the West. Disappointed by President Polk's failure to win the whole of Oregon for the United States, Douglas became an ardent supporter of the administration upon the outbreak of war with Mexico.

Appointed to the U.S. Senate in 1847, Douglas im-mediately became chairman of the Committee on Territories. In this post, he encountered the active demand of Northern political groups that Congress prevent the extension of slavery, while Southerners were equally insistent that citizens should not be prevented from taking slaves into the territories. Douglas was acutely conscious of these opposing forces. His wife, Martha Denny Martin, had upon her father's death inherited some 150 slaves; there were those who interpreted Douglas's subsequent career by this economic interest. On the other hand, the center of gravity in Illinois politics was shifting from the southern and central counties, originally settled by people from the South, to the northern counties settled by Yankees. In 1847 Douglas took up residence in Chicago and identified himself with the city's commercial interests. Through his efforts the revised Illinois Central Railroad Bill passed Con-gress in 1850. In 1850 also, Douglas and Congress-man McClernand drafted the bills providing terri-torial governments for Utah and New Mexico which promised that, when they came to be admitted as states, they should be admitted with or without slavery as their constitutions should prescribe. Though Douglas was absent when the vote on the Fugitive-Slave Bill was taken, he approved of the Act and de-fended it in a speech at Chicago.

Young men of his generation seemed drawn to Douglas. As the presidential candidate of "Young America" in 1852, he gave Cass and Buchanan sup-

porters some concern although he was unsuccessful. Re-elected senator in 1852, the death of his wife at that time changed his character; he seemed bitter and morose, and grew careless in personal habits.

Territorial problems now returned to the fore. The speedy organization of the vast territory of Nebraska concerned Missouri politicians, settlers already in the region and promoters of a Pacific railway. Under pressure of many conflicting interests, the Commit-tee on Territories produced a bill (January 1854) with a report stating that the Compromise of 1850 had established the principle that questions of slavery in the territories should be left to the people resid-ing therein. A Southern attempt explicitly to repeal the Missouri Compromise by amendment to the new bill led to the Kansas-Nebraska Bill which provided for two new territories instead of one and declared the Act of 1820 "superseded." Subsequently the phrase was altered to "inoperative and void." In ensuing debates Douglas coined the phrase "popular sovereignty," to describe the new principle of de-cision. Independent Democrats in Congress claimed that Douglas's position was motivated by presidential ambition; yet Douglas had nothing to gain by sub-serviency to the South. Though an opportunist, Doug-las had taken his stand on what he believed was a fundamental principle—self-determination. He failed to gauge the attachment of Northern Democrats to "a compact binding in moral force" for over thirty years. Though the bill was contested in the House, the master mind in its passage was Douglas. As a result anti-slavery Democrats were driven to join anti-slavery Whigs or Free-Soilers; also, the fierce con-test between pro-slavery and free-state settlers for control of Kansas ensued. Douglas blamed the break-down of the popular sovereignty principle in Kansas on the activities of organizations from outside the territory who had interfered in its domestic concerns, citing the peaceful contrast of Nebraska.

At the convention of 1856 Douglas was a leading contender for the presidency. When Buchanan re-ceived a majority, Douglas withdrew his name and in the campaign unreservedly supported the candidate.

In 1857 the Lecompton convention adopted a con-stitution for Kansas which in effect guaranteed the right of property in slaves in the territory. Free-state people had secured control of the territorial legis-lature, and it was evident that in a fair test the pro-slavery constitution would be rejected. Convinced that Buchanan favored the Lecompton constitution, Douglas declared he would oppose administration policy. He denounced the Lecompton constitution as a travesty of popular sovereignty, thus indicating his separation from the pro-slavery faction of his party.

Douglas was opposed by Abraham Lincoln in his 1858 campaign for re-election to the Senate. The famous series of debates in which the candidates engaged widened Douglas's breach with the dominant faction of his party by forcing him to deny the full force of the Dred Scott decision as interpreted by the national administration. Douglas won the election, but he was deposed by fellow Democrats from chairmanship of the Committee on Territories. Though he supported party policies where he could, he was eventually forced to declare opposition to any congressional intervention to protect slavery in the territories.

When the Democratic convention of 1860 met at Charleston, S.C., in April, Douglas led the balloting for the presidency but did not command two-thirds of the votes. When the convention reconvened at Baltimore two months later, Southern delegations withdrew and Douglas was nominated by acclamation. The bolters nominated John C. Breckinridge. Douglas had hoped to win the South and enough free states to insure election, but by midsummer a Democratic victory seemed impossible. His efforts were bent upon reorganizing the Democratic party and quashing disunion. The popular vote in 1860 was a personal triumph for Douglas, for he alone among the candidates drew votes from every section of the country and his total vote fell only 489,495 short of Lincoln's.

In the last weeks of Buchanan's administration, Douglas worked for compromise. He urged Lincoln to call a national convention for amendment of the Constitution so as to forbid the federal government from interfering with the domestic institution of slavery in the states. It is to his credit that Douglas gave total support to Lincoln in the early days of his administration. After the outbreak of the Civil War, Douglas on Lincoln's advice left Washington to rouse the people of the Northwest to the seriousness of the crisis. Soon after delivering a moving speech at Springfield, Ill. (April 25, 1861), Douglas was stricken with typhoid fever and died.

DOUGLAS, WILLIAM (*b. Plainfield, Conn., 1742/3; d. Northford, Conn., 1777*), merchant, Revolutionary sailor and soldier. Served with credit in Montgomery's Canadian expedition, 1775, and in the defense of New York, 1776.

DOUGLAS, WILLIAM LEWIS (*b. Plymouth, Mass., 1845; d. 1924*), shoe manufacturer. From small beginnings at Brockton, Mass., 1876, Douglas built a business controlling 117 retail shoe stores throughout the country. He was Democratic governor of Massachusetts, 1905–06.

DOUGLASS, DAVID BATES (*b. Pompton, N.J., 1790; d. Geneva, N.Y., 1849*), engineer, soldier, teacher. Planned (1834–36) the Croton water supply system which served New York City for 75 years; planned and laid out Greenwood Cemetery, Brooklyn, N.Y.; taught science and engineering at West Point, New York University and Hobart College.

DOUGLASS, FREDERICK (*b. Tuckahoe, Md., 1817?; d. 1895*), abolitionist, orator, journalist. Son of an unknown white father and a slave who had some Indian blood, he was named Frederick Augustus Washington Bailey but assumed the name of Douglass after escaping from slavery in 1838. In 1841 he successfully addressed a Massachusetts Anti-Slavery Society convention and was employed as its agent. To answer those who doubted that a man of his abilities could ever have been a slave, he wrote his *Narrative of the Life of Frederick Douglass* (1845). Later, he founded a newspaper, the *North Star*, labored continuously for justice to his race and assisted other social reforms including woman suffrage.

DOUGLASS, WILLIAM (*b. Gifford, Scotland, c. 1691; d. 1752*), physician. Settled in Boston, Mass., 1718. His account of a scarlet fever epidemic (published, 1736) was the first adequate clinical description of the disease; he was author also of a history of colonial settlement and a treatise on colonial currency.

DOVE, DAVID JAMES (*b. Portsmouth, England, c. 1696; d. Philadelphia, Pa., 1769*), Philadelphia schoolmaster, pamphleteer. The first person in Pennsylvania (perhaps in the colonies) to offer higher education for women, Dove came to Philadelphia in 1750 and taught there and in Germantown until his death.

DOW, HENRY (*b. Ormsby, England, 1634; d. Hampton, N.H., 1707*), soldier, lawyer. Came to America as a child. Residing in Hampton, N.H. *post* 1644, he held a great number of town and provincial offices.

DOW, HERBERT HENRY (*b. Belleville, Canada, 1866; d. Rochester, Minn., 1930*), chemist. Came to the United States as an infant. Graduated Case School of Applied Science, 1888; here began his interest in brine analysis. He patented a method for obtaining bromine from brine and in 1892 operated the first commercially successful American electrochemical plant at Midland, Mich. The Dow Chemical Co. was chartered in 1897 for the production of chlorine and bleaching powder. Dow products later developed from brines included insecticides, salicylates, magnesium, the first synthetic indigo in the Western Hemisphere and the first production of iodine in the United States. [*Supp. 1*]

DOW, LORENZO (*b. Coventry, Conn., 1777; d. Georgetown, Md., 1834*), evangelist. An itinerant eccentric, tentatively connected with the Methodists, Dow preached throughout the colonies and in England and Ireland, 1794–1834.

DOW, LORENZO (*b. Sumner, Maine, 1825; d. New York, N.Y., 1899*), inventor, businessman. Obtained the first patent for a waterproof cartridge, 1861. He later developed and marketed type-distributing and type-setting machines invented by his son Alexander.

DOW, NEAL (*b. Portland, Maine, 1804; d. Portland, 1897*), temperance reformer, Union soldier, mayor of Portland. Father of the "Maine Law" (1851, 1858), a prohibition measure.

DOWELL, GREENSVILLE (*b. Albemarle Co., Va., 1822; d. Galveston, Texas, 1881*), surgeon. Remembered for his monograph *Yellow Fever and Malarial Diseases . . .* (1876) which suggested that the disease was transmitted by mosquitoes. Practicing principally in Texas *post* 1853, he developed a radical cure for hernia and designed a number of surgical instruments.

DOWIE, JOHN ALEXANDER (*b. Edinburgh, Scotland, 1847; d. 1907*), founder of the Christian Catholic Apostolic Church in Zion. Came to America, 1888. His sect, centered in Zion City (near Chicago), claimed 50,000 members scattered throughout the world before his self-exposure and downfall, 1903–05.

DOWLING, AUSTIN (*b. New York, N.Y., 1868; d. St. Paul, Minn., 1930*), Roman Catholic clergyman. Bishop of Des Moines, Iowa, 1912–19; archbishop of St. Paul, Minn., 1919–30. [*Supp. 1*]

DOWNER, ELIPHALET (*b. Norwich, now Franklin, Conn., 1744; d. Brookline, Mass., 1806*), physician. Revolutionary army and navy surgeon.

DOWNER, SAMUEL (*b. Dorchester, Mass., 1807; d. 1881*), manufacturer. With Joshua Merrill and the Atwood brothers, introduced hydrocarbon lubricating and illuminating oils on a wide scale in America.

DOWNES, JOHN (*b. Canton, Mass., 1784; d. Charlestown, Mass., 1854*), naval officer. First lieutenant of the *Essex* during her memorable cruise, 1812–13. Led first American engagement in Orient, the attack on Quallah Battoo, Sumatra, 1832.

DOWNEY, JOHN (*b. Germantown, Pa., c. 1765; d. Harrisburg, Pa., 1826*), educator. His 1797 plan for a state educational system was ahead of its time, but was later commended by Henry Barnard.

DOWNEY, JUNE ETTA (*b. Laramie, Wyo., 1875; d. 1932*), psychologist. Pioneer in the field of personality measurement. [*Supp. 1*]

DOWNING, ANDREW JACKSON (*b. Newburgh, N.Y., 1815; d. 1852*), landscape gardener, architect, horticulturist. Author of the classic *A Treatise on the Theory and Practice of Landscape Gardening* (1841) which established him as America's authority on "rural art." His *Cottage Residences* (1842) adapted his theories to the needs of humbler folk; *The Fruits and Fruit Trees of America* (1845) was the most complete treatise of its kind at that time. In 1846 Downing became editor of the *Horticulturist*, a new periodical. Increasingly interested in architecture,

Downing, with Calvert Vaux, designed and constructed many estates. The first great American landscape gardener, Downing "made over the face of rural America."

DOWNING, CHARLES (*b. Newburgh, N.Y., 1802; d. 1885*), pomologist, horticulturist, author. Brother of Andrew J. Downing.

DOWNING, GEORGE (*b. Dublin, Ireland, 1623; d. 1684*), baronet, diplomat, member of Parliament. Nephew of John Winthrop. A graduate of the first class (1642) at Harvard, he left New England, 1645. Downing Street, London, is named for him.

DOWSE, THOMAS (*b. Charlestown, Mass., 1772; d. 1856*), bibliophile. Collected a remarkable library which he donated to the Massachusetts Historical Society.

DOYLE, ALEXANDER (*b. Steubenville, O., 1857; d. Boston, Mass., 1922*), sculptor. Designer of a vast number of public monuments.

DOYLE, ALEXANDER PATRICK (*b. San Francisco, Calif., 1857; d. San Francisco, 1912*), Roman Catholic clergyman, Paulist. Editor, *Catholic World*, 1893–1904; co-founder and rector of Apostolic Mission House at Catholic University, Washington, D.C.

DOYLE, JOHN THOMAS (*b. New York, N.Y., 1819; d. San Mateo, Calif., 1906*), lawyer. Graduated Georgetown (D.C.), 1838. Secured restitution from Mexico of proceeds from Spanish colonial "Pious Fund."

DOYLE, SARAH ELIZABETH (*b. Providence, R.I., 1830; d. Providence, 1922*), educator. Promoted the establishment of the Women's College in Brown University.

DRAKE, ALEXANDER WILSON (*b. Westfield, N.J., 1843; d. New York, N.Y., 1916*), wood-engraver. Art director of the *Century Magazine*, and a leading figure in the development of American illustration.

DRAKE, BENJAMIN (*b. Mays Lick, Ky., 1795; d. 1841*), lawyer, editor, biographer. Brother of Daniel Drake. Author of *Cincinnati in 1826*, an account which encouraged immigration to Ohio and is still a valuable source; also of *Tales and Sketches from the Queen City* (1838) and lives of Black Hawk, W. H. Harrison, and Tecumseh.

DRAKE, CHARLES DANIEL (*b. Cincinnati, O., 1811; d. 1892*), lawyer, jurist. Son of Daniel Drake. Leader of the radical faction which controlled Missouri from 1865 to 1871. U.S. senator, Republican, 1867–70; thereafter chief justice, U.S. Court of Claims until 1885.

DRAKE, DANIEL (*b. near Plainfield, N.J., 1785; d. Cincinnati, O., 1852*), physician. Raised in Kentucky; studied medicine at Cincinnati, 1800–04, and practiced there with distinction for the greater part of his life. A teacher of medicine at several institutions,

Drake expressed ideals of medical education far ahead of his time. He served at various times as president of the Ohio Medical College, which he founded. He was author of *Notices Concerning Cincinnati* (1810), *Picture of Cincinnati in 1815* (1815) and his principal work, *A Systematic Treatise . . . on the Principal Diseases of the Interior Valley of North America* (1850, 1854).

DRAKE, EDWIN LAURENTINE (*b. Greenville, N.Y., 1819; d. Bethlehem, Pa., 1880*), railroad conductor, pioneer petroleum industrialist. In 1857 he visited properties, near Titusville, Pa., of the Pennsylvania Rock Oil Co., in which he owned stock. He studied salt-well drilling operations, leased land and formed the Seneca Oil Co., for exploitation of the properties. In 1859 he struck oil at a depth of 69 feet. This was the first time petroleum was tapped at its source and the first proof of oil reservoirs within the earth's surface. Drake developed the use of pipe driven to bed-rock to keep clay and quicksand from the drill hole.

DRAKE, FRANCES ANN DENNY (*b. Schenectady, N.Y., 1797; d. near Louisville, Ky., 1875*), actress. Sometimes called the "Star of the West"; the "tragedy queen" of the American stage, 1824–36.

DRAKE, FRANCIS MARION (*b. Rushville, Ill., 1830; d. Centerville, Iowa, 1903*), railroad builder, Union soldier, philanthropist. Removed to Iowa as a child. Promoter and official of several Iowa railroads. Republican governor of Iowa, 1896–97. His donation facilitated incorporation of Drake University, 1881.

DRAKE, FRANCIS SAMUEL (*b. Northwood, N.H., 1828; d. Washington, D.C., 1885*), historian. Son of Samuel G. Drake. Author, among other works, of an excellent *Dictionary of American Biography* (1872) and *Tea Leaves* (1884).

DRAKE, JOHN BURROUGHS (*b. Lebanon, O., 1826; d. 1895*), hotel man. Prospered as Chicago, Ill., hotel keeper, 1855–95. Won national fame at Grand Pacific Hotel.

DRAKE, JOSEPH RODMAN (*b. New York, N.Y., 1795; d. New York, 1820*), poet. Friend of Fitz-Greene Halleck, with whom he collaborated in *The Croaker Poems* (1819); a selection of his work appeared in *The Culprit Fay and Other Poems* (1835).

DRAKE, SAMUEL (*b. England, 1768; d. Oldham Co., Ky., 1854*), pioneer actor-manager of the West. Came to America, 1810. Drake brought the first really talented company beyond Pittsburgh and established the drama in Louisville, Lexington and Frankfort, Ky.

DRAKE, SAMUEL ADAMS (*b. Boston, Mass., 1833; d. Kennebunkport, Maine, 1905*), historian. Son of Samuel G. Drake.

DRAKE, SAMUEL GARDNER (*b. Pittsfield, N.H., 1798; d. 1875*), antiquarian, historian. Author, among other works, of *Indian Biography* (1832), enlarged as *Book of the Indians* (1841). Editor of several classic source works on New England.

DRAPER, ANDREW SLOAN (*b. Westford, N.Y., 1848; d. 1913*), lawyer, politician, educator. Elected first commissioner of education of New York State, 1904, Draper laid the basis of the state's present Department of Education.

DRAPER, EBEN SUMNER (*Milford, now Hopedale, Mass., 1858; d. Greenville, S.C., 1914*), cotton-machinery manufacturer. Republican governor of Massachusetts, 1909–10.

DRAPER, HENRY (*b. Prince Edward Co., Va., 1837; d. 1882*), astronomer, pioneer in astronomical photography. Son of John W. Draper. Graduated New York University, M.D., 1858. Secured his first spectrum photograph of a star, 1872; he also photographed the spectra of the moon, Jupiter and Venus. In 1874 Draper organized the photographic work of the government expedition to observe the transit of Venus.

DRAPER, IRA (*b. Dedham, Mass., 1764; d. Saugus, Mass., 1848*), textile-machinery inventor, manufacturer. Known as the inventor of the first rotary loom temple, a device which allowed one weaver to attend two looms.

DRAPER, JOHN (*b. Boston, Mass., 1702; d. Boston, 1762*), printer, journalist. Father of Richard Draper. Publisher of the *Boston News-Letter*, 1733–62.

DRAPER, JOHN WILLIAM (*b. St. Helen's, England, 1811; d. 1882*), chemist, author. Studied chemistry, London University; emigrated to America, *ante* 1834. Graduated M. D., University of Pennsylvania, 1836. Taught at Hampden-Sidney College and at New York University. Distinguished in chemical and physical research, he was also a pioneer in American photography and in promotion of long-distance telegraphy. Among his many books were the influential but now outdated *History of the Intellectual Development of Europe* (1863) and *History of the Conflict between Religion and Science* (1874).

DRAPER, LYMAN COPELAND (*b. New York State, 1815; d. Madison, Wis., 1891*), historian, collector, librarian. Resolving at the age of 23 to devote his life to writing biographies of Western heroes and to seek from their living contemporaries data to make his narratives complete, Draper journeyed extensively to find pioneer survivors, whose reminiscences, with other documentary material, filled a long series of manuscript volumes. In addition he collected account books, letters, diaries, etc., which supplemented his frontier researches. All of his materials, known as the Draper Collection, were bequeathed to the Wisconsin State Historical Society whose secretary he was, 1854–86, and were the foundation of its great historical library. He was also founder and first editor of *Wisconsin Historical Collections*.

DRAPER, MARGARET GREEN (*fl. 1750–1807*), wife of Richard Draper. Published *The Massachusetts Gazette and Weekly News-Letter*, post 1774. Strongly Loyalist, she left Boston in 1776.

DRAPER, RICHARD (*b. Boston, Mass., 1726/7; d. Boston, 1774*), printer. Son of John Draper. Succeeded father as publisher of *Boston News-Letter*, 1762, and continued it under subsequent titles, *The Boston Weekly News-Letter and New England Chronicle* and *The Massachusetts Gazette and Boston News-Letter* and others.

DRAPER, WILLIAM FRANKLIN (*b. Lowell, Mass., 1842; d. Washington, D.C., 1910*), Union soldier, manufacturer, diplomat. Grandson of Ira Draper. Partner and principal executive in the family firm manufacturing textile machinery. Congressman, Republican, from Massachusetts, 1892–97; U.S. ambassador to Italy, 1897–1900.

DRAYTON, JOHN (*b. near Charleston, S.C., 1766; d. Charleston, 1822*), South Carolina jurist, legislator, author. Son of William H. Drayton. Governor of South Carolina, 1800–02; 1808–10. Responsible for establishment of South Carolina College, 1801, opened 1805. Author of *A View of South Carolina* (1802), *Memoirs of the American Revolution* (1821).

DRAYTON, PERCIVAL (*b. South Carolina, 1812; d. Washington, D.C., 1865*), naval officer. Son of William Drayton (1776–1846). Unionist in Civil War, in which he served under Du Pont and Farragut, rising to chief of Bureau of Navigation, 1865.

DRAYTON, THOMAS FENWICK (*b. South Carolina, 1808; d. Florence, S.C., 1891*), planter, Confederate brigadier. Son of William Drayton (1776–1846). Graduated West Point, 1828. Friend of Jefferson Davis; president of Charleston and Savannah Railroad, 1853–61.

DRAYTON, WILLIAM (*b. Magnolia Plantation, South Carolina, 1732; d. 1790*), jurist. Chief justice of East Florida, 1763–77; first U.S. judge, district of South Carolina, 1789–90.

DRAYTON, WILLIAM (*b. St. Augustine, East Florida, 1776; d. Philadelphia, Pa., 1846*), lawyer, soldier. Son of William Drayton (1732–1790). Congressman, Democrat, from South Carolina, 1825–33; a foe of nullification.

DRAYTON, WILLIAM HENRY (*b. near Charleston, S.C., 1742; d. Philadelphia, Pa., 1779*), Revolutionary leader. Cousin of William Drayton (1732–1790). Educated in England, Drayton returned to South Carolina, 1764, and became a planter. He entered the Assembly in 1765. In 1769 he published articles denouncing the non-importation movement and de-

fending the right of the individual to ignore rules established without legal authority. He then went to England, where he was received as a champion of British rights. Returning to Carolina, he became a member of the Council of the province, 1772–75. In 1775 he assumed leadership of the revolutionary movement in Carolina. Elected chief justice of South Carolina in 1776, he represented the state in the Continental Congress after 1778.

DRESEL, OTTO (*b. Geisenheim, Germany, c. 1826; d. 1890*), concert-pianist, composer. Came to America, 1848. Resided in Boston, post 1852; was for many years a force in that city's musical life.

DRESSLER, MARIE (*b. Cobourg, Canada, 1871; d. 1934*), stage and screen comedian. Her greatest success was on the screen in *Anna Christie* (1930) and as "Tugboat Annie" (1933). [*Supp.* 1]

DREW, DANIEL (*b. Carmel, N.Y., 1797; d. 1879*), capitalist, speculator. Enlisted in War of 1812 to earn the $100 paid for substitutes. Became a cattle drover and horse trader. With capital supplied by Henry Astor, Drew extended his operations westward, being the first to drive cattle from Ohio, Kentucky and Illinois across the Alleghanies. In 1834 he entered the steamboat business in competition with Cornelius Vanderbilt. In 1844 he entered Wall St., where he became known as a crafty independent operator and amasser of money. Becoming director of the Erie Railroad in 1857, he shamelessly manipulated stock. His greatest business battle was the "Erie War" with Vanderbilt, 1866–68, which he waged in alliance with Jay Gould and James Fisk. *Post* 1870 his luck failed him and he went bankrupt.

DREW, GEORGIANA EMMA. [See Barrymore, Georgiana Emma Drew, 1856–1893.]

DREW, JOHN (*b. Dublin, Ireland, 1827; d. Philadelphia, Pa., 1862*), actor. Father of one of the most noted stage families of the United States; made American debut, New York, 1842.

DREW, JOHN (*b. Philadelphia, Pa., 1853; d. San Francisco, Calif., 1927*), actor. Son of John Drew (1827–1862) and Louisa L. Drew. Made his debut in Philadelphia, 1873; joined Augustin Daly's New York company, 1875; later accompanied his brother-in-law, Maurice Barrymore, in barnstorming. Drew acted exclusively with Daly's company, 1879–92; his Petruchio, opposite Ada Rehan's Kate, in *The Taming of the Shrew* was a high point of Daly's productions. Starred for the first time in Clyde Fitch's *Masked Ball*, 1892; for two decades thereafter he was managed by Charles Frohman. Best known for ease, grace and skill in high comedy acting, Drew played an important part in the growth of the modern American theatre.

DREW, LOUISA LANE (*b. London, England, 1820; d. Larchmont, N.Y., 1897*), actress, theatrical manager. Wife of John Drew (1827–1862); mother of John Drew (1853–1927) and Georgiana Drew Barrymore. Herself a versatile actress, she managed the Arch Street Theatre, Philadelphia, 1861–92.

DREXEL, ANTHONY JOSEPH (*b. Philadelphia, Pa., 1826; d. Carlsbad, Germany, 1893*), philanthropist, banker. Son of Francis M. Drexel. Partner in his father's brokerage house at 21, he guided the successful development of Drexel and Co. in the post-Civil War period. Founded the Drexel Institute, Philadelphia.

DREXEL, FRANCIS MARTIN (*b. Dornbirn, Austria, 1792; d. 1863*), artist, banker. Came to America, 1817. Established brokerage office at Louisville, Ky., 1837, which became the famous Philadelphia banking house of Drexel & Co.

DREXEL, JOSEPH WILLIAM (*b. Philadelphia, Pa., 1833; d. 1888*), banker, philanthropist. Son of Francis M. Drexel. Partner in Drexel, Harjes and Co., Paris; also Drexel, Morgan and Co., New York.

DRINKER, CATHARINE ANN. [See JANVIER, CATHARINE ANN, 1841–1922.]

DRINKWATER, JENNIE MARIA (*b. Yarmouth, Maine, 1841; d. 1900*), writer of juvenile fiction. Originator of the Shut-in-Society, *c.* 1874, for promoting correspondence to invalids.

DRIPPS, ISAAC L. (*b. Belfast, Ireland, 1810; d. 1892*), inventor, engineer. Mechanical superintendent, Camden & Amboy Railroad; later of Pennsylvania Railroad. Built the first freight-car truck of the diamond-framed pattern.

DRISLER, HENRY (*b. Staten Island, N.Y., 1818; d. 1897*), educator. Graduated Columbia, 1839, and was associated thereafter with Columbia as professor, dean and acting president. Jay professor of Greek, 1867–94, he was co-editor of a number of lexicons and textbooks with Charles Anthon and others.

DROMGOOLE, WILLIAM ALLEN (*b. Murfreesboro, Tenn., 1860; d. 1934*), author and journalist. Writer of fiction about the Negroes and mountaineers of Tennessee and also stories for children, Miss Dromgoole was a feature writer for the *Nashville Banner* post 1904. [*Supp. 1*]

DROPSIE, MOSES AARON (*b. Philadelphia, Pa., 1821; d. 1905*), lawyer. Public spirited and philanthropic, Dropsie left his entire estate for the founding of the Philadelphia college for Hebrew studies which today bears his name.

DROWN, THOMAS MESSINGER (*b. Philadelphia, Pa., 1842; d. Bethlehem, Pa., 1904*), chemist. Graduated M.D., University of Pennsylvania, 1862. Made advanced studies at Yale, Harvard and in Germany. Taught at Lafayette College and Massachusetts Institute of Technology; president, Lehigh University, 1895–1904.

DRUILLETTES, GABRIEL (*b. France, 1610; d. Quebec, Canada, 1681*), Jesuit missionary. Came to Canada, 1643; ministered to Abenakis and later to Western tribes. Author of an account of his diplomatic visits to New England, 1648 and 1651.

DRUMGOOLE, JOHN CHRISTOPHER (*b. Granard, Ireland, 1816; d. New York, N.Y., 1888*), Roman Catholic clergyman. Came to America, 1824. Devoted himself to reclaiming incorrigible children; founded Mission of the Immaculate Virgin, New York City and Staten Island.

DRURY, JOHN BENJAMIN (*b. Rhinebeck, N.Y., 1838; d. New Brunswick, N.J., 1909*), Reformed Dutch clergyman, editor.

DRYDEN, JOHN FAIRFIELD (*b. Temple Mills, Maine, 1839; d. 1911*), pioneer of industrial insurance in America. Founded Prudential Insurance Co., 1875. U.S. senator, Republican, from New Jersey, 1902–07.

DUANE, ALEXANDER (*b. Malone, N.Y., 1858; d. 1926*), ophthalmologist. Son of James C. Duane. Graduated Union, 1878; M.D., College of Physicians and Surgeons, New York, 1881.

DUANE, JAMES (*b. New York, N.Y., 1733; d. Schenectady, N.Y., 1797*), jurist. Admitted to the bar, 1754. A conservative throughout the pre-revolutionary period in New York, he was elected to the Continental Congress, 1774, and served on the committee which wrote the statement of rights of the colonists, being largely responsible for its mild tone; served in Congress almost continuously until 1783. As mayor of New York, 1784–89, he was chiefly concerned with rehabilitating the city. Became first federal judge of the district of New York, 1789.

DUANE, JAMES CHATHAM (*b. Schenectady, N.Y., 1824; d. 1897*), military and civil engineer. Grandson of James Duane. Graduated West Point, 1848. Largely responsible for design of bridges and siege works as chief engineer, Army of the Potomac. Retired as brigadier-general and chief of engineers, U.S. Army, 1888.

DUANE, WILLIAM (*b. near Lake Champlain, N.Y., 1760; d. Philadelphia, Pa., 1835*), journalist, politician. After a stormy youth in Ireland, India and England, he returned to America, 1796, and joined Benjamin Franklin Bache in publishing the *Aurora.* Under Duane, *post* 1798, this newspaper became the most powerful Jeffersonian organ. Energetic, radical and fearless, Duane materially assisted Jefferson's election in 1800. Disappointed of his hopes for advancement, he continued to edit his paper until 1822.

DUANE, WILLIAM (*b. Philadelphia, Pa., 1872; d. Devon, Pa., 1935*), physicist. Graduated at University of Pennsylvania, 1892; A.M., Harvard, 1895; Ph.D.,

Berlin, 1897. Studied radioactivity in Madame Curie's laboratory, 1907–13. On his return to the United States, worked at Harvard and with the Cancer Commission until 1934. Devised standards of measurement for dosage in the biological application of radioactivity; his proposals were internationally accepted in 1928. His most important single discovery was the "Duane-Hunt law" which states that there is a sharp upper limit to the frequency of X-rays emitted from a target under electron bombardment. [*Supp. 1*]

DUANE, WILLIAM JOHN (*b. Clonmel, Ireland, 1780; d. Philadelphia, Pa., 1865*), lawyer. Son of William Duane. Associated with father on the *Aurora* newspaper; author of numerous pamphlets on local affairs. Secretary of the treasury, 1833–35; dismissed from office for refusal to aid Jackson's bank policy.

DUBBS, JOSEPH HENRY (*b. Lehigh Co., Pa., 1838; d. 1910*), clergyman of Reformed Church (German), church historian. Professor of history, Franklin and Marshall, 1875–1910.

DUBOIS, AUGUSTUS JAY (*b. Newton Falls, O., 1849; d. 1915*), civil engineer. Professor of engineering, Sheffield Scientific School, 1884–1915. His *Elements of Graphical Statics . . .* (1875) was the first comprehensive work on this subject to appear in the United States.

DUBOIS, JOHN (*b. Paris, France, 1764; d. New York, N.Y., 1842*), Roman Catholic clergyman. Came to America, 1791. After successful missionary career in frontier Maryland, established Mt. St. Mary's at Emmitsburg, Md., 1807. Consecrated bishop of New York, 1826, he experienced great difficulties in coping with the lay trustee system.

DU BOIS, WILLIAM EWING (*b. Doylestown, Pa., 1810; d. Philadelphia, Pa., 1881*), numismatist.

DuBOSE, WILLIAM PORCHER (*b. near Winnsboro, S.C., 1836; d. Sewanee, Tenn., 1918*), Episcopal clergyman, theologian. A professor and chaplain, University of the South, 1871–1918; also held administrative posts. In the field of philosophy of the Christian religion, Du Bose was the foremost thinker in the Episcopal Church in America.

DU BOURG, LOUIS GUILLAUME VALENTIN (*b. Cap Français, Santo Domingo, 1766; d. Besançon, France, 1833*), Roman Catholic clergyman. Arriving in Baltimore, Md., 1794, he joined Sulpicians. President, Georgetown College, 1796–98; head of St. Mary's College, Baltimore, c. 1800–12, he encouraged Elizabeth Ann Seton in foundation of Sisters of Charity. Appointed Administrator Apostolic of New Orleans, c. 1812, he was consecrated bishop, 1815, but because of difficulties with local clergy governed from St. Louis, Mo., 1817–20. During his stay in St. Louis and later at New Orleans, he was responsible for extensive building of churches and seminaries and the introduction of teaching orders of nuns and

priests. He resigned his see February 1825 and returned to Europe the following year.

DUBUQUE, JULIEN (*b. St. Pierre les Brecquets, Canada, 1762; d. Iowa, 1810*), first white settler of Iowa. As early as 1785 was at Prairie du Chien, Wis.; won permission in 1788 from a band of Fox Indians to work lead mines in the Iowa country.

DU CHAILLU, PAUL BELLONI (*b. France, 1835; d. St. Petersburg, Russia, 1903*), African explorer. Came to America, 1852. Traveled through tropical Africa, 1856–59, 1863–65. Author of *Explorations and Adventures in Equatorial Africa* (1861), *Stories of the Gorilla Country* (1868) and other books.

DUCHÉ, JACOB (*b. Philadelphia, Pa., 1737/8; d. Philadelphia, 1798*), Anglican clergyman, Loyalist. Chaplain of Continental Congress. Author of *Caspipina's Letters* (1774; published in periodical form, 1772), sermons and other works. Renounced revolutionary sympathies, 1777.

DUCHESNE, ROSE PHILIPPINE (*b. Grenoble, France, 1769; d. St. Charles, Mo., 1852*), teacher, pioneer. Coming to America in 1818 as a religious of the Society of the Sacred Heart, she founded schools of that society in Missouri and Louisiana; also served as a missionary to Indians in Kansas.

DUDLEY, BENJAMIN WINSLOW (*b. Spotsylvania Co., Va., 1785; d. near Lexington, Ky., 1870*), surgeon. Graduated M.D., University of Pennsylvania, 1806; studied also in London. Practiced in Kentucky until 1853. Known for his operation for bladder stone in which he was more successful than any surgeon until that time.

DUDLEY, CHARLES BENJAMIN (*b. Oxford, N.Y., 1842; d. 1909*). Chemist to the Pennsylvania Railroad Co. after 1875, he was the first person to apply chemistry to railroad economy, efficiency and safety problems.

DUDLEY, CHARLES EDWARD (*b. Stafford, England, 1780; d. Albany, N.Y., 1841*), politician. Often mayor of Albany and a loyal member of the "Albany Regency," he served as U.S. senator, Democrat, from New York, 1829–33.

DUDLEY, EDWARD BISHOP (*b. Onslow Co., N.C., 1789; d. Wilmington, N.C., 1855*), businessman, politician. Congressman, Democrat, from North Carolina, 1829–31; Whig governor, 1837–40. Founder and president of the Wilmington & Weldon Railroad.

DUDLEY, JOSEPH (*b. Roxbury, Mass., 1647; d. Roxbury, 1720*), politician. Son of Thomas Dudley. Graduated Harvard, 1665. Served in the General Court, 1673–76, and, after King Philip's War, in the upper house of the legislature until 1684. When the Massachusetts Charter was revoked, Dudley became president of the Council and governor of Massachusetts, New Hampshire and the King's Province.

Replaced by Andros in 1686, he helped enforce unpopular laws passed under the new governor, thus winning New England's hatred. After a brief period as chief of the Council of New York (1691–92) and some years abroad, Dudley became governor of Massachusetts in 1702. He immediately entered upon a struggle with the General Court over salary and prerogatives which continued until his retirement, 1715.

DUDLEY, PAUL (*b. Roxbury, Mass., 1675; d. Roxbury, 1751*), jurist. Son of Joseph Dudley. Massachusetts attorney-general, 1702–18; judge of superior court, 1718–45; chief justice, 1745–51. Founder of Dudleian lectures at Harvard.

DUDLEY, THOMAS (*b. Northampton, England, 1576; d. Roxbury, Mass., 1653*), governor of the colony of Massachusetts Bay. Steward to the Earl of Lincoln, parishioner of John Cotton, Dudley emigrated to Massachusetts, 1630, on the *Arbella*. Deputy-governor under Gov. Winthrop, he resented Winthrop's move of the colony from Newtown to Boston and fixed his own residence at Roxbury. Throughout his life he was almost constantly in public office. He was elected governor in 1634, 1640, 1645, and 1650. Dogmatic, austere, Dudley dominated the community by sheer strength of will.

DUDLEY, WILLIAM RUSSEL (*b. Guilford, Conn., 1849; d. 1911*), botanist. Taught at Cornell, Indiana and Leland Stanford. Active in conservation; founder of the Dudley Herbarium.

DUER, JOHN (*b. Albany, N.Y., 1782; d. Staten Island, N.Y., 1858*), jurist. Son of William Duer. Served on commission to revise New York statutes, 1825–27; judge, superior court, New York City, 1849–58.

DUER, WILLIAM (*b. Devonshire, England, 1747; d. New York, N.Y., 1799*), merchant, financier. Settled in America, *post* 1773. A patriot, he served in the New York constitutional convention, 1776, and on the Committee of Public Safety. Member of the Continental Congress, 1777–79. Grown rich, he entered on extensive speculations and was instrumental in establishing the Bank of New York, 1784. Secretary to the Board of the Treasury *post* 1786, and briefly assistant secretary of the U.S. Treasury, 1789–90, he continued personal dealings and was prime mover in the Scioto land speculation and others. His insolvency and arrest for debt in 1792 precipitated New York's first financial panic.

DUER, WILLIAM ALEXANDER (*b. Rhinebeck, N.Y., 1780; d. Morristown, N.J., 1858*), jurist, educator. Son of William Duer; grandson of Gen. William Alexander. Judge, N.Y., supreme court, 1822–29; president, Columbia College, 1829–42.

DUFF, MARY ANN DYKE (*b. London, England, 1794; d. New York, N.Y., 1857*), actress. Made American debut, 1810, at Boston; at her best in tragedy, appeared mainly in the South *post* 1835.

DUFFIELD, GEORGE (*b. Lancaster Co., Pa., 1732; d. Philadelphia, Pa., 1790*), Presbyterian clergyman. A "New Side" Presbyterian, he was chaplain of the Pennsylvania militia and also to the Continental Congress; later pastor, Third Church, Philadelphia.

DUFFIELD, GEORGE (*b. Strasburg, Pa., 1794; d. Detroit, Mich., 1868*), Presbyterian clergyman. Grandson of George Duffield (1732–1790). Pastor at Carlisle, Pa., dismissed for views expressed in *Spiritual Life: or, Regeneration* (1832), he had a successful ministry thereafter in Detroit, Mich.

DUFFIELD, SAMUEL AUGUSTUS WILLOUGHBY (*b. Brooklyn, N.Y., 1843; d. 1887*), Presbyterian clergyman, hymnologist. Grandson of George Duffield (1794–1868).

DUFFY, FRANCIS PATRICK (*b. Cobourg, Canada, 1871; d. New York, N.Y., 1932*), Roman Catholic clergyman, chaplain of the "Fighting 69th" New York regiment in World War I. [*Supp. 1*]

DUFOUR, JOHN JAMES (*b. Chatelard, Switzerland, c. 1763; d. Vevay, Ind., 1827*), pioneer viticulturist. Came to America, 1796, and set up vineyards in Kentucky which failed; later his vineyard colony merged with another at Vevay, Ind. He wrote *The American Vine Dresser's Guide* (1826).

DUGANNE, AUGUSTINE JOSEPH HICKEY (*b. Boston, Mass., 1823; d. New York, N.Y., 1884*), journalist. Author of adventure stories, popular manuals, plays, dime novels and other miscellaneous writings, of which *Parnassus in Pillory* (1851) and *Camp and Prisons* (1865) have some value.

DUGDALE, RICHARD LOUIS (*b. Paris, France, 1841; d. 1883*), social economist. Came to America, 1851. Attended night classes at Cooper Union, and, interested in sociological subjects, worked for the Prison Association of New York, *post* 1868. Struck with the consanguinity of many criminals, he used private funds to study one large family connection and published "The Jukes, A Study in Crime, Pauperism, Disease and Heredity" (1875) in a Prison Association report. Dugdale believed inheritance was more important in determining character than environment.

DUGUÉ, CHARLES OSCAR (*b. New Orleans, La., 1821; d. Paris, France, 1872*), Creole poet and dramatist, educator.

DUHRING, LOUIS ADOLPHUS (*b. Philadelphia, Pa., 1845; d. Philadelphia, 1913*), dermatologist. Published several pioneer works on dermatology, among them a *Practical Treatise on Diseases of the Skin* (1877), the first American textbook in the field.

DUKE, BASIL WILSON (*b. Scott Co., Ky., 1838; d. 1916*), lawyer, Confederate soldier. Served with

John Hunt Morgan's "Lexington Rifles"; published *History of Morgan's Cavalry* (1867).

DUKE, BENJAMIN NEWTON (*b. near Durham, N.C., 1855; d. New York, N.Y., 1929*), industrialist. Brother of James B. Duke, with whom he was associated in business; active *post* 1906 in Southern railroad, power and manufacturing enterprises. Benefactor of Duke University.

DUKE, JAMES BUCHANAN (*b. near Durham, N.C., 1856; d. 1925*), industrialist. Just after the Civil War, Washington Duke and his sons Benjamin and James began to retail tobacco off their own farm; by 1889 the firm was producing more than half the cigarettes sold in the United States. Backed by Eastern financiers, James B. Duke monopolized the American retail tobacco trade, merging competitors into a series of combines which bore at last the title of the American Tobacco Co. In 1911, the Supreme Court ordered Duke's company dissolved as in restraint of trade; its constituents then continued business as normal competitors. Duke created the Southern Power Co. to develop the water-power of the Southern Piedmont; in 1924 he assigned these holdings in trust for Duke University and for other charitable purposes.

DULANY, DANIEL (*b. Queen's Co., Ireland, 1685; d. Annapolis, Md., 1753*), lawyer. Emigrated to Maryland, 1703. As attorney-general and a member of the Maryland Legislative Assembly, he led the fight against the proprietary government for introduction of English statutes into colony law, c. 1722–32. Thereafter, he held a number of high provincial offices.

DULANY, DANIEL (*b. Annapolis, Md., 1722; d. Baltimore, Md., 1797*), lawyer. Son of Daniel Dulany (1685–1753). Educated at Eton, Cambridge and the Middle Temple. Opposed popular measures as a member of Maryland Assembly. In Stamp Act crisis, issued *Considerations on the Propriety of Imposing Taxes in the British Colonies* (1765) in support of colonial representation, yet later opposed American revolutionary action and was deprived of his property as a Loyalist.

DULUTH, DANIEL GREYSOLON, Sieur (*b. St. Germain-en-Laye, France, 1636; d. Montreal, Canada, 1710*), explorer. Cousin of Henry de Tonty. Visited Montreal about 1674 and returned to France. He soon came back to Montreal and in 1678 set out to explore Lake Superior and routes westward. He succeeded in reconciling the Chippewa and Sioux who barred the way, meeting their chiefs near the site of present Duluth, Minn. 1679; he also made alliance with the Sioux and took possession of their territory for Louis XIV. From 1680 to 1690 Duluth made several futile efforts to explore westward from Lake Superior; however, no one did more to establish French control over the Northwest. He retired about 1695 and spent his last years in Montreal. One

of the great French explorers, Duluth sought not gain but knowledge in his travels.

DUMMER, JEREMIAH (*b. Newbury, Mass., 1645; d. 1718*), silversmith, engraver, portrait-painter, magistrate. A leading citizen of Boston, he produced some of the finest ecclesiastical and convivial silver pieces of his period.

DUMMER, JEREMIAH (*b. Boston, Mass., c. 1679; d. Plaistow, England, 1739*), colonial agent, author. Son of Jeremiah Dummer (1645–1718). Graduated Harvard, 1699; studied in Utrecht until 1703. Returning to Massachusetts, he found no occupation there and went to England where he remained and prospered at the law. Became the Massachusetts colonial agent, 1710; also agent for Connecticut, 1712. He persuaded Elihu Yale to bestow money on the college which bears his name. In 1715, when Parliament attacked colonial charters, Dummer wrote his *Defence of the New England Charters* (printed in 1721). His refusal to endorse complaints made by the colony against Gov. Shute led to dismissal as Massachusetts agent, 1721. He remained agent for Connecticut until 1730.

DUN, ROBERT GRAHAM (*b. Chillicothe, O., 1826; d. 1900*). Began as employee of Tappan's Mercantile Agency, New York, 1850; became sole owner of the credit rating agency, 1859, which he conducted as R. G. Dun and Co.

DUNBAR, CHARLES FRANKLIN (*b. Abington, Mass., 1830; d. 1900*), editor, economist. First professor of political economy at Harvard, c. 1869–1900, he edited the *Quarterly Journal of Economics,* the first American periodical exclusively devoted to economic science. He was active also in the general administration of the university.

DUNBAR, MOSES (*b. Wallingford, Conn., 1746; d. near Hartford, Conn., 1777*), only person ever executed in Connecticut for treason. A Loyalist and an Episcopalian, he was convicted of recruiting for the British service.

DUNBAR, PAUL LAURENCE (*b. Dayton, O., 1872; d. Dayton, 1906*), poet. Both his parents had been slaves in Kentucky. Printed at his own expense his first book of poems, *Oak and Ivy* (1893). His second book, *Majors and Minors* (1895), was reviewed enthusiastically by W. D. Howells. *Lyrics of Lowly Life* (1896) was introduced by Howells who described Dunbar as the first man of African descent and American training to feel Negro life esthetically and express it lyrically.

DUNBAR, ROBERT (*b. Carnbee, Scotland, 1812; d. Buffalo, N.Y., 1890*), engineer, inventor. Raised in Canada. Expert in the design and construction of grain elevators, he contributed to Buffalo's development as a major grain market after his removal to that city in 1834.

DUNBAR, WILLIAM (*b. near Elgin, Scotland, 1749; d. near Natchez, Miss., 1810*), planter, scientist. Coming to America in 1771, Dunbar established a plantation in the then British province of West Florida, 1773; after destruction of this plantation by a series of raids and other misfortunes, he built another near Natchez in 1792. Prospering through scientific improvements in farming methods, he was soon able to devote much time to scientific investigation. First surveyor general of his area and its first meteorological observer, he was a friend and correspondent of Jefferson and a member of the American Philosophical Society. At Jefferson's request, Dunbar with George Hunter explored the Oachita River country (1804) and was the first to give a scientific account of the Hot Springs; in 1805, he was appointed to explore the region bordering on the Red River.

DUNCAN, ISADORA (*b. San Francisco, Calif., 1878; d. Nice, France, 1927*), dancer. The first in modern times to make her profession a creative art and a medium of esthetic expression. Author of the autobiography *My Life* (1927) and *The Art of the Dance* (1928).

DUNCAN, JAMES (*b. Kincardine Co., Scotland, 1857; d. 1928*), labor leader. Came to America, *c.* 1880. A long-time associate of Samuel Gompers, Duncan played a prominent part in the American Federation of Labor during its formative period and was its first vice-president, 1900–28. [*Supp. 1*]

DUNCAN, JOSEPH (*b. Paris, Ky., 1794; d. Jacksonville, Ill., 1844*), farmer, politician. Removed to Illinois, 1818. Congressman, Democrat, 1827–34; governor, 1834–38. Subsequently an unsuccessful Whig candidate for the governorship, he was a consistent advocate of public education.

DUNCAN, ROBERT KENNEDY (*b. Brantford, Canada, 1868; d. 1914*), chemist. A well-known popular interpreter of science, he advocated a system of industrial fellowships and inspired the foundation of the Mellon Institute of Industrial Research at University of Pittsburgh.

DUNGLISON, ROBLEY (*b. Keswick, England, 1798; d. Philadelphia, Pa., 1869*), medical writer, teacher. Made studies in Edinburgh, Paris, London and Erlangen. Came to America, 1825. Taught at Universities of Virginia and Maryland, and was professor at Jefferson Medical College, 1836–68. A voluminous writer and attractive lecturer, he was a pioneer in systematic teaching of physiology.

DUNHAM, HENRY MORTON (*b. North Bridgewater, Mass., 1853; d. 1929*), composer, organist, educator. Teacher at New England Conservatory of Music, 1875–1929. Published two books on organ technique. His organ sonatas are widely known.

DUNIWAY, ABIGAIL JANE SCOTT (*b. near Groveland, Ill., 1834; d. 1915*), leader of the woman suffrage movement in the Pacific Northwest. Removed to Oregon, 1852. Engaged in business in Portland, she edited a newspaper, *The New Northwest*, 1871–87, in support of equal rights for women, thereafter continuing her efforts through political action.

DUNLAP, JOHN (*b. Strabane, Ireland, 1747; d. Philadelphia, Pa., 1812*), printer. Came to America *c.* 1757. Publisher of *The Pennsylvania Packet*, post 1771, which became (1784) the first daily newspaper in the United States. Also printed first broadside Declaration of Independence and the Constitution of the United States.

DUNLAP, ROBERT PINCKNEY (*b. Brunswick, Maine, 1794; d. Brunswick, 1859*), lawyer. Democratic governor of Maine, 1834–38; instrumental in obtaining prison reforms, an insane asylum and the first geological survey of Maine.

DUNLAP, WILLIAM (*b. Perth Amboy, N.J., 1766; d. New York, N.Y., 1839*), playwright, theatrical manager, painter, historian. Showing early artistic promise, Dunlap studied briefly under Benjamin West in London, returning to America *c.* 1787 fired with a new interest, the stage. For numerous plays written and adapted between this period and about 1805, he has an important place in the history of American drama. Between 1796 and 1805, he was proprietor and manager of New York's John Street and Park theatres but met with indifferent financial reward and eventual bankruptcy. Turning again to painting, he served also as assistant to the new manager of the Park Theatre, 1806–11, was employed by the government and had some success as a portrait painter. After 1821, he exhibited a series of subject paintings, and in 1826 helped found the National Academy of Design. In addition to all this he was author of various valuable biographies and histories. These include *Memoirs of George Fred. Cooke* (1813); *Life of Charles Brockden Brown* (1815); *History of the American Theatre* (1832); and *History of the Rise and Progress of the Arts of Design in the United States* (1834).

DUNLOP, JAMES (*b. Chambersburg, Pa., 1795; d. Baltimore, Md., 1856*), lawyer. Author of *The General Laws of Pennsylvania, 1700–1846* (1847).

DUNMORE, JOHN MURRAY, Earl of (*b. Scotland, 1732; d. Ramsgate, England, 1809*), colonial administrator. Appointed governor of New York, 1770; eleven months after arrival in October, was appointed governor of Virginia. At first popular, Dunmore offended patriots, 1773, by dissolving House of Burgesses for proposing a committee of correspondence on colonial grievances; in 1774, he again dissolved the House after a dispute over Boston Port Bill. Despite these local difficulties he called out militia to engage hostile Shawnees on frontier of the province and led with Andrew Lewis a successful campaign (1774) against Cornstalk known as "Lord Dunmore's War." As revolutionary activity increased in Virginia, he opposed it by force rather than finesse, undertaking several abortive raids against patriot forces in the fall and winter of 1775. In July 1776 he returned to England.

DUNN, CHARLES (*b. Bullitt's Old Lick, Ky., 1799; d. Mineral Point, Wis., 1872*), lawyer, jurist. Removed to Illinois, 1819. Chief justice of territory of Wisconsin, 1836–48; a Democrat, he also served in the Wisconsin legislature, 1853–56.

DUNN, WILLIAM McKEE (*b. Hanover, Ind., 1814; d. Fairfax Co., Va., 1887*), lawyer, Union soldier. Judge-advocate general, U.S. Army, 1875–81.

DUNN, WILLIAMSON (*b. near Crow's Station, Ky., 1781; d. 1854*), Indiana pioneer, soldier. Removed to present Hanover, Ind., 1809. Served in important public offices, and in the state legislature; gave land to establish Hanover College and Wabash College.

DUNNE, FINLEY PETER (*b. Chicago, Ill., 1867; d. New York, N.Y., 1936*), author, humorist. While working on the Chicago *Post* in 1892 he wrote some Irish dialect pieces, his protagonist being "Colonel McNeery," modeled after an actual Chicago saloon keeper. Increasingly Dunne used the character as a vehicle for his social and political observations; on Oct. 7, 1893, his spokesman became "Mr. Martin Dooley." The genial bartender, with his homely democratic philosophy, his tolerance, his dislike of sham, became increasingly popular. Dooley's first appearance in book form, *Mr. Dooley in Peace and War* (1898), was an instant success at home and abroad. Half a dozen collections of Dooley pieces followed. In 1900 Dunne moved to New York, where he became a contributor to *Collier's,* the *American Magazine,* and other publications. [*Supp.* 2]

DUNNING, ALBERT ELIJAH (*b. Brookfield, Conn., 1844; d. Brookline, Mass., 1923*), Congregational clergyman. Secretary of the Congregational Sunday School and Publishing Society, 1881–89; editor, *The Congregationalist,* 1889–1911.

DUNNING, WILLIAM ARCHIBALD (*b. Plainfield, N.J., 1857; d. 1922*), historian. Graduated Columbia, 1881; Ph.D., 1885. Taught history at Columbia. A founder of the American Historical Association, Dunning was among the first to make a scholarly investigation of the Civil War and Reconstruction.

DUNSTER, HENRY (*b. Bury, England, 1609; d. Scituate, Mass., 1658/9?*), first president of Harvard College, 1640–54. Established rules of admission and of granting degrees; shaped college according to form of English universities. Resigning because of Baptist principles, he served as minister in Scituate.

DUNWOODY, WILLIAM HOOD (*b. Westtown, Pa., 1841; d. Minneapolis, Minn., 1914*), merchant miller, financier. During 1877, established permanent trade in flour and wheat between Europe and America; present U.S. export flour business is result of his work. Endowed the Dunwoody Industrial Institute, Minneapolis.

DU PONCEAU, PIERRE ÉTIENNE (*b. St.-Martin, France, 1760; d. Philadelphia, Pa., 1844*), lawyer, author. Came to America, 1777, as secretary to Baron Steuben and served in Revolution as aide to Steuben and Greene. Admitted to the bar in 1785, he became America's leading expert on international law and practice. Author of various legal treatises and valuable early works on history and philology, particularly of the Indians.

DU PONT, ALFRED IRÉNÉE (*b. near Wilmington, Del., 1864; d. Jacksonville, Fla., 1935*), manufacturer. Grandson of Eleuthère I. du Pont. With cousins Thomas C. and Pierre S. du Pont, incorporated the family powder company in 1902.

[*Supp.* 1]

DU PONT, ELEUTHÈRE IRÉNÉE (*b. Paris, France, 1771; d. Philadelphia, Pa., 1834*), manufacturer. Worked under Lavoisier at French royal powder works. Came to America, 1799, with father, Pierre Samuel du Pont de Nemours, a publisher and a member of the physiocratic school of economists. After making a study of American gunpowder manufacture and noting the poor quality of the powder produced, Irénée decided that a small efficient plant would yield substantial profit. Securing machinery from France, he established a powder works near Wilmington, Del., 1802. The War of 1812 assured success of the enterprise.

DU PONT, HENRY (*b. Wilmington, Del., 1812; d. 1889*), manufacturer. Son of Eleuthère Irénée du Pont. Graduated West Point, 1833. Presided over the family firm, 1850–89, expanding its activities through the Civil War and after.

DU PONT, HENRY ALGERNON (*b. near Wilmington, Del., 1838; d. 1926*), Union soldier, industrialist. Son of Henry du Pont. Graduated West Point, 1861. Congressional Medal winner in Civil War. Entered family business, 1878, and in 1899 brought to fruition his plan to incorporate it so as to retain family control. U.S. senator from Delaware, 1906–17.

DU PONT, SAMUEL FRANCIS (*b. Bergen Point, N.J., 1803; d. Philadelphia, Pa., 1865*), naval officer. Son of Victor du Pont. Appointed midshipman, 1815. During the Mexican War, commanded Commodore Stockton's flagship and later sloop *Cyane* in California operations. For two decades thereafter he was concerned with improvements in naval education, national defense, lighthouse maintenance, and service personnel efficiency. He was promoted captain, 1855. Assigned to command South Atlantic blockading squadron, 1861, he occupied Port Royal, South Carolina, November 1861, in a notable fleet action against shore defenses; also occupied Beaufort and Tybee Island. Promoted rear admiral, July 1862. After failure to take Charleston, 1863, he was relieved by Adm. John A. Dahlgren and began a long controversy with Secretary of the Navy Welles over responsibility for the failure.

DU PONT, THOMAS COLEMAN (*b. Louisville, Ky., 1863; d. 1930*), capitalist. Merged all military powder plants in super-holding company, E. I. du Pont de Nemours Co.; interested financially in many industries. Cousin of Alfred I. Du Pont. [*Supp. 1*]

DU PONT, VICTOR MARIE (*b. Paris, France, 1767; d. Philadelphia, Pa., 1827*), diplomat, manufacturer. Brother of Eleuthère I. du Pont. Attaché to the first French legation in the United States, 1787; second secretary of the legation, 1791. French consul-general in the United States, 1798. Settled in America, 1800; for a time, tried to establish a commission business. After a land development project in New York failed, he became the active director of woolen-mills erected by his brother.

DUPRATZ, ANTOINE SIMON LE PAGE (*fl. 1718–1758*), pioneer, historian. Author of *Histoire de la Louisiane* (1758).

DUPUY, ELIZA ANN (*b. Petersburg, Va., 1814; d. New Orleans, La., 1881*), novelist.

DURAND, ASHER BROWN (*b. Jefferson Village, N.J., 1796; d. Jefferson Village, 1886*), engraver, painter. Apprenticed to Peter Maverick, 1812; met Samuel Waldo who instructed him in portrait work. In partnership with Maverick, engraved Trumbull's "Signing of the Declaration of Independence" (1820–23), which established his reputation. His engraving of Vanderlyn's "Ariadne" created a stir in American artistic circles. Durand also produced many superior engraved portraits of eminent men and also banknote designs which established a tradition still apparent in our currency. *Post* 1836, he became a professional painter, producing illustrations for books and landscapes greatly esteemed in their time. Durand was identified with every contemporary movement to foster American arts.

DURAND, CYRUS (*b. Jefferson Village, N.J., 1787; d. Irvington, N.J., 1868*), engraver, inventor. To execute his brother Asher B. Durand's designs for banknotes, he invented several machines for ruling geometrical patterns.

DURAND, ÉLIE MAGLOIRE (*b. Mayenne, France, 1794; d. 1873*), pharmacist, botanist. Came to America, 1816. Conducted a celebrated drugstore in Philadelphia, 1825–52. Made extensive botanical collections which he presented to the Paris Jardin des Plantes, the Philadelphia Academy of Natural Sciences and other public institutions. He also wrote memoirs of F. A. Michaux and Thomas Nuttall.

DURANT, CHARLES FERSON (*b. New York, N.Y., 1805; d. 1873*), aeronaut, scientist. The first professional American aeronaut; made balloon flights in New York, 1830–33; also at Albany, Baltimore and Boston.

DURANT, HENRY (*b. Acton, Mass., 1802; d. Oakland, Calif., 1875*), Congregational clergyman. Graduated Yale, 1827. Held pastorate in Byfield, Mass., and was principal of Dummer Academy until 1853 when he removed to California to conduct a school in Oakland. First president, 1870–72, University of California, which he helped to found. Twice mayor of Oakland.

DURANT, HENRY FOWLE (*b. Hanover, N.H., 1822; d. 1881*), lawyer, evangelist. Successful at the Boston bar, he became a revivalist preacher *c.* 1864 and gave his fortune to found Wellesley College, whose early development he guided.

DURANT, THOMAS CLARK (*b. Lee, Mass., 1820; d. North Creek, N.Y., 1885*), a financier and builder of the Union Pacific Railroad. With Henry Farnam, built several Midwestern railroads; alone sponsored 1863 surveys of routes for the railroad to the Pacific. Became vice-president of the Union Pacific, 1863, and was chief manager of the railroad until 1869. When New York capitalists failed to subscribe funds for the road, Durant organized and was president of the Crédit Mobilier, a funding organization, 1864. A struggle between Boston and New York capitalists for control of the Crédit Mobilier and the road now ensued. Durant, although ousted from the Crédit Mobilier, continued to supervise construction. Two weeks after he joined Leland Stanford in driving the "last spike," May 10, 1869, he was dropped from the directorate of the road.

DURANT, THOMAS JEFFERSON (*b. Philadelphia, Pa., 1817; d. Washington, D.C., 1882*), lawyer, politician. Practiced in New Orleans. A Unionist throughout the Civil War, he was distinguished for his successful argument in the Slaughterhouse Cases, 1873.

DURBIN, JOHN PRICE (*b. Bourbon Co., Ky., 1800; d. New York, N.Y., 1876*), Methodist clergyman. Secretary of the Missionary Society, 1850–72.

DURELL, EDWARD HENRY (*b. Portsmouth, N.H., 1810; d. Schoharie, N.Y., 1887*), jurist. Removed to New Orleans, La., 1837, where he practiced and held local office. A Unionist and U.S. judge, 1863–74, he issued the famous 1872 "midnight order" declaring the Louisiana Democratic electoral board illegal and so enabling the Republicans to win control of the state government.

DURFEE, JOB (*b. Tiverton, R.I., 1790; d. Tiverton, 1847*), jurist, author. Graduated Brown, 1813. Justice, supreme court of Rhode Island, 1833–35; chief justice, 1835–47.

DURFEE, THOMAS (*b. Tiverton, R.I., 1826; d. Providence, R.I., 1901*), jurist. Son of Job Durfee. Graduated Brown, 1846. Justice, supreme court of Rhode Island, 1865–75; chief justice, 1875–91. His *Treatise on the Law of Highways* (1857) was a standard work.

DURFEE, WILLIAM FRANKLIN (*b. New Bedford, Mass., 1833; d. 1899*), engineer, inventor. Supervised at Wyandotte, Mich., 1864, the manufacture of the first Bessemer steel produced in America; expert also in copper refining, wrought-iron casting and machinery design. Cousin of Zoheth S. Durfee.

DURFEE, ZOHETH SHERMAN (*b. New Bedford, Mass., 1831; d. Providence, R.I., 1880*), inventor, manufacturer. Led to believe that William Kelly was the real inventor of the "Bessemer process," Durfee (with Capt. E. B. Ward) gained control of Kelly's patents, 1861. With Ward and a cousin, William F. Durfee, he formed the Kelly Pneumatic Process Co. In 1864 he gained American control of Robert Mushet's invention for using spiegeleisen as a recarburizing agent. In 1865 persons holding license under Bessemer's patents joined with Durfee in the Pneumatic Steel Association; Durfee was its secretary and treasurer until his death. He originated the use of the cupola instead of a reverberatory furnace for melting pig iron for the converter charge. Interested throughout his life in manufacturing steel, Durfee protected Kelly's interests.

DURHAM, CALEB WHEELER (*b. Tunkhannock, Pa., 1848; d. Peekskill, N.Y., 1910*), engineer, inventor. Invented, 1880, the Durham System for house drainage, using screw-jointed pipe to provide a tight, rigid installation.

DURIVAGE, FRANCIS ALEXANDER (*b. Boston, Mass., 1814; d. 1881*), author, journalist, playwright.

DURKEE, JOHN (*b. Windham, Conn., 1728; d. Norwich, Conn., 1782*), Revolutionary soldier. Led Connecticut emigrants to Wyoming Valley, Pa., and settled Wilkes-Barre, 1769.

DURRETT, REUBEN THOMAS (*b. Henry Co., Ky., 1824; d. Louisville, Ky., 1913*), lawyer, historian. Practiced in Louisville, 1850–80; thereafter built up a magnificent library on Western history and founded the Filson Club, 1884.

DURRIE, DANIEL STEELE (*b. Albany, N.Y., 1819; d. Madison, Wis., 1892*). Librarian of the State Historical Society of Wisconsin *post* 1856; with Lyman Draper built up an outstanding collection of historical sources there.

DURYEA, CHARLES EDGAR (*b. near Canton, Ill., 1861; d. Philadelphia, Pa., 1938*), inventor, automobile manufacturer. Began his career in the bicycle trade, inventing several devices, and launching his own business in Peoria, Ill., moving later to Springfield, Mass. By 1891 he had designed a motor-driven carriage and a gas engine, and with his brother J. Frank built the first successful American car; it was demonstrated in Springfield in September 1893. An improved car, largely of Frank's design, won several races at home and abroad, 1895–96. The Duryea Motor Wagon Co. made the first sale of an American built automobile in 1896. The brothers parted company in 1898. Charles Duryea later organized the Duryea Power Co., manufacturing until 1914 a three-cylinder car. His brother developed the Stevens-Duryea (1903–14). [*Supp. 2*]

DURYEA, HARMANUS BARKULO (*b. Brooklyn, N.Y., 1863; d. Saranac Lake, N.Y., 1916*), yachtsman, breeder of race horses.

DURYÉE, ABRAM (*b. New York, N.Y., 1815; d. New York, 1890*), merchant, Union soldier. Colonel, 5th New York Regiment (Duryée Zouaves) in Civil War.

DU SIMITIÈRE, PIERRE EUGÈNE (*b. Geneva, Switzerland, c. 1736; d. Philadelphia, Pa., 1784*), artist, antiquary.

DUSSER de BARENNE, JOANNES GREGORIUS (*b. Brielle, Netherlands, 1885; d. Boston, Mass., 1940*), physiologist. M.D., University of Amsterdam, 1909; came to America, 1930. Professor at Yale, 1930–40. Pioneering investigator of the functional divisions and interrelations of the cerebral cortex. [*Supp. 2*]

DUSTIN, HANNAH (*b. Haverhill, Mass., 1657*), pioneer. Survivor of Indian raid on Haverhill, 1697; escaped after herself killing and scalping ten Indians.

DUTTON, CLARENCE EDWARD (*b. Wallingford, Conn., 1841; d. Englewood, N.J., 1912*), Union soldier, geologist. On detail to U.S. Geological Survey, 1875–90, Dutton studied plateau region of Utah and Arizona; was leading advocate of doctrine of isostasy.

DUTTON, HENRY (*b. Watertown, Conn., 1796; d. New Haven, Conn., 1869*), jurist. Kent professor of law at Yale, *post* 1847.

DUTTON, SAMUEL TRAIN (*b. Hillsboro, N.H., 1849; d. 1919*), educator. Graduated Yale, 1873. A national figure in education, he was superintendent of schools, New Haven, Conn., and Brookline, Mass.; professor of administration, Teachers College, Columbia, 1900–15.

DUVAL, WILLIAM POPE (*b. near Richmond, Va., 1784; d. Washington, D.C., 1854*), lawyer, politician. First judge, superior court of East Florida, 1821; civil governor, 1822–34. Outstanding achievement was the peaceable removal of Seminole Indians to South Florida.

DUVALL, GABRIEL (*b. Prince George's Co., Md., 1752; d. Prince George's Co., 1844*), Revolutionary soldier, jurist. Admitted to the bar, 1778. Elected to Maryland House of Delegates, 1787; congressman, Democratic-Republican, from Maryland, 1794–96. Became first comptroller of the treasury, 1802. Appointed to the U.S. Supreme Court by President Madison, 1811, he remained in office until 1835. Although supporting Marshall's constitutional views generally, he dissented from the chief justice in *Trustees of Dartmouth College* vs. *Woodward.*
[*Supp.* 1]

DUVENECK, FRANK (*b. Covington, Ky., 1848; d. Cincinnati, O., 1919*), painter, etcher, sculptor, teacher. Trained as ecclesiastical decorator in Cincinnati; studied at Royal Academy, Munich, 1870–72 and 1875–77. Early celebrated for technical skill and emotional quality in his work. As a teacher successively in Munich, Florence and Venice, his influence on a generation of American painters was great and good. Returning to America, 1888, he continued his fruitful career as teacher in Cincinnati. Several sculptures, among them a monument to his wife, indicate Duveneck's talent in this field. It was said of him that he had the greatest talent of the brush in his generation.

DUYCKINCK, EVERT AUGUSTUS (*b. New York, N.Y., 1816; d. New York, 1878*), editor, critic. Graduated Columbia, 1835. Edited two outstanding literary magazines, *Arcturus*, 1840–42, and the *Literary World*, 1847 and 1848–53. With brother George, edited *Cyclopædia of American Literature*, 1855.

DUYCKINCK, GEORGE LONG (*b. New York, N.Y., 1823; d. New York, 1863*). Brother and literary associate of Evert A. Duyckinck; active in Episcopal Sunday School work.

DWENGER, JOSEPH (*b. in/near Stallotown, O., 1837; d. Fort Wayne, Ind., 1893*), Roman Catholic clergyman. Ordained, 1859; member of Congregation of the Most Precious Blood. Bishop of Fort Wayne, 1872–93, he built up a highly efficient parochial school system there.

DWIGHT, BENJAMIN WOODBRIDGE (*b. New Haven, Conn., 1816; d. 1889*), educator, Presbyterian clergyman. Brother of Theodore W. Dwight.

DWIGHT, EDMUND (*b. Springfield, Mass., 1780; d. 1849*), merchant, manufacturer, philanthropist. Established three manufacturing centers in the Connecticut Valley at Chicopee Falls, Chicopee and Holyoke; erected cotton mills. Promoted Western Railroad from Worcester to Albany. Helped devise Massachusetts School Law of 1837; patron of Horace Mann.

DWIGHT, FRANCIS (*b. Springfield, Mass., 1808; d. 1845*), lawyer, educator. Published *District School Journal of the State of New York, post* 1840, the organ of the state common-school system.

DWIGHT, HARRISON GRAY OTIS (*b. Conway, Mass., 1803; d. near Bennington, Vt., 1862*). Resided chiefly in Constantinople as "missionary to Armenians," 1834–62; one of the first American students of Armenian.

DWIGHT, HENRY OTIS (*b. Constantinople, Turkey, 1843; d. Roselle, N.J., 1917*), Congregational missionary, editor. Son of Harrison G. O. Dwight. Author of books on Turkey; editor, *Turkish and English Lexicon* (1890) of Sir James Redhouse, and of reference works on missions.

DWIGHT, JOHN SULLIVAN (*b. Boston, Mass., 1813; d. Boston, 1893*), music critic, editor. Graduated Harvard, 1832; Harvard Divinity School, 1836; studied and translated German poetry; spent short time in the ministry. Joined Brook Farm, 1841, and while there contributed musical and other articles to the *Harbinger*. Founded, 1852, *Dwight's Journal of Music*, which for nearly thirty years exerted an unparalleled influence on the formation of musical taste in America. Long associated with Harvard Musical Association, he was instrumental in the establishment of a professorship of music at Harvard.

DWIGHT, NATHANIEL (*b. Northampton, Mass., 1770; d. Oswego, N.Y., 1831*), physician, educator. Brother of Timothy Dwight (1752–1817).

DWIGHT, SERENO EDWARDS (*b. Fairfield, Conn., 1786; d. Philadelphia, Pa., 1850*), educator, Congregational clergyman. Son of Timothy Dwight (1752–1817). Minister at Park Street Church, Boston, 1817–26; edited writings of Jonathan Edwards, his great-grandfather (1830).

DWIGHT, THEODORE (*b. Northampton, Mass., 1764; d. New York, N.Y., 1846*), lawyer, author, editor. Brother of Timothy Dwight (1752–1817). Practiced law principally in Hartford, Conn.; was one of "Connecticut Wits." Served as secretary to the Hartford Convention, 1814, and in 1833 published its journal.

DWIGHT, THEODORE (*b. Hartford, Conn., 1796; d. 1866*), author, educator. Son of Theodore Dwight (1764–1846). Graduated Yale, 1814. A prolific writer and espouser of numerous "causes."

DWIGHT, THEODORE WILLIAM (*b. Catskill, N.Y., 1822; d. Clinton, N.Y., 1892*), lawyer, educator. Grandson of Timothy Dwight (1752–1817). Professor of law, Hamilton College, 1846–58; first professor at Columbia Law School, 1858, and its warden, 1878–91. Emphasized fundamental principles in teaching of law.

DWIGHT, THOMAS (*b. Boston, Mass., 1843; d. 1911*), anatomist. M.D., Harvard, 1867. Taught at Harvard and Bowdoin; succeeded O. W. Holmes as

Parkman professor of anatomy, Harvard; served 1883–1911. Dwight's chief contributions related to meticulous studies of anatomical variations of the skeleton and joints.

DWIGHT, TIMOTHY (*b. Northampton, Mass., 1752; d. New Haven, Conn., 1817*), Congregational clergyman, author, president of Yale College, 1795–1817. His mother, Mary Edwards Dwight, daughter of Jonathan Edwards, was a woman of remarkable character and mental ability, to whom Dwight said he owed all that he was. Prepared by her for college, he entered Yale at thirteen and graduated, 1769. He returned to Yale, 1771, to remain six years as an able and popular tutor.

In 1774 he united with the college church and turned to the study of theology. An early interest in literature was evinced by his *Dissertation on the History, Eloquence, and Poetry of the Bible* delivered upon receiving his master's degree in 1772; he was later to be a prolific member of the literary group known as the "Connecticut" or "Hartford Wits." In service, 1777–79, as chaplain of Gen. S. H. Parson's Connecticut Continental Brigade, he resigned to take charge of family affairs in Northampton, where for the next five years he managed two large farms, supplied churches and established a school for both sexes.

In 1783 he became pastor of the Congregational church at Greenfield Hill, Conn.; during his twelve years there his fame as educator, preacher, author and man of affairs spread. Again he established a school for both sexes, which eventually drew students from the Middle and Southern states as well as New England. In 1785 he published *The Conquest of Canaan*, the first epic poem, according to Dwight, to appear in America. Tedious to modern readers, it increased his contemporary prestige. His *Greenfield Hill* (1794) imitated 18th century English formal descriptive verse; it purported to contribute to moral improvement and to demonstrate to Europeans that America offered material for native poetry. A rigid Calvinist and staunch Federalist, Dwight energetically opposed the prevalent rise of democracy and infidelity. His satiric *Triumph of Infidelity, a Poem* (1788) uncorked vials of abuse on Voltaire, Hume and others. Dwight's views were also set forth in many sermons and addresses.

In 1795, upon the death of Ezra Stiles, Dwight was elected president of Yale. For more than 21 years he administered the college with great ability and exerted an extraordinary influence over the students. The most conspicuous intellectual figure in New England, he was dubbed "Pope Dwight." From his administration Yale dates her modern era. Narrow in his view of life and political and social doctrines, he appeared somewhat bigoted and uncharitable. His literary work was not original. Theologically indebted to Jonathan Edwards, Dwight outlined his own system in *Theology, Explained and Defended* (1818–19). His *Travels in New England and New York* (1821–22), written to refute foreign misrepresentations of America, is an astonishingly varied collection of descriptions of natural, agricultural, political, religious and social conditions, and of statistical information.

DWIGHT, TIMOTHY (*b. Norwich, Conn., 1828; d. 1916*), Congregational clergyman, educator. Grandson of Timothy Dwight (1752–1817). Graduated Yale, 1849. Professor of sacred literature, Yale Divinity, 1858–86; president, Yale University, 1886–98; in which time a successful expansion and reorganization of the various schools of the university took place.

DWIGHT, WILLIAM (*b. Springfield, Mass., 1831; d. Boston, Mass., 1888*), manufacturer, Union soldier. Rose to division command under P. H. Sheridan in Virginia, 1864, after gallant service in the Peninsula (1861–62) and in the Western campaigns (1863) under N. P. Banks.

DYAR, HARRISON GRAY (*b. New York, N.Y., 1866; d. Washington, D.C., 1929*), entomologist. Graduated Massachusetts Institute of Technology, 1889; Ph.D., Columbia, 1895. Chief interest, lepidoptera; his main work, *The Mosquitoes of North and Central America and the West Indies* (1912–17).

DYE, WILLIAM McENTYRE (*b. Pennsylvania, 1831; d. Muskegon, Mich., 1899*), soldier. Graduated West Point, 1853. Served with distinction in Union Army. Staff officer of the Egyptian army, 1873–78; military adviser to Korea, 1888–99.

DYER, ALEXANDER BRYDIE (*b. Richmond, Va., 1815; d. 1874*), soldier. Graduated West Point, 1837. In ordnance service, *post* 1838. Commanded U.S. arsenal, Springfield, Mass., 1861–64; chief of ordnance, U.S. Army, 1864–74.

DYER, ELIPHALET (*b. Windham, Conn., 1721; d. Windham, 1807*), jurist. Prominent in affairs of the Susquehanna Co., 1753–83; member of the Continental Congress; chief justice of Connecticut, 1789–93.

DYER, ISADORE (*b. Galveston, Tex., 1865; d. New Orleans, La., 1920*), physician. Graduated Tulane, M.D., 1889; taught there, 1905–20, and was dean, 1908–20. A successful dermatologist and one of the foremost leprologists of his time.

DYER, LOUIS (*b. Chicago, Ill., 1851; d. 1908*), classical scholar, writer, lecturer. Graduated Harvard, 1874. Associated with Oxford University, *post* 1893.

DYER, MARY (*d. Boston, Mass., 1660*), Quaker preacher and martyr.

DYER, NEHEMIAH MAYO (*b. Provincetown, Mass., 1839; d. 1910*), naval officer. Volunteered in U.S. Navy, 1862. Remaining in service, he was promoted captain, 1897, and commanded U.S.S. *Baltimore* at Manila Bay. Retired as rear-admiral, 1901.

DYLANDER, JOHN (*b. Sweden, c. 1709; d. Southwark, Philadelphia, Pa., 1741*), Lutheran clergyman. Pastor, Gloria Dei Church, Philadelphia, 1737–41.

DYMOND, JOHN (*b. Canada, 1836; d. New Orleans, La., 1922*), Louisiana sugar-planter, inventor, editor.

DYOTT, THOMAS W. (*b. England, 1771; d. Philadelphia, Pa., 1861*), patent medicine king, welfare worker, temperance advocate. Came to Pennsylvania *c.* 1795. The largest dealer in patent medicines in America, Dyott operated the Kensington Glass Works, *post* 1833. He also engaged in eccentric reform activities, including operation of a personal bank maintained entirely on his own credit. Imprisoned briefly after his financial failure in 1836, he returned to his drug-store and again acquired considerable wealth.

EADS, JAMES BUCHANAN (*b. Lawrenceburg, Ind., 1820; d. Nassau, Bahama Islands, 1887*), engineer, inventor. Became a purser on a Mississippi River steamboat, 1838; invented a diving bell, which he patented, and in 1842 formed a partnership to engage in steamboat salvage. A student of the laws which governed the Mississippi's flow and determined its deposits, Eads in 1856 proposed to Congress to remove all snags and wrecks from the Mississippi, Missouri, Arkansas, and Ohio rivers and to keep their channels open for some years; the bill, however, died in the Senate.

Summoned to Washington by Lincoln in 1861 to advise upon the best methods of utilizing Western rivers for attack and defense, Eads proposed a fleet of armor-plated, steam-propelled gunboats. He contracted to construct seven such vessels ready for armament in 65 days; despite chaotic conditions, the boats were built. In the course of the war he built 14 armored gunboats and armed and built other vessels.

In 1865 a bill was introduced into Congress authorizing construction of a bridge across the Mississippi at St. Louis, Mo. The project was declared impracticable, but Eads's plan for the bridge was approved and construction was successfully completed in 1874. That year Eads proposed to Congress to open a mouth of the Mississippi and maintain the channel at the sole risk of himself and his associates. The proposition was accepted. In 1879 the project was completed, Eads having devised a system of jetties which caused the river to deposit its sediments where he wanted them. His reports and articles during this work are probably unsurpassed in value as engineering expositions on controlling the flow of water and correct river improvement.

In opposition to the Panama Canal Eads proposed a ship railway; from 1880 until his death he worked on this project. He selected a route by way of the Tehuantepec Isthmus, 2000 miles shorter than the Panama route, and offered to build the railway at his own expense provided the government would guarantee a dividend of 6% for 15 years when it was proved practical. A bill embodying his suggestion passed the House but failed in the Senate.

An engineer of international reputation, Eads advised American and foreign municipalities and governments. His improvement at the mouth of the Mississippi placed him in the foremost rank of hydraulic engineers as his great bridge at St. Louis placed him in the first rank of bridge engineers.

EAGELS, JEANNE (*b. Kansas City, Mo., 1894; d. New York, N.Y., 1929*), actress. Best known for her performance as Sadie Thompson in *Rain*, 1922–26.

EAKINS, THOMAS (*b. Philadelphia, Pa., 1844; d. Philadelphia, 1916*), painter, sculptor, teacher. Attended Pennsylvania Academy of Fine Arts; studied in Paris at École des Beaux-Arts under J. L. Gérôme, Léon Bonnat and the sculptor A. A. Dumont. While in Spain in 1869 Eakins was impressed by the work of the great Spanish realists, especially Velasquez, Ribera, Goya and Herrera. Returned to Philadelphia, 1870; studied anatomy at Jefferson Medical College. Knowledge of anatomy brought him the opportunity to teach at the Pennsylvania Academy, where he became dean and was for many years its principal instructor. He also taught at the Art Students' League. Eakins worked unsparingly, painting many portraits and eventually more elaborate compositions. Among these the "Clinic of Dr. Gross," completed in 1875, is generally regarded as his masterpiece. In this painting is displayed the masterly drawing of the human figure in repose or action which is his chief title to fame. Among many other pictures may be mentioned the "Clinic of Dr. Agnew," "Between Rounds," "Chess Players," "The Pair-Oared Shell," "The Biglen Brothers Turning the Stakeboat," and a long series of fishing subjects.

The virility of his nature appears in his selection of subjects and his strength of characterization. He was able to reveal in each portrait not only an individual personality but a racial type. "The Thinker," for example, unique in its plainness, is a penetrating study of a native type. Eakins's sense of the dignity and worth of common things and people suggests analogies with the work of Walt Whitman, Winslow Homer and Ralph Waldo Emerson.

EAMES, CHARLES (*b. New Braintree, Mass., 1812; d. 1867*), lawyer, diplomat. Successful in concluding a treaty with the Hawaiian Government in 1849, Eames later practiced international law in Washington, D.C.

EAMES, WILBERFORCE (*b. Newark, N.J., 1855; d. New York, N.Y., 1937*), librarian, bibliographer. Specialist in Americana, New York Public Library, 1895–1937. [*Supp. 2*]

EARHART, AMELIA MARY (*b. Atchison, Kans., 1897; d. 1937*), aviator. Made first solo flights *c.* 1921; was the first woman passenger on a transatlantic flight, June 1928. In May 1932 she made the trip alone, establishing a record of 14 hours, 56 minutes. She followed three record-breaking transcontinental flights (1932–33) by making the first solo flight from Hawaii to the U.S. mainland, January 1935, and the first non-stop flight from Mexico City to Newark, N.J., May 1935. In July 1937 she and her navigator, Frederick Noonan, were lost after leaving New Guinea on the last lap of a globe-circling flight. [*Supp. 2*]

EARLE, ALICE MORSE (*b. Worcester, Mass., 1853; d. Hempstead, N.Y., 1911*). Author of a number of valuable studies in colonial costume and customs.

EARLE, JAMES (*b. Paxton, Mass., 1761; d. Charleston, S.C., 1796*), portrait painter. Brother of Ralph Earle. Ranked by contemporaries with Copley and Trumbull, Earle spent his professional life in London, England, and Charleston, S.C.

EARLE, MORTIMER LAMSON (*b. New York, N.Y., 1864; d. 1905*), classical scholar, educator. Taught at Barnard, Bryn Mawr and Columbia; known for archaeological discoveries as well as paleographical and bibliographical knowledge before his untimely death.

EARLE, PLINY (*b. Leicester, Mass., 1762; d. 1832*), cotton-machinery manufacturer. Invented and patented, 1803, a machine for making wool and cotton cards.

EARLE, PLINY (*b. Leicester, Mass., 1809; d. 1892*), physician, psychiatrist. Son of Pliny Earle (1762–1832). A co-founder of the American Medical Association, Earle led his contemporaries in study of psychiatric institutions and in treatment of the insane.

EARLE, RALPH (*b. Shrewsbury, Mass., 1751; d. 1801*), painter. Brother of James Earle. Designer of crude views of battles at Lexington and Concord engraved by Amos Doolittle; led a rambling life in England and America. Celebrated for portraits of uneven quality.

EARLE, RALPH (*b. Worcester, Mass., 1874; d. Worcester, 1939*), naval officer, educator. Graduated Annapolis, 1896. Chief, Bureau of Ordnance (as rear admiral), 1916–19. Responsible for arming navy in World War I, he developed and procured mines for North Sea blockage and suggested use of naval guns on railroad cars on Western Front, 1918. [*Supp. 2*]

EARLE, THOMAS (*b. Leicester, Mass., 1796; d. 1849*), lawyer. Son of Pliny Earle (1762–1832). Led agitation for reform of the constitution of Pennsylvania, *ante* 1837.

EARLY, JOHN (*b. Bedford Co., Va., 1786; d. Lynchburg, Va., 1873*), Methodist clergyman. Helped found Randolph-Macon College. Active in formation of Methodist Episcopal Church, South, he served as bishop, 1854–66.

EARLY, JUBAL ANDERSON (*b. Franklin Co., Va., 1816; d. Lynchburg, Va., 1894*), lawyer, Confederate soldier. Graduated West Point, 1837. Admitted Virginia bar, 1840. Though against secession in 1861, he joined the Confederate Army and for the next three years served with the Army of Northern Virginia, rising to lieutenant-general; after June 1864 he was in independent command in the Shenandoah Valley. From this position his forces threatened Washington and obstructed communications between the capital and the West. He was defeated by Sheridan at Cedar Creek, occasion of the famous "ride." After the war, Early remained a loyal, "unreconstructed" Confederate.

EARLY, PETER (*b. Madison Co., Va., 1773; d. Greensboro, Ga., 1817*), politician, judge. Removed to Georgia, 1795. As governor of Georgia, 1813–15, he supported the War of 1812 and vetoed an unwise stay-law for relief of debtors.

EASLEY, RALPH MONTGOMERY (*b. Schuyler Co., Ill., 1856; d. Rye, N.Y., 1939*), reformer. Founded National Civic Federation, 1900, to improve relations of capital and labor. [*Supp. 2*]

EAST, EDWARD MURRAY (*b. Du Quoin, Ill., 1879; d. Boston, Mass., 1938*), plant geneticist. Graduated University of Illinois, B.S., 1901; M.S., 1904; Ph.D. 1907. Trained as a chemist, he became interested in genetics through researches, 1900–04, to improve Indian corn for animal nutrition. As agronomist at Connecticut Agricultural Experiment Station, 1904–08, East continued his corn experiments. Together with independent investigations by George Harrison Shull, they led to the development of hybrid corn, a new method of seed production revolutionizing corn growing throughout the world. East also did important theoretical studies of Mendelian heredity in corn, of self- and cross-incompatibility, species hybridization, cytoplasmic heredity, and heretosis. In 1909 he joined the Bussey Institution of Harvard University. [*Supp. 2*]

EASTMAN, ARTHUR MacARTHUR (*b. Gilmanton, N.H., 1810; d. 1877*), firearms manufacturer. During the Civil War Eastman made a fortune turning old arms into cavalry carbines. He promoted a direct ocean cable between Europe and the United States which was successfully completed in 1875.

EASTMAN, CHARLES GAMAGE (*b. Fryeburg, Maine, 1816, d. Montpelier, Vt., 1860*), journalist, politician, poet. *Post* 1846, editor of *Montpelier* (Vt.) *Patriot.*

EASTMAN, ENOCH WORTHEN (*b. Deerfield, N.H., 1810; d. 1885*), Iowa lawyer and public official.

EASTMAN, GEORGE (*b. Waterville, N.Y., 1854; d. Rochester, N.Y., 1932*), inventor, manufacturer, philanthropist. Convinced before 1879 of the commercial prospects for photographic dry plates, he invented a machine for coating plates and began their manufacture. After experimenting, 1884, with transparent and flexible film, he marketed the first Kodak, using paper-backed film, 1888. With aid of Henry Reichenbach, he prepared transparent film, 1889, and introduced a daylight-loading film, 1891. The Eastman Co., reorganized as the Eastman Kodak Co., 1893, was remarkably successful, owing largely to Eastman's aggressive fight to control the market in photographic goods. Among the objects of Eastman's philanthropies, on which were spent well over $75-000,000, were the University of Rochester and its various schools, Massachusetts Institute of Technology, Hampton and Tuskegee Institutes. [*Supp.* 1]

EASTMAN, HARVEY GRIDLEY (*b. near Waterville, N.Y., 1832; d. Denver, Colo., 1878*), businessman, politician, promoter. Founded Eastman's National Business College, Poughkeepsie, N.Y., 1859, which aided in development of that town.

EASTMAN, JOHN ROBIE (*b. Andover, N.H., 1836; d. 1913*). One of several astronomers (among them Newcomb and Hall) who established the reputation of the Naval Observatory; served there, 1862–98.

EASTMAN, TIMOTHY CORSER (*b. Croydon, N.H., 1821; d. Tarrytown, N.Y., 1893*), cattle merchant, meat packer. A pioneer in shipping cattle, other livestock and especially dressed meat in commercial quantities to England and Scotland. His first shipment of dressed meat abroad was made in October, 1875.

EASTMAN, WILLIAM REED (*b. New York, N.Y., 1835; d. 1925*), engineer, Presbyterian clergyman. Entering upon a career in library work at 55 years of age, he became a leading authority on library buildings and equipment.

EASTON, JOHN (*b. c. 1625; d. Newport, R.I., 1705*), governor of Rhode Island, 1690–95. Son of Nicholas Easton. Author of a *Narrative of the Causes which led to Philip's Indian War* (published 1858).

EASTON, NICHOLAS (*b. Wales, 1593; d. Newport, R.I., 1675*), governor of Rhode Island, 1672–74. Came to America, 1634. Built the first house in Newport, 1639, removing there eventually from Massachusetts after involvement in Antinomian controversy.

EATON, AMOS (*b. Chatham, N.Y., 1776; d. Troy, N.Y., 1842*), scientist, educator. Graduated Williams, 1799. Author of *Manual of Botany for the Northern States* (1817). Lecturer on scientific subjects; professor at Rensselaer Institute, 1824–42.

EATON, BENJAMIN HARRISON (*b. near Zanesville, O., 1833; d. 1904*), agriculturist, pioneer in irrigation. Settled near present Windsor, Colo., 1864; developed and irrigated extensive holdings in Colorado.

EATON, DANIEL CADY (*b. Fort Gratiot, Mich., 1834; d. New Haven, Conn., 1895*), botanist. Author of *The Ferns of North America* (1877–80) and numerous shorter works; professor of botany, Yale, 1864–95.

EATON, DORMAN BRIDGMAN (*b. Hardwick, Vt., 1823; d. 1899*), lawyer, civil-service reformer. Entitled to share with G. W. Curtis and Carl Schurz honor of securing national recognition for merit system.

EATON, HOMER (*b. Enosburg, Vt., 1834; d. Madison, N.J., 1913*), Methodist clergyman. Agent, Methodist Book Concern, 1889–1913.

EATON, JOHN (*b. Sutton, N.H., 1829; d. 1906*), educator. Graduated Dartmouth, 1854. Organized Freedmen camps, 1862–65. U.S. commissioner of education, 1870–86.

EATON, JOHN HENRY (*b. North Carolina, 1790; d. Washington, D.C., 1856*), lawyer, politician. Settled in Tennessee, c. 1808. U.S. senator, Democrat, from Tennessee, 1818–29; strong supporter of Andrew Jackson. Appointed secretary of war, 1829, he resigned in 1831 after Washington society's refusal to accept his second wife, Peggy O'Neale, disrupted Jackson's cabinet. Eaton was governor of Florida, 1834–35, and minister to Spain, 1836–40.

EATON, JOSEPH ORIEL (*b. Newark, O., 1829; d. Yonkers, N.Y., 1875*), painter.

EATON, MARGARET L. O'NEILL. [See O'NEALE, MARGARET L., 1796–1879.]

EATON, NATHANIEL (*b. Coventry, England, c. 1609; d. Southwark, London, England, 1674*), first head of Harvard College. Brother of Samuel and Theophilus Eaton. Emigrated to Massachusetts, 1637, where he was welcomed for his learning and made head (though not president) of Harvard College. He was soon in trouble, charged with withholding food from the students and with beating his usher. Removed from office, fined, and excommunicated by the church, he fled Boston for Virginia, and later returned to England.

EATON, SAMUEL (*b. Cheshire, England, 1596?; d. England, 1664/5*), clergyman. Brother of Theophilus and Nathaniel Eaton. Became colleague of John Davenport at New Haven, Conn., 1637. Returned to England, c. 1640.

EATON, THEOPHILUS (*b. Stony Stratford, England, 1590; d. New Haven, Conn., 1658*), merchant, colonizer. Brother of Samuel and Nathaniel Eaton. A successful merchant in London and an original patentee of the Massachusetts Co., he emigrated in 1637 with his old schoolmate John Davenport and others, including his brothers, to Boston. Eaton's group, the wealthiest and, commercially, the ablest which had up to that time gone to America, established their own independent colony at what is now New Haven (located, 1637–38, organized 1639). Thenceforth Eaton and Davenport ruled the colony. Eaton was elected civic governor and was annually re-elected until his death. His attempt to establish a fur trading post on the Delaware occasioned conflict with the Dutch of New Amsterdam. His administration of the colony, however, was marked by wisdom, justice, firmness and prudence.

EATON, WILLIAM (*b. Woodstock, Conn., 1764; d. Brimfield, Mass., 1811*), army officer, diplomat. Graduated Dartmouth, 1790; commissioned captain, U.S. army, 1792. Appointed U.S. consul to Tunis, 1798, he renegotiated an unsatisfactory treaty with aid of James L. Cathcart; at Cathcart's suggestion also, he urged on Congress in 1804 a scheme to win peace with Tripoli by reinstating an exiled Pasha. His venture suddenly countermanded after he had led a spectacular march with a motley army from Alexandria, Egypt, to Derna, Eaton returned to America where he made many political enemies by his complaints about his treatment.

EATON, WYATT (*b. Philipsburg, Canada, 1849; d. Newport, R.I., 1896*), painter. A friend of the French painter Millet, who influenced him, Eaton is known for his portraits of distinguished American and Canadian contemporaries.

EBERLE, EDWARD WALTER (*b. Denton, Texas, 1864; d. Washington, D.C., 1929*), naval officer. Graduated Annapolis, 1885. Wrote the first modern manual of naval gun and torpedo drills, first instructions for wireless on naval vessels. Superintendent at Annapolis, 1915–19, he was promoted rear-admiral, 1919, and was chief of naval operations, 1923–27.

EBERLE, JOHN (*b. Hagerstown ?, Md., 1787; d. Lexington, Ky., 1838*), physician. Author of *Treatise on the Materia Medica and Therapeutics* (1823) and *Notes of Lectures on Theory and Practice of Medicine* (1834). Founder of Jefferson Medical College (1824) where he taught, 1825–30; taught also at Transylvania and Medical College of Ohio.

ECHOLS, JOHN (*b. Lynchburg, Va., 1823; d. Staunton, Va., 1896*), lawyer, Confederate major-general. For many years an official and director of the Chesapeake & Ohio Railway.

ECKART, WILLIAM ROBERTS (*b. Chillicothe, O., 1841; d. Palo Alto, Calif., 1914*), engineer. Associated with B. F. Isherwood during Civil War and after in marine propeller design and other marine engineering projects; specialized in mining machinery design; pioneered in high-head long-distance transmission power plants.

ECKELS, JAMES HERRON (*b. Princeton, Ill., 1858; d. Chicago, Ill., 1907*), lawyer, financier. Efficient comptroller of the currency, 1893–97; presi-

dent, Commercial National Bank of Chicago, 1897–1907.

ECKERT, THOMAS THOMPSON (*b. St. Clairsville, O., 1825; d. Long Branch, N.J., 1910*), telegrapher. Organized and supervised U.S. military telegraph during Civil War; later administrator of telegraph companies controlled by Jay Gould and others, he was president of Western Union, 1893–1900.

ECKFORD, HENRY (*b. Irvine, Scotland, 1775; d. in Turkey, 1832*), ship builder. Settled in New York City, 1796. Ships of his design were famous for strength and speed. Built the *Robert Fulton* which made first successful steam voyage from New York to New Orleans and Havana (1822).

ECKSTEIN, JOHN (*b. ? Mecklenburg, Germany, c. 1750; d. ? Philadelphia, Pa., c. 1817*), painter, sculptor, engraver.

EDDIS, WILLIAM (*fl. 1769–77*), Maryland Loyalist. Secretary to Gov. Robert Eden. Author of *Letters from America, Historical and Descriptive* (1792).

EDDY, CLARENCE (*b. Greenfield, Mass., 1851; d. Chicago, Ill., 1937*), organist. [*Supp. 2*]

EDDY, DANIEL CLARKE (*b. Salem, Mass., 1823; d. Martha's Vineyard, Mass., 1896*), Baptist clergyman. Know-Nothing speaker of Massachusetts lower house, 1854.

EDDY, HARRISON PRESCOTT (*b. Millbury, Mass., 1870; d. Montreal, Canada, 1937*), sanitary engineer. A leader in the development of water supply and purification, and of sewage treatment. Author, with Leonard Metcalf, of *American Sewerage Practice* (1914–15). [*Supp. 2*]

EDDY, HENRY TURNER (*b. Stoughton, Mass., 1844; d. 1921*), mathematician, physicist. Applied his learning to engineering problems; taught at University of Tennessee, Cornell, Princeton, Cincinnati, Minnesota. President, Rose Polytechnic Institute, 1891–94.

EDDY, MARY MORSE BAKER (*b. Bow, N.H., 1821; d. Chestnut Hill, Mass., 1910*), founder of the Christian Science Church.

EDDY, THOMAS (*b. Philadelphia, Pa., 1758; d. 1827*), insurance broker. Promoted reforms of prisons, hospitals, schools, and penal code of New York; supported DeWitt Clinton's Erie Canal project.

EDEBOHLS, GEORGE MICHAEL (*b. New York, N.Y., 1853; d. 1908*), surgeon. Graduated Fordham, 1871; M.D., College of Physicians and Surgeons, 1875. Specialized in gynecology; originated Edebohls's operation for Bright's disease.

EDEN, CHARLES (*b. England, 1673; d. Bertie Co., N.C., 1722*), colonial governor of North Carolina, 1714–22; last person to receive title of "Landgrave" under John Locke's constitution for Carolina.

EDEN, ROBERT (*b. Durham, England, 1741; d. Annapolis, Md., 1784*), colonial governor of Maryland, 1768–76. His skillful diplomacy and moderation won him friends among the colonial gentry; created a baronet, 1776, he resided in England during the Revolution.

EDES, BENJAMIN (*b. Charlestown, Mass., 1732; d. Boston, Mass., 1803*), journalist. With John Gill, founded *Boston Gazette and Country Journal*, 1755, organ of Massachusetts patriots. His fortunes declined after the Revolution.

EDES, ROBERT THAXTER (*b. Eastport, Maine, 1838; d. Springfield, Mass., 1923*), physician. Graduated Harvard, 1858; M.D., Harvard Medical, 1861. Specialized on diseases of nervous system; foreshadowed modern treatment of psychoneuroses.

EDESON, ROBERT (*b. New Orleans, La., 1868; d. 1931*), actor. Played with Frohman's Empire Theatre company; leading man to Maude Adams and other stars; one of the first stage stars to go into motion pictures. [*Supp. 1*]

EDGAR, CHARLES (*b. Metuchen, N.J., 1862; d. Miami, Fla., 1922*), lumberman. Helped develop lumber areas of upper Midwest and Southern pine districts. Invented band saw with teeth on both edges.

EDGERTON, ALFRED PECK (*b. Plattsburg, N.Y., 1813; d. Hicksville, O., 1897*) businessman, politician. Long active as a "Bourbon" Democrat in Ohio and Indiana politics.

EDGERTON, SIDNEY (*b. New York, N.Y., 1818; d. 1900*), lawyer. Congressman, Republican, from Ohio, 1858–62; chief justice of Idaho, 1863; active in establishment of Montana territory and its first territorial governor, 1864.

EDGREN, AUGUST HJALMAR (*b. Vermland, Sweden, 1840, d. Stockholm, Sweden, 1903*), soldier, linguist. Volunteered Union Army in Civil War; after the war, taught abroad, returning 1870 to graduate Cornell, A.B., 1871; Ph.D., Yale, 1874. Taught subsequently in Sweden and at University of Nebraska. Specialist in Sanskrit, Germanic and Romance languages.

EDISON, THOMAS ALVA (*b. Milan, O., 1847; d. West Orange, N.J., 1931*), inventor. Raised in Michigan, contrary to popular legend, in a "prosperous, changing and beautiful environment." Slow in school, inept in mathematics, he was an avid reader and by age ten had developed a strong taste for chemistry. As a youth, established a profitable business selling newspapers, candy, etc., on railroad trains; became a telegraph operator, 1863; went to work for Western Union in Boston, Mass., 1868. During all this time he had continued to read and experiment in chemistry and in applications of electricity to telegraphy;

in 1869, he patented his first invention, an electrographic vote recorder, and also took out patents for an improved stock-ticker. In the same year he took an excellent position in New York as general manager of the Laws Gold Indicator Co.; he also entered partnership with two others in an "electrical engineer" consultation business. His share of the profits of this partnership when it was bought out in 1870 permitted him to set up his own shop and devote himself with a staff of assistants (who later became famous on their own account) to improvements in telegraphy. In 1874, he made quadruplex telegraphy practicable; in 1875 invented a resonator for analyzing sound waves; in 1876, devised the carbon telephone transmitter. Also in 1876, he moved his laboratory to Menlo Park, N.J.; in 1877, he invented the phonograph, his greatest single achievement from the viewpoint of inventive imagination.

In 1879 he made commercially practicable the incandescent lamp, although he did not invent it. He introduced improvements vital to its common use and cheap production and was responsible for the system by which widely distributed lamps were empowered from central stations, an immense engineering achievement. Edison made his first and only scientific discovery, the "Edison effect," in 1883, whereby he demonstrated that the incandescent lamp could be used as a valve admitting negative but not positive electricity. Seeing no practical use for such a valve, Edison abandoned it, but it was to become later the basis for the vacuum tube so essential to modern radio. In 1891, he patented a "kinetoscope," an apparatus for exhibiting photographs of moving objects. It had no projector or screen. In 1895 Thomas Armat invented a machine which would project a picture from film to screen, and in the following year Edison acquired the patent, a fact which erroneously caused contemporaries to give him credit for it. Edison did however do much for the organization and standardization of the motion picture industry.

In 1887 Edison had moved his laboratory to West Orange. He had put in motion the many commercial companies for manufacturing and selling his many inventions, companies which later were consolidated into the Edison General Electric Co., and later the General Electric Co. Having organized the companies, he lost interest in them and turned to investigation of the fluoroscope, ore-mill machinery, magnetic separation of iron, the storage battery, and railway signaling. He devised a dictating machine and mimeograph, and during World War I conducted research on torpedo mechanisms, flame throwers, and submarine periscopes.

Because Edison was the idol of the press of his day, it may be some time before the Edison myth can be divorced from the Edison fact. Edison was for the most part a trial-and-error inventor who scorned scientific theory and mathematical study which might have saved him time. He had an infinite capacity for hard work, could dispense with regular hours of sleep, and was able to keep two or more parallel trains of thought in motion at the same time. His mind could register and conjecture with new information on some remote subject without losing the main thread of his thinking on a current problem. The sensitiveness of genius seems to have been lacking in him, and he wasted little time on the art of living. Seeking devices adapted to abundant commercial use, his approach to invention was economic. Although his technical triumphs seem less brilliant in mid-century than in the era when his pioneer work was done, he must be judged with a consciousness of that era and of the society which acclaimed his gifts. [*Supp.* 1]

EDMANDS, JOHN (*b. Framingham, Mass., 1820; d. Philadelphia, Pa., 1915*), librarian, bibliographer. Graduated Yale, 1847. Librarian, Philadelphia Mercantile Library, 1856–1915. Author of a classification system (1883).

EDMONDS, FRANCIS WILLIAM (*b. Hudson, N.Y., 1806; d. Westchester Co., N.Y., 1863*), businessman, genre painter.

EDMONDS, JOHN WORTH (*b. Hudson, N.Y., 1799; d. New York, N.Y., 1874*), jurist. Brother of Francis W. Edmonds. Justice of state supreme court, 1847–52. Published annotated N.Y. *Statutes at Large* (1863), a standard reference.

EDMUNDS, GEORGE FRANKLIN (*b. near Richmond, Vt., 1828; d. Pasadena, Calif., 1919*), lawyer. Practiced in Vermont, *post* 1849; argued successfully against constitutionality of income tax in *Pollock vs. Farmers' Loan and Trust Co.*, 1895. As U.S. senator, Republican, from Vermont, 1866–91, made important contributions in domestic legislation. Supported radical Reconstructionists; arranged procedural rules for President Johnson's impeachment; secured adoption of Electoral Count Act of 1887; championed Thurman Act of 1878; was principal author of Sherman Anti-Trust Act, 1890; advocated civil service reform. A Republican reform candidate for presidential nomination in 1884, he drew support of independents away from Blaine. After Fessenden's death, Edmunds was generally considered ablest constitutional lawyer in Congress.

EDWARDS, BELA BATES (*b. Southampton, Mass., 1802; d. Athens, Ga., 1852*), Congregational clergyman, editor. Co-founder of *Bibliotheca Sacra*, 1842, and editor, 1844–52. Taught at Andover Theological Seminary.

EDWARDS, CHARLES (*b. Norwich, England, 1797; d. 1868*), lawyer, author. Settled in New York City after graduation, Cambridge University; studied law. Standing counsel to British consulate-

general, New York. Author of, among other works, *Edwards' Chancery Reports* (1833–51).

EDWARDS, CLARENCE RANSOM (*b. Cleveland, O., 1860; d. Boston, Mass., 1931*), army officer. Nephew of Oliver Edwards. Graduated West Point, 1883. Successful administrator of Bureau of Insular Affairs; commanded 26th Division in World War I. Retired as major-general, 1922. [*Supp.* 1]

EDWARDS, HENRY WAGGAMAN (*b. New Haven, Conn., 1779; d. 1847*), lawyer. Grandson of Jonathan Edwards (1703–1758). Congressman, Democratic-Republican, from Connecticut, 1819–23; U.S. senator, 1823–27; governor, 1833, 1835–38.

EDWARDS, JOHN (*b. London, England, c. 1671; d. Boston, Mass., 1746*), early American silversmith. Emigrated to Boston *ante* 1689.

EDWARDS, JOHN (*b. Stafford Co., Va., 1748; d. Bourbon Co., Ky., 1837*), planter. Removed to Lincoln Co., Ky., 1780; to Bourbon Co., 1785. Led in Kentucky's struggle for independence and statehood; opposed Spanish conspiracy, 1787–88. U.S. senator, 1792–95.

EDWARDS, JONATHAN (*b. East Windsor, Conn., 1703; d. Princeton, N.J., 1758*), Congregational clergyman, theologian, philosopher. Son of Timothy and Esther Stoddard Edwards. Entered Yale College, 1716, where his mind was formed by the idealism of John Locke and the new science of Newton. For Edwards, however, Newton's world of natural law was not a lifeless mechanism, but was made up of bodies the substance of which was "the infinitely exact, and precise, and perfectly stable Idea, in God's mind . . ." Reason could interpret the orderly related facts of Newton's science, but excellency—consisting in greatness and beauty, the consent or love of being to being—had to be apprehended independent of intellectual reason. The apprehension of divine beauty was God's redemptive disclosure of himself to the privileged elect.

After graduation, 1720, two years of theological study and a short pastorate in New York, in 1726 Edwards took over parish duties in Northampton, Mass., as a colleague of his grandfather, the Rev. Solomon Stoddard. Edwards's emphasis on divine majesty, on personal conversion, and on salvation through supernatural illumination rather than through intellectual effort or "moral sincerity" estranged him from his relatives and congregation. He feared that their tendency to Arminian theology would diminish the doctrinal differences between the Congregational Church and the Church of England. He expressed his views in *God Glorified in the Work of Redemption* (1731) and in *A Divine and Supernatural Light, Immediately Imparted to the Soul by the Spirit of God* (1734). One result of his fiery sermons was the Northampton revival of 1734–35. His *Faithful Narrative of the Surprising Work of God in the*

Conversion of Many Hundred Souls in Northampton (1737) prepared the ground for Whitefield's "Great Awakening" of 1740–42, the excesses of which and its resulting social and religious divisions prompted Edwards to set down his mature analysis of piety and his psychology of religion. In his *Treatise Concerning Religious Affections* (1746) he described the mind as having two activities: understanding and will. Both must receive light; the former through intellectual study, the latter through a delight in holiness. The resulting birth of a love of God changes the soul's nature. It now shares in the divine light, in the character of Christ. His theology led Edwards to demand a more rigorous criterion for church membership than many of his colleagues and parishioners were willing to accept. From December 1748 to June 1750 he was involved in a dispute with the Standing Committee of his church. The dispute resulted in Edwards's resignation. After a year of occasional service in Northampton, he went as missionary to the Indians at Stockbridge.

This new activity did not lessen the hardships to which he was exposed. To reduce his financial obligations, his wife and children sold their needlework in Boston. Old animosities of his Northampton days reasserted themselves in Stockbridge when Ephraim Williams, a relative of the Stoddard family, sought to oust Edwards from his church in order to escape the preacher's censure of his greed and intrigues. Edwards, however, prevailed in this struggle, and enjoyed the confidence and support of settlers, Indians, commissioners, and the legislature. With his *Freedom of the Will* (1754) Edwards renewed his campaign against Arminianism and revealed himself as the first great philosophic intelligence in American history. The essay maintained the doctrine of unconditional predestination together with the freedom of the mind to act out its choice. Moral responsibility lies in the choice, not in the course of the choice. Liberty means only that man can do what he wills, but, as appears from the fact of divine foreknowledge, volitions are determined. In *The Great Christian Doctrine of Original Sin Defended* (1758), a reply to the English dissenter John Taylor's rejection of Adam's sin, Edwards demonstrated that man's identity is constituted by God with Adam's; that man is born depraved; that sin is infinite, for it is sin against infinite being. In "The Nature of True Virtue" (1765), Edwards reiterated that although all men possess a "natural conscience" which makes them approve justice and benevolence and perceive their beauty, only those whose conscience is enlightened by saving grace may love and taste this beauty. Natural virtues are spurious and rest on self-love. Disinterested love belongs to God and the redeemed. Edwards's esthetic appreciation, his delight as a lover of beauty, finally found expression in his pantheistic, mystic essay, "Concerning the Ends for which God Created the World" (1755). Here he described the universe as an exfoliation of God; an emanation, not a creation out of nothing. The end, therefore, is the manifestation of Himself, the creation of the supreme artist.

Edwards's service in Stockbridge came to an end with his call to the presidency of the College of New Jersey at Princeton. Beginning in January 1758 he conducted a seminar course in theology for seniors until March 22, when he died of the after-effects of a smallpox inoculation. Thus came to a close the life of America's first philosopher; of a theologian admired by many for the saintliness of his disciplined character, and hated by others for his pitiless logical consistency. Edwards had created the first great religious revival of modern times; had intensified the power of Calvinism to stem the tide of the world's new thought; had fused the iron logic of that system with a rapture of mystic communion; and had initiated a New England Theology as a new chapter in the history of doctrine.

EDWARDS, JONATHAN (*b.* Northampton, Mass., 1745; *d.* Schenectady, N.Y., 1801), Congregational clergyman, theologian. Son of Jonathan Edwards (1703–1758). Graduated Princeton, 1765. After long pastorate in New Haven, Conn., served as president, Union College, 1799–1801. His writings carried his father's doctrine a step further toward "progressive orthodoxy."

EDWARDS, JULIAN (*b.* Manchester, England, 1855; *d.* 1910), composer. Came to America, 1888. Best known for light operas and for the song "My Own United States."

EDWARDS, JUSTIN (*b.* Westhampton, Mass., 1787; *d.* Bath Alum Springs, Va., 1853), Congregational clergyman. Writer of pamphlets and tracts on temperance; president, Andover Theological Seminary, 1836–42.

EDWARDS, MORGAN (*b.* Trevethin Parish, Monmouthshire, England, 1722; *d.* Pencader, Del., 1795), pastor of Philadelphia Baptist Church, 1761–71. Collected and published manuscripts relating to American Baptist history.

EDWARDS, NINIAN (*b.* Montgomery Co., Md., 1775; *d.* Belleville, Ill., 1833), lawyer. Removed to Kentucky, 1795. Governor of Illinois Territory, 1809–18; U.S. senator from state of Illinois, 1818–24; governor of Illinois, 1826–30. Lacking in judgment, he lost early prestige as spokesman for interests of settlers.

EDWARDS, NINIAN WIRT (*b.* Frankfort, Ky., 1809; *d.* 1889), lawyer, merchant. Son of Ninian Edwards. Brother-in-law of Mary Todd Lincoln. First Illinois superintendent of public instruction, 1854–57, he also served in both houses of the legislature.

EDWARDS, OLIVER (*b.* Springfield, Mass., 1835; *d.* 1904), Union brigadier-general, businessman, inventor. Removed to Warsaw, Ill., 1856. Conspicuous for bravery at Spotsylvania and Winchester.

EDWARDS, PIERPONT (*b. Northampton, Mass., 1750; d. 1826*), lawyer, politician. Son of Jonathan Edwards (1703–1758). Directed drafting of liberal 1818 Connecticut constitution; federal district judge in Connecticut, 1806–26.

EDWARDS, TALMADGE (*b. England, 1747; d. Johnstown, N.Y., 1821*), tanner. Originated American glove and mitten industry and the "oil-tan" method for preparing buckskin.

EDWARDS, WELDON NATHANIEL (*b. Northampton Co., N.C., 1788; d. 1873*), planter. Congressman, Democrat, from North Carolina, 1815–27. Thereafter prominent in the state legislature as a conservative, he presided over the first secession meeting at Goldsboro, March 1861.

EDWARDS, WILLIAM (*b. Elizabethtown, N.J., 1770; d. Brooklyn, N.Y., 1851*), tanner, inventor. Grandson of Jonathan Edwards (1703–1758). Founder of the hide and leather industry in the United States. Persevering in the face of repeated business failures, he greatly improved the tanning process through inventions, such as rollers for preparing leather, a hide mill for softening dry leather and an improved sole leather tanning process.

EDWARDS, WILLIAM HENRY (*b. Hunter, N.Y., 1822; d. 1909*), entomologist, lawyer, businessman. Grandson of William Edwards. Author of *Voyage up the Amazon* (1847) and a classic study, *The Butterflies of North America* (1868–97).

EDWIN, DAVID (*b. Bath, England, 1776; d. Philadelphia, Pa., 1841*), stipple engraver. Came to America, 1797. Worked with Edward Savage and Gilbert Stuart, and for Philadelphia magazines; reputed to be America's "first good engraver of the human countenance."

EELLS, DAN PARMELEE (*b. Westmoreland, N.Y., 1825; d. Cleveland, O., 1903*), banker, capitalist. President, Commercial National Bank of Cleveland, 1868–97.

EGAN, MAURICE FRANCIS (*b. Philadelphia, Pa., 1852; d. Brooklyn, N.Y., 1924*), journalist, diplomat. Graduated La Salle College (Phila.), 1873. Professor at Notre Dame and Catholic universities; was "unofficial adviser" to Presidents McKinley and T. Roosevelt. Served as minister to Denmark, 1907–18.

EGAN, MICHAEL (*b. Ireland?, 1761; d. Philadelphia, Pa., 1814*), Roman Catholic clergyman. A learned Franciscan, his brief term as first bishop of Philadelphia (1810–14) was marred by internal strife and a contest for authority with the trustees of the parishes.

EGAN, PATRICK (*b. Ballymahon, Ireland, 1841; d. New York, N.Y., 1919*), politician, diplomat. A political refugee to America in 1883, he settled in Lincoln, Neb., and engaged in the grain and milling business. A Republican, and friend of James G. Blaine, he served ably as U.S. minister to Chile.

EGGLESTON, EDWARD (*b. Vevay, Ind., 1837; d. Joshua's Rock, Lake George, N.Y., 1902*), clergyman, novelist, historian. Methodist pastor and Bible agent in Indiana and Minnesota, 1856–66; removed to Evanston, Ill., and became a journalist. Resident in Brooklyn, N.Y., 1870–79, where he was pastor of nonsectarian Church of Christian Endeavor, 1874–79, he won fame for a series of popular novels which had an important influence in turning American fiction toward realism. These included: *The Hoosier Schoolmaster* (1871); *The Circuit Rider* (1874); *Roxy* (1878); *The Graysons* (1888). Shifting his interest to history, he planned to write a history of life in the United States but completed only two volumes: *The Beginners of a Nation* (1896) and *The Transit of Civilization* (1901). The emphasis in these books on cultural development helped advance this then-neglected view of the historian's function.

EGGLESTON, GEORGE CARY (*b. Vevay, Ind., 1839; d. New York, N.Y., 1911*), lawyer, Confederate soldier, journalist. Brother of Edward Eggleston. Post 1870, worked on various New York newspapers as editor, including the *Evening Post*, the *Commercial Advertiser* and the *World*. Author of stories for boys, novels of ante-bellum Virginia life, *The History of the Confederate War* (1910), and several volumes of recollections.

EGLE, WILLIAM HENRY (*b. Lancaster Co., Pa., 1830; d. 1901*), Pennsylvania historian, physician. Edited second and third series of *Pennsylvania Archives*; developed state library as a research center.

EGLESTON, THOMAS (*b. New York, N.Y., 1832; d. 1900*), mineralogist. Founded School of Mines, Columbia University, 1864; preserved New York's Washington Square for recreational purposes; author of *The Metallurgy of Silver, Gold and Mercury in the U.S.* (1887–90).

EHNINGER, JOHN WHETTEN (*b. New York, N.Y., 1827; d. Saratoga Springs, N.Y., 1889*), genre painter, illustrator. Studied in Düsseldorf and Paris under Leutze and Couture.

EHRLICH, ARNOLD BOGUMIL (*b. Wlodawa, Polish Russia, 1848; d. 1919*), Bible exegete, Hebrew scholar. Came to America, 1878. His works, published in Germany, are the most comprehensive and valuable contributions to Old Testament scholarship made in America.

EICHBERG, JULIUS (*b. Düsseldorf, Germany, 1824; d. 1893*), violinist, teacher, composer. Came to America, 1857. Founded Boston Conservatory of Music; wrote *The Doctor of Alcantara* (1862) and other light operas.

EICHHOLTZ, JACOB (*b. Lancaster, Pa., 1776; d. 1842*), painter. Produced portraits in the style of Sully and Stuart, also landscapes and historical groups.

EICKEMEYER, RUDOLF (*b. Altenbamberg, Germany, 1831; d. 1895*), inventor, manufacturer. Came to America, 1850. Invented and patented hat-making machinery which gradually revolutionized the hat-making industry throughout the world. Later he carried out experiments in electricity and produced improved armatures and generators, also the first direct-connected railway motor. In 1892 his business was consolidated with the General Electric Co. He was the discoverer and first employer of Charles P. Steinmetz.

EIDLITZ, CYRUS LAZELLE WARNER (*b. New York, N.Y., 1853; d. 1921*), architect. Son of Leopold Eidlitz. Designed many important buildings, among them Dearborn Station, Chicago, the Buffalo, N.Y., Library, and the *N.Y. Times* Building, Times Square, New York City.

EIDLITZ, LEOPOLD (*b. Prague, Bohemia, 1823; d. 1908*), architect. Came to America, 1843. Designed many churches and other buildings in the Gothic style, his most successful being Christ Church, St. Louis, Mo.; redesigned state capitol at Albany, N.Y.

EIELSEN, ELLING (*b. Vossestranden, Norway, 1804; d. Chicago, Ill., 1883*), Norwegian lay preacher. Came to America, 1839. Preached on the Midwestern frontier; founded Norwegian Evangelical Lutheran Church of North America, 1846.

EIGENMANN, CARL H. (*b. Flehingen, Germany, 1863; d. California, 1927*), ichthyologist, educator. Came to America, 1877. Graduated Indiana University, 1886; Ph.D., 1889. Taught at Indiana University; founded its Graduate School and served as dean. Specialized in fishes of South America. Author of *Cave Vertebrates of America* (1909).

EILERS, FREDERIC ANTON (*b. Laufenselden, Germany, 1839; d. 1917*), metallurgist, leader in American lead-silver smelting. Came to America, 1859. Made theoretical as well as mechanical advances in Western smelting operations and furnace design.

EIMBECK, WILLIAM (*b. Brunswick, Germany, 1841; d. Washington, D.C., 1909*), geodetic engineer. Came to America, 1857. Originated duplex base apparatus for triangulation; carried out triangulation of the 39th parallel, 1878–96; engineer, U.S. Coast Survey, 1871–1906.

EINHORN, DAVID (*b. Dispeck, Germany, 1809; d. New York, N.Y., 1879*), rabbi. Came to America, 1855; served congregations in Baltimore, Philadelphia and New York. The leading theologian of the reform Judaism of his generation in America.

ELBERT, SAMUEL (*b. Prince William Parish, S.C., 1740; d. Savannah, Ga., 1788*), Revolutionary soldier, merchant. Removed to Georgia in early youth. Governor of Georgia, 1785.

ELDER, SAMUEL JAMES (*b. Hope, R.I., 1850; d. 1918*), lawyer, authority on copyright.

ELDER, SUSAN BLANCHARD (*b. Fort Jessup, La., 1835; d. Cincinnati, O., 1923*), author. In many biographies, stories, poems, and dramas expressed her devotion to the South and the Catholic Church.

ELDER, WILLIAM (*b. Somerset, Pa., 1806; d. Washington, D.C., 1885*), physician, writer. Contributed to Free-Soil papers; in *Questions of the Day: Economic and Social* (1871), popularized the economic theories of Henry C. Carey.

ELDER, WILLIAM HENRY (*b. Baltimore, Md., 1819; d. Cincinnati, O., 1904*), Roman Catholic clergyman. Ordained Rome, 1846. Served as professor of theology, Mt. St. Mary's, Emmitsburg, Md., 1846–57. Consecrated bishop of Natchez, 1857; archbishop of Cincinnati, 1883.

ELDRIDGE, SHALOR WINCHELL (*b. West Springfield, Mass., 1816; d. Lawrence, Kans., 1899*), Kansas leader, Union soldier, businessman.

ELIOT, CHARLES (*b. Cambridge, Mass., 1859; d. 1897*), landscape architect, author. Son of Charles W. Eliot. Active in establishing Boston Metropolitan Park Commission, 1892; associated with Frederick Law Olmsted under whom he had studied.

ELIOT, CHARLES WILLIAM (*b. Boston, Mass., 1834; d. Northeast Harbor, Maine, 1926*), educational leader. Son of Samuel A. Eliot. Graduated Harvard, 1853; taught there as tutor in mathematics and as assistant professor of mathematics and chemistry, 1854–63. Introduced first written examinations; emphasized laboratory work and elective as well as compulsory instruction. After a trip to Europe during which he made a first-hand study of European methods of education, he returned in 1865 as professor of chemistry at Massachusetts Institute of Technology. His concept of education as embodied in two articles in the *Atlantic Monthly*, 1869, won him the favorable notice of the Harvard Corporation and he was chosen president of Harvard, 1869.

His forty-year tenure transformed the College into a modern university. Primarily an administrator, rather than a scholar or teacher, Eliot concentrated all undergraduate studies in the college, and around it grouped the professional schools and research centers. His policy was to give the University coherence by drawing its parts into organic relationship, so that they might then be given a larger autonomy under their own deans and faculties. The bachelor's degree was made prerequisite for all graduate and professional studies. He encouraged the teaching of private classes for women by Harvard faculty members, a venture which in 1894 resulted in the founding of Radcliffe College. Eliot greatly improved the quality of the faculty, recruiting good men from all over the United States and from abroad; he also introduced the system of sabbatical leaves and French and German exchange professorships, raised salaries and inaugurated retirement allowances for professors.

Eliot's most radical reform in the College was the development of the "elective system." This necessitated a wide offering of graded courses in each subject among which the student was free to make his choice, thus to develop self-reliance and be governed in his degree work by interest rather than compulsion. Since 1825, preceding presidents had endeavored to implement this policy; Eliot made it almost fully effective by the year 1894. One of Eliot's projects, the three-year college course, encountered difficulties and was not formally adopted. His interest in the elective system led Eliot to pay considerable attention to admission requirements and to the need for improving the work done in secondary and primary schools. He participated in the work of the New England Association of Colleges and Preparatory Schools and in the National Education Association, of which he became president in 1903. He also prepared the report of the "Committee of Ten" of the NEA (1892) which formulated standard programs for secondary instruction and charged the secondary schools with the task of preparing all their students for college. The report prepared the way for the organization in 1901 of the Board of College Entrance Examinations. Eliot believed that only an enriched secondary school curriculum could free the colleges for their proper task. As a believer in freedom as an indispensable condition for the learning process and in training of the senses, the body, and the imagination, Eliot favored the "progressive" schools.

Eliot's influence was exerted strongly on the Graduate Schools of the University. In 1872 the degrees of Master of Arts, Doctor of Science, and Doctor of Philosophy were established; in 1890 followed the Graduate School of Arts and Sciences, organized under the same faculty as that of the College and the Scientific School. Eliot transformed the Divinity School from a denominational training school for ministers into a non-sectarian institution of higher learning. But his most notable contributions were made with the reforms of the Law School and the School of Medicine. Under Dean C. C. Langdell, a two-year course (1872) and later (1877–78) a three-year course, with admission and graduation examinations, were required of all law students. Adoption of the "case system" was the principal reform in law-school methods of instruction. By 1883, opposition to these innovations lost its effectiveness. In like manner, the low standards of the Medical School were raised. In 1871, a three-year course,

laboratory work, and written examinations were inaugurated, and clinical instruction and internships were gradually made available at the Boston hospitals. By 1892, a four-year course was obligatory.

After retirement from the presidency in 1909, Eliot continued his active public career in the cause of American education as an overseer of Harvard College (1910–16), as a member of the General Education Board and as a trustee of the Rockefeller Foundation and of the Carnegie Foundation for the Advancement of Teaching. In politics Eliot was independent with a leaning towards the Democratic party; in religion he was a Unitarian. He held an optimistic philosophy which put a premium on individual liberty and considered the essence of democratic freedom to consist in the maintenance of social mobility so as to insure equal opportunities for all. In his annual *Reports of the President of Harvard College* Eliot left a forty-year documentary record of the history of American education. His views on education may be found also in *Educational Reform* (1898); on politics and social issues in *American Contributions to Civilization* (1897); on religion in *The Religion of the Future* (1909), and in *The Durable Satisfactions of Life* (1910). He was also editor of the widely sold *Harvard Classics,* a collection illustrative of his statement that anyone could acquire a liberal education by reading fifteen minutes a day from great books which would fit on a "five-foot shelf." During the 40 years of Eliot's presidency the enrollment figures of Harvard College and its affiliated schools rose from approximately 1,000 students and 60 teachers to 4,000 students and 600 teachers. During the same period Harvard's endowment increased from 2¼ million dollars to over 20 millions.

ELIOT, JARED (*b. Guilford, Conn., 1685; d. Killingworth, Conn., 1763*), Congregational clergyman, physician. Grandson of John Eliot. Graduated Yale, 1706. Pastor of Killingworth (now Clinton), Conn., 1708–63; became the leading physician in New England. Discovered local black beach sand to be a valuable iron ore; also developed ore beds in northwestern Connecticut. Together with Ezra Stiles, Eliot introduced silk culture into Connecticut. Author of *Essay on the invention . . . of making . . . Iron from black Sea Sand* (1762) and a widely read and esteemed *Essay on Field Husbandry in New England* (1748–59). Yale College owes him its earliest bequest for the permanent endowment of the library.

ELIOT, JOHN (*b. Widford, England, 1604; d. Roxbury, Mass., 1690*), missionary to the Indians. A graduate of Cambridge University and influenced by Thomas Hooker, Eliot came to Massachusetts in 1631 and served as pastor and teacher in Roxbury. He preached first to the Indians in 1646. Recognizing the desire of the Indians to live by themselves, he founded the first town of native Christians at Natick,

1651; by 1674, fourteen such self-governing communities had been set up with a population of about 1,100. King Philip's War reduced this number to four towns, and the "praying Indians" gradually dwindled away. Eliot's celebrated translation of the Bible into the Indian language, the first Bible printed in North America, was published in 1661 (New Testament) and 1663 (Old Testament). His book *The Christian Commonwealth* (1659) was suppressed by the Massachusetts government for its republican sentiments.

ELIOT, SAMUEL (*b. Boston, Mass., 1821; d. Beverly Farms, Mass., 1898*), historian, educator, philanthropist. President, Trinity College, Hartford, Conn., 1860–64. Devoted rest of life to educational, religious, and eleemosynary institutions in Boston.

ELIOT, SAMUEL ATKINS (*b. Boston, Mass., 1798; d. Cambridge, Mass., 1862*), statesman, man of letters. Father of Charles W. Eliot. Mayor of Boston, 1837–39; served in legislature, and briefly in Congress where he supported Compromise of 1850. Promoted Boston musical life.

ELIOT, WILLIAM GREENLEAF (*b. New Bedford, Mass., 1811; d. Pass Christian, Miss., 1887*), Congregational clergyman, founder of Washington University, St. Louis, Mo.

ELKIN, WILLIAM LEWIS (*b. New Orleans, La., 1855; d. New Haven, Conn., 1933*), astronomer. Studied at Stuttgart, Germany; Ph.D., University of Strassburg, 1880. Director of Yale Observatory, 1896–1910; increased substantially the fund of information regarding stellar distances. [*Supp. 1*]

ELKINS, STEPHEN BENTON (*b. Perry Co., O., 1841; d. 1911*), lawyer. Union soldier, industrialist. Raised in Westport, Mo.; graduated University of Missouri, 1860. Began law practice in New Mexico, 1864; was elected to territorial legislature and appointed successively territorial district attorney, attorney general, and U.S. district attorney. Elected Republican delegate to Congress, 1872 and 1874–77. Was founder and president of the Santa Fé First National Bank, and held considerable Colorado land and coal properties. *Post* 1890, he was a resident of West Virginia where he had many industrial interests. Elkins entered national politics as a supporter of James G. Blaine. He served as U.S. secretary of war, 1891–95, and as Republican senator from West Virginia, 1895–1911. As head of the interstate commerce committee he was author of the anti-rebate act of 1903 and co-author of the Mann-Elkins Act of 1910.

ELKINS, WILLIAM LUKENS (*b. near Wheeling, W. Va., 1832; d. Philadelphia, Pa., 1903*), oil promoter, capitalist. Refined first gasoline; organized gas and street railway companies in Philadelphia and other cities.

ELLERY, FRANK (*b. Newport, R.I., 1794; d. Castleton, Vt., 1871*), naval officer. Grandson of William Ellery.

ELLERY, WILLIAM (*b. Newport, R.I., 1727; d. Newport, 1820*), lawyer, politician, signer of the Declaration of Independence from Rhode Island. Grandfather of Frank Ellery, W. E. Channing (1780–1842) and R. H. Dana. An expert committeeman on commercial and naval affairs as a member of Congress, 1776–86 (failed of election 1780 and 1782). Collector of customs at Newport, 1790–1820.

ELLET, CHARLES (*b. Penn's Manor, Pa., 1810; d. Cairo, Ill., 1862*), civil engineer. Designed and built innovating and important suspension bridges over the Schuylkill at Fairmount (1842) and over the Ohio at Wheeling (1849). Urged in *The Mississippi and Ohio Rivers* (1853) flood and navigation control of western rivers through dams and reservoirs. In 1854 built the Virginia Central track across the Blue Ridge. In *Coast and Harbour Defences* (1855), proposed construction of "ram-boats"; in 1862 led a fleet of nine ram-boats down the Mississippi and received surrender of Memphis. During this action he was mortally wounded. Ellet was recognized here and abroad as one of the great engineers of his time.

ELLET, ELIZABETH FRIES LUMMIS (*b. Sodus Point, N.Y., 1818; d. New York, N.Y., 1877*). Author of, among other works, *Domestic History of the American Revolution* (1850) and *Queens of American Society* (1867). Proficient as translator and critic of French, German and Italian literature.

ELLICOTT, ANDREW (*b. Bucks County, Pa., 1754; d. West Point, N.Y., 1820*), Revolutionary soldier, surveyor, mathematician. In 1784, aided in completing Pennsylvania-Maryland boundary begun by Mason and Dixon; also served on survey of western and northern Pennsylvania boundary and of islands in the Ohio and Allegheny. Determined southwestern boundary of New York, 1789; from 1791 to 1793 surveyed what was to become the District of Columbia. His revised plan of the "Federal City" (1792) was a redrawn version of L'Enfant's original design. After surveying in Pennsylvania, Georgia and on the United States–Florida frontier, Ellicott served as professor of mathematics at West Point, 1813–20.

ELLICOTT, JOSEPH (*b. Bucks Co., Pa., 1760; d. 1826*), engineer, land agent. Brother and associate of Andrew Ellicott. Served as the Holland Land Company's agent in western New York, 1800–21. Founded Buffalo, N.Y.

ELLIOT, DANIEL GIRAUD (*b. New York, N.Y., 1835; d. 1915*), zoologist. Founded American Ornithologists' Union; author of *Review of the Primates* (1912).

ELLIOT, JAMES (*b. Gloucester, Mass., 1775; d. 1839*), politician, lawyer, soldier. Federalist congressman from Vermont, 1803–09. Author of *Poetical and Miscellaneous Works* (1798).

ELLIOT, JONATHAN (*b. near Carlisle, England, 1784; d. 1846*), editor, publicist. Came to America, 1802. Produced the *Gazette,* first daily evening paper in Washington, D.C., 1814. Best known as publisher of *Debates . . . on the Adoption of the Federal Constitution* (1827–30, 1845) and *Diplomatic Code of the United States* (1827, 1834).

ELLIOTT, AARON MARSHALL (*b. Wilmington, N.C., 1844; d. 1910*), philologist. A pioneer in scientific study of modern languages and literatures as professor of Romance languages at Johns Hopkins University. Established the Modern Language Association, 1883.

ELLIOTT, BENJAMIN (*b. Charleston, S.C., 1787; d. Charleston, 1836*), lawyer. Nephew of Charles Pinckney; law partner of Robert Y. Hayne. Collaborated in a pioneer defense of slavery, *A Refutation of the Calumnies, etc.* (1822) with E. C. Holland.

ELLIOTT, CHARLES (*b. Co. Donegal, Ireland, 1792; d. Mt. Pleasant, Ia., 1869*), Methodist clergyman, editor, historian.

ELLIOTT, CHARLES BURKE (*b. Morgan Co., O., 1861; d. 1935*), lawyer, jurist, writer. Associate justice, supreme court of the Philippines, 1909; member of Philippine Commission, 1910–12. [*Supp. 1*]

ELLIOTT, CHARLES LORING (*b. Scipio, N.Y., 1812; d. Albany, N.Y., 1868*), painter. His portraits of many famous 19th century Americans are marked by firm drawing, clean color and a natural likeness.

ELLIOTT, JESSE DUNCAN (*b. Hagerstown, Md., 1782; d. Philadelphia, Pa., 1845*), naval officer. As commander of *Niagara* during the battle of Lake Erie, 1813, he was accused of failure to come to the aid of Commodore Perry's flagship, and a thirty-year controversy ensued. James Fenimore Cooper ably defended Elliott, but Admiral Mahan reached conclusions favorable to Perry. Elliott subsequently held many commands and died as commandant of the Philadelphia navy yard.

ELLIOTT, JOHN (*b. Lincolnshire, England, 1858; d. Charleston, S.C., 1925*), painter. Best known for murals in Boston Public Library and Washington, D.C., National Museum, and for his distinguished portraits.

ELLIOTT, MAXINE (*b. Rockland, Maine, 1871; d. near Cannes, France, 1940*), actress. Changed name from Jessie Carolyn Dermot. A famous beauty and an astute business woman, she starred in drawing-room comedies. [*Supp. 2*]

ELLIOTT, SARAH BARNWELL (*b. Georgia, 1848; d. Sewanee, Tenn., 1928*), author, suffragist leader. Shares with Charles Egbert Craddock credit for introducing realistic Southern mountaineer characters into literature.

ELLIOTT, STEPHEN (*b. Beaufort, S.C., 1771; d. 1830*), botanist, banker, U.S. senator. Co-founder of the *Southern Review,* 1828; author of *Sketch of the Botany of South Carolina and Georgia* (1821–24).

ELLIOTT, WALTER HACKETT ROBERT (*b. Detroit, Mich., 1842; d. Washington, D.C., 1928*), lawyer, Union soldier, Roman Catholic priest of the Paulist Congregation. Co-founder, Apostolic Mission House at Catholic University, Washington, D.C.; was a celebrated missionary. Author of *Life of Father Hecker* (1891) and other works.

ELLIOTT, WASHINGTON LAFAYETTE (*b. Carlisle, Pa., 1825; d. San Francisco, Calif., 1888*), soldier. Son of Jesse D. Elliott. Served in Mexico, on Western frontier, and rose to Union major-general of cavalry during Civil War.

ELLIOTT, WILLIAM (*b. Beaufort, S.C., 1788; d. Charleston, S.C., 1863*), planter. Author of *Carolina Sports by Land and Water* (1846) and *Letters of Agricola* (1852).

ELLIS, CALVIN (*b. Boston, Mass., 1826; d. 1883*), physician. Graduated Harvard, 1846; M.D., Harvard Medical, 1849. As dean of Harvard Medical School, *post* 1869, he carried out the reform program of Charles W. Eliot, and made important contributions to scientific medical diagnosis.

ELLIS, EDWARD SYLVESTER (*b. Geneva, O., 1840; d. Cliff Island, Maine, 1916*). Author of *Seth Jones, or the Captive of the Frontier* (1860) and other dime novels, biographies and histories under many pen-names.

ELLIS, GEORGE EDWARD (*b. Boston, Mass., 1814; d. Boston, 1894*), Unitarian clergyman, historian, editor. Professor of theology at Harvard; president of Massachusetts Historical Society, 1885–94.

ELLIS, GEORGE WASHINGTON (*b. Weston, Mo., 1875; d. 1919*), lawyer, sociologist. While secretary of American legation in Liberia, 1902–10, made scientific study of West African tribes; author of *Negro Culture in West Africa* (1914) and other works marked by originality and insight.

ELLIS, HENRY (*b. Ireland, 1721; d. Naples, Italy, 1806*), hydrographer. Searched unsuccessfully for Northwest Passage; active and able royal governor of Georgia, 1757–60.

ELLIS, JOB BICKNELL (*b. near Potsdam, N.Y., 1829; d. Newfield, N.J., 1905*), botanist, mycologist. Graduated Union College, 1851. His *North American Pyrenomycetes* (1892) spread his fame among botanists throughout the world.

ELLIS, JOHN WASHINGTON (*b. Williamsburg, O., 1817; d. New York, N.Y., 1910*), merchant, banker. Headed First National of Cincinnati, 1863–69, and Winslow, Lanier and Co., 1870–83.

ELLIS, JOHN WILLIS (*b. Rowan Co., N.C., 1820; d. Raleigh, N.C., 1861*), lawyer. Served in legislature and as judge of superior court. As Democratic governor of North Carolina, 1858–61, he favored secession; called for volunteers to resist Northern invasion.

ELLIS, POWHATAN (*b. Amherst Co., Va., 1790; d. Richmond, Va., 1863*), jurist, diplomat. Removed to Mississippi, 1816; served on supreme court there, 1818–25, and as U.S. senator, Democrat, 1825–32. U.S. minister to Mexico, 1839–42.

ELLIS, SETH HOCKETT (*b. Martinsville, O., 1830; d. Waynesville, O., 1904*), farmer, politician. Organized first Ohio Grange, 1872, and was active in the movement thereafter. Union Reform party candidate for U.S. presidency, 1900.

ELLSWORTH, ELMER EPHRAIM (*b. Malta, N.Y., 1837; d. Alexandria, Va., 1861*), soldier. Commanded a volunteer Zouave unit in Chicago, Ill.; entered Abraham Lincoln's office as a law clerk, 1860, and was active in the presidential campaign. In 1861, he recruited a Zouave regiment from New York volunteer firemen and was first man of note killed in Civil War.

ELLSWORTH, HENRY LEAVITT (*b. Windsor, Conn., 1791; d. Fair Haven, Conn., 1858*), lawyer, agriculturist. Son of Oliver Ellsworth. Appointed, 1832, as commissioner to superintend resettlement of Indian tribes south and west of Arkansas. As first U.S. commissioner of patents, 1835–45, Ellsworth obtained a congressional appropriation for Morse's telegraph, and made his office assume many functions of an agricultural bureau. Removing to Lafayette, Ind., he became one of the largest landowners in the West and a pioneer advocate of the use of agricultural machinery.

ELLSWORTH, HENRY WILLIAM (*b. Windsor, Conn., 1814; d. New Haven, Conn., 1864*), lawyer, diplomat. Son of Henry L. Ellsworth. Served as chargé d'affaires to Sweden and Norway, 1845–49.

ELLSWORTH, OLIVER (*b. Windsor, Conn., 1745; d. 1807*), statesman, jurist. Graduated Princeton (College of New Jersey), 1766. Admitted to the bar, 1771; opened an office in Hartford, Conn., 1775. By 1780 he had become a member of the Governor's Council, and subsequently served on the state supreme court of errors, on the superior court, and as state's attorney. During the Revolution he acted as a member of Connecticut's Committee of the Pay Table, as delegate to the Continental Congress from 1777 to 1783, and as a member of the Connecticut Council of Safety. As a delegate to the Constitutional Convention, Ellsworth took a prominent part in working out the "Connecticut compromise," and ably defended the plan against the large-state delegates. He favored state rather than national payment of representatives and a three-fifths ratio in counting slaves as a basis of both taxation and representation. He opposed the abolition of the foreign slave-trade. His "Letters of a Landholder" printed in the *Connecticut Courant* (1787–88) and widely circulated urged ratification of the new Constitution.

Intimately familiar with organizational and administrative affairs, he enjoyed a predominant position among his colleagues as U.S. senator from Connecticut, 1789–96. He reported the first set of Senate rules, considered a plan for printing a journal, reported back from conference the first twelve amendments, framed the measure which admitted North Carolina and devised the non-intercourse act that forced Rhode Island into the Union. He reported a bill for government of the territory south of the Ohio, drew up the first bill regulating the consular service, and vigorously defended Hamilton's plans for funding the national debt and for incorporating a bank of the United States. His most important single contribution was his draft of the bill organizing the federal judiciary. In the words of John Adams, Ellsworth was "the firmest pillar of his [Washington's] administration."

Ellsworth resigned from the Senate in 1796 to become chief justice of the United States. He did not excel as a judge. His decisions were marked by common sense but by no great legal learning, and his skill in advocacy which had established him at the bar and in the Senate was of little use in purely judicial business. In 1799 he reluctantly became one of a commission to France to improve American relations with that country. He and his colleagues, W. R. Davie and William Vans Murray, were obliged to accept terms from Napoleon which neither conformed to their hopes nor to their instructions; Ellsworth felt, however, that a possible war with France had been thereby avoided. Broken in health, he resigned from his office as chief justice and, on returning to the United States in the spring of 1801, retired to his home in Windsor.

ELLSWORTH, WILLIAM WOLCOTT (*b. Windsor, Conn., 1791; d. Hartford, Conn., 1868*), lawyer. Son of Oliver Ellsworth. Congressman, Whig, from Connecticut, 1829–34; governor, 1838–42; judge of state supreme court, 1847–61.

ELMER, EBENEZER (*b. Cedarville, N.J., 1752; d. Bridgeton, N.J., 1843*), physician, Revolutionary surgeon, New Jersey legislator.

ELMER, JONATHAN (*b. Cedarville, N.J., 1745; d. 1817*), physician, Revolutionary patriot, jurist. Brother of Ebenezer Elmer. Gave up promising medical career for politics; served in Congress, 1776–78;

1781–84; 1787–88. Elected U.S. senator, Federalist, from New Jersey in 1789, he served until 1791. He was surrogate of Cumberland County for many years.

ELMER, LUCIUS QUINTIUS CINCINNATUS (*b. Bridgeton, N.J., 1793; d. 1883*), jurist, legislator. Son of Ebenezer Elmer. Prominent in New Jersey Assembly as independent Democrat; U.S. attorney for New Jersey, 1824–29. Later congressman and New Jersey attorney-general, he was a justice of state supreme court, 1852–59; 1861; 1862–69.

ELMORE, FRANKLIN HARPER (*b. Laurens District, S.C., 1799; d. Washington, D.C., 1850*), banker. Disciple of J. C. Calhoun; served briefly as representative and as U.S. senator from South Carolina.

ELSBERG, LOUIS (*b. Iserlohn, Prussia, 1836; d. 1885*), laryngologist. Came to America, 1849. Graduated Jefferson Medical College, 1857. Studied his specialty at Vienna and pioneered in it thereafter in New York. Author of *Laryngoscopal Surgery* (1865).

ELSON, LOUIS CHARLES (*b. Boston, Mass., 1848; d. Boston, 1920*), music critic, lecturer. Taught theory at New England Conservatory of Music; author of *History of American Music* (1904).

ELWELL, FRANK EDWIN (*b. Concord, Mass., 1858; d. Darien, Conn., 1922*), sculptor. Patronized by Louisa M. Alcott and Daniel C. French; studied in Paris and Ghent. Versatile author of many public monuments and portrait statues.

ELWELL, JOHN JOHNSON (*b. near Warren, O., 1820; d. Cleveland, O., 1900*), physician, lawyer, Union soldier, editor. Specialized in and taught medical jurisprudence; wrote standard text, *Medico-Legal Treatise on Malpractice and Medical Evidence* (1860).

ELWYN, ALFRED LANGDON (*b. Portsmouth, N.H., 1804; d. Philadelphia, Pa., 1884*), physician. Student of history, philology, botany; philanthropist. Author of *Glossary of Supposed Americanisms* (1859).

ELZEY, ARNOLD (*b. Somerset Co., Md., 1816; d. Baltimore, Md., 1871*), soldier. Graduated West Point, 1837. Fought in Seminole and Mexican wars; as a Confederate officer, he led final and successful charge of Kirby Smith's brigade at first battle of Manassas. Promoted major-general, 1864, after severe wounding at Cold Harbor, he commanded in Richmond and was later chief of artillery, Army of Tennessee.

EMBREE, ELIHU (*b. Washington Co., Tenn., 1782; d. 1820*), iron manufacturer, Abolitionist. Became leader of Tennessee Manumission Society, editor of *Manumission Intelligencer* (1819) and of the *Emancipator* (1820).

EMBURY, EMMA CATHERINE (*b. New York, N.Y., c. 1806; d. 1863*), author, leader of a literary *salon*. Her verse suffered from vagueness of imagery and conventionality of theme.

EMBURY, PHILIP (*b. Ballingrane ?, Ireland, c. 1728; d. near East Salem, N.Y., 1773*), Methodist preacher, carpenter. Came to America, 1760. Reputed to have been the first Methodist preacher in America (1766, New York City).

EMERSON, BENJAMIN KENDALL (*b. Nashua, N.H., 1843; d. Amherst, Mass., 1932*), educator, geologist. Taught at Amherst and Smith Colleges.
[*Supp. 1*]

EMERSON, EDWARD WALDO (*b. Concord, Mass., 1844; d. Concord, 1930*), physician, author. Edited works and journals of his father, Ralph Waldo Emerson; author of *Emerson in Concord* (1889) and other books.

EMERSON, ELLEN RUSSELL (*b. New Sharon, Maine, 1837; d. 1907*), ethnologist. Author of *Indian Myths* (1884) and *Masks, Heads, and Faces* (1891).

EMERSON, GEORGE BARRELL (*b. Wells, Maine, 1797; d. Newton, Mass., 1881*), educator. Graduated Harvard, 1817. Headed a Boston private school, 1823–55; helped organize American Institute of Instruction. Published survey of Massachusetts trees and shrubs.

EMERSON, GOUVERNEUR (*b. near Dover, Del., 1795; d. Philadelphia, Pa., 1874*), physician, agriculturist.

EMERSON, JAMES EZEKIEL (*b. Norridgewock, Maine, 1823; d. Columbus, O., 1900*), machinist, inventor. Patented the inserted-tooth circular saw, a steel-making process, saw-making machinery, and a steel scabbard for bayonets.

EMERSON, JOSEPH (*b. Hollis, N.H., 1777; d. Wethersfield, Conn., 1833*), Congregational clergyman, educator. Conducted a noteworthy seminary for young women, 1816–33; Zilpah Grant and Mary Lyon were among its graduates.

EMERSON, MARY MOODY (*b. Concord, Mass., 1774; d. Brooklyn, N.Y., 1863*), aunt of Ralph Waldo Emerson, whose education she supervised and on whom she had a strong influence.

EMERSON, OLIVER FARRAR (*b. near Wolf Creek, Iowa, 1860; d. Ocala, Fla., 1927*), philologist. Taught at Cornell and Western Reserve; wrote extensively on English language and literature.

EMERSON, RALPH (*b. Andover, Mass., 1831; d. 1914*), inventor, manufacturer. Produced agricultural machines in association with John H. Manny; developed knitting concerns in Rockford, Ill. Founded Emerson Institute for education of Negro children at Mobile, Ala.

EMERSON, RALPH WALDO (*b. Boston, Mass., 1803; d. Concord, Mass., 1882*), essayist, poet. Son of William Emerson and Ruth Haskins Emerson; descendant of Peter Bulkeley. Orphaned of his father, 1811, he grew up under strong influence of his aunt, Mary Moody Emerson. Attended Boston Latin School; enrolled at Harvard College, 1817. Helped support himself there as messenger, waiter, and tutor. Among professors who influenced him were George Ticknor, Edward Everett and Edward Tyrrel Channing. Emerson became a member of the Pythologian Club, a literary society, and graduated as class poet in 1821. From his junior year at the college dates the earliest extant volume of his journals, in which he noted his ideas and sensations and which served through life as the quarry from which he drew his lectures and books. During the next four years he taught school; in 1825 he entered the Harvard Divinity School. He soon found that his strength lay in his oratorical ability and in the exercise of "moral imagination," rather than in reasoning and the defense of church dogma. He was beset by doubts concerning the latter and suffered from ill health. Nevertheless, he was "approbated to preach" in 1826 and gave occasional sermons in churches in Boston and other New England towns. In 1829 he became minister of the Second Church of Boston and held this position until the summer of 1832 when he refused to administer the Lord's Supper in the accepted fashion. During this period he enjoyed a few happy months of married life which ended with the death of the first Mrs. Emerson (Ellen Tucker) in February, 1831.

Emerson's break with the ministry and recurring poor health prompted him to set off on a journey to Italy, England and Scotland where he met, among others, Coleridge, Wordsworth and Carlyle. From his visit with Carlyle dates their correspondence of nearly forty years. His European sojourn brought Emerson into direct contact with men and ideas which stimulated his reason and imagination. If liberal American Unitarianism, eighteenth century republicanism, and British philosophical skepticism had cleansed his mind of traditional dogmas, German idealism and Goethean, as well as English, transcendentalism provided the materials and incentives for his future work. These currents of thought together with insights derived from Montaigne, Plato, and Swedenborg turned Emerson's attention to a deliberate observation of nature. He strove to establish an original relationship with the visible universe, spending a portion of each day in the woods and along the rivers, seeking to effect a marriage between his thoughts and sensations. He presented the results of his endeavors in his first book, *Nature* (1836). Nature, Emerson declared, was man's greatest teacher. Being the dress God wears, it taught lessons of usefulness and beauty, it had its own language and, being always moral, carried its own discipline.

Emerson enjoyed the company of like-minded friends, the so-called Transcendentalists, among whom were Orestes Brownson, Theodore Parker, Bronson Alcott, Margaret Fuller, and James Freeman Clarke. While he was working on *Nature,* Emerson continued preaching every Sunday in different churches, and also began his career as a lecturer. His *Journals,* in which he entered his thoughts, fancies and speculations as they occurred to him, provided the materials for his lectures on natural history, biography, English literature, and other topics; the lectures themselves were later published in very little altered form in his *Essays* (published 1841 and 1844). He now made his home in Concord, and in 1835 married his second wife, Lydia Jackson. He settled down to a daily routine of writing, walking, and enjoying the company of his friends, among whom he also counted Henry David Thoreau, Jones Very, and Nathaniel Hawthorne. In 1837 he delivered his famous Phi Beta Kappa address at Harvard, *The American Scholar,* called by Oliver Wendell Holmes "our intellectual Declaration of Independence." It urged an original relation of the American scholar to philosophy and the arts, and it repudiated American reliance on the culture of Europe and the ancient world. In 1838 Emerson's Divinity School Address at Cambridge declared the Church dead and the ministry outmoded; he called for an end to the scholar's dependence on the Church as an institution, and for a new revelation commensurate to the present age. Emerson's indictment roused the antagonism of many churchmen and made Emerson *persona non grata* at Harvard for almost thirty years. In 1840 Emerson became a regular contributor to the Transcendentalist magazine, *The Dial;* in 1842 he became its editor. Unsympathetic with "practical" reform aspects of the magazine's program, he emphasized poetry and metaphysics. Believing that reforms must spring from the hearts and minds of individuals, he remained cool to the communal reform efforts of his friends and to such projects as Brook Farm and Fruitlands. He did, however, speak on behalf of the Abolitionist cause.

Going to England on a lecture tour in 1847, he found himself famous there; he renewed his friendship with Carlyle and made the acquaintance of all the literary notables of the time. His reactions to England and her people were expressed in lectures later (1856) published as *English Traits.* The need to make money for his support by lecturing was not altogether to his taste; he continued, however, to travel the circuit, extending his trips well to the West. Meanwhile, he had published *Poems* (1847) which, with *May-Day and Other Pieces* (1867), ranks him in the poetic company of Poe, Whitman and Emily Dickinson. His output was uneven, but at his best he produced an intellectual poetry burning with what he himself called "aromatic fire."

In 1850, he published *Representative Men*, based on lectures delivered five years previously; in 1855, he was among the first to recognize Walt Whitman's genius. Emerson's chief mental occupation during the 1850's, however, was politics, and his journals are filled with comment on the great issues which were dividing the nation. He became bolder in his criticism of slavery and of those who defended it.

Immediately preceding the Civil War, he formed about him a group of men for monthly discussions which was known as the Saturday Club; it numbered Longfellow, Hawthorne, Motley, Dana, Agassiz, O. W. Holmes and others. He also took pleasure in the outdoor excursions of the Adirondack Club.

After 1866, Emerson did nothing new, although he continued to lecture, and, in some measure, to write. His poem "Terminus" expresses his mood at this time, and five years thereafter (1871) began the slow erosion of physical and mental powers which marked his declining years. During this period appeared *Parnassus* (1874), an anthology of English poetry which had pleased him, and *Letters and Social Aims* (1876).

Emerson's fame at home and abroad rests on the fact that he had something of importance to say and that he said it with a beautiful, aphoristic freshness. His doctrine that men are exalted creatures, that instinct is to be obeyed, that the soul is a sensible reality, and that man is capable of all things if he but stand erect and go alone is an ideal doctrine, but he clothed it in a durable style and enforced it with a rare power of observation and a subtle sense of humor. His stylistic excellencies will be found most marked in the concluding paragraph of the chapter "Illusions" in *The Conduct of Life* (1860). Few American intellectuals have been more picturesque; none holds a solider position in the history of American life, for the impact of his shining, energizing personality is still strong.

EMERSON, WILLIAM (*b. Concord, Mass., 1769; d. 1811*), Unitarian clergyman, father of Ralph Waldo Emerson. Graduated Harvard, 1789. Pastor, First Church, Boston, 1799 until his death. Served as chaplain of the state senate, as editor of the *Monthly Anthology,* and was a founder of the Anthology Club from whose library grew the Boston Athenaeum.

EMERTON, EPHRAIM (*b. Salem, Mass., 1851; d. 1935*), educator, historian. Professor at Harvard; specialist in Renaissance and Reformation history; emphasized cultural aspects of history in original and influential textbooks as also in scholarly monographs. [*Supp.* 1]

EMERTON, JAMES HENRY (*b. Salem, Mass., 1847; d. 1930*), naturalist, arachnologist, artist. Authority on the taxonomy and habits of spiders. [*Supp.* 1]

EMERY, ALBERT HAMILTON (*b. Mexico, N.Y., 1834; d. Glenbrook, Conn., 1926*), engineer, inventor. Consultant and designer of testing machinery;

made principal contribution in ordnance, and hydraulic pressure measuring devices.

EMERY, CHARLES EDWARD (*b. Aurora, N.Y., 1838; d. 1898*), engineer. Consultant to U.S. Navy on steam engines, also to Coast Survey and Coast Guard; chief engineer and manager, N.Y. Steam Co., *post* 1879.

EMERY, HENRY CROSBY (*b. Ellsworth, Maine, 1872; d. at sea, 1924*), economist, businessman. Son of Lucilius A. Emery. Graduated Bowdoin, 1892; Ph.D., Columbia, 1896. Taught at Yale; was chairman of Tariff Board, 1909–13; *post* 1915 worked as financier in Russia and China.

EMERY, LUCILIUS ALONZO (*b. Carmel, Maine, 1840; d. 1920*), jurist. Introduced coordinated system of equity pleading and chancery rules in Maine; justice of state supreme court, 1883–1911 (chief justice, *post* 1906).

EMERY, STEPHEN ALBERT (*b. Paris, Maine, 1841; d. Boston, Mass., 1891*), teacher, composer. Taught harmony, piano, composition and theory at New England Conservatory and Boston University; author of *Elements of Harmony* (1879).

EMMET, THOMAS ADDIS (*b. Cork, Ireland, 1764; d. New York, N.Y., 1827*), lawyer. Brother of Robert Emmet, the Irish patriot. Graduated Trinity College, Dublin, 1782; M.D., Edinburgh, 1784. After study at the Temple, was admitted to Irish bar, 1790. Became an Irish national idol for activities on behalf of Society of United Irishmen. After arrest, 1798–1802, he was exiled to the Continent; emigrated, 1804, to the United States. Over opposition of Federalist lawyers Emmet was admitted to the New York bar where he was very successful. In 1812 he served as state attorney-general.

EMMET, THOMAS ADDIS (*b. near Charlottesville, Va., 1828; d. 1919*), physician. Grandson of Thomas A. Emmet (1764–1827). Graduated Jefferson Medical College, 1850. Practiced at Emigrants' Refuge Hospital, N.Y., and later with J. Marion Sims at the Woman's Hospital. Devised Emmet's operation for the repair of tears in the womb; wrote *Principles and Practice of Gynaecology* (1879). Recognized as outstanding surgeon in America and Europe. Made an important collection of American prints and autographs. An ardent advocate of Irish home rule, Emmet wrote a vitriolic indictment of England, *Ireland Under English Rule* (1903), and was president of the Irish National Federation of America.

EMMETT, BURTON (*b. Lee, Ill., 1871; d. Melfa, Va., 1935*), advertising executive, book and print collector. [*Supp.* 1]

EMMETT, DANIEL DECATUR (*b. Mt. Vernon, O., 1815; d. Mount Vernon, 1904*), one of the originators of the "Negro Minstrel" troupe, 1842–43. Author of "Old Dan Tucker" (*c.* 1831); "Dixie" (1859); and other minstrel songs.

EMMONS, EBENEZER (*b. Middlefield, Mass., 1799; d. Brunswick Co., N.C., 1863*), geologist, physician, teacher. State geologist of North Carolina, *post* 1851.

EMMONS, GEORGE FOSTER (*b. Clarendon, Vt., 1811; d. Princeton, N.J., 1884*), naval officer. Active in Wilkes's Exploring Expedition and on Pacific Coast, 1838–50. Author of *The Navy of the United States . . . 1775–1853* (1853). Served with ability on Gulf blockade in Civil War. Retired as rear-admiral, 1873.

EMMONS, NATHANAEL (*b. East Haddam, Conn., 1745; d. Franklin, Mass., 1840*), Congregational clergyman, conservative theologian.

EMMONS, SAMUEL FRANKLIN (*b. Boston, Mass., 1841; d. 1911*), geologist, mining engineer. Participated in geological exploration of 40th Parallel and later Western surveys; author of *Geology and Mining Industry of Leadville, Colo.* (1886).

EMORY, JOHN (*b. Spaniard's Neck, Md., 1789; d. near Reisterstown, Md., 1835*), Methodist clergyman. Held pastorates in Philadelphia and Baltimore Conferences; was agent of Methodist Book Concern; elected bishop, 1832.

EMORY, WILLIAM HEMSLEY (*b. Queen Annes Co., Md., 1811; d. 1887*), soldier. Graduated West Point, 1831. As topographical engineer, participated in Northeastern boundary survey; served with Army of the West in Mexican War. Chief astronomer in survey of California-Mexico boundary, 1848–53; commissioner and astronomer under Gadsden Treaty, 1854–57. During Civil War, held brigade, division and corps commands with high distinction. Author, among others, of *Notes of a Military Reconnaissance from Fort Leavenworth to San Diego* (1848) and *Report on the U.S. and Mexican Boundary Survey* (1857–59). Retired as brigadier-general, regular army, 1876.

EMOTT, JAMES (*b. Poughkeepsie, N.Y., 1771; d. 1850*), New York jurist, legislator, Federalist congressman.

EMOTT, JAMES (*b. Poughkeepsie, N.Y., 1823; d. Poughkeepsie, 1884*), jurist, banker. Son of James Emott (1771–1850). First mayor of Poughkeepsie, Whig, 1854; judge, New York supreme court, 1856–64. Active in exposure of "Tweed Ring."

ENDECOTT, JOHN (*b. Chagford, England, c. 1589; d. Boston, Mass., 1665*), governor of Massachusetts. An incorporator of the Massachusetts Bay colony, he was in charge of the first settlement from their arrival at Naumkeag (Salem), Sept. 1628, until the main body of the company arrived in the summer of 1630 and John Winthrop took over as governor. Endecott ruled with sternness and efficiency; he helped organize an independent church after the model of the Pilgrims at Plymouth, and deported two members of his colony who declined to accept Separatism. After Winthrop's succession, Endecott served as his assistant and in military capacities; he was again governor in 1644, 1649, 1651–53, 1655–64. A punitive expedition against the Indians which he led in 1636 proved a complete failure and did much to bring on the Pequot War. Intolerant of religious opinions other than his own, in his persecution of the Quakers he showed himself bloodthirsty and brutal. He was interested in education, urged the establishment of a free school at Salem and became an overseer of Harvard College. As a public servant Endecott was capable, honest, although unable to conceive of any public good other than as he saw it. In his religious and social views he was a thoroughgoing Puritan, stern and irascible, a man of iron will and little human sympathy.

ENDICOTT, CHARLES MOSES (*b. Danvers, Mass., 1793; d. 1863*), sea-captain, antiquarian. Author of the useful and important *Sailing Directions for the Pepper Ports on the West Coast of Sumatra* (1833).

ENDICOTT, JOHN. [See ENDECOTT, JOHN, *c.* 1589–1665.]

ENDICOTT, MORDECAI THOMAS (*b. Mays Landing, N.J., 1844; d. Washington, D.C., 1926*), naval engineer. Chief of Bureau of Yards and Docks, 1898–1907; completed floating dry dock *Dewey*, largest of its time.

ENDICOTT, WILLIAM CROWNINSHIELD (*b. Salem, Mass., 1826; d. Boston, Mass., 1900*), jurist. Judge, supreme judicial court of Massachusetts, 1873–82; as secretary of war, 1885–89, distinguished himself through his work with the Endicott Board of Fortifications on Atlantic Coast defence work.

ENELOW, HYMAN GERSON (*b. Kovno, Russia, 1877; d. at sea, 1934*), rabbi. Came to America, 1893. Graduated Hebrew Union College, 1898. Held pastorates in Kentucky and at Temple Emanu-el, New York City. Author of scholarly works and patron of scholars. [*Supp. 1*]

ENGELHARDT, ZEPHYRIN (*b. Bilshausen, Germany, 1851; d. Santa Barbara, Calif., 1934*), Roman Catholic clergyman, Franciscan. Came to America as an infant. Missionary to the Indians. Author of *The Franciscans in California* (1897), *Missions and Missionaries of California* (1908–16) and many other works. [*Supp. 1*]

ENGELMANN, GEORGE (*b. Frankfurt-am-Main, Germany, 1809; d. St. Louis, Mo., 1884*), physician, botanist, pioneer meteorologist. Graduated Würzburg, M.D., 1831. Came to America, 1832; practiced in St. Louis, Mo., *post* 1835. Made important contributions to grape culture. His botanical monographs were published in collected form, 1887.

ENGELMANN, GEORGE JULIUS (*b. St. Louis, Mo., 1847; d. Boston, Mass., 1903*), gynecologist, obstetrician. Son of George Engelmann. Studied medicine in Germany, Austria, France, and England; practiced and taught in St. Louis and Boston. Made extensive researches of Indian mounds in Missouri.

ENGLAND, JOHN (*b. Cork, Ireland, 1786; d. Charleston, S.C., 1842*), Roman Catholic clergyman. Active in Irish nationalist movements and a highly articulate democrat, he was consecrated first bishop of Charleston, S.C., 1820. An indefatigable preacher and vehement controversialist, he roused the spirit of his diocese, instituted a democratic constitution for its guidance by lay and clerical delegates, opened the Philosophical and Classical Seminary of Charleston, (an innovating school), brought in Irish Ursulines for the education of girls, and unsuccessfully sought to open a school for free Negroes. For practical reasons he accepted slavery as an institution. He was a prolific writer and lecturer, the first priest to address the House of Representatives and a prime mover in calling the Provincial Councils of Baltimore. In 1833–37 he served as apostolic delegate to Haiti. His greatest achievement was the founding of the *United States Catholic Miscellany* (1822–61), the first distinctly Catholic paper in America.

ENGLIS, JOHN (*b. New York, N.Y., 1808; d. 1888*), shipbuilder. His Hudson River, Long Island Sound and Great Lakes steamboats were known for speed and grace of line.

ENGLISH, ELBERT HARTWELL (*b. Madison Co., Ala., 1816; d. 1884*), Arkansas lawyer and jurist.

ENGLISH, GEORGE BETHUNE (*b. Cambridge, Mass., 1787; d. Washington, D.C., 1828*), writer, soldier, linguist. Graduated Harvard, 1807. Served as officer of U.S. Marines; turned Mahometan and served in Egyptian army; secret U.S. agent in Levant, 1823–27. Versatile but erratic.

ENGLISH, JAMES EDWARD (*b. New Haven, Conn., 1812; d. New Haven, 1890*), clock and brass manufacturer. Congressman, Democrat, 1861–65; U.S. senator, 1875–76; governor of Connecticut, 1867, 1868 and 1870.

ENGLISH, THOMAS DUNN (*b. in or near Philadelphia, Pa., 1819; d. Newark, N.J., 1902*), editor, politician, playwright. Remembered for his poem "Ben Bolt" (1843).

ENGLISH, WILLIAM HAYDEN (*b. Lexington, Ind., 1822; d. Indianapolis, Ind., 1896*), lawyer, banker. Congressman, Democrat, from Indiana, 1852–60; author of "English Bill" (1858). Democratic candidate for vice-presidency, 1880. Author of *Life of Gen. George Rogers Clark* (1896).

ENNEKING, JOHN JOSEPH (*b. Minster, O., 1841; d. Boston, Mass., 1916*), landscape and figure painter. A romanticist and impressionist, Enneking has been called the interpreter of New England in painting as was Edward MacDowell in music.

ENSLEY, ENOCH (*b. near Nashville, Tenn., 1836; d. 1891*), planter, manufacturer, economist. A pioneer in industrial development of the South. Author of *What Should Be Taxed . . .* (1873), a novel and important work, very far in advance of its time.

ENTWISTLE, JAMES (*b. Paterson, N.J., 1837; d. Paterson, 1910*), naval engineer. Fleet engineer under Commodore George Dewey at Manila Bay, 1898.

EPPES, JOHN WAYLES (*b. near Petersburg, Va., 1773; d. Buckingham Co., Va., 1823*), lawyer. Nephew of Thomas Jefferson. Congressman, (Democrat) Republican, from Virginia, 1803–11; 1813–15. U.S. senator, 1817–19. Upheld Jefferson's policies against John Randolph of Roanoke's factional group.

ERICSSON, JOHN (*b. Vermland, Sweden, 1803; d. New York, N.Y., 1889*), engineer, inventor. Received early training as cadet in Swedish corps of mechanical engineers; worked in London, England, 1826–38, where he perfected many mechanical inventions and improvements, among others a steam fire-engine, a steam locomotive, and the screw propeller for steam vessels. Came to America, 1839, intending a short visit; remaining, he became a citizen. Prolific, versatile, but incapable of working closely with others, he designed power-plants for all purposes, including fire-engines, hot-air stationary engines and the first screw-propelled man-of-war, U.S.S. *Princeton*. The Civil War brought him fame as designer of the iron-clad, turreted, propeller-driven warship *Monitor*. After the war he developed the forerunner of the modern torpedo boat or destroyer.

ERLANGER, ABRAHAM LINCOLN (*b. Buffalo, N.Y., 1860; d. 1930*), theatrical booking agent, manager, producer. Developed modern centralized booking system; with Klaw, Charles Frohman, and others organized Theatrical Syndicate, 1896, which was denounced as a monopoly.

ERNST, HAROLD CLARENCE (*b. Cincinnati, O., 1856; d. 1922*), bacteriologist. Graduated Harvard, 1876; Harvard Medical, 1880; studied bacteriology under Koch. Gave first (1885) lectures on bacteriology at Harvard Medical School; was professor of his specialty there, 1895–1922.

ERNST, OSWALD HERBERT (*b. near Cincinnati, O., 1842; d. Washington, D.C., 1926*), soldier, engineer. Graduated West Point, 1864. Specialist in river and harbor improvement; supervised digging of deep-sea channel to Galveston, Texas; was member of original Isthmian Canal Commission.

ERRETT, ISAAC (*b. New York, N.Y., 1820; d. 1888*), Disciples of Christ clergyman, author. Editor of *The Christian Standard*, 1866–88.

ERSKINE, JOHN (*b. Strabane, Ireland, 1813; d. Atlanta, Ga., 1895*), jurist. Came to America as a child; settled in Georgia, 1855. A foe of secession, he was federal judge in Georgia, 1866–83, where his integrity and fairness won him public confidence and respect.

ERSKINE, ROBERT (*b. Dunfermline, Scotland, 1735; d. 1780*), geographer, hydraulic engineer. Came to America, 1771, as representative of British interests in the American Iron Co. By 1775 his sympathies for the colonials led to a commission as captain in the New Jersey militia; in 1777 he was named geographer and surveyor-general to the Continental Army. Erskine's maps of the seat of war were important contributory factors in Washington's ultimate victory.

ERVING, GEORGE WILLIAM (*b. Boston, Mass., 1769; d. New York, N.Y., 1850*), diplomat. Served with ability in U.S. legations at London, Madrid, and Copenhagen; initiated negotiations which culminated in treaty of 1819 with Spain.

ESBJÖRN, LARS PAUL (*b. Delsbo, Sweden, 1808; d. Sweden, 1870*), Lutheran clergyman. Came to America, 1849, with emigrant party; was pastor of settlement at Andover, Ill. First president of Augustana Seminary, Chicago, 1860–63, he is regarded as the founder of the Swedish Lutheran Church in the United States.

ESCALANTE, SILVESTRE VELEZ DE (*fl. 1768–1779*), Franciscan missionary, explorer. Born in Spain, Escalante sailed for New Spain in 1768 and served as missionary in Sonora, and at the Laguna and Zuñi pueblos, New Mexico. He is celebrated for two exploring expeditions and the reports which he made on them. The first (1775) took him from Zuñi to the Moqui (Hopi) pueblos; the second, which had as object the opening of direct communication between Santa Fé and Monterey, California, was performed in 1776. Leaving Santa Fé in July, Escalante and Fray Francisco Dominguez traveled northwest to Utah Lake and thence southwest to Black Rock Springs where a fall of snow discouraged their passage over the sierras. They returned to Santa Fé on Jan. 2, 1777, by way of the Colorado River, the Moqui towns, and Zuñi.

ESHER, JOHN JACOB (*b. Baldenheim, Alsace, 1823; d. 1901*), bishop of the Evangelical Church, 1863–1901.

ESPEJO, ANTONIO DE (*fl. 1581–1583*), Spanish merchant in Mexico. After prospecting for ores in the Pueblo Indian region, he stimulated an interest in the territory by his reports which culminated in the conquest of New Mexico under Juan de Oñate.

ESPY, JAMES POLLARD (*b. Pennsylvania, 1785; d. Cincinnati, O., 1860*), educator, meteorologist. Developed convectional theory of precipitation; first used telegraphic bulletins as basis for weather forecasting. Author of *Philosophy of Storms* (1841).

ESTABROOK, JOSEPH (*b. Lebanon, N.H., 1793; d. Anderson Co., Tenn., 1855*), educator. Graduated Dartmouth, 1815. President, East Tennessee College (later University of Tennessee), 1834–50.

ESTAUGH, ELIZABETH HADDON (*b. Southwark, England, c. 1680; d. Haddonfield, N.J., 1762*), Quaker founder of "a home in the wilderness for travelling ministers" at Haddonfield, 1701.

ESTERBROOK, RICHARD (*b. Liskeard, England, 1813; d. Camden, N.J., 1895*), manufacturer. Organized Esterbrook steel pen company, 1858; was its president, 1858–95.

ESTERLY, GEORGE (*b. Plattekill, N.Y., 1809; d. Hot Springs, S.D., 1893*), inventor, manufacturer. Patented first successful American harvesting machine, 1844, a horse-pushed "header" which won gold medal at 1848 fair of Chicago Mechanics Institute. Subsequently patented a mowing machine, plow, hand-rake reaper, the first sulky cultivator, a seeder, and a self-rake reaper. Erected his own manufacturing plant at Whitewater, Wis., 1858; produced twine binders and mowers; built up a large export trade. In 1892 moved his plant to Minneapolis, Minn., where it failed in the panic of 1893.

ESTES, DANA (*b. Gorham, Maine, 1840; d. Boston, Mass., 1909*), bookseller, publisher. Partner in Boston firms of Estes and Lauriat and Dana Estes and Co.

ESTEY, JACOB (*b. Hinsdale, N.H., 1814; d. 1890*), pioneer American organ manufacturer. *Post* 1850, developed small melodeon-manufacturing shop into one of the world's largest organ companies.

ETTWEIN, JOHN (*b. Freudenstadt, Germany, 1721; d. Bethlehem, Pa., 1802*), Moravian bishop. Came to America, 1754, as spiritual adviser to children of Moravians; undertook missionary work among Indians in middle and southern colonies; in 1766 was appointed assistant to Bishop Nathanael Seidel at Bethlehem, Pa. In 1772, he led party of Christian Indians to David Zeisberger's settlement in Tuscarawas Valley, Ohio. Known as a Loyalist he was temporarily imprisoned during Revolution. Successfully negotiated with Continental Congress and Pennsylvania Assembly over refusal of Moravians to bear arms and to subscribe to the Test Oath; served devotedly as chaplain, Continental Army hospital at Bethlehem, 1776–77. In 1785, he prevailed upon Congress and upon the Pennsylvania Assembly to establish reservations for converted Indians. Chosen bishop in 1784, he presided over the Moravian Church of

North America until his death and ranks as one of its greatest leaders.

EUSTIS, GEORGE (*b. Boston, Mass., 1796; d. New Orleans, La., 1858*), jurist. Nephew of William Eustis. Louisiana chief justice, 1846–52; held other state offices. Encouraged development of Louisiana educational system.

EUSTIS, GEORGE (*b. New Orleans, La., 1828; d. Cannes, France, 1872*), statesman, diplomat. Son of George Eustis (1796–1858). Secretary to Confederate legation at Paris, France, during Civil War.

EUSTIS, HENRY LAWRENCE (*b. Boston, Mass., 1819; d. Cambridge, Mass., 1885*), engineer, soldier. Graduated Harvard, 1838; West Point, 1842. Resigned army, 1849, to become professor of engineering, Harvard, where he taught until his death. Commanded 10th Massachusetts Regiment, 1862–64.

EUSTIS, JAMES BIDDLE (*b. New Orleans, La., 1834; d. Newport, R.I., 1899*), lawyer, statesman, Confederate soldier, diplomat. Son of George Eustis (1796–1858). U.S. senator from Louisiana, Democrat, 1877–79 and 1885–91. Ambassador to France.

EUSTIS, WILLIAM (*b. Cambridge, Mass., 1753; d. Boston, Mass., 1825*), Revolutionary army surgeon, statesman. Graduated Harvard, 1772. Congressman, (Democrat) Republican, from Massachusetts, 1801–05 and 1820–23; secretary of war, 1809–12; minister to Holland, 1814–18; governor of Massachusetts, 1823–25.

EVANS, ANTHONY WALTON WHYTE (*b. New Brunswick, N.J., 1817; d. 1886*), civil engineer. Graduated Rensselaer Polytechnic, 1836. Won fame as builder of railroads in Chile and Peru.

EVANS, AUGUSTA JANE (*b. Columbus, Ga., 1835; d. Mobile, Ala., 1909*). Author of turgid and sentimental novels including the best-seller *St. Elmo* (1866).

EVANS, CHARLES (*b. Boston, Mass., 1850; d. 1935*), librarian, bibliographer. Author of *American Bibliography* (1903–34). [*Supp. 1*]

EVANS, CLEMENT ANSELM(*b. Stewart Co., Ga., 1833; d. Atlanta, Ga., 1911*), lawyer, Confederate soldier, Methodist clergyman, historian. Commander-in-chief of United Confederate Veterans; edited *Confederate Military History* (1899).

EVANS, EDWARD PAYSON (*b. Remsen, N.Y., 1831; d. New York, N.Y., 1917*), man of letters. An expatriate to Germany, he wrote scholarly works on many abstruse subjects.

EVANS, EVAN (*b. Carnoe, Wales, 1671; d. Harford Co., Md., 1721*), Anglican clergyman. Second rector of Christ Church, Philadelphia, 1700–18; strengthened influence of Church of England in America.

EVANS, FREDERICK WILLIAM (*b. Leominster, England, 1808; d. Mount Lebanon, N.Y., 1893*), reformer, Shaker elder. Brother of George H. Evans. Edited radical reform publications with his brother before becoming prominent Shaker leader.

EVANS, GEORGE (*b. Hallowell, Maine, 1797; d. 1867*), lawyer. Congressman, Whig, from Maine, 1829–41; U.S. senator, 1841–47. Expert in public finance.

EVANS, GEORGE ALFRED (*b. Brooklyn, N.Y., 1850; d. 1925*), physician. Graduated Bellevue Medical College, 1873. Pioneered in sanatorium and climatic treatment of pulmonary tuberculosis; wrote *Handbook of Historical and Geographical Phthisiology* (1888).

EVANS, GEORGE HENRY (*b. Bromyard, England, 1805; d. Granville, N.J., 1856*), reformer. Brother of Frederick W. Evans. Came to America, 1820. Influenced by Thomas Paine's writings, Evans edited a series of papers which were the first labor papers in America. These were *The Man* (Ithaca, N.Y., c. 1822); *Working Man's Advocate* (New York, 1829–45); *Daily Sentinel* and *Young America* (between 1837 and 1853). Championed working men's parties and advocated agrarian principles similar to those of Henry George. Opposed doctrines of Fourier and Owen with principles developed from Paine's and Jefferson's individualism and natural rights doctrines. Advocated right of every man to an inalienable homestead, abolition of laws for collection of debts and imprisonment for debt, abolition of chattel and wage slavery, equal rights for women.

EVANS, HENRY CLAY (*b. Juniata Co., Pa., 1843; d. Chattanooga, Tenn., 1921*), industrialist. Raised in Wisconsin. Settled in Chattanooga, 1870, and prospered in car-building industry. Served as mayor of Chattanooga, as organizer of its school system; was prominent in national Republican politics.

EVANS, HUGH DAVEY (*b. Baltimore, Md., 1792; d. Baltimore, Md., 1868*), lawyer, Protestant Episcopal lay theologian, editor, author.

EVANS, JOHN (*fl. 1703–1731*), deputy governor of Pennsylvania, 1703–07. His riotous living, aggressive Anglicanism and policy of military preparedness antagonized the Quaker Assembly and led to his removal.

EVANS, JOHN (*b. Waynesville, O., 1814; d. 1897*), physician, railroad builder. Prominent in his profession in Indiana and as professor of obstetrics at Rush Medical College, Chicago, he was also an investor in real estate and railroads. Evanston, Ill., was named for him. He took a leading part in founding of Northwestern University where he endowed two chairs. Removing to Denver, he was territorial governor of Colorado, 1862–65; he supported churches and founded Colorado Seminary which later became

University of Denver. The Denver Pacific, South Park, and Denver & New Orleans railroads which saved the city from isolation were promoted by him.

EVANS, LAWRENCE BOYD (*b. Radnor, O., 1870; d. Washington, D.C., 1928*), lawyer. Taught history and public law at Tufts College; published legal case books; codified navigation laws for U.S. Shipping Board.

EVANS, LEWIS (*b. Llangwnadl Parish, Wales, c. 1700; d. New York, N.Y., 1756*), geographer. In 1749 published "A Map of Pennsylvania, New-Jersey, New-York, And the Three Delaware Counties," which traced the major emigration roads through Lancaster, York and Carlisle. His best-known map, "A General Map of the Middle British Colonies in America" (1755), was published with an "Analysis" stressing the importance of the Ohio region, was used by Braddock in his campaign and was generally accepted as standard authority in settling boundary disputes.

EVANS, NATHAN GEORGE (*b. Marion, S.C., 1824; d. Midway, Ala., 1868*), Confederate general. Graduated West Point, 1848. On frontier service with cavalry, 1848–60. Displayed courage and leadership at first Bull Run and Ball's Bluff, but later showed little fitness for command.

EVANS, NATHANIEL (*b. Philadelphia, Pa., 1742; d. Haddonfield, N.J., 1767*), Anglican clergyman, poet. Belonged to Philadelphia group of Francis Hopkinson and Thomas Godfrey; his works collected in *Poems on Several Occasions* (1772) were edited by William Smith (1727–1803).

EVANS, OLIVER (*b. near Newport, Del., 1755; d. New York, N.Y., 1819*), inventor, America's first steam-engine builder. Apprenticed to a wagon-maker; studied mathematics and mechanics; early determined to develop and extend the use of the steam-engine. First worked at perfecting a machine for making card teeth for carding wool; then at improving flour-mill machinery. His improvements (*c.* 1785) made hand operations unnecessary, but were universally scorned by millers at the time. By 1802 Evans produced his first stationary high-pressure steam-engine; in the following year he set up in business as engine builder. He established the Mars Iron Works, 1807; in 1817 he designed and constructed the engine and boilers for Fairmount Waterworks in Philadelphia. By the time of his death fifty of his engines were in operation on the Atlantic Coast. He never received sufficient pecuniary assistance to build his proposed "steam carriage" on which he worked for many years or to develop his ideas on steam propulsion for boats.

EVANS, ROBLEY DUNGLISON (*b. Floyd Court House, Va., 1846; d. 1912*), naval officer, "Fighting Bob." Commanded U.S.S. *Iowa* at Santiago, 1898; commisioned rear-admiral, 1901; commanded U.S. fleet on round-the-world cruise, 1907.

EVANS, THOMAS (*b. Philadelphia, Pa., 1798; d. Philadelphia, 1868*), Quaker minister and editor. Wrote and edited extensively in defense of orthodox doctrine and towards reconciliation of Hicksites.

EVANS, THOMAS WILTBERGER (*b. Philadelphia, Pa., 1823; d. Paris, France, 1897*), dentist, philanthropist. Pupil of Dr. John De Haven White. Practiced in Baltimore, Md., and Lancaster, Pa., removing to Paris, *c.* 1848, and opening his own office there, 1850. Beginning as dentist to Napoleon III, he came to know and serve the principal royal families of Europe; built up a private fortune; became an amateur diplomat. Aided Empress Eugénie in her escape from Paris, 1870. Provided ambulance and medical services at his own expense during Crimean and Franco-Prussian wars; established first American paper in Paris. His technical contributions to dentistry were considerable, and he left his fortune to establish an Institute and Museum which are today the Dental School of the University of Pennsylvania.

EVANS, WALTER (*b. Barren Co., Ky., 1842; d. 1923*), jurist, Union soldier. Congressman, Republican, from Kentucky, 1895–99; helped formulate Dingley Tariff. U.S. judge for district of Kentucky, *post* 1899.

EVANS, WARREN FELT (*b. Rockingham, Vt., 1817; d. 1889*), clergyman, disciple of Phineas P. Quimby as a mental healer.

EVANS, WILLIAM THOMAS (*b. Clough-Jordan, Ireland, 1843; d. 1918*), New York City dry-goods merchant, patron of American art.

EVARTS, JEREMIAH (*b. Sunderland, Vt., 1781; d. Charleston, S.C., 1831*), lawyer, philanthropist. Edited the *Panoplist* (Boston, 1810–21); opposed policy of transferring Indians to Western reservations; a founder of American Board of Commissioners for Foreign Missions.

EVARTS, WILLIAM MAXWELL (*b. Boston, Mass., 1818; d. New York, N.Y., 1901*), lawyer, statesman. Son of Jeremiah Evarts; grandson of Roger Sherman. Graduated Yale, 1837; admitted to New York bar, 1841. Formed partnership, 1842, with Charles E. Butler in a firm which later included Charles F. Southmayd, Joseph H. Choate and Charles C. Beaman. Early successful in private practice, Evarts entered public life as assistant U.S. attorney for the southern district of New York, 1849–53.

His public career included service as chairman of the New York delegation to the 1860 Republican National Convention, and as secretary to the Union Defense Committee. He went to England in 1863 and in 1864 to halt, if possible, the building and equipping of Confederate navy vessels. In 1867 he was a member of the judiciary committee of the New York state constitutional convention; from July 1868 to March 1869, he was attorney-general in

President Johnson's cabinet; for ten years after 1870 he was president of the New York City Bar Association. In this capacity he fought for reform and against the corruption of the "Tweed Ring." He served as President Hayes's secretary of state, 1877–81; as delegate to the Paris Monetary Conference; and as U.S. senator from New York, 1885–89, until his health and eyesight failed.

Evarts's legal career ran parallel to and was interspersed between events of his career as a statesman. Among the many outstanding causes in which he was engaged were *People vs. Draper,* in which he successfully sustained the right of the legislature to create a new metropolitan police district; the case of the Savannah privateers; the prosecution of Jefferson Davis for treason (1867); the Bank Tax, Legal Tender, and Cotton Tax cases before the Supreme Court; and his appearance in the Springbok Case before the Mixed Commission on British and American claims (1873). Evarts's fame, however, rests on his success in three cases of national and international importance. His eloquence prevented the required two-thirds vote for conviction in the impeachment of President Johnson (1868); his courteous and conciliatory attitude won the respect of the British participants during the Geneva arbitration negotiations (1871–72); and his argument reaffirming the constitutional power of the states to regulate casting and counting of votes prevailed in the Hayes-Tilden presidential dispute (1876–77).

EVE, JOSEPH (*b. Philadelphia, Pa., 1760; d. Augusta, Ga., 1835*), inventor, scientist, poet.

EVE, PAUL FITZSIMONS (*b. near Augusta, Ga., 1806; d. Nashville, Tenn., 1877*), surgeon. Graduated University of Pennsylvania, M.D., 1828; studied also in London and Paris. Taught surgery at Medical College of Georgia and at Nashville; served as Confederate army surgeon; credited with being first American to perform hysterectomy.

EVERENDON, WALTER (*d. 1725*), colonial gunpowder manufacturer. First man to make powder in America; overseer of Neponset, Mass., mill which supplied powder for prosecution of King Philip's war (1675–76).

EVERETT, ALEXANDER HILL (*b. Boston, Mass., 1790; d. Canton, China, 1847*), editor, diplomat. Brother of Edward Everett. Served in diplomatic posts in Russia, Holland, Spain, Cuba and China. Edited *North American Review,* 1830–35.

EVERETT, CHARLES CARROLL (*b. Brunswick, Maine, 1829; d. 1900*), theologian. Graduated Bowdoin, 1850. Author of *Science of Thought* (1869); dean of Harvard Divinity School, 1878–1900.

EVERETT, DAVID (*b. Princeton, Mass., 1770; d. Marietta, O., 1813*), lawyer, journalist. Author of *Common Sense in Dishabille* (1799); a play, *Daran-*zel (performed 1798, 1800; published, 1800), and other works.

EVERETT, EDWARD (*b. Dorchester, Mass., 1794; d. Boston, Mass., 1865*), Unitarian clergyman, educator, statesman, orator. Graduated Harvard, 1811; was first American to receive Ph.D. degree at Göttingen (1817); taught Greek literature at Harvard; edited *North American Review.* Congressman, Independent, from Massachusetts, 1825–35; Whig governor, 1836–39. American minister to Court of St. James, 1841–45; president of Harvard College, 1846–49; U.S. secretary of state, 1852–53; senator from Massachusetts, 1853–54. An ardent Unionist, he compromised himself by not voting on the Kansas-Nebraska bill, and resigned his seat. Ran for vice-president on Constitutional Union ticket, 1860. Spent last four years of his life speaking in support of the Union; shared platform with Lincoln at Gettysburg, November 19, 1863. A brilliant and magnetic public speaker, he was given to making compromises either because of personal ambition or because of a strain of timidity in his character.

EVERETT, ROBERT (*b. Gronant, Wales, 1791; d. 1875*), Congregational clergyman, publisher. Emigrated to Oneida Co., N.Y., 1823. Advocating abolition and prohibition, he won most of the Welsh Congregationalists in America for the Republican party.

EVERMANN, BARTON WARREN (*b. Albia, Iowa, 1853; d. Berkeley, Calif., 1932*), ichthyologist. Graduated University of Indiana, 1886; Ph.D., 1891. Associated with U.S. Bureau of Fisheries, 1891–1914. His principles of conservation prevented extinction of Alaska fur seal. Author of *Fishes of North and Middle America* (1896–1900) and other works.
[*Supp.* 1]

EWBANK, THOMAS (*b. Durham, England, 1792; d. New York, N.Y., 1870*), inventor, manufacturer, author. Came to America, 1819. As U.S. commissioner of patents, 1849–52, he filled his annual reports with useful essays on historical aspects and industrial applications of inventions.

EWELL, BENJAMIN STODDERT (*b. Georgetown, D.C., 1810; d. 1894*), Confederate soldier, educator. Son of Thomas Ewell. Graduated West Point, 1832. Professor of mathematics at several colleges; chief-of-staff to Gen. J. E. Johnston. President of William and Mary College, 1854–61, 1865–88; president emeritus thereafter. Preserved the college from extinction during his post-bellum service.

EWELL, JAMES (*b. near Dumfries, Va., 1773; d. Covington, La., 1832*), physician. Introduced vaccination in Savannah, Ga.; author of *Planter's and Mariner's Medical Companion* (1807); practiced in Washington, D.C., and New Orleans, La.

EWELL, RICHARD STODDERT (*b. Georgetown, D.C., 1817; d. near Spring Hill, Tenn., 1872*), Confederate soldier. Son of Thomas Ewell. Graduated West Point, 1840. Served in Mexican War, and with distinction as brigade, division and corps commander in Civil War under Jackson and Lee. Promoted lieutenant-general, 1863, he commanded II Corps in the Gettysburg and Wilderness campaigns; he subsequently commanded the defenses of Richmond.

EWELL, THOMAS (*b. near Dumfries, Va., 1785; d. Centerville, Va., 1826*), physician, businessman. Brother of James Ewell. Edited first American edition of Hume's *Essays* (1817); author of *The American Family Physician* (1824).

EWER, FERDINAND CARTWRIGHT (*b. Nantucket, Mass., 1826; d. 1883*), Episcopal clergyman. After an early career as a California journalist (editor, *The Pioneer*, 1854, and others), he was ordained, 1858, and became a leading exponent of Anglo-Catholicism. He served as rector of parishes in New York City *post* 1862.

EWING, CHARLES (*b. Bridgeton, N.J., 1780; d. 1832*), jurist. Graduated Princeton, 1798. Practiced law in Trenton, N.J.; was chief justice of New Jersey supreme court, 1824–32.

EWING, FINIS (*b. Bedford Co., Va., 1773; d. 1841*), farmer, chief founder of Cumberland Presbyterian Church, 1810. Pastor in Kentucky, Tennessee and Missouri; helped shape doctrines of his sect.

EWING, HUGH BOYLE (*b. Lancaster, O., 1826; d. near Lancaster, 1905*), lawyer, Union soldier. Son of Thomas Ewing (1789–1871); foster-brother of W. T. Sherman. Attended West Point; practiced law in St. Louis, Mo., Leavenworth, Kans., and Washington, D.C. Division commander in Civil War. U.S. minister to Holland, 1866–70.

EWING, JAMES (*b. Lancaster Co., Pa., 1736; d. Hellam, Pa., 1806*), Revolutionary soldier, Pennsylvania legislator and official.

EWING, JAMES CARUTHERS RHEA (*b. Rural Valley, Pa., 1854; d. Princeton, N.J., 1925*), Presbyterian missionary in India, 1879–1922. Principal, Forman College, Lahore, 1888–1918; officer of Panjab University.

EWING, JOHN (*b. East Nottingham, Md., 1732; d. Norristown, Pa., 1802*), Presbyterian clergyman. Pastor, First Church, Philadelphia. Provost of University of Pennsylvania and professor of natural philosophy there *post* 1779, he enjoyed high contemporary repute as a scholar and scientist.

EWING, THOMAS (*b. near West Liberty, Va., 1789; d. Lancaster, O., 1871*), lawyer. Raised in Athens Co., O.; graduated Ohio University, 1815. Became one of the ablest and most successful lawyers in the West. U.S. senator, Whig, from Ohio, 1831–36, 1850–51; U.S. secretary of treasury, 1841, resigning in contest with President Tyler over recharter of a national bank; secretary of interior, 1849–50. Supported Lincoln; opposed post-war Reconstruction policies.

EWING, THOMAS (*b. Lancaster, O., 1829; d. 1896*), Union soldier, lawyer. Son of Thomas Ewing (1789–1871). Distinguished in fighting in Missouri and Kansas, 1863–64. Leader of Greenback wing of Democratic party, 1870–81.

EYTINGE, ROSE (*b. Philadelphia, Pa., 1835; d. Amityville, N.Y., 1911*), actress, author, teacher. Acted with companies of E. Booth, J. W. Wallack, Augustin Daly; principal success in *Antony and Cleopatra*, produced by her own company, New York, 1877.

EZEKIEL, MOSES JACOB (*b. Richmond, Va., 1844; d. Rome, Italy, 1917*), sculptor, Confederate soldier. Graduated Virginia Military Institute, 1866. Studied at Royal Academy, Berlin. Among his many works are the Jefferson monument at Louisville, Ky., and the Confederate monument at Arlington Cemetery. Skilful and prolific, he was knighted by both Germany and Italy.

FABER, JOHN EBERHARD (*b. Stein, Bavaria, 1822; d. 1879*), pencil manufacturer. Extended family business to America, *c.* 1848; opened factory here, 1861. First to attach rubber erasers to pencils.

FACCIOLI, GIUSEPPE (*b. Milan, Italy, 1877; d. Pittsfield, Mass., 1934*), mechanical and electrical engineer. Came to America *c.* 1900; was associated thereafter principally with William Stanley and General Electric Co. in design and development of alternating current machinery and high-tension transmission apparatus. [*Supp. 1*]

FACKLER, DAVID PARKS (*b. Kempsville, Va., 1841; d. Richmond, Va., 1924*), actuary. Graduated College of the City of New York, 1859. Made notable improvements in life insurance practice; served as consulting actuary to private companies and governmental investigating committees.

FAESCH, JOHN JACOB (*b. Canton of Basle, Switzerland, 1729; d. 1799*), ironmaster, government contractor. Came to America, 1764. Had charge of Mt. Hope furnaces in New Jersey. Cast shot for Continental Army.

FAGAN, JAMES FLEMING (*b. Clark Co., Ky., 1828; d. 1893*), planter, Confederate soldier. Raised in Arkansas. Served in Mexican War and in western campaigns of Civil War; was major-general at surrender.

FAGES, PEDRO (*fl. 1767–1796*), first *commandante* and later governor of Alta California. Accompanied Portolá, 1770, to Monterey; explored San Francisco

Bay; as governor, 1782–91, encouraged fur trade, erection of missions and presidios, education of Indians.

FAGET, JEAN CHARLES (*b. New Orleans, La., 1818; d. New Orleans, 1884*), physician. Graduated in medicine at Paris, 1844; practiced in New Orleans. Discovered (1859) a conclusive sign of diagnosis for yellow fever; was made Chevalier of Legion of Honor.

FAHNESTOCK, HARRIS CHARLES (*b. Harrisburg, Pa., 1835; d. 1914*), banker. Directed New York branch of Jay Cooke & Co., 1866–73; on its failure, he became a vice-president and organizer of the First National Bank of New York.

FAIR, JAMES GRAHAM (*b. near Belfast, Ireland, 1831; d. San Francisco, Calif., 1894*), forty-niner, financier. Came to America as a boy of twelve. Derived fortune from Consolidated Virginia mine of the Comstock Lode.

FAIRBANK, CALVIN (*b. Allegany, now Wyoming, Co., N.Y., 1816; d. Angelica, N.Y., 1898*), Methodist clergyman, abolitionist, "underground railway" agent.

FAIRBANKS, CHARLES WARREN (*b. near Unionville Center, O., 1852; d. 1918*), lawyer. Graduated Ohio Wesleyan, 1872. Practiced as railway attorney in Indianapolis, Ind.; was temporary chairman and key-note speaker of convention which nominated McKinley. As U.S. senator, Republican, from Indiana, 1897–1904, he served on foreign relations committee, advocated comprehensive plans for internal improvements, was American chairman of Joint High Commission, 1898. Was vice-president, 1905–09; chairman of Republican platform committee, 1912; and "favorite son" candidate for presidential nomination in 1908 and 1916.

FAIRBANKS, DOUGLAS (*b. Denver, Colo., 1883; d. Santa Monica, Calif., 1939*), motion-picture actor and producer. Changed name from Douglas Ulman. Best known for his costume adventure films, *The Three Musketeers, Robin Hood,* etc. [*Supp. 2*]

FAIRBANKS, ERASTUS (*b. Brimfield, Mass., 1792; d. 1864*), manufacturer. Brother of Thaddeus Fairbanks. Headed E. & T. Fairbanks & Co., a firm which he founded with his two brothers and which enjoyed world-wide reputation for the quality of its platform scales. Whig governor of Vermont, 1852–53, his stand on temperance lost him re-election. Running on the Republican ticket, 1860, he returned as governor and ably mobilized the state to support the federal war effort.

FAIRBANKS, HENRY (*b. St. Johnsbury, Vt., 1830; d. 1918*), Congregational clergyman, inventor, manufacturer. Son of Thaddeus Fairbanks. Graduated Dartmouth, 1853. Taught natural philosophy at Dartmouth, 1860–69; patented scales and pulp-manu-

facturing machines; also invented an alternating current electric generator.

FAIRBANKS, THADDEUS (*b. Brimfield, Mass., 1796; d. St. Johnsbury, Vt., 1886*), inventor. Cofounder with Erastus and Joseph Fairbanks, his brothers, of the E. & T. Fairbanks iron-foundry, 1823, later famous as scale manufacturers. Inventor of improved plows, stoves and a machine for dressing flax and hemp, he was granted a patent for the first platform scale, 1831. He later invented draft mechanism for furnaces, a hot-water heater and a feed-water heater. With his brothers, he founded and endowed St. Johnsbury Academy.

FAIRCHILD, BLAIR (*b. Belmont, Mass., 1877; d. 1933*), composer. Influenced by Widor and César Franck. [*Supp. 1*]

FAIRCHILD, CHARLES STEBBINS (*b. Cazenovia, N.Y., 1842; d. Cazenovia, 1924*), lawyer, financier. New York state attorney-general under Governor S. J. Tilden; prosecuted "Canal Ring" frauds. U.S. secretary of the treasury, 1887–89.

FAIRCHILD, GEORGE THOMPSON (*b. Brownhelm, O., 1838; d. Columbus, O., 1901*), educator. Graduated Oberlin, 1862, 1865. President, Kansas Agricultural College, 1879–97.

FAIRCHILD, JAMES HARRIS (*b. Stockbridge, Mass., 1817; d. 1902*), educator. Graduated Oberlin, 1838, 1841. A professor at Oberlin, 1841–98, and president of the college, 1866–89.

FAIRCHILD, LUCIUS (*b. Portage Co., O., 1831; d. Madison, Wis., 1896*), Union soldier, diplomat. Republican governor of Wisconsin, 1866–72. Consul at Liverpool, consul-general at Paris; U.S. minister to Spain, 1880–82. National Commander, G.A.R., 1886.

FAIRCHILD, MARY SALOME CUTLER (*b. Dalton, Mass., 1855; d. 1921*), librarian. Pioneer in professional library training at New York State Library School, Albany, 1889–1905.

FAIRFAX, DONALD McNEILL (*b. Virginia, 1821; d. Hagerstown, Md., 1894*), naval officer. Supervised capture of Confederate agents Mason and Slidell from the *Trent*, 1861. Retired as rear-admiral, 1881.

FAIRFAX, THOMAS (*b. Leeds Castle, Kent, England, 1693; d. "Greenway Court," Shenandoah Valley, Va., 1781*), sixth Lord Fairfax of Cameron, proprietor of the Northern Neck of Virginia. Came first to Virginia, 1735–37, to protect his property from efforts of the Virginia Assembly to narrow its boundaries; returning in 1747, he settled in the Shenandoah Valley, 1752. Served as justice of the peace and county lieutenant and was an early friend to George Washington. The only resident peer in America, he was accorded all the privileges of Virginia citizens and was never molested during the Revolution.

FAIRFIELD, EDMUND BURKE (*b. Parkersburg, Va., 1821; d. Oberlin, O., 1904*), Baptist and Congregational clergyman, educator. Second chancellor of University of Nebraska, 1876–82, he resigned over a Fundamentalist-Modernist controversy among the faculty in which he stood for the older modes of thought.

FAIRFIELD, JOHN (*b. Saco, Maine, 1797; d. 1847*), lawyer, politician. Congressman, Democrat, from Maine, 1835-38; U.S. senator, 1843–47. As Maine governor, 1838–39 and 1841–42, he clashed with Great Britain over northeastern boundary dispute.

FAIRFIELD, SUMNER LINCOLN (*b. Warwick, Mass., 1803; d. New Orleans, La., 1844*), teacher, poet. Author of *The Last Night of Pompeii* (1832), and others; editor, the *North American Magazine*, 1832–38.

FAIRLAMB, JAMES REMINGTON (*b. Philadelphia, Pa., 1838; d. Ingleside, N.Y., 1908*), composer, organist.

FALCKNER, DANIEL (*b. Langen-Reinsdorf, Saxony, 1666; d. New Jersey (?), c. 1741*), Lutheran clergyman. Brother of Justus Falckner. Came to America, 1694. Agent for Frankfort Land Co., proprietors of Germantown, Pa.; organized first German Lutheran congregation in Pennsylvania.

FALCKNER, JUSTUS (*b. Langen-Reinsdorf, Saxony, 1672; d. 1723*), Lutheran clergyman. Brother of Daniel Falckner. Came to America, 1700, and was ordained at Philadelphia, 1703. Ministered thereafter to Dutch and German Lutheran congregations in New York, East Jersey and western Long Island.

FALK, OTTO HERBERT (*b. Wauwatosa, Wis., 1865; d. Milwaukee, Wis., 1940*), soldier, industrialist. President, Allis-Chalmers Manufacturing Co., 1913–32. [*Supp. 2*]

FALKNER, ROLAND POST (*b. Bridgeport, Conn., 1866; d. New York, N.Y., 1940*), economist, statistician. Graduated Wharton School of Finance, University of Pennsylvania, 1885; Ph.D., University of Halle, 1888. Joining the Wharton School faculty, 1888–1900, he became probably first American professor to teach statistics full time. Statistician, subcommittee of U.S. Senate Finance Committee investigating prices and wages, 1891, he made its findings an important milestone in economic statistics. A keen analyst with a gift for expression, Falkner divided his later career between government and private service. [*Supp. 2*]

FALLOWS, SAMUEL (*b. Pendleton, England, 1835; d. Chicago, Ill., 1922*), Union soldier, Methodist clergyman, bishop of Reformed Episcopal Church, 1876–1922.

FANEUIL, PETER (*b. New Rochelle, N.Y., 1700; d. Boston, Mass., 1743*), merchant. Donor of Faneuil Hall, Boston.

FANNIN, JAMES WALKER (*b. Georgia, c. 1804; d. Goliad, Texas, 1836*), colonel in Texas army. Removed to Texas, 1834. Active in the revolutionary movement, he successfully carried out missions at Gonzales, Concepcion, and west of Trinity River, 1835. Overtaken near Goliad by Gen. Urrea's force, he was defeated, March 19, 1836, and captured. On order of Santa Anna, 330 men of Fannin's force, including Fannin himself, were shot.

FANNING, ALEXANDER CAMPBELL WILDER (*b. Boston, Mass., 1788; d. Cincinnati, O., 1846*), soldier. Graduated West Point, 1812. Served in War of 1812 and Seminole campaigns of 1818 and 1835–39. Brevetted colonel for gallantry on the Withlacoochee, December 1835; defended Camp Monroe, February 1837.

FANNING, DAVID (*b. Beech Swamp, Va., c. 1755; d. Canada, 1825*), North Carolina Loyalist and partisan leader. Author of *Narrative of Col. David Fanning* (written 1790; first published 1861).

FANNING, EDMUND (*b. Suffolk Co., N.Y., 1739; d. London, England, 1818*), lawyer, North Carolina Loyalist. Graduated Yale, 1757. A favorite of Gov. Tryon, he won a North Carolina reputation for avarice and immorality; commanded King's American Regiment of Foot during the Revolution.

FANNING, EDMUND (*b. Stonington, Conn., 1769; d. New York, N.Y., 1841*), sea-captain, explorer, promoter. Brother of Nathaniel Fanning. Discovered Fanning's Islands in the Pacific; promoted South Sea trade.

FANNING, JOHN THOMAS (*b. Norwich, Conn., 1837; d. 1911*), hydraulic engineer. Author of *A Practical Treatise on Water Supply Engineering* (1877). Designed water supply and purification systems for Minneapolis, Des Moines, Omaha, Birmingham, Ala., and many other American cities.

FANNING, NATHANIEL (*b. Stonington, Conn., 1755; d. Charleston, S.C., 1805*), privateersman, naval officer. Won fame as captain of the maintop during the *Bonhomme Richard's* fight with the *Serapis*, 1779. Author of *Narrative of the Adventures of an American Naval Officer* (1806), later published as *Memoirs of the Life of Captain Nathaniel Fanning* (1808).

FANNING, TOLBERT (*b. Cannon Co., Tenn., 1810; d. 1874*), Disciples of Christ minister, educator, editor.

FARABEE, WILLIAM CURTIS (*b. Washington Co., Pa., 1865; d. 1925*), anthropologist, ethnologist. Graduated Waynesburg, 1894; Ph.D., Harvard, 1903. Taught at Harvard and University of Pennsylvania; carried out important field studies in South America.

FARAN, JAMES JOHN (*b. Cincinnati, O., 1808; d. 1892*), lawyer, politician, editor. Held state offices and was congressman, Democrat, from Ohio, 1845–49. A proprietor and editor of the *Cincinnati Enquirer*, 1844–81.

FARGO, WILLIAM GEORGE (*b. Pompey, N.Y., 1818; d. Buffalo, N.Y., 1881*), expressman. Was messenger and agent for Pomeroy & Co., express firm between Albany and Buffalo; became messenger and co-owner of Wells & Co., first express concern west of Buffalo, 1844, and secretary of first American Express Co., 1850. Helped organize Wells, Fargo & Co. for express service to California, 1852. By 1855 the company controlled Western express business, carrying gold dust, mail, packages, and passengers and conducting banking services. After a series of mergers, Wells, Fargo and associated express companies were united as the American Express Co., 1873, with Fargo as president. He also served as Democratic mayor of Buffalo, 1862–66.

FARIBAULT, JEAN BAPTISTE (*b. Berthier, Canada, 1775; d. St. Paul, Minn., 1860*), pioneer fur and lead trader. Influential with the Sioux, he preserved peace on the Minnesota frontier.

FARLEY, HARRIET (*b. Claremont, N.H., 1817; d. New York, N.Y., 1907*), editor, author. Edited the *Lowell Offering*, 1842–45, 1848–50, publishing contributions from girl-workers in Lowell, Mass., mills.

FARLEY, JOHN MURPHY (*b. Newtown-Hamilton, Ireland, 1842; d. New York, N.Y., 1918*), Roman Catholic clergyman. Came to America, 1864. Ordained Rome, 1870; served as secretary to Archbishop McCloskey; succeeded him as archbishop of New York, 1902. Created cardinal, 1911.

FARLOW, WILLIAM GILSON (*b. Boston, Mass., 1844; d. 1919*), botanist. Graduated Harvard, 1866. Studied under Asa Gray and De Bary; laid foundation of American phytopathology; built up Harvard's cryptogamic herbarium and library.

FARMAN, ELBERT ELI (*b. New Haven, N.Y., 1831; d. 1911*), jurist, diplomat. Graduated Amherst, 1855. Served as consul-general and judge of the international mixed tribunals in Egypt, 1876–84.

FARMER, FANNIE MERRITT (*b. Boston, Mass., 1857; d. 1915*), educator. Director, Boston Cooking School, 1891–1902, and of her own school. Editor, *Boston Cooking School Cook Book* (1896).

FARMER, FERDINAND (*b. Swabia, Germany, 1720; d. Philadelphia, Pa., 1786*), Jesuit priest. Came to America, 1752; changed his name from Steinmeyer. Served in Lancaster, Pa., 1752–58; thereafter worked as missionary out of St. Joseph's parish, Philadelphia. In 1775, he is believed to have organized first Catholic congregation in New York City.

FARMER, HANNAH TOBEY SHAPLEIGH (*b. Berwick, Maine, 1823; d. Eliot, Maine, 1891*), philanthropist. Wife of Moses G. Farmer.

FARMER, JOHN (*b. Chelmsford, Mass., 1789; d. Concord, N.H., 1838*), apothecary, antiquarian, genealogist. A *Genealogical Register of the First Settlers of New England* (1829) is his most important work.

FARMER, JOHN (*b. Halfmoon, N.Y., 1798; d. 1859*), surveyor, cartographer. Mapped states of Michigan and Wisconsin, also city of Detroit.

FARMER, MOSES GERRISH (*b. Boscawen, N.H., 1820; d. Chicago, Ill., 1893*), teacher, inventor, pioneer American electrician. Devised machine for printing paper window shades; in 1845 started experiments with electricity, and in 1847 exhibited a practical miniature electric train. Accepted position with new electric telegraph line in Massachusetts between Boston and Worcester, 1848; shortly thereafter took charge of Boston and Newburyport telegraph. Was superintendent of first American electric fire-alarm system in Boston, 1851–53, a system which he had developed in association with Dr. William F. Channing. Devised the duplex and quadruplex telegraph, 1855; in 1856 succeeded in depositing aluminum electrolytically. Invented an incandescent electric lamp, 1858–59, and patented in 1866 the "self-exciting" dynamo, lighting thereby a Cambridge, Mass., residence with forty of his incandescent lamps arranged in multiple series. As electrician at the U.S. Torpedo Station, Newport, R.I., 1872–81, he greatly advanced the art of torpedo warfare for the U.S. Navy. Thereafter he acted as consulting electrician for the U.S. Electric Light Co. of New York, giving his attention chiefly to electric power generation and distribution. Interested always in discovering the principles that made his inventions work, he did not profit greatly from any of them.

FARNAM, HENRY (*b. Scipio, N.Y., 1803; d. 1883*), engineer, philanthropist. Built Michigan Southern and other railroads to Chicago, also the Rock Island bridge across the Mississippi; president of Chicago & Rock Island, 1854–63.

FARNAM, HENRY WALCOTT (*b. New Haven, Conn., 1853; d. New Haven, 1933*), economist, philanthropist, reformer. Son of Henry Farnam. Taught at Yale; active in Civil Service reform.
[*Supp. 1*]

FARNHAM, ELIZA WOODSON BURHANS (*b. Rensselaerville, N.Y., 1815; d. Milton-on-the-Hudson, N.Y., 1864*), philanthropist. Author of *Woman and Her Era* (1864).

FARNHAM, RUSSEL (*b. Massachusetts, 1784; d. St. Louis, Mo., 1832*), fur-trader. One of the "Astorians" of the 1810 expedition. Traveled across Siberia on foot, 1814–16; managed Astor's American Fur Co. on upper Mississippi, 1817–19; thereafter farmed in Missouri.

FARNHAM, THOMAS JEFFERSON (*b. Vermont ?, 1804; d. San Francisco, Calif., 1848*), lawyer, traveler. Author of *Travels in the Great Western Prairies* (1841), describing his 1839 journey across the continent to Oregon.

FARNSWORTH, ELON JOHN (*b. Green Oak, Mich., 1837; d. near Gettysburg, Pa., 1863*), Union soldier. Rose from lieutenant to brigadier-general in two years. Killed leading a gallant cavalry charge near Little Round Top.

FARNSWORTH, JOHN FRANKLIN (*b. Eaton, Canada, 1820; d. Washington, D.C., 1897*), lawyer, politician, Union soldier. Raised in Michigan; removed to Illinois, 1842. Congressman, Republican, from Illinois, 1857–61, 1863–73. An active Radical during the Reconstruction era.

FARNUM, DUSTIN LANCY (*b. Hampton Beach, N.H., 1874; d. 1929*), actor. Famous for his portrayal of *The Virginian*, 1904, and other romantic roles; later became screen actor.

FARRAGUT, DAVID GLASGOW (*b. Campbell's Station, Tenn., 1801; d. Portsmouth, N.H., 1870*), naval officer. Son of George Farragut. Appointed midshipman, 1810; one year later he saw his first sea duty on the *Essex* under Commodore David Porter, his foster-father. During the War of 1812 the young midshipman was made master of one of the *Essex's* prizes; after creditable service during the *Essex's* losing fight with the *Phoebe* and *Cherub* in the harbor of Valparaiso, 1814, he was taken prisoner. Served in the Mediterranean, 1815–20; accompanying his naval schoolmaster Charles Folsom to the latter's post as consul to Tunis, he learned to speak French, Italian, Spanish and Arabic. Serving, 1822–24, in the West Indies against pirates, he obtained his first command of a naval vessel, the *Ferret*. A lieutenant from 1825 to 1841, he conveyed Lafayette to France on the frigate *Brandywine;* served on the sloop *Vandalia* off the coast of Brazil and on the sloop *Natchez* on her visit to Charleston, S.C., during the nullification controversy. In 1838, he commanded the *Erie* on a mission to protect American citizens and property in Mexico during the Franco-Mexican war. On duty on the Brazil station, 1841, he was made commander; he took over the sloop *Decatur*, 1842. During the Mexican War, in disfavor with his commodore, he commanded the *Saratoga* on routine blockade duties. Commissioned captain, 1855, while establishing Mare Island navy yard in California, he returned east in 1859 and took command of the *Brooklyn*.

At home in Norfolk, Va., on waiting orders, 1860–61, Farragut left the state the day after the Virginia Convention had passed its secession ordinance, and was assigned at first to an unimportant post at the New York navy yard. Appointed in January 1862 to command of the West Gulf Blockading Squadron, Farragut was responsible for the area between St. Andrew's Bay, Fla., and the Rio Grande; he had confidential orders to reduce the defenses guarding New Orleans and to take the city. Arriving at Ship Island late in February, on April 18 he began operations with his fleet of seventeen vessels and a mortar flotilla by bombarding Fort Jackson. The bombardment appearing ineffective, Farragut, against orders, decided to run by Fort Jackson and Fort St. Philip before they were reduced. He was successful, all but three of his ships passing the forts. He destroyed eleven of the enemy's vessels and took New Orleans without further bloodshed.

This victory made him the Navy's leading officer, earned him a Congressional resolution of thanks and a commission as the first American rear-admiral. He continued up the Mississippi and passed the defenses of Vicksburg, but on finding that place impregnable to naval attack returned to blockade duty in the Gulf. By the end of 1862, he held the whole of the Gulf Coast within the limits of his command except for Mobile.

After varying success and a furlough in 1863, he hoisted his flag again on the *Hartford* and returned to the Gulf. On August 5, 1864, he led his fleet against the defenses at the entrance to Mobile Bay, forcing his way over the mines with which the passage was sown and inspiring his men with his famous cry: "Damn the torpedoes!" Fort Gaines and Fort Morgan surrendered soon after the dispersal of the supporting Confederate flotilla. Mobile Bay was the crowning event of Farragut's career. He had reached a position as pre-eminent in the American Navy as that of Nelson had been in the British. On December 23, 1864, he was made vice-admiral; on July 26, 1866, he was commissioned admiral, a grade especially created for him.

The closing months of the Civil War saw Farragut on leave of absence to recover his health and on a mission to guard the James River. After the war, he commanded the European Squadron on a goodwill tour, 1867–68, and in 1869 visited the Mare Island navy yard. He died on a visit to the commandant of the Portsmouth, N.H., navy yard. Farragut was a master of every detail of his profession. His superiority lay in his mental and moral qualities, his courage, initiative, judgment, and willingness to accept responsibility.

FARRAGUT, GEORGE (*b. Ciudadela, Minorca, 1755; d. Point Plaquet, Miss., 1817*), mariner. Naval and army officer in the American Revolution and War of 1812. Father of David G. Farragut.

FARRAND, LIVINGSTON (*b. Newark, N.J., 1867; d. New York, N.Y., 1939*), psychologist, anthropologist, public health administrator. Graduated Princeton, 1888; M.D., College of Physicians and Surgeons, 1891. After graduate work in physiological psychology at Cambridge, England, and Berlin, he taught psychology, and, later, anthropology, at Columbia, 1893–1913, meanwhile serving (1905–14) as executive secretary of the National Tuberculosis Association. He was president, University of Colorado, 1914–19, and after heading the American Red Cross for two years, he became president of Cornell, 1921–37. A pioneer in the field of public health education, he was especially active in developing the medical schools of the universities he so ably served.

[*Supp.* 2]

FARRAR, EDGAR HOWARD (*b. Concordia, La., 1849; d. Biloxi, Miss., 1922*), lawyer. Authority on municipal and corporation law; reformed New Orleans city government.

FARRAR, JOHN (*b. Lincoln, Mass., 1779; d. Cambridge, Mass., 1853*), mathematician, physicist, astronomer. Graduated Harvard, 1803, and taught there, 1805–1836; translated French scientific literature for textbook use.

FARRAR, TIMOTHY (*b. New Ipswich, N.H., 1788; d. Boston, Mass., 1874*), jurist. Daniel Webster's law partner; author of a report on the Dartmouth College Case (1819); excelled as legislative draftsman.

FARRER, HENRY (*b. London, England, 1843; d. Brooklyn, N.Y., 1903*), etcher, landscape-painter. Came to America, 1863.

FARRINGTON, WALLACE RIDER (*b. Orono, Maine, 1871; d. 1933*), newspaperman, governor of Hawaii, 1921–29. [*Supp.* 1]

FARWELL, CHARLES BENJAMIN (*b. Mead Creek, N.Y., 1823; d. Lake Forest, Ill., 1903*), businessman, politician. Brother of John V. Farwell, and his partner in business. Served without distinction as Republican congressman and U.S. senator from Illinois.

FARWELL, JOHN VILLIERS (*b. Steuben Co., N.Y., 1825; d. Chicago, Ill., 1908*), merchant. Raised in Illinois. Entered dry-goods business in Chicago, 1844; organized John V. Farwell and Co., 1865, Chicago's leading wholesale firm before rise of Marshall Field.

FASSETT, CORNELIA ADÈLE STRONG (*b. Owasco, N.Y., 1831; d. Washington, D.C., 1898*), portrait and figure painter. Pursued successful career in Chicago, Ill., and Washington.

FASSETT, JACOB SLOAT (*b. Elmira, N.Y., 1853; d. Vancouver, Canada, 1924*), lawyer, financier. Anti-machine Republican. As New York state legislator, 1883–91, headed exposé of city corruption; was congressman, 1905–11. Edited *Elmira Advertiser,* 1879–96.

FAULK, ANDREW JACKSON (*b. Milford, Pa., 1814; d. Yankton, S.D., 1898*), lawyer, journalist, post-trader. Governor of Dakota territory, 1866–68.

FAULKNER, CHARLES JAMES (*b. Martinsburg, present W. Va., 1806; d. Martinsburg, 1884*), lawyer.

Congressman, Democrat, from Virginia, 1851–59; from West Virginia, 1875–77. U.S. minister to France, 1859–61. Served in Confederate forces as staff officer to Gen. T. J. Jackson.

FAULKNER, CHARLES JAMES (*b. Martinsburg, Va., 1847; d. Martinsburg, W. Va., 1929*), lawyer. Son of Charles J. Faulkner (1806–1884). U.S. senator, Democrat, from West Virginia, 1887–99. Framed first general law (1888–89) against food and drug adulteration.

FAUNCE, WILLIAM HERBERT PERRY (*b. Worcester, Mass., 1859; d. Providence, R.I., 1930*), Baptist clergyman. Taught at Chicago, Harvard, Yale; liberal and able president of Brown University, 1899–1929.

FAUQUIER, FRANCIS (*b. England, 1704 ?; d. Williamsburg, Va., 1768*), lieutenant-governor of Virginia. Director of the South Sea Co.; fellow of the Royal Society, 1753; writer on economics. Was appointed lieutenant-governor of Virginia, 1758, a position which made him governor in fact. His administration was marked by tact and skill in dealing with the colonists and a realistic independence of orders given him by the British Board of Trade.

FAVERSHAM, WILLIAM ALFRED (*b. London, England, 1868; d. Bay Shore, N.Y., 1940*), actor. Came to America, 1886. Replaced Henry Miller as leading man of Frohman's Empire Theatre company, 1892, and was successful as romantic lead; achieved greatest success in *The Squaw Man,* 1905–08.

[*Supp.* 2]

FAVILL, HENRY BAIRD (*b. Madison, Wis., 1860; d. 1916*), physician. Graduated Rush Medical College, 1883, where he later taught. Specialized in internal medicine; had large Chicago practice and enjoyed nation-wide reputation.

FAWCETT, EDGAR (*b. New York, N.Y., 1847; d. London, England, 1904*), author. Satirized New York society in some thirty-five tepid novels and plays. *The Buntling Ball* (1884), a Gilbertian essay in verse, is metrically clever.

FAY, EDWARD ALLEN (*b. Morristown, N.J., 1843; d. 1923*), educator of the deaf. Graduated University of Michigan, 1862. Associated with Gallaudet College, 1866–1920. Author of *Concordance of the Divina Commedia* (1888) and a study of *Marriages of the Deaf in America* (1898).

FAY, EDWIN WHITFIELD (*b. Minden, La., 1865; d. Texas, 1920*), classical scholar. Professor of Latin at Washington and Lee, 1893–99, and thereafter at University of Texas.

FAY, JONAS (*b. Westborough, Mass., 1737 n.s.; d. Bennington, Vt., 1818*), physician, politician. Removed to Vermont, 1766, and was active in independence and statehood movements of Vermont settlers, 1772–1785.

FAY, THEODORE SEDGWICK (*b. New York, N.Y., 1807; d. Berlin, Germany, 1898*), author, diplomat. Miscellaneous writer for the *New York Mirror, post* 1828. Left America, 1833; served as secretary of legation at London and Berlin, 1837–53, and as minister to Switzerland, 1853–61. Author of *Norman Leslie* (1835) and other books.

FAYERWEATHER, DANIEL BURTON (*b. Stepney, Conn., 1822; d. 1890*), leather merchant. Bequeathed entire estate unconditionally to a score of American colleges.

FAYSSOUX, PETER (*b. Charleston, S.C. ?, 1745; d. 1795*), physician, surgeon. Graduated M.D., Edinburgh, 1769. Served as senior physician with South Carolina forces in Revolution; first president of South Carolina Medical Society, 1790–92.

FEARN, JOHN WALKER (*b. Huntsville, Ala., 1832; d. Hot Springs, Va., 1899*), lawyer, diplomat. Nephew of Leroy P. Walker.

FEATHERSTON, WINFIELD SCOTT (*b. near Murfreesboro, Tenn., 1819; d. Holly Springs, Miss., 1891*), lawyer, Confederate soldier. Congressman, Democrat, from Mississippi, 1847–51; rose to brigadier-general in Civil War. Was a leader, 1874–78, in overthrow of Ames regime in Mississippi.

FEBIGER, CHRISTIAN (*b. Fünen, Denmark, 1746; d. Philadelphia, Pa., 1796*), Revolutionary soldier. Came to America, 1772. Served with ability in all theatres of the war, retiring, 1783, as brigadier-general. Treasurer of Pennsylvania, 1789–96.

FECHTER, CHARLES ALBERT (*b. London, England, 1824; d. near Quakertown, Pa., 1879*), actor. Successful as innovating actor-manager on French, English and American stages, 1848–70. His later career was unhappy.

FEE, JOHN GREGG (*b. Bracken Co., Ky., 1816; d. Berea, Ky., 1901*), Abolitionist, founder of Berea College (1855).

FEEHAN, PATRICK AUGUSTINE (*b. Killenaule, Ireland, 1829; d. Chicago, Ill., 1902*), Roman Catholic clergyman. Came to America, 1852; was ordained that year in St. Louis, Mo. Consecrated bishop of Nashville, 1865; archbishop of Chicago, 1880. A man of great ability and charity.

FEKE, ROBERT (*b. Oyster Bay, N.Y., c. 1705; d. Bermuda, c. 1750*), portrait-painter. A clever draftsman and catcher of likenesses, Feke resided in Newport, R.I., but is known to have worked also in Boston and Philadelphia.

FELCH, ALPHEUS (*b. Limerick, Maine, 1804; d. Ann Arbor, Mich., 1896*), lawyer. Removed to Michigan, 1833. Held state offices, and was Democratic governor, 1846–47; U.S. senator, 1847–53.

FELL, JOHN (*b. New York, N.Y., 1721; d. Coldenham, N.Y., 1798*), merchant, Revolutionary patriot. Member of Continental Congress from New Jersey, 1778–80; judge, court of common pleas, 1766–74, 1776–86.

FELS, JOSEPH (*b. Halifax Co., Va., 1854; d. 1914*), soap manufacturer. Devoted time and fortune to world-wide spread of Henry George's Single Tax doctrine.

FELSENTHAL, BERNHARD (*b. Münchweiler, Bavaria, 1822; d. 1908*), rabbi. Came to America, 1854. Associated with Zion Congregation, Chicago. A leading figure of Reform Judaism in the Middle West, he became a fervent advocate of Zionism.

FELT, JOSEPH BARLOW (*b. Salem, Mass., 1789; d. 1869*), antiquarian, New England historian.

FELTON, CORNELIUS CONWAY (*b. Newbury, Mass., 1807; d. Chester, Pa., 1862*), classical scholar. Graduated Harvard, 1827. Professor of Greek, Harvard, 1832–60; regent of that university, 1849–57, and president, 1860–61. Author of school texts and *Greece: Ancient and Modern* (1867).

FELTON, REBECCA LATIMER (*b. near Decatur, Ga., 1835; d. Atlanta, Ga., 1930*), writer. Wife of William H. Felton. First woman U.S. senator; held 2-day *ad interim* appointment in 1922.

FELTON, SAMUEL MORSE (*b. Newbury, Mass., 1809; d. 1889*), civil engineer. Brother of Cornelius C. Felton. Graduated Harvard, 1834. Built and managed the Fitchburg Railroad; became president of the Philadelphia, Wilmington & Baltimore, 1851, and made it one of the country's best-equipped and most profitable roads. Rendered inestimable service in Civil War transportation of Union troops. Was a developer and director of the Pennsylvania Railroad and later of the Northern Pacific.

FELTON, WILLIAM HARRELL (*b. Oglethorpe Co., Ga., 1823; d. Cartersville, Ga., 1909*), Methodist preacher, physician, farmer, reform politician. As independent legislator and congressman, fought Democratic "ring rule" in Georgia *post* 1874.

FENDALL, JOSIAS (*b. c. 1620; d. c. 1687*), colonial governor of Maryland, 1656–60. Attempted overthrow of proprietary government, 1659–60; was later influential among supporters of Nathaniel Bacon and was associate of John Coode.

FENGER, CHRISTIAN (*b. Breininggaard, Denmark, 1840; d. Chicago, Ill., 1902*), surgeon, pathologist. After practice in Europe and Egypt, came to America, 1877, and won fame as a teacher at Chicago's medical schools and at Cook County Hospital. His students numbered some of the greatest names in modern surgery and pathology.

FENN, WILLIAM WALLACE (*b. Boston, Mass., 1862; d. 1932*), Unitarian clergyman, theologian. Professor, Harvard Divinity School, and Dean, 1906–22. [*Supp. 1*]

FENNELL, JAMES (*b. London, England, 1766; d. 1816*), actor. Came to America, 1793. His invariable success as an actor in Philadelphia and New York alternated with his failures as a promoter of salt-works, schools and other enterprises.

FENNER, ARTHUR (*b. Providence, R.I., 1745; d. Providence, 1805*). Anti-Federalist governor of Rhode Island, 1790–1805.

FENNER, BURT LESLIE (*b. Rochester, N.Y., 1869; d. Croton-on-Hudson, N.Y., 1926*), architect. Partner in McKim, Mead and White, 1906–26.

FENNER, CHARLES ERASMUS (*b. Jackson, Tenn., 1834; d. New Orleans, La., 1911*), Confederate soldier, jurist. Associate justice, Louisiana supreme court, 1880–94. Active trustee of Tulane University and of Peabody Educational Fund.

FENNER, JAMES (*b. Providence, R.I., 1771; d. 1846*), politician. Son of Arthur Fenner. U.S. senator from Rhode Island, 1804–07; governor, 1807–11, 1824–31, and 1843–45.

FENNO, JOHN (*b. Boston, Mass., 1751 o.s.; d. Philadelphia, Pa., 1798*), editor. Published and edited the Federalist *Gazette of the United States* (New York, 1789; Philadelphia, 1790–98) with the aid of Alexander Hamilton as contributor and patron.

FENOLLOSA, ERNEST FRANCISCO (*b. Salem, Mass., 1853; d. London, England, 1908*), poet, student of Oriental art. Author of *Epochs of Chinese and Japanese Art* (1912) and translations of verse and dramas published posthumously by his literary executor, Ezra Pound.

FENTON, REUBEN EATON (*b. Carroll, N.Y., 1819; d. Jamestown, N.Y., 1885*), lumberman, politician, banker. As Democratic congressman from New York, 1853–55, seceded from his party over the slavery issue; in 1855 presided over first Republican state convention. Served as Republican congressman, 1857–64, and as governor of New York, 1864–68; built up a powerful political machine. While U.S. senator, 1869–75, he broke with Roscoe Conkling over control of state patronage and was forced out of power.

FENWICK, BENEDICT JOSEPH (*b. near Leonardtown, Md., 1782; d. Boston, Mass., 1846*), Roman Catholic clergyman, Jesuit. Ordained, 1808; served at St. Peter's, New York City, 1809–17, and as president of Georgetown College, 1817–18. After a few years in Charleston, S.C., he served again as president of Georgetown, 1822–25. Consecrated bishop of Boston, 1825, he founded *The Jesuit* (now *The Boston Pilot*), 1829, and administered his diocese with great energy and success.

FENWICK, EDWARD DOMINIC (*b. St. Mary's Co., Md., 1768; d. Wooster, O., 1832*), Roman Catholic clergyman, Dominican. Consecrated first bishop of Cincinnati, 1822. Founded American mother-house of Dominican order in Springfield, Ky.

FENWICK, GEORGE (*b. England, 1603; d. England, 1656/7*), colonist. Patentee of part of Connecticut. Resident at Saybrook, 1639–45.

FENWICK, JOHN (*b. Bynfield, England, 1618; d. 1683*), colonist. A Cromwellian trooper turned Quaker, he advocated a Quaker colony in America and was assigned West Jersey in trust for the purpose; he planted first Quaker settlement on the Delaware at Salem, 1675.

FENWICKE, JOHN. [See FENWICK, JOHN, 1618–1683.]

FERGUSON, ALEXANDER HUGH (*b. Manilla, Canada, 1853; d. Chicago, Ill., 1911*), surgeon. Taught in Canada, and in Chicago *post* 1894; devised method of treating hernia and improved cleft palate operations.

FERGUSON, ELIZABETH GRAEME (*b. Philadelphia, Pa., 1737; d. Montgomery Co., Pa., 1801*), poet, translator. Acted as go-between in British intrigues during Revolution.

FERGUSON, THOMAS BARKER (*b. near Charleston, S.C., 1841; d. Boston, Mass., 1922*), Confederate soldier, scientist, diplomat. Carried out valuable researches in fish propagation.

FERGUSON, WILLIAM JASON (*b. Baltimore, Md., 1844; d. Baltimore, 1930*), actor. Sole eyewitness of Lincoln's assassination, 1865.

FERGUSON, WILLIAM PORTER FRISBEE (*b. Delhi, N.Y., 1861; d. 1929*), clergyman, journalist, militant Prohibitionist.

FERNALD, CHARLES HENRY (*b. Fernald's Point, Maine, 1838; d. 1921*), entomologist. Professor at Massachusetts Agricultural College, 1886–1910. One of first Americans who taught entomology systematically; led fight against gipsy moth in New England.

FERNALD, JAMES CHAMPLIN (*b. Portland, Maine, 1838; d. Upper Montclair, N.J., 1918*), Baptist clergyman, author. Edited *English Synonyms and Antonyms* (1896, 1914).

FERNOW, BERNHARD EDUARD (*b. Inowrazlaw, Germany, 1851; d. Toronto, Canada, 1923*), forester, author, teacher. Trained in Prussian forest service; came to America, 1876; was U.S. pioneer of scientific forestry. Managed Cooper-Hewitt timber lands in Pennsylvania; in 1882 helped organize American Forestry Congress; in 1886 became chief, Division of Forestry, U.S. Department of Agriculture. Advocated special studies of trees, federal and state protection laws, and the present system of National Forests.

Shaped federal forest reserve law of 1897. Organized first American collegiate school of forestry at Cornell University, 1898; inaugurated forestry work at Pennsylvania State College, 1906; became head of forestry department, University of Toronto, 1907. Author of *Economics of Forestry* (1902), *A Brief History of Forestry* (1907), *The Care of Trees* (1910) and many government circulars.

FERNOW, BERTHOLD (*b. Inowrazlaw, Germany, 1837; d. Togus, Maine, 1908*), historian, archivist, Union soldier. Specialist in documentary sources for New York and the middle colonies.

FERREL, WILLIAM (*b. Fulton Co., Pa., 1817; d. 1891*), meteorologist. Internationally known for "Essay on the Winds and the Currents of the Ocean" (1856); worked for U.S. Coast and Geodetic Survey.

FERRERO, EDWARD (*b. Granada, Spain, 1831; d. New York, N.Y., 1899*), dancing master, Union soldier.

FERRIS, GEORGE WASHINGTON GALE (*b. Galesburg, Ill., 1859; d. 1896*), civil engineer. Graduated Rensselaer Polytechnic, 1881. Specialist in steel testing and inspection; invented the Ferris Wheel.

FERRIS, ISAAC (*b. New York, N.Y., 1798; d. 1873*), Reformed Dutch clergyman. Active on foreign mission board of his church; chancellor of University of the City of New York, 1852–70.

FERRIS, JEAN LÉON GÉRÔME (*b. Philadelphia, Pa., 1863; d. Philadelphia, 1930*), historical painter. Nephew of Edward, Peter and Thomas Moran; studied under Christian Schussele, and in France, Spain and England. His studies from American history excel in fidelity and accuracy of detail.

FERRIS, WOODBRIDGE NATHAN (*b. near Spencer, N.Y., 1853; d. Washington, D.C., 1928*), educator. Founded Ferris Institute, Big Rapids, Mich.; Democratic governor of Michigan, 1913–17; U.S. senator, 1923–28.

FERRY, ELISHA PEYRE (*b. Monroe, Mich., 1825; d. 1895*), lawyer, Union soldier. Governor of Washington Territory, 1872–80; first governor of state of Washington, 1890–93.

FERRY, ORRIS SANFORD (*b. Bethel, Conn., 1823; d. 1875*), lawyer, Union soldier. Congressman, Republican, from Connecticut, 1859–61, and U.S. senator, 1866–75, shifting from radical views to a moderate position on Reconstruction.

FERRY, THOMAS WHITE (*b. Mackinac Island, Mich., 1827; d. Grand Haven, Mich., 1896*), businessman. U.S. senator, Republican, from Michigan, 1871–83; financial expert; president *pro tempore* of the Senate during Hayes-Tilden electoral count, 1877.

FERSEN, HANS AXEL, Count Von (*b. Stockholm, Sweden, 1755; d. Sweden, 1810*), soldier, statesman. Aide-de-camp to Rochambeau in America, 1780–83; attempted to rescue French royal family, 1791, by flight to Varennes.

FESS, SIMEON DAVIDSON (*b. Allen Co., O., 1861; d. Washington, D.C., 1936*), educator. Graduated Ohio Northern, 1889; LL.B., 1894. President, Antioch College, 1907–17. Congressman, Republican, from Ohio, 1913–23; U.S. senator, 1923–35. A conservative leader of the "Old Guard" and an ardent prohibitionist, he opposed President Wilson's policies and later attacked progressive spirits in his own party, vehemently supporting the regimes of Presidents Harding, Coolidge and Hoover. Solemn, superior and long-winded, he won respect for his sincerity. [*Supp. 2*]

FESSENDEN, FRANCIS (*b. Portland, Maine, 1839; d. 1906*), lawyer, Union major-general, biographer of his father, William Pitt Fessenden.

FESSENDEN, JAMES DEERING (*b. Portland, Maine, 1833; d. 1882*), lawyer, Union brigadier-general, Maine official and legislator. Son of William Pitt Fessenden.

FESSENDEN, REGINALD AUBREY (*b. East Bolton, Canada, 1866; d. Bermuda, 1932*), inventor, pioneer in radio communication. Educated in Canada, gave up a career in education because of his interest in science. Removed to New York *ca.* 1886. Worked for Thomas A. Edison, Westinghouse Electric Co., and taught at the University of Pittsburgh where he concentrated on wireless communication. Formed the National Electric Signalling Co., 1902. Believed wireless telephony to be practicable if a continuous flow of high frequency vibrations were developed; achieved success with an alternator on a frequency of 50,000 cycles, and in 1906 sent out, it is believed, the first broadcast of speech and music ever made. Established two-way transatlantic telegraphic communication, 1906. He is credited also with invention of heterodyne reception, with the fathometer and with the radio compass. [*Supp. 1*]

FESSENDEN, SAMUEL (*b. Fryeburg, Maine, 1784; d. 1869*), lawyer, Abolitionist. Father of William Pitt Fessenden.

FESSENDEN, THOMAS GREEN (*b. Walpole, N.H., 1771; d. Boston, Mass., 1837*), poet, journalist, inventor. Graduated Dartmouth, 1796. Contributed under pen-name "Simon Spunkey" to Dennie's *Farmer's Weekly Museum*; practiced law. In England, 1801–04, as agent and promoter of inventions, he there published a satire *Terrible Tractoration* (1803) and a volume of *Original Poems* (1804; reprinted at Philadelphia, 1806). Returning to Boston, he wrote *Democracy Unveiled* (1805), a virulent Hudibrastic attack on Jefferson; edited a partisan Federalist magazine. During law practice in Brattleboro, Vt., 1809–22, he also edited local newspapers and compiled legal and other works. Established *New England Farmer* (1822) and other agricultural periodicals; invented a portable hot-water stove. Served as Whig in Massachusetts General Court. Was most important American verse satirist between John Trumbull and James Russell Lowell.

FESSENDEN, WILLIAM PITT (*b. Boscawen, N.H., 1806; d. Portland, Maine, 1869*), lawyer, politician, financier. Son of Samuel Fessenden. Graduated Bowdoin, 1823; admitted to Maine bar, 1827; became one of the state's outstanding lawyers. Entered public life with election to the state legislature on anti-Jackson ticket, 1831; active as a Whig, he accompanied Daniel Webster on a Western tour in 1837, but later (1852) opposed Webster's presidential nomination. Elected again to Maine legislature, 1839, he was Whig Congressman, 1841–43; he returned to the legislature in 1845–46, 1853–54. His rise to national fame began when the anti-slavery faction of the Maine legislature elected him to the U.S. Senate in 1854. There he quickly became known through his eloquent opposition to the Kansas-Nebraska bill, and in 1857 began his notable ten-year service on the Senate's finance committee. In poor health, and given to displays of irritability, with a reputation for harshness and austerity, Fessenden was one of the Senate's greatest debaters and intellectual forces. As chairman of the finance committee after 1861, he earned a permanent place among America's public financiers. He consistently tried to administer the finances of the Civil War economically and efficiently. He opposed many popular personal and sectional projects and protested against the issue of legal-tender notes, although he later admitted that they presented the only resource available at the time. He foresaw the need for increased taxation and at the beginning of the war proposed the levy of an income tax. Appointed secretary of the treasury, 1864, during his one year of service Fessenden stood firm against further inflation, raised the interest rate on government bonds and marketed yet another great loan through Jay Cooke and Company.

Re-elected to the Senate, 1865, he became chairman of the Joint Committee on Reconstruction. A Radical Reconstructionist, he believed in the power of Congress to change the South's form of government, to punish, to exact security and to take entire charge of the defeated section. He was not, however, an extremist, and opposed part of the Confiscation Act and the attempt to expel Sen. Garrett Davis for treasonable acts. In the impeachment of President Johnson, he held that impeachment was a judicial process to be motivated by manifestly impeachable offenses and not a device for the summary removal of an unpopular, ill-advised executive. Although he disapproved of President Andrew Johnson's policies and conduct, he thought him free of impeachable offenses and so voted, refusing to bow to the opinions and wishes of his constituents in the matter. He courageously faced a storm of popular disapproval in the confident hope that events would justify his course. His death occurred before his term ended.

FETTERMAN, WILLIAM JUDD (*b. c. 1833; d. near Lodge Trail Ridge, Wyo., 1866*), soldier. Ambushed and killed with his command of eighty men by Indian chief Red Cloud while leading a foolhardy attack out of Fort Phil Kearny.

FEW, IGNATIUS ALPHONSO (*b. near Augusta, Ga., 1789; d. Athens, Ga., 1845*), Methodist clergyman. Founder and first president, Emory College.

FEW, WILLIAM (*b. near Baltimore, Md., 1748; d. Fishkill-on-the-Hudson, N.Y., 1828*), statesman, Revolutionary soldier, banker. Raised in North Carolina; removed to Georgia, 1776. Georgia delegate to Continental Congress and member of Constitutional Convention; U.S. senator from Georgia, 1789–93. Removed to New York, 1799, and engaged in banking.

FEW, WILLIAM PRESTON (*b. Sandy Flat, S.C., 1867; d. Durham, N.C., 1940*), educator. Graduated Harvard, 1893; Ph.D., 1896. President, Trinity College, Durham, N.C., 1910–24, and first president of its successor, Duke University. [*Supp. 2*]

FEWKES, JESSE WALTER (*b. Newton, Mass., 1850; d. Forest Glen, Md., 1930*), zoologist, ethnologist. Graduated Harvard, 1875; Ph.D., 1877. Founded the *Journal of American Ethnology and Archaeology*. Became associated with Bureau of American Ethnology, 1895. Introducing zoological methods to archaeology, Fewkes intensively studied Hopi cults as well as pioneering in exploration and conservation of Southwest cliff dwellings and pueblos. Became chief of Bureau, 1918; received international recognition. Among his many contributions to anthropology was his demonstration of value of study of living tribes in solving problems of their past.

FFOULKE, CHARLES MATHER (*b. Quakertown, Pa., 1841; d. New York, N.Y., 1909*), wool merchant. Collector of and authority on tapestries.

FFRENCH, CHARLES DOMINIC (*b. Galway, Ireland, 1775; d. 1851*), Roman Catholic clergyman, Dominican. *Post* 1812, attended missions in New Brunswick (Canada), New York, New Jersey and New England; pastor at Lawrence, Mass., *post* 1846.

FIELD, BENJAMIN HAZARD (*b. Yorktown, N.Y., 1814; d. New York, N.Y., 1893*), merchant, philanthropist. Benefactor and officer of New York Home for Incurables, 1866–93; helped found New York Free Circulating Library.

FIELD, CHARLES WILLIAM (*b. Woodford Co., Ky., 1828; d. Washington, D.C., 1892*), Confederate soldier, engineer. Graduated West Point, 1849. Served with cavalry on Southwest frontier. As major-general, commanded Hood's old Texas division, 1864–65. Inspector-general of Egyptian army, 1875–77.

FIELD, CYRUS WEST (*b. Stockbridge, Mass., 1819; d. 1892*), merchant, capitalist, promoter of first Atlantic cable. Son of David D. Field (1781–1867). Retiring from business as paper merchant, 1852, he turned to promotion of an Atlantic cable *post* 1854. In association with Peter Cooper and others, and with advice of M. F. Maury and S. F. B. Morse, Field formed a company to build cable between Newfoundland and Ireland. After many reverses and a partial success in 1858, a fully serviceable cable was in operation by 1866. Field also promoted New York elevated railroads, and with Jay Gould developed the Wabash Railroad. A man of courage and vision, he was easily deceived and his last years were saddened by financial reverses.

FIELD, DAVID DUDLEY (*b. East Guilford, Conn., 1781; d. Stockbridge, Mass., 1867*), Congregational clergyman, historian. Minister at Haddam and Stockbridge, Conn. Father of four celebrated Americans: David Dudley, Cyrus West, Stephen Johnson, and Henry Martyn Field.

FIELD, DAVID DUDLEY (*b. Haddam, Conn., 1805; d. 1894*), lawyer. Son of David D. Field (1781–1867). Attended Williams College; admitted to New York bar, 1828; became partner of Robert Sedgwick. Long active in politics as anti-slavery Democrat, briefly as a Republican, and *post* 1865 as a Democrat again, Field's career was primarily that of a lawyer and law reformer. He was outstanding in the years following the Civil War as counsel in great constitutional cases, defending L. P. Milligan before the Supreme Court in 1867, and contending successfully that military courts were without jurisdiction as long as civilian courts were open. Likewise he won arguments on usurpations of constitutional rights in the Cummings, McCardle and Cruikshank cases. During the Erie Railroad litigation of 1869, Field was counsel for Jay Gould and James Fisk, and was accused of unprofessional conduct; the committee on grievances of the New York City bar delivered a damaging report on Field but its recommendations were not adopted. Field's connection with "Boss" Tweed, a co-director of Erie with Gould and Fisk, also laid him open to adverse criticism.

Field served with distinction as counsel for Samuel J. Tilden in the 1876 election dispute; also in the case of *New York vs. Louisiana* before the Supreme Court, 1882. His permanent fame, however, derives from his fight for codification of municipal and international law. He inspired and personally shaped reformed political, penal and civil procedural codes for New York; in 1881 the Penal Code was adopted. The Civil Code involved Field in a bitter fight in which he almost singlehandedly engaged the New York bar. His work has been recognized by

wide adoption of his codes both in the United States and abroad. In 1872 he published a *Draft Outline of an International Code,* whose second edition (1876) carried an added part on relations in time of war. In 1873 Field helped found the Association for the Reform and Codification of the Law of Nations and was active in furthering the movement until the end of his life.

FIELD, EUGENE (*b. St. Louis, Mo., 1850; d. Chicago, Ill., 1895*), author. Attended Williams, Knox College and University of Missouri. Worked as newspaperman in Missouri and on Denver, Colo., *Tribune,* 1873–83. Joined staff of Chicago *Morning News* (renamed *Record,* 1890) with which he remained until his death. His practical jokes, his practice of attributing poems to embarrassed notables and his uproarious reporting of imaginary events distinguished his column "Sharps and Flats," in which much of his verse originally appeared. As whimsical in his life as in his writings, he was a student of Horace and a bibliophile, and the character of his column set a higher standard for American journalism. His poems are at their best ("Little Boy Blue," "Wynken, Blynken, and Nod") sentimental and pathetic; at their worst, jejune and repetitive. Among his books are: *The Tribune Primer* (1882); *Culture's Garland* (1887); *A Little Book of Western Verse* (1889); *Second Book of Verse* (1892); *The Holy Cross and Other Tales* (1893); and a selection from *Sharps and Flats* (1900).

FIELD, HENRY MARTYN (*b. Stockbridge, Mass., 1822; d. 1907*), Presbyterian clergyman. Son of David D. Field (1781–1867). Author of popular travel books and biographies of his brothers, David Dudley and Cyrus West Field; owned and edited the *Evangelist.*

FIELD, HERBERT HAVILAND (*b. Brooklyn, N.Y., 1868; d. 1921*), zoologist, bibliographer. Studied at Harvard, Freiburg, Leipzig, Paris; established "Concilium Bibliographicum," Zurich, 1895, international center for indexing zoological literature.

FIELD, JOSEPH M. (*b. Dublin, Ireland ?, 1810; d. Mobile, Ala., 1856*), actor, playwright, journalist. Brought to America in infancy. Played in West and South.

FIELD, KATE. [See FIELD, MARY KATHERINE KEEMLE, 1838–1896.]

FIELD, MARSHALL (*b. near Conway, Mass., 1834; d. 1906*), merchant. Removed to Chicago, 1856; was clerk and salesman for dry-goods firm of Cooley, Wadsworth & Co.; became general manager, 1861, and a partner, 1862. Associated with Levi Z. Leiter and Potter Palmer in retail and wholesale firm of Field, Palmer and Leiter until 1867; with Leiter and his own brothers in Field, Leiter and Co. until 1881, when Leiter withdrew and it became Marshall Field and Co. Under his able management, his shop won a reputation for quality merchandise and honest dealing. Like A. T. Stewart and John Wanamaker, Field promoted new trends in merchandising. Prices were marked plainly; sales were for cash or on short credit; goods could be bought on approval and exchanged; large stocks were acquired in anticipation of demand and a demand was then created. Field bought his goods on a world-wide scale and manufactured many of them in his own factories. He was a master of detail, a diplomat in employee relations and shrewd in his choice of able assistants.

FIELD, MARY KATHERINE KEEMLE (*b. St. Louis, Mo., 1838; d. Honolulu, Hawaii, 1896*), journalist, author, lecturer, actress. Daughter of Joseph M. Field. Friend of the Brownings, George Eliot, Anthony Trollope and other distinguished Victorians.

FIELD, MAUNSELL BRADHURST (*b. Peekskill, N.Y. ?, 1822; d. New York, N.Y., 1875*), lawyer. Served in U.S. Paris legation and as president of U.S. commission to Paris Exhibition, 1855. Did valuable service as assistant in U.S. Treasury Dept., 1861–65. Author of *Memories* (1874).

FIELD, RICHARD STOCKTON (*b. White Hill, N.J., 1803; d. Princeton, N.J., 1870*), lawyer, jurist. Grandson of Richard Stockton. Developed New Jersey's educational system; defended Lincoln's suspension of *habeas corpus* as U.S. senator, 1862; federal judge, New Jersey district, 1863–70.

FIELD, ROBERT (*b. England, c. 1769; d. Jamaica, B.W.I., 1819*), painter of portraits in oil, miniaturist, engraver. Led successful professional and social life in Philadelphia, Washington, Baltimore, Boston, 1794–1808; in Halifax, N.S., 1808–16.

FIELD, ROSWELL MARTIN (*b. St. Louis, Mo., 1851; d. Morristown, N.J., 1919*), journalist. Brother of Eugene Field; collaborator with him in *Echoes from the Sabine Farm* (1891, 1892).

FIELD, STEPHEN DUDLEY (*b. Stockbridge, Mass., 1846; d. Stockbridge, 1913*), electrical engineer, inventor. Nephew of Cyrus W. Field. Active in telegraphy in California, 1863–79, during which time he developed many improvements. Thereafter, designed and built electric railroads; designed a superior stock ticker; invented and installed submarine quadruplex telegraph.

FIELD, STEPHEN JOHNSON (*b. Haddam, Conn., 1816; d. 1899*), jurist. Son of David D. Field (1781–1867). Graduated Williams, 1837; studied law with brother David D. Field and with John Van Buren; admitted to bar, 1841. Removed to California, 1849; became alcalde of Marysville; served in state legislature, where he drafted state civil and criminal practice acts. Elected to state supreme court, 1857, he became known and respected for his pragmatism and disregard for common law notions, his defense of the power of the legislature to legislate for the general welfare and to adopt measures for the protection of labor. A Union Democrat, he was appointed U.S. circuit judge at San Francisco and U.S. Supreme Court justice in 1863.

In contrast to his previous pragmatism, Field's constitutional position became increasingly doctrinaire. He held the dualistic thesis of "a national government for national purposes, local governments for local purposes," each sovereign in its sphere, neither dependent upon or subordinate to the other in any degree. The Court could define the spheres of local and national government only acting judicially and as mere mouthpiece of the Constitution. His second major tenet was his natural rights doctrine derived from the contemporary discussion of freedmen's rights, from the individualism of the classical school of economics and from his own Western experience. The two articles of his creed were not always compatible. Among the noteworthy cases in which Field spoke for the Court were the Test Oath Cases, *Paul vs. Virginia, The Daniel Ball,* Tarbles' Case, *Pennoyer vs. Neff, Escanaba Bridge & Transportation Company vs. Chicago, Barbier vs. Connelly, Gloucester Ferry Company vs. Pennsylvania,* and *Chae Chan Ping vs. United States.* Among his most important contributions were his dissents in the Slaughterhouse Cases and in *Munn vs. Illinois.* Field's work as California circuit judge contributed the most dramatic chapters to his career. His defiance of local anti-Chinese feeling, and other considerations, thwarted his hopes of a Democratic presidential nomination. He retired from the bench in 1897.

FIELD, THOMAS WARREN (*b. Onondaga Hill, N.Y., 1821; d. Brooklyn, N.Y., 1881*), author. Edited several valuable historical works, in particular *An Essay Towards an Indian Bibliography* (1873).

FIELD, WALBRIDGE ABNER (*b. Springfield, Vt., 1833; d. 1899*), jurist. Graduated Dartmouth, 1855. Served as assistant to the U.S. attorney-general; as congressman, Republican, from Massachusetts, 1877–78, 1878–80; and as justice of Massachusetts supreme judicial court, 1881–99 (chief justice *post* 1890).

FIELDS, ANNIE ADAMS (*b. Boston, Mass., 1834; d. 1915*), Boston hostess, author. Wife of James T. Fields. Wrote memoirs of the literary people whom she entertained, a life of her husband and other works.

FIELDS, JAMES THOMAS (*b. Portsmouth, N.H., 1817; d. Boston, Mass., 1881*), publisher. Head of Ticknor & Fields; editor of *Atlantic Monthly,* 1861–70; author of poems, essays and *Yesterdays with Authors* (1872).

FIFER, JOSEPH WILSON (*b. near Staunton, Va., 1840; d. Bloomington, Ill., 1938*), politician, Union soldier. Republican governor of Illinois, 1889–93.
[*Supp.* 2]

FILENE, EDWARD ALBERT (*b. Salem, Mass., 1860; d. Paris, France, 1937*), merchant, reformer. Transformed a small family business into a large Boston department store which earned him a fortune, although he lost control of its management in 1928 and was unable to realize his ambition to make it a cooperative enterprise. Idealistic in public affairs, he organized with Lincoln Steffens and others the "Boston 1915" civic reform group, and was a pioneer in the chamber of commerce movement. His most permanent contributions were his development of credit unions, and his sponsorship of the Twentieth Century Fund, 1919, a fact-gathering organization specializing in the economic field, to which he left the bulk of his fortune. [*Supp. 2*]

FILLEBROWN, THOMAS (*b. Winthrop, Maine, 1836; d. 1908*), dentist. Practiced in Boston, Mass. Professor of operative dentistry and oral surgery at Harvard, 1883–1904; author of *A Textbook of Operative Dentistry* (1889).

FILLMORE, JOHN COMFORT (*b. near Franklin, Conn., 1843; d. Taftville, Conn., 1898*), musician, theorist, educator. Authority on music of American Indians.

FILLMORE, MILLARD (*b. Locke, N.Y., 1800; d. Buffalo, N.Y., 1874*), president of the United States. Grew up on the then New York frontier, a farmer's son; was admitted to bar, 1823; moved to Buffalo, 1830. Elected Anti-Masonic representative to the legislature, 1828; in 1834, following lead of his mentor Thurlow Weed, he became a Whig. Served in Congress, 1833–35, 1837–43; as chairman of the Ways and Means Committee, he took a leading part in framing tariff of 1842. The support of Henry Clay's followers helped him win nomination for vice-president in 1848. Shortly after his inauguration Fillmore broke with Weed and was reconciled with Daniel Webster with whom he had had a difference. Fillmore presided over the great slavery debate of 1850 in the Senate with firmness and fairness. Slow in announcing his support for Clay and Webster on the compromise bill of 1850, he appointed Webster as secretary of state on his succession to the presidency after Zachary Taylor's death, and otherwise demonstrated his alliance with the moderate Whigs who favored compromise. When he signed the Fugitive Slave Law in the fall of 1850, he exposed himself to violent abuse by the Abolitionists. Fillmore lost the 1852 Whig presidential nomination to Gen. Winfield Scott. In 1856, nominated by the Know-Nothings, he ran a poor third to Buchanan and Frémont. Always for conciliation as against coercion, he opposed Lincoln's conduct of the Civil War; he supported McClellan in the 1864 presidential campaign and was sympathetic to President Andrew Johnson's policies.

FILSON, JOHN (*b. East Fallowfield Township, Pa., c. 1747; d. on Little Miami River, O., 1788*), explorer, historian. Author of *Discovery, Settlement, and Present State of Kentucke* (1784) which contained the first appearance of Daniel Boone's so-called autobiography, and the first map of Kentucky. The map was also issued separately.

FINCH, FRANCIS MILES (*b. Ithaca, N.Y., 1827; d. 1907*), jurist. Associate judge, New York court of appeals; wrote popular poems "Nathan Hale" (1853) and "The Blue and the Gray" (1867).

FINCK, HENRY THEOPHILUS (*b. Bethel, Mo., 1854; d. 1926*), author. Music critic for the *Nation*, 1881–1924.

FINDLAY, JAMES (*b. Franklin Co., Pa., 1770; d. Cincinnati, O., 1835*), soldier. Removed to Cincinnati, O., *ante* 1798. Was first U.S. marshal of Ohio and mayor of Cincinnati, 1805–06, 1810–11. Commended for service in War of 1812, he was later major-general of state militia. Congressman, Democrat, 1825–33.

FINDLEY, WILLIAM (*b. North Ireland, 1741; d. Westmoreland Co., Pa., 1821*), Revolutionary soldier, politician. Came to America, 1763; settled near Waynesboro, Pa., and worked as weaver, teacher, and farmer. At close of Revolution, removed to a farm near present Latrobe, Pa. Active as Anti-Federalist in local and state politics; opposed ratification of the Constitution and Hamilton's financial policies; served in U.S. Congress, 1791–99, 1803–17; in the Pennsylvania senate, 1799–1803. Upon his recommendation the first standing congressional committee, that of Ways and Means, was appointed. As spokesman of the frontier he encouraged and later helped settle the Whiskey Insurrection of 1794.

FINE, HENRY BURCHARD (*b. Chambersburg, Pa., 1858; d. 1928*), mathematician. Graduated Princeton, 1880; Ph.D., Leipzig, 1885; specialized in logic of mathematics. Professor of mathematics, Princeton, 1891–1928; dean of faculty, 1903–12; dean of scientific departments, 1909–28.

FINK, ALBERT (*b. Lauterbach, Germany, 1827; d. New York, 1897*), railroad engineer, pioneer in U.S. railway economics and statistics. Came to America, 1849. Invented Fink bridge truss, *c.* 1852. As construction engineer, Louisville & Nashville Railroad, *post* 1857, built Green River bridge near Louisville, then second largest iron bridge in North America. Carried out successful reconstruction of the road after the Civil War; became general superintendent, 1865, and vice-president, 1869. Built mile-long Ohio River bridge at Louisville, the world's longest truss bridge. His 1874 report on costs of transportation is considered the foundation stone of U.S. rail economics. Resigning from the Louisville and Nashville, 1875, he served as commissioner of Southern Railway & Steamship Association and of New York City Trunk Line Association.

FINLAY, CARLOS JUAN (*b. Camagüey, Cuba, 1833; d. 1915*), physician. Educated in France; graduated M.D., Jefferson Medical College, 1855, and University of Havana, 1857. Spent most of his professional career in Havana. Declared the mosquito to be the probable transmitting agent of yellow fever in a paper read in 1881; his theory was received with indifference. His view was triumphantly confirmed by the findings of the Reed Board, 1900.

FINLAY, HUGH (*b. Scotland, c. 1731; d. 1801*), colonial postmaster. Developed postal service in Quebec, New England and Maritime Provinces; postmaster-general of British North America, 1787–99.

FINLEY, JAMES BRADLEY (*b. North Carolina, 1781; d. Ohio, 1856*), Methodist preacher. Raised in frontier Ohio. Was one of the West's most distinguished evangelical pioneers *post* 1810; co-founder of Wyandot Indian Mission.

FINLEY, JOHN HUSTON (*b. near Grand Ridge, Ill., 1863; d. New York, N.Y., 1940*), educator, editor, author. Graduated, 1887, Knox College, Galesburg, Ill.; returned as president, 1892. He subsequently filled with distinction the following posts: editor of *Harper's Weekly*, 1899–1900; a chair of politics at Princeton, 1900–03; president of City College of New York, 1903–13; New York State Commissioner of Education, 1913–21; associate editor, 1921–37, and editor-in-chief, 1937–38, of the *New York Times*. A man of disciplined mind, cultured taste, and active conscience, he was the author of eight books and many articles in the fields of education, politics, and the humanities. [*Supp.* 2]

FINLEY, MARTHA FARQUHARSON (*b. Chillicothe, O., 1828; d. Elkton, Md., 1909*), author of popular juvenile "series." Wrote the immortal *Elsie Dinsmore* (1868).

FINLEY, ROBERT (*b. Princeton, N.J., 1772; d. 1817*), Presbyterian clergyman, educator. Organizer of the American Colonization Society, 1816; president of University of Georgia, 1817.

FINLEY, SAMUEL (*b. Co. Armagh, Ireland, 1715; d. Philadelphia, Pa., 1766*), Presbyterian clergyman. Came to America, 1734. Friend and fellow worker of Gilbert Tennent, and a notable evangelistic preacher in the "Great Awakening," 1740–43. Pastor at Nottingham, Pa., 1744–61; president of College of New Jersey (Princeton), 1761–66.

FINN, FRANCIS JAMES (*b. St. Louis, Mo., 1859; d. Cincinnati, O., 1928*), Roman Catholic clergyman, Jesuit, educator. Author of *Percy Wynn* (1889); *Tom Playfair* (1892) and other long-popular stories of Catholic schoolboys.

FINN, HENRY JAMES WILLIAM (*b. Sydney, Canada, 1787; d. Long Island Sound, 1840*), actor, playwright, journalist. Raised in New York City. Made stage debut in England; first American appearance, 1817, at Philadelphia. Excelled as eccentric comedian. Author of various melodramas and satires and of the *American Comic Annual* (1831).

FINNEY, CHARLES GRANDISON (*b. Warren, Conn., 1792; d. Oberlin, O., 1875*), revivalist, educator. Raised in frontier New York. Abandoned practice of law after a highly emotional conversion; studied theology; was ordained as Presbyterian minister, 1824. Conducted extraordinary revivals in Middle and Eastern States; became pastor in New York City, 1832. Withdrew from the Presbytery, and was associated, *post* 1837, with Oberlin College, serving as its president, 1851–66, and from 1835 to 1872 as pastor of Oberlin's First Congregational Church. A New School Calvinist whose "Oberlin theology" was frequently attacked as tending towards Arminianism and Perfectionism, he objected to popular amusements as hindrances to maintenance of "revival pitch" in churches and opposed the use of tobacco, tea and coffee.

FINOTTI, JOSEPH MARIA (*b. Ferrara, Italy, 1817; d. Colorado, 1879*), Roman Catholic clergyman, bibliographer. Was literary editor of Boston *Pilot*; compiled *Bibliographia Catholica Americana, Pt. I, 1784–1820* (1872).

FIRESTONE, HARVEY SAMUEL (*b. Columbiana, O., 1868; d. Miami Beach, Fla., 1938*), rubber manufacturer. Organized Firestone Tire and Rubber Co., 1900, catering to the growing automobile market; by 1913 the company's annual sales were $15,000,000. Firestone weathered the post-1919 depression by cutting prices and wages; he expanded production and introduced the balloon tire, 1923. To circumvent the rise in British crude rubber prices *post* 1924, he acquired extensive rubber plantations in Liberia, assuming an important role in the country's affairs. [*Supp.* 2]

FISCHER, EMIL FRIEDRICH AUGUST (*b. Brunswick, Germany, 1838; d. Hamburg, Germany, 1914*), singer. Principal bass at New York Metropolitan Opera, 1885–98; at his best in Wagnerian roles.

FISH, CARL RUSSELL (*b. Central Falls, R.I., 1876; d. Madison, Wis., 1932*), historian. Graduated Brown, 1897; Ph.D., Harvard, 1900. Taught at University of Wisconsin, *post* 1900. Author of *The Development of American Nationality*, a textbook, (1913), *The Rise of the Common Man* (1927) and other works marked by originality and an emphasis on human and social aspects. [*Supp.* 1]

FISH, HAMILTON (*b. New York, N.Y., 1808; d. 1893*), statesman. Son of Nicholas Fish. Graduated Columbia, 1827; admitted to the bar, 1830. Congressman, Whig, from New York, 1843–45; governor of New York, 1849–51. As governor, established statewide free schools; extended canal system; expressed hostility towards extension of slavery. While U.S. senator, 1851–57, won no special distinction. Joined Republican party with no enthusiasm. Served on N.Y. Union Defense Committee during Civil War and as federal commissioner for relief of prisoners.

Appointed U.S. secretary of state, 1869, he acted until 1877 with efficiency, caution and patience. His most notable achievement was the settlement of the so-called *Alabama* claims against Great Britain for damages suffered by Northern commerce during the Civil War through the action of Confederate cruisers fitted out or supplied in British ports. By the Treaty of Washington, 1871, these claims were arbitrated by a tribunal at Geneva which in 1872 levied damages to the amount of $15,500,000 against Great Britain.

Fish faced difficulties over Cuba throughout his term. An insurrection in Cuba had obliged Fish to press claims on Spain for redress of injuries to Americans, and to contend with Americans who wanted the United States to recognize the Cuban rebels as belligerents and intervene in their favor. Fish persuaded President Grant in 1869 to declare unjustified any recognition of belligerency, and in 1871 reached an agreement for a joint commission to decide on American claims. In 1873 a new crisis arose when Spanish authorities in Cuba executed the captain, crew members and passengers of the *Virginius*, a steamer under American registry but belonging to the Cuban revolutionary committee in New York. Fish succeeded in adjusting the affair peacefully, and in 1874 secured the *Virginius* indemnity claims; in 1875 he instructed the U.S. minister to Spain to warn her of possible international intervention if the Cuban insurrection continued. Spain complied at last with all American demands and on the quelling of the revolt in 1876 the discussion over Cuba ended.

Other achievements during Fish's tenure as secretary of state concerned the protection of interests of North German citizens in France during the Franco-Prussian War; the recognition by Bismarck of the right to pass sealed dispatches through the German lines around Paris; the agreement of both belligerents to refrain from extending hostilities to the Far East; the protection of American rights in China; and the signing of a treaty of commercial reciprocity with Hawaii in 1875. His efforts to secure agreements with Colombia and Nicaragua for an interoceanic canal failed.

FISH, NICHOLAS (*b. New York, N.Y., 1758; d. 1833*), Revolutionary officer, lawyer. Lifelong friend of Alexander Hamilton; distinguished in Saratoga and Yorktown campaigns; an active Federalist politician.

FISH, PRESERVED (*b. Portsmouth, R.I., 1766; d. New York, N.Y., 1846*), merchant, ship-owner. A founder, 1815, of Fish & Grinnell, foremost New York shipping firm; president, Tradesman's Bank, 1836–46.

FISH, STUYVESANT (*b. New York, N.Y., 1851; d. 1923*), railroad executive, banker. Son of Hamilton Fish. Successfully managed Illinois Central Railroad as president, *post* 1887, until ousted by E. H. Harriman interests, 1906.

FISHBACK, WILLIAM MEADE (*b. Jeffersonton, Va., 1831; d. Fort Smith, Ark., 1903*), lawyer. Removed to Arkansas, 1858. Unionist in Civil War, but turned against carpetbaggers. Governor of Arkansas, Democrat, 1893–95.

FISHER, ALVAN (*b. Needham, Mass., 1792; d. Dedham, Mass., 1863*), painter. Brother of John D. Fisher. Specialized in rural landscapes and portraits.

FISHER, CLARA (*b. London, England, 1811; d. Metuchen, N.J., 1898*), actress, singer. Began career as child star in London; in America, *post* 1827, became one of the country's most finished stage artists, retiring in 1889. Author of an autobiography (1897).

FISHER, CLARK (*b. Levant, Maine, 1837; d. 1903*), naval engineer. Graduated Rensselaer Polytechnic, 1858. Served in U.S. Navy, 1859–71, resigning as chief engineer, after experiments proving value of oil as fuel. A prolific inventor, 1874–91, as head of Eagle Anvil Works.

FISHER, DANIEL WEBSTER (*b. Arch Spring, Pa., 1838; d. Washington, D.C., 1913*), Presbyterian clergyman. President of Hanover College, 1879–1907.

FISHER, EBENEZER (*b. Charlotte, Maine, 1815; d. Canton, N.Y., 1879*), Universalist clergyman, educator. Principal of the theological school, St. Lawrence University, 1858–79.

FISHER, FREDERICK BOHN (*b. Greencastle, Pa., 1882; d. Detroit, Mich., 1938*), Methodist clergyman. Active in missions *post* 1910, he was bishop of Calcutta, India, 1920–30. [*Supp.* 2]

FISHER, GEORGE JACKSON (*b. North Castle, N.Y., 1825; d. 1893*), physician, book-collector. Practiced at Ossining, N.Y.

FISHER, GEORGE PARK (*b. Wrentham, Mass., 1827; d. 1909*), Congregational clergyman, historian. Graduated Brown, 1847; Andover Theological Seminary, 1851. Studied in Germany. Professor of divinity, Yale, 1854–61; of history, Yale Divinity School, 1861–1901, and dean, 1895–1901. Author of numerous works on history and theology.

FISHER, GEORGE PURNELL (*b. Milford, Del., 1817; d. Washington, D.C., 1899*), lawyer. Judge of supreme court, District of Columbia, 1863–70; presided over first trial of John Surratt.

FISHER, HARRISON (*b. Brooklyn, N.Y., 1875; d. New York, N.Y., 1934*), illustrator and magazine-cover artist. Creator of the Harrison Fisher girl, "supernally beautiful and starry eyed." Collections of his drawings were published in book form, 1907–14. [*Supp.* 1]

FISHER, JOHN DIX (*b. Needham, Mass., 1797; d. Boston, Mass., 1850*), physician. Brother of Alvan Fisher. Graduated Harvard Medical School, 1825; studied in Paris. One of the first in America to use auscultation. Inspired New England Asylum, 1829, later the Perkins Institute for the Blind.

FISHER, JOSHUA FRANCIS (*b. Philadelphia, Pa., 1807; d. 1873*), humanitarian. A founder and life-long trustee of Pennsylvania Institution for the Blind. Advocated sympathetic understanding of Southern problems, reform of the representative system.

FISHER, PHILIP. [See Copley, Thomas, 1595-*c.* 1652.]

FISHER, SIDNEY GEORGE (*b. Philadelphia, Pa., 1809; d. Philadelphia, 1871*), lawyer, author.

FISHER, SYDNEY GEORGE (*b. Philadelphia, Pa., 1856; d. Essington, Pa., 1927*), lawyer, historian. Son of Sidney G. Fisher. Graduated Trinity (Hartford, Conn.), 1879. Author of many historical studies, notably *The Evolution of the Constitution* (1897); *The True Benjamin Franklin* (1899); and *The Struggle for American Independence* (1908).

FISHER, THEODORE WILLIS (*b. Westboro, Mass., 1837; d. 1914*), psychiatrist.

FISHER, WALTER LOWRIE (*b. Wheeling, W. Va., 1862; d. Winnetka, Ill., 1935*), lawyer, reformer. Son of Daniel W. Fisher. Practiced in Chicago, *post* 1889. Leader in movement to conserve U.S. natural resources; secretary of the interior, 1911–13. [*Supp. 1*]

FISK, CLINTON BOWEN (*b. western New York, 1828; d. New York, N.Y., 1890*), banker, Union soldier. Opened school for Negro freedmen, 1866, which later became Fisk University; presidential candidate on Prohibition party ticket, 1888.

FISK, JAMES (*b. Greenwich, Mass., 1763; d. Swanton, Vt., 1844*), lawyer, politician. Congressman, (Democrat) Republican, from Vermont, 1805–09, 1811–15; served as Vermont federal collector of revenue, 1818–26.

FISK, JAMES (*b. Bennington, Vt., 1834; d. New York, N.Y., 1872*), capitalist, speculator. Began his career as a boastful, flashy peddler and jobber; in 1866 founded brokerage house of Fisk & Belden with support of Daniel Drew. Drawn into the "Erie War" of 1868 between Drew and Cornelius Vanderbilt, Fisk broke Vanderbilt's attempt to corner Erie stock and with Jay Gould came to control the Erie Railroad. With Drew and Gould, he launched a campaign in 1868 to tighten credit and raise price of gold; their raids on U.S. Express Co. and Albany & Susquehanna RR. stock culminated in an attempted gold corner on Black Friday, September 1869, which reacted disastrously on the nation's business.

FISK, WILBUR (*b. Brattleboro, Vt., 1792; d. Middletown, Conn., 1839*), Methodist clergyman, educator. Dispelled indifference of eastern Methodists toward education; first president, Wesleyan University, Middletown, Conn., 1830–39.

FISKE, AMOS KIDDER (*b. Whitefield, N.H., 1842; d. 1921*), editor, author. Staff member of *New York Times*, 1869–71, 1878–97; of *Journal of Commerce*, 1902–19.

FISKE, DANIEL WILLARD (*b. Ellisburg, N.Y., 1831; d. 1904*), scholar, librarian, book-collector. Student of Icelandic civilization, newspaperman, book-dealer, diplomat, Fiske lived in Italy *post* 1883. He was a principal benefactor of Cornell University library.

FISKE, FIDELIA (*b. Shelburne, Mass., 1816; d. Shelburne, 1864*), missionary to the Nestorians. Graduated Mt. Holyoke Seminary, 1842. Improved condition of women in Persia on tour of duty, 1843–58; wrote *Recollections of Mary Lyon* (1866).

FISKE, GEORGE CONVERSE (*b. Roxbury Highlands, Mass., 1872; d. 1927*), classicist, educator. Graduated Harvard, 1894; Ph.D., 1900. Taught at University of Wisconsin, 1901–27; authority on Roman satire; author of *Lucilius and Horace* (1920) and other works.

FISKE, HALEY (*b. New Brunswick, N.J., 1852; d. 1929*), insurance official, lawyer. Brother of Stephen Fiske. Graduated Rutgers, 1871. Became vice-president of Metropolitan Life Insurance Co., 1891; was instrumental in placing control of company in hands of policy-holders, in making payments of bonuses to the insured, in initiating a highly successful national health campaign and in directing the company's capital into housing developments. By 1919, when he became president, the company was recognized as the world's largest financial institution.

FISKE, JOHN (*b. Salem, Mass., 1744; d. 1797*), naval commander, merchant. Captain in the Massachusetts navy during the Revolution; commanded the brigantines *Tyrannicide* and *Massachusetts* on successful cruises, 1776–77.

FISKE, JOHN (*b. Hartford, Conn., 1842; d. Gloucester, Mass., 1901*), philosopher, historian. Born Edmund Fisk Green. Precocious as a linguist. Graduated Harvard, 1863; as a student, became disciple of Herbert Spencer and published articles on evolution in *North American Review*. Lectured on philosophy and history at Harvard and in Boston; in 1872 became assistant librarian at Harvard and published his first book, *Myths and Myth-Makers*. In 1874 followed *The Outlines of Cosmic Philosophy*. After resignation from Harvard, 1879, he became a popular lecturer on history both in the United States and abroad. Profound neither as a thinker nor a scholar, he was America's chief exponent of evolution and remarkable in the field of history chiefly for the lucid freedom of style in his many books.

FISKE, MINNIE MADDERN (*b. New Orleans, La., 1865; d. 1932*), actress. Christened Marie Augusta Davey. Made her stage appearance at age 3 as "Little Minnie Maddern"; New York debut, 1870; continued to act on and off Broadway until 1890 when she married Harrison Grey Fiske and retired. In 1893 she returned in *Hester Crewe.* Continued with *A Doll's House, Tess of the D'Urbervilles, Becky Sharp, Salvation Nell* and acted in and directed many others. During the 1920's she toured the country as Mrs. Malaprop in *The Rivals.* One of the most potent forces in the American theatre for realism on the stage, she won fame for her grasp of character, intellectual acuteness, emotional sensitivity and ability as a director. [*Supp. 1*]

FISKE, STEPHEN RYDER (*b. New Brunswick, N.J., 1840; d. 1916*), journalist, theatrical manager. Brother of Haley Fiske.

FITCH, ASA (*b. Salem, N.Y., 1809; d. 1879*), physician, entomologist. State entomologist of New York, 1854–70; issued important annual reports on crop pests. Fitch's appointment gave official recognition to applied entomology and represented the first great practical step taken in the United States to investigate the problem of insect damage.

FITCH, CLYDE. [See FITCH, WILLIAM CLYDE, 1865–1909.]

FITCH, JOHN (*b. Windsor Township, Conn., 1743; d. Bardstown, Ky., 1798*), metal craftsman, inventor. After an unhappy boyhood and various employments, set up brass shop in East Windsor, 1764; lost money in unsound investments; after further financial setbacks abandoned his family and shop, 1769. Built up profitable brass and silversmith business in Trenton, N.J., which was wiped out by the Revolution. Entered military service; took charge of Trenton gun factory; profited by selling provisions to the Continental Army and invested in Virginia land-warrants. While surveying along the Ohio, 1780, acquired 1600 acres in Kentucky. Captured by Indians, 1782, he was turned over to the British and held prisoner in Canada. After his exchange, settled in Bucks Co., Pa., but organized a land company and surveyed in the Northwest Territory, 1783 and 1785. His projects failed with the adoption of the federal government's township system.

After 1785, Fitch devoted all his attention to inventing a steamboat. Obtained exclusive privileges for use of his proposed boat from Pennsylvania, New York, Delaware and Virginia; was given financial support by prominent Philadelphia citizens. Launched his first boat successfully on the Delaware near Philadelphia, 1787; his second, a 60-foot paddle-wheeler, 1788. With this vessel, he carried thirty passengers on numerous round trips between Philadelphia and Burlington, N.J. Despite public indifference, Fitch built a third boat in 1790 providing

regular service on the Delaware. Received American (1791) and French patents, but lost financial support when his fourth boat was wrecked before completion. After a futile effort to get backing in France, he returned to America, destitute and ill. Built a four-passenger, screw-propelled steamboat in New York, 1796, but failing once again to win financial support he moved to Kentucky where he died.

FITCH, SAMUEL (*b. Lebanon, Conn., 1724; d. London, England, 1799*), lawyer, Boston Loyalist.

FITCH, THOMAS (*b. Norwalk, Conn., c. 1700; d. 1774*), lawyer. Graduated Yale, 1721. Colonial governor of Connecticut, 1754–66; defeated for re-election, 1766, because of his support of the Stamp Act by taking the oath required in it, he published a pamphlet justifying his conduct.

FITCH, WILLIAM CLYDE (*b. Elmira, N.Y., 1865; d. Châlons-sur-Marne, France, 1909*), playwright. Graduated Amherst, 1886. Wrote *Beau Brummell* for Richard Mansfield (produced, 1890). Many other original plays and adaptations from foreign sources were written by Fitch in rapid succession, all marked by his strong sense of "theater" and skill in suiting the taste of the period. *The Moth and the Flame* and *Nathan Hale* opened to great acclaim at the same time in Philadelphia and Chicago, 1898. Other successes followed, notably *Barbara Frietchie* (1898); *The Climbers* (1901); *Captain Jinks* (1901); *The Truth* (1907); and *The City* (1909).

FITLER, EDWIN HENRY (*b. Philadelphia, Pa., 1825; d. near Philadelphia, 1896*), cordage manufacturer. Mayor of Philadelphia, 1887–91.

FITTON, JAMES (*b. Boston, Mass., 1805; d. Boston, 1881*), Roman Catholic clergyman. Missionary in New England, 1827–43, he later held pastorates in Providence and Newport, R.I. and in East Boston, Mass. In 1842, he gave Bishop Fenwick the site of Holy Cross College, Worcester, Mass.

FITZ, HENRY (*b. Newburyport, Mass., 1808; d. New York, N.Y., 1863*), telescope maker.

FITZ, REGINALD HEBER (*b. Chelsea, Mass., 1843; d. 1913*), pathologist, clinician. Graduated Harvard, B.A., 1864; M.D., 1868. Studied at Vienna, and under Virchow at Berlin. Taught at Harvard Medical School, *post* 1870, and was visiting physician to Massachusetts General Hospital. His paper "Perforating Inflammation of the Vermiform Appendix" (1886) named appendicitis, provided its diagnosis, proved its origin and advocated radical surgery for its cure. It ranks as a classic of modern medicine. In a second major contribution Fitz described acute pancreatitis. Earliest of Virchow's students to return to America, Fitz was first to introduce the microscopic study of diseased tissue, greatly influenced scientific pathology and advanced rational therapeusis.

FITZGERALD, DESMOND (*b. Nassau, Bahamas, 1846; d. 1926*), hydraulic engineer. Raised in Providence, R.I. Supervised Boston water reservoirs, 1873–1903; did important research work on evaporation and coloration of water.

FITZGERALD, EDWARD (*b. Limerick, Ireland, 1833; d. Hot Springs, Ark., 1907*), Roman Catholic clergyman. Came to America, 1849; ordained, 1857. Served as pastor at Columbus, O. Consecrated bishop of Little Rock, 1867, and served until 1906. Voted *non placet* on doctrine of infallibility at Vatican Council, 1870.

FITZGERALD, EDWIN. [See FOY, EDDIE, 1856–1928.]

FITZGERALD, FRANCIS SCOTT KEY (*b. St. Paul, Minn., 1896; d. Hollywood, Calif., 1940*), novelist. Reflected in his work his admiration for wealth as a means of realizing "the promises of life," and his distrust of the insensitivity of the rich.

Entering Princeton in 1913, he achieved some social and literary success but fell behind scholastically, dropped out for a year, and finally left in 1917 to enlist in the army. Training in Alabama, he became engaged to Zelda Sayre. They were married in 1920, on the success of his first novel, *This Side of Paradise* (1920). This first book about "the Jazz Age" made Fitzgerald famous and momentarily rich. Following *The Beautiful and Damned* (1922) and an unsuccessful play, *The Vegetable* (1923), Fitzgerald wrote *The Great Gatsby* (1925), his most brilliant book though a financial failure.

The Fitzgeralds lived in Europe from 1924 to 1930, when Zelda's mental breakdown brought them back to America. Fitzgerald then began his long, losing struggle against his wife's insanity, his own drinking and their increasing debts. *Tender Is the Night* (1934), deeply moving but unsuited to the taste of the 1930's, was a financial and critical failure. His fear that his talent was dead, revealed in *The Crack-Up* (1945), led Fitzgerald to Hollywood as a movie writer in 1937. Before his death he had partially finished *The Last Tycoon* (1941). Of his 160 short stories, four volumes were collected: *Flappers and Philosophers* (1921), *Tales of the Jazz Age* (1922), *All the Sad Young Men* (1926), and *Taps at Reveille* (1935). [*Supp. 2*]

FITZGERALD, OSCAR PENN (*b. Caswell Co., N.C., 1829; d. Monteagle, Tenn., 1911*), Methodist bishop, author.

FITZGERALD, THOMAS (*b. New York, N.Y., 1819; d. London, England, 1891*), editor, playwright. Published Philadelphia *Evening City Item*; campaigned for local progressive reforms.

FITZGIBBON, CATHERINE. [See IRENE, SISTER, 1823–96.]

FITZHUGH, GEORGE (*b. Prince William Co., Va., 1806; d. Huntsville, Texas, 1881*), lawyer, sociologist. Author of regular articles in *DeBow's Review*, 1857–67, and of *Sociology for the South* (1854). Defended slavery as better suited than socialism to overcome evils of *laissez-faire*.

FITZHUGH, WILLIAM (*b. Bedford, England, 1651; d. Stafford Co., Va., 1701*), lawyer. Came to Virginia, c. 1670; was successful as lawyer and merchant. His extant letters give valuable insights into business procedures of a Virginia capitalist between 1679 and 1699.

FITZPATRICK, BENJAMIN (*b. Greene Co., Ga., 1802; d. 1869*), lawyer, planter. Removed to Mississippi Territory, 1816; settled near Montgomery, Ala. As Democratic governor of Alabama, 1841–45, reformed state banking system. U.S. senator from Alabama, 1848 and 1853–61; declined nomination for vice-president on Douglas ticket, 1860.

FITZPATRICK, JOHN BERNARD (*b. Boston, Mass., 1812; d. Boston, 1866*), Roman Catholic clergyman. Studied at Collège de Montreal and at Saint-Sulpice, Paris; ordained, 1840. Consecrated coadjutor of Boston, 1844, he succeeded to the see, 1846. An intellectual and an able administrator, he raised standards of clerical training and prepared his diocese to handle the great wave of Irish immigration.

FITZPATRICK, JOHN CLEMENT (*b. Washington, D.C., 1876; d. Washington, 1940*), curator of manuscripts, Library of Congress, 1897–1928. Editor, collected writings of George Washington (39 vols., 1931–44). [*Supp. 2*]

FITZPATRICK, MORGAN CASSIUS (*b. Tuscaloosa, Ala., 1868; d. Gallatin, Tenn., 1908*), lawyer, educator. Tennessee Democratic leader and legislator; effective state superintendent of public instruction, 1899–1903.

FITZPATRICK, THOMAS (*b. Co. Cavan, Ireland, c. 1799; d. Washington, D.C., 1854*), trapper, guide, Indian agent. Came to America, *ante* 1816. Served as second in command under Jedediah S. Smith in effective discovery of South Pass, 1824; became partner in Rocky Mountain Fur Co., 1830, with James Bridger, Milton Sublette and others. After decline of fur trade, served as guide, accompanying the Bidwell-Bartleson pioneer emigrant train (1841), the White-Hastings Oregon party (1842), Frémont's second expedition (1843–44), Kearny's expedition to South Pass and J. W. Abert's expedition (1845) and Kearny's Army of the West (1846). As agent of the Upper Platte and Arkansas Indian agency, *post* 1846, Fitzpatrick was in charge of Cheyennes, Arapahos and some Sioux. He negotiated the Indian treaties signed at the Fort Laramie Council (1851) which he helped to arrange, and also peace treaties with the Comanches, Kiowas and Kiowa Apaches at

Fort Atkinson (1853). The Indians called him "Broken Hand"; they trusted and respected him. His contemporaries considered him the greatest of the "mountain men."

FITZSIMMONS, ROBERT PROMETHEUS (*b. Helston, England, 1862; d. Chicago, Ill., 1917*), pugilist. Raised in New Zealand. Came to California, 1890, and won middleweight title, 1891. Defeated Jim Corbett for heavyweight title, 1897; lost it to J. J. Jeffries, 1899.

FITZSIMMONS, or FITZSIMONS, THOMAS (*b. Ireland, 1741; d. Philadelphia, Pa., 1811*), merchant, Revolutionary soldier and patriot. Emigrated to Philadelphia in youth. Served in Confederation Congress, in Pennsylvania legislature, and in Federal Convention (1787). Congressman, Federalist, from Pennsylvania, 1789–95. Active in establishment of Bank of North America, 1781, he was a founder of Insurance Company of North America.

FLAD, HENRY (*b. near Heidelberg, Germany, 1824; d. Pittsburgh, Pa., 1898*), engineer, inventor, Union soldier. Came to America, 1849; worked on railway construction. Associated after Civil War with St. Louis, Mo., public improvements. A prolific inventor.

FLAGET, BENEDICT JOSEPH (*b. Contournat, France, 1763; d. 1850*), Roman Catholic clergyman, Sulpician. Came to America after French Revolution; worked at Vincennes, at Georgetown College and at St. Mary's College, Baltimore. Consecrated bishop of Bardstown (later Louisville), Ky., 1810; save for a year's interlude served until his death as bishop and active missionary.

FLAGG, AZARIAH CUTTING (*b. Orwell, Vt., 1790; d. 1873*), editor, politician. Democratic assemblyman, secretary of state, state comptroller in New York; comptroller of New York City, 1852–59; a man of "unassailable integrity."

FLAGG, EDMUND (*b. Wiscasset, Maine, 1815; d. 1890*), author, lawyer, journalist, diplomat. His roving life was spent in the Middle West, in Berlin, Vienna, Venice and at last on a farm in Virginia.

FLAGG, GEORGE WHITING (*b. New Haven, Conn., 1816; d. 1897*), genre painter. Nephew of Washington Allston. Studied in London, Paris and Italy. Retired after many years' New York residence to Nantucket, Mass., 1879.

FLAGG, JARED BRADLEY (*b. New Haven, Conn., 1820; d. New York, N.Y., 1899*), portrait painter, Episcopal clergyman. Brother of George W. Flagg. Author of *Life and Letters of Washington Allston* (1892) whose nephew he was.

FLAGG, JOSIAH (*b. Woburn, Mass., 1737; d. c. 1795*), musician. Established liaison between New England psalmody and classical musical forms; introduced the anthem to the English colonies. Author

of *A Collection of the best Psalm Tunes* (1764) and *Sixteen Anthems* (1766).

FLAGG, JOSIAH FOSTER (*b. Boston, Mass., 1788; d. 1853*), dentist, anatomical artist, early experimenter in use of dental porcelain. Graduated Boston Medical College, 1815; practiced in Boston. Designed traction apparatus, extracting forceps and in 1833 made first "mineral teeth."

FLAGG, THOMAS WILSON (*b. Beverly, Mass., 1805; d. Cambridge, Mass., 1884*), naturalist, author.

FLAGLER, HENRY MORRISON (*b. Hopewell, N.Y., 1830; d. West Palm Beach, Fla., 1913*), capitalist, promoter. A grain merchant in Bellevue and Cleveland, O., he became an associate of John D. Rockefeller and his partner in Standard Oil Co. Active *post* 1883 in Florida development. Organized Florida East Coast Railway which reached Miami, 1896; built a string of resort hotels along the line and transformed beaches and swamps into playgrounds. Completed railroad line to Key West, 1912; dredged Miami harbor; established steamship services to Key West and Nassau where he also opened hotels.

FLAGLER, JOHN HALDANE (*b. Cold Spring, N.Y., 1836; d. Greenwich, Conn., 1922*), pipe and tube manufacturer, capitalist.

FLANAGAN, WEBSTER (*b. Claverport, Ky., 1832; d. Texas, 1924*), merchant, cattle-breeder, Confederate soldier. Republican officeholder and, *post* 1890, leader of Republican party in Texas.

FLANAGIN, HARRIS (*b. Roadstown, N.J., 1817; d. 1874*), lawyer. Settled in Arkansas, 1837; practiced at Greenville and Arkadelphia. Confederate governor of Arkansas, 1862–65.

FLANDERS, HENRY (*b. Plainfield, N.H., 1824; d 1911*), lawyer. Practiced in Philadelphia, Pa., *post* 1853, specializing in admiralty work. Author of works on maritime law, fire insurance and legal biography.

FLANDRAU, CHARLES EUGENE (*b. New York, N.Y., 1828; d. St. Paul, Minn., 1903*), jurist, soldier, author. Removed to St. Paul, 1853; settled at Traverse des Sioux, 1854. Was member of Minnesota constitutional convention and justice of the state supreme court; defended frontier during Sioux outbreak, 1862.

FLANDRAU, CHARLES MACOMB (*b. St. Paul, Minn., 1871; d. St. Paul, 1938*), essayist and traveler. Son of Charles E. Flandrau. Best known for his unorthodox, penetrating account of Mexican life and character: *Viva Mexico* (1908). [Supp. 2]

FLANNERY, JOHN (*b. Nenagh, Ireland, 1835; d Savannah, Ga., 1910*), Confederate soldier, banker, cotton-factor. Came to America, 1851; settled in Savannah, 1854. Head of John Flannery and Co.; president of Southern Bank and of Cotton Exchange.

FLATHER, JOHN JOSEPH (*b. Philadelphia, Pa.,* *1862; d. 1926*), mechanical engineer. Graduated Sheffield Scientific School, 1885. Taught at Lehigh, at Purdue, and at University of Minnesota; national authority on transmission and measurement of power.

FLEEMING, JOHN. [See FLEMING, JOHN, fl. 1764–1800.]

FLEET, THOMAS (*b. Shropshire, England, 1685;* *d. Boston, Mass., 1758*), printer. Came to Boston, *c.* 1712. Publisher of *Boston Evening-Post,* 1735–58.

FLEGENHEIMER, ARTHUR (*b. New York, N.Y.,* *1902; d. Newark, N.J., 1935*), gangster, better known as Dutch Schultz. Rose to power as a bootlegger; killed in a gang war. [*Supp. 1*]

FLEISCHMANN, CHARLES LOUIS (*b. near Buda-* *pest, Hungary, 1834; d. 1897*), yeast manufacturer, capitalist, philanthropist.

FLEMING, ARETAS BROOKS (*b. near Middleton,* [W.] *Va., 1839; d. 1923*), jurist, coal operator. Democratic governor of West Virginia, 1890–93.

FLEMING, ARTHUR HENRY (*b. Halton Co., Ont.,* *Canada, 1856; d. Pasadena, Calif., 1940*), lumber magnate. Removed to the United States, 1879. Founder and chief benefactor (with his wife, Clara Huntington Fowler) of California Institute of Technology. [*Supp. 2*]

FLEMING, JOHN (*fl. 1764–1800*), printer, Loyalist. Born in Scotland; arrived in Boston, Mass., 1764. In partnership with John Mein, published *Boston* *Chronicle,* chief Tory organ, Dec. 1767–June 1770; was officially proscribed and banished, 1778.

FLEMING, JOHN (*b. Mifflin Co., Pa., 1807; d.* *Ayr, Nebr., 1894*), Presbyterian clergyman. Missionary to Creeks, Weas, Chippewas, Ottawas; first to reduce Creek language to writing, *c.* 1834.

FLEMING, WALTER LYNWOOD (*b. Brundidge,* *Ala., 1874; d. 1932*), educator, historian. Graduated Alabama Polytechnic Institute, 1896; Ph.D., Columbia, 1904. Specialist in Civil War and Reconstruction history. Taught at West Virginia, Louisiana State and Vanderbilt universities [*Supp. 1*]

FLEMING, WILLIAM (*b. Jedburgh, Scotland, 1729;* *d. Montgomery Co., Va., 1795*), physician, soldier, statesman. Came to America, 1755. Served in the Forbes and Abercromby campaigns and others; practiced medicine at Staunton, Va., 1763–68. Wounded at battle of Point Pleasant. Was member of Virginia Senate and Council and acting governor, 1781.

FLEMING, WILLIAM MAYBURY (*b. Danbury,* *Conn., 1817; d. New York, N.Y., 1866*), actor, manager, Union soldier.

FLEMING, WILLIAMINA PATON STEVENS (*b.* *Dundee, Scotland, 1857; d. 1911*), astronomer. Came to America, 1878. At Harvard College Observatory, pioneered in analysis of photographs of stellar spectra, discovered 10 *novae* and over 200 variable stars.

FLETCHER, ALICE CUNNINGHAM (*b. Cuba,* *1838; d. Washington, D.C. ?, 1923*), ethnologist, pioneer student of Indian music. Authoritative interpreter of religious and social observances of North American Indians; author of *The Omaha Tribe* (1911) and many other studies.

FLETCHER, BENJAMIN (*b. London, England,* *1640; d. near Boyle, Ireland, 1703*), soldier. Colonial governor of New York, 1692–98, and briefly of Pennsylvania; allied himself with conservative elements; accused of excessive land grants and protection of pirates; replaced by Earl of Bellomont. [*Supp. 1*]

FLETCHER, CALVIN (*b. Ludlow, Vt., 1798; d.* *Indianapolis, Ind., 1866*), lawyer, banker. First lawyer to practice in Indianapolis, where he settled in 1821.

FLETCHER, DUNCAN UPSHAW (*b. Sumter Co.,* *Ga., 1859; d. Washington, D.C., 1936*), lawyer, politician. Removed to Jacksonville, Fla., 1881. U.S. senator, Democrat, from Florida, 1909–36; sponsored the Fletcher-Rayburn Act, 1934, creating the Securities and Exchange Commission. [*Supp. 2*]

FLETCHER, HORACE (*b. Lawrence, Mass., 1849,* *d. Copenhagen, Denmark, 1919*), writer and lecturer on nutrition. A successful, world-traveling salesman, he preached a gospel of health through thorough chewing of food.

FLETCHER, JAMES COOLEY (*b. Indianapolis,* *Ind., 1823; d. Los Angeles, Calif., 1901*), Presbyterian clergyman, missionary, diplomat. Son of Calvin Fletcher. Served in South America, Portugal, Italy; co-author of *Brazil and the Brazilians* (1857).

FLETCHER, RICHARD (*b. Cavendish, Vt., 1788,* *d. 1869*), jurist. Graduated Dartmouth, 1806. A noted jury lawyer, he became a leading Massachusetts practitioner; successfully contested Harvard's claim to an exclusive franchise over Charles River bridge.

FLETCHER, ROBERT (*b. Bristol, England, 1823;* *d. Washington, D.C., 1912*), medical scholar, bibliographer. Member of Royal College of Surgeons, 1844. Came to America, 1847; practiced at Cincinnati, O.; was field and hospital surgeon in Civil War. Assistant to John S. Billings in preparing great *Catalogue of Surgeon-General's Library,* 1876–95, he succeeded Billings as editor. Was co-editor of *Index Medicus,* 1879–95, and sole editor thereafter; author also of pioneer papers on medical history.

FLETCHER, ROBERT (*b. New York, N.Y., 1847; d.* *Hanover, N.H., 1936*), engineering educator. Graduated West Point, 1868. First director, 1871–1918, of Thayer School of Engineering of Dartmouth.

[*Supp.* 2]

FLETCHER, THOMAS CLEMENT (*b. Herculaneum, Mo., 1827; d. Washington, D.C., 1899*), lawyer, Union soldier, Republican governor of Missouri, 1865–69.

FLETCHER, WILLIAM ASA (*b. Plymouth, N.H., 1788; d. 1852*), jurist. Attorney-general of Michigan Territory and circuit judge; served as first chief justice of state supreme court, 1836–42.

FLETCHER, WILLIAM BALDWIN (*b. Indianapolis, Ind., 1837; d. Orlando, Fla., 1907*), physician. Son of Calvin Fletcher. Taught at Indiana medical institutions; as superintendent of Indiana Central Hospital for the Insane, introduced many reforms.

FLICK, LAWRENCE FRANCIS (*b. Cambria Co., Pa., 1856; d. Philadelphia, Pa., 1938*), physician, pioneer tuberculosis specialist. M.D., Jefferson Medical College, Philadelphia, 1879. President, 1901–35, White Haven Sanatorium, Luzerne Co., Pa.; president, 1903–10, Henry Phipps Institute, Philadelphia.

[*Supp.* 2]

FLICKINGER, DANIEL KUMLER (*b. Sevenmile, O., 1824; d. Columbus, O., 1911*), clergyman of United Brethren in Christ. Directed church missions in Africa and Germany.

FLINT, ALBERT STOWELL (*b. Salem, Mass., 1853; d. 1923*), astronomer. Graduated Harvard, 1875, and studied at Princeton with C. A. Young. Did valuable work at Washburn Observatory, University of Wisconsin, 1889–1920.

FLINT, AUSTIN (*b. Petersham, Mass., 1812; d. 1886*), physician, one of the most eminent American practitioners and teachers of his century. Graduated Harvard, M.D., 1833. Practiced in Boston briefly, and in Buffalo, N.Y. Taught at Rush Medical College, Chicago; founded Buffalo Medical College, 1847; lectured at University of Louisville and at New Orleans Medical College. Helped found Bellevue Hospital Medical College at New York, 1861, where he taught; also taught at Long Island College Hospital. Was active as hospital physician, teacher, textbook author and consultant; in 1883–84 served as president of American Medical Association. Published first text on diagnosis of respiratory diseases in 1856, of which eighth edition appeared in 1920 as *A Manual of Physical Diagnosis*. His classic work, *A Treatise on the Principles and Practice of Medicine*, appeared first in 1866 and was many times reissued and revised.

FLINT, AUSTIN (*b. Northampton, Mass., 1836; d. 1915*), physician, physiologist, alienist. Son of Austin Flint (1812–1886). Associated with father in teaching in Buffalo, New Orleans, New York; author of *The Physiology of Man* (1867–73).

FLINT, CHARLES LOUIS (*b. Middleton, Mass., 1824; d. Hillman, Ga., 1889*), lawyer, agriculturist. Secretary of Massachusetts Board of Agriculture, 1853–80; helped found Massachusetts Institute of Technology and Massachusetts Agricultural College.

FLINT, CHARLES RANLETT (*b. Thomaston, Maine, 1850; d. Washington, D.C., 1934*), industrial capitalist with international connections who provided guns and munitions to foreign governments. Known as "the father of trusts," he arranged many business mergers in the United States, 1892–1928. [*Supp.* 1]

FLINT, TIMOTHY (*b. near North Reading, Mass., 1780; d. Salem, Mass., 1840*), missionary, writer. Graduated Harvard, 1800. Pastor at Lunenburg, Mass., 1802–14; served as missionary in New Hampshire, Ohio, Missouri, Arkansas, 1815–25. Published the *Western Monthly Review* (Cincinnati, O., 1827–30); for brief period, edited the *Knickerbocker; or New-York Monthly Magazine*. Wrote romanticized, melodramatic stories of the Western border: *Francis Berrian* (1826); *Life and Adventures of Arthur Clenning* (1828); *Shoshonee Valley* (1830); *George Mason, the Young Backwoodsman* (1829). He was author also of *Recollections of the Last Ten Years . . . in the Valley of the Mississippi* (1826); *The History and Geography of the Mississippi Valley* (1832); *Indian Wars of the West* (1833); and *The Biographical Memoir of Daniel Boone* (1833). He edited *The Personal Narrative of James O. Pattie* (1831).

FLINT, WESTON (*b. Wyoming Co., N.Y., 1835; d. 1906*), librarian, government official. Graduated Union College, 1860. Held various government positions; prepared catalogue of U.S. Patent Office library; helped organize U.S. Civil Service Commission.

FLORENCE, THOMAS BIRCH (*b. Philadelphia, Pa., 1812; d. Washington, D.C., 1875*), politician, editor. Congressman, Democrat, from Pennsylvania, 1851–61. Championed temperance; was popular among workmen as "the widow's friend."

FLORENCE, WILLIAM JERMYN (*b. Albany, N.Y., 1831; d. Philadelphia, Pa., 1891*), actor. Born Bernard Conlin. Comedian, excelling in dialect parts and impersonation; considered among the six leading comedians of his time for skill in vivid drawing of character.

FLOWER, BENJAMIN ORANGE (*b. Albion, Ill., 1858; d. Boston, Mass., 1918*), editor, social reformer. Grandson of George Flower. Edited many reform periodicals, among them *The Arena* (Boston); wrote numerous books; became virulently anti-Catholic and edited *The Menace*.

FLOWER, GEORGE (*b. Hertford, England, 1788; d. Grayville, Ill., 1862*), pioneer. Son of Richard Flower. With Morris Birkbeck, promoted settlement of English and Scandinavian immigrants in Edwards Co., Ill.; resisted introduction of slavery into Illinois.

FLOWER, LUCY LOUISA COUES (*b. Boston, Mass., 1837; d. Coronado, Calif., 1921*), educator. Engaged in philanthropic work in Chicago; member of city school board and trustee of University of Illinois.

FLOWER, RICHARD (*b. England, 1761; d. Albion, Ill., 1829*), reformer, Illinois pioneer. Father of George Flower. Came in 1819 to settlement made in Edwards Co., Ill., by his son and Morris Birkbeck. Founded probably first library in Illinois; negotiated sale of village and lands of Harmony, Ind., to Robert Owen.

FLOWER, ROSWELL PETTIBONE (*b. Theresa, N.Y., 1835; d. Long Island, N.Y., 1899*), banker, stockbroker, politician. Began as jeweler and postmaster at Watertown, N.Y.; admitted to New York Stock Exchange, 1873. A Democrat of wealth, he served as congressman from New York, 1881–83; in 1884 and 1885 respectively Tammany Hall unsuccessfully suggested him as presidential candidate and for governor to offset influence of Grover Cleveland. Returning to Congress, 1889–92, from 1892 to 1895 he served as governor of New York. In 1896 he headed the New York delegation of gold Democrats at the Indianapolis convention and vigorously protested his party's "surrender to Populism and Anarchy." Always a person of importance in his party, he was denounced by opponents as a "flamboyant millionaire."

FLOY, JAMES (*b. New York, N.Y., 1806; d. New York, 1863*), Methodist Episcopal clergyman, editor, hymnologist.

FLOYD, JOHN (*b. Floyd Station, Ky., 1783; d. 1837*), surgeon. Graduated in medicine, University of Pennsylvania, 1806. Congressman, Democrat, from Virginia, 1817–29, he was first to propose occupation and territorial organization of Oregon, 1821. As governor of Virginia, 1830–34, he came to defend state sovereignty and the pro-slavery cause.

FLOYD, JOHN BUCHANAN (*b. Smithfield, Va., 1806; d. near Abingdon, Va., 1863*), lawyer. Son of John Floyd. Graduated South Carolina College, 1829. Entered Virginia Assembly, 1847; served as state-rights but anti-secession Democratic governor, 1849–52; re-entered Assembly, 1855. Secretary of war in Buchanan's cabinet, 1857–Dec. 29, 1860, he resigned over Buchanan's refusal to order evacuation of Fort Sumter, but was subsequently accused of transferring an excessive number of arms from Northern to Southern arsenals and of having tolerated abstraction of Indian trust funds. After Virginia's secession he raised and commanded a volunteer brigade for the Confederate Army. Dismissed by President Davis for abandoning his post at Fort Donelson, 1862, he was commissioned major-general by the Virginia Assembly.

FLOYD, WILLIAM (*b. Brookhaven, N.Y., 1734; d. Westernville, N.Y., 1821*), landowner, signer of the Declaration of Independence from New York. Member of Continental Congress, 1774–77, 1778–83; of national Congress, 1789–91. Active also in New York legislature. Lacking brilliance and unusual distinction, he was valued for his reliability and common sense.

FLÜGEL, EWALD (*b. Leipzig, Germany, 1863; d. 1914*), philologist. Ph.D., Leipzig, 1885. Professor at Stanford *post* 1892, he planned and partly executed a historical dictionary of the Chaucerian vocabulary.

FLYNT, JOSIAH. [See WILLARD, JOSIAH FLINT, 1869–1907.]

FOGG, GEORGE GILMAN (*b. Meredith Center, N.H., 1813; d. Concord, N.H., 1881*), lawyer, editor, diplomat. Founded and edited *Independent Democrat* (Concord). Served as U.S. minister to Switzerland, 1861–65.

FOLGER, CHARLES JAMES (*b. Nantucket, Mass., 1818; d. 1884*), jurist. Moved to Geneva, N.Y., as a boy. Served as New York state senator, and was judge of court of appeals; as secretary of treasury in President Arthur's cabinet, reduced public debt and put department offices under Civil Service rules.

FOLGER, HENRY CLAY (*b. New York, N.Y., 1857; d. Brooklyn, N.Y., 1930*), lawyer, capitalist. Graduated Amherst, 1879. Long associated with Standard Oil Co., he was president, Standard Oil Co. of New York, 1911–23. Founded and endowed Folger Shakespeare Library, Washington, D.C.

FOLGER, PETER (*b. Norwich, England, 1617; d. 1690*), grandfather of Benjamin Franklin. Came to Massachusetts, *c.* 1635; settled on Nantucket, 1663, and as teacher and Indian interpreter was island's "indispensable citizen." Author of *A Looking Glass for the Times* (1676).

FOLGER, WALTER (*b. Nantucket, Mass., 1765; d. Nantucket, 1849*), lawyer, jurist, scientist. Built "Folger's astronomic clock," 1788–90, a mechanical marvel; discovered process of annealing wire; served in Massachusetts General Court and as congressman, Democrat, 1817–21.

FOLIN, OTTO KNUT OLOF (*b. Asheda, Sweden, 1867; d. 1934*), biological chemist. Came to America, 1882. Worked on a farm to put himself through school. Graduated University of Minnesota, 1892; studied also in Germany and Sweden; Ph.D., University of Chicago, 1898. For seven years worked at McLean Hospital, Waverly, Mass.; *post* 1907, headed the department of biological chemistry at Harvard School of Medicine. His investigations illuminated the laws governing the composition of normal urine and the fields of the intermediate stages in protein metabolism. He studied part played in health and disease by creatine, creatinine, and uric acid; created methods for the accurate quantitation of the constituents of urine and blood. These methods soon were in general use throughout the world in determining the diagnosis and progress of disease and the effects of treatment. [*Supp. 1*]

FOLK, JOSEPH WINGATE (*b. Brownsville, Tenn., 1869; d. New York, N.Y., 1923*), lawyer. Graduated Vanderbilt University Law School, 1890. Practiced corporation law in St. Louis, Mo. Elected that city's chief law-enforcing officer, 1900, he conducted a series of exposures of alliance there between corrupt business and corrupt politics, 1901–02. Supported by rural counties and opposed by city politicians, he was elected Democratic governor of Missouri, 1905, and continued his reforming policies in that office until 1909. Served as chief counsel for Interstate Commerce Commission in first Wilson administration; returned to private law practice after defeat for U.S. senate seat, 1918.

FOLLEN, CHARLES (*b. Giessen, Germany, 1796; d. Long Island Sound, 1840*), first professor of German literature at Harvard, Abolitionist, Unitarian clergyman. Came to America, 1824. Taught at Harvard, 1825–35; lectured on law, gave lessons in gymnastics, wrote linguistic textbooks, literary readers, theological and philosophical essays. His vigorous defense of the Abolitionists and his "Address to the People of the United States," drafted at the New England Anti-Slavery Society's first convention, caused his severance from Harvard.

FOLLEN, ELIZA LEE CABOT (*b. Boston, Mass., 1787; d. 1860*), author. Prominent in Sunday-school movement and as a Massachusetts Abolitionist. Wife of Charles Follen.

FOLLEN, KARL THEODOR CHRISTIAN. [See FOLLEN, CHARLES, 1796–1840.]

FOLLETT, MARY PARKER (*b. Quincy, Mass., 1868; d. Boston, Mass., 1933*), vocational guidance counselor. Author of *The New State* (1918) and *Creative Experience* (1924). [*Supp. 1*]

FOLSOM, CHARLES (*b. Exeter, N.H., 1794; d. Cambridge, Mass., 1872*), librarian, teacher, editor. Served as U.S. Navy chaplain and instructor, later as tutor and librarian at Harvard and as librarian of Boston Athenaeum, 1846–56.

FOLSOM, GEORGE (*b. Kennebunk, Maine, 1802; d. Rome, Italy, 1869*), lawyer, antiquarian. Editor and librarian, American Antiquarian Society and New-York Historical Society; translated *Dispatches of Hernando Cortez* (1843).

FOLSOM, NATHANIEL (*b. Exeter, N.H., 1726; d. 1790*), Revolutionary soldier, New Hampshire politician.

FOLWELL, SAMUEL (*b. c. 1768; d. Philadelphia, Pa., 1813*), miniature painter, engraver.

FOLWELL, WILLIAM WATTS (*b. Romulus, N.Y., 1833; d. 1929*), educator, Union soldier. First president of University of Minnesota, 1869–84; thereafter librarian and professor of political science. Author of *History of Minnesota* (1921–30).

FONDA, JOHN H. (*b. Watervliet, N.Y., c. 1797; d. Prairie du Chien, Wis., c. 1868*), frontiersman, soldier. Led a wandering life along frontier from Texas to Green Bay, 1819–31; his reminiscences of early Wisconsin published, 1868.

FONT, PEDRO (*d. Pitique, Sonora, Mexico, 1781*), Franciscan missionary, cartographer. Accompanied de Anza's expedition to San Francisco, Calif., 1775–76; left graphic account of the journey.

FOOT, SAMUEL AUGUSTUS (*b. Cheshire, Conn., 1780; d. Cheshire, 1846*), merchant, farmer, politician. Graduated Yale, 1797. A Democratic legislator and congressman, he was U.S. senator, 1827–33; in 1829, he offered a resolution on public lands which led to Webster-Hayne debate. Served as governor of Connecticut, 1834–35.

FOOT, SOLOMON (*b. Cornwall, Vt., 1802; d. Washington, D.C., 1866*), lawyer, politician. Served in Vermont legislature. As Whig (later Republican) senator from Vermont, 1850–66, excelled as presiding officer through tact and knowledge of parliamentary law.

FOOTE, ANDREW HULL (*b. New Haven, Conn., 1806; d. New York, N.Y., 1863*), naval officer. Son of Samuel A. Foot. Appointed midshipman, 1822. When first lieutenant on U.S.S. *Cumberland*, enforced temperance on shipboard; was largely responsible for abolishment of grog ration in navy, 1862. After duty along African coast, wrote *Africa and the American Flag* (1854); supported agitation against slave-traffic. As commander of U.S.S. *Portsmouth* in China, 1856–58, led retaliatory raid on four barrier forts below Canton. Commanding naval operations on upper Mississippi, 1861–62, he was at reduction of Fort Henry and Fort Donelson; was wounded in the latter engagement. After fall of Island No. 10 in spring of 1862, he was relieved of duty afloat for reasons of health and promoted rear admiral.

FOOTE, ARTHUR WILLIAM (*b. Salem, Mass., 1853; d. Boston, Mass., 1937*), composer. A typical member of the New England group, his simple lyric forms, romantic in feeling, were rooted in classical tradition. [*Supp. 2*]

FOOTE, HENRY STUART (*b. Fauquier Co., Va., 1804; d. Nashville, Tenn., 1880*), lawyer, Mississippi Democratic politician. A personal and political enemy of Jefferson Davis, Foote opposed secession sentiment in his state as U.S. senator, 1847–52, and as governor of Mississippi, 1852–54. After the triumph of the state-rights faction, he removed first to California, then to Tennessee. After failure of his attempts to make peace, 1861, he resided for a time in Europe. Called the "Vallandigham of the South," he was author of *The War of the Rebellion* (1866), *Casket of Reminiscences* (1874) and other books.

FOOTE, JOHN AMBROSE (*b. Archbald, Pa., 1874; d. Washington, D.C., 1931*), physician, pediatrician. M.D., Georgetown, 1906; thereafter taught at Georgetown Medical School; dean, 1929–31. [*Supp.* 1]

FOOTE, LUCIUS HARWOOD (*b. Winfield, N.Y., 1826; d. San Francisco, Calif., 1913*), lawyer, diplomat. Active in Republican politics in California; U.S. minister to Korea, 1883–85.

FOOTE, SAMUEL AUGUSTUS. [See Foot, Samuel Augustus, 1780–1846.]

FOOTE, WILLIAM HENRY (*b. Colchester, Conn., 1794; d. Romney, W. Va., 1869*), Presbyterian clergyman. Author of *Sketches of North Carolina, Historical and Biographical* (1846) and *Sketches of Virginia, Historical and Biographical* (1850, 1855). [*Supp.* 1]

FORAKER, JOSEPH BENSON (*b. near Rainsboro, O., 1846; d. 1917*), lawyer, Union soldier, politician. Began law practice, Cincinnati, O., 1869; was judge of superior court. Republican governor of Ohio, 1886–90. As U.S. senator, 1896–1908, he was recognized as an outstanding constitutional lawyer and party leader; a supporter of McKinley's policies, he consistently opposed the policies of Theodore Roosevelt. Disclosure of questionable financial ties with Standard Oil led to his resignation in 1908.

FORBES, EDWIN (*b. New York, N.Y., 1839; d. Flatbush, N.Y., 1895*), painter, etcher, writer. Studied with Arthur F. Tait. As Civil War staff artist for *Leslie's*, sketched camp life and battlefields; published *Life Studies of the Great Army* (1876).

FORBES, JOHN (*b. Pittencrieff, Scotland, 1710; d. Philadelphia, Pa., 1759*), British officer. Came to America, 1757, as colonel of the 17th Foot; was promoted brigadier-general in America only. Commanded expedition against Fort Duquesne, 1758. Contending with unenthusiastic supporters, continual rainfalls, and his own mortal illness, he penetrated the western Pennsylvania wilderness; cut a road by way of Bedford and Ligonier and over Laurel Hill which later became major emigration highway; safeguarded line of communication by building regularly spaced blockhouses. Upon his arrival the French evacuated Fort Duquesne, and Forbes raised the British flag over the site on Nov. 25, 1758.

FORBES, JOHN (*b. Scotland, 1740?; d. England, 1783*), Church of England clergyman. First and for many years only English clergyman licensed in East Florida where he served, 1764–83, also holding high judicial offices in the province.

FORBES, JOHN (*b. Scotland, 1769; d. Cuba, 1823*), merchant. Agent for, and *post* 1792 a partner in, Panton, Leslie and Co., trading with the Creeks, Choctaws and Cherokees on the Spanish-Indian frontier; secured "Forbes purchase," land grant on Appalachicola River from Spain and the Indians, 1804 and 1811.

FORBES, JOHN MURRAY (*b. St. Augustine, Fla., 1771; d. Buenos Aires, Argentina, 1831*), lawyer, diplomat. Son of John Forbes (1740–1783). John Quincy Adams's most trusted agent in southern South America; served as agent for commerce, secretary of legation and chargé d'affaires at Buenos Aires, 1820–31.

FORBES, JOHN MURRAY (*b. Bordeaux, France, 1813; d. 1898*), merchant, capitalist. Grandson of John Forbes (1740–1783). Began business career in China; *post* 1846, turned to railroad building and management. With others bought and completed Michigan Central Railroad; financed roads which later became the Chicago, Burlington & Quincy; built the Hannibal & St. Joseph. During Civil War helped organize Negro regiments in Massachusetts; advised Navy Department; built a cruiser; organized Loyal Publication Society. After the war, was member of Republican national executive committee. Forbes brought into railroad business sound methods of finance and a broad view of its relation to the public interest.

FORBES, ROBERT BENNET (*b. Jamaica Plain, Mass., 1804; d. 1889*), sea-captain, China merchant, ship-owner, writer. Brother of John M. Forbes (1813–1898). Began career in employ of his uncles (James and Thomas H. Perkins) in the China trade; as head of Russell & Co., at Canton, 1839, during opium war refused to join British boycott of the port. Part-owned or constructed 68 vessels; invented "Forbes rig"; early acquired screw-driven, iron steamers. Commanded ship carrying food from Boston to Ireland in famine of 1847; supported coastal life-saving work; built Union warships during Civil War. Author of numerous pamphlets on China and on nautical subjects and a volume of *Personal Reminiscences* (1876).

FORBES, STEPHEN ALFRED (*b. Silver Creek, Ill., 1844; d. 1930*), entomologist, naturalist. After service in Union army, studied at Rush Medical; *post* 1872, worked at Museum of State Natural History, Normal, Ill; became director of State Laboratory of Natural History. Professor of zoology and entomology, University of Illinois, 1884–1921; state entomologist, 1882–1917. His more than 500 publications cover many diverse branches of biology. He was the first writer and teacher in America to stress the study of ecology, the earliest and leading American hydrobiologist, and a pioneer student of the foods of birds and fishes.

FORBUSH, EDWARD HOWE (*b. Quincy, Mass., 1858; d. 1929*), ornithologist. Author of *The Gypsy Moth* (1896); *Birds of Massachusetts and Other New England States* (1925, 1927), and other works.

FORCE, MANNING FERGUSON (*b. Washington, D.C., 1824; d. 1899*), Union soldier, jurist. Son of Peter Force. Brevetted major-general in recognition of "especial gallantry before Atlanta"; was judge of superior court of Cincinnati, O., 1877–87.

FORCE, PETER (*b. near Passaic Falls, N.J., 1790; d. 1868*), printer, publisher, archivist, historian. Whig mayor of Washington, D.C., 1836–40. Principally famous for collecting and publishing a series of reprints of rare pamphlets on colonial history, *Tracts and Other Papers, etc.* (1836–46) and for the monumental volumes known as *American Archives*, a most important collection of original materials on American history, originally planned to cover from the 17th century through 1789. Only nine volumes, covering the years 1774–76, appeared (1837–53).

FORD, DANIEL SHARP (*b. Cambridge, Mass., 1822; d. 1899*), printer. Edited and published *Youth's Companion, post* 1857, building it into the country's most successful family journal. Bequeathed funds for construction of Boston's Ford Hall.

FORD, GEORGE BURDETT (*b. Clinton, Mass., 1879; d. New York, N.Y., 1930*), architect, city planner. Worked in office of George S. Post. Sponsored a program of urban development in which esthetic considerations played a large role. [*Supp. 1*]

FORD, GORDON LESTER (*b. Lebanon, Conn., 1823; d. Brooklyn, N.Y., 1891*), lawyer, businessman, collector of Americana.

FORD, HENRY JONES (*b. Baltimore, Md., 1851; d. Blue Ridge Summit, Pa., 1925*), newspaper editor, publicist, historian. Author of *The Rise and Growth of American Politics* (1898) and other works; professor of politics at Princeton; confidential agent of President Woodrow Wilson and member of Interstate Commerce Commission.

FORD, JACOB (*b. Morristown, N.J., 1738; d. Morristown, 1777*), Revolutionary soldier, powder-maker, ironmaster. With father, cast shot and shell for Washington's army; operated powder-mill by Whippanong River.

FORD, JOHN BAPTISTE (*b. Danville, Ky., 1811; d. 1903*), inventor, manufacturer. Learned saddler's trade in Greenville, Ind.; operated general store, woodworking plant, foundry and rolling-mill. During Civil War built and operated river steamboats; turned to plate-glass manufacture at New Albany, Ind., 1863; lost his fortune in depression of 1873. Established Ford Plate Glass Co. at Creighton, near Pittsburgh, Pa., 1884, and made second large fortune; with his sons, controlled Pittsburgh Plate Glass Co. Established Michigan Alkali Co. at Wyandotte, Mich.; helped develop gas deposits near Pittsburgh.

FORD, JOHN THOMSON (*b. Baltimore, Md., 1829; d. 1894*), theatre manager. Built Baltimore Grand Opera house; managed theatres in Baltimore, Washington, Alexandria, Richmond.

FORD, PATRICK (*b. Galway, Ireland, 1835; d. Brooklyn, N.Y., 1913*), journalist. Came to America as a child. Editor of *Irish World* (New York), *post* 1870; a vehement advocate of complete Irish independence.

FORD, PAUL LEICESTER (*b. Brooklyn, N.Y., 1865; d. New York, N.Y., 1902*), historian, novelist. Son of Gordon L. Ford. Precociously expert, he began bibliographical researches in his father's library of Americana; reprinted many volumes of rare historical materials; produced bibliographical studies among others on Noah Webster, Charles Chauncy, Alexander Hamilton, Benjamin Franklin. He also edited the writings of John Dickinson and Thomas Jefferson and wrote popular works such as *The True George Washington* (1896) and *The Many-Sided Franklin* (1899). Among his successful works of fiction were *The Honorable Peter Stirling* (1894), *Janice Meredith* (1899), and *The Great K. and A. Train Robbery* (1897). Inherited wealth, restless energy, and a gift of painstaking concentration made possible Ford's impressive labors.

FORD, THOMAS (*b. Fayette Co., Pa., 1800; d. Peoria, Ill., 1850*), lawyer, jurist. As governor of Illinois, Democrat, 1842–46, he saved the state's credit by avoiding debt repudiation; he also secured removal of the Mormons in the interest of peace. Author of *History of Illinois* (1854).

FORDNEY, JOSEPH WARREN (*b. near Hartford City, Ind., 1853; d. 1932*), lumberman. Congressman, Republican, from Michigan, 1899–1923. An ardent protectionist, he gave name to the Fordney-McCumber Tariff of 1922, the climax of his legislative career. [*Supp. 1*]

FORDYCE, JOHN ADDISON (*b. Guernsey Co., O., 1858; d. New York, N.Y., 1925*), dermatologist, syphilologist. Graduated Adrian College, 1878; M.D., Northwestern, 1881; M.D., Berlin, 1888; studied also in Vienna and Paris. Practiced and taught in New York; organized first adequate American training center for dermatologists.

FOREPAUGH, ADAM (*b. Philadelphia, Pa., 1831; d. 1890*), showman. Began his circus career in 1864; by 1880 was most formidable rival of Barnum's Greatest Show on Earth.

FORESTER, FRANK. [See HERBERT, HENRY WILLIAM, 1807–1858.]

FORESTI, ELEUTARIO FELICE (*b. Conselice, Papal States, 1793; d. Genoa, Italy, 1858*), educator. Exiled from Italy as member of the Carbonari, came to America, 1836. Professor of Italian at Columbia and New York Universities, 1839–56; appointed U.S. consul to Genoa, 1858.

FORGAN, JAMES BERWICK (*b. St. Andrews, Scotland, 1852; d. 1924*), banker. Vice-president, 1892–1900, and president, *post* 1900, First National Bank, Chicago, Ill.

FORMAN, DAVID (*b. Monmouth Co., N.J., 1745; d. on shipboard, 1797*), Revolutionary soldier. Commanded Jersey militia at battle of Germantown; while suppressing armed Loyalists in Jersey, earned reputation for brutality.

FORMAN, JOSHUA (*b. Pleasant Valley, N.Y., 1777; d. Rutherfordton, N.C., 1848*), lawyer, businessman. Graduated Union College, 1798. Practiced law at present Syracuse, N.Y., of which he is recognized as founder. Was early advocate of Erie Canal and author of New York's Safety Fund plan (1828–29) insuring redemption of bank-notes.

FORMAN, JUSTUS MILES (*b. LeRoy, N.Y., 1875; d. aboard* Lusitania, *1915*), author.

FORNEY, JOHN WIEN (*b. Lancaster, Pa., 1817; d. 1881*), Philadelphia journalist, politician. Author of *Anecdotes of Public Men* (1873, 1881).

FORNEY, MATTHIAS NACE (*b. Hanover, Pa., 1835; d. New York, N.Y., 1908*), engineer, editor, inventor. Designed tank locomotive, 1866, used on urban elevated railroads; edited railroad journals. Author of *Catechism of the Locomotive* (1875) and other works.

FORNEY, WILLIAM HENRY (*b. Lincolnton, N.C., 1823; d. 1894*), lawyer, Confederate brigadier-general. Practiced law in Jacksonville, Ala. Congressman, Democrat, from Alabama, 1875–93.

FORREST, EDWIN (*b. Philadelphia, Pa., 1806; d. Philadelphia, 1872*), earliest American-born actor of the first rank. Made his debut at Walnut St. Theatre, Philadelphia, Nov. 1820; spent his apprenticeship in frontier theatres and at New Orleans. Supported Edmund Kean at Albany, N.Y., 1825, and received encouragement and advice from him. Forrest's appearance as Othello at New York's Park Theatre, 1826, launched him as a successful, popular star. His aggressive nationalism, his animal vigor and sonorous voice gained him the love of the less critical public, and enabled him to amass a small fortune and to give over $20,000 in prizes for native dramas and plays. Visiting England, 1845, he played Macbeth in London, where he had been previously well received, and was hissed. Believing the English actor Macready to be responsible, Forrest hissed Macready in Edinburgh shortly thereafter and stirred up a hornet's nest of passions. When Macready came to America in 1848–49, American audiences took sides in the actors' rivalry and interpreted it as a struggle of democracy versus Anglomania. Macready was howled down at his farewell appearance at New York's Astor Place Opera House on May 8, 1849, by a riotous mob of Forrest's adherents. When the Englishman was persuaded to try again on May 10, mob violence broke out which was quelled by the militia after much bloodshed. This shadow on Forrest's reputation was followed by scandalous divorce proceedings which dragged on from 1851 to 1869. Although he continued to enjoy financial success, he now alternated between periods of acting and of brooding withdrawal in his Philadelphia home. After 1865, he became increasingly crippled by sciatica and the public turned to younger actors. Forrest's strength was his vigorous rendering of strong-willed, elemental characters; his weakness lay in his egocentric passions, his vanity and arrogance.

FORREST, FRENCH (*b. St. Mary's Co., Md., 1796; d. Georgetown, D.C., 1866*), naval officer. Distinguished in the Mexican War at Alvarado and at Vera Cruz landing; as a Confederate officer, commanded Norfolk Navy Yard, 1861–62, and the James River squadron, 1863–64.

FORREST, NATHAN BEDFORD (*b. Bedford Co., Tenn., 1821; d. Memphis, Tenn., 1877*), Confederate general. A self-made wealthy plantation owner, Forrest enlisted as private in Confederate Army, 1861; having raised and equipped a mounted battalion, he was appointed lieutenant-colonel. Avoided capture at Fort Donelson, 1862, by leading his troops through a gap in the Union encirclement. Brigadier-general after July 1862, he carried out daring and tactically brilliant raids behind Union lines, in 1864 penetrating as far north as Paducah, Ky. Defeated superior force at Brice's Cross Roads, Miss., June 1864; commanded Confederate cavalry in Nashville campaign. Promoted lieutenant-general, February 1865, he met final defeat at Selma, Ala., in April and surrendered in May. His reputation as courageous soldier and superior cavalry leader is darkened by his failure to prevent the massacre of Negro soldiers at Fort Pillow, 1864.

FORSYTH, JOHN (*b. Fredericksburg, Va., 1780; d. Washington, D.C., 1841*), lawyer, statesman. Graduated Princeton, 1799. Attorney-general of Georgia, 1808; congressman, Democrat, from Georgia, 1813–18 and 1823–27; U.S. senator, 1818 and 1829–34; U.S. secretary of state, 1834–41. Served also as minister to Spain, 1819–22; secured ratification of treaty of 1819. Was governor of Georgia, 1827–29. Repudiating early state-rights leanings, he became staunch supporter of President Jackson. Voted against the tariff of 1832, but challenged authority of Georgia's nullification convention and helped to defeat its purposes. Voted for Force Bill; justified Jackson's stand on Bank issue. As secretary of state, secured French indemnity payments owing under treaty of 1831; stalled on issue of Texas recognition and annexation. A diplomat and courtier, Forsyth was a gifted orator and powerful debater.

FORSYTH, JOHN (*b. Newburgh, N.Y., 1810; d. Newburgh, 1886*), Associate Reformed clergyman, professor. Pastor in Philadelphia and Newburgh; taught languages, history, theology at Newburgh Seminary, Princeton, Rutgers, West Point.

FORSYTH, THOMAS (*b. Detroit, 1771; d. St. Louis, Mo., 1833*), Indian agent, explorer. Fur-trader in Michigan and Illinois; as agent to Potawatomi, Sauk and Foxes, helped maintain peace along the frontier, 1812–30. He was half-brother of John Kinzie.

FORTEN, JAMES (*b. Philadelphia, Pa., 1766; d. Philadelphia, 1842*), sail-maker. One of the foremost American Negroes of his time. Served in Continental Navy; became prominent Philadelphia businessman and an active philanthropist.

FORTESCUE, CHARLES LeGEYT (*b. York Factory, Canada, 1876; d. Pittsburgh, Pa., 1936*), electrical engineer, inventor. His contributions to power transmission include the method of symmetrical components for checking polyphase alternating current systems and a method of protecting lines against lightning. [*Supp. 2*]

FORTIER, ALCÉE (*b. St. James Parish, La., 1856; d. 1914*), educator, author, historian. Professor of Romance languages at Tulane University. Author of a classic *History of Louisiana* (1904); also textbooks and works on Creole history and customs.

FORWARD, WALTER (*b. Old Granby, Conn., 1786; d. Pittsburgh, Pa., 1852*), lawyer. Congressman, Democrat, from Pennsylvania, 1822–25; advocated high tariff. Played important part in forming Whig party, 1834. U.S. secretary of treasury, 1841–43, he was in constant disagreement with President John Tyler.

FORWOOD, WILLIAM HENRY (*b. Brandywine Hundred, Del., 1838; d. Washington, D.C., 1915*), army medical officer. Saw extensive field service during Civil War and on western reconnaissances, 1879–83; taught surgery at Army Medical School, 1893–1898; headed hospitals at Montauk Point, N.Y., Savannah, Ga., and San Francisco, Calif., 1898–1901. Retired in 1902 after brief tenure as surgeon-general.

FOSDICK, CHARLES AUSTIN (*b. Randolph, N.Y., 1842; d. Hamburg, N.Y., 1915*), author. Writing under the pen-name of Harry Castlemon, he produced many popular "series" of boys' books, beginning with *Frank, the Young Naturalist* (1864). Appealed

through his brisk, realistic descriptions and Northern patriotism.

FOSDICK, WILLIAM WHITEMAN (*b. Cincinnati, O., 1825; d. Cincinnati, 1862*), lawyer, author.

FOSS, CYRUS DAVID (*b. Kingston, N.Y., 1834; d. Philadelphia, Pa., 1910*), Methodist Episcopal clergyman. President of Wesleyan University, Middletown, Conn., 1875–80; as bishop, *post* 1880, traveled widely on missionary tours around the world.

FOSS, SAM WALTER (*b. Candia, N.H., 1858; d 1911*), poet, journalist. Graduated Brown, 1882. Worked as editor and humorous columnist on Massachusetts newspapers; *post* 1898 was librarian in Somerville, Mass. Best known for poem "The House by the Side of the Road" in *Dreams in Homespun* (1898).

FOSTER, ABIEL (*b. Andover, Mass., 1735; d. 1806*), Congregational clergyman. Actively supported Revolution; served in New Hampshire legislature. As congressman from New Hampshire, 1789–91 and 1795–1803, was staunch Federalist.

FOSTER, ABIGAIL KELLEY (*b. Pelham, Mass., 1810; d. 1887*), Abolitionist lecturer, woman's rights advocate. Wife of Stephen S. Foster.

FOSTER, BENJAMIN (*b. North Anson, Maine, 1852; d. New York, N.Y., 1926*), landscape-painter, art critic. Studied with Abbott Thayer and in Paris. An individual depicter of the quiet, meditative moods of nature.

FOSTER, CHARLES (*b. Fostoria, O., 1828; d. Fostoria, 1904*), merchant. Republican congressman from Ohio, 1871–79; governor of Ohio, 1880–84; U.S. secretary of the treasury, 1891–93. Efficient in office but unspectacular.

FOSTER, CHARLES JAMES (*b. Bicester, England, 1820; d. Astoria, N.Y., 1883*), sports editor. Came to America, 1848. Authority on history of the turf; wrote for *Porter's* (later *Wilkes's*) *Spirit of the Times*.

FOSTER, DAVID SKAATS (*b. Utica, N.Y., 1852; d. 1920*), merchant. Author of facile, sentimental novels crowded with action and superficial humor.

FOSTER, EPHRAIM HUBBARD (*b. near Bardstown, Ky., 1794; d. 1854*), prominent Nashville, Tenn., lawyer and Whig leader. U.S. senator, 1838–39 and 1843–45; voted against admission of Texas.

FOSTER, FRANK HUGH (*b. Springfield, Mass., 1851; d. 1935*), Congregational clergyman, theologian. Graduated Harvard, 1873; Ph.D., Leipzig, 1882. Author of many books including *A Genetic History of the New England Theology* (1907).

[*Supp. 1*]

FOSTER, FRANK PIERCE (*b. Concord, N.H., 1841; d. 1911*), physician, immunologist, editor. Graduated College of Physicians and Surgeons, New York,

1862. Pioneered in use of animal lymph as vaccine; edited *New York Medical Journal*, 1880–1911; compiled *Illustrated Encyclopedic Medical Dictionary* (1888–94).

FOSTER, GEORGE BURMAN (*b. Alderson, W. Va., 1858; d. 1918*), Baptist clergyman, educator. Professor at McMaster University and University of Chicago; an articulate liberal in theology, he regarded religion as something experimental and almost wholly pragmatically sanctioned.

FOSTER, HANNAH WEBSTER (*b. Boston, Mass., 1759; d. Montreal, Canada, 1840*). Author of *The Coquette: or, The History of Eliza Wharton* (1797), a widely read *roman à clef;* also of *The Boarding School* (1798).

FOSTER, JOHN (*b. Dorchester, Mass., 1648; d. Dorchester, 1681*), printer, earliest wood-engraver in English America. Chief among some ten woodcuts attributed to him are a portrait of Richard Mather, a 1677 map of New England and a view of Boston and Charlestown.

FOSTER, JOHN GRAY (*b. Whitefield, N.H., 1823; d. 1874*), army officer, engineer. Graduated West Point, 1846. Author of an important journal and reports of the attack on Fort Sumter where he was serving as captain, 1861. He held important field commands in the Union army and was promoted major-general, 1862.

FOSTER, JOHN PIERREPONT CODRINGTON (*b. New Haven, Conn., 1847; d. 1910*), tuberculosis specialist. Graduated Yale, 1869; M.D., Yale, 1875. Practiced and taught at Yale; was first in America to experiment with Koch's tuberculin; advocated rest and fresh air cures.

FOSTER, JOHN WATSON (*b. Pike Co., Ind., 1836; d. 1917*), lawyer, Union soldier, diplomat. Graduated Indiana University, 1855. Practiced at Evansville, Ind., and *post* Civil War edited *Evansville Daily Journal.* U.S. minister to Mexico, 1873–80; to Russia, 1880–81; to Spain, 1883–84. Acted as U.S. agent in Bering Sea arbitration, and was secretary of state, 1892–93. Author of *A Century of American Diplomacy: 1776–1876* (1900), *Diplomatic Memoirs* (1909) and other works.

FOSTER, JUDITH ELLEN HORTON (*b. Lowell, Mass., 1840; d. 1910*), lawyer, temperance reformer. Practiced in Clinton, Iowa.

FOSTER, LAFAYETTE SABINE (*b. Franklin, Conn, 1806; d. 1880*), lawyer. Graduated Brown, 1828. Practiced at Norwich, Conn.; edited *Norwich Republican.* U.S. senator, Whig, from Connecticut, 1855–67. Justice, state superior court, 1870–76.

FOSTER, MURPHY JAMES (*b. near Franklin, La., 1849; d. New Orleans, La., 1921*), lawyer. Served in state senate, 1880–92, and led fight against renewal of Louisiana Lottery charter. Was Democratic governor of Louisiana, 1892–1900; U.S. senator, 1900–13.

FOSTER, RANDOLPH SINKS (*b. Williamsburg, O., 1820; d. 1903*), Methodist Episcopal clergyman. Held pastorates in western Virginia and Ohio, and in and about New York City; was author of popular books on Methodist beliefs. President of Northwestern University, 1857–60; of Drew Theological Seminary, 1870–72; elected bishop, 1872.

FOSTER, ROBERT SANFORD (*b. Vernon, Ind., 1834; d. Indianapolis, Ind., 1903*), Union soldier. Held brigade and divisional commands in eastern theater of the Civil War, rising to rank of brigadier-general in able but unspectacular service.

FOSTER, ROGER SHERMAN BALDWIN (*b. Worcester, Mass., 1857; d. 1924*), lawyer. Graduated Yale, 1878; Columbia Law School, 1880. Practiced in New York City, specializing in tax law, corporation law and constitutional cases. Drafted New York Tenement House Act, 1895; expressed decisive opinion (1892) in Homestead trials. Author, among other books, of *Commentaries on the Constitution* (1895) which established his reputation as an authority on constitutional law.

FOSTER, STEPHEN COLLINS (*b. Pittsburgh, Pa., 1826; d. New York, N.Y., 1864*), composer. Began life as a bookkeeper in his brother's office at Cincinnati, O. After publication of "Louisiana Belle," "O Susanna," "Uncle Ned," and "Away Down South" in *Songs of the Sable Harmonists* (1848), he turned to music for a livelihood. In writing songs for the then popular Negro Minstrel troupes, Foster found his best medium. In 1851, he sold to E. P. Christy the privilege of singing his songs from manuscript before their formal appearance, reserving to himself all publication rights. Among his greatest songs were "The Old Folks at Home" (1851), "Massa's in the Cold Ground," (1852), "My Old Kentucky Home" and "Old Dog Tray" (both 1853) and "Old Black Joe" (1860). Foster probably visited the South only once. Living in New York after 1860 he wrote ceaselessly, but his music grew reiterative and commonplace and he spent his last years in poverty. His best songs gave permanent expression to the nostalgic melancholy of the American Negro and remain a valuable contribution to the folk-literature of American music.

FOSTER, STEPHEN SYMONDS (*b. Canterbury, N.H., 1809; d. 1881*), farmer, reformer. Graduated Dartmouth, 1838. Was associated with extremist wing of Abolitionists and second only to W. L. Garrison in activity in early years of agitation. Author of *The Brotherhood of Thieves* (1843), a vitriolic attack on organized religion.

FOSTER, THEODORE (*b. Brookfield, Mass., 1752; d. Providence, R.I., 1828*), lawyer, antiquarian. Rhode

Island legislator and jurist. U.S. senator, Federalist, 1790–1803.

FOSTER, THOMAS JEFFERSON (*b. Pottsville, Pa., 1843; d. Scranton, Pa., 1936*), journalist. Founder, 1901, of the International Correspondence Schools. [*Supp. 2*]

FOULK, GEORGE CLAYTON (*b. Marietta, Pa., 1856; d. Kyoto, Japan, 1893*), naval officer, diplomat. Graduated Annapolis, 1876. Served under great stress and with ability as naval attaché and head of American mission in Korea, 1885–87; later taught mathematics at Kyoto.

FOULKE, WILLIAM DUDLEY (*b. New York, N.Y., 1848; d. 1935*), lawyer, leader in civic reform. LL.B., Columbia, 1871. Practiced in New York City and *post c.* 1876 in Richmond, Ind.; gave special attention to civil service reform and woman suffrage; was associate of Lucius B. Swift and his biographer. [*Supp. 1*]

FOWKE, GERARD (*b. near Maysville, Ky., 1855; d. 1933*), archeologist. Author of *Archaeological History of Ohio; the Mound Builders and the Later Indians* (1902) and *The Evolution of the Ohio River* (1933). [*Supp. 1*]

FOWLE, DANIEL (*b. Charlestown, Mass., 1715; d. 1787*), printer. In partnership with Gamaliel Rogers, 1740–50, published at Boston a number of books and *The American Magazine and Historical Chronicle* (1743–46); also published *The Independent Advertiser*, a weekly newspaper, 1748–50. Fowle removed to Portsmouth, N.H., 1756, and was the first printer in New Hampshire.

FOWLE, WILLIAM BENTLEY (*b. Boston, Mass., 1795; d. Medfield, Mass., 1865*), bookseller, educator. Nephew of William Bentley. Organized a monitorial school in Boston, 1821, in which he introduced blackboards, map drawing, written spelling lessons, and abolished corporal punishment. In 1823 took charge of Female Monitorial School which probably was first American school to have adequate scientific apparatus, and where he introduced study of vocal and instrumental music, calisthenics, needlework. Wrote more than fifty textbooks and gave scientific lectures. Was publisher, and from 1848 to 1852 editor, of Horace Mann's *Common School Journal;* served as one of Mann's ablest assistants in the Teachers' Institute.

FOWLER, CHARLES HENRY (*b. Burford, Canada, 1837; d. 1908*), Methodist Episcopal clergyman. Gifted administrator and preacher, he was president of Northwestern University, 1873–77, and editor of *Christian Advocate,* 1876–80. Active in missionary work, he was elected bishop, 1884.

FOWLER, FRANK (*b. Brooklyn, N.Y., 1852; d. 1910*), painter, critic. Studied under Edwin White and Carolus Duran; excelled in portraits.

FOWLER, GEORGE RYERSON (*b. New York, N.Y., 1848; d. 1906*), surgeon. Graduated Bellevue Hospital Medical College, 1871. Specialized in abdominal surgery; author of classic *Treatise on Appendicitis* (1894) and *Treatise on Surgery* (1906). Introduced class instruction in first aid.

FOWLER, JOSEPH SMITH (*b. Steubenville, O., 1820; d. Washington, D.C., 1902*), educator, lawyer, Unionist. U.S. senator from Tennessee, 1866–71. Supported Reconstruction acts but voted against President Johnson's impeachment on grounds that the action was a plot of "mere politicians"; supported Greeley in 1872.

FOWLER, ORIN (*b. Lebanon, Conn., 1791; d. Washington, D.C., 1852*), Congregational clergyman, politician. Pastor in Plainfield, Conn., and Fall River, Mass. As congressman, Free-Soil Whig, from Massachusetts, 1849–52, advocated temperance laws, cheap postage.

FOWLER, ORSON SQUIRE (*b. Cohocton, N.Y., 1809; d. near Sharon Station, Conn., 1887*), phrenologist. An immensely popular lecturer and writer of inordinate self-conceit, he happily interwove scientific facts with popular superstitions and personal fancy.

FOX, CHARLES KEMBLE (*b. Boston, Mass., 1833; d. New York, N.Y., 1875*), actor. Brother of George W. L. Fox with whose career he was closely associated.

FOX, GEORGE WASHINGTON LAFAYETTE (*b. Boston, Mass., 1825; d. Cambridge, Mass., 1877*), actor, manager. An excellent comedian and the greatest pantomimist of his time, he had his principal success in a series of fantasies about "Humpty Dumpty," *post* 1868.

FOX, GILBERT (*b. England, 1776; d. 1807?*), engraver, actor, singer. Came to Philadelphia as assistant to Edward Trenchard, 1795; taught drawing; as singer, induced Joseph Hopkinson to write "Hail, Columbia," 1798.

FOX, GUSTAVUS VASA (*b. Saugus, Mass., 1821; d. New York, N.Y., 1883*), naval officer, assistant secretary of the navy, 1861–66. Appointed midshipman, 1841. Resigned from navy, 1856, to enter business as mill agent. Suggested plan for relief of Fort Sumter, February 1861; evacuated Major Anderson and garrison in April. As assistant secretary, *post* August 1861, suggested D.G. Farragut as commander of New Orleans expedition; was early advocate of *Monitor;* gave indispensable support to Gideon Welles.

FOX, HARRY (*b. Westfield, Mass., 1826; d. Salt Lake City, Utah, 1883*), contractor, railroad constructor. Removed to Chicago, Ill., 1856, where he was a leader in the topographical improvement of the city.

FOX, JOHN WILLIAM (*b. Stony Point, Ky., 1863; d. Big Stone Gap, Va., 1919*), novelist. Described life of Kentucky mountaineers in *A Cumberland Vendetta* (1895); *The Little Shepherd of Kingdom Come* (1903); *Trail of the Lonesome Pine* (1908); and other very popular works.

FOX, MARGARET (*b. Canada, 1833; d. Brooklyn, N.Y., 1893*), medium. Raised in upper New York State. Produced "spirit" rappings with her toes; admitted her trickery, 1888, but retracted her confession and continued to practice until her death.

FOX, RICHARD KYLE (*b. Belfast, Ireland, 1846; d. Red Bank, N.J., 1922*), journalist. Came to America, 1874. Made *National Police Gazette* America's most lurid journal; then gradually transformed it into an intelligent sports and theatrical paper.

FOX, WILLIAMS CARLTON (*b. St. Louis, Mo., 1855; d. New York, N.Y., 1924*), diplomat. Served in Germany, Persia, Greece, Ecuador; published *Diplomatic and Consular Review;* was director of Pan American Union.

FOXALL, HENRY (*b. Monmouthshire, England, 1758; d. Handsworth, England, 1823*), iron-founder. Came to America, 1797. Operated Columbian Foundry at Georgetown, D.C., 1800–15; produced heavy guns and shot for the government and rendered valuable service in War of 1812.

FOY, EDDIE (*b. New York, N.Y., 1856; d. Kansas City, Mo., 1928*), comedian. Born Edwin Fitzgerald. Raised in Chicago, Ill. His career led him from Western towns and mining camps to stardom as eccentric farceur; played vaudeville with his children, 1913–23.

FRALEY, FREDERICK (*b. Philadelphia, Pa., 1804; d. Philadelphia, 1901*), merchant, banker. Co-founder of Franklin Institute; president of American Philosophical Society, 1880–1901.

FRANCHÈRE, GABRIEL (*b. Montreal, Canada, 1786; d. St. Paul, Minn., 1863*), fur-trader. As employee of John Jacob Astor, sailed on the *Tonquin* from New York to the Columbia River, 1810–11; helped found Astoria. Returned overland to Montreal, 1814; acted as Astor's agent there and at Sault Ste. Marie. Later established his own fur-trading company in New York. Franchère's published reminiscences of Astoria (*Relation d'un Voyage à la Côte du Nord Ouest de l'Amérique Septentrionale*, Montreal, 1820) were utilized by Sen. Benton during the Oregon controversy, 1846. Washington Irving relied on them as source for his *Astoria.*

FRANCIS, CHARLES SPENCER (*b. Troy, N.Y., 1853; d. 1911*), editor, diplomat. Son of John M. Francis whom he succeeded as owner and editor of the Troy *Times.* An important figure in state and national Republican politics, he served as U.S. minister to Greece, Roumania and Servia, and as ambassador to Austria-Hungary.

FRANCIS, CHARLES STEPHEN (*b. Boston, Mass., 1805; d. Tarrytown, N.Y., 1887*), New York City bookseller, publisher, 1826–70.

FRANCIS, CONVERS (*b. Menotomy, Mass., 1795; d. 1863*), Unitarian clergyman, educator. Graduated Harvard, 1815. Succeeded Henry Ware as professor at Harvard Divinity School, 1842–63; an outstanding theologian, he early utilized German scholarship.

FRANCIS, DAVID ROWLAND (*b. Richmond, Ky., 1850; d. 1927*), grain merchant. Democratic mayor of St. Louis, Mo., 1885–89; governor of Missouri, 1889–93; secretary of the interior, 1896. Defended creation of forest reserves. Served under great stress as U.S. ambassador to Russia, 1916–18.

FRANCIS, JAMES BICHENO (*b. Southleigh, England, 1815; d. Lowell, Mass., 1892*), hydraulic engineer. Came to America, 1833. Helped construct Stonington Railroad. Built locomotives for the "Proprietors of the Locks and Canals on the Merrimack River"; as company's chief engineer and general manager *post* 1837, developed water-power facilities at Lowell, Mass., and contributed heavily to Lowell's rise as industrial center. Designed mixed-flow turbine; published *The Lowell Hydraulic Experiments* (1855). Also devised a pioneer fire-protection water system for Lowell and hydraulic lifts for gates on Pawtucket Canal.

FRANCIS, JOHN BROWN (*b. Philadelphia, Pa., 1791; d. Warwick, R.I., 1864*), merchant. Grandson of John Brown (1736–1803). Anti-Masonic and Democratic governor of Rhode Island, 1833–38; U.S. senator, 1844–45. Strongly influenced education in Rhode Island.

FRANCIS, JOHN MORGAN (*b. Prattsburg, N.Y., 1823; d. 1897*), editor, publicist, diplomat. Father of Charles Spencer Francis. As proprietor-editor of the *Times* of Troy, N.Y., *post* 1851, supported Republican party from its beginnings; served as U.S. minister to Greece, to Portugal and to Austria-Hungary.

FRANCIS, JOHN WAKEFIELD (*b. New York, N.Y., 1789; d. New York, 1861*), physician. Graduated Columbia, 1809; studied medicine with David Hosack and was first graduate (1811) of College of Physicians and Surgeons, New York. Was the city's leading obstetrician and active in all phases of the city's social and literary life.

FRANCIS, JOSEPH (*b. Boston, Mass., 1801; d. Cooperstown, N.Y., 1893*), inventor, manufacturer. Early interested in unsinkable boats, he patented an unsinkable life-boat, 1838, which had great commercial success. In 1845 he received a patent for use of corrugated metal in all types of boat construction; later he adapted this technique for manufacture of water-tight army wagons. Extending his business to Europe, he built a fleet of light-draft corrugated iron steamers for use on Aral Sea. Author of a *History of Life-Saving Appliances* (1885).

FRANCIS, PAUL JAMES (*b. Millington, Md., 1863; d. Graymoor, N.Y., 1940*), Episcopal clergyman, Roman Catholic priest. Founded the Society of the Atonement under the Franciscan rule, 1898; entered the Roman Catholic Church with his friars, 1909.

[*Supp. 2*]

FRANCIS, SAMUEL WARD (*b. New York, N.Y., 1835; d. Newport, R.I., 1886*), physician, author, inventor. Son of John W. Francis. Patented a number of devices, including a "printing machine" which anticipated the typewriter.

FRANCIS, TENCH (*b. Ireland, date unknown; d. Philadelphia, Pa., 1758*), lawyer. Came to America *ante* 1720 as attorney for Lord Baltimore; removed from Talbot Co., Md., to Philadelphia, 1738, and became leader of Pennsylvania bar. Attorney-general of Pennsylvania, 1741–55.

FRANCKE, KUNO (*b. Kiel, Germany, 1855; d. Cambridge, Mass., 1930*), historian, philologist. Came to America, 1884, as instructor in German at Harvard; professor of German culture, Harvard, 1896–1917. Author of *Social Forces in German Literature* (1896); founded Harvard Germanic Museum.

FRANK, GLENN (*b. Queen City, Mo., 1887; d. near Greenleaf, Wis., 1940*), editor, publicist. Graduated Northwestern University, 1912; became executive assistant to its president, then a research assistant to the reform-minded Boston merchant Edward A. Filene. Associate editor and editor-in-chief, *Century* magazine, 1919–25; an optimistic advocate of social reform. As president of the University of Wisconsin, he initiated the Experimental College, 1927–32, and the Short Course in Agriculture. Increasingly critical of the New Deal, he fell into disfavor with the dominant La Follette faction and with the university's board of regents, and was dismissed in 1937. He was seeking the Republican nomination for U.S. senator, when he died in an automobile accident.

[*Supp. 2*]

FRANK, TENNEY (*b. near Clay Center, Kans., 1876; d. Oxford, England, 1939*), classical scholar. Graduated University of Kansas, 1898; Ph.D., Chicago, 1903. Taught Latin at Bryn Mawr, 1904–19, and Johns Hopkins, 1919–39. His fresh and revealing interpretations of Roman civilization combine the disciplines of history, literature and archeology. His books include biographies of Vergil (1922), Catullus and Horace (1928), *History of Rome* (1923) and *Economic History of Rome to the End of the Republic* (1920). He planned, edited and wrote two volumes of the series *An Economic Survey of Ancient Rome*, one of the first large cooperative enterprises in American classical scholarship. [*Supp. 2*]

FRANKLAND, LADY AGNES SURRIAGE (*b. Marblehead, Mass., 1726; d. Chichester, England, 1783*), Boston social figure. Wife of Sir Charles Henry Frankland; heroine of a "rags-to-riches" romance which has served as basis for a poem by O. W. Holmes and a novel by E. L. Bynner.

FRANKLIN, BENJAMIN (*b. Boston, Mass., 1706; d. Philadelphia, Pa., 1790*), printer, author, philanthropist, inventor, statesman, diplomat, scientist. Son of Josiah and Abiah (Folger) Franklin. Attended Boston Grammar School and George Brownell's school for writing and arithmetic; at age ten was employed in his father's business of tallow chandler and soap boiler; at twelve was apprenticed in the printing shop of his brother James. Repeated quarrels with James led Benjamin to leave Boston for Philadelphia where he arrived in October 1723.

He had already gone far in that close application to study and self-improvement which was one secret of his success. He had read Bunyan, Plutarch, Defoe, Cotton Mather, Tryon on "vegetable diet," Cocker's arithmetic, Seller on navigation, Locke's *Essays*, Shaftesbury and Collins, Xenophon's *Memorabilia*. He improved his style by rewriting essays in Addison's *Spectator* from memory and checking them against the originals. He was delighted when his brother printed in the *New England Courant* essays which Benjamin had slipped beneath the door of the shop under the pen-name of Silence Dogood.

At Philadelphia, Benjamin obtained employment as a printer; was urged by Governor Keith to set up a shop of his own. On Keith's promise of money to buy equipment, Benjamin went to London, 1724; Keith's promise unfulfilled, he found work as a printer, and wrote *A Dissertation on Liberty and Necessity* (1725), a refutation of Wollaston's *Religion of Nature Delineated*. Back in Philadelphia in 1726, he became by 1730 the sole owner of a printing business and of *The Pennsylvania Gazette*. He married Deborah Read in the same year and devoted himself to business until 1748. His thrift and industry won him prosperity; the chief reasons for his success, however, were his capacity for making influential friends, his uncanny instinct for advertising himself and his paper and above all, the sense, novelty, and charm of his writings. His almanac, sold as *Poor Richard's* (1732–57) and credited to a supposititious "Richard Saunders," abounded with homely aphorisms which Franklin pilfered and adapted from everywhere, and made the author's name a household word throughout the colonies.

Franklin's efforts at self-improvement led him to study French, Spanish, Italian, and Latin; in the "Junto," a debating club which he had founded in 1727, he perfected himself in the arts of oral persuasion. He regarded religion as a useful sanction for the practice of virtue. He believed in one God who made all things and governs the world through His providence; who is to be worshipped by adoration, prayer, and thanksgiving; who will certainly reward virtue and punish vice, and to whom the most acceptable service consists in doing good to men. Franklin believed in the immortality of the soul, and devised a list of thirteen useful virtues: Temperance, Silence, Order, Resolution, Frugality, Industry, Sincerity, Justice, Moderation, Cleanliness, Tranquillity, Chastity, and Humility. He assiduously devoted himself to practicing one virtue a week, and went through "a course compleat in 13 weeks, and four courses a year." The outward expressions of his passion for improvement were his promotion of a city police force; of improved paving, cleaning, and lighting of streets; of a circulating library; of the American Philosophical Society (founded 1743); of a city hospital (1751); of an Academy for the Education of Youth. He served as clerk of the Pennsylvania Assembly, 1736–51, as member for Philadelphia, 1751–64; he was deputy postmaster at Philadelphia, 1737–53, and jointly with William Hunter deputy postmaster-general for the colonies, 1753–74.

His interest in science ("natural philosophy") was awakened probably in England. As early as 1737 he was writing in the *Gazette* on earthquakes; by 1741 he had invented the "Pennsylvania Fireplace," a stove with an open fire-box which heated rooms better at less expense. Every sort of natural phenomenon interested him and called forth some ingenious idea. Feeling that he had a sufficient income from real estate and through a partnership arrangement with David Hall, his printing-house foreman, he turned in 1748 to full-time occupation with "philosophical studies and amusements." His leisure lasted only six years but during this time he made those electrical experiments on which his fame as a scientist rests. He had become interested in electricity *c.* 1743; thereafter his correspondence is filled with the record of his varied experiments. He was not the first to suggest the identity of lightning and electricity, but in a letter of 1750 proposed a method of testing the theory by erecting an iron rod on a high tower or steeple. The famous kite experiment, performed in the summer of 1752 and described by Franklin in a letter in the *Pennsylvania Gazette* (Oct. 19), was a simpler employment of the same method. *Experiments and Observations on Electricity . . . by Mr. Benjamin Franklin* (London, 1751, and reprinted with additions in 1753) embodied the results and method of his experiments, was translated into French, and won him general recognition. Harvard and Yale gave him the degree of Master of Arts, 1753; William and Mary, 1756.

Public affairs claimed him thereafter. He had represented Pennsylvania at the Albany Congress, 1754, where his "Plan of Union" was considered to have "too much prerogative in it" for the taste of the colonial assemblies, and was judged too democratic in England. In 1757, he went to England to present to Parliament the grievance of the Pennsylvania Assembly against the proprietors of the province, notably the claim of the Penn heirs to be exempt from taxation. This matter was settled in 1760 but Franklin remained in England, becoming intimate with Collinson, Priestley, Strahan and others, and corresponding with Lord Kames, and Hume, the philosopher. He received degrees of LL.D. from St. Andrews, 1759, and D.C.L. from Oxford, 1762.

He returned reluctantly to Philadelphia, 1762, but was soon sent again to London to obtain recall of the Pennsylvania charter, an effort submerged in the controversy over the Stamp Act. Perceiving the intransigence of the British government, Franklin advised the colonists to accept the tax and even arranged for a friend to become tax collector in Philadelphia. This and his own purchase of stamped paper exposed him to much ill-will, but his prestige was restored when the news of his "examination" in February 1766 before the House of Commons reached Philadelphia. Franklin's answers to his questioners portrayed the tax as contrary to custom and as administratively impracticable both on account of the country's circumstances and the settled opposition of the people.

Reappointed in 1766 as agent in London for Pennsylvania, Franklin became in effect ambassador extraordinary for the colonies; he was also appointed agent for Georgia (1768), New Jersey (1769), and Massachusetts (1770). He saw his task as the reconciliation of the colonies with Great Britain, but after the passing of the coercive acts (1774) he began to despair of any reconciliation. His ideas on American rights became more precise and radical. In 1765 he had not doubted the right of Parliament to levy the Stamp Tax. In 1766 he had defended the distinction between internal and external taxes. By 1768 he was convinced, however, "that no middle doctrine can be well maintained . . ." Either Parliament had the power to make all laws, or it had no power to make any. In 1770 he rejected the term "supreme authority of Parliament" and urged the theory that the colonies and England were united only in having a common sovereign. Although he deprecated violence, he agreed with Samuel Adams that good relations could not be re-established until the repeal of the duty on tea; he welcomed the establishment of committees on correspondence; he distrusted Gov. Thomas Hutchinson and sought to discredit him in England. Turning to satire as a means of checking what he considered anti-American excesses, he published his "Edict by the King of Prussia," and the "Rules by which a Great Empire may be reduced to a Small one." These did more to aggravate than to compose the troubles, as did the affair of the "Hutchinson Letters." By the agency of Franklin, letters in which the Governor of Massachusetts had advocated drastic measures on the ground that "there must be an abridgement of what are called English Liberties," were printed in Boston and circulated in London. The ensuing furore caused Franklin to suffer public denunciation and abuse and to lose his office as deputy postmaster-general. Supported by his friends and his own conviction of having carried out "one of the best actions of his life," he remained in England, aiding Pitt in his fruitless efforts at conciliation until he left for America in March 1775. Elected a member of the second Continental Congress, he sketched a Plan of Union for the colonies; organized the Post Office; served on the commissions which vainly sought Canadian cooperation, and which advised Washington on defense. He served also on the committee appointed to draft the Declaration of Independence, prepared instructions for Silas Deane, colonial commissioner to France, and in December 1776 himself arrived in France as one of three commissioners to negotiate a treaty.

He was received by the French people as the personification of all the ideas dear to the Age of the Enlightenment. His simplicity of dress and manners, his wit and wisdom, his natural courtesy, all endeared him to his hosts and made him the object of unmeasured adulation. While he and his colleagues negotiated with foreign minister Vergennes, his mere presence in France intensified popular enthusiasm for the Americans and made it increasingly difficult for France to avoid a rupture with Great Britain.

Treaties of commerce and defensive alliance were signed between France and the United States in February 1778. Throughout the negotiations Franklin had to contend with annoying difficulties contrived by Arthur Lee, his fellow commissioner with Silas Deane. Lee took it upon himself to prove the supposed incompetence and venality of his colleagues and of the French agent Beaumarchais with whom they dealt. Besides suffering Lee's "magisterial snubbings and rebukes," Franklin carried the chief burden of the negotiations with Vergennes, served as consul, judge of admiralty, and director of naval affairs, and negotiated for the exchange of prisoners in England. His task was made easier when on September 14, 1778, Congress appointed him as sole plenipotentiary. Now Franklin found time again to write scientific articles, to correspond with Madame Helvétius and Madame Brillon, and to publish satires and bagatelles for the amusement of his friends. Throughout the next three years his chief tasks were to obtain loans of money from France, to mollify creditors, and to meet the innumerable bills of exchange which were drawn on him by Congress, ship owners, and others engaged in the Revolutionary War. His offered resignation was declined by Congress, March, 1781; in June, he, John Jay, and John Adams were appointed to negotiate a peace with Great Britain. Awaiting the arrival of his colleagues, Franklin began preliminary conversations and proposed as a basis of negotiation (1) independence, (2) cession of the Mississippi Valley, (3) fishing rights

"on the banks of Newfoundland, and elsewhere." He rejected British claims for recovery of debts and Congressional compensation for American Loyalists, but indicated a willingness to consider the second demand favorably if Britain should cede Canada. He kept Vergennes informed of every step in the negotiations. British naval successes and the arrival of Jay, however, injected new factors into the negotiations and strengthened the hands of the British commissioners. Franklin broke the deadlock which resulted by an American counterclaim for war damages, and on November 30 the preliminaries of a treaty were signed. In the interest of harmony Franklin had yielded to his colleagues on his previous agreement to keep the French government informed of the negotiations because Adams and Jay were convinced that France and Spain were conspiring to restrict the boundaries of the United States to the Alleghenies. Vergennes penned a formal protest, but Franklin replied that although a point of courtesy had been neglected, the agreement had not been broken since there would be no peace between England and America until France had concluded hers. The final and definitive peace having been signed on September 3, 1783, Franklin asked Congress for recall in December, but did not receive notice until May 1785.

Home in America, he served as president (1785–88) of the executive council of Pennsylvania, and in May 1787, at the age of 81, took his seat in the Constitutional Convention. None of his cardinal ideas was accepted, but his personality and genial humor proved invaluable in soothing tempers and in suggesting compromises. The Constitution, as it finally emerged, was not all to his liking. Reminding himself and his colleagues of human fallibility, Franklin urged nevertheless that it be unanimously adopted. The last five years of his life he spent in his home near Market Street, Philadelphia. He carried on a large correspondence, enjoyed conversations with his friends and many visitors, and, as his last public act, signed a memorial to Congress for the abolition of slavery. He died on April 17, 1790, and was buried in Christ Church Burial Ground.

Franklin spoke the language of the Enlightenment philosophers, but with a homely accent, a tang of his native soil. His humor was neither brilliant nor corrosive; rather it was genial and kindly, even if cynical. He accepted without question and expressed without effort all the characteristic ideas and prepossessions of his century—its aversion to "superstition" and "enthusiasm" and mystery; its dislike of dim perspectives; its healthy, clarifying scepticism; its passion for freedom and its humane sympathies; its preoccupation with the world that is evident to the senses; its profound faith in common sense, in the efficacy of reason for the solution of human problems and the advancement of human welfare. His pragmatic habit of thought made him shun the ideal conceptions of the philosophers; insatiably curious, knowing neither inhibitions nor repressions, he accepted serenely the world as it was and brought to its understanding and mastery rare common sense, genuine disinterestedness, and a cool, flexible intelligence fortified by exact knowledge and chastened and humanized by practical experience. Rising from poverty to affluence, from obscurity to fame, he was equally at ease with rich and poor, the cultivated and the untutored; he spoke with equal facility the language of vagabonds and kings, politicians and philosophers, men of letters, kitchen girls, and *femmes savantes*. The whole world was his field of activity. He was indeed the most universal and cosmopolitan spirit of his age, a true citizen of the world, and yet remained throughout his life more pungently American than any of his famous countrymen. The secret of Franklin's amazing capacity for assimilating experience lay perhaps in his final refusal to commit himself completely to any issue or cause. No one enterprise ever absorbed all his energies. In all of Franklin's dealings with men and affairs, genuine, sincere, loyal as he surely was, one feels that he is nevertheless not wholly committed; some thought remains uncommunicated; some penetrating observation is held in reserve. Was there not, on that placid countenance, even at the signing of the great Declaration, the bland smile which seems to say: This is an interesting, alas even a necessary game; and we are playing it well, according to all the rules; but men being what they are it is perhaps best not to inquire too curiously what its ultimate significance may be. This characteristic is plain in his famous *Autobiography*, which is anything but a frank revelation of self, valuable as it may be for other reasons. Science alone commanded his unreserved service, for Nature met him on equal terms. She did not conceal a stupendous cosmic joke in her affairs, as Franklin seemed to suspect lay hidden in the affairs of men. In his character, therefore, as scientist the essential quality of Franklin appears to best advantage. As a literary artist, he possessed rare merit and was master of a style distinguished for clarity, precision, and pliable adhesion to the form and pressure of the idea to be conveyed.

FRANKLIN, BENJAMIN (*b. Belmont Co., O., 1812; d. Anderson, Ind., 1878*), minister of the Disciples of Christ. A prominent evangelist, he edited the *American Christian Review*, 1856–78, and became spokesman of conservative Disciples.

FRANKLIN, EDWARD CURTIS (*b. Geary City, Kans., 1862; d. Stanford, Calif., 1937*), chemist. Graduated University of Kansas, 1888; M.S., 1890; attended University of Berlin, 1890–91, and received his doctorate from Johns Hopkins, 1894. An unusually effective teacher, he was professor of chemistry at Kansas, 1899–1903, when he went to Stanford University for the remainder of his career. Here Franklin made pioneering investigations in developing the ammonia system of acids, bases, and salts, from which he synthesized and compiled data on many new compounds, and developed new concepts of the structure and relationship of nitrogenous compounds. His monograph *The Nitrogen System of Compounds* (1935) is one of the classics of American chemistry. [*Supp. 2*]

FRANKLIN, FABIAN (*b. Eger, Hungary, 1853; d. New York, N.Y., 1939*), mathematician, journalist, publicist. Came to America as an infant. Graduated, Columbian College, 1869; Ph.D., Johns Hopkins, 1880; taught mathematics there until 1895, when, increasingly interested in public affairs, he became editor of the *Baltimore News*. From 1908 to 1917 he was co-editor of the New York *Evening Post* and of the *Nation*. He found his true profession in publicizing his convictions in editorials, articles, pamphlets, and books. A fervent believer in internationalism, personal liberty, low tariffs, women's rights, and *laissez-faire* in government, he championed Woodrow Wilson's policies and the Allied cause in World War I, and vehemently opposed prohibition and New Deal bureaucracy. [*Supp. 2*]

FRANKLIN, JAMES (*b. Boston, Mass., 1696/7; d. Newport, R.I., 1735*), printer. Brother of Benjamin Franklin (1706–1790). Published *New England Courant*, 1721–26, a lively, secular paper which offended official dignity; started *Rhode Island Gazette*, 1732.

FRANKLIN, JESSE (*b. Orange Co., Va., 1760; d. North Carolina, 1823*), Revolutionary soldier, politician. U.S. senator, (Democrat) Republican, from North Carolina, 1799–1805 and 1807–13; governor, 1821.

FRANKLIN, PHILIP ALBRIGHT SMALL (*b. Ashland, Md., 1871; d. Locust Valley, N.Y., 1939*), shipping executive. Associated with International Mercantile Marine Co., 1903–36; president, *post* 1921. Chairman, Shipping Control Committee in World War I. [*Supp. 2*]

FRANKLIN, WILLIAM (*b. 1731; d. 1813*), last royal governor of New Jersey. Reared in household of his father, Benjamin Franklin (1706–1790); became comptroller of General Post Office and clerk of Pennsylvania Provincial Assembly; went to England with his father, 1757, studied at Middle Temple and was admitted to bar. Named governor of New Jersey, 1763, he supported improvement of roads and agriculture and laws mitigating imprisonment for debt. In Stamp Act controversy, he upheld British view and became estranged from his countrymen and his father. Arrested 1776 by the Jersey Provincial Congress, he was exchanged, 1778; soon thereafter, he returned to England where he died.

FRANKLIN, WILLIAM BUEL (*b. York, Pa., 1823; d. Hartford, Conn., 1903*), soldier, business executive. Graduated West Point, 1843; served in topographical engineers. A division and corps commander, 1861–62, he was blamed for the Union debacle at Fredericksburg and sent to subordinate commands in the Southwest. He was manager of Colt's Firearms Co. from his resignation from the army in 1866 until 1888.

FRANZ, SHEPHERD IVORY (*b. Jersey City, N.J., 1874; d. California, 1933*), physiological psychologist. Graduated Columbia, 1894; Ph.D., 1899. Noted for his discoveries in brain localization, brain action and the rehabilitation of persons suffering from brain injuries. [*Supp. 1*]

FRASCH, HERMAN (*b. Gaildorf, Germany, 1851?; d. Paris, France, 1914*), pharmacist, chemical engineer, inventor. Came to America, 1868. Developed the Frasch process for desulfurizing petroleum, 1885–94. Also patented processes for producing white lead directly from galena, for producing sodium carbonate from salt and, most important of all, for mining sulfur by superheated water. His Union Sulphur Co. wrested control of the world sulfur supply from the Anglo-Sicilian monopoly and made the United States an exporter of sulfur.

FRASER, CHARLES (*b. 1782; d. 1860*), miniature painter. A Charleston, S.C., lawyer and man of letters, his fame rests on his portraits, noted for their subtle, uncompromising, yet sympathetic characterization.

FRAUNCES, SAMUEL (*b. West Indies, c. 1722; d. Philadelphia, Pa., 1795*). Post 1762, kept New York tavern in former De Lancey house; was steward of Washington's presidential households in New York and Philadelphia, 1789–94.

FRAYNE, HUGH (*b. Scranton, Pa., 1869; d. New York, N.Y., 1934*), labor leader. General organizer of the American Federation of Labor, 1901–34; conservative; created a better public understanding of the objectives of labor movement. [*Supp. 1*]

FRAZEE, JOHN (*b. Rahway, N.J., 1790; d. Compton Mills, R.I., 1852*), sculptor. From unlettered bricklayer, became stone-cutter and sculptor of bust-portraits of famous contemporaries. His portrait of John Wells in St. Paul's Church, New York, was the first marble bust carved in this country by a native.

FRAZER, JOHN FRIES (*b. Philadelphia, Pa., 1812; d. Philadelphia, 1872*), scientist, teacher. Editor, *Journal of the Franklin Institute*, 1850–66. Assistant to Alexander D. Bache, whom he succeeded as professor of natural philosophy, University of Pennsylvania, serving 1844–72.

FRAZER, OLIVER (*b. Jessamine Co., Ky., 1808; d. Lexington, Ky., 1864*), portrait-painter. Studied with M. H. Jouett and Thomas Sully and in Europe. His work was marked by simplicity of line and firmness of texture.

FRAZER, PERSIFOR (*b. Chester Co., Pa., 1736; d. Chester Co., 1792*), Revolutionary soldier, iron-master, merchant.

FRAZER, PERSIFOR (*b. Philadelphia, Pa., 1844; d. 1909*), geologist, metallurgist. Son of John F. Frazer. Graduated University of Pennsylvania, 1862, and attended Royal School of Mines, Freiberg, Germany. Member of Hayden Survey of Colorado and J. P. Lesley's geological survey of Pennsylvania. A prolific writer on science and a handwriting expert.

FRAZIER, CHARLES HARRISON (*b. Germantown, Pa., 1870; d. North Haven, Maine, 1936*), neurological surgeon. M.D., University of Pennsylvania, 1892; studied in Germany under Virchow, 1895–96. Taught at University of Pennsylvania. Pioneer in surgery of the trigeminal nerve and of the spinal cord for relief of pain. [*Supp. 2*]

FREAR, WILLIAM (*b. Reading, Pa., 1860; d. 1922*), agricultural chemist, educator. Graduated Bucknell, 1881. Taught at Pennsylvania State College. His greatest work was done in lifetime service with federal and state committees on food and drug standards.

FREAS, THOMAS BRUCE (*b. near Newark, O., 1868; d. 1928*), chemist. Developed the art of laboratory control at University of Chicago. Invented special thermostats and Freas ovens for maintenance of constant temperatures; experimented with a sun-motor.

FREDERIC, HAROLD (*b. Utica, N.Y., 1856; d. Henley-on-Thames, England, 1898*), journalist, novelist. London correspondent for *New York Times, post* 1884. Author of ten books of fiction, including *In the Valley* (1890), *The Copperhead* (1893), and a study in spiritual deterioration (his masterpiece) *The Damnation of Theron Ware* (1896).

FREEDMAN, ANDREW (*b. New York, N.Y., 1860; d. 1915*), capitalist. Organizer of insurance companies and a promoter of the first New York subway. Left his estate to found a home for aged couples.

FREEMAN, BERNARDUS (*b. Netherlands ?, date unknown; d. 1741*), Reformed Dutch clergyman. Ordained 1700 as pastor of Albany, N.Y., but served at Schenectady and Long Island. Often involved in controversies; preached successfully to the Mohawks and translated religious texts for their use.

FREEMAN, FREDERICK KEMPER (*b. Culpeper Co., Va., 1841; d. Georgia, 1928*), Confederate soldier, journalist. Nephew of James L. Kemper. Editor with his brother Legh of the *Frontier Index,* a newspaper published 1866–69 at successive railheads of the Union Pacific.

FREEMAN, JAMES (*b. Charlestown, Mass., 1759; d. Newton, Mass., 1835*), first Unitarian minister of King's Chapel, Boston, 1787–1826.

FREEMAN, JAMES EDWARDS (*b. Indian Island, N.B., Canada, 1808; d. Rome, Italy, 1884*), genre painter. Studied with William Dunlap and at National Academy of Design, New York. Lived in Italy, *post* 1836. His work was richly colored but largely sentimental.

FREEMAN, JOHN RIPLEY (*b. West Bridgton, Maine, 1855; d. Providence, R.I., 1932*), hydraulic engineer. [*Supp. 1*]

FREEMAN, MARY ELEANOR WILKINS (*b. Randolph, Mass., 1852; d. Metuchen, N.J., 1930*), writer. Through stories in the Harper publications, *post* 1883, she became known as one of the chief exponents of New England rural life. The flat, inland scenery of eastern Massachusetts formed the background of tales which were collected in *A Humble Romance* (1887), *A New England Nun* (1891) and many other volumes. She tried other kinds of writing but without her success in the short story of country life, where she identified herself completely with her material and wrote with subtle and dispassionate objectivity at a time when sentimentality was popular.

FREEMAN, NATHANIEL (*b. Dennis, Mass., 1741; d. 1827*), physician, lawyer, Revolutionary patriot. Practiced in Barnstable Co., Mass.

FREEMAN, THOMAS (*b. Ireland, date unknown; d. Huntsville, Ala., 1821*), civil engineer, astronomer. Came to America, 1784. Accompanied Andrew Ellicott on survey of boundary between United States and Spain, 1797. Explored the Arkansas and Red Rivers, 1806; mapped Tennessee-Alabama boundary, 1807; fought land speculation as U.S. surveyor of Southern public lands, 1811–21.

FREER, CHARLES LANG (*b. Kingston, N.Y., 1856; d. 1919*), capitalist. Active in organization of American Car and Foundry Co. Donated Freer Gallery, Washington, D.C., which holds his own unique collections of J. M. Whistler's work, ancient glazed pottery and oriental art.

FRELINGHUYSEN, FREDERICK (*b. near Somerville, N.J., 1753; d. 1804*), lawyer, Revolutionary soldier. Grandson of Theodorus J. Frelinghuysen. Graduated College of New Jersey (Princeton), 1770. Served in Continental Congress, New Jersey state legislature, and in the U.S. Senate, 1793–96.

FRELINGHUYSEN, FREDERICK THEODORE (*b. Millstone, N.J., 1817; d. Newark, N.J., 1885*), statesman. Grandson of Frederick Frelinghuysen. Graduated Rutgers, 1836. Attorney-general of New Jersey, 1861–66; U.S. senator, Republican, from New Jersey, 1866–69, 1871–77. Achieved commanding influence, especially with the "Stalwarts"; supported President Johnson's impeachment.

Succeeding Blaine as secretary of state (1881–85) he pursued a less aggressive foreign policy; favored closer reciprocal commercial relations with Latin America; vigorously supported American commercial interests in Germany and France; negotiated for a naval base at Pearl Harbor; opened up treaty relations with Korea; authorized United States participation in the Berlin Conference, 1884. Always considerate of the rights of other nations, he aimed to create a feeling of generous good will in diplomatic relations.

FRELINGHUYSEN, THEODORE (*b. Franklin Township, N.J., 1787; d. New Brunswick, N.J., 1862*), lawyer. Son of Frederick Frelinghuysen. Graduated Princeton, 1804. Attorney-general of New Jersey, 1817–29; U.S. senator, Whig, 1829–35. Opposed Indian removals; was respected for integrity. President, Rutgers College, 1850–62, after service as chancellor of present New York University, 1839–50.

FRELINGHUYSEN, THEODORUS JACOBUS (*b. Lingen, Germany, 1691; d. c. 1748*), Reformed Dutch clergyman. Came to America, 1719, to serve in Raritan Valley, N.J. A master revivalist, triumphant in controversy with New York clergymen, he did much to invoke the Great Awakening in the Middle Colonies.

FRÉMONT, JESSIE BENTON (*b. near Lexington, Va., 1824; d. Los Angeles, Calif., 1902*), writer. Daughter of Thomas Hart Benton. Married John Charles Frémont, 1841; assisted him in writing his reports and in all crises of his career. Contributed regularly to periodicals, *post* 1871.

FRÉMONT, JOHN CHARLES (*b. Savannah, Ga., 1813; d. New York, N.Y., 1890*), explorer, politician, soldier. A precocious youth born out of wedlock, Frémont was raised in Charleston, S.C. Through influence of Joel Poinsett, he was appointed to an instructorship in the navy, resigning to become a second lieutenant in the U.S. Topographical Corps. After assisting in survey of a projected Charleston-Cincinnati railroad, and a reconnaissance of the Cherokee country in 1837–38, he joined J. H. Nicollet's expedition to the upper Mississippi and Missouri Rivers, acquiring expert training in astronomical, topographical and geographical observation.

Through this work he met Thomas Hart Benton, who gave him a new vision of Western exploration and expansion to the Pacific. Alarmed by the mutual attachment of Frémont and his daughter Jessie, Benton had Frémont sent to explore the Des Moines River. Secretly married at Washington, D.C. upon Frémont's return in October 1841, the couple were reconciled to Benton who became Frémont's patron and with others planned his first important expedition to examine the Oregon Trail, and to report on rivers, mountains, fertility, positions for forts and the nature of the mountains in Wyoming.

With Kit Carson as guide, Frémont left the Kansas River in June 1842, traveled by way of the Platte and South Pass and explored the Wind River Range. Back in Washington by October, he composed with his wife's expert literary help a report (published 1843) which showed zest for adventure and descriptive sparkle and gave him a wide popular reputation.

The departure of his second expedition, May 1843, with Thomas Fitzpatrick as guide, was hastened by a message from Jessie Frémont, who suppressed a War Department order requiring Frémont to return to Washington. Failing to blaze a new trail through northern Colorado, he followed the Oregon Trail, explored Great Salt Lake and pushed on to the Columbia River. He then struck off through Oregon to Pyramid Lake and into Nevada, reaching the Carson River in January 1844, and daring to cross the Sierra into California, where he refitted at Sutter's Fort. He returned to St. Louis, Mo., in August 1844 after forming a clear impression of the weakness of the Mexican hold on California. He and Jessie collaborated on a second vivid report.

Frémont's third expedition set out in 1845 as war with Mexico was imminent. He desired to participate in conquering California and claimed in his *Memoirs* (1887) that Benton and George Bancroft intended his scientific force to turn into a military body in case of war. Guided once again by Kit Carson, he went West by way of Great Salt Lake and the so-called "Hastings Cutoff," blazed a new trail across Nevada and took his men to Monterey and San Jose, Calif. When ordered by Mexican officials to leave, he hoisted the American flag. Moving north, he was overtaken in May 1846 by news that war was expected in a few days and hastened to the Sacramento Valley, where he inspired discontented American settlers to begin the "Bear Flag revolt" and in June gave them armed support. With his "California Battalion," he helped in the capture of Los Angeles in August, and in its final capture in January 1847. Involved in the quarrel of Commodore Stockton and Gen. S. W. Kearny, he sided with Stockton who appointed him civil governor of California. When Kearny was proved to be in command, he arrested Frémont on charges of mutiny and insubordination. A Washington court martial found him guilty, and though President Polk remitted the penalty, Frémont resigned from the service.

A midwinter expedition in 1848–49 at the expense of Benton and others seeking a Pacific railroad route proved a disastrous venture. Frémont after much hardship reached California, settled in Monterey and began to develop the Mariposa estate recently acquired for him by U.S. consul Thomas Larkin. In a short time he was wealthy through gold mined on the estate and real estate operations in San Francisco. He made a fifth exploring expedition to the mountains in 1853–54. Meanwhile, he had served as U.S. senator from California, September 1850—March 1851.

Frémont's explorations and court martial had made him a national figure. Nominated for the presidency by the new Republican party in June 1856, with W. L. Dayton as vice-presidential candidate, he lost to James Buchanan. Returning to California, he devoted himself to his mines at Mariposa.

His first Civil War appointment was as major general commanding the department of the West, with headquarters at St. Louis. Blamed for federal defeats at Wilson's Creek and Lexington, and justly accused of extravagance, he lost Lincoln's confidence by refusing to rescind a rash proclamation of Aug. 30, 1861, in which he declared the property of rebel Missourians confiscated and their slaves emancipated. He was investigated and removed, to the dismay of radical anti-slavery men; in deference to these, Lincoln appointed Frémont in March 1862 to command the mountain department in western Virginia. Here he was outgeneralled by Stonewall Jackson in May and June. Placed subordinate in command to Gen. John Pope, Frémont resigned.

Frémont's prosperity and popularity declined thereafter. He left public life, failed in business, was saved from poverty by his wife's activities as an author. His whole later career was a tragic anti-climax; his achievements as an explorer remain justly famous. The reports of his earlier expeditions were of particular value in publicizing the fertility of the plains country and the Northwest, and in supplying trustworthy information for emigrants.

FRENCH, AARON (*b. Wadsworth, O., 1823; d. 1902*), inventor, manufacturer. Began life as a blacksmith; manufactured first steel springs for railroad cars at Pittsburgh, Pa., *post 1862*; invented and put into use light-weight coiled and elliptic steel springs.

FRENCH, ALICE (*b. Andover, Mass., 1850; d. Davenport, Iowa, 1934*), author. Under pen-name "Octave Thanet," wrote realistic stories of life in the Midwest and South. Among her books were *Stories of a Western Town* (1893) and *A Book of True Lovers* (1897). [*Supp. 1*]

FRENCH, DANIEL CHESTER (*b. Exeter, N.H., 1850; d. Stockbridge, Mass., 1931*), sculptor. Mainly self-taught, he was helped by Louisa M. Alcott, William Morris Hunt, John Quincy Adams Ward, and William Rimmer. His first important commission was the "Minute Man" memorial, unveiled at Concord, Mass., 1875. On return after two years' study in Italy, he worked in Washington, D.C. on sculptural groups for the St. Louis Custom House, the Philadelphia Court House, and the Boston Post Office. He was also commissioned to do busts of Emerson and Bronson Alcott. When Emerson saw French's portrayal of him, he said, "That is the face I shave." In 1884 French designed the seated statue of John Harvard at Cambridge.

Post 1888 his work was prolific, and its rich variety continued until he was eighty. For the World's Columbian Exposition, 1893, he designed "The Republic" and submitted also his "Death Staying the Hand of the Young Sculptor." As the leading American sculptor he was selected to design what was to become the monumental figure of Abraham Lincoln for the Memorial in Washington, D.C.

French's work was modeled on reality but with a touch of idealism subtly interposed; it has poetic feeling and perfection of execution. Probably no other American sculptor has won such appreciative response from the general public. [*Supp.* 1]

FRENCH, EDWIN DAVIS (*b. North Attleboro, Mass., 1851; d. Saranac Lake, N.Y., 1906*), engraver on silver; a master of copperplate engraving of bookplates.

FRENCH, LUCY VIRGINIA SMITH (*b. Accomac Co., Va., 1825; d. McMinnville, Tenn., 1881*), author of romantic novels and poems; literary editor of several Southern periodicals.

FRENCH, WILLIAM HENRY (*b. Baltimore, Md., 1815; d. Washington, D.C., 1881*), soldier. Graduated West Point, 1837. Served in Florida and Mexican wars; in Civil War, rose to command III Corps, Army of the Potomac, until failure at Mine Run in 1863 cost him Gen. Meade's confidence.

FRENCH, WILLIAM MERCHANT RICHARDSON (*b. Exeter, N.H., 1843; d. Chicago, Ill., 1914*), secretary and director, Art Institute of Chicago, 1879–1914. Brother of Daniel C. French.

FRENEAU, PHILIP MORIN (*b. New York, N.Y., 1752; d. near Middletown Point, N.J., 1832*), poet, editor, mariner. Graduated College of New Jersey (Princeton), 1771, a classmate of James Madison and H. H. Brackenridge. Collaborated with the latter on a poem "The Rising Glory of America" (published 1772). With the coming of the Revolution he became fiercely active, publishing within a few months eight pamphlet satires, including *General Gage's Soliloquy* and *General Gage's Confession* (1775). An opening as secretary to a planter took him to the West Indies, and in the next three years there he wrote his most significant poems, "Santa Cruz," "The Jamaica Funeral," "The House of Night." The latter, written before the opening of the romantic period in Europe, has all the elements of the new romanticism and places Freneau as a pioneer in the movement.

Returning to find the Revolution in full career, he went to sea; taken by the British, he suffered the brutal imprisonment described in *The British Prison Ship: A Poem* (1781). Exchanged and working in Philadelphia, Pa., he helped edit the *Freeman's Journal,* satirizing the "insolent foe" and writing much patriotic poetry. He took to the sea again in 1784 as master of a brig, surviving storms and shipwreck and writing sea poems. No other American poet has known the ocean so well or pictured it more graphically.

In 1789 he began editing the New York *Daily Advertiser,* which he made an important newspaper. With Jefferson's support and encouragement, he edited the *National Gazette* in Philadelphia, 1791–93, effectively opposing John Fenno's pro-Hamilton *Ga-*

zette of the United States. A passionate Democrat, Freneau more than any other early journalist quickened this spirit in the new republic. After service as editor of the *Jersey Chronicle* and the New York *Time-Piece,* he gave up journalism and spent the rest of his life either at sea or on his New Jersey farm.

Freneau's poems were published in collected form in 1786, 1788, 1795, 1809 and 1815. He was the most significant poetic figure in America before William Cullen Bryant.

FREUND, ERNST (*b. New York, N.Y., 1864; d. Chicago, Ill., 1932*), lawyer, professor of law at Columbia and University of Chicago. Excelled in drafting uniform statutes for acceptance by legislative bodies. [*Supp.* 1]

FREY, JOSEPH SAMUEL CHRISTIAN FREDERICK (*b. Mainstockheim, Bavaria, 1771; d. Pontiac, Mich., 1850*), clergyman. Converted from Judaism, 1798, he came to America, 1816. As a preacher and agent for "The American Society for Meliorating the Condition of the Jews," he traveled extensively in the United States.

FRICK, HENRY CLAY (*b. West Overton, Pa., 1849; d. 1919*), steel manufacturer, capitalist. A coke millionaire at the age of 30, Frick became chairman of Carnegie Brothers in 1889 and reorganized the steel business by building connecting railroads, improving operating methods, employing capable young men and exploiting labor. He bought out Duquesne Steel, Carnegie's chief competitor, and by 1890 controlled the world's largest coke and steel operation. The notorious Homestead, Pa., strike (1892) brought much criticism on Frick. A key man in forming the U.S. Steel Corporation, 1901, and a director of many enterprises, he gratified a youthful taste for art by collecting old masters, now housed in the Frick Museum, New York City.

FRIDAY (*b. Kansas-Colorado plains, c. 1822; d. Wyoming, 1881*), Arapaho sub-chief. Sent to school in St. Louis, Mo., by Thomas Fitzpatrick, he returned to Indian life; a famous hunter and leader, he remained friendly to the whites.

FRIEDENWALD, AARON (*b. Baltimore, Md., 1836; d. Baltimore, 1902*), physician, ophthalmologist. Practiced in Baltimore; professor of diseases of eye and ear in College of Physicians and Surgeons; co-founder and first president, Maryland Ophthalmological Society.

FRIEDLAENDER, ISRAEL (*b. Kovel, Russian Poland, 1876; d. Kamenetz-Podolsk, Russia, 1920*), Semitist. Educated at Warsaw, Berlin, Strassburg; called to New York, 1903, to chair of Biblical literature and exegesis in Jewish Theological Seminary of America. Interested in historical relations between Islam and Judaism, he published many scholarly works. An ardent worker for Jewish education and for Zionism, he felt it his duty to go to the war-and-revolution-torn Ukraine in 1920 as commissioner of the Joint Distribution Committee of America. He was murdered there by Bolshevik soldiers.

FRIES, FRANCIS (*b. Salem, N.C., 1812; d. 1863*), manufacturer. One of a group which sought to implant industry in the ante-bellum South, he built and operated woolen and cotton mills at Salem *post 1836*.

FRIES, JOHN (*b. Montgomery Co., Pa., c. 1750; d. Bucks Co., Pa., 1818*), insurgent. An itinerant auctioneer, militia captain, and general rural favorite, he led the Pennsylvania Germans in opposition to the federal property tax of 1798. Assessors were ordered out of Bucks Co. and Capt. Fries with a band of followers ejected collectors and liberated federal prisoners. President John Adams sent a force of cavalry and militia in March 1799 to quell the rioters. Fries was arrested, tried for treason in Philadelphia and twice sentenced to death. President Adams pardoned him against the advice of his cabinet.

FRIESEKE, FREDERICK CARL (*b. Owosso, Mich., 1874; d. Plagny-Château, France, 1939*), painter. His impressionist, essentially orthodox paintings were well received in America and Europe. [*Supp. 2*]

FRIEZE, HENRY SIMMONS (*b. Boston, Mass., 1817; d. Ann Arbor, Mich., 1889*), professor of Latin. Graduated Brown, 1841. Thrice acting president of the University of Michigan (1869–71, 1880–82, 1887–88), he taught at Michigan *post 1854*.

FRISBIE, LEVI (*b. Ipswich, Mass., 1783; d. 1822*), educator. Graduated Harvard, 1802. Blind from early manhood, he was a teacher of Latin at Harvard, 1805–17, and thereafter Alford Professor of Natural Religion.

FRISSELL, HOLLIS BURKE (*b. South Amenia, N.Y., 1851; d. 1917*), Presbyterian clergyman. Chaplain of Hampton Institute, 1880–93; principal, 1893–1917.

FRITSCHEL, CONRAD SIGMUND (*b. Nürnberg, Germany, 1833; d. Dubuque, Iowa, 1900*), Lutheran clergyman, theologian. Came to America, 1854; helped constitute Evangelical Synod of Iowa. He and his brother Gottfried were principal professors at Wartburg Seminary.

FRITSCHEL, GOTTFRIED LEONHARD WILHELM (*b. Nürnberg, Germany, 1836; d. Mendota, Ill., 1889*), Lutheran clergyman, editor, theologian. Came to America, 1857. Served as colleague of his brother Conrad at Wartburg Seminary and defended its theological position (that of Wilhelm Löhe) against attacks of Missouri Synod.

FRITZ, JOHN (*b. Chester Co., Pa., 1822; d. 1913*), mechanical engineer, ironmaster. Starting as blacksmith and mechanic, he learned all phases of the iron business. As superintendent of Cambria Iron Works,

Johnstown, Pa., he raised the mill from bankruptcy, designing solid new machinery and introducing new techniques. He resigned in 1860 to become superintendent and chief engineer for the Bethlehem Iron Co. Fritz was one of a group which revolutionized the steel industry by applying the Bessemer process to American practice. Other outstanding improvements tried out in the Bethlehem plant were open-hearth furnaces, the Thomas basic process and the Whitworth forging press. He was first recipient of the John Fritz Medal, established in his honor, 1902.

FRIZELL, JOSEPH PALMER (*b. Barford, Canada, 1832; d. Dorchester, Mass., 1910*), hydraulic engineer. Assistant to James B. Francis and trained by him. Author of *Water Power, an Outline, etc.* (1900), the first practical book on the subject published in the United States, he had been engaged *post 1868* in government work and general practice.

FROHMAN, CHARLES (*b. Sandusky, O., 1860; d. aboard Lusitania, 1915*), theatrical manager. Acting first as advance agent to road companies, Frohman became an independent manager, 1883; then opened a booking office which was the basis of what later became the "Theatrical Syndicate." *Shenandoah* (1889) was his first independent success. He engaged John Drew as nucleus of his Empire Stock Co. which developed star figures such as Maude Adams, William Faversham, Ethel Barrymore. "The Napoleon of the drama," he produced plays by Belasco, Clyde Fitch, Augustus Thomas, Somerset Maugham and many others, introducing Sir James Barrie to the American public with Maude Adams in *The Little Minister* (1897). The Barrie-Adams-Frohman combination scored success after success, notably with *Peter Pan*. Frohman was noted for the tasteful lavishness of his productions and for the complete trust to be put in his pledged word.

FROHMAN, DANIEL (*b. Sandusky, O., 1851; d. New York, N.Y., 1940*), theatrical manager and producer. Brother of Charles Frohman. Organized Lyceum Theatre (New York) stock company, 1887. A pioneer in motion-picture production. [*Supp. 2*]

FROST, ARTHUR BURDETT (*b. Philadelphia, Pa., 1851; d. Pasadena, Calif., 1928*), illustrator, humorist. Trained as a wood-engraver and lithographer, his illustrating career began with wood-engravings for "Max Adeler's" (Charles H. Clark) *Out of the Hurly Burly* (1874); by 1900 he was probably the country's most popular illustrator.

Frost's illustrations cover a wide range, but his true talent was for American folk pictures—comic line sketches in story sequence, or finished illustrations in pen and ink, oils or water-color. Selections of his humorous sketches appeared in *Stuff and Nonsense* (1884); *The Bull Calf* (1892); *Carlo* (1913). His more formal illustrations appeared in *Scribner's*, *Harper's* and *Collier's*; a selection of these was published in *A Book of Drawings* (1904). His best-known drawings were for Joel Chandler Harris's *Uncle Remus* books (1892–1918).

FROST, EDWIN BRANT (*b. Brattleboro, Vt., 1866; d. Chicago, Ill., 1935*), astronomer. Graduated Dartmouth, 1885. Director, Yerkes Observatory, 1905–32. His most important work dealt with the spectra of the stars. [*Supp. 1*]

FROST, HOLLOWAY HALSTEAD (*b. Brooklyn, N.Y., 1889; d. Kansas City, Mo., 1935*), naval officer. Graduated Annapolis, 1910. Specialist in naval strategy and tactics, he wrote and lectured extensively on these subjects. [*Supp. 1*]

FROST, WADE HAMPTON (*b. Marshall, Va., 1880; d. Baltimore, Md., 1938*), epidemiologist. M.D., University of Virginia, 1903. Medical officer, U.S. Public Health Service, 1905–28; professor of epidemiology and public health, Johns Hopkins, 1919–38.
[*Supp. 2*]

FROTHINGHAM, ARTHUR LINCOLN (*b. Boston, Mass., 1859; d. Princeton, N.J., 1923*), scholar, educator. Professor of archaeology at Princeton, 1886–1905. Founded *American Journal of Archaeology,* 1885; wrote prolifically on archaeological subjects.

FROTHINGHAM, NATHANIEL LANGDON (*b. Boston, Mass., 1793; d. 1870*), Unitarian clergyman. Graduated Harvard, 1811. Pastor of the First Church, Boston, 1815–50; an intellectual, much admired by R. W. Emerson, he was author of hymns, metrical translations from Latin and German literature, sermons and other works.

FROTHINGHAM, OCTAVIUS BROOKS (*b. Boston, Mass., 1822; d. Boston, 1895*), Unitarian and independent clergyman. Son of Nathaniel L. Frothingham. Pastor, Third Congregational Unitarian Society, New York, 1859–79, and a founder and first president of the Free Religious Association (Boston), he was considered the intellectual heir of Theodore Parker.

FROTHINGHAM, PAUL REVERE (*b. Jamaica Plain, Mass., 1864; d. 1926*), Unitarian clergyman. Nephew of Octavius B. Frothingham.

FROTHINGHAM, RICHARD (*b. Charlestown, Mass., 1812; d. 1880*), historian, businessman, legislator. Managing editor of the *Boston Post*, 1852–65; author of meticulously accurate studies of local history, including *History of the Siege of Boston* (1848), and *The Rise of the Republic* (1872).

FRY, BIRKETT DAVENPORT (*b. Kanawha Co., Va., now W. Va., 1822; d. Richmond, Va., 1891*), lawyer, cotton manufacturer, Confederate brigadier-general.

FRY, JAMES BARNET (*b. Carrollton, Ill., 1827; d. Newport, R.I., 1894*), soldier, writer. Graduated West Point, 1847. Organized Bureau of the Provost-Marshal-General, 1863, after outstanding field service at first Bull Run, Shiloh and Perryville. His conduct of the Bureau until 1866 was the occasion of celebrated debate in Congress between J. G. Blaine and Roscoe Conkling. He served thereafter in the Adjutant General's department. Published much military history.

FRY, JOSHUA (*b. Crewkerne, England, c. 1700; d. Will's Creek, now Cumberland, Md., 1754*), mathematics professor, surveyor, pioneer. Came to Virginia, *ante* 1720. Member of the House of Burgesses; commander of the militia, 1754. Author, with Peter Jefferson, of a celebrated "Map of the Inhabited Parts of Virginia" (1751).

FRY, RICHARD (*fl. 1731–1741*), paper-maker, bookseller. In Boston jail for debt, he sent to the legislature in 1739 a scheme for a chain of factories to provide New England with a wide variety of products.

FRY, WILLIAM HENRY (*b. Philadelphia, Pa., 1815; d. Santa Cruz, W.I., 1864*), composer, journalist. First successful American opera composer; his *Leonora* was produced in Philadelphia and New York, 1845, and revived, 1858.

FRYE, JOSEPH (*b. Andover, Mass., 1711/12; d. 1794*), soldier. At siege of Louisburg, 1744/45; on Kennebec expedition, 1754; survived massacre at Fort William Henry, 1757; served briefly in Revolution. Grantee of Fryeburg, Maine, which was named in his honor, 1777.

FRYE, WILLIAM PIERCE (*b. Lewiston, Maine, 1831; d. Lewiston, 1911*), lawyer. Great-great-grandson of Joseph Frye. As congressman, Republican, from Maine, 1871–81, established himself both as a debater and an industrious committee worker. Chosen U.S. senator, 1881, he served until death as a Senate wheel horse, was one of the Old Guard under Roosevelt and Taft, long Chairman of the Committee on Commerce and a member of the Foreign Relations Committee. An ardent expansionist, he was also a constant supporter of measures to revive the American merchant marine.

FUERTES, ESTEVAN ANTONIO (*b. San Juan, P.R., 1838; d. 1903*), engineer, educator. Dean, civil engineering department of Cornell University, 1873–1902; built it into a great technical school, devising courses, installing laboratories, making his idealism and enthusiasm widely felt.

FUERTES, LOUIS AGASSIZ (*b. Ithaca, N.Y., 1874; d. 1927*), artist-naturalist. Son of Estevan A. Fuertes. Illustrated most of the leading bird-books published, 1896–1927, with paintings and sketches of extraordinary accuracy.

FULLER, ANDREW S. (*b. Utica, N.Y., 1828; d. 1896*), horticulturist, editor. Pioneer in strawberry cross-breeding. Author of *Illustrated Strawberry Culturist* (1862); *The Small Fruit Culturist* (1867); *The*

Nut Culturist (1896); and other works. An indefatigable experimenter.

FULLER, GEORGE (*b. Deerfield, Mass., 1822; d. Brookline, Mass., 1884*), painter. Pupil of Henry Kirke Brown; studied also at National Academy of Design. After a number of years of wandering and artist-life, settled at Deerfield as a farmer, 1860–75. Forced back to his profession by financial pressure, he entered on the finest period of his work, producing his masterpiece "Winifred Dysart" in 1881. An elusive, mystical quality distinguishes all his painting.

FULLER, GEORGE WARREN (*b. New York, N.Y., 1868; d. 1934*), engineer. Graduated Massachusetts Institute of Technology, 1890; studied at University of Berlin. An expert in water supply and purification, sewerage and sewage treatment. [*Supp.* 1]

FULLER, HENRY BLAKE (*b. Chicago, Ill., 1857; d. 1929*), novelist. His early work was divided between use of romantic materials from his European travels, as in *The Chevalier of Pensieri-Vani* (1890, under pseudonym "Stanton Page"), and *The Chatelaine of La Trinité* (1892), and realistic studies of the raw Middle West. Of the latter, *The Cliff-Dwellers* (1893) and *With the Procession* (1895) are outstanding. His subsequent work expressed his disgust with developing trends in our national culture, culminating in a revival of creativity shortly before his death. *Gardens of This World* and *Not on the Screen,* written in the last year of his life, were published posthumously.

FULLER, HIRAM (*b. Halifax, Mass., 1814; d. Paris, France, 1880*), journalist. Partner of George P. Morris and Nathaniel P. Willis in conducting the *New York Mirror,* 1843–44; continuing as owner-manager of the *Evening Mirror,* he lost all support by pro-Southern utterances and expatriated himself on outbreak of the Civil War.

FULLER, JOHN WALLACE (*b. Harston, England, 1827; d. Toledo, O., 1891*), businessman, Union soldier. Came to America as a child. Colonel, 27th Ohio; brigadier-general, commanding "Fuller's Brigade" in western campaigns and on the Atlanta and Carolina campaigns.

FULLER, JOSEPH VINCENT (*b. Knoxville, Tenn., 1890; d. 1932*), historical editor in research section, U.S. State Department. Graduated Harvard, 1914; Ph.D., 1921. Edited diplomatic correspondence of the United States relating to World War I. [*Supp.* 1]

FULLER, LEVI KNIGHT (*b. Westmoreland, N.H., 1841; d. 1896*), inventor, manufacturer. Long associated with Estey Organ Co. Republican governor of Vermont, 1892–94.

FULLER, LOIE (*b. Fullersburg, Ill., 1862; d. 1928*), dancer. Her "serpentine" dance brought success *post* 1891. Experimenting with possibilities latent in harmonies of light, color and movement, she developed a school in Paris; was especially popular in Europe.

FULLER, MARGARET. [See FULLER, SARAH MARGARET, 1810–1850.]

FULLER, MELVILLE WESTON (*b. Augusta, Maine, 1833; d. Sorrento, Maine, 1910*), jurist. Graduated Bowdoin, 1853. Removed to Chicago, Ill., 1856, where he practiced law. Dignity, courtesy, moderation, learning, distinct personality marked him at the bar and on the bench. A strong Democrat, on his appointment as chief justice of U.S. Supreme Court by President Cleveland in 1888, he inclined toward strict construction of all governmental powers and insisted that Congress's powers were derivable only from specific grants, reasonably construed. He was consistent in support of traditional rights of person and property against the tendency toward regulation and limitation which marked his time.

FULLER, RICHARD (*b. Beaufort, S.C., 1804; d. Baltimore, Md., 1876*), Baptist clergyman, apologist for slavery.

FULLER, ROBERT MASON (*b. Schenectady, N.Y., 1845; d. 1919*), physician, pharmacist. Graduated Albany Medical School, 1865. Originated and worked out the principle of the tablet triturate, also the use of the camera in teaching and in forensic medicine.

FULLER, SARAH MARGARET (*b. Cambridgeport, Mass., 1810; d. at sea, 1850*), journalist, critic, social reformer. Forced in her education by her strenuous father, she began her friendships with intellectual leaders like F. H. Hedge, James Freeman Clarke and W. H. Channing at an early age and was accepted in the transcendentalist circle on a par with Alcott and Thoreau. After several years of teaching, she started her famous "conversations" in 1839 with a group of ladies from cultivated Boston society who met at Elizabeth Peabody's; from their discussions derived *Woman in the Nineteenth Century* (1845), a work often compared to Mary Wollstonecraft's. It touched on all issues of the woman's movement but was too philosophical for the militant enthusiasts.

With R. W. Emerson and George Ripley, Margaret edited the transcendentalist *Dial.* Invited by Horace Greeley to join the *New York Tribune,* she won a reputation as one of the best American critics. Going to Europe, 1846, she visited Carlyle, Wordsworth and others, and met Mazzini. Settling in Rome, 1847, she joined in the revolution of 1848. Angelo Ossoli, an Italian *marchese* whom she married at some time during her Italian sojourn, fought with the republican army. Margaret assisted in the organization of hospitals, writing occasionally to the *Tribune* to describe the siege of Rome, 1849.

When the French suppressed the Roman Republic in July, Margaret fled to Florence with Ossoli and their son, now about a year old; she spent the winter writing a history of the Roman Revolution. In May 1850, the family sailed from Leghorn for America.

All drowned when the vessel went down off Fire Island, N.Y. An invalid most of her life and a better talker than a writer, Margaret worked prodigiously. Although her eccentricities offended many, her noble and generous personality impressed itself upon her generation. Her critical writings were published in *Papers on Literature and Art* (1846) and in the edition of her works by Horace Greeley (1869).

FULLER, THOMAS CHARLES (*b. Fayetteville, N.C., 1832; d. Raleigh, N.C., 1901*), lawyer, Confederate soldier. Member of Confederate Congress. Justice of court of private land claims dealing with former Mexican territory, 1891–1901.

FULLERTON, GEORGE STUART (*b. Fatehgarh, India, 1859; d. Poughkeepsie, N.Y., 1925*), "new realist" philosopher. Taught at University of Pennsylvania, and was dean of Graduate School; later a research professor at Columbia. Author of *System of Metaphysics* (1904), *The World We Live In* (1912) and other scholarly works.

FULTON, JUSTIN DEWEY (*b. Earlville, N.Y., 1828; d. Somerville, Mass., 1901*), Baptist clergyman. Fanatical opponent of slavery, drink, woman suffrage, the drama and Roman Catholicism.

FULTON, ROBERT (*b. Lancaster Co., Pa., 1765; d. New York, N.Y., 1815*), artist, civil engineer, inventor. As a boy, showed genius for drawing; learned gunsmithing; provided mechanical aid and decorative designs much in demand with gunmakers. Went to Philadelphia, 1782; successfully painted portraits, miniatures, landscapes; also made mechanical drawings. Journeying to London, 1786, for his health, he did not return for twenty years.

Friendship with the Duke of Bridgewater and Lord Stanhope encouraged him to devote full time to engineering projects for internal improvements and the devising of mechanical equipment, especially for canals. He patented machines for sawing marble, spinning flax, twisting hemp rope and a "doubly inclined plane" for raising and lowering canal boats which was used in England and the United States. He invented a dredge for cutting channels, wrote many pamphlets and *A Treatise on the Improvement of Canal Navigation* (1796), profusely illustrated by himself and containing complete computations of construction and operating costs. He also designed cast-iron low-cost aqueducts and bridges.

From 1797 to 1806 Fulton devoted himself principally to the development of the submarine mine and torpedo. Aided by Joel Barlow, he experimented at Brest; then, to support himself in France, obtained French patents on his canal improvements and saw his plans for the Paris-Dieppe canal adopted. He also painted probably the first panorama, "L'Incendie de Moscow." About 1799 the Directory rejected his torpedo plans. Following Napoleon's appointment of a commission to examine his schemes, Fulton built a

remarkably successful diving boat, *Nautilus*, which descended 25 feet, steered easily under water, could stay down 4½ hours. After trials, Napoleon authorized Fulton to proceed against British ships, but when a summer's reconnoitering of the coast brought no British prizes, the French lost interest and Fulton received no pay or expense money.

The British government now made overtures to Fulton, but although he proved the value of his submarine by blowing up a brig near Deal, he failed against the French fleet and his invention was not adopted. During all these negotiations and experiments Fulton kept the United States officially informed.

Fulton now entered into an agreement with Robert R. Livingston to construct a steamboat to navigate between New York and Albany. After one boat launched on the Seine sank because of the weight of machinery (1803), Fulton built a successful steamboat which proceeded upstream at 4½ mph. He then ordered an engine from Boulton & Watt for the *Clermont* to be built in New York by Charles Brown. She was 133 feet long, 18 feet broad, 7 feet deep. The Watt engine was placed forward of a 20-foot boiler set in brickwork and housed over. Two side paddle-wheels propelled the boat up the Hudson to Albany and back in five days, August 17–22, 1807, the *Clermont* being actually under way only 62 hours.

After the success of the *Clermont*, Fulton was busy establishing commercial lines and directing the building of seventeen other steamboats, a torpedo-boat and a ferryboat. He designed a steam warship for New York harbor defense, authorized for construction in 1814; called *Fulton the First*, it was a large vessel, 156 feet long and carrying thirty 32-pounders. During his last years Fulton experimented with firing guns under water. Commonly called the "inventor" of the steamboat, he was rather the man who devised for it a practical design and demonstrated its commercial value.

FULTON, ROBERT BURWELL (*b. Sumter Co., Ala., 1849; d. New York, N.Y., 1919*), educator. Graduated University of Mississippi, 1869. Taught there, and served as chancellor, 1892–1906. Developed system of affiliated high schools; extended curriculum; added three professional schools.

FUNK, ISAAC KAUFFMAN (*b. Clifton, O., 1839; d. 1912*), Lutheran clergyman, publisher, editor. Founded Funk & Wagnalls Co., 1877, with A. W. Wagnalls. Projected and edited the *Literary Digest* and *A Standard Dictionary of the English Language*.

FUNSTON, FREDERICK (*b. New Carlisle, O., 1865; d. 1917*), soldier. Raised in Kansas; trained as botanist. Served in Cuban insurrection, 1896–97; commanded a regiment in the Philippines, 1899–1900; received the Congressional Medal and became brigadier-general of volunteers. With a small party, he captured Aguinaldo, the insurrectionist leader, in March 1901 and was transferred to the regular army as brigadier-general. Commanded the department of California during San Francisco earthquake, 1906; commanded the force sent to hold Vera Cruz, 1914, and was military governor there. Promoted major-general in November 1914, he commanded thereafter on the Mexican border.

FURLOW, FLOYD CHARLES (*b. Americus, Ga., 1877; d. New York, N.Y., 1923*), engineer. Graduated Georgia School of Technology, 1897. Chief engineer, later president, Otis Elevator Co. Inventor of many devices which brought electric elevators to high efficiency.

FURMAN, JAMES CLEMENT (*b. Charleston, S.C., 1809; d. near Greenville, S.C., 1891*), Baptist clergyman. President, Furman University, 1852–79. Son of Richard Furman.

FURMAN, RICHARD (*b. Esopus, N.Y., 1755; d. 1825*), Baptist clergyman, educator. Raised in South Carolina; ordained 1774, he took an active part in the Revolution. A Federalist in politics, Furman also favored strong central authority in his church and was its outstanding leader in the South. He led the movement to found a collegiate school for the Baptist ministry and Furman University, founded a short time after his death, was named for him.

FURNAS, ROBERT WILKINSON (*b. near Troy, O., 1824; d. Lincoln, Neb., 1905*), agriculturist, Union soldier. Removed to Nebraska, 1856; edited *Nebraska Advertiser*. Republican governor of Nebraska, 1873–75. Noteworthy for a lifelong devotion to the advancement of agriculture and education.

FURNESS, HORACE HOWARD (*b. Philadelphia, Pa., 1833; d. Wallingford, Pa., 1912*), lawyer, Shakespeare scholar. Son of William H. Furness. Graduated Harvard, 1854. Edited the New Variorum Shakespeare, 1871 to his death.

FURNESS, HORACE HOWARD (*b. Philadelphia, Pa., 1865; d. 1930*), Shakespeare scholar. Son of Horace H. Furness (1833–1912). Co-editor, New Variorum Shakespeare, *post* 1901; succeeded his father as editor of the project.

FURNESS, WILLIAM HENRY (*b. Boston, Mass., 1802; d. 1896*), Unitarian clergyman. Pastor, Unitarian church in Philadelphia, 1825–75; thereafter emeritus. Active in anti-slavery movement, and a pioneer American student of German literature.

FURST, CLYDE BOWMAN (*b. Williamsport, Pa., 1873; d. 1931*), educator. Known for his work with Carnegie Foundation for the Advancement of Teaching; secretary, *post* 1911. Put teachers' pension systems on sound basis. [*Supp. 1*]

FURUSETH, ANDREW (*b. near Romedal, Norway, 1854; d. Washington, D.C., 1938*), labor leader.

Changed name from Anders Andreassen. Came to America, 1880. President, International Seamen's Union, 1908–38; crusader for seamen's rights; his ideas embodied in La Follette Seamen's Act, 1915.

[*Supp. 2*]

FUSSELL, BARTHOLOMEW (*b. Chester Co., Pa., 1794; d. Chester Springs, Pa., 1871*), physician, Abolitionist. Active cooperator in the "underground railroad."

GABB, WILLIAM MORE (*b. Philadelphia, Pa., 1839; d. Philadelphia, 1878*), paleontologist. Studied with James Hall. Served on Geological Survey of California (Whitney's), 1861–64; worked also in Mexico, Santo Domingo and Costa Rica.

GABRILOWITSCH, OSSIP (*b. St. Petersburg, Russia, 1878; d. Detroit, Mich., 1936*), concert pianist, orchestra conductor. Son-in-law of Samuel L. Clemens. Settled in America, 1914. Director, Detroit Symphony Orchestra, 1918–35. [*Supp. 2*]

GADSDEN, CHRISTOPHER (*b. Charleston, S.C., 1724; d. 1805*), merchant, Revolutionary leader. Member of South Carolina Assembly, 1757–84. In the Stamp Act Congress, 1765, Gadsden argued for colonial union and against recognition of Parliament's authority. As leader of the radicals, his integrity, zeal and courage made him an invaluable champion; the Charleston mechanics followed him enthusiastically. Delegate to the First and Second Continental Congresses, he left in 1776 to serve in the South Carolina forces. The climax of his career came in 1778 when he and William H. Drayton secured the disestablishment of the church and popular election of senators in the South Carolina constitution adopted that year. He was among the few Carolina legislators who opposed confiscation of Loyalist property.

GADSDEN, JAMES (*b. Charleston, S.C., 1788; d. Charleston, 1858*), soldier, politician. Grandson of Christopher Gadsden. Settled in Florida, 1822–39. As president of the South Carolina Railroad Co., 1840–50, he hoped to form the Southern railroads into one system connected by a route to the Pacific along the southern U.S. frontier. This would make the West tributary to the South and inaugurate direct trade with Europe. He promoted this idea through a series of so-called railroad and commercial conventions but realized that purchase of Mexican territory was necessary to secure the most practicable westward route. As minister to Mexico under President Pierce, Gadsden was authorized to buy as much border land as possible for $50,000,000. The Gadsden Purchase was the result of this offer (1853–54).

GAFFNEY, MARGARET. [See HAUGHERY, MARGARET GAFFNEY, c. 1814–1882.]

GAGE, FRANCES DANA BARKER (*b. Marietta, O., 1808; d. Greenwich, Conn., 1884*), reformer, author.

Popular speaker and writer on slavery, temperance, women's rights.

GAGE, LYMAN JUDSON (*b. Deruyter, N.Y., 1836; d. San Diego, Calif., 1927*), banker. Removed to Chicago, Ill., 1855; was associated *post* 1868 with First National Bank there, and served as its president, 1891–97. Prominent in moves to reconcile capital and labor, and as director of Chicago Exposition, 1893, he accepted the post of secretary of the treasury from McKinley after staunchly defending the gold standard in the 1896 campaign. During the Spanish-American War he added greatly to his financial reputation, and was influential in securing passage of the Act establishing the gold standard, March 14, 1900. He resigned the secretaryship in 1902.

GAGE, MATILDA JOSLYN (*b. Cicero, N.Y., 1826; d. Chicago, Ill., 1898*), woman's suffrage leader. Co-author with Elizabeth Cady Stanton and Susan B. Anthony of *History of Woman Suffrage* (1881–86).

GAGE, THOMAS (*b. Firle, England, 1721; d. 1787*), soldier, last royal governor of Massachusetts. Came to America, 1754. Fought with distinction on Braddock's expedition and in later campaigns of French and Indian War; was commander-in-chief in North America, 1763–73. He succeeded Thomas Hutchinson as governor of Massachusetts, 1774, to find the quarrel with the English government in a high state of aggravation, the Boston Port Bill having just been announced. Gage's attempts to seize military stores from the colonists resulted in the outbreak of hostilities at Lexington and Concord, April 1775, and the subsequent siege of Boston. He left Boston for England on Oct. 10, 1775.

GAILLARD, DAVID DU BOSE (*b. Fulton, S.C., 1859; d. Baltimore, Md., 1913*), engineer, soldier. Graduated West Point, 1884. Served on commission re-establishing Mexican boundary; surveyed Portland Channel; commanded regiment of engineers in Spanish-American War. Published valuable standard work, *Wave Action in Relation to Engineering Structures* (1904). In 1907, he was put in charge of dredging and excavation on the Panama Canal by Gen. Goethals. He energetically organized his areas, presently taking charge of central division, which included cutting through the continental divide. Gaillard progressed in spite of great earth slides and other discouragements, until in July 1913, within sight of the end of the work, he broke under the strain and never recovered.

GAILLARD, EDWIN SAMUEL (*b. near Charleston, S.C., 1827; d. 1885*), surgeon, medical journalist. Founder and editor, *Richmond Medical Journal* and *American Medical Weekly*.

GAILLARD, JOHN (*b. St. Stephen's Parish, S.C., 1765; d. Washington, D.C., 1826*), planter. U.S. senator, (Democrat) Republican, from South Carolina, 1805–26.

GAILLARDET, THÉODORE FRÉDÉRIC (*b. Auxerre, France, 1808; d. Plessis-Bouchard, France, 1882*), journalist, author. As owner-editor, 1840–48, revivified the *Courrier des États-Unis* and gave it national standing as a newspaper for Franco-Americans.

GAILOR, THOMAS FRANK (*b. Jackson, Miss., 1856; d. Sewanee, Tenn., 1935*), Episcopal clergyman. Long associated with University of the South, Sewanee, Tenn. Consecrated Bishop of Tennessee, 1893. [*Supp. 1*]

GAINE, HUGH (*b. Belfast, Ireland, 1726/27; d. New York, N.Y., 1807*), printer, bookseller. Came to America, 1745. Founded the *New-York Mercury*, 1752, and kept the paper going through denominational and Revolutionary difficulties until 1783; was official New York printer for city and province *post* 1768.

GAINES, EDMUND PENDLETON (*b. Culpeper Co., Va., 1777; d. New Orleans, La., 1849*), soldier. Brother of George S. Gaines. In War of 1812, covered the American retreat at Chrysler's Field; conducted defense of Fort Erie. Fought against Creeks and Seminoles; in Black Hawk War; and in Florida War, 1835. In command of the western department at outbreak of Mexican War, he was court-martialed for raising troops in defiance of War Department reprimands. Defending himself skillfully and vehemently, he was exonerated and later commanded the eastern department. Fiery and unrestrained, he cherished a lifelong feud with Gen. Winfield Scott and the U.S. War Department.

GAINES, GEORGE STROTHER (*b. Stokes Co., N.C., c. 1784; d. Mississippi, 1873*), Alabama pioneer, Indian agent, merchant, planter. Brother of Edmund P. Gaines. His fair dealing, kindness, adroitness as agent to the Choctaws, 1805–19, won their trade and friendship. His services to pioneers of Mississippi Territory were inestimable. Gainesville, Ala., was named for him.

GAINES, JOHN POLLARD (*b. Augusta Co., Va., 1795; d. near Salem, Ore., 1857*), lawyer, soldier. Raised in Kentucky. Served in War of 1812 and Mexican War; was congressman, Whig, from Kentucky, 1847–49. Appointed governor of Oregon Territory, he served 1850–53. His single term was marked by disputes, principally over the choice of Salem or Oregon City for the capital.

GAINES, REUBEN REID (*b. Sumter Co., Ala., 1836; d. 1914*), lawyer, Confederate soldier. Removed to Texas, 1868. Chief justice, supreme court of Texas, 1894–1911.

GAINES, WESLEY JOHN (*b. Wilkes Co., Ga., 1840; d. Atlanta, Ga., 1912*), bishop of the African Methodist Episcopal Church. An able organizer and financial agent, and a promoter of Negro education.

GALBERRY, THOMAS (*b. Naas, Ireland, 1833; d. New York, N.Y., 1878*), Roman Catholic clergyman. Came to America as a child. Graduated Villanova, 1851. Ordained as Augustinian, 1856. Was rector of Villanova, 1872–75, and Augustinian provincial. Consecrated bishop of Hartford, 1876.

GALBREATH, CHARLES BURLEIGH (*b. near Leetonia, O., 1858; d. Columbus, O., 1934*), Ohio State librarian. Author of *History of Ohio* (1925) and other works. [*Supp. 1*]

GALE, BENJAMIN (*b. Jamaica, N.Y., 1715; d. 1790*), physician, political writer. Studied with Jared Eliot at Killingworth, Conn.; succeeded him in practice there. Wrote a valuable paper on smallpox; associated with David Bushnell in early submarine work.

GALE, ELBRIDGE (*b. Bennington, Vt., 1824; d. 1907*), Baptist clergyman, horticulturist. Professor, Kansas State Agricultural College; removed to Florida, 1884, where he raised fruits and succeeded in propagating the Mulgoba mango.

GALE, GEORGE WASHINGTON (*b. Stanford, N.Y., 1789; d. 1861*), Presbyterian clergyman, educator. Graduated Union, 1814. Founded Oneida Institute, Whitesboro, N.Y., 1827; also Knox College, Galesburg, Ill., 1837. Both schools were at first operated on the principle of instruction for students in return for manual labor.

GALE, ZONA (*b. Portage, Wis., 1874; d. Chicago, Ill., 1938*), journalist, novelist. Her best work was done in studies in regional realism such as *Birth* (1918), *Miss Lulu Bett* (1920). The latter, dramatized (1921), won a Pulitzer Prize. [*Supp. 2*]

GALES, JOSEPH (*b. Eckington, England, 1761; d. Raleigh, N.C., 1841*), printer, journalist, reformer. Friend of Joseph Priestley. Fled England, 1794, after advocating principles of Thomas Paine and defending French Revolution. Founded Raleigh, N.C., *Register*, 1799; compiled first two volumes *Annals of Congress* (1834).

GALES, JOSEPH (*b. Eckington, England, 1786; d. 1860*), journalist. Son of Joseph Gales (1761–1841). Sole reporter of U.S. Senate proceedings, 1807–20. Proprietor with W. W. Seaton of *National Intelligencer*, most valuable source of Congressional debates to 1833. Published *Annals of Congress* (1834–56) and *American State Papers* (1832–61).

GALL (*b. on Moreau River, S. Dak., c. 1840; d. Oak Creek, S. Dak., 1894*), Hunkpapa Sioux war chief. Military leader at Little Big Horn, 1876; later opposed Sitting Bull, became friend of whites, urged education on Indians.

GALLAGHER, HUGH PATRICK (*b. Killygordon, Ireland, 1815; d. San Francisco, Calif., 1882*), Roman Catholic clergyman. Came to America, 1837. Invited to California, 1852, by Bishop Alemany, he became colorful "Father Hugh" of mining camps, frontier towns; was organizer of parishes, schools, orphanages, hospitals.

GALLAGHER, WILLIAM DAVIS (*b. Philadelphia, Pa., 1808; d. Louisville, Ky., 1894*), editor, poet, public official. Raised in Ohio. Associated with many short-lived periodicals and newspapers, 1826–39; with the *Cincinnati Gazette*, 1839–50. His principal claim to remembrance is as a poet, among the first of his section, and influential there in encouraging literary expression. His work was collected in *Erato* (three issues, 1835–37); *Miami Woods* (1881); and in his own anthology, *Selections from the Poetical Literature of the West* (1841).

GALLATIN, ABRAHAM ALFONSE ALBERT (*b. Geneva, Switzerland, 1761; d. Astoria, N.Y., 1849*), statesman, diplomat. Early orphaned son of an aristocratic family, Gallatin developed Rousseauistic and republican sympathies and emigrated to America, 1780. At first trading in Maine, he later tutored in French at Harvard; in 1784 he set up a store at Clare's Farm on the Pennsylvania frontier near where he had sunk his patrimony in an extensive and unprofitable land purchase. He began his political career as a radical member of the 1788 Harrisburg conference called to consider revision of the U.S. Constitution and introduced radical resolutions. At the 1789–90 convention to revise the Pennsylvania constitution, he contributed notably to discussions of suffrage, representation, taxation and the judiciary. In the state legislature, 1790–92, he prepared the reports and bills of many committees and became leader in financial legislation. Elected to the U.S. Senate, 1793, he was ousted by the Federalists, who for political reasons challenged him on the inadequate time he had been a citizen. During the brief time he sat in the Senate, he angered Hamilton by calling for a detailed statement of the government's finances down to Jan. 1, 1794. Returning home to Fayette Co., 1794, he found western Pennsylvania seething with the "Whiskey Rebellion," provoked by the excise bill of 1791. Gallatin courageously faced an armed mob and succeeded in persuading the revolutionary committee to peaceable submission, thus helping to prevent what amounted to civil war.

As congressman, (Democrat) Republican, from Pennsylvania, 1795–1801, Gallatin showed an unrivaled grasp of constitutional and international law and great power of argument; he became leader of the minority, but his signal service was in matters of finance, though hindered by Federalist opposition. His insistence on the strict accountability of the Treasury Department to Congress caused the creation of the Ways and Means Committee. He also urged that no moneys be spent except for the purposes for which they had been appropriated.

Appointed secretary of the treasury on Jefferson's

accession in 1801 and holding the post until 1814, Gallatin was not content to be a mere financier. He shaped his policy to further the political and social ends which he envisaged as the destiny of the United States. He felt that the nation, highly favored by geographical position and natural resources, would prosper through industry and commerce; without oppressive taxation, therefore, the government could look forward to a surplus to devote to national projects for education and internal improvements. Despite much British and French vexation of American commerce, an inefficient Navy Department, bitter Senate opposition, indifferent support from Jefferson and scarcely any from Madison, all government expenses including interest on stock for the Louisiana purchase had been met, and the treasury surplus was $1,000,000 at the end of Jefferson's first administration.

Gallatin's policies and his calculations for paying off the public debt were wrecked by the events of 1807–13. He had to enforce the Embargo by drastic means and extend internal taxes. His plea for the Bank of the United States did not save its charter, and the issue of paper money by state banks brought about a suspension of specie payments outside New England. Senate opposition became so bitter that he asked the President to send him on a mission to Russia and left for St. Petersburg in May 1813.

For the next ten years Gallatin was abroad in the diplomatic service. As a member of the peace commission at Ghent, 1814, Gallatin not only prepared drafts on the most important points in dispute with Great Britain, but with great skill maintained some harmony between John Quincy Adams and Henry Clay, his fellow-commissioners, who clashed over sectional interests. Henry Adams has called the treaty signed at Ghent (December 1814) "the special and peculiar triumph of Mr. Gallatin." Before revisiting the United States in the fall-winter of 1815, Gallatin worked to conclude a favorable British-American commercial treaty. Declining to return to the Treasury, he became U.S. minister to France where he worked conscientiously in a diplomatic deadlock, 1816–23, unable to press claims for injury done to American commerce by the Napoleonic decrees. He did assist the American minister in London in negotiating the treaty of 1818 which stabilized our relations with Great Britain for a time.

Repelled by the tone of politics at home, Gallatin retired to his home in Pennsylvania until 1826 when he undertook a successful term as U.S. minister to London. When he returned in November, 1827, the commercial treaties of 1815 and 1818 had been renewed, joint occupation of Oregon was to be continued indefinitely, the northeast Canadian boundary was to be settled by the arbitration of the friendly King of the Netherlands. Urged by John Jacob Astor, Gallatin served as president (1831–39) of the new National Bank in New York, using his great influence in banking circles to hasten return to specie payments after the panic of 1837.

The services of this great financier, diplomat and statesman have never been adequately recognized by his adopted country. He never paraded his patriotism, which was sincere and abiding. He never sought to ingratiate himself with the multitude. His appeal was always to men's reason and judgment, not to their emotions and prejudices. No prospect of political preferment or threat of personal loss could tempt or frighten him from what he felt to be the path of duty, honor and truth. He was the author also of several pamphlets on currency and on tariffs and was a pioneer in study of American ethnology.

GALLAUDET, EDWARD MINER (*b. Hartford, Conn., 1837; d. 1917*), educator of the deaf. Son of Thomas H. Gallaudet. First principal of the Washington, D.C., school for the deaf, which became Gallaudet College, named after his father.

GALLAUDET, THOMAS (*b. Hartford, Conn., 1822; d. 1902*), teacher, Episcopal clergyman. Son of Thomas H. Gallaudet. Established church for the deaf in New York, 1852, the center of his tireless and widespread missionary work on their behalf.

GALLAUDET, THOMAS HOPKINS (*b. Philadelphia, Pa., 1787; d. 1851*), educator of the deaf. Graduated Yale, 1805. Studied instructional methods at the Institut Royal des Sourds-Muets, Paris, under Abbé Sicard, 1815; returned with the brilliant teacher Laurent Clerc. Together they raised money for the first free American school for the deaf, established at Hartford, Conn., 1817. As principal, 1817–30, Gallaudet trained men who established similar schools. He worked also for Negro education, public normal schools, manual training in public schools and higher education for women.

GALLIER, JAMES (*b. Ravensdale, Ireland, 1798; d. at sea, 1868*), architect. Came to New York, 1832; removed to New Orleans, 1834. With James H. Dakin, responsible for the introduction into New Orleans of buildings strongly influenced by Greek Revival.

[*Supp. 1*]

GALLINGER, JACOB HAROLD (*b. Cornwall, Canada, 1837; d. 1918*), physician. Practiced in Concord, N.H. Became power in Republican party, serving as New Hampshire legislator, as congressman, 1885–89, and as U.S. senator, 1891–1918. The embodiment of "stand-pattism," he was active in legislation to improve the District of Columbia.

GALLITZIN, DEMETRIUS AUGUSTINE (*b. The Hague, Netherlands, 1770; d. Loretto, Pa., 1840*), Roman Catholic clergyman. Son of a distinguished Russian diplomat, he was converted to Catholicism, 1787; coming to America, 1792, he entered St. Mary's Seminary, Baltimore, Md., and was ordained, 1795. Founded Catholic colony at Loretto, Pa., 1799, on frontier at the summit of the Alleghanies, persevering against poverty and local opposition. Receiving only a fraction of his expected patrimony from Europe, accepting no salary, and slow to collect land payments from his settlers, he ran into difficulties, although widely known and respected. A public appeal in 1827 brought aid from many sources, and Gallitzin endured every privation in order to pay back his creditors. His *Defence of Catholic Principles* (1816) went through many editions; in this as in his other works he was a model of tolerant controversy.

GALLOWAY, BEVERLY THOMAS (*b. Millersburg, Mo., 1863; d. Washington, D.C., 1938*), pioneer plant pathologist, agricultural research administrator. With U.S. Department of Agriculture, 1887–1933; chief, Bureau of Plant Industry, 1901–13. [*Supp. 2*]

GALLOWAY, CHARLES BETTS (*b. Kosciusko, Miss., 1849; d. Jackson, Miss., 1909*), Methodist Episcopal, South, clergyman. Pastor at Jackson and Vicksburg, Miss.; as bishop, *post* 1886, made extensive missionary tours in the Orient and South America; was a noted orator.

GALLOWAY, JOSEPH (*b. West River, Md., c. 1731; d. England, 1803*), colonial statesman, Loyalist. Rose early to eminence at Philadelphia bar; member of Pennsylvania Assembly, 1756–64, 1766–76. An able politician, he served interests of his own merchant class. As speaker of the Assembly, 1766–75, he attempted to restore harmony with England, believing that difficulties were basically constitutional and could be solved by provision of a written imperial constitution. Conscience, legalism and pride forbade his adherence to the American cause although he was a delegate to the First Continental Congress. Going over to the British, he was of great service to Gen. Howe. He went to England, 1778, where he became spokesman for the American Loyalists. His many tracts and pamphlets are important sources for the history of the Revolution.

GALLOWAY, SAMUEL (*b. Gettysburg, Pa., 1811; d. Columbus, O., 1872*), educator, lawyer, congressman. Reconstructed the entire Ohio school system, 1844–50, raising teaching standards, organizing teachers' institutes, inspiring educators and public to fresh vigor and interest.

GALLUP, JOSEPH ADAMS (*b. Stonington, Conn., 1769; d. Woodstock, Vt., 1849*), physician, teacher. Graduated Dartmouth Medical College, 1798. Established clinical school of medicine at Woodstock, Vt., with free infirmary to give students bedside instruction (1827), an innovation in medical teaching.

GALLY, MERRITT (*b. near Rochester, N.Y., 1838; d. Brooklyn, N.Y., 1916*), Presbyterian clergyman, inventor. Patented the "Universal" job-printing press, 1869; also a linotype machine, a system of multiplex telegraphy, a long-distance telephone repeater and devices for automatic musical instruments.

GÁLVEZ, BERNARDO de (*b. Macharaviaya, Spain, 1746; d. Mexico, 1786*), captain-general of Louisiana and the Floridas. Appointed governor of Louisiana, 1776, he strove to weaken the British by supplying arms to American frontier rebels and seizing British ships. When Spain entered the war, 1778, he reduced every British post in West Florida, enabling Spain to secure both Floridas at the peace settlement of 1783. In taking Pensacola (1781), he crossed the bar alone under the guns of the British fort in a small ship, the *Galveztown;* for this feat he was named Count de Gálvez and Viscount de Galveztown. He was also promoted to be captain-general of Cuba, and in 1785 was made viceroy of New Spain.

GAMBLE, HAMILTON ROWAN (*b. Winchester, Va., 1798; d. 1864*), lawyer, jurist. Removed to Missouri, 1818. Presiding judge at first Dred Scott suit, he dissented in Scott's favor. As provisional governor, Unionist, 1861–64, he labored to save Missouri for the Union.

GAMBRELL, JAMES BRUTON (*b. Anderson, S.C., 1841; d. Dallas, Tex., 1921*), Baptist clergyman, editor, educator. President, Mercer University, 1893–96; secretary, Baptist General Convention of Texas, 1896–1918.

GAMMON, ELIJAH HEDDING (*b. present Lexington, Maine, 1819; d. 1891*), Methodist clergyman, farm machinery manufacturer. Removed to Illinois, 1851. *Post* 1858, became a leader in promotion, manufacture and distribution of harvesters, acquiring rights to sale of the machine devised by Charles W. and William W. Marsh. He was later a partner of William Deering. Devoting much of his wealth to religious and educational purposes, he founded and endowed Gammon Theological Seminary at Atlanta, Ga.

GANNETT, EZRA STILES (*b. Cambridge, Mass., 1801; d. 1871*), Unitarian clergyman, editor. Assisted William E. Channing at Federal St. Church, Boston; succeeded him as pastor. Active in organizing American Unitarian Association, 1825; vigorously opposed the Transcendental movement.

GANNETT, HENRY (*b. Bath, Maine, 1846; d. 1914*), chief geographer, U.S. Geological Survey, 1882–1914. Graduated Lawrence Scientific School, Harvard, 1869. Topographer to Hayden Survey of Colorado and Wyoming; geographer to tenth, eleventh and twelfth U.S. censuses, and assisted in Philippine, Cuban and Porto Rican censuses. Helped establish U.S. Geographic Board, 1890, to eliminate confusion in place names and served as its chairman; aided in forming the National Geographic Society, the Geological Society of America, the Association of American Geographers. His work was characterized by zeal for exactitude; under him the maps of the Survey achieved their high perfection.

GANNETT, WILLIAM CHANNING (*b. Boston, Mass., 1840; d. 1923*), Unitarian clergyman, writer. Son of Ezra S. Gannett. Held pastorates in Illinois, Minnesota, and *post* 1889 at Rochester, N.Y. An extreme liberal.

GANO, JOHN (*b. Hopewell, N.J., 1727; d. 1804*), Baptist clergyman, Continental Army chaplain. Pastor at Morristown, N.J., and at New York City, 1762–88. Thereafter preached in Kentucky and North Carolina.

GANO, STEPHEN (*b. New York, N.Y., 1762; d. 1828*), Baptist clergyman. Son of John Gano. Pastor at Providence, R.I., 1793–1828. An energetic pastor of liberal views, he was also active in community and educational affairs.

GANSEVOORT, LEONARD (*b. Albany, N.Y., 1751; d. 1810*), New York legislator, judge. Brother of Peter Gansevoort. Treasurer, Albany Committee of Correspondence; member of New York Provincial Congresses; prominent to the end of his life in state politics.

GANSEVOORT, PETER (*b. Albany, N.Y., 1749; d. 1812*), Revolutionary soldier. Brother of Leonard Gansevoort. Received thanks of Congress for brave defense of Fort Schuyler against British under St. Leger, 1777.

GANSS, HENRY GEORGE (*b. Darmstadt, Germany, 1855; d. Lancaster, Pa., 1912*), Roman Catholic clergyman, composer. Came to America as an infant. Graduated St. Vincent's College, Latrobe, Pa., 1876, and was pastor in small Pennsylvania towns. His high character, scholarship and ecclesiastical music made him influential in the church and the musical world.

GANTT, HENRY LAURENCE (*b. Calvert Co., Md., 1861; d. 1919*), engineer, industrial leader. Graduated Johns Hopkins, 1880; Stevens Institute of Technology, 1884. Associated with Frederick W. Taylor in pioneer scientific management. Among his major contributions was a paper, "Training Workmen in Habits of Industry and Cooperation" (1908), in which he broke with Taylor's ideas; also *Work, Wages and Profits* (1913) and *Industrial Leadership* (1916). Gantt devised the "Gantt Chart," a widely used analytical presentation of the mechanism of management.

GARAKONTHIE, DANIEL (*b. c. 1600; d. Onondaga village (N.Y.), 1676*), Iroquois chief, councillor of the Onondaga and of the confederacy. Friendly to the French, he rescued many white captives from Indian torture and death.

GARCELON, ALONZO (*b. Lewiston, Maine, 1813; d. Medford, Mass., 1906*), physician, farmer, Union soldier, railroad president, editor. Democratic governor of Maine, 1879–80.

GARCÉS, FRANCISCO TOMÁS HERMENEGILDO (*b. Villa Morata del Conde, Aragon, 1738; d. junction of the Colorado and the Gila, 1781*), Spanish missionary-explorer. Assigned to San Xavier del Bac, 1768. Made four expeditions to points on Gila and Colorado Rivers, 1768–74; on the last, he accompanied de Anza to California, and joined him again on the exploration of 1775. He was killed by Indians while founding pueblo missions.

GARDEN, ALEXANDER (*b. Birse, Scotland, c. 1730; d. London, England, 1791*), physician, naturalist. Graduated Aberdeen, M.D., 1753. Emigrated soon after to Prince William Parish, S.C. Interested in fauna and flora of the region where he practiced, he exchanged notes and specimens with other naturalists; his voluminous correspondence with Linnaeus and John Ellis, the British naturalist, forms a precious scientific document. Ellis named the flower *Gardenia* after him. Garden was elected to the Royal Societies of Upsala and London. A Loyalist, he left America for England, 1783.

GARDEN, ALEXANDER (*b. Charleston, S.C., 1757; d. 1829*), Revolutionary soldier, planter. Son of Alexander Garden (c. 1730–1791). His *Anecdotes of the Revolutionary War* (1822) and *Anecdotes, etc., Second Series* (1828) are valuable and entertainingly written sources.

GARDENER, HELEN HAMILTON (*b. Winchester, Va., 1853; d. Washington, D.C., 1925*), author, suffragette, first woman member of U.S. Civil Service Commission.

GARDINER, SIR CHRISTOPHER (*fl. 1630–1632*), agent and spy of Sir Ferdinando Gorges. Preceded the Puritans in 1630 to Massachusetts Bay; arrested by them and imprisoned, he appeared as witness in Gorges's attempt to break the Massachusetts charter, 1632/33.

GARDINER, HARRY NORMAN (*b. Norwich, England, 1855; d. Northampton, Mass., 1927*), philosopher. Came to America, 1874. Graduated Amherst, 1878. Studied at Göttingen, Heidelberg, and Leipzig. Professor of philosophy at Smith, 1884–1924. Author of *Feeling and Emotion—A History of Theories* (1937). [*Supp. 1*]

GARDINER, JAMES TERRY (*b. Troy, N.Y., 1842; d. 1912*), engineer. Chief topographer, U.S. Geological Survey of 40th Parallel, 1866–73; pioneered (1880–86) in public health by establishing proper sewerage systems in New York State; was later a leader in the coal industry.

GARDINER, JOHN (*b. Boston, Mass., 1737; d. at sea, 1793*), lawyer. Son of Silvester Gardiner. Called to English bar, 1761; an ardent Whig, he was counsel for John Wilkes. After practicing for some years at St. Christopher, B.W.I., he returned to Boston, 1783, and settled in Maine. Representative for Pownalboro in the General Court, he was a zealous democrat and law reformer.

GARDINER, JOHN SYLVESTER JOHN (*b. Haverfordwest, England, 1765; d. Harrowgate, England, 1830*), Episcopal clergyman. Son of John Gardiner. Came to America, 1783. Minister at Trinity Church, Boston, Mass., 1792–1830; pastor, *post* 1805. Conducted a classical school; president, Anthology Club; a founder of Boston Athenaeum and author of *Remarks on the Jacobiniad* (1795).

GARDINER, LION (*b. England, 1599; d. Easthampton, N.Y., 1663*), colonist, military engineer. Sent to Connecticut to fortify and protect the new colony, he built Saybrook fort, 1636; was co-commander in Pequot War; became proprietor of Gardiner's Island.

GARDINER, ROBERT HALLOWELL (*b. Bristol, England, 1782; d. 1864*), agriculturist. Grandson and heir of Silvester Gardiner whose surname he assumed. Came to America, 1792. Developed model Maine farm; fostered agricultural societies; founded Gardiner (Maine) Lyceum, 1821, forerunner of American agricultural and technical schools.

GARDINER, SILVESTER (*b. South Kingston, R.I., 1708; d. Newport, R.I., 1786*), physician, Loyalist, landowner. Practiced in Boston. *Post* 1753, was chief promoter of Kennebec Company, developing a huge grant of land in Maine. Founder of Pittston and Gardiner, Maine.

GARDNER, CALEB (*b. Newport, R.I., 1739; d. 1806*), merchant, Revolutionary soldier. Celebrated for piloting French fleet into Newport, July 1780.

GARDNER, CHARLES KITCHEL (*b. Morris Co., N.J., 1787; d. 1869*), journalist. Author of a manual of infantry tactics and *A Dictionary of all Officers in the Army of the U.S.: 1789–1853* (1853).

GARDNER, GILSON (*b. Chicago, Ill., 1869; d. Washington, D.C., 1935*), journalist. [*Supp. 1*]

GARDNER, HENRY JOSEPH (*b. Dorchester, Mass., 1818; d. Milton, Mass., 1892*), dry-goods merchant. Prominent organizer in Know-Nothing party and its successful candidate for governor of Massachusetts, 1855–58.

GARDNER, ISABELLA STEWART (*b. New York, N.Y., 1840; d. Boston, Mass., 1924*), art collector, social leader. Married John Lowell Gardner, 1860. Witty, exuberant, clever, she dazzled and often shocked Boston society. Began buying works of art, 1867; was influenced by Charles E. Norton and Edward S. Morse, and aided by Bernard Berenson. To house and display her superb collections, she built Fenway Court, 1899–1903, an Italianate structure known as "Mrs. Jack Gardner's Palace." Here she continued her lifelong entertainment of artists, musicians and visiting celebrities, and on her death left it "for the education and enjoyment of the public forever."

GARDNER, JOHN LANE (*b. Boston, Mass., 1793; d. Wilmington, Del., 1869*), soldier. Served in War of 1812, Florida War; commanded a regiment in Mexico and was twice brevetted. Superseded as commander at Fort Moultrie, 1861, he retired as colonel.

GAREY, THOMAS ANDREW (*b. Cincinnati, O., 1830; d. 1909*), horticulturist. Outstanding in development of citrus industry in southern California, *post* 1865; introduced and promoted fruit varieties, including the Eureka lemon.

GARFIELD, JAMES ABRAM (*b. Cuyahoga Co., O., 1831; d. Elberon, N.J., 1881*), teacher, Union soldier, president of the United States. Attended Western Reserve Eclectic Institute, Hiram, O.; graduated Williams, 1856. Elected to Ohio Senate, 1859, he became known as an effective speaker and an anti-slavery man. Helped raise 42nd Ohio Volunteer Infantry, 1861; commanded it so ably that he was given a brigade by Gen. Buell and justified the choice by winning a victory at Middle Creek, Ky., 1862. Served as chief of staff in the Army of the Cumberland, 1863; was much praised for his conduct at Chickamauga and made a major-general.

Elected by a heavy Republican majority from the 19th Ohio district, he entered the House of Representatives, 1863, and sat in Congress until November 1880. He took an important place on the Military Affairs Committee and later served on the Appropriations and Ways and Means Committees, training himself in public finance and opposing "greenback" and excessive tariff legislation. Touched by the Crédit Mobilier and DeGolyer paving contract scandals, he yet managed to win re-election to Congress. When James G. Blaine entered the Senate, 1876, Garfield became House minority leader. He had been an active agent in the election of R. B. Hayes who asked him to postpone his own senatorial ambitions and continue as Republican leader in the lower chamber. Elected to the U.S. senate in 1880, he never took his seat. As head of Ohio delegation to the 1880 Republican convention and manager for John Sherman, who sought the presidential nomination, he blocked the path of the "Stalwarts," pressing for a third term for Grant, and also Blaine's supporters. A deadlock ensued. On the 35th ballot, Wisconsin votes were shifted to Garfield, and his nomination became unanimous in a stampede. Not until September, however, did Grant's partisans decide to recognize the candidate. Blaine bore no malice nor did Sherman at that time. Garfield and his vice-presidential running-mate, Chester A. Arthur, carried the country, 214 electoral votes to 155.

Garfield attempted to build a conciliation cabinet with Blaine as secretary of state; however, his recognition of the "Stalwarts" was less than they desired, and a bitter wrangle ensued over patronage. Garfield stood firm in his determination to maintain the independence of the president in matters of appointment, and the "star route" scandal in the Post Office discredited his opponents.

Before his administration could proceed much further, he was shot on July 2, 1881, by a disappointed office seeker, Charles J. Guiteau.

GARLAND, AUGUSTUS HILL (*b. Tipton Co., Tenn., 1832; d. Washington, D.C., 1899*), lawyer, Confederate congressman and senator. Governor of Arkansas, Democrat, 1874–77; U.S. senator, 1877–85; attorney-general under Cleveland, 1885–89. Worked industriously for tariff and civil service reform.

GARLAND, HAMLIN (*b. near West Salem, Wis., 1860; d. Los Angeles, Calif., 1940*), novelist. Raised on small farms, first in Wisconsin, then in Iowa, where he early experienced the dehumanizing drudgery of farm life that he later depicted in his novels. His family moved to Dakota Territory in 1881, but Garland came East, settling in Boston in 1884. Association with W. D. Howells, and a trip back to Iowa and Dakota, encouraged Garland to write some short stories of middle-western farm life. A collection appeared as *Main-Travelled Roads* (1891). Hailed by Howells as an advance in American realism, the book was not widely read, nor were three novels indicting social injustices, published in 1892. In 1893 Garland moved to Chicago, where he remained until his removal to New York in 1916. The lack of success of *Crumbling Idols* (1894), a collection of critical essays, and *Rose of Dutcher's Coolly* (1895), a farm novel, led Garland to write a series of Indian-country romances, stereotyped in character and arbitrarily motivated. Finally in 1913 he resumed work on an autobiographical account of his youth. Serialized in *Collier's Weekly* and published as *A Son of the Middle Border* (1917), it was recognized as a major contribution to America's knowledge of her recent history. *A Daughter of the Middle Border* (1921), a Pulitzer Prize winner, and two other sequels, were equally successful. In *A Son of the Middle Border* and *Main-Travelled Roads,* Garland achieves his place as a realistic recorder of a particular aspect of his time and of its spirit. [*Supp. 2*]

GARLAND, LANDON CABELL (*b. Nelson Co., Va., 1810; d. Nashville, Tenn., 1895*), educator. President, Randolph-Macon College, 1836–46, and of University of Alabama, 1855–65. Chancellor, Vanderbilt University, 1875–93, which incorporated his plan for a theological seminary for the Methodist Episcopal Church, South.

GARLICK, THEODATUS (*b. Middlebury, Vt., 1805; d. 1884*), plastic surgeon, sculptor, pioneer in pisciculture. Practiced in Ohio, *post* 1834. Invented orthopedic procedures, fashioned surgical instruments, made anatomical models, medallions, busts. Experimented with artificial breeding of trout.

GARMAN, CHARLES EDWARD (*b. Limington, Maine, 1850; d. 1907*), educator. Graduated Amherst, 1872. Taught philosophy there, 1881–1907.

GARMAN, SAMUEL (*b. Indiana Co., Pa., 1843; d. 1927*), zoologist. Pupil of Agassiz; curator of fishes, Harvard Museum of Comparative Zoology; a foremost authority on sharks, skates and rays.

GARNER, JAMES WILFORD (*b. Pike Co., Miss., 1871; d. 1938*), political scientist, expert on international law. Ph. D., Columbia, 1902. Taught at University of Illinois, 1904–38. [*Supp. 2*]

GARNET, HENRY HIGHLAND (*b. New Market, Md., 1815; d. Liberia, 1882*), Presbyterian clergyman. Born a slave, he was educated at Oneida Institute. Became a noted anti-slavery speaker and the leading Negro Abolitionist before the rise of Frederick Douglass.

GARNETT, ALEXANDER YELVERTON PEYTON (*b. Essex Co., Va., 1819; d. Rehoboth Beach, Del., 1888*), physician. M.D., University of Pennsylvania, 1841. Prominent Confederate medical officer and personal physician to Jefferson Davis. Later greatly esteemed in Washington, D.C., he worked fearlessly to improve standards of medical ethics.

GARNETT, JAMES MERCER (*b. Essex Co., Va., 1770; d. Essex Co., 1843*), agriculturist, educator. Congressman, Democrat, from Virginia, 1805–09; partisan of John Randolph. Wrote many articles on agricultural reform; advocated seed selection, fertilizers, crop rotation. Conducted girls' and boys' schools, urged a state school system.

GARNETT, JAMES MERCER (*b. Aldie, Va., 1840; d. 1916*), philologist, Confederate soldier. Grandson of James M. Garnett (1770–1843). A painstaking and erudite scholar, he was acclaimed for the first American translation of *Beowulf* (1882) and other translations from Anglo-Saxon.

GARNETT, MUSCOE RUSSELL HUNTER (*b. Essex Co., Va., 1821; d. Essex Co., 1864*), lawyer, statesman. Grandson of James M. Garnett (1770–1843). Strict constructionist and defender of slavery; congressman from Virginia, 1856–61, and member of Confederate Congress.

GARNETT, ROBERT SELDEN (*b. Essex Co., Va., 1819; d. Carrick's Ford, Va., 1861*), soldier. Nephew of James M. Garnett (1770–1843). Graduated West Point, 1841. Fought with distinction through Mexican War; commanded Puget Sound and Yakima expeditions, 1855–58. Commanded Confederate forces in northwestern Virginia, 1861; was killed in action.

GARRARD, JAMES (*b. Stafford Co., Va., 1749; d. Mt. Lebanon, Bourbon Co., Ky., 1822*), Baptist clergyman, politician. Removed to Kentucky, 1783; was minister at church at Cooper's Run; helped organize other Baptist congregations. Represented Fayette and Bourbon Counties in conventions to achieve Kentucky statehood; served as (Democrat) Republican governor, 1796–1804, but did not distinguish himself in office.

GARRARD, KENNER (*b. Kentucky, 1828; d. Cincinnati, O., 1879*), Union soldier. Graduated West Point, 1851. After distinguished service in all theaters of the Civil War, resigned as major-general, 1866.

GARREAU, ARMAND (*b. Cognac, France, 1817; d. New Orleans, La., 1865*), French novelist, journalist. Resident in New Orleans, *c*. 1839–49, *c*. 1858–65. Contributed extensively to New Orleans and French newspapers, wrote several romantic-historical novels, including *Louisiana* (1849).

GARRETSON, AUSTIN BRUCE (*b. Winterset, Iowa, 1856; d. Cedar Rapids, Iowa, 1931*), labor leader. Officer in railway engineers' union; helped bring about the eight-hour day on railroads. [*Supp. 1*]

GARRETSON, JAMES EDMUND (*b. Wilmington, Del., 1828; d. Lansdowne, Pa., 1895*), dentist. M.D., University of Pennsylvania, 1859. Professor and dean, Philadelphia Dental College. Originator of oral surgery as a specialty; author of *A System of Oral Surgery* (1873, and many later editions) and other works.

GARRETT, EDMUND HENRY (*b. Albany, N.Y., 1853; d. Needham, Mass., 1929*), painter, illustrator, etcher.

GARRETT, JOHN WORK (*b. Baltimore, Md., 1820; d. 1884*), railroad executive, banker. Son of Robert Garrett. President, Baltimore and Ohio Railroad, 1858–84; freed the road of political control and gave it efficient management. In the Civil War, the railroad was a main objective of Southern attack and only Garrett's extraordinary skill and energy prevented its abandonment. The first rail movement of troops in history, the transfer of 20,000 men from the Potomac to Chattanooga, 1863, was a triumph for Garrett. After the war, he secured direct routes to Pittsburgh and Chicago and a line to New York.

GARRETT, ROBERT (*b. Lisburn, Ireland, 1783; d. 1857*), merchant, financier. Came to America as a child; settled in Baltimore, Md., 1800. Alert to that city's business possibilities and energetic in civic enterprises, Garrett established faster transportation to capture Western trade, developed own banking house for foreign commerce.

GARRETT, THOMAS (*b. Upper Darby, Pa., 1789; d. Wilmington, Del., 1871*), merchant, Abolitionist. Fearless and resourceful, he helped about 2700 slaves to escape north.

GARRETT, WILLIAM ROBERTSON (*b. Williamsburg, Va., 1839; d. 1904*), Confederate soldier, educator, historian. Graduated William and Mary, 1858. Held numerous educational posts, including Tennessee superintendency of education; dean, Peabody College for Teachers, 1899–1904. Was especially interested in state teachers' institutes and associations.

GARRETTSON, FREEBORN (*b. Maryland, 1752; d. 1827*), itinerant Methodist minister. Admired by John Wesley and Asbury, he traveled for more than fifty years *post* 1776; his outstanding work was in extension of Methodism in New York State.

GARRIGAN, PHILIP JOSEPH (*b. Cavan, Ireland, 1840; d. 1919*), Roman Catholic clergyman. Came to America as a child. Vice-rector, Catholic University; first bishop of Sioux City, Iowa, 1902–19.

GARRISON, CORNELIUS KINGSLAND (*b. Fort Montgomery, N.Y., 1809; d. New York, N.Y., 1885*), financier. Steamship magnate, banker, he carried on financial operations of great variety and magnitude. Accomplished remarkable reforms as mayor of San Francisco, 1853–57.

GARRISON, FIELDING HUDSON (*b. Washington, D.C., 1870; d. Baltimore, Md., 1935*), medical historian, bibliographer. Collaborated on *Index* of surgeon general's library. Author of *An Introduction to the History of Medicine* (1913). [*Supp. 1*]

GARRISON, LINDLEY MILLER (*b. Camden, N.J., 1864; d. Seabright, N.J., 1932*), lawyer. Graduated University of Pennsylvania, 1885; admitted to the bar, 1886. Practiced in Camden and Jersey City, N.J., 1904–12. U.S. secretary of war, 1913–16. After outbreak of World War I Garrison stressed the need for a large regular army. President Wilson, who seemed to agree, refused to condemn the Hay Bill, which repudiated Garrison's plan, and Garrison resigned. Garrison's clash with Wilson focused public attention on the unpreparedness of the country and contributed to the National Defense Act of 1916. [*Supp. 1*]

GARRISON, WILLIAM LLOYD (*b. Newburyport, Mass., 1805; d. New York, N.Y., 1879*), reformer, dominant figure in fight against Negro slavery. A printer and editor by trade, Garrison met Benjamin Lundy *c*. 1828, and was moved by him to devote himself to the Abolition movement. Was one of earliest Abolitionists to demand "immediate and complete emancipation"; denounced slavery and slave-owners harshly and violently in platform speeches and in the weekly *Genius of Universal Emancipation*. Founded *The Liberator*, 1831, in which for thirty-five years he employed his one weapon of denunciation against the slave power. Its opening manifesto contained the famous words: "I am in earnest—I will not equivocate—I will not excuse—I will not retreat a single inch—and *I will be heard.*" A founder of the American Anti-Slavery Society, 1833, pacifist and non-resistant by conviction, he braved persecution and threat of bodily harm without fear. His gift for antagonizing extended even to his friends and supporters; to conservatives and the orthodox clergy he was a thorn in the flesh. On July 4, 1854, he publicly burned a copy of the Constitution, exclaiming, "So perish all compromises with tyranny." When the Civil War concluded the Abolitionist crusade, Garrison gave his full attention to other reforms in which he had been interested, notably woman suffrage, prohibition and the improvement of the American Indian. An extremist in all things, he inspired more than he led and is remembered more for his courage and tenacity than for his ideas.

GARRISON, WILLIAM RE TALLACK (*b. Goderich, Canada, 1834; d. Long Branch, N.J., 1882*), financier. Son of Cornelius K. Garrison. Identified with marine and rail transportation interests, he achieved complete unification of New York City elevated railways in Manhattan Railway Co., 1879.

GARRY, SPOKANE (*b. present Spokane Co., Wash., 1811; d. 1892*), Indian missionary, teacher, peace advocate. Leader among Columbia River basin tribes, he promoted peaceful white settlement; later tried to protect his people against white aggression.

GARTRELL, LUCIUS JEREMIAH (*b. Wilkes Co., Ga., 1821; d. 1891*), lawyer, Confederate brigadier-general, politician. As legislator, and as congressman, Democrat, from Georgia, 1857–61, he championed ultra-Southern views and was an advocate of secession. After the war he became noted as a criminal lawyer.

GARVEY, MARCUS MOZIAH (*b. St. Ann's Bay, Jamaica, B.W.I., 1887; d. London, England, 1940*), Negro leader. Came to America, 1916. Chauvinistic, demagogic organizer of the Universal Negro Improvement Association, which flourished in the U.S., 1917–22. [*Supp. 2*]

GARVIN, LUCIUS FAYETTE CLARK (*b. Knoxville, Tenn., 1841; d. Lonsdale, R.I., 1922*), physician. Graduated Amherst, 1862; M.D., Harvard Medical School, 1867. Advocate of Henry George's Single Tax theory, he served for many years in the Rhode Island legislature, and as Democratic governor of that state, 1903–05.

GARY, ELBERT HENRY (*b. near Wheaton, Ill., 1846; d. 1927*), corporation lawyer, financier. Built up a wide practice in Illinois; removed to New York City, 1898, as president of Federal Steel Co. J. P. Morgan entrusted him with major role in organization of U. S. Steel Corp., and Gary dominated its policies until his death; he was chairman of the board, 1903–27. He followed a conservative but fair policy, keeping within the anti-trust laws, paying fair wages and striving for social amelioration, though he insisted upon the open shop. He was much criticized for his unwillingness to negotiate with organized labor which led to the strike of 1919, yet it was said in his defense that he had early introduced schemes for pensions and purchase of stock by employees. Gary, Ind., was named for him.

GARY, JAMES ALBERT (*b. Uncasville, Conn., 1833; d. Baltimore, Md., 1920*), cotton manufacturer, banker, Republican politician. U.S. postmaster general, 1897–98.

GARY, MARTIN WITHERSPOON (*b. Cokesbury, S.C., 1831; d. 1881*), lawyer, Confederate brigadier-general, planter. *Post* 1876, a South Carolina legislator; favored the "straightout policy."

GASKILL, HARVEY FREEMAN (*b. Royalton, N.Y., 1845; d. 1889*), inventor, engineer. Met need for higher steam economy and larger pumping capacity by inventing first crank and fly-wheel high duty pumping engine for waterworks, 1882.

GASS, PATRICK (*b. Falling Springs, Pa., 1771; d. 1870*), soldier, explorer. Author of *Journal of the Voyages and Travels of a Corps of Discovery, etc.* (Pittsburgh, 1807, and many later editions), the first published account by a member of the Lewis and Clark expedition.

GASSON, THOMAS IGNATIUS (*b. Sevenoaks, England, 1859; d. Montreal, Canada, 1930*), Jesuit priest, educator. Came to America, 1872; became a Catholic, 1874; ordained, 1891. As president, 1907–14, moved and rebuilt Boston College. Reorganized Georgetown University graduate school; helped develop Loyola College, Montreal.

GASTON, JAMES McFADDEN (*b. near Chester, S.C., 1824; d. Atlanta, Ga., 1903*), surgeon. Served in Confederate hospitals; lived and practiced in Brazil, 1865–83. Returning to Atlanta, Ga., he taught very successfully at Southern Medical College.

GASTON, WILLIAM (*b. New Bern, N.C., 1778; d. Raleigh, N.C., 1844*), jurist. Attended Georgetown; graduated College of New Jersey (Princeton), 1796; studied law with F. X. Martin. Served as Federalist legislator; as congressman, North Carolina, 1813–17, his speeches in support of the Bank of the U.S. and in opposition to the Loan Bill won him national reputation. Popular opposition in North Carolina to the state supreme court was overcome in 1833 by electing Gaston chief justice, although as a Catholic he was supposedly barred by the 32nd article of the state constitution. Later he labored in constitutional convention to have all religious restrictions on office-holding removed. Gaston's opinions displayed profound learning, clarity, vigor and a broad humanitarian spirit. He sought to mitigate the harshness of the slave code and delivered two masterful opinions on the subject.

GASTON, WILLIAM (*b. Killingly, Conn., 1820; d. Boston, Mass., 1894*), lawyer. Graduated Brown, 1840. Served in Massachusetts legislature; was Democratic mayor of Boston, 1871–72; governor of Massachusetts, 1875–76.

GATES, FREDERICK TAYLOR (*b. Maine, N. Y., 1853; d. Phoenix, Ariz., 1929*), Baptist clergyman, business executive. Graduated University of Rochester, 1877; Rochester Th. Seminary, 1880. As secretary of Baptist Education Society, he arranged conference of leading Baptist educators and laymen to formulate plan for reconstituted University of Chicago which won support of the elder John D. Rockefeller. In 1893 Gates became Rockefeller's business associate and a guiding force in many enterprises, notably in developing iron-ore projects in Minnesota. Gates's greatest achievement lay in education and philanthropy. He was president of the General Education Board, first of the Rockefeller foundations, and he conceived the idea of the Rockefeller Institute for Medical Research. Analyzing appeals for aid flowing in to Rockefeller's office, Gates developed the principles and policies which led to establishment of the Rockefeller Foundation.

GATES, GEORGE AUGUSTUS (*b. Topsham, Vt., 1851; d. 1912*), minister, educator. Graduated Dartmouth, 1873; Andover Seminary, 1880. President of Iowa (now Grinnell) College, 1887–1900; of Pomona College, 1901–08; of Fisk University, 1909–12.

GATES, HORATIO (*b. Maldon, England, c. 1728/29; d. New York, N.Y., 1806*), Revolutionary soldier. Godson of Horace Walpole. Entered the British army at an early age, served in Nova Scotia, 1749–50; in Virginia, 1755; was wounded in Braddock's defeat before Fort Duquesne. Served under Monckton in the conquest of Martinique, 1761. After retirement in England *post* 1764, was advised by George Washington about land in Virginia, and in 1772 moved to a plantation in Berkeley Co.

Gates was drawn to the patriot cause by his personal revolt against the English caste system. Commissioned brigadier-general in the Continental Army, in July 1775 he was at Cambridge, Mass., as adjutant-general, organizing the miscellaneous units besieging Boston, showing himself a capable administrator, a loyal and indefatigable supporter of Washington. Commissioned major-general in May 1776, he went to command the troops of the broken invasion of Canada who were retreating to Crown Point and Ticonderoga. Here a conflict arose with Gen. Philip Schuyler over command of the northern department which was not settled until Gates relieved Schuyler, August 1777, in time to oppose Burgoyne's expedition. Gates and Benedict Arnold, the dramatic figure of the fighting at Freeman's Farm and Bemis Heights, quarreled over what Arnold regarded as Gates's lack of initiative and failure to appreciate Arnold's services in the victory of Saratoga. Criticism of Gates for not notifying Congress and Washington more promptly of the victory was owing to his dilatory messenger and adjutant, James Wilkinson, who was also responsible for a worsening of relations between Gates and Washington in the affair of Gen. Thomas Conway's letter of October 11, 1777. According to Wilkinson, with whom Gates subsequently fought a duel, Gates publicized in his headquarters a letter from Conway criticizing Washington and complaining of the mismanagement of the war. Gates's undignified insistence, first that the letter had been stolen,

then that it was a forgery, disgusted Washington; Gates's friends in Congress, who were engaged in a scheme to have him supersede Washington, dropped the matter.

Gates commanded the northern and eastern departments, 1778–79. Called in June 1780 to command the southern department, then in straits because of the surrender of Lincoln at Charleston, he raised troops and opposed Cornwallis at Camden, S.C. In a disastrous defeat on August 16, he tried vainly to rally the fleeing militia who made up more than half his army. Gates was relieved by Nathanael Greene. Congress voted an inquiry into Gates's conduct, but charges were never pressed. Congress repealed its resolve, 1782, ordering Gates to take such command as Washington should direct.

In 1783 he returned home to Virginia and remained there until 1790 when, old doubts about social inequality again besetting him, he emancipated his slaves and moved to an estate on the then outskirts of New York City. Unpopular with many of the best officers in the army, his character was contradictory. At times vigorous and able, at other times he seems to have been wavering and indecisive.

GATES, JOHN WARNE (*b. near Turner Junction, Ill., 1855; d. Paris, France, 1911*), promoter, speculator. Known as "Bet-you-a-million" Gates. Starting with the manufacture and promotion of barbed wire, he formed through a series of consolidations the American Steel and Wire Co., 1898; became head of the U.S. wire industry. Restless, imaginative and more interested in floating companies than running them, he was a daring speculator, feared on the Stock Exchange. A manipulation of the Louisville & Nashville Railroad, which he secretly acquired and resold at a fancy price to J. P. Morgan, ended in his virtual ostracism from New York finance. Thereafter, he removed to Port Arthur, Texas, organized the Texas Company and controlled the town's industries.

GATES, Sir THOMAS (*b. Colyford, England; d. Netherlands, 1621*), soldier, governor of Virginia. An investor in the Virginia Company, Gates sailed in June 1609 with a fleet of settlers for Virginia. His ship, separated from the others in a storm, landed in the Bermudas. He reached Virginia at last in May 1610, to find the colonists in deplorable condition but was prevented from taking them back to England by the arrival of Lord De La Warr, who took over the government from Gates. Returning to England, Gates worked to gain support and settlers for the colony. With a large company he reached Jamestown again in August 1611, resumed the government in a discouraging time, and laid the foundations for the colony's prosperity before his final departure in the spring of 1614.

GATLING, RICHARD JORDAN (*b. Hertford Co., N.C., 1818; d. 1903*), inventor. Devised and manufactured farm tools. The Gatling gun, a repeating weapon which he patented in 1862, made him world famous.

GATSCHET, ALBERT SAMUEL (*b. Saint Beatenberg, Switzerland, 1832; d. 1907*), linguist, ethnologist. European trained, he came to America, 1868; worked as ethnologist in U.S. Geological Survey and Bureau of Ethnology, *post* 1877, on classification of Indian tribes by linguistic families. Author, among other books, of *The Klamath Indians* (1890).

GATTI-CASAZZA, GIULIO (*b. Udine, Italy, 1869; d. Ferrara, Italy, 1940*), general manager of La Scala opera, Milan, 1898–1908; of the Metropolitan Opera, New York, 1908–35. [*Supp. 2*]

GAUL, WILLIAM GILBERT (*b. Jersey City, N.J., 1855; d. New York, N.Y., 1919*), painter, illustrator. Ablest American military painter; notable for vivid, accurate Civil War scenes, and for studies of Indians and cowboys.

GAUT, JOHN McREYNOLDS (*b. Cleveland, Tenn., 1841; d. 1918*), lawyer. Practiced in Nashville, Tenn. Was authority on law in its relations to church organizations and property; became general counsel to the Presbyterian Church in the United States, 1906.

GAVIN, FRANK STANTON BURNS (*b. Cincinnati, O., 1890; d. New York, N.Y., 1938*), Episcopal clergyman, historian. An Anglo-Catholic, and active in ecumenical movements. Professor at General Theological Seminary, New York, *post* 1923. [*Supp. 2*]

GAY, EBENEZER (*b. Dedham, Mass., 1696; d. Hingham, Mass., 1787*), Congregational clergyman. Pastor at Hingham, 1718–87. A precursor of the Unitarian movement in New England.

GAY, FREDERICK PARKER (*b. Boston, Mass., 1874; d. New Hartford, Conn., 1939*), bacteriologist. Graduated Harvard, 1897; M.D., Johns Hopkins, 1901. Studied also at University of Pennsylvania and Pasteur Institute, Brussels. Professor of pathology, University of California at Berkeley, 1910–23, where he developed bacteriology and immunology as separate disciplines; *post* 1923, professor of bacteriology at Columbia University. Gay's early investigations dealt with the serological phenomena accompanying infection and immunity. Later studies included the phenomenon of anaphylaxis, typhoid fever, the pathogenesis and chemotherapy of hemolytic streptococcus infections, tissue immunity, and virus infections. [*Supp. 2*]

GAY, SYDNEY HOWARD (*b. Hingham, Mass., 1814; d. 1888*), journalist. Great-grandson of Ebenezer Gay. Editor, *American Anti-Slavery Standard*, 1843–57; managing editor, *New York Tribune*, through Civil War, and of *Chicago Tribune*, 1867–71. Author of W. C. Bryant's *History of the United States*.

GAY, WINCKWORTH ALLAN (*b. West Hingham, Mass., 1821; d. West Hingham, 1910*), landscape painter. Brother of Sidney H. Gay. Studied with R. W. Weir, and in Paris with Constant Troyon. Among the first Americans to work in the then new "naturalist" style of landscape painting as practiced by his master and other contemporaries.

GAYARRÉ, CHARLES ÉTIENNE ARTHUR (*b. New Orleans, La., 1805; d. 1895*), lawyer, legislator, historian. Author of *Histoire de la Louisiane* (1846–47), largely a series of documentary extracts. His accurate and readable history of Louisiana in English appeared in four volumes issued in 1848, 1852, 1854 and 1866.

GAYLE, JOHN (*b. Sumter District, S.C., 1792; d. 1859*), lawyer. Democratic governor of Alabama, 1831–35. Under his leadership, the state rejected nullification, upheld the Union. Turning Whig, Gayle served in Congress, 1847–49, and thereafter was a federal district judge.

GAYLER, CHARLES (*b. New York, N.Y., 1820; d. Brooklyn, N.Y., 1892*), playwright. Wrote some 200 tragedies, comedies, melodramas, operettas, exploiting topical material.

GAYLEY, JAMES (*b. Lock Haven, Pa., 1855; d. New York, N.Y., 1920*), engineer, metallurgist, inventor. Graduated Lafayette, 1876. Manager, Edgar Thomson Steel Works; became managing director of Carnegie Steel, 1897. Called "father of American blast furnace practice," he instituted economies of fuel consumption; invented and introduced new appliances, such as the bronze cooling-plate for furnace walls, a casting apparatus for use with the Bessemer converter and, most important, the dry air blast (perfected 1894–1911).

GAYLORD, WILLIS (*b. Bristol, Conn., 1792; d. Camillus, N.Y., 1844*), agricultural writer. Editor, *Genesee Farmer* and *Cultivator;* did much to advance New York State agriculture. With Luther Tucker, wrote *American Husbandry* (1840).

GAYNOR, WILLIAM JAY (*b. near Oriskany, N.Y., 1849; d. on shipboard, 1913*), jurist, mayor of New York City, 1909–13. Noted for reforms in local politics and severe dealing from the bench.

GAYOSO DE LEMOS, MANUEL (*b. Spain, c. 1752; d. Louisiana, 1799*). Appointed governor of Natchez District, 1787, he served 1789–97. Endeavored to separate the West from the United States with the aid of James Wilkinson and Kentucky dissidents; acted vigorously in defense of Spanish rights. As governor of Louisiana, 1797–99, excluded Americans, encouraged commerce, prepared for invasion by the United States.

GEAR, JOHN HENRY (*b. Ithaca, N.Y., 1825; d. 1900*), businessman. Removed to Iowa as a boy. After service in legislature, was Republican governor of

Iowa, 1878–82; congressman, 1887–91, 1893–95; U.S. senator, 1895–1900.

GEARY, JOHN WHITE (*b. near Mount Pleasant, Pa., 1819; d. 1873*), engineer, soldier. Active militia officer; led assault on Chapultepec in Mexican War. Chosen to establish postal service in California, Geary arrived in San Francisco, 1849; superseded by a Whig postmaster, he was elected "first *alcalde*," and in 1850, first mayor. He was active in making California a free state and was chairman of the Democratic Territorial Committee but he returned to Pennsylvania in 1852. Declining the governorship of Utah, he accepted that of Kansas Territory, where he found virtual civil war on his arrival in September 1856. He disbanded the pro-slavery militia, organized his own and within three weeks could report "Peace now reigns in Kansas." The enmity of the pro-slavery group (an overwhelming majority in the legislature) and the refusal of Gen. Persifor Smith to supply more troops so discouraged him, however, that he resigned in March 1857. On the outbreak of the Civil War, Geary became colonel of the 28th Pennsylvania, fought with distinction in many campaigns and was brevetted major-general. Becoming a Republican, he served as governor of Pennsylvania, 1867–73, battling often with the legislature, striving to reduce the state debt and safeguard the treasury. He advocated a general insurance law, state control of gas companies, safeguards for public health. He also urged that taxes be shifted from business to land to encourage business growth.

GEDDES, JAMES (*b. near Carlisle, Pa., 1763; d. 1838*), civil engineer. An early producer of salt in Syracuse, N.Y., region. His 1809 report of a survey to the N.Y. legislature established the route adopted later for Erie Canal, of which he was one of the engineers, 1816–22.

GEDDES, JAMES LORAINE (*b. Edinburgh, Scotland, 1827; d. 1887*), soldier, college administrator. Raised in Canada. Distinguished in British service and as Union brigadier-general. Officer at Iowa State College, *post* 1870.

GEERS, EDWARD FRANKLIN (*b. Wilson Co., Tenn., 1851; d. Wheeling, W. Va., 1924*), turfman. World's leading racing driver of his period.

GELLATLY, JOHN (*b. New York, N.Y., 1853; d. New York, 1931*), businessman, art collector.

[*Supp. 1*]

GEMÜNDER, AUGUST MARTIN LUDWIG (*b. Ingelfingen, Germany, 1814; d. New York, N.Y., 1895*), and his brother George (*b. 1816; d. 1899*), emigrated to America, 1846, and were pioneer makers in the United States of the finest violins; they had no contemporary superiors. *Post* 1852, they worked in New York City.

GENET, EDMOND CHARLES (*b. France, 1763; d. 1834*), diplomat. A precocious scholar and fashionably liberal in his ideas, Genet succeeded his father in 1781 as *premier commis* of the bureau of interpretation, department of foreign affairs at Versailles. By the time he was 25, he had made the rounds of the most important courts in Europe. After he was expelled as chargé d'affaires at St. Petersburg, 1792, the Girondist ministry of France appointed him minister plenipotentiary to the United States, where he hoped to press French rights to fit out privateers under the treaties of 1778, a matter of current concern to Washington and his advisers. Arriving at Charleston, S.C., April 1793, he journeyed to Philadelphia, Pa. where he was first made welcome by Jefferson and other French sympathizers. His efforts soon made him a storm center of politics. He worked in South Carolina with dissatisfied local politicians; sent André Michaux to Kentucky to encourage an expedition down the Mississippi to take Louisiana from Spain; planned to send the French fleet to recapture St. Pierre and Miquelon and so provoke a rebellion in Canada. These energetic enterprises proved abortive. He had, however, stimulated the formation of local Jacobin clubs which soon spread and contributed to the growth of the Democratic-Republican party. Recalled home at request of U.S. government, he remained in this country, becoming a citizen. He settled on Long Island, N.Y., 1794; *c.* 1800, he moved to a farm in Rensselaer Co., N.Y.

GENIN, JOHN NICHOLAS (*b. New York, N.Y., 1819; d. 1878*), hatter, merchant. A pioneer in the use of novel advertising methods, he built up a large clothing business, starting with a hat shop adjoining Barnum's museum in New York City.

GENTH, FREDERICK AUGUSTUS (*b. Wächtersbach, Germany, 1820; d. 1893*), analytical chemist. Studied at Heidelberg, Giessen and Marburg. Came to America, 1848. At his Philadelphia laboratory, 1850–70, he devoted himself to research, commercial analysis and the instruction of special students; was professor of chemistry, University of Pennsylvania, 1872–88. Peerless in accuracy and industry, expert in minerals, Genth discovered 23 new mineral species, and published 102 investigations—over 70 on mineral topics. Another group of studies on fertilizers arose from his work with the Pennsylvania Board of Agriculture. His most important work was a study of ammonia-cobalt bases. It was begun in 1847; a preliminary paper was published, 1851; subsequently it was developed jointly with Wolcott Gibbs and issued as a Smithsonian monograph, 1856.

GENUNG, JOHN FRANKLIN (*b. Willseyville, N.Y., 1850; d. 1919*), Baptist clergyman. Graduated Union, 1870; Ph.D., Leipzig. Beloved teacher of rhetoric at Amherst College, 1882–1917; published Biblical and literary studies, and *Working Principles of Rhetoric* (1901).

GEORGE, HENRY (*b. Philadelphia, Pa., 1839; d. New York, N.Y., 1897*), journalist, economist, reformer. After brief schooling, George began work at fourteen but read widely, particularly in poetry. Shipped out to Australia and India, 1855–56. Learned to set type. Sailed to San Francisco, Calif., 1857–58; worked as compositor, storekeeper, prospector. Penniless and jobless, he married Annie Fox, 1861. The desperate years which followed gave him a burning personal knowledge of poverty which was reflected in all he afterward did and wrote. Starting as printer on the San Francisco *Times*, 1866, he rose to managing editor, 1868.

In that same year he visited New York City, where he was struck with the "shocking contrast between monstrous wealth and debasing want." Why did progress have its twin in poverty? Returning to California, he became editor of the Oakland *Transcript*, 1869. He believed he had found the answer to his question in the monopolization of land and natural resources, and published a pamphlet, *Our Land and Land Policy* (1871), which contained the essentials of the philosophy he afterwards expanded. It was several years before George could continue writing, but in 1877 he started *Progress and Poverty*, the definitive statement of his thesis: that as all men have an equal right to apply their labor to natural resources, economic rent is robbery, and, by the necessity of paying economic rent, labor, capital and enterprise receive less return than is their due. To cure this condition, it is not necessary to distribute land; it is necessary only to take economic rent in taxation, abolishing all other contributions to government. This will insure the smooth working of natural economic laws, which, thus freed, will make for an equitable sharing of wealth; monopoly, being grounded in appropriation of land values, will disappear, and so economic society will not be subject to the recurrent seizures called industrial depressions.

This theory, known in George's version as the Single Tax, had been anticipated by the 18th-century Physiocrats, by the two Mills, and Marx, Spencer and others in the 19th century; but George had never read their works and gave his own statement a singular force and beauty.

Published first in an author's edition of 500 copies (1879), *Progress and Poverty* was published in a trade edition (1880) and soon attracted wide notice. George now became a propagandist. He moved to New York; published *The Irish Land Question* (1881); spent a year in Ireland and England speaking, writing and becoming a public figure. In 1883 he made a triumphal lecture tour in Britain and in 1884 another. He published *Social Problems* (1883) and *Protection or Free Trade* (1886).

Backed by labor, he ran for mayor of New York in a spectacular campaign, 1886. Following his defeat, he organized Land and Labor Clubs throughout the country and began publishing the weekly *Standard*. After intervening years of intense activity he ran again for mayor, 1897, but illness and strain brought on his death before election day.

GEORGE, HENRY (*b. Sacramento, Calif., 1862; d. 1916*), journalist. Son of Henry George (1839–1897). His father's intimate helper; editor of the *Standard*, 1887–92; author of *Life of Henry George* (1900).

GEORGE, JAMES ZACHARIAH (*b. Monroe Co., Ga., 1826; d. 1897*), soldier, jurist. Raised in Mississippi. U.S. senator, Democrat, from Mississippi, 1881–97. Defended 1890 Mississippi constitution in the Senate, also workmen's right to organize.

GEORGE, WILLIAM REUBEN (*b. West Dryden, N.Y., 1866; d. near Freeville, N.Y., 1936*), businessman, philanthropist. Founded, 1895, the George Junior Republic, an innovation in institutional self-government for adolescents. [*Supp. 2*]

GERARD, JAMES WATSON (*b. New York, N.Y., 1794; d. 1874*), lawyer, philanthropist. Graduated Columbia, 1811; admitted to bar, 1816. Early began work in behalf of juvenile offenders; procured incorporation in 1824 of the Society for the Reformation of Juvenile Delinquents, whose House of Refuge was the first institution of its kind in the United States. Devoted himself to many other social causes. In later years his greatest services were in behalf of popular education.

GERHARD, WILLIAM WOOD (*b. Philadelphia, Pa., 1809; d. 1872*), physician. Graduated Dickinson, 1826; M.D., University of Pennsylvania, 1830; studied also in Paris. Famous for first distinguishing (1837) typhus from typhoid fever, Gerhard also published a series of papers on the pathology of smallpox, pneumonia in children, tuberculous meningitis.

GERHART, EMANUEL VOGEL (*b. Freeburg, Pa., 1817; d. Lancaster, Pa., 1904*), German Reformed theologian. President, Franklin and Marshall College, 1854–66; Mercersburg Theological Seminary, 1868–1904. Strongly influenced doctrinal development of his church.

GERICKE, WILHELM (*b. Gratz, Austria, 1845; d. 1925*), musician. Conductor and director of Boston Symphony Orchestra, 1884–89, 1898–1906.

GERONIMO (*b. southern Arizona, 1829; d. Fort Sill, Okla., 1909*), Chiricahua Apache warrior. Indian name, "Goyathlay." Not a Chiricahua by birth, he assumed virtual leadership of the tribe. Their forced removal to San Carlos on the Gila, 1876, started him raiding; after an interval as a farmer, 1877–79, he led other forays in 1880 and 1882–83. He began his bloodiest, most spectacular campaign in May 1885. For ten months he raided outlying settlements until, followed into Mexico, he surrendered on March 27, 1886, only to escape again two nights later. He was not recaptured until early in September. He and his band were imprisoned in Florida and Alabama; later they became orderly farmers and stock-raisers at Fort Sill.

GERRISH, FREDERIC HENRY (*b. Portland, Maine, 1845; d. 1920*), surgeon. M.D., Bowdoin, 1869; taught anatomy and surgery there *post* 1875.

GERRY, ELBRIDGE (*b. Marblehead, Mass., 1744; d. Washington, D.C., 1814*), statesman. Graduated Harvard, 1762; entered family shipping business. Elected to General Court, 1772. An ardent follower of Samuel Adams, he was member of Mass. committee of correspondence, of the First and Second Provincial Congresses and of the committee of safety. He was active in raising troops and efficient in procuring all manner of supplies for the provincial army. Delegate to the Second Continental Congress, he was an industrious member of the Treasury Board and an early advocate of separation from Great Britain. He signed both the Declaration of Independence and the Articles of Confederation.

As the Revolutionary war continued, his experience and faithful attendance made him increasingly valuable in Congress. In foreign policy he opposed the French alliance but was an implacable enemy of England. He worked hard to provide army supplies. Frowning on profiteering, he tried to enforce on others (and observed himself) the schedule of fair prices fixed by the New Haven convention of 1778. Opposed in Congress on this point in 1780, he absented himself for three years, engaging successfully in trade and privateering at home. After the peace, Gerry returned to Congress where he attempted to carry the stern republicanism of the 1770's into a period when altered problems required other qualities for solution. His colleagues appreciated his gentlemanliness, profited by his attention to detail, never questioned his integrity. On the other hand, he frequently changed his mind, showed an "obstinacy that will risk great things to secure small ones," and suspected the motives of others. At the Federal Convention of 1787, he began by advocating strong, centralized government; ended by opposing the Constitution because it did not square with theoretical republicanism. His inconsistency made a bad impression. He continually preached compromise but disliked the compromise as made and declared the Constitution to be "full of vices." Gerry was doubtless sincere in fearing the Constitution would fail to secure liberty, and he probably expected ratification to fail. He was disgruntled by the result. Elected to Congress, 1789, after declaring he would support the Constitution, he continued to pursue an inconsistent course, supporting now the Anti-Federalist position, now the Federalist. He retired from Congress, 1793.

In 1797, Gerry was appointed member of the "X.Y.Z." mission to France because John Adams wanted a non-party man joined with Marshall and Pinckney. His conduct throughout was mistaken. He allowed Talleyrand to negotiate with him singly and in secret and remained in Paris when his indignant colleagues departed, believing that the Directory would declare war if he left. On his return to America in October 1798, the Federalists snubbed him but the Massachusetts Republicans, sharing his belief that he had prevented war with France, put him up unsuccessfully for governor in 1800 and each year thereafter until 1804. In 1810, however, he was elected governor and served until April 1812. His second term was immortalized by the "Gerrymander" bill in which the state was redistricted so as to give to the Republicans a number of state senators in excess of their voting strength. Elected vice-president on the ticket with James Madison, 1812, Gerry entered into the social life of Washington with zest, but he was in frail health and died November 23, 1814.

GERRY, ELBRIDGE THOMAS (*b. New York, N.Y., 1837; d. 1927*), lawyer, philanthropist. Grandson of Elbridge Gerry. Graduated Columbia, 1857. Energetic legal adviser to the American Society for the Prevention of Cruelty to Animals; procured enabling and subsequent legislation for the New York Society for the Prevention of Cruelty to Children, incorporated 1875, first of its kind in the world. Gerry studied all the phases of child rescue and gradually devoted all his time to the Society, molding policy and directing activities as president (1879–1901) in the face of bitter opposition.

GERSHWIN, GEORGE (*b. Brooklyn, N.Y., 1898; d. Beverly Hills, Calif., 1937*), composer. His first influential music teacher, Charles Hambitzer, recognizing the youth's latent talents, advised him to study harmony and attend concerts. In 1913 Gershwin left high school to work as staff pianist for the Remick music publishing firm. By 1916 one of the many popular songs he had written was published and another appeared in the *Passing Show of 1916*. In 1918 Max Dreyfus, head of the publishing firm of Harms, engaged Gershwin simply to write songs and show them to him. Gershwin's career advanced rapidly. In 1919 he had his first smash song hit, "Swanee," and wrote the score for a musical comedy *La, La Lucille*. From 1920 to 1924 he wrote the music for the annual *George White's Scandals*.

In 1922 Gershwin wrote *Blue Monday*, a one-act opera in the jazz idiom, which was performed once in the *Scandals* but withdrawn because of its somber mood. However, its conductor, Paul Whiteman, was deeply impressed. At his request Gershwin wrote a new symphonic-jazz work, *Rhapsody in Blue*, which Whiteman introduced at a concert in February 1924. It made the young composer famous and wealthy, and opened up new horizons for jazz. Other notable concert compositions by Gershwin followed: *Concerto in*

F (1925), commissioned by the New York Symphony Society; *Three Piano Preludes* (1926); *An American in Paris* (1928); *Second Rhapsody* (1932); *Cuban Overture* (1932); *Variations on I Got Rhythm* (1934); and, perhaps his most enduring work, *Porgy and Bess* (1935).

Meanwhile Gershwin was also writing scores (his brother Ira writing most of the lyrics) for Broadway stage productions and Hollywood films. His best musical comedies were *Lady Be Good* (1924), *Tip Toes* (1925), *Oh Kay* (1926), *Funny Face* (1927), *Strike Up the Band* (1929), *Girl Crazy* (1930), and *Of Thee I Sing* (1931, the first musical comedy to win the Pulitzer Prize). Gershwin's music is filled with verve, spontaneity, excitement; it is American music to the core. Its continued growth in popularity and artistic stature mark Gershwin as one of the most significant creative figures that American music has produced. [*Supp.* 2]

GERSTER, ARPAD GEYZA CHARLES (*b. Kassa, Hungary, 1848; d. 1923*), surgeon. M.D., Vienna, 1872. Came to America, 1873. An early partisan of the antiseptic technique, he published the first textbook in America on the new surgery, *Rules of Aseptic and Antiseptic Surgery* (1888). This epochmaking book contained some of the earliest half-tone pictures made from Gerster's own plates. He was professor of surgery at the New York Polyclinic, 1882–94; he became professor of clinical surgery at Columbia, 1916. A superior diagnostician, he excelled in post-operative care.

GERSTLE, LEWIS (*b. Ichenhausen, Germany, 1824; d. 1902*), California pioneer, capitalist. Came to America, 1847; settled in California, 1850. Promoter and director of many business enterprises; president of the Alaska Commercial Co.

GETTY, GEORGE WASHINGTON (*b. Georgetown, D.C., 1819; d. Maryland, 1901*), soldier. Graduated West Point, 1840. Fought in Mexican War; served with distinction in Army of the Potomac, 1861–65, especially at siege of Suffolk, Va., 1863.

GEYER, HENRY SHEFFIE (*b. Frederick, Md., 1790; d. 1859*), lawyer. Removed to St. Louis, Mo., c. 1816. Eminent in land-title litigation; played prominent part in Missouri struggle for statehood. U.S. senator, Whig, from Missouri, 1851–59. Attorney for defendant slave-owner in Dred Scott case.

GHERARDI, BANCROFT (*b. Jackson, La., 1832; d. Stratford, Conn., 1903*), naval officer. Nephew of George Bancroft. Graduated U.S. Naval Academy, 1852. Commended for conduct at Mobile Bay, 1864. Held series of naval posts; rose to rear admiral and command of North Atlantic Squadron, 1889–92.

GHOLSON, SAMUEL JAMESON (*b. Madison Co., Ky., 1808; d. Aberdeen, Miss., 1883*), jurist, legislator,

Confederate soldier. Federal district judge in Mississippi, 1839–61.

GHOLSON, THOMAS SAUNDERS (*b. Gholsonville, Va., 1808; d. Savannah, Ga., 1868*), Virginia lawyer and jurist. Confederate congressman.

GHOLSON, WILLIAM YATES (*b. Southampton Co., Va., 1807; d. 1870*), lawyer, jurist. Practiced in Mississippi, 1834–44; removing to Cincinnati, O., he won reputation for legal learning and integrity.

GIBAULT, PIERRE (*b. Montreal, Canada, 1737; d. New Madrid, Spanish Louisiana, 1804*), Roman Catholic clergyman. Vicar-general of Illinois mission country, 1769–90. After George Rogers Clark's capture of Kaskaskia, 1778, encouraged French settlers there and at Vincennes to assist the American cause.

GIBBES, ROBERT WILSON (*b. Charleston, S.C., 1809; d. 1866*), physician, author. Son of William H. Gibbes. Graduated South Carolina College, 1827; M.D., Medical College of South Carolina, 1830. Worked as assistant to Thomas Cooper, and won national reputation; his 1842 treatise "On Typhoid Pneumonia" revolutionized treatment. Proprietor and editor, Columbia, S.C., *South Carolinian.*

GIBBES, WILLIAM HASELL (*b. Charleston, S.C., 1754; d. Charleston, 1834*), lawyer, Revolutionary soldier. Rendered important services as master-in-equity, 1783–1825.

GIBBON, JOHN (*b. near Holmesburg, Pa., 1827, d. Baltimore, Md., 1896*), soldier. Graduated West Point, 1847. Author of *Artillerist's Manual* (1860). As brigadier-general, commanded the Union "Iron Brigade" at Second Bull Run, South Mountain, Antietam; raised to divisional command, he was wounded at Fredericksburg and Gettysburg. Commanding the new XXIV Corps, 1865, he was named to the commission which arranged details of Lee's surrender. After the war he served mainly in the West. He commanded the expedition which rescued the Custer survivors, 1876, and in 1877 pursued and defeated the Nez Percés under Chief Joseph.

GIBBONS, ABIGAIL HOPPER (*b. Philadelphia, Pa., 1801; d. 1893*), teacher, philanthropist. Daughter of Isaac T. Hopper; wife of James S. Gibbons. An active Abolitionist, she engaged in many other forms of humanitarian work, including relief of crippled and blind children and Civil War nursing. Her most important accomplishment was as president of the Women's Prison Association.

GIBBONS, FLOYD (*b. Washington, D.C., 1887; d. near Stroudsburg, Pa., 1939*), war correspondent, radio commentator. [*Supp.* 2]

GIBBONS, HERBERT ADAMS (*b. Annapolis, Md., 1880; d. Grunslee, Austria, 1934*), journalist, foreign correspondent. [*Supp.* 1]

GIBBONS, JAMES (*b. Baltimore, Md., 1834; d. Baltimore, 1921*), Roman Catholic prelate. Graduated St. Charles College, 1858; studied at St. Mary's Seminary, Baltimore; ordained, 1861. As a local pastor, he soon showed unusual powers. During the Civil War he was chaplain at Fort McHenry, ministering to Federals and Confederates alike. Appointed secretary to Archbishop Spalding of Baltimore, 1865, he attracted general notice at the Second Plenary Council of Baltimore, 1866, and was nominated Vicar Apostolic of North Carolina. Consecrated bishop of Adramyttum, 1868; bishop of Richmond, 1872.

In attendance at Vatican Council, Rome, 1870, he was impressed by the difficulties of Church-State relations in Europe as compared with the ease of relations in the United States under the American system. An able administrator, popular with people of all creeds, he was made archbishop-coadjutor of Baltimore with right of succession in 1877 only five months before Archbishop J. R. Bayley's death. He then became head of the oldest U.S. archdiocese, the first native of the city to be appointed to the See. He took an active part in civic and humanitarian movements, acquired a wide Washington acquaintance. His exposition of Catholic doctrine, *The Faith of Our Fathers* (1877), leapt into popularity. Sharing the belief of Pope Leo XIII that the future of the Church would be among democratic peoples, Gibbons organized the Third Plenary Council of Baltimore, 1884, and presided as Apostolic Delegate. The decrees of the Council have guided the Catholic Church in the United States since, and were strong in support of American civil institutions. The Catholic University at Washington, D.C., was also established as an outcome of this Council, and Gibbons was head of its board of trustees until his death.

In 1886, Leo XIII made Gibbons the second American cardinal. At his installation in Rome he declared that the progress of the Catholic Church in the United States was due in large part to American liberty. Sympathizing with labor's aspirations, he obtained Roman assurance that the Knights of Labor would not be condemned as a secret society; he also succeeded in preventing ecclesiastical condemnation of Henry George's *Progress and Poverty*. Back in Baltimore, he was hailed as a champion of labor and representative of American principles. He threw all his influence against the so-called "Cahensly Movement" for the appointment of U.S. Catholic bishops on the basis of representation of national immigrant groups. He was in favor of early blending of immigrants with the native population and especially opposed to transplantation of European differences. Through his efforts also, the controversy over "Americanism" in doctrine was exposed as an error and ended. In 1911 at a celebration of his jubilee as cardinal, Gibbons received honors never before accorded any American churchman. His greatest influence was shown as a far-sighted leader and administrator and in promoting the spirit of religious toleration.

GIBBONS, JAMES SLOAN (*b. Wilmington, Del., 1810; d. New York, N.Y., 1892*), Abolitionist, banker. Son of William Gibbons (1781–1845). Author of works on banking and taxation, and of the famous Civil War song, "We Are Coming, Father Abraham."

GIBBONS, THOMAS (*b. near Savannah, Ga., 1757; d. New York, N.Y., 1826*), lawyer, politician. Mayor of Savannah, 1791–92, 1794–95, 1799–1801; federal judge in Georgia. Removing North, he began running steamboats from Elizabethtown, N.J., to New York City, 1818, competing with Aaron Ogden, who had purchased rights to the route from the holders of the New York monopoly on steam navigation in state waters granted to Robert Livingston and Robert Fulton in 1803. Ogden secured an injunction; Gibbons appealed; the case was carried to the Supreme Court in 1824, and Chief Justice John Marshall handed down his famous decision declaring the New York monopoly with all others of its kind null and void.

GIBBONS, WILLIAM (*b. Bear Bluff, S.C., 1726; d. 1800*), lawyer, Revolutionary patriot. Practiced in Savannah, Ga.; led in opposition to the Crown there. Member of the Provincial Congress, the Committee of Safety, and of the Continental Congress, 1784–86.

GIBBONS, WILLIAM (*b. Philadelphia, Pa., 1781; d. 1845*), physician. Practiced in Wilmington, Del. Interested in Negro emancipation and education.

GIBBS, GEORGE (*b. Newport, R.I., 1776; d. near Astoria, N.Y., 1833*), friend of science. His mineral collection, the largest and most valuable in the country, was deposited at Yale, 1810. Friend and encourager of the elder Benjamin Silliman, Gibbs inspired founding of *American Journal of Science*.

GIBBS, GEORGE (*b. near Astoria, N.Y., 1815; d. New Haven, Conn., 1873*), ethnologist. Son of George Gibbs (1776–1833); brother of Oliver W. Gibbs. Graduated Harvard, 1838. Studied natural history and geology of Northwest, and the languages and traditions of its Indians. Author of Indian language studies and of *Memoirs of the Administrations of Washington and John Adams* (1846).

GIBBS, GEORGE (*b. Chicago, Ill., 1861; d. New York, N.Y., 1940*), engineer. Nephew of Oliver W. Gibbs. Graduated Stevens Institute, 1882. Associated with Samuel M. Vauclain of Baldwin Locomotive Works, and George Westinghouse, in the development of electric locomotives, *post* 1897. He represented the Westinghouse companies abroad in the electrification of railways in London and Liverpool. From 1901 he played an important part in the electrification of American railways, in particular of the New York Central, Pennsylvania, and Long Island lines leading into New York City. He was consulting engineer for the first New York City subway, and designed and patented the first all-steel subway passenger car. [*Supp. 2*]

GIBBS, JAMES ETHAN ALLEN (*b. Rockbridge Co., Va., 1829; d. Raphine, Va., 1902*), inventor. Patented (1857) chain- and lock-stitch devices and a twisted loop rotary hook which with his partner, James Willcox, he marketed as the Willcox and Gibbs sewing-machine.

GIBBS, JOSIAH WILLARD (*b. Salem, Mass., 1790; d. 1861*), Orientalist, philologist. Graduated Yale, 1809. Professor of sacred literature at Yale Divinity School, 1826–61.

GIBBS, JOSIAH WILLARD (*b. New Haven, Conn., 1839; d. New Haven, 1903*), mathematician, physicist. Son of Josiah W. Gibbs (1790–1861). Graduated Yale, 1858; Ph.D., 1863; studied at Paris, Berlin and Heidelberg, 1866–69. Appointed professor of mathematical physics at Yale, 1871, a post he held for 32 years. Few undergraduates were equipped to profit from Gibbs's advanced lectures, and despite his world-wide reputation he did not draw many graduate students to New Haven. His influence on science came chiefly from his writings.

In his first two scientific papers (1873) he made an exhaustive study of geometrical methods of representing by diagrams the thermodynamic properties of homogeneous substances and established a point of view for his later work. His great memoir "On the Equilibrium of Heterogeneous Substances" appeared in two parts in 1876 and 1878 in the *Transactions of the Connecticut Academy of Arts and Sciences*. This epochal work with its later supplementary monographs provided the basic theory for a new branch of science, physical chemistry. Many years passed before some of Gibbs's theoretical developments were experimentally verified, and even today his suggestions have not been exhausted by experimenters.

Gibbs was occupied between 1880 and 1884 with modifying the work of Hamilton in quaternions and of Grassman on geometric algebra into a system of vector analysis especially suited to the need of mathematical physicists which he printed privately (1881, 1884) for his students and friends. The whole was not published until 1901. Between 1882 and 1889, besides completing the second part of the vector analysis, Gibbs developed his own electrical theory of optics which he set forth in articles in the *American Journal of Science* (April, June, 1882; February, 1883; June, 1888; February, 1889).

His last great work, *Elementary Principles in Statistical Mechanics,* appeared in 1902 in the Yale Bicentennial series. Gibbs's English style was perfection—brief, precise, free from dogmatic statements, not given to ornamentation, fascinating in its inexorable logic. Little is known of Gibbs's methods of work. He left few notes and would appear to have composed mainly from ideas carried in his head. At the time of his death he had three pieces of work in mind: re-edition and amplification of his work on thermodynamics; some developments of multiple algebra on which he had an original point of view; a revision of the method used in his theory of orbits published in 1889.

Gibbs received many medals and honorary degrees, belonged to many learned societies at home and abroad. He lived quietly with his sister and her husband and never married. His personality was unassuming and self-contained, dignified, without the least taste of austerity. He gave generously of his time and thought to simple family and household problems, to encouragement of earnest students and to regular university duties. He had none of the peculiarities popularly associated with genius. The scientific world is still expounding, amplifying and applying his ideas.

GIBBS, OLIVER WOLCOTT (*b. New York, N.Y., 1822; d. 1908*), chemist. Son of George Gibbs (1776–1833); brother of George Gibbs (1815–1873). Graduated Columbia, 1841; M.D., College of Physicians and Surgeons, 1845; studied also in Germany and France. Professor at N.Y. City College (Free Academy), 1849–63; Rumford Professor at Harvard, 1863–87. Directed Lawrence Scientific School laboratory, inspiring his students with zeal for research and introducing laboratory methods which he had learned in Europe. His chief work was with inorganic compounds, analytical methods, physiological chemistry. With F. A. Genth he conducted classical researches into the nature of the complex compounds of cobalt; his work on the platinum metals was of equal importance. A later series of researches established the nature of the complex acids formed by vanadium, tungsten, molybdenum, phosphorus, arsenic and antimony.

GIBBS, WOLCOTT. [See GIBBS, OLIVER WOLCOTT, 1822–1908.]

GIBSON, GEORGE (*b. Lancaster, Pa., 1747; d. Fort Jefferson, Northwest Terr., 1791*), Revolutionary soldier. Brother of John Gibson. Agent for gunpowder purchase at New Orleans, 1776; killed on St. Clair's expedition.

GIBSON, JOHN (*b. Lancaster, Pa., 1740; d. Braddock's Field, Pa., 1822*), frontier soldier. Brother of George Gibson. Indian trader at Fort Pitt. Reported the famous speech of Chief Logan, publicized by Thomas Jefferson; served on frontier during Revolution. Secretary of Indiana Territory, 1800–16.

GIBSON, JOHN BANNISTER (*b. Westover Mills, Pa., 1780; d. Philadelphia, Pa., 1853*), jurist. Justice of Pennsylvania supreme court, 1816–53, and chief justice, *post* 1827, he was the dominant figure of the state judiciary, distinguished for breadth of view, independence, originality and masterful opinions. In hearing over 6000 cases and delivering reasons for judgment in more than 1200, he profoundly influenced the development of Pennsylvania law. His opinions range over the whole legal field, those on constitutional problems commanding the greatest respect.

GIBSON, PARIS (*b. Brownfield, Maine, 1830; d. 1920*), Montana pioneer, conservationist. Introduced sheep farming in northern Montana, 1879; planned city of Great Falls; was closely connected with waterpower, coal mining and railroad development. U.S. senator, Democrat, 1901–05.

GIBSON, RANDALL LEE (*b. Woodford Co., Ky., 1832; d. Hot Springs, Ark., 1892*), lawyer, planter, Confederate soldier. Congressman, Democrat, from Louisiana, 1875–83; U.S. senator, 1883–92. Worked in Congress to improve Mississippi navigation; was chief agent in founding Tulane University.

GIBSON, WALTER MURRAY (*b. at sea en route from England, 1823; d. 1888*), adventurer, politician. Raised in New York and New Jersey; early orphaned. After a fantastic career in Central America, Sumatra and in Utah as an adviser to Brigham Young, settled in Hawaii, 1861. Opposing non-natives there, he became premier of the kingdom, 1882, and was deposed in revolution of 1887.

GIBSON, WILLIAM (*b. Baltimore, Md., 1788; d. Savannah, Ga., 1868*), surgeon. Graduated Edinburgh, M.D., 1809; studied also with Bell and Cooper in London. Organized University of Maryland's medical department, and taught there, 1811–19; professor of surgery, University of Pennsylvania, 1819–55.

GIBSON, WILLIAM HAMILTON (*b. Newtown, Conn., 1850; d. Washington, Conn., 1896*), artist, naturalist, popularizer of nature study.

GIDDINGS, FRANKLIN HENRY (*b. Sherman, Conn., 1855; d. Scarsdale, N.Y., 1931*), sociologist, educator. Attended Union College; became first a teacher, then a journalist. Specialized in statistical investigations of social problems. Taught at Bryn Mawr, 1888–94; went to Columbia, 1894, as professor of sociology and served until 1931. His first volume to attract widespread attention was *The Principles of Sociology* (1896); in eleven subsequent volumes he shaped social research and the concepts and teaching of sociology. A disciple of Herbert Spencer and an influential propagandist for the scientific method, he helped to bring sociology out of the theoretical and into the scientific stage. [*Supp. 1*]

GIDDINGS, JOSHUA REED (*b. Bradford Co., Pa., 1795; d. Montreal, Canada, 1864*), lawyer, Abolitionist. Raised in Ashtabula Co., O. Congressman, Whig, Free-Soil, from Ohio, 1839–54; Republican, 1854–58. A militant crusader against slavery, he opposed the annexation of Texas, the Mexican War and the compromise on the Oregon boundary. His program called

for freedom in the Territories, opposition to disunion, and, if war resulted, use of the president's war powers to emancipate all slaves. Lincoln, who had been a student of his speeches, appointed him consul-general to Canada, 1861.

GIDEON, PETER MILLER (*b. near Woodstock, O., 1820; d. 1899*), pioneer pomologist. Settled, 1858, on Gideon's Bay, Lake Minnetonka, Minn., where he worked to develop fruit hardy enough to withstand the rigors of northern winters. After many setbacks, he produced from seed of the Siberian crab the "Wealthy" apple, first noticed in the *Western Farmer*, 1869. In quest of a variety with equal size and flavor but with a tougher skin, he also developed "Peter" and "Gideon."

GIDLEY, JAMES WILLIAMS (*b. Springwater, Iowa, 1866; d. 1931*), vertebrate paleontologist. Graduated Princeton, 1898. Associated with U.S. National Museum, *post* 1905. Authority on the history and development of fossil horses in America. [*Supp. 1*]

GIESLER-ANNEKE, MATHILDE FRANZISKA (*b. Lerchenhausen, Germany, 1817; d. 1884*), author, German revolutionary, reformer. Married Fritz Anneke, 1847. Came to America, *ca.* 1850. Conducted a girls' school in Milwaukee, Wis., 1865–84.

GIFFORD, ROBERT SWAIN (*b. Naushon Island, Mass., 1840; d. New York, N.Y., 1905*), landscapepainter, etcher. Teacher for many years at Cooper Union. His most congenial subject, the Buzzard's Bay, Massachusetts, area, may be seen in such spacious, melancholy paintings as "Dartmouth Moors."

GIFFORD, SANFORD ROBINSON (*b. Greenfield, N.Y., 1823; d. New York, N.Y., 1880*), landscapepainter. Inspired by work of Thomas Cole and F. E. Church; studied with John Rubens Smith. His paintings show some of the scenic manner of Turner, and his work is differentiated from that of other men of the Hudson River School by a more subtle perception of values, a greater interest in air and light. Emotional content, glowing color mark his sunny and cheerful landscapes.

GIHON, ALBERT LEARY (*b. Philadelphia, Pa., 1833; d. 1901*), naval surgeon.

GILBERT, ANNE HARTLEY (*b. Rochdale, England, 1821; d. 1904*), dancer, character actress. Came to America, 1849. Played in Western companies, and was a member of Augustin Daly's company, 1869–99. One of "Big Four" which included James Lewis, John Drew and Ada Rehan.

GILBERT, CASS (*b. Zanesville, O., 1859; d. Brockenhurst, England, 1934*), architect. Attended Massachusetts Institute of Technology, 1878–79; worked as surveyor; traveled in England, France and Italy; worked as draftsman in office of McKim, Mead and White. Entered partnership as architect in St. Paul, Minn., December 1882; won first success with Minnesota State Capitol, 1896. Removing to New York City, he was successful competitor for design of U.S. Customs House, New York, and was soon engaged in other large work including the Woolworth Building (completed 1913).

In 1910 he was appointed a member of the National Commission of Fine Arts, and through the prestige of this position secured Washington commissions for the U.S. Treasury Annex, 1918–19, the Chamber of Commerce, 1924, and the Supreme Court Building. Other important commissions included the St. Louis Public Library, the New York Life Insurance Building, New York City, and the George Washington Memorial Bridge.

Gilbert's achievement was diversified, generally successful, and often monumental. His early designs showed a leaning to the Romanesque; in his later work he turned to the American concept of the Classic. Although his designs were somewhat heavy and uninspired, with little originality, they were generally safe and commonly approved. It is remarkable that one man working without partners could accomplish so much and do it so well. [*Supp. 1*]

GILBERT, CHARLES HENRY (*b. Rockford, Ill., 1859; d. 1928*), zoölogist. Professor at Leland Stanford, 1891–1925. Participated in intensive investigations of fishes in the waters of the United States, British Columbia, the North Pacific, Hawaii, Japan.

GILBERT, ELIPHALET WHEELER (*b. New Lebanon, N.Y., 1793; d. Philadelphia, Pa., 1853*), Presbyterian clergyman. Pastor at Wilmington, Del., and later in Philadelphia. President of Newark College (now University of Delaware), 1834 and 1841–47.

GILBERT, GROVE KARL (*b. Rochester, N.Y., 1843; d. 1918*), geologist. Graduated University of Rochester, 1862. Worked with J. S. Newberry on geological survey of Ohio, and with the Wheeler Survey, 1871–74. Joined J. W. Powell in U.S. geological and geographical surveys, and continued with the consolidated surveys until 1918. His *magnum opus* was a monograph on the extinct Lake Bonneville of Nevada and Utah. He also investigated the life history of the Niagara River and recent earth movements in the Great Lakes region. His study of the "Coon Butte" crater in Arizona illustrates his deliberate, detailed, judicial method. He was unquestionably one of the best-balanced and most philosophical of American geologists.

GILBERT, HENRY FRANKLIN BELKNAP (*b. Somerville, Mass., 1868; d. 1928*), composer. Studied with Edward MacDowell. The first American composer whose work was wholly indigenous, he developed a mature, original style shown in ballet, opera and orchestral pieces.

GILBERT, JOHN (*b. Logan, Utah, 1897; d. Beverly Hills, Calif., 1936*), film actor. Star of *The Big Parade* (1925), *Flesh and the Devil* (1927), and others; his popularity waned with talking films.

[*Supp. 2*]

GILBERT, JOHN GIBBS (*b. Boston, Mass., 1810; d. 1889*), actor. Member of Tremont Theatre stock company, Wallack's and Joseph Jefferson's companies. Famous for elderly roles, his greatest being Sir Anthony Absolute.

GILBERT, LINDA (*b. Rochester, N.Y., 1847; d. Mt. Vernon, N.Y., 1895*), philanthropist. The "Prisoners' Friend," she established the Gilbert Library and Prisoners' Aid Society to provide prison libraries and help ex-convicts obtain employment.

GILBERT, RUFUS HENRY (*b. Guilford, N.Y., 1832; d. 1885*), physician, Union soldier, inventor. Convinced that overcrowding in cities created ill health, he projected the New York City Elevated Railway as a means of providing rapid transit and spreading out the city's population.

GILBERT, SEYMOUR PARKER (*b. Bloomfield, N.J., 1892; d. New York, N.Y., 1938*), lawyer, financier. Graduated Rutgers, 1912; Harvard Law School, 1915. Assistant secretary of U.S. treasury, 1920–23. Appointed agent-general for reparation payments, 1924, he directed with tact and ability the economic rehabilitation of Germany under the Dawes Plan. From 1931 until his death, he was a partner in J. P. Morgan & Co. [*Supp. 2*]

GILBERT, WILLIAM LEWIS (*b. Northfield, Conn., 1806; d. Oshawa, Canada, 1890*), capitalist, clock manufacturer, philanthropist.

GILCHRIST, ROBERT (*b. Jersey City, N.J., 1825; d. 1888*), lawyer, Union soldier. Attorney-general of New Jersey, 1869–75. An authority on constitutional law, he defined rights of Negroes to vote in state, drew up riparian-rights act.

GILCHRIST, WILLIAM WALLACE (*b. Jersey City, N.J., 1846; d. Easton, Pa., 1916*), organist, composer. Founder and conductor, Philadelphia Symphony Society and Philadelphia Mendelssohn Club.

GILDER, JEANNETTE LEONARD (*b. Flushing, N.Y., 1849; d. New York, N.Y., 1916*), journalist. Sister of Richard W. and William H. Gilder.

GILDER, RICHARD WATSON (*b. Bordentown, N.J., 1844; d. New York, N.Y., 1909*), editor, poet. Managing editor, *Scribner's Monthly*, 1870–81; editor, *Century Magazine*, 1881–1909. Active in many civic and social movements. An ardent worker for international copyright, civil service reform, better city government, he performed a notable public service in 1894 as chairman of New York State's Tenement House Committee. Author of *The New Day* (1876) and other volumes of only adequate verse, he published collections of his poetry in 1894 and 1908.

GILDER, WILLIAM HENRY (b. Philadelphia, Pa., 1838; d. 1900), journalist. Brother of Jeannette L. and Richard W. Gilder.

GILDERSLEEVE, BASIL LANNEAU (b. Charleston, S.C., 1831; d. Baltimore, Md., 1924), philologist, Confederate soldier, author, editor. Graduated Princeton, 1849; Ph.D., Göttingen, 1853. Professor of Greek, University of Virginia, 1856–76; University Professor of Greek, Johns Hopkins, 1876–1915. Author of many monographs, of a Latin Grammar (1867), of masterly editions of Persius (1875), Justin Martyr (1877), and of Pindar (1885). Of his great work Syntax of Classical Greek, Part I appeared in 1900; Part II (with C. W. E. Miller) appeared in 1911. The American Journal of Philology, which he founded in 1880 and edited until 1920, printed many of his articles on Attic syntax.

GILES, CHAUNCEY (b. Charlemont, Mass., 1813; d. 1893), Swedenborgian clergyman, teacher, editor. Held pastorates in Cincinnati, O., New York City, and Philadelphia, Pa., 1853–93.

GILES, WILLIAM BRANCH (b. Amelia Co., Va., 1762; d. Amelia Co., 1830), lawyer, statesman. Graduated Princeton, 1781; studied law under George Wythe at William and Mary. Congressman, Democratic-Republican, from Virginia, 1790–98 and 1801; U.S. senator, 1804–15; governor of Virginia, 1827–30. Spurred inquiry into Hamilton's conduct of the Treasury, 1793; opposed the Jay Treaty. Favoring Madison's election, 1808, he then opposed him; he vented his hostility also on Gallatin and Monroe. Post 1809 he was a "War Hawk," but bitterly criticized the administration during the War of 1812. Personal animosity often marred his judgment and rendered his career not only erratic but destructive.

GILL, JOHN (b. Charlestown, Mass., 1732; d. 1785), printer, journalist. With Benjamin Edes, printed and published the radical Boston Gazette, 1755–75; the Boston Tea Party set forth from their office. Post 1776, Gill published the Continental Journal.

GILL, LAURA DRAKE (b. Chesterville, Maine, 1860; d. Berea, Ky., 1926), educator, pioneer in vocational placement. Started first vocational bureau for college women, Boston, Mass., 1910.

GILL, THEODORE NICHOLAS (b. New York, N.Y., 1837; d. Washington, D.C., 1914), zoölogist. Long associated with George Washington University and with the Smithsonian. Never a field worker, in matters of taxonomy he was easily first in the world. Among his important papers are "Arrangement of the Families of Mollusks" (1871), "Arrangement of the Families of Mammals" (1872), "Arrangement of the Families of Fishes" (1872), "A Comparison of Antipodal Faunas" (1893). His published memoirs on fishes alone number 388 titles, and he contributed many articles to American encyclopedias and lexicons. Himself an encyclopedia of science, he knew how to make technical phraseology plain to laymen.

GILLAM, BERNHARD (b. Banbury, England, 1856; d. Canajoharie, N.Y., 1896), political cartoonist. Came to America as a child. His "tattooed man" cartoons of James G. Blaine were influential in 1884 campaign. As director of Judge, 1886–96, his work had strong influence on political opinion.

GILLEM, ALVAN CULLEM (b. Jackson Co., Tenn., 1830; d. near Nashville, Tenn., 1875), soldier. Graduated West Point, 1851. Served effectively against Confederates in Kentucky and Tennessee, 1861–65; was prominent in reorganizing Tennessee civil government, 1865. As commander, 4th Military District, he was criticized by Northern radicals for refusal to execute reconstruction policies harshly.

GILLESPIE, ELIZA MARIA. [See ANGELA, MOTHER, 1824–1887.]

GILLESPIE, MABEL (b. St. Paul, Minn., 1867; d. Boston, Mass., 1923), labor leader. Executive secretary, Boston Women's Trade Union League; active in minimum-wage legislation and in unionizing women workers post 1909.

GILLESPIE, WILLIAM MITCHELL (b. New York, N.Y., 1816; d. New York, 1868), first professor of civil engineering at Union College, 1845–68. Graduated Columbia, 1834; studied also in France. An unusually effective teacher, he believed engineers should be familiar with the humanities.

GILLET, RANSOM HOOKER (b. New Lebanon, N.Y., 1800; d. 1876), lawyer, Democratic politician, New York congressman and federal official. Partner and protégé of Silas Wright.

GILLETT, EZRA HALL (b. Colchester, Conn., 1823; d. 1875), Presbyterian clergyman, educator, author. Pastor in Harlem, N.Y., 1845–70. Professor of political science, New York University, 1870–75. Official historian of his church.

GILLETT, FREDERICK HUNTINGTON (b. Westfield, Mass., 1851; d. 1935), lawyer. Graduated Harvard Law School, 1877. U.S. congressman, Republican, from Massachusetts, 1893–1925; a leader in the reform of appropriations procedure resulting in the Budget Act, 1921; impartial and tactful speaker of the House, 1919–25; U.S. senator, 1925–31.

[Supp. 1]

GILLETTE, FRANCIS (b. Bloomfield, Conn., 1807; d. Hartford, Conn., 1879), farmer, businessman. Graduated Yale, 1829. U.S. senator, Whig and Free-Soil, from Connecticut, 1854–55. Active in formation of state Republican party; vigorously supported Abolition, temperance, education.

GILLETTE, KING CAMP (b. Fond du Lac, Wis., 1855; d. Calif., 1932), inventor, manufacturer. Invented safety razor, c. 1895; organized Gillette Razor Co., 1901. [Supp. 1]

GILLETTE, WILLIAM HOOKER (b. Hartford, Conn., 1853; d. Hartford, 1937), actor, dramatist. Son of Francis Gillette. Famous principally for creating role of Sherlock Holmes (1899). [Supp. 2]

GILLIAM, DAVID TOD (b. Hebron, O., 1844; d. 1923), surgeon, gynecologist. Practiced in Columbus, O.; taught at several medical schools there. Devised the Gilliam operation (1899) for relief of backward displacement of the uterus, as well as other new techniques and instruments.

GILLISS, JAMES MELVILLE (b. Georgetown, D.C., 1811; d. 1865), naval officer, astronomer. Placed in charge of the Depot of Charts and Instruments, 1836, Gilliss made observations for evaluation of findings of the Wilkes Exploring Expedition seldom equaled for accuracy; he also planned and equipped the first U.S. Naval Observatory, 1842–44. His "Astronomical Observations" (1846) was the first such volume to be published in America, as was his first catalogue of stars. He headed a South American expedition to determine anew the solar parallax, 1849–52, and was finally given charge of the Naval Observatory in 1861.

GILLISS, WALTER (b. Lexington, Ky., 1855; d. 1925), printer. With his brothers, directed the Gilliss Press, 1871–1908, specializing in designing and making books distinguished for care in production and classic taste.

GILLMAN, HENRY (b. Kinsale, Ireland, 1833; d. Detroit, Mich., 1915), archaeologist, scientist. Came to America, 1850. Assisted in U.S. survey of Great Lakes, 1851–69, and held other government posts. U.S. consul at Jerusalem, 1886–91. Did important work on mound-builder culture study.

GILLMORE, QUINCY ADAMS (b. Black River, O., 1825; d. Brooklyn, N.Y., 1888), soldier, military engineer. Graduated West Point, 1849, and later taught there. In Civil War, gave brilliant service to the Union, rising to rank of major-general of regulars. Among his outstanding feats were the reduction of Fort Pulaski, Ga., by rifled cannon fire, the reduction of Morris Island and the retaking of Fort Sumter. His most important post-war service was as president, Mississippi River Commission, 1879. He was author of a number of technical treatises.

GILLON, ALEXANDER (b. Rotterdam, Holland, 1741; d. "Gillon's Retreat," S.C., 1794), Charleston merchant, Revolutionary financial and naval agent for South Carolina.

GILMAN, ARTHUR (b. Alton, Ill., 1837; d. 1909), author, editor, educator. Proposed (1878) and served as executive secretary of the "Harvard Annex" for higher education of women. On its incorporation as Radcliffe College, 1893, he became regent.

GILMAN, ARTHUR DELEVAN (b. Newburyport, Mass., 1821; d. 1882), architect. Designed Boston City Hall, New York Equitable Building, New York State Capitol; important as one of the first American architectural eclectics.

GILMAN, CAROLINE HOWARD (b. Boston, Mass., 1794; d. Washington, D.C., 1888), writer, poet. Wife of Samuel Gilman. Edited early children's paper, Southern Rosebud (1832); author of Recollections of a Southern Matron (1836) and many other popular works.

GILMAN, CHARLOTTE PERKINS STETSON (b. Hartford, Conn., 1860; d. Pasadena, Calif., 1935), social reformer, lecturer. Daughter of Frederick B. Perkins. Author of Women and Economics (1898) and other books. [Supp. 1]

GILMAN, DANIEL COIT (b. Norwich, Conn., 1831; d. Norwich, 1908), educator. Graduated Yale, 1852. Spent years 1853–55 abroad; was enlisted by James D. Dana to write plan (1856) for what was to be the Sheffield Scientific School at Yale. Here he served as professor of physical and political geography; through his efforts it was the first institution to use funds derived from the Morrill Act. He declined presidency of the University of Wisconsin, 1867, and that of the University of California, 1870, but became president of the latter in 1872. Hampered by politics at Berkeley, he showed so much ability that he was called to be first president of Johns Hopkins University, 1875, recommended for the post by Presidents Eliot of Harvard, A. D. White of Cornell, and Angell of Michigan. Johns Hopkins was still largely unformed but under the will of the founder was free to develop without legislative supervision.

Gilman's conception was clear and complete from the start. "Everywhere," he said, "the real efficiency of a college is admitted to consist, not chiefly in buildings, nor in sites, nor in apparatus, but in the number and character of the teachers." For a year he searched in Europe and America for the men who were to do a unique piece of creative work in Baltimore. The new university was to put emphasis on graduate study; its students would be already grounded in culture and informed with scholarly purpose; the chief inspiration was to be the freedom of thinking and teaching on which Gilman insisted from the very start. In 1876 at the opening of the university, the address was given by T. H. Huxley, who seconded Gilman's central thought of staking all on personality. "It has been my fate," he said, "to see great educational funds fossilize into mere bricks and mortar in the petrifying springs of architecture, with nothing left to work the institution they were intended to support." Gilman had studied the methods of like institutions in Europe and America, but the ultimate product bore the stamp of his own personality rather than that of any particular university system, and the soul of the whole organism was research.

The Johns Hopkins Medical School, Gilman's second great contribution to the educational development of America, was deferred by the suspension of common stock dividends by the Baltimore & Ohio Railroad whose shares formed the bulk of the endowment. Gilman persevered, however, and in 1893 the school opened with William H. Welch, William Osler, William S. Halstead and Howard A. Kelly on the faculty. Standards of admission were high. Gilman wisely insisted that all matters pertaining to medical instruction should come under the university, while actual care of the sick, clinical opportunities, and residence within the hospital were the responsibility of the Johns Hopkins Hospital.

Gilman retired from the presidency in 1902, but threw himself into the work of founding the projected Carnegie Institution of Washington of which Carnegie wished him to be president. Finding, however, that he did not have a free hand in unifying the forces of the institution, he resigned the presidency after three years. He was one of the original trustees of the John F. Slater Fund and its president from 1893 until his death, a trustee of the Peabody Educational Fund and of the Russell Sage Foundation.

GILMAN, JOHN TAYLOR (*b. Exeter, N.H., 1753; d. 1828*), financier. Brother of Nicholas Gilman. Federalist governor of New Hampshire, 1794–1805, 1813–16.

GILMAN, LAWRENCE (*b. Flushing, N.Y., 1878; d. Franconia, N.H., 1939*), music critic. Nephew of Daniel C. Gilman. On staff of *New York Tribune* (later *Herald Tribune*), 1923–39. [*Supp. 2*]

GILMAN, NICHOLAS (*b. Exeter, N.H., 1755; d. Philadelphia, Pa., 1814*), politician. Brother of John T. Gilman. Congressman, Federalist, from New Hampshire, 1789–97; U.S. senator, (Democrat) Republican, 1805–14.

GILMAN, SAMUEL (*b. Gloucester, Mass., 1791; d. Kingston, Mass., 1858*), Unitarian clergyman, author. Graduated Harvard, 1811. Minister of Second Independent Church, Charleston, S.C., *post* 1819; published poems and translations. Wrote "Fair Harvard," 1836.

GILMER, FRANCIS WALKER (*b. Albemarle Co., Va., 1790; d. 1826*), lawyer, author. Grandson of Dr. Thomas Walker. Procured professors, books, equipment for new University of Virginia on mission to Great Britain at Thomas Jefferson's request, 1824.

GILMER, GEORGE ROCKINGHAM (*b. Broad River Settlement, Ga., 1790; d. Georgia, 1859*), lawyer, congressman. Democratic governor of Georgia, 1829–31, 1837–39. Author of *Sketches of Some of the First Settlers of Upper Georgia* (1855).

GILMER, JOHN ADAMS (*b. Guilford Co., N.C., 1805; d. 1868*), lawyer, legislator. Congressman, Whig, from North Carolina, 1857–61. An outstanding

Southern Unionist who strongly opposed secession, he declined a place in Lincoln's cabinet and urged withdrawal of federal troops from Southern forts. He later sat in Confederate Congress.

GILMER, THOMAS WALKER (*b. Albemarle Co., Va., 1802; d. 1844*), legislator, statesman. Whig governor of Virginia, 1840–41; congressman, 1841–43; secretary of the navy, 1844. Killed in gun explosion on U.S.S. *Princeton.*

GILMOR, HARRY (*b. near Baltimore, Md., 1838; d. 1883*), soldier. Daring Confederate cavalry raider.

GILMORE, JAMES ROBERTS (*b. Boston, Mass., 1822; d. Glens Falls, N.Y., 1903*), cotton-shipper. Writer under pseudonym "Edmund Kirke" of superficial sketches of the South at war. With James F. Jaquess, undertook unofficial mission (July 1864) from Lincoln to Jefferson Davis, seeking peace terms.

GILMORE, JOSEPH ALBREE (*b. Weston, Vt., 1811; d. 1867*), railroad executive, legislator. Republican governor of New Hampshire, 1863–65.

GILMORE, JOSEPH HENRY (*b. Boston, Mass., 1834; d. Rochester, N.Y., 1918*), Baptist clergyman, teacher. Professor of rhetoric, University of Rochester, 1868–1908; author of textbooks, and of the hymn "He Leadeth Me."

GILMORE, PATRICK SARSFIELD (*b. near Dublin, Ireland, 1829; d. St. Louis, Mo., 1892*), bandmaster. Came to America, *c.* 1849. Originator of monster band concerts.

GILMOUR, RICHARD (*b. Glasgow, Scotland, 1824; d. St. Augustine, Fla., 1891*), Roman Catholic clergyman. Came to America as a child. A convert to Catholicism, 1842; consecrated bishop of Cleveland, O., 1872. An aggressive leader and upholder of episcopal prerogatives, he ruled his rapidly growing diocese with a strong hand.

GILPIN, CHARLES SIDNEY (*b. Richmond, Va., 1878; d. Eldridge Park, N.J., 1930*), printer, actor. Managed first Negro stock company in New York City, 1916. His great triumph was the title role in Eugene O'Neill's *Emperor Jones* which he created in November 1920.

GILPIN, EDWARD WOODWARD (*b. Wilmington, Del., 1803; d. Dover, Del., 1876*), jurist. Attorney-general of Delaware, 1840–50; upheld Negro rights in *The State vs. James Whittaker.* Chief justice of Delaware, 1857–76.

GILPIN, HENRY DILWORTH (*b. Lancaster, England, 1801; d. 1860*), Philadelphia lawyer and author. Brother of William Gilpin. U.S. attorney, eastern district of Pennsylvania, 1831–37; U.S. attorney-general, 1840–41.

GILPIN, WILLIAM (*b. Brandywine, Pa., 1813; d. Denver, Colo., 1894*), soldier, lawyer, editor. Accompanied J. C. Frémont on 1843 expedition; served with Doniphan's Missouri volunteers in Mexican War. First territorial governor of Colorado, 1861–62, he helped save Colorado for the Union.

GINN, EDWIN (*b. Orland, Maine, 1838; d. Winchester, Mass., 1914*), textbook publisher. Founded Ginn & Co., 1867. Endowed World Peace Foundation.

GINTER, LEWIS (*b. New York, N.Y., 1824; d. Richmond, Va., 1897*), tobacconist, philanthropist.

GIRARD, CHARLES FRÉDÉRIC (*b. Mülhausen, Alsace, 1822; d. Neuilly-sur-Seine, France, 1895*), zoölogist, physician. Came to America as assistant to Louis Agassiz, 1847. At Smithsonian Institution, 1850–60, he was chief author of reports on fishes and reptiles collected by Wilkes and Pacific Railroad exploring expeditions.

GIRARD, STEPHEN (*b. Bordeaux, France, 1750; d. Philadelphia, Pa., 1831*), merchant, financier, philanthropist. Served as master in French merchant marine and for Thos. Randall and Son of New York, 1773–76; settled in Philadelphia after the British left that city and established himself in the West Indian, Asian and European trade. Commerce to him was a subject of vast speculative possibilities to which he brought great industry, initiative, a genius for detail and a knowledge of sea markets and political conditions acquired through personal experience and careful study of the reports of his agents. Branching out into banking, real estate, insurance, he grew rich. A strong supporter of the First United States Bank, he served on the committee which petitioned for renewal of the bank's charter in 1810. When Congress refused, Girard bought the bank building and started the "Bank of Stephen Girard" as a private venture. With David Parish and John Jacob Astor, Girard arranged with treasury secretary Gallatin to take over the unsubscribed portion of the U.S. loan for the War of 1812 and dispose of it to the public. This action restored public confidence and averted financial crisis. After the war, Girard rendered a similar service by taking over \$3,000,000 worth of stock in the Second U.S. Bank.

In the yellow fever epidemic at Philadelphia, 1793, Girard volunteered to superintend the Bush Hill fever hospital, where he nursed the sick day and night. He served Philadelphia in many ways, leaving in his will over \$6,000,000 in trust to the city for educating poor white orphan boys. Girard College is the monument to this generosity. He also left sums to Pennsylvania for internal improvements.

GIRARDEAU, JOHN LAFAYETTE (*b. near Charleston, S.C., 1825; d. Columbia, S.C., 1898*), Presbyterian clergyman, theologian. Ministered to Negroes in Charleston, 1853–60; served as Confederate chaplain; was professor of theology, Columbia Seminary, 1875–95.

GIRSCH, FREDERICK (*b. Büdingen, Germany, 1821; d. Mt. Vernon, N.Y., 1895*), bank-note engraver.

GIRTY, SIMON (*b. near Harrisburg, Pa., 1741; d. near Amherstburg, Canada, 1818*), "the Great Renegade." An Indian captive, 1756–59, he was employed as an interpreter at Fort Pitt, 1759–74. Served as scout in Dunmore's War and as interpreter for Continental forces, 1776. With Alexander McKee and others, he deserted the American cause in March 1778 and fled to Detroit, where Lieutenant-Governor Hamilton used him as interpreter. Active in many forays against the frontier settlers, he was notoriously savage and cruel, encouraging the torture of captives. He remained among the tribes in the Ohio country, opposing any peace with the Americans, and participated in many battles, including St. Clair's defeat and Fallen Timbers.

GIST, CHRISTOPHER (*b. Maryland, c. 1706; d. South Carolina or Georgia, 1759*), explorer, soldier. The first white American to explore carefully the Ohio River lands and northeastern Kentucky (1750–51), preceding Daniel Boone by 18 years, his reports show keen observation of topography and native customs; his plats and surveys have been much praised. On a mission to Fort Le Boeuf, 1753–54, Gist twice saved George Washington's life. He was with Washington in the defeat of Jumonville, 1754, at the surrender of Fort Necessity and on the Braddock campaign.

GIST, MORDECAI (*b. near Reisterstown, Md., 1742/43; d. South Carolina, 1792*), Revolutionary soldier. Nephew of Christopher Gist. This devoted patriot served throughout the war, rising to brigadier-general, 1779. The dying De Kalb praised his conduct in the Battle of Camden.

GIST, WILLIAM HENRY (*b. Charleston, S.C., 1807; d. Union District, S.C., 1874*), planter, legislator. As governor of South Carolina, 1858–60, he pressed for secession and directed the legislature's proceedings to accomplish it after Lincoln's election.

GLACKENS, WILLIAM JAMES (*b. Philadelphia, Pa., 1870; d. Westport, Conn., 1938*), painter, illustrator. Worked as an artist-reporter on various Philadelphia newspapers, meanwhile studying painting at Pennsylvania Academy of the Fine Arts under Robert Henri. Later, did magazine and book illustrating in New York; concentrated on painting, *post* 1905. One of "The Eight"; helped organize and was president of Society of Independent Artists; was chairman, Selection Committee of the "Armory Show." Although frequently a spokesman for the vanguard of American artists, Glackens was always a painter of gay, pleasant, and elegant scenes, his glowing luminous impressionism suggesting some of Renoir's coloristic tendencies.
[*Supp. 2*]

GLADDEN, WASHINGTON (*b. Pottsgrove, Pa., 1836; d. Columbus, O., 1918*), Congregational clergyman, early proponent of the "social gospel." Graduated Williams, 1859. Held pastorates in New York, Massachusetts, and in Columbus, O., 1882–1918. Influenced by F. W. Robertson and Horace Bushnell. Active as a popularizer of the new trends in Biblical criticism, he is more famous, however, for application of fundamental religious principles to social relations in such books as *Working People and their Employers* (1876), *The Christian Way* (1877), *Applied Christianity* (1886), *Social Salvation* (1902), *The Church and Modern Life* (1908). He held that the church's chief business is to Christianize the social order, not by use of force or endorsing a particular program but by inspiring individuals with love of justice and the spirit of service.

GLADWIN, HENRY (*b. Stubbing Court, near Chesterfield, England, 1729; d. Stubbing Court, 1791*), British soldier. Best known for his brilliant defense of Detroit in Pontiac's War, 1763–64, he had previously fought under Braddock and Gage. He refused to serve in the Revolutionary War.

GLASS, FRANKLIN POTTS (*b. Centreville, Ala., 1858; d. Birmingham, Ala., 1934*), manager, *Montgomery Advertiser*, 1886–1915; editor, *Birmingham News*, 1910–20; publisher, *Montgomery Advertiser*, 1927–34. A forceful, independent journalist. [*Supp.* 1]

GLASS, HUGH (*fl. 1823–1833*), trapper. Joined Ashley's Missouri River expedition, 1823. Returning to the mouth of the Yellowstone in August with Andrew Henry's party, he was terribly injured by a grizzly bear. His death momentarily expected, he was left in charge of James Bridger and a certain Fitzgerald. They took his rifle and equipment and rejoined the party, reporting him dead and buried. Regaining some strength, Glass began crawling toward Fort Kiowa, more than 100 miles away. He reached it and recuperated, vowing vengeance. He forgave Bridger because of his youth; later, after recovering his favorite rifle, he abated his wrath against Fitzgerald. Glass was subsequently the hero of many encounters with Indians. He is believed to have been killed by Blackfeet on the upper Yellowstone.

GLASS, MONTAGUE MARSDEN (*b. Manchester, England, 1877; d. 1934*), author. Came to America, 1890. Creator of the characters "Potash and Perlmutter" who were famous for a generation in story, stage and motion pictures. [*Supp.* 1]

GLEASON, FREDERIC GRANT (*b. Middletown, Conn., 1848; d. 1903*), composer, organist. Studied with Dudley Buck and in Germany. *Post* 1877, taught and worked in Chicago, Ill.

GLEASON, KATE (*b. Rochester, N.Y., 1865; d. Rochester, 1933*), business woman, philanthropist. An energetic promoter and leader in the development of gear-cutting machinery and home-building projects. [*Supp.* 1]

GLEAVES, ALBERT (*b. Nashville, Tenn., 1858; d. Haverford, Pa., 1937*), naval officer. Graduated Annapolis, 1877. Authority on ordnance and hydrography; in charge of Atlantic convoy operations, World War I. During his command of Destroyer Force, a successful method of refueling at sea was devised. [*Supp.* 2]

GLENN, HUGH (*b. Berkeley Co., Va., 1788; d. Cincinnati, O., 1833*), trader, army contractor. With Jacob Fowler, conducted first successful trading expedition to Mexican provinces, from Verdigris River to Santa Fe, 1821–22.

GLIDDEN, CHARLES JASPER (*b. Lowell, Mass., 1857; d. 1927*), telephone pioneer, motorist, aviator. Directed test of long-distance telephony for Alexander Graham Bell, 1876; organized first telephone exchange at Lowell, Mass., 1877, which gave satisfactory service with one of first multiple switchboards. The Lowell Company and other Massachusetts companies established by Glidden, William A. Ingham and associates were the nucleus of New England Telephone Co. Successful in this and other telephone operations, Glidden turned his attention to motoring and aviation, organizing the first round-the-world motor tour, and establishing the Glidden trophy, 1905. He made 46 balloon ascensions and was prominent in early air meets. President of World's Board of Aeronautical Commissioners, he also edited *Aeronautical Digest*, 1921–24.

GLIDDEN, JOSEPH FARWELL (*b. Charleston, N.H., 1813; d. 1906*), farmer, inventor, capitalist. Removed *c.* 1844 to De Kalb, Ill.; managed large Illinois and Texas farms. Invented and patented, 1874, a basic improvement in barbed wire fencing which made its manufacture feasible and successful.

GLOVER, JOHN (*b. Salem, Mass., 1732; d. Marblehead, Mass., 1797*), Revolutionary soldier. Commanded troop transports in retreat from Long Island; ferried army across Delaware to Trenton, 1776. Promoted brigadier-general, 1777, he retired after extensive further service in 1782.

GLOVER, SAMUEL TAYLOR (*b. Virginia, 1813; d. 1884*), lawyer. Raised in Kentucky; removed to Missouri, 1837; practiced in Palmyra and St. Louis. Devoted to emancipation; prominent in retaining Missouri in the Union, 1861–65; leading constitutional lawyer of his time in the West.

GLOVER, TOWNEND (*b. Rio de Janeiro, Brazil, 1813; d. Baltimore, Md., 1883*), artist, earliest government entomologist. Educated in England and Germany; came to America, 1836. Served as insect expert in Bureau of Agriculture, 1854–78.

GLUCK, ALMA (b. Bucharest, Roumania, 1884; d. New York, N.Y., 1938), operatic and concert soprano. Came to America as a child. [Supp. 2]

GLYNN, JAMES (b. Philadelphia, Pa., 1801; d. New Haven, Conn., 1871), naval officer. His reports after rescue of American sailors held captive in Japan, 1849, helped prepare the way for Commodore M. C. Perry's mission, 1853–54.

GLYNN, MARTIN HENRY (b. Kinderhook, N.Y., 1871; d. Albany, N.Y., 1924), journalist, lawyer, politician. Graduated Fordham, 1894. Edited Albany Times-Union, post 1895. Astute state comptroller, 1906–08. As Democratic governor of New York, 1913–14, he instituted workmen's compensation law and statewide primary elections.

GMEINER, JOHN (b. Baernau, Bavaria, 1847; d. 1913), Roman Catholic priest, author. Came to America as a child; raised and educated in Wisconsin. An authority on German emigrants, he opposed "Cahenslyism," expressed a stout Americanism, as teacher and pastor in Wisconsin and Minnesota.

GOBRECHT, CHRISTIAN (b. Hanover, Pa., 1785; d. Philadelphia, Pa., 1844), die-sinker, engraver to the U.S. Mint in Philadelphia, post 1836.

GODBE, WILLIAM SAMUEL (b. London, England, 1833; d. Brighton, Utah, 1902), merchant, mine operator, Mormon convert and dissenter. Came to Salt Lake City, 1851. Disfellowshipped by Mormons, 1869, for advocating development of mining industry, he championed liberal attitude in his Utah Magazine and Salt Lake Tribune.

GODDARD, CALVIN LUTHER (b. Covington, N.Y., 1822; d. Worcester, Mass., 1895), inventor. Patented (1866) and marketed indispensable machine for extracting burrs and dust from wool.

GODDARD, JOHN (b. Dartmouth, Mass., 1723/24; d. Newport, R.I., 1785), leading Newport cabinet-maker. Produced unequaled pieces in Santo Domingo mahogany, especially secretaries and knee-hole desks. Probably originated the "block front" which he perfected.

GODDARD, LUTHER MARCELLUS (b. Palmyra, N.Y., 1840; d. 1917), lawyer. Practiced in Leavenworth, Kans., 1865–78; thereafter in Leadville and Denver, Colo. As district judge, and judge of Colorado supreme court, his common-sense decisions and masterly opinions largely developed into its present form the state law dealing with prospecting and mining claims.

GODDARD, MORRILL (b. Auburn, Maine, 1865; d. Naskeag Point, Maine, 1937), journalist. Grandson of Anson P. Morrill. Innovator of the sensational "Sunday Supplement" with pictures and comics. City editor and Sunday editor, New York World, 1885–95; first editor of the American Weekly. [Supp. 2]

GODDARD, PAUL BECK (b. Baltimore, Md., 1811; d. Philadelphia, Pa., 1866), physician, anatomist, pioneer in photography. Discovered and exhibited in 1839 use of vapor of bromine on silvered plate, perfecting Daguerre's process. Obtained first instantaneous pictures by heliographic process.

GODDARD, PLINY EARLE (b. Lewiston, Maine, 1869; d. 1928), ethnologist. Graduated Earlham College, 1892; served as lay missionary to Hupa tribe in California. Became outstanding authority in Athapascan; wrote intensive, uniformly valuable studies, principally of Indian languages; was associated post 1909 with American Museum of Natural History, New York.

GODDARD, WILLIAM (b. New London, Conn., 1740; d. Rhode Island, 1817), printer, Whig journalist. Pioneer printer of Providence, R.I. (1762); published Pennsylvania Chronicle, 1767–74; established Maryland Journal, 1773, at Baltimore.

GODDU, LOUIS (b. St. Césaire, Canada, 1837; d. Winchester, Mass., 1919), inventor of shoe-manufacturing machines.

GODEFROY, MAXIMILIAN (fl. 1806–1824), painter, architect, military engineer. Came to America, 1805. Designed St. Mary's Seminary chapel, Baltimore, Md., 1807, first Gothic revival church built in America; also the Unitarian Church and fortifications in Baltimore (1814–17), and Richmond, Va., Court House (1816).

GODEY, LOUIS ANTOINE (b. New York, N.Y., 1804; d. Philadelphia, Pa., 1878), publisher of Godey's Lady's Book, post 1830, and other magazines.

GODFREY, BENJAMIN (b. Chatham, Mass., 1794; d. Godfrey, Ill., 1862), sea-captain, merchant, financier, philanthropist. Made and lost several fortunes in Mexico and New Orleans, La. Settled in Alton, Ill., 1832; ruined state bank by using money in speculative schemes to develop Alton. Founded Monticello Female Academy, 1838.

GODFREY, THOMAS (b. Philadelphia, Pa., 1704; d. 1749), glazier, mathematician, true inventor of Hadley's quadrant. His natural, uneducated genius for mathematics, astronomy and optics was encouraged by James Logan. In 1730 Godfrey invented and made a quadrant improved over Davis's which was then in general use. Godfrey's quadrant was tried in Delaware Bay, and Capt. Wright carried it to Jamaica, where "he showed and explained it to several Englishmen, among whom was a nephew of Hadley's." The Royal Society being about to reward James Hadley for inventing a similar quadrant in 1734, Gov. Logan wrote and claimed recognition for Godfrey.

GODFREY, THOMAS (b. Philadelphia, Pa., 1736; d. Wilmington, N.C., 1763), poet, playwright. Son of Thomas Godfrey (1704–1749). Under the tutelage of

William Smith he joined a group of young men (including Benjamin West and Francis Hopkinson) who pioneered in painting, music and drama in the middle colonies. He wrote Cavalier love songs, pastorals and a long poem *The Court of Fancy* (published 1762), but is remembered for the *Prince of Parthia*, a romantic tragedy which he wrote c. 1758–59 for David Douglass's American Company. The first drama written by a native American to be produced on the professional stage (Philadelphia, 1767), it had already been published in his *Juvenile Poems* (1765).

GODKIN, EDWIN LAWRENCE (*b. Moyne, Ireland, 1831; d. Brixham, England, 1902*), journalist. Came to America, 1856, after experience as a correspondent in Hungary and the Crimea. Edited the *Nation* from its foundation in 1865. Noted for range of scholarship and breadth of view, the influence of the paper was out of all proportion to its circulation. Godkin was also editor-in-chief of the New York *Evening Post*, 1883–1900. By his entire independence of party and fearless treatment of public questions, Godkin won a unique place in the American journalism of his time.

GODMAN, JOHN DAVIDSON (*b. Annapolis, Md., 1794; d. 1830*), naturalist, anatomist. Edited *Western Quarterly Reporter* (Cincinnati, O., 1822), the first medical journal published west of Alleghanies; author of *American Natural History* (1826–28), first original treatise on this subject, and *Rambler of a Naturalist* (1833).

GODOWSKY, LEOPOLD (*b. Soshly, Lithuania, 1870; d. New York, N.Y., 1938*), concert pianist, composer. Taught in the United States, 1891–1900; settled here, 1914. [*Supp. 2*]

GODWIN, PARKE (*b. Paterson, N.J., 1816; d. 1904*), editor, author. Associated (1836–81) with N.Y. *Evening Post*, later editor of *Commercial Advertiser*. Edited reference works and the collected works of his father-in-law, William Cullen Bryant (1883–84).

GOEBEL, WILLIAM (*b. Carbondale, Pa., 1856; d. Kentucky, 1900*), lawyer, legislator. Raised in Covington, Ky. Credited with the passing of much reform legislation as a Democratic state senator, 1887–99, he was sponsor of the bitterly denounced Goebel Election Law of 1898. He secured nomination for governor, 1899, by a series of political maneuvers which greatly increased the number of his enemies. An exciting campaign resulted in a contested election and Goebel's murder on January 30, 1900. The legislature declared him legally elected governor before his death.

GOERZ, DAVID (*b. Neu Bereslow, South Russia, 1849; d. California, 1914*), Mennonite clergyman. Came to America, 1873; settled in Kansas. Excelled as organizer and missioner.

GOESSMANN, CHARLES ANTHONY (*b. Naumburg, Germany, 1827; d. 1910*), chemist. Ph.D., Göt-

tingen, 1852. Came to America, 1857, and worked in sugar and salt refining. Professor at Massachusetts Agricultural College, 1868–1907, he helped shape the policies of this new type of college and developed its experiment station.

GOETHALS, GEORGE WASHINGTON (*b. Brooklyn, N.Y., 1858; d. 1928*), engineer, soldier, builder of the Panama Canal. Graduated West Point, 1880. Previously assigned to important canal, river and harbor works, he was appointed by President Theodore Roosevelt chief engineer of the Panama Canal, 1907, with full authority and responsibility for every phase of the work. Tact and intelligence were needed to combat civilian prejudice against an army man; moreover, 30,000 employees of many nationalities had to be housed, fed, amused and kept healthy. Offices, messes, quarters, machine shops, cold-storage plants, schools, recreation centers were built. Departments of sanitation, accounting and supply and a complete judicial system were instituted. Labor troubles and landslides delayed the work, but persistently and patiently, Goethals and his assistants overcame gigantic engineering and personnel problems. He devoted time every day to hearing complaints of employees, no matter how trivial, and built up in them a dedication to the project and an *esprit de corps* which has probably never been surpassed. Starting in an atmosphere of opposition, Goethals ended his construction days on the Isthmus with the respect and even veneration of his helpers.

The Panama Canal was opened to world commerce in August 1914. Goethals remained as governor of the Canal Zone until the latter part of 1916, having been made a major-general by special act of Congress. He retired in November 1916 at his own request but was recalled in December 1917 as acting quartermaster-general, and given additional duty as director of purchase, storage and traffic, supervising transport of all supplies and movement of all troops throughout the first World War. He returned voluntarily to the retired list, 1919, but served as consulting engineer on many important works, including the Inner Harbor Navigation Canal of New Orleans, Columbia Basin Irrigation Project, East Bay Municipal Utility District of Oakland, California, and the New York-New Jersey Port and Harbor Development Commission.

GOETSCHIUS, JOHN HENRY (*b. Berneck, Switzerland, 1718; d. New Jersey, 1774*), Reformed Dutch clergyman. Came to America, 1735. Belligerent minister of Long Island and New Jersey churches, he supported the Coetus party, which wished to be free from control of the Classis of Amsterdam.

GOETZ, GEORGE. [See CALVERTON, VICTOR FRANCIS, 1900–1940.]

GOETZ, GEORGE WASHINGTON (*b. Milwaukee, Wis., 1856; d. 1897*), metallurgist, consultant to large steel and iron companies. Pioneered in gas analysis, mechanical puddling, and the "basic" process which he was first to use successfully in America.

GOFF, EMMET STULL (*b. Elmira, N.Y., 1852; d. 1902*), horticulturist. Noted for research in economic entomology, plant pathology and physiology, and for experiments with fungicides, insecticides, he was also an effective professor of horticulture at University of Wisconsin, 1889–1902.

GOFF, JOHN WILLIAM (*b. Co. Wexford, Ireland, 1848; d. 1924*), jurist. Came to America as a child. Counsel for Lexow Committee, 1893, which investigated corruption in New York City police department. Last recorder of New York, 1894–1906; New York supreme court justice, 1906–19.

GOFFE, WILLIAM (*d. 1679?*), Parliamentary soldier, regicide. Fled with Edward Whalley to New England, 1660. He moved secretly from place to place and probably died in Hartford, Conn.

GOFORTH, WILLIAM (*b. New York, N.Y., 1766; d. Cincinnati, O., 1817*), physician. Removed to Kentucky, 1788; *post* 1800, was leading physician in Cincinnati. Teacher of Daniel Drake, he was probably the first to vaccinate in the Northwest Territory (1801).

GOING, JONATHAN (*b. Reading, Vt., 1786; d. 1844*), Baptist clergyman, educator. Graduated Brown, 1809. With John M. Peck planned American Baptist Home Mission Society, 1832, and served as its secretary. President of college at Granville, O., later Denison University, 1837–44.

GOLDBECK, ROBERT (*b. Potsdam, Prussia, 1839; d. St. Louis, Mo., 1908*), pianist, teacher, prolific composer.

GOLDBERGER, JOSEPH (*b. Austria, 1874; d. Washington, D.C., 1929*), medical research worker. Came to America as a child. M.D., Bellevue Hospital Medical College, 1895. Served in U.S. Public Health Service, and *post* 1904 with Hygienic Laboratory, Washington. Directed pellagra research campaign, 1913–25, which practically freed Southern public institutions of the disease.

GOLDENWEISER, ALEXANDER ALEXANDROVICH (*b. Kiev, Russia, 1880; d. Portland, Oreg., 1940*), anthropologist. [*Supp. 2*]

GOLDER, FRANK ALFRED (*b. near Odessa, Russia, 1877; d. Stanford, Calif., 1929*), historian. Came to America as a child. Graduated Bucknell, 1898; Ph.D., Harvard, 1909. Authority on Alaska, Russian expansion in Pacific. Professor of history, Stanford; director, Hoover War Library.

GOLDIN, HORACE (*b. near Vilna, Poland, 1873; d. London, England, 1939*), internationally known magician, innovator of "Sawing a Woman in Half." [*Supp. 2*]

GOLDMAN, EMMA (*b. Kovno, Lithuania, 1869; d. Toronto, Canada, 1940*), anarchist editor and propagandist, lecturer, literary critic. Resided in the U.S. from 1885 until her deportation to Russia in 1919. [*Supp. 2*]

GOLDMAN, MAYER C. (*b. New Orleans, La., 1874; d. New York, N.Y., 1939*), lawyer. Lifetime advocate of a public defender in criminal cases. [*Supp. 2*]

GOLDMARK, RUBIN (*b. New York, N.Y., 1872; d. New York, 1936*), pianist, composer, music teacher. Studied at Vienna Conservatory, and at New York's National Conservatory under Joseffy and Dvořák. Director, Colorado College Conservatory, 1895–1901; of the department of theory of New York College of Music, 1911–24; and of the composition department of Juilliard School, 1924–36. Goldmark influenced a number of students who later became distinguished composers and performers. His own compositions reflect his idealism and thorough craftsmanship. His orchestral works include *Hiawatha* (1900), *Samson* (1914), *Gettysburg Requiem* (1919), *Negro Rhapsody* (1922), and *Call of the Plains* (*c. 1932*). [*Supp. 2*]

GOLDSBOROUGH, CHARLES (*b. near Cambridge, Md., 1765; d. near Cambridge, 1834*), lawyer, legislator. Congressman, Federalist, 1805–17; last Federalist governor of Maryland, 1818–19.

GOLDSBOROUGH, LOUIS MALESHERBES (*b. Washington, D.C., 1805; d. 1877*), naval officer. Commanded Atlantic and North Atlantic Blockading Squadrons, *post* 1861; commanded fleet which, with Burnside's troops, captured Roanoke Island and destroyed Confederate fleet, 1862; was later criticized for ineffectiveness at Drewry's Bluff. Retired in 1873 as rear-admiral.

GOLDSBOROUGH, ROBERT (*b. near Cambridge, Md., 1733; d. near Cambridge, 1788*), lawyer, legislator, member of Continental Congress, 1774–75.

GOLDSMITH, MIDDLETON (*b. Port Tobacco, Md., 1818; d. Rutland, Vt., 1887*), physician, surgeon. Graduated N.Y. College of Physicians and Surgeons, 1840. With his father, introduced practice of lithotrity. Taught surgery at Castleton, Vt. and Louisville, Ky. During Civil War, as Union Army surgeon devised a bromine treatment for gangrene which was generally adopted.

GOLDTHWAITE, GEORGE (*b. Boston, Mass., 1809; d. 1879*), jurist. Removed to Montgomery, Ala., *c.* 1826. Read law with brother, Henry B. Goldthwaite, and achieved success as lawyer and planter. Unsympathetic to slavery, he opposed but accepted secession. Served as U.S. senator, Democrat, from Alabama, 1871–77.

GOLDTHWAITE, HENRY BARNES (*b. Concord, N.H., 1802; d. 1847*), lawyer. Brother of George Goldthwaite. Removed to Alabama, *c.* 1817; won distinction as lawyer in Mobile, and as Alabama supreme court justice *post* 1836.

GOMPERS, SAMUEL (*b. London, England, 1850; d. 1924*), labor leader. Apprenticed to a cigar-maker; came to America, 1863; joined Cigarmakers' Union, 1864. Attended Cooper Union lectures, but got the most important part of his education in the skilled cigarmakers' shops where books, papers and magazines were purchased from a common fund and the workmen took turns reading aloud. Ferdinand Laurrell, a one-time leader of the Scandinavian Marxist Socialist organization, interpreted the Communist Manifesto for Gompers, taught him the "Marx of trade unionism" and warned him against joining the Socialist movement. Gompers went to Socialist meetings, was admitted to the inner circle of a group of European refugees, *die Zehn Philosophen.* From this group "came the purpose and the initiative that finally resulted in the present American labor movement."

In 1877, local American cigarmakers' unions carried on a prolonged and fruitless strike against the tenement house sweating system. Gompers and Strasser led in a reorganization of the cigarmakers, Strasser becoming the international president or traveling organizer, Gompers president of Local 144. In this reorganization, they made international officers supreme over local unions, greatly increased membership dues to build up a fund, concentrated control of that fund in the national officers, and adopted, or prepared to adopt, sickness, accident and unemployment benefits. The cigarmakers' union became a model for others, and in 1881 the "Federation of Organized Trades and Labor Unions of the United States of America and Canada" was formed, reorganized in 1886 as the American Federation of Labor and operating on a unique basis of principles. Elected president of the new Federation, Gompers remained official head of the American labor movement, except for one year, until his death. The power he exerted may be called "moral," a term which in his interpretation signified organized consent to collective action. He believed that drastic methods would not bring education and solidarity; that it was persuasion, not dictation, that unionized. Gompers's moral influence with the executives of each national union was founded on their knowledge that no "dual union" would be allowed to displace them. Gompers was well aware of the limits beyond which labor organization could not go. Labor could not lift itself as a body into another status. For this reason Gompers was always against theorizers and intellectuals in the organization of labor. Amid all the differences in America of religion, race, language, politics, there was only one direction toward which labor should unite—more wages, more leisure, more liberty. Labor must struggle by collective action toward better living, better citizenship.

Although Gompers held that labor is always right,

his conviction that labor could never displace the capitalist in management enabled him to negotiate with capitalists. He felt too that labor could not compete with politicians, that its role in politics was to bargain for immunity from interference by legislatures, courts and executives so that it could use its own power in collective bargaining. With the expansion of the American Federation of Labor, Gompers became an important public figure. President Wilson appointed him to the Council of National Defense and to the Commission on International Labor Legislation at the Peace Conference. During the first World War he was an implacable foe of pacifism and organized a War Committee on Labor. His autobiography, *Seventy Years of Life and Labor* (1925), is an authoritative and important account of the rise and growth of American trade unionism.

GONZALES, AMBROSE ELLIOTT (*b. Colleton Co., S.C., 1857; d. 1926*), newspaper publisher, writer of Negro dialect stories. His liberal paper, the Columbia, S.C., *State,* opposed the Tillman regime, *post* 1891, fought for reforms, and achieved a national reputation.

GOOCH, Sir WILLIAM (*b. Yarmouth, England, 1681; d. Bath, England, 1751*), colonial governor of Virginia, 1727–49. Favorably regarded by colonists, he staunchly defended them and tried to improve tobacco export conditions.

GOOD, ADOLPHUS CLEMENS (*b. West Mahoning, Pa., 1856; d. Efulen, Cameroons, 1894*), Presbyterian missionary to Africa, naturalist. Unusually effective in his work, he journeyed far into interior; prepared a Bulu primer and translated Gospels into Bulu.

GOOD, JAMES ISAAC (*b. York, Pa., 1850; d. Philadelphia, Pa., 1924*), German Reformed clergyman. Graduated Lafayette, 1872; Union Theological, 1875. Pastor and seminary professor; his greatest work was as historian of the Reformed Church. He discovered documents, collected a notable library, published over twenty books.

GOOD, JEREMIAH HAAK (*b. Rehrersburg, Pa., 1822; d. Tiffin, O., 1888*), German Reformed clergyman. Uncle of James I. Good. Studied at Marshall College and Mercersburg. Pastor in Ohio; taught at Heidelberg College. Professor of theology and president, Heidelberg Theological Seminary, 1869–87.

GOOD, JOHN (*b. Co. Roscommon, Ireland, 1841; d. 1908*), inventor, manufacturer of rope. Came to America as a child; raised in Brooklyn, N.Y. Granted more than 100 patents for rope-making machinery, 1869–1908, he revolutionized this hitherto hand industry.

GOODALE, GEORGE LINCOLN (*b. Saco, Maine, 1839; d. 1923*), physician, botanist. Son of Stephen L. Goodale. Graduated Amherst, 1860; M.D., Harvard and Bowdoin, 1863. Taught at Harvard and was Fisher Professor of Natural History, 1888–1909. Stimulated interest in plant physiology, economic botany and in Harvard Botanical Garden and Museum which he developed.

GOODALE, STEPHEN LINCOLN (*b. South Berwick, Maine, 1815; d. Saco, Maine, 1897*), agriculturist. Secretary of Maine Board of Agriculture; stimulated scientific approach to all phases of agricultural practice.

GOODALL, HARVEY L. (*b. Lunenburg, Vt., 1836; d. 1900*), journalist. Founded Chicago *Sun* in 1869, and *Drovers' Journal*, pioneer livestock market paper, in 1873.

GOODALL, THOMAS (*b. Dewsbury, England, 1823; d. 1910*), woolen manufacturer, originator of the horse blanket. Came to America, 1846. His mills at Sanford, Maine, were first in country to make carriage robes, mohair, plushes, kersey blankets.

GOODE, GEORGE BROWN (*b. New Albany, Ind., 1851; d. 1896*), ichthyologist, museum administrator, assistant secretary of Smithsonian Institution. Graduated Wesleyan (Conn.), 1870. Author of monographs and books on his speciality and of histories of the Smithsonian (1895 and 1897).

GOODE, JOHN (*b. Bedford Co., Va., 1829; d. 1909*), lawyer, Confederate soldier and congressman, statesman. Congressman, Democrat, from Virginia, 1875–81; president, Virginia Constitutional Convention, 1901–02.

GOODE, JOHN PAUL (*b. near Stewartville, Minn., 1862; d. Little Point Sable, Mich., 1932*), geographer. Graduated University of Minnesota, 1889; Ph.D., University of Pennsylvania, 1901. Taught at University of Chicago, 1903–28. Made his principal reputation as a cartographer in a series of maps for school use which set new standards in design and craftsmanship, and a school atlas. His projections embodied three new devices: the principle of "interruption" in a map grid applied to a sinusoidal projection (1916); a homolosine projection, using the sinusoidal from the equator to nearly 40° north and south, and homolographic thence to the poles (1923); and a polar equal-area projection in which continental lobes were deployed radially from the North Pole (1928). [*Supp. 1*]

GOODELL, HENRY HILL (*b. Constantinople, Turkey, 1839; d. on shipboard, 1905*), educator. Son of William Goodell (1792–1867). Graduated Amherst, 1862. Taught at Massachusetts Agricultural College, 1867–86; president, 1886–1905.

GOODELL, WILLIAM (*b. Templeton, Mass., 1792; d. Philadelphia, Pa., 1867*), Congregational clergyman; missionary to Near East, 1823–65. Laid foundation for American Board's work in Turkey with mission at Constantinople; translated Bible into Armeno-Turkish.

GOODELL, WILLIAM (*b. Coventry, N.Y., 1792; d. Janesville, Wis., 1878*), reformer, Abolitionist. Edited a great number of temperance and anti-slavery publications; founded Liberty League, 1847, which opposed slavery, monopoly, tariffs, liquor, war and secret societies.

GOODENOW, JOHN MILTON (*b. Westmoreland, N.H., 1782; d. New Orleans, La., 1838*), jurist. Removed to Ohio, 1811; admitted to bar, 1813. Successfully opposed Judge Benjamin Tappan's view that, in absence of specific state legislation, crimes under English common law should be held as crimes by Ohio courts.

GOODHUE, BENJAMIN (*b. Salem, Mass., 1748; d. 1814*), merchant, legislator. Congressman, Federalist, from Massachusetts, 1789–96; U.S. senator, 1796–1800. Cousin of Timothy Pickering.

GOODHUE, BERTRAM GROSVENOR (*b. Pomfret, Conn., 1869; d. 1924*), architect. Studied in office of James Renwick, New York City; as a draftsman, soon gained reputation for remarkable facility. Joined new firm of Ralph Adams Cram and Francis Wentworth in Boston, 1889; later he became a partner. Working in the style of the English Gothic revival and influenced by Morris and the Arts and Crafts movement, Goodhue did book design and type design at this period as well as ecclesiastical buildings. This first period of his career culminated in the group of buildings at West Point, commissioned, 1903. The superb rugged chapel was Goodhue's particular work, and the group gave a powerful impetus to the adoption of Gothic forms in college architecture.

Goodhue removed to New York c. 1903; the Cram partnership was dissolved in 1913. The detail of St. Thomas's Church, Fifth Avenue, New York, was largely Goodhue's work. His characteristic romantic spirit and design formulae appear in the Chapel of the Intercession, and St. Vincent Ferrer, New York, designed by himself. In St. Bartholomew's, New York, and the University of Chicago Chapel he added Byzantine elements.

As Goodhue grew older he grew dissatisfied with medievalism. The invention of re-enforced concrete turned him toward modernism. "I dream," he wrote, "of something very much bigger and finer and more modern and more suited to present day civilization than any Gothic church could possibly be." In practice he turned toward a kind of classicism shown in the Nebraska Capitol. Essentially a belated romanticist and eclectic, Goodhue was influenced by many styles. He died before achieving a vitally creative modernity.

GOODHUE, JAMES MADISON (*b. Hebron, N.H., 1810; d. 1852*), lawyer, editor. Graduated Amherst, 1833. Removed to Wisconsin, and to St. Paul, Minn., 1849, where he published the *Minnesota Pioneer*, first newspaper in the territory. An outstanding frontier figure, he promoted immigration, urged settlement of Indian lands, sharply criticized conditions in rapidly growing St. Paul.

GOODLOE, DANIEL REAVES (*b. Louisburg, N.C., 1814; d. Warrenton, N.C., 1902*), journalist, Abolitionist, politician. Edited the *National Era* in succession to Gamaliel Bailey; author, among many other writings, of *Inquiry into the Causes which have retarded the Accumulation of Wealth . . . in the Southern States* (1846).

GOODLOE, WILLIAM CASSIUS (*b. Madison Co., Ky., 1841; d. Lexington, Ky., 1889*), politician. Grandnephew, and for a time secretary, of Cassius M. Clay. Helped organize Kentucky Republican party; killed in a sensational fight with political rival, Armistead M. Swope.

GOODMAN, CHARLES (*b. Philadelphia, Pa., 1796; d. Philadelphia, Pa., 1835*), stipple-engraver, lawyer. Taught by David Edwin; gave up engraving and dissolved partnership with Robert Piggot, 1819.

GOODMAN, KENNETH SAWYER (*b. Chicago, Ill., 1883; d. 1918*), playwright. Graduated Princeton, 1906. Specialist in one-act play form. His first book *Quick Curtains* (1915) included "The Game of Chess" and others popular with "little theatres." Plays in which he collaborated with Ben Hecht were published in *The Wonder Hat* (1925).

GOODNIGHT, CHARLES (*b. Macoupin Co., Ill., 1836; d. 1929*), cattleman. Removed to Texas, 1846; was cattle-handler, guide, scout, and a member of the Frontier Regiment, Texas Rangers, during Civil War. Post-war, he established ranches in New Mexico and Colorado. With Oliver Loving, he laid out the Goodnight Cattle Trail from Belknap, Texas, to Fort Sumner, N.M., 1866; he also blazed the Goodnight-Loving Trail into Wyoming, and the New Goodnight Trail from Alamogordo Creek, N.M., to Granada, Colo., 1875. With John George Adair, he developed the JA Ranch in the Texas Panhandle, which soon after the forming of their partnership in 1877 embraced nearly 1,000,000 acres and 100,000 head of cattle. Also in 1877, he ran a cattle trail from the JA Ranch to Dodge City, Kans. In extensive breeding experiments he developed one of America's finest beef herds and a large buffalo herd. Goodnight originated in 1880 and dominated the first Panhandle stockmen's association which policed trails, introduced purebred cattle, systematized range work, kept order.

GOODNOUGH, XANTHUS HENRY (*b. Brookline, Mass., 1860; d. Waterford, Maine, 1935*), sanitary engineer. [*Supp. 1*]

GOODNOW, FRANK JOHNSON (*b. Brooklyn, N.Y., 1859; d. Baltimore, Md., 1939*), political scientist. Graduated Amherst, 1879; Columbia Law School, 1882. Taught at Columbia, 1883–1914; president,

Johns Hopkins, 1914–29. A pioneer in the study of public administration. [*Supp. 2*]

GOODNOW, ISAAC TICHENOR (*b. Whitingham, Vt., 1814; d. near Manhattan, Kans., 1894*), teacher, Kansas pioneer. Led a company of Free-Soil colonists who founded Manhattan, 1855. Helped establish college there which became Kansas State Agricultural College, 1863.

GOODRICH, ALFRED JOHN (*b. Chilo, O., 1847; d. Paris, France, 1920*), musical theorist, composer, teacher, writer.

GOODRICH, BENJAMIN FRANKLIN (*b. Ripley, N.Y., 1841; d. Manitou Springs, Colo., 1888*), physician, rubber manufacturer. In partnership with J. P. Morris, bought Hudson River Rubber Co., 1867; despite lack of success here and at another small rubber factory at Melrose, N.Y., Goodrich persevered, moving the business to Akron, O., 1870–71. Continued lack of working capital and of local confidence in his enterprise hindered progress until 1880 when adequate backing was secured from G. W. Crouse.

GOODRICH, CHARLES AUGUSTUS (*b. Ridgefield, Conn., 1790; d. Hartford, Conn., 1862*), Congregational clergyman, author. Brother of Samuel G. Goodrich. Wrote many informational and children's books; his *History of the United States* (1822) went through more than 150 editions.

GOODRICH, CHAUNCEY (*b. Durham, Conn., 1759; d. 1815*), lawyer. Son of Elizur Goodrich (1734–1797). Graduated Yale, 1776. Congressman, Federalist, from Connecticut, 1795–1801; U.S. senator, 1807–13; lieutenant-governor, Connecticut, 1813–15. Prominent at Hartford Convention, 1814.

GOODRICH, CHAUNCEY (*b. Hinsdale, Mass., 1798; d. Burlington, Vt., 1858*), bookseller, publisher, horticulturist. Greatly encouraged and improved fruit-growing in Vermont and northern New York.

GOODRICH, CHAUNCEY (*b. Hinsdale, Mass., 1836; d. 1925*), Congregational clergyman. Nephew of Chauncey Goodrich (1798–1858). Missionary to China, 1865–1925. Leader of committee which translated Bible into Mandarin (published 1919), he also published valuable Chinese language studies.

GOODRICH, CHAUNCEY ALLEN (*b. New Haven, Conn., 1790; d. New Haven, 1860*), Congregational clergyman, educator, lexicographer. Son of Elizur Goodrich (1761–1849). Graduated Yale, 1810; was professor of rhetoric there *post* 1817. Author of several textbooks, he helped in the 1847 revision of the *Dictionary* by Noah Webster whose daughter he had married, 1816.

GOODRICH, ELIZUR (*b. Wethersfield, Conn., 1734; d. Durham, Conn., 1797*), Congregational clergyman. Graduated Yale, 1752. Pastor at Durham, Conn., 1756–97. Biblical scholar, ardent Whig, keen astronomer, he was greatly interested in Yale and a member of its Corporation, *post* 1776.

GOODRICH, ELIZUR (*b. Durham, Conn., 1761; d. New Haven, Conn., 1849*), lawyer, Federalist politician. Son of Elizur Goodrich (1734–1797); brother of Chauncey Goodrich (1759–1815). Mayor of New Haven, 1803–22. Secretary of Yale, 1818–46.

GOODRICH, FRANK BOOTT (*b. Boston, Mass., 1826; d. Morristown, N.J., 1894*), journalist, playwright. Son of Samuel G. Goodrich. Author of superficial popular books; as dramatist, collaborated with John Brougham, Dion Boucicault and others.

GOODRICH, SAMUEL GRISWOLD (*b. Ridgefield, Conn., 1793; d. New York, N.Y., 1860*), author, publisher, known by pen-name "Peter Parley." Grandson of Elizur Goodrich (1734–1797); brother of Charles A. Goodrich. Mainly self-educated. After several unsuccessful ventures, removed to Boston, 1826, where he published and save for two years edited *The Token*, best of the American "annuals." The first of the Peter Parley books, *The Tales of Peter Parley about America* (1827), was followed by more than a hundred others. In these books, which sold by the millions, a kindly, omniscient old gentleman converses with a group of priggishly inquiring children, and instruction is given a thin sugar-coating of fiction. Goodrich's claim to have written all the books which bear his name as author is doubtful.

GOODRICH, SARAH. [See GOODRIDGE, SARAH, 1788–1853.]

GOODRICH, WILLIAM MARCELLUS (*b. Templeton, Mass., 1777; d. Boston, Mass., 1833*), organ builder.

GOODRIDGE, SARAH (*b. Templeton, Mass., 1788; d. Boston, Mass., 1853*), miniature painter. Sister of William M. Goodrich. Originally self-taught, she improved her technique with help from Gilbert Stuart, 1820–24. Her best work was done before 1840.

GOODRIDGE, WILLIAM MARCELLUS. [See GOODRICH, WILLIAM MARCELLUS, 1777–1833.]

GOODSELL, DANIEL AYRES (*b. Newburg, N.Y., 1840; d. New York, N.Y., 1909*), Methodist clergyman. A force for tolerance in his church, he was made a bishop in 1888.

GOODSPEED, THOMAS WAKEFIELD (*b. near Glens Falls, N.Y., 1842; d. 1927*), Baptist clergyman, educational leader. Graduated University of Rochester, 1863; Rochester Theological, 1866. With Frederick T. Gates, helped in founding University of Chicago; was secretary of its board of trustees, 1890–1912, and author of its history.

GOODWIN, DANIEL RAYNES (*b. North Berwick, Maine, 1811; d. Philadelphia, Pa., 1890*), Episcopal clergyman. Graduated Bowdoin, 1832; attended Andover Theological Seminary. A professor at Bowdoin, 1835–53, he was ordained to the Episcopal priesthood, 1848. He served as president of Trinity College, Hartford, Conn., 1853–60, and as provost of University of Pennsylvania, 1860–68.

GOODWIN, ELIJAH (*b. Champaign Co., O., 1807; d. near Cleveland, O., 1879*), minister of the Disciples of Christ. As pioneer preacher, traveled and preached widely and energetically in Indiana and Illinois. Edited *Christian Record*, 1847–48, 1859–66.

GOODWIN, HANNIBAL WILLISTON (*b. Taughannock, N.Y., 1822; d. 1900*), Episcopal clergyman, inventor. Graduated Union College, 1848; General Theological Seminary, 1851. Served parishes in New Jersey and California. Received patent in 1898 for invention of celluloid photographic film.

GOODWIN, ICHABOD (*b. North Berwick, Maine, 1794; d. Portsmouth, N.H., 1882*), merchant, financier, railroad executive. Brother of Daniel R. Goodwin. Whig New Hampshire legislator, and Republican governor, 1859–61.

GOODWIN, JOHN NOBLE (*b. South Berwick, Maine, 1824; d. Paraiso Springs, Calif., 1887*), lawyer, politician. Graduated Dartmouth, 1844. As territorial governor of Arizona, 1863–65, Goodwin showed great tact and ability in conciliating factions, guiding the first legislature and maintaining a stable government.

GOODWIN, NATHANIEL CARLL (*b. Boston, Mass., 1857; d. 1919*), actor. An impulsive, wayward, much-married personality, "Nat" Goodwin failed in Shakespearean roles but succeeded in contemporary plays, especially those he produced with his second wife Maxine Elliott as co-star.

GOODWIN, WILLIAM WATSON (*b. Concord, Mass., 1831; d. 1912*), Hellenist. Graduated Harvard, 1851; Ph.D., Göttingen, 1855. Eliot Professor of Greek Literature at Harvard, 1860–1901. Always zealous for high scholarly standards, as Harvard expanded from college to university Goodwin fought the battle for Greek with wit, clarity and good nature. His book on Greek syntax (1860) gave new life to American methods of studying Greek. He published a widely used elementary Greek grammar, an excellent *Greek Reader* (1871), translations of *Plutarch's Morals*, the *Birds* and *Clouds* of Aristophanes and other important studies and textbooks. The Greek constitutional and artistic achievements interested him profoundly, and he gave a course on Greek law. He was a founder of the Archaeological Institute of America and first director of the American School of Classical Studies in Athens.

GOODYEAR, CHARLES (*b. New Haven, Conn., 1800; d. New York, N.Y., 1860*), inventor. Became interested in rubber, 1834, while designing an improved inflating valve for a rubber life preserver. The rubber industry, after a mushroom growth, *post* 1830, had collapsed because no process was known to prevent India rubber from melting, sticking and decomposing in heat. Goodyear began experiments enthusiastically, kneading into raw rubber every conceivable material. Despite a succession of failures and the most extreme poverty, he continued undaunted. In June 1837 he obtained Patent No. 240, in which he claimed to eliminate adhesive properties of rubber by superficial application of the metals, especially nitric acid with copper or bismuth. In 1838 he began new experiments, combining Nathaniel M. Hayward's method of spreading sulfur on rubber to eliminate stickiness with his own process. Vulcanization was discovered when a mass of sulfur and rubber mixture, dropped accidentally on a hot stove by Goodyear, did not melt. Further experiments with mixes and baking temperatures were made with great difficulty. After three years, however, he produced a uniform product, and in 1844 received his celebrated Patent No. 3,633. Goodyear was so deeply in debt that he had to sell licenses and establish royalties for use of vulcanization at absurdly low figures.

In 1851 Goodyear went to Europe to extend his patent and designed a magnificent exhibit in London with everything made of rubber—furniture, floor-covering, jewelry, books. Napoleon III conferred on him the Grand Medal of Honor and the Cross of the Legion of Honor for a similar exhibit in Paris, 1855. Foreign patents were granted him in all countries except England, yet despite all his efforts he died in debt.

GOODYEAR, CHARLES (*b. Germantown, Pa., 1833; d. 1896*), industrialist. Son of Charles Goodyear (1800–1860). President of the American Shoe-tip Co. *c.* 1860, he was convinced of the feasibility of producing a completely machine-made shoe. To this end he purchased patents for stitching machines, encouraged the invention of new ones and manufactured them himself. Though his experts made progress in inventing machines, the demand for them was small. With the help of Jonathan Munyon, a consolidation with Goodyear's competitor Gordon McKay was effected. *Post* 1880, McKay took care of the turned-shoe business, Goodyear of the welt-shoe business, and Munyon successfully marketed both products.

GOODYEAR, WILLIAM HENRY (*b. New Haven, Conn., 1846; d. 1923*), archaeologist, museum curator, author. Son of Charles Goodyear (1800–1860). Proved that deviation, rather than mathematical regularity, was the traditional practice in architecture before modern times.

GOOKIN, DANIEL (*b. England or Ireland, 1612; d. 1686/87*), colonist, soldier, magistrate. Removed from Virginia to Massachusetts, 1644; was for many years Assistant to the General Court. His efforts on the Indians' behalf were second only to John Eliot's.

GOOLD, WILLIAM A. (*b. near Glasgow, Scotland, 1830; d. 1912*), coal miner, prospector, operator.

Came to America, 1852. Identified *post* 1854 with development of the coal industry in Alabama.

GORDIN, JACOB (*b. Mirgorod, Russia, 1853; d. Brooklyn, N.Y., 1909*), playwright. Came to America, 1891. Characteristically Russian in his approach to the theatre, he wrote many successful plays for the Yiddish theatres in New York.

GORDON, ANDREW (*b. Putnam, N.Y., 1828; d. Philadelphia, Pa., 1887*), Presbyterian clergyman. Instituted successful Presbyterian mission in the Punjab, India, 1855.

GORDON, GEORGE ANGIER (*b. Oyne, Scotland, 1853; d. 1929*), Congregational clergyman, author. Came to America, 1871. Graduated Harvard, 1881. Minister of Old South Church, Boston, Mass., 1884–1929; an outstanding champion of religious freedom and theological progress in American Congregationalism.

GORDON, GEORGE BYRON (*b. New Perth, P.E.I., Canada, 1870; d. 1927*), archaeologist. Director of University Museum, Philadelphia; specialist in American anthropology.

GORDON, GEORGE HENRY (*b. Charlestown, Mass., 1823; d. 1886*), soldier, lawyer. Graduated West Point, 1846. Served with credit in Mexican War and at Western frontier posts; resigned from army, 1854. Returning 1861 to Union Army, he rose to major-general, 1865. Author of a three-volume history of Civil War campaigns he had experienced.

GORDON, GEORGE PHINEAS (*b. Salem, N.H., 1810; d. Norfolk, Va., 1878*), printer, inventor. Began experimenting *c.* 1835 on improvement of presses for card printing; took out the first of more than fifty patents, 1851. He invented and manufactured the "Yankee" and "Firefly" presses, and in 1858 the highly successful "Franklin," later called the "Gordon," job press.

GORDON, GEORGE WASHINGTON (*b. Giles Co., Tenn., 1836; d. 1911*), Confederate brigadier-general, lawyer. Distinguished in Civil War service, in particular at battle of Franklin, he practiced law, served as Indian agent, and was congressman, Democrat, from Tennessee, 1907–11.

GORDON, JAMES (*b. Monroe Co., Miss., 1833; d. Okolona, Miss., 1912*), planter, legislator, Confederate soldier. Captured on return from mission to England, 1864, he escaped to Canada and was accused groundlessly of complicity in the murder of Abraham Lincoln.

GORDON, JOHN BROWN (*b. Upson Co., Ga., 1832; d. Miami, Fla., 1904*), lawyer, Confederate lieutenant-general, statesman. The idol of Georgia for forty years and the state's most important military figure, Gordon began service, 1860, as elected captain of a company of mountaineers; he had no previous military experience. His personality and genius for war won him the title "Chevalier Bayard of the Confederate Army." After the war, Gordon was in the thick of the fight to restore home rule to Georgia. He was U.S. senator, Democrat, from Georgia, 1873–80 and 1891–97; governor of Georgia, 1886–90. He represented the rising commercial and industrial, rather than the agrarian, spirit in the state. His *Reminiscences of the Civil War* (1903) is an important source.

GORDON, LAURA DE FORCE (*b. North East, Pa., 1838; d. San Joaquin Co., Calif., 1907*), lawyer, suffragist. Settled in California, *c.* 1868; founded and edited newspapers in Stockton. Active in securing legislation permitting women to practice law in the state, she was one of first (1879) women admitted to California bar and to practice before the U.S. Supreme Court.

GORDON, WILLIAM (*b. Hitchin, England, 1728; d. Ipswich, England, 1807*), Congregational clergyman, author. Came to America, 1770. As pastor at Roxbury, Mass., was a strong Whig and served as chaplain to Provincial Congress. Collected materials for a history of the Revolution; professing to doubt American reception of an "impartial" work, he published it in England, 1788. Modern research has discovered it to be a plagiarism from the *Annual Register*.

GORDON, WILLIAM FITZHUGH (*b. Germanna, Va., 1787; d. Albemarle Co., Va., 1858*), lawyer, Virginia legislator. As congressman, Democrat, from Virginia, 1830–35, introduced the bill (1834) which later led to establishment of an independent U.S. treasury.

GORDON, WILLIAM WASHINGTON (*b. Screven Co., Ga., 1796; d. 1842*), lawyer. Graduated West Point, 1815. As president, Central Railroad of Georgia, supervised its planning and construction under great difficulties, 1836–42.

GORDY, JOHN PANCOAST (*b. near Salisbury, Md., 1851; d. New York, N.Y., 1908*), educator. Professor of history of education and American history at New York University, 1901–08.

GORGAS, JOSIAH (*b. Dauphin Co., Pa., 1818; d. Tuscaloosa, Ala., 1883*), soldier, educator. Father of William C. Gorgas. Graduated West Point, 1841. An ordnance specialist, he married Amelia, daughter of John Gayle, while in command of the U.S. arsenal near Mobile, Ala., 1853. His Southern marriage and his dislike of Abolitionists led him to resign his federal commission, and in April 1861 he was appointed Confederate chief of ordnance. There was no manufacturing arsenal in the Confederate States, only one foundry capable of casting cannon and but two small powder mills. Available cannon were outmoded as were most of the small-arms. Cavalry and infantry

equipment was practically non-existent. Because of the blockade, the import of munitions was uncertain; the armies relied chiefly on local manufactures and captured items. Gorgas, with the aid of a remarkable staff of subordinates, established armories at Richmond, Va., and Fayetteville, N.C.; arsenals at Charleston, Augusta, Macon, Atlanta, Columbus, Selma, Baton Rouge, Little Rock and other places; a cannon foundry and a central laboratory at Macon; a powder mill at Augusta. Lead, iron and copper were mined and saltpetre made. By 1863, Gorgas's bureau was operating with high efficiency; despite enormous difficulties, he supplied arms and ammunition to the very end of the war. After the collapse of the Confederacy, he managed an Alabama iron works. In 1869, he joined the staff of the University of the South at Sewanee, Tenn., becoming professor of engineering and vice-chancellor. Elected president of the University of Alabama, 1878, he resigned because of ill health.

GORGAS, WILLIAM CRAWFORD (*b. near Mobile, Ala., 1854; d. England, 1920*), sanitarian. Son of Josiah Gorgas. Unable to obtain appointment to West Point, Gorgas joined the Army Medical Corps in 1880 after graduation from the University of the South, 1875, and Bellevue Hospital Medical College, 1879. Early in his career, he survived an attack of yellow fever at Fort Brown, Texas; thereafter he was in demand for posts where yellow fever was rife. Placed in charge of a yellow fever camp at Siboney, Cuba, in 1898 and soon made chief sanitary officer of Havana, he applied the conventional methods of control: segregation of the sick, quarantine of infected localities and general cleanliness. In spite of his efforts, the incidence of the disease grew worse. Following proof by the board headed by Walter Reed that the *Stegomyia* mosquito, later named *Aedes Aegypti*, was the yellow fever carrier, Gorgas set about to destroy the breeding places of the insect. Within a few months Havana was rid of mosquitoes and fever.

From 1902–04, promoted colonel in recognition of his Cuban achievement, Gorgas studied the sanitary problems of the Panama Canal area. He arrived there with his staff in 1904 when actual work commenced on the Isthmus. Although aware that French failure with the canal project had been caused by disease, the American Canal Commissions were disinclined to support adequate preventive measures. A visitation of yellow fever in late 1904 brought Gorgas some support, but the first two Commissions made determined efforts to discredit and supplant him. President Theodore Roosevelt, however, directed active support of his mosquito-control work and after visiting Panama in 1906 made Gorgas a member of the Commission. Temporarily he had a free hand, but when George W. Goethals became chief engineer in 1908, he attacked Gorgas's sanitary work on the grounds of its cost. In spite of these difficulties, Gorgas rid the Canal Zone of yellow fever, made the cities of Colon and Panama models of sanitation and came to be regarded as the foremost sanitary expert in the world. He was appointed U.S. Army surgeon-general in 1914. After service during the first World War, he retired as a major-general. Commissioned by the International Health Board to investigate yellow fever on the west coast of Africa, he was stricken en route and died in Queen Alexandra Hospital, Millbank, England.

GORHAM, JABEZ (*b. Providence, R.I., 1792; d. 1869*), silversmith, merchant. Founder of Gorham Manufacturing Co.; first American silversmith to use machinery in that industry.

GORHAM, JOHN (*b. Boston, Mass., 1783; d. Boston, 1829*), physician. Erving Professor of Chemistry at Harvard, 1816–27. Taught with conspicuous success, and was author of *The Elements of Chemical Science* (1819–20), a standard textbook for many years.

GORHAM, NATHANIEL (*b. Charlestown, Mass., 1738; d. 1796*), merchant, Massachusetts patriot and legislator. President of Continental Congress, 1786; active in Federal Convention, 1787. With Oliver Phelps, purchased the so-called Genesee Country in New York, 1788, for development and settlement.

GORMAN, ARTHUR PUE (*b. Woodstock, Md., 1839; d. Washington, D.C., 1906*), politician. Protégé of Stephen A. Douglas. Maryland legislator, 1869–79; president, Chesapeake and Ohio Canal Co.; U.S. senator, Democrat, 1881–99, 1903–06. Conducted Cleveland's campaigns in 1884 and 1892, but opposed his policies.

GORMAN, WILLIS ARNOLD (*b. near Flemingsburg, Ky., 1816; d. St. Paul, Minn., 1876*), lawyer. Removed to Indiana, 1835; practiced in Bloomington. After service in Mexican War, was congressman, Democrat, from Indiana, 1849–53; governor of Minnesota Territory, 1853–57. Interrupted successful practice of law at St. Paul to serve as Union brigadier-general, 1861–64.

GORRIE, JOHN (*b. Charleston, S.C., 1803; d. Apalachicola, Fla., 1855*), physician, pioneer in mechanical refrigeration. Conceived the idea of artificially cooling the air of sick rooms and hospitals to cure and prevent fever, *c.* 1839; by 1845 was giving his whole time to the problem. From artificially cooling air he turned to artificial ice-making and accomplished it by 1850 with machinery of his own design. Patent No. 8080, granted him in May 1851, was presumably the first U.S. patent on mechanical refrigeration. Gorrie had no capital, and his failure to raise funds for the manufacture of his machinery induced a nervous collapse from which he never recovered.

GORRINGE, HENRY HONEYCHURCH (*b. Barbados, B.W.I., 1841; d. New York, N.Y., 1885*), naval officer. Engineered and directed transportation of obelisk Cleopatra's Needle from Egypt to New York City, 1879–80.

GORTON, SAMUEL (*b. Gorton, near Manchester, England, c. 1592; d. Warwick, R.I., 1677*), colonist, founder of Gortonites. His unorthodox religious beliefs brought him into conflict with authorities in Massachusetts Bay, Plymouth, and Newport, 1637–44. He denied the doctrine of the Trinity, denied the fitness of any paid person to be a minister, and also denied the actual existence of heaven and hell. After being several times imprisoned and banished, Gorton sought redress in England. Returning to America, 1648, he bore a letter from the Earl of Warwick ordering Massachusetts to leave him unmolested at Shawomet, R.I., which he renamed Warwick, and where he lived peaceably the rest of his life.

GOSNOLD, BARTHOLOMEW (*fl. 1572–1607*), navigator, colonizer. Made a landfall in the *Concord* on the southern Maine coast, 1602; standing southward, he landed on a foreland which he named Cape Cod, traversed Nantucket Sound, erected a small fort on Cuttyhunk, and searched for a western passage. On returning to England with a cargo of furs, cedar and sassafras, Gosnold tried to interest others in American settlement. Late in 1606 he sailed as vice-admiral of the fleet in command of the *God Speed* which carried 52 of the Virginia Company pioneers; they landed at Cape Henry in April 1607. As a member of the council for the colony, he opposed the selection of the island site in the James River for a settlement but was overruled and there Jamestown was founded. He died there in August that same year.

GOSS, JAMES WALKER (*b. Albemarle Co., Va., 1812; d. Piedmont, Va., 1870*), minister of the Disciples of Christ, educator.

GOSTELOWE, JONATHAN (*b. Passyunk, Pa., 1744; d. Philadelphia, Pa., 1795*), cabinetmaker, Revolutionary soldier. Worked in mahogany and walnut, displaying considerable originality at a time when English models were paramount.

GOTSHALL, WILLIAM CHARLES (*b. St. Louis, Mo., 1870; d. 1935*), engineer, specialist in electric railroad work. [*Supp. 1*]

GOTTHEIL, GUSTAV (*b. Pinne, Prussia, 1827; d. 1903*), rabbi. Ministered at Temple Emanu-El, New York, 1873–99. Outstanding in the transition of Reform Jewry from German to American standards.

GOTTHEIL, RICHARD JAMES HORATIO (*b. Manchester, England, 1862; d. New York, N.Y., 1936*), Semitics scholar. Son of Gustav Gottheil. Came to America, 1873. Graduated Columbia, 1881; Ph.D., Leipzig, 1886. Taught at Columbia, 1886–1936; chief, Oriental Division, N.Y. Public Library, 1896–1936; Zionist leader. [*Supp. 2*]

GOTTSCHALK, LOUIS MOREAU (*b. New Orleans, La., 1829; d. Tijuca, Brazil, 1869*), pianist, composer. Trained in Paris; a pupil and friend of Berlioz, with whom he later gave a series of concerts. Chopin commented favorably on his debut in 1845. Successful European tours included a triumph in Madrid, 1851, where the Queen of Spain decorated him. In 1853 he returned to America. Brilliant New York seasons followed and equal success in tours throughout the United States, Canada, Panama and South America. A prolific composer, largely in bravura style, he is remembered today as a performer, decidedly the best American pianist and one of the greatest of his period.

GOUCHER, JOHN FRANKLIN (*b. Waynesburg, Pa., 1845; d. 1922*), Methodist clergyman, philanthropist. Pastor in Baltimore, Md. A principal benefactor of Woman's College of Baltimore (later Goucher College) and its second president, 1890–1908. Supported many Far Eastern missions.

GOUDY, WILLIAM CHARLES (*b. Indiana, 1824; d. 1893*), lawyer. Raised in Jacksonville, Ill.; admitted to bar, 1847; removed to Chicago, 1859. Authority on real property law, expert also in commercial and constitutional law, he was retained in much heavy railroad litigation.

GOUGE, WILLIAM M. (*b. Philadelphia, Pa., 1796; d. Trenton, N.J., 1863*), U.S. treasury official, writer. Author, among other works, of *Short History of Money and Banking in the United States* (1833) in which he opposed banks, paper money and corporations.

GOUGH, JOHN BARTHOLOMEW (*b. Sandgate, England, 1817; d. Frankford, Pa., 1886*), temperance lecturer.

GOULD, AUGUSTUS ADDISON (*b. New Ipswich, N.H., 1805; d. 1866*), physician, conchologist. Son of Nathaniel D. Gould. Graduated Harvard, 1825; M.D., Harvard Medical School, 1830. Author with Louis Agassiz of *Principles of Zoology* (1848), he was a constant contributor to scientific journals, writing chiefly on mollusks. His *Report on the Invertebrata of Massachusetts* (1841) was chief among his contributions to American science; for it, he penned beautiful illustrations. He also studied and reported on the mollusks obtained by the Wilkes Exploring Expedition and edited the first two volumes of Amos Binney's *Terrestrial Air-Breathing Mollusks*. No one except Thomas Say was more influential in developing the study of American conchology.

GOULD, BENJAMIN APTHORP (*b. Lancaster, Mass., 1787; d. Boston, Mass., 1859*). Graduated Harvard, 1814. As principal of Boston Latin School, 1814–28, he made the school famous. Resigning for reasons of health, he became a successful merchant.

GOULD, BENJAMIN APTHORP (*b. Boston, Mass., 1824; d. Cambridge, Mass., 1896*), astronomer. Son of Benjamin A. Gould (1787–1859). Graduated Harvard, 1844; studied also at Berlin and Göttingen. Founded *Astronomical Journal*, 1849; was in charge of longitude department, U.S. Coast Survey, 1852–67. His observations of the stars in the southern heavens comprise his greatest work. This private project led to the establishment of a national observatory at Córdoba, Argentina, 1870. There, with unfaltering devotion and energy, aided by a corps of enthusiastic assistants, in the short space of fifteen years he prepared zone catalogues of 73,160 stars and a general catalogue of 32,448 stars. He brought back photographs of the southern clusters in 1885, and their measurement and reduction occupied much of the last ten years of his life.

GOULD, EDWARD SHERMAN (*b. Litchfield, Conn., 1805; d. New York, N.Y., 1885*), author. Son of James Gould. Wrote novels, sketches, comedies; also *Good English; or Popular Errors in Language* (1867).

GOULD, ELGIN RALSTON LOVELL (*b. Oshawa, Canada, 1860; d. near North Bay, Canada, 1915*), economist, reformer. Made important studies of production costs, wages and family budgets for U.S. Department of Labor, 1887–92.

GOULD, GEORGE JAY (*b. 1864; d. Mentone, France, 1923*), financier, railroad executive. Son, and unsuccessful successor, of Jay Gould.

GOULD, GEORGE MILBRY (*b. Auburn, Maine, 1848; d. Atlantic City, N.J., 1922*), ophthalmologist, medical journalist. Friend and patron of Lafcadio Hearn.

GOULD, HANNAH FLAGG (*b. Lancaster, Mass., 1789; d. Newburyport, Mass., 1865*), poet. Sister of Benjamin A. Gould (1787–1859).

GOULD, JAMES (*b. Branford, Conn., 1770; d. 1838*), jurist, law teacher. Graduated Yale, 1791. In 1798, on completing course at Tapping Reeve's Litchfield, Conn., law school, he became Reeve's associate and had sole charge of the school, 1820–33.

GOULD, JAY (*b. Roxbury, N.Y., 1836; d. 1892*), financier. As a youth, learned rudiments of surveying and showed precocious skill in money-making. Keen-witted and unscrupulous, he traded first as a tanner and leather-merchant and began speculating in railroads *post* 1860. His operations became spectacular when in 1867 with James Fisk he became a director of the Erie Railroad, of which Daniel Drew was treasurer and controlling agent. In the ensuing struggle for control with Cornelius Vanderbilt, Gould supplied the strategic imagination. Defying a court injunction, Gould, Fisk and Drew broke Vanderbilt's attempted corner by flinging 50,000 Erie shares on the market in March 1868. Gould, by lavish bribes,

357

then effected passage of a bill by the New York legislature legalizing the recent issue of Erie stock and forbidding union of the Erie and the New York Central. To the Gould-Fisk partnership were added Peter B. Sweeney and William M. Tweed as directors, Drew having withdrawn. They looted the Erie by huge stock-watering measures, carried out a daring raid on the credit, produce and export markets, and in the fall of 1869 attempted to corner the gold market, bringing on the disastrous panic of Black Friday (September 24). This excited general indignation and litigation commenced over the sale of fraudulent Erie stock. After Fisk's death and the overthrow of the Tweed Ring, Gould was ejected from control of the Erie in March 1872. Between 1874 and 1879 he juggled control of the Union Pacific, Kansas Pacific, Denver Pacific, Central Pacific and Missouri Pacific railroads. By threatening to extend the Kansas Pacific so as to form a new transcontinental railroad, he compelled the Union Pacific to consolidate with Kansas Pacific at par, then sold his Kansas Pacific stock, clearing an estimated $10,000,000. By 1890 he owned half of the railroad mileage in the Southwest. He also owned the New York *World*, 1879–83, was practically full owner of the New York City elevated railways by 1886, and controlled the Western Union Telegraph Co. Working almost to the end, he died of tuberculosis. As a young man, he had written *History of Delaware County, and Border Wars of New York* (1856). His hobby was gardening.

GOULD, NATHANIEL DUREN (*b. Bedford, Mass., 1781; d. Boston, Mass., 1864*), conductor, music teacher. Author of *Church Music in America* (1853).

GOULD, ROBERT SIMONTON (*b. Iredell Co., N.C., 1826; d. Austin, Texas, 1904*), jurist, Confederate soldier. Raised in Alabama; removed to Texas, 1850. Associate justice, state supreme court, 1874–82, and briefly chief justice. Professor of law, University of Texas, 1883–1904.

GOULD, THOMAS RIDGEWAY (*b. Boston, Mass., 1818; d. Florence, Italy, 1881*), sculptor.

GOULDING, FRANCIS ROBERT (*b. Midway, Ga., 1810; d. Roswell, Ga., 1881*), Presbyterian clergyman. Author of many books for boys, of which *Robert and Harold* (1852), later titled *The Young Marooners on the Florida Coast*, was extremely popular here and abroad.

GOUPIL, RENÉ (*b. Anjou, France, c. 1607; d. Ossernenon, near present Auriesville, N.Y., 1642*), Jesuit lay brother, martyr. Companion of Father Isaac Jogues; slain by Iroquois after capture while journeying to the Huron missions. Beatified, 1925; canonized, 1930.

GOVAN, DANIEL CHEVILETTE (*b. Northampton Co., N.C., 1829; d. 1911*), planter, Confederate brigadier-general. Raised in Mississippi; settled in Arkansas, *post* 1853. Described by his division commander,

P. R. Cleburne, as one of the best officers in the Confederate service.

GOVE, AARON ESTELLUS (*b. Hampton Falls, N.H., 1839; d. 1919*), educator, Union soldier. Graduated Illinois State Normal School, 1861. As Denver superintendent of schools, 1874–1904, he was educational leader and shaper of school policies in Colorado.

GOWANS, WILLIAM (*b. Lanarkshire, Scotland, 1803, d. New York, N.Y., 1870*), bibliophile, bookseller, publisher. Came to America, 1821. Starting with a book-stall on Chatham Street, New York, he was from 1863 to his death the "Antiquarian of Nassau Street" celebrated among collectors for the range of his stock and his interest in Americana.

GOWEN, FRANKLIN BENJAMIN (*b. Mount Airy [Philadelphia], Pa., 1836; d. Washington, D.C., 1889*), lawyer, president of the Philadelphia & Reading Railroad. Procured investigation and trials of the "Molly Maguires," secret Pennsylvania terrorists, 1875–77.

GRABAU, JOHANNES ANDREAS AUGUST (*b. Olvenstedt, Prussia, 1804; d. 1879*), Lutheran clergyman. Persecuted in Germany, he came as pastor of an emigrant group which settled in Buffalo, N.Y., 1839. Organized Buffalo Synod and founded Martin Luther Seminary.

GRÄBNER, AUGUST LAWRENCE (*b. Frankentrost, Mich., 1849; d. St. Louis, Mo., 1904*), Lutheran theologian, historian. Professor in Wisconsin and Concordia Seminaries.

GRACE, WILLIAM RUSSELL (*b. Queenstown, Ireland, 1832; d. 1904*), international merchant, capitalist. With his brother Michael, developed a prosperous trading firm in Callao, Peru. Organized W. R. Grace & Co., New York City, 1865, originally formed to serve as correspondent for the Peru company. As confidential adviser to the Peruvian government, between 1875 and 1879 Grace handled equipment of the army and navy, furnished munitions during war with Chile, 1879. After the unsuccessful outcome of the war he took over the Peruvian national debt, receiving huge concessions in return for funding it. The Grace firm opened offices in practically every Latin-American country, establishing world-wide contacts in banking, importing and exporting, and steamship operation. William R. Grace served as reform mayor of New York City, 1880–88.

GRACIE, ARCHIBALD (*b. New York, N.Y., 1832; d. Petersburg, Va., 1864*), Confederate soldier. Graduated West Point, 1854. Resigned commission, 1856, to enter business at Mobile, Ala. Served with first Alabama troops to enter Confederate service; promoted brigadier-general, 1862.

GRADLE, HENRY (*b. Friedberg, Germany, 1855; d. Santa Barbara, Calif., 1911*), ophthalmologist.

Came to America, 1868. M.D., Northwestern University, 1874; studied also in Europe. Professor at Northwestern, 1879–1906. Author of *Bacteria and the Germ Theory of Disease* (1883), the first book in English to deal with this subject.

GRADY, HENRY WOODFIN (*b. Athens, Ga., 1850; d. Atlanta, Ga., 1889*), journalist, orator. Graduated University of Georgia, 1868. After newspaper experience in Georgia and New York, he was loaned money by Cyrus W. Field to buy a fourth interest in the Atlanta (Ga.) *Constitution*, 1879. With his unerring sense for news, zeal for ordered progress, faculty for writing in accord with popular taste, he did much to shatter post-bellum despair in the South. He encouraged development of local resources, diversification of crops; he also convinced his readers of the need for manufacturing and for a logical adjustment of the Negro problem. His address, "The New South," delivered first in New York City, December 1886, expressed the gist of his creed and helped allay the last of intersectional animosities.

GRAEBNER, AUGUST LAWRENCE. [See GRÄBNER, AUGUST LAWRENCE, 1849–1904.]

GRAESSL, LAWRENCE (*b. Ruemannsfelden, Bavaria, 1753; d. Philadelphia, Pa., 1793*), Roman Catholic clergyman. Came to America, 1787, on urging of Rev. Ferdinand Farmer; served as assistant at St. Mary's, Philadelphia, and as missionary in Pennsylvania, Delaware, New Jersey. Chosen coadjutor to Bishop John Carroll, Father Graessl died of yellow fever before the formal appointment arrived.

GRAFF, FREDERIC (*b. Philadelphia, Pa., 1817; d. Philadelphia, 1890*), engineer. Son of Frederick Graff, whom he succeeded as chief engineer of the Philadelphia water department.

GRAFF, FREDERICK (*b. Philadelphia, Pa., 1774; d. Philadelphia, 1847*), civil engineer. Associated with Philadelphia water system, 1797–1847; superintendent, *post* 1805. Responsible for the hydraulic system employed, virtually a pioneer effort.

GRAFFENRIED, CHRISTOPHER, Baron de (*b. Bern, Switzerland, 1661; d. Bern, 1743*), adventurer, colonizer. Combined with Franz Ludwig Michel and Georg Ritter to bring Swiss emigrants and exiled German Palatines as colonists to North Carolina, 1710. A town, New Bern, was laid out but the colony suffered a series of misfortunes. Graffenried secured a patent from Gov. Spotswood of Virginia for lands on the upper Potomac in hope of finding silver and transplanting the New Bern settlers, but as Michel would not support the project and his own resources were exhausted, Graffenried returned to Bern, 1713.

GRAFLY, CHARLES (*b. Philadelphia, Pa., 1862; d. Philadelphia, Pa., 1929*), sculptor. Trained at Pennsylvania Academy of Fine Arts and in Paris, he won reputation as a sculptor of imaginative groups, portraitist and teacher. Among his finest works are the "Pioneer Mother Monument" designed 1915 for a location in San Francisco, Calif., and the heroic General Meade Memorial in Washington, D.C. Probably the foremost American sculptor of male portrait busts. Occupied the chair of sculpture at Pennsylvania Academy and Boston Museum of Fine Arts.

GRAFTON, CHARLES CHAPMAN (*b. Boston, Mass., 1830; d. Fond du Lac, Wis., 1912*), Episcopal clergyman. High Churchman; ordained, 1858. Associated in establishing Society of St. John the Evangelist (Cowley Fathers); founded Sisterhood of the Holy Nativity. Rector, Church of the Advent, Boston, Mass., 1872–88. Bishop of Fond du Lac, 1889–1912.

GRAHAM, CHARLES KINNAIRD (*b. New York, N.Y., 1824; d. Lakewood, N.J., 1889*), Union brigadier-general, civil engineer.

GRAHAM, DAVID (*b. London, England, 1808; d. Nice, France, 1852*), lawyer. Brought to America as an infant. Author of *Treatise on the Practice of the Supreme Court of New York* (1832), a masterly text; one of the ablest New York advocates of his time.

GRAHAM, EDWARD KIDDER (*b. Charlotte, N.C., 1876; d. 1918*), educator. Graduated University of North Carolina, 1898. Taught in English department there, 1899–1913. As dean, acting president, and president, 1914–18, he gave the university its characteristic social-mindedness, training students and public to consider state and community problems. The advances in education, health, public welfare and industry which North Carolina made, 1910–30, were owing in large measure to the ideas which Graham urged.

GRAHAM, ERNEST ROBERT (*b. Lowell, Mich., 1866; d. 1936*), architect. Construction supervisor for the Chicago firm of Burnham and Root, *post* 1888; partner, 1894–1912. In 1917, with three former Burnham associates, established partnership of Graham, Anderson, Probst and White. The firm became the leading architects of commercial America, executing such notable commissions in Chicago as the Wrigley Building, Union Station, Post Office, Civic Opera, and Merchandise Mart, as well as civic and commercial buildings in other cities. Their work was predominantly classical in character, reflecting Daniel Burnham's influence. Graham's function was chiefly that of organizer and administrator. [*Supp. 2*]

GRAHAM, GEORGE REX (*b. Philadelphia, Pa., 1813; d. Orange, N.J., 1894*), editor, publisher. Issued first number of *Graham's Magazine* in January 1841, replacing the insipid contents then usual with a variety of original fiction, light essays, verse, biography, travel, art criticism, book notices, editorial chat and tasteful engravings. He paid writers with unprecedented liberality and had a distinguished staff which included Edgar Allan Poe, R. W. Griswold and

Bayard Taylor. Success was immediate. Graham lived lavishly for a time but his prosperity was short. By 1848 he had lost control of *Graham's*, though he remained editor. He bought back the magazine in 1850, but he lacked energy and it no longer flourished. He sold out for good in 1853.

GRAHAM, ISABELLA MARSHALL (*b. Lanarkshire, Scotland, 1742; d. 1814*), teacher, philanthropist. Settled in New York City, 1789, where she conducted a school. Active in charity, she promoted societies for relief of widows and orphans which were among earliest formed in America.

GRAHAM, JAMES (*d. Morrisania, N.Y., 1700/01*), provincial official. Came to New York, 1678. Served as an alderman of the city and its first recorder, as attorney-general and a judge of the province, and as speaker of the first General Assembly of the province.

GRAHAM, JAMES DUNCAN (*b. Prince William Co., Va., 1799; d. Massachusetts, 1865*), army engineer. Graduated West Point, 1817. First assistant on S. H. Long's expedition to the Rockies, 1819–21. Distinguished himself in national border surveys, especially joint demarcation of United States and British provinces. Discovered lunar tide on Great Lakes.

GRAHAM, JOHN (*b. Scotland, c. 1718; d. Naples, Italy, 1795*), merchant, planter, Loyalist. Came to Georgia, 1753. Served on Council of province; was chosen lieutenant-governor, 1776; in England, 1776–79; resided in Georgia during British occupancy, 1779–82. After a short stay in East Florida, resided in London.

GRAHAM, JOHN (*b. Dumfries, Va., 1774; d. Washington, D.C., 1820*), diplomat. Secretary of Orleans Territory; Thomas Jefferson's confidential agent in thwarting of Aaron Burr's western designs. Chief clerk, U.S. Department of State, 1807–17; minister to Portugal, 1819.

GRAHAM, JOHN ANDREW (*b. Southbury, Conn., 1764; d. 1841*), lawyer. Practiced in New York City *post* 1805, mainly in criminal courts. Forced amendment of code, outlawing use of evidence obtained by private examination of accused persons without aid of counsel.

GRAHAM, JOSEPH (*b. Chester Co., Pa., 1759; d. 1836*), Revolutionary soldier, legislator. Removed to North Carolina as a child. After the Revolution, engaged in iron-mining in Lincoln Co., N.C.

GRAHAM, SYLVESTER (*b. West Suffield, Conn., 1794; d. Northampton, Mass., 1851*), reformer. Began as a temperance lecturer *c.* 1830, but was soon preaching on Biblical subjects, health, personal hygiene and comparative anatomy. He advocated coarsely ground whole wheat (Graham) flour for bread, hard mattresses, open bedroom windows, cold showers, looser and lighter clothing, daily exercise,

vegetables, fresh fruits, rough cereals, pure drinking water and cheerfulness at meals. He had many adherents, among them Horace Greeley, but his frankness shocked many others. Emerson referred to him as the "poet of bran bread and pumpkins" and he was widely lampooned. His influence waned *post* 1840.

GRAHAM, WILLIAM ALEXANDER (*b. Lincoln Co., N.C., 1804; d. Saratoga Springs, N.Y., 1875*), lawyer, statesman. Son of Joseph Graham. Graduated University of North Carolina, 1824. State legislator, 1833–40; U.S. senator, Whig, from North Carolina, 1840–43; governor, 1845–49. He was an excellent administrator. As secretary of the navy, 1850–52, he reorganized the coastal survey and the personnel of the navy, encouraged the exploration of the Amazon and supported Perry's expedition to Japan.

After running for vice-president on Gen. Winfield Scott's ticket, 1852, Graham returned home and was leader of the moderates in the state until his death. He condemned secession, and his position was so strong nationally that in 1860 New York and Pennsylvania electors were urged to vote for him in the electoral college so as to avert dissolution of the Union. When war came, he ceased to be a Union man, although as a Confederate senator, 1864, he worked toward peace. He remained always a trusted adviser in his state.

GRAHAM, WILLIAM MONTROSE (*b. District of Columbia, 1834; d. Annapolis, Md., 1916*), soldier. Son of James D. Graham. Artilleryman, with extensive record of able service in Army of the Potomac, on frontier duty and in Spanish-American war.

GRANDGENT, CHARLES HALL (*b. Dorchester, Mass., 1862; d. Cambridge, Mass., 1939*), Romance philologist. Graduated Harvard, 1883; studied also at Leipzig, Paris and in Spain. Professor of Romance languages, Harvard, 1886–89, 1896–1932. Author of an excellent edition of the *Divina Commedia* (1933).
[*Supp. 2*]

GRANGER, ALFRED HOYT (*b. Zanesville, O., 1867; d. Roxbury, Conn., 1939*), architect. Grandnephew of William T. and John Sherman. Graduated Kenyon, 1887; studied at Boston Technical Institute and in Paris. Employed in office of successors to Henry H. Richardson; practiced *post* 1893 in Cleveland, Chicago and Philadelphia. Designer of Euclid Heights (Cleveland) and of the La Salle Street Station, Chicago; also of many other railroad stations in the West. An eclectic in design. [*Supp. 2*]

GRANGER, FRANCIS (*b. Suffield, Conn., 1792; d. Canandaigua, N.Y., 1868*), lawyer, legislator. Son of Gideon Granger. Prominent in New York Anti-Masonic movement; congressman, Whig, from New York, 1835–41, 1842–43. U.S. postmaster-general, 1841.

GRANGER, GIDEON (*b. Suffield, Conn., 1767; d. Canandaigua, N.Y., 1822*), lawyer, politician. As

Connecticut legislator, took prominent part in passage of Common School Law, 1795; *post* 1798, led Democratic-Republican minority in the state. Became postmaster-general, 1801, and successfully directed an expanding service until 1814.

GRANGER, GORDON (*b. Joy, N.Y., 1822; d. Santa Fé, N.M., 1876*), soldier. Graduated West Point, 1845. Served in Mexican War and at Western frontier posts. As major-general of volunteers, he rose to greatness in September 1863, when his surprise attack at Chickamauga drove back the Confederate forces encircling General Thomas's corps and saved the Union Army from annihilation.

GRANT, ALBERT WESTON (*b. East Benton, Maine, 1856; d. Philadelphia, Pa., 1930*), naval officer. Graduated Annapolis, 1877. In command of Atlantic Fleet submarine flotilla, 1915–17, he built up its efficiency, provided training schools, established submarine bases at New London, Conn., and Coco Solo, Panama.

GRANT, ASAHEL (*b. Marshall, N.Y., 1807; d. Mosul, Turkey, 1844*), physician. Presbyterian missionary to the Nestorians of western Persia, 1835–44.

GRANT, CLAUDIUS BUCHANAN (*b. Lebanon, Maine, 1835; d. St. Petersburg, Fla., 1921*), Michigan jurist. Graduated University of Michigan, 1859. State circuit judge, 1881–89, celebrated for stern prosecution of criminals; judge of state supreme court, 1889–1910, and chief justice, 1898–99, 1908.

GRANT, FREDERICK DENT (*b. St. Louis, Mo., 1850; d. New York, N.Y., 1912*), soldier. Son of Ulysses S. Grant. Graduated West Point, 1871. Resigned from army, 1881, to enter business; served as U.S. minister to Austria-Hungary, 1889–93, and as commissioner of police, New York City, 1895–97. Distinguished in Philippine insurrection, 1899–1902, he thereafter held territorial commands as regular major-general.

GRANT, GEORGE BARNARD (*b. Gardiner, Maine, 1849; d. Pasadena, Calif., 1917*), mechanical engineer. Graduated Lawrence Scientific School of Harvard, 1873. Invented "Grant's Difference Engine," a successful calculating machine (exhibited at Philadelphia, 1876); was a founder of the American gear-cutting industry.

GRANT, JAMES BENTON (*b. Russell Co., Ala., 1848; d. Excelsior Springs, Mo., 1911*), metallurgist, banker. Prominent in Denver's civic and business life, he served as Colorado's first Democratic governor, 1883–85.

GRANT, JOHN THOMAS (*b. Greene Co., Ga., 1813; d. Atlanta, Ga., 1887*), capitalist. *Post* 1844, he developed one of greatest plantations in Georgia; also executed railway-building contracts throughout the South. After the Civil War, he took a prominent part in the growth of Atlanta as a business center.

GRANT, LEWIS ADDISON (*b. Winhall, Vt., 1829; d. 1918*), lawyer, Union soldier. Awarded Congressional Medal for action as brigade-commander, Salem Heights, Va., 1863. Practiced law, *post* 1867, in Iowa and at Minneapolis, Minn. Assistant secretary of war, 1890–93.

GRANT, MADISON (*b. New York, N.Y., 1865; d. New York, 1937*), lawyer, naturalist, advocate of immigration restriction. Author of *The Passing of the Great Race* (1916). [*Supp. 2*]

GRANT, PERCY STICKNEY (*b. Boston, Mass., 1860; d. Mount Kisco, N.Y., 1927*), Episcopal clergyman. Graduated Harvard, 1883; Episcopal Seminary, Cambridge, 1886. Ordained, 1887. Controversial rector of the Church of the Ascension, New York, 1893–1924.

GRANT, ROBERT (*b. Boston, Mass., 1852; d. Boston, 1940*), jurist, novelist. Graduated Harvard, 1873; Ph.D., 1876; Harvard Law School, 1879. Author of *Unleavened Bread* (1900), *The Chippendales* (1909) and other works of a reforming tendency. [*Supp. 2*]

GRANT, ULYSSES SIMPSON (*b. Point Pleasant, O., 1822; d. Mount McGregor, N.Y., 1885*), general of the armies, president of the United States. Son of Jesse Root Grant, a tanner, and Hannah Simpson. Baptized Hiram Ulysses Grant, he accepted the name by which he is known on entry at West Point, 1839, although it was an error of the congressman who appointed him. Upon graduation, 1843, rated as the best rider at the academy, he was assigned for duty with the 4th Infantry. He joined Gen. Zachary Taylor's army in Texas, 1845. Disliking military life and out of sympathy with aims of the Mexican War, he yet distinguished himself at Monterey. Transferred to Gen. Scott's army, he marched to Mexico City and was mentioned for bravery. He married Julia Dent, 1848. In 1852 he left for the West Coast with his regiment and by his energy and resource prevented even greater loss of life than did occur in a terrible crossing of the Isthmus of Panama. Stationed first at Fort Vancouver, he was promoted to captain, 1853, and transferred to the dreary frontier post at Humboldt Bay, Calif. Lonely for his wife and children whom he saw no prospect of supporting on his pay, he began to drink; warned by his commanding officer, he resigned from the army.

Unsuccessful in various occupations, the outbreak of the Civil War found him a clerk in his brothers' leather shop at Galena, Ill. His application to Washington for duty got no reply. Appointed colonel of the 21st Illinois Volunteers in June 1861, to his own surprise he was raised to brigadier-general in August and given command of a district with headquarters at Cairo, Ill. Nearby Columbus, Ky., was the western end of a line held by Gen. A. S. Johnston to protect the Confederate supply depot at Nashville, Tenn. The line was strong in the flanks, but Fort Henry and

Fort Donelson in the center were weak, and Grant proposed their capture to Gen. H. W. Halleck.

Grant took Fort Henry early in February 1862. On February 13, he invested Donelson. A Confederate sortie drove back the Union right and center, but Grant attacked with his left and at the end of a day's fighting possessed the outer line of Confederate trenches. To a request for an armistice, he made his famous reply, "No terms except an unconditional and immediate surrender." The North greeted this victory joyfully, and Lincoln named Grant a major-general of volunteers. The advance of Buell's force as well as Grant's caused the Confederates to concentrate at Corinth, Miss. Grant ordered a concentration of all his forces save one division at Pittsburg Landing. Although both Grant and his lieutenant, W. T. Sherman, knew that a superior Confederate force was only 22 miles away, they established no line of defense, set up no reconnaissance system and prepared no plan of action. The night before the battle of Shiloh, Grant telegraphed Halleck, "I have scarcely the faintest idea of an attack . . . being made upon us. . . ." Early in the morning of April 6, 1862, the Confederates attacked and in desperate fighting drove the Union lines steadily back. Grant encouraged his men but failed to direct the battle. The next day, Union reinforcements having arrived, the Confederates were forced to retreat toward Corinth. No major battle of the Civil War displayed less generalship or more courage on the part of the enlisted men than Shiloh. A storm of denunciation followed, but Lincoln refused to relieve Grant, saying: "I can't spare this man—he fights."

Grant redeemed himself in the Vicksburg campaign where he was at his best. By capturing Vicksburg, the Union Army would control the Mississippi and the Confederacy's only remaining railroad leading east from the river. After the failure of his first try in Nov. 1862, Grant planned and executed in April 1863 one of the boldest movements in modern warfare. Abandoning his communications, he interposed his inferior force between the armies of J. E. Johnston and Pemberton, defeated both and laid siege to Vicksburg, which surrendered on the 4th of July. Ten days later, Port Hudson surrendered and the Confederacy was cut in two. Promoted to major-general in the regular army, Grant proceeded in October to the relief of Rosecrans's army, shut up in Chattanooga. He opened up a supply line and set about at once to drive Gen. Bragg from the approaches to the city. On November 24, Hooker took the Confederate position on Lookout Mountain; that day and the next, Sherman and Thomas seized Missionary Ridge. Bragg was driven back to Dalton, Ga., where he intrenched. Grant received the thanks of Congress, a gold medal, the rank of lieutenant-general and command of all the Union armies.

As general-in-chief, Grant devised a sound strategy, provided a unity of plan and a concentration of effort.

His aim was to cut the Confederacy into fragments; to engage all its armies at the same time; to destroy those armies by following them wherever they might go. He began simultaneous, coordinated movements: Meade's Army of the Potomac against Lee's army in Virginia; Butler's Army of the James against Lee's communications and Richmond; Sherman's Army of the Tennessee against J. E. Johnston's army and Atlanta.

Meade's army, hoping to pass Lee in the dense thickets of the Wilderness, was caught in a terrible battle there on May 5–7, 1864. Undeterred by appalling losses, Grant determined to march by Lee's right flank and interpose between him and Richmond. After Spotsylvania, North Anna, and more terrific losses at Cold Harbor, Grant realized he could not dislodge Lee from his position. By June 12, the Wilderness campaign had ended. Though Lee was undefeated and Grant outmaneuvered, the policy of attrition had worn down the enemy and robbed him of any initiative.

Grant withdrew from Lee's front and crossed the James River in a brilliant maneuver. Lee, deceived for four days, at last realized what was happening and brought his army south of Richmond. The long siege of Petersburg, Va., which followed left the Confederates drained of strength and in desperate need of food and transport. Meanwhile Sherman was on the march through the rich lands of Georgia. Lee abandoned Petersburg on April 2, 1865, and marched west, hoping to join J. E. Johnston, but Grant paralleled the march and blocked the retreat with cavalry. At Appomattox Court House on April 9, Lee surrendered the Army of Northern Virginia on Grant's magnanimous terms. Johnston surrendered to Sherman on April 26 and the Civil War was over.

Congress revived the rank of general, unused since 1799, and it was conferred on Grant, who served directly under Secretary of War Stanton and the president. Grant assumed the secretary's duties when Stanton was suspended by President Johnson in 1867; when the Senate restored Stanton, Grant surrendered the secretaryship thereby winning Johnson's bitter enmity.

The inevitable Republican presidential nominee in 1868, Grant had no real party affiliation, disliked politics as he disliked war, and was reluctant to give up the lifetime salary of general. He accepted, however, and was elected. He ran his office like an army headquarters, for this was the only method he knew. His choice of cabinet officers was poor, and he passed around other posts with no reference to the Republican party or to popular feeling. On the positive side, however, he took steps to restore the public credit, fought inflation, and frustrated the efforts of gold gamblers and currency raiders. With the exception of his scheme to annex the Dominican Republic in 1869, he supported Secretary of State Hamilton Fish in a firm and wise foreign policy.

In the North and West, a Liberal Republican movement based on disapproval of Reconstruction policies and on a demand for reform in the national administration was growing in influence. Its first objective was the defeat of Grant in 1872, but Grant was easily re-elected. Much galling criticism attended his second term. He dismissed capable advisers and continued to show a naive bad taste in his choice of personal associates. His defense of friends caught red-handed in graft and other corrupt practices further hurt his own reputation. Failing to understand why people did not wish him to undertake a third term, he retired without complaint and traveled with his family in Europe, 1877–79. Put forward for the nomination in 1880 by the Republican "Old Guard," he lost to James A. Garfield.

Grant's last years were overshadowed by poverty, misfortune, calumny and illness. His income failed; he was exploited in business and humiliated by bankruptcy. Shortly before his death, his friends succeeded in reviving his office of general for his benefit. His *Personal Memoirs* (1885–86), one of the most successful of American books and a primary historical source, was written by him in the sickroom during the last year of his life.

GRASS, JOHN (*b. on the Grand River, S.D., 1837; d. near Fort Yates, S.D., 1918*), a chief of the Blackfoot (Sihasapa) Sioux. Warrior name, Charging Bear. Early distinguished as an orator, and in battle with the Crows and Mandans, he urged his people to take up settled occupations and strongly opposed war with the whites. After the conflicts of 1876–77 his influence became dominant. He defended Indian rights in many treaty councils and served for years as chief justice of the Court of Indian Offenses at Fort Yates.

GRASSELLI, CAESAR AUGUSTIN (*b. Cincinnati, O., 1850; d. 1927*), manufacturing chemist, banker, philanthropist. Expanded activities of the family business, the Grasselli Chemical Co.; was one of the captains of industry who made Cleveland, O., a manufacturing center.

GRASTY, CHARLES HENRY (*b. Fincastle, Va., 1863; d. London, England, 1924*), editor, publisher, newspaper owner. Warred against municipal corruption in Baltimore (Md.) *News* and *Sun*, 1892–1914. Toured war fronts, 1917, as special correspondent of *New York Times*.

GRATIOT, CHARLES (*b. Lausanne, Switzerland, 1752; d. 1817*), pioneer trader. Came to Canada, 1769. Settled at Cahokia in the Illinois country, 1777; with Father Pierre Gibault helped George Rogers Clark secure allegiance of the Illinois settlers. Removed to St. Louis, Mo., 1781, and married half-sister of Col. Auguste Chouteau. Associated *post* 1795 to his death with the first John Jacob Astor, he was the most widely known of the St. Louis traders.

GRATZ, BARNARD (*b. Langensdorf, Upper Silesia, 1738; d. Baltimore, Md., 1801*), merchant. Brother of Michael Gratz and his partner in business. Came to Philadelphia, Pa., 1754. As a "merchant venturer" did pioneer service in opening the then West to trade. Laid cornerstone of first Philadelphia synagogue, 1782.

GRATZ, MICHAEL (*b. Langensdorf, Upper Silesia, 1740; d. Philadelphia, Pa., 1811*), merchant. Came to Philadelphia, Pa., 1759. Like his brother and partner, Barnard Gratz, he was active in coast and Western trade and a supporter of the American cause in the Revolution.

GRATZ, REBECCA (*b. Philadelphia, Pa., 1781; d. 1869*), philanthropist. Daughter of Michael Gratz. Traditionally the original of Rebecca in Scott's *Ivanhoe*. Devoted her life to good causes. Helped found Philadelphia Orphan Society, 1815, and was its secretary for forty years; founded Hebrew Sunday School Society, 1838, first of its kind in the United States, and served as president until 1864; inspired founding of the Jewish Foster Home.

GRAU, MAURICE (*b. Brünn, Austria, 1849; d. 1907*), theatrical and operatic impresario, best known for his brilliant management of the Metropolitan Opera, New York, 1898–1903.

GRAUPNER, JOHANN CHRISTIAN GOTTLIEB (*b. Verden, Hanover, Prussia, 1767; d. Boston, Mass., 1836*), musician. First oboist in Haydn's London orchestra, 1791–92, he emigrated to Canada, 1793. Settling finally in Boston, Mass., 1796, he opened a music store where he sold instruments, gave lessons and published music. Gathering together amateur and professional instrumentalists, he organized the Phil-harmonic Society in 1810 or 1811 and directed its Saturday evening sessions. It became the finest of contemporary American orchestras. In response to demand for a permanent choral society, Graupner, Thomas Smith Webb and Asa Peabody organized the Handel and Haydn Society, which gave its first concert in King's Chapel on Christmas, 1815.

GRAVENOR, JOHN. [See ALTHAM, JOHN, 1589–1640.]

GRAVES, FREDERICK ROGERS (*b. Auburn, N.Y., 1858; d. Shanghai, China, 1940*), Episcopal clergyman. Missionary in China, *post* 1881. Consecrated Bishop of Shanghai, 1893; resigned, 1937. [*Supp. 2*]

GRAVES, JAMES ROBINSON (*b. Chester, Vt., 1820; d. Memphis, Tenn., 1893*), Baptist clergyman. Brother of Zuinglius C. Graves. Edited *Tennessee Baptist*; established Southern Baptist Sunday-School Union and Southern Baptist Publication Society. Author of *The Great Iron Wheel* (1855), a very popular tirade against Methodism.

GRAVES, JOHN TEMPLE (*b. Abbeville Co., S.C., 1856; d. Washington, D.C., 1925*), journalist, popular lecturer.

GRAVES, ROSEWELL HOBART (*b. Baltimore, Md., 1833; d. China, 1912*), Southern Baptist missionary in South China, 1856–1912.

GRAVES, WILLIAM PHILLIPS (*b. Andover, Mass., 1870; d. 1933*), gynecologist. Graduated Harvard Medical School, 1899. Chief surgeon, Hospital for Women, Brookline, Mass., 1908–33; professor, Harvard Medical, 1911–32. Author of *Gynecology* (1916). [*Supp.* 1]

GRAVES, WILLIAM SIDNEY (*b. Mount Calm, Texas, 1865; d. Shrewsbury, N.J., 1940*), army officer. Graduated West Point, 1889; appointed, 1909, to the General Staff; promoted to major-general, 1918. In 1918–20, commanded American Expeditionary Force in Siberia. His troops achieved the limited objective of deterring Japan from dismembering Russia's Far Eastern possessions. Graves wrote of his controversial mission in *America's Siberian Adventure* (1931). [*Supp.* 2]

GRAVES, ZUINGLIUS CALVIN (*b. Chester, Vt., 1816; d. 1902*), educator. Brother of James R. Graves. First president of Mary Sharp College, Winchester, Tenn., 1850–96, where he maintained a degree of scholastic integrity nearly unique among U.S. women's schools of that period.

GRAVIER, JACQUES (*b. Moulins, France, 1651; d. Mobile, colony of Louisiana, 1708*), Jesuit priest. Came to Canada, 1685. Assistant to Father Allouez on mission to the Illinois, 1688–89; on Allouez's death in the latter year, became vicar-general of the mission, ministering to Kaskaskia, Peoria and Miami tribes. Superior of Western missions, *c.* 1696–1699, and in Louisiana colony, 1700–02, he returned to the Illinois where he labored until 1705.

GRAY, ASA (*b. Sauquoit, N.Y., 1810; d. Cambridge, Mass., 1888*), botanist. Graduated Fairfield (N.Y.) Medical School, 1831; influenced in choice of botany as a life-work by James Hadley, Lewis C. Beck, John Torrey. Between 1831 and 1835, Gray made a series of botanical journeys, taught, served as Torrey's assistant. His first independent publication, the *North American Gramineae and Cyperaceae* (1834–35) was followed by *Elements of Botany* (1836). He became curator of the N.Y. Lyceum of Natural History and collaborated with Torrey on their *Flora of North America* (published, 1838–40, 1841–43). Having accepted the professorship of botany at the University of Michigan, then organizing, he went to Europe, 1838, to purchase books for the University and to study type-specimens of American plants for the *Flora*. He never assumed his duties at the University of Michigan. In 1842 his *Botanical Text-Book* (later called *Structural Botany*) was published, the first of

many editions. Its lucid text and telling illustrations from pen drawings by Isaac Sprague became the model for many imitations. He became Fisher Professor of Natural History at Harvard in the summer of 1842 and held the chair until his death. At Cambridge he created the Harvard department of botany and trained many eminent botanists of the next generation. To the *American Journal of Science* he contributed reviews, bibliographical notes, news items, and short biographies which constitute an authoritative, readable, detailed history of botany extending over fifty years. His important textbooks—*First Lessons in Botany and Vegetable Physiology* (1857); *How Plants Grow* (1858); *Field, Forest and Garden Botany* (1868); *How Plants Behave* (1872); and another *Elements of Botany* (1887)—did immense service in popularizing botany.

Gray was a pioneer and master in the field of plant geography. His monograph on the botany of Japan and its relations to that of the North Temperate Zone (1859) probably did more than any other one production to give Gray his world-wide reputation. His greatest achievement, however, was his elaboration of the descriptive botany of North America. Most of his more than 350 books, monographs and shorter papers deal with portions of this vast subject. Most notable were the *Manual of the Botany of the Northern United States* (1848)—the most widely used of all his books—; *Genera Florae Americae Boreali-Orientalis Illustrata;* and *Synoptical Flora of North America.* He also elaborated the collections of the Wilkes Exploring Expedition (Vol. XV, 1854–57; Vol. XVII, 1874). In such work Gray was at the height of his genius.

Charles Darwin wrote Gray the famous letter (Sept. 5, 1857) in which he first outlined his theory of the evolution of species by means of natural selection. Gray became Darwin's chief American advocate but, wiser than others in his time, refused to accept Darwinism as a sort of scientific religion and reached conclusions about variations which looked forward to the discoveries of Mendel and De Vries.

Gray received honorary degrees from Oxford, Cambridge and Aberdeen. He was a founder of the National Academy of Sciences; president, 1863–73, of the American Academy of Arts and Sciences; president, 1872, of the American Association for the Advancement of Science; regent, 1874–88, of the Smithsonian Institution. He belonged to many learned and scientific societies, ranging from the Royal Society of London to the Polk County Agricultural Society of Iowa. Everywhere he was beloved for his simplicity, good humor and friendliness, as well as revered for qualities that made him one of the great botanists of the world.

GRAY, CARL RAYMOND (*b. Princeton, Ark., 1867; d. Washington, D.C., 1939*), railway executive. President, Great Northern, 1912–14; Western Maryland,

1914–19; Union Pacific, 1920–37. Director, federal Railroad Administration, World War I. [*Supp. 2*]

GRAY, ELISHA (*b. Barnesville, O., 1835; d. near Boston, Mass., 1901*), inventor. Partner with E. M. Barton in Gray & Barton, 1872–*c.* 1874; retired to devote whole time to electrical research. He had already invented an automatic self-adjusting telegraphic relay, a telegraph switch and annunciator, a private telegraph line printer, a telegraphic repeater. From his system of electro-harmonic telegraphy for transmitting musical tones (patented, 1875) grew the idea of transmitting vocal sounds. On Feb. 14, 1876, Gray filed a caveat with the Patent Office a few hours after Alexander Graham Bell filed a patent application for a speaking telephone. A bitter infringement battle followed; Bell's patent was sustained. Gray continued to invent electrical devices and obtained some seventy patents of which the most important was the telautograph (1888, 1891).

GRAY, FRANCIS CALLEY (*b. Salem, Mass., 1790; d. 1856*), Harvard benefactor, lawyer, Massachusetts legislator. Son of William Gray.

GRAY, GEORGE (*b. New Castle, Del., 1840; d. 1925*), jurist. Graduated Princeton, 1859. Attorney-general of Delaware, 1879–85; U.S. senator, Democrat, 1885–99; U.S. circuit court judge, 1899–1914. His reputation rests on his skill and tact as an arbitrator both in domestic and international disputes. Perhaps the outstanding accomplishment of his later career was the successful settlement of the Pennsylvania coal strike of 1902.

GRAY, GEORGE ALEXANDER (*b. Mecklenburg Co., N.C., 1851; d. 1912*), cotton manufacturer. Developed Gastonia, N.C., *post* 1888, into an important cotton town.

GRAY, HENRY PETERS (*b. New York, N.Y., 1819; d. 1877*), portrait and genre painter. Pupil of Daniel Huntington. Worked according to strict academic canons.

GRAY, HORACE (*b. Boston, Mass., 1828; d. 1902*), jurist. Grandson of William Gray. Graduated Harvard, 1845; admitted to the bar, 1851. An original Free-Soiler, interested in pre-Civil War political conflicts, Gray was appointed associate justice of the Massachusetts supreme judicial court, 1864. In 1873 he became chief justice and during eighteen years on the bench wrote far more than his share of the court's published opinions. Appointed to the U.S. Supreme Court, 1881, he was pre-eminent in his knowledge of former decisions and of the history and development of legal doctrine. His judicial opinions were characterized by a critical and chronological examination of all important decisions bearing on the question at issue.

GRAY, ISAAC PUSEY (*b. Chester Co., Pa., 1828; d. Mexico, 1895*), lawyer, Union soldier. Raised in Ohio; removed to Indiana, 1855. Republican state legislator, 1868–72; Democratic governor of Indiana, 1880–81, 1885–89; U.S. minister to Mexico, 1893–95.

GRAY, JOHN CHIPMAN (*b. Brighton, Mass., 1839; d. 1915*), lawyer, Union soldier, author, teacher. Grandson of William Gray. Graduated Harvard, 1859; Harvard Law School, 1861. Entered partnership in Boston with John C. Ropes, *c.* 1866. Lecturer, Harvard Law School, 1869–75. Appointed the Story Professor of Law, 1875, he was transferred to Royall Professor, 1883, and held that chair until 1913 when he retired. Gray became the most brilliant exponent of the new case system of legal instruction. He was also the foremost U.S. authority on the law of real property. Among his few but outstanding books were: *The Rule against Perpetuities* (1886); *Select Cases . . . on the Law of Property* (1888–92); and *The Nature and Sources of the Law* (1909).

GRAY, JOHN PURDUE (*b. Center Co., Pa., 1825; d. 1886*), physician, alienist. M.D., University of Pennsylvania, 1849. As superintendent, New York State Lunatic Asylum, Utica, 1854–86, Gray became known as the leading alienist of his day in America. More than any other one man he improved conditions for the insane, insisting on fresh air and exercise, abandoning as far as possible mechanical restraint and solitary feeding, and revolutionizing asylum construction. His asylum became a sort of post-graduate school for training alienists.

GRAY, JOSEPH W. (*b. Bridport, Vt., 1813; d. 1862*), journalist. Owner and editor of the Cleveland *Plain Dealer*, 1842–62. A witty, trenchant writer and a pioneer in use of cartoons.

GRAY, ROBERT (*b. Tiverton, R.I., 1755; d. at sea, 1806*), navigator, fur-trader. Sailing from Boston, September 1787, in the sloop *Lady Washington*, with the *Columbia* under Capt. John Kendrick, Gray made the Northwest coast, succeeded to command of the *Columbia*, gathered a cargo of sea-otter skins and returned home by way of China, arriving at Boston harbor in August 1790. He had sailed almost 42,000 miles and had carried the American flag around the world for the first time. After a refit, the *Columbia* sailed again in September 1790, arriving at Vancouver Island in June 1791. In the spring of 1792, Gray sailed his ship through the difficult passage at the mouth of the Columbia River and made an effectual discovery of that river; this later served as foundation of the U.S. claim to Oregon. He returned home again by way of China, arriving at Boston, July 1793.

GRAY, WILLIAM (*b. Lynn, Mass., 1750, o.s.; d. Boston, Mass., 1825*), merchant, shipowner. Prospered in privateering during Revolution; was among first Salem merchants to trade with Russia, China, India. Broke with Federalists on the Embargo issue, 1808; was (Democrat) Republican lieutenant-governor of Massachusetts, 1810–12.

GRAYDON, ALEXANDER (*b. Bristol, Pa., 1752; d. Philadelphia, Pa., 1818*), Revolutionary soldier. Author of *Memoirs of a Life . . .* (1811), one of the best-known and most valuable historical sources for the Revolutionary period.

GRAYSON, WILLIAM (*b. Prince William Co., Va., 1736?; d. Dumfries, Va., 1790*), lawyer, Revolutionary soldier. Aide to George Washington, and on active service, 1776–79; commissioner of Board of War, 1779–81. Served in Virginia legislature; member, Continental Congress, 1785–87. Opposed Federal Constitution as inimical to Southern interests. U.S. senator, Anti-Federal, from Virginia, 1789–90.

GREATHOUSE, CLARENCE RIDGEBY (*b. Kentucky, c. 1845; d. Seoul, Korea, 1899*), lawyer, diplomat. Legal adviser to Korean government, 1890–99.

GREATON, JOHN (*b. Roxbury, Mass., 1741; d. Roxbury, 1783*), trader, Revolutionary soldier. Distinguished at siege of Boston, and as colonel, 24th Continental Infantry. Promoted brigadier-general, 1783. One of the memorialists to Congress on dissatisfaction of army, 1782.

GREATON, JOSEPH (*b. London, England, 1679; d. Bohemia, Md., 1753*), Jesuit priest. Came to America, *c.* 1720; first Roman Catholic pastor in Pennsylvania, 1729–49. Built St. Joseph's Church, Philadelphia.

GREELEY, HORACE (*b. Amherst, N.H., 1811; d. 1872*), editor, political leader. Learned printer's trade as apprentice in office of *Northern Spectator*, East Poultney, Vt.; came to New York City as journeyman 1831; formed partnership in printing shop with F. V. Story, 1833, later with Jonas Winchester. Founded with Winchester, 1834, the *New Yorker*, a nonpartisan, literary and news weekly which achieved a good circulation but lost money. Married Mary Y. Cheney, 1836. Augmented his income by writing for Whig newspapers and edited the *Jeffersonian* (1838), a Whig campaign weekly which ran a year and exercised real influence. Greeley acquired important political friendships, notably with Thurlow Weed and William H. Seward, and in 1840 published a second Whig weekly, the *Log Cabin*, which gained unprecedented success.

As no Whig penny paper existed in New York, nor any paper offering a choice between the sensationalism of Bennett's *Herald* and the staidness of Bryant's *Evening Post*, Greeley launched his *New York Tribune* on April 10, 1841. After a few anxious days, subscriptions poured in. Greeley labored tirelessly and had the efficient aid of Thomas McElrath as business manager to give the establishment system and to free the editor from routine. The *Tribune* was the best all-round paper in the city by 1846. Its energy in news-gathering, good taste, high moral standards and intellectual appeal set a new standard.

Editorials were vigorous but temperate, political news exact, book reviews numerous.

Greeley's own radical views were expressed fearlessly in his paper. He was an egalitarian, despising and fearing monopoly of any kind and class dominance; he espoused Fourierism and the agrarian movement; he supported cooperative shops and labor unions, opposed capital punishment, urged restrictions on liquor-selling. A free-trader by conviction, he supported high tariffs as the best means to that end, an apparent paradox. Assisted by a liberal, versatile staff, which included Charles A. Dana, Margaret Fuller, Bayard Taylor, George Ripley and J. S. Pike, he made the *Tribune* a popular teacher, champion and moral leader with unrivaled national influence. The greatest element in this success was Greeley's own moral earnestness and interpretive and editorial gifts. Throughout the 1850's, the paper concentrated on the Free-Soil movement. Greeley opposed slavery as immoral and uneconomic; the fight over the Kansas-Nebraska Bill aroused his greatest eloquence. Among the first editors to join the Republican party, he insisted on the importance of the Union; he had no patience with W. L. Garrison's secessionist views and strongly attacked Know-Nothingism.

As a public figure Greeley was regarded with a mixture of admiration and affectionate amusement. His mild, pink face, fringed by throat whiskers, his broad-brimmed hat, white overcoat, crooked cravat, his shambling gait and absent-minded manner were widely caricatured. His naïveté on many subjects, his homely wisdom on others appealed to millions. Some of his phrases, like "Go West, young man," were universally current. By signing many editorials and frequently appearing in public as a lecturer, he gave his work a direct appeal unusual in journalism. His principal defect of character was a thirst for political office which led him to unwise and undignified actions.

At the coming of the Civil War, he supported the Union energetically; his primary demand was that no concessions be made to slavery. Allying himself with the radical anti-slavery element, he warred against Democrats and moderates. He opposed Lincoln's policy of conciliating the border states, demanded early emancipation. His reputation and influence were injured by his hesitation to support Lincoln in 1864. His peace activities of 1864–65 were even more ill advised and gave people a poor opinion of his judgment. His radical views extended to Reconstruction policies as well; he believed in full Negro equality and indorsed the 14th and 15th Amendments, yet he favored general amnesty, advocated Jefferson Davis's release from custody and signed his bond.

At first a supporter of U. S. Grant, by 1870 Greeley was critical of the president's public policies and of his support of the Conkling-Cornell machine in New York. Gradually convinced that Grant's administration was demoralized and corrupt, Greeley and the *Tribune* declared against renomination in September 1871; Greeley also encouraged the movement for a new party. As the Liberal Republican movement grew and a coalition with the Democrats seemed possible, he agreed to be a presidential candidate and was nominated by the Liberal Republicans at Cincinnati, O., in May 1872. A dispirited Democratic convention indorsed Greeley but many Democrats bolted. The campaign was exceptionally abusive. Greeley took the merciless attacks on himself much to heart. After a strenuous speaking tour in which he urged full reconciliation of North and South for achievement of reforms, he carried only six states and was profoundly hurt by the feeling that he was "the worst beaten man who ever ran for high office." Shortly after the campaign, Greeley's wife died. The final blow came when on returning to the *Tribune* he found Whitelaw Reid firmly in charge and realized he had practically, if not nominally, lost the editorship which had been his lifelong pride. His body and mind broke and he died insane.

GREELY, ADOLPHUS WASHINGTON (*b. Newburyport, Mass., 1844; d. Washington, D.C., 1935*), soldier, explorer, scientist, author. Rose from private to brevet major in important Civil War engagements; remained in army and became major-general, 1906. Commanded U.S. expedition for study of Arctic weather and climate, 1881–84; of the ill-fated *Proteus* expedition to Lady Franklin Bay, only six of the participants reached home. Although Greely was at first blamed for the failure, he eventually was honored for his sound judgment under trying conditions. His book *Three Years of Arctic Service* (1885) was a popular account of the adventure. [*Supp. 1*]

GREEN, ALEXANDER LITTLE PAGE (*b. Sevier Co., Tenn., 1806; d. 1874*), Methodist clergyman. Influential in locating Southern Methodist publishing houses in Nashville, Tenn., 1854.

GREEN, ANDREW HASWELL (*b. Worcester, Mass., 1820; d. New York, N.Y., 1903*), lawyer. Partner of Samuel J. Tilden. Commissioner and planner of Central Park, New York City; as N.Y.C. Comptroller, 1871–76, straightened out city finances. Conceived and carried through consolidation of "Greater New York."

GREEN, ANNA KATHARINE. [See Rohlfs, Anna Katharine Green, 1846–1935.]

GREEN, ASA (*b. Ashby, Mass., 1789; d. c. 1837*), physician, novelist, bookseller. Author of *The Perils of Pearl Street* (1834) and other satires.

GREEN, ASHBEL (*b. Hanover, N.J., 1762; d. Philadelphia, Pa., 1848*), Presbyterian clergyman. Son of Jacob Green (1722–1790). Graduated College of New Jersey (Princeton), 1783. Minister of Second Presbyterian Church, Philadelphia, 1787–1812; held many offices in the work of his denomination, and was author of its 1818 declaration against slavery. Composed the plan of Princeton Theological Seminary; served as president of Princeton, 1812–22.

GREEN, BARTHOLOMEW (*b. Cambridge, Mass., 1666; d. Boston, Mass., 1732*), printer, journalist. Chief printer in New England, 1692–1732; printed *Boston News-Letter, post* 1704.

GREEN, BENJAMIN EDWARDS (*b. Elkton, Ky., 1822; d. near Dalton, Ga., 1907*), lawyer, diplomat, promoter. Son of Duff Green. After diplomatic experience in Mexico and the West Indies, associated himself in his father's enterprises and was active in industrial development of Georgia. Wrote and translated works on currency and economics.

GREEN, BERIAH (*b. Preston, Conn., 1795; d. Whitesboro, N. Y., 1874*), Congregational clergyman, Abolitionist. President of Philadelphia convention which formed American Anti-Slavery Society, 1833; president, Oneida Institute, 1833–43.

GREEN, DUFF (*b. Woodford Co., Ky., 1791; d. near Dalton, Ga., 1875*), journalist, politician, industrial promoter. Prospered as land speculator and merchant in St. Louis, Mo., *post* 1816; admitted to bar, he built up a large practice and was among most influential members of Missouri constitutional convention. Removing to Washington, D.C., 1825, he became editor-publisher of the *United States Telegraph*, an outstanding Democratic leader and a member of Jackson's "Kitchen Cabinet." He followed J. C. Calhoun in his split with Jackson; however, although a radical state-rights man, he opposed extreme nullification views. In 1832, he supported Henry Clay and thereafter stood with the Whigs. In England, 1842–44, he served as an unofficial U.S. agent, seeking to secure commercial treaties, lower duties, direct trade with the South. An expansionist, he welcomed the Mexican War; both before and after the Civil War (during which he conducted iron works for the Confederacy), he was engaged in developing coal and iron lands and railroads. In the post-bellum period, he was especially active in raising capital for reconstruction of the South's economy.

GREEN, FRANCES HARRIET WHIPPLE (*b. Smithfield, R.I., 1805; d. Oakland, Calif., 1878*), author, reformer. Active on behalf of temperance, labor, suffrage, abolition, spiritualism.

GREEN, FRANCIS (*b. Boston, Mass. 1742 o.s.; d. Medford, Mass., 1809*), soldier, merchant, Loyalist. First American to write on methods for instructing the deaf and dumb (1783, 1801).

GREEN, FRANCIS MATHEWS (*b. Boston, Mass., 1835; d. Albany, N.Y., 1902*), naval officer, hydrographer. Grandson of Francis Green. Led expeditions (1876–82) to West Indies, South and Central America, China, Japan and East Indies to determine longitude by exchange of telegraphic time signals.

GREEN, GABRIEL MARCUS (*b. New York, N.Y., 1891; d. 1919*), mathematician. Graduated College of the City of New York, 1911; Ph.D., Columbia, 1913. Author of a work on projective differential geometry and other papers which showed great promise.

GREEN, HENRY WOODHULL (*b. Lawrenceville, N.J., 1804; d. 1876*), jurist. Brother of John C. Green. Graduated Princeton, 1820; practiced law in Trenton, N.J. Outstanding as chief justice, New Jersey supreme court, 1846–60; chancellor, and judge of prerogative court, 1860–66.

GREEN, HETTY HOWLAND ROBINSON (*b. New Bedford, Mass., 1834; d. New York, N.Y., 1916*), financier. In managing a large, inherited fortune, she became known as a Wall Street "character." Although she negotiated several "bull" movements, notably in railroad stocks, her Wall Street business was principally lending money. Shrewd and eccentric, the newspapers gave her an exaggerated reputation as a miser.

GREEN, HORACE (*b. Chittenden, Vt., 1802; d. Sing Sing, now Ossining, N.Y., 1866*), laryngologist. Graduated Castleton Medical College, M.D., 1825. First American throat specialist. Discovered value of applying silver nitrate solutions locally in catarrhal inflammation of the pharynx and larynx. Author of *Treatise on Diseases of the Air Passages* (1846), a pioneer work.

GREEN, JACOB (*b. Malden, Mass., 1722; d. 1790*), Presbyterian clergyman, physician. Father of Ashbel Green. Pastor at Hanover, N.J., 1746–90. An outspoken patriot in the Revolution. Leader of "Associated Presbytery" movement, 1780.

GREEN, JACOB (*b. Philadelphia, Pa., 1790; d. Philadelphia, 1841*), chemist, naturalist. Son of Ashbel Green. Graduated University of Pennsylvania, 1807. Professor of chemistry, Princeton, 1818–22; at Jefferson Medical College, 1825–41. An excellent teacher and author of useful textbooks.

GREEN, JAMES STEPHENS (*b. near Rectortown, Va., 1817; d. 1870*), lawyer. Settled in Lewis Co., Mo., *c.* 1836; practiced in Monticello. Protégé of Thomas H. Benton, he served in Congress, 1847–51; he led the Democratic revolt in 1849 which broke Benton's hold on the party in Missouri. As U.S. senator, 1857–61, he was recognized as one of the ablest spokesmen for the Breckinridge Democracy.

GREEN, JOHN (*b. Worcester, Mass., 1835; d. St. Louis, Mo., 1913*), ophthalmologist.

GREEN, JOHN CLEVE (*b. Lawrenceville, N.J., 1800; d. New York, N.Y., 1875*), China merchant, financier, philanthropist. Head of Russell and Co.,

most powerful American house in the China trade, 1834–39; a heavy investor in the railroad enterprises of his old Canton partner, J.M. Forbes. Benefactor of Princeton and Lawrenceville School.

GREEN, JONAS (*b. Boston, Mass., 1712; d. Annapolis, Md., 1767*), printer, journalist. Great-grandson of Samuel Green. Removed to Maryland, 1738, where he became printer to the Province. Established the *Maryland Gazette*, 1745. His typographical masterpiece was Thomas Bacon's *Laws of Maryland* (1765).

GREEN, JOSEPH (*b. probably Boston, Mass., 1706; d. London, England, 1780*), merchant, Loyalist. Author of witty occasional satires in verse.

GREEN, LEWIS WARNER (*b. near Danville, Ky., 1806; d. 1863*), Presbyterian clergyman, educator. Graduated Centre College, 1824; studied also in Germany, 1834–36. President of Hampden-Sydney College, 1848–56; Transylvania University, 1856–57; Centre College, 1858–63.

GREEN, NATHAN (*b. Salem, Mass., 1787?; d. New York, N.Y., 1825*), privateersman. Commanded the *Grand Turk* of Salem, which shares with the *America* (also of Salem) the honor of being the most successful privateer in the War of 1812.

GREEN, NORVIN (*b. New Albany, Ind., 1818; d. 1893*), physician, legislator. Raised in Kentucky. Among first to conceive of a national consolidation of telegraph lines; formed North American Telegraph Co., 1857; Western Union Telegraph Co., 1866; served as president, Western Union, 1878–93.

GREEN, SAMUEL (*b. England, 1615; d. Cambridge, Mass., 1701/02*), printer. Came to Massachusetts, *c.* 1633. Succeeded Stephen Day as manager of the Cambridge press and colony printer.

GREEN, SAMUEL ABBOTT (*b. Groton, Mass., 1830; d. 1918*), physician, author. Practiced in Boston. First Massachusetts physician to volunteer, he was distinguished throughout the Civil War in field and hospital service. Prominent in Massachusetts Historical Society, he served as its librarian, 1868–1918.

GREEN, SAMUEL BOWDLEAR (*b. Chelsea, Mass., 1859; d. 1910*), horticulturist. Graduated Massachusetts Agricultural College, 1879. Professor of horticulture and forestry, University of Minnesota, 1892–1910; active in Minnesota experiment station work and author of textbooks.

GREEN, SAMUEL SWETT (*b. Worcester, Mass., 1837; d. 1918*), librarian. Brother of John Green. Graduated Harvard, 1858. Pioneered in modern practice at Worcester Free Library, 1871–1909.

GREEN, SETH (*b. Monroe Co., N.Y., 1817; d. 1888*), pioneer fish culturist. Made fish breeding a recognized and practical art; transported live shad to the Pacific coast, 1871; experimented with hatching salmon, sturgeon and other fish.

GREEN, THOMAS (*b. New London, Conn., 1735; d. New Haven, Conn., 1812*), printer, editor. Great-great-grandson of Samuel Green. Established *Connecticut* (now *Hartford*) *Courant*, 1764; *Connecticut Journal and New Haven Post Boy*, 1767.

GREEN, WILLIAM (*b. Fredericksburg, Va., 1806; d. 1880*), lawyer. Practiced *post* 1827 in Culpeper Co.; *post* 1855 in Richmond, where he stood at head of the Virginia bar for legal learning.

GREEN, WILLIAM HENRY (*b. Groveville, N.J., 1825; d. 1900*), Presbyterian clergyman, Hebrew scholar. Nephew of John C. and Henry W. Green. Graduated Lafayette, 1840; Princeton Theological Seminary, 1846. Professor at Princeton Seminary, 1851–1900; also its acting president for 17 years. Scholarly leader in America of the ultraconservative school of Biblical criticism.

GREENE, ALBERT GORTON (*b. Providence, R.I., 1802; d. Cleveland, O., 1868*), poet, jurist, book-collector. Author of "Old Grimes" (1818) and other poems.

GREENE, CHARLES EZRA (*b. Cambridge, Mass., 1842; d. Ann Arbor, Mich., 1903*), civil engineer, teacher. Graduated Harvard, 1862; Massachusetts Institute of Technology, 1868. Held chair of civil engineering, University of Michigan, *post* 1872; dean, College of Engineering, *post* 1895. First to apply graphical methods of analysis to problems of roofs, bridges and arches.

GREENE, CHRISTOPHER (*b. Warwick, R.I., 1737; d. Westchester Co., N.Y., 1781*), Revolutionary soldier. Cited for gallant defense of Fort Mercer against Hessian attack, October 1777.

GREENE, DANIEL CROSBY (*b. Roxbury, Mass., 1843; d. 1913*), Congregational clergyman. Graduated Dartmouth, 1864; Andover Theological, 1869. Missionary to Japan, 1869–1913.

GREENE, EDWARD LEE (*b. Hopkinton, R.I., 1843; d. Washington, D.C., 1915*), botanist. Taught at University of California, 1885–95; at Catholic University, 1895–1904. Associate of the Smithsonian, 1904–11. A controversial, picturesque scholar, unexcelled in field knowledge of North American flora.

GREENE, FRANCES HARRIET WHIPPLE. [See GREEN, FRANCES HARRIET WHIPPLE, 1805–1878.]

GREENE, FRANCIS VINTON (*b. Providence, R.I., 1850; d. New York, N.Y., 1921*), soldier, historian, engineer. Son of G. S. Greene (1801–99). Graduated West Point, 1870. Commanded second Philippine expedition, 1898. His *The Russian Army and Its Campaigns in Turkey in 1877–78* (1879) is the standard authority on its subject.

GREENE, GEORGE SEARS (*b. Apponaug, R.I., 1801; d. Morristown, N.J., 1899*), soldier, civil engineer. Graduated West Point, 1823. The high point of his career as brigade commander, 1862–66, was his holding of Culp's Hill at Gettysburg against repeated Confederate attacks. Worked extensively in New York City on water supply, elevated railways, laying out new streets. He was the father of Francis V., Samuel D., and George S. Greene (1837–1922).

GREENE, GEORGE SEARS (*b. Lexington, Ky., 1837; d. 1922*), civil engineer. Son of George S. Greene (1801–1899). Studied with his father; early devised a drifting head for transits and other improvements in surveying instruments. Notable for his work on the sea-wall around Manhattan Island and his original method in constructing the New York Chelsea piers.

GREENE, GEORGE WASHINGTON (*b. East Greenwich, R.I., 1811; d. East Greenwich, 1883*), author, educator. Grandson of Gen. Nathanael Greene, whose life he wrote; held first chair of American history to be established in the United States (Cornell University, 1871).

GREENE, NATHANAEL (*b. Potowomut [Warwick], R.I., 1742; d. near Savannah, Ga., 1786*), Revolutionary general. Brought up as a member of the Society of Friends; employed as a young man in the family business of iron-founding. Denied officer-status in a local militia company he had helped organize, he served as a private, 1774–75. Appointed brigadier-general by Rhode Island Assembly, May 1775; commissioned Continental brigadier, June 1775. Served through siege of Boston and commanded army of occupation after evacuation by British, March 1776. Assumed charge of defences of New York City, May 1776. Promoted major-general in August, he was ill during the British attack on Long Island that same month. Subsequent to battle of Harlem Heights, he was given command of the troops in New Jersey with headquarters at Fort Lee. His advice to hold Fort Washington (taken by the British in November, 1776) has been sharply criticized by historians.

Greene ably led left column at battle of Trenton, then wintered with the army at Morristown. In March 1777, he held conference about the army with Congress at Washington's request. After the battle of Brandywine Greene's skillful disposition of troops insured the safe withdrawal of the army and saved the artillery. There is no evidence that he was at fault in the defeat at Germantown where he led the left column.

Succeeding Thomas Mifflin as quartermaster-general, March 2, 1778, Greene reorganized the department, insisting on monthly returns from his deputies and the appointment of trusted friends, John Cox and Charles Pettit, to assist him. He established an efficient system of depots so as to draw on the fertile middle states for forage and on New England for manufactured goods. At the battle of Monmouth, June 1778, Greene led the right; in July he assisted with preparations to drive the British from Rhode Island; with Gen. Sullivan he won a victory there in late August. Greene's exertions as quartermaster greatly reduced the army's suffering in winter quarters at Middlebrook, N.J., 1778–79.

Attacked by Congress at Mifflin's instigation in the spring of 1780 for permitting dishonesty on the part of his subordinates, Greene replied indignantly. When his enemies in Congress adopted a new quartermaster plan of Timothy Pickering's in July, Greene resigned as quartermaster and returned to the line. Appointed to command in the South, October 1780, after Gates's defeat at Camden, S.C., Greene set out on his greatest campaign.

Realizing that the Camden disaster had been due to failure of supplies, Greene in nine days provided a medical department, engineers, artillery, clothing, every detail of equipment, and a cavalry force without which Gates had had inadequate intelligence. He went on to secure the cooperation of the local authorities in Virginia and North Carolina and reorganized Gates's army. Unlike Gates, he showed tact and ability in handling such able if independent officers as Henry Lee, Daniel Morgan and William Washington as well as the various partisan corps in the area. The tide turned definitely in January 1781, when Morgan gained a striking victory over Tarleton at Cowpens. Greene's general policy was typical of successful American strategy in the Revolution, which was to withdraw as far as the enemy would pursue and, when he had outrun his communications, to follow and worry him on his retreat. The British under Cornwallis gained costly victories at Guilford Court House and Hobkirk's Hill but were maneuvered out of Camden, which the patriot army entered in triumph. Greene captured the British posts in the South one by one until by December 1781 only Charleston remained. Under siege for a year, the town was evacuated on December 14, 1782.

Greene pledged his own fortune for the support of his army, 1782–83, and had to indorse the paper of John Banks, a contractor, to keep the men from starving. When Banks later went bankrupt, Greene became involved in debts he could not pay and was obliged to sell his estates. In 1785 he established himself near Savannah, Ga., at Mulberry Grove, the confiscated property of the Loyalist John Graham, where he died.

GREENE, NATHANIEL (*b. Boscawen, N.H., 1797; d. Boston, Mass., 1877*), Boston newspaper editor, Democratic politician and officeholder, linguist.

GREENE, SAMUEL DANA (*b. Cumberland, Md., 1840; d. Portsmouth, N.H., 1884*), naval officer. Son of George S. Greene (1801–1899). Graduated Annapolis, 1859. Executive officer of U.S.S. *Monitor* from her launching until she sank. Gunnery officer in fight with *Merrimac*.

GREENE, SAMUEL STILLMAN (*b. Belchertown, Mass., 1810; d. 1883*), educator. Founder of Rhode Island College of Education; long on faculty of Brown University. His progressive ideas on teaching were embodied in many successful textbooks on English grammar.

GREENE, WILLIAM (*b. Warwick, R.I., 1695/96; d. Warwick, 1758*), colonial governor of Rhode Island, 1743–45; 1746–47; 1748–55; 1757–58.

GREENE, WILLIAM (*b. Warwick, R.I., 1731; d. Warwick, 1809*), legislator, jurist. Son of William Greene (1695/96–1758). Governor of Rhode Island, 1778–86.

GREENE, WILLIAM CORNELL (*b. Chappaqua, N.Y., 1851; d. Cananea, Mexico, 1911*), promoter. After a youth as cowboy, Indian fighter and prospector in Arizona, Greene settled as a rancher in the San Pedro valley. Convinced that La Cananea, a tract of land in Sonora, Mexico, contained mineral deposits, he filed mining claims, obtained possession, and raised capital for several operating companies, the last being Greene Consolidated Copper Co. Shrewdly appealing to the small investor and exercising his genius for writing prospectuses, he prospered exceedingly *post* 1900, and very rich copper ores were discovered on his claims. His own speculations and raids by other financiers severely affected him, however, and his fall was rapid. In 1906, Amalgamated Copper and other interests forced formation of a new company, Greene-Cananea-Consolidated, from which he was soon squeezed out. The panic of 1907 finished his fortunes.

GREENER, RICHARD THEODORE (*b. Philadelphia, Pa., 1844; d. Chicago, Ill., 1922*), educator, lawyer. The first Negro to receive a degree from Harvard (1870), he taught at University of South Carolina, 1873–77, and in law department of Howard University, of which he became dean, 1879. He began to practice law in Washington, D.C., 1882. A fluent speaker, he argued against Frederick Douglass, recommending Southern freedmen to go West and take up fertile land. He served as chief examiner of the New York City civil-service board, 1885–90, as U.S. consul at Bombay, and as U.S. commercial agent at Vladivostok.

GREENHALGE, FREDERIC THOMAS (*b. Clitheroe, England, 1842; d. Boston, Mass., 1896*), lawyer. Came to America, 1855. Practiced in Lowell, Mass., where he held several offices. Congressman, Republican, from Massachusetts, 1889–91, he served with zeal and independence as governor of Massachusetts *post* 1894.

GREENHOW, ROBERT (*b. Richmond, Va., 1800; d. San Francisco, Calif., 1854*), physician, linguist, historian. Author of *The History of Oregon and California* (1844), a pioneer work based on original sources.

GREENLAW, EDWIN ALMIRON (*b. Flora, Ill., 1874; d. 1931*), educator. Graduated Northwestern, 1897; Ph.D., Harvard, 1904. Taught at Adelphi College; headed English Department, University of North Carolina, 1914–25, and was dean of graduate school; Osler Professor of English at Johns Hopkins, 1925–31. Authority on Spenser. [*Supp.* 1]

GREENLEAF, BENJAMIN (*b. Haverhill, Mass., 1786; d. 1864*), educator. Graduated Dartmouth, 1813. Author of the *National Arithmetic* (1836) and other popular mathematical textbooks.

GREENLEAF, HALBERT STEVENS (*b. Guilford, Vt., 1827; d. Charlotte, N.Y., 1906*), industrialist, Union soldier. Partner in lock factory of Sargent and Greenleaf, Rochester, N.Y. Congressman, Democrat, from New York, 1883–85, 1891–93.

GREENLEAF, MOSES (*b. Newburyport, Mass., 1777; d. 1834*), map-maker, jurist, author. Brother of Simon Greenleaf. Removed to Maine, 1790; was active in the settlement of the district's interior. His 1815 map of Maine with its accompanying volume of statistics was influential in promoting Maine statehood; his *Survey of the State of Maine* (1829) is one of the most important books relating to Maine history.

GREENLEAF, SIMON (*b. Newburyport, Mass., 1783; d. 1853*), lawyer, author. Brother of Moses Greenleaf. Educated at Newburyport Latin School; read law in office of Ezekiel Whitman; admitted to bar, 1806; practiced until 1818 at Standish and Gray, Maine. Removing to Portland, he at once took place as one of the town's most learned practitioners and served as reporter of the Maine supreme court, 1820–32. Appointed Royall Professor of Law at Harvard, 1833, he held the chair until 1846 when he succeeded Joseph Story as Dane Professor. His health declining in 1848, he retired as emeritus. Under the dual leadership of Greenleaf and Story, the Harvard Law School rose to national eminence. Greenleaf's learned *Treatise on the Law of Evidence* (1842–53) became in its completed form the foremost American authority. His revision of *Cruise's Digest of the Law of Real Property* (1849–50) superseded the English original in the United States.

GREENLEAF, THOMAS (*b. Abington, Mass., 1755; d. New York, N.Y., 1798*), printer, journalist. Removed to New York City, 1785; published *New-York Journal;* founded the *Argus,* 1795, in support of Aaron Burr's party and against the Federalists.

GREENOUGH, HENRY (*b. Newburyport, Mass., 1807; d. 1883*), architect, painter. Brother of Horatio and Richard S. Greenough.

GREENOUGH, HORATIO (*b. Boston, Mass., 1805; d. Somerville, Mass., 1852*), sculptor. Brother of Henry and Richard S. Greenough. Washington Allston guided his art studies. After graduation from Harvard, 1825, he went to Rome where he began serious study of sculpture and had aid of Thorwaldsen. Home within a year with malaria, he modeled from life an excellent likeness of John Quincy Adams and other portraits. In 1828 he returned to Italy and settled in Florence. An early commission from James Fenimore Cooper was a small marble group called "Chanting Cherubs." The nudity of the cherubs raised much American protest to which Greenough returned a spirited defense. In 1831 he modeled a bust of Lafayette. American travelers gave him small commissions, and he produced several groups, busts and figures. Commissioned, 1833, to do a statue of Washington to be placed in the U.S. Capitol, for nearly eight years he gave himself to what he believed the crowning work of his career. The colossal, half-draped marble figure, poetically treated, proved too heavy for the Capitol floor and was placed outside, where it met the gibes of an unappreciative public. It was the first colossal group in marble by an American. A second colossal group, "The Rescue," executed 1837–51, was placed on a buttress of the Capitol portico.

Greenough returned home and settled at Newport, R.I., 1851. His importance lies in his influence, rather than in the artistic merit of his work. He dedicated himself to his art with the utmost earnestness and did much to dignify it in the minds of Americans. He was author of *Aesthetics in Washington* (1851).

GREENOUGH, JAMES BRADSTREET (*b. Portland, Maine, 1833; d. 1901*), lawyer, philologist. Taught Latin at Harvard, *post* 1865; was the first to teach Sanskrit and comparative philology there. Author of *Analysis of the Latin Subjunctive* (1870), and (with Joseph H. Allen) of a famous Latin grammar. Edited many texts.

GREENOUGH, RICHARD SALTONSTALL (*b. Jamaica Plain, Mass., 1819; d. Rome, Italy, 1904*), sculptor. Brother of Henry and Horatio Greenough.

GREENUP, CHRISTOPHER (*b. probably Loudoun Co., Va., c. 1750; d. Blue Lick Springs, Ky., 1818*), lawyer. Removed to Kentucky near end of the Revolution. Congressman from Kentucky, 1792–97; Democratic governor, 1804–08.

GREENWALD, EMANUEL (*b. near Frederick, Md., 1811; d. Lancaster, Pa., 1885*), Lutheran clergyman. Pastor in Ohio, 1831–54; in Easton, Pa., 1854–67; thereafter at Lancaster, Pa. A conservative, he opposed revivals and other innovations.

GREENWAY, JOHN CAMPBELL (*b. Huntsville, Ala., 1872; d. New York, N.Y., 1926*), mining engineer. Specialist in Southwest copper mining.

[*Supp.* 1]

GREENWOOD, GRACE. [See LIPPINCOTT, SARAH JANE CLARKE, 1823–1904.]

GREENWOOD, ISAAC (*b. Boston, Mass., 1702; d. Charleston, S.C., 1745*). Graduated Harvard, 1721. At instance of Thomas Hollis, was appointed professor of mathematics at Harvard, 1727; served in that capacity, 1728–38. His *Arithmetick, Vulgar and Decimal* (1729) was first textbook of its kind in English by a native American.

GREENWOOD, JOHN (*b. Boston, Mass., 1760; d. New York, N.Y., 1819*), dentist. Grandson of Isaac Greenwood. Apprenticed to a cabinetmaker, he established himself in New York City as a dentist, 1784–85. He is credited with originating the foot-power drill, spiral springs to hold plates of artificial teeth in position, the use of porcelain in the manufacture of teeth. Two sets which he made for George Washington are still in existence and are remarkable examples of dental skill.

GREENWOOD, MILES (*b. Jersey City, N.J., 1807; d. Cincinnati, O., 1885*), ironmaster. Established Eagle Iron Works at Cincinnati, 1832; was early advocate of a paid steam fire department. The first steam fire-engine in the United States was made in his factory by Shawk and Latta (in use, May 1852).

GREER, DAVID HUMMELL (*b. Wheeling, W. Va., 1844; d. New York, N.Y., 1919*), Episcopal clergyman. Rector at Covington, Ky., and Providence, R.I.; at St. Bartholomew's, New York City, 1888–1903. Consecrated coadjutor-bishop of New York, 1904, he succeeded to the see, 1908. A conservative broad churchman.

GREER, JAMES AUGUSTIN (*b. Cincinnati, O., 1833; d. Washington, D.C., 1904*), naval officer. Graduated U.S. Naval Academy, 1854. After a widely varied career, retired as rear-admiral, 1895.

GREGG, ANDREW (*b. near Carlisle, Pa., 1755; d. Bellefonte, Pa., 1835*), farmer, politician. Congressman, (Democrat) Republican, from Pennsylvania, 1791–1807; U.S. senator, 1807–13. Strong supporter of agrarian interests.

GREGG, DAVID McMURTRIE (*b. Huntingdon, Pa., 1833; d. 1916*), Union soldier. Grandson of Andrew Gregg. Graduated West Point, 1855. Most conspicuous among the exploits which made Gen. U. S. Grant consider him one of the best cavalry generals in the Union Army was his defeat of J. E. B. Stuart's charge against Meade's extreme right at Gettysburg, July 3, 1863.

GREGG, JOHN (*b. Lawrence Co., Ala., 1828; d. near Richmond, Va., 1864*), lawyer, Confederate soldier. Removed to Texas, c. 1852. Commanded Texas brigade, formerly Hood's, in Longstreet's corps, 1864.

GREGG, JOSIAH (*b. Overton Co., Tenn., 1806; d. California, 1850*), Santa Fé trader, author. He made frequent journeys from Independence, Mo., to Santa Fé, 1831–41. A close observer, he kept copious notes of everything that interested him. His book *Commerce of the Prairies* (1844) enjoyed immediate success and is a classic of the frontier. Gregg joined Wool's army at San Antonio, 1846, and saw service in Mexico. In 1849 he made his last trip to Santa Fé, journeying thence to California and the Trinity mines. He died of hunger and exposure after crossing the Coast Range with an exploring party.

GREGG, MAXCY (*b. Columbia, S.C., 1814; d. Fredericksburg, Va., 1862*), lawyer, politician, Confederate brigadier-general. Grandson of Jonathan Maxcy. South Carolina state-rights leader and ardent secessionist.

GREGG, WILLIAM (*b. Monongalia Co., Va., now W. Va., 1800; d. Edgefield District, S.C., 1867*), father of Southern cotton manufacturing. A watchmaker and silversmith, retired from business, he established himself in Charleston, S.C., 1838. With leisure to think, he became convinced that South Carolina and the whole South should abandon devotion to a staple agriculture and develop cotton manufacturing. Industrial communities, as he saw it, would provide new markets for local products and give employment to unpropertied whites who had been rendered superfluous by the slave system. Embodying his ideas in *Essays on Domestic Industry* (1845), he gave them practical effect by founding Graniteville, near Aiken, S.C., 1846. Using native labor and materials, he erected a mill and provided comfortable housing for his work-force, thus creating the first typical Southern cotton-mill village and setting an example followed elsewhere in the South. The enterprise was highly successful, owing mainly to Gregg's insistence on specializing in a small range of product for sale direct from the mill in a national or world market. Highly solicitous for his employees, he was a pioneer in improving the condition of the poor whites.

GREGG, WILLIS RAY (*b. Phoenix, N.Y., 1880; d. Chicago, Ill., 1938*), meteorologist. Graduated Cornell, 1903. In service of U.S. Weather Bureau, 1904–38; specialist in aeronautical meteorology. [*Supp. 2*]

GREGORY, CASPAR RENÉ (*b. Philadelphia, Pa., 1846; d. Neufchatel-sur-Aisne, France, 1917*), New Testament scholar. Graduated University of Pennsylvania, 1864; Princeton Theological Seminary, 1870. Taught at University of Leipzig, 1884–1914; prepared a celebrated edition of the Greek New Testament, *Novum Testamentum Graece* (Leipzig, 1884, 1890, 1894).

GREGORY, CHARLES NOBLE (*b. Unadilla, N.Y., 1851; d. 1932*), lawyer, educator. Brother of Stephen S. Gregory. Admitted to the Wisconsin bar, 1872. Dean of Law, at University of Iowa, 1901–11; at George Washington University, 1911–14. [*Supp. 1*]

GREGORY, DANIEL SEELYE (*b. Carmel, N.Y., 1832; d. 1915*), Presbyterian clergyman, educator, editor. Held many pastorates; president of Lake Forest University, 1878–86; managing editor of *Standard Dictionary of the English Language*, 1889–95.

GREGORY, ELIOT (*b. New York, N.Y., 1854?; d. 1915*), painter, essayist, dilettante.

GREGORY, JOHN MILTON (*b. Sand Lake, N.Y., 1822; d. Washington, D.C., 1898*), Baptist clergyman, educational leader. Graduated Union, 1846. First regent (president) of University of Illinois, 1867–80, he labored enthusiastically to make it a true university, not a vocational school.

GREGORY, SAMUEL (*b. Guilford, Vt., 1813; d. Boston, Mass., 1872*), pioneer in medical education of women. Founded in 1848 and directed the Boston Female Medical School, later merged in Boston University School of Medicine.

GREGORY, STEPHEN STRONG (*b. Unadilla, N.Y., 1849; d. 1920*), Chicago lawyer. Raised in Madison, Wis. Outstanding trial counsel; represented Eugene Debs and American Railway Union in case arising out of Pullman strike. Brother of Charles N. Gregory.

GREGORY, THOMAS WATT (*b. Crawfordsville, Miss., 1861; d. New York, N.Y., 1933*), lawyer. Graduated Law School, University of Texas, 1885. Practiced in Texas. Was prominent in Democratic politics and helped nominate Woodrow Wilson, 1912. As U.S. attorney-general, 1914–19, he ably managed the vastly expanded Department of Justice during World War I. [*Supp. 1*]

GREIST, JOHN MILTON (*b. Crawfordsville, Ind., 1850; d. 1906*), inventor, manufacturer. Devised and made efficient sewing-machine attachments for tucking, ruffling and the like.

GRELLET, STEPHEN (*b. Limoges, France, 1773; d. Burlington, N.J., 1855*), minister of the Society of Friends. Came to America, 1795. Undertook missionary journeys over practically all Europe and the United States.

GRESHAM, WALTER QUINTIN (*b. near Lanesville, Ind., 1832; d. Washington, D.C., 1895*), soldier, jurist, statesman. Union major-general of volunteers in Civil War; won respect and friendship of U.S. Grant, who appointed him district judge for Indiana. Was frequently mentioned as a presidential possibility along with his rival for Indiana Republican leadership, Benjamin Harrison. As postmaster-general under President Arthur, 1883–84, he worked many reforms. Prominent in Republican conventions of 1884 and 1888, he grew outspoken in opposition to his party's tariff policy; he supported the Democrats, 1892. As U.S. secretary of state, 1893–95, he proved strong and independent, but he lacked a far-reaching knowledge of foreign affairs and left no enduring mark on American foreign policy.

GREW, THEOPHILUS (*d. Philadelphia, Pa., 1759*), mathematician, astronomer. First professor of mathematics at the College and Academy of Philadelphia, 1750–59.

GREY, ZANE (*b. Zanesville, O., 1872; d. Altadena, Calif., 1939*), prolific and popular author of Western romances, sport and outdoor adventure stories, and juveniles. Among these are *Riders of the Purple Sage* (1912); *Wanderer of the Wasteland* (1923); *West of the Pecos* (1937). [*Supp. 2*]

GRIDLEY, CHARLES VERNON (*b. Logansport, Ind., 1844; d. Kobe, Japan, 1898*), naval officer. Graduated U.S. Naval Academy, 1863. As captain of U.S.S. *Olympia*, began the battle of Manila Bay, 1898, on receiving Commodore Dewey's command, "You may fire when you are ready, Gridley."

GRIDLEY, JEREMIAH (*b. Boston, Mass., 1701/02; d. Brookline, Mass., 1767*), Massachusetts lawyer. His most famous case was the action over the legality of the Writs of Assistance in 1761; as government counsel, he was opposed by James Otis.

GRIDLEY, RICHARD (*b. Boston, Mass., 1710/11; d. Stoughton, now Canton, Mass., 1796*), military engineer, iron smelter. Headed artillery at siege of Louisburg, 1745; commanded provincial artillery, on Crown Point expedition, 1755; also built Lake George fortifications. Commanded provincial artillery at Quebec, 1759. Chief engineer, Massachusetts forces, and chief of artillery, 1775; chief engineer, Continental Army, 1775–76, and of the eastern department, 1777–80.

GRIER, ROBERT COOPER (*b. Cumberland Co., Pa., 1794; d. Philadelphia, Pa., 1870*), jurist. Graduated Dickinson College, 1812. As associate justice of the U.S. Supreme Court, 1846–70, his opinions were characterized by concision, clarity, freedom from bias, and citation of few but carefully chosen authorities. He made no concessions to popularity.

GRIERSON, BENJAMIN HENRY (*b. Pittsburgh, Pa., 1826; d. Omena, Mich., 1911*), Union soldier. Enlisting as a private, 1861, he became colonel, 6th Illinois Cavalry, and in 1863 commander of a cavalry brigade. In April and May 1863, he executed his famous raid from La Grange, Tenn., to Baton Rouge, La., piercing the heart of the Confederacy and destroying railroads and stores. "Grierson's Raid" was of great service to Grant in the reduction of Vicksburg. Retired as regular brigadier-general, 1890.

GRIERSON, FRANCIS (*b. Birkenhead, England, 1848; d. Los Angeles, Calif., 1927*), musician, author. Came to America as infant; was raised in Illinois and St. Louis, Mo. As Jesse Shepard, had unique musical success in Europe, 1869–80. Changing his name, he embarked on a literary career and produced a series of extraordinary books of which the most notable is

The Valley of Shadows (1909). He has been described as "a philosophical mystic."

GRIEVE, MILLER (*b. Edinburgh, Scotland, 1801, d. Milledgeville, Ga., c. 1878*), journalist, diplomat. Came to America, 1817. Edited the Milledgeville *Southern Recorder*, 1833–53, unofficial but influential Whig organ.

GRIFFES, CHARLES TOMLINSON (*b. Elmira, N.Y., 1884; d. 1920*), composer, pianist, teacher. Studied in Berlin; was influenced in study of composition by Humperdinck. On his return to America, 1908, he was piano teacher, organist, choirmaster at Hackley School, Tarrytown, N.Y., where he remained until his untimely death. His first works were songs in German romantic style. Gradually developing his own style, influenced at times by Oriental idioms, he attained wide recognition by the Boston Symphony's 1919 performance of "The Pleasure-Dome of Kubla Khan," a symphonic poem. His other large works include "Poem" for flute and orchestra, two sketches on Indian themes for string quartet, and a piano sonata.

GRIFFIN, APPLETON PRENTISS CLARK (*b. Wilton, N.H., 1852; d. 1926*), librarian, bibliographer. Advancing from "runner" to librarian in the Boston Public Library, he joined the staff of the Library of Congress, 1897, became chief bibliographer, 1900, and served as chief assistant librarian, 1908–26.

GRIFFIN, CHARLES (*b. Granville, O., 1825; d. Galveston, Texas, 1867*), Union soldier. Graduated West Point, 1847. A vigorous, bellicose, indiscreet artilleryman, Griffin rose to corps command on sheer merit and *post* 1866 to command of the military district of Texas.

GRIFFIN, CYRUS (*b. Richmond Co., Va., 1748; d. Yorktown, Va., 1810*), jurist, legislator. Last president of Continental Congress, *post* January 1788. As federal judge for the district of Virginia, 1789–1810, he presided over Aaron Burr's trial for treason.

GRIFFIN, EDWARD DORR (*b. East Haddam, Conn., 1770; d. Newark, N.J., 1837*), Congregational clergyman. Graduated Yale, 1790. As president of Williams College, 1821–36, he revitalized the institution in every way.

GRIFFIN, EUGENE (*b. Ellsworth, Maine, 1855; d. Schenectady, N.Y., 1907*), electrical engineer, soldier, manufacturer. Graduated West Point, 1875. Author of a government report (1888) which hastened use of electricity in street-cars and for railways. Officer in General Electric and Thomson-Houston companies.

GRIFFIN, MARTIN IGNATIUS JOSEPH (*b. Philadelphia, Pa., 1842; d. 1911*), journalist, historian. A meticulous gatherer of facts about Catholic elements in U.S. history. [*Supp. 1*]

GRIFFIN, ROBERT STANISLAUS (*b. Fredericksburg, Va., 1857; d. Washington, D.C., 1933*), naval officer. Graduated Annapolis, 1878. Chief, Bureau of Steam Engineering, U.S. Navy, 1913–21; responsible for the construction, repair and outfitting of the enormously expanded World War I Navy. [*Supp. 1*]

GRIFFIN, SIMON GOODELL (*b. Nelson, N.H., 1824; d. Keene, N.H., 1902*), Union brigadier-general, New Hampshire legislator.

GRIFFIN, SOLOMON BULKLEY (*b. Williamstown, Mass., 1852; d. 1925*), journalist. Managing editor, *Springfield* (Mass.) *Daily Republican*, 1878–1919.

GRIFFING, JOSEPHINE SOPHIE WHITE (*b. Hebron, Conn., 1814; d. 1872*), reformer. Ardent, practical worker for Abolition and woman's suffrage; active in formation of the Freedman's Bureau.

GRIFFIS, WILLIAM ELLIOT (*b. Philadelphia, Pa., 1843; d. 1928*), Congregational clergyman, educator. Graduated Rutgers, 1869; Union Theological Seminary, 1877. Interpreter of Japan to America. Author of more than fifty books of which *The Mikado's Empire* (1876) and *Corea: The Hermit Nation* (1882) are outstanding.

GRIFFITH, BENJAMIN (*b. Cardigan, Wales, 1688; d. 1768*), Baptist clergyman. Came to America, 1710; pastor in Montgomery Co., Pa., 1722–68. His manuscript record of the several churches comprised in the Philadelphia Association is one of the most important sources for early American Baptist history.

GRIFFITH, GOLDSBOROUGH SAPPINGTON (*b. Harford Co., Md., 1814; d. Baltimore, Md., 1904*), merchant, prison reformer, philanthropist.

GRIFFITH, WILLIAM (*b. Boundbrook, N.J., 1766; d. Burlington, N.J., 1826*), lawyer, legal writer. Expert on New Jersey land titles.

GRIFFITHS, JOHN WILLIS (*b. New York, N.Y., 1809?; d. Brooklyn, N.Y., 1882*), naval architect. Established American shipbuilding on a scientific basis through his writings: *A Treatise on Marine and Naval Architecture* (1849); *The Ship-builder's Manual* (1853); *The Progressive Shipbuilder* (1874–75). Content to let others build, he specialized in design, showing amazing versatility. The first "extreme clipper ship" *Rainbow* (launched 1845) and the famous *Sea Witch* (1846) were his work. They proved the fastest ships afloat and strongly affected the subsequent development of the American clipper. Griffiths's influence on steamship design was also important. He incorporated new features, including a straight bow, in the *Arctic, Baltic* and *Pacific,* the fastest, finest steamships of the early 1850's.

GRIGGS, EVERETT GALLUP (*b. Chaska, Minn., 1868; d. Tacoma, Wash., 1938*), lumberman. Proponent of industrial cooperation, reforestation and other advanced policies. [*Supp. 2*]

GRIGGS, JOHN WILLIAM (*b. near Newton, N.J., 1849; d. 1927*), lawyer, statesman. Graduated Lafayette, 1868. After able service in the New Jersey legislature, he was Republican governor of that state, 1896–98; U.S. attorney-general, 1898–1901; member of the Permanent Court at the Hague, 1901–12.

GRIGSBY, HUGH BLAIR (*b. Norfolk, Va., 1806; d. probably "Edgehill," Charlotte Co., Va., 1881*), newspaper editor, Virginia historian.

GRIM, DAVID (*b. Zweibrücken, Bavaria, 1737; d. New York, N.Y., 1826*), tavern-keeper, merchant, antiquarian. Came to New York as a child. Noted for pen-and-ink sketches with descriptive notes of early New York City landmarks.

GRIMES, ABSALOM CARLISLE (*b. Jefferson Co., Ky., 1834; d. St. Louis, Mo., 1911*), Mississippi River pilot, Confederate mail-runner. Partner in Mark Twain's brief service with the Confederate armed forces, 1861. Author of a volume of reminiscences (published 1926).

GRIMES, JAMES STANLEY (*b. Boston, Mass., 1807; d. Evanston, Ill., 1903*), erratic philosopher, lecturer. An early evolutionist, opposed to spiritualism, but an ardent student of phrenology and mesmerism.

GRIMES, JAMES WILSON (*b. Deering, N.H., 1816; d. Burlington, Iowa, 1872*), lawyer, legislator. Removed to Iowa, 1836. As Whig governor of Iowa, 1854–58, he established many state institutions, including free schools, and virtually remade the state; he also made it staunchly Republican. U.S. senator, 1859–69, his refusal to vote for President Johnson's impeachment (1868) was crucial in the outcome of the trial and cost Grimes his political popularity.

GRIMKÉ, ANGELINA EMILY (1805–1879.) [See Grimké, Sarah Moore, 1792–1873.]

GRIMKÉ, ARCHIBALD HENRY (*b. near Charleston, S.C., 1849; d. Washington, D.C., 1930*), lawyer, author, publicist. Nephew of Sarah M. Grimké. Graduated Lincoln University, 1870; Harvard Law School, 1874. A Negro, Grimké was a lifelong crusader against race discrimination; he was president of the American Negro Academy, 1903–16, and was author of numerous pamphlets and books, including biographies of William Lloyd Garrison and Charles Sumner.

GRIMKÉ, JOHN FAUCHERAUD (*b. Charleston, S.C., 1752; d. Long Branch, N.J., 1819*), Revolutionary soldier, South Carolina jurist and legislator. A stern, unpopular judge, he did his best work as a legal compiler in the period of legal reform following the Revolution. He was author, among other books, of *Public Laws of . . . South Carolina* (1790).

GRIMKÉ, SARAH MOORE (*b. Charleston, S.C., 1792; d. Hyde Park, Mass., 1873*) and her sister, **ANGELINA EMILY** (*b. Charleston, S.C., 1805; d. Hyde Park, Mass., 1879*), Abolitionists, advocates of woman's rights. Daughters of John F. Grimké; sisters of Thomas S. Grimké. Dissatisfied with slavery, they left their home in Charleston for Philadelphia, turned Quakers, found themselves increasingly in sympathy with Abolition. Angelina's forceful *Appeal to the Christian Women of the South* (1836) was publicly burned in South Carolina. She began to address small groups of women and was joined by Sarah. Their subsequent appearances on the lecture platform aroused great enthusiasm, especially in New England. Opposition to women speaking in public led them to defend woman's rights as well as Abolition, and they effectively championed both causes. Angelina married Theodore Dwight Weld, 1838.

GRIMKÉ, THOMAS SMITH (*b. Charleston, S.C., 1786; d. 1834*), lawyer, legislator, educator, reformer. Brother of Sarah M. and Angelina E. Grimké; son of John F. Grimké. Graduated Yale, 1807. An ardent pacifist, he also conceived a radical plan of education which was grounded in religion and utilitarianism. As early as 1832, he advocated manual training in the schools and an extended treatment of science, modern history and modern literature.

GRINNELL, FREDERICK (*b. New Bedford, Mass., 1836; d. New Bedford, 1905*), industrialist, engineer. Patented (1881) the automatic fire-extinguisher sprinkler which bears his name; invented also an automatic fire-alarm system.

GRINNELL, GEORGE BIRD (*b. Brooklyn, N.Y., 1849; d. New York, N.Y., 1938*), naturalist, conservationist. Graduated Yale, 1870; Ph.D., 1880. Editor, *Forest and Stream*, 1876–1911; author, among others, of *The Cheyenne Indians* (1923), *Blackfoot Lodge Tales* (1892); founder, Audubon Society, 1886.

[*Supp. 2*]

GRINNELL, HENRY (*b. New Bedford, Mass., 1799; d. 1874*), New York merchant, philanthropist. Brother of Joseph and Moses H. Grinnell. Financed Arctic expeditions, one of which discovered Grinnell Land; a founder of American Geographical and Statistical Society.

GRINNELL, HENRY WALTON (*b. New York, N.Y., 1843; d. St. Augustine, Fla., 1920*), naval officer. Son of Henry Grinnell. Served in Civil and Spanish-American wars; served in and helped develop Japanese Navy, 1868–98.

GRINNELL, JOSEPH (*b. New Bedford, Mass., 1788; d. New Bedford, 1885*), merchant, financier. Brother of Henry and Moses H. Grinnell. Established textile industry in New Bedford. Congressman, Whig, from Massachusetts, 1843–51.

GRINNELL, JOSIAH BUSHNELL (*b. New Haven, Vt., 1821; d. 1891*), Congregational clergyman, Abolitionist, railroad promoter. Settled in Iowa, 1854; founded town of Grinnell, Iowa, and Grinnell College.

Friend of Lincoln and Horace Greeley, who addressed the historic "Go West, young man" advice to him.

GRINNELL, MOSES HICKS (*b. New Bedford, Mass., 1803; d. 1877*), New York merchant, shipowner, philanthropist, public official. Brother of Henry and Joseph Grinnell.

GRISCOM, CLEMENT ACTON (*b. Philadelphia, Pa., 1841; d. near Philadelphia, 1912*), financier, shipowner. Organized International Mercantile Marine Co.; earlier developed such revolutionary steps in shipbuilding as twin screws, transverse bulkheads, watertight compartments.

GRISCOM, JOHN (*b. Hancock's Bridge, N.J., 1774; d. 1852*), teacher, chemist, philanthropist. Publicized value of iodine in goiter treatment and other chemical discoveries. Helped establish House of Refuge, New York, first U.S. reformatory.

GRISWOLD, ALEXANDER VIETS (*b. Simsbury, Conn., 1766; d. Boston, Mass., 1843*), Episcopal clergyman. Consecrated first and only bishop of Eastern Diocese, 1811; extended his church's influence through all New England.

GRISWOLD, JOHN AUGUSTUS (*b. Nassau, N.Y., 1818; d. Troy, N.Y., 1872*), iron manufacturer, congressman. Made plates and machinery for the *Monitor* and other ships of her class; controlled use of Bessemer patents in America, *post* 1864, in association with John F. Winslow and others.

GRISWOLD, MATTHEW (*b. Lyme, Conn., 1714; d. Lyme, 1799*), jurist, Revolutionary patriot. Deputy governor and chief justice of Connecticut, 1769–84; governor, 1784–86.

GRISWOLD, ROGER (*b. Lyme, Conn., 1762; d. 1812*), lawyer, politician. Son of Matthew Griswold. Congressman, Federalist, from Connecticut, 1795–1805; as governor of Connecticut, 1811–12, denied command of state militia to federal officers.

GRISWOLD, RUFUS WILMOT (*b. Benson, Vt., 1815; d. New York, N.Y., 1857*), journalist, anthologist. Associated with many newspapers and periodicals; compiled, edited, or wrote upwards of forty volumes. His most substantial original work was *The Republican Court* (1855); he grew conspicuous and influential as editor of *The Poets and Poetry of America* (1842) and other popular anthologies. He is best remembered as literary executor and editor of Edgar Allan Poe, in which capacity he incorporated all the current scandal about Poe together with many errors into an inexcusable memoir (1850). Griswold's last years were made miserable by disease, scandal and domestic trouble.

GRISWOLD, STANLEY (*b. Torrington, Conn., 1763; d. Shawneetown, Illinois Territory, 1815*), Congregational clergyman, editor, politician. Partisan of Jefferson. Secretary of Michigan Territory, 1805–08; U.S. senator from Ohio, 1809–10; U.S. circuit judge, Illinois Territory, 1810–15.

GRISWOLD, WILLIAM McCRILLIS (*b. Bangor, Maine, 1853; d. Seal Harbor, Maine, 1899*), bibliographer. Son of Rufus W. Griswold, whose valuable correspondence he edited, 1898.

GROESBECK, WILLIAM SLOCUM (*b. near Schenectady, N.Y., 1815; d. Cincinnati, O., 1897*), Ohio lawyer, congressman. Outstanding among defense counsel for Pres. Andrew Johnson in impeachment trial, 1868.

GRONLUND, LAURENCE (*b. Denmark, 1846; d. New York, N.Y., 1899*), lawyer, Socialist writer and lecturer. Came to America, 1867. Author, among other works, of *The Cooperative Commonwealth* (1884), first comprehensive work in English on Socialism.

GROS, JOHN DANIEL (*b. Webenheim, Bavaria, 1738; d. Canajoharie, N.Y., 1812*), German Reformed clergyman, philosopher. Came to America, 1764; held numerous pastorates and served as New York militia chaplain in Revolution. Professor of German, geography, and moral philosophy, Columbia College, *post* 1784; served also as a trustee, 1787–92.

GROSE, WILLIAM (*b near Dayton, Ohio, 1812; d. Newcastle, Ind., 1900*), lawyer, Indiana legislator. Conspicuous among Indiana's Civil War leaders; had excellent combat record as regimental and brigade commander.

GROSEILLIERS, MEDART CHOUART, Sieur de (*fl. 1625–1684*), explorer. Born at Charly-Saint-Cyr, France, he came to Canada in 1637 or 1641 as assistant in Jesuit mission to Hurons. Formed a fur-trading partnership, 1654, with brother-in-law, Pierre Radisson. Heavily fined and their furs confiscated after an unlicensed journey to the Far West, 1658–60, they entered the service of England. Their joint expedition of 1668, in which Groseilliers alone reached Hudson Bay and secured a cargo of furs, resulted in the organization of the Hudson's Bay Co., 1670. Groseilliers eventually returned to French allegiance and settled down in Canada where, prior to 1698, it is thought, he died.

GROSS, CHARLES (*b. Troy, N.Y., 1857; d. 1909*), educator, historian. Graduated Williams, 1878; Ph.D., Göttingen, 1883. Taught history at Harvard. Author of *The Gild Merchant* (1890) and the monumental *Sources and Literature of English History from the Earliest Times to about 1485* (1900).

GROSS, SAMUEL DAVID (*b. near Easton, Pa., 1805; d. Philadelphia, Pa., 1884*), surgeon, teacher, author. Graduated Jefferson Medical College, 1828; began practice in Philadelphia. Was author of several translations from French and German, including Tavernier's *Elements of Operative Surgery* (1829), first treatise on operative surgery published in America, and an original work, *Treatise on the Anatomy, Physiology, and Diseases and Injuries of the Bones and Joints* (1830). Became professor of pathological anatomy at Cincinnati Medical College, 1835. Gross's *Elements of Pathological Anatomy* (1839) was the first effort in English to present the subject systematically, and long the chief authority on it. Elected professor of surgery, University of Louisville, 1840, he became the most celebrated surgeon of the South. In 1856 he was appointed professor of surgery at Jefferson Medical College. His contributions to medical literature were numerous and important. *A Practical Treatise on the Diseases and Injuries of the Urinary Bladder, the Prostate Gland, and the Urethra* (1851) became the accepted authority and a standard textbook. His third pioneer work, *A Practical Treatise on Foreign Bodies in Air Passages* (1854), was the first attempt to systematize knowledge on that subject. His *System of Surgery, Pathological, Diagnostic, Therapeutic and Operative* (1859) is one of the greatest surgical treatises ever written. Translated into several languages, it had enormous influence on surgical thought.

Outstanding in practice as in precept, particularly noted for operating for bladder stone, he was one of the first to insist on the proper plan of suturing intestinal wounds and restoring damaged intestines by resection, and of suturing tendons and nerves. He invented a number of instruments and was a founder of numerous medical societies, including the American Medical Association and the American Surgical Society.

GROSS, SAMUEL WEISSELL (*b. Cincinnati, O., 1837; d. Philadelphia, Pa., 1889*), surgeon, author, teacher. Son of Samuel D. Gross. Graduated Jefferson Medical College, 1857, where he succeeded father as professor of surgery, 1882. With W. S. Halsted and others, developed present-day radical operation for cancer.

GROSSCUP, PETER STENGER (*b. Ashland, O., 1852; d. at sea, 1921*), jurist. Prominent Chicago lawyer; federal district judge, 1892–98; judge, circuit court of appeals, 1899–1911. Issued injunction in Chicago railway strike, 1894; was friendly to trusts.

GROSSET, ALEXANDER (*b. Windsor Mills, Canada, 1870; d, Riverside, Conn., 1934*), publisher. Founder of Grosset and Dunlap, reprint publishers; president of the firm, 1900–34. [*Supp.* 1]

GROSSMANN, GEORG MARTIN (*b. Grossbieberau, Germany, 1823; d. Waverly, Iowa, 1897*), Lutheran clergyman. Came to America, 1852. Helped organize German Lutheran Synod of Iowa, 1854, and served as its president until 1893.

GROSSMANN, LOUIS (*b. Vienna, Austria, 1863; d. Detroit, Mich., 1926*), rabbi. Came to America as a child. Graduated University of Cincinnati, 1884, and Hebrew Union College, 1884, where he served as

professor, 1898–1921. Pioneer in modernizing Jewish religious education.

GROSVENOR, CHARLES HENRY (*b. Pomfret, Conn., 1833; d. 1917*), lawyer, Union soldier. Raised in Athens Co., O. As congressman, Republican, from Ohio, 1885–1907, he was renowned as a bitter partisan debater.

GROSVENOR, EDWIN PRESCOTT (*b. Constantinople, Turkey, 1875; d. New York, N.Y., 1930*), lawyer. Graduated Amherst, 1897; Columbia Law School, 1904. Prosecutor of anti-trust violations as assistant U.S. attorney-general, 1908–13, his principal achievements were in proceedings against the Kentucky night-riders and against the "bathtub trust." In *U.S. vs. Standard Sanitary Manufacturing Co.*, he won from the Supreme Court a decision which prevents extension of a patent monopoly beyond the invention or process described in the patent, a landmark in the development of anti-trust law. A member of the firm of Cadwalader, Wickersham and Taft, *post* 1914, he successfully defended the Fur Dealers Association against the government, and thereby clarified the law affecting trade associations.

GROSVENOR, JOHN. [See ALTHAM, JOHN, 1589–1640.]

GROSVENOR, WILLIAM MASON (*b. Ashfield, Mass., 1835; d. 1900*), journalist, publicist. Editor, *St. Louis Democrat;* associate of Joseph Pulitzer and Carl Schurz in Liberal Republican movement. Economics editor, *New York Tribune*, 1875–1900; editor of *Dun's Review post* 1893. His strictly impartial advice on tariff acts and financial policy was sought frequently by federal officials.

GROTE, AUGUSTUS RADCLIFFE (*b. Liverpool, England, 1841; d. Hildesheim, Germany, 1903*), entomologist. Came to America as a child. A born naturalist, he described over 2000 new species of American *Lepidoptera;* his published entomological bibliography includes 201 titles.

GROUARD, FRANK (*b. Paumotu Islands, South Pacific, 1850; d. St. Joseph, Mo., 1905*), army scout. Son of a missionary and a native mother; raised in California. Prisoner of the Sioux, 1869–75; scouted in Wyoming, Montana and the Dakotas, 1876–95.

GROVER, CUVIER (*b. Bethel, Maine, 1828; d. Atlantic City, N.J., 1885*), Union soldier. Brother of La Fayette Grover. Graduated West Point, 1850. Lifelong army career included exploration in Far West, divisional command in Civil War, and frontier duty.

GROVER, LA FAYETTE (*b. Bethel, Maine, 1823; d. Portland, Oreg., 1911*), lawyer, politician, manufacturer. Brother of Cuvier Grover. Removed to Oregon, 1851; was active in territorial politics. As partisan Democratic governor of Oregon, 1871–77, was a key figure in disputed presidential election of 1876. Represented his state in U.S. House and was U.S. senator, 1877–83.

GROW, GALUSHA AARON (*b. Ashford, Conn., 1822; d. 1907*), lawyer, politician. Raised in western Pennsylvania. Graduated Amherst, 1844; became law partner of David Wilmot. Congressman, Democrat, from Pennsylvania, 1851–55; Independent and Republican, 1855–63; Republican, 1893–1901. A frontiersman, his immediate and continuing interest was in public lands. He became one of the most outspoken of the new Republicans in the turbulent sessions preceding the Civil War. During his term as speaker of the House of Representatives (1861–63), he saw the homestead measure, for which he had so long labored, enacted into law. Out of office thirty years, he returned to Congress a picturesque veteran still interested in extending homestead legislation and acquiring new territory.

GRUBE, BERNHARD ADAM (*b. near Erfurt, Germany, 1715; d. Bethlehem, Pa., 1808*), Moravian missionary. Came to America, 1748. Worked among Delaware Indians of Pennsylvania; minister at Gnadenhütten and Head's Creek; later pastor at Lititz, and elsewhere in Pennsylvania.

GRUENING, EMIL (*b. Hohensalza, E. Prussia, 1842; d. New York, N.Y., 1914*), pioneer ophthalmologist and otologist, teacher. Came to America, 1862. Graduated N.Y. College of Physicians and Surgeons, 1867; postgraduate student, London, Paris and Berlin. Made pioneer contributions in surgery of the eye, brain abcess, mastoid; practiced and taught in New York City.

GRUND, FRANCIS JOSEPH (*b. Klosterneuburg, Austria, 1798; d. Philadelphia, Pa., 1863*), author, journalist, politician. [*Supp. 1*]

GRUNDY, FELIX (*b. Virginia, 1777; d. 1840*), lawyer, jurist. Raised in Kentucky, where he served as legislator and appeals judge. Removed to Tennessee, 1807, and was Democratic congressman, 1811–15; U.S. senator, 1829–38, 1839–40; U.S. attorney-general, 1838–39.

GUE, BENJAMIN F. (*b. Greene Co., N.Y., 1828; d. Des Moines, Iowa, 1904*), Iowa legislator and lieutenant-governor, journalist. Removed to Iowa, 1852. Author of *History of Iowa* (1903).

GUÉRIN, ANNE-THÉRÈSE (*b. Étables, France, 1798; d. 1856*). In religion, Mother Theodore, educator. Foundress of Sisters of Providence of Saint Mary-of-the-Woods, Ind., 1840; established first women's academy in the state.

GUERNSEY, EGBERT (*b. Litchfield, Conn., 1823; d. 1903*), physician, medical journalist. M.D., University of the City of New York, 1846. Attempted to bring homeopathy into harmony with the old school of medicine.

GUESS, GEORGE. [See Sequoyah, 1770–1843.]

GUFFEY, JAMES McCLURG (*b. Sewickley Township, Pa., 1839; d. 1930*), oil producer. One of largest landowners, producers and operators in U.S., individually and in partnership with John H. Galey, 1880–1905.

GUGGENHEIM, DANIEL (*b. Philadelphia, Pa., 1856; d. near Port Washington, N.Y., 1930*), capitalist, philanthropist. Son of Meyer Guggenheim. Headed American Smelting and Refining Co., also the miscellaneous corporations which in the Guggenheim plan of operation clustered about the central enterprise. One of the foremost representatives of American industrial imperialism, he developed Bolivian tin mines, Yukon gold mines, Belgian Congo diamond fields and rubber plantations, copper mines in Alaska, Utah, Chile, also Chilean nitrate fields. He helped plan the "Guggenheim strategy," *viz.* integration of smelting and refining with exploration for and control of sources of supply. Among his notable philanthropies, in the tradition of his father, were the Daniel and Florence Guggenheim Foundation and the Daniel Guggenheim Fund for the Promotion of Aeronautics.

GUGGENHEIM, MEYER (*b. Langnau, Switzerland, 1828; d. Palm Beach, Fla., 1905*), financier. Came to America, *c.* 1847. Built up import firm of M. Guggenheim's Sons, specializing in Swiss embroideries; became interested in mining and smelting, 1887, and by 1891 had thrown his entire fortune into the new venture. Besides his own abilities, his chief resources were seven sons whom he had trained in business tactics, thus enabling him to maintain personal control of large-scale enterprises. His great success came in 1901; after a severe struggle he gained control of the American Smelting and Refining Co., a trust composed of the country's largest metal-processing plants. His policies were carried on by his sons, among them Daniel Guggenheim who vastly extended the firm's activities.

GUIGNAS, MICHEL (*b. Condom, France, 1681; d. Quebec, Canada, 1752*), Jesuit priest. Came to Canada, 1716. Missionary to the Sioux in Minnesota and Wisconsin, 1727–28, 1731–37.

GUILD, CURTIS (*b. Boston, Mass., 1827; d. 1911*), journalist, author. Editor-manager of Boston *Commercial Bulletin*, 1859–98; financial authority, antiquarian; founded Bostonian Society.

GUILD, CURTIS (*b. Boston, Mass., 1860; d. 1915*), son of Curtis Guild (1827–1911) and associated with him on *Commercial Bulletin*. Republican governor of Massachusetts, 1905–07; ambassador to Russia, 1911–13. As governor, initiated labor and other reforms; enjoyed great respect and popularity.

GUILD, LA FAYETTE (*b. Tuscaloosa, Ala., 1825; d. Marysville, Calif., 1870*), army medical officer.

Graduated University of Alabama, 1845; M.D., Jefferson Medical College, 1848. Joined the army medical service, 1849. Confederate surgeon and inspector of hospitals, 1861; medical director of Lee's Army of Northern Virginia, 1862–65. His service was marked by intelligence, industry and initiative of a high order. Following the war he went to Mobile, Ala., broken in health, thence to San Francisco, 1869, in hopes of improvement. [*Supp.* 1]

GUILD, REUBEN ALDRIDGE (*b. West Dedham, Mass., 1822; d. Providence, R.I., 1899*), librarian of Brown University, 1847–93. A founder of American Library Association.

GUILFORD, NATHAN (*b. Spencer, Mass., 1786; d. Cincinnati, O., 1854*), lawyer. Graduated Yale, 1812. Settled in Cincinnati, O., 1816. Devoted life to fight for free schools in Ohio; published school textbooks. Public school superintendent, Cincinnati, 1850–52.

GUINEY, LOUISE IMOGEN (*b. Boston, Mass., 1861; d. Chipping Campden, England, 1920*), essayist, poet. Author, among other books, of *Songs at the Start* (1884) and *Happy Ending* (her selected poems, 1909, 1927); her sympathetic critical sense and exquisite prose style are best displayed in *A Little English Gallery* (1894) and *Patrins* (1897). Cavalier England was her country of the mind.

GUITERAS, JUAN (*b. Matanzas, Cuba, 1852; d. Matanzas, 1925*), physician, medical teacher. Made valuable contributions to knowledge of tropical medicine; associate of W. C. Gorgas, C. J. Finlay and Walter Reed in yellow fever study.

GULICK, JOHN THOMAS (*b. Waimea, Hawaii, 1832; d. Honolulu, 1923*), Congregational missionary to Japan and China, naturalist. Graduated Williams, 1859. Brother of Luther H. Gulick (1828–1891). Formulated hypothesis that evolution is divergent through influence of segregation.

GULICK, LUTHER HALSEY (*b. Honolulu, Hawaii, 1828; d. Springfield, Mass., 1891*), Congregational clergyman. Brother of John T. Gulick. Medical missionary in Caroline Islands, China, Japan, Spain, Italy, Turkey, Bohemia.

GULICK, LUTHER HALSEY (*b. Honolulu, Hawaii, 1865; d. Maine, 1918*), specialist in physical education; author. Son of Luther H. Gulick (1828–1891). Graduated M.D., University of the City of New York, 1889. Active in Y.M.C.A. work; helped devise game of basketball; founded Camp Fire Girls; promoted school hygiene and physical education.

GUMMERE, FRANCIS BARTON (*b. Burlington, N.J., 1855; d. 1919*), philologist. Son of Samuel J. Gummere. Graduated Haverford, 1872; Ph.D., Freiburg, 1881. Taught at Haverford, 1887–1919; distinguished prosodist. Best known for theory of communal origin of English and Scottish ballads.

GUMMERE, JOHN (*b. near Willow Grove, Pa., 1784; d. 1845*), mathematician. Author of *Treatise on Surveying* (1814); headed a successful school at Burlington, N.J., 1814–33 and *post* 1843.

GUMMERE, SAMUEL JAMES (*b. Rancocas, N.J., 1811; d. 1874*), educator. Son of John Gummere. President, Haverford College, 1862–74; nationally known as mathematician and astronomer.

GUMMERE, SAMUEL RENÉ (*b. Trenton, N.J., 1849; d. Wimbledon, England, 1920*), lawyer, diplomat. Played important role in "Perdicaris incident," Morocco, 1904. First U.S. minister to Morocco, 1905–09. Brother of William S. Gummere.

GUMMERE, WILLIAM STRYKER (*b. Trenton, N.J., 1850; d. Newark, N.J., 1933*), lawyer, jurist. Brother of Samuel R. Gummere. Judge, New Jersey supreme court, 1895–1933; chief justice, *post* 1901. [*Supp.* 1]

GUNN, FREDERICK WILLIAM (*b. Washington, Conn., 1816; d. Washington, Conn., 1881*), schoolmaster. Graduated Yale, 1837. Unconventional, strongly individualistic founder of "The Gunnery" school (1850).

GUNN, JAMES NEWTON (*b. Springfield, O., 1867; d. 1927*), pioneer industrial and production engineer. Perfected tab type index card and vertical file; assisted in organization of Harvard Business School.

GUNNISON, JOHN WILLIAMS (*b. Goshen, N.H., 1812; d. near Sevier Lake, Utah, 1853*), army engineer. Graduated West Point, 1837. Engaged in surveys in Georgia and in lake region of Northwest; in 1849 was topographical engineer with Stansbury survey exploring a central route to the Pacific. Author of *The Mormons, or Latter-Day Saints, in the Valley of the Great Salt Lake* (1852). Assigned in 1853 to explore a westward route by way of the Grand and Green River valley to the Santa Clara, he and six of his party were killed by Pahvant Indians who raided their camp.

GUNSAULUS, FRANK WAKELEY (*b. Chesterville, O., 1856; d. Chicago, Ill., 1921*), Congregational clergyman, author. Pastor in Chicago *post* 1887; notable preacher; collector of books and art. A founder and president of Armour Institute of Technology.

GUNTER, ARCHIBALD CLAVERING (*b. Liverpool, England, 1847; d. New York, N.Y., 1907*), playwright, novelist, publisher. Came to America as a child; raised in San Francisco, Calif. His novels had a great contemporary popularity, 1887–94. *Mr. Barnes of New York* (1887) sold more than a million copies.

GUNTHER, CHARLES FREDERICK (*b. Wildberg, Germany, 1837; d. 1920*), candy manufacturer, rarebook collector, Chicago civic and political leader. Came to America as a child. Made numerous popular confectionery inventions, including the caramel.

GUNTON, GEORGE (*b. Chatteris, England, 1845; d. New York, N.Y., 1919*), editor, economist. Emigrated to Fall River, Mass., 1874; edited *Labor Standard*. Author of *Wealth and Progress* (1887); editor, *Social Economist* (later *Gunton's Magazine*), 1891–1904. His views on wages and hours of labor influenced direction of economic thought in America.

GURLEY, RALPH RANDOLPH (*b. Lebanon, Conn., 1797; d. Washington, D.C., 1872*), philanthropist. Devoted life to American Colonization Society; was expert on Liberia and African colonization.

GURNEY, EPHRAIM WHITMAN (*b. Boston, Mass., 1829; d. 1886*), educator. Graduated Harvard, 1852; taught there *post* 1857, and was first dean of faculty, 1870–86. Aided Charles W. Eliot in his transformation of Harvard into a great university.

GUROWSKI, ADAM (*b. Kalisz, Poland, 1805; d. Washington, D.C., 1866*), author, agitator. Exiled from Poland, he was influenced in Paris by Fourier and the St. Simon group; later he was a propagandist for Panslavism. Came to America, 1849; worked for the New York *Tribune*. Served as adviser to W. H. Seward, 1861; was author of a *Diary* (1862) which criticized Lincoln and Seward, and praised Stanton. [*Supp. 1*]

GUTHE, KARL EUGEN (*b. Hanover, Germany, 1866; d. Ashland, Oreg., 1915*), physicist. Graduated University of Marburg, Ph.D., 1892, the year he came to America. Taught at universities of Iowa and Michigan; dean of Graduate School, Michigan.

GUTHERZ, CARL (*b. Schöftland, Switzerland, 1844; d. Washington, D.C., 1907*), artist. Came to America as a child; raised in Cincinnati, O., and Memphis, Tenn. Muralist, influenced by Puvis de Chavannes; executed ceiling of House Reading Room, Library of Congress.

GUTHRIE, ALFRED (*b. Sherburne, N.Y., 1805; d. Chicago, Ill., 1882*), engineer. Son of Samuel Guthrie. Instituted (1852) a federal system of steamboat inspection; served as first head of enforcement bureau.

GUTHRIE, GEORGE WILKINS (*b. Pittsburgh, Pa., 1848; d. Tokyo, Japan, 1917*), lawyer, diplomat. Reform mayor of Pittsburgh, 1906–09. As ambassador to Japan, 1913–17, he calmed intense anti-American feeling provoked by California Alien Land Bill.

GUTHRIE, JAMES (*b. Bardstown, Ky., 1792; d. Louisville, Ky., 1869*), lawyer, railroad promoter. Served in Kentucky legislature, 1827–41; strong advocate of state internal improvements. Grew rich through real estate investment and promotion of macadam roads and railways; founded University of Louisville. As U.S. secretary of treasury, 1853–57, he was a ruthless reformer and highly effective. A Unionist, he put his Louisville and Nashville Railroad at the disposal of federal troops, 1861–65, a decisive factor in the conquest of the Southwest. Served as U.S. senator, Democrat, from Kentucky, 1865–68.

GUTHRIE, SAMUEL (*b. Brimfield, Mass., 1782; d. Sacketts Harbor, N.Y., 1848*), chemist, physician. Invented "percussion pill" and lock to explode it, replacing flint-lock musket. Discovered chloroform, 1831, antedating independent discoveries by Soubeiran and Liebig.

GUTHRIE, WILLIAM DAMERON (*b. San Francisco, Calif., 1859; d. Lattingtown, N.Y., 1935*), lawyer. Authority on constitutional law and Ruggles Professor at Columbia, 1913–22. Argued many leading cases before Supreme Court. [*Supp. 1*]

GUY, SEYMOUR JOSEPH (*b. London, England, 1824; d. 1910*), portrait and genre painter. Came to America, 1854; worked in New York. Best known for his pictures of child-life, genuine in sentiment.

GUYOT, ARNOLD HENRY (*b. Boudevilliers, Switzerland, 1807; d. 1884*), geographer. Graduated University of Berlin, Ph.D., 1835. Urged by J. R. L. Agassiz, he came to America, 1848; taught at Princeton, 1854–84. Made important contributions to glacial study; began U.S. weather station system; was author of pioneer textbooks and the classic *The Earth and Man* (1849); emphasized topography in teaching geography.

GWIN, WILLIAM McKENDREE (*b. Sumner Co., Tenn., 1805; d. New York, N.Y., 1885*), lawyer, physician, politician. Graduated Transylvania, M.D., 1828; practiced in Mississippi. Removed to California, 1849. Represented San Francisco district in California constitutional convention; served as U.S. senator, Democrat, 1850–61. On outbreak of the Civil War he was arrested as a Southern sympathizer; released, he engaged in a scheme to establish settlers from the South in Sonora and Chihuahua, Mexico, which was rejected by Emperor Maximilian, 1864. Arrested again, 1865, he was held prisoner at Fort Jackson for eight months. He died in obscurity.

GWINNETT, BUTTON (*b. Down Hatherly, England, c. 1735; d. near Savannah, Ga., 1777*), signer of the Declaration of Independence, Georgia merchant and planter. Settled in Savannah, Ga., 1765. Member of the Continental Congress, 1776–77, he was president (governor) of Georgia in March–April, 1777. He was killed in a duel with Lachlan McIntosh.

HAAN, WILLIAM GEORGE (*b. near Crownpoint, Ind., 1863; d. Washington, D.C., 1924*), soldier. Graduated West Point, 1889. Distinguished in Spanish-American War and in World War I as major-general commanding 32nd "Red Arrow" Division.

HAARSTICK, HENRY CHRISTIAN (*b. Hohenhameln, Germany, 1836; d. St. Louis, Mo., 1919*), businessman. Came to America as a child. Pioneer in Mississippi river barge transportation after Civil War.

HAAS, JACOB JUDAH AARON de (*b. London, England, 1872; d. New York, N.Y., 1937*), journalist, Zionist leader. Came to America, 1902. Associate of Theodor Herzl, and of Louis D. Brandeis whom he brought actively into the movement. [*Supp. 2*]

HABBERTON, JOHN (*b. Brooklyn, N.Y., 1842; d. Glen Ridge, N.J., 1921*), author, editor. Wrote stories of ordinary people and everyday life; remembered exclusively for *Helen's Babies* (1876).

HABERSHAM, ALEXANDER WYLLY (*b. New York, N.Y., 1826; d. Annapolis, Md., 1883*), naval officer, tea and coffee merchant. Great-grandson of James Habersham.

HABERSHAM, JAMES (*b. Beverley, England, 1712 o.s.; d. New Brunswick, N.J., 1775*), merchant, planter, colonial official. Emigrated to Georgia, 1738, with his friend George Whitefield with whom he established Bethesda Orphanage, one of the first in America. Organized firm of Harris & Habersham, 1744, the first commercial enterprise in the colony. An outspoken advocate of slavery, he developed large rice plantations after introduction of slaves to Georgia, 1749. A leader in the political life of the colony, he held many offices and acted as governor, 1771–73. He was a staunch Loyalist in the years leading up to the Revolution.

HABERSHAM, JOSEPH (*b. Savannah, Ga., 1751; d. 1815*), merchant, Revolutionary patriot. Son of James Habersham. Associated in business with Joseph Clay. Ardently espoused the American cause; served in provincial congress and as colonel in the Continental Army. Was delegate to the Continental Congress, 1785–86, and to the Georgia convention which ratified the Federal Constitution, 1788. Served as postmaster-general, 1795–1801. He is said to have raised and exported the first cotton shipped from America.

HACK, GEORGE (*b. Cologne, Germany, c. 1623; d. Virginia, c. 1665*), merchant, physician, colonist. Partner of Augustine Herrman in one of largest tobacco trading companies at New Amsterdam; ruined by British Navigation Act, 1651, he returned to practice of medicine.

HACKETT, FRANK WARREN (*b. Portsmouth, N.H., 1841; d. Portsmouth, 1926*), lawyer, writer. One of Henry Adams's Washington intimates.

HACKETT, HORATIO BALCH (*b. Salisbury, Mass., 1808; d. 1875*), New Testament scholar. Graduated Amherst, 1830; Andover Theological Seminary, 1834. Taught at Newton and Rochester theological seminaries. Active in American Bible Revision Committee; advocate of scientific exegesis.

HACKETT, JAMES HENRY (*b. New York, N.Y., 1800; d. Jamaica, N.Y., 1871*), character actor. Debut at New York Park Theater, 1826. Famous for his portrayal of Falstaff. Founded first American-born theatrical family; helped develop American types of comedy character.

HACKETT, JAMES KETELTAS (*b. Wolfe Island, Canada, 1869; d. Paris, France, 1926*), actor. Son of James H. Hackett. Leading man in romantic "cloak and sword" plays, 1896–1908.

HACKLEY, CHARLES HENRY (*b. Michigan City, Ind., 1837; d. 1905*), lumberman. *Post* 1856, identified with Muskegon, Mich.; a principal benefactor of that city.

HADDOCK, CHARLES BRICKETT (*b. Salisbury, N.H., 1796; d. West Lebanon, N.H., 1861*), Congregational clergyman, educator. Nephew of Daniel Webster. Professor at Dartmouth, 1819–50; partisan of public school education in New Hampshire.

HADDON, ELIZABETH. [See ESTAUGH, ELIZABETH HADDON, *c. 1680–1762.*]

HADFIELD, GEORGE (*b. Leghorn, Italy, c. 1764; d. Washington, D.C., 1826*), architect. Came to America, 1795, as superintendent of construction, U.S. Capitol; dismissed, 1798. Designed "Arlington" (later the home of R. E. Lee) and a number of public buildings in Washington, D.C.

HADLEY, ARTHUR TWINING (*b. New Haven, Conn., 1856; d. Kobe, Japan, 1930*), economist, president of Yale University, 1899–1921. Son of James Hadley. Graduated Yale, 1876. After a year of graduate study at Yale and two years at University of Berlin, he joined the Yale faculty as tutor. In 1883 he began to teach political science which became his specialty; he served as professor of political science in the college, the graduate school, and the Sheffield Scientific School. From 1892 to 1895 he was dean of the graduate school. His first book, *Railroad Transportation, Its History and Its Laws* (1885), was the earliest comprehensive study of the subject in the United States and established him as an authority in the field. He began his public career as expert witness before the Senate committee that drafted the Interstate Commerce Law in the same year and from 1885 to 1887 was commissioner of labor statistics in the state of Connecticut, publishing two reports that extended his reputation as an economist. While a brilliant and stimulating teacher at Yale, he contributed many articles on railroading and economics to various publications. His second book, *Economics—An Account of the Relations between Private Property and Public Welfare* (1896), was widely used as a text.

In May 1899 he became president of Yale. Though his classroom duties were terminated, audiences on both sides of the Atlantic were given an opportunity to hear him through various lectureships. He gave the Lowell Institute lectures, Boston, 1902; in 1907, he was Roosevelt professor of American history at the

University of Berlin. In 1914 he lectured at Oxford. During his administration Yale developed into a great national university. New enterprises inaugurated during his term of office included the School of Forestry, the University Press, the *Yale Review*, and Yale-in-China. His administration gave Yale a vastly increased endowment and an unprecedented number of new buildings.

In 1921, having seen the university through the difficult period of World War I, he retired from the presidency. He had many interests to keep him occupied. He had been chairman of the Railroad Securities Commission, established by Congress in 1910, and of the commission, commonly called by his name, appointed by President Taft in 1911 to investigate the conditions of the railroads out of which came the railway valuation act of 1913. He was an active director of a number of railroads. He died while on a tour around the world.

HADLEY, HENRY KIMBALL (*b. Somerville, Mass., 1871; d. New York, N.Y., 1937*), composer, conductor. Received musical education from his father and at the New England Conservatory; also studied in Germany. Conducted successively the Seattle, San Francisco, New York Philharmonic and Manhattan Symphony orchestras, 1909–32. A prolific composer, his works include five symphonies, four operas, numerous other orchestral works, chamber music, recital songs and some particularly effective choral music. His work derives from the "Boston group" (musicians schooled in the German tradition of classicism and romanticism) with Hadley's own admixture of geniality and vigor. He was a leader in promoting the interests of American composers. [*Supp.* 2]

HADLEY, HERBERT SPENCER (*b. Olathe, Kans., 1872; d. 1927*), lawyer. Attorney-general, 1905–09, and Republican governor of Missouri, 1909–13. Chancellor of Washington University. Helped start movement for reform of American criminal justice.

HADLEY, JAMES (*b. Fairfield, N.Y., 1821; d. 1872*), philologist. Father of Arthur T. Hadley. Graduated Yale, 1842; was professor of Greek there, 1851–72.

HA-GA-SA-DO-NI. [See DEERFOOT, 1828–1897.]

HAGEN, HERMANN AUGUST (*b. Königsberg, Germany, 1817; d. 1893*), entomologist. Author of *Bibliotheca Entomologica* (1862–63). First man to hold a chair confined to entomology in any college in the United States (at Harvard *post* 1870).

HAGER, JOHN SHARPENSTEIN (*b. near Morristown, N.J., 1818; d. San Francisco, Calif., 1890*), lawyer, judge, California legislator. Removed to California, 1849. U.S. senator, anti-monopoly Democrat, 1873–75.

HAGGERTY, MELVIN EVERETT (*b. Bunker Hill, Ind., 1875; d. Minneapolis, Minn., 1937*), educational psychologist, specialist in intelligence and achievement tests. Graduated Indiana, 1902; Ph.D., Harvard, 1910. Dean, College of Education, University of Minnesota, 1920–37. [*Supp.* 2]

HAGGIN, JAMES BEN ALI (*b. Harrodsburg, Ky., 1827; d. Newport, R.I., 1914*), lawyer, rancher, stock-breeder, capitalist. Removed to California, 1850; practiced law with Lloyd Tevis. Controlled over 100 mines, Alaska to Peru; developed extensive California irrigation projects.

HAGNER, PETER (*b. Philadelphia, Pa., 1772; d. 1850*), third auditor of the Treasury, 1817–49. Known as "watchdog of the Treasury," he rendered valuable service in settlement of important claims against the government.

HAGOOD, JOHNSON (*b. Barnwell Co., S.C., 1829; d. Barnwell Co., 1898*), lawyer, planter, Confederate soldier. Graduated Citadel, 1847. Governor of South Carolina, 1880–82. Helped rebuild the state after Civil War; was leader in development of agriculture and education.

HAGUE, ARNOLD (*b. Boston, Mass., 1840; d. 1917*), geologist. Brother of James D. Hague. Assistant, C. King's Survey of Fortieth Parallel; thereafter with U.S. Geological Survey. Supervised survey of Yellowstone National Park, *post* 1883.

HAGUE, JAMES DUNCAN (*b. Boston, Mass., 1836; d. Stockbridge, Mass., 1908*), mining engineer. Brother of Arnold Hague. Contributed classic third volume, *Mining Industry* (1870), to report of Geological Survey of Fortieth Parallel.

HAGUE, ROBERT LINCOLN (*b. Lincoln, R.I., 1880; d. New York, N.Y., 1939*), shipbuilder, ship operator. Manager, marine department, Standard Oil Co. of New Jersey, 1920–37; was later a vice-president and director. A leader in modern tanker design, especially of ships convertible to naval auxiliaries. [*Supp.* 2]

HAHN, GEORG MICHAEL DECKER (*b. Klingenmünster, Bavaria, 1830; d. Washington, D.C., 1886*), lawyer, editor, Louisiana Unionist. Came to America as a child. Practiced law in New Orleans. Congressman, Republican, 1863 and 1885–86; first Republican governor of Louisiana, 1864–65.

HAID, LEO (*b. near Latrobe, Pa., 1849; d. 1924*), Roman Catholic clergyman, Benedictine. Elected abbot of Belmont Abbey, N.C., 1885; consecrated vicar-apostolic of North Carolina, 1888.

HAIGHT, CHARLES COOLIDGE (*b. New York, N.Y., 1841; d. Garrison-on-Hudson, N.Y., 1917*), architect. Graduated Columbia, 1861; studied in office of E. T. Littell. Adapted English collegiate Gothic to school architecture in America; designed, among others, the General Theological Seminary buildings (New York City) and a number of buildings at Yale and Hobart.

HAIGHT, HENRY HUNTLY (*b. Rochester, N.Y., 1825; d. San Francisco, Calif., 1878*), lawyer. Removed to California, 1850, where he was Democratic governor, 1868–72. Among important acts of his term was establishment of University of California (1868).

HAILMANN, WILLIAM NICHOLAS (*b. Glarus, Switzerland, 1836; d. California, 1920*), educator. Came to America, 1852. Leader of the kindergarten movement in the United States. Among his numerous publications, his expositions of Froebel's doctrines are outstanding.

HAINES, CHARLES GLIDDEN (*b. Canterbury, N.H., 1792; d. New York, N.Y., 1825*), lawyer, author, politician. Private secretary to De Witt Clinton. Published one of first American law journals, *United States Law Journal and Civilian Magazine* (1822–23).

HAINES, DANIEL (*b. New York, N.Y., 1801; d. 1877*), jurist. As Democratic governor of New Jersey, 1843–44, 1848–51, he built up educational system and improved governmental machinery of the state. He was a justice of the state supreme court, 1852–66.

HAINES, LYNN (*b. Waseca, Minn., 1876; d. 1929*), publicist, journalist. Editor and executive secretary, National Voters' League.

HAISH, JACOB (*b. near Karlsruhe, Germany, 1826; d. De Kalb, Ill., 1926*), contractor, inventor, manufacturer. Came to America as a boy. Invented "S" barbed wire, patented 1875; was long in litigation with assignees of Joseph F. Glidden's patents.

HALDEMAN, SAMUEL STEMAN (*b. Locust Grove, Pa., 1812; d. Chickies, Pa., 1880*), naturalist, geologist, philologist. First professor of comparative philology, University of Pennsylvania, 1868–80; wrote extensively on orthography, etymology, orthoepy.

HALDERMAN, JOHN A. (*b. Fayette Co., Ky., 1833; d. Atlantic City, N.J., 1908*), judge, Union soldier, Kansas legislator, diplomat. Consul-general and minister resident to Siam, 1880–85, where he introduced postal and telegraph systems.

HALE, BENJAMIN (*Newburyport, Mass., 1797; d. Newburyport, 1863*), Congregational and Episcopal clergyman, educator. Third president of Geneva College, N.Y. (later Hobart), 1836–58; an educational liberal in sympathy with movement to substitute modern languages for classics.

HALE, CHARLES (*b. Boston, Mass., 1831; d. 1882*), journalist, Massachusetts legislator. Son of Nathan Hale (1784–1863); brother of Edward E. and Lucretia P. Hale. Consul-general to Egypt, 1864–70; assistant U.S. secretary of state, 1872–74.

HALE, CHARLES REUBEN (*b. Lewistown, Pa., 1837; d. Cairo, Ill., 1900*), Episcopal clergyman. Consecrated bishop of Cairo, Ill., coadjutor to the bishop of Springfield, 1892. A High-churchman, distinguished for scholarship.

HALE, DAVID (*b. Lisbon, Conn., 1791; d. 1849*), journalist. Cousin of Nathan Hale (1784–1863). Co-owner with Gerard Hallock of *New York Journal of Commerce, post* 1831; initiated new methods of news gathering.

HALE, EDWARD EVERETT (*b. Boston, Mass., 1822; d. Boston, 1909*), author, Unitarian clergyman. Son of Nathan Hale (1784–1863); nephew of Edward Everett. Graduated Harvard, 1839. Minister to South Congregational Church, Boston, 1856–99. Published in the *Atlantic Monthly* (December, 1863) "The Man Without A Country," one of the best short stories written by an American. In the vast bulk of his writings, *A New England Boyhood* (1893, 1900), *James Russell Lowell and His Friends* (1899) and *Memories of a Hundred Years* (1902) deserve special mention. He was chaplain of the U.S. Senate, 1903–09.

HALE, EDWARD JOSEPH (*b. near Fayetteville, N.C., 1839; d. 1922*), journalist, Confederate soldier. Editor, *Fayetteville Observer,* c. 1866–1913. Consul at Manchester, England, 1885–89; minister to Costa Rica, 1913–19.

HALE, EDWIN MOSES (*b. Newport, N.H., 1829; d. 1899*), homeopathic physician and teacher of medicine. Practiced in Michigan and Chicago, Ill.

HALE, ENOCH (*b. Westhampton, Mass., 1790; d. 1848*), physician. Brother of Nathan Hale (1784–1863). Graduated Harvard, M.D., 1813. Practiced in Gardiner, Maine, and Boston; author of the important *Observations on the Typhoid Fever of New England* (1839).

HALE, EUGENE (*b. Turner, Maine, 1836; d. Washington, D.C., 1918*), lawyer, politician, Maine legislator. Admitted to bar, 1857. Congressman, Republican, from Maine, 1869–79; authority on naval affairs and public expenditure; friend of James G. Blaine. U.S. senator, 1881–1911, a conservative and supporter of high tariff, he opposed measures for social and political reform. Hale did work of utmost importance in developing the modern Navy, but after the Spanish-American War his naval enthusiasm declined because of his dislike of American imperialism. His contempt for every progressive idea of the time made him unpopular in the country at large after 1901. After retirement from politics he was a member of the National Monetary Commission.

HALE, GEORGE ELLERY (*b. Chicago, Ill., 1868; d. Pasadena, Calif., 1938*), astronomer. Graduated Massachusetts Institute of Technology, 1890. Taught astrophysics at University of Chicago *post* 1892, and planned and directed the Yerkes Observatory there. His most important role was as initiator and director, 1904–23, of Mount Wilson Observatory, near Pasadena, Calif., where he performed many pioneering investigations, among them his discovery of magnetic fields in sunspots. He persuaded the Rockefeller Foundation to establish a 200-inch telescope on Palomar Mountain, Calif., 1928. Hale's bibliography of 450 titles covers a wide range of subjects but deals mainly with solar research; his eminence was international. [*Supp. 2*]

HALE, HORATIO EMMONS (*b. Newport, N.H., 1817; d. 1896*), lawyer, ethnologist. Son of Sarah J. B. Hale. On Wilkes Exploring Expedition, 1838–42, he collected data comprised in monumental *Ethnography and Philology* (Vol. VI of the Expedition Report, 1846). His subsequent work aided development of anthropology.

HALE, JOHN PARKER (*b. Rochester, N.H., 1806; d. 1873*), lawyer, politician, diplomat. Graduated Bowdoin, 1827. U.S. district attorney, 1834–41; congressman, Democrat, from Maine, 1843–45. Read out of the party for anti-slavery views, he was elected to the U.S. Senate, 1846, as an independent and served until 1853. Made his most notable speech in reply to Webster on Compromise of 1850; secured abolition of flogging and of the grog ration in the navy. Was presidential candidate of the Free-Soil party, 1852. Returned to the U.S. Senate, 1855, he was re-elected, 1858, for a six-year term as a Republican and was chairman of the naval affairs committee. Involved in an influence-peddling scandal, he failed of renomination. While minister to Spain, 1865–69, he was charged with moral delinquencies involving the Queen and abuse of his importation franchise, and was recalled.

HALE, LOUISE CLOSSER (*b. Chicago, Ill., 1872; d. Los Angeles, Calif., 1933*), actress, author. Excelled as player of character roles and as writer of travel books. [*Supp. 1*]

HALE, LUCRETIA PEABODY (*b. Boston, Mass., 1820; d. Boston, 1900*), author. Daughter of Nathan Hale (1784–1863); sister of Edward E. and Charles Hale. Remembered for *The Peterkin Papers* (1880) and *The Last of the Peterkins* (1886).

HALE, NATHAN (*b. Coventry, Conn., 1755; d. New York, 1776*), "Martyr Spy" of the Revolutionary War. Graduated Yale, 1773; was noted for physical and literary prowess. Taught school in Connecticut, 1773–75. Commissioned lieutenant, July 1775; served at siege of Boston and was promoted captain, January 1776. With Knowlton's Rangers in defense of New York, April to September, 1776. When Washington needed information on the strength and designs of the British after the defeat on Long Island, Hale volunteered to get it. Assuming the role of a schoolmaster with his college diploma for credentials, he accomplished his mission on Long Island. Returning to the American position on Harlem Heights, he had almost reached his own lines when he was apprehended as a spy. That he was betrayed by his Tory cousin Samuel Hale, British Deputy Commissioner of Prisoners, was the belief of the times and of his family. Military sketches and notes having been found on his person, Hale declared his name, rank, and mission. Without trial, Gen. Howe gave orders for his execution. At the gallows on the morning of Sept. 22, 1776, Hale made a "spirited and sensible speech" concluding with the memorable words, "I only regret that I have but one life to lose for my country."

HALE, NATHAN (*b. Westhampton, Mass., 1784; d. 1863*), journalist. Nephew of Nathan Hale (1755–1776); father of Charles, Edward E. and Lucretia P. Hale. Edited *Boston Daily Advertiser*, 1814–54; one of first Americans to introduce editorial articles as a regular feature; helped found *North American Review*, 1815; was active in New England railroad promotion.

HALE, PHILIP (*b. Norwich, Vt., 1854; d. Boston, Mass., 1934*), musician, critic. Music critic and columnist on staff of the *Boston Herald*, 1903–33; author of program notes of the Boston Symphony Orchestra. [*Supp. 1*]

HALE, PHILIP LESLIE (*b. Boston, Mass., 1865; d. Boston, 1931*), figure painter, critic, teacher. Son of Edward E. Hale. Author of *Jan Vermeer of Delft* (1913).

HALE, ROBERT SAFFORD (*b. Chelsea, Vt., 1822; d. 1881*), lawyer. Practiced in Elizabethtown, N.Y.; was a Republican member of 39th and 43rd Congresses, and U.S. agent and counsel before American-British Mixed Claims Commission, 1871–73.

HALE, SARAH JOSEPHA BUELL (*b. Newport, N.H., 1788; d. Philadelphia, Pa., 1879*), author, editor. After publication of a novel, *Northwood* (1827), she removed at instance of John Lauris Blake to Boston to edit the *Ladies' Magazine*, first significant publication of its kind. When Louis A. Godey bought it out in 1837, she became literary editor of his famous *Lady's Book* and helped make it the best known of American women's periodicals. Throughout her life she fought for better education for American women, guided their taste and constantly set forth their duties and privileges. Of all the work in her 36 published volumes, the poem "Mary's Lamb" (in *Poems for Our Children*, 1830) is best remembered.

HALE, WILLIAM BAYARD (*b. Richmond, Ind., 1869; d. Munich, Germany, 1924*), Episcopal clergyman, journalist. Early admirer of Woodrow Wilson whose campaign biography he wrote in 1912 and whose *The New Freedom* (1914) he edited. Exposed (1918) as undercover German propaganda adviser in United States.

HALE, WILLIAM GARDNER (*b. Savannah, Ga., 1849; d. Stamford, Conn., 1928*), classical scholar. Graduated Harvard, 1870; studied at Leipzig and

Göttingen. Professor of Latin, Cornell, 1880–92; University of Chicago, 1892–1919. First director, American School of Classical Studies, Rome. Discovered lost Catullus manuscript.

HALL, ABRAHAM OAKEY (*b. Albany, N.Y., 1826; d. New York, N.Y., 1898*), lawyer, politician, journalist. Known as "Elegant Oakey." Graduated New York University, 1844. New York county district attorney, 1855–58, 1862–68. Previously and successively a Whig, a Know-Nothing and a Republican, he joined Tammany Hall, 1864. As mayor of New York City, 1868–72, he acted as the mountebank of the "Tweed Ring" covering up ugly facts by his wit and debonair manner. Conducting his own defense, he was acquitted of implication with Tweed, 1872. City editor of the New York *World*, 1879–82, he was later London representative of the *New York Herald* and the New York *Morning Journal*. He wrote a number of books and plays, *The Crucible* (1878) being his best claim to dramatic distinction.

HALL, ARETHUSA (*b. Norwich, Mass., 1802; d. Northampton, Mass., 1891*), educator, author. Cofounder of the Brooklyn Heights Seminary.

HALL, ARTHUR CRAWSHAY ALLISTON (*b. Binfield, England, 1847; d. Burlington, Vt., 1930*), Episcopal clergyman, member of Cowley Fathers. Came to America, 1874. Consecrated bishop of Vermont, 1894. Widely known canonist and writer, active in Christian unity work.

HALL, ASAPH (*b. Goshen, Conn., 1829; d. Annapolis, Md., 1907*), astronomer. Largely self-taught. Worked at Harvard Observatory, 1858–62; at U.S. Naval Observatory, 1862–91. His most spectacular observation was his discovery in 1877 of the two satellites of Mars. Among his 500 published papers are masterly investigations of the orbits of various satellites and of double stars, the mass of Mars and of Saturn's rings, the perturbations of the planets, the advance of Mercury's perihelion, the parallax of the sun, and solutions of mathematical problems these investigations brought up. After 1896, he taught celestial mechanics at Harvard.

HALL, BAYNARD RUSH (*b. Philadelphia, Pa., 1798; d. Brooklyn, N.Y., 1863*), Presbyterian clergyman, educator. Author of a frontier classic *The New Purchase* (1843, under pseudonym "Robert Carlton"), *Frank Freeman's Barber Shop* (1852) and other books.

HALL, BOLTON (*b. Armagh, Ireland, 1854; d. Thomasville, Ga., 1938*), lawyer, reformer. Son of John Hall. Came to America as a boy; graduated Columbia Law School, 1888. Author of many books and pamphlets on tax and other reforms of which the most successful was *Three Acres and Liberty* (1907). [*Supp. 2*]

HALL, CHARLES CUTHBERT (*b. New York, N.Y., 1852; d. 1908*), Presbyterian clergyman. Graduated Williams, 1872. Pastor, First Presbyterian Church, Brooklyn, N.Y., 1877–97; president, Union Theological Seminary, 1897–1908.

HALL, CHARLES FRANCIS (*b. Rochester, N.H., 1821; d. in Arctic, 1871*), explorer. Went alone to Frobisher Bay area and searched for traces of Sir John Franklin's party, 1860–62; described his expedition in *Arctic Researches, and Life among the Esquimaux* (London, 1864; New York, 1865). Supported by Henry Grinnell, he left in 1864 on a five-year trip to the north end of Hudson Bay. With aid of Congress and a naval vessel, the *Polaris*, he departed in 1871 for a trip to the North Pole, reaching 82° 11′ N., 61° W., the most northerly point then attained by any vessel. Among the important geographic results of this expedition was the disclosure of the way to the North Pole. With similar limited resources no man has surpassed Hall in Arctic explorations.

HALL, CHARLES HENRY (*b. Augusta, Ga., 1820; d. Brooklyn, N.Y., 1895*), Episcopal clergyman. Rector, Church of the Epiphany, Washington, D.C., 1856–69, and of Holy Trinity, Brooklyn. Conducted funeral of friend Henry Ward Beecher.

HALL, CHARLES MARTIN (*b. Thompson, O., 1863; d. 1914*), chemist, manufacturer. Graduated Oberlin, 1885. Encouraged by college chemistry professor, F. F. Jewett, Hall discovered the only commercially successful process of making aluminum (patent applied for, 1886; granted, 1889). When the Cowles Smelting Co. gave up an option they had taken on his patent, he secured backing from the Mellons; as Pittsburgh Reduction Co., he began producing fifty pounds of aluminum daily at Kensington, Pa., 1888. Cowles later brought suit against him for stealing the process, but the U.S. circuit court approved Hall's originality in an 1893 decision. His achievement brought aluminum into general use.

HALL, DAVID (*b. Edinburgh, Scotland, 1714; d. Philadelphia, Pa., 1772*), printer, bookseller. Came to America, 1743, as journeyman in Benjamin Franklin's shop. Was Franklin's partner, 1748–66, and carried on the business as Hall and Sellers after Franklin sold his interest, 1766.

HALL, DOMINICK AUGUSTIN (*b. c. 1765; d. New Orleans, La., 1820*), lawyer. Practiced in Charleston, S.C. As federal judge in Louisiana, 1804–20, he fined Andrew Jackson $1000 for overriding writ of *habeas corpus*, 1815.

HALL, EDWIN HERBERT (*b. Great Falls, Maine, 1855; d. Cambridge, Mass., 1938*), physicist. Graduated Bowdoin, 1875; Ph.D., Johns Hopkins, 1880. Taught physics at Harvard, 1881–1921. His Ph.D. thesis was upon an effect he had discovered—a particular interaction between an electric current and a magnetic field that had been sought unsuccessfully by others, including the director of his graduate studies, Henry Augustus Rowland. The Hall effect, hailed as "a discovery comparable with the greatest made by Faraday," was Hall's major activity for the rest of his life, as he worked to fit it and other related effects and phenomena into a unified theoretical picture. [*Supp. 2*]

HALL, FITZEDWARD (*b. Troy, N.Y., 1825; d. 1901*), philologist. Graduated Rensselaer Polytechnic, 1842; Harvard, 1846. In India as teacher and inspector of public instruction, 1846–62; became professor of Sanskrit, Hindustani and Indian jurisprudence at King's College, London, 1862, and served until 1869. Edited H. H. Wilson's translation of *The Vishńu Puráná* (1864–77). Hall was the first American to edit a Sanskrit text (in 1852); his activity in editing and writing was prodigious. As much an authority on English philology as on Sanskrit, he wrote extensively in that field as well and was a valued contributor to the *Oxford English Dictionary* and other cooperative works.

HALL, FLORENCE MARION HOWE (*b. Boston, Mass., 1845; d. High Bridge, N.J., 1922*), author, lecturer. Daughter of Samuel G. and Julia Ward Howe.

HALL, GEORGE HENRY (*b. Manchester, N.H., 1825; d. 1913*), genre painter.

HALL, GRANVILLE STANLEY (*b. Ashfield, Mass., 1844; d. 1924*), psychologist, philosopher, educator. Graduated Williams, 1867; was influenced there by John Bascom. Entered Union Theological Seminary but left in 1868 for study in Germany. Returned to America, 1871; taught at Antioch College, 1872–76; took Ph.D. at Harvard, 1878. Following further study in Germany and development of a course on pedagogy at Harvard, he was made professor of psychology and pedagogics at Johns Hopkins where he continued his researches in experimental psychology, 1883–88, and built up a circle of disciples including John Dewey and Joseph Jastrow. In 1887 he founded the *American Journal of Psychology* and in 1891 became first president of the newly formed American Psychological Association.

Hall attracted wide attention by his article "The Moral and Religious Training of Children" (1882), and by his first study, *The Contents of Children's Minds* (1883). By 1888 he was perhaps the foremost educational critic in the country, a reputation which led to his selection as president of newly founded Clark University, Worcester, Mass. Dissension soon arose between the founder, Jonas G. Clark, and the administration, though the trustees stood unanimously by Hall and gave him full support on all occasions until he resigned in 1919. During these difficult years he devoted himself to the new child-study movement which his writings had inaugurated. *The Pedagogical Seminary* which he founded in 1891 became its organ. His own interest culminated in *Adolescence, Its Psychology and Its Relation to Physiology, Anthropology, Sociology, Sex, Crime, Religion and Education* (1904), a digest of all the literature on that subject. In 1893 he returned to the classroom as head of the Clark psychology department, lecturing on a wide range of subjects including the history of philosophy. Publication of *Educational Problems* (1911) marked a return of his interest from education to psychology, a phase which resulted in *Founders of Modern Psychology* (1912), dealing as much with philosophy as psychology. Hall's place in American psychology is much disputed. In education he made a great impression on his own generation. Through his personality and ideas, he influenced the country's schools more profoundly than any other theorists except W. T. Harris and John Dewey. Hall's original point of view is better described in George E. Partridge, *Genetic Philosophy of Education* (1912) than in any work of his own.

HALL, HAZEL (*b. St. Paul, Minn., 1886; d. Portland, Oreg., 1924*), poet.

HALL, HENRY BRYAN (*b. London, England, 1808; d. Morrisania, N.Y., 1884*), engraver, portrait painter. Came to America, *c.* 1850. Founded H. B. Hall and Sons, engravers of portraits of American historical figures, notably plates of Washington.

HALL, HILAND (*b. Bennington, Vt., 1795; d. Springfield, Mass., 1885*), jurist. Congressman, Whig, from Vermont 1833–43; Republican governor, 1858–60. Author of *The History of Vermont* (1868), an important work.

HALL, ISAAC HOLLISTER (*b. Norwalk, Conn., 1837; d. 1896*), lawyer, Orientalist. Graduated Hamilton, 1859. An outstanding Syriac scholar, he was also one of first to translate an entire Cypriot inscription. Collaborated with L. P. di Cesnola on Metropolitan Museum catalogs of Cypriot art.

HALL, JAMES (*b. Carlisle, Pa., 1744; d. Bethany, N.C., 1826*), Presbyterian clergyman. Removed to North Carolina as a child. Graduated College of New Jersey (Princeton), 1774. Chaplain in American Revolution; pastor at Bethany, N.C., and neighboring towns, 1776–1826. Established first Protestant mission in lower Mississippi Valley at Natchez, 1800.

HALL, JAMES (*b. Philadelphia, Pa., 1793; d. Cincinnati, O., 1868*), author, jurist, banker. Brother of John E. Hall; son of Sarah E. Hall. Commended for bravery in War of 1812, after which he served with Decatur's expedition against Algiers. Removed to Shawneetown, Ill., 1820, to practice law and edit *Illinois Gazette;* contributed as jurist, state treasurer, and promoter of education to the development of the state, 1820–32. Established the *Illinois Monthly*

Magazine, 1830, first literary periodical west of Ohio, to which he contributed half the contents. When its successor, the *Western Monthly Magazine*, lost most of its subscribers in 1835 because of Hall's vigorous defense of Catholics against Lyman Beecher's *A Plea for the West*, Hall withdrew to become cashier of the Commercial Bank, Cincinnati, where he had moved in 1833. In 1853 he became the bank's president. He is remembered chiefly as one of the most important recorders and interpreters of pioneer history, life, and legend in Illinois and the Ohio Valley. Of his many published works, probably the most valuable are *Legends of the West* (1832) and *Sketches of History, Life and Manners in the West* (1834, 1835); he collaborated with T. L. McKenney in the celebrated *History of the Indian Tribes of North America* (1836–42; 1884).

HALL, JAMES (*b. Hingham, Mass., 1811; d. 1898*), geologist, paleontologist. Graduated Rensselaer Polytechnic, 1832. His report, *Geology of New York: Part IV, Comprising the Survey of the Fourth Geological District* (1843), became a classic in geological literature. In 1843 he began a fifty-year study of the state's paleontology, embodied in *New York State Natural History Survey: Paleontology* (8 vols. in 13, 1847–94). Served as state geologist of Iowa, 1855–58, and of Wisconsin, 1857–60. Became director of New York State Museum, 1866, and state geologist, 1893. His lifework lay in domain of stratigraphic geology and invertebrate paleontology. His contribution was invaluable; his influence, world-wide.

HALL, JOHN (*b. Co. Armagh, Ireland, 1829; d. Bangor, Ireland, 1898*), Presbyterian clergyman. Came to America, 1867; served thereafter as influential pastor of Fifth Avenue Presbyterian Church, New York City.

HALL, JOHN ELIHU (*b. Philadelphia, Pa., 1783; d. Philadelphia, 1829*), lawyer, editor. Brother of James Hall (1793–1868). Published *American Law Journal* (Baltimore, Md., 1808–17) and a number of useful legal treatises; edited the *Port Folio*, 1816–27, also Dennie's *Lay Preacher* (1817).

HALL, LUTHER EGBERT (*b. near Bastrop, La., 1869; d. 1921*), lawyer, jurist. Democratic governor of Louisiana, 1912–16. A reformer, he reduced patronage, freed the public schools from politics, and bonded state debt.

HALL, LYMAN (*b. Wallingford, Conn., 1724; d. Burke Co., Ga., 1790*), physician. Removed to New England settlement at Sunbury, Ga.; was active in Revolutionary cause and served in Continental Congress; was a signer of the Declaration of Independence. Elected Georgia governor, 1783, he initiated chartering of the state university.

HALL, NATHAN KELSEY (*b. Skaneateles, N.Y., 1810; d. 1874*), jurist. Law partner of Millard Fillmore; U.S. postmaster-general, 1850–52; federal judge, Northern District of New York, 1852–74.

HALL, SAMUEL (*b. Medford, Mass., 1740; d. Boston, Mass., 1807*), printer. Apprentice to his uncle, Daniel Fowle. Established first printing-house, Salem, Mass., 1768; published intensely Whig *Essex Gazette*, 1768–75; published also *New England Chronicle*, *Salem Gazette* and *Massachusetts Gazette*.

HALL, SAMUEL (*b. Marshfield, Mass., 1800; d. 1870*), East Boston shipbuilder. Built *Surprise*, 1850, the first Massachusetts clipper; also *John Gilpin, R.B. Forbes* and other celebrated vessels.

HALL, SAMUEL READ (*b. Croydon, N.H., 1795; d. 1877*), Congregational clergyman, educator. Established a teacher-training school at Concord, Vt., 1823; later another at Phillips Academy, Andover. Was a founder of American Institute of Instruction, Boston, 1830.

HALL, SARAH EWING (*b. Philadelphia, Pa., 1761; d. Philadelphia, 1830*), essayist. Daughter of John Ewing; mother of James Hall (1793–1868) and John E. Hall. Contributor to the *Port Folio*, 1801–27; author of *Conversations on the Bible* (1818).

HALL, SHERMAN (*b. Weathersfield, Vt., 1800; d. Sauk Rapids, Minn., 1879*), Congregational clergyman. Missionary to Chippewa Indians in southern Lake Superior region, 1831–54.

HALL, THOMAS (*b. Philadelphia, Pa., 1834; d. 1911*), inventor, patent attorney. Devised a pioneer typewriter, patented 1867; also the single-keyed "Hall Typewriter" (1880), sewing-machine attachments, an improved mill-grinder and other machinist's tools.

HALL, THOMAS SEAVEY (*b. Upper Bartlett, N.H., 1827; d. Meriden, Conn., 1880*), wool manufacturer, inventor. Perfected a system of electric automatic signals for railroads, patented first in 1867. His most important invention, the electric inclosed disc, or "banjo," signal was patented, 1869. Later he worked out signals for drawbridges and in 1879 devised a method for highway-crossing protection. The first installation of his automatic block-signalling system was made on a line of the Eastern Railroad of Massachusetts, 1871. The principles Hall developed still prevail in railroad-signalling practice.

HALL, WILLARD (*b. Westford, Mass., 1780; d. Wilmington, Del., 1875*), jurist, legislator. Removed to Delaware, 1803; served as federal district judge, 1823–71. Author of Delaware school law of 1829; a lifelong advocate of free public education.

HALL, WILLARD PREBLE (*b. Harper's Ferry, Va., 1820; d. 1882*), lawyer, soldier, congressman. Graduated Yale, 1839. Removed to Missouri, 1840; practiced law at Sparta and St. Joseph, Mo. Served with distinction under Col. A. W. Doniphan in Mexican War. A

Unionist, he was lieutenant-governor of Missouri, 1861–64, and provisional governor, 1864–65.

HALL, WILLIAM WHITTY (*b. Paris, Ky., 1810; d. New York, N.Y., 1876*), Presbyterian clergyman, physician, pioneer editor of popular health magazines. Author of many rather dubious publications; edited *Hall's Journal of Health*, 1854–76.

HALLAM, LEWIS (*b. England, c. 1740; d. Philadelphia, Pa., 1808*), theatrical manager. Came to America with his father's theatrical company which first appeared in *The Merchant of Venice* at Williamsburg, Va., Sept. 15, 1752, a date which begins the continuous history of the American theatre. After two years' playing in American cities, the company was in Jamaica, B.W.I., 1754–58. When they returned to the American colonies, Lewis Hallam was leading man, undertaking such roles as Hamlet, which he was probably the first to present in this country, and Romeo to his mother's Juliet. Forced back to Jamaica by the Revolution, the so-called "American company" returned after the war with Hallam as manager. In 1785 he began a stormy partnership with John Henry, a rival manager, playing principally in New York and Boston. Henry in 1794 sold his interest to John Hodgkinson, an even greater source of discord. William Dunlap, a third partner *post* 1796, tried to act as mediator, but Hallam withdrew from the management, 1797, continuing his connection only as a salaried actor. Parsimonious, crafty, quarrelsome, often the source of his own troubles, Hallam was not a good manager; as an actor, however, he was admired for many years, playing every important character in the dramas then current. His forte was high comedy.

HALLECK, FITZ-GREENE (*b. Guilford, Conn., 1790; d. Guilford, 1867*), poet. Employed, 1811–49, as confidential clerk to Jacob Barker and the first John Jacob Astor. Author, with his friend Joseph Rodman Drake, of "Croaker & Co.," satires on local celebrities which appeared anonymously in N.Y. *Evening Post*, 1819. Halleck published *Fanny*, a social satire, in 1819 (enlarged edition, 1821), and collected his poems in *Alnwick Castle*, 1827. Editions of his work with a few additional poems were numerous; in 1865, his *Young America* was published. He was a gifted talker. Though Thomas Campbell was his literary ideal, his poems show more the influence of Byron and Scott. Overrated by his contemporaries, his best work such as "Marco Bozzaris" and his tributes to Drake and Robert Burns gives him a secure niche among minor American poets.

HALLECK, HENRY WAGER (*b. Westernville, N.Y., 1815; d. Louisville, Ky., 1872*), soldier, lawyer, capitalist. Graduated Union College, 1837; West Point, 1839. After a trip to Europe, 1844, he wrote a "Report on the Means of National Defense," which brought him an invitation to give the Lowell lectures in Boston; these were published as *Elements of Military Art and Science* (1846). On his way to service in California, 1846, he translated Jomini's *Vie Politique et Militaire de Napoléon* (published, 1864). Active in both military and civil affairs in California, 1847–53, and already distinguished as an engineer, he studied law, resigning his captaincy, 1854, to head the principal law firm in the state. He published two books on mining law and in 1861 *International Law, or Rules Regulating the Intercourse of States in Peace and War*, widely used as a textbook.

Eminently successful in law and business, he was commissioned major-general, 1861, and in November went to St. Louis to succeed Frémont in command of the Department of Missouri. His prestige enhanced by the success of his subordinates, U. S. Grant, Foote and Pope, his area of command was enlarged in March 1862 into the Department of the Mississippi. The next month he took the field before Corinth, Miss., for his only active campaign, a partial failure through his overcaution. He became military adviser to Lincoln with the title general-in-chief, July 1862. Cold, impersonal and impartial, nicknamed "Old Brains," he antagonized both politicians and his own subordinates. Devoting his time to details, he lost sight of the need to follow out a grand strategy. Halleck's deficiencies as supreme commander could be painted very black, but it is impossible now to reconstruct the difficulties of what he termed his "political Hell." Dependent on dispatches for knowledge of the battlefields, he was an office general without opportunity to obliterate his mistakes by victories in the field. In March 1864, he was made chief of staff, a demotion he took in good part, fulfilling his duties with unflagging energy. After Appomattox he commanded the Military Division of the James, the Military Division of the Pacific, and in 1869, his last post, the Division of the South. Halleck gave up much when he re-entered the army in 1861. Thrust against his will into a treacherous position, he was victim of his limitations.

HALLET, ÉTIENNE SULPICE (*b. Paris, France, 1755; d. New Rochelle, N.Y., 1825*), architect. Came to America, c. 1786–88. Submitted a variety of designs in competition for a federal Capitol building, 1791–92; was commissioned to revise plans of the winner, William Thornton, and supervise erection of the building. His name appears as "Stephen Hallette" on the cornerstone laid at Washington, Sept. 18, 1793, though he was shortly dismissed from his post. In one of Hallet's rejected designs, he created the type of capitol which was to prevail in America: a building with a tall central dome and wings for the two legislative houses; in another, he was first to adopt the classic hemicycle for a modern legislative hall.

HALLET, STEPHEN. [See HALLET, ÉTIENNE SULPICE, 1755–1825.]

HALLETT, BENJAMIN (*b. Barnstable, Mass., 1760; d. 1849*), owner of packet lines. Founder *c.* 1815 of the "Bethel Movement" for religious and social work among seamen in port cities.

HALLETT, BENJAMIN FRANKLIN (*b. Osterville, Mass., 1797; d. 1862*), editor, politician. Son of Benjamin Hallett. Militant, liberal editor of *Providence Journal*, 1821–28, and *Boston Advocate*, 1831–38, he later as editor of *Boston Post* became conservative and a docile Democratic party man.

HALLETT, MOSES (*b. Galena, Ill., 1834; d. 1913*), jurist. Chief justice, Colorado Territory supreme court, 1866–77; federal judge, Colorado district, 1877–1906; first dean, University of Colorado Law School.

HALLIDIE, ANDREW SMITH (*b. London, England, 1836; d. San Francisco, Calif., 1900*), engineer, inventor. Emigrated to California, 1853. Designed and built wire suspension bridges and flumes; produced in 1858 the first wire rope made on the Pacific Coast. Invented a rigid suspension bridge and perfected the "Hallidie ropeway" to carry freight over canyons, 1867. Devised, 1871, and installed, 1873, the endless moving cable and mechanical gripping device employed to pull streetcars up San Francisco's hillsides. He was active also in municipal affairs, reform movements and education.

HALLOCK, CHARLES (*b. New York, N.Y., 1834; d. Washington, D.C., 1917*), journalist, author, scientist. Son of Gerard Hallock. Founded *Forest and Stream* magazine, 1873; wrote extensively on outdoor life.

HALLOCK, GERARD (*b. Plainfield, Mass., 1800; d. New Haven, Conn., 1866*), journalist. Brother of William A. Hallock. Graduated Williams, 1819. After editing papers in Boston and New York, became editor of *New York Journal of Commerce*, 1828, of which he and David Hale became proprietors, 1831. A pioneer in the cooperative news-gathering movement, he resigned his editorship, 1861.

HALLOCK, WILLIAM ALLEN (*b. Plainfield, Mass., 1794; d. 1880*), first secretary of the American Tract Society, 1825–70, and director of all its activities.

HALLOWELL, BENJAMIN (*b. Montgomery County, Pa., 1799; d. Sandy Spring, Md., 1877*), educator, minister of the Society of Friends. Conducted his own preparatory school, Alexandria, Va., 1824–58; first president of Maryland Agricultural College, 1859.

HALLOWELL, RICHARD PRICE (*b. Philadelphia, Pa., 1835; d. 1904*), wool merchant. A leader in antislavery agitation in Philadelphia and Boston.

HALPINE, CHARLES GRAHAM (*b. Oldcastle, Ireland, 1829; d. 1868*), journalist, poet, Union soldier, politician. Came to America, 1851. Member of literary group that included Fitz-Hugh Ludlow and Fitz-James O'Brien. His popular Civil War satires were gathered in *Miles O'Reilly His Book* (1864).

HALSEY, FREDERICK ARTHUR (*b. Unadilla, N.Y., 1856; d. New York, N.Y., 1935*), mechanical engineer. Graduated Cornell, 1878. Devised industrial profit-sharing plan known as the Halsey premium payment plan; influential editor of the *American Machinist*, 1894–1911. [*Supp. 1*]

HALSEY, JOHN (*b. Boston, Mass., 1670; d. Madagascar, 1716*), South Sea pirate.

HALSEY, THOMAS LLOYD (*b. Providence, R.I., c. 1776; d. Providence, 1855*), merchant. U.S. consul in Buenos Aires, 1814–18; supplied arms to South American rebels; dismissed from post for privateer activity.

HALSTEAD, MURAT (*b. Butler Co., O., 1829; d. 1908*), journalist, war correspondent. Editor of *Cincinnati Commercial*, post 1853 to 1884; wrote graphic accounts of political conventions, 1860; covered Civil and Franco-Prussian wars. Later edited Brooklyn, N.Y., *Standard-Union*.

HALSTED, GEORGE BRUCE (*b. Newark, N.J., 1853; d. New York, N.Y., 1922*), mathematician, educator. Graduated Princeton, 1875; Ph.D., Johns Hopkins, 1879. Did much to make non-Euclidean geometry theories known in the United States. Taught at Princeton, University of Texas, and at a number of other schools.

HALSTED, WILLIAM STEWART (*b. New York, N.Y., 1852; d. 1922*), surgeon. Graduated Yale, 1874; N.Y. College of Physicians and Surgeons, 1877. Probably his greatest contribution was his early development of an operative technique concerned with preserving the power of the patient's tissues to resist weakening and infection. His second great service was his discovery, 1884, that a whole region of the body could be anaesthetized by injecting cocaine into the nerve. As professor of surgery at Johns Hopkins Hospital, 1890–1922, he trained many distinguished surgeons who owe their careers to his stimulus and example. The range and quality of his later work may be studied in *Surgical Papers by William Stewart Halsted* (1924).

HAMBIDGE, JAY (*b. Simcoe, Canada, 1867; d. 1924*), artist. Advanced theory in "The Natural Basis of Form in Greek Art" (1902) that the "principle of proportion" found in nature's symmetrical forms was used consciously in Greek art and involved a "dynamic" symmetry as opposed to "static" symmetry based on pattern properties of two-dimensional figures. His published works include *Dynamic Symmetry* (1917), an explanation of the mathematical background of his theory, and *The Parthenon and Other Greek Temples: Their Dynamic Symmetry* (1924).

HAMBLETON, THOMAS EDWARD (*b. Maryland, 1829; d. Baltimore, Md., 1906*), Confederate blockade runner, Baltimore financier and traction magnate.

HAMBLIN, JOSEPH ELDRIDGE (*b. Massachusetts, 1828; d. New York, N.Y., 1870*), insurance broker, Union brevet major-general.

HAMBLIN, THOMAS SOWERBY (*b. London, England, 1800; d. New York, N.Y., 1853*), actor. Came to America, 1825. Managed Bowery Theatre, New York, 1830–53, except for interruptions when fire twice destroyed it.

HAMER, THOMAS LYON (*b. Northumberland Co., Pa., 1800; d. Mexico, 1846*), lawyer, Ohio legislator, soldier. Congressman, Democrat, from Ohio, 1833–39. Died as division commander in Mexico under Zachary Taylor. Appointed U.S. Grant to West Point.

HAMILTON, ALEXANDER (*b. in or near Edinburgh, Scotland, 1712; d. Annapolis, Md., 1756*), physician, social historian. Came to America, 1738. Author of an *Itinerarium* (written 1744, published 1907), descriptive of a tour through the Northern colonies and sharply observant of the manners of the period.

HAMILTON, ALEXANDER (*b. Nevis, Leeward Islands, 1755 or 1757; d. New York, N.Y., 1804*), statesman. Came to New York, 1772; entered King's College (now Columbia University), 1773. His college career interrupted by the stirrings of the Revolution, he entered into the pamphlet wars of the day with *A Full Vindication of the Measures of Congress, etc.* (December 1774) and continued the debate in a reply to Samuel Seabury entitled *The Farmer Refuted* (1775), both brilliant expressions of a moderate point of view. Commissioned to command an artillery company early in 1776, he fought in the fall campaign on Long Island, at Harlem Heights and White Plains, was in the New Jersey retreat, and at Trenton and Princeton. He became secretary and aide-de-camp to Washington on March 1, 1777, with rank of lieutenant-colonel. In this position of great responsibility he became the general's trusted adviser and did much to systematize the handling of business at headquarters. He also drafted a series of important reports on the defects of the military system. Between 1777 and 1781, his correspondence with various colonial leaders reveals the growth of his political ideas and the incisiveness of his thought. Though a staunch believer in representative government (then widely distrusted), he insisted from the first that it must act through a highly centralized authority. In a letter of 1780 to James Duane, he made the first proposal for a constitutional convention; also in 1780 he married Elizabeth, daughter of Gen. Philip Schuyler. After a quarrel with Washington (February 1781), in which Hamilton's conduct does him discredit, he resigned from the staff but through Washington's magnanimity was appointed to head an infantry regiment. At Yorktown he conducted a brilliant attack on one of the principal British redoubts.

The fighting over, he went to Albany, N.Y., read law and was admitted to the bar. In 1783, after one term in the Continental Congress, he retired to private life and opened a law office in New York City, continuing active in the movement for a strong federal government. As a New York delegate to the Annapolis commercial convention, 1786, he secured adoption of a resolution recommending a convention of representatives from all the states to meet in Philadelphia the following May to devise provisions "necessary to render the Constitution of the Federal Government adequate to the exigencies of the Union." It was one of the most adroit of all his strokes. A member of the New York legislature of 1787, he made one of his greatest speeches to secure the state's adherence to an impost measure asked by Congress. Named a delegate from New York to the Philadelphia Convention, his federalist zeal was offset by the state-rights obscurantism of his colleagues, Robert Yates and John Lansing. His role at Philadelphia was not of great importance, but his work at home in New York was. He opened the fierce newspaper war over adoption of the Constitution in July 1787 and then planned the "Federalist" series, a magnificent sequence of expository and argumentative articles, the greater part of which he wrote either alone or in collaboration with James Madison. At the New York convention for ratification of the Constitution (Poughkeepsie, 1788), with irresistible speeches he led the successful fight for adoption, one of the few instances in American history of the decision of a deliberative body being changed by sheer power of sustained argument. He sat again in the Continental Congress in 1788 and was much in the foreground until the new government was organized, April 1789.

Appointed secretary of the treasury in September, he devised a plan for establishing the nation's credit on a sound basis which was presented to the House on Jan. 14, 1790. This famous document is one of his greatest state papers. He argued that the government should pay not only the foreign debt, but also fund the domestic debt at par value though many holders of public securities had bought them cheaply for speculation. He also argued that the federal government should assume debts contracted during the Revolution by the states. Several schemes for funding the debt on a basis that would postpone full interest charges were offered by Hamilton. To provide annual operating revenue, he proposed to levy import duties and an excise. His plans met fierce opposition. He carried the bill for assumption of state debts to success at last by his famous bargain with Jefferson and Madison for location of the national capital. The funding and assumption measures became law on Aug. 4, 1791. Meanwhile, Dec. 13, 1790, he had presented his plan for an excise on spirits; the next day, his plan for a national bank; and on Jan. 28, 1791, his report on the establishment of a mint. All three proposals were accepted. As a capstone to his financial and economic structure he presented his report on manufactures at the winter session of 1791–92; its cardinal feature was the proposal of protection for infant industries either by import duties or bounties. Whatever critics may say of Hamilton's system, he must be credited with creating public credit out of a void, putting the government on a firm financial foundation, and giving the country adequate banking and currency facilities and important new industries. If only because he went further than any member of the government in exercising the powers of the Constitution, he must rank as one of the boldest and most farsighted of the nation's founders.

Hamilton's aggressiveness and his belief that he was in effect prime minister of Washington's cabinet led to improper interference with other departments and accentuated party divisions which arose from differences in principles. Hamilton and Thomas Jefferson were natural antagonists; each truly believed that the policies of the other would destroy the government. The struggle between them reached a point of great bitterness. Hamilton encouraged John Fenno to establish the *Gazette of the United States* in 1789; in October 1791, Philip Freneau's *National Gazette* appeared under Jefferson's aegis; both were propaganda organs. The attacks on Hamilton's policies culminated in the House in the presentation by William B. Giles of nine resolutions of censure whose defeat early in 1793 vindicated Hamilton. The wars of the French Revolution and the arrival of Genet as envoy in April 1793 added fuel to the party flames. Despite the old alliance with France, Hamilton won Washington over to a policy of strict neutrality between France and Great Britain, maintained close relations with the British envoy and had John Jay sent to London to negotiate a trade treaty with England. He carefully controlled Jay's work in the interests of his domestic financial policy. The breach between Jefferson and Hamilton widened. Jefferson resigned as secretary of state in December 1793 and tried to discredit Hamilton's party by connecting it with speculation at home and British interests abroad; in home affairs, however, Hamilton's place was secure. When the Whiskey Rebellion occurred in 1794, he played the chief role in its suppression, taking the field with the punitive force, since he regarded the rebellion as an opportunity for the federal government to show its strength. Forced to resign from the cabinet in January 1795 because of personal financial pressures, he still did much to advise Washington and helped draft the final form of his Farewell Address.

Hamilton remained out of civil office thereafter, but continued to be a major figure in the country's life and was eminently successful as a lawyer. On bad terms with John Adams throughout his administration, he attempted to meddle in administration affairs by influencing members of Adams's cabinet. When war threatened with France in 1798, through Washington's influence Hamilton was appointed inspector-general of the provisional army. His plans for mo-

bilization and the conquest of Louisiana and Florida were dissipated when Adams ended the tension by sending a new minister to France. Later, hearing that Adams accused him of being under British influence, Hamilton harshly arraigned Adams as unfit for the presidency in a letter which was published by the Democrat-Republicans and went through a number of printings in 1800. It was a serious blunder and a surrender to personal irritation without excuse. Yet after this pettiness he magnificently rose above it on two important occasions. In the presidential election of 1800, when the Jefferson-Aaron Burr tie went into the House, Hamilton, in opposition to other Federalists, exerted his influence for Jefferson. When Burr sought the governorship of New York in 1804 and it was suspected, if he were victorious, that he would join with New England malcontents in forming a Northern Confederacy, Hamilton took the offensive and succeeded in getting Burr defeated. Thirsting for revenge, and on the pretext that Hamilton had expressed a "despicable opinion of him," Burr challenged Hamilton to a duel which occurred at Weehawken, N.J., July 11, 1804. Mortally wounded, Hamilton died the next day.

Certain of Hamilton's acts which arose from passion and errors in judgment may be counted against him, but apart from these, his character was of the highest and his patriotism unquestioned. His power as an orator was great but he chose to exert it on select bodies of influential men, not on the multitude whose political capacities he distrusted. His intellect was incisive, logical and amazingly quick but wanting in subtlety and the higher imagination. His political principles probably laid a clearer impress on the Republic than those of any other single man. As a cabinet member he worked to go beyond the Constitution in invigorating the government and hence proclaimed his doctrine of implied powers which, as developed under John Marshall and since, has tremendously strengthened the national sovereignty. Believing in a powerful federal authority, he thought much of governmental strength, but little of liberty. He believed in governmental measures for helping whole classes grow prosperous, but paid no attention to the aspirations of the individual for greater happiness and opportunity. A hard, efficient realist, his work was invaluable to the nation at the time, but his narrow aristocratic ideas needed correction from the doctrines of Jefferson and Lincoln.

HAMILTON, ALLAN McLANE (*b. Williamsburg, N.Y., 1848; d. Great Barrington, Mass., 1919*), physician, alienist. Grandson of Alexander Hamilton (1757–1804); also of Louis McLane. Graduated N.Y. College of Physicians and Surgeons, 1870. Pioneer in neurology; expert witness in homicide cases.

HAMILTON, ANDREW (*b. Scotland; d. Perth Amboy, N.J., 1703*). Settled in America, 1686. Governor of East and West Jersey, 1692–97, 1699–1702.

Deputy-governor of Pennsylvania, 1701–03; as deputy postmaster-general of America, *post* 1692, helped organize first postal system.

HAMILTON, ANDREW (*d. "Bush Hill," Philadelphia, Pa., 1741*), lawyer, legislator. Came to America toward end of 17th century. Practiced first in Maryland; appointed attorney-general of Pennsylvania, 1717; held numerous other offices. His title to fame is his successful defense in 1735 of John Peter Zenger, publisher of the New York *Weekly Journal*, against a charge of seditious libel brought by the New York authorities. In a masterful speech, Hamilton persuaded the jury, at peril to themselves, to render a "general verdict" on both law and facts at a time when "good law" reduced their role to determining the fact of publication, the libelous character of the words being left as a question of law to the judges. The issue at stake was the freedom of the press as the only orderly means of resistance to an arbitrary, unscrupulous executive.

HAMILTON, ANDREW JACKSON (*b. Madison Co., Ala., 1815; d. 1875*), lawyer, legislator. Removed to Texas, 1847. Unionist leader in Texas and congressman; provisional governor, 1865–66; member of Texas supreme court.

HAMILTON, CHARLES SMITH (*b. Western, N.Y., 1822; d. Milwaukee, Wis., 1891*), soldier. Graduated West Point, 1843. Distinguished in Mexican War; resigned commission, 1853, to enter business; in Civil War served as colonel, 3rd Wisconsin, and rose to corps command and rank of major-general in Western campaigns.

HAMILTON, EDWARD JOHN (*b. Belfast, Ireland, 1834; d. 1918*), Presbyterian clergyman, philosopher. Came to America as a boy. Taught at Hanover (Ind.), Princeton and Hamilton colleges; worked and published in fields of epistemology, logic, metaphysics, ethics. His most ambitious book was *The Human Mind* (1883).

HAMILTON, FRANK HASTINGS (*b. Wilmington, Vt., 1813; d. 1886*), surgeon. Graduated Union, 1830; M.D., University of Pennsylvania, 1835. Practiced and taught at Buffalo, N.Y., and New York City. Civil War medical officer, Union Army. Instituted healing of old ulcers by skin grafting.

HAMILTON, GAIL. [See DODGE, MARY ABIGAIL, 1833–1896.]

HAMILTON, JAMES (*b. probably Accomac Co., Va., c. 1710; d. 1783*), lieutenant-governor of Pennsylvania, 1748–54, 1759–63. Son of Andrew Hamilton (d. 1741). Supported proprietors in colonial difficulties, particularly in their political clashes with back country; neither opposed nor supported American Revolution.

HAMILTON, JAMES (*b. Charleston, S.C., 1786; d. Gulf of Mexico, 1857*), lawyer, statesman. Partner of James L. Petigru. Congressman, Democrat, from South Carolina, 1822–29; leader in Jacksonian opposition to John Q. Adams's administration, in anti-tariff movement, and in state-rights movement; nullificationist. As governor of South Carolina, 1830–32, he called a popular convention on the passage of the 1832 tariff act. Calhoun was the intellectual theorist of nullification, but Hamilton interpreted it to the people of the state and won them to it. When the ordinance was passed, he retired from the governorship to command the state's troops. After organizing an armed force of 27,000 men, he changed his mind on nullification and favored the compromise that secured tariff reduction. No more a force in politics, he turned to business and later played an important part in the struggle of Texas for independence.

HAMILTON, JAMES ALEXANDER (*b. New York, N.Y., 1788; d. New York, 1878*), lawyer, politician. Son of Alexander Hamilton (1757–1804). At first a Tammany partisan and a follower of Jackson and Van Buren, *post* 1840 he was identified with the Whig and Republican parties.

HAMILTON, JOHN WILLIAM (*b. Weston, Va., 1845; d. Boston, Mass., 1934*), Methodist clergyman. Bishop in California and New England, 1900–16; chancellor of the American University, Washington, D.C., 1916–22. [*Supp. 1*]

HAMILTON, PAUL (*b. South Carolina, 1762; d. 1816*), Revolutionary soldier, planter, legislator. Democrat-Republican governor of South Carolina, 1804–06. As secretary of the navy, 1809–12, he was powerless in face of the refusal of Congress to vote funds for his department.

HAMILTON, PETER (*b. Harrisburg, Pa., 1817; d. Mobile, Ala., 1888*), lawyer, legislator. Graduated Princeton, 1835; admitted to Alabama bar, 1838. A leader of conservative Democrats during Reconstruction, he played a great part in restoring Alabama's transportation and credit.

HAMILTON, SCHUYLER (*b. New York, N.Y., 1822; d. New York, 1903*), soldier, engineer. Grandson of Alexander Hamilton (1757–1804). Graduated West Point, 1841. Distinguished for Mexican War service and as staff and field officer in Civil War.

HAMILTON, WILLIAM THOMAS (*b. Hagerstown, Md., 1820; d. Hagerstown, 1888*), lawyer, legislator. Congressman, Democrat, from Maryland, 1849–55. Sympathetic to the South but anti-secession. As U.S. senator, 1869–75, opposed radical Reconstruction; as Democratic governor of Maryland, 1880–84, fought without success for economy and political reform.

HAMILTON, WILLIAM THOMAS (*b. England, 1822; d. Columbus, Mont., 1908*), trapper, Indian trader, scout. Came to America as a child; raised in St. Louis, Mo. Author of *My Sixty Years on the Plains* (ed. E. T. Sieber, 1905).

HAMLIN, ALFRED DWIGHT FOSTER (*b. near Constantinople, Turkey, 1855; d. 1926*), architect. Son of Cyrus Hamlin. Taught at Columbia University, *post* 1887; influenced teaching of history of architecture and ornament in American schools; author of standard textbooks.

HAMLIN, CHARLES (*b. Hampden, Maine, 1837; d. Bangor, Maine, 1911*), Union brigadier-general, lawyer, businessman. Son of Hannibal Hamlin. Pioneer in organizing building and loan associations.

HAMLIN, CHARLES SUMNER (*b. Boston, Mass., 1861; d. Washington, D.C., 1938*), lawyer. Graduated Harvard, 1883; LL.B., 1886. Member of the Federal Reserve Board, 1914–36, and its first governor, 1914–16. [*Supp. 2*]

HAMLIN, CYRUS (*b. near Waterford, Maine, 1811; d. 1900*), missionary, educator. Graduated Bowdoin, 1834; Bangor Theological Seminary, 1837. Worked in Turkey, 1838–60, 1861–77. Founded Robert College at Bebek, Turkey, 1863, and was its president until 1877; president, Middlebury College (Vt.), 1880–85.

HAMLIN, EMMONS (*b. Rome, N.Y., 1821; d. Boston, Mass., 1885*), inventor, manufacturer of organs and pianos. Revolutionized "voicing" of organ reeds, increasing variety of stops. Partner, *post* 1854, with Henry Mason in Mason & Hamlin Organ Co.

HAMLIN, HANNIBAL (*b. Paris Hill, Maine, 1809; d. 1891*), lawyer, politician. As a Jacksonian Democrat, he represented Hampden in the Maine legislature, serving three terms as speaker, and was a member of Congress, 1843–47. In his first terms as U.S. senator, 1848–57, he wrote important legislation on steamboat inspection and ship-owners' liability. Becoming a Republican, he resigned from the Senate in January 1857 to become governor of Maine for a few weeks; resigning the governorship, he returned to the Senate. Widely prominent in the anti-slavery contest, he was a logical running-mate for Abraham Lincoln in 1860 and served as vice-president during Lincoln's first term. Failing of renomination, 1864, he returned to politics on re-election to the U.S. Senate where he served, 1869–81. He supported the Radical group in reconstruction matters and Republican principles in economic issues. He was minister to Spain, 1881–82.

HAMLIN, WILLIAM (*b. Providence, R.I., 1772; d. Providence, 1869*), engraver. His interest to collectors of American prints is chiefly historical.

HAMLINE, LEONIDAS LENT (*b. Burlington, Conn., 1797; d. 1865*), Methodist clergyman and bishop in Ohio and Iowa; helped found Hamline University.

HAMMER, WILLIAM JOSEPH (*b. Cressona, Pa., 1858; d. New York, N.Y., 1934*), electrical engineer. Associate of Thomas A. Edison; as chief engineer of the English Edison Co., built the world's first central station for incandescent electric lighting, Holborn, London, 1882. [*Supp. 1*]

HAMMERSTEIN, OSCAR (*b. Germany, c. 1847; d. New York, N.Y., 1919*), inventor, composer, theatrical manager, opera impresario. Came to America, *ante* 1865.

HAMMETT, HENRY PINCKNEY (*b. Greenville Co., S.C., 1822; d. 1891*), cotton manufacturer. Founded Piedmont Manufacturing Co., 1873; its success inspired confidence in practicability of manufacturing cotton in the South.

HAMMETT, SAMUEL ADAMS (*b. Jewett City, Conn., 1816; d. Brooklyn, N.Y., 1865*), merchant, author. His first book, *A Stray Yankee in Texas* (1853, published under pseudonym, "Philip Paxton"), was a noteworthy contribution to literature of the Southwestern frontier.

HAMMON, JUPITER (*b. c. 1720; d. c. 1800*), poet. An African slave, resident in Long Island, N.Y., and Hartford, Conn., his first poem was written late in 1760 and antedates by several years that of Phillis Wheatley, commonly regarded as the first Negro voice in American literature.

HAMMOND, CHARLES (*b. near Baltimore, Md., 1779; d. 1840*), lawyer, journalist. Removed to Ohio, 1810; became leader of Ohio bar. Edited *Cincinnati Gazette*, 1825–40, making it one of most influential papers in the West. He was also an Ohio legislator and was reporter of the state supreme court *post* 1823.

HAMMOND, EDWARD PAYSON (*b. Ellington, Conn., 1831; d. Hartford, Conn., 1910*), evangelist. Influenced William Booth, founder of Salvation Army.

HAMMOND, EDWIN (*b. Middlebury, Vt., 1801; d. 1870*), Merino sheep-breeder.

HAMMOND, GEORGE HENRY (*b. Fitchburg, Mass., 1838; d. Detroit, Mich., 1886*), meat packer, pioneer (*c. 1868*) in the use of refrigerator cars.

HAMMOND, JABEZ DELANO (*b. New Bedford, Mass., 1778; d. Cherry Valley, N.Y., 1855*), lawyer, politician. Author of *The History of Political Parties in the State of New-York* (Auburn, N.Y., 1842 and Syracuse, N.Y., 1848).

HAMMOND, JAMES BARTLETT (*b. Boston, Mass., 1839; d. St. Augustine, Fla., 1913*), inventor, manufacturer. Invented the Hammond typewriter, patented 1880.

HAMMOND, JAMES HENRY (*b. Newberry District, S.C., 1807; d. 1864*), lawyer, planter. Graduated South Carolina College, 1825. Early advocate of nullification; Southern nationalist; constant proponent of secession. Considered his attack on the state bank his greatest achievement as Democratic governor of South Carolina, 1842–44. The chief event of his career as U.S. senator, 1857–60, during which he began to doubt the wisdom of secession, was his reply to W. H. Seward, 1858, in which he advanced his theory that Southern slaves and Northern workers were "mudsills of society," and declared, "You dare not make war on cotton . . . Cotton is king."

HAMMOND, JOHN HAYS (*b. San Francisco, Calif., 1855; d. Gloucester, Mass., 1936*), mining engineer. Graduated Sheffield Scientific School, 1876; Royal School of Mines, Freiberg, Saxony, 1879; soon earned a reputation as a mine valuation expert. In South Africa on an assignment, 1893, he became chief consulting engineer for Cecil Rhodes and took part in the abortive "Jameson Raid" against the Kruger government, 1896. On his return to America, 1899, he acquired many important clients, including the Guggenheims. After 1907 his chief interest was in politics and public affairs, especially in the cause of peace. [*Supp.* 2]

HAMMOND, NATHANIEL JOB (*b. Elbert Co., Ga., 1833; d. 1899*), lawyer. Leader of Georgia bar; Congressman, Democrat, 1879–87; strong supporter of Georgia educational institutions.

HAMMOND, PERCY HUNTER (*b. Cadiz, O., 1873; d. New York, N.Y., 1936*), drama critic. Wrote with distinction for the *Chicago Tribune*, 1908–21; *New York Tribune* and *Herald Tribune*, 1921–36. "Dramatic criticism," he once wrote, "is the venom of contented rattlesnakes." [*Supp.* 2]

HAMMOND, SAMUEL (*b. Farnham's Parish, Va., 1757; d. 1842*), Revolutionary soldier, merchant, Missouri territorial official. Organized first bank in St. Louis. Removed to South Carolina, 1824.

HAMMOND, WILLIAM ALEXANDER (*b. Annapolis, Md., 1828; d. Washington, D.C., 1900*), neurologist. Graduated M.D., University of City of New York, 1848; U.S. army surgeon, 1849–59. Appointed surgeon-general, 1862, he accomplished many reforms but clashed with Secretary of War Stanton and was dismissed, 1864. Became a leader in practice of neurology, then in its infancy, and taught at a number of schools until 1888. A prolific writer, his *Treatise on Diseases of the Nervous System* (1871) was described as the "first text-book on nervous diseases in English." He founded and edited a number of medical journals and was a pioneer in modern treatment of mental and nervous diseases in the United States.

HAMMOND, WILLIAM GARDINER (*b. Newport, R.I., 1829; d. St. Louis, Mo., 1894*), lawyer, legal educator. Graduated Amherst, 1849; studied at Heidelberg. Settled in Des Moines, Iowa, *post* 1860. As chancellor, law school of University of Iowa, and dean, law school of Washington University, his teaching methods approached the case system of study later introduced at Harvard. He was leading contemporary American authority on the history of the common law.

HAMPTON, WADE (*b. Halifax Co., Va., 1751 or 1752; d. Columbia, S.C., 1835*), planter, Revolutionary soldier. As major-general in War of 1812, commanded on Lake Champlain but resigned 1813 after dispute with Gen. James Wilkinson. Reputed wealthiest planter in America.

HAMPTON, WADE (*b. Charleston, S.C., 1818; d. Columbia, S.C., 1902*), planter, statesman, Confederate soldier. Grandson of Wade Hampton (1751/52–1835). Graduated South Carolina College, 1836. As a member of state legislature, he was conservative on questions of Southern policy. Though he had not favored secession, he gave himself and his resources to the Confederacy from the outset, offering his cotton to be exchanged in Europe for arms and raising troops at his own expense. Serving first as an infantry officer, he was wounded at Bull Run and Seven Pines. He became a cavalry officer, July 1862. After September, as second in command, he served in all major movements of Gen. J. E. B. Stuart and became major-general, 1863. After Stuart's death (May 1864), Hampton commanded the Confederate cavalry corps. Promoted lieutenant-general early in 1865, he covered J. E. Johnston's retreat and on Johnston's surrender proposed unsuccessfully to join Jefferson Davis and continue resistance from Texas. When a drastic Reconstruction policy was instituted, Hampton came out of retirement and joined in the protests against Republican rule, *post* 1868. In 1876, as a "straight-out" Democrat, he was elected governor. His greatest contribution toward restoration of white supremacy in his state was his influence in avoiding general armed conflict, particularly between the election and the withdrawal of U.S. troops (Apr. 10, 1877) when the Democrats were permitted to take over the government. In 1878 he was re-elected governor. Shortly afterward he was made U.S. senator and served until 1891. From 1876 to 1890 the name Wade Hampton was the symbol of the South Carolina political regime, conservative in tradition and practices and of the old rather than the new South. Opposition arose, led by Benjamin R. Tillman, which represented the farmer and artisan strata of society, and Hampton was defeated for re-election to the Senate.

HAMTRAMCK, JOHN FRANCIS (*b. Fort Wayne, Ind., 1798; d. Shepherdstown, [W.] Va., 1858*), soldier, planter, jurist. Graduated West Point, 1819. Indian agent for Osage Indians, 1826–31. Fought in War of 1812 and Mexican War.

HANAFORD, PHOEBE ANN COFFIN (*b. Nantucket Island, 1829; d. Rochester, N.Y., 1921*), Universalist minister, author. First woman to be regularly ordained in New England.

HANBY, BENJAMIN RUSSEL (*b. Rushville, O., 1833; d. 1867*), song writer. Composer of "Darling Nelly Gray" and "Ole Shady, the Song of the Contraband" (1861), a favorite of the Northern armies.

HANCHETT, HENRY GRANGER (*b. Syracuse, N.Y., 1853; d. Siasconset, Mass., 1918*), pianist, music teacher, author. Inventor of the "sostenuto" or third tone-sustaining pedal now used on all grand pianos.

HANCOCK, JOHN (*b. Braintree, Mass., 1736/37; d. Quincy, Mass., 1793*), merchant, politician. Nephew of Thomas Hancock. Graduated Harvard, 1754. Entered his uncle's mercantile firm; became a partner in 1763, and headed it *post* 1764. In 1768, a riot ensued when his sloop *Liberty* was seized for smuggling wine; the episode and an unsuccessful Crown prosecution were important in the prelude to the Revolution and added to Hancock's local popularity. He was elected to the General Court, 1769, and headed the Boston committee of patriots, 1770. Samuel Adams soon became a determining influence in his life, and he became an idol of the populace. President of the Massachusetts Provisional Congress, 1774–75, he was the richest if not the most intelligent New Englander on the patriot side; he was elected president of the Second Continental Congress and signed the Declaration of Independence. Not realizing his limitations, he desired to be made commander-in-chief of the army. Congress thwarted him by appointing Washington, a slight Hancock never forgave. He resigned the presidency of the Congress in 1777; though still a member, he spent much time in Boston, more interested in local than national politics. In command of a Massachusetts contingent in a Rhode Island action, 1778, his performance was neither able nor creditable. As treasurer of Harvard College, 1773–77, he gave that institution infinite trouble. In 1780 he was elected first governor of Massachusetts state. He served until 1785 when, in the face of troubles culminating in Shays's Rebellion, he had an attack of gout and resigned. After the rebellion, he was again elected governor. In 1788, presiding at the state convention to ratify the Federal Constitution, he maneuvered matters so as to appear popular peacemaker at the divided meeting. He was serving his ninth term as governor when he died.

HANCOCK, JOHN (*b. Jackson Co., Ala., 1824; d. Austin, Texas, 1893*), Texas Unionist, lawyer. Partner of Andrew J. Hamilton; expert in land laws. Congressman, Democrat, from Texas, 1871–77, 1883–85.

HANCOCK, THOMAS (*b. present Lexington, Mass., 1703; d. Boston, Mass., 1764*), merchant, army supplier. Uncle of John Hancock.

HANCOCK, WINFIELD SCOTT (*b. Montgomery Square, Pa., 1824; d. Governors Island, N.Y., 1886*), soldier. Graduated West Point, 1844. Served in Mexican War, Seminole War, and at various Western posts until 1861. Commissioned brigadier-general in that year and major-general, 1862, he distinguished himself at Fredericksburg and Chancellorsville; at Gettysburg, he won fame as one of the Civil War's great soldiers, selecting the field and diverting Lee from immediate attack. On the second day of Gettysburg he thwarted Lee's nearly successful attack on the Union flank; on July 3 he repulsed the Confederate thrust at the federal center. His volunteer rank was confirmed in the regular army, 1866; thereafter, he commanded various army departments. Democratic presidential candidate in 1880, he was defeated by Garfield.

HAND, DANIEL (*b. East Guilford, Conn., 1801; d. 1891*), merchant in Augusta, Ga., and Charleston, S.C. Established Daniel Hand Educational Fund for Colored People, 1888.

HAND, EDWARD (*b. King's Co., Ireland, 1744; d. near Lancaster, Pa., 1802*), physician, Revolutionary soldier. Came to America, 1767, as army surgeon; settled in Lancaster, *post* 1774. Brevet major-general, 1783, after outstanding service.

HANDERSON, HENRY EBENEZER (*b. Orange, O., 1837; d. Cleveland, O., 1918*), physician, medical historian.

HANDY, ALEXANDER HAMILTON (*b. Princess Anne, Md., 1809; d. Canton, Miss., 1883*), Mississippi jurist.

HANNA, MARCUS ALONZO (*b. New Lisbon, O., 1837; d. 1904*), capitalist, politician. A partner in father's grocery and commission firm in Cleveland, O., 1862. Married Charlotte Rhodes, daughter of a Cleveland coal and iron merchant, 1864, and in 1867 transferred all his interests to expansion of new firm of Rhodes & Co. Reorganized the firm as M. A. Hanna & Co., 1885; meantime, he had helped organize the Union National Bank, and had become owner of the *Cleveland Herald* and of the Cleveland Opera House. Quick to see interrelation of business and politics as necessary under new industrialism, he entered politics; by organizing Cleveland businessmen in support of Garfield, 1880, he became an important figure in Ohio Republican politics. Hanna successfully promoted his friend William McKinley for governor in 1891 and got him re-elected in 1893. He then launched the McKinley boom for president and in 1894–95 withdrew from business to devote his energies to the pre-convention maneuvers which brought about McKinley's nomination on the first ballot at the St. Louis convention, 1896. Hanna became chairman of the Republican national committee, giving that body new importance; he raised the unprecedented amount of $3,500,000 in a highly organized campaign which included regular assessments on business institutions and assured McKinley's election. Hanna succeeded John Sherman as U.S. senator from Ohio, 1897. He played an active part in the Republican congressional campaign of 1898 and was an important presidential adviser, particularly in employment of federal patronage to strengthen the party. In 1900, again national chairman, he played a great part in McKinley's re-election. Thereafter, he took a more active role in the Senate, revealing qualities of statesmanship. When Theodore Roosevelt became president on McKinley's death, September 1901, Hanna continued as a presidential adviser and, as chairman of the conciliation committee, National Civic Federation, helped settle disputes in the anthracite coal industry. Hanna believed in the right of labor to organize as a corollary to his advocacy of big business and organized capital, and because it was easier and more efficient to deal with labor's responsible spokesmen than with a mass of employees. Re-elected to the Senate, 1903, he died the following year. Hanna played politics according to the rules without any of the instincts of the reformer. In 1902 he declared himself champion of "Stand-pattism," which carried all the connotations of reactionary politics.

HANNEGAN, EDWARD ALLEN (*b. Hamilton Co., O., 1807; d. St. Louis, Mo., 1859*), lawyer. Congressman, independent Democrat, from Indiana, 1833–37; U.S. senator, 1843–49. An aggressive expansionist.

HANSEN, GEORGE (*b. Hildesheim, Germany, 1863; d. Berkeley, Calif., 1908*), horticulturist, landscape architect. Came to America, 1887. Active in reclamation of exploited central Sierra region of California, 1889–96.

HANSEN, MARCUS LEE (*b. Neenah, Wis., 1892; d. Redlands, Calif., 1938*), historian. Taught at University of Illinois. Pioneer student of American immigration; author of *The Atlantic Migration* (ed. A. M. Schlesinger, 1940). [*Supp. 2*]

HANSON, ALEXANDER CONTEE (*b. Annapolis, Md., 1749; d. Annapolis, 1806*), jurist. Son of John Hanson. Chancellor of Maryland, 1789–1806. Author of *Remarks on the Proposed Plan of a Federal Government* (1787) and various legal works.

HANSON, ALEXANDER CONTEE (*b. Annapolis, Md., 1786; d. near Elkridge, Md., 1819*), lawyer, editor. Son of Alexander C. Hanson (1749–1806). Graduated St. John's College, 1802. An extreme Federalist; founded *Federal Republican*, Baltimore, 1808. On June 22, 1812, because of an editorial hostile to Madison and the war, a mob destroyed the newspaper building; Hanson secured a new building and made it into an arsenal; on July 28 a member of the mob was killed in an attack on it. That night the offending Federalists within were brutally beaten in the jail where they had consented to go for protection. Among them were Hanson, Gen. J. L. Lingan and Gen. Henry Lee. In reaction to this Republican terrorism, Hanson was elected to Congress (1812), and served as U.S. senator, 1817–19.

HANSON, JOHN (*b. Charles Co., Md., 1721; d. Prince Georges Co., Md., 1783*), Revolutionary leader. Member of Maryland Assembly, 1757–79; a strong proponent of every revolutionary measure preceding the war. Served in Continental Congress, 1780–82, and as president of Congress under the Articles of Confederation, Nov. 5, 1781–1782. With Daniel Carroll, succeeded in securing relinquishment of claims of Virginia and other states to unsettled territory extending westward to the Mississippi.

HANSON, OLE (*b. near Union Grove, Wis., 1874; d. Los Angeles, Calif., 1940*), politician, real-estate dealer. Removed to Seattle, Wash., 1902, where as mayor, 1919, he broke a general strike which had paralyzed the city. [*Supp. 2*]

HANSON, ROGER WEIGHTMAN (*b. Winchester, Ky., 1827; d. 1863*), Confederate brigadier-general. Known as "Old Flintlock"; mortally wounded at Murfreesboro, Tenn.

HAPGOOD, ISABEL FLORENCE (*b. Boston, Mass., 1850; d. New York, N.Y., 1928*), translator, journalist. Introduced works of Tolstoy, Gogol, Turgenev and other European authors to English-speaking world.

HAPGOOD, NORMAN (*b. Chicago, Ill., 1868; d. New York, N.Y., 1937*), publicist, reformer. Graduated Harvard, A.B., 1890; LL.B., 1893. Associate of Lincoln Steffens on N.Y. *Commercial Advertiser*, 1897–1902; editor, *Collier's Weekly*, during progressive reform era, 1902–12. [*Supp. 2*]

HAPPER, ANDREW PATTON (*b. Washington Co., Pa., 1818; d. Wooster, O., 1894*), Presbyterian missionary. Worked mainly in Canton, China, 1844–84, and again in 1888–91 when he founded Canton Christian College.

HARADEN, JONATHAN (*b. Gloucester, Mass., 1744; d. Salem, Mass., 1803*), Revolutionary naval officer and privateersman. Commanded *Tyrannicide*, 1777–78; *General Pickering*, 1778–81; *Julius Caesar*, 1782.

HARAHAN, JAMES THEODORE (*b. Lowell, Mass., 1841; d. 1912*), railroad official. Pioneer in public relations aspect of railroad management. After Civil War service, held responsible posts with many roads; was president of Illinois Central, 1906–11.

HARAHAN, WILLIAM JOHNSON (*b. Nashville, Tenn., 1867; d. Clifton Forge, Va., 1937*), railroad executive. Son of James T. Harahan. President, Chesapeake and Ohio, 1920–29 and 1935–37; also of Nickel Plate and Pere Marquette railways, 1935–37.
[*Supp. 2*]

HARASZTHY DE MOKCSA, AGOSTON (*b. Futtak, Hungary, c. 1812; d. near Corinto, Nicaragua, 1869*), pioneer. Came to America, 1840; founded Sauk City, Wis. Removed to California, 1849, and imported first European grapevines, 1852. Planted first large California vineyard in Sonoma Valley, 1858.

HARBAUGH, HENRY (*b. Washington Township, Pa., 1817; d. Mercersburg, Pa., 1867*), German Reformed clergyman. Author of folk poetry in Pennsylvania-German dialect; popularized "Mercersburg theology."

HARBEN, WILLIAM NATHANIEL (*b. Dalton, Ga., 1858; d. New York, N.Y., 1919*), novelist.

HARBY, ISAAC (*b. Charleston, S.C., 1788; d. New York, N.Y., 1828*), journalist, playwright. A founder of Reformed Society of Israelites in Charleston, earliest American movement of its kind.

HARDEE, WILLIAM JOSEPH (*b. Camden Co., Ga., 1815; d. Wytheville, Va., 1873*), Confederate soldier. Graduated West Point, 1838. Served ably in Mexican War and as commandant of cadets, West Point, 1856–61. Author of a textbook on infantry tactics. Identified through Civil War with Army of Tennessee, he rose by merit to lieutenant-general, 1862. Noted for personal bravery.

HARDENBERGH, HENRY JANEWAY (*b. New Brunswick, N.J., 1847; d. 1918*), architect. Trained in office of Detlef Lienau; designed old Waldorf and Astoria hotels, also the Plaza Hotel, New York. The Fine Arts building, New York (1896), is characteristic of his best work.

HARDENBERGH, JACOB RUTSEN (*b. Rosendale, N.Y., 1736; d. 1790*), Dutch Reformed clergyman, Revolutionary patriot, first president of Rutgers College, 1786–90. A leader of the Coetus faction, advocating independence from the church in Holland, he brought about chartering of Queens (now Rutgers) College, 1766.

HARDEY, Mother MARY ALOYSIA (*b. Piscataway, Md., 1809; d. Paris, France, 1886*), religious of the Society of the Sacred Heart. Co-founder of the first Eastern convent of her congregation at New York, 1841; established many other foundations and served as a provincial and assistant-general of the Society.

HARDIE, JAMES ALLEN (*b. New York, N.Y., 1823; d. Washington, D.C., 1876*), Union major-general. Graduated West Point, 1843. Served in Mexican War and in California, Oregon and at Eastern posts. A very able staff officer with the Army of the Potomac in the Civil War, he was later chief of the Inspector-General's office.

HARDIN, BEN (*b. Westmoreland Co., Pa., 1784; d. 1852*), lawyer. Nephew of John Hardin. Raised near Springfield, Ky. Practiced law *post* 1808 in Bardstown, Ky. An active Kentucky legislator and a congressman, Whig, for five terms between 1815 and 1837.

HARDIN, CHARLES HENRY (*b. Trimble Co., Ky., 1820; d. 1892*), lawyer, Missouri legislator, philanthropist. Democratic reform governor of Missouri, 1875–77.

HARDIN, JOHN (*b. Fauquier Co., Va., 1753; d. at site of Hardin, O., 1792*), Revolutionary soldier, Indian fighter. Settled in present Washington Co., Ky., 1786. Served thereafter, until his murder by the Miamis, on every punitive expedition into Indian territory with the exception of St. Clair's.

HARDIN, JOHN J. (*b. Frankfort, Ky., 1810; d. in battle of Buena Vista, Mexico, 1847*), lawyer, soldier. Son of Martin D. Hardin. Settled in Jacksonville, Ill., c. 1831. Rival of Abraham Lincoln for Whig leadership in Illinois legislature and for election to Congress, 1845–46.

HARDIN, MARTIN D. (*b. Pennsylvania, 1780; d. 1823*), lawyer. Son of John Hardin. Raised in Kentucky and practiced in Frankfort; served in state legislature and briefly as U.S. senator, National Democrat, 1816–17.

HARDING, ABNER CLARK (*b. East Hampton, Conn., 1807; d. Monmouth, Ill., 1874*), lawyer, financier, railroad builder, Union soldier. Removed to Illinois, 1838. Congressman, Republican, from Illinois, 1865–69.

HARDING, CHESTER (*b. Conway, Mass., 1792; d. Boston, Mass., 1866*), portrait painter. After a varied career as chair maker, drum manufacturer, tavern keeper, and itinerant house and sign painter, Harding settled as a self-schooled portrait painter in Paris, Ky. His success there and later in St. Louis, Mo., Washington, D.C., and Northampton, Mass., encouraged him to attempt Boston. There, after six busy months of "Harding fever" (a term coined by Gilbert Stuart whose popularity was momentarily eclipsed), he earned enough to go to England, 1823, where he had a great social success. Finding that his family were not received in the circles where he moved, he returned to Boston, 1826, and settled permanently at Springfield, Mass. His portraits of American celebrities, ranging in time from Daniel Boone to W. T. Sherman, are now in most important collections.

HARDING, GEORGE (*b. Philadelphia, Pa., 1827; d. 1902*), patent lawyer. Son of Jesper Harding. Prominent in litigation over Morse telegraph, McCormick reaper, and a series of cases involving manufacture of fat acids and glycerin.

HARDING, JESPER (*b. Philadelphia, Pa., 1799; d. Philadelphia, 1865*), printer, publisher. Editor-proprietor of *Pennsylvania* (later *Philadelphia*) *Inquirer*, post 1829; was largest printer of Bibles in the United States.

HARDING, ROBERT (*b. Nottinghamshire, England, 1701; d. 1772*), Jesuit priest. Entered Society of Jesus, 1722; worked as missionary in Maryland, 1732–49; pastor, St. Joseph's, Philadelphia, 1749–72. Prominent in civic and intellectual life of Pennsylvania.

HARDING, SETH (*b. Eastham, Mass., 1734; d. Schoharie, N.Y., 1814*), naval officer. In June 1776, commanding brig *Defence*, he took 3 British transports in Massachusetts Bay, providing Washington with badly needed military stores; later commanded *Oliver Cromwell, Confederacy*.

HARDING, WARREN GAMALIEL (*b. Caledonia, now Blooming Grove, O., 1865; d. San Francisco,*

Calif., 1923), newspaper publisher, politician, president of the United States. Purchased the weekly Marion, O., *Star*, 1884; as the town grew and prospered, so did the paper. Florence Kling De Wolfe, a widow whom he married, 1891, helped him transform it into a daily. Harding grew in importance too, becoming director of local corporations. Genial, "community-minded," he fitted the small-town environment in every respect. A state senator, Republican, 1898–1902, through the efforts of Harry M. Daugherty he was elected lieutenant-governor of Ohio, 1903. At the close of his undistinguished term he retired from politics until 1910 when he was defeated for governor. Always friendly to the machine elements of his party, and celebrated for the kind of empty oratory that pleased the unthinking, he was elected U.S. senator, 1914, under Daugherty's guidance. During six years in the Senate he was a safe conservative member, a defender of big business and attached to standard Republican policies.

National reaction from tensions of World War I made Harding with his conservative, cautious nationalism, limited ideas and amiable temperament a potential presidential candidate. Daugherty, at the head of the Ohio Republican machine, began a campaign in his behalf. Nominated at Chicago, June 1920, through agreement of a little two-o'clock-in-the-morning group of Republican senators, he was elected 29th president over the Democrat James M. Cox after a confused and equivocal campaign. His cabinet was a strange mixture of distinguished men, mediocrities, and politicians largely unfit for their offices, such as Daugherty (attorney-general) and Albert M. Fall (secretary of the interior). His policies were less his own than those of the Republican Senate leaders and the three strongest cabinet members, Charles E. Hughes, Andrew Mellon and Herbert Hoover. Soft mentally, he bowed to authority; moreover, his close associates were an inferior, predatory and disreputable set. His tariff policy, his reduction of taxes policy and his handling of labor and farm problems were all misguided, but his worst single error was his failure to guard the public domain from marauders who acted with the connivance of Secretary of the Interior Fall. In the preliminary steps to calling the Washington Conference, November 1921 (the one memorable achievement of his administration), Harding responded to rather than led Congress.

By spring 1923, difficulties were thickening fast around the president. The administration's legislative program was crippled by a precarious Republican congressional majority; the farm block of radical Republicans held a balance of power with resultant political confusion. Rumors of corruption, extortion, and wholesale looting in high places, and the existence of an illegitimate child added to Harding's anxieties. In June 1923, the president, his wife and a large party set off on a transcontinental tour. Returning from Alaska in July after receipt of a long message in code

which deeply disturbed him, he was taken ill in San Francisco and died there on August 2. After a few months, a series of public investigations, of which the chief was an inquiry by the committee under Sen. Thomas J. Walsh into leases to private parties of naval oil reserves by Secretary Fall, revealed how Harding had been victimized by treachery and corruption in his administration. Fall was sent to prison; Attorney-General Daugherty escaped prison by a hair; others resigned under fire. These exposures, continuing for several years, disclosed a looseness and dishonesty in government which paralleled the post-Civil War era. A heavy responsibility for Harding's record, however, falls upon the party and the nation which elected a man of moderate abilities, weak judgment and lack of vigilance to so exacting an office. It was his cruel misfortune to be lifted to a post beyond his powers.

HARDING, WILLIAM PROCTER GOULD (*b. Greene Co., Ala., 1864; d. 1930*), banker. Grandson of Chester Harding. Federal Reserve Board governor, 1916–22, during difficult period of war and postwar instability. Author of *The Formative Period of the Federal Reserve System* (1925).

HARDING, WILLIAM WHITE (*b. Philadelphia, Pa., 1830; d. Philadelphia, 1889*), publisher. Son of Jesper Harding. Succeeded him as publisher of *Philadelphia Inquirer*, 1859, and built it into a model journal. He was also identified with first attempts to make paper from wood.

HARDY, ARTHUR SHERBURNE (*b. Andover, Mass., 1847; d. Woodstock, Conn., 1930*), mathematician, novelist, diplomat.

HARDY, SAMUEL (*b. Isle of Wight Co., Va., c. 1758; d. New York, N.Y., 1785*), lawyer, statesman. Member of Virginia House of Delegates and of Privy Council; briefly lieutenant-governor of Virginia, 1782. Virginia delegate to Continental Congress, 1783–85.

HARDY, WILLIAM HARRIS (*b. Collirene, Ala., 1837; d. Gulfport, Miss., 1917*), lawyer, jurist, journalist. Promoted New Orleans and Northeastern, and Gulf and Ship Island railroads to develop the Mississippi pine belt and Gulf Coast regions. Founded Hattiesburg and Gulfport.

HARE, GEORGE EMLEN (*b. Philadelphia, Pa., 1808; d. Philadelphia, 1892*), Episcopal clergyman, educator. Graduated Union, 1826; ordained, 1830; pastor in Princeton, N.J., and Philadelphia. Headmaster, Academy of Protestant Episcopal Church, Philadelphia, 1846–57; headed, *post* 1857, institution which became Divinity School of Protestant Episcopal Church, Philadelphia.

HARE, JOHN INNES CLARK (*b. 1816; d. Philadelphia, Pa., 1905*), Philadelphia jurist. Son of Robert Hare. Made important contribution to establishment of equity as general system in Pennsylvania.

HARE, ROBERT (*b. Philadelphia, Pa., 1781; d. 1858*), chemist, teacher. Studied with James Woodhouse; friend and associate of Benjamin Silliman. His important inventions included the oxy-hydrogen blowpipe (1801), the calorimotor, the use of the mercury cathode in electrolysis, and an electric furnace. He also did pioneer work on the constitution of salts.

HARE, WILLIAM HOBART (*b. Princeton, N.J., 1838; d. Atlantic City, N.J., 1909*), Episcopal clergyman. Son of George E. Hare; nephew of John H. Hobart. *Post* 1872, missionary bishop in the Sioux country north of Niobrara River; his diocese was later limited to South Dakota.

HARGROVE, ROBERT KENNON (*b. Pickens Co., Ala., 1829; d. Nashville, Tenn., 1905*), bishop of Methodist Episcopal Church, South; president, board of trust, Vanderbilt University, 1889–1905.

HARKNESS, ALBERT (*b. Mendon, Mass., 1822; d. 1907*), classical scholar. Graduated Brown, 1842; Ph.D., University of Bonn, 1854. Professor of Greek at Brown, 1855–92. Author of Latin textbooks, notably *Latin Grammar* (1865; revised, 1898). A founder of American School of Classical Studies, Athens.

HARKNESS, EDWARD STEPHEN (*b. Cleveland, O., 1874; d. New York, N.Y., 1940*), philanthropist. Son of S. V. Harkness, an associate and partner of John D. Rockefeller, Sr. As president of the family-established Commonwealth Fund, Edward Harkness directed many grants in the fields of health and education. He was largely responsible for the establishment of the Columbia-Presbyterian Medical Center, New York, financing the affiliation of the two institutions, giving the land for the site, and endowing the hospital. His interest in the decentralization of large educational institutions led to vast gifts for that purpose to Harvard, Yale, and Phillips Exeter Academy. His British benefactions included establishing the Pilgrim Trust. [*Supp. 2*]

HARKNESS, WILLIAM (*b. Ecclefechan, Scotland, 1837; d. Jersey City, N.J., 1903*), astronomer. Came to America as a child. Associated with U.S. Naval Observatory, 1862–99; was director, *post* 1894.

HARLAN, JAMES (*b. Harlan Station, Ky., 1800; d. 1863*), lawyer, legislator. Congressman, Whig, from Kentucky, 1835–39; held many state offices, including secretary of state and attorney-general; opposed secession.

HARLAN, JAMES (*b. Clark Co., Ill., 1820; d. 1899*), lawyer, teacher, college president. Raised on Indiana frontier; settled in Iowa, 1845. U.S. senator, Free-Soil, 1855–61; Republican, 1861–65, 1867–73. During inept term as U.S. secretary of the interior, 1865–66, dismissed Walt Whitman from Indian Office in economy move.

HARLAN, JOHN MARSHALL (*b. Boyle Co., Ky., 1833; d. 1911*), jurist. Son of James Harlan (1800–1863). Graduated Centre College, 1850. Elected county court judge, 1858, his only judicial position prior to Supreme Court appointment. Southern by tradition, a Whig and a slave-holder, he raised and commanded the 10th Kentucky Volunteer Infantry and served on the Union side from 1861 until his father's death in 1863; thereafter until 1867 he served as Kentucky attorney-general. Firm for the Union, he was a bitter critic of Lincoln's administration; after 1866, however, he cast his lot with the radical Republicans. In 1871 and 1875 he was defeated for governor. Heading the Kentucky delegation to the Republican National Convention in 1876, he threw its support to R. B. Hayes. As a reward, President Hayes named him to the U.S. Supreme Court where he assumed his seat Dec. 11, 1877. His tenure until 1911 made him a participant in the constitutional controversies of a third of a century. During this time he wrote the opinion of the Court in 703 cases. His legal philosophy was built on an almost religious reverence for the Constitution; he believed that the Constitution—and all legislation—should be construed in accordance with the framers' intention and the dictates of common sense. He tried to hold an even course between strong nationalism and state rights, a balance of conflicting pressures evident in his opinions on specific constitutional problems. His famous dissent (1895) in the income-tax cases (*Pollock vs. Farmer's Loan and Trust Co.*, 158 U.S., 601) was a protest against what he regarded as impairment of the vital power of national taxation. But he also believed that firm protection should be given the police power of the states. Therefore, he dissented in a series of cases, including the famous "original package case," in which the states' power to keep intoxicating liquor from being shipped in through channels of interstate commerce was cut down or denied. He supported this principle also in his dissent from the Court's judgment in *Lochner vs. New York*.

A stern defender of civil liberty, Harlan believed that the constitutional guarantees in its behalf should be strictly construed. This is apparent in his numerous opinions interpreting the clause forbidding impairment of contracts by states or municipalities. He had profound reverence for the jury system and its attributes. For him the Constitution "followed the flag," and he could not conceive of any American territory being deprived protection of the fundamental law. He rendered valiant service in helping discredit the "natural rights" philosophy which Justice Field had struggled to engraft upon American constitutional law and resented with all his vigor what seemed to him judicial legislation.

His first dissent like his last ones, written a few months before his death in the Standard Oil and American Tobacco Co. cases, were all strong denunciations of judicial legislation. It is as the "great dissenter," vigorous, uncompromising, often bitter, that he will be remembered; altogether he dissented in 316 cases. Justice Harlan served as an American representative in the Bering Sea arbitration with Great Britain, 1892, and lectured on constitutional law at Columbian (George Washington) University, 1889–1910.

HARLAN, JOSIAH (*b. Chester County, Pa., 1799; d. San Francisco, Calif., 1871*), physician, soldier, adventurer. Brother of Richard Harlan. Recounted his exploits as secret agent and Afghan general in *A Memoir of India and Afghanistan* (1842).

HARLAN, RICHARD (*b. Philadelphia, Pa., 1796; d. New Orleans, La., 1843*), naturalist, physician. Brother of Josiah Harlan. His major interests were zoölogy and vertebrate paleontology. A prolific writer, his most notable work was *Fauna Americana* (1825), first systematic treatise on American mammals.

HARLAND, HENRY (*b. St. Petersburg, Russia, 1861; d. San Remo, Italy, 1905*), novelist. Raised in New York City. Editor, *The Yellow Book* (London), 1894–97; author, among other works, of *As It Was Written* (under pseudonym, "Sidney Luska," 1885), *The Cardinal's Snuff Box* (1900) and *My Friend Prospero* (1904).

HARLAND, MARION. [See TERHUNE, MARY VIRGINIA, 1830–1922.]

HARLAND, THOMAS (*b. England, 1735; d. 1807*), watch and clock maker, silversmith. Established in Norwich, Conn., *post* 1773. Eli Terry was one of his apprentices.

HARLOW, JEAN (*b. Kansas City, Mo., 1911; d. Los Angeles, Calif., 1937*), "platinum blonde" motion-picture actress; star of *Hell's Angels* (1930), *Bombshell* (1933). [*Supp. 2*]

HARMAR, JOSIAH (*b. Philadelphia, Pa., 1753; d. 1813*), soldier. An able Revolutionary officer, he served as commander of the U.S. Army, 1784–91. His 1790 campaign against the Indians in the Maumee valley was a failure.

HARMON, DANIEL WILLIAMS (*b. Bennington, Vt., 1778; d. Montreal, Canada, 1845*), fur trader, explorer. Recorded his experiences as employee and partner of the North-West Co. in *Journal of Voyages and Travels in the Interior of North America* (1820).

HARMON, JUDSON (*b. Newtown, O., 1846; d. Cincinnati, O., 1927*), jurist. Graduated Denison, 1866; Cincinnati Law School, 1869. Practiced in Cincinnati. U.S. attorney-general, 1895–97; Democratic governor of Ohio, 1909–13. An able, conservative reformer.

HARNDEN, WILLIAM FREDERICK (*b. Reading, Mass., 1812; d. 1845*), pioneer expressman. Began parcel service between New York and Boston, 1839; prospered and opened European offices for shipping

and exchange. Facilitated movement of 100,000 immigrants to United States.

HARNETT, CORNELIUS (*b. probably Chowan Co., N.C., 1723?; d. Wilmington, N.C., 1781*), Revolutionary statesman, "the Samuel Adams of North Carolina." Member of the Assembly, 1754–75; president of N.C. Provincial Congress, 1776; put state on war basis. Served three terms in Continental Congress.

HARNEY, BENJAMIN ROBERTSON (*b. near Middleboro, Ky., 1871; d. Philadelphia, Pa., 1938*), early composer of "ragtime music," which he played and sang in vaudeville. His "You've Been a Good Old Wagon" (1895) was probably the first piece of ragtime to be printed. [*Supp. 2*]

HARNEY, WILLIAM SELBY (*b. Haysboro, Tenn., 1800; d. Orlando, Fla., 1889*), soldier. Commissioned lieutenant in 1st Infantry, 1818. Served on numerous expeditions against Florida Indians. Promoted colonel, 1846, he was ranking cavalry officer under Gen. Scott who tried, unsuccessfully, to remove Harney from his command. Harney displayed brilliant, heroic leadership in the war with Mexico. Stationed later in the Platte country, he defeated the Sioux at Sand Hill. Given command of the Department of Oregon and promoted brigadier, 1858, he was soon recalled because of anti-British proclivities and commanded the Department of the West at St. Louis until 1861. Suspected of Southern sympathies, he was superseded and given no active duty during the Civil War. He was retired in 1863.

HARPER, FLETCHER (*b. Newtown, New York, 1806; d. 1877*), printer, publisher. With James, John, and Joseph Wesley Harper, was partner in Harper & Brothers. Created *Harper's Weekly* (1857), which exerted strong political influence; also *Harper's Bazar* (1867).

HARPER, IDA HUSTED (*b. Fairfield, Ind., 1851; d. Washington, D.C., 1931*), journalist, author. Historian of woman's suffrage movement in which she was prominent.

HARPER, JAMES (*b. Newtown, New York, 1795; d. 1869*), printer, publisher. Started printing business in 1817 which, with his brothers Fletcher, John and Joseph Wesley Harper as partners, was first known as J. and J. Harper and as Harper & Brothers, *post* 1833. Originated *Harper's New Monthly Magazine* (1850). Elected reform mayor, New York City, 1844.

HARPER, JOHN (1797–1875). [See HARPER, JAMES, 1795–1869.]

HARPER, JOHN LYELL (*b. Harpersfield, N.Y., 1873; d. Niagara Falls, N.Y., 1924*), mechanical and electrical engineer, specialist in hydroelectric work. Graduated Cornell, 1897. Chief engineer, Niagara Falls Hydraulic Power & Manufacturing Co., *post* 1904; chief engineer, Niagara Falls Power Co., *post* 1918. His most important achievement was designing and constructing the company's hydroelectric power plant in the gorge below the Falls, largest in the world at that time. He served as chief engineer of other companies and patented several electric furnaces, one being the Harper Electric Furnace for commercial firing of ceramic materials.

HARPER, JOSEPH WESLEY (1801–1870). [See HARPER, JAMES, 1795–1869.]

HARPER, ROBERT FRANCIS (*b. New Concord, O., 1864; d. London, England, 1914*), Assyriologist. Brother of William R. Harper. Graduated University of Chicago, 1883; Ph.D., Leipzig, 1886. Taught at Yale and University of Chicago. Edited monumental *Assyrian and Babylonian Letters Belonging to the Kouyunjik Collections of the British Museum* (14 vols., 1892–1914).

HARPER, ROBERT GOODLOE (*b. near Fredericksburg, Va., 1765; d. Baltimore, Md., 1825*), lawyer, Federalist politician. Graduated Princeton, 1785. Practiced law and entered politics in South Carolina; served in legislature and as congressman, 1795–1801. Elected as a (Democrat) Republican, he almost immediately shifted allegiance and became leader of the Federalists, publishing in 1797 his *Observations on the Dispute Between the U.S. and France.* He married Catherine, daughter of Charles Carroll, 1801, and moved to Baltimore where he was a successful lawyer, prominent in civic affairs. An original member of the American Colonization Society, he was influential in selecting Africa as the place for the Society's colony and suggested Liberia and Monrovia as names for the colony and its capital.

HARPER, WILLIAM (*b. Antigua, 1790; d. 1847*), South Carolina legislator and nullification leader, judge. Graduated South Carolina College, 1808. Chancellor of Missouri Territory and state, 1819–23; chancellor of South Carolina, 1828–30, 1835–47. Author of nullification ordinance at 1832 convention. His *Memoir on Slavery* (1837) is regarded as one of the most important pro-slavery arguments.

HARPER, WILLIAM RAINEY (*b. New Concord, O., 1856; d. 1906*), Hebraist, educator. Brother of Robert F. Harper. Graduated Muskingum College, 1870; Ph.D., Yale, 1874. After work at Masonic College, Macon, Tenn., and Denison University, he taught Semitic languages at Baptist Union Theological Seminary, Chicago, 1879–86. Prominent in work at Chatauqua, *post* 1885, he gave a summer course there and was president of the college of liberal arts for several years. As a teacher at Yale, 1886–90, he multiplied his activities and won a national reputation as teacher, lecturer, organizer and editor. When, with John D. Rockefeller's encouragement, the new University of Chicago was established, Harper was named president. Before accepting the position he made plain his conception of the new university and his own position in the conflict between orthodoxy and modernism,

stipulating that there should be entire academic freedom. His plans included university extension, a university press, university affiliations, division of the year into four quarters, distinction of the two upper years of undergraduate school as the senior college, faculty control of athletics, concentration on a few studies at a time, emphasis on graduate study and research. He expounded his ideas in numerous addresses, the most significant being collected in *The Trend in Higher Education* (1905). A volume of talks to students, *Religion and the Higher Life* (1904), reveals much of his inner self and beliefs. His works on *The Priestly Element in the Old Testament* (1902) and *The Prophetic Element in the Old Testament* (1905) illustrate his enormous industry. His colleagues recognized him as a sound, if not greatly creative Semitic scholar, and a very great teacher who contributed much to the revival of Hebrew scholarship. His *Critical and Exegetical Commentary on Amos and Hosea* (1905) was favorably reviewed by experts.

From 1892 to his death, Harper's life was inseparable from that of the University of Chicago. Within two or three years he assembled a brilliant faculty, established a working library and had an adequate university functioning. He also did what few university presidents have ever done—taught full time as chairman of his department. The demands on his vitality were terrific. His days were filled with administrative problems, "campaigns" for endowment, mediation between a faculty to which he had promised full freedom and alarmed sectarians, and the swift continuous growth of the University. Though Harper was a sturdy man, no constitution could endure a regimen of incessant work, no vacations, little sleep, irregular diet and a perpetual round of dinners and speeches. An appendicitis operation revealed a cancerous infection, and in January 1906, he died.

Like all strong executives, Harper wished to have his own way because it seemed to him the efficient way; but he was always ready to listen to the other side, and was flexible in adapting himself to modifications of his plans. His was a dominating but not a domineering personality. Though a devout Christian, he remained despite calumny a champion of the rights of higher criticism.

HARPSTER, JOHN HENRY (*b. Centerhall, Pa., 1844; d. Philadelphia, Pa., 1911*), Lutheran clergyman. Missionary to India, 1872–76, 1893–1901, 1902–09.

HARPUR, ROBERT (*b. Ballybay, Ireland, 1731?; d. 1825*), educator, Revolutionary patriot, New York legislator. Professor of mathematics, librarian, tutor, King's College, New York, 1761–75; secretary, Regents of University of State of New York, 1784–87; clerk of board of trustees, Columbia College, 1787–95. Member, N.Y. Assembly, 1777–84. Founded Harpursville, N.Y.

HARRAH, CHARLES JEFFERSON (*b. Philadelphia, Pa., 1817; d. Philadelphia, 1890*), promoter, capitalist. Prominent in business in Philadelphia, and in Brazil (1843–73) where he built shipyards, railroads, and established first telegraph company, first street railroad and first public school.

HARRELL, JOHN (*b. Perquimans Co., N.C., 1806; d. 1876*), Methodist clergyman, educator. Labored *post* 1831 in western Arkansas and Indian Territory.

HARRIGAN, EDWARD (*b. New York, N.Y., 1845; d. New York, 1911*), playwright, actor, producer. Began career in California, c. 1867. Made New York début, 1870; joined Anthony Cannon ("Tony Hart,") in the famous firm of Harrigan and Hart, 1872. The most famous of Harrigan's productions began with *The Mulligan Guards* (1873). The Mulligan cycle of burlesque on Irish and German immigrant types and life had its best expression in *Cordelia's Aspirations* (1883) and *Dan's Tribulations* (1884). Besides variety sketches he wrote 39 plays, in all of which he acted the leading part. The many charming songs interspersed through his plays were set to music by his father-in-law, Dave Braham.

HARRIMAN, EDWARD HENRY (*b. Hempstead, N.Y., 1848; d. 1909*), railroad executive, capitalist. Son of an Episcopal clergyman. A Wall St. office-boy at fourteen, he bought a seat on the N.Y. stock exchange seven years later. In 1879 he married Mary Averell, whose father was an Ogdensburg, N.Y., banker and president of a railroad. This relationship aroused Harriman's interest in transportation; he began his career as rebuilder of bankrupt railroads with the Lake Ontario Southern, successfully reorganizing it, 1881–82. In 1883 he entered the Illinois Central directorate and was vice-president by 1887, a dominant influence in its financial policy. In 1895 he joined in the syndicate which reorganized the Union Pacific, and by 1898 was chairman of the executive committee; from then on his word was law on the Union Pacific system. He was responsible for restoring the physical efficiency of the road, spending $25,000,-000 on rails and rolling stock. In 1903 he became president of the Union Pacific, after fully restoring it both physically and financially. In 1901 he had begun buying into the Southern Pacific until the Union Pacific controlled 46% of the stock; this carried control of that corporation and ownership of its subsidiary, the Central Pacific, which would make possible an efficient system to the Pacific Coast. He strengthened the financial and operating conditions of both roads and evolved a brilliant administrative organization for the combined system. To secure an entrance into Chicago, he began his fight with James J. Hill of the Northern Pacific for control of the Chicago, Burlington & Quincy. Outgeneraled by Hill, Harriman began buying stock of the Northern Pacific which now held a half-interest in the Burlington. The Hill-Harriman struggle for the Northern Pacific resulted in the stock market panic of May 9, 1901. The issue was settled by organization of the Northern Securities Co. to take over the stocks of the Great Northern and the Northern Pacific with the Harriman interests represented on the board of the holding company.

When the Northern Securities Co. was condemned by the Supreme Court in 1904 for effecting a combination in restraint of trade, Harriman sold his interests in the Northwestern roads and emerged with a profit of over $50,000,000. His purchase of stocks of other railways led to an investigation of the Harriman lines by the Interstate Commerce Commission, 1906–07. The reorganization of the Chicago & Alton in 1899 was cited as an example of how a road may be drained of its resources for the benefit of insiders. The Commission's report also revealed the range of Harriman's holdings and the extent to which the Union Pacific served as a holding company for securities of other transportation companies. From the standpoint of public welfare, his offense was his use of the resources of the Union Pacific speculatively to purchase other securities instead of devoting them to the road as an agency of transportation.

Harriman's influence extended beyond railroads into banks and insurance companies. He owned a steamship line to the Orient. He was a director of the Equitable Life Assurance Society and was one of those responsible for the change in its ownership and control in 1905. The investigation which followed this change, together with the Interstate Commerce Commission report, made him in popular opinion a personification of all the evils of the existing monopolistic business situation and subjected him to a storm of abuse. Characterized as the last great individualist and the last figure of an epoch, his genius as an administrator made him one of the great railway builders of all time. Self-confident, dominant, cold and ruthless, he spared neither friend nor foe if they blocked his plans.

HARRIMAN, WALTER (*b. Warner, N.H., 1817; d. Concord, N.H., 1884*), Universalist clergyman, businessman, Union soldier. Republican governor of New Hampshire, 1867–69.

HARRINGTON, CHARLES (*b. Salem, Mass., 1856; d. Lynton, England, 1908*), Boston sanitarian, educator. Graduated Harvard, 1878; Harvard Medical School, 1881, where he taught hygiene, *post* 1885. Through his writings, he did much to arouse interest in preventive medicine.

HARRINGTON, MARK WALROD (*b. Sycamore, Ill., 1848; d. 1926*), astronomer, meteorologist, educator. First civilian chief of U.S. Weather Bureau, 1891–95. Established *American Meteorological Journal*, 1884; author of *About the Weather* (1899).

HARRINGTON, SAMUEL MAXWELL (*b. Dover, Del., 1803; d. Philadelphia, Pa., 1865*), Delaware jurist and railroad promoter.

HARRINGTON, THOMAS FRANCIS (*b. Lowell, Mass., 1866; d. 1919*), physician, hygienist. Graduated Harvard Medical School, 1888; practiced in Lowell and Boston. Author of a standard history, *The Harvard Medical School* (1905). Pioneer of hygienic physical culture in public schools.

HARRIS, BENJAMIN (*fl. 1673–1716*), bookseller, publisher, author, first American journalist. After a career in London where he was associated with Shaftesbury and the Whigs as an anti-Catholic and anti-court propagandist, he came to New England, 1686. Successful as bookseller and publisher in Boston, he brought out on Sept. 25, 1690, the first newspaper printed in America, *Publick Occurrences Both Foreign and Domestick,* remarkable because the news was chiefly American. The first issue was suppressed by the governor and the council "because not licensed." Sometime before 1690, Harris had published *The New England Primer,* one of the most popular and influential books ever printed in America. Established as the leading publisher and bookseller of 17th-century America, he returned to London, 1695, and was active as journalist and publisher until 1716.

HARRIS, CALEB FISKE (*b. Warwick, R.I., 1818; d. Moosehead Lake, Maine, 1881*), merchant, bibliophile. The American poetry collection formed by him was presented to Brown University Library, 1884.

HARRIS, CHAPIN AARON (*b. Pompey, N.Y., 1806; d. Baltimore, Md., 1860*), dentist, editor. One of the founders of dentistry as an organized profession; practiced in Baltimore from 1839 until his death. Author of *The Dental Art, a Practical Treatise on Dental Surgery* (1839), perhaps the most popular dental textbook ever written. With several New York dentists, established in 1839 the world's first dental periodical, the *American Journal of Dental Science.* With Horace H. Hayden, organized the world's first dental college, the Baltimore College of Dental Surgery, chartered 1840. Harris helped organize the first national dental association, the American Society of Dental Surgeons, also in 1840. His many valuable articles and books include *A Dictionary of Dental Science, Biography, Bibliography and Medical Terminology* (1849).

HARRIS, CHARLES KASSELL (*b. Poughkeepsie, N.Y., 1865; d. New York, N.Y., 1930*), song writer, music publisher. Composed many sentimental popular ballads, of which the most famous were "After the Ball" (1892) and "Break the News to Mother" (1897).

HARRIS, DANIEL LESTER (*b. Providence, R.I., 1818; d. Springfield, Mass., 1879*), engineer, Massachusetts legislator. Notable in railroad and bridge construction; president, Connecticut River Railroad, c. 1855–79.

HARRIS, ELISHA (*b. Westminster, Vt., 1824; d. 1884*), pioneer sanitarian. Graduated College of Physicians and Surgeons, New York, 1849. Practiced in New York; was superintendent of New York quarantine hospital; helped organize U.S. Sanitary Commission, 1861. Designed a hospital car to relieve Civil War wounded and also originated an effective national system of records of death and burial of soldiers. Served as registrar of records of New York's board of health and sanitary superintendent of the city. In 1869 he organized the first free public vaccination service. He was an organizer of the American Public Health Association, 1872, becoming president in 1877. In 1880 he was appointed secretary of the new New York State Board of Health and state superintendent of vital statistics.

HARRIS, GEORGE (*b. East Machias, Maine, 1844; d. 1922*), Congregational minister, educator. Nephew of Samuel Harris. Professor of theology, Andover Theological Seminary, 1883–99; president, Amherst College, 1899–1912.

HARRIS, GEORGE WASHINGTON (*b. Allegheny City, Pa., 1814; d. 1869*), humorist. Raised in Knoxville, Tenn. A metal craftsman and engineer by profession, he contributed humorous sketches post 1843 to Porter's *Spirit of the Times.* His *Sut Lovingood Yarns* (1867) and many uncollected humorous sketches delineate the localisms, dialect, thoughts, and superstitions of the East Tennessee mountain people.

HARRIS, IRA (*b. Charleston, N.Y., 1802; d. Albany, N.Y., 1875*), jurist, New York legislator, legal educator. Justice, state supreme court, 1847–59; U.S. senator, Republican, from New York, 1861–67.

HARRIS, ISHAM GREEN (*b. near Tullahoma, Tenn., 1818; d. 1897*), lawyer, Confederate soldier, politician. Congressman, Democrat, from Tennessee, 1849–53. As governor of that state, 1857–63 (and nominally until 1865), he urged secession and committed Tennessee to the Confederacy by a series of legislative maneuvers, 1861. Post 1867, he practiced law in Memphis. Elected to the U.S. Senate, 1877, he served until his death.

HARRIS, JAMES ARTHUR (*b. near Plantsville, O., 1880; d. St. Paul, Minn., 1930*), botanist, biometrician. Raised in Kansas. Graduated University of Kansas, 1901; Ph.D., Washington University, St. Louis, 1903. Botanical investigator, Station for Experimental Evolution, Carnegie Institution of Washington, 1907–24; head of botany department, University of Minnesota, 1924–30. Adapted exact techniques of physics and chemistry to study of plant geography. Collaborated with Bureau of Plant Industry, U.S. Department of Agriculture, 1918–30, on problems of cotton and cereal growing in arid and semi-arid regions. Interested early in the application of mathematics to biology, he became America's leading exponent of and contributor to biometric theory and practice. His papers, numbering over 300 titles, include topics pertaining to almost every field of the biological sciences.

HARRIS, JOEL CHANDLER (*b. near Eatonton, Ga., 1848; d. Atlanta, Ga., 1908*), journalist, author. Learned to set type on the weekly *Countryman*, published near his home by the planter Joseph A. Turner. Turner lent him books, schooled him in writing and gave him the run of the plantation, whence came his sympathetic knowledge of the Negro dialect and folkways. After varied newspaper experience, 1864–76, Harris was on the staff of the *Atlanta Constitution*, 1876–1900. He published *Uncle Remus: His Songs and His Sayings* in 1880. This volume and its continuation *Nights with Uncle Remus* (1883) are among the unforgettable books of American literature. A whole cycle of Uncle Remus books followed. He also produced several volumes of children's stories, a few poems, magazine articles and many short stories which were republished in book form, the best of which appear in the collections *Mingo and Other Sketches in Black and White* (1884) and *Free Joe and Other Georgian Sketches* (1887).

HARRIS, JOHN (*b. Harris Ferry, Pa., 1726; d. Harrisburg, Pa., 1791*), Revolutionary soldier, Indian trader. Founder of Harrisburg, Pa.

HARRIS, JOHN WOODS (*b. Nelson Co., Va., 1810; d. Galveston, Texas, 1887*), lawyer. Graduated University of Virginia, 1837. Removed to Texas, 1837. Served in Congress of the Texas Republic, where he had profound influence in framing the laws; was later first attorney-general of the State of Texas.

HARRIS, JOSEPH (*b. Shrewsbury, England, 1828; d. near Rochester, N.Y., 1892*), scientific agriculturist, editor. Came to America, 1849. Edited *Genesee Farmer;* partner of Orange Judd in *American Agriculturist*. Among his books are *Harris on the Pig* (1870) and *Talks on Manures* (1878).

HARRIS, MAURICE HENRY (*b. London, England, 1859; d. 1930*), rabbi. Came to America, c. 1878. Graduated Columbia, 1887; Ph.D., 1889. Minister of Hand in Hand Synagogue (later Temple Israel), New York; a founder of Jewish Institute of Religion; active in social work.

HARRIS, MERRIMAN COLBERT (*b. Beallsville, O., 1846; d. Aoyama, Japan, 1921*), missionary bishop of Methodist Episcopal Church. In Japan, 1873–86; established Pacific Coast and Hawaiian missions, 1886–1904; bishop of Japan and Korea, 1904–16.

HARRIS, MIRIAM COLES (*b. Dosoris, N.Y., 1834; d. Pau, France, 1925*), author. Her many novels, popular in the late 19th century, are all of the same melodramatic type. Her reputation rests on *Rutledge* (1860).

HARRIS, NATHANIEL HARRISON (*b. Natchez, Miss., 1834; d. Malvern, England, 1900*), lawyer, Confederate brigadier-general.

HARRIS, ROLLIN ARTHUR (*b. Randolph, N.Y., 1863; d. 1918*), oceanographer, mathematician. Graduated Cornell, 1885; Ph.D., 1888. Entered U.S. Coast and Geodetic Survey as computer, 1890. Author of the valuable "Manual of Tides" which appeared serially in the Survey Reports, 1894–1907.

HARRIS, SAMUEL (*b. East Machias, Maine, 1814; d. Litchfield, Conn., 1899*), Congregational clergyman, theologian, educator. Graduated Bowdoin, 1833; studied at Andover Theological Seminary, 1835–38. Professor, Bangor (Maine) Seminary, 1855–67. President of Bowdoin, 1867–71. Resigned to become Dwight professor of systematic theology, Yale Divinity School, 1871–95. Author of *The Philosophical Basis of Theism* (1883), which made a deep impression, and *The Self-Revelation of God* (1887), which carried his philosophical argument into the domain of doctrinal theology; also of *God: The Creator and Lord of All* (1896). He occupied a transitional position between the old dialectical New England theology and the more modern school.

HARRIS, THADDEUS MASON (*b. Charlestown, Mass., 1768; d. 1842*), Unitarian clergyman, author, editor. Graduated Harvard, 1787. Pastor of First Church in Dorchester, Mass., 1793–1836. Librarian, Harvard College, 1791–93, and of Massachusetts Historical Society, 1837–42.

HARRIS, THADDEUS WILLIAM (*b. Dorchester, Mass., 1795; d. 1856*), entomologist, librarian. Son of Thaddeus M. Harris. Graduated Harvard, 1815; M.D., 1820. Interest in entomology inspired by W. D. Peck. Librarian, Harvard College, 1831–56. Became a member of the scientific commission to make a geological and botanical survey of Massachusetts, 1837; from this experience came his classic *Report on the Insects of Massachusetts Injurious to Vegetation* (1841 and later revisions). Probably no 19th-century American work on natural history was better done and the trend of American entomology toward the practical stems from it. Harris's bibliography covers 120 titles on entomological subjects and eight other titles. He is generally considered the father of economic entomology in the United States.

HARRIS, THOMAS LAKE (*b. Fenny Stratford, England, 1823; d. New York, N.Y., 1906*), Universalist clergyman, spiritualist. Founded "Brotherhood of the New Life" and its colony "The Use," located first in New York and *post* 1875 at Santa Rosa, Calif.

HARRIS, TOWNSEND (*b. Sandy Hill, N.Y., 1804; d. New York, N.Y., 1878*), merchant, politician, diplomat. As president, New York City Board of Education, 1846–48, he managed the legislation for College of City of New York. Appointed consul-general to Japan, 1855, and minister-resident, 1859, he negotiated earliest U.S. treaties with Japan, 1857–58. Honest and moderate as he showed himself, no foreigner in the East ever so quickly attained such influence over the government of an Oriental people. He resigned his post in 1860.

HARRIS, WILEY POPE (*b. Pike Co., Miss., 1818; d. Jackson, Miss., 1891*), lawyer, judge, congressman.

HARRIS, WILLIAM (*b. Springfield, Mass., 1765; d. 1829*), Episcopal clergyman. Graduated Harvard, 1786. Rector, St. Mark's-in-the-Bowery, New York City, 1802–16. President, Columbia College, 1811–29.

HARRIS, WILLIAM ALEXANDER (*b. Loudoun Co., Va., 1841; d. Chicago, Ill., 1909*), Confederate soldier, engineer, stockman. Imported Scotch Shorthorns and bred a famous herd near Lawrence, Kans.; Congressman, Populist and Democrat, from Kansas, 1893–95; U.S. senator, 1897–1903.

HARRIS, WILLIAM LITTLETON (*b. Elbert Co., Ga., 1807; d. Memphis, Tenn., 1868*), Mississippi jurist.

HARRIS, WILLIAM LOGAN (*b. near Mansfield, O., 1817; d. Brooklyn, N.Y., 1887*), Methodist clergyman. Secretary of General Conferences, 1856–72; elected bishop, 1872; served as secretary to the board of bishops.

HARRIS, WILLIAM TORREY (*b. near North Killingly, Conn., 1835; d. Providence, R.I., 1909*), educator, philosopher. Attended Yale; began to teach in public schools, St. Louis, Mo., 1857, and was appointed superintendent, 1868. After dabbling in mesmerism, spiritualism and phrenology, he took up study of Hegel under influence of Henry C. Brokmeyer; found life-work in exposition of Hegel's thought and application of his principles especially to education. Founded *Journal of Speculative Philosophy*, 1867, in which German thought was critically presented and in which Royce, Peirce, James and Dewey made debuts as writers. Harris helped establish the Concord (Mass.) School of Philosophy, 1880. After its failure, as U.S. commissioner of education, 1889–1906, he labored to put education on a psychological basis and to relate schools to other departments of institutional life. His *Introduction to the Study of Philosophy* (1889) is the best approach to his views.

HARRISON, ALEXANDER. [See HARRISON, THOMAS ALEXANDER, 1853–1930.]

HARRISON, BENJAMIN (*b. Charles City Co., Va., 1726?; d. 1791*), planter, Revolutionary statesman. Grandson of Robert Carter of Corotoman. Member, Virginia House of Burgesses, 1749–74; of Continental Congress, 1774–77; of Virginia House of Delegates, 1777–81. A signer of the Declaration of Independence. Governor of Virginia, 1781–84. Re-elected to the House of Delegates, he served until his death.

HARRISON, BENJAMIN (*b. North Bend, near Cincinnati, O., 1833; d. Indianapolis, Ind., 1901*), lawyer, statesman, president of the United States. Grandson of William H. Harrison. Graduated Miami University, 1852. Settled in Indianapolis, Ind., 1854; practiced law; entered politics as a Republican. Elected city attorney, 1857; elected, 1860 and 1864, reporter of Indiana supreme court. Colonel of the 70th Indiana Infantry, 1862, he rose to brigade rank on merit; after the Civil War he returned to his profession and built up a lucrative practice, maintaining interest in public affairs and local philanthropy, but regarded as austere and cold in personal relationships. An ardent radical Republican during Johnson's presidency, he fought for sound money and helped keep Indiana Republicans from supporting "Greenback" doctrines. Defeated for governor in 1876, he drew national attention; as chairman of the Indiana delegation to the Republican National Convention, 1880, he played a leading role in James A. Garfield's nomination. A member of the U.S. Senate, 1881–87, he was chairman of the committee on territories and generally aligned himself with the moderate, progressive group of his party. He supported railroad regulation, labor legislation, protective tariff and increased pensions.

Harrison's friends began in 1887 a campaign which secured him the Republican presidential nomination at Chicago in 1888. He set a precedent by conducting a "front porch" campaign, making many short speeches to visiting delegations. He received in the electoral college 233 votes to 169 for Grover Cleveland (although the latter's popular plurality was 100,000), and became the 23rd president of the United States. James G. Blaine was named secretary of state, but most of the other cabinet appointees were little known in national politics, and some were obnoxious to the reform element in the Republican party. Appreciative of the forces sweeping the nation into imperialism, Harrison took pride in the navy of steel ships being built under Secretary Benjamin Tracy and in his own policy of building a merchant marine. The Pan-American Congress was brilliantly conducted by Blaine, who also pushed American claims in Samoa and received credit for the result although his hand was guided by the president. Civil-service reform proved troublesome to Harrison. Though elected on a reform platform, the hunger of his party for office was great. His attempt at a middle course aroused the antipathy of reformers and politicians alike, for which he suffered in the 1892 campaign. His repugnance to wield the "big stick" caused him to avoid policies distinct from those his party advocated in Congress, and he was not skillful in arousing public opinion in support of legislation he desired. His reserved manner limited his influence with congressmen of his party which from 1888 to 1891 was in the hands of leaders he could not control. Important laws passed during his administration included the McKinley Tariff Act (in which he insisted on a reciprocity provision), the Sherman Silver Act and the Sherman Anti-Trust Act. As a result of Republican legislation and general economic conditions, the federal treasury surplus disappeared and the panic of 1893 was foreshadowed. Moved to seek renomination in 1892 in resentment of the virulent hostility of the Republican bosses, Harrison was soundly defeated by Cleveland. The enmity of labor, the apathy of the Republican bosses, resentment of the McKinley Tariff, and many other factors contributed to his defeat. No other ex-president, however, resumed the practice of law so successfully as Harrison. He was senior counsel for Venezuela before the arbitration tribunal in Paris (1899) in the boundary dispute with England, presenting a masterly closing argument. During his last years he gave his influence to the liberal side of national and international problems, condemned extremes of imperialism and emphasized the obligations of wealth.

HARRISON, BIRGE. [See HARRISON, LOVELL BIRGE, 1854–1929.]

HARRISON, CARTER HENRY (b. near Lexington, Ky., 1825; d. 1893), lawyer, businessman, politician. Graduated Yale, 1845. Grew wealthy in Chicago, Ill., real estate ventures. Elected Cook Co. commissioner, 1871; congressman, Democrat, 1874 and 1876. Elected five times mayor of Chicago, 1879, 1881, 1883, 1885, and 1893 when he was shot and killed by a disappointed office seeker. A successful businessman, witty and a liberal, he won support from both propertied and working classes.

HARRISON, CHARLES CUSTIS (b. Philadelphia, Pa., 1844; d. Philadelphia, 1929), financier, educator. Amassed a fortune in sugar refining. As provost, University of Pennsylvania, 1894–1910, he contributed greatly to its expansion and improvement. He served in later years as president of the University Museum and made possible its archeological expeditions.

HARRISON, CONSTANCE CARY (b. Fairfax Co., Va., 1843; d. Washington, D.C., 1920), novelist. As Mrs. Burton Harrison, wrote Flower de Hundred (1890) and many other popular tales; also an autobiographical volume, Recollections Grave and Gay (1911).

HARRISON, ELIZABETH (b. Athens, Ky., 1849; d. San Antonio, Texas, 1927), kindergartner. President, National Kindergarten and Elementary College, Chicago. Author of A Study of Child Nature (1890).

HARRISON, FAIRFAX (b. New York, N.Y., 1869; d. Baltimore, Md., 1938), lawyer. Son of Burton and Constance C. Harrison. President, Southern Railway, 1913–37. [Supp. 2]

HARRISON, GABRIEL (b. Philadelphia, Pa., 1818; d. Brooklyn, N.Y., 1902), theatrical manager, actor, author, painter. Friend of Edgar A. Poe. A force in

dramatic, musical and art life of Brooklyn, N.Y., 1848–88.

HARRISON, GEORGE PAUL (b. near Savannah, Ga., 1841; d. 1922), lawyer, Confederate brigadier-general, Alabama legislator and congressman.

HARRISON, GESSNER (b. Harrisonburg, Va., 1807; d. 1862), teacher, classicist. Graduated University of Virginia, 1828, and served there as professor of ancient languages, 1828–59. The first American college teacher to recognize science of comparative grammar.

HARRISON, HENRY BALDWIN (b. New Haven, Conn., 1821; d. New Haven, 1901), lawyer, Connecticut legislator. Graduated Yale, 1846. Republican governor of Connecticut, 1885–87.

HARRISON, HENRY SYDNOR (b. Sewanee, Tenn., 1880; d. Atlantic City, N.J., 1930), newspaperman, novelist. Graduated Columbia, 1900. Editorial writer, Richmond Times-Dispatch. Author of best-selling Queed (1911), V. V.'s Eyes (1913) and other works.

HARRISON, JAMES (b. Bourbon Co., Ky., 1803; d. 1870), merchant, trader, developer of Missouri mineral resources. Organized the American Iron Mountain Co., 1843, which became one of world's largest iron producers.

HARRISON, JAMES ALBERT (b. Pass Christian, Miss., 1848; d. Charlottesville, Va., 1911), philologist. Professor of languages at Randolph-Macon, Washington and Lee, and University of Virginia; an American pioneer in Old-English scholarship; editor in chief of Virginia Edition of E. A. Poe (1902).

HARRISON, JOHN (b. Philadelphia, Pa., 1773; d. Philadelphia, 1833), first (1801) manufacturing chemist in the United States.

HARRISON, JOSEPH (b. Philadelphia, Pa., 1810; d. Philadelphia, 1874), mechanical engineer. Served as apprentice to a steam-engine builder; after varied working experience, became a partner in Eastwick & Harrison, locomotive manufacturers, first to design a practical 8-wheel engine. In 1839 Harrison patented a method for equalizing weight on the driving wheels and made the forward truck flexible so as to meet irregular undulations on rails. The Gowan and Marx engine, built by the firm in 1841, pulled 101 loaded coal-cars, an unprecedented feat at that time. Eastwick and Harrison removed their plant to St. Petersburg, Russia, where, in association with Thomas Winans, they completed a huge railroad contract for the Russian government, 1844–51. Harrison returned home in 1852; the sectional Harrison Steam Boiler, which he patented 1859, marked an era in reduction of danger from explosion.

HARRISON, LOVELL BIRGE (b. Philadelphia, Pa., 1854; d. 1929), landscape painter. Brother of Thomas A. Harrison. Studied at Pennsylvania Academy of

Fine Arts, and in Paris with Carolus-Duran and Cabanel. Specialized in urban subjects and winter scenes; founded the Woodstock, N.Y., art colony.

HARRISON, PETER (*b. York, England, 1716; d. New Haven, Conn., 1775*), merchant, architect. Came to Newport, R.I., 1740; engaged in agriculture and trade with his brother, Joseph. In 1761 they moved to New Haven where Peter became collector of customs, 1768. A cultivated amateur of the arts, he made maps of Cape Breton and Newport, 1745, and assisted in the fortification of Newport, 1746. The Redwood Library (1748–50), the Brick Market (1761), and the Synagogue (1762–63), all in Newport; King's Chapel, Boston (1749–54); and Christ Church, Cambridge (1761) were built from his designs and justify his claim to being the most notable architect of colonial America. His buildings were exceptional in America of that time for their purity of detail and monumental qualities.

HARRISON, RICHARD BERRY (*b. London, Canada, 1864; d. 1935*), lecturer, teacher, actor. Created the memorable part of "de Lawd" in Marc Connelly's *The Green Pastures*, 1930. [*Supp. 1*]

HARRISON, THOMAS ALEXANDER (*b. Philadelphia, Pa., 1853; d. Paris, France, 1930*), marine and figure painter. Brother of Lovell B. Harrison. Studied at Pennsylvania Academy of Fine Arts, and in Paris with J. L. Gérôme and Bastien-Lepage.

HARRISON, WILLIAM HENRY (*b. Charles City Co., Va., 1773; d. Washington, D.C., 1841*), soldier, statesman, president of the United States. Son of Benjamin Harrison (1726?–1791). Attended Hampden-Sidney College; studied medicine briefly under Benjamin Rush. In August 1791, following his father's death he entered the army and was commissioned ensign in the 1st Infantry. Serving in the Northwest Territory against the Indians, he became a lieutenant and aide-de-camp to Anthony Wayne. After the Treaty of Greenville, 1795, he remained on garrison duty at North Bend and Ft. Washington (Cincinnati). In 1795 he married Anna Symmes, daughter of John Cleves Symmes. On resigning from the army, 1798, he was appointed secretary of the Northwest Territory and was elected first delegate to Congress, 1799. There, as chairman of the committee on public lands, he obtained passage of the act dividing the Northwest Territory into the territories of Ohio and Indiana. He was appointed governor of Indiana in May 1800. Instructed to win the confidence of the Indians and secure justice for them from the settlers, he was also urged to obtain cession of as much land as possible for the government. Harrison did his best, but the two aims of the government were irreconcilable. During his term, he obtained Indian grants of millions of acres in the present states of Indiana and Illinois, but the Indians' resentment of the invading settlers increased. An Indian confederacy under the

Shawnee warrior Tecumseh and his brother, the Prophet, began to develop in 1805. Tecumseh's aim was to bind all tribes into an agreement to sell no more land. When Harrison, by the Treaty of Fort Wayne, 1809, secured some 2½ million acres on the Wabash River, Tecumseh warned him that he would oppose occupation, and the Indians encamped in force near the point where Tippecanoe Creek empties into the Wabash. On Nov. 6, 1811, with a force of about 1000 men, Harrison encamped near the Indian village at Tippecanoe and was attacked next morning by the Shawnees. Though Harrison was able to take possession of their settlement, his losses were heavy and by spring the Indians became bold again. Convinced of the necessity of a general war against the Indians, Harrison urged his plans upon President Madison, but the War of 1812 ended such an idea. He received no regular command at the start of the war, but participated as a brevet major-general of Kentucky militia in an action which relieved Fort Wayne, August 1812. Finally, in September he received notice of his appointment as regular brigadier-general and supreme commander of the Army of the Northwest.

The task before him was great. The British held Mackinac, Chicago and Detroit. Harrison had to train and equip an army and transport it across Ohio before winter. His initial mistake was his undertaking a difficult campaign with raw troops. He tried to move his forces in three divisions north through Ohio so as to concentrate at Miami Rapids, but impassable roads and faulty communications proved fatal to such a plan. Gen. James Winchester, on the left wing, reached the rendezvous first and attempted an unsupported advance; at Frenchtown on Jan. 22, 1813, his force was overcome by the British. For six months thereafter, based on Fort Meigs, Harrison pursued a defensive policy, trying to build a force for another offensive. Perry's victory over the British fleet on Lake Erie (Sept. 10, 1813) was a factor of great strategic importance. Harrison felt able to take the offensive. On September 27 he occupied Malden and two days later reoccupied Detroit. Pursuing the retreating British under Procter, Harrison overtook and defeated them at the Thames River in early October. Procter fled and Tecumseh was killed; the British did not again attempt offensive operations in that quarter. Tecumseh's death and the surrender of the Indian allies brought about pacification of most of the Indians of the Northwest. Harrison had been promoted major-general in March 1813, and in the same month had been replaced as governor of Indiana by Thomas Posey. On his resignation from the army in May 1814, he returned to his farm in North Bend, O., and engaged in several unfortunate commercial enterprises. Congressman from Ohio, 1816–19, he was in no sense an outstanding figure in the House. As U.S. senator, 1825–28, he was chiefly distinguished by his work as chairman of the military affairs committee. In

May 1828, he was appointed minister to Colombia through the influence of Henry Clay whose political follower he was. Arriving in Bogotá, February 1829, he meddled in the local revolutionary situation and was recalled that summer, not because of his behavior, but because President Jackson desired the place for one of his own supporters.

For some years after his return from Colombia, Harrison encountered a series of financial reverses and family misfortunes. He kept up his interest in politics, however, and in 1836 was an unsuccessful anti-Van Buren candidate for president. In 1840 he was selected over Henry Clay by the Whigs as their presidential candidate. The election of 1840 is famous because of its emphasis on emotional and demagogic appeal. The Whigs drew up no political platform, but emphasized Harrison's military record and alleged frontier character. "Tippecanoe and Tyler too" was the campaign slogan and, the general was pictured seated before a log cabin with a barrel of cider beside him. Elected by a landslide electoral vote, Harrison was inaugurated 9th president of the United States amid tremendous enthusiasm. One month later he died of pneumonia.

HARRISON, WILLIAM POPE (*b. Savannah, Ga., 1830; d. Columbus, Ga., 1895*), Methodist clergyman, editor.

HARRISSE, HENRY (*b. Paris, France, 1829; d. Paris, 1910*), lawyer, bibliographer, historian of the discovery of America. Author, among other works, of *Bibliotheca Americana Vetustissima* (1866), a monumental study of printed books relating to America before 1550. [*Supp.* 1]

HARROD, BENJAMIN MORGAN (*b. New Orleans, La., 1837; d. New Orleans, 1912*), engineer, Confederate soldier. A leading hydraulic engineer and expert on levee construction; member, Mississippi River Commission and Panama Canal Commission; city engineer, New Orleans.

HARROD, JAMES (*b. Big Cove, Pa., 1742; d. 1793*), pioneer, soldier. Founded the first settlement in Kentucky at Harrodsburg, 1774. Took an active part in the war in the West, serving in Bowman's expedition against Chillicothe, 1779, and in George Rogers Clark's invasion of the Shawnee country, 1782.

HARSHBERGER, JOHN WILLIAM (*b. Philadelphia, Pa., 1869; d. Philadelphia, 1929*), botanist, naturalist. Graduated University of Pennsylvania, 1892; Ph.D., 1893. Taught biology and botany at Pennsylvania, 1893–1929. Author, among many other works, of the *Phytogeographic Survey of North America* (1911).

HARSHE, ROBERT BARTHOLOW (*b. Salisbury, Mo., 1879; d. Chicago, Ill., 1938*), artist, teacher. Director, Chicago Art Institute, 1921–38. [*Supp.* 2]

HART, ABRAHAM (*b. Philadelphia, Pa., 1810; d. Long Branch, N.J., 1885*), publisher. Partner in Carey and Hart, 1829–49; continued until 1854 under his own name.

HART, CHARLES HENRY (*b. Philadelphia, Pa., 1847; d. New York, N.Y., 1918*), lawyer, art expert. Authority on historical portraiture; made a special study of work of Gilbert Stuart.

HART, EDMUND HALL (*b. Manchester Bridge, N.Y., 1839; d. 1898*), pioneer Florida horticulturist. Settled at Federal Point, Fla., 1867, as citrus fruit grower; introduced the Valencia orange there. The Choice banana was also an important product of his breeding.

HART, EDWARD (*b. Doylestown, Pa., 1854; d. 1931*), chemist, educator, editor. Ph.D., Johns Hopkins, 1879. Taught at Lafayette College, 1880–1924. Designed a widely used nitric acid condenser; founded and managed the Chemical Publishing Co. [*Supp.* 1]

HART, GEORGE OVERBURY (*b. Cairo, Ill., 1868; d. New York, N.Y., 1933*), painter, etcher. Known as "Pop" Hart. An accomplished draftsman and colorist, he traveled widely recording his sensitive impressions of scenes and people. [*Supp.* 1]

HART, HASTINGS HORNELL (*b. Brookfield, O., 1851; d. 1932*), social worker, penologist. A commanding figure in his field; drafted the juvenile court law for Cook County, Ill., the first law of its kind in the world. [*Supp.* 1]

HART, JAMES MacDOUGAL (*b. Kilmarnock, Scotland, 1828; d. Brooklyn, N.Y., 1901*), landscape painter. Brother of William Hart. Came to America as a child. Studied at Düsseldorf and made great success in New York *post* Civil War, supplying the new-rich with paintings they could understand.

HART, JAMES MORGAN (*b. Princeton, N.J., 1839; d. Washington, D.C., 1916*), lawyer, philologist. Son of John S. Hart. Graduated Princeton, 1860; J.U.D., Göttingen, 1864. Professor of English, University of Cincinnati, 1876–90; Cornell, 1890–1907. Author of *German Universities: A Narrative of Personal Experience* (1874) and other works.

HART, JOEL TANNER (*b. near Winchester, Ky., 1810; d. Florence, Italy, 1877*), sculptor. Self-taught, Hart was at his best in portrait busts.

HART, JOHN (*b. Stonington, Conn., 1711?; d. 1779*), farmer, New Jersey signer of the Declaration of Independence. Member of New Jersey Assembly, 1761–71; of Jersey Provincial Congress, 1774–76; of Continental Congress, 1776. Speaker of the first Assembly of the state of New Jersey.

HART, JOHN SEELY (*b. Stockbridge, Mass., 1810; d. 1877*), educator, editor. Raised in Pennsylvania. Graduated Princeton, 1830; Princeton Theological

Seminary, 1834. Principal, Philadelphia Central High School, and State Normal School, Trenton, N.J. Taught also at Princeton. Founder and first editor (1859–71) of the *Sunday School Times.*

HART, SAMUEL (*b. Saybrook, Conn., 1845; d. 1917*), Episcopal clergyman, theologian. Graduated Trinity College, Hartford, Conn., 1866; Berkeley Divinity School, 1869. Taught at both institutions; was dean of Berkeley *post* 1908. Author of *History of the American Book of Common Prayer* (1910).

HART, VIRGIL CHITTENDEN (*b. Lorraine, N.Y., 1840; d. Burlington, Canada, 1904*), Methodist clergyman. Missionary to China, 1866–87; 1891–1900.

HART, WILLIAM (*b. Paisley, Scotland, 1823; d. 1894*), painter. Brother of James MacDougal Hart. Came to America as a child. Though thin and crude, his work has some of the freshness of the primitive. He was a portraitist, and a landscapist of the "Hudson River" school.

HARTE, BRET. [See HARTE, FRANCIS BRETT, 1836–1902.]

HARTE, FRANCIS BRETT (*b. Albany, N.Y., 1836; d. London, England, 1902*), author. Removed to California, 1854; his early experiences there as clerk, teacher, newspaperman were the basis of his literary work. Variously employed in San Francisco, 1860–68, he contributed verse and prose to the *Golden Era* and the *Californian* and published three books: *Outcroppings* (1865, but dated 1866), an anthology of California verse; *The Lost Galleon* (1867), a collection of his own poems; and a volume of parodies, *Condensed Novels* (1867). The work for which he is remembered, the short-stories of California life which pointed out the way to a whole school of "local color" writers, appeared between 1868, when he became editor of the *Overland Monthly,* and 1871 when he deserted the West for the East and Europe. The best of these are found in *The Luck of Roaring Camp and Other Sketches* (1870); in the same year appeared his most celebrated poem "The Heathen Chinee." After his removal eastward, his life as lecturer, journalist, consul, and finally hack story-writer in London, was a study in debt and declining fortunes. His one great achievement was the application of simple, well-tested story formulas to novel material.

HARTLEY, FRANK (*b. Washington, D.C., 1856; d. 1913*), surgeon. Graduated Princeton, 1877; M.D., Columbia, 1880, where he was teacher and professor, *post* 1886. Devised intracranial method for curing trigeminal neuralgia by bisecting ganglion of the trigeminal nerve.

HARTLEY, JONATHAN SCOTT (*b. Albany, N.Y., 1845; d. 1912*), sculptor. Studied at Royal Academy, London; also at Rome and Paris. Famous for portraits of men.

HARTLEY, THOMAS (*b. Colebrookdale, Berks Co., Pa., 1748; d. 1800*), lawyer, Revolutionary soldier. Commanded 1st Pennsylvania Brigade; led 1778 expedition to avenge Wyoming Massacre. Congressman, Federalist, 1789–1800.

HARTNESS, JAMES (*b. Schenectady, N.Y., 1861; d. 1934*), tool builder, inventor. Associated *post* 1889 with Jones & Lamson Co.; devised many lathe improvements and was active in standardization of screw threads. Republican governor of Vermont, 1921–23.
[*Supp.* 1]

HARTRANFT, CHESTER DAVID (*b. Frederick, Pa., 1839; d. Wolfenbüttel, Germany, 1914*), Reformed Dutch Church clergyman, educator. President, Hartford Theological Seminary, 1888–1903.

HARTRANFT, JOHN FREDERICK (*b. near Fagleysville, Pa., 1830; d. 1889*), lawyer, Union soldier, politician. Republican governor of Pennsylvania, 1873–79; noted for his attempt to solve industrial labor problems by armed force.

HARTSHORNE, HENRY (*b. Philadelphia, Pa., 1823; d. Tokyo, Japan, 1897*), physician. Graduated Haverford, 1839; M.D., University of Pennsylvania, 1845. Versatile but unstable, he held an extraordinary number of medical and teaching positions.

HARTSUFF, GEORGE LUCAS (*b. Tyre, N.Y., 1830; d. New York, N.Y., 1874*), soldier. Graduated West Point, 1852. Served as Union brigade and corps commander; retired as major-general, 1871.

HARTWIG, JOHANN CHRISTOPH (*b. Thüringen, Germany, 1714; d. Clermont, N.Y., 1796*), Lutheran clergyman. Came to America, 1746; served congregations in Hudson Valley until 1748 when he became a nomad, ranging from Maine to Virginia. A friend of Henry M. Mühlenberg, he established Hartwick Seminary.

HARTZELL, JOSEPH CRANE (*b. Moline, Ill., 1842; d. Blue Ash, O., 1928*), Methodist clergyman. Pastor, New Orleans, La., 1870–81; active in Freedmen's Aid Society, 1883–96; missionary bishop for Africa, 1896–1916.

HARVARD, JOHN (*b. London, England, 1607; d. Charlestown, Mass., 1638*), benefactor of Harvard University. Graduated Emmanuel College, Cambridge, B.A., 1631/32; M.A., 1635. Sailed to New England not earlier than May 29, 1637; admitted an inhabitant at Charlestown, Mass., August 1, 1637; became teaching elder of the church at Charlestown. John Harvard left half his estate, a sum estimated at between £400 and £800, and his library of about 400 volumes to the college founded by the colony in the fall of 1636. The General Court named the college after him on March 13, 1638/39.

HARVEY, "COIN." [See HARVEY, WILLIAM HOPE, 1851–1936.]

HARVEY, GEORGE BRINTON McCLELLAN (*b. Peacham, Vt., 1864; d. Dublin, N.H., 1928*), political journalist. Grew wealthy through connections with William C. Whitney and other Wall St. figures. Edited *North American Review* and *Harper's Weekly;* was president of Harper and Brothers, 1900–15. Promoted both Woodrow Wilson and Warren G. Harding for presidency. Ambassador to Great Britain, 1921–23.

HARVEY, HAYWARD AUGUSTUS (*b. Jamestown, N.Y., 1824; d. Orange, N.J., 1893*), inventor, manufacturer. Secured 125 patents on a wide variety of mechanical inventions. The Harvey Process for treating armor plate brought him world-wide reputation.

HARVEY, Sir JOHN (*d. 1646*), sea captain. Governor and captain-general of Virginia, serving 1630–35 and 1637–39. Returned to England, 1641. [*Supp.* 1]

HARVEY, LOUIS POWELL (*b. East Haddam, Conn., 1820; d. Savannah, Tenn., 1862*), businessman, legislator. Raised in Ohio; removed to Wisconsin, 1841. Union-Republican governor of Wisconsin, 1861–62.

HARVEY, WILLIAM HOPE (*b. Buffalo, W. Va., 1851; d. Monte Ne, Ark., 1936*), promoter, publicist. Proponent, through "Coin's Financial Series," of free coinage of silver at a ratio of 16 to 1. Number 3 of this pamphlet series, *Coin's Financial School* (1894), had wide circulation and influence. [*Supp.* 2]

HARVIE, JOHN (*b. Albemarle Co., Va., 1742; d. near Richmond, Va., 1807*), Revolutionary patriot, Virginia statesman, financier.

HASBROUCK, ABRAHAM BRUYN (*b. Kingston, N.Y., 1791; d. Kingston, 1879*), lawyer. Graduated Yale, 1810. As president of Rutgers, 1840–50, his administration was marked by increasing independence of the college from ecclesiastical (Reformed Dutch) control.

HASBROUCK, LYDIA SAYER (*b. Warwick, N.Y., 1827; d. Middletown, N.Y., 1910*), writer, lecturer. Advocated temperance, woman's suffrage, dress reform; edited the *Sibyl*, a fortnightly reform paper, 1856–64.

HASCALL, MILO SMITH (*b. Le Roy, N.Y., 1829; d. Chicago, Ill., 1904*), soldier, lawyer, banker. Graduated West Point, 1852. Brigade and division commander in Union Army, 1862–64.

HASELTINE, JAMES HENRY (*b. Philadelphia, Pa., 1833; d. Rome, Italy, 1907*), sculptor. Spent most of his life abroad; produced allegorical works pseudoclassic in type and busts of well-known contemporaries including Longfellow.

HASELTON, SENECA (*b. Westford, Vt., 1848; d. 1921*), jurist. Graduated University of Vermont, 1871; LL.B., University of Michigan, 1875. Practiced in Burlington, Vt. U.S. minister to Venezuela, 1894–95. Served on Vermont supreme court, 1902–06, 1908–19.

HASENCLEVER, PETER (*b. Remscheid, Prussia, 1716; d. 1793*), iron manufacturer. Resided in America, 1764–68. Established extensive works in New Jersey, New York and elsewhere for mining and smelting, also for producing potash; engaged in raising flax and hemp. After initial success, the mismanagement of his partners in England and America left him stripped of his properties and loaded with debts.

HASKELL, CHARLES NATHANIEL (*b. Leipsic, O., 1860; d. Oklahoma City, Okla., 1933*), lawyer, railway and telephone promoter. Removed to Oklahoma, 1901. First governor of state of Oklahoma, Democrat, 1907–11. [*Supp.* 1]

HASKELL, DUDLEY CHASE (*b. Springfield, Vt., 1842; d. Washington, D.C., 1883*), legislator, politician. Removed to Kansas, 1855. Congressman, Republican, from Kansas, 1877–83; an ardent protectionist.

HASKELL, ELLA LOUISE KNOWLES (*b. Northwood Ridge, N.H., 1860; d. Montana, 1911*), lawyer, Populist politician, crusader for equal rights for women. Graduated Bates College, 1884. Admitted to Montana bar, 1889, by special legislative act.

HASKELL, ERNEST (*b. Woodstock, Conn., 1876; d. near Bath, Maine, 1925*), painter, etcher, lithographer. An unusually versatile artist, mainly self-taught, he is best known as an etcher.

HASKET, ELIAS (*b. Salem, Mass., 1670; d. 1739?*), sea-captain. Governor of New Providence, Bahamas, 1701. The people revolted, imprisoned him and returned him to New York after a four-month tenure of office.

HASKINS, CHARLES HOMER (*b. Meadville, Pa., 1870; d. Cambridge, Mass., 1937*), historian. Graduated Johns Hopkins, A.B., 1887; Ph.D., 1890. Taught at Johns Hopkins, 1889–92; Wisconsin, 1892–1902; and Harvard, 1902–31. Dean of Harvard graduate school, 1908–24. A leading medievalist of his generation, and an outstanding teacher, especially of graduate students, Haskins's work centered on Norman institutions and on the transmittal of Greek and Arabic learning to Western Europe. *Norman Institutions* (1918), *Studies in the History of Mediaeval Science* (1924) and *Studies in Mediaeval Culture* (1929) sum up his work in these fields. He was a prominent member of the group of presidential advisers known as "The Inquiry," 1917. As delegate to the Paris Peace Conference, 1918–19, Haskins advanced the solution eventually adopted for the Saar. [*Supp.* 2]

HASSAM, FREDERICK CHILDE (*b. Dorchester, Mass., 1859; d. East Hampton, N.Y., 1935*), artist. A brilliant exponent of the Impressionist school.

[*Supp.* 1]

HASSARD, JOHN ROSE GREENE (*b. New York, N.Y., 1836; d. 1888*), journalist. Graduated Fordham, 1855. Served literary apprenticeship with George Ripley. Essayist, music critic with *New York Tribune*, 1866–88. His numerous writings include an authoritative biography of Archbishop John Hughes of New York (1866).

HASSAUREK, FRIEDRICH (*b. Vienna, Austria, 1831; d. Paris, France, 1885*), journalist, lawyer, diplomat, politician. Emigrated to America, 1849; published German newspaper at Cincinnati, O.; active in Republican politics. Served with distinction as American minister to Ecuador, 1861–64, 1865–66.

HASSELQUIST, TUVE NILSSON (*b. Hasslaröd, Sweden, 1816; d. 1891*), Lutheran clergyman, editor, educator. Came to America, 1852, as pastor at Galesburg, Ill. Ablest leader, most versatile personality of Swedish Lutheran Church in America. President, Augustana College and Seminary, 1863–91.

HASSLER, FERDINAND RUDOLPH (*b. Aarau, Switzerland, 1770; d. Philadelphia, Pa., 1843*), geodesist, mathematician. Came to America, 1805. Nominated to superintend a survey of the United States coast, 1807, he did not receive formal appointment until 1816 when he began work. In 1818 civilians were restricted from the survey, and it came to a virtual halt until 1832 when Hassler again became superintendent and served until his death. The work of the Coast Survey to the present day follows his plan; his field work was of such high precision that it still forms part of the basic network.

HASTINGS, CHARLES SHELDON (*b. Clinton, N.Y., 1848; d. 1932*), physicist. Graduated Sheffield Scientific School, 1870; Ph.D., Yale, 1873. Professor of physics, Sheffield, 1884–1915. A specialist in optics and spectroscopy, he was celebrated for his theory of achromatic lenses, and for contributions to the microscope, including the Aplanat magnifier. [*Supp.* 1]

HASTINGS, SAMUEL DEXTER (*b. Leicester, Mass., 1816; d. Evanston, Ill., 1903*), businessman, Wisconsin legislator and public official, reformer.

HASTINGS, SERRANUS CLINTON (*b. Jefferson Co., N.Y., 1814; d. 1893*), jurist. Removed to Iowa, 1837; to California, 1849. Was first chief justice of California supreme court. Gave endowment to establish Hastings' College of Law at San Francisco, 1878.

HASTINGS, THOMAS (*b. Washington, Conn., 1784; d. New York, N.Y., 1872*), hymn-writer, hymn-book editor, composer. Devoted his life to church music; composed about 1000 tunes, the best of that time in America except for Lowell Mason's.

HASTINGS, THOMAS (*b. New York, N.Y., 1860; d. Mineola, N.Y., 1929*), architect. Grandson of Thomas Hastings (1784–1872). Graduated École des Beaux-Arts, Paris, 1884, where he met John Carrère with whom he formed a celebrated partnership, 1886.

Interested in city planning, he designed the industrial town for the United States Steel Co. at Duluth, Minn. His interest in city beautification is exemplified by his treatment of the Plaza in New York City. The Memorial Amphitheatre in the national cemetery, Arlington, Va., is one of many monuments he designed. Hastings believed in a scholarly, respectful attitude toward the past and in the importance to modern American architecture of the classic tradition.

HASTINGS, WILLIAM WIRT (*b. Delaware District, Cherokee Nation, later Oklahoma, 1866; d. Muskogee, Okla., 1938*), lawyer. Congressman, Democrat, from Oklahoma, 1915–21, 1923–35. A leader in legislation to protect Indian rights. [*Supp.* 2]

HASWELL, ANTHONY (*b. Portsmouth, England, 1756; d. Bennington, Vt., 1816*), printer, editor, ballad writer. Came to Boston, Mass., as a boy; was apprentice to Isaiah Thomas. Published newspapers at Worcester and Springfield, Mass.; published the *Vermont Gazette* at Bennington *post* 1783.

HASWELL, CHARLES HAYNES (*b. New York, N.Y., 1809; d. 1907*). First engineer to be appointed in U.S. Navy, 1836; chief engineer, 1844–52. Worked thereafter as a consultant. Author of *Mechanic's and Engineer's Pocket Book* (1842; 74th ed., 1913) and other works.

HATCH, EDWARD (*b. Bangor, Maine, 1832; d. Fort Robinson, Nebr., 1889*), Union soldier. Colonel, 2nd Iowa Cavalry, 1862–64; participated in Grierson's raid, 1863; rose to major-general of volunteers. Commissioned colonel, 9th U.S. Cavalry, 1866; served in Arizona and New Mexico.

HATCH, JOHN PORTER (*b. Oswego, N.Y., 1822; d. New York, N.Y., 1901*), Union soldier. Graduated West Point, 1845. Served in Mexican War, in Oregon, Texas and New Mexico; as brigade commander in Civil War, received Medal of Honor for conduct at South Mountain. Retired, 1886, as colonel of 2nd U.S. Cavalry.

HATCH, RUFUS (*b. Wells, Maine, 1832; d. 1893*), financier, promoter. Removed to Rockford, Ill., 1851; was in business there and in Chicago. *Post* 1864, a New York stockbroker and speculator, he is said to have coined the phrase, "lambs of Wall Street."

HATCH, WILLIAM HENRY (*b. near Georgetown, Ky., 1833; d. 1896*), lawyer, politician, Confederate soldier. Removed to Hannibal, Mo., 1854, where he practiced law. As congressman, Democrat, from Missouri, 1879–95, his chief interest was agricultural legislation; he served during several sessions as chairman of Committee on Agriculture and successfully sponsored the Bureau of Animal Industry Act (1884), the first oleomargarine act (1886), and a meat inspection act (1890). His greatest service was in establishment of federal aid for agricultural experiment stations by the Hatch Act, 1887. He was a leader in agitation to raise the Department of Agriculture to cabinet status.

HATCHER, WILLIAM ELDRIDGE (*b. Bedford Co., Va., 1834; d. Fork Union, Va., 1912*), Baptist clergyman, author. Pastor for many years at Grace Street Baptist Church, Richmond, Va.

HATFIELD, EDWIN FRANCIS (*b. Elizabeth, N.J., 1807; d. Summit, N.J., 1883*), Presbyterian clergyman, hymnologist. New York City pastor; stated clerk of New School Church, 1846–70, and of united church thereafter. Moderator, General Assembly, 1883.

HATHORNE, WILLIAM (*b. Binfield, England, c. 1607; d. Salem, Mass., 1681*), merchant, colonial official. Emigrated with John Winthrop, 1630; settled in Salem, 1636. Speaker, Massachusetts General Court, 1644–50; commissioner, New England Confederacy, 1650–53; held many other offices, civil and military. Ancestor of Nathaniel Hawthorne.

HATTON, FRANK (*b. Cambridge, O., 1846; d. 1894*), journalist. Removed to Iowa, 1866; *post* 1874, published the influential *Burlington Daily Hawk-Eye;* was editor and publisher, *Washington Post*, 1889–94. As assistant postmaster-general, 1881–84, created special-delivery system; was postmaster-general for a brief period, 1884–85.

HAUGEN, GILBERT NELSON (*b. Plymouth Township, Wis., 1859; d. Norwood, Iowa, 1933*), farmer, businessman. Raised in Iowa. Congressman, Republican, from Iowa, 1899–1933. Chairman of the committee on agriculture for many years. Co-author of McNary-Haugen bill for relief of farm surpluses.

[*Supp. 1*]

HAUGEN, NILS PEDERSON (*b. Modum, Norway, 1849; d. Madison, Wis., 1931*), lawyer. Came to Wisconsin as a child. Congressman, Republican, from Wisconsin, 1887–95. As a tax commissioner, 1900–21, aided Gov. Robert M. La Follette in reform.

[*Supp. 1*]

HAUGHERY, MARGARET GAFFNEY (*b. Cavan, Ireland, c. 1814; d. New Orleans, La., 1882*), philanthropist. Came to America, *c.* 1822; settled in New Orleans, *c.* 1836; operated a dairy and a bakery. Established and sustained three orphanages for 600 children and did numerous other charities.

HAUGHTON, PERCY DUNCAN (*b. Staten Island, N.Y., 1876; d. New York, N.Y., 1924*), football coach, broker. Graduated Harvard, 1899, where he played varsity tackle and kicking fullback, earning a reputation as one of the outstanding kickers of all time. Successfully coached Cornell, 1899–1900. As coach at Harvard, 1908–16, he produced winning teams and wrought rules and strategy changes which revolutionized the game. He was coach at Columbia, 1923–24.

HAUK, MINNIE (*b. New York, N.Y., 1852?; d. Lake Lucerne, Switzerland, 1929*), dramatic soprano. Debut at Brooklyn, N.Y., 1866, in *Sonnambula;* was internationally famous, 1868–95. America's first *Carmen*, she also sang in American premières of *Roméo et Juliette* and *Manon.*

HAUPT, HERMAN (*b. Philadelphia, Pa., 1817; d. Jersey City, N.J., 1905*), civil engineer, author, inventor. Graduated West Point, 1835. Engaged in railroad construction; wrote *General Theory of Bridge Construction* (1851). After work for Pennsylvania Railroad, he began construction of the Hoosac tunnel, 1856, and developed in 1858 a pneumatic drill superior to any in use to that time. Served as chief of construction and transportation on U.S. military railroads, 1862–63. After the Civil War he held important positions with a number of railroads and other firms. Throughout his career he was a voluminous writer on technical subjects.

HAUPT, PAUL (*b. Görlitz, Germany, 1858; d. 1926*), philologist, Assyriologist. Ph.D., Leipzig, 1878. Taught at Göttingen; was Spence Professor of Semitic Languages and director of the Oriental Seminary, Johns Hopkins, 1883–1926. A prolific author, his bibliography includes 522 titles. Few men have had wider accurate knowledge of Semitic languages and dialects. His contribution to Biblical criticism was, however, inferior to his work in Assyriology and Semitic philology. He was in his time the chief interpreter of the Gilgamesh Epic.

HAUSER, SAMUEL THOMAS (*b. Falmouth, Ky., 1833; d. 1914*), miner, capitalist. After early training as railroad surveyor, he prospected in Idaho and Montana, 1862–63; thereafter, he bought silver mines and built first silver-ore reduction furnace in Montana. He operated coal mines, built toll roads, telegraph lines, railroads and organized banks in the Territory; he also planned the first large irrigation project in Montana, and was one of the first to engage in large-scale stock raising there. He served as territorial governor, 1885–86.

HAVELL, ROBERT (*b. Reading, England, 1793; d. Tarrytown, N.Y., 1878*), engraver, painter. Resided in America, 1839–78. Engraved in aquatint and colored all but ten of the plates in the folio *Birds of America* by J. J. Audubon, completed in 1838. The success of the work owed much to Havell's genius.

HAVEMEYER, HENRY OSBORNE (*b. New York, N.Y., 1847; d. 1907*), sugar refiner, capitalist. Cousin of William F. Havemeyer. President of the "sugar trust," the American Sugar Refining Co. and its predecessor company, 1887–1907.

HAVEMEYER, WILLIAM FREDERICK (*b. New York, N.Y., 1804; d. New York, 1874*), sugar refiner, capitalist. Graduated Columbia, 1823. Formed a partnership in a refinery, 1828; retired, wealthy, 1842.

Democratic mayor of New York City, 1845 and 1848. Turning his attention to business, he had coal and railroad interests and was president of the Bank of North America and the New York Savings Bank until 1861. Elected reform mayor, 1872, after outstanding services as an unmasker of the "Tweed Ring," his term was a tragedy. His appointment of police commissioners, previously guilty of public offenses, astounded the city. He wrangled constantly with the Board of Aldermen. A petition sent Gov. John A. Dix for Havemeyer's removal was ineffectual, however, because there was no evidence of the mayor's personal corruption or dishonesty.

HAVEN, ALICE B. [See HAVEN, EMILY BRADLEY NEAL, 1827–1863.]

HAVEN, EMILY BRADLEY NEAL (*b. Hudson, N.Y., 1827; d. Mamaroneck, N.Y., 1863*), author, editor. Wife of Joseph C. Neal. Editor, *Neal's Saturday Gazette and Lady's Literary Museum,* 1847–53; contributor to *Sartain's* and *Graham's* magazines and to *Godey's Lady's Book.* After second marriage to Samuel L. Haven, continued work as Alice B. Haven.

HAVEN, ERASTUS OTIS (*b. Boston, Mass., 1820; d. Salem, Oreg., 1881*), educator, Methodist clergyman and bishop. Graduated Wesleyan University, 1842. Editor, *Zion's Herald,* 1856–63. President, University of Michigan, 1863–69, and of Northwestern University, 1869–72; Chancellor of Syracuse University, 1874–80.

HAVEN, GILBERT (*b. Malden, Mass., 1821; d. Malden, 1880*), abolitionist, Methodist clergyman. Cousin of Erastus O. Haven. Editor, *Zion's Herald,* 1867–72. As bishop at Atlanta, Ga., 1872–80, he energetically and courageously pressed freedmen's claims to racial equality.

HAVEN, HENRY PHILEMON (*b. Norwich, Conn., 1815; d. 1876*), whaling merchant, capitalist. An outstanding Sunday-school superintendent at Second Congregational Church, New London, Conn., 1858–76.

HAVEN, JOSEPH (*b. Dennis, Mass., 1816; d. 1874*), Congregational clergyman, teacher, scholar. Graduated Amherst, 1835, and taught philosophy there, 1851–58. Professor of theology, Chicago Theological Seminary, 1858–70; of philosophy, University of Chicago, 1873–74. A gifted teacher.

HAVENS, JAMES SMITH (*b. Weedsport, N.Y., 1859; d. Rochester, N.Y., 1927*), lawyer, Democratic congressman.

HAVERLY, CHRISTOPHER (*b. near Bellefonte, Pa., 1837; d. Salt Lake City, Utah, 1901*), "Col. Jack H. Haverly," theatrical manager. He began his career by purchasing a variety theatre in Toledo, O., 1864; his first minstrel show opened in Adrian, Mich., in the same year. Thereafter he organized minstrel troupes and acquired theatres all over America. His most famous show was Haverly's Mastodon Minstrels, organized 1878, with which he toured England and Germany, 1880–81. In 1884 his most brilliant company failed in London and his fortunes declined. A daring speculator in stocks and the greatest minstrel manager in America, he died in obscurity.

HAVERLY, JACK H. [See HAVERLY, CHRISTOPHER, 1837–1901.]

HAVILAND, CLARENCE FLOYD (*b. Spencertown, N.Y., 1875; d. Cairo, Egypt, 1930*), physician, psychiatrist.

HAVILAND, JOHN (*b. Gundenham Manor, Somersetshire, England, 1792; d. Philadelphia, Pa., 1852*), architect. Came to America, 1816. Designed many buildings in Philadelphia. His most notable work was his creation of the modern prison on the "radiating plan" as exemplified in Eastern State Penitentiary at Cherry Hill, Philadelphia.

HAWES, CHARLES BOARDMAN (*b. Clifton Springs, N.Y., 1889; d. 1923*). Author of *The Dark Frigate* (1923) and other tales of adventure.

HAWKINS, BENJAMIN (*b. Warren Co., N.C., 1754; d. Crawford Co., Ga., 1816*), planter, Indian agent. French interpreter on Washington's staff, 1776–79. Member of Confederation Congress, 1781–84, 1786–87; U.S. senator, Federalist, from North Carolina, 1789–95. As Indian commissioner, he negotiated treaties with Cherokees (1785), Choctaws and Chickasaws (1786) and with the Creeks the important treaty of Coleraine (1796). Washington then appointed him agent to the Creeks and general superintendent of all Indians south of the Ohio. His headquarters were first at Fort Hawkins near Macon, Ga., later at the "Old Agency" on Flint River. Known as "Beloved Man of the Four Nations," he semicivilized the Creeks by teaching them agriculture and won their liking and respect. The War of 1812 ruined the work to which he had sacrificed a great part of his life.

HAWKINS, DEXTER ARNOLD (*b. Canton, Maine, 1825; d. Groton, Conn., 1886*), lawyer, educator, political reformer. Champion of public schools, instrumental in establishing national Department of Education, 1867.

HAWKINS, RUSH CHRISTOPHER (*b. Pomfret, Vt., 1831; d. 1920*), lawyer, Union soldier. Practiced law in New York City; commanded 9th New York Volunteers (Hawkins Zouaves), 1861–63. Presented his superb collection of incunabula to the Annmary Brown Memorial, Providence, R.I.

HAWKS, FRANCIS LISTER (*b. New Bern, N.C., 1798; d. 1866*), lawyer, Episcopal clergyman, historian. Grandson of John Hawks. Held a number of pastorates in the North and the South; was first president, University of Louisiana, 1844–49; published a number of valuable works on the history of the church in the United States.

HAWKS, JOHN (*b. Dragby, England, 1731; d. New Bern, N.C., 1790*), architect. Came to America, 1764, as designer and builder of the governor's palace at New Bern; completed in 1770, it was one of the finest structures in colonial America. After holding various local offices, Hawks served as first auditor of North Carolina, 1784–90.

HAWLEY, GIDEON (*b. Stratfield (Bridgeport) Conn., 1727; d. Mashpee, Mass., 1807*), Congregational clergyman. Graduated Yale, 1749. Missionary under Jonathan Edwards at Stockbridge, 1752–54; among Six Nations on New York frontier, 1754–56; and as permanent preacher to Mashpees, 1758–1807.

HAWLEY, GIDEON (*b. Huntington, Conn., 1785; d. 1870*), lawyer. Graduated Union College, 1809. Became successful Albany, N.Y., lawyer and a pioneer in New York railroad development, but his most notable service was in education. From 1812 to 1821, as first superintendent of public instruction for New York State, he laid foundations for the public elementary school system. From 1814 to 1841 he was secretary of the Board of Regents, who guided the development of private academies; he served as a member of the Board of Regents of the University of the State of New York, 1842–70. He was largely responsible for establishing the first normal school in the state at Albany.

HAWLEY, JAMES HENRY (*b. Dubuque, Iowa, 1847; d. 1929*), lawyer, Idaho legislator. Governor of Idaho, 1911–13. Nationally prominent as prosecutor of W. D. Haywood and other labor officials for murder of Gov. Steunenberg.

HAWLEY, JOSEPH (*b. Northampton, Mass., 1723; d. Northampton, 1788*), lawyer. Grandson of Solomon Stoddard. Graduated Yale, 1742. Influential in dismissal of his cousin Jonathan Edwards from his church, 1749–50. Guiding spirit of the Revolution in the Connecticut Valley.

HAWLEY, JOSEPH ROSWELL (*b. Stewartville, N.C., 1826; d. Washington, D.C., 1905*), editor, Union soldier. Graduated Hamilton College, 1847. Helped organize Republican party in Connecticut, 1856. Editor, Hartford *Evening Press*, 1857–61; rose to major-general in Civil War; editor, *Hartford Courant*, 1867. Elected governor of Connecticut, 1866, he was in politics to the end of his life, serving three times as congressman *post* 1868, and as U.S. senator, 1881–1905. A consistent, able conservative.

HAWORTH, JOSEPH (*b. Providence, R.I., 1855?; d. 1903*), actor. Début with Ellsler's stock company, Cleveland, *c.* 1873. Supported Barrett, Edwin Booth, McCullough, Modjeska; was reputed an intellectually superior performer of serious roles.

HAWTHORNE, CHARLES WEBSTER (*b. Lodi, Ill., 1872; d. Baltimore, Md., 1930*), painter. Studied at Art Students League, New York, and with William M. Chase. Established Cape Cod School of Art, Provincetown, Mass.

HAWTHORNE, JULIAN (*b. Boston, Mass., 1846; d. 1934*), author. Son of Nathaniel Hawthorne; brother of Rose H. Lathrop. [*Supp. 1*]

HAWTHORNE, NATHANIEL (*b. Salem, Mass., 1804; d. Plymouth, N.H., 1864*), novelist. Descended from a New England line that began with William Hathorne who came to Massachusetts in 1630, and included a judge of the Salem witchcraft trials and several sea-captains. His father's death, 1808, and his mother's consequent withdrawal from society caused him to grow up in habits of solitude. By the age of 14, he was widely read in novels and romances of all kinds, and in the works of the classic authors, French and English. On graduation from Bowdoin, 1825, he settled down in Salem, devoting a dozen years to making himself a man of letters. Yearly he struck out on a kind of wary summer vagabondage, traveling through other districts of New England, across New York to Niagara, and perhaps even so far as Detroit. His *American Note-Books* show him to have used his eyes and ears on his travels, as do many of his tales and sketches. Everywhere he was attentive to manners and customs. He continued to read extensively, particularly in the early history of New England, aiming to enliven and warm the cold record by reconstructing typical "moments of drama . . . clashes between the parties and ideas which divided the old New England." Though a descendent of the Puritans, he seemed to sympathize with humane and expansive rebels against the order of austerity and orthodoxy. That this was less an historical than a moral position is indicated by the theme of egotism stressed in his short stories. Solitary by habit, he deeply feared that solitude which ends in egotism and is in turn encouraged and deepened by it. Egotism leads to pride; pride by different roads leads always away from nature. Aside from the stories he wrote between 1825 and 1837, there are no events to mark his life in that period. In 1828 he issued, at his own expense and anonymously, the undistinguished novel *Fanshawe*. Though unsuccessful, it got him a publisher, Samuel G. Goodrich of Boston, just then founding an annual, the *Token*, which with the *New England Magazine* was to be Hawthorne's chief publishing outlet. *Twice-Told Tales* (1837), a collection of short masterpieces, marked the end of his years of solitary experiment. Thereafter he wrote with increasing reputation and in 1842 published a second series of *Twice-Told Tales*.

The need of money did as much as anything else to end Hawthorne's career of solitude. He served for seven months during 1836 as editor of Goodrich's *American Magazine of Useful and Entertaining*

Knowledge and wrote or compiled the whole of every issue. He compiled *Peter Parley's Universal History* (1837), a piece of hackwork which sold over a million copies. For children he wrote *Grandfather's Chair* (1841), *Famous Old People* (1841), *Liberty Tree* (1841), *Biographical Stories for Children* (1842) and, later, two of the lasting triumphs of their mode, *A Wonder-Book for Girls and Boys* (1852) and *Tanglewood Tales for Girls and Boys* (1853). With the help of Franklin Pierce, he was employed as weigher and gager in the Boston Custom House, 1839–41. He then went to live at West Roxbury with the Transcendentalists who had founded Brook Farm; after an intermittent year of residence he left, satisfied that the association was not for him. After his marriage to Sophia Peabody of Salem in July 1842, he moved to the Old Manse at Concord. Profoundly happy with his wife, he was not distracted by the presence nearby of the most distinguished group who have ever come together in a single American village. Alcott bored him; he heard Emerson with interest but without the customary reverence; only with Thoreau did he arrive at anything like intimacy. His story collection *Mosses from an Old Manse* (1846) contained an introductory paper describing this pastoral interlude. Pressed for money, he moved to Salem, 1845, and was appointed surveyor of the port; in 1849, when the Democrats went out of power, he was dismissed. Forced into private life, he produced within the next three years the novels which brought his art to its peak.

The novels marked no break with the tales. In style, tempo, themes, Hawthorne proceeded much as he had always done. Only the dimensions were different. *The Scarlet Letter* (1850) is a succession of moments of drama from the lives of the principal characters, bound together by a continuity of mood and firmness of central idea which lift the story to a region more spacious than 17th-century Salem. The novel portrays a clash between elements opposed in old New England, and also, at the same time, the universal clash between egotism and nature with which Hawthorne had dealt in his shorter stories. *The House of the Seven Gables* (1851) is an extended description of such households as he dealt with in many of his sketches. The house, like the household of his own youth, was withdrawn, solitary, declining, haunted by an ancestral curse. Into the story he distilled all the representative qualities of decadent New England without, however, bringing in that New England complacency which made a virtue out of decay and refused to admit the existence of evil in adversity. In *The Blithedale Romance* (1852) he turned to the contemporary world. The setting was more or less what he remembered of Brook Farm. His thesis was that philanthropy, of his character Hollingsworth's sort, is only another egotism which may bring the philanthropist into tragic conflict with nature. *The Scarlet Letter* was written at Salem; he

wrote *The House of the Seven Gables* at Lenox in the Berkshires, where he made the acquaintance of Herman Melville, then writing *Moby Dick* at Pittsfield. Here, also, he collected *The Snow Image and Other Twice-Told Tales* (1851) and wrote *A Wonder-Book*. In 1851 he moved to West Newton, Mass., where the third novel was completed; as the novels put money at his command, he bought a house in Concord. After writing with much labor and out of obligation for many favors a campaign *Life of Franklin Pierce* (1852), Hawthorne was appointed U.S. consul at Liverpool, where he served conscientiously, 1853–57. During 1858 and early 1859 he lived in Italy. Here he began *The Marble Faun* (1860) which he completed in England before returning to Concord, 1860.

The four years after his return to America, except for his shrewd, slily satirical commentary on England, *Our Old Home* (1863), saw nothing further by him. He experimented with four ideas (published posthumously and unfinished as *The Ancestral Footstep, Septimius Felton, Dr. Grimshaw's Secret,* and *The Dolliver Romance*), but he could not fuse or complete them. His imagination was dissolving; his vitality was breaking up. The Civil War weighed upon him, as did the illness of his daughter Una, and Thoreau's death in 1862. He could not survive his era of New England or endure the tumult of its passing. In May 1864, enfeebled and discouraged, he set out from Concord for a carriage trip with his friend Pierce. At Plymouth, N.H., he died in his sleep. Mourned as a classic figure, he has ever since been so regarded.

HAWTHORNE, ROSE. [See Alphonsa, Mother, 1851–1926.]

HAY, CHARLES AUGUSTUS (*b. York, Pa., 1821; d. Gettysburg, Pa., 1893*), Lutheran clergyman. Nephew of John Gottlieb Morris. Professor of theology, German and Hebrew at Gettysburg Seminary, 1844–48, 1865–93.

HAY, GEORGE (*b. Williamsburg, Va., 1765; d. 1830*), jurist, Virginia legislator. Son-in-law of James Monroe. As U.S. attorney for district of Virginia, conducted prosecution of Aaron Burr for treason. Later a federal judge in eastern Virginia, he was an able political writer on the Jeffersonian side.

HAY, JOHN MILTON (*b. Salem, Ind., 1838; d. New Hampshire, 1905*), poet, journalist, historian, statesman. Graduated Brown, 1858. Entered his uncle's law office, Springfield, Ill., 1859. John G. Nicolay, a young friend, persuaded Abraham Lincoln to hire Hay as assistant private secretary. Daily relations with Lincoln during more than four years of national peril gave Hay a wide experience of men and issues and an abiding sense of Lincoln's greatness. In 1864 Hay became assistant adjutant-general in the army on detail to the White House. Appointed secretary to the American legation in Paris, March 1865, Hay was influenced by John Bigelow to revive his early ambition to be a writer. In 1867–68 he was chargé d'affaires at Vienna; in June 1869 he became secretary of legation at Madrid, where he collected impressions which he later published as *Castilian Days* (1871). Returning to New York in 1870, he accepted a position as editorial writer and night editor on the *New York Tribune;* in January 1874, he married the wealthy Clara Stone, daughter of Amasa Stone of Cleveland. Within a year he quit journalism and removed to Cleveland to assist his father-in-law in financial matters and to continue his own literary efforts. His best-known verses, "Little Breeches" and "Jim Bludso," after appearing in the *Tribune,* were included in *Pike County Ballads and Other Pieces* (1871) and sounded an original and virile note in American poetry. He published anonymously *The Bread-Winners* (1884), a satirical novel which attacked labor unions and defended economic individualism. With John Nicolay he was author of *Abraham Lincoln: A History* (10 vols., 1890), a cooperative work which required ten years of labor. It is a monument to Lincoln and an invaluable narrative of the history of his presidency based on original sources.

Removing to Washington, D.C., 1878, as assistant secretary of state, Hay formed his most important friendship, that with Henry Adams. He had no opportunity to hold office again *post* 1880 until his help to William McKinley's campaign won him appointment as ambassador to Great Britain, 1897. With the outbreak of the Spanish-American War, April 1898, all of Hay's resources were used successfully to secure Great Britain's goodwill. Accepting the post of U.S. secretary of state, he took office in September 1898. An imperialist in his dealings with Spain, he supported President McKinley in his determination that the Philippines should become American. In 1899 he made his proposal to the European powers that a declaration should be made in favor of the "Open Door," or equal trade opportunity for all in China. This policy (actually formulated by W. W. Rockhill) was largely an illusion, but his China policy in 1900 during the Boxer Rebellion was masterful and helped China escape dissolution. It is also to his credit that the United States did not shamefully abrogate the Clayton-Bulwer treaty in 1900, and the successful 1903 settlement of the Alaskan boundary dispute with Canada was his work. He suffered some disappointment in his efforts to clear the way for the Panama Canal by treaties and was in ill-health for several years before his death in office.

HAY, MARY GARRETT (*b. Charlestown, Ind., 1857; d. New Rochelle, N.Y., 1928*), civic worker. Active in woman's suffrage and prohibition movements.

HAY, OLIVER PERRY (*b. near Hanover, Ind., 1846; d. 1930*), paleontologist. Indiana University, Ph.D., 1884. Associated with Field Museum, American Museum of Natural History, Carnegie Institution. Author of notable *Bibliography and Catalogue of the Fossil Vertebrata of North America* (1902), supplemented by *Second Bibliography and Catalogue . . .* (1929–30).

HAYDEN, AMOS SUTTON (*b. Youngstown, O., 1813; d. Collamer, O., 1880*), minister of Disciples of Christ, educator. Brother of William Hayden. A founder and first principal of Hiram College.

HAYDEN, CHARLES (*b. Boston, Mass., 1870; d. New York, N.Y., 1937*), financier, philanthropist. Founded brokerage firm of Hayden, Stone & Co., 1892. Established Hayden Foundation to aid youth work; principal donor of Hayden Planetarium, New York City. [*Supp. 2*]

HAYDEN, CHARLES HENRY (*b. Plymouth, Mass., 1856; d. Belmont, Mass., 1901*), landscape painter.

HAYDEN, EDWARD EVERETT (*b. Boston, Mass., 1858; d. Baltimore, Md., 1932*), naval officer, meteorologist. Graduated Annapolis, 1879. Established system of correcting the observatory time-signal transmission on the basis of barometric pressure and temperature. [*Supp. 1*]

HAYDEN, FERDINAND VANDIVEER (*b. Westfield, Mass., 1829; d. 1887*), geologist. Graduated Oberlin, 1850; M.D., Albany Medical College, 1853. Influenced by James Hall, went on exploration of Dakota badlands with F. B. Meek, 1853; continued surveys unofficially and as member of Warren expedition (1856–57) and Raynolds survey (1859). Served as surgeon with Union Army, 1861–65; was professor of geology, University of Pennsylvania, 1865–72. Surveyed Nebraska Territory, 1867; in so doing, laid the foundation for U.S. Geological Survey as it exists today. *Post* 1872, Hayden devoted full time to geological and natural-history surveys in the West and Southwest which were outstanding pioneer studies; the act of Congress which set aside the public reservation known as Yellowstone National Park was a result of his efforts. Subsequent to consolidation of government survey work under Clarence King (1879), he took rank as geologist and worked chiefly in Montana.

HAYDEN, HIRAM WASHINGTON (*b. Haydenville, Mass., 1820; d. Waterbury, Conn., 1904*), brass-manufacturer. Son of Joseph S. Hayden. Invented pioneer kettle-making machinery by die process, 1851; took out many patents on brass lamp burners.

HAYDEN, HORACE H. (*b. Windsor, Conn., 1769; d. Baltimore, Md., 1844*), dentist, geologist. Began life as architect; removed to New York City, 1792, where he studied dentistry with the help of John Greenwood; began practice of dentistry in Baltimore *c.* 1800. With Chapin A. Harris and others, established first dental college in the world, the Baltimore College of Dental Surgery (chartered 1840), and was its first president. He also helped organize the American Society of Dental Surgeons, 1840.

HAYDEN, JOSEPH SHEPARD (*b. Foxborough, Mass., 1802; d. Waterbury, Conn., 1877*), inventor and manufacturer of button-making machinery.

HAYDEN, WILLIAM (*b. Westmoreland Co., Pa., 1799; d. Chagrin Falls, O., 1863*), pioneer evangelist of the Disciples of Christ. Brother of Amos S. Hayden.

HAYES, AUGUSTUS ALLEN (*b. Windsor, Vt., 1806; d. 1882*), chemist. Studied chemistry at Dartmouth under James F. Dana. Removed to Boston, 1828, and was director of a chemical plant, consulting chemist to dyeing, bleaching, gas-making and smelting firms, and state assayer of Massachusetts. Quicker methods for smelting iron and refining copper were devised by him. His 1837 study of fuel economy in generating steam led to improvements in furnace and boiler construction; his investigations for the Navy Department on the use of copper sheathing in building vessels led to extensive study of the composition of sea water. Among other practical effects of his constant research was a process for manufacturing saltpeter used by the U.S. Navy in the Civil War.

HAYES, CHARLES WILLARD (*b. Granville, O., 1858; d. Washington, D.C., 1916*), geologist. Associated with U.S. Geological Survey, 1887–1911; thereafter engaged in oil prospecting in Mexico. An able administrator, he took particular interest in physiography.

HAYES, EDWARD CARY (*b. Lewiston, Maine, 1868; d. 1928*), sociologist. Ph.D., University of Chicago, 1902. Established department of sociology, University of Illinois, 1907. His theoretical outlook will be found in "Sociological Construction Lines," *American Journal of Sociology*, March 1905–July 1906. [*Supp. 1*]

HAYES, ISAAC ISRAEL (*b. Chester Co., Pa., 1832; d. 1881*), physician, Arctic explorer. Graduated M.D., University of Pennsylvania, 1853; surgeon with the second Arctic expedition of Elisha K. Kane, 1853–55. Hayes described his own early explorations and experiences in *An Arctic Boat Journey* (1860) and *The Open Polar Sea* (1867). During the Civil War he was an army surgeon at Satterlee Hospital, Philadelphia. A third voyage to the Arctic, 1869, provided materials for *The Land of Desolation* (1871); he also wrote an account of his adventures for children, *Cast Away in the Cold* (1868).

HAYES, JOHN LORD (*b. South Berwick, Maine, 1812; d. Cambridge, Mass., 1887*), lawyer, scientist, tariff lobbyist for wool industry.

HAYES, PATRICK JOSEPH (*b. New York, N.Y., 1867; d. Monticello, N.Y., 1938*), Roman Catholic clergyman. Graduated Manhattan College, 1888; or-

dained priest, 1892. As archbishop of New York, 1919–38, he unified Catholic charitable efforts in the city. He was made cardinal, 1924. [*Supp. 2*]

HAYES, RUTHERFORD BIRCHARD (*b. Delaware, O., 1822; d. Fremont, O., 1893*), lawyer, statesman, president of the United States. Graduated Kenyon College, 1842; read law for a few months in an office at Columbus, O., and studied for a year and a half at Harvard Law School. Began practice in Lower Sandusky (later Fremont), O., 1845; opened an office in Cincinnati, 1850, where he prospered. He married Lucy Webb, 1852. At first a Whig, he became a moderate Republican; he believed that war could and should be averted, even by compromising on slavery. When the Civil War began, he helped recruit men, became a major in the 23rd Ohio and later commanded the regiment. His military service was varied and capable but not distinguished; he was commissioned brigadier in 1864 and brevetted major-general of volunteers, 1865. Elected to Congress 1864, though he did not leave his military duties to campaign, he took his seat late in 1865. His best work was as chairman of the library commission. Re-elected in 1866, his career was brief; in June 1867, he resigned from Congress to accept Republican nomination for governor of Ohio. Elected after an arduous campaign, he carried through important prison reforms and a measure for better supervision of charities and was re-elected, 1869. His reputation as a courageous, liberal and wise administrator grew, and some of his addresses were widely reported and read. An astute politician, though he sympathized with many aims of the Liberal Republicans, he refused to leave his party in 1872 and campaigned for Grant. Elected governor again in 1875 in a campaign which made him a national figure and "available" for the next presidential nomination, he was awarded it at the Republican National Convention, Cincinnati, 1876. His nomination satisfied the different factions of the party and did much to hold it together. The first returns on November 7 seemed to show that the Democrat, Samuel J. Tilden, had won the election. Hayes's hopes revived next day when Zachariah Chandler sent out his telegram "Hayes has 185 votes and is elected." When it became clear that the result hinged on contested returns from South Carolina, Florida, Louisiana and Oregon, Hayes was opposed to any attempt at compromise, as he believed himself "justly and legally" elected. As a result of Carl Schurz's arguments, he consented to the creation of an Electoral Commission to examine the vote and determine the result. There is evidence that as the work of the Commission approached its close, especially after Louisiana's votes were counted for Hayes, Republican party agents made commitments to the Southern Democrats who cared less about the presidency than the restoration of white rule in the contested states of the South. On March 2, 1877, Hayes was awarded the presidency, with 185 electors to Tilden's 184.

Hayes's administration was notable for his policy of Southern pacification, his attention to reform and his insistence on conservative treatment of financial questions. His first important measure was to carry out "the bargain" which had ended the contested election by withdrawing Federal troops from the South. Though he was fiercely attacked by many Republican leaders, the wisdom of his course was shown by the immediate end of violence and establishment of relative prosperity and contentment at the South. The restoration of full autonomy to the one-time Confederate states was his greatest achievement. He continued to excite hostility among the "Stalwarts" of his own party by his measures of civil-service reform. With his encouragement, Secretary Carl Schurz at once reformed the Interior Department and other department heads took similar action. After an investigation of the New York Custom House, Hayes issued orders forbidding partisan control of the revenue service and all political assessments upon revenue officers. When Chester A. Arthur, collector at New York, and A. B. Cornell, naval officer, defied these orders, Hayes, after a long fight, had them removed. Facing an unsatisfactory monetary situation, Hayes insisted on resumption of specie payments; his determined stand helped prevent the Senate from passing the bill to postpone resumption, but did not defeat the Bland-Allison Bill. He did not fully understand the social and economic problems of the time and did nothing to strike at the root of business distress and labor troubles, but showed firmness in vetoing a popular Chinese exclusion bill as a violation of the Burlingame treaty, and in combating congressional usurpation of the Executive's powers. Gradually his conscientiousness and responsiveness to moral forces impressed the nation and he became genuinely esteemed. Believing that a president could most effectively discharge his duties by refusing to think of a second term, he had expressed at his nomination his determination to serve but one term. He returned to his "Spiegel Grove" estate near Fremont, O., in March 1881, to spend his remaining years, devoting much time to his library, filling many speaking engagements, and enlisting in a variety of humanitarian causes.

HAYES, WILLIAM HENRY (*b. Cleveland, O.?, 1829; d. at sea, 1877*), trader, swindler, adventurer, commonly known as Bully Hayes. Famous for his rascality through the Pacific and South Sea islands.

HAYFORD, JOHN FILLMORE (*b. Rouse's Point, N.Y., 1868; d. 1925*), geodesist. Graduated C.E., Cornell, 1889. Worked in U.S. Coast and Geodetic Survey and headed engineering school, Northwestern University. Established existence and applications of isostasy.

HAYGOOD, ATTICUS GREEN (*b. Watkinsville, Ga., 1839; d. 1896*), bishop of Methodist Episcopal Church, South, educator. President, Emory College, 1875–84. Resigned to act as agent of Slater Fund to aid Negro education.

HAYGOOD, LAURA ASKEW (*b. Watkinsville, Ga., 1845; d. Shanghai, China, 1900*), Methodist missionary to China, *post* 1884. Sister of Atticus G. Haygood.

HAYNE, ISAAC (*b. Colleton District, S.C., 1745; d. Charleston, S.C., 1781*), Revolutionary soldier. Condemned and hung by the British as a spy without benefit of trial, an event which produced a long controversy.

HAYNE, PAUL HAMILTON (*b. Charleston, S.C., 1830; d. 1886*), poet. Nephew of Robert Y. Hayne. Edited *Russell's Magazine*, 1857–60. Threnodist of the Southern ante-bellum regime whose ideals he illustrated in his poetry; his best single volume, *Legends and Lyrics* (1872).

HAYNE, ROBERT YOUNG (*b. Colleton District, S.C., 1791; d. Asheville, N.C., 1839*), lawyer, legislator, railroad president. Studied in Charleston office of Langdon Cheves and acquired a large practice. Elected to the South Carolina legislature, 1814, he became speaker in 1818 for one year. After two years as state attorney-general, he was elected U.S. senator, Democratic-Republican, in 1822 and again in 1828. His chief endeavor was to check the heightening of protective tariff rates. In 1830, after Daniel Webster shifted with New England from low to high tariff and from strict to broad construction of the Constitution, Hayne was his natural opponent. Foot's resolution to restrain public land sales gave occasion for a trial of eloquence. Thos. H. Benton, for the West, opposed the resolution. Hayne, alert to the Southern need of an alliance with the West, supported Benton. Webster replied to Hayne. The forensic duel began in mid-January, 1830, and covered a broad range of topics. Hayne indorsed the doctrine of nullification, arguing that the U.S. Constitution was a compact between the several states and the federal government. Webster showed that the federal government was not a party to such a compact. In 1832 when the crisis came, Hayne resigned his seat and became governor of South Carolina, to give Calhoun a place on the Senate floor. He played a leading role in the convention which adopted the nullification ordinance, and as governor defended the state's policy with vigor, yet with temperance. To Jackson's proclamation he replied in similar form defiantly, and summoned the state to furnish 10,000 troops to repel invasion. But when Clay proposed his compromise, Hayne readily concurred and rescinded the ordinance. After one term as governor, and a year as Charleston's mayor, Hayne's main interest became the project of a railroad to tap the Ohio Valley traffic at Cincinnati, make Charleston rival of New York, and bind the South and the West together. In 1836 the Louisville, Cincinnati, & Charleston Railroad Co. was formed with Hayne as president. Subscriptions to stock did not meet expectations and the panic of 1837 completed the work of ruin. Only a loan by the South Carolina legislature enabled the corporation to survive long enough to build a few miles of track.

HAYNES, JOHN (*b. Essex, England, 1594?; d. Hartford, Conn., 1653/54*). Came to Massachusetts, 1633; settled at Newtown (Cambridge). As governor of Massachusetts, 1635, banished Roger Williams. Removing to Connecticut, 1637, he was chosen the colony's first governor under the Fundamental Orders, 1639, and elected every alternate year thereafter until his death.

HAYNES, JOHN HENRY (*b. Rowe, Mass., 1849; d. North Adams, Mass., 1910*), archeologist. Graduated Williams, 1876. Did important work in excavations at Nippur; acted as first American consul at Bagdad, 1888.

HAYS, ALEXANDER (*b. Franklin, Pa., 1819; d. 1864*), soldier. Graduated West Point, 1844. Served in occupation of Texas and Mexican War. Returning to the army, 1861, after retirement, 1848, he served gallantly in the Civil War and was killed in action at the battle of the Wilderness.

HAYS, HARRY THOMPSON (*b. Wilson Co., Tenn., 1820; d. New Orleans, La., 1876*), lawyer, Confederate major-general. Brother of John C. Hays.

HAYS, ISAAC (*b. Philadelphia, Pa., 1796; d. Philadelphia, 1879*), physician, ophthalmologist. Graduated M.D., University of Pennsylvania, 1820. Editor, *post* 1827, of the valuable *American Journal of the Medical Sciences*. One of first to detect astigmatism and to study color blindness.

HAYS, JOHN COFFEE (*b. Little Cedar Lick, Tenn., 1817; d. near Piedmont, Calif., 1883*), soldier, surveyor. Went to Texas as a volunteer to help in the revolution, 1836. Served four years on the frontier against hostile Mexicans and Indians and was made captain of a Ranger company, 1840, rising to major for gallantry and efficiency. A colonel of Texas volunteer cavalry in the Mexican War, he won especial distinction at Monterey. In 1849 he went to California, and after serving as sheriff of San Francisco, 1850–53, and a single term as state surveyor-general, he entered the real-estate business. He also had large banking, public service, and industrial interests in Oakland.

HAYS, WILLIAM JACOB (*b. New York, N.Y., 1830; d. New York, 1875*), painter of animals. Studied drawing with John Rubens Smith. Visited the West, 1860, and produced a number of works of historic as well as artistic value. His "The Wounded Buffalo" is one of the best animal paintings ever executed by an American.

HAYS, WILLIAM SHAKESPEARE (*b. Louisville, Ky., 1837; d. Louisville, 1907*), ballad writer, composer.

HAYWARD, GEORGE (*b. Boston, Mass., 1791; d. 1863*), surgeon. First to employ ether anesthesia during a major operation, 1846. Graduated Harvard, 1809; M.D., University of Pennsylvania, 1812. Practiced in Boston, and was professor of surgery, Harvard Medical School, 1835–49. His medical writings are of considerable importance.

HAYWARD, NATHANIEL MANLEY (*b. Easton, Mass., 1808; d. Colchester, Conn., 1865*), inventor, manufacturer. Subjected rubber-coated cloth to sulphur fumes to bleach it and found that it did not soften, thus achieving its partial vulcanization. Patenting his process, 1839, he sold it to Charles Goodyear for $1,000. Hayward owned various businesses thereafter, and in 1843 engaged in manufacturing rubber shoes for which he had devised a method of giving luster. He helped organize the Hayward Rubber Co., 1847, was its manager until 1854, and president, 1855–65.

HAYWOOD, JOHN (*b. Halifax Co., N.C., 1762; d. near Nashville, Tenn., 1826*), jurist, historian. Self-taught, and successful as lawyer and judge in North Carolina, he removed to Tennessee, *c.* 1807, where he prospered and served as state supreme court judge, 1816–26. With Robert Cobbs he compiled *The Statute Laws of the State of Tennessee* (1831). A pioneer in the field of history in the Southwest, his books *The Natural and Aboriginal History of Tennessee* (1823) and *The Civil and Political History of Tennessee* (1823) are of high authority.

HAYWOOD, WILLIAM DUDLEY (*b. Salt Lake City, Utah, 1869; d. Russia, 1928*), labor agitator. Officer in Western Federation of Miners; advocated industrial unionism and violence in labor disputes; presided over founding convention of I.W.W., 1905, and held office in that organization. Acquitted after trial for complicity in murder of Idaho governor, F. R. Steunenberg (1906–07). Jumped bail after conviction for sedition, 1918, and resided *post* 1921 in Soviet Russia.

HAZARD, AUGUSTUS GEORGE (*b. South Kingstown, R.I., 1802; d. Enfield, Conn., 1868*), merchant. Principal owner and president, 1843–68, of the Hazard Powder Co. with departments in practically every state in the Union.

HAZARD, EBENEZER (*b. Philadelphia, Pa., 1744; d. 1817*), editor, businessman, scholar. Graduated College of New Jersey (Princeton), 1762. As surveyor-general of the U.S. Post Office, 1776–82, he traveled extensively and collected source materials of early American history. His term as postmaster-general, 1782–89, was one of the few in which the post office paid its way. His pioneer *Historical Collections*

(1792–94) contain documents relating to the discovery and colonization period of America and records of the New England Confederation edited with conscientious skill.

HAZARD, JONATHAN J. (*b. Narragansett, R.I., c. 1744; d. Verona, N.Y., post 1824*), Rhode Island political leader.

HAZARD, ROWLAND GIBSON (*b. South Kingstown, R.I., 1801; d. 1888*), woolen manufacturer, author. Brother of Thomas R. Hazard.

HAZARD, SAMUEL (*b. Philadelphia, Pa., 1784; d. Germantown, Pa., 1870*), editor, antiquarian. Son of Ebenezer Hazard.

HAZARD, THOMAS (*b. Rhode Island, 1720; d. South Kingstown, R.I., 1798*), Abolitionist. Nicknamed "College Tom." One of first of Society of Friends to work actively against slavery.

HAZARD, THOMAS ROBINSON (*b. South Kingstown, R.I., 1797; d. near Newport, R.I., 1886*), agriculturist, manufacturer, social reformer. Grandson of Thomas Hazard. Nicknamed "Shepherd Tom." Author of *Recollections of Olden Times,* and *The Jonny-Cake Letters* (1882, 1915).

HAZELIUS, ERNEST LEWIS (*b. Neusalz, Prussia, 1777; d. Lexington, S.C., 1853*), Lutheran clergyman. Came to America, 1800. Taught theology, *post* 1807, in several Moravian and Lutheran seminaries.

HAZELTINE, MAYO WILLIAMSON (*b. Boston, Mass., 1841; d. Atlantic City, N.J., 1909*), lawyer, journalist. Literary editor, New York Sun, 1878–1909.

HAZELTON, GEORGE COCHRANE (*b. Boscobel, Wis., 1868; d. 1921*), actor, lawyer, playwright, novelist. Co-author, with J. Harry Benrimo, of *The Yellow Jacket* (1912).

HAZELWOOD, JOHN (*b. England, c. 1726; d. 1800*), Revolutionary naval officer. Active in planning defense of the Hudson and Delaware rivers; especially distinguished before Philadelphia, Oct. 1777.

HAZEN, ALLEN (*b. Hartford, Vt., 1869; d. Miles City, Mont., 1930*), hydraulic and sanitary engineer. With Gardner S. Williams, developed Williams and Hazen pipe-flow formula. [*Supp. 1*]

HAZEN, HENRY ALLEN (*b. Sirur, India, 1849; d. Washington, D.C., 1900*), meteorologist. Came to America, 1859. Graduated Dartmouth, 1871. Associated with U.S. Weather Bureau and its predecessor agencies *post* 1881.

HAZEN, MOSES (*b. Haverhill, Mass., 1733; d. Troy, N.Y., 1803*), Revolutionary soldier. A veteran of the French and Indian War and a resident of Canada at outbreak of the Revolution, Hazen took part in Montgomery's attack on Quebec but quarreled with Benedict Arnold. Later as colonel of a Canadian regiment in Continental service, he served with it under Washington's command at various times, 1776–81. He was promoted brigadier-general, 1781.

HAZEN, WILLIAM BABCOCK (*b. Vermont, 1830; d. 1887*), soldier. Graduated West Point, 1855. Served in Oregon and Texas, and rose to colonel in regular army and major-general of volunteers during the Civil War. As an officer on the frontier, *post* 1865, Hazen denounced exaggerated claims of Western land promoters and revealed corruption in the post-trader system which led to Secretary of War Belknap's resignation, 1876. In 1880 Hazen became brigadier-general and chief signal officer in the War Department, a post which included managing the Weather Bureau and involved him in a humiliating controversy. For censuring Secretary of War Lincoln for failure to send a third relief party to find A. W. Greely's expedition stranded in the Arctic since 1881, Hazen was court-martialed and reprimanded, 1885.

HEADLEY, JOEL TYLER (*b. Walton, N.Y., 1813; d. Newburgh, N.Y., 1897*), author. Brother of Phineas C. Headley. Graduated Union, 1839. Prolific, superficial and popular, he produced over thirty biographies, histories and travel books. *Napoleon and his Marshals* (1846) reached a 50th edition, 1861. *Washington and his Generals* was another resounding success.

HEADLEY, PHINEAS CAMP (*b. Walton, N.Y., 1819; d. Lexington, Mass., 1903*), Presbyterian clergyman. Brother of Joel T. Headley and like him a facile writer of inspirational biographies.

HEALY, GEORGE PETER ALEXANDER (*b. Boston, Mass., 1813; d. Chicago, Ill., 1894*), portrait painter. Encouraged by Thomas Sully; studied in Paris under Gros where he made his first success. Painted hundreds of portraits as well as historical and genre subjects. "Webster's Reply to Hayne" is his best-known historical composition.

HEAP, SAMUEL DAVIES (*b. Carlisle, Pa., 1781; d. Tunis, 1853*), naval surgeon. Consul at Tunis, 1823–53, except for brief intervals. Negotiated a treaty, 1824, which replaced the treaty of 1797 with Tunis and which stood without amendment for eighty years.

HEARD, AUGUSTINE (*b. Ipswich, Mass., 1785; d. Ipswich, 1868*), sea captain, merchant. Partner in Samuel Russell & Co. and in its successor firm Augustine Heard & Co., Canton, China. Through maintenance of high ethical standards, the firm was highly regarded by Chinese and prospered, 1840–65.

HEARD, DWIGHT BANCROFT (*b. Boston, Mass., 1869; d. Arizona, 1929*), investment banker, farmer. Nephew of Franklin F. Heard. Removed to the Southwest, 1894, and exerted a dominating influence on Arizona affairs after settling in Phoenix. A leader in movement resulting in U.S. Reclamation Act, 1902, and in all phases of the development of Arizona as territory and state.

HEARD, FRANKLIN FISKE (*b. Wayland, Mass., 1825; d. Boston, Mass., 1889*), legal author. Graduated Harvard, 1848. Author of over twenty legal treatises now largely superseded but valuable to the profession in their time. Among these were *A Treatise on Libel and Slander* (1860), the first American work on this subject, and *Equity Pleading* (1882).

HEARN, LAFCADIO (*b. Santa Maura Island, Greece, 1850; d. Japan, 1904*), author. Son of C. B. Hearn, surgeon-major in the British Army, and Rosa Tessima, a Greek. After an unhappy childhood in Ireland, Hearn arrived in New York, 1869, friendless, half-blind, and morbidly shy. Beset by poverty and hardship there and in Cincinnati, he began work for the *Cincinnati Enquirer*, 1873, and became a successful reporter. Commissioned by the *Cincinnati Commercial* to report politics in New Orleans, 1877, he was dismissed and almost died of dengue fever and starvation before he got work on the New Orleans *Item*. The *Times-Democrat* assigned him, 1881, to write a Sunday feature of translations from the French and Spanish, and his initial book, *One of Cleopatra's Nights* (1882), a very able rendering of six stories by Theo. Gautier, was a result of this work. His articles on strange and exotic subjects were collected in *Stray Leaves from Strange Literatures* (1884). *Gombo Zhèbes* (1885), a collection of proverbs in French Negro patois, followed. *Some Chinese Ghosts*, an exquisitely written group of Oriental legends, appeared in 1887. Hearn lived precariously in Martinique, 1887–89, and produced *Two Years in the French West Indies* (1890), still the most perfect picture of the islands that has been painted; he also wrote *Youma* (1890), a novel of the slave rebellion there. Early in 1890 he went to Japan, married a Japanese girl and became a Japanese citizen under the name of Koizumi Yakumo. He taught at various schools and in 1894 was given the chair of English literature, Imperial University of Tokio, which he occupied until 1903. Among the twelve books which he wrote during this period are *Glimpses of Unfamiliar Japan* (1894) and the posthumous *Japan: An Attempt at Interpretation* (1904), the summation of all his sympathetic and acute observation of his adopted country. Of all modern writers in English, his prose was possibly the most polished, exact and lyrical, but he was deficient in breadth of view, knowledge of human nature and ordinary common sense.

HEARST, GEORGE (*b. near Sullivan, Mo., 1820; d. Washington, D.C., 1891*), mining prospector, mine owner, publisher. Father of William Randolph Hearst. Crossed the plains on foot to California, 1850. Engaged in quartz mining and later in placer mining. By 1859, speculating in Nevada strikes, he laid the foundation of a great fortune. His interests spread to other states and to Mexico; his famous holdings, among them the Ophir, Homestake and Anaconda mines, made him a multimillionaire. In 1880 he acquired the San Francisco *Daily Examiner*. Appointed as a Democrat to the U.S. Senate in March 1886 to fill an unexpired term, in 1888 he was elected for the full term as senator from California.

HEARST, PHOEBE APPERSON (*b. Missouri, 1842; d. 1919*), philanthropist. Wife of George Hearst.

HEATH, JAMES EWELL (*b. probably Northumberland Co., Va., 1792; d. 1862*), author, state auditor of Virginia, 1819–49. Published *Edgehill, or The Family of the Fitzroyals* (1828); gave important assistance to *Southern Literary Messenger* during its first year, 1834.

HEATH, PERRY SANFORD (*b. Muncie, Ind., 1857; d. 1927*), newspaperman, politician. For directing publicity in McKinley's 1896 campaign, he was appointed first assistant postmaster-general and installed the rural free-delivery system. He resigned in 1900 and was later censured for the character of some of his appointees.

HEATH, THOMAS KURTON. [See McINTYRE, JAMES, 1857–1937.]

HEATH, WILLIAM (*b. Roxbury, Mass., 1737; d. Roxbury, 1814*), Revolutionary soldier. Active in pre-Revolutionary committees and the Massachusetts Provincial Congress. Served with credit before Boston but, although promoted major-general, 1777, proved inept in the field. Commanded Eastern district, 1777–79, and lower Hudson, 1779–83. Author of *Memoirs* (1798), an important source work.

HEATHCOTE, CALEB (*b. Derbyshire, England, 1665/66; d. 1720/21*), merchant, statesman, churchman. Came to New York, 1692; appointed to the governor's council, he served on it, except 1698–1702, until his death. Prospering as a contractor and farmer of Westchester Co. taxes, he was colonel of militia, 1692–1720, and a county judge. He took up residence in Westchester borough town, 1696, and was its mayor for life. Heathcote patented many large tracts of land including the "Great Nine Partners" tract and the Manor of Scarsdale (1701), the last manor granted in the British Empire. He was mayor of New York, 1711–13. A devoted churchman, he aided the partial establishment of Anglicanism in New York and led in founding Trinity Parish. He set up Episcopal worship in Westchester, Rye, New Rochelle, Eastchester and Yonkers and was chiefly responsible for planting episcopacy in Connecticut.

HEATON, JOHN LANGDON (*b. Canton, N.Y., 1860; d. Brooklyn, N.Y., 1935*), newspaper editor, writer. Brilliant editorial writer for New York *World*, 1900–31. [*Supp. 1*]

HÉBERT, LOUIS (*b. Iberville Parish, La., 1820; d. St. Martin Parish, La., 1901*), engineer, Confederate brigadier-general. Graduated West Point, 1845. Cousin of Paul O. Hébert.

HÉBERT, PAUL OCTAVE (*b. Iberville Parish, La., 1818; d. New Orleans, La., 1880*), engineer, Confederate brigadier-general. Graduated West Point, 1840. Participated in all important battles of Mexican War. Democratic governor of Louisiana, 1853–56.

HECK, BARBARA (*b. Ballingrane, Ireland, 1734; d. Augusta, Canada, 1804*), "Mother of Methodism in America." Came to New York, 1760. Inspired Philip Embury to preach, 1766, thus beginning the Wesleyan movement in America.

HECKER, FRIEDRICH KARL FRANZ (*b. Eichtersheim, Germany, 1811; d. Summerfield, Ill., 1881*), German revolutionist, Union soldier, farmer.

HECKER, ISAAC THOMAS (*b. New York, N.Y., 1819; d. New York, 1888*), Roman Catholic priest, founder of the Paulists. Under influence of Orestes Brownson, studied philosophy, engaged in early labor and reform activities; was at Brook Farm, 1843; lived with Thoreau family. Became a Roman Catholic, 1844; was ordained a Redemptorist priest in London, 1849. Missionary to German immigrants in America, 1851–57, he was dismissed from the order for urging need of an English-speaking Redemptorist house. In 1858, with papal approval he founded the Paulist order in New York and served as its superior until his death. Father Hecker conceived of the Catholic Church as essentially democratic, hence uniquely suited to democratic America. He founded the *Catholic World*, 1865. Among his books were *Questions of the Soul* (1852) and *Aspirations of Nature* (1857).

HECKEWELDER, JOHN GOTTLIEB ERNESTUS (*b. Bedford, England, 1743; d. Bethlehem, Pa., 1823*), missionary of the Moravian Church to the Indians of Ohio. Came to America, 1754. Served as a messenger to frontier Indian settlements, 1763–71. In his regular mission work as assistant to David Zeisberger, 1771–86, he lived with the Moravian Christian Indians, protecting them as they were forced westward. He served the U.S. government on commissions to arrange peace treaties with the frontier Indians, 1792–93, and recorded his views of Indian life in a number of important publications through which the story of colonial Indian affairs in the Ohio country received a proper perspective in history.

HECTOR, FRANCISCO LUIS. [See CARONDELET, FRANCISCO LUIS HECTOR, BARON DE, *c. 1748–1807*.]

HEDDING, ELIJAH (*b. Pine Plains, N.Y., 1780; d. Poughkeepsie, N.Y., 1852*), Methodist Episcopal bishop, 1824–52. One of foremost agents in extending Methodism in New England. Instrumental in founding *Zion's Herald*, Boston, 1823, earliest Methodist periodical.

HEDGE, FREDERIC HENRY (*b. Cambridge, Mass., 1805; d. Cambridge, 1890*), Unitarian clergyman, professor at Harvard. Son of Levi Hedge. Had early education in Germany; graduated Harvard, 1825. With R. W. Emerson and George Ripley, organized Transcendentalist group and imbued it with his own enthusiasm for German philosophy. Of his numerous publications, the most important is *Prose Writers of Germany* (1848), which helped to introduce German literature to America.

HEDGE, LEVI (*b. Warwick, Mass., 1766; d. 1844*), philosopher. Graduated Harvard, 1792; taught there, *post* 1795. His *Elements of Logick* (1816) was a remarkably clear, practical textbook which was far in advance of its time.

HEENAN, JOHN CARMEL (*b. West Troy, N.Y., 1835; d. Green River Station, Wyo., 1873*), pugilist, the "Benicia Boy."

HEGEMAN, JOHN ROGERS (*b. Brooklyn, N.Y., 1844; d. Mamaroneck, N.Y., 1919*), president, Metropolitan Life Insurance Co., 1891–1919.

HEILPRIN, ANGELO (*b. Sátoralja-Ujhely, Hungary, 1853; d. New York, N.Y., 1907*), geologist, paleontologist. Son of Michael Heilprin. Came to America as a child. Famous as a traveler, his explorations included Mexico, Alaska, British Guiana, North Africa, the West Indies, and the Arctic with Peary, 1891–92.

HEILPRIN, MICHAEL (*b. Piotrkow, Poland, 1823; d. 1888*), scholar, writer, encyclopaedia expert. Came to America, 1856. Began lifelong encyclopaedia work on *New American Cyclopaedia*, 1858; was a valued contributor to the *Nation*.

HEINEMANN, ERNST (*b. Brunswick, Germany, 1848; d. Fort Wadsworth, N.Y., 1912*), woodengraver.

HEINRICH, ANTONY PHILIP (*b. Schönbüchel, Bohemia, 1781; d. New York, N.Y., 1861*), composer. Came to America, 1805. Led a wandering, erratic life, here and abroad. Published *The Dawning of Music in Kentucky* (1820), a collection of his compositions. He was presumably the first composer to essay "Americanism" in music, and to build a great part of his amazing output on American subjects.

HEINRICH, MAX (*b. Chemnitz, Germany, 1853; d. 1916*), concert baritone. Came to America, 1873. A pioneer in cultivating taste for German *Lieder*.

HEINTZELMAN, SAMUEL PETER (*b. Manheim, Pa., 1805; d. Washington, D.C., 1880*), soldier. Graduated West Point, 1826. Distinguished for gallantry in Mexican War and on Far West frontier duty. As division and corps commander under McClellan, 1862, he lacked initiative and magnified difficulties; his subsequent Civil War service was administrative. Retired as major-general, 1869.

HEINTZELMAN, STUART (*b. New York, N.Y., 1876; d. Hot Springs, Ark., 1935*), army officer. Grandson of Samuel P. Heintzelman. Graduated West Point, 1899. Served in Philippine insurrection and Boxer uprising; chief of staff, II Army, World War I. Skilled in training of officers. Promoted major-general, 1931. [*Supp. 1*]

HEINZ, HENRY JOHN (*b. Pittsburgh, Pa., 1844; d. Pittsburgh, 1919*), manufacturer of prepared food. Founded F. and J. Heinz, 1876 (H. J. Heinz Co., 1888); was a pioneer in the pure-food movement in America; invented advertising slogan "57 Varieties."

HEINZE, FREDERICK AUGUSTUS (*b. Brooklyn, N.Y., 1869; d. Saratoga Springs, N.Y., 1914*), copper miner, speculator. Graduated Columbia School of Mines, 1889. Engaged in successful operations at Butte, Mont., 1892–1906. Lost epic struggle for control of the industry to the Amalgamated Copper Co.

HEINZEN, KARL PETER (*b. Grevenbroich, Rhenish Prussia, 1809; d. 1880*), German revolutionist, journalist, satirist. Resided in America *post* 1850; settled in Boston, 1859. Most intellectual of the German revolutionist exiles, his work became known only to a few. Editor of a radical weekly, the *Pionier*, 1854–79.

HEISS, MICHAEL (*b. Pfahldorf, Bavaria, 1818; d. Milwaukee, Wis., 1890*), Roman Catholic clergyman. Studied under Görres, Döllinger and Moehler at Munich. Came to America, 1842, and served as pastor and missionary to Germans in Wisconsin. First bishop of La Crosse, 1868–80; archbishop of Milwaukee, 1880–90. Helped establish Catholic University, Washington, D.C.

HELBRON, PETER (*b. Hilbringen, Germany, 1739; d. Carlisle, Pa., 1816*), Roman Catholic clergyman, Capuchin. Came to Pennsylvania, 1787. Pastor in Philadelphia, 1791–96. His later missionary journeys covered all western Pennsylvania and as far as Buffalo; he organized the first congregation at Pittsburgh.

HELFFENSTEIN, JOHN ALBERT CONRAD (*b. Mosbach, Germany, 1748; d. Germantown, Pa., 1790*), German Reformed clergyman. Came to America, 1772; won fame for the eloquence and pungency of his sermons. Served congregations at Lancaster and Germantown, Pa., 1772–90.

HELLER, MAXIMILIAN (*b. Prague, Bohemia, 1860; d. 1929*), rabbi. Came to America, 1879. Graduated University of Cincinnati, 1882; Hebrew Union College, 1884. Pastor of Temple Sinai, New Orleans, 1887–1927. A leader in reform movements and an early Zionist, he was also professor of Hebrew language and literature at Tulane University, 1912–28.

HELM, CHARLES JOHN (*b. Hornellsville, N.Y., 1817; d. Toronto, Canada, 1868*), U.S. consul-general, 1858–61, and later Confederate agent at Havana, Cuba.

HELM, JOHN LARUE (*b. near Elizabethtown, Ky., 1802; d. 1867*), lawyer, Kentucky legislator. Whig governor of Kentucky, 1850–51; Democratic governor-elect, 1867. President, Louisville and Nashville Railroad, 1854–60.

HELMER, BESSIE BRADWELL (*b. Chicago, Ill., 1858; d. Battle Creek, Mich., 1927*), lawyer, editor, publisher. An important figure in the growth of the American Association of University Women.

HELMPRAECHT, JOSEPH (*b. Niederwinkling, Bavaria, 1820; d. New York, N.Y., 1884*), Roman Catholic clergyman, Redemptorist. Came to America, 1843; served German congregations in Baltimore, Md., Buffalo, N.Y., and elsewhere. American provincial of his order, 1865–77.

HELMUTH, JUSTUS HENRY CHRISTIAN (*b. Helmstedt, Germany, 1745; d. 1825*), Lutheran clergyman. Came to America, 1769. Pastor at Lancaster, Pa., 1769–79; co-pastor of St. Michael's and Zion's, Philadelphia, 1779–1820. Founded *Evangelisches Magazin*, 1812, first Lutheran Church paper in the United States.

HELMUTH, WILLIAM TOD (*b. Philadelphia, Pa., 1833; d. 1902*), surgeon. Great-grandson of Justus H. C. Helmuth. An important figure in teaching and practice of homeopathy in St. Louis, Philadelphia, and New York; edited several homeopathic journals; contributed extensively to literature of medicine and surgery.

HELPER, HINTON ROWAN (*b. Rowan, now Davie, Co., N.C., 1829; d. Washington, D.C., 1909*), author, businessman. Published *The Impending Crisis* (1857), a brief in behalf of non-slaveholding Southern whites in which he attributed the South's economic backwardness to impoverishment of free labor by slavery. Furiously attacked in the South, the book caused a greater sensation than *Uncle Tom's Cabin* and was a powerful contributing cause of the Civil War. Helper was consul at Buenos Aires, 1861–66. Interested in commercial relations with South America, he tried to promote a railroad from Hudson Bay to the Strait of Magellan and almost monomaniacally sacrificed everything to this dream. He died, despondent, by suicide.

HEMENWAY, MARY PORTER TILESTON (*b. New York, N.Y., 1820; d. 1894*), philanthropist. Aided freedmen; instituted sewing, cooking, gymnastics in Boston schools; contributed lavishly to save Old South Meeting House, Boston, and to promote study of American history and ethnology.

HEMMETER, JOHN CONRAD (*b. Baltimore, Md., 1863; d. Baltimore, 1931*), physiologist, musical composer. Made early, possibly first, use of Roentgen rays to study the stomach; invented method of intubating the duodenum. M.D., University of Maryland, 1884; Ph.D., Johns Hopkins, 1890.

HEMPEL, CHARLES JULIUS (*b. Solingen, Germany, 1811; d. 1879*), homeopathic physician, author, translator. Came to America, 1835. Graduated M.D., University of the City of New York, 1845. Author of *A New and Comprehensive System of Materia Medica and Therapeutics* (1859).

HEMPHILL, JOHN (*b. near Blackstock, S.C., 1803; d. 1862*), Texan jurist. Removed to Texas, 1838. Chief-justice of Texas supreme court, 1840–58, he was called "the John Marshall of Texas" for his wisdom in reconciliation of the civil and common law systems there. He served as U.S. senator, 1858–61.

HEMPHILL, JOSEPH (*b. Thornbury Township, Pa., 1770; d. 1842*), lawyer, Philadelphia jurist. Congressman, Federalist, from Pennsylvania, 1801–03; Democrat, 1819–27, 1829–31. Opponent of slavery.

HEMPL, GEORGE (*b. Whitewater, Wis., 1859; d. 1921*), philologist. Graduated University of Michigan, 1879; Ph.D., Jena, 1889. Taught at Michigan, 1889–1906; at Leland Stanford, 1907–21. Published extensively on etymology and usage; studied American dialects.

HENCHMAN, DANIEL (*b. Boston, Mass., 1689; d. 1761*), merchant, colonial bookseller, importer and manufacturer whose records shed a valuable light on colonial commerce. Maternal grandfather of John Hancock. [*Supp.* 1]

HENCK, JOHN BENJAMIN (*b. Philadelphia, Pa., 1815; d. Montecito, Calif., 1903*), engineer, educator. Supervised, at first with W. S. Whitwell, the filling-in, planning and paving of Boston's Back Bay, 1855–81. Head of civil engineering department, Massachusetts Institute of Technology, 1865–81.

HENDEL, JOHN WILLIAM (*b. Dürkheim, Germany, 1740; d. Philadelphia, Pa., 1798*), German Reformed clergyman. Came to America, 1765. Held pastorates at Lancaster, Tulpehocken and Philadelphia, Pa.

HENDERSON, ARCHIBALD (*b. Granville Co., N.C., 1768; d. Salisbury, N.C., 1822*), lawyer. Son of Richard Henderson. Congressman, Federalist, from North Carolina, 1799–1803; was one of the ablest lawyers of his time.

HENDERSON, CHARLES RICHMOND (*b. Covington, Ind., 1848; d. Charleston, S.C., 1915*), Baptist clergyman, sociologist. After pastorates in Terre Haute, Ind., and Detroit, he served as university chaplain and sociology professor at the University of Chicago, 1892–1915. Many of his books and articles were of pioneer importance in penology, industrial insurance and industrial legislation. They include *Introduction to the Study of the Dependent, Defective and Delinquent Classes* (1893); *Modern Methods of Charity* (1904); *Industrial Insurance in the United States* (1907).

HENDERSON, DANIEL McINTYRE (*b. Glasgow, Scotland, 1851; d. Baltimore, Md., 1906*), bookseller, poet. Came to America, 1873. Proprietor, University Book Store, Baltimore. Author of *Poems, Scottish and American* (1888); *A Bit Bookie of Verse* (1905).

HENDERSON, DAVID BREMNER (*b. Old Deer, Scotland, 1840; d. Dubuque, Iowa, 1906*), Iowa pioneer, Union soldier, lawyer. Came to America as a child; raised in Illinois and Fayette Co., Iowa. Congressman, Republican, from Iowa, 1883–1903; speaker of House, 1899–1903. An ardent "stand-patter."

HENDERSON, JAMES PINCKNEY (*b. Lincoln Co., N.C., 1808; d. Washington, D.C., 1858*), lawyer, first governor of Texas. Fought in Texan War for independence and Mexican War. Attorney-general of Texas Republic and secretary of state; performed important service as Texas agent to England and France, 1837–39. Governor, 1846–47; U.S. senator, 1857–58.

HENDERSON, JOHN (*b. Bridgeton, N.J., 1795; d. Pass Christian, Miss., 1857*), lawyer. Removed as a young man to Mississippi. U.S. senator, Whig, from Mississippi, 1839–45. Stood trial, 1851, for his support of Lopez in filibustering expeditions against Spanish authorities in Cuba.

HENDERSON, JOHN BROOKS (*b. Danville, Va., 1826; d. Washington, D.C., 1913*), lawyer. Removed to Missouri as a child. Served as Democrat in state legislature; was in 1861 one of most influential antisecession forces in Missouri. Appointed U.S. senator, 1862, he was elected for a full term as a Republican, 1863. He quickly became prominent, served on important committees and was responsible for much of the Civil War financial legislation. His great test of courage came in the impeachment trial of President Johnson. A severe critic of Johnson, he voted "not guilty," and was denounced by the Missouri radicals. He returned to practice law in St. Louis and in 1889 retired to Washington, D.C.

HENDERSON, LEONARD (*b. Granville Co., N.C., 1772; d. 1833*), jurist. Son of Richard Henderson. Judge of North Carolina superior court, 1808–16; supreme court, 1818–33; chief justice, 1829–33. Had great influence as a teacher, conducting a law school in connection with his law office.

HENDERSON, PETER (*b. Pathhead, Scotland, 1822; d. 1890*), horticulturist, seed merchant. Came to America, 1843. Established New York seed and garden supply house, Peter Henderson & Co. Among his numerous books were: *Gardening for Profit* (1866); *Gardening for Pleasure* (1875, 1888); *Henderson's Hand Book of Plants* (1881). He also exerted great influence in his field through a very large personal correspondence.

HENDERSON, RICHARD (*b. Hanover Co., Va., 1735; d. Nutbush Creek, Granville Co., N.C., 1785*), lawyer, North Carolina jurist. As early as 1764, organized Richard Henderson & Co., a land company, with Daniel Boone as agent, and by 1769 was projecting a colony in Kentucky. In 1773, Henderson retired from his judgeship of the superior court to give full time to Western colonization projects, organizing the Louisa (renamed the Transylvania) Company, 1774. In 1775, he signed a treaty at Sycamore Shoals with the Cherokees giving him title to a tract between the Kentucky and Cumberland rivers. Preceded by the trail-blazing Boone, Henderson went through Cumberland Gap and established the first settlement of his projected colony at Boonesborough. North Carolina and Virginia objected to the colony within their chartered limits, and the Revolution ended any chance of English support for the legality of the enterprise. Later, in 1779–80, Henderson promoted colonization in western Tennessee, establishing a settlement at French Lick, later Nashville.

HENDERSON, THOMAS (*b. Freehold, N.J., 1743; d. Freehold, 1824*), physician, Revolutionary soldier. Held many political offices in New Jersey, including acting-governor; was a Federalist congressman, 1795–97.

HENDERSON, WILLIAM JAMES (*b. Newark, N.J., 1855; d. New York, N.Y., 1937*), outstanding music critic of the *New York Times*, 1887–1902, and of the New York *Sun*, 1902–37. [*Supp. 2*]

HENDRICK (*b. c. 1680; d. at battle of Lake George, 1755*), Mohawk sachem. His Indian name, Tiyanoga. As spokesman for the Mohawks, his friendship was cultivated by William Johnson and the English colonial governors. Active in his efforts to hold the Six Nations to the English interest against the French menace, he represented his tribe at the numerous councils between the English and the Six Nations which culminated in the Albany Congress of 1754. There he delivered the greatest speech of his career, taking the English to task for neglecting their border defenses and leaving the Mohawks exposed to French reprisals. In the summer of 1755, he lost his life while leading a force of Mohawks in William Johnson's expedition against Crown Point.

HENDRICK, ELLWOOD (*b. Albany, N.Y., 1861; d. New York, N.Y., 1930*), chemist, broker, author.

HENDRICKS, THOMAS ANDREWS (*b. near Zanesville, O., 1819; d. Indianapolis, Ind., 1885*), lawyer, Indiana legislator. Nephew of William Hendricks. Raised in Shelby Co., Ind. Congressman, Democrat, from Indiana, 1851–55; commissioner, general land office, 1855–59. As U.S. senator from Indiana, 1863–69, won prominence as a leader of the Democratic opposition, a constant critic of every administration policy. He supported Johnson's plan of reconstruction but opposed the 14th and 15th Amendments. Governor of Indiana, 1873–77, one of the first Democratic governors of a Northern state after the Civil War. Vice-president of the United States, 1885.

HENDRICKS, WILLIAM (*b. Ligonier, Pa., 1782; d. Madison, Ind., 1850*), lawyer, Indiana legislator. Removed to Indiana, 1813; was congressman, Democrat, 1816–22, and governor of Indiana, 1822–25. As U.S. senator, 1825–37, he was interested especially in development of roads and canals, and in the cession of public lands to the individual states.

HENDRIX, EUGENE RUSSELL (*b. Fayette, Mo., 1847; d. Kansas City, Mo., 1927*), clergyman of Methodist Episcopal Church, South. Was engaged mainly in administrative work; bishop, 1886–1927. Brother of Joseph C. Hendrix. First president, Federal Council of Churches of Christ in America, 1908–12.

HENDRIX, JOSEPH CLIFFORD (*b. Fayette, Mo., 1853; d. Brooklyn, N.Y., 1904*), banker. Brother of Eugene R. Hendrix. Congressman, Democrat, from New York, 1893–95. President, National Bank of Commerce, New York, 1900–03.

HENEY, FRANCIS JOSEPH (*b. Lima, N.Y., 1859; d. Santa Monica, Calif., 1937*), lawyer. Raised in San Francisco. Practiced first in Arizona Territory; *post* 1895 in California. Prosecuted Oregon land frauds, 1903, and Abe Ruef, 1906–08. Progressive politician, pro-labor, he was long at feud with Hiram Johnson. [*Supp. 2*]

HENING, WILLIAM WALLER (*b. probably Spotsylvania Co., Va., 1767/68; d. Richmond, Va., 1828*), legal writer. Edited *The Statutes at Large; Being a Collection of all the Laws of Virginia* (13 vols., 1809–23), at instance of Thomas Jefferson.

HENKEL, PAUL (*b. Rowan Co., N.C., 1754; d. New Market, Va., 1825*), Lutheran clergyman. The greatest Lutheran home missionary of his generation; traveled each year through Virginia, North Carolina, Tennessee, Kentucky, Ohio and Indiana.

HENLEY, ROBERT (*b. Williamsburg, Va., 1783; d. Sullivan's Island, S.C., 1828*), naval officer. Second in command to Commodore Macdonough at battle of Lake Champlain, September 1814, he aggressively commanded the brig *Eagle*.

HENNEPIN, LOUIS (*b. Ath, Flemish province of Hainaut, 1640; d. post 1701*), Recollect friar. Missionary in Canada, 1675–82. Accompanied La Salle, 1679, on his expedition through the Great Lakes into the Illinois country; explored the upper Mississippi, 1680. Captured by Sioux, he was rescued by Duluth after traveling over much of Minnesota. On his return to France, he published *Description de la Louisiane* (Paris, 1683), called "the most minute of all narratives of early American exploration." Two later books, *Nouveau Voyage* (Antwerp, 1696) and *Nouvelle Découverte* (Utrecht, 1697), the latter of which appeared in English as *A New Discovery* (1698), also deal with his North American travels but are filled with false claims. His works have charm and graphic quality but are marred by his garrulity, vanity, mendacity and appropriating without credit what others had written. He was in Rome in 1701; after that no trace of him has been found.

HENNESSY, JOHN (*b. Bulgaden, Ireland, 1825; d. Dubuque, Iowa, 1900*), Roman Catholic clergyman. Came to America, 1847. Ordained, St. Louis, Mo., 1850. Bishop of Dubuque, 1866–93; archbishop, 1893–1900. Staunch advocate of parochial schools.

HENNESSY, WILLIAM JOHN (*b. Thomastown, Ireland, 1839; d. 1917*), painter, illustrator. Came to America as a child. Successful landscape and genre painter, he made his mark particularly as an illustrator of the works of Tennyson, Longfellow, Whittier and other 19th-century classic authors.

HENNI, JOHN MARTIN (*b. Misanenga, Switzerland, 1805; d. Milwaukee, Wis., 1881*), Roman Catholic clergyman. Came to America, 1828. Ordained 1829; was pastor in Cincinnati, O. Founded *Wahrheitsfreund*, Cincinnati, 1837, first American German Catholic newspaper. Consecrated bishop of Milwaukee, 1844; archbishop, 1875.

HENNINGSEN, CHARLES FREDERICK (*b. probably Belgium, 1815; d. Washington, D.C., 1877*), soldier, author. Fought in Spain, Caucasus, Hungary; came to America with Kossuth, 1851. Joined William Walker in filibuster to Nicaragua, 1856. Colonel 59th Virginia Infantry, 1861–62. Wrote extensively on historical and cultural subjects.

HENNY, DAVID CHRISTIAAN (*b. Arnhem, Netherlands, 1860; d. 1935*), hydraulic engineer. Came to America, 1884. Authority on the construction of dams and inventor of the "Henny shear joint" used at Boulder and Grand Coulee dams. [*Supp. 1*]

HENRI, ROBERT (*b. Cincinnati, O., 1865; d. New York, N.Y., 1929*), painter, teacher. Studied at Pennsylvania Academy of Fine Arts under T. P. Anschutz and in Paris under Bouguereau and Fleury. Taught successfully at Women's School of Design, Philadelphia, Pa., the Art Students League and other schools, laying emphasis on visual honesty, avoiding imitation and being true to one's self. Associated with John Sloan, A. B. Davies, George Luks, Maurice Prendergast, Shinn, Glackens and Lawson in the group of realists known as "The Eight." *The Art Spirit* (1923) was compiled from Henri's essays and classroom notes; like his painting, the writing is sketchy but vital. The chief merit of his art is its naturalness and spontaneity.

HENROTIN, CHARLES (*b. Belgium, 1843; d. Chicago, Ill., 1914*), banker. Brother of Fernand Henrotin. Came to America as a child. A leader in organizing the Chicago Stock Exchange, he was its first president, 1882–84.

HENROTIN, FERNAND (*b. Brussels, Belgium, 1847; d. 1906*), surgeon. Brother of Charles Henrotin. Came to America as an infant. Graduated Rush Medical School, 1868. A founder of the Chicago Polyclinic. Achieved international reputation in the field of operative gynecology and contributed to its literature.

HENRY, ALEXANDER (*b. New Brunswick, N.J., 1739; d. Montreal, Canada, 1824*), fur trader, explorer in the Great Lakes and Northwest area, 1760–76. Author of *Travels and Adventures* (1809). [*Supp. 1*]

HENRY, ANDREW (*b. York Co., Pa., c. 1775; d. Harmony Township, Mo., 1833*), fur trapper, lead miner. Removed to Missouri, 1800, and engaged in lead mining. Joined with Manuel Lisa, Pierre Chouteau and others in St. Louis Missouri Fur Co., 1809. Left that year for the upper Missouri country and in 1810 was with Pierre Ménard in first organized invasion of the Three Forks region. That winter, after crossing the continental divide, he and his party descended Henry's Fork of the Snake River, the first American trappers to operate west of the Rockies. The venture was a failure and Henry returned to his lead mines, 1811. In 1822 he joined W. H. Ashley's first trapping expedition and spent the ensuing two years adventurously in the Western mountains. Discouraged by his lack of success, in 1824 he returned once again to St. Louis and his lead mines. He figures largely in the early annals of the frontier. Few trappers had wider renown as a hero.

HENRY, CALEB SPRAGUE (*b. Rutland, Mass., 1804; d. 1884*), Congregational and Episcopal clergyman, educator, author.

HENRY, EDWARD LAMSON (*b. Charleston, S.C., 1841; d. Ellenville, N.Y., 1919*), historical painter. Studied at Pennsylvania Academy of Fine Arts and in Paris under Gleyre and Courbet. Primarily an illustrator in oils, his pictures were accurate in the most minute detail. His major interest was in the life and customs of the United States, 1800–50.

HENRY, JOHN (*b. Dublin, Ireland, 1746; d. 1794*), actor, theatrical manager. A member of the so-called "Old American" company and later a partner of Lewis Hallam, 1785–94.

HENRY, JOHN (*b. Dorchester Co., Md., 1750; d. Dorchester Co., 1798*), lawyer. Maryland delegate to the Continental Congress, 1778–81, 1784–87; state senator, 1781–84; U.S. senator from Maryland, 1789–97; governor of Maryland, 1798.

HENRY, JOHN (*fl. 1807–1820*), adventurer. His secret reports on U.S. public opinion to the governor-general of Canada, written in 1809, were sold to President Madison for $50,000 in 1811. Their publication influenced the declaration of war in 1812.

HENRY, JOSEPH (*b. Albany, N.Y., 1797; d. Washington, D.C., 1878*), investigator in physics, first secretary and director of the Smithsonian Institution. A graduate of Albany Academy, Henry worked as schoolteacher, private tutor, and surveyor before appointment as professor of mathematics at Albany Academy, 1826. He then took up research in the new field of the relation of electric currents to magnetism. His first notable success was the improvement of William Sturgeon's electromagnet. Henry's method of making magnets was at once adopted everywhere, and the electromagnets of the present day are precisely like those he designed. Discovering a difference in effect when coils were joined in parallel to the battery or successively in a series, he called these two types "quantity" and "intensity" magnets and pointed out as early as January 1831 in the *American Journal of Science* that the intensity magnet was the type to be used in the electromagnetic telegraph. By experiment in 1830 he had discovered the principle of self-induction but, failing to publish his findings, was anticipated by Faraday's announcement of the discovery made independently in 1831. The modern unit of inductance is called the Henry in honor of his research. While at Albany, Henry invented an electromagnetic motor, a little machine he called a "philosophical toy." In 1832 he became professor of natural philosophy at Princeton. His researches, 1838–42, on the induction of a current by another current anticipated modern developments in the science of electricity, notably the action of transformers. In his experiments with inductive effect from a Leyden-jar discharge, he came very near the fundamentals of wireless telegraphy. He is usually credited with discovering the oscillatory nature of a discharge through a spiral. He collaborated with Stephen Alexander in investigating solar radiation and the heat of sun spots and was also greatly interested in capillarity and the cohesion of liquids.

In 1846 he left Princeton to become the first secretary and director of the Smithsonian Institution. The development of the Institution followed the course marked out for it in his first report to the Board of Regents. In that report and afterward, he urged upon the Regents and upon Congress the importance of relieving the Institution of the burden of supporting the museum, art gallery, and library, so freeing the Smithson fund to promote and publish original research. As time went on, his wisdom in regard to these matters was recognized. His duties left him little time for further research in pure science. As director he initiated various enterprises, among them the system of receiving weather reports by telegraph and basing predictions on them. He helped organize the American Association for the Advancement of Science; he was an original member of the National Academy of Sciences and its president, 1868–78. He received many honorary degrees and honorary elections to scientific and literary societies. The Smithsonian Institution published *The Scientific Writings of Joseph Henry* (1886).

HENRY, MORRIS HENRY (*b. London, England, 1835; d. 1895*), physician, surgeon. Came to America, 1852. Graduated University of Vermont, M.D., 1860. Served as a naval surgeon in Civil War. Founded *American Journal of Syphilography and Dermatology*, 1870, a pioneer effort to bring awareness of importance of knowledge of skin and venereal diseases.

HENRY, O. [See PORTER, WILLIAM SYDNEY, 1862–1910.]

HENRY, PATRICK (*b. Hanover Co., Va., 1736; d. Red Hill Plantation, Charlotte Co., Va., 1799*), lawyer, Revolutionary statesman, orator. Brought up among frontier farmers; educated at home. After failure as storekeeper and planter, he was licensed to practice law, 1760; opened an office at Hanover Courthouse and won immediate success. The case which brought him fame throughout the colony was one in the Parson's Cause series, 1763. Defending the constitutionality of the vestrymen's right to fix the price of tobacco with which the clergy of the established church were paid, Henry discoursed less upon the law in question than upon the clergy's declining to observe the law of their "country," and above all upon the encroachment of the Crown on the rights of Virginia freemen. On May 20, 1765, he became a member of the House of Burgesses and at once was engaged in a controversy over illegal use by the treasurer of the colony of paper money issued to support the recent war. He caused a strong alignment of the western and northern counties against the tidewater region. In arguing against the Stamp Act, May 1765, Henry offered seven radical resolutions in a speech which closed with his famous comparison, "Caesar had his Brutus—Charles the first, his Cromwell—and George the third—may profit by their example." The resolutions were publicized in the other colonies and became the basis for violent agitation from Boston to Charleston. Leader of a new party, between 1765 and 1770 Henry was as complete a master of public life in Virginia as Samuel Adams was in Massachusetts. The Townshend Acts and the efforts at resistance which followed them enabled Henry to consolidate the opposition to Great Britain. In May 1774, Gov. Dunmore dissolved the Assembly for declaring a day of prayer in sympathy with the closing of the port of Boston. The members assembled at Raleigh Tavern under Henry's leadership to ask all the colonies to meet in a continental congress and to call a Virginia convention, Aug. 1, 1774. At this convention, Henry and six others were chosen delegates to the First Continental Congress at Philadelphia. There he took an active part, always leaning toward radical measures and showing strong nationalist tendencies. On Mar. 20, 1775, at an assembly meeting in Richmond, he offered three resolutions, one of which provided for military defense of the colony. On this occasion he uttered his famous saying: "Give me liberty, or give me death." The colony was armed. In May 1775, after forcing Gov. Dunmore to restore to the colony the gunpowder he had seized at Williamsburg, Henry went to the Second

Continental Congress at Philadelphia but returned to Virginia in August to help put an army in the field. Appointed colonel of the first regiment, he was superseded in command by political opponents in the Assembly. Resigning his commission, February 1776, he went home to Hanover County. In May, at the Third Revolutionary Convention, he helped draft a new constitution for Virginia and on its completion in June was elected governor. He was twice re-elected. As governor he sent George Rogers Clark in 1778 on a military mission to the Illinois country which resulted in expulsion of the British from the Northwest. In 1778–79, when there was intrigue to remove Washington from his command, Henry sent him evidence which defeated the movement. In 1779 Henry retired to Henry County and was succeeded in the governorship by his friend Thomas Jefferson.

In 1781 Henry joined in the criticism of Jefferson's conduct and began the feud which lasted the rest of their lives. To the surprise of his followers, he urged restoration of property to the Loyalists, 1783, proposed an onerous tariff and opposed Madison's proposal to disestablish the church. As governor again, 1784–86, he opposed a treaty with Spain, seeing in it an alignment of the trading states against the South. He declined election to the Federal Convention. At the Virginia ratifying convention in October 1788, he vigorously led those opposed to adopting the new constitution. As his life drew on to an end, he became increasingly conservative. In October 1795 he refused Washington's offer of the office of secretary of state; three months later, when he also declined the position of chief justice, he made a speech declaring his admiration for Washington which created a sensation and led to fierce party warfare in Virginia. In January 1799, at Washington's request, Henry consented to become a Federalist candidate for the Virginia House of Delegates. He was elected, but death in June prevented his ever taking his seat.

HENRY, ROBERT (*b. Charleston, S.C., 1792; d. 1856*), Presbyterian and Episcopal clergyman, educator. From 1818 to 1856, except for a brief interval, he served South Carolina College, now University of South Carolina, as professor of various subjects and on several occasions as president.

HENRY, WILLIAM (*b. West Caln, Chester Co., Pa., 1729; d. 1786*), gunsmith, Revolutionary patriot. Established a firearms factory at Lancaster, Pa., 1750, which brought him a fortune. An enthusiastic student of science, he made experiments with steam, and by 1763 completed a stern-wheel steamboat. Although its trial on Conestoga Creek was unsuccessful, he was the first person in America to make such an experiment and later encouraged Robert Fulton. Among others whom he aided was Benjamin West. He devised labor-saving machines for his gun factory, invented a screw augur and perfected a steam-heating

system. He held important civil and military offices in Pennsylvania. Elected to the Continental Congress in 1784, he died in office.

HENRY, WILLIAM ARNON (*b. near Norwalk, O., 1850; d. San Diego, Calif., 1932*), agriculturist. As professor of agriculture, University of Wisconsin, and dean of its College of Agriculture, he stressed value of silage and promoted efficient methods of livestock-raising. Author of *Feeds and Feeding* (1898).

[*Supp.* 1]

HENRY, WILLIAM WIRT (*b. Charlotte Co., Va., 1831; d. 1900*), lawyer, historian. Author of *Patrick Henry: Life, Correspondence and Speeches* (1891), a still valuable biography of his grandfather.

HENSHALL, JAMES ALEXANDER (*b. Baltimore, Md., 1836; d. Cincinnati, O., 1925*), physician, naturalist. Associated with U.S. Bureau of Fisheries, 1896–1917. Published many books and articles on fish and fishing.

HENSHAW, DAVID (*b. Leicester, Mass., 1791; d. 1852*), businessman, politician. Leader of Massachusetts Democrats, 1821–37, 1843–50. Secretary of the navy, July 1843 to February 1844.

HENSHAW, HENRY WETHERBEE (*b. Cambridge, Mass., 1850; d. Washington, D.C., 1930*), ornithologist, ethnologist. Naturalist, Wheeler Survey, 1872–79; associated with Bureau of Ethnology, 1879–93; chief, Bureau of Biological Survey, 1910–16. Contributed important papers on ornithology and ethnology to scientific journals.

HENSON, JOSIAH (*b. Charles Co., Md., 1789; d. Dresden, Canada, 1883*), Negro slave, active in the service of his race, reputed original of Uncle Tom in H. B. Stowe's *Uncle Tom's Cabin*. With his wife and children escaped to Ontario, Canada, 1830. Tried to develop a Negro community there which failed because of an agent's incompetence. Published *The Life of Josiah Henson . . . Narrated by Himself* (1849); it appeared in subsequent editions with introductory material by H. B. Stowe.

HENTZ, CAROLINE LEE WHITING (*b. Lancaster, Mass., 1800; d. Marianna, Fla., 1856*). Author of a number of plays and novels including *Aunt Patty's Scrap Bag* (1846) and *The Planter's Northern Bride* (1854).

HEPBURN, ALONZO BARTON (*b. Colton, N.Y., 1846; d. 1922*), lawyer, banker, philanthropist. As a member of the New York legislature, he wrote the "Hepburn Report," 1879, a landmark in railroad history which influenced the Federal Interstate Commerce Act, 1887. He engaged in lumber and land operations, 1883–89, the foundation of his later fortune, was U.S. bank examiner in New York City, 1889–92, and comptroller of the currency, 1892–93. After holding several important posts in New York banks, he became vice-president of the Chase National

Bank, 1899. He was its president, 1904–11, and was chairman of boards, 1911–22. He became an important international figure, playing a significant role in international diplomacy and finance. Of his many important writings, *A History of Currency in the United States: with a Brief Description of the Currency Systems of All Commercial Nations* (1915) is a classic. His philanthropies were widespread.

HEPBURN, JAMES CURTIS (*b. Milton, Pa., 1815; d. East Orange, N.J., 1911*), Presbyterian medical missionary. Graduated Princeton, 1832; University of Pennsylvania, M.D., 1836. In Malaya and China, 1843–45; in Japan, 1859–92.

HEPBURN, WILLIAM PETERS (*b. Wellsville, O., 1833; d. Clarinda, Iowa, 1916*), lawyer, Union soldier, politician. Raised in Iowa. As congressman, Republican, from Iowa, 1881–87, an opponent of "pork barrel" legislation and advocate of military pensions. He was solicitor of the treasury, 1889–93. In 1892 he was again a congressional candidate and was elected for eight consecutive terms. For 14 years chairman of the interstate and foreign commerce committee and 10 years on the Pacific railroads committee, his work culminated in the Hepburn Rate Law, 1906, his principal achievement. He was also joint author and leading advocate of the Pure Food and Drug Act of 1906.

HEPWORTH, GEORGE HUGHES (*b. Boston, Mass., 1833; d. 1902*). Unitarian and Congregational clergyman, journalist.

HERBERMANN, CHARLES GEORGE (*b. Saerbeck, Germany, 1840; d. New York, N.Y., 1916*), editor, educator, scholar. Came to America as a boy. Graduated St. John's College (Fordham), 1858. Professor of Latin, College of the City of New York, 1869–1914. Editor-in-chief, *The Catholic Encyclopedia*, 1905–13.

HERBERT, HENRY WILLIAM (*b. London, England, 1807; d. New York, N.Y., 1858*), writer. Graduated Caius College, Cambridge, 1830. Came to America, 1831. A classical scholar, he taught in New York City private schools. His literary output was prodigious and varied. He edited periodicals, made many translations from the French, wrote historical romances and histories. Under the pseudonym "Frank Forester," he began in 1839 in the *American Turf Register* the series of writings on field sports which constitute his chief claim to fame. Among his sporting books are *The Warwick Woodlands* (1845), *My Shooting Box* (1846), *Frank Forester's Field Sports* (London, 1848; New York, 1849), *Frank Forester's Horse and Horsemanship, etc.* (1857).

HERBERT, HILARY ABNER (*b. Laurensville, S.C., 1834; d. Tampa, Fla., 1919*), lawyer, Confederate soldier. Congressman, Democrat, from Alabama, 1877–93; secretary of the navy, 1893–97. Responsible for overcoming congressional opposition to a large navy.

HERBERT, VICTOR (*b. Dublin, Ireland, 1859; d. 1924*), musician. Came to America, 1886, with European reputation as a cellist. Played at Metropolitan Opera and with New York Philharmonic orchestra, and was later conductor of Pittsburgh Symphony. In 1894, with *Prince Ananias* he began his career as a composer of light opera. There followed a long list of immediately successful works which included *The Fortune Teller* (1898), *Babes in Toyland* (1903), *Mlle. Modiste* (1905), *The Red Mill* (1906) and *Naughty Marietta* (1910). He also wrote the musical scores for the Ziegfeld Follies of 1919, 1921 and 1924. His *Natoma* (1911) remains musically one of the best American grand operas. His non-dramatic compositions include a wide variety of musical forms. He attained a popularity which no other American composer had won despite the inadequate librettos with which he worked. He was a founder of the American Society of Composers, Authors and Publishers.

HERDIC, PETER (*b. Fort Plains, N.Y., 1824; d. New York, N.Y., 1888*), lumberman. Patented, 1880, an improved vehicle, the "Herdic," for city and interurban transportation.

HERFORD, OLIVER BROOKE (*b. Sheffield, England, 1863; d. New York, N.Y., 1935*), author, illustrator, wit. Came to America as a boy. Contributed to *Century Magazine, Life, Harper's Weekly* and others. Author of *An Alphabet of Celebrities* (1899), *The Rubáiyát of a Persian Kitten* (1904), *Cupid's Cyclopedia* (1910) and numerous other books.

[*Supp. 1*]

HERING, CARL (*b. Philadelphia, Pa., 1860; d. Philadelphia, 1926*), electrical engineer. Son of Constantine Hering.

HERING, CONSTANTINE (*b. Oschatz, Saxony, 1800; d. Philadelphia, Pa., 1880*), physician, a founder of homeopathy in the United States. Educated at Dresden and Leipzig; M.D., Würzburg, 1826. Came to America, 1833. Founder of Hahnemann Medical College, Philadelphia, 1867. Author of *Guiding Symptoms* (10 vols., 1878–91).

HERING, RUDOLPH (*b. Philadelphia, Pa., 1847; d. New York, N.Y., 1923*), pioneer sanitary engineer. Son of Constantine Hering. Graduated Royal Polytechnic School, Dresden, Germany, 1867. After working as civil engineer, he was assistant city engineer at Philadelphia, 1876–80. Because of yellow fever in American cities, the National Board of Health sent him to Europe to study sewage disposal. His *Report on European Sewerage Systems* (1881) was the first comprehensive American writing in the field and for years the chief work on sanitary engineering. On his return he began his practice as consulting sanitary engineer and made reports for over 250 cities and towns in North and South America on water

429

supply and sewage disposal. He wrote extensively on hydraulics for technical journals.

HERKIMER, NICHOLAS (*b. near Herkimer, N.Y., 1728; d. near Oriskany, N.Y., 1777*), Revolutionary officer. Appointed chairman, Committee of Safety of Tryon County and a brigadier-general of militia; charged with defense of the Mohawk Valley; led a force against Sir John Johnson, 1776. In August 1777, marching with 800 men to relieve Fort Schuyler, under attack by Gen. St. Leger's force of Tories and Indians, he was ambushed near Oriskany in a heavily wooded ravine. The battle, long and desperate, was one of the bloodiest of the Revolution, and Herkimer was severely wounded. The Americans retreated, taking him to his home where he died within a fortnight. The battle has been variously described as victory or defeat for either side.

HERMAN, LEBRECHT FREDERICK (*b. Güsten, Germany, 1761; d. Pottstown, Pa., 1848*), German Reformed clergyman. Came to America, 1786; held various Pennsylvania pastorates. Wielded far-reaching influence over his denomination by founding the famous "Swamp College" in his home at Pottstown.

HERNDON, WILLIAM HENRY (*b. Greensburg, Ky., 1818; d. 1891*), lawyer. Became Abraham Lincoln's junior partner, 1844, and worked thereafter to further Lincoln's political ambitions. His claim to fame is as Lincoln's biographer. After Lincoln's death, Herndon traveled in Kentucky and Indiana gathering personal reminiscences of Lincoln's boyhood. He gave these stories freely to other biographers who made scanty acknowledgment of their debt. As an old man he published (with Jesse W. Weik) *Herndon's Lincoln: The True Story of a Great Life* (1889; revised, 1892). The work met savage criticism, but recent opinion acquits Herndon of serious blunders and endorses his attempt to keep Lincoln human and save him from too uncritical an apotheosis.

HERNDON, WILLIAM LEWIS (*b. Fredericksburg, Va., 1813; d. at sea, 1857*), naval officer. Saw active service in Mexican War and was for a time attached to the Naval Observatory. Detached, 1851, to explore Amazon River system, he reported his findings in *Exploration of the Valley of the Amazon* (1853–54). Lost with his ship, *Central America*, in storm off Cape Hatteras.

HERNE, JAMES A. (*b. Cohoes, N.Y., 1839; d. New York, N.Y., 1901*), actor, playwright. Changed name from James Ahern when he became professional actor, 1859. Played in support of J. B. Booth, Edwin Booth, Forrest and others; toured country as leading man for Lucille Western. His real talents first showed themselves in San Francisco where with David Belasco he wrote *Hearts of Oak*, produced 1879, a play unusual in its day for its simple, genuine sentiment. *Drifting Apart*, produced New York, 1888, was a second pioneering effort in realism. *Margaret Fleming*, pro-

duced by the author, 1890, was written in the spirit of the new Continental naturalist playwrights. A story of marital infidelity, its reality shocked audiences. *Shore Acres*, realistic in method but full of homely sentiment, was first produced in Chicago, 1892; Herne played it successfully for five years. *Griffith Davenport*, produced 1899, a tragic domestic drama of the Civil War, was unsuccessful on the stage; it was succeeded by *Sag Harbor*, a return to the mood of *Shore Acres*, first acted in Boston, 1899, with great success. Subsequent developments in the modern American theatre owe much to his pioneering efforts in realism.

HEROLD, DAVID E. [See BOOTH, JOHN WILKES, 1838–1865.]

HERON, MATILDA AGNES (*b. Co. Londonderry, Ireland, 1830; d. 1877*), actress. Came to Philadelphia, Pa., as a child. American debut at Walnut Street Theater, 1851. Famed for her interpretation of the title role of *Camille* post 1857.

HERON, WILLIAM (*b. Cork, Ireland, 1742; d. 1819*), teacher, surveyor, Revolutionary spy. Member of the Connecticut Assembly, 1778–82, he supplied military intelligence to Oliver De Lancey, British secret service head. His duplicity was not discovered until long after his death.

HERR, HERBERT THACKER (*b. Denver, Colo., 1876; d. Philadelphia, Pa., 1933*), mechanical engineer, inventor. Designed safety-braking devices for railroads, improvements in engines and turbines and a remote-control device whereby ship engines might be operated from the bridge. [*Supp. 1*]

HERR, JOHN (*b. West Lampeter, Pa., 1781; d. Humberstone, Canada, 1850*), founded Reformed Mennonites, 1812.

HERRESHOFF, JAMES BROWN (*b. near Bristol, R.I., 1834; d. New York, N.Y., 1930*), chemist, inventor. Brother of John B. and Nathanael Herreshoff. Patented many inventions, as various as a sliding seat for rowboats, 1860, and an apparatus for measuring specific heat of gases, 1872; perfected the fin keel for racing yachts.

HERRESHOFF, JOHN BROWN (*b. near Bristol, R.I., 1841; d. 1915*), shipbuilder, yacht designer. Brother of James B. and Nathanael Herreshoff, with whom, in 1874, he devised an improved tubular marine boiler. The brothers formed the Herreshoff Manufacturing Co., 1878, John handling finance and construction, Nathanael the drafting, engineering and experimentation. Original in their designs and building methods, they were among the first to build yachts over molds, keel upward, with double skins and iron floors and knees. Among their triumphs in sailing craft design were the *Gloriana* (1891), and the *America's* Cup defenders, *Vigilant, Defender, Columbia, Reliance*. The *Resolute's* victory in 1920 gave the Herreshoffs a record of 18 winners in 20 starts against the fastest English yachts.

HERRESHOFF, NATHANAEL GREENE (*b. Bristol, R.I., 1848; d. Bristol, 1938*), naval architect, marine engineer, shipbuilder. Brother of James B. and John B. Herreshoff; the latter's partner in Herreshoff Manufacturing Co. From the 1890's to 1924, the leading U.S. yacht designer. [*Supp. 2*]

HERRICK, EDWARD CLAUDIUS (*b. New Haven, Conn., 1811; d. New Haven, 1862*), librarian, scientist. Yale librarian, 1843–58; treasurer, 1852–62.

HERRICK, MYRON TIMOTHY (*b. Huntington, O., 1854; d. Paris, France, 1929*), lawyer, banker, diplomat. Admitted to the bar, 1878, practiced in Cleveland. Engaged in successful business ventures; became director of several railroads and trust companies; was elected president of American Bankers Association, 1901. Meanwhile he had entered politics, become a friend of William McKinley, and been influential in his election, 1896. Republican governor of Ohio, 1904–06. From 1907 to 1912, while still interested in politics, Herrick was chiefly engaged in large financial transactions and reorganized several railroads. Though he had refused McKinley's offers to make him secretary of the treasury or ambassador to Italy, in 1912 he accepted appointment by President Taft as ambassador to France. Staying on until December 1914 at President Wilson's request, he became a symbol of American good will in a time of French national peril, and was decorated with the Legion of Honor by the French government. During a second term as ambassador to France, 1921–29, the problems of financial settlement resulting from the war, 1914–18, presented many difficulties with which he was particularly fitted to deal. Criticism of the United States caused him much unhappiness, but he served to remind the French of past American kindness, and personally did much to ease the situation. He died in the embassy building which he had purchased and presented to the U.S. government.

HERRICK, ROBERT WELCH (*b. Cambridge, Mass., 1868; d. St. Thomas, V.I., 1938*), novelist, educator. Graduated Harvard, 1890. Taught at Massachusetts Institute of Technology and University of Chicago. Author of controversial novels of urban middle-class life which include *The Web of Life* (1900), *The Common Lot* (1904) and *Together* (1908). [*Supp. 2*]

HERRICK, SOPHIA McILVAINE BLEDSOE (*b. Gambier, O., 1837; d. 1919*), editor, author. Daughter of Albert T. Bledsoe. Contributor to *Southern Review*, 1868–78; assistant editor, *Scribner's* and *Century* magazines, 1879–1906.

HERRING, AUGUSTUS MOORE (*b. Covington, Ga., 1867; d. Brooklyn, N.Y., 1926*), pioneer in aviation. Made early experiments with gliders; associated with Samuel P. Langley, 1895; with Octave Chanute, 1896. Applied for a patent on an engine-powered flying machine, 1896. Though the Patent Office found twenty new claims in his design, he had no working model, and the application was rejected. The Herring-Curtiss Co. was formed to build airplanes, c. 1909, Herring contributing his patent applications and attempting to revive the 1896 claim. After a second denial of Herring's petition, the Herring-Curtiss Co. was the unsuccessful defendant in a famous 1910 infringement suit by the Wright brothers.

HERRING, JAMES (*b. London, England, 1794; d. Paris, France, 1867*), portrait painter. Published, in collaboration with J. B. Longacre, *The National Portrait Gallery* (1834–39) which includes some of his own portrait work.

HERRING, SILAS CLARK (*b. Salisbury, Vt., 1803; d. 1881*), safe-manufacturer.

HERRMAN, AUGUSTINE (*b. Prague, Bohemia, c. 1605; d. Maryland, 1686*), colonial cartographer, merchant, land-holder. Served in North and South America for Dutch West India Co.; was agent for Peter Gabry & Sons, 1644–51, at New Amsterdam. In partnership with George Hack, became largest tobacco exporter in America. Ruined by Peter Stuyvesant, Herrman went to Maryland, 1659, and became a citizen of that colony, 1666. His outstanding achievement is the map *Virginia and Maryland as it is Planted and Inhabited This Present Year 1670 . . .* [*by*] *Augustin Herrman Bohemiensis*, for which he spent ten years making the surveys. Lord Baltimore rewarded Herrman by granting him over 13,000 acres in northeastern Maryland.

HERRMANN, ALEXANDER (*b. Paris, France, 1844; d. 1896*), magician. Became an American citizen, 1876. Enjoyed world-wide fame.

HERRON, FRANCIS JAY (*b. Pittsburgh, Pa., 1837; d. New York, N.Y., 1902*), youngest major-general in Civil War, commissioned 1862 after brilliant service with the 1st and 9th Iowa regiments in Missouri and Arkansas.

HERRON, GEORGE DAVIS (*b. Montezuma, Ind., 1862; d. Munich, Germany, 1925*), Congregational clergyman, Socialist. Influential in founding Rand School, New York City, 1906. American representative to Prinkipo Conference.

HERSCHEL, CLEMENS (*b. Boston, Mass., 1842; d. Glen Ridge, N.J., 1930*), hydraulic engineer. Graduated Lawrence Scientific School, Harvard, 1860; studied at Karlsruhe Technical School. Became chief engineer of the Holyoke Co., c. 1879; constructed the Holyoke testing flume which marked the beginning of scientific study of water turbines, and invented the Venturi meter, a device without moving parts to measure the flow of water in pipes.

HERTER, CHRISTIAN (*b. Stuttgart, Germany, 1840; d. 1883*), designer. Came to America, 1860. Head of Herter Brothers, interior decorators, *post* 1870. An influential figure in American art after the Civil War when millionaires' "palaces" were rising in the principal cities of the United States.

HERTER, CHRISTIAN ARCHIBALD (*b. Glenville, Conn., 1865; d. 1910*), physician, biochemist. Son of Christian Herter. Graduated College of Physicians and Surgeons, New York, M.D., 1885. His chief contribution, beyond his *On Infantilism* (1908) and other writings, was the foundation of lectureships for European scientists at Johns Hopkins and Bellevue.

HERTY, CHARLES HOLMES (*b. Milledgeville, Ga., 1867; d. Savannah, Ga., 1938*), chemist. Graduated University of Georgia, 1886; Ph.D., Johns Hopkins, 1890. Taught at universities of Georgia and North Carolina. His later researches (especially on pine products) and his publicizing of the chemical industry contributed substantially to the South's industrial development. [*Supp. 2*]

HESS, ALFRED FABIAN (*b. New York, N.Y., 1875; d. 1933*), pediatrician, pathologist. Graduated Harvard, 1897; M.D., College of Physicians and Surgeons, New York, 1901. After studying abroad, began practice in New York City. Made classic studies of scurvy in infants, devising tests and therapy. Popularized the use of pasteurized milk formulas for infants supplemented with antiscorbutic substances, as well as a supplement of fresh orange juice. Discovered that irradiation of certain foodstuffs caused the formation of antirachitic vitamin D (1924). With Adolf Windaus, identified provitamin D (1927). An outstanding investigator and leader in improving pediatric practice. [*Supp. 1*]

HESSELIUS, GUSTAVUS (*b. Folkarna, Sweden, 1682; d. Philadelphia, Pa., 1755*), portrait painter, organ builder. Came to Philadelphia, 1711; resided in Maryland, *c.* 1718–33. His altar-piece "The Last Supper" for St. Barnabas's Church, Prince Georges Co., Md. (1721), was first public art commissioned in colonies.

HESSELIUS, JOHN (*b. probably Prince Georges Co., Md., 1728; d. near Annapolis, Md., 1778*), portrait painter. Son of Gustavus Hesselius. Influenced by John Wollaston. Probably the most prolific painter of the pre-Revolutionary period, his known portraits number nearly a hundred.

HESSOUN, JOSEPH (*b. Vrcovice, Bohemia, 1830; d. St. Louis, Mo., 1906*), Roman Catholic clergyman. Came to St. Louis, Mo., 1865. A national, as well as clerical, leader of emigrant Czechs in the Midwest; pastor, journalist, founder of abbeys.

HETH, HENRY (*b. Chesterfield Co., Va., 1825; d. Washington, D.C., 1899*), soldier. Cousin of Gen. George Pickett. Graduated West Point, 1847. Served in the Mexican War and in the West. Resigned his commission, 1861; entered Confederate service and served in West Virginia, Kentucky and Tennessee. Promoted major-general, 1863, his most conspicuous action was at Gettysburg where accidental contact of his division with a superior Union force precipitated that battle.

HEWAT, ALEXANDER (*b. Scotland, c. 1745; d. London?, England, c. 1829*), Presbyterian clergyman, historian. Came to America, 1763; served as pastor in South Carolina until 1775. Author of *An Historical Account of . . . South Carolina and Georgia* (1779), the first history of South Carolina.

HEWES, JOSEPH (*b. Kingston, N.J., 1730; d. Philadelphia, Pa., 1779*), businessman, North Carolina legislator and signer of Declaration of Independence. Removed to Edenton, N.C., in the late 1750's. As member of Continental Congress, 1774–77, 1779, he was outstanding as executive head of Continental Navy.

HEWES, ROBERT (*b. Boston, Mass., 1751; d. Boston, 1830*), glassmaker, fencing instructor, bonesetter. Helped organize Essex Glass Works, Boston, 1787, for years the leading cylinder or window-glass firm in America.

HEWETT, WATERMAN THOMAS (*b. Miami, Mo., 1846; d. London, England, 1921*), educator, editor. Graduated Amherst, 1869; studied in Germany and Holland; Ph.D., Cornell, 1879. Professor of German, Cornell, 1879–1910. A pioneer of modern language study, at his best as textbook editor.

HEWIT, AUGUSTINE FRANCIS (*b. Fairfield, Conn., 1820; d. New York, N.Y., 1897*), Roman Catholic clergyman, Paulist. Graduated Amherst, 1839. Influenced by the Oxford Movement, he was converted to Catholicism, 1846, and was ordained, 1847. With Isaac Hecker and others, formed the Paulist congregation; edited *Catholic World*, 1869–74; succeeded Father Hecker as Paulist superior, 1888. A prolific writer, for years one of the foremost Catholic apologists in America.

HEWITT, ABRAM STEVENS (*b. Haverstraw, N.Y., 1822; d. Ringwood, N.J., 1903*), iron manufacturer, statesman, philanthropist. Graduated Columbia, 1842. There he formed a friendship with Edward Cooper, son of Peter Cooper who turned over to their partnership of Cooper & Hewitt his own iron works at Trenton. Pioneers in making iron beams and girders, they were successful from the start. In 1862 Hewitt erected at Weston, N.J., the first American open-hearth furnace. Here he produced for the U.S. government all the gun-barrel material it needed at bare production cost, and in 1870 produced the first steel of commercial value in the United States. As the iron and steel industry grew, Cooper, Hewitt & Co. expanded with it, and Hewitt became a force in financial and industrial affairs acting as executive of many corporations. In 1855 he married Peter Cooper's daughter Sarah. When Peter Cooper established Cooper Union, Hewitt took a leading part in the undertaking and for over forty years directed all its financial and educational details. In 1871, with Samuel J. Tilden and Edward Cooper, he joined in a campaign against the "Tweed Ring," and helped reorganize Tammany Hall; he served as congressman, Democrat, from New York, 1875–87, except for one term, winning a position of authority on questions of labor, finance, and national resources. Chairman of the Democratic National Committee, 1876. In 1886 he defeated Henry George and Theodore Roosevelt for the mayoralty of New York City. His vigorous administration was notable for reforms and improvements, which included the plan for the municipal construction of the rapid transit railroad. His reforms and intolerance of partisanship led to a break with Tammany Hall and he retired from politics. The last ten years of his life were devoted to the public interest, especially in education and charity.

HEWITT, JAMES (*b. Dartmoor, England, 1770; d. Boston, Mass., 1827*), violinist, composer. Came to America, 1792. His many compositions included the quasi-opera *Tammany or the Indian Chief* (1794), which became a symbol of Republican protest against the Federalists.

HEWITT, JOHN HILL (*b. New York, N.Y., 1801; d. Baltimore, Md., 1890*), journalist, musician, poet. Son of James Hewitt.

HEWITT, PETER COOPER (*b. New York, N.Y., 1861; d. Paris, France, 1921*), scientist, inventor. Son of Abram S. Hewitt; grandson of Peter Cooper. Educated at Columbia College and Stevens Institute. He is best known for his invention in 1903 of the mercury vapor lamp, bearing his name, which has been widely adopted for industrial illumination. His other inventions include a static converter or rectifier, an electrical interrupter, and a wireless receiver. He was a pioneer in developing hydro-airplanes and highspeed motor boats. Early interested in the problem of helicopters, he built a successful one in 1918. Appointed to the Naval Consulting Board in 1915, he designed an aerial torpedo. He had large business interests and was director in a number of corporations.

HEYDT, HANS JÖST. [See HITE, JOST, *d. 1760*.]

HEYER, JOHN CHRISTIAN FREDERICK (*b. Helmstedt, Germany, 1793; d. Philadelphia, Pa., 1873*), Lutheran clergyman. Came to America *c.* 1807. Held pastorates in Pennsylvania, Maryland and Minnesota; was for many years a missionary to India, founding the first foreign mission of his church, 1842.

HEYWARD, DuBOSE (*b. Charleston, S.C., 1885; d. Tryon, N.C., 1940*), poet, novelist, dramatist. His

novel *Porgy* (1924) was the basis of a successful play (1927) and a folk opera as *Porgy and Bess* (1935). [*Supp. 2*]

HEYWARD, THOMAS (*b. St. Helena's Parish, S.C., 1746; d. 1809*), Revolutionary soldier, planter, jurist, signer of Declaration of Independence from South Carolina.

HEYWOOD, EZRA HERVEY (*b. Princeton, Mass., 1829; d. Boston, Mass., 1893*), radical pamphleteer. Graduated Brown, 1856. Active Abolitionist, Civil War pacifist. With his wife, wrote and printed an astonishing amount of propaganda on marriage reform, women's rights, labor reform and others. Edited a monthly journal of reform, *The Word*, 1872–93.

HEYWOOD, LEVI (*b. Gardner, Mass., 1800; d. 1882*), chair manufacturer. Invented many new manufacturing methods for use in his factory, in particular, a machine for bending wood and another for the manipulating of rattan in furniture.

HIACOOMES (*b. c. 1610; d. 1690*), Pokanauket Indian preacher of Edgartown, Martha's Vineyard, Mass. First convert of the younger Thomas Mayhew, 1643, he aided conversion of other Indians and was ordained in 1670.

HIBBARD, FREEBORN GARRETTSON (*b. New Rochelle, N.Y., 1811; d. 1895*), Methodist clergyman.

HIBBEN, JOHN GRIER (*b. Peoria, Ill., 1861; d. near Rahway, N.J., 1933*), Presbyterian clergyman, philosopher, educator. Graduated Princeton, 1882; Ph.D., 1893. Taught logic at Princeton, 1891–1912; succeeded Woodrow Wilson as president of the university, 1912–32. After the controversies of Wilson's administration, Hibben gave the university peace and academic freedom, greatly expanding it. He combined a rare talent for conciliation with a robust tenacity to principle. His educational philosophy is revealed in *A Defense of Prejudice* (1911). In philosophy his most enduring contribution is *The Philosophy of the Enlightenment* (1910). [*Supp. 1*]

HIBBEN, PAXTON PATTISON (*b. Indianapolis, Ind., 1880; d. 1928*), diplomat, journalist. Graduated Princeton, 1903. Embassy secretary in Russia, Colombia, Mexico, Chile, Netherlands. Actively sympathetic with Russian Revolution.

HIBBINS, ANN (*d. Boston, Mass., 1656*), witch. Executed because she had "more wit than her neighbors," according to later opinion.

HICHBORN, PHILIP (*b. Charlestown, Mass., 1839; d. Washington, D.C., 1910*), naval officer. Rose from apprentice shipwright to be chief of Navy's Bureau of Construction, 1893–1901. Invented Franklin lifebuoy and Hichborn balanced turrets for battleships. Retired as rear-admiral, 1901.

HICKENLOOPER, ANDREW (*b. Hudson, O., 1837; d. 1904*), engineer, Union soldier. Supervised engineering at siege of Vicksburg; brevet brigadier-general, 1865. Later a power in business and political life of Cincinnati, O.

HICKOK, JAMES BUTLER (*b. Troy Grove, Ill., 1837; d. Deadwood, Dakota Territory, 1876*), stage driver, soldier, scout, and U.S. marshal, commonly known as "Wild Bill." Removed to Kansas, 1855. Achieved fame as gun fighter while driving over Santa Fe and Oregon Trails; rendered invaluable service as Union scout and spy in Missouri and in campaigns against Western Indians after the Civil War. As deputy and marshal in turbulent Kansas frontier communities, notably Hays City and Abilene, he controlled the lawless elements by courage and skill. After touring the East with Buffalo Bill Cody, 1872–73, he settled in Deadwood where he was murdered by Jack McCall. Quiet in manner and greatly admired, Hickok never killed a man except in self-defense or in line of duty.

HICKOK, LAURENS PERSEUS (*b. Bethel, Conn., 1798; d. Amherst, Mass., 1888*), clergyman, philosopher. Graduated Union, 1820. Taught in Western Reserve and Auburn seminaries and at Union College where he was president, 1866–68. As philosopher, the ablest American dialectician of his day; *Rational Psychology* (1849) was his most important work.

HICKOK, "WILD BILL." [See HICKOK, JAMES BUTLER, 1837–1876.]

HICKS, ELIAS (*b. Hempstead Township, N.Y., 1748; d. Jericho, N.Y., 1830*), Quaker preacher, leader of the 1827–28 separation in the Society of Friends. Inclined to extreme Quietism, the inward light became for him the all-important and central feature of religion. By 1815, he was clearly the principal exponent of liberal views within the Society of Friends and opposed doctrinal definition. Both then and later, the term "Hicksite" has been used to designate his following.

HICKS, JOHN (*b. Auburn, N.Y., 1847; d. San Antonio, Texas, 1917*), Oshkosh, Wis., editor, diplomat.

HICKS, THOMAS (*b. Newtown, Pa., 1823; d. Trenton Falls, N.Y., 1890*), painter. Studied at Pennsylvania Academy and in Paris under Couture. Of present interest mainly because of the distinguished persons he portrayed.

HICKS, THOMAS HOLLIDAY (*b. Dorchester Co., Md., 1798; d. Washington, D.C., 1865*), politician. Know-Nothing governor of Maryland, 1857–61. Hindered secessionist movement in Maryland until arrival of Union troops. U.S. senator, 1862–65.

HIESTER, DANIEL (*b. Upper Salford Township, Pa., 1747; d. 1804*), farmer, Revolutionary patriot, businessman. Congressman, Anti-Federalist, from Pennsylvania, 1789–96; from Maryland, 1801–04.

HIESTER, JOSEPH (*b. Bern Township, Pa., 1752; d. Reading, Pa., 1832*), merchant, Revolutionary soldier. Cousin of Daniel Hiester. Served in Pennsylvania legislature, and as congressman, 1797–1805, 1815–20. An Independent Republican, he was described by Jefferson as "disinterested, moderate and conscientious." He was governor of Pennsylvania, 1820–23.

HIGGINS, FRANK WAYLAND (*b. Rushford, N.Y., 1856; d. 1907*), businessman, New York legislator. Republican governor of New York, 1905–07; promoted insurance legislation, election and taxation reforms.

HIGGINSON, FRANCIS (*b. Claybrooke, England, 1586; d. Salem, Mass., 1630*), clergyman. Graduated Jesus College, Cambridge, 1610; M.A., 1613. Ordained 1614, he became a nonconformist through association with Thomas Hooker and other Puritans and emigrated to New England, 1629. As religious teacher of Salem (Naumkeag) settlement, he drew up its confession of faith and the covenant of the church. He was author also of *New-Englands Plantation* (1630), a valuable source.

HIGGINSON, HENRY LEE (*b. New York, N.Y., 1834; d. 1919*), banker, Union soldier. Partner in Lee, Higginson & Co., Boston. Founded the Boston Symphony Orchestra, 1881, and was its sole underwriter until 1918. Benefactor also of numerous colleges and schools.

HIGGINSON, JOHN (*b. Claybrooke, England, 1616; d. 1708*), clergyman. Son of Francis Higginson, with whom he came to Salem, Mass., as a boy. Religious teacher and pastor at Guilford, Conn.; pastor, Salem, Mass., *post* 1660. Held a high place among Massachusetts clergy.

HIGGINSON, NATHANIEL (*b. Guilford, Conn., 1652; d. London, England, 1708*), merchant. Son of John Higginson. Graduated Harvard, 1670. Entered service of East India Co., 1683. First mayor of Madras, 1688; governor of Fort Saint George, 1692–98. Returned to England, 1700.

HIGGINSON, STEPHEN (*b. Salem, Mass., 1743; d. 1828*), Boston merchant, Revolutionary privateer. Descendant of Francis Higginson.

HIGGINSON, THOMAS WENTWORTH (*b. Cambridge, Mass., 1823; d. Cambridge, 1911*), reformer, author, Unitarian minister, Union soldier. Grandson of Stephen Higginson. Graduated Harvard, 1841; was early advocate of woman suffrage and a violent opponent of slavery; supported disunion movement and participated in riots connected with return of fugitive slave Anthony Burns, 1854. As colonel of the first Negro regiment in the Union Army, he served in South Carolina, 1862–64. A prominent "magazinist" thereafter, he wrote most frequently for *Atlantic Monthly*. He aided in the discovery of Emily Dickinson and her poetry and was author of a number of books, among them *Life in a Black Regiment* (1870) and *Atlantic Essays* (1871).

HIGINBOTHAM, HARLOW NILES (*b. near Joliet, Ill., 1838; d. 1919*), merchant, philanthropist. Partner and associate of Marshall Field; president of World's Columbian Exposition, 1893; director of museums; benefactor to Chicago charities.

HILDRETH, RICHARD (*b. Deerfield, Mass., 1807; d. Florence, Italy, 1865*), lawyer, historian. Graduated Harvard, 1826. Editor and writer, *Boston Daily Atlas*, 1832–38. An active Whig in 1840, an advocate of temperance and abolition, he was author of numerous tracts; also *Banks, Banking and Paper Currencies* (1840) and a novel *The Slave: or Memoirs of Archy Moore* (1836). Engaged in writing his *History of the United States, post* 1844, he published its six volumes, 1849–52. Competent and accurate in detail, his major work is heavy in style and influenced by an unconscious tendency toward socialism.

HILDRETH, SAMUEL CLAY (*b. Independence, Mo., 1866; d. New York, N.Y., 1929*), turfman. Trainer of Zev, Purchase, Grey Lag and other great champions.

HILDRETH, SAMUEL PRESCOTT (*b. Methuen, Mass., 1783; d. Marietta, O., 1863*), physician, naturalist, historian. Began practice in Ohio, 1806. Collected and preserved the oral traditions and papers of Ohio pioneers.

HILGARD, EUGENE WOLDEMAR (*b. Zweibrücken, Bavaria, 1833; d. 1916*), geologist, authority on soils. Son of Theodor E. Hilgard. Came to America as a boy. Studied in Philadelphia, Zürich, Freiberg; Ph.D., Heidelberg, 1853. As director of Mississippi geological survey, published *Geology and Agriculture of the State of Mississippi* (1860, issued 1866). After Civil War, taught at University of Mississippi and again directed the state survey; was one of the first to recognize relation of soil-analysis to agriculture. Professor of agriculture and director of Agricultural Experiment Station at University of California, Berkeley, *post* 1875, he exerted great influence on application of scientific knowledge to agriculture. His *Geology of the Mississippi Delta* (1870) has become a classic; almost as famous is his *Soils, Their Formation, Properties, Composition, and Relations to Climate and Plant Growth in Humid and Arid Regions* (1906).

HILGARD, JULIUS ERASMUS (*b. Zweibrücken, Bavaria, 1825; d. Washington, D.C., 1891*), geodesist. Son of Theodor E. Hilgard. Came to America as a boy. Associated *post* 1844 with U.S. Coast Survey; superintendent, 1881–85. Active in scientific organizations and in the introduction here of the metric system.

HILGARD, THEODOR ERASMUS (*b. Marnheim, Bavaria, 1790; d. Heidelberg, Germany, 1873*).

Father of Eugene W. and Julius E. Hilgard. A prominent lawyer and justice in Germany, he emigrated to Belleville, Ill., 1836, where he became a successful farmer and land speculator.

HILL, AMBROSE POWELL (*b. Culpeper, Va., 1825; d. near Petersburg, Va., 1865*), soldier. Graduated West Point, 1847. Served briefly in Mexican War, and Seminole campaigns. Resigned from U.S. army, 1861, to join Virginia's forces. Promoted major-general, May 1862, he participated in all Lee's major battles, opening the Seven Days battle and meeting his death in combat at close of the siege of Petersburg. He served with Jackson at Cedar Mountain, Second Bull Run and Harper's Ferry; by rapid marching from Harper's Ferry to Sharpsburg (Antietam), he re-enforced and saved Lee's yielding right wing. Hill shared in Jackson's famous flanking movement at Chancellorsville. As lieutenant-general (promoted, May 1863), he commanded all the Confederate forces during the first day's fighting at Gettysburg. Genial and affectionate in private life, he was a restless and impetuous soldier.

HILL, BENJAMIN HARVEY (*b. Jasper Co., Ga., 1823; d. Atlanta, Ga., 1882*), lawyer, legislator. Opposed secession, but became Davis spokesman in Confederate Senate, 1861–65; was a moderate Southern spokesman as Georgia congressman, Democrat, 1875–77, and U.S. senator, 1877–81.

HILL, DANIEL HARVEY (*b. York District, S.C., 1821; d. Charlotte, N.C., 1889*), soldier, educator. Graduated West Point, 1842. After service in Mexican War, resigned to become professor of mathematics at Washington College, and later at Davidson College. Rose to lieutenant-general in Confederate service, 1861–65; published Southern regional journals; served as president, University of Arkansas, 1877–84.

HILL, DAVID BENNETT (*b. Montour Falls, N.Y., 1843; d. near Albany, N.Y., 1910*), lawyer, New York legislator. A machine politician and strict party man, he possessed a genius for organization and became recognized leader of the Democratic party in his state. As governor, 1885–91, he showed great administrative efficiency; as U.S. senator from New York, 1892–97, he won a fight with Pres. Grover Cleveland over the control of the New York patronage but was otherwise undistinguished. Aspirant for the presidency in 1892, his high-handed actions to block Cleveland in the Democratic Convention helped, rather than hindered, his rival secure the nomination. He opposed free-silver in the Convention of 1896. After W. J. Bryan's nomination, he wrote: "I am a Democrat still—very still."

HILL, DAVID JAYNE (*b. Plainfield, N.J., 1850; d. Washington, D.C., 1932*), educator, diplomat, publicist. Graduated Bucknell, 1874. Taught at Bucknell, and was president, 1879–88; president, University of

Rochester, 1888–95. Assistant U.S. secretary of state, 1898–1903. Served, 1903–11, as U.S. minister successively in Switzerland, Netherlands and Germany. Author of *A History of Diplomacy* (1905, 1906, 1914) and other works. [*Supp.* 1]

HILL, FRANK ALPINE (*b. Biddeford, Maine, 1841; d. 1903*), educator. Graduated Bowdoin, 1862. As secretary of board of education of Massachusetts *post* 1894, he worked for more expert supervision of schools and higher qualifications for teachers.

HILL, FREDERIC STANHOPE (*b. Boston, Mass., 1805; d. 1851*), actor, playwright. Two of his adaptations of French melodramas (*The Six Degrees of Crime* and *The Shoemaker of Toulouse,* 1834), became stock pieces for the American theatre of his day.

HILL, FREDERICK TREVOR (*b. Brooklyn, N.Y., 1866; d. 1930*), New York lawyer, novelist. Author of *Lincoln, the Lawyer* (1906).

HILL, GEORGE HANDEL (*b. 1809; d. Saratoga Springs, N.Y., 1849*), actor, commonly known as "Yankee" Hill. Popular comedian in America and England, *post* 1832. Unsurpassed in Yankee character parts.

HILL, GEORGE WILLIAM (*b. New York, N.Y., 1838; d. West Nyack, N.Y., 1914*), mathematician. Graduated Rutgers, 1859. His important contributions to mathematical astronomy were published by the Carnegie Institution, 1905–07.

HILL, HENRY BARKER (*b. Waltham, Mass., 1849; d. 1903*), chemist. Son of Thomas Hill (1818–1891). Graduated Harvard, 1869. Professor at Harvard, *post* 1874, he specialized in organic chemistry and qualitative analysis; made distinguished researches in uric acid and in furaldehyde derivatives.

HILL, ISAAC (*b. Cambridge, Mass., 1789; d. Washington, D.C., 1851*), New Hampshire political leader. Editor, *New Hampshire Patriot,* 1809–29; U.S. senator, Democrat, from New Hampshire, 1831–36; governor of New Hampshire, 1836–39. A member of Andrew Jackson's "kitchen cabinet."

HILL, JAMES (*b. Kittery, Maine, 1734; d. 1811*), soldier in colonial and Revolutionary wars, shipbuilder, New Hampshire landowner and legislator.

HILL, JAMES JEROME (*b. near Rockwood, Canada, 1838; d. St. Paul, Minn., 1916*), railroad executive, financier. Settled in St. Paul, 1856. Worked as clerk for a line of Mississippi River steamboats, as a freight agent and as agent for the St. Paul and Pacific Railroad. Operated Northwestern Fuel Co., 1875–78. Began his rise with Norman W. Kittson in the Red River Transportation Co., freighting to Fort Garry (Winnipeg). Purchased, 1878, the bankrupt St. Paul and Pacific Railroad in association with Kittson, Donald A. Smith (later Lord Strathcona) and George Stephen (later Lord Mount Stephen);

through Hill's able management and a wise policy of extension and reconstruction, the opulent Great Northern system was created out of it. Hill served as general manager, 1879–81; vice-president, 1881–82; president, 1882–1907; chairman, 1907–12. Hill's belief that the competition of the less successful Northern Pacific was uneconomical, as well as dangerous to his own line, led to his acquisition of stock in that property after formal unification had been enjoined by the courts, 1896. To assure an entrance for the lines into Chicago and St. Louis, Hill and J. P. Morgan, acting for the Great Northern and Northern Pacific respectively, bought 97% of the share capital of the Chicago, Burlington and Quincy. E. W. Harriman, denied participation in the Burlington, sought to win control of the vulnerable Northern Pacific by purchase of its shares on the open market, thus precipitating the stock market panic of May 9, 1901. Harriman established a minority interest on the Northern Pacific board in a resulting compromise. The Northern Securities Co., a holding company designed to act virtually as trustee for Hill's far-flung railroad interests, was declared illegal by Supreme Court decision, 1904.

Under Hill's management, his railroad system was the only transcontinental carrier which weathered all financial storms and maintained an uninterrupted dividend record. His success was owing to unceasing watchfulness and attention to detail. He built his lines where he knew that traffic would flow; he selected routes with favorable grades; he held operation costs to a minimum; he was a pioneer in recognizing the value of adequate terminal facilities. The Great Northern made its way without land grants or government aid, and was among the first to run agricultural demonstration trains with expert lecturers. The great part which Hill played in the settling and development of the Northwest brought him the sobriquet of "empire builder."

HILL, JOHN (*b. London, England, 1770; d. near West Nyack, N.Y., 1850*), engraver, aquatinter. Came to America, 1816. Celebrated for the craftsmanship of his *Landscape Album* (1820, after Joshua Shaw) and the *Hudson River Portfolio* (1828, after W. G. Wall).

HILL, JOHN HENRY (*b. New York, N.Y., 1791; d. Athens, Greece, 1882*), Episcopal clergyman, missionary to Greece *post* 1832. With his wife, founded in Athens the leading girls' school in the Greek-speaking world.

HILL, JOSEPH ADNA (*b. Stewartstown, N.H., 1860; d. 1938*), statistician. Graduated Harvard, 1885; Ph.D., University of Halle, 1892. Associated with U.S. Bureau of the Census, *post* 1898; chief of statistical research, 1933–38. [*Supp.* 2]

HILL, JOSHUA (*b. Abbeville District, S.C., 1812; d. 1891*), lawyer. Practiced in Madison, Ga. Congressman, Know-Nothing, 1857–61; opposed secession, declined to participate in Civil War. Worked for radical reconstruction policies, and was U.S. senator, Republican, from Georgia, 1868–73.

HILL, LOUIS CLARENCE (*b. Ann Arbor, Mich., 1865; d. Los Angeles, Calif., 1938*), civil and hydraulic engineer. Specialist in design and construction of dams and irrigation projects. As chief engineer, U.S. Reclamation Service, supervised Roosevelt Dam (Arizona), Laguna Dam and Colorado Basin project, 1906–14; later served as consultant. [*Supp. 2*]

HILL, NATHANIEL PETER (*b. Montgomery, N.Y., 1832; d. 1900*), metallurgist. Replaced amalgamation process for reducing Colorado ores with smelting process, 1868, thus inaugurating great era of Rocky Mountain mining. Settled in Colorado, 1871, and was U.S. senator, 1879–85.

HILL, RICHARD (*b. Maryland, c. 1673; d. Philadelphia, Pa., 1729*), merchant. Settled in Philadelphia, c. 1700. Was four times mayor of that city, an intimate of William Penn and associate justice of the provincial supreme court.

HILL, ROBERT ANDREWS (*b. Iredell Co., N.C., 1811; d. Oxford, Miss., 1900*), judge, anti-secessionist, moderate reconstructionist. Raised in Tennessee; removed to Mississippi, 1855. Neutral in Civil War, he was U.S. district judge, 1866–91.

HILL, THOMAS (*b. New Brunswick, N.J., 1818; d. Waltham, Mass., 1891*), Unitarian clergyman, scientist. Graduated Harvard, 1843. President of Antioch College, 1859–62; of Harvard, 1862–68, where he introduced elective system and encouraged advanced scientific investigation.

HILL, THOMAS (*b. Birmingham, England, 1829; d. Raymond, Calif., 1908*), landscape painter. Came to America as a child. Studied at Pennsylvania Academy. Settled in California c. 1870. Emphasized romantic elements of Western scenery.

HILL, URELI CORELLI (*b. probably Connecticut, c. 1802; d. Paterson, N.J., 1875*), violinist, music teacher. First president, and a founder of Philharmonic Society of New York, 1842.

HILL, WALTER BARNARD (*b. Talbot Co., Ga., 1851; d. 1905*), lawyer, educator. Chancellor, University of Georgia, 1899–1905, in which period he expanded the university's plant and instituted a state college of agriculture.

HILL, WILLIAM (*b. Ireland, 1741; d. York, S.C., 1816*), ironmaster, Revolutionary soldier, politician. Came to America c. 1761; settled in York Co., S.C., 1762. Operated important mines and ironworks both during and after Revolution; served with distinction as soldier under Gen. Sumter.

HILLARD, GEORGE STILLMAN (*b. Machias, Maine, 1808; d. near Boston, Mass., 1879*), lawyer, orator. A man of talent, friend of Charles Sumner and Nathaniel Hawthorne, he failed of eminence through too great versatility. Author of *Six Months in Italy* (1853).

HILLEBRAND, WILLIAM FRANCIS (*b. Honolulu, Hawaii, 1853; d. 1925*), chemist. After extensive study in the United States, at Heidelberg (Ph.D., 1875) and elsewhere in Germany, he joined the U.S. Geological Survey as chemist, 1880, soon establishing a reputation for accuracy in analysis. He was first to publish a consistent outline for complete analysis of silicate rock. His work with uraninite led to significant discoveries of his own and of other scientists. Hillebrand's term of service as chief chemist of the Bureau of Standards, 1908–1925, was particularly noteworthy.

HILLEGAS, MICHAEL (*b. Philadelphia, Pa., 1729; d. Philadelphia, 1804*), merchant, Revolutionary patriot. His considerable fortune was acquired from a business inherited from his father and his own ventures into sugar refining, iron manufacturing and, finally, banking. He performed his patriotic service as treasurer, in turn, of the Philadelphia Committee of Safety, the Province of Pennsylvania, and as U.S. treasurer, 1777–89. During the Revolution he contributed a large part of his fortune to the support of the army.

HILLHOUSE, JAMES (*b. Montville, Conn., 1754; d. New Haven, Conn., 1832*), lawyer, politician, Revolutionary soldier. Congressman, Federalist, from Connecticut, 1791–96; U.S. senator, 1796–1810. Member of Hartford Convention. Administered Connecticut schools fund with great ability. Treasurer, Yale College, 1782–1832.

HILLHOUSE, JAMES ABRAHAM (*b. New Haven, Conn., 1789; d. New Haven, 1841*), poet. Son of James Hillhouse. Graduated, Yale, 1808. Author of *Hadad* (1825), a blank verse drama, and other works issued in collected form (1839).

HILLIARD, FRANCIS (*b. Cambridge, Mass., 1806; d. Worcester, Mass., 1878*), legal writer. Abandoned active practice of law to write and publish treatises on numerous and widely separated legal subjects embodying American decisions and showing the extent to which they followed English Common Law. His treatise *The Law of Torts* (1859) was the first work in English on the subject. All of his works were compilations. First in the field, however, they made litigation less difficult and costly.

HILLIARD, HENRY WASHINGTON (*b. Fayetteville, N.C., 1808; d. Atlanta, Ga., 1892*), lawyer, Confederate soldier. Congressman, Whig, from Alabama, 1845–51. Opposed William L. Yancey in political debates, 1840–60; opposed secession, but supported Confederacy on ground that coercion of a state was wrong. Minister to Brazil, 1877–81.

HILLIS, DAVID (*b. Washington Co., Pa., 1788; d. 1845*), Indiana pioneer, judge, Indian fighter, legislator. Removed to Madison, Ind., c. 1808.

HILLIS, NEWELL DWIGHT (*b. Magnolia, Iowa, 1858; d. 1929*), pastor of Plymouth Church, Brooklyn, N.Y., 1899–1924.

HILLMAN, THOMAS TENNESSEE (*b. Montgomery Co., Tenn., 1844; d. Atlantic City, N.J., 1905*), Alabama industrialist. In association with H. F. DeBardeleben, built first iron furnace in Birmingham, Ala., 1880; was promoter of consolidations in Alabama steel and coal industries.

HILLQUIT, MORRIS (*b. Riga, Russia, 1869; d. 1933*), Socialist leader, lawyer, author. Came to New York City, 1886; joined the Socialist Labor party; led anti-De Leon faction. Graduated New York University Law School, 1893. Took an active part in trade-union organizations, especially of Jewish garment workers. Opposed American participation in World War I on Socialist grounds; polled high Socialist vote in mayoralty campaign, 1917. Active as attorney in espionage cases and labor cases. Acted as legal adviser to the Soviet Government Bureau in the United States until 1919. Frequently an unsuccessful candidate for public office; long subject to tuberculosis. Author of *History of Socialism in the United States* (1903) and other works. [*Supp.* 1]

HILLS, ELIJAH CLARENCE (*b. Arlington, Ill., 1867; d. 1932*), Romance philologist, educator. [*Supp.* 1]

HILLYER, JUNIUS (*b. Wilkes Co., Ga., 1807; d. Decatur, Ga., 1886*), lawyer, Georgia Congressman, Democrat, 1851–55; solicitor of U.S. treasury, 1857–61. In letters to Howell Cobb, Jan.–Feb. 1861, he warned that border states would not secede.

HILPRECHT, HERMAN VOLRATH (*b. Hohenerxleben, Germany, 1859; d. 1925*), Assyriologist. Came to America, 1886. Professor and curator at University of Pennsylvania, 1887–1911; resigned his post after a controversy which involved John H. Haynes. Author of *Old Babylonian Inscriptions, Chiefly from Nippur* (1893, 1896).

HIMES, CHARLES FRANCIS (*b. Lancaster Co., Pa., 1838; d. Baltimore, Md., 1918*), educator. Graduated Dickinson College, 1855; taught the sciences there, 1865–96. Authority on photography. His elective laboratory courses were among first (1865) offered by American colleges.

HIMES, JOSHUA VAUGHAN (*b. North Kingstown, R.I., 1805; d. Elk Point, S.D., 1895*), Adventist and Episcopal clergyman.

HINDMAN, THOMAS CARMICHAEL (*b. Knoxville, Tenn., 1828; d. Arkansas, 1868*), lawyer, Confederate major-general. Raised in Mississippi; removed to Helena, Ark., 1856. Severely wounded in Atlanta campaign; murdered by an assassin after vigorously opposing Reconstruction government.

HINDMAN, WILLIAM (*b. Dorchester Co., Md., 1743; d. Baltimore, Md., 1822*), lawyer, Revolutionary patriot. Congressman, Federalist, from Maryland, 1793–99; U.S. senator, 1800–01.

HINDS, ASHER CROSBY (*b. Benton, Maine, 1863; d. Washington, D.C., 1919*), journalist, politician. Parliamentarian of Congress, 1895–1911. Author of monumental *Hinds' Precedents of the House of Representatives* (1907–1908).

HINE, CHARLES DE LANO (*b. Vienna, Va., 1867; d. New York, N.Y., 1927*), railroad official, organizational expert for American railroads. Author of *Modern Organization: An Exposition of the Unit System* (1912).

HINE, LEWIS WICKES (*b. Oshkosh, Wis., 1874; d. Hastings-on-Hudson, N.Y., 1940*), photographer. Specialized in creating social documents; his photographs (1907–14) for Child Labor Committee helped bring legislative reforms. Pioneer in industrial photography. [*Supp.* 2]

HINES, WALKER DOWNER (*b. Russellville, Ky., 1870; d. Merano, Italy, 1934*), lawyer. Assistant director and director, U.S. Railroad Administration, 1917–20; adviser on railroads to foreign governments. [*Supp.* 1]

HINMAN, ELISHA (*b. Stonington, Conn., 1734; d. Stonington, 1805*), naval officer, privateer in American Revolution.

HINMAN, GEORGE WHEELER (*b. Mount Morris, N.Y., 1864; d. Winnetka, Ill., 1927*), editor, educator. Graduated Hamilton College, 1884; Ph.D., Heidelberg, 1888. On staff New York *Sun*, 1888–98; editor, Chicago *Inter Ocean*, 1898–1912.

HINMAN, JOEL (*b. Southbury, Conn., 1802; d. 1870*), Connecticut legislator and jurist.

HINSDALE, BURKE AARON (*b. near Wadsworth, O., 1837; d. Atlanta, Ga., 1900*), educator. President, Hiram College, 1870–82; superintendent, Cleveland public schools, 1882–86; professor of education, University of Michigan, *post* 1888.

HIRES, CHARLES ELMER (*b. near Roadstown, N.J., 1851; d. Haverford, Pa., 1937*), soft-drink manufacturer, popularizer of root beer. [*Supp.* 2]

HIRSCH, EMIL GUSTAV (*b. Luxemburg, 1851; d. 1923*), rabbi. Came to America as a boy. Graduated University of Pennsylvania, 1872; studied also at Berlin, Leipzig. Ministered in Philadelphia, Baltimore, Louisville; in Chicago *post* 1880. Professor at University of Chicago, *post* 1892. An editor of the *Jewish Encyclopedia* and active civic leader, he was the Jewish apostle to the non-Jewish world.

HIRSCHENSOHN, CHAIM (*b. Safed, Palestine, 1857; d. New York, N.Y., 1935*), rabbi. Came to America, 1903. Pastor in Hoboken, N.J. Active in movements for popularizing Hebrew, he was a dedicated Zionist. [*Supp. 1*]

HIRST, BARTON COOKE (*b. Philadelphia, Pa., 1861; d. Philadelphia, 1935*), obstetrician, author. Graduated M.D., University of Pennsylvania, 1883; studied also in Germany and Austria. Professor of obstetrics, University of Pennsylvania, 1889–1927, and in graduate school, 1927–35. [*Supp. 1*]

HIRST, HENRY BECK (*b. Philadelphia, Pa., 1817; d. Philadelphia, 1874*), poet, lawyer. Eccentric author of *The Coming of the Mammoth* (1845), *Endymion* (1848) and other works.

HIRTH, WILLIAM ANDREW (*b. Tarrytown, N.Y., 1875; d. Columbia, Mo., 1940*), journalist. Removed to Missouri as a child. Publisher, the *Missouri Farmer;* organized Missouri Farmers' Assn., 1917; advocate of the McNary-Haugen farm-surplus plan.
[*Supp. 2*]

HISE, ELIJAH (*b. Allegheny Co., Pa., 1801; d. Russellville, Ky., 1867*), lawyer, jurist, diplomat. Raised in Kentucky. Negotiated controversial canal treaty with Nicaragua, 1849, while on mission to Guatemala.

HITCHCOCK, CHARLES HENRY (*b. Amherst, Mass., 1836; d. Honolulu, Hawaii, 1919*), geologist. Son of Edward Hitchcock (1793–1864). Professor at Dartmouth, 1868–1908, and administrator of New Hampshire geological survey, 1868–78.

HITCHCOCK, EDWARD (*b. Deerfield, Mass., 1793; d. 1864*), geologist, educator, Congregational clergyman. Professor of science, Amherst, *post* 1825; president, 1845–55. Along with his academic duties, he conducted two geological surveys of Massachusetts; after long investigation, ascribed the sandstone "bird tracks," found in the Connecticut Valley, to dinosauric origin; served as Vermont state geologist, 1856–61. Outstanding among his books were *Elementary Geology* (1840), *Report on Geology of Vermont* (1861) and *Illustrations of Surface Geology* (1857).

HITCHCOCK, EDWARD (*b. Amherst, Mass., 1828; d. 1911*), educator. Son of Edward Hitchcock (1793–1864). M.D., Harvard, 1853. First professor of physical education in an American college (Amherst, 1861–1911).

HITCHCOCK, ENOS (*b. Springfield, Mass., 1744; d. Providence, R.I., 1803*), Congregational clergyman, Revolutionary Army chaplain. Author of numerous works including two early didactic novels, *Memoirs of the Bloomsgrove Family* (1790) and *The Farmer's Friend* (1793).

HITCHCOCK, ETHAN ALLEN(*b. Vergennes, Vt., 1798; d. Sparta, Ga., 1870*), soldier, author. Graduated West Point, 1817. Served on the frontiers, in the Florida war and with distinction on Winfield Scott's staff in Mexico. His integrity and intelligence brought him often into conflict with his superiors. Retired, 1855, he was commissioned major-general of volunteers, 1861, and rendered valuable service in Union Army during Civil War. He wrote extensively on scientific subjects, philosophy and alchemy.

HITCHCOCK, ETHAN ALLEN (*b. Mobile, Ala., 1835; d. Washington, D.C., 1909*), businessman. Brother of Henry Hitchcock. An important figure in American steel and glass manufacturing, when he first entered political life, 1897. His friendship with President McKinley led to his appointment as minister to Russia and, in 1898, as secretary of the interior, which office he retained under Theodore Roosevelt. As secretary, he was a vigorous and persistent conservationist. He instituted legal proceedings against officials in the Land Office and secured 126 convictions. He withdrew mineral lands from sale, helped institute reclamation projects and protected the Five Tribes in their possession of oil lands. It was claimed and denied that Roosevelt welcomed his resignation, 1907.

HITCHCOCK, FRANK. [See MURDOCH, FRANK HITCHCOCK, d. 1872.]

HITCHCOCK, FRANK HARRIS (*b. Amherst, O., 1867; d. Tucson, Ariz., 1935*), lawyer, politician. Managed presidential campaign of William H. Taft, 1908. Postmaster-general, 1909–12. His businesslike and forward-looking policies included establishment of the first air-mail route and the parcel-post system.
[*Supp. 1*]

HITCHCOCK, GILBERT MONELL (*b. Omaha, Nebr., 1859; d. Washington, D.C., 1934*), politician. Son of Phineas W. Hitchcock. Publisher, Omaha *World Herald.* Congressman, Democrat, from Nebraska, 1903–05, 1907–11; U.S. senator, 1911–23. Spoke and wrote in support of Treaty of Versailles; opposed Senator Lodge's amendments. [*Supp. 1*]

HITCHCOCK, HENRY (*b. Alabama, 1829; d. St. Louis, Mo., 1902*), lawyer, Union soldier. Brother of Ethan Allen Hitchcock (1835–1909). Organized law school of Washington University (St. Louis, Mo.) and served as its first dean.

HITCHCOCK, JAMES RIPLEY WELLMAN (*b. Fitchburg, Mass., 1857; d. New York, N.Y., 1918*), journalist, publishers' editor, author. Art-critic for *New York Tribune,* 1882–90. Editorial adviser to D. Appleton and Co., and Harper and Brothers.

HITCHCOCK, PETER (*b. Cheshire, Conn., 1781; d. Painesville, O., 1853*), Ohio jurist and legislator. Graduated Yale, 1801. Removed to Ohio, 1806.

HITCHCOCK, PHINEAS WARRENER (*b. New Lebanon, N.Y., 1831; d. 1881*), lawyer. Removed to Nebraska, 1857; practiced in Omaha. Was territorial delegate, Republican, 1865–67; U.S. senator, 1871–77.

HITCHCOCK, RAYMOND (*b. Auburn, N.Y., 1865; d. Beverly Hills, Calif., 1929*), actor, comedian.

HITCHCOCK, RIPLEY. [See HITCHCOCK, JAMES RIPLEY WELLMAN, 1857–1918.]

HITCHCOCK, ROSWELL DWIGHT (*b. East Machias, Maine, 1817; d. Somerset, Mass., 1887*), Congregational clergyman, educator. Graduated Amherst, 1836. Professor of religion, Bowdoin, 1852–55; professor of church history, Union Theological Seminary, New York, 1855–87.

HITE, JOST (*b. Strasbourg, Alsace; d. Virginia, 1760*), colonizer. Came to America, 1710; promoted settlement in New York and Pennsylvania; colonized area near Winchester, Va., *post* 1732. Litigation with Lord Fairfax over titles to the Virginia grants continued for more than fifty years.

HITT, ROBERT ROBERTS (*b. Urbana, O., 1834; d. Newport, R.I., 1906*), reporter, diplomat. Congressman, Republican, from Illinois, 1883–1906; chairman, House foreign affairs committee, 1889–91, 1895–1905. Able but unspectacular.

HITTELL, JOHN SHERTZER (*b. Jonestown, Pa., 1825; d. 1901*), journalist, author, statistician. Brother of Theodore H. Hittell. Removed to California, 1849. On staff of the *Alta California*, 1853–80. Author of *The Resources of California* (1863), *A History of the City of San Francisco, and Incidentally of the State of California* (1878) and other works.

HITTELL, THEODORE HENRY (*b. Marietta, Pa., 1830; d. 1917*), California lawyer, land-title expert. Brother of John S. Hittell. Removed to California, 1856. Author of important legal works; also *The Adventures of James Capen Adams* (1860) and the *History of California* (1885–1897).

HOADLEY, DAVID (*b. Waterbury, Conn., 1774; d. Waterbury, 1839*), architect. The North Church in New Haven, the Samuel Russell mansion in Middletown, and many other houses through Connecticut displayed the intuitive genius of this self-taught craftsman and master of styles.

HOADLEY, JOHN CHIPMAN (*b. Martinsburg, N.Y., 1818; d. 1886*), engineer, designer and manufacturer of steam-engines and mill machinery. Author of *The Portable Steam-Engine* (1863) and *Steam-Engine Practice in the United States* (1884).

HOADLY, GEORGE (*b. New Haven, Conn., 1826; d. Watkins, N.Y., 1902*), lawyer, Ohio jurist. Nephew of Theodore D. Woolsey. Raised in Ohio; studied law in office of Salmon P. Chase. Democratic governor of Ohio, 1884–86.

HOAG, JOSEPH (*b. Oblong, N.Y., 1762; d. Charlotte, Vt., 1846*), Quaker preacher. Opposed teaching of Elias Hicks; allied himself with "Wilburites" in New York.

HOAR, EBENEZER ROCKWOOD (*b. Concord, Mass., 1816; d. 1895*), lawyer, jurist. Brother of George F. Hoar; son of Samuel Hoar. Graduated Harvard, 1835; Harvard Law School, 1839. Coined the slogan "Conscience Whig" (1845) but joined the Free Soil party, 1848, and finally became a Republican. When he was called by President Grant to become attorney-general, 1869, he had served on the Massachusetts supreme judicial court for a decade. His demand that federal judgeships not be treated as patronage cost him a seat on the Supreme Court, the Senate refusing confirmation. He retired from the cabinet, 1870.

HOAR, GEORGE FRISBIE (*b. Concord, Mass., 1826; d. 1904*), lawyer, statesman. Son of Samuel Hoar. Graduated Harvard, 1846; Harvard Law School, 1849. Closely associated with founding of Republican party in Massachusetts; was congressman, 1869–77, and U.S. senator, 1877–1904. He was on the congressional electoral commission which settled the Hayes-Tilden controversy and voted for the Republican candidates. In Congress he was considered an able committeeman, and was a respected authority on the judiciary, Civil War claims and privileges and elections. A formidable, successful debater, both at the bar and in Congress, he upheld in speech and conduct the highest traditions of his profession. The bent of his mind was liberal; apparently he did not appreciate the social and economic developments which had changed the party of Abraham Lincoln to that of Mark Hanna and William McKinley.

HOAR, LEONARD (*b. Gloucester, England, c. 1630; d. Boston, Mass., 1675*), clergyman, scholar. Came to New England as a boy. Graduated Harvard, 1647, and returned to England where he became M.A., Cambridge, 1654, and M.D., 1671. Called to presidency of Harvard, 1672–75, he incurred violent opposition of fellows and undergraduates. Among other reforms, he tried to introduce experimental sciences into Harvard curriculum.

HOAR, SAMUEL (*b. Lincoln, Mass., 1778; d. 1856*), lawyer, Massachusetts congressman, opponent of slavery. Father of Ebenezer R. and George F. Hoar.

HOARD, WILLIAM DEMPSTER (*b. Munnsville, N.Y., 1836; d. Fort Atkinson, Wis., 1918*), editor, educational leader. Removed to Wisconsin, 1857. Founded *Hoard's Dairyman*, 1885, a paper which circulated in every American state and most foreign countries. Introduced alfalfa in Wisconsin; pioneered in use of tuberculin test for cattle; urged use of silos; founded Wisconsin Dairyman's Association and was an organizer of Northwestern Dairyman's Association, 1872. Governor of Wisconsin, 1888–91.

HOBAN, JAMES (b. Callan, Ireland, c. 1762; d. Washington, D.C., 1831), architect, contractor. Emigrated to Philadelphia, ante 1785. Designed old state capitol in Columbia, S.C., 1790–91. Moved to the new Federal City, 1792, and took part in competition for the proposed public buildings there. Designed the White House, supervised its construction and rebuilt it after its destruction by the British in 1814. Among his later works were the State and War offices, begun 1818.

HOBART, GARRET AUGUSTUS (b. Long Branch, N.J., 1844; d. Paterson, N.J., 1899), lawyer. New Jersey legislator, corporation director. Vice-president of the United States, 1897–99.

HOBART, JOHN HENRY (b. Philadelphia, Pa., 1775; d. Auburn, N.Y., 1830), Episcopal clergyman. Graduated College of New Jersey (Princeton), 1793; A.M., 1796. Installed assistant minister, Trinity Parish, New York, 1801; elected assistant bishop of New York, 1811. His ability, energy in controversy, and devotion to his creed made him a prominent religious figure. In 1816 he was chosen both rector of Trinity and diocesan of New York. He established a society for training ministers, 1806, which later developed into General Theological Seminary, where he taught theology. He succeeded in awakening the loyalty of both clergy and laity in a church which had suffered loss of prestige during the Revolution and the early years of the nation.

HOBART, JOHN SLOSS (b. Fairfield, Conn., 1738; d. New York, N.Y., 1805), Revolutionary patriot. Landowner in Suffolk Co., Long Island; member, N.Y. Provincial Congress. Justice of N.Y. supreme court, 1777–98; U.S. senator from New York, 1798; U.S. district judge, 1798–1805.

HOBBS, ALFRED CHARLES (b. Boston, Mass., 1812; d. Bridgeport, Conn., 1891), lock expert, manufacturer, mechanical engineer, designer of machine tools.

HOBSON, EDWARD HENRY (b. Greensburg, Ky., 1825; d. Cleveland, O., 1901), businessman, Union brigadier-general. Leader of 1863 expedition which pursued Confederate General John H. Morgan for 900 miles through Kentucky and Ohio; captured a major portion of the raider's command.

HOBSON, RICHMOND PEARSON (b. Greensboro, Ala., 1870; d. New York, N.Y., 1937), naval officer. Graduated Annapolis, 1889. Won fame for sinking collier Merrimac in Santiago, Cuba, channel, 1898; resigned, 1903. Congressman, Democrat, from Alabama, 1907–15. [Supp. 2]

HOCH, AUGUST (b. Basel, Switzerland, 1868; d. San Francisco, Calif., 1919), psychiatrist. M.D., University of Maryland, 1890; studied extensively abroad. Taught at Cornell Medical School, 1905–17.

HODGE, ARCHIBALD ALEXANDER (b. Princeton, N.J., 1823; d. 1886), Presbyterian clergyman. Son of Charles Hodge. Graduated Princeton, 1841; Princeton Theological Seminary, 1845, where he taught theology, 1877–86. A severely orthodox writer whose class lectures and theological discussions were audacious, brilliant and humorous.

HODGE, CHARLES (b. Philadelphia, Pa., 1797; d. 1878), Presbyterian clergyman, theologian. Graduated Princeton, 1815; Princeton Theological Seminary, 1819, where he was instructor and professor, 1820–78. Advocated the Calvinistic theology as stated by the Westminster divines and supported it by Scriptural interpretation. He maintained his position with skill at the time when Calvinism was disintegrating and evolutionary ideas were becoming increasingly powerful. His learned, able controversial writings and success in awakening minds explain his fame as teacher and leader; he was a powerful conservative force on Presbyterianism and on other churches. Systematic Theology (1872–1873) and Discussions in Church Polity (published posthumously) were of outstanding importance among his many books. He contended against the Presbyterian "New School" views and opposed slavery while deprecating Abolitionist policy.

HODGE, HUGH LENOX (b. Philadelphia, Pa., 1796; d. 1873), obstetrician. Brother of Charles Hodge. Professor of obstetrics, University of Pennsylvania, 1835–63; designer of obstetrical instruments; author of The Principles and Practice of Obstetrics (1864).

HODGE, WILLIAM THOMAS (b. Albion, N.Y., 1874; d. near Greenwich, Conn., 1932), actor, playwright. Famous for characterization of slow-speaking, good-humored, astute, American rustic.

[Supp. 1]

HODGEN, JOHN THOMPSON (b. Hodgenville, Ky., 1826; d. St. Louis, Mo., 1882), surgeon. Professor and dean, St. Louis Medical College, 1864–82. Developed a splint for fracture of the femur and other surgical aids.

HODGES, GEORGE (b. Rome, N.Y., 1856; d. 1919), Episcopal clergyman. Influenced by Kingsley and Maurice, he became advocate of the "social gospel" while active minister and as dean of Episcopal Theological Seminary, Cambridge, Mass., post 1894.

HODGES, HARRY FOOTE (b. Boston, Mass., 1860; d. Lake Forest, Ill., 1929), military engineer. Graduated West Point, 1881. Supervised important work on Ohio, Missouri and Mississippi rivers; served in Porto Rico, 1898–99, and was chief engineer in Cuba under Gen. Leonard Wood. Assigned to Panama, 1907, he performed notable service as engineer in charge of design of locks, dams and regulating works on the Canal. He trained and commanded the 76th

Division in World War I, retiring as major-general, 1921.

HODGKINSON, JOHN (*b. England, c. 1767; d. near Bladensburg, Md., 1805*), actor, theatrical manager. Trained in English provincial theatres; came to America, 1792. Maneuvered John Henry and Lewis Hallam out of management of their New York company; uneasy partner of William Dunlap, 1797; later played in Dunlap's company and at Charleston, S.C. As an actor, his peculiar province was low comedy, but he was equally capable in high comedy, tragedy and operatic roles.

HODGSON, WILLIAM BROWN (*b. Georgetown, D.C., 1801; d. New York, N.Y., 1871*), U.S. consular officer, Orientalist. World-pioneer in studies of the Berber languages. [*Supp. 1*]

HOE, RICHARD MARCH (*b. New York, N.Y., 1812; d. Florence, Italy, 1886*), inventor, manufacturer. Son of Robert Hoe (1784–1833). In 1830, he assumed responsibility, together with his cousin, Matthew Smith, for the Hoe printing-press-building establishment. His interest in experimentation led to vast improvements and great prosperity for an already famous company. Hoe was the dominant force in management and active director of policy for more than fifty years. Among his inventions or adaptations were the large cylinder press and the type-revolving press (1847) which caused an immediate revolution in newspaper printing. *Post* 1871, he helped to develop the web press.

HOE, ROBERT (*b. Hoes, England, 1784; d. New York, N.Y., 1833*), founder of R. Hoe & Co., makers of printing presses. Father of Richard M. Hoe. Came to America, 1803. His improved cylinder press succeeded in displacing presses imported from England.

HOE, ROBERT (*b. New York, N.Y., 1839; d. London, England, 1909*), manufacturer, bibliophile. Grandson of Robert Hoe (1784–1833); nephew of Richard M. Hoe. Succeeded his uncle as head of R. Hoe & Co., 1886. Undeterred by unsuccessful experiments, the firm went on to produce a double supplement press, the quadruple newspaper press, then the sextuple machine. A 96-page press for newspapers was perfected, 1901, along with rotary art presses and color presses. Collector of a celebrated library, Hoe was founder and first president of Grolier Club and a founder of Metropolitan Museum of Art.

HOECKEN, CHRISTIAN (*b. Tilburg, Belgium, 1808; d. Missouri River, near mouth of the Platte, 1851*), Jesuit missionary to Kickapoo and Potawatomi Indians in Kansas and Iowa; associate of P. J. De Smet. Came to America, 1833. Composed a grammar and dictionary of the Kickapoo language, and prayer-books and catechisms in Potawatomi language.

HOEN, AUGUST (*b. Höhn, Germany, 1817; d. Baltimore, Md., 1886*), lithographer, map printer. Came to America, 1835; joined cousin in establishment of a firm in Baltimore which developed into A. Hoen & Co. Soon established a reputation in his specialty, lithographing maps and illustrating publications of government bureaus and of Congress. The maps and illustrations in J. C. Frémont's reports (1845 and 1846) and the color charts in U.S. Geological Survey reports were considered outstanding achievements. Hoen produced first colored show cards in this country, 1839. Hoen's research laboratory made important contributions in the field of map symbolism and developed many new processes, the most notable being "Lithokaustic" (1860), which was greatly favored by illustrators and producers of trade labels.

HOENECKE, GUSTAV ADOLF FELIX THEODOR (*b. Brandenburg, Germany, 1835; d. 1908*), Lutheran clergyman. Came to America, 1863. Conservative president and professor at Evangelical Lutheran Seminary, Milwaukee, Wis.

HOFF, JOHN VAN RENSSELAER (*b. Mount Morris, N.Y., 1848; d. 1920*), army medical officer. Graduated Union, 1871; M.D., Columbia, 1874. A pioneer in establishing proper military rank and status for army doctors.

HOFFMAN, CHARLES FENNO (*b. New York, N.Y., 1806; d. Harrisburg, Pa., 1884*), editor, poet. Author of a number of books including *A Winter in the West* (1835) and *Greyslaer* (1839).

HOFFMAN, DAVID (*b. Baltimore, Md., 1784; d. New York, N.Y., 1854*), lawyer. As professor of law, University of Maryland, at various times between 1823 and 1843, he outlined a course of legal study (1817 and 1836) that was, according to Justice Joseph Story, the most perfect yet offered. Hoffman's basic requirements were systematic reading of legal and social literature, the study of statutes and forms, and an insistence on pleadings in genuine practice courts. His teachings were in advance of the practice of his time and were poorly patronized.

HOFFMAN, DAVID MURRAY (*b. New York, N.Y., 1791; d. Flushing, N.Y., 1878*), jurist. Nephew of Josiah O. Hoffman. Graduated Columbia, 1809. Distinguished commentator on chancery practice and procedure in New York; pioneer commentator on the revision of the New York Code.

HOFFMAN, EUGENE AUGUSTUS (*b. New York, N.Y., 1829; d. 1902*), Episcopal clergyman. Graduated Rutgers, 1847; General Theological Seminary, New York, 1851. Dean of that seminary, 1879–1902, where his efficient administration brought prosperity and success.

HOFFMAN, JOHN THOMPSON (*b. Sing Sing, N.Y., 1828; d. Wiesbaden, Germany, 1888*), lawyer, Tammany politician. Mayor of New York City, 1865–68; governor of New York, 1869–73. His popularity served as a screen for the Tweed Ring which he later repudiated.

HOFFMAN, JOSIAH OGDEN (*b. Newark, N.J., 1766; d. 1837*), lawyer. Leader of Federalist party in N.Y. Assembly, 1791–1797. Associate judge, N.Y. superior court, 1828–37.

HOFFMAN, OGDEN (*b. New York, N.Y., 1793; d. New York, 1856*), lawyer. Son of Josiah O. Hoffman. Graduated Columbia, 1812. Served under Commodore Decatur, 1812–16. Practiced in New York City, *post* 1826. District attorney, N.Y. County, 1829–35; congressman, Whig, from New York, 1837–41. Opposed Jackson's stand on U.S. Bank; became in Congress an outstanding enemy of the Sub-Treasury Bill. U.S. attorney, N.Y. southern district, 1841–45; N.Y. State attorney-general, 1853–55. Hoffman's brilliance was clearly evidenced as trial attorney; he was considered the outstanding criminal lawyer of his generation.

HOFFMAN, RICHARD (*b. Manchester, England, 1831; d. Mt. Kisco, N.Y., 1909*), concert pianist, composer, teacher. Came to America, 1847. Accompanied Jenny Lind in her first American concerts.

HOFFMAN, WICKHAM (*b. New York, N.Y., 1821; d. Atlantic City, N.J., 1900*), Union soldier, diplomat, lawyer. Son of David M. Hoffman. Able staff officer throughout Civil War; secretary in important legations, 1866–83; U.S. minister to Denmark, 1883–85.

HOFFMANN, FRANCIS ARNOLD (*b. Herford, Germany, 1822; d. near Jefferson, Wis., 1903*), Lutheran clergyman, banker. Came to America *c.* 1840. Agricultural writer under name of Hans Buschbauer. Settled thousands of immigrants on land of Illinois Central. Lieutenant-governor, Republican, of Illinois, 1861–65.

HOFMAN, HEINRICH OSCAR (*b. Heidelberg, Germany, 1852; d. 1924*), metallurgist. Came to America, 1882. Professor, Massachusetts Institute of Technology, *post* 1889. His *Metallurgy of Lead and the Desilverization of Base Bullion* (1892, 1918) became a standard work.

HOGAN, JOHN (*b. Mallow, Ireland, 1805; d. 1892*), Methodist preacher, businessman, Missouri politician.

HOGE, MOSES (*b. Cedargrove, Va., 1752; d. 1820*), Presbyterian clergyman, educator. President, Hampden-Sydney College, 1807–20. His teaching resulted in founding of Union Theological Seminary in Virginia. A moderate Evangelical.

HOGE, MOSES DRURY (*b. Hampden-Sydney, Va., 1819; d. Richmond, Va., 1899*), Presbyterian clergyman. Grandson of Moses Hoge. Pastor, Second Presbyterian Church, Richmond, Va., 1845–99. Ran blockade during Civil War to bring Bibles for Confederate soldiers.

HOGG, GEORGE (*b. Cramlington, England, 1784; d. Allegheny City, Pa., 1849*), merchant, glass manufacturer, operator of lake and river shipping. Came to America as a young man. A pioneer in field of chain stores, wholesale and retail.

HOGG, JAMES STEPHEN (*b. near Rusk, Texas, 1851; d. 1906*), lawyer. Texas attorney-general, 1887–91; Democratic governor of Texas, 1891–95. Curbed abuses of corrupt corporations, railroads and land companies.

HOGUE, WILSON THOMAS (*b. Lyndon, N.Y., 1852; d. 1920*), clergyman and bishop of the Free Methodist Church. President, Greenville College, Illinois, 1892–1904.

HOGUN, JAMES (*b. Ireland; d. Haddrell's Point, S.C., 1781*), Revolutionary soldier. Settled in Halifax Co., N.C., *c.* 1751. As brigadier-general, commanded North Carolina brigade under Washington and Lincoln; taken prisoner at Charleston, S.C., 1780.

HOHFELD, WESLEY NEWCOMB (*b. Oakland, Calif., 1879; d. Alameda, Calif., 1918*), legal scholar. Graduated University of California, 1901; Harvard Law School, 1904. Served as professor of law at Stanford, 1905–14; at Yale, 1914–18. His greatest work was a series of monographs published posthumously, *Fundamental Legal Conceptions as Applied in Judicial Reasoning* (1919, 1923), setting forth the ideas of legal analysis which later became known as the Hohfeld System. Although subjected to much discussion, his terminology was adopted in substance by the American Law Institute.

HOISINGTON, HENRY RICHARD (*b. Vergennes, Vt., 1801; d. Centerbrook, Conn., 1858*), Congregational clergyman. Missionary to Ceylon, 1833–49. Principal, Batticotta Seminary, Ceylon. Translated Tamil religious texts and treatise on Hindu astronomy.

HOKE, ROBERT FREDERICK (*b. Lincolnton, N.C., 1837; d. Raleigh, N.C., 1912*), businessman, Confederate soldier. Rose from second lieutenant, 1861, to major-general, 1864; served mainly with Lee's army and was highly regarded by that general.

HOLABIRD, WILLIAM (*b. Amenia Union, N.Y., 1854; d. Evanston, Ill., 1923*), architect. Resigning from West Point, 1875, he moved to Chicago and was employed as a draftsman by William Le Baron Jenney. In association, *post* 1883, with Martin Roche, he took the lead among Chicago architects. Confronted with the demand for a building with profitable floor space, to be constructed on a narrow building lot, the firm designed the first office building in the world to utilize throughout its façades the principles of skeleton construction. This building at La Salle and Madison Streets, completed 1888, established the use of skeleton construction in high buildings. This achievement and the introduction of multiple deep basements were outstanding contributions of Holabird & Roche to the science of structural engineering.

HOLBROOK, ALFRED (*b. Derby, Conn., 1816; d. Lebanon, O., 1909*), pioneer in professional teacher training in Middle West. Son of Josiah Holbrook. Established Lebanon (O.) University, 1855, to democratize college education and reduce cost to students.

HOLBROOK, FREDERICK (*b. near East Windsor, Conn., 1813; d. Brattleboro, Vt., 1909*), scientific farmer. Republican governor of Vermont, 1861–63.

HOLBROOK, JOHN EDWARDS (*b. Beaufort, S.C., 1794; d. Norfolk, Mass., 1871*), physician, zoölogist, Confederate medical officer. Graduated Brown, 1815; M.D., University of Pennsylvania, 1818. Practiced at Charleston, S.C., and taught at South Carolina Medical College. Author of *North American Herpetology* (1836, 1838), rearranged systematically in five volumes (1842). He also published *Ichthyology of South Carolina* (1855, 1860), an abbreviation of his proposed series on the fishes of the Southern states.

HOLBROOK, JOSIAH (*b. Derby, Conn., 1788; d. near Lynchburg, Va., 1854*), educational reformer, originator of movement known as the American Lyceum. Graduated Yale, 1810. An itinerant lecturer on science, he began the organization, *post* 1826, of community enterprises for mutual improvement and the establishment of museums and libraries. These town lyceums were established throughout the country and became a typical feature of American community life for half a century. The training of teachers was an important phase of his program.

HOLCOMB, AMASA (*b. Southwick, Mass., 1787; d. Southwick, 1875*), instrument maker. Produced telescopes, *c.* 1835, with focal length of 14 feet; experimented with photographic cameras.

HOLCOMB, SILAS ALEXANDER (*b. Gibson Co., Ind., 1858; d. Bellingham, Wash., 1920*), lawyer, Populist politician. Settled in Nebraska, 1879. Governor of that state, 1895–99; state supreme court judge, 1899–1905. Conservative leader of a radical party and a popular and successful administrator.

HOLCOMBE, CHESTER (*b. Winfield, N.Y., 1844; d. Rochester, N.Y., 1912*), Presbyterian clergyman, missionary to China, 1869–76. Became interpreter, secretary and acting chargé at Peking; helped draft treaty with China, 1880, and first American treaty with Korea, 1882.

HOLCOMBE, HENRY (*b. Prince Edward Co., Va., 1762; d. Philadelphia, Pa., 1824*), Baptist clergyman in South Carolina, Georgia and Philadelphia, Pa.

HOLCOMBE, JAMES PHILEMON (*b. Powhatan Co., Va., 1820; d. Capon Springs, W. Va., 1873*), lawyer, writer on legal subjects. Professor of law, University of Virginia, 1851–61. Confederate congressman, 1862–64; secret agent in Canada, 1864, with C. C. Clay and Jacob Thompson.

HOLCOMBE, WILLIAM HENRY (*b. Lynchburg, Va., 1825; d. New Orleans, La., 1893*), homeopathic physician, authority on yellow fever. Brother of James P. Holcombe.

HOLDEN, EDWARD SINGLETON (*b. St. Louis, Mo., 1846; d. 1914*), astronomer. Graduated West Point, 1870. Assistant at Naval Observatory, 1873–81, associate of Simon Newcomb; director, Lick Observatory, 1888–97; librarian, West Point, 1901–14. A man of many talents and wide achievement.

HOLDEN, HALE (*b. Kansas City, Mo., 1869; d. New York, N.Y., 1940*), lawyer. President, Chicago, Burlington & Quincy Railroad, 1914–18, 1920–29; chairman, Southern Pacific, 1932–39; a notable railway statesman. [*Supp. 2*]

HOLDEN, LIBERTY EMERY (*b. Raymond, Maine, 1833; d. 1913*), financier, mine owner, proprietor of *Cleveland Plain Dealer, post* 1884.

HOLDEN, OLIVER (*b. Shirley, Mass., 1765; d. Charlestown, Mass., 1844*), carpenter, land owner, preacher, writer and composer of hymns. His *Union Harmony* (1793) contains forty of his compositions including his "Coronation."

HOLDEN, WILLIAM WOODS (*b. Orange Co., N.C., 1818; d. 1892*), journalist. Editor, *North Carolina Standard, post* 1843. Governor of North Carolina, 1868–70, when he was impeached for arbitrary action and protection of corrupt elements. A political chameleon, he began as a Whig and was in succession Democrat, Unionist, Republican.

HOLDER, CHARLES FREDERICK (*b. Lynn, Mass., 1851; d. Pasadena, Calif., 1915*), naturalist, sportsman. Son of Joseph B. Holder. Author of popular works on zoology. Founded "Tournament of Roses," Pasadena; developed tuna fishing as a sport.

HOLDER, JOSEPH BASSETT (*b. Lynn, Mass., 1824; d. 1888*), marine zoologist, physician, author. As U.S. army surgeon at Ft. Jefferson, Fla., he made important studies of coral formation.

HOLDREGE, GEORGE WARD (*b. New York, N.Y., 1847; d. Omaha, Nebr., 1926*), Western railroad builder, agricultural promoter. [*Supp. 1*]

HOLLADAY, BEN (*b. Carlisle Co., Ky., 1819; d. Portland, Ore., 1887*), stagecoach master, financier. Starting as Indian trader in Kansas, he expanded operations by supplying Kearny's Army of the West during the Mexican War; later traded with Mormon settlements in Utah and drove cattle to California market. On bankruptcy of Russell, Majors and Waddell, he bought their freight lines and organized the Holladay stagecoach empire which served an area stretching from the Missouri River to the Golden Gate until 1866. After losses by Indian raiding and aware of coming railroad dominance, he sold out to Wells, Fargo and Co. and turned first to ocean transport and then to promoting and constructing the Oregon Central Railroad. The failure of this railroad, after the panic of 1873, broke his financial power.

HOLLAND, CLIFFORD MILBURN (*b. Somerset, Mass., 1883; d. Battle Creek, Mich., 1924*), civil engineer, leader in field of subaqueous construction. Graduated Harvard, 1905; B.S. in civil engineering, 1906. Recommended and constructed the New Jersey-New York vehicular tunnel which bears his name.

HOLLAND, EDMUND MILTON (*b. 1848; d. Chicago, Ill., 1913*), actor, character comedian. Son of George Holland.

HOLLAND, EDWIN CLIFFORD (*b. Charleston, S.C., c. 1794; d. Charleston, 1824*), author. His *Odes, Naval Songs and Other Poems* (Charleston, 1813) marked the beginning of romantic poetry in South Carolina.

HOLLAND, GEORGE (*b. London, England, 1791; d. New York, N.Y., 1870*), comedian. Made American début, Bowery Theatre, New York, 1827; especially popular in the South. Was with Wallack's company in New York, 1855–67. Refusal of a fashionable church to conduct his funeral was the occasion for the naming of "The Little Church Around the Corner."

HOLLAND, JOHN PHILIP (*b. Liscanor, Ireland, 1840; d. Newark, N.J., 1914*), inventor. While in Ireland, he conceived the idea of a submarine, hoping that it might be used as a means of gaining Irish independence, an idea he retained after emigration to the United States, 1873. The American Fenian Society financed the building of a submarine, the *Fenian Ram* (1881), which embodied the chief principles of the modern submarine in balance, control and compensation of weight lost in torpedo discharge. Holland's designs for submarines to be built by the Navy Department were uniformly unsuccessful. In 1898, he launched the *Holland*, built by him according to his design and without official meddling, which was successful and clearly demonstrated the practical value of submarines. It was purchased by the Navy Department, 1900.

HOLLAND, JOSEPH JEFFERSON (*b. New York, N.Y. 1860; d. Falmouth, Mass., 1926*), actor. Son of George Holland.

HOLLAND, JOSIAH GILBERT (*b. Belchertown, Mass., 1819; d. 1881*), editor. Abandoned practice of medicine, 1848; associated with Samuel Bowles in editorship of *Springfield Republican*, 1850– c. 1868. Editor, *Scribner's Monthly* post 1870, and of the *Century Magazine*, 1881. Author of popular but now forgotten books.

HOLLAND, WILLIAM JACOB (*b. Jamaica, B.W.I., 1848; d. Pittsburgh, Pa., 1932*), naturalist, educator, Presbyterian clergyman. Director, Carnegie Museum of Pittsburgh, 1898–1922. Sponsored fossil explora-

tions in the West. Author of *The Butterfly Book* (1898) and *The Moth Book* (1903). [*Supp. 1*]

HOLLANDER, JACOB HARRY (*b. Baltimore, Md., 1871; d. 1940*), economist. Graduated Johns Hopkins, 1891; Ph.D., 1894. Taught at Johns Hopkins, 1894–1940. Served as government adviser in revising Puerto Rico finances, 1900–01, and as financial adviser to Dominican Republic, 1905–10. Built up labor seminar at Johns Hopkins. [*Supp. 2*]

HOLLERITH, HERMAN (*b. Buffalo, N.Y., 1860; d. Washington, D.C., 1929*), inventor of tabulating machines. Graduated School of Mines, Columbia, 1879. Became an assistant in the Census of 1880; this work brought him in contact with John Shaw Billings from whom came the suggestion for a machine to do the mechanical work of tabulating population statistics. Invented machines to record statistical items by means of electrical current through a system of punched holes in non-conducting material. These were first used in the Census of 1890 and subsequently improved. Organized the Tabulating Machine Co., 1896, which after consolidations became known as the International Business Machines Corp. [*Supp. 1*]

HOLLEY, ALEXANDER LYMAN (*b. Lakeville, Conn., 1832; d. Brooklyn, N.Y., 1882*), mechanical engineer, metallurgist. Graduated Brown, 1853. While in college, drew plans of locomotives and invented a steam cut-off; after practical experience in locomotive plants, became publisher of *Holley's Railroad Advocate*, 1855–57. Thereafter, until the end of his life, he continued to write technical articles, but was progressively more involved in original engineering work. In 1863 he bought American rights to the Bessemer process and was able to reconcile the conflicting claims under the Bessemer and Kelly processes and construct an improved steel mill at Troy, N.Y., 1865. He planned other steel mills and was recognized as the foremost steel-plant engineer in the United States and the "father of modern American steel manufacture."

HOLLEY, HORACE (*b. Salisbury, Conn., 1781; d. at sea, 1827*), Unitarian minister, educator. Brother of Myron Holley. Graduated Yale, 1803. Minister, Hollis Street Church, Boston, 1809–18; outstanding president, Transylvania University, 1818–27.

HOLLEY, MARIETTA (*b. Jefferson Co., N.Y., 1836; d. 1926*), humorist, woman's rights advocate. Author of *My Opinions and Betsy Bobbet's* (1873) and many other books and magazine articles in which as Samantha, "Josiah Allen's wife," her droll, homely humor delighted countless readers.

HOLLEY, MYRON (*b. Salisbury, Conn., 1779; d. 1841*), editor, Abolitionist. Brother of Horace Holley. Treasurer, Erie Canal Commission; a leader in the anti-Masonic movement. Largely responsible for formation of Liberty party, 1840; edited *Rochester Freeman,* (N.Y.), 1839–41.

HOLLICK, CHARLES ARTHUR (*b. Staten Island, N.Y., 1857; d. 1933*), engineer, paleobotanist. Associated for many years with N.Y. Botanical Garden. [*Supp. 1*]

HOLLIDAY, CYRUS KURTZ (*b. near Carlisle, Pa., 1826; d. 1900*), businessman. Removed to Kansas, 1854; builder and promoter of Topeka. He secured charter and federal land grants for the Atchison, Topeka & Santa Fe Railroad; served for a time as its president and was a director until his death.

HOLLINGWORTH, LETA STETTER (*b. near Chadron, Nebr., 1886; d. New York, N.Y., 1939*), psychologist. Taught at Teachers College, Columbia, 1919–39; studied individual and group differences, particularly of subnormal and gifted children, and adolescents. [*Supp. 2*]

HOLLINS, GEORGE NICHOLS (*b. Baltimore, Md., 1799; d. Baltimore, 1878*), naval officer. Resigned from U.S. Navy, 1861, to enter Confederate service. Commanded Confederate flotilla at New Orleans, 1861, and all naval forces on upper Mississippi, 1862. His advice was ignored in Confederate defense of New Orleans.

HOLLIS, IRA NELSON (*b. Mooresville, Ind., 1856; d. Cambridge, Mass., 1930*), naval engineer, educator. Graduated Annapolis, 1878. Resigned from U.S. Navy, 1893. Harvard professor of mechanical engineering, 1893–1913; president, Worcester Polytechnic Institute, 1913–25.

HOLLISTER, GIDEON HIRAM (*b. Washington, Conn., 1817; d. 1881*), lawyer. Author of *Mount Hope* (1851) and *Kinley Hollow* (1882).

HOLLOWAY, JOHN (*b. England, c. 1666; d. Virginia, 1734*), colonial official, lawyer, jurist. Despite doubts of his character, he succeeded in practice in Virginia *post c.* 1700, and was long a member of the House of Burgesses (speaker for 14 years), and treasurer of the colony, 1723–34.

HOLLOWAY, JOSEPH FLAVIUS (*b. Uniontown, O., 1825; d. Buffalo, N.Y., 1896*), mechanical engineer. Designed and built machinery for steam craft on Great Lakes, the Mississippi, and for ocean-going vessels of all types.

HOLLS, FREDERICK WILLIAM. [See HOLLS, GEORGE FREDERICK WILLIAM, 1857–1903.]

HOLLS, GEORGE FREDERICK WILLIAM (*b. Zelienople, Pa., 1857; d. New York, N.Y., 1903*), lawyer, publicist. Aroused President McKinley's interest in Hague International Peace Conference and converted German opposition into support of International Court.

HOLLY, JAMES THEODORE (*b. Washington, D.C., 1829; d. Port-au-Prince, Haiti, 1911*), Episcopal clergyman. A leader in Negro Emigration Conventions, 1854 and 1856. Led emigration of free Negroes to Haiti, 1861; consecrated Protestant Episcopal bishop of Haiti, 1874.

HOLLYER, SAMUEL (*b. London, England, 1826; d. 1919*), engraver, etcher. Settled permanently in America, 1866. Published series of antiquarian etchings in *Prints of Old New York* (1904).

HOLMAN, JESSE LYNCH (*b. near Danville, Ky., 1784; d. 1842*), Baptist clergyman, Indiana pioneer and legislator. Federal judge in Indiana, 1834–42.

HOLMAN, WILLIAM STEELE (*b. near Aurora, Ind., 1822; d. 1897*), lawyer, jurist. Congressman, Democrat, from Indiana, 1859–65, 1867–77, 1881–95, 1897. Powerful in debate and skilled as a parliamentarian, he expressed the philosophy of Jeffersonian agrarianism in an age dominated by railroad operators, industrial magnates and leaders of high finance. Denounced by some for his "hay-seed statesmanship," Holman was hailed by others as "The Watch-dog of the Treasury" and "The Great Objector" to excess appropriations.

HOLME, THOMAS (*b. probably Yorkshire, England, 1624; d. Philadelphia Co., Pa., 1695*). Came to America, 1682, as surveyor-general of Pennsylvania. Laid out site of Philadelphia; drafted *A Map of the Province of Pennsilvania* (published London *c.* 1687) and also an earlier map or plot of Philadelphia, first printed in *A Letter from William Penn . . . to the Committee of the Free Society of Traders* (1683).

HOLMES, ABIEL (*b. Woodstock, Conn., 1763; d. Cambridge, Mass., 1837*), Congregational clergyman, historian. Graduated Yale, 1783. Pastor, First Church, Cambridge, Mass., 1792–1829. He is best known as father of Oliver Wendell Holmes (1809–1894) and as author of *American Annals* (1805), the first serious attempt at an orderly history of America.

HOLMES, BAYARD TAYLOR (*b. North Hero, Vt., 1852; d. Fairhope, Ala., 1924*), surgeon. Raised in Minnesota. Graduated, M.D., Chicago Homeopathic College, 1884; Chicago Medical College, 1888. Professor of pathology and surgery, University of Illinois, 1892–1908. Socialist candidate for mayor of Chicago, 1895.

HOLMES, DANIEL HENRY (*b. New York, N.Y., 1851; d. Hot Springs, Va., 1908*), poet, musician, lawyer.

HOLMES, DAVID (*b. York Co., Pa., 1770; d. near Winchester, Va., 1832*), lawyer. Congressman, (Democrat) Republican, from Virginia, 1797–1809; governor of Mississippi Territory, 1809–17; of State of Mississippi, 1817–20 and 1826; U.S. senator from Mississippi, 1820–25. Instrumental in occupation of

Baton Rouge district and in annexation, 1812, of Mobile district by Americans.

HOLMES, EZEKIEL (*b. Kingston, Mass., 1801; d. 1865*), editor, physician, agriculturist. Graduated Brown, 1821; M.D., Bowdoin, 1824. While an undergraduate, he showed an early interest in botany and mineralogy; shortly afterward he discovered the important tourmaline deposit on Mount Mica in Maine. He served as instructor in agriculture and as principal of Gardiner Lyceum, also lectured on scientific subjects at Waterville College, Maine. Settled permanently in Winthrop, Maine, 1832. Started the first farm journal in Maine, 1833, thus embarking on his real mission, the promotion of scientific agriculture in that state. He was instrumental in the establishment of the University of Maine and stimulated American settlement in the disputed Aroostook area.

HOLMES, GEORGE FREDERICK (*b. Straebrock, British Guiana, 1820; d. Virginia, 1897*), educator, scholar. Educated in England; settled in America, 1837. Contributor to *Southern Literary Messenger*. First president, University of Mississippi, 1848; professor of history and political economy, University of Virginia, 1857–97.

HOLMES, ISAAC EDWARD (*b. Charleston, S.C., 1796; d. Charleston, 1867*), lawyer, politician. Vehement opponent of abolition; nullificationist. Congressman, Democrat, from South Carolina, 1839–51. In California, 1851–61; returned to Charleston and was a zealous Confederate.

HOLMES, ISRAEL (*b. Waterbury, Conn., 1800; d. 1874*), Connecticut brass manufacturer. Associated with firms of Holmes and Hotchkiss, Waterbury Brass Co., Holmes, Booth and Atwood, and others. Active in construction of Naugatuck Railroad.

HOLMES, JOHN (*b. Kingston, Mass., 1773; d. Portland, Maine, 1843*), lawyer. Graduated Brown, 1796. Removed to Maine, 1799, and was successful in land-title practice. Opposed Daniel Webster and Hopkinson in Dartmouth College case. Represented Maine in Congress and was active in separation of Maine from Massachusetts, 1816–20. U.S. senator, Democrat, later Whig, from Maine, 1821–27, 1828–33. U.S. attorney, Maine district, 1841–43.

HOLMES, JOSEPH AUSTIN (*b. Laurens, S.C., 1859; d. Denver, Colo., 1915*), mining engineer. Graduated Cornell, 1881. Professor of geology, University of North Carolina, 1882–92; state geologist, 1891–1904. His testing of fuels in public demonstration at St. Louis World's Fair, 1904, led to an appointment to head testing laboratories of the U.S. Geological Survey; his advocacy of conservation of mineral resources and mine safety gained him promotion to first director of Bureau of Mines, 1910. His "safety first" campaign was responsible for installation of equipment and devices that reduced the accident rate throughout American industry.

HOLMES, MARY JANE HAWES (*b. Brookfield, Mass., 1825; d. Brockport, N.Y., 1907*), popular novelist. Among her books were *Tempest and Sunshine* (1854), *Lena Rivers* (1856), *Ethelyn's Mistake* (1869) and other sentimental tales of small town life.

HOLMES, NATHANIEL (*b. Peterborough, N.H., 1815; d. Cambridge, Mass., 1901*), Missouri jurist. Royall Professor of Law, Harvard, 1868–72. Enthusiast for the Baconian authorship of Shakespeare's plays.

HOLMES, OLIVER WENDELL (*b. Cambridge, Mass., 1809; d. Boston, Mass., 1894*), essayist, poet, teacher of anatomy. Son of Abiel Holmes. Graduated Harvard, 1829; achieved early popularity as a poet. His "Old Ironsides," published in the *Boston Daily Advertiser*, 1830, was copied widely by other newspapers and reprinted and distributed on hand-bills to help save U.S.S. *Constitution* from destruction. His collected early *Poems* appeared in 1836. Deciding upon a medical career, Holmes had studied at Harvard and in Paris under Louis and Larrey; graduated M.D. from Harvard, 1836, he became a teacher and lecturer rather than a practitioner. He wrote, among other medical pieces, a noteworthy and controversial article on "The Contagiousness of Puerperal Fever" (1843) and became deservedly famous for his lectures on anatomy and other medical subjects at Harvard (as Parkman Professor, 1847–82) and as a lyceum lecturer. Meanwhile, he continued to produce verse and literary prose. His twelve Lowell Institute lectures on the English poets (1853) were concluded, each time, with an original poem, a practice later adopted in his *Autocrat* articles. His total production as poet occupied 300 double-column pages in the *Collected Works* of 1895. It contains verse that may be classified as the poetic, the merely fanciful, the deftly humorous and the *vers d'occasion;* in this last group, the various Class of 1829 poems reveal his gifts as a weaver of felicitous after-dinner verses at their best. Holmes was a brilliant and indefatigable conversationalist with a boundless intellectual curiosity which caused his fellow member of the Saturday Club, James Russell Lowell, to assess correctly his possibilities as an essayist. The first installment of *The Autocrat of the Breakfast Table* appeared in the first issue of *The Atlantic Monthly* under Lowell's editorship (November 1857) and marked the entrance of Holmes into the field of witty "dramatized *causerie*" which he proceeded to make his own. The *Autocrat* essays were published as a book in 1858; *The Professor at the Breakfast Table* (1860) and *The Poet at the Breakfast Table* (1872) were not equal to their prototype. Holmes's best serious poem "The Chambered Nautilus" appeared in the *Autocrat;* his masterpiece in light-verse "The Deacon's Masterpiece, or the Wonderful One-Hoss-Shay" appeared in another installment of the original series and has been called "a parable of the breakdown of Calvinism." In the field of fiction Holmes was not so successful, although his first novel *Elsie Venner* (1861) foreshadowed later psychological fiction. Many successively enlarged editions of his poems appeared between 1836 and 1895, and among the mass of his published travel notes, memorial addresses and other works may be singled out his biographies of *John L. Motley* (1879) and *R. W. Emerson* (1885). His ability to give universal interest to local Boston scenes and topics is the secret of his appeal. A rationalist and a wit, he was in lifelong revolt against the Calvinist view of life which had shadowed his boyhood. He was the father of Justice Oliver Wendell Holmes of the U.S. Supreme Court.

HOLMES, OLIVER WENDELL (*b. Boston, Mass., 1841; d. 1935*), jurist. Son of Oliver Wendell Holmes (1809–1894) and Amelia Lee Jackson. Descended from a long line of New Englanders among whom were Dorothy Quincy and Anne Bradstreet, he was deeply rooted in the Puritan tradition.

Volunteering for the infantry in April 1861, before his graduation from Harvard that year, he was commissioned second lieutenant in July. He served until July 1864 with the 20th Massachusetts. Wounded three times, he was mustered out with the rank of captain. Returning to Boston as a military hero, he shocked patriotic sentimentalists by speaking of war as an "organized bore," but useful so "that we may realize that our comfortable routine is no eternal necessity of things . . . in this time of individualist negations." After his graduation from Harvard Law School, 1866, he visited in England, making friendships with Leslie Stephen, James Bryce, Frederick Pollock and others. Admitted to the bar, 1867, he practiced in Boston, working with feverish intensity to become a master in his calling. He was editor of the *American Law Review*, 1870–73, worked to bring Kent's *Commentaries* up to date and lectured on law at Harvard. In 1872 he married Fanny Bowditch Dixwell whose influence on his life and career must be measured in any account of him.

In his early writings he canvassed issues which are vital to a society devoted to justice according to law. What are the sources of law and what are its sanctions? What are the ingredients, conscious or unconscious, of adjudication? What are the wise demands of precedent and when should the judicial process feel unbound by its past? These were some of the inquiries which guided Holmes's investigations at a time when law was generally treated as a body of settled doctrine from which answers to the new problems of industrialized society were to be derived by logical deduction. While judges boasted a want of philosophy, Holmes realized that decisions are functions of some juristic philosophy,

and that awareness of the considerations moving beneath the surface of logical form is the prime requisite of a civilized system of law. He was conscious of the role of the unconscious more than a generation before Freud began to influence modern psychology, and a half a century before Ogden and Richards wrote *The Meaning of Meaning*. He systematized these pioneer contributions in *The Common Law* (1881), which is a classic in the sense that its stock of ideas has been absorbed and become part of common juristic thought. "The life of the law," he wrote, "has not been logic: it has been experience."

Called to Harvard Law School, 1882, as Weld Professor of Law, he became a justice of the supreme judicial court of Massachusetts in 1883. His Massachusetts opinions (nearly 1300) if brought together would constitute the most comprehensive and philosophic body of American law for any period of its history. He became chief justice of Massachusetts in 1899, and although his opinions in labor cases (e.g., *Vegelahn vs. Guntner*) disturbed the conservatism of Boston, they were in part the influences which led Pres. Theodore Roosevelt to appoint Holmes to the U.S. Supreme Court, 1902. He served until Jan. 12, 1932.

He came to the Court at a time when legislative activity reflected changing social conceptions stimulated by technological development. Probably no man on the Court was ever freer of emotional commitments which might compel him to translate his own economic or social views into constitutional commands. His disbelief in ultimate answers to social questions permitted him to exhibit judicial function at its purest. Social development could be an effective process of trial and error only when there was the fullest possible opportunity for the free play of the mind. To Holmes, the Constitution was not a literary document or an occasion for juggling with words but a framework of great governmental powers to be exercised for great public ends. Expressing his opinions with stinging brevity, he was unimpressed by what are called great cases. "My keenest interest is excited . . . by little decisions . . . which have in them . . . the germ of some wider theory . . . some profound interstitial change in the very tissue of law." In deciding cases his aim was "to strike the jugular," to omit in his expression of opinion all but essentials.

Some of his weightiest utterances are dissents that have shaped history, written with "cold Puritan passion": *Adair vs. United States; Hammer vs. Dagenhart; U.S. vs. Schwimmer; Tyson & Bro. vs. Banton; Baldwin vs. Missouri.* Some of his most powerful opinions were written in his ninth decade. After his retirement, he continued his life in Washington and Beverly Farms until March 6, 1935, and was buried on his birthday in Arlington Cemetery. Without explanation he left the bulk of his estate to the nation, the largest unrestricted gift ever made to it.

Because Holmes disciplined himself against any kind of parochialism in his thinking, he is a significant figure in the history of civilization, not merely a commanding American legal figure. He is unsurpassed in the depth of his penetration into the nature of the judicial process and in the originality of its exposition. He early rejected legal principles as absolutes. Looking beneath their formulations, he saw them as expressions of conflicting or overlapping social policies; the vital judicial issue, therefore, was apt to be their accommodation and decisions became essentially a matter of drawing lines. [Supp. 1]

HOLMES, THEOPHILUS HUNTER (b. Sampson Co., N.C., 1804; d. Cumberland Co., N.C., 1880), Confederate soldier. West Point classmate of Jefferson Davis, 1829. Cited for bravery in Mexican War; ineffective lieutenant-general in Confederate Army, 1862–64.

HOLMES, WILLIAM HENRY (b. near Cadiz, O., 1846; d. 1933), archeologist, artist. Served with the Hayden Survey, 1872–77; U.S. Geological Survey, 1880–84; American Bureau of Ethnology, 1889–94. Curator of anthropology, Field Museum, Chicago, 1894–97; Smithsonian Institution, 1897–1920. In 1902, he succeeded J. W. Powell as chief of Bureau of American Ethnology. Director, National Gallery of Art, 1920–32. Author of Handbook of Aboriginal American Antiquities (1919) which became the standard treatise on the subject. [Supp. 1]

HOLSEY, LUCIUS HENRY (b. near Columbus, Ga., c. 1842; d. 1920), an organizer (1870) and bishop (1873) of the Colored Methodist Episcopal Church. Born a slave and self-educated, he founded a number of schools and colleges for his people.

HOLST, HERMANN EDUARD von (b. Fellin, Russia [Esthonia], 1841; d. Freiburg, Baden, Germany, 1904), historian. Graduated Heidelberg, Ph.D., 1865. Came to America, 1867. Returned to Europe as professor at Strassburg, 1872–74, and at Freiburg, 1874–92. Head of history department, University of Chicago, 1892–99. His voluminous Constitutional and Political History of the United States (1873–92) emphasized the moral influence of slavery on American history.

HOLT, EDWIN MICHAEL (b. Orange Co., N.C., 1807; d. Alamance Co., N.C., 1884), cotton manufacturer. First Southern manufacturer to dye yarn; introduced the "Alamance Plaids."

HOLT, HENRY (b. Baltimore, Md., 1840; d. 1926), publisher. Graduated Yale, 1862. Established firm of Leypoldt and Holt, 1866, later Henry Holt and Co.

HOLT, JOHN (b. Williamsburg, Va., 1721; d. 1784), printer, journalist, Revolutionary patriot. Learned the printing art at Williamsburg; moved north, 1754, to become part owner with James Parker and editor of papers in New Haven and New York. He acquired full ownership of the New-York Gazette and Weekly Post-Boy, 1762 (later, The New-York Journal, Parker resuming the Gazette title, 1766). Active as a Whig printer, Holt left New York on the eve of the British occupation, 1776, a procedure which he repeated in New Haven and Danbury, Conn., and Kingston, N.Y.; on each removal his property was destroyed by the enemy. He returned to New York City, 1783, and edited The Independent New-York Gazette and its successors. He was interested also in improving the delivery service for newspapers, in postal reforms, and book-selling.

HOLT, JOSEPH (b. Breckenridge Co., Ky., 1807; d. Washington, D.C., 1894), lawyer, politician. Postmaster-general, 1859–61; secretary of war, 1861. Sympathetic at first to Southern sentiments, after South Carolina's secession he became a leading Kentucky Unionist. As judge-advocate general, 1862–75, Holt used military commissions effectively in prosecuting citizens accused of disloyalty, the Vallandigham and Milligan cases being notable examples. His prosecution of the alleged assassins of President Lincoln brought him great popularity, but disclosures of perjury on the part of government witnesses and the charge that he had suppressed important evidence favorable to Mrs. Surratt brought him into disfavor.

HOLT, LUTHER EMMETT (b. Webster, N.Y., 1855; d. Peking, China, 1924), pediatrician. Graduated M.D., College of Physicians and Surgeons, New York, 1880. First practiced his specialty at the New York Infant Asylum and similar institutions. The Babies Hospital of New York (founded 1887) was, medically speaking, his creation. A teacher by nature, he served as professor at the Polyclinic Hospital and the College of Physicians and Surgeons. As author of popular medical books, he reached a vast audience; his The Care and Feeding of Children (1894) and The Diseases of Infancy and Childhood (1896) made "Dr. Holt" a household word. Osler alone in the United States exercised a comparable educational influence.

HOLTEN, SAMUEL (b. Salem Village [Danvers], Mass., 1738; d. Danvers, 1816), physician. Massachusetts legislator and Revolutionary leader; member of Continental Congress, 1778–87. Strongly opposed ratification of Federal Constitution.

HOLYOKE, EDWARD AUGUSTUS (b. Marblehead, Mass., 1728; d. Salem, Mass., 1829), physician. Graduated Harvard, 1746. A promoter of medical education in Massachusetts, among his students were N. W. Appleton and James Jackson. Experience, in his view, was the key to medical knowledge.

HOLYOKE, SAMUEL (*b. Boxford, Mass., 1762; d. Concord, N.H., 1820*), teacher, composer of "Arnheim" and other music. Compiled *Harmonia Americana* (1791), the *Columbian Repository of Sacred Harmony* (1802) and other collections of hymns.

HOMER, WINSLOW (*b. Boston, Mass., 1836; d. 1910*), painter. Apprenticed to Bufford, the Boston lithographer, 1855; set up his own studio in Boston, 1857, and New York, 1858, selling drawings to *Ballou's Pictorial* and to *Harper's Weekly. Harper's* sent him to Washington, 1861, to make drawings of Lincoln's inauguration; thereafter, he sketched camp scenes and early engagements during the Peninsular campaign, and on his return to New York began to paint pictures of war subjects which were exhibited at the National Academy of Design, 1863. He was made an Academician, 1865. *Post* 1867, he produced mainly rural *genre* and landscapes until a stay in England, 1881–82, brought a change in his art. He became increasingly concerned with the drama of the sea. Turning his back on the city, he settled at Prout's Neck, Scarboro, Maine, 1884, and except for seasonal expeditions to Florida, Nassau, Cuba or Bermuda, lived there until death. From the Maine coast came outstanding works such as "The Life Line" (actually started in England), "The Fog Warning," "Banks Fishermen," the stirring deep-sea classic "Eight Bells," and "A Summer Night." The haunting "Gulf Stream" and "Searchlight, Harbor Entrance, Santiago de Cuba" were products of his stays in southern climes. Both in water-colors and in oils, Homer's method and style were those of a man who had something to say and who employed no surplus rhetoric; he drove straight to the mark. He echoed no other painter and his work is wholly personal and American. Pre-eminent as a realistic marine painter, he is never prosaic; his work throbs with the essential elements of poetry, with deep feeling and a sense of the dignity and heroism of man.

HOMES, HENRY AUGUSTUS (*b. Boston, Mass., 1812; d. 1887*). Graduated Amherst, 1830. Missionary to Turkey, 1836–54. Librarian, New York State Library, 1854–87. Author of papers on library administration and historical subjects.

HONE, PHILIP (*b. New York, N.Y., 1780; d. New York, 1851*), auctioneer, diarist. Whig leader; mayor of New York City, 1825; promoter of cultural and commercial enterprises. Principally remembered for his diary (covering 1828–51; first published, in part, 1889) which furnishes a useful view of New York life in its period.

HONTAN, LOUIS-ARMAND DE LOM D'ARCE, Baron de la. [See LAHONTAN, LOUIS ARMAND DE LOM D'ARCE, 1666–*c.* 1713.]

HOOD, JAMES WALKER (*b. Kennett Township, Pa., 1831; d. 1918*), bishop, African Methodist Episcopal Zion Church (ordained, 1872). First Negro to preside over the Ecumenical Conference; assistant superintendent of public instruction, North Carolina, 1868–70.

HOOD, JOHN BELL (*b. Owingsville, Ky., 1831; d. New Orleans, La., 1879*), Confederate soldier. Graduated West Point, 1853; served in California and Texas. As Confederate brigadier-general, March 1862, he commanded the "Texas Brigade" which won high reputation on the Peninsula and at Antietam. As major-general, October 1862, he was division commander under Longstreet at Gettysburg and directed Longstreet's Corps at Chickamauga. Lee wrote President Davis that Hood was "a bold fighter" but expressed doubt about his qualifications for high command; yet Hood (promoted lieutenant-general, Feb. 1864) was named to replace Gen. J. E. Johnston as leader of the Confederate Army defending Atlanta. Uniformly unsuccessful in this command, he experienced a disastrous defeat at Nashville, December 1864, and was relieved. His subsequent career in Texas and New Orleans was marked by misfortune.

HOOD, RAYMOND MATHEWSON (*b. Pawtucket, R.I., 1881; d. Stamford, Conn., 1934*), architect. Graduated Massachusetts Institute of Technology, 1903; École des Beaux-Arts, 1911. After working for Cram, Goodhue and Ferguson, and other architects, opened office in New York, 1914. Joined J. M. Howells in 1922 competition for Chicago Tribune building and won; its strong composition and late-Gothic detail won immediate acclaim. In 1929, had misgivings about traditional styles and joined the "modernists." His conversion was expressed in the American Radiator building, New York, the Beaux-Arts Apartments and, in association with Kenneth Murchison, the New York Daily News building. His last great work was in connection with Rockefeller Center in New York, whose final form owed much to his influence. [*Supp. 1*]

HOOD, WASHINGTON (*b. Philadelphia, Pa., 1808; d. Bedford Springs, Pa., 1840*), army officer, topographical engineer. Graduated West Point, 1827. His map of Oregon Territory (compiled 1838) was used as justification for occupation of that territory by the United States.

HOOKER, ELON HUNTINGTON (*b. Rochester, N.Y., 1869; d. Pasadena, Calif., 1938*), civil engineer, industrialist. Founded Hooker Electrochemical Co., 1909, producers of chlor-alkali chemicals and plastics. [*Supp. 2*]

HOOKER, ISABELLA BEECHER (*b. Litchfield, Conn., 1822; d. Hartford, Conn., 1907*), leading advocate of rights for women. Daughter of Lyman Beecher. Promoter of Connecticut law granting married women equal property rights (1877).

HOOKER, JOSEPH (*b. Hadley, Mass., 1814; d. Garden City, N.Y., 1879*), soldier. Graduated West Point, 1837. Served in Florida War, on Canadian border and as adjutant at West Point. Distinguished for gallantry and efficiency in Mexican War through part of Taylor's campaign and most of Scott's, he was brevetted lieutenant-colonel at Chapultepec. His testimony in the Pillow-Scott controversy gained for Hooker the hostility of Gen. Scott, and he resigned, 1853, to engage in various occupations at Sonoma, Calif., and in Oregon. He returned to service in 1861, as brigadier-general of volunteers. During the Peninsular campaign, 1862, he gained the sobriquet of "Fighting Joe" and promotion to major-general of volunteers. He was effective as a corps commander at South Mountain and at Antietam, where he was wounded. Returning to active duty, he participated in the assault on Fredericksburg and in the open criticism of Gen. Burnside. Appointed commander of the Army of the Potomac in Burnside's place, January 1863, he was defeated by Lee at Chancellorsville, May 2-4, 1863, despite a 2 to 1 superiority. The indecision which caused his defeat may be explained in part by the injury he sustained during the course of the battle. He declined to admit defeat and managed to protect Washington and Baltimore from Lee's invading army as it swept into Pennsylvania. Gen. Halleck's refusal to send re-enforcements from Harper's Ferry was, he concluded, a breach of faith in him, and Hooker asked to be relieved of his command although the decisive battle at Gettysburg was in immediate prospect. Transferred to the Department of the Cumberland, he served under Thomas and Sherman in all the decisive battles from Chattanooga to the fall of Atlanta. After McPherson's death, Sherman's refusal to award his command to Hooker brought another request for relief from duty, 1864. Thereafter he commanded several northern departments of the army, retiring as regular major-general, 1868.

HOOKER, PHILIP (*b. Rutland, Mass., 1766; d. Albany, N.Y., 1836*), architect. Removed to Albany, N.Y., as a child and was associated with that city until his death, transforming it architecturally *post* 1796 from a Dutch frontier town to the semblance of a New England city. His work derived from Mangin, McComb and Bulfinch; little of it remains unaltered at the present writing.

HOOKER, SAMUEL COX (*b. Brenchley, England, 1864; d. Brooklyn, N.Y., 1935*), chemist. Trained abroad; came to America, 1885. Specialist in the chemistry of sugar. [*Supp.* 1]

HOOKER, THOMAS (*b. probably Marfield, England, 1586?; d. Hartford, Conn., 1647*), Congregational clergyman. Graduated Emmanuel College, Cambridge, 1608; was a fellow there, 1609-18. Developed Puritan leanings there and as rector of Esher, Surrey, *post* 1620. As lecturer at St. Mary's, Chelmsford, 1626-30, his preaching was popular and attracted the enmity of Archbishop Laud. Hooker then opened a school at Little Baddow with John Eliot as assistant. Summoned, nevertheless, to appear before the High Commission, 1630, Hooker forfeited bond and escaped to Holland, whence he returned to England briefly in 1633 before sailing for New England in company with John Cotton and Samuel Stone. Arriving at Boston, September 1633, Hooker quickly established himself as a popular pastor at Newtown; as dissension deepened between his flock and the rest of the Bay Colony, he led the 1636 migration of most of his congregation to Hartford in the Connecticut valley. At the Synod called in 1637 for the purpose of condemning the Hutchinsonian and other heresies, Hooker proposed to John Winthrop a New England Confederation, but his long cherished plan was not to assume tangible form until 1643. A born democrat, he had much to do with framing the "Fundamental Orders" or constitution of Connecticut, 1639. He was a prolific author of sermons; his introduction to his posthumously published *A Survey of the Summe of Church Discipline* (1648) is considered as clear an exposition of Congregationalism as has ever been given.

HOOKER, WILLIAM (*fl. 1804-1846*), engraver, map-maker in Newburyport, Mass., and New York, N.Y. Associated with Edmund M. Blunt as engraver of charts for *American Coast Pilot* and maps of the New York area.

HOOKER, WORTHINGTON (*b. Springfield, Mass., 1806; d. 1867*), physician. Graduated Yale, 1825; M.D., Harvard, 1829. Practiced in Norwich, Conn., until 1852; thereafter at New Haven. Professor in Yale Medical School; author, *Rational Therapeutics* (1857).

HOOPER, JESSIE ANNETTE JACK (*b. Winneshiek Co., Iowa, 1865; d. Oshkosh, Wis., 1935*), suffragist. Active in League of Women Voters and world peace societies. [*Supp.* 1]

HOOPER, JOHNSON JONES (*b. Wilmington, N.C., 1815; d. Richmond, Va., 1862*), humorist, Alabama journalist, early portrayer of Southern frontier types. Created a celebrated character whose exploits appeared in newspapers and in collected form as *Some Adventures of Captain Simon Suggs, Late of the Tallapoosa Volunteers* (Philadelphia, 1846).

HOOPER, LUCY HAMILTON (*b. Philadelphia, Pa., 1835; d. Paris, France, 1893*), editor, journalist.

HOOPER, SAMUEL (*b. Marblehead, Mass., 1808; d. Washington, D.C., 1875*), merchant, Massachusetts legislator. Congressman, Republican, from Massachusetts, 1861-75. Advocated issue of legal tender notes and establishment of a national banking system;

post 1865, he urged contraction of greenbacks and was prominent in framing the 1873 currency act.

HOOPER, WILLIAM (*b. Boston, Mass., 1742; d. Hillsboro, N.C., 1790*), lawyer. Practiced in North Carolina *post* 1764. Member of Continental Congress, 1775–77. Signer of Declaration of Independence. Opposed democratic tendencies as North Carolina legislator.

HOOVER, CHARLES FRANKLIN (*b. Miamisburg, O., 1865; d. Cleveland, O., 1927*), physician, diagnostician. Professor of medicine in Western Reserve University, *post* 1907. Prominent as consultant in cardio-respiratory, neurological and hepatic diseases.

HOOVER, JAMES MATTHEWS (*b. Greenvillage, Pa., 1872; d. Kuching, Borneo, 1935*), Methodist missionary to Malaya. [*Supp. 1*]

HOPE, JAMES BARRON (*b. Norfolk, Va., 1829; d. 1887*), poet, newspaperman, Confederate soldier.

HOPE, JOHN (*b. Augusta, Ga., 1868; d. Atlanta, Ga., 1936*), educator. Of mixed white and Negro blood, Hope might have lived in the white world but chose to devote himself primarily to the education of Negro youth. Graduated Brown University, 1894. Professor of classics, Atlanta Baptist College (later Morehouse College), in 1906 he became its president. A great schoolmaster and able administrator, Hope became president of Atlanta University, 1929, when Atlanta became the first Negro graduate school, after affiliation with Morehouse and Spelman colleges. His advocacy through many national Negro organizations of complete equality for the Negro was made on an intellectual rather than an emotional basis. [*Supp. 2*]

HOPKINS, ARTHUR FRANCIS (*b. Pittsylvania Co., Va., 1794; d. Mobile, Ala., 1865*), lawyer, planter, jurist. Prominent in Alabama Whig party; president, Mobile and Ohio Railway; state agent for Alabama hospitals during Civil War.

HOPKINS, CYRIL GEORGE (*b. near Chatfield, Minn., 1866; d. Gibraltar, 1919*), agricultural chemist, inventor. Graduated South Dakota Agricultural College, 1890; Ph.D., Cornell, 1898. Professor of agronomy, University of Illinois, 1900–19. Devised the "Illinois System" of permanent soil fertility.

HOPKINS, EDWARD (*b. Shrewsbury, England, 1600; d. London, England, 1657*), merchant. Emigrated to New England, 1637, with Theophilus Eaton and John Davenport; settled in Hartford, Conn. Elected many times governor or deputy-governor of Connecticut between 1639 and 1654. Returned to England *c.* 1653. Benefactor to educational institutions in New England.

HOPKINS, EDWARD AUGUSTUS (*b. Pittsburgh, Pa., 1822; d. Washington, D.C., 1891*), naval officer, journalist. Promoter of trade between United States and Latin America. Established steam navigation on Paraná River; built a railroad between Buenos Aires and San Fernando. Son of Bishop John H. Hopkins.

HOPKINS, EDWARD WASHBURN (*b. Northampton, Mass., 1857; d. Madison, Conn., 1932*), Orientalist, philologist. Author of *The Religions of India* (1895), *Epic Mythology* (1915), etc. [*Supp. 1*]

HOPKINS, ESEK (*b. Scituate, R.I., 1718; d. Providence, R.I., 1802*), sea captain, commander-in-chief of the Continental Navy, 1775–77. Brother of Stephen Hopkins. An able, energetic seaman, he was impatient and critical as a commander. Regarding his orders from Congress to attack the British ships off Virginia and Carolina as discretionary, he led his command of eight small vessels on an expedition to New Providence, Bahamas, early in 1776; it was on the whole a successful enterprise. Uncertainty of pay by Congress discouraged recruiting, so that Hopkins was unable to man his vessels on his return. He was plagued also by insubordination and criticism of his inactivity. The British blockaded his ships in Narragansett Bay, December 1776, and Congress suspended him in March 1777 for acting unwisely and speaking slightingly of authorities in Philadelphia. A loyal patriot, he continued to serve the American cause in his native Rhode Island.

HOPKINS, ISAAC STILES (*b. Augusta, Ga., 1841; d. 1914*), Methodist clergyman, educator. Initiated technological instruction at Emory College as president, 1884–88; first president, Georgia School of Technology, 1888–96.

HOPKINS, JAMES CAMPBELL (*b. Rutland Co., Vt., 1819; d. 1877*), lawyer. Removed to Wisconsin, 1856. He helped arrange the Wisconsin code of legal procedure, and was federal judge, western Wisconsin district, 1870–77.

HOPKINS, JOHN BURROUGHS (*b. Providence, R.I., 1742; d. 1796*), naval officer. Son of Esek Hopkins. Captain and squadron leader, Continental Navy, 1775–79. Cruised as successful privateer, 1780 and 1781.

HOPKINS, JOHN HENRY (*b. Dublin, Ireland, 1792; d. 1868*), Episcopal clergyman. Came to America as a boy. Successful as ironmaster and lawyer, he abandoned his practice of law when elected rector by Trinity Episcopal Church, Pittsburgh, Pa., 1823. After a year as assistant at Trinity Church, Boston, (1831), he became rector of St. Paul's Church, Burlington, Vt., and first bishop of Vermont, 1832. As presiding bishop *post* 1865, he played a leading role in effecting the reunion of the northern and southern members of the Episcopal communion. A High Churchman and a student of patristic literature, he was author of many books.

HOPKINS, JOHNS (*b. Anne Arundel Co., Md., 1795; d. Baltimore, Md., 1873*), merchant, philanthropist. Accumulated a vast fortune as commission merchant, note-broker and warehouseman; was director and largest individual stockholder in Baltimore and Ohio Railroad; became president of the Baltimore Merchants' Bank and director of several others. His interests extended also to life and fire insurance companies and steamship lines. Under his will (1870) he left the bulk of his fortune—some seven million dollars—for the establishment of the university and hospital which bear his name today.

HOPKINS, JULIET ANN OPIE (*b. Jefferson Co., Va., 1818; d. Washington, D.C., 1890*). Wife of Arthur F. Hopkins. Director of Confederate hospitals in Virginia and Alabama.

HOPKINS, LEMUEL (*b. Naugatuck, Conn., 1750; d. Hartford, Conn., 1801*), physician, satirist, one of "Hartford Wits." Removed to Hartford, 1784, where he practiced until his death, specializing in treatment of tuberculosis by a method far in advance of his day. Author of pro-Federalist satires in collaboration with John Trumbull, Richard Alsop, Theodore Dwight and Joel Barlow.

HOPKINS, MARK (*b. Stockbridge, Mass., 1802; d. 1887*), philosopher, theologian, educator. Graduated Williams, 1824. Except for a brief experience as medical student and doctor, he spent the major portion of his adult life at Williams College, as tutor, 1825–27, as professor of moral philosophy, 1830–87, and as president also, 1836–72. He was not a great scholar or an original thinker although he did evolve an ingenious, rather labored philosophy, over which he had reflected deeply. His fame rests on his skill as a teacher who encouraged his students to make good use of their minds.

HOPKINS, SAMUEL (*b. Waterbury, Conn., 1721; d. Newport, R.I., 1803*), Congregational clergyman, theologian. Graduated Yale, 1741. Pastor at Great Barrington, Mass., 1743–69; at First Church, Newport, R.I., 1770–1803. One of first Congregational ministers to denounce slavery. Chiefly remembered for the profound influence which his philosophy (called Hopkinsianism) had on New England thought. His teachings were presented finally in complete and logical form in his *System of Doctrines Contained in Divine Revelation, Explained and Defended* (1793). His principle that disinterested benevolence should be the motive of the individual possessed great ethical value; his conception of a universe steadily set toward the greatest happiness for all had real spiritual grandeur. An associate of Jonathan Edwards in earlier years, he influenced, in his turn, the youthful William Ellery Channing.

HOPKINS, SAMUEL (*b. Albemarle Co., Va., 1753; d. near Henderson, Ky., 1819*), Revolutionary soldier, lawyer, Kentucky legislator.

HOPKINS, STEPHEN (*b. Providence, R.I., 1707; d. Providence, 1785*), farmer, surveyor, merchant. Brother of Esek Hopkins. Served Rhode Island as assemblyman, chief-justice, governor (1755–68, excepting three years); was a staunch advocate of colonial rights. While chief-justice he not only refused to apprehend those accused in the *Gaspée* affair, 1772, but suffered no executive officer in the colony to do it. His newspaper, the *Providence Gazette*, founded to express colonial sentiment, published his own early argument for American home rule: *The Rights of the Colonies Examined* (1764; in pamphlet form, 1765). As member of Continental Congress, 1774–76, he signed the Declaration of Independence and served on the committee selected to draw up the Articles of Confederation. As a public-spirited citizen, he fostered literary and scientific enterprises and became first chancellor of Rhode Island College.

HOPKINSON, FRANCIS (*b. Philadelphia, Pa., 1737; d. Philadelphia, 1791*), statesman, judge, author, musician. Received the first diploma from the College of Philadelphia, 1757. Achieved early success as musician and composer; contributed poetry to the *American Magazine* and others, 1757–72. After ill success in business, he rose rapidly in the legal profession *post* 1773, was appointed a member of the Governor's Council, 1774, and in 1776 was elected to the Continental Congress. A signer of the Declaration of Independence, he served as chairman of the Navy Board, 1776–78, and as treasurer of loans, 1778–81. He was effective also as a witty, satiric essayist and poet. *A Pretty Story* (1774) presented American grievances in allegory; *A Letter to Lord Howe* (1777) protested brutality to noncombatants. Among his satires were also *The Battle of the Kegs* (1778), *Date Obolum Bellesario* (1778) and *Advertisement* (1781). As a graphic artist, he used his talents to design official seals and, in 1777, the American flag. A judge of admiralty, 1779–89, and a federal judge for Pennsylvania thereafter, Hopkinson continued to write and to follow up his musical interests. His most notable essays of this later period were the allegory "The New Roof" (1787) in support of the Federal Constitution, and "Modern Learning" (1784); the *Columbian Magazine* and the *American Museum* published his new works *post* 1786 and republished many of his earlier works. His book *Seven Songs* (1788) is probably the first book of music published by an American composer. A collected edition of his literary work was published as *The Miscellaneous Essays and Occasional Writings* (1792).

HOPKINSON, JOSEPH (*b. Philadelphia, Pa., 1770; d. Philadelphia, 1842*), lawyer, jurist. Son of Francis

Hopkinson. Graduated University of Pennsylvania, 1786. Congressman, Federalist, from Pennsylvania, 1815–19; federal judge, 1828–42. Author of "Hail Columbia," first sung in Philadelphia, 1798.

HOPPER, De WOLF (*b. New York, N.Y., 1858; d. Kansas City, Mo., 1935*), actor, light-opera singer. Known for his rich bass voice, his 10,000 recitations of "Casey at the Bat," and his many marriages.

[*Supp.* 1]

HOPPER, ISAAC TATEM (*b. Deptford, N.J., 1771; d. New York, N.Y., 1852*), Quaker Abolitionist, prison reformer. A foremost promoter of the "Underground" method of aiding runaway slaves; operated in Philadelphia and New York, 1800–52.

HOPPIN, AUGUSTUS (*b. Providence, R.I., 1828; d. Flushing, N.Y., 1896*). Popular as magazine and book illustrator, 1852–85. His works include drawings for Curtis's *Potiphar Papers* (1853), Shillaber's *Mrs. Partington* (1854) and Holmes's *Autocrat of the Breakfast Table* (1858).

HOPPIN, JAMES MASON (*b. Providence, R.I., 1820; d. New Haven, Conn., 1906*), Congregational clergyman. Brother of William W. Hoppin. Professor, Yale Divinity School, 1861–79; taught history of art at Yale School of Fine Arts, 1879–99.

HOPPIN, JOSEPH CLARK (*b. Providence, R.I., 1870; d. 1925*), archeologist, collector. Graduated Harvard, 1893; Ph.D., Munich, 1896. Author of *A Handbook of Attic Red-Figured Vases* (1919) and *Greek Black-Figured Vases* (1924) which are standard reference books.

HOPPIN, WILLIAM WARNER (*b. Providence, R.I., 1807; d. 1890*), lawyer. Brother of James M. Hoppin. Know-Nothing governor of Rhode Island, 1854–56.

HOPWOOD, AVERY (*b. Cleveland, O., 1882; d. Juan-les-Pins, France, 1928*), playwright. Graduated University of Michigan, 1905. Wrote, entirely or in collaboration, 18 successful Broadway plays which include *The Bat* (1920) and *Getting Gertie's Garter* (1921).

HORLICK, WILLIAM (*b. Ruardean, England, 1846; d. Racine, Wis., 1936*), food manufacturer, philanthropist. Innovator (1887) of malted milk.

[*Supp.* 2]

HORN, EDWARD TRAILL (*b. Easton, Pa., 1850; d. Philadelphia, Pa., 1915*), Lutheran clergyman. Pastor in Philadelphia and Reading, Pa., and in Charleston, S.C. Active member of committee which prepared the Lutheran Common Service (1888) and the *Common Service Book* (1917).

HORN, GEORGE HENRY (*b. Philadelphia, Pa., 1840; d. Beesley's Point, N.J., 1897*), entomologist, physician. Graduated M.D., University of Pennsylvania, 1861. Associated with J. L. Le Conte in *The Classification of the Coleoptera of North America* (1883); became world authority on the coleoptera.

HORN, TOM (*b. near Memphis, Mo., 1860; d. Cheyenne, Wyo., 1903*), government scout, interpreter, Wyoming stock detective. Helped negotiate surrender of Geronimo, 1886; controversial figure in Wyoming cattlemen-rustler warfare.

HORNADAY, WILLIAM TEMPLE (*b. near Plainfield, Ind., 1854; d. Stamford, Conn., 1937*), naturalist, conservationist. First director, New York Zoological Park, 1896–1926. [*Supp.* 2]

HORNBLOWER, JOSEPH COERTEN (*b. Belleville, N.J., 1777; d. Newark, N.J., 1864*), lawyer. Son of Josiah Hornblower. Chief-justice, New Jersey supreme court, 1832–46. Wrote important decisions on law of remainders and disqualifications of jurors; in *State vs. Sheriff of Burlington* (1836), held that Congress had no right to pass a fugitive slave law.

HORNBLOWER, JOSIAH (*b. Staffordshire, England, 1729 n.s.; d. 1809*), engineer, mine operator, New Jersey legislator. Came to America, 1753. Assembled first steam engine in America at copper mine near Belleville, N.J., 1753–55.

HORNBLOWER, WILLIAM BUTLER (*b. Paterson, N.J., 1851; d. Litchfield, Conn., 1914*), jurist. Grandson of Joseph C. Hornblower; nephew of Joseph P. Bradley. Graduated Princeton, 1871; LL.B., Columbia, 1875. Practiced successfully in New York. Appointed to U.S. Supreme Court by President Cleveland, 1893, but his nomination was blocked by David B. Hill on partisan political grounds.

HORNER, HENRY (*b. Chicago, Ill., 1878; d. Winnetka, Ill., 1940*), jurist. Judge, probate court, Cook Co., 1914–32; Democratic governor of Illinois, 1932–40. Able and effective depression governor; foe of machine politics. [*Supp.* 2]

HORNER, WILLIAM EDMONDS (*b. Warrenton, Va., 1793; d. Philadelphia, Pa., 1853*), physician, anatomist. Graduated M.D., University of Pennsylvania, 1814. Teacher and professor of anatomy, University of Pennsylvania, 1816–53; dean, medical department, 1822–52. Author of *A Treatise on Pathological Anatomy* (1829), first work on this subject to appear in America.

HORR, GEORGE EDWIN (*b. Boston, Mass., 1856; d. 1927*), Baptist clergyman. Editor, New England Baptist weekly, the *Watchman*, post 1901; president, Newton Theological Institution, 1908–25.

HORROCKS, JAMES (*b. Wakefield, England, c. 1734; d. Oporto, Portugal, 1772*), Episcopal clergyman, educator. Graduated Trinity College, Cambridge, 1755. Came to America c. 1761. President, College of William and Mary, post 1764, a controversial choice. Commissary of bishop of London;

member of the Council of Virginia. Advocated an American episcopate, 1771.

HORSFIELD, THOMAS (*b. near Bethlehem, Pa., 1773; d. 1859*), explorer, naturalist. Graduated M.D., University of Pennsylvania, 1798. Was many years in Java as army surgeon. Curator, East India Company Museum, London, 1820–59. His most important monograph was the beautifully illustrated *Plantae Javanicae Rariores* (1838–1852).

HORSFORD, EBEN NORTON (*b. Moscow, N.Y., 1818; d. Cambridge, Mass., 1893*), chemist. Graduated Rensselaer Polytechnic, 1838. Taught chemistry at Lawrence Scientific School, whose laboratory was among first to teach analytical chemistry systematically to individual students, 1847–63; engaged thereafter in chemical research for industry.

HORSMANDEN, DANIEL (*b. Purleigh, England, 1694; d. Flatbush, N.Y., 1778*), last chief-justice of New York Province. Studied law at Middle and Inner Temple, London. Settled in New York, 1731. Held numerous civil and judicial offices, 1733–46. An active member of the DeLancey faction, Horsmanden was stripped of his offices by Gov. Clinton, 1747. He managed a financial and political recovery, becoming councilman, member of the New York supreme court, 1753, and chief-justice, 1763. He achieved popularity when he ruled (1765) against any appeals from supreme court to the governor and council except on error in law. He was author of *A Journal of the Proceedings in the Detection of the Conspiracy, etc.* (1744), an account of the so-called Negro Plot of 1741.

HORTON, SAMUEL DANA (*b. Pomeroy, O., 1844; d. Washington, D.C., 1895*), lawyer, economist. Son of Valentine B. Horton. Graduated Harvard, 1864; LL.B., 1868. Lifelong crusader for theory that silver could be restored to importance through formation of international monetary union.

HORTON, VALENTINE BAXTER (*b. Windsor, Vt., 1802; d. 1888*), lawyer. Pioneer bituminous coal operator in Ohio; deviser of "Condor" towboats. Congressman, Whig and Republican, from Ohio, 1855–59, 1861–63. Organized a salt combine which was regarded as an early example of a trust.

HOSACK, ALEXANDER EDDY (*b. New York, N.Y., 1805; d. 1871*), pioneer urological surgeon. Son of David Hosack. Author of classic paper on removal of sensitive tumors from female urethra (*New York Journal of Medicine,* 1839).

HOSACK, DAVID (*b. New York, N.Y., 1769; d. 1835*), physician, teacher. Graduated Princeton, 1789; studied medicine under Samuel Bard, Benjamin Rush and others. Professor of botany and materia medica, Columbia, 1795–1811; taught practice and theory of medicine at College of Physicians and Surgeons, 1811–26. In practice in New York, he was one of the first American surgeons to use the stethoscope and to advocate vaccination; he was also instrumental in founding Bellevue Hospital. With his pupil and partner John W. Francis, he established the *American Medical Register,* 1810; the Elgin Botanical Garden was founded at his home in Hyde Park, N.Y. He was also prominent in the cultural and social life of New York City.

HOSHOUR, SAMUEL KLINEFELTER (*b. Heidelburg, York Co., Pa., 1803; d. Indianapolis, Ind., 1883*), clergyman, Lutheran and Disciples. Removed to Indiana, 1835, where he was a pioneer educator.

HOSMER, FREDERICK LUCIAN (*b. Framingham, Mass., 1840; d. 1929*), Unitarian clergyman, hymn writer.

HOSMER, HARRIET GOODHUE (*b. Watertown, Mass., 1830; d. 1908*), sculptor. Studied in Boston, at St. Louis University, and under John Gibson at Rome, Italy, 1852–59. Her best-known work, a statue of Zenobia, was shown in London, 1862; her pseudo-classic statue of Thomas H. Benton was placed in St. Louis, Mo., 1868. Famous in her day, she had a genius for friendship and a great zest for living.

HOSMER, HEZEKIAH LORD (*b. Hudson, N.Y., 1814; d. San Francisco, Calif., 1893*), jurist. Removed to Ohio, 1830, where he practiced law and journalism *post* 1835. Controversial chief-justice of Montana Territory, 1864–68. Held minor offices in California *post* 1872.

HOSMER, JAMES KENDALL (*b. Northfield, Mass., 1834; d. Minneapolis, Minn., 1927*), Unitarian clergyman, educator, popular historian.

HOSMER, TITUS (*b. Middletown, Conn., 1737; d. 1780*), lawyer, Connecticut state legislator, Revolutionary statesman, patron of literature.

HOSMER, WILLIAM HOWE CUYLER (*b. Avon, N.Y., 1814; d. Avon, 1877*), lawyer, poet, Union soldier. Versified Seneca Indian legends.

HOTCHKISS, BENJAMIN BERKELEY (*b. Watertown, Conn., 1826; d. Paris, France, 1885*), inventor, ordnance manufacturer. Supplied Union Army cannon projectiles, 1861–65; patented machine gun, 1872; perfected magazine rifle, 1875. Considered the leading artillery engineer of his time.

HOTCHKISS, HORACE LESLIE (*b. Auburn, N.Y., 1842; d. San Antonio, Texas, 1929*), financier, New York stock broker. Promoted stock quotation ticker through Gold and Stock Telegraph Co., 1867–71; organized American District Telegraph Co., 1871.

HOTZ, FERDINAND CARL (*b. Wertheim, Germany, 1843; d. Chicago, Ill., 1909*), ophthalmologist. Graduated M.D., Heidelberg, 1865. Establishing a practice in Chicago, 1869, he performed the first plastic operation for the entropion and the first recorded mastoid operation in Chicago. Internationally renowned for plastic surgery of the eye, he taught at Rush Medical College and at Presbyterian Hospital *post* 1898.

HOUDINI, HARRY (*b. Appleton, Wis., 1874; d. Detroit, Mich., 1926*), magician, author. Family name, Ehrich Weiss; celebrated for sensational feats as escape artist.

HOUGH, CHARLES MERRILL (*b. Philadelphia, Pa., 1858; d. New York, N.Y., 1927*), jurist. U.S. district and circuit court judge in New York, 1906–27. Authority on maritime law.

HOUGH, EMERSON (*b. Newton, Iowa, 1857; d. 1923*), journalist. Author of the *Singing Mouse Stories* (1895), the *Mississippi Bubble* (1902) and many other popular novels. His *The Covered Wagon* (1922) became a famous motion picture. He was a lifelong propagandist for conservation and for the national park idea.

HOUGH, FRANKLIN BENJAMIN (*b. Martinsburg, N.Y., 1822; d. 1885*), forester. Graduated Union, 1843; Western Reserve, M.D., 1848. Practiced medicine at Somerville, N.Y., was army surgeon during Civil War. Served as superintendent of 1870 U.S. Census. The Census revealing a need for publicizing rapid depletion of the country's forest reserves, Hough submitted a series of reports on this subject to the federal government even before his appointment as forestry agent in the Department of Agriculture, 1876. Traveling widely through the United States and Europe, he investigated forestry systems and embodied his findings in official reports, books and pamphlets. His activities paved the way for the successful conservation movement of later years.

HOUGH, GEORGE WASHINGTON (*b. Tribes Hill, N.Y., 1836; d. 1909*), astronomer, inventor of astronomical and meteorological instruments. Made systematic study of surface details of Jupiter as director of Dearborn Observatory, 1879–1909; he also discovered and measured difficult double stars.

HOUGH, THEODORE (*b. Front Royal, Va., 1865; d. Charlottesville, Va., 1924*), physiologist. Graduated Johns Hopkins, 1886; Ph.D., 1893. Taught at Massachusetts Institute of Technology, Simmons College, and University of Virginia; dean of medicine, University of Virginia, 1916–24; an authority on the medical school curriculum.

HOUGH, WALTER (*b. Morgantown, W. Va., 1859; d. 1935*), anthropologist. Graduated West Virginia University, 1883; Ph.D., 1894. Served for many years with the U.S. National Museum; was head curator at his death. Made extensive researches in the Southwest, and was author of a wide range of technical articles. [*Supp. 1*]

HOUGH, WARWICK (*b. Loudoun Co., Va., 1836; d. St. Louis, Mo., 1915*), lawyer, Confederate soldier. Justice, supreme court of Missouri, 1874–84; circuit court judge, 1900–06.

HOUGHTON, DOUGLASS (*b. Troy, N.Y., 1809; d. 1845*), geologist, physician. Graduated Rensselaer Polytechnic, 1829. Removed to Michigan, 1830; was surgeon-botanist on H. R. Schoolcraft's 1831 expedition to the sources of the Mississippi. Professor of geology, University of Michigan, 1838–45; mayor of Detroit, 1842–43.

HOUGHTON, GEORGE HENDRIC (*b. Deerfield, Mass., 1820; d. New York, N.Y., 1897*), Episcopal clergyman. Founded the New York City parish of the Transfiguration, 1849, known as "The Little Church around the Corner." Active in charity.

HOUGHTON, HENRY OSCAR (*b. Sutton, Vt., 1823; d. North Andover, Mass., 1895*), publisher. Established H. O. Houghton & Co., 1852, printers; merged publishing branch of Hurd and Houghton with J. R. Osgood & Co., 1878, becoming Houghton Mifflin and Company, 1880.

HOUK, LEONIDAS CAMPBELL (*b. near Boyds Creek, Tenn., 1836; d. 1891*), lawyer, Tennessee Unionist and soldier, jurist. Congressman, Republican, from Tennessee, 1879–91. Early advocate of equal rights for former Confederates.

HOURWICH, ISAAC AARONOVICH (*b. Vilna, Russia, 1860; d. New York, N.Y., 1924*), statistician, lawyer. Came to America, 1890. Author of controversial *Immigration and Labor* (1912).

HOUSE, EDWARD HOWARD (*b. Boston, Mass., 1836; d. Tokyo, Japan, 1901*), journalist, musician. Japan's first foreign publicist. Editor, *Tokyo Times*, 1877.

HOUSE, EDWARD MANDELL (*b. Houston, Texas, 1858; d. New York, N.Y., 1938*), presidential adviser, known as "Colonel House." Active, 1892–1902, in Texas politics as campaign manager and adviser to Gov. James S. Hogg and his successors. Vigorously supporting Woodrow Wilson's candidacy, 1912, House became the president's most intimate adviser and chief deputy. Primarily interested in foreign affairs, House attempted conciliatory negotiations before and during World War I and he set up an advisory group, "The Inquiry," to formulate peace strategy and policies. Thrown in the shadow by Wilson's presence at the Paris peace talks and more realistic and conciliatory than the president, House broke off relations with Wilson over the conduct of negotiations, June 1919. No other American of his time was on such close terms with so many men of international fame. [*Supp. 2*]

HOUSE, HENRY ALONZO (*b. Brooklyn, N.Y., 1840; d. Bridgeport, Conn., 1930*), inventor, manufacturer. Nephew of Royal E. House. Patented a machine to work buttonholes, 1862, and other sewing-machine inventions. Designed a steam motor-car, 1866; aided building of Maxim steam flying machine, 1896.

HOUSE, ROYAL EARL (*b. Rockland, Vt., 1814; d. Bridgeport, Conn., 1895*), inventor. Exhibited a printing telegraph, 1844 (patented, 1846) which had extensive standard use; constructed profitable range of telegraph lines; was first to employ stranded wire and also designed a glass screw-socket insulator.

HOUSE, SAMUEL REYNOLDS (*b. Waterford, N.Y., 1817; d. Waterford, 1899*), physician, Presbyterian clergyman. Medical missionary in Siam, 1846–52; superintendent of a boys' school in Bangkok, which popularized Western education, 1852–1876.

HOUSTON, DAVID FRANKLIN (*b. Monroe, N.C., 1866; d. New York, N.Y., 1940*), educator, businessman. President, Texas A.&M., 1902–05; University of Texas, 1905–08. U.S. secretary of agriculture, 1913–20, and secretary of treasury, 1920–21. Brought into politics by Edward M. House, he enlarged and reorganized the Department of Agriculture; his conservative policies at the Treasury were blamed for declining farm prices, 1920. [*Supp. 2.*]

HOUSTON, EDWIN JAMES (*b. Alexandria, Va., 1847; d. Philadelphia, Pa., 1914*), educator, electrical engineer. Pioneer in laboratory method of instruction in sciences at Central H.S., Philadelphia. Inventor, with Elihu Thomson, of an improved system of arc lighting, patented 1881. Author, with A. E. Kennelly, of probably the first elementary electrical textbooks (1895–1906).

HOUSTON, GEORGE SMITH (*b. Williamson Co., Tenn., 1811; d. 1879*), lawyer, politician. Raised in Alabama. Congressman, Democrat and Unionist, 1841–49, 1851–61. Opposed secession; refused to serve in Confederate Army. Reform Democratic governor of Alabama, 1874–78; U.S. senator, 1878–79.

HOUSTON, HENRY HOWARD (*b. Wrightsville, Pa., 1820; d. Philadelphia, Pa., 1895*), railroad executive. Innovated through freight-car service over Pennsylvania and Lake Shore systems; promoted the Union Line and the Empire Line.

HOUSTON, SAMUEL (*b. Rockbridge Co., Va., 1793; d. Huntsville, Texas, 1863*), lawyer, soldier, statesman. Grew up in vicinity of Maryville, Tenn., only a few miles from the Cherokee country; acquired a liking and sympathetic appreciation for Indian life which he retained throughout his career. Served under Andrew Jackson against the Creeks, 1813–14; was wounded at battle of Horseshoe Bend, 1814. Tall and handsome, he had a natural gift for stump-speaking. Resigning from the army, 1818, he studied law and was chosen district attorney for the Nashville district. In 1827, he was elected governor of Tennessee on an internal improvements platform after serving, 1823–27, as a Democratic congressman. His wife leaving him for reasons undivulged, he resigned

the office and became an Indian trader and adopted son of the Cherokees, 1829. He traded on the Verdigris near Fort Gibson, 1829–34. A confidante of the Indians, he represented them on several missions to Washington. After 1835, Texas commanded both his interest and his services; during that year he assumed command of the Texan army of 400 men, which he managed to expand and improve. Houston's withdrawal before the Mexican invaders under Santa Anna was unpopular, but his surprise attack at Buffalo Bayou on the San Jacinto, Apr. 21, 1836, overthrew the Mexicans and established the fame of the Texas commander. Elevated to the presidency of the republic, 1836, he secured recognition of the new nation. Houston was sent to the Texas Congress, after the expiration of this first presidential term, where he opposed the expensive, expansionist policy of Pres. Mirabeau B. Lamar. Elected president again, 1841, he restored Texas's finances. When it was clear that annexation was popular and possible, Houston accepted it, despite earlier doubts of its wisdom. As U.S. senator from the State of Texas, 1846–59, he became a strong Unionist and an increasingly lonely figure among his Southern colleagues. Defeated for re-election to the Senate, 1858, he was elected governor of Texas, 1859. He opposed secession and refused to recognize the authority of the Secession Convention, but resigned his office when the Convention's action was sustained by the voters, 1861. The hero of San Jacinto refused to take an oath of allegiance to the Confederacy since, in his opinion, Texas had resumed the status of an independent nation.

HOUSTON, WILLIAM CHURCHILL (*b. c. 1746; d. Frankford, Pa., 1788*), lawyer, teacher, Revolutionary leader in New Jersey. Taught at Princeton, 1768–83; practiced law in Trenton, N.J., thereafter.

HOUSTOUN, JOHN (*b. near Waynesboro, Ga., 1744; d. near Savannah, Ga., 1796*), Revolutionary leader, jurist. Governor of Georgia, 1778 and 1784.

HOVE, ELLING (*b. Northwood, Iowa, 1863; d. 1927*), Lutheran clergyman. Professor of theology, Luther Seminary, St. Paul, Minn., 1901–26. His *Christian Doctrine* (1930) puts him in front rank of Lutheran theologians in America.

HOVENDEN, THOMAS (*b. Dunmanway, Ireland, 1840; d. near Norristown, Pa., 1895*), historical and genre painter. Came to America, 1863. Studied in New York, and in Paris under Cabanel. Taught in Pennsylvania Academy; among his pupils was Robert Henri. "The Last Moments of John Brown" is his best-known work.

HOVEY, ALVAH (*b. Greene, N.Y., 1820; d. 1903*), Baptist clergyman. Graduated Dartmouth, 1844; Newton Theological Institution, 1848. Taught at Newton, 1849–1903; served as president, 1868–98.

HOVEY, ALVIN PETERSON (*b. near Mount Vernon, Ind., 1821; d. 1891*), jurist, Union major-general. Credited by Grant with key victory at Champion's Hill during Vicksburg campaign. Minister to Peru, 1865–70; Republican governor of Indiana, 1889–91.

HOVEY, CHARLES EDWARD (*b. Thetford, Vt., 1827; d. Washington, D.C., 1897*), educator, Union major-general, lawyer. Graduated Dartmouth, 1852. An outstanding Illinois school official, 1854–61; founder of normal school near Bloomington. Practiced law in Washington, D.C., *post* 1865.

HOVEY, CHARLES MASON (*b. Cambridge, Mass., 1810; d. 1887*), horticulturist. With his brother Phineas, established a nursery at Cambridge, Mass., 1832. Here, by a definite plan of plant breeding, he originated the Hovey strawberry (1834) and also became well known as an authority on a variety of fruits and ornamentals. He achieved national fame as editor of *The Magazine of Horticulture, Botany, and all Useful Discoveries, etc.*, 1835–68. He was author of *Fruits of America*, which he published in parts, 1847–1856.

HOVEY, RICHARD (*b. Normal, Ill., 1864; d. New York, N.Y., 1900*), poet. Son of Charles E. Hovey. Graduated Dartmouth, 1885. Author of Dartmouth verse; also of a series of poetic dramas on Arthurian themes. Translated Maeterlinck's dramas. In collaboration with Bliss Carman, published *Songs from Vagabondia* (1894), of which a second series appeared in 1896, and a final volume, *Last Songs*, in 1901.

HOWARD, ADA LYDIA (*b. Temple, N.H., 1829; d. Brooklyn, N.Y., 1907*), educator. Graduated Mount Holyoke Seminary, 1853. First president of Wellesley College, 1875–81.

HOWARD, BENJAMIN (*b. Virginia, 1760; d. St. Louis, Mo., 1814*), soldier, Kentucky legislator and congressman. Governor of District of Louisiana, 1810–12; of Territory of Missouri, 1812–13.

HOWARD, BENJAMIN CHEW (*b. near Baltimore, Md., 1791; d. Baltimore, 1872*), lawyer. Son of John E. Howard. Graduated Princeton, 1809. Congressman, Democrat, from Maryland, 1829–33, 1835–39. Reporter of U.S. Supreme Court Reports covering period 1843–62. These volumes were models of clarity, diction and thoroughness.

HOWARD, BLANCHE WILLIS (*b. Bangor, Maine, 1847; d. Munich, Germany, 1898*), popular novelist.

HOWARD, BRONSON CROCKER (*b. Detroit, Mich., 1842; d. 1908*), journalist, playwright. First president, American Dramatist's Club. Author of many successful plays, too closely keyed to the taste of his generation to have survived as literature. Among them were *Saratoga* (1870), *The Henrietta* (1887) and *Shenandoah* (1888).

HOWARD, CHARLES PERRY (*b. Harvel, Ill., 1879; d. Colorado Springs, Colo., 1938*), labor leader. President, International Typographical Union, 1923–24, 1926–38; first secretary, Committee (later Congress) for Industrial Organization, 1935. [*Supp. 2*]

HOWARD, GEORGE ELLIOTT (*b. Saratoga, N.Y., 1849; d. 1928*), teacher, scholar. Graduated University of Nebraska, 1876. Professor of history at University of Nebraska, 1879–91; at Stanford University, 1891–1901. Returning to Nebraska, 1904, he was head of political science and sociology departments and taught until 1924. Author of *History of Matrimonial Institutions* (1904).

HOWARD, JACOB MERRITT (*b. Shaftsbury, Vt., 1805; d. Detroit, Mich., 1871*), lawyer, politician. Removed to Detroit, 1832, where he practiced law. An organizer of Republican party, he served as U.S. senator from Michigan, 1862–71; an outspoken Radical, he favored extreme punishment for the South.

HOWARD, JOHN EAGER (*b. Baltimore Co., Md., 1752; d. 1827*), Revolutionary soldier. Federalist governor of Maryland, 1788–91; U.S. senator, 1796–1803; vice-presidential candidate, 1816.

HOWARD, OLIVER OTIS (*b. Leeds, Maine, 1830; d. Burlington, Vt., 1909*), Union soldier. Graduated West Point, 1854, where he served as instructor in mathematics. Promoted brigadier-general of volunteers, 1861; in the regular army, 1864. Retired as major-general, regular army, 1894. Medal of Honor winner for valor at Fair Oaks, a general officer during major Civil War campaigns, Howard's military reputation has been the subject of controversy. Military critics assign him blame for Union failures at Chancellorsville and during the first day of Gettysburg, although his personal courage has never been questioned. As commissioner of the Freedmen's Bureau, 1865–72, he was charged with inefficiency and over-enthusiasm. Instrumental in founding Howard University, he served as its president, 1869–74. He commanded the 1877 expedition against the Nez Percés and in 1878 went against the Bannocks and Paiutes.

HOWARD, SIDNEY COE (*b. Oakland, Calif., 1891; d. near Tyringham, Mass., 1939*), dramatist. Graduated University of California, 1915; student in Harvard's famous "47 Workshop." His most successful independent plays, the Pulitzer Prize-winning *They Knew What They Wanted* (1924), *The Silver Cord* (1926), and *Alien Corn* (1933), demonstrate his skill in dealing realistically with the problems and characters of middle-class society. *Yellow Jack* (1934, written with Paul de Kruif) was a strikingly original documentary; *The Late Christopher Bean* (1932, from René Fauchois) and *Dodsworth* (1934) were successful stage adaptations by Howard. He also wrote several notable screen plays, including *Arrowsmith*

(1932), *Dodsworth* (1936) and *Gone with the Wind* (1939). [*Supp.* 2]

HOWARD, TIMOTHY EDWARD (*b. near Ann Arbor, Mich., 1837; d. 1916*), jurist, Indiana legislator. Graduated Notre Dame, 1862. Justice and chief-justice, Indiana supreme court; professor of law, University of Notre Dame, 1906–1916.

HOWARD, VOLNEY ERSKINE (*b. Oxford Co., Maine, 1809; d. Santa Monica, Calif., 1889*), lawyer. Removed to Mississippi, 1832. Editor of *Howard's Reports* of decisions of Mississippi appeals court, 1834–43. Served as Texas legislator and congressman; removed to California, 1853, where he unsuccessfully opposed the Vigilantes. He served later as district attorney and judge in Los Angeles.

HOWARD, WILLIAM ALANSON (*b. Hinesburg, Vt., 1813; d. Washington, D.C., 1880*), lawyer, politician. Removed to Detroit, Mich., 1840. Congressman, Republican, from Michigan, 1855–61; was later a land commissioner for railroads. He was governor of Dakota Territory, 1878–80.

HOWARD, WILLIAM TRAVIS (*b. Cumberland Co., Va., 1821; d. Narragansett Pier, R.I., 1907*), gynecologist. Graduated Jefferson Medical College, 1844. Taught at University of Maryland for many years. First to use Tarnier's forceps successfully in the United States; devised the bivalve, or Howard, speculum.
[*Supp.* 1]

HOWE, ALBION PARRIS (*b. Standish, Maine, 1818; d. Cambridge, Mass., 1897*), soldier. Graduated West Point, 1841. Artillery officer in Scott's Mexican campaign and in Army of Potomac campaigns. Retired, 1882, as colonel of 4th Artillery.

HOWE, ANDREW JACKSON (*b. Paxton, Mass., 1825; d. 1892*), surgeon. Graduated Harvard, 1853; M.D., Worcester Medical Institute, 1855. Practiced in Cincinnati, O., *post* 1856. Author of *Art and Science of Surgery* (1876) and many other works.

HOWE, EDGAR WATSON (*b. Wabash Co., Ind., 1853; d. near Atchison, Kans., 1937*), journalist. Editor, Atchison *Daily Globe*, 1877–1911; *E. W. Howe's Monthly*, 1911–33. Author of *The Story of a Country Town* (1883). [*Supp.* 2]

HOWE, ELIAS (*b. Spencer, Mass., 1819; d. Brooklyn, N.Y., 1867*), inventor. Apprenticed in cotton-machinery and hemp-carding machine factories, 1835–37. Later, while apprentice and machinist with Ari Davis, Boston maker of watches and scientific apparatus, inspired by a random suggestion, he set to work to invent a sewing machine. By 1845 he had devised and constructed a successful machine whose eye-pointed needle worked in conjunction with a lower thread-loaded shuttle; this shuttle was thrown, accurately and at proper intervals, through loops of thread made by the upper needle—thus making the desired lock-stitch. Securing a patent, 1846, he found no interest in his machine by U.S. manufacturers. After one was sold in England to William Thomas, together with all British rights, Howe was induced to enter Thomas's employ, only to break with him after eight months. Returning to America, Howe found that unauthorized manufacturers were infringing his patent; with his partner, George W. Bliss, he waged a long but successful law suit against the pirates, his patent being declared basic, 1854.

HOWE, FREDERIC CLEMSON (*b. Meadville, Pa., 1867; d. Oak Bluffs, Mass., 1940*), lawyer, reformer. Associated with Tom L. Johnson in Cleveland, O., reforms. Removed to New York, 1910. Author, among other books, of *The City: the Hope of Democracy* (1905). [*Supp.* 2]

HOWE, FREDERICK WEBSTER (*b. Danvers, Mass., 1822; d. Providence, R.I., 1891*), mechanical engineer, inventor. Designed first commercially exploited universal milling-machine, 1850; also many machine tools of basic design used today.

HOWE, GEORGE (*b. Dedham, Mass., 1802; d. 1883*), Presbyterian clergyman. Professor of Biblical literature, Columbia, (S.C.), Theological Seminary, 1831–83; author of *History of the Presbyterian Church in South Carolina* (1870–1883).

HOWE, GEORGE AUGUSTUS (*b. England, c. 1724; d. foot of Lake George, N.Y., 1758*), third Viscount Howe, British soldier. Commissioned ensign, 1st Foot Guards, 1745; rose rapidly because of his high connections and his own natural aptitude for the military profession. Appointed colonel, 3rd Battalion of the Royal Americans (60th), he made the campaign of 1757 in upper New York; in September 1757, he became colonel of the 55th Regiment and led an abortive winter expedition against the French at Ticonderoga, February 1758. Accepting the peculiarities of war in the wilderness, he increased the efficiency of his British soldiers by cropping their hair and cutting down their hats and coats. Highly regarded by Pitt, as brigadier-general he served as Abercromby's second in command in the summer strike against Ticonderoga, 1758. When he was shot by French skirmishers on July 6, it was said that "the soul of the army seemed to expire." Massachusetts erected a tablet to his memory in Westminster Abbey.

HOWE, HENRY (*b. New Haven, Conn., 1816; d. 1893*), historian. Editor and publisher of a series of *Historical Collections* of New York (1841), New Jersey (1844), Virginia (1845), Ohio (1847), and other sections of the country which still have value for their first-hand narratives and anecdotes and original drawings of subjects treated.

HOWE, HENRY MARION (*b. Boston, Mass., 1848; d. Bedford Hills, N.Y. 1922*), metallurgist, designer of manufacturing plants, teacher. Son of Samuel G.

Howe and Julia Ward Howe. His books on the metallurgy of steel (1890) and cast-iron (1916) have been called epoch-making.

HOWE, HERBERT ALONZO (*b. Brockport, N.Y., 1858; d. 1926*), astronomer. Dean, University of Denver, *post* 1891. He discovered double stars, remeasured positions of faint nebulae and engaged in research on Kepler's problem.

HOWE, JOHN IRELAND (*b. Ridgefield, Conn., 1793; d. Birmingham, Conn., 1876*), physician. Inventor of a rotary pin-making machine (patented 1841).

HOWE, JULIA WARD (*b. New York, N.Y., 1819; d. Middletown, R.I., 1910*), poet, reformer, hostess to Boston reform leaders of the Civil War period, leader in woman's suffrage and peace movements. Granddaughter of Samuel Ward (1756–1832); daughter of Samuel Ward (1786–1839); wife of Samuel G. Howe. She produced her celebrated "Battle Hymn of the Republic" after a visit to a camp near Washington, D.C. in autumn, 1861. It was first printed in the *Atlantic Monthly*, February 1862.

HOWE, LOUIS McHENRY (*b. Indianapolis, Ind., 1871; d. Washington, D.C., 1936*), journalist. Political mentor and secretary to Franklin D. Roosevelt, 1913–30. [*Supp. 2*]

HOWE, LUCIEN (*b. Standish, Maine, 1848; d. 1928*), ophthalmologist. Nephew of Albion P. Howe. Graduated Bowdoin, 1870; studied medicine at Harvard, Bellevue and in Scotland and Germany. Founded Buffalo Eye and Ear Infirmary, 1876. Donor, Howe laboratory for ophthalmic research at Harvard; author, N.Y. Howe Law, obliging application of prophylactic to eyes of newborn children.

HOWE, MARK ANTHONY DeWOLFE (*b. Bristol, R.I., 1808; d. 1895*), Episcopal clergyman. Graduated Brown, 1828. Ordained, 1833, he served as pastor in and about Boston, and was rector of St. Luke's, Philadelphia, 1846–71; bishop of Central Pennsylvania, 1871–95.

HOWE, ROBERT (*b. Brunswick Co., N.C., 1732; d. 1786*), Revolutionary major-general, planter. Unpopular commander of Southern Department, 1776–78, he retained the confidence of Gen. Washington who employed him in various capacities until 1783.

HOWE, SAMUEL (*b. Belchertown, Mass., 1785; d. 1828*), lawyer, Massachusetts jurist.

HOWE, SAMUEL GRIDLEY (*b. Boston, Mass., 1801; d. 1876*), reformer. Husband of Julia Ward Howe. Graduated Brown, 1821; M.D., Harvard, 1824. Participated in Greek revolution of 1827–29. Pioneer in education of the blind; his program at Perkins Institute in Massachusetts became a model for others. Active in public-school promotion, in prison reform and in aiding the feeble-minded. An Abolitionist, he

supported the Free Soilers in Kansas and aided and abetted the plots of John Brown.

HOWE, TIMOTHY OTIS (*b. Livermore, Maine, 1816; d. Kenosha, Wis., 1883*), lawyer, politician. Removed to Green Bay, Wis., 1845. Judge, state supreme court, 1850–53. U.S. senator, Republican, from Wisconsin, 1861–79; U.S. postmaster-general, 1881–83. An early advocate of emancipation.

HOWE, WILLIAM (*b. Spencer, Mass., 1803; d. Springfield, Mass., 1852*), inventor. Uncle of Elias Howe. Designed and patented (1840) a bridge truss with wooden diagonals and vertical iron ties in single or double systems which was used widely up to the development of the iron bridge.

HOWE, WILLIAM F. (*b. Boston, Mass., 1828; d. New York, N.Y., 1902*), lawyer. Educated in England; admitted to the bar in New York City, 1859. *Post* 1869, in partnership with Abraham H. Hummel, became notorious, as well as famous, in criminal court practice.

HOWE, WILLIAM HENRY (*b. Ravenna, O., 1846; d. Bronxville, N.Y., 1929*), landscape and cattle painter, follower of Troyon.

HOWE, WILLIAM WIRT (*b. Canandaigua, N.Y., 1833; d. New Orleans, La., 1909*), Union soldier, lawyer. Became leading New Orleans attorney *post* 1865 and a nationally recognized authority on the civil code.

HOWELL, CLARK (*b. Barnwell Co., S.C., 1863; d. Atlanta, Ga., 1936*), newspaper editor, political leader. Associated *post* 1884 with the *Atlanta Constitution*, at that time controlled by his father, Evan Park Howell, and edited by Henry W. Grady. As managing editor, *post* 1889, and editor-in-chief, *post* 1897, Clark Howell championed Southern industrialization, diversification of agriculture, improvement of education, free silver and a just resolution of racial problems. Active in state Democratic politics, Howell served in the state assembly, 1886–91, and senate, 1900–06. He was appointed to national commissions by Presidents Harding, Hoover, and Franklin D. Roosevelt. [*Supp. 2*]

HOWELL, DAVID (*b. Morristown, N.J. 1747; d. 1824*), lawyer. Taught at Rhode Island College (Brown) *post* 1766; was president, 1791–92. Served also as state attorney-general, state judge, and federal judge (1812–1824).

HOWELL, EVAN PARK (*b. Warsaw, Ga., 1839; d. Atlanta, Ga., 1905*), Confederate soldier, lawyer, editor. Associated with the *Atlanta Constitution*, 1876–97, which he and his associates made the most important Southern newspaper.

HOWELL, JAMES BRUEN (*b. near Morristown, N.J., 1816; d. 1880*), lawyer, political journalist, called "Horace Greeley of Iowa." Raised in Ohio;

settled in Iowa c. 1842. Editor of newspapers in Des Moines and Keokuk, 1845–70. A pronounced Radical Republican.

HOWELL, JOHN ADAMS (*b. Bath, N.Y., 1840; d. Warrenton, Va., 1918*), naval officer. Graduated Annapolis, 1858. Promoted rear-admiral, 1898. Invented the Howell torpedo c. 1885, first to use a gyroscopic device; also invented torpedo-launching apparatus, a disappearing gun carriage and high-explosive shells.

HOWELL, RICHARD (*b. Delaware, 1754; d. 1802*), Revolutionary patriot, soldier and intelligence agent. Federalist governor of New Jersey, 1793–1801.

HOWELL, ROBERT BOYTÉ CRAWFORD (*b. Wayne Co., N.C., 1801; d. 1868*), leading Baptist clergyman in Virginia and Nashville, Tenn.

HOWELL, THOMAS JEFFERSON (*b. near Pisgah, Mo., 1842; d. Portland, Oreg., 1912*), Oregon pioneer, botanist. Discoverer of the weeping spruce; author of *Flora of Northwest America* (1897–1903), the text of which he set in type himself.

HOWELLS, WILLIAM DEAN (*b. Martin's Ferry, O., 1837; d. 1920*), author. Learned printer's trade in his father's country newspaper offices, read diligently, went to common school when he could. Master of no language or no literature in the strict scholar's sense, he was an outstanding example of self-education; his early years are reflected in his *A Boy's Town* (1890) and *My Literary Passions* (1895). Was reporter and editorial writer on *Ohio State Journal*, Columbus, O., 1856–61; published (with John J. Piatt) *Poems by Two Friends* (1860). A successful "campaign biography" of Lincoln, 1860, led to his appointment as consul in Venice, Italy, 1861–65. Returning to America, Howells published *Venetian Life* (1866), served briefly on staff of the *Nation,* and became sub-editor of the *Atlantic Monthly* (1866–71) and editor-in-chief, 1871–81. James Russell Lowell, his friend, felt that he had assimilated completely all that was good in the refined social life of Cambridge; certainly he found a natural affinity there, but the hard-working, firm-fibered Westerner in him survived also. His novels published while he lived in Cambridge (among others, *A Chance Acquaintance,* 1873; *The Lady of the Aroostook,* 1879) are in the main comedies of the incongruities of manners, urbane, subtle in psychology and humorous. *Post* 1881, he put off the Bostonian quiet and applied himself in fiction to a wider range of more aggressive themes. *A Modern Instance* (1882) and *A Woman's Reason* (1883) are departures, as is his masterpiece *The Rise of Silas Lapham* (1885) in which the old cultured Boston consorts with untutored wealth; thereafter, influenced by his reading of Continental novelists, Howells's work is progressively realistic. His theory of art may be studied in *Criticism and Fiction* (1891); his realism may be summarized in the dictum that everything real in human nature is valuable and that nothing unreal has value except by way of sportive interlude. His ideal novelist-realist is a moralist too, tasteful and cultivated, who uses the helps of a realistic approach to enrich the process and not to pervert the result.

Howells lived in New York *post* 1891. The range of his subjects during his middle life expanded in two directions: to the use of art itself as theme, and to examination of the economic or class problems of the time. *A Hazard of New Fortunes* (1890), *The Quality of Mercy* (1892), *The Story of a Play* (1898) illustrate these interests; *A Traveler from Altruria* (1894) and other works illustrate an unpartisan, undogmatic socialist trend in his thinking. His abilities did not age with the man. *The Landlord at Lion's Head* (1897) and *The Son of Royal Langbrith* (1904) are among the most vital of his books.

Howells also published five volumes of short tales, thirty-one remarkable closet-dramas, eleven books of travel, two more books of verse, numerous volumes of literary criticism and miscellanies, and several books of reminiscence of which *Literary Friends and Acquaintance* (1900) and *My Mark Twain* (1910) are outstanding. Honored by many colleges and universities, he was first president of the American Academy of Arts and Letters.

HOWISON, GEORGE HOLMES (*b. Montgomery Co., Md., 1834; d. 1916*), philosopher. Graduated Marietta College, 1852; Lane Seminary, 1855. While teaching political economy in St. Louis, Mo., became philosopher under influence of H. C. Brokmeyer and W. T. Harris. Taught at Massachusetts Institute of Technology, Harvard, University of Michigan; organized philosophy department, University of California, and taught there, 1884–1909.

HOWLAND, ALFRED CORNELIUS (*b. Walpole, N.H., 1838; d. Pasadena, Calif., 1909*), artist.

HOWLAND, EMILY (*b. Sherwood, N.Y., 1827; d. 1929*), promoter of education for Negroes; founder of school for Negroes in Northumberland Co., Va. Educational leader in New York State; advocated woman's suffrage, temperance, world peace.

HOWLAND, GARDINER GREENE (*b. Norwich, Conn., 1787; d. New York, N.Y., 1851*), merchant. Partner with his brother in New York firm of G. G. & S. Howland, 1816–34; promoter, New York & Harlem and Hudson River railroads.

HOWLAND, JOHN (*b. New York, N.Y. 1873; d. 1926*), pediatrician. Graduated Yale, 1894; M.D., New York University, 1897. Associated as an intern with Luther E. Holt, whose assistant he became, 1901; studied also in Vienna and under Czerny in Strassburg where he laid foundations for subsequent research concerning nutritional disorders of infancy. After teaching at Washington University, St. Louis,

Mo., he became professor of pediatrics at Johns Hopkins Medical School, 1912, and held that post until his death. He devoted himself to the study of the chemical aspects of disease and developed a clinic at Johns Hopkins which became the first pediatric clinic in this country. His noteworthy research included studies of chloroform poisoning, chemical and energy metabolism of sleeping children, infantile tetany, acidosis and rickets. He proved, with Edward A. Park, the effectiveness of cod-liver oil in rickets.

HOWLEY, RICHARD (*b. probably Liberty Co., Ga., 1740; d. Savannah, Ga., 1784*), Revolutionary patriot. Georgia's governor during occupation by British army; member of Continental Congress, 1780–82; chief justice of Georgia, 1782–83.

HOWRY, CHARLES BOWEN (*b. Oxford, Miss., 1844; d. Washington, D.C., 1928*), jurist, Confederate soldier. Justice, Court of Claims, 1897–1915; a man of wide learning whose decisions were often monographs on points of special knowledge.

HOWZE, ROBERT LEE (*b. Overton, Texas, 1864; d. Columbus, O., 1926*), soldier. Graduated West Point, 1888. Cited or decorated for service in Indian Wars, 1890–91, in Cuban and Philippine campaigns, Mexican border expedition, and Meuse-Argonne Offensive where he commanded 38th Division. Promoted major-general, 1922.

HOXIE, ROBERT FRANKLIN (*b. Edmeston, N.Y., 1868; d. 1916*), economist, teacher.

HOXIE, VINNIE REAM (*b. Madison, Wis., 1847; d. Washington, D.C., 1914*), sculptor, Washington hostess. Of moderate talent, she made statues of Lincoln, Sequoyah and Farragut, (sited in Washington, D.C.); her sitters for portraits included many famous persons of the Civil War era.

HOXIE, WILLIAM DIXIE (*b. Brooklyn, N.Y., 1866; d. at sea, 1925*), marine engineer. Associated with Babcock and Wilcox Co. *post* 1889. Improved water-tube and express-type boilers for use on war and commercial ships; built them by mass production methods.

HOYME, GJERMUND (*b. Vestre Slidre, Norway, 1847; d. Eau Claire, Wis., 1902*), Lutheran clergyman. Came to America as a child. Pastor at Eau Claire, 1876–1902. First president, United Norwegian Lutheran Church of America, 1890–1902; labored to unite all the Norwegian Lutheran Synods.

HOYT, ALBERT HARRISON (*b. Sandwich, N.H., 1826; d. 1915*), antiquarian. An efficient editor and learned contributor to the quarterly *Register* of the New England Historic Genealogical Society.

HOYT, CHARLES HALE (*b. Concord, N.H., 1860; d. Charlestown, N.H., 1900*), playwright. A writer of farces and satires, 1882–98, of which *A Trip to Chinatown* (1891) and *The Texas Steer* (1890) are typical.

HOYT, HENRY MARTYN (*b. Kingston, Pa., 1830; d. 1892*), lawyer, politician, Union soldier. As Republican governor of Pennsylvania, 1879–83, he reduced state debt, prosecuted railroads for rate discrimination, promoted state institutions for youthful offenders.

HOYT, JOHN WESLEY (*b. near Worthington, O., 1831; d. 1912*), educator. Removed to Wisconsin, 1857. Governor of Wyoming Territory, 1878–82; first president, state university of Wyoming, 1887–90; advocate of a national university.

HUBBARD, DAVID (*b. Old Liberty, Va., c. 1792; d. Pointe Coupée Parish, La., 1874*), politician, lawyer. Raised in Tennessee; removed to Alabama c. 1819, where he was prominent as a state-rights Democratic legislator and congressman, and champion of the poor whites.

HUBBARD, ELBERT (*b. Bloomington, Ill., 1856; d. at sea, 1915*), author, founder of the Roycroft Shops, editor of *The Philistine,* lecturer. An American disciple of William Morris, whose theories he turned to rather crass practical account, Hubbard is best remembered for his *Message to Garcia* (1899).

HUBBARD, FRANK McKINNEY (*b. Bellefontaine, O., 1868; d. 1930*), humorist, caricaturist. Known as "Kin" Hubbard. Created the character "Abe Martin," whose rustic humor had a vast audience in American newspapers *post* 1904.

HUBBARD, GARDINER GREENE (*b. Boston, Mass., 1822; d. Washington, D.C., 1897*), lawyer. Graduated Dartmouth, 1841. Became interested in educating the deaf because of his daughter's affliction; this led to association with Alexander G. Bell *post* 1871, to interest in Bell's invention and to development of the telephone industry. Hubbard acted as business head of the early telephone companies and instituted policy of renting rather than selling telephones. Resident in Washington, *post* 1879, he devoted his energies to educational and scientific enterprises. He was founder and first president (1888–97) of the National Geographic Society.

HUBBARD, GURDON SALTONSTALL (*b. Windsor, Vt., 1802; d. 1886*), fur trader, merchant, pioneer meat packer. An apprentice in the fur trade, 1818–23, he became superintendent of American Fur Company's posts in the Illinois country and eventual owner of all the company's interests in Illinois. Hubbard was the last "bartering fur trader" in Illinois and its first purchaser of surplus hogs and other livestock for packing in Chicago. He played a leading role not only in expanding Lake shipping but also in promoting the Canal Bill (1836) which made Chicago the pivotal point for commerce of the Mississippi Valley. His interests grew along with his city, even to banking and insurance; he was ruined, however, by the Chicago fire of 1871.

HUBBARD, HENRY GRISWOLD (*b. Middletown, Conn., 1814; d. 1891*). First (*c. 1841–42*) manufacturer in the United States to reduce India rubber to thread and weave it into webbing by machinery.

HUBBARD, HENRY GUERNSEY (*b. Detroit, Mich., 1850; d. 1899*), entomologist. Graduated Harvard, 1873; influenced in study of entomology by H. A. Hagen, C. R. Osten Sacken, E. A. Schwarz. Acquired an estate in Florida *c.* 1879, and there began successful investigations of insects injurious to cotton and oranges; published *Insects Affecting the Orange* (1885), the most careful study made at the time and the standard since. His fame rests on this work and the "Riley-Hubbard emulsion" he developed as pest preventive.

HUBBARD, JOHN (*b. probably Readfield, Maine, 1794; d. Hallowell, Maine, 1869*), physician. Graduated Dartmouth, 1816; M.D., University of Pennsylvania, 1822. As Democratic governor of Maine, 1849–53, he signed the celebrated Maine Law (1851), outlawing liquor traffic; advocated free lands in Maine, agricultural schools, reform schools, education for women.

HUBBARD, JOSEPH STILLMAN (*b. New Haven, Conn., 1823; d. New Haven, 1863*), astronomer. Associated *post* 1845 with Naval Observatory. Contributed important works to *Astronomical Journal*, including masterly calculations on orbit of 1843 comet.

HUBBARD, KIN. [See HUBBARD, FRANK MCKINNEY, 1868–1930.]

HUBBARD, LUCIUS FREDERICK (*b. Troy, N.Y., 1836; d. Minneapolis, Minn., 1913*), editor, businessman, Union soldier. Removed to Red Wing, Minn., where he founded the *Republican* newspaper, 1857. Republican governor of Minnesota, 1882–87; acted to prevent discriminatory freight rates and unfair grading of wheat.

HUBBARD, RICHARD BENNETT (*b. Walton Co., Ga., 1832; d. 1901*), lawyer, Confederate soldier. Graduated Mercer College, 1851. Settled in Tyler, Texas, *c.* 1854. Democratic governor of Texas, 1876–79; U.S. minister to Japan, 1885–89.

HUBBARD, RICHARD WILLIAM (*b. Middletown, Conn., 1816; d. 1888*), landscape painter. Studied under Samuel F. B. Morse and Daniel Huntington.

HUBBARD, THOMAS HAMLIN (*b. Hallowell, Maine, 1838; d. 1915*), Union soldier, lawyer. Son of John Hubbard. Graduated Bowdoin, 1857; admitted to New York bar, 1861. Beginning as manager of Mark Hopkins interests in Southern Pacific, 1888, he was associated thereafter with other railroads here

and abroad and was president, International Banking Corp. *post* 1904.

HUBBARD, WILLIAM (*b. England, c. 1621; d. Ipswich, Mass., 1704*), Congregational clergyman, historian. Came to America as a child. Graduated Harvard, 1642. Ordained minister at Ipswich, 1658, he served as pastor until 1703. Author of *Narrative of the Troubles with the Indians* (1677) and *A General History of New England*, used in manuscript by Cotton Mather, Thomas Prince and others for information concerning early New England, but not itself published until 1815.

HUBBELL, JOHN LORENZO (*b. Pajarito, N. Mex., 1853; d. 1930*). Navajo Reservation post trader, and a trusted friend to Navajos and Hopis for whose work he built up a world market. [*Supp. 1*]

HUBBS, REBECCA (*b. Burlington Co., N.J., 1772; d. 1852*), traveling Quaker preacher. Resided in Woodstown, N.J.; accredited a minister, 1807; visited meetings in her own state, Pennsylvania and the Middle West.

HUBER, GOTTHELF CARL (*b. Hubli, India, 1865; d. 1934*), anatomist, educator. Son of a Swiss missionary family; brought to America, 1871. Graduated University of Michigan medical school, 1887; studied also in Berlin and Prague. Taught anatomy, histology and embryology at Michigan; *post* 1927, was dean of the graduate school. An authority on the sympathetic nervous system, and probably the first American to employ Ehrlich's methylene blue technique. Using the Born method, he made first wax-plate reconstruction of a complete uriniferous tubule; demonstrated that practically all the blood to the parenchyma of the kidney passes through a second capillary plexus. [*Supp. 1*]

HUBERT, CONRAD (*b. Minsk, Russia, 1855; d. Cannes, France, 1928*), inventor. Changed name from Akiba Horowitz. Successful in Russia as distiller. Came to New York, 1890. Patented various electrical devices, and in 1902 secured basic patents for electric flashlight; organized successful American Ever-Ready Co.; left his estate to charity.

HUBNER, CHARLES WILLIAM (*b. Baltimore, Md., 1835; d. Atlanta, Ga., 1929*) poet, Confederate soldier. His critical volume *Representative Southern Poets* (1906) is his best work.

HUDDE, ANDRIES (*b. Kampen, Netherlands, 1608; d. Apoquenamingh, 1663*), surveyor. Emigrated to New Netherland, 1629; was for a time Dutch commander on the Delaware.

HUDSON, CHARLES (*b. Marlboro, Mass., 1795; d. Lexington, Mass., 1881*), clergyman. Editor, *Boston Daily Atlas*; congressman, Whig, from Massachusetts, 1841–49; held many Massachusetts offices, both elective and appointive. Active as contributor to reports of Massachusetts Historical Society.

HUDSON, DANIEL ELDRED (*b. Nahant, Mass., 1849; d. Notre Dame, Ind., 1934*), Roman Catholic clergyman. Joined congregation of the Holy Cross, 1871. Editor of *Ave Maria* magazine, 1875–1929. [*Supp.* 1]

HUDSON, EDWARD (*b. County Wexford, Ireland, 1772; d. Philadelphia, Pa., 1833*), Irish patriot, dentist. Trained in his profession in Ireland, where he was a friend and adviser of Thomas Moore. Came to America, 1803; practiced in Philadelphia, 1810–33, setting high professional standards.

HUDSON, FREDERIC (*b. Quincy, Mass., 1819; d. Concord, Mass., 1875*) journalist. Organizer of N.Y. *Herald*'s news coverage of the Civil War; author of *Journalism in the United States* (1873). Associated with the *Herald*, 1837–66, Hudson was considered an outstanding gatherer of news and the father of modern American journalism. [*Supp.* 1]

HUDSON, HENRY (*d. post June 23, 1611*), English navigator. Hudson sailed May 1, 1607 o.s. on his so-called "First Voyage," made for the English Muscovy Co. in the *Hopewell,* which took him to the coast of Greenland and to Spitzbergen. The Muscovy Co. sent him again in 1608 to seek a northeast passage to the Orient between Spitzbergen and Novaya Zemlya; becalmed for a time, he found it impossible to get through the ice-pack. His famous "Third Voyage" was financed by the Dutch East India Co., once again for the purpose of finding a northeast passage. Hudson sailed from Amsterdam early in the spring of 1609 on the *Halve Maen* (*Half Moon*) with a mixed Dutch-English crew of 18. After rounding the North Cape, he was so discouraged by icebergs and snow storms that he despaired of reaching Novaya Zemlya. He decided to disregard his instructions and, after consulting with his crew, sailed westward for America, of whose coast he had been informed by Capt. John Smith. Beset by Atlantic gales the *Half Moon* arrived off Newfoundland without a foremast; Hudson repaired her on the Maine coast and sailed to the southward of Chesapeake Bay, then back up the coast for exploration. He entered Delaware Bay and River but soon concluded that it would not lead to China; then, coasting the Jersey shore, he anchored early in September 1609 in the Lower Bay of New York. Ten days later he stopped at Manhattan, and on Sept. 13–19 sailed slowly up the river which bears his name, to anchor near the site of Albany. After a month of exploring in the pleasant valley, he sailed the *Half Moon* back across the Atlantic. Hudson was detained at Dartmouth, England, and forbidden to sail again in other than English employ; his reports and papers, however, were despatched to Amsterdam during the winter, and an account of the voyage was published. English adventurers staked Hudson's last voyage. Sailing in the *Discovery* in April 1610, Hudson sighted the coast of Greenland in June; he passed the strait which bears his name by August 2, observing next day "a Sea to the Westward" (Hudson Bay) which he explored until the *Discovery* was hauled ashore for the winter on November 1. New explorations were started or in prospect when the ice broke the next spring, but the half-starved crew seized their captain at the instigation of the deposed mate Robert Juet, and set Hudson, his son, and seven others adrift in a shallop "without food, drink, fire, clothing, or other necessaries" on June 23, 1611.

HUDSON, HENRY NORMAN (*b. Cornwall, Vt., 1814; d. 1886*), Shakespearian scholar, Episcopal clergyman, Union Army chaplain. Edited "Harvard Edition" of Shakespeare (1880–81).

HUDSON, MARY CLEMMER AMES. [See Clemmer, Mary, 1839–1884.]

HUDSON, THOMSON JAY (*b. Windham, O., 1834; d. Detroit, Mich., 1903*), journalist, lecturer. Author of the *Law of Psychic Phenomena* (1893).

HUDSON, WILLIAM SMITH (*b. near Derby, England, 1810; d. 1881*), mechanical engineer, inventor. Came to America, 1835. Superintendent of Rogers Locomotive Works, Paterson, N.J.; invented many improvements on locomotives including the radius bar and the double-end locomotive.

HUGER, BENJAMIN (*b. Charleston, S.C., 1805; d. Charleston, 1877*), soldier. Son of Francis K. Huger. Graduated West Point, 1825. Chief of ordnance under Gen. Scott in Mexican War. A Confederate major-general, he was criticized for dilatory tactics in the Peninsular campaign and for Confederate disaster at Roanoke Island, 1862.

HUGER, DANIEL ELLIOTT (*b. South Carolina, 1779; d. 1854*), jurist, South Carolina Unionist. Nephew of Isaac and John Huger. U.S. senator from South Carolina, 1843–45.

HUGER, FRANCIS KINLOCH (*b. Charleston, S.C., 1773; d. Charleston, 1855*), physician, artillery officer during War of 1812. Nephew of Isaac and John Huger. In association with J. E. Bollman, attempted to liberate Lafayette from Olmütz prison; was captured and imprisoned.

HUGER, ISAAC (*b. Limerick plantation, S.C., 1742/43; d. 1797*), Revolutionary brigadier-general. Led important commands at Guilford Court House and Hobkirk's Hill.

HUGER, JOHN (*b. Limerick plantation, S.C., 1744; d. 1804*), Revolutionary leader. Brother of Isaac Huger. Member, South Carolina Council of Safety *post* 1775; first secretary of state of South Carolina.

HUGGINS, MILLER JAMES (*b. Cincinnati, O., 1879; d. 1929*), lawyer, baseball player. Second-baseman for Cincinnati Reds and St. Louis Cardinals. As manager, New York Yankees, 1918–29, rose to national prominence as builder of championship teams.

HUGHES, CHARLES FREDERICK (*b. Bath, Maine, 1866; d. Chevy Chase, Md., 1934*), naval officer. Graduated Annapolis, 1888. Commanded *U.S.S. New York*, Adm. Rodman's flagship, 1916–18; active in North Sea. Fleet commander, 1926–27; chief of naval operations, 1927–30. [*Supp.* 1]

HUGHES, CHRISTOPHER (*b. Baltimore, Md., 1786; d. Baltimore, 1849*), wit, diplomat. Secretary, American Peace Commission, Ghent, 1814; secretary and chargé in Sweden, Norway and the Netherlands, 1816–45.

HUGHES, DAVID EDWARD (*b. London, England, 1831; d. London, 1900*), inventor. Came to America as a child; educated in Virginia and Kentucky. While teaching music, experiments with tuning forks and synchronism led him into telegraphic experimentation, in particular, telegraphic printing. His printing telegraph device, patented 1856, was eventually combined with that of Royal E. House. Hughes became European representative of the company which owned the merged patents and secured adoption of his improved device by the principal European countries, devoting his time to further experimentation in London *post* 1877. Abroad, Hughes is credited with invention of the microphone (1878), and the induction balance (1879).

HUGHES, DUDLEY MAYS (*b. Twiggs Co., Ga., 1848; d. 1927*), farmer. Congressman, Democrat, from Georgia, 1909–17; co-author of Smith-Hughes Bill (Vocational Education Act), 1917; active in other measures for agricultural improvement.

HUGHES, GEORGE WURTZ (*b. Elmira, N.Y., 1806; d. near Annapolis, Md., 1870*), topographical engineer, soldier, railroad official, congressman. Served on staff of Gen. J. E. Wool in Mexican War and as governor, Jalapa Province; surveyed route for railroad across Isthmus of Panama, 1849.

HUGHES, HECTOR JAMES (*b. Centralia, Pa., 1871; d. 1930*), civil engineer. Graduated Harvard, 1894; Lawrence Scientific School, 1899. Taught hydraulics at Harvard *post* 1902; was professor of engineering *post* 1914, and dean, Harvard Engineering School, 1920–30.

HUGHES, HENRY (*d. Port Gibson, Miss., 1862*), lawyer, Confederate soldier. Defender of slavery as "warranteeism"; author of *Treatise on Sociology* (1854) and other writings.

HUGHES, HOWARD ROBARD (*b. Lancaster, Mo., 1869; d. Houston, Texas, 1924*), inventor and manufacturer of oil industry equipment. Devised cone-type rock drill and improvements for which he obtained basic patents, 1909.

HUGHES, JAMES (*b. Hamstead, Md., 1823; d. Bladensburg, Md., 1873*), lawyer, Indiana legislator. Practiced in Indiana *post* 1842. A Democrat, he followed proslavery leadership of Jesse Bright until 1860 when he became a vehement Republican. Judge, U.S. Court of Claims, 1859–64.

HUGHES, JOHN JOSEPH (*b. Annaloghan, Ireland, 1797; d. New York, N.Y., 1864*), Roman Catholic clergyman. Apprenticed to a gardener; came to America, 1817; worked as a gardener in Maryland. Admitted to seminary at Mt. St. Mary's College, Emmitsburg, Md., 1820. Showing marked ability in study of theology under Simon W. G. Bruté, Hughes was ordained priest, 1826. As pastor of old St. Mary's Church, Philadelphia, he entered into controversies with leading Protestant clergymen over prevalent nativism, notably against Rev. John Breckinridge (1833); he was also successful in settling difficulties over trusteeism, founded the *Catholic Herald*, and was favored for elevation to the sees of Philadelphia and Cincinnati. However, on nomination of the Council at Baltimore, he was consecrated as coadjutor-bishop of New York, 1838. Although he did not succeed to formal command of the diocese until 1842, he immediately took control and won the respect and support of the vastly increasing Irish and German immigrant population.

While Hughes managed the temporal concerns of the diocese with skill, his principal value in his time was as a fighter for Catholic rights; he ended trusteeism in New York by securing state legislation permitting a vesting of church property in the bishop or his appointees, and through his efforts, political as well as polemic, the public schools were secularized after a bitter fight. His assurance that he would protect Catholic institutions by force, if necessary (1844), compelled an inactive mayor to keep New York nativist rioters under control. He committed his people to the development of a parochial school system, brought several orders of religious into the diocese to staff schools and hospitals, and founded St. John's College (now Fordham), 1841. Active in Irish famine relief, he urged the American Irish to avoid Irish politics and give their first allegiance to the United States; in opposing the movement of immigrants westward and advising them to stay on the seaboard, he made his greatest error.

When New York was raised to an archdiocese, 1850, Hughes was named archbishop, receiving the pallium on April 3, 1851. In his correspondence with Southern prelates, he denounced attempts to justify secession, and on outbreak of the Civil War served President Lincoln as an unofficial agent in Paris, Dublin and Rome, promoting the Union cause. His personal plea to the rioters during the Draft Riots, 1863, did much to end the disorder. A man of unbending will, a firm clerical disciplinarian, Hughes fought openly for what he believed was right. When he was wrong, he erred in a large way. Yet he succeeded in turning a bewildered, apologetic mass of immigrant people, groping toward active citizenship, into a militant, instructed group aware of their right to social and economic advancement.

HUGHES, PRICE (*d. near mouth of Alabama River, 1715*), frontier adventurer. Came to America *c.* 1712, concerned with a scheme of Welsh colonization in South Carolina; as a volunteer Indian agent, traveled widely among Cherokees; developed project for British province of Annarea on the Mississippi to supplant French influence. Led a trade offensive, 1713–15, seeking to detach Choctaws and others from French, and intrigued with Indians from Illinois to the Gulf of Mexico. Seized by the French, Hughes was imprisoned for a time at Mobile; released, he was slain by a band of Tohome Indians.

HUGHES, ROBERT BALL (*b. London, England, 1806; d. Boston, Mass., 1868*), sculptor. Came to America, 1828 or 1829. His statue of Alexander Hamilton for New York's Merchants' Exchange, 1835, is believed the first marble portrait carved in the United States; his bronze of Nathaniel Bowditch, 1847, was the first bronze statue to be cast here.

HUGHES, ROBERT WILLIAM (*b. Powhatan Co., Va., 1821; d. near Abingdon, Va., 1901*), editor, jurist. State's rights advocate in *Richmond Examiner* and *Washington Union;* was hostile to Jefferson Davis. Later edited Republican papers and served as federal judge, eastern district of Virginia, 1874–98.

HUIDEKOPER, FREDERIC (*b. Meadville, Pa., 1817; d. Meadville, 1892*), Unitarian clergyman. Son of Harm J. Huidekoper. Professor of New Testament and church history, Meadville Theological School, 1844–77. Early interested in higher criticism, but basically conservative.

HUIDEKOPER, HARM JAN (*b. Hoogeveen, Holland, 1776; d. 1854*), businessman, theologian. Came to America, 1796; employed by Holland Land Co. and its agent in Meadville, Pa., he became an extensive landholder in that area. Founded Meadville Theological School, 1844.

HULBERT, ARCHER BUTLER (*b. Bennington, Vt., 1873; d. Colorado Springs, Colo., 1933*), historian. Projected and edited *Historic Highways Series*, 1902–05. Edited the records of the Ohio Company, 1917. Author of the *Forty-niners* (1931) and many other books. [*Supp. 1*]

HULBERT, EDWIN JAMES (*b. Sault Ste. Marie, Mich., 1829; d. Rome, Italy, 1910*), surveyor, mining engineer. Nephew of Henry R. Schoolcraft. Discovered (1858–59) the Calumet conglomerate, copper-bearing deposits in northern Michigan which were developed as Calumet and Hecla mine.

HULL, ISAAC (*b. Huntington, now Shelton, Conn., 1773; d. Philadelphia, Pa., 1843*), naval officer. Nephew and adopted son of William Hull. Appointed lieutenant, U.S. Navy, 1798; served in naval war with France and in attacks on Tripoli (1804) and Derne (1805); promoted captain, 1806. Commanded U.S.S. *Constitution*, 1810–12, and was outstanding in action with H.M.S. *Guerrière*, Aug. 19, 1812. After long sea service and command of several shore stations, hauled down his flag as commodore, July 1841.

HULL, JOHN (*b. England, 1624; d. Boston, Mass., 1683*), merchant, goldsmith. Came to New England, 1635; prospered in his own trade and as a merchant. As mint-master, coined first Massachusetts shillings; served as treasurer of the colony and in other civic capacities.

HULL, WILLIAM (*b. Derby, Conn., 1753; d. Newton, Mass., 1825*), soldier. Participated actively and almost continuously in all the major campaigns of the Revolutionary army in the North, winning the commendations of Washington and Congress. A leading Massachusetts Jeffersonian, he was appointed governor of Michigan Territory, 1805, and was so energetic in securing land cessions as to incur the enmity of the Indians. In the War of 1812, he was persuaded against his wishes to become brigadier-general of the newly raised army charged with defense of Michigan and invasion of Canada. Because of faulty strategy, for which he was partly responsible, and his excessive concern for noncombatants he abandoned the Canadian offensive, withdrew to Detroit, and surrendered the post and army without a blow on Aug. 16, 1812.

HULLIHEN, SIMON P. (*b. Northumberland Co., Pa., 1810; d. 1857*), plastic surgeon, dentist. Practiced in Canton, O., *post* 1832; removed to Wheeling, Va. (now W. Va.), 1834. Improved operative techniques for cleft-palate, harelip, deformities of lower jaw, nose, lips; stressed scientific training for dental practitioners.

HUMBERT, JEAN JOSEPH AMABLE (*b. Rouvray, France, 1755; d. New Orleans, La., 1823*), distinguished French general exiled by Napoleon. Established residence in New Orleans, 1814; served bravely under Jackson in the Battle of New Orleans.

HUME, ROBERT ALLEN (*b. Byculla, India, 1847; d. Brookline, Mass., 1929*), Congregational clergyman. Missionary at Ahmednagar, India, 1874–1926; founded United Divinity College there.

HUME, WILLIAM (*b. Waterville, Maine, 1830; d. 1902*), pioneer in salmon industry. With his brothers and Andrew Hapgood, Hume started the salmon canning industry along Sacramento and Columbia rivers, 1864–65.

HUMES, THOMAS WILLIAM (*b. Knoxville, Tenn., 1815; d. Knoxville, 1892*), Episcopal clergyman. Reopened East Tennessee University as president, 1866; remained president after it became University of Tennessee, 1869–83.

HUMISTON, WILLIAM HENRY (*b. Marietta, O., 1869; d. 1923*), musician, critic. Assistant-conductor, New York Philharmonic Society; best known as authority on life and works of Bach and Wagner.

HUMMEL, ABRAHAM HENRY (*b. Boston, Mass., 1850; d. London, England, 1926*), New York lawyer. Devious partner of William F. Howe in their notorious criminal law practice. Convicted of conspiracy, 1905, and imprisoned for one year, Hummel left for England, 1908, where he lived thereafter.

HUMPHREY, HEMAN (*b. Canton, Conn., 1779; d. 1861*), Congregational clergyman. Graduated Yale, 1805. Pastor at Fairfield, Conn., and Pittsfield, Mass. Advocate of temperance. President, Amherst College, 1823–45.

HUMPHREYS, ALEXANDER CROMBIE (*b. Edinburgh, Scotland, 1851; d. 1927*), mechanical engineer, educator. Came to America as a child. Designer and constructor of gas plants in all parts of the world; president, Stevens Institute of Technology, 1902–27.

HUMPHREYS, ANDREW ATKINSON (*b. Philadelphia, Pa., 1810; d. 1883*), soldier, scientist. Grandson of Joshua Humphreys. Graduated West Point, 1831; served in Seminole War; appointed lieutenant, Corps of Topographical Engineers, 1838. Served in Coast Survey and for a time worked on survey of Mississippi delta; during 1854–55, supervised explorations and surveys for transcontinental railroad routes. Renewed his Mississippi River work, 1857, in association with Henry L. Abbot; their joint *Report upon the Physics and Hydraulics of the Mississippi River* (1861) has been basis for later flood control and improvements. Humphreys served with great distinction under McClellan in the Peninsular campaign, and was a divisional commander at Antietam and Fredericksburg; at Gettysburg, his division resisted Longstreet's attack on the afternoon of July 2 (1863). Thereafter as major-general he served as chief of staff, Army of the Potomac, until November 1864, when Grant chose him to command the II Corps. From 1866 until his retirement, 1879, he was chief of the Corps of Engineers, U.S. Army.

HUMPHREYS, BENJAMIN GRUBB (*b. Claiborne Co., Miss., 1808; d. 1882*), planter, Mississippi legislator, Confederate brigadier-general. First elected post-bellum governor of Mississippi, serving 1865–68, he was ejected from office by federal military authority.

HUMPHREYS, DAVID (*b. Derby, Conn., 1752; d. 1818*), soldier, diplomat, merchant, poet. Graduated Yale, 1771. Served with energy and ability in the Revolutionary War, acting as aide-de-camp to Washington whose close friend he became, and rising to rank of lieutenant-colonel. Was secretary to the American commercial treaty commission in France and England, 1784–86; served as a secret U.S. intelligence agent at London, Lisbon and Madrid, 1790; as commissioner for Algerine affairs, *post* 1793; and as minister to Spain, 1796–1801. Settling in Boston on his return from abroad, he interested himself in the breeding of merino sheep and in mills for cloth manufacture at Humphreysville, Conn. Nature endowed him with the habit of success in everything but poetry; his verses are conscientious, aspiring and leaden; they may be read, along with his *Life of Israel Putnam* and other writings, in his *Miscellaneous Works* (1804). He is associated, with his college contemporaries John Trumbull and Joel Barlow and others, with America's first literary coterie, the "Hartford Wits."

HUMPHREYS, JAMES (*b. Philadelphia, Pa., 1748; d. Philadelphia, 1810*), Loyalist printer and publisher. Published first American *Works of Laurence Sterne* (1774), also the Tory *Pennsylvania Ledger*, 1775–76 and December 1777–May 1778. Removing to New York first and later to Nova Scotia, he returned to Philadelphia, 1797, and was employed until his death in book printing.

HUMPHREYS, JOSHUA (*b. Haverford Township, Pa., 1751; d. 1838*), ship-builder, naval architect. A leader in his profession by 1776, Humphreys fitted out at his Philadelphia shipyard the Continental fleet which sailed that year under Esek Hopkins. After passage of the act of 1794 providing for a naval force of six frigates, Humphreys suggested improved radical designs which were adopted in building the *United States, Constitution, Chesapeake, Constellation, President* and *Congress;* the *United States* was built under his personal supervision. Longer, broader, lower in the water, carrying more canvas than any vessels of their class afloat and superior in fire power, these ships became famous for their speed and individual accomplishments. Humphreys served as first U.S. naval constructor, 1794–1801.

HUMPHREYS, MILTON WYLIE (*b. Greenbrier Co., W. Va., 1844; d. Charlottesville, Va., 1928*), Confederate soldier, scholar. Professor of Latin and Greek at universities of Washington and Lee, Vanderbilt, Texas; and at University of Virginia, 1887–1912. Classical philologist, linguist.

HUMPHREYS, WEST HUGHES (*b. Montgomery Co., Tenn., 1806; d. near Nashville, Tenn., 1882*), jurist. Tennessee attorney-general and state supreme court reporter, 1839–51; edited *Humphreys' Reports* (1841–1851). Federal judge, Tennessee, 1853–62, he was impeached for accepting a Confederate commission as district judge.

HUNEKER, JAMES GIBBONS (*b. Philadelphia, Pa., 1860; d. 1921*), musician, critic of art and literature. Author of *Chopin; the Man and His Music* (1900) and many other volumes of critical essays marked by wit, insight and enthusiasm for new developments in the arts.

HUNNEWELL, HORATIO HOLLIS (*b. Watertown, Mass., 1810; d. 1902*), Boston banker, railroad financier and specialist in foreign exchange, horticulturist.

HUNNEWELL, JAMES (*b. Charlestown, Mass., 1794; d. 1869*), sea captain, merchant. Sailed a 49-ft. schooner, the *Missionary Packet*, laden with merchandise and missionaries around Cape Horn to Honolulu, 1825–26. Established an Hawaiian commercial house later known as C. Brewer and Co.

HUNT, ALFRED EPHRAIM (*b. East Douglas, Mass., 1855; d. Philadelphia, Pa., 1899*), metallurgist, engineer. Son of Mary H. H. Hunt. Organized pioneer testing laboratory for metals in Pittsburgh; instrumental in developing Hall process for reduction of aluminum.

HUNT, BENJAMIN WEEKS (*b. Chappaqua, N.Y., 1847; d. 1934*), horticulturist. Removed to Eatonton, Ga., *c.* 1876. Developed livestock farm and was active in eradicating tick menace; his farm and garden became in effect an experiment station where he worked with many varieties of fruit.

[*Supp.* 1]

HUNT, CARLETON (*b. New Orleans, La., 1836; d. New Orleans, 1921*), lawyer, Confederate soldier. Professor and dean, law department, University of Louisiana; a founder of American Bar Association, 1878.

HUNT, CHARLES WALLACE (*b. Candor, N.Y., 1841; d. Staten Island, N.Y., 1911*), mechanical engineer, manufacturer. Developed and manufactured automatic coal-handling system, patented 1872; a pioneer in bucket conveying and industrial railway systems; constructed coal terminals for industry and government.

HUNT, FREEMAN (*b. Quincy, Mass., 1804; d. 1858*), publisher. Edited *Merchants' Magazine and Commercial Review, post* 1839; it was known *post* 1850 as *Hunt's Merchants' Magazine*. Author of *American Anecdotes* (1830), *Lives of American Merchants* (1858) and other books.

HUNT, GAILLARD (*b. New Orleans, La., 1862; d. 1924*), able official of State Department and Library of Congress, 1887–1924. Editor of *Writings of James Madison* (1900–10), *Journals of the Continental Congress* (1910–22); author of biographies of Madison and Calhoun; also of *The Department of State* (1914) and *Life in America One Hundred Years Ago* (1914). Son of William H. Hunt.

HUNT, GEORGE WYLIE PAUL (*b. Huntsville, Mo., 1859; d. Phoenix, Ariz., 1934*), businessman, politician, Arizona legislator. Democratic governor of Arizona, 1912–19, 1923–29, 1931–33. A friend of labor, a masterly politician and almost a legend in the Southwest. [*Supp.* 1]

HUNT, HARRIOT KEZIA (*b. Boston, Mass., 1805; d. 1875*), pioneer woman physician, reformer. Began practicing medicine *c.* 1834 without formal training; was twice denied admission to Harvard Medical School; advocated woman's suffrage, temperance, abolition.

HUNT, HENRY JACKSON (*b. Detroit, Mich., 1819; d. Washington, D.C., 1889*), soldier. Graduated West Point, 1839. Commended for gallantry, Mexican War. With W. F. Barry and W. H. French, wrote revised light artillery tactics, adopted 1860. A distinguished artillery officer in all major campaigns, Army of the Potomac; at Gettysburg, instrumental in securing the Peach Orchard for the Federals and in breaking Pickett's charge.

HUNT, ISAAC (*b. Bridgetown, Barbados, c. 1742; d. England, 1809*), author, Church of England clergyman. Father of Leigh Hunt. Graduated Philadelphia Academy, 1763. Effective lampooner of Pennsylvania authorities, 1764–65. As Loyalist writer and lawyer, threatened with tar and feathers, 1775, at which time he escaped to England and took orders.

HUNT, MARY HANNAH HANCHETT (*b. Canaan, Conn., 1830; d. 1906*), temperance reformer, educator, author of temperance textbooks. Successful in securing state laws requiring teaching of hygiene and temperance in all public schools.

HUNT, NATHAN (*b. Guilford Co., N. C., 1758; d. 1853*), Quaker preacher and mystic. Opposed slavery; founded New Garden School, 1837, now Guilford College.

HUNT, RICHARD MORRIS (*b. Brattleboro, Vt., 1827; d. 1895*), architect. Brother of William M. Hunt. His artistic interests stimulated by association with his own talented family, he started architectural study in Geneva, Switzerland, at 16. Admitted to the Beaux-Arts, 1846, during his nine-year residence in Paris he worked with Couture and the sculptor Antoine Barye. He returned to America, 1855, and took his first job as draftsman, under T. U. Walter, during construction of additions to the Capitol, Washington, D.C. He opened his first studio in New York, but did not feel ready to enter upon a career as architect in that city until 1868 after further study in Paris.

A law-suit against a cheating client brought his name to the attention of wealthy New Yorkers. Newport, R.I., houses designed for Ogden Goelet, Cornelius Vanderbilt, Oliver H. P. Belmont and Mrs. William Vanderbilt were successful efforts; the most ambitious of all his country houses was "Biltmore," at Asheville, N.C. (1890), which he designed in the French Renaissance style. The Fifth Ave., New York, town houses of Elbridge T. Gerry, John Jacob Astor and William K. Vanderbilt came from the office of Hunt; the Vanderbilt residence, at Fifth Ave. and Fifty-second St., was called his masterpiece. Many important public buildings were constructed from his designs: among them, the main portion of the New York Metropolitan Museum, the old Lenox Library Building, the Naval Observatory in Washington, the Administration Building at Chicago World's Fair (1893) and the base of the Statue of Liberty. Hunt was an outspoken advocate of better training methods for architects and for the need among them of a general artistic education as well as technical training. Establishing a studio in his own office, he actually taught some of the men who later carried on his tradition.

HUNT, ROBERT (b. c. 1568; d. Jamestown, Va., 1608), Church of England clergyman. Chaplain of the Jamestown expedition; sailed with the expedition Dec. 19, 1606. A zealous minister, he was overcome by the physical hardships of the new settlement.

HUNT, ROBERT WOOLSTON (b. Fallsington, Pa., 1838; d. Chicago, Ill., 1923), metallurgist, Union soldier. Established at Cambria Iron Co., the first analytical laboratory to form an integral part of an iron works, 1860; pioneer in manufacture of Bessemer steel in America; producer of first commercial order for steel rails, 1867; developed automatic rail mills.

HUNT, THEODORE WHITEFIELD (b. Metuchen, N.J., 1844; d. 1930), educator. Graduated Princeton, 1865. Taught English at Princeton post 1868, becoming professor emeritus in 1918. A pioneer in reintroduction of Old English studies into American college curricula.

HUNT, THOMAS STERRY (b. Norwich, Conn., 1826; d. 1892), chemist, geologist. With geological survey of Canada, 1847–72; professor of geology, Massachusetts Institute of Technology, 1872–78. Published papers on many phases of theoretical chemistry, especially on diatomic molecules of gaseous elements and on structure of compounds of the water type.

HUNT, WARD (b. Utica, N.Y., 1810; d. 1886), lawyer, New York jurist. Appointed a justice of the U.S. Supreme Court, 1872, he served actively until the end of 1878. Thereafter a paralytic, he was on inactive status until pensioned by Congress, 1882.

HUNT, WASHINGTON (b. Windham, N.Y., 1811; d. New York, N.Y., 1867), lawyer, politician. Whig governor of New York, 1851–53.

HUNT, WILLIAM GIBBES (b. Boston, Mass., 1791; d. 1833), journalist. Graduated Harvard, 1810.

Settled at Lexington, Ky., 1815. As editor, *Western Review and Miscellaneous Magazine,* Lexington, Ky., 1819–21, he was literary spokesman of the Ohio Valley region. He later was editor and publisher of the *Nashville Banner* (Tenn.) and successors.

HUNT, WILLIAM HENRY (b. Charleston, S.C., 1823; d. in Russia, 1884), jurist. Practiced law in New Orleans, La., 1844–78. Successively a Whig and a Know-Nothing, he was a Southern Unionist, 1860–65. A Republican during Reconstruction, he served as judge of U.S. Court of Claims, 1878–81, as secretary of the navy, 1881, and as minister to Russia, 1882–84.

HUNT, WILLIAM MORRIS (b. Brattleboro, Vt., 1824; d. Isles of Shoals, N.H., 1879), painter. Brother of Richard M. Hunt. The eldest child in an artistic family, he learned to draw at an early age. After living in southern France and Rome, he entered the Düsseldorf Academy of Art, 1845. In France, 1846–56, he studied with Thomas Couture, mastering that artist's famous method. Jean François Millet's friendship and association became a major factor in the career of the young American. Hunt's style of painting eventually became a composite of Couture's method plus Millet's ponderous virility, on which was superimposed his own serious and ardent nature. On returning to America, Hunt set up his studio finally in Boston. Ahead of his time in taste, Hunt was dissatisfied with his own progress although he made Boston conscious of Millet, Corot, Rousseau and the other Barbizon painters, and provided a market for them in America before they were accepted in France. His solid worth as a painter is demonstrated in his portraits of Chief-Justice Shaw, Francis Gardner and Mrs. Charles Francis Adams. His large murals at the Capitol in Albany, N.Y., were the most important and perhaps the best that had been done here up to that time.

HUNT, WILSON PRICE (b. Hopewell, N.J., 1782?; d. 1842), fur trader, merchant. Removed to St. Louis, Mo., 1804; ran a general store there until 1809. As partner, Pacific Fur Co., he went westward in 1810, establishing winter camp near present St. Joseph, Mo., in September. On April 21, 1811, he and his party started up the Missouri River as far as the Arikara villages. Thereafter they traveled to the Snake River overland. Hunt's attempt to navigate that turbulent stream forced the expedition to divide. The various groups reached Astoria, after extreme privation, early in 1812. After two years of unsatisfactory activity on the Pacific Coast and in the Sandwich Islands, during which the post at Astoria was lost to the British, he returned to St. Louis and became prosperous in general business.

HUNTER, ANDREW (b. York Co., Pa., 1751; d. Washington, D.C., 1823), Presbyterian chaplain in both army and navy. Commended by Washington for conduct at battle of Monmouth; first chaplain-schoolmaster in U.S. Navy, 1811–23; taught also in College of New Jersey (Princeton).

HUNTER, DAVID (*b. Washington, D.C., 1802; d. Washington, 1886*), Union soldier. Son of Andrew Hunter; nephew of Richard Stockton. Graduated West Point, 1822. Served at Midwestern posts and in Mexican War. During the Civil War, in which he rose to major-general, his principal success was in the taking of Fort Pulaski, Ga., 1862, and at Piedmont, Shenandoah Valley, 1864. He was president of the military commission which tried Lincoln's assassins.

HUNTER, ROBERT (*b. Hunterston, Scotland; d. Jamaica, B.W.I., 1734*), colonial governor. Distinguished himself as soldier under Marlborough. Appointed lieutenant-governor of Virginia, 1707, he was captured en route and imprisoned in France. Released, he was appointed governor of New York and New Jersey, 1709. Arriving New York City, 1710, he served until 1719. He was a successful administrator and one of the few popular royal governors in American colonial history. In furtherance of his defense of the frontiers against the French, Hunter endeavored to influence neighboring colonies to lend assistance and instituted an express between Boston and Albany, possibly the first organized postal service in the English colonies. A man of wit, he was author, with Lewis Morris, of *Androborus* (1714), a satiric farce and the first play known to have been written and printed in British America. He served as governor of Jamaica, 1727–34.

HUNTER, ROBERT MERCER TALIAFERRO (*b. Essex Co., Va., 1809; d. near Lloyds, Va., 1887*), lawyer, statesman. Nephew of James M. Garnett. Studied law with Henry St. George Tucker; admitted to the bar, 1830. After service in the Virginia legislature, and in Congress as a States-Rights Whig (he was speaker of the House for a single term), Hunter's particularism became pronounced as did his devotion to John C. Calhoun's principles. When he returned to Congress, 1845, it was as a Democrat; from 1847–61 he was U.S. senator from Virginia. He wavered, 1850–61, between his natural conservatism and a spirited defense of Southern interests when threatened. He served the Confederacy briefly as secretary of state, July 1861–February 1862, and as a senator. With A. H. Stephens and J. A. Campbell, he attended the Hampton Roads conference, 1865. After the war, he aided the local conservatives and was treasurer of Virginia, 1874–80.

HUNTER, THOMAS (*b. Ardglass, Ireland, 1831; d. New York, N.Y., 1915*), educator. Came to America, 1850. Famous teacher and principal, P.S. No. 35 in New York City; organized first evening high school, 1866; founded Normal College of New York City, 1869, now called Hunter College in his honor.

HUNTER, WALTER DAVID (*b. Lincoln, Nebr., 1875; d. El Paso, Texas, 1925*), entomologist. Graduated University of Nebraska, 1895. Served with great ability as director of U.S. Department of Agriculture investigation of the boll weevil and other cotton pests, 1901–25.

HUNTER, WHITESIDE GODFREY (*b. near Belfast, Ireland, 1841; d. Louisville, Ky., 1917*), physician, Union soldier, Kentucky legislator and Republican congressman from Kentucky. Minister to Guatemala and Honduras, 1897–1903.

HUNTER, WILLIAM (*b. Newport, R.I., 1774; d. 1849*), lawyer, Rhode Island legislator. U.S. senator, Federalist, from Rhode Island, 1812–21; chargé d'affaires and minister to Brazil, 1834–45.

HUNTER, WILLIAM C. (*b. Kentucky, 1812; d. Nice, France, 1891*), merchant. Worked in Canton, China, 1825–44, latterly as a partner in Russell and Co. Author of several excellent accounts of life in the Canton "Factories."

HUNTINGTON, COLLIS POTTER (*b. Harwinton, Conn., 1821; d. 1900*), railroad magnate, capitalist. Began life as a peddler; kept a store at Oneonta, N.Y., 1842–49. Removing to California, he set up a retail and jobbing business at Sacramento; under the name of Huntington & Hopkins, it soon became a prosperous enterprise. Exploiting, *post* 1860, the opportunity presented by Theodore D. Judah's proposal for a railroad to cross the Sierra Nevada as part of a transcontinental route, he joined Leland Stanford, Charles Crocker and Mark Hopkins in financing a survey of the route and in securing government support. This so-called Huntington group won exclusive control, 1863, when Judah died. Eastern capital was secured by the activities of Huntington in New York; Stanford acted as president of the company; Crocker took charge of construction. The railroad known as the Central Pacific was completed to a junction with the Union Pacific, 1869. Thereafter, Huntington's group became involved in even greater enterprises, for which he secured capital from both private investors and the government. Railway lines were expanded in California, thence to El Paso and New Orleans. The Central Pacific was actually overshadowed by this new enterprise known as the Southern Pacific Co. (organized as such, 1884). Huntington was active in discouraging government aid to competing lines to the Pacific Coast. An active, profane, and cynical advocate of his company's interest before Congress, he was a firm believer in the power of money to influence legislation. In 1890 he displaced Leland Stanford as president of the Southern Pacific; meanwhile he had extended his control over transportation companies in eastern America and on the high seas. He was greatly interested in developing the Chesapeake & Ohio and, as his wealth increased, became more and more outstanding in the business world. Vindictive, sometimes untruthful, he was a persistent opponent of the idea that his railroads were to any degree burdened with obligations to the public.

HUNTINGTON, DANIEL (*b. New York, N.Y., 1816; d. 1906*), painter. Brother of Jedediah V. Huntington; grandson of Jedediah Huntington. Encouraged in art by Charles L. Elliott; studied with Samuel F. B. Morse and Henry Inman. His subjects, when not portraits, were historic in nature and moral in character.

HUNTINGTON, ELISHA (*b. Topsfield, Mass., 1796; d. 1865*), physician, long-time mayor of Lowell, Mass., where he practiced *post c. 1825*.

HUNTINGTON, FREDERIC DAN (*b. Hadley, Mass., 1819; d. Hadley, 1904*), Unitarian and Episcopal clergyman. Resigned his Harvard professorship and post as college preacher, 1860, and was ordained to the Episcopal priesthood, 1861. Organized Emmanuel Church, Boston; consecrated bishop of Central New York, 1869; founded St. John's School, Manlius, N.Y.

HUNTINGTON, HENRY EDWARDS (*b. Oneonta, N.Y., 1850; d. Philadelphia, Pa., 1927*), railroad executive, financier, founder of Huntington Library and Art Gallery, philanthropist. Nephew of Collis P. Huntington, with whom he was associated in business. Developed San Francisco and Los Angeles street railways. After his uncle's death, 1900, he sold his Southern Pacific control to E. H. Harriman. Disposing of later Southern California interurban developments, 1910, he turned his energies to electric power and real estate. An enthusiastic collector of books and art, he acquired many famous collections both in America and Europe, now housed at San Marino, Calif., for public use.

HUNTINGTON, JABEZ (*b. Norwich, Conn., 1719; d. 1786*), merchant, Connecticut legislator. Revolutionary major-general and commander of Connecticut militia, 1777–79.

HUNTINGTON, JEDEDIAH (*b. Norwich, Conn., 1743; d. 1818*), merchant, Revolutionary brigadier-general. Son of Jabez Huntington. Collector, port of New London, 1789–1818.

HUNTINGTON, JEDEDIAH VINCENT (*b. New York, N.Y., 1815; d. Pau, France, 1862*), novelist, editor. Grandson of Jedediah Huntington; brother of Daniel Huntington. A convert to Catholicism, 1849. Author of *Lady Alice* (1849), *Rosemary* (1860) and other novels.

HUNTINGTON, MARGARET JANE EVANS (*b. Utica, N.Y., 1842; d. 1926*), educator. Raised in Minnesota. Professor of English and dean, Carleton College, 1874–1908. Organizer, Minnesota Federation of Women's Clubs, 1895; vice-president, General Federation, 1898. Leader in library and missionary organizations.

HUNTINGTON, SAMUEL (*b. Windham, Conn., 1731; d. Norwich, Conn., 1796*), lawyer, Connecticut legislator and jurist, signer of Declaration of Independence. Member, Continental Congress, 1775–84; president of Congress, 1779–81; governor of Connecticut, 1786–96.

HUNTINGTON, SAMUEL (*b. Coventry, Conn., 1765; d. Painesville, O., 1817*), jurist, Ohio legislator. Nephew and adopted son of Samuel Huntington (1731–1796). Graduated Yale, 1785. Removed to Ohio *c.* 1801. (Democrat) Republican governor of Ohio, 1808–10, he represented the conservative element of his party.

HUNTINGTON, WILLIAM EDWARDS (*b. Hillsboro, Ill., 1844; d. 1930*), Methodist clergyman. Nephew of Frederic D. Huntington. Graduated University of Wisconsin, 1870; B.D., Boston University, 1873, and Ph.D., 1882. Dean, Boston University, 1882–1904; president, 1904–11; dean, graduate school, 1911–17.

HUNTINGTON, WILLIAM REED (*b. Lowell, Mass., 1838; d. 1909*), Episcopal clergyman. Son of Elisha Huntington. Graduated Harvard, 1859; studied theology under Frederic D. Huntington. Rector, All Saints, Worcester, Mass., 1862–83; Grace Church, New York City, 1883–1909. A leader in revision of Prayer Book (1892). The unity of Christendom was the dominant interest of his life and thought.

HUNTON, EPPA (*b. Fauquier Co., Va., 1822; d. Richmond, Va., 1908*), lawyer, Confederate brigadier-general. U.S. congressman, Democrat, from Virginia, 1873–81; U.S. senator, 1892–95.

HUNTON, WILLIAM LEE (*b. Morrisburg, Canada, 1864; d. 1930*), Lutheran clergyman, editor, author.

HURD, JOHN CODMAN (*b. Boston, Mass., 1816; d. Boston, 1892*), publicist. Graduated Yale, 1836. His legal treatise *Law of Freedom and Bondage in the United States* (1858, 1862) is unexcelled as a study of chattel slavery in its constitutional and statutory aspects.

HURD, NATHANIEL (*b. Boston, Mass., 1730; d. 1777*), silversmith, engraver chiefly of bookplates.

HURLBERT, WILLIAM HENRY (*b. Charleston, S.C., 1827; d. Cadenabbia, Italy, 1895*), journalist. Graduated Harvard, 1847. Staff writer for *Putnam's Magazine* and *New York Times*, ante 1861; war and foreign correspondent; editor, *New York World*, 1876–83. Brilliant but erratic.

HURLBUT, JESSE LYMAN (*b. New York, N.Y., 1843; d. Bloomfield, N.J., 1930*), Methodist clergyman, editor, author. Associated *post* 1875 with the Chautauqua movement.

HURLBUT, STEPHEN AUGUSTUS (*b. Charleston, S.C., 1815; d. Lima, Peru, 1882*), lawyer, Union major-general, Illinois legislator. Accused of corruption while commanding in Louisiana, 1864. Inept minister to Colombia and Peru. First commander Grand Army of the Republic, 1866–68.

HURLEY, EDWARD NASH (*b. Galesburg, Ill., 1864; d. Chicago, Ill., 1933*), industrialist. Organized Standard Pneumatic Tool Co., 1896, manufacturing the first piston air drills; successful also in other businesses. Served on Federal Trade Commission, 1915–17, and was chairman of U.S. Shipping Board and president of Emergency Fleet Corporation, 1917–19. Hurley's achievement made possible the transportation of the U.S. Army and supplies to Europe in World War I. [*Supp. 1*]

HURST, JOHN FLETCHER (*b. near Salem, Md., 1834; d. 1903*), Methodist clergyman. Graduated Dickinson College, 1854. Professor, Drew Seminary, and president, 1873–80. Elected bishop, 1880. Founded American University, Washington, D.C., and was chancellor, 1891–1901. Author of *History of the Christian Church* (1897–1900).

HUSBANDS, HERMON (*b. probably Cecil Co., Md., 1724; d. 1795*), farmer, leader of the North Carolina Regulators, 1768–71.

HUSE, CALEB (*b. Newburyport, Mass., 1831; d. Highland Falls, N.Y., 1905*), soldier. Graduated West Point, 1851. Because of Southern associations, entered Confederate Army, 1861; acted as arms purchasing agent in Europe. Returning to the United States, 1868, he conducted a successful preparatory school for West Point *post* 1876.

HUSK, CHARLES ELLSWORTH (*b. Shabbona, Ill., 1872; d. Laredo, Texas, 1916*), physician. Graduated Chicago College of Physicians and Surgeons, 1898. Worked mainly in Mexico. As municipal health officer of Santa Barbara, State of Chihuahua, he instituted campaigns against smallpox and worked until death with the anti-typhus commission sent by Mt. Sinai Hospital, New York, to study the disease.

HUSMANN, GEORGE (*b. Meyenburg, Prussia, 1827; d. Napa, Calif., 1902*), viticulturist. Came to America as a boy. Operated vineyards in Missouri; taught pomology and forestry at the State University, Columbia, Mo. Removed to California, 1881. His reputation as viticulturist was second only to that of Nicholas Longworth.

HUSSEY, CURTIS GRUBB (*b. near York, Pa., 1802; d. 1893*), physician, merchant. Raised in Ohio; practiced in Indiana. Settled in Pittsburgh, 1840. Opened first Lake Superior copper mine *c.* 1843. Engaged in copper rolling and perfected, *post* 1859, the "direct process" for manufacturing crucible steel.

HUSSEY, OBED (*b. Maine, 1792; d. 1860*), inventor. Acting on a suggestion made to him *c.* 1830, he worked on a device to cut grain, perfecting its design in Baltimore, Md., and starting construction of

a full-sized reaper at Cincinnati, O., 1832–33. Successfully employed in the harvest of 1833, the Hussey reaper was patented in December of that year, six months before the issue of the McCormick reaper patent. Bitter competition developed between Hussey and McCormick. Improvements were made to both machines, but Hussey's refusal to purchase improvement inventions made by others led to the decline of his business and its sale in 1858.

HUSSEY, WILLIAM JOSEPH (*b. Mendon, O., 1862; d. 1926*), astronomer. Director of observatories, University of Michigan and La Plata, Argentina; discovered nearly 1400 double stars.

HUSTING, PAUL OSCAR (*b. Fond du Lac, Wis., 1866; d. 1917*), lawyer. Democratic legislator who supported La Follette's Progressive program in Wisconsin; U.S. senator, 1915–17; conservationist.

HUSTON, CHARLES (*b. Philadelphia, Pa., 1822; d. Coatesville, Pa., 1897*), physician. Partner in Lukens Iron and Steel Mills; one of first steel manufacturers to make scientific studies of the properties of his product; recommended standard tests for boiler-plate (1877).

HUTCHINS, HARRY BURNS (*b. Lisbon, N.H., 1847; d. 1930*), lawyer, educator. Graduated University of Michigan, 1871; taught history there, 1872–76, and law, 1884–87. First dean, Cornell Law School, 1887–95; dean, University of Michigan Law School, 1895–1910. Outstanding president, University of Michigan, 1910–20.

HUTCHINS, THOMAS (*b. Monmouth Co., N.J., 1730; d. Pittsburgh, Pa., 1789*), military engineer. Officer in Pennsylvania colonial forces, 1757–59; in regular British service until 1780. Produced important maps and travel journals, among them *A Topographical Description of Virginia, Pennsylvania, Maryland, and North Carolina* (London, 1778) and *An Historical . . . Description of Louisiana and West-Florida* (Phila., 1784). During the American Revolution, he declined a British majority, was imprisoned in England, and escaped to France whence he came to Charleston, S.C., 1781, and served under Gen. Greene. Appointed "Geographer to the United States," July 1781, he surveyed Pennsylvania–Virginia and New York–Massachusetts boundaries. In charge of surveys under the Ordinance of 1785, he ran the famous "east-west line" and drew the plats of the first ranges, 1786–87.

HUTCHINSON, ANNE (*b. Alford, England, 1591; d. Pelham Bay, N.Y., 1643*), pioneer, religious liberal. Born Anne Marbury; married William Hutchinson, 1612. Emigrated to Massachusetts Bay colony, 1634. Advocated preaching of a "covenant of grace," i.e., religion based on the individual's direct intuition of God's grace and love; her criticism of the Massachusetts clergy and assertions of her own doctrine caused her to be labeled an antinomian. Supported at first by John Cotton, John Wheelwright and Henry Vane, a synod of the churches denounced her views; thereafter the General Court sentenced her to banishment after a travesty of a trial. Early in the spring of 1638, she removed with her family to Aquidneck (Rhode Island); after her husband's death in 1642, she removed first to Long Island and then to the New York mainland on the shore of what is now Pelham Bay. There, in August or September 1643, she and all but one of her household were murdered by Indians.

HUTCHINSON, BENJAMIN PETERS (*b. Middleton, Mass., 1829; d. 1899*), meat packer, commodity speculator. Settled in Chicago, Ill., 1858; prospered in Civil War demand for pork products. *Post* 1876, took lead in organizing "call market" for dealing in futures; attempted numerous "corners" and was successful with September wheat, 1888; he declined in fortunes *post* 1890.

HUTCHINSON, CHARLES LAWRENCE (*b. Lynn, Mass., 1854; d. 1924*), Chicago banker, merchant. Son of Benjamin P. Hutchinson, in whose office he was trained. President of Chicago Board of Trade, 1888; of Corn Exchange Bank, 1886–98. Sponsor and president, Chicago Art Institute; chairman, Fine Arts Committee, World's Columbian Exposition; active in planning and carrying out Chicago lake front improvement, 1907–22; treasurer, University of Chicago, 1893–1924.

HUTCHINSON, JAMES (*b. Wakefield, Bucks Co., Pa., 1752; d. Philadelphia, Pa., 1793*), physician, Revolutionary patriot. Surgeon-general of Pennsylvania, 1778–84; died while fighting yellow-fever epidemic.

HUTCHINSON, THOMAS (*b. Boston, Mass., 1711; d. England, 1780*), merchant, colonial official. Great-great-grandson of Anne Hutchinson. Graduated Harvard, 1727, and by systematic reading obtained a wide and exact knowledge of history and literature. Served in Massachusetts legislature, 1737–49; was speaker, 1746–48. Represented the province in England, 1740–41, pressing claims against New Hampshire; strongly opposed a "soft" currency and the Land Bank scheme (1740–41) whose collapse ruined the elder Samuel Adams and turned Adams's son into Hutchinson's bitter enemy. In 1749, owing to Hutchinson's persistence, a stable Massachusetts currency was established. Now a leader among the conservative class, he was chosen to the Council and thereafter sat continuously until 1766. Appointed judge of probate and justice of common pleas, he represented the province at the Albany Congress, 1754, and was named lieutenant-governor, 1758; in 1760, he became chief-justice. Although he merited these multiple offices, he could be, and was, rightly charged with having appropriated too many salaried posts;

his appointment to chief-justice angered and alienated James Otis. Although he opposed the Sugar Act and the Stamp Act as harmful to empire trade, he was too much of a "prerogative man" to deny the right of Parliament to govern and tax the colonies as it saw fit; the popular leaders, therefore, concluded that he was subservient to ministerial pressure, and the feeling against him led to the sack of his house by a Boston mob (August 26, 1765) during which he barely escaped with his life. The experience left him embittered and convinced him that more strenuous measures were needed to reduce the "common sort" to obedience.

Dropped from the Council, 1766, he served as acting-governor, 1769–71, received his commission as governor, 1771, and served in that office until 1774. Following his instructions without question, he became more and more unpopular, yet he tended to ascribe his troubles and the disturbed state of the province to the machinations of James Otis and Samuel Adams rather than to an aroused public feeling. After a cessation of controversy, 1770–72, his wrangling with the legislature over trivialities revived the revolutionary spirit as much as any overt acts of its proponents; his position became untenable after publication of his letters to friends in England (published with Benjamin Franklin's agency, 1773) which revealed that he was secretly urging the use of sterner measures by the British government.

Succeeded *pro tem.* by Gen. Gage as governor, Hutchinson went to England in 1774, expecting to return. Homesick for New England, he never saw it again. Honorable and kindly, he was also unusually attached to property although scrupulously honest in his dealings with it. Among his writings, his *History of the Colony of Massachusetts Bay* (Boston, 1764 and 1828; London, 1765) is outstanding.

HUTCHINSON, WOODS (*b. Selby, England, 1862; d. Brookline, Mass., 1930*), physician. Emigrated with family to Iowa as a boy. Graduated Penn College, 1880; M.D., University of Michigan, 1884. Practiced and taught in Des Moines, Iowa, and New York City; author of books and syndicated articles on medicine for the layman, with emphasis on preventive medicine.

HUTSON, RICHARD (*b. Beaufort District, S.C., 1748; d. Charleston, S.C., 1795*), jurist, Revolutionary patriot. Justice of state chancery court, 1784–93; senior chancellor, 1791–93.

HUTTON, FREDERICK REMSEN (*b. New York, N.Y., 1853; d. New York, 1918*), engineer. Graduated Columbia, 1873; Columbia School of Mines, E.M., 1876; Ph.D., Columbia, 1881. Taught engineering at Columbia, 1877–1907; head of mechanical engineering department, 1892–1907. Author of widely used textbooks in his field.

473

HUTTON, LAURENCE (*b. New York, N.Y., 1843; d. 1904*), editor, bibliophile, dramatic critic. Author of dramatic biographies and ephemeral essays on literature.

HUTTON, LEVI WILLIAM (*b. Batavia, Iowa, 1860; d. 1928*), mine-operator, philanthropist. Early orphaned, Hutton went West *c.* 1878 and made a fortune *post* 1901 in Idaho mines and Spokane, Wash., real-estate. Founded the Hutton Settlement for underprivileged children, 1917.

HYATT, ALPHEUS (*b. Washington, D.C., 1838; d. 1902*), zoologist, palaeontologist, Union soldier. Influenced in his career by Louis Agassiz, S. H. Scudder, A. E. Verrill; graduated Harvard, B.S., 1862. In charge *post* 1865 of fossil cephalopods at Museum of Comparative Zoology, Cambridge, Mass.; a great part of his research work was done in this collection. Assisted in founding Peabody Academy of Sciences and *American Naturalist*, of which he was an editor, 1867–71; associated in several capacities with Boston Society of Natural History, 1870–1902. Taught zoology and palaeontology at Massachusetts Institute of Technology and at Boston University; helped found marine biological laboratory at Woods Hole, Mass. Hyatt's main interest in all his work was based on his desire to discover the laws which governed the development of the individual and the evolution of groups. Among his many technical monographs were "Genesis of the Arietidae" (1889), dealing with cephalopods, and "Phylogeny of an Acquired Characteristic" (1894), which discussed stages in development and their controlling laws.

HYATT, JOHN WESLEY (*b. Starkey, N.Y., 1837; d. Short Hills, N.J., 1920*), inventor. After experimentation with nitrocellulose as a foundation for plastics, he discovered celluloid-molding process and designed special machinery for its manufacture (first patent, July 12, 1870). Also patented a process for filtration and purification of water, and in 1891–92 devised a widely used type of roller-bearing. Among his other inventions were a sugar-cane mill, a multiple-stitch sewing machine and a machine for cold rolling and straightening steel shafting.

HYDE, EDWARD (*b. England, c. 1650; d. North Carolina, 1712*), colonial official. Designated deputy-governor of North Carolina, 1709; on arrival in Virginia, 1710, learned that Gov. Tynte had died and assumed governorship. His action was approved by the Lords Proprietors, 1710, and by the Privy Council, 1711. He resolved political divisions in the colony and died while preparing to subdue an outbreak of the Tuscarora Indians.

HYDE, EDWARD. [See CORNBURY, EDWARD HYDE, VISCOUNT, 1661–1723.]

HYDE, HELEN (*b. Lima, N.Y., 1868; d. Pasadena, Calif., 1919*), artist. Spent early life in California and lived many years in Japan. Worked as color etcher and was an American pioneer in making woodblock prints after Japanese manner.

HYDE, HENRY BALDWIN (*b. Catskill, N.Y., 1834; d. 1899*), founded, and was dominant personality in, the Equitable Life Assurance Society, 1859–99; served as president *post* 1874.

HYDE, JAMES NEVINS (*b. Norwich, Conn., 1840; d. Prouts Neck, Maine, 1910*), physician, U.S. Navy surgeon. Graduated Yale, 1861; M.D., University of Pennsylvania, 1869. Pioneer specialist in dermatology; practiced in Chicago, Ill., and taught his specialty at Rush Medical College *post* 1873. Author of *Practical Treatise on Diseases of the Skin* (1883).

HYDE, WILLIAM DeWITT (*b. Winchendon, Mass., 1858; d. 1917*), Congregational clergyman, educator. Graduated Harvard, 1879; Andover Theological Seminary, 1882. Professor of philosophy, Bowdoin; president of the college, 1885–1917.

HYER, ROBERT STEWART (*b. Oxford, Ga., 1860; d. 1929*), scientist. Graduated Emory College, 1881. Professor of science, Southwestern University (Georgetown, Texas), 1882–1911; president, 1898–1911. As first president, Southern Methodist University, 1911–20, Hyer planned the campus, supervised erection of buildings and procured an endowment.

HYLAN, JOHN FRANCIS (*b. near Hunter, N.Y., 1868; d. Forest Hills, N.Y., 1936*), lawyer, politician. Democratic mayor of New York City, 1917–24; supported by William Randolph Hearst. [*Supp. 2*]

HYRNE, EDMUND MASSINGBERD (*b. South Carolina, 1748; d. St. Bartholomew's Parish, S.C., 1783*), Revolutionary soldier, distinguished in campaigns under Sumter and Greene.

HYSLOP, JAMES HERVEY (*b. Xenia, O., 1854; d. Upper Montclair, N.J., 1920*), philosopher, psychologist, investigator of psychic phenomena.

IBERVILLE, PIERRE LE MOYNE, Sieur de (*b. Montreal, Canada, 1661; d. Havana, Cuba, 1706*), explorer, soldier. Brother of Jean, Sieur de Bienville. After a decade of service at sea with the French royal navy, Iberville returned to his native Canada and in 1686 joined in an expedition against the British trading posts in James Bay. He made further military expeditions to the north in 1689, 1691, 1694 and 1697; meanwhile he had gone as a volunteer on the French raid against Schenectady, N.Y., 1690, and led the successful attacks on Pemaquid and on Fort St. John's, Newfoundland, 1696. His broad vision of New France led him on to succeed where LaSalle had failed. In 1698 he founded a new colony, Louisiana, at the mouth of the Mississippi which Bienville supervised after his death from fever during a campaign against the West Indies. Iberville has been called "the first great Canadian."

IDDINGS, JOSEPH PAXON (*b. Baltimore, Md., 1857; d. Montgomery Co., Md., 1920*), geologist, petrologist. Graduated Sheffield Scientific School, Yale, 1877; served with U.S. Geological Survey in association with Arnold Hague, 1880–95. Made reputation in survey of Yellowstone National Park. A leader in American petrology, he taught that subject at University of Chicago, 1895–1908.

IDE, HENRY CLAY (*b. Barnet, Vt., 1844; d. St. Johnsbury, Vt., 1921*), lawyer, Vermont legislator, diplomat. Successful U.S. commissioner and chief-justice in Samoa; member of Philippine Commission, 1900–06, in charge of finance and justice; governor-general of Philippines, April to September, 1906. U.S. minister to Spain, 1909–13.

IGLESIAS, SANTIAGO (*b. La Coruña, Spain, 1872; d. Washington, D.C., 1939*), Puerto Rican labor leader and resident commissioner in Congress, 1933–39. Emigrated to Puerto Rico from Cuba, 1896. A Socialist, he worked closely with Samuel Gompers and the A.F. of L. [*Supp. 2*]

IK MARVEL. [See MITCHELL, DONALD GRANT, 1822–1908.]

ILLINGTON, MARGARET (*b. Bloomington, Ill., 1879; d. Miami Beach, Fla., 1934*), actress. Wife of Daniel Frohman; after divorce, 1909, married Edward J. Bowes. [*Supp. 1*]

ILPENDAM, JAN JANSEN VAN. [See VAN ILPENDAM, JAN JANSEN, *c. 1595–1647.*]

IMBER, NAPHTALI HERZ (*b. Zloczow, Polish Galicia, 1856; d. 1909*), Hebrew poet. Lived in the United States, 1892–1909, mainly on New York's East Side. Author, among many other works, of the national anthem "Hatikvah."

IMBERT, ANTOINE (*b. Calais, France; d. New York, N.Y. ?, c. 1835*), marine artist, lithographer. Came to America *c.* 1824; established first New York lithographic establishment. Printer and publisher of A. J. Davis "Views of Public Buildings, etc.," 1826–28, and of maps, caricatures and other works.

IMBODEN, JOHN DANIEL (*b. near Staunton, Va., 1823; d. Damascus, Va., 1895*), Confederate brigadier-general. Played important part in first battle of Bull Run, 1861; conducted "Imboden Raid," 1863, securing cattle and horses for Gettysburg campaign; covered Confederate retreat from Gettysburg. After the war, pioneered in encouraging development of Virginia resources by foreign and domestic capital.

IMLAY, GILBERT (*b. Monmouth Co., N.J., c. 1754; d. probably on island of Jersey, C.I., 1828*), adventurer, author. Speculated in Kentucky land, 1784–85; fled court jurisdiction to Europe. Published *A Topographical Description of the Western Territory of North America* in London, England, 1792; also a novel *The Emigrants* (1793). Plotted with Brissot's party in Paris to seize Spanish Louisiana. Was father, by Mary Wollstonecraft, of Fanny Imlay (born, 1794).

INGALLS, JOHN JAMES (*b. Middleton, Mass., 1833; d. Las Vegas, N. Mex., 1900*), lawyer, Kansas legislator. Graduated Williams, 1855. Removed to Kansas, 1858; became celebrated for denunciatory oratory. Not so much the controlling leader of the Republican party in Kansas as its figurehead, he served as U.S. senator, 1873–91.

INGALLS, MARILLA BAKER (*b. Greenfield Centre, N.Y., 1828; d. 1902*), Baptist missionary to Burma, 1851–56 and post 1858.

INGALLS, MELVILLE EZRA (*b. Harrison, Maine, 1842; d. Hot Springs, Va., 1914*), lawyer. As railroad executive, was associated with Vanderbilt interests; headed "Big Four" line, 1889–1905, and Chesapeake & Ohio, 1888–1900.

INGALS, EPHRAIM FLETCHER (*b. Lee Center, Ill., 1848; d. 1918*), physician, pioneer in bronchoscopy. Graduated Rush Medical College, 1871, and taught there for the remainder of his life; as comptroller post 1898, was largely responsible for affiliation of the college with the University of Chicago.

INGERSOLL, CHARLES JARED (*b. Philadelphia, Pa., 1782; d. 1862*), lawyer, Pennsylvania legislator and congressman, author. Son of Jared Ingersoll (1749–1822). In political life, he was a Democrat and champion of causes which were unpopular in his own environment; he strongly opposed extremists on both sides of the slavery controversy. His writings include a tragedy *Edwy and Elgiva* (produced at Philadelphia, 1801); an anti-British *View of the Rights and Wrongs, Power and Policy of the United States* (1808); *Inchiquin, the Jesuit's Letters* (1810), a declaration of our literary, social and moral independence which was widely discussed; another play, *Julian: A Tragedy* (1831); and a history of the War of 1812.

INGERSOLL, EDWARD (*b. Philadelphia, Pa., 1817; d. Germantown, Pa., 1893*), lawyer, legal writer. Son of Charles J. Ingersoll.

INGERSOLL, JARED (*b. Milford, Conn., 1722; d. New Haven, Conn., 1781*), lawyer, public official, Loyalist. London agent for Connecticut, 1758–61 and 1764–65; opposed Stamp Act, but accepted post as stamp master for Connecticut which he was compelled by force to resign; judge of vice-admiralty post 1768, he officiated at Philadelphia, 1771–75. Paroled at New Haven, 1777–81.

INGERSOLL, JARED (*b. New Haven, Conn., 1749; d. Philadelphia, Pa., 1822*), jurist. Son of Jared Ingersoll (1722–1781). Distinguished as a lawyer, he was of counsel in many of the early leading cases before the U.S. Supreme Court; he was also a member of the Continental Congress and a delegate to the Federal Convention, 1787. The attorney-general of Pennsylvania, 1790–99 and 1811–17, he held a number of other offices both in the state and in Philadelphia municipal government.

INGERSOLL, ROBERT GREEN (*b. Dresden, N.Y., 1833; d. Dobbs Ferry, N.Y., 1899*), lawyer, Union soldier, professional agnostic and lecturer. Characterized James G. Blaine as the "plumed knight" in presidential nominating speech, 1876.

INGERSOLL, ROBERT HAWLEY (*b. Delta, Mich., 1859; d. Denver, Colo., 1928*), merchant, manufacturer. Introduced and promoted sale of the famous "dollar Ingersoll" watch.

INGERSOLL, ROYAL RODNEY (*b. Niles, Mich., 1847; d. La Porte, Ind., 1931*), naval officer. Graduated Annapolis, 1868. As ordnance specialist, took prominent part in reform of naval gunnery *post* 1900; was chief of staff to Adm. R. D. Evans in world cruise, 1907–08; retired as rear-admiral, 1909.

INGERSOLL, SIMON (*b. Stanwich, Conn., 1818; d. 1894*), inventor. Patented the Ingersoll rock drill, 1871, and various improvements to it, 1873–93; sold his rights for a nominal sum.

INGHAM, CHARLES CROMWELL (*b. Dublin, Ireland, 1796; d. New York, N.Y., 1863*), portrait painter, miniaturist. Worked in New York City, 1816–63; his work was rich in coloring, weak in line.

INGHAM, SAMUEL DELUCENNA (*b. near New Hope, Pa., 1779; d. Trenton, N.J., 1860*), paper manufacturer, politician. Congressman, Democrat, from Pennsylvania, 1813–18 and 1823–29; U.S. secretary of the treasury, 1829–31. Resigned in the controversy over Mrs. John H. (Peggy O'Neale) Eaton. Later, helped develop Pennsylvania anthracite fields.

INGLE, RICHARD (*b. England, 1609; d. post 1653*), rebel, pirate. Came first to the colonies as a tobacco merchant *c.* 1631; appeared in Maryland as master of ship *Eleanor*, March 1641/42. He was arrested and his ship *Reformation* seized on warrant of high treason, January 1643/44, but Maryland juries refused to convict. Under Parliamentary letters-of-marque, Ingle raided Maryland early in 1644/45, compelling Gov. Calvert to flee into Virginia; professing to act as protector of Protestant rights, he pillaged the province before returning to England.

INGLIS, ALEXANDER JAMES (*b. Middletown, Conn., 1879; d. 1924*), educator. Graduated Wesleyan University (Conn.), 1902; Ph.D., Teachers College, Columbia, 1911. Professor of education at Rutgers and Harvard; made important surveys of the educational systems of South Dakota, Washington, Indiana and Virginia.

INGLIS, CHARLES (*b. Donegal, Ireland, 1734; d. Halifax, Canada, 1816*), Anglican clergyman, Loyalist.

Came to America, *c.* 1755, as a teacher; was ordained in London, England, 1758, and returned to serve as missionary in Dover, Del., 1759–65. As assistant to the rector of Trinity Church, New York City, 1765–77, Inglis worked with Rev. Thomas B. Chandler for establishment of an American episcopate. After the outbreak of Revolution, he answered Paine's *Common Sense* with *The True Interest of America Impartially Stated* (1776). Succeeding Rev. Samuel Auchmuty as rector of Trinity, 1777, he continued to write against the American cause over the pen-name "Papinian." He departed for England, 1783, and was consecrated first bishop of Nova Scotia, 1787.

INGRAHAM, DUNCAN NATHANIEL (*b. Charleston, S.C., 1802; d. Charleston, 1891*), naval officer. Nephew of Joseph Ingraham. Compelled release of Koszta at Smyrna, 1853; served in Confederate Navy, 1861–65.

INGRAHAM, EDWARD DUFFIELD (*b. Philadelphia, Pa., 1793; d. Philadelphia, 1854*), lawyer, legal writer and editor.

INGRAHAM, JOSEPH (*b. Boston, Mass., 1762; d. at sea, 1800*), navigator, Northwest Coast trader. Mate under Capt. John Kendrick and Capt. Robert Gray on the *Columbia*, 1787–90; as captain of the *Hope*, 1791–93, discovered the Washington Islands in the Marquesas; lost on the U.S.S. *Pickering*.

INGRAHAM, JOSEPH HOLT (*b. Portland, Maine, 1809; d. Holly Springs, Miss., 1860*), Episcopal clergyman, author. A writer of many blood-and-thunder novels, among which *Lafitte* (1836) may be singled out, Ingraham also produced an interesting regional study *The South-West, by a Yankee* (1835), and three religious romances which enjoyed great popularity. These were *The Prince of the House of David* (1855); *The Pillar of Fire* (1859); *The Throne of David* (1860).

INGRAHAM, PRENTISS (*b. Adams Co., Miss., 1843; d. 1904*), Confederate soldier, soldier of fortune. Son of Joseph H. Ingraham. After an adventurous life, became one of the most prolific writers for Beadle's dime-novel factory; principally remembered as the friend and literary celebrant of Buffalo Bill (William F. Cody).

INMAN, GEORGE (*b. Boston, Mass., 1755; d. St. George, Grenada, B.W.I., 1789*), Loyalist, British soldier.

INMAN, HENRY (*b. Utica, N.Y., 1801; d. 1846*), portrait, landscape and genre painter. Brother of John Inman. Apprentice and assistant to John Wesley Jarvis. Except for Gilbert Stuart, few American portraitists have had a more distinguished list of sitters than Inman. He died as he was at work on the first of a series of historical paintings for the Capitol, Washington, D.C. Facile and exact in drawing, Inman's work was likened to that of Sir Thomas

Lawrence but it is often commonplace and at times meretricious.

INMAN, HENRY (*b. New York, N.Y., 1837; d. Topeka, Kans., 1899*), Union soldier, journalist. Son of Henry Inman (1801–1846). Author of *The Old Santa Fe Trail* (1897) and other books of frontier adventure.

INMAN, JOHN (*b. Utica, N.Y., 1805; d. 1850*), journalist. Brother of Henry Inman (1801–1846). An editor of Morris's *New York Mirror*, of the New York *Commercial Advertiser* and other newspapers and periodicals; associate of the Knickerbocker group of writers.

INMAN, JOHN HAMILTON (*b. Dandridge, Tenn., 1844; d. New Canaan, Conn., 1896*), cotton merchant, financier. Brother of Samuel M. Inman. Promoted Southern industrial development, notably railroads, through provision of Northern capital.

INMAN, SAMUEL MARTIN (*b. Jefferson Co., Tenn., 1843; d. Atlanta, Ga., 1915*), cotton merchant, financier, philanthropist. Brother of John H. Inman. An organizer and director of the Southern Railway system. Benefactor of Georgia School of Technology and many other educational institutions.

INNES, HARRY (*b. Caroline Co., Va., 1752 o.s.; d. 1816*), lawyer. Brother of James Innes. Removed to Kentucky, 1785; served as U.S. district judge, Kentucky, 1789–1816. Threatened with impeachment for possible implication in schemes of Aaron Burr, James Wilkinson and Benjamin Sebastian, 1806.

INNES, JAMES (*b. Caroline Co., Va., 1754; d. Philadelphia, Pa., 1798*), lawyer, orator, Revolutionary soldier, Virginia legislator. Considered equal of Patrick Henry in addressing popular groups, he served as Virginia attorney-general *post* 1786 and was also a Jay Treaty commissioner.

INNESS, GEORGE (*b. Newburgh, N.Y., 1825; d. Bridge of Allan, Scotland, 1894*), landscape painter. Pupil of Régis Gignoux in New York City; set up his own studio, 1845; spent a year in Italy, 1847–48, and made numerous trips abroad thereafter. Strongly influenced by Rousseau, Corot, Daubigny. Beginning as a follower of the scenic and literal "Hudson River" school, his style underwent a steady development in direction of lyricism and individuality through Barbizon influence and his own recognition of value of suggestion in portraying nature. In his later work the poetic intensity of his temperament dominated; by common consent he came to occupy first place among American landscapists. His best work has a power and charm which defy analysis.

INNOKENTÏĬ (*b. near Irkutsk, Siberia, 1797; d. 1879*), Alaska pioneer and missionary, Russian Orthodox monk and bishop. In secular life, Ioann Evsieevich Popov-Veniamïnov, he took his name in religion when he became a monk, 1839. Previously he had served as pastor at Unalaska and Sitka, 1823–38, making valuable scientific and linguistic studies as well. Returning to Alaska, 1841, as bishop of Kamchatka and the Kurile and Aleutian islands, he was raised to archbishop, 1850; *post* 1853, his work centered more on the mainland in the Amur River region, and in 1868 he was called to Moscow to receive appointment as metropolitan.

INSHTATHEAMBA. [See BRIGHT EYES, 1854–1903.]

INSKIP, JOHN SWANEL (*b. Huntingdon, England, 1816; d. Ocean Grove, N.J., 1884*), Methodist clergyman. Came to America as a child. Served in Philadelphia, Ohio and New York conferences. A leader in the "holiness movement" and promoter of camp-meetings *post* 1864.

INSULL, SAMUEL (*b. London, England, 1859; d. Paris, France, 1938*), public utility magnate. Became Thomas A. Edison's private secretary on coming to America, 1881; advanced to presidency of Chicago Edison Co., 1892. Initiated many new techniques and concepts which became basic economic principles of the electric power industry. By 1907 Chicago's electricity was entirely Insull-operated; soon thereafter he pioneered in unified rural electrification. In the 1920's Insull turned to large-scale public financing of his utilities holdings, which included gas and traction interests. He became overextended financially and the Insull empire collapsed in 1932. His receivership became a political issue and he fled to Europe. On return to America, he was tried on mail fraud, bankruptcy and embezzlement charges, and acquitted. [*Supp. 2*]

ĬOASAF (*b. Strazhkovo, Russia, 1761; d. at sea between Unalaska and Kodiak, 1799*), Alaska pioneer and missionary, Russian Orthodox monk and bishop. In secular life, Ivan Ilyich Bolotov. First Russian missionary to Aleutians and Alaska, serving at Kodiak, 1794–c.1797; consecrated bishop of Kodiak at Irkutsk, Siberia, 1799, he died returning to his diocese.

IOOR, WILLIAM (*b. St. George's Parish, S.C.; fl. 1780–1830*), playwright. Author of *Independence* (first performed Charleston, S.C., 1805, published 1805); *The Battle of Eutaw Springs* (published 1807, first recorded production at Philadelphia, Pa., 1813). These were early examples of the American comedy of manners and of patriotic drama.

IREDELL, JAMES (*b. Lewes, England, 1751; d. Edenton, N.C., 1799*), jurist, statesman. Comptroller of customs at Edenton, 1768–74; collector of the port, 1774–76. Active in the Revolutionary cause. Served also as state attorney-general, 1779–81, and collected and revised all state acts in force (revisal issued, 1791). A strong partisan of the new federal constitution, he issued over signature "Marcus" in 1788 his *Answers to Mr. Mason's Objections to the New Con-*

stitution, and was floor leader of the Federalists in the North Carolina ratifying convention. Associate justice of the U.S. Supreme Court, 1790–99, he had no superior on that bench as a constitutional lawyer. His most notable opinions were given in *Calder vs. Bull* (that a legislative act unauthorized by, or in violation of, the Constitution was void) and in *Chisholm vs. Georgia* (an enunciation, directly or by implication, of all the leading principles of state-rights doctrine).

IRELAND, JOHN (*b. near Millerstown, Ky., 1827; d. Seguin, Texas, 1896*), lawyer, Confederate soldier, Texas legislator. Removed to Texas, 1853. Democratic governor of Texas, 1883–87.

IRELAND, JOHN (*b. Burnchurch, Ireland, 1838; d. St. Paul, Minn., 1918*), Roman Catholic clergyman. Came to America, 1849, settling with his family in St. Paul, Minn., 1853. Graduated Séminaire de Meximieux, France, and the Scholasticat à Montbel; ordained St. Paul, 1861. Chaplain, 5th Minnesota Volunteers, 1862–63. Made pastor, St. Paul Cathedral, 1867; consecrated coadjutor-bishop of St. Paul, 1875; succeeded to the see, 1884, and was named archbishop, 1888. Waged war against political corruption and the liquor interests; organized total abstinence societies; participated actively in civic affairs. Was an advocate of Western settlement by immigrants and encouraged them to move out of the slums of Eastern cities through his Catholic Colonization Bureau. Strongly supported Catholic University, Washington, D.C.; opposed retention of native languages by immigrants, notably the Germans, and any appointment of bishops on racial grounds as attempts to foster foreignism in the United States for European political reasons. With Cardinal Gibbons and others, defended right of labor to organize, yet insisted on labor's recognition of its obligations as well. Projected Faribault plan of parochial school support, 1891. Maintained a strong liberal attitude in task of reconciling the spirit of the age with religion. A Republican in politics, he was an adviser and friend of Presidents McKinley and Theodore Roosevelt.

IRELAND, JOSEPH NORTON (*b. New York, N.Y., 1817; d. Bridgeport, Conn., 1898*), businessman. Author of *Records of the New York Stage: 1750–1860* (1866–67), a valuable work of research.

IRENE, Sister (*b. London, England, 1823; d. 1896*), Sister of Charity, philanthropist. In secular life, Catherine Fitzgibbon. Came to America as a child; entered Roman Catholic community of Sisters of Charity, 1850. First directress, New York Foundling Hospital, 1869–96, and an innovator in methods of foundling care.

IRVINE, JAMES (*b. Philadelphia, Pa., 1735; d. Philadelphia, 1819*), Revolutionary soldier, Pennsylvania legislator.

IRVINE, WILLIAM (*b. near Enniskillen, Ireland, 1741; d. Philadelphia, Pa., 1804*), surgeon, Revolutionary brigadier-general. Practiced medicine *post* 1764 at Carlisle, Pa.; served in Continental Army, 1776–83. Advised purchase by Pennsylvania of the "triangle" tract which gave the state an outlet to Lake Erie; served in both Continental and federal congresses; active as an arbitrator and as commander of state troops in quelling Whiskey Rebellion, 1794.

IRVINE, WILLIAM MANN (*b. Bedford, Pa., 1865; d. 1928*), educator. Graduated Princeton, A.B., 1888; Ph.D., 1891. Headmaster, Mercersburg Academy, 1893–1928.

IRVING, JOHN BEAUFAIN (*b. Charleston, S.C., 1825; d. 1877*), portrait, genre and historical painter. Pupil of Leutze at Düsseldorf; strongly influenced by work of Meissonier; worked in New York City after the Civil War.

IRVING, JOHN DUER (*b. Madison, Wis., 1874; d. 1918*), mining geologist. Son of Roland D. Irving. Graduated Columbia, A.B., 1896; Ph.D., 1899. Worked with U.S. Geological Survey, 1899–1907, mainly in South Dakota and Colorado; taught at Wyoming, Lehigh and Yale universities; died in service during World War I.

IRVING, JOHN TREAT (*b. New York, N.Y., 1812; d. 1906*), lawyer, author. Nephew of Washington Irving.

IRVING, PETER (*b. New York, N.Y., 1772; d. 1838*), physician, journalist. Brother of Washington Irving and William Irving; an important formative influence on Washington Irving. Owner-editor, New York *Morning Chronicle,* 1802; also *The Corrector,* 1804. Lived abroad, 1809–36, and served his famous younger brother as companion and adviser during European sojourns.

IRVING, PIERRE MUNRO (*b. New York, N.Y., 1803; d. 1876*), lawyer. Son of William Irving; nephew and biographer of Washington Irving. Assisted his uncle in collecting materials for *Astoria* (1836) and managed his financial and literary affairs *post* 1846.

IRVING, ROLAND DUER (*b. New York, N.Y., 1847; d. 1888*), geologist, mining engineer. Grandson of John Duer; related on father's side to Washington Irving. Graduated Columbia, School of Mines, 1869. Taught geology at University of Wisconsin *post* 1870, made important surveys of iron- and copper-bearing rocks, Lake Superior region; was an American pioneer in genetic petrography.

IRVING, WASHINGTON (*b. New York, N.Y., 1783; d. Tarrytown, N.Y., 1859*), author. Brother of Peter and William Irving. Superficially educated in various New York City schools, but quick to observe and learn and precocious in sensibility, Irving studied drawing with Archibald Robertson as a youth and stole away from the Scottish Covenanting atmosphere of his home to attend secretly the little theater in John St. Soon wearying of the law, his chosen profession, he wrote for his brother Peter's newspapers (contributing *The Letters of Jonathan Oldstyle* to the *Morning Chronicle*), went in society, traveled. His health beginning to fail, he toured France and Italy (May 1804—March 1806), returning home with restored health and a series of notes of backgrounds, observations and anecdotes. In 1807–08, he was a moving spirit in the publication of *Salmagundi*, a whimsical periodical miscellany of essays, fables and verse which commented on life in New York and in which he was associated with his brother William and James Kirke Paulding. While engaged on the first of his books to bring him fame, the comic *A History of New York* (1809), allegedly by Diedrich Knickerbocker, Irving suffered the loss of his betrothed, Matilda Hoffman. Thereafter, for six years he was restless, engaging in hackwork, dabbling in politics and serving briefly as aide-de-camp to Gov. Daniel Tompkins of New York.

From 1815 to 1832, Irving was in Europe. At first in Liverpool, England, and until 1818 assisting in the English branch of his brothers' business, he realized the romantic dreams of his boyhood in the English landscape, English houses and the English way of life; a visit to Sir Walter Scott at Abbotsford, 1817, stimulated his desire to write, fixed in him a predilection for legendary themes and introduced him to German literature. Compelled to earn his own living by the failure of his brothers' firm, 1818, he composed the essays and tales of *The Sketch Book*, publishing them in New York in part-issues (1819, 1820) and in London collectively (1820). Success was immediate in both countries. Irving, under his pen-name "Geoffrey Crayon" found himself a distinguished and sought-after man of letters, admired for his style and for the apparent originality of such stories as "Rip Van Winkle" and "The Legend of Sleepy Hollow." *Bracebridge Hall* (1822) increased his reputation, even if its sketches pictured an English way of life that had no existence save in the author's romantic imagination. He spent the period between July 1822 and August 1823 in a pleasant but unfruitful tour of Germany; the succeeding nine months he spent in Paris. After the failure of his *Tales of a Traveller* (1824), he made a further sojourn in France while he sought vainly for a means of retrieving his literary reputation and his financial stability. Early in 1826, he went to Madrid, Spain, as attaché in the U.S. embassy and with the purpose of translating the collection of scholarly documents on the life of Christopher Columbus gathered and published by Don Martín Fernández de Navarrete. Skillfully adapting these materials, he produced his charming and popular *History of the Life and Voyages of Christopher Columbus* (1828); meanwhile, fascinated by the country and its history, he made notes for his *Chronicle of the Conquest of Granada* (1829) and *The Alhambra* (1832). Between 1829 and 1832, he served as secretary of the U.S. legation in London, England.

On his return to his native land, he was greeted as the supreme figure in American letters, went much in society, established himself in his "Sunnyside" home near Tarrytown, N.Y., but found himself restless. Profiting by current literary fashion, he produced a series *The Crayon Miscellany* (*A Tour on the Prairies; Abbotsford and Newstead Abbey; Legends of the Conquest of Spain;* all 1835). *Astoria* (1836) and *The Adventures of Captain Bonneville* (1837) were written from materials furnished by John J. Astor and from Bonneville's papers; they were frankly hackwork. His readjustment to American life was imperfect and he welcomed his appointment, 1842, as U.S. minister to Spain. After four years of competent service in the troubled Spain of the Regency, he returned to quiet "Sunnyside," there to end his career with the issue of the pleasant but tame *Oliver Goldsmith* (1849), *Mahomet and His Successors* (1849–50), *Wolfert's Roost* (1855) and a five-volume life of George Washington which he had conceived of in 1825 and whose last volume appeared in the year of his death. His life and career were notable for a marked, if limited, literary talent and the coincidence of that talent with the formative years of American letters.

IRVING, WILLIAM (*b. New York, N.Y., 1766; d. 1821*), poet, merchant, politician. Patron of his brother Washington Irving. Contributed verse to *Salmagundi*, 1807–08. Congressman, Democrat, from New York, 1814–19.

IRWIN, GEORGE LE ROY (*b. Fort Wayne, Mich., 1868; d. off Port of Spain, Trinidad, 1931*), soldier. Graduated West Point, 1889. Served in Philippines, Cuba and Mexico; identified with use and development of modern field artillery. Particularly distinguished in France, 1918, commanding the 57th F.A. Brigade; promoted major-general, 1928.

IRWIN, MAY (*b. Whitby, Canada, 1862; d. New York, N.Y., 1938*), actress and music-hall entertainer, popularizer of many ragtime songs. Real name, Ada Campbell. Appeared in one of earliest motion pictures, a close-up filmed for Edison's Vitascope, 1895.
[*Supp.* 2]

ISAACS, ABRAM SAMUEL (*b. New York, N.Y., 1851; d. Paterson, N.J., 1920*), educator, editor. Son of Samuel M. Isaacs. Graduated New York University, 1871; Ph.D., 1878, after studies at Breslau. Editor, N.Y. *Jewish Messenger*, 1878–1903. Professor of Hebrew and German, New York University.

ISAACS, SAMUEL MYER (*b. Leeuwarden, Netherlands, 1804; d. 1878*), rabbi. Educated in England;

came to New York City, 1839, where he held a pastorate until his death and was renowned as an orthodox teacher. Founder and editor, *Jewish Messenger*, 1857–78.

ISHAM, SAMUEL (*b. New York, N.Y., 1855; d. Easthampton, N.Y., 1914*), landscape, figure, and genre painter. Author of authoritative *History of American Painting* (1905).

ISHERWOOD, BENJAMIN FRANKLIN (*b. New York, N.Y., 1822; d. New York, 1915*), mechanical engineer, naval architect. Entered Engineer Corps, U.S. Navy, 1844; promoted chief engineer, 1848. Published *Engineering Precedents* (1859), the first systematic attempt to ascertain distribution of energy and losses in steam engines and boilers by actual measurements under operating conditions; author also of *Experimental Researches in Steam Engineering* (1863, 1865) which became a standard text and a new basis for further experimental research. Isherwood was first chief, Navy Bureau of Steam Engineering, 1862–70, and responsible for design and construction of propulsion machinery for the expanded Civil War Navy. He retired as chief engineer (commodore), 1884.

ISOM, MARY FRANCES (*b. Nashville, Tenn., 1865; d. 1920*), librarian. Made Portland, Oreg., Public Library an important community institution; established libraries in camps and war hospitals, 1917–18.

IVERSON, ALFRED (*b. probably Liberty Co., Ga., 1798; d. Macon, Ga., 1873*), lawyer, Georgia legislator and jurist. As U.S. senator, Democrat, 1855–61, represented a radical position on Southern rights and was an early advocate of secession.

IVES, CHAUNCEY BRADLEY (*b. Hamden, Conn., 1810; d. Rome, Italy, 1894*), sculptor.

IVES, ELI (*b. New Haven, Conn., 1778; d. 1861*), physician. Graduated Yale, 1799. Influential in establishing the medical school at Yale, he taught materia medica and botany there, 1813–29, 1852–61. He was professor of medical practice, 1829–52.

IVES, FREDERIC EUGENE (*b. near Litchfield, Conn., 1856; d. Philadelphia, Pa., 1937*), inventor. Devised (1885) the crossline-screen halftone process for photoengraving, which, with later technical improvements, came into general use. Ives also invented the modern short-tube binocular microscope, the parallax stereogram, and many important processes relating to three-color printing and color photography.

[*Supp.* 2]

IVES, HALSEY COOLEY (*b. Montour Falls, N.Y., 1847; d. London, England, 1911*), artist, teacher, art-museum administrator. Began in 1874, at St. Louis, Mo., a free drawing class which developed into the St. Louis Museum and School of Fine Arts; headed

art department at Chicago (1893) and St. Louis (1904) world's fairs.

IVES, JAMES MERRITT (*b. New York, N.Y., 1824; d. 1895*), partner of Nathaniel Currier in Currier & Ives, lithographers of popular prints; directed the firm's art staff.

IVES, JOSEPH CHRISTMAS (*b. New York, N.Y., 1828; d. New York, 1868*), explorer, soldier. Graduated West Point, 1852. Assistant to A. W. Whipple in Pacific Railroad survey, 1853–54; commanded exploration of Colorado River, 1857–58, of which his report is a classic of description. He served the Confederate Army as engineer and presidential aide-de-camp.

IVES, LEVI SILLIMAN (*b. Meriden, Conn., 1797; d. 1867*), Episcopal bishop of North Carolina, 1831–52. Influenced by Oxford Movement, he resigned his see and became a Catholic, serving thereafter as teacher at Fordham and other Catholic institutions.

IVINS, ANTHONY WOODWARD (*b. Toms River, N.J., 1852; d. Utah, 1934*), Mormon leader.

[*Supp.* 1]

IVINS, WILLIAM MILLS (*b. Freehold, N.J., 1851; d. 1915*), lawyer, political reformer. In practice in New York City *post* 1873, he fought for election law and municipal government reform, also for effective control of public utilities.

IZARD, GEORGE (*b. near London, England, 1776; d. Arkansas, 1828*), soldier. Son of Ralph Izard. Educated in military schools in England, Germany and France; entered U.S. Army *c.* 1797. Senior American general, Canadian border, 1814; resigned over interference from War Department. Territorial governor of Arkansas, 1825–28.

IZARD, RALPH (*b. near Charleston, S.C., 1741/42; d. near Charleston, 1804*), rice and indigo planter, Revolutionary patriot, diplomat. Grandson of Robert Johnson. Resided in London, 1771–76; after outbreak of Revolution, moved to Paris and was appointed U.S. commissioner to Tuscany. Insisting on his equal status with other American representatives in France, he was repeatedly checked by Franklin, but was friendly with Arthur Lee. Recalled, 1779, he persuaded Washington to put Gen. Greene in command of Southern Army. A strong Federalist, he supported the new Constitution; he was U.S. senator, from South Carolina, 1789–95.

JACK, CAPTAIN. [See CAPTAIN JACK, 1837?–1873.]

JACKMAN, WILBUR SAMUEL (*b. Mechanicstown, O., 1855; d. 1907*), educator. Graduated Harvard, 1884. Pioneer teacher of nature studies in elementary schools; advocate of reform in teaching methods; dean, College of Education, University of Chicago, 1901–04.

JACKSON, ABRAHAM REEVES (*b. Philadelphia, Pa., 1827; d. 1892*), physician, pioneer gynecologist, Union surgeon. Practiced in Chicago, Ill., *post* 1870. Founder and surgeon-in-chief, Woman's Hospital of Illinois. Immortalized by Mark Twain as witty doctor in *Innocents Abroad*.

JACKSON, ABRAHAM VALENTINE WILLIAMS (*b. New York, N.Y., 1862; d. New York, 1937*), Orientalist, philologist. Graduated Columbia, 1883; Ph.D., 1886; studied also in Germany. Taught at Columbia, 1886–1937. Specialist in Indo-Iranian languages and literature. [*Supp. 2*]

JACKSON, ANDREW (*b. Waxhaw Settlement, S.C., 1767; d. "The Hermitage," Nashville, Tenn., 1845*), soldier, seventh president of the United States. His father, an emigrant from the north of Ireland in 1765, died shortly before Andrew's birth. His brother Hugh was killed in 1779; he and his brother Robert took part in the battle of Hanging Rock, were taken by the British, and suffered smallpox in prison from which Robert died. The death of his mother, 1781, left him alone in the world. He began to study law at Salisbury, N.C., but devoted more time to horse-racing and carousing with his friend John McNairy than to Blackstone. In 1788 he and McNairy removed to Jonesboro, Tenn.; they settled in Nashville, then a stockaded log village, late in the fall. Jackson's landlady, the widow of Col. John Donelson, had a daughter Rachel who had made an unfortunate marriage. After her divorce, Jackson married her; a technical flaw in their marriage led to a long-lived scandal.

Jackson soon became prosecutor for the district (then still part of North Carolina); on erection of the territorial government, his appointment was renewed in 1791. Among other land speculations in which he engaged at the time, he bought the Hermitage tract which was thereafter his home. In 1796 he was delegate to the convention which framed Tennessee's first constitution and was elected representative in Congress; he owed his rise to the favor of Sen. William Blount. On Blount's expulsion, 1797, Jackson secured a place in the U.S. Senate, but resigned it in April 1798 and was elected a superior judge of Tennessee. He became major-general of Tennessee militia, 1802, thus provoking the enmity of John Sevier. Jackson resigned from the bench, 1804, and lived the life of a planter until the War of 1812, when, given command of the Tennessee militia expedition against the Creek Indians, he defeated them at Horseshoe Bend, 1814. Commissioned major-general, U.S. Army, he defended New Orleans against the British, defeating the invaders Jan. 8, 1815, and becoming a national figure. Tall, slender, narrow-faced, kind to friends and implacable to enemies, he was able, when he chose, to restrain his high temper or play it up for the sake of effect. Although he denied he sought office, it was clear that he was

a presidential possibility. His chances were somewhat dashed by his rash invasion of Spanish Florida, 1818, and his hanging of two British subjects for inciting Indian hostility on the border. After the excitement died down and Florida had been acquired by the United States, Jackson served as its first territorial governor for six months in 1821.

The Panic of 1819 had left hordes of debtors in the West and state banks whose paper money issues were to assist the needy had been established. Jackson opposed the bank in Tennessee, aligning himself with the conservatives even though the great popular movement which bears his name was already getting under way. Thanks to a committee including William B. Lewis, John H. Eaton and John Overton, Jackson's nomination for the presidency was moved by the Tennessee legislature in 1822. A wave of revulsion against the older school of politicians was rising all through the country; in consequence, at the 1824 election, Jackson received the highest popular vote as against Henry Clay, John Q. Adams and W. H. Crawford. However, a majority electoral vote was lacking; the election being thrown into the House of Representatives, Clay's admirers supported Adams, who became president. Sending up a cry of "corrupt bargain," Jackson's friends campaigned in a crusading spirit, issuing no program, asserting no principles, their sole aim the vindication of "Old Hickory." In 1828, supported by Martin Van Buren of New York and by the followers of Crawford in Virginia and Georgia, Jackson swept to victory; John C. Calhoun was elected vice-president. For the first time the great mass of Americans had been aroused to active interest in politics; they demanded a share of the spoils, and the new administration satisfied them by removing government employees wholesale and replacing them with its friends. Early in its course the administration ran into trouble over the refusal of the Cabinet ladies to receive the wife of John H. Eaton, secretary of war. A more basic trouble was the tariff measure of 1828 which aroused South Carolina's resistance to a protection policy and led to the nullification struggle which climaxed 1830–32 and revealed Jackson as no friend to state rights. Jackson had also, in his first message to Congress, opposed renewal of the charter of the Bank of the United States, but appeared to favor establishment of a government-owned bank with limited operations. The efforts of Clay and Nicholas Biddle to hasten recharter of the Bank turned the question into the leading issue of the 1832 campaign. The president's anti-Bank stand appeared democratic and was popular. Jackson was re-elected over Clay, defeating his opposition even in New England. Van Buren succeeded Calhoun in the vice-presidency, as he had earlier succeeded him in Jackson's confidence.

Immediately after election, the tariff of 1832 brought the nullification question to a head. South

Carolina forbade collection of the tariff duties; Jackson swore to uphold the law by force, if necessary. Clay's compromise tariff of 1833 averted the danger. In order to prevent exercise of power by the Bank (which had until 1836 to live), Jackson withdrew from it all federal deposits and distributed them to state banks. Although he thus humbled the "money power," this and his specie circular, July 1836, in part precipitated panic in 1837. The administration's diplomatic history was highly successful; Indian removals west of the Mississippi were accomplished; the British West Indies were opened to trade; and U.S. claims against France were finally paid. Jackson's dictation of the choice of Martin Van Buren to succeed him alienated many of his friends who joined with the Clay-Adams forces to form the Whig party.

Under Jackson, the nation and the office of president grew stronger. No theorist, he met issues as they arose and was unconscious of his inconsistencies. He had little understanding of the democratic movement named for him and he supported it primarily because it supported him. He was not interested in the will of the people unless it coincided with his own, yet the common man believed in him implicitly and remained his faithful follower. Veering for expediency's sake between strict and liberal constructionism, he left the Democratic party with a heritage of strict-constructionism. The partisan alignment established in his day persisted for many years; even to the present time, the Democratic party retains some of the principles which he adopted. After seeing Van Buren elected and inaugurated, he retired to "The Hermitage" where his strength gradually failed; there he died and was buried.

JACKSON, CHARLES (*b. Newburyport, Mass., 1775; d. 1855*), lawyer. Brother of James Jackson (1777–1867) and Patrick T. Jackson. Graduated Harvard, 1793; read law with Theophilus Parsons. Judge, Massachusetts supreme court, 1813–23; chairman, commission to revise Massachusetts statutes, 1833–35.

JACKSON, CHARLES SAMUEL (*b. Middlesex Co., Va., 1860; d. 1924*). Emigrating to Oregon, 1880, he became proprietor of a newspaper at Pendleton; settling in Portland, 1902, he built up the successful *Oregon Daily Journal* as the recognized Democratic organ in the area.

JACKSON, CHARLES THOMAS (*b. Plymouth, Mass., 1805; d. 1880*), chemist, geologist. Graduated Harvard Medical School, 1829, after study with James Jackson and Walter Channing. Studied also in Paris at the Sorbonne and the École des Mines. Established an experimental laboratory at Boston, 1836. Conducted important geological surveys of Maine, Massachusetts, Rhode Island and New Hampshire. Claimed prior discovery of electric telegraph in controversy with S. F. B. Morse. Suggested possible use of ether to W. T. G. Morton, 1846, later claiming to be true discoverer of surgical anaesthesia.

JACKSON, CLAIBORNE FOX (*b. Fleming Co., Ky., 1806; d. near Little Rock, Ark., 1862*), businessman, Missouri legislator. Pro-slavery opponent of Thomas H. Benton *post* 1846; Democratic governor of Missouri, 1860–61.

JACKSON, DAVID (*b. Oxford, Pa., 1747?; d. Philadelphia, Pa., 1801*), physician, apothecary, Revolutionary patriot. First graduate in medicine, College of Philadelphia (later University of Pennsylvania), 1768; associated, 1793, with David Rittenhouse and others in organizing first U.S. Democratic society.

JACKSON, EDWARD PAYSON (*b. Erzerum, Turkey, 1840; d. 1905*), educator. Son of missionary parents; served as instructor in science, Boston Latin School, 1877–1904, showing much originality in methods.

JACKSON, GEORGE K. (*b. Oxford, England, 1758; d. 1822*), organist, music teacher, composer. Came to America, 1796; settled in Boston, Mass., *c.* 1815, after serving at St. George's, New York City, and was organist at King's Chapel, Trinity and St. Paul's.

JACKSON, GEORGE THOMAS (*b. New York, N.Y., 1852; d. New York, 1916*), physician. Brother of Samuel M. Jackson. An outstanding specialist in dermatology, which he taught at Woman's Medical College and at the College of Physicians and Surgeons, New York.

JACKSON, HALL (*b. Hampton, N.H., 1739; d. 1797*), physician, surgeon. Practiced in Portsmouth, N.H., after study in London, England; specialized in smallpox. Chief surgeon, New Hampshire troops in Continental Army, 1775–83. Was among first to raise foxglove (digitalis) in America.

JACKSON, HELEN MARIA FISKE HUNT (*b. Amherst, Mass., 1830; d. 1885*), author, better known as Helen Hunt Jackson, or as "H. H." A neighbor and schoolmate of Emily Dickinson, Helen Fiske married Edward B. Hunt, 1852. After the death of her husband and children, she was encouraged to write by T. W. Higginson, publishing her first book *Verses* in 1870 and becoming a valued contributor of stories and essays to the magazines. After her marriage to William S. Jackson, 1875, she resided in Colorado Springs, Colo. Her novel *Mercy Philbrick's Choice* (1876) is said to deal with the life of Emily Dickinson; her *A Century of Dishonor* (1881) and the very popular *Ramona* (1884) reflect her passionate espousal of the cause of the Indians against mistreatment by the U.S. government.

JACKSON, HENRY ROOTES (*b. Athens, Ga., 1820; d. 1898*), jurist, diplomat, Confederate brigadier-general. Nephew of James Jackson (1757–1806). U.S. minister to Austria, 1853–58; to Mexico, 1885–86. Supporter of Joseph E. Brown in Georgia politics.

JACKSON, HOWELL EDMUNDS (*b. Paris, Tenn., 1832; d. near Nashville, Tenn., 1895*), jurist. Brother of William H. Jackson. U.S. senator, Democrat, from Tennessee, 1881–86; federal judge, 6th circuit, 1886–91; first presiding judge, circuit court of appeals at Cincinnati, 1891–93. Justice, U.S. Supreme Court, 1893–95.

JACKSON, JAMES (*b. Moreton Hampstead, England, 1757; d. Washington, D.C., 1806*), lawyer, Revolutionary soldier, Georgia legislator. Emigrated to Georgia c. 1772; studied law with George Walton after outstanding service with Georgia state troops. Bitter opponent of Yazoo land frauds. U.S. senator, independent (Democrat) Republican, 1793–95, 1801–06; governor of Georgia, 1798–1801.

JACKSON, JAMES (*b. Newburyport, Mass., 1777; d. 1867*), physician. Brother of Charles and Patrick T. Jackson. Graduated Harvard, 1796; attended Harvard Medical School (M.B., 1802; M.D., 1809); was apprentice to Edward A. Holyoke and studied in London, England, with Cline and Astley Cooper. Began practice in Boston, Mass., 1800; was one of first in America to investigate vaccination in a scientific spirit. Hersey Professor at the reorganized Harvard Medical School, 1812–33, he was largely responsible for founding Massachusetts General Hospital. His *Letters to a Young Physician* (1855) is a medical classic.

JACKSON, JAMES (*b. Jefferson Co., Ga., 1819; d. Atlanta, Ga., 1887*), jurist, Georgia legislator. Grandson of James Jackson (1757–1806).

JACKSON, JAMES CALEB (*b. Manlius, N.Y., 1811; d. Dansville, N.Y., 1895*), Abolitionist editor, reformer, hydropathic physician.

JACKSON, JOHN ADAMS (*b. Bath, Maine, 1825; d. Pracchia, Italy, 1879*), sculptor of portrait busts and ideal figures in the pseudo-classic manner.

JACKSON, JOHN BRINCKERHOFF (*b. Newark, N.J., 1862; d. Switzerland, 1920*), diplomat, lawyer. Graduated Annapolis, 1883. Secretary of legation and embassy, Berlin, 1890–1902; U.S. minister to Greece, 1902–07. Served thereafter as minister to Cuba, Persia, Roumania, Servia and Bulgaria, resigning in 1913; was special aide to U.S. embassy at Berlin 1915–17.

JACKSON, JOHN DAVIES (*b. Danville, Ky., 1834; d. Danville, 1875*), physician, Confederate surgeon. Reviewed and vindicated (1873) the claim of Ephraim McDowell to recognition as pioneer in ovariotomy and abdominal surgery.

JACKSON, JOHN GEORGE (*b. near Buckhannon, [W.] Va., 1777; d. 1825*), surveyor, jurist, Virginia legislator. Congressman, (Democrat) Republican, from Virginia, 1803–10, 1813–17; first U.S. judge for Western District of Virginia, 1819–25;

active in developing Virginia's natural resources. Brother-in-law of James Madison.

JACKSON, MERCY RUGGLES BISBE (*b. Hardwick, Mass., 1802; d. 1877*), homeopathic physician. Adjunct professor of diseases of children, Boston University Medical School, 1873–77.

JACKSON, MORTIMER MELVILLE (*b. Rensselaerville, N.Y., 1809; d. 1889*), jurist. Removed to Wisconsin, 1838; served as territorial attorney-general, 1841–45, and as a state circuit and supreme court judge, 1848–53. As U.S. consul at Halifax, Canada, 1861–82, Jackson did outstanding service during the Civil War and in later adjustment of the disputes over fisheries.

JACKSON, PATRICK TRACY (*b. Newburyport, Mass., 1780; d. Beverly, Mass., 1847*), merchant, financier. Brother of Charles Jackson and James Jackson (1777–1867). With Nathan Appleton, Francis Cabot Lowell and others, organized Boston Manufacturing Co., 1813, whose Waltham mill on the Charles River was probably the first in which all operations for turning raw cotton into finished cloth were done in one factory. Jackson was prime mover in founding Lowell, Mass., 1820. He also built the Boston & Lowell Railroad, and was active in Boston realty speculation.

JACKSON, SAMUEL (*b. Philadelphia, Pa., 1787; d. Philadelphia, 1872*), physician. Son of David Jackson. Graduated University of Pennsylvania, 1808; taught physiology there, 1827–63.

JACKSON, SAMUEL MACAULEY (*b. New York, N.Y., 1851; d. 1912*), Presbyterian clergyman, church historian. Brother of George T. Jackson. Disciple of Philip Schaff and his associate in the *Dictionary of the Bible* (1880) and the several editions of the Schaff-Herzog *Encyclopedia*. Author also of numerous works including *Huldreich Zwingli* (1901).

JACKSON, SHELDON (*b. Minaville, N.Y., 1834; d. Asheville, N.C., 1909*), Presbyterian clergyman. Pastor in Minnesota; missionary in Rocky Mountain states. Missionary in Alaska, and first U.S. superintendent of public instruction there, 1885–1909. Introduced domesticated reindeer into Alaska, 1892.

JACKSON, THOMAS JONATHAN (*b. Clarksburg, Va., now W. Va., 1824; d. Guiney's Station, Va., 1863*), "Stonewall" Jackson, Confederate soldier. Graduated West Point, 1846. Became major by brevet within 18 months after distinguished Mexican War service at Vera Cruz, Cerro Gordo, Chapultepec; resigned from army, February 1852; became professor of artillery tactics and natural philosophy at Virginia Military Institute, Lexington, Va. A devout Presbyterian, grave and slightly stiff in his public manner, Jackson took no part in public affairs prior to the Civil War beyond that of commanding the cadet corps at the hanging of John

Brown, 1859. He deplored the prospect of war which he described as the "sum of all evils."

Ordered to Richmond, April 21, 1861, with part of the cadet corps, he was soon sent to Harper's Ferry as colonel of infantry; on June 17, 1861, he was made brigadier-general. Bringing his command to high efficiency, he sustained a Union assault at a critical moment during the first battle of Bull Run, thus winning his famous sobriquet from Brig.-Gen. B. E. Bee. Promoted major-general, Oct. 7, 1861, Jackson assumed command in the Shenandoah Valley. Gen. J. E. Johnston's retreat to the line of the Rappahannock early in March 1862 forced Jackson to abandon Winchester, Va., and enter upon his celebrated "Valley Campaign" which many critics regard as the most remarkable display of strategic science and tactics in all American military history. Marching up the Valley, Jackson turned on his pursuer, the federal force under Maj.-Gen. James Shields, and was defeated with heavy loss at Kernstown on March 23. Criticism of Jackson as irresponsibly reckless failed to take into account the effect of his action in alarming the federal command and causing the retention of force in northern and western Virginia which would otherwise have supported McClellan's attack on Richmond. In further development of this strategy, Jackson continued on the offensive, attacking the federal force under Brig.-Gen. N. P. Banks at Front Royal on May 23, driving it back through Winchester to the Potomac and threatening the safety of Washington. Menaced in the rear from both east and west by superior forces, Jackson withdrew rapidly up the Valley and engaged each opponent separately; the force under Frémont was checked at Cross Keys on June 8, and Shields's advanced guard was defeated at Port Republic on June 9.

Meanwhile, Gen. R. E. Lee had succeeded to command of the forces defending Richmond. An admirer of Jackson, Lee summoned him to join in the Seven Days' Campaign late in June, but Jackson's failures at Beaver Dam Creek and White Oak Swamp were disappointing. After an inconclusive action at Cedar Run, Aug. 9, Jackson was detached and executed the most famous of all his marches, destroying the federal base at Manassas Junction, Aug. 27, holding off the enemy at Groveton, and on Aug. 30–31 sharing in the offensive against Gen. Pope at the second battle of Bull Run which permitted Lee to carry the war into the enemy's country. By this time, Jackson was a legend. Eccentric in behavior and appearance, he was known as "Old Jack" to his adoring soldiers, but his trusted lieutenant, Ewell, was convinced that he was insane.

Leading Lee's advance into Maryland, Jackson took Harper's Ferry, Sept. 15, 1862, and distinguished himself at Antietam (Sept. 17) and at Fredericksburg. Promoted lieutenant-general, Oct. 10, he now commanded one of the two corps into which the Army of Northern Virginia had been divided. On renewal of the federal offensive in the spring of 1863, Jackson in concert with Lee planned to attack the rear of Gen. Hooker's advanced guard as it lay near Chancellorsville. Before dawn on May 2, he began the last of his great marches and near sunset surprised the rear of the Union right, so threatening Hooker's line that a retreat was inevitable. Returning from the front in the dusk, Jackson was severely wounded by the fire of his own men and died of pneumonia eight days later. Although his career in high field command was limited to less than 25 months, he is listed by all critics among the greatest American soldiers.

JACKSON, WILLIAM (*b. Cumberland, England, 1759; d. Philadelphia, Pa., 1828*), Revolutionary soldier, public official. Came to America as a youth; raised in South Carolina. Served as aide to Gen. Benjamin Lincoln, and as secretary to John Laurens on European mission, 1781. Was secretary to Federal Convention, 1787, and personal secretary to President Washington, 1789–91. Thereafter was employed in business, in the customs, and in journalism.

JACKSON, WILLIAM (*b. Newton, Mass., 1783; d. 1855*), tallow chandler, promoter of Massachusetts railroads, Massachusetts legislator and congressman.

JACKSON, WILLIAM HICKS (*b. Paris, Tenn., 1835; d. Belle Meade, Tenn., 1903*), Confederate general, planter, stock-breeder. Brother of Howell E. Jackson. Graduated West Point, 1856. After outstanding services in Mississippi, Tennessee and the defense of Atlanta, in which he rose to divisional command, Jackson returned to manage family plantations. *Post* 1868, he was associated in development of the famous Belle Meade thoroughbred horse farm.

JACOB, RICHARD TAYLOR (*b. Oldham Co., Ky., 1825; d. 1903*), Kentucky soldier, Unionist.

JACOBI, ABRAHAM (*b. Hartum-in-Minden, Germany, 1830; d. 1919*), pediatrician. Graduated Bonn, M.D., 1851. After two years' imprisonment for revolutionary activity, escaped and made his way to England; settled in New York, N.Y., c. 1855. Identifying himself from the first with treatment of infants' and children's diseases, he won international fame in his specialty. He became the first professor of diseases of children in this country at New York Medical College, 1860, and established there the first free clinic for such diseases; from 1870 until 1902 he was professor of pediatrics, College of Physicians and Surgeons, New York. He was a prolific contributor to medical journals and the author of several books.

JACOBI, MARY CORINNA PUTNAM (*b. London, England, 1842; d. 1906*), physician. Daughter of George P. Putnam; wife of Abraham Jacobi. Graduated Female Medical College of Pennsylvania, 1864; École de Médicine, Paris, France, 1871, the second woman to receive its degree. Served as professor, Woman's Medical College, New York, 1871–88. The leading woman physician of her generation.

JACOBS, HENRY EYSTER (*b. Gettysburg, Pa., 1844; d. Philadelphia, Pa., 1932*), Lutheran clergyman, theologian. Professor at Gettysburg College, 1870–83; professor, dean and president, Lutheran Theological Seminary, Philadelphia, *post* 1883. Had strong influence in the liturgical development of Lutheran bodies in the United States. [*Supp.* 1]

JACOBS, JOSEPH (*b. Sydney, New South Wales, 1854; d. 1916*), historian, folklorist. Graduated St. John's College, Cambridge, 1876; studied in Berlin; won early fame for Jewish anthropological and historical studies. Was editor of numerous and valuable collections of fairy tales. *Post* 1900, Jacobs lived in the United States where he served as revising editor of the *Jewish Encyclopedia* and was editor of the *American Hebrew*, 1913–16.

JACOBS, JOSEPH (*b. Jefferson, Ga., 1859; d. 1929*), pharmacist, drugstore chain proprietor, collector of works by and about Robert Burns.

JACOBS, MICHAEL (*b. near Waynesboro, Pa., 1808; d. Gettysburg, Pa., 1871*), Lutheran clergyman. Professor of mathematics and science, Gettysburg College, 1832–66.

JACOBS, WILLIAM PLUMER (*b. York Co., S.C., 1842; d. 1917*), Presbyterian clergyman. Pastor in Clinton, S.C., *post* 1864; founded Thornwell Orphanage, 1875, and Clinton College (later Presbyterian College of South Carolina), 1880.

JACOBSON, JOHN CHRISTIAN (*b. Burkhall, Denmark, 1795; d. 1870*), Moravian bishop, educator. Came to America, 1816; taught at Nazareth and Bethlehem, Pa., and at Salem, N.C.; brought European standards to Moravian education.

JACOBY, LUDWIG SIGMUND (*b. Altstrelitz, Germany, 1813; d. St. Louis, Mo., 1874*), Methodist clergyman. Came to America, 1838; was converted to Methodism in Cincinnati, O., 1839; worked among Germans in upper Mississippi valley, 1841–48. Evangelized in Germany, 1849–71.

JADWIN, EDGAR (*b. Honesdale, Pa., 1865; d. Canal Zone, 1931*), soldier, engineer. Graduated West Point, 1890. Assistant to G. W. Goethals in Panama Canal construction; built channel through Gatun Lake, Gatun Dam, and breakwater at Atlantic terminus. As brigadier-general, 1917–18, Jadwin supervised vast wartime construction projects in France; he served as chief of engineers, 1926–29, retiring as lieutenant-general.

JAMES, CHARLES (*b. near Northampton, England, 1880; d. 1928*), chemist. Came to America *c.* 1906. Professor at University of New Hampshire, 1906–28. Won international recognition for his work in study of rare earths.

JAMES, CHARLES TILLINGHAST (*b. West Greenwich, R.I., 1805; d. Sag Harbor, N.Y., 1862*), engineer. Expert in textile machinery construction; advocate of steam power for cotton mills. U.S. senator, Democrat, from Rhode Island, 1851–57.

JAMES, DANIEL WILLIS (*b. Liverpool, England, 1832; d. 1907*), merchant, philanthropist. Born of U.S. parents resident in England; educated in England and Scotland. Came to America, 1849; became partner in Phelps, Dodge & Co., 1854. A lifelong, anonymous donor to charities, in particular to the Children's Aid Society and Union Theological Seminary, New York.

JAMES, EDMUND JANES (*b. Jacksonville, Ill., 1855; d. Covina, Calif., 1925*), economist, educator. Graduated University of Halle, Ph.D., 1877. Taught at Wharton School, University of Pennsylvania, and University of Chicago; founded American Academy of Political and Social Science, 1889–90. Served as president, Northwestern University, 1902–04; University of Illinois, 1904–19.

JAMES, EDWARD CHRISTOPHER (*b. Ogdensburg, N.Y., 1841; d. 1901*), lawyer, Union soldier. Practiced in New York City *post* 1882; a notable cross-examiner in all types of cases.

JAMES, EDWIN (*b. Weybridge, Vt., 1797; d. Rock Spring, Iowa, 1861*), physician, explorer, naturalist. Graduated Middlebury, 1816; studied botany and geology with John Torrey and Amos Eaton at Albany, N.Y. Surgeon-naturalist on Stephen H. Long's expedition to explore region between Mississippi and Rocky Mountains, 1820. Author of *Account of an Expedition from Pittsburgh to the Rocky Mountains* (1822–23), the official record of the survey. Later, as army surgeon at Prairie du Chien and Mackinac, James studied and wrote on the Indian languages; he settled near Burlington, Iowa, *c.* 1838.

JAMES, GEORGE WHARTON (*b. Gainsborough, England, 1858; d. 1923*), author, lecturer. Came to America, 1881; was a Methodist minister in California and Nevada until 1889. Thereafter he became widely known as an enthusiast for the history and spirit of the Southwest and as a friend of the Indians.

JAMES, HENRY (*b. Albany, N.Y., 1811; d. Cambridge, Mass., 1882*), author, lecturer, philosopher. Father of Henry James (1843–1916) and William James. Graduated Union, 1830. Employed Swedenborg's interpretation of Christianity as a framework for his own speculations; was intimate with Horace Greeley, Albert Brisbane and the New York Fourierist circle, also with R. W. Emerson, Thomas Carlyle and other leaders in the thought of his time.

JAMES, HENRY (*b. New York, N.Y., 1843; d. London, England, 1916*), novelist. Son of Henry James (1811–1882); brother of William James. Educated in accordance with his father's theory that children destined to cosmopolitanism should not be allowed to take root in any religion, political system, ethical code or set of personal habits. From boyhood he interested himself in the sensitive observation of subtle human relationships; constantly on the move, he was able to form impressions in a variety of American cities and abroad in Geneva, London, Paris, Boulogne and Bonn. Mathematics and drawing interested him at the outset, but while residing at Cambridge, Mass., he was influenced by Charles E. Norton and William D. Howells to a gradual awareness of his vocation in literature. Kept from service in the Civil War by physical infirmity, he felt himself cast in the role of a spectator on life. Between 1865 and 1869 he wrote criticism for the *Nation* and stories for the *Atlantic Monthly* and the *Galaxy* magazines; his early fiction derived from Hawthorne and Balzac and inclined to melodrama. The earliest story to reveal James's essential traits and his predominant theme of a raw traveler making contact with older cultures was "A Passionate Pilgrim" (*Atlantic Monthly*, 1871). In 1875 he left America for Paris but felt himself too much a foreigner there; in 1876 he settled for good in England. An overconsciousness of national qualities and a too great concern with superficial elements of international differences appear in the works produced during the first period of his European residence; only *The Portrait of a Lady* (1881) rises clearly above these prepossessions. *Roderick Hudson* (1876), *The American* (1877), *Daisy Miller* (1879), *An International Episode* (1879), all suffer despite their merits from the author's concern with matters which are not of first importance for a novelist.

Moving as he did in a world withdrawn from the rougher phases of life, he grew more and more absorbed in his special society. He had conceived of himself as writing in a cosmopolitan capital but having elsewhere a vast native province to draw upon, much as Turgenev drew on Russia; gradually, however, he lost this sense of America as a spiritual reservoir. *The Princess Casamassima* (1886) indicated how far James had gone in his saturation with English life and is the high point of his idealization of it. *The Tragic Muse* (1890) is more critical of the world of leisure and fashion, and here James sets forth his concept of the aristocracy of art and artists as more important and more desirable than anything in those "dense categories of dark arcana" which he had gone to Europe to penetrate. Except for *Daisy Miller,* none of his books had had popular acclaim either in England or America; a personal resentment dictated his siding with fellow-artists against the public, and the years 1886–96 saw this resentment grow and finally surrender to a kind of philosophic stoicism. During these years he confined himself largely to unsuccessful plays, distinguished critical essays and short narratives of unique delicacy, skill and beauty. *The Author of Beltraffio* (1885), *The Aspern Papers* (1888), *The Lesson of the Master* (1892) and *Embarrassments* (1896) contain what he himself described as a "multitude of pictures of my time."

After this decade, reconciled to the fact that his art was for the few, he settled down to practice it as he pleased, to write without conflict in his own way for his own audience. *The Two Magics* (1898) contained "The Turn of the Screw." It was preceded by *The Spoils of Poynton* (1897) and *What Maisie Knew* (1897), and followed by the three novels in which he brought his art to its peak: *The Wings of the Dove* (1902), *The Ambassadors* (1903) and *The Golden Bowl* (1904). Again and again in his later books he dealt with the adventures of exquisite souls in a rough world and their defeat by vulgarity and vice.

James traveled in America, 1904–05; the fruit of his observations was *The American Scene* (1907). The New York edition of his works, 1907–1909, presented a selection of what he judged his best with the addition of prefaces which throw valuable light on the art of fiction. His three autobiographical works, *A Small Boy and Others* (1913), *Notes of a Son and Brother* (1914) and *The Middle Years* (1917) are of great importance for an understanding of James. The first World War ended his career; as a gesture of sympathy with his long-loved England, he became a British citizen, 1915.

In his meticulous examinations of motives, atmospheres and backgrounds, James did not seek deliberately to be obscure. Obscurity and esoteric reputation were his destiny, not his design. He had set out to identify and represent certain subtle relationships which he had perceived binding men and women together in the human picture before his eyes, and he would not call it his fault if his perceptions proved to be more delicate than those of the reading public at large.

He must be thought of as something more than a merely Anglo-Saxon phenomenon. Balzac and Turgenev furnished the examples in which he found what his own art needed to employ or avoid. His originality lay, first, in his choice of his terrain, that international triangle which has London, Paris and New York at its points and which embraces a homogeneous civilization which before James had never had a great novelist concerned with it as entity and whole. He was original too in his attitude toward the English-American novel as an art form; he found it an unconscious and left it a fully conscious form of art. By example, and in his critical writings, he called attention to the finer details of craftsmanship, generalized the practices of individuals into principles, and brought the whole art of the novel into the region of esthetics. His influence upon numerous followers, in Europe and in America, has been weighty and persistent.

JAMES, JESSE WOODSON (*b. near Kearney, Mo., 1847; d. St. Joseph, Mo., 1882*), desperado, train-robber. With his brother Alexander Franklin (Frank) James, was a member of Confederate guerrillas under W. C. Quantrill; became leader of a gang of robbers which included Coleman Younger, 1866. They operated successfully until 1876, when all but Jesse and Frank were killed in an attempted holdup of bank at Northfield, Minn. Led a new gang of outlaws, 1879–81; was shot from behind by Robert Ford, a member of his band.

JAMES, LOUIS (*b. Tremont, Ill., 1842; d. Helena, Mont., 1910*), actor. Made début, Louisville, Ky., 1864. Accomplished his best work under management of Augustin Daly, 1871–75; played in support of Edwin Booth, Lawrence Barrett and many others.

JAMES, OLLIE MURRAY (*b. Crittenden Co., Ky., 1871; d. 1918*), lawyer, politician. Congressman from Kentucky, Democrat, 1903–12; U.S. senator, 1912–18. One of the most popular campaign orators of his day.

JAMES, THOMAS (*b. Maryland, 1782; d. Monroe City, Ill., 1847*), trapper, Santa Fé trader. Author of *Three Years Among the Indians and Mexicans* (1846), an important source for early frontier history.

JAMES, THOMAS CHALKLEY (*b. Philadelphia, Pa., 1766; d. Philadelphia, 1835*), physician. Grandson of Thomas Chalkley. Graduated University of Pennsylvania, B.M., 1787; awarded doctor's degree, 1811. Served as ship's surgeon; studied in England under Dr. John Hunter and the famous obstetricians Osborne and John Clark, and also in Edinburgh. Gave first regular course on obstetrics at Philadelphia, 1802; served as obstetrician, Pennsylvania Hospital, 1810–32; by teaching and example, laid firm foundation for practice of scientific obstetrics in America.

JAMES, THOMAS LEMUEL (*b. Utica, N.Y., 1831; d. 1916*), businessman, newspaper publisher. Highly efficient postmaster, New York City, 1873–81; as postmaster-general, 1881, helped put end to Star Route frauds.

JAMES, THOMAS POTTS (*b. Radnor, Pa., 1803; d. Cambridge, Mass., 1882*), wholesale pharmacist, botanist. Specialized in study of mosses; with C. L. Lesquereux, prepared classic *Manual of North American Mosses* (1884).

JAMES, WILLIAM (*b. New York, N.Y., 1842; d. Chocorua, N.H., 1910*), philosopher, psychologist. Eldest son of Henry James (1811–1882); brother of Henry James (1843–1916). Influenced by father's preoccupation with problems of life and religion, he was exposed to an irregular, intermittent education but frequented art galleries and theatres, and observed life in many European cities. Entered studio of William M. Hunt, Newport, R.I., 1860, and worked with John LaFarge; although talented as painter, he decided to pursue a scientific career and entered Lawrence Scientific School, 1861, thus beginning his lifelong association with Harvard. After studying chemistry under Charles W. Eliot and comparative anatomy under Jeffries Wyman, he entered Harvard Medical School, 1864, but interrupted studies to participate in a zoological expedition to the Amazon basin, directed by Louis Agassiz. He acquired from Wyman and Agassiz his respect for facts and first-hand observation, which became a fixed element in his intellectual composition. Failure of health interrupted his medical study; he occupied himself in studying experimental physiology in Germany, 1867–68. This was a period of indecision and discouragement for the young student; he became convinced that his poor health eliminated any prospect of sustained laboratory work. Re-entering Harvard Medical School, he received his degree, 1868, but felt unable to engage in medical practice. Another, more prolonged period of ill health and nervous depression followed, but his readings in the fields of the sciences, literature and philosophy would have taxed the capacity of any well person. In 1870, Charles Renouvier's *Traité de Psychologie Rationelle* delivered him from his melancholia and philosophic doubt.

Accepting an instructorship in physiology in Harvard College, 1872, for the next ten years he taught comparative anatomy, comparative physiology, and hygiene. At that time the theory of evolution was the central topic in the field of biology, and psychology had received a new impulse from increased knowledge of the physiology of the senses and nervous system. James offered a course entitled "Relations between Physiology and Psychology," 1875, established the first psychology laboratory in America, and in 1880 became assistant professor of philosophy. He began work on his *Principles of Psychology*, 1878, published 12 years later. Sections of this work were first published in learned journals and given in lectures; the immense popularity of the *Principles* was due mainly to the author's learning and skillful use of citation and his success in giving an adequate summary of the state of the science of psychology at the end of the 19th century. An abridged edition was for many years the most popular textbook on the subject in America. James's *Talks to Teachers on Psychology* (1899) spread the vogue of his ideas and gave powerful impulse to the new subject of educational psychology. In 1884, two articles of great importance had been contributed by James to *Mind*. The first presented for the first time his insistence on the continuity of the stream of consciousness. The second expressed the so-called "James-Lange Theory" of emotion.

After 1890 there was a gradual shift in emphasis in James's teaching and writing from psychology to philosophy. As a philosopher, he was solicited on the one side by religion and on the other by science. Firmly stationed on the side of empiricism by temperament, he was aware of the need for a new empiricism freed from associationism. He had accepted the Shadworth Hodgson dictum that "realities are only what they are known as"; repelled by Hodgson's determinism, he concluded that conscious experience must be supplemented by freedom of the will. Experience may be considered knowledge, but James held that it must be supplemented by faith to satisfy man's moral and emotional nature. His first step toward a philosophy was to reject the pretensions and negations of science. The affirmation of man's freedom was, to James, a first step in the cogitative as well as moral life. Renouvier's belief that natural processes really begin and end discontinuously had suggested, to the troubled younger James, that a nature so consistent with novelty and creativity implied also free will. His philosophy now developed into a more radical union of empiricism and voluntarism. His ideas, originally published in articles, appeared in book form as *The Will to Believe and Other Essays* (1897). This volume presented reasons for a firm belief in freedom, in the triumph of righteousness and in the God which guarantees this belief. In *Varieties of Religious Experience* (1902), he presented a masterly exposition of the data of conversion, saintliness and other characteristics of man's religious life. The most important effect of this book was to shift the emphasis from religious dogmas and external forms to the unique states of mind associated with it. In 1904–05 he published the articles later issued as *Essays in Radical Empiricism* (1912); in 1907 he published his famous *Pragmatism,* a doctrine adumbrated in the concluding chapter of his *Principles of Psychology.* The meaning of an idea, says James, consists in the particular consequences to which it leads. Truth should properly be applied as a term, not to reality, but to our beliefs about it. A particular truth must be about something in particular; secondly, it must "work," that is, satisfy the purpose for which it was adopted. He defended this position and its corollaries in *The Meaning of Truth* (1909). James's effort to give a systematic statement of his metaphysics was published as *A Pluralistic Universe* (1909).

Although this volume is popular in style, it affords the best and the final synopsis of his *Weltanschauung* and of his general philosophical orientation. He pays his respects to Hegel and to the absolutists generally, setting forth the failure of their arguments, and the "thinness" of their results. To reject the absolute does not imply the rejection of every hypothesis of a "superhuman consciousness." But instead of the dialectical method used by the Hegelians to establish such a consciousness, James commended the method of empirical

analogy and free speculation used by Fechner in his doctrine of an "earth-soul"; and, instead of a superhuman consciousness that is in some unintelligible sense "all-embracing," James proposed that it should be finite like human consciousness. In that case it may without contradiction have those relations to an environment other than itself, and that freedom from evil, which have in fact always been attributed to it by the religious worshipper. It was far from James's intention to increase the distance between man and God. Man is a part, or is capable under certain conditions of becoming a part, of an enveloping spiritual life; and that life is like his own—different in degree, but similar in kind. The probability of such a hypothesis is supported by the mystical state, and by allied abnormal and supernormal experiences to which modern psychology has called attention, as well as by the moral and emotional demands which it satisfies. James ends upon the note of pluralism, in which the "each" is preferred to the "all," and the world is a "multiverse"; which corresponds to the actual appearances of things and satisfies the creed of individualism and freedom, but without that complete disintegration that has usually been supposed to be the only alternative to monism. This was James's solution of that problem which he had set himself at the beginning of his philosophical career, the union, namely, of the empirical temper and method of science with the essential ideals and beliefs of religion.

James is commonly grouped with Jonathan Edwards and R. W. Emerson as a leader in American thought, a distinction owing in great part to his cosmopolitanism and to his literary style. His style is that of a brilliant talker, concrete, witty, and giving the effect of spontaneity. As a person, he was humorous and totally lacking in either self-consciousness or self-righteousness. He responded warmly to humanity in all its forms. He has been fortunate in that the direction of his thought coincided with that of his posterity. The application of an empirical study of human nature to human affairs; a shift of emphasis in philosophy from pure intellect to perception; a recognition of the significance of religious experience; an acknowledgment of the play of will and feeling in formation of belief; these are a few of the major items in the record of James's permanent achievement. He continued to teach at Harvard until January 1907.

JAMESON, HORATIO GATES (*b. York, Pa., 1778; d. New York, N.Y., 1855*), Baltimore, Md., physician, surgeon, teacher. Founded Washington Medical College (Baltimore, 1827–51).

JAMESON, JOHN ALEXANDER (*b. Irasburgh, Vt., 1824; d. Hyde Park, Ill., 1890*), jurist. Practiced law in Illinois *post* 1853; judge, chancery division, superior court of Chicago (later Cook Co.), 1865–

83. Author of *The Constitutional Convention* (1867), an exhaustive historical study.

JAMESON, JOHN FRANKLIN (*b. Somerville, Mass., 1859; d. Washington, D.C., 1937*), historian. Graduated Amherst, 1879; Ph.D., Johns Hopkins, 1882. After teaching at Johns Hopkins, Brown, and Chicago universities, he was director, 1905–28, of the department of historical research of the Carnegie Institution. Here he led the campaign for a National Archives building, and directed the publication of guides to foreign archives and of many significant American historical documents. A leader in American historical scholarship, Jameson was chief of the Manuscripts Division of the Library of Congress, 1928–37; managing editor, 1895–1901, 1905–28 of the *American Historical Review;* and, as chairman of the Committee of Management, a guiding spirit in the planning and execution of the *Dictionary of American Biography.* [*Supp. 2*]

JAMISON, CECILIA VIETS DAKIN HAMILTON (*b. Yarmouth, Canada, 1837; d. Roxbury, Mass., 1909*), portrait painter, author.

JAMISON, DAVID (*b. Scotland, 1660; d. New York, N.Y. ?, 1739*), lawyer. Came to America as a bondsman, 1685. Defended Francis Makemie for preaching without license, 1707; was chief-justice of New Jersey, 1711–23, also recorder of New York City and acting attorney-general *post* 1712. Active in establishing Church of England in New York.

JAMISON, DAVID FLAVEL (*b. Orangeburg District, S.C., 1810; d. 1864*), planter, South Carolina legislator, author. Friend of William Gilmore Simms. President, South Carolina secession convention.

JANAUSCHEK, FRANZISKA MAGDALENA ROMANCE (*b. Prague, Bohemia, 1830; d. Amityville, N.Y., 1904*), actress, better known as Fanny Janauschek. A leading German tragedienne, she came to America, 1867, playing in German; in 1870 she began her career in English under Augustin Daly's management, acting in *Mary Stuart* at the New York Academy of Music. *Post* 1880, she made the United States her home. Unable to adapt her heroic style of acting to changing tastes, she gradually lost favor with American audiences.

JANES, LEWIS GEORGE (*b. Providence, R.I., 1844; d. Eliot, Maine, 1901*), lecturer, teacher. Associated with the Ethical Association and other free religious groups. Author of *Health and a Day* (1901).

JANEWAY, EDWARD GAMALIEL (*b. New Brunswick, N.J., 1841; d. Summit, N.J., 1911*), physician. Graduated Rutgers, 1860; M.D., College of Physicians and Surgeons, New York, 1864. Professor of pathological anatomy, Bellevue; later held chair of principles and practice there, and was dean, 1898–1905, after consolidation with New York University. A notable diagnostician and consultant.

JANEWAY, THEODORE CALDWELL (*b. New York, N.Y., 1872; d. 1917*), physician. Son of Edward G. Janeway. Distinguished professor and innovator in methods at New York University, College of Physicians and Surgeons (New York), and Johns Hopkins. Made special studies of tuberculosis.

JANIN, LOUIS (*b. New Orleans, La., 1837; d. Santa Barbara, Calif., 1914*), mining engineer. Trainer and mentor, among others, of Herbert Hoover and John Hays Hammond.

JANNEY, ELI HAMILTON (*b. Loudoun Co., Va., 1831; d. Alexandria, Va., 1912*). Inventor of the modern railroad car-coupler. Basic patents were granted him, 1868 and 1873; his device became standard by agreement of the railroads, 1888.

JANNEY, OLIVER EDWARD (*b. Washington, D.C., 1856; d. Baltimore, Md., 1930*), physician, Quaker reformer and philanthropist.

JANNEY, SAMUEL McPHERSON (*b. Loudoun Co., Va., 1801; d. 1880*), educator, Hicksite Quaker minister. Author of lives of William Penn (1852) and George Fox (1853), and a history of the Society of Friends.

JANSEN, REINIER (*b. Alkmaar, Holland; d. Philadelphia, Pa., 1706 n.s.*), merchant. Came to Pennsylvania, 1698. Operated a printing-press for the Society of Friends in Philadelphia, his first imprints bearing the date 1699.

JANSON, KRISTOFER NAGEL (*b. Bergen, Norway, 1841; d. 1917*), poet, novelist, Unitarian clergyman. Served as Unitarian missionary in Minnesota, 1879–80 and 1881–93, returning to Norway in the latter year.

JANSSENS, FRANCIS (*b. Tilburg, North Brabant, 1843; d. at sea, 1897*), Roman Catholic clergyman. Graduated Louvain; ordained, 1867. Came to America, 1868, and was pastor in Richmond, Va. Bishop of Natchez, Miss., 1881–88; archbishop of New Orleans, 1888–97.

JANVIER, CATHARINE ANN DRINKER (*b. Philadelphia, Pa., 1841; d. Merion, Pa., 1922*), painter, author. Wife of Thomas A. Janvier. Enthusiast for Provençal culture and literature.

JANVIER, MARGARET THOMSON (*b. New Orleans, La., 1844; d. Moorestown, N.J., 1913*), author. Sister of Thomas A. Janvier. Wrote, under pseudonym of Margaret Vandegrift, a variety of juvenile stories and verses.

JANVIER, THOMAS ALLIBONE (*b. Philadelphia, Pa., 1849; d. New York, N.Y., 1913*), journalist. Author, among other books, of *Color Studies* (1885); *The Aztec Treasure House* (1890); *In Old New York* (1894); *At the Casa Napoleon* (1914). A graceful and sympathetic observer of New York

City's 19th century Bohemia, Janvier was also a student and admirer of the literature of Provence.

JAQUESS, JAMES FRAZIER (*b. near Evansville, Ind., 1819; d. St. Paul, Minn., 1898*), Methodist clergyman, Union soldier. Made two unsuccessful attempts to end Civil War by peace missions to Jefferson Davis, 1863 and 1864.

JARRATT, DEVEREUX (*b. New Kent Co., Va., 1733; d. Dinwiddie Co., Va., 1801*), Episcopal clergyman. Rector of Bath Parish, (Dinwiddie Co.), 1763–1801. An advocate of vital religion, he was friendly to the early American Methodists.

JARVES, DEMING (*b. Boston, Mass., 1790; d. Boston, 1869*), inventor, leader in American glass industry. Partner in New England Glass Co., Boston and Sandwich Glass Co., Cape Cod Glass Co.; attempted to claim credit for invention of pressed-glass machine, 1826–27; developed red-lead manufactory; a brilliant experimenter in color compounding and technical innovation.

JARVES, JAMES JACKSON (*b. Boston, Mass., 1818; d. Switzerland, 1888*), journalist, critic, pioneer art collector. Son of Deming Jarves. Traveled widely as young man; edited *Polynesian*, first newspaper published in Hawaii, 1840–48. Settling in Florence, Italy, he began career as art critic and collector early in the 1850's. His important collection of early Italian masters became Yale's property, 1871, and is today regarded as priceless. Jarves's declared purpose was the "diffusion of artistic knowledge and aesthetic taste in America." Among his many books were *Scenes and Scenery in California* (1844); *Art Studies* (1861); *The Art Idea* (1864, 1865).

JARVIS, ABRAHAM (*b. Norwalk, Conn., 1739 o.s.; d. 1813*), Episcopal clergyman. Graduated Yale, 1761. Rector at Middletown, Conn. Consecrated bishop of Connecticut, 1797.

JARVIS, CHARLES H. (*b. Philadelphia, Pa., 1837; d. Philadelphia, 1895*), concert pianist, teacher.

JARVIS, EDWARD (*b. Concord, Mass., 1803; d. Dorchester, Mass., 1884*), physician, alienist, statistician. Reformer of procedures in U.S. Census.

JARVIS, JOHN WESLEY (*b. South Shields, England, 1781; d. New York, N.Y., 1839*), portrait painter. Came to America as a child. Encouraged in art by Matthew Pratt and others; apprenticed to print publisher Edward Savage, in whose shop he learned drawing and engraving from David Edwin. Successful as painter of portraits in New York City, Baltimore, Md., Charleston, S.C., and New Orleans, La.; prodigiously facile, his work is uneven in quality. Extravagant and reckless, he died in poverty.

JARVIS, THOMAS JORDAN (*b. Jarvisburg, N.C., 1836; d. 1915*), lawyer, Confederate soldier, North Carolina legislator. Gave strong and progressive leadership as Democratic governor of North Carolina, 1879–85. U.S. minister to Brazil, 1885–89.

JARVIS, WILLIAM (*b. Boston, Mass., 1770; d. 1859*), Boston merchant. U.S. consul at Lisbon, Portugal, 1802–11. Introduced Merino sheep in large numbers to the United States and effected their distribution throughout the country.

JARVIS, WILLIAM CHAPMAN (*b. Fortress Monroe, Va., 1855; d. Willet's Point, N.Y., 1895*), physician, pioneer laryngologist and rhinologist. Graduated University of Maryland, M.D., 1875; did post-graduate work at Johns Hopkins. Devised a famous "snare" which revolutionized treatment of intranasal tumors, 1881. Professor at New York University *post* 1886. His career was marked by a long series of innovations in diagnosis and treatment of nasal and laryngeal diseases.

JASPER, WILLIAM (*b. near Georgetown, S.C., c. 1750; d. near Savannah, Ga., 1779*), Revolutionary soldier. Enlisted, and appointed sergeant, in the 2nd South Carolina Infantry under William Moultrie, 1775; distinguished himself during British bombardment of Fort Sullivan (now Fort Moultrie), June 1776, recovering flag after it had been shot down, and remounting it over the fort in face of heavy fire. Declining a commission because of his lack of education, he was made a scout and performed valuable service under Generals Moultrie, Marion and Lincoln. Accompanying the latter and D'Estaing in the assault on Savannah, 1799, he was killed planting his regiment's colors upon an enemy redoubt.

JASTROW, MARCUS (*b. Rogasan, Posen, Poland, 1829; d. Philadelphia, Pa., 1903*), rabbi, lexicographer. Educated in Poland and Germany; imprisoned and exiled by the Russians for patriotic Polish activities. Came to America, accepting a call from Congregation Rodeph Shalom, Philadelphia, 1866. His militant conservative Judaism soon engaged him in controversy with reform Judaism. He helped organize Maimonides College, where he taught religion and Jewish history, and made his synagogue a center of conservative Judaism. After 1876, he concentrated on his monumental *Dictionary of the Targumim, the Talmud Babli and Yerushalmi and the Midrashic Literature* (1886–1903), illustrative of a millennium of Hebrew and Aramaic literature. His declining years found Jastrow fervently espousing Herzlian Zionism.

JASTROW, MORRIS (*b. Warsaw, Poland, 1861; d. Philadelphia, Pa., 1921*), Semitic scholar. Son of Marcus Jastrow. Graduated University of Pennsylvania, 1881; Ph.D., Leipzig, 1884. Taught at University of Pennsylvania, 1892–1921. One of the most influential Orientalists of his time; author of *Religion Babyloniens und Assyriens* (1905, 1912) and other works in English on related subjects which revealed rare skill in linguistics, criticism and literary insight.

JAY, ALLEN (*b. Mill Creek, O., 1831; d. Richmond, Ind., 1910*), Quaker preacher, educator. Contributed greatly to Quaker revival, late 19th century; developed endowment of Earlham College and other Quaker schools.

JAY, Sir JAMES (*b. New York, N.Y., 1732; d. Springfield, N.J., 1815*), physician. Brother of John Jay (1745–1829). Suspected, 1782, of working against American independence.

JAY, JOHN (*b. New York, N.Y., 1745; d. Bedford, N.Y., 1829*), statesman. Brother of James Jay; sixth son of Peter and Mary (Van Cortlandt) Jay and thus a scion of two of colonial New York's wealthiest and most influential families. His father was a leading merchant who carefully guided his upbringing and education under private tutors. Bookish and pious, Jay early developed the aristocratic self-confidence and self-satisfaction which characterized his later career. Graduating from King's College, 1764, he prepared for the bar in a New York law office, where he evidenced the powerful and stubborn mental qualities, along with a lucidity of literary expression, which already marked him as a man of unusual force and intellectual ability.

Jay practiced law from 1768 until the American Revolution, which embarked him on a career of public service. He was one of New York's delegates to the first and second Continental Congresses, where he reflected the interests of conservative colonial merchants who opposed independence through fear that it might precipitate a social upheaval and democratic rule. As member of New York provincial congress, he supported the Declaration of Independence unreservedly and helped ratify it. He then guided the framing of New York's constitution and served as state chief justice until 1779. Resuming his seat in the Continental Congress, December 1778, Jay was elected its president, holding that position until chosen minister plenipotentiary to Spain nine months later. Jay began his diplomatic career with a mission which was hopeless from the start. His two chief points, according to the Spanish foreign minister, Floridablanca, were: "Spain, recognize our independence; Spain, give us more money." Jay obtained a small loan, but Spain had no intention of recognizing America's independence.

In the spring of 1782, Jay was summoned to Paris to join Franklin on the joint commission to negotiate peace with Great Britain. His participation in this secret negotiation remains controversial. His insistence that the British representative, Richard Oswald, be given powers to treat with representatives of the "United States of America" rather than the "Colonies" may have wrecked Franklin's prospect of gaining the cession of Canada. Distrusting French foreign minister Vergennes, Jay privately communicated with the British prime minister, thereby delaying negotiations until events in Europe had greatly strengthened Brit-

ain's bargaining position. Whether the British government would have agreed to Franklin's proposal regarding Canada is questionable; but Jay's victory in a matter of form was of dubious value.

Jay and John Adams then convinced Franklin that they should sign preliminary articles of peace without Vergennes's knowledge. This was a violation of their instructions to negotiate only with the full confidence of the French ministry but not technically a violation of the Franco-American treaty of alliance, for the peace was not to become effective until France had also made terms with Britain. France could not make peace until Spain agreed, and the American preliminaries undoubtedly helped bring Spain into line. France and Spain separately signed preliminaries of peace with Great Britain on Jan. 20, 1783.

Declining new diplomatic appointments in order to return to his law practice, Jay came home in July 1784 to discover that he had been drafted by Congress as secretary of foreign affairs. He retained this position until Jefferson became secretary of state in the new federal government, 1790. During his six-year tenure, Jay labored mostly over relations with Britain and Spain. The former retained the Northwest Posts in violation of the peace treaty; Spain occupied territory claimed by the United States and in addition closed the Mississippi to navigation by Americans. Protracted negotiations between Jay and Gardoquí, the Spanish minister, failed when Congress rejected a proposed treaty which would have denied Americans the navigation of the Mississippi for 25 years—a project which earned Jay the lasting distrust of the West and South.

Seriously handicapped by the weakness of government under the Confederation, Jay became one of the strongest advocates of a new constitution. In 1787 he joined with Hamilton and Madison and contributed five of the "Federalist" papers. Under the new government, he became the first chief justice of the United States, presiding over the Supreme Court during its first five formative years. His most important case was *Chisholm vs. Georgia*, in which he pointed out that the Constitution specifically gave a citizen of one state the right to sue another state, and that suability and state sovereignty were incompatible. This vigorous exposition of nationalism so alarmed several of the states that the 11th Amendment was quickly added to the Constitution.

Still chief justice, Jay was sent to dissipate the war crisis with Britain which arose in 1794 mainly over continuing occupation of the Northwest Posts and increasing British depredations on American commerce. Since Hamilton's new credit system depended on tariff revenue, and as nine-tenths of it came from British imports, the Federalists were determined to avert a British war and even to prevent adoption of a Republican-sponsored program of commercial retaliation which might have suspended all intercourse. Jay, undercut by disclosures made by Hamilton to the British minister at Philadelphia, eventually signed a treaty which failed to uphold America's neutral rights under international law and thereby led to a serious crisis with France. Jay's Treaty (1794), which might more appropriately be called Hamilton's Treaty, provided for the evacuation of the Northwest Posts and for the establishment of mixed claims commissions to dispose of other mutual grievances. Jay and his treaty were enormously unpopular, but the Senate ratified it and history has justified it as a necessary evil.

Jay returned home to find himself again drafted for another post, that of governor of New York. Nominated and elected *in absentia* in 1795, he served two terms, for a total of six years. He gave his state an upright, conservative administration and thereafter retired to private life, preferring not to involve himself in the imminent Federalist debacle of 1800. His last public act bore witness to his uncompromising moral rectitude. Knowing that the newly elected Republican legislature would choose Jeffersonian electors, Hamilton asked Jay to summon the expiring Federalist legislature to choose Federalists, but Jay merely noted on his friend's letter: "Proposing a measure for party purposes which I think it would not become me to adopt." An able man, but not a genius, he brought intellectual vigor and moral tone into every office which he held.

JAY, JOHN (*b. New York, N.Y., 1817; d. 1894*), lawyer. Grandson of John Jay (1745–1829). Active in the anti-slavery movement and civil-service reform; an organizer of the Republican party in New York. U.S. minister to Austria, 1869–74.

JAY, PETER AUGUSTUS (*b. Elizabeth Town, N.J., 1776; d. 1843*), New York lawyer. Son of John Jay (1745–1829); served him as secretary during 1794 mission to England.

JAY, WILLIAM (*b. New York, N.Y., 1789; d. 1858*), jurist. Son of John Jay (1745–1829). Active in anti-slavery and other reform movements. Author of *The Life of John Jay* (1833) and other books.

JAYNE, HORACE FORT (*b. Philadelphia, Pa., 1859; d. 1913*), biologist. Graduated M.D., University of Pennsylvania, 1882; studied at Leipzig and Jena. Heir to a patent medicine fortune, he was professor of biology, dean, and a benefactor of the University of Pennsylvania; also director, Wistar Institute, 1894–1904.

JEANES, ANNA T. (*b. near Philadelphia, Pa., 1822; d. 1907*), Quaker philanthropist. Among many other benefactions, established Negro Rural School Fund *c.* 1907.

JEFFERS, WILLIAM NICHOLSON (*b. Swedesboro, N.J., 1824; d. Washington, D.C., 1883*), naval officer, ordnance expert. Graduated Naval Academy, 1846. Commanded U.S.S. *Monitor* in James River operations

post Merrimac battle. Chief of Bureau of Ordnance, 1873–81.

JEFFERSON, CHARLES EDWARD (*b. Cambridge, O., 1860; d. Fitzwilliam, N.H., 1937*), Congregational clergyman. Pastor in Chelsea, Mass., and at Broadway Tabernacle Church, New York, 1898–1930. A conspicuous Protestant liberal. [*Supp. 2*]

JEFFERSON, JOSEPH (*b. Plymouth, England, 1774; d. Harrisburg, Pa., 1832*), actor. Came to America, 1795; made New York debut, 1796. A pillar of Philadelphia's Chestnut Street Theatre, 1803–30.

JEFFERSON, JOSEPH (*b. Philadelphia, Pa., 1829; d. Palm Beach, Fla., 1905*), actor. Grandson of Joseph Jefferson (1774–1832). Debut at Washington, D.C., 1833, with "Jim Crow" Rice. In 71 years on the stage, Jefferson gained fame and fortune and became one of the best-loved figures in American life. His genius as a comedian was instantly recognized with his first appearance as Rip in Boucicault's version of *Rip Van Winkle* in 1865. From that time until his death, Jefferson in *Rip Van Winkle* provided a practical ideal of dramatic entertainment drawn from native sources, and humor, pathos, even poetry, extracted from the common lot. He succeeded Edwin Booth as president of the Players' Club, 1893, and hence as America's premier actor. Among other parts in which he was celebrated were Asa Trenchard (*Our American Cousin*), Caleb Plummer (*The Cricket on the Hearth*) and Bob Acres (*The Rivals*).

JEFFERSON, THOMAS (*b. Goochland, now Albemarle, Co., Va., 1743; d. "Monticello," Albemarle Co., Va., 1826*), statesman, diplomat, author, scientist, architect, apostle of freedom and enlightenment.

Jefferson's father, Peter Jefferson, was of good stock but not wealthy; a surveyor, he had moved from Henrico Co. to Goochland, where he patented 1000 acres on the Rivanna River and by 1734 was a magistrate. He married Jane Randolph, first cousin of his friend William Randolph of "Tuckahoe," thus connecting himself with perhaps the most distinguished family of the province and assuring the social standing of his children. He helped Joshua Fry continue the boundary line between Virginia and North Carolina and with him made the first accurate map of Virginia. From his father, Jefferson doubtless acquired much of his zest for exploring and drawing.

Jefferson was tutored privately until 1760, when he entered the College of William and Mary, graduating 1762. There, Dr. William Small aroused the scientific interest which remained active all his life and introduced him to the "familiar table" of Gov. Francis Fauquier and to George Wythe, Virginia's most noted teacher of law, under whom Jefferson prepared himself for practice. A recognized and companionable member of the close-knit social group of the children of Virginia's great families, his natural seriousness soon asserted itself and he early formulated a stern code of personal conduct and disciplined himself to rigorous study habits. His legal preparation was thorough and, admitted to the bar in 1767, he was quite successful until he ceased practicing on the eve of the Revolution.

In 1772 Jefferson married Martha Wayles Skelton, a widow who, in their ten years of married life, bore him six children, of whom only three survived her and only two (Martha and Mary) reached maturity. Jefferson settled his bride at Monticello, the mountaintop home begun in 1770 and whose construction was to extend over a generation. The 5000 acres left him by his father were doubled in 1774, when he received from his father-in-law's estate holdings practically equivalent to his own. With these, however, came a huge debt from whose effects he never entirely escaped. All through his long lifetime he was most methodical in recording everything connected with his plantations.

Jefferson served in the House of Burgesses from 1769 until it ceased to function in 1775. Not an effective public speaker, he performed best in committees, employing his marked talents as a literary draftsman. A member of the aggressive anti-British group, he was active in creating the Virginia Committee of Correspondence and in subsequent anti-British moves of the House. His most notable contribution to the Revolutionary cause before 1776 was his *A Summary View of the Rights of British America,* composed for the Virginia convention of 1774 and containing his views regarding the colonies' relationship to England. Denying all parliamentary authority over the colonies, he insisted that the King, to whom the colonies had voluntarily submitted, supplied the only political tie with Great Britain. Emphasizing "rights as derived from the laws of nature," he advocated freedom of trade in articles Britain could not use and the relinquishment of all British claims in regard to taxation.

Sent to Congress by the Virginia convention in 1775, he was elected to the committee to draft a declaration of independence after the introduction of Richard Henry Lee's resolution on June 7, 1776. His reputation of a masterly pen was one reason for his selection as its major draftsman. John Adams and Franklin, and Congress itself, made changes in his draft of the Declaration, but its composition belongs indisputably to Jefferson. The doctrines are essentially those of John Locke, the source of current revolutionary philosophy. No believer in absolute equality, Jefferson believed in government by popular consent which would insure the inalienable rights of man, including the pursuit of happiness rather than of property as an end in itself. Notable for its clarity and felicity of expression, the Declaration is Jefferson's noblest literary monument.

In September 1776 Jefferson left Congress to further the "reformation" of Virginia and served in the House of Delegates from October 1776 until his election as governor in June 1779. He favored the end of the artificial aristocracy of wealth and birth and its replacement by one of talent and virtue, supported by an enlightened electorate. Assuming the leadership of the progressives in the House, he deserves the chief credit for an unparalleled program of reform and an almost unequaled record of legislative achievement. Succeeding in abolishing land-holding in fee-tail, he moved the revision of the laws. For two years he labored with a committee of five, eventually producing a report comprising 126 bills, of which at least 100 were eventually enacted in substance. Primogeniture was abolished in 1785 and his Bill for Establishing Religious Freedom, passed in 1786, he regarded as one of his greatest contributions to humanity. His educational bills were unsuccessful, but he may properly be termed the architect of Virginia government.

The qualities which accounted for Jefferson's preeminence as a legislative leader and prophet were of little avail as executive. Hesitant and reluctant in the exercise of authority, as war-governor he was also handicapped by constitutional limitations and the diminution of the state's resources. Re-elected in 1780, he managed well enough until the British invasion of Virginia in the spring of 1781. Early in June, he was succeeded in the governorship by Gen. Thomas Nelson after his virtual abdication. Meeting later at Staunton, the Assembly ordered an investigation of charges that he had been lacking in military precaution and expedition, but he was formally vindicated and a resolution of thanks finally adopted. Retired from public life, Jefferson found leisure to organize the memoranda concerning Virginia which he had made over many years. In 1782–83 he enlarged them; in 1785 the *Notes on the State of Virginia* were printed in France, laying the foundation of his fame as a universal scholar. Along with unbounded optimism regarding his country's future, his picture of 18th-century Virginia included strictures on slavery and on Virginia's government.

Seeking relief from the woe caused by the death of his wife, 1782, Jefferson accepted an appointment as peace commissioner to Europe. The mission became unnecessary, but the next year he was elected to Congress, where he performed notable service (advocated adoption of the dollar unit; anticipated Ordinance of 1787 in report of March 22, 1784) until appointed, 1784, to assist Franklin and Adams in Paris in negotiating treaties of commerce.

In 1785 Congress appointed Jefferson to succeed Franklin as U.S. minister to France. He unsuccessfully contended against French commercial exclusiveness, negotiated the Consular Convention of 1788, and reported home in detail on the course of the French Revolution till his departure in October 1789. Intimate and sympathetic with the moderate reformers, he deplored the violence of the Revolution's later phases but remained convinced that it had done more good than ill. He left Europe convinced of the value of American cultivation of France as a counterpoise to Britain, and believing that Britain and Spain could be made to pay for American neutrality in future European conflicts, from which therefore the United States would greatly benefit. From his observations abroad, he had gained an emotional stimulus and returned to his own country much strengthened in his civic faith.

Before he reached his beloved Monticello in December, Jefferson received Washington's offer of the secretaryship of state which, despite his distaste for political strife, he accepted on patriotic grounds. Although he regarded the government of the Confederation as "without comparison the best existing or that ever did exist," he favored the movement to strengthen it and approved the new Constitution, objecting mainly to the absence of a bill of rights, soon remedied. At first he strove to cooperate with Alexander Hamilton, who had already assumed first place among Washington's counselors, but he soon concluded that Hamilton was aiming at a monarchy. His subsequent statement that he was duped into trading approval of Hamilton's assumption policy for the location of the capital on the Potomac is unconvincing, as his contemporary letters show that he regarded some compromise as essential to peace and unity.

The first serious difference between Jefferson and Hamilton came over the use of commercial discrimination against Britain to force her to surrender the Northwest Posts and grant commercial privileges. Jefferson supported a movement to this end, led in Congress by James Madison; Hamilton's influence against the measure, based on his fear of losing revenue from British imports, defeated it. Soon after, at Washington's request, the two men presented opinions on the constitutionality of a national bank. Jefferson argued that Hamilton's bill assumed powers not enumerated by the Constitution and thus committed himself to a narrow and literal interpretation of that instrument which he later found in practice would have rendered the government feeble and inflexible. By mid-1792 the hostility between the two men, sharpened by Hamilton's constant interference in Jefferson's domain of foreign affairs, had become implacable. Hamilton published a series of ferocious anonymous attacks on his colleague in the newspapers. Jefferson's friends defended him, but he himself refrained from newspaper controversy. He probably had a part, however, in drafting the resolutions of William Branch Giles which were severely critical of Hamilton's conduct of the Treasury.

Jefferson's hostility to Hamilton stemmed from the conviction that the latter's system "flowed from principles adverse to liberty, and was calculated to undermine and demolish the republic, by creating an influence of his department over the members of the legislature." At the earnest insistence of George Washington, who valued and utilized both his subordinates, Jefferson agreed to remain in office only until the end of 1793. The outbreak of general war in Europe (Feb. 1793) brought a series of crises. Jefferson, like Washington and Hamilton, believed neutrality was imperative but was determined that his country should not oppose the principles of the French Revolution. He kept the word "neutrality" out of Washington's proclamation, April 1793, and persuaded the president to receive the new French minister Edmond Genet without qualification, though he agreed with Hamilton in refusing to anticipate payments on the debt to France. He welcomed Genet and rejoiced in the popular enthusiasm for democracy which Genet kindled; he came near conniving in the Frenchman's projected expeditions against Louisiana. Eventually, however, he lost patience with Genet and joined in asking his recall. He failed to solve the problems of British relations and pronounced the subsequent Hamilton-inspired Jay Treaty an ignominious surrender of American rights. Equally unsuccessful in negotiations with Spain, the objectives he sought were attained in the treaty of 1795.

Believing his second retirement (Dec. 31, 1793) final, Jefferson devoted himself to the continual improvement of Monticello and to agriculture. Early in 1795 he told Madison that the "little spice of ambition" he once had was gone, but he remained the symbol of anti-Hamilton and Republican political faith and did not refuse the presidential nomination in 1796. He would serve if elected so as "to put our vessel on her republican tack before she should be thrown too much to leeward of her true principles." He was surprisingly content to run second to Adams in the presidential race, whom perhaps he regarded as the only barrier to Hamilton. The vice-president's salary, which he undoubtedly needed, and the relative leisure the position afforded, were welcome but he played no part in the administration, which Hamilton continued to dominate.

Federalists continued to regard him as the personification of the Republican party and seized every opportunity, notably the "Mazzei letter" incident (1797), to vilify him. He approved Monroe's conduct in France and privately condemned the "X.Y.Z. frenzy," which the Federalists aggravated to discredit the Republicans. When the Alien and Sedition Acts were passed, menacing his most cherished ideals, he drafted the Kentucky Resolutions of 1798 while Madison supplied similar resolutions in Virginia. Though the constitutional doctrines contained in the famous Resolutions later gave comfort to proponents of nullification, their purpose was to denounce the offensive laws as an unconstitutional attack upon individual freedom. In fact, they constituted a somewhat extravagant party platform, pointing to the coming election.

Federalist dissensions contributed to a Republican victory in 1800, to which Jefferson was anything but indifferent. Due to the electoral machinery, he and Aaron Burr received an identical vote, but the Federalist House eventually yielded to Republican preference and to its own grudging feeling that Jefferson was the safer man and elected him president. His election, variously interpreted since then, was immediately significant by its vindication of political opposition and its repudiation of a reactionary regime. Walking from his boarding-house to the uncompleted Capitol to take the oath of office from his cousin and inveterate political foe, Chief Justice John Marshall, Jefferson felt that the danger of monarchy was now removed; his benevolent first inaugural address wooed the more moderate Federalists into acceptance of the majority will. In keeping with his views of the negative function of government, he lived in the Executive Mansion in sartorial indifference and dispensed generous but informal hospitality, to the consternation of tradition-bound diplomats.

Madison, the secretary of state, and Albert Gallatin, who as secretary of the treasury carried out his economy program with considerable success, were his chief collaborators. It was to Robert R. Livingston and Monroe that Jefferson gave chief credit for the outstanding accomplishment of his administration, the purchase of Louisiana, 1803. Hearing of the retrocession of Louisiana to France by Spain, Jefferson had written to Livingston that the possessor of New Orleans was the natural enemy of the United States and even felt compelled to consider a rapprochement with Britain in order to preserve the open navigation on the Mississippi which was secured by the purchase. The problem of constitutional powers bothered him, for he was aware that broad construction of the Constitution would void a major safe-guard against tyranny, but overwhelming public approval crowned his pragmatic statesmanship. Aware of inconsistency in this matter, he seems to have viewed the achievement with little pride. His handling of the Florida question was inept and diminished his influence on Congress; on the other hand, he acted with force and success against the Barbary powers.

Triumphantly re-elected, 1804, the difficulties facing Jefferson in his second administration as a neutral during a ruthless European war were probably unsolvable. After 1805, the United States stood in an intolerable position between British Orders in Council and Napoleonic decrees. Even after the *Chesapeake* incident, 1807, Jefferson remained committed to peaceful diplomacy and economic coercion to maintain American rights. The Embargo (December 1807) and the Non-Importation Act, however, though daring measures, were practical failures. Convinced that the Embargo had not received a fair trial, he nevertheless yielded to a rebellious Congress and signed the Non-Intercourse Act, March 1, 1809, just before he left office.

During the remaining years of his life, spent in continuing financial stringency, Jefferson never ventured far from Monticello, maintaining a voluminous correspondence with friends in America and Europe, where his reputation as a patron of learning continued high, and devoting much time to promoting popular education, which he regarded as a guarantor of freedom. He tirelessly promoted a liberal, modern university for his "country," Virginia, and attended every stage of the formation of the University of Virginia with a paternal care. Upon his death, appropriately on the fiftieth anniversary of the Declaration of Independence, this most enigmatic and probably most versatile of great Americans was buried at Monticello, under a stone describing him as he wished to be remembered—as the author of the Declaration of Independence and the Virginia statute for religious freedom, and the father of the University of Virginia.

The popularity and political success of Jefferson, whose diffidence and lack of spectacular qualities would have constituted in a later day an insuperable handicap, and whose relative freedom from personal ambition makes it impossible to characterize him as a demagogue, was due in part to his identification of himself with causes for which time was fighting, and also to his remarkable sensitiveness to fluctuations in public opinion, combined with an ability to utilize and to develop agencies of popular appeal. As a practical politician he worked through other men, whom he energized and who gave him to an extraordinary degree their devoted cooperation. His unchallenged leadership was due, not to self-assertiveness and imperiousness of will, but to the fact that circumstances had made him a symbolic figure, and that to an acute intelligence and unceasing industry he joined a dauntless and contagious faith.

Over the course of his public life this earnest advocate of a free press was one of its principal victims. Long regarded in ecclesiastical circles, especially in New England, as the embodiment of foreign infidelity, he was also charged by the Federalist press with cowardice, drunkenness, sexual immorality and plain dishonesty. These largely groundless charges were widely believed, especially by the "better sort of people." In fact, Jefferson was anything but an infidel and had he lived a generation later would have been more at home in New England liberal religious circles than anywhere else in America.

During his lifetime Jefferson received international honors for scholarship. Although much of this was owing to his political prominence, he could properly claim the reputation of scholar. He served as president of the American Philosophical Society from 1797 until 1815. Modern scholars have recognized Jefferson as an American pioneer in numerous branches of science, notably paleontology, ethnology, geography, and botany. Living before the age of specialization, he was for his day a careful investigator, no more credulous than his learned contemporaries, and notable among them for his effort in all fields to attain scientific exactitude. In state papers he is commonly the lawyer, pleading a cause; in the heat of political controversy he doubtless compromised his intellectual ideals and certainly indulged in exaggeration; but his procedure in arriving at his fundamental opinions, the habits of his life, and his temperament were essentially those of a scholar. As secretary of state, he was in effect the first commissioner of patents and the first patent examiner. He himself invented or adapted to personal uses numerous ingenious devices, the best known of which is his polygraph.

He was at home in French, Italian, and Spanish, as well as Greek and Latin. He owned one of the best private collections of paintings and statuary in the country, and has been termed "the first American connoisseur and patron of the arts." Besides the Virginia state capitol, "Monticello," and the original buildings of the University of Virginia, he designed wholly or in part numerous Virginia houses, among them his own "Poplar Forest," "Farmington," "Edgemont," "Barboursville," and perhaps the middle section of "Brandon." Before the advent of professional architects in America, he began to collect books on architecture and discovered Palladio, from whom his careful and extensive observations abroad never weaned him. He did more than any other man to stimulate the classical revival in America. His own work, while always ingenious, is academic, precise, and orderly, but, because of the fortunate necessity of using brick and wood, the new creation was a blend, with a pleasing domesticity.

Few other American statesmen have been such careful and unremitting students of political thought and history as was Jefferson, or have been more concerned with ultimate ends. Yet he has left no treatise on political philosophy, and all general statements about his theoretical position are subject to qualification. It is impossible to grant eternal validity to the "principles" adduced by him to support his position in particular circumstances; he was always more interested in applications than in speculation, and he was forced to modify his own philosophy in practice. A homely aristocrat in manner of life and personal tastes, he distrusted all rulers and feared the rise of an industrial proletariat, but, more than any of his eminent contemporaries, he trusted the common man, if measurably enlightened and kept in rural virtue. Although pained and angered when the press made him the victim of its license, he was a passionate advocate of human liberty and laid supreme stress on the individual. Although he clearly realized the value of union, he emphasized the importance of the states and of local agencies of government. An intellectual internationalist, he gave whole-hearted support to the policy of political isolation, and anticipated the development on the North American continent of a dominant nation, unique in civilization. He is notable, not for his harmony with the life of his age, but rather for his being a step or several steps ahead of it; no other American more deserves to be termed a major prophet, a supreme pioneer. A philosophical statesman rather than a political philosopher, he contributed to democracy and liberalism a faith rather than a body of doctrine.

JEFFERY, EDWARD TURNER (*b. Liverpool, England, 1843; d. New York, N.Y., 1927*), railroad executive. Came to America as a child. General manager, Illinois Central; controversial president, Denver & Rio Grande, 1891–1912; involved in Western Pacific fiasco, 1905–13.

JEFFREY, JOSEPH ANDREW (*b. Clarksville, O., 1836; d. Columbus, O., 1928*), banker, manufacturer of coal-mining machinery.

JEFFREY, ROSA GRIFFITH VERTNER JOHNSON (*b. Natchez, Miss., 1828; d. Lexington, Ky., 1894*), poet, novelist.

JEFFRIES, BENJAMIN JOY (*b. Boston, Mass., 1833; d. 1915*), ophthalmic surgeon. Grandson of John Jeffries. Writer of a treatise on color blindness (1879) which was long the standard authority.

JEFFRIES, JOHN (*b. Boston, Mass., 1744/45; d. 1819*), physician, scientist. Graduated Harvard, 1763; M.D., Aberdeen, 1770. A Loyalist with service on the British side during the Revolution, he became interested in aerostation while in England c. 1782–90, and made two balloon ascents with the French aeronaut Blanchard. The first was over London, November 1784; the second carried him across the English Channel, January 1785. Jeffries made observations of temperature, pressure, and humidity, constituting the first scientific data of the free air, to a height of 9309 feet. He returned to Boston c. 1790 where he practiced medicine.

JEMISON, MARY (*b. at sea, en route to Philadelphia from Belfast, 1743; d. Buffalo Creek Reservation, N.Y., 1833*), "the White Woman of the Genesee." Was captured in Pennsylvania and adopted by Indians, 1758. In 1762 she was taken to the Seneca tribal home on the Genesee River near present Geneseo, N.Y. Twice married to Indians, in 1797 she was granted a large tract of land near Castile, N.Y.; her land-title was confirmed by the New York legislature, 1817, when she was also naturalized. One of the most extensive landholders in the region, she became a tradition in western New York, largely through publication of her story as told to James Everett Seaver. *A Narrative of the Life of Mrs. Mary Jemison* (1824) was one of the most popular Indian "captivities."

JENCKES, JOSEPH. [See JENKS, JOSEPH, 1602–1683.]

JENCKES, JOSEPH (*b. probably near Hammersmith, England, 1632; d. 1717*), founder of Pawtucket, pioneer iron manufacturer of Rhode Island. Came to America c. 1650. Set up sawmill and forge near Pawtucket Falls, 1671. Son of Joseph Jenks.

JENCKES, JOSEPH (*b. Pawtucket, R.I., 1656; d. 1740*), surveyor. Son of Joseph Jenckes (1632–1717).

Deputy governor of Rhode Island, 1715–27; governor, 1727–31. Opposed excessive issue of paper currency.

JENCKES, THOMAS ALLEN (*b. Cumberland, R.I., 1818; d. 1875*), jurist, Rhode Island legislator. Graduated Brown, 1838; rose rapidly in the field of patent litigation. Congressman, Republican, from Rhode Island, 1863–71. Among the earliest proponents of civil-service reform, he successfully campaigned for a national bankruptcy law, and initiated competitive examinations for admission to West Point.

JENIFER, DANIEL OF ST. THOMAS (*b. Charles Co., Md., 1723; d. Annapolis, Md., 1790*), Maryland political leader. Nephew of John Hanson. Held many colonial offices; active in Revolutionary cause; member, Continental Congress, 1778–82. Played minor part in Federal Convention, 1787; advocated three year term for members of the national House of Representatives.

JENKINS, ALBERT GALLATIN (*b. Cabell Co., Va., now W. Va., 1830; d. near Cloyd's Mountain, Va., 1864*), lawyer, farmer. Congressman, Democrat, from Virginia, 1857–61. As Confederate brigadier-general, commanded cavalry raid into Ohio, August–September 1862. Died as result of surgery after a severe wound.

JENKINS, CHARLES JONES (*b. Beaufort District, S.C., 1805; d. 1883*), jurist, Georgia legislator. Governor of Georgia, 1865–68. Removed for refusing compliance with Reconstruction acts of 1867.

JENKINS, EDWARD HOPKINS (*b. Falmouth, Mass., 1850; d. New Haven, Conn., 1931*), agricultural chemist. Graduated Yale, 1872; Ph.D., 1879; studied also in Germany. Introduced shade-grown tobacco into Northern states among other achievements during lifelong association with Connecticut Agricultural Experiment Station.

JENKINS, HOWARD MALCOLM (*b. Gwynedd, Pa., 1842; d. 1902*), newspaper editor, historical writer. As editor-in-chief of the *Friends' Intelligencer*, became a distinguished Quaker leader. Wrote extensively on Pennsylvania history.

JENKINS, JAMES GRAHAM (*b. Saratoga Springs, N.Y., 1834; d. Milwaukee, Wis., 1921*), lawyer. Grandson of Reuben H. Walworth. Moved to Milwaukee, 1857, soon after his admission to the bar. A Democratic leader in Wisconsin, he served as U.S. district judge, eastern district of Wisconsin, 1888–93, and as U.S. circuit judge, 1893–1905. His name is associated with two important cases: *Pillsbury vs. Pillsbury Washburn Company, Ltd.*, in which his decision involving unfair competition remains a landmark of American jurisprudence; and the so-called Northern Pacific receivership (*Farmers Loan and Trust Co. vs. Northern Pacific*), in which a strike order he granted, later affirmed by the Supreme Court, involved him in a controversy with Congress. He was dean of the law school, Marquette University, 1908–15.

JENKINS, JOHN (*b. probably East Greenwich, Conn., 1728; d. Orange Co., N.Y., 1785*), pioneer, surveyor. Leading spirit in efforts by Susquehanna Co. of Connecticut to settle Wyoming Valley in Pennsylvania, 1762–69. Driven from the valley, 1778.

JENKINS, JOHN (*b. New London, Conn., 1751 o.s.; d. Exeter, Pa., 1827*), Revolutionary soldier, pioneer, surveyor. Son of John Jenkins (1728–1785). Leader of the Connecticut settlers of the Wyoming Valley after his father's retirement. Helped plan Gen. Sullivan's campaign against the Indians, 1779.

JENKINS, JOHN STILWELL (*b. Albany, N.Y., 1818; d. Syracuse, N.Y., 1852*), lawyer, newspaper editor. Compiled many historical popularizations and abridgments of longer works.

JENKINS, MICAH (*b. Edisto Island, S.C., 1835; d. 1864*), Confederate soldier. Commanded 5th South Carolina and Palmetto Sharpshooters; promoted brigadier-general, 1862; commanded Hood's division at Chickamauga; killed at the Wilderness.

JENKINS, NATHANIEL (*b. Boston, Mass., 1812; d. 1872*), inventor, manufacturer. Developed rubber compound packing for water faucets, steam valves; invented the Jenkins valve (patented 1868).

JENKINS, THORNTON ALEXANDER (*b. Orange Co., Va., 1811; d. 1893*), naval officer, lighthouse expert. Chief, Bureau of Navigation, 1865–69. Commanded U.S.S. *Hartford* at Port Hudson, March 1863; retired as rear-admiral, 1873.

JENKS, GEORGE CHARLES (*b. London, England, 1850; d. 1929*), journalist. Came to America, 1872. As writer of dime novels *post* 1886, was one of group which produced the endless adventures of Nick Carter and Diamond Dick.

JENKS, JEREMIAH WHIPPLE (*b. St. Clair, Mich., 1856; d. New York, N.Y., 1929*), economist, teacher. Graduated University of Michigan, 1878; Ph.D., Halle, 1885. Taught at Indiana, Cornell and New York universities. First American academic economist to serve extensively on government boards and commissions, Jenks was influential in shaping legislation on trusts, immigration, and the white-slave trade; he also advised foreign governments on currency and other economic problems.

JENKS, JOSEPH (*b. probably Colnbrook, England, 1602; d. Saugus, Mass., 1683 n.s.*), inventor. Father of Joseph Jenckes (1632–1717). A skilled iron-worker, Jenks was induced to come to America, 1642, to assist in establishing the first iron works near Lynn, Mass., but he soon occupied himself with original projects. His reputation caused his selection to cut dies for the first coins minted in Boston and to build the first fire engine. In his own forge, Jenks in 1655 produced a scythe of a new, improved type which has long remained standard.

JENKS, TUDOR STORRS (*b. Brooklyn, N.Y., 1857; d. 1922*), lawyer. Author of a large number of juvenile books; associate editor of *St. Nicholas*, 1887–1902.

JENKS, WILLIAM (*b. Newton, Mass., 1778; d. 1866*), Congregational clergyman, antiquarian. Graduated Harvard, 1797. Pastor in Bath, Maine; later, a Boston pioneer in religious work among seamen. An outstanding Biblical and Oriental scholar, he was author of *Comprehensive Commentary on the Holy Bible* (1835–1838) and other works.

JENNEY, WILLIAM LE BARON (*b. Fairhaven, Mass., 1832; d. Los Angeles, Calif., 1907*), architect, inventor, Union soldier. Studied art and architecture in France. After serving as an engineer throughout the Civil War on staffs of Generals Grant and Sherman, he established himself in Chicago as an architect, 1868. For the Home Insurance Building in Chicago, he devised a method of skeleton construction in which each story was carried independently on columns. This building (1883–84) was the first high building to use such a method as the basic principle of its design; as such it was the first skyscraper. Jenney also introduced the use of Bessemer steel beams in building construction.

JENNINGS, JAMES HENNEN (*b. Hawesville, Ky., 1854; d. 1920*), mining engineer. Graduated Lawrence Scientific School, 1877. Instituted the cyanide process for recovering gold which made South Africa's Rand district profitable.

JENNINGS, JOHN (*b. probably Philadelphia, Pa., c. 1738; d. Philadelphia, 1802*), public official, Revolutionary soldier. A prominent figure in the Pennamite War in Pennsylvania against settlers from Connecticut, 1761 and 1769.

JENNINGS, JONATHAN (*b. either Hunterdon Co., N.J., or Rockbridge Co., Va., 1784; d. near Charlestown, Ind., 1834*), lawyer. Removed to Northwest Territory, 1806. Territorial delegate to Congress from Indiana, 1809–15; first governor of Indiana, 1816–22; congressman, 1823–31.

JEROME, CHAUNCEY (*b. Canaan, Conn., 1793; d. 1868*), clock maker, inventor. Devised the "bronze looking-glass clock" *c.* 1825; invented a one-day brass clock movement *c.* 1838.

JEROME, WILLIAM TRAVERS (*b. New York, N.Y., 1859; d. New York, 1934*), lawyer. Anti-Tammany foe of corruption; assistant to J. W. Goff, 1894; controversial and unconventional but effective district attorney in New York City, 1901–09. [Supp. 1]

JERVIS, JOHN BLOOMFIELD (*b. Huntington, N.Y., 1795; d. Rome, N.Y., 1885*), engineer. Began his career on the survey for the Erie Canal, rising rapidly to section engineer and then superintendent. Became associated with the projected Delaware & Hudson canal and railway system, 1825; built the railroad, drawing up the specifications for all equipment including the first locomotive to run in America. This was the "Stourbridge Lion," tested Aug. 1829. For the Mohawk & Hudson Railway, he invented the four-wheel, "bogie" truck used on the locomotive "Experiment," 1832. As chief engineer of the Chenango (N.Y.) Canal, he did original work in determining the amount of rainfall available to supply artificial reservoirs for the upper levels. He was chief engineer of the Croton Aqueduct and consulting engineer for the Boston water supply; he also directed construction of the Hudson River Railroad, the Michigan Southern, the Chicago & Rock Island and others.

JESSE, RICHARD HENRY (*b. Lancaster Co., Va., 1853; d. 1921*), educator. Graduated University of Virginia, 1875. Taught at Tulane. President of University of Missouri, 1891–1907, where he established pioneer schools of education and journalism.

JESSUP, HENRY HARRIS (*b. Montrose, Pa., 1832; d. Beirut, Syria, now Lebanon, 1910*), Presbyterian missionary to Syria, 1855–1910. A founder of the present American University of Beirut, 1866.

JESUP, MORRIS KETCHUM (*b. Westport, Conn., 1830; d. 1908*), capitalist, philanthropist. Made his fortune in New York City in banking before retiring in 1884 to sponsor philanthropies. An original incorporator of the American Museum of Natural History (1868) in which he was primarily interested, he gave it a total of $2,000,000 and supported many of its scientific investigations. He contributed to Peary's discovery of the North Pole, aided the New York conservation movement which resulted in the Adirondack Preserve, was a supporter of the Audubon Society, and gave assistance to many educational institutions, particularly the American University at Beirut and the Union Theological Seminary in New York.

JESUP, THOMAS SIDNEY (*b. Berkeley Co., Va., now W. Va., 1788; d. Washington, D.C., 1860*), soldier. Entered the U.S. Army, 1808; served with distinction in War of 1812. In December 1814 he was sent to Connecticut to watch the Hartford Convention and was able to dispel President Madison's fears concerning secession. In 1818 he began an unequaled 42 years as quartermaster-general of the army and soon organized that department on a sound military and business basis. His service as quartermaster-general was interrupted during the Seminole War by field commands, 1836–38; he was wounded in 1838. Resuming his duties in Washington, he served until his death. *Post* 1828, he held rank of major-general.

JETER, JEREMIAH BELL (*b. Bedford Co., Va., 1802; d. 1880*), Baptist clergyman, editor. Pastor in Richmond, Va., 1836–49, 1852–70. A leader in organizing the Southern Baptist Convention, 1845.

JEWELL, HARVEY (*b. Winchester, N.H., 1820; d. 1881*), lawyer. Brother of Marshall Jewell. Whig and Republican leader in Massachusetts; appointed by

President Grant to Court of Commissioners of Alabama Claims (1875–76); practiced in Boston.

JEWELL, MARSHALL (*b. Winchester, N.H., 1825; d. 1883*), leather belting manufacturer, capitalist. Brother of Harvey Jewell. Republican governor of Connecticut, 1869–70; 1871–73. U.S. minister to Russia, 1873–74; efficient U.S. postmaster-general, 1874–76.

JEWETT, CHARLES COFFIN (*b. Lebanon, Maine, 1816; d. Braintree, Mass., 1868*), bibliographer, librarian. Brother of John P. Jewett. Published first extended collection of statistics on American libraries at Smithsonian Institution, 1851; projected a union catalogue, 1852; directed Boston Public Library, 1858–68.

JEWETT, CLARENCE FREDERICK (*b. Claremont, N.H., 1852; d. New York, N.Y., 1909*), projector of historical works. Best known for fostering Justin Winsor's *Narrative and Critical History of America* (1886–1889).

JEWETT, DAVID (*b. New London, Conn., 1772; d. 1842*), naval officer. Served in U.S. Navy, 1799–1801; entered Argentine service, 1815; *post* 1822 was in naval service of Brazil.

JEWETT, HUGH JUDGE (*b. Harford Co., Md., 1817; d. Augusta, Ga., 1898*), lawyer, Ohio legislator. Held executive posts in various Midwestern railroads; successful reorganizer of the Erie, 1874–84.

JEWETT, JOHN PUNCHARD (*b. Lebanon, Maine, 1814; d. Orange, N.J., 1884*), publisher. Brother of Charles C. Jewett. An Abolitionist, he brought out *Uncle Tom's Cabin* in book form, 1852, but was thereafter relatively unsuccessful.

JEWETT, MILO PARKER (*b. St. Johnsbury, Vt., 1808; d. 1882*), educational pioneer. Graduated Dartmouth, 1828. Largely responsible for the establishment of Vassar College, of which he was first president, 1861–67. Thereafter he served in several Wisconsin educational posts.

JEWETT, SARAH ORNE (*b. South Berwick, Maine, 1849; d. 1909*), author. Taught by her father to observe every detail of her surroundings, she possessed at the outset of her career an almost complete knowledge of her environment. Beginning with her first real success, *Deephaven* (1877), and continuing to the classic *The Country of the Pointed Firs* (1896), she gave permanence through her writings to a disappearing order of New England, the remote provincial life which had lingered a few years after the dissolution of the West Indian trade before being engulfed by the new civilization of smoke and steam. The artistic discipline displayed in her sketches of villages and villagers is possibly the most impressive quality in her achievement.

JEWETT, WILLIAM (*b. East Haddam, Conn., 1792; d. Jersey City, N.J., 1874*), portrait painter. Worked in partnership with his teacher, Samuel L. Waldo.

JEWETT, WILLIAM CORNELL (*b. New York, N.Y., 1823; d. Geneva, Switzerland, 1893*), publicist. Known as "Colorado Jewett." Gained notoriety by his efforts to end the Civil War through European intervention; arranged Niagara Falls meeting between Horace Greeley and Confederate commissioner J. P. Holcombe, July 1864.

JOCELYN, NATHANIEL (*b. New Haven, Conn., 1796; d. 1881*), portrait painter, bank-note engraver. Teacher of, among others, Thomas Rossiter and William O. Stone.

JOGUES, ISAAC (*b. Orleans, France, 1607; d. Ossernenon, now Auriesville, N.Y., 1646*), Jesuit missionary, martyr. Came to Canada, 1636. Began mission among Huron Indians on Georgian Bay. Captured by hostile Iroquois, 1642, together with René Goupil, he was tortured and kept a slave for a year, until rescued by the Dutch at Fort Orange. Repatriated to France, he was honored by the queen regent and the pope, but soon returned to his labors in Canada. After visiting the Iroquois as an ambassador of the governor, he obtained permission to undertake a mission to the Mohawks, who killed him on his arrival at one of their villages. He was beatified, 1925; canonized, 1930.

JOHNS, CLAYTON (*b. New Castle, Del., 1857; d. Boston, Mass., 1932*), composer. Prominent in music circles of Boston. [*Supp. 1*]

JOHNS, JOHN (*b. New Castle, Del., 1796; d. 1876*), Episcopal clergyman. Son of Kensey Johns (1759–1848). Graduated Princeton, 1815; ordained, 1819; pastor at Frederick and Baltimore, Md. Assistant bishop of Virginia, 1842–62; bishop, 1862–76. President of College of William and Mary, 1849–54.

JOHNS, KENSEY (*b. West River, Md., 1759; d. 1848*), Delaware jurist. Studied law with Samuel Chase and George Read. Served, 1799–1830, as chief justice of the supreme court of Delaware; was chancellor, 1830–32.

JOHNS, KENSEY (*b. New Castle, Del., 1791; d. Sussex, Del., 1857*), Delaware jurist, congressman. Son of Kensey John (1759–1848). Graduated Princeton, 1810; studied law with his uncle Nicholas Van Dyke. Chancellor of Delaware, 1832–57.

JOHNSEN, ERIK KRISTIAN (*b. near Stavanger, Norway, 1863; d. St. Paul, Minn., 1923*), Lutheran theologian. Came to America, 1892. Professor at Red Wing Seminary; and at Luther Theological Seminary, St. Paul, Minn., 1900–23.

JOHNSON, ALEXANDER BRYAN (*b. Gosport, England, 1786; d. 1867*), Utica, N.Y., banker. Came to America, 1801. Wrote extensively on a variety of subjects ranging from religion to finance.

499

JOHNSON, ALEXANDER SMITH (*b. Utica, N.Y., 1817; d. Nassau, Bahama Islands, 1878*), New York jurist. Son of Alexander B. Johnson. Held several state and federal judicial posts, including U.S. circuit judge, 2nd Judicial Circuit, 1875–78.

JOHNSON, ALLEN (*b. Lowell, Mass., 1870; d. Washington, D.C., 1931*), teacher and writer of history, biographer. Graduated Amherst, 1892; Ph.D., Columbia, 1899. Studied also at Leipzig and Paris. Editor of the *Chronicles of America* (1918–1921) and first editor of the *Dictionary of American Biography*. Professor of history at Grinnell College, Bowdoin, and Yale.

JOHNSON, ANDREW (*b. Raleigh, N.C., 1808; d. near Carter Station, Tenn., 1875*), seventeenth president of the United States. The younger son of a bank porter and sexton who died leaving his sons in poverty, Johnson removed to Tennessee, 1826; settled finally at Greeneville, Tenn. Self-educated, ambitious, he gradually accumulated a small estate by thrift in his management of the tailor shop he established. Neat in appearance and courteous, he was a powerful speaker, though in his early years often crude in thought and diction.

Championship of the working men of Greeneville against the aristocratic element brought about Johnson's election as alderman and then mayor. Beginning in 1835, he was successively representative to the Tennessee legislature; state senator; Democratic congressman, 1843–53; governor of Tennessee, 1853–57, and U.S. senator, 1857–62. Johnson's ability rather than the support of others advanced him; although a Jacksonian Democrat who nearly always voted with his party, Johnson quarreled with so many Democratic leaders that he lacked friends.

Johnson favored a change to the "white basis" of representation instead of the standard count of five slaves as three whites (East Tennessee had relatively few slaves) and supported the formation of East Tennessee into a new state. Yet he claimed orthodoxy regarding slavery and frequently denounced the Abolitionists. He favored the election of federal judges and of senators by popular vote, and the abolition of the electoral college in presidential elections. He became the special advocate of the "homestead" law for the granting of public lands to actual settlers, skillfully appealing to the interest of the laboring classes of the East as well as the frontier states. Throughout his life, he manifested a strong dislike of superiority claimed by right of wealth or birth and was a consistent friend of labor.

In 1860, the Tennessee delegation presented Johnson's name for the presidential nomination. After the split in the Democratic party, he supported Breckinridge and Lane, while favoring compromise between North and South. While the South Carolina secession convention was meeting in December 1860, Johnson declared for the Union in the Senate; when the other

Southern senators withdrew, he alone remained. The North at once welcomed him as a powerful ally in the tradition of Jackson, while Southern extremists denounced him as a traitor. In the special session of July 1861, Johnson introduced a successful resolution declaring the war to be only for the defense and maintenance of the supremacy of the Constitution and the Union. During the following winter, he devoted much time to the joint committee on conduct of the war.

Early in 1862, President Lincoln appointed Johnson military governor of Tennessee, which was in Confederate hands with Unionist East Tennessee overrun by Confederates and under martial law. After Grant's victories in secessionist West Tennessee, Johnson began his efforts at reconstruction. Constantly at odds with Union military authorities, he succeeded in restoring civil government by state action after the defeat of the Confederate armies. By 1865, a constitutional convention adopted amendments abolishing slavery which were later ratified by popular vote. Meanwhile, in recognition of the services of Southern Unionists and to help relieve the party of its sectional character, the National Union Convention nominated Johnson as Lincoln's vice-presidential running mate, 1864. Exhaustion and ill health were responsible for Johnson's being under the influence of liquor when he took the oath of office, giving malice something later to feed upon. The day after Lincoln's assassination, April 15, 1865, Johnson took the oath of office and announced that he would retain Lincoln's cabinet and continue Lincoln's policies.

At first Johnson shared the vindictive Northern rage at the assassination, reportedly stating: "Treason must be made infamous, and traitors must be impoverished." Soon freed of hysteria, however, Johnson began to execute Lincoln's plan for re-establishing government in the states that had seceded. He issued a general proclamation of amnesty, excepting 14 classes of persons requiring special pardons; he also issued a proclamation for the establishment of loyal government in North Carolina and followed it by similar proclamations for other of the seceded states. Supervised by Johnson's provisional governors, elections for state conventions were held, new constitutions adopted, and state governments organized through the legislatures. Ordinances of secession were repealed, slavery abolished, the 13th Amendment ratified by all Southern states except Mississippi, and Confederate state debts repudiated. The extension of suffrage to the Negro was left a power belonging exclusively to the states.

Johnson addressed Congress in December 1865 in a conciliatory spirit, holding that acts of secession had been null and void and that the Southern states should be invited back into the Union, their ratification of the 13th Amendment serving as a pledge of perpetual loyalty and peace. But some radical Republican congressmen led by Thaddeus Stevens, who believed that the Southern states should rejoin the Union as new states or remain conquered provinces, were determined to block Johnson's plan. Stevens secured the establishment of the joint committee of 15—the "Central Directory" of the radicals—which was to dominate Reconstruction and institute reform by force.

The war-expanded power of the executive, altruistic concern for the freedmen, and the threat to the Republican party's control of the government by the return of larger Democratic representations to Congress from the Southern states, all combined to make inevitable a struggle between Congress and a president who was a Southerner and a state-rights Democrat. The Civil Rights Act, designed to provide federal protection of the civil rights of freedmen, was passed over Johnson's veto, April 9, 1866, and was followed by the 14th Amendment. Strengthened in the elections of 1866, the radicals passed over the president's veto the Reconstruction Act of 1867 and a succession of supplementary acts, including a Tenure of Office Act forbidding the president to remove any Senate-approved office holder without the Senate's concurrence.

During a congressional recess in August 1867, Johnson defied the Tenure of Office Act by attempting to oust War Secretary E. M. Stanton, the radicals' informer and adviser within the president's cabinet. The attempt failed, an effort to secure a judicial test of the Act miscarried and the radicals used the incident to introduce impeachment proceedings against Johnson by the House of Representatives. With Chief Justice Chase presiding, the Senate, sitting as a court of impeachment, began the president's trial, since characterized as a "solemn theatrical fiasco," in March 1868. Attorney-general Stanbery had resigned his post to lead Johnson's defense, while the notorious Gen. Ben Butler and Thaddeus Stevens played leading parts for the prosecution. Impeachment failed in May by one vote (35–19), seven Republicans voting with the Democrats.

The National Union Republican convention had already nominated Gen. U. S. Grant as its presidential candidate and Johnson had made no effort to secure the Democratic nomination, though he received 65 votes on the first ballot. Returning to Tennessee after a bitter valedictory on leaving office, March 1869, Johnson was drawn again into state politics and in 1874 became a successful candidate for the U.S. Senate. He returned to the Senate on March 5, 1875, but within five months suffered a fatal paralytic attack while visiting a daughter in Tennessee. His last public utterance was a Senate speech in which he attacked Grant's Reconstruction policies in Louisiana and closed with the plea: "Let peace and prosperity be restored to the land. May God bless this people; may God save the Constitution."

JOHNSON, BENJAMIN PIERCE (*b. Canaan, N.Y., 1793; d. 1869*), lawyer, agriculturist. Long-time of-

ficer of New York State Agricultural Society and representative of that state at international exhibitions.

JOHNSON, BRADLEY TYLER (*b. Frederick, Md., 1829; d. Amelia, Va., 1903*), lawyer, Virginia legislator, Confederate brigadier-general of cavalry. Practiced law in Richmond, Va., and Baltimore, Md., after the Civil War.

JOHNSON, BUSHROD RUST (*b. Belmont Co., O., 1817; d. Brighton, Ill., 1880*), educator, soldier. Graduated West Point, 1840. As Confederate brigadier-general, commanded at Fort Henry; escaped after fall of Fort Donelson. Distinguished at Chickamauga and in defense of Richmond, 1864–65.

JOHNSON, BYRON BANCROFT (*b. Norwalk, O., 1864; d. St. Louis, Mo., 1931*). President of the American League of Professional Base Ball Clubs, 1900–27; established World Series.

JOHNSON, CAVE (*b. near Springfield, Tenn., 1793; d. Clarksville, Tenn., 1866*), lawyer. Congressman, Democrat, from Tennessee, 1829–37, 1839–45. Postmaster-general, 1845–49, under President Polk, to whom he was confidential friend and adviser; introduced use of postage stamps. Active in support of James Buchanan for presidency.

JOHNSON, CHAPMAN (*b. Louisa Co., Va., 1779; d. Richmond, Va., 1849*), Virginia lawyer and legislator. Championed democratic western against aristocratic eastern Virginia in constitutional convention, 1829–30.

JOHNSON, DAVID BANCROFT (*b. La Grange, Tenn., 1856; d. Rock Hill, S.C., 1928*), educator. Founder and president, 1886–1928, of Winthrop College at Rock Hill, a woman's state college originally established to train teachers.

JOHNSON, EASTMAN. [See JOHNSON, JONATHAN EASTMAN, 1824–1906.]

JOHNSON, EDWARD (*b. Canterbury, England, 1598; d. Woburn, Mass., 1672*), colonial chronicler. Emigrated to Boston, 1630. Author of *The Wonder-Working Providence of Sion's Saviour in New England*, published in London, 1654, as *A History of New England*. The book was written to encourage the friends of the colonies by stories of marvelous evidences of success.

JOHNSON, EDWARD (*b. Salisbury, Va., 1816; d. Richmond, Va., 1873*), soldier, farmer. Graduated West Point, 1838. Resigned captaincy in U.S. Army, 1861; as Confederate brigadier-general (1861) and major-general (1863), served until capture at Nashville, 1864. Particularly distinguished at the Wilderness and Spotsylvania.

JOHNSON, EDWIN FERRY (*b. Essex, Vt., 1803; d. New York, N.Y., 1872*), civil engineer. One of foremost railroad engineers of his day. Promoter and chief engineer of Northern Pacific Railroad which he had advocated as early as 1854.

JOHNSON, ELIAS HENRY (*b. Troy, N.Y., 1841; d. Philadelphia, Pa., 1906*), Baptist theologian. Professor at Crozier Seminary and a leader in organizing the Baptist Congress.

JOHNSON, ELIJAH (*b. probably New Jersey, c. 1780; d. Monrovia, Liberia, 1849*), pioneer settler and one of the founders of Liberia, 1820. Commander of the colony's defense force and associate of Jehudi Ashmun in its early government.

JOHNSON, ELLEN CHENEY (*b. Athol, Mass., 1829; d. London, England, 1899*), educator, prison reformer. Campaigned for separate women's prisons; made Sherborn (Mass.) Reformatory a model institution as superintendent, 1884–99.

JOHNSON, FRANKLIN (*b. Frankfort, O., 1836; d. Brookline, Mass., 1916*), Baptist clergyman, author, educator. Scholarly writer and contributor to theological publications; professor of church history at University of Chicago, 1892–1908.

JOHNSON, GUY (*b. Ireland, c. 1740; d. London, England, 1788*). Northern superintendent of Indian affairs, 1774–82, Loyalist. Son-in-law of Sir William Johnson. Organized Iroquois to fight on British side during American Revolution.

JOHNSON, HELEN LOUISE KENDRICK (*b. Hamilton, N.Y., 1844; d. New York, N.Y., 1917*), author, educator, anti-suffragist.

JOHNSON, HENRY (*b. Gardiner, Maine, 1855; d. Brunswick, Maine, 1918*), teacher at Bowdoin College, poet. His most important works were translations, particularly Dante's *Divine Comedy* in blank verse (1915).

JOHNSON, HERSCHEL VESPASIAN (*b. Burke Co., Ga., 1812; d. 1880*), jurist. Democratic governor of Georgia, 1853–57; accepted 1860 Democratic vice-presidential nomination; opposed secession but served in Confederate senate, 1862–65. Denied seat in U.S. Senate, 1866. A consistent moderate state-rights man of sound judgment and high integrity.

JOHNSON, JAMES (*b. Orange Co., Va., 1774; d. 1826*), soldier. Removed to Kentucky as a boy. Hero of battle of the Thames, 1813, where he served under his brother, Richard M. Johnson.

JOHNSON, JAMES WELDON (*b. Jacksonville, Fla., 1871; d. Wiscasset, Maine, 1938*), lawyer, author, educator. Graduated Atlanta University, 1894. Removed to New York City, 1901; with his brother, J. Rosamond Johnson, collaborated on some 200 popular songs for their own song-and-dance act and for other shows. Served as U.S. consul in Venezuela and Nicaragua, 1906–12. A key figure in National Association for the Advancement of Colored People, 1916–30, Johnson did much to secure Negro rights by his literary and organizational talents. He had wide influence upon other Negro writers and in winning respect for the Negro's contribution to American culture. He was author of *The Autobiography of an Ex-Colored Man* (1912), *Fifty Years and Other Poems* (1917), *God's Trombones* (1927), *Along This Way* (1933) and other books of high merit. [*Supp. 2*]

JOHNSON, Sir JOHN (*b. Mohawk Valley, N.Y., 1742; d. Montreal, Canada, 1830*), Loyalist. Son of Sir William Johnson. Was knighted, 1765; inherited his father's baronetcy and estates, 1774, along with post of major-general of New York militia. At outbreak of Revolution, he fled to Montreal. Commissioned lieutenant-colonel, he raised the "Royal Greens," and served with St. Leger in 1777. During 1778–81, he led raids in upper New York, thoroughly devastating the country. Johnson was commissioned "Superintendent General and Inspector General of the Six Nations Indians and those in the province of Quebec," in 1782. As compensation for confiscated property, the British government granted him land in Canada, where he continued to influence Indian affairs and promoted relief measures for Loyalists.

JOHNSON, JOHN ALBERT (*b. near St. Peter, Minn., 1861; d. 1909*), newspaper editor. Democratic governor of Minnesota, 1904–09. Beloved in his state, he attracted national attention as a public speaker and Chautauqua lecturer.

JOHNSON, JOHN BUTLER (*b. near Marlboro, O., 1850; d. Pier Cove, Mich., 1902*), civil engineering professor, Washington University, St. Louis, 1883–99. Dean of Engineering, University of Wisconsin, 1899–1902. Wrote several widely used engineering reference books and made important studies of strength of timber.

JOHNSON, JOHN GRAVER (*b. Philadelphia, Pa., 1841; d. Philadelphia, 1917*), lawyer, art collector. Argued many important cases before the Supreme Court as attorney for trusts. Built up an extraordinary collection of paintings which he left to the city of Philadelphia.

JOHNSON, JONATHAN EASTMAN (*b. Lovell, Maine, 1824; d. 1906*), portrait and genre painter. Began his career in Boston at the age of 16 in Bufford's lithograph shop. By 1845 he was in Washington, D.C., drawing crayon portraits of statesmen and government officials. Studied with Leutze at Düsseldorf, 1849–51; traveled; declined position as Dutch court painter. Returned to New York, 1858; soon gained a reputation which continued to grow. Traveling in the South to study Negro life, he painted some of his most successful genre pictures, including his "Old Kentucky Home," exhibited in Paris, 1867, and Philadelphia, 1876. His portraits of many eminent Americans were similarly notable for human interest and sound technical qualities of color, drawing and composition.

JOHNSON, JOSEPH (*b. Mount Pleasant, S.C., 1776; d. Pineville, S.C., 1862*), physician. Brother of William Johnson (1771–1834). Practiced in Charleston where he was active in civic life and a leader of the Union party. Author of *Traditions . . . of the American Revolution in the South* (1851) and other works.

JOHNSON, JOSEPH FRENCH (*b. Hardwick, Mass., 1853; d. 1925*), educator, writer on finance. As dean of New York University School of Commerce, 1903–25, he brought it to a high degree of success, developing night-school courses and generally instituting a more practical training for business.

JOHNSON, LEVI (*b. Herkimer Co., N.Y., 1786; d. 1871*), ship-builder and trader. Initiator of regular navigation on Great Lakes at Cleveland, O. *post* 1814.

JOHNSON, MAGNUS (*b. near Karlstad, Sweden, 1871; d. Litchfield, Minn., 1936*), farmer, agrarian reformer. Came to America, 1891. U.S. senator, Farmer-Labor, from Minnesota, 1923–24; congressman, 1933–35. [*Supp. 2*]

JOHNSON, MARMADUKE (*d. Boston, Mass., 1674*), printer. Came to Massachusetts, 1660. With Samuel Green, printed John Eliot's Indian translation of the Bible, 1663.

JOHNSON, Sir NATHANIEL (*b. Kibblesworth, England, c. 1645; d. Carolina, 1713*), colonial official. Governor of Carolina, 1702–08; active in defense of colony during Queen Anne's War; encouraged Indian trade and helped establish Church of England in Carolina.

JOHNSON, OLIVER (*b. Peacham, Vt., 1809; d. Brooklyn, N.Y., 1889*), anti-slavery leader, editor. Close associate of William L. Garrison and a founder of New England Anti-Slavery Society; active also in movements for world peace and women's rights.

JOHNSON, REVERDY (*b. Annapolis, Md., 1796; d. Annapolis, 1876*), constitutional lawyer, diplomat. Graduated St. John's College, Annapolis, 1811; admitted to bar, 1815; practiced in Baltimore, Md. His most famous case was *Dred Scott vs. Sanford;* he was allegedly the major influence in the Supreme Court's decision. He served as U.S. senator from Maryland, Whig, 1845–49, and was briefly attorney-general under President Taylor. He later became a Union Democrat and worked for reconciliation of North and South. Returning to the Senate, 1863, he generally supported Presidents Lincoln and Johnson, although called "trimmer" because of his inconsistencies. He worked effectively against Johnson's impeachment. As U.S. minister to Great Britain, 1868–69, he negotiated a series of agreements on financial claims and other points in dispute which were not ratified but served as bases for later treaties.

JOHNSON, RICHARD MENTOR (*b. Beargrass, now Louisville, Ky., 1780; d. 1850*), lawyer, soldier. Admitted to the bar, 1802. Congressman, (Democrat) Republican, from Kentucky, 1807–19; Democrat, 1829–37; U.S. senator from Kentucky, 1819–29. Won military reputation at battle of the Thames, War of 1812, where he is said to have killed Tecumseh. An intimate friend and on occasion personal agent of Andrew Jackson, whom he often supported despite contrary personal views, his nomination as Van Buren's running-mate was dictated by Jackson but his vice-presidential career, 1837–41, was inconspicuous.

JOHNSON, RICHARD W. (*b. near Smithland, Ky., 1827; d. St. Paul, Minn., 1897*), Union soldier. Graduated West Point, 1849; served mainly in Texas and Indian Territory. Distinguished as brigade and division commander in Tennessee and Georgia campaigns, 1863–64. *Post* 1867, he served as professor of military science at the universities of Missouri and Minnesota.

JOHNSON, ROBERT (*b. England, c. 1676; d. 1735*), popular colonial governor of Carolina, 1717–19, and first royal governor of South Carolina, 1731–35. He was son of Sir Nathaniel Johnson.

JOHNSON, ROBERT UNDERWOOD (*b. Washington, D.C., 1853; d. New York, N.Y., 1937*), editor, poet. Associate editor, *Century Magazine*, 1881–1909; editor, 1909–13. Co-editor, *Battles and Leaders of the Civil War* (1887). Director, Hall of Fame, *post* 1919; secretary, American Academy of Arts and Letters. [*Supp. 2*]

JOHNSON, ROBERT WARD (*b. Scott Co., Ky., 1814; d. 1879*), lawyer. Nephew of James and Richard M. Johnson. Removed to Little Rock, Ark., 1835. Congressman, Democrat, from Arkansas, 1847–53; U.S. senator, 1853–61. Served in Confederate Senate.

JOHNSON, SAMUEL (*b. Guilford, Conn., 1696; d. Stratford, Conn., 1772*), minister of the Church of England in colonial Connecticut, president of King's College, New York, 1754–63. Ranks with Jonathan Edwards as one of the two most important exponents of the idealist philosophy in colonial America. First ordained a Congregationalist pastor, he took orders in the Church of England, 1723, serving a small mission in Stratford, Conn., 1724–54, and leading the Church of England movement in New England. On retirement from King's College, he resumed duties as rector at Stratford. Among his works were *Ethices Elementa* (1746), augmented, 1752, with a new section under title *Elementa Philosophica*.

JOHNSON, SAMUEL (*b. Salem, Mass., 1822; d. 1882*), independent liberal preacher, author. Friend of Samuel Longfellow. Too radical an individualist ever to affiliate with any denomination, his associations were Unitarian and his philosophy thoroughly Transcendentalist.

JOHNSON, SAMUEL WILLIAM (*b. Kingsboro, N.Y., 1830; d. 1909*), agricultural chemist. Studied at Yale where John P. Norton encouraged his interest in chemistry; also at Leipzig and Munich. Professor, analytical chemistry, Yale, *post* 1856. Author of the classic volumes *How Crops Grow* (1868) and *How Crops Feed* (1870). His lectures and his publications greatly influenced the development of scientific agriculture in America. He became the founder of agricultural regulatory work in this country and was the leader in the movement leading to the establishment of agricultural experiment stations, directing Connecticut's new state experiment station at New Haven, 1877–99.

JOHNSON, SETH WHITMORE (*b. Middle Haddam, Conn., 1811; d. 1907*), ship builder. Removed to Cleveland, O., 1834. Successor of Levi Johnson (no kin) as a pioneer in the Great Lakes ship-building industry.

JOHNSON, THOMAS (*b. Calvert Co., Md., 1732; d. near Frederick, Md., 1819*), lawyer, Maryland legislator. Elected, 1774, to represent Maryland in the Continental Congress; placed Washington's name in nomination for command of army, 1775. Though not in Philadelphia when the Declaration of Independence was adopted, he voted in Annapolis, July 6, 1776, to separate Maryland from the mother country. He served in the state convention of 1776 which framed Maryland's declaration of rights and constitution. Elected first governor of Maryland, 1777, he served until November 1779. In 1791 Washington, his friend and business associate, appointed him to the Supreme Court and to the board of commissioners of the Federal City. He resigned as associate justice of the Supreme Court, 1793, and in 1795 refused the secretaryship of state.

JOHNSON, TOM LOFTIN (*b. Blue Spring, Ky., 1854; d. 1911*), inventor, street-railroad operator, steel producer, congressman. Influenced by Henry George. As mayor of Cleveland, O., 1901–09, he made it the best governed city in America. Proponent of municipal traction ownership, public ownership of railroads and woman's suffrage, he was perhaps the most outstanding city executive America has produced and was certainly the most spectacular in American life, 1890–1910.

JOHNSON, VIRGINIA WALES (*b. Brooklyn, N.Y., 1849; d. 1916*), novelist, writer of travel books.

JOHNSON, Sir WILLIAM (*b. Smithtown, Ireland, 1715; d. near present Johnstown, N.Y., 1774*), Mohawk valley pioneer, colonial superintendent of Indian affairs. Came to America *c.* 1738; assumed charge of an estate in the lower Mohawk River valley of New York which was owned by his uncle, Sir Peter Warren. He soon purchased a tract of his own, set up a store to trade with the Indians and other settlers and laid the foundations of a large fortune. He became intimately acquainted with the neighboring tribes of the Six Nations, particularly the Mohawks. During King George's War, 1744–48, he was largely responsible for preventing the Six Nations from supporting the French. Gov. Clinton made him colonel of the Six Nations, 1746, transferring to him the conduct of Indian affairs. In 1750 he was appointed a member of the Council of New York and soon after resigned his management of Indian affairs. The Indians in attendance at the Albany Congress (1754) requesting his reappointment as agent, Gen. Braddock gave him in 1755 the "sole Management & direction of the Affairs of the Six Nations of Indians & their Allies" and command of an expedition against Crown Point. At Lake George a French and Indian force under Dieskau attacked him and was defeated. Though he failed to capture Crown Point, he had warded off the French threat to the Northern colonies; the King made him a baronet, and commissioned him once again colonel of the Six Nations and "Sole Agent and Superintendent of the said Indians and their Affairs." In 1759 he commanded the force which captured Niagara and in 1760 accompanied Amherst's expedition against Montreal.

Henceforth, Johnson worked to create a centralized and independent Indian department and to centralize control of the fur trade, ideals which were never realized and could only have been of temporary effect in stabilizing the westward rush of settlement and preventing white encroachment on hunting grounds reserved to the Indians.

An imperialist unquestionably loyal to the Crown, Johnson was a man of energy and versatility. He aided in opening the Mohawk valley to settlement; his services in helping to drive the French from North America were invaluable; and he did much to facilitate the difficult transition from French to English rule north of the Ohio following the conquest of Canada. He had also shown interest in the Indians for their own sake, aiding projects for their education and religious training.

JOHNSON, WILLIAM (*b. Middletown, Conn., 1769; d. 1848*), law reporter. Associated with Chancellor Kent in the work of New York's supreme court and court of chancery; his reports distinguished by accuracy and good sense.

JOHNSON, WILLIAM (*b. Charleston, S.C., 1771; d. Brooklyn, N.Y., 1834*), jurist. Brother of Joseph Johnson. Studied law with Charles Cotesworth Pinckney; served in South Carolina legislature, 1794–98, and as judge of the state court of common pleas until 1806, when President Jefferson appointed him associate justice of the U.S. Supreme Court. Though personally and politically close to Jefferson, his legal opinions leaned toward Federalism; however, he opposed the strong views of Marshall and Story, as well as the doctrines of secession and nullification. Among his ablest opinions was his dissent in *Fletcher* vs. *Peck.*

JOHNSON, WILLIAM BULLEIN (*b. Beaufort Co., S.C., 1782; d. Greenville, S.C., 1862*), Baptist preacher, pioneer educator in South Carolina. President of the Southern Baptist Convention, 1845–52; helped found present Furman University and Johnson Female University.

JOHNSON, WILLIAM RANSOM (*b. Warren Co., N.C., 1782; d. Mobile, Ala., 1849*), known as "The Napoleon of the Turf." Leading horse-breeder and -racer of his generation; Southern manager, North-South matches, 1823–34.

JOHNSON, WILLIAM SAMUEL (*b. Stratford, Conn., 1727; d. 1819*), statesman, jurist. Son of Samuel Johnson (1696–1772). Graduated Yale, 1744. Without formal training, he became a leader at the Connecticut bar. He represented Stratford in the house of representatives, 1761, 1765; in 1766 he became the first Anglican ever elected to the Council.

Though Johnson's conservative background made the problems of the Revolutionary era particularly difficult, he was a member of the Stamp Act Congress and later served as Connecticut's colonial agent in London, 1767–71. In 1771 he was re-elected to the Council and made judge of the superior court. Elected to the Continental Congress, 1774, he declined to serve, believing the Congress would "tend to widen the breach already much too great between the parent state and her colonies." After the radical party gained control in Connecticut, he went into political retirement.

From 1785 to 1787 he served in the Confederation Congress, exercising more influence than any other Connecticut delegate. The crowning event of his career was the Federal Convention, where he was one of the most generally respected members. He contributed greatly to the compromise on representation, was one of two Connecticut signers of the Constitution and worked effectively for ratification, emphasizing that the federal system formed "one new nation out of the individual States." He became one of the first two senators from Connecticut, but resigned in 1791.

In 1787 Johnson had become the first president of Columbia College, bringing to the post the prestige of his distinguished public career, a reputation for scholarship, and a paternal interest in young men. By the close of his administration in 1800, when he retired on account of ill health, the college was on a sound footing.

JOHNSON, WILLIAM WOOLSEY (*b. Owego, N.Y., 1841; d. 1927*), mathematician. Professor at the U.S. Naval Academy, 1881–1921; one of the best-known expository mathematicians of his time and author of a number of textbooks and monographs.

JOHNSON, WILLIS FLETCHER (*b. New York, N.Y., 1857; d. 1931*), journalist. Graduated New York University, 1879. Associated with the *New York Tribune*, 1880–1931, in many editorial capacities.

JOHNSTON, ALBERT SIDNEY (*b. Washington, Ky., 1803; d. 1862*), soldier. Graduated West Point, 1826. Served in the Black Hawk War but resigned his commission, 1834, because of his wife's illness. Thereafter, went to Texas, became commander of the Texan army, 1837, and was secretary of war of the Republic of Texas, 1838–40. During the Mexican War he was colonel in the U.S. Army; he later commanded the Department of Texas. As brevet brigadier-general he served as commander of the punitive expedition against the Mormons, 1858–60. Assigned to command of the Department of the Pacific, he resigned when Texas seceded. Appointed general in the Confederate Army, commanding the Western Department, he suffered a series of apparent reverses before routing the Federals at the first day of Shiloh, where he was fatally wounded. His loss was regarded as a mortal blow to the Confederacy.

JOHNSTON, ALEXANDER (*b. Brooklyn, N.Y., 1849; d. 1889*), historian, professor of jurisprudence and political economy at the College of New Jersey (Princeton), 1883–89. A prolific writer, he was author of the popular *History of American Politics* (1879).

JOHNSTON, ANNIE FELLOWS (*b. Evansville, Ind., 1863; d. 1931*), author of books for children, notably the series which began with *The Little Colonel* (1895).

JOHNSTON, AUGUSTUS (*b. Amboy, N.J., c. 1730; d. c. 1790*), lawyer. Attorney-general for the colony of Rhode Island, 1757–1766. Served as stamp-distributor, 1765, and was later interned as a Loyalist.

JOHNSTON, DAVID CLAYPOOLE (*b. Philadelphia, Pa., 1799; d. Dorchester, Mass., 1865*), engraver, lithographer, actor. Achieved a reputation for his comic sketches, modeled after the English caricaturist George Cruikshank, but pointedly satiric on American themes and excellently drawn.

JOHNSTON, GABRIEL (*b. Scotland, 1699; d. 1752*), journalist. Co-editor, *The Craftsman*, post 1726. Royal governor of North Carolina, 1734–52. His tenure was featured by a long controversy over quit-rents, causing practical rebellion of the whole colony.

JOHNSTON, GEORGE BEN (*b. Tazewell, Va., 1853; d. Richmond, Va., 1916*), surgeon. M.D., University of the City of New York, 1876; professor, Medical College of Virginia, 1884–1914. Virginia pioneer in antiseptic operations; also contributed much information to surgery of the kidney and spleen.

JOHNSTON, HENRIETTA (*d. 1728/29, buried Charleston, S.C.*), artist. Probably the first woman painter in North America; painted pastel portraits, mostly of colonial South Carolina grandees. Little is known of her lineage and education.

JOHNSTON, HENRY PHELPS (*b. Trebizond, Turkey, 1842; d. 1923*), educator, Union soldier, historian. Born of missionary parents; graduated Yale, 1862. Taught history at the College of the City of New York, 1879–1916. Author of *The Campaign of 1776* (1878), *The Battle of Harlem Heights* (1897); edited correspondence and public papers of John Jay.

JOHNSTON, JOHN (*b. New Galloway, Scotland, 1791; d. Geneva, N.Y., 1880*), agriculturist. Came to America, 1821; started farming near Geneva. Known as "father of American tile-draining" because of his introduction (1835) of this technique of underdraining land. He was among the first to employ other new methods of cultivation: the use of lime and plaster, the surface application of manure, the purchase of oil meal for feeding cattle and sheep, and early cutting of hay.

JOHNSTON, JOHN TAYLOR (*b. New York, N.Y., 1820; d. 1893*), railroad executive, art collector. First president of the Metropolitan Museum of Art, New York; benefactor of New York University.

JOHNSTON, JOSEPH EGGLESTON (*b. Prince Edward Co., Va., 1807; d. Washington, D.C., 1891*), soldier, Confederate general. Son of Peter Johnston. Graduated West Point, 1829. Served in Florida campaign, 1838, and in the Mexican War; appointed quartermaster-general and brigadier-general, 1860. Resigning from the U.S. Army when Virginia seceded, he was named Confederate brigadier-general. His leadership and tactical skill at the first battle of Bull Run, July 1861, won him promotion to general and the command in northern Virginia. Passive in conducting defense of Richmond, spring 1862, his excellent plan of counterattack failed in May because of his faulty supervision of subordinates. Assigned in November 1862 to command Confederate forces in Tennessee and Mississippi, his failure to supersede ineffective subordinate generals contributed to loss of Vicksburg. He then commanded the Confederate withdrawal from Chattanooga to Atlanta, where he was relieved in July 1864 for failing to arrest Sherman's advance. Reassigned to the Army of the Tennessee, February 1865, he surrendered to Sherman on April 26. He served as congressman from Virginia, 1879–81, and in 1885 became a U.S. commissioner of railroads.

JOHNSTON, JOSEPH FORNEY (*b. Lincoln Co., N.C., 1843; d. Washington, D.C., 1913*), lawyer, Confederate soldier, businessman. Removed to Alabama *c*. 1861. Studied law with William H. Forney; was identified with development of Birmingham, Ala. Democratic governor of Alabama, 1896–1900; U.S. senator, 1907–13.

JOHNSTON, JOSIAH STODDARD (*b. Salisbury, Conn., 1784; d. on Red River above Alexandria, La., 1833*), Louisiana jurist and legislator. Half-brother of Albert S. Johnston. Graduated Transylvania, 1802; studied law with William T. Barry of Lexington, Ky.; removed to Louisiana, 1805. A supporter of Henry Clay, he served as congressman from Louisiana, 1821–23; U.S. senator, 1823–33.

JOHNSTON, MARY (*b. Buchanan, Va., 1870; d. near Warm Springs, Va., 1936*), novelist. Best known as author of popular historical novels about Virginia and the Civil War, which include *To Have and to Hold* (1900), *The Long Roll* (1911), *Cease Firing* (1912), and *The Great Valley* (1926). [*Supp. 2*]

JOHNSTON, PETER (*b. Osborne's Landing on James River, Va., 1763; d. 1831*), Revolutionary soldier, Virginia legislator and circuit judge. Strenuously advocated Virginia Resolutions of 1798 in House of Delegates. Father of Joseph E. Johnston.

JOHNSTON, RICHARD MALCOLM (*b. near Powelton, Ga., 1822; d. 1898*), lawyer, educator. Graduated Mercer University, 1841. Taught at University of Georgia, 1857–61; conducted a successful school for boys near Sparta, Ga., 1862–67. Encouraged by his friend Sidney Lanier, he wrote *Dukesboro Tales* (1871), *Old Times in Middle Georgia* (1897) and other sensitive and perceptive sketches of life in his native state.

JOHNSTON, ROBERT MATTESON (*b. Paris, France, 1867; d. Cambridge, Mass., 1920*), historian, author. Graduated Pembroke College, Cambridge, England, 1889. Came to America, 1902; taught, mainly at Harvard, 1902–20. Specialist in military history and the French Revolution.

JOHNSTON, SAMUEL (*b. Dundee, Scotland, 1733; d. 1816*), lawyer, Revolutionary leader. Nephew of Gabriel Johnston. Came to America as an infant. North Carolina legislator; governor, 1787–89; U.S. senator, 1789–93. A legalist, of vigorous intellect and strong convictions, he was a central figure in North Carolina during the Revolution and led the conservative faction in the period of constitutional reorganization which ensued.

JOHNSTON, SAMUEL (*b. Shelby, N.Y., 1835; d. Buffalo, N.Y., 1911*), inventor. Patented rake and reel improvements for harvesters, 1863 and 1865; practically all reapers in the world were altered to use the Johnston system. In 1868 he established a factory at Syracuse, N.Y., to manufacture his harvester rake but later moved it to Brockport, N.Y. In addition to his work on harvesters, he patented rotary and disc harrows and devised new metal-working processes, cold rolling mills, rolled forging mills and casting machinery.

JOHNSTON, THOMAS (*b. Boston, Mass., c. 1708; d. 1767*), organ-builder, topographical engraver.

JOHNSTON, WILLIAM ANDREW (*b. Pittsburgh, Pa., 1871; d. Chicago, Ill., 1929*), journalist. Wrote mystery novels, humorous books; was active in New

York City civic and welfare work. Associated with *New York World*, 1900–27.

JOHNSTON, WILLIAM HARTSHORNE (*b. Cincinnati, O., 1861; d. Nice, France, 1933*), army officer. Retired as major-general, 1925; distinguished in service in Philippines and World War I. [*Supp. 1*]

JOHNSTON, WILLIAM HUGH (*b. Westville, N.S., Canada, 1874; d. Washington, D.C., 1937*), labor leader. Came to America as a boy. President, 1912–26, International Association of Machinists; socialist; proponent of industrial unionism and political action by labor. [*Supp. 2*]

JOHNSTON, WILLIAM PRESTON (*b. Louisville, Ky., 1831; d. Lexington, Va., 1899*), lawyer, Confederate soldier, educator. Son of Albert S. Johnston. Aide-de-camp to Jefferson Davis, 1862–65. Taught at Washington and Lee University, 1867–77; served as president of Louisiana State University, 1880–83, and of Tulane University *post* 1884.

JOHNSTON, ZACHARIAH (*b. near Staunton, Va., 1742; d. 1800*), farmer, Virginia legislator, Revolutionary soldier. Active in fight for Virginia's "Act for Establishing Religious Freedom," 1786; also in Virginia ratification of the federal Constitution.

JOHNSTONE, JOB (*b. Fairfield District, S.C., 1793; d. Newberry, S.C., 1862*), South Carolina jurist, advocate of nullification.

JOLINE, ADRIAN HOFFMAN (*b. Sing Sing, N.Y., 1850; d. 1912*), N.Y. lawyer, book and autograph collector. Specialized in railroad and trust practice. Author of *The Diversions of a Book-lover* (1903) and other works on his hobbies.

JOLLIET, LOUIS (*b. near Beaupré, Canada, 1645; d. 1700*), explorer. Traveled to Lake Superior region, 1669; met Father Jacques Marquette at Sault Ste. Marie; on journey back, was first to pass down Great Lakes by way of Detroit River into Lake Erie. Was chosen, 1672, to find "the great Western river"; collaborated with Father Marquette on plans; traveled by canoe to the upper Fox River, where guides showed them the portage to the Wisconsin River, which carried them to the Mississippi. They floated south to the Arkansas River, returning by way of the Illinois and Des Plaines rivers and portaging at the site of Chicago. In 1697 Jolliet was appointed royal hydrographer for Canada. His fame rests on his services in opening the Great Lakes and the Mississippi Valley to civilization and has been overshadowed by Marquette's because of his loss of his notes and journals, 1674, when returning from his great voyage of discovery.

JONES, ABNER (*b. Royalston, Mass., 1772; d. Exeter, N.H., 1841*), physician. Led a movement for undenominational Christianity in New England, *post* 1801, which had theological affiliations with the later "Christian Connection."

JONES, ALEXANDER (*b. North Carolina, c. 1802; d. 1863*), author, news reporter, physician. Filed first news message by telegraph from New York to Washington, 1846; pioneered in organizing cooperative press service and market reporting by wire among American cities.

JONES, ALFRED (*b. Liverpool, England, 1819; d. New York, N.Y., 1900*), line engraver. Came to America as a young man. Invented a process for producing directly from a photograph a plate that could be printed with type.

JONES, ALLEN (*b. Halifax Co., N.C., 1739; d. Northampton Co., N.C., 1807*), Revolutionary soldier, planter, North Carolina legislator. Brother of Willie Jones yet a strong Federalist.

JONES, AMANDA THEODOSIA (*b. East Bloomfield, N.Y., 1835; d. Junction City, Kans., 1914*), author, inventor. Patented, 1873, the Jones Preserving Process for fruit and meat; also patented a liquid fuel burner, 1880.

JONES, ANSON (*b. Great Barrington, Mass., 1798; d. Houston, Tex., 1858*), physician, Texas legislator. Settled in Texas, 1833; served at San Jacinto. Texas secretary of state, 1841; last president of Republic of Texas, 1844–46.

JONES, BENJAMIN FRANKLIN (*b. Claysville, Pa., 1824; d. 1903*), leader in the iron and steel industry. Founded Jones & Lauth, 1851, which became Jones & Laughlin, 1857.

JONES, CALVIN (*b. Great Barrington, Mass., 1775; d. near Bolivar, Tenn., 1846*), physician, North Carolina legislator, planter. Removed to North Carolina, 1795; retired to Tennessee, 1832.

JONES, CATESBY AP ROGER (*b. Fairfield, Va., 1821; d. Selma, Ala., 1877*), naval officer. Nephew of Thomas ap Catesby Jones. Assisted in perfecting Dahlgren gun. Commanded the Confederate ironclad *Merrimac* in her duel with the *Monitor*, March 1862; supervised Confederate gun works, Selma, Ala.

JONES, CHARLES COLCOCK (*b. Savannah, Ga., 1831; d. Augusta, Ga., 1893*), lawyer, historian. Brother of Joseph Jones (1833–1896). Author of *History of Georgia* (1883) and other works.

JONES, DAVID (*b. New Castle Co., Del., 1736; d. 1820*), Baptist clergyman, chaplain in Revolution and War of 1812. Pastor in New Jersey and Pennsylvania. Author of, among other works, *A Journal of Two Visits to Some Nations of Indians . . . in the Years 1772 and 1773* (1774).

JONES, DAVID RUMPH (*b. Orangeburg District, S.C., 1825; d. Richmond, Va., 1863*), Confederate major-general. Graduated West Point, 1846. Supposedly hauled down the national colors at Ft. Sumter.

JONES, ERNEST LESTER (*b. East Orange, N.J., 1876; d. 1929*). Director, U.S. Coast and Geodetic Survey, 1915–29.

JONES, EVAN WILLIAM (*b. Monmouthshire, Wales, 1852; d. Portland, Oreg., 1908*), mechanical engineer. Came to America as a child. Invented mechanical underfeed stoker for boiler furnaces.

JONES, FRANK (*b. Barrington, N.H., 1832; d. Portsmouth, N.H., 1902*), brewer, capitalist. Chief promoter and first president, Portsmouth & Dover Railroad, subsequently Boston & Maine; served as president of the latter, 1889–92 and 1893.

JONES, GABRIEL (*b. near Williamsburg, Va., 1724; d. Augusta Co., Va., 1806*), lawyer, adviser and executor for Lord Fairfax. King's attorney on Virginia frontier, 1745–75; sponsored George Washington's entry into public life, 1758.

JONES, GEORGE (*b. near York, Pa., 1800; d. Philadelphia, Pa., 1870*), Episcopal clergyman, naval chaplain, author. First chaplain of U.S. Naval Academy, 1851; accompanied Commodore Perry to Japan.

JONES, GEORGE (*b. Poultney, Vt., 1811; d. 1891*), newspaper publisher. Co-founder of the *New York Times*, 1851. Was responsible for overthrowing the "Tweed Ring" and was the first conspicuous business-type newspaper proprietor.

JONES, GEORGE HEBER (*b. Mohawk, N.Y., 1867; d. Miami, Fla., 1919*), Methodist clergyman. Missionary in Korea, 1887–1909.

JONES, GEORGE WALLACE (*b. Vincennes, Ind., 1804; d. 1896*), pioneer miner, merchant, legislator. Michigan Territory delegate to Congress, 1835; secured organization of Wisconsin Territory, 1836, and of Iowa Territory. U.S. senator, Democrat, from Iowa, 1848–59; U.S. minister to New Granada, 1859–61. A representative of the Southern point of view, he lost influence in Iowa *post* 1854.

JONES, HARRY CLARY (*b. New London, Md., 1865; d. 1916*), physical chemist. Established at Johns Hopkins University, 1895, the first distinctive department of physical chemistry in America; specialized on hydrates in solution.

JONES, HERSCHEL VESPASIAN (*b. Jefferson, N.Y., 1861; d. 1928*), journalist, bibliophile. Associated with *Minneapolis Journal*, 1885–1928, as editor, publisher and owner. Collected three notable libraries.

JONES, HILARY POLLARD (*b. Hanover Co., Va., 1863; d. Washington, D.C., 1938*), naval officer. Graduated Annapolis, 1884. Commander-in-chief, U.S. Fleet, 1922–23; adviser at naval conferences at Geneva (1927) and London (1930). [*Supp. 2*]

JONES, HUGH (*b. c. 1670; d. 1760*), Anglican clergyman, mathematician, historian. Came to Virginia, 1716; taught at William and Mary. Author of *The Present State of Virginia* (1724) and *A Short English Grammar* (1724), the first English grammar written in America. Was pastor in Virginia and Maryland; rector, 1731–60, of St. Stephen's, Cecil Co., Md.

JONES, HUGH BOLTON (*b. Baltimore, Md., 1848; d. New York, N.Y., 1927*), landscape painter.

JONES, JACOB (*b. near Smyrna, Del., 1768; d. Philadelphia, Pa., 1850*), physician, naval officer. Appointed midshipman, 1799; served in Tripolitan War; commanded the *Wasp* in its victory over the British *Frolic*, 1812.

JONES, JAMES CHAMBERLAYNE (*b. near the Davidson and Wilson county lines, Tenn., 1809; d. near Memphis, Tenn., 1859*), farmer. Whig governor of Tennessee, 1841–45; U.S. senator, 1851–57.

JONES, JAMES KIMBROUGH (*b. Marshall Co., Miss., 1829; d. Washington, D.C., 1908*), lawyer, Arkansas legislator. Congressman, Democrat, from Arkansas, 1879–85; U.S. senator, 1885–1903; advocated tariff reform and free silver.

JONES, JEHU GLANCY (*b. Caernarvon Township, Pa., 1811; d. Reading, Pa., 1878*), Episcopal clergyman, lawyer. Congressman, Democrat, from Pennsylvania, 1851–53, 1854–58; helped his friend Buchanan obtain the Democratic nomination for president, 1856. U.S. minister to Austria, 1858–61.

JONES, JENKIN LLOYD (*b. Wales, 1843; d. 1918*), Unitarian clergyman. Came to America as an infant; raised in Wisconsin. Principal pastorate in Chicago, Ill.; editor, 1880–1918, of *Unity*, religious weekly dedicated to "Freedom, Fellowship and Character in Religion." Accompanied the Ford Peace Ship Mission, 1915–16.

JONES, JOEL (*b. Coventry, Conn., 1795; d. 1860*), lawyer. Practiced in Easton and Philadelphia, Pa.; Pennsylvania district court judge, 1835–47. First president, Girard College, 1848–49.

JONES, JOHN (*b. Jamaica, N.Y., 1729; d. 1791*), surgeon. Received most of his medical education abroad, obtaining his degree, 1751, at the University of Rheims. He became a successful lithotomist in New York, served as surgeon throughout the French and Indian War, and in 1767 became professor of surgery and obstetrics at King's College when its medical department was organized. He petitioned for the charter of New York Hospital, 1770, and became one of its attending physicians. Too frail for active service, he helped organize the medical department of the Continental Army. More important was his authorship (1775) of the first surgical textbook written in the American colonies (*Plain . . . Remarks on the Treatment of Wounds and Fractures*). He practiced in Philadelphia, Pa., *post* 1780. A personal friend of

George Washington, he was Benjamin Franklin's personal physician.

JONES, JOHN B. (*b. Fairfield District, S.C., 1834; d. Texas, 1881*), Confederate soldier. Appointed major of Texas Rangers Frontier Battalion, 1874; cleared out Indians and badmen from Red River to Rio Grande; broke up Sam Bass gang, 1878. Adjutant-general of Texas, 1879–81.

JONES, JOHN BEAUCHAMP (*b. Baltimore, Md., 1810; d. Burlington, N.J., 1866*), journalist. Author of many novels, including a minor classic of the frontier, *Wild Western Scenes* (1841); was author also of *A Rebel War Clerk's Diary* (1866).

JONES, JOHN PAUL (*b. Kirkbean, Scotland, 1747; d. Paris, France, 1792*), merchant captain, naval officer. Known as John Paul until about 1773. At outbreak of Revolution, went to Philadelphia where, through influence of Joseph Hewes and Robert Morris, he was commissioned lieutenant, 1775. He served on the *Alfred*, first U.S. naval vessel to fly the Continental flag, and was at capture of New Providence, 1776. Given command of the *Providence*, 1776, he was promoted captain and on one cruise captured 16 prizes. In June 1777 Congress gave him command of the *Ranger,* and the marine committee ordered him to France, to report to the American commissioners at Paris. In April 1778 he began raids on English ports and shipping from his base at Brest. In February 1779 the French king placed under his command a wornout East Indiaman of 40 guns, which he renamed the *Bonhomme Richard* in honor of Benjamin Franklin. That summer Jones sailed with a small squadron around Ireland and Scotland, taking 17 prizes. Off Flamborough Head, Yorks., on September 23 he fell in with a large British Baltic convoy escorted by the *Serapis*, 44 guns, and the *Countess of Scarborough,* 20 guns. Jones maneuvered the outclassed *Bonhomme Richard* alongside the *Serapis* and, in one of the most desperate and sanguinary seafights in naval history, forced the Britisher to surrender, though his own ship was so badly damaged she sank two days later. Putting in to neutral Holland, where the French government took possession of the prizes, prisoners and fleet, except for the *Alliance* to which Jones transferred his flag, he returned to L'Orient early in 1780 after a short cruise off Spain. At Paris, Jones was received as a popular hero; overstaying his time, he sailed for Philadelphia, arriving in February 1781 after an absence of more than three years. He was then chosen to command the *America*, the first and only 74-gun ship in the Continental Navy, then building at Portsmouth, N.H. After more than a year supervising the construction, Jones launched the vessel, which was then presented to the French government.

Out of the Navy in 1783, Jones was recommended by Congress to the American minister at Paris as agent to solicit payment for prizes taken by his ships. He last visited America in 1787, when Congress resolved unanimously to present him with a gold medal to commemorate his brilliant services. He was the only Continental naval officer so honored. Returning to France, he was offered a commission in the Russian navy, then fighting the Turks, by the Empress Catherine. As rear-admiral, he commanded the sail squadron on the Black Sea, May–October 1788. Because of the jealousies and intrigues of rivals, Jones's experience in Russia was unhappy and he returned to Paris, 1790.

No longer a popular hero, Jones lived comfortably in Paris, though in declining health. On June 1, 1792, Jefferson as secretary of state wrote that President Washington had appointed him commissioner to treat with Algiers on peace and ransoming of prisoners. Before the letter reached Paris, however, he was dead. He was buried in Paris, but in 1905 what are thought to be his remains were brought to Annapolis and in 1913 entombed in the crypt of the Naval Academy chapel.

JONES, JOHN PERCIVAL (*b. Herefordshire, England, 1829; d. 1912*), miner, California legislator. Raised in Cleveland, O. Removed to California, 1849; made fortune in Crown Point mine, Nevada. U.S. senator, Republican, from Nevada, 1873–1903; author of an important report on bimetallism, 1877–79.

JONES, JOHN PETER (*b. Wrexham, Wales, 1847; d. Hartford, Conn., 1916*), Congregational clergyman. Missionary in India, 1878–1914.

JONES, JOHN TAYLOR (*b. New Ipswich, N.H., 1802; d. Bangkok, Siam, 1851*), Baptist clergyman. First American missionary to Siam (1833–51); prepared a Siamese grammar and translated the New Testament from the Greek into Siamese.

JONES, JOHN WILLIAM (*b. Louisa Court House, Va., 1836; d. Columbus, Ga., 1909*), Baptist clergyman, Confederate soldier. Author of *Personal Reminiscences . . . of Gen. Robert E. Lee* (1874) and *Life and Letters of Robert Edward Lee* (1906).

JONES, JOHN WINSTON (*b. Amelia Co., Va., 1791; d. 1848*), lawyer. Congressman, Democrat, from Virginia, 1835–45; speaker of the House, 1843–45.

JONES, JOSEPH (*b. King George Co., Va., 1727; d. 1805*), Revolutionary statesman, jurist. Uncle of James Monroe. Particularly remembered for preventing Virginia's revocation of the cession of the Northwest Territory to the United States.

JONES, JOSEPH (*b. Liberty Co., Ga., 1833; d. New Orleans, La., 1896*), physician, sanitarian. Brother of Charles C. Jones. Graduated Princeton, 1853; M.D., University of Pennsylvania, 1856. Taught at University of Louisiana *post* 1872. As president of the state board of health, 1880–84, and thereafter as a private citizen, he engaged in a thankless struggle for the sanitary improvement of New Orleans.

JONES, JOSEPH STEVENS (*b. Boston, Mass., 1809; d. Boston, 1877*), physician, dramatist, actor. Won transitory and largely local fame as the author of about 150 plays.

JONES, LEONARD AUGUSTUS (*b. Templeton, Mass., 1832; d. 1909*), jurist, legal writer. Published an exhaustive exposition of the law of securities; also a manual on conveyancing (1886) widely used and known as "Jones Legal Forms." Judge of the Massachusetts land court *post* 1898.

JONES, MARY HARRIS (*b. Cork, Ireland, 1830; d. Silver Spring, Md., 1930*), labor leader known and beloved as "Mother Jones." Came to America as a child; raised in Canada. Active in U.S. labor movement, 1871–1923, as organizer and orator.

JONES, NOBLE WYMBERLEY (*b. near London, England, c. 1724; d. Savannah, Ga., 1805*), physician, planter, Georgia patriot and legislator. Came to Georgia as a youth; was patronized by Gen. Oglethorpe. Opposed British colonial policy *post* 1765, serving as member of provincial congresses and of the Council of Safety.

JONES, SAMUEL (*b. Fort Hill, Long Island, N.Y., 1734; d. 1819*), lawyer, New York legislator. With Richard Varick, published a basic revision of New York statutes; was recorder of New York City, 1789–96, and comptroller, 1797–1800.

JONES, SAMUEL (*b. New York, N.Y., 1770; d. Cold Spring, Long Island, N.Y., 1853*), New York jurist. Son of Samuel Jones (1734–1819). Chancellor of New York, 1826–28; state supreme court justice, 1847–49.

JONES, SAMUEL MILTON (*b. Carnarvonshire, Wales, 1846; d. 1904*), inventor, manufacturer, reformer. Came to America as an infant. Made a fortune in manufacture of oil-well machinery. In his factory at Toledo, O., instituted reforms such as the eight-hour day, a minimum wage and vacations with pay; was called "Golden Rule" Jones; advocated trade unionism, a cooperative insurance plan and sick benefits. He believed that the state should assume ownership of trusts which are logical outgrowths of modern business competition and should operate them for all the people. Elected mayor of Toledo, 1897, he served until his death in 1904. During his administration, he established civil service, an eight-hour day and a minimum wage for city employees. [*Supp.* 1]

JONES, SAMUEL PORTER (*b. Chambers Co., Ala., 1847; d. 1906*), itinerant Methodist evangelist. Operated throughout the country, 1872–1906, and was perhaps the foremost American public speaker of his type in his generation.

JONES, SYBIL (*b. Brunswick, Maine, 1808; d. near Augusta, Maine, 1873*), Quaker preacher. One of the principal factors in the great Quaker revival, 1840–80.

JONES, THOMAS (*b. Fort Neck, South Oyster Bay, N.Y., 1731; d. Hoddesdon, England, 1792*), jurist, Loyalist. Author of *History of New York during the Revolutionary War*, a biased Tory work which was not published until 1879. Son-in-law of Chief Justice James de Lancey, he became a judge of the New York supreme court in 1773. Persecuted during the Revolution, he removed to England in 1781.

JONES, THOMAS AP CATESBY (*b. Westmoreland Co., Va., 1790; d. Sharon, Va., 1858*), naval officer. Appointed midshipman, 1805. Distinguished at New Orleans, La., Dec. 14, 1814, for opposing entrance of British into Lake Borgne; seized Monterey, Calif., October 1842, in advance of war with Mexico; commanded Pacific squadron during war with Mexico. Court-martialed, 1850, but restored, 1853.

JONES, THOMAS GOODE (*b. Macon, Ga., 1844; d. Montgomery, Ala., 1914*), Confederate soldier, Alabama legislator. Democratic governor of Alabama, 1890–94; federal district judge, 1901–14; opponent of B. B. Comer over railroad legislation.

JONES, THOMAS P. (*b. Herefordshire, England, 1774; d. Washington, D.C., 1848*), editor, *Journal of the Franklin Institute*, 1826–48. As editor and U.S. patent office official, he gave valuable encouragement to the development of genuinely useful inventions and exposed unworthy projects.

JONES, WALTER (*b. Northumberland Co., Va., 1776; d. Washington, D.C., 1861*), lawyer. Studied law with Bushrod Washington; served as U.S. attorney, for District of Columbia, 1802–21. Practicing with distinguished success in Washington, D.C., he was of counsel in many famous cases including *McCulloch vs. Maryland*, the Girard Will case and the litigation over the will of Daniel Clark. A founder of the American Colonization Society (1816), he later strongly opposed secession.

JONES, WESLEY LIVSEY (*b. near Bethany, Ill., 1863; d. 1932*), lawyer. Removed to State of Washington, 1889. Congressman, Republican, from Washington, 1899–1909; U.S. senator, 1909–32. [*Supp.* 1]

JONES, WILLIAM (*b. Newport, R.I., 1753; d. 1822*), merchant. Revolutionary soldier and Federalist governor of Rhode Island, 1811–17. Defied national government over War of 1812 and other policies.

JONES, WILLIAM (*b. Philadelphia, Pa., 1760; d. Bethlehem, Pa., 1831*), Revolutionary soldier and privateersman, merchant. Hopelessly inefficient as secretary of the navy and of the treasury, 1813–14, and as first president of the second United States Bank, 1816–19.

JONES, WILLIAM (*b. Sac and Fox Indian reservation in present Oklahoma, 1871; d. Philippine Islands, 1909*), Indian ethnologist. Graduated Harvard, 1900; Ph.D., Columbia, 1904. Made major contributions to knowledge of Algonquian language and lore.

JONES, WILLIAM ALFRED (*b. New York, N.Y., 1817; d. Norwich Town, Conn., 1900*), author. A critic admired by Poe and Irving, Jones did not bear out his early promise. Served as librarian at Columbia University, 1851–65. His *Characters and Criticisms* (1857) contains the bulk of his work.

JONES, WILLIAM PALMER (*b. Adair Co., Ky., 1819; d. Nashville, Tenn., 1897*), physician, psychiatrist. President, medical faculty, University of Tennessee, 1876–96.

JONES, WILLIAM PATTERSON (*b. Philadelphia, Pa., 1831; d. Fullerton, Nebr., 1886*), educator and U.S. consul in China, 1862–68. Founded Northwestern Female College (later absorbed by Northwestern University), 1855, at which he introduced teaching methods far in advance of his time. Among his students were Frances E. Willard and May W. Sewall.

JONES, WILLIAM RICHARD (*b. Hazleton, Pa., 1839; d. Pittsburgh, Pa., 1889*), engineer, Union soldier, steelman. Became assistant to superintendent, Cambria Iron Co., Johnstown, Pa., 1872; later went to Pittsburgh as master mechanic, Edgar Thomson Steel Co. Became general superintendent of the company at Braddock, Pa., 1875; *post* 1888 was also consulting engineer to Carnegie, Phipps & Co. Characterized as "probably the greatest mechanical genius that ever entered the Carnegie shops," he patented numerous devices and processes, including the Jones mixer, 1889. His pre-eminence, however, rested primarily on his ability as a manager of men, demonstrated most notably in rescue work during the Johnstown Flood.

JONES, WILLIE (*b. Northampton Co., N.C., c. 1741; d. Raleigh, N.C., 1801*), Revolutionary leader, planter, merchant. A man of wide influence and an ardent supporter of colonial rights from the beginning of the quarrel with the mother country. An important member of each of the provincial congresses, he served on the committee to draft a North Carolina constitution and has been credited with its authorship. Undisputed leader of the dominant democratic element in North Carolina, he served frequently in the legislature. Declining election to the federal convention, he led the successful opposition to the federal Constitution in the North Carolina convention of 1788, fearing it would check the development of political democracy, to which, though an aristocrat, he was passionately attached. He was a brother of Allen Jones.

JORDAN, DAVID STARR (*b. near Gainesville, N.Y., 1851; d. Stanford University, Calif., 1931*), described himself as naturalist and explorer first, teacher second, and minor prophet of Democracy third. He taught botany while still an undergraduate at Cornell University from which he graduated, 1872. After further study, including a brief period under the elder Agassiz and the publication of his *Manual of the Vertebrates of the Northern U.S.* (1876), he went to Indiana University, 1879, as head of the natural science department and became president, 1885. In 1891 he became first president of Leland Stanford University. He had become the greatest living authority on ichthyology, and was always to be a student of the problems of geographic distribution of animal and plant species. He introduced the "major-professor" system and other innovations in higher education at both Indiana and Stanford, chose and trained outstanding faculties, was able in financial administration, and yet found time to serve frequently on government and private special commissions. After 1898 he became an indefatigable crusader for international peace. He retired from the presidency of Stanford, 1913, becoming chancellor.

JORDAN, EBEN DYER (*b. Boston, Mass., 1857; d. West Manchester, Mass., 1916*), merchant. Head of Jordan, Marsh & Co.; as patron of music, aided the New England Conservatory of Music and contributed much to establishing opera in Boston.

JORDAN, EDWIN OAKES (*b. Thomaston, Maine, 1866; d. Lewiston, Maine, 1936*), bacteriologist, sanitarian. Graduated Massachusetts Institute of Technology, 1888; Ph.D., Clark University, 1892. Headed division of hygiene and bacteriology at University of Chicago where he taught, 1892–1933. Jordan made important contributions to public health, investigating water pollution and water-borne disease, food poisoning, and influenza. His efforts helped secure for Chicago high-grade diphtheria antitoxin and a clean and pasteurized milk supply. [*Supp. 2*]

JORDAN, JOHN WOOLF (*b. Philadelphia, Pa., 1840; d. 1921*), librarian, editor, antiquary. Librarian, Historical Society of Pennsylvania, 1903–21; edited many important manuscript sources for *Pennsylvania Magazine of History and Biography*, of which he was editor, 1887–1921.

JORDAN, KATE (*b. Dublin, Ireland, 1862; d. Mountain Lakes, N.J., 1926*), novelist, playwright.

JORDAN, THOMAS (*b. Luray, Va., 1819; d. 1895*), soldier, journalist. Graduated West Point, 1840. Served as Gen. Beauregard's chief of staff, 1862–65; later led Cuban insurgents. Conducted *Financial and Mining Record*, New York City, 1870–92.

JORDAN, WILLIAM GEORGE (*b. New York, N.Y., 1864; d. 1928*), editor, author. Campaigned for educational reform.

JOSEFFY, RAFAEL (*b. Hunfalu, Hungary, 1852; d. New York, N.Y., 1915*), concert pianist, teacher, editor. Studied at Budapest, Leipzig, and in Berlin under

Tausig; came to America, 1879. Excelled in playing Bach and Mozart, introduced Brahms's works in America; edited, among others, the *Complete Works of Chopin* (1915).

JOSEPH (*b. probably Wallowa Valley, Oreg., c. 1840; d. Nespelim, Colville reservation, Wash., 1904*), Nez Percé chief. Generally regarded as the greatest of Indian strategists. As leader of the "non-treaty" Nez Percés, who refused to recognize the 1863 agreement ceding their lands and confining them to a reservation in Idaho, Joseph was drawn into hopeless resistance. Recognizing that his 200 warriors were no match for the military power opposed to him, he planned escape with women and children to Canada. In 1877, he led a brilliant retreat more than 1000 miles through Montana, Idaho and Yellowstone Park, eluding one U.S. Army under Gen. O. O. Howard, defeating another under Gen. John Gibbon at Big Hole, Mont.; and finally surrendering after a five-day siege only 30 miles from safety. Noted for his humaneness in warfare, he thereafter gave his efforts to help his people learn peaceful ways.

JOSSELYN, JOHN (*fl. 1638–1675*), traveler and writer. Author of two volumes dealing with New England, based on his observations during two visits there in 1638–39 and 1663–71. *New-Englands Rarities Discovered*, published 1672, was the first systematic account of botanical species of the region. *An Account of Two Voyages to New-England* (1674) was a rather strange compound of scientific lore, suggestions for settlers, bits of local history, and much general observation.

JOUBERT DE LA MURAILLE, JAMES HECTOR MARIE NICHOLAS (*b. Saint Jean d'Angely, France, 1777; d. 1843*), Roman Catholic clergyman, Sulpician. Came to Baltimore, Md., *c.* 1805; ordained, 1810; taught at St. Mary's College. Founded the Oblate Sisters of Providence, Baltimore, Md., 1828.

JOUETT, JAMES EDWARD (*b. near Lexington, Ky., 1826; d. Sandy Spring, Md., 1902*), naval officer. Son of Matthew H. Jouett. Served in Mexican War and was distinguished as captain of U.S.S. *Metacomet* on blockade duty, Gulf of Mexico, 1863–65. Recipient of Farragut's "Damn the torpedoes!" order at Mobile Bay, 1864.

JOUETT, JOHN (*b. Albemarle Co., Va., 1754; d. 1822*), Revolutionary patriot. Out-raced Tarleton's British horse, 1781, to save Gov. Jefferson and the Virginia legislature from capture at Charlottesville. Removed to Kentucky, 1782, where he became a stock-breeder and legislator.

JOUETT, MATTHEW HARRIS (*b. near Harrodsburg, Ky., 1787; d. Lexington, Ky., 1827*), portrait painter. Son of John Jouett. Studied with Gilbert Stuart; worked extensively in the South.

JOUTEL, HENRI (*b. Rouen, France, c. 1645; d. Rouen, post 1723*), soldier. Was La Salle's lieutenant and the journalist of his last expedition to America and of his last days and death. He joined La Salle, 1684, in an expedition to form a settlement at the mouth of the Mississippi. They reached the Gulf of Mexico but missed the river mouth, landed in Matagorda Bay on the Texas coast, and began a colony. La Salle made several efforts to find the Mississippi, but early in 1687 he was murdered by conspirators among his own men. Joutel and La Salle's brother and nephew were allowed to escape, crossed what is now Arkansas, and eventually reached Quebec by way of the Mississippi and Tonty's Fort on the Illinois River. Joutel returned to France, 1688. In 1713 he published an account of his adventures, issued in English, 1714, as *A Journal of the Last Voyage Performed by M. de la Sale.*

JOY, AGNES ELIZA. [See SALM SALM, AGNES ELIZA JOY, PRINCESS, 1840–1912.]

JOY, HENRY BOURNE (*b. Detroit, Mich., 1864; d. Grosse Pointe Farms, Mich., 1936*), financier and industrialist. Son of James F. Joy. General manager, 1903–09, and president, 1909–16, Packard Motor Car Co. [*Supp. 2*]

JOY, JAMES FREDERICK (*b. Durham, N.H., 1810; d. Detroit, Mich., 1896*), lawyer, Western railroad builder. Removed to Detroit, 1836; was active in financing the Michigan Central and organizing Chicago, Burlington and Quincy. Constructed the "Joy System," the first important Western railroad combination.

JOY, THOMAS (*b. probably Hingham, England, c. 1610; d. 1678*), architect, builder. Came to Boston, Mass., *c.* 1636 o.s. Designed and built the first "statehouse" in Boston, 1657, and considerably influenced early Boston architecture.

JOYCE, ISAAC WILSON (*b. Hamilton Co., O., 1836; d. Minnesota, 1905*), Methodist clergyman. Rode circuits and held pastorates in Indiana and Ohio, 1858–88; elected bishop, 1888. Noted as a preacher and revivalist.

JOYNES, EDWARD SOUTHEY (*b. Accomac Co., Va., 1834; d. 1917*), Southern educator, Confederate official, textbook writer. Exerted important influence *post* 1880 in upbuilding of schools and colleges, particularly in Virginia, Tennessee and South Carolina.

JUDAH, SAMUEL (*b. New York, N.Y., 1798; d. 1869*), lawyer, Indiana legislator. Graduated Rutgers, 1816. Removed to Indiana, 1818; settled in Vincennes, where he practiced until his death.

JUDAH, SAMUEL BENJAMIN HELBERT (*b. New York, N.Y., c. 1799; d. New York, 1876*), lawyer. Author of several plays and dramatic poems and of the libelous satire *Gotham and the Gothamites* (1823).

JUDAH, THEODORE DEHONE (*b. Bridgeport, Conn., 1826; d. New York, N.Y., 1863*), engineer, railroad builder. Initiated and successfully promoted the first realized plan for constructing a railroad across the Sierra Nevada, 1862; associated with C. P. Huntington, Leland Stanford and others in Central Pacific Railroad Co.

JUDD, EDWARD STARR (*b. Rochester, Minn., 1878; d. Chicago, Ill., 1935*), surgeon. M.D., University of Minnesota, 1902. Lifelong associate at Mayo Clinic. Outstanding in field of abdominal surgery.
[*Supp. 1*]

JUDD, GERRIT PARMELE (*b. Paris, N.Y., 1803; d. 1873*), physician, Hawaiian statesman. Went to Hawaii as medical missionary, 1827; became trusted adviser of the Hawaiian king, serving in the highest offices of state, 1842–53.

JUDD, NORMAN BUEL (*b. Rome, N.Y., 1815; d. 1878*), railroad lawyer, diplomat. Removed to Chicago, Ill., 1836, and was first city attorney; served also in state legislature. Managed Lincoln's campaign for Republican nomination, 1860; was U.S. minister to Prussia, 1861–65.

JUDD, ORANGE (*b. near Niagara Falls, N.Y., 1822; d. Chicago, Ill., 1892*), agricultural editor and publisher. A pioneer in relating chemistry to agriculture, he became joint editor of the *American Agriculturist*, 1853, and was owner and publisher as well as editor by 1856; he also was agricultural editor of the *New York Times*. After the Civil War he published *Hearth and Home* and a number of agricultural books. He devised the crop-reporting percentage system later adopted by nearly all nations. A benefactor of Wesleyan University, he made possible the establishment there of the first of the State Agricultural Experiment Stations serving Connecticut. *Post* 1884 he edited the *Prairie Farmer* and the *Orange Judd Farmer*. He also pioneered (1857) in the raising of sorghum.

JUDD, SYLVESTER (*b. Westhampton, Mass., 1813; d. 1853*), Unitarian clergyman. Propagated his idea of the "birthright church" and other religious and social views as pastor in Augusta, Maine. Author of *Margaret* (1845), *Richard Edney* (1850), novels of New England life. An idealist, he opposed war, Abolitionism and capital punishment.

JUDGE, THOMAS AUGUSTINE (*b. South Boston, Mass., 1868; d. Washington, D.C., 1933*), Roman Catholic clergyman, Vincentian. Active as missionary; founded Missionary Servants of the Most Holy Trinity and a similar community of nuns. [*Supp. 1*]

JUDGE, WILLIAM QUAN (*b. Dublin, Ireland, 1851; d. 1896*), lawyer, theosophist. Came to America as a boy. Established branches of the Theosophical Society in every large American city; remained loyal to Mme. Blavatsky after her exposure.

JUDSON, ADONIRAM (*b. Malden, Mass., 1788; d. at sea, 1850*), Baptist missionary. Graduated Brown, 1807; was a leader in movement resulting in forming of American Board of Commissioners for Foreign Missions. Going to Calcutta in 1812 as a Congregationalist missionary to Burma, he became a Baptist. He later reached Rangoon, where he set about learning Burmese and eventually translated the Bible into Burmese (completed 1834) and completed his *Dictionary, English and Burmese* (1849). He had married twice, enjoying marital associations remarkable for their intellectual and spiritual compatibility, before his return to America in 1845, when he married once more. The following year he returned to Maulmain, which had earlier become the center of American Baptist activities in Burma.

JUDSON, ADONIRAM BROWN (*b. Maulmain, Burma, 1837; d. 1916*), surgeon. Son of Adoniram Judson. Graduated Brown, 1859; M.D., Jefferson Medical College, 1865; M.D., College of Physicians and Surgeons, N.Y., 1868. Served in Civil War as naval surgeon. Specialized in orthopedic surgery in New York; was instrumental in forming the American Orthopedic Association, 1887.

JUDSON, ANN HASSELTINE (*b. Bradford, Mass., 1789; d. Amherst, Burma, 1826*), missionary to Burma, first wife of Adoniram Judson. Author of *Account of the American Baptist Mission to the Burman Empire* (1823).

JUDSON, EDWARD (*b. Maulmain, Burma, 1844; d. 1914*), Baptist clergyman. Son of Adoniram Judson. After a teaching career and a pastorate at Orange, N.J., became pastor of Berean Baptist Church, New York City, 1881; as pastor of Judson Memorial Church, New York City, *post* 1890, made it a laboratory for readjusting relations of city churches with their communities.

JUDSON, EDWARD ZANE CARROLL (*b. Stamford, N.Y., 1823; d. Stamford, 1886*), adventurer. Led a roving and discreditable career. *Post* 1846, composed hundreds of dime novels under pseudonym Ned Buntline. He was the friend and exploiter of Buffalo Bill Cody.

JUDSON, EGBERT PUTNAM (*b. Syracuse, N.Y., 1812; d. San Francisco, Calif., 1893*), inventor and manufacturer of explosives. Patented Giant Powder, 1873; also a less shattering explosive for railroad construction, marketed as "Judson's RRP."

JUDSON, EMILY CHUBBUCK (*b. Eaton, N.Y., 1817; d. Hamilton, N.Y., 1854*), writer, Baptist missionary. Author of a number of works under penname "Fanny Forester." Third wife of Adoniram Judson, whom she married in 1846 and accompanied to Burma.

JUDSON, FREDERICK NEWTON (*b. St. Mary's, Ga., 1845; d. St. Louis, Mo., 1919*), corporation lawyer, legal writer. Raised in Connecticut; began legal practice in St. Louis, Mo., 1873. Victoriously defended strikers in Wabash Railroad Case, 1903; served on many state and national commissions.

JUDSON, HARRY PRATT (*b. Jamestown, N.Y., 1849; d. 1927*), educator. Graduated Williams, 1870. Was dean and professor, and later president (1906–23), University of Chicago.

JUDSON, SARAH HALL BOARDMAN (*b. Alstead, N.H., 1803; d. St. Helena Island, 1845*), missionary to Burma. Second wife of Adoniram Judson whom she married in 1834.

JUENGLING, FREDERICK (*b. Leipzig, Saxony, 1846; d. New York, N.Y., 1889*), wood-engraver. Came to America, 1866. Won international recognition as a leading American wood-engraver of the "new school" of his art.

JUILLIARD, AUGUSTUS D. (*b. at sea en route from France to America, 1836; d. 1919*), textile merchant, capitalist, patron of music. An active supporter of Metropolitan Opera, New York; established Juilliard Foundation to promote music education.

JULIA, SISTER (*b. Inver, Ireland, 1827; d. Peabody, Mass., 1901*), educator. Name in religion of Susan McGroarty. Came to America as a child; raised in Cincinnati, O.; entered congregation of sisters of Notre Dame de Namur. Founded many convents and schools, including Trinity College for women, Washington, D.C.

JULIAN, GEORGE WASHINGTON (*b. near Centerville, Ind., 1817; d. Irvington, Ind., 1899*), Abolitionist leader. Entered Indiana legislature, 1845, as a Whig and began to attack slavery in newspaper articles. Elected to Congress as a Free-Soiler, 1848, he opposed the Compromise of 1850 and lost his seat in that year. He helped organize the Republican party, 1856. Re-elected to Congress as a Republican, 1860, he urged Emancipation, contributed to passage of Homestead Act (1862) and served on committee on conduct of the war; he helped draw articles of impeachment against President Johnson, 1867. Failing of renomination, 1870, he joined the Liberal Republican movement, supporting Horace Greeley, 1872, and S. J. Tilden, 1876. He published several books and articles championing reform and was surveyor-general of New Mexico under President Cleveland.

JUMEL, STEPHEN (*b. France, c. 1754; d. New York, N.Y., 1832*), wine merchant. Remembered chiefly as husband of the charming but unscrupulous Mme. Jumel who later married Aaron Burr.

JUNE, JENNIE. [See Croly, Jane Cunningham, 1829–1901.]

JUNEAU, SOLOMON LAURENT (*b. L'Assomption, near Montreal, Canada, 1793; d. Menominee Indian reservation, 1856*), founder of Milwaukee, Wis., which grew from his trading agency, established there, 1818.

JUNGMAN, JOHN GEORGE (*b. Hockenheim, Germany, 1720; d. Bethlehem, Pa., 1808*), Moravian missionary. Came to America as a boy; joined Bethlehem community, 1743. Taught and preached among Indians on Pennsylvania, Connecticut and Ohio frontiers, 1746–85.

JUNKIN, GEORGE (*b. Cumberland Co., Pa., 1790; d. Philadelphia, Pa., 1868*), Presbyterian clergyman, educator. First president of Lafayette College, 1832–41 and 1844–48; served also as president of Miami University, Ohio (1841–44) and Washington College, Lexington, Va. (1848–61). An uncompromising "Old School" leader.

KAFER, JOHN CHRISTIAN (*b. Trenton, N.J., 1842; d. Trenton, 1906*), engineer, educator. Served in U.S. Navy at sea, 1863–68; instructor, steam engineering at Annapolis, 1868–74, 1876–82; assistant to chief, Bureau of Steam Engineering, U.S. Navy.

KAH-GE-GA-GAH-BOWH. [See Copway, George, 1818– c. 1863.]

KAHN, JULIUS (*b. Kuppenheim, Germany, 1861; d. 1924*), actor, lawyer. Came to California as a child. Congressman, Republican, from California, for 12 terms between 1898 and 1924. An advocate of military preparedness, he was author of the Selective Draft Act of 1917.

KAHN, OTTO HERMAN (*b. Mannheim, Germany, 1867; d. New York, N.Y., 1934*), banker, art patron. Came to America, 1893. Became partner in Kuhn, Loeb & Co., 1897. [*Supp. 1*]

KAISER, ALOIS (*b. Szobotist, Hungary, 1840; d. 1908*), cantor, composer. Pupil of Solomon Sulzer, Vienna; came to Baltimore, Md., 1866, where he was cantor of Oheb Shalom synagogue. He was the leading American exponent of the modification of the Jewish musical tradition by German oratorio and operatic standards.

KALANIANAOLE, JONAH KUHIO (*b. Kauai, Hawaii, 1871; d. 1922*), delegate to Congress from Hawaii, 1902–22. A native prince, he exerted a great influence in reconciling the Hawaiians to their loss of independence as a nation.

KALB, JOHANN (*b. Hüttendorf, Germany, 1721; d. Camden, S.C., 1780*), Revolutionary general known as Baron de Kalb. After leaving home at 16, he appears, 1743, as Lieutenant Jean de Kalb of a regiment of French infantry. He served throughout the War of the Austrian Succession and the Seven Years' War, and in 1764 retired as lieutenant-colonel to live near Paris. In 1768 he traveled in the British colonies in America for about four months on a secret mission of observation for the Duc de Choiseul. Made a

French brigadier-general, 1776, he was soon engaged by Silas Deane as major-general. With his protégé Lafayette and other companions, he sailed to America, arriving in 1777 to discover that Congress refused to ratify Deane's contracts. Congress, however, received Lafayette as major-general and eventually elected Kalb to a new major-generalship. He saw some action before Philadelphia and spent the winter at Valley Forge. Constantly with the army until 1780, he was ordered on April 3rd of that year to relieve Charleston, S.C., then under siege. In North Carolina he was joined by the new commander for the South, Gen. Gates, who, despite his advice, determined to march to Camden, S.C., to attack the British. In the sudden encounter with Lord Cornwallis's army, Gates's militia fled. Kalb repeatedly charged the enemy, finally falling, mortally wounded.

KALISCH, ISIDOR (*b. Krotoschin, Posen, Prussia, 1816; d. Newark, N.J., 1886*), reform rabbi. Came to America, 1849. Held many pastorates; by his writing contributed greatly to the shaping of reform Judaism in America, combatting both radical reform and orthodox Judaism.

KALISCH, SAMUEL (*b. Cleveland, O., 1851; d. 1930*), jurist. Son of Isidor Kalisch. Graduated Columbia Law School, 1870; practiced in Newark, N.J. Justice, supreme court of New Jersey, 1911–30; active in Democratic politics and in reform.

KAMAIAKAN (*b. near present Lewiston, Idaho, c. 1800; d. c. 1880*), Yakima chief. Organized Indian resistance to cession of Yakima lands, 1856–58.

KANE, ELISHA KENT (*b. Philadelphia, Pa., 1820; d. Havana, Cuba, 1857*), naval officer, physician. Son of John K. Kane. Graduated University of Pennsylvania, M.D., 1842. Served as U.S. Navy surgeon; *post* 1850 attached to U.S. Coast Survey. Medical officer to first Grinnell Arctic expedition; commanded the second, 1853–55. Pioneer of the American route to North Pole. Author, *Arctic Explorations* (1856).

KANE, JOHN (*b. West Calder, Scotland, 1860; d. 1934*), landscape painter. Came to America, 1879. Worked as laborer and house painter. Received first recognition, 1927, as important figure in modern art.
[*Supp. 1*]

KANE, JOHN KINTZING (*b. Albany, N.Y., 1795; d. Philadelphia, Pa., 1858*), jurist. Graduated Yale, 1814; studied law with Joseph Hopkinson; admitted to the bar, 1817, and practiced in Philadelphia. Assisted President Andrew Jackson in preparation of state papers, particularly in fight against Bank of the U.S. Judge, U.S. district court in Pennsylvania, 1846–58.

KANE, THOMAS LEIPER (*b. Philadelphia, Pa., 1822; d. Philadelphia, 1883*), lawyer, Union major-general, Abolitionist. Son of John K. Kane.

KAPP, FRIEDRICH (*b. Hamm, Westphalia, Germany, 1824; d. Berlin, Germany, 1884*), publicist, historian. Resided in America, 1850–70. Helped unite German-Americans in support of the Union, 1860–65; wrote valuable studies in American history.

KASSON, JOHN ADAM (*b. Charlotte, Vt., 1822; d. Washington, D.C., 1910*), lawyer, diplomat. Congressman, Republican, from Iowa, 1863–66; 1873–77; 1881–84. Was effective U.S. minister to Austria-Hungary, 1877–81, and represented this country in numerous foreign negotiations thereafter as special envoy. Had important part in framing Republican platform, 1860.

KATTE, WALTER (*b. London, England, 1830; d. New York, N.Y., 1917*), civil engineer. Came to America, 1849. One of the world's foremost railroad and bridge construction engineers; supervised Eads bridge, St. Louis, Mo., and New York Central right-of-way construction, Park Avenue, New York City.

KATZER, FREDERIC XAVIER (*b. Ebensee, Upper Austria, 1844; d. Fond du Lac, Wis., 1903*), Roman Catholic clergyman. Came to America, 1864; was seminary professor in Milwaukee, Wis., *post* 1866, and an official in that diocese. Bishop of Green Bay, 1886–90; archbishop of Milwaukee, 1891–1903. Opposed Bennett law.

KAUFFMAN, CALVIN HENRY (*b. Lebanon Co., Pa., 1869; d. 1931*), botanist, mycologist. Taught at University of Michigan *post* 1904. Author of many major monographs and *The Agaricaceae of Michigan* (1918).

KAUTZ, AUGUST VALENTINE (*b. Ispringen, Germany, 1828; d. Seattle, Wash., 1895*), soldier. Came to America as an infant; raised in Ohio. Graduated West Point, 1852. Civil War brigade and division commander of cavalry; breveted major-general, 1865. Served principally in West and Southwest thereafter until retirement, 1892.

KAVANAGH, EDWARD (*b. Damariscotta Mills, District of Maine, 1795; d. 1844*), lawyer, Maine legislator, diplomat. Democratic governor of Maine, 1843. As commissioner, helped negotiate Maine boundary with Webster and Ashburton.

KAY, EDGAR BOYD (*b. Warriors Mark, Pa., 1860; d. Washington, D.C., 1931*), educator, sanitary engineer. Taught engineering at Union, Cornell and University of Alabama. Invented the U.S. Standard Incinerator; was recognized as a leader in sanitation and incineration.

KAYE, FREDERICK BENJAMIN (*b. New York, N.Y., 1892; d. Boston, Mass., 1930*), scholar, author. Graduated Yale, 1914; Ph.D., 1917. Professor of English at Northwestern University; achieved international reputation for scholarship in neo-classical English literature (late 17th, early 18th century).

KEAGY, JOHN MILLER (*b. Strasburg, Pa., 1792; d. 1837*), physician, educator. Influenced movement toward professionalizing education in Pennsylvania and shaping it according to the ideas of Pestalozzi.

KEANE, JAMES JOHN (*b. Joliet, Ill., 1857; d. 1929*), Roman Catholic clergyman. Pastor in St. Paul and Minneapolis; bishop, Cheyenne, Wyo., 1902–11; archbishop of Dubuque, 1911–29.

KEANE, JOHN JOSEPH (*b. Ballyshannon, Ireland, 1839; d. Dubuque, Iowa, 1918*), Roman Catholic clergyman. Came to Baltimore, Md., as a child. Graduated St. Mary's Seminary; ordained, 1866. Appointed bishop of Richmond, Va., 1878, he did much to promote the project of a Catholic university, and when one was founded at Washington, D.C., 1889, he served as its first rector until the end of 1896. Stationed in Rome, 1897–99, he returned to serve as archbishop of Dubuque, 1900–11. He was gifted as an orator.

KEARNEY, DENIS (*b. Oakmount, Ireland, 1847; d. Alameda, Calif., 1907*), labor agitator. Settled in San Francisco *c.* 1868. Was leader in organizing Workingmen's Party of California, 1877 (often called the Kearney movement) and served as its president.

KEARNY, FRANCIS (*b. Perth Amboy, N.J., 1785; d. Perth Amboy, 1837*), engraver in line and aquatint. Brother of Lawrence Kearny; nephew of James Lawrence. Worked in Philadelphia, 1810–33.

KEARNY, LAWRENCE (*b. Perth Amboy, N.J., 1789; d. Perth Amboy, 1868*), naval officer. Brother of Francis Kearny; nephew of James Lawrence. Appointed midshipman, 1807; promoted captain, 1832. While commanding the East India Squadron, initiated the Open Door Policy in China by actions at Canton, 1842; facilitated conclusion of first Sino-American treaty, 1844.

KEARNY, PHILIP (*b. New York, N.Y., 1814; d. Chantilly, Va., 1862*), soldier. Nephew of Stephen W. Kearny. Prevented by family opposition from entering West Point; graduated Columbia, 1833. Commissioned second lieutenant, 1st Dragoons, 1837, he served on the frontier; studied at French cavalry school, Saumur, and saw action in Algiers, 1840. Returning to America, he was aide to Gen. Macomb and Winfield Scott. Commanding Scott's bodyguard in Mexican War, he lost his left arm at Churubusco. Resigning from the U.S. Army, 1851, he won the cross of the Legion of Honor for service with Napoleon III's cavalry, Italian campaign, 1859. Returning home at outbreak of Civil War, he was named brigadier-general, 1861, and major-general, 1862; he participated in at least twelve engagements in the Virginia campaigns and was killed while reconnoitering a new position. Gen. Scott called him "a perfect soldier." The divisional shoulder patch, now in general use, was introduced by Kearny.

KEARNY, STEPHEN WATTS (*b. Newark, N.J., 1794; d. St. Louis, Mo., 1848*), soldier. Cousin of Lawrence Kearny. Commissioned first lieutenant, 13th Infantry, 1812; distinguished at Queenston Heights; promoted captain, 1813. Except for an occasional detail in the East, he served exclusively on the Western frontier, 1819–46, becoming brigadier-general commanding Army of the West, 1846. In the war with Mexico, he set out from Fort Leavenworth and occupied Santa Fé, N. Mex., in August 1846; striking for California, he was blocked by superior forces at San Pasqual but relieved by U.S. troops sent by Com. R. F. Stockton with whom he later quarreled over the chief command. In concert with Stockton, he took Los Angeles early in 1847; thereafter he quarreled also with John C. Frémont, whom he deposed as civil governor of California and ordered court-martialed. Kearny then served briefly as civil governor of Vera Cruz and of Mexico City. He was the uncle of Philip Kearny. Fort Kearny (Kearney), Neb., was named for him.

KEARSLEY, JOHN (*b. Greatham, England, 1684; d. 1772*), physician, architect, teacher. Came to America, 1711; settled in Philadelphia, Pa., 1717. Maintained a medical office called "the first college" of Pennsylvania and trained many physicians; designed, financed and built Christ Church, Philadelphia.

KEATING, JOHN McLEOD (*b. Kings Co., Ireland, 1830; d. Gloucester, Mass., 1906*), journalist. Came to America, 1848. Edited newspapers in Memphis, Tenn., 1859–91, notably the *Memphis Appeal*.

KEATING, JOHN MARIE (*b. Philadelphia, Pa., 1852; d. Colorado Springs, Colo., 1893*), physician. Grandson of René La Roche. Graduated University of Pennsylvania, M.D., 1873. Practiced, taught and wrote principally on obstetrics and children's diseases.

KEATING, WILLIAM HYPOLITUS (*b. Wilmington, Del., 1799; d. London, England, 1840*), mineralogical chemist, educator, businessman. Geologist of Stephen H. Long's 1823 expedition, of which he wrote *Narrative of an Expedition to the Source of St. Peter's River, . . .* (1824). He helped inaugurate the Franklin Institute of Pennsylvania.

KEDZIE, ROBERT CLARK (*b. Delhi, N.Y., 1823; d. 1902*), physician, chemist, sanitarian. Raised in Michigan. Associated *post* 1863 with the Michigan State Agricultural College and in public health work.

KEEFE, DANIEL JOSEPH (*b. Willowsprings, Ill., 1852; d. Elmhurst, Ill., 1929*), labor leader, industrial arbitrator. Dominant figure in National (now International) Longshoremen's Association, 1892–1908; U.S. commissioner-general of immigration, 1908–13.

KEELER, JAMES EDWARD (*b. La Salle, Ill., 1857; d. 1900*), astronomer. Devised many improvements and made many important spectroscopic studies at Lick Observatory; was director at Lick *post* 1898.

KEELER, RALPH OLMSTEAD (*b. on site of present Custar, O., 1840; d. at sea, 1873*), journalist, foreign correspondent. Author of autobiographical *Vagabond Adventures* (1870) and other works.

KEELEY, LESLIE E. (*b. St. Lawrence Co., N.Y., 1832; d. Los Angeles, Calif., 1900*), physician. Graduated Rush Medical College, 1864; practiced at Dwight, Ill. Exploited commercially the "Keeley Cure" for chronic alcoholism and drug addiction.

KEELY, JOHN ERNST WORRELL (*b. probably Philadelphia, Pa., 1827; d. 1898*), inventor and imposter. Claimed discovery of a new physical force; organized Keely Motor Co. *post* 1874 to exploit it; mulcted thousands of trusting investors.

KEEN, MORRIS LONGSTRETH (*b. Philadelphia, Pa., 1820; d. near Stroudsburg, Pa., 1883*), inventor, wood-pulp manufacturer. Patented several papermaking processes; established American Wood Paper Co., 1863.

KEEN, WILLIAM WILLIAMS (*b. Philadelphia, Pa., 1837; d. 1932*), surgeon. M.D., Jefferson Medical, 1862. Served as Union medical officer. Was professor of surgery at his alma mater, 1889–1907. Said to have performed the first (1887) successful operation for brain tumor in the United States. Co-author and editor of numerous works. [*Supp. 1*]

KEENAN, JAMES FRANCIS (*b. Dubuque, Iowa, 1858; d. 1929*), character actor, better known as Frank Keenan. Particularly popular as a "road star," and active in motion pictures, 1915–29.

KEENE, JAMES ROBERT (*b. Chester, England, 1838; d. 1913*), stock-market speculator, turfman. Came to America as a boy; made fortune on San Francisco Exchange, 1866–76. Later acted as market manipulator in New York for the Havemeyers, J.P. Morgan, James J. Hill.

KEENE, LAURA (*b. England, c. 1826; d. 1873*), actress. Trained in Mme. Vestris's company; came to America, 1852, as member of James W. Wallack's New York company. Enjoyed brilliant success as comedy star; was a pioneer woman theatre manager in New York, 1855; encouraged native authors. Played at Ford's Theatre, Washington, D.C., on night Lincoln was assassinated.

KEENE, THOMAS WALLACE (*b. New York, N.Y., 1840; d. Castleton, Staten Island, N.Y., 1898*), actor. Made countrywide tours in Shakespeare repertory, 1880–98, playing in the old, robust style of an earlier day.

KEENER, WILLIAM ALBERT (*b. Augusta, Ga., 1856; d. New York, N.Y., 1913*), lawyer, educator. Graduated Emory, 1874; Harvard Law School, 1877. Was distinguished professor of law at Harvard and Columbia; helped reorganize law teaching on case-system for which he edited a series of standard textbooks. Dean, Columbia Law School, 1891–1901.

KEEP, HENRY (*b. Adams, N.Y., 1818; d. New York, N.Y., 1869*) financier. *Post* 1850, was one of the boldest and most successful Wall Street operators in railroad stocks.

KEEP, ROBERT PORTER (*b. Farmington, Conn., 1844; d. Farmington, 1904*), educator. Graduated Yale, 1865; Ph.D., 1869. Progressive principal, Free Academy of Norwich, Conn., 1885–1902.

KEHEW, MARY MORTON KIMBALL (*b. Boston, Mass., 1859; d. 1918*), leader in constructive social movements, especially for women in industry; was moving spirit of Women's Educational and Industrial Union, 1892–1918.

KEIFER, JOSEPH WARREN (*b. near Springfield, O., 1836; d. 1932*), lawyer, Union soldier. Congressman, Republican, from Ohio, 1877–85, 1905–11. Served as mediocre speaker of the House, 1881–83. [*Supp. 1*]

KEIMER, SAMUEL (*b. London, England, 1688; d. Barbados, B.W.I., c. 1739*), printer. Emigrated to Philadelphia, Pa., 1722; employed Benjamin Franklin in his shop, 1723, and at a later period. Removed to Barbados after bankruptcy, 1729.

KEITH, BENJAMIN FRANKLIN (*b. Hillsboro Bridge, N.H., 1846; d. Palm Beach, Fla., 1914*), theatre owner, vaudeville manager. Presented first "continuous performance" shows in America at Gaiety Theatre, Boston, Mass., *post* 1883; organized Keith Circuit; partner in Keith and Proctor *post* 1906. Raised standard of taste in vaudeville entertainment.

KEITH, GEORGE (*b. Peterhead, Scotland, c. 1638; d. England, 1716*), founder of "Christian Quakers," schoolmaster, Anglican missionary. Became a Quaker, 1664; was associated with Quaker founders, Fox, Penn and Barclay. Appointed New Jersey surveyor-general c. 1685, he settled in Philadelphia, Pa., 1689; was headmaster of the school founded there by William Penn. Critical of Quaker failure to appreciate Christ, he entered into controversy with Quaker leaders, his followers becoming known as "Christian Quakers" or "Keithians." Disowned by the Quakers, he took Anglican orders, 1700, and worked as a missionary in America, 1702–04.

KEITH, JAMES (*b. near Warrenton, Va., 1839; d. 1918*), Confederate soldier, jurist. Virginia circuit judge; president, state supreme court of appeals, 1895–1916; exercised a paramount influence on Virginia jurisprudence.

KEITH, MINOR COOPER (*b. Brooklyn, N.Y., 1848; d. 1929*), capitalist, Central American railroad builder and banana planter. A founder of United Fruit Co.

KEITH, Sir WILLIAM (*b. probably Peterhead, Scotland, 1680; d. London, England, 1749*), royal customs official. Governor of Pennsylvania and Delaware, 1717–26; espoused popular interests against the proprietors. Advised British government on colonial matters after his return to England, 1728.

KEITH, WILLIAM (*b. Old Meldrum, Scotland, 1839; d. 1911*), landscape painter, engraver. Came to America as a boy. Removed, 1859, to California whose scenery was theme of his numerous paintings. Friend of George Inness, John Burroughs, John Muir, he painted with poetic intensity and a wealth of color.

KEITT, LAWRENCE MASSILLON (*b. Orangeburg District, S.C., 1824; d. Cold Harbor, Va., 1864*), lawyer. Congressman, Democrat, from South Carolina, 1853–60; a "tempestuous" radical slavery leader and secessionist. Killed as colonel, 20th South Carolina Volunteers.

KELLER, ARTHUR IGNATIUS (*b. New York, N.Y., 1867; d. New York, 1924*), painter, book and magazine illustrator.

KELLER, MATHIAS (*b. Ulm, Württemberg, 1813; d. Boston, Mass., 1875*), composer, song-writer. Came to America, 1846. Author of a number of Civil War anthems and other patriotic compositions.

KELLERMAN, KARL FREDERIC (*b. Göttingen, Germany, 1879; d. Washington, D.C., 1934*), plant physiologist. Born of American parents; graduated Cornell, 1900. Served in Bureau of Plant Industry, U.S. Department of Agriculture *post* 1901; developed *Journal of Agricultural Research*. Among many programs which he directed was that in which the Oriental citrus canker disease was brought under control in the United States, the first instance of a substantially complete eradication of a widespread destructive bacterial plant disease. [*Supp. 1*]

KELLEY, ALFRED (*b. Middlefield, Conn., 1789; d. 1859*), lawyer, Ohio legislator, canal and railroad builder. His many enterprises deeply affected the material welfare of Ohio, especially Cleveland where he settled, 1810; he resided in Columbus, O., *post* 1830. He founded Ohio's state canal system, saved its public credit (1841–43), and was author of its system of banking and taxation.

KELLEY, FLORENCE (*b. Philadelphia, Pa., 1859; d. 1932*), social worker. Daughter of William D. Kelley. Member of the Hull-House group in Chicago and the Henry Street Settlement in New York; helped establish U.S. Children's Bureau. [*Supp. 1*]

KELLEY, HALL JACKSON (*b. Northwood, N.H., 1790; d. 1874*), teacher, surveyor. Became obsessed *c.* 1829 with a plan for colonizing Oregon; incorporated American Society for Encouraging the Settlement of the Oregon Territory, 1831, enlisting prospective emigrants, of whom only Nathaniel J. Wyeth

actually made the journey. Traveling to Mexico and thence to California, Kelley himself reached Fort Vancouver, October 1834. Cared for during the winter by a Hudson's Bay Co. official, he was transported home by sea, returning to Boston, 1836. Subsequently, he wrote a "Memoir" (published with Caleb Cushing's report on Oregon in *House Report No. 101, 25 Cong., 3 Sess., App.*), and many petitions for reimbursement of his losses. An impressive fanatic with some real ability, he exerted appreciable influence in favor of American occupation of Oregon.

KELLEY, JAMES DOUGLAS JERROLD (*b. New York, N.Y., 1847; d. New York, 1922*), naval officer. Graduated Annapolis, 1868. Writer on yachting and maritime history; wireless pioneer.

KELLEY, OLIVER HUDSON (*b. Boston, Mass., 1826; d. Washington, D.C., 1913*), farmer, land speculator, founder of the Grange. Removed to Minnesota, 1849; became an enthusiastic advertiser of its advantages to settlers. As clerk in U.S. Bureau of Agriculture, 1864–66, he traveled in Minnesota and the South, surveying agricultural conditions. Conceiving the idea of organizing farmers into a fraternal organization, in the winter of 1867 he founded and became secretary of the National Grange of the Patrons of Husbandry. The depression of the 1870's and the order's usefulness in the fight against monopolies caused farmers to join in numbers; by 1874 there were over 20,000 granges. Kelley resigned as secretary, 1878.

KELLEY, WILLIAM DARRAH (*b. Philadelphia, Pa., 1814; d. Washington, D.C., 1890*), Philadelphia jurist, politician. Congressman, Republican, from Pennsylvania, 1861–90; was called "Pig Iron" because of his high protectionist sentiments. He was also an advocate of inflationary financial policies.

KELLOGG, ALBERT (*b. New Hartford, Conn., 1813; d. Alameda, Calif., 1887*), physician, botanist. Settled in California, 1849; practiced in San Francisco. Wrote first botanical account of California's *silvas*.

KELLOGG, CLARA LOUISE (*b. Sumterville, S.C., 1842; d. New Hartford, Conn., 1916*), dramatic soprano. Trained in America. Made New York début in Verdi's *Rigoletto* as Gilda, 1861; identified with role of Marguerite in *Faust*.

KELLOGG, EDWARD (*b. Norwalk, Conn., 1790; d. Brooklyn, N.Y., 1858*), businessman, financial reformer. Invented the "interconvertible bond plan of financial reform"; was the intellectual father of Greenbackism. Author of *Labor and Other Capital* (1849).

KELLOGG, ELIJAH (*b. Portland, Maine, 1813; d. 1901*), Congregational clergyman. Author, among other works, of "Spartacus to the Gladiators" (published 1846 in E. Sargent's *School Reader*) and a number of excellent adventure stories for boys of which *Lion Ben* (1869) is representative.

KELLOGG, FRANK BILLINGS (*b. Potsdam, N.Y., 1856; d. St. Paul, Minn., 1937*), lawyer. Raised in Minnesota. Law partner of Cushman K. Davis *post* 1887; active in "trust busting," 1905–12, notably in compelling dismemberment of Standard Oil. U.S. senator, Republican, from Minnesota, 1917–23; U.S. ambassador to Great Britain, 1923–25; secretary of state, 1925–29; co-signer of Kellogg-Briand Pact outlawing war, 1928. [*Supp. 2*]

KELLOGG, MARTIN (*b. Vernon, Conn., 1828; d. Berkeley, Calif., 1903*), Congregational clergyman. Graduated Yale, 1850. Taught *post* 1861 at present University of California; was also dean, 1869–85, and president, 1893–99.

KELLOGG, SAMUEL HENRY (*b. Quogue, N.Y., 1839; d. Landour, India, 1899*), Presbyterian clergyman. Missionary to India for various tours of duty, 1864–99; compiled a monumental *Grammar of the Hindi Language* and other works.

KELLOGG, WILLIAM PITT (*b. Orwell, Vt., 1830; d. Washington, D.C., 1918*), lawyer, Union soldier. Conspicuous as a Carpet-bag politician after the Civil War. Served as U.S. senator from Louisiana, 1868–72, 1877–83; also as controversial Republican governor, 1873–77.

KELLY, ALOYSIUS OLIVER JOSEPH (*b. Philadelphia, Pa., 1870; d. 1911*), physician, pathologist. Graduated La Salle College, 1888; M.D., University of Pennsylvania, 1891; studied also in Vienna. Instructor and professor of medicine, University of Pennsylvania, 1896–1911; occupied a high position in medical literature as editor and writer; taught also at University of Vermont and at Woman's Medical College of Pennsylvania.

KELLY, EDMOND (*b. Blagnac, France, 1851; d. near Nyack, N.Y., 1909*), lawyer, political reformer, sociologist.

KELLY, EUGENE (*b. Co. Tyrone, Ireland, 1808; d. 1894*), banker, philanthropist. Came to America as a young man. Prospered in California, 1850–57; conducted private bank in New York City thereafter. A founder and benefactor of Catholic University.

KELLY, JOHN (*b. New York, N.Y., 1822; d. 1886*), New York politician and congressman. Became dictator of Tammany Hall after the "Tweed Ring" had discredited it; ruled it autocratically, 1873–82.

KELLY, LUTHER SAGE (*b. Geneva, N.Y., 1849; d. Paradise, Calif., 1928*), army scout, known as "Yellowstone Kelly." His memoirs of service in the old West were published in 1926.

KELLY, MICHAEL J. (*b. Troy, N.Y., 1857; d. Boston, Mass., 1894*), baseball player, known as "King Kelly" and the "Ten Thousand Dollar Beauty." Popular idol of the Chicago White Stockings; object of the slogan, "Slide, Kelly, slide!"

KELLY, MYRA (*b. Dublin, Ireland, 1875; d. Torquay, England, 1910*), teacher. Came to America as a child. Author of *Little Citizens* (1904), *Little Aliens* (1910) and other stories about immigrant children she knew while teaching on New York's East Side.

KELLY, WILLIAM (*b. Pittsburgh, Pa., 1811; d. Louisville, Ky., 1888*), original inventor of the "air-boiling process," later known as the Bessemer process, of steel making. With his brother, purchased Kentucky iron-ore land and a furnace and developed the Suwanee Iron Works & Union Forge, manufacturing sugar kettles. Worrying over high costs of production of wrought iron and a diminishing charcoal supply, he noticed one day that the air-blast in his furnace blowing on molten iron with no charcoal covering raised the iron to white heat. Further experiments revealed that the carbon contained in molten cast-iron could be employed under air-blast as a fuel, and in burning out could make the molten mass much hotter. Failing to convince his relatives and customers of the significance of his discovery, he began building the first of seven experimental converters which he secretly constructed between 1851 and 1856. Though the Englishman Henry Bessemer was granted a U.S. patent on the same process in 1856, Kelly convinced patent officials of his priority and on June 23, 1857, was granted a patent and declared to be the original inventor. He later interested Daniel J. Morrell in his process and was encouraged to work it out at the Cambria Iron Works, Johnstown, Pa. An eighth experimental converter was a failure, but on a second trial succeeded; for the first time soft steel could be made cheaply and in the large quantities necessary for rails and other products of the great "Steel Age" just beginning. Steel under the Kelly patent was first blown commercially at the Wyandotte Iron Works near Detroit, Mich., in the fall of 1864.

KELPIUS, JOHANN (*b. near Schässburg, Transylvania, 1673; d. 1708*), mystic. Saintly leader of a community established near Germantown, Pa., 1694, to await the Millennium.

KELSEY, FRANCIS WILLEY (*b. Ogden, N.Y., 1858; d. 1927*), classicist, archaeologist. Graduated University of Rochester, 1880. Professor of Latin, University of Michigan, 1889–1927; instituted its *Studies: Humanistic Series* and organized its Near Eastern expeditions.

KELSEY, RAYNER WICKERSHAM (*b. Western Springs, Ill., 1879; d. Haverford, Pa., 1934*), Quaker minister, teacher. Professor of history at Haverford College *post* 1911. [*Supp. 1*]

KELTON, JOHN CUNNINGHAM (*b. Delaware Co., Pa., 1828; d. Washington, D.C., 1893*), soldier. Graduated West Point, 1851. Served on frontier duty and as instructor at West Point; was a staff officer to Gen. H. W. Halleck, 1861–65. Inventor of many improvements for the service rifle and revolver; adjutant-general, U.S. Army, 1889–92.

KEMBLE, FRANCES ANNE (*b. London, England, 1809; d. London, 1893*), actress, author. A member of one of the great English stage families, Fanny Kemble came to America, 1832, on tour with her father and won high acclaim as Bianca in *Fazio,* as Juliet, and especially as Julia in *The Hunchback.* She married Pierce Butler, a wealthy American in 1834 and retired from the theatre, a profession she acutely disliked despite her success. In 1835 she published *Journal of a Residence in America,* a record of her tour which criticized American customs; during a winter on her husband's Georgia plantation (1838–39), she kept a second journal expressive of her revulsion at slavery. This appeared as a book in 1863 and was issued to influence British public opinion on the Civil War. Meanwhile, she climaxed estrangement from her husband by leaving him, 1846; after a brief return to the stage and a divorce, 1849, she entered on a highly successful career of public readings from Shakespeare which she continued until 1869.

KEMBLE, GOUVERNEUR (*b. New York, N.Y., 1786; d. Cold Spring, N.Y., 1875*), cannon founder, congressman. Established the West Point Foundry at Cold Spring, N.Y., 1818. He was a friend of Washington Irving and J. K. Paulding.

KEMEYS, EDWARD (*b. Savannah, Ga., 1843; d. Georgetown, D.C., 1907*), sculptor. First American to specialize in animal sculpture; self-taught, he studied his subjects in natural habitats.

KEMP, JAMES (*b. Keith Hall, Aberdeenshire, Scotland, 1764; d. 1827*), Episcopal clergyman. Graduated Marischal College, Aberdeen, 1786. Came to America as a tutor, 1787; ordained at Philadelphia, 1789; rector at Great Choptank, Md., 1790–1813. Assistant bishop and bishop of Maryland, 1814–27.

KEMP, JAMES FURMAN (*b. New York, N.Y., 1859; d. Great Neck, N.Y., 1926*), geologist, mining engineer. Professor of geology, Columbia University, 1892–1926; specialist in study of ore deposition and alteration.

KEMP, JOHN (*b. Auchlossan, Scotland, 1763; d. New York, N.Y., 1812*), educator. Came to America, 1783, on graduation from Marischal College, Aberdeen. Professor, Columbia College, New York, 1785–1812; taught mathematics, geography and the natural sciences. Influenced De Witt Clinton in projecting Erie Canal.

KEMP, ROBERT H. (*b. Wellfleet, Mass., 1820; d. Charlestown, Mass., 1897*), shoe dealer. Director of "Old Folks' Concerts" of sacred music, originally given at Reading, Mass.

KEMPER, JACKSON (*b. Pleasant Valley, N.Y., 1789; d. Delafield, Wis., 1870*), Episcopal clergyman. Graduated Columbia, 1809; ordained, 1814; served first in Philadelphia parish. Developed early interest in West, making missionary journeys into frontier Pennsylvania, Virginia and Ohio; visited Indian Mission near Green Bay, Wis., 1834. Elected missionary bishop of "the Northwest," 1835, he was until 1859 a familiar and beloved figure throughout Missouri, Indiana, Wisconsin and Iowa. In 1854 he became diocesan of Wisconsin, devoting himself exclusively to that see *post* 1859. He established seven dioceses, founded three colleges to train clergymen, opened numerous schools and academies and planted the Episcopal Church firmly in the Northwest.

KEMPER, JAMES LAWSON (*b. Madison Co., Va., 1823; d. Orange Co., Va., 1895*), lawyer, Virginia legislator, Confederate major-general. Democratic governor of Virginia, 1874–77, he provided an administration marked by independence and integrity.

KEMPER, REUBEN (*b. probably Loudoun or Fauquier Co., Va., date unknown; d. Natchez, Miss., 1827*), controversial figure on the West Florida border, associated 1800–02 with John Smith (*c. 1735–c. 1824*). Led filibustering attempts to subvert Spanish rule, 1804 and 1810.

KEMPFF, LOUIS (*b. near Belleville, Ill., 1841; d. Santa Barbara, Calif., 1920*), naval officer. Attended Naval Academy, 1857–61; served on Civil War blockade duty. As senior American naval officer at Taku during Boxer troubles (1900), refused to join attack of international fleet on Chinese forts.

KEMPSTER, WALTER (*b. London, England, 1841; d. Milwaukee, Wis., 1918*), physician, psychiatrist. Came to America as a boy. Graduated Long Island College Hospital, 1864, after Civil War service. Practiced in Milwaukee *post* 1884.

KENDALL, AMOS (*b. Dunstable, Mass., 1789; d. 1869*), journalist. Graduated Dartmouth, 1811. Migrated to Kentucky, 1814; edited *Argus of Western America* at Frankfort, 1816–29; helped carry Kentucky for Andrew Jackson in 1828. For the next twelve years Kendall was closely identified with the Jacksonian regime, as treasury auditor, as postmaster-general, but most importantly as a member of the "Kitchen Cabinet." The most capable and successful of Jackson's administrators, he prepared many public papers, including the veto message of July 10, 1832, and other documents relative to Jackson's war on the Bank of the United States. Engaged in journalism and farming, 1840–45, he entered in the latter year on a new phase of his career as business agent of Samuel F. B. Morse, by 1859 becoming a rich man. A vigorous War Democrat, 1860–65, he devoted the closing years of his life to church work and to the school for mutes now called Gallaudet College. His "Letter to Rutherford" (1868) was a keen and searching criticism of Republican policy toward the South.

KENDALL, GEORGE WILKINS (*b. Mount Vernon, N.H., 1809; d. Texas, 1867*), journalist. Learned printing in Vermont and worked in Washington, D.C., and New York City before going south about 1832. He founded the first cheap daily in New Orleans, the *Picayune*, whose first number appeared in January 1837. His instinct for news and ardor for adventure led him to join the ill-fated 1841 raid into Mexico which he chronicled in the widely read *Narrative of the Texan Santa Fé Expedition* (1844). He campaigned through the *Picayune* for war with Mexico; when it came, he attached himself to the army. The *Picayune* became famous for its war news, and "Mr. Kendall's express" often out-sped government dispatches. His *The War between the United States and Mexico* (1851) is celebrated for its splendid illustrations by Nebel.

KENDRICK, ASAHEL CLARK (*b. Poultney, Vt., 1809; d. 1895*), scholar, classicist. Graduated Hamilton, 1831. Taught Greek language and literature at present Colgate University, 1831–50, and at University of Rochester, 1850–88; developed a new method for its study.

KENDRICK, JOHN (*b. Harwich, Mass., c. 1740; d. Honolulu Harbor, Hawaii, 1794*), navigator, Revolutionary privateersman, trader. Commanded expedition of *Columbia* and *Lady Washington* from Boston to Nootka, 1787–89, in association with Robert Gray. First to fly the American flag in Japan, 1791; traded between the Northwest Coast and the Orient, 1789–94. Killed by accidental cannon fire.

KENDRICK, JOHN BENJAMIN (*b. Cherokee Co., Tex., 1857; d. near Sheridan, Wyo., 1933*), rancher. Democratic governor of Wyoming, 1915–17; U.S. senator, 1917–33. [*Supp. 1*]

KENEDY, PATRICK JOHN (*b. New York, N.Y., 1843; d. 1906*), Catholic book-seller and publisher. Directed present firm of P. J. Kenedy & Sons, New York, 1866–1904.

KENNA, JOHN EDWARD (*b. Kanawha Co., Va., now W. Va., 1848; d. 1893*), lawyer. Congressman, Democrat, from W. Virginia, 1877–83; U.S. senator, 1883–93. Championed federal railroad regulation and aid for slack-water navigation on the Kanawha.

KENNAN, GEORGE (*b. Norwalk, O., 1845; d. 1924*), explorer, journalist. Author of *Tent Life in Siberia* (1870) and *Siberia and the Exile System* (1891), which were important original contributions to the world's knowledge of Russia.

KENNEDY, ARCHIBALD (*b. Scotland, 1685; d. 1763*), British colonial official. Came to New York *ante* 1710. Served as collector of customs and member of the Council; was author of pamphlets dissenting from the methods of British mercantilist policy.

KENNEDY, JOHN DOBY (*b. Camden, S.C., 1840; d. Camden, 1896*), lawyer, Confederate brigadier-general, South Carolina legislator. Helped restore white supremacy after the Civil War.

KENNEDY, JOHN PENDLETON (*b. Baltimore, Md., 1795; d. Newport, R.I., 1870*), author, statesman. Wrote three outstanding pieces of fiction: *Swallow Barn* (under pseudonym "Mark Littleton," 1832), *Horse-Shoe Robinson* (same pseudonym, 1835) and *Rob of the Bowl* (1838). He was author also of *Memoirs of the Life of William Wirt* (1842) and various minor works. He served as congressman, Whig, from Maryland, 1838 and 1841–45. As secretary of the navy, 1852–53, he organized four important expeditions, including Com. Perry's to Japan. He strove to prevent secession and supported the Union but favored "amnesty and forgiveness" after the Civil War.

KENNEDY, JOHN STEWART (*b. Blantyre, Scotland, 1830; d. 1909*), capitalist, philanthropist. Settled in America, 1857, as banking partner of Morris K. Jesup; important in Western railroad-building as head of J. S. Kennedy and Co., 1868–83.

KENNEDY, JOSEPH CAMP GRIFFITH (*b. Meadville, Pa., 1813; d. 1887*), statistician. Superintendent of the censuses of 1850 and 1860. Helped organize the First International Statistical Congress (Brussels, 1853).

KENNEDY, ROBERT PATTERSON (*b. Bellefontaine, O., 1840; d. Columbus, O., 1918*), Union brigadier-general, lawyer, Republican congressman. Lieutenant-governor of Ohio, 1886–87.

KENNEDY, WILLIAM SLOANE (*b. Brecksville, O., 1850; d. West Yarmouth, Mass., 1929*), biographer, anthologist. Intimate friend of Walt Whitman; author of *Reminiscences of Walt Whitman* (1896) and other volumes on the poet and his work.

KENNELLY, ARTHUR EDWIN (*b. Colaba, India, 1861; d. Boston, Mass., 1939*), electrical engineer. Left school at 13 to work in office of Society of Telegraph Engineers, London; studied physics in his spare time. Worked for Eastern Telegraph Co. as operator and in submarine cable work, 1876–86. In 1887 he came to the United States and was chief electrical assistant to Thomas A. Edison until 1894. After some years as consulting engineer in partnership with Edwin J. Houston, Kennelly in 1902 became professor of engineering at Harvard, retiring in 1930. He also taught at Massachusetts Institute of Technology.

Kennelly contributed to electrical engineering as an originator, but especially as an interpreter. His careful choice of nomenclature, clarity of exposition and meticulous mathematical presentations made possible the general use of abstruse methods of analysis by many in his profession. For example, in the field of circuit theory Kennelly's paper on impedance (1893) crystallized the application of the so-called imaginary and complex variables to alternating currents, and led to the wide use of complex numbers in analyzing alternating-current phenomena. Similarly, his application of complex hyperbolic functions to the solution of line problems advanced the development of electrical engineering by many years. In 1902 Kennelly proposed the theory that the conducting properties of the ionized rarefied upper atmosphere reflected electromagnetic waves. The theory, also advanced by the English physicist and electrician Oliver Heaviside, was later verified experimentally. Kennelly's publications included twenty-eight books and over 350 technical papers. [*Supp. 2*]

KENNER, DUNCAN FARRAR (*b. New Orleans, La., 1813; d. New Orleans, 1887*), sugar planter, Louisiana legislator. Originated an unsuccessful project, 1864–65, to obtain recognition of the Confederacy by England and France in return for abolition of slavery.

KENNICOTT, ROBERT (*b. New Orleans, La., 1835; d. Fort Nulato, Alaska, 1866*), naturalist, explorer. A founder (1856) of Chicago Academy of Sciences; collected fauna from British North America and Alaska which became part of its collections.

KENRICK, FRANCIS PATRICK (*b. Dublin, Ireland, 1796; d. 1863*), Roman Catholic clergyman. Brother of Peter R. Kenrick. Came to America after ordination in Rome, 1821; worked in Kentucky. Bishop-coadjutor and bishop of Philadelphia, 1830–51; became archbishop of Baltimore, 1851. Effective in fight against trusteeism (1831) and against nativism, 1844; noted as preacher and scholar.

KENRICK, PETER RICHARD (*b. Dublin, Ireland, 1806; d. 1896*), Roman Catholic clergyman. Brother of Francis P. Kenrick. Came to America, 1833; was pastor in Philadelphia, Pa., and vicar-general of the diocese. Bishop-coadjutor of St. Louis, Mo., 1841–43; bishop, 1843–47; archbishop thereafter until *c.* 1891. A prominent opponent of infallibility at Vatican Council, 1870.

KENRICK, WILLIAM (*b. Newton, Mass, 1789; d. Newton, 1872*), nurseryman. Author of *The New American Orchardist* (1833).

KENSETT, JOHN FREDERICK (*b. Cheshire, Conn., 1816; d. 1872*), landscape painter, engraver. Associate of A. B. Durand, John W. Casilear, T. P. Rossiter and Benjamin Champney; studied in Paris, England and Italy, 1840–47. Painted somewhat thin, atmospheric canvases imbued with the sincerest love of nature.

KENT, CHARLES FOSTER (*b. Palmyra, N.Y., 1867; d. 1925*), Biblical scholar, educator. Graduated Yale, 1889; Ph.D., 1891. Taught at University of Chicago, Brown and Yale. Founded National Council on Religion in Higher Education. Made the results of modern Biblical study widely accessible in a number of readable popular books.

KENT, EDWARD (*b. Concord, N.H., 1802; d. Bangor, Maine, 1877*), lawyer, Maine legislator and jurist. Whig governor of Maine, 1838–39 and 1841–42.

KENT, JAMES (*b. Fredericksburgh, now Southeast, N.Y., 1763; d. New York, N.Y., 1847*), jurist, legal commentator. Graduated Yale, 1781. Earlier, his reading of *Blackstone's Commentaries* had inspired him to become a lawyer. After three years in the Poughkeepsie law office of Attorney-Gen. Egbert Benson, Kent was admitted to the New York bar and practiced in Poughkeepsie until 1793, when he removed to New York City. He had already established political affiliations with Federalist leaders and become an admirer of Alexander Hamilton. Though three times elected to the New York Assembly, his political influence was exerted through judicial office. Stoutly conservative, he fought always for the rights of the individual as distinguished from those of the people. Briefly in financial straits, in December 1793 he secured appointment as first professor of law at Columbia College. The failure of his courses to attract students led him to resign early in 1798, shortly after Gov. Jay appointed him a judge of the New York supreme court. He became chief justice of the court, 1804, and chancellor of the New York court of chancery, 1814.

Kent's record as judge is to be found in the three sets of law reports published by William Johnson. His reports span the years 1799–1823, and preserve a line of decisions in law and equity which are basic in American jurisprudence. As chancellor, Kent was practically the creator of equity jurisdiction in the United States. "I took the court," he wrote, "as if it had been a new institution, and never before known in the United States. I had nothing to guide me, and was left at liberty to assume all such English Chancery powers and jurisdiction as I thought applicable under our Constitution. This gave me grand scope, and I was checked only by the revision of the Senate, or Court of Errors." At a time when English law and legal institutions were regarded here with distrust, Kent preserved their best features and justified his work by his own high standard of integrity and judicial conduct.

Forced to retire as chancellor by New York constitutional provision in 1823, he accepted reappointment to the law professorship at Columbia. He delivered three courses of lectures (1824–26) before again abandoning a task which he disliked. Urged by his son, he began the rewriting and expansion of his law lectures into a work on which his reputation rests no less firmly than on his judicial decisions, the *Commentaries on American Law* (1826–28, 1830). Many times revised, the *Commentaries* was of fundamental importance and still remains the foremost American institutional legal treatise.

KENT, JOSEPH (*b. Calvert Co., Md., 1779; d. near Bladensburg, Md., 1837*), physician. Congressman from Maryland, Federalist, 1811–15; (Democrat) Republican, 1819–26. National Republican leader and friend of Henry Clay *post* 1824, he served as governor of Maryland, 1826–28, and as U.S. senator, 1833–37.

KENT, WILLIAM (*b. Philadelphia, Pa., 1851; d. Gananoque, Canada, 1918*), mechanical engineer. Established Pittsburgh Testing Laboratory *c.* 1882, the pioneer commercial physical testing laboratory. Author of *Mechanical Engineers' Pocket-Book* (1895) first handbook of the modern type.

KENTON, SIMON (*b. probably Fauquier Co., Va., 1755; d. near Zanesfield, O., 1836*), frontiersman, Indian fighter. Hunted along the Ohio until 1774, when he served as a scout in Dunmore's War. Settled in Boonesborough, Ky., 1775; was appointed a scout by Daniel Boone and participated in all local encounters with the Indians. Accompanied George R. Clark to Kaskaskia, 1778, and scouted on the Little Miami; captured, he was taken to Detroit by the British but escaped to scout for Clark again in 1780 and 1782. Established himself at Maysville, Ky., 1785; served with Wayne's expedition, 1794. Removing to Ohio, 1798–99, he was made brigadier-general of militia, 1805. In the War of 1812 he fought with Gen. Shelby's Kentuckians at the battle of the Thames. His latter years were spent in poverty.

KENYON, WILLIAM SQUIRE (*b. Elyria, O., 1869; d. Maine, 1933*), lawyer, jurist. Raised in Iowa. U.S. senator, progressive Republican, from Iowa, 1911–22. Supported labor; *post* 1918, organized and led "farm bloc" of Western and Southern senators. As U.S. circuit judge, 1922–33, he cancelled the Teapot Dome leases. [*Supp.* 1]

KEOKUK (*b. Sauk village on Rock River, Ill., c. 1790; d. Sauk Agency, Franklin Co., Kans., probably 1848*), Sauk war leader. Succeeded Black Hawk as chief; consistently aided government Indian policy.

KEPHART, EZEKIEL BORING (*b. Clearfield Co., Pa., 1834; d. 1906*), United Brethren clergyman, educator. Brother of Isaiah L. Kephart. President, Western College, Western, Iowa, 1868–81; rendered his greatest service as bishop of the United Brethren Church, 1881–1905.

KEPHART, ISAIAH LAFAYETTE (*b. Clearfield Co., Pa., 1832; d. 1908*), United Brethren clergyman. Brother of Ezekiel B. Kephart. Editor, the *Religious Telescope*, 1887–1908.

KEPPEL, FREDERICK (*b. Tullow, Ireland, 1845; d. 1912*), print-dealer, art-critic. Emigrated to Canada, 1862; removed to Utica, N.Y., 1864; thence to New York City where he opened his first print shop, 1868.

KEPPLER, JOSEPH (*b. Vienna, Austria, 1838; d. New York, N.Y., 1894*), caricaturist. Came to America, 1867. Founded several German comic papers, achieving success with *Puck*, 1876 (issued also in English *post* 1877), for which he lithographed cartoons in colors and provided an exuberant German flavor and satirical sense in comment on public affairs.

KERBY, WILLIAM JOSEPH (*b. Lawler, Iowa, 1870; d. Washington, D.C., 1936*), Roman Catholic clergyman, sociologist. Graduated Loras College, 1889; ordained 1892. Pupil of Thomas J. Bouquillon at Catholic University of America; Ph.D., Louvain, 1897. Taught sociology at Catholic University, 1897–1936. His interest in social reform led him to organize National Conference of Catholic Charities, 1910, of which he was secretary, 1910–18. For participating in social welfare conferences and advocating legislative reforms Kerby was sometimes criticized, but he in turn criticized "Catholic isolationism." His efforts led to the founding (1921) of the National Catholic School of Social Service. He was a pioneer in arousing the American Catholic social conscience. [*Supp. 2*]

KERENS, RICHARD C. (*b. Kilberry, Ireland, 1842; d. Merion, Pa., 1916*), railroad builder, Republican politician. Came to America as an infant. After Civil War service with Union Army, prospered in Southern overland mail contract hauling, 1866–76; thereafter in West Virginia and other railroads. *Post* 1876, he was influential and active in Missouri politics.

KERFOOT, JOHN BARRETT (*b. Dublin, Ireland, 1816; d. Meyersdale, Pa., 1881*), Episcopal clergyman. Came to America as a child; was protegé of William A. Muhlenberg. Principal of St. James Hall, Md., 1842–64; briefly president, Trinity College. First bishop of Pittsburgh, 1866–81.

KERLIN, ISAAC NEWTON (*b. Burlington, N.J., 1834; d. 1893*), pioneer psychiatrist. Graduated University of Pennsylvania, M.D., 1856. Made important contributions toward understanding and care of the mentally deficient; superintended the Pennsylvania Training School at Elwyn.

KERN, JOHN WORTH (*b. Alto, Ind., 1849; d. Asheville, N.C., 1917*), lawyer, Indiana legislator. U.S. senator, Democrat, from Indiana, 1911–17; a leader of the progressives and a fighter for social justice.

KERNAN, FRANCIS (*b. Wayne, now Tyrone, N.Y., 1816; d. 1892*), lawyer, New York legislator. Practiced in Utica, N.Y. Associate of Samuel J. Tilden in breaking the Tweed Ring. Denied governorship by religious prejudice, he served as U.S. senator, Democrat, from New York, 1875–81.

KERNEY, JAMES (*b. Trenton, N.J., 1873; d. Baltimore, Md., 1934*), editor of *Trenton Evening Times*, *post* 1903; adviser and friend of Woodrow Wilson. [*Supp. 1*]

KERR, JOHN GLASGOW (*b. near Duncansville, O., 1824; d. 1901*), Presbyterian missionary, physician. Headed Medical Missionary Society's hospital at Canton, China, 1855–98; pioneered there in treatment of the insane.

KERR, WALTER CRAIG (*b. St. Peter, Minn., 1858; d. 1910*), engineer. Graduated Cornell, 1879. Moving spirit in organizing Westinghouse, Church, Kerr and Co., first firm to undertake entire contracts for construction of large engineering properties.

KERR, WASHINGTON CARUTHERS (*b. Guilford Co., N.C., 1827; d. Asheville, N.C., 1885*), geologist. As North Carolina state geologist c. 1865–82, produced the state survey map, 1882, and advertised North Carolina resources.

KERSHAW, JOSEPH BREVARD (*b. Camden, S.C., 1822; d. Camden, 1894*), Confederate major-general, South Carolina legislator, jurist. Commanded "Kershaw's Brigade" with Army of Northern Virginia and also in Tennessee campaign, 1863–64.

KESTER, PAUL (*b. Delaware, O., 1870; d. Lake Mohegan, N.Y., 1933*), playwright. Brother of Vaughan Kester; cousin of William D. Howells. Romantic author of such hits as *Sweet Nell of Old Drury* (1900) and *When Knighthood Was in Flower* (1901). [*Supp. 1*]

KESTER, VAUGHAN (*b. New Brunswick, N.J., 1869; d. Fairfax Co., Va., 1911*), journalist. Author of *The Prodigal Judge* (1911) and other fiction significant for depiction of frontier types and accurate rendering of their idiom. Brother of Paul Kester.

KETTELL, SAMUEL (*b. Newburyport, Mass., 1800; d. Malden, Mass., 1855*), author. Hack writer for Samuel G. Goodrich. Edited *Specimens of American Poetry* (1829), the first comprehensive anthology of native verse.

KEY, DAVID McKENDREE (*b. Greene Co., Tenn., 1824; d. Chattanooga, Tenn., 1900*), lawyer, Confederate soldier. U.S. senator, Democrat, from Tennessee, 1875–77; U.S. postmaster-general, 1877–80; U.S. district judge, east and middle Tennessee, 1880–94.

KEY, FRANCIS SCOTT (*b. "Terra Rubra," present Carroll Co., Md., 1779; d. Baltimore, Md., 1843*), lawyer. Nephew of Philip B. Key. Wrote "The Star Spangled Banner" during British naval bombardment of Fort McHenry, Baltimore, September 1814.

KEY, PHILIP BARTON (*b. near Charlestown, Md., 1757; d. Georgetown, D.C., 1815*), lawyer, Maryland legislator, jurist. Loyalist soldier during the Revolution; congressman, Federalist, from Maryland, 1807–13. Uncle of Francis S. Key.

KEYES, EDWARD LAWRENCE (*b. Fort Moultrie, Charleston, S.C., 1843; d. 1924*), surgeon. Son of Erasmus D. Keyes. Graduated Yale, 1863; M.D., New York University, 1866; associate of William H. Van Buren; professor at Bellevue, New York City. An American pioneer in dermatology and in male genito-urinary surgery; wrote papers of international importance on syphilis treatment.

KEYES, ELISHA WILLIAMS (*b. Northfield, Vt., 1828; d. Madison, Wis., 1910*), lawyer, politician. Postmaster of Madison, 1861–82, 1898–1910. Autocratic chairman of Wisconsin Republican central committee, 1867–1877.

KEYES, ERASMUS DARWIN (*b. Brimfield, Mass., 1810; d. Nice, France, 1895*), soldier, businessman. Graduated West Point, 1832. Performed a wide variety of services in the West and South until 1861. As brigadier-general, commanded IV Corps in Peninsular Campaign and was promoted major-general, 1862. Resigning 1864, he entered business in San Francisco, Calif. Author of *Fifty Years' Observation of Men and Events* (1884).

KEYT, ALONZO THRASHER (*b. Higginsport, O., 1827; d. Cincinnati, O., 1885*), physician, physiologist. Graduated Medical College of Ohio, M.D., 1848. Made many important contributions to knowledge of blood circulation; perfected clinical methods of diagnosis of circulatory diseases.

KICKING BIRD (*d. 1875*), Kiowa chief. Accepted reservation life in Oklahoma; kept most of his tribe at peace in south plains outbreaks, 1873–74.

KIDD, WILLIAM (*b. Greenock, Scotland, c. 1645; d. London, England, 1701*), "Captain Kidd," the most celebrated pirate in English literature. A ship-owner and sea captain in New York by 1690, Kidd rendered England and the colony useful service in the West Indies and elsewhere during King William's war with France. Since the war had precluded sending a man-of-war to protect East India Co. shipping in the Red Sea and the Indian Ocean, William III authorized the outfitting of a private expedition for the purpose, at the same time appointing the Earl of Bellomont governor of New England with special instructions to suppress piracy. Bellomont signed an agreement with Kidd on October 10, 1695, whereby Kidd accepted command of an expedition for which Bellomont undertook to raise four-fifths of the necessary investment; the net profits were to be similarly divided. Bellomont's partners were high-placed Whig members of British society; their names were kept from public knowledge. Kidd then obtained the 34-gun *Adventure Galley* and sailed for New York from Plymouth in April 1696; he filled out his crew in New York and began his mission against the pirates in September.

By spring he had reached the Comoro Islands, having avoided the pirate-infested eastern coast of Madagascar and without capturing a prize. Now, threatened by a mutinous crew, he became a pirate and determined to plunder the ships he had been sent to protect. After taking a few small vessels, he captured the rich Armenian merchantman *Quedagh Merchant* early in 1698. Scuttling his own ship, he continued his activities aboard the *Quedagh;* in September 1698, he left Madagascar for the West Indies, where he arrived in April 1699 and learned that he had been already proclaimed a pirate. Protesting his innocence, he went to Boston; after failing to convince Bellomont of his innocence, Kidd was sent to London. Tried and found guilty of murder and five instances of piracy on clear and weighty evidence, he was hanged and his property confiscated by the Crown.

KIDDER, DANIEL PARISH (*b. South Pembroke, now Darien, N.Y., 1815; d. Evanston, Ill., 1891*), Methodist clergyman, educator. Organized the Sunday School work of his church; taught at Methodist seminaries.

KIDDER, FREDERIC (*b. New Ipswich, N.H., 1804; d. Melrose, Mass., 1885*), businessman, local historian.

KIEFT, WILLEM (*b. Amsterdam, Holland, 1597; d. in shipwreck on the Welsh coast, 1647*), fifth governor of New Netherland, 1637–45. On arriving at New Amsterdam, 1638, he assumed absolute control in order to reform the dilapidated colony, but his administration is principally noted for the cruel massacre of the Indians and their retaliatory destruction of outlying settlements. Between 1639 and 1644 there were only five months of peace. In 1642 he dissolved the Board of Twelve Men and prohibited public meetings. After the murder of eighty Indians in February 1643, the people elected a new Board which complained to the States-General in Holland. Kieft was replaced by Peter Stuyvesant.

KIENTPOOS. [See CAPTAIN JACK, 1837?–1873.]

KIER, SAMUEL M. (*b. Indiana Co., Pa., 1813; d. Pittsburgh, Pa., 1874*), industrialist, pioneer oil refiner. Owned and operated canal boats on the Pennsylvania State Canal; *post* 1850, developed refined oil by a distillation process for use as illuminant.

KILBOURNE, JAMES (*b. New Britain, Conn., 1770; d. Worthington, O., 1850*), surveyor, Episcopal clergyman, Ohio pioneer. As congressman, introduced the first Homestead Bill, 1814; was early prominent as a Whig leader.

KILBY, CHRISTOPHER (*b. Boston, Mass., 1705; d. Dorking, England, 1771*), merchant, colonial agent.
[Supp. 1]

KILDAHL, JOHAN NATHAN (*b. Beitstaden, Norway, 1857; d. St. Paul, Minn., 1920*), Lutheran clergyman. Came to America as a boy. Worked to unite Lutheran bodies; became vice-president of United Norwegian Lutheran Church of America and was professor of dogmatics at St. Paul Seminary.

KILMER, ALFRED JOYCE (*b. New Brunswick, N.J., 1886; d. near Seringes, France, 1918*), poet, critic, soldier. Graduated Columbia, 1908. Author, among other works, of *Trees and Other Poems* (1914). Convert to Roman Catholicism, 1913. By death in battle, became for Americans a symbol of soldierly courage and poetic idealism.

KILPATRICK, HUGH JUDSON (*b. near Deckertown, N.J., 1836; d. Santiago, Chile, 1881*), soldier, diplomat. Graduated West Point, 1861. Rose to major-general in almost continuous brilliant service as Union cavalry commander in Civil War; initiated raid on Richmond to rescue captives from Libby Prison, 1863. U.S. minister to Chile, 1865–68 and 1881.

KILTY, WILLIAM (*b. London, England, 1757; d. Annapolis, Md., 1821*), Revolutionary army surgeon, jurist. Came to America *ante* 1775. Compiled *The Laws of Maryland* (1799–1800) and supplementary works; was chancellor of Maryland, 1806–21.

KIMBALL, GILMAN (*b. New Chester, now Hill, N.H., 1804; d. 1892*), surgeon. Graduated Dartmouth, M.D., 1827; studied also in Paris. Practiced in Lowell, Mass., *post* 1830. A pioneer in difficult gynecological and traumatic surgery.

KIMBALL, HEBER CHASE (*b. Sheldon, Vt., 1801; d. Utah, 1868*), Mormon leader. Joined the church, 1832; was ordained one of its twelve apostles, 1835; served as missionary in England and accompanied first migration to Utah, 1847. Was one of Brigham Young's chief counselors.

KIMBALL, NATHAN (*b. Fredericksburg, Ind., 1823?; d. Ogden, Utah, 1898*), physician. Served in Mexican War. Colonel, 14th Indiana, in Civil War, he was promoted brigadier-general after defeat of Stonewall Jackson at Kernstown, 1862; he won distinction also at Antietam, Fredericksburg and Vicksburg, and commanded a division in Atlanta campaign. *Post* 1873, he served as surveyor-general of Utah and postmaster of Ogden.

KIMBALL, RICHARD BURLEIGH (*b. Plainfield, N.H., 1816; d. New York, N.Y., 1892*), lawyer, author. Founded Kimball, Texas; headed first Texas railroad, 1854–60.

KIMBALL, SUMNER INCREASE (*b. Lebanon, Maine, 1834; d. Washington, D.C., 1923*), lawyer, public official. Organizer of the U.S. life-saving service; served as its general superintendent, 1878–1915.

KIMBALL, WILLIAM WIRT (*b. Paris, Maine, 1848; d. 1930*), naval officer. Graduated U.S. Naval Academy, 1869. A specialist in ordnance, he was a friend of John P. Holland and an early promoter of submarines; he commanded the first U.S. torpedo boat flotilla, 1897–98, and (as rear-admiral) the Nicaragua Expedition, 1909–10.

KING, ALBERT FREEMAN AFRICANUS (*b. Oxfordshire, England, 1841; d. Washington, D.C., 1914*), physician. Came to America as a boy. Graduated from National Medical College, Washington, D.C., 1861; M.D., University of Pennsylvania, 1865. Taught obstetrics at National Medical College, 1870–1914; pioneered in linking mosquito to malaria, 1882.

KING, AUSTIN AUGUSTUS (*b. Sullivan Co., Tenn., 1802; d. St. Louis, Mo., 1870*), lawyer, jurist, Missouri legislator and congressman. Grandson of John Sevier. An ardent Jacksonian Democrat and member of Sen. Benton's wing of the party in Missouri, he served as governor, 1848–52.

KING, BASIL. [See KING, WILLIAM BENJAMIN BASIL, 1859–1928.]

KING, CHARLES (*b. New York, N.Y., 1789; d. Frascati, Italy, 1867*), merchant. Son of Rufus King (1755–1827); brother of James G. and John A. King. Editor, *New York American*, 1823–45; president of Columbia College, 1849–64. His administration marked the conscious beginning of Columbia University with the broadening of curriculum and addition of professional schools.

KING, CHARLES WILLIAM (*b. probably New York, N.Y., c. 1809; d. at sea, 1845*), merchant. Grandson of Samuel King. Spent almost whole life *post* 1826 in Canton, China; visualized more clearly than any other contemporary American the significance and complicated relationships of Eastern Asia.

KING, CLARENCE (*b. Newport, R.I., 1842; d. Arizona, 1901*), geologist, mining engineer. Nephew of Charles W. King. Graduated Yale, 1862. Worked in Nevada and California in association with James T. Gardiner and W. H. Brewer, 1863–66. His survey of an area about 100 miles in width over the Cordilleran ranges from eastern Colorado to the California boundary line was undertaken between 1867 and 1877. His 7-volume *Report of the Geological Exploration of the Fortieth Parallel* (1870–80), reached perhaps the highest standard yet attained by government publications. He introduced into mapping the system of denoting topography by contour lines and extensively used the laboratory in the solution of geophysical problems. In 1878 Congress combined all the Western surveys in a U.S. Geological Survey under King. After organizing the new survey, he resigned in 1881 and entered private engineering practice. His close friends included Henry Adams, John Hay, John La Farge and William Dean Howells. His literary gifts were displayed in his book of sketches *Mountaineering in the Sierra Nevada* (1872).

KING, DAN (*b. Mansfield, Conn., 1791; d. 1864*), physician, pamphleteer. Prominent in the Rhode Island suffrage movement *c.* 1837–41. Author of *The Life and Times of Thomas Wilson Dorr* (1859).

KING, EDWARD LEONARD (*b. Bridgewater, Mass., 1873; d. Fort McPherson, Ga., 1933*), soldier. Graduated West Point, 1896. Distinguished in the Philippines and in World War I; active in army school system, commanding at Cavalry School and at General Staff School. [*Supp.* 1]

KING, EDWARD SKINNER (*b. Liverpool, N.Y., 1861; d. 1931*), astronomer. Graduated Hamilton, 1887. Associated with the Harvard Observatory, 1887–

1931; author of *Photographic Photometry* (1912) and *Manual of Celestial Photography* (1931).

KING, EDWARD SMITH (*b. Middlefield, Mass., 1848; d. 1896*), journalist, foreign and war correspondent. Author, among other books, of *The Great South* (1875); literary discoverer of George W. Cable.

KING, FRANKLIN HIRAM (*b. near Whitewater, Wis., 1848; d. 1911*), agricultural scientist, educator. Devised the round silo; was author of various works on soils and ventilation, and of *Farmers of Forty Centuries* (1911), the best account of soil management in the Orient.

KING, GRACE ELIZABETH (*b. New Orleans, La., 1851; d. 1932*). Author of fiction and historical studies on Creole and Southern themes which include *Monsieur Motte* (1888) and *Balcony Stories* (1893).

KING, HENRY (*b. Salem, O., 1842; d. 1915*), journalist, Union soldier. As editor of the *St. Louis Globe-Democrat*, 1897–1915, made it a great conservative force in American journalism.

KING, HENRY CHURCHILL (*b. Hillsdale, Mich., 1858; d. Oberlin, O., 1934*), theologian. President of Oberlin College, 1903–27. [*Supp.* 1]

KING, HENRY MELVILLE (*b. Oxford, Maine, 1838; d. 1919*), Baptist clergyman. Pastor in Roxbury, Mass., Albany, N.Y., and Providence, R.I.; was eminent in his denomination's educational and missionary fields.

KING, HORATIO (*b. Paris, Maine, 1811; d. Washington, D.C., 1897*), editor, lawyer, postal official.

KING, JAMES GORE (*b. New York, N.Y., 1791; d. 1853*), financier, railroad president. Son of Rufus King (1755–1827); brother of Charles and John A. King. Associated with firm of Prime, Ward and King, New York bankers, *post* 1824. Secured British loan of specie for relief of panic of 1837.

KING, JOHN (*b. New York, N.Y., 1813; d. North Bend, O., 1893*), physician. A founder of the eclectic school of medicine; author of *The American Dispensatory* (1852) and other works.

KING, JOHN ALSOP (*b. New York, N.Y., 1788; d. Jamaica, N.Y., 1867*), lawyer, farmer. Son of Rufus King (1755–1827); brother of Charles and James G. King. As a politician, was allied in turn with the Democrats, Anti-Masons, National Republicans, Whigs and Republicans; served as New York legislator, congressman, and as Republican governor, 1857–59.

KING, JOHN PENDLETON (*b. near Glasgow, Ky., 1799; d. Summerville, Ga., 1888*), lawyer. Removed to Georgia *c.* 1817; served as U.S. senator, Democrat, 1833–37. As cotton manufacturer and railroad president, was one of the constructive industrial leaders in the ante-bellum South.

KING, JONAS (*b. near Hawley, Mass., 1792; d. 1869*), Congregational clergyman. Conducted a mission in Greece *post* 1830.

KING, PRESTON (*b. Ogdensburg, N.Y., 1806; d. New York, N.Y., 1865*), lawyer, politician, New York legislator. Congressman, Democrat, 1843–47, and Free Soiler, 1849–53; U.S. senator, Republican, 1857–63. An important figure in the Republican party organization *post* 1856.

KING, RICHARD (*b. Orange Co., N.Y., 1825; d. 1885*), steamboat captain. Founded the King Ranch in Nueces Co., Texas, 1852. The original tract of 75,000 acres had grown to more than half a million at the time of his death.

KING, RUFUS (*b. Scarboro, Maine, 1755; d. Jamaica, N.Y., 1827*), lawyer, Federalist statesman. Father of Charles, James G., and John A. King. Graduated Harvard, 1777; studied law under Theophilus Parsons at Newburyport, Mass., where he practiced *post* 1780. As a Massachusetts congressman, 1784–86, he renewed Jefferson's original suggestion prohibiting slavery in the Northwest Territory; his motion was later incorporated in the Ordinance of 1787. Probably the most eloquent orator in the Constitutional Convention, he urged a vigorous central government and contributed powerfully to the Constitution's ratification by Massachusetts.

Having married Mary Alsop, the daughter of a wealthy New York merchant, King moved to that city *c.* 1786, was elected to the N.Y. Assembly and was chosen by the legislature to serve as U.S. senator, 1789. He became the ablest Federalist in the Senate, upholding Alexander Hamilton in all his financial measures, earnestly defending Jay's 1794 Treaty with England, and winning re-election to the Senate, 1795. Hamilton recommended him in 1796 to succeed Thomas Pinckney as U.S. minister to Great Britain. Said to have been one of the most effective representatives the United States ever had at London, he remained there until relieved at his own request in 1803. Federalist candidate for vice-president, 1804, he retired to Jamaica, Long Island, after his defeat, but ran unsuccessfully a second time with C. C. Pinckney in 1808. Opposed like all his party to the War of 1812, he returned to the U.S. Senate in 1813 to become opposition leader; later he supported measures for defense. In 1816 he was the last Federalist candidate for president. Re-elected to the U.S. Senate in 1820, he worked to secure a halt to further extension of slavery and proposed a plan for emancipation and resettlement of Negroes. Declining re-election at the end of his term, he was prevailed upon by President John Quincy Adams to become minister to Great Britain once again. Shortly after his arrival in Liverpool, 1825, however, he became ill. Returning home, he died within a year.

KING, RUFUS (*b. New York, N.Y., 1814; d. 1876*), soldier, editor, diplomat. Son of Charles King; grandson of Rufus King (1755–1827). Graduated West Point, 1833. Edited *Milwaukee* (Wis.) *Sentinel,* 1845–61; was one of first regents, University of Wisconsin. Organized famous "Iron Brigade," 1861; commanded a Union division, 1862; resigned from army because of illness, 1863. U.S. minister to Papal States, 1863–67.

KING, SAMUEL (*b. Newport, R.I., 1748; d. Newport, 1819*), portrait painter, maker of nautical instruments, teacher of art.

KING, SAMUEL ARCHER (*b. Tinicum, Pa., 1828; d. Philadelphia, Pa., 1914*), aeronaut. Made first balloon ascent, Philadelphia, 1851; labored to prove feasibility of Atlantic crossing by balloon.

KING, SAMUEL WARD (*b. Johnston, R.I., 1786; d. 1851*), physician. As Whig governor of Rhode Island, 1840–43, played colorless role in suppression of the so-called Dorr's Rebellion.

KING, THOMAS BUTLER (*b. Palmer, Mass., 1800; d. Waresboro, Ga., 1864*), lawyer, planter, Georgia legislator. Nephew of Zebulon Butler. Settled in Georgia, 1823. Congressman, Whig, 1839–43, 1845–49. U.S. collector at San Francisco, Calif., 1851–52.

KING, THOMAS STARR (*b. New York, N.Y., 1824; d. 1864*), Unitarian clergyman, lyceum lecturer. Pastor in Charlestown and Boston, Mass., 1846–60; in San Francisco, Calif., 1860–64. His eloquence is credited as a prime factor in keeping California loyal to the Union.

KING, WILLIAM (*b. Scarboro, Maine, 1768; d. 1852*), ship-owner, Maine legislator. Half-brother of Rufus King (1755–1827). *Post* 1800, a resident of Bath, Maine, he amassed a large fortune, was a leader in the movement for separation of Maine from Massachusetts and served as Maine's first governor, 1820–21.

KING, WILLIAM BENJAMIN BASIL (*b. Charlottetown, P.E.I., Canada, 1859; d. Cambridge, Mass., 1928*), Episcopal clergyman, popular novelist. Rector in Canada and at Christ Church, Cambridge, Mass., 1892–1900; author thereafter of some twenty novels and the widely read *The Conquest of Fear* (1921).

KING, WILLIAM RUFUS DEVANE (*b. Sampson Co., N.C., 1786; d. Dallas Co., Ala., 1853*), planter, statesman. Congressman, (Democrat) Republican, from North Carolina, 1811–16; U.S. senator, Democrat, from Alabama, 1820–44; an ardent follower of Andrew Jackson. After competent service as U.S. minister to France, 1844–46, King returned to the Senate in 1848; he resigned in 1852 after election as vice-president of the United States.

KING OF WILLIAM, JAMES (*b. Georgetown, D.C., 1822; d. San Francisco, Calif., 1856*), journalist. Removed to California, 1848; prospered as a San Francisco banker, 1849–53; served as executive member, first Vigilante committee. As editor-publisher of the *Evening Bulletin* after Oct. 8, 1855, King attacked in blistering language and by name the corrupt elements in the city's business and political life. His murder by J. P. Casey on May 14, 1856, brought about the revival of the Vigilantes.

KINGSBURY, JOHN (*b. South Coventry, Conn., 1801; d. 1874*), educator. Graduated Brown, 1826. Principal of an innovating girl's high school in Providence, R.I., 1828–59; active also in improvement of Rhode Island public schools. President, Washington Insurance Co., Providence, R.I., *post* 1859.

KINGSFORD, THOMAS (*b. Wickham, Kent, England, 1799; d. Oswego, N.Y., 1869*), inventor, manufacturer. Came to America, 1831; became superintendent of starch factory. Perfected process for producing cornstarch, 1842; produced it for food purposes, 1850.

KINGSLEY, CALVIN (*b. Annsville, N.Y., 1812; d. Beirut, Syria, 1870*), Methodist bishop, educator.

KINGSLEY, DARWIN PEARL (*b. near Alburg, Vt., 1857; d. 1932*), insurance executive. President of New York Life Insurance Co., 1907–30. [*Supp. 1*]

KINGSLEY, ELBRIDGE (*b. Carthage, O., 1842; d. Brooklyn, N.Y., 1918*), wood engraver, landscape painter.

KINGSLEY, JAMES LUCE (*b. Scotland, Conn., 1778; d. 1852*), educator. Graduated Yale, 1799. First professor of languages at Yale, appointed 1805 and serving until 1851; *post* 1835, devoted himself exclusively to Latin.

KINGSLEY, NORMAN WILLIAM (*b. Stockholm, N.Y., 1829; d. Warren Point, N.J., 1913*), dentist. Practiced in New York, N.Y., *post* 1852. *Post* 1858, specialized in oral deformities. Perfected gold obturator and soft-rubber artificial velum for cleft palates; author of *A Treatise on Oral Deformities* (1880), for many years the standard textbook on orthodontia.

KINKEAD, EDGAR BENTON (*b. Beverly, O., 1863; d. Atlanta, Ga., 1930*), jurist. Judge, common pleas court of Ohio, 1908–30; a prolific writer on legal subjects, particularly in field of procedure; professor of law, Ohio State University.

KINLOCH, CLELAND (*b. Charleston, S.C., 1760; d. "Acton" in High Hills of Santee, 1823*), rice planter. Among first to adopt Dupont system of flooding rice-fields by tidal movement; built and improved one of the first tidal rice-pounding mills.

KINLOCH, ROBERT ALEXANDER (*b. Charleston, S.C., 1826; d. Charleston, 1891*), surgeon, teacher of surgery at Medical College of South Carolina.

KINNE, LA VEGA GEORGE (*b. Syracuse, N.Y., 1846; d. Des Moines, Iowa, 1906*), Iowa jurist, teacher of law and Democratic political leader.

KINNERSLEY, EBENEZER (*b. Gloucester, England, 1711; d. Philadelphia, Pa., 1778*), Baptist clergyman, educator. Came to America as a child. Raised in Lower Dublin, Pa., he was educated by his father. His experiments in electricity were second in importance only to Franklin's; he published a syllabus of his lectures on the subject in 1764 as *A Course of Experiments in . . . Electricity* and was the inventor of an electrical air thermometer. He taught English and oratory in the College of Philadelphia, 1753–73.

KINNEY, ELIZABETH CLEMENTINE DODGE STEDMAN (*b. New York, N.Y., 1810; d. 1889*), poet, essayist. Daughter of David L. Dodge; mother by her first marriage of Edmund C. Stedman; married William B. Kinney, 1841.

KINNEY, WILLIAM BURNET (*b. Speedwell, N.J., 1799; d. New York, N.Y., 1880*), journalist, diplomat. Literary adviser, Harper and Bros., 1825–35; editor, Newark, N.J., *Daily Advertiser;* U.S. chargé d'affaires at Turin, Italy, 1850–53. Resided thereafter in Turin and Florence until 1865 when he returned to America. Associate of the Browning circle at Florence.

KINNICUTT, LEONARD PARKER (*b. Worcester, Mass., 1854; d. Worcester, 1911*), chemist, educator. Graduated Massachusetts Institute of Technology, 1875; studied under Bunsen at Heidelberg and specialized in organic chemistry at Bonn. Taught at Worcester Polytechnic *post* 1882; was authority on sewage disposal and sanitation of air, water and gas.

KINO, EUSEBIO FRANCISCO (*b. Segno, Italy, c. 1645; d. Magdalena River Mission, Mexico, 1711*), Jesuit missionary, explorer, cartographer. Entered Jesuit order at Freiburg, 1665; assigned to Mexican missions, 1678; arrived in Vera Cruz, 1681. After early experience in Lower California, 1683–85, Kino worked in present northern Sonora and southern Arizona. Between 1687 and 1711, from headquarters at Mission Dolores, he founded missions in the San Miguel, Magdalena, Altar, Sonóita, Santa Cruz and San Pedro river valleys. On his missionary journeys he discovered and wrote the first description of the Casa Grande; as a result of two expeditions which he made to the lower Colorado River, he determined that California was a peninsula and not an island. His autobiography appears in *Kino's Historical Memoir of Pimería Alta* (edited by H. E. Bolton, 1919).

KINSELLA, THOMAS (*b. Co. Wexford, Ireland, 1832; d. Brooklyn, N.Y., 1884*), journalist. Came to America, 1849. Editor, *Brooklyn Daily Eagle,* 1861–84; helped organize Liberal Republican movement, 1871–72.

KINSEY, JOHN (*b. Burlington, N.J., 1693; d. Burlington, 1750, o.s.*), lawyer, New Jersey and Pennsylvania legislator. Chief justice, supreme court of Pennsylvania, 1743–50; leader of the Quaker party in Pennsylvania Assembly; prepared first compilation of New Jersey laws, 1732.

KINTPUASH. [See CAPTAIN JACK, 1837?–1873.]

KINZIE, JOHN (*b. Quebec, Canada, 1763; d. Chicago, Ill., 1828*), fur trader. Changed name from McKenzie. Traded on Maumee and St. Joseph rivers *post* 1781; removed to site of present Chicago, 1804.

KIP, WILLIAM INGRAHAM (*b. New York, N.Y., 1811; d. 1893*), Episcopal clergyman, author. Graduated Yale, 1831; General Theological Seminary, New York, 1835. Consecrated missionary bishop of California, 1853, he accepted the election of the diocese, 1857, and served until his death. As rector of Grace Church, San Francisco, 1862, he established it as his cathedral, the first cathedral of the Episcopal Church in America.

KIRBY, EPHRAIM (*b. Litchfield Co., Conn., 1757; d. Fort Stoddart, Mississippi Territory, 1804*), lawyer, law reporter, Revolutionary soldier, Connecticut legislator. Edited *Reports of Cases Adjudged in the Superior Court and Court of Errors of the State of Connecticut, 1785–1788* (1789), the first fully developed volume of law reports to be published in the United States.

KIRBY, GEORGE HUGHES (*b. Goldsboro, N.C., 1875; d. 1935*), psychiatrist. M.D., Long Island College Medical School, 1899. Director of New York State Psychiatric Institute, 1917–31. [*Supp. 1*]

KIRBY, J. HUDSON (*b. off Sandy Hook, aboard ship as his parents were emigrating to America, 1819; d. London, England, 1848*), actor. Made début at Walnut Street Theatre, Philadelphia, *c.* 1837. A favorite of the gallery gods at the Bowery and Chatham Theatres, New York City, for his strenuous style; origin of the slogan, "Wake me up when Kirby dies."

KIRBY-SMITH, EDMUND (*b. St. Augustine, Fla., 1824; d. Sewanee, Tenn., 1893*), Confederate soldier, educator. Grandson of Ephraim Kirby. Graduated West Point, 1845; fought under Taylor and Scott in Mexican War. After teaching mathematics at West Point and service on the frontier, he resigned on the secession of Florida. Commissioned Confederate colonel of cavalry, 1861, he was promoted brigadier-general in June, was wounded at first Bull Run, and as major-general commanded a division under Beauregard. After the campaign for Nashville, 1862, where he acted with Bragg's force, cleared Cumberland Gap and occupied Lexington, Ky., he was made lieutenant-general. In February 1863, he took command of the Trans-Mississippi Department. Cut off after the fall of Vicksburg, he became virtual civil and military ruler of the area, administering it ably and repelling Union efforts at invasion. Promoted general, 1864, he surrendered the Confederacy's last military force

on June 2, 1865. He became president of University of Nashville, 1870; *post* 1875, he taught mathematics at University of the South.

KIRCHHOFF, CHARLES WILLIAM HENRY (*b. San Francisco, Calif., 1853; d. near Asbury Park, N.J., 1916*), mining engineer, metallurgist. Chief editor, *Iron Age*, 1889–1910; made it the recognized authority on the American iron and steel industry.

KIRCHMAYER, JOHN (*b. Bavaria, c. 1860; d. Cambridge, Mass., 1930*), wood-carver. Came to America *c.* 1895. An outstanding artist and craftsman, patronized by Stanford White, Ralph A. Cram and other architects.

KIRK, EDWARD NORRIS (*b. New York, N.Y., 1802; d. Boston, Mass., 1874*), clergyman, revivalist. Pastor of Presbyterian and Congregational churches in New York and Massachusetts; at Mount Vernon Church, Boston, *post* 1842.

KIRK, JOHN FOSTER (*b. Fredericton, N.B., Canada, 1824; d. 1904*), author, editor. Secretary and research assistant to William H. Prescott, 1848–59. Kirk's *History of Charles the Bold* (1864–68) won high praise from contemporaries; he served as editor of *Lippincott's Magazine*, 1870–86, and helped prepare *Lippincott's New Dictionary*.

KIRKBRIDE, THOMAS STORY (*b. Pennsylvania shore of Delaware River opposite Trenton, N.J., 1809; d. 1883*), physician, psychiatrist. M.D., University of Pennsylvania, 1832. Made major contributions as superintendent, Pennsylvania Hospital for the Insane, 1840–83.

KIRKLAND, CAROLINE MATILDA STANSBURY (*b. New York, N.Y., 1801; d. New York, 1864*), author. Granddaughter of Joseph Stansbury. A resident on the Midwest frontier *c.* 1831–43, she wrote vivid sketches of the pioneers in *A New Home— Who'll Follow* (1839, under pseudonym of Mrs. Mary Clavers) and *Forest Life* (1842). Her later works were commonplace.

KIRKLAND, JAMES HAMPTON (*b. Spartanburg, S.C., 1859; d. Magnetawan, Canada, 1939*), educator. Ph.D., Leipzig, 1885. Chancellor, Vanderbilt University, 1893–1937. [*Supp. 2*]

KIRKLAND, JOHN THORNTON (*b. near Little Falls, N.Y., 1770; d. Boston, Mass., 1840*), Congregationalist and Unitarian clergyman. Son of Samuel Kirkland. Graduated Harvard, 1789. As president of Harvard, 1810–28, he gave the college a university status during an administration known as Harvard's "Augustan Age"; introduced lecture method and the first electives. A man of broad culture, he was one of the founders of the *Monthly Anthology* and the Boston Athenaeum.

KIRKLAND, JOSEPH (*b. Geneva, N.Y., 1830; d. 1894*), Chicago businessman, lawyer, writer. Son of

Caroline M. S. Kirkland. A factor in development of realism in American fiction. Author of, among other works, *Zury* (1885); *The McVeys* (1888); *The Captain of Company K* (1891).

KIRKLAND, SAMUEL (*b. Norwich, Conn., 1741; d. 1808*), Congregationalist clergyman. Father of John T. Kirkland. Missionary to the Senecas, 1764–66; to the Oneidas, 1766–1808. Helped prevent Lord Dunmore's War (1774–75) from becoming a general Indian uprising. Through his efforts, the Oneidas and Tuscaroras remained neutral during the Revolution; Kirkland also served as chaplain at Fort Stanwix and to Gen. Sullivan's expedition, 1779. After the Miamis' victory over St. Clair, 1791, Kirkland helped keep the Six Nations friendly to the United States. He obtained a charter for an academy (later Hamilton College) for the coeducation of white and Indian boys in 1793.

KIRKMAN, MARSHALL MONROE (*b. Morgan Co., Ill., 1842; d. Chicago, Ill., 1921*), railroad executive. Comptroller, Chicago and North Western R.R., 1881–1910; standardized railroad accounting; author of many pamphlets and books on all phases of the railroad business.

KIRKPATRICK, ANDREW (*b. Minebrook, N.J., 1756; d. New Brunswick, N.J., 1831*), jurist. Studied law in office of William Paterson. A judicial conservative, he was associate justice, New Jersey supreme court, 1798–1804, and chief justice, 1804–24.

KIRKWOOD, DANIEL (*b. Harford Co., Md., 1814; d. Riverside, Calif., 1895*), astronomer. Taught at Indiana University and Leland Stanford. Established connection between comets and meteors (1861, 1867, 1873) among many other contributions to mathematical astronomy.

KIRKWOOD, SAMUEL JORDAN (*b. Harford Co., Md., 1813; d. Iowa City, Iowa, 1894*), lawyer, miller. Settled in Iowa, c. 1855. Republican governor of Iowa, 1859–63, 1875–77; U.S. senator, 1866–67, 1877–81; secretary of the interior, 1881–82. Crushed Iowa "Copperhead" movement, 1862–63.

KIRLIN, JOSEPH LOUIS JEROME (*b. Philadelphia, Pa., 1868; d. 1926*), Roman Catholic clergyman. Pastor in Philadelphia; author of devotional works and *Catholicity in Philadelphia* (1909), a diocesan history.

KIRTLAND, JARED POTTER (*b. Wallingford, Conn., 1793; d. Rockport, O., 1877*), physician, naturalist, Ohio legislator. A founder of Cleveland Medical College, 1843, and a member of its faculty until 1864. Made important studies of zoology of Ohio.

KITCHIN, CLAUDE (*b. near Scotland Neck, N.C., 1869; d. Wilson, N.C., 1923*), lawyer. Brother of William W. Kitchin. Congressman, Democrat, from North Carolina, 1901–23; was reputed the most pow-

erful debater in the House; chairman, ways and means committee and majority leader, 1915–19.

KITCHIN, WILLIAM WALTON (*b. near Scotland Neck, N.C., 1866; d. Scotland Neck, 1924*), lawyer. Brother of Claude Kitchin. Congressman, Democrat, from North Carolina, 1897–1909; governor of North Carolina, 1909–13. Anti-trust and anti-machine in politics, he worked to satisfy the economic needs of the common man.

KITTSON, NORMAN WOLFRED (*b. Chambly, Canada, 1814; d. 1888*), fur-trader. Associate of James J. Hill in Red River steamboating and in reorganization of St. Paul and Pacific R.R., 1878–79.

KLAUDER, CHARLES ZELLER (*b. Philadelphia, Pa., 1872; d. Philadelphia, 1938*), architect. Specialist in college architecture. Designed Dining Hall-Holder Hall group at Princeton, 1916, and University of Pittsburgh, 1934. [*Supp. 2*]

KLAW, MARC (*b. Paducah, Ky., 1858; d. Sussex, England, 1936*), theatrical booking agent, manager, producer. With his partner, Abraham L. Erlanger, and others, organized the Theatrical Syndicate *post* 1896. [*Supp. 2*]

KLEIN, BRUNO OSCAR (*b. Osnabrück, Germany, 1858; d. 1911*), pianist, composer. Settled in New York, N.Y., 1884, after touring the U.S. in concert, 1878–83. Church organist and teacher of piano, he composed numerous works for piano and instrumental groups; also church music and an opera *Kenilworth*.

KLEIN, CHARLES (*b. London, England, 1867; d. aboard* Lusitania, *1915*), dramatist. Came to America as actor, 1883. Author of *The Auctioneer* (1901), *The Music Master* (1904), *The Lion and the Mouse* (1905) and many other ephemeral plays concerned with contemporary life in the United States.

KLEIN, JOSEPH FREDERIC (*b. Paris, France, 1849; d. Bethlehem, Pa., 1918*), mechanical engineer. Came to America as a child. Graduated Sheffield Scientific School, Yale, 1871. Created and developed engineering school at Lehigh University *post* 1881.

KLINE, GEORGE (*b. Germany, c. 1757; d. Carlisle, Pa., 1820*), frontier newspaper editor and book publisher. Settled in Carlisle, 1785. In the same year, established *The Carlisle Gazette*, first newspaper in Pennsylvania published west of the Susquehanna River.

KLINGELSMITH, MARGARET CENTER (*b. Portland, Maine, 1859; d. 1931*), lawyer, author. Librarian, Biddle Law Library, University of Pennsylvania, 1899–1931.

KLIPPART, JOHN HANCOCK (*b. near Canton, O., 1823; d. 1878*), agricultural writer. Secretary, Ohio State Board of Agriculture, 1856–78; edited its superior series of reports.

KLIPSTEIN, LOUIS FREDERICK (*b. Winchester, Va., 1813; d. Florida, 1878*), philologist. First American to publish works on Anglo-Saxon, including a *Grammar* (1848) and a number of texts.

KLOPSCH, LOUIS (*b. Lübben, Germany, 1852; d. 1910*), publisher, humanitarian. Came to America as a child. Prospered as manager of a press syndicate. As editor and proprietor of the *Christian Herald post* 1890, made the paper a medium of American bounty to the needy throughout the world.

KNAB, FREDERICK (*b. Würzburg, Bavaria, 1865; d. 1918*), landscape painter, entomologist. Came to America as a boy. Made important discoveries in biology of Northern mosquitoes; a co-author of *The Mosquitoes of North and Central America and the West Indies* (1912–17).

KNABE, VALENTINE WILHELM LUDWIG (*b. Kreuzburg, Prussia, 1803; d. 1864*), piano manufacturer. Came to America, 1833. Established reputation as one of best piano-makers by 1860; virtually controlled ante-bellum piano business in the Southern states from headquarters in Baltimore, Md.

KNAPP, BRADFORD (*b. Vinton, Iowa, 1870; d. Lubbock, Texas, 1938*), agriculturist, educator, lawyer. President, Oklahoma Agricultural and Mechanical College, 1923–28, Alabama Polytechnic Institute, 1928–32, Texas Technological College, 1932–38.

[*Supp. 2*]

KNAPP, GEORGE (*b. Montgomery, N.Y., 1814; d. at sea, returning from Europe, 1883*), journalist. Raised in St. Louis, Mo. Worked on the *Missouri Republican, post* 1826, becoming one of its proprietors, 1837.

KNAPP, HERMAN (*b. near Wiesbaden, Germany, 1832; d. Mamaroneck, N.Y., 1911*), ophthalmologist. Graduated University of Giessen, M.D., 1854; was pupil of Helmholtz and later taught at Heidelberg. Resided and practiced in New York, N.Y., *post* 1868; taught at New York University and at College of Physicians and Surgeons, New York. Established Ophthalmic and Aural Institute which was his clinic; founded *Archives of Ophthalmology and Otology.*

KNAPP, MARTIN AUGUSTINE (*b. Spafford, N.Y., 1843; d. 1923*), lawyer. Practiced in Syracuse, N.Y.; specialized in transportation problems. Served on Interstate Commerce Commission, 1897–1916; was federal circuit judge assigned to Commerce Court, 1910–13, and U.S. circuit court of appeals justice thereafter.

KNAPP, PHILIP COOMBS (*b. Lynn, Mass., 1858; d. 1920*), neurologist. Graduated Harvard, 1878; Harvard Medical School, 1883. An American pioneer in his field, he published in 1891 the first U.S. treatise on the pathology, diagnosis and treatment of brain tumors. He taught at Harvard, 1888–1913.

KNAPP, SAMUEL LORENZO (*b. Newburyport, Mass., 1783; d. Hopkinton, Mass., 1838*), lawyer, politician, writer. Author, among much ephemera, of *Lectures on American Literature* (1829), an early attempt to weigh critically the national literary output.

KNAPP, SEAMAN ASAHEL (*b. Schroon Lake, N.Y., 1833; d. Washington, D.C., 1911*), agriculturist, educator. Removed to Iowa c. 1867. Drafted first experiment-station bill, 1882 (introduced in Congress by C. C. Carpenter). Developed rice industry in the Southwest *post* 1886; inaugurated the Farmer's Cooperative Demonstration Work in the Department of Agriculture as part of fight against the boll weevil.

KNAPP, WILLIAM IRELAND (*b. Greenport, N.Y., 1835; d. Paris, France, 1908*), teacher, scholar. Graduated Colgate, 1860. Taught modern languages at Colgate, Vassar, Yale; first professor of Romance languages at University of Chicago, 1892–95. Was biographer and editor of George Borrow.

KNEASS, SAMUEL HONEYMAN (*b. Philadelphia, Pa., 1806; d. Philadelphia, 1858*), civil engineer, architect. Son of William Kneass; brother of Strickland Kneass. Trained in office of William Strickland. Primarily a railroad and canal builder, he helped construct the Philadelphia and Wilmington R.R., the Delaware and Schuylkill Canal and many other major projects.

KNEASS, STRICKLAND (*b. Philadelphia, Pa., 1821; d. 1884*), civil engineer, Pennsylvania Railroad official. Son of William Kneass; brother of Samuel H. Kneass to whom he served for a time as assistant. As chief engineer and surveyor of Philadelphia, 1855–70, he designed a new drainage system for the city, and also bridges over the Schuylkill River.

KNEASS, WILLIAM (*b. Lancaster, Pa., 1780; d. Philadelphia, Pa., 1840*), engraver, die-sinker. Did superior work for the *Port-Folio* and *Analectic* magazines; employed *post* 1824 by the U.S. Mint.

KNEELAND, ABNER (*b. Gardner, Mass., 1774; d. near Farmington, Iowa, 1844*), Universalist clergyman, anti-theist. Leader of the Boston, Mass., "First Society of Free Enquirers"; lectured and wrote on rationalism; edited *Boston Investigator*, 1831–c.1834, first American rationalist journal.

KNEELAND, SAMUEL (*b. Boston, Mass., 1697; d. 1769*), printer. Nephew of Bartholomew Green. Publisher, *Boston Gazette, or Weekly Advertiser,* 1741–55, which he had printed at intervals *post* 1720; for many years the official provincial printer.

KNEELAND, SAMUEL (*b. Boston, Mass., 1821; d. Hamburg, Germany, 1888*), Boston physician, zoölogist, teacher.

KNEELAND, STILLMAN FOSTER (*b. South Stukely, Canada, 1845; d. 1926*), lawyer. Admitted to bar, Albany, N.Y., 1869; practiced in New York City *post* 1872 as authority on commercial law.

KNEISEL, FRANZ (*b. Bucharest, Rumania, 1865; d. 1926*), violinist, teacher. Studied at Bucharest and Vienna conservatories; came to America, 1855, as principal violinist, Boston Symphony. Formed Kneisel Quartet for chamber music, 1885.

KNICKERBOCKER, HERMAN (*b. probably Albany, N.Y., 1779; d. Brooklyn, N.Y., 1855*), lawyer, jurist, New York legislator. A leading citizen of Troy, N.Y.

KNIGHT, AUSTIN MELVIN (*b. Ware, Mass., 1854; d. Washington, D.C., 1927*), naval officer. Graduated Annapolis, 1873. Author of *Modern Seamanship* (1901). As admiral commanding U.S. Asiatic fleet, 1917, was in charge of early American operations at Vladivostok and in Siberia.

KNIGHT, DANIEL RIDGWAY (*b. Philadelphia, Pa., 1840; d. Rolleboise par Bonniers, France, 1924*), painter. Studied at Pennsylvania Academy; also in Paris with Charles Gleyre and Meissonier. Resided in France *post* 1872. Received international recognition for story-telling paintings of French life.

KNIGHT, EDWARD COLLINGS (*b. Collingswood, N.J., 1813; d. Cape May, N.J., 1892*), wholesale grocer, capitalist. Established Southwark Sugar Refinery in Philadelphia; invented "Knight" railroad sleeping-car, 1859.

KNIGHT, EDWARD HENRY (*b. London, England, 1824; d. Bellefontaine, O., 1883*), mechanical expert, Patent Office official, patent attorney. Settled in Cincinnati, O., 1845. Author of *Knight's American Mechanical Dictionary* (1874–76 and 1882–84) and other works on various subjects.

KNIGHT, FREDERICK IRVING (*b. Newburyport, Mass., 1841; d. 1909*), physician, laryngologist. Graduated Yale, 1862; M.D., Harvard, 1866; worked with Austin Flint and Henry I. Bowditch. Taught at Harvard Medical School, 1872–92; was clinical professor of laryngology *post* 1886. A pioneer in early days of the war against tuberculosis.

KNIGHT, HENRY COGSWELL (*b. probably Newburyport, Mass., 1789; d. Rowley, Mass., 1835*), writer, Episcopal clergyman. His poems in *The Cypriad* (1809) and *The Broken Harp* (1815) have curious parallels with Blake and Coleridge. He was author also of *Letters from the South and West* (1824).

KNIGHT, JONATHAN (*b. Bucks Co., Pa., 1787; d. East Bethlehem, Pa., 1858*), civil engineer. Self-educated. Employed on extension of the National Road to Wheeling, Va. (now W.Va.), and *post* 1825 to Illinois; surveyed route of Baltimore and Ohio R.R. and was its chief engineer, 1829–42.

KNIGHT, JONATHAN (*b. Norwalk, Conn., 1789; d. 1864*), physician. A founder of the American Medical Association and of Yale Medical School. Connecticut's leading surgeon *post* 1838.

KNIGHT, LUCIAN LAMAR (*b. Atlanta, Ga., 1868; d. Clearwater, Fla., 1933*), Georgia historian, archivist. [*Supp. 1*]

KNIGHT, RIDGWAY. [See KNIGHT, DANIEL RIDGWAY, 1840–1924.]

KNIGHT, SARAH KEMBLE (*b. Boston, Mass., 1666; d. probably New London, Conn., 1727*), teacher, diarist. Author of a classic account of New England colonial manners and idiom (*c.* 1704) which first appeared as *The Journals of Madam Knight . . .*, New York, 1825.

KNOTT, ALOYSIUS LEO (*b. near Newmarket, Md., 1829; d. 1918*), lawyer, Maryland legislator. Practiced in Baltimore, Md., *post* 1855. Helped form Conservative-Democratic party, 1866, and in ensuing legislative session took lead in freeing Maryland from military rule. Was dean, Baltimore Law School, 1905–*c.*1918.

KNOTT, JAMES PROCTOR (*b. near Raywick, Ky., 1830; d. Lebanon, Ky., 1911*), lawyer. Congressman, Democrat, from Kentucky, 1867–71, 1875–83; governor of Kentucky, 1883–87; professor and first dean, Centre College law school, 1894–1901.

KNOWLES, LUCIUS JAMES (*b. Hardwick, Mass., 1819; d. Washington, D.C., 1884*), inventor, steam-pump and loom manufacturer.

KNOWLTON, CHARLES (*b. Templeton, Mass., 1800; d. 1850*), physician. Graduated Dartmouth, M.D., 1824. Author of *Fruits of Philosophy* (1832), an early and influential work in favor of birth-control.

KNOWLTON, FRANK HALL (*b. Brandon, Vt., 1860; d. Ballston, Va., 1926*), paleontologist, pioneer paleobotanist, author. Graduated Middlebury, 1884. Associated with U.S. National Museum and U.S. Geological Survey. Advanced an original hypothesis on evolution of geologic climates, 1919.

KNOWLTON, MARCUS PERRIN (*b. Wilbraham, Mass., 1839; d. Springfield, Mass., 1918*), lawyer, jurist. Graduated Yale, 1860. Justice, supreme court of Massachusetts, 1887–1911; effective and distinguished as chief justice, *post* 1902.

KNOWLTON, THOMAS (*b. West Boxford, Mass., 1740; d. Harlem Heights, New York, N.Y., 1776*), Revolutionary soldier. Veteran of Seven Years' War. As captain, Ashford Company, protected line of colonial retreat at Bunker Hill; was commissioned major, 20th Continentals, Jan. 1, 1776, and commanded a celebrated raid into Charlestown, Mass., on Jan. 8, 1776. Organized "Knowlton's Rangers" late in August after promotion to lieutenant-colonel; was killed at battle of Harlem Heights, Sept. 16.

KNOX, GEORGE WILLIAM (*b. Rome, N.Y., 1853; d. Seoul, Korea, 1912*), Presbyterian clergyman. Missionary to Japan, 1877–93; served as seminary professor in Tokyo. Professor of philosophy and history of religions, Union Theological Seminary, New York, 1899–1911.

KNOX, HENRY (*b. Boston, Mass., 1750; d. near Thomaston, Maine, 1806*), bookseller, soldier. As second-in-command, Boston Grenadier Corps, made special study of military science and engineering, 1772–75; rose rapidly in American army after volunteering, June 1775; was close friend and adviser of George Washington. As colonel of artillery, brought captured guns from Ticonderoga for use in terminal stage of siege of Boston; his services thereafter were given in almost every Northern operation of the Revolution, and his handling of the artillery received general praise. Promoted major-general in November 1781; conceived and organized Society of the Cincinnati, May 1783; chosen secretary of war by Congress, 1785. Confirmed in that post under the new Constitution, he served until 1794.

KNOX, JOHN JAY (*b. Augusta, N.Y., 1828; d. New York, N.Y., 1892*), financier, U.S. treasury official. Comptroller of the currency, 1872–84.

KNOX, PHILANDER CHASE (*b. Brownsville, Pa., 1853; d. Washington, D.C., 1921*), lawyer. Graduated Mount Union College, Ohio, 1872. Became one of the country's ablest corporation lawyers and was appointed U.S. attorney-general, 1901, by his friend President McKinley. An active and successful prosecutor of anti-trust cases, he resigned the office, 1904, to accept appointment as U.S. senator, Republican, from Pennsylvania. In 1909, he was appointed President Taft's secretary of state, retiring in March 1913. He reorganized his department; extended the merit system; conducted foreign relations by "dollar diplomacy," first in the Far East and then in Latin America. He extended the Monroe Doctrine to apply to aggressions of Asian nations and settled the Bering Sea and North Atlantic fisheries controversies. Returning to the Senate, 1917, he helped lead the fight against the Treaty of Versailles.

KNOX, SAMUEL (*b. Ireland, 1756; d. 1832*), Presbyterian clergyman, educator. Settled in Maryland *c.* 1795; held pastorates and taught at Bladensburg, Frederick and elsewhere. Campaigned (1799) for a uniform system of national education with state colleges and a national university.

KNOX, THOMAS WALLACE (*b. Pembroke, N.H., 1835; d. New York, N.Y., 1896*), traveler, journalist, war and foreign correspondent.

KOBBÉ, GUSTAV (*b. New York, N.Y., 1857; d. near Bay Shore, N.Y., 1918*), music critic, music historian. Author of *Wagner's Life and Works* (1890) and a number of other less important books in general and musical literature.

KOBER, GEORGE MARTIN (*b. Alsfeld, Germany, 1850; d. 1931*), physician. Came to America, 1866. Served as U.S. Army hospital aide; graduated Georgetown University, M.D., 1873; was army surgeon until 1886. Gave up practice, 1893, to engage in public welfare work; was dean of medical department, Georgetown, 1901–28.

KOCHERTHAL, JOSUA von (*b. Bretten, Germany, 1669; d. 1719*), Lutheran clergyman. Leader of the Palatine emigration to the province of New York, 1708 and 1710.

KOEHLER, ROBERT (*b. Hamburg, Germany, 1850; d. Minneapolis, Minn., 1917*), painter. Came to America as a child. As director, Minneapolis School of Fine Arts, 1893–1917, was a pioneer in art instruction and appreciation in the Northwest.

KOEHLER, SYLVESTER ROSA (*b. Leipzig, Germany, 1837; d. Littleton, N.H., 1900*), museum curator, writer, artist. Built up print department of Boston Museum of Fine Arts as curator *post* 1887.

KOEMMENICH, LOUIS (*b. Elberfeld, Germany, 1866; d. 1922*), musician. Came to America, 1890. Served as conductor of New York Oratorio Society and other choral groups; composed songs and choruses.

KOENIG, GEORGE AUGUSTUS (*b. Willstätt, Baden, Germany, 1844; d. 1913*), chemist, mineralogist. Came to America, 1868. Taught at University of Pennsylvania and Michigan College of Mines; discovered thirteen new species of minerals; developed a number of improved processes for treatment of ores.

KOERNER, GUSTAVE PHILIP. [See KÖRNER, GUSTAV PHILIPP, 1809–1896].

KOHLER, ELMER PETER (*b. Egypt, Pa., 1865; d. Boston, Mass., 1938*), organic chemist. Graduated Muhlenberg, 1886; Ph.D., Johns Hopkins, 1892. Distinguished teacher at Bryn Mawr, 1892–1912, and Harvard, 1912–14, 1919–38. [*Supp. 2*]

KOHLER, KAUFMANN (*b. Fürth, Bavaria, 1843; d. New York, N.Y., 1926*), rabbi. Early mastered Talmudic knowledge. At universities of Munich, Berlin and Erlangen (Ph.D., 1867), broke with orthodox Judaism. Called to congregation Beth-El in Detroit, he came to America, 1869; in 1879 he became rabbi of Temple Beth-El, New York. Continuing his battle against conservative and orthodox critics, he particularly attacked Alexander Kohut's definition of traditional Judaism. Kohler called the Pittsburgh Conference which adopted the radical Pittsburgh Platform (1885), later accepted as a statement of principles by American reform Judaism. In 1903 he became president of Hebrew Union College, Cincinnati, and served until 1921. A productive, mature scholar, he was author of many monographs and books, of which the principal was *Jewish Theology* (1918).

KOHLER, MAX JAMES (*b. Detroit, Mich., 1871; d. Long Lake, N.Y., 1934*), lawyer, publicist, author. Son of Kaufmann Kohler; grandson of David Einhorn. Authority on immigration law; defender and protector of immigrants and minority rights. [*Supp.* 1]

KOHLER, WALTER JODOK (*b. Sheboygan, Wis., 1875; d. Kohler, Wis., 1940*), manufacturer of plumbing fixtures. Republican governor of Wisconsin, 1928–30; opposed by the La Follettes. Built model industrial town of Kohler, Wis.; opposed trade unions.

[*Supp.* 2]

KOHLMANN, ANTHONY (*b. Kaiserberg, Alsace, 1771; d. 1836*), Jesuit priest, educator, missionary. Worked in America, 1806–24. Administered diocese of New York, 1808–14; was president of Georgetown College, 1818–20; taught at Gregorian University, Rome, *post* 1824. Defendant in celebrated legal action ensuring secrecy of confession made to a priest.

KOHLSAAT, HERMAN HENRY (*b. Albion, Ill., 1853; d. Washington, D.C., 1924*), restaurateur, editor. An influential Republican, publisher of several Chicago newspapers *post* 1891, including the *Inter-Ocean* and the *Times-Herald;* claimed authorship of Republican gold plank, 1896.

KOHUT, ALEXANDER (*b. Félegyháza, Hungary, 1842; d. New York, N.Y., 1894*), rabbi, lexicographer. Graduated Jewish Theological Seminary, Breslau, 1867; Ph.D., University of Leipzig, 1870. Elected to the Hungarian parliament, 1885, he was called the same year to Ahawath Chesed Congregation, New York. Shocked by the vagaries of radical reform Judaism in America, he established his leadership of conservative Jewry in a series of sermons on "The Ethics of the Fathers." Reform, led by Kaufmann Kohler, replied with the Pittsburgh Program. Kohut then organized the Jewish Theological Seminary of America, 1887, where he was professor of Talmud. He published his encyclopedic modern version of the *Aruch Hashalem,* 1878–92; it was reissued, 1926.

KOHUT, GEORGE ALEXANDER (*b. Stuhlweissenberg, Hungary, 1874; d. 1933*), rabbi, scholar. Son of Alexander Kohut. Came to America as a boy. Promoter of Jewish intellectual activities in many fields.

[*Supp.* 1]

KOLB, DIELMAN (*b. Palatinate, Germany, 1691; d. 1756*), Mennonite preacher. Came to America, 1717; throve in Pennsylvania as weaver and farmer; assisted Swiss and German emigration to America.

KOLB, REUBEN FRANCIS (*b. Eufaula, Ala., 1839; d. Montgomery, Ala., 1918*), planter, Confederate soldier, farm leader. Fought for a progressive democracy in Alabama against the so-called "Organized Democrats" *post* 1890.

KOLLE, FREDERICK STRANGE (*b. Hanover, Germany, 1872; d. New York, N.Y., 1929*), physician. Came to America as a youth. Graduated Long Island College Hospital, M.D., 1893. Pioneer in radiography

and modern plastic surgery; author of *Plastic and Cosmetic Surgery* (1911).

KOLLOCK, SHEPARD (*b. Lewes, Del., 1750; d. Philadelphia, Pa., 1839*), journalist, Revolutionary patriot. Nephew and apprentice of William Goddard. Published *New Jersey Journal* at various places *post* 1779 up to 1818; issued numerous books at New York, N.Y., and Elizabeth, N.J.

KOOPMAN, AUGUSTUS (*b. Charlotte, N.C., 1869; d. Étaples, France, 1914*), painter, etcher.

KOOWESKOWE. [See Ross, JOHN, *c.* 1790–1866].

KOREN, JOHN (*b. Washington Prairie, near Decorah, Iowa, 1861; d. at sea, 1923*), Lutheran clergyman, statistician. Son of Ulrik V. Koren. Expert special agent, Bureau of the Census, 1903–12; worked for better data in criminal statistics.

KOREN, ULRIK VILHELM (*b. Bergen, Norway, 1826; d. 1910*), Norwegian Lutheran clergyman. Came to America, 1853. Was influential in Norwegian Synod (president, 1894–1910); pastor at Washington Prairie, Iowa, 1853–1910.

KÖRNER, GUSTAV PHILIPP (*b. Frankfurt-am-Main, Germany, 1809; d. 1896*), jurist, statesman, historian. Came to America, 1833; settled in Belleville, Ill., where he practiced law. Was state supreme court judge, 1845–50, and lieutenant-governor of Illinois, Democrat, 1852–56. Joining Republican party, 1856, he influenced German-Americans to follow his example. A close friend of Abraham Lincoln. Served as U.S. minister to Spain, 1862–64; later in life, wrote on history of German influence in the United States and composed a valuable autobiography.

KOŚCIUSZKO, TADEUSZ ANDRZEJ BONAWENTURA (*b. Palatinate of Breesc, Grand Duchy of Lithuania, 1746; d. Switzerland, 1817*), Revolutionary soldier, Polish patriot. Graduated Royal School, Warsaw, as captain, 1769; received further training in engineering and artillery at Mézières, France. Stirred by the American Revolution, he came to America, 1776, and soon was commissioned colonel of engineers, Continental Army. He contributed greatly to the victory over Burgoyne at Saratoga, 1777; designed works at West Point, 1778–80; served with Greene in the South, 1780–83. Promoted brigadier-general, 1783, he returned to Europe, 1784. In 1792 and 1794 he led the Poles in their resistance to the Russians. Becoming liberal dictator of Poland in the latter year, he was defeated at Maciejowice in October. He revisited America, 1797–98, after imprisonment by the Russians, and spent the rest of his life in exile working for Polish freedom.

KOYL, CHARLES HERSCHEL (*b. Amherstburg, Canada, 1855; d. Evanston, Ill., 1931*), civil engineer. Pioneer in treatment of industrial water supplies, especially in connection with railroad operations.

KRAEMER, HENRY (*b. Philadelphia, Pa., 1868; d. 1924*), botanist, pharmacognosist. Graduated Girard College, 1883; Philadelphia College of Pharmacy, 1889. Taught at Northwestern, at Philadelphia College of Pharmacy and University of Michigan; edited and reported for pharmaceutical publications.

KRANTZ, PHILIP. [See ROMBRO, JACOB, 1858–1922.]

KRAPP, GEORGE PHILIP (*b. Cincinnati, O., 1872; d. 1934*), educator. Graduated Wittenberg College, 1894; Ph.D., Johns Hopkins, 1899. Professor of English language at Columbia for many years. Author of *The Pronunciation of Standard English in America* (1919), *The English Language in America* (1925) and many scholarly texts. [*Supp. 1*]

KRAUS, JOHN (*b. Nassau, Germany, 1815; d. New York, N.Y., 1896*), educator. Came to America, 1851. As an official of U.S. Bureau of Education, 1867–73, promoted Froebel's kindergarten theory; *post* 1873, with wife Maria Kraus-Boelté, conducted a seminar for kindergarten teachers.

KRAUS-BOELTÉ, MARIA (*b. Hagenow, Germany, 1836; d. Atlantic City, N.J., 1918*), educator, Froebel kindergarten disciple. Came to America, 1872. Established, with her husband John Kraus, the Normal Training Kindergarten and its model schools, New York City, *c.* 1873.

KRAUSKOPF, JOSEPH (*b. Ostrowo, Prussia, 1858; d. 1923*), rabbi, leader in reform Judaism. Came to America as a boy. Graduated Hebrew Union College, 1883. Engaged in innumerable public activities, especially in Philadelphia, Pa., where he ministered *post* 1887. Founded National Farm School at Doylestown, Pa., 1896.

KRAUTH, CHARLES PHILIP (*b. New Goshenhoppen, Pa., 1797; d. 1867*), Lutheran clergyman. First president of Pennsylvania (now Gettysburg) College, 1834–50; professor in Gettysburg Theological Seminary, 1850–67.

KRAUTH, CHARLES PORTERFIELD (*b. Martinsburg, Va., now W.Va., 1823; d. Philadelphia, Pa., 1883*), Lutheran clergyman, theologian, educator, author. Son of Charles P. Krauth. Graduated Gettysburg Theological Seminary, 1841. Champion of reaction of U.S. Lutheranism from a developing American type of liberalism to an older European form of confessional conservatism. As editor-in-chief of *Lutheran and Missionary*, as first professor of "systematic divinity" at the new (1864) theological seminary at Mt. Airy (Philadelphia), for almost 20 years, and through his writings, especially *The Conservative Reformation and Its Theology* (1871), he influenced a generation of American Lutheran ministers.

KREHBIEL, CHRISTIAN (*b. Weierhof, Palatinate, Germany, 1832; d. near Halstead, Kans., 1909*), Mennonite preacher. Came to America *c.* 1850; resided in Iowa and Illinois. Responsible for establishment of Mennonite immigrant settlements in Kansas *post* 1872; active in charitable work.

KREHBIEL, HENRY EDWARD (*b. Ann Arbor, Mich., 1854; d. 1923*), music critic, historian, author, lecturer. Associated with New York *Tribune*, 1880–1923; edited A. W. Thayer's *Life of Beethoven* (1921); wrote numerous original works of criticism.

KREZ, KONRAD (*b. Landau, Rhenish Bavaria, 1828; d. Milwaukee, Wis., 1897*), lawyer, Union soldier, Wisconsin legislator, poet in the German language. Emigrated to America, 1851.

KRIMMEL, JOHN LEWIS (*b. Ebingen, Germany, 1789; d. near Germantown, Pa., 1821*), painter. Came to America, 1810. Painted portraits and humorous genre pieces of American scenes, types and occasions.

KROEGER, ADOLPH ERNST (*b. Schwabstedt, Duchy of Schleswig, 1837; d. St. Louis, Mo., 1882*), journalist. Came to America as a child. A minor figure in the St. Louis philosophical movement, he translated some of Fichte's works.

KROEGER, ERNEST RICHARD (*b. St. Louis, Mo., 1862; d. 1934*), musician, composer, conductor, teacher. Son of Adolph E. Kroeger. [*Supp. 1*]

KROGER, BERNARD HENRY (*b. Cincinnati, O., 1860; d. Wianno, Mass., 1938*), businessman. Founded in Cincinnati a chain of grocery stores extending through the Middle West and into the South.

[*Supp. 2*]

KROL, BASTIAEN JANSEN (*b. Harlingen, Friesland, 1595; d. 1674*), Dutch colonial official. Commissary and director at Fort Orange (Albany, N.Y.) at various periods, 1626–*c.* 1643.

KRUELL, GUSTAV (*b. near Düsseldorf, Germany, 1843; d. San Luis Obispo, Calif., 1907*), wood engraver. Came to America, 1873. Was particularly successful in portraiture.

KRUESI, JOHN (*b. Speicher, Switzerland, 1843; d. Schenectady, N.Y., 1899*), mechanical expert, inventor. Came to America, 1870. Was associated with Thomas A. Edison *post* 1871 and responsible for mechanical execution of many of his ideas. Devised system of underground electric cables; superintended Edison Machine Works, 1886–95.

KRÜSI, JOHANN HEINRICH HERMANN (*b. Yverdon, Switzerland, 1817; d. Alameda, Calif., 1903*), educator. Came to America, 1854. Did notable work in Object Teaching at Oswego (N.Y.) State Normal School, 1862–87.

KUGELMAN, FREDERICK BENJAMIN. [See KAYE, FREDERICK BENJAMIN, 1892–1930.]

KUHN, ADAM (*b. Germantown, Pa., 1741; d. Philadelphia, Pa., 1817*), physician, botanist. Pupil of Linnaeus at Upsala; M.D., University of Edinburgh, 1767. Practiced and taught in Philadelphia *post* 1768.

KUHN, JOSEPH ERNST (*b. Leavenworth, Kans., 1864; d. San Diego, Calif., 1935*), army officer. Graduated West Point, 1885; entered Engineer Corps. President of Army War College, 1917; commanded 79th Division, World War I. Retired as major-general. [*Supp.* 1]

KUMLER, HENRY (*b. Lancaster Co., Pa., 1775; d. near Trenton, O., 1854*), bishop of the United Brethren in Christ. Removed to Ohio, 1819; was largely responsible for the planting and nurture of United Brethren churches in southwestern Ohio.

KUNZ, GEORGE FREDERICK (*b. New York, N.Y., 1856; d. 1932*), authority on gems and ancient jewelry. [*Supp.* 1]

KUNZE, JOHN CHRISTOPHER (*b. Artern on the Unstrut, Saxony, 1744; d. New York, N.Y., 1807*), Lutheran clergyman. Came to America, 1770, as coadjutor to Henry M. Muhlenberg at Philadelphia; was pastor in New York *post* 1784. Advocate of training in English for Lutheran clergymen; prepared first Lutheran hymn book in the English language (1795).

KUNZE, RICHARD ERNEST (*b. Altenburg, Germany, 1838; d. near Phoenix, Ariz., 1919*), eclectic physician, naturalist. Came to America c. 1854. Specialized *post* 1896 in study of Southwest reptiles and flora, especially cactus.

KURTZ, BENJAMIN (*b. Harrisburg, Pa., 1795; d. Baltimore, Md., 1865*), Lutheran clergyman. Editor, *Lutheran Observer*, 1833–58; a leader of evangelical "American Lutheranism."

KUSKOV, IVAN ALEKSANDROVICH (*b. Totma, Vologda Government, Russia, 1765; d. Totma, 1823*). Assistant to A. A. Baranov in Alaska, *post* 1791. Founder (1812) and first manager of the Russian settlement called "Fort Ross" in California; returned to Russia, 1822.

KYLE, DAVID BRADEN (*b. Cadiz, O., 1863; d. 1916*), laryngologist. Professor of laryngology, Jefferson Medical College, 1904–16; wrote a widely used textbook on nose and throat diseases.

KYLE, JAMES HENDERSON (*b. near Xenia, O., 1854; d. Aberdeen, S. Dak., 1901*), Congregational clergyman. U.S. senator, Populist-Republican, from South Dakota, 1891–1901; chairman of National Industrial Commission.

KYNETT, ALPHA JEFFERSON (*b. Adams Co., Pa., 1829; d. Harrisburg, Pa., 1899*), Methodist clergyman, reformer, prohibitionist.

LA BARGE, JOSEPH (*b. St. Louis, Missouri Territory, 1815; d. St. Louis, Mo., 1899*), Missouri River navigator, fur-trader.

LA BORDE, MAXIMILIAN (*b. Edgefield, S.C., 1804; d. Columbia, S.C., 1873*), physician, writer, educator. Associated for over 50 years with South Carolina College as student, trustee and professor; wrote *History of South Carolina College* (1859).

LACEY, JOHN (*b. Buckingham, Pa., 1755; d. New Mills, now Pemberton, N.J., 1814*), Revolutionary soldier, public official in Pennsylvania and New Jersey.

LACEY, JOHN FLETCHER (*b. near New Martinsville, Va., now W.Va., 1841; d. Oskaloosa, Iowa, 1913*), Union soldier, lawyer. Congressman, Republican, from Iowa, 1889–91, 1893–1907; a strong conservative, he opposed Gov. A. B. Cummins's progressive "Iowa Idea."

LACHAISE, GASTON (*b. Paris, France, 1882; d. 1935*), sculptor. Studied at École des Beaux Arts with G. J. Thomas. Came to America, 1906. His work distinguished by its robust, earthy, exaggerated anatomies and candid, opulent voluptuousness.

[*Supp.* 1]

LACKAYE, WILTON (*b. Loudoun Co., Va., 1862; d. 1932*), actor. Changed name from William A. Lackey. Made debut in New York, 1883. One of the most illustrious stage villains; remembered for his brilliant Svengali in *Trilby*. [*Supp.* 1]

LACLEDE, PIERRE (*b. Bedous, lower Pyrenees, France, c. 1724; d. Mississippi River near mouth of the Arkansas, 1778*), trader. Came to New Orleans, 1755; founded St. Louis, Mo., 1764.

LACOCK, ABNER (*b. Cub Run, near Alexandria, Va., 1770; d. near Freedom, Pa., 1837*), farmer, Pennsylvania legislator. Congressman, Democrat, 1811–13; U.S. senator, 1813–19. An early advocate of state-built canals to connect the Delaware and Ohio rivers.

LACY, DRURY (*b. Chesterfield Co., Va., 1758; d. Philadelphia, Pa., 1815*), educator, Presbyterian clergyman. Graduated Hampden-Sydney College, 1788; served as its acting president, 1789–97. Established his own academy nearby, 1797, and taught many students later eminent in the professions.

LACY, ERNEST (*b. Warren, Pa., 1863; d. 1916*), lawyer, playwright, educator. Pioneered in developing rational public speaking and debating in Philadelphia public schools.

LADD, CATHERINE (*b. Richmond, Va., 1808; d. near Winnsboro, S.C., 1899*), South Carolina schoolmistress, writer of fugitive verse.

LADD, EDWIN FREMONT (*b. Starks, Maine, 1859; d. 1925*), chemist. Removed to Fargo, N.D., 1890; active in state and national fight against adulterated food. U.S. senator, Republican and Non-Partisan, from North Dakota, 1921–25.

LADD, GEORGE TRUMBULL (*b. Painesville, O., 1842; d. 1921*), Congregational clergyman, psychologist, philosopher. Maintained a connection with Yale University, 1881–1921, interpreting and systematizing the work of German post-Kantian idealists and helping introduce study of psychology as an experimental science grounded in physiology.

LADD, JOSEPH BROWN (*b. Newport, R.I., 1764; d. 1786*), physician, poet. Author of *Poems of Arouet* (1786), which show influence of English pre-romantics. Practiced in Charleston, S.C., *post* 1783.

LADD, WILLIAM (*b. Exeter, N.H., 1778; d. Portsmouth, N.H., 1841*), sea captain, farmer. Founded American Peace Society, 1828; prophesied the development of international organization in his *Essay on a Congress of Nations* (1840).

LADD, WILLIAM SARGENT (*b. Holland, Vt., 1826; d. 1893*), merchant, banker. Removed to Portland, Ore., 1851. Became leading promoter of transportation and industrial enterprises in the Pacific Northwest, particularly in Portland.

LADD-FRANKLIN, CHRISTINE (*b. Windsor, Conn., 1847; d. 1930*), logician, psychologist. Graduated Vassar, 1869; qualified for Ph.D., Johns Hopkins, 1882. Married Fabian Franklin, 1882. Made a major original contribution to logic, the "antilogism," 1883; developed a controversial color theory, 1892. Lectured at Johns Hopkins and Columbia.

LAEMMLE, CARL (*b. Laupheim, Germany, 1867; d. Beverly Hills, Calif., 1939*), pioneer exhibitor, distributor, and producer of motion pictures. Founder and head, 1912–36, of Universal Pictures. [*Supp. 2*]

LA FARGE, CHRISTOPHER GRANT (*b. Newport, R.I., 1862; d. Saunderstown, R.I., 1938*), architect. Son of John La Farge. Designer, with George Lewis Heins, of original Romanesque plans for Cathedral of St. John the Divine, New York, and of many other buildings. [*Supp. 2*]

LA FARGE, JOHN (*b. New York, N.Y., 1835; d. Providence, R.I., 1910*), painter, worker in stained glass, writer. Graduated Mount St. Mary's College, Emmitsburg, Md., 1853; trifled with legal studies; went to Paris, 1856, where relatives introduced him into the stimulating French literary world and he studied painting briefly under Thomas Couture. Thereafter he toured northern Europe, studying the paintings of the old masters. Returning to America, 1858, he practiced painting at Newport, R.I., with William M. Hunt. Married Margaret Mason Perry, 1860. Disqualified for Civil War service, he turned his mind to studies of light and color. His "Paradise Valley" (1866–68) reveals the influence of his discoveries; it anticipated the formula of Monet and the French impressionists who had yet to make their impact upon American art. His early work included landscapes, flowers and a few figure subjects; he also did magazine illustrations marked by imagination and technical skill.

Invited by H. H. Richardson, builder of Trinity Church, Boston, to decorate the interior, 1876, La Farge produced a scheme of murals astonishingly unified and of great warmth and dignity. This was the forerunner of other important commissions, including "The Ascension" in the Church of the Ascension, New York City, the greatest mural painting of a religious subject produced anywhere in his time. He was also much occupied with work in stained glass, and it was owing to his genius and invention that one of the noble crafts of the Middle Ages was revived in America and lifted to a high plane. His Watson Memorial window won him the Legion of Honor at the Paris Exposition, 1889. In his glass work, his ability as designer and colorist came uniquely into its own. La Farge visited Japan with his friend Henry Adams and later went with him to the South Seas, recording what he saw and his own thoughts in *An Artist's Letters from Japan* (1897) and *Reminiscences of the South Seas* (1912). He was author also of a number of works on art and artists. In his many-sided activity, La Farge maintained an intellectuality which gave balance to everything he did and enriched his work with subtle implications and overtones. His sensibility was matched by the delicate French precision with which he defined his thought, either in words or in the language of art. He could work with complete simplicity, or in the grand style, as the theme required it. He was the first American master of the fusion of decorative art with architecture, a colorist and designer who developed remarkable powers in collaboration with builders.

LAFAYETTE, MARIE JOSEPH PAUL YVES ROCH GILBERT DU MOTIER, Marquis de (*b. chateau of Chavaniac, Auvergne, France, 1757; d. Paris, France, 1834*), statesman, soldier. Descended from notable and ancient French families. His father was killed, 1759, in the Seven Years' War; his mother died in 1770. Shy and awkward, yet eager to follow his family's military tradition, he entered the King's Musketeers, 1771, and was promoted captain shortly after his marriage, 1774, to Marie Adrienne Françoise de Noailles, an heiress of one of the old régime's most powerful families. At a dinner in honor of the Duke of Gloucester in August 1775, his imagination was stirred by the Duke's sympathetic talk of the American insurgents. Sensing the possibility of avenging France's defeat in the Seven Years' War, moved by romantic enthusiasm for regeneration of society, and hopeful of satisfying his own love of *la gloire*, he decided to help the Americans. Withdrawing from active service with the army, June 1776, he undertook through Silas Deane and Arthur Lee to serve in the colonies without pay. He sailed for America on April 20, 1777. Commissioned major-general by Congress on July 31, he met Gen. George Washington in Philadelphia who virtually adopted him and attached him to his staff. Slightly wounded at the Brandywine in September, he took command on December 1 of the division of Virginia light troops. During the winter at Valley Forge he won the title of "the soldier's friend." He was a valuable liaison officer between the American army and the French force under D'Estaing during and after the unsuccessful operation against Newport, R.I., in August 1778.

In January 1779, he left for France with an elegant sword voted him by Congress and a letter of appreciation to Louis XVI. Acclaimed and consulted in Paris and Versailles, he acquiesced in Rochambeau's appointment to lead a French expeditionary army and returned to America, April 1780, to prepare for its arrival. Congress restored him to his old command, and he served Washington as intermediary with Rochambeau at Newport during conferences with the French general in September. Going with Washington to West Point, he served on the court-martial after Benedict Arnold's treason and voted for André's death. After leading an unsuccessful campaign to capture Arnold at Hampton Roads, March 1781, he was ordered south to join Greene and reached Richmond just in time to prevent its capture by the British. He retreated slowly northward before Cornwallis's advancing army, but after meeting Wayne's force at Rapidan River he turned on Cornwallis, who retired to the coast. He then held Cornwallis in check until the arrival of Washington's and Rochambeau's armies and De Grasse's fleet which resulted in the British surrender at Yorktown, Oct. 19, 1781, and the virtual end of Revolutionary military operations.

In December, Lafayette sailed for France, to enter on a long, eventful and rather checkered career which belongs to French rather than American history. He re-visited the United States in 1784, and again, on President Monroe's invitation, in 1824, when he made an epochal tour of the country. His grave in Picpus Cemetery in Paris was covered with earth from Bunker Hill.

LAFEVER, MINARD (*b. Morristown, N.J., 1798; d. Williamsburg [Brooklyn], N.Y., 1854*), architect. Established in New York *post* 1828. Did much miscellaneous work, but is famous for Gothic churches built after 1835 in Brooklyn, of which his masterpieces are Holy Trinity (1844–47) and Church of the Saviour (1844). His chief influence on American architecture came more from his books, of which the best-known are *The Modern Builder's Guide* (1833), *The Beauties of Modern Architecture* (1835) and *The Architectural Instructor* (1856). [*Supp. 1*]

LAFFAN, WILLIAM MACKAY (*b. Dublin, Ireland, 1848; d. 1909*), journalist, art connoisseur. Came to America, 1868; worked on San Francisco, Calif., and Baltimore, Md., papers. *Post* 1877, he became successively dramatic critic, publisher, and proprietor of the New York *Sun*. He was also chief art adviser to J. P. Morgan, Sr., and Henry Walters.

LAFFITE, JEAN (*b. probably Bayonne, France, c. 1780; d. c. 1821*), adventurer, outlaw. Established in New Orleans by 1809, he became chief of Barataria Bay pirates *c.* 1810; operated out of Galveston *post* 1817. A shrewd, successful merchant on the Spanish Main as well as the last of the great freebooters, he was responsible for the service of many of his followers in the defense of New Orleans, Dec. 1814– Jan. 1815.

LA FLESCHE, SUSETTE. [See BRIGHT EYES, 1854–1903.]

LA FOLLETTE, ROBERT MARION (*b. Primrose, Wis., 1855; d. Washington, D.C., 1925*), governor of Wisconsin, U.S. senator, Progressive candidate for president, was born to the hard labor of pioneer poverty. He worked his way into, and through, the University of Wisconsin, graduating in 1879. After studying law a few months, he was admitted to the bar. He married a classmate, Belle Case, who earned a law degree from the state university, 1885, and worked with him in law and politics; it became a tradition that her sound judgment was the family's most valuable asset. In 1880 he was elected district attorney of Dane County and on renomination in 1882 was the only Republican elected in the county. In 1884 he was elected to Congress and twice re-elected. Still relatively a conservative, he was defeated in the Democratic landslide of 1890.

In 1891 La Follette broke with Sen. Philetus Sawyer, state Republican leader, claiming that Sawyer had attempted through him to bribe a judge in a corruption suit against several former state treasurers. Thereafter, he increasingly opposed the party bosses and developed a vision of a new political system. During the years before his inauguration as governor in 1901 he elaborated a reform program: direct-primary nominations protected by law; the equalization of taxation of corporate property with that of other property; the regulation of railroad charges; and the erection of commissions of experts to regulate railroads. He failed to win the Republican nomination for governor in 1896 and 1898, but in 1900 he was nominated by acclamation and elected. His associates in the state government, however, were "Stalwart Republicans" who had surrendered nothing. He took office committed to direct-primary legislation, tax reform, and railroad control, measures partly reminiscent of Populism and partly anticipatory of Progressivism. Attacking the Republican leaders as greedy and corrupt, he created a lasting party schism; his Stalwart legislature refused to implement his platform. He took his case to the people and was so successful that his chief lieutenant became speaker of the Assembly in 1903. By 1905 the "Wisconsin Idea" of reform was a reality in prospect, and La Follette was elected to the U.S. Senate, to be thrice re-elected. His program made his state a model. A surprising number of his reforms were adopted nationally, while the regulatory commissions and technical experts he advocated changed to some extent the whole aspect of American government.

La Follette hoped to succeed Theodore Roosevelt whom he regarded as a lukewarm reformer; he feared that the unrestrained greed of businessmen would drive the nation into Socialism and must be checked. In 1912 he was the logical leader of liberal, insurgent Republicans openly at war with the party leadership. The revolt against Taft no longer appeared hopeless, but many of La Follette's supporters seized on a pretext to switch to Roosevelt at the Progressive Convention in Chicago and La Follette was shunted aside. He never forgave Roosevelt for what he considered a betrayal. Supporting the Democrats on many occasions, he opposed Wilson's 1916–17 diplomatic course and voted against war with Germany. He supported all the other war measures, however, and sought to make the war a charge on the current income of the rich rather than upon posterity. He opposed joining the League of Nations and the World Court. In 1924, at the highest point of his prestige, he decided to run independently for president as a Progressive with the hope of throwing the election into the House of Representatives where the insurgents might determine the choice. He received one-sixth of the votes cast.

LAFON, THOMY (*b. New Orleans, La., 1810; d. New Orleans, 1893*), Negro financier, philanthropist. Bequeathed the bulk of his large estate to charitable and educational institutions in New Orleans.

LAGUNA, THEODORE DE LEO DE (*b. Oakland, Calif., 1876; d. Hardwick, Vt., 1930*), philosopher. Taught at Bryn Mawr College, 1907–30; characterized his philosophy as "The Way of Opinion." He denied existence of truth in general, holding that there are only truths of particular propositions; he also denied validity of induction.

LAHONTAN, LOUIS-ARMAND DE LOM D'ARCE, Baron de (*b. Lahontan, France, 1666; d. probably Hanover, Germany, c. 1713*), soldier, explorer. Came to Canada, 1683; served in La Barre's and Denonville's expeditions against Iroquois; was commandant at Fort St. Joseph on St. Clair River and explored farther westward beyond Mackinac. Deserted the French service, 1693, after assignment to Newfoundland. Author of *Nouveaux Voyages, etc.* (The Hague, 1703), a well-written and popular mixture of fact and fiction about New France and the western country which exerted a strong influence on the literature of France and England and contributed to the growth of 18th century primitivism.

LAIMBEER, NATHALIE SCHENCK (*b. New York, N.Y., 1882; d. New York, 1929*), banker, financial writer.

LALOR, ALICE. [See TERESA, MOTHER, 1766–1846.]

LAMAR, GAZAWAY BUGG (*b. Richmond Co., Ga., 1798; d. New York, N.Y., 1874*), ship owner, banker, cotton merchant. Introduced the first iron steamship in American waters (the *John Randolph*, Savannah, Ga., 1834); was an incorporator of the Iron Steamboat Co. of Augusta, 1835. Removed to New York City, 1845, where he became president of the Bank of the Republic; remained in New York as Confederate intelligence agent until after the Civil War began. Back in Savannah, he engaged in banking and blockade running. When Gen. Sherman occupied Savannah, Lamar immediately took the oath of allegiance to save his property; later imprisoned on bribery charges, he was released by President Johnson.

LAMAR, JOSEPH RUCKER (*b. Elbert Co., Ga., 1857; d. Washington, D.C., 1916*), jurist. Attended University of Georgia; graduated Bethany College, W.Va., 1877. Admitted to Georgia bar, 1878, he practiced in Augusta and rose rapidly in his profession. As one of three commissioners appointed, 1893, to recodify the laws of Georgia, he undertook the major task of preparing the civil code. Appointed associate justice of state supreme court, 1904, after two years he resigned. In 1911 he became an associate justice of the U.S. Supreme Court. His decisions were terse, clear and just; among them, *Gompers vs. Bucks Stove Co.* and *U.S. vs. Midwest Oil Co.* were outstanding. He served as a U.S. commissioner to the Niagara Falls mediation conference to adjust U.S.-Mexican difficulties in May-June 1914.

LAMAR, LUCIUS QUINTUS CINCINNATUS (*b. Putnam Co., Ga., 1825; d. Macon, Ga., 1893*), lawyer, statesman. Nephew of Mirabeau B. Lamar. Graduated Emory College, 1845; admitted to the bar in Georgia, 1847. Settled permanently in Mississippi, 1855; was congressman, Democrat, 1857–60. Although conservative by temperament, he was determined to preserve what he considered the rights of the Southern states and drafted and reported the Mississippi ordinance of secession. Appointed Confederate special commissioner to Russia after military service, 1861–62, he spent several months in London and Paris, 1863, but was recalled before going to St. Petersburg. For a period after the end of the Civil War, he practiced law and taught at University of Mississippi. Elected to Congress, 1872, he labored to achieve sectional reconciliation and good will; as U.S. senator, 1877–85, he continued to impress the country with the desire of the new South to serve the interests of a common nationality and was outstanding as an orator. He was an able secretary of the interior, 1885–87. Appointed to the U.S. Supreme Court late in 1887, he served with great distinction until his death.

LAMAR, MIRABEAU BUONAPARTE (*b. Warren Co., Ga., 1798; d. Richmond, Texas, 1859*), statesman, planter. Uncle of Lucius Q. C. Lamar. Early active in Georgia politics; edited *Columbus* (Ga.) *Enquirer.* Removed to Texas, 1836; commanded cavalry at San Jacinto; served as secretary of war in provisional cabinet of President Burnet. Elected vice-president of Texas, 1836; served as president of the republic, December 1838–December 1841. Originally opposed to U.S. annexation, he planned a comprehensive system of education; began successful negotiations for recognition by France, England and Holland; founded city of Austin, 1840. He was, however, unable to solve the growing financial problems of Texas and failed to gain recognition of the republic's independence by Mexico. His career after his presidency was relatively uneventful.

LAMB, ISAAC WIXOM (*b. Hartland, Mich., 1840; d. Perry, Mich., 1906*), Baptist clergyman. Patented, 1863, the first successful flat (as contrasted to circular) knitting machine to be designed in the United States. *Post* 1869, he was engaged in pastoral work in Michigan.

LAMB, JOHN (*b. New York, N.Y., 1735; d. 1800*), Revolutionary patriot, soldier, merchant. An active leader of the Sons of Liberty *post* 1765, Lamb was commissioned captain of artillery in July 1775, and served under Gen. Richard Montgomery in the invasion of Canada that year. Described as "very turbulent and troublesome," he was wounded, captured and paroled; exchanged in 1777, he was made colonel of 2nd Continental Artillery. Promoted brigadier-general, 1783, he became collector of customs at port of New York, 1784. Although an anti-Federalist, his appointment was confirmed under the new Constitution, and he served in the post of collector until his resignation, 1797, by reason of a defalcation by his deputy.

LAMB, MARTHA JOANNA READE NASH (*b. Plainfield, Mass., 1829; d. New York, N.Y., 1893*), author. Her principal work was the popular and still valuable *History of the City of New York* (1877–81); she was distinguished also as editor of the *Magazine of American History*, 1883–93.

LAMBDIN, JAMES REID (*b. Pittsburgh, Pa., 1807; d. near Philadelphia, Pa., 1889*), portrait painter, miniaturist. Pupil of Thomas Sully. Long associated with Artists' Fund Society, Philadelphia, and with Pennsylvania Academy of the Fine Arts.

LAMBERT, LOUIS ALOISIUS (*b. Charleroi, Pa., 1835; d. Newfoundland, N.J., 1910*), Roman Catholic clergyman, author. Ordained 1859 for diocese of Alton, Ill.; served as Civil War chaplain, 18th Illinois Infantry; was pastor for many years at Waterloo, N.Y. Wrote effectively against fashionable infidelism of Robert G. Ingersoll and was first American Catholic apologist to reach a wide audience outside his own communion; edited New York *Freeman's Journal*, 1894–1910. Engaged in controversy with Bishop Bernard J. McQuaid.

LAMBERTON, BENJAMIN PEFFER (*b. Cumberland Co., Pa., 1844; d. Washington, D.C., 1912*), naval officer. Graduated U.S. Naval Academy, 1864. Was chief of staff to Com. Dewey at battle of Manila Bay, 1898; retired as rear-admiral, 1906.

LAMBING, ANDREW ARNOLD (*b. Manorville, Pa., 1842; d. Wilkinsburg, Pa., 1918*), Roman Catholic clergyman, pastor in western Pennsylvania, historian of the Catholic Church in that area.

LAMBUTH, JAMES WILLIAM (*b. Alabama, 1830; d. Kobe, Japan, 1892*), clergyman, Methodist Episcopal Church, South. Graduated University of Mississippi, 1851. Missionary to China and Japan, *post* 1854.

LAMBUTH, WALTER RUSSELL (*b. Shanghai, China, 1854; d. Yokohama, Japan, 1921*), bishop, Methodist Episcopal Church, South. Son of James W. Lambuth. Graduated Emory and Henry College, 1875; M.D., Vanderbilt, 1877; M.D., Bellevue Hospital Medical College, New York, 1881. Missionary to China; with his father, inaugurated missionary work of his church in Japan, 1885–86. Returning to the United States, 1891, he was general secretary, Board of Missions, 1894–1910. Elected bishop, 1910, he superintended mission work in Brazil and projected a new field in tropical Africa.

LAMME, BENJAMIN GARVER (*b. near Springfield, O., 1864; d. Pittsburgh, Pa., 1924*), engineer, inventor. Graduated Ohio State, M.E., 1888. Joined Westinghouse Electric Co., 1889, and was that organization's chief engineer at the time of his death. A master of analytical work and computing, he became an outstanding designer of electrical machinery. He was a leader in development of motors for railways, a pioneer in designing rotary converters and among the first to produce a commercially successful induction motor. He transformed the ideas of Nikola Tesla into commercial form and was the creator of the single-phase railway system.

LAMON, WARD HILL (*b. Frederick Co., Va., 1828; d. near Martinsburg, W.Va., 1893*), lawyer. Settled in Danville, Ill., 1847; associate and friend of Abraham Lincoln. As U.S. marshal of District of Columbia, 1861–65, he was a conspicuous Washington figure. Law partner of Jeremiah S. Black, 1865–79. Lamon's *Life of Abraham Lincoln* (1872) was written by Chauncey F. Black and based chiefly upon material which Lamon bought from W. H. Herndon.

LAMONT, DANIEL SCOTT (*b. Cortland Co., N.Y., 1851; d. Millbrook, N.Y. 1905*), New York state official, politician, financier. Private secretary to President Grover Cleveland, 1885–89; prospered in street-railway ventures as employee of William C. Whitney. Served effectively as secretary of war, 1893–97, and was thereafter vice-president of Northern Pacific Railway Co. and a close associate of James J. Hill.

LAMONT, HAMMOND (*b. Monticello, N.Y., 1864; d. New York, N.Y., 1909*), educator, journalist. Graduated Harvard, 1886. Taught English at Harvard and Brown; was managing editor, New York *Evening Post*, 1900–09; editor, the *Nation*, 1906–09. Author of *English Composition* (1906).

LA MOUNTAIN, JOHN (*b. Wayne Co., N.Y., 1830; d. 1870*), aeronaut. Became interested early in ballooning; with O. A. Gager and John Wise, constructed balloon *Atlantic* in which they flew from St. Louis, Mo., to Henderson, N.Y., July 1–2, 1859, longest air voyage on record to that date. La Mountain served as a balloon observer with the Army of the Potomac in the Civil War.

LAMOUREUX, ANDREW JACKSON (*b. Iosco, Mich., 1850; d. Ithaca, N.Y., 1928*), journalist. Edited liberal *Rio News*, English newspaper in Rio de Janeiro, Brazil, *post* 1877. Returned to the United States, 1902, and was for many years reference librarian, College of Agriculture, Cornell University.

LAMPSON, Sir CURTIS MIRANDA (*b. New Haven, Vt., 1806; d. London, England, 1885*), merchant. Removed to London, 1830; grew wealthy as an importer. Created a baronet, 1866, for his ten years' work in financing and seeing through to eventual success the Atlantic Cable project.

LAMY, JOHN BAPTIST (*b. Lempdes, France, 1814; d. Santa Fé, N. Mex., 1888*), Roman Catholic clergyman. Ordained at Clermont-Ferrand, 1838; volunteered for mission work in lower Ohio, 1839. Appointed vicar-apostolic of New Mexico, 1850; named bishop of Santa Fé, 1853, and archbishop, 1875. Overcame resentment of turbulent native Catholics against an American bishop and performed long journeys of great difficulty in doing the work of his vast diocese; resigned his see, 1885. Willa Cather's *Death Comes for the Archbishop* (1927) is based on the records of his career.

LANDAIS, PIERRE (*b. St. Malo, France, c. 1731; d. New York, N.Y., 1820*), naval officer. After long service in French Navy, accepted captain's commission in Continental Navy, 1777; commanded frigate *Alliance*, 1778–79. Moody, indecisive and jealous, he was formally accused by John Paul Jones of insubordination and treachery during action with British off Flamborough Head, 1779. Court-martialed and discharged from the service, January 1781, he later served creditably with the French Navy. He returned to New York City, 1797, where he lived thereafter in poverty, pressing his claims against the government for prize money and restitution of rank.

LANDER, EDWARD (*b. Salem, Mass., 1816; d. Washington, D.C., 1907*), jurist. Brother of Frederick W. Lander. Graduated Harvard, 1835; LL.B., 1839. Removed to Indianapolis, Ind., 1841. Served as justice of supreme court, Washington Territory, 1853–58; engaged in controversy over supremacy of civil law with Gov. I. I. Stevens.

LANDER, FREDERICK WEST (*b. Salem, Mass., 1821; d. in camp on Cacapon River, Va., 1862*), engineer, explorer, Union soldier. Brother of Edward Lander. After work on Eastern railroad surveys, Lander led or participated in five Western survey expeditions which included I. I. Stevens' survey of a Northern route for a Pacific Railroad, 1853; the exploration of a feasible route for a railway from the Mississippi via South Pass to Puget Sound, 1854; he served as superintendent and chief engineer of the overland wagon road, 1855–59. Appointed brigadier-general of volunteers, 1861, he was cited for gallantry in operations on the upper Potomac and died while preparing to move his force into the Shenandoah Valley to assist Banks's campaign.

LANDER, JEAN MARGARET DAVENPORT (*b. Wolverhampton, England, 1829; d. Lynn, Mass., 1903*), actress. Wife of Frederick W. Lander. Made American début in New York City as child prodigy, 1838; was first American "Camille" (1853).

LANDIS, HENRY ROBERT MURRAY (*b. Niles, O., 1872; d. Bryn Mawr, Pa., 1937*), physician. Graduated Amherst, 1894; M.D., Jefferson Medical College, 1897. Pioneer investigator (Phipps Institute, Philadelphia) of tuberculosis among Negroes, and of silicosis and anthracosis. Professor at University of Pennsylvania *post* 1910. Co-author *Diseases of the Chest, etc.* (1917). [*Supp. 2*]

LANDON, MELVILLE DE LANCEY (*b. Eaton, N.Y., 1839; d. Yonkers, N.Y., 1910*), journalist, humorous lecturer and writer under pseudonym "Eli Perkins."

LANDRETH, DAVID (*b. Philadelphia, Pa., 1802; d. Bristol, Pa., 1880*), agriculturist. Proprietor *post* 1828 of nursery and seed business established by his father, 1784; was active in agricultural societies.

LANE, FRANKLIN KNIGHT (*b. near Charlottetown, Canada, 1864; d. Rochester, Minn., 1921*), lawyer, statesman. Removed as a child to California; was raised in Napa and Oakland. Attended University of California, 1884–86, and Hastings College of Law; was admitted to bar, 1888. After a brief, unsuccessful period as a newspaper publisher and editor, he practiced law in San Francisco. Served three terms as Democratic city and county attorney; won national notice in vigorous but unsuccessful campaigns for governor of California and mayor of San Francisco, 1902 and 1903. Appointed to Interstate Commerce Commission, 1905, he served with outstanding ability, 1906–13; his decisions largely determined the constitutional powers of the government in the regulation of common carriers. As secretary of the interior in President Wilson's cabinet, 1913–20, Lane favored conservation, worked to develop Alaska and pressed for a more liberal Indian policy. He was notable also for his ability to inspire in his subordinates his own enthusiasm for honest public service.

LANE, GEORGE MARTIN (*b. probably Northampton, Mass., 1823; d. 1897*), classicist. Graduated Harvard, 1846; Ph.D., Göttingen, 1851. Professor of Latin, Harvard, 1851–94. A notable teacher. Author of *Latin Pronunciation* (1871) and an important *Latin Grammar* (1898). Hero of the "Lay of the Lone Fishball."

LANE, HENRY SMITH (*b. near Sharpsburg, Ky., 1811; d. 1881*), lawyer, banker. Removed to Crawfordsville, Ind., 1834. Congressman, Whig, from Indiana, 1840–43. As Republican, presided over national convention, 1856, and was U.S. senator from Indiana, 1861–67.

LANE, HORACE M. (*b. Readfield, Maine, 1837; d. São Paulo, Brazil, 1912*), physician. Presbyterian missionary educator in Brazil *post* 1886; organized Mackenzie College, São Paulo, 1891.

LANE, JAMES HENRY (*b. probably Lawrenceburg, Ind., 1814; d. 1866*), soldier, Kansas political leader. Served creditably in Mexican War; was Democratic lieutenant-governor of Indiana, 1849–53, and congressman, 1853–55. Emigrating to Kansas Territory, he joined Free-State movement and soon was directing its campaign to unite all anti-slavery factions and secure a "free" constitution preliminary to statehood. President of Topeka constitutional convention, he emerged from the crisis of the so-called Wakarusa War as a radical. In late summer, 1856, he led "Lane's Army of the North" into Kansas in atrocious attacks on pro-slavery strongholds; when the Free-State party won control of the Assembly, he was elected major-general of the militia. Elected to the U.S. senate, he served from 1861 until his death by suicide. Meanwhile, he was a pioneer in advocating emancipation of Negroes and their use as soldiers, and was a strong supporter of Lincoln.

LANE, JAMES HENRY (*b. Mathews Court House, Va., 1833; d. 1907*), Confederate brigadier-general, educator. Graduated Virginia Military Institute, 1854; University of Virginia, 1857. Served with Lee's army throughout Civil War. Taught at several schools, and was professor of civil engineering at Alabama Polytechnic Institute, 1882–1907.

LANE, JOHN (*b. Fairfax Co., Va., 1789; d. Vicksburg, Miss., 1855*), Methodist clergyman, merchant. A founder of Vicksburg, Miss., as administrator of estate of Newet Vick, his father-in-law.

LANE, JOSEPH (*b. Buncombe Co., N.C., 1801; d. Oregon, 1881*), soldier, governor, legislator. Raised in Henderson Co., Ky. Settled in Vanderburg Co., Ind., 1820; prospered as farmer and flatboat merchant; was frequently elected to the legislature. One of the Mexican War's outstanding heroes, he won a brevet of major-general. Commissioned governor of Oregon Territory, 1848, he resigned in 1850 to be chosen delegate to Congress. Re-elected three times, he became U.S. senator, 1859, on Oregon's admission as a state. In 1860 he ran for vice-president on the Breckinridge ticket as an avowed partisan of secession, and his public career was ended. One of the ablest men of his time in the West, he was an independent thinker on public questions. His alleged connection with the "Pacific Republic" scheme to aid the Confederacy is legend rather than fact.

LANE, LEVI COOPER (*b. near Somerville, O., 1830; d. 1902*), surgeon. Graduated Jefferson Medical College, 1851. Associated with his uncle Elias S. Cooper in San Francisco, Calif., 1859–64; was considered leading surgeon on Pacific Coast. Benefactor of Medical College of Pacific, where he taught.

LANE, Sir RALPH (*b. England, c. 1530; d. Dublin, Ireland, 1603*), colonist. Accompanied Sir Richard Grenville to Virginia, 1585; commanded the settlement on Roanoke Island until it was abandoned the following year.

LANE, TIDENCE (*b. near Baltimore, Md., 1724; d. 1806*), pioneer Baptist minister of Tennessee. Organized Buffalo Ridge Church in present Washington Co. *c.* 1779; was pastor at Bent Creek, 1785–1806.

LANE, WALTER PAYE (*b. Co. Cork, Ireland, 1817; d. Marshall, Texas, 1892*), soldier, merchant. Came to America as a child; was raised in Fairview, O. Served in Texan war of independence and as a Confederate brigadier.

LANE, WILLIAM CARR (*b. Fayette Co., Pa., 1789; d. St. Louis, Mo., 1863*), physician. First mayor of St. Louis, 1823; re-elected many times. Governor of New Mexico Territory, 1852.

LANG, BENJAMIN JOHNSON (*b. Salem, Mass., 1837; d. Boston, Mass., 1909*), musician, organist at Old South and King's Chapel, Boston. Conductor of the Apollo Club, the Cecilia Society and the Handel and Haydn Society; introduced much new music as pianist and orchestra leader.

LANG, HENRY ROSEMAN (*b. St. Gall, Switzerland, 1853; d. 1934*), philologist. Came to America *c.* 1875. Ph.D., University of Strassburg, 1892. Taught Romance languages, Yale, 1893–1922. His many publications deal mainly with Portuguese and Spanish literature of the earlier periods. [*Supp. 1*]

LANGDELL, CHRISTOPHER COLUMBUS (*b. New Boston, N.H., 1826; d. Cambridge, Mass., 1906*), lawyer, legal author. Attended Harvard College and Law School, 1851–54; practiced law in New York City, 1854–70. Called to Harvard, 1870, to become Dane Professor (afterwards dean) in the Law School, he introduced striking changes, requiring examinations for the law degree and training his students to use original authorities for their derivation and understanding of legal principles. For teaching by his case method, he edited and published *A Selection of Cases on the Law of Contracts* (1871), *A Selection of Cases on Sales of Personal Property* (1872) and *Cases on Equity Pleading* (1875). At first opposed by the bar and other law school teachers, his method gained popularity, particularly through the use of it by William A. Keener and James B. Ames.

LANGDON, COURTNEY (*b. Rome, Italy, 1861; d. Providence, R.I., 1924*), educator. Son of William C. Langdon. Taught modern and Romance languages at Lehigh and Cornell, and at Brown University *post* 1890. Published translation of Dante's *Divine Comedy* (1918–21).

LANGDON, JOHN (*b. Portsmouth, N.H., 1741; d. 1819*), merchant, Revolutionary patriot, politician. Brother of Woodbury Langdon. Organized and financed Stark's expedition against Burgoyne, 1777; was speaker of New Hampshire legislature and member of Continental Congress. Governor of New Hampshire, 1785, 1788, 1805–08, 1810–11; U.S. senator, (Democrat) Republican, 1789–1801.

LANGDON, SAMUEL (*b. Boston, Mass., 1723; d. Hampton Falls, N.H., 1797*), Congregational clergyman. President of Harvard, 1774–80, appointed as a "zealous whig" to counterbalance pro-British college officers.

LANGDON, WILLIAM CHAUNCY (*b. Burlington, Vt., 1831; d. Providence, R.I., 1895*), patent lawyer, Episcopal clergyman. Graduated Transylvania University, 1850; ordained, 1859. Took lead in founding American Confederation of Y.M.C.A., 1854, and was first general secretary. Resided in Europe as rector of Episcopal churches in Rome, Florence and Geneva, 1859–62, 1865–76. A partisan of Christian reunion.

LANGDON, WOODBURY (*b. Portsmouth, N.H., 1738 or 1739; d. 1805*), merchant, New Hampshire legislator and official. Brother of John Langdon.

LANGE, ALEXIS FREDERICK (*b. Lafayette Co., Mo., 1862; d. 1924*), educator. Director and dean, University of California School of Education; originated junior high school movement; helped begin junior college movement.

LANGE, LOUIS (*b. Hesse, Germany, 1829; d. St. Louis, Mo., 1893*), printer, periodical editor. Came to America *c.* 1846; settled in St. Louis, 1859. His German language publications, *Die Abendschule* and *Die Rundschau*, had wide influence.

LANGFORD, NATHANIEL PITT (*b. Westmoreland, N.Y., 1832; d. St. Paul, Minn., 1911*), businessman, explorer, first superintendent of Yellowstone National Park. Removed to St. Paul, 1854. Joined Fisk's Northern Overland Expedition to Salmon River gold fields, 1862; at Bannack, Mont., was an organizer of

Vigilantes for law administration and enforcement as described in his *Vigilante Days and Ways* (1890). He is best known for his early (1870) exploration of the Yellowstone Park area and his pioneer description of it in *Diary of the Washburn Expedition to the Yellowstone and Fire Hole Rivers* (1905). His articles and political efforts helped bring about creation of the area as a national park, 1872. He served without pay as its superintendent, 1872–76, and preserved the natural wonders from exploitation and misuse.

LANGLADE, CHARLES MICHEL DE [See DE LANGLADE, CHARLES MICHEL, 1729–1801.]

LANGLEY, JOHN WILLIAMS (*b. Boston, Mass., 1841; d. Ann Arbor, Mich., 1918*), chemist, educator. Brother of Samuel P. Langley. Graduated Lawrence Scientific School, Harvard, 1861. Taught at present Pittsburgh University, at Michigan and at Case School; engaged in chemical and metallurgical research in iron and steel.

LANGLEY, SAMUEL PIERPONT (*b. Roxbury, Mass., 1834; d. Aiken, S.C., 1906*), scientist, aviation research pioneer, author, third secretary of the Smithsonian Institution. Brother of John W. Langley. Read omnivorously; attended several private schools and graduated from Boston High School, 1851; had no college training. Engaged in engineering and architectural work, 1851–64. After a tour of Europe visiting scientific institutions with his brother, 1864–65, he took charge of the small observatory at the U.S. Naval Academy during 1866. He then went to Western University of Pennsylvania as professor of physics and astronomy and director of the Allegheny Observatory, where he remained 20 years.

As an astronomer, his great achievement was in the field of spectral measurements of solar and lunar radiation. He invented the bolometer, 1878, with which he began an epoch-making series of experiments on the distribution of radiation in the solar spectrum, the transparency of the atmosphere to the different solar rays and the enhancement of their intensity at high altitudes and even outside the atmosphere altogether. In an expedition to Mt. Whitney, California, 1881, he was able to amplify his findings on the solar constant. Thereafter, he made studies of the lunar spectrum and did considerable popular lecturing and writing on astronomical subjects; his *The New Astronomy* (1888) became a classic in astronomical literature.

In 1887 Langley went to the Smithsonian Institution, becoming secretary the same year and remaining until his death. He early established the National Zoological Park and the Astrophysical Observatory, where he carried forward his studies of solar radiation and observation of solar eclipses. Before leaving Allegheny Observatory, he had begun the series of investigations into the possibilities of flight in heavier-than-air machines which he continued with conspicuous results at Washington. The greatness of his contribution to aviation depends on his pioneering laboratory investigations and successful long-distance flights of large power-driven models (1896), and also on the fact that one of his reputation should have adventured in a field so much ridiculed at the time. Persuaded to undertake with Charles M. Manly the construction of a man-carrying airplane, Langley abandoned his efforts after the mechanical failure of their machine in trials during October and December 1903.

LANGSTON, JOHN MERCER (*b. Louisa Co., Va., 1829; d. 1897*), lawyer, educator, diplomat. Graduated Oberlin, 1849; Oberlin theological department, 1853. Admitted to the Ohio bar, 1854, he was nominated and elected clerk of Brownhelm Township, 1855, probably the first Negro chosen to an elective office in the United States. After service as inspector-general of the Freedmen's Bureau, 1868, he was professor of law and dean at Howard University, 1869–76. Appointed U.S. minister to Haiti, 1877, he remained in the diplomatic and consular service until 1885. He was thereafter president of Virginia Normal and Collegiate Institute and served a single term as Republican congressman from Virginia, 1889–91.

LANGSTROTH, LORENZO LORRAINE (*b. Philadelphia, Pa., 1810; d. Dayton, O., 1895*), Congregational clergyman, educator, apiarist. Invented the moveable-frame beehive, which revolutionized method of keeping bees.

LANGWORTHY, EDWARD (*b. in or near Savannah, Ga., c. 1738; d. Baltimore, Md., 1802*), Revolutionary patriot, educator. Georgia member of Continental Congress, 1777–79; published *Memoirs of the Life of the Late Charles Lee* (London, 1792).

LANGWORTHY, JAMES LYON (*b. Windsor, Vt., 1800; d. Dubuque, Iowa, 1865*), lead miner, Iowa pioneer. Prospected near site of Dubuque, 1830; settled there, 1833, and was prominent in its civic affairs and development.

LANIER, JAMES FRANKLIN DOUGHTY (*b. Washington, N.C., 1800; d. New York, N.Y., 1881*), lawyer, financier. Raised in Eaton, O.; removed to Madison, Ind., 1817. A successful lawyer, he became largest shareholder in new State Bank of Indiana, 1833, and was president of its Madison branch. As it was one of the few banks in the Mississippi Valley to weather the panic of 1837, Lanier and the other officers won high repute. He later went to Europe and arranged to restore Indiana's shaken financial credit. In 1848 he moved to New York, where he helped found Winslow, Lanier & Co., a pioneer firm in the floating of railway securities. During the Civil War, he advanced large sums to the State of Indiana to equip and support troops.

LANIER, SIDNEY (*b. Macon, Ga., 1842; d. Lynn, N.C., 1881*), poet, musician, critic. Musically precocious, Lanier graduated from Oglethorpe University,

1860. He had intended to fit himself for teaching by study at a German university, but on the outbreak of the Civil War, enlisted in the Confederate Army. Captured in 1864, he spent four dreary months in a federal prison (described in *Tiger-Lilies*, 1867). Already consumptive, his next eight years were a tragic experience as he moved restlessly from one occupation to another; in 1873 his father agreed to help him devote himself to the "two sublime arts" music and poetry. He played the flute in the Peabody Orchestra, Baltimore, and his poems "Corn" and "The Symphony," published in *Lippincott's Magazine*, 1875, marked the definite beginnings of his poetic career. Thereafter he continued to produce verses written in accordance with his theories of identity between the technical laws of music and poetry until his early death. His works include *The Science of English Verse* (1880) and *The English Novel* (1883), fruit of his 1879 lectureship at Johns Hopkins; his poems were published in a small book in 1877 and were issued in collected form, 1884.

LANIGAN, GEORGE THOMAS (*b. St. Charles, on the Richelieu River, Canada, 1845; d. Philadelphia, Pa., 1886*), journalist, humorist. Author of the celebrated "Threnody for the Ahkoond of Swat."

LANMAN, CHARLES (*b. Monroe, Mich., 1819; d. Georgetown, D.C. 1895*), writer, amateur explorer, artist. Author of *Private Life of Daniel Webster* (1852) and many other books.

LANMAN, JOSEPH (*b. Norwich, Conn., 1811; d. Norwich, 1874*), naval officer. Served in Mexican War and Civil War; as commodore, led second division of Porter's squadron in attacks on Fort Fisher, 1864–65. Retired as rear-admiral, 1872.

LANSING, GULIAN (*b. Lishaskill, N.Y., 1825; d. Cairo, Egypt, 1892*), Associate Reformed Church and United Presbyterian clergyman. Missionary to Syria and Egypt *post* 1850.

LANSING, JOHN (*b. Albany, N.Y., 1754; disappeared, New York City, 1829*), jurist. Admitted to practice in Albany, 1775. Served six terms in N.Y. Assembly, 1780–88; was a member of Congress, 1784–85, and mayor of Albany, 1786–90. A delegate to the Philadelphia Convention, 1787, with Alexander Hamilton and Robert Yates, he and Yates withdrew on grounds that the convention was exceeding its authority by drafting a new constitution rather than amending the Articles of Confederation. As a member of New York ratifying convention in 1788, he opposed the federal constitution. He was justice of the N.Y. supreme court, 1790–1801, and chief justice in 1798; named chancellor of New York, 1801, he retired, 1814. Although he owed his political preferment to the Clinton faction, he remained a man of independent mind.

LANSING, ROBERT (*b. Watertown, N.Y., 1864; d. Washington, D.C., 1928*), lawyer. Graduated Amherst, 1886; was admitted to the bar, 1889. His marriage to the daughter of John W. Foster in 1890 brought him into the international field where he won distinction; from 1892 to 1914 he served frequently as U.S. counsel or agent on international arbitration tribunals. He helped found American Society of International Law (1906) and was an editor of its *Journal*, 1907–28. He became counselor for the State Department, 1914, and succeeded William J. Bryan as secretary, serving 1915–20. President Wilson decided major policy himself and handled delicate negotiations informally through Edward M. House, but he and Lansing worked in outward harmony until the Peace Conference. Lansing's view that the proposed League of Nations was unimportant brought about estrangement, and when Lansing held cabinet meetings during the President's illness, Wilson demanded his resignation.

LANSTON, TOLBERT (*b. Troy, O., 1844; d. Washington, D.C., 1913*), lawyer, inventor. Worked in U.S. Patent Office, 1865–87; was granted patents on variety of devices, 1870–83. In 1887, he patented the monotype machines for composing printing type; he received further patents for improvements, 1896, 1897, 1899, 1900, 1902, 1910. His perfected machines were introduced commercially, 1897.

LAPHAM, INCREASE ALLEN (*b. Palmyra, N.Y., 1811; d. Oconomowoc, Wis., 1875*), canal builder and engineer, pioneer Wisconsin scientist. Removed from Ohio to Milwaukee, Wis., 1836, as assistant to Byron Kilbourn in surveying, platting, and promoting the area. Made some of the first and best maps of Wisconsin and wrote on the state's geology, mineralogy and Indian remains. The U.S. Weather Bureau was established at his insistence, 1869.

LAPHAM, WILLIAM BERRY (*b. Greenwood, Maine, 1828; d. Togus, Maine, 1894*), physician. Expert local historian and genealogist of Maine.

LARAMIE, JACQUES (*b. probably Canada; d. on Laramie River, Wyo., 1821*), pioneer trapper. Entered the unknown country of southeastern Wyoming *c.* 1819; reputed to be first white man to visit upper course of the Laramie River. In the legendry of the West, he became an important figure, but little factual information about him has been discovered.

LARCOM, LUCY (*b. Beverly, Mass., 1824; d. Boston, Mass., 1893*), author, teacher. Contributed first to the *Operative's Magazine* of Lowell, Mass., *c.* 1840, and to its successor the *Lowell Offering and Magazine*. Her verses were popular and were published collectively in 1869 and 1884, but her *New England Girlhood* (1889) has greater value as literature and social history. She was co-editor with her friend John G. Whittier of several successful verse anthologies.

LARD, MOSES E. (*b. Bedford Co., Tenn., 1818; d. Lexington, Ky., 1880*), minister of Disciples of Christ, editor.

LARDNER, JAMES LAWRENCE (*b. Philadelphia, Pa., 1802; d. Philadelphia, 1881*), naval officer. Appointed midshipman, 1820; retired as rear-admiral. A type of the navy career man, active in varied service, 1820–72.

LARDNER, RINGGOLD WILMER (*b. Niles, Mich., 1885; d. East Hampton, N.Y., 1933*), journalist, author. Known as Ring Lardner. Began career, 1905, as sports reporter in South Bend, Ind.; thereafter worked on several Chicago papers and wrote a successful sports column for the *Chicago Tribune*, 1913–19. Began contributing "Jack Keefe" letters about baseball to the *Saturday Evening Post c.* 1914; they were later published in book form as *You Know Me Al* (1916) and others. He was author also of *Treat 'Em Rough* (1918) and *The Real Dope* (1919). His broad humor later grew mordant and ironical in *How to Write Short Stories* (1924), *The Love Nest* (1926) and *Round Up* (1929). Accuracy in using the vernacular, humor, and the exposure of dullness and sham through self-revelation by the characters of his stories, are the outstanding virtues of his work.

[*Supp.* 1]

LARKIN, JOHN (*b. Newcastle-upon-Tyne, England, 1801; d. New York, N.Y., 1858*), Roman Catholic clergyman, Sulpician and Jesuit. Ordained Baltimore, Md., 1827; entered Society of Jesus in Kentucky, 1840. Taught at Fordham (St. John's College), 1846; founded Xavier School, New York City, 1847; was president of Fordham, 1851–53.

LARKIN, THOMAS OLIVER (*b. Charlestown, Mass., 1802; d. 1858*), merchant, diplomatic agent. Removed to California, 1832; played a part in the machinations preliminary to the U.S. acquisition of California. He served as U.S. consul at Monterey, 1844–48; confidential agent, 1846–48; naval store-keeper, 1847–48; navy agent, 1847–49. He watched British and French diplomatic agents closely, fearful of their designs on California *post* 1844. James Buchanan's secret dispatch of October 1845 appointed him "confidential agent in California," under authority of which he launched a propaganda campaign to separate California from Mexico in furtherance of President Polk's expansionist policy.

LARNED, JOSEPH GAY EATON (*b. Thompson, Conn., 1819; d. New York, N.Y., 1870*), lawyer, industrialist. Inventor, promoter and manufacturer of steam fire engines, 1856–63.

LARNED, JOSEPHUS NELSON (*b. Chatham, Canada, 1836; d. Buffalo, N.Y., 1913*), librarian, journalist. Pioneered at Buffalo, N.Y., library in use of Dewey system and other improvements. Author of *History for Ready Reference* (1894–95) and *The Literature of American History* (1902).

LARNED, WILLIAM AUGUSTUS (*b. Summit, N.J., 1872; d. New York, N.Y., 1926*), lawn tennis champion. Among first ten U.S. players, 1892–1912; a master of ground-strokes.

LaROCHE, RENÉ (*b. Philadelphia, Pa., 1795; d. 1872*), physician, musician. M.D., University of Pennsylvania, 1820. An erudite and prolific writer on medical subjects; his *Yellow Fever* (1855) is a classic treatise.

LA RONDE, LOUIS DENIS, Sieur de (*b. Quebec, Canada, 1675; d. Quebec, 1741*), French naval officer. Accompanied Iberville to Hudson's Bay, 1697, and to Louisiana, 1700–01. Discovered copper in Lake Superior region, c. 1734.

LARPENTEUR, CHARLES (*b. near Fontainebleau, France, 1807; d. Harrison Co., Iowa, 1872*), fur trader. Came to America as a boy. His autobiography, *Forty Years a Fur Trader on the Upper Missouri* (1898), is a valuable primary historical source.

LARRABEE, CHARLES HATHAWAY (*b. Rome, N.Y., 1820; d. California, 1883*), lawyer, Union soldier, Wisconsin jurist and Democratic congressman. Helped frame constitutions for Wisconsin (1847) and Washington (1877–78).

LARRABEE, WILLIAM (*b. Ledyard, Conn., 1832; d. 1912*), businessman, Iowa legislator. Removed to Iowa, 1853. Forceful Republican governor of Iowa, 1886–90; early proponent of railroad regulation by law. Author of *The Railroad Question* (1893).

LARRABEE, WILLIAM CLARK (*b. Cape Elizabeth, Maine, 1802; d. Indiana, 1859*), Methodist clergyman, educator, editor. First state superintendent, Indiana public school system, 1852–54, 1856–58.

LARRAZOLO, OCTAVIANO AMBROSIO (*b. Allende, Mexico, 1859; d. Albuquerque, N. Mex., 1930*), jurist, educator, political leader. Republican governor of New Mexico, 1918–21; U.S. senator, 1929–30. Long-time champion of native Spanish-Americans.

LARRÍNAGA, TULIO (*b. Trujillo Alto, P.R., 1847; d. Santurce, P.R., 1917*), engineer, architect, government official. Second resident commissioner for Puerto Rico in the United States, 1905–11.

LARSEN, PETER LAURENTIUS (*b. Christiansand, Norway, 1833; d. Decorah, Iowa, 1915*), Norwegian Lutheran clergyman, educator. Came to America, 1857. *Post* 1863, associated with Luther College as professor and president.

LARSON, LAURENCE MARCELLUS (*b. Spjutøy, Norway, 1868; d. Urbana, Ill., 1938*), historian. Came to America as a child. Graduated Drake University, 1894; Ph.D., Wisconsin, 1902. Taught at University of Illinois, 1907–37. Specialist in the interaction between the cultures of northern and western Europe.
[*Supp. 2*]

LA SALLE, ROBERT CAVELIER, Sieur de (*b. Rouen, France, 1643; d. on Brazos River, Texas, above mouth of the Navasota, 1687*), explorer. Entered the Society of Jesus as a novice; not liking its discipline, he left the Society, 1665. His elder brother, a Sulpician, having gone to Montreal, Robert followed him there in the summer of 1666. He at first lived the life of a pioneer farmer in New France, but in the summer of 1669 sold his seigniory and went exploring to Niagara, the western shores of Lake Ontario, and by his own statement to the Ohio; on this expedition he first met Louis Jolliet. His activities from 1669 to 1673 are not known.

Count de Frontenac, appointed governor of New France, 1672, on arriving at Quebec encouraged La Salle to present his hopes for a western empire to the authorities at Paris. When La Salle returned to Canada, 1675, he brought a grant of Fort Frontenac on Lake Ontario as a seigniory and exclusive permission for trade there. Three years thereafter, he journeyed again to France and obtained a patent permitting him to explore and exploit the regions of the West. Back in Canada in the summer of 1678, he and Frontenac began extensive preparations for that task. In the fall of 1679, La Salle, in concert with his lieutenant Henri de Tonty, explored Lake Michigan to St. Joseph River and proceeded by the Kankakee and Illinois rivers to Lake Peoria, where they built Fort Crêvecoeur, January 1680. Thence La Salle sent three men, including Father Louis Hennepin, to explore the upper Mississippi, himself returning to Fort Frontenac on foot. Going back to the Illinois country in late autumn, he found the ruins of Fort Crêvecoeur, whence all had fled before an Iroquois invasion. La Salle and Tonty were reunited in June 1681 at Mackinac; they returned to the Illinois country and rebuilt their fort, this time on the upper Illinois River near present Ottawa. From here they set out early in 1682 to explore the Mississippi River to its mouth. On their arrival at the Gulf of Mexico on April 9, they took possession of the entire river valley for the king of France and named it Louisiana in his honor. This was the climax of La Salle's career.

Frontenac was replaced in 1682 by Governor de la Barre, who deprived La Salle of many of his concessions and privileges. Having returned to France, La Salle re-established his position at the French Court, and on July 24, 1684, sailed at the head of an expedition of four ships and 200 colonists to plant a settlement at the mouth of the Mississippi. The expedition missed its mark and landed on the Texas coast. While La Salle was seeking an overland route to the Mississippi River, his men mutinied and murdered him. In many respects an heroic figure, he was a dreamer with magnificent ideas and hopes. His vision of a great French empire in the heart of the continent, and his accomplishments as an explorer and publicity agent, all merit praise. His failures, however, reflected his lack of administrative ability and his habit of uncertainty of judgment at critical moments.

LASATER, EDWARD CUNNINGHAM (*b. Goliad Co., Texas, 1860; d. Ardmore, Okla., 1930*), cattleman, land developer. Served briefly under Herbert Hoover on U.S. Food Administration, 1917; differed violently with Hoover's policies. A fighter for reforms in both politics and business practices, Lasater was also an authority on range problems.

LATANÉ, JOHN HOLLADAY (*b. Staunton, Va., 1869; d. New Orleans, La., 1932*), historian, educator. Graduated Johns Hopkins, 1892; Ph.D., 1895. Professor of history, Randolph-Macon, 1898–1902; Washington and Lee University, 1902–1913; Johns Hopkins, *post* 1913. His chief interest was in the problems of international relations; he was a champion of the ideas and policies of Woodrow Wilson. His books and numerous articles reflected his keen interest in the contemporary world. Aside from three widely used textbooks which he wrote, his most influential work was *America as a World Power: 1897–1907* (1907). [*Supp. 1*]

LATHAM, MILTON SLOCUM (*b. Columbus, O., 1827; d. 1882*), lawyer, financier. Removed to California, 1850. Democratic congressman, 1853–55; collector of port of San Francisco, 1855–57; governor of California, Jan. 9–14, 1860; U.S. senator, 1860–63. Suggested independence for California in event of dissolution of Union (April 1860).

LATHBURY, MARY ARTEMISIA (*b. Manchester, N.Y., 1841; d. East Orange, N.J., 1913*), teacher, author of juvenile stories and verses, hymn-writer.

LATHROP, FRANCIS AUGUSTUS (*b. at sea en route to Honolulu, 1849; d. Woodcliffe Lake, N.J., 1909*), mural painter. Brother of George P. Lathrop. Student of Whistler and Madox Brown; associate of Burne-Jones and William Morris. Noted for his wall panels, mosaics and stained-glass windows.

LATHROP, GEORGE PARSONS (*b. near Honolulu, Hawaii, 1851; d. New York, N.Y., 1898*), author, editor. Brother of Francis A. Lathrop; husband of Mother Alphonsa (Rose Hawthorne). Active in work of American Copyright League and a founder of Catholic Summer School of America.

LATHROP, JOHN (*b. Boston, Mass., 1772; d. Georgetown, D.C., 1820*), lawyer, poet, educator.

LATHROP, JOHN HIRAM (*b. Sherburne, N.Y., 1799; d. Columbia, Mo., 1866*), pioneer in Mid-West higher education. Graduated Yale, 1819. Served *post* 1841 as president of universities of Missouri, Wisconsin and Indiana.

LATHROP, JULIA CLIFFORD (*b. Rockford, Ill., 1858; d. 1932*), social worker. Graduated Vassar, 1880. Entered social work in association with Jane Addams at Hull House, Chicago; was first woman member, Illinois Board of Public Charities, 1893–1909. She took an active part in many movements for social improvement including the mental hygiene movement, the establishment of juvenile courts, and woman suffrage. Appointed chief of federal Children's Bureau, 1912, she served until 1921 and made her department a strong force for regulation of child labor, assistance to working mothers and all manner of welfare legislation. [*Supp. 1*]

LATHROP, ROSE HAWTHORNE. [See ALPHONSA, MOTHER, 1851–1926.]

LATIL, ALEXANDRE (*b. New Orleans, La., 1816; d. 1851*), Louisiana poet. A victim of leprosy; author of *Les Ephémères* (1841).

LATIMER, MARY ELIZABETH WORMELEY (*b. London, England, 1822; d. Baltimore, Md., 1904*), writer. Settled in the United States *c.* 1845. Author of numerous popular studies of 19th century European history.

LA TOUR, LE BLOND de (*b. France, late 17th century; d. New Orleans, La., 1723*), engineer. Came to province of Louisiana, 1720; as engineer-in-chief, planned Biloxi, Miss., and supervised development of New Orleans.

LATROBE, BENJAMIN HENRY (*b. Fulneck, England, 1764; d. New Orleans, La., 1820*), architect, engineer. Grandson of Henry Antes. Spent his boyhood in England and his youth in Germany, where he received an excellent education. Returning to England *c.* 1786, he studied both architecture and engineering under outstanding masters. Emigrated to Norfolk, Va., 1796; was soon employed on important works. In 1797, among other projects, he designed the penitentiary to be built at Richmond, one of the earliest to adopt the principle of solitary confinement. In December 1798 he settled in Philadelphia, where he designed and supervised the construction of a new building for the Bank of Pennsylvania (completed 1801); this building has been termed the first monument of the Greek revival in America. Also in 1798, he wrote and published a pamphlet advocating a city water supply (the first in America); work was begun on it in March 1799 with Latrobe as engineer. This water system functioned successfully, 1801–15; it was superseded by a larger plant designed by one of Latrobe's pupils. In 1801 and 1802 he supervised the improvement of the Susquehanna River, clearing the channel for downstream navigation from Columbia to tidewater; he also designed several large homes in and about Philadelphia.

As early as 1800 Latrobe was at work on designs for the federal government. Some of these plans were not accepted, but President Jefferson came to think highly of his work, and created for Latrobe in 1803 the post of surveyor of U.S. public buildings. His first task was to build the Capitol's south wing. Latrobe and Jefferson found themselves in bitter conflict with William Thornton, who had won the original competition for the design in 1792–93 and balked at necessary changes. Jefferson and Latrobe eventually carried their point and brought the building to a worthy completion. For the east basement vestibule, Latrobe designed in 1809 his "American order" of maize, promptly christened by admiring members of Congress the "corn-cob capitals." Meanwhile he had worked on the President's house, on the Washington City Canal, and *post* 1804 as "engineer of the Navy Department" had done work at the yards in Washington, New York and elsewhere. He built fireproof vaults for the State Department, 1810, and drew plans for the Marine Hospital in Washington, 1812.

During these years he also executed an increasing flood of private commissions. He designed churches, including the Catholic Cathedral in Baltimore, Md., college buildings, beautiful homes. It was his custom to draw plans for religious and educational buildings free of charge. On the outbreak of the War of 1812 and the suspension of his government work, Latrobe entered partnership with Robert Fulton, Robert R. Livingston and Nicholas I. Roosevelt to build a steamboat adapted to navigation of the Ohio River above the falls, but increasing costs and the death of Fulton brought this work to a close. Latrobe lost all of his private means in this venture and was left with many debts. In the spring of 1815 he was invited to return to Washington and take charge of the rebuilding of the Capitol, a task he resigned in 1817. Harassed by his debts, he took advantage of the new insolvency act, 1818, and then removed to Baltimore where he had several commissions awaiting him.

As early as 1809, Latrobe had been consulted about a water supply for New Orleans. In 1810 he sent his son, Henry, to pursue the project. The work was delayed by the war, and the son died of yellow fever in 1817, his task unfinished. The father determined to go to New Orleans and finish it, but he too was attacked by fever and died on Sept. 3, 1820, soon after he reached Louisiana.

Latrobe found architecture in America a polite accomplishment of gentleman amateurs; he left it a profession, with professional standards and practices, largely in the hands of his own pupils. Few American architects before the great organizations of the past generation have had so wide and varied a practice. Apprenticeship in his office constituted the first important professional training in engineering and architecture in America. He was a good linguist; he drew with facility and accuracy, and his reports on engineering and architectural projects are models of technical exposition.

LATROBE, BENJAMIN HENRY (*b. Philadelphia, Pa., 1806; d. Baltimore, Md., 1878*), lawyer, civil engineer. Son of Benjamin H. Latrobe (1764–1820). Obtained a position in the engineer corps of the Baltimore and Ohio Railroad, 1831; an excellent mathematician, he became assistant to Jonathan

Knight, chief engineer of the road. The Thomas Viaduct at Relay, Md., was his design. *Post* 1842, he was chief engineer in succession to Knight and had charge of building many miles of difficult track, including the extensions to the Ohio River and to Pittsburgh. He was the first to employ the present type of railroad ferry (1835), originated the "ton mile" work unit, served as consultant in the planning of the first transcontinental railroads, and was a member of the committee to which Roebling submitted the plans of the Brooklyn Bridge.

LATROBE, CHARLES HAZLEHURST (*b. Baltimore, Md., 1834; d. Baltimore, 1902*), civil engineer, Confederate soldier. Son of Benjamin H. Latrobe (1806–1878). A specialist in bridge construction, noted for the structural beauty of his work.

LATROBE, JOHN HAZLEHURST BONEVAL (*b. Philadelphia, Pa., 1803; d. Baltimore, Md., 1891*), lawyer, inventor, public servant. Son of Benjamin H. Latrobe (1764–1820). Studied law with Robert G. Harper. Helped draft charter of the Baltimore and Ohio Railroad, 1827; served as its legal adviser *post* 1828 and was widely recognized as a railroad and patent attorney. He was also of help to S. F. B. Morse in installation of first telegraph, invented the Latrobe stove, was active in many philanthropic societies, including the American Colonization Society, and practiced the arts of painting and design.

LATTA, ALEXANDER BONNER (*b. near Chillicothe, O., 1821; d. Ludlow, Ky., 1865*), machinist. Made many improvements on locomotives; invented and manufactured steam fire engines, 1852–60, supplying his first engine to Cincinnati, O., 1852.

LATTIMORE, WILLIAM (*b. near Norfolk, Va., 1774; d. Amite Co., Miss., 1843*), physician, Mississippi territorial delegate to Congress. Played a major role in establishing boundary line between Mississippi and Alabama, 1817.

LAUDONNIÈRE, RENÉ GOULAINE de (*fl. 1562–1582*), a French Huguenot who was sent to establish a colony in Florida, is little known except for the narratives of his expedition. Jean Ribaut's lieutenant in the establishment of Charlesfort (now Port Royal, S.C.), 1562, Laudonnière established Fort Caroline on St. John's River, 1564, and was in command when the Spanish under Menendez attacked it, Sept. 20, 1565. Most of the French were massacred, but the wounded Laudonnière eventually made his way back to France. His account of the Florida expeditions is contained in his *L'Histoire notable de la Floride* (Paris, 1586), translated the following year by Hakluyt.

LAUFER, BERTHOLD (*b. Cologne, Germany, 1874; d. Chicago, Ill., 1934*), Sinologist. Studied at Berlin, and at Leipzig where he received the Ph.D. degree, 1897. Came to America, 1898. Associated with

American Museum of Natural History, New York, and Columbia University, 1898–1908, he became staff member of the Field Museum, Chicago, Ill., and curator of anthropology there. The outstanding Sinologist in the United States, he was concerned chiefly with the cultural exchanges between the Chinese and other peoples prior to the 19th century. His long list of publications includes work on Far Eastern linguistics, art, religion, magic; his most important monographs were *Sino-Iranica* (1919) and *Jade* (1912).

[*Supp.* 1]

LAUGHLIN, JAMES LAURENCE (*b. Deerfield, O., 1850; d. Jaffrey, N.H., 1933*), economist. Graduated Harvard, 1873; won Ph.D., 1876, for work under Henry Adams in Anglo-Saxon law. Taught political economy at Harvard, 1878–88. After a brief interval at Cornell, he became professor and head of department of political economy, University of Chicago, 1892, and served until 1916. Founder of the *Journal of Political Economy*, his classroom work was overshadowed by his seminar for doctoral candidates. Author of a number of books of which *The History of Bimetallism in the United States* (1886) and *The Principles of Money* (1903) were oustanding, Laughlin strongly influenced much federal legislation; he was responsible for preparation of the *Report of the Monetary Commission of the Indianapolis Convention* (1898) and was prominent in the educational campaign leading to the Federal Reserve Act (1913). His monetary theory shows a tendency toward propaganda against silver and paper money; although he saw the growing importance of credit, which he described as "a refined system of barter," he insisted that the price of an article is arrived at by comparing its value with that of the gold standard.

[*Supp.* 1]

LAUNITZ, ROBERT EBERHARD SCHMIDT VON DER (*b. Riga, Russia, 1806; d. 1870*), sculptor. Came to America *c.* 1828. Served as journeyman to John Frazee; later was his partner in monument and stone-carving firm. Taught Thomas Crawford.

LAURANCE, JOHN (*b. near Falmouth, England, 1750; d. New York, N.Y., 1810*), Revolutionary soldier, lawyer. Came to America, 1767. Son-in-law of Alexander Macdougall. Judge advocate-general on Washington's staff, 1777–82. Congressman, Federalist, from New York, 1789–93; U.S. senator, 1796–1800.

LAURENS, HENRY (*b. Charleston, S.C., 1724; d. South Carolina, 1792*), merchant, planter, Revolutionary statesman. Probably the leading merchant of Charleston, Laurens gradually withdrew from commerce *post* 1764 and concentrated his attention on his plantations and on the political events of the period. Accepted as a leader of the Revolutionary movement in the South, he took a middle ground between radicals like Gadsden and conservatives who favored little if any action. His "constitutional stubbornness" against the policies of the British ministry was heightened by his disgust with the corruption of the British ruling class as observed by him during a stay in London, 1771–74. Returning home late in 1774, within a month he was elected to the first Provincial Congress and thereafter was active in all early phases of the Revolution in his section; he took part in the successful defense of Charleston, June 1776. A year later he took his seat in the Continental Congress and served nearly three years, part of the time as president. On many important committees, he demonstrated great ability and high patriotism; at times however he resorted to partisan maneuvers and was hampered in legislative and diplomatic activity by his tendency to be self-righteous and over-sensitive. On his way abroad to negotiate a treaty with the Dutch, he was captured by the British in September 1780, confined to prison and treated harshly. Exchanged for Lord Cornwallis, 1782, he joined Franklin, John Adams and Jay in Paris and was responsible for several wise stipulations in the preliminary articles of peace. For the next year-and-a-half he acted as a sort of unofficial minister to England, returning to New York in August 1784. After making his report to Congress, he returned to his home on Cooper River. Broken in health, saddened by the death of his son John, his wealth reduced by the heavy property losses he had suffered, he lived on for seven years, the recipient of honors and public recognition.

LAURENS, JOHN (*b. Charleston, S.C., 1754; d. South Carolina, 1782*), Revolutionary soldier, diplomat. Son of Henry Laurens. Served on a military mission to France, 1780–81; killed in a nameless skirmish against British partisans.

LAURIE, JAMES (*b. near Edinburgh, Scotland, 1811; d. Hartford, Conn., 1875*), civil engineer. Came to America *c.* 1833. Active in American railroad building; first president, American Society of Civil Engineers, 1852.

LA VÉRENDRYE, PIERRE GAULTIER DE VARENNES, Sieur de (*b. Three Rivers, Canada, 1685; d. Canada, 1749*), soldier, explorer. Served in Canada and Europe, returning to Canada, 1711. Assigned to a frontier post north of Lake Superior, 1726, he heard from the Indians accounts of lands to the far west and the routes thither. Between 1731 and 1734, after securing permission to explore at his own expense, Vérendrye and his sons set up forts in the region west and north of Lake Superior. Persistence in the face of great discouragements enabled him to become between 1738 and 1744 the discoverer of Manitoba, of the Dakotas, the western plains of Minnesota, the northwest territories of Canada and probably part of Montana. His labors opened up a vast region to French fur traders and pointed the way to the overland route to the Pacific.

LAW, ANDREW (*b. Milford, Conn., 1748/49; d. Cheshire, Conn., 1821*), composer and teacher of sacred music. Author or compiler of widely published hymnals.

LAW, EVANDER McIVOR (*b. Darlington, S.C., 1836; d. 1920*), Confederate major-general, educator. Founded South Florida Military Institute.

LAW, GEORGE (*b. Jackson, now Shushan, N.Y., 1806; d. New York, N.Y., 1881*), contractor, financier. Founded with Marshall O. Roberts the U.S. Mail Steamship Co., 1847; later active in Panama Railroad and in New York City horse-car lines. A prominent Know-Nothing politician.

LAW, JOHN (*b. New London, Conn., 1796; d. Evansville, Ind., 1873*), lawyer, Indiana jurist and congressman. Grandson of Richard Law. Author of *Colonial History of Vincennes* (1858); prosecuted Francis Vigo's claims.

LAW, JONATHAN (*b. Milford, Conn., 1674; d. 1750*), lawyer, Connecticut jurist. Deputy-governor of Connecticut, 1724–41; governor, 1741–50; an able conservative.

LAW, RICHARD (*b. Milford, Conn., 1733; d. New London, Conn., 1806*), Revolutionary patriot, Connecticut legislator and jurist. Son of Jonathan Law. Editor, with Roger Sherman, of *Acts and Laws of the State of Connecticut* (1784).

LAW, SALLIE CHAPMAN GORDON (*b. Wilkes Co., N.C., 1805; d. Memphis, Tenn., 1894*), organizer of Confederate hospital and relief services.

LAWLEY, GEORGE FREDERICK (*b. London, England, 1848; d. South Boston, Mass., 1928*), yacht builder. Came to America as a child. Built *America's* Cup defenders *Puritan* (1885), *Mayflower* (1886) and many other vessels.

LAWRANCE, JOHN. [See LAURANCE, JOHN, 1750–1810.]

LAWRANCE, URIAH MARION (*b. Winchester, O., 1850; d. Portland, Oreg., 1924*), businessman. Promoter of organized Sunday School activity.

LAWRENCE, ABBOTT (*b. Groton, Mass., 1792; d. 1855*), merchant, manufacturer, philanthropist. Brother of Amos and William Lawrence. Partner in Boston firm of A. and A. Lawrence, *post* 1814. During its first decade the firm was chiefly interested in the importation of English manufactures; gradually it began to deal in cottons and woolens manufactured in New England and in 1830 commenced the making, as well as the sale, of domestic textiles. Associating themselves with the Lowells, Appletons, Jacksons, and other rising manufacturers, the Lawrences were active in the development of New England industry. Abbott Lawrence took the lead in founding the great textile city that bears the family name, 1845, and in establishing there the mills that made Lawrence the principal rival of Lowell, Mass., founded a quarter century earlier. He was also a leader in New England railroad promotion and in the construction of municipal water works. His ability and public spirit made him a chief spokesman for Boston merchants and manufacturers in political and business discussions. A prominent member of the Whig party, he served in Congress, attended national conventions, and was a leading candidate for the vice-presidential nomination in 1848. Refusing the offer of cabinet posts by President Taylor, he served as U.S. minister to Great Britain, 1849–52. Strongly opposed to slavery, he was a man of firm religious principles. Among his principal benefactions were the founding of chairs at Harvard for the teaching of science and the endowment of the Lawrence Scientific School there.

LAWRENCE, AMOS (*b. Groton, Mass., 1786; d. 1852*), merchant. Brother of Abbott and William Lawrence. Original partner in A. and A. Lawrence. Retired in 1831 and devoted himself chiefly to philanthropy.

LAWRENCE, AMOS ADAMS (*b. Boston, Mass., 1814; d. 1886*), merchant, philanthropist. Son of Amos Lawrence. Graduated Harvard, 1835. Principal partner in Mason & Lawrence, selling agents for several of the largest textile mills in the country, Lawrence also engaged independently in textile manufacturing, notably in the field of knit goods. Active in many philanthropic enterprises, he established Lawrence University (Appleton, Wis.), and also a college at Lawrence, Kans., which became the nucleus for the state university. The success of the New England Emigrant Aid Society was largely owing to his efficiency as treasurer, yet despite his early zeal against slavery, he opposed the Republicans in 1856 and 1860, supported the Constitutional Union party and worked for the Crittenden compromise. When the Civil War broke out he loyally supported the administration.

LAWRENCE, GEORGE NEWBOLD (*b. New York, N.Y., 1806; d. New York, 1895*), ornithologist, wholesale druggist.

LAWRENCE, JAMES (*b. Burlington, N.J., 1781; d. at sea off Boston, Mass., 1813*), naval officer. Appointed midshipman, 1798; promoted lieutenant, 1802. Distinguished in war with Tripoli, 1801–05, as second in command of two daring operations: Porter's boat attack on Tripoli; the burning of the *Philadelphia*. In the War of 1812, commanding the *Hornet*, he defeated and sank HMS *Peacock* on Feb. 24, 1813; soon after, he was promoted captain and ordered to relieve the commander of the *Chesapeake* at Boston. Disobeying specific orders with respect to *Chesapeake's* mission, he put to sea on June 1 to engage HMS *Shannon*, then blockading Boston. In an action that lasted less than fifteen minutes, the *Shannon* was victorious and Lawrence was mortally wounded. His words, "Don't give up the ship," said to have been uttered when he was carried below, became a popular slogan.

LAWRENCE, RICHARD SMITH (*b. Chester, Vt., 1817; d. Hartford, Conn., 1892*), gunsmith. Inventor of machine tools for large-scale manufacture of rifles and carbines.

LAWRENCE, WILLIAM (*b. Groton, Mass., 1783; d. 1848*), merchant. Brother of Abbott and Amos Lawrence. A director of the Suffolk Bank System, 1818–48.

LAWRENCE, WILLIAM (*b. Mount Pleasant, O., 1819; d. Kenton, O., 1899*), Ohio jurist and legislator. As congressman, Republican, from Ohio, 1865–71, 1873–77, he was virtual author of the law creating the Department of Justice, drafted the law granting homesteads to Civil War veterans from reserved sections of railroad land-grants, and secured indemnification of the government by the railroads for public lands improperly granted them (1876).

LAWRENCE, WILLIAM BEACH (*b. New York, N.Y., 1800; d. 1881*), lawyer, public official, writer on international law.

LAWRIE, ALEXANDER (*b. New York, N.Y., 1828; d. Lafayette, Ind., 1917*), landscape and portrait painter.

LAWS, SAMUEL SPAHR (*b. Ohio Co., Va., 1824; d. Asheville, N.C., 1921*), Presbyterian clergyman, educator. Invented the stock-market "ticker" for reporting sales. Was president, among other institutions, of University of Missouri, 1876–89. A scholar of remarkable versatility.

LAWSON, ALEXANDER (*b. Ravenstruthers, Scotland, 1773; d. Philadelphia, Pa., 1846*), line engraver. Came to America, 1794. Established reputation by engraving plates for Alexander Wilson's *American Ornithology* (1808–14) and for the continuation by C. L. Bonaparte (1825–33).

LAWSON, ERNEST (*b. San Francisco, Calif., 1873; d. Miami Beach, Fla., 1939*), painter. Studied with John H. Twachtman and J. A. Weir. One of "The Eight," 1908; a sponsor of the Armory Show, 1913. His style, based on impressionism, was characterized by glowing color and thick impasto. [*Supp. 2*]

LAWSON, JAMES (*b. Glasgow, Scotland, 1799; d. Yonkers, N.Y., 1880*), accountant, insurance expert. Came to America, 1815. A lifelong amateur in literature and friend to literary men.

LAWSON, JOHN (*b. England; d. North Carolina, 1711*), pioneer, associate of Christopher de Graffenried in settlement of New Bern, N.C. Author of *A New Voyage to Carolina, etc.* (1709), useful for study of Indian life and customs.

LAWSON, LEONIDAS MERION (*b. Nicholas Co., Ky., 1812; d. Cincinnati, O., 1864*), physician, teacher

of medicine. Author of *Phthisis Pulmonalis* (1861), a valuable treatise.

LAWSON, THOMAS (*b. Virginia, c. 1781 or 1785; d. Norfolk, Va., 1861*), surgeon. In U.S. Army service *post* 1811; a forceful and efficient surgeon-general, 1836–61. Lawson obtained military rank for members of the medical department and was responsible for the publication of valuable statistical reports on army sickness and mortality.

LAWSON, THOMAS WILLIAM (*b. Charlestown, Mass., 1857; d. 1925*), stockbroker, speculator. Associated with Standard Oil interests; author of the exposé *Frenzied Finance* (1904–05).

LAWSON, VICTOR FREEMONT (*b. Chicago, Ill., 1850; d. 1925*), journalist. Proprietor, *Chicago Daily News*, 1876–88; proprietor and editor thereafter. President, Associated Press, 1894–1900. A powerful influence in civic reform.

LAWTON, ALEXANDER ROBERT (*b. Beaufort District, S.C., 1818; d. Clifton Springs, N.Y., 1896*), Confederate brigadier-general, lawyer, Georgia legislator. Graduated West Point, 1839; Harvard Law School, 1842. A leading Georgia secessionist, Lawton served ably in the field, 1861–63, and as Confederate quartermaster-general, 1863–65. Thereafter he was in the first rank of the national bar and served as U.S. minister to Austria, 1887–89.

LAWTON, HENRY WARE (*b. near Toledo, O., 1843; d. San Mateo, P.I., 1899*), soldier. Raised in Fort Wayne, Ind. Medal of Honor winner for gallantry at Atlanta in Civil War; served in frontier Indian wars; received surrender of Geronimo, 1886. Commanded 2nd Division, V Corps, at Santiago, Cuba, 1898, as major-general of volunteers; was killed in action during Philippine Insurrection.

LAY, BENJAMIN (*b. Colchester, England, 1677; d. near Abington, Pa., 1759*), Quaker reformer. Settled in Pennsylvania, 1731. Made dramatic, eccentric protests against slavery.

LAY, HENRY CHAMPLIN (*b. Richmond, Va., 1823; d. Baltimore, Md., 1885*), Episcopal clergyman. Rector in Huntsville, Ala., he was chosen missionary bishop for Arkansas and Indian Territory, 1859, and served until 1869. Thereafter he was bishop of Easton (Maryland).

LAY, JOHN LOUIS (*b. Buffalo, N.Y., 1832; d. New York, N.Y., 1899*), inventor. While in Union naval service, 1861–65, Lay perfected the torpedo used to destroy Confederate ram *Albemarle*, October 1864; he later received patents for an electrically driven torpedo, the vessel from which it could be launched and other devices. *Post* 1870, he lived mainly in Europe.

LAZARUS, EMMA (*b. New York, N.Y., 1849; d. 1887*), poet. Author of *Poems and Translations* (1866, 1867), *Admetus and Other Poems* (1871), *Songs of* *a Semite* (1882), translations from Heinrich Heine and other literary work. A sonnet written by her was placed on the pedestal of the Statue of Liberty, 1886. *Post* 1881, she became a prominent defender of Judaism and an organizer of relief efforts for Jewish immigrants.

LAZEAR, JESSE WILLIAM (*b. Baltimore Co., Md., 1866; d. Quemados, Cuba, 1900*), physician. Johns Hopkins, A.B., 1889; Columbia, M.D., 1892; studied also at Pasteur Institute, Paris. Showed great promise in bacteriological research. Appointed assistant surgeon in the army, 1900, he was a member of the Yellow Fever Commission in Cuba with Walter Reed, James Carroll and Aristides Agramonte. His death from the fever, after being bitten by an infected mosquito, went far to convince the Commission that they were on the right path to proof of the mosquito transmission theory and effective control of the disease.

LEA, HENRY CHARLES (*b. Philadelphia, Pa., 1825; d. Philadelphia, 1909*), publisher, historian. Son of Isaac Lea; grandson of Mathew Carey. Active in family publishing firm and in movements for municipal and civil-service reform. Author of a number of important scholarly studies which include *A History of the Inquisition of the Middle Ages* (1888), *The Moriscos of Spain* (1901) and *A History of the Inquisition of Spain* (1906–07).

LEA, HOMER (*b. Denver, Colo., 1876; d. near Los Angeles, Calif., 1912*), soldier. Removed to China, 1899; rose to general's rank in Chinese army and was a confidential adviser to Sun Yat Sen. Author of *The Valor of Ignorance* (1909), a warning against Japanese aggression.

LEA, ISAAC (*b. Wilmington, Del., 1792; d. 1886*), malacologist, publisher. Son-in-law of Mathew Carey; father of Henry C. and Mathew C. Lea. Partner in M. Carey and Sons and successor firms, 1821–51.

LEA, MATHEW CAREY (*b. Philadelphia, Pa., 1823; d. Philadelphia, 1897*), chemist. Son of Isaac Lea; grandson of Mathew Carey. A pioneer in photochemistry, he also made important studies in the platinum metals and was an active investigator in the domain of pure physics.

LEACH, ABBY (*b. Brockton, Mass., 1855; d. 1918*), classicist. Professor of Greek at Vassar, 1889–1918.

LEACH, DANIEL DYER (*b. Bridgewater, Mass., 1806; d. 1891*), Episcopal clergyman, educator. Superintendent of schools in Providence, R.I., 1855–83; pioneer in modern public-school administration; author of many widely used elementary school textbooks.

LEACH, SHEPHERD (*b. Easton, Mass., 1778; d. Easton, 1832*), iron founder, capitalist.

LEAMING, JACOB SPICER (*b. near Madisonville, O., 1815; d. 1885*), farmer, seedsman. Developed the famous "Leaming corn," 1856.

LEAMING, JEREMIAH (*b. near Durham, Conn., 1717; d. New Haven, Conn., 1804*), Episcopal clergyman, Loyalist. First choice of Connecticut clergy for consecration as bishop, 1783.

LEAMING, THOMAS (*b. Cape May Co., N.J., 1748; d. Philadelphia, Pa., 1797*), Revolutionary soldier, lawyer, merchant.

LEAR, TOBIAS (*b. Portsmouth, N.H., 1762; d. Washington, D.C., 1816*), consular officer. Graduated Harvard, 1783. George Washington's confidant and secretary, 1785–93, 1798–99. U.S. consul to Santo Domingo, 1801–02; U.S. consul-general at Algiers, 1803–12. His conduct of affairs with Morocco, Algiers and Tunis was able; his 1805 treaty with Tripoli, however, was harshly criticized. On his return home, Lear was made an accountant in the war department. He committed suicide, 1816.

LEARNED, EBENEZER (*b. Oxford, Mass., 1728; d. Oxford, 1801*), Revolutionary soldier. Colonel, 3rd Continental Infantry; led entry into Boston after siege, 1776; held brigade command in Saratoga campaign. Resigned commission for physical disability, March 1778.

LEARNED, MARION DEXTER (*b. near Dover, Del., 1857; d. 1917*), philologist, historian, editor. Head of German department, University of Pennsylvania, *post* 1895.

LEARY, JOHN (*b. St. John, N.B., Canada, 1837; d. Riverside, Calif., 1905*), lawyer, capitalist. Removed to Seattle, Wash., 1869; became a leader in industrial and commercial development of Puget Sound area.

LEASE, MARY ELIZABETH CLYENS (*b. Ridgway, Pa., 1853; d. Callicoon, N.Y., 1933*), Populist leader in Kansas, 1890–96, professional radical, lecturer.
[*Supp.* 1]

LEAVENWORTH, FRANCIS PRESERVED (*b. Mt. Vernon, Ind., 1858; d. 1928*), astronomer. A distinguished teacher at Haverford College and University of Minnesota.

LEAVENWORTH, HENRY (*b. New Haven, Conn., 1783; d. on Washita River, near junction with the Red, 1834*), lawyer, soldier. Entered U.S. Army at start of War of 1812, rising to rank of colonel; *post* 1819, was almost continuously on frontier service. He built Forts Snelling and Leavenworth and was for a time post commander at Jefferson Barracks; he was put in command of the entire southwestern frontier in 1834. While making an effort to negotiate peace among the warring Indian tribes of the region, he was stricken with bilious fever and died. A man of broad and varied culture, he holds a place second only to Henry Atkinson in the military annals of the early frontier.

LEAVITT, DUDLEY (*b. Exeter, N.H., 1772; d. 1851*), almanac-maker, mathematician, author, teacher.

LEAVITT, ERASMUS DARWIN (*b. Lowell, Mass., 1836; d. Cambridge, Mass., 1916*), mechanical engineer. Associated with Calumet and Hecla Mining Co., 1874–1904; specialized in pumping and mining machinery design.

LEAVITT, FRANK McDOWELL (*b. Athens, O., 1856; d. Scarsdale, N.Y., 1928*), mechanical engineer, inventor. Graduated Stevens Institute of Technology, 1875; was associated with E.W. Bliss & Co., *post* 1884. Over 300 patents were granted him between 1875 and 1921; he perfected much sheet-metal-working machinery and was the first to build a successful automatic tin-can body-making machine. Most of his attention *post* 1900 was given to the improvement of torpedoes. His last engineering work was the design for an aircraft steam boiler.

LEAVITT, HENRIETTA SWAN (*b. Lancaster, Mass., 1868; d. 1921*), astronomer. Graduated Radcliffe, 1892; joined staff of Harvard Observatory, 1902; became head of department of photographic stellar photometry. Discovered more than 2400 variable stars and made measurements of sequences of stars.

LEAVITT, HUMPHREY HOWE (*b. Suffield, Conn., 1796; d. Springfield, O., 1873*), Ohio federal jurist, legislator.

LEAVITT, JOSHUA (*b. Heath, Mass., 1794; d. 1873*), Congregational clergyman, Abolitionist. Graduated Yale, 1814. An active journalist and supporter of many reform movements; office editor of the *Independent*, 1848–73.

LEAVITT, MARY GREENLEAF CLEMENT (*b. Hopkinton, N.H., 1830; d. Boston, Mass., 1912*), educator, temperance reformer. As a result of her efforts as traveling representative, the W.C.T.U. became a world organization.

LE BRUN, NAPOLÉON EUGÈNE HENRY CHARLES (*b. Philadelphia, Pa., 1821; d. 1901*), architect. Studied under Thomas U. Walter; practiced in Philadelphia *post* 1841, in New York City *post* 1864. In partnership with sons, designed many notable churches and civic buildings; his Metropolitan Life Building, New York City (1889–1909) was an early success in skyscraper design.

LECHFORD, THOMAS (*fl. 1629–1642*), lawyer. Emigrated from England to Boston, Mass., 1638. The first professional lawyer in Massachusetts Bay, he was held in low esteem by the clergy and returned to England, 1641. Author of *Plain Dealing: or, Newes from New-England* (1642).

LE CLEAR, THOMAS (*b. Owego, N.Y., 1818; d. Rutherford Park, N.J., 1882*), portrait and genre painter, particularly effective as a portraitist of men.

LeCONTE, JOHN (*b. Liberty Co., Ga., 1818; d. 1891*), physician, scientist. Brother of Joseph Le Conte; cousin of John L. LeConte. Professor of physics at several universities, notably at University of California *post* 1869, where he served also as president, 1875–81. Made important acoustical studies.

LeCONTE, JOHN LAWRENCE (*b. New York, N.Y., 1825; d. 1883*), entomologist, physician. Cousin of John and Joseph LeConte. M.D., N.Y. College of Physicians and Surgeons, 1846. Interested in the geographic distribution of species, he made numerous studies and wrote a variety of monographs relative to the subject; he was the first biologist to map faunal areas of western part of the United States. His patient and original investigations may be said to have culminated in his monographic revision of the *Rhynchophora* (1876) and his *Classification of the N.A. Coleoptera* (1883). In addition to studies in entomology, Le Conte published essays dealing with mineralogy, geology, radiates, recent fossil mammals and ethnology. He was recognized at home and abroad as the greatest entomologist America had produced.

LeCONTE, JOSEPH (*b. Liberty Co., Ga., 1823; d. Yosemite Valley, Calif., 1901*), physician, geologist. Brother of John LeConte; cousin of John L. LeConte. M.D., N.Y. College of Physicians and Surgeons, 1845. Taught at Georgia University and College of South Carolina; professor of geology, University of California, 1869–96. Author of numerous articles on a wide variety of scientific topics.

LEDERER, JOHN (*fl. 1668–1671*), traveler, explorer. Came to Virginia from Germany, 1668; made several journeys into western Virginia and North Carolina, 1669–70. Author of *The Discoveries of John Lederer, etc.* (London, 1672).

LE DUC, WILLIAM GATES (*b. Wilkesville, O., 1823; d. Hastings, Minn., 1917*), agriculturist, Union soldier, railroad promoter. Settled in St. Paul, Minn., 1850; was active in development of the region. Secured first charter for a railway in Minnesota territory, 1853; was first miller to manufacture and introduce flour made from Minnesota spring wheat, 1856. U.S. commissioner of agriculture, 1877–81.

LEDYARD, JOHN (*b. Groton, Conn., 1751; d. Cairo, Egypt, 1789*), explorer. Nephew of William Ledyard. Went to sea *c.* 1773; joined Capt. James Cook in expedition, 1776. At Nootka Sound, 1778, realized vast possibilities of northwest fur trade. On arrival in London late in 1780, he was confined to barracks two years for refusal to fight against Americans. Returning home, December 1782, he tried to obtain means for a sailing venture to Northwest Coast. Journeyed to Spain, June 1784, and to France; received encouragement from Thomas Jefferson and John Paul Jones but all projects failed. Proposed to walk across Siberia, for which he sought passport from Russians who refused it. Went to Hamburg, 1786, then by way of Norway, Sweden and Lapland to St. Petersburg. Permitted to go on from there in 1787, he was arrested in Siberia by order of Empress Catherine and brought back. Engaged in London to explore sources of Niger River, he reached Cairo where he died. Author of *A Journal of Captain Cook's Last Voyage* (1783).

LEDYARD, WILLIAM (*b. Groton, Conn., 1738; d. Groton, 1781*), Revolutionary soldier. Uncle of John Ledyard. Killed after his heroic defense of Fort Griswold, Connecticut, against a superior British force.

LEE, ALFRED (*b. Cambridge, Mass., 1807; d. Wilmington, Del., 1887*), Episcopal clergyman. Consecrated first bishop of Delaware, 1841. A strong Evangelical, he served as presiding bishop, 1884–87.

LEE, ANN (*b. Manchester, England, 1736; d. Watervliet, N.Y., 1784*), foundress of Shakers in America, 1774–76.

LEE, ARTHUR (*b. Westmoreland Co., Va., 1740; d. Middlesex Co., Va., 1792*), diplomat. Great-grandson of Richard Lee. Brother of Richard H., Francis L. and William Lee. M.D., University of Edinburgh, 1764. Began practice of medicine, Williamsburg, Va., 1766; went to London, 1768, and studied law at Lincoln's Inn and Middle Temple. Admitted to bar, 1775. Chosen agent of Massachusetts in London, 1770, he wrote *An Appeal to the Justice and Interests of the People of Great Britain* (1774), followed in the next year by the *Second Appeal*. Associated, 1776, in Paris with Benjamin Franklin and Silas Deane as a commissioner to seek foreign aid, he went to Spain, 1777, and to Berlin where he was refused recognition. Returning to Paris, he commenced making complaints against his colleagues and out of his fervid imagination convinced himself that Franklin, Deane and others were plundering the public. In consequence, Deane was recalled, and Congress split into hostile factions, comprised of the supporters of Lee and the supporters of Deane. Lee was superseded, 1779. On return to America, he was elected to the Virginia House of Delegates, 1781, then to the Continental Congress in which he served until 1784.

LEE, CHARLES (*b. Dernhall, England, 1731; d. Philadelphia, Pa., 1782*), soldier of fortune, Revolutionary general. Served in America, 1755–61; with British in Portugal, 1762–63; and as soldier of fortune in Poland. Returned to America, 1773; took up land in Berkeley Co., Va., 1775. Vehement in support of patriot cause, he was made major-general, Continental Army, 1775. He served during siege of Boston, at New York, and in the South, returning to Washington's army just before battle of White Plains, October 1776. After White Plains, he was posted with his division at Philipsburg, N.Y. Consistent with his view that Americans could not stand in pitched battle against the British, he was slow to rejoin main army, explaining that he could do better by hanging on British flanks and harassing them. Taken prisoner in his New Jersey headquarters by British in December 1776, Lee was kept in New York for a year. During this time he became intimate with Sir William Howe

and presented to him a plan detailing how Americans might best be defeated. Lee's purpose in doing this has long been a subject of controversy. Exchanged, 1778, he went to York, Pa., in May and appeared before Congress. He returned to the army at Valley Forge just before the Monmouth campaign. His withdrawal of his forces during battle of Monmouth caused a rout of the Americans which was stopped only by Washington's prompt action. Courtmartialed, July-August 1778, Lee was found guilty of disobeying orders, misbehavior in face of the enemy and disrespect to the Commander-in-Chief. Suspended from the army for twelve months, he intrigued with Congress and otherwise conducted himself with so much enmity to Washington that he was challenged to a duel and wounded by Col. John Laurens. Retiring to his Virginia estate, July 1779, he was dismissed from the army, January 1780, in consequence of an insulting letter to Congress. One of the most contradictory characters in American history, Lee had an exaggerated sense of his own ability and great luck in impressing his own view of himself upon other people. On the credit side of his character, he was extremely generous to his friends and considerate of his soldiers.

LEE, CHARLES (*b. Prince William Co., Va., 1758; d. near Warrenton, Va., 1815*), jurist. Brother of Henry Lee (1756–1818) and Richard B. Lee. Graduated College of New Jersey, 1775. Federalist attorney-general of the United States, 1795–1801; one of defense lawyers in trial of Aaron Burr and in impeachment of Judge Chase.

LEE, CHARLES ALFRED (*b. Salisbury, Conn., 1801; d. 1872*), physician, teacher of medicine. Author of *Catalogue of Medicinal Plants . . . in the State of New York* (1848).

LEE, ELIZA BUCKMINSTER (*b. Portsmouth, N.H., c. 1788; d. 1864*), writer. Sister of Joseph S. Buckminster. Author of family biographies and religious works and of popular translations from the German.

LEE, FITZHUGH (*b. Fairfax Co., Va., 1835; d. Washington, D.C., 1905*), soldier. Nephew of Robert E. Lee. Graduated West Point, 1856; commissioned in cavalry. Resigned from U.S. Army, 1861; commissioned lieutenant in Confederate Army, 1861; promoted brigadier-general, July 1862. Lee's reconnaissance before Chancellorsville was largely responsible for Jackson's success in that battle; he was promoted major-general, 1863, and is generally ranked among the best dozen cavalry officers born in America. Engaged in farming after the Civil War, he was elected governor of Virginia, 1885, served until 1890, and did much to secure continued Democratic control of Virginia government. Consul-general to Havana, Cuba, 1896–98, he was commissioned major-general of volunteers, May 1898, and fought in the Spanish-American War.

LEE, FRANCIS LIGHTFOOT (*b. Westmoreland Co., Va., 1734; d. Richmond Co., Va., 1797*), Virginia legislator, Revolutionary patriot. Brother of Richard H., Arthur and William Lee. Member of the Continental Congress, 1775–79, and a signer of the Declaration of Independence.

LEE, FREDERIC SCHILLER (*b. Canton, N.Y., 1859; d. Waverly, S.C., 1939*), physiologist. Graduated St. Lawrence University, 1878; Ph.D., Johns Hopkins, 1885. Spent a year in Karl Ludwig's physiology laboratory, Leipzig. Taught physiology at College of Physicians and Surgeons, Columbia University, 1891–1938; helped extend physiology courses into other fields besides medicine. Lee was best known for his studies of fatigue, particularly in its application to industrial occupations. As a result of his investigations he became an advocate of the eight-hour working day as conducive to more and better work. [*Supp. 2*]

LEE, GEORGE WASHINGTON CUSTIS (*b. Fortress Monroe, Va., 1832; d. Fairfax Co., Va., 1913*), soldier, educator. Son of Robert E. Lee. Graduated West Point, 1854; assigned to engineers. Served in Confederate Army, 1861–65, notably as aide-de-camp on staff of Pres. Jefferson Davis. President of Washington and Lee University, 1871–97.

LEE, HANNAH FARNHAM SAWYER (*b. Newburyport, Mass., 1780; d. 1865*), author of miscellaneous works, including tracts on thrift and self-improvement.

LEE, HENRY (*b. Prince William Co., Va., 1756; d. Cumberland Island, Ga., 1818*), soldier, statesman. Better known as "Light-Horse Harry" Lee. Brother of Richard B. and Charles Lee (1758–1815); father of Robert E. Lee. Graduated College of New Jersey (Princeton), 1773. Won fame in Revolution as commander of irregular cavalry known as "Lee's Legion"; sent south to aid Nathaniel Greene, 1780, his subsequent story is the entire history of the campaign in the South. He was particularly effective at Guilford Courthouse, March 1781, and at Eutaw Springs, September 1781; he was present at the siege of Yorktown and at the surrender of Cornwallis. Active after the war as a Federalist politician in Virginia, he served as governor, 1792–95, and in 1794 was chosen to command the army assembled to put down Whiskey Rebellion in Pennsylvania. Resolutions offered by John Marshall on Washington's death, 1799, were drawn up by Lee and contained the description "first in war, first in peace and first in the hearts of his countrymen." Harassed by debt *post* 1800, he was seriously injured in the Baltimore riot, 1812, during his attempt to help Alexander C. Hanson defend the Federalist press in that city against a mob. He was author of *Memoirs of the War in the Southern Department, etc.* (1812).

LEE, HENRY (*b. Beverly, Mass., 1782; d. 1867*), Boston merchant, publicist. Brother-in-law of James (1777–1867), Charles, and Patrick T. Jackson. Author of "Boston Report" (1827) opposing tariff increases; leader in free-trade movement.

LEE, HENRY (*b. Westmoreland Co., Va., 1787; d. Paris, France, 1837*), soldier, Virginia legislator. Son of Henry Lee (1756–1818); half-brother of Robert E. Lee. Graduated William and Mary, 1808. Served in War of 1812; was an active writer for newspapers in Andrew Jackson's behalf. Author of *Observations on the Writings of Thomas Jefferson* (1832).

LEE, IVY LEDBETTER (*b. Cedartown, Ga., 1877; d. New York, N.Y., 1934*), publicity expert. Adviser on public relations to leading industrialists, *post* 1904. His clients included the Pennsylvania Railroad, John D. Rockefeller, Bethlehem Steel Co. and the Guggenheim interests. [*Supp. 1*]

LEE, JAMES MELVIN (*b. Port Crane, N.Y., 1878; d. 1929*), magazine editor, teacher of journalism. Author of *History of American Journalism* (1917).

LEE, JAMES WIDEMAN (*b. Rockbridge, Ga., 1849; d. 1919*), Methodist clergyman, editor. Held pastorates in St. Louis, Mo., and Atlanta, Ga. Author of *The Religion of Science* (1912).

LEE, JASON (*b. Stanstead, Canada [then considered part of Vermont], 1803; d. Stanstead, 1845*), Methodist missionary, Oregon pioneer. Chosen to head a mission to the Flathead Indians, 1833, Lee left Independence, Mo., in April 1834 in company with N. J. Wyeth's second expedition. The missionary group arrived at Fort Vancouver in September, and on abandonment of the Flathead project settled in October some ten miles northwest of the present city of Salem, Oreg. Additional missionary settlers came in June 1837, and missions were established in the Clatsop country and at The Dalles on the Columbia River. Lee journeyed overland to the East in 1838, presented a settlers' petition for territorial organization to the authorities at Washington and addressed many Methodist groups for support of his mission; he returned to Oregon by sea with additional missionary-settlers in May, 1840. A decline in missionary effort and a concentration on building up the material side of the settlements ensued, with Lee in a leading role as promoter, developer, advocate of Americanization; he presided over the meeting for territorial organization held at Champoeg, Feb. 7, 1841, and was influential in bringing about completion of a provisional government, July 5, 1843. Returning East, 1844, he learned en route that he had been superseded in his mission post. His character and his influence on early Oregon have been themes of much controversy.

LEE, JESSE (*b. Virginia, 1758; d. near Hillsborough, Md., 1816*), Methodist preacher, apostle of Methodism in New England. Author of *A Short History of the Methodists in the United States of America* (1810).

LEE, JOHN DOYLE (*b. Kaskaskia, Ill., 1812; d. Mountain Meadows, Utah, 1877*), Mormon elder. Tried and executed for his part in the Mountain Meadows Massacre, 1857.

LEE, JOSEPH (*b. Brookline, Mass., 1862; d. Cohasset, Mass., 1937*), social worker, "father of American playgrounds." Cousin of Richard C. Cabot. President of Playground Association of America (later National Recreation Association), 1910–37. [*Supp. 2*]

LEE, LUTHER (*b. Schoharie, N.Y., 1800; d. Flint, Mich., 1889*), Methodist clergyman, Abolitionist. First president of Wesleyan Methodist Connection, elected 1844. Returned to the parent church, 1867.

LEE, PORTER RAYMOND (*b. Buffalo, N.Y., 1879; d. Englewood, N.J., 1939*), social worker. Director, New York School of Social Work, 1916–38. [*Supp. 2*]

LEE, RICHARD (*d. 1664*), Virginia planter and legislator; ancestor of the Lees of Virginia. Emigrated *c.* 1641; settled in York Co.; removed to Northumberland Co. *c.* 1651.

LEE, RICHARD BLAND (*b. Prince William Co., Va., 1761; d. Washington, D.C., 1827*), planter, Virginia legislator. Brother of Henry (1756–1818) and Charles Lee (1758–1815). Congressman, Federalist, from Virginia, 1789–95. His change of vote, 1789, secured Hamilton necessary votes to put through assumption bill and to create District of Columbia.

LEE, RICHARD HENRY (*b. Westmoreland Co., Va., 1732; d. Chantilly, Va., 1794*), lawyer, Virginia legislator, Revolutionary statesman. Brother of Arthur, Francis L. and William Lee. Educated by private tutors and in English schools, he entered the Virginia House of Burgesses, 1758, where he opposed the spread of slavery and acted with Patrick Henry on many issues. His opposition to the Stamp Act placed him at once in the forefront of the defenders of colonial rights. In February 1766, he drew the citizens of his own county into the "Westmoreland Association," binding themselves to import no British goods until the Stamp Act should be repealed. He opposed the Townshend Acts even more firmly, branding them "arbitrary, unjust, and destructive of that mutual beneficial connection which every good subject would wish to see preserved." As early as 1768 he was advocating committees for intercolonial correspondence. Between 1768 and 1773, with Patrick Henry and Thomas Jefferson, he was active in the radical wing of the House of Burgesses.

Elected to the First Continental Congress, Lee was attracted to John Adams and formed a life-long friendship with Samuel Adams. He was a member of many of the most important committees and was among the foremost proponents of strong measures against England. Openly advocating independence in the spring of 1776, Lee was chosen to move the independence resolutions in Congress. On June 13, 1776,

he left Philadelphia to take part in forming the new state government in Virginia; returning to Congress, he furthered the idea of confederation by urging Virginia's surrender of her claim to Western lands. In foreign affairs he supported his brother Arthur in the latter's controversy with Silas Deane.

He left Congress in 1779 and was active in Virginia's public affairs, strangely enough on the conservative side. Elected to Congress, 1784, he played an important role in passage of the Northwest Ordinance but refused to attend the Constitutional Convention, and led in Virginia's opposition to the new Constitution. His *Letters of the Federal Farmer* (1787, 1788) became an anti-Federal textbook. He served in the U.S. Senate 1789–92, his chief concern being for the ideas embodied in the Bill of Rights.

LEE, ROBERT EDWARD (*b. "Stratford," Westmoreland Co., Va., 1807; d. Lexington, Va., 1870*), soldier. Son of Henry Lee (1756–1818); half-brother of Henry Lee (1787–1837). Two strong influences affected him in childhood: the sense of responsibility engendered by need to care for a sickly mother, and mingled admiration and pity for his father—a great soldier who had never been able to cope adequately with civilian life. Quick in his studies at school, he graduated second in his West Point class, without a single demerit, 1829. The years that followed his commission as second lieutenant of engineers were such as might have been spent by any young officer of that service who combined a fine presence with social graces, exemplary conduct, energy, and ability. In 1831 he married Mary Ann Randolph Custis, a descendant of Martha Washington. The marriage was a happy one. Association with the Washington traditions at the Custis home, "Arlington," made his father's old commander Lee's ideal; he seems consciously to have emulated Washington in his bearing and in his conception of duty.

Lee's first important independent assignment (July 1837) was to be superintending engineer over river and harbor work at St. Louis, Mo. On the outbreak of the Mexican War he was ordered to San Antonio, Texas, as assistant engineer to Gen. John E. Wool. He won much praise for his reconnaissance work at Buena Vista. Transferred to Gen. Winfield Scott's Vera Cruz expedition, Lee distinguished himself in nearly every engagement from Vera Cruz to Chapultepec. In 1855, after further duty in fortress construction and a tour as superintendent at West Point, Lee was glad to change from the staff to the line as lieutenant-colonel of the 2nd Cavalry. When the secession movement began, Lee had no sympathy with it, yet he was fixed in the belief that he could never bear arms against his native state. When he was offered field command of the U.S. Army, April 18, 1861, he refused acceptance; two days later, on learning to his sorrow that the Virginia convention had voted for secession, he resigned from the army.

Virginia chose Lee as commander of her forces on

April 23; he accepted and threw all his energies into organizing her defense. For a time, he served as military consultant to Pres. Jefferson Davis with the rank of general; in operations against a threatened invasion from western Virginia he lost popular reputation; from November 1861 to March 1862, he organized the South Atlantic seaboard defense. Returning to Richmond as military adviser to Davis, he worked out in concert with T. J. Jackson a plan to cripple Gen. McClellan's plans to besiege that city. On June 1, 1862, Lee succeeded Gen. Joseph E. Johnston, wounded the previous day, in command of the field force which Lee promptly named the "Army of Northern Virginia." During the next 34 months, the odds against Lee were to be always 3 to 2 and sometimes 3 to 1, yet seldom was he in a more precarious position than when he took command. McClellan, with 100,000 Union men, was but seven miles from Richmond. Three separate forces were threatening T. J. Jackson in the Valley of Virginia. Jackson won two quick actions and dispelled the threat; Lee took the offensive and in the Seven Days' Battles drove the Federals back on Washington. This campaign was the most important period in Lee's military education. Strategically sound in principle though demanding too much of untrained officers, the campaign was tactically bad. It taught Lee the necessity of simpler methods and organization. Ridding himself of inefficient division commanders, and with his first display of skill in the difficult military art of troop-movement, Lee outmaneuvered Gen. John Pope and with T. J. Jackson's help routed him at the second battle of Bull Run, August 30, 1862. Lee might have smashed Pope's army, but he yielded to Gen. James Longstreet's stubbornness and disclosed for the first time his one great weakness as field commander—his inability to work with unwilling subordinates. Longstreet insisted on a day's delay in the general assault; a further day was lost in regrouping after the battle; and a rainstorm at Chantilly on the afternoon of September 1 then kept Lee from overtaking the fleeing Pope.

During the invasion of Maryland in September 1862, Lee made his only serious blunder in logistics in miscalculating the time required for troop movements. In spite of this, he was able to retreat to Virginia after the bloody fight at Antietam, Sept. 17, 1862. Reorganizing his forces, he awaited the next Federal move. In offensive operations against Lee, Gen. A. E. Burnside was badly whipped at Fredericksburg on Dec. 13, and Gen. Joseph Hooker was beaten at Chancellorsville on May 2–4, 1863, in the most brilliant of Lee's victories. Lee suffered a serious loss in the latter battle, however, when T. J. "Stonewall" Jackson was mortally wounded. Lee had worked in complete understanding with Jackson, whom he regarded as a perfect executive officer, and he was never able to replace him. The next month, June 1863, Lee made his second and final invasion of

the North. He was met by Gen. George Meade at Gettysburg, Pa., and suffered his worst defeat in the crucial battle of July 1, 2 and 3. Defective staff work, Ewell's caution, J. E. B. Stuart's absence, Longstreet's obduracy, all help to explain the defeat. Lee assumed full responsibility, however, and sought unsuccessfully to resign.

Lee was never again able to take the offensive. On May 4, 1864, Gen. U. S. Grant with a force twice that of Lee's army crossed the Rapidan and headed for Richmond. For the next eleven months Lee was always on the defensive. He fought brilliantly and doggedly, but the Confederate cause grew ever more hopeless. Short of artillery, low on all supplies including food and munitions, plagued by the impossible task of replacing manpower in numbers and staff officers in quality, Lee fought on. Intuitively sensing Grant's maneuvers, constructing excellent field fortifications, but never able to catch Grant on the move or to attack the Federals in detail, he repulsed Grant's attacks time after time. On Feb. 6, 1865, Lee became general-in-chief of all the Confederate armies, but it was too late. He evacuated Petersburg and Richmond, Va., on April 2–3, and on April 9, reduced to 7,800 men able to bear arms, he surrendered at Appomattox Court House.

In September 1865, Lee became president of Washington College in Lexington, Va. He rebuilt the college, shunned publicity and set an example of obedience to civil authority. His supreme interest was in restoring the economic, cultural and political life of the South and in him the South still sees the embodiment of all its best ideals.

Lee's place in history is that of a great soldier and a Christian gentleman in the widest sense of that term. Self-control was second nature to him. As soldier, he excelled as a strategist; his reputation is not dependent on able seconding of his plans by Stonewall Jackson. Lee devised; Jackson executed. Lee's one great weakness was his inability to persuade stubborn, contrary minds to accept his view of a situation and achieve his purpose. His strategical power sprang from his ability to put himself in his opponents' place, to analyze military intelligence and to make accurate judgments of the strength of opposing forces.

LEE, SAMUEL PHILLIPS (*b. Fairfax Co., Va., 1812, d. Silver Spring, Md., 1897*), naval officer. Grandson of Richard Henry Lee. Remained loyal to Union; was distinguished at attack on New Orleans, 1862, and in both passages of Vicksburg by Union fleet. Commanding blockade squadron off Virginia and North Carolina, 1862–64, he is credited with placing second cordon of blockade ships at sea to intercept runners who had escaped first cordon. Promoted rear-admiral, 1870, he retired in 1873.

LEE, STEPHEN DILL (*b. Charleston, S.C., 1833; d. Vicksburg, Miss., 1908*), Confederate soldier, educator. Grandson of Thomas Lee. Graduated West Point, 1854. Commissioned captain in Confederate Army, 1861, he rose to lieutenant-general (1864) after distinguished service, principally with cavalry and in the western campaigns *post* 1862. After the war, he was active in the Mississippi legislature and served as president, Mississippi A. and M. College, 1880–99.

LEE, THOMAS (*b. Charleston, S.C., 1769; d. Charleston, 1839*), jurist, banker. Grandson of Jeremiah Theus. Became president, Bank of South Carolina, 1817; was appointed federal judge for South Carolina district, 1823; held both offices until his death. Opposed nullification.

LEE, THOMAS SIM (*b. Prince George's Co., Md., 1745; d. 1819*), planter, Revolutionary patriot. Great-grandson of Richard Lee. Governor of Maryland, 1779–83 and 1792–94.

LEE, WILLIAM (*b. Westmoreland Co., Va., 1739; d. 1795*), merchant, diplomat. Brother of Richard H., Francis L. and Arthur Lee. Resident in London *post* 1768, he was made alderman of that city, 1775, the only American who ever held that office. Appointed joint commercial agent at Nantes, France, 1777; became involved in controversy between Silas Deane and his brother Arthur Lee. The unratified treaty of commerce between the United States and Holland which he proposed was the ostensible cause of war between England and Holland. He was later unsuccessful in efforts to secure recognition of the United States by Prussia and Austria. In 1783, he returned to Virginia.

LEE, WILLIAM GRANVILLE (*b. Laprairie, Ill., 1859; d. Cleveland, O., 1929*), labor leader. Official in Brotherhood of Railroad Trainmen *post* 1895; president, 1909–28.

LEE, WILLIAM HENRY FITZHUGH (*b. Arlington, Va., 1837; d. near Alexandria, Va., 1891*), Confederate soldier, politician. Son of Robert E. Lee. Served in Confederate cavalry, 1861–65. Promoted brigadier-general, 1862, major-general, 1864, he was a cool, scientific fighting man who had the perfect confidence of his men. Congressman, Democrat, from Virginia, 1887–91.

LEE, WILLIAM LITTLE (*b. Sandy Hill, N.Y., 1821; d. Hawaii, 1857*), jurist. Removed to Hawaii, 1846; became chief justice, superior court of law and equity, 1847; drafted Hawaiian penal code, 1850. Lee was one of the little group of statesmen who created the Hawaiian constitutional monarchy.

LEEDS, DANIEL (*b. Leeds, England, 1652; d. Burlington, N.J., 1720*), surveyor, almanac maker. Came to America in third quarter of seventeenth century; settled in Burlington, N.J., 1677; appointed surveyor general, Province of West Jersey, 1682. He was also

a member of the assembly and of the governor's council and author of pamphlets attacking the Quakers.

LEEDS, JOHN (*b. Talbot Co., Md., 1705; d. Wade's Pt., Md., 1790*), mathematician, astronomer. Served on joint commission to mark off boundary between Maryland and Pennsylvania, 1762–68. Appointed surveyor general of Maryland *c.* 1766, he served until his death, excepting the period of the Revolutionary War, when his Loyalist sympathies caused his suspension from office.

LEES, ANN. [See LEE, ANN, 1736–1784.]

LEESER, ISAAC (*b. Neuenkirchen, Prussia, 1806; d. 1868*), rabbi, author. Came to America, 1824; served congregation Mikveh Israel, Philadelphia, 1829–50. Headed faculty of Maimonides College. A strong advocate of traditional Jewish doctrine.

LEETE, WILLIAM (*b. Dodington, England, c. 1613; d. Hartford, Conn., 1683*), colonist. Came to America, 1639. Was a founder of Guilford, Conn.; held numerous colonial offices and was deputy governor, New Haven Colony, 1658–61; governor, 1661–64. After acceptance of Connecticut Charter by New Haven, Leete served as deputy governor, Connecticut Colony, 1669–76, governor, 1676–83.

LEFEVERE, PETER PAUL (*b. Roulers, Belgium, 1804; d. Detroit, Mich., 1869*), Roman Catholic clergyman. Came to America, 1828; ordained, St. Louis, Mo., 1831. Worked among immigrants in northeastern Missouri, southern Iowa, western Illinois. Consecrated bishop of Detroit, Mich., 1841. Associated with Bishop J. L. Spalding in founding American College at Louvain.

LEFFEL, JAMES (*b. Botetourt Co., Va., 1806; d. Springfield, O., 1866*), manufacturer, inventor. Raised in Ohio. Patented an improved water wheel, 1845; perfected double turbine wheel, patented 1862.

LEFFERTS, GEORGE MOREWOOD (*b. Brooklyn, N.Y., 1846; d. 1920*), laryngologist. Son of Marshall Lefferts. M.D., N.Y. College of Physicians and Surgeons, 1870. Studied laryngology in London, Paris and Vienna; practiced in New York *post* 1873; taught at College of Physicians and Surgeons, 1874–1904.

LEFFERTS, MARSHALL (*b. Brooklyn, N.Y., 1821; d. 1876*), engineer. Associated with many early telegraph companies; became president, Gold and Stock Telegraph Co., 1871.

LEFFLER, ISAAC (*b. Washington Co., Pa., 1788; d. Chariton, Iowa, 1866*), lawyer, Virginia and Iowa legislator. Brother of Shepherd Leffler. Presided over meeting at Burlington, Iowa, 1837, at which resolutions were adopted for establishment of Iowa Territory.

LEFFLER, SHEPHERD (*b. Washington Co., Pa., 1811; d. 1879*), lawyer, Iowa legislator. Brother of

Isaac Leffler. Congressman, Democrat, from Iowa, 1846–51.

LEFFMANN, HENRY (*b. Philadelphia, Pa., 1847; d. 1930*), chemist. Graduated Jefferson Medical College, 1869. Distinguished as a teacher of chemistry in Philadelphia medical schools and colleges, he served also as port physician of Philadelphia and made numerous contributions to chemical literature.

LEFLORE, GREENWOOD (*b. Jackson, Miss., 1800; d. 1865*), Choctaw chief, Mississippi planter and legislator, Unionist.

LEGARÉ, HUGH SWINTON (*b. Charleston, S.C., 1797; d. 1843*), lawyer, South Carolina legislator. Graduated South Carolina College, 1814; studied also in Edinburgh and Paris. Associated with Stephen Elliott as editor, *Southern Review*, 1828–32. Fought J. C. Calhoun over issue of nullification, although himself a believer in states' rights and an opponent of protective tariffs. Served as U.S. chargé d'affaires in Belgium, 1832–36. On his return home, he served briefly in Congress; identified himself with Whig party and was active in campaign of 1840. Appointed U.S. attorney-general by President Tyler, 1841, he served with distinction until death.

LeGENDRE, CHARLES WILLIAM (*b. Ouillins, France, 1830; d. Seoul, Korea, 1899*), Union soldier, diplomat. U.S. consul at Amoy, China, 1866–72. Served as foreign adviser to Japanese government, 1872–75; as adviser to the King of Korea, 1890–99.

LEGGE, ALEXANDER (*b. Dane Co., Wis., 1866; d. Hinsdale, Ill., 1933*), manufacturer. Associated, *post* 1891, with the antecedent firms of International Harvester Co., of which he was elected president, 1922. During World War I, he served as chief assistant to Bernard M. Baruch on the War Industries Board and was manager of the Allied Purchasing Commission. [*Supp. 1*]

LEGGETT, MORTIMER DORMER (*b. near Ithaca, N.Y., 1821; d. 1896*), Ohio lawyer, Union soldier. U.S. commissioner of patents, 1871–74. First president of Brush Electric Co., *post* 1884.

LEGGETT, WILLIAM (*b. New York, N.Y., 1801; d. 1839*), journalist. Midshipman in U.S. Navy, 1822–26; part owner and assistant editor under William Cullen Bryant of N.Y. *Evening Post*, 1829–36. Combative, energetic and independent, he became oracle of radical Democrats, writing in support of free trade, direct taxation, the right of working men to organize, and abolition. His collected political writings were published, 1840. After leaving the *Post*, he edited the *Plaindealer* (1837) and a daily paper, the *Examiner*.

LEGLER, HENRY EDUARD (*b. Palermo, Italy, 1861; d. 1917*), journalist, librarian. Came to America as a boy; was raised in La Crosse, Wis. Secretary, Milwaukee school board, 1890–1904; distinguished as

secretary, Wisconsin Free Library Commission, 1904–09; directed Chicago Public Library system, 1909–17.

LEHMAN, ARTHUR (*b. New York, N.Y., 1873; d. New York, 1936*), investment banker. Partner, *post* 1901, in Lehman Brothers; played large part in the firm's rise to major status. [*Supp. 2*]

LEHMANN, FREDERICK WILLIAM (*b. Prussia, 1853; d. St. Louis, Mo., 1931*), lawyer. Came to America as a child. Practiced first in Iowa and *post* 1890 in St. Louis, Mo. U.S. solicitor-general, 1910–12. Independent in politics, learned and witty.

LEIB, MICHAEL (*b. Philadelphia, Pa., 1760; d. 1822*), physician, Pennsylvania legislator. Congressman, (Democrat) Republican, 1799–1806; U.S. senator, 1809–14. Collaborated with William Duane as political dictator of Philadelphia *post* 1796; his violence and avarice, however, soon wrecked the Jeffersonian party in Pennsylvania. He later opposed Thomas McKean, Gallatin's fiscal policies, and James Madison's administration.

LEIDY, JOSEPH (*b. Philadelphia, Pa., 1823; d. 1891*), naturalist, foremost American anatomist of his time. M.D., University of Pennsylvania, 1844. Professor of anatomy, University of Pennsylvania, 1853–91. Distinguished as an anatomist, he was scarcely less at home in other fields of science, notably vertebrate paleontology and parasitology. A tireless worker, he was nearly devoid of any ambition but for the collection of facts; he was not given to theory and disliked controversy. Among his numerous published works were *Elementary Treatise on Human Anatomy* (1861), his monograph "On the Extinct Mammalia of Dakota and Nebraska" (1869) and his *Fresh Water Rhizopods of North America* (1879).

LEIGH, BENJAMIN WATKINS (*b. Chesterfield Co., Va., 1781; d. 1849*), lawyer, Virginia legal codifier and legislator. As U.S. senator from Virginia, 1834–36, he refused to obey the legislature's order to vote for expunging of censure of Andrew Jackson over removal of government deposits from the Bank of the United States and denounced the measure in outstanding speeches. His integrity cost him his political career.

LEIGHTON, WILLIAM (*fl. 1825–1868*), glass-maker. Employed by New England Glass Co., Cambridge, Mass., he hit upon an original formula for ruby glass *c.* 1849. Removing to Wheeling, W. Va., 1863, he worked at a new formula for lime-flint glass which he produced, 1864.

LEIPER, THOMAS (*b. Strathaven, Scotland, 1745; d. Delaware Co., Pa., 1825*), tobacco merchant, Revolutionary soldier.

LEIPZIG, NATE (*b. Stockholm, Sweden, 1873; d. New York, N.Y., 1939*), magician. Came to America as a boy; was raised in Detroit, Mich. Internationally recognized as the most skillful sleight-of-hand performer of his time. [*Supp. 2*]

LEIPZIGER, HENRY MARCUS (*b. Manchester, England, 1854; d. 1917*), educator, lecturer. Came to America as a boy. Graduated College of the City of New York, 1873; LL.B., Columbia, 1875. Superintendent, Hebrew Technical Institute, 1884–91; assistant superintendent of schools, New York City, 1891–96. Thereafter, he supervised public evening lectures given in the schools, a work which he had inaugurated.

LEISHMAN, JOHN G. A. (*b. Pittsburgh, Pa., 1857; d. Nice, France, 1924*), steel manufacturer, diplomat. Associated with Carnegie interests. U.S. minister to Switzerland, 1897–1900; to Turkey, 1900–09, rising to ambassador, 1906. U.S. ambassador to Italy, 1909–11; to Germany, 1911–13.

LEISLER, JACOB (*b. Frankfort, Germany, 1640; d. New York, N.Y., 1691*), soldier, merchant. Came to New Amsterdam, 1660. Married a wealthy widow, 1663; became thereby associated with leading Dutch families, among them the Bayards and Van Cortlandts. Soon numbered among richest men in the colony, he was at odds with his wife's relatives over his claim for a share of her first husband's estate. The Revolution of 1688 in England becoming known in New York, Leisler at head of the militia seized the fort at New York. On the flight of Lt.-Gov. Francis Nicholson, Leisler on his own authority proclaimed William and Mary. Acting as leader of various discontented elements in the colony and named commander-in-chief, Aug. 1689, by a committee of safety representing his faction in New York, he governed the province by military force until the arrival of the officially appointed new governor, Sloughter, in March 1691. Tried for his arbitrary seizure of authority and refusal to give it up at the first demand of the new governor, he was condemned to death for treason and executed with his son-in-law and aid, Jacob Milborne. The bitter feeling aroused by Leisler's career and fate was long a factor in New York politics.

LEITER, JOSEPH (*b. Chicago, Ill., 1868; d. Chicago, 1932*), capitalist. Son of Levi Z. Leiter. Attempted a corner in wheat, 1897–98, which failed disastrously; was notable for the numerous litigations in which he engaged. [*Supp. 1*]

LEITER, LEVI ZEIGLER (*b. Leitersburg, Md., 1834; d. 1904*), merchant. Removed to Springfield, O., 1854; to Chicago, Ill., 1855. Serving as a clerk in a firm of wholesale dry-goods merchants, he met Marshall Field, 1856. Both men became partners in the concern, leaving it in 1865 to establish firm of Field, Palmer & Leiter. The new firm prospered remarkably under Field's direction as merchant, Leiter's as credit manager. Retiring from the firm, 1881, a wealthy man, Leiter risked his fortune on the continued growth of Chicago and increased it in Chicago real estate. He was active in the promotion and support of cultural institutions in the city.

LE JAU, FRANCIS (*b. Angers, France, 1665; d. 1717*), Anglican clergyman, educator. Rector of Goose Creek parish, S.C., *post* 1706. Interested himself in education of Negroes and Indian slaves and exposed cruel practices against them.

LELAND, CHARLES GODFREY (*b. Philadelphia, Pa., 1824; d. Florence, Italy, 1903*), writer. Graduated Princeton, 1845; studied also at Heidelberg and Munich. Active in New York and Philadelphia journalism, 1849–69; resided in Europe, 1869–79, and *post* 1884. His published books cover a wide range of subjects, all written with ability and zest. He is remembered particularly for his translations of Heinrich Heine, for the humorous dialect poems collected in *The Breitmann Ballads* (1871) and his numerous works on gypsy lore and language. A genial giant of a man, he was interested to the end of his life in anything mysterious or occult.

LELAND, GEORGE ADAMS (*b. Boston, Mass., 1850; d. Boston, 1924*), physician, otologist, educator. M.D., Harvard Medical School, 1878; made special studies in laryngology and otology at Vienna, Heidelberg and elsewhere in Europe. Professor of laryngology, Dartmouth Medical School, 1893–1914.

LELAND, JOHN (*b. Grafton, Mass., 1754; d. Cheshire, Mass., 1841*), Baptist clergyman. As minister at Orange, Va., 1777–91, played a prominent part in disestablishing Episcopal Church in Virginia; similarly, as minister in Cheshire, Mass., *post* 1791, he labored for the complete disestablishment of the Congregational Standing Order. He obtained considerable celebrity, 1801, when he traveled to Washington to present Thomas Jefferson with a mammoth cheese made by the women of Cheshire.

LEMKE, PETER HENRY (*b. Rhena, Mecklenburg, 1796; d. Carrolltown, Pa., 1882*), Roman Catholic clergyman. A convert to Catholicism, 1824, he was ordained priest, 1826. Volunteering for the American missions, he came to New York, 1834, and by his own choice was assigned to assist Demetrius A. Gallitzin in his Pennsylvania backwoods mission. Inspiring Boniface Wimmer to make the first settlement of Benedictines in Pennsylvania, 1846, Lemke himself joined the Benedictines, 1851. Departing for Kansas, 1855, he took up land near Atchison, where subsequently was established St. Benedict's Abbey. Returning to Pennsylvania, 1858, he served as missionary and pastor until his retirement *c.* 1876.

LEMMON, JOHN GILL (*b. Lima, Mich., 1832; d. 1908*), botanist, teacher. After Civil War service, removed to California, 1866. Self-educated, he made botanical explorations of wide areas of California, Nevada and Arizona, and was encouraged by Asa Gray. Two of his reports as botanist of the California board of forestry, "Pines of the Pacific Slope" (1888) and "Conebearers of California" (1890), attracted world-wide attention. His many booklets and pamphlets helped to prepare public opinion for an established forestry policy which came after his death.

LeMOYNE, FRANCIS JULIUS (*b. Washington, Pa., 1798; d. 1879*), physician, reformer. Early American advocate of cremation.

LE MOYNE, JEAN BAPTISTE. [See BIENVILLE, JEAN BAPTISTE LE MOYNE, Sieur de, 1680–1768.]

LE MOYNE, PIERRE. [See IBERVILLE, PIERRE LE MOYNE, Sieur d', 1661–1706.]

LE MOYNE, WILLIAM J. (*b. Boston, Mass., 1831; d. Inwood-on-Hudson, N.Y., 1905*), actor, master of the art of make-up.

LENEY, WILLIAM SATCHWELL (*b. London, England, 1769; d. near Montreal, Canada, 1831*), engraver. Came to America *c.* 1805. Worked in New York City for publishers and as bank-note engraver up to 1820.

L'ENFANT, PIERRE CHARLES (*b. Paris, France, 1754; d. Prince George's Co., Md., 1825*), soldier, engineer. Son of one of the "painters in ordinary to the King in his Manufacture of the Gobelins," L'Enfant received some instruction in both engineering and architecture. Coming to America, 1777, as a volunteer engineer in Continental service, he served at his own expense. Wounded while leading an American column in the advance on Savannah, Oct. 9, 1779, he was taken prisoner on fall of Charleston, S.C., May 1780. Exchanged early in 1782, he was promoted major by special act of Congress and retired from the army, January 1784.

One of the early members of the Society of the Cincinnati, L'Enfant designed its insignia and diploma, and was charged by Washington to have the designs executed abroad. Here, for perhaps the first time, one of his major defects appeared. Blessed with great enthusiasm and imagination, he had little business sense or judgment, and the work proved to be overly expensive. Returning to New York, he found increasing occupation for his artistic talents; among other commissions, he converted the old City Hall into Federal Hall, temporary seat of the new national government *post* 1789.

L'Enfant now received his great opportunity, and proved himself worthy of it in imagination and prophetic foresight if not in discretion. Called on by Washington to survey the site and make the plan for the new Federal City, he submitted his complete design to the President, August 1791. The plan was greatly influenced by the layout of Versailles. L'Enfant set about at once to clear the principal sites and avenues, but difficulties arose over the scope of his activities and his refusal to heed suggestions. On Feb. 27, 1792, he was informed that his services were at

an end. The city of Washington grew slowly through the 19th century, and often not in accord with L'Enfant's plan. His genius was justified, however, when the Park Commission of 1901 endorsed the merits of his original design and recommended its restoration and extension.

Alexander Hamilton and Robert Morris retained their faith in L'Enfant, and each secured commissions for him. In almost every case, L'Enfant conceived brilliantly but wrought so well and so expensively that the task was never completed. Robert Morris, bankrupt, plaintively wrote of the house L'Enfant began for him, "A much more magnificent house than I ever intended to have built." Subsequently, L'Enfant planned some fortifications for the government and was offered a professorship at West Point (1812) which he declined. He died forgotten and in poverty.

LENKER, JOHN NICHOLAS (*b. Sunbury, Pa., 1858; d. 1929*), Lutheran clergyman, historian. A leader in the pan-Lutheran movement.

LENNON, JOHN BROWN (*b. Lafayette Co., Wis., 1850; d. Bloomington, Ill., 1923*), labor leader, temperance reformer. Settled in Denver, Colo., 1869; was active in organizing tailor's union. Held office in his own local and in the national union; was treasurer, American Federation of Labor, 1890–1917.

LENNOX, CHARLOTTE RAMSAY (*b. New York, possibly in Albany, 1720; d. London, England, 1804*), novelist, dramatist, translator. Removed to England *c.* 1735. A London "bluestocking," she was a friend of Samuel Johnson, Samuel Richardson and Henry Fielding. Author, among other books, of *The Female Quixote* (1752) and *Shakespear Illustrated* (1753), an early study of Shakespeare's sources.

LENOX, JAMES (*b. New York, N.Y., 1800; d. New York, 1880*), merchant, real estate investor, book collector. Graduated Columbia, 1818. Ranks with John Carter Brown and George Brinley as a pioneer in collecting Americana. His splendid Lenox Library is now part of New York Public Library.

LENTHALL, JOHN (*b. District of Columbia, 1807; d. Washington, D.C., 1882*), naval architect. Chief, U.S. Navy bureau of construction, 1853–71. Responsible for design of wooden steam frigates of *Merrimac* class; able, blunt and incorruptible.

LEONARD, CHARLES LESTER (*b. Easthampton, Mass., 1861; d. 1913*), physician. M.D., University of Pennsylvania, 1889; also studied abroad for three years. Became interested in X-rays, 1896; was perhaps the first to demonstrate the presence of stones in the kidney by means of this agent (1898). His powers of observation and interpretation were almost uncanny; he was a prolific writer on X-ray technique, a generous teacher and a founder or officer of many medical societies. Excessive exposure to X-rays caused serious ulcers on his hands and eventually induced cancer, from which he died.

LEONARD, DANIEL (*b. Norton, Mass., 1740; d. London, England, 1829*), lawyer, Massachusetts colonial legislator, Loyalist. Graduated Harvard, 1760. Practiced law in Taunton, Mass.; served as member of the General Court. Appointed a mandamus councilor, 1774, he was forced to flee his home by his Whig neighbors and go to Boston. A series of articles by him in defense of Crown policies was published in the *Massachusetts Gazette*, 1774–75, over signature "Massachusettensis." Removing to Halifax, N.S., 1776, and later to England, he was appointed chief justice of Bermuda, a post which he held, 1782–1806. Eventually he became dean of English barristers.

LEONARD, GEORGE (*b. Plymouth, Mass., 1742; d. New Brunswick, Canada, 1826*), Loyalist. Directed Loyalist privateering during the Revolution; associated with life and politics of New Brunswick, *post* 1783.

LEONARD, HARRY WARD (*b. Cincinnati, O., 1861; d. New York, N.Y., 1915*), electrical engineer, inventor. Graduated Massachusetts Institute of Technology, 1883. Worked with Thomas A. Edison in introduction of central-station power systems; established Ward Leonard Electric Co., 1894. Among his numerous inventions are the first electric train-lighting system, patented 1889; a system of motor control, patented 1891; an electric elevator-control device, patented 1892; the double-arm circuit-breaker, patented 1902.

LEONARD, HELEN LOUISE. [See RUSSELL, LILLIAN, 1861–1922.]

LEONARD, LEVI WASHBURN (*b. Bridgewater, Mass., 1790; d. Exeter, N.H., 1864*), Unitarian clergyman, educator. Pastor in Dublin, N.H., *post* 1820; a dominant figure in the life of that town.

LEONARD, ROBERT JOSSELYN (*b. San José, Calif., 1885; d. 1929*), educator. Graduated State Normal School, San José, 1904; Ph.D., Columbia, 1923. Specialist in vocational and adult education. Taught at University of Indiana, University of California, and at Teachers College, Columbia University, where he directed the school of education and organized the first course in college administration.

LEONARD, STERLING ANDRUS (*b. National City, Calif., 1888; d. Madison, Wis., 1931*), educator. Graduated University of Michigan, 1908; Ph.D., Columbia, 1928. Professor of English, University of Wisconsin, 1920–31. Author of textbooks in composition.

LEONARD, WILLIAM ANDREW (*b. Southport, Conn., 1848; d. Gambier, O., 1930*), Episcopal clergyman. Held pastorates in Brooklyn, N.Y., and Washington, D.C. Consecrated bishop of Ohio, 1889.

LEONARD, ZENAS (*b. near Clearfield, Pa., 1809; d. Sibley, Mo., 1857*), trapper, author. His *Narrative of the Adventures of Zenas Leonard* (1839) is a highly valuable contemporary depiction of trapper life and early Western travel.

LE PAGE DU PRATZ, ANTOINE SIMON. [See DUPRATZ, ANTOINE SIMON LE PAGE, fl. 1718–1758.]

LE ROUX, BARTHOLOMEW (*b. probably Amsterdam, Holland, c. 1665; d. New York, N.Y., 1713*), goldsmith and silversmith. Settled in New York *ante* 1687; held numerous city offices.

LE ROUX, CHARLES (*b. New York, N.Y., 1689; d. New York, 1745*), engraver, silversmith. Son of Bartholomew Le Roux. Official silversmith, New York City, 1720–43; active in New York City politics and in the Reformed Dutch Church.

LÉRY, JOSEPH GASPARD CHAUSSE-GROS de (*b. Canada, 1721; d. Quebec, Canada, 1797*), engineer. Employed, 1743–59, in fortification work in Canada; author of nine travel journals descriptive of his journeys to Detroit, the Ohio country and elsewhere.

LESCHI (*b. on Nisqually River in present state of Washington, date unknown; d. 1858*), Nisqualli chief. Commanded rebel Indian forces west of the Cascades, 1855. On failure of the uprising, he received amnesty but was twice tried on a charge of murder, convicted (March 1857) and hanged January 1858.

LESLEY, J. PETER. [See LESLEY, PETER, 1819–1903.]

LESLEY, PETER (*b. Philadelphia, Pa., 1819; d. 1903*), Presbyterian clergyman, geologist. Taught at University of Pennsylvania, *post* 1859; dean of Towne Scientific School, *post* 1875. State geologist of Pennsylvania, 1873–87; superintended issue of 77 volumes of reports, with auxiliary atlas volumes, and also a final report in three volumes, 1892–95. Author also of *A Manual of Coal* (1856), *The Iron Manufacturer's Guide* (1859) and works on philology and philosophy.

LESLIE, CHARLES ROBERT (*b. London, England, 1794; d. London, 1859*), painter, author. Brother of Eliza Leslie. Brought to America as a child; raised in Philadelphia, Pa. Returning to London, 1811, he studied under Fuseli and Benjamin West; was roommate of Samuel F. B. Morse. Highly successful and able in genre painting, Leslie took his subjects from the works of classic English authors, notably Shakespeare, Sterne, Goldsmith and Fielding. A Royal Academician, he came to the United States, 1833, as teacher of drawing at West Point; after a few months he returned to England and in 1847 became professor of painting, Royal Academy. Author of *A Handbook for Young Painters* (1855); also *Memoirs of the Life of John Constable* (1843).

LESLIE, ELIZA (*b. Philadelphia, Pa., 1787; d. Gloucester, N.J., 1858*), author. Sister of Charles R. Leslie. A prolific writer of books on domestic economy and stories for young people.

LESLIE, FRANK (*b. Ipswich, England, 1821; d. 1880*), wood-engraver, pioneer publisher of illustrated journals. Christened Henry Carter; came to America, 1848. Employed in Boston on *Gleason's Pictorial* and in New York on the *Illustrated News*, he devised method of rapid wood-block engraving whereby current events could be pictured the day following their occurrence. After two unsuccessful attempts, 1854 and 1855, he brought out first issue of *Frank Leslie's Illustrated Newspaper*, Dec. 15, 1855. The newspaper was particularly effective in its coverage of the Civil War; its artists were found wherever the campaigns were hottest. Leslie published a number of other journals and was successful up to about 1877; however, he died bankrupt.

LESLIE, MIRIAM FLORENCE FOLLINE (*b. New Orleans, La., c. 1836; d. 1914*), author, publisher. Widow of Frank Leslie, whom she married, 1874. Assuming management of her husband's business, together with his debts, she was highly successful as manager and editor of the Leslie publications. A flamboyant figure in the life of her time, she left the bulk of her fortune to the cause of woman suffrage.

LESQUEREUX, LEO (*b. Fleurier, Switzerland, 1806; d. Columbus, O., 1889*), paleobotanist. Came to America, 1848, a recognized authority on peat bogs and an associate of J. L. R. Agassiz and Arnold H. Guyot. Became recognized authority on coal plants and on entire Appalachian coal field.

LESTER, CHARLES EDWARDS (*b. Griswold, Conn., 1815; d. Detroit, Mich., 1890*), Presbyterian clergyman, journalist, author.

LESUEUR, CHARLES ALEXANDRE (*b. Le Havre, France, 1778; d. Le Havre, 1846*), artist, naturalist. Came to America, 1816, as traveling companion and co-worker of William Maclure. While employed as teacher and engraver in Philadelphia, Pa., 1817–25, Lesueur served also as curator of the Academy of Natural Sciences. Consenting to join the projected community at New Harmony, Ind., Lesueur set out from Pittsburgh with Thomas Say, Gerard Troost, Robert Dale Owen and others, arriving in January 1826. At the community he taught drawing, engraved the plates for Say's works. He made extensive study trips up and down the Mississippi valley, 1826–37, returning to France, 1837. Lesueur was the first to study the fishes of the Great Lakes of North America and one of the first systematic zoologists to work in this country.

LE SUEUR, PIERRE (*b. Artois, France c. 1657; d. at sea c. 1705*), explorer, trader. Came to Canada, 1679. Traded among the Sioux on the upper Mississippi River *post* 1681; was responsible for securing peace between Sioux and Chippewa, 1695.

LETCHER, JOHN (*b. Lexington, Va., 1813; d. 1884*), lawyer, newspaper editor, politician. Congressman, Democrat, from Virginia, 1851–59. As member of ways and means committee, he was an opponent of government spending and was known as "Honest John, Watchdog of the Treasury." Elected governor of Virginia, 1859, he opposed secession until Lincoln's call for troops to coerce seceding states. A zealous supporter of the Confederate war effort, he resumed practice of law after 1865 and served in the Virginia legislature, 1875–76 and 1876–77.

LETCHER, ROBERT PERKINS (*b. Goochland Co., Va., 1788; d. 1861*), lawyer, Kentucky legislator. Congressman, from Kentucky, 1823–35; supporter of Henry Clay. Whig governor of Kentucky, 1840–44; U.S. minister to Mexico, 1849–52.

LETCHWORTH, WILLIAM PRYOR (*b. Brownville, N.Y., 1823; d. 1910*), businessman, philanthropist. Labored *post* 1869, by private and public effort, to improve condition of New York State dependent and delinquent children, epileptics and the insane poor.

LETTERMAN, JONATHAN (*b. Canonsburg, Pa., 1824; d. 1872*), military surgeon. M.D., Jefferson Medical College, 1849; appointed assistant surgeon, U.S. Army, 1849. Served on frontiers until start of Civil War. As medical director, Army of the Potomac, 1862–64, he completely reorganized field medical service, created mobile hospital organization, instituted ambulance service. His basic plan has influenced medical service in every modern army.

LEUPP, FRANCIS ELLINGTON (*b. New York, N.Y., 1849; d. Washington, D.C., 1918*), journalist. Outstanding as a Washington correspondent, 1885–1904; active and able U.S. Indian commissioner, 1905–09.

LEUTZE, EMANUEL (*b. Gmünd, Württemberg, 1816; d. Washington, D.C., 1868*), historical and portrait painter. Came to America as an infant; was raised in Fredericksburg, Va. and in Philadelphia, Pa. Studied and worked in Düsseldorf, Germany, 1841–59. Famous for large historical compositions dealing with American history, such as his "Washington Crossing the Delaware." Though full of anachronisms, few modern historical pictures have been more popular in the United States.

LEVENE, PHOEBUS AARON THEODORE (*b. Sagor, Russia, 1869; d. New York, N.Y., 1940*), biochemist. M.D., Imperial Military Medical Academy, St. Petersburg, 1891. Came to America, 1892. Staff member, Rockefeller Institute for Medical Research, 1905–40, and head of its division of chemistry.
[Supp. 2]

LEVER, ASBURY FRANCIS (*b. near Springhill, S.C., 1875; d. Lexington Co., S.C., 1940*), politician. Congressman, Democrat, from South Carolina, 1901–19. A sponsor of important farm legislation as chairman of the House Committee on Agriculture, 1913–19.
[Supp. 2]

LEVERETT, JOHN (*b. Boston, England, 1616; d. Boston, Mass., 1679*), governor of Massachusetts, 1673–79. Emigrated to New England, 1633. In England, 1644–48, as officer in Parliamentary army. Held numerous colony offices, both political and military; opposed activities of Edward Randolph.

LEVERETT, JOHN (*b. 1662; d. 1724*), educator, lawyer. Grandson of John Leverett (1616–1679). Graduated Harvard, 1680; in 1685, was appointed fellow and tutor. After disagreement with the Mathers, Leverett was dropped from the College, 1700, and practiced law. His rise was rapid; he served as provincial councillor, judge of the superior court, judge of probate. In 1707 he became the first lawyer and judge to hold the Harvard presidency. His tenure was marked by liberal policy and progressive action which included a liberalized curriculum, enlarged student body, increased physical plant and endowment. He was long engaged in a clerico-political battle against the Mathers and their allies; his victory did much to assist religious and intellectual freedom at Harvard.

LEVERING, JOSEPH MORTIMER (*b. Hardin Co., Tenn., 1849; d. 1908*), Moravian bishop, historian. Author of *A History of Bethlehem, Pennsylvania, 1741–1892* (1903).

LEVERMORE, CHARLES HERBERT (*b. Mansfield, Conn., 1856; d. Berkeley, Calif., 1927*), educator, peace advocate. Founder and president of Adelphi College, Brooklyn, N.Y., 1896–1912; won Bok Peace Award, 1924.

LEVIN, LEWIS CHARLES (*b. Charleston, S.C., 1808; d. 1860*), lawyer. Settled in Philadelphia, 1838. Know-Nothing editor and congressman.

LEVINS, THOMAS C. (*b. Drogheda, Ireland, 1789; d. 1843*), Roman Catholic clergyman. Came to America as Jesuit *c.* 1822; left the Society and became diocesan priest in New York, 1825. Active in early Catholic journalism. Suspended, 1834, he worked as an engineer until resumption of clerical office, 1841.

LEVY, JOSEPH LEONARD (*b. London, England, 1865; d. 1917*), rabbi. Came to America, 1889; served congregations in Sacramento, Calif., and Philadelphia, Pa.; rabbi of Temple Rodeph Shalom, Pittsburgh, Pa., 1901–17. A leader of Reform Judaism and in community social welfare.

LEVY, LOUIS EDWARD (*b. Stenowitz, Bohemia, 1846; d. 1919*), photo-chemist. Came to America as a boy. Inventor, with his brother Max, of the Levy half-tone screen, patented 1893.

LEVY, MAX (*b. Detroit, Mich., 1857; d. Allenhurst, N.J., 1926*), photo-engraver. Brother of Louis E. Levy, with whom he worked on invention of half-tone screen. Patented the hemocytometer, 1917.

LEVY, URIAH PHILLIPS (*b. Philadelphia, Pa., 1792; d. New York, N.Y., 1862*), naval officer. Served on merchant ships, 1802–11; commissioned sailing master, 1812. His long service in the navy was punctuated with quarrels and difficulties, but he rose to rank of Flag Officer, 1860.

LEWELLING, HENDERSON. [See LUELLING, HENDERSON, 1809–1878.]

LEWELLING, LORENZO DOW (*b. Salem, Iowa, 1846; d. 1900*), Quaker reformer, teacher, public servant. Nephew of Henderson Luelling. Populist governor of Kansas, 1893–95.

LEWIS, ALFRED HENRY (*b. Cleveland, O., c. 1858; d. New York, N.Y., 1914*), journalist. Author of *Wolfville* (1897), *Wolfville Nights* (1902) and other popular tales of cowboy life.

LEWIS, ANDREW (*b. Ireland, 1720; d. 1781*), soldier, Revolutionary patriot. Came to America as a boy; raised near Staunton, Va. Defeated Indians in battle of Point Pleasant, 1774; served as Continental brigadier-general, 1776–77.

LEWIS, ARTHUR (*b. London, England, 1846; d. New York, N.Y., 1930*), actor, theatrical manager.

LEWIS, CHARLES BERTRAND (*b. Liverpool, O., 1842; d. Brooklyn, N.Y., 1924*), humorist, printer, Detroit and New York newspaper editor. Wrote under pen-name "M. Quad."

LEWIS, CHARLTON THOMAS (*b. West Chester, Pa., 1834; d. Morristown, N.J., 1904*), Methodist clergyman, classicist, editor, lawyer.

LEWIS, DIOCLESIAN (*b. near Auburn, N.Y., 1823; d. 1886*), temperance reformer, pioneer in physical culture. Author of *New Gymnastics*, 1862; founder of Boston Normal Institute for Physical Education.

LEWIS, DIXON HALL (*b. probably Dinwiddie Co., Va., 1802; d. New York, N.Y., 1848*), lawyer, Alabama legislator. Leader of state-rights faction in Alabama; congressman, Democrat, 1829–44; U.S. senator, 1844–48. Opposed protective tariffs and internal improvements by the federal government.

LEWIS, EDMUND DARCH (*b. Philadelphia, Pa., 1835; d. Philadelphia, 1910*), landscape painter, collector of art objects.

LEWIS, ELLIS (*b. Lewisberry, Pa., 1798; d. 1871*), lawyer. Pennsylvania supreme court justice, 1851–57; chief justice *post* 1854.

LEWIS, ENOCH (*b. Radnor, Pa., 1776; d. 1856*), mathematician, educator. Author of textbooks, and of miscellaneous works applying Quaker principles to moral and political issues; founded and edited *Friends' Review*, 1847–56.

LEWIS, ESTELLE ANNA BLANCHE ROBINSON (*b. near Baltimore, Md., 1824; d. London, England, 1880*), poet and magazine writer under pen-names, "Stella" and "Sarah A. Lewis." A friend and admirer of Edgar Allan Poe.

LEWIS, EXUM PERCIVAL (*b. Edgecombe Co., N.C., 1863; d. 1926*), physicist, educator. Graduated Columbian University (present George Washington), 1888; Ph.D., Johns Hopkins, 1895, specializing in spectroscopy under H. A. Rowland. Taught physics at University of California *post* 1895, becoming full professor, 1908. He published no books, but was the author of papers on diverse subjects; many of his chief contributions related to the spectra of gases under various conditions of excitation, purity, etc. He was a pioneer in infra-red and far ultra-violet spectroscopy and did work also in study of ionization and conductivity of gases.

LEWIS, FIELDING (*b. Gloucester Co., Va., 1725; d. Fredericksburg, Va., c. 1782*), Revolutionary patriot. Brother-in-law of George Washington.

LEWIS, FRANCIS (*b. Llandaff, Wales, 1713; d. 1802*), New York merchant. Came to New York, 1738; prospered as businessman and government contractor. Active in pre-Revolutionary agitation; New York delegate to Continental Congress, 1775–79; signed Declaration of Independence.

LEWIS, FRANCIS PARK (*b. Hamilton, Ontario, Canada, 1855; d. Port Jefferson, N.Y., 1940*), ophthalmologist. Student of Herman Knapp; practiced in Buffalo, N.Y. Pioneer in development of organized efforts to prevent blindness. [*Supp. 2*]

LEWIS, ISAAC NEWTON (*b. New Salem, Pa., 1858; d. Hoboken, N.J., 1931*), soldier, inventor. Graduated West Point, 1884; ordnance expert. Patented Lewis depression position finder, 1891, and the Lewis machine gun, 1911; also fire-control systems and torpedo improvements.

LEWIS, JAMES (*b. Troy, N.Y., 1837; d. West Hampton, N.Y., 1896*), actor. Born James Lewis Deming; a principal comedian with Augustin Daly's company *post* 1869.

LEWIS, JAMES HAMILTON (*b. Danville, Va., 1863; d. Washington, D.C., 1939*), lawyer. Removed to Seattle, Wash., c. 1885; served as congressman, Democrat, from Washington, 1897–98. Resident in Chicago, Ill., *post* 1903, he was U.S. senator, Democrat, from Illinois, 1913–19, 1931–39. Despite a deliberately cultivated eccentricity of dress and manner, Lewis was an excellent parliamentary tactitian (twice serving as majority whip) and a supporter of the New Deal. [*Supp. 2*]

LEWIS, JOHN FRANCIS (*b. near Port Republic, Va., 1818; d. Rockingham Co., Va., 1895*), planter, lawyer, Virginia Unionist. U.S. senator, Republican-Conservative, 1870–75; helped overthrow rule of William Mahone, 1889.

LEWIS, JOSEPH HORACE (*b. near Glasgow, Ky., 1824; d. 1904*), lawyer, Confederate brigadier-general,

Kentucky legislator and congressman. Judge, Kentucky court of appeals, 1881–99.

LEWIS, LAWRENCE (*b. Philadelphia, Pa., 1856; d. near West Chester, Pa., 1890*), lawyer, author of valuable studies in Pennsylvania legal history.

LEWIS, MERIWETHER (*b. Albemarle Co., Va., 1774; d. central Tennessee, 1809*), explorer, soldier. Raised in upper Georgia, where he became an expert hunter and early showed both scientific and literary tastes; studied under private tutors in Virginia, 1787–92. Served in militia during Whiskey Rebellion; entered regular army as ensign, May 1795. Appointed President Jefferson's private secretary (1801) after duty on the Western frontiers he arrived in Washington soon after the inauguration and took up residence in the White House.

The discussions and councils to which he was witness were a liberal education for the President's young friend. Exploration for a land route to the Pacific Ocean was often discussed, and Jefferson proposed to Congress a journey of discovery on Jan. 18, 1803. Lewis made the estimate of expenses and Congress quickly appropriated the $2500 he thought necessary. Jefferson's high opinion of Lewis's qualifications to lead such an expedition determined his choice and was later stated in Jefferson's memoir written for the 1814 history of the enterprise. Lewis chose William Clark as his companion officer and their names and fame are inseparably united.

Mustering in Illinois, the men enlisted for the journey were drilled for their work during the winter of 1803–04. In the spring of 1804, the expedition started up the Missouri River. Successfully evading Sioux efforts to block progress, Lewis and Clark wintered in the Mandan villages in North Dakota where they secured the services of Sacajawea as guide to the upper river. They resumed travel on April 7, 1805. By August they were at the head of navigation but Sacajawea obtained horses to cross the divide from her Shoshone relatives. Arriving at the Columbia River, they built canoes and descended to the ocean. They spent the winter at Fort Clatsop, not far from Astoria, and returned overland to St. Louis on Sept. 23, 1806, to the great joy of the entire nation, which had long given them up for lost.

The abilities of Lewis and Clark complemented each other in an unusual manner, yet Lewis was the ultimate authority on every question. On his resignation from the army after making his report in Washington, he was appointed governor of Louisiana. He was successful in his brief administration there. En route to Washington in October 1809, he met a mysterious death which is still the subject of scholarly controversy. His observations and journals display his intellectual ardor and scientific spirit; they form, together with those of William Clark, the basis of the *History of the Expedition* (Phila., 1814; ed. Nicholas Biddle and Paul Allen).

LEWIS, MORGAN (*b. New York, N.Y., 1754; d. New York, 1844*), Revolutionary soldier, jurist, political leader. Son of Francis Lewis. Graduated College of New Jersey (Princeton), 1773. Married Gertrude, daughter of Robert R. Livingston, 1779, an alliance which furthered his career in New York politics; served as state attorney-general and as justice and chief justice of state supreme court. Elected governor, 1804, he proved unable to navigate in deep political waters and alienated the powerful Clinton faction. He failed of re-election. After service as major-general in the War of 1812, he passed the rest of his long life in relatively private activity.

LEWIS, ORLANDO FAULKLAND (*b. Boston, Mass., 1873; d. 1922*), social worker, penologist, author of professional studies and of short-stories.

LEWIS, SAMUEL (*b. Falmouth, Mass., 1799; d. 1854*), lawyer, educator. Leader, *post* 1826, in founding free public school system of Ohio; first Ohio superintendent of common schools, 1837–39. Anti-slavery leader and an organizer of the Liberty party.

LEWIS, TAYLER (*b. Northumberland, N.Y., 1802; d. 1877*), lawyer, educator, Orientalist. Graduated Union, 1820. Professor of Greek, University of the City of New York, 1838–50; professor of Greek, Oriental languages and Bible at Union, 1850–77.

LEWIS, WILFRED (*b. Philadelphia, Pa., 1854; d. at sea, 1929*), mechanical engineer. Graduated Massachusetts Institute of Technology, 1875. An expert in the mechanics of gears. [*Supp. 1*]

LEWIS, WILLIAM (*b. near Edgemont, Pa., 1751, o.s.; d. Philadelphia, Pa., 1819*), lawyer, Pennsylvania Federalist legislator. Counsel for John Fries, 1799.

LEWIS, WILLIAM BERKELEY (*b. Loudoun Co., Va., 1784; d. near Nashville, Tenn., 1866*), planter, politician. Friend and supporter of Andrew Jackson; a member of the "Kitchen Cabinet." A Unionist in the Civil War.

LEWIS, WILLIAM DAVID (*b. Christiana, Del., 1792; d. near Florence, N.J., 1881*), merchant, banker. Resided in Russia, 1814–24; translated poems of Pushkin and other Russian writers (published 1849).

LEWIS, WILLIAM GASTON (*b. Rocky Mount, N.C., 1835; d. Goldsboro, N.C., 1901*), engineer, Confederate brigadier-general.

LEWIS, WINSLOW (*b. Wellfleet, Mass., 1770; d. Boston, Mass., 1850*), sailor, lighthouse designer and builder.

LEWISOHN, ADOLPH (*b. Hamburg, Germany, 1849; d. near Upper Saranac Lake, N.Y., 1938*), capitalist, art collector, philanthropist. Came to America, 1867, joining New York branch of his family's Hamburg importing business. Recognizing the importance of copper in the commercial future of electricity, Adolph and his brother Leonard formed the Montana Copper Co., 1879, and subsequently organized the United Metals Selling Co. and the American Smelting & Refining Co. Conducting his affairs independently *post* 1901, Adolph Lewisohn was president of copper mines in Tennessee, Arizona and South America, and senior member of Adolph Lewisohn & Sons, a brokerage and investment house. He devoted himself chiefly, *post* 1916, to philanthropy, prison reform, music and the collection of modern French paintings. [*Supp. 2*]

LEXOW, CLARENCE (*b. Brooklyn, N.Y., 1852; d. 1910*), lawyer, New York legislator. As Republican chairman of a state senate special committee, he gave his name to a famous investigation of corruption in New York City, 1894, which was actually managed by John W. Goff.

LEYNER, JOHN GEORGE (*b. Boulder Co., Colo., 1860; d. Littleton, Colo., 1920*), inventor, manufacturer. Devised and marketed many improvements in mining machinery, notably a compressed air rock-drilling machine (patented 1899), the hollow drill or "jackhammer" (*ante* 1902), and a drill-sharpening machine.

LEYPOLDT, FREDERICK (*b. Stuttgart, Germany, 1835; d. 1884*), publisher, book-trade bibliographer. Came to America, 1854. Published translations and textbooks; was in partnership with Henry Holt, 1866–68. Founded *Publishers' Weekly*, 1873; the *Library Journal*, 1876; was also responsible for *Publishers' Trade List Annual*.

L'HALLE, CONSTANTIN de (*d. Detroit, Mich., 1706*), Roman Catholic missionary. Came to Canada, 1696. A Recollect priest, he served as chaplain at Detroit from about 1703 until his death.

L'HOMMEDIEU, EZRA (*b. Southold, N.Y., 1734; d. Southold, 1811*), lawyer, New York legislator, agriculturist. Brother-in-law of William Floyd. Continuously in public service from 1775 until his death, he was the principal author of the measure establishing the reconstituted University of the State of New York, 1787.

LIBBEY, EDWARD DRUMMOND (*b. Chelsea, Mass., 1854; d. 1925*), glass manufacturer, philanthropist. Founded Libbey Glass Co. at Toledo, O., 1888. Developed business framework for exploitation of glass-making inventions of Michael J. Owens. Principal benefactor of Toledo Museum of Art.

LICK, JAMES (*b. Fredericksburg, Pa., 1796; d. 1876*), piano maker, California real-estate investor. Came to California *ante* 1848. Left the bulk of his estate for charitable and educational purposes, notably for creation of the Lick Observatory.

LIE, JONAS (*b. Moss, Norway, 1880; d. New York, N.Y., 1940*), painter. Came to America as a boy; studied at National Academy of Design and at Art Students League, New York. Artistically a traditionalist, he aimed "not to symbolize nature, but in portraying nature to impart a sense of what is within and beyond." [Supp. 2]

LIEB, JOHN WILLIAM (*b. Newark, N.J., 1860; d. New York, N.Y., 1929*), mechanical engineer. Graduated Stevens Institute of Technology, 1880. Worked with Thomas A. Edison on pioneer electric-lighting power plants, 1881–82; was in Italy, 1882–94, as chief engineer and later as manager and technical director of the Italian Edison Co. Returning to New York, Lieb held many responsible positions in the various Edison companies until his death. Under his direction, some of the earliest experiments were undertaken in parallel operation of large direct-driven alternators and in long-distance transmission of high-tension alternating current by underground cables. In his later career, he directed all research and development work for the New York Edison and affiliated companies.

LIEBER, FRANCIS (*b. Berlin, Germany, 1800; d. 1872*), political scientist, reformer, educator. Fought as a schoolboy under Blücher at Waterloo; graduated Jena, Ph.D., 1820. Volunteered to aid Greeks in war of liberation, 1822; was tutor in Rome to son of the historian Niebuhr, 1823. Persecuted as a liberal in Prussia, he came to America, 1827, and won success as editor of the *Encyclopedia Americana* (1829–33). Lieber became professor of history and political economy at South Carolina College, 1835, and wrote the first systematic works on political science as such that had appeared in America up to that time. They won him high contemporary reputation; the best known of them was *On Civil Liberty and Self-Government* (1853). In 1857 he was appointed to a chair in Columbia College; in 1865, he transferred to Columbia Law School where he remained for the rest of his life. His *Code for the Government of Armies* (1863) was long standard as a basis of international understanding on the conduct of war.

LIEBLING, EMIL (*b. Pless, Germany, 1851; d. 1914*), pianist, teacher, composer. Came to America, 1867. Studied in Europe, 1873–76, under Liszt and others. A brilliant interpreter of Bach, Chopin, and Beethoven.

LIENAU, DETLEF (*b. Ütersen, Germany, 1818; d. New York, N.Y., 1887*), architect. Came to America, 1848. Fortunate in his American social connections, Lienau developed a very large practice, 1849–85, designing domestic, industrial and educational buildings. His work was basically eclectic and influenced by the Parisian examples of his student days, but it was restrained and marked always by excellent planning, good composition and thoroughness.

[Supp. 1]

LIGGETT, HUNTER (*b. Reading, Pa., 1857; d. San Francisco, Calif., 1935*), soldier. Graduated

West Point, 1879. After efficient service at Western frontier posts and in the Spanish-American War and Philippine insurrection, he reached rank of lieutenant-colonel, 1909. Marked by superiors for his consistent application to professional studies, on graduation from Army War College, 1910, he was detailed to the general staff and selected as a director of the War College. Promoted colonel, 1912, he was made president of the College and less than a year later became a brigadier-general. Promoted major-general, March 1917, he preceded his men of the 41st Division to France. After a period of observation duty on the Western Front, he took command of the I Army Corps, January 1918. His Corps participated in the Champagne-Marne operation in July and in the counteroffensive known as the Second Battle of the Marne. In the reduction of St. Mihiel salient during mid-September and in the Meuse-Argonne offensive, September–November, his men were highly effective in defeating a stubborn, experienced enemy. On assignment to command of the I Army, October 1918, he was promoted lieutenant-general. Under his command, the Army broke the Hindenburg Line and forced the Germans to withdraw across the Meuse. Gen. John J. Pershing cited Liggett as conspicuous for personality, leadership and efficiency. Thereafter, he commanded the Army of Occupation until it was disbanded, July 1919. He retired in 1921. [Supp. 1]

LIGGETT, WALTER WILLIAM (*b. Benson, Minn., 1886; d. Minneapolis, Minn., 1935*), journalist, editor. After a varied and restless career on many newspapers in many places, Liggett published (1932–35) the *Mid-West American*, a small personal weekly paper which contained almost unrestrained attacks on Minnesota state, county and city officials, denouncing their alleged connections with crime. He was shot to death by unknown assassins. [Supp. 1]

LIGHTBURN, JOSEPH ANDREW JACKSON (*b. near West Newton, Pa., 1824; d. West Virginia, 1901*), farmer, Union brigadier-general, Baptist clergyman. Resident in Lewis Co., W. Va., post 1840.

LIGON, THOMAS WATKINS (*b. Prince Edward Co., Va., 1810; d. near Ellicott City, Md., 1881*), lawyer, Maryland legislator. Congressman, Democrat, 1845–49; governor of Maryland, 1853–57. Opposed Know-Nothingism at expense of his own political future.

LILE, WILLIAM MINOR (*b. Trinity, Ala., 1859; d. Hallsboro, Va., 1935*), lawyer. Professor of law, University of Virginia, 1893–1932; dean of department of law, post 1904. [Supp. 1]

LILIENTHAL, MAX (*b. Munich, Bavaria, 1815; d. Cincinnati, O., 1882*), rabbi. University of Munich, Ph.D., 1837. Came to America, 1845. Pastor in Cincinnati post 1855; strove to promote good will between Jews and Christians; helped to found Hebrew

Union College and Union of American Hebrew Congregations.

LINCECUM, GIDEON (*b. Hancock Co., Ga., 1793; d. Washington Co., Texas, 1874*), frontier physician, naturalist. Early in life a merchant and Indian trader; practiced in vicinity of Columbus, Miss., 1830–48; settled in Texas, 1848. Made special studies of the mound-building ant.

LINCOLN, ABRAHAM (*b. Hardin, now Larue, Co., Ky., 1809; d. Washington, D.C., 1865*), sixteenth president of the United States. Thomas Lincoln, his father, was a powerful, barely literate, unambitious frontiersman. Nancy Hanks, his mother, was of uncertain paternity; there is little reliable evidence concerning her. She seems to have had some intellectual vigor and has been described as spiritually inclined, affectionate and amiable.

When Abraham Lincoln was seven, the family moved to the Indiana woods, spending the first winter in a rough lean-to, known as a "half-faced camp," in what is now Spencer County. Here, in October 1818, his mother died of fever. Thomas Lincoln soon married Sarah Bush Johnston, a Kentucky widow who brought her own three children to live in the floorless cabin. This stepmother, a woman of energy and ambition, improved the living conditions and closely supervised the lives of the children. From reminiscences of friends and neighbors, recorded much later, we may reconstruct a fairly definite picture of Lincoln as an easy-going backwoods youth—tall, strong and ungainly—who did his stint of hard labor on the homestead, performed odd jobs for neighbors, shunned the vociferous camp-meetings of the time, avoided membership in the church and used his leisure for self-improvement by the reading of a few good books. He attended school whenever possible, but his entire schooling probably did not exceed one year. Somehow he grew up without the usual frontier vices although he was uncommonly sociable.

In 1830 the Lincolns moved to Illinois, settling on the Sangamon River not far from Decatur. Abraham helped move, build the new cabin, clear the land and fence it. He remained through the next winter, and then left home to shift for himself. He assisted one Denton Offutt in building a flatboat and navigating it to New Orleans; on his return to Illinois, he settled at the village of New Salem. Here, he spent six picturesque and formative years (1831–37), managing a mill, conducting a store which left him burdened with debt, all in all eking out a scanty living. He read law meanwhile, studied grammar, widened his acquaintance and increased his ability to work with people. His skill in sports, especially wrestling, gave him stature among the rough frontiersmen. In 1834 he was elected to the Illinois legislature and served four terms (1834–41), becoming a power in the minority Whig party. In

1836 he was licensed to practice as an attorney; in 1837 he moved to Springfield. At New Salem occurred Lincoln's over-romanticized engagement to Ann Rutledge, who died in 1835; in Springfield he met the vivacious, popular and socially prominent Mary Todd. Confused testimony, much of it attributable to W. H. Herndon, surrounds their courtship. They were married on Nov. 4, 1842. In spite of Mary's atrocious temper and Abraham's diffidence, untidiness, and lack of dignity, their marriage seems to have been a happy one, their love for each other deep and sincere. Of their four sons, only Robert Todd Lincoln grew to manhood.

Abraham Lincoln served in Congress, 1847–49, the only Whig elected from Illinois. He did not move among the great in Washington, nor did he rise above the obscurity of the average congressman. Supporting the official Whig line, he joined in the attack on the Mexican War and President Polk's policies and so antagonized the Illinois voters that he did not even try for a second term. He campaigned for Zachary Taylor for president in 1848, but there is evidence that he had little influence, even in his own district in Illinois. His return to Springfield was the ebb point of his life: politically unpopular, in debt, his law practice diminished.

Within three or four years, however, Lincoln rose by merit to the front rank of lawyers in his own state. He was associated with capable partners: John Todd Stuart first; then Stephen T. Logan; finally William H. Herndon. In practice before the state supreme court and in the federal courts, he showed qualities that mark the outstanding attorney: a searching thoroughness of investigation, a familiarity with pertinent judicial doctrines, and a knack of so stating a legal question as to brush away its technicalities and get at the core of the controversy. In his journeys on circuit, he rebuilt his popularity and extended it among all classes of people. His important cases included defenses of the Illinois Central R.R. against county taxes and of the McCormick Reaper Co. against patent infringement.

The Lincoln of the prairies was a man of marked individuality. Standing six feet four, with uncommon length of arms and legs, his figure loomed in any crowd, while the rugged face bespoke a pioneer origin and an early life of toil and poverty. In a head not overlarge, each feature was rough and prominent; his face showed deep hollows and heavy shadows. The craggy brow, tousled hair, drooping eyelids, melancholy gray eyes, large nose and chin, heavy lips, and sunken, wrinkled cheeks produced an effect not easily forgotten. He was fond of droll yarns and skilled in telling them. Indifferent to social niceties, he was thought to lack "dignity." He was conservative in his attitude on the slavery question and disliked abolition doctrines. As a stump speaker, he was outstanding.

In the agitation that swept the country on the

repeal of the Missouri Compromise, Lincoln emerged from political inactivity and launched upon a new and larger career. Still calling himself a Whig, he competed unsuccessfully for the U.S. senatorship from Illinois in 1855. The next year he identified himself with the new Republican party, wherein he rose rapidly to leadership and received considerable support for the vice-presidential nomination with Frémont. The senatorial election of 1858 was a major turning point in Lincoln's career. Obtaining the Republican nomination to oppose Stephen A. Douglas, he waged an astute campaign. In a carefully prepared speech of acceptance at Springfield on June 16, he made the oft-quoted statement: "A house divided against itself cannot stand. I believe this government cannot endure permanently, half-slave and half-free." After trailing Douglas in the early weeks, Lincoln challenged him to a series of public debates. Between August 21 and October 15, the seven "joint debates" which were held captured the imagination not only of Illinois but of large segments of the nation. In them, Lincoln was conservative; he disavowed abolition doctrines, but shrewdly pointed up the inconsistencies of his opponent's position on slavery.

The Republicans carried the majority of the voting population, but as a result of previous gerrymandering the Democrats were able to organize the state legislature and elect Douglas. Lincoln, however, emerged as a national figure and was increasingly mentioned for the presidency during the next year. It was as a presidential candidate that he delivered his New York speech at Cooper Union, Feb. 27, 1860, in which he formulated the issues on which the Republicans could do battle. He spoke with the greatest clarity, eloquence and dignity.

A combination of factors led to Lincoln's success in the 1860 Republican convention at Chicago. He was so free from radicalism, had been so careful to avoid offense, and yet withal so skillful in inspiring enthusiasts, that he proved to be precisely the type of candidate to which a convention turns after others have proved unavailable. On the third ballot, the delegates stampeded to Lincoln, who became the convention's choice amid scenes of wild excitement. In the fury of the ensuing campaign, with the Democratic party split between North and South and disunion threatened in case of Republican success, Lincoln remained quietly at Springfield. He made little effort to reassure the South. Chosen president, Nov. 6, 1860, by a considerable majority in the electoral college, he received only a minority of the popular vote.

In the critical interval between his election and his inauguration, Lincoln continued his policy of silence, making no speeches and avoiding public statements as to his policy, even as disunion was effected by formation of a Southern Confederacy. To measures of compromise proposed in Congress, he gave scant encouragement. On Feb. 11, 1861, Lincoln left Springfield for Washington. His speeches en route did little to reassure the skeptical East and, by making it clear that the government would resist secession, had a distinctly unfavorable effect in the South. His secret night ride into the capital (occasioned by rumors of a plot against his life) humiliated his friends and was a subject of ridicule for his opponents. In a conciliatory inaugural address, although he denounced secession as anarchy, he disclaimed any intention of interfering with slavery in the states.

Inexperienced in management of great affairs, untrained in executive functions requiring vigorous action, the new president was soon borne down by pressure of miscellaneous duties and of a horde of office-seekers, although the Fort Sumter crisis was crying out for solution, and peace or war hung in the balance. Meanwhile, W. H. Seward, secretary of state, was arrogating authority and making promises to the Southern leaders which the administration could not possibly keep, thereby laying Lincoln open to the suspicion of bad faith. After some vacillation and much muddling, deciding that Fort Sumter should not be surrendered, he attempted to send food to the garrison without aggressively strengthening it. The South chose to regard this as an act of war.

Since Congress did not convene until July 1861, Lincoln met the issue with a series of purely executive measures. Treating the conflict as a massive "insurrection," he summoned the militia, proclaimed a blockade, suspended *habeas corpus* and undertook a multifold series of military measures. As the war progressed, Lincoln extended his executive powers until many called him a dictator; in general, however, he acted with restraint against disloyal elements and used the suspension of *habeas corpus* more as a preventive precaution than as a punitive weapon. Many difficulties beset the administration. There was continual friction within the cabinet, opposition in Congress and from the "radicals" of the Republican party, hysterical demands by the abolitionists, bitter attacks in the press and a constant revelation of profiteering and graft. It is in his reaction to these difficulties and in his constant effort to keep the spirit of vindictiveness out of war policy that we find the measure of Lincoln's qualities as president: his unaffected kindness, his fairness toward opponents, his poise, humor and largeness of soul, his refusal to get angry, his ability to maintain that well-tempered morale which is indispensable in a leader of a desperate cause. Lax as an administrator, he was able to keep the disparate elements of his administration in approximate harmony.

The military phase of his task was a sore problem. Inadequate organization, undue state interference with troops, confusion and experimentation in the central control of the army, jealousy and petty strife in the higher command, a poor system of manpower procurement, and constant interference by Congress, were only a few of the factors that contributed to the months of Union defeat in the field. The pressure of military responsibility thrust on Lincoln was more than any president of a republic should bear, and his search for a winning general is a painful story. His undeniable blunders in military matters were attributable to political pressure or unsatisfactory human material; they were partly offset by his attention to the Western phases of the war and his final support of U. S. Grant in face of withering criticism. Moderate politicians were very often disappointed by his "pliancy" in yielding to distasteful measures of the radical Congress, yet the radicals never in any sense controlled him. He was an adept in yielding on relatively minor points in order to make a firm stand on major issues. His policy toward slavery illustrates his reluctance to form hasty conclusions, or to take hasty and overemphatic action. The Emancipation Proclamation (Jan. 1, 1863) was the result of much thought and was issued when Lincoln considered it wise and expedient. It did not abolish slavery, nor did it declare slavery an evil; it appeared only a half-measure, yet it did change the moral character of the war at home and had great effect on European opinion of the Union cause. Lincoln gave little direct attention to foreign affairs, delegating this work in the main to Secretary Seward.

His manners as president remained much what they had always been—homely and unconventional. His melancholy deepened as the war ground on and he sought eagerly for relaxation in rough jokes and the repetition of favorite passages from literature. He made few public addresses but most of these were effective—notably his two inaugurals, the Gettysburg Address (Nov. 19, 1863), and his last speech delivered at Washington, D.C. on April 11, 1865. He was also able to influence public opinion by means of letters, written to individuals or delegations but intended for publication.

His renomination in 1864, though opposed, was finally unanimous in convention. The first strength of a popular campaign to replace him was sapped by the news of the fall of Atlanta. He was re-elected by a popular majority of more than 400,000 over the Democrat, Gen. George B. McClellan.

At his second inauguration, March 4, 1865, Lincoln delivered a brief address which ranks among his greatest state papers. Refusing to blame the South for the war, he counseled his countrymen to leniency. More than a year before, he had promoted organization of "loyal" governments in the seceded states, requiring that they abolish slavery but standing ready to welcome them back into the Union even though their "loyal" nucleus constituted no more than 10% of their voters in 1860. Later he had killed by pocket veto the Wade-Davis bill providing for severe punitive measures against the South. In several informal peace negotiations, he had insisted only on reunion and the end of slavery; on collateral issues he had shown great generosity, even to compensation of slaveholders for their property loss. On the last day of his life, the subject of Southern reconstruction was considered in a cabinet meeting and a project considered which resembled the plan later announced (May 29, 1865) by Pres. Andrew Johnson. The war, meanwhile, had to all intents and purposes ended with the surrender of Gen. R. E. Lee.

With opposition growing in his own party and threatening the ruin of his generous plans for reunion, Lincoln was removed by assassination which silenced all criticism. At Ford's Theater, Washington, D.C., he was shot by John Wilkes Booth and died the next morning, April 15, 1865. (Details will be found under the entry, *Booth, John Wilkes*). The early crystallization of the Lincoln tradition was illustrated by Edwin M. Stanton's comment, "Now he belongs to the ages!"

In even the shortest list of American liberal leaders, Abraham Lincoln takes eminent place. Liberalism with him was no garment; it was of the fiber of his mind. His hold upon the affections of his own people has not been due merely to the fact that he, a backwoods lad, rose to the highest office in the land. It is doubtful whether any other leader of the North could have matched him in dramatizing the Civil War to the popular mind, in shaping language to his purpose, in smoothing personal difficulties by a magnanimous touch or a tactful gesture, in avoiding domestic and international complications, in persisting courageously in the face of almost unendurable discouragements, in maintaining war morale while refusing to harbor personal malice against the South. His political philosophy was close akin to the creed of Thomas Jefferson. Not inappropriately, he has become a symbol both of American democracy and of the Union.

LINCOLN, BENJAMIN (*b. Hingham, Mass., 1733; d. 1810*), farmer, Massachusetts legislator, Revolutionary major-general. Served in provincial military forces *post* 1755; appointed brigadier-general, February 1776, and major-general, May 1776. Commissioned major-general in the Continental service, February 1777. His maneuvers on Burgoyne's flank prepared way for victory at Saratoga by cutting enemy line of communication with Canada. Appointed to command of American forces in the Southern department, September 1778, he failed in operations before Savannah, Ga.; shut up in Charleston, S.C., he was captured with his whole army, May 1779. Exchanged, November 1779, he commanded under Washington in the neighborhood of New York, 1780, and took part in the Yorktown campaign. He served as secretary of war, 1781–83, and *c.* Jan. 1, 1787, was appointed to lead Massachusetts troops in suppression of Shays's Rebellion. His plea for leniency to the rebels was disregarded by the legislature. Thereafter he served on several federal commissions and as lieutenant-governor of Massachusetts, 1788. He was collector of the port of Boston, 1789–1809.

LINCOLN, ENOCH (*b. Worcester, Mass., 1788; d. Augusta, Maine, 1829*), lawyer, Maine politician. Son of Levi Lincoln (1749–1820). Removed to District of Maine, 1812. Congressman, (Democrat) Republican, from that part of Massachusetts, 1818–20; from Maine as a state, 1820–26. Governor of Maine, 1827–29. A popular and efficient executive.

LINCOLN, JOHN LARKIN (*b. Boston, Mass., 1817; d. 1891*), educator, Latinist. Graduated Brown, 1836; studied also at Halle and Berlin. Professor of Latin at Brown *post* 1845; made his teaching of Latin a medium for appreciation of beauty in all literatures.

LINCOLN, LEVI (*b. Hingham, Mass., 1749; d. Worcester, Mass., 1820*), lawyer, Massachusetts legislator. Graduated Harvard, 1772. Early successful as a trial lawyer, he was of counsel, 1781, in three cases which involved the question of the right to hold a Negro in slavery; a supreme court decision upholding the contentions of Lincoln and Caleb Strong was regarded as a landmark in the struggle against slavery. A leader of the Massachusetts (Democrat) Republicans, Lincoln served as U.S. attorney-general, 1801–04; in *Letters to the People, by a Farmer* (1802), he assailed political activity of the clergy. Lieutenant-governor of Massachusetts, 1807–08, he was offered a place on the U.S. Supreme Court, 1812, which he refused because of failing eyesight.

LINCOLN, LEVI (*b. Worcester, Mass., 1782; d. Worcester, 1868*), lawyer, politician. Son of Levi Lincoln (1749–1820). Graduated Harvard, 1802. Active in state politics as a (Democrat) Republican, he served several terms in the legislature; having become a National Republican, he was elected governor of Massachusetts, 1825, and re-elected annually until 1834. As governor he showed notable executive capacity and a liberal point of view. Entering the national House of Representatives, 1834, he served until 1841 as congressman from Massachusetts.

LINCOLN, MARY JOHNSON BAILEY (*b. South Attleboro, Mass., 1844; d. 1921*), teacher. First principal, Boston Cooking School, 1879–85; author of *Mrs. Lincoln's Boston Cook Book* (1884) and other works on domestic economy.

LINCOLN, MARY TODD (*b. Lexington, Ky., 1818; d. Springfield, Ill., 1882*), wife of Abraham Lincoln. Resident in Springfield *post* 1839, she lived with her sister, who was daughter-in-law of Gov. Ninian Edwards. She was married to Lincoln Nov. 4, 1842, and within limits of her unstable temperament, was a devoted wife. *Post* 1871, her mental instability became more pronounced owing to the successive losses of husband and children; adjudged insane, she was later declared competent and after some years of foreign travel died in the home of Mrs. Edwards.

LINCOLN, ROBERT TODD (*b. Springfield, Ill., 1843; d. 1926*), lawyer, businessman, diplomat. Son of Abraham and Mary Todd Lincoln. Graduated Harvard, 1864. Practiced at the Chicago bar *post* 1867. U.S. secretary of war, 1881–85; U.S. minister to Great Britain, 1889–93. On his return, he continued as counsel for leading business firms and was for a time president of the Pullman Co.

LINCOLN, RUFUS PRATT (*b. Belchertown, Mass., 1840; d. 1900*), physician, laryngologist, Union soldier. Graduated Amherst, 1862; M.D., Harvard Medical School, 1868. Practiced in New York in partnership with Willard Parker; later specialized in intranasal surgery.

LIND, JOHN (*b. Kånna, Sweden, 1854; d. 1930*), lawyer. Emigrated to Minnesota as a boy. Congressman, Republican, from Minnesota, 1887–93; Democrat, from Minnesota, 1903–05. Democratic governor of Minnesota, 1899–1901. Despite party designations, Lind was an independent progressive. He served as Pres. Woodrow Wilson's agent in overturning the Huerta government in Mexico, 1913.

LINDABURY, RICHARD VLIET (*b. near Peapack, N.J., 1850; d. 1925*), New Jersey corporation lawyer.

LINDBERG, CONRAD EMIL (*b. Jönköping, Sweden, 1852; d. 1930*), Lutheran clergyman. Came to America, 1871. A leader in the Augustana Synod of his church, he taught theology at its Rock Island, Ill., seminary *post* 1890. He served from 1901 to 1910 as the seminary's vice-president; as dean, 1920–30.

LINDBERGH, CHARLES AUGUSTUS (*b. Stockholm, Sweden, 1859; d. 1924*), lawyer, politician. Father of Charles A. Lindbergh (1902—). Came to America as an infant; raised near Melrose, Minn. Graduated University of Michigan Law School, 1883; practiced in Little Falls, Minn. Congressman, Republican, from Minnesota, 1907–17. An active and able progressive reformer, he was temporarily unpopular for denouncing war propaganda, 1916–17.

LINDE, CHRISTIAN (*b. near Copenhagen, Denmark, 1817; d. Oshkosh, Wis., 1887*), pioneer Wisconsin physician. A political refugee, Linde emigrated to the vicinity of Oshkosh, 1842, where he planned to establish a landed estate. Called on to treat neighboring settlers and Indians, he resumed practice. A skillful surgeon as well as a busy practitioner, he is credited with discovering the value of animal tendons for surgical sutures.

LINDENKOHL, ADOLPH (*b. Niederkaufungen, Germany, 1833; d. 1904*), cartographer, oceanographer. Came to America, 1852. Associated as draftsman with the U.S. Coast and Geodetic Survey, 1854–

1904, he executed many distinguished maps and made the first transverse polyconic map of the United States.

LINDENTHAL, GUSTAV (*b. Brünn, Moravia, Austria, 1850; d. 1935*), civil engineer. Came to America, 1874. Reputed by 1890 to be one of the great bridge builders of his time; among his principal works are the Queensboro Bridge over the East River, New York, and the railway bridge over Hell Gate. [*Supp. 1*]

LINDERMAN, HENRY RICHARD (*b. Pike Co., Pa., 1825; d. 1879*), physician. Chief clerk, Philadelphia mint, 1853–65; director, Philadelphia mint, 1867–69. First director, Bureau of the Mint, 1873–79.

LINDGREN, WALDEMAR (*b. Kalmar, Sweden, 1860; d. Brookline, Mass., 1939*), geologist. Came to America, 1883. Chief geologist, U.S. Geological Survey, 1911–25; headed department of geology, Massachusetts Institute of Technology, 1912–33. Advocated hydrothermal theory of ore deposition. [*Supp. 2*]

LINDHEIMER, FERDINAND JACOB (*b. Frankfurt-am-Main, Germany, 1801; d. New Braunfels, Texas, 1879*), botanist. Came to America, 1834; fought in Texan war for independence; edited a German newspaper at New Braunfels, 1852–70. Encouraged by George Engelmann, he undertook systematic collection of Texas botanical specimens.

LINDLEY, CURTIS HOLBROOK (*b. Marysville, Calif., 1850; d. 1920*), lawyer, jurist. Authority on mining law; author of *Treatise on the American Law Relating to Mines and Mineral Lands* (1897).

LINDLEY, DANIEL (*b. Washington Co., Pa., 1801; d. 1880*), Presbyterian clergyman. Missionary to South Africa, 1835–59 and 1862–73. Principally active among the Zulus. [*Supp. 1*]

LINDLEY, JACOB (*b. Washington Co., Pa., 1774; d. Connellsville, Pa., 1857*), Presbyterian clergyman. Graduated College of New Jersey (Princeton), 1800. Active *post* 1805 in founding Ohio University at Athens; served in its preparatory department as instructor and on college faculty, 1822–28.

LINDSAY, NICHOLAS VACHEL (*b. Springfield, Ill., 1879; d. Springfield, 1931*), poet. Known as Vachel Lindsay. Studied first for the ministry, then for a career in art. In 1906, unable to obtain work, he tramped through the South distributing poems in exchange for bed and board; this experience was basis for his later *A Handy Guide for Beggars* (1916). His first volume of poems, *General William Booth Enters into Heaven* (1913), attracted little attention. *The Congo and Other Poems* (1914) met with wide popular success by reason of its technical innovations, notably a new ragtime poetic music, a blend of speech and song expressive of the energetic idealism of the period. His later books were notably uneven and seemed almost parodies of his better work.

LINDSAY, VACHEL. [See LINDSAY, NICHOLAS VACHEL, 1879–1931.]

LINDSAY, WILLIAM (*b. near Lexington, Va., 1835; d. 1909*), lawyer, Kentucky jurist and legislator, Confederate soldier. U.S. senator, Democrat, from Kentucky, 1893–1901.

LINDSEY, WILLIAM (*b. Fall River, Mass., 1858; d. Boston, Mass., 1922*), textile manufacturer, author.

LINDSLEY, JOHN BERRIEN (*b. Princeton, N.J., 1822; d. Nashville, Tenn., 1897*), physician, Presbyterian clergyman, educator. Son of Philip Lindsley. Graduated University of Nashville, 1839; M.D., University of Pennsylvania, 1843. Organized medical department, University of Nashville, 1850, first school of its kind south of Ohio River; was chancellor of the University, 1855–70. Active in public health and educational work.

LINDSLEY, PHILIP (*b. near Morristown, N.J., 1786; d. Nashville, Tenn., 1855*), Presbyterian clergyman, educator. Graduated College of New Jersey (Princeton), 1804. Taught languages at Princeton, and served as acting president but in 1823 declined election to presidency. President, University of Nashville, 1825–50.

LINING, JOHN (*b. Scotland, 1708; d. 1760*), physician, pioneer physiologist. Came to South Carolina, *c.* 1730. Practiced in Charleston; made a study of yellow fever and sent abroad earliest account (1748) from America of its symptoms and pathology (published Edinburgh, 1753). Reports made by him on the effect of climatic conditions upon his own metabolism (published by the Royal Society in London, 1743 and 1745) were the first published records of the weather in America. Lining was also an early experimenter in electricity.

LINN, JOHN BLAIR (*b. Shippensburg, Pa., 1777; d. 1804*), Presbyterian clergyman, poet. Brother-in-law of Charles Brockden Brown. Graduated Columbia, 1795. Among the numerous publications of this minor poet were *The Poetical Wanderer* (1796), *The Powers of Genius* (1801, 1802), *Valerian* (1805).

LINN, LEWIS FIELDS (*b. near Louisville, Ky., 1795; d. Missouri, 1843*), physician, authority on Asiatic cholera. Practiced in southeastern Missouri. U.S. senator, Democrat, from Missouri, 1833–43. A sincere exponent of Manifest Destiny. His bill providing for the occupation and settlement of Oregon passed the Senate on Feb. 28, 1843.

LINN, WILLIAM ALEXANDER (*b. Deckertown, now Sussex, N.J., 1846; d. 1917*), journalist, author. Associated as editor with N.Y. *Evening Post, post* 1871, he became managing editor, 1891, and retired, 1900. Under his editorship, the paper was celebrated for the reliability of its news.

LINTNER, JOSEPH ALBERT (*b. Schoharie, N.Y., 1822; d. Rome, Italy, 1898*), manufacturer, entomologist. Appointed New York State entomologist, 1880, he was famous for thoroughness of his annual reports.

LINTON, WILLIAM JAMES (*b. London, England, 1812; d. New Haven, Conn., 1897*), wood-engraver. Came to America, 1866, after a notable career as artist and radical political reformer. Engraved illustrations for a number of books, many after his own designs; opposed the "new school" of American wood-engravers. Author of *The History of Wood-Engraving in America* (1882).

LIPMAN, JACOB GOODALE (*b. Friedrichstadt, Russia, 1874; d. New Brunswick, N.J., 1939*), soil scientist, agricultural educator. Came to America, 1888. Graduated Rutgers, 1898; Ph.D., Cornell, 1903. Meanwhile he had organized (1901) a department of soil chemistry and bacteriology at the New Jersey Agricultural Experiment Station, and had taught agricultural chemistry at Rutgers. As director, *post* 1911, of the Experiment Station, and first dean (*post* 1915) of the N.J. State College of Agriculture at Rutgers, Lipman attracted international acclaim as a scientist and administrator. He founded (1916) and edited *Soil Science*, which became the outstanding journal of its kind in the world. Of his more than one hundred published studies on soil bacteriology and agronomy, many were of a pioneering nature. [*Supp. 2*]

LIPPARD, GEORGE (*b. Chester Co., Pa., 1822; d. Philadelphia, Pa., 1854*), novelist, journalist. Author of a number of fantastic works which include: *The Monks of Monk Hall* (1844), reprinted as *The Quaker City* (1845); *Washington and His Generals* (1847); *Washington and His Men* (1850); *New York: Its Upper-Ten and Lower Million* (1854). An enemy of capitalism, he originated a political philosophy and a religion of his own.

LIPPINCOTT, JAMES STARR (*b. Philadelphia, Pa., 1819; d. Greenwich, N.J., 1885*), horticulturist, meteorologist, agricultural writer.

LIPPINCOTT, JOSHUA BALLINGER (*b. Juliustown, N.J., 1813; d. Philadelphia, Pa., 1886*), publisher. Founder of J. B. Lippincott & Co., 1836; was interested also in banking, insurance and railroads.

LIPPINCOTT, SARA JANE CLARKE (*b. Pompey, N.Y., 1823; d. New Rochelle, N.Y., 1904*), author. Pseudonym, "Grace Greenwood." Contributed widely to magazines; was one of the first women in the United States to become a regular newspaper correspondent. Among her many books, *Greenwood Leaves* (1850) is representative.

LIPPITT, HENRY (*b. Providence, R.I., 1818; d. 1891*), cotton manufacturer, financier. Governor of Rhode Island, 1875–77.

LIPSCOMB, ABNER SMITH (*b. Abbeville District, S.C., 1789; d. 1856*), lawyer. Alabama legislator and jurist, 1811–38. Removed to Texas *c.* 1839; served as secretary of state, Republic of Texas, and was influential in framing the Texas state constitution, 1845. Justice, Texas supreme court, 1845–56.

LIPSCOMB, ANDREW ADGATE (*b. Georgetown, D.C., 1816; d. Athens, Ga., 1890*), Methodist clergyman. Chancellor, University of Georgia, 1860–74.

LISA, MANUEL (*b. New Orleans, La., 1772; d. St. Louis, Mo., 1820*), fur trader. Removed to St. Louis, Mo., *c.* 1790; held a Spanish patent for monopoly of trade with the Osages. Led expedition up Missouri River, 1807–08, during which he placed a trading house at mouth of Big Horn River and built fort later known as Fort Manuel, first structure of its kind on upper Missouri. Joined with Andrew Henry, Pierre Chouteau and others in Missouri Fur Co., 1808; was appointed, 1814, to post of sub-agent for Indian tribes on the Missouri above mouth of Kansas River. Between 1807 and his death, he made some 13 trips on the Missouri, amounting to about 26,000 miles of river travel.

LIST, GEORG FRIEDRICH (*b. Reutlingen, Germany, 1789; d. Tyrol, Austria, 1846*), journalist, economist. An influential German liberal and a friend of Lafayette, List emigrated to America, 1825. Settling in Reading, Pa., 1826, he very ably edited the *Readinger Adler*. One of the foremost advocates of the protectionist movement, he achieved national recognition for his *Outlines of American Political Economy* (1827) and other publications. Turning his attention to business, he developed anthracite deposits near Tamaqua, Pa., and organized, 1828, the progenitor of the modern Reading Railroad. Returning to Europe in 1831 as a consular official, he divided his energies between literary work and the promotion of a German railway system. List's theory of productive forces, of the economic importance of nations as against the individualism of Adam Smith, and his application of the historical method, all advanced the study of economics. He ranks next to Alexander Hamilton as the most constructive thinker among the early advocates of protectionism in America.

LISTEMANN, BERNHARD (*b. Schlotheim, Germany, 1841; d. 1917*), violinist, conductor, educator. Studied at Leipzig Conservatory, and at Vienna under Joseph Joachim and Henry Vieuxtemps. Came to America, 1867; founded Boston Philharmonic Club, 1875, from which grew Boston Philharmonic Orchestra; served briefly as concert master, Boston Symphony. Removed to Chicago, 1893, where he had successful career as teacher and performer.

LITCHFIELD, ELECTUS BACKUS (*b. Delphi Falls, N.Y., 1813; d. 1889*), financier, railroad builder. Built up, with aid of his two brothers, a remarkable network of railroads in Michigan, Indiana, Ohio and Illinois, the most impressive organization of its kind before the Civil War. Overextended when the panic of 1857 occurred, the Litchfields lost control of their system in subsequent reorganization; thereafter they turned to development of street railways and real estate in Brooklyn, N.Y. The St. Paul & Pacific Railroad, built by the Litchfields *post* 1862, after many vicissitudes was sold by them to James J. Hill; its lines became nucleus of the Great Northern system. Brooklyn's famous Prospect Park was constructed on land purchased from the Litchfields.

LITTELL, ELIAKIM (*b. Burlington, N.J., 1797; d. Brookline, Mass., 1870*), publisher. *Littell's Living Age* (founded 1844) and his earlier *Museum* (1822–43) reprinted materials from European periodicals and brought foreign thought to the attention of Americans during the early period of development of our national culture.

LITTELL, SQUIER (*b. Burlington, N.J., 1803; d. Bay Head, N.J., 1886*), physician, ophthalmic surgeon. Brother of Eliakim Littell.

LITTELL, WILLIAM (*b. New Jersey, 1768; d. 1824*), Kentucky lawyer and compiler of law books. Author also of *Epistles of William* (1806), a series of satirical essays on prominent men of the time, and *Political Transactions In and Concerning Kentucky* (1806).

LITTLE, ARTHUR DEHON (*b. Boston, Mass., 1863; d. Northeast Harbor, Maine, 1935*), chemical engineer. A recognized leader in paper technology, he was an organizer and partner in Arthur D. Little, Inc., the largest unendowed commercial industrial research laboratory in the U.S. [*Supp. 1*]

LITTLE, CHARLES COFFIN (*b. Kennebunk, Maine, 1799; d. 1869*), publisher. Associated with James Brown (1800–1855) in firm of Little, Brown & Co.; supervised legal publications of the firm.

LITTLE, CHARLES JOSEPH (*b. Philadelphia, Pa., 1840; d. 1911*), Methodist clergyman, theologian, educator. Graduated University of Pennsylvania, 1861; taught at Dickinson College and Syracuse University. Professor of church history, Garrett Biblical Institute, 1891–95; president of the Institute, 1895–1911.

LITTLE, CHARLES SHERMAN (*b. Webster, N.H., 1869; d. Thiells, N.Y., 1936*), psychiatrist. M.D., Dartmouth, 1896. First superintendent, 1910–36, of Letchworth Village in Rockland Co., N.Y., pioneering school for the feebleminded. [*Supp. 2*]

LITTLE, GEORGE (*b. Marshfield, Mass., 1754; d. Weymouth, Mass., 1809*), naval officer. Served in Massachusetts navy during the Revolution. Appointed, 1799, captain in U.S. Navy, he served with great distinction in command of frigate *Boston* during naval war with France.

LITTLE CROW V (*b. c. 1803; d. near Hutchinson, Minn., 1863*), chief of Mdewakanton Sioux. A drunkard and habitual liar but a persuasive orator, he was chiefly responsible for the Minnesota outbreak of the Sioux in August–September 1862.

LITTLE TURTLE (*b. on Eel River, northwest of Ft. Wayne, Ind., c. 1752; d. Ft. Wayne, 1812*), Miami Indian chief. Tribal name, Michikinikwa. A principal leader at defeat of Gen. Harmar, 1790, and of Gen. St. Clair, 1791. Led attack on Ft. Recovery, 1794. Thereafter counseling peace, he lost his leadership in council, and his prestige among his people declined. He is, however, credited with keeping the Miami from joining the confederacy of Tecumseh.

LITTLEFIELD, GEORGE WASHINGTON (*b. Panola Co., Miss., 1842; d. 1920*), cattleman, banker, Confederate soldier. Raised in Gonzales Co., Texas. Engaged in trail driving cattle *post* 1871; established cattle ranch near Tascosa, 1877. Locating on the Pecos River in New Mexico, 1882, and soon ranging some 40,000 head of cattle, he spread the fame of his LFD brand the length of the West. Removing to Austin, Texas, 1883, he organized the American National Bank, 1890, of which he served as president until his death. He was a generous supporter of historical research and a benefactor of the University of Texas.

LITTLEJOHN, ABRAM NEWKIRK (*b. Florida, N.Y., 1824; d. Williamstown, Mass., 1901*), Episcopal clergyman. Consecrated bishop of Long Island, 1869. Secured interest of Alexander T. Stewart in building Cathedral Church of the Incarnation, Garden City, N.Y., 1885.

LITTLEPAGE, LEWIS (*b. Hanover Co., Va., 1762; d. Fredericksburg, Va., 1802*), adventurer. Educated at College of William and Mary. Served with Spanish army in siege of Gibraltar, 1782; was confidential emissary of Stanislaus II Poniatowski, King of Poland, 1786–95. Returned to Virginia, 1801.

LITTLETON, MARTIN WILEY (*b. Roane Co., Tenn., 1872; d. 1934*), lawyer, Democratic politician. Self-educated, Littleton resided in Brooklyn, N.Y., *post* 1897, where his rise as legal practitioner, particularly in criminal practice, was rapid. He received national notice for his speech nominating Alton B. Parker for the presidency at the Democratic convention, St. Louis, Mo., 1904. [*Supp. 1*]

LIVERIGHT, HORACE BRISBIN (*b. Osceola Mills, Pa., 1886; d. 1933*), bond salesman, theatrical producer, publisher. Partner in Boni & Liveright, 1918–30. A vivid figure in the literary world of the 1920's, he was first publisher to take interest in works of Eugene O'Neill and helped advance reputations of Ben Hecht, Theodore Dreiser and others. [*Supp. 1*]

LIVERMORE, ABIEL ABBOT (*b. Wilton, N.H., 1811; d. Wilton, 1892*), Unitarian clergyman. President, Theological School, Meadville, Pa., 1863–90.

LIVERMORE, ARTHUR (*b. Londonderry, N.H., 1766; d. Campton, N.H., 1853*), lawyer, New Hampshire legislator, congressman and jurist. Son of Samuel

Livermore (1732–1803), brother of Edward St. L. Livermore.

LIVERMORE, EDWARD ST. LOE (*b. Portsmouth, N.H., 1762; d. Tewksbury, Mass., 1832*), lawyer, New Hampshire jurist and Federalist congressman. Son of Samuel Livermore (1732–1803), brother of Arthur Livermore.

LIVERMORE, GEORGE (*b. Cambridge, Mass., 1809; d. 1865*), wool merchant, book collector.

LIVERMORE, MARY ASHTON RICE (*b. Boston, Mass., 1820; d. Melrose, Mass., 1905*), teacher, woman's rights advocate, reformer. Active in work of U.S. Sanitary Commission. Author of *My Story of the War* (1888) and *The Story of My Life* (1897).

LIVERMORE, SAMUEL (*b. Waltham, Mass., 1732; d. Holderness, N.H., 1803*), lawyer, New Hampshire legislator and jurist. Father of Edward St. L. and Arthur Livermore. Practiced law in Portsmouth, N.H., *post c.* 1757; served as judge-advocate in Admiralty and attorney-general of province, 1769–74. Elected state attorney-general, 1776, he continued to hold state office almost continuously until his death. He served as U.S. congressman from New Hampshire, 1789–93; elected to the U.S. Senate, 1793, he resigned, 1801, because of failing health.

LIVERMORE, SAMUEL (*b. Concord, N.H., 1786; d. Florence, Ala., 1833*), lawyer, legal writer. Son of Edward St. L. Livermore. Graduated Harvard, 1804. Successful as a lawyer in New Orleans *post* 1822, Livermore wrote the first American work on agency and auctions (1811); also the first American work on the conflict of laws (1828).

LIVINGSTON, EDWARD (*b. Columbia Co., N.Y., 1764; d. Dutchess Co., N.Y., 1836*), lawyer, statesman. Son of Robert R. Livingston (1718–1775). Graduated College of New Jersey (Princeton), 1781; studied law at Albany under John Lansing. Practiced law in New York City *post* 1785. Congressman, (Democrat) Republican, from New York, 1795–1801. Acting (1801–03) simultaneously as U.S. attorney for New York and as mayor of New York City, he was held responsible for the defalcation of an agent and gave up all his own property to be sold in order to make restitution of the loss to the Treasury. Removing to New Orleans, La., 1804, he began practice of the law there, struggling meanwhile under a weight of private as well as public debt. Falsely accused of abetting Aaron Burr in his 1806 activities, Livingston no sooner cleared himself of these charges before he was brought into controversy with President Jefferson over the rights to certain alluvial lands at New Orleans which Livingston claimed. Dispossessed of the property, he published pamphlets on the subject and complained of his treatment in the courts and before Congress.

As chairman of the New Orleans committee of public defense, Livingston organized the people of Louisiana in their resistance to British invasion, 1814. At the battle of New Orleans he served Andrew Jackson as aide-de-camp, interpreter and adviser. Commissioned, 1821, to revise the Louisiana penal law, he completed a code in 1825 which aimed at the prevention rather than the punishment of crime. Although it was not adopted, the publication of the code brought him wide fame. As a Democrat, he represented the New Orleans district in the U.S. House of Representatives, 1823–29, and was chosen by the legislature to be U.S. senator, 1829–31. As U.S. secretary of state, 1831–33, he drafted the celebrated 1832 proclamation to the South Carolina nullifiers; he also secured an admission by the French Government in 1831 of the justice of American claims for spoliation under the Berlin and Milan decrees. His last public service was as U.S. minister to France, 1833–35.

LIVINGSTON, HENRY BROCKHOLST (*b. New York, N.Y., 1757; d. Washington, D.C., 1823*), lawyer, Revolutionary soldier. Son of William Livingston (1723–1790). Graduated College of New Jersey (Princeton), 1774. Justice, New York supreme court, 1802–06; justice, U.S. Supreme Court, 1807–23. Opinions written by Livingston dealt mainly with questions of maritime and commercial law; his decisions on the circuit court were considered more noteworthy than those he made on the Supreme bench.

LIVINGSTON, JAMES (*b. probably Montreal, Canada, 1747; d. Schuylerville, N.Y., 1832*), Revolutionary soldier, New York legislator. Responsible, 1780, for failure of H.M.S. *Vulture* to wait for Major André, thus contributing to his later capture.

LIVINGSTON, JOHN HENRY (*b. near Poughkeepsie, N.Y., 1746; d. New Brunswick, N.J., 1825*), Dutch Reformed clergyman, educator. Graduated Yale, 1762; doctor of theology, University of Utrecht, 1770. Professor of theology to the General Synod, 1784–1825; president of Queens College (now Rutgers University), 1810–25. A principal factor in guiding the Dutch Reformed Church to a complete and independent American organization.

LIVINGSTON, JOHN WILLIAM (*b. New York, N.Y., 1804; d. New York, 1885*), naval officer.

LIVINGSTON, PETER VAN BRUGH (*b. Albany, N.Y., 1710; d. Elizabethtown, N.J., 1792*), merchant, Revolutionary patriot. Brother of Philip Livingston and William Livingston (1723–1790). Graduated Yale, 1731. Made a fortune in privateering and government contracting during French wars. Followed lead in New York politics of his brother William, of John M. Scott and William Smith, Jr.

LIVINGSTON, PHILIP (*b. Albany, N.Y., 1716; d. York, Pa., 1778*), New York legislator, Revolutionary patriot, signer of the Declaration of Independence.

Brother of Peter Van B. Livingston and William Livingston (1723–1790). Graduated Yale, 1737. Among the first to advocate founding of King's College (Columbia) to which he was a benefactor; also helped organize N.Y. Society Library, 1754, and N.Y. Chamber of Commerce, 1768. In politics, he supported the Whig Presbyterian faction against the Anglicans as represented by the De Lancey interest but was not so intense a partisan as his brother William. A member of the New York provincial congress, he served also in the Continental Congress, 1774–78, where he was active in committee work. Too dignified and austere to win popularity, he pledged his personal credit to maintain confidence in the Congress and was honored in his own generation for ability and integrity.

LIVINGSTON, ROBERT (*b. Ancrum, Roxburghshire, Scotland, 1654; d. 1728*), landowner, trader, New York legislator. Raised in Rotterdam, Holland, where his father was pastor of a Presbyterian congregation; came to New England, 1673; appeared in Albany, N.Y., 1674. Appointed town clerk and secretary of the board of commissioners for Indian affairs, he came to have influence with the successive governors of the province. By careful purchase of Indian claims to lands along the Hudson, and by his marriage to the widowed sister of Peter Schuyler, he rose in fortune and prominence. He secured a patent raising his landholdings into the manor and lordship of Livingston, 1686. Among other activities in which he engaged were government contracting and tax-farming as well as private trade with the Indians and French. As speaker of the New York Assembly, 1718–25, he showed a marked tendency to support the Assembly in its frequent quarrels with the royal governor. Grasping and shrewd, he was also a courtier and diplomat of no mean ability.

LIVINGSTON, ROBERT R. (*b. New York, 1718; d. 1775*), jurist, New York legislator, Revolutionary patriot. Grandson of Robert Livingston. A leader of the Whig interest, he was ready to go as far as necessary to assure the economic welfare of the colonies but was opposed to revolution merely for the sake of abstract principle. During the Stamp Act controversy, he was chairman of the New York committee of correspondence and author of the address to the King presented by the Stamp Act Congress.

LIVINGSTON, ROBERT R. (*b. New York, N.Y., 1746; d. 1813*), lawyer, diplomat, agriculturist. Son of Robert R. Livingston (1718–1775); brother of Edward Livingston. Graduated King's College (Columbia), 1765. Admitted to the bar, 1770; practiced at first in partnership with John Jay. Member of Continental Congress, 1775–76, 1779–81, 1784–85. Serving on the congressional committee appointed to draft a declaration of independence, he considered the course inexpedient and was one of the principal speakers for its postponement. Few members of Congress were

more conscientious or more in demand as committee members; of his many reports, the most important was that of Dec. 14, 1779, describing the financial problems of the general government and urging methods of solving them. From August 1781 until May 1783, he served as secretary of the newly created Department of Foreign Affairs. In this office he set up a system for business and arranged for the dissemination of news to all departments, innovations which marked an advance in the development of American executive machinery. Throughout his life he was also deeply involved in New York affairs, helping to govern the state in the period after British withdrawal, to settle boundary disputes with Massachusetts and Vermont and active on the committee to draft first New York constitution, 1777. He held post of chancellor of New York State, 1777–1801. Excepting Alexander Hamilton, no individual contributed more toward New York's ratification of the Federal Constitution. Irked by what he considered the slights of the administration, he became a (Democrat) Republican sometime *ante* 1791. As U.S. minister to France, 1801–04, he scored the greatest diplomatic success recorded in American history by seizing the opportunity offered the United States for the purchase of Louisiana. After his retirement, he conducted agricultural experiments and was a pioneer in the import of Merino sheep and the use of gypsum as fertilizer. His technical as well as financial aid made possible the experiments of Robert Fulton in France and later the success of the steamboat *Clermont* on the Hudson.

LIVINGSTON, WILLIAM (*b. Albany, N.Y., 1723; d. Elizabethtown, N.J., 1790*), lawyer, New York legislator. Grandson of Robert Livingston; brother of Philip and Peter Van B. Livingston; father-in-law of John Jay. Graduated Yale, 1741; studied law under James Alexander and William Smith (1697–1769). Like his brothers a leader in opposition to New York conservatives and an advocate of Whig principles, he was an intense and impatient partisan. The 1751 proposal to place the new King's College of New York under trustees of Episcopalian sentiment and sympathy appeared to him the first step toward establishment of the Anglican Church; his views were ably presented in the weekly publication *Independent Reflector* (1752), in the "Watch Tower" column in the *New York Mercury*, and in other satirical publications. After the 1769 defeat of the Whigs in the New York Assembly, he removed to an estate near Elizabethtown, N.J., quickly rising to a position of leadership in New Jersey. He was a member of the First Continental Congress and of the Second Continental Congress until June 5, 1776, when for a brief period he commanded the New Jersey militia. Elected first governor of New Jersey, 1776, he served until his death. A delegate to the Federal Convention, 1787, he supported the New Jersey plan and worked for a compromise that would be acceptable. Among his contemporaries, he was honored for a high moral courage, for wit and for a sense of social responsibility.

LIVINGSTONE, WILLIAM (*b. Dundas, Ontario, Canada, 1844; d. 1925*), Great Lakes shipowner and operator; Detroit, Mich., newspaper owner and banker.

LLOYD, ALFRED HENRY (*b. Montclair, N.J., 1864; d. 1927*), philosopher. Graduated Harvard, 1886; studied also in Germany. Taught at University of Michigan, 1891–1927; served also as dean of graduate school, *post* 1915. Author of *Dynamic Idealism* (1898), *Philosophy of History* (1899) and *The Will to Doubt* (1907), an answer to William James.

LLOYD, DAVID (*b. Manafon, Wales, c. 1656; d. Chester, Pa., 1731 o.s.*), lawyer, Pennsylvania legislator. Commissioned by William Penn attorney-general of Pennsylvania, 1686, he was soon appointed clerk of county and provincial courts and began in 1694 his long intermittent career as speaker of the Assembly. Removed from his position as attorney-general, 1700, he became an enemy of Penn and of James Logan and was recognized leader of the anti-proprietary party *post* 1703. He served as chief justice of Pennsylvania, 1717–31. Long regarded as a quarrelsome demagogue, he is today represented as a pioneer in the fight for democratic principles in America, because of his steady resistance to the efforts of the governors and council to control the judiciary and encroach upon the powers of the Assembly.

LLOYD, EDWARD (*b. Talbot Co., Md., 1744; d. 1796*), Maryland legislator, Revolutionary patriot.

LLOYD, EDWARD (*b. Talbot Co., Md., 1779; d. Annapolis, Md., 1834*), landowner, Maryland legislator. Son of Edward Lloyd (1744–1796). Congressman, (Democrat) Republican, from Maryland, 1806–09; governor of Maryland, 1809–11; U.S. senator, 1819–26.

LLOYD, HENRY DEMAREST (*b. New York, N.Y., 1847; d. 1903*), journalist, lawyer, opponent of monopoly. Author of the "Story of a Great Monopoly" (*Atlantic Monthly*, March 1881) and *Wealth against Commonwealth* (1894), he was the first and perhaps the best of the "muckrakers." Resident in Chicago, Ill., and its vicinity *post* 1873, he engaged in constant struggle for the rights of labor and made world-wide studies of social experiments. He formally joined the Socialist party in 1903.

LLOYD, JAMES (*b. Oyster Bay, N.Y., 1728; d. Boston, Mass., 1810*), pioneer obstetrician and surgeon. Apprenticed in medicine at Boston, Mass.; studied in London, England, with leading surgeons. On his return to Boston, 1752, he introduced new methods of surgery there and was the first physician to practice midwifery in America.

LLOYD, JOHN URI (*b. North Bloomfield, N.Y., 1849; d. Van Nuys, Calif., 1936*), pharmacist, plant chemist, drug manufacturer, novelist. Active proponent of Eclectic school of medicine. Author, among other works, of *Stringtown on the Pike* (1900).

[*Supp. 2*]

LLOYD, MARSHALL BURNS (*b. St. Paul, Minn., 1858; d. Menominee, Mich., 1927*), inventor of machines for weaving wire and wicker.

LLOYD, THOMAS (*b. Dolobran, Wales, 1640 o.s.; d. Philadelphia, Pa., 1694 o.s.*), physician, politician. A Quaker, he emigrated to Philadelphia, 1683, and served as president of the provincial council, 1684–88, 1690–91. Appointed deputy-governor of Pennsylvania, 1691, he was superseded, 1693. An opponent of usurpation of power by the executive branch of the government, he was the ablest and most popular political leader of his time in Pennsylvania.

LOCHMAN, JOHN GEORGE (*b. Philadelphia, Pa., 1773; d. Harrisburg, Pa., 1826*), Lutheran clergyman. Took leading part in organization of the General Synod at Frederick, Md., 1821, and was chosen its president.

LOCKE, DAVID ROSS (*b. Vestal, N.Y., 1833; d. Toledo, O., 1888*), journalist, political satirist. Pseudonym, "Petroleum V. Nasby." His attacks on Copperheads and Democrats, *post* March 1861, were admired by Abraham Lincoln. Numerous collections of his satirical letters appeared in book form, beginning with *The Nasby Papers* (1864). Marked by humor, aggressive malice and merciless insistence on a few points, "Nasby's" satires have not survived their own day. For many years, Locke was editor of the *Toledo Blade*, in which he owned a controlling interest.

LOCKE, JOHN (*b. Lempster, N.H., 1792; d. Cincinnati, O., 1856*), physician, scientist, inventor. M.D., Yale, 1819. Settling in Cincinnati, O., c. 1822, he conducted a girls' school there until 1835 and was professor of chemistry, Medical College of Ohio, 1835–53. During this time Locke was also employed in geological surveying for Ohio and for the federal government. He was inventor of a number of instruments, notably his so-called electromagnetic chronograph (1844–48), a device which completely changed the art of determining longitudes.

LOCKE, MATTHEW (*b. 1730; d. near Salisbury, N.C., 1801*), Revolutionary patriot, North Carolina legislator. Congressman, radical Jeffersonian Republican, from North Carolina, 1793–99.

LOCKE, RICHARD ADAMS (*b. East Brent, England, 1800; d. Staten Island, N.Y., 1871*), journalist. Emigrated to New York City, 1832. As a writer for the New York *Sun*, he was author of the celebrated "Moon Hoax" (August 1835).

LOCKHART, CHARLES (*b. Cairn Heads, Scotland, 1818; d. 1905*), pioneer oil producer. Came to America, 1836. A successful oil producer *post* 1853, he leased land in Oil Creek soon after the discovery at Titusville, Pa., 1859, and built up a large export trade. With an associate, he built the Brilliant Refinery (first important refinery erected) and also the Atlantic Refinery in Philadelphia. He was an early partner in Standard Oil.

LOCKREY, SARAH HUNT (*b. Philadelphia, Pa., 1863; d. 1929*), surgeon, worker for woman suffrage.

LOCKWOOD, BELVA ANN BENNETT (*b. Royalton, N.Y., 1830; d. 1917*), teacher, lawyer, suffragist. Admitted to the Washington, D.C., bar, 1873, she was first woman admitted to practice before U.S. Supreme Court, 1879. As nominee of the National Equal Rights party, 1884 and 1888, she was the first woman candidate for the presidency of the United States.

LOCKWOOD, JAMES BOOTH (*b. Annapolis, Md., 1852; d. Cape Sabine, E. Ellesmere Island, Canada, 1884*), army officer, Arctic explorer. Commissioned second-lieutenant, U.S. Army, 1873; served at various posts in the West. Volunteered, 1881, for duty with Greely Expedition, on which he distinguished himself in the explorations and in particular during the winter of starvation at Cape Sabine.

LOCKWOOD, RALPH INGERSOLL (*b. Greenwich, Conn., 1798; d. New York, N.Y., 1858?*), lawyer, expert in equity practice. Author of several works on law and of two novels: *Rosine Laval* (1833), and *The Insurgents* (1835) which deals with Shays's Rebellion.

LOCKWOOD, ROBERT WILTON (*b. Wilton, Conn., 1861; d. 1914*), portrait and flower painter. Studied with John La Farge and at Art Students League, N.Y.; studied also in Paris and Munich. Worked in Boston, Mass., *post* 1896.

LOCKWOOD, SAMUEL DRAKE (*b. Poundridge, N.Y., 1789; d. Batavia, Ill., 1874*), jurist. Removed to Illinois, 1818; held various state offices, 1821–24. Justice, Illinois supreme court, 1825–48. A man of great reputation in his state, Lockwood was a principal contributor to the revision of the Illinois statutes, 1826–29.

LOCKWOOD, WILTON. [See LOCKWOOD, ROBERT WILTON, 1861–1914.]

LOCY, WILLIAM ALBERT (*b. Troy, Mich., 1857; d. 1924*), zoologist. Taught at Northwestern University *post* 1896. Author of numerous important scientific papers, he wrote three studies in the historical development of biology: *Biology and Its Makers* (1908), *The Main Currents of Zoology* (1918) and *Growth of Biology* (1925).

LODGE, GEORGE CABOT (*b. Boston, Mass., 1873; d. 1909*), poet. Son of Henry Cabot Lodge. Published, among other books, *The Song of the Wave* (1898), *Cain, a Drama* (1904), *Herakles* (1908). His collected *Poems and Dramas* were published, 1911, in which year appeared a biography of him by Henry Adams.

LODGE, HENRY CABOT (*b. Boston, Mass., 1850; d. Cambridge, Mass., 1924*), lawyer, politician, author. Great-grandson of George Cabot. Graduated Harvard, 1871; Harvard Law School, 1874. At invitation of Henry Adams, worked as assistant editor, *North American Review*, 1873–76. Received first degree of Ph.D. granted by Harvard in political science, 1876. Author of *Life and Letters of George Cabot* (1877), *Alexander Hamilton* (1882), *Daniel Webster* (1882) and *George Washington* (1888). Although he continued to write, his works were marred by increasing partisanship.

After service as a Republican in the Massachusetts legislature and a failure to secure nomination for Congress, 1882, he managed the 1883 Republican gubernatorial campaign in Massachusetts with political adroitness of a high order. Delegate to the Republican National Convention, 1884, he worked with Theodore Roosevelt to prevent choice of James G. Blaine, but put aside his principles to support the national ticket in the campaign. Elected to Congress, 1886, he spoke often and effectively and became notable in the House of Representatives before his first term was finished. Serving in the House until 1893, he outraged practical politicians by championing civil service reform. Chosen U.S. senator, January 1893, by the Massachusetts legislature, his hold on the post was never thereafter seriously in doubt until his death, with the exception of 1911 at the time of the Progressive upheaval. Lodge helped draft the Sherman Anti-Trust Law, 1890, the Pure Food and Drugs Law, and several tariff measures—in particular the tariff of 1909. He was a thoroughgoing protectionist and an opponent of free silver. He viewed all proposals for compulsory international arbitration or disarmament with suspicion, supported the taking of the Philippines, and assisted Roosevelt's successful intrigue in Panama. He voted against the direct election of senators, opposed womans' suffrage and voted against adoption of the Eighteenth Amendment.

Lodge's judgment on international affairs was highly valued by Theodore Roosevelt. Early finding a place on the Foreign Relations Committee, he did not become chairman until late in his career, when his leadership in the fight against ratification of the Peace Treaty and Covenant, 1919, made him a national figure. He was convinced that his opposition to the coupling of the treaty of peace with a guarantee of United States participation in the proposed League of Nations (which in principle he approved) represented majority American opinion and that President Wilson was opposing the popular will. His part in effecting the rejection of the League gained for him at the time both admiration and bitter resentment. Lodge was one of those who were chiefly responsible for the nomination of Warren G. Harding. An excellent practical politician, he was not always scrupulous in his choice of means provided they served his end; he was rarely receptive to reform proposals of any sort and was ruthlessly vindictive toward those whom he opposed or disliked.

LOEB, JACQUES (*b. Mayen, Germany, 1859; d. Bermuda, 1924*), physiologist. Came to America, 1891. Taught at Bryn Mawr and University of Chicago; accepted a call to University of California, 1902; was a member of Rockefeller Institute for Medical Research, 1910–24. Author of the "tropism" theory of behavior. Made pioneer experiments in artificial fertilization.

LOEB, JAMES (*b. New York, N.Y., 1867; d. Murnau, Bavaria, Germany, 1933*), banker, philanthropist. Graduated Harvard, 1888. After working in family banking firm of Kuhn, Loeb & Co., 1888–1901, he devoted himself to artistic pursuits and numerous philanthropies; *post* 1905, he resided abroad. His outstanding contribution to humanistic studies was the Loeb Classical Library, founded in 1910, which provided competently edited texts and translations of Greek and Latin literature in convenient pocket size. [*Supp. 1*]

LOEB, LOUIS (*b. Cleveland, O., 1866; d. Canterbury, N.H., 1909*), painter. Studied at Art Students League, N.Y., and in Paris under J. L. Gérôme. Illustrated with rare taste and skill works by Mark Twain, F. Marion Crawford and others.

LOEB, MORRIS (*b. Cincinnati, O., 1863; d. New York, N.Y., 1912*), chemist. Graduated Harvard, 1882; Ph.D., Berlin, 1887; studied the new field of physical chemistry at Heidelberg and Leipzig. An American pioneer in physical chemistry, he taught at Clark University and New York University *post* 1890 and was author of a number of papers, notably on molecular weights. He was a benefactor of Harvard.

LOEB, SOPHIE IRENE SIMON (*b. Rovno, Russia, 1876; d. New York, N.Y., 1929*), social worker, journalist. Came to America as a child; was raised in McKeesport, Pa. As reporter and unselfish lobbyist, she secured more constructive welfare legislation than any other woman in America of her time.

LOEFFLER, CHARLES MARTIN (*b. Mülhausen, Alsace, 1861; d. Medfield, Mass., 1935*), violinist, composer. Came to America, 1881, bearing a letter of introduction from his teacher, Joseph Joachim, to Leopold Damrosch, who employed him in his concerts. Associated with the Boston Symphony Orchestra, 1882, Loeffler devoted his major attention to it until he retired to teach and compose, 1903. Although his musical idiom was so Gallic in spirit that it can hardly be considered American in character, it represented something rare at a time when the best American composers excepting MacDowell were largely academic. Loeffler was an independent thinker, an artistic hermit; his sparkling and colorful scores were polished to a refinement which approached perfection. Among his numerous works are *Pagan Poem* (first

composed, 1901, but taking its final form, 1907) and *Hora Mystica* (1916). [*Supp. 1*]

LOEW, MARCUS (*b. New York, N.Y., 1870; d. Glen Cove, N.Y., 1927*), theatre owner, motion-picture pioneer.

LOEWENTHAL, ISIDOR (*b. Posen, Prussia, c. 1827; d. Peshawar, India, 1864*), Presbyterian missionary. Came to America, 1846, as a political refugee. Graduated Lafayette, 1848; Princeton Theological Seminary, 1851. Worked in India *post* 1855.

LOGAN, BENJAMIN (*b. Augusta Co., Va., c. 1743; d. Shelby Co., Ky., 1802*), Kentucky pioneer, Indian fighter. Joined with other frontiersmen in settlement of Transylvania colony, 1775; was a leader in retaliatory expeditions against Ohio Indians, 1778, 1780, 1782. Throughout the Revolution the most influential and trusted of Kentucky leaders, he failed to hold his position after the peace and occupied a minor place in public life.

LOGAN, CORNELIUS AMBROSE (*b. Deerfield, Mass., 1832; d. Los Angeles, Calif., 1899*), physician, Union army surgeon, politician. Son of Cornelius Ambrosius Logan; cousin of John A. Logan. Removed to Kansas, 1857. As first president, Kansas State Medical Society, he worked *post* 1867 to raise standards of the profession and quality of medical instruction in the state. U.S. minister to Chile, 1873–77 and 1882–85, he served also as minister resident to Central American states, 1879–82.

LOGAN, CORNELIUS AMBROSIUS (*b. probably Baltimore, Md., 1806; d. near Marietta, O., 1853*), actor, dramatist, manager.

LOGAN, DEBORAH NORRIS (*b. 1761; d. "Stenton," near Germantown, Pa., 1839*), historian. Granddaughter of Isaac Norris; wife of George Logan. Preserved, deciphered, copied and annotated Logan family papers at "Stenton"; these were later published by Historical Society of Pennsylvania.

LOGAN, GEORGE (*b. "Stenton," near Germantown, Pa., 1753; d. "Stenton," 1821*), physician, Pennsylvania legislator. Grandson of James Logan (1674–1751). M.D., University of Edinburgh, 1779; studied also in Paris where he enjoyed close friendship with Benjamin Franklin. On return to Philadelphia, 1780, he applied himself to study of improved methods of farming and was a founder of Philadelphia Society for Promotion of Agriculture. He served in Pennsylvania legislature as a friend and follower of Thomas Jefferson. A strict Quaker and a friend to peace, he attempted, at his own expense and on his own authority, to bring about better understanding with France, 1798. This mission was the object of much hostile criticism; in consequence of it, on Jan. 30, 1799, Congress passed the so-called "Logan Act" forbidding private citizens to undertake diplomatic negotiations without official sanction. He served as U.S. senator, (Democrat) Republican, from Pennsylvania, 1801–07.

LOGAN, JAMES (*b. Lurgan, Ireland, 1674; d. near Germantown, Pa., 1751*), colonial statesman, scholar. Became William Penn's secretary, 1699; was his confidential adviser and the counselor of his descendants for more than fifty years. Emigrating to Pennsylvania, 1699, he served as secretary of the Province and clerk of the Provincial Council, 1701–17. Supervisor of the Penn family interests in Pennsylvania, Logan was a voting member of the Council, 1702–47; he became in time its senior member and president. Among numerous executive and judicial posts which he held was that of chief justice of the Supreme Court, 1731–39. He amassed a fortune in land investment and in trade with the Indians. Subsequent to his retirement from the Council, he lived at the estate which he had established at "Stenton," near Germantown. Botany was his special field of interest in science; he was a friend of John Bartram and his botanical investigations were recognized by Linnaeus. He published two works of scholarship: *Cato's Moral Distiches, Englished* (1735) and *M.T. Cicero's Cato Major* (1744), the latter of which is considered the finest specimen of printing from Franklin's press.

LOGAN, JAMES (*b. probably Shamokin, now Sunbury, Pa., c. 1725; d. 1780*), Mingo orator. Son of Shikellamy. Early a friendly collaborator of the whites, Logan turned against his former friends after the Yellow Creek massacre, April 1774, in which members of his family were killed. More successful in his retaliatory raids against the settlements than were Cornstalk and his warriors, Logan refused to become reconciled after the battle of Point Pleasant, November 1774. During the Revolution he was active on behalf of the British at Detroit. He became famous through Jefferson's use (in *Notes, on the State of Virginia,* edition of 1800) of an alleged reply which he made to John Gibson and from extensive newspaper quotation of the speech prior to this publication.

LOGAN, JAMES HARVEY (*b. near Rockville, Ind., 1841; d. Oakland, Calif., 1928*), California jurist, horticulturist. Developed the loganberry *c.* 1881.

LOGAN, JOHN ALEXANDER (*b. Jackson Co., Ill., 1826; d. Washington, D.C., 1886*), lawyer, Union soldier, politician. Congressman, Democrat, from Illinois, 1859–61. Entering the Civil War as colonel, 31st Illinois, he was made brigadier-general after Fort Donelson and major-general after Vicksburg, and succeeded to command of the Army of the Tennessee, 1864. Relieved of this command on recommendation of Gen. W. T. Sherman because of what Sherman termed his active political interests and his contempt for logistics, Logan, after discharge from the army, 1865, returned to political life, serving as congressman, Republican, from Illinois, 1867–71, and as U.S. senator, 1871–77 and 1879–86. He ran as Republican

candidate for the vice-presidency, 1884. A regulation stalwart Republican, he associated himself with all matters of veteran relief; the idea of Memorial Day was conceived by him and he inaugurated it, May 30, 1868.

LOGAN, OLIVE (*b. Elmira, N.Y., 1839; d. Banstead, England, 1909*), actress, lecturer, journalist. Daughter of Cornelius Ambrosius Logan; sister of Cornelius Ambrose Logan.

LOGAN, STEPHEN TRIGG (*b. Franklin Co., Ky., 1800; d. Springfield, Ill., 1880*), jurist, Illinois legislator. Grandnephew of Benjamin Logan. Removed to Springfield, Ill., *c.* 1833; was law partner of Abraham Lincoln, 1841–44.

LOGAN, THOMAS MULDRUP (*b. Charleston, S.C., 1808; d. Sacramento, Calif., 1876*), sanitarian, climatologist. M.D., Medical College of South Carolina, 1828. Practiced in Charleston and in New Orleans, La., before removing to Sacramento, Calif., 1850. Active in public health work, he made complete studies of the epidemiology of California.

LOGAN, THOMAS MULDRUP (*b. Charleston, S.C., 1840; d. New York, N.Y., 1914*), Confederate brigadier-general, lawyer, capitalist. Nephew of Thomas M. Logan (1808–1876). *Post* 1878, organized and managed a railway system in the South which adopted its present name, the Southern Railway, 1894. Worked for many years on development and promotion of the telautograph.

LOGUEN, JERMAIN WESLEY (*b. Davidson Co., Tenn., c. 1813; d. Saratoga Springs, N.Y., 1872*), Negro leader. Escaped from slavery, *c.* 1835, to Canada where he began his education. Settling in Syracuse, N.Y., *c.* 1840, he became one of the local managers of the Underground Railroad; he was an associate of Gerrit Smith and John Brown. Loguen held several pastorates in the African Methodist Episcopal Zion Church and was elected a bishop, 1868.

LOMAX, JOHN TAYLOE (*b. Caroline Co., Va., 1781; d. Fredericksburg, Va., 1862*), Virginia jurist. First professor of law at University of Virginia, 1826–30; later a judge of the state circuit court.

LOMAX, LUNSFORD LINDSAY (*b. Newport, R.I., 1835; d. Washington, D.C., 1913*), Confederate major-general. Graduated West Point, 1856. After hard and effective Civil War service, he was a farmer near Warrenton, Va., 1865–85, and president of Virginia Agricultural and Mechanical College, 1885–99. He worked on the compilation of official records of the Union and Confederate Armies (published as *War of the Rebellion* by the War Department), 1899–1905.

LOMBARD, WARREN PLIMPTON (*b. West Newton, Mass., 1855; d. Ann Arbor, Mich., 1939*), physiologist. Graduated Harvard, 1878; M.D., Harvard, 1881. Taught at Columbia and Clark universities, and at University of Michigan, 1892–1923. Made important studies of the knee-jerk reflex, of fatigue, blood pressure and metabolism; devised special apparatus for delicate measurements. [*Supp. 2*]

LONDON, JACK (*b. San Francisco, Calif., 1876; d. Sonoma Co., Calif., 1916*), writer, novelist. Spent his youth in acute poverty; read voraciously in public library but had major part of his education along the Oakland waterfront. Worked successively, when he did work, as seaman aboard a sealing vessel, as a jute mill hand and as a janitor; was for a while a hobo, at which time he roamed over eastern part of the United States. Returning to Oakland, he attended high school, became a Socialist, spent a brief time at University of California, Berkeley. During 1897–98, he joined the gold rush to the Klondike. On his return, unable to get a job of any sort, he worked furiously at writing and was successful in selling a story of the Yukon to the *Overland Monthly*, December 1898. During the next year he published eight stories in the magazine. Acceptance by the *Atlantic Monthly* of "An Odyssey of the North" in July 1899 and publication of his volume of collected stories, *The Son of the Wolf* (1900), convinced London that he now had his vocation. Between 1899 and 1903, he wrote extensively and successfully for periodicals. He also published eight volumes, five of which dealt with the Klondike. In Europe briefly, 1902, he was engaged January–June 1904 as a correspondent in the Russo-Japanese War. Thereafter, except for a long cruise in the South Seas, California was his home and his ranch his chief interest. His vast output of some fifty books contains, besides fiction, volumes of Socialist propaganda and miscellaneous essays. Several of his books are autobiographical: *The Road* (1907), *Martin Eden* (1909) and *John Barleycorn* (1913). The best of his fiction is for the most part taken direct from firsthand experience, either in the Far North or at sea. Almost all his writing, masterful in swift and vivid depiction of action, deals with the primitive and reversion to savagery. His insistence is constant upon the importance of brute force. *The Call of the Wild* (1903), *The Sea Wolf* (1904), *White Fang* (1906), together with the works already cited, are representative of London's work.

LONDON, MEYER (*b. Suwalki Province, Russian Poland, 1871; d. New York, N.Y., 1926*), Socialist, labor leader. Emigrated to New York City, 1891. Admitted to the bar, 1898. Opposing Socialist leadership of Daniel DeLeon, London became one of the founders of the Socialist Party of America. His activity as legal counsel and adviser to unions in the "needle trades" made his influence felt in the entire labor movement. Congressman, Socialist, from New York, 1915–19 and 1921–23, he advocated numerous useful reforms, but was consistent with his principles in voting against the declaration of war, 1917, and the conscription laws. An enemy to communism in theory

and practice, he vigorously denounced the allied policy towards Russia immediately after the Russian Revolution on grounds that it had rallied the Russian people to support of the Bolshevists.

LONESOME CHARLEY. [See REYNOLDS, CHARLES ALEXANDER, *c. 1842–1876.*]

LONG, ARMISTEAD LINDSAY (*b. Campbell Co., Va., 1825; d. Charlottesville, Va., 1891*), Confederate brigadier-general. Graduated West Point, 1850. Served as military secretary to Gen. Robert E. Lee, 1861–63, and as brigadier-general, commanding artillery, 1863–65. Author of *Memoirs of Robert E. Lee* (1886), a valuable source book.

LONG, CHARLES CHAILLÉ. [See CHAILLÉ-LONG, CHARLES, *1842–1917.*]

LONG, CRAWFORD WILLIAMSON (*b. Danielsville, Ga., 1815; d. Athens, Ga., 1878*), surgeon, pioneer anaesthetist. Graduated Franklin College (University of Georgia), 1835; M.D., University of Pennsylvania, 1839. Practiced *post* 1841 in rural Georgia, removing in 1850 to Athens, Ga. Performed eight operations with the help of sulphuric ether *ante* September 1846, the earliest in 1842. He did not publish his experience with ether, however, until December 1849, when a controversy had already arisen over the claims of W. T. G. Morton to priority in anaesthesia.

LONG, HUEY PIERCE (*b. near Winnfield, La., 1893; d. Baton Rouge, La., 1935*), politician. Son of a landowning farmer, Long came from a culturally meager background, which was most strongly marked by Baptist evangelicalism and a Populistic animosity toward the wealthy. In his early career as a traveling salesman, he acquired canvassing experience which was later to be a political advantage. After eight months of study at Tulane University Law School, he passed a special bar examination, May 1915, and began practice at Winnfield. Elected railroad commissioner, 1918, he was re-elected, 1924, and served as chairman of the Louisiana commission now known as the Public Service Commission, 1921–26. In this post he performed highly creditable services in control of utilities and attracted widespread attention by furious attacks upon the Standard Oil Co.

Defeated for governorship in 1924, Long renewed his candidacy in 1928, and became governor in May of that year. As governor, he aroused violent opposition. Charges of improper influence upon legislators through patronage and the use of state funds for personal expenditures brought about his impeachment at a special session of the legislature, 1929. He escaped conviction on a technicality, meanwhile claiming that he was being persecuted by Standard Oil. Between 1930 and 1934, Long ruled Louisiana by an alliance with the old regular Democrats. Retaining the governorship after his 1930 election as U.S. senator, in order to prevent succession of a hostile lieutenant-governor, he expanded his highway program, began construction of a $5,000,000 capitol and sponsored the growth of Louisiana State University. He entered the U.S. Senate, January 1932. Appearing to many Americans primarily a country clown who carried out his nickname "Kingfish," Long brought with him a serious program for the redistribution of wealth; when the Senate rejected drastic tax proposals, he resigned his committee posts in rebellion against the Democratic leader, Joseph T. Robinson. Pres. F. D. Roosevelt's refusal to support Long's proposed redistribution of wealth or to satisfy his expectations of patronage caused Long loudly to denounce Roosevelt by August 1933, although he had campaigned for him a year earlier.

By January 1934, in disfavor with the federal administration and having lost the support of the old regular Democratic machine in Louisiana, Long brought about a reorganization of the Louisiana legislature whereby he created the most complete absolutism that has ever existed in a state of the United States. Local government was abolished and Long was given control of the appointment of every employee in the state, of the militia, of the judiciary, the election officials and the tax-assessing bodies. To his decrees there was no redress, either electoral or legal. In January 1934, he organized a Share-Our-Wealth Society which promised homestead allowances and minimum annual income for every American family. This economically fallacious scheme he used as a goad for the administration in Washington, declaring in 1935 that he would bolt the party if Roosevelt were renominated and announcing his own candidacy in August of that year. On a visit to the Louisiana state capitol in the fall for a special session of his legislature, despite the constant protection of bodyguards, he was shot by Dr. Carl A. Weiss on the night of Sept. 8 and died two days later.

Ruthless, violent and unprincipled, Long was possibly emotionally sincere in championing the cause of the underdog. Flagrantly corrupt, his campaign for the improvement of Louisiana was administered with relative efficiency. His rise was aided by the ineffectuality of his opponents who might have been more polite but were certainly not more ethical than he. He found his opportunity as spokesman of a long-standing agrarian discontent that flared up in the ill wind of the great depression. [Supp. 1]

LONG, JAMES (*b. North (?) Carolina, c. 1793; d. Mexico, 1822*), military adventurer. Attempted to open Texas to American settlement, 1819. Proclaimed a republic at Nacogdoches with himself as president and commander-in-chief, June 23. After a period of military alliance with Mexican revolutionary leaders, he was killed while on a visit of negotiation to Mexico City.

LONG, JOHN DAVIS (*b. Buckfield, Maine, 1838; d. Hingham, Mass., 1915*), lawyer, Massachusetts legislator. Republican governor of Massachusetts, 1880–

82; congressman, 1883–89. Appointed secretary of the navy, 1897, he served until 1902 with tact and ability; here as in his governorship he showed himself an efficient if unspectacular administrator.

LONG, JOHN HARPER (*b. near Steubenville, O., 1856; d. 1918*), chemist. Graduated University of Kansas, 1877; studied chemistry in Germany, receiving D.Sc., 1879, from Tübingen. Professor of chemistry, Northwestern University, *post* 1881. Did extensive work on treatment of sewage and on the influence on health of alum, sodium benzoate and other adulterants. This latter work was of great benefit in administration of the later Food and Drugs Act. He was author of many textbooks and research papers.

LONG, JOHN LUTHER (*b. Hanover, Pa., 1861; d. Philadelphia, Pa., 1927*), writer, dramatist. His short story "Madame Butterfly" (*Century Magazine,* January 1898) was basis for David Belasco's dramatization (produced, March 1900) and for the libretto of Puccini's opera.

LONG, JOSEPH RAGLAND (*b. Charlottesville, Va., 1870; d. Boulder, Colo., 1932*), lawyer, legal writer. Professor of law, Washington and Lee University, 1902–23; University of Colorado, 1923–32.

[Supp. 1]

LONG, STEPHEN HARRIMAN (*b. Hopkinton, N.H., 1784; d. Alton, Ill., 1864*), explorer, engineer. Graduated Dartmouth, 1809. Entered army as second lieutenant of engineers, 1814, and continued with the topographical engineers throughout remainder of his life, becoming chief of the corps and colonel, 1861. Commanding an expedition to the Rocky Mountains, 1820, he discovered the peak which bears his name, journeyed south to neighborhood of Colorado Springs, headed east by way of the Arkansas and its tributaries. *Account of an Expedition from Pittsburgh to the Rocky Mountains* (1822–23) by Edwin James contains a vivid narrative of the journey. In 1823, Long examined the sources of the Minnesota River and the adjacent northern boundary of the United States, as described in *Narrative of an Expedition to the Source of the St. Peter's River, etc.* (1824) by W. H. Keating. Thereafter, Long worked as consulting engineer for various railroad enterprises; in association with Jonathan Knight, he selected the route for the Baltimore & Ohio.

LONGACRE, JAMES BARTON (*b. Delaware Co., Pa., 1794; d. Philadelphia, Pa., 1869*), line and stipple engraver. His chief work is found in the series of volumes entitled *The National Portrait Gallery of Distinguished Americans* (published 1834–39 in association with James Herring). He was chief engraver, U.S. Mint, *post* 1844.

LONGFELLOW, ERNEST WADSWORTH (*b. Cambridge, Mass., 1845; d. Boston, Mass., 1921*), painter. Son of Henry Wadsworth Longfellow.

LONGFELLOW, HENRY WADSWORTH (*b. Portland, Maine, 1807; d. Cambridge, Mass., 1882*), poet. Son of Stephen Longfellow; grandson of Peleg Wadsworth. Published verses as early as his 13th year. Graduated Bowdoin, 1825. Offered professorship of modern languages at Bowdoin on condition he study abroad, he spent years 1826–29 in France, Spain, Italy and Germany. While professor at Bowdoin, 1829–35, he prepared textbooks and contributed essays and sketches to magazines. He married Mary S. Potter, September 1831; she died four years later. Having accepted professorship of modern languages and belles-lettres at Harvard, 1835, Longfellow went abroad and made extensive study of German literature before returning home, 1836. Taking up residence in the Craigie House, Cambridge, he worked hard at his teaching but went much into society, an immaculate jaunty figure. Among his friends were Cornelius C. Felton, Charles Sumner, George S. Hillard; *post* 1837, his relations with Nathaniel Hawthorne were increasingly friendly. Published *Hyperion*, a semi-autobiographical romance, 1839; also, *Voices of the Night*, his first book of verse, in the same year.

In July 1843, he married Frances Elizabeth Appleton, daughter of a Boston merchant. For a number of years thereafter his outward life flowed on pleasantly and placidly; he resigned his professorship, 1854, giving his whole time to study and work in poetry. The tragic death of his wife, July 1861, left the care and upbringing of their six children to him. His grief over his loss persisted for many years, during which he continued to work and to achieve an international reputation which few poets have won. The gentleness and sweetness of Longfellow's character have always received due emphasis, although he was afflicted lifelong with an extreme nervous sensibility. He worked steadily so far as moods allowed and with a conscientious craftsmanship; he could never "twang off a lyric" at will or mechanically grind out a long poem. Longfellow's writings belong to the Romantic Movement in its milder phases; they have nothing of the storm-and-stress mood except in *Hyperion*. Except for the abolition of slavery (which inspired his *Poems on Slavery*, 1842), social reforms did not much interest him. His unspeculative nature and his Unitarian faith combined to save him alike from the theological struggles of his contemporaries Tennyson and Arnold, and from the paganism of Swinburne. His technical indebtedness to Goldsmith and Keats is plain, but the example of Wordsworth may have quickened his sympathy with common men and women. The strongest single foreign influence on him was that of Goethe and the German romantic lyrists; his use of hexameters, an innovation in American verse, was doubtless due to their success in German narrative poems. When Longfellow fails as a poet it is usually because he has turned to preaching in verse or because he insists on pinning a moral to an incident or a portrait which requires none. His nature poetry is often purely sensuous; his sea poems have a rare felicity and his ballads are spirited. Of all his contributions to our culture, his interpretation of the Old World to the New is perhaps his greatest. His long poems are too often "literary" and smell of the library, but the pictures of American life in his popular short poems are truthful and vivid. His later poems have much more merit than is commonly recognized; the thought is broader and maturer, the style often has more distinction and strength. Longfellow was particularly effective in the sonnet form. Among the many books which he published during his lifetime, the principal are: *Hyperion* (1839), *Voices of the Night* (1839), *Ballads and Other Poems* (1842), *Evangeline* (1847), *The Song of Hiawatha* (1855), *The Courtship of Miles Standish* (1858), *Tales of a Wayside Inn* (1863), *The Divine Comedy of Dante Alighieri* (a translation, issued 1865–67), *Kéramos and Other Poems* (1878), *Ultima Thule* (1880), *In the Harbor* (1882).

LONGFELLOW, SAMUEL (*b. Portland, Maine, 1819; d. Portland, 1892*), Unitarian clergyman, teacher. Son of Stephen Longfellow; brother of Henry Wadsworth Longfellow, whose biography he wrote (published, 1886–87).

LONGFELLOW, STEPHEN (*b. Gorham, Maine, 1776; d. 1849*), lawyer, Massachusetts legislator. Graduated Harvard, 1798. Father of Henry Wadsworth and Samuel Longfellow.

LONGFELLOW, WILLIAM PITT PREBLE (*b. Portland, Maine, 1836; d. East Gloucester, Mass., 1913*), architect, writer on architecture. Nephew of Henry Wadsworth Longfellow.

LONGLEY, ALCANDER (*b. Oxford, O., 1832; d. Chicago, Ill., 1918*), printer, social reformer. Early adopted Fourieristic ideas. After several attempts to organize utopian colonies along the line of cooperatives, he turned to communism and made five essays at establishing a Communist society in Missouri, 1868–85. He publicized his program in *The Communist*, published irregularly *post* 1868; its name was changed to *The Altruist*, 1885, and he continued its publication until 1917.

LONGSTREET, AUGUSTUS BALDWIN (*b. Augusta, Ga., 1790; d. Oxford, Miss., 1870*), lawyer, Methodist clergyman, educator. Son of William Longstreet; uncle of James Longstreet. Published anonymously a series of sketches called "Georgia Scenes" in Milledgeville and Augusta newspapers *post* 1827. Humorous, often crudely realistic, and dealing with life in Georgia as Longstreet knew it, the sketches were at once widely popular and are among the earliest examples in America of the humor later manifested by Mark Twain, Bret Harte and Joel C. Harris. They appeared in book form, still anonymously, at Augusta, 1835; in 1840 a New York edition appeared under the author's name. Longstreet served as president, Emory College, 1839–48; of Centenary College, Louisiana, 1849; of University of Mississippi, 1849–56; of University of South Carolina, 1857–65. A vigorous proponent of secession, the actuality of the Civil War dismayed him, although he wrote extensively *post* 1865 to prove that the South had always been right and the North always wrong.

LONGSTREET, JAMES (*b. Edgefield District, S.C., 1821; d. Gainesville, Ga., 1904*), soldier. Nephew of Augustus B. Longstreet. Graduated West Point, 1842; saw action in Mexican War with Zachary Taylor until after battle of Monterrey; served then with Scott in campaign against Mexico City. Commissioned Confederate brigadier-general, 1861, his excellent leadership at first battle of Bull Run brought him promotion to major-general and command of a division under J. E. Johnston. He enhanced his prestige at Yorktown and Williamsburg, but diminished it by tardiness at Seven Pines. During the Seven Days' Battles, June–July 1862, he won R. E. Lee's entire confidence.

At the second battle of Bull Run, Longstreet maneuvered well but delayed a day in taking the offensive. Examined in detail, his reasons for the delay are defensible and may be valid, but his general attitude showed for the first time the greatest defect of his military character. Though he was vigorous and effective when his judgment approved the plans of his superior, he was slow to yield his own opinions and equally slow to move when he thought his commander's course was wrong. Fighting well at Antietam, he failed to impress in his first semi-independent command southeast of Richmond, and was not present at Chancellorsville. The reasons for Confederate defeat at Gettysburg will be long argued but Longstreet's delays on July 2 and 3, 1863, were certainly among them. After further service in Georgia and Tennessee, he returned to Virginia in April 1864 and executed excellent defensive fighting during the last year of the war.

Longstreet prospered in business for a time after the war. Ostracized socially when he became a Republican, for 35 years he held a series of federal political appointments. His differences with Lee, the Southern idol, and the claims made in *From Manassas to Appomattox* (1896), his military autobiography, brought him much unpopularity in the South. He had military weaknesses, but excelled as a combat officer and was an almost ideal corps commander.

LONGSTREET, WILLIAM (*b. near Allentown, N.J., 1759; d. Augusta, Ga., 1814*), inventor. Experimented with a steam engine *c.* 1780; adapted it to operate cotton gins, sawmills and boats in Georgia, *post* 1788.

LONGWORTH, NICHOLAS (*b. Newark, N.J., 1782; d. 1863*), lawyer, landowner, horticulturist. Settled in Cincinnati, O., *c.* 1803. His practice of accepting land for legal fees brought him great wealth in time. He devoted himself *post* 1828 to grape culture and wine

manufacture; he also introduced new varieties of the strawberry and the raspberry.

LONGWORTH, NICHOLAS (*b. Cincinnati, O., 1869; d. 1931*), lawyer, Ohio legislator. Great-grandson of Nicholas Longworth (1782–1863). Graduated Harvard, 1891. Congressman, Republican, from Ohio, 1909–13, 1915–31; Republican floor leader of the House, 1923–25, and speaker, 1925–31. A strong protectionist and a partisan Republican, he served as speaker with complete fairness and tact. He married Alice Roosevelt, daughter of Theodore Roosevelt, February 1906.

LONGYEAR, JOHN MUNROE (*b. Lansing, Mich., 1850; d. 1922*), surveyor, capitalist. Best known for his part in opening and developing the Menominee and Gogebic iron ranges and for his promotion of the "Longyear Process" for using low-grade ores.

LOOMIS, ARPHAXED (*b. Winchester, Conn., 1798; d. 1885*), lawyer, New York legislator. A member, with David Graham and David D. Field, of the N.Y. commission for legal reform which produced Code of Civil Procedure, effective July 1848.

LOOMIS, CHARLES BATTELL (*b. Brooklyn, N.Y., 1861; d. Hartford, Conn., 1911*), journalist, humorous lecturer.

LOOMIS, DWIGHT (*b. Columbia, Conn., 1821; d. near Waterbury, Conn., 1903*), lawyer, Connecticut legislator and congressman. Judge, superior court of Connecticut, 1864–75; supreme court of errors, 1875–91. Served thereafter as state referee.

LOOMIS, ELIAS (*b. Connecticut, 1811; d. New Haven, Conn., 1889*), mathematician, astronomer, benefactor of Yale. Graduated Yale, 1830. Taught at Yale, Western Reserve, Princeton, New York University; exerted his greatest influence through excellent textbooks on natural philosophy, astronomy, the calculus and other subjects.

LOOMIS, ELMER HOWARD (*b. Vermillion, N.Y., 1861; d. 1931*), physicist. Graduated Madison (now Colgate) University, 1883; Ph.D., University of Strassburg, 1893. Taught physics at Princeton, 1894–1929.

LOOMIS, MAHLON (*b. Oppenheim, N.Y., 1826; d. Terre Alta, W. Va., 1886*), dentist. *Post* 1860, experimented with electricity; carried on two-way communication without wires for distance of 18 miles between two mountains in Virginia, 1868. Unable to find financial backing for exploitation of his device, he died in distress.

LOOP, HENRY AUGUSTUS (*b. Hillsdale, N.Y., 1831; d. Lake George, N.Y., 1895*), portrait and figure painter. Studied in New York City under Henry P. Gray; *post* 1857 studied in Paris under Thomas Couture. Worked in New York City *post* 1860.

LOOS, CHARLES LOUIS (*b. Woerth-sur-Sauer, Lower Alsace, France, 1823; d. 1912*), clergyman of the Disciples of Christ, educator. Came to America as a boy; raised in Ohio. Graduated Bethany College, 1846. Held several pastorates; taught at Bethany, 1858–80; president of Kentucky University, 1880–97.

LOPEZ, AARON (*b. Portugal, 1731; d. near Providence, R.I., 1782*), colonial merchant. Emigrated to Newport, R.I., 1752. Prospering in the coastwise and West Indies trade, by 1775 he had interest in over thirty ships.

LORAS, JEAN MATHIAS PIERRE (*b. Lyons, France, 1792; d. 1858*), Roman Catholic clergyman. A seminary professor and president in France, he came to America, 1829, and served seven years in the diocese of Mobile, Ala. Consecrated bishop of Dubuque, 1837, he administered the new diocese, which reached then from the northern boundary of Missouri to Canada and from the Mississippi River to the Missouri, with great ability and devotion.

LORD, ASA DEARBORN (*b. Madrid, N.Y., 1816; d. Batavia, N.Y., 1875*), teacher, educational leader. Superintendent of schools, Columbus, O., 1847–56; organized first public high school in Columbus; published a variety of educational journals. *Post* 1856, specialized in education of the blind.

LORD, CHESTER SANDERS (*b. Romulus, N.Y., 1850; d. Garden City, N.Y., 1933*), editor, educator. Associated *post* 1872 with New York *Sun*, Lord received editorial training from Charles A. Dana and became managing editor of the newspaper, 1881. Except for a brief period, he continued at this post until his retirement, 1913. Selecting his staff with scrupulous care, he built up a group of brilliant writers who were particularly effective in reporting human interest features of any story and "making literature out of news." Under Lord, the *Sun* became a pioneer school of journalism whose graduates were accepted anywhere. As a regent of the University of the State of New York, 1897–1904, 1909–21, and as chancellor *post* 1921, he played an important part in shaping and supervising New York educational policies.

[*Supp. 1*]

LORD, DANIEL (*b. Stonington, Conn., 1795; d. 1868*), lawyer. Beginning as an attorney for the first John Jacob Astor, he became the favorite counsel of influential New York businessmen.

LORD, DAVID NEVINS (*b. Franklin, Conn., 1792; d. 1880*), New York merchant, theologian. Brother of Eleazar Lord.

LORD, ELEAZAR (*b. Franklin, Conn., 1788; d. Piermont, N.Y., 1871*), businessman, author of books on currency and banking, theological writer. Brother of David N. Lord. President of the Erie Railroad, 1833, 1839–41, 1844–45; lobbyist for the protective tariff.

LORD, HENRY CURWEN (*b. Cincinnati, O., 1866; d. 1925*), astronomer. Grandson of Nathan Lord. Grad-

uated University of Wisconsin, 1889. Long associated with Ohio State University and with its observatory.

LORD, HERBERT MAYHEW (*b. Rockland, Maine, 1859; d. Washington, D.C., 1930*), financial administrator. Director and chief of finance for U.S. War Department, 1917–22; director of the budget, 1922–29.

LORD, JOHN (*b. Portsmouth, N.H., 1810; d. Stamford, Conn., 1894*), historical lecturer. Nephew of Nathan Lord. Graduated Dartmouth, 1833. Author of a number of books of which *Beacon Lights of History* (a series, 1884–96) are the best known.

LORD, NATHAN (*b. So. Berwick, Maine, 1792; d. 1870*), Congregational clergyman, educator. Graduated Bowdoin, 1809; Andover Theological Seminary, 1815. Pastor at Amherst, N.H., 1816–28; president of Dartmouth, 1828–63. An able executive and disciplinarian, he stood for ideas and attitudes which were rapidly passing. His support of slavery as a divinely ordained institution not to be questioned brought him widespread censure and compelled his resignation from office.

LORD, OTIS PHILLIPS (*b. Ipswich, Mass., 1812; d. 1884*), lawyer, Massachusetts Whig legislator, jurist.

LORD, WILLIAM PAINE (*b. Dover, Del., 1839; d. 1911*), lawyer, Union soldier, Oregon jurist. Settled in Salem, Oreg., 1868. Served as justice, state supreme court, 1880–94; Republican governor of Oregon, 1895–99. U.S. minister to the Argentine Republic, 1899–1902. Compiled *Lord's Oregon Laws* (1910).

LORD, WILLIAM WILBERFORCE (*b. Madison Co., N.Y., 1819; d. New York, N.Y., 1907*), Episcopal clergyman, Confederate chaplain. Held several pastorates in the South, notably rectorate of Christ Church, Vicksburg, Miss., 1854–63.

LOREE, LEONOR FRESNEL (*b. Fulton City, Ill., 1858; d. West Orange, N.J., 1940*), railroad executive. President, Baltimore & Ohio Railroad, 1901–03; president, Delaware and Hudson Company, 1907–38.

[*Supp. 2*]

LORILLARD, PIERRE (*b. New York, N.Y., 1833; d. New York, 1901*), merchant, breeder of race horses, developer of Tuxedo Park, N.Y.

LORIMER, GEORGE CLAUDE (*b. Edinburgh, Scotland, 1838; d. Aix-les-Bains, France, 1904*), Baptist clergyman. Came to America as an actor *c.* 1855. Highly effective as preacher and pastor, notably at Tremont Temple, Boston, Mass., 1873–79 and 1891–1901.

LORIMER, GEORGE HORACE (*b. Louisville, Ky., 1867; d. Wyncote, Pa., 1937*), editor. Became literary editor, 1898, of the *Saturday Evening Post*, "an elderly and indisposed magazine" which had just been purchased by Cyrus H. K. Curtis. As editor-in-chief, 1899–1936, Lorimer made the *Post* an extraordinarily successful magazine, interpreting the America of his time to Americans, with a particular accent on conservatism and the role of business. By his policy of prompt decision and payment on acceptance, he attracted a great variety of first-rate writers of fiction and discovered many new talents. [*Supp.* 2]

LORIMER, WILLIAM (*b. Manchester, England, 1861; d. Chicago, Ill., 1934*), Illinois political boss. Came to America as a child. Adept at political organization, Lorimer cultivated the immigrant population of Cook County and became a power in the state Republican party; he was elected congressman, 1894, re-elected in 1896 and 1898 and after a defeat in 1900, served from 1903 until 1909. Chosen U.S. senator by the Illinois legislature, 1909, he was accused, 1910, of obtaining his seat by corrupt means and ousted, July 1912, after a series of investigations which substantiated the charge. [*Supp.* 1]

LORIMIER, PIERRE LOUIS (*b. Lachine, Canada, 1748; d. 1812*), Indian trader. Established at a post in the present Shelby Co., O., *post* 1769, he led Shawnee and Delaware Indians against American frontiers during Revolutionary War. Settled near present St. Mary's, Mo., 1787. Founded town of Cape Girardeau, Mo., 1808.

LORING, CHARLES HARDING (*b. Boston, Mass., 1828; d. Hackettstown, N.J., 1907*), naval officer. Holding rank of chief engineer, 1861, he was made fleet engineer on North Atlantic station; later became inspector of iron-clad steamers under construction, which included supervision over "monitors." A report in whose preparation he shared brought about abandonment of wooden naval ships, 1881. Appointed U.S. Navy engineer-in-chief, with rank of rear-admiral, 1884, he resigned in the following year.

LORING, CHARLES MORGRIDGE (*b. Portland, Maine, 1832; d. Minneapolis, Minn., 1922*), businessman. Removing to Minneapolis, Minn., 1860, he became nationally known as a worker for civic betterment through his planning of parks and playgrounds in that city *post* 1864.

LORING, EDWARD GREELY (*b. Boston, Mass., 1837; d. New York, N.Y., 1888*), ophthalmologist. Began study of medicine, 1859, in Italy; M.D., Harvard Medical School, 1864. Practiced mainly in New York. His greatest contribution to medicine was his improvement of the ophthalmoscope; he brought out the first practical instrument of the type, *c.* 1869, and a further improved form of it, 1874. He was author of *A Text Book on Ophthalmoscopy* (1886, 1891).

LORING, ELLIS GRAY (*b. Boston, Mass., 1803; d. 1858,*) Boston lawyer, anti-slavery advocate, liberal.

LORING, FREDERICK WADSWORTH (*b. Boston, Mass., 1848; d. 1871*), journalist. Graduated Harvard, 1870. As correspondent for *Appletons' Journal*, 1871, Loring was killed by Apaches between Wickenburg

and La Paz, Ariz., while returning from his coverage of the Wheeler Expedition.

LORING, GEORGE BAILEY (*b. No. Andover, Mass., 1817; d. 1891*), physician, Massachusetts legislator. Congressman, Republican, from Massachusetts, 1877–81; served with intelligent ability as U.S. commissioner of agriculture, 1881–85. Founded New England Agricultural Society, 1864, and served as its president until 1889. U.S. minister to Portugal, 1889–90.

LORING, JOSHUA (*b. Boston, Mass., 1716; d. Highgate, England, 1781*), Loyalist, captain in British navy. Commanded operations on Lakes George, Champlain and Ontario, 1759–60; participated in capture of Quebec and subsequent conquest of Canada. Removed to England after evacuation of Boston, 1776.

LORING, JOSHUA (*b. Hingham, Mass., 1744; d. Berkshire, England, 1789*), Loyalist. Son of Joshua Loring (1716–1781). After service in the army, 1761–68, he held various offices under the Crown and was one of the addressers to Gov. Hutchinson and Gen. Gage. Appointed vendue-master and auctioneer, October 1775, Loring went with the Royal army to Halifax, March 1776; appointed British commissary of prisoners early in 1777, he made himself detested by the colonial leaders who charged him with excessive cruelty. Banished from Massachusetts, he spent the last years of his life in England.

LORING, WILLIAM WING (*b. Wilmington, N.C., 1818; d. New York, N.Y., 1886*), soldier. Raised in Florida. Served against Seminoles and with distinction as commander of the Mounted Rifles in campaign from Vera Cruz to Mexico City, 1847. He also commanded the 1849 march of the Mounted Rifles to Oregon and headed the Oregon department, 1849–51. After service in Texas and New Mexico and in the Mormon Expedition, 1858–59, he resigned from the army, 1861, and was commissioned brigadier-general in the Confederate service. Promoted to major-general, 1862, he served as a corps commander in Georgia, Mississippi and Tennessee; in April 1865, serving under Gen. J. E. Johnston in the Carolinas, he surrendered to W. T. Sherman. Entering the army of the Khedive of Egypt, 1869, as brigadier-general, he rose to rank of general of division and Pasha before mustering out, 1879, and returning to the United States.

LOSKIEL, GEORGE HENRY (*b. Angermuende, Courland, Russia, 1740; d. Bethlehem, Pa., 1814*), bishop of the Moravian Church. Consecrated bishop, 1802, he came to Bethlehem, Pa., in that year to take charge of the work of the Church in North America. He was first of Moravian bishops to strive for Americanization and a separate polity from the European establishment.

LOSSING, BENSON JOHN (*b. Beekman, N.Y., 1813; d. 1891*), wood engraver, author. A prolific writer and editor of popular books on American history, among them the *Pictorial Field Book of the Revolution* (1850–52) and the *Pictorial Field Book of the War of 1812* (1868).

LOTHROP, ALICE LOUISE HIGGINS (*b. Boston, Mass., 1870; d. Newtonville, Mass., 1920*), social worker, expert in disaster relief.

LOTHROP, DANIEL (*b. Rochester, N.H., 1831; d. 1892*), publisher. Established D. Lothrop & Co., 1868, at Boston, Mass. Specialized in juvenile books and periodicals; founded *Wide Awake* (1875).

LOTHROP, GEORGE VAN NESS (*b. Easton, Mass., 1817; d. Detroit, Mich., 1897*), lawyer. Removed to Michigan, 1839; practiced in Detroit. U.S. minister to Russia, 1885–88.

LOTHROP, HARRIETT MULFORD STONE (*b. New Haven, Conn., 1844; d. San Francisco, Calif., 1924*), author of books for children under pen-name "Margaret Sidney." Married Daniel Lothrop, 1881. Of her many works, *Five Little Peppers and How They Grew* (1881) was the most popular.

LOTHROPP, JOHN (*b. Yorkshire, England, 1584; d. Barnstable, Mass., 1653*), Nonconformist clergyman. Came to New England, 1634. Served as pastor at Scituate, 1635–39, and thereafter at Barnstable, Mass.

LOTTA [See CRABTREE, CHARLOTTE, 1847–1924.]

LOUCKS, HENRY LANGFORD (*b. Hull, Canada, 1846; d. Clearlake, S. Dak., 1928*), agrarian politician. Homesteaded, 1884, in Deuel Co., Dakota Territory. Active in reform movements on behalf of farmers of his section, he organized them into the Independent political party (later identified with the Populist party) which played an important part in South Dakota and national politics *post* 1890. He was a leader in the National Farmers' Alliance and a strong advocate of temperance.

LOUDON, SAMUEL (*b. probably Ireland, c. 1727; d. near Middletown Point, N.J., 1813*), merchant, printer. Came to America *ante* 1753. Published *The New York Packet* (January 1776–August 1776) at New York City, and (January 1777–1783) at Fishkill, N.Y. As state printer, he printed first New York State constitution (Fishkill, 1777); also several issues of state paper money. When the British removed from New York City, he returned there and continued his printing business along with a bookshop and circulating library.

LOUDOUN, JOHN CAMPBELL, Fourth Earl of (*b. Loudoun Castle, Ayrshire, Scotland, 1705; d. Loudoun Castle, 1782*), British soldier. A veteran field officer and a major-general, he accepted the post of commander-in-chief of all forces in North America, January 1756, together with the sinecure post of governor-general of Virginia. He had a dual task: to mold the

British forces in North America into an efficient fighting unit and to unite the colonies in support of the war with France and her colonies (French and Indian War) then raging. Successful as a trainer of troops and organizer of military services, his insistence on his authority and his outbursts of temper alienated many colonial representatives. His military campaigns were completely unsuccessful and he was recalled, December 1757. He later commanded with better success in Portugal, 1762–63, and was promoted general in 1770.

LOUGHRIDGE, ROBERT McGILL (*b. Laurensville, S.C., 1809; d. Waco, Texas, 1900*), Presbyterian clergyman, educator. Raised in Alabama. Worked as a missionary among the Creek Indians, 1843–61 and 1881–88.

LOUNSBURY, THOMAS RAYNESFORD (*b. Ovid, N.Y., 1838; d. 1915*), Union soldier, educator, philologist. Graduated Yale, 1859. Professor of English, Sheffield Scientific School, 1871–1906. A brilliant and unconventional teacher, Lounsbury taught his students to recognize in literature the record of a life as real as their own. As a scholar, he was recognized internationally as a master in several fields of English language and literature; in the latter part of his career he showed an increasing interest in questions of spelling, pronunciation and usage. His scholarship was marked by common sense, regard for fact and an unshakable sense of values. Among his books were *History of the English Language* (1879, 1894, 1907); *James Fenimore Cooper* (1882); and *Studies in Chaucer* (1892), one of the most important works in its field to appear in the 19th century.

LOVE, ALFRED HENRY (*b. Philadelphia, Pa., 1830; d. 1913*), merchant, radical pacifist. Founded the Universal Peace Union, 1866, and served as its president until his death.

LOVE, EMANUEL KING (*b. near Marion, Ala., 1850; d. 1900*), Baptist clergyman. Graduated Augusta (Ga.) Institute, 1877. His most distinctive work and greatest influence came while pastor, First African Baptist Church, Savannah, Ga., 1885–1900. He was especially interested in securing liberal education for Negroes.

LOVE, ROBERTUS DONNELL (*b. near Irondale, Mo., 1867; d. St. Louis, Mo., 1930*), journalist. Author of *The Rise and Fall of Jesse James* (1926).

LOVEJOY, ASA LAWRENCE (*b. Groton, Mass., 1808; d. Portland, Oreg., 1882*), lawyer, Oregon legislator. Nephew of Abbott Lawrence. Visited Oregon, 1842; accompanied Marcus Whitman on his famous ride eastward, 1842–43. A founder of the city of Portland, Lovejoy was long active in Oregon public life after his settlement there in fall, 1843.

LOVEJOY, ELIJAH PARISH (*b. Albion, Maine, 1802; d. Alton, Ill., 1837*), Abolitionist martyr. Brother of Owen Lovejoy. After studying for the ministry, he served as editor of a Presbyterian weekly, the *St. Louis Observer*, 1833–36, making the paper a vehement voice against slavery, intemperance and "popery." St. Louis, Mo., river port for the lower South, was not the place for such a newspaper. Rather than moderate his tone, Lovejoy moved to Alton, Ill., 1836, and edited the *Alton Observer* as an active Abolitionist organ. Harassed by destruction of his printing press several times, Lovejoy was shot dead in defense of yet another press which had been sent him by the Ohio Anti-Slavery Society.

LOVEJOY, OWEN (*b. Albion, Maine, 1811; d. 1864*), Congregational clergyman, Abolitionist, Illinois legislator. Brother of Elijah P. Lovejoy. Urged Abraham Lincoln as early as 1854 to assume leadership of the new political movement which became the Republican party; remained Lincoln's loyal supporter and friend until his death. He served as congressman, Republican, from Illinois, 1857–64.

LOVELACE, FRANCIS (*b. England, c. 1621; d. probably Woodstock, England, 1675*), colonial governor. Brother of the English poet Richard Lovelace. Appointed governor of New York, 1667, he arrived in the colony, March 1668. A conscientious tolerant man, Lovelace interested himself in better transportation by land and by water and in regulation of trade. He instituted the first New York merchants' exchange and promoted shipbuilding; the first continuous post road between New York and Boston under a postmaster was one of his numerous innovations. While he was visiting in Connecticut, New York was retaken by a Dutch naval force, July–August 1673; held responsible for negligence in this matter, he was recalled and suffered persecution and imprisonment.

LOVELAND, WILLIAM AUSTIN HAMILTON (*b. Chatham, Mass., 1826; d. Lakeside, Colo., 1894*), merchant, Colorado legislator. After a wandering youth, he settled in Colorado, 1859, where he prospered as a merchant and real estate investor; he was also owner of the Denver *Rocky Mountain News*, promoter of the Colorado Central Railroad, and a leader in the Democratic party.

LOVELL, JAMES (*b. Boston, Mass., 1737; d. Windham, Maine, 1814*), schoolmaster, politician. Son of John Lovell. Graduated Harvard, 1756. Delivered first Boston Massacre oration, 1771; arrested as an American spy by the British, 1775, he spent a year as prisoner in Halifax. As delegate to the Continental Congress, 1777–82, he was a zealous partisan of Gen. Horatio Gates and a participant in the so-called Conway Cabal. He was also one of the congressional group which was opposed to Benjamin Franklin and Silas Deane. A useful member of Congress in many ways, and diligent in foreign affairs committee work, he was too fond of intrigue for its own sake. *Post* 1789, he served as naval officer for Boston district.

LOVELL, JOHN (*b. Boston, Mass., 1710; d. Halifax, Nova Scotia, 1778*), schoolmaster, Loyalist. Graduated Harvard, 1728. Master of the South Grammar or Latin School, Boston, 1734–75.

LOVELL, JOHN EPY (*b. Colne, England, 1795; d. Milwaukee, Wis., 1892*), educator. Came to America *ante* 1822, in which year he started a successful Lancasterian school in New Haven, Conn. He was author of a number of textbooks, in particular *The United States Speaker* (1833).

LOVELL, JOSEPH (*b. Boston, Mass., 1788; d. 1836*), surgeon. Grandson of James Lovell. Graduated Harvard, 1807; Harvard Medical School, 1811. Entering U.S. Army, 1812, as surgeon, 9th Infantry, he made a reputation in administration of hospitals. Appointed surgeon-general, 1818, on establishment of the army medical department, he held that office until his death. A man of vision and scholarship, he will be remembered for his aid to William Beaumont in the latter's study of gastric physiology and for his institution of a system of quarterly reports of weather and of the incidence of disease.

LOVELL, MANSFIELD (*b. Washington, D.C., 1822; d. 1884*), soldier, civil engineer. Son of Joseph Lovell. Graduated West Point, 1842. After service in Mexican War and on the frontiers, he resigned from army, 1854, worked as engineer in iron works, and served as New York City street commissioner. Appointed major-general, Confederate Army, 1861, he was put in command of the garrison at New Orleans, La. Held responsible for the evacuation and loss of that city, April 1862, although absolved of blame by a military court, he received no further important commands.

LOVERING, JOSEPH (*b. Charlestown, Mass., 1813; d. 1892*), educator. Graduated Harvard, 1833. Hollis professor of mathematics and natural philosophy, Harvard, 1838–88. Secretary, American Association for Advancement of Science, 1854–73; president, American Academy of Arts and Sciences, 1880–92.

LOVETT, ROBERT SCOTT (*b. near San Jacinto, Texas, 1860; d. 1932*), lawyer. Protégé and confidant of E. H. Harriman, Lovett served as general counsel and as president of the Southern Pacific and Union Pacific railroads. [*Supp. 1*]

LOVETT, ROBERT WILLIAMSON (*b. Beverly, Mass., 1859; d. Liverpool, England, 1924*), orthopedic surgeon, medical writer. Graduated Harvard, 1881; Harvard Medical School, 1885. *Post* 1899, he concentrated on work in Boston Children's Hospital; taught his specialty at Harvard Medical School; was a leader in orthopedic restoration for victims of infantile paralysis. His crowning work, prepared in cooperation with his friend Sir Robert Jones, was *Orthopedic Surgery* (1923).

LOVEWELL, JOHN (*b. Dunstable, Mass., now part of Nashua, N.H., 1691; d. near "Lovewell's Pond" on Saco River, Maine, 1725*), Indian fighter. Killed on the third of his punitive expeditions against the Pequawkets in Maine. Lovewell and the sad fate of his company were subjects for several early ballads.

LOW, ABIEL ABBOT (*b. Salem, Mass., 1811; d. Brooklyn, N.Y., 1893*), merchant. Served as clerk and partner, Russell & Co., Canton, China, 1833–40. A profitable enterprise engaged in with the mandarin Houqua enabled Low to begin business in New York on his own account. The firm of A. A. Low & Brothers soon gained leading position in tea and silk trade with China and Japan; Low also shared in financing the first Atlantic cable and in the building of the Chesapeake and Ohio Railroad through West Virginia.

LOW, FREDERICK FERDINAND (*b. Frankfort, now Winterport, Maine, 1828; d. San Francisco, Calif., 1894*), merchant, banker. Emigrated to California, 1849; was successful as a merchant in San Francisco and Marysville. Congressman, Union Republican, from California, 1862–63; governor of California, 1863–67. As governor, much credit is due him for the later founding of University of California and for preserving the site of Golden Gate Park. He served as U.S. minister to China, 1870–74.

LOW, ISAAC (*b. near New Brunswick, N.J., 1735; d. Isle of Wight, England, 1791*), merchant. A delegate to the Stamp Act Congress, 1765, and representative of moderate opinion against the policy of the English ministry, Low served as a delegate from New York to the First Continental Congress but showed himself hostile to independence and, unlike his brother Nicholas Low, went over to the British, 1776. He was a founder of the N.Y. Chamber of Commerce.

LOW, JOHN GARDNER (*b. Chelsea, Mass., 1835; d. 1907*), painter. Designer and manufacturer of art tiles and other ceramic products.

LOW, JULIETTE GORDON (*b. Savannah, Ga., 1860; d. Savannah, 1927*), founder (1912) of the Girl Scouts of America.

LOW, NICHOLAS (*b. near New Brunswick, N.J., 1739; d. New York, N.Y., 1826*), merchant, land speculator, New York legislator. Brother of Isaac Low.

LOW, SETH (*b. Brooklyn, N.Y., 1850; d. Bedford Hills, N.Y., 1916*), merchant, political reformer. Son of Abiel A. Low. Graduated Columbia, 1870. A partner in his father's business, 1876–87, Low served as mayor of the then city of Brooklyn, N.Y., 1881–1885. He introduced the merit system in the municipal service, reduced the city debt and completely reformed the public school system. Standing for a separation of local and national politics, Low disclaimed the Republican label as mayor, although he was a Republican, and refused to support the candidacy of James G. Blaine in 1884. As the president of Columbia,

1890–1901, he reorganized graduate and professional instruction and brought into association with the university Teachers College, Barnard and the College of Physicians and Surgeons; he was also responsible for the purchase of the new site on Morningside Heights, 1892. Victorious as independent candidate for New York City mayoralty, 1901, his administration marked a brief era of civic reform, but he failed of re-election, 1903. An active philanthropist, he worked to improve the condition of the Negro and labor-capital relations.

LOW, WILL HICOK (*b. Albany, N.Y., 1853; d. Bronxville, N.Y., 1932*), artist. Studied in Paris, 1872–77, with Gérôme and Carolus-Duran; was friend of Robert Louis Stevenson. Outstanding as a decorative painter, Low was author of *A Chronicle of Friendships* (1908) and *A Painter's Progress* (1910). [*Supp.* 1]

LOWE, CHARLES (*b. Portsmouth, N.H., 1828; d. 1874*), Unitarian clergyman. Helped organize National Conference, American Unitarian Association, 1865; served as the Association's first executive secretary, 1865–71.

LOWE, RALPH PHILLIPS (*b. Warren Co., O., 1805; d. Washington, D.C., 1883*), lawyer. Settled in Iowa, 1840. Rep. governor of Iowa, 1858–60; justice, supreme court of Iowa, 1860–68, acting in 1860 and 1866–68 as chief justice.

LOWE, THADDEUS SOBIESKI COULINCOURT (*b. Jefferson Mills, N.H., 1832; d. Pasadena, Calif., 1913*), aeronaut, meteorologist. Chief of aeronautic section, Army of the Potomac, 1861–63, he made valuable air observations and was first in the United States to take photographs from a balloon. After the Civil War he became interested in manufacture of artificial ice, constructing a plant for this purpose as early as 1866; he also made several later improvements in the manufacture of gas and coke.

LOWELL, AMY (*b. Brookline, Mass., 1874; d. Brookline, 1925*), poet, critic. Granddaughter of Abbott Lawrence; sister of Abbott L. and Percival Lowell; descendant of John Lowell (1769–1840). Educated at private schools; traveled extensively. The supreme interest of her life *post* 1902 was the art of poetry. Alive to the new movements at that time, she turned from the more or less conventional tendencies of her earliest attempts at literature to work of a markedly original character both in verse and prose. Having met Ezra Pound in England, 1913, she became associated with the Imagist school whose work she endeavored to publicize in the United States. *Post* 1914, her poems are phrased in free verse or, as she preferred to call it, "unrhymed cadence." The principles on which she worked were defined in the preface to her *Sword Blades and Poppy Seed* (1914); this volume also contained her experiments in what she termed "polyphonic prose." Later in her career her work showed the influence of her studies in Chinese and Japanese poetry. From 1915 until her death, she lectured and gave readings from her work, defending her poetic creed and technique with great vigor and verve. During these years she was the most striking figure in contemporary American letters, her serene independence of conventional opinion and her Elizabethan outspokenness occasioning considerable comment. Her important publications besides that already cited are her first book, *A Dome of Many-Coloured Glass* (1912), *Can Grande's Castle* (1918), *Pictures of the Floating World* (1919), *Legends* (1921) and her most important critical work, *John Keats* (1925).

LOWELL, EDWARD JACKSON (*b. Boston, Mass., 1845; d. Cotuit, Mass., 1894*), historian. Grandson of Francis C. Lowell. Graduated Harvard, 1867. Author, among other books, of *The Eve of the French Revolution* (1892).

LOWELL, FRANCIS CABOT (*b. Newburyport, Mass., 1775; d. Boston, Mass., 1817*), textile manufacturer. Son of John Lowell (1743–1802). Graduated Harvard, 1793. During a journey to England, 1810, he studied textile machinery in Lancashire; on return to America, 1812, he determined to establish a cotton factory. Forming the Boston Manufacturing Co. with his brother-in-law, Patrick T. Jackson, he purchased land at Waltham, Mass., and designed and built (with the aid of Paul Moody) necessary spinning machinery and a practical power loom. When the factory was in complete operation *c.* 1814, it was believed to be the first mill in the world which combined all operations of converting raw cotton into finished cloth.

LOWELL, GUY (*b. Boston, Mass., 1870; d. Madeira Islands, 1927*), architect. Son of Edward J. Lowell. Graduated Harvard, 1892; department of architecture, Massachusetts Institute of Technology, 1894. Received diploma, École des Beaux-Arts, Paris, 1899; had immediate success on his return to America. Among his notable works are the buildings at Phillips Academy, Andover, Mass., and the New York County Court House, designed 1913. A confirmed classicist, Lowell also engaged in landscape architecture.

LOWELL, JAMES RUSSELL (*b. Cambridge, Mass., 1819; d. Cambridge, 1891*), poet, educator, public servant, foremost American man of letters in his time. Grandson of John Lowell (1743–1802); brother of Robert T. S. Lowell. Graduated Harvard, 1838; Harvard Law School, 1840. Married Maria White, 1844, whose enthusiasm for the anti-slavery movement and for poetry inspired and encouraged him; her influence is noted in his early publications, *A Year's Life* (1841) and *Poems* (1844). His first book of literary criticism, *Conversations on Some of the Old Poets*, was published, 1845. He had made his debut as an editor in *The Pioneer*, a magazine published briefly in 1843. In the year 1848 Lowell published *Poems: Second Series;* the rollicking critical satire, *A Fable for Critics;* the first volume of *The Biglow Papers;*

and *The Vision of Sir Launfal.* All of this work was highly competent and some of it was brilliant, yet there was truth in Margaret Fuller's criticism that "his great facility at versification has enabled him to fill the ear with a copious stream of pleasant sound. But his verse is stereotyped; his thought sounds no depth." In *The Biglow Papers* Lowell reproduced Yankee dialect with extreme exactness, and his satiric criticism of the national government in its conduct of the Mexican War was remarkably telling. Nearly twenty years later the second series of *The Biglow Papers* (written, 1864; first published in book form in the United States, 1867) dealt with equal skill with the Civil War. These satires may be regarded as his most distinctive contribution to the literature of his time.

Dealt a desolating blow by the death of his wife, 1853, Lowell busied himself with writing for the magazines and with much social bustle. He succeeded H. W. Longfellow as Smith professor of French and Spanish and professor of belles-lettres at Harvard, 1855, and, in 1857, became editor of the *Atlantic Monthly*. Nominally he held his Harvard chair from 1855 to 1886, when he became emeritus for the remainder of his life; actually there were several intermissions in his teaching. He left the *Atlantic Monthly*, 1861, but renewed editorial work, 1864, in association with Charles E. Norton, in conduct of the *North American Review*. The emphasis in his work shifted from creation to criticism more and more as his career went on, although in his "Ode Recited at the Harvard Commemoration, July 21, 1865" (first published, *Atlantic Monthly*, September 1865) he attained a high point in his own poetic achievement and produced a work which stands in the front rank of its genre. Highly rated as a critic in his own day, his stature has diminished with the passage of the years; the scholar of today finds him highly impressionistic and only analytic under pressure of challenge. *Among My Books* (1870), *My Study Windows* (1871) and *Among My Books*, second series (1876), were all gatherings of literary essays, most of which had appeared in the *Atlantic* and the *North American Review*. The books which he published subsequent to 1876 did not materially affect his place in American letters. Lowell's permanent reputation as poet or prose writer has suffered because of his extraordinary versatility and cleverness—the very qualities which gave him so great an influence in his own time.

His career as a public servant began with his service as U. S. minister to Spain, 1877–80. Adapting himself to his new profession with skill and zest, he moved on to England, serving as U.S. minister to the Court of St. James, 1880–85. Despite an earlier literary antipathy to England and the English, Lowell performed a notable mission of good will as our minister in London, showing himself an excellent public speaker both on formal and informal occasions. Among his many addresses, one of the best is "Democracy," Oct. 6, 1884. Lowell's second wife, Frances Dunlap, whom he had married, 1857, died shortly before his return to America at the end of his service in London.

LOWELL, JOHN (*b. Newburyport, Mass., 1743; d. Roxbury, Mass., 1802*), Massachusetts legislator, jurist. U.S. judge, district of Massachusetts, 1789–1801; chief judge, first circuit, 1801–02. Father (by successive marriages) of John (1769–1840) and Francis C. Lowell; grandfather of James R. and Robert T. S. Lowell.

LOWELL, JOHN (*b. Newburyport, Mass., 1769; d. 1840*), lawyer, Federalist political writer. Son of John Lowell (1743–1802); half-brother of Francis C. Lowell. Graduated Harvard, 1786. His many vigorous pamphlets and letters to the press won him the title of the "Boston Rebel," but were of influence only in New England.

LOWELL, JOHN (*b. Boston, Mass., 1799; d. Bombay, India, 1836*), businessman. Son of Francis C. Lowell. Founder of the Lowell Institute, to which he left half of his estate in trust.

LOWELL, JOHN (*b. Boston, Mass., 1824; d. 1897*), lawyer. Grandson of John Lowell (1769–1840); grandson also of Francis C. Lowell. Graduated Harvard, 1843; Harvard Law School, 1845. Independent, learned and courteous as U.S. judge, district of Massachusetts, 1865–78, and as judge for the first circuit, 1878–84. Particularly effective in commercial, marine and bankruptcy cases.

LOWELL, JOSEPHINE SHAW (*b. West Roxbury, Mass., 1843; d. 1905*), philanthropist, reformer. Sister of Robert G. Shaw; married nephew of James Russell Lowell, 1863. First woman appointed to New York State Board of Charities; founder of Charity Organization Society; one of the organizers of the Consumer's League.

LOWELL, PERCIVAL (*b. Boston, Mass., 1855; d. 1916*), astronomer, businessman. Grandson of Abbott Lawrence; brother of Abbott L. and Amy Lowell. Graduated Harvard, 1876. Successful in business, he spent the years 1883–93 in travel in the Far East both as private citizen and diplomat; his books, *Chöson—The Land of the Morning Calm* (1885) and *Soul of the Far East* (1888), show remarkable insight into the Oriental mind. He devoted himself to astronomy subsequent to the early 1890's and built an observatory near Flagstaff, Ariz., where he and a staff of astronomers carried on a most valuable program of research *post* 1894.

LOWELL, ROBERT TRAILL SPENCE (*b. Boston, Mass., 1816; d. 1891*), Episcopal clergyman, author. Brother of James R. Lowell. Graduated Harvard, 1833. Pastor in Newfoundland and at churches in New York and New Jersey. Headmaster, St. Mark's School, 1869–73; professor of Latin, Union College, 1873–79. Author, among other books, of *The New Priest in Conception Bay* (1858) and *Poems* (1864).

LOWERY, WOODBURY (*b. New York, N.Y., 1853; d. Taormina, Sicily, 1906*), lawyer, legal editor, historian. Grandson of Levi Woodbury. Graduated Harvard, 1875. Author of *The Spanish Settlements Within the Present Limits of the United States, 1513–61* (1901, 1905). Bequeathed his valuable collection of early maps to the Library of Congress.

LOWNDES, LLOYD (*b. Clarksburg, Va., 1845; d. 1905*), lawyer, financier. Practiced *post* 1867 at Cumberland, Md. Congressman, Republican, from Maryland, 1873–75; Republican governor of Maryland, 1896–1900.

LOWNDES, RAWLINS (*b. St. Kitts, B.W.I., 1721; d. 1800*), lawyer, South Carolina legislator. Raised in Charleston, S.C., where he practiced *post* 1754. A conservative, he hoped that the American colonies would be satisfied with a redress of grievances, yet he served on the local revolutionary committees and was a member of the legislative council, 1776–78 and president of the state of South Carolina, 1778. A member of the legislature after the Revolution, he opposed ratification of the Constitution because he considered it "ruinous to the liberty of America."

LOWNDES, WILLIAM (*b. Colleton Co., S.C., 1782; d. at sea, 1822*), planter, South Carolina legislator. Son of Rawlins Lowndes. Congressman, (Democrat) Republican, from South Carolina, 1811–22. With Langdon Cheves, John C. Calhoun and others, formed nucleus of the "War Hawks." A very able congressional debater, he spoke with particular effectiveness in the debate over Missouri, 1820. Highly respected by his contemporaries, he was nominated by the South Carolina legislature for the presidency in December, 1821.

LOWREY, MARK PERRIN (*b. McNairy Co., Tenn., 1828; d. Middleton, Tenn., 1885*), Baptist clergyman, Confederate brigadier-general.

LOWRIE, JAMES WALTER (*b. Shanghai, China, 1856; d. Paotingfu, China, 1930*), Presbyterian clergyman. Grandson of Walter Lowrie. Missionary to China *post* 1883.

LOWRIE, WALTER (*b. Edinburgh, Scotland, 1784; d. New York, N.Y., 1868*), businessman, Pennsylvania legislator. Came to America as a boy. U.S. senator, Democrat, from Pennsylvania, 1819–25; outspoken opponent of slavery and of cash-sale basis for public lands. Secretary of the Senate, 1825–36, he became secretary of the Board of Foreign Missions of the Presbyterian Church in 1836 and served with great efficiency and success until 1868.

LOWRY, HIRAM HARRISON (*b. near Zanesville, O., 1843; d. Peking, China, 1924*), Methodist clergyman. Missionary to China *post* 1867; superintendent of North China mission, 1873–93; head of Peking University, 1893–1918.

LOWRY, ROBERT (*b. Chesterfield District, S.C., 1830; d. Jackson, Miss., 1910*), lawyer, Confederate brigadier-general. Raised in Tennessee and Mississippi. Governor of Mississippi, Democrat, 1882–90.

LOWRY, THOMAS (*b. Logan Co., Ill., 1843; d. 1909*), lawyer, capitalist. Settled in Minneapolis, Minn., 1867. Active *post* 1875 in local rapid transit and other transportation interests.

LOY, MATTHIAS (*b. Cumberland Co., Pa., 1828; d. Columbus, O., 1915*), Lutheran clergyman, theologian, leader in the Ohio Synod.

LOYD, SAMUEL (*b. Philadelphia, Pa., 1841; d. 1911*), better known as Sam Loyd, composer of chess problems and inventor of puzzles and games including "Pigs in Clover" and "Parchesi."

LOZIER, CLEMENCE SOPHIA HARNED (*b. Plainfield, N.J., 1813; d. 1888*), homeopathic physician, feminist. Founded New York Medical College and Hospital for Women, 1863; the school was later merged with New York Homeopathic Medical College.

LUBBOCK, FRANCIS RICHARD (*b. Beaufort, S.C., 1815; d. 1905*), rancher, businessman, politician, Confederate soldier. Removed to Texas, 1836; served as clerk of Texas Congress and comptroller of the republic, 1837. Democratic lieutenant-governor of Texas, 1857–59; governor, 1861–63. During his term he mobilized the state's manpower and resources in support of the Confederacy; at its close, he served as a staff officer in the Confederate Army and was one of those captured with President Davis, May 1865. Elected state treasurer of Texas, 1878, he held office until his retirement, 1891.

LUBIN, DAVID (*b. Klodowa, Russian Poland, 1849; d. Rome, Italy, 1919*), agriculturist. Came to America as a child; removed to California, 1865; returned East. Went West again to Sacramento, Calif., 1874, where he built up the largest mail-order merchandising business on the Pacific Coast. Leader of a revolt of the fruit-growers against discriminatory railroad rates and other evils including protective tariffs, he later campaigned successfully for creation of an international agricultural organization which was effected, 1910, under a treaty ratified by 46 nations.

LUCAS, ANTHONY FRANCIS (*b. Spalato, Austria, 1855; d. 1921*), Austrian naval officer, geologist, engineer. Came to America, 1879; became American citizen and engaged first in lumbering, then as consulting engineer. His examination of low mounds, or "domes," in Gulf Coastal Plain areas of Louisiana and Texas led him to believe they were natural reservoirs of petroleum. Prosecuting his investigations, he brought in the famous Spindletop oil strike near Beaumont, Texas, Jan. 10, 1901.

LUCAS, DANIEL BEDINGER (*b. near Charles Town, Va., 1836; d. 1909*), West Virginia legislator, jurist, Confederate soldier. Author of a quantity of poetry and some minor dramas.

LUCAS, ELIZA. [See PINCKNEY, ELIZA LUCAS, 1722–1793.]

LUCAS, FREDERIC AUGUSTUS (*b. Plymouth, Mass., 1852; d. 1929*), naturalist. Associated with Henry A. Ward at Rochester, N.Y., 1871–82; held curatorial posts at U.S. National Museum, 1882–1904; curator, Brooklyn Museum, 1904–11; director, American Museum of Natural History, New York City, 1911–29. Had lasting influence on conduct of American museums; stressed the teaching function of exhibits.

LUCAS, JAMES H. (*b. Pittsburgh, Pa., 1800; d. 1873*), St. Louis banker, capitalist. Son of John B. C. Lucas.

LUCAS, JOHN BAPTISTE CHARLES (*b. Pont-Audemer, France, 1758; d. St. Louis, Mo., 1842*), Pennsylvania legislator, Missouri jurist. Came to America, 1784. Congressman, (Democrat) Republican, from Pennsylvania, 1803–05. Appointed U.S. judge for northern district of Louisiana, 1805, he removed to St. Louis, Mo., and served on the bench until 1820; also a member of the commission for land titles, he acquired as much real estate as he could and died possessed of large property.

LUCAS, JONATHAN (*b. Cumberland, England, 1754; d. 1821*), millwright. Came to Charleston, S.C., c. 1790. As rice planters were then handicapped by slow, expensive methods necessary to remove the husks from the grain, Lucas designed tide-mill machinery by which three persons could beat 16 to 20 barrels of rice on a single tide. He and his son later developed many improvements in his mill, including the first steam rice mill (1817). In all essentials, later rice mills adhered to his plans, and the rice industry owed as much to him as the cotton industry to Eli Whitney.

LUCAS, JONATHAN (*b. England, 1775; d. Surrey, England, 1832*), millwright. Son and assistant of Jonathan Lucas (1754–1821); accompanied him to South Carolina c. 1790. Patented a machine for rice-cleaning without pounding by pestles, 1808, which was adopted with great success in England.

LUCAS, ROBERT (*b. Shepherdstown, Va., 1781; d. near Iowa City, Iowa, 1853*), surveyor, farmer, Ohio legislator. Democratic governor of Ohio, 1832–36; governor and superintendent of Indian affairs, territory of Iowa, 1838–41. Served as member of the 1844 Iowa constitutional convention.

LUCE, STEPHEN BLEECKER (*b. Albany, N.Y., 1827; d. Newport, R.I., 1917*), naval officer. Appointed midshipman, 1841; served in varied sea and shore duty until assignment just before the Civil War as head of department of seamanship, U.S. Naval Academy, Newport, R.I. His book *Seamanship* (1863) became standard treatise on the subject. After serving in commands at sea, 1863–65, he was commandant of midshipmen, U.S. Naval Academy, Annapolis, 1866–69, and occupied with various training duties thereafter until 1884. During all this time he worked in the face of marked opposition to secure better training for naval officers and advocated establishment of a school for advanced studies. Promoted commodore, 1881, Luce was appointed first president of the Naval War College on its establishment, 1884, at Newport, R.I. With Capt. A. T. Mahan as lecturer, the College struggled on, providing officers with instruction in history, international law and higher command, "teaching the navy to think." Commissioned rear-admiral, 1886, Luce retired in 1889.

LUDELING, JOHN THEODORE (*b. New Orleans, La., 1827; d. near Monroe, La., 1891*), Louisiana jurist, Unionist. Republican chief justice of Louisiana, 1868–77.

LUDLOW, DANIEL (*b. New York, N.Y., 1750; d. Skaneateles, N.Y., 1814*), merchant. A Loyalist during the Revolution, Ludlow built up a very large importing trade as Daniel Ludlow & Company, 1790–1808. Active in the organization of the Manhattan Company, 1799, he was chosen its first president and served until 1808 when he fell into financial difficulties.

LUDLOW, FITZ HUGH (*b. New York, N.Y., 1836; d. Geneva, Switzerland, 1870*), writer. Author, among other works, of *The Hasheesh Eater* (1857), an autobiographical work strongly influenced by DeQuincey.

LUDLOW, GABRIEL GEORGE (*b. probably New York City, 1736; d. 1808*), Loyalist soldier. Half-brother of Daniel Ludlow; brother of George D. Ludlow. *Post* 1784, a councilor of the province of New Brunswick, Canada.

LUDLOW, GEORGE DUNCAN (*b. probably New York City, 1734; d. near Fredericton, New Brunswick, Canada, 1808*), Loyalist, jurist. Brother of Gabriel G. Ludlow; half-brother of Daniel Ludlow. Justice, supreme court of New York Colony, 1769–78; chief justice, province of New Brunswick, 1784–1808.

LUDLOW, NOAH MILLER (*b. New York, N.Y., 1795; d. St. Louis, Mo., 1886*), actor, theatrical manager. *Post* 1815, played through Kentucky and Tennessee; a company formed by him gave the first performances in English by professionals in New Orleans, La., 1817. He was in partnership with Sol Smith, 1835–53, and assisted in management of theatres in Mobile, St. Louis, Cincinnati, New Orleans. Author of *Dramatic Life as I Found It* (1880).

LUDLOW, ROGER (*fl. 1590–1664*), lawyer. Little is known of Ludlow's early life. He was baptized at Dinton, Wiltshire, England, 1590; entered Balliol College, Oxford, 1610; was admitted to the Inner Temple, 1612. He arrived at Massachusetts Bay, May 30, 1630, aboard the *Mary and John*. One of the founders of Dorchester, he took an active part in early government of the colony and was elected deputy-governor, 1634. Removing, 1635, to the new Connecticut River settlements, he presided at Windsor, April 1636, over the first court held in Connecticut. He is credited with having drafted the Fundamental Orders adopted by the colony, January 1638/39. He was author also of "Ludlow's Code," the first gathering together of Connecticut laws, issued 1650. Having settled at Fairfield, 1639, Ludlow resided there until 1654, when he returned to England and took office as a member of the parliamentary commission for seizing forfeited lands in Ireland. He resided in Dublin, 1654–64; the time and place of his death are unknown.

LUDLOW, THOMAS WILLIAM (*b. New York, N.Y., 1795; d. Yonkers, N.Y., 1878*), lawyer, financier. A founder of New York Life Insurance Co., 1845; first president, Panama Railroad Co., 1849; also a promoter of other railroads including the Illinois Central.

LUDLOW, WILLIAM (*b. Islip, N.Y., 1843; d. Convent Station, N.J., 1901*), soldier, engineer. Graduated West Point, 1864. In a single year of Civil War service with the Union Army, he won brevets up to lieutenant-colonel for services in the Georgia campaign and in the Carolinas. As chief engineer, Department of Dakota, 1872–76, he made important surveys of Yellowstone National Park and the Black Hills country. After a wide experience in engineering work *post* 1876, Ludlow as brigadier-general commanded the first brigade in the attack on El Caney, Cuba, 1898. Commissioned major-general of volunteers, September 1898, he was made military governor of Havana and served until May 1900; he also saw extensive service during the Philippine insurrection.

LUDLOWE, ROGER. [See LUDLOW, ROGER, fl. 1590–1664.]

LUDWELL, PHILIP (*fl. 1660–1704*), planter, Virginia councilor. Born in Somersetshire, England, he emigrated to Virginia *c.* 1660 and acquired estates in James City County. Led resistance to Lord Howard of Effingham, 1686–87; went to England, 1689, to present the charges of the Burgesses against Howard; was chosen governor of the northern part of Carolina by the Lords Proprietors, December 1689. In 1691 his commission was altered to make him governor of the entire province of Carolina. Effective in restoring a state of comparative peace in the colony, he was recalled, 1694, and ultimately returned to England where he died.

LUDWICK, CHRISTOPHER (*b. Giessen, Germany, 1720; d. Philadelphia, Pa., 1801*), baker, philanthropist. Settled in Philadelphia, 1754. An active patriot, he caused hundreds of Hessians to desert the British, 1776. Congress appointed him superintendent of bakers, Continental Army, May 1777; in this capacity he served until the end of the war. Prospering thereafter in business, he left his entire fortune for the education of poor children.

LUELLING, HENDERSON (*b. Randolph Co., N.C., 1809; d. San José, Calif., 1878*), nurseryman. Transported by ox-team a stock of young trees and shrubs from Iowa to near present Portland, Oreg., April–November 1847. After success in operations there, he removed to vicinity of Oakland, Calif., 1854.

LUFBERY, RAOUL GERVAIS VICTOR (*b. Clermont, France, 1885; d. Maron, France, 1918*), aviator, American ace in World War I. Son of an American father; raised in France. After a roving life, enlisted in French air force, December 1914; having qualified as a pilot, he joined the *Escadrille Lafayette*, May 1916, and was officially credited with 17 victories. Commissioned major, U.S. Army air force, January 1918, he was shot down in combat.

LUKEMAN, HENRY AUGUSTUS (*b. Richmond, Va., 1871; d. New York, N.Y., 1935*), sculptor. Worked in studio of Launt Thompson and as assistant to Daniel Chester French. Among his many works, the statue of Manu on the Appellate Court House, New York City, and the relief of Gen. Robert E. Lee on Stone Mountain, Georgia, are notable. [*Supp. 1*]

LUKENS, REBECCA WEBB PENNOCK (*b. Coatesville, Pa., 1794; d. Coatesville, 1854*), iron manufacturer. Headed Brandywine Rolling Mill *post* 1825, becoming first woman in United States to engage in iron industry.

LUKS, GEORGE BENJAMIN (*b. Williamsport, Pa., 1867; d. New York, N.Y., 1933*), painter. Studied at Pennsylvania Academy of the Fine Arts and in Düsseldorf, London and Paris; was an ardent admirer of Rembrandt and Franz Hals. Adventurous, turbulent, he painted anything from circus wagons to comic strips for a living; the serious work of Luks dealt with the common life about him, particularly the colorful life of New York's East Side. Reacting from fashionable Impressionism, he associated himself with the group of painters known derisively as the "ash-can school." Though his output was uneven, all of his pictures show an inescapable vitality. [*Supp. 1*]

LULL, EDWARD PHELPS (*b. Windsor, Vt., 1836; d. 1887*), naval officer. Graduated U.S. Naval Academy, 1855. Served with credit in Union Navy during Civil War; thereafter had a varied experience as explorer and surveyor, notably in Nicaragua.

LUMBROZO, JACOB (*fl. 1656–1665*), physician, planter, merchant. Born in Lisbon of Jewish ancestry, he emigrated first to Holland, and from Holland to Maryland, 1656. One of the first Jews to settle in Maryland and the first physician to practice there.

LUMMIS, CHARLES FLETCHER (*b. Lynn, Mass., 1859; d. 1928*), journalist, author. Removed to Los Angeles, Calif., 1885; to New Mexico, 1888; lived among Pueblo Indians, and was associated in ethnological work with Adolph Bandelier. Through his books, *The Land of Poco Tiempo* (1893), *The Spanish Pioneers* (1893) and others, he aroused interest in the romantic history of the Southwest. Founded the Southwest Museum, Los Angeles.

LUMPKIN, JOSEPH HENRY (*b. Oglethorpe Co., Ga., 1799; d. 1867*), lawyer. Brother of Wilson Lumpkin. Graduated College of New Jersey (Princeton), 1819. Practiced mainly in Athens, Ga. Chief justice, supreme court of Georgia, 1845–67. During his tenure he and his associates, by the wisdom of their decisions, firmly established their court in the good graces of the people of Georgia who had traditionally opposed any court of review.

LUMPKIN, WILSON (*b. Pittsylvania Co., Va., 1783; d. Athens, Ga., 1870*), lawyer, planter, Georgia legislator. Brother of Joseph H. Lumpkin. Congressman, Democrat, 1815–17, 1827–31; governor of Georgia, 1831–35; U.S. senator, 1837–41. An extreme staterights advocate.

LUNA Y ARELLANO, TRISTAN de (*fl. 1530–1561*), Spanish explorer. Came to New Spain *c.* 1530; served as captain under Francisco Coronado. Appointed governor and captain-general of Florida, he led the ill-fated expedition which attempted a settlement around Pensacola Bay, 1559–61.

LUNDEEN, ERNEST (*b. Beresford, S. Dak., 1878; d. near Lovettsville, Va., 1940*), lawyer, Minnesota legislator. Congressman, Republican, from Minnesota, 1917–19; Farmer-Labor, 1933–36. U.S. senator, Farmer-Labor, 1936–40. A progressive isolationist, humorless and independent, Lundeen was in domestic affairs to the left of the New Deal, favoring nationalization of banks, high taxes and a broad program of unemployment insurance. [*Supp. 2*]

LUNDIE, JOHN (*b. Arbroath, Scotland, 1857; d. New York, N.Y., 1931*), engineer. Came to America *c.* 1880. Laid out first low-level drainage system for Chicago; was connected with water-supply projects elsewhere. Established Lundie formula for train resistance; designed first combined electric hoist and tractor (telpher) *c.* 1898.

LUNDIN, CARL AXEL ROBERT (*b. Venersborg, Sweden, 1851; d. 1915*), optician. Came to America, 1873. Became chief instrument-maker for Alvan Clark & Sons, Cambridgeport, Mass.; in that post worked on many of the largest telescope lenses made in his time.

LUNDY, BENJAMIN (*b. Sussex Co., N.J., 1789; d. Illinois, 1839*), Abolitionist. A saddler of Quaker stock, Lundy removed to Ohio, 1815. An ardent antislavery agitator subsequent to 1815, he traveled widely in search of a place where freed Negroes might be colonized, meanwhile publishing *post* 1821 an Abolitionist paper, *The Genius of Universal Emancipation;*

it ceased publication, 1835. Between 1836 and 1838, Lundy published *The National Enquirer* in opposition to what he claimed were plots of slaveholders to take Texas from Mexico; in March 1838 this paper became *The Pennsylvania Freeman*. Lundy revived *The Genius of Universal Emancipation* in Illinois in 1839 shortly before his death. He was the most active figure in the anti-slavery movement during the 1820's, and his enlistment of W. L. Garrison as an associate (1828) brought to the cause its chief protagonist.

LUNT, GEORGE (*b. Newburyport, Mass., 1803; d. 1885*), lawyer, journalist, author. Editor, *Boston Daily Courier*, 1857–63.

LUNT, ORRINGTON (*b. Bowdoinham, Maine, 1815; d. Evanston, Ill., 1897*), businessman, philanthropist. Removed to Chicago, Ill., 1842, where he prospered in various mercantile activities. Active in establishment of Northwestern University.

LURTON, HORACE HARMON (*b. Newport, Ky., 1844; d. Atlantic City, N.J., 1914*), lawyer, Confederate soldier, jurist. Practiced at Clarksville, Tenn., 1867–86. Justice, supreme court of Tennessee, 1886–93; chief justice, 1893. U.S. circuit judge, 1893–1909. During service on the federal bench, his abilities impressed the presiding judge of the circuit, William H. Taft. Appointed by Taft a justice of U.S. Supreme Court, 1909, Lurton served ably until his death. A strict constitutionalist, he had little sympathy with those who wished to adjust the machinery of government to changing conditions of life and thought by judicial interpretation.

LUSK, GRAHAM (*b. Bridgeport, Conn., 1866; d. 1932*), physiologist. Son of William T. Lusk. Graduated School of Mines, Columbia, 1887; Ph.D., Munich, 1891. Taught physiology at Yale, New York University and Cornell. His studies in animal and clinical calorimetry extended over a period of 44 years and dealt with a great variety of topics such as basal metabolism, specific dynamic action of various foodstuffs and the like. His book *The Elements of the Science of Nutrition* (1906) had a marked influence on medical research in the United States and in promoting an appreciation of the value of laboratory methods in explaining the inner processes in disease. [*Supp. 1*]

LUSK, WILLIAM THOMPSON, (*b. Norwich, Conn., 1838; d. 1897*), obstetrician, Union soldier. Graduated Bellevue Hospital Medical College, 1864; studied also at Edinburgh and Vienna. Junior partner of Benjamin F. Barker, 1866–73; professor of obstetrics, Bellevue, 1871–97; held numerous hospital appointments. His classic work *The Science and Art of Midwifery* (1882) was considered the most learned textbook of the day in English.

LUTHER, SETH (*fl. 1817–1846*), carpenter, pioneer labor reformer. Born probably in Providence, R.I., Luther traveled widely through the United States,

1817–30. His first pamphlet, *An Address to the Working-men of New England* (1832), was an attack on the abuses of the incipient factory system. In the following year he published *An Address on the Right of Free Suffrage* and in 1834 *An Address on the Origin and Progress of Avarice*. His deadly sincerity and biting sarcasm made his pamphlets valuable weapons in the labor movement.

LUTKIN, PETER CHRISTIAN *b. Thompsonville, Wis., 1858; d. Evanston, Ill., 1931*), musical composer and conductor, educator. As professor of music and dean of school of music, Northwestern University, *post* 1891 (dean, *post* 1897), he developed the school into one of the important musical institutions of the country. He also established the Chicago North Shore Festival Association, 1908, of which he was the choral conductor until 1930.

LYALL, JAMES (*b. Auchterardar, Scotland, 1836; d. New York, N.Y., 1901*), inventor, manufacturer. Came to New York, N.Y., as a small child. Invented a positive-motion loom (patented, 1868, 1871, 1872) which abolished use of picking sticks and permitted great widths of fabric to be woven. Lyall made other improvements in textile machinery and in machines for manufacture of jute twine; he also patented a new type of woven fabric for pneumatic tires and fire hose, 1893–96.

LYDSTON, GEORGE FRANK (*b. Jacksonville, Calif., 1857; d. Los Angeles, Calif., 1923*), physician. Graduated Bellevue Hospital Medical School, 1879; practiced in Chicago, Ill., *post* 1881. A specialist in genito-urinary surgery, he wrote vehemently on many subjects. He was the Peck's Bad Boy of the medical profession of his time and engaged in a number of intra-professional controversies.

LYMAN, ALBERT JOSIAH (*b. Williston, Vt., 1845; d. 1915*), Congregational clergyman. Pastor at Milford, Conn., 1869–73; at South Church, Brooklyn, N.Y., 1874–1915. A man of practical ability rather than a theologian, he was a leader in Congregationalism through many years.

LYMAN, BENJAMIN SMITH (*b. Northampton, Mass., 1835; d. Philadelphia, Pa., 1920*), geologist, mining engineer. As general geologist for the Japanese government, 1873–80, he discovered many coal and other mineral deposits in Japan and assisted in their development.

LYMAN, CHESTER SMITH (*b. Manchester, Conn., 1814; d. New Haven, Conn., 1890*), Congregational clergyman, astronomer, physicist. Graduated Yale, 1837. Traveling widely in search of health, he worked in Hawaii and in California. His letter, published in *American Journal of Science and Arts* (September 1848), is said to be the first credible account of the discovery of gold in California received in the East. As professor of physics and astronomy, Sheffield Scientific School, *post* 1859, he invented a number of instruments for demonstrating physical theory and also the first combined transit and zenith instrument for determining latitude by Talcott's method. His journal of his travels was published as *Around the Horn to the Sandwich Islands and California* (1924).

LYMAN, JOSEPH BARDWELL (*b. Chester, Mass., 1829; d. Richmond Hill, N.Y., 1872*), lawyer, Confederate soldier, agriculturist. After the Civil War, as agricultural editor of several newspapers and periodicals, notably the N.Y. *Weekly Tribune*, he impressed on American farmers the need of sustaining home manufactures and of diversifying crops.

LYMAN, PHINEAS (*b. near Durham, Conn., 1715; d. 1774*), lawyer, Connecticut legislator. Graduated Yale, 1738. Commanding Connecticut provincial troops during the Seven Years' War, he won reputation of being ablest general in Northern colonies and aided in defeat of the French at Lake George, 1755. Accompanied Amherst against Crown Point, 1759; later commanded at Ticonderoga. In 1762, he led all the provincial troops on expedition to Havana. *Post* 1763, he planned a series of colonies for discharged provincial soldiers along the Mississippi, especially at the mouth of the Ohio.

LYMAN, THEODORE (*b. Boston, Mass., 1792; d. 1849*), Massachusetts legislator, author, philanthropist. Graduated Harvard, 1810. A Federalist and opponent of John Q. Adams, Lyman became a supporter of Andrew Jackson *post* 1828, but soon cooled in his affection for the Democrats. He served as mayor of Boston, 1834–35, an able but undistinguished term of office during which he was bitterly assailed by the Abolitionists.

LYMAN, THEODORE (*b. Waltham, Mass., 1833; d. Nahant, Mass., 1897*), Union soldier, zoölogist. Son of Theodore Lyman (1792–1849). Graduated Harvard, 1855. Worked under Louis Agassiz in Lawrence Scientific School. Recognized as an authority on the Ophiuridae. Served on state Fisheries Commission and in other civic capacities; was an original trustee and later treasurer of the Museum of Comparative Zoölogy.

LYNCH, ANNA CHARLOTTE. [See BOTTA, ANNA CHARLOTTE LYNCH, 1815–1891.]

LYNCH, CHARLES (*b. near present Lynchburg, Va., 1736; d. Virginia, 1796*), Virginia legislator, planter, Revolutionary patriot. Presiding over an extralegal court in Bedford Co., Va., during the Revolution, Lynch gave his name to the use of summary unauthorized process in punishing lawlessness.

LYNCH, JAMES DANIEL (*b. Boydton, Va., 1836; d. Sulphur Springs, Texas, 1903*), Confederate soldier, author of numerous works on the history of Mississippi and Texas.

LYNCH, JAMES MATHEW (*b. Manlius, N.Y., 1867; d. Syracuse, N.Y., 1930*), labor leader. As president, International Typographical Union, 1900–14, 1924–26, he won for its members the eight-hour day (1906–08), established an old-age pension system, provided better apprentice education and greatly strengthened its financial position. He served on the New York State Industrial Commission, 1915–21.

LYNCH, JOHN ROY (*b. Concordia Parish, La., 1847; d. Chicago, Ill., 1939*). A Negro, Lynch served as congressman from Mississippi, 1873–77, 1882–83. He was active in Republican politics through 1900, and was chosen temporary chairman of the national Republican convention, 1884. After service as a U.S. army officer, 1901–11, he practiced law in Chicago.
[*Supp. 2*]

LYNCH, PATRICK NEESON (*b. Clones, Ireland, 1817; d. Charleston, S.C., 1882*), Roman Catholic clergyman. Came to America as an infant; was raised in Cheraw, S.C. Ordained in Rome, 1840, he served as pastor in Charleston *post* 1845, and was consecrated bishop of Charleston, 1858. A successful administrator and a forceful preacher and writer, he carried a letter from President Davis to Pope Pius IX, 1863, expressing desire of the Confederacy for peace. After the Civil War, he was an effective promoter of better feeling between North and South.

LYNCH, ROBERT CLYDE (*b. Carson City, Nev., 1880; d. near Richmond, Ky., 1931*), physician. M.D., Tulane University, 1903; also made studies of the eye, ear, nose and throat in France, Germany and England. Taught rhinology and otolaryngology at Tulane *post* 1911; developed radical frontal sinus operation known as the "Lynch operation" and was first to make successful moving pictures of larynx and vocal cords.

LYNCH, THOMAS (*b. Berkeley Co., S.C., 1727; d. Annapolis, Md., 1776*), planter, South Carolina legislator. With Christopher Gadsden and John Rutledge, represented South Carolina in Stamp Act Congress, 1765, at New York City; also served as member of First and Second Continental Congresses, 1774–76.

LYNCH, THOMAS (*b. Winyaw, S.C., 1749; d. at sea?, 1779*), planter. Son of Thomas Lynch (1727–1776). Educated at Eton and Cambridge and at the Middle Temple (1764–72). A member of the Second Continental Congress, 1776–77, he was a signer of the Declaration of Independence, but soon became an invalid and retired from public life.

LYNCH, WILLIAM FRANCIS (*b. Norfolk, Va., 1801; d. Baltimore, Md., 1865*), naval officer. Appointed midshipman, 1819. Author of *Official Report of the U.S. Expedition to Explore the Dead Sea and the River Jordan* (1852), which dealt with investigations he had made in 1848 and described in an earlier popular work (1849). He served in the Confederate navy during the Civil War.

LYNDE, BENJAMIN (*b. Salem, Mass., 1700; d. Salem, 1781*), Massachusetts colonial legislator and jurist. Graduated Harvard, 1718. Justice, Massachusetts superior court, 1746–72; presided over trial of British soldiers involved in Boston Massacre.

LYNDE, FRANCIS (*b. Lewiston, N.Y., 1856; d. near Chattanooga, Tenn., 1930*), novelist. Drew on his early life experiences on Western railroads in *David Vallory* (1919), *The Wreckers* (1920) and other works.

LYNDS, ELAM (*b. Litchfield, Conn., 1784; d. South Brooklyn, N.Y., 1855*), prison administrator. Originator of so-called Auburn system of prison keeping.

LYON, CALEB (*b. Lyonsdale, N.Y., 1821; d. Staten Island, N.Y., 1875*), politician, New York legislator and congressman. A polished misfit as second territorial governor of Idaho, 1864–66.

LYON, DAVID GORDON (*b. Benton, Ala., 1852; d. 1935*), educator, Orientalist. Graduated Howard College, 1875; attended Southern Baptist Theological Seminary, Louisville, Ky; Ph.D., Leipzig, 1882. Inaugurated teaching of Assyriology in the United States, 1882, at Harvard, where he taught Semitic languages and history until his retirement, 1922. [*Supp. 1*]

LYON, FRANCIS STROTHER (*b. Stokes Co., N.C. 1800; d. Demopolis, Ala., 1882*), lawyer, Alabama politician. Nephew of George S. Gaines. Congressman, Whig, from Alabama, 1835–39; served also in the Confederate Congress, 1861–65. His principal public service was as liquidator of the involved Bank of the State of Alabama, *post* 1844, when by shrewd management he saved the state from bankruptcy and many of the bank's creditors from ruin.

LYON, HARRIS MERTON (*b. Santa Fé, N. Mex., 1883; d. 1916*), journalist. Graduated University of Missouri, 1905. His short fiction as contained in *Sardonics* (1908) and *Graphics* (1913) displayed literary powers of a high order.

LYON, JAMES (*b. Newark, N.J., 1735; d. 1794*), Presbyterian clergyman, psalmodist. Pastor, principally at Machias, Maine. Author of *Urania* (Philadelphia, probably 1761; second edition, 1767).

LYON, JAMES BENJAMIN (*b. Pennsylvania Furnace, Pa., 1821; d. 1909*), Pittsburgh glass manufacturer. First to make pressed glass the chief output of his factory, *post* 1849.

LYON, MARY (*b. Buckland, Mass., 1797; d. 1849*), educator. Studied in academies at Ashfield and Amherst, Mass.; attended Byfield Seminary, 1821. After 13 years of practical teaching, she conceived of a permanent female college which would not be beyond the scope of girls of moderate means, and set about to achieve it. She opened Mount Holyoke Seminary in November 1837, at South Hadley, Mass., with a curriculum based on that followed at Amherst College. Her contribution to the education of women was threefold: the opening to women of the highest educational opportunities; the conviction that these opportunities should be used as preparation for service; the conception of such education as the development of all the powers of an individual.

LYON, MATTHEW (*b. Co. Wicklow, Ireland, 1750; d. Spadra Bluff, Ark., 1822*), Revolutionary soldier, Vermont and Kentucky legislator. Came to America, 1765; was an indentured servant in Connecticut; removed to Vermont, 1774. A leading businessman, he was elected congressman, (Democrat) Republican, from Vermont, 1797. Insulted and badgered by Federalists, his retaliation on Roger Griswold on the floor of the House, Jan. 30, 1798, was probably the first personal encounter of its kind. Prosecuted under the Sedition Act, Lyon served four months in jail, October 1798—January 1799, and was fined; re-elected triumphantly to Congress, he continued his vigorous opposition to John Adams's administration and cast the decisive vote of Vermont for election of Thomas Jefferson. Removing to Kentucky, 1801, at the head of a colony, he soon became a political power there and served as congressman, 1803–11. In his many able speeches he denounced anti-democratic tendencies but opposed the War of 1812.

LYON, NATHANIEL (*b. Ashford, Conn., 1818; d. near Wilson's Creek, Mo., 1861*), Union brigadier-general. Graduated West Point, 1841. After serving in Mexican War, and in California, he was stationed in Kansas, 1854–61. Assigned, February 1861, to the St. Louis (Mo.) Arsenal, he took command in May of all local Union forces and by constant pressure against the Confederates did much to hold Missouri for the Union. He was killed in action.

LYON, THEODATUS TIMOTHY (*b. Lima, N.Y., 1813; d. 1900*), pomologist, businessman. Removed to Michigan as a youth; engaged in pioneer railroad building there. Although self-taught, he came to be considered the most critical and accurate of American pomologists. Removing to South Haven, Mich., 1874, he assembled a collection of fruit varieties which was an important factor in the rapid development of orcharding in that region.

LYON, WILLIAM PENN (*b. Chatham, N.Y., 1822; d. Edenvale, Calif., 1913*), lawyer, Union soldier, Wisconsin legislator and jurist.

LYONS, PETER (*b. Co. Cork, Ireland ?, 1734/35; d. Hanover Co., Va., 1809*), Virginia lawyer and jurist. Licensed to practice in Virginia county courts, 1756; served as plaintiff's attorney in the "Parsons' Cause." Appointed judge of general court of Virginia, 1779, he served as president of the court, *post* 1803.

LYSTER, HENRY FRANCIS LE HUNTE (*b. Co. Wexford, Ireland, 1837; d. 1894*), physician, Union

Army surgeon. Came to America as an infant. Graduated University of Michigan, A.B., 1858; M.D., 1860. Practiced and taught mainly in Detroit, Mich.

LYTLE, WILLIAM HAINES (*b. Cincinnati, O., 1826; d. Chickamauga, Tenn., 1863*), lawyer, Union brigadier-general, Ohio legislator. Author of *Poems* (1894). Killed in action.

LYTTELTON, WILLIAM HENRY (*b. England, 1724; d. Hagley, Worcestershire, England, 1808*), colonial official, author. Appointed governor of South Carolina, 1755, he caused renewed Indian war along the borders of the colony by his high-handed detention of Cherokee chiefs who had come on a peace mission, 1759. In April 1760, he left the colony to assume the governorship of Jamaica.

MAAS, ANTHONY J. (*b. Bainkhausen, Westphalia, Germany, 1858; d. Poughkeepsie, N.Y., 1927*), Roman Catholic clergyman, Jesuit educator. Came to America *c.* 1877. Provincial of Jesuit Maryland–New York province, 1912–18, he spent most of his life as a seminary professor.

MABERY, CHARLES FREDERIC (*b. New Gloucester, Maine, 1850; d. Portland, Maine, 1927*), chemist. Graduated Lawrence Scientific School, 1876; Sc.D., 1881. Taught at Case School, Cleveland, O., 1883–1911. Authority on petroleum and on the electric furnace.

MABIE, HAMILTON WRIGHT (*b. Coldspring, N.Y., 1845; d. 1916*), lawyer, editor, essayist. Associated with the *Christian Union* (*post* 1893, the *Outlook*), 1879–1916.

McADAMS, CLARK (*b. near Otterville, Ill., 1874; d. St. Louis, Mo., 1935*), journalist, conservationist. Associated in a number of capacities from reporter to editor with the *St. Louis Post–Dispatch*, 1898–1935. [*Supp. 1*]

McAFEE, JOHN ARMSTRONG (*b. Marion Co., Mo., 1831; d. 1890*), Presbyterian clergyman, educator. Co-founder of Park College, of which he was president, 1875–90.

McAFEE, ROBERT BRECKINRIDGE (*b. present Mercer Co., Ky., 1784; d. Mercer Co., 1849*), lawyer, Kentucky legislator. Author of *A History of the Late War in the Western Country* (1816).

MACALESTER, CHARLES (*b. Campbeltown, Scotland, 1765; d. 1832*), merchant, shipowner. Emigrated to Philadelphia, Pa., *ante* 1786. Designer of the ship *Fanny* (*c.* 1800), fastest merchant vessel of her day.

MACALESTER, CHARLES (*b. Philadelphia, Pa., 1798; d. Philadelphia, 1873*), banker. Son of Charles Macalester (1765–1832). Philadelphia agent and correspondent for George Peabody. Donated site of Macalester College, Minneapolis, Minn., 1873.

McALEXANDER, ULYSSES GRANT (*b. Dundas, Minn., 1864; d. Portland, Oreg., 1936*), army officer. Graduated West Point, 1887. Awarded Silver Star for gallantry in action in Santiago campaign, 1898. Known as the "Rock of the Marne," following his brilliant conduct as colonel commanding 38th Infantry in the Surmelin Valley, France, July 15–16, 1918. McAlexander retired as major-general, 1924. [*Supp. 2*]

MacALISTER, JAMES (*b. Glasgow, Scotland, 1840; d. at sea, 1913*), educator. Came to America as a boy. Graduated Brown, 1856. Notably successful as superintendent of public schools in Milwaukee, Wis., and Philadelphia, Pa.; developed programs of industrial training. President, Drexel Institute, 1890–1913.

McALLISTER, CHARLES ALBERT (*b. Dorchester, N.J., 1867; d. New York, N.Y., 1932*), marine engineer. Chief engineer, Revenue-Cutter Service, 1902–16; U.S. Coast Guard, 1916–19. As vice-president and president of American Bureau of Shipping *post* 1919, he took a leading part in agitation for government support of American merchant marine.

McALLISTER, HALL (*b. Savannah, Ga., 1826; d. near San Rafael, Calif., 1888*), lawyer. Son of Matthew H. McAllister; brother of Samuel W. McAllister. Practiced with great success in San Francisco, Calif., *post* 1849.

McALLISTER, MATTHEW HALL (*b. Savannah, Ga., 1800; d. San Francisco, Calif., 1865*), lawyer, Georgia legislator. Father of Hall and Samuel W. McAllister. U.S. circuit judge in California, 1855–62.

McALLISTER, SAMUEL WARD (*b. Savannah, Ga., 1827; d. 1895*), lawyer, leader of New York society. Son of Matthew H. McAllister; brother of Hall McAllister. On the strength of a fortune made at San Francisco in partnership with his father and brother, 1850–52, he removed to New York and by the late 1860's had made himself arbiter of the post-Civil War "new money" society of New York. He originated the phrase the "Four Hundred" *c.* 1892, to describe the numerical limits of the city's social world.

McALPINE, WILLIAM JARVIS (*b. New York, N.Y., 1812; d. New Brighton, N.Y., 1890*), civil engineer. Apprenticed to John B. Jervis, 1827, he succeeded his teacher in 1836 as chief engineer of the eastern division of the Erie Canal. In this post and later as chief engineer of the government dry dock, Brooklyn, N.Y., he established himself as one of the leading engineers of his time. He served as engineer-in-charge and as consultant for many railroads; planned water supply systems for Chicago, San Francisco and many smaller cities; was in charge of some of the greatest bridge projects of the time. He superintended construction of the New York State Capitol, Albany, 1873, and later built Riverside Drive, New York City.

McANALLY, DAVID RICE (*b. Grainger Co., Tenn., 1810; d. 1895*), Methodist clergyman, educator. Editor, *St. Louis Christian Advocate*, 1851–95.

McANDREW, WILLIAM (*b. Ypsilanti, Mich., 1863; d. Mamaroneck, N.Y., 1937*), educator. Graduated University of Michigan, 1886. A vigorous, if not always popular, administrator, McAndrew made a notable reputation as principal of Pratt Institute, Brooklyn, N.Y., and as organizer of a girls' technical high school (Washington Irving), New York City. He served as associate superintendent of New York City schools, 1914–24. Called to Chicago, Ill., 1924, as superintendent of schools, he fell foul of Mayor W. H. Thompson ("Big Bill"); his dismissal, 1927, was subsequently overruled by the courts. A colorful personality, he stood out as one of the most rugged individualists in public education. [*Supp. 2*]

MacARTHUR, ARTHUR (*b. Springfield, Mass., 1845; d. Milwaukee, Wis., 1912*), soldier. Father of Douglas MacArthur. Raised in Wisconsin. Served with 24th Wisconsin Infantry throughout Civil War; recipient of many honors for gallantry, including the Medal of Honor, he entered the regular army as second-lieutenant, 1866, and served mainly on Western frontier duty up to 1898. After outstanding service in Philippine Islands, 1898–99, MacArthur was military governor of the Islands, 1900–01. On his return to the United States, he held various departmental commands, retiring, 1909, with the rank of lieutenant-general. [*Supp. 1*]

McARTHUR, DUNCAN (*b. Dutchess Co., N.Y., 1772; d. near Chillicothe, O., 1839*), surveyor, land speculator, Ohio legislator. Raised in the vicinity of Pittsburgh, Pa.; settled near Chillicothe, O., 1796. As brigadier-general in War of 1812, he defended Fort Meigs; he succeeded to command of army in the Northwest, 1814. Anti-Jackson governor of Ohio, 1830–32.

McARTHUR, JOHN (*b. Bladenock, Scotland, 1823; d. Philadelphia, Pa., 1890*), architect. Came to America as a child; apprenticed to a carpenter in Philadelphia, Pa. Self-taught, he was established in his profession by winning a competition for design of House of Refuge, Philadelphia, 1848. His most notable work was the Philadelphia City Hall which he designed, 1869.

McARTHUR, JOHN (*b. Erskine, Scotland, 1826; d. 1906*), manufacturer, Union major-general. Emigrated to Chicago, Ill., 1849, where he became a partner in Excelsior Iron Works; rose to colonel in the militia. Promoted brigadier-general, 1862, he distinguished himself at Shiloh and in Vicksburg campaign; his attack against Hood's left wing at Nashville, December 1864, turned the battle into a Confederate rout.

MacARTHUR, ROBERT STUART (*b. Dalesville, Canada, 1841; d. Daytona Beach, Fla., 1923*), Baptist clergyman. Graduated University of Rochester, 1867; Rochester Theological Seminary, 1870. Pastor, Calvary Baptist Church, New York City, 1870–1911. President, Baptist World Alliance, *post* 1911.

McARTHUR, WILLIAM POPE (*b. Ste. Genevieve, Mo., 1814; d. at sea off Panama, 1850*), naval officer, hydrographer. Nephew of Lewis F. Linn. Detailed to U.S. Coast Survey, 1840, he participated in surveys of the Gulf Coast, and commanded the first scientific reconnaissance of the Pacific Coast from Monterey to the Columbia River, 1848–50.

MACAULEY, EDWARD YORKE. [See McCauley, Edward Yorke, 1827–1894.]

McAULEY, JEREMIAH (*b. Ireland, c. 1839; d. New York, N.Y., 1884*), reformed criminal. Conducted Water St. Mission, New York City, 1872–82; a second mission on West 32nd Street, 1882–84. Author of *Transformed, or the History of a River Thief* (1876).

McAULEY, THOMAS (*b. Ireland, 1778; d. 1862*), Presbyterian clergyman, educator. Came to America *ante* 1799. Graduated Union, 1804; taught there, 1805–22; thereafter held pastorates in New York City and Philadelphia. A leader of the "new-school" party in his church, he was a founder of Union Theological Seminary (New York City), 1835, and its first president, 1836–40.

McBAIN, HOWARD LEE (*b. Toronto, Canada, 1880; d. 1936*), political scientist. Raised in Richmond, Va. Graduated Richmond College, 1900; Ph.D., Columbia, 1907. Taught at George Washington University and University of Wisconsin. At Columbia *post* 1913, he held chairs of Municipal Science and Constitutional Law and was dean of graduate faculties, 1929–36. Among his books, *The Law and the Practice of Municipal Home Rule* (1916) and *The Living Constitution* (1927) were outstanding. [*Supp. 2*]

McBRYDE, JOHN McLAREN (*b. Abbeville, S. C., 1841; d. New Orleans, La., 1923*), agriculturist, educator, Confederate soldier. While professor of agriculture, University of Tennessee, 1879–82, his 1880 report on application of scientific methods to agriculture marked an epoch in the history of Southern husbandry. President of South Carolina College, 1882–91, he reorganized the College and expanded it into a modern university. He accepted the presidency of Virginia Agricultural and Mechanical College, 1891, and by 1907 turned a moribund institution into a high-grade polytechnic institute. He became president emeritus, 1907. Few Southern college executives contributed more to the cause of education along so many different lines.

McBURNEY, CHARLES (*b. Roxbury, Mass., 1845; d. Brookline, Mass., 1913*), surgeon. Graduated Harvard, 1866; M.D., College of Physicians and Surgeons, New York, 1870; made postgraduate studies in surgery at Vienna, Paris and London. Taught surgery at College of Physicians and Surgeons, 1880–1907, and was a leader in the diagnosis and treatment of appendicitis. First described his diagnostic pressure point known as "McBurney's point" in the *New York Medical Journal,* December 1889; developed "McBurney's incision," 1894.

McBURNEY, ROBERT ROSS (*b. Castle-Blayney, Ireland, 1837; d. Clifton Springs, N.Y., 1898*), Young Men's Christian Association secretary. Came to America, 1854. *Post* 1865, he was a principal factor in Y.M.C.A. growth and organization in North America and throughout the world.

McCABE, CHARLES CARDWELL (*b. Athens, O., 1836; d. New York, N.Y., 1906*), Methodist clergyman. Became nationally known as chaplain, 122nd Ohio Volunteers in the Civil War; lectured widely on his experiences in Libby Prison. Gifted as a money-raiser and promoter, he was active in extension work and missions, *post* 1868; elected bishop, 1896.

McCABE, JOHN COLLINS (*b. Richmond, Va., 1810; d. Chambersburg, Pa., 1875*), Episcopal clergyman, Confederate chaplain. A frequent contributor to the *Southern Literary Messenger* and an intimate friend of Edgar A. Poe.

McCABE, WILLIAM GORDON (*b. Richmond, Va., 1841; d. 1920*), schoolmaster, Confederate soldier. Son of John C. McCabe. Conducted the University School, 1865–1901, at Petersburg, and later at Richmond, Va.

McCAFFREY, JOHN (*b. Emmitsburg, Md., 1806; d. Emmitsburg, 1881*), Roman Catholic clergyman, educator. Associated all his life with Mount St. Mary's College, Emmitsburg, as professor, rector and governor. A sound, conservative theologian, he was responsible for the training of no small proportion of the hierarchy; his *Catechism of Christian Doctrine* (1865) was widely used in elementary school classes.

McCAINE, ALEXANDER (*b. Ireland, c. 1768; d. Augusta, Ga., 1856*), clergyman, controversialist. Emigrated to Charleston, S.C., *c.* 1788; *post* 1797, rode circuits in the Carolinas and Virginia. Withdrew from the ministry, 1806, but later re-entered it. A strong opponent of episcopacy, he was a leader in founding the Methodist Protestant Church, 1830.

McCALEB, THEODORE HOWARD (*b. Pendleton District, S.C., 1810; d. "Hermitage Plantation," Miss., 1864*), jurist, educator. Studied law under Rufus Choate in Salem, Mass. Removed to New Orleans, 1832, where he practiced. Appointed U.S. judge for the District of Louisiana, 1841, he served until 1861. One of the original members of the law school faculty of the University of Louisiana (present Tulane), he taught admiralty and international law there, 1847–64.

McCALL, EDWARD RUTLEDGE (*b. Beaufort, S.C., 1790; d. Bordentown, N.J., 1853*), naval officer.

Appointed midshipman, 1808. Took over command of U.S.S. *Enterprise,* September 1813, when her captain was killed in the taking of H.M.S. *Boxer.* Performed mainly shore duties thereafter until he went on waiting orders as captain, 1835.

McCALL, JOHN AUGUSTINE (*b. Albany, N.Y., 1849; d. 1906*), insurance official. After rapid advancement in New York State department of insurance, he became comptroller of Equitable Life Insurance Co., New York, 1885, succeeding to presidency of New York Life Insurance Co., 1892. Although the company made great progress under McCall, revelations of irregularities in its management which were made during the New York State insurance investigation of 1905 compelled his resignation.

McCALL, SAMUEL WALKER (*b. East Providence, Pa., 1851; d. 1923*), lawyer, Massachusetts legislator. Graduated Dartmouth, 1874; practiced law in Boston. Congressman, Republican, from Massachusetts, 1893–1913. A strict constitutionalist and enemy of paternalism, he acted with independence in Congress and at the height of Theodore Roosevelt's popularity pointed out dangers of executive encroachment. As Republican governor of Massachusetts, 1916–18, he supported Woodrow Wilson's policies and advocated ratification of Versailles Treaty. He was author of *Thaddeus Stevens* (1898) and *The Life of Thomas Brackett Reed* (1914).

McCALLA, BOWMAN HENDRY (*b. Camden, N.J., 1844; d. Santa Barbara, Calif., 1910*), naval officer. Graduated U.S. Naval Academy, 1864. After varied sea service and shore duty, he distinguished himself in the landing at Guantanamo, Cuba, 1898, and was promoted captain. After aiding in suppressing Philippine insurrection, 1899, he commanded the American force which marched to Peking during the Boxer uprising in 1900. Promoted rear-admiral, 1903, he retired, 1906.

McCALLA, WILLIAM LATTA (*b. Jessamine Co., Ky., 1788; d. near Bayou Bidal Church, La., 1859*), Presbyterian clergyman, controversialist. A militant leader of the "old-school" party.

McCALLUM, DANIEL CRAIG (*b. Renfrewshire, Scotland, 1815; d. 1878*), engineer. Emigrated to Rochester, N.Y., as a boy. Originated and patented an inflexible arched truss bridge, 1851; specialized thereafter in bridge construction. Appointed military director of railroads, 1862, with rank of colonel in the Union Army, he superintended operation and repair of more than 2,000 miles of railroad, and bossed a construction corps of some 10,000 men. One of his most important achievements was the supplying of Gen. W. T. Sherman's army during the Atlanta campaign. At the end of the war he received a brevet of major-general.

MacCAMERON, ROBERT (*b. Chicago, Ill., 1866; d. New York, N.Y., 1912*), figure and portrait painter.

Raised in rural Wisconsin, he studied at the Y.M.C.A. in Chicago, Ill. and was successful as an illustrator. *Post* 1889 he resided in France, studied under J. L. Gérôme, and won critical recognition and success, 1904–07. His best work was done in the portrayal of the unfortunate and destitute.

McCANN, ALFRED WATTERSON (*b. Pittsburgh, Pa., 1879; d. 1931*), journalist, pure-food reformer.

McCANN, WILLIAM PENN (*b. Paris, Ky., 1830; d. New Rochelle, N.Y., 1906*), naval officer. Distinguished *post* 1848 in general service; promoted commodore, 1887; retired, 1892.

McCARREN, PATRICK HENRY (*b. East Cambridge, Mass., 1847; d. 1909*), politician, New York legislator. Succeeded Hugh McLaughlin as Democratic boss of Brooklyn, N.Y., 1903; thereafter fought successfully to keep Tammany from securing control of Brooklyn.

McCARROLL, JAMES (*b. Lanesboro, Ireland, 1814; d. 1892*), journalist, dramatist. Emigrated to Canada *c.* 1831. Active toward the end of his life in New York City journalism.

McCARTEE, DIVIE BETHUNE (*b. Philadelphia, Pa., 1820; d. San Francisco, Calif., 1900*), Presbyterian medical missionary. M.D., University of Pennsylvania, 1840. Missionary to China, 1843–72, during which time he served also in U.S. consular offices. Professor of law and science, Imperial University at Tokyo, Japan, 1872–77. Thereafter he enjoyed a varied career as diplomat and missionary executive.

McCARTHY, CHARLES (*b. Brockton, Mass., 1873; d. Prescott, Ariz., 1921*), political scientist, publicist. Graduated Brown, 1896; Ph.D., University of Wisconsin, 1901. Organized at Madison, Wis., for the use of legislators, the first official reference library and bill-drafting bureau in the United States, which he directed until his death. Author of *The Anti-Masonic Party* (1903) and *The Wisconsin Idea* (1912).

McCARTNEY, WASHINGTON (*b. Westmoreland Co., Pa., 1812; d. Easton, Pa., 1856*), lawyer, mathematician, Pennsylvania educator and jurist.

McCAULEY, CHARLES STEWART (*b. Philadelphia, Pa., 1793; d. Washington, D.C., 1869*), naval officer. Nephew of Comm. Charles Stewart. As commandant of Norfolk, Va., navy-yard, 1860–61, he scuttled the ships therein and abandoned the post without a defense after secession of the state of Virginia. Censured for this single questionable action in a long, honorable career, he was retired in 1862.

MacCAULEY, CLAY (*b. Chambersburg, Pa., 1843; d. Berkeley, Calif., 1925*), Unitarian clergyman, Union soldier. Graduated Princeton, 1864; Presbyterian Theological Seminary of the Northwest, 1867. Held numerous pastorates; made studies of Seminole Indians of Florida; served as missionary in Japan, 1889–1920.

McCAULEY, EDWARD YORKE (*b. Philadelphia, Pa., 1827; d. Canonicut Island, Narragansett Bay, R.I., 1894*), naval officer, Egyptologist. Nephew of Charles S. McCauley.

McCAULEY, MARY LUDWIG HAYS (*b. near Trenton, N.J., 1754; d. 1832*), Revolutionary heroine, better known as "Molly Pitcher." While carrying water to soldiers at battle of Monmouth, June 28, 1778, she took her husband's place when he fell overcome by the heat and served his gun ably through the rest of the battle.

McCAUSLAND, JOHN (*b. St. Louis, Mo., 1836; d. Mason Co., W. Va., 1927*), Confederate brigadier-general. Graduated Virginia Military Institute, 1857. On a raid into Pennsylvania, he burned the town of Chambersburg, July 30, 1864, under specific orders from Gen. Jubal Early.

McCAW, JAMES BROWN (*b. Richmond, Va., 1823; d. Richmond, 1906*), physician, educator. Supervised Confederate Chimborazo Hospital, the largest in use during the Civil War; was associated, *post* 1865, as professor and dean, with Medical College of Virginia.

McCAWLEY, CHARLES GRYMES (*b. Philadelphia, Pa., 1827; d. Rosemont, Pa., 1891*), soldier. Appointed second-lieutenant, U.S. Marine Corps, 1847, he served with great ability and gallantry in both Mexican and Civil Wars. Made colonel-commandant of Marine Corps, 1876, he retired, 1891.

McCAWLEY, CHARLES LAURIE (*b. Boston, Mass., 1865; d. 1935*), soldier, Marine officer. Son of Charles G. McCawley. Served in Cuba during Spanish-American War and in Philippine insurrection; military aide to Pres. Theodore Roosevelt. Commissioned colonel, 1913, and brigadier-general, 1916, he served as quartermaster, U.S. Marine Corps, 1913–29. [*Supp. 1*]

McCAY, CHARLES FRANCIS (*b. Danville, Pa., 1810; d. Baltimore, Md., 1889*), mathematician, actuary. Brother of Henry K. McCay. Graduated Jefferson College, 1829. Taught mathematics and science at Lafayette College, at University of Georgia, and at South Carolina College, where he was president, 1855–57. Thereafter, he was active as a banker and as consulting actuary to life insurance companies. He prepared what is believed to have been the first "select and ultimate" table of life insurance mortality in the United States, 1887.

McCAY, HENRY KENT (*b. Northumberland Co., Pa., 1820; d. 1886*), lawyer, Confederate soldier. Brother of Charles F. McCay. Removed to Georgia *c.* 1839. Justice, Georgia supreme court, 1868–75; U.S. judge, northern district of Georgia, 1882–86.

McCLAIN, EMLIN (*b. Salem, O., 1851; d. 1915*), lawyer, Iowa jurist. Professor of law, State Univ. of Iowa, 1881–1901; justice, Iowa supreme court, 1901–13. Author of a number of authoritative texts and annotations on Iowa law.

McCLATCHY, CHARLES KENNY (*b. Sacramento, Calif., 1858; d. near Sacramento, 1936*), journalist. Editor of the *Sacramento Bee, post* 1884, also co-owner; an outspoken independent progressive.

[*Supp.* 2]

McCLELLAN, GEORGE (*b. Woodstock, Conn., 1796; d. 1847*), anatomist, surgeon. Graduated Yale, 1816; M.D., University of Pennsylvania, 1819. Founded Jefferson Medical College, Philadelphia, 1825, at which he taught until 1839; helped establish Pennsylvania College medical school at Gettysburg. Made early use of clinical methods in teaching.

McCLELLAN, GEORGE (*b. Philadelphia, Pa., 1849; d. 1913*), anatomist, physician. Grandson of George McClellan (1796–1847). Graduated University of Pennsylvania, 1869; Jefferson Medical College, 1870. Founded Pennsylvania School of Anatomy and Surgery, 1881, and taught there with great success until 1898. He taught anatomy also at Pennsylvania Academy of the Fine Arts and Jefferson Medical College. Author of *Regional Anatomy* (1891, 1892).

McCLELLAN, GEORGE BRINTON (*b. Philadelphia, Pa., 1826; d. Orange, N.J., 1885*), soldier. Son of George McClellan (1796–1847); cousin of Henry B. McClellan. Graduated West Point, 1846; was assigned to the Engineers. Serving in Gen. Winfield Scott's command during the war with Mexico, he was often mentioned in dispatches and won brevet of captain. Assistant instructor in military engineering, West Point, 1848–51, he went in March 1852 with R. B. Marcy's expedition to explore sources of the Red River in Arkansas; thereafter, he undertook varied duties until his appointment as captain of cavalry, 1855. He was detailed in April 1855 as a member of a board sent to study European military systems. While abroad he made a complete study of the siege of Sevastopol and on his return proposed a new type of cavalry saddle which was then adopted and remained standard. Resigning his commission, January 1857, he became chief engineer of the Illinois Central Railroad and in 1860, president of the Ohio and Mississippi Railroad.

Appointed major-general of Ohio Volunteers, April 23, 1861, he was named (as of date May 3) major-general of the regular army in command of the Department of the Ohio. His prompt action in his Department helped keep Kentucky and western Virginia in the Union; his success in the campaign of Rich Mountain led to his appointment to command the Division of the Potomac. Arriving in Washington on July 26, after the defeat at Bull Run, he found the troops in utter confusion but with great energy began their reorganization and retraining. On retirement of Gen. Winfield Scott in November, McClellan became general-in-chief in his place. Overestimating the strength of the Confederates, McClellan refused to make any decisive move despite the impatience of

President Lincoln, with whom he disagreed also on the proper strategy to employ. Lincoln believed that the army should move directly against the Confederates at and about Manassas; McClellan urged that he should transport the army by water to the lower Rappahannock and advance on Richmond from the east. Lincoln consented at last to such a move by way of Fortress Monroe but imposed conditions to maintain the security of the city of Washington. Relieved as general-in-chief, McClellan took the field with his Army of the Potomac early in April 1862 but was hampered by the withdrawal of McDowell's corps for the defense of Washington.

On the advance from Fortress Monroe, McClellan was delayed for a month before Yorktown but then moved up the peninsula toward Richmond. Further delays were caused by heavy rains and impassable roads; on the Chickahominy River there was another long delay. The first Union troops to cross had heavy fighting at Seven Pines on May 31, 1862, and at Fair Oaks on June 1, but a position almost at the gates of Richmond was occupied and entrenched. The arrival of Confederate Gen. T. J. Jackson in support of Gen. R. E. Lee encouraged the Confederate command to attack McClellan's army on the left bank of the river, June 26. After a Union defeat at Gaines's Mill, the Confederate pursuit was finally checked at Malvern Hill on July 1. This ended the campaign known as the Seven Days' Battles, and the Union Army established itself at Harrison's Landing. McClellan in dispatches charged failure of support from Washington, insisting that he was outnumbered and demanding for a further offensive a greater reinforcement than the President or Gen. Halleck was willing to provide. On August 3, the Army of the Potomac was ordered withdrawn and its troops were assigned to Gen. Pope's Army of Virginia. After Pope's defeat at the second battle of Bull Run, McClellan was called upon again to reorganize the army and defend Washington. Pope's retreating soldiers received him with enthusiasm and between September 1 and September 13 he restored their morale. Learning that the Confederates were much scattered, he moved to take advantage of this but too slowly. Lee succeeded in concentrating his forces and was able to avoid destruction in the fierce battles of South Mountain and Antietam (Sept. 17, 1862). McClellan, overcautious as ever, permitted Lee to withdraw his army across the Potomac and did not follow until late in October. Superseded by Gen. Burnside at Warrenton, Va., on November 7, he was never again employed in the field.

Nominated as Democratic candidate for the presidency, 1864, he ran on a peace platform but carried only the states of New Jersey, Delaware and Kentucky against Abraham Lincoln. He held various employments as an engineer thereafter, and from January 1878 to January 1881 served as governor of New Jersey. An excellent linguist and a scholar of his military profession, he was also well informed in archeological research and exploration. As a soldier, he took the best of care of his men and had the faculty of inspiring confidence and loyalty in them. His concepts of strategy and of tactics were clear and sound, but he was never satisfied with what he had; he could always see the way in which he might make an improvement if he were given time, and he took time at the expense of losing opportunity. He accepted too readily the strength estimates given him by his intelligence service, which consistently placed the number of Confederates too high. It should be remembered that up until the time of the Civil War he had held no actual field commands. It is probable that he came to supreme command too early in his career. Robert E. Lee, who was very well aware of McClellan's deficiencies, set him down as the best commander who faced him during the war.

McCLELLAN, GEORGE BRINTON (*b. Dresden, Saxony, 1865; d. Washington, D.C., 1940*), politician, educator. Son of George B. McClellan (1826–1885). Graduated Princeton, 1886. A sachem and prominent orator of Tammany Hall, McClellan was elected president of the New York City board of aldermen, 1892, and served as a congressman from New York, 1895–1903. Running against Seth Low for mayor of New York, 1903, McClellan won easily and served until 1909; *post* 1905, he showed a pronounced independence of Tammany and accomplished a program of public works with efficiency and imagination. His flouting of Charles F. Murphy, the Tammany boss, cost him any further chances he might have had for political preferment. He served as professor of economic history at Princeton, 1912–31. He was author, among other books, of *The Oligarchy of Venice* (1904) and *Venice and Bonaparte* (1931). [*Supp. 2*]

McCLELLAN, HENRY BRAINERD (*b. Philadelphia, Pa., 1840; d. 1904*), Confederate soldier, educator. Cousin of George B. McClellan (1826–1885). Graduated Williams, 1858. Entering the Confederate Army as a private, 1861, he rose to rank of major and served as chief of staff to Generals J. E. B. Stuart and Wade Hampton. He was principal of Sayre Female Institute, Lexington, Ky., 1870–1904.

McCLELLAN, ROBERT (*b. near Mercersburg, Pa., 1770; d. Missouri, 1815*), Indian trader, scout. Won rank of lieutenant for bravery in Gen. Anthony Wayne's campaign of 1794–95; was active in Indian trade on the upper Missouri, 1807–10. Accompanied Pacific Fur Co. expedition to Astoria, 1811–13.

McCLELLAND, ROBERT (*b. Greencastle, Pa., 1807; d. Detroit, Mich., 1880*), lawyer, Michigan legislator. Removed to Monroe, Mich., 1833; was active in organizing the new state government and the Democratic party there. Served as congressman, Democrat, from Michigan, 1843–49; became chief lieutenant of Lewis Cass. As governor of Michigan, 1851–53, he brought his fellow Michigan Democrats to endorse the compromise measures of 1850. Appointed U.S. secretary of the interior, 1853, he reorganized the department, reduced corruption and waste in the land, Indian and pension bureaus, and called for special legislation to prevent reoccurrence of difficulties. None of his major recommendations were adopted by Congress. A conservative, he joined W. L. Marcy in urging President Pierce to follow a neutral policy in Kansas. *Post* 1857, he practiced law in Detroit.

McCLENAHAN, HOWARD (*b. Port Deposit, Md., 1872; d. Winter Park, Fla., 1935*), educator. Taught physics at Princeton, 1897–1925; was made dean of the college, 1912. Served as secretary of Franklin Institute, Philadelphia, 1925–35. [*Supp. 1*]

McCLERNAND, JOHN ALEXANDER (*b. near Hardinsburg, Ky., 1812; d. Springfield, Ill., 1900*), lawyer, Illinois legislator, Union soldier. Raised in Illinois; admitted to the bar, 1832. A staunch Jacksonian, he hated Abolitionists. As congressman, 1843–51, 1859–61, he urged conciliation between the sections and popular sovereignty as a remedy for the slavery crisis. Leaving Congress on the outbreak of the Civil War, he accepted a brigadier-general's commission and by vigor and personal bravery rose to major-general, March 1862. Ambitious, tactless, he disliked West Pointers and was critical of Gen. U. S. Grant in letters to President Lincoln and to Gen. Halleck. Unauthorized by Grant, with navy support he reduced Arkansas Post, January 1863, and continued to conduct himself independently. Charged by Grant with tardiness and responsibility for heavy loss in the Vicksburg campaign, he was ordered back to Illinois, June 1863, but early in 1864 regained command of the XIII Corps scattered between New Orleans and the Rio Grande. Sickness prevented his participation in the Red River expedition, April 1864, and he resigned his commission in November.

McCLINTOCK, EMORY (*b. Carlisle, Pa., 1840; d. 1916*), mathematician, actuary. Son of John M'Clintock. Associated for many years as actuary with Northwestern Life Insurance Co. of Milwaukee and Mutual Life Insurance Co. of New York, he was at the head of his profession in his time.

McCLINTOCK, JAMES HARVEY (*b. Sacramento, Calif., 1864; d. Sawtelle, Calif., 1934*), Arizona journalist, soldier. Commanded a troop of Roosevelt's Rough Riders, 1898; was active in Arizona National Guard activities. [*Supp. 1*]

M'CLINTOCK, JOHN (*b. Philadelphia, Pa., 1814; d. 1870*), Methodist clergyman, educator. Taught at Dickinson College, 1836–48; editor, *Methodist Quarterly Review*, 1848–56. First president, Drew Theological Seminary, 1867–70. Co-editor, with Dr. James Strong, of celebrated *Cyclopoedia of Biblical, Theological and Ecclesiastical Literature*, 1853–70.

McCLINTOCK, OLIVER (*b. Pittsburgh, Pa., 1839; d. 1922*), Pittsburgh merchant, political reformer. Led fight (c. 1885–1895) against corrupt political ring headed by Christopher L. Magee.

McCLOSKEY, JOHN (*b. Brooklyn, N.Y., 1810; d. near Yonkers, N.Y., 1885*), Roman Catholic clergyman, first American cardinal. Graduated Mount St. Mary's College, Emmitsburg, Md., 1828; attended Gregorian University, Rome, 1835–37. Consecrated coadjutor to Bishop John Hughes of New York, March 1844, he was a conservative dependable counselor; on erection of Albany, N.Y., into a separate see in 1847, McCloskey was given charge of that diocese. Succeeding as archbishop of New York on the death of Hughes, 1864, he continued in a conservative course. During his incumbency there was great progress in the building of charitable institutions; owing largely to his efforts St. Patrick's Cathedral was completed and made ready for dedication, May 1879. Created cardinal, March 1875, he continued active in the management of the New York archdiocese until 1884.

McCLOSKEY, WILLIAM GEORGE (*b. Brooklyn, N.Y., 1823; d. 1909*), Roman Catholic clergyman. First rector of the American College in Rome, 1859–68; bishop of Louisville, Ky., 1868–1909.

McCLURE, ALEXANDER KELLY (*b. Sherman's Valley, Pa., 1828; d. 1909*), newspaper editor, Pennsylvania Republican legislator, lawyer. Helped switch Pennsylvania vote to Abraham Lincoln at Republican convention, Chicago, 1860. As chairman of state committee, perfected organization of Republican machine in Pennsylvania. Chairman, Liberal Republican delegation from Pennsylvania, 1872.

McCLURE, ALEXANDER WILSON (*b. Boston, Mass., 1808; d. Canonsburg, Pa., 1865*), Congregational and Dutch Reformed clergyman, editor.

McCLURE, GEORGE (*b. near Londonderry, Ireland, c. 1770; d. Elgin, Ill., 1851*), merchant, soldier. Came to America c. 1790; removed to Bath, N.Y., c. 1793. Serving as brigadier-general of New York militia in War of 1812, he was responsible for burning of Newark, Canada, which brought about British reprisals against Buffalo, N.Y.

McCLURG, ALEXANDER CALDWELL (*b. Philadelphia, Pa., 1832; d. St. Augustine, Fla., 1901*), bookseller, publisher, Union soldier. Cousin of Joseph W. McClurg. Graduated Miami University, Ohio, 1853. Removed to Chicago, Ill., 1859. After winning recognition as an able staff officer in Western campaigns, 1862–65, he built up in Chicago one of the leading bookselling businesses in the Middle West.

McCLURG, JAMES (*b. near Hampton, Va., c. 1746; d. Richmond, Va., 1823*), physician, Revolutionary soldier. As a Virginia delegate to the federal convention, 1787, McClurg advocated a life tenure for the executive and strove to keep the executive as far removed from legislative control as possible.

McCLURG, JOSEPH WASHINGTON (*b. St. Louis Co., Mo., 1818; d. Lebanon, Mo., 1900*), merchant, Republican politician. Cousin of Alexander C. McClurg. As congressman, Republican, from Missouri, 1863–68, he became an ardent disciple of Thaddeus Stevens and a strenuous supporter of carpetbag policies. During his term as governor of Missouri, 1869–71, he was dominated by Charles D. Drake and other Radical Republicans; the memory of the proscriptions which he sponsored was responsible for Democratic success in Missouri over the following thirty years.

McCOMAS, LOUIS EMORY (*b. near Williamsport, Md., 1846; d. 1907*), lawyer. Congressman, Republican, from Maryland, 1883–91; justice, supreme court of District of Columbia, 1892–99; U.S. senator from Maryland, 1899–1905. Active in congressional committee work, he was especially interested in currency problems, the suppression of alien contract labor, civil service reform and anti-trust legislation.

McCOMB, JOHN (*b. New York, N.Y., 1763; d. 1853*), architect. Began independent practice, 1790; won competition for design of New York City Hall, 1802, in association with Joseph F. Mangin; superintended execution of the design until completion, 1812. Thereafter, McComb designed many churches and public buildings in New York City which illustrated the persistence of American colonial tradition, with strong British influence, into the 19th century.

McCONNEL, JOHN LUDLUM (*b. present Scott Co., Ill., 1826; d. 1862*), lawyer, novelist. Author, among other works, of *Talbot and Vernon* (1850), *The Glenns* (1851) and *Western Characters: or Types of Border Life* (1853), which are of value as studies of life on the frontier.

McCONNELL, IRA WELCH (*b. Schell City, Mo., 1871; d. 1933*), engineer. C. E., Cornell, 1897. Worked with U.S. Reclamation Service, 1903–09 and later with private firms as an irrigation and hydraulics expert. Associated, *post* 1918, with Dwight P. Robinson & Co., Inc., and United Engineers & Constructors, Inc., in many large projects here and abroad.

[*Supp.* 1]

McCOOK, ALEXANDER McDOWELL (*b. Columbiana Co., O., 1831; d. Dayton, O., 1903*), soldier. Graduated West Point, 1852. As divisional commander, Army of the Ohio, he performed outstanding service at Corinth, Nashville and Shiloh; commanding XIV and later XX Corps in Army of the Cumberland, he was relieved in October 1863, for failure at Chickamauga, but was exonerated by a military court. After the Civil War he performed varied military service in the West. Promoted major-general, 1894, he retired the following year.

McCOOK, ANSON GEORGE (*b. Steubenville, O., 1835; d. New York, N.Y., 1917*), lawyer, Union soldier. Brother of Edward M., Henry C. and John J.

McCook; cousin of Alexander McD. McCook. For service in many engagements in all theatres of the Civil War, he received brevet of brigadier-general of volunteers, 1865. In practice in New York *post* 1873, he served creditably as a Republican congressman from that state, 1877–83; was secretary of the U.S. Senate, 1884–93. For many years he was editor of the *Daily Register*, later the *New York Law Journal*.

McCOOK, EDWARD MOODY (*b. Steubenville, O., 1833; d. Chicago, Ill., 1909*), lawyer, Union brigadier-general, financier. Brother of Anson G., Henry C. and John J. McCook; cousin of Alexander McD. McCook. An outstanding cavalry commander in Army of the Cumberland, he performed his most brilliant exploit by cutting off Atlanta from reinforcement when under siege. After the war, he held several federal administrative and diplomatic posts, including governorship of Territory of Colorado (1869–73, 1874–75). Thereafter, he was very successful as a financier.

McCOOK, HENRY CHRISTOPHER (*b. New Lisbon, O., 1837; d. 1911*), Presbyterian clergyman, naturalist. Brother of Anson G., Edward M. and John J. McCook; cousin of Alexander McD. McCook. Held pastorates in Midwest and at Tabernacle Presbyterian Church, Philadelphia, Pa., 1870–1902. Author of many valuable technical papers on spiders and ants, he published a number of popular works as well on natural history subjects and also *The Latimers* (1897), a story of the Whiskey Rebellion.

McCOOK, JOHN JAMES (*b. New Lisbon, O., 1843; d. 1927*), Episcopal clergyman, Union soldier, educator. Brother of Edward M., Anson G. and Henry C. McCook; cousin of Alexander McD. McCook. Rector at St. John's Church, East Hartford, Conn., 1868–1927; taught at Trinity College, Hartford, 1883–1923.

McCORD, DAVID JAMES (*b. St. Matthew's Parish, S.C., 1797; d. 1855*), lawyer, South Carolina legislator. Under his editorship *post* 1823, the *Columbia Telescope* became the most violent of all nullification newspapers. He edited Volumes VI to X of the *Statutes at Large of South Carolina* (1839–42).

McCORD, LOUISA SUSANNA CHEVES (*b. Charleston, S.C., 1810; d. Charleston, 1879*), writer. Daughter of Langdon Cheves; second wife of David J. McCord. Contributor of conservative pro-slavery essays to ante-bellum Southern journals.

McCORMACK, JOSEPH NATHANIEL (*b. near Howard's Mill, Ky., 1847; d. Louisville, Ky., 1922*), physician. M.D., Miami University, 1870. As a member of Kentucky State Board of Health, and as its secretary, 1883–1913, he won national reputation in public health work, particularly in rural districts. Brought about rehabilitation of the American Medical Association during his chairmanship of the Association's committee on organization, 1899–1913.

McCORMICK, CYRUS HALL (*b. Rockbridge Co., Va., 1809; d. Chicago, Ill., 1884*), inventor, manufacturer. Son of Robert McCormick. After his father's abandonment of plan to perfect a reaping machine, Cyrus McCormick constructed a crude machine on different principles, which was successful in use on his home farm in the fall of 1831. After introducing improvements, he exhibited his machine on several farms near Lexington, Va., 1832; on hearing of similar work by Obed Hussey, 1833, he took out a patent for his reaper, June 21, 1834. *Post* 1837, McCormick turned seriously to exploitation of his invention. After unfortunate experiences with licensees, he erected his own factory in Chicago, Ill., 1847, closed out other manufacturing contracts, and by 1850 had succeeded in building up a national business. Although he had to compete against Hussey's reaper and at least thirty other rival manufacturers, by hard work and constant improvement of his machine he managed to hold his premier place among reaping machine manufacturers. McCormick was a pioneer in modern business methods. He was among the first to introduce use of field trials, guarantees and testimonials in advertising, deferred payments for merchandise, also to promote the invention and use in his factory of labor-saving machinery. He was an active benefactor of the Presbyterian Church and took a part in Democratic party councils until his death.

McCORMICK, CYRUS HALL (*b. Washington, D.C., 1859; d. Lake Forest, Ill., 1936*), farm-machinery manufacturer. Son of Cyrus H. McCormick (1809–1884). After serving as assistant to his father, he became president of McCormick Harvesting Machine Co., 1884. In 1902, with William Deering and other industry leaders, he brought about organization of the International Harvester Co. of which he became president and continued in the presidency until 1918, when he assumed chairmanship of board of directors. Under his direction the company defended itself against a succession of rugged anti-trust suits, expanded its research departments and instituted numerous employee benefits. [*Supp. 2*]

McCORMICK, JOSEPH MEDILL (*b. Chicago, Ill., 1877; d. Washington, D.C., 1925*), journalist, politician. Son of Robert S. McCormick; grandson of Joseph Medill. Graduated Yale, 1900. Associated all his life with the family newspaper, *Chicago Tribune;* shared in ownership of several Cleveland, O., newspapers. An ardent follower of Theodore Roosevelt, he returned to the Republican party, 1914, and served as congressman from Illinois, 1917–19, and as U.S. senator, 1919–25. He opposed the League of Nations and the Versailles Treaty; sponsored the bill providing for creation of the Bureau of the Budget, 1921. He also encouraged the proposed "Great Lakes to Gulf waterway" and favored the child-labor amendment.

McCORMICK, LEANDER JAMES (*b. Rockbridge Co., Va., 1819; d. Chicago, Ill., 1900*), manufacturer, philanthropist. Son of Robert McCormick; brother of Cyrus H. McCormick (1809–1884). Aided his father and brother in construction of reapers. *Post* 1849, he supervised the manufacturing department of the McCormick Harvesting Machine Co.

McCORMICK, MEDILL. [See McCORMICK, JOSEPH MEDILL, 1877–1925].

McCORMICK, RICHARD CUNNINGHAM (*b. New York, N.Y., 1832; d. Jamaica, N.Y., 1901*), journalist, businessman, politician. Acted as war correspondent for New York newspapers in the Crimea and with Army of the Potomac, 1861–62. An early and enthusiastic Republican, he was appointed secretary of Arizona Territory, 1863, and governor, 1866. He served as territorial delegate to Congress, 1869–75. A progressive and intelligent executive, he urged improvement of communications, development of agriculture along with mining, a conservation policy and humane treatment of the Indians.

McCORMICK, ROBERT (*b. Rockbridge Co., Va., 1780; d. Rockbridge Co., 1846*), inventor. Father of Leander J. and Cyrus H. McCormick (1809–1884). After developing and patenting a number of agricultural implements which included a hempbrake and a threshing machine, he abandoned a twenty-year effort to devise a power implement for reaping grain in 1831. His son, Cyrus H. McCormick, was inspired by his efforts to invent in that same year a workable reaper which the father manufactured, *post* 1837, on a contract basis.

McCORMICK, ROBERT SANDERSON (*b. Rockbridge Co., Va., 1849; d. Chicago, Ill., 1919*), diplomat. Grandson of Robert McCormick; nephew of Leander J. and Cyrus H. McCormick (1809–1884). U.S. ambassador to Austria-Hungary, 1902; to Russia, 1902–05; to France, 1905–07.

McCORMICK, SAMUEL BLACK (*b. Westmoreland Co., Pa., 1858; d. near Pittsburgh, Pa., 1928*), Presbyterian clergyman, educator. Graduated Washington and Jefferson College, 1880. President, Coe College, 1897–1904. Chancellor, Western University of Pennsylvania (University of Pittsburgh), 1904–20, he was responsible for its great expansion and modernization both in scope and physical plant.

McCORMICK, STEPHEN (*b. Auburn, Va., 1784; d. 1875*), inventor, manufacturer. Invented, *ante* 1816, a cast-iron plow on which he took out his first patent, 1819. His plow, made of detachable parts, consisted of a cast-iron mould board, to the bottom of which was fastened an adjustable wrought-iron point whereby the furrow was deepened and the soil more thoroughly pulverized. Manufactured chiefly between 1826 and 1850, McCormick's plows were widely used in Virginia and other Southern states.

McCOSH, ANDREW JAMES (*b. Belfast, Ireland, 1858; d. 1908*), surgeon. Son of James McCosh. Came to America as a boy. Graduated Princeton, 1877; M.D., N.Y. College of Physicians and Surgeons, 1880. Long associated with New York Presbyterian Hospital, he was a professor of surgery at New York Polyclinic and at College of Physicians and Surgeons. His published papers cover every department of major surgery and he was an outstanding operator.

McCOSH, JAMES (*b. Ayrshire, Scotland, 1811; d. Princeton, N.J., 1894*), Presbyterian clergyman, philosopher. Educated at Glasgow and Edinburgh universities. Licensed to preach by the Established Church of Scotland, 1834, he was one of those who seceded from it to set up the Free Church of Scotland, thereby sacrificing his living and his prospects. Independent in philosophy as he was in church polity, McCosh reacted against his first teacher, William Hamilton, and adopted the intuitionism of Reid and the Scottish school. His first book, a critique of John Stuart Mill, led to his appointment as professor of logic and metaphysics, Queen's College, Belfast, Ireland, a post which he held, 1852–68. Firmly established as a philosopher by his work at Belfast, McCosh accepted the presidency of the College of New Jersey (Princeton), 1868. During his twenty years' administration, the faculty was strengthened; a balanced system of elective studies and graduate work was instituted; schools of science, philosophy and art were organized; fellowships and other means for stimulating research were provided; and the physical plant of the university was greatly extended. During the early 1870's, President McCosh stood almost alone among U.S. ministers in defense of the doctrine of evolution, insisting that the doctrine was not directly or by implication a denial of God. He became president emeritus, 1888.

McCOY, ELIJAH (*b. Canada, 1843; d. Eloise, Mich., 1929*), inventor. A Negro, McCoy engaged in mechanical work at an early age and soon showed marked inventive talent. Resident in Ypsilanti, Mich., c. 1870, he began experiments with lubricators for steam engines and obtained six patents for lubricating devices, 1872–76. McCoy is regarded as the pioneer in devising means for steady supply of oil to machinery in intermittent drops from a cup. Active in Detroit, Mich., 1882–1926, he received 44 additional patents, which included a locomotive steam dome, a wheel tire and an improved airbrake lubricator.

McCOY, ISAAC (*b. near Uniontown, Pa., 1784; d. Louisville, Ky., 1846*), Baptist missionary, Indian agent. In his *Remarks on the Practicability of Indian Reform* (1827), he advanced a plan to remove Eastern Indians west of the Mississippi River and to form an Indian state for them. Appointed U.S. agent to assist Indians in their westward migration, 1830, he surveyed, or caused to be surveyed, most of the Indian reservations in Kansas and the Cherokee Outlet in Oklahoma but his plan for a separate state never materialized.

McCOY, JOSEPH GEATING (*b. Sangamon Co., Ill., 1837; d. Kansas City, Mo., 1915*), pioneer cattleman. Founded terminal point for cattle drives at Abilene, Kans., 1867; established cattle drives to Cottonwood Falls and to Wichita; helped open Chisholm Trail. Author of *Historic Sketches of the Cattle Trade* (1874), an important source work.

MacCRACKEN, HENRY MITCHELL (*b. Oxford, O., 1840; d. Orlando, Fla., 1918*), Presbyterian clergyman, educator. Graduated Miami University, 1857; studied also at Princeton Theological Seminary and universities of Tübingen and Berlin. *Post* 1881, he turned from pastoral to educational work. Becoming professor of philosophy, University of the City of New York (present New York University), 1884, he was appointed vice-chancellor, 1885, and chancellor, 1891. Between 1885 and 1910, MacCracken completely transformed and greatly expanded New York University, removing the college to University Heights, establishing a graduate school and schools of pedagogy and commerce, and bringing the medical school in combination with Bellevue Hospital Medical College under direct control of the University council.

McCRADY, EDWARD (*b. Charleston, S.C., 1833; d. 1903*), lawyer, Confederate officer, South Carolina legislator. Author of *The History of South Carolina* (1897, 1899, 1901, 1902). Despite its neglect of manuscript sources and its pedestrian style, this work (which covers 1670–1783) is one of the best narrative histories which exist for any of the original commonwealths.

McCRAE, THOMAS (*b. Guelph, Canada, 1870; d. Philadelphia, Pa., 1935*), physician. Graduated University of Toronto, 1891; M.B., 1895; M.D., 1903. Associated with Johns Hopkins Hospital, 1896–1912; professor of medicine, Jefferson Medical College, 1912–35. Joint author with William Osler in revisions of *The Principles and Practice of Medicine.* [*Supp.* 1]

McCRARY, GEORGE WASHINGTON (*b. near Evansville, Ind., 1835; d. 1890*), lawyer, Iowa legislator. Congressman, Republican, from Iowa, 1869–77; U.S. secretary of war, 1877–79; U.S. circuit judge, Eighth Judicial Circuit, 1879–84.

McCREARY, JAMES BENNETT (*b. Madison Co., Ky., 1838; d. Richmond, Ky., 1918*), lawyer, Confederate soldier, Kentucky legislator. Democratic governor of Kentucky, 1875–79 and 1911–15; congressman from Kentucky, 1885–97 and U.S. senator, 1903–09. A sound money Democrat, McCreary favored international bimetallism; as governor he strove for liberal reforms.

McCREERY, CHARLES (*b. near Winchester, Ky., 1785; d. West Point, Ky., 1826*), pioneer Kentucky physician. Practiced in Hartford, Ky., *post* 1810; performed first U.S. operation for complete extirpation of the clavicle, 1813.

McCREERY, JAMES WORK (*b. Indiana Co., Pa., 1849; d. 1923*), lawyer, Colorado legislator, authority on irrigation law.

McCULLAGH, JOSEPH BURBRIDGE (*b. Dublin, Ireland, 1842; d. St. Louis, Mo., 1896*), journalist, Union soldier. Came to America *c.* 1853. Won repute as a Civil War correspondent and as Washington correspondent for Cincinnati, O., papers; worked later in Chicago and St. Louis. Editor of *St. Louis Globe-Democrat*, 1875–96.

McCULLOCH, BEN (*b. Rutherford Co., Tenn., 1811; d. Elkhorn Tavern, Ark., 1862*), surveyor, soldier. Served in Texas army at battle of San Jacinto. Settled at Gonzales, 1838; became one of the most popular figures in Texas as an Indian-fighting ranger; commanded a company of rangers with Zachary Taylor's army in Mexican War. In California, 1849–52; U.S. marshal, coast district of Texas, 1853–59. Commissioned brigadier-general, Confederate Army, he commanded at battle of Wilson's Creek, August 1861. Died in battle at Elkhorn Tavern.

McCULLOCH, HUGH (*b. Kennebunk, Maine, 1808; d. Prince George's Co., Md., 1895*), lawyer, banker. Removed to Fort Wayne, Ind., 1833; won high reputation for management of State Bank of Indiana in panics of 1837 and 1857. Visiting Washington, D.C., 1862, to oppose projected national banking legislation, he was asked by Salmon P. Chase in March 1863 to accept office as comptroller of currency and launch the new system himself. Successful in this task because of his influence with existing state banks, McCulloch held office until March 1865 when he became secretary of the U.S. treasury, serving until 1869. He at once recommended retirement of wartime U.S. notes and return to the gold standard. Failing to get congressional support for his policy, McCulloch concentrated on reduction of the funded public debt, readjustment of public revenue and reintroduction of federal taxation in the South. Active in banking *post* 1869, he served again as secretary of the treasury, October 1884–March 1885. During his second term he warned the nation of the peril to its currency inherent in the Silver Coinage Act of 1878.

McCULLOCH, OSCAR CARLETON (*b. Fremont, O., 1843; d. Indianapolis, Ind., 1891*), Congregational clergyman. Pastor of Plymouth Church, Indianapolis, *post* 1877, he founded or organized practically all the philanthropic enterprises created in that city during the time of his pastorate.

McCULLOUGH, ERNEST (*b. Staten Island, N.Y., 1867; d. 1931*), structural engineer, specialist in use of reinforced concrete and structural steel. Edited a number of technical periodicals *post* 1909 and wrote extensively on engineering subjects.

McCULLOUGH, JOHN (*b. near Coleraine, Ireland, 1832; d. Philadelphia, Pa., 1885*), actor. Came to America, 1847; made professional debut, Arch Street Theatre, Philadelphia, August 1857. His rise in his profession was slow but steady, the result of close study and hard work. Chosen by Edwin Forrest to act second parts, 1861, he traveled with Forrest several seasons and was then partner with Lawrence Barrett in management of the California Theatre, San Francisco. He acted as sole manager, 1870–75. Successor to Forrest in "strong" characters, his talent was always effective though it fell short of genius.

McCULLOUGH, JOHN GRIFFITH (*b. Newark, Del., 1835; d. New York, N.Y., 1915*), lawyer, railroad executive, politician. Removed to California *c.* 1859; served in California legislature and as state attorney-general, 1863–67. Associated with his father-in-law, Trenor W. Park, in the Panama Railroad, McCullough removed to Bennington, Vt., in the 1870's. He was associated, 1895, with the successful reorganization of the Erie Railroad. Prominent in Republican politics, he served in the Vermont legislature and was governor of that state, 1902–04.

McCUMBER, PORTER JAMES (*b. Crete, Ill., 1858; d. 1933*), lawyer, North Dakota legislator. U.S. senator, Republican, from North Dakota, 1899–1923. Active in passage of national Food and Drugs Act; as chairman of Senate Finance Committee, was sponsor of the Fordney-McCumber Tariff. [*Supp. 1*]

McCURDY, RICHARD ALDRICH (*b. New York, N.Y., 1835; d. Morristown, N.J., 1916*), lawyer, insurance official. Held various posts in Mutual Life Insurance Co.; was president, 1885–1905. Escaped criminal prosecution for improper use of company funds subsequent to investigation of life insurance companies by New York legislature, 1905–06.

McCUTCHEON, GEORGE BARR (*b. near Lafayette, Ind., 1866; d. New York, N.Y., 1928*), novelist. Author, among other books, of the best-selling romances *Graustark* (1901), *Brewster's Millions* (1902) and *Beverly of Graustark* (1904).

McDANIEL, HENRY DICKERSON (*b. Monroe, Ga., 1836; d. Monroe, 1926*), lawyer, Confederate soldier, Georgia legislator, industrialist. Labored, *post* 1865, for restoration of home rule and for material rehabilitation of Georgia. Democratic governor of Georgia, 1883–86, in which time he reduced the state bonded debt and the tax rate, he was for many years chairman of the board of trustees, University of Georgia.

McDILL, JAMES WILSON (*b. Monroe, O., 1834; d. Creston, Iowa, 1894*), lawyer, Iowa jurist. Removed to Afton, Iowa, 1857. As congressman, Re-

publican, from Iowa, 1873–77, he did useful service on Pacific Railroad and public lands committees. Appointed in 1878 to the railroad commission created to implement Iowa's Granger Laws, he served (except for brief period in which he filled a U.S. Senate vacancy) until 1886. Influential in creation of Interstate Commerce Commission, he served on it, 1892–94.

MACDONALD, CHARLES BLAIR (*b. Niagara Falls, Canada, 1856; d. Southampton, N.Y., 1939*), golfer, golf-course designer, stockbroker. [*Supp. 2*]

McDONALD, CHARLES JAMES (*b. Charleston, S.C., 1793; d. Marietta, Ga., 1860*), Georgia jurist and legislator. Democratic governor of Georgia, 1839–43; justice of Georgia supreme court, 1855–59. Restored Georgia's credit after panic of 1837. An advocate of secession, he led the Georgia delegation to Nashville Convention, 1850, and with Rhett, Barnwell and Colquitt attempted to commit the convention to extreme measures.

MacDONALD, JAMES WILSON ALEXANDER (*b. Steubenville, O., 1824; d. Yonkers, N.Y., 1908*), sculptor. Won reputation, 1854, for a marble portrait bust of Thomas H. Benton. Removing from St. Louis, Mo., where he had done his early work, he settled permanently in New York City, 1865. His portrait statues and busts of celebrated contemporaries were valued for their realistic correctness. He often signed his works "Wilson MacDonald."

McDONALD, JOHN BARTHOLOMEW (*b. Fermoy, Ireland, 1844; d. New York, N.Y., 1911*), contractor. Came to America as a child; rose to front rank among railroad constructors, 1870–90. His most remarkable achievement was the Baltimore belt-line railroad, 1890–94; he was also builder of the first New York City subway, 1900–10.

McDONALD, JOSEPH EWING (*b. Butler Co., O., 1819; d. Indianapolis, Ind., 1891*), lawyer, politician, Indiana congressman and attorney-general. A consistent but fair critic of the Lincoln administration, he helped reorganize the Democratic party in his state after the Civil War and served as U.S. senator from Indiana, 1875–81. An advocate of hard money and a protective tariff, he served on the committee investigating the disputed Hayes-Tilden election, 1876.

MacDONALD, RANALD (*b. Ft. George [Astoria], Oreg., 1824; d. near Toroda, Wash., 1894*), adventurer. An Indian half-breed, MacDonald ran away to sea, 1841, and in 1848, entered the kingdom of Japan by stratagem. Seized and imprisoned, he taught English to Japanese government interpreters. Rescued, 1849, he lived thereafter a wandering life in Australia, Canada and the United States.

McDONOGH, JOHN (*b. Baltimore, Md., 1779; d. 1850*), merchant, philanthropist. Removed to New Orleans, La., *c.* 1800, where he traded successfully and built up a large estate in land. Retiring from business, 1817, he worked out a practical plan whereby his slaves might achieve their own emancipation. He left his property for the foundation of schools in New Orleans and Baltimore.

MACDONOUGH, THOMAS (*b. The Trap, present Macdonough, Del., 1783; d. at sea, 1825*), naval officer. Entered the navy as midshipman, 1800; distinguished himself in the war with Tripoli, taking part under Stephen Decatur in burning of the *Philadelphia;* promoted lieutenant, 1807. Ordered to command the fleet on Lake Champlain, he arrived at the lake early in October 1812 and worked under great difficulties to fit out ships and maintain superiority over the enemy. By the spring of 1814 he had built or otherwise obtained a superior fleet of 13 small vessels (flagship *Saratoga,* 26 guns) but by September the enemy had regained the advantage, a strong British army cooperating with British ships having advanced to the vicinity of Plattsburg. By superior tactics, Macdonough defeated the invading squadron on September 11 in one of the most decisive engagements ever fought by the American navy. His victory caused the enemy's army to retreat into Canada and upset the British plan to claim sovereignty over the Great Lakes. Promoted captain for his services at Plattsburg, he held various other sea and shore commands. His health, which had been seriously impaired in the War of 1812, declined rapidly in the last year of his life. He died aboard a merchantman while returning home from his command in the Mediterranean.

McDOUGAL, DAVID STOCKTON (*b. Chillicothe, O., 1809; d. San Francisco, Calif., 1882*), naval officer. While commanding USS *Wyoming* in search of Confederate cruiser *Alabama* in Far Eastern waters, McDougal destroyed Japanese land batteries and armed vessels at Shimonoseki, July 16, 1863, because of local violation of treaty pledges to the United States.

McDOUGALL, ALEXANDER (*b. Islay, Scotland, 1732; d. New York, N.Y., 1786*), merchant, Revolutionary agitator and soldier. Emigrated to New York as a child. Came into prominence, 1769, as author of a broadside attacking the General Assembly which was declared libelous. Called by his supporters the "Wilkes of America," he whipped up New York City public opinion in favor of the colonial cause, 1774–75. Appointed colonel of the 1st New York regiment, 1775, he was made a Continental brigadier-general, 1776, and major-general, 1777. His most important military service was in the Highlands of the Hudson where he commanded during most of the war; he succeeded Benedict Arnold as commander at West Point. Increasingly conservative as he grew older, he was an organizer and first president of the Bank of New York and president of the New York Society of the Cincinnati from its organization until his death.

McDOUGALL, ALEXANDER (*b. Islay, Scotland, 1845; d. Duluth, Minn., 1923*), Great Lakes mariner, shipbuilder, inventor. Came to Canada as a boy; *post* 1871, was a resident of Duluth, Minn. Patented basic design for "whaleback" freight vessels, 1881; *post* 1888, engaged in their construction. McDougall built the first steel-ship yard in the Northwest, 1892, and founded the city of Everett, Wash.; he patented (1888–1900) forty inventions pertaining to ship construction, ore and grain loading apparatus and dredging machinery. Between 1903 and 1907 he perfected and patented a successful process for washing and cleaning sand iron ores; he later brought suit for infringement of this process against a subsidiary of the U.S. Steel Corp.

McDOUGALL, FRANCES HARRIET. [See GREEN, FRANCES HARRIET WHIPPLE, 1805–1878.]

McDOUGALL, WILLIAM (*b. Chadderton, England, 1871; d. Durham, N.C., 1938*), psychologist. Studied physiology, anatomy, and anthropology for B.A. degree (1894) at Cambridge University and went on to win medical degrees there, 1897. His interest turning to psychology, after further study at Cambridge and Göttingen he taught psychology at University College, London, and at Oxford *post* 1904, simultaneously conducting his own researches, principally in the psycho-physics of vision. He published *An Introduction to Social Psychology* (1908) in which he described human action in terms of basic, inherited instincts. McDougall became professor of psychology at Harvard, 1920. Here he incurred the hostility of the press and of American psychologists by his lectures on national eugenics (published, 1921, as *Is America Safe for Democracy?*) in which, on the basis of army mental tests, he proclaimed the superiority of the Nordic race and made class distinctions in mental endowment. In *Outline of Psychology* (1923) and *Modern Materialism and Emergent Evolution* (1929), he developed a "hormic" psychology based on the concept that purposive action is "a form of causal efficiency distinct in nature from all mechanistic causation."

McDougall taught at Duke University *post* 1927. During his last 17 years he experimented, inconclusively, to prove the inheritance of acquired characteristics. His support of indeterminism and free will in an era of deterministic behaviorism and his unpopular theories of race obscured his contributions during his lifetime, but later acceptance of his theories of instinct, of innate capacities, of purposive action, and of the dynamic nature of mental processes mark him as one of the most original and productive of twentieth-century psychologists. Other books by McDougall include: *Body and Mind, A History and a Defense of Animism* (1911), *The Group Mind* (1920), *Outline of Abnormal Psychology* (1926), *The Energies of Men* (1932) and *Psycho-Analysis and Social Psychology* (1936). [Supp. 2]

McDOWELL, CHARLES (*b. Winchester, Va., c. 1743; d. 1815*), Revolutionary soldier, partisan leader in North Carolina. Brother of Joseph McDowell. His initiative and that of Isaac Shelby brought together the force which made possible an American victory at King's Mountain, October 1780.

MacDOWELL, EDWARD ALEXANDER (*b. New York, N.Y., 1861; d. New York, 1908*), musician, composer. Studied with Teresa Carreño and Paul Desvernine; at Paris Conservatory, 1876–78; at Wiesbaden, 1878–79. Entering Frankfort Conservatory, he studied composition with Joachim Raff and piano with Carl Heymann. Recommended by Heymann to succeed him, MacDowell was denied the post on grounds of youth and inexperience; he served as head piano teacher at the Darmstadt Conservatory, 1881. Franz Liszt approved his first concerto (*opus* 15) and recommended his First Modern Suite (*opus* 10) for a program at Zurich, 1882. Publishing two of his suites, 1883, he turned seriously to composition. He visited America to wed former Frankfort pupil Marian Nevins, 1884. Residing in and near Wiesbaden, 1885–88, he produced such works as the second concerto (*opus* 23) and "Lancelot and Elaine"; he also stored up inspiration for many later compositions.

MacDowell returned to America, 1888, with his reputation established; he composed, taught and performed successfully in Boston, Mass., 1888–96. To this period belong his "Indian Suite," "Sonata Eroica" and "Woodland Sketches." As his more serious works were played by orchestras here and abroad, he gained more acclaim than any previous American musician. Appointed to the newly created chair of music at Columbia University, 1896, he assumed that his function was to train musicians. Trying "to make music function in the academic community," he grew disillusioned over college students' inadequate musical background and the reluctance of his colleagues to recognize the value of the arts. He resigned his chair, 1904, after failure of his plan to establish an independent faculty of fine arts. In addition to his academic work, he conducted the Mendelssohn Glee Club, gave occasional performances, taught private pupils and continued to compose. To this period belong his Norse Sonata (*opus* 57) and his Keltic Sonata (*opus* 59), many of his finest songs and a suite for stringed orchestra which he left unfinished. In failing health *post* 1905, he found his happiest refuge in his farm at Peterboro, N.H.

MacDowell's music is highly original and extremely colorful. The popularity of some of his small things such as "To a Wild Rose" has obscured his large qualities, but musicians have always shown respect for the orchestral works, for the greater piano pieces, especially the sonatas, for the second concerto and for the best of the songs. In all his work the quality is lyrical. He turned away deliberately from the extreme experimentation of the music of his day.

McDOWELL, EPHRAIM (*b. Rockbridge Co., Va., 1771; d. Danville, Ky., 1830*), physician. Raised in Kentucky. Made first studies of medicine in Staunton, Va.; attended lectures at University of Edinburgh, 1793–94. Returning to America, 1795, without a degree, he settled in Danville and became known as best surgeon west of Philadelphia. McDowell was not a writer and did not even keep case notes; the five cases upon which he performed pioneer ovariotomy were described by him very inadequately in the *Eclectic Repertory* as late as April 1817 and October 1819, although descriptive of operations performed as early as 1809. Justly considered the founder of abdominal surgery, McDowell by 1829 had performed ovariotomy 12 times with but a single death and had repeatedly performed radical operations for nonstrangulated hernia. He also performed at least 32 operations for bladder stone without a death.

McDOWELL, IRVIN (*b. Columbus, O., 1818; d. San Francisco, Calif., 1885*), soldier. Graduated West Point, 1838. Served on Canadian frontier, at the Military Academy and as aide-de-camp to Gen. Wool in Mexican War; he was on headquarters staff duty, 1848–61. Highly regarded by Gen. Winfield Scott, he was promoted brigadier-general, 1861, and assigned to command of the troops assembled south of the Potomac, later known as the Army of the Potomac. Forced by political pressure to attempt a dislodgement of Confederate forces at Manassas Junction, Va., he undertook the brief campaign which ended in the first federal disaster at Bull Run. Superseded by Gen. George B. McClellan, he remained with the army as a division commander and later a corps commander. Later in 1862 his force was separated from McClellan's command and designated as the Army of the Rappahannock. Commanding the III Corps of Gen. Pope's Army of Virginia, McDowell was severely criticized and relieved of command for his actions at the second battle of Bull Run (August 1862). Exonerated by a court of inquiry, he was never afterwards employed in the field. He retired as major-general, 1882. Able, energetic, honest, McDowell had never held a command of his own, even of a company, until he took over the Army of the Potomac. His failure at the first battle of Bull Run (which came very near being a success) may have been owing to his tendency to defer too much to the views of subordinates as well as to his inexperience in field command.

McDOWELL, JAMES (*b. Rockbridge Co., Va., 1795; d. near Lexington, Va., 1851*), planter, Virginia legislator, orator. An early opponent of slavery as a cause of national dissension, he also opposed nullification. As Democratic governor of Virginia, 1843–46, he devoted himself largely to problems of internal improvements. Elected congressman from Virginia, 1846, to fill out an unexpired term, he served until his death.

McDOWELL, JOHN (*b. Cumberland, present Franklin Co., Pa., 1751; d. Franklin Co., 1820*), lawyer, educator. Graduated College of Philadelphia, 1771. First principal or head, St. John's College, Annapolis, 1789–1806; professor of natural philosophy and provost, University of Pennsylvania, 1806–10.

McDOWELL, JOHN (*b. Bedminster, N.J., 1780; d. 1863*), Presbyterian clergyman. Graduated College of New Jersey (Princeton), 1801. Pastor at Elizabethtown, N.J., 1804–33, and at Philadelphia churches thereafter. A loyal supporter of the Old School party.

McDOWELL, JOSEPH (*b. Winchester, Va., 1756; d. 1801*), Revolutionary soldier, North Carolina legislator. Brother of Charles McDowell. Commanded his brother's troops at battle of King's Mountain, October 1780. A leader of the (Democrat) Republican party in western North Carolina, he served as congressman, 1797–99.

MacDOWELL, KATHERINE SHERWOOD BONNER (*b. Holly Springs, Miss., 1849; d. Holly Springs, 1883*), short story writer, novelist under pseudonym "Sherwood Bonner."

McDOWELL, MARY ELIZA (*b. Cincinnati, O., 1854; d. Chicago, Ill., 1936*), settlement house founder. Head, University of Chicago Settlement, 1894–1929. [*Supp. 2*]

McDOWELL, WILLIAM FRASER (*b. Millersburg, O., 1858; d. Washington, D.C., 1937*), Methodist clergyman. Bishop *post* 1904; a noted preacher and leader in Methodist reunion. [*Supp. 2*]

McDUFFIE, GEORGE (*b. probably Columbia Co., Ga., 1790; d. Sumter District, S.C., 1851*), lawyer, South Carolina legislator. Congressman, Democrat, from South Carolina, 1821–34; governor of South Carolina, 1834–36; U.S. senator, 1842–46. Entering Congress as a strong nationalist, McDuffie was soon attacking the tariff and opposing internal improvements. Holding that the tariff affected cotton growers most unfairly because it subtracted from their profits by forcing them to sell their produce in exchange for a reduced purchasing power, he argued that the Southern planters in paying import duties on what they purchased gave to the government or to Northern manufacturers forty out of every hundred bales of cotton they produced. His speech of May 19, 1831 at Charleston is frequently said to have brought John C. Calhoun to open advocacy of nullification. Delegate to the nullification convention, 1832, he wrote the address to the people of the other states in which, after severely condemning the protective tariff, he warned the states that secession might well follow. He stated that if the federal government employed force South Carolina would rather be "the cemetery of freemen, than the habitation of slaves." A ready, eloquent and sensational debater,

his speeches were characterized by their sound and fury and extravagance of phrase. John Q. Adams said of him that he had a "gloomy churlishness" in his character; this may well have been caused by a chronic dyspepsia from which he suffered. In the first session of the Nineteenth Congress he made furious charges of a "corrupt bargain" between John Q. Adams and Henry Clay and proposed a constitutional amendment which would provide for direct election of a president in order to prevent a recurrence of the situation which had resulted in the election of Adams. He broke off relations with Andrew Jackson on the questions of nullification and the recharter of the U.S. Bank. After the expiration of his term as governor, he began to lose influence in South Carolina while Calhoun gained it.

McELRATH, THOMAS (*b. Williamsport, Pa., 1807; d. 1888*), publisher. Partner of Horace Greeley in publication of the *New York Tribune;* was its efficient business manager, 1841–57.

McELROY, JOHN (*b. Enniskillen, Ireland, 1782; d. Frederick, Md., 1877*), Roman Catholic clergyman, Jesuit. Came to America, 1803; entered Society of Jesus, 1806. Pastor at Frederick, Md., 1822–46; Mexican War chaplain; pastor of St. Mary's Church, Boston, Mass. A forceful preacher and retreat-master.

McELROY, JOHN (*b. Greenup Co., Ky., 1846; d. 1929*), journalist, Union soldier. Author of *Andersonville* (1879), descriptive of his prison experiences, *The Struggle for Missouri* (1909), and other books. Held editorial posts in Chicago, Ill. and Toledo, O.; editor-publisher of the *National Tribune* (Washington, D.C.).

McELWAIN, WILLIAM HOWE (*b. Charlestown, Mass., 1867; d. 1908*), shoe manufacturer. Without knowledge of the work of F. W. Taylor, McElwain applied principles of scientific management in his factories *post* 1900, thereby obtaining largest output of product in the shoe industry, 1908.

McENERY, SAMUEL DOUGLAS (*b. Monroe, La., 1837; d. New Orleans, La., 1910*), jurist, Confederate soldier, politician. Democratic governor of Louisiana, 1881–88; justice, state supreme court, 1888–96; U.S. senator, 1897–1910.

McENTEE, JERVIS (*b. Rondout, N.Y., 1828; d. Rondout, 1891*), landscape painter. Studied with Frederick E. Church. Noted for winter and autumn scenes of a marked poetic character.

McFADDEN, LOUIS THOMAS (*b. Troy, Pa., 1876; d. New York, N.Y., 1936*), banker. Congressman, Republican, from Pennsylvania, 1915–35; co-author of controversial McFadden-Pepper Act (1927), liberalizing powers of the national banks. [*Supp. 2*]

McFARLAND, JOHN THOMAS (*b. Mount Vernon, Ind., 1851; d. Maplewood, N.J., 1913*), Methodist clergyman, educator. President, Iowa Wesleyan, 1884–91. *Post* 1904, he edited Methodist Sunday-school literature which he reformed and liberalized.

McFARLAND, SAMUEL GAMBLE (*b. Washington Co., Pa., 1830; d. Canonsburg, Pa., 1897*), Presbyterian clergyman. Missionary to Siam, 1860–78; principal of royal school at Bangkok, 1878–96.

McFARLAND, THOMAS BARD (*b. near Mercersburg, Pa., 1828; d. San Francisco, Calif., 1908*), lawyer. Removed to California, 1850. Held several district judgeships; justice, supreme court of California, 1886–1908.

MACFARLANE, CHARLES WILLIAM (*b. Philadelphia, Pa., 1850; d. Philadelphia, 1931*), engineer, builder, author of a number of works in philosophy and economics. Chief theoretical work was *Value and Distribution* (1899), an exposition of the Austrian School.

MACFARLANE, ROBERT (*b. Rutherglen, Scotland, 1815; d. Brooklyn, N.Y., 1883*), dyer. Came to America, 1835. Editor, *Scientific American*, 1848–65; author of works on dyeing and marine propulsion by steam.

McFAUL, JAMES AUGUSTINE (*b. Larne, Ireland, 1850; d. 1917*), Roman Catholic clergyman. Came to America as an infant. Served *post* 1877 as curate and pastor in numerous New Jersey parishes and was consecrated bishop of Trenton, 1894. He interested himself particularly in work among immigrant Poles, Hungarians and Italians, was liberal in spirit, took an active part in municipal and state reforms.

McFERRIN, JOHN BERRY (*b. Rutherford Co., Tenn., 1807; d. Nashville?, 1887*), Methodist clergyman. Editor, *Southwestern Christian Advocate*, 1840–58. Active thereafter in missionary work and as agent for the publishing interests of his denomination which he restored to solvency, 1878–87. Author of *History of Methodism in Tennessee* (1869–73).

MacGAHAN, JANUARIUS ALOYSIUS (*b. Perry Co., O., 1844; d. Constantinople, Turkey, 1878*), war correspondent. Cousin of Gen. Philip Sheridan. His reporting of Turkish massacres in Bulgaria, 1876, for the London *Daily News,* prepared British sentiment to approve war between Russia and Turkey which resulted in Bulgarian independence.

McGARRAH, GATES WHITE (*b. near Monroe, N.Y., 1863; d. New York, N.Y., 1940*), banker. Chairman, Chase National Bank, 1926–27; first president, Bank for International Settlements, 1930–33. [*Supp. 2*]

McGARVEY, JOHN WILLIAM (*b. Hopkinsville, Ky., 1829; d. Lexington, Ky., 1911*), Disciples of Christ clergyman, educator, writer. A strong conservative influence in his sect.

McGEE, WILLIAM JOHN (*b. near Farley, Iowa, 1853; d. 1912*), geologist, hydrologist, anthropologist. Associated with U.S. Geological Survey, 1883–94, he conducted important studies of the Atlantic Coastal Plain. He was chief ethnologist, Bureau of American Ethnology, 1893–1903. Thereafter he served on the Inland Waterways Commission and supervised a study of U.S. water resources for the Department of Agriculture.

McGEEHAN, WILLIAM O'CONNELL (*b. San Francisco, Calif., 1879; d. 1933*), journalist, sports columnist. Began career on San Francisco newspapers; removed to New York, 1914, where he wrote for *New York Herald-Tribune* and its predecessor papers. His work was notable for literary quality and turn of satire; he coined memorable phrases such as "the cauliflower industry" and "the manly art of modified murder" as definitions of boxing. [*Supp. 1*]

McGHEE, CHARLES McCLUNG (*b. Monroe Co., Tenn., 1828; d. Knoxville, Tenn., 1907*), Confederate soldier, financier, executive of Tennessee railroads.

McGIFFERT, ARTHUR CUSHMAN (*b. Sauquoit, N.Y., 1861; d. Dobbs Ferry, N.Y., 1933*), Presbyterian clergyman, historian. Graduated Western Reserve, 1882; Union Theological Seminary, New York, 1885. Ph.D., University of Marburg, Germany, 1888. Taught church history at Lane Theological Seminary and at Union Theological Seminary; president, Union Theological, 1917–26. Author of ten books covering the development of Christian religious ideas, among them, *A History of Christianity in the Apostolic Age* (1897) and *A History of Christian Thought* (1932–33).
[*Supp. 1*]

McGIFFIN, PHILO NORTON (*b. Washington, Pa., 1860; d. New York, N.Y., 1897*), naval officer. Graduated Annapolis, 1882. Honorably discharged, 1884, he took a commission in the Chinese navy, 1885, serving as naval constructor and professor of gunnery and seamanship. As executive officer but in fact commander of the battleship *Chen Yuen,* he fought with rare skill a losing action off the Yalu River, Sept. 17, 1894, compelling the retreat of the Japanese main squadron.

McGILL, JOHN (*b. Philadelphia, Pa., 1809; d. 1872*), Roman Catholic clergyman, lawyer. Raised in Kentucky; served there as curate and pastor until 1850 when he was consecrated bishop of Richmond, Va. Although opposed to slavery, he was a Confederate sympathizer; he did notable work in the reconstruction of his diocese subsequent to the Civil War.

McGILLIVRAY, ALEXANDER (*b. c. 1759; d. Pensacola, Fla., 1793*), Creek Indian chieftain, Loyalist. From 1784 to his death, McGillivray's career possessed international significance. His immediate purpose was to form a confederation of Southern Indians and, with the aid of Spain or perhaps Great

Britain, compel the United States to restore the Indian boundary line as it existed in 1773; in other words, to evacuate a large part of Georgia, Tennessee and Kentucky. Trusting to Spanish support, he precipitated a war along the American frontier from Georgia to the Cumberland, 1786; his power was at height, 1787, when the attacks of his warriors almost succeeded in destroying the stations on the Cumberland River. McGillivray signed a peace treaty at New York, August 1790, which was satisfactory to the United States but it failed of Indian approval. Influenced by British arguments and Spanish money, McGillivray repudiated the Treaty of New York in July 1792. He died during the progress of further negotiations for formation of a confederation of Southern Indians in alliance with Spain against the United States.

McGILVARY, DANIEL (*b. Moore Co., N.C., 1828; d. Chieng-mai, Siam, 1911*), Presbyterian clergyman. Missionary in Siam, 1858–1911, he was known as "the Apostle to the Lao."

McGIVNEY, MICHAEL JOSEPH (*b. Waterbury, Conn., 1852; d. Thomaston, Conn., 1890*), Roman Catholic clergyman. Leader in organizing (January 1882) the Knights of Columbus which he served as national chaplain until his death.

McGLOTHLIN, WILLIAM JOSEPH (*b. near Gallatin, Tenn., 1867; d. Gastonia, N.C., 1933*), Baptist clergyman, professor of church history. President, Furman University, 1919–33. [*Supp. 1*]

McGLYNN, EDWARD (*b. New York, N.Y., 1837; d. Newburgh, N.Y., 1900*), Roman Catholic clergyman, social reformer. Educated in New York City schools and at College of the Propaganda, Rome, Italy; ordained, Rome, 1860. Active in charitable and humanitarian affairs, McGlynn was appointed pastor of St. Stephen's parish (New York City), 1866. Becoming acutely aware of the disruption of morals attributable to unemployment and poverty, he became an adherent of Henry George and accepted the Single-Tax doctrine as a fundamental remedy for social evils. His active part in George's 1886 campaign for mayor of New York City brought him into open conflict with Archbishop M. A. Corrigan. Suspended from exercise of his priestly functions, he was removed from his pastorate, January 1887, and summoned to Rome to explain views which he had propagated upon the land question. His refusal to go, on advice of counsel, coupled with a misunderstanding over his failure to reply to the summons, resulted in his excommunication in July 1887. For five years following this censure he continued to defend the Single-Tax doctrine; in December 1892, after a review of his teachings and of the facts, he was reinstated. Thereafter, as pastor of St. Mary's Church at Newburgh, N.Y., he was a frequent speaker at Single-Tax meetings and made it quite clear that Rome

had not required him to retract his views on the ownership of land.

McGOVERN, JOHN (*b. Troy, N.Y., 1850; d. Chicago, Ill., 1917*), journalist, Chicago editor.

McGOWAN, SAMUEL (*b. Laurens District, S.C., 1819; d. Abbeville, S.C., 1897*), lawyer, South Carolina legislator, Confederate brigadier-general. Justice, South Carolina supreme court, 1879–93.

McGRATH, JAMES (*b. Co. Tipperary, Ireland, 1835; d. Albany, N.Y., 1898*), Roman Catholic clergyman, Oblate. Came to Canada, 1856. After extensive missionary service in Canada and the United States, he was appointed pastor at St. John's, Lowell, Mass., 1870, erected there the Church of the Immaculate Conception in 1872, and was elected first provincial of the American province of the Oblate Fathers, 1883. He served for ten years.

McGRAW, JOHN HARTE (*b. Penobscot Co., Maine, 1850; d. 1910*), lawyer. Removed to Seattle, Wash., 1876. Republican governor of Washington, 1893–97. His term was a stormy period of strikes and riots which he handled with skill and courage; he fought hard against legislative extravagance.

McGRAW, JOHN JOSEPH (*b. Truxton, N.Y., 1873; d. New Rochelle, N.Y., 1934*), baseball player, manager. Celebrated for his work at third base for Baltimore, 1891–99, McGraw served as manager of the New York Giants, 1902–32. In that time he won ten National League pennants and three World Series. [*Supp. 1*]

McGREADY, JAMES (*b. western Pennsylvania, c. 1758; d. Henderson Co., Ky., 1817*), Presbyterian preacher, revivalist. Raised in Guilford Co., N.C. Pastor in Orange Co., N.C., c. 1790–96, he removed in the latter year to Kentucky where he conducted a series of revivals in Logan Co., 1797–99. These were the forerunners of the Great Revival of 1800. After a period of alliance with the Cumberland Presbytery, McGready returned to orthodoxy and founded pioneer churches in southern Indiana, 1811–16, preaching almost up to his death.

McGROARTY, SUSAN. [See JULIA, SISTER, 1827–1901.]

McGUFFEY, WILLIAM HOLMES (*b. Washington Co., Pa., 1800; d. 1873*), educator, compiler of school readers. Raised near Youngstown, O.; graduated Washington College, 1826; was licensed to preach in the Presbyterian church, 1829. Professor of languages, Miami University, 1826–36; president, Cincinnati College, 1836–39; president, Ohio University, 1839–43; professor of moral philosophy, University of Virginia, 1845–73. Associated with Samuel Lewis and others in promoting common school education in Ohio, he continued his interest in public schools throughout his life. He is most widely known for his series of *Eclectic Readers* for elementary schools. These books, the first and second of which were published in 1836, the third and fourth in 1837, the fifth added in 1844 and the sixth in 1857, went through edition after edition, were revised and enlarged and reached a sale of more than 120,000,000 copies. Their influence contributed much to the shaping of the American mind in the 19th century.

McGUIRE, CHARLES BONAVENTURE (*b. Dungannon, Ireland, 1768; d. Pittsburgh, Pa., 1833*), Roman Catholic clergyman, Franciscan. After a life of adventure and peril during the French Revolution and after, he volunteered for the American missions and arrived in Pennsylvania, 1817. Cosmopolitan and highly educated, he served as pastor in Pittsburgh, Pa., *post* 1820.

McGUIRE, HUNTER HOLMES (*b. Winchester, Va., 1835; d. Richmond, Va., 1900*), surgeon. Commissioned a Confederate medical officer, 1861, he was chief surgeon of "Stonewall" Jackson's commands until the latter's death; he was also Jackson's personal physician. Subsequently he served as surgeon and medical director under Gens. Ewell and Early, and was professor of surgery, Virginia Medical College, 1865–78. Active in establishment of the College of Physicians and Surgeons, Richmond, Va., 1893, he was its president and professor of surgery at the time of his death.

McGUIRE, JOSEPH DEAKINS (*b. Washington, D.C., 1842; d. 1916*), lawyer, anthropologist. Expert in aboriginal technology.

MACHEBEUF, JOSEPH PROJECTUS (*b. Riom, France, 1812; d. 1889*), Roman Catholic clergyman. Accompanied J. B. Lamy to Cincinnati, O., 1839, and worked as a missionary in northern Ohio until 1850 when he went with Lamy to New Mexico to serve him as assistant and vicar-general. A prodigy for work, Machebeuf traveled widely through the Southwest on missionary tours in addition to serving as pastor in the cathedral at Santa Fé. *Post* 1860, he worked in Colorado and Utah, building churches in Denver, Central City and other towns, besides establishing chapels in the new agricultural villages which were springing up in those territories. Consecrated vicar apostolic of Colorado and Utah, 1868, he was made bishop, 1887.

MACHEN, JOHN GRESHAM (*b. Baltimore, Md., 1881; d. Bismarck, N. Dak., 1937*) Presbyterian clergyman, theologian. Suspended (1935) from the ministry as a schismatic, he formed, with others, the Orthodox Presbyterian Church. [*Supp. 2*]

McHENRY, JAMES (*b. Ballymena, Ireland, 1753; d. Fayetteville, Md., 1816*), physician, Revolutionary soldier, Maryland legislator. Came to America, 1771; studied medicine in Philadelphia with Benjamin Rush;

served as surgeon, 5th Pennsylvania, 1776–77. Appointed secretary to Gen. George Washington, 1778, he served on Lafayette's staff in a similar capacity and continued in active service until 1781. Congressman from Maryland, 1783–86, he was a strong campaigner for adoption of the federal Constitution by Maryland. As U.S. secretary of war, 1796–1800, he supported Alexander Hamilton on all major matters of policy.

McHENRY, JAMES (*b. Larne, Ireland, 1785; d. Larne, 1845*), physician, poet, novelist. Resident in Baltimore, Md., Pittsburgh and Philadelphia, Pa., 1817–43. Author of several American historical tales. A conservative poet and critic, he was at his best in *The Pleasures of Friendship* (1822).

McILVAINE, CHARLES PETTIT (*b. Burlington, N.J., 1799; d. Florence, Italy, 1873*). Protestant Episcopal clergyman. Graduated Princeton, 1816; ordained, 1823; served parishes in Washington, D.C., and Brooklyn, N.Y. His theology was strongly evangelical, alienating some high-churchmen. Consecrated bishop of Ohio, 1832, he ably administered Kenyon College and was a strenuous opponent of tractarian doctrine. Sent to England at Lincoln's request during the *Trent* affair crisis, 1861, he was able to win friends for the American cause among the higher clergy. His best-known printed works were *Evidences of Christianity* (1832) and *Oxford Divinity* (a defense of evangelical doctrines, 1841).

McILWAINE, RICHARD (*b. Petersburg, Va., 1834; d. Richmond, Va., 1913*), Presbyterian clergyman, Confederate chaplain. President, Hampden-Sydney College, 1883–1904.

McINTIRE, SAMUEL (*b. Salem, Mass., 1757; d. Salem, 1811*), architect, wood-carver. Designed the classical Peirce house (a notable contribution to Salem architecture), 1779, and won the lifelong patronage of merchant prince Elias H. Derby. Noted for boldness and simplicity of design, his Doric and Ionic porticoes and pilasters came to adorn many of Salem's leading homes. McIntire commenced public and semi-public building with a Concert Hall, 1782, and the Salem Court House, 1785; in 1792 he submitted an able plan (not unlike that later used for the White House) for the Federal Capitol. Speedily recognizing and adopting the style of Charles Bulfinch, McIntire displayed in all his works a refined and delicate elegance. Many of the ornaments —grape sprays, eagles, cornucopias and the baskets of fruit which became almost a hallmark—he carved himself. Early dwellings which showed the Bulfinch influence (and that of the Adam brothers) were the Nathan Read house and, in Waltham, the home of Theodore Lyman. When Mrs. E. H. Derby demanded a house in the new fashion, he combined features in drawings by Bulfinch and several New York architects, and drafted final plans for what came to be called the "Mansion." This palatial dwelling (1795–98), its front modeled after the Provost's House in Dublin, was to contemporaries perhaps McIntire's masterpiece, although it was razed for newer buildings a few years after his death. Following their parents' deaths the Derby children had McIntire build or remodel homes for them; "Oak Hill," for Mrs. Nathaniel West, in Peabody, Mass., rivaled even the "Mansion" in ornateness. Other clients came to him; the Cook and Gardner houses (1804–05) are among his finest works, and his remodeled parlor in the Peirce house is considered a superb example of the Adam style. He built or reconstructed several Salem churches, and designed the gateways to Washington Square. His later structures (including the Woodbridge and Tucker houses and numerous business buildings) were all of brick; they seemed to reveal the restraint of growing classicism with their sober, almost austere, treatment, but his homes and furniture continued to display elaborate wood carvings and furniture work.

McINTOSH, JOHN BAILLIE (*b. Florida, 1829; d. 1888*), Union soldier. Served in U.S. Navy during Mexican War. As brigadier-general of cavalry, distinguished himself at Kelly's Ford, 1863, at Gettysburg, and at Winchester, 1864.

McINTOSH, LACHLAN (*b. Raits, Scotland, 1725; d. Savannah, Ga., 1806*), Revolutionary soldier. Came to America as a boy; raised in Georgia. As brigadier-general, Continental, he commanded at Fort Pitt 1778–79, and fought in southern theater, 1779–80. Suspended from service by George Walton's influence, he was vindicated by Congress, 1784. Killed Button Gwinnett in duel, 1777.

McINTOSH, WILLIAM (*b. present Carroll Co., Ga., c. 1775; d. Carroll Co., 1825*), Creek chieftain. Son of a British agent and an Indian woman, McIntosh led friendly Lower Creeks against British and Indians in War of 1812. He served as U.S. brigadier-general under Jackson against the Seminoles, 1817–18, and cooperated with his cousin, Gov. George M. Troup, to remove Indians from western Georgia. His faction signed treaty of land cession, 1825. The Upper Creeks protested his disinterestedness, and when the treaty was approved they raided his home and killed him. McIntosh's life epitomized the tragedy of the half-breed friendly to whites and viewed by Indians as a renegade.

McINTYRE, JAMES (*b. Kenosha, Wis., 1857; d. near Southampton, N.Y., 1937*) and **THOMAS KURTON HEATH** (*b. Philadelphia, Pa., 1853; d. Poquott, L.I., N.Y., 1938*), blackface comedians, partners in a variety act for more than fifty years. Their celebrated skit *The Ham Tree* was made into a musical revue, 1906. [*Supp. 2*]

McINTYRE, OSCAR ODD (*b. Plattsburg, Mo., 1884; d. New York, N.Y., 1938*), journalist. His syndicated column, "New York Day by Day," appeared in more than five hundred newspapers and brought "Broadway to Main Street." [*Supp. 2*]

McIVER, CHARLES DUNCAN (*b. Moore Co., N.C., 1860; d. 1906*), Southern educator. Graduated University of North Carolina, 1881. A zealous advocate of teacher training, universal public education and women's higher education, he served as president, North Carolina College for Women, 1892–1906. He was also secretary, Southern Education Board.

MACKAY, CLARENCE HUNGERFORD (*b. San Francisco, Calif., 1874; d. New York, N.Y., 1938*), capitalist, philanthropist, society leader. Son of John W. Mackay. [*Supp. 2*]

McKAY, DONALD (*b. Shelburne Co., Nova Scotia, 1810; d. Hamilton, Mass., 1880*), shipbuilder, master builder of the clipper. Emigrated to New York, N.Y., 1827; became shipwright, working among others for Jacob Bell. Entered partnership at Newburyport, Mass., 1841, to build packet ships; established shipyard at East Boston, Mass., 1844. In December 1850, he launched the *Stag Hound*, his first clipper, and in April 1851 the *Flying Cloud* which made San Francisco in less than 90 days' passage from New York. Among other famous clippers from McKay's yard were *Sovereign of the Seas* (1852), *Great Republic* (1853), *James Baines* and *Lightning* (1854–55). The last two vessels were also world record holders for speed under sail. McKay not only designed his ships but oversaw every detail of construction; he had an innate sense of beauty and proportion. An early advocate of steam screw naval ironclads of the largest class, he was not successful in urging their construction on the government. *Glory of the Seas* (1869) was his last great sailing ship.

McKAY, GORDON (*b. Pittsfield, Mass., 1821; d. Newport, R.I., 1903*), industrialist, inventor. Grandson of Samuel Dexter. Purchased Lyman Blake patent for sewing shoe soles to uppers, 1859, and improved it to stitch around toes and heels. Obtained Civil War shoe contracts; manufactured and leased his machines on royalty to other manufacturers. With royalties from over sixty factories, he soon became a millionaire. Retiring from business in 1895, he engaged in philanthropies which included an institute for educating Negro boys and a trust fund for Harvard.

MACKAY, JAMES (*b. Kildonan, Scotland, c. 1759; d. 1822*), explorer, fur trader. Emigrated to Canada, c. 1776. Explored Louisiana Territory for Spain, 1795–97, preparing maps later used by Lewis and Clark.

McKAY, JAMES IVER (*b. Bladen Co., N.C., 1792; d. Goldsboro, N.C., 1853*), planter, North Carolina legislator. Influential debater as congressman, Democrat, 1831–49; famous, while Ways and Means Committee chairman, for insistence on rigid governmental economy.

MACKAY, JOHN WILLIAM (*b. Dublin, Ireland, 1831; d. London, England, 1902*), miner, capitalist. Came to New York, N.Y., as a boy; removed to California, 1851. Became expert in timbering Nevada mines. Joined with James G. Fair and others, 1868, in scheme to make low-grade ore pay by reworking Comstock Lode with up-to-date equipment. Reinvesting profits in nearby mines, the group struck the "Big Bonanza," 1873. Mackay became overnight the most spectacular success in Western mining. He acquired real estate, became a banker and railroad director. Forming the Commercial Cable Co., 1883, and the Postal Telegraph Co., 1886, he made his greatest constructive contribution by breaking the Jay Gould-Western Union communications monopoly.

MacKAYE, JAMES MORRISON STEELE (*b. Buffalo, N.Y., 1842; d. Timpas, Colo., 1894*), playwright, actor, inventor. Wrote *Hazel Kirke* (produced 1880); introduced stage and lighting innovations; preached drama's social values. Established first U.S. dramatic school at old Lyceum Theater, New York City.

MacKAYE, STEELE. [See MacKAYE, JAMES MORRISON STEELE, 1842–1894.]

McKEAN, JOSEPH BORDEN (*b. New Castle, Del., 1764; d. Philadelphia, Pa., 1826*), Pennsylvania jurist. Son of Thomas McKean. Attorney-general of Pennsylvania, 1800–08; Philadelphia district judge, 1817–26, presiding for much of this time. Promoted coalition of Federalists and moderate (Democrat) Republicans, 1805.

McKEAN, SAMUEL (*b. Huntingdon Co., Pa., 1787; d. West Burlington, Pa., 1841*), merchant, Pennsylvania legislator. Congressman, Democrat, 1823–29; U.S. senator, 1833–39. High-tariff advocate; opposed the U.S. Bank, but voted to restore deposits; enemy of anti-slavery agitation.

McKEAN, THOMAS (*b. Chester Co., Pa., 1734; d. Philadelphia, Pa., 1817*), lawyer, statesman, signer of the Declaration of Independence. Entered political life shortly after admission to the bar, 1754; became clerk of the Delaware Assembly, 1757; served as member of Assembly, 1762–79. Noted for radical opposition to the Stamp Act, he led movement in Delaware for a Continental Congress and represented the state in Congress almost continuously throughout the Revolution. An advocate of independence by early 1776, he sent for Caesar Rodney to break a tie vote so that Delaware's delegation would approve Lee's motion of July 1. He supported the Articles of Confederation in Congress and presided briefly (1781) over that body.

While active in Delaware politics McKean had established a home in Philadelphia, and there his interests turned. Increasingly conservative, he opposed Pennsylvania's radical constitution of 1776, though he served as chief justice under it, 1777–99 (for

a time holding Delaware offices simultaneously). Strongly favoring the Constitution, and noted for decisions stressing judicial integrity, Francophile sentiments led him into the Jeffersonian ranks and he was nominated for governor of Pennsylvania, 1799. Elected after a bitter fight, he removed enemies from office and fastened the spoils system upon Pennsylvania. Despite (Democrat) Republican divisions occasioned by editor William Duane's domination of the party and McKean's defense of executive and judicial prerogatives, he was re-elected, 1802. When radicals demanded a new state constitution, moderates rallied behind him and he was again elected, 1805. McKean then turned on his (Democrat) Republican foes, dismissing them from office and appointing Federalist supporters; this produced charges of nepotism (his son had been attorney-general since 1800) and abuse of power. Libel suits against his accusers led to counter-demands for impeachment, but these charges were skillfully postponed by the legislature. He retired from office, 1808. Stormy petrel of Pennsylvania politics, McKean furthered education and internal improvements but his chief accomplishment was the prevention of excesses of radicalism in his state.

McKEAN, WILLIAM WISTER (*b. Philadelphia, Pa., 1800; d. near Binghamton, N.Y., 1865*), naval officer. Son of Joseph B. McKean; cousin of Franklin Buchanan. Headed Naval Asylum for instructing midshipmen, Philadelphia, 1843–44; recommended founding of naval school at Annapolis.

McKEE, JOHN (*b. Rockbridge Co., Va., 1771; d. near Boligee, Ala., 1832*), Indian agent, Alabama congressman. Cousin of Sam Houston. Cherokee and Choctaw agent; pacified tribes during Creek War. Furthered trans-Mississippi removal of Five Civilized Tribes *post* 1815.

McKEEN, JOSEPH (*b. Londonderry, N.H., 1757; d. Brunswick, Mass. [Maine], 1807*), Congregational clergyman. Graduated Dartmouth, 1774; eminent pastor, Beverly, Mass., 1785–1802. First president, Bowdoin College, 1802–07.

MACKELLAR, PATRICK (*b. Scotland, 1717; d. Minorca, 1778*), British military engineer. Accompanied Braddock's expedition, 1755; captured at Oswego, 1756. Exchanged, he directed siege operations at Louisbourg and was Wolfe's chief engineer at Quebec, 1759.

MacKELLAR, THOMAS (*b. New York, N.Y., 1812; d. 1899*), printer, type-founder, poet. As partner in MacKellar, Smiths and Jordan, Philadelphia, Pa., *post* 1860, he made that firm the leading American manufactory of type. He edited and printed the *Typographic Advertiser*, 1855–84, and his textbook, *The American Printer* (1866), went through many editions.

McKELWAY, ST. CLAIR (*b. Columbia, Mo., 1845; d. 1915*), newspaperman. Edited *Albany Argus*, 1878–84; *Brooklyn (N.Y.) Daily Eagle*, 1884–1915. He closely identified the latter paper with Brooklyn, yet gave it national standing.

McKENDREE, WILLIAM (*b. King William Co., Va., 1757; d. Sumner Co., Tenn., 1835*), first American-born Methodist bishop. Served as soldier in the Revolution. Converted to Methodism *c.* 1776, he was appointed, 1788, a helper circuit preacher; ordained deacon, 1790, and elder, 1791. Under James O'Kelly's influence he joined a movement to limit bishops' powers, but close association with Bishop Francis Asbury changed his views. He served on various circuits for many years and became a leader in the trans-Allegheny revival movement. Elected bishop, 1808, he introduced practice of episcopal addresses at conferences and the consulting of elders in appointments.

McKENNA, CHARLES HYACINTH (*b. Fallalea, Ireland, 1835; d. Jacksonville, Fla., 1917*), Roman Catholic clergyman, Dominican. Came to America, 1851. A powerful missionary preacher and ascetical writer, he was associated with the growth of the Holy Name Society and the Rosary Confraternity.

McKENNA, JOSEPH (*b. Philadelphia, Pa., 1843; d. Washington, D.C., 1926*), California legislator, congressman, jurist. U.S. attorney-general, 1897. Justice, U.S. Supreme Court, 1898–1925. Branded as pro-railroad, his appointment was widely criticized but his record on the bench won approval for sound, if slow, judgment and social vision.

McKENNAN, THOMAS McKEAN THOMPSON (*b. Dragon Neck, Del., 1794; d. Reading, Pa., 1852*), lawyer. Congressman, Whig, from Pennsylvania, 1831–39 and 1842–43. U.S. secretary of interior, 1850. President, Hempfield Railroad (eventually absorbed by Baltimore and Ohio).

McKENNEY, THOMAS LORAINE (*b. Hopewell, Md., 1785; d. New York, N.Y., 1859*), businessman, author. Much-criticized superintendent of Indian trade, 1816–22; headed U.S. Bureau of Indian Affairs, 1824–30; was joint commissioner with Lewis Cass at Treaty of Butte des Morts, 1827. Author of text to *History of the Indian Tribes of North America* (with James Hall, 1836–44), *Memoirs* (1846), and other works.

McKENZIE, ALEXANDER (*b. New Bedford, Mass., 1830; d. 1914*), Congregational clergyman. Pastor, First Church, Cambridge, Mass., 1867–1914. Affirmative preaching and civic-mindedness gave him influence comparable to that of colonial ministers.

MACKENZIE, ALEXANDER SLIDELL (*b. New York, N.Y., 1803; d. 1848*), naval officer, author of travel books and naval biographies. Brother of John Slidell. As commander of brig *Somers*, he executed son of secretary of war for mutiny (December 1842).

MACKENZIE, DONALD (*b. Scotland, 1783; d. Mayville, N.Y., 1851*), fur trader. Partner with John Jacob Astor in Pacific Fur Co., 1810. With Wilson P. Hunt, led overland adventurers to Fort Astoria, 1812; sold post to North West Co., 1814. Later served as governor of Red River Colony for Hudson's Bay Co.

MACKENZIE, GEORGE HENRY (*b. North Kessock, Scotland, 1837; d. New York, N.Y., 1891*), chessplayer, British and U.S. (Union) army officer. American (1871–80) and world (1887) chess champion.

MACKENZIE, JAMES CAMERON (*b. Aberdeen, Scotland, 1852; d. New York, N.Y., 1931*), Presbyterian clergyman, educator. Graduated Lafayette, 1878. Organizer and headmaster, Lawrenceville School, 1882–99. Established "Upper House" system, giving older boys greater freedom in preparation for college.

MACKENZIE, JOHN NOLAND (*b. Baltimore, Md., 1853; d. Baltimore, 1925*), physician, pioneer laryngologist. M.D., University of Virginia, 1876; studied also at Metropolitan Throat Hospital (N.Y.), Munich and Vienna. Chief of clinic at London Throat Hospital, he helped Sir Morell Mackenzie prepare *Manual of the Diseases of the Throat and Nose* (1880–84). Founded Baltimore Eye, Ear and Throat Charity Hospital; was surgeon at University of Maryland Hospital, 1887–97, and at Johns Hopkins Hospital, 1889–1912, and professor at their associated medical schools. Mackenzie edited various medical journals and wrote numerous papers on laryngo-rhinology (particularly on vaso-motor neuroses of the nose, on sinuses, and on laryngeal cancer), opposing excessive surgery for nose and throat conditions.

MACKENZIE, KENNETH (*b. Ross and Cromarty shire, Scotland, 1797; d. St. Louis, Mo., 1861*), fur trader, merchant. Joined North West Co. (Canada), 1816; organized Columbia Fur Co., St. Louis, Mo., 1822. Associated with American Fur Co. *post* 1827, he built Fort Union and administered the Upper Missouri trade until 1834. Thereafter, he engaged in various business concerns in St. Louis.

MACKENZIE, MURDO (*b. Co. Ross, Scotland, 1850; d. Denver, Colo., 1939*), cattleman. Came to America, 1885. Manager, Matador Land and Cattle Co., 1891–1911 and 1922–37; managed Brazil Land, Cattle and Packing Co. (at São Paulo), 1912–18.

[Supp. 2]

MACKENZIE, RANALD SLIDELL (*b. New York, N.Y., 1840; d. Staten Island, N.Y., 1889*), soldier. Son of Alexander S. Mackenzie. Graduated West Point, 1862. Assigned to engineer corps, he was brevetted seven times for gallantry in eastern Civil War campaigns, attaining divisional command as a cavalry officer; Grant considered him the "most promising young officer in the army." After the Civil War, as colonel of the 4th Cavalry, Mackenzie campaigned in western Texas and opened the Staked Plains area to white settlement. He pacified hostiles in Indian Territory and vanquished Sioux bands at Chadron Creek, also Dull Knife's Cheyennes in the Big Horn Mountains after Custer's death, 1876. He fought with marked success against the Utes, 1879–81, and in New Mexico and Arizona. He retired for disability as brigadier-general, 1884. Perhaps our ablest Indian fighter, Mackenzie avoided publicity but was recognized as a master tactician by army colleagues.

MACKENZIE, ROBERT SHELTON (*b. Co. Limerick, Ireland, 1809; d. Philadelphia, Pa., 1881*), journalist. Came to America, 1852. A pioneer European correspondent, he served as literary and foreign editor for the Philadelphia *Press*, 1857–78; he was author of a number of popular biographies and an able editor of literary *causeries.*

McKENZIE, ROBERT TAIT (*b. Almonte, Canada, 1867; d. Philadelphia, Pa., 1938*), physician, sculptor. Graduated McGill, 1889; M.D., 1892. Director of physical education (1904–31) and professor of physical therapy, University of Pennsylvania. [*Supp.* 2]

MACKENZIE, WILLIAM (*b. Philadelphia, Pa., 1758; d. Philadelphia, 1828*), merchant, book collector. Bequeathed many rare examples of early printing to Philadelphia institutions.

MACKEY, ALBERT GALLATIN (*b. Charleston, S.C., 1807; d. Old Point Comfort, Va., 1881*), physician. Author of Masonic histories, manuals and the *Encyclopedia of Freemasonry* (1874).

McKIM, CHARLES FOLLEN (*b. Isabella Furnace, Pa., 1847; d. St. James, L.I., N.Y., 1909*), architect. Son of James M. McKim. Educated in Philadelphia public schools, at Lawrence Scientific School (Harvard), and in Paris at L'École des Beaux Arts, 1867–70. On his return, he worked in Henry H. Richardson's office, New York City. Forming a partnership with William Rutherford Mead, 1878, he was joined by Stanford White, 1879. Convinced that Wren's modified classical style of architecture (as brought over by English colonists and exhibited by Charles Bulfinch in his work) was best suited for American homes and public buildings, McKim and his firm consistently maintained this doctrine, although a tendency toward the Italian Renaissance was also shown in some work. They broke with the Richardson tradition because they felt that his style was brilliant but undisciplined. McKim's own method was first to study a proposed structure's purpose, then to consider its exterior. Members of the firm cooperated on design and details after determination of a basic plan. Their reputation established by a group of Italian Renaissance buildings for Henry Villard on Madison Ave., New York,

N.Y., the firm was commissioned to design the Boston Public Library (1887). This structure, with its classical exterior and its perfect siting, was McKim's first masterpiece; he envisaged its murals and sculpture as essential parts of the building rather than mere adornment, and enjoyed the collaboration on details of Augustus Saint-Gaudens and the leading artists of the time. The Columbian Exposition at Chicago (1893), which helped set American architectural patterns for years and ushered in the city-planning movement, owed much of its effectiveness to McKim's designs. In 1901 he participated in plans for developing Washington, D.C., assuming responsibility for the area between the Capitol and the Potomac. His White House restoration (1902–03) showed respect for the spirit and good work of capable predecessors. Columbia University's Morningside Heights campus, with subordinate brick buildings surrounding a monumental stone library, demonstrated McKim's ingenious use of terrain. Many critics, however, consider New York's University Club his finest achievement. He designed New York's Morgan Library and Pennsylvania Railway Station (then the world's largest building erected at one time), both in 1903; in each case he persuaded strong-willed clients to accept his own concept of the finished structure. The office of McKim, Mead and White was widely recognized as America's outstanding training school for young architects. Ever-modest, aware of his own limited training, McKim's fondest dream was to found an American Academy in Rome where artists of promise might study amid masterpieces of all time; supported by him and by other private contributions, the idea became an eventual reality. The deaths of White (1906) and Saint-Gaudens (1907) broke his closest ties; overwork led him to retire, 1908, acclaimed the preeminent American architect of his day.

McKIM, ISAAC (*b. Philadelphia, Pa., 1775; d. Washington, D.C., 1838*), Baltimore merchant, Maryland legislator and congressman. Helped organize Baltimore & Ohio Railroad; built the *Ann McKim* (1832), prototype of later Yankee clipper ships.

McKIM, JAMES MILLER (*b. Carlisle, Pa., 1810; d. Orange, N.J., 1874*), Presbyterian clergyman, abolitionist leader. Helped form American Anti-Slavery Society, 1833; was active thereafter in work for the abolition cause and for freedmen. Father of Charles F. McKim.

McKINLEY, ALBERT EDWARD (*b. Philadelphia, Pa., 1870; d. Germantown, Pa., 1936*), historian. Professor of history, University of Pennsylvania, 1915–36; editor and a founder (1909) of the magazine which became *Social Studies.* [*Supp.* 2]

McKINLEY, CARLYLE (*b. Newnan, Ga., 1847; d. 1904*), journalist, essayist, poet. Correspondent, associate editor, Charleston, S.C., *News and Courier, post* 1875. An optimistic Southern romantic.

McKINLEY, JOHN (*b. Culpeper Co., Va., 1780; d. Louisville, Ky., 1852*), lawyer, Alabama legislator. U.S. senator, Democrat, from Alabama, 1826–31; congressman, 1833–35. Hard-working and conscientious justice of the U.S. Supreme Court, 1837–52.

McKINLEY, WILLIAM (*b. Niles, O., 1843; d. Buffalo, N.Y., 1901*), president of the United States. Of Scotch-Irish stock, McKinley was educated at Allegheny College; he taught briefly in a rural school before enlisting in the 23rd Ohio Volunteer Infantry, with which he served throughout the Civil War. Mustered out as major by brevet, he studied law in Ohio and at Albany (N.Y.) Law School, commencing practice in Canton, O., immediately following admission to the bar, 1867.

McKinley's political career began with his election as Stark Co. prosecuting attorney, 1869. In 1871 he married Ida Saxton, to whom he remained devoted despite her later chronic invalidism. An active supporter of his old regimental commander, Rutherford B. Hayes, in Ohio politics, McKinley was a successful Republican candidate for Congress, 1876, and served (though unseated in 1882 by a Democratic House) for seven terms (1877–91). A leading supporter of the protective tariff (to him no tool of privilege but a sound national policy), he grew in public stature and was given a place on the Ways and Means Committee, 1880. As chairman of the Committee on Resolutions at the Republican National Convention, 1888, he was steadfast in support of John Sherman for the presidency, protesting votes cast for himself. Although the Sherman movement failed, McKinley gained the friendship of Marcus A. Hanna, a Cleveland businessman with funds to spend for furthering the policy of protection. McKinley, in 1889–90 the chairman of the Ways and Means Committee, was largely responsible for the tariff act bearing his name. Its higher rates proved unpopular and he lost his congressional seat in the 1890 Democratic landslide. With Hanna's aid, however, he was elected governor of Ohio, 1891, and re-elected, 1893; the governorship served as his sounding board and point of vantage in attaining the Republican presidential nomination.

Uninjured politically after Hanna and others raised money (1893) to redeem notes he had endorsed for a friend, McKinley held the commanding position in his party after the death of James G. Blaine. Unfortunately for him, protection was being overshadowed as an issue by free silver, on which his record was ambiguous. Despite this, Hanna obtained McKinley's nomination in 1896 on a prearranged gold platform, and during the campaign against the Democrat William J. Bryan, the Republican orators played on Eastern fear of a devalued dollar. McKinley's placid, uncommitted "front-porch campaign" avoided mistakes. Improved agricultural conditions helped secure his election to the presidency with 271 electoral votes against 176 for Bryan. He received more than 7 million popular votes out of about 14 million cast.

Orthodox and at first undistinguished, McKinley's conciliatory "businessman" administration (never appreciably ahead of public opinion) enjoyed good relations with Congress. A special session immediately (1897) enacted the Dingley Tariff, but establishment of the gold standard had to be deferred as the Cuban question demanded increasing attention. Secretary of State John Sherman proved inadequate in handling problems arising from the insurrection there. McKinley soon had either to defy popular clamor and the party jingoists or lead America into a war he personally opposed. He referred the matter to a Congress enthusiastic for war with Spain; the ensuing conflict found him acting as "his own chief of staff" because of an incompetent secretary of war. Luckily Spain was weak, and presidential embarrassments over military mobilization, supply and management soon gave way to problems of the peace. Reluctant at first to annex any territory, he came to believe that the retention of the Philippines was demanded by the people and by the very dictates of conscience. Encouraged by an improvement in the economy, a strengthened Republican congressional majority adopted the gold standard, 1900, and legislated for the government of the newly acquired insular possessions. The armed forces were reorganized. Negotiations commenced for unilateral construction of an Isthmian canal. The Platt Amendment to the Army Act of 1901 (providing for intervention in Cuba) heralded the legal beginnings of a new imperialism. The new Secretary of State John Hay's "Open Door" policy of equal trading privileges in China, and intervention during the Boxer Rebellion there, demonstrated that the nation was now irrevocably involved in the world-wide rivalry among the great powers.

Imperialism proved a tame issue in 1900. McKinley was easily re-elected and the administration was soon strengthened by Supreme Court decisions upholding his territorial policies. Booming business might have had some misgivings after McKinley's Buffalo speech of Sept. 5, 1901, which appeared to suggest lowered tariffs; next day, however, the president was shot by an anarchist and on his death eight days later was succeeded by Vice-President Theodore Roosevelt. Kindly and well-meaning, McKinley inspired an unusual affection among his associates which persisted long after his death, but he was essentially a "party" man and a follower.

McKINLEY, WILLIAM BROWN (*b. Petersburg, Ill., 1856; d. Martinsville, Ind., 1926*), utility operator, philanthropist, politician. Developed the Illinois Traction System, largest electric interurban system in the world, *c.* 1900–10. Elected to Congress as a Republican from Illinois, 1904, he served until 1921 with the exception of the years 1913–15, always regular in his support of Republican policies. As U.S. senator, 1921–26, he became a warm advocate of world peace. McKinley was widely esteemed for generosity toward charitable causes and notably as a benefactor of the University of Illinois. [*Supp.* 1]

McKINLY, JOHN (*b. north Ireland, 1721; d. Wilmington, Del., 1796*), physician, Revolutionary legislator. Came to Delaware *ante* 1747. Chosen first president (governor) of Delaware, February 1777, he was captured by the British a few months later, imprisoned, and paroled, 1778. Resuming the practice of medicine, he took no further part in politics.

McKINSTRY, ALEXANDER (*b. Augusta, Ga., 1822; d. Mobile, Ala., 1879*), lawyer, Confederate soldier, Alabama legislator and lieutenant-governor. Identified himself with the Radical party *post* 1865.

McKINSTRY, ELISHA WILLIAMS (*b. Detroit, Mich., 1825; d. San José, Calif., 1901*), jurist. Removed to California, 1849; held district and county judgeships. Justice of the California supreme court, 1873–88. Delivered opinion of the court in many important cases, including *Ex Parte Wall* (48 *Cal.* 279).

McKNIGHT, ROBERT (*b. Augusta Co., Va., c. 1789; d. 1846*), Santa Fé trader, copper-miner. Joined Santa Fé trading expedition from St. Louis, Mo., without passports, 1812; was seized at Santa Fé and imprisoned in Mexico for nine years. Denied aid or redress by the U.S., he settled in Mexico after a brief visit home in 1822 and an expedition with Thomas James.

MACKUBIN, FLORENCE (*b. Florence, Italy, 1861; d. Baltimore, Md., 1918*), portrait and miniature painter.

McLANE, ALLAN (*b. Philadelphia, Pa., 1746; d. Wilmington, Del., 1829*), Revolutionary soldier. Celebrated as a scout and as commander of small raiding parties. U.S. marshal of Delaware, 1789–97; U.S. customs collector at Wilmington, 1797–1829.

McLANE, LOUIS (*b. Smyrna, Del., 1786; d. Baltimore, Md., 1857*), lawyer, statesman, diplomat. Son of Allan McLane. Attended Newark College (Del.); studied law under James A. Bayard. As congressman, (Democrat) Republican, from Delaware, 1817–27, he as a rule upheld the party program, yet championed the Bank of the United States. As U.S. senator, 1827–29, he supported Andrew Jackson. Appointed U.S. minister to Great Britain, 1829, he negotiated a West Indian trade agreement and returned to become U.S. secretary of the treasury, 1831. Differing with Jackson over the recharter of the Bank, McLane was shifted to secretary of state, 1833. He advocated stern measures in French spoliation claims, ably reorganized departmental procedures, but failed to adjust Northeast Boundary question with Great Britain. Resigning in 1834, he held several canal and railroad

presidencies. As U.S. minister to Great Britain, 1845–46, he negotiated the Oregon boundary compromise. An efficient executive, he was frequently precipitate and uncooperative.

McLANE, ROBERT MILLIGAN (*b. Wilmington, Del., 1815; d. Paris, France, 1898*), lawyer, soldier, politician, diplomat. Son of Louis McLane. Congressman, Democrat, from Maryland, 1847–51. U.S. commissioner to China and Japan, 1853–54. As U.S. minister to Mexico, 1859–60, he recognized the Juarez government there but his treaty was not ratified. Subsequent to the Civil War, he served again in Congress, 1879–83, and was advocate of lower tariffs; he was also governor of Maryland, 1884–85, and U.S. minister to France, 1885–89.

McLAREN, WILLIAM EDWARD (*b. Geneva, N.Y., 1831; d. 1905*), Episcopal clergyman. A Presbyterian missionary and pastor, 1860–72, he was ordained to the Episcopal priesthood, October 1872. Consecrated bishop of Illinois (later Chicago), 1875, he was a leader of the High-Church party.

McLAUGHLIN, HUGH (*b. Brooklyn, N.Y., c. 1826; d. 1904*), political boss. Maintained at least partial, sometimes complete, control of Brooklyn, N.Y., Democratic machine, 1862–1903.

McLAUGHLIN, JAMES (*b. Avonmere, Ontario, Canada, 1842; d. Washington, D.C., 1923*), Indian agent. Removed to Minnesota, 1863; joined U.S. Indian service, 1871. As agent at Devils Lake and Standing Rock, he won the confidence of the Sioux and their acceptance of land cessions and education. *Post* 1895, he served as Indian reservation inspector and negotiator for the Interior Department. His book *My Friend the Indian* (1910) is an important study.

McLAURIN, ANSELM JOSEPH (*b. Brandon, Miss., 1848; d. 1909*), lawyer, legislator. U.S. senator, Democrat, from Mississippi, 1894–95, 1901–09. Governor of Mississippi, 1896–1900.

MACLAURIN, RICHARD COCKBURN (*b. Lindean, Scotland, 1870; d. 1920*), physicist. After a distinguished career at Cambridge University (England) and in New Zealand, he served briefly at Columbia University as professor of mathematical physics, 1908–09. Chosen president, Massachusetts Institute of Technology in 1909, he directed that institution through a vast program of expansion until his death. He also played a leading part in organizing the Students Army Training Corps, 1917–18.

McLAWS, LAFAYETTE (*b. Augusta, Ga., 1821; d. 1897*), soldier. Graduated West Point, 1842. Served in Mexican War and on the Western frontier. Entering the Confederate service, 1861, he became major-general, May 1862, commanded a division in all the larger operations of Lee's army, 1862–63, and was outstanding at Antietam and Fredericksburg. Relieved of command and court-martialed for failure in the Confederate attempt to relieve Knoxville, Tenn., he was exonerated; commanding the defense of Savannah, Ga., he failed in his efforts to oppose Gen. W. T. Sherman's operations, 1864.

MACLAY, EDGAR STANTON (*b. Foochow, China, 1863; d. Washington, D.C., 1919*), journalist. Son of Robert S. Maclay. Author of works on naval history.

MACLAY, ROBERT SAMUEL (*b. Concord, Pa., 1824; d. San Fernando, Calif., 1907*), Methodist clergyman. Missionary in China, Korea and Japan, 1847–88; founded colleges in Foochow and Tokyo.

MACLAY, SAMUEL (*b. Franklin Co., Pa., 1741; d. Buffalo Valley, Pa., 1811*), surveyor, landowner, Revolutionary patriot, Pennsylvania legislator. Brother of William Maclay. As congressman, (Democrat) Republican, 1795–97, Maclay favored France and opposed the Jay Treaty; in U.S. Senate, 1803–09, he was a consistent supporter of the administration.

MACLAY, WILLIAM (*b. Chester Co., Pa., 1734; d. Harrisburg, Pa., 1804*), lawyer, soldier, legislator. Brother of Samuel Maclay. Served in French and Indian War on Pennsylvania frontier. Laid out town of Sunbury, Pa., 1772; settled in Harrisburg, Pa., 1786. After holding numerous state offices, he was active in the first U.S. Congress, 1789–91, as senator from Pennsylvania. Maclay's private journal (not published until 1880) is of the greatest importance since it is the only continuous report of Senate deliberations of that period. His diary reveals Maclay to have been a stout antagonist of Alexander Hamilton's program and a strong defender of the agricultural interest. His comments on all the leaders of that time including Washington are invaluable sidelights on the contest over interpretation of the new Constitution, the funding of the debt, the tariff, enlivened with a caustic wit.

MACLAY, WILLIAM BROWN (*b. New York, N.Y., 1812; d. 1882*), lawyer, editor. As a member of the New York Assembly, 1839–41, he obtained passage of an act which gave New York City full benefit of the state law providing for publicly supported, publicly controlled schools. A consistent Jacksonian Democrat, he served five terms in Congress between 1843 and 1859, advocating reduced postal rates, the distribution of public lands in the form of gratuitous homesteads and the annexation of Texas. He was a vigorous opponent of the Know-Nothings.

McLEAN, ANGUS WILTON (*b. Robeson Co., N.C., 1870; d. Washington, D.C., 1935*), lawyer, businessman. As Democratic governor of North Carolina, 1925–29, he brought all state departments and agencies under centralized executive fiscal control, he also took effective steps against lynching. [*Supp.* 1]

McLEAN, ARCHIBALD (*b. near Summerside, P.E.I., Canada, 1849; d. Battle Creek, Mich., 1920*), clergyman and missionary executive of the Disciples of Christ.

MacLEAN, GEORGE EDWIN (*b. Rockville, Conn., 1850; d. Washington, D.C., 1938*), Congregational clergyman, educator. Professor of English, University of Minnesota, 1883–95; chancellor, University of Nebraska, 1895–99; president, State University of Iowa, 1899–1911. [*Supp.* 2]

MACLEAN, JOHN (*b. Glasgow, Scotland, 1771; d. Princeton, N.J., 1814*), chemist. Studied at Glasgow, Edinburgh, London and Paris. Emigrated to America, 1795. At suggestion of Benjamin Rush, settled in Princeton, N.J., where he served the then College of New Jersey as professor of chemistry and natural history, 1795–1812. He was the first professor of chemistry in any American college other than a medical institution. Benjamin Silliman regarded him as his earliest master in chemistry.

McLEAN, JOHN (*b. Morris Co., N.J., 1785; d. 1861*), politician, jurist. Raised in Kentucky and Ohio. McLean was largely self-educated; admitted to the Ohio bar, 1807, he began practice in Lebanon. As congressman, Democrat, from Ohio, 1813–16, he vigorously supported the war against England. After service as judge, supreme court of Ohio, 1816–22, and a brief period as commissioner of the land office, McLean became U.S. postmaster-general, 1823, and won a national reputation as an able administrator. Appointed a justice of the U.S. Supreme Court, 1829, he served until his death. Fearless, able and conscientious, he was not a great judge, but his circuit decisions were seldom reversed. In the famous Dred Scott case, he dissented from the majority of the Court and in an opinion of his own held that slavery had its origins merely in force and was contrary to right. During his long term on the bench, he was frequently mentioned as a presidential possibility.

MACLEAN, JOHN (*b. Princeton, N.J., 1800; d. Princeton, 1886*), Presbyterian clergyman, educator. Son of John Maclean (1771–1814); nephew of William Bainbridge. Graduated College of New Jersey (Princeton), 1816. Taught at Princeton *post* 1818, handling at various times mathematics, natural philosophy and languages; founded Alumni Association of Nassau Hall, 1826. Appointed vice-president of the College, 1829, Maclean acted in effect as dean and was an effective force in improving the standards of the school. Elected president, 1853, he remained in office until 1868. The profits of his book *History of the College of New Jersey* (1877) were left by him to found scholarships for poor students.

McLEAN, WALTER (*b. Elizabeth, N.J., 1855; d. Annapolis, Md., 1930*), naval officer. Graduated Annapolis, 1876. Admiral Dewey's supply and communications officer at Manila, 1898; commanded Norfolk navy yard and Hampton Roads base, World War I.

McLEAN, WILLIAM LIPPARD (*b. Mount Pleasant, Pa., 1852; d. Germantown, Pa., 1931*), newspaper publisher, philanthropist. Published the Philadelphia *Evening Bulletin, post* 1895; made it noted for honesty, independence. Helped reorganize Associated Press, 1900.

McLELLAN, ISAAC (*b. Portland, Maine, 1806; d. 1899*), sportsman. Author of *Poems of the Rod and Gun* (1886), *Haunts of Wild Game* (1896).

McLEOD, ALEXANDER (*b. Mull, Inner Hebrides, Scotland, 1774; d. 1833*), Reformed Presbyterian clergyman. Came to America, 1792. Graduated Union, 1798. Pastor in New York City, *post* 1800. An eloquent preacher and opponent of slavery.

McLEOD, HUGH (*b. New York, N.Y., 1814; d. Dumfries, Va., 1862*), soldier. Raised in Georgia; graduated West Point, 1835. Resigning from the army, he removed to Texas, 1836, and served in the army of that republic. Commissioned brigadier-general, 1841, he headed the ill-fated expedition sent to Santa Fé in that year to open a trade route. A minor office holder thereafter and a member of the legislature, he was chiefly known for his violent tirades against Sam Houston. He died while in Confederate service as colonel of the 1st Texas Infantry.

McLEOD, MARTIN (*b. near Montreal, Canada, 1813; d. near Fort Snelling, Minn., 1860*), fur trader, Minnesota pioneer and legislator.

McLOUGHLIN, JOHN (*b. Rivière du Loup, Quebec, Canada, 1784; d. 1857*), fur trader, physician. As chief factor of the Hudson's Bay Co., he took charge of the Columbia District where he remained in control, 1824–46. *Post* 1825, Fort Vancouver (within present city of Vancouver, Wash.) was the capital of his far-flung domain. Obliged to monopolize and exploit the fur trade in his area as completely as possible, McLoughlin was generally successful in keeping peace among the numerous Indian tribes and in preventing American competition from affecting the interests of his company. Merciless as a business competitor, he gave all his rivals personally the most generous treatment; by extending credit to the early American settlers for supplies and provisions, he kept many of them from perishing. This humane attitude and his encouragement of missionaries brought on him the censure of his superiors. Retiring from the Hudson's Bay Co., 1846, he failed to make good a claim for lands which he had improved, and it was not until 1862 that his heirs were able to secure the property. A man of extraordinary dignity and appearance, McLoughlin was known to the Indians as the White Eagle.

MACLURE, WILLIAM (*b. Ayr, Scotland, 1763; d. near Mexico City, 1840*), merchant, geologist, patron of science. Settled in America *c.* 1796; became a U.S. citizen *ante* 1803. After making observations throughout the entire United States east of the Mississippi, Maclure produced a geological map of the country, the first of its scope, which was published with an explanatory text in Volume I of the *Transactions* of the American Philosophical Society and appeared in a revised form, 1817 and 1818. He was president of the Academy of Natural Sciences of Philadelphia, 1817–40, and presented to the Academy the greater part of his valuable library and collections of specimens; he was also responsible for the introduction of Pestalozzian methods of education in America. Becoming interested in Robert Owen's projected community at New Harmony, Ind., he persuaded a number of other scientists to accompany him there, where he hoped to test out a plan for a great agricultural school. After the failure of Owen's venture, Maclure spent most of the rest of his life in Mexico.

McMAHON, BERNARD (*b. Ireland, date unknown; d. Philadelphia, Pa., 1816*), horticulturalist. Emigrating to America, 1796, McMahon settled in Philadelphia where he conducted a seed and general nursery business in a shop which served as a club or meeting place for the prominent botanists of the time. He was author of the first notable American horticultural book, *American Gardener's Calendar* (1806).

McMAHON, JOHN VAN LEAR (*b. Cumberland, Md., 1800; d. Cumberland, 1871*), lawyer, Maryland legislator. Author of *Historical View of the Government of Maryland* (1831).

McMANES, JAMES (*b. Co. Tyrone, Ireland, 1822; d. Philadelphia, Pa., 1899*), Philadelphia Republican politician. Held dominant position, 1866–81, in city politics.

McMASTER, GUY HUMPHREYS (*b. Clyde, N.Y., 1829; d. 1887*), New York jurist, poet.

McMASTER, JAMES ALPHONSUS (*b. Duanesburg, N.Y., 1820; d. New York, N.Y., 1886*), journalist, lawyer. An associate of Isaac Hecker and Clarence Walworth, McMaster was received into the Catholic Church, 1845, and served as editor of the independent Catholic paper, the *Freeman's Journal*, 1847–86. Courageous and able, McMaster made his paper an outstanding organ even though his utter frankness brought upon him at times the criticism of the clergy, of the laity and of Irish activists. A picturesque editor of the old school, McMaster was bitter and prejudiced, stubborn in support of principle, firm in friendship.

McMASTER, JOHN BACH (*b. Brooklyn, N.Y., 1852; d. Darien, Conn., 1932*), historian. Graduated College of the City of New York, 1872. Practiced engineering and taught it at Princeton, 1877–83; professor of American history, University of Pennsylvania, 1883–

1920. McMaster is remembered for his monumental *History of the People of the United States* in eight volumes, published at irregular intervals between 1883 and 1913. The earlier volumes in particular hold a unique place in the field of social and economic history which up until their publication had been so largely neglected for war and politics. Working independently and at firsthand from many contemporary sources, McMaster made effective use of newspapers, magazines, memoirs, narratives of travel and letters. His contribution to history included also a number of excellent textbooks which, like his larger works, showed originality and breadth of conception.

McMATH, ROBERT EMMET (*b. Varick, N.Y., 1833; d. Webster Groves, Mo., 1918*), civil engineer. A specialist in river hydraulics, he is best known for the formula which he devised to help in determining proper size for storm-water sewers (1886).

McMICHAEL, MORTON (*b. Bordentown, N.J., 1807; d. Philadelphia, Pa., 1879*), journalist, Whig and Republican politician. Edited several magazines including *Godey's Lady's Book;* also edited and managed Philadelphia *North American,* 1847–79. Held many local offices in Philadelphia, including the mayoralty, 1866–69.

McMILLAN, JAMES (*b. Hamilton, Canada, 1838; d. 1902*), manufacturer, financier. Removed to Detroit, Mich., 1855; managed successful freight-car building company; was partner of John S. Newberry in varied transport and manufacturing enterprises. As state committee chairman, he reorganized the Michigan Republican party, 1886, and was thereafter its effectual leader. Serving as U.S. senator, 1889–1902, he was a member of an influential informal conservative group of senators who determined Republican policies *post* 1890. McMillan promoted the Great Lakes "20-foot channel" and also secured adequate channel entrances to Atlantic harbors. As member of the Senate Committee on the District of Columbia, he secured creation of a notable commission for the development of Washington, D.C.; the resulting "McMillan Plan" (based on L'Enfant's plan of 1792) was the basis for subsequent improvements in the capital.

McMILLAN, JAMES WINNING (*b. Clark Co., Ky., 1825; d. Washington, D.C., 1903*), Union soldier. Organized 21st Indiana Infantry, 1861; resigned from service, 1865, as brevet major-general of volunteers. A brave, tenacious and able brigade commander.

McMILLIN, BENTON (*b. Monroe Co., Ky., 1845; d. 1933*), lawyer, Tennessee legislator. Congressman, Democrat, from Tennessee, 1879–99; governor of Tennessee, 1899–1903. U.S. minister to Peru, 1913–19; to Guatemala, 1919–22. As congressman, favored free silver and advocated an income tax; as governor, reduced the state debt and instituted factory inspection and minimum working age laws. [*Supp. 1*]

McMINN, JOSEPH (*b. Chester Co., Pa., 1758; d. 1824*), Tennessee pioneer and legislator. Governor of Tennessee, 1815–21; a just and benevolent U.S. agent to the Cherokees, 1823–24.

MacMONNIES, FREDERICK WILLIAM (*b. Brooklyn, N.Y., 1863; d. New York, N.Y., 1937*), sculptor. Began as studio boy to Augustus Saint-Gaudens who instructed him and encouraged him to enter night classes at the National Academy of Design and the Art Students League; at twenty he went to Paris to study under Alexandre Falguière at the École des Beaux Arts. By 1891 MacMonnies' work was known at home and abroad; in that year he became the first American to win a medal at the Paris Salon for his statues "J.S.T. Stranahan" and "Nathan Hale" (the latter for New York's City Hall Park). In 1893 Saint-Gaudens chose MacMonnies to design and execute a large fountain for the Chicago World's Fair. The sculptor created a symbolic ship of state, bearing Columbia and many other elaborate figures, which was the sensation of the Fair. Other notable commissions included two fountains for the New York Public Library, "Sir Henry Vane" for the Boston Public Library, "Shakespeare" for the Library of Congress, and, in Grand Army Plaza, Brooklyn, N.Y., two groups and a quadriga for the Memorial Arch. His lovely but pagan "Bacchante" was rejected by staid Boston, and the later "Civic Virtue" aroused a similar controversy in New York. Most ambitious was his war memorial at Meaux, France, his gift to his second country, 1926. Noted for its vigor, ardor, and boldness, MacMonnies' art, as Lorado Taft observed, ". . . is essentially plastic. He delights in the 'feel' of the clay, and he handles it like a magician." [*Supp. 2*]

McMURRICH, JAMES PLAYFAIR (*b. Toronto, Canada, 1859; d. Toronto, 1939*), biologist, anatomist. Professor of anatomy at University of Michigan, 1894–1907; at University of Toronto, 1907–30. First dean (1922–30) of School of Graduate Studies at Toronto. [*Supp. 2*]

McMURRY, FRANK MORTON (*b. near Crawfordsville, Ind., 1862; d. Quaker Hill, N.Y., 1936*), educator. Graduated Jena, Ph.D., 1889. Exponent of Herbartian pedagogy; professor of elementary education, Teachers College, Columbia University, 1898–1926. [*Supp. 2*]

McMURTRIE, WILLIAM (*b. near Belvidere, N.J., 1851; d. New York, N.Y., 1913*), chemist. Associated with Department of Agriculture, 1871–82; *post* 1888, chemist and official of Royal Baking Powder Co. His 1880 report on the foreign beet-sugar industry was instrumental in starting manufacture of that product in the United States.

McNAIR, ALEXANDER (*b. present Juniata Co., Pa., 1775; d. 1826*), merchant. Settled in St. Louis, Mo.,

1804; held many public offices there. Defeated William Clark for governorship of Missouri, 1820, in the first state election; served until 1824.

McNAIR, FRED WALTER (*b. Fennimore, Wis., 1862; d. near Buda, Ill., 1924*), mathematician, educator. Graduated University of Wisconsin, 1891. President, Michigan College of Mines, 1899–1924. Assisted in developing a gun-fire director for battleships during World War I.

McNAIR, FREDERICK VALLETTE (*b. Jenkintown, Pa., 1839; d. Washington, D.C., 1900*), naval officer. Appointed midshipman, 1853; received commendation for notable Civil War service; was assigned thereafter to positions of unusual responsibility. Promoted rear-admiral, 1898, he held the superintendency of U.S. Naval Academy, 1898–1900.

MACNAUGHTAN, MYRA KELLY. [See KELLY, MYRA, 1875–1910.]

McNEILL, DANIEL (*b. Charlestown, Mass., 1748; d. Boston, Mass., 1833*), Revolutionary privateersman, naval officer. As captain of privateer *General Mifflin*, he took thirteen prizes, 1778–1779. Commissioned captain, U.S. Navy, 1798, he served until 1802, commanding the *Portsmouth* and the frigate *Boston*.

McNEILL, GEORGE EDWIN (*b. Amesbury, Mass., 1837; d. Somerville, Mass., 1906*), labor leader. Active in eight-hour-day movement, 1863–74, as speaker, writer and organizer for appropriate legislation. The Knights of Labor adopted his declaration of labor principles, 1874. McNeill drafted a plan for cooperation of the Knights with the American Federation of Labor, 1886; when this failed he joined the Federation whose nonpolitical program appealed to him. He arbitrated a number of labor disputes, edited the Boston *Labor Leader* and wrote several books. His *The Labor Movement* (1887) was the first systematic history of American labor organizations.

McNEILL, HECTOR (*b. Co. Antrim, Ireland, 1728; d. at sea, 1785*), Revolutionary naval officer, privateersman. Came to Boston, Mass., as a child. Commanded frigate *Boston* in John Manley's squadron, 1777; was court-martialed and dismissed from the service for conduct during action with H.M.S. *Rainbow*, July 7, 1777.

McNEILL, JOHN HANSON (*b. Hardy Co., Va., 1815; d. Harrisonburg, Va., 1864*), livestock raiser, Confederate partisan. Removed to Missouri, 1848. Served in Missouri campaigns, 1861–62. Captured and imprisoned, he escaped to western Virginia where he organized the McNeill Partisan Rangers, an independent command which engaged in successful raiding activities against Union forces.

McNEILL, WILLIAM GIBBS (*b. Wilmington, N.C., 1801; d. Brooklyn, N.Y., 1853*), civil engineer. Gradu-

ated West Point, 1817. In association with George W. Whistler, McNeill worked on the projection of most new railways in the eastern United States, 1828–37.

MacNEVEN, WILLIAM JAMES (*b. Co. Galway, Ireland, 1763; d. New York, N.Y., 1841*), physician. Educated at universities of Prague and Vienna; practiced in Dublin *post* 1784. After imprisonment for Irish revolutionary activities *post* 1798, he served briefly in the French army and in 1805 came to New York City where he was successful in practice and as a teacher in the College of Physicians and Surgeons, 1808–26.

McNULTY, FRANK JOSEPH (*b. Londonderry, Ireland, 1872; d. Newark, N.J., 1926*), labor leader. As president, International Brotherhood of Electrical Workers, 1903–19, McNulty succeeded in raising its membership from the condition of a nonskilled labor group and in furthering the settlement of disputes by negotiation instead of by strikes.

McNUTT, ALEXANDER (*b. probably Londonderry, Ireland, c. 1725; d. c. 1811*), colonial land promoter. Came to America *ante* 1753; settled near Staunton, Va. Promoted settlement of Irish Protestants and others in Nova Scotia; helped foment rebellion there, 1778–81.

MACOMB, ALEXANDER (*b. Detroit, 1782; d. Washington, D.C., 1841*), soldier. Commissioned cornet and second lieutenant, U.S. Army, 1799; re-commissioned, 1801; commissioned first lieutenant, Corps of Engineers, 1802. One of the first student officers to be trained at West Point, Macomb remained on duty there until 1805 when he was promoted captain and engaged thereafter until 1812 on coast fortifications in the Carolinas and Georgia. Made colonel of artillery, 1812, he served in minor capacities on the Canadian frontier until 1814 when he was promoted brigadier-general and stationed with his brigade in the Lake Champlain region. His defense of Plattsburg, N.Y., against a superior British invading force, Sept. 11, 1814, was skillfully conducted, but the retreat of the British was probably due rather to the destruction of their supporting fleet by U.S. naval forces under Thomas Macdonough and resultant danger to their communications than to the effectiveness of the small American army. Engaged in various types of service, 1814–21, in the latter year he became head of the Corps of Engineers. In 1828 he was designated senior major-general and commanding general of the U.S. Army, a position which he filled until his death. His ability was primarily of the organizing, systematizing kind which the army of his day greatly needed.

MACOMBER, MARY LIZZIE (*b. Fall River, Mass., 1861; d. Boston, Mass., 1916*), painter of symbolic decorative panels and portraits.

MACON, NATHANIEL (*b. Edgecomb, now Warren, Co., N.C., 1758; d. Warren Co., 1837*), lawyer, North Carolina legislator, Revolutionary soldier. A follower of Willie Jones, Macon opposed the Federal Convention and advocated rejection of the U.S. Constitution. Congressman, (Democrat) Republican, from North Carolina, 1791–1815, and U.S. senator, 1815–28, he was for years the outstanding leader of his party in the House and served as speaker, 1801–07. A supporter in its entirety of the foreign policy of the Jefferson and Madison administrations, Macon as chairman of the Foreign Relations Committee, 1809, reported the two celebrated bills which bear his name although he was the author of neither. He opposed recharter of the U.S. Bank in 1811 and 1816, voted against any form of protective tariff, and opposed a policy of internal improvements; he was also an earnest defender of slavery and voted against the Missouri Compromise. Important as he was in Congress for many years, he was not a constructive force but a negative radical, rural and local-minded.

McPHERSON, EDWARD (*b. Gettysburg, Pa., 1830; d. 1895*), Pennsylvania journalist and political statistician. Congressman, Republican, from Pennsylvania, 1859–63; clerk of the House of Representatives, 1863–75, 1881–83, 1889–91. Author of several political histories of the period *post* 1861; also of the *Political Manual* (1866–69) and the *Handbook of Politics* (biennially, 1868 through 1894).

McPHERSON, JAMES BIRDSEYE (*b. Sandusky Co., O., 1828; d. near Atlanta, Ga., 1864*), Union soldier. Graduated West Point, 1853; was assigned to Corps of Engineers. After service at start of Civil War as aide to Gen. H. W. Halleck, McPherson was chief engineer in U. S. Grant's Tennessee campaign, 1862, and from that time on was constantly in the field. Promoted brigadier-general and major-general, 1862, he served with particular distinction in the campaigns which led up to the taking of Vicksburg. Assuming command of the Army of the Tennessee, March 1864, McPherson led it through the entire subsequent campaign up to the fortifications of Atlanta where he met his death in action. Recognized as one of the ablest generals in the Union Army, McPherson welcomed responsibility and service.

McPHERSON, LOGAN GRANT (*b. Circleville, O., 1863; d. New York, N.Y., 1925*), railway statistician and economist.

McPHERSON, SMITH (*b. near Mooresville, Ind., 1848; d. Redoak, Iowa, 1915*), lawyer, jurist. Iowa attorney-general, 1881–85; federal judge, southern district of Iowa, 1900–15. An able active judge, his decisions were markedly conservative.

McQUAID, BERNARD JOHN (*b. New York, N.Y., 1823; d. Rochester, N.Y., 1909*), Roman Catholic clergyman. Held various pastorates in New Jersey; was consecrated bishop of Rochester, 1868. A zealous reforming prelate, McQuaid ruled his diocese ably but exactingly; he was particularly notable because of his ardor for the establishment of parochial schools and for his conflicts of opinion with more liberal Catholic prelates and clergymen of his time. A rigid canonist and conservative, he opposed secret societies, Irish patriotic groups and the Knights of Labor.

McQUILLEN, JOHN HUGH (*b. Philadelphia, Pa., 1826; d. Philadelphia, 1879*), dentist. Graduated Jefferson Medical College, M.D., 1852. Helped organize American Dental Association, 1859; founded Philadelphia Dental College, 1863, and served there as dean and professor until death. Edited *Dental Cosmos,* 1865–72.

McRAE, DUNCAN KIRKLAND (*b. Fayetteville, N.C., 1820; d. Brooklyn, N.Y., 1888*), lawyer, Confederate soldier. U.S. consul at Paris, 1853–57. Disabled by wounds, he resigned command of 5th North Carolina regiment, 1862, to serve abroad in the succeeding year as a successful purchasing and commercial agent for his state. *Post* 1865, he practiced law principally in Memphis, Tenn.

McRAE, MILTON ALEXANDER (*b. Detroit, Mich., 1858; d. La Jolla, Calif., 1930*), publisher. Associate of James E. and Edward W. Scripps in development of newspapers and newspaper chains. The Scripps-McRae Press Association, formed in 1897, of which he was president, later developed into the United Press.

McRAE, THOMAS CHIPMAN (*b. Union Co., Ark., 1851; d. 1929*), lawyer, politician. Congressman, Democrat, from Arkansas, 1886–1903, McRae held important committee posts and worked for conservation policies, for the recovery of public lands, and for the imposition of a graduated income tax. As Democratic governor of Arkansas, 1921–25, he was successful in abolishing a number of useless offices and instituting a systematic and economical financial administration.

McREYNOLDS, SAMUEL DAVIS (*b. Bledsoe Co., Tenn., 1872; d. Washington, D.C., 1939*), lawyer, Tennessee jurist. Congressman, Democrat, from Tennessee, 1923–39. Advocated limiting immigration, 1924; was chairman of Foreign Affairs Committee *post* 1932. Served most ably as administration spokesman on neutrality legislation, 1935–37. [*Supp. 2*]

MacSPARRAN, JAMES (*b. probably Co. Derry, Ireland, 1693; d. South Kingston, R.I., 1757*), Presbyterian and Anglican clergyman. Served briefly as a minister of the Congregational church, Bristol, R.I., 1718. Refused ordination because of Cotton Mather's enmity, MacSparran returned to England, was ordained in the Church of England (1720) and came out to America again as a missionary of the Society for the Propagation of the Gospel in Foreign Parts.

Arriving at Narragansett, R.I., in April 1721, he proved to be one of the ablest of the missionaries sent to America by the Society. He served as rector of St. Paul's parish and ministered to the surrounding country thereafter until his death. He was author, among other works, of *America Dissected* (1753), an account of the colonies in a series of letters to friends.

McTAMMANY, JOHN (*b. Kelvin Row, Scotland, 1845; d. Stamford, Conn., 1915*), inventor, Union soldier. Came to America, 1862. Conceived the idea of the player-piano, 1863, embodying such elements as a flexible sheet on rolls, a wind motor, foot pedals and other important features suitable for organs as well as pianos. After 13 years of experimentation, he filed a caveat but neglected to obtain a patent and his invention was extensively pirated. After long and costly litigation which reduced him to poverty, he was declared the original inventor, 1880, and received patents, 1881. In 1892, McTammany received a basic patent for a pneumatic registering voting machine employing a perforated roll. The first machine to be used in an election, it was adopted in several states but its manufacture provided little or no return to the inventor.

McTYEIRE, HOLLAND NIMMONS (*b. Barnwell Co., S.C., 1824; d. Nashville, Tenn., 1889*), clergyman and bishop of the Methodist Episcopal Church, South. The chief agent in the founding of Vanderbilt University, Bishop McTyeire served as president of the University's board of trust, 1873–89.

MACUNE, CHARLES WILLIAM (*b. Kenosha, Wis., 1851; d. Fort Worth, Texas, 1940*), farm leader. Drifted about the country *post* 1865, ranching, cattle driving, house painting, and studying law and medicine. Settling in Milam Co., Texas, *c.* 1885, he soon became a leader in the Farmers' Alliance, merging the Texas Alliance with other state farm groups. By 1890 Macune was president of an organization of more than a million members. Moving to Washington, D.C., he edited the Alliance's weekly newspaper, pressing for farm credit legislation. Charged with undermining the Populist cause, Macune dropped out of the Alliance in 1893. From 1900 to 1918 he was a Methodist preacher in Texas. [*Supp. 2*]

MacVEAGH, CHARLES (*b. West Chester, Pa., 1860; d. near Santa Barbara, Calif., 1931*), lawyer, diplomat, philanthropist. Son of Isaac W. MacVeagh. Graduated Harvard, 1881; practiced corporation law in New York, N.Y., *post* 1886. U.S. ambassador to Japan, 1925–29. [*Supp. 1*]

MacVEAGH, FRANKLIN (*b. near Phoenixville, Pa., 1837; d. 1934*), lawyer, businessman. Brother of Isaac W. MacVeagh. Removed to Chicago, 1866, where he engaged in the wholesale grocery business and was active in civic reform movements. Independent in his political thinking, MacVeagh left the Republican party,

1884, but rejoined it in reaction to the policies of William Jennings Bryan; however, he supported Alfred E. Smith, 1928. As U.S. secretary of the treasury, 1909–13, MacVeagh reorganized his department in the direction of efficiency and economy and provided a spark of progressivism in an otherwise conservative cabinet. [*Supp. 1*]

MacVEAGH, ISAAC WAYNE (*b. near Phoenixville, Pa., 1833; d. 1917*), lawyer. Brother of Franklin MacVeagh; son-in-law of Simon Cameron. Graduated Yale, 1853. Appointed U.S. minister resident in Turkey, 1870, he resigned, 1871, in protest against political conditions under the Grant administration and began a lifelong career of "insurgency" by opposing the Cameron Republican machine in Pennsylvania. Active under President R. B. Hayes in bringing an end to Reconstruction in Louisiana, he served briefly as U.S. attorney-general, 1881. MacVeagh's growing interest in civil service and other reforms impelled him to leave the Republican party and to support Grover Cleveland in the campaign of 1892. During a two-year term as U.S. ambassador to Italy *post* December 1893, he preserved good relations despite Italian excitement over treatment of their immigrant compatriots in the United States at the time. Subsequent to 1897, he practiced law, continued his interest in reforms, and was as persistent a nonconformist in the Democratic party as he had been in the Republican. He served as chief counsel for the United States in the Venezuela arbitration, 1903.

MacVICAR, MALCOLM (*b. Dunglass, Scotland, 1829; d. 1904*), Baptist clergyman, educator. Came to Canada as a child; graduated University of Rochester, 1859. Notably successful as a teacher in upstate New York, he organized and administered state normal schools in New York and Michigan. Returning to his ministerial profession in 1881, he taught at and headed several Baptist colleges and was superintendent of the educational work of the American Baptist Home Mission Society.

McVICKAR, JOHN (*b. New York, N.Y., 1787; d. New York, 1868*), Episcopal clergyman, economist. Graduated Columbia, 1804; studied theology with John H. Hobart; was ordained, 1812. A teacher at Columbia, 1817–64, McVickar was one of the earliest professors of political economy in the United States, treating the subject as a branch of moral philosophy. He was author of a life of John H. Hobart and of an important economic essay *Hints on Banking* (1827), among other works.

McVICKAR, WILLIAM NEILSON (*b. New York, N.Y., 1843; d. Beverly Farms, Mass., 1910*), Episcopal clergyman. Graduated Columbia, 1865; General Theological Seminary, New York, 1868. An intimate friend of Phillips Brooks, he was rector of Holy Trinity, Philadelphia, 1875–97. Elected coadjutor bishop of Rhode Island, 1897, he succeeded as bishop, 1903.

McVICKER, JAMES HUBERT (*b. New York, N.Y., 1822; d. 1896*), actor, theatrical manager. A specialist in Yankee comedy parts, McVicker made his most notable success as a manager in Chicago, Ill., *post* 1857. His stock companies were among the best in the United States.

MacWHORTER, ALEXANDER (*b. New Castle Co., Del., 1734 o.s.; d. Newark, N.J., 1807*), Presbyterian clergyman, Revolutionary patriot. Pastor at Newark, N.J., 1759–1807.

MACY, JESSE (*b. near Knightstown, Ind., 1842; d. 1919*), philosopher, political scientist. Professor at Grinnell College (Iowa), 1870–1912. Advocated teaching of government in public schools by observation of the workings of local government, also application of scientific method to study of politics.

MACY, JOHN ALBERT (*b. Detroit, Mich., 1877; d. Stroudsburg, Pa., 1932*), editor, critic, poet. Graduated Harvard, 1899. A Socialist iconoclast, he is remembered for his *The Spirit of American Literature* (1913), a plea for realism and for a profounder examination of American life by American writers.

MACY, JOSIAH (*b. Nantucket, Mass., 1785; d. Rye, N.Y., 1872*), merchant captain. Founder of New York shipping and commission firm of Josiah Macy & Son, 1828.

MACY, VALENTINE EVERIT (*b. New York, N.Y., 1871; d. near Phoenix, Ariz., 1930*), capitalist, philanthropist. Performed notable service as a public official in Westchester Co., N.Y.

MADDEN, JOHN EDWARD (*b. Bethlehem, Pa., 1856; d. New York, N.Y., 1929*), Kentucky horse breeder. Leading American breeder of winning thoroughbred racers, 1916–27; outstanding among his horses were Zev and Princess Doreen.

MADDEN, MARTIN BARNABY (*b. Darlington, England, 1855; d. Washington, D.C., 1928*), politician. Came to America as a child; was raised in Cook Co., Ill., where he prospered as a quarryman. Active in Republican politics *post* 1889, he broke with the Cook Co. machine, 1897, and helped destroy it. As congressman, 1905–28, he was in the main a party regular but served with ability as member and chairman of the appropriations committee *post* 1919.

MADISON, DOLLY PAYNE (*b. present Guilford Co., N.C., 1768; d. Washington, D.C., 1849*), hostess. Raised in Hanover Co., Va.; married John Todd, Jr., a lawyer, 1790; was widowed, 1793. Married James Madison, 1794. She became a social figure of the first importance when her husband assumed U.S. secretaryship of state in 1801; acting as hostess for President Jefferson, who was a widower, her charm and social gifts served to relieve the excessive plainness of the Jeffersonian social regime. Her friendliness, her

remarkable memory of persons and their interests and her unfailing tact were of great service to her husband also during his terms as president. From Madison's retirement, 1817, until his death, 1836, she remained with him at Montpelier living the busy, hospitable life of the mistress of the plantation. In 1837 she returned to Washington and became again a noted and honored figure there until her own death.

MADISON, JAMES (*b. near Staunton, Va., 1749; d. 1812*), Episcopal clergyman, Revolutionary patriot, educator. Cousin of James Madison (1750/51–1836). Graduated William and Mary, 1771. Ordained in England, 1775, he was elected president of William and Mary, 1777, and held this office until his death. Noted among the scientific men of his day, he made surveys from which was made the *Map of Virginia* (1807), commonly known as "Madison's Map" and standard for many years. Under his leadership, the College of William and Mary was brought to a high degree of efficiency; its reorganization and revival after the chaotic period of the Revolution were owing to him. Consecrated first bishop of Virginia, 1790, he was hampered in his efforts to rebuild the church by the pressure of his duties at the college; this and other factors resulted in a gradual weakening of the Episcopal Church in Virginia in the time of his episcopate.

MADISON, JAMES (*b. Port Conway, Va., 1750/51; d. "Montpelier," Orange Co., Va., 1836*), president of the United States. Descendant of independent but not wealthy ancestors, Madison attended school in Virginia and graduated from the College of New Jersey (Princeton), 1771. A diligent student, especially of history and government, he continued another year at Princeton after graduation studying Hebrew and ethics. After a period of melancholy depression following on his return to Virginia, he was aroused to activity by the political struggle with the mother country and by the local controversy over religious toleration. Elected to the Orange Co. Committee of Safety, he was chosen a member of the Virginia convention, 1776, where he served on the committee which framed the Constitution and Declaration of Rights. His chief contribution was a resolution which made the free exercise of religion a matter of right rather than of toleration. A member of the first Assembly under the new Constitution, Madison was elected to the governor's Council, 1778, and in 1780 was chosen a delegate to the Continental Congress. Almost constantly in attendance, March 20, 1780–December 1783, he was a consistent advocate of a federal revenue to be raised by duties on imports; he supported Virginia's claims to Western territory against the assaults of the smaller states; he was instrumental in working out the compromise of September 1783 by which Congress accepted Virginia's cession of the Northwest. When a change of the basis of state contributions from land values to population numbers was urged, he suggested the three-to-five "federal" ratio of free persons to slaves which was later incorporated in the U.S. Constitution.

On returning to Virginia, December 1783, he took up the study of law. Elected within a few months to the House of Delegates, he led in efforts to develop the state's resources, to improve commerce, to complete disestablishment of the Anglican church and to block paper money legal-tender laws; he favored communications to the West, Kentucky statehood, and the natural right of the West to the use of the Mississippi River outlet. He failed in his efforts to achieve a public school system, to honor debts to British creditors, and to insure payment of Virginia's obligations to the federal government. As he saw clearly that the effectual regulation of commerce and the securing of commercial concessions from foreign nations depended on the adoption by the states of a united commercial policy, he urged that the Assembly grant Congress the power to regulate commerce and he took a prominent part in bringing about the inter-state conferences which led through the Annapolis Convention, 1786, to the Federal Convention at Philadelphia, 1787. Once again a congressman, February to May 1787, Madison fought the Jay-Gardoqui agreement that the United States should forego the right to use the Mississippi River.

Named a member of the Virginia delegation to the Philadelphia Convention, 1787, Madison was fearful that its failure would be disastrous to the United States and he set forth constructive preliminary suggestions in letters to Thomas Jefferson, Edmund Randolph and George Washington in March and April 1787. His principal proposals were: (1) A change in the principle of representation which would give the large states a more just influence; (2) The arming of the national government with positive and complete authority in all cases which required uniformity; (3) A negative in all cases whatsoever on the legislative acts of the states, perhaps to be lodged in the less numerous House of the legislature; (4) The extension of the national supremacy to the judiciary departments; (5) A legislature of two Houses with differing terms of office; (6) A national executive; (7) An article expressly guaranteeing the tranquillity of the states against internal as well as external dangers; (8) An express declaration of the right of coercion; (9) Ratification obtained from the people and not merely from the authority of state legislatures. These suggestions were in substance embodied in resolutions drawn up by the Virginia delegates and submitted to the Convention on May 29, known thereafter as the Virginia Plan. Madison became the acknowledged leader of the group in the Convention which favored a strong central government. While many of his ideas failed of adoption, his influence upon the work of the Convention was so great that he may aptly be described as the "master-builder of the Constitution." His most conspicuous quality was perhaps his prac-

tical sense which sought solutions to problems in the realm of past experience rather than in untried theories. Madison was also the chief recorder of the Convention's proceedings; although he was not official secretary of the body, his "Journal of the Federal Convention" (first published, 1840) is by far the most complete record of the proceedings.

Although convinced that the new Constitution would neither sufficiently strengthen the national government nor prevent "local mischiefs," Madison threw himself energetically into the fight for its adoption; among his efforts to overcome opposition was his share in the series of essays published in several New York newspapers over the signature of "Publius," which were later collected and published as *The Federalist* (1788). These celebrated essays, in which he cooperated with Alexander Hamilton and John Jay, have long been accepted as an authoritative exposition of the new Constitution and Madison's share in them was particularly noteworthy. His combination of faith in popular government with a clear-eyed realization that a popular majority can be quite as tyrannical as any monarch is not the least of his virtues. He also emphasized the dual nature of the new government (federal in the extent of its powers, national in their operation) and stressed the idea that the legislative, executive and judicial branches must not be entirely distinct but must be interrelated if they were to form effective checks on one another. In the Virginia ratifying convention, Madison upheld the Constitution against Patrick Henry and George Mason and overthrew their oratory and arguments with quiet but cogent reasoning. Although Henry attempted to block his election to the first Congress, Madison from the beginning participated in the new government, taking a leading part during the first session in the passage of revenue legislation, in the creation of the executive departments and in the framing of the first ten amendments to the Constitution. In the second session and thereafter, Madison was increasingly critical of Hamilton's financial measures; from being an ardent Federalist he became leader of the opposition, the Jeffersonian or (Democrat) Republican party. Wholly out of sympathy with the pro-British trend of Hamilton's policy, his sympathies in the European conflicts which arose at the time of the French Revolution were with France. He opposed assumption of the state debts by the federal Treasury; he opposed creation of the United States Bank; he criticized Washington's Neutrality Proclamation, 1793; he advocated harsh retaliation against British violations of American rights; he voted against the measures for putting the Jay Treaty into effect.

Madison's marriage to Dolly Payne Todd, September 1794, was the beginning of an extraordinarily happy domestic life. After two more years in Congress, he voluntarily retired from public service, March 1797, expecting to devote his time to scientific farming and the pleasures of rural life. However, repressive legislation initiated by the Federalists against critics of their administration (the Alien and Sedition Acts) brought him back into politics. The chief answer to the Federalist policy was the resolutions drawn up by Madison and Jefferson in 1798 and adopted by the Virginia and Kentucky legislatures respectively. The state-rights doctrine of these resolutions was to become a matter of controversy; Madison himself in defending them against hostile criticism, 1799, stated that they were mere expressions of opinion. Later, when the South Carolina nullifiers appealed to the authority of the resolutions as supporting their doctrine, Madison denied this and explained that he and Jefferson had proposed no more than cooperation among the states for securing the repeal of laws or the amendment of the Constitution.

Madison returned to a prominent position in public life when President Jefferson was elected, 1800. Appointed U.S. secretary of state in March 1801, and at once confirmed by the Senate, he was opposed from the outset by a hostile faction headed by William Duane of Pennsylvania and W. B. Giles of Virginia, joined later by John Randolph of Roanoke and by Robert and Samuel Smith of Maryland. The principal foreign policy problems which confronted him arose from the relation of the United States to the war between Great Britain and Napoleonic France and to the disregard by both belligerents of the rights of neutrals on the high seas. Madison believed that peace with both warring nations was possible, resting that faith in part upon the supposed vital need each had for the goods and services of the United States. He played only a formal part in the purchase of Louisiana, 1803. On the renewal of the European war, 1803, after the brief respite of the Peace of Amiens, American commerce and seamen were again subjected to mistreatment by Great Britain and France. Madison's diplomatic notes were able presentations of the legal arguments against the British Orders in Council and the French imperial decrees, but their ineffectiveness was aptly summed up by John Randolph when he characterized one of Madison's treatises as "a shilling pamphlet hurled against eight hundred ships of war." American exasperation was guided by President Jefferson and Madison into the ineffectual Embargo Act, December 22, 1807, which closed American ports and forbade American ships to go to sea. When this measure was repealed, March 1, 1809, administration proposals for a war against both Great Britain and France were defeated in Congress.

Jefferson had chosen Madison as his successor in the presidency. There was little opposition to the choice and Madison entered upon his new duties, March 4, 1809. Observers at the inauguration noted that he appeared care-worn, aging, spiritless and exhausted. He was to have in the presidency eight difficult years and considerable tragedy. Necessary changes in the cabinet added strength to the faction that had opposed him from his entrance into the administra-

tion. Foreign relations steadily grew worse. After holding out a promise to trade with whichever belligerent would repeal its obnoxious measures, Congress, in May 1810, resolved to trade with both; it authorized the president, if either France or Great Britain should reform its practices, to revive non-intercourse against the other. On the strength of what appeared to be an assurance from Napoleon that the objectionable decrees were revoked insofar as they affected the United States, Madison on November 2, 1810, naively issued a proclamation of non-intercourse against Great Britain. This error was not the only cause of war in 1812. Indian outbreaks in the Ohio Valley were ascribed to British intrigues; the West raised a cry that the British must be driven from Canada and their Spanish allies from Florida. Pressure for war was at its height, November 1811 to June 1812. In his message of November 5, 1811, Madison had warned Congress of the danger and had counseled preparations; in a special message of June 1, 1812, he advised a declaration of war against Great Britain, assigning as principal causes the impressment of American seamen, interference with American trade and the incitement of the Indians to border hostilities. Acting upon the president's advice in the June message, Congress declared war on June 18. Congress had neglected to follow Madison's previous counsel to put the United States into a state of preparation, however, and the president despite his many admirable qualities was not the man to lead his country through such an ordeal. Six months of failure ensued before the War and Navy Departments were cleared of incompetent executives; another year went by before men of talent in the army found their way to the top. Federalists opposed the war; Northern (Democrat) Republicans and Madison's personal enemies within his own party thwarted the administration's efforts to seize what remained of the Floridas. Southerners, including James Monroe the secretary of state, felt little enthusiasm for the conquest of Canada and the creation of more Northern states.

The war along the Canadian border was mismanaged until the summer of 1814 and by the time the army became competent it was too late for victory. Great Britain had disposed of Napoleon and could give the United States her undivided attention. Moreover, a few weeks after the declaration of the war, it was learned that Great Britain had in fact repealed the Orders in Council; the war might have been halted then in August 1812 had the war spirit in the West been less powerful. An offer of the British government to negotiate directly with the United States led in time to negotiations at Ghent from August to December 1814 and a treaty of peace was signed, December 24, 1814, on the basis of the surrender of occupied territory only. Thus, not a single declared aim of the war was attained although the city of Washington had been captured and the president and his family forced to flee to the woods. Victories during the closing months of the conflict, however, at Plattsburg, N.Y., and Fort Erie, and in particular at New Orleans, gave an illusion of glory and sent "Mr. Madison's War" down to posterity in school histories as an American triumph. The Hartford Convention held by the New England Federalists in the closing months of the war weighed heavily upon Madison who regarded it properly as a gesture of sedition. The end of the war marked the end of the Federalists as a party, but many of their principles were adopted by the (Democrat) Republicans. Madison shared partially in this conversion. He signed a bill providing for a new Bank of the United States and also the Tariff Act of 1816; he also approved measures strengthening the permanent military and naval establishments. His retirement from the presidency, March 4, 1817, brought his political career to a close except for his share in the Virginia Constitutional Convention, 1829. He supported Thomas Jefferson in the founding of the University of Virginia, of which he became rector after Jefferson's death, 1826. He was interested in the work of the American Colonization Society as the most eligible solution of the Negro problem. During the controversy over nullification, he denied the validity of those doctrines and of the doctrine of peaceful secession, maintaining the general beneficence of the Constitution and Union which he had done so much to create. As the years went by, he was under the necessity of reducing his scale of living and selling part of his farm because of straitened circumstances. The most important work of his later years was the arrangement and preparation for publication of his notes on the Federal Convention.

A small man, Madison was never impressive in appearance. A poor public speaker, he was a delightful conversationalist. His work as architect of the U.S. Constitution overshadowed in importance and success his labors as secretary of state and president. A note entitled "Advice to my Country" which was found among his papers after his death concluded as follows: "The advice nearest to my heart and deepest in my convictions is, that the Union of the states be cherished and perpetuated. Let the open enemy of it be regarded as a Pandora with her box opened, and the disguised one as the serpent creeping with his deadly wiles into paradise."

MAEDER, CLARA FISHER. [See FISHER, CLARA, 1811–1898.]

MAES, CAMILLUS PAUL (*b. Courtrai, Belgium, 1846; d. 1915*), Roman Catholic clergyman. Came to America, 1869; worked as missionary and pastor in Michigan. Consecrated bishop of Covington, Ky., 1885, he was active in promoting the American College at Louvain, and Catholic University, Washington, D.C.

MAFFITT, DAVID (*d. Philadelphia, Pa., 1838*), privateersman in the War of 1812, commanding schooner *Atlas* and brig *Rattlesnake*.

MAFFITT, JOHN NEWLAND (*b. at sea, between Dublin and New York, 1819; d. near Wilmington, N.C., 1886*), naval officer. Appointed midshipman, 1832; served on detached duty with Coast Survey, 1842–58. Resigning from U.S. Navy, 1861, he was commissioned lieutenant in the Confederate Navy and performed with brilliance as commander of combat ships and in blockade-running. Among his principal exploits were his 1862 run of the cruiser *Florida* from Nassau to Mobile, and his final trip in the blockade-runner *Owl* (1865) in which he sought harbor for his cargo all the way from Wilmington to Galveston.

MAGEE, CHRISTOPHER LYMAN (*b. Pittsburgh, Pa., 1848; d. 1901*), politician, political agent for Pennsylvania Railroad and other business interests. Controlled the politics of Pittsburgh and Allegheny Co. with scarcely a break, 1882–99; post 1876, he sat as a delegate in every Republican national convention.

MAGIE, WILLIAM JAY (*b. Elizabeth, N.J., 1832; d. Elizabeth, 1917*), lawyer, New Jersey legislator and jurist. Justice of the state supreme court, 1880–97; chief justice, 1897–1900. New Jersey chancellor, 1900–08.

MAGILL, EDWARD HICKS (*b. Bucks Co., Pa., 1825; d. New York, N.Y., 1907*), educator. Graduated Brown, 1852. President of Swarthmore College, 1871–89. His administration of Swarthmore as a coeducational institution was successful and constitutes his chief service. He founded, 1887, the College Association of Pennsylvania which in time became the Association of Colleges and Preparatory Schools of the Middle States and Maryland.

MAGINNIS, MARTIN (*b. Wayne Co., N.Y., 1841; d. Los Angeles, Calif., 1919*), Union soldier, Montana politician and Democratic congressman.

MAGOFFIN, BERIAH (*b. Harrodsburg, Ky., 1815; d. Harrodsburg, 1885*), lawyer, farmer. Active in Kentucky Democratic politics post 1839; elected governor of Kentucky, 1859. Taking office on the eve of secession, Magoffin did what he could to prevent Democratic disruption at the Charleston Convention; he then favored Crittenden Compromise. He refused Lincoln's call for troops, April 15, 1861, and a week later refused Davis's call for troops though he secretly permitted Confederate recruiting in Kentucky. After the state's proclaimed neutrality was broken many times by both sides, the Confederates invaded Kentucky; Magoffin vetoed a resolution of the legislature calling upon him to order the Confederates out. His subsequent opposition to the predominant Union sentiment of the state resulted in his loss of power and he resigned, August 1862. His advocacy after the Civil War of Kentucky's ratification of the Thirteenth Amendment and the granting of civil rights to Negroes lost him the friendship of many Democrats.

MAGOFFIN, JAMES WILEY (*b. Harrodsburg, Ky., 1799; d. San Antonio, Texas, 1868*), trader, Texas pioneer. Brother of Beriah Magoffin. Traded extensively with Mexico where he resided, 1825–44; by clever diplomacy, assisted U.S. Army capture of Santa Fé, August 1846; resided in Texas *post* 1847.

MAGONIGLE, HAROLD VAN BUREN (*b. Bergen Heights, N.J., 1867; d. Vergennes, Vt., 1935*), architect, sculptor, critic. Studied in offices of Calvert Vaux, Charles C. Haight, and McKim, Mead & White. Celebrated for design of a series of important memorials beginning with the McKinley Memorial, 1904, and climaxing in the Liberty War Memorial, Kansas City, Mo., 1923. He also designed a great deal of important residential work. [*Supp.* 1]

MAGOON, CHARLES EDWARD (*b. Steele Co., Minn., 1861; d. Washington, D.C., 1920*), lawyer. After outstanding service as a law-officer of the War Department, 1899–1904, Magoon served on the Isthmian Canal Commission, as governor of the Canal Zone, 1905–06, and as provisional governor of Cuba, 1906–09. In all his assignments he was noted for his tact and ability to handle complicated economic problems.

MAGOUN, GEORGE FREDERIC (*b. Bath, Maine, 1821; d. 1896*), Congregational clergyman, educator. Graduated Bowdoin, 1841. President of Iowa (Grinnell) College, 1862–84.

MAGRATH, ANDREW GORDON (*b. Charleston, S.C., 1813; d. Charleston, 1893*), jurist. Graduated South Carolina College, 1831; studied law in office of James L. Petigru. As judge, U.S. district court, 1856–60, he raised that court from a position of disfavor in the state to one of distinction. He opposed secession as inexpedient when advocated by R. B. Rhett, 1852; on Lincoln's election, however, he accepted view that there were sufficient grounds for separation and that the welfare of South Carolina required her secession. During service as South Carolina secretary of state, 1860–61, he directed much of the official correspondence over disposition of Fort Sumter. Some of his decisions as judge of the Confederate district courts in South Carolina, 1861–64, ran counter to the policy of the Richmond government and lost him its favor. Chosen governor of South Carolina by the legislature, 1864, he took an extreme state-rights position within the Confederacy. Arrested in May 1865, he was imprisoned for a short time; on his release, he resumed the practice of law.

MAGRUDER, GEORGE LLOYD (*b. Washington, D.C., 1848; d. Washington, 1914*), physician. Grad-

uated Gonzaga College, 1868; M.D., Georgetown, 1870. Professor, dean and treasurer of Georgetown Medical School *post* 1871. Magruder was a strong influence in promoting sanitary conditions in Washington, in particular, a pure water supply and effective regulation of the sale of milk.

MAGRUDER, JOHN BANKHEAD (*b. Winchester, Va., 1810; d. Houston, Texas, 1871*), soldier. Graduated West Point, 1830. Served in occupation of Texas and in Seminole war; in Mexican War, commanded light artillery of Pillow's division. Nicknamed "Prince John" for his devotion to society. Magruder resigned his commission, March 1861, to accept appointment as colonel, Confederate Army. His handling of troops on the Virginia Peninsula up to the spring of 1862 won him promotion to major-general; his failures during the Seven Days' Battles around Richmond seriously hampered Lee's operations against McClellan. Transferred to command of the district of Texas, October 1862, he was reasonably successful in small operations. At the close of hostilities, refusing to seek parole, Magruder went to Mexico and became a major-general under Maximilian.

MAGRUDER, JULIA (*b. Charlottesville, Va., 1854; d. Richmond, Va., 1907*), novelist, short-story writer. Niece of John B. Magruder.

MAGUIRE, CHARLES BONAVENTURE. [See Mc-GUIRE, CHARLES BONAVENTURE, 1768–1833.]

MAHAN, ALFRED THAYER (*b. West Point, N.Y., 1840; d. Washington, D.C., 1914*), naval officer, historian. Son of Dennis H. Mahan. Graduated U.S. Naval Academy, 1859. After Civil War service mainly on blockade duty, Mahan followed a routine of sea and shore duty until 1885 when he was promoted captain. Appointed lecturer on tactics and naval history at the newly established Naval War College, Newport, R.I., he delivered his first lectures in the autumn of 1886. Succeeding Admiral Luce as president, 1886–89, he supported the College against the hostility of the secretary of the navy and the indifference of the service itself. He published his lectures in 1890 as *The Influence of Sea Power Upon History, 1660–1783*. The book won immediate recognition, far greater in Europe than in America, and with its successor *The Influence of Sea Power Upon the French Revolution and Empire, 1793–1812* (1892) made him world famous. Mahan's power of generalization, his ability to subordinate details to the central theme and to indicate the significance of events for later times made him the first "philosopher of sea power." He served a second term as president of the Naval War College, 1892–93, and retired, 1896. He returned to duty, 1898, to serve as a member of the strategy board directing naval operations in the Spanish-American War. Mahan wrote a number of other books, among them his memoirs *From Sail to Steam* (1907). Few other historians have so widely influenced the policies of their own time as did Mahan; however, there will always be a question how much his success was due to the value of his books as propaganda for naval expansion already under way in Great Britain, Germany and the United States.

MAHAN, ASA (*b. Vernon, N.Y., 1799; d. Eastbourne, England, 1889*), Congregational clergyman. Graduated Hamilton, 1824; Andover Theological Seminary, 1827. First president of Oberlin College, 1835–50, he required that the college receive students without discrimination as to color or sex. He served also as president of Adrian College, 1860–71.

MAHAN, DENNIS HART (*b. New York, N.Y., 1802; d. by drowning in Hudson River, 1871*), soldier, educator. Half-brother of Milo Mahan; father of Alfred T. Mahan. Graduated West Point, 1824; studied also in French army engineering school, Metz. Associated almost all his life with West Point as professor of civil and military engineering, Mahan was best known as the author of pioneering textbooks on fortification, outpost duty and general engineering.

MAHAN, MILO (*b. Suffolk, Va., 1819; d. Baltimore, Md., 1870*), Episcopal clergyman, educator. Half-brother of Dennis H. Mahan. Professor of ecclesiastical history, General Theological Seminary, New York, 1851–64; thereafter, rector, St. Paul's Church, Baltimore. Author of church histories.

MAHONE, WILLIAM (*b. Southampton Co., Va., 1826; d. Washington, D.C., 1895*), railroad executive, Confederate major-general, politician. Graduated Virginia Military Institute, 1847. President of the Norfolk-Petersburg Railroad. At the outbreak of the Civil War, Mahone proved himself an able field commander and capable administrator; he was particularly distinguished during July 1864 in the Wilderness and at the Crater. Following the war he organized the lines which later became the Norfolk and Western Railroad and developed a strong following in the state legislature. In 1879, he organized and led the "Readjusters" who advocated a partial repudiation of the state's debt and popular social and economic legislation. Frowned on by the regular party machines and by the wealthy, this movement swept the state, 1879 and 1881. Elected to the U.S. Senate, 1880, Mahone traded his vote for offices and committee assignments, thereby angering the Democrats. By his control of state and federal patronage, he built a political machine which thereafter dominated the Republican party in Virginia of which he was absolute boss.

MAILLY, WILLIAM (*b. Pittsburgh, Pa., 1871; d. 1912*), journalist, Socialist. National secretary, Socialist party, 1903–05.

MAIN, JOHN HANSON THOMAS (*b. Toledo, O., 1859; d. 1931*), educator. Ph.D., Johns Hopkins, 1892. Taught Greek in Iowa (Grinnell) College; served as acting president, 1900–02, as dean, 1902–06, and as president of Grinnell, 1906–31. [*Supp. 1*]

MAISCH, JOHN MICHAEL (*b. Hanau, Germany, 1831; d. 1893*), pharmacist. Came to America *c.* 1850. Able manager of U.S. Army Laboratory, 1863–65; professor, Philadelphia College of Pharmacy, 1866–93, eventually becoming dean. Editor, *American Journal of Pharmacy,* 1871–93, and author of *A Manual of Organic Materia Medica* (1882).

MAJOR, CHARLES (*b. Indianapolis, Ind., 1856; d. 1913*), popular novelist, lawyer. Author, among other books, of the best-selling *When Knighthood Was in Flower* (1898) and *Dorothy Vernon of Haddon Hall* (1902).

MAJORS, ALEXANDER (*b. near Franklin, Ky., 1814; d. Chicago, Ill., 1900*), freight-line operator, promoter of the Pony Express. Raised in Missouri, Majors began freighting from Independence, Mo., to Santa Fé, 1848; *c.* 1855, he entered partnership with William H. Russell; in 1858, the partnership became Russell, Majors & Waddell. The firm took over operation of a daily stagecoach line from Fort Leavenworth to Denver, 1859, afterwards including in their schedules Atchison, Kans., Salt Lake City, Fort Kearney and Fort Laramie. On April 3, 1860, they established the famous Pony Express which lasted only 18 months and was a financial failure. The firm itself failed in 1861.

MA-KA-TAI-ME-SHE-KIA-KIAK. [See Black Hawk, 1767–1838.]

MAKEMIE, FRANCIS (*b. near Ramelton, Ireland, c. 1658; d. 1708*), Presbyterian clergyman, regarded as chief founder of the Presbyterian Church in America. Arriving in Maryland, 1683, Makemie worked as an evangelist there and in North Carolina and Virginia and also in Barbados. Settling in Virginia, 1698, he secured a license to preach and thus became the first dissenting minister licensed under the Toleration Act; he labored as well in Maryland. In 1706, Makemie united with two young ministers who had come to Maryland through his agency, and also with four others, to form the first American presbytery. He was arrested in January 1707 and imprisoned six weeks for preaching in the colony of New York without a license. His vigorous defense of himself brought about legislation which made another such persecution impossible in New York.

MALBONE, EDWARD GREENE (*b. Newport, R.I., 1777; d. Savannah, Ga., 1807*), miniature painter. Self-taught, Malbone began business in Providence, R.I., 1794; his earliest work shows the use of fine stipple for modeling the face and scrupulous regard to detail in finish, costume and background painting. His success in Providence was followed by continuing success in Boston, 1796–98, and at New York and Philadelphia, 1798–99. In the autumn of 1800 he went to Charleston, S.C. His technique by this time had changed from a stiff, detailed style to a freer method in which delicate interwoven lines of color performed the double function of creating form as well as providing color. He visited London in 1801 where his work won the praise of Benjamin West. A third style becomes recognizable in his painting on his return to Charleston in December 1801; the same delicate lines of color are used in painting the face but the stroke is even freer and somewhat broader. Subtle transitions give the effect of smoothness and the size of the ivory becomes larger. Malbone spent most of the years 1804 and 1805 in Boston, returning once more to Charleston in December 1805; during the following March, he contracted tuberculosis and was forced to give up painting. His genius as a technician is undisputed; his continual and thoughtful experimentation is one of his chief claims to superiority over other miniature painters.

MALCOLM, DANIEL (*b. Georgetown, Maine, 1725; d. Boston, Mass., 1769*), Revolutionary patriot, merchant, sea captain. A leader in Boston of overt defiance of British trade regulations, 1766–68.

MALCOLM, JAMES PELLER (*b. Philadelphia, Pa., 1767; d. England, 1815*), engraver, author, Loyalist. Removing to England *c.* 1787, Malcolm became an engraver of illustrative plates for magazines and an industrious compiler of books on antiquarian subjects.

MALCOM, DANIEL. [See MALCOLM, DANIEL, 1725–1769.]

MALCOM, HOWARD (*b. Philadelphia, Pa., 1799; d. Philadelphia, 1879*), Baptist clergyman, educator. President of Georgetown (Kentucky) College, 1840–49; of Lewisburg (Bucknell) University, 1851–57; of Hahnemann Medical College, 1874–79. Author of a number of books including the popular *Dictionary of Important Names, Objects and Terms Found in the Holy Scriptures* (1830).

MALCOM, JAMES PELLER. [See MALCOLM, JAMES PELLER, 1767–1815.]

MALL, FRANKLIN PAINE (*b. near Belle Plaine, Iowa, 1862; d. Baltimore, Md., 1917*), anatomist, embryologist. M.D., University of Michigan, 1883; made further studies at Heidelberg and Leipzig. Fellow in pathology and later instructor at Johns Hopkins Hospital, Mall taught anatomy at Clark University, 1889–92. After a brief service in the new University of Chicago as professor of anatomy, he returned to Baltimore as head of the department of anatomy, Johns Hopkins Medical School. He was appointed, in addition, director of the department of embryology of the Carnegie Institution, Washington, 1914. Mall vitalized the study of anatomy in America. In medical educa-

tion, he stood for freedom of curriculum, concentration of courses, broad electives; his department of anatomy at Johns Hopkins was the first to bring into one discipline cytology, histology, embryology and adult structure. His own researches were numerous and important; he first traced the embryologic origin of the thymus gland, added to knowledge of the structure and function of the intestines, introduced the idea of histological units in organs and worked out the muscular system of the heart.

MALLARY, ROLLIN CAROLAS (*b. Cheshire, Conn., 1784; d. Baltimore, Md. 1831*), lawyer. Congressman from Vermont, 1820–31. As chairman, House committee on manufactures, he reported Tariff of Abominations, 1828, and was largely responsible for its passage.

MALLERY, GARRICK (*b. Wilkes-Barre, Pa., 1831; d. 1894*), lawyer, Union soldier, ethnologist. On staff of Bureau of Ethnology, 1879–94, Mallery wrote notable papers on Indian pictography and sign-language.

MALLET, JOHN WILLIAM (*b. near Dublin, Ireland, 1832; d. Virginia, 1912*), chemist. Highly trained in Ireland and Germany, Mallet came to America, 1853. He was professor of chemistry, Alabama University, 1855–60, and made an exhaustive scientific study of cotton culture (published 1862). After serving as general superintendent of Confederate ordnance laboratories, 1862–65, he returned to teaching, retiring as professor emeritus, University of Virginia, 1908.

MALLINCKRODT, EDWARD (*b. near St. Louis, Mo., 1845; d. St. Louis, 1928*), chemical manufacturer, philanthropist.

MALLORY, STEPHEN RUSSELL (*b. Trinidad, c. 1813; d. Pensacola, Fla., 1873*), lawyer. Raised in Florida where he practiced law *post c.* 1840. As U.S. senator, Democrat, from Florida, 1851–60, he was active in congressional naval reform; in February 1861, he was named Confederate secretary of the navy. Vehement and forceful, Mallory employed the talents of John M. Brooke and others so well that the Confederacy, which started without ships or yards, was able to prevent penetration of the Virginia rivers by the U.S. Navy; also, he encouraged development of torpedoes and submarines. He failed, however, in his efforts to build up a sizable ironclad fleet. After the war and a brief imprisonment, he resumed his law practice.

MALONE, SYLVESTER (*b. Trim, Ireland, 1821; d. Brooklyn, N.Y., 1899*), Roman Catholic clergyman. Came to America, 1839; ordained, New York, 1844. An outstanding Williamsburg (Brooklyn), N.Y., pastor, he was a Republican and a strong Civil War Unionist. Later a pro-labor liberal and civic reformer, he served as a regent of the University of the State of New York, 1894–99.

MALONE, WALTER (*b. DeSoto Co., Miss., 1866; d. Memphis, Tenn., 1915*), Tennessee circuit court judge, poet. Wrote *Songs of North and South* (1900) and epic *Hernando De Soto* (1914).

MALONEY, MARTIN (*b. near Thurles, Ireland, 1847; d. Spring Lake, N.J., 1929*), industrialist, public utilities operator, philanthropist.

MALTER, HENRY (*b. near Sabno, Galicia, Austria, 1864; d. 1925*), scholar, teacher. Graduated Heidelberg, Ph.D., 1894; studied also at Berlin and made special rabbinical studies. Came to America, 1900. Professor of Jewish philosophy and Oriental languages, Hebrew Union College, Cincinnati, O., 1900–07; professor of rabbinical language and literature, Dropsie College, Philadelphia, Pa., 1909–25. Author, among other works, of *Saadia Gaon* (1921); projected a method for creation of a critical text of the Talmud.

MANATT, JAMES IRVING (*b. Millersburg, O., 1845; d. Providence, R.I., 1915*), classicist. Professor of Greek literature and history, Brown, 1893–1915. Co-author of *The Mycenaean Age* (1897).

MANDERSON, CHARLES FREDERICK (*b. Philadelphia, Pa., 1837; d. at sea, returning to America, 1911*), lawyer, Union soldier. Practiced law first in Canton, O., and *post* 1869 in Omaha, Nebr. As U.S. senator, Republican, from Nebraska, 1883–95, advocated nationally built highways; on leaving office, became general solicitor for Burlington Railroad.

MANEY, GEORGE EARL (*b. Franklin, Tenn., 1826; d. Washington, D.C., 1901*), lawyer, Confederate brigadier-general, diplomat. U.S. minister resident to Colombia, 1881–82; to Bolivia, 1882–89; to Paraguay, 1889–90. He served thereafter until 1894 in Paraguay with rank of envoy extraordinary and minister plenipotentiary.

MANGIN, JOSEPH FRANÇOIS (*fl. 1794–1818*), engineer, architect. Came to New York from France at an undetermined date, possibly as a refugee from the Revolution; served *post* 1795 as chief engineer of New York fortifications and as one of the city's surveyors, in which capacity he produced the official city map (published, 1803). He is best known for his connection with the New York City Hall; his share in the design of this work is still a matter of controversy. His only other known important work was the design for the first St. Patrick's Cathedral, Mott Street (built, 1809–15).

MANGUM, WILLIE PERSON (*b. Orange, now Durham, Co., N.C., 1792; d. 1861*), lawyer, jurist. Congressman, Democrat, from North Carolina, 1823–27; U.S. senator, Democrat, 1831–35. Breaking with Andrew Jackson over the Force Bill and the removal of federal deposits from the U.S. Bank, Mangum subsequently identified himself with the Whig party and served again in the U.S. Senate as a Whig, 1841–53.

As president *pro tempore* of the Senate, May 1842—March 1845, he served as an acting vice-president of the United States. An astute politician and effective debater, he was known for his power as a campaign speaker; owing in part to his urging, Daniel Webster made his celebrated 7th of March speech.

MANIGAULT, ARTHUR MIDDLETON (*b. Charleston, S.C., 1824; d. Georgetown Co., S.C., 1886*), soldier, merchant, planter. Descendant of Pierre Manigault. Served in Mexican War. In Confederate service, 1861–64, he was mainly with the armies in the West and was promoted brigadier-general, April 1863.

MANIGAULT, GABRIEL (*b. Charleston, S.C., 1704; d. Charleston, 1781*), merchant, planter, Revolutionary patriot, South Carolina legislator. Son of Pierre Manigault.

MANIGAULT, PETER (*b. Charleston, S.C., 1731; d. London, England, 1773*), lawyer. Son of Gabriel Manigault. Studied law at the Inner Temple; was called to the English bar, 1754. In practice at Charleston, 1754–73, he served as a member of the South Carolina Assembly, 1755–72. During the last seven years of his membership, he was speaker.

MANIGAULT, PIERRE (*b. La Rochelle, France, date unknown; d. Charleston, S.C., 1729*), merchant. Removed to Charleston from London, England, *c.* 1695. Starting as a brandy distiller, he branched out into general trade and died wealthy.

MANLEY, JOHN (*b. probably Boston, Mass., c. 1734; d. Boston, 1793*), naval officer. Commanding schooner *Lee*, he captured in November 1775 the first valuable prize taken by Americans in the Revolutionary War, the brigantine *Nancy*, laden with a cargo of military stores. Appointed captain, Continental Navy, April 1776, Manley was made prisoner aboard frigate *Hancock*; exchanged, March 1778, he commanded successful privateers, was twice captured and exchanged, and in 1783 (again a naval officer, commanding the frigate *Hague*) took the last valuable prize to be taken by a Continental ship.

MANLEY, JOSEPH HOMAN (*b. Bangor, Maine, 1842; d. 1905*), lawyer, journalist, Maine legislator. Editor and half-owner of the *Maine Farmer*, *post* 1878. Chairman, Republican national committee, 1896–1904. James G. Blaine's closest political friend.

MANLY, BASIL (*b. near Pittsboro, N.C., 1798; d. Greenville, S.C., 1868*), Baptist clergyman, educator. Held pastorates in South Carolina, principally in Charleston; helped found Furman University; president, University of Alabama, 1837–55. As pastor in Montgomery, Ala., he delivered prayer at inauguration of Jefferson Davis, February 1861.

MANLY, BASIL (*b. Edgefield District, S.C., 1825; d. Louisville, Ky., 1892*), Baptist clergyman, educator.

Son of Basil Manly (1798–1868). Held numerous pastorates; helped organize Southern Baptist Theological Seminary, Greenville, S.C., 1859, and served it as professor at various times, 1859–92.

MANLY, CHARLES MATTHEWS (*b. Staunton, Va., 1876; d. 1927*), mechanical engineer. Grandson of Basil Manly (1798–1868). Graduated Furman University, 1896; M.E., Cornell, 1898. Associated with Samuel P. Langley in his early aeronautical experiments, Manly served as pilot in the unfortunate trials of Langley's machine, October and December 1903. His permanent contribution to aviation, however, was his design and construction of a five-cylinder water-cooled radial gasoline engine of 52 horsepower weighing only 125 pounds; this engine has been characterized as the first modern aircraft engine. Manly also invented and patented, 1902, the Manly Drive, a hydraulic device for transmitting power at variable speeds from a constant-speed motor.

MANLY, JOHN MATTHEWS (*b. Sumter Co., Ala., 1865; d. Tucson, Ariz., 1940*), philologist. Grandson of Basil Manly (1798–1868). Graduated Furman University, 1883; Ph.D., Harvard, 1890. Taught at Brown, 1890–98; first head, department of English, University of Chicago, 1898–1933. Notable as Chaucer scholar; with Edith Rickert, edited critical edition of *Canterbury Tales* (1940). [*Supp.* 2]

MANN, AMBROSE DUDLEY (*b. Hanover Court House, Va., 1801; d. Paris, France, 1889*), lawyer, diplomat. An active and efficient consular representative and special American agent in central Europe, 1842–53, and an assistant U.S. secretary of state, 1853–56, Mann became increasingly identified thereafter with the fight for Southern rights and the economic independence of the South. As a Confederate commissioner, in England and Belgium, 1861–65, he showed himself credulous and lacking in penetration.

MANN, HORACE (*b. Franklin, Mass., 1796; d. Yellow Springs, O., 1859*), lawyer, Massachusetts legislator, educator. After an unhappy childhood marked by poverty and repression and by the ignorance and stultifying methods of district schoolmasters, Mann began to prepare himself for college in 1816. Graduating from Brown University, 1819, he studied law, was admitted to the bar, 1823, and practiced with great success at Dedham and Boston, Mass. until 1837. Meanwhile, he served in the Massachusetts legislature, as a member of the House, 1827–33, and of the Senate, 1833–37. As president of the Senate, 1836–37, he signed the epoch-making education bill which became a law, April 20, 1837. This bill provided for a state board of education which was empowered to appoint a secretary. Through the influence of Edmund Dwight, Mann was appointed to this post. Between 1837 and 1848, when he resigned the secretaryship, he almost completely transformed the decaying Massachusetts public school system. His first task

was to arouse and educate public opinion with reference to the purpose, value and needs of public education. He organized, therefore, annual educational conventions in every county which were attended by teachers, school officials and the public and which were addressed by civic leaders and men of intellectual distinction. To improve the teaching profession, he brought about the establishment of teachers' institutes and of the first three state normal schools in the United States. He also started and edited a semi-monthly magazine, the *Common School Journal* and prepared a series of annual reports which widely influenced American opinion on public education.

Progress was amazing. A six-months' minimum school year was established, educational appropriations were doubled, fifty new high schools were founded, curricula and methods were revamped and teachers' salaries were greatly increased. Mann's efforts, especially his advocacy of nonsectarian instruction and his commendation of German and Swiss educational methods, produced bitter opposition but his proposals triumphed.

Resigning his school post, 1848, he served in Congress as an anti-slavery Whig, 1848–53; he was defeated as Free-Soil candidate for governor, 1852. He served *post* 1853 as president, also professor of a variety of subjects, at Antioch College. Mismanagement, insufficient funds, and dissension caused sale of the college for debt, 1859; exhausted, Mann died shortly thereafter. Interested in numerous humanitarian reforms, Mann was at his best in achieving a revival of American public school education.

MANN, JAMES (*b. Wrentham, Mass., 1759; d. Governor's Island, N.Y., 1832*), army surgeon. Served with 4th Massachusetts regiment, 1779–82; headed medical department on Northern frontier, War of 1812. Author of *Medical Sketches of the Campaigns of 1812, 13, 14* (1816).

MANN, JAMES ROBERT (*b. near Bloomington, Ill., 1856; d. 1922*), lawyer. Congressman, Republican, from Illinois, 1897–1922; an effective if excessively "stand pat" minority leader, 1912–18. Among the major measures with which he was associated were the Mann-Elkins Act, the Pure Food and Drug Act of 1906, the Mann Act, and the resolution providing for the woman-suffrage amendment.

MANN, LOUIS (*b. New York, N.Y., 1865; d. 1931*), actor, playwright. Celebrated in dialect roles.

MANN, MARY TYLER PEABODY (*b. Cambridge, Mass., 1806; d. Jamaica Plain, Mass., 1887*), educator. Sister of Elizabeth P. Peabody; married Horace Mann, 1843. Collaborated with and influenced profoundly her husband's life and thought. Author of *Life and Works of Horace Mann* (1865–68).

MANN, NEWTON (*b. Cazenovia, N.Y., 1836; d. Chicago, Ill., 1926*), Unitarian clergyman, early advocate of Darwinism. Held principal pastorates in Rochester, N.Y. and Omaha, Nebr.

MANN, WILLIAM JULIUS (*b. Stuttgart, Germany, 1819; d. Boston, Mass., 1892*), Lutheran clergyman. Came to America, 1845, at urging of Philip Schaff; held pastorates in Philadelphia, Pa. Professor, Philadelphia Lutheran Theological Seminary, 1864–84. Author of *Life and Times of Henry Melchior Mühlenberg* (1887).

MANNERS, JOHN HARTLEY (*b. London, England, 1870; d. New York, N.Y., 1928*), actor, dramatist. Author, among other plays, of *Peg O' My Heart*, produced first in 1912.

MANNING, DANIEL (*b. Albany, N.Y., 1831; d. 1887*), journalist, politician, banker. Became part-owner of the *Albany Argus*, 1865. Virtually succeeded Samuel J. Tilden as leader of the New York Democratic party, 1877. Grover Cleveland was greatly indebted to Manning for his nomination as New York governor and for his first nomination to the presidency. Appointed U.S. secretary of the treasury, 1885, he served with great ability and loyally endorsed Cleveland's views. His resignation in 1887, allegedly owing to ill health, was actually caused by Cleveland's resentment of Tilden's desire to be the power behind the throne; as Manning was Tilden's friend, he was therefore proscribed.

MANNING, JAMES (*b. Piscataway, N.J., 1738; d. Providence, R.I., 1791*), Baptist clergyman. Graduated College of New Jersey (Princeton), 1762. Elected president of the new Rhode Island College, 1765, he served until his death and showed administrative ability of a high order in his management of the school both at Warren, R.I., and at Providence. Serving also as pastor of the First Baptist Church in Providence, he took a firm stand (along with Isaac Backus and others) against the oppression suffered by Baptists under the "Standing Order" in Connecticut and Massachusetts.

MANNING, RICHARD IRVINE (*b. Camden District, S.C., 1789; d. Philadelphia, Pa., 1836*), planter. Governor of South Carolina, 1824–26, Manning attached himself to the Union party *post* 1826 and was one of the leaders of the opposition to nullification. As a congressman, 1834–36, he supported Henry L. Pinckney's 1836 gag resolution.

MANNING, RICHARD IRVINE (*b. Sumter Co., S.C., 1859; d. Columbia, S.C., 1931*), planter, South Carolina legislator. Grandson of Richard I. Manning (1789–1836). A progressive Democrat and an opponent of the faction led by B. R. Tillman, Manning served as governor of South Carolina, 1915–19, and gave the state its most notable administration since the time of Wade Hampton. Among other constructive acts, he emphasized law enforcement and the suppression of lynching, set up a board of labor conciliation, a tax commission, a board of welfare, and reformed state care of the insane and feeble-minded.

MANNING, ROBERT (*b. Salem, Mass., 1784; d. 1842*), businessman, pomologist. Uncle of Nathaniel Hawthorne. Established a pomological garden at Salem in 1823 with the aim of securing specimens of all varieties of fruits hardy enough to withstand the Massachusetts climate. At the time of his death he possessed the finest collection of fruit trees in America and one of the best in the world. He helped found the Massachusetts Horticultural Society and was author of the *Book of Fruits* (1838). To him, more than to any other man of his time, the fruit-growers of America were indebted for the introduction of new and choice varieties, for correcting the nomenclature of fruits, and for identifying many varieties.

MANNING, THOMAS COURTLAND (*b. Edenton, N.C., 1825; d. New York, N.Y., 1887*), lawyer, Confederate soldier. Practiced in Louisiana *post* 1855; chief justice, Louisiana supreme court, 1877–80. Appointed, 1882, to the newly constituted supreme bench of Louisiana, he served until 1886 when he was appointed U.S. minister to Mexico.

MANNING, VANNOY HARTROG (*b. Horn Lake Depot, Miss., 1861; d. 1932*), topographer. Served *post* 1885 with U.S. Geological Survey. Transferring to the newly created Bureau of Mines, 1910, he succeeded Joseph A. Holmes as director of the Bureau in 1915 and served until 1920. Under his direction, the Bureau did notable research and other work for the U.S. War Department, 1917–18; resultant from this work were a wide variety of chemical weapons, the production of better airplane motor fuels, and the production of helium gas for use in lighter-than-air craft.

MANSELL, WILLIAM ALBERT (*b. Moradabad, India, 1864; d. Bareilly, India, 1913*), Methodist clergyman. Missionary and educator in India *post* 1889.

MANSFIELD, EDWARD DEERING (*b. New Haven, Conn., 1801; d. near Morrow, O., 1880*), lawyer. Son of Jared Mansfield. Graduated West Point, 1819; College of New Jersey (Princeton), 1822. Practiced law in Cincinnati, O., *post* 1825, and was associated with Benjamin Drake in newspaper publications there. A promoter of Cincinnati and its area, he was co-author with Drake of *Cincinnati in 1826* (1827), a valuable study of the locality which greatly affected immigration thereto.

MANSFIELD, JARED (*b. New Haven, Conn., 1759; d. New Haven, 1830*), mathematician, physicist. A school teacher in New Haven, 1786–1802, he was brought into prominence by his book *Essays, Mathe-*

matical and Physical (1801) which is considered to be the first book of original mathematical researches by a native American. Appointed captain of engineers, U.S. Army, by President Jefferson, 1802, he was professor of mathematics and natural philosophy at West Point, 1802–03 and 1812–28. He was surveyor general of the United States, 1803–12, assigned to service in the survey of Ohio and the Northwest Territory.

MANSFIELD, JOSEPH KING FENNO (*b. New Haven, Conn., 1803; d. near Sharpsburg, Md., 1862*), military engineer. Nephew of Jared Mansfield. Graduated West Point, 1822. Served with the highest distinction in Mexican War as chief engineer of the army under Gen. Zachary Taylor; was inspector-general of the army, 1853–61. Commissioned brigadier-general, regular army, 1861, and major-general of volunteers, July 1862, Mansfield commanded the Union XII Corps at the battle of Antietam where he was mortally wounded.

MANSFIELD, RICHARD (*b. New Haven, Conn., 1723; d. Derby, Conn., 1820*), Episcopal clergyman, Loyalist. Rector, St. James Church, Derby, 1748–1820. First Episcopalian to receive degree of Doctor of Divinity from Yale (1792).

MANSFIELD, RICHARD (*b. Berlin, Germany, 1854; d. New London, Conn., 1907*), actor. Son of a London wine merchant and a noted opera singer mother, Mansfield resided in Boston, Mass., 1872–77. Returning to London in the latter year, he sang in touring Gilbert and Sullivan companies and played small parts in London and the provinces. His U.S. professional debut was in New York, September 1882, in the operetta *Les Manteaux Noirs;* his first success was as Baron Chevrial in *A Parisian Romance,* also 1882. Failing in an early attempt as a manager, he reached the rank of star in legitimate drama in 1886. Thereafter until the end of his life he was his own manager and producer. He first acted his most spectacular role, that of "Dr. Jekyll and Mr. Hyde," in May 1887 at the Boston Museum. In London, March 1889, he made his Shakespearean debut as Richard III and brought the production to the United States that autumn. Among his other outstanding roles were "Beau Brummell," "Shylock," "Cyrano de Bergerac," "Monsieur Beaucaire." He produced *Arms and the Man* at the Herald Square Theatre, New York, September 1894, the first play by G. B. Shaw ever seen in America. In October 1906 he began his season in Chicago with the first American production of Ibsen's *Peer Gynt.* Although Mansfield represented more brilliantly and persistently than any actor of his day the romantic tradition and the grand style in plays and playing, he also helped usher in a new and different era in the history of drama. His performances in Shaw plays were as mordantly modern as the plays themselves. He had a splendid voice under perfect command yet he indulged in numerous eccentricities of speech. In addition to his natural gifts as a mime, he had a certain electric quality which informed all his characterizations from the wistful young prince of *Old Heidelberg* to his portrayal of Brutus haunted by remorse. High-strung, nervous, always carrying the whole weight of his productions, Mansfield was not popular with his fellow actors but he was at bottom a generous and kindly man.

MANSON, OTIS FREDERICK (*b. Richmond, Va., 1822; d. Richmond, 1888*), physician, Confederate surgeon. Graduated medical department, Hampden-Sydney College, 1840; practiced in rural North Carolina until 1862. Early observing importance of malaria as causative agent and complicating force in other diseases, he presented his findings to the profession in numerous controversial writings. Professor of pathology and physiology, Medical College of Virginia, 1869–82.

MANTELL, ROBERT BRUCE (*b. Irvine, Scotland, 1854; d. Atlantic Highlands, N.J., 1928*), actor. Made American debut at Albany, N.Y., November 1878, in Madame Modjeska's company. Was identified with the American stage *post* 1884, principally as an interpreter of Shakespeare. His interpretations depended more upon force of action and vigor of voice than upon intellectual subtlety.

MAPES, CHARLES VICTOR (*b. New York, N.Y., 1836; d. 1916*), agricultural chemist, manufacturer. Son of James J. Mapes; brother of Mary Mapes Dodge. A pioneer in developing fertilizers adapted to the peculiar needs of different crops and different soils.

MAPES, JAMES JAY (*b. Maspeth, N.Y., 1806; d. New York, N.Y., 1866*), agriculturalist, chemist. Edited *The Working Farmer,* 1849–63, in which he published results of his experimental farming and stressed the scientific principles underlying his practice. Among other contributions to agriculture, he developed a formula for nitrogenized superphosphate which was probably the first complete plant food among artificial fertilizers used in the United States.

MAPPA, ADAM GERARD (*b. Delft, Holland, 1754; d. present Trenton, N.Y., 1828*), soldier, typefounder. Came to New York City, 1789, and established the first type foundry in that place. After its failure, he removed to Oneida Co., N.Y., where he farmed and acted as agent of the Holland Land Co. *post* 1794.

MARBLE, ALBERT PRESCOTT (*b. Vassalboro, Maine, 1836; d. 1906*), educator. Graduated Waterville (now Colby) College, 1861. His success as superintendent of public schools in Worcester, Mass., and in Omaha, Nebr., resulted in his appointment as superintendent of New York City high schools, 1896. He was author of *Sanitary Conditions for School Houses* (1891).

MARBLE, DANFORTH (*b. East Windsor, Conn., 1810; d. Louisville, Ky., 1849*), actor. Skillful in roles requiring Yankee dialect, he scored his greatest success in *Sam Patch,* written especially for him by E. H. Thompson, 1836.

MARBLE, MANTON MALONE (*b. Worcester, Mass., 1835; d. England, 1917*), journalist. Editor and owner, N.Y. *World,* 1862–76, Marble opposed many of the policies of the Lincoln administration and was later active in exposing the Tweed Ring. He was credited with having written the Democratic national platform in 1876 and 1884.

MARBURY, ELISABETH (*b. New York, N.Y., 1856; d. 1933*), author's agent, theatrical producer. Beginning as agent for Frances H. Burnett, Miss Marbury came in time to be representative of the most celebrated dramatists of her day; among her clients were Sardou, Rostand, Oscar Wilde, Bernard Shaw, Somerset Maugham, J. M. Barrie. She pioneered also in production of the "revue," or intimate type of musical comedy. [*Supp. 1*]

MARBUT, CURTIS FLETCHER (*b. Verona, Mo., 1863; d. Harbin, Manchuria, 1935*), geologist, soil expert. Associated *post* 1905 with the Bureau of Soils, U.S. Department of Agriculture, Marbut was a leader in mapping the soils of the United States and with others developed an international system of soil study known as pedology. His most extensive publication was *Soils of the United States* (1935). [*Supp. 1*]

MARCH, ALDEN (*b. Sutton, Mass., 1795; d. Albany, N.Y., 1869*), surgeon, anatomist, teacher of surgery. Practiced at Albany *post* 1820; held principal teaching appointments at Vermont Academy of Medicine and Albany Medical College.

MARCH, FRANCIS ANDREW (*b. Worcester Co., Mass., 1825; d. 1911*), philologist. Graduated Amherst, 1845. After several years in legal study and practice, he became a tutor at Lafayette College and in 1857 was appointed professor of the English language and comparative philology there, a post which he held until his retirement, 1906. March seems to have been the first to apply scientific methods of exegesis to the classroom study of English literary monuments; his chief title to fame, however, rests on his researches in the field of English historical grammar. He was author of *A Comparative Grammar of the Anglo-Saxon Language* (1870), a piece of research of the first rank; he also did much valuable work in English lexicography.

MARCH, FRANCIS ANDREW (*b. Easton, Pa., 1863; d. Easton, 1928*), lexicographer. Son of Francis A. March (1825–1911). Taught English at Lafayette College *post* 1882; served on staffs of *Century* and *Standard* dictionaries; edited *A Thesaurus Dictionary of the English Language* (1902).

MARCHAND, JOHN BONNETT (*b. Greensburg, Pa., 1808; d. Carlisle, Pa., 1875*), naval officer. Appointed midshipman, 1828; retired as commodore, 1870, after varied service mainly at sea. Commanded *U.S.S. Lackawanna* on blockade duty in Gulf of Mexico, 1863–64.

MARCHANT, HENRY (*b. Martha's Vineyard, Mass., 1741; d. Newport, R.I., 1796*), lawyer, Revolutionary patriot, Continental Congressman. U.S. district judge in Rhode Island, 1790–96.

MARCOU, JULES (*b. Salins, France, 1824; d. Cambridge, Mass., 1898*), geologist. Made collections in America for Paris Jardin des Plantes, 1848–50; *post* 1860, was employed as field geologist in Western surveys and at Harvard Museum of Comparative Zoology. Author of many articles and books, including a life of his mentor Louis Agassiz (1895).

MARCY, HENRY ORLANDO (*b. Otis, Mass., 1837; d. 1924*), surgeon, gynecologist, Union medical officer. Graduated Harvard Medical School, 1864; studied also in Berlin, London, and at Edinburgh where he became first American pupil of Joseph Lister. Practicing in Boston, Mass., and *post* 1880 in Cambridge, Marcy was notable in introduction of Lister's methods here, as a pioneer in antiseptic treatment of wounds, and as the developer of absorbable animal sutures.

MARCY, RANDOLPH BARNES (*b. Greenwich, Mass., 1812; d. West Orange, N.J., 1887*), soldier. Graduated West Point, 1832. Served on Michigan and Wisconsin frontier; saw Mexican War service in Texas; was on active duty in the Southwest, 1847–57. Opened new trail, Fort Smith to Santa Fé, 1849; led exploration to headwaters of Red and Canadian rivers, 1852. Made a famous winter march through the Rockies, 1857–58, to reprovision A. S. Johnston's army operating against Mormons in Utah. Served as chief-of-staff to son-in-law, Gen. George B. McClellan, in Civil War Peninsular and Antietam campaigns. Retired as brigadier-general, 1881. Author of valuable official reports on his explorations in the Red-Canadian region; also of *The Prairie Traveler* (1859) and two volumes of reminiscences.

MARCY, WILLIAM LEARNED (*b. Sturbridge, present Southbridge, Mass., 1786; d. Ballston, N.Y., 1857*), lawyer, statesman. A graduate of Brown, 1808, he removed to Troy, N.Y., where he read law and was admitted to the bar, 1811. Active in support of Jeffersonian principles, Marcy held local and state offices. He became friendly *c.* 1818 with Martin Van Buren and helped to organize the dominant Democratic political group known as the "Albany Regency." Skillful in restraining the rise of public debt as New York state comptroller, 1823–29, he served with marked ability as a justice of the state supreme court, 1829–31. As U.S. senator, December 1831–December

1832, he defended Van Buren's appointment as minister to London, stating that he could see nothing wrong in the rule that "to the victor belong the spoils of the enemy," whence the term "spoils system" as used in American politics. Outstanding as governor of New York, 1833–38, Marcy organized the state's first geological survey, settled the boundary dispute with New Jersey, refused to extradite Abolitionists for Southern trial but reprobated Abolitionism. He was an effective conciliator in disputes over Mexican Claims, 1840–42, and as secretary of war, 1845–49, won national prestige despite a controversy with Gen. Winfield Scott.

Appointed secretary of state by President Pierce, Marcy handled with distinction a series of great issues between 1853 and 1857. He was responsible for negotiation of 24 treaties, the largest number ratified within an administration up to that time; among them, the Gadsden (1853), the Reciprocity (with Great Britain, 1854), and treaties with the Netherlands (1855) and Denmark (1857) were most significant. During Marcy's term, three delicate cases involving international relations were settled: the Koszta case with Austria; the *Black Warrior* case with Spain; the Patrice Dillon case with France. In the matter of the sensational Ostend Manifesto (published in March 1855), Marcy was indirectly at fault for putting trust in Pierre Soulé and John Y. Mason who were bent on acquiring Cuba by any means for Southern interests. Reckoned among the nation's foremost men at the time of his death, he ranks among the ablest of our secretaries of state.

MARDEN, CHARLES CARROLL (*b. Baltimore, Md., 1867; d. 1932*), philologist. Graduated Johns Hopkins, 1889; Ph.D., 1894. Taught Hispanic studies at Johns Hopkins, Princeton, University of Chicago; edited medieval texts.

MARDEN, ORISON SWETT (*b. near Thornton, N.H., 1850; d. 1924*), hotel operator, journalist. Publicized "the will to succeed" in various books and in his magazine *Success* (1897–1912, 1918–24).

MARÉCHAL, AMBROSE (*b. near Orléans, France, 1764; d. 1828*), Roman Catholic clergyman, Sulpician. Served as missioner and seminary teacher in Maryland, 1792–1803; after returning to France, was recalled to St. Mary's Seminary, Baltimore, 1812. As archbishop of Baltimore, 1817–28, he administered his archdiocese with zeal and firmness and showed himself wholly American in sympathies; during his term, the Baltimore Cathedral was completed (1821).

MAREST, PIERRE GABRIEL (*b. Laval, France, 1662; d. Kaskaskia Mission, 1714*), Roman Catholic clergyman, Jesuit, pioneer priest in Illinois.

MARETZEK, MAX (*b. Brünn, Austria, present Czecho-Slovakia, 1821; d. Staten Island, N.Y., 1897*), composer, conductor. First successful impresario of Italian opera in New York, 1848–79.

MARGOLIS, MAX LEOPOLD (*b. Merech, Russia, 1866; d. 1932*), Biblical scholar, educator. Studied in Warsaw and Berlin; came to America, 1889; graduated Columbia, Ph.D., 1891. Essentially a philologist, he taught Semitic languages at Hebrew Union, University of California and Dropsie College, and was author of a number of scholarly works on the Bible.

MARIGNY, BERNARD (*b. New Orleans, La., 1785; d. New Orleans, 1868*), planter, Louisiana legislator. Putative introducer of game of "craps" to the United States c. 1802.

MARION, FRANCIS (*b. probably St. John's Parish, Berkeley Co., S.C., c. 1732; d. St. John's Parish, 1795*), planter, Revolutionary soldier, South Carolina legislator. Nicknamed the "Swamp Fox." Served against the Cherokees, 1759 and 1761; appointed captain, 2nd South Carolina Regiment, 1775. After service in and near Charleston, he commanded the regiment in attack on Savannah, 1779. Detailed by Gen. Gates to command militia between Santee and Pedee rivers, after the American disaster at Camden (1780) Marion prevented effective organization of South Carolina Tories and disrupted British communications by guerrilla operations. At the battle of Eutaw Springs (1781), he led the militia and was thereafter Gen. Greene's chief aide for outpost duty until the evacuation of Charleston.

MARKHAM, CHARLES HENRY (*b. Clarksville, Tenn., 1861; d. Altadena, Calif., 1930*), railroad executive. President, Illinois Central, 1911–18 and 1919–26; improved facilities and service; began modernization of Chicago terminal and yards.

MARKHAM, EDWIN (*b. Oregon City, Oreg., 1852; d. Staten Island, N.Y., 1940*), poet. Author of "The Man with the Hoe," one of the most popular poems of all time, first published in *San Francisco Examiner*, and issued separately in a special supplement to that newspaper on January 15, 1899. [*Supp. 2*]

MARKHAM, WILLIAM (*b. England, c. 1635; d. Philadelphia, Pa., 1704*), Pennsylvania official. Cousin of William Penn. As deputy-governor, arrived at present Chester, Pa., 1681; presided over first provincial council; helped select site of Philadelphia; reverted to office of councilor at Penn's arrival, 1682. Served thereafter as provincial secretary, 1685–91; as deputy-governor of Lower Counties, 1691–93; as lieutenant-governor or governor of both Pennsylvania and the Lower Counties (Delaware), 1693–99. Probably the chief author of the "Frame of Government."

MARKOE, ABRAHAM (*b. St. Croix, V.I., 1727; d. Philadelphia, Pa., 1806*), capitalist, Revolutionary patriot. Removed to Philadelphia, c. 1770; organized Philadelphia Light Horse (First Troop), 1774.

MARKOE, PETER (*b. St. Croix, V.I., c. 1752; d. Philadelphia, Pa., 1792*), poet, dramatist. Son of

Abraham Markoe. Author of *The Patriot Chief* (published 1784, a tragedy); *Miscellaneous Poems* (1787); *The Times* (1788, a satire); *The Reconciliation* (1790, an early comic opera), and other works.

MARKS, AMASA ABRAHAM (*b. Waterbury, Conn., 1825; d. Sound Beach, Conn., 1905*), inventor and manufacturer of improved artificial limbs.

MARKS, ELIAS (*b. Charleston, S.C., 1790; d. Washington, D.C., 1886*), physician, educator. Founded South Carolina Female Institute, 1828, for higher education of women.

MARLING, ALFRED ERSKINE (*b. Toronto, Canada, 1858; d. 1935*), real-estate operator. President, H. S. Ely & Co., New York, 1904–31. [*Supp. 1*]

MARLING, JOHN LEAKE (*b. Nashville, Tenn., 1825; d. Nashville, 1856*), journalist, diplomat. Editor, Nashville *Gazette* and *Daily Union;* opposed secessionist sentiment at Nashville Convention, 1850. U.S. minister-resident in Guatemala, 1854–56.

MARMADUKE, JOHN SAPPINGTON (*b. near Arrow Rock, Mo., 1833; d. Jefferson City, Mo., 1887*), Confederate major-general, businessman. Graduated West Point, 1857; served with infantry in Utah and New Mexico. Entering Confederate service, 1861, he was distinguished at Shiloh and later in small but effective actions in Arkansas and western Missouri. As Democratic governor of Missouri, 1885–87, he secured needed legislation for regulation of railroads.

MARQUAND, ALLAN (*b. New York, N.Y., 1853; d. New York, 1924*), art historian. Son of Henry G. Marquand. Graduated Princeton, 1874; Ph.D., Johns Hopkins, 1880. Taught at Princeton *post* 1881 and was director and patron of the department of art and archaeology there. Author of many scholarly studies; also of *Greek Architecture* (1909), and of a monumental series of catalogues of sculptures by the Della Robbia family.

MARQUAND, HENRY GURDON (*b. New York, N.Y., 1819; d. 1902*), capitalist, philanthropist. Benefactor of the Metropolitan Museum of Art (New York) and of Princeton University; president, Metropolitan Museum, 1889–1902.

MARQUETT, TURNER MASTIN (*b. Clark Co., O., 1829; d. Lincoln, Nebr., 1894*), lawyer, Nebraska territorial legislator and attorney for the Burlington Railroad.

MARQUETTE, JACQUES (*b. Laon, France, 1637; d. at mouth of Pere Marquette River, near present Ludington, Mich., 1675*), Jesuit missionary, explorer. Came to Quebec, 1666; learned Indian languages at Three Rivers; appointed to mission among the Ottawa Indians, 1668. After wintering at Sault Ste. Marie, he went to the mission of La Pointe at Chequamegon Bay on the south shore of Lake Superior where he first encountered Indians from the Illinois country. In the summer of 1671, he founded the mission of St. Ignace on the north shore of the Straits of Mackinac; there, in December 1672, he encountered for the second time Louis Jolliet, who brought him news that the governor had commissioned them both to go in search of a great river to the westward, of which Marquette had already heard from the Illinois Indians. They set forth in May 1673 by way of Green Bay and Fox River, portaged to the Wisconsin, and on June 17, 1673, reached the Mississippi. Turning their canoes southward, they reached the mouth of the Arkansas by mid-July; there, learning that the river entered the Gulf of Mexico and that Spaniards were on the lower river, they turned back. They reached Lake Michigan by the Illinois River and the Chicago portage, coasted the lake shore, and rested at the mission of St. Francis Xavier at DePere. Marquette remained there for more than a year, recruiting his health and writing his journal. In October 1674, he set out to found a mission among the Illinois Indians. After suffering many hardships and serious illness, Marquette reached the Illinois village, spent Easter of 1675 there, but died on his way back to the mission of St. Ignace. Marquette is the most renowned of all the Jesuit missionaries in the West, in part because of his early death and saintly nature, in part because he and Jolliet were the first to follow the course of the Mississippi River and to make their journey known by journals, maps and letters.

MARQUIS, DON(ALD ROBERT PERRY) (*b. Walnut, Ill., 1878; d. Forest Hills, N.Y., 1937*), journalist, humorist. Worked on Washington, D.C., and Atlanta, Ga., newspapers, 1899–1909; in New York City thereafter. Wrote "Sun Dial" column in N.Y. *Evening Sun,* 1913–22. Author of *archy and mehitabel* (1927), also volumes of fiction, light verse and several plays, all of a high order. Called "a belated Elizabethan."

[*Supp. 2*]

MARQUIS, JOHN ABNER (*b. Dinsmore, Pa., 1861; d. New York, N.Y., 1931*), Presbyterian clergyman, educator. President, Coe College, 1909–20; secretary, Presbyterian Board of Home Missions, 1917–23, and of National Missions *post* 1923.

MARRIOTT, WILLIAMS McKIM (*b. Baltimore, Md., 1885; d. San Francisco, Calif., 1936*), biochemist, pediatrician. Graduated University of North Carolina, 1904; M.D., Cornell, 1910. Taught biochemistry at Washington University Medical School, 1910–14. Wishing to apply biochemistry to medical problems, he became aide to Dr. John Howland in pediatrics department, Johns Hopkins Medical School. Their joint work on acidosis in infancy won international recognition, as did Marriott's later work at Washington University, where he returned as professor of pediatrics, 1917. Here he discovered the cause of "alimentary intoxication" and revolutionized infant feeding by introducing simplified procedures and inexpensive ingredients such as evaporated milk and corn syrup. [*Supp. 2*]

MARSH, CHARLES WESLEY (*b. near Trenton, Ontario, Canada, 1834; d. 1918*), inventor, manufacturer, editor. Settled with his parents in De Kalb Co., Ill., 1849. With his brother William, he patented first practical hand-binding harvester, 1858. After the failure of companies which he set up to manufacture his machine, Marsh became editor of the *Farm Implement News,* 1885, and later president of the company which published it.

MARSH, FRANK BURR (*b. Big Rapids, Mich., 1880; d. Dallas, Texas, 1940*), historian. Graduated University of Michigan, 1902; Ph.D., 1906. Taught at University of Texas, 1910–40; author of *The Founding of the Roman Empire* (1922) and other works. [*Supp. 2*]

MARSH, GEORGE PERKINS (*b. Woodstock, Vt., 1801, d. Vallombrosa, Italy, 1882*), lawyer, diplomat. Cousin of James Marsh. Graduated Dartmouth, 1820; admitted to bar, 1825; practiced in Burlington, Vt. As congressman, Whig, from Vermont, 1843–49, he supported high tariffs and opposed slavery and the Mexican War. Serving as U.S. minister to Turkey, 1849–54, he arranged for the departure of Kossuth to America and acted with fairness but discretion in the cases of Jonas King and Martin Koszta. Appointed first U.S. minister to the kingdom of Italy, 1860, he served there with success for the remainder of his life. Marsh was a conscientious and erudite scholar in many fields. Notable among his books was *Man and Nature* (1864), revised as *The Earth as Modified by Human Action* (1874), which has been described as "the fountainhead of the conservation movement."

MARSH, GRANT PRINCE (*b. Chautauqua Co., N.Y., 1834; d. Bismarck, N.D., 1916*), Mississippi and Missouri river pilot and steamboat captain, friend of Mark Twain.

MARSH, JAMES (*b. Hartford, Vt., 1794; d. Burlington, Vt., 1842*), philosopher, educator. Cousin of George P. Marsh. Graduated Dartmouth, 1817. During his presidency of the University of Vermont, 1826–33, that institution became a leader in educational reform both in New England and in the Middle West. His edition of Coleridge's *Aids to Reflection* (1829) with its preliminary essay was read with enthusiasm by Emerson and other young intellectuals of the period and had a strong influence upon the Transcendentalist movement.

MARSH, JOHN (*b. Wethersfield, Conn., 1788; d. Brooklyn, N.Y., 1868*), Congregational clergyman, temperance reformer.

MARSH, JOHN (*b. South Danvers, Mass., 1799; d. near Martinez, Calif., 1856*), physician, adventurer, California pioneer.

MARSH, OTHNIEL CHARLES (*b. Lockport, N.Y., 1831; d. New Haven, Conn., 1899*), paleontologist. Nephew of John Marsh (1799–1856). Graduated Yale, 1860; did graduate work in science there and studied at Berlin, Breslau and Heidelberg, 1863–66. He returned from Germany to become America's first professor of paleontology, holding that chair at Yale, 1866–99. Organizing numerous scientific expeditions (at first financed by his own means, augmented by an inheritance from a maternal uncle, George Peabody), he uncovered almost unlimited fossil material in Nebraska, Wyoming, Colorado and California. He actually accumulated fossils more rapidly than he could study them, and his published bibliography is less comprehensive than might be expected. Besides many papers in the *American Journal of Science,* he wrote the monographs *Odontornithes* (1880) and *Dinocerata* (1884); his best single paper was the *Introduction and Succession of Vertebrate Life in America* (1877); other works had only just been begun at his death. Marsh was the first to describe remains of fossil serpents and flying reptiles in western North America; American museums owe to his almost compulsive collecting the fact that they now often have fossil skeletons as complete as those of animals now living. In 1882 Marsh was appointed vertebrate paleontologist to the U.S. Geological Survey. President of the National Academy of Sciences, 1883–95, recipient of foreign awards, he put the collection and preparation of vertebrate fossils upon a truly scientific basis.

MARSH, SYLVESTER (*b. Campton, N.H., 1803; d. Concord, N.H., 1884*), inventor, meat-packer, grain dealer. Invented devices for handling and drying grain and meal; devised and constructed cog-wheel railroad up Mount Washington, N.H. (1869).

MARSH, WILLIAM WALLACE (*b. near Trenton, Ontario, Canada, 1836; d. Sycamore, Ill., 1918*), inventor, manufacturer. Removed as a boy to De Kalb Co., Ill. Partner with his brother, Charles W. Marsh, in the invention and manufacture of the first practical hand-binding harvester.

MARSHALL, BENJAMIN (*b. Huddersfield, England, 1782; d. Troy, N.Y., 1858*), merchant, cotton textile manufacturer. Came to America, 1803; settled in New York, N.Y., and engaged in import-export trade. A partner with Jeremiah Thompson and others in the Black Ball Line, 1817–33, Marshall was thereafter principally concerned with the manufacture of high-quality cotton goods at Utica and Troy, N.Y.

MARSHALL, CHARLES HENRY (*b. Nantucket Island, 1792; d. New York, N.Y., 1865*), sea captain, shipping executive. Commanded packet ships of the

Black Ball Line, 1822–34; served thereafter as New York City agent of that line and became its principal owner.

MARSHALL, CHRISTOPHER (*b. probably Dublin, Ireland, 1709; d. Philadelphia, Pa., 1797*), pharmacist, Revolutionary patriot. Came to America *c.* 1727; settled in Philadelphia. Best known for the *Diary* which he kept during the Revolution, one of the most valuable sources for the period. Published in part in 1839 and 1849, the comprehensive edition is that of 1877.

MARSHALL, CLARA (*b. West Chester, Pa., c. 1848; d. 1931*), physician. Graduated Woman's Medical College of Pennsylvania, 1875; practiced for many years in Philadelphia, Pa. Joining the faculty of her alma mater immediately after graduation, she remained there as professor until 1923 and served also as dean, 1888–1917. The success of the school was owing largely to her energy and enthusiasm.

MARSHALL, DANIEL (*b. Windsor, Conn., 1706; d. 1784*), pioneer "Separate Baptist" preacher. Brother-in-law of Shubael Stearns. Leading a wandering life *post* 1744, Marshall settled on Kiokee Creek, Ga., 1771, where he founded the first Baptist church in that state, 1772.

MARSHALL, HENRY RUTGERS (*b. New York, N.Y., 1852; d. 1927*), architect, writer on aesthetics. Executive secretary, New York City Municipal Art Commission, 1914–27.

MARSHALL, HUMPHREY (*b. Fauquier Co., Va., 1760; d. Lexington, Ky., 1841*), lawyer, Kentucky landowner and legislator. Nephew of Thomas Marshall; cousin of John and Louis Marshall. U.S. senator, Federalist, from Kentucky, 1795–1801. Instrumental in exposing motives of Aaron Burr, 1806. Author of *The History of Kentucky* (1812, 1824).

MARSHALL, HUMPHREY (*b. Frankfort, Ky., 1812; d. Louisville, Ky., 1872*), soldier, lawyer, diplomat. Grandson of Humphrey Marshall (1760–1841); nephew of James G. Birney. Graduated West Point, 1832, but resigned his commission a year later. Served with credit in the Mexican War. Congressman, Whig, from Kentucky, 1849–52; U.S. minister to China, 1853–54; congressman, Know-Nothing, 1855–59. Commissioned a Confederate brigadier-general, 1861, he resigned his commission, 1863, because he could not secure an independent command. He served in the second Confederate Congress, 1864–65.

MARSHALL, HUMPHRY (*b. Chester Co., Pa., 1722 o.s.; d. Chester Co., 1801*), botanist. Cousin of John Bartram. Proprietor of a notable botanic garden at Marshallton, Pa.; author of *Arbustrum Americanum, the American Grove* (1785), which has been called the first truly indigenous botanical essay to be published in the Western Hemisphere.

MARSHALL, JAMES FOWLE BALDWIN (*b. Charlestown, Mass., 1818; d. Weston, Mass., 1891*), merchant, educator. In business at Honolulu, Hawaii, 1838–59; as representative of Hawaiian native government, helped foil British annexation attempt, 1843. Returning to Boston, he engaged in Civil War service and after the war joined Samuel C. Armstrong at Hampton Institute where he served as resident trustee and in other capacities, 1870–84.

MARSHALL, JAMES MARKHAM (*b. Fauquier Co., Va., 1764; d. Fauquier Co., 1848*), landholder, Kentucky legislator. Son of Thomas Marshall; brother of John and Louis Marshall; son-in-law of Robert Morris. Acquired large holdings by purchase of Fairfax estates in the Northern Neck section of Virginia.

MARSHALL, JAMES WILSON (*b. Hunterdon Co., N.J., 1810; d. near Coloma, Calif., 1885*), mechanic, discoverer of gold in California. Starting westward in search of adventure and fortune *c.* 1831, Marshall settled for a brief period in Indiana and Illinois and for a longer time near Fort Leavenworth. His health failing, he struck out along the Oregon Trail, 1844, wintered at Fort Hall and reached the Willamette Valley in the spring. Early in July 1845, Marshall reached Sutter's Fort, site of the present city of Sacramento, after traveling across the Klamath Mountains under guidance of James Clyman. Entering partnership with John A. Sutter for construction and operation of a sawmill near Sutter's Fort on the south fork of the American River, Marshall began operations only to discover early in 1848 that the tail-race would have to be deepened. During excavation for this purpose, gold was discovered on Jan. 24, 1848. The discovery was kept secret for a short time, but the news soon got out and by the end of the year settlers were pouring in from all the neighboring regions. The discovery of gold by Marshall was an epoch-making event but it brought only misfortune to the discoverer.

MARSHALL, JOHN (*b. near Germantown, Va., 1755; d. Philadelphia, Pa., 1835*), lawyer, chief justice of the United States, principal founder of judicial review and of the American system of constitutional law. Son of Thomas Marshall; brother of James M. and Louis Marshall (1773–1866); related on his mother's side to William Randolph. Raised on the sparsely-settled Virginia frontier, Marshall attributed much of his own success in life to the example and teaching of his father who was a man of superior ability and force of character. Tutored by his father and a local clergyman, Marshall learned early to enjoy the Latin classics and the English literature popular in that time, notably the moral essays of Alexander Pope. His father was one of the subscribers to the first (1772) American edition of Blackstone's *Commentaries*, and it is likely that John Marshall began his self-education in the law about that time. The eldest of 15 children, he grew up in an environment of thrift and mutual helpfulness; the careless dress, love of debate and easy "slouching" manners characteristic of his later life were natural consequences of his upbringing in a frontier society. Helping to raise his brothers and sisters developed in him a skill in putting his own ideas into the minds of others unconscious of his purpose, a skill later the distinctive feature of his leadership of the Supreme Court. His youthful view on politics was that of his father, which was in turn the view of Patrick Henry.

A member of the Culpeper minutemen, John Marshall was mustered into the 3rd Virginia Continental Regiment, July 30, 1776, and rose to captain in service (among other engagements) at the Brandywine, Germantown and Monmouth; he was also at Valley Forge and participated in the taking of Stony Point. While awaiting a new command in 1780, he studied law briefly at the College of William and Mary under George Wythe; this was his only institutional instruction of any sort.

Mustered out of the service, 1781, he was elected to the state assembly, 1782, married Mary Ambler, January 1783, and soon afterward began practice in Richmond, Va. He was soon recognized as a leading attorney. Since British legal precedents were in disfavor following the Revolution, while there were as yet few if any American precedents, what was chiefly demanded of counsel was not learning but a capacity for absorbing material suited to the immediate occasion and then of spinning it out in a web of argumentation. Marshall developed much skill in making his daily practice in court educate him in the law, and he was able to inform himself from the knowledge displayed by his adversaries. Impressed with the need for a strong central government by his army experiences, and now as an assemblyman disgusted with the way state legislatures ignored treaty obligations and encouraged interstate commercial wars, Marshall became an eager advocate of constitutional reform. Through his efforts in the Virginia Assembly, 1787, the U.S. Constitution was submitted to the state ratifying convention without hampering instructions with respect to amendments. In the ratifying convention itself he argued for adoption, significantly stressing the concept of judicial review as a preventive of abuse of power by Congress. Strong in support of Washington's administration and of the financial measures of Alexander Hamilton, Marshall became the recognized Federalist leader in Virginia; in 1797, he served as one of the XYZ commissioners to France. Elected to Congress, 1799, he refused nomination as secretary of war but accepted appointment as secretary of state under John Adams, May 12, 1800.

Nominated to the post of chief justice of the United States, Jan. 20, 1801, Marshall took his seat on February 4 after a reluctant confirmation by the Senate. He continued as secretary of state until the end of the Adams administration though he did not draw the salary of that office; he served as chief justice until his death. A contemporary described him at this time as "tall, meager, emaciated, inelegant in dress, attitudes, gesture, of swarthy complexion, his countenance pervaded with great good humour and hilarity." He enjoyed, according to the same biographer, the faculty of developing a subject by a single glance of his mind. Another contemporary comments upon his "simplicity of manners and convivial habits," also, on his indolence. He may well have appeared indolent to the casual view, but the fresh energy of mind with which he met the larger occasions of his career is one of his most striking characteristics. Contrary to the previous procedure of the Supreme Court whereby the justices frequently delivered their opinions one after the other, the new chief justice spoke "for the Court," beginning with the August term, 1801. One of the last acts of the Adams administration had been to enlarge the lower federal judicial establishment; one of the early acts of the Jefferson administration was to abolish these new courts (April 1802). At the same time in order to prevent any judicial test of the constitutionality of the Repeal Act, Congress postponed the next term of the Supreme Court to February 1803. Marshall, seeing in the action of Congress a dangerous challenge to the prestige of the Supreme Court and to the principle that it was the final authoritative interpreter of the Constitution, took the first opportunity to vindicate the Court's authority. This opportunity was the celebrated case of *Marbury vs. Madison* which came before the Court in February 1803, and in which Federalist appointees to abolished judicial posts requested an order compelling the secretary of state to deliver their commissions of office. Marshall's opinion in this case was a very cleverly contrived document. While conceding that Marbury was entitled to the remedy he sought, Marshall, speaking for the Court, held that the Court could not award the remedy, since to do so would be to assume original jurisdiction in a case not within the categories enumerated by the Constitution. He avoided a direct clash with President Jefferson over the matter while at the same time he read him a lecture on his legal duty. By holding the constitutional enumeration of cases in which the Supreme Court has original jurisdiction to be exclusive, he put a spoke in Republican plans to abolish the lower federal judiciary and parcel out its jurisdiction between the Supreme Court and the state courts. Most important of all, by holding Section 13 of the Judiciary Act of September 1789 to be unconstitutional, he brought to the support of the Union the important proposition that the Constitution has one final interpreter, at the same time seizing for the Supreme Court its greatest prerogative—the right of judicial review. After acting with a little less than courage during the impeachment trial of Judge Samuel Chase, 1804, Marshall seized the opportunity of the trial of Aaron Burr, 1807, for a renewed attack against the administration of President Jefferson. Marshall's conduct of the proceedings from start to finish was one prolonged baiting of the president whose unholy zeal to hang Burr fairly exposed him to such treatment. In the process of saving Burr's neck, however, Marshall permitted the whole common-law view of treason as a conspiracy to be junked with the monstrous result that it becomes impossible to convict the procurer of a treason who is canny enough to leave the overt acts to his agents and dupes. Meantime Marshall had been busying himself in his leisure time with writing *The Life of George Washington* (1804–07), a hastily written and badly proportioned work which was celebrated in its own time but which recent scholarship has shown to be meretricious.

Since the sittings of the Supreme Court until 1827 were fairly brief, none of the justices resided in Washington; they took lodgings during term time, sometimes all in the same boarding house and living in the closest intimacy. These circumstances allowed Marshall to bring to bear upon his associates all his charm of personality and superiority in debate, thus further establishing his dominant position. In his great decisions subsequent to *Marbury vs. Madison*, he set forth a body of constitutional doctrine which possesses internal consistency to a notable extent and which may be summarized generally as follows. The Constitution was the act of the people of the United States, although in bringing about its establishment they naturally made such use of existing governmental machinery as convenience dictated. It springs therefore from the ultimate source of authority in the country and possesses such characteristics as this authority chose to stamp upon it. By its own terms it is law and supreme law, wherefore its provisions control all governments and governmental agencies within the territory of the United States. Furthermore, being law, it is directly enforcible by courts in the decision of cases. Indeed, its clear intention is to designate the Supreme Court as the one final authoritative expositor of its terms; and while the Court has no will of its own apart from that of the law, it is none the less under obligation always to remember that "it is a constitution" which it is expounding, and that this Constitution was "intended to endure for ages to come" and hence to be "adapted to the various *crises* of human affairs." Especially should a narrow rendition of its terms be avoided when questions of the advancement of national unity and power or of the security of private, especially property rights, are involved. These were the interests which had suffered most acutely at the hands of the states during the period of the Confederation and concern for which had brought about the convention that framed the Constitution. By the same token state power must be sternly repressed whenever it entrenches upon the field of powers delegated by the Constitution to "the government of all" or when it menaces the principles on which public and private faith depends. The designated organ to effect these ends is the Supreme Court.

The immediate target, indeed, of all Marshall's great opinions following 1809 was furnished by the pretensions of state legislatures, the seat then as in 1787 of localizing and democratic tendencies. His system of constitutional doctrine has continued the vehicle to the present time both of his ingrained conservatism and of his love of the Union.

Marshall's further basic constitutional opinions are to be read in the following cases: *Fletcher vs. Peck* (6 *Cranch*, 87), *McCulloch vs. Maryland* (4 *Wheaton*, 316), *Sturges vs. Crowninshield* (17 *U.S.*, 122), and *Dartmouth College vs. Woodward* (17 *U.S.*, 518), all three delivered at the single term of 1819; *Cohens vs. Virginia* (6 *Wheaton*, 264), given in the 1821 term; *Gibbons vs. Ogden* (9 *Wheaton*, 1) and *Osborn vs. U.S. Bank* (22 *U.S.*, 738), rendered in 1825; *Brown vs. Maryland* (25 *U.S.*, 419) and *Ogden vs. Saunders* (25 *U.S.*, 213, Marshall's sole dissenting opinion in the constitutional field), rendered in 1827.

A constantly increasing group of Americans, however, began to find Marshall's reading of the Constitution less and less acceptable. The slogan of the day was "state rights" or "state sovereignty," and one of the most notable spokesmen against Marshall's views was John Taylor of Caroline who spoke for the dissidents in Virginia. There was hardly a congressional session *post* 1821 in which some proposal for weakening the Court, or at least Marshall's influence over it, was not made. He made a few concessions to the spirit of the hour, but returned to his strong position in *Craig vs. Missouri* (4 *Peters*, 410) and *Worcester vs. Georgia* (6 *Peters*, 515). With respect to the latter of these opinions, the word ran round that President Jackson had declared "John Marshall has made his decision, now let him enforce it"; Marshall saw the Union crumbling in such developments as these and in the contemporary Nullification movement in South Carolina. His life's work was seemingly being destroyed. However, when in 1833 Joseph Story published his *Commentaries on the Constitution of the United States,* Marshall saw his version of the Constitution systematized therein and given its historical setting.

While official propriety forbade that Marshall should express himself publicly on political issues, it is known from his correspondence that he would have welcomed the Federalist nomination for the presidency in 1812 and that in 1832 he was hoping against hope for the election of Henry Clay so that Andrew Jackson would not have the appointment of his own successor. When Jackson was elected, he determined to stick it out to the end and did so. He took a leading role in the Virginia constitutional convention, 1829, and it was due to his and Madison's efforts that manhood suffrage was defeated and that the oligarchic system of county justices was fastened upon the state more tightly than ever.

MARSHALL, LOUIS (*b. Fauquier Co., Va., 1773; d. Woodford Co., Ky., 1866*), physician, educator. Son of Thomas Marshall; brother of James M. and John Marshall. As president, Washington College (now Washington and Lee University), 1830–34, his effort to develop individualism among the students by a total absence of discipline failed to succeed. Later he taught at Transylvania University and at other schools in Kentucky. A man of great intellectual attainment, he was eccentric in manners and speech.

MARSHALL, LOUIS (*b. Syracuse, N.Y., 1856; d. Zurich, Switzerland, 1929*), lawyer, publicist, Jewish leader. Completed the course at Columbia Law School in a single year (1876–77); was admitted to the bar, 1878. Practiced in New York City *post* 1894 as a member of the firm of Guggenheimer, Untermyer & Marshall. In his practice before the U.S. Supreme Court no contemporary succeeded so frequently as Marshall in striking down measures which violated the federal or state constitutions; he was particularly interested in cases involving discrimination against minorities, corporate abuses and the rights of immigrants. Active in the American Jewish Committee, he served as its president from 1912 until his death; he was also one of the reorganizers of the Jewish Theological Seminary and served as chairman of its board of directors. At the Paris Peace Conference, 1919, he cooperated with the committee on new states in drafting anti-discrimination clauses for insertion into the treaties with Poland, Rumania and other East European states. He was also a leader in the Zionist movement.

MARSHALL, THOMAS (*b. Westmoreland Co., Va., 1730; d. 1802*), surveyor, Virginia and Kentucky pioneer and legislator, Revolutionary soldier. Father of James M., John and Louis Marshall (1773–1866). Removed to the Virginia frontier *c.* 1754; to the Kentucky frontier, 1783. A friend of George Washington and a man of marked intellectual stature, Marshall had a strong formative influence on the mind of his son John, the later chief justice.

MARSHALL, THOMAS ALEXANDER (*b. Kentucky, 1794; d. Louisville, Ky., 1871*), jurist, Kentucky legislator. Son of Humphrey Marshall (1760–1841). Congressman, Whig, from Kentucky, 1831–35; held orthodox Whig opinions. As justice, Kentucky court of appeals, 1835–56, he was twice named chief justice of that court. A Unionist during the Civil War, he served briefly as chief justice of the state court of appeals, 1866–67.

MARSHALL, THOMAS RILEY (*b. North Manchester, Ind., 1854; d. Washington, D.C., 1925*), lawyer, statesman, wit. Graduated Wabash College, 1873. Admitted to the bar, 1875, he practiced for

many years at Columbia City, Ind. A loyal Democrat ("Democrats, like poets, are born not made," he once said), he supported his party for many years without any desire to hold office. Elected governor of Indiana, 1908, he opposed "dry" legislation, pushed an extensive program of labor and social enactments through the legislature, and tried to secure adoption of a much-needed new state constitution. Nominated for the vice-presidency on the Woodrow Wilson ticket, 1912, Marshall was elected and was re-elected, 1916, the first vice-president in nearly a century to succeed himself. Presiding over the Senate with grace and tact, he exerted personal influence most effectively on behalf of many administration measures; he was perhaps the most popular vice-president that the United States has ever had. Generous, kindly and tolerant, he possessed a never-failing sense of humor. Among his most quoted remarks were: "What this country needs is a really good 5 cent cigar"; also "It's got so it's as easy to amend the Constitution of the United States as it used to be to draw a cork."

MARSHALL, WILLIAM EDGAR (*b. New York, N.Y., 1837; d. New York, 1906*), portrait painter, engraver. Best known for his portrait of Abraham Lincoln, painted from photographs and descriptions, which had enormous circulation as an engraving. Marshall helped many struggling painters, notably Albert P. Ryder.

MARSHALL, WILLIAM LOUIS (*b. Washington, Ky., 1846; d. Washington, D.C., 1920*), soldier, engineer. Served in 10th Kentucky Cavalry, 1862–63; graduated West Point, 1868. As assistant to G. M. Wheeler in exploration of the Rocky Mountains, 1872–76, he discovered Marshall Pass and also the gold placers in the Marshall Basin, San Miguel River, Colo. After working on river improvement projects in the South, 1876–84, he was placed in charge of river and harbor improvements in Wisconsin and Illinois. In his construction of the Hennepin Canal, 1890–99, he pioneered in the use of concrete masonry; at New York City, 1899–1908, he completed the Ambrose Channel, the extension of Governor's Island, and also improved the coast defenses. Commissioned chief of engineers, July 1908, with the rank of brigadier-general, he retired from active service, 1910.

MARSHALL, WILLIAM RAINEY (*b. Boone Co., Mo., 1825; d. Pasadena, Calif., 1896*), Union soldier, Minnesota pioneer. Republican governor of Minnesota, 1866–70.

MARTIN, ALEXANDER (*b. Hunterdon Co., N.J., 1740; d. Rockingham Co., N.C., 1807*), lawyer, planter, Revolutionary soldier, North Carolina legislator. Removed to North Carolina *c.* 1757 where he held judicial offices under the Crown. Resigning his commission as a Continental colonel, 1777, he was active during the rest of the Revolution as a North Carolina legislator and as acting governor, 1781–82. A moderate Federalist *ante* 1790, he was elected governor in 1782 and re-elected, 1783 and 1784; again elected governor, 1789, he served through 1792. A master of the art of conciliation, he drifted with the current of opinion in the General Assembly. He served as U.S. senator, (Democrat) Republican, 1793–99.

MARTIN, ARTEMAS (*b. Steuben Co., N.Y., 1835; d. Washington, D.C., 1918*), mathematician. Publisher and editor of the *Mathematical Visitor, 1877–94,* and of the *Mathematical Magazine, 1882–1913;* associated *post* 1885 with U.S. Coast and Geodetic Survey; authority on early mathematical textbooks.

MARTIN, EDWARD SANDFORD (*b. near Auburn, N.Y., 1856; d. New York, N.Y., 1939*), poet, essayist. A regular contributor to *Life, Scribner's Magazine, Harper's Weekly.* Author of *A Little Brother of the Rich* (1890) and other books. [*Supp. 2*]

MARTIN, ELIZABETH PRICE (*b. Philadelphia, Pa., 1864; d. 1932*), civic leader, philanthropist. Granddaughter of Eli K. Price (1797–1884). Active in Pennsylvania welfare movements and in Republican politics; founded Garden Club of America. [*Supp. 1*]

MARTIN, FRANÇOIS-XAVIER (*b. Marseilles, France, 1762; d. New Orleans, La., 1846*), jurist. Came to America *c.* 1780; settled in New Bern, N.C., where he built up a printing and publishing business. Admitted to the bar, 1789, he wrote or edited a variety of law texts, was successful in practice and was employed by the state to make his well-known "Revisal" of the *Laws of the State of North Carolina.* Appointed a federal judge for Mississippi Territory, 1809, he was transferred to the Territory of Orleans, 1810. He was the first attorney-general of Louisiana (1813) and in 1815 became a judge of the state supreme court. Named chief justice, 1836, he retired, 1846. Martin played a great part in creating a jurisprudence for Louisiana out of the tangle of French, Spanish and Anglo-American codes which applied there. He began to publish reports of cases decided by the courts, 1811, and continued them until 1830; he also published poorly written and badly arranged historical studies of Louisiana and North Carolina.

MARTIN, FRANKLIN HENRY (*b. Ixonia, Wis., 1857; d. Phoenix, Ariz., 1935*), surgeon. Graduated Chicago Medical College, 1880. An American pioneer in aseptic surgery and in a number of gynecological operations, Martin founded *Surgery, Gynecology and Obstetrics,* 1905, and served as its editor-in-chief until his death. He was largely instrumental in forming the American College of Surgeons, 1913. [*Supp. 1*]

MARTIN, FREDERICK TOWNSEND (*b. Albany, N.Y., 1849; d. London, England, 1914*), lawyer, philanthropist. Author, among other works, of *The Passing of the Idle Rich* (1911).

MARTIN, HENRY AUSTIN (*b. London, England, 1824; d. Boston, Mass., 1884*), physician, surgeon. Came to America as a boy. Graduated Harvard Medical School, 1845, and practiced thereafter in Roxbury, Mass. His principal service to American medicine arose from his study of vaccination and conditions essential for standardizing its procedure.

MARTIN, HENRY NEWELL (*b. Newry, Ireland, 1848; d. Yorkshire, England, 1896*), physiologist. Educated at University of London and at Cambridge University; served as assistant to T. H. Huxley, 1874. As professor of biology, Johns Hopkins, 1876–93, he laid down broad foundations for instruction and research in the biological sciences there. He held that physiology should be studied without regard to its applications to medicine, as a pure science absolutely independent of so-called practical affiliation. His own researches were mainly in the field of cardiac physiology.

MARTIN, HOMER DODGE (*b. Albany, N.Y., 1836; d. St. Paul, Minn., 1897*), landscape painter. Largely self-schooled, Martin was a practicing landscapist at the age of 16. Following Thomas Cole's predilection for wild scenery and large spaces, for some twenty years he tramped on sketching tours through the Adirondacks, the Catskills and the Berkshires. Removing to New York City, 1865, he began to change his style of painting, simplifying his compositions by eliminating needless detail and experimenting with recondite colors. His work in the new style, although a vast improvement over the old, was considered eccentric by contemporaries and his patronage fell off. Further refinement in handling and tonality followed a trip to England, 1876, during which he met Whistler and was somewhat influenced by him. Never properly supported by his serious work, Martin eked out his living by magazine illustration. A residence in France, 1882–86, brought about a further change in Martin's style; his scale grew more intimate and less panoramic, his method grew richer and somewhat impressionistic. Misfortune continued to dog him after his return to America, but despite failing eyesight and the onset of a fatal sickness he filled the few years left of his life with the creation of masterpieces. Within a few years of his death, deep in debt, his erstwhile unsalable paintings had become the sensation of the art market. A poet in his painting, drawing from the contemplation of nature a soothing and noble melancholy, Martin is the most distinguished American artist in the imaginative tradition of landscape painting, although he lacked the vigorous construction of George Inness at his best and of Winslow Homer.

MARTIN, JAMES GREEN (*b. Elizabeth City, N.C., 1819; d. Asheville, N.C., 1878*), soldier, lawyer. Graduated West Point, 1840. Served with distinction in the Mexican War and on the Western frontier. Resigning his commission in June 1861, he performed brilliant service in the preparation, training and arming of North Carolina militia. Appointed Confederate brigadier-general, May 1862, he held commands principally in North Carolina until the end of the war.

MARTIN, JOHN ALEXANDER (*b. Brownsville, Pa., 1839; d. 1889*), journalist, Union soldier. Removed to Kansas, 1857; *post* 1858 edited the Atchison *Champion*. Long prominent in the Republican party, Martin served as governor of Kansas, 1885–89. He made prohibition the settled policy of the Republican party in the state, advocated legal reforms, opposed excessive state financing of railroads and monopolies.

MARTIN, JOHN HILL (*b. Philadelphia, Pa., 1823; d. 1906*), lawyer, Pennsylvania local historian.

MARTIN, JOSIAH (*b. 1737; d. London, England, 1786*), British army officer. Commissioned royal governor of North Carolina, 1771, he was soon in conflict with the Assembly over a number of issues on which his commission would not permit him to yield. Fleeing from New Bern, he took refuge aboard a British ship in Cape Fear River, July 1775. After the failure of several of his plans for recapturing the colony, he served as a volunteer under Clinton and Cornwallis in the Carolina campaigns, 1779–81.

MARTIN, LUTHER (*b. near New Brunswick, N.J., c. 1748; d. New York, N.Y., 1826*), lawyer, Revolutionary patriot. Graduated College of New Jersey (Princeton), 1766. Taught school in Maryland and Virginia; admitted to the bar in Virginia, 1771, he practiced in Maryland until the outbreak of the Revolution. As attorney-general of Maryland, 1778–1805, he resided in Baltimore. A delegate to the Federal Convention at Philadelphia, he opposed the plan for a strong central government and later made a futile effort to prevent Maryland's ratification of the Constitution. Because of his bitter enmity against Thomas Jefferson, Martin allied himself with the Federalist party and aided Justice Samuel Chase in his impeachment trial, 1804; in 1807, he was one of the lawyers who defended Aaron Burr at his treason trial. Serving again as Maryland attorney-general, 1818–22, Martin, in his last important case (*McCulloch vs. State of Maryland*), opposed Daniel Webster, William Pinkney and William Wirt. Ruined by drink and extravagance, Martin died in the house of Aaron Burr. Eminent as a lawyer, an opponent of slavery, and a generous loyal friend, Martin was his own worst enemy—"the rollicking, witty, audacious attorney-general of Maryland . . . drunken, generous, slovenly, grand; bulldog of Federalism . . . the notorious reprobate genius."

MARTIN, THOMAS COMMERFORD (*b. London, England, 1856; d. Pittsfield, Mass., 1924*), scientific writer. Came to America *c.* 1877; served as assistant in laboratory of Thomas A. Edison, 1877–79. Edited the *Electrical Engineer* and the *Electrical World*, 1883–1909; was author of a number of books and articles on electricity and inventions.

MARTIN, THOMAS STAPLES (*b. Scottsville, Va., 1847; d. 1919*), lawyer, politician. U.S. senator, Democrat, from Virginia, 1895–1919. A conservative of great personal integrity, Martin led the Democratic "machine" in Virginia. Majority floor leader, 1917–19, he also served as chairman of the Committee on Appropriations during World War I.

MARTIN, VICTORIA CLAFLIN WOODHULL. [See WOODHULL, VICTORIA CLAFLIN, 1838–1927.]

MARTIN, WILLIAM ALEXANDER PARSONS (*b. Livonia, Ind., 1827; d. Peking, China, 1916*), Presbyterian clergyman. Missionary and educator in China *post* 1850.

MARTIN, WILLIAM THOMPSON (*b. Glasgow, Ky., 1823; d. Natchez, Miss., 1910*), lawyer, Confederate major-general of cavalry, Mississippi legislator and railroad builder.

MARTINDALE, JOHN HENRY (*b. Hudson Falls, N.Y., 1815; d. Nice, France, 1881*), lawyer, Union soldier. Graduated West Point, 1835. Practiced law *post* 1838 in Batavia and Rochester, N.Y. During the Civil War, Martindale took an active part in training volunteer regiments, served with credit as governor of the District of Columbia and in the field, and rose to corps command before his resignation for ill health in the fall of 1864.

MARTINY, PHILIP (*b. Strasbourg, Alsace, France, 1858; d. New York, N.Y., 1927*), sculptor. Coming to America as a young man, Martiny worked as a carver under Augustus Saint-Gaudens and won reputation as the foremost decorative sculptor of the day for his work for the Agricultural Building at the Chicago World's Fair, 1893. Thereafter he received numerous commissions from McKim, Mead and White and other architects. Among his noted works are the high-relief marble carvings of the balustrade, entrance hall, Library of Congress; the Soldiers' and Sailors' Monument, Jersey City, N.J.; the south pair of bronze doors, St. Bartholomew's Church, New York City; the World War I Memorials in Abingdon Square and Chelsea Park, New York City; the cornice and entrance figures of the New York City Hall of Records.

MARTY, MARTIN (*b. Schwyz, Switzerland, 1834; d. St. Cloud, Minn., 1896*), Roman Catholic clergyman, Benedictine. Came to the monastery at St. Meinrad, Ind., 1860; was chosen its first mitred abbot, 1870. Led a group of Benedictines to work among the Sioux at Standing Rock agency, 1873. Vicar apostolic of the territory of Dakota, 1880–90; first bishop of Sioux Falls, 1890–95. Bishop of St. Cloud, Minn. *post* 1895.

MARTYN, SARAH TOWNE SMITH (*b. Hopkinton, N.H., 1805; d. New York, N.Y., 1879*), author. Editor of religious and reform publications.

MARVEL, IK. [See MITCHELL, DONALD GRANT, 1822–1908.]

MARVIN, DUDLEY (*b. Lyme, Conn., 1786; d. Ripley, N.Y., 1852*), lawyer. Congressman, National Republican (Adams Democrat), from New York, 1823–29. Coming under the influence of Henry Clay, he became a Whig and advocated a protective tariff and the limitation of slavery. Again in Congress as a Whig, 1847–49, he defended the right of the federal government to exclude slavery from the territories acquired from Mexico.

MARVIN, ENOCH MATHER (*b. present Warren Co., Mo., 1823; d. 1877*), Methodist clergyman. Pastor of several congregations in Missouri, 1855–62; served as Confederate Army chaplain. Stationed at Marshall, Texas, after the Civil War, he was elected bishop, Methodist Episcopal Church South, 1866.

MARWEDEL, EMMA JACOBINA CHRISTIANA (*b. near Göttingen, Germany, 1818; d. San Francisco, Calif., 1893*), leader in the kindergarten movement. Came to America c. 1869. Established kindergartens and kindergarten normal classes in Washington, D.C., and at various places in California. The recognition which California gained as a leader in the kindergarten movement was largely the result of her work.

MARZO, EDUARDO (*b. Naples, Italy, 1852; d. New York, N.Y., 1929*), composer, organist, teacher of music. Settled in the United States, 1869. After touring the country for a number of years as director of opera and concert companies and as accompanist of leading solo artists, Marzo devoted himself *post* 1882 to composition, voice teaching and his work as a church organist in New York.

MASCHKE, HEINRICH (*b. Breslau, Germany, 1853; d. Chicago, Ill., 1908*), mathematician. Studied at Heidelberg, Berlin and at Göttingen. Came to America, 1891, as an electrical technician; taught mathematics at University of Chicago *post* 1892. His original work in pure mathematics dealt with the theory of finite groups of linear substitutions and the theory of quadratic differential quantics.

MASON, ARTHUR JOHN (*b. Melbourne, Australia, 1857; d. 1933*), engineer, inventor, agriculturalist. Came to America, 1881. Invented and designed excavating and ore-handling machinery; *post* 1910, experimented extensively on mechanized systems for agriculture which would guard against soil erosion.
[*Supp.* 1]

MASON, CHARLES (*b. Pompey, N.Y., 1804; d. 1882*), jurist. Graduated West Point, 1829; was admitted to New York bar, 1832. Removed to present Burlington, Iowa, 1837. On the organization of the territory of Iowa in 1838 he was appointed chief justice of the supreme court and served until early in 1847. A member of the commission which drafted

the 1851 Iowa Code, he served for a time as a county judge. After acting as federal commissioner of patents, 1853–57, he engaged in the practice of patent law.

MASON, CLAIBOURNE RICE (*b. Chesterfield Co., Va., 1800; d. Swope's Station, Va., 1885*), contractor, Confederate soldier, bridge and railroad construction engineer. Showed great resourcefulness as a military bridge constructor while serving with Gen. T. J. Jackson's commands.

MASON, FRANCIS (*b. York, England, 1799; d. Burma, 1874*), Baptist clergyman. Came to America, 1818. Prepared for the ministry at Newton Theological Institution; was missionary to Burma *post* 1831.

MASON, FRANK STUART (*b. Weymouth, Mass., 1883; d. Boston, Mass., 1929*), musician. Taught at New England Conservatory of Music and elsewhere in Massachusetts with notable success.

MASON, GEORGE (*b. England, c. 1629; d. Virginia, c. 1686*), Virginia legislator and official. The first mention of Mason in the colonial records is in a patent for land in Westmoreland Co., March 1655. He later secured other large tracts of adjacent lands and was active in the defense of the government of the colony. He is chiefly remembered as an Indian fighter and as the precipitator of events culminating in Bacon's Rebellion.

MASON, GEORGE (*b. Fairfax Co., Va., 1725; d. Fairfax Co., 1792*), planter, statesman, political philosopher. Fourth in descent from George Mason (*c. 1629–c. 1686*). Privately tutored, 1736–39, Mason educated himself in the main by avid reading in his uncle's library; although never licensed as an attorney, he was a notably competent counsel on questions of public law throughout his life. Settling at "Gunston Hall," a new house which was completed to his taste in 1758, Mason personally managed his large and practically self-sufficient plantation; he also held county, town and parish offices. Becoming a member of the Ohio Company, 1752, he served as its treasurer until 1773; in the latter year when the Crown abrogated the Ohio Company's rights and regranted the area they covered to a Pennsylvania group, Mason produced his first major state paper in protest. He shunned office in the colonial government prior to the Revolution allegedly because of chronic ill health, but most probably because of the low rating he put upon human nature acting in committee. Off-stage, however, he played a highly important part in the revolutionary movement *post* 1765. He drafted the non-importation Association which Virginia adopted at the time of the dispute over the Townshend duties; he wrote the Fairfax Resolves of July 1774, which were accepted ultimately by the Continental Congress as a definition of the constitutional position of the colonies as against the

Crown; he exerted a constant word-of-mouth influence over all with whom he came in contact, and these included George Washington, Thomas Jefferson and others of the Virginia dynasty.

Serving on the Committee of Safety, which took over the executive powers vacated by Governor Dunmore, 1775, Mason achieved his outstanding contribution as a constitutionalist by framing the Declaration of Rights, 1776, and the major part of the constitution of Virginia. The Declaration of Rights was drawn upon by Jefferson in the first part of the Declaration of Independence, became the basis for the first ten amendments to the U.S. Constitution and had a considerable influence in France at the time of the French Revolution. Between 1776 and 1780, Mason was in the forefront of legislative activity, a close collaborator of Jefferson, Patrick Henry and George Wythe. He was responsible in large degree for the securing of the Northwest Territory through the efforts of George Rogers Clark, and it was he who sketched the plan out of which grew the cession by Virginia to the United States of her western lands and also Jefferson's ordinance for their government.

Disgusted at the conduct of public affairs *post* 1781, Mason went into retirement. His return to the Assembly, 1786, was motivated by his wish to prevent Virginia from indulging in further orgies of inflation and his growing conviction, despite his lifelong attachment to state-rights, that the Articles of Confederation were an inadequate basis for the central government. A member of the Federal Convention, he was one of the five most frequent speakers in the debates at Philadelphia and exerted on the Constitution a marked constructive influence. Until the final days of the Convention, he fought for the inclusion of certain clauses and the exclusion of others which he regarded as respectively essential and evil. Deciding not to sign the final document, he campaigned against ratification of the Constitution in the Virginia Convention, 1788. Mason's insistence on the necessity of a Bill of Rights bore fruit in the first ten amendments. The eleventh amendment, 1798, testified to the correctness of his criticism of one part of the judiciary article. His principal reason for refusing to sign the Constitution, however, was that it incorporated a compromise between the New England states and those of the extreme South on the tariff and the slave trade; his opposition to slavery was perhaps the most consistent feature of his public career and the Civil War served later as a sad justification of his views. More than perhaps any other American statesman of the period, Mason represented the rationalistic spirit, the Enlightenment in its American manifestation.

MASON, HENRY (*b. Brookline, Mass., 1831; d. Boston, Mass., 1890*), piano manufacturer. Son of Lowell Mason; brother of William Mason (1829–1908).

Founded the Mason & Hamlin Co. with Emmons Hamlin, 1854.

MASON, JAMES MURRAY (*b. Georgetown, D.C., 1798; d. near Alexandria, Va., 1871*), lawyer, Virginia legislator. Grandson of George Mason (1725–1792). Congressman, Democrat, from Virginia, 1837–39; U.S. senator, 1847–61. Long associated with the Southern-rights wing of the Democratic party, Mason was influenced particularly by John C. Calhoun. He drafted the Fugitive Slave Law of 1850 and considered the dispute between the North and the South to be a basically uncompromisable conflict between two social and economic systems, one of which was agrarian and the other industrial. His high social position, his ten years as chairman of the Senate Foreign Relations Committee and his friendship with Jefferson Davis resulted in his appointment as Confederate diplomatic commissioner to England, 1861. En route to his post on board the *Trent*, he and his colleague John Slidell, who was bound to France on a similar mission, were seized by a U.S. ship-of-war. This action very nearly caused a war between Great Britain and the United States. On his release from confinement at Boston, Jan. 1, 1862, Mason proceeded to England where he cultivated the leading members of the House of Lords and the Commons, the great merchants and manufacturers and the newspapermen; he also acted as central agent for the various naval and military purchasing agents of the Confederacy. He was, however, never received officially by the British government. After the Civil War, Mason lived for a time in Canada, returning to Virginia, 1868.

MASON, JEREMIAH (*b. Lebanon, Conn., 1768; d. Boston, Mass., 1848*), lawyer, New Hampshire legislator. Graduated Yale, 1788; studied law with Simeon Baldwin and with Stephen R. Bradley. Practiced in Portsmouth, N.H., *post* 1797. U.S. senator, Federalist, from New Hampshire, 1813–17. Removed to Boston, Mass., 1832. Associated with Daniel Webster in the so-called Dartmouth College Case, Mason was considered by Webster and by Rufus Choate and Joseph Story as one of the greatest lawyers of his time.

MASON, JOHN (*b. England, c. 1600; d. Norwich, Conn., 1672*), colonial soldier and magistrate. Came to Massachusetts *ante* 1633; was a leader in the migration thence to found Windsor on the Connecticut River, 1635. He is remembered principally for his part in the victory over the Pequot Indians near the Mystic River, 1637. His history of the war was printed in *A Relation of the Troubles that Have Hapned in New England* (1677) by Increase Mather; it was reprinted by Thomas Prince under the title *A Brief History of the Pequot War* (1736).

MASON, JOHN (*b. Orange, N.J., 1858; d. Stamford, Conn., 1919*), actor. Grandson of Lowell Mason. Gifted with much self-possession and a wonderful sense of timing, Mason played with great success *post*

1879, notably with the Boston Museum company and with the Lyceum Theatre company, New York.

MASON, JOHN MITCHELL (*b. New York, N.Y., 1770; d. New York, 1829*), clergyman, educator. Held Associate Reform and Presbyterian pastorates; established forerunner of Union Theological Seminary, N.Y., 1804. Provost, Columbia College, 1811–16; president, Dickinson College, 1821–24.

MASON, JOHN YOUNG (*b. Greensville Co., Va., 1799; d. 1859*), lawyer, Virginia legislator, diplomat. Congressman, Democrat, from Virginia, 1831–37; secretary of the navy, 1844 and 1846–49; U.S. attorney-general, 1845–46. As congressman, supported Jacksonian measures with exception of the Force Bill; introduced bill recognizing independence of Texas. While undistinguished U.S. minister to France, 1853–59, he joined with James Buchanan and Pierre Soulé in signing the Ostend Manifesto, October 1854.

MASON, JONATHAN (*b. Boston, Mass., 1756; d. Boston, 1831*), lawyer, Massachusetts legislator. Graduated College of New Jersey (Princeton), 1774; read law with John Adams and Josiah Quincy. U.S. senator, Federalist, from Massachusetts, 1800–03; congressman, 1817–20. Was member of syndicate which developed Beacon Hill section of Boston *post* 1795; was also active in development of Dorchester.

MASON, LOWELL (*b. Medfield, Mass., 1792; d. Orange, N.J., 1872*), musical educator, hymnwriter. Resident in Savannah, Ga., 1812–27; thereafter until 1851, identified with musical life of Boston, Mass., where he was president of Handel and Haydn Society, founder of Boston Academy of Music (1833), and promoter of musical education for public school children and for the general public. He was author of *Boston Handel and Haydn Society's Collection of Church Music* (1822); *Manual of Instruction* (1834, for teaching music by Pestalozzian methods); more than fifty books of tunes, sacred and secular. Not a great composer, Mason is remembered for "From Greenland's Icy Mountains" and "Nearer, My God, to Thee"; his chief importance, however, was in his service to musical education as teacher and method-planner and as an originator of the musical "convention" for training of teachers.

MASON, LUTHER WHITING (*b. Turner, Maine, 1828; d. Buckfield, Maine, 1896*), music teacher. Supervised public school musical instruction in Louisville, Ky., Cincinnati, O., Boston, Mass.; edited "National System" of music-charts and books; organized teaching of music in Japanese public schools, 1879–82.

MASON, OTIS TUFTON (*b. Eastport, Maine, 1838; d. Washington, D.C., 1908*), ethnologist, educator. Associated *post* 1872 with Smithsonian Institution; as its curator of ethnology *post* 1884, classified and regulated National Museum; was author of numerous papers on aboriginal technology.

MASON, RICHARD BARNES (*b. Fairfax Co., Va., 1797; d. Jefferson Barracks, Mo., 1850*), soldier. Great-grandson of George Mason (1725–1792). Commissioned in regular army, 1817; served in Black Hawk War; as colonel, 1st Dragoons, served under Gen. S. W. Kearny in conquest of New Mexico and California, 1846. Somewhat hidebound during his term as civil and military governor of California, 1847–49, Mason was author of the most authentic story of the discovery of California gold (in his report at Monterey, Aug. 17, 1848).

MASON, SAMUEL (*b. Virginia, c. 1750; d. 1803*), desperado, river pirate. Headed gang at Cave-in-Rock (Ohio River), 1797; thereafter pillaged travelers on Natchez Trace and on lower Mississippi until his murder by an accomplice.

MASON, STEVENS THOMSON (*b. Stafford Co., Va., 1760; d. Philadelphia, Pa., 1803*), lawyer, Virginia legislator. Son of Thomson Mason; nephew of George Mason (1725–1792). As U.S. senator, (Democrat) Republican, from Virginia, 1794–1803, Mason was a strong partisan and achieved notoriety for publishing an abstract of the terms of Jay's Treaty while it was still under consideration by the Senate.

MASON, STEVENS THOMSON (*b. Loudoun Co., Va., 1811; d. New York, N.Y., 1843*), lawyer, politician. Grandson of Stevens T. Mason (1760–1803). Raised in Kentucky. Succeeded father as secretary of Michigan Territory, 1831; pressed movement for statehood; by intransigence over boundary with Ohio, secured Upper Peninsula for Michigan. As first governor of Michigan, 1836–40, followed a liberal policy on civic rights and education, but was held accountable for failing to check speculation and for the hardships following the panic of 1837.

MASON, THOMSON (*b. Prince William Co., Va., 1733; d. 1785*), lawyer, Revolutionary patriot, Virginia legislator. Brother of George Mason (1725–1792).

MASON, WALT (*b. Columbus, Canada, 1862; d. La Jolla, Calif., 1939*), journalist, newspaper humorist. His widely syndicated "prose poems" first appeared in the *Emporia* (Kans.) *Gazette*, 1907. [Supp. 2]

MASON, WILLIAM (*b. Mystic, Conn., 1808; d. Taunton, Mass., 1883*), inventor, manufacturer. Designed and built specialized power looms; patented the self-acting mule for spinning cotton, 1840 and 1846. Began manufacture of high quality locomotives, 1852; also produced tubular-spoke car wheels.

MASON, WILLIAM (*b. Boston, Mass., 1829; d. New York, N.Y., 1908*), musician. Son of Lowell Mason. Studied in Boston and abroad; was pupil of Franz

Liszt. Founded (with Theodore Thomas) Mason-Thomas chamber music recital series, 1855–56. An outstanding teacher, he was author of *Touch and Technic* and other piano textbooks.

MASON, WILLIAM ERNEST (*b. Franklinville, N.Y., 1850; d. 1921*), lawyer. Raised in Iowa; practiced law in Chicago, Ill., *post* 1872. Congressman, Republican, from Illinois, 1887–91, 1917–21; U.S. senator, 1897–1903. Independent, anti-machine proponent of intervention in Cuba, 1898; later fought imperialism, and in 1917 opposed U.S. entry into World War I.

MASQUERIER, LEWIS (*b. Paris, Ky., 1802; d. probably New York, N.Y., date unknown*), pioneer in phonetic spelling, anarchic agrarian reformer. An early disciple of George H. Evans. Author of *The Phonotypic Spelling and Reading Manual* (1867), as well as earlier pamphlets on phonetics; author also of *Sociology* (1877).

MASSASSOIT (*date of birth unknown; d. 1661*), chief of the Wampanoag Indians. Native name, Ousamequin (Yellow Feather). Resided mainly at Pokanoket (Mount Hope), near Bristol, R.I.; father of Metacomet (King Philip). Accompanied Samoset and Squanto to Plymouth, March 1621, and there negotiated a peace treaty with the settlers which he never broke.

MASSEY, GEORGE BETTON (*b. Kent Co., Md., 1856; d. 1927*), physician, pioneer in electro-therapeutics. Practiced in Philadelphia, Pa., *post* 1879.

MASSEY, JOHN EDWARD (*b. Spotsylvania Co., Va., 1819; d. 1901*), Baptist clergyman, Virginia legislator. A founder of the "Readjuster" movement, Massey rebelled against leadership of William Mahone and aided in restoration of a liberalized Democratic régime.

MASSON, THOMAS LANSING (*b. Essex, Conn., 1866; d. Glen Ridge, N.J., 1934*), humorist. Managing editor, *Life*, 1893–1922. [*Supp. 1*]

MAST, PHINEAS PRICE (*b. Lancaster Co., Pa., 1825; d. Springfield, O., 1898*), inventor and manufacturer of farm machinery. Published *Farm and Fireside* (*post* 1879); also *Woman's Home Companion*.

MASTERSON, WILLIAM BARCLAY (*b. Iroquois Co., Ill., 1853; d. New York, N.Y., 1921*), frontier peace officer, gambler, sports writer. Commonly known as "Bat" Masterson. Worked as buffalo hunter and contractor; won fame for bravery at battle of Adobe Walls, June 1874; served as U.S. Army scout. Between 1876 and 1885, Masterson was marshal or sheriff in a number of frontier towns, including Dodge City, Deadwood, and Tombstone. After his removal to New York City, 1902, he worked as sports writer and editor, N.Y. *Morning Telegraph*.

MASTIN, CLAUDIUS HENRY (*b. Huntsville, Ala., 1826; d. Mobile, Ala., 1898*), surgeon. M.D., University of Pennsylvania, 1849. Served in Confederate Army medical branch, 1861–65. Devised instruments for genito-urinary surgery; pioneered in use of metallic sutures. Practiced principally in Mobile.

MASURY, JOHN WESLEY (*b. Salem, Mass., 1820; d. New York, N.Y., 1895*), paint manufacturer, inventor. Devised metal paint containers which made feasible the marketing of ready-mixed paints; also invented an improved mill (patented 1870) for fine grinding of colors.

MATEER, CALVIN WILSON (*b. Cumberland Co., Pa., 1836; d. Tsingtao, China, 1908*), Presbyterian clergyman, educator. Missionary to China *post* 1863; author of *Mandarin Lessons* (1892) and other textbooks.

MATHER, COTTON (*b. Boston, Mass., 1662/63; d. Boston, 1727/28*), Puritan clergyman, scholar, author. Son of Increase Mather; grandson of Richard Mather and John Cotton. Influenced profoundly as a boy by his family tradition of leadership in the church, sensitive and self-conscious, Mather was more popular at Harvard with his tutors than with his classmates. Graduating, 1678, he took the degree of M.A., 1681, and was ordained, 1685, at the Boston Second Church where he held office for the rest of his life, serving as his father's colleague until 1723. A tract written by him, *The Declaration of the Gentlemen, Merchants, and Inhabitants of Boston* (1689), served as the manifesto of the insurgents against the rule of Sir Edmund Andros. Elected a fellow of Harvard, 1690, he was recognized in spite of his youth as one of the most eminent divines in New England. The accession of a new governor, Sir William Phips, 1692, gave Cotton Mather an opportunity for exerting political influence; he wrote in defense of the new (1691) Massachusetts charter and of Phips's acts as governor. Despite the common opinion of Mather's actions during the Massachusetts witchcraft prosecution of 1692, he had in fact endeavored to impose on the court a fairer set of evidential rules than were employed and he had also suggested milder punishments. As earlier writings of his, however, had excited the public mind on the subject of witchcraft, and as he uttered no public protest against the trials or the sentences and indeed defended some of the verdicts in his book *Wonders of the Invisible World* (1693), he must be assigned a sufficient share of the blame.

Popular dissatisfaction with the new charter, a general weakening of clerical dominance in New England and Mather's own too frequent arrogance of tone combined to lessen his popularity and political influence. Finding that he could not manage Joseph Dudley who had become governor, 1702, Mather endeavored to oust him but was unsuccessful. Passed over several times in the choice of a president for Harvard, he came to look upon Yale as the hope of the Congregational education in which he believed. Despite frustrated ambitions, failure in politics and the loss of personal popularity, he remained a leader in the church; he projected societies for various good causes —the maintenance of peace, the building of churches in poor communities, the relief of needy clergymen and the like. He set up and supported a school for the education of slaves and gave generously of money and time to the poor.

His tireless activity as a writer gave him reputation abroad as well as at home. When smallpox broke out in Boston, 1721, he interested Dr. Zabdiel Boylston in innoculation and defended ably in print what seemed to him a beneficent medical practice. The greater part of his more than 450 books was published *post* 1692; his works reveal him an able editor, a historian, an amateur in many fields of knowledge and a prose writer with a definite theory of style. His *Magnalia Christi Americana* (published, London, 1702) was the mightiest American literary achievement up to its time; his *Bonifacius* (1710) under its later title as *Essays to do Good* had great popularity and was praised by Benjamin Franklin.

Constantly overworking himself, plagued by domestic tragedies, vain, unstable and pedantic, Cotton Mather was consistently more tolerant in deed than in word and his tolerance grew as he aged. None of the charges made against his honesty in money matters and even his sexual morality has ever been substantiated. Essentially a conservative, he was always torn between allegiance to inherited ideals and the realization that the newer time demanded new standards. Though bred in Calvinism, he expounded in his *Christian Philosopher* (1721) doctrines which represent a step toward deism. However unlovable he may appear at the present, he commands respect for his studiousness, his industry and for his self-forgetfulness in his work.

MATHER, FRED (*b. present Rensselaer, N.Y., 1833; d. near Lake Nebagomain, Wis., 1900*), pisciculturist. Supervised New York State hatchery, Cold Spring Harbor, N.Y., 1883–95, where he developed and improved methods of propagation; was author of a number of technical works as well as popular books on outdoor life.

MATHER, INCREASE (*b. Dorchester, Mass., 1639; d. Boston, Mass., 1723*), Puritan clergyman, politician, author. Son of Richard Mather; father of Cotton Mather. Graduated Harvard, 1656; M.A., Trinity College, Dublin, 1658. Served as Puritan pastor in Devonshire, as chaplain to the garrison at Guernsey and in several other posts in England. Returning to Boston, Mass., September 1661, he became teacher of the Second Church, 1664. In 1681, he refused to leave his congregation to accept the offered presidency of Harvard. Drawn into politics by the crisis produced by the *quo warranto* issued against the Massachusetts charter, 1683, he exhorted the citizens of Boston not to submit to the king. Appointed acting president of

Harvard, 1685, and a year afterwards rector, he encouraged the study of science and showed willingness to make the college something more than a training school for ministers; at the same time, he resisted successfully all efforts to undermine its Congregationalism.

In 1688, he was chosen to take petitions to the king from the Congregational churches in Massachusetts requesting the return of the charter. In London at the fall of James II and the accession of William III, Mather gave assurances of New England's loyalty to the new king and secured the exception of Massachusetts from Andros's rule. Appointed an official agent from Massachusetts, 1690, he and his fellow agents accepted a new charter framed by William III which, while it took away the colonists' right to elect their own governors, preserved most of the power of the representative assembly elected by the voters. Mather was given by the king the privilege of nominating the governor and also all other officers to be appointed for the first year of the new government. He thus secured unique influence in Massachusetts politics.

On his return to Boston, May 1692, with Sir William Phips, the royal governor whom he had nominated, Mather found himself the object of a campaign of opposition and discredit conducted by Elisha Cooke and others who regarded the old charter as the foundation of Massachusetts liberties and who resented the political influence of Mather and his family. His enemies centered their attack in an attempt to oust him from the rectorship at Harvard. During the celebrated Salem witchcraft trials, Increase Mather, like his son Cotton, was slow to make a public protest even though he disapproved of the type of evidence admitted. In October, however, Increase wrote and issued the most outspoken and the earliest public utterance issued in New England against the practices of the witchcraft court—*Cases of Conscience Concerning Evil Spirits*. It was first circulated in manuscript, perhaps even printed, before the end of 1692 although the printed version bears the date 1693.

His political prestige, like Cotton Mathers's, declined *post* 1692 and for the same reasons. He was committed to the new charter which he had helped to obtain and he was a supporter of Gov. Phips whom he had nominated; he shared in their unpopularity. Surrendering his presidency of Harvard, 1701, he continued to exercise his ministry and to write. He took less of a part in politics although he shared in his son's unsuccessful campaign against Gov. Dudley. Increase Mather was unequaled in reputation and power by any native-born American Puritan of his generation. Hot-tempered, self-confident, favoring an ecclesiastical oligarchy, he was yet charitable and sometimes even conciliatory; in civil affairs, he argued for the preservation of democratic institutions. As an author his style was simple and direct, but without brilliance. Among his many books and pamphlets, the most interesting of them today are his political tracts written in connection with his agency in London and his two histories: *A Brief History of the Warr with the Indians* (1676); and *A Relation of the Troubles Which Have Hapned in New-England by Reason of the Indians There* (1677).

MATHER, RICHARD (*b. Lowton, Lancashire, England, 1596; d. Dorchester, Mass., 1669*), Puritan clergyman, author. Father of Increase Mather; grandfather of Cotton Mather. Originally a schoolmaster at Toxteth Park, now part of Liverpool, he began to preach there in November 1618. Ordained soon afterwards, he developed Puritan tendencies but continued to preach at Toxteth and elsewhere in Lancashire until 1633 when he was suspended from his ministry. Removing to Boston, Mass., 1635, he became teacher of the church in Dorchester, August 1636, and continued to minister there until his death. He was, from the first, a leader of Massachusetts Congregationalism; his *Church-Government and Church-Covenant Discussed* (1643) was the first elaborate defense and exposition of the New England theory of the church to be put forth in print. He was a collaborator with John Eliot and Thomas Welde in *The Whole Booke of Psalmes* (1640), better known as the "Bay Psalm Book"; he also wrote the original draft of the "Cambridge Platform" which, amended and adopted by a synod at Cambridge, 1646, was for many years the basic document of New England Congregationalism. Richard Mather's practical approach to ecclesiastical affairs was shown in his advocacy of the Half-Way Covenant which permitted a limited church membership to those who gave no acceptable proof of spiritual regeneration.

MATHER, SAMUEL (*b. Boston, Mass., 1706; d. Boston, 1785*), Congregational clergyman, author. Son of Cotton Mather. Graduated Harvard, 1723. Chosen pastor at the Second Church, Boston, 1732, he was dismissed, 1741; a number of his congregation withdrawing with him, he established a new church where he ministered until his death. The last of the Mather dynasty, Samuel Mather had neither wide public influence nor preaching skill. He published a number of books and pamphlets which displayed erudition rather than distinction or intellectual strength.

MATHER, SAMUEL (*b. Cleveland, O., 1851; d. 1931*), iron merchant, financier. Son of Samuel L. Mather. Associated *post* 1873 with the numerous interests controlled by his family, notably, the Cleveland Iron Mining Co. and its successors and subsidiaries. He was a benefactor of Kenyon College, of Western Reserve University and of the Cleveland Community Fund.

MATHER, SAMUEL HOLMES (*b. Washington, N.H., 1813; d. 1894*), lawyer, banker. Removed to Cleveland, O., 1835. Helped organize Cleveland Society for Savings, 1849; served it from the first as secretary and chief officer, and was president *post* 1884.

MATHER, SAMUEL LIVINGSTON (*b. Middletown, Conn., 1817; d. Cleveland, O., 1890*), capitalist. Removing to Cleveland, O., as an agent for his family and other interests who owned land in Ohio, he helped organize the Cleveland Iron Mining Co. *c.* 1850, and by 1853 had become the driving force in the organization. The beginning of the city of Cleveland's industrial prominence may be attributed to Mather's company more than to any other single enterprise; his foresight and business ability in developing the ore lands in the Lake Superior region and improving the means of shipping their product revolutionized the iron industry in the United States. In 1869, Mather became president and treasurer of the company and held these offices until his death.

MATHER, STEPHEN TYNG (*b. San Francisco, Calif., 1867; d. Brookline, Mass., 1930*), organizer of the National Park Service. Graduated University of California, 1887; achieved success as a borax company executive. Named an assistant U.S. secretary of the interior, 1915, he was assigned to coordinate the 14 national parks under a single bureau; at Secretary Franklin K. Lane's insistence, he became director of the newly created National Park Service and served from 1917 to 1929. He secured definition of national parks as areas of the highest scenic value, to be preserved forever in their primitive condition. He opposed attempts to include tracts of lesser scenic importance, educated America in national park ideals, and established and maintained service standards.

MATHER, WILLIAM WILLIAMS (*b. Brooklyn, Conn., 1804; d. Columbus, O., 1859*), geologist. Graduated West Point, 1828; taught there, and at the University of Louisiana and Ohio University. Directed geological surveys of Ohio, Kentucky and New York, 1836–44.

MATHESON, WILLIAM JOHN (*b. Elkhorn, Wis., 1856; d. at sea, 1930*), chemist, financier. Active in American production of synthetic dyes; headed National Aniline & Chemical Co. and helped organize Allied Chemical & Dye Corp. Established, 1927, a fund for an international study of encephalitis.

MATHEWS, ALBERT (*b. New York, N.Y., 1820; d. Lake Mohonk, N.Y., 1903*), lawyer, author. Wrote minor essays, legends and fiction under pen-name "Paul Siogvolk."

MATHEWS, CORNELIUS (*b. Port Chester, N.Y., 1817; d. New York, N.Y., 1889*), author. Graduated University of the City of New York (New York University), 1834. A regular contributor to the *Knickerbocker Magazine* and other periodicals, he founded and edited with his friend E. A. Duyckinck the monthly, *Arcturus* (1840–1842).

MATHEWS, GEORGE (*b. Augusta Co., Va., 1739; d. Augusta, Ga., 1812*), Revolutionary soldier, politician. Removed to Georgia, 1785; served as governor of Georgia, 1787, as congressman, and as governor again, 1793–96. Falling into disfavor because of his connection with the Yazoo Act and suspected connection with the Blount Conspiracy, Mathews returned to prominence in 1810. Employed in official negotiations for transfer of West Florida, he continued irregular activities in East Florida on the failure of his primary mission. These included the stirring up of an insurrection and its support from nearby Georgia. The "insurgents" declared independence of Spain and between March and June 1812 occupied portions of the province. They had come within sight of St. Augustine before Secretary of State James Monroe disavowed the whole proceeding.

MATHEWS, HENRY MASON (*b. Greenbrier Co., Va., 1834; d. Lewisburg, W. Va., 1884*), lawyer, Confederate soldier. Democratic governor of West Virginia, 1877–81.

MATHEWS, JOHN (*b. Charleston, S.C., 1744; d. 1802*), lawyer, Revolutionary patriot and legislator. Governor of South Carolina, 1782–83; chancellor, 1784–91; judge of the court of equity, 1791–97.

MATHEWS, JOHN ALEXANDER (*b. Washington, Pa., 1872; d. Scarsdale, N.Y., 1935*), metallurgist, expert in steel alloys. [*Supp. 1*]

MATHEWS, SAMUEL (*b. England c. 1600; d. Virginia, 1660*), colonial planter. Came to Virginia, 1622; became a member of the council, 1623; was leader of the council in a revolt against the governor, Sir John Harvey, 1635. A Puritan and an early convert to the cause of the British Parliament, he became governor of Virginia, March 1658, and served with honesty and ability until his death.

MATHEWS, WILLIAM (*b. Waterville, Maine, 1818; d. Forest Hills, Mass., 1909*), journalist, teacher. Author of a number of works of literary criticism and of *Getting on in the World* (1873).

MATHEWS, WILLIAM SMYTHE BABCOCK (*b. Loudon, N.H., 1837; d. Denver, Colo., 1912*), music-teacher and author. Identified with music in Chicago, Ill., 1867–1910; raised standards of musical education in the West.

MATHEWSON, CHRISTOPHER (*b. Factoryville, Pa., 1880; d. Saranac, N.Y., 1925*), baseball player. Pitcher, New York Giants, 1900–16; won 511 games in National League career. Celebrated for sportsmanship; improved tone of professional baseball by encouraging employment of college-trained players.

MATIGNON, FRANCIS ANTHONY (*b. Paris, France, 1753; d. Boston, Mass., 1818*), Roman Catholic clergyman, Sulpician. Came to America, 1792.

Pastor in Boston, Mass., *post* 1792. His scholarship, kindness, humility did much to make Catholicism acceptable in New England.

MATLACK, TIMOTHY (*b. Haddonfield, N.J., c. 1734; d. Philadelphia, Pa., 1829*), merchant, Revolutionary patriot, Pennsylvania official. Assistant secretary of Continental Congress; probably engrossed Declaration of Independence. Active in forming Society of Free Quakers, 1781.

MATTESON, JOEL ALDRICH (*b. Watertown, N.Y., 1808; d. Chicago, Ill., 1873*), businessman, Illinois legislator. Removed to Illinois *c.* 1833. As Democratic governor of Illinois, 1853–57, Matteson reduced state debt, introduced free schools. Implicated (1858) in theft and refunding of state canal warrants, he devoted his efforts thereafter to railroad operation and banking.

MATTESON, TOMPKINS HARRISON (*b. Peterboro, N.Y., 1813; d. Sherburne, N.Y., 1884*), genre and portrait painter. Used patriotic or American country life themes; painted "Spirit of '76," "The First Sabbath of the Pilgrims" and other popular works.

MATTHEW, WILLIAM DILLER (*b. St. John, New Brunswick, Canada, 1871; d. San Francisco, Calif., 1930*), vertebrate paleontologist. Graduated University of New Brunswick, 1889; Ph.B., School of Mines, Columbia, 1893, and Ph.D., Columbia, 1895. Associated *post* 1895 with American Museum of Natural History; argued against existence of former land bridges between continents.

MATTHEWS, BRANDER. [See MATTHEWS, JAMES BRANDER, 1852–1929.]

MATTHEWS, CLAUDE (*b. Bethel, Ky., 1845; d. 1898*), stock-breeder. Democratic governor of Indiana, 1893–97; used state troops to restore order in coal-miners' and Pullman strikes; reformed state tax laws.

MATTHEWS, FRANKLIN (*b. St. Joseph, Mich., 1858; d. 1917*), journalist. Reporter, editor, correspondent, New York Sun, 1890–1912; thereafter, teacher of journalism, Columbia University.

MATTHEWS, JAMES BRANDER (*b. New Orleans, La., 1852; d. New York, N.Y., 1929*), educator, dramatist, critic. Graduated Columbia, 1871; Columbia Law School, 1873. Active in literary life of United States and England *post* 1880; intimate of major writers of the 1880's and 1890's; associate in authorship with Henry C. Bunner and Laurence Hutton. Taught literature and drama at Columbia, 1892–1924, and was author of many critical works in addition to plays and fiction.

MATTHEWS, JOHN (*b. London, England, 1808; d. 1870*), manufacturer and inventor of soda-water dispensing machinery. Emigrated to New York, N.Y., c. 1832.

MATTHEWS, JOSEPH MERRITT (*b. Philadelphia, Pa., 1874; d. San Diego, Calif., 1931*), chemist, textile expert. Author of, among other works, *The Textile Fibres* (1904).

MATTHEWS, NATHAN (*b. Boston, Mass., 1854; d. Boston, 1927*), lawyer, city official, reformer. As Democratic mayor of Boston, 1891–95, he demonstrated the need of a strong executive in municipal government for securing effective reforms; he advocated department consolidations, civil service, and a remodeled charter.

MATTHEWS, STANLEY (*b. Cincinnati, O., 1824; d. Washington, D.C., 1889*), lawyer, Union soldier, Ohio legislator and jurist. Graduated Kenyon College, 1840. As U.S. attorney in Ohio southern district, 1858–61, he gained unpopularity for fugitive-slave law enforcement; during Civil War he resigned colonelcy of 51st Ohio to become judge of Cincinnati's superior court, 1863–65. He won national attention as counsel for the electoral commission of 1877, contending that Congress should not go behind returns of state electors. U.S. senator, Republican, from Ohio, 1877–79, he was responsible for the "Matthews Resolution" of 1878 making silver legal tender. Appointed U.S. Supreme Court justice in 1881 after being earlier rejected by the Senate, he demonstrated fairness and ability during a period of expanding federal authority through liberal constitutional interpretations of the commerce clause and government borrowing powers.

MATTHEWS, WASHINGTON (*b. Killiney, Ireland, 1843; d. Washington, D.C., 1905*), army surgeon, ethnologist. Came to America as an infant; was raised in Iowa. M.D., University of Iowa, 1864. Serving in Western frontier posts, he became an authority on the Indians of the plains and the Southwest. Author of numerous papers, notably *Navaho Legends* (1897); pioneered in physical anthropology.

MATTHEWS, WILLIAM (*b. Aberdeen, Scotland, 1822; d. Brooklyn, N.Y., 1896*), bookbinder, scholar. Came to America, 1843. Celebrated for craftsmanship and learning, he headed the bindery of D. Appleton and Co., 1853–90.

MATTHIESSEN, FREDERICK WILLIAM (*b. Altona, Germany, 1835; d. La Salle, Ill., 1918*), metallurgist. Came to America, 1857. Pioneered in U.S. commercial production of zinc, 1858; built first zinc rolling-mill in America at La Salle, 1866; founded Western Clock Manufacturing Co.

MATTICE, ASA MARTINES (*b. Buffalo, N.Y., 1853; d. New York, N.Y., 1925*), mechanical engineer. Graduated in engineering, U.S. Naval Academy, 1874; taught engineering at Annapolis and with John C. Kafer developed course in mechanical drawing there. After service at sea, worked with George W. Melville on design of machinery for new naval vessels. Resign-

ing from the navy, 1890, he worked as machine designer and engineer for a number of corporations including Westinghouse, Allis-Chalmers and Remington Arms.

MATTISON, HIRAM (*b. Norway, N.Y., 1811; d. Jersey City, N.J., 1868*), Methodist clergyman, controversialist, reformer.

MATTOCKS, JOHN (*b. Hartford, Conn., 1777; d. 1847*), lawyer, Vermont legislator and congressman. Anti-slavery Whig governor of Vermont, 1843–44. An important figure at the Vermont bar, he tried to establish Thanksgiving Day on December 25.

MATTOON, STEPHEN (*b. Champion, N.Y., 1816; d. Marion, O., 1889*), Presbyterian clergyman. With Samuel R. House, founded Presbyterian mission in Siam where he served, 1847–65. First U.S. consul at Bangkok, 1856–59.

MATTSON, HANS (*b. Skåne, Sweden, 1832; d. 1893*), Minnesota pioneer, Union soldier, emigration agent. Came to America, 1851; removed from Illinois to Minnesota Territory as leader of a group of Swedish immigrants, 1853. Remained to the end of his life a power among Swedish-Americans.

MATZELIGER, JAN ERNST (*b. Dutch Guiana, 1852; d. Lynn, Mass., 1889*), inventor. Born of a white father and a Negro mother, he emigrated to the United States *c.* 1872. Between 1880 and 1883, he invented and developed a lasting machine which made it possible to manufacture shoes completely by machinery.

MAURAN, JOHN LAWRENCE (*b. Providence, R.I., 1866; d. Peterboro, N.H., 1933*), architect. Graduated Massachusetts Institute of Technology, 1889. Organized his own firm in St. Louis, Mo., 1900; conducted a large and varied practice there. [*Supp. 1*]

MAURY, DABNEY HERNDON (*b. Fredericksburg, Va., 1822; d. Peoria, Ill., 1900*), Confederate soldier. Nephew of Matthew F. Maury. Graduated West Point, 1846. Served with credit in Mexican War; taught at West Point, 1847–52; served thereafter in Texas and New Mexico until 1861 when he entered the Confederate Army. Promoted major-general, November 1862, he became commander of the district of the Gulf, July 1863, and served in this capacity for the rest of the war. He organized the Southern Historical Society, 1868, was author of *Recollections of a Virginian* (1894), and served as U.S. minister to Colombia, 1885–89.

MAURY, FRANCIS FONTAINE (*b. near Danville, Ky., 1840; d. 1879*), surgeon. Graduated Centre College, 1860; M.D., Jefferson Medical College, 1862. Chief surgeon, Philadelphia Hospital, *post* 1865; performed many complex operations for the first time in America; headed surgical clinic at Jefferson Medical College.

MAURY, MATTHEW FONTAINE (*b. near Fredericksburg, Va., 1806; d. Lexington, Va., 1873*), naval officer, oceanographer. Raised in Tennessee. Appointed midshipman, 1825, he saw extensive service at sea; promoted lieutenant, 1836, in the same year he published his *A New Theoretical and Practical Treatise on Navigation* which met with immediate favor. Assigned to harbor survey duty, he published a number of articles under the pen-name "Harry Bluff," 1838, which scored inefficiency in the navy and suggested specific reforms. Appointed superintendent of the Depot of Charts and Instruments, 1842, he began a series of researches on winds and currents; in 1847, he issued his *Wind and Current Chart of the North Atlantic* which was followed in the next year by explanatory sailing directions in *Abstract Log for the Use of American Navigators*. Demonstration of the practical utility of these charts and sailing directions secured for Maury the cooperation of many seamen in noting the winds and currents they encountered in various regions. By 1853, a uniform system of recording oceanographic data which he advocated was adopted for naval vessels and merchant ships of the whole world by a congress at Brussels, Belgium. On the basis of data now coming in from all quarters, Maury revised his previous charts and drew up another for the Indian Ocean. Great savings of time and money resulted from the shorter passages made possible by Maury's researches. He published *The Physical Geography of the Sea* (1855), now recognized as the first textbook of modern oceanography, and served as a consultant in the laying of the Atlantic Cable.

Deeply interested in the development of Southern commerce, Maury hoped for the opening of the Amazon Valley to free trade, believing that one effect of such a measure would be to draw slaves from the United States to Brazil. As antagonism mounted between North and South, he favored conciliation; however, on the secession of Virginia, he resigned from the U.S. Navy and accepted a commission as commander in the navy of the Confederate States. His world-wide reputation made him an effective spokesman for the Southern cause during his service as agent in England, 1862–65; he was also instrumental in securing warships for the Confederacy and was engaged in a series of experiments with electric mines. At the end of the war, Maury sought service with Mexico but returned to England, 1866. Accepting the professorship of meteorology in the Virginia Military Institute, 1868, he served in that capacity and as a lecturer until his death.

MAUS, MARION PERRY (*b. Burnt Mills, Md., 1850; d. New Windsor, Md. 1930*), soldier, celebrated Indian fighter. Graduated West Point, 1874. Served in campaigns against the Sioux, the Nez Percé and the Apaches; received the Congressional Medal of Honor for his actions in the Geronimo campaign, 1885–86.

After a further career of exceptionally varied duties, he retired as brigadier-general, 1913.

MAVERICK, PETER (*b. New York, N.Y., 1780; d. New York, 1831*), engraver, one of the founders of the National Academy of Design.

MAVERICK, SAMUEL (*c. 1602–c. 1676*), colonist. Came from England to America *c.* 1624, settling on Boston Bay; welcomed John Winthrop and his party, 1630; was described by John Josselyn as "the only hospitable man in all the country." Became a freeman of the colony of Massachusetts, 1632, but joined in protest against limitation of citizenship to church members and other violation of civil and religious rights, 1646–47. Removing from Massachusetts *c.* 1650, he returned to England *c.* 1660 where he recommended a more rigid supervision of the colonies. He revisited Massachusetts in 1664, as one of four royal commissioners sent out to hear and determine complaints.

MAXCY, JONATHAN (*b. Attleborough, Mass., 1768; d. Columbia, S.C., 1820*), Baptist clergyman. Brother of Virgil Maxcy. Graduated Rhode Island College (Brown University), 1787, and served as president of that institution, 1792–1802. After a brief term as president of Union College, he became first president of the University of South Carolina, 1804. Able and broadly tolerant, Maxcy introduced the study of the sciences and also recommended establishment of chairs of law and political economy.

MAXCY, VIRGIL (*b. Attleborough, Mass., 1785; d. aboard U.S.S. Princeton, 1844*), lawyer, Maryland legislator, diplomat. Brother of Jonathan Maxcy. Graduated Brown, 1804; studied law with Robert G. Harper. First solicitor of U.S. Treasury, 1830–37; U.S. chargé d'affaires at Brussels, Belgium, 1837–42. Killed by explosion of a gun aboard the *Princeton* while a guest of President John Tyler.

MAXEY, SAMUEL BELL (*b. Tompkinsville, Ky., 1825; d. Eureka Springs, Ark., 1895*), lawyer, Confederate major-general, friend of the Indians. Graduated West Point, 1846; after service in Mexican War, resigned his commission. Removed to Paris, Texas, 1857. On the outbreak of the Civil War, he organized the 9th Texas Infantry and after active engagement in the campaigns of 1862–63 in Tennessee and Mississippi, was appointed commander in Indian territory, December 1863. Organizing three brigades of Indians, he persuaded them that victory for the South was essential to their own safety and gained their goodwill as no other Texan had done since the days of Sam Houston. As U.S. senator, Democrat, from Texas, 1875–87, he advocated economy but did not fail to obtain appropriations for Texas projects; he was among the first to favor individual farms as the ultimate solution of the Indian question.

MAXIM, HIRAM PERCY (*b. Brooklyn, N.Y., 1869; d. La Junta, Colo., 1936*). Son of Hiram S. Maxim. Inventor of the "silencer" for gunfire, and many electrical devices; developed gas- and electric-powered automobiles for the Pope Manufacturing Co., Hartford, Conn., 1895–1907. [*Supp. 2*]

MAXIM, HIRAM STEVENS (*b. near Sangerville, Maine, 1840; d. Streatham, England, 1916*), Anglo-American inventor, engineer. Brother of Hudson Maxim. As a youth he learned and practiced several trades. Turning to engineering, he worked with machines for illuminating gas, invented a locomotive headlight and devised a process for equalizing carbon deposit on incandescent lamp filaments. Residing in England *post* 1881, he made scores of inventions, notably the automatic Maxim Gun (1883). This first efficient weapon of its class loaded, fired, and ejected cartridges by using the recoil of the barrel as each shot was fired. In 1894 he built an airplane that lifted itself from the ground, but its steam engine proved too heavy for practicable use.

MAXIM, HUDSON (*b. Orneville, Maine, 1853; d. 1927*), inventor, explosives expert. Brother of Hiram S. Maxim. Supplemented irregular schooling with training in science and engineering; entered a partnership in the job-printing business, also selling writing style charts and colored ink powders. *Real Pen-Work Self-Instructor* (1881), published by his firm, was highly successful. After studying manufacture of French smokeless gunpowder at his brother's gun factory in England, he returned to the U.S. in 1888 and became its first American producer; his plant and patents were sold to the Du Pont Co. (1897) for whom he became consultant. He had earlier produced a safer dynamite, and now perfected the armor-piercing high explosive "Maximite." Among his other inventions were a device for driving torpedoes, an automobile, improved cartridges and a process for manufacturing calcium carbide.

MAXWELL, AUGUSTUS EMMETT (*b. Elberton, Ga., 1820; d. Chipley, Fla., 1903*), lawyer, Florida legislator. Raised in Alabama; removed to Tallahassee, Fla., 1845, where he entered politics. After inconspicuous service as congressman from Florida, 1853–57, he resumed practice of law and served throughout the Civil War as member of the Confederate Senate. A law partner of Stephen R. Mallory, *post* 1866, he became a Florida circuit judge, 1877, and served in various judicial posts until 1891.

MAXWELL, DAVID HERVEY (*b. Garrard Co., Ky., 1786; d. Bloomington, Ind., 1854*), physician, Indiana legislator. Chiefly remembered for his long and unflagging interest in Indiana higher education.

MAXWELL, GEORGE TROUP (*b. Bryan Co., Ga., 1827; d. Jacksonville, Fla., 1897*), physician, Florida legislator, Confederate soldier.

MAXWELL, HUGH (*b. Paisley, Scotland, 1787; d. New York, N.Y., 1873*), lawyer, New York Whig politician. Came to America as a child. District-attorney, New York County, 1817–18 and 1821–29.

MAXWELL, LUCIEN BONAPARTE (*b. Kaskaskia, Ill., 1818; d. Fort Sumner, N. Mex., 1875*), frontiersman, rancher. Grandson of Pierre Menard. Friend of Kit Carson and hunter for John C. Frémont's first expedition. Maxwell married, 1842, the heiress of the vast Beaubien-Miranda tract in New Mexico. An active and valuable member of Frémont's force in the events culminating in the conquest of California, 1845–46, he then settled down to the management of his father-in-law's estate. In 1864, he became sole owner of what has ever since been known as the Maxwell Grant, later the subject of much litigation. Brave and self-reliant as a hunter and Indian fighter, Maxwell was improvident and unwise in handling his business affairs.

MAXWELL, SAMUEL (*b. Lodi, N.Y., 1825; d. Fremont, Nebr., 1901*), lawyer, Nebraska legislator. Justice of Nebraska supreme court, 1873–94, he served much of the time as chief justice. Originally a Republican, he took up Populist doctrines and was elected with Populist help to Congress where he served, 1897–99.

MAXWELL, WILLIAM (*b. near Newtown Stewart, Ireland, c. 1733; d. Lansdown, N.J., 1796*), Revolutionary soldier, New Jersey legislator. Came to America as a boy; settled with his parents in present Warren Co., N.J. Served in British and provincial regiments during French and Indian War; at its close, was attached to British commissary at Mackinac with rank of colonel. Returning to New Jersey, 1774, he was a member of the Provincial Congress, 1775, served on the expedition against Canada, 1776, and was commissioned brigadier-general by Congress, October 1776. He resigned from the army, July 1780, after performing notable service as a soldier, particularly at the battle of Monmouth and in Gen. Sullivan's campaign against the Six Nations in Pennsylvania and New York, 1779.

MAXWELL, WILLIAM (*b. New York or New Jersey, c. 1755; d. Greene Co., O., 1809*), printer. Removed to Lexington, Ky., 1792, where he published several pamphlets; removing again to Cincinnati, O., he issued the first number of *The Centinel of the North-Western Territory*, Nov. 9, 1793, which he published weekly until 1796. He was publisher also of the *Laws of the Territory of the United States, Northwest of the Ohio* (1796), since known as the "Maxwell Code," the first book published in the Northwest Territory.

MAXWELL, WILLIAM (*b. Norfolk, Va., 1784; d. near Williamsburg, Va., 1857*), lawyer, Virginia legislator. Graduated Yale, 1802. President, Hampden-Sydney College, 1838–44.

MAXWELL, WILLIAM HENRY (*b. Stewartstown, Ireland, 1852; d. 1920*), educator, journalist. Graduated Queen's College, Galway, 1872. Came to America, 1874. Associate superintendent of schools, Brooklyn, N.Y., 1882–87; superintendent, 1887–98. Superintendent of schools, New York City, 1898–1917. Promoted vocational education, building of playgrounds; raised requirements for teachers and established them on civil service.

MAY, EDWARD HARRISON (*b. Croydon, England, 1824; d. Paris, France, 1887*), historical and portrait painter. Came to America as a boy. Studied under Daniel Huntington and with Thomas Couture in Paris. Among examples of his elaborate compositions are the "Last Days of Christopher Columbus" (1861) and "Milton Dictating to his Daughters" (1883).

MAY, SAMUEL JOSEPH (*b. Boston, Mass., 1797; d. 1871*), Unitarian clergyman, reformer. Advocated temperance, women's rights, improved popular education, international peace; was an ardent Abolitionist and active agent of the Underground Railroad. Held pastorates in Connecticut, Massachusetts, and Syracuse, N.Y.

MAY, SOPHIE. [See CLARKE, REBECCA SOPHIA, 1833–1906.]

MAYER, ALFRED GOLDSBOROUGH. [See MAYOR, ALFRED GOLDSBOROUGH, 1868–1922.]

MAYER, ALFRED MARSHALL (*b. Baltimore, Md., 1836; d. 1897*), physicist. Nephew of Brantz Mayer; protégé of Joseph Henry. Taught at various colleges and was professor at Stevens Institute of Technology, 1871–97. Leading American authority on acoustics.

MAYER, BRANTZ (*b. Baltimore, Md., 1809; d. Baltimore, 1879*), lawyer, author. A founder of Maryland Historical Society, 1844. Author of *Mexico as It Was and as It Is* (1844), *Captain Canot* (1854), and other volumes on Mexican and Maryland history.

MAYER, CONSTANT (*b. Besançon, France, 1829; d. Paris, France, 1911*), artist. Worked in New York, N.Y., 1857–95; was noted for competent but commonplace genre paintings, portraits.

MAYER, EMIL (*b. New York, N.Y., 1854; d. New York, 1931*), laryngologist. M.D., New York University, 1877; associated with N.Y. Eye and Ear Infirmary and Mount Sinai Hospital. Pioneer in submucous resection of the nasal septum; made valuable report on local anaesthesia (1926).

MAYER, LEWIS (*b. Lancaster, Pa., 1783; d. York, Pa., 1849*), German Reformed clergyman. Founded denomination's first theological seminary, Carlisle, Pa., 1829 (later Marshall College, Mercersburg).

MAYER, PHILIP FREDERICK (*b. New York, N.Y., 1781; d. 1858*), Lutheran clergyman. Graduated Columbia, 1799; studied theology with John C. Kunze. Pastor, St. John's Church, Philadelphia, Pa., 1806–58.

MAYES, EDWARD (*b. near Jackson, Miss., 1846; d. 1917*), lawyer, professor of law. Chancellor, University of Mississippi, 1889–92. Author of a number of works, including a life of his father-in-law, Lucius Q. C. Lamar (1896).

MAYES, JOEL BRYAN (*b. near present Cartersville, Ga., 1833; d. 1891*), Cherokee chief, Confederate soldier, stock breeder. Raised in Indian Territory (Oklahoma). Justice, Cherokee supreme court; worked for his tribe's educational and material betterment.

MAYHEW, EXPERIENCE (*b. Chilmark, Martha's Vineyard, Mass., 1673 n. s.; d. 1758*). Grandson of Thomas Mayhew (*c. 1621–1657*). Outstanding missionary to Martha's Vineyard Indians, 1694–1758; translated Psalms into native tongue. Author of *Indian Converts* (1727) and *Grace Defended* (revealing modified Calvinist beliefs, 1744).

MAYHEW, JONATHAN (*b. Chilmark, Martha's Vineyard, Mass., 1720; d. Boston, Mass., 1766*), clergyman. Son of Experience Mayhew. Graduated Harvard, 1744. Pastor of West Church, Boston, 1747–66. Vigorous as thinker and writer, he preached a rational and practical religion, rejecting the Trinitarian view and Calvinistic predestinarianism. He detested episcopacy, condemning Anglican mission activities in the colonies; he was also a stanch supporter of civil liberty against arbitrary rule. Influencing such patriot leaders as James Otis, Josiah Quincy and the Adamses, he recommended (1766) that the Massachusetts lower house send out circular letters to further intercolonial cooperation in defense of their rights. Able as a pamphleteer in religious and political controversy, he was a harbinger of the American Revolution.

MAYHEW, THOMAS (*b. Wiltshire, England, 1593; d. Martha's Vineyard, Mass., 1682*), colonial governor, missionary. Settled in Medford, Mass., *ante* 1632. Purchased (1641) present-day Dukes and Nantucket counties (Mass.); settling in Martha's Vineyard, 1646, he served there as chief magistrate and governor.

MAYHEW, THOMAS (*b. England, c. 1621; d. at sea, en route for England, 1657*), Congregational clergyman, first English missionary to the Indians of New England. Son of Thomas Mayhew (1593–1682). Came to America with his father *ante* 1632; led first settlers to his father's purchase of Martha's Vineyard, 1642. Serving also as pastor of the settlement, he turned his attention to the Indian inhabitants of the Vineyard and islands adjacent; his first convert was made in 1643, three years before John Eliot began work. Devoting almost his entire time to missionary activities, he neglected his personal concerns and paid the expenses of his mission out of his private purse.

MAYNARD, CHARLES JOHNSON (*b. West Newton, Mass., 1845; d. West Newton, 1929*), taxidermist, naturalist. Author of *Naturalist's Guide* (1870), *The Birds of Florida* (1872–78), *Manual of North American Butterflies* (1891) and many other useful works.

MAYNARD, EDWARD (*b. Madison, N.Y., 1813; d. Washington, D.C., 1891*), dental surgeon. Practiced in Washington, D.C., *post* 1836. A profound research student, as early as 1836 he announced the existence of dental fevers; he was the first to fill teeth with gold foil (1838) and to introduce the practice into Europe (1845). He was also inventor of many improvements in dental instruments and was professor of theory and practice of dentistry, Baltimore College of Dental Surgery, *post* 1857. Maynard's work in improving firearms was equally notable. He patented the Maynard tape primer, 1845, and in 1851, an improvement in breech-loading rifles which, with the subsequent improvements he made, brought about adoption of the Maynard rifle throughout the world.

MAYNARD, GEORGE WILLIAM (*b. Brooklyn, N.Y., 1839; d. Boston, Mass., 1913*), mining engineer.

MAYNARD, GEORGE WILLOUGHBY (*b. Washington, D.C., 1843; d. New York, N.Y., 1923*), portrait, figure and mural painter. Son of Edward Maynard. An assistant to John LaFarge in the decoration of Trinity Church, Boston, Maynard painted a number of important decorative murals in New York and Boston public buildings. His principal work was the exterior decoration of the Agricultural Building at the Chicago World's Fair, 1893; he also painted the Pompeian panels in the second-floor corridors of the Library of Congress, Washington.

MAYNARD, HORACE (*b. Westboro, Mass., 1814; d. 1882*), lawyer, Tennessee Unionist. Removed to Tennessee, 1838. Congressman, Whig and Know-Nothing, from Tennessee, 1857–63; attorney-general of Tennessee, 1863–65. Returning to Congress, July 1866, he aligned himself with the radical Republicans and served until 1875. He was U.S. minister to Turkey, 1875–80, and U.S. postmaster-general briefly in the last months of President Hayes's administration.

MAYO, AMORY DWIGHT (*b. Warwick, Mass., 1823; d. Washington, D.C., 1907*), Unitarian clergyman, educator, promoter of public education in the Southern states.

MAYO, FRANK (*b. Boston, Mass., 1839; d. near Grand Island, Nebr., 1896*), actor. Stage name of Frank McGuire. Made debut at Adelphi Theatre, San Francisco, 1856; New York debut, 1865. One of the most popular actors on the American stage, Mayo was effective in classical roles but at his best in American character parts, particularly in the title roles in *Davy Crockett* and the stage version of *Puddin'head Wilson*.

MAYO, HENRY THOMAS (*b. Burlington, Vt., 1856; d. Portsmouth, N.H., 1937*), naval officer. Graduated Annapolis, 1876. Rose through the grades to rear-admiral, 1913. Central figure in "Tampico Incident" with Mexico, 1914, Mayo's firm stand was backed by the Wilson administration and he became vice-admiral, 1915. From 1916 through World War I, Mayo served as commander-in-chief, Atlantic Fleet. He was regarded in the navy as restrained, judicious, and the most competent flag officer of his time. [*Supp. 2*]

MAYO, MARY ANNE BRYANT (*b. near Battle Creek, Mich., 1845; d. 1903*), teacher, pioneer Grange and Farmer's Institute worker.

MAYO, SARAH CARTER EDGARTON (*b. Shirley, Mass., 1819; d. Gloucester, Mass., 1848*), author. Wife of Amory D. Mayo. Editor, *The Rose of Sharon: A Religious Souvenir* (1840–48).

MAYO, WILLIAM (*b. Wiltshire, England, c. 1684; d. 1744*), surveyor. Emigrated to Barbados *ante* 1712; removed to Virginia *c.* 1723. Associated with William Byrd (1674–1744) in survey of Virginia-North Carolina boundary, 1728; accompanied Byrd in the founding of Richmond and Petersburg, Va.; made a general map of the Fairfax proprietary.

MAYO, WILLIAM JAMES (*b. Le Sueur, Minn., 1861; d. Rochester, Minn., 1939*), and **CHARLES HORACE** (*b. Rochester, Minn., 1865; d. Chicago, Ill., 1939*), surgeons, founders of the Mayo Clinic. Second and third sons of William W. Mayo. After William's graduation from the University of Michigan medical school in 1883 and Charles's from the Chicago Medical College in 1888, they joined their father and gradually took over his large practice. When Rochester, Minn., acquired a new hospital, 1889, the Drs. Mayo were the entire medical staff, giving them control of the only adequate surgical facilities in an area comprising several states. At this time new methods of antiseptic surgery, based on the principles of Joseph Lister, were making many ailments amenable to cure, and a stream of new operations were being developed in the hospitals and clinics of Europe and America. The Mayo brothers made a point of traveling every year to study the new surgical techniques, bringing them back to Rochester; they were especially adept at synthesizing and refining the surgical methods they had learned from others. Their reports of improved techniques and remarkable results were at first hardly believed, but skeptical Eastern doctors were convinced by observing the volume and quality of the Mayo surgery, and Rochester became world famous. As the number of patients grew to exceed their personal capacities, the Mayo brothers engaged new men to help them, choosing the best qualified doctors they could find and providing them with opportunities for travel and study. Thus the Mayo Clinic evolved, a group of some two hundred trained specialists engaged in the cooperative private practice of medicine. Before their retirement the Mayos changed the Clinic from a partnership to an independent, self-governing association. In 1915 the brothers, wishing to provide a planned course of graduate study leading to an advanced degree in medicine, established the Mayo Foundation for Medical Education and Research. Originally endowed with $1,500,000 (eventually with $2,500,000), the Foundation became affiliated with the University of Minnesota. The brothers were completely unlike in personality. Dr. Will was reserved, imperturbable, decisive, the chief in fact as well as in name; Dr. Charlie's supreme gift was the common touch. Each appreciated the complementary strengths of the other, and their phenomenal success was won as a team. [Supp. 2]

MAYO, WILLIAM KENNON (b. Drummondtown, Va., 1829; d. Washington, D.C., 1900), naval officer. Nephew of Abel P. Upshur. Appointed midshipman, 1841, Mayo saw active service throughout the Mexican War and performed several tours of duty as instructor in the U.S. Naval Academy. Remaining loyal to the Union in the Civil War, he engaged effectively in blockade duty. He retired as commodore, 1886.

MAYO, WILLIAM STARBUCK (b. Ogdensburg, N.Y., 1811; d. New York, N.Y., 1895), physician. Graduated College of Physicians and Surgeons, New York, 1832; practiced mainly in New York City. Mayo is remembered principally for his novels which had a large contemporary success; they include Kaloolah (1849), The Berber (1850) and Never Again (1873).

MAYO, WILLIAM WORRALL (b. Manchester, England, 1819; d. Rochester, Minn., 1911), surgeon. Came to America c. 1845. Father of William J. and Charles H. Mayo. M.D., University of Missouri, 1854. Removing in 1855 to St. Paul, Minn., he took part in the further organization of the territory and became within a decade the leading physician and surgeon in and about Rochester, Minn. A liberal Democrat, he took an active interest in politics, serving as mayor of Rochester several times and as state senator twice.

MAYO-SMITH, RICHMOND (b. Troy, O., 1854; d. New York, N.Y., 1901), statistician, economist. Graduated Amherst, 1875; was drawn to economics and allied subjects by John W. Burgess. Taught political science at Columbia University, 1877–1901, with marked success in both graduate and undergraduate courses. His course in statistics, said to be the first given in an American university, provided training for many subsequently distinguished statisticians. His Statistics and Sociology (1895) contained one of the first systematic applications of statistics to social problems; his Statistics and Economics (1899) was designed to show what economic problems could be treated by statistical inquiry. He was author also of

many scholarly papers on statistics and economics including Emigration and Immigration (1890).

MAYOR, ALFRED GOLDSBOROUGH (b. near Frederick, Md., 1868; d. Dry Tortugas, Fla., 1922), biologist. Son of Alfred M. Mayer. Graduated Stevens Institute of Technology, 1889, as an engineer; accompanied Alexander Agassiz on scientific voyages. After engaging in curatorial work in several museums, he served, 1904–22, as organizer and director of the Carnegie Institution's marine laboratory at Dry Tortugas, Fla. His own researches included studies of butterflies, jellyfishes and the formation of coral reefs. He was author, among other works, of Medusae of the World (1910).

MAYTAG, FREDERICK LOUIS (b. Elgin, Ill., 1857; d. Los Angeles, Calif., 1937), pioneer manufacturer of washing machines. Began business, 1907; organized Maytag Co., 1909. [Supp. 2]

MAZUREAU, ÉTIENNE (b. France, 1777; d. New Orleans, La., 1849), lawyer, Louisiana legislator. Settled in New Orleans, 1804; was law partner of Edward Livingston. Appointed attorney-general of Louisiana, 1815, he held that position repeatedly but not successively throughout his life.

MAZZEI, PHILIP (b. Poggio-a-Caiano, Italy, 1730; d. Pisa, Italy, 1816), physician, merchant, horticulturist. A wine merchant in London for a number of years, he removed to Virginia, 1773, to introduce there the culture of grapes, olives and other fruits. Settling on a plantation east of Charlottesville, adjoining Jefferson's "Monticello," he became an ardent supporter of the Revolutionary movement in Virginia. Sent abroad in June 1779 by Patrick Henry to borrow money for the Commonwealth of Virginia, he was unsuccessful in the mission but busied himself in gathering political and military information which he sent to Gov. Jefferson. Mazzei returned to America late in 1783; disappointed in hopes of a consular office, he sailed for Europe in June 1785, never to return. Thereafter, he was in the service of the King of Poland, and post 1802, a pensioner of the Emperor of Russia. Among his writings was Récherches historiques et politiques sur les États-Unis de l'Amérique septentrionale (1788) which was based in part on materials furnished by Thomas Jefferson. An indiscreet letter to him from Jefferson written on April 24, 1796, became famous in the history of American political controversy.

MAZZUCHELLI, SAMUEL CHARLES (b. Milan, Italy, 1806; d. 1864), Roman Catholic clergyman, Dominican. Came to America, 1828; ordained at Cincinnati, O., 1830. Served as a missionary to the Canadians and Indians in the neighborhood of Mackinac and Green Bay; built the first church in the area of Prairie du Chien, 1835; served the settlements of Galena and Dubuque. Acted as vicar-general to

Bishop Loras. Founded Sinsinawa Mound College, 1845; founded a congregation of teaching sisters, the Dominican Congregation of the Most Holy Rosary. Father Mazzuchelli was also the architect of the county courthouse at Galena, built the bishop's residence in Dubuque and designed the first Iowa capitol at Iowa City.

MEAD, CHARLES MARSH (*b. Cornwall, Vt., 1836; d. 1911*), Congregational clergyman, Biblical scholar and reviser.

MEAD, EDWIN DOAK (*b. Chesterfield, N.H., 1849; d. Boston, Mass., 1937*), reformer, author. Cousin of William R. and Larkin G. Mead. Editor, *New England Magazine* (1890–1901); edited *Old South Leaflets*. [*Supp. 2*]

MEAD, ELWOOD (*b. near Patriot, Ind., 1858; d. Washington, D.C., 1936*), irrigation engineer. Graduated Purdue, 1882; C.E., Iowa State College, 1883. In 1890, as a government engineer in Wyoming, he helped secure and administered a state water law which became a model for the West. He headed the U.S. Office of Irrigation Investigation, 1899–1907, and spent the years 1907–15 in Australia inaugurating a program of water conservation and reclamation. As head of California's Land Settlement Board, 1917–23, he initiated cooperative group settlements on newly irrigated tracts. He directed the U.S. Bureau of Reclamation *post* 1924. [*Supp. 2*]

MEAD, GEORGE HERBERT (*b. South Hadley, Mass., 1863; d. 1931*), educator, philosopher. Graduated Oberlin, 1883; Harvard, 1888. Studied also at universities of Berlin and Leipzig. Taught philosophy at University of Michigan, 1891–94, and at University of Chicago *post* 1894. Developed concept that human thinking and the characteristically human forms of social activity are aspects of the same fundamental process, the development of communication. Though Mead emphasized the philosophical implications of his social psychology and in particular its congruence with pragmatic speculation, his description and analysis of the relations between individual and social development have been useful to sociologists who disregarded or rejected the accompanying philosophy. [*Supp. 1*]

MEAD, LARKIN GOLDSMITH (*b. Chesterfield, N.H., 1835; d. Florence, Italy, 1910*), sculptor. Nephew of John H. Noyes; brother of William R. Mead. Among his many works in the pseudo-classic style are the statues of "Vermont" and "Ethan Allen" for the capitol at Montpelier, Vt., and also the Lincoln Monument at Springfield, Ill.

MEAD, WILLIAM RUTHERFORD (*b. Brattleboro, Vt., 1846; d. Paris, France, 1928*), architect. Graduated Amherst, 1867; studied architecture in New York and in Florence, Italy, where he lived with his brother, Larkin G. Mead. Returning to America, 1872, he became associated with Charles F. McKim and Stanford White in professional practice. Mead managed the office, often conceived the basic scheme of the plan and acted as efficient critic of the work of both his creative partners.

MEADE, GEORGE (*b. Philadelphia, Pa., 1741; d. Philadelphia, 1808*), merchant, Revolutionary patriot. Brother-in-law and partner in business of Thomas FitzSimons. Instrumental in building of St. Mary's Church, Philadelphia, one of the oldest Catholic churches there.

MEADE, GEORGE GORDON (*b. Cadiz, Spain, 1815; d. Philadelphia, Pa., 1872*), soldier. Son of Richard W. Meade, U.S. naval agent in Spain. Graduated West Point, 1835; served in Seminole War; resigned commission, 1836. After working as a civilian engineer, 1836–42, he applied for reinstatement in the army. As lieutenant, Topographical Engineer Corps, he helped survey the northeastern boundary, constructed lighthouses on Delaware Bay, fought under Taylor and Scott in the Mexican War. Further lighthouse work and Great Lakes surveys occupied him until the Civil War, when he became brigadier-general of Pennsylvania volunteers, August 1861. His brigade worked on the Washington defenses and participated in McClellan's Peninsular campaign, in which Meade was seriously wounded at Glendale. He rejoined his command before full recovery, fighting at Second Bull Run and displaying ability as temporary division and corps commander in the Antietam campaign. Following the Fredericksburg disaster, December 1862, as major-general he commanded V Corps, which acquitted itself well at Chancellorsville, May 1863.

When Lee again invaded the North, Meade was awakened early in the morning of June 28 with orders to take command of the Army of the Potomac. Protesting the order, unfamiliar with Gen. Joseph Hooker's previous plans, he began gathering his forces along the Emmitsburg-Hanover line to defend Washington and Baltimore. Advance elements of the hostile armies collided by accident near Gettysburg, Pa., on July 1, and Meade concentrated his troops in a strong defensive position to repulse the Confederates in what is usually considered the Civil War's decisive battle (July 1–3, 1863). Despite his own recent assumption of command and the exhaustion of his men, he has been criticized for not counter-attacking and for permitting Lee's escape; indisputably, however, he avoided mistakes that conceivably could have lost the war. Commander of the Army of the Potomac throughout the remaining hostilities, Meade was subordinated to Gen. U. S. Grant *post* March 1864, and his functions were thenceforward tactical in nature. Notwithstanding the anomalous situation and his own high-strung temperament, he loyally and competently carried out Grant's orders. Promoted major-general in the regular army, August 1864, he commanded the Military Division of the Atlantic, 1865–68, and the 3rd Military District in the South, 1868–69, where his firm justice made almost tolerable the difficult Reconstruction administration. Serving again as commander, Military Division of the Atlantic at Philadelphia (where he beautified Fairmount Park), he died at his post. Never popular, undiplomatic but of absolute honesty, he was a sound, steadfast commander.

MEADE, RICHARD KIDDER (*b. Nansemond Co., Va., 1746; d. Frederick Co., Va., 1805*), Revolutionary soldier, aide-de-camp to Gen. George Washington, 1777–83.

MEADE, RICHARD WORSAM (*b. Chester Co., Pa., 1778; d. Washington, D.C., 1828*), merchant. Son of George Meade; father of George G. and Richard W. Meade (1807–1870). U.S. naval agent at the port of Cadiz, Spain, 1806–16.

MEADE, RICHARD WORSAM (*b. Cadiz, Spain, 1807; d. 1870*), naval officer. Son of Richard W. Meade (1778–1828); brother of George G. Meade.

MEADE, RICHARD WORSAM (*b. New York, N.Y., 1837; d. Washington, D.C., 1897*), naval officer. Son of Richard W. Meade (1807–1870). Graduated U.S. Naval Academy, 1856. Commanded naval battalion which subdued Draft Riots in New York City, July 1863. After long and varied service at sea and on shore, he retired as rear-admiral, 1895.

MEADE, ROBERT LEAMY (*b. Washington, D.C., 1841; d. Lexington, Mass., 1910*), officer, U.S. Marine Corps. Son of Richard W. Meade (1807–1870). Graduated U.S. Naval Academy, 1856. Made prisoner in unsuccessful night attack upon Fort Sumter, Sept. 8, 1863; he was exchanged after 15 months' imprisonment. After service in the Spanish-American War as fleet marine officer, North Atlantic Squadron, he was promoted colonel, 1899, and in 1900, took part in the China Relief Expedition. He retired as brigadier-general, 1903.

MEADE, WILLIAM (*b. Frederick, later Clarke, Co., Va., 1789; d. 1862*), Episcopal clergyman, third bishop of the Diocese of Virginia. Son of Richard K. Meade. Graduated College of New Jersey (Princeton), 1808. A principal factor in the revival of the Episcopal Church in Virginia *post* 1814, he was elected assistant bishop of Virginia, 1829, and from 1841 until his death was bishop of the diocese which included the present states of Virginia and West Virginia. Bishop Meade was the leader of the Low-Church party in his denomination. Although opposed to secession in principle, he went with his state when Virginia seceded. He became presiding bishop of the Protestant Episcopal Church in the Confederate States. Among his numerous writings the best known is *Old Churches, Ministers, and Families of Virginia* (1857).

MEAGHER, THOMAS FRANCIS (*b. Waterford, Ireland, 1823; d. near Fort Benton, Mont., 1867*), politician, lawyer, Union soldier. A leader in the Young Ireland movement, he was arrested for sedition and banished to Tasmania, 1849. Escaping to New York City, 1852, he was naturalized, studied and practiced law and became a leader among the Irish-Americans. At the outbreak of the Civil War, he organized a volunteer Zouave company (later part of the 69th New York); he became commander of the famed Irish Brigade, February 1862. When the Brigade was so decimated as to be non-effective (after Chancellorsville), he resigned his commission; recommissioned brigadier-general early in 1864, he took over command of the district of Etowah and was mustered out of the service with the coming of peace. Appointed territorial secretary of Montana, 1865, he arrived there in October and served for a year as temporary governor. He was drowned while making a reconnaissance on the Missouri River.

MEANS, GASTON BULLOCK (*b. Blackwelder's Spring, N.C., 1879; d. Springfield, Mo., 1938*), private detective, swindler. His notorious career culminated in a ransom money swindle in the Lindbergh kidnapping case. [*Supp. 2*]

MEANY, EDMOND STEPHEN (*b. East Saginaw, Mich., 1862; d. 1935*), educator, Washington legislator, Seattle journalist. [*Supp. 1*]

MEARNS, EDGAR ALEXANDER (*b. Highland Falls, N.Y., 1856; d. Washington, D.C., 1916*), army surgeon, naturalist. His principal contribution was made as a gatherer of materials in the Southwest, the Philippines and Africa for the use of specialists in systematic zoology and botany.

MEARS, DAVID OTIS (*b. Essex, Mass., 1842; d. 1915*), Congregational and Presbyterian clergyman, prohibitionist, Anti-Saloon League organizer.

MEARS, HELEN FARNSWORTH (*b. Oshkosh, Wis., 1872; d. New York, N.Y., 1916*), sculptor. Acted as assistant to Augustus Saint-Gaudens. Created statue of Frances Willard in the U.S. Capitol, Washington, and also "the Fountain of Life" at the St. Louis Exposition, 1904.

MEARS, JOHN WILLIAM (*b. Reading, Pa., 1825; d. Clinton, N.Y., 1881*), Presbyterian clergyman, educator. A "New School" minister in New Jersey, Maryland and Delaware; served as professor of philosophy, Hamilton College, 1871–81.

MEARS, OTTO (*b. Courland, Russia, 1840; d. Pasadena, Calif., 1931*), Colorado pioneer. Emigrated to California as a boy; established a sawmill and a gristmill at Conejos, Colo., 1865. Beginning with a road over Poncho Pass, he constructed a series of toll roads to the newly opened mining districts in Colorado, operated freighting outfits and pack trains over them, and constructed also the Rio Grande Southern and the Silverton Northern railroads in southwestern Colorado.

MEASE, JAMES (*b. Philadelphia, Pa., 1771; d. Philadelphia, 1846*), physician. Graduated University of Pennsylvania, 1787; M.D., 1792. Although he wrote, edited or compiled several medical works, he is principally remembered for his *Picture of Philadelphia* (1811) and for his pioneering *Geological Account of the United States* (1807).

MEASON, ISAAC (*b. probably Virginia, 1742; d. 1818*), pioneer ironmaster west of the Alleghenies. Settled in western Pennsylvania *c.* 1771; established Union Furnace on Dunbar Creek *c.* 1791; financed first mill for puddling and rolling bar iron in Pennsylvania, 1816.

MECHEM, FLOYD RUSSELL (*b. Nunda, N.Y., 1858; d. 1928*), lawyer, educator. Admitted to the Michigan bar, 1879; practiced in Battle Creek and in Detroit until 1893. Taught law at University of Michigan, 1892–1903, and at University of Chicago, 1903–28. Internationally known as an authority on agency, partnership, sales and corporations, he was author of *Treatise on the Law of Agency* (1889), *Treatise on the Law of Sale of Personal Property* (1901) and a number of other important text and case books. In a period when contemporary thought was submerging the individual for the sake of "social good," Mechem held firmly that the important ultimate values were individual and not social.

MECOM, BENJAMIN (*b. Boston, Mass., 1732; place and date of death unknown*), printer. Nephew of Benjamin Franklin. After apprenticeship to James Parker of New York City, Mecom managed his uncle's printing office in Antigua, 1752–56; he worked in Boston, Mass., 1757–62. Failing thereafter in New York, New Haven and Philadelphia, he removed to Burlington, N.J., 1774, where he was employed by Isaac Collins.

MEDARY, MILTON BENNETT (*b. Philadelphia, Pa., 1874; d. Philadelphia, 1929*), architect. Graduated University of Pennsylvania, 1894; apprentice in office of Frank Miles Day. Noted for his use of Gothic, he designed among other structures the Washington Memorial Chapel, Valley Forge, and the carillon tower at Mountain Lake, Fla. He served also as a member of several commissions for the development of Washington, D.C.

MEDARY, SAMUEL (*b. Montgomery Co., Pa., 1801; d. Columbus, O., 1864*), editor, Ohio legislator. Removed to Ohio, 1825; edited the *Ohio Sun* and the *Ohio Statesman;* became Democratic party dictator in Ohio, supporting the annexation of Texas, the reoccupation of Oregon, the Mexican War. Governor of Minnesota Territory (1857–58) and of Kansas Territory (1858–60), he favored the Lecompton Constitution for Kansas and vetoed a bill prohibiting slavery there. Returning to Ohio, he edited the *Crisis,* opposed the Civil War, and was an active "Peace Democrat."

MEDILL, JOSEPH (*b. near St. John, New Brunswick, Canada, 1823; d. San Antonio, Texas, 1899*), journalist. Raised in Stark Co., O., Medill studied law and was admitted to the bar, 1846. With his three younger brothers, he bought the *Coshocton Whig,* 1849; within two years he removed to Cleveland and established there the *Daily Forest City,* later the *Cleveland Leader.* Possibly the first man to advocate use of the name Republican for a new anti-slavery party, he was a founder of that party, and in the winter of 1854–55 bought an interest in the *Chicago Tribune,* making that paper a Republican organ. He played an important part in the campaign of 1856, and in 1860 strongly promoted the nomination of Abraham Lincoln. An active supporter of the Republican Civil War policy, Medill favored emancipation and the confiscation of Southern property and continually urged more radical courses of action on the administration, both during the war and in the Reconstruction period which followed. Acquiring a majority of the stock of the *Tribune,* 1874, he remained actively in charge of the paper until the day of his death.

MEEHAN, THOMAS (*b. England, 1826; d. 1901*), botanist. Emigrated to Philadelphia, Pa., 1848; establishing nurseries at Upper Germantown, Pa., *c.* 1853, he was successful in business. Author of the *American Handbook of Ornamental Trees* (1853) and *The Native Flowers and Ferns of the United States* (1878–80); edited gardening magazines.

MEEK, ALEXANDER BEAUFORT (*b. Columbia, S.C., 1814; d. 1865*), lawyer, Alabama legislator, author. A leader *post* 1853 in founding Alabama's public school system.

MEEK, FIELDING BRADFORD (*b. Madison, Ind., 1817; d. Washington, D.C., 1876*), paleontologist. After serving as assistant to David Dale Owen and James Hall, Meek was associated *post* 1858 with Ferdinand V. Hayden and worked with him on his surveys in Nebraska, Wyoming and the Rocky Mountain regions.

MEEK, JOSEPH L. (*b. Washington Co., Va., 1810; d. Hillsboro, Oreg., 1875*), Oregon pioneer. Removed to St. Louis, Mo., 1828; was employed as a trapper, 1829–40. Journeying to Oregon, 1840, he settled as a farmer on the Willamette. A dominating influence in the Champoeg convention of May 2, 1843, he was sheriff of the territory and elected to the legislature in 1846 and 1847. Appointed special messenger to Washington after the Whitman massacre, he set out on Jan. 4, 1848, and reached the capital in May. Appointed U.S. marshal by President Polk after the passage of the Oregon bill in August, Meek lost his office when the Pierce administration came in. A natural leader of great courage, he failed to obtain high office because of his lack of education and excess of humor.

MEEKER, EZRA (*b. near Huntsville, O., 1830; d. Seattle, Wash., 1928*), Oregon and Washington pioneer. Emigrated from Indiana to Oregon, 1851–52; was a farmer most of his life near Puyallup on Puget Sound. *Post* 1906, he gave his time to commemorative marking of the Oregon Trail.

MEEKER, JOTHAM (*b. Hamilton Co., O., 1804; d. near Ottawa, Kans., 1855*), Baptist missionary, printer. Printed first pamphlet and first book in what is now Kansas, near present Kansas City, Kans., March 1834.

MEEKER, MOSES (*b. New Haven, N.J., 1790; d. Shullsburg, Wis., 1865*), lead-miner, physician. Developed lead deposits in Fevre River region, Ill., 1823; removed to Iowa Co., Wis., *post* 1832, where he erected one of the first smelting furnaces in the territory, 1837.

MEEKER, NATHAN COOK (*b. Euclid, O., 1817; d. White River Reservation, Colo., 1879*), journalist, Indian agent. A disciple of Fourierism and a lecturer on the subject, Meeker led a roving life until *c.* 1865, when he joined the staff of the *New York Tribune* as agricultural editor. Supported by Horace Greeley and the *Tribune*, he organized and set up a cooperative agricultural colony known as the Union Colony, December 1869, siting it the next year at Greeley, Colo. Accepting appointment as agent at White River Reservation, 1878, he attempted to carry out his ideas of the proper method of managing Indians. The Utes, hostile to his plans, massacred him together with the other white men at the agency.

MEERSCHAERT, THÉOPHILE (*b. Russignies, Belgium, 1847; d. 1924*), Roman Catholic clergyman. Came to America, 1872; worked as a missionary in Mississippi and was vicar general, diocese of Natchez, 1887–91. Made vicar apostolic of Indian Territory, 1891, he became first bishop of Oklahoma, 1905, and served until his death.

MEES, ARTHUR (*b. Columbus, O., 1850; d. New York, N.Y., 1923*), choral and orchestral conductor, organist, teacher of music.

MEGAPOLENSIS, JOHANNES (*b. 1603; d. New York, 1670*), Reformed Dutch clergyman. After serving in parishes in Holland, 1634–42, he came to America as minister to the colony at Rensselaerswyck; he served there until 1649. A charitable man and a friend to the Indians, he rescued the Jesuit Father Jogues from captivity, 1642. At the persuasion of Gov. Peter Stuyvesant and the Council, he removed to New Amsterdam as minister, in which post he continued until his death.

MEGRUE, ROI COOPER (*b. New York, N.Y., 1883; d. 1927*), dramatist. Graduated Columbia, 1903. Author of popular topical dramas including *Under Cover* (first produced Boston, 1913), *It Pays to Advertise* (1914) and *Under Fire* (1915).

MEIGGS, HENRY (*b. Catskill, N.Y., 1811; d. Peru, 1877*), lumber merchant, railroad builder. Removed to California, 1849, and prospered in San Francisco during the first boom there. Absconded, October 1854, leaving behind him debts of almost a million dollars. Gaining reputation as superintendent of Chilean railroads, he undertook construction of railroads in Peru *post* 1868 and by a combination of ruthlessness and executive genius produced works which remain among the engineering wonders of the world. Before the Peruvian lines were completed, however, both the nation and the builder were bankrupt.

MEIGS, ARTHUR VINCENT (*b. Philadelphia, Pa., 1850; d. Philadelphia, 1912*), physician. Brother of William M. Meigs. M.D., University of Pennsylvania, 1871; studied also in Vienna. By patient analysis of milks, he succeeded in modifying cow's milk so as to make it generally wholesome for infants.

MEIGS, CHARLES DELUCENA (*b. St. George, Bermuda, 1792; d. Hamanassett, Pa., 1869*), physician. Son of Josiah Meigs. Graduated University of Georgia, 1809; studied medicine privately and at University of Pennsylvania. Practiced in Philadelphia; was professor of obstetrics, Jefferson Medical College, 1841–61. Author of *The Philadelphia Practice of Midwifery* (1838) and other works.

MEIGS, JAMES AITKEN (*b. Philadelphia, Pa., 1829; d. 1879*), physician, anthropologist. Graduated Jefferson Medical College, 1851. A general practitioner in Philadelphia, he became especially noted for his work in obstetrics; he also taught physiology in several Philadelphia schools.

MEIGS, JOHN (*b. near Pottstown, Pa., 1852; d. near Pottstown, 1911*), educator. Graduated Lafayette, 1871. Associated, *post* 1876, with the Hill School as director and teacher; developed it into one of the most extensive and best-equipped schools in the United States.

MEIGS, JOHN FORSYTH (*b. Philadelphia, Pa., 1818; d. 1882*), physician. Son of Charles D. Meigs; brother of Montgomery C. Meigs. M.D., University of Pennsylvania, 1838. Assisted his father in practice, later specializing in pediatrics. Author of *A Practical Treatise on the Diseases of Children* (1848).

MEIGS, JOSIAH (*b. Middletown, Conn., 1757; d. Washington, D.C., 1822*), lawyer, editor, educator, public official. Father of Charles D. Meigs; brother of Return J. Meigs (1740–1823). Graduated Yale, 1778. Edited *New Haven Gazette*, 1784–88, in which appeared many of the literary productions of the

"Hartford Wits." Resident in Bermuda, 1789–94, he returned to be professor of mathematics and science at Yale but resigned in 1800 because of the excessive Federalist tone of the university. Removing to Georgia, he served as president of the state university, 1801–10. Appointed surveyor-general of the United States, 1812, he was made commissioner of the General Land Office, 1814, and from 1819 until his death, was president of the Columbian Institute.

MEIGS, MONTGOMERY CUNNINGHAM (*b. Augusta, Ga., 1816; d. Washington, D.C., 1892*), soldier, engineer. Son of Charles D. Meigs; brother of John F. Meigs. Graduated West Point, 1836. Transferring from the artillery to the engineer corps, he carried through a number of important federal projects, including the Washington Aqueduct and the building of the wings and dome of the Capitol at Washington, D.C. Promoted to brigadier-general, May 1861, he served throughout the Civil War as quartermaster-general, Union army, with splendid efficiency and complete integrity. "Without him," said W. H. Seward, "the national cause must have been lost or deeply imperiled. "

MEIGS, RETURN JONATHAN (*b. Middletown, Conn., 1740; d. Cherokee Agency, Tenn., 1823*), Revolutionary soldier, Ohio pioneer. Brother of Josiah Meigs. U.S. agent to the Cherokees *post* 1801.

MEIGS, RETURN JONATHAN (*b. Middletown, Conn., 1764; d. Marietta, O., 1824*), Ohio pioneer, politician. Son of Return J. Meigs (1740–1823). Removed to Marietta, O., 1788; held several posts under the territorial government and served as chief justice of the state supreme court, 1803–04. After representing Ohio in the U.S. Senate, 1808–10, he was elected governor by a fusion of Federalists and conservative (Democrat) Republicans. Re-elected, 1812, he resigned in March 1814 to accept the post of U.S. postmaster general in which he served rather inefficiently until 1823.

MEIGS, RETURN JONATHAN (*b. near Winchester, Ky., 1801; d. Washington, D.C., 1891*), lawyer. Nephew of Return J. Meigs (1764–1824). Removing to Tennessee *c.* 1823, he practiced in Nashville, served as attorney-general of the state and as U.S. attorney, and was co-author of the *Code of Tennessee* (1858). A Whig in politics, he was prominent in the encouragement of educational, cultural and economic movements for improvement of Tennessee. Loyal to the Union, he left the state, 1861. Appointed clerk of the supreme court of the District of Columbia, 1863, he continued in this office until his death.

MEIGS, WILLIAM MONTGOMERY (*b. Philadelphia, Pa., 1852; d. 1929*), lawyer, historian. Son of John F. Meigs; brother of Arthur V. Meigs. Author of numerous articles on the courts and the U.S. Constitution, he also produced scholarly biographies of Josiah Meigs (1887), Thomas Hart Benton (1904) and John C. Calhoun (1917).

MELCHERS, GARI (*b. Detroit, Mich., 1860; d. Falmouth, Va., 1932*), landscape, genre and portrait painter. Studied at Düsseldorf and Paris. Grounded in habits of fine draftsmanship and sound design, Melchers expressed his own candid character in his work whose unforced, deeply felt quality won him many honors here and abroad.

MELISH, JOHN (*b. Methven, Scotland, 1771; d. Philadelphia, Pa., 1822*), merchant, traveler, geographer. After several periods of extensive travel in the United States, Melish settled in Philadelphia, 1811. His *Travels in the United States of America, etc.* (1812) was praised for its truthfulness and accuracy; he was also author of numerous statistical and descriptive accounts of regions of the United States illustrated with his own maps. His most notable undertaking was *The State Map of Pennsylvania* (1822).

MELL, PATRICK HUES (*b. Walthourville, Ga., 1814; d. Athens, Ga., 1888*), Baptist clergyman, educator, Confederate soldier. Professor of classics at Mercer College, 1841–55; at University of Georgia, 1856–88. Served also as vice-chancellor and chancellor of the university.

MELL, PATRICK HUES (*b. Penfield, Ga., 1850; d. Fredericksburg, Va., 1918*), scientist, educator. Son of Patrick H. Mell (1814–1888). Graduated University of Georgia, 1871; Ph.D., 1880. Taught geology and botany at State College, Auburn, Ala.; directed Alabama weather service, originating system of weather signals long in use by U.S. Weather Bureau; was associated with and for a time directed Alabama Agricultural Experiment Station. President, Clemson College, 1902–10. Distinguished for his work in hybridizing cotton and on the climatology of Alabama.

MELLEN, CHARLES SANGER (*b. Lowell, Mass., 1851; d. Concord, N.H., 1927*), railroad executive. After training in the business and traffic departments of New England railroads, he became general manager, New York and New England Railroad, 1892. Under the influence of J. Pierpont Morgan, he became president of the Northern Pacific, 1897, improving the physical aspects of that road during his term. Appointed president, New York, New Haven and Hartford Railroad, 1903, he won notoriety for that road by his monopolistic policies and by his neglect of adequate maintenance for which he was censured in a report of the Interstate Commerce Commission (*Sen. Doc. 543, 63 Cong., 2 Sess.*).

MELLEN, GRENVILLE (*b. Biddeford, Maine, 1799; d. New York, N.Y., 1841*), author, minor poet.

MELLEN, PRENTISS (*b. Sterling, Mass., 1764; d. Portland, Maine, 1840*), lawyer. A leading attorney in Biddeford and later Portland, District of Maine, Mellen served in the executive council of Massachusetts and as U.S. senator from Massachusetts, 1818–20. In 1820, when Maine became a state, he was named chief justice of the Maine supreme court and held office until 1834.

MELLETTE, ARTHUR CALVIN (*b. Henry Co., Ind., 1842; d. Pittsburg, Kans., 1896*), lawyer, journalist, Indiana legislator. Removing to Dakota Territory, 1879, he was active in movements toward statehood, was named governor of Dakota Territory, 1889, and in the same year was elected first governor of the state of South Dakota. He served until 1893 with ability and economy.

MELLON, ANDREW WILLIAM (*b. Pittsburgh, Pa., 1855; d. Southampton, N.Y., 1937*), industrialist, financier, art collector. Son of Thomas and Sarah Jane (Negley) Mellon. A lawyer who had also served as judge of the common pleas court of Allegheny Co., Thomas Mellon established a private banking house in Pittsburgh, 1869. Andrew Mellon attended public schools and the Western University of Pennsylvania (later the University of Pittsburgh) and in 1874 entered the family bank. Judge Mellon, recognizing his son's financial talents, transferred ownership of T. Mellon & Sons to Andrew, 1882. Quick to grasp opportunities to supply capital in a growing industrial area, Andrew Mellon was especially adept at assessing the worth of new ideas and fostering enterprises that others neglected. His backing of the inventor of the electrolytic process of aluminum manufacture resulted in formation of the Aluminum Co. of America, with the Mellons as principal stockholders. Similar support brought him stock control of the Carborundum Co. Other enterprises which he helped to establish included the Gulf Oil Corp., the Union Steel Co. and the American organization of the German inventor Heinrich Koppers. T. Mellon & Sons was incorporated as the Mellon National Bank, with Andrew Mellon as president, 1902. Other Pittsburgh banks soon joined with Mellon, forming one of the great financial powers of the nation.

A generous contributor to the Republican machine in Pennsylvania, Mellon became increasingly interested in national politics through his close friend and legal counsel Philander C. Knox. When Warren G. Harding became president in 1920, he accepted Knox's advice that Mellon be made secretary of the treasury. Though hardly one citizen in a thousand had heard of the retiring Pittsburgh banker, Mellon became the dominant figure in the Harding and Coolidge administrations. His immense wealth and technical expertness in complex financial matters impressed a nation embarking on perhaps the most materialistic period in its history. Mellon emphasized economy and tax reduction, based on his belief that business was the mainspring of national well-being and that it would prosper in proportion to the lightening of its

tax-load, thus bringing benefits that would filter down to workingmen and farmers. Although his initial tax program, favoring repeal of the excess profits tax and cuts in taxes on high incomes, aroused violent controversy, many of its objectives were attained. Prosperity and peace helped him in a steady lowering of the national debt, a reduction of federal spending and further reduction of income tax rates. He was applauded by upper and middle income groups but assailed by Democrats and progressive Republicans, and also by veterans and farmers for his opposition to veterans' bonus and farm relief legislation. His program of settlements of World War I debts with foreign nations was less successful. Remittances by the one-time Allies to the United States depended on payments to them of German reparations, which in turn depended on loans from the United States. Yet this country recognized no connection between reparations and debt and refused to lower tariffs to permit European debtors to dispose of goods which would help finance their payments. Eventually the debt settlement problem was engulfed in the great depression and the later World War, but Mellon in his time showed no great imagination or foresight in this area. Neither did he foresee the depression or take precautionary measures. It could even be asked whether his policies, favoring rapid accumulation and investment, had not stimulated stock market speculation and inflation. Hoover and Mellon met the depression by emphasizing retrenchment. By 1931 large borrowings became necessary and Mellon was increasingly criticized. His under-secretary, Ogden L. Mills, replaced him in February 1932, and Mellon accepted the ambassadorship to Great Britain, which post he occupied, gracefully but uneventfully, until March 1933. His later years were marked by an unpleasant tax wrangle over an alleged underpayment of some $2,000,000 on his 1931 income tax. Mellon carried his case to the Board of Tax Appeals, which soon after his death unanimously vindicated his actions, although on other technical grounds it added $485,809 to his 1931 tax.

Over the years Mellon had acquired one of the world's great art collections. In 1937 he announced the gift of his collection to the nation, together with funds to erect a building and establish a $5,000,000 endowment. Construction of the National Gallery of Art (Washington, D.C.) began before his death.

[*Supp. 2*]

MELSHEIMER, FRIEDRICH VALENTIN (*b. Negenborn, Duchy of Brunswick, 1749; d. Hanover, Pa., 1814*), Lutheran clergyman, entomologist. Coming to America as chaplain with the Brunswick forces hired by the British to serve in the Revolution, he was taken prisoner at the battle of Bennington, August 1777. He became pastor of several small Lutheran congregations in Dauphin Co., Pa., 1779, and later held pastorates at Manheim, New Holland and Hanover, Pa. His book *Catalogue of Insects of Pennsylvania* (Hanover, 1806) was the first volume published on the entomology of North America.

MELTZER, SAMUEL JAMES (*b. Ponevyezh, Russia, 1851; d. 1920*), physician, physiologist. M.D., University of Berlin, 1882. Came to New York, N.Y., 1883, where he practiced until 1906. His experimental work in physiology won him wide recognition; *post* 1906, he served as head, department of physiology and pharmacology, Rockefeller Institute of Medical Research.

MELVILLE, DAVID (*b. Newport, R.I., 1773; d. Newport, 1856*), pewterer, inventor. After experimentation with use of gas for illumination, Melville received first U.S. patent for apparatus for making coal gas, March 1813. His efforts to turn his invention to practical account met with no success.

MELVILLE, GEORGE WALLACE (*b. New York, N.Y., 1841; d. Philadelphia, Pa., 1912*), naval officer. Entered Engineer Corps, U.S. Navy, 1861. Served as chief engineer of *Tigress*, 1873, in search for crew of the *Polaris;* again volunteered for Arctic service, 1879, as chief engineer of the *Jeannette*. During her two years icebound in the Arctic Ocean, Melville's energy and skill were largely responsible for keeping the vessel afloat. After she sank, the lifeboat which he commanded was one of the two which reached Siberia, and he was the only boat commander to survive and bring his crew to safety. He later led a fruitless expedition in search of George W. DeLong and finally succeeded in finding and burying his dead shipmates. In 1884, he served as chief engineer of the *Thetis* in the Greely relief expedition. Appointed chief of the Bureau of Steam Engineering, 1887, he served until 1903. Among innovations which he introduced, often in opposition to conservative opinion, were the water-tube boiler and the triple-screw system; he superintended design of the machinery of 120 ships and was influential in merging the Engineer Corps with the Line. He retired as rear-admiral, 1903.

MELVILLE, HERMAN (*b. New York, N.Y., 1819; d. New York, 1891*), author. Melville's paternal grandfather, Maj. Thomas Melville of Boston, was the model for O. W. Holmes's poem "The Last Leaf"; his maternal grandfather was Gen. Peter Gansevoort, famous for defense of Fort Stanwix in the Revolution. Left in care of his unsympathetic mother when his bankrupt father died, 1831, Melville had scant schooling at the Albany Academy but read much in his father's library. Commencing work, 1834, he was a bank clerk, assistant in his brother's fur store, farmhand, schoolteacher. In 1837 he shipped as cabinboy on a New York-Liverpool voyage, returning with a taste for the sea and experiences which influenced much of his later writing. After more teaching, he shipped out of Fairhaven, Mass., aboard the whaler *Acushnet* (1841), deserting with a shipmate at the

Marquesas Islands 18 months later. After struggling through the jungle, he spent an idyllic month among friendly cannibals in beautiful Typee valley, escaping to Tahiti on an Australian whaler. There he worked for a time as a field laborer and studied the island life; eventually he enlisted in the U.S. Navy on the frigate *United States* and returned to Boston, 1844.

His nearly four years' wandering had made him a romantic figure and furnished material for his greatest books. He commenced writing immediately and the success of *Typee* (1846), based on his Marquesas experience, convinced him that destiny had intended him for a literary career. This book and *Omoo* (1847), which fictionalized the Tahitian episode, made him famous but also a target of criticism for his attacks on missionaries. In 1847, Melville married Elizabeth, daughter of Lemuel Shaw, chief justice of Massachusetts; removing to New York, he continued writing. *Mardi* (1849), *Redburn* (1849), and *White-Jacket* (1850)—all created from his South Seas adventures and naval service—appeared in rapid succession. He visited England and France briefly and then purchased "Arrowhead" farm in Pittsfield, Mass., where he became a friend of Nathaniel Hawthorne and completed his classic *Moby Dick* (1851). This marked his peak; the autobiographical *Pierre* (1852) revealed the strain and soul-searching bred of his youthful disappointments and family troubles and also inaugurated a gradual decline of his literary powers. Overworked, seeking religious solace, he visited the Holy Land, 1856–57, tried unavailingly to obtain a consulship and took to lecturing to supplement his income. *Moby Dick* did not sell well and was misunderstood by the critics; the plates and unsold copies of his books were destroyed by fire, 1853. His later volumes were largely ignored, though *Israel Potter* (1855), a Revolutionary novel, was distinguished by excellent writing about the sea and by remarkable characterizations of Benjamin Franklin and John Paul Jones. He turned to writing poetry, much of it obscure, and withdrew almost completely from society and the literary life. Working as a customs inspector in New York, 1866–85, he completed a remarkable short novel, *Billy Budd*, shortly before his death. It was not published until 1924. Virtually forgotten in America (though not in England) for seven decades, his mastery of prose became recognized *c*. 1920, partially as a result of a sudden vogue for South Seas travel books.

Moby Dick, with its haunting allegory of the great whale's pursuit, is considered Melville's masterpiece, but all his earlier works show vivid portraiture, well-organized observations, enthusiasm, and a good, classical style. He was the first literary artist to write of Polynesia, glorifying the virtues of primitive man and providing unforgettable pictures of island life. *Mardi* departs from the reporting of *Typee* and *Omoo* and employs the background of the earlier books to tell of a quest for happiness. It contains many pages of profound speculation as well as symbolic beauty and has been likened in structure and intention to the work of Rabelais. *The Piazza Tales* (1856) contains some grimly powerful sketches, notably "Benito Cereno" (the most successful of Melville's shorter works) and "The Encantadas." *The Confidence Man* (1857) is a muddled satire on commercialism. The value of Melville's poetry is in process of reassessment; neglected for a long time, *Battle Pieces* (1866) is now recognized as important and the subjective *Clarel* (1876) is significant in reflecting the theological strivings of the age. Melville wrote nothing entirely devoid of quality, but his supreme work was *Moby Dick,* whose rhythm and epic qualities bear comparison with the great Scandinavian sagas.

MEMBRÉ, ZENOBIUS (*b. Bapaume, France, 1645; d. 1687?*), Roman Catholic missionary, Recollect. Assigned to Canada, 1675, Membré went to Fort Frontenac, 1678; he ministered to La Salle's men on their expedition (1679–80) to the site of present-day Peoria, Ill. There (at Fort Crêvecoeur) Membré and Henri Tonty escaped from an Iroquois attack, rejoining La Salle at Mackinac, 1681, and accompanying him to the mouth of the Mississippi (1681–82). Returning to France with La Salle, Membré was made superior of the Recollect missionaries who accompanied La Salle in his attempt to found a settlement at the Mississippi's mouth, 1684. Missing its objective, the expedition built Fort Saint Louis (Lavaca Bay, Texas); there Membré died presumably, since the colony perished at some time after La Salle's departure in 1687. Membré's detailed journals were incorporated in *Premier Établissement de la Foy dans la Nouvelle France* (1691) by Chrétien Le Clercq; they give details of La Salle's expeditions not to be found elsewhere.

MEMMINGER, CHRISTOPHER GUSTAVUS (*b. Nayhingen, Duchy of Würtemberg, 1803; d. Charleston, S.C., 1888*), lawyer, South Carolina legislator. Came to Charleston, S.C., in infancy; graduated South Carolina college, 1819. Practiced law in Charleston; opposed nullification, 1830–32. As a state legislator, he urged laws requiring specie payments by banks; gained reputation as sound financier; also improved public school system in Charleston and the state. Earlier a foe of secession, he advocated joint Southern defensive measures following John Brown's raid. A member of the committee which drafted the Confederacy's provisional constitution, he was named Confederate secretary of the treasury, 1861. Disliking paper money, he was forced to issue treasury notes when Confederate bonds sold slowly. Comprehensive tax laws were enacted too late; military reverses depreciated the currency, requiring still more notes; funding schemes failed because of the Union blockade and for other reasons. Although Memminger is customarily blamed for the Confederacy's credit collapse, probably no financier could have averted it. He resigned his post, June 1864.

MENARD, MICHEL BRANAMOUR (*b. Laprairie, Lower Canada, 1805; d. Galveston, Texas, 1856*), Indian trader, Texas pioneer. Nephew of Pierre Menard. Removed to Kaskaskia, Ill., 1823, as employee of his uncle, trading among Delawares and Shawnees; was adopted by Shawnees and elected a chief. Going southward with them to Arkansas, Louisiana and Texas, he settled at Nacogdoches where he prospered as trader and land operator; in 1833, he settled as miller and trader on Menard Creek above Liberty on the Trinity River. A signer of the Texas Declaration of Independence, 1836, he helped draft the Texas Constitution and served in the Texas Congress. An able businessman and authority on land titles, he founded the city of Galveston, claiming its site in 1834 and organizing a company for its development, 1838.

MENARD, PIERRE (*b. St. Antoine, Quebec, Canada, 1766; d. Kaskaskia, Ill., 1844*), fur-trader, merchant, statesman. Removed to Vincennes, Ind., *c. 1787;* was employed by Francis Vigo. Opened a store in Kaskaskia, 1791. Active as a militia officer, as a county judge (1801–11) and as a delegate to the Indiana legislature (1803–09), Menard was a partner in the St. Louis Missouri Fur Co. *post* 1809; with Andrew Henry he led the first organized invasion of trappers to the Three Forks of the Missouri, 1810. He served as first president of the Illinois legislative council, 1812–18, and as first lieutenant-governor of the state of Illinois.

MÉNARD, RENÉ (*b. Paris, France, 1605; d. probably present Taylor Co., Wis., 1661*), Roman Catholic missionary, Jesuit. Came to Canada, 1640; ministered first to the Hurons; attempted an Iroquois mission, 1656–58. First Jesuit missionary to the Ottawa near Lake Superior, 1660–61.

MENDEL, LAFAYETTE BENEDICT (*b. Delhi, N.Y., 1872; d. 1935*), physiological chemist. Graduated Yale, 1891; Ph.D., 1893. Began a teaching career of 42 years at Yale as assistant in the chemistry laboratory of Sheffield Scientific School, 1893; was appointed Sterling Professor of Physiological Chemistry, 1921. Celebrated for his work in nutrition, he was, with Thomas B. Osborne, one of the first in America to recognize the existence of vitamins and their relation to health and disease. Equally far-reaching was their joint work on the nutritive value of the different food proteins, the differences in content of amino acids in proteins and their effect on growth. [*Supp.* 1]

MENDENHALL, CHARLES ELWOOD (*b. Columbus, O., 1872; d. 1935*), physicist. Son of Thomas C. Mendenhall. Graduated Rose Polytechnic, 1894; Ph.D., Johns Hopkins, 1898. After teaching briefly at Williams College, he became assistant professor of physics, University of Wisconsin, 1901, and remained at Wisconsin as professor and chairman of the department until his death. His research interests were so extremely broad that he was called "one of the few remaining natural philosophers". His investigations were concerned with gravity measurements, galvanometer design, melting-point determinations and radiation. He originated the V wedge black body, of great value in certain problems in pyrometry.

[Supp. 1]

MENDENHALL, THOMAS CORWIN (b. near Hanoverton, O., 1841; d. Ravenna, O., 1924), physicist, educator. Largely self-educated, he taught mathematics and science in Ohio high schools; as physics professor at Ohio State University, 1873–78 and 1881–84, he helped popularize science in the Midwest and organized and directed the state weather bureau. He held the chair of physics at the Imperial University, Tokyo, Japan, 1878–81. Serving as president, Rose Polytechnic Institute, 1886–89, he became superintendent of the U.S. Coast and Geodetic Survey where he developed improved means for measuring gravity and inaugurated high scholastic standards as prerequisite for entry into the Survey's technical force. Resigning, 1894, he served as president of Worcester Polytechnic Institute until 1901. Mendenhall made a number of significant contributions to science, especially in seismology, gravity and electricity.

MENDES, FREDERIC DE SOLA (b. Montego Bay, Jamaica, B.W.I., 1850; d. New Rochelle, N.Y., 1927), rabbi, author. Brother of Henry P. Mendes. Graduated London University, 1869; Ph.D., Jena, 1871. Came to America, 1873, and ministered in New York City; established and edited (1879–85) American Hebrew magazine. Conservative theologically, he opposed radical reform Judaism.

MENDES, HENRY PEREIRA (b. Birmingham, England, 1852; d. Mount Vernon, N.Y., 1937), rabbi. Brother of Frederic De S. Mendes. Minister to Congregation Shearith Israel, New York City, 1877–1920; co-founder, Jewish Theological Seminary of America, 1887; first president, Union of Orthodox Jewish Congregations; an early supporter of Zionism. [Supp. 2]

MENEELY, ANDREW (b. West Troy, now Watervliet, N.Y., 1802; d. West Troy, 1851), bellfounder. Established a foundry, 1826, whose work won international reputation.

MENÉNDEZ DE AVILÉS, PEDRO (b. Avilés, Spain, 1519; d. Santander, Spain, 1574), naval officer, Florida colonizer. Appointed captain-general of Spain's Indies fleet, 1554, he was commissioned in 1565 to resist French encroachments in Florida. He surprised and scattered Jean Ribaut's fleet off St. John's River in August, commenced a fort at St. Augustine in September, and reduced Fort Caroline. Capturing many survivors from the wrecked French fleet including Ribaut, he killed them after exacting their unconditional surrender. Between 1565 and 1572, he built two other posts in Florida, explored the coast, and attempted to evangelize the Indians (with whom he dealt honorably), but received little help from Cuba or Spain for his settlements. Successful in establishing Spanish power in Florida, he is remembered chiefly for his massacre of the French captives.

MENETREY, JOSEPH (b. Freiburg, Switzerland, 1812; d. St. Ignatius Mission, Mont., 1891), Roman Catholic missionary, Jesuit. Came to Oregon, 1847; ministered to Indians, miners and settlers in Idaho, Washington and Montana.

MENEWA (fl. 1814–1835), half-breed Creek chief. Famed for Tennessee border raids; as second chief of his people, commanded at battle of Horseshoe Bend (1814); killed William McIntosh (1825) for ceding tribal lands.

MENGARINI, GREGORY (b. Rome, Italy, 1811; d. Santa Clara, Calif., 1886), Roman Catholic missionary, Jesuit, educator. Came to America, 1840; accompanied Pierre de Smet to St. Mary's Mission, Idaho, 1841, where he served until 1850. He compiled several Indian language dictionaries and a Flathead grammar, and helped found College of Santa Clara in California, first collegiate institution on the Pacific slope.

MENKEN, ADAH ISAACS (b. probably Milneburg, La., 1835?; d. Paris, France, 1868), actress, poet. Uninhibited beauty of the mid-nineteenth-century stage; famed in Mazeppa. Author of Infelicia (collected poems, 1868); noted for marriages, divorces, and friendships with major literary figures of the time.

MENOCAL, ANICETO GARCIA (b. Cuba, 1836; d. New York, N.Y., 1908), naval officer, civil engineer. Graduated Rensselaer Polytechnic, 1862. An engineer officer in the U.S. Navy, 1874–98, he engaged officially and privately in surveys and negotiations for an interoceanic canal in Panama and Nicaragua. He favored Nicaraguan route.

MENOHER, CHARLES THOMAS (b. Johnstown, Pa., 1862; d. 1930), soldier. Graduated West Point, 1886. Commanded 42nd (Rainbow) Division, World War I; as chief of Air Service, 1919–22, was troubled by controversy with Col. William Mitchell. Retired as major-general, 1926.

MERCER, CHARLES FENTON (b. Fredericksburg, Va., 1778; d. Fairfax Co., Va., 1858), lawyer, businessman, Virginia legislator. Son of James Mercer. Congressman, Federalist and Whig, from Virginia, 1817–39; favored free Negro colonization, suppression of slave trade, internal improvements.

MERCER, HENRY CHAPMAN (b. Doylestown, Pa., 1856; d. Doylestown, 1930), archeologist, antiquarian, inventor.

MERCER, HUGH (*b. Aberdeenshire, Scotland, c. 1725; d. near Princeton, N.J., 1777*), physician, Revolutionary soldier. Educated at University of Aberdeen, Mercer joined the Jacobite army in 1745 and was present at the battle of Culloden. Emigrating to America *c.* 1746, he settled near present Mercersburg, Pa., where he practiced his profession. During the French and Indian War, he served gallantly in the line and, as commandant at Fort Pitt, conducted important negotiations for peace with the Six Nations and other tribes. At the suggestion of George Washington, Mercer removed his practice to Fredericksburg, Va. after the war. Elected colonel, 3rd Virginia Regiment, January 1776, he was named brigadier-general by the Continental Congress in June. Commanding the Flying Camp in northern New Jersey, he accompanied Washington's army on its retreat across the state in the fall of 1776 and led a brigade at the battle of Trenton. Attempting to rally his disordered command at the battle of Princeton, Jan. 3, 1777, he was mortally wounded.

MERCER, JAMES (*b. Stafford Co., Va., 1736; d. Richmond, Va., 1793*), Revolutionary patriot, Virginia jurist. Half-brother of John F. Mercer.

MERCER, JESSE (*b. Halifax Co., N.C., 1769; d. Butts Co., Ga., 1841*), Baptist clergyman. Raised in Wilkes Co., Ga., he was ordained there, 1789, and held a number of frontier pastorates. A tactful leader in his denomination, he was a benefactor of Mercer University which was named in his honor.

MERCER, JOHN FRANCIS (*b. Stafford Co., Va., 1759; d. Philadelphia, Pa., 1821*), Revolutionary soldier, Virginia and Maryland legislator. Half-brother of James Mercer. After serving as a member of Congress from Virginia, 1782–85, he removed to Anne Arundel Co., Md. As delegate from Maryland to the Federal Convention, 1787, he strongly opposed the centralizing character of the U.S. Constitution and spoke and voted against its ratification. Congressman, (Democrat) Republican, from Maryland, 1791–94, he was chosen governor of Maryland, 1801, and served until 1803.

MERCER, LEWIS PYLE (*b. Kennett Square, Pa., 1847; d. Cincinnati, O., 1906*), Swedenborgian clergyman. Active in the ministry *post* 1870, notably in Detroit, Mich., Chicago, Ill., and Cincinnati.

MERCER, MARGARET (*b. Annapolis, Md., 1791; d. near Leesburg, Va., 1846*), anti-slavery worker, educator. Daughter of John F. Mercer.

MERCIER, CHARLES ALFRED (*b. McDonogh, La., 1816; d. New Orleans, La., 1894*), physician, Creole author. Brother-in-law of Pierre Soulé. Founder of the Athénée Louisianais, 1876.

MERCUR, ULYSSES (*b. Towanda, Pa., 1818; d. Wallingford, Pa., 1887*), Pennsylvania jurist. As congressman, Republican, from Pennsylvania, 1865–72, he was an active advocate of extreme Reconstruction measures. Justice, supreme court of Pennsylvania, 1872–83; chief justice, 1883–87.

MEREDITH, EDWIN THOMAS (*b. near Avoca, Iowa, 1876; d. 1928*), journalist, publisher. Founded *Successful Farming*, 1902; *Better Homes and Gardens*, 1922. Forced a reform in the type of advertising handled by farm papers; served as U.S. secretary of agriculture, 1920–21.

MEREDITH, SAMUEL (*b. Philadelphia, Pa., 1741; d. Mount Pleasant Township, Pa., 1817*), Revolutionary soldier, financier, Pennsylvania legislator. Brother-in-law of George Clymer. First treasurer of the United States, 1789–1801.

MEREDITH, WILLIAM MORRIS (*b. Philadelphia, Pa., 1799; d. Philadelphia, 1873*), lawyer, Pennsylvania legislator and official. A leading Whig, Meredith was U.S. secretary of the treasury, March 1849—July 1850; in his annual report for 1849 he set forth an elaborate argument for the protective tariff. He served as attorney-general of Pennsylvania, 1861–67.

MERGENTHALER, OTTMAR (*b. Hachtel, Germany, 1854; d. Baltimore, Md., 1899*), maker of watches and scientific instruments, inventor of the linotype. Came to America, 1872. Completed the first direct-casting linotype, July 1884; received first patent for it, August 1884; with associates, organized National Typographic Co. for its manufacture, 1885. The first of 12 machines made by the company for the *New York Tribune* was used to compose a part of the issue of the paper on July 3, 1886. After resigning from the manufacturing company in 1888, Mergenthaler continued to add to the value of his invention by devising more than fifty patented improvements to it.

MERGLER, MARIE JOSEPHA (*b. Mainstockheim, Bavaria, 1851; d. Los Angeles, Calif., 1901*), physician. Came to America as a child. Graduated Woman's Medical College, Chicago, Ill., 1879; practiced medicine *post* 1881 in Chicago. Taught gynecology at Woman's Medical College and at Northwestern University; was notable for her success in abdominal surgery.

MERRIAM, AUGUSTUS CHAPMAN (*b. Leyden, N.Y., 1843; d. Athens, Greece, 1895*), philologist, archeologist. Graduated Columbia, 1866. *Post* 1868, taught Greek and Latin at Columbia; *post* 1876, taught Greek only; appointed professor of Greek archeology and epigraphy, Columbia, 1890. A productive scholar, Merriam was author of a number of research monographs which won him international reputation.

MERRIAM, CHARLES (*b. West Brookfield, Mass., 1806; d. 1887*), publisher. Established a printing house and bookshop in Springfield, Mass., 1831, which became G. & C. Merriam, 1832. Acquiring the rights to publish Noah Webster's *American Dictionary of the English Language* in 1843, the Merriams with the editorial assistance of Chauncey A. Goodrich republished the work in unabridged revised form with the greatest success.

MERRIAM, HENRY CLAY (*b. Houlton, Maine, 1837; d. Portland, Maine, 1912*), soldier. Serving in the Union Army, 1862–65, Merriam received the Congressional Medal for bravery in leading assault at Fort Blakely, April 1865. Commissioned major, 1866, he served on the Western frontiers, rising to the rank of brigadier-general, June 1897. He organized the Philippines Expeditionary Force, 1898, suppressed labor riots at Coeur d'Alène mines, 1899, and retired as major-general, 1901 (1903).

MERRIAM, WILLIAM RUSH (*b. Wadham's Mills, N.Y., 1849; d. Fort Sewall, Fla., 1931*), banker, Minnesota legislator. Raised in St. Paul, Minn. Republican governor of Minnesota, 1889–93; highly efficient director of the Twelfth Census, 1899–1903.

MERRICK, EDWIN THOMAS (*b. Wilbraham, Mass., 1808; d. New Orleans, La., 1897*), lawyer. Admitted to Ohio bar, 1833; practiced in Clinton, La., *post* 1838. Chief justice of Louisiana, 1855–65.

MERRICK, FREDERICK (*b. Wilbraham, Mass., 1810; d. Delaware, O., 1894*), Methodist clergyman, educator. Identified with Ohio Wesleyan University *post* 1843 as professor of science and moral philosophy, as president, 1860–73, and as lecturer on religion thereafter.

MERRICK, PLINY (*b. Brookfield, Mass., 1794; d. 1867*), lawyer, Massachusetts jurist and legislator. Senior counsel to Prof. John W. Webster at his trial for the murder of Dr. George Parkman, 1850. Judge, state supreme judicial court, 1853–64.

MERRICK, SAMUEL VAUGHAN (*b. Hallowell, Maine, 1801; d. Philadelphia, Pa., 1870*), engine manufacturer, railroad executive. An early promoter of the Pennsylvania Railroad Co., Merrick served as its first president, 1847–49.

MERRILL, DANIEL (*b. Rowley, Mass., 1765; d. Sedgwick, Maine, 1833*), Congregational and Baptist clergyman, Revolutionary soldier. Took the lead (1813) in securing charter and land grant for "Maine Literary and Theological Association," later Colby College.

MERRILL, ELMER TRUESDELL (*b. Millville, Mass., 1860; d. Santa Barbara, Calif., 1936*), Episcopal clergyman, educator, classicist, church historian. Graduated Wesleyan University, 1881; studied also at Yale and at University of Berlin. His two principal teaching positions were at Wesleyan (professor of

Latin, 1888–1905) and at University of Chicago, 1908–25. He was best known for his work on Catullus and the younger Pliny. [*Supp. 2*]

MERRILL, GEORGE EDMANDS (*b. Charlestown, Mass., 1846; d. Hamilton, N.Y., 1908*), Baptist clergyman. Graduated Harvard, 1869. After holding pastorates in several Massachusetts cities and in Colorado, he served as president of Colgate University, 1901–08.

MERRILL, GEORGE PERKINS (*b. Auburn, Maine, 1854; d. Auburn, 1929*), geologist. Graduated University of Maine, 1879. Joining the staff of the U.S. National Museum, 1881, he remained there the rest of his life, becoming head curator, 1897, and developing the department of geology and paleontology into one of the great collections of the world. Merrill was also a pioneer in research on building-stones and the processes of rock-weathering, on meteorites and on the history of American physical geology. He was author, among other works, of *A Treatise on Rock, Rock-weathering and Soils* (1897), *Non-metallic Minerals* (1904) and *The First One Hundred Years of American Geology* (1924).

MERRILL, JAMES CUSHING (*b. Cambridge, Mass., 1853; d. Washington, D.C., 1902*), army surgeon, ornithologist. Librarian, U.S. Surgeon-General's office, 1897–1902.

MERRILL, JAMES GRISWOLD (*b. Montague, Mass., 1840; d. Mountain Lakes, N.J., 1920*), Congregational clergyman, educator. After holding a number of pastorates, Merrill served as editor of the *Christian Mirror*; he became professor of logic and dean at Fisk University, 1898. Named acting president of the University in 1899, he served as president, 1901–08. Among his outstanding achievements in office were the improvement of the endowment, confirmation of the policy of having a bi-racial faculty and promotion of the Fisk Jubilee Singers.

MERRILL, JOSHUA (*b. Duxbury, Mass., 1820; d. 1904*), chemist, pioneer oil refiner. Partner and successor of Samuel Downer. Developed many important technological processes, among them the invention (1869) of a method of distilling by steam without partial decomposition, thereby producing less odorous paraffine lubricating oils.

MERRILL, SAMUEL (*b. Peacham, Vt., 1792; d. Indianapolis, Ind., 1855*), lawyer, Indiana official and legislator. Removed to Vevay, Ind., 1816. Successful in business and public life, particularly as president of the State Bank of Indiana, Merrill purchased a bookstore, 1850, which became a constituent of the Bowen-Merrill, later the Bobbs-Merrill, publishing company.

MERRILL, SELAH (*b. Canton Center, Conn., 1837; d. near East Oakland, Calif., 1909*), Congregational clergyman, archeologist. U.S. consul at Jerusalem,

1882–1907, except during President Cleveland's two terms; author of *Ancient Jerusalem* (1908).

MERRILL, STEPHEN MASON (*b. near Mount Pleasant, O., 1825; d. Keyport, N.J., 1905*), Methodist clergyman. A Midwest leader of his denomination, Merrill was elected bishop, 1872, and made his headquarters thereafter in St. Paul, Minn., and Chicago, Ill. He was celebrated for his encyclopedic knowledge of Methodist law.

MERRILL, STUART FITZRANDOLPH (*b. Hempstead, N.Y., 1863; d. Versailles, France, 1915*), French symbolist poet. Raised in Paris and educated there, he returned to live in New York City, 1884–89, but resided in France thereafter save for occasional visits. The only book which he wrote in English was *Pastels in Prose* (1890, with a preface by W. D. Howells).

MERRILL, WILLIAM BRADFORD (*b. Salisbury, N.H., 1861; d. 1928*), newspaper editor and manager. Managing editor, Philadelphia *Press*, 1884–91; *New York Press*, 1891–1901; New York *World*, 1901–08. Attracting the attention of William R. Hearst because of his financial abilities, Merrill became manager of the *New York American,* 1908, and in 1917 was made general manager of all the Hearst papers. He retired in 1927.

MERRILL, WILLIAM EMERY (*b. Fort Howard, Wis., 1837; d. 1891*), soldier, engineer. Graduated West Point, 1859. Served with distinction as a military engineer throughout the Civil War and as chief engineer of the Division of the Missouri; *post* 1870, he devoted himself mainly to river and harbor improvement work. Originated (1878–79) the idea of canalizing the Ohio River from Pittsburgh to its mouth; inaugurating the project in 1879, he worked on it until his death.

MERRIMON, AUGUSTUS SUMMERFIELD (*b. Cherryfields, N.C., 1830; d. 1892*), lawyer, North Carolina politician, U.S. senator and jurist.

MERRITT, ANNA LEA (*b. Philadelphia, Pa., 1844; d. London, England, 1930*), painter, etcher.

MERRITT, ISRAEL JOHN (*b. New York, N.Y., 1829; d. New York, 1911*), salvage expert, inventor. Patented (1865) a pontoon device for raising sunken vessels by displacement, which completely revolutionized the salvage business.

MERRITT, LEONIDAS (*b. Chautauqua Co., N.Y., 1844; d. Duluth, Minn., 1926*), prospector. Raised in Oneota, Minn. After working as lumberman and iron prospector, Merritt with his brothers located deposits of iron ore in the Mesabi Range, 1887. The brothers organized the Mountain Iron Co. to exploit their find, July 1890, and secured the financial participation of John D. Rockefeller. In 1893, Rocke-

feller obtained full control of the mining and transportation enterprises initiated by the Merritts.

MERRITT, WESLEY (*b. New York, N.Y., 1834; d. Natural Bridge, Va., 1910*), soldier. Raised in Illinois. Graduated West Point, 1860. Served as aide-de-camp to Gen. P. St. G. Cooke, 1861; promoted captain, 1862; commissioned brigadier-general of volunteers, 1863. Commanded reserve cavalry at Gettysburg; following continual service in Virginia rose to brevet rank of major-general. After frontier service in the West, 1866–79, he was superintendent at West Point, 1882–87. Commissioned brigadier-general, regular army, 1887, he commanded successively the departments of Missouri, Dakota, Missouri again and the Department of the East. In command of the first Philippine expedition, 1898, supported by Adm. Geo. Dewey, he took the city of Manila in August in a campaign complicated by the presence of the Philippine insurgent army. After a short tour as military governor of the Philippines, Merritt resumed his old command of the Department of the East and retired as major-general, 1900.

MERRY, ANN BRUNTON (*b. London, England, 1769; d. Alexandria, Va., 1808*), actress, theatrical manager. Made debut at Bath, England, 1785; married Robert Merry, a minor poet, 1791. Came to America as member of Philadelphia Company, 1796. Widowed, she married Thomas Wignell, director of the Philadelphia Theatre, 1803; on his death, she married William Warren, 1806. A woman of great charm and integrity, Mrs. Merry was one of the really notable players on the early American stage.

MERRY, WILLIAM LAWRENCE (*b. New York, N.Y., 1842; d. Battle Creek, Mich., 1911*), sea captain, merchant. Principal protagonist for Nicaragua Isthmian Canal, 1890–95; served as U.S. minister to Nicaragua, Costa Rica and El Salvador, 1897–1907, remaining as minister to Costa Rica until 1911.

MERVINE, WILLIAM (*b. Philadelphia, Pa., 1791; d. Utica, N.Y., 1868*), naval officer. Headed landing detachment of marines and sailors at Monterey, Calif., July 1846; in October, commanded landing party which engaged the Mexicans near Los Angeles. Commanded Gulf Blockading Squadron, May–September, 1861. Retired as rear-admiral, 1866.

MERZ, KARL (*b. Bensheim, Germany, 1836; d. Wooster, O., 1890*), musician, teacher of music. Came to America, 1854. After teaching at various towns in Pennsylvania and Virginia, Merz directed musical studies at Oxford Female College, Ohio, 1861–82, and at Wooster University, 1882–90. He was author of a number of musical textbooks and of *Music and Culture* (1890).

MESERVE, NATHANIEL (*b. Newington, N.H., c. 1705; d. Louisbourg, Cape Breton Is., Canada, 1758*), shipwright, colonial soldier. Constructed frigate

America at Portsmouth, N.H., 1749; served as master-constructor under Loudoun and Amherst, 1756–58.

MESSER, ASA (*b. Methuen, Mass., 1769; d. Providence, R.I., 1836*), Baptist clergyman, educator. Graduated Rhode Island College, 1790. After teaching there, 1791–1802, Messer was made president and served until 1826. During his term, the institution made sure progress, Nicholas Brown became its patron, and its name was changed to Brown University. Messer resigned because of antagonism aroused by his alleged Arianism.

MESSLER, THOMAS DOREMUS (*b. Somerville, N.J., 1833; d. Cresson, Pa., 1893*), railway executive. Evolved the "Messler System" of railroad accounting, 1857, while auditor of the Pittsburgh, Fort Wayne and Chicago Railway.

MESSMER, SEBASTIAN GEBHARD (*b. Goldach, Switzerland, 1847; d. Goldach, 1930*), Roman Catholic clergyman. Educated at University of Innsbrück, Austria. Came to America, 1871; taught theology and canon law at Seton Hall College until 1889 and at Catholic University of America, 1889–91. Consecrated bishop of Green Bay, 1892, he became archbishop of Milwaukee, 1903. A broadminded man, sympathetic with labor and trade unionism, he upheld progressive reforms and was notable for his encouragement of educational institutions.

METCALF, HENRY HARRISON (*b. Newport, N.H., 1841; d. 1932*), New Hampshire editor. Published a number of Democratic newspapers and also the *Granite Monthly*, 1877–1919.

METCALF, JOEL HASTINGS (*b. Meadville, Pa., 1866; d. Portland, Maine, 1925*), Unitarian clergyman, astronomer.

METCALF, THERON (*b. Franklin, Mass., 1784; d. 1875*), Massachusetts jurist. Graduated Brown, 1805. Practiced in Massachusetts *post* 1808, principally at Dedham. Compiled *Reports of Cases Argued . . . Supreme Judicial Court of Massachusetts* (1841–50); served on Massachusetts supreme bench, 1848–65.

METCALF, WILLARD LEROY (*b. Lowell, Mass., 1858; d. 1925*), landscape and figure painter.

METCALF, WILLIAM (*b. Pittsburgh, Pa., 1838; d. Pittsburgh, 1909*), metallurgist, steel manufacturer. Graduated Rensselaer Polytechnic, 1858. As general superintendent, Fort Pitt Foundry, 1859–65, he supervised production of more than three thousand heavy guns for the United States, no one of which was ever reported as failing in service. Thereafter he was associated with the Crescent Steel Works and the Braeburn Steel Co. He was one of the first practical experts to stress the importance of mechanical treatment and heat treatment of steel as compared with chemical composition, and also the different effects of different kinds of tests of strength.

METCALFE, SAMUEL LYTLER (*b. near Winchester, Va., 1798; d. Cape May, N.J., 1856*), chemist, physician. Author of the *Kentucky Harmonist* (1820) and *A Collection of Some of the Most Interesting Narratives of the Indian Warfare in the West* (1821); also *Caloric* (1837, 1843), an elaborate study of the nature of heat.

METCALFE, THOMAS (*b. Fauquier Co., Va., 1780; d. Nicholas Co., Ky., 1855*), stone-mason, Kentucky politician and legislator. A strong exponent of Western democracy while a Kentucky congressman, 1819–28, he followed Henry Clay in voting for John Q. Adams, 1825. Nominated for governor by the Adams-Clay convention, 1827, he was elected and served, 1828–32. As governor, he endorsed protective tariffs, federal aid for internal improvements; he denounced nullification and Jackson's general policy. As U.S. senator, Whig, from Kentucky, 1848–49, he denounced secession, declaring that Kentucky would uphold the Union.

METTAUER, JOHN PETER (*b. Prince Edward Co., Va., 1787; d. 1875*), physician, surgeon. M.D., University of Pennsylvania, 1809. Entering practice in his native county, he continued to work there except for brief intervals until his death. A daring and original surgeon, he was a pioneer in genito-urinary surgery and in lithotomy was regarded as second only to Benjamin W. Dudley. He first performed an operation for vesico-vaginal fistula in August 1838, and was called by J. Marion Sims one of two men who "stand out in bold relief amongst those who have devoted some time" to such surgery. In 1837 Mettauer organized Prince Edward Medical Institute which became the medical department of Randolph-Macon College, 1847. Eccentric but respected, he wore on all occasions, even while operating, a high stove-pipe hat; his daughter said she had never seen him without it, and he left instructions that he be buried in it.

METZ, CHRISTIAN (*b. Neuwied, Prussia, 1794; d. Amana, Iowa, 1867*), founder of the Christian-Communist community of Amana. Leader *post* 1823 of a German pietist sect, Metz emigrated with his followers to America *c.* 1842, settling at Ebenezer near Buffalo, N.Y. Seeking cheaper land and greater seclusion, he led his brethren westward to Iowa in 1854 where, with extraordinary executive ability and sincere piety, he presided over the most successful experiment in communal living attempted in 19th century America.

MEYER, GEORGE VON LENGERKE (*b. Boston, Mass., 1858; d. 1918*), banker, Massachusetts legislator, diplomat. Graduated Harvard, 1879. Active in Republican politics, Meyer was appointed U.S. ambassador to Italy, 1900; he served with success in this post and was the means by which Pres. Theodore Roosevelt's peace proposals were presented to the Czar of Russia, 1905. As U.S. postmaster-general,

1907–09, Meyer served with ability and efficiency, as also in the post of secretary of the navy, 1909–13.

MEYER, HENRY CODDINGTON (*b. Hamburg, Germany, 1844; d. Montclair, N.J., 1935*), dealer in plumbing fixtures, Union soldier, pioneer in sanitary engineering. Founded *Plumber and Sanitary Engineer,* 1877, which after various changes of title, became the *Engineering Record,* 1890. [*Supp.* 1]

MEYER, MARTIN ABRAHAM (*b. San Francisco, Calif., 1879; d. San Francisco, 1923*), rabbi, Semitic scholar. Ministered at Albany and Brooklyn, N.Y.; served Temple Emanu El, San Francisco, *post* 1910. Active in philanthropy and as Zionist.

MEZES, SIDNEY EDWARD (*b. Belmont, Calif., 1863; d. Altadena, Calif., 1931*), educator. Graduated University of California, 1884; Ph.D., Harvard, 1893; taught philosophy at University of Texas *post* 1894, serving also as dean, and as president, 1908–14. As president of the College of the City of New York, 1914–27, he oversaw it during a period of extraordinary growth and was responsible for the establishment of its schools of technology, business and education. At the request of his brother-in-law, Edward M. House, and by direction of Pres. Woodrow Wilson, he brought together the body of experts known as "The Inquiry," 1917. This group, which collected data that might be needed eventually at the Peace Conference, was later constituted at Paris under Mezes as a special research section. A good part of the credit for the able service which these men rendered both before and during the negotiations at Paris belongs to Mezes who selected and trained them.

MIANTONOMO (*d. near Norwich, Conn., 1643*), Narragansett Indian chief. Nephew of Canonicus. Gave aid to the English in the Pequot War, 1637; in March 1638, signed deed to William Coddington and his associates for the island of Rhode Island.

MICHAËLIUS, JONAS (*b. Grootebroek, Holland, 1584; date and place of death unknown*). Came to New Amsterdam, 1628, as first minister of the Dutch Reformed Church to serve there. After conflict with Peter Minuit and the members of the Council, Michaëlius returned to Holland, 1632, and denounced them to the West India Co. as oppressors and frauds.

MICHAUX, ANDRÉ (*b. Versailles, France, 1746; d. Madagascar, 1802*), explorer, silviculturist. After extensive travels in Europe and the Near East, Michaux came to New York, 1785, directed by the French government to make a study of forest trees of North America. Between the year of his arrival and 1793 he made collecting journeys in the southern Appalachians, in Spanish Florida, in the Carolina mountains, in the Bahamas and in Canada, even visiting the vicinity of Hudson Bay. A supporter of the French Revolu-

tion, he acted as an emissary from Edmond C. Genet to George Rogers Clark, 1793; he traveled extensively in the Midwest, 1793–96, before returning to France. His manuscript journals, crude and laconic in form, remained unpublished until 1889.

MICHAUX, FRANÇOIS ANDRÉ (*b. Versailles, France, 1770; d. France, 1855*), silviculturist, traveler, botanist. Son of André Michaux. Accompanied his father to America; resided in New York and vicinity and in Charleston, S.C., 1785–90. Returning to France, he became an ardent partisan of the French Revolution. Coming again to America, 1801, commissioned by the French government to sell the tree nurseries which his father had established in the United States, he traveled extensively through Ohio, Kentucky, Tennessee and the Carolinas before going back to France, 1803. Michaux made another voyage of travel and study in the United States, 1806–09. He was author of, among other books, *Voyage à l'ouest des monts Alléghanys* (Paris, 1804; in English, London, 1805) and *Histoire des Arbres forestiers de l'Amérique Septentrionale* (Paris, 1810–13). The second book is better known as *The North American Sylva;* it was later supplemented by Thomas Nuttall.

MICHEL, VIRGIL GEORGE (*b. St. Paul, Minn., 1890; d. Collegeville, Minn., 1938*), Roman Catholic clergyman, Benedictine, philosopher, educator. Organized liturgical movement in America; founded (1925) and edited *Orate Fratres.* [*Supp.* 2]

MICHEL, WILLIAM MIDDLETON (*b. Charleston, S.C., 1822; d. 1894*), physician, Confederate surgeon. Graduated École de Médecine, Paris, 1845; Medical College of the State of South Carolina, 1846. Opened Summer Medical Institute of Charleston, 1847, in which he lectured on anatomy, physiology and obstetrics until 1860. Professor of physiology and histology, Medical College of South Carolina, 1868–94.

MICHELSON, ALBERT ABRAHAM (*b. Strelno, Prussia, 1852; d. Pasadena, Calif., 1931*), physicist. Came to America as a child; raised in California and Nevada. Graduated Annapolis, 1873. After serving as instructor in physics and chemistry there, 1875–79, Michelson studied at the universities of Berlin, Heidelberg and Paris. He was professor of physics at Case School, 1883–89, at Clark University, 1889–92, and was head of the department of physics, University of Chicago, 1892–1931. Michelson also served on international scientific committees, received eleven honorary degrees and numerous medals, and was member or officer of the world's leading scientific societies. His major work dealt with light; 68 of his eighty significant papers were on that subject. His experiments in measuring velocity of light demonstrated ingenuity, unusual precision; the general confidence in his integrity and ability was so great that his self-checked results were invariably accepted. His other studies in light concerned optical interference. Like other experts, he first believed that light consists of electromagnetic wave motion carried through ether, and that its velocity could serve as a constant for measuring cosmical motions. His experiments refuted this point of view and resulted in new basic theories leading to the relativity concept. Michelson's echelon spectroscope gave direct evidence of the effect of heat upon molecular motion and disclosed the effect of a magnetic field upon a source of radiation. He developed a method for measuring diameters of stars, adopted wave length of cadmium light as a standard measuring unit, determined earth's rigidity and viscosity to be comparable to that of steel, and established a center for producing high-grade diffraction gratings.

MICHENER, EZRA (*b. Chester Co., Pa., 1794; d. near Toughkenamon, Pa., 1887*), physician, botanist. M.D., University of Pennsylvania, 1818. Invented apparatus for treatment of femur fractures; was one of first physicians to use ergot as a uterine tonic.

MICHIE, PETER SMITH (*b. Brechin, Scotland, 1839; d. West Point, N.Y., 1901*), Union soldier. Came to America as a child; was raised in Cincinnati, O. Graduated West Point, 1863. Received brevet of brigadier-general for able Civil War service. Instructor in science at West Point, 1867–1901, he was author of a number of textbooks on mechanics, physics and astronomy.

MICHIKINIKWA. [See LITTLE TURTLE, *c.* 1752–1812.]

MICHLER, NATHANIEL (*b. Easton, Pa., 1827; d. Saratoga Springs, N.Y., 1881*), Union officer. Graduated West Point, 1848. Performed notable work as a topographical engineer and as a builder of defensive fortifications throughout the Civil War. He was regarded as one of the leading military topographers of his time. [*Supp.* 1]

MIDDLETON, ARTHUR (*b. Charleston, S.C., 1681; d. 1737*), South Carolina official and legislator. Headed movement in Assembly to overthrow control of proprietors, 1716–19. President of the Council under Gov. Francis Nicholson and later under Gov. Johnson, he administered the colony as acting governor, 1725–29. In constant difficulties with the legislature over currency disputes, he was effective in subduing Indian troubles on the border and in counteracting French influence. His acquisitiveness and earlier revolutionary activity, however, embarrassed him in his appeals for loyal support from the Assembly.

MIDDLETON, ARTHUR (*b. "Middleton Place," near Charleston, S.C. 1742; d. Goose Creek, S.C., 1787*), Revolutionary leader. Son of Henry Middleton (1717–1784). Read law at the Middle Temple, London, returning in 1763 to serve as justice of the peace and as a member of the South Carolina Assembly.

Active *post* 1772 in all the movements toward revolution, Middleton was elected to the Continental Congress, 1776, and was a signer of the Declaration of Independence. He continued to be elected to Congress but was irregular in his attendance and left little mark on the records of that body.

MIDDLETON, HENRY (*b. probably "The Oaks," near Charleston, S.C., 1717; d. 1784*), planter, South Carolina legislator. Son of Arthur Middleton (1681–1737). A great landowner, a churchman and a conservative, he became a leader in opposition to British policy *post* 1770. Chosen to represent South Carolina in the Continental Congress, July 1774, he became second president of the Congress and served, October 1774—May 1775. A moderate, hoping for accommodation with Britain, he resigned from Congress, February 1776. He continued public service as president of the congress of South Carolina, of the legislative council, and *post* January 1779, of the newly created state senate. After the surrender of Charleston, 1780, he "took protection" under the British but lost no reputation thereby.

MIDDLETON, HENRY (*b. London, England, 1770; d. Charleston, S.C. 1846*), South Carolina legislator, diplomat. Son of Arthur Middleton (1742–1787). Served as governor of South Carolina, 1810–12, as congressman, 1815–19, and then as U.S. minister to Russia. As minister, he negotiated the convention of 1824 to regulate Pacific trade and fisheries. Returning to the United States in 1830, he became a leader of the Union party in opposition to Calhoun's nullification policy.

MIDDLETON, JOHN IZARD (*b. near Charleston, S.C., 1785; d. Paris, France, 1849*), painter, archeologist. Son of Arthur Middleton (1742–1787). Author and illustrator of *Grecian Remains in Italy* (London, 1812).

MIDDLETON, NATHANIEL RUSSELL (*b. Charleston, S.C., 1810; d. Charleston, 1890*), planter, educator. Great-grandson of Henry Middleton (1717–1784). Graduated College of Charleston, 1828; served as its president, 1857–80.

MIDDLETON, PETER (*b. Scotland; d. New York, N.Y., 1781*), physician. M.D., University of St. Andrews, 1752. Practiced in New York City *post* 1752 in which year (or possibly later) he and Dr. John Bard made in New York one of the first dissections of a human body for the purposes of medical instruction on record in America. A founder of the Medical School of King's College (Columbia), 1767, Middleton taught physiology, pathology and materia medica there. He was also one of the incorporators of New York Hospital, 1771.

MIDDLETON, THOMAS COOKE (*b. Philadelphia, Pa., 1842; d. Villanova, Pa., 1923*), Roman Catholic clergyman, Augustinian. Identified for most of his life with Villanova College, he was a founder and first president (1884–90) of the American Catholic Historical Society.

MIELATZ, CHARLES FREDERICK WILLIAM (*b. Breddin, Germany, 1860; d. New York, N.Y., 1919*), etcher. Came to America as a child; studied at the Chicago School of Design. Celebrated for his renderings of picturesque corners in New York City.

MIELZINER, MOSES (*b. Schubin, Posen, Germany, 1828; d. Cincinnati, O., 1903*), rabbi, educator. Educated by his father and at University of Berlin; Ph.D., University of Giessen, 1859. Came to America, 1865. After ministering for a short time in New York and conducting a private boys' school there, he became professor of the Talmud at Hebrew Union College, 1879, and held that chair until his death. Chairman of the committee of editors of the *Union Prayerbook* (1892–94) and author of a number of works, Mielziner served as president of Hebrew Union, 1900–03.

MIFFLIN, LLOYD (*b. Columbia, Pa., 1846; d. Columbia, 1921*), painter, poet. Studied art with Thomas Moran and at Düsseldorf, Germany. Author of a number of volumes of verse in the sonnet form from which he made a selection, *Collected Sonnets* (1905).

MIFFLIN, THOMAS (*b. Philadelphia, Pa., 1744; d. Lancaster, Pa., 1800*), merchant, Pennsylvania legislator, Revolutionary soldier. Graduated College of Philadelphia (University of Pennsylvania), 1760. Conspicuous in opposition to British policy *post* 1765, he was one of the youngest and most radical members of the first Continental Congress and helped to draft the Association of 1774. Entering military service, 1775, he was read out of meeting by his fellow Quakers. Appointed Washington's aide-de-camp, June 1775, he became quartermaster-general of the Continental Army in August and held that post except for a brief period until March 1778. Promoted major-general, February 1777, he assisted in the defense of Philadelphia. Involved in the congressional plot to advance Gen. Gates over Gen. Washington, Mifflin aided the cabal as a member of the board of war but soon disclaimed all part in it. He then met criticism of his record as quartermaster with a demand for a formal inquiry which was never made. He resigned definitely from military service, August 1778, and turned to state politics. A member of Congress, 1782–84, he served as its president, December 1783–June 1784; a member of the Federal Convention, 1787, he was a strong supporter of the new U.S. Constitution. During three terms as (Democrat) Republican governor of Pennsylvania, 1790–99, he sympathized with Jeffersonian ideas, openly favored the French and, after first evading action in the Whiskey Insurrection, later called for speedy action against the insurgents. His last three years as governor were marked by increasing negligence and laxity. He died penniless.

MIFFLIN, WARNER (*b. Accomac Co., Va., 1745; d. near Camden, Del., 1798*), farmer, Quaker reformer, anti-slavery worker.

MIGNOT, LOUIS REMY (*b. Charleston, S.C., 1831; d. Brighton, England, 1870*), landscape painter. Studied in Holland, 1851–55; was associate and follower of Frederick E. Church. Sympathetic to the Confederacy, Mignot resided abroad *post* 1862.

MILBURN, WILLIAM HENRY (*b. Philadelphia, Pa., 1823; d. Santa Barbara, Calif., 1903*), Methodist clergyman. Rode circuit in Illinois, 1843–44; held numerous pastorates in both North and South; was chaplain of Congress four times.

MILES, EDWARD (*b. Yarmouth, England, 1752; d. Philadelphia, Pa., 1828*), miniature painter. Court painter in both England and Russia. Miles's work was distinguished for good drawing and exquisiteness of finish. Coming to Philadelphia, Pa., 1807, he worked there as a drawing master thereafter.

MILES, GEORGE HENRY (*b. Baltimore, Md., 1824; d. near Emmitsburg, Md., 1871*), poet, playwright, educator.

MILES, HENRY ADOLPHUS (*b. Grafton, Mass., 1809; d. Hingham, Mass., 1895*), Unitarian clergyman. Author of *Lowell as It Was and Is* (1845), a rosy picture of the development of industry at that place.

MILES, JOHN. [See MYLES, JOHN, *c. 1621–1683.*]

MILES, MANLY (*b. Homer, N.Y., 1826; d. probably Lansing, Mich., 1898*), physician, naturalist, agriculturist. Raised in Michigan. Graduated Rush Medical College, 1850. Held first chair of practical agriculture in the United States (Michigan State, 1865–74); served later as professor of agriculture at University of Illinois and at Massachusetts Agricultural College. A constant collector of natural history specimens, he was author of several books, chief among which were *Stock Breeding* (1879), *Silos, Ensilage and Silage* (1889) and *Land Drainage* (1892).

MILES, NELSON APPLETON (*b. near Westminster, Mass., 1839; d. Washington, D.C., 1925*), soldier. Volunteering at outbreak of Civil War, he was commissioned captain of infantry and served through the Peninsular campaign on Gen. O. O. Howard's staff. For gallantry at Fair Oaks (May 31–June 1, 1862), he won promotion to lieutenant-colonel of the 61st New York Volunteers; he was made colonel in September. Distinguished at Antietam, Fredericksburg, Chancellorsville, the Wilderness and at Petersburg, Miles was promoted brigadier-general of volunteers, May 1864; in October 1865, he was made major-general, commanding the II Army Corps. Commissioned colonel, regular army, July 1866, he assumed command of the 5th Infantry, 1869. Thereafter, he served against the hostile Indians west of the Mississippi until 1891.

Notable among his Indian campaigns were those against the Nez Percé (1877) and against the Apaches under Geronimo (1886). Promoted major-general, 1890, he commanded the troops which quelled the riots accompanying the Pullman strike at Chicago, 1894. Becoming by seniority commander-in-chief of the army, 1895, Miles directed organization and training of troops for the Spanish-American War and led the force which pacified Puerto Rico. Advanced to lieutenant-general, 1901, he retired, 1903.

MILES, RICHARD PIUS (*b. Prince George's Co., Md., 1791; d. Nashville, Tenn., 1860*), Roman Catholic clergyman, Dominican. Raised in Kentucky. After service as a missionary-pastor in Ohio *post* 1828, he became a superior in his order, 1833, and was elected provincial, 1837. Consecrated first bishop of Nashville, 1838, he served ably until his death.

MILES, WILLIAM PORCHER (*b. Walterboro, S.C., 1822; d. Ascension Parish, La., 1899*), educator, sugar planter, politician. Graduated College of Charleston, 1842; taught mathematics there, 1843–55. Conservative Democratic mayor of Charleston, 1855–57, Miles served as congressman from South Carolina, 1857–60. Eloquent in support of slavery and secession, he was chairman of the foreign relations committee of the South Carolina secession convention, signed the ordinance of secession and was one of the three commissioners who arranged the terms of surrender of Fort Sumter. He represented the Charleston district in the Confederate Congress during its entire existence. President of the University of South Carolina, 1880–82, he resigned to manage his father-in-law's extensive sugar plantations.

MILHOLLAND, INEZ. [See BOISSEVAIN, INEZ MILHOLLAND, 1886–1916.]

MILLEDGE, JOHN (*b. Savannah, Ga., 1757; d. near Augusta, Ga., 1818*), lawyer, Georgia legislator, Revolutionary soldier. Congressman, (Democrat) Republican, from Georgia, 1792–93, 1795–99, 1801–02; governor of Georgia, 1802–06; U.S. senator, 1806–09. A principal benefactor of the University of Georgia and donor of its site.

MILLEDOLER, PHILIP (*b. Rhinebeck, N.Y., 1775; d. Staten Island, N.Y., 1852*), clergyman, educator. Graduated Columbia, 1793; studied theology under John D. Gros. Held Presbyterian and Dutch Reformed pastorates in New York and Philadelphia; was professor of theology at Dutch Reformed Seminary, New Brunswick, N.J., 1825–40, and simultaneously, president of Rutgers College.

MILLER, CHARLES HENRY (*b. New York, N.Y., 1842; d. New York, 1922*), physician, landscape painter, etcher. Distinguished for his studies of Long Island scenery.

MILLER, CHARLES RANSOM (*b. Hanover Center, N.H., 1849; d. 1922*), journalist. Graduated Dartmouth, 1872. Served on staff of *Springfield Daily Republican;* was associated in a number of capacities with the *New York Times, post* 1875, and editor-in-chief of that paper, 1883–1922. His editorial style was marked by strong conviction, forceful reasoning and clarity.

MILLER, CINCINNATUS HINER (*b. Liberty, Ind., 1839; d. 1913*), poet, known as Joaquin Miller. Raised in Oregon, he led a drifting life through the mining camps of northern California c. 1856–59; thereafter, he taught school, practiced law, dabbled in journalism and served as a county judge in Oregon until 1870, when two volumes of verse which he had published, *Specimens* (1868) and *Joaquin et al* (1869), attracted some attention in literary circles in San Francisco. Journeying to London, England, he was taken up by the critics there as a genuine phenomenon of the American West. His *Songs of the Sierras* (1871) won high praise from the British despite its cheap rhythms and mock-Byronism. After traveling abroad for some time and publishing a number of other works of verse and prose, he returned to America and settled permanently in Oakland, Calif., 1886. He published his complete poetical works in 1897.

MILLER, EDWARD (*b. near Dover, Del., 1760; d. New York, N.Y., 1812*), physician. Brother of Samuel Miller (1769–1850). M.D., University of Pennsylvania, 1789; removed to New York City, 1796, where he practiced thereafter. He was a co-founder with Samuel L. Mitchill and E. H. Smith of the *Medical Repository* (1797) and gave aid in establishment of the New York College of Physicians and Surgeons (1807) which he served as its first professor of the practice of medicine.

MILLER, EMILY CLARK HUNTINGTON (*b. Brooklyn, Conn., 1833; d. Northfield, Minn., 1913*), author. Helped secure charter for Evanston College for Ladies, 1871. After the college had been united with Northwestern University, Mrs. Miller taught English literature there and was dean of women, 1891–98.

MILLER, EZRA (*b. near Pleasant Valley, N.J., 1812; d. Mahwah, N.J., 1885*), civil engineer. Patented (1863–1865) a railroad-car platform coupler and buffer which was widely used before superseded by the Janney coupler.

MILLER, GEORGE (*b. Pottstown, Pa., 1774; d. Union Co., Pa., 1816*), Evangelical Association preacher and compiler of that sect's Book of Discipline (1809).

MILLER, HARRIET MANN (*b. Auburn, N.Y., 1831; d. Los Angeles, Calif., 1918*), naturalist, author. Under pen-name "Olive Thorne Miller," wrote a number of excellent studies of bird life of which *In Nesting Time* (1888) is typical.

MILLER, HEINRICH. [See MILLER, JOHN HENRY, 1702–1782.]

MILLER, HENRY (*b. Glasgow, Ky., 1800; d. Louisville, Ky., 1874*), physician. A leading obstetrician and gynecologist, Miller taught at Louisville Medical College and at its predecessor institutions; he was author of *Principles and Practice of Obstetrics* (1858).

MILLER, HENRY (*b. London, England, 1860; d. New York, N.Y., 1926*), actor, theatrical manager. Came as a boy to Canada; made stage debut *c.* 1878; was strongly influenced by Dion Boucicault's example. Miller's career falls into three main divisions: his connection as leading man with the Empire Theatre stock company, New York City, in the early nineties; his period as a Broadway star, 1899–1906; and finally his success as actor-manager *post* 1906. His productions of William V. Moody's *The Great Divide* (1906) and *The Faith Healer* (1910), together with C. R. Kennedy's *The Servant in the House* (1908), exhibited his varied talents at their climax and represented a great artistic advance for the American theatre.

MILLER, JAMES RUSSELL (*b. Harshaville, Pa., 1840; d. Philadelphia, Pa., 1912*), Presbyterian clergyman. Editorial superintendent, Presbyterian Board of Publication, 1887–1912.

MILLER, JOAQUIN. [See MILLER, CINCINNATUS HINER, 1839–1913.]

MILLER, JOHN (*b. Berkeley Co., Va., now W.Va., 1781; d. near Florissant, Mo., 1846*), journalist, soldier. Removed to Ohio, 1803; served in War of 1812 as colonel, 19th U.S. Infantry; resigned from army, 1818, and in 1821 became register of the land office at Franklin, Mo. Democratic governor of Missouri, 1825–32, he advocated a well-organized militia, withdrawal of state paper money from circulation, protection of trade and travel on the Santa Fé Trail, the encouragement of educational activities, and the exclusion by the federal government of all British traders from the fur trading regions of the Rocky Mountains. As congressman, 1837–43, he worked for improvement of river navigation and opposed the growing tendency toward sectionalism.

MILLER, JOHN (*b. Princeton, N.J., 1819; d. Princeton, 1895*), Presbyterian clergyman, Confederate chaplain. Son of Samuel Miller (1769–1850). Withdrew from Presbyterian Church, 1877, on doctrinal grounds; served as pastor of an independent congregation at Princeton, 1880–95.

MILLER, JOHN FRANKLIN (*b. South Bend, Ind., 1831; d. Washington, D.C., 1886*), lawyer, Indiana legislator, Union major-general. Collector of the port of San Francisco, 1865–69; able president, Alaska Commercial Co., 1869–81. As U.S. senator, Republican, from California, 1881–86, his name is linked with efforts to modify the Burlingame Treaty with China and also with the Exclusion Bill of 1882.

MILLER, JOHN HENRY (*b. Rheden, Germany, 1702; d. Bethlehem, Pa., 1782*), printer, editor. After several brief stays in America *post* 1741, Miller set up a printing establishment in Philadelphia, 1760. Publisher of a German language newspaper, he also published a yearly German almanac and, among other books, Thomas Godfrey's *Juvenile Poems* (1765). His newspaper, by a fortunate accident, was the first to announce the adoption of the Declaration of Independence (*Pennsylvanische Staatsbote,* issue of July 5, 1776).

MILLER, JOHN PETER (*b. probably Zweibrücken, Germany, 1709; d. Ephrata, Pa., 1796*), German Reformed clergyman. Came to Philadelphia, Pa., 1730; was ordained in that year by three Presbyterian ministers; was minister to German congregations on the Pennsylvania frontier *post* 1731. Coming under influence of Johann C. Beissel, Miller renounced the Reformed Church, 1735, and after living a while as a hermit, joined Beissel at the Ephrata Community. Miller succeeded Beissel as head of the community, 1768.

MILLER, JONATHAN PECKHAM (*b. Randolph, Vt., 1796; d. Montpelier, Vt., 1847*), lawyer, Vermont legislator. Volunteer soldier in the Greek revolutionary army, 1824–26; anti-slavery advocate.

MILLER, KELLY (*b. Winnsboro, S.C., 1863; d. Washington, D.C., 1939*), educator. Son of a free Negro father and a slave mother, Miller graduated from Howard University, 1886. After further study of mathematics, physics and astronomy with Simon Newcomb and also at Johns Hopkins, he taught at Howard, 1890–1934. He served as dean, 1907–18, and *post* 1918 devoted most of his time to sociology. As a writer and lecturer on behalf of the Negro, he directed his arguments to the reason and conscience of his fellow-Americans; as a theorist on Negro education, he took a middle course in the controversy between proponents of "higher" as opposed to "industrial" emphasis. [*Supp.* 2]

MILLER, KEMPSTER BLANCHARD (*b. Boston, Mass., 1870; d. Pasadena, Calif., 1933*), engineer. Graduated Cornell, 1893. An expert in telephone design, construction and operation, Miller also designed and built several hydroelectric plants and was the designer of the New York City fire-alarm system.

[*Supp.* 1]

MILLER, LESLIE WILLIAM (*b. Brattleboro, Vt., 1848; d. Martha's Vineyard, Mass., 1931*), painter, educator. Organized the School of Industrial Art,

Philadelphia, Pa.; made it one of the leading institutions in its field as its director, 1880–1920.

MILLER, LEWIS (*b. Greentown, O., 1829; d. New York, N.Y., 1899*), inventor, farm-implement manufacturer. Conceiving the idea of combining recreation with some form of education, in 1874 he invited John H. Vincent to join him in organizing a general assembly, as distinct from a Sunday-school teachers' assembly, to meet on Lake Chautauqua, N.Y. This was the beginning of the Chautauqua movement, a pioneer force in adult education.

MILLER, OLIVE THORNE. [See MILLER, HARRIET MANN, 1831–1918.]

MILLER, OLIVER (*b. Middletown, Conn., 1824; d. Ellicott City, Md., 1892*), jurist. Admitted to the Maryland bar, 1850, he became reporter of the state court of appeals, 1852, and established a reputation as editor of *Maryland Reports* (1853–62). Elected chief judge of the fifth judicial circuit of Maryland, 1867, he served until 1892. His opinions are among the best known in the judicial annals of Maryland.

MILLER, PETER. [See MILLER, JOHN PETER, 1709–1796.]

MILLER, SAMUEL (*b. near Dover, Del., 1769; d. 1850*), Presbyterian clergyman, educator, author. Brother of Edward Miller. Educated chiefly at home; attended University of Pennsylvania. Ordained, 1793, he served as collegiate pastor in New York City until 1809 and was sole pastor of the Wall Street congregation until 1813. Thereafter he was professor of church history, Princeton Theological Seminary, of which he had been a founder. His writings covered a broad range; chief among them was the very important *Brief Retrospect of the Eighteenth Century* (1803). Long the official historian of the Presbyterian General Assembly, he became its moderator, 1806.

MILLER, SAMUEL (*b. Lancaster, Pa., 1820; d. Bluffton, Mo., 1901*), horticulturist. His best-known plant contribution is perhaps the Captain Jack strawberry; most of his plant-breeding work was practiced with grapes. He was particularly notable for his generous disinterested efforts in testing types and varieties sent him by their owners.

MILLER, SAMUEL FREEMAN (*b. Richmond, Ky., 1816; d. Washington, D.C., 1890*), physician, lawyer. M.D., Transylvania, 1838; practiced medicine in neighborhood of Barbourville, Ky. After studying law and admission to the Knox Co. bar, 1847, he found the pro-slavery atmosphere of that section uncongenial and removed to Keokuk, Iowa, 1850. There he practiced law with success and engaged in the organization of the Republican party. Appointed an associate justice of the U.S. Supreme Court, 1862, he was strong in support of the national authority, upholding the constitutionality of the loyalty oath in *Ex parte Garland* and voting with the majority in the Legal Tender Cases. Yet within the limits of common sense, he upheld the rights of the individual and the need to maintain an ample autonomy for state governments. He was strong in his belief that it was not the function of federal courts to sit in judgment on state courts expounding state law. Always more concerned with the practical result of a decision than with its doctrinal basis, he was disposed to let no technicality stand in the way of what seemed just. The dominant personality on the bench in his time, he sometimes showed a blunt impatience with lesser minds and with futile arguments.

MILLER, STEPHEN DECATUR (*b. Lancaster District, S.C., 1787; d. Raymond, Miss., 1838*), lawyer, South Carolina legislator, representative and senator. As a member of Congress, 1817–19, he became a convert to the nullification doctrine of J. C. Calhoun and did much to inflame the state against Congress while governor, 1829–30. As U.S. senator, anti-Jackson Democrat, 1831–33, he opposed the 1832 Tariff and was active in the state nullification conventions.

MILLER, WARNER (*b. Hannibal, N.Y., 1838; d. New York, N.Y., 1918*), paper manufacturer, politician. Congressman, "Half Breed" Republican, from New York, 1878–81; U.S. senator, 1881–87. Favored Chinese exclusion, development of the U.S. merchant marine, and the protective tariff.

MILLER, WEBB (*b. near Pokagon, Mich., 1892; d. London, England, 1940*), journalist, foreign correspondent. Appointed to staff of United Press, 1916, for excellent free-lance work during Pancho Villa incident on Mexican border. Covered World War I; managed U.P. Paris and London bureaus; was general European news manager of U.P., *post* 1930. Author of *I Found No Peace* (1936). [*Supp. 2*]

MILLER, WILLIAM (*b. Pittsfield, Mass., 1782; d. Hampton, N.Y., 1849*), farmer, leader of the Adventists, or "Millerites." Raised in Washington Co., N.Y. Preached doctrine that Christ's second coming would take place in 1843 or 1844. Publicized by Joshua V. Himes, Miller drew a large following from the orthodox Protestant churches; he headed the Adventist Church at its founding, 1845.

MILLER, WILLIAM HENRY HARRISON (*b. Augusta, N.Y., 1840; d. Indianapolis, Ind., 1917*), lawyer. Practiced in Indiana *post* 1865; was partner of Benjamin Harrison. As U.S. attorney-general, 1889–93, Miller's advice was largely responsible for the excellence of President Harrison's federal bench appointments. An impartial and vigorous law officer, Miller was held in high respect by his subordinates.

MILLER, WILLIAM SNOW (*b. Sterling, Mass., 1858; d. Madison, Wis., 1939*), anatomist, medical

historian. M.D., Yale, 1879; studied also with Francis Delafield and Franklin P. Mall; attended University of Leipzig and Johns Hopkins Medical School. Taught at University of Wisconsin, 1892–1924. Author of an important study *The Lung* (1937) which summarized his lifelong research on the anatomy of that organ.
[*Supp.* 2]

MILLER, WILLOUGHBY DAYTON (*b. near Alexandria, O., 1853; d. Newark, O., 1907*), dentist. Graduated University of Michigan, 1875; studied also at universities of Edinburgh and Berlin; D.D.S., University of Pennsylvania, 1879. Practiced in Germany, 1879–1907, where he received high scholarly and professional honors and was recognized as one of the leading dental authorities and bacteriologists of his day. Among results of his research was the demonstration that tooth tissue is destroyed by fermentative acids formed by bacteria in the mouth; also findings on the action of diseased teeth as foci of infection and the etiology of dental erosion. Accepting appointment as dean, Dental College, University of Michigan, he died before he took up his duties.

MILLET, FRANCIS DAVIS (*b. Mattapoisett, Mass., 1846; d. at sea aboard* Titanic, *1912*), painter, illustrator, journalist. Graduated Harvard, 1869; studied art at Royal Academy, Antwerp, and also at Rome and Venice. Correspondent, Russo-Turkish War, 1877; associate of E. A. Abbey, John S. Sargent, Henry James in colony at Broadway, England; director of decorations of White City, Chicago World's Fair, 1893; correspondent in Philippines, 1899. Director, American Academy in Rome, 1911–12.

MILLIGAN, ROBERT (*b. Co. Tyrone, Ireland, 1814; d. Lexington, Ky., 1875*), Disciples of Christ clergyman, educator. Came to America as a child; raised in Ohio. Taught at Washington College (Pa.), Indiana University, Bethany College; president, Kentucky University, 1859–65.

MILLIGAN, ROBERT WILEY (*b. Philadelphia, Pa., 1843; d. Annapolis, Md., 1909*), naval officer. Chief engineer of U.S.S. *Oregon* on famous cruise around South America, 1898, and in battle of Santiago. Retired as rear admiral, 1905.

MILLINGTON, JOHN (*b. near London, England, 1779; d. Richmond, Va., 1868*), engineer, educator. Came to America, *c.* 1833, after distinguished career as scientist and teacher of science. Taught engineering and the sciences at William and Mary, the University of Mississippi, and Memphis (Tenn.) Medical College. Author, among other works, of *Elements of Civil Engineering* (1839).

MILLS, ANSON (*b. near Thorntown, Ind., 1834; d. Washington, D.C., 1924*), Union Army officer, Indian fighter, inventor. As surveyor in Texas, 1857–61, made original plat of El Paso and gave city its name; patented (1866) and manufactured first cartridge belt adopted by U.S. Army.

MILLS, BENJAMIN (*b. Worcester Co., Md., 1779; d. Frankfort, Ky., 1831*), lawyer, Kentucky legislator. Associate justice, Kentucky court of appeals, 1820–28; opposed legislature's dissolution of court during contest over debtor relief in 1820's.

MILLS, BENJAMIN FAY (*b. Rahway, N.J., 1857; d. Grand Rapids, Mich., 1916*), interdenominational evangelist.

MILLS, CHARLES KARSNER (*b. Philadelphia, Pa., 1845; d. Philadelphia, 1931*), neurologist. M.D., University of Pennsylvania, 1869; Ph.D., 1871. Taught at Pennsylvania, 1877–1915; was professor of neurology emeritus thereafter. Created famed "Philadelphia school of neurology"; was president of the American Neurological Association, 1887 and 1924. Author of *The Nervous System and Its Diseases* (1898).

MILLS, CLARK (*b. Onondaga Co., N.Y., 1810; d. Washington, D.C., 1883*), sculptor, pioneer bronze founder. His monument to Andrew Jackson, the first large equestrian statue to be cast here in bronze, stands in Lafayette Square, Washington, D.C. With this statue (dedicated in 1853) virtually began the industry of bronze casting in the United States. Mills thereafter created a replica of the Jackson piece for New Orleans (dedicated in 1856), an equestrian statue of Washington for the capital city in 1860, and a bronze casting of Crawford's colossal "Liberty" for the Capitol dome (dedicated in 1863). Numerous portrait busts by him include those of Calhoun, Webster and Crittenden.

MILLS, CYRUS TAGGART (*b. Paris, N.Y., 1819; d. Oakland, Calif., 1884*), Presbyterian missionary to Ceylon and Hawaii, educator, businessman. Administered (with wife Susan Mills) Oahu College near Honolulu; founded Mills Seminary near Oakland, Calif., 1871.

MILLS, DARIUS OGDEN (*b. North Salem, N.Y., 1825; d. 1910*), merchant, banker, philanthropist. From the post of cashier in a Buffalo, N.Y., bank, Mills removed to California in 1849 and founded the bank of D. O. Mills & Co. at Sacramento, 1850. Accumulating a fortune, 1850–60, he served as president of the Bank of California at San Francisco, 1864–73; he resumed the presidency in 1875 to reorganize the bank after difficulties caused by his successor, W. C. Ralston. Residing in New York City *post* 1878, Mills became an investor and director in Eastern banking, railway and industrial concerns. To his many benefactions was added in 1888 financial support of the "Mills Hotels" where people of low income could get inexpensive board and lodging.

MILLS, ELIJAH HUNT (*b. Chesterfield, Mass., 1776; d. Northampton, Mass., 1829*), lawyer, Massachusetts legislator. Congressman, Federalist, from Massachusetts, 1815–19; U.S. senator, 1820–27.

MILLS, ENOS ABIJAH (*b. near Kansas City, Kans., 1870; d. Colorado, 1922*), naturalist, author, conservationist. Creator of Rocky Mountain National Park. [*Supp.* 1]

MILLS, HIRAM FRANCIS (*b. Bangor, Maine, 1836; d. Hingham, Mass., 1921*), hydraulic and sanitary engineer. Graduated Rensselaer Polytechnic, 1856. As chief engineer at Lowell and Lawrence, Mass., Mills initiated far-reaching experiments on sewage, water purification and hydraulics. His work, among other effects, reduced the threat of typhoid fever and advanced the development of the turbine.

MILLS, LAWRENCE HEYWORTH (*b. New York, N.Y., 1837; d. 1918*), Episcopal clergyman, Iranian scholar. Resident abroad *post* 1872. Distinguished student of the Avesta; professor of "Zend Philology," Oxford University, England, 1897–1918.

MILLS, OGDEN LIVINGSTON (*b. Newport, R.I., 1884; d. New York, N.Y., 1937*), lawyer, New York legislator. Grandson of Darius O. Mills; nephew of Whitelaw Reid. Graduated Harvard, 1905; LL.B., 1907. Congressman, Republican, from New York, 1921–27. Exerted substantial influence on fiscal policies of Coolidge and Hoover administrations as assistant secretary of the treasury, 1927–32. Succeeding Andrew Mellon as secretary in February 1932, Mills continued Mellon's general policies until his retirement, 1933. [*Supp.* 2]

MILLS, ROBERT (*b. Charleston, S.C., 1781; d. Washington, D.C., 1855*), architect, engineer. Unique among native Americans of his era, Mills undertook regular training for the career of a professional architect with James Hoban, with Thomas Jefferson at "Monticello," and with Benjamin H. Latrobe in whose office he served as draftsman and clerk from 1803 to 1808. From Latrobe, the father of the Greek revival in America, he received not only his knowledge of Greek forms, but also his principles of professional practice and scientific engineering skill. During his period of training, Mills shared an architectural prize for a South Carolina College building (1802) and designed (1804) the "Circular" Congregational Church in Charleston.

In independent practice in Philadelphia, 1808–17, Mills designed or helped to engineer several churches and public structures in that city and in Richmond, Va. Entering the winning design for the first important public monument to Geo. Washington (Baltimore, Md., 1814), he resided in Baltimore, 1817–20, supervising construction of the colossal Doric column, first of its type. Commissions for Baltimore churches followed, together with the presidency of the city water company.

In 1820 Mills returned to Charleston to become a member of the Board of Public Works of his native state. He is referred to in public documents of that period as "State Engineer and Architect" and as "Civil and Military Engineer of the State." South Carolina had entered on an extensive scheme of internal improvements, with annual appropriations exceeding $100,000, spent chiefly on roads and on river and canal development. To his interest in the latter subject Mills had already testified in his *Treatise on Inland Navigation,* published in 1820 before his departure from Baltimore. Extensive works were built under his direction on the Saluda, Broad and Catawba rivers with numerous locks, and the rivers and bays were connected by several canals. The Board of Public Works had charge also of the public buildings of the state. Those erected from 1820 to 1830 were after designs made by Mills or revised by him; they included the Fireproof Record Building in Charleston, a wing of the Charleston prison planned for solitary confinement, and the State Hospital for the Insane at Columbia which embodied many modern and humane ideas. While in Charleston, Mills issued a number of valuable publications relative to his state: *Internal Improvement of South Carolina* (1822); an accurate *Atlas of the State of South Carolina* (1825); and *Statistics of South Carolina* (1826).

With the cessation of state appropriations for public works in 1830 Mills removed to Washington, D.C. A stanch Jacksonian as he had been a loyal Jeffersonian, he had hopes of federal employment, which were not disappointed. In 1836 he was appointed "Architect of Public Buildings," a position he held until 1851. In this office, he designed three of the principal 19th century buildings in Washington: the Treasury, the Patent Office, and the Post Office. The crowning success of his life was his victory in competition (1836) for the design of the Washington Monument at the capital.

Mills is outstanding as our first native-born professional architect, and as one of the chief exponents of the Greek revival. His works now appear a little stereotyped and arid, but very sober, competent, and dignified—contributing to that austere tradition still powerful in American architectural style.

MILLS, ROBERT (*b. Todd Co., Ky., 1809; d. Galveston, Texas, 1888*), merchant, planter. Removed to Texas, 1830, where in partnership with his brothers he built up a great trading and banking business. Bankrupt, 1873, he died in poverty.

MILLS, ROGER QUARLES (*b. Todd Co., Ky., 1832; d. Corsicana, Texas, 1911*), lawyer, Confederate soldier. Congressman, Democrat, from Texas, 1873–92; U.S. senator, 1892–99. Author of the Mills bill (1887) providing for tariff reduction; an advocate of governmental economy and lower taxes.

MILLS, SAMUEL JOHN (*b. Torringford, Conn., 1783; d. at sea, 1818*), Congregational clergyman, father of American Protestant foreign missionary work. Chiefly responsible for formation of American

Board of Commissioners for Foreign Missions, c. 1810, and of the American Bible Society, 1816.

MILLS, SUSAN LINCOLN TOLMAN (*b. Enosburg, Vt., 1826; d. Oakland, Calif., 1912*), missionary, educator. Wife of Cyrus T. Mills. President, Mills College, 1890–1909.

MILLSPAUGH, CHARLES FREDERICK (*b. Ithaca, N.Y., 1854; d. 1923*), physician, botanist. Nephew of Ezra Cornell. A noted botanical specimen collector and artist-naturalist, he served as curator of botany, Field Museum, Chicago, Ill., 1893–1923.

MILMORE, MARTIN (*b. Co. Sligo, Ireland, 1844; d. Boston Highlands, Mass., 1883*), sculptor. Came to Boston, Mass., as a child; was a protégé of Thomas Ball. A good but unimaginative workman, Milmore did his most significant work on the Soldiers' and Sailors' Monument, erected on Boston Common, 1877.

MILNER, JOHN TURNER (*b. Pike Co., Ga., 1826; d. Newcastle, Ala., 1898*), civil engineer, industrialist. Served as city surveyor, San Jose, Calif., 1849–54. Removing to Alabama, he built the Montgomery and West Point Railroad and, on the basis of an 1858 survey, projected a railroad through the coal and iron region from Decatur, Ga. to Elyton, Ala. Construction was suspended during the Civil War. After the war, despite political opposition, Milner and his associates successfully completed the line according to their original plan and formed the Elyton Land Co., which in 1871 founded Birmingham. Milner was also associated with first production of coke pig iron in Birmingham, 1876.

MILNER, MOSES EMBREE. [See CALIFORNIA JOE, 1829–1876.]

MILNER, THOMAS PICTON. [See PICTON, THOMAS, 1822–1891.]

MILROY, ROBERT HUSTON (*b. Washington Co., Ind., 1816; d. Olympia, Wash., 1890*), lawyer, Union major-general, Indian agent. Held field command throughout Civil War, mainly in western Virginia where he suppressed guerrilla warfare ruthlessly; supervised Indian affairs in the state of Washington, 1872–85.

MILTON, JOHN (*b. Jefferson Co., Ga., 1807; d. 1865*), lawyer. Removed to Jackson Co., Fla., 1846, where he resided until his death. As Democratic governor of Florida, 1861–65, he was a vigorous defender of state rights against the Confederate government, at the same time giving it maximum military and economic support.

MINER, ALONZO AMES (*b. Lempster, N.H., 1814; d. Boston, Mass., 1895*), Universalist clergyman, anti-slavery and temperance reformer. President of Tufts College, 1862–74.

MINER, CHARLES (*b. Norwich, Conn., 1780; d. near Wilkes-Barre, Pa., 1865*), journalist, Pennsylvania legislator. Editor and proprietor of a number of Pennsylvania newspapers *post* 1802, Miner served as a Federalist congressman from Pennsylvania, 1825–29. He is remembered principally for his humorous sketches published as a book under the title *Essays from the Desk of Poor Robert the Scribe* (1815) in which the phrase "to have an axe to grind" was first used; he was author also of a standard *History of Wyoming* (1845) and in other of his writings did much to popularize use of anthracite coal.

MINER, MYRTILLA (*b. Brookfield, N.Y., 1815; d. Washington, D.C., 1864*), promoter of Negro education. Founded a normal school for free Negro girls, 1851, in Washington, D.C.

MING, JOHN JOSEPH (*b. Gyswyl, Switzerland, 1838; d. Parma, O., 1910*), Roman Catholic clergyman, Jesuit, sociologist. Came to America, 1872; taught in various Jesuit schools, and at St. Louis University where he gained recognition as a pioneer Catholic sociologist.

MINNIGERODE, LUCY (*b. near Leesburg, Va., 1871; d. Virginia, 1935*), nurse. Superintendent of the department of nurses, U.S. Public Health Service, 1919–35. [*Supp. 1*]

MINOR, BENJAMIN BLAKE (*b. Tappahannock, Va., 1818; d. Richmond, Va., 1905*), lawyer, educator. LL.B., William and Mary, 1839; practiced mainly in Richmond. As editor, *Southern Literary Messenger*, 1843–47, he identified that magazine with Southern writers and Southern views. After service as president, University of Missouri, 1860–62, he engaged in teaching, public lecturing and business in Missouri, returning to Richmond, 1889.

MINOR, JOHN BARBEE (*b. Louisa Co., Va., 1813; d. 1895*), legal educator and author. Brother of Lucian Minor. Established high reputation of law school of University of Virginia as professor there *post* 1845. Author, among other works, of the *Institutes of Common and Statute Law* (1875–95).

MINOR, LUCIAN (*b. Louisa Co., Va., 1802; d. 1858*), temperance advocate, lawyer, teacher of law. Brother of John B. Minor. Author of *Reasons for Abolishing the Liquor Traffic* (1853).

MINOR, RALEIGH COLSTON (*b. Charlottesville, Va., 1869; d. Charlottesville, 1923*), lawyer, author. Son of John B. Minor. Teacher of law at University of Virginia *post* 1893. His principal subjects were real property, constitutional law, conflict of laws and international law. He stands as one of America's three pioneers in the field of private international law. In 1901 he achieved international recognition through the publication of his *Conflict of Laws*, an American legal classic, which clarified the existing chaotic condition of that difficult branch of jurisprudence. Among his other books were *The Law of Tax Titles in Virginia* (1898), *The Law of Real Property* (1908), and *A Republic of Nations* (1918), in which he advocated prevention of war through a supranational union of nations.

MINOR, ROBERT CRANNELL (*b. New York, N.Y., 1839; d. Waterford, Conn., 1904*), landscapist. Studied in Antwerp and Paris. Deeply influenced by Diaz and the Barbizon School, he excelled in painting the New York and Connecticut countryside.

MINOR, VIRGINIA LOUISA (*b. Goochland Co., Va., 1824; d. St. Louis, Mo., 1894*), woman suffragist. Early in 1867, she led in organization of the Woman Suffrage Association of Missouri (the first organization in the world to make its exclusive aim that of enfranchising women) of which she was elected president. Denied suffrage in Missouri, 1872, she sued for damages in the circuit court at St. Louis. Although her feeble legal case met with defeat here as well as later in the U.S. Supreme Court when Chief Justice Waite's elaborate opinion (21 *Wallace*, 177, 178) upheld the Missouri decisions, the publicity accompanying it contributed to the ultimate victory of woman suffrage.

MINOT, CHARLES SEDGWICK (*b. Boston, Mass., 1852; d. 1914*), biologist, educator. Graduated Massachusetts Institute of Technology, 1872; Sc.D., Harvard, 1878. Taught embryology in Harvard Medical School, 1880–1914. Author of *Human Embryology* (1892); made prolonged studies of senility.

MINOT, GEORGE RICHARDS (*b. Boston, Mass., 1758; d. Boston, 1802*), Massachusetts jurist, historian. Graduated Harvard, 1778. Served with ability as clerk of first Massachusetts house of representatives after adoption of new state constitution, 1780; also as secretary of the Massachusetts convention ratifying the Federal Constitution, 1788. His fame as historian comes from his *History of the Insurrection in Massachusetts* (Shays's Rebellion), published first in 1788, and his *Continuation of* (Thomas Hutchinson's) *History of the Province of Massachusetts Bay, from the Year 1748* (1798, 1803).

MINTO, WALTER (*b. Cowdenknowes, Scotland, 1753; d. Princeton, N.J., 1796*), mathematician. Came to America, 1786. Professor of mathematics and natural philosophy, College of New Jersey (Princeton), 1787–1796.

MINTURN, ROBERT BOWNE (*b. New York, N.Y., 1805; d. New York, 1866*), merchant. Beginning work in the counting house of Preserved Fish and Joseph Grinnell, 1829, Minturn became a partner upon their retirement in 1832. Renamed Grinnell, Minturn & Co., the firm became one of the greatest of the New York commercial houses, extending its influence into almost

all parts of the world and sharing leadership in American shipowning with the Welds of Boston. The greatest of the clippers, Donald McKay's *Flying Cloud,* sailed under the Grinnell, Minturn house flag.

MINTY, ROBERT HORATIO GEORGE (*b. Co. Mayo, Ireland, 1831; d. Jerome, Ariz., 1906*), Union brigadier-general, railroad official. Emigrated to Michigan, 1853, after service as British officer. Rose to division command in cavalry; helped capture Jefferson Davis.

MINUIT, PETER (*b. Wesel, Duchy of Cleves, 1580; d. off St. Christopher, West Indies, 1638*), first official director-general of the Dutch colony of New Netherland, governor of New Sweden. Through his purchase of Manhattan Island (1626) from the Indian sachems for trinkets valued at 60 guilders ($24), the accomplished fact of Dutch occupation received a semblance of legality which the West India Company was eager to acquire. Minuit made New Amsterdam the rallying point for other Dutch settlements and instituted peaceful relations with Plymouth Colony. Embroiled in a quarrel with Jonas Michaëlius and other Dutch Reformed ministers and with the provincial secretary, he was dismissed in 1631. He next was chosen to lead a Swedish company which established New Sweden (1638), building Fort Christina where Wilmington, Del., now stands.

MIRÓ, ESTEBAN RODRÍGUEZ (*b. Catalonia, 1744; d. Spain, 1795*), Spanish governor of Louisiana. His administration, which began with his appointment as acting governor in 1782 and included the intendancy after 1788, encouraged commerce and agriculture; his conduct toward the United States and its frontiersmen was not so aggressive, independent, or venal as sometimes described. Toward the Southern Indians, whom he sought to control through Alexander McGillivray, his policy was purely defensive. His notorious intrigue with James Wilkinson was begun on the initiative of the latter and carried on (as were all important matters in which Miró acted) under minute orders from Madrid. His term ended in 1791.

MITCHEL, JOHN (*b. Camnish, Ireland, 1815; d. 1875*), journalist, Irish nationalist. An advocate of armed resistance to England *post* 1845, he escaped to America, 1853, from Van Diemen's Land where he had been transported for treason. Constantly engaged in journalistic and other intrigue against the English, he was a Confederate sympathizer during the Civil War and served as editor of the *Richmond Enquirer* and also of the *Richmond Examiner*, 1862–65. After further essays in journalism, revolution and politics, he returned to Ireland, 1875. A man who cared nothing for liberty in the abstract or humanity at large, Mitchel was motivated throughout his life by a desire for vengeance against England.

MITCHEL, JOHN PURROY (*b. Fordham, N.Y., 1879; d. Lake Charles, La., 1918*), lawyer, politician.

Grandson of John Mitchel. Graduated Columbia, 1899; New York Law School, 1901. After making his name as a special investigator into conduct of borough officials in New York City, 1906, Mitchel had a spectacular rise in city politics culminating in his election as mayor on a Fusion ticket, 1913. Embarking on a program of municipal reform and ignoring party ties, he and his administration became increasingly unpopular. Defeated for re-election, 1917, he was killed while training for World War I service in the air corps.

MITCHEL, ORMSBY MacKNIGHT (*b. Morganfield, Ky., 1809; d. Beaufort, S.C., 1862*), astronomer, educator, Union major-general. Graduated West Point, 1829. Taught mathematics and astronomy at Cincinnati (O.) College; by his lectures and writings, stimulated establishment of observatories at Harvard, Washington, D.C., Cincinnati, O. Commanded Department of the Ohio, 1861; was later subordinate to Gen. D. C. Buell. Promoted major-general of volunteers, 1862, for brilliant capture of Huntsville, Ala., in April. Died of yellow fever soon after assuming command of X Army Corps and the Department of the South.

MITCHELL, ALEXANDER (*b. Ellon, Aberdeenshire, Scotland, 1817; d. New York, N.Y. 1887*), banker, railroad builder, politician. Came to America, 1839, engaging first in the insurance business at Milwaukee, Wis. By 1861, one of the principal bankers in that state, Mitchell served with great success as president of the Chicago, Milwaukee and St. Paul Railroad, 1865–87; he served also as congressman, Democrat, from Wisconsin, 1871–75.

MITCHELL, DAVID BRYDIE (*b. Perthshire, Scotland, 1766; d. Milledgeville, Ga., 1837*), lawyer, Georgia legislator. Emigrated to Georgia, 1783. Active in the state militia, he served as (Democrat) Republican governor, 1809–13, and 1815–17; he was a liberal supporter of internal improvement, education and frontier defense. As agent to the Creek Indians, 1817–21, he concluded the land-cession treaty of 1818.

MITCHELL, DAVID DAWSON (*b. Louisa Co., Va., 1806; d. 1861*), fur trader, soldier. Built Fort Mackenzie, 1832; settled in St. Louis, Mo., 1840. Except for an interval of conspicuous service in the Mexican War, he served as U.S. superintendent of Indian affairs, central division, 1841–53.

MITCHELL, DONALD GRANT (*b. Norwich, Conn., 1822; d. near New Haven, Conn., 1908*), author, agriculturist. Grandson of Stephen M. Mitchell. Graduated Yale, 1841. Under pseudonym "Ik Marvel," he wrote a number of contemporaneously popular works which included *Reveries of a Bachelor* (1850), *Dream Life* (1851), and *My Farm of Edgewood* (1863). *Post* 1855, he devoted a great deal of time to arousing his countrymen to a sense of beauty in farming, home-building and town-planning.

MITCHELL, EDWARD CUSHING (*b. East Bridgewater, Mass., 1829; d. 1900*), Baptist clergyman, Old Testament scholar. Grandson of Nahum Mitchell. Active in furthering the higher education of Negroes, notably at Leland University where he was president, 1887–1900.

MITCHELL, EDWARD PAGE (*b. Bath, Maine, 1852; d. New London, Conn., 1927*), journalist, editor. Graduated Bowdoin, 1871. After apprenticeship on Boston, Mass., and Maine newspapers, Mitchell joined the staff of the New York *Sun* on invitation of Charles A. Dana in October 1875. He remained with the *Sun* until his death as editorial writer and policy-maker, and as editor-in-chief, 1903–20.

MITCHELL, EDWIN KNOX (*b. Locke, O., 1853; d. Hartford, Conn., 1934*), Presbyterian clergyman. A pupil of Adolf Harnack, Mitchell was professor of ancient and early church history, Hartford Theological Seminary *post* 1892. He translated Harnack's *Outlines of the History of Dogma* (1893) and was author of other scholarly works in his field. [*Supp. 1*]

MITCHELL, ELISHA (*b. Washington, Conn., 1793; d. Mitchell's Falls, N.C., 1857*), Presbyterian clergyman, geologist, botanist. Graduated Yale, 1813. Professor of mathematics and the sciences, University of North Carolina, 1818–57. His activity in exploring and surveying much of the state is commemorated in Mount Mitchell, highest peak in the eastern United States, which he was the first to measure.

MITCHELL, GEORGE EDWARD (*b. present Elkton, Md., 1781; d. Washington, D.C., 1832*), physician, Maryland legislator, soldier. Remembered for his brilliant defense of Fort Oswego, N.Y., 1814. Congressman, Democrat, from Maryland, 1823–27 and 1829–32. Author of resolutions honoring Lafayette and inviting him to visit America, 1824.

MITCHELL, HENRY (*b. Nantucket, Mass., 1830; d. New York, N.Y., 1902*), engineer, hydrographer. Son of William Mitchell (1791–1869); brother of Maria Mitchell. Associated with U.S. Coast Survey, 1849–88, he specialized in tide and current investigations in North Atlantic harbors and came to be recognized as the leading American hydrographer. He was author of *Tides and Tidal Phenomena* (1868) and numerous other works.

MITCHELL, HINCKLEY GILBERT THOMAS (*b. Lee, N.Y., 1846; d. 1920*), Methodist clergyman, educator, Hebrew scholar. Graduated Wesleyan University, 1873; Boston University school of theology, 1876; Ph.D., Leipzig, 1879. Taught Hebrew at Boston University and at Tufts College; was attacked as champion of the higher criticism and for Unitarian tendencies.

MITCHELL, ISAAC (*b. near Albany, N.Y., c. 1759; d. Poughkeepsie, N.Y., 1812*), journalist. Author of "Alonzo and Melissa," an early American piece of fiction, first published in the Poughkeepsie, N.Y., *Political Barometer,* June 1804 through October 30, 1804. The tale was published in book form as *The Asylum, or Alonzo and Melissa* (1811); a pirated edition (also 1811) was issued at Plattsburg, N.Y.

MITCHELL, JAMES TYNDALE (*b. near Belleville, Ill., 1834; d. Philadelphia, Pa., 1915*), Pennsylvania jurist. Edited *American Law Register* (1863–88) and *Weekly Notes of Cases* (1875–99). After holding several Philadelphia judgeships, he served as justice of the Pennsylvania supreme court, 1888–1910, sitting as chief justice, 1903–10. Described once as "a brake on the wheels of progress," Mitchell's principal positive influence was in connection with legal procedure on which he was an authority.

MITCHELL, JOHN (*b. probably in the British Isles, date unknown; d. England, 1768*), physician, botanist, cartographer. Practiced medicine successfully at Urbanna, Va., 1735–46; thereafter he resided chiefly in or near London, England. Mitchell's method of treating yellow fever was practiced later by Benjamin Rush in Philadelphia; he was a correspondent of Cadwallader Colden and Benjamin Franklin. He wrote with versatility on several scientific subjects but his most important work was his *Map of the British and French Dominions in North America, etc.* which he began to make in 1750 and published at London, 1755. This *Map* was many times reprinted, copied and plagiarized and because of its subsequent use in scores of diplomatic and other controversies (including the peace negotiations at the end of the American Revolution) is considered the most important map in American history.

MITCHELL, JOHN (*b. Braidwood, Ill., 1870; d. New York, N.Y., 1919*), labor leader. Began work in coal mines at the age of 12; joined Knights of Labor, 1885. Joined United Mine Workers, 1890, and helped lead the union in its first victorious national strike, 1897. President of the United Mine Workers, 1898–1908, he won national celebrity for his tact and ability in the anthracite coal strike, Pennsylvania, 1902.

MITCHELL, JOHN AMES (*b. New York, N.Y., 1845; d. Ridgefield, Conn., 1918*), artist, author. Founded *Life* magazine, 1883, whose success was owing largely to Mitchell's ability as editor to anticipate trends in American popular thought and give expression to them in humorous form.

MITCHELL, JOHN HIPPLE (*b. Washington Co., Pa., 1835; d. 1905*), lawyer, politician. Settled in Oregon, 1860. Served intermittently as U.S. senator, Republican, from Oregon, 1872–1905. An adroit, disreputable, and very popular political leader.

MITCHELL, JOHN KEARSLEY (*b. Shepherdstown, Va., now W. Va., 1793; d. 1858*), physician, chemist, physiologist. M.D., University of Pennsylvania, 1819.

Practiced in Philadelphia; was professor of medicine, Jefferson Medical College, 1841–58.

MITCHELL, JONATHAN (*b. Halifax, England, 1624; d. 1668*), Congregational clergyman. Came to America as a boy; graduated Harvard, 1647. Pastor at Cambridge, Mass., *post* 1650, he was a leading advocate of the "Half-Way Covenant."

MITCHELL, LANGDON ELWYN (*b. Philadelphia, Pa., 1862; d. Philadelphia, 1935*), playwright. Son of Silas W. Mitchell. Author of a number of once-popular plays, which included *Becky Sharp* (produced, New York, 1899) and *The New York Idea* (produced, New York, 1906). [*Supp. 1*]

MITCHELL, LUCY MYERS WRIGHT (*b. Urumiah, Persia, 1845; d. Lausanne, Switzerland, 1888*), missionary, historian. Born of missionary parents; resided mainly abroad. Author of *A History of Ancient Sculpture* (1883).

MITCHELL, MARGARET JULIA (*b. New York, N.Y., 1837; d. New York, 1918*), actress, known generally as Maggie Mitchell. Made debut in New York, June 1851; was long a favorite actress, especially in the South. Famous for performance in title role of *Fanchon the Cricket.*

MITCHELL, MARIA (*b. Nantucket, Mass., 1818; d. Lynn, Mass., 1889*), astronomer, educator. Daughter of William Mitchell (1791–1869); sister of Henry Mitchell. First professor of astronomy at Vassar College *post* 1865.

MITCHELL, NAHUM (*b. East Bridgewater, Mass., 1769; d. Plymouth, Mass., 1853*), Massachusetts legislator and jurist, composer. Co-editor of the "Bridgewater Collection" of hymns, first published in 1802; author of *History of the Early Settlement of Bridgewater* (1840).

MITCHELL, NATHANIEL (*b. near Laurel, Del., 1753; d. Laurel, 1814*), Revolutionary soldier, Delaware legislator and public official. Governor of Delaware, 1805–08.

MITCHELL, ROBERT BYINGTON (*b. Mansfield, O., 1823; d. Washington, D.C., 1882*), lawyer, Union brigadier-general. Settled at Paris, Kans., 1856; was a conservative Free-State man. His governorship of New Mexico Territory, 1866–69, was marked by quarrels with the legislature over his alleged arbitrary rule.

MITCHELL, SAMUEL AUGUSTUS (*b. Bristol, Conn., 1792; d. Philadelphia, Pa., 1868*), geographer, publisher of geographical works.

MITCHELL, SILAS WEIR (*b. Philadelphia, Pa., 1829; d. 1914*), physician, neurologist, author. Son of John K. Mitchell. Graduated Jefferson Medical College, 1850; began practice as assistant to his father;

served as Union Army surgeon. Mitchell's contributions to medical literature covered many different fields; his 119 papers included studies in neurology, pharmacology, physiology and toxicology. He devoted over forty years of service to Philadelphia Orthopaedic Hospital; under his influence it became a center for the treatment of nervous disorders. He was distinguished also in the field of literature, particularly in fiction. Among his novels the following are outstanding: *Roland Blake* (1886); *Hugh Wynne* (1898); *The Adventures of François* (1899); *Constance Trescott* (1905).

MITCHELL, STEPHEN MIX (*b. Wethersfield, Conn., 1743; d. Wethersfield, 1835*), Connecticut legislator and jurist. U.S. senator, Federalist, from Connecticut, 1793–95. Judge of Hartford County court, 1779–93; of state superior court, 1795–1814 (chief justice *post* 1807).

MITCHELL, THOMAS DUCHÉ (*b. Philadelphia, Pa., 1791; d. 1865*), physician. M.D., University of Pennsylvania, 1812. Taught medicine and chemistry in a number of schools in Pennsylvania, Ohio and Kentucky.

MITCHELL, WILLIAM (*b. Nantucket, Mass., 1791; d. Poughkeepsie, N.Y., 1869*), teacher, businessman, amateur astronomer. Father of Henry and Maria Mitchell.

MITCHELL, WILLIAM (*b. Billquay, England, 1798; d. 1856*), actor, dramatist. Made American debut in New York, 1836. As manager of New York's Olympic Theatre, 1839–50, Mitchell devised a type of burlesque entertainment, topical in character, which was highly successful.

MITCHELL, WILLIAM (*b. New York, N.Y., 1801; d. Morristown, N.J., 1886*), lawyer. Elected judge of the New York supreme court, 1849, he became presiding justice of that court, 1854, and continued to preside until retirement in 1857.

MITCHELL, WILLIAM (*b. Welland Co., Ontario, Canada, 1832; d. Lake Alexandria, Minn., 1900*), railroad official, jurist. Minnesota district court judge, 1874–81; learned and liberal judge of the Minnesota supreme court, 1881–99.

MITCHELL, WILLIAM (*b. Nice, France, 1879; d. New York, N.Y., 1936*), army officer, aviator. Grandson of Alexander Mitchell; raised in Milwaukee, Wis. Left college, 1898, to enlist in war with Spain. Commissioned in regular army, 1901, Mitchell was associated with Signal Corps duty. He learned to fly, 1916, and for a while commanded the tiny aviation section of the Signal Corps. Planner of the A.E.F. aviation program, 1917, he made a brilliant record in World War I as pilot and strategist, advancing in rank to brigadier-general. Appointed assistant chief of the Air Service, 1919, he sought to secure a greater autonomy for military aviation and was increasingly outspoken in his criticism of the role of the navy in national defense. The significance of bombing tests conducted by him against surface ships in July and September 1921, became a national issue. Branded a trouble-maker, he was relieved of his post, 1925. In September 1925, Mitchell, by a public statement attacking the War and Navy Departments, precipitated his court-martial; found guilty, he was sentenced to a five-year suspension but on Feb. 1, 1926, resigned from the army. He continued to propagate his ideas while a civilian, and the significant results of his long campaign were the Army Air Force of World War II and the Department of Defense established in 1947. [*Supp. 2*]

MITCHILL, SAMUEL LATHAM (*b. North Hempstead, N.Y., 1764; d. 1831*), physician, New York legislator. Studied medicine in New York City with Samuel Bard; M.D., Edinburgh, 1786. Active all his life in the progress of medical education and the sciences, Mitchill served as congressman, (Democrat) Republican, from New York, 1801–04, 1810–13; he was U.S. senator, 1804–09. Characterized by contemporaries as "a living encyclopedia" and "a chaos of knowledge," he made no epoch-making discoveries and his theories were often erroneous; he was, however, sincere and amiable and did his best to popularize scientific inquiry.

MITTEN, THOMAS EUGENE (*b. Brighton, England, 1864; d. near Milford, Pa., 1929*), street-railway official. Came to America as a boy; was raised in Indiana. After a successful career in the Midwest, he headed the Philadelphia Rapid Transit Co. *post* 1911. Under investigation at the time of his death, his management was described as "a colossal conspiracy against the taxpayers."

MIX, TOM (*b. Mix Run, Pa., 1880; d. near Florenze, Ariz., 1940*), cowboy, motion-picture star. An outstanding box-office attraction, *c.* 1916–28. [*Supp. 2*]

MIXTER, SAMUEL JASON (*b. Hardwick, Mass., 1855; d. Grand Junction, Tenn., 1926*), surgeon. Graduated Massachusetts Institute of Technology, 1875; M.D., Harvard, 1879. On the staff of Massachusetts General Hospital, 1886–1926, Mixter made important contributions to neurological surgery, to the technique of skin-grafting and to surgery for intestinal obstruction.

MIZNER, ADDISON (*b. Benicia, Calif., 1872; d. Palm Beach, Fla., 1933*), architect, adventurer. Mainly self-trained, Mizner arrived in New York City, 1904; there, with the aid of wealthy contacts provided by Stanford White and others, he commenced practice but without immediate success. Removing to Palm Beach, Fla., 1918, he succeeded in making his personal vision of Spanish art and architecture the fashionable style for ambitious Florida house-builders in the boom era *post* World War I. After his triumphs at Palm Beach, he and his brother Wilson Mizner developed Boca Raton as a resort. His prosperity ended with the collapse of the Florida land bubble. [*Supp.* 1]

MODJESKA, HELENA (*b. Cracow, Poland, 1840; d. East Newport, Calif., 1909*), Polish-American actress. The reigning actress of Poland, 1868–76, she came to America, learned to speak English in six months, and began in 1877 a long series of successful theatrical tours in a wide range of parts. In Polish she had a repertoire of over a hundred roles; in English she played nine heroines of Shakespeare from Juliet to Cleopatra, and such well-known parts as "Adrienne," "Camille," "Mary Stuart," and, for the first time in America, Ibsen's "Nora."

MODJESKI, RALPH (*b. Cracow, Poland, 1861; d. Los Angeles, Calif., 1940*), bridge engineer. Son of Helena Modjeska. [*Supp.* 2]

MOELLER, HENRY (*b. Cincinnati, O., 1849; d. 1925*), Roman Catholic clergyman. Archbishop of Cincinnati, 1904–1925; a skilled administrator and promoter of education.

MOFFAT, DAVID HALLIDAY (*b. Washingtonville, N.Y., 1839; d. New York, N.Y., 1911*), capitalist. Settled in Denver, Colo., 1860; prospered as banker and as investor in mining properties, farm lands and Denver real estate. Although he promoted and financed a number of Colorado railroads, his name is associated principally with the Denver, Northwestern & Pacific.

MOFFAT, JAMES CLEMENT (*b. Glencree, Scotland, 1811; d. Princeton, N.J., 1890*), Presbyterian clergyman, church historian, educator. Came to America, 1833. Graduated Princeton, 1835; taught thereafter at Princeton, at Lafayette and at Miami University until 1852 when he returned to Princeton as professor of classics. Appointed professor of church history at Princeton, 1861, he continued to teach until the year before his death.

MOFFETT, CLEVELAND LANGSTON (*b. Boonville, N.Y., 1863; d. Paris, France, 1926*), journalist. Author of mystery stories and of a number of successful plays of an ephemeral nature.

MOFFETT, WILLIAM ADGER (*b. Charleston, S.C., 1869; d. aboard dirigible Akron off New Jersey coast, 1933*), naval officer. Graduated Annapolis, 1890. Served with great distinction at Manila, 1898; at Vera Cruz, Mexico, 1914; and as a training officer in World War I. As rear-admiral and chief of the Bureau of Aeronautics, 1921–33, he was largely responsible by his vision, enthusiasm and sound policies for the high efficiency and morale of U.S. naval aviation. [*Supp.* 1]

MOHR, CHARLES THEODORE (*b. Esslingen, Württemberg, 1824; d. Asheville, N.C., 1901*), botanist, pharmacist. Came to America, 1848; settled in Mobile, Ala., 1857. His extensive and important studies were embodied in several official reports and principally in *Plant Life of Alabama* (1901).

MOÏSE, PENINA (*b. Charleston, S.C., 1797; d. 1880*), poet. Her most characteristic work is found in *Hymns Written for the Use of Hebrew Congregations* (1856).

MOLDEHNKE, EDWARD FREDERICK (*b. Insterburg, East Prussia, 1836; d. Watchung, N.J., 1904*), Lutheran clergyman. Came to America, 1861, as missionary in Wisconsin and Minnesota. Pastor, Zion and St. Peter's Church, New York City, 1871–1904.

MOLDENKE, RICHARD GEORGE GOTTLOB (*b. Watertown, Wis., 1864; d. Plainfield, N.J., 1930*), metallurgist. Son of Edward F. Moldehnke (*sic*). Stimulated scientific study of foundry problems, especially in gray-iron industry; wrote *The Principles of Iron Founding* (1917).

MOLLENHAUER, EMIL (*b. Brooklyn, N.Y., 1855; d. Boston, Mass., 1927*), violinist. Conductor of Boston Festival Orchestra; also of the Handel and Haydn Society, 1899–1927. A talented, versatile, conservative musician.

MÖLLHAUSEN, HEINRICH BALDUIN (*b. near Bonn, Germany, 1825; d. Berlin, Germany, 1905*), traveler, author, artist. Came to America, 1849; led roving life in region of Kaskaskia River, Ill.; joined expedition of Duke of Württemberg to the Rocky Mountains, 1851. After a brief return to Germany, he served as topographer to Lieutenant A. W. Whipple's division of the Pacific Railroad survey, 1853–54. In the years 1857 and 1858 he went out as assistant on the exploration and survey of the Colorado River headed by Lieutenant J. C. Ives. The sketches which he drew as illustrations to the reports of these expeditions rank high as documents of the topography of the old West. After his return to Germany, 1858, he produced a great number of novels and novelettes which deal with Indian and emigrant life in the West; among them are *Der Halbindianer* (1861) and *Das Mormonenmädchen* (1864).

MOLYNEUX, ROBERT (*b. near Formby, England, 1738; d. 1808*), Roman Catholic clergyman, Jesuit. Coming to America, 1771, he served on the Maryland missions and succeeded Robert Harding as pastor in Philadelphia, Pa., 1773. He served twice as president of Georgetown College and was named American superior of the Society of Jesus, 1805.

MOMBERT, JACOB ISIDOR (*b. Cassel, Germany, 1829; d. Paterson, N.J., 1913*), Episcopal clergyman. A pastor for many years *post* 1859 in Pennsylvania and New Jersey, Mombert was author of several learned theological works, some popular biographies and a *History of Lancaster County* (1869).

MONCKTON, ROBERT (*b. probably England, 1726; d. 1782*), British lieutenant-general. Came to Nova Scotia, 1752. With a small force of regulars and a large number of New England militia, he took Fort Beauséjour in June, 1755, and was active in removal of the French inhabitants of the island southward. He commanded in Nova Scotia during Amherst's siege of Louisburg, 1758, and was appointed second-in-command of the Quebec Expedition of 1759. Governor of New York, 1761–63, he commanded the successful expedition against Martinique which resulted in the surrender of that island, February 1762. Offered the chief command in North America, 1773, he refused it.

MONCURE, RICHARD CASSIUS LEE (*b. Stafford Co., Va., 1805; d. Stafford Co., 1882*), lawyer, Virginia legislator and jurist. Judge, state supreme court of appeals, 1851–65; presiding judge, 1870–82. Outstanding in equity cases.

MONDELL, FRANK WHEELER (*b. St. Louis, Mo., 1860; d. Washington, D.C., 1939*), lawyer, mine operator. Settled in Wyoming *c.* 1888 and pioneered there in development of oil and coal deposits. Congressman, Republican, from Wyoming, 1895–97, 1899–1923. As congressman, and as floor leader *post* 1919, Mondell was a model of unenlightened conservatism. [*Supp. 2*]

MONETTE, JOHN WESLEY (*b. near Staunton, Va., 1803; d. Louisiana, 1851*), physician, historian. Author of the monumental *History of the Discovery and Settlement of the Valley of the Mississippi, etc.* (1846).

MONEY, HERNANDO DE SOTO (*b. Holmes Co., Miss., 1839; d. Mississippi, 1912*), lawyer, newspaper editor, Confederate soldier. Congressman, Democrat, from Mississippi, 1875–85 and 1893–97; U.S. senator, 1897–1911. A singularly independent figure in Congress, Money was a leader in the destruction of the "star route" system of mail handling and held a number of important committee assignments.

MONIS, JUDAH (*b. Algiers or Italy, 1683; d. Northborough, Mass., 1764*), Hebrew scholar, educator. Educated in Jewish schools of Leghorn and Amsterdam; settled in New York, 1715/16, as a merchant; removed to Massachusetts *ante* 1720. Monis was the first Jew to receive a Harvard degree (M.A., 1720); he was the first Harvard teacher to bear the title of instructor (taught Hebrew, 1722–60); and he was author of the first Hebrew grammar published in America (Cambridge, 1735).

MONROE, HARRIET (*b. Chicago, Ill., 1860; d. Arequipa, Peru, 1936*), poet. Founder, and editor (1912–36), of *Poetry: A Magazine of Verse*, which became a principal vehicle of 20th-century movements in poetry. [*Supp. 2*]

MONROE, JAMES (*b. Westmoreland Co., Va., 1758; d. New York, N.Y., 1831*), statesman, president of the United States. His parents were respectable but not distinguished Virginians. At sixteen he entered the College of William and Mary but his academic career was interrupted by the Revolution, in which he participated during the campaigns of 1777 and 1778, rising from lieutenant to major and receiving a wound at the battle of Trenton. From 1780 to 1783 he studied law with Thomas Jefferson and formed the close and fruitful friendship that lasted until Jefferson's death.

The first phase of Monroe's political career, 1782–94, saw him established as a strong member of the anti-Federalist faction. Guided by caution, strong localism, and fear of centralization, he served successively in the Virginia legislature (1782, 1787–90?), the Confederation Congress (1783–86), the Annapolis conference of 1786, the Virginia convention to ratify the federal Constitution (1788), and as U.S. senator from Virginia, 1790–94. His opposition to the Constitution before its ratification seems to have reflected the strong sectional sentiment of his district and his suspicion that a strengthened federal government would give up the American claim to navigation of the Mississippi. As a senator he drew even closer to Jefferson and severely criticized the Washington administration. He opposed the Bank of the United States and the appointments of Gouverneur Morris and John Jay as U.S. ministers, and he took a leading and somewhat equivocal part in the senatorial investigation of Alexander Hamilton's handling of the public funds.

Upon his appointment as minister to France (1794), Monroe began his career as an important but seldom successful diplomat. Though at the outset of his mission he was relatively successful in securing redress for the grievances of American commerce and the hardships suffered by American citizens, he soon suffered from what the French considered to be the Anglophile policy of the American administration as evidenced in the Jay Treaty and in other actions. During his last year in France he satisfied neither the authorities in Paris nor those at home. Recalled in 1796, he published a vindication of his mission, *A View of the Conduct of the Executive in the Foreign Affairs of the United States* (1797). He served as governor of Virginia, 1799–1802. He returned to France early in 1803 to cooperate with Robert R. Livingston in the discussions that led to the Louisiana Purchase. The next year found him in Madrid with Charles Pinckney to negotiate for the cession of the eastern Floridas, an almost impossible task that, under discourteous treatment from the Spanish government, he had to abandon. Another extremely difficult assignment was given him in 1805—the settlement of a number of vexing disputes between the United States and Great Britain. The resulting treaty (1806) did not outlaw the practice of impressment of seamen by Britain and was so unsatisfactory to Jefferson and Madison that it never reached the Senate. He was associated in this negotiation with William Pinkney.

Monroe's career in politics was renewed with his unsuccessful candidacy against James Madison for the presidency in 1808. The confidence of his Virginia supporters was never shaken by his diplomatic defeats and discomfitures. Refraining from criticizing Madison's administration and avoiding factional disputes within the (Democrat) Republican party in his home state, he was brought to a reconciliation with Madison, who offered him in 1811 the post of secretary of state. Meanwhile, he had served briefly as governor of Virginia again, from January to March 1811. Disappointed as secretary in his hopes for a reconciliation with Great Britain, Monroe seems to have been convinced by December 1811, that war would come. When it did in June 1812, he was in a measure involved in General George Mathews's unsavory attempt to revolutionize West Florida, which activity he was compelled to disavow. Although he continued to justify the war because of British impressments even after the obnoxious British Orders in Council were withdrawn, he was willing with Madison to accept Russian mediation in 1813. He had little influence upon the peace negotiations, but he can be partly credited with the selection of the very able American delegation at Ghent. Throughout the war Monroe had strong presidential ambitions. American military victories at Plattsburg and New Orleans enhanced his personal prestige because he was also holding the post of secretary of war (August, 1814–March, 1815). In the congressional caucus of 1816, with administration support, he won the presidency by only eleven votes over William H. Crawford.

He had now reached the summit of his ambition. As chief executive, he showed a capacity for administration and for accurately interpreting the national mood. Few great domestic political issues confronted him in eight years of office. His policies were marked by a characteristic middle-of-the-road viewpoint, notably with regard to internal improvements, in the advocacy of which he modified his earlier strict constructionism ("Views on the Subject of Internal Improvements," 1822, and "Survey Act," 1824). Although his sympathies were naturally with the South in the struggle over the admission of Missouri (1819–20), his conception of his presidential duties led him to abstain from all interference with the Missouri bill until he reluctantly signed it, undoubtedly the most momentous act of his administration. Despite the economic depression of 1819, Monroe had been almost unanimously re-elected to the presidency in 1820. Political strength came through his abandonment of his earlier sectionalism and his choice of excellent advisers—J. C. Calhoun, William Wirt, W. H. Crawford, and particularly John Quincy Adams to whom he gave

large discretion while maintaining presidential supervision over foreign affairs.

In the field of foreign policy, several important settlements were made during his presidency: the Rush-Bagot agreement for limitation of armaments on the Great Lakes, 1817; liquidation of the Newfoundland and Labrador fisheries dispute, 1818; joint-occupation of the Northwest, and (following Andrew Jackson's invasion of Florida, during which Monroe maintained a somewhat equivocal silence) the acquisition of Florida, 1819. Out of his slow recognition (March 1822) of the independence of the revolted Spanish colonies, grew the events leading to his famous message of December 2, 1823, enunciating what has come to be known as the Monroe Doctrine. Both the initiative and the responsibility for the famous declaration belong to Monroe, but the principle that the American continents were no longer subject to European colonization owes its origin to John Q. Adams. Upon leaving the presidency Monroe returned to private life in Virginia, became a visitor of the University of Virginia (1828), and was president of the Virginia constitutional convention (1829–30) wherein he supported the conservatives on suffrage and slavery.

Lacking high imagination, unpretentious in appearance, far from brilliant in speech, without any genuine graces, Monroe yet attained distinction. "Untiring application and indomitable perseverance" were a part of his character. Although the tribute to the soundness of his judgment which was applied to the rising Virginia politician by his wide circle of admirers seems not wholly deserved, it is difficult not to accept it with regard to his years in the presidency. By the Doctrine which bears his name, he is indissolubly connected with one of the major dogmas of American foreign policy. While he promulgated nothing very novel, he consolidated and fortified existing views and gave expression to a growing popular sentiment in striking form. No colorless personality could have left behind him so favorable a judgment on the part of so many persons of such diverse views and temperaments as did Monroe. Less intellectual than either Jefferson or Madison, he surpassed them both as an administrator. If he can never be assigned a place among the really great men who have held the presidency, he must be numbered among the more useful and the more successful.

MONTAGUE, ANDREW JACKSON (b. Campbell Co., Va., 1862; d. Urbanna, Va., 1937), lawyer, Reforming Democratic governor of Virginia, 1902–06; congressman, 1913–37. Made a strong effort as governor to destroy the machine headed by Thomas S. Martin. [Supp. 2]

MONTAGUE, HENRY JAMES (b. Staffordshire ?, England, 1843; d. San Francisco, Calif., 1878), actor. Stage name of Henry Mann. Made American debut at Wallack's Theatre, New York, 1874, and was an immediate success as a "leading man."

MONTEFIORE, JOSHUA (*b. London, England, 1762; d. St. Albans, Vt., 1843*), lawyer, author, British officer. Emigrated to America at end of the War of 1812; practiced law, settling eventually in Vermont.

MONTGOMERY, DAVID HENRY (*b. Syracuse, N.Y., 1837; d. Cambridge, Mass., 1928*), writer of history textbooks, benefactor of Harvard.

MONTGOMERY, EDMUND DUNCAN (*b. Edinburgh, Scotland, 1835; d. near Hempstead, Texas, 1911*), physician, philosopher. Came to America, 1870; settled in Texas, 1872. Author of *Philosophical Problems in the Light of Vital Organization* (1907).

MONTGOMERY, GEORGE WASHINGTON (*b. Alicante, Spain, 1804; d. Washington, D.C., 1841*), diplomat, consular official, translator of Washington Irving's works into Spanish.

MONTGOMERY, JAMES (*b. Ashtabula Co., O., 1814; d. Mound City, Kans., 1871*), Campbellite minister, Jayhawker, Union soldier.

MONTGOMERY, JOHN BERRIEN (*b. Allentown, N.J., 1794; d. Carlisle, Pa., 1873*), naval officer. Appointed midshipman, 1812; saw long and varied services at sea. Commanding U.S.S. *Portsmouth*, he raised American flag at San Francisco, July 9, 1846. Retired as captain, 1861, he served throughout Civil War as commodore on shore duty and was promoted rear-admiral, 1866.

MONTGOMERY, RICHARD (*b. Co. Dublin, Ireland, 1738; d. Quebec, Canada, 1775*), soldier. Served in French and Indian War with British regular forces; sold his commission, 1772, and settled in New York; married Janet, daughter of Robert R. Livingston (1718–1775). In full sympathy with the colonial cause, Montgomery was elected a member of the New York Provincial Congress, 1775; in June of the same year, he was appointed a Continental brigadier-general. Appointed second-in-command to Gen. Philip Schuyler in the expedition against Canada, he took full command on Schuyler's illness, captured Montreal and in December, joined the force under Gen. Benedict Arnold at Point-aux-Trembles. The combined forces then laid siege to Quebec. Montgomery was killed on the last day of the year during the American assault on that city. He was a capable soldier of high personal character.

MONTGOMERY, THOMAS HARRISON (*b. New York, N.Y., 1873; d. 1912*), zoologist, educator. Taught at universities of Pennsylvania and Texas; noted for brilliant cytological investigations and studies of heredity.

MONTGOMERY, WILLIAM BELL (*b. Fairfield District, S.C., 1829; d. Mississippi, 1904*), agriculturist. Introduced new grasses and cattle breeds to Mississippi. Founded *Live Stock Journal*, 1875.

MONTRÉSOR, JAMES GABRIEL (*b. Fort William, Scotland, 1702; d. Teynham, Kent, England, 1776*), British military engineer. Served in America, 1754–60, as chief engineer to the forces; was skillful in adapting European systems of fortifications to frontier conditions.

MONTRÉSOR, JOHN (*b. Gibraltar, 1736; d. England, 1799*), British military engineer. Son of James G. Montrésor with whom he came to America, 1754. Saw extensive scouting service in French and Indian War and Pontiac's War. Worked on surveying details and on improvement of fortifications at New York, Boston and Philadelphia *post* 1766; commissioned chief engineer in America, 1775. During the Revolution, the British made little use of his long and valuable experience and he returned to England, 1778.

MOOD, FRANCIS ASBURY (*b. Charleston, S.C., 1830; d. Waco, Texas, 1884*), Methodist Episcopal (South) clergyman, educator.

MOODY, DWIGHT LYMAN (*b. Northfield, Mass., 1837; d. Northfield, 1899*), evangelist. Accompanied by the organist and singer Ira D. Sankey, he preached to millions throughout urban America and the British Isles between 1873 and 1899. A layman of great business ability with early experience as a successful shoe salesman, Moody inspired businessmen as well as ministers. Unacademic, he yet commanded the admiring cooperation of university people. He founded Northfield Seminary (1879) and Mount Hermon School (1881), and stimulated Young Men's Christian Associations on college campuses as well as in Chicago where, in 1860, he had resigned from business to become an independent city missionary. He believed in personal evangelism; his preaching was direct, forceful, intimate, with emphasis on God's fatherly love.

MOODY, JAMES (*b. New Jersey, 1744; d. Weymouth, N.S., Canada, 1809*), British spy during American Revolution. Rejecting the compulsory state oath of allegiance, 1777, Moody fled from Sussex Co. to Bergen Co., N.J., where he enlisted in Gen. Cortlandt Skinner's Loyalist brigade and served, 1777–81. He spied on the troops of Washington, Sullivan, and Gates, achieving some small but spectacular successes, and was engaged in various abortive schemes to capture patriot officials and their public papers. After capture, 1780, and imprisonment, he escaped and was promoted to lieutenant, 1781. With impaired health he visited England, where he published a *Narrative* (1782, 1783) of his sufferings and exertions.

MOODY, PAUL (*b. Newbury, Mass., 1779; d. Lowell, Mass., 1831*), inventor of a number of valuable improvements in cotton-mill machinery. Associated *post* 1814 with Francis C. Lowell.

MOODY, WILLIAM HENRY (*b. Newbury, Mass., 1853; d. Haverhill, Mass., 1917*), lawyer, cabinet officer, jurist. Graduated Harvard, 1876; studied law in office of Richard H. Dana, Jr. Served with ability as district attorney, eastern district of Massachusetts, 1890–95; was congressman, Republican, from Massachusetts, 1895–1902. His service as member of the Appropriations Committee won him notice of President Theodore Roosevelt who became his close friend. Appointed U.S. secretary of the navy, 1902, he succeeded Philander C. Knox in 1904 as U.S. attorney-general. Roosevelt's anti-trust activities reached their high point while Moody held this post (1904–06) and the President described his work as comparable to that of any other man who had ever held the office. His anti-trust activities aroused opposition to his appointment to the U.S. Supreme Court but he was confirmed by the Senate in December 1906. Before his resignation because of ill health, 1910, Moody wrote a number of opinions of which the principal were his dissent in the Employer's Liability cases and his majority opinion in *Twining vs. State of New Jersey*.

MOODY, WILLIAM VAUGHN (*b. Spencer, Ind., 1869; d. Colorado Springs, Colo., 1910*), poet, playwright, educator. Graduated Harvard, 1893; A.M., 1894. Taught English at University of Chicago, 1895–99 and 1901–07. Moody's lyric poetry as well as his dramas were written out of moral conviction and mental necessity; he was constantly striving to come to grips with the spirit of the age and to express his insights with force and beauty. He succeeded in his prose dramas in expressing philosophic ideas in contemporary terms and in bringing to the American theatre new spiritual values. His first published book was a drama in verse *A Masque of Judgment* (1900); he next published *Poems* (1901) and another essay in poetic drama *The Fire-Bringer* (1904). His play *The Great Divide* (produced 1906) was at once recognized as an important advance in American drama and he moved to leadership among contemporary American dramatists with *The Faith Healer* (produced, Cambridge, Mass., 1909 and New York, 1910). Moody's early death cut short a career that might have risen to greatness for he was a thinker as well as a conscientious artist.

MOON, PARKER THOMAS (*b. New York, N.Y., 1892; d. New York, 1936*), historian. Graduated Columbia, 1913; Ph.D., 1921. A specialist in international relations, Moon taught at Columbia *post* 1915. [*Supp. 2*]

MOONEY, JAMES (*b. Richmond, Ind., 1861; d. 1921*), ethnologist. Associated with the Bureau of American Ethnology, 1885–1921, Mooney was a sympathetic and able student of American Indian language, folklore and material culture, in particular that of the Cherokees and the Kiowa. He took an active part in preparation of the *Handbook of American Indians* (edited, F. W. Hodge, 1907–10).

MOONEY, WILLIAM (*b. probably New York, N.Y., 1756; d. New York, 1831*), upholsterer, politician. A leader in founding the New York Tammany Society, 1786, he was chosen its first grand sachem, 1789.

MOORE, ADDISON WEBSTER (*b. Plainfield, Ind., 1866; d. London, England, 1930*), philosopher. Graduated DePauw University, 1890; Ph.D., University of Chicago, 1898. A teacher at the University of Chicago thereafter until his retirement as professor emeritus, 1929, Moore allied himself with the Chicago school of instrumental pragmatism of which John Dewey was the creator. The most complete statement of his point of view is in *Pragmatism and Its Critics* (1910).

MOORE, ALFRED (*b. New Hanover Co., N.C., 1755; d. Bladen Co., N.C., 1810*), planter, Revolutionary soldier, jurist. Son of Maurice Moore. North Carolina attorney-general, 1782–91; shared leadership of the North Carolina bar with William R. Davie. Appointed associate justice of U.S. Supreme Court, 1799, he resigned, 1804.

MOORE, ANDREW (*b. near Staunton, Va., 1752; d. 1821*), lawyer, Revolutionary soldier, Virginia legislator. A leader in politics in the Valley section of Virginia, Moore was a principal supporter of James Madison; he served as congressman, (Democrat) Republican, 1789–99, 1804; U.S. senator, 1804–09. He was largely instrumental in the permanent establishment of the school which later became Washington and Lee University.

MOORE, ANNIE AUBERTINE WOODWARD (*b. Montgomery Co., Pa., 1841; d. Madison, Wis., 1929*), musician, student of Scandinavian music.

MOORE, BARTHOLOMEW FIGURES (*b. Halifax Co., N.C., 1801; d. 1878*), lawyer, North Carolina legislator and Unionist. A leader in the state convention of 1865–66, he was author of the 1866 constitution which failed of ratification.

MOORE, BENJAMIN (*b. Newtown, N.Y., 1748; d. Greenwich Village, N.Y., 1816*), Episcopal clergyman, Loyalist. Served without distinction as president *pro tempore* of King's College (Columbia), 1775–84, and as actual president of Columbia, 1801–11. Accepting the rectorship of Trinity Church, New York City, 1800, he was consecrated bishop of New York, 1801. Incapacitated by paralysis, 1811, his duties as bishop were assumed by his assistant, John H. Hobart.

MOORE, CHARLES HERBERT (*b. New York, N.Y., 1840; d. Winchfield, England, 1930*), artist, educator. Taught principles of art at Harvard, 1874–1909; was first curator of Fogg Art Museum and its director, 1896–1909. Author, among other works, of *Development and Character of Gothic Architecture* (1890).

MOORE, CLARENCE LEMUEL ELISHA (*b. Bainbridge, O., 1876; d. 1931*), mathematician. Graduated

Ohio State, 1901; Ph.D., Cornell, 1904. Taught at Massachusetts Institute of Technology *post* 1904. Noted for his work in geometry, he was one of the first American mathematicians to recognize the importance of the methods of Ricci in the geometry of hyperspace.

MOORE, CLEMENT CLARKE (*b. New York, N.Y., 1779; d. Newport, R.I., 1863*), Hebrew scholar, poet. Son of Benjamin Moore. Graduated Columbia, 1798. A principal benefactor of the General Theological Seminary, New York City, Moore taught there, 1823–50. He is chiefly remembered for his ballad "A Visit from St. Nicholas," first published in the *Troy Sentinel*, Dec. 23, 1823, several times reprinted thereafter, and included in a collection of Moore's verse, *Poems* (1844).

MOORE, CLIFFORD HERSCHEL (*b. Sudbury, Mass., 1866; d. 1931*), classicist, professor of Greek and Latin. Graduated Harvard, 1889; Ph.D., University of Munich, 1897. Taught at Harvard, 1898–1931. *Post* 1918, he served with outstanding ability as dean of the Harvard Graduate School and of the Faculty of Arts and Sciences.

MOORE, EDWARD MOTT (*b. Rahway, N.J., 1814; d. Rochester, N.Y., 1902*), surgeon, teacher of medicine. Made original contributions in studies of fracture and dislocation; was first president, New York State Board of Health. M.D., University of Pennsylvania, 1838. Practiced and taught in a number of places, principally in Buffalo and Rochester, N.Y.

MOORE, EDWIN WARD (*b. Alexandria, Va., 1810; d. New York, N.Y., 1865*), naval officer. Served in U.S. Navy, 1825–39, when he accepted command of the navy of the Republic of Texas. After four years of stirring service against Mexico in the Gulf, he was suspended from command (1843) and spent much of the rest of his life prosecuting claims against the governments of Texas and of the United States.

MOORE, ELIAKIM HASTINGS (*b. Marietta, O., 1862; d. 1932*), mathematician. Graduated Yale, 1883; Ph.D., 1885; studied also at Berlin and Göttingen. Taught mathematics at Yale and Northwestern universities; headed department of mathematics at University of Chicago *post* 1892. Under his leadership, the department became one of the leading centers in America for teaching and research. His interest in integral equations led to the formulation of his so-called General Analysis, a theory which included as special cases the classical integral equation theory and numerous other chapters of mathematics. Far ahead of his time, he set forth ideas which other writers have rediscovered and developed since his death. [*Supp. 1*]

MOORE, ELY (*b. near Belvidere, N.J., 1798; d. Lecompton, Kans., 1860*), printer, labor leader. Elected president of newly formed New York City General Trades' Union, 1833; edited its official organ, the *National Trades' Union;* was chairman of national convention of trade unions, New York, 1834. Running as a unionist with Tammany Hall support, he served as congressman from New York, 1835–39. Removing to Kansas *c.* 1850, he held various federal offices until his death.

MOORE, FRANK (*b. Concord, N.H., 1828; d. Waverly, Mass., 1904*), author, editor. Son of Jacob B. Moore; brother of George H. Moore. Edited a number of useful compilations which include *Songs and Ballads of the American Revolution* (1856), *Diary of the American Revolution* (1859–60), and *The Rebellion Record* (1861–68).

MOORE, GABRIEL (*b. Stokes Co., N.C., 1785?; d. probably Caddo, Texas, 1845?*), lawyer, Alabama legislator. Removed to Huntsville, then in Mississippi Territory, *c.* 1810. A leader of the Jacksonian faction, he served as congressman from Alabama, 1821–29, and as governor of the state, 1829–31. He advocated the graduation system for the sale of public lands and opposed nullification; locally, he supported beginning of canal construction around Muscle Shoals and the opening of the state university. While U.S. senator, 1831–37, he broke with the Jackson forces and so ended his political career.

MOORE, GEORGE FLEMING (*b. Elbert Co., Ga., 1822; d. Washington, D.C., 1883*), lawyer, Confederate soldier. Settled in Texas, 1846. Associate justice and chief justice, Texas supreme court, 1862–67, 1874–81. An independent and courageous judge, he excelled in equity cases.

MOORE, GEORGE FOOT (*b. West Chester, Pa., 1851; d. 1931*), theologian, Orientalist, historian of religions. Studied at Yale and Union Theological Seminary; was Presbyterian pastor at Zanesville, O., 1878–83; Old Testament professor at Andover Theological Seminary, 1884–1901; professor of the history of religion at Harvard, 1902–28. Eminent here and abroad as a critical scholar in the fields of Hebrew and the Old Testament, he was assistant editor of the *Andover Review* (1884–93) and editor of the *Harvard Theological Review* (1908–14, 1921–31). His chief works include: *Critical and Exegetical Commentary on Judges* (1895), *History of Religions* (1913–19), and *Judaism in the First Centuries of the Christian Era* (1927–30).

MOORE, GEORGE HENRY (*b. Concord, N.H., 1823; d. 1892*), librarian, historian, bibliographer. Son of Jacob B. Moore; brother of Frank Moore. Active in work of New-York Historical Society, 1841–91; superintendent of Lenox Library, New York, N.Y., *post* 1872.

MOORE, Sir HENRY (*b. Vere, Jamaica, B.W.I., 1713; d. New York, 1769*), colonial official. Educated at Eton and University of Leyden. Served successively as member of Jamaica assembly, as councilman and as secretary of the island; was acting governor, 1756–62, in which time he quelled a Negro insurrection. Created baronet, 1764, he was appointed governor of New York, 1765, and served until his death. Patient and conciliatory during the Stamp Act disturbances, he was accused of "caressing the demagogues." Thereafter, he devoted time to settlement of boundary disputes with neighboring provinces and to Indian policy; his controversy with the New York Assembly over their failure to pass the Quartering Bill led to the prorogation of the Assembly, December 1766, and to the restraining act, signed by the King in the summer of 1767.

MOORE, JACOB BAILEY (*b. Andover, N.H., 1797; d. Bellows Falls, Vt., 1853*), New Hampshire journalist, printer. Brother of John W. Moore; father of George H. and Frank Moore. Removed to New York City, 1839. After holding federal offices in Washington, D.C., and New Hampshire, he was elected librarian of New-York Historical Society, 1848. He resigned in 1849 to set up the U.S. post office in California and served as deputy postmaster, San Francisco, 1850–53.

MOORE, JAMES (*b. probably Ireland, date unknown; d. Charleston, S.C., 1706*), Indian trader, colonial official. Settled at Charleston *c.* 1675; was soon prominent in movements of protest against the proprietors. Elected governor of South Carolina by the council, 1700, he served until 1703. Ambitious and adventurous, he led the force which besieged St. Augustine during Queen Anne's War.

MOORE, JAMES (*b. New Hanover Co., N.C., 1737; d. Wilmington, N.C., 1777*), Revolutionary soldier, North Carolina provincial legislator. Brother of Maurice Moore. Directed American maneuvers in campaign ending in victory at Moore's Creek Bridge, February 1776.

MOORE, JAMES (*b. probably Virginia, 1764; d. Lexington, Ky., 1814*), Episcopal clergyman, educator. Removed to Kentucky *ante* April 1792; was ordained to Episcopal Ministry, 1794. Served *post* 1792 as principal of Transylvania Seminary and of Kentucky Academy; headed both schools when united under name of Transylvania University, 1799–1804. Became first resident Episcopal rector in Kentucky, 1809.

MOORE, JAMES EDWARD (*b. Clarksville, Pa., 1852; d. 1918*), surgeon. M.D., Bellevue Hospital Medical College, 1873. Practiced in Minneapolis, Minn., *post* 1882; taught orthopedics and clinical surgery at University of Minnesota from 1888 until his death. Author of *Orthopedic Surgery* (1898).

MOORE, JOHN (*b. England, c. 1659; d. Philadelphia, Pa., 1732*), colonial official. Emigrated *c.* 1680 to South Carolina where he held provincial offices; removed to Philadelphia *c.* 1696. Appointed advocate of the court of vice-admiralty for Pennsylvania and West Jersey, 1698, he and his friend, Robert Quarry, who was the judge of this court, were closely associated in leadership of the Anglican party and in efforts to enforce the acts of trade and navigation. King's attorney-general for Pennsylvania, 1700–04, Moore continued to serve in lucrative provincial posts until his death despite his opposition and disloyalty to the proprietors and unpopularity with the people of Pennsylvania. He belongs in the same class with Edward Randolph, Joseph Dudley and other early American Tories who combined a lust for office with a sincere devotion to the cause of imperial unity.

MOORE, JOHN (*b. Rosmead, Ireland, 1834; d. 1901*), Roman Catholic clergyman. Emigrated to Charleston, S.C., 1848; ordained in Rome, 1860; served as curate and rector in Charleston, 1860–77. Able and liberal bishop of St. Augustine, Fla., 1877–1901.

MOORE, JOHN TROTWOOD (*b. Marion, Ala., 1858; d. Nashville, Tenn., 1929*), journalist. Resident in Tennessee *post* 1885. Author of *The Bishop of Cottontown* (1906), *Uncle Wash, His Stories* (1910), *The Gift of the Grass* (1911) and other authentic, regional novels, tales and verse.

MOORE, JOHN WEEKS (*b. probably Andover, N.H., 1807; d. Manchester, N.H., 1889*), printer, newspaper publisher, editor of musical journals and collections. Brother of Jacob B. Moore.

MOORE, MAURICE (*b. New Hanover Co., N.C., 1735; d. 1777*), North Carolina jurist and provincial legislator, Revolutionary patriot. Brother of James Moore (1737–1777); father of Alfred Moore. Initially sympathetic toward the Regulator movement, he served as a judge at the special court in Hillsboro that sentenced 12 Regulators to death after the battle of Alamance (May 1771). Thereafter, however, he opposed Gov. Tryon's policy toward the insurgents and actively promoted a policy of leniency toward their leaders. A member of several important committees in the patriot interest *post* 1775, he was too conservative to approve actual separation from Great Britain.

MOORE, NATHANIEL FISH (*b. Newtown, N.Y., 1782; d. 1872*), scholar, librarian, author, educator. Nephew of Benjamin Moore. Graduated Columbia, 1802; taught classical languages there, 1817–35, and served as president, 1842–49.

MOORE, NICHOLAS. [See MORE, NICHOLAS, d. 1689.]

MOORE, PHILIP NORTH (*b. Connersville, Ind., 1849; d. St. Louis, Mo., 1930*), mining engineer. Did important work in stimulating production of strategic minerals through War Minerals Committee, 1917.

MOORE, RICHARD BISHOP (*b. Cincinnati, O., 1871; d. Lafayette, Ind., 1931*), chemist. Son of William T. Moore. Educated mainly abroad; studied under William Ramsay at London, 1886–90, and became interested in rare gases and radium. After teaching chemistry at several institutions, he entered U.S. government service, 1911, and went with the Bureau of Mines as physical chemist, 1912. In government service until 1923, he supervised preparation of the first radium salts produced in the United States, was among the first to advocate use of helium in balloons and airships, and as chief chemist of the Bureau, *post* 1919, organized the cryogenic laboratory in Washington and directed work of reducing the cost of helium production. *Post* 1926, he served as professor of chemistry and dean of the school of science at Purdue University.

MOORE, RICHARD CHANNING (*b. New York, N.Y., 1762; d. Lynchburg, Va., 1841*), Episcopal clergyman, physician. Zealous and strongly evangelical, he was consecrated bishop of Virginia, 1814, and served until his death. Together with John H. Hobart and Alexander V. Griswold, he is credited with reconstructing the Episcopal Church in the United States both in spirit and in character.

MOORE, SAMUEL PRESTON (*b. Charleston, S.C., 1813; d. Richmond, Va., 1889*), army surgeon. Graduated Medical College of South Carolina, 1834; commissioned, U.S. Army assistant surgeon, 1835. After long service on the Western frontiers and in the Mexican War, he resigned his commission early in 1861 and accepted the post of surgeon-general of the Confederate Army in which he served until 1865. Strict and exacting, he did the best he could in a most difficult task.

MOORE, THOMAS OVERTON (*b. Sampson Co., N.C., 1804; d. near Alexandria, La., 1876*), planter. Removed to Louisiana, 1829, where he became an important sugar grower. As Democratic governor of Louisiana, 1860–64, he led in making his state a member of the Confederacy and in securing its resources for Confederate use even after the Union seizure of New Orleans and its neighborhood.

MOORE, THOMAS PATRICK (*b. Charlotte Co., Va., 1796?; d. Harrodsburg, Ky., 1853*), lawyer, soldier in War of 1812 and Mexican War, Kentucky politician and legislator. An ardent Jacksonian, he served as U.S. minister to Colombia, 1829–33, where he obtained important commercial concessions for the United States.

MOORE, VERANUS ALVA (*b. Hounsfield, N.Y., 1859; d. 1931*), pathologist, leader in veterinary science. Graduated Cornell, 1887; M.D., Columbian

(now George Washington University) Medical School, 1890. Professor of comparative pathology, bacteriology and meat inspection in the veterinary college at Cornell, 1896–1929, he also held the position of dean, 1908–29. Under his administration the college became outstanding and Moore won international reputation in his fields. His researches were of incalculable value to the livestock industry.

MOORE, WILLIAM (*b. Philadelphia, Pa., 1699; d. near Valley Forge, Pa., 1783*), Pennsylvania provincial legislator and jurist. Son of John Moore (*c. 1659–1732*). Opposed Quaker-dominated Assembly over frontier defense, 1755–58; was a passive Loyalist during Revolution.

MOORE, WILLIAM (*b. Philadelphia, Pa., c. 1735; d. Philadelphia, 1793*), merchant, Revolutionary patriot. Vice-president (1779–1781) and president (1782) of Pennsylvania supreme executive council. A conservative constitutionalist, he was a jealous guardian of executive privilege and was active in promoting plans to solve Pennsylvania's financial difficulties.

MOORE, WILLIAM HENRY (*b. Utica, N.Y., 1848; d. New York, N.Y., 1923*), lawyer, capitalist, promoter. After successful practice of corporation law in partnership with his brother in Chicago, Moore turned *post* 1887 to the development and exploitation of industrial mergers. The first important venture of the Moore brothers, who continued to work together, was the reorganization of the Diamond Match Co. in whose stock they formed a pool; after much manipulation and publicity the price of the stock was forced up with the intention of unloading it at top price on the unwary. Failure of this scheme resulted in the closing of the Chicago Exchange, August 1896. Forced out of Diamond Match, Moore organized a merger of various biscuit and cracker companies into the National Biscuit Co., 1898, which was immensely successful, achieving as it did a monopoly control of 90% of the nation's business in that commodity. Turning to the steel industry, he organized in rapid succession (1898–99) the American Tin Plate Co., the National Steel Co., and the American Steel Hoop Co. Although the stock of all three companies was plentifully watered and represented anticipated profits rather than actual properties, it was over-subscribed. After failure in attempting to buy the Carnegie-Frick properties, the Moores created the American Sheet and Steel Co., 1900, and the American Can Co., 1901. When J. P. Morgan succeeded in buying out Carnegie and launching the new U.S. Steel Corp., 1901, the Moore companies were included in the merger and their sale brought the brothers enormous wealth. Later activities of the Moores in railroad properties were equally daring and unscrupulous. Their looting of the Rock Island system resulted in their arraignment by the Interstate Commerce Commission, 1916.

MOORE, WILLIAM THOMAS (*b. Henry Co., Ky., 1832; d. Orlando, Fla., 1926*), clergyman of the Disciples of Christ, educator, promoter of missionary work.

MOORE, ZEPHANIAH SWIFT (*b. Palmer, Mass., 1770; d. 1823*), Congregational clergyman, educator. Graduated Dartmouth, 1793; served as pastor at Leicester, Mass., 1797–1811. Professor of learned languages at Dartmouth, 1811–15, he was then elected president of Williams College, a post which he filled with high efficiency until 1821. Chosen as first president of Amherst College, he saw that institution successfully under way before his death in office.

MOOREHEAD, WILLIAM GALLOGLY (*b. near Rix Mills, O., 1836; d. Xenia, O., 1914*), United Presbyterian clergyman, Biblical scholar. Taught at Xenia Theological Seminary, and served as its president, 1899–1914.

MOORHEAD, JAMES KENNEDY (*b. Halifax, Pa., 1806; d. Pittsburgh, Pa., 1884*), canal builder, pioneer in commercial telegraphy, politician. President *post* 1846 of Monongahela Navigation Co.; president, Atlantic and Ohio Telegraph Co. and subsidiary companies *post* 1853. Congressman, Republican, from Pennsylvania, 1859–69.

MOOSMÜLLER, OSWALD WILLIAM (*b. Aidling, Bavaria, 1832; d. Wetaug, Ill., 1901*), Roman Catholic clergyman, Benedictine. Came to America, 1852; was educated at St. Vincent's Abbey, Latrobe, Pa.; ordained, 1856. Led an active, wandering life here and abroad during which he held many positions as an official of his order and as missionary and army chaplain. Organized Cluny monastery, Wetaug, Ill., 1892.

MORAIS, SABATO (*b. Leghorn, Italy, 1823; d. 1897*), rabbi of Mikveh Israel congregation, Philadelphia, Pa., 1851–97. A founder of the Jewish Theological Seminary, New York City, 1886, he served it as president of the faculty and professor of the Bible until his death.

MORAN, BENJAMIN (*b. Chester Co., Pa., 1820; d. England, 1886*), diplomat. Served as clerk, secretary and chargé d'affaires at the U.S. legation in London, 1853–74, and as U.S. minister-resident to Portugal, 1874–76. On discontinuance of his office, he became chargé d'affaires at Lisbon, resigning in 1882. Moran's journal (covering 1857–74) provides invaluable material on contemporary relations between United States and Great Britain. A staunch Unionist, Moran played no little part in preventing open rupture with Great Britain during the Civil War.

MORAN, DANIEL EDWARD (*b. Orange, N.J., 1864; d. Mendham, N.J., 1937*), civil engineer, specialist in foundation work. [*Supp. 2*]

MORAN, EDWARD (*b. Bolton, England, 1829; d. 1901*), marine painter. Brother of Peter and Thomas Moran. Came to America, 1844; worked as a weaver; was encouraged to paint by several landscapists in Philadelphia. Removing to New York City, 1872, he was a conspicuous figure in the art life there until his death. His important group of 13 large paintings illustrating salient episodes in American history is owned by the Pennsylvania Museum of Art and betrays influence of the British painters Turner and Stanfield.

MORAN, PETER (*b. Bolton, England, 1841; d. Philadelphia, Pa., 1914*), landscape and animal painter, etcher. Brother of Edward and Thomas Moran. Came to America as a child; studied with his elder brothers who had become established as painters. Won high repute in field of animal painting and as one of the best American workers in etching and dry point of his time.

MORAN, THOMAS (*b. Bolton, England, 1837; d. Santa Barbara, Calif., 1926*), landscape painter, etcher. Brother of Edward and Peter Moran. Came to America as a child; was apprenticed to a wood engraver in Philadelphia. Began to paint under tutelage of his brother Edward. In England, 1862, he copied Turner's pictures whose influence remained with him throughout his life. After a later European tour on the continent, he returned to the United States and in 1871 accompanied the U.S. Geological Expedition under F. V. Hayden to the Yellowstone region; in 1873, he made a second exploration to the Grand Canyon of the Colorado. Panoramic landscapes of the Yellowstone and Colorado canyons which he painted were purchased by Congress and are of importance as the first adequate pictorial records of the scenery of those then unfamiliar regions. His success with these and similar Far West subjects was owing in large measure to his assimilation of the grand style of Turner with its daring color, visible atmosphere and splendor of effect. He did excellent work also as an illustrator, and was an etcher and original lithographer of more than common merit.

MORAWETZ, VICTOR (*b. Baltimore, Md., 1859; d. Charleston, S.C., 1938*), lawyer, specialist in railroad and corporation law. [*Supp. 2*]

MORDECAI, ALFRED (*b. Warrenton, N.C., 1804; d. Philadelphia, Pa., 1887*), soldier, engineer. Graduated West Point, 1823. After serving with great ability as an engineer and ordnance expert, he resigned from the army in May 1861 on the conscientious ground that he could fight against neither his country nor his state. Thereafter, he worked as an engineer in railroad construction and as an official of canal and coal companies controlled by the Pennsylvania Railroad.

MORDECAI, MOSES COHEN (*b. Charleston, S.C., 1804; d. Baltimore, Md., 1888*), merchant, shipowner, Charleston official and South Carolina legislator. Removed to Baltimore, Md., 1865, where he recouped losses suffered in the Civil War.

MORE, NICHOLAS (*b. England, date unknown; d. Moreland Township, Philadelphia Co., Pa., 1689*), Pennsylvania jurist. Emigrated to Pennsylvania, 1682. Appointed chief justice of Pennsylvania and the lower counties (Delaware), 1684, he became involved in a dispute with the Assembly which ended in the first impeachment trial in American history, May 1685. The provincial council refusing to sanction the impeachment proceedings, he was retained in office and in 1686 was appointed one of five commissioners who were to act as the executive of the province. His health failed and he was unable to serve.

MORE, PAUL ELMER (*b. St. Louis, Mo., 1864; d. Princeton, N.J., 1937*), literary critic, philosopher. Graduated Washington University, 1887; A.M., 1892. A.M., Harvard, 1893. After teaching for a short time, he retired to Shelburne, N.H., for two years of study and meditation (1898–1900). He then became successively literary editor of the *Independent* and the N.Y. *Evening Post*, and editor (1904–14) of the *Nation*. From 1914 until his retirement in 1934, he gave lectures and graduate seminars at Princeton University. His penetrating, judicial essays in criticism are embodied in the *Shelburne Essays* (8 volumes, 1904–21) and *New Shelburne Essays* (3 volumes, 1928–36). Associated in the public mind with his lifelong friend Irving Babbitt as a leader of the crusade for the "New Humanism," More regarded himself as the spokesman of enduring tradition in literature; he sought to evaluate given authors in relation to the stream of historical tendency. His final position in religious philosophy was a sort of working compromise between Platonism and Christianity. [*Supp. 2*]

MOREAU DE SAINT-MÉRY, MÉDÉRIC-LOUIS-ÉLIE (*b. Fort Royal, Martinique, 1750; d. Paris, France, 1819*), publisher, historian, French Revolutionary politician. Resident in Philadelphia, Pa., 1794–98, as a refugee from Revolutionary excesses in Paris, he set up as a bookseller and stationer; his shop became the rendezvous of the French émigrés, notably Volney, Talleyrand, LaRochefoucauld-Liancourt and the Duke of Orleans. He published in excellent style a number of books and pamphlets written by him or by his friends, among them his own two books on the history of Santo Domingo. Threatened with deportation under the Alien Bill, he returned to France in August 1798, where he was prominent as a diplomat and official in the earlier days of Napoleon's rule.

MOREAU-LISLET, LOUIS CASIMIR ELISABETH (*b. Cap Français, Santo Domingo, 1767; d. New Orleans, La., 1832*), Louisiana jurist and legislator. Co-author of several valuable works on the criminal and civil law of Louisiana.

MOREHEAD, CHARLES SLAUGHTER (*b. Nelson Co., Ky., 1802; d. near Greenville, Miss., 1868*), lawyer, Kentucky legislator. Congressman, Whig, from Kentucky, 1847–51; governor, Know-Nothing, 1855–59. Approved Kentucky neutrality, 1861; was imprisoned briefly, 1861, for his public criticism of cutting off trade with the South.

MOREHEAD, JAMES TURNER (*b. near Shepherdsville, Ky., 1797; d. Covington, Ky., 1854*), lawyer, Kentucky legislator. National Republican governor of Kentucky, 1834–36; U.S. senator, Whig, 1841–47. A consistent supporter of the policies of Henry Clay.

MOREHEAD, JOHN MOTLEY (*b. Pittsylvania Co., Va., 1796; d. 1866*), lawyer, North Carolina legislator and railroad promoter. Whig governor of North Carolina, 1841–45.

MOREHOUSE, HENRY LYMAN (*b. Stanfordville, N.Y., 1834; d. Brooklyn, N.Y., 1917*), Baptist clergyman, promoter of Baptist home mission work.

MORELL, GEORGE WEBB (*b. Cooperstown, N.Y., 1815; d. Scarborough, N.Y., 1883*), engineer, lawyer, Union major-general. Grandson of Samuel B. Webb.

MOREY, SAMUEL (*b. Hebron, Conn., 1762; d. Fairlee, Vt., 1843*), lumberman, contractor, inventor. Built and operated several vessels driven by steam, 1793–97; claimed that his ideas were stolen by Robert Fulton. Received one of first American patents for an internal combustion engine, 1826.

MORFIT, CAMPBELL (*b. Herculaneum, Mo., 1820; d. near London, England, 1897*), pioneer industrial chemist. Taught applied chemistry at University of Maryland, 1854–58; assisted James C. Booth in preparing *The Encyclopedia of Chemistry* (1850) and was sole author of a number of technical treatises on fertilizers, the manufacture of paper and soap, and oil refining. Resided in England *post* 1861.

MORFORD, HENRY (*b. New Monmouth, N.J., 1823; d. 1881*), journalist. Author of a number of successful travel guides; also, of *The Rest of Don Juan* (1846), a continuation of Byron's poem, and of three novels which attempted to express the mood of the Civil War. These were *Shoulder-Straps* (1863), *The Days of Shoddy* (1863), and *The Coward* (1864).

MORGAN, ABEL (*b. Cardiganshire, South Wales, 1673; d. Pennsylvania, 1722*), Baptist clergyman. Emigrated to Philadelphia, 1712; became a leader among Pennsylvania Baptists and also established churches in Delaware and New Jersey. Author of the first real concordance to the Welsh Bible, published posthumously (1730).

MORGAN, CHARLES (*b. Killingworth, now Clinton, Conn., 1795; d. New York, N.Y., 1878*), shipping magnate, railroad owner. Built up successful line of steamers plying to Gulf ports of the United States and to Mexico *post* 1835; with C. K. Garrison, engaged in a commercial war against Cornelius Vanderbilt and George Law to secure control of the Nicaragua Transit, 1853–55. After profiting heavily by the Civil War, Morgan started the Morgan Line from New York to New Orleans and extended his activities to include Texas railroads. By the time of his death, he had established a virtual monopoly of Texas transportation.

MORGAN, CHARLES HILL (*b. Rochester, N.Y., 1831; d. Worcester, Mass., 1911*), engineer. Designed an automatic machine for making paper bags, 1860, whose success placed paper-bag manufacturing on a commercial footing for the first time. With Fred H. Daniels, patented improvements in wire-rolling mills which were combined in the Morgan Mill. Founded Morgan Construction Co. for manufacture of rolling-mill machinery, 1891.

MORGAN, DANIEL (*b. probably Hunterdon Co., N.J., 1736; d. 1802*), Revolutionary soldier. Removed as a youth to the Shenandoah Valley of Virginia; accompanied Braddock's expedition as an independent wagoner, 1755; served as lieutenant in Pontiac's War. Commissioned captain of Virginia riflemen, June 1775, he was taken prisoner during the ill-fated assault on Quebec in that year. Exchanged in autumn, 1776, he commanded a corps of sharpshooters, distinguishing himself particularly in the Saratoga campaign. Resigning from the army, July 1779, in a dispute over promotion, he returned to active service, 1780. As brigadier-general commanding the troops in western North Carolina, he won the decisive victory of Cowpens, January 1781. Later a large landowner in western Pennsylvania and Virginia, he assisted in suppressing the Whiskey insurrection, 1794.

MORGAN, EDWIN BARBER (*b. Aurora, N.Y., 1806; d. Aurora, 1881*), merchant, philanthropist. Cousin of Edwin D. Morgan. Associated with Henry Wells in the express business, he was first president of Wells, Fargo, 1852; he was active also in the U.S. Express Co. and in the American Express Co. As a stockholder of the *New York Times*, he supported editor George Jones in the fight against Boss Tweed, 1871. He was a principal benefactor of Wells College and of Auburn Theological Seminary.

MORGAN, EDWIN DENISON (*b. Washington, Mass., 1811; d. New York, N.Y., 1883*), merchant, banker, New York legislator. Cousin of Edwin B. Morgan. As Republican governor of New York, 1859–63, he displayed independence and statesmanship, improving New York's credit and giving maximum support to the Lincoln administration in the Civil War. He served with ability as U.S. senator, 1863–69, and was a generous benefactor of Williams College, Union Theological Seminary, and several New York City hospitals.

MORGAN, EDWIN VERNON (*b. Aurora, N.Y., 1865; d. Brazil, 1934*), diplomat. Grandson of Edwin

B. Morgan. After serving as a teacher of history, 1893–98, Morgan formally entered the U.S. diplomatic service, 1900. Among the numerous posts which he held, he was most effective as U.S. minister to Brazil, 1912–33. [*Supp.* 1]

MORGAN, GEORGE (*b. Philadelphia, Pa., 1743; d. near Washington, Pa., 1810*), land-speculator, Indian agent. Brother of John Morgan. Partner *post* 1763 in trading firm of Baynton, Wharton and Morgan, representing it in the Illinois country; named secretary-agent of the Indiana Company with headquarters at Fort Pitt, 1776. Served during the Revolution as Indian agent for the United States in the middle department and as deputy commissary-general of purchases for the western district, resigning in 1779. Founded colony of New Madrid in present Missouri, 1789. Refused overtures of Aaron Burr to join him in his Western schemes.

MORGAN, GEORGE WASHINGTON (*b. Washington Co., Pa., 1820; d. Fortress Monroe, Va., 1893*), lawyer, diplomat, soldier. Removed to Mount Vernon, O., 1843. Received brevet of brigadier-general for gallantry in Mexican War; served as U.S. consul at Marseilles, 1856–58, and as U.S. minister to Lisbon, 1858–61. Commissioned Union brigadier-general, November 1861, he rose to division and corps command in the Western campaigns of the Civil War before his resignation, June 1863. As congressman, Democrat, from Ohio, 1867–68 and 1869–73, he opposed harsh reconstruction measures.

MORGAN, JAMES DADA (*b. Boston, Mass., 1810; d. Quincy, Ill., 1896*), merchant, banker, Union soldier. Removed to Quincy, Ill., 1834; served with credit in Mexican War. Entering Civil War as colonel of 10th Illinois Infantry, he received brevet of major-general, March 1865, for saving the left wing of Sherman's army at Bentonville, N.C.

MORGAN, JAMES MORRIS (*b. New Orleans, La., 1845; d. 1928*), Confederate naval officer. Half-brother of Philip H. Morgan. Author of *Recollections of a Rebel Reefer* (1917).

MORGAN, JOHN (*b. Philadelphia, Pa., 1735; d. Philadelphia, 1789*), physician. Brother of George Morgan. Graduated College of Philadelphia (University of Pennsylvania), 1757; served medical apprenticeship under John Redman and studied under outstanding medical men in England and Italy; M.D., University of Edinburgh, 1763. Proposed establishment of a medical school in connection with College of Philadelphia, 1765; on adoption of the project, was appointed professor of the theory and practice of medicine there. In line with this work, he published his classic *Discourse upon the Institution of Medical Schools in America* (1765) in which he advocated separating the functions of physician, surgeon and apothecary. Elected by Congress director-general of hospitals and chief physician of the American army, October 1775, he made a drastic reorganization of the medical department and by his exacting methods provoked the jealousy and antagonism of his subordinates. After a curtailment of his authority in October 1776, he was removed from his posts, January 1777. Publishing a vindication of his conduct, he withdrew from public life, confining himself to his private practice and his duties as professor and as physician at the Pennsylvania Hospital.

MORGAN, JOHN HUNT (*b. Huntsville, Ala., 1825; d. Greenville, Tenn., 1864*), businessman, Confederate raider. Early in 1862, as captain of cavalry he began his famous raids in Tennessee and Kentucky during which he harassed the Union Army by penetrating its lines, capturing men and trains, and destroying supplies. His rapidity in action, his dispersal of his command after securing his objectives, and his policy of avoiding fighting wherever possible account for his remarkable success. His most memorable raid took place in July 1863 through part of Ohio. Although it ended in his capture, it saved east Tennessee to the Confederacy for several months. After his escape from Ohio State Penitentiary at Columbus, Morgan was assigned to command the Department of Southwest Virginia in April 1864. He organized an efficient force, raided Kentucky in June, but was killed in action while preparing to attack Union forces near Knoxville.

MORGAN, JOHN PIERPONT (*b. Hartford, Conn., 1837; d. Rome, Italy, 1913*), banker, connoisseur of art. Son of Junius S. Morgan; grandson of John Pierpont. Entered father's firm in London, 1856; returned to New York, 1857, to work for American representatives of George Peabody & Co.; acted as New York agent for father's firm, 1860–64. Member of firm of Dabney, Morgan & Co., 1864–71; formed firm of Drexel, Morgan & Co., with Anthony J. Drexel, 1871. Closely associated with correspondent firms in Philadelphia, Paris and London, the firm (*post* 1895 known as J. P. Morgan & Co.) became one of the most powerful banking houses in the world.

J. P. Morgan, although he engaged in several dubious pieces of business during the Civil War period, was essentially an organizer and stabilizing force in business. His prominence may be said to date from 1873, when, by securing a division of a U.S. treasury loan between a Morgan syndicate and one organized by Jay Cooke, he broke the monopoly of that financier in the refunding operations of the government. After Cooke's failure, the Morgan firm became dominant in government financing and managed a long series of railroad and other corporate reorganizations with a view to the restoration of faith abroad in American securities. Morgan was also able to establish some community of interest among railroads hitherto engaged in ruthless and wasteful competition. His efforts were particularly valuable in the reorgani-

zations required after the panic of 1893, although the methods which he employed resulted in a vast concentration of power in his own hands. In 1895, on extremely harsh terms, he formed a syndicate which effectually halted a drain of gold from the reserves of the U.S. treasury. One of his most daring and imperial undertakings was the formation of the U.S. Steel Corp., 1901, which, although heavily overcapitalized, proved highly successful to investors. Among his less successful activities were the International Mercantile Marine (1902) and his struggle for control of the Northern Pacific Railroad with Edward H. Harriman. Morgan's personal influence was a decisive factor in overcoming the money panic of 1907 and after Harriman's death Morgan stood without a rival in the public mind as the symbol of financial power.

Investigated by Congress, 1912, he emerged with unimpaired personal credit and prestige. His statements under examination that "the first requisite of credit is character" and that he "would not lend money to a man he didn't trust" were characteristic of him. Implicit faith was reposed in his word; his very physique was commanding and he dealt in ultimatums. He was capable of violent dislikes as well as likes, but despite his prejudices he was gifted in choosing talented partners. He was a ruthless force making for centralized control of industry and credit, yet on the other hand he contributed to corporate stability. He was not interested in social reform nor did he care for public opinion; he had an instinctive shrinking from personal publicity. As a collector of books and art, he displayed good personal taste and the same powers of imagination and instant decision which marked his business career. A major benefactor of the Metropolitan Museum of Art, New York, he left his superb personal library to be administered as a public reference library. An enthusiastic yachtsman and traveler, he was also one of the most active lay members of the Episcopal Church.

MORGAN, JOHN TYLER (*b. Athens, Tenn., 1824; d. 1907*), lawyer, Confederate brigadier-general. Raised in Calhoun Co., Ala., he studied law with William P. Chilton. In 1855, he removed to Selma, Ala., where he resided until his death. As U.S. senator, Democrat, from Alabama, 1877–1907, he advocated state-rights views with independence and courage, fought to reclaim unearned land grants which the railroads were holding, sponsored legislation in support of education, and was long identified with the fight for an Isthmian Canal over the Nicaragua route. He was a strong expansionist and an ardent supporter of free silver.

MORGAN, JUNIUS SPENCER (*b. West Springfield, Mass., 1813; d. Monte Carlo, Monaco, 1890*), international banker. Father of John Pierpont Morgan. After business experience in Hartford and Boston, Morgan became a partner (1854) in the London international banking firm of George Peabody & Co.; on Peabody's retirement, 1864, Morgan headed the firm under the name of J. S. Morgan & Co. until his own death. The remark "Never sell a bear on the United States" is attributed to him.

MORGAN, JUSTIN (*b. near West Springfield, Mass., 1747; d. Woodstock, Vt., 1798*), schoolteacher. In return for a debt, Morgan accepted (1795) the colt which was the progenitor of the breed known as the "Morgan horse."

MORGAN, LEWIS HENRY (*b. near Aurora, N.Y., 1818; d. 1881*), lawyer, New York legislator, ethnologist, anthropologist. Graduated Union, 1840. Author of a number of pioneering books based on serious scientific study which include *The League of the . . . Iroquois* (1851), *Systems of Consanguinity and Affinity of the Human Family* (in Smithsonian Contributions to Knowledge, vol. XVII, 1871), *Ancient Society* (1877, 1878) and *Houses and House-Life of the American Aborigines* (1881). He was author also of a number of monographs and of *The American Beaver* (1868). He has been called the "father of American anthropology."

MORGAN, MATTHEW SOMERVILLE (*b. London, England, 1839; d. New York, N.Y., 1890*), artist, correspondent, cartoonist. Worked in America, 1870–90; famous for Civil War cartoons in London *Fun*.

MORGAN, MORRIS HICKY (*b. Providence, R.I., 1859; d. 1910*), classicist. Graduated Harvard, 1881; Ph.D., 1887. Taught classical languages and philology at Harvard, 1887–1910; translator-editor, *Vitruvius, the Ten Books on Architecture* (1914).

MORGAN, PHILIP HICKY (*b. Baton Rouge, La., 1825; d. New York, N.Y., 1900*), jurist, diplomat. Half-brother of James M. Morgan; nephew of Thomas M. T. McKennan. Opposed secession; as Louisiana supreme court judge, 1873–76, upheld reconstruction policies. A judge of the international court in Egypt, 1877–80, he served as U.S. minister to Mexico, 1880–85.

MORGAN, THOMAS JEFFERSON (*b. Franklin, Ind., 1839; d. 1902*), Union brigadier-general, Baptist clergyman. Active *post* 1872 in educational work, he was U.S. commissioner of Indian affairs, 1889–93; thereafter he was corresponding secretary, American Baptist Home Mission Society, until his death.

MORGAN, WILLIAM (*b. probably Culpeper Co., Va., 1774?; d. possibly in vicinity of Batavia, N.Y., 1826?*), central figure in the anti-Masonic agitation, 1826–38. Morgan's disappearance and alleged murder just before publication of his book *Illustrations of Masonry*, an exposé of the secrets of freemasonry, had a profound effect on the politics of the time.

MORIARITY, PATRICK EUGENE (*b. Dublin, Ireland, 1804; d. Chestnut Hill, Pa., 1875*), Roman Catholic clergyman, Augustinian, temperance reformer. Came to Philadelphia, Pa., 1839; was pastor of St. Augustine's Church there and superior of Augustinian mission work. Founded Villanova College, 1842.

MORINI, AUSTIN JOHN (*b. Florence, Italy, 1826; d. Rome, Italy, 1909*), Roman Catholic clergyman, Servite. Came to the United States in 1870 to establish a foundation for the Servites in the diocese of Green Bay, Wis.; established Servite mother house in Chicago, Ill., 1874.

MORISON, GEORGE SHATTUCK (*b. New Bedford, Mass., 1842; d. 1903*), engineer, lawyer. Regarded at the time of his death as the leading bridge engineer in America and internationally renowned as a railway and waterway expert, Morison received his engineering training as principal assistant to Octave Chanute. Active in consulting practice *post* 1880, he was responsible for the building of more than a score of great railroad bridges over the principal rivers of this country; his work in bridging the Missouri River at some nine points is considered his outstanding achievement. He was a pioneer in the use of steel for bridge construction.

MORLEY, EDWARD WILLIAMS (*b. Newark, N.J., 1838; d. West Hartford, Conn., 1923*), chemist, physicist. Professor of natural history and chemistry at Western Reserve University, 1869–1906, Morley displayed great ingenuity in constructing apparatus and in making accurate measurements. His *magnum opus* was a study of densities of oxygen and hydrogen and the ratio in which they combine to form water (*Smithsonian Contributions*, No. 980, 1895). He made studies of the variation of the oxygen content of the atmosphere by which he substantiated the Loomis-Morley hypothesis of oxygen deficiency at times of high atmospheric pressure. He collaborated with A. A. Michelson in development of the interferometer and in subsequent experiments to measure lengths in terms of the wave-length of light. Morley also determined the velocity of light in a magnetic field (with Dayton C. Miller), and studied thermal expansion of air, nitrogen, oxygen, and carbon dioxide, devising a new form of manometer for this purpose.

MORLEY, FRANK (*b. Woodbridge, England, 1860; d. Baltimore, Md., 1937*), mathematician. Graduated King's College, Cambridge, 1884; Sc.D., 1898. Came to America, 1887, to join faculty of Haverford College where he remained until 1900; he then transferred to Johns Hopkins where he taught until his retirement, 1928. He was a specialist in application of complex numbers to the treatment of problems of plane geometry. [*Supp.* 2]

MORLEY, MARGARET WARNER (*b. Montrose, Iowa, 1858; d. Washington, D.C., 1923*), teacher. Wrote pioneering grade-school textbooks on nature study; those on sex and birth, such as *Song of Life* (1891), shocked contemporaries.

MORPHY, PAUL CHARLES (*b. New Orleans, La., 1837; d. New Orleans, 1884*), lawyer, chess player. After a brilliant campaign in Europe, 1858–59, Morphy was recognized as chess champion of the world and an unparalleled genius of the game. Disappointed in a normal career, he virtually ceased play in 1864.

MORRELL, BENJAMIN (*b. Rye, N.Y., 1795; d. Mozambique, 1839*), sealing-ship captain, explorer. Author of *A Narrative of Four Voyages to the South Sea* (1832).

MORRIL, DAVID LAWRENCE (*b. Epping, N.H., 1772; d. Concord, N.H., 1849*), Congregational clergyman, physician, New Hampshire legislator. U.S. senator, (Democrat) Republican, from New Hampshire, 1817–23; governor of New Hampshire, 1824–27. A moderate anti-slavery advocate, he vigorously disapproved the Missouri Compromise. He was an unusual combination of scholar and man of affairs.

MORRILL, ANSON PEASLEE (*b. Belgrade, Maine, 1803; d. Augusta, Maine, 1887*), woollen-mill owner. Brother of Lot M. Morrill. Breaking with the Democratic party on the issues of slavery and temperance, Morrill was elected governor of Maine in 1854 by a fusion of Whigs, Free-Soilers and temperance Democrats. Re-elected, 1855, by a popular plurality, he was set aside by the Democratic state senate. He served as congressman, Republican, from Maine, 1861–63, and later headed the Maine Central Railroad.

MORRILL, EDMUND NEEDHAM (*b. Westbrook, Maine, 1834; d. San Antonio, Texas, 1909*), businessman, Union soldier, Kansas legislator. Removed to Kansas, 1857. As congressman, Republican, from Kansas, 1883–91, he devoted his time almost exclusively to pension legislation; as anti-Populist Republican governor of Kansas, 1895–97, he met problems of the local farmers arising from drought and high rates of mortgage interest with the statement: "When the government has protected the individual in his life and property he ought to hustle for himself to get bread."

MORRILL, JUSTIN SMITH (*b. Strafford, Vt., 1810; d. Washington, D.C., 1898*), merchant, farmer, politician. Elected to the U.S. House of Representatives, 1854, as an anti-slavery Whig, he began an unbroken service of 12 years in the House and almost 32 years in the U.S. Senate to which he was first elected, 1866. In the House he became an important member of the ways and means committee, of which he served as chairman, 1865–67; in the Senate he served as a member of the committee on finance of which he was chairman, 1877–79, 1881–93, and 1895–98. A conscientious and fair-minded protectionist and an au-

thority on finance, he was influential throughout his congressional career in tariff legislation, especially in the acts of 1861 and 1883; he consistently opposed inconvertible money and financial inflation. Morrill made his greatest contribution in the Land-Grant College Act, first introduced in 1857 and vetoed by Buchanan but signed in a similar form by Abraham Lincoln, 1862. He was responsible also for an amplification of federal aid to education by grants of public lands in 1890, when he introduced the so-called Second Morrill Act.

MORRILL, LOT MYRICK (*b. Belgrade, Maine, 1812; d. Portland, Maine, 1883*), lawyer, Maine legislator. Brother of Anson P. Morrill. After achieving power in the Democratic party in Maine, he left the party formally in 1856 in protest against its platform of that year. Republican governor of Maine, 1858–61, he was U.S. senator, 1861–March 1869, and September 1869–July 1876. A strong adherent of congressional Reconstruction, he served briefly as U.S. secretary of the treasury at the end of President Grant's second term and was thereafter collector of customs at Portland, Maine.

MORRIS, ANTHONY (*b. London, England, 1654; d. 1721*), Quaker leader and minister, brewer, Pennsylvania jurist. Mayor of Philadelphia, 1703–04.

MORRIS, ANTHONY (*b. Philadelphia, Pa., 1766; d. near Georgetown, D.C., 1860*), merchant, Pennsylvania legislator. Unofficial U.S. representative to Spain, 1810–14; suggested purchase of East and West Florida, as eventually realized in Treaty of 1819.

MORRIS, CADWALADER (*b. Philadelphia, Pa., 1741 o.s.; d. Philadelphia, 1795*), merchant, Revolutionary patriot. Aided establishment of Pennsylvania Bank, 1780; a founder and a director (1781–87) of the Bank of North America.

MORRIS, CASPAR (*b. Philadelphia, Pa., 1805; d. 1884*), physician, Philadelphia philanthropist. Aided in planning of Johns Hopkins Hospital, Baltimore.

MORRIS, CHARLES (*b. Woodstock, Conn., 1784; d. 1856*), naval officer. Appointed midshipman, 1799; assisted Stephen Decatur in destruction of frigate *Philadelphia*, 1803; promoted to captain after exemplary service as first-lieutenant of U.S.S. *Constitution* in War of 1812. After further sea duty, he served at various times *post* 1823 as a member of the Board of Navy Commissioners; *post* 1844 he headed the Bureau of Construction and the Bureau of Ordnance. He was called by Admiral Farragut the "ablest sea officer of his day."

MORRIS, CLARA (*b. Toronto, Canada, 1848; d. New Canaan, Conn., 1925*), actress. Raised in Cleveland, O.; made first stage appearance there, 1862. Later famous with Daly's company and on the road as the most prominent emotional actress on the American stage, she was able, despite distinctly limited abilities, to play with great effect on the feelings of her audiences.

MORRIS, EDMUND (*b. Burlington, N.J., 1804; d. Burlington, 1874*), newspaper editor, agricultural writer.

MORRIS, EDWARD DAFYDD (*b. Utica, N.Y., 1825; d. Columbus, O., 1915*), Presbyterian clergyman. Held responsible teaching and other positions at Lane Theological Seminary, Cincinnati, O., *post* 1863; was a vigorous exponent of New School theology.

MORRIS, EDWARD JOY (*b. Philadelphia, Pa., 1815; d. Philadelphia, 1881*), lawyer, Pennsylvania legislator, diplomat. Congressman, Whig, from Pennsylvania, 1843–45; congressman, Republican, 1857–61. U.S. minister to Turkey, 1861–70. Author, among other books, of *Notes of a Tour through Turkey, Greece, Egypt, etc.* (1842).

MORRIS, ELIZABETH (*b. probably England, c. 1753; d. Philadelphia, Pa., 1826*), actress. Known on the stage as Mrs. Owen Morris. Made first American stage appearance, Philadelphia, 1772, with the American Company. Joined Wignell's company, 1791; shared in first Boston, Mass. theatrical season, 1792; was associated mainly with Chestnut St. Theatre, Philadelphia, 1794–1810. Mrs. Morris was regarded in her time as the greatest attraction on the American stage and was especially effective in high comedy.

MORRIS, GEORGE POPE (*b. Philadelphia, Pa., 1802; d. 1864*), journalist, poet. Founded *New-York Mirror*, 1823, which he published until 1842; founded the *New Mirror*, 1843, edited by himself and Nathaniel P. Willis, but discontinued, 1844; was associated also with Willis in the *Home Journal post* 1846 (original title, the *National Press*). General Morris, as he was known in his day, was a writer of popular song lyrics; his most famous individual poem is "Woodman, Spare that Tree." He was author also of a volume of prose sketches, *The Little Frenchman and His Water Lots* (1839). His verses were published in numerous editions.

MORRIS, GEORGE SYLVESTER (*b. Norwich, Vt., 1840; d. Ann Arbor, Mich., 1889*), educator, philosopher. Taught at University of Michigan *post* 1870; was a champion of Kantian idealism. His point of view may be regarded as akin to that of W. T. Harris and the St. Louis Hegelians and to English philosophers like T. H. Green and F. H. Bradley.

MORRIS, GOUVERNEUR (*b. Morrisania, N.Y., 1752; d. 1816*), statesman, diplomat. Grandson of Lewis Morris (1671–1746); half-brother of Lewis (1726–98) and Richard Morris. Brilliance, the influence of his prominent landed New York family, unfailing self-assurance, and remarkable social aptitude all combined to make a political career inevitable

for him. But for the constant interruptions of politics and diplomacy, he could have achieved the foremost rank of lawyers in his day, as attested by his successful practice in New York City after graduation from King's College, 1768, and admission to the bar, 1771. Originally a conservative and reluctant to countenance a break with Great Britain, after the clash at Lexington he showed himself a nationalist before the birth of the nation, seeking to resolve tension between radicals and loyalists in the New York provincial congress (May 1775) and appealing for a united front in support of the Continental Congress at Philadelphia. In July 1776, he sat in the New York State constitutional convention and, with John Jay and Robert R. Livingston, drafted the frame of government (1777) that lasted nearly fifty years. Thereafter he served diligently on the Council of Safety.

During his membership in the Continental Congress, 1778–79, Morris turned his talents and soundness of judgment to financial, military, and diplomatic matters, chairing several leading committees and drafting many important foreign policy documents. His army inspection trip to Valley Forge, 1778, brought him close to Washington, to whom he remained devoted for life. Defeated for re-election to the Continental Congress, 1779, he transferred his citizenship to Pennsylvania, resumed the practice of law, and cultivated polite society in Philadelphia. His articles on Continental finances in the *Pennsylvania Packet* (February–April, 1780) led Robert Morris, the new superintendent of finance (not a relative), to request his service as assistant. In this position, 1781–85, the younger Morris initially planned our decimal coinage system. As Pennsylvania delegate to the Constitutional Convention, 1787, he participated frequently in debate, favoring strong, centralized government in the hands of the rich and well-born, with suffrage limited to freeholders. Although Morris loyally accepted the compromises embodied in the U.S. Constitution (which he wrote out in its final form), his cynical contempt for democracy barred him from high office under it. Consequently, he forsook public life to attend to various commercial ventures, purchased the family mansion at Morrisania, N.Y., and returned there to live, 1788. Soon, as business agent for Robert Morris, he left for Europe where, in pursuit of business, diplomatic duties, and recreational travel, he remained for nearly a decade.

Arriving in Paris, February 1789, he saw the French Revolution begin. His fame as a founder of the American Republic had preceded him and his affability, family connections, command of French, and intellectual versatility opened all doors to him. After Jefferson's return to America in late 1789, Morris was the most influential American in Paris and he worked to improve Franco-American business and financial relations. Freedom from diplomatic responsibility allowed him to criticize and counsel without offense. His voluminous diary of the early Revolutionary period (first published, 1888) is highly informative.

Named U.S. minister to France by President Washington, 1792, Morris was almost rejected by the Senate, owing to his sympathy with the French monarchy and his unsuccessful commercial negotiations at London, 1790–91. No one at Paris, however, could have represented the United States better than Morris did in the stormy years, 1792–94. He weathered the Terror with dignity and courage. Recalled, 1794, in return for Washington's dismissal of "Citizen" Edmond Genet, he remained abroad until 1798. After serving as Federalist senator from New York, 1800–02, he retired to his Morrisania estate to cultivate his friends and nurse his hatred of Republicans and their measures.

MORRIS, JOHN GOTTLIEB (*b. York, Pa., 1803; d. Lutherville, Md., 1895*), Lutheran clergyman. Held several pastorates in Baltimore, Md., 1827–73; founded *Lutheran Observer* (1831) and also the Lutheran Historical Society. A notable student, Morris was librarian of the Peabody Institute, 1860–65.

MORRIS, LEWIS (*b. near New York, N.Y., 1671; d. near Trenton, N.J., 1746*), colonial landowner and official, first lord of the manor of Morrisania, N.Y. (erected, 1697). Holder of numerous offices in colonial New York and New Jersey, Morris's principal services were given as chief justice of the supreme court of New York Province, 1715–33 and as governor of New Jersey, 1738–46. Long involved in provincial political disputes, Morris strongly opposed unscrupulous Crown officials such as the governors Lord Cornbury and William Cosby, and in general served with great contentiousness and ability as a champion of the popular cause against the so-called "court party." As governor of New Jersey, his administration was marked by bitter, wordy quarrels with the Assembly over taxation, support of the militia, bills of credit and validity of land titles.

MORRIS, LEWIS (*b. Morrisania, N.Y., 1726; d. Morrisania, 1798*), landowner, statesman, third and last lord of the manor of Morrisania. Grandson of Lewis Morris (1671–1746); half-brother of Gouverneur Morris. Graduated Yale, 1746. Active in provincial politics *post* 1762, he grew increasingly critical of British policy, secured appointment of deputies from Westchester Co. to the New York provincial convention in April 1775, and served as a New York delegate to the Continental Congress, 1775–76. Absent from Philadelphia when the Declaration of Independence was finally adopted, he signed it for New York late in 1776. As congressman, he was particularly effective in handling of Indian affairs. Brigadier-general of the militia of Westchester Co., N.Y., he served also as county judge, 1777–78, and was intermittently a member of the New York State senate from 1777 until 1790.

MORRIS, LEWIS RICHARD (*b. Scarsdale, N.Y., 1760; d. Springfield, Vt., 1825*), landowner, Vermont legislator. Son of Richard Morris. Congressman, Federalist, from Vermont, 1797–1803. His abstention from voting allowed Thomas Jefferson's election as president by the House of Representatives, February 1801.

MORRIS, LUZON BURRITT (*b. Newtown, Conn., 1827; d. 1895*), lawyer, Connecticut legislator. Democratic governor of Connecticut, 1893–95.

MORRIS, MARY PHILIPSE (1730–1825). [See MORRIS, ROGER, 1727–1794.]

MORRIS, NELSON (*b. Hechingen, Germany, 1838; d. Chicago, Ill., 1907*), stock breeder, meat packer. Came to America as a boy. Settling in Chicago, he worked in the Union Stock Yards and soon rose to a leading position in the live-cattle trade. A pioneer in transporting dressed beef from Chicago to the Atlantic seaboard, he opened one of the first packing houses in the Chicago Stock Yards, owned a number of large cattle ranches, and established packing plants also in Missouri and Kansas.

MORRIS, MRS. OWEN. [See MORRIS, ELIZABETH, *c.* 1753–1826.]

MORRIS, RICHARD (*b. probably Morrisania, N.Y., 1730; d. Scarsdale, N.Y., 1810*), jurist. Brother of Lewis Morris (1726–1798); half-brother of Gouverneur Morris. Graduated Yale, 1748. Judge of the vice-admiralty court having jurisdiction over New York, Connecticut and New Jersey, 1762–75; succeeded John Jay as chief justice, New York supreme court, 1779; retired from public life, 1790.

MORRIS, RICHARD VALENTINE (*b. Morrisania, N.Y., 1768; d. Morrisania, 1815*), naval officer, diplomat. Son of Lewis Morris (1726–1798). Unsuccessful negotiator with Barbary powers as commodore commanding Mediterranean squadron, 1802–03. Author of *A Defence of the Conduct of Commodore Morris* (1804).

MORRIS, ROBERT (*b. in or near Liverpool, England, 1734; d. Philadelphia, Pa., 1806*), financier of the American Revolution. Joined his father, a tobacco exporter, in Maryland, *c.* 1747. After brief schooling in Philadelphia he went into service of the Willings, shipping merchants, and rose to partnership in their firm, 1754. To Willing, Morris & Co., and its successors under other names, he gave his interest for 39 years and, for a large part of that period, his active direction. His prudence and resolution brought him wealth and to the firm a leading position in the trade of Philadelphia and America. The house concentrated upon importing British manufactures, exporting American goods, shipowning, and a general exchange and banking business.

Morris's public career began when he signed the non-importation agreement of 1765, opposing the

Stamp Act. Uncommitted to the "Patriot" cause as late as 1774, he became a leader in it with the battle of Lexington, April 1775. A member of the Council of Safety, appointed by the Pennsylvania Assembly, June 30, 1775, his commercial experience was of immediate use in the committee charged with procuring munitions and he frequently acted as its banker. In Benjamin Franklin's absence he presided over the Council. In November 1775, the Assembly sent Morris as delegate to the Continental Congress. He signed the Declaration of Independence in August 1776, after initial disapproval. Throughout his term in Congress he provided strong financial leadership, especially after Congress fled from Philadelphia in December 1776, when he remained to carry on committee work, buying supplies and borrowing money despite appalling difficulties, and providing Washington and his lieutenants the moral support and material assistance without which the army must have been dispersed. Morris profited greatly as a middleman from the deals which he directed through his committee for the procurement of munitions and naval armaments. He did this, however, at great personal financial risk and without lessening his colleagues' confidence in him. John Adams wrote: "He . . . no doubt pursues mercantile ends, which are always gain; but he is an excellent Member of our Body." Morris signed the Articles of Confederation on behalf of Pennsylvania, March 1778. Ineligible for re-election to Congress, he was elected to the Pennsylvania Assembly, November 1778. Attacks upon him in 1779 by Thomas Paine for improper commercial enterprises in public office, and upon his firm by Henry Laurens for fraud, diminished his political popularity although he and the firm were acquitted by a congressional investigating committee.

With the Treasury empty, credit gone, and the Union a "rope of sand," Congress recognized that a financial dictator was needed and chose Morris to be superintendent of finance, February 1781. Accepting the unique office with stipulations that he might retain his private commercial connections and could control the personnel of his department, Morris initiated a program which included the laying of federal taxes in specie to be used in paying interest on the debt; requisitions from the states to be used to carry on the war; a possible loan from France; and vigilant economy. To save expense to the government he himself accepted the agency of marine. He assumed the task of buying all supplies for the armies; he used notes which circulated only upon his own credit; he pressed the states for their cash contributions; he put vigor, as well as order, into civil administration. Continuously he was driven to greater risks and to daring financial sleight-of-hand. Disgusted with the impotence of Congress and with the states' failure to meet obligations, Morris resigned in September 1784, but not before he had financed the victorious Yorktown campaign, formed the Bank of North America (January 1782) with a French loan, and under-

gone severe press abuse for his announced wish to resign.

His remaining years in public office saw him a member of the Pennsylvania General Assembly (1785–86), a delegate to the Annapolis Convention (1786), a member of the Constitutional Convention (1787) with Federalist convictions, and U.S. senator from Pennsylvania, 1789–95. *Post* 1785, he held a monopoly of the American tobacco trade with France. His financial downfall came when extensive land speculations in which he was engaged collapsed, and his prestige was demolished when a small creditor caused him to be confined (February 1798—August 1801) in the Philadelphia debtors' prison. Broken in body and spirit, he died a nearly forgotten and much pitied man.

MORRIS, ROBERT (*b. New Brunswick, N.J., c. 1745; d. New Brunswick, 1815*), jurist. Natural son of Robert H. Morris. Chief justice, New Jersey supreme court, 1777–79; federal judge, New Jersey district, 1789–1815.

MORRIS, ROBERT (*b. near Boston, Mass., 1818; d. La Grange, Ky., 1888*), Masonic writer and lecturer.

MORRIS, ROBERT HUNTER (*b. Morrisania, N.Y., c. 1700; d. Shrewsbury, N.J., 1764*), jurist, politician. Son of Lewis Morris (1671–1746). Chief justice of New Jersey, 1738–64, Morris was a belligerent defender of the Royal prerogative and of property rights. Despite his absence as governor of Pennsylvania, 1754–56, and during a long visit to England, 1757–58, he was never considered to have surrendered his commission as chief justice.

MORRIS, ROGER (*b. England, 1727; d. Yorkshire, England, 1794*), British soldier, Loyalist. Came to America, 1755; served with credit in the French and Indian War; married Mary Philipse, heiress of Frederic Philipse, 1758. His American property, which came to him by his marriage, was confiscated by an act of attainder of the New York state legislature soon after the outbreak of the Revolution. He left America permanently in 1783.

MORRIS, THOMAS (*b. Berks Co., Pa., 1776; d. 1844*), lawyer, Ohio legislator. Raised near Clarksburg, now in West Virginia; removed to Ohio, 1795. A partisan of Andrew Jackson, Morris served as U.S. senator from Ohio, 1833–39; he was an opponent of lotteries, monopolies, imprisonment for debt and the extension of slavery. His speech defending the Abolitionists against the charges of Henry Clay, made on Feb. 9, 1839, ended his political career, but he was active in the campaign of 1844 as vice-presidential nominee of the Liberty party.

MORRIS, THOMAS ARMSTRONG (*b. Nicholas Co., Ky., 1811; d. San Diego, Calif., 1904*), engineer, Union brigadier-general, Indiana canal and railroad builder.

MORRIS, WILLIAM HOPKINS (*b. New York, N.Y., 1827; d. Long Branch, N.J., 1900*), Union major-general. Son of George P. Morris. Graduated West Point, 1851. Author of several works on infantry tactics.

MORRISON, JOHN IRWIN (*b. near Chambersburg, Pa., 1806; d. Knightstown, Ind., 1882*), educator, promoter of public school legislation in Indiana.

MORRISON, NATHAN JACKSON (*b. Sanbornton, now Franklin, N.H., 1828; d. Wichita, Kans., 1907*), Congregational clergyman, educator. President, Olivet (Michigan) College, 1864–1872; Drury College, Springfield, Mo., 1873–1888; Fairmont Institute, Wichita, Kans., 1895–1907.

MORRISON, WILLIAM (*b. Doylestown, Pa., 1763; d. Kaskaskia, Ill., 1837*), merchant. Removed to Kaskaskia *ante* August 1790 where he built up a flourishing trading business; was first U.S. citizen to attempt opening trade with Santa Fé, New Mexico, 1804; joined Pierre Menard in backing Manuel Lisa for upper Missouri venture, 1807. Led political faction opposed to William H. Harrison in Old Northwest.

MORRISON, WILLIAM McCUTCHAN (*b. near Lexington, Va., 1867; d. Luebo, Congo Free State, 1918*), Southern Presbyterian clergyman, missionary to the Congo. Denounced treatment of natives by Congo government and its concessionary companies; supplied part of data to Mark Twain for *King Leopold's Soliloquy* (1905).

MORRISON, WILLIAM RALLS (*b. near Waterloo, Ill., 1824?; d. Waterloo, 1909*), lawyer, Union soldier. Congressman, Democrat, from Illinois, 1863–65, 1873–87. Popularized idea of tariff reform by introducing generally unsuccessful bills in Congress which called for abandonment of protection principle. As member of the Interstate Commerce Commission, 1887–97 (chairman *post* 1892), he conducted a vigorous but temporarily unsuccessful campaign against railroad privilege and attacked discriminations and rebates.

MORRISSEY, JOHN (*b. Templemore, Ireland, 1831; d. 1878*), gambler, prize fighter, politician. Came to Canada as a child; was raised in Troy, N.Y. Claimed heavyweight championship of the world after beating Yankee Sullivan in 37 rounds at Boston Four Corners, N.Y., October 1853; defeated John C. Heenan in Canada, October 1858. Profiting by financial advice given him by Cornelius Vanderbilt, he made successful speculations and grew wealthy. He served two terms in Congress, 1867–71, and served also in the New York legislature. *Post* 1870, he occupied himself principally with gambling and race-track interests in Saratoga, N.Y.

MORROW, DWIGHT WHITNEY (*b. Huntington, W. Va., 1873; d. Englewood, N.J., 1931*), lawyer, banker, diplomat. Graduated Amherst, 1895; Columbia Law School, 1899. Successful in corporation

law practice through his ability to find common ground on which claims of divergent interests could be resolved, Morrow, among other public services, drafted New Jersey's workmen's compensation law of 1911 and effected reforms in administration of penal institutions. Associated with J. P. Morgan & Co., 1914–27, he served during World War I as adviser to the Allied Transport Council and was awarded the Distinguished Service Medal for rationalizing the Allied tonnage situation. He effected the restoration of the Cuban economy *post* 1920, was chairman of the Aircraft Board whose 1926 report led to separate control for military and commercial aviation, and as U.S. ambassador to Mexico, 1927–30, restored harmonious U.S. relations with that republic; he also resolved difficulties between the Mexican government and the Roman Catholic Church. He was U.S. senator, Republican, from New Jersey, 1930–31.

MORROW, EDWIN PORCH (*b. Somerset, Ky., 1877; d. Frankfort, Ky., 1935*), lawyer. Nephew of William O. Bradley. Republican governor of Kentucky, 1919–23. [*Supp. 1*]

MORROW, JEREMIAH (*b. near Gettysburg, Pa., 1771; d. near Lebanon, O., 1852*), surveyor, farmer, Ohio legislator. Removed to Ohio, 1794; was leader in movement for statehood. Congressman, (Democrat) Republican, from Ohio, 1803–13; U.S. senator, 1813–19; governor of Ohio, 1822–26. Expert in matters pertaining to the public lands, he advocated the sale of land in smaller units, also cash payments and lower prices; as governor, he inaugurated the state canal-building program and was influential in establishing the public school system. A supporter of John Q. Adams, 1828, he later became a Whig and as such served again in Congress, 1840–43.

MORROW, PRINCE ALBERT (*b. Mount Vernon, Ky., 1846; d. 1913*), physician, dermatologist, sociologist. Nephew of Thomas V. Morrow. M.D., New York University, 1874; began practice in New York City, 1875. A specialist in diseases of the skin, he taught this subject at New York University, 1882–90. Early recognizing the social, moral and economic problems brought about by venereal diseases, he labored to overcome prejudice against open discussion of them and to arouse greater public interest in their prevention.

MORROW, THOMAS VAUGHAN (*b. Fairview, Ky., 1804; d. Cincinnati, O., 1850*), physician, pioneer in eclectic medicine. Studied under Wooster Beach; practiced at Hopkinsville, Ky.; helped to found and taught at eclectic medical schools in Ohio. First president, National Eclectic Medical Association, 1848.

MORROW, WILLIAM W. (*b. near Milton, Ind., 1843; d. San Francisco, Calif., 1929*), California jurist, congressman. Removed to California, 1859. Federal district judge in California, 1891–97; circuit judge, 1897–1923.

MORSE, ANSON DANIEL (*b. Cambridge, Vt., 1846; d. Amherst, Mass., 1916*), educator. Brother of Harmon N. Morse. Graduated Amherst, 1871; taught political science and history there, 1876–1907. Author of *Parties and Party Leaders* (1923) and a number of articles on the theory of political action by parties.

MORSE, CHARLES WYMAN (*b. Bath, Maine, 1856; d. Bath, 1933*), financial promoter, speculator. His American Ice Co., formed 1899, was one of the earlier and more flagrant instances of corrupt promotion in the American trust movement. After this primary success, turning to banking and shipping, he made a number of rapid consolidations of individual firms, either through peaceful or forceful penetration. Pyramiding assets and forming syndicates to float the over-capitalized stock of his consolidated companies, he managed to obtain before 1907 close to a monopoly of Atlantic coastal shipping and also won control of a number of New York banks. After the Morse banks had become the storm center of the panic of 1907, Morse was indicted for criminal misapplication of funds and sentenced to a 15-year term in Atlanta Penitentiary, November 1908. Released from jail two years later through fraud and collusion, Morse re-entered Wall Street. He found a golden opportunity on the U.S. entrance into World War I, when he accepted contracts for construction of merchant vessels and borrowed the money to build them from the government. In the shadow of an indictment for conspiracy to defraud the government in these matters, Morse went to Europe, 1922. Arrested on his attempt to return to the United States, he became subject to two indictments but was acquitted of criminal charges. The government won heavy judgments against him, however, in civil suits.

MORSE, EDWARD SYLVESTER (*b. Portland, Maine, 1838; d. 1925*), zoologist, authority on Japanese art. Director, Peabody Museum, Salem, Mass., *post* 1880; curator, Japanese pottery collection, Boston Museum of Fine Arts *post* 1892.

MORSE, FREEMAN HARLOW (*b. Bath, Maine, 1807; d. Surbiton, England, 1891*), carver of figureheads for ships, politician. Congressman, Whig, from Maine, 1843–45; congressman, Republican, 1857–61. U.S. consul at London, England, 1861–70.

MORSE, HARMON NORTHROP (*b. Cambridge, Vt., 1848; d. Chebeague, Maine, 1920*), organic chemist. Brother of Anson D. Morse. Graduated Amherst, 1873; Ph.D., Göttingen, 1875. Taught chemistry at Johns Hopkins, 1876–1916. Devised new methods of quantitative analysis; made extended research on permanganic acid and its salts *post* 1896. Developed electrolytic method for depositing semipermeable membranes which he used for accumulating accurate experimental data on osmotic pressure of aqueous solutions.

MORSE, HENRY DUTTON (*b. Boston, Mass., 1826; d. Jamaica Plain, Mass., 1888*), diamond cutter. The first American to learn the technique of diamond-cutting, Morse invented machinery for sawing and polishing stones and cut the first modern full-fashioned brilliants with 56 facets.

MORSE, JEDIDIAH (*b. Woodstock, Conn., 1761; d. New Haven, Conn., 1826*), Congregational clergyman. Graduated Yale, 1783; served briefly as tutor at Yale; was pastor, First Church, Charlestown, Mass., 1789–1819. Opposed Unitarian and other heresies in the Congregational churches; edited the *Panoplist* (1805–10); was a founder of Andover Theological Seminary. The pamphlet *American Unitarianism* (1815) issued by him but extracted from another work resulted in driving many Unitarian churches from the Congregational fold. As conservative in politics as in religion, Morse was a strong Federalist and contributed to the popular hysteria aroused in the United States during the 1790's by the events of the French Revolution. He is best remembered, however, as the "father of American geography." His *Geography Made Easy* (1784) was the first geography to be published in the United States and went through many editions, as did its larger successor *The American Geography* (1789). During Morse's lifetime, his geographies virtually monopolized their field in the United States. He was father of Samuel F. B. and Sidney E. Morse.

MORSE, JOHN LOVETT (*b. Taunton, Mass., 1865; d. Newton, Mass., 1940*), pediatrician. Graduated Harvard, 1887; Harvard Medical School, 1891. As a teacher at Harvard Medical School and in his work at Boston Children's Hospital, Morse was one of the pioneers in the development of pediatrics as a specialty. [*Supp. 2*]

MORSE, JOHN TORREY (*b. Boston, Mass., 1840; d. Needham, Mass., 1937*), biographer, editor, lawyer. Graduated Harvard, 1860. Projected and edited the "American Statesmen" series (34 volumes, 1882–1916). [*Supp. 2*]

MORSE, SAMUEL FINLEY BREESE (*b. Charlestown, Mass., 1791; d. New York, N.Y., 1872*), artist, inventor. Son of Jedidiah Morse. Graduated Yale, 1810. Studied painting under Washington Allston and at the Royal Academy of London, 1811–15. Returning to America, he found that portraits were the only works of art which Americans would buy; he achieved initial successes as a portraitist in Charleston, S.C., where he spent the winters, 1818–21, and in New York City, where he made his headquarters *post* 1823. The general excellence of his portraits is high, displaying insight into character and a free and delicate technique; his landscapes and subject-pictures are fewer in number and for the most part cold and unimaginative. Leading spirit among the founders of the National Academy of Design, Morse served as its first president, 1826–42. Despite his success in the intellectual and art circles of New York, his income was small and irregular. After spending the years 1829–32 in European travel and study, he returned to New York to accept a nominal post as professor of painting and design in New York University and to engage in some extremely ill-judged Nativist and anti-Catholic agitation. He abandoned painting as a profession c. 1837.

Morse's preoccupation with the telegraph dates from October 1832, when a conversation with Charles T. Jackson aboard ship suggested to Morse's mind the concept of an electro-magnetic recording telegraph for the rapid transmission of intelligence. What he knew of electricity at this time was solely what he had learned in attending a course of lectures on the subject given by James F. Dana, 1827; he was ignorant of Joseph Henry's discoveries in electro-magnetism and of the several European experiments which were being conducted with electro-magnetic needle telegraphs. The essential features of Morse's invention as set down in his 1832 notebook were (1) a sending apparatus to transmit signals by the closing and opening of an electric circuit; (2) a receiving apparatus operated by an electro-magnet to record the signals as dots and spaces on a strip of paper moved by clockwork; (3) a code translating the dots and spaces into numbers and letters. From this original concept, Morse brought his invention through elaboration to eventual simplicity. Early in the process, he noticed that signals could also be read by ear and worked out an efficient sounder. The code, too, went through a series of changes before it became the "Morse Code." Initially the inventor did not dream of the telegraph as a convenience; it was to be government controlled and used only for communications of great importance. In consequence, he wasted a great deal of time devising a semi-secret code that required the use of a huge dictionary for translation. With the assistance of Leonard Dunnell Gale and Joseph Henry, Morse finally reduced his invention to practical working form and he filed a caveat for it in the patent office, 1837. In the same year, he took Alfred Vail into partnership with him. Several years of discouragement followed, in which Morse was denied European patent protection for his work, before Congress voted an appropriation for an experimental line from Washington to Baltimore in 1843. The line was built by Ezra Cornell and on May 24, 1844, Morse sent over it the famous greeting "What hath God wrought!" The further development of the telegraph was neglected by the government, however, and left to private enterprise. With the help of Amos Kendall as business manager, Morse ultimately became rich as a result of the practical exploitation of his invention despite much litigation in which his rights were challenged and during which he lost the friendship of Joseph Henry.

MORSE, SIDNEY EDWARDS (*b. Charlestown, Mass., 1794; d. 1871*), inventor, author. Son of Jedidiah Morse; brother of Samuel F. B. Morse.

MORTIMER, MARY (*b. Trowbridge, England, 1816; d. Milwaukee, Wis., 1877*), educator, pioneer in higher education of women. In collaboration with Catharine E. Beecher, Miss Mortimer instituted the Milwaukee Female College, 1850–51.

MORTON, CHARLES (*b. Cornwall, England, 1626/27; d. 1698*), Puritan clergyman, schoolmaster. Came to Boston, Mass., 1686, after serving *post 1666* as master of the famous Dissenting academy at Newington Green. Named minister at Charlestown, Mass., he was elected a fellow of Harvard, 1692, and vice-president of the college, 1697.

MORTON, CHARLES GOULD (*b. Cumberland, Maine, 1861; d. San Francisco, Calif., 1933*), soldier. Graduated West Point, 1883. After serving in a number of posts abroad and at home, Morton rose to rank of major-general, May 1917. Appointed to command the 29th Division in July, he trained the unit and actively commanded it in France, 1918–19. His successful operations east of Verdun prevented an increase of German strength between the Argonne and the Meuse and aided the American offensive there (September to November 1918). [*Supp. 1*]

MORTON, GEORGE (*b. Nottinghamshire, England, 1585; d. Plymouth, Mass., 1624*), Pilgrim father. Converted when very young by William Brewster, he was a member of the Scrooby congregation before their emigration, was one of the financial mainstays of the Pilgrims at Leyden, and was probably chief Pilgrim agent during the absence of Robert Cushman. He changed his name to George Mourt c. 1619. Receiving the reports sent in the ship *Fortune* from Plymouth, 1622, he published them in London as *A Relation or Iournall of the beginning and proceedings of the English Plantation setled at Plimoth in New England*, which is still the only contemporary account of the *Mayflower* voyage and the first months of the Plymouth colony. He came to Plymouth and settled, 1623.

MORTON, HENRY (*b. New York, N.Y., 1836; d. 1902*), scientist, Biblical archaeologist. Graduated University of Pennsylvania, 1857. As first president of Stevens Institute of Technology, 1870–1902, Morton developed the first curriculum in mechanical engineering in America. He was widely known as a research chemist and physicist.

MORTON, JAMES ST. CLAIR (*b. Philadelphia, Pa., 1829; d. Petersburg, Va., 1864*), military engineer. Son of Samuel G. Morton. Graduated West Point, 1851. Expert in fortification work, he served during the Civil War as chief engineer of the Army of the Ohio and the Army of the Cumberland; he was killed in action, June 17, 1864, while chief engineer of the IX Army Corps.

MORTON, JOHN (*b. Ridley, Pa., c. 1724; d. 1777*), surveyor, farmer, Pennsylvania provincial legislator and jurist. Signer of the Declaration of Independence as a Pennsylvania delegate to the Continental Congress, 1774–77; active on a number of important congressional committees.

MORTON, JULIUS STERLING (*b. Adams, N.Y., 1832; d. Lake Forest, Ill., 1902*), agriculturist, Nebraska politician. Raised in Michigan; removed to Nebraska, 1854, where he edited the *Nebraska City News* and became a leader in territorial affairs. He was secretary of Nebraska Territory, 1858–61, and was thereafter repeatedly a candidate for office on the Democratic ticket. His appointment as U.S. secretary of agriculture, 1893–97, was owing as much to his standing as a practical agriculturist as it was to his orthodox Democratic record. The annual celebration of Arbor Day was brought about at his suggestion.

MORTON, LEVI PARSONS (*b. Shoreham, Vt., 1824; d. 1920*), banker. Congressman, Republican, from New York, 1879–81; U.S. minister to France, 1881–85; vice-president of the United States, 1889–93. Independent of party pressure while presiding over the Senate, he showed the same characteristic as governor of New York, 1895–97; a firm and moderate advocate of civil-service reform, he consistently refused to accept the domination of Thomas C. Platt.

MORTON, MARCUS (*b. Freetown, Mass., 1784; d. Taunton, Mass., 1864*), lawyer. Congressman, Democrat, from Massachusetts, 1817–21; lieutenant-governor of Massachusetts, 1824–25; judge, Massachusetts supreme court, 1825–40. A perennial Democratic candidate for governor of Massachusetts (1828–43), he was successful only in 1839 and 1842. An advocate of governmental economy, he was ahead of his time in his championship of the working man, his distrust of over-large corporations and his advocacy of shorter working hours.

MORTON, MARCUS (*b. Taunton, Mass., 1819; d. Andover, Mass., 1891*), jurist. Son of Marcus Morton (1784–1864). Held a number of Massachusetts judicial positions, 1858–90; was chief justice, supreme judicial court, 1882–90.

MORTON, NATHANIEL (*b. Leyden, Netherlands, 1613; d. Plymouth, Mass., 1685 o.s.*), Pilgrim father. Son of George Morton. Came to Plymouth, 1623; was reared in family of William Bradford, his uncle by marriage. As secretary of the colony and keeper of the records, 1647–85, Morton handled much of the routine work of government and probably drafted most of the colony's laws. Custodian of Bradford's papers after his death, Morton was an authority on Pilgrim history and was author-editor of *New Englands Memoriall* (printed at Cambridge, 1669).

MORTON, OLIVER PERRY (*b. Salisbury, Ind., 1823; d. Indianapolis, Ind., 1877*), lawyer, politician. Rose rapidly to leadership of Wayne Co. bar, serving railway interests. Left Democratic party over Kansas-Nebraska Bill and helped form the Republican party along national lines. As governor of Indiana, 1861–67, he was reputedly the ablest and most energetic of the Civil War state executives in the West, arousing the people of Indiana to enthusiastic support of the war and thwarting the plots of Copperhead elements by any means that worked. Elected to the U.S. Senate, 1867, he served there until his death as an uncompromising supporter of "thorough" Reconstruction. A contender for the Republican presidential nomination, 1876, he lost the nomination because of his tendency to favor soft-money, his strict partisanship, and the state of his health (he had been a paralytic since 1865). Incorruptible in money matters, he was distinctly of his time in his fanatical devotion to party and his intolerance of opposition.

MORTON, PAUL (*b. Detroit, Mich., 1857; d. 1911*), businessman. Son of Julius S. Morton. Appointed U.S. secretary of the navy, 1904, he resigned, 1905, following exposure of his part in illegal rebate practices while an officer of the Santa Fé railroad. Thereafter, he engaged in the rehabilitation of the Equitable Life Assurance Association, New York.

MORTON, SAMUEL GEORGE (*b. Philadelphia, Pa., 1799; d. Philadelphia, 1851*), physician, naturalist. M.D., University of Pennsylvania, 1820; M.D., Edinburgh, 1823. Morton's researches extended through the fields of medicine, geology, paleontology, zoology; his monograph describing fossils brought back by the Lewis and Clark Expedition (published 1834) has been called the starting point of all systematic work on American fossils. He was author of a number of other works including *Human Anatomy* (1849) and exercised a marked influence upon the mind of Louis Agassiz.

MORTON, SARAH WENTWORTH APTHORP (*b. Boston, Mass., 1759; d. Quincy, Mass., 1846*), poet. Her stilted and derivative didactic poems, which enjoyed a great repute in their own time, appeared widely in American periodicals over her pseudonym "Philenia." Her published books included *Ouâbi* (1790), *Beacon Hill* (1797) and *The Virtues of Society* (1799).

MORTON, THOMAS (*fl. 1622–1647*), adventurer. Came to Wessagusset (Mass.) probably in 1622; settled in limits of present Quincy, Mass., after a trip back to England and a return with the Wollaston Company. Established at "Merry Mount," he led a licentious and convivial life in the intervals of his work as fur trader. He was soon anathema to the Plymouth Pilgrims for this and also for selling guns to the Indians. Three times arrested and twice deported to England, he paid his compliments to New

England in his satiric book *New English Canaan* (1637).

MORTON, WILLIAM JAMES (*b. Boston, Mass., 1845; d. Miami, Fla., 1920*), neurologist. Son of William T. G. Morton. Made extensive investigations in electro-therapeutics; was one of first physicians in America to use X-ray in treatment of skin disorders and cancerous growths (1902–07).

MORTON, WILLIAM THOMAS GREEN (*b. Charlton, Mass., 1819; d. New York, N.Y., 1868*), dentist. Practicing in Boston, Mass., 1842–44, Morton became acquainted with the Boston chemist and researcher Charles T. Jackson. In July 1844, at Jackson's suggestion, he employed ether in drops as a local anaesthetic during the filling of a tooth. After testing the effect of inhalation of sulphuric ether on animal subjects and on himself, he made his first attempt to use it in the treatment of a human patient on Sept. 30, 1846. Public notice of the incident appeared in the *Boston Daily Journal* of October 1. Other successful extractions followed. With the encouragement of Henry J. Bigelow and John C. Warren, ether was first used successfully in a surgical operation at the Massachusetts General Hospital, Oct. 16, 1846, when Warren removed a vascular tumor from a patient. The next day, again under Morton's supervision, Dr. George Hayward also operated with equal success. During the next two weeks a disagreement arose as to the advisability of continuing the procedure, since Morton was not a medical man and refused to tell the composition of his anaesthetic agent. The difficulties were finally overcome and the discovery was first announced by Henry J. Bigelow on Nov. 18, 1846, in the *Boston Medical and Surgical Journal*.

Seeking at once to secure profit from his discovery, Morton applied for a patent to protect his rights, refusing to reveal that the anaesthetic agent was sulphuric ether and designating it only by the name "letheon." Letters patent were issued to him (and to Charles T. Jackson, whom he had been forced to include by legal advisers) in November, 1846, for a period of fourteen years. Morton, however, adamantly insisted that the discovery was entirely his. A congressional appropriations bill to compensate him for the discovery was blocked by supporters of the claims of Jackson, Horace Wells, and Crawford W. Long; subsequent deliberations of congressional committees and subcommittees were drawn out for nearly two decades and the last twenty years of Morton's life brought him only honor without riches and the perpetual torment of controversy and litigation. Although others shared in the discovery, Morton's independent action, the experiments he made upon his own initiative, and his assumption of entire responsibility for the outcome make him the true discoverer of ether for surgical use. Important among his little-known writings are: *Remarks on the Proper Mode of Administering Sulphuric Ether by Inhalation* (1847) and a brochure *On the Physiological Effects of Sulphuric Ether, and its Superiority to Chloroform* (Boston, 1850).

MORWITZ, EDWARD (*b. Danzig, Prussia, 1815; d. Philadelphia, Pa., 1893*), physician, publisher. Settled in Philadelphia, 1852, where he practiced, published several German-language newspapers, and organized the Newspaper Union, the most extensive German distributor of "patent-inside" material in the United States.

MOSBY, JOHN SINGLETON (*b. Edgemont, Va., 1833; d. Washington, D.C., 1916*), lawyer, Confederate ranger. A cavalry officer, Mosby operated (January 1863—April 1865) in Virginia and Maryland under partisan ranger law; he rose to a colonelcy. Among his spectacular successes were the capture of Gen. Stoughton at Fairfax Court House (March 1863), raids on Chantilly (April 1863) and Point of Rocks, Md. (July 4, 1864), and the "greenback raid" (Oct. 14, 1864), when he seized $168,000, dividing it among his men to buy new uniforms and equipment, as was his custom. Mosby personally never received any of the loot but the Union forces regarded him and his men as robbers. After the war he joined the Republican party, was U.S. consul at Hong Kong, 1878–85, and an assistant attorney for the Department of Justice, 1904–10. He published *Mosby's War Reminiscences* (1887) and other works.

MOSCOSO DE ALVARADO, LUIS de (*fl. 1530–1543*), second in command under Hernando de Soto during conquest of Florida. After de Soto's death early in 1542, Moscoso led the survivors of the expedition back to Mexico City.

MOSELEY, EDWARD AUGUSTUS (*b. Newburyport, Mass., 1846; d. Washington, D.C., 1911*), lawyer, advocate of railway safety laws. Secretary, Interstate Commerce Commission, 1887–1911.

MOSER, CHRISTOPHER OTTO (*b. Dallas, Texas, 1885; d. 1935*), organizer of farm groups, scientific dairy farmer. Becoming interested in cotton cooperatives *c.* 1920, he was responsible for organization of the American Cotton Growers Exchange and served it as president, 1925–30. [*Supp. 1*]

MOSES, BERNARD (*b. Burlington, Conn., 1846; d. 1930*), political scientist, historian. Pioneer in research study of Hispanic-American history. Graduated University of Michigan, 1870; Ph.D., Heidelberg, 1873. Taught at University of California, 1876–1930 (emeritus *post* 1910).

MOSES, FRANKLIN J. (*b. Sumter District, S.C., 1838; d. Winthrop, Mass., 1906*), lawyer, editor, Confederate soldier and official, Scalawag. Turning Republican, 1867, he entered on an opportunistic career of fraud and extravagance. A corrupt legislator and public official, he reached the climax of his unscrupulous course as governor of South Carolina, 1872–74. Turning state's evidence against former associates to save himself from prison, he slipped thereafter into obscurity.

MOSES, MONTROSE JONAS (*b. New York, N.Y., 1878; d. 1934*), dramatic critic, editor. Graduated College of the City of New York, 1899. After serving as critic and editor on a number of periodicals, Moses devoted himself to free lance writing *post* 1919. An authority on the history and traditions of the American theatre, he edited the plays of Clyde Fitch, produced a number of valuable anthologies of American and foreign drama, and wrote several critical biographies of figures in the theatre. [*Supp. 1*]

MOSESSOHN, DAVID NEHEMIAH (*b. Ekaterinoslav, Russia, 1883; d. 1930*), lawyer, businessman. Came to America as a child; was raised in Portland, Oreg. LL.B., University of Oregon, 1902. Practiced in New York City *post* 1918. Planned organization of Associated Dress Industries, 1918; was appointed its executive director, and *post* 1923 was its executive chairman. Distinguished as an impartial arbitrator in industrial disputes, Mosessohn was a leader in Jewish affairs and edited the *Jewish Tribune*, 1926–30.

MOSHER, ELIZA MARIA (*b. Cayuga Co., N.Y., 1846; d. Brooklyn, N.Y., 1928*), physician, educator, pioneer in physical education of women. M.D., University of Michigan, 1875. Professor of physiology and hygiene, Vassar College; professor of hygiene and first dean of women, University of Michigan, 1896–1902.

MOSHER, THOMAS BIRD (*b. Biddeford, Maine, 1852; d. Portland, Maine, 1923*), publisher of the "Mosher Books," beautifully printed, inexpensive editions of little-known masterpieces.

MOSKOWITZ, BELLE LINDNER ISRAELS (*b. New York, N.Y., 1877; d. New York, 1933*), welfare worker, political leader, authority on factory legislation. Trusted adviser on social and economic problems of Alfred E. Smith. [*Supp. 1*]

MOSLER, HENRY (*b. New York, N.Y., 1841; d. New York, 1920*), genre painter. His "Le Retour" (1879) was the first painting by an American to be bought for the Luxembourg Museum, Paris.

MOSS, FRANK (*b. Coldspring, N.Y., 1860; d. 1920*), lawyer, reformer. Counsel for Society for the Prevention of Crime *post* 1887. Associate of Howard Crosby and Charles H. Parkhurst in attacks against Tammany Hall and vice conditions in New York, he later acted as counsel to the Lexow and Mazet investigating committees and as an assistant district attorney under Charles Whitman, 1909–14.

MOSS, JOHN CALVIN (*b. near Bentleyville, Pa., 1838; d. 1892*), printer, pioneer commercial photoengraver. Perfected his process *c.* 1870; worked in New York City, 1871–92.

MOSS, LEMUEL (*b. Boone Co., Ky., 1829; d. New York, N.Y., 1904*), Baptist clergyman, editor, educator. Taught at Bucknell University and at Crozer Theological Seminary; was president of (old) Chicago University, 1874, and of Indiana State University, 1875–84.

MOST, JOHANN JOSEPH (*b. Augsburg, Germany, 1846; d. Cincinnati, O., 1906*), anarchist. Edited *Die Freiheit post* 1878. Expelled from the German Socialist party, 1880, for his extreme anarchist views, he came to New York City in 1882, where he continued to edit his paper and became leader of the most radical faction of the American anarchists. He dictated the declaration of principles adopted by the Pittsburgh convention of 1883 which became the doctrine of communist anarchism in America.

MOTLEY, JOHN LOTHROP (*b. Dorchester, Mass., 1814; d. England, 1877*), historian, diplomat. Attended Round Hill School where George Bancroft was one of his teachers; graduated Harvard, 1831; made further studies in Germany and traveled in Great Britain and on the continent. Returning to Boston, 1835, he worked at writing and published two novels: *Morton's Hope* (1839) and *Merrymount* (written *c.* 1839, published 1849). After a brief service as secretary of legation at St. Petersburg, Russia, he decided *c.* 1847 on the field of history that was to be his interest for the rest of his life, the attainment of independence by the Netherlands. Encouraged by W. H. Prescott, Motley entered on a lengthy research into his chosen subject and after numerous difficulties and disappointments, published *The Rise of the Dutch Republic* (London and New York, 1856). It had an immediate and great success which it owed to its picturesque, dramatic narrative of a striking series of events and the enthusiasm which it showed for liberty; however, Motley's warm, partisan prejudices lessened the value of the work as history and it remains a brilliant, personal interpretation of its subject. He next produced the *History of the United Netherlands* (1860, 1867, London; 1861, 1868, New York) and *The Life and Death of John of Barneveld* (1874) which completed his project but were lacking in the dramatic interest of the earlier work. Happy and reasonably successful as U.S. minister to Austria, 1861–67, Motley resigned under pressure from Washington occasioned by circumstances not of his making. Appointed U.S. minister to Great Britain, 1869, he was unsuccessful in pressing the *Alabama* claims. He was dismissed by President Grant in 1870 not so much for his failure as because he was a friend of Charles Sumner with whom the president was at odds.

MOTON, ROBERT RUSSA (*b. Amelia Co., Va., 1867; d. Capahosic, Va., 1940*), Negro educational administrator. Graduated Hampton Institute, 1890. Served Hampton in many administrative capacities, 1890–1915; was principal, Tuskegee Institute, 1915–35.

[*Supp. 2*]

MOTT, GERSHOM (*b. Lamberton, N.J., 1822; d. 1884*), businessman, Union major-general. Earned special recognition as a divisional commander in the battles of the Wilderness and Spotsylvania Court House, May–June 1864.

MOTT, JAMES (*b. North Hempstead, N.Y., 1788; d. Brooklyn, N.Y., 1868*), businessman, Quaker reformer, Abolitionist. Married Lucretia Coffin (Mott), 1811.

MOTT, LUCRETIA COFFIN (*b. Nantucket, Mass., 1793; d. 1880*), reformer, Quaker preacher. Cousin of Isaac and John Coffin; married James Mott, 1811. Aligned like her husband with the liberal or Hicksite group of the Society of Friends, she traveled extensively to speak at Quaker meetings in different parts of the country. Her most notable work was connected with the questions of woman's rights and anti-slavery; with Elizabeth Cady Stanton, she was a chief promoter of the convention at Seneca Falls, N.Y., 1848, where the U.S. woman's rights movement was formally launched.

MOTT, VALENTINE (*b. Glen Cove, N.Y., 1785; d. New York, N.Y., 1865*), surgeon. M.D., Columbia, 1806; studied also in London and Edinburgh under Astley Cooper and other noted surgeons. Taught surgery at various times at Columbia, at Rutgers Medical College, at the New York College of Physicians and Surgeons and at the University of the City of New York (New York University). A bold, original surgeon of international repute, he was the first to tie the innominate artery (1818) and successfully tied the common iliac artery (1827) for an aneurism of the external iliac; he was also one of the first to perform a successful amputation of the hip joint, to excise the jaw for necrosis and to resect and suture veins.

MOULTON, ELLEN LOUISE CHANDLER (*b. Pomfret, Conn., 1835; d. Boston, Mass., 1908*), minor poet and author of juvenile stories.

MOULTON, RICHARD GREEN (*b. Preston, England, 1849; d. Tunbridge Wells, England, 1924*), educator, author. An enthusiastic and inspiring lecturer on literature, Moulton taught at the University of Chicago, 1892–1919.

MOULTRIE, JOHN (*b. Charleston, S.C., 1729; d. Shropshire, England, 1798*), physician, planter, lieutenant-governor of East Florida, Loyalist. Brother of William Moultrie.

MOULTRIE, WILLIAM (*b. Charleston, S.C., 1730; d. 1805*), planter, Revolutionary general, South Carolina legislator. Brother of John Moultrie. A leader in the military affairs of South Carolina *post* 1762, Moultrie conducted a successful defense of the fort on Sullivan's Island, Charleston Harbor, June 28, 1776. Promoted brigadier-general in the Continental service, he operated independently in South Carolina after the fall of Savannah in December 1778, and de-feated a British force at Beaufort, February 1779. After effective action that saved Charleston, S.C., from capture, May 1779, he was taken prisoner a year later with the garrison of that city when it fell. Exchanged, February 1782, he served till the end of the war, being made major-general, October 1782. As governor of South Carolina, 1785–87, he worked for re-establishment of the state's credit, for better organization of the militia, and for improvement of internal navigation. Re-elected governor, 1792, he retired to private life at the end of his term.

MOUNT, WILLIAM SIDNEY (*b. Setauket, N.Y., 1807; d. Stony Brook, N.Y., 1868*), genre and portrait painter, notable for the honesty and craftsmanship of his work. His genre pieces of country life on Long Island are valuable pictorial documents of his time.

MOURT, GEORGE. [See MORTON, GEORGE, 1585–1624.]

MOUTON, ALEXANDER (*b. present Lafayette Parish, La., 1804; d. 1885*), planter, Louisiana legislator. U.S. senator, Democrat, from Louisiana, 1837–42; governor, 1843–46. Mouton put the state on a sound financial basis while governor; he was later a secessionist and sustained heavy loss by the Civil War.

MOWATT, ANNA CORA OGDEN (*b. Bordeaux, France, 1819; d. Twickenham, England, 1870*), actress, author. Granddaughter of Uzal Ogden. Raised and educated in New York City, she married James Mowatt, a New York lawyer, 1834. A writer of verse and dramatic pieces since childhood, she published her first book *Pelayo* under the pseudonym "Isabel" in 1836, and attacked its critics in *Reviewers Reviewed.* After financial reverses she began a career as a public reader of poetry at Boston, October 1841; obliged to give up work because of recurrent illness, 1842, she became a devotee of Mesmerism and turned for financial support to general journalism and fiction writing. Her most important imaginative work was *Fashion: or, Life in New York,* a play first produced at the Park Theatre, New York, March 24, 1845, and first published, 1850. It was a farce-comedy satirizing the pretensions of the New York new-rich of its period. In September 1847, her *Armand,* a romantic historical play, was first produced in New York where it met with favor as later in London. It was first published in 1849. Meanwhile, Mrs. Mowatt had made a highly successful debut as an actress in *The Lady of Lyons* (New York, 1845) and until 1853 acted in most important American cities and in England with E. L. Davenport as her leading man. Her *Autobiography of an Actress* appeared in 1854; in the same year she made her final appearance on the stage in New York and (her husband having died, 1851) married William F. Ritchie, editor of the *Richmond Enquirer.* Active in her retirement as a writer and in the movement for the purchase and preservation of Mount

Vernon, she separated from her husband, 1861, and lived thereafter abroad.

MOWBRAY, GEORGE MORDEY (*b. Brighton, England, 1814; d. North Adams, Mass., 1891*), pioneer oil refiner, inventor of explosives. Came to America, 1854. Removed to Titusville, Pa., 1859, where he produced the first refined oil and was the first to use nitroglycerin for the shooting of dormant wells. *Post* 1866, he turned his attention to the manufacture of nitroglycerin and did valuable work in the development of celluloid.

MOWBRAY, HENRY SIDDONS (*b. Alexandria, Egypt, 1858; d. Washington, Conn., 1928*), figure and mural painter. Nephew and adopted son of George M. Mowbray. Made early success in Paris after study there in atelier of Léon Bonnat. Returning to the United States, 1886, he settled in New York City, removing to Washington, Conn., 1907. Recipient of many honors, Mowbray was most famous for his mural work in private mansions and public and commercial buildings. His most important and brilliant work was the decoration of the library of the University Club of New York.

MOWER, JOSEPH ANTHONY (*b. Woodstock, Vt., 1827; d. New Orleans, La., 1870*), Union major-general. Entered army at outbreak of Mexican war as private of engineers; was commissioned second lieutenant, 1855, and had risen to rank of captain, 1861. His combat record during the Civil War was one rarely equalled in the American army. Twelve times cited for conspicuous bravery, in particular during the Vicksburg campaign, he was promoted major-general of volunteers, August 1864. He headed a division under W. T. Sherman in Georgia and commanded the XX Corps in the Carolina campaign.

MOWRY, WILLIAM AUGUSTUS (*b. Uxbridge, Mass., 1829; d. 1917*), educator. As principal of the English and Classical School, Providence, R.I., he became a national authority on practical pedagogy and a leader in the Teachers' Institute movement.

MOXHAM, ARTHUR JAMES (*b. Neath, South Wales, 1854; d. Great Neck, N.Y., 1931*), steel manufacturer. Came to America, 1869. Organized Birmingham (Ala.) Rolling-Mill Co., 1878; removed to Johnstown, Pa. c. 1883, where, in partnership with Tom L. Johnson, he came to control a great part of the business in girder-rails. After merging of his company in the U.S. Steel Corp., 1901, Moxham was associated with the duPont Powder Co. He became president of the Aetna Explosives Co., 1914.

MOXOM, PHILIP STAFFORD (*b. Markham, Ont., Canada, 1848; d. 1923*), Baptist and Congregationalist clergyman, prominent preacher. Held pastorates in Cleveland, O., and Boston and Springfield, Mass.

MOYLAN, STEPHEN (*b. Cork, Ireland, 1737; d. Philadelphia, Pa., 1811*), merchant, Revolutionary

soldier. Settled in Philadelphia, 1768. Recommended to George Washington by John Dickinson for patriotic zeal, he was appointed muster-master general of the army at Cambridge, Mass., August 1775, and served later as quartermaster-general. He organized and commanded a regiment of light dragoons *post* April 1777, succeeded Casimir Pulaski in command of the American cavalry, March 1778, and retired in 1783 as brevet brigadier-general.

MOZIER, JOSEPH (*b. Burlington, Vt., 1812; d. Faido, Switzerland, 1870*), sculptor. Resided and worked in Rome, Italy, *post* 1845.

MUDGE, ENOCH (*b. Lynn, Mass., 1776; d. Lynn, 1850*), Methodist clergyman. First native New Englander to enter the Methodist ministry (1793), Mudge held many pastorates and as a member of the Massachusetts legislature, 1811–12 and 1815–16, aided in the passage of the "religious freedom bill."

MUDGE, JAMES (*b. West Springfield, Mass., 1844; d. Malden, Mass., 1918*), Methodist clergyman. Great-nephew of Enoch Mudge. Missionary to India (1873–83) and Massachusetts pastor.

MUHLENBERG, FREDERICK AUGUSTUS (*b. Lancaster, Pa., 1818; d. Reading, Pa., 1901*), Lutheran clergyman, educator. Great-grandson of Henry M. Muhlenberg. First president, Muhlenberg College, 1867–76.

MUHLENBERG, FREDERICK AUGUSTUS CONRAD (*b. Trappe, Pa., 1750; d. Lancaster, Pa., 1801*), Lutheran clergyman, politician. Son of Henry M. Muhlenberg; brother of John P. G. and Gotthilf H. E. Muhlenberg. A member of the Continental Congress and of the Pennsylvania Assembly, Muhlenberg presided over the Pennsylvania ratification convention, 1787. Congressman, Federalist, from Pennsylvania, 1789–97, he served as speaker of the House of Representatives in the First Congress. Displaced in the Second Congress, he was re-elected speaker on organization of the Third Congress by the help of (Democrat) Republican votes. He abandoned the Federalist party c. 1799.

MÜHLENBERG, GOTTHILF HENRY ERNEST (*b. Trappe, Pa., 1753; d. Lancaster, Pa., 1815*), Lutheran clergyman, botanist. Son of Henry M. Muhlenberg; brother of John P. G. and Frederick A. C. Muhlenberg. Pastor at Philadelphia, 1774–79; at Lancaster, Pa., 1780–1815. First president of Franklin College, 1787. Author of a number of valuable papers descriptive of his botanical field work.

MUHLENBERG, HENRY AUGUSTUS PHILIP (*b. Lancaster, Pa., 1782; d. 1844*), Lutheran clergyman, politician, diplomat. Son of Gotthilf H. E. Muhlenberg. Pastor at Reading, Pa., 1803–28. Congressman, Democrat, from Pennsylvania, 1829–38, a loyal, intelligent supporter of Andrew Jackson. First U.S. minister to Austria, 1838–40.

MÜHLENBERG, HENRY MELCHIOR (*b. Einbeck, Hanover, 1711; d. New Providence [Trappe], Pa., 1787*), Lutheran clergyman, virtual founder of the Lutheran church in America. Graduated in theology at Göttingen, 1738; ordained, Leipzig, 1739. Offered a call to the United Congregations (Philadelphia, New Providence, New Hanover) in Pennsylvania, by G. A. Francke of the Halle Waisenhaus where he had taught, 1738–39, Muhlenberg accepted the proposal. Rumors in Germany of Count von Zinzendorf's efforts at church union among the Germans in Pennsylvania prompted him to take the post. After conferring with Johann Martin Boltzius in Georgia, Muhlenberg arrived in Philadelphia, Nov. 25, 1742. He found his Philadelphia congregation split and his rural congregations known by the sinister vernacular names of "Die Trappe" and "Der Schwamm." Received skeptically, he gradually won support of intelligent parishioners and was duly installed. Conflict with Zinzendorf, deplorable but inevitable, was fortunately brief. Muhlenberg saw his task, almost from the beginning, not as the serving of three isolated congregations, but as the planting of a church, and to that great enterprise he brought high talents. His intellect was clear and vigorous, though not original; he had the necessary physical stamina to withstand long days in the saddle; his Biblical and theological scholarship was sound; his personal religious life was mellowed by a mild type of Pietism. He was a good linguist, spoke Latin with ease, and learned to preach in English and Dutch with amazing rapidity. To his fundamental pastoral and missionary zeal he added a genius for organization. Nominally, he remained pastor of the United Congregations until almost the close of his life but he soon made them the nucleus of an organization that spread rapidly wherever German Lutherans had settled in the middle colonies. Through his efforts, Lutheran congregations came to realize the need for closer organization and the first convention of the Evangelical Lutheran Ministerium of Pennsylvania was held at Philadelphia, Aug. 26, 1748. Muhlenberg remained the revered leader of a highly intelligent, constantly expanding Lutheran society in Pennsylvania. He formally resigned his rectorship of St. Michael's and Zion's in Philadelphia, 1779.

MUHLENBERG, JOHN PETER GABRIEL (*b. Trappe, Pa., 1746; d. Philadelphia, Pa., 1807*), Lutheran pastor, Revolutionary soldier, politician. Son of Henry M. Muhlenberg; grandson of John Conrad Weiser. Receiving Anglican orders from the bishop of London, 1772, he was pastor of the German Lutheran congregation at Woodstock, Va., until 1776; *post* 1774, he was associated with the leaders of the Revolutionary party and served in the House of Burgesses. Having raised and commanded a Virginia regiment composed of Shenandoah Germans, he was commissioned brigadier-general in the Continental Army, February 1777. Distinguished as a brigade commander at Brandywine, Germantown and Monmouth, he supported Wayne in the assault on Stony Point, 1779, and served through 1780 as second-in-command to Baron von Steuben. On Oct. 14, 1781, he commanded the American brigade that stormed one of the two British redoubts at Yorktown. Leaving the army as brevet major-general, he was elected to the Council of Pennsylvania, 1784, was vice-president of the state, 1785–88, and was influential in securing early adoption of the U.S. Constitution. He served as representative-at-large, (Democrat) Republican, 1789–91, and as congressman from Montgomery Co., Pa., 1793–95, 1799–1801. Elected to the U.S. Senate, February, 1801, he resigned a month later. He was collector of customs for Philadelphia, 1802–07.

MUHLENBERG, WILLIAM AUGUSTUS (*b. Philadelphia, Pa., 1796; d. New York, N.Y., 1877*), Episcopal clergyman, educator. Grandson of Frederick A. C. Muhlenberg. Graduated University of Pennsylvania, 1815; ordained, 1820; held pastorates at Lancaster, Pa., and Flushing, N.Y. Founded and headed Flushing Institute and St. Paul's College which served as models for subsequent educational institutions under Christian auspices. Retiring from educational enterprises, 1843, he became rector of the Church of the Holy Communion, New York, 1846; among the philanthropic works which stemmed from this parish were the Episcopal Sisterhood of the Holy Communion and St. Luke's Hospital, New York. The "Memorial" presented to the Episcopal bishops, 1853, requesting liturgical reform and other innovations, was drafted by Muhlenberg. Resigning his rectorship in 1858, he gave all his time thereafter to St. Luke's Hospital and to an experiment in Christian communal life on Long Island which was called St. Johnsland.

MUIR, CHARLES HENRY (*b. Erie, Mich., 1860; d. 1933*), army officer. Graduated West Point, 1885. Distinguished for gallantry in Spanish-American War; commanded 28th Division in France, 1918–19. Retired as major-general, 1924. [*Supp.* 1]

MUIR, JOHN (*b. Dunbar, Scotland, 1838; d. Los Angeles, Calif., 1914*), naturalist, explorer, conservationist. Came to America as a boy; was raised in Wisconsin and attended the University of Wisconsin where chemistry and geology were his major interests. After extensive travel on foot through the Midwest, he arrived in California, 1868. Six years of study and exploration in Yosemite Valley were followed by equivalent work in Nevada, Utah, the Northwest and Alaska. On all his excursions, he kept a journal in which he noted his observations and illustrated them with sketches. After spending the decade, 1881–91, in securing a competence by fruit-ranching, Muir devoted the rest of his life to travel and study. The principal objects of his interest were glaciers and forests; he was the first to demonstrate the origin of Yosemite Valley by glacial erosion and discovered and described many great glaciers in Alaska. The establishment of Yosemite National Park by Congress, 1890, was largely owing to propaganda written by him and Robert U. Johnson. A similar campaign based on Muir's observation of the wastage of the national forest resources, also the general trend of his lecturing and writing, 1891–1903, played an influential part in securing conservation laws. Muir was author, among other books, of *The Mountains of California* (1894); *Stickeen* (1909); *The Yosemite* (1912); *The Story of My Boyhood and Youth* (1913) and *A Thousand Mile Walk to the Gulf* (1916).

MULDOON, WILLIAM (*b. Caneadea, N.Y., 1852; d. 1933*), wrestler, police officer, expert physical trainer. [*Supp. 1*]

MULFORD, ELISHA (*b. Montrose, Pa., 1833; d. Cambridge, Mass., 1885*), Episcopal clergyman, educator. Author of *The Nation* (1870) in which he attempted to show that the nation is an organism responding in its total life to ethical ideals.

MULFORD, PRENTICE (*b. Sag Harbor, N.Y., 1834; d. Sheepshead Bay, N.Y., 1891*), journalist, comic lecturer. Creator of the system of popular philosophy known as "New Thought."

MULHOLLAND, ST. CLAIR AUGUSTIN (*b. Lisburn, Ireland, 1839; d. 1910*), Union major-general. Came to America as a boy; was raised in Philadelphia, Pa. Fighting with distinction, 1861–65, he rose to brigade command and won the Congressional Medal of Honor for covering the withdrawal of the Army of the Potomac across the Rappahannock River after the battle of Chancellorsville. After the Civil War, he served as chief of police of Philadelphia (1868–71) and as U.S. pension agent in the same city.

MULHOLLAND, WILLIAM (*b. Belfast, Ireland, 1855; d. Los Angeles, Calif., 1935*), engineer. Came to America c. 1872; removed to California, 1877. Superintendent and chief engineer of the Los Angeles, Calif., waterworks, he provided water supply facilities keeping pace with that city's enormous growth. [*Supp. 1*]

MULLAN, JOHN (*b. Norfolk, Va., 1830; d. Washington, D.C., 1909*), explorer, army officer. Graduated St. John's College, Annapolis, 1847; West Point, 1852. Associated with I. I. Stevens in exploring railroad route from St. Paul to the Pacific, 1853–54; discovered Mullan Pass. Acting as chief of construction for a military road from Fort Benton on the Missouri to Walla Walla, Wash., he distinguished himself in battle with Indians at Four Lakes, September 1858, and elsewhere. After completion of the road, 1863, Mullan resigned from the army. Failing in several attempts at business, he was successful in practice of law at San Francisco, Calif., and Washington, D.C.

MULLANY, JAMES ROBERT MADISON (*b. New York, N.Y., 1818; d. 1887*), naval officer. Appointed midshipman, 1832, he retired as rear-admiral, 1874, after a long and varied career; he won particular distinction in command of U.S.S. *Oneida* at battle of Mobile Bay, August 1864.

MULLANY, PATRICK FRANCIS. [See AZARIAS, BROTHER, 1847–1893.]

MÜLLER, WILHELM MAX (*b. Gliessenberg, Bavaria, 1862; d. Wildwood, N.J., 1919*), Orientalist, Egyptologist. Taught Hebrew and Greek at Reformed Episcopal Seminary, Philadelphia, Pa., *post* 1890; was latterly assistant professor of Egyptology at University of Pennsylvania.

MULLIGAN, CHARLES J. (*b. Co. Tyrone, Ireland, 1866; d. Chicago, Ill., 1916*), sculptor. Came to America c. 1883; studied with Lorado Taft. Succeeded Taft as head of department of sculpture, Art Institute, Chicago.

MULLIKEN, SAMUEL PARSONS (*b. Newburyport, Mass., 1864; d. 1934*), chemist. Graduated Massachusetts Institute of Technology, 1887; Ph.D., Leipzig, 1890. Taught chemistry at Clark University and at Bryn Mawr and worked in private laboratory of Oliver W. Gibbs; *post* 1895, taught at Massachusetts Institute of Technology, specializing in courses in organic chemistry. He was author of the monumental work *A Method for the Identification of Pure Organic Compounds, etc.* (1904–22). [*Supp. 1*]

MULLINS, EDGAR YOUNG (*b. Franklin Co., Miss., 1860; d. Louisville, Ky., 1928*), Baptist clergyman, educator. President, Southern Baptist Theological Seminary, 1899–1928; president, Baptist World Alliance, 1923–28.

MULRY, THOMAS MAURICE (*b. New York, N.Y., 1855; d. New York, 1916*), contractor, banker, philanthropist. A leader in the Society of St. Vincent de Paul and in many other local and national charitable undertakings.

MUMFORD, JAMES GREGORY (*b. Rochester, N.Y., 1863; d. 1914*), surgeon, author. Practiced in Boston; was for many years on staff of Massachusetts General Hospital.

MUNDÉ, PAUL FORTUNATUS (*b. Dresden, Germany, 1846; d. New York, N.Y., 1902*), physician. Came to America as a child. M.D., Harvard, 1866. After seven years' military and civilian practice in Europe, Mundé practiced in New York City where, as teacher at New York Polyclinic and gynecologist to Mt. Sinai Hospital, he exerted a powerful influence on the course of the gynecological specialty in America.

MUNDELEIN, GEORGE WILLIAM (*b. New York, N.Y., 1872; d. Chicago, Ill., 1939*), Roman Catholic clergyman. Graduated Manhattan College, 1889; made theological studies at St. Vincent Seminary, Latrobe, Pa., and in Rome where he was ordained, 1895. After twenty years of varied service in the diocese of Brooklyn, N.Y., he succeeded as archbishop of Chicago, 1915. He was elevated to the cardinalate, 1924. Outspoken in his social views, Mundelein supported labor and the New Deal, opposed Hitler and the isolationist Rev. Charles E. Coughlin. Noted for his administrative talents, he initiated and supported much building on behalf of the church, in particular St. Mary of the Lake Seminary at Mundelein, Ill.

[*Supp. 2*]

MUNFORD, ROBERT (*b. Prince George Co., Va., date unknown; d. Mecklenburg Co., Va., 1784*), Revolutionary soldier, dramatist. Nephew of Theodorick Bland, Sr. Author of *A Collection of Plays and Poems* (1798) which contains his excellent translation of the first book of Ovid's *Metamorphoses* and his satiric drama *The Candidates*, which introduces probably the first use of a Negro as a character in American drama.

MUNFORD, WILLIAM (*b. Mecklenburg Co., Va., 1775; d. 1825*), Virginia lawyer and legislator. Son of Robert Munford, whose poetic and dramatic works he edited, 1798. Studied law under George Wythe. Served as clerk of the House of Delegates, 1811–25; co-reporter with W. W. Hening of the decisions of the Virginia supreme court of appeals, 1806–10. After Hening's death, Munford continued as reporter until 1821. His literary works appeared as *Poems and Compositions in Prose* (1798); his blank verse translation of Homer's *Iliad* was not published until 1846.

MUNGER, ROBERT SYLVESTER (*b. Rutersville, Texas, 1854; d. Birmingham, Ala., 1923*), inventor and manufacturer of cotton-gin machinery. The Munger System for pneumatic handling of cotton was a revolutionary improvement over the old system; first patented, 1892, it was quickly adopted throughout the cotton states and through the world generally.

MUNGER, THEODORE THORNTON (*b. Bainbridge, N.Y., 1830; d. 1910*), Congregational clergyman. After holding a number of pastorates, Munger served as minister of the United Church, New Haven, Conn., *post* 1885. He was author of a number of books including *The Freedom of Faith* (1883) and *Horace Bushnell, Preacher and Theologian* (1899).

MUNN, ORSON DESAIX (*b. Monson, Mass., 1824; d. 1907*), publisher. Joined Alfred E. Beach in purchase of *Scientific American*, 1846, and was associated with the publication and its correlative activities thereafter until his death.

MUÑOZ-RIVERA, LUIS (*b. Barranquitas, Puerto Rico, 1859; d. Santurce, Puerto Rico, 1916*), poet,

editor, Puerto Rican political leader. Elected resident commissioner from Puerto Rico to the United States, 1910.

MUNRO, DANA CARLETON (*b. Bristol, R.I., 1866; d. New York, N.Y., 1933*), historian. Graduated Brown, 1887; made graduate studies at Strassburg, Freiburg-im-Breisgau and University of Pennsylvania. Taught medieval and European history at Pennsylvania and at University of Wisconsin; professor of medieval history, Princeton, 1915–33. Author of *The Middle Ages* (1902), Munro made his chief contribution in the incentive he gave others to produce work of high quality.

MUNRO, GEORGE (*b. West River, Nova Scotia, 1825; d. 1896*), publisher. Removed to New York City, 1856; clerked in firm of Beadle & Adams, dime-novel publishers. Prospered *post* 1866 as publisher of a number of cheap series of which the most successful was the "Seaside Library"; he was also publisher of the *Fireside Companion*, a family paper, and of the manifold adventures of *Old Sleuth* and *Old Cap Collier*. The success of his reprints of British works on which no royalty was paid helped hasten passage of the international copyright law.

MUNRO, HENRY (*b. Scotland, 1730; d. Edinburgh, Scotland, 1801*), Presbyterian and Episcopal clergyman, army chaplain, Loyalist. Came first to America, 1757; worked as a Church of England missionary along the New York frontier, 1765–76; joined British forces in Canada, 1777. Munro married Eve, sister of John Jay, 1766.

MUNROE, CHARLES EDWARD (*b. East Cambridge, Mass., 1849; d. Forest Glen, Md., 1938*), chemist. Graduated Harvard, 1871. Taught at Harvard, at the U.S. Naval Academy and at George Washington University. A pioneer in American chemical engineering, he was the outstanding explosives expert of his time; he was the discoverer of smokeless powder and of the so-called "Munroe Effect."

[*Supp. 2*]

MUNSELL, JOEL (*b. Northfield, Mass., 1808; d. Albany, N.Y., 1880*), printer, antiquarian. Edited and published at Albany, in addition to newspapers and periodicals, a number of important collections of historical source material relating to the early wars and settlements of America.

MUNSEY, FRANK ANDREW (*b. Mercer, Maine, 1854; d. New York, N.Y., 1925*), publisher, financier. Removed to New York City, 1882; began successful career in that year with the *Golden Argosy*, a magazine for boys and girls. Living for his business and for success alone, Munsey founded or purchased magazines, and later, newspapers, with cold-blooded zeal, merging or destroying them if they failed to earn well. He was also a fortunate speculator in Wall St., was owner of a chain of grocery stores, and engaged in banking. Failing in his operations in the field of daily journalism more often than he succeeded, he kept his papers clean and respectable, if dull; his publications reflected the viewpoint of the average, prosperous American concerned with his own affairs and his own personal success. His career illustrated dramatically the trend toward consolidation, combination and decreasing competition which has become the most striking phase of the newspaper business.

MUNSON, THOMAS VOLNEY (*b. near Astoria, Ill., 1843; d. Denison, Texas, 1913*), viticulturist, horticulturist. Gave hundreds of new horticultural varieties to the world by hybridization and selection experiments; was author, among other outstanding works on grapes, of *Foundations of American Grape Culture* (1909).

MUNSON, WALTER DAVID (*b. Cheshire, Conn., 1843; d. 1908*), shipowner. Founded the Munson Line, 1873 (incorporated, 1899) which grew to be the largest freighting organization in the American coastal trade.

MÜNSTERBERG, HUGO (*b. Danzig, Germany, 1863; d. Cambridge, Mass., 1916*), psychologist. Studied under Wilhelm Wundt at University of Leipzig, where he graduated, Ph.D., 1885; he graduated also as M.D. at Heidelberg, 1887, and taught philosophy and psychology at Freiburg, 1887–97. On leave of absence from Freiburg, 1892–95, he headed the psychological laboratory at Harvard on the invitation of William James; associating himself permanently with Harvard, 1897, he taught there until his death.

Münsterberg paved the way for the more extensive use of psychology in industry, medicine, the arts and education; he may justly be called one of the pioneers in the field of applied psychology. In philosophy, he was an idealist of the type of Fichte. In psychology, he believed that the causal law held good for mental phenomena insofar as these were correlated with physiological processes. When, however, he considered the mental from the viewpoint of values, he believed in freedom. His chief contribution to theoretical psychology was probably his "action theory," which defined attention in terms of the openness of the nerve paths to the muscles of adjustment. His insistence upon the motor response as an essential factor of consciousness makes him a forerunner of modern behaviorism.

MURAT, ACHILLE (*b. Paris, France, 1801; d. Tallahassee, Fla., 1847*), author. Son of Joachim Murat and Caroline Buonaparte Murat, Achille became crown prince of Naples, 1808. Deprived by the fall of the French Empire and under suspicion in Europe, he came to New York, 1823, and settled near Tallahassee, Fla., 1827. His three books on the United States, if not as philosophic as the work of De

Tocqueville are often more graphic; of them, the most important is *Esquisse morale et politique des États-Unis, etc.* (1832).

MURDOCH, FRANK HITCHCOCK (*b. Chelsea, Mass., 1843; d. Philadelphia, Pa., 1872*), actor. Nephew of James E. Murdoch. Associated *post* 1861 with Mrs. Drew at Arch St. Theatre, Philadelphia; wrote *Davy Crockett* for Frank Mayo (produced, Rochester, N.Y., 1872), the most popular of all the plays on this theme.

MURDOCH, JAMES EDWARD (*b. Philadelphia, Pa., 1811; d. near Cincinnati, O., 1893*), actor, lecturer, teacher of elocution. Excelled as a light comedian.

MURDOCK, JAMES (*b. Westbrook, Conn., 1776; d. Columbus, Miss., 1856*), Congregational clergyman, scholar and author. Graduated Yale, 1797. Taught at University of Vermont, 1815–19; was professor of ecclesiastical history, Andover Theological Seminary, 1819–28.

MURDOCK, JOSEPH BALLARD (*b. Hartford, Conn., 1851; d. 1931*), naval officer. Graduated Annapolis, 1870; specialized in the sciences, particularly in applied electricity. Promoted rear-admiral, 1909, he commanded the Asiatic Fleet, 1911–12, and ably protected American interests during the Chinese revolution of that period.

MUREL, JOHN A. [See MURRELL, JOHN A., fl. 1804–1844.]

MURFEE, JAMES THOMAS (*b. Southampton Co., Va., 1833; d. 1912*), Alabama educator. Graduated Virginia Military Institute, 1853. Taught at University of Alabama *post* 1860; served as president, Howard College, 1871–1887; was superintendent, Marion (Ala.) Military Institute, 1887–1906.

MURFREE, MARY NOAILLES (*b. near Murfreesboro, Tenn., 1850; d. Murfreesboro, 1922*), novelist, short-story writer. Better known under her pen-name "Charles Egbert Craddock," she had a virile, robust, forthright style well suiting her masculine pseudonym. The Cumberland Mountains, where she spent many summers, were the scene of her first short stories, *In the Tennessee Mountains* (1884). The volume created a literary sensation and was followed until the mid-1890's by some eleven further collections of stories about the locale and its inhabitants. With simplicity, originality, graphic descriptions, and in a singularly rhythmical prose, she revealed the lonely, frustrated lives of mountaineers. *Post* 1900, she produced a quantity of historical fiction which included *A Spectre of Power* (1903), *The Frontiersmen* (1904), and *The Amulet* (1906).

MURIETTA (MURIETA), JOAQUIN. [See MURRIETA, JOAQUIN, c. 1832–1853.]

715

MURPHEY, ARCHIBALD DE BOW (*b. Caswell Co., N.C., 1777?; d. 1832*), North Carolina jurist, legislator, reformer. Advocated without success internal improvements and aids to navigation; also urged reform of the criminal code, abolition of imprisonment for debt and the colonization of free Negroes. His *Report on Education* (1817) offered the first definite plan for public education submitted in North Carolina. A scholar and idealist, he was too advanced for his place and time.

MURPHY, CHARLES FRANCIS (*b. New York, N.Y., 1858; d. New York, 1924*), saloon-keeper, political boss. Tactful, shrewd and reticent leader of Tammany Hall, 1902–24; brought that organization by the time of his death to its highest point of prestige and power.

MURPHY, DOMINIC IGNATIUS (*b. Philadelphia, Pa., 1847; d. Stockholm, Sweden, 1930*), government official. Served in Pension Office, Washington, D.C., *post* 1871; rose to commissioner of pensions, 1896. Secretary, Isthmian Canal Commission, 1904–05; was U.S. consul thereafter in numerous European posts, serving with particular distinction as consul-general at Sofia, Bulgaria, 1915–19.

MURPHY, EDGAR GARDNER (*b. Fort Smith, Ark., 1869; d. 1913*), Episcopal clergyman. A strong liberal force in Montgomery, Ala., while a pastor there, he withdrew from the ministry, 1903, to serve as publicist for reform of race relations and improvement of education in the South and to secure child-labor legislation. Author of *Problems of the Present South* (1904) and other works.

MURPHY, FRANCIS (*b. Tagoat, Co. Wexford, Ireland, 1836; d. Los Angeles, Calif., 1907*), temperance reformer, evangelist.

MURPHY, FRANKLIN (*b. Jersey City, N.J., 1846; d. Palm Beach, Fla., 1920*), varnish manufacturer, Union soldier. An early advocate of profit-sharing and pension systems for employees, he instituted numerous social, political and administrative reforms as Republican governor of New Jersey, 1902–05.

MURPHY, FREDERICK E. (*b. near Troy, Wis., 1872; d. New York, N.Y., 1940*), newspaper publisher. Graduated Notre Dame, 1893. Long associated with the *Minneapolis Tribune*, Murphy served it as publisher and president *post* 1921. He was an authority on scientific agriculture and farm economics.

[*Supp. 2*]

MURPHY, HENRY CRUSE (*b. Brooklyn, N.Y., 1810; d. Brooklyn, 1882*), lawyer, politician, scholar. Graduated Columbia, 1830. Democratic mayor of Brooklyn, 1842; congressman, 1843–45, 1847–49; U.S. minister to the Netherlands, 1857–61. He served with ability and integrity from 1861 to 1873 in the New York senate, but his ambitions for higher office were blocked by the fact that he belonged to a minority faction of a minority party. He drafted and secured passage of the legislation necessary for building the Brooklyn Bridge; he was president of the private company which began the enterprise and of the corporation which succeeded it. Collector of a famous library of rare Americana, he edited, translated and published important works relating to the early history of New Netherland.

MURPHY, ISAAC (*b. near Pittsburgh, Pa., 1802; d. Madison Co., Ark., 1882*), lawyer, Arkansas Unionist. As provisional governor and governor of Arkansas, 1864–68, Murphy avoided commitment to radical Republican policies and gave the state an honest, economical government.

MURPHY, JOHN (*b. Omagh, Co. Tyrone, Ireland, 1812; d. Baltimore, Md., 1880*), publisher. Came to America as a boy. Founded John Murphy & Co., specializing in publication of Catholic books, 1837; engaged also in commercial printing and law-book publishing.

MURPHY, JOHN BENJAMIN (*b. near Appleton, Wis., 1857; d. Mackinac Island, Mich., 1916*), surgeon. Graduated Rush Medical College, 1879; made graduate studies in Vienna. Practicing in Chicago, he held teaching positions at Northwestern University and Rush Medical College; he served as chief of surgical staff, Mercy Hospital *post* 1895, and was an attending surgeon at Cook County Hospital. One of the first surgeons to investigate the cause and treatment of peritonitis following appendicitis, he produced the "Murphy button," 1892, a device which revolutionized gastro-intestinal surgery; he also advanced surgical knowledge of every region of the abdomen. Later, devoting himself to study of surgery of the lungs, of the nervous system and of bones and joints, he was pre-eminent as a teacher of clinical surgery and was the recipient of many professional honors.

MURPHY, JOHN FRANCIS (*b. Oswego, N.Y., 1853; d. New York, N.Y., 1921*), landscape painter. Self-taught; opened New York City studio, 1875; enjoyed a career of gradually increasing popularity *post* 1880. The chief merit of his work is its poetic sentiment; his small early canvases are among his best productions.

MURPHY, JOHN W. (*b. New Scotland, N.Y., 1828; d. Philadelphia, Pa., 1874*), bridge engineer. Graduated Rensselaer Polytechnic, 1847. As assistant to Squire Whipple, he devised a modification of Whipple's truss bridge; he also developed a testing machine for determining elasticity of construction materials.

MURPHY, MICHAEL CHARLES (*b. Westboro, Mass., 1861; d. Philadelphia, Pa., 1913*), pioneer athletic trainer. Successful track coach and trainer at Yale and University of Pennsylvania; coached American Olympic teams of 1908 and 1912. Introduced crouching start for sprinters.

MURPHY, WILLIAM SUMTER (*b. South Carolina, 1796?; d. Galveston, Texas, 1844*), lawyer, Ohio militia officer. U.S. chargé d'affaires to Texas, 1843–44. An ardent annexationist, he acted mainly as an intermediary between Secretary of State Upshur and President Sam Houston.

MURPHY, WILLIAM WALTON (*b. Ernestown, Canada, 1816; d. 1886*), consular officer. Raised in Ovid, N.Y.; removed to Michigan *c.* 1835 where he became prominent in Free-Soil and Republican politics. As U.S. consul-general in Frankfort, Germany, 1861–69, Murphy skillfully blocked Confederate attempts at recognition and fund raising.

MURRAY, ALEXANDER (*b. Chestertown, Md., 1754 or 1755; d. near Philadelphia, Pa., 1821*), naval officer, Revolutionary privateersman, merchant. Appointed captain, July 1798, he served with credit in the naval war with France and later as commander of U.S.S. *Constellation* in the blockade of Tripoli. He was commanding officer at Philadelphia, 1808–21.

MURRAY, DAVID (*b. Bovina, N.Y., 1830; d. New Brunswick, N.J., 1905*), educator. Graduated Union, 1852; professor of mathematics and astronomy at Rutgers College, 1863–73; helped establish Japanese educational system as superintendent of educational affairs in Japan, 1873–79. Secretary, Regents of the University of the State of New York, 1880–89.

MURRAY, JAMES ORMSBEE (*b. Camden, S.C., 1827; d. Princeton, N.J., 1899*), Presbyterian clergyman, educator. Raised in Ohio; graduated Brown, 1850, and Andover Theological Seminary, 1854. Held pastorates in Massachusetts and New York; taught English literature at Princeton *post* 1875 and served as first dean of the Princeton faculty *post* 1883.

MURRAY, JOHN (*b. near Lancaster, Pa., 1737; d. New York, N.Y., 1808*), Quaker merchant. Brother of Robert Murray with whom he was in partnership in New York City *post* 1753. President of New York Chamber of Commerce, 1798–1806. Murray, with Thomas Eddy, instituted movement for formation of a free school in New York, 1805.

MURRAY, JOHN (*b. Alton, England, 1741; d. Boston, Mass., 1815*), founder of Universalism in America. Bred up in strict Calvinism, Murray came first under the influence of Wesleyanism and then of George Whitefield. Convinced of the truth of James Relly's doctrine of universal redemption, he set forth for America, 1770, and began a two-year career of itinerant evangelism in New Jersey. Invited to New England, 1772, he won the admiration of prominent laymen and the hostility of the orthodox clergy. Befriended by Winthrop Sargent, a prosperous shipowner of Gloucester, Mass., Murray became minister of the Independent Church of Christ at Gloucester, 1779; after much persecution, he and his congregation finally obtained legal recognition as a Church. He served as pastor of a Universalist society in Boston, 1793–1809.

MURRAY, JOHN GARDNER (*b. Lonaconing, Md., 1857; d. Atlantic City, N.J., 1929*), Episcopal clergyman. Ordained, 1894, he held pastorates in Birmingham, Ala., and Baltimore, Md.; elected bishop coadjutor of Maryland, he succeeded to the bishopric, 1911. In October 1925, he became presiding bishop of the Episcopal Church, the first to hold this office through election.

MURRAY, JOSEPH (*b. Queen's Co., Ireland, c. 1694; d. New York, N.Y., 1757*), lawyer. Emigrated to New York early in life, appearing at the bar there in 1718. He later attended the Middle Temple in London (admitted 1725). On his return *c.* 1728 to New York, he appeared in most of the leading cases in his generation. He appears to have had a principal share in amending and completing the draft of the Montgomerie Charter and his "Opinion Relating to the Courts of Justice in the Colony of New York" (appended to William Smith's *Opinion*, published in 1734) is one of the few really important contributions to legal history written in the American colonies. He argued in this work against the claim that courts of law can be established only by statute and set forth the view that "fundamental courts" are a part of the constitution of England. Associated with the so-called DeLancey faction, Murray served as a New York delegate at the Albany Congress, 1754.

MURRAY, JUDITH SARGENT STEVENS (*b. Gloucester, Mass., 1751; d. near Natchez, Miss., 1820*), author. Wife of John Murray (1741–1815); sister of Winthrop Sargent. A contributor to Boston periodicals *post* 1784, Mrs. Murray produced her most important work in the series of essays entitled "The Gleaner," which appeared in the *Massachusetts Magazine*, 1792–94. She was author also of two plays, *The Medium, or Virtue Triumphant* and *The Traveller Returned*, produced in Boston, 1795 and 1796 respectively. Her collected works were published by subscription at Boston as *The Gleaner* (1798); she also edited her husband's works.

MURRAY, LINDLEY (*b. present Dauphin Co., Pa., 1745; d. York, England, 1826*), grammarian. Son of Robert Murray. Studied law with John Jay in office of Benjamin Kissam; acquired extensive practice among Quakers; was successful as a N.Y. merchant, 1779–83. Removing to England, 1784, he remained there until his death. Murray's fame rests on his school textbooks of which the *English Grammar* (1795, fully revised, 1818) was for many years to grammar what Hoyle was to card-playing. He was author also of a number of miscellaneous works of a religious nature.

MURRAY, LOUISE SHIPMAN WELLES (*b. Athens, Pa., 1854; d. 1931*), archaeologist, local historian. Founder and director of Tioga Point Museum.

MURRAY, ROBERT (*b. Scotland, 1721; d. 1786*), Quaker merchant. Brother of John Murray (1737–1808). Brought to America as a child, Murray was raised in Dauphin Co., Pa.; he was engaged with his brother in general trade in New York *post* 1753 and represented the firm in England, 1767–75. Although he was a British sympathizer during the Revolution, his wife intentionally or unintentionally saved Putnam's division of Washington's army in September 1776 after the landing at Kip's Bay by delaying pursuing British officers at her country house (Murray Hill).

MURRAY, THOMAS EDWARD (*b. Albany, N.Y., 1860; d. Southampton, N.Y., 1929*), consulting engineer, inventor. Associated in technical capacities *post* 1887 with utility companies operated by Anthony N. Brady, he removed to New York City, 1895, to consolidate and manage electric power properties in Brooklyn and Manhattan. As general director of the New York and Brooklyn Edison companies, Murray was responsible for the building of the principal power stations supplying New York City and was also designer and builder of power plants in many other American cities. His inventive genius secured for him over 1100 patents which touch upon almost every phase of industry. He held high corporate positions in the Edison companies and organized and directed several corporations of his own for the manufacture of devices invented by him.

MURRAY, WILLIAM VANS (*b. Cambridge, Md., 1760; d. near Cambridge, 1803*), diplomat. Studied law at the Middle Temple, England; began practice in Maryland, 1787; served as congressman, Federalist, from Maryland, 1791–97. Appointed U.S. minister to the Netherlands in 1797, he made The Hague the channel for restoring diplomatic negotiations with France after the XYZ affair, 1798. Appointed U.S. commissioner to treat with the French Directory, he and his fellow commissioners, Oliver Ellsworth and W. R. Davie, found themselves confronted with Napoleon Bonaparte who had overthrown the Directory. After negotiating from February to October 1800, Murray and his fellows obtained a less than satisfactory convention which, however, allayed previous misunderstandings and disputes. Resigning his post at The Hague, September 1801, Murray returned to the United States. He was author of *Political Sketches* (1787).

MURRELL, JOHN A. (*b. probably Tennessee, 1804; d. Pikesville, Tenn., post 1844*), outlaw, active in the Old Southwest, 1823–44. Beginning his career as a highway robber and horse thief, he created a criminal organization for disposition of spoils and later for Negro stealing.

MURRIETA, JOAQUIN (*b. probably Sonora, Mexico, c. 1832; d. near Tulare Lake, Calif., 1853*), brigand, most noted of California bandits, 1849–53. Strongly anti-American.

MURROW, JOSEPH SAMUEL (*b. Jefferson Co., Ga., 1835; d. Oklahoma, 1929*), Baptist clergyman. Missionary *post* 1857 to the Creeks, Seminoles and Choctaws in Indian Territory (later Oklahoma).

MUSICA, PHILIP MARIANO FAUSTO (*b. New York, N.Y., 1884; d. Fairfield, Conn., 1938*), swindler. Under alias of "F. Donald Coster," he was the principal factor in the McKesson & Robbins fraud, 1930–38. [*Supp. 2*]

MUSIN, OVIDE (*b. near Liège, Belgium, 1854; d. Brooklyn, N.Y., 1929*), violinist, composer. After a notable career as a concert artist, he established a school of violin playing in New York City, 1908; his compositions were for the most part brilliant virtuoso pieces.

MUSSEY, ELLEN SPENCER (*b. Geneva, O., 1850; d. Washington, D.C., 1936*), lawyer, feminist, social reformer. [*Supp. 2*]

MUSSEY, REUBEN DIMOND (*b. Pelham, N.H., 1780; d. Boston, Mass., 1866*), surgeon. Graduated Dartmouth, 1803; M.B., Dartmouth, 1805; M.D., University of Pennsylvania, 1809. Taught medical subjects at Dartmouth and other eastern schools, 1814–38; professor of surgery, Medical College of Ohio, 1838–52; professor of surgery, Miami Medical College, Cincinnati, 1852–57. An early user of chloroform and ether as anaesthetics; was particularly interested in temperance reform.

MUYBRIDGE, EADWEARD (*b. Kingston-on-Thames, England, 1830; d. England, 1904*), pioneer in motion photography. Came to America as a young man; was photographer for U.S. Coast and Geodetic Survey. Employed by Leland Stanford, Muybridge, by a series of photographs in silhouette made at Palo Alto, Calif., 1872, proved that at certain times all four feet of a running horse are off the ground. His book *The Horse in Motion* (1878) excited world-wide interest. Thereafter he worked in animal locomotion photography throughout his lifetime, and developed the zoopraxiscope (1879) by which he successfully reproduced moving figures in large size on a screen. Results of his later experiments were published in eleven volumes as *Animal Locomotion, etc.* (1887).

MYER, ALBERT JAMES (*b. Newburgh, N.Y., 1829; d. Buffalo, N.Y., 1880*), army surgeon. Graduated Hobart, 1847; M.D., Buffalo Medical College, 1851. An enthusiastic experimenter in signal devices, he was appointed to organize and command the U.S. Army Signal Corps, June 1861. After extensive military field service in Virginia, he succeeded in securing the formal establishment of the Signal Corps, March 3,

1863, together with his own appointment as chief signal officer and colonel. Friction with the War Department caused his relief in November 1863, but an act of Congress of July 1866, reorganized the Signal Corps and restored Myer to his post and rank which he held until his death. Myer was responsible for the establishment of the U.S. Weather Bureau under direction of the Signal Corps, February 1870. Two months before his death, he was promoted brigadier-general.

MYERS, ABRAHAM CHARLES (*b. Georgetown, S.C., 1811; d. Washington, D.C., 1889*), soldier. Graduated West Point, 1833; served in the Seminole wars and with distinction in the Mexican War; thereafter, until 1861, he was stationed in the quartermaster service at various Southern posts. As quartermaster-general of the Confederate Army, 1861–63, he worked with personal honesty and efficiency in a situation of monumental difficulty. Unable to overcome the inefficiency of his subordinates, he was superseded.

MYERS, JEROME (*b. Petersburg, Va., 1867; d. New York, N.Y., 1940*), painter. Studied at Cooper Union and the N.Y. Art Students League. An associate of the New York realist school, Myers painted the everyday life of New Yorkers, particularly the residents of the lower East Side and Greenwich Village; after working in an early, rather dark impressionist manner, he developed a gay and sparkling method in his later work. [*Supp. 2*]

MYLES, JOHN (*b. probably Herefordshire, England, c. 1621; d. Swansea, Mass., 1683*), pioneer Baptist clergyman. A leader among Welsh Baptists, Myles emigrated to New England in 1662 and became pastor of one of the earliest Baptist churches in America at Rehoboth in Plymouth Colony, 1663. He removed, with his church, to the present site of Swansea, 1667, where he served as pastor with an interlude as acting pastor of the First Baptist Church in Boston.

MYRICK, HERBERT (*b. Arlington, Mass., 1860; d. Bad Nauheim, Germany, 1927*), editor and publisher of agricultural periodicals. Crusaded for post office improvement, farmers' cooperatives, federal farm legislation.

NACK, JAMES M. (*b. New York, N.Y., 1809; d. 1879*), poet. A deaf mute, Nack won celebrity for his work in the years, 1827–60, principally because of his triumph over his physical handicap. Among his numerous books, imitative of Scott and Byron, were *The Legend of the Rocks* (1827) and *The Romance of the Ring and Other Poems* (1859).

NADAL, EHRMAN SYME (*b. Greenbrier Co., Va., now W. Va., 1843; d. Princeton, N.J., 1922*), journalist, essayist, public official.

NAIRNE, THOMAS (*b. probably Scotland, date unknown; d. South Carolina, 1715*), planter, South Carolina legislator, Indian agent. First mentioned in South Carolina records, 1698, as landowner on St. Helena Island, he acquired influence over the Indians that made him the most remarkable frontier figure of the South in the period of Queen Anne's War. Active in efforts to regulate the Indian trade among the Yamasee and to Christianize them, he became leader of the country party in the Assembly and clashed vigorously with Sir Nathaniel Johnson, the governor of the colony. Under the Indian Act, 1707, he served as the first provincial Indian agent. An active Carolina expansionist, he was burned at the stake after attempting a parley with the discontented Yamasee.

NAISMITH, JAMES (*b. Almonte, Canada, 1861; d. Lawrence, Kans., 1939*), professor of physical education, originator of basketball. Graduated McGill University, 1887; Presbyterian College, Montreal, 1890. While attending the Y.M.C.A. Training School in Springfield, Mass., Naismith invented the game of basketball in 1891 as a project to interest young athletes during the winter season. He taught in the physical education department, University of Kansas, 1898–1937. [*Supp. 2*]

NANCRÈDE, CHARLES BEYLARD GUÉRARD de (*b. Philadelphia, Pa., 1847; d. Ann Arbor, Mich., 1921*), surgeon. Grandson of Paul J. G. de Nancrède. M.D., University of Pennsylvania, 1869; M.D., Jefferson Medical College, 1883. After successful practice in Philadelphia, Nancrède was appointed professor of surgery, University of Michigan, 1889, and held that position for the remainder of his life; he taught also during the summer months at Dartmouth Medical College *post* 1887.

NANCRÈDE, PAUL JOSEPH GUÉRARD de (*b. near Fontainebleau, France, 1761; d. Paris, France, 1841*), soldier, teacher, bookseller and printer. Served as a private in the Soissonnais regiment of Rochambeau's army, 1780–83. Returning to America, 1785, he was instructor in French at Harvard, 1787–98, and published the first French school text composed especially for use in American colleges, *L'Abeille Françoise* (1792). He published also a French newspaper, the *Courier de Boston*, 1789, and from 1796 to 1804 published a number of French and English books from his shop in Boston, mainly in the genre of Rousseau. After a residence in France, 1804–12, he returned to the United States and transferred his business from Boston to Philadelphia.

NANUNTENOO. [See CANONCHET, d. 1676.]

NAPTON, WILLIAM BARCLAY (*b. near Princeton, N.J., 1808; d. 1883*), jurist. Removed to Missouri, 1832; was judge of the state supreme court, 1839–51, 1857–61, 1873–80. A pro-slavery state-rights Democrat, Napton made lasting contributions to the jurisprudence of commercial law, land titles and equity.

NARVÁEZ, PÁNFILO de (*b. Valladolid, Spain, c. 1478; d. near Matagorda Bay, 1528*), Spanish conquistador. Came to West Indies early in the 16th century; served first in Jamaica. As chief captain of Diego Velásquez, Narváez participated ruthlessly in the pacifying and settling of Cuba. Commissioned by Velásquez to seize or kill Cortés and supersede him as captain-general of Mexico, he was defeated by Cortés, May 23, 1520, lost an eye, and was imprisoned until 1521. Acquiring concessions in Florida, he sailed thence from Spain in June 1527. He arrived, accidentally and off-course, to the west of Tampa Bay and took possession of Florida for the King of Spain, April 16, 1528. Separated from his ships, he and 300 men trekked overland, fruitlessly hunting for riches amid the hostile Indians. Beset by great difficulties, he was drowned as his expedition was cruising in improvised boats along the Gulf Coast in search of Mexico.

NASBY, PETROLEUM V. [See LOCKE, DAVID ROSS, 1833–1888.]

NASH, ABNER (*b. Amelia Co., Va., c. 1740; d. New York, N.Y., 1786*), lawyer, Revolutionary patriot, North Carolina legislator. Prominent *post* 1774 in the movement toward revolution, Nash served as speaker of the first North Carolina House of Commons and as speaker of the state senate, 1779. As governor, 1780–81, he quarreled with the legislature over its usurpation of his executive powers; as a member of Congress, 1782–85, he advocated a strong federal government.

NASH, ARTHUR (*b. Tipton Co., Ind., 1870; d. Cincinnati, O., 1927*), clergyman, clothing manufacturer. Originator of the "golden rule" plan of copartnership with workers. Author of *The Golden Rule in Business* (1923).

NASH, CHARLES SUMNER (*b. Granby, Mass., 1856; d. 1926*), Congregational clergyman. After pastoral and educational experience in the East, Nash removed to Oakland, Calif., 1891, as professor of homiletics and pastoral theology, Pacific Theological Seminary. He served the school as dean, 1906–11, as president, 1911–20, and as president emeritus until his death. Under his leadership, the Seminary became undenominational, 1912, and in 1916, changed its name to Pacific School of Religion.

NASH, DANIEL (*b. present Great Barrington, Mass., 1763; d. Burlington, N.Y., 1836*), Episcopal clergyman. A successful missionary on the western New York frontier *post* 1797, Father Nash, as he was known, was the supposed prototype for "Reverend Mr. Grant" in J. F. Cooper's *The Pioneers*.

NASH, FRANCIS (*b. Amelia Co., Va., c. 1742; d. Kulpsville, Pa., 1777*), Revolutionary soldier. Brother of Abner Nash. Mortally wounded in battle of Germantown, October 1777, while commanding Continental North Carolina brigade. Nashville, Tenn., was named in his honor.

NASH, FREDERICK (*b. New Bern, N.C., 1781; d. 1858*), North Carolina jurist and legislator. Son of Abner Nash. Graduated College of New Jersey (Princeton), 1799; commenced law practice in New Bern, 1801, but removed to Hillsboro, 1807. Served as state superior court judge, 1818–26, 1836–44; as state supreme court judge, 1844–58 (chief justice *post* 1852).

NASH, HENRY SYLVESTER (*b. Newark, O., 1854; d. 1912*), Episcopal clergyman. *Post* 1882, taught literature and interpretation of the New Testament at Episcopal Theological School, Cambridge, Mass.

NASH, SIMEON (*b. South Hadley, Mass., 1804; d. Gallipolis, O., 1879*), Ohio jurist. Author of *Pleadings and Practice under the Civil Code* (1856), a major contribution to the jurisprudence of his state.

NASON, ELIAS (*b. Wrentham, Mass., 1811; d. 1887*), Congregational clergyman, educator, lecturer. Author of a number of books and pamphlets principally on American colonial and religious history.

NASON, HENRY BRADFORD (*b. Foxboro, Mass., 1831; d. 1895*), educator. Graduated Amherst, 1855; Ph.D., Göttingen, 1857. Professor of natural history, Rensselaer Polytechnic Institute, 1858–66; professor of chemistry and natural science, 1866–95. An expert in analytic procedures, Nason introduced a number of improvements in the process of treating crude oil as adviser to the Standard Oil Co., 1880–90.

NASSAU, ROBERT HAMILL (*b. near Norristown, Pa., 1835; d. Ambler, Pa., 1921*), Presbyterian clergyman, linguist. Missionary in West Africa, 1861–1906. Author of a number of works dealing with African religion and society including *Fetichism in West Africa* (1904).

NAST, THOMAS (*b. Landau, Germany, 1840; d. Guayaquil, Ecuador, 1902*), cartoonist. Brought to New York City as a child, he attended public schools and the National Academy of Design; he received much personal instruction from Alfred Fredericks. Engaged as a staff artist on *Frank Leslie's Illustrated Newspaper* at the age of 15, Nast left that paper in 1859 to join the *New York Illustrated News* as artist-correspondent. As a staff-member and contributor to *Harper's Weekly*, 1862–86, he received a free hand in choice of subjects and method of treatment and vigorously advanced the art of political caricature. His Civil War period cartoons were vastly influential and made him, in Abraham Lincoln's words, "our best recruiting sergeant." Always a fierce partisan, Nast employed his art in support of the Radical Republicans; his attacks on the "Tweed Ring," 1869–72, contributed much to its overthrow. He made Horace Greeley ludicrous in the campaign of 1872, defended Hayes against Tilden, and forsook the Republicans only when James G. Blaine was nominated. He invented the symbolic Democratic donkey and Republican elephant, both becoming fixed in his pictures, 1874. Financially unfortunate in his later years, he died as U.S. consul at Guayaquil.

NAST, WILLIAM (*b. Stuttgart, Germany, 1807; d. 1899*), Methodist clergyman. Came to America, 1828. Active, *post* 1835, as missionary to Germans in Ohio and adjoining states; was a founder of German Wallace College, Berea, O.

NATION, CARRY AMELIA MOORE (*b. Garrard Co., Ky., 1846; d. Leavenworth, Kans., 1911*), temperance agitator. An ignorant, unbalanced, and contentious woman of vast energies, afflicted with an hereditary paranoia, she was subjected to early hardships that fused all her great physical and emotional powers into a flaming enmity toward liquor and its corrupt purveyors. From her first saloon-smashing ventures at Medicine Lodge, Kans., she carried her campaign to Wichita (1900), where her distinctive weapon, the hatchet, was first used, and then on to many of the principal American cities. Arrested thirty times for "disturbing the peace," she paid fines from sales of souvenir hatchets, lecture tours, and stage appearances. Her autobiography was published, 1904.

NAVARRE, PIERRE (*b. Detroit, Mich., 1790?; d. near Toledo, O., 1874*), frontiersman. Pensioned for legendary exploits as scout of William Henry Harrison's army in campaigns of 1813–14; fur trader in Old Northwest.

NEAGLE, JOHN (*b. Boston, Mass., 1796; d. Philadelphia, Pa., 1865*), portrait painter. Studied with Bass Otis; was encouraged by Thomas Sully whose niece he married. Successful as a portraitist in Philadelphia, his picture "Pat Lyon the Blacksmith" (1826) added greatly to his reputation; his portrait of Gilbert Stuart is the best existing likeness of that artist.

NEAL, DAVID DALHOFF (*b. Lowell, Mass., 1838; d. Munich, Germany, 1915*), painter. After study in Munich under von Piloty and other masters, he produced many popular historical canvases including "The First Meeting of Mary Stuart and Rizzio" and "Oliver Cromwell Visiting Mr. John Milton." The later years of his life were devoted to portrait work.

NEAL, JOHN (*b. Falmouth, now Portland, Maine, 1793; d. Portland, 1876*), author, editor. Resident in Baltimore, Md., 1815–23, Neal produced a prodigious amount of literary work, editing for brief periods the *Baltimore Telegraph* and the *Portico*, compiling a large part of *A History of the American Revolution* (1819) credited to Paul Allen, and publishing several narrative poems, a verse tragedy and five novels

which included *Logan* (1822), *Seventy-Six* (1823) and *Randolph* (1823). While resident in England, 1824–27, Neal was a contributor to the chief British periodicals. Among the most important of his works of this period were a critical appraisal of American authors entitled "American Writers" (in *Blackwood's Magazine*, September 1824–February 1825) and *Brother Jonathan* (published by Blackwood as a book, 1825). On his return to America, he settled in Portland, Maine, and was active in many fields, publishing three more novels and as a magazine editor encouraging young contributors, among them John G. Whittier and Edgar A. Poe. *Post* 1840, he devoted himself to business and civic interests but continued to write voluminously and to speak in behalf of numerous causes. His autobiography *Wandering Recollections* (1869) is invaluable as self-portraiture of this talented but hasty and over-enthusiastic man.

NEAL, JOSEPH CLAY (*b. Greenland, N.H., 1807; d. 1847*), Philadelphia journalist, humorist. Author of *Charcoal Sketches* (1838), *In Town and About* (1843), *Peter Ploddy, and Other Oddities* (1844) and *Charcoal Sketches: Second Series* (1848).

NEALE, LEONARD (*b. near Port Tobacco, Md., 1746; d. Baltimore, Md., 1817*), Roman Catholic clergyman, Jesuit. As president of Georgetown College, 1799–1806, he transformed the school from an academy into an excellent classical college. Consecrated bishop-coadjutor of Baltimore, 1800, he established a community of nuns in Georgetown which was affiliated in 1816 with the Visitation Order. Succeeding to the archbishopric of Baltimore, 1815, he served until his death.

NEEDHAM, JAMES (*b. England, date unknown; d. on the Yadkin River, near the Occaneechi Village, 1673*), explorer. Came to the southern Carolina settlement from Barbados, 1670; became a planter on the Ashley River. Exploring in search of a passage by water to the southwest from the present site of Petersburg, Va., 1673, Needham reached the main Cherokee village and was, so far as is known, the first Englishman to penetrate the country of the over-hill Cherokees.

NEEF, FRANCIS JOSEPH NICHOLAS (*b. Soultz, Alsace, 1770; d. New Harmony, Ind., 1854*), educator. Trained by Pestalozzi in Switzerland, Neef was persuaded to come to Philadelphia by William Maclure and arrived there, 1806. He established near Philadelphia the first Pestalozzian school in the United States *c.* 1808, and maintained a school at Louisville, Ky., 1814–26. Neef conducted the educational program in the community at New Harmony from 1826 until the failure of that venture two years later.

NEELY, THOMAS BENJAMIN (*b. Philadelphia, Pa., 1841; d. 1925*), Methodist clergyman and bishop. A conservative, learned authority on Methodist polity and doctrine, Neely opposed Methodist unification, the granting of autonomy to the churches in mission lands and other liberalizing tendencies.

NEF, JOHN ULRIC (*b. Herisau, Switzerland, 1862; d. Carmel, Calif., 1915*), chemist. Came to America as a boy; was raised in western Massachusetts. Graduated Harvard, 1884; Ph.D., Munich, 1886. Professor of chemistry at Purdue, 1887–89, and at Clark University, 1889–92; organized and headed department of chemistry, University of Chicago, 1892–1915. Author of much pioneer work in organic chemistry, Nef made outstanding researches on the structure of quinone.

NEGLEY, JAMES SCOTT (*b. East Liberty, Pa., 1826; d. Plainfield, N.J., 1901*), Union major-general, horticulturist, railroad executive. A veteran of the Mexican War and long active in the Pennsylvania militia, Negley fought in the western campaigns of the Civil War with conspicuous skill and gallantry until Chickamauga, when he was relieved of command on charges of desertion and cowardice of which a court of inquiry cleared him. Entering business in Pittsburgh, Pa., he served as congressman, Republican, from Pennsylvania, 1869–75 and 1885–87.

NEHRLING, HENRY (*b. Herman, Wis., 1853; d. 1929*), ornithologist, horticulturist. Author of *North American Birds* (1889–93).

NEIDHARD, CHARLES (*b. Bremen, Germany, 1809; d. Philadelphia, Pa., 1895*), pioneer homeopathist. Stepson of Georg F. List. Came to America, 1825; after studies at the University of Pennsylvania, he completed his education at Leipzig and Jena. Returning to America, 1836, he practiced homeopathic medicine in Philadelphia and was a founder of the Hahnemann Medical College, 1839.

NEIGHBORS, ROBERT SIMPSON (*b. Virginia, 1815; d. Fort Belknap, Texas, 1859*), Texas pioneer, Indian agent. Removed to Texas, probably 1833. After holding a captaincy in the Texas army and imprisonment by the Mexicans, 1842–44, his concern with the Indians began in 1845 when he became the Texas agent for the Lipan and Tonkawa tribes; he also treated with the Comanche and other wild tribes. Commissioned U.S. agent for Texas Indians, 1847, he was instructed to keep them friendly and away from settlements and intoxicating liquors. He performed his difficult task well in view of the inadequacy of the laws and the encroachments of the white settlers but he was removed from office, 1849. His reports constitute the most reliable information extant on Texas tribes, especially the Comanche, for the period of his activity. Reappointed in 1853, he served until his murder by an outlaw.

NEILL, EDWARD DUFFIELD (*b. Philadelphia, Pa., 1823; d. 1893*), Presbyterian clergyman, educa-

tor, historian. Brother of John and Thomas H. Neill. President, Macalester College, 1874–84. Author of studies on the colonization of Maryland and Virginia and of a *History of Minnesota* (1858). First superintendent of public instruction for Minnesota Territory, 1851–53.

NEILL, JOHN (*b. Philadelphia, Pa., 1819; d. Philadelphia, 1880*), surgeon, teacher of surgery. Brother of Edward D. and Thomas H. Neill. Distinguished organizer of military hospitals in Pennsylvania during the Civil War.

NEILL, THOMAS HEWSON (*b. Philadelphia, Pa., 1826; d. Philadelphia, 1885*), soldier. Brother of Edward D. and John Neill. Graduated West Point, 1847. Received brevet of major-general of volunteers for services in eastern campaigns, 1861–65; after serving with the 6th Cavalry in Indian campaigns, 1870–75, he was commandant at West Point, 1875–79. Thereafter, until retirement in 1883, he was colonel, 6th Cavalry.

NEILL, WILLIAM (*b. near McKeesport, Pa., 1778 or 1779; d. 1860*), Presbyterian clergyman, educator. As pastor at Cooperstown, N.Y., 1805–09, Neill was tutor to James Fenimore Cooper; thereafter he served in a variety of pastorates, was president of Dickinson College, 1824–29, and was a director of Princeton Theological Seminary from its founding.

NEILSON, JOHN (*b. Raritan Landing, N.J., 1745; d. New Brunswick, N.J., 1833*), merchant, Revolutionary soldier, New Jersey jurist and legislator.

NEILSON, WILLIAM GEORGE (*b. Philadelphia, Pa., 1842; d. Philadelphia, 1906*), mining engineer, locomotive builder. Pioneer in the bauxite industry *post* 1883. Helped establish Adirondack Mountain Reserve, 1888.

NELL, WILLIAM COOPER (*b. Boston, Mass., 1816; d. Boston, 1874*), Negro author, anti-slavery worker. First Negro to hold a federal government post (1861).

NELSON, CHARLES ALEXANDER (*b. Calais, Maine, 1839; d. 1933*), librarian, bibliographer, indexer. Graduated Harvard, 1860. Worked on catalogues of the New York Astor Library, the Howard Memorial Library of New Orleans, the Newberry Library of Chicago; was deputy librarian, Columbia University, 1893–1909.

NELSON, DAVID (*b. near Jonesboro, Tenn., 1793; d. Oakland, Ill., 1844*), Presbyterian clergyman, educator, Abolitionist. Expelled from the state of Missouri, 1836, for anti-slavery preaching.

NELSON, EDWARD WILLIAM (*b. Amoskeag, N.H., 1855; d. 1934*), naturalist. Made pioneer field studies *post* 1877 of the biology and ethnology of vast areas of country from arctic Alaska into Mexico; his work in Alaska was particularly notable. He was chief of the Bureau of Biological Survey, U.S. Department of Agriculture, 1916–27. [*Supp. 1*]

NELSON, HENRY LOOMIS (*b. New York, N.Y., 1846; d. New York, 1908*), journalist, teacher. *Post* 1878, Nelson was Washington, D.C., correspondent of the *Boston Post*, the New York *World* and other papers; he was editor of *Harper's Weekly*, 1894–98. Wells Professor of Political Science at Williams College, 1902–08, he was a supporter of the gold standard, a free-trader, an anti-imperialist, and a fighter for civil-service reform.

NELSON, HUGH (*b. York Co., Va., 1768; d. Albemarle Co., Va., 1836*), planter, lawyer, Virginia legislator and jurist. Son of Thomas Nelson. Congressman, (Democrat) Republican, from Virginia, 1811–23. A close friend and adviser of Thomas Jefferson and James Monroe. U.S. minister to Spain, 1823–25.

NELSON, JOHN (*b. England, 1654; d. 1734*), New England merchant and statesman. Nephew and heir of Sir Thomas Temple who was proprietor and governor of Nova Scotia, 1656–70. Nelson came to Boston, Mass., *c.* 1670 and engaged in fur trade in the Kennebec country. An opponent of Edward Randolph and Sir Edmund Andros and also of William Phips, he kept up a continuous propaganda with the Board of Trade in London for the expulsion of the French from North America.

NELSON, JULIUS (*b. Copenhagen, Denmark, 1858; d. 1916*), biologist, authority on oyster culture. Came to America as a child; was raised in Wisconsin. Graduated University of Wisconsin, 1881; Ph.D., Johns Hopkins, 1888. Served *post* 1888 as professor of biology at Rutgers and biologist of the New Jersey Agricultural Experiment Station.

NELSON, KNUTE (*b. Evanger, Norway, 1843; d. 1923*), lawyer, Union soldier, Wisconsin and Minnesota legislator. Congressman, Republican, from Minnesota, 1883–89; governor of Minnesota, 1893–95; U.S. senator, 1895–1923. Nelson's Republican conservatism was modified by sympathy for a low tariff and for a federal income tax; among the more notable measures ascribed to him are the Nelson bankruptcy act (1898) and the act creating the Department of Commerce and Labor (1902).

NELSON, NELSON OLSEN (*b. Lillesand, Norway, 1844; d. 1922*), Union soldier, manufacturer, promoter of profit-sharing. Came to rural Missouri as a child. Founded (1877) N. O. Nelson Manufacturing Co., St. Louis, Mo., makers of building and plumbing supplies, which became one of the largest concerns of its kind in the world. Long interested in problems of labor, he was arbitrator of the Gould railroad lines strike, 1886. After study of basic causes of industrial disharmony, he grew convinced of the practicability

of profit-sharing and introduced it into his own plant, 1886. Failing to understand that its success was more personal than institutional, he founded a model cooperative community, Leclaire, near Edwardsville, Ill., 1890, and later extended his ideas to a low-profit, cooperative grocery store chain, centered in New Orleans, La., which went bankrupt, 1918.

NELSON, RENSSELAER RUSSELL (*b. Cooperstown, N.Y., 1826; d. 1904*), lawyer, jurist. Son of Samuel Nelson. Removed to St. Paul, Minnesota Territory, 1850, where he served as associate justice, supreme court, 1857–58, and as U.S. district judge for Minnesota, 1858–96.

NELSON, REUBEN (*b. New York, N.Y., 1818; d. New York, 1879*), Methodist clergyman, educator. Principal, Wyoming Seminary, Kingston, Pa., 1844–71; thereafter, served as publishing agent, Methodist Book Concern, New York.

NELSON, ROGER (*b. Frederick Co., Md., 1759; d. Frederick, Md., 1815*), Revolutionary soldier. Fought with credit at battles of Camden, Guilford Court House, Eutaw Springs and Yorktown. A practicing lawyer after the Revolution, he served in the Maryland legislature and as congressman, (Democrat) Republican, 1804–10.

NELSON, SAMUEL (*b. Hebron, N.Y., 1792; d. Cooperstown, N.Y., 1873*), jurist. Graduated Middlebury College, 1813; studied law in upstate New York. Appointed judge of the sixth New York circuit, 1823, he held this post until 1831, when he was appointed associate justice, New York supreme court; he acted as chief justice, 1837–45. Named an associate justice of the U.S. Supreme Court, 1845, Nelson served until his retirement, November 1872. He became one of the most useful and hard working members of the Court and a recognized authority on admiralty and maritime law, international law, patent law and conflict of laws. His training as a common-law lawyer and judge made him somewhat less willing than some of his colleagues to blaze new trails in judicial review and constitutional interpretation. Unspectacular, he was logical, lucid and brief. His unwillingness to play politics under the guise of constitutional interpretation was illustrated by his attitude in the Dred Scott case; in writing the first opinion, before the Court decided to widen the scope of the case, Nelson denied the Court's jurisdiction in the matter and omitted as irrelevant all consideration of the validity of the Missouri Compromise Act of 1820. During the Civil War, he was a conservative, loyal Democrat who doubted the constitutionality of coercing the Southern states, looked askance at what appeared to him to be unwarranted accretions of power to the executive and military branches of government, and was one of the original majority denying validity of the Legal Tender Acts. He was named a member of the Joint High Commission to negotiate settlement of the *Alabama* claims, 1871.

NELSON, THOMAS (*b. Yorktown, Va., 1738; d. Hanover Co., Va., 1789*), merchant, Revolutionary patriot, signer of the Declaration of Independence. Son of William Nelson (1711–1772). Governor of Virginia, 1781, the first conservative to hold that office. Nelson ruined his own personal fortune by his generosity in the American cause; he gave security for Virginia's loan of 1780 and financed equipment of the state troops.

NELSON, THOMAS HENRY (*b. near Maysville, Ky., c. 1823; d. Terre Haute, Ind., 1896*), lawyer. Brother of William Nelson (1824–1862). Removed to Indiana, 1844; became a Whig leader, a friend of Abraham Lincoln, and a founder of the Republican party in the Middle West. Served ably as U.S. minister to Chile, 1861–66; to Mexico, 1869–73.

NELSON, WILLIAM (*b. near Yorktown, Va., 1711; d. Yorktown, 1772*), merchant, planter. Member of the Virginia Council, 1744–72; acting governor, October 1770—August 1771. Took leading part in opposing British pre-Revolutionary taxation policy.

NELSON, WILLIAM (*b. near Maysville, Ky., 1824; d. Louisville, Ky., 1862*), naval officer, Union soldier. Brother of Thomas H. Nelson. Appointed midshipman, 1840; served in Mexican War and with Mediterranean squadron. Commissioned brigadier-general of volunteers, 1861, Nelson organized Unionist troops in Kentucky and fought with credit at Shiloh, at Corinth and in the advance against Chattanooga, receiving promotion to major-general, 1862. He was shot dead by Jefferson C. Davis while preparing the defenses of Louisville.

NELSON, WILLIAM (*b. Newark, N.J., 1847; d. Matamoras, Pa., 1914*), lawyer, New Jersey historian. Principal editor of *Archives of the State of New Jersey*; author of a number of works on the local history of that state.

NELSON, WILLIAM ROCKHILL (*b. Fort Wayne, Ind., 1841; d. 1915*), journalist. Owner-publisher *post* 1880 of *Kansas City Evening Star*, Nelson made his paper a family journal in the best sense, independent alike in politics and advertising policy. He and his paper were responsible for many Kansas City (Mo.) reforms and civic improvements.

NERINCKX, CHARLES (*b. Herffelingen, Belgium, 1761; d. Ste. Geneviève, Mo., 1824*), Roman Catholic clergyman. Came to America, 1804; joined Stephen T. Badin as a missionary in Kentucky, 1805, serving there with great zeal until 1824. He was founder of the Sisters of Loretto (Kentucky), 1812.

NESBITT, JOHN MAXWELL (*b. Loughbrickland, Ireland, c. 1730; d. Philadelphia, Pa., 1802*), merchant,

Revolutionary patriot. Emigrated to Philadelphia, 1747. Cooperated with Robert Morris in sustaining of public credit, 1780. Director of the Bank of North America, 1781–92, and first president of the Insurance Company of North America, 1792–96.

NESMITH, JAMES WILLIS (*b. New Brunswick, Canada, 1820; d. 1885*), lawyer, Oregon pioneer and legislator. Removed as a youth to the Midwest; to Oregon, 1843. U.S. senator, Douglas Democrat, 1861–67, he sacrificed his career by his friendship for Andrew Johnson.

NESMITH, JOHN (*b. Londonderry, N.H., 1793; d. Lowell, Mass., 1869*), merchant, textile manufacturer, temperance reformer. Lieutenant-governor of Massachusetts, 1862–63.

NETTLETON, ALVRED BAYARD (*b. Delaware Co., O., 1838; d. Chicago, Ill., 1911*), Union soldier, journalist. Publicity man for Jay Cooke in his Northern Pacific operations.

NETTLETON, ASAHEL (*b. Killingworth, Conn., 1783; d. East Windsor, Conn., 1844*), Congregational evangelist. Graduated Yale, 1809. A strict Calvinist, Nettleton evangelized eastern Connecticut, 1811–22, later working in Virginia and in England. He was strongly opposed to the revival methods of Charles G. Finney.

NETTLETON, EDWIN S. (*b. near Medina, O., 1831; d. Denver, Colo., 1901*), engineer. Joined the Greeley Colony, 1870; surveyed townsite of Greeley, Colo., and laid out its irrigation ditches. Later, working for private companies and for the state, he planned and built a number of irrigation systems in Colorado, Wyoming and Idaho.

NEUENDORFF, ADOLPH HEINRICH ANTON MAGNUS (*b. Hamburg, Germany, 1843; d. New York, N.Y., 1897*), musician, conductor, impresario. Came to New York City as a boy; made debut as concert pianist, 1859. Pioneered in American productions of Wagner's operas.

NEUMANN, JOHN NEPOMUCENE (*b. Prachatitz, Bohemia, 1811; d. Philadelphia, Pa., 1860*), Roman Catholic clergyman, Redemptorist. Ordained, New York City, 1836, after making studies in Europe; joined Redemptorists, 1840. After service as a missionary and as a pastor in Pittsburgh, Pa., and Baltimore, Md. (where he acted as vice-provincial of his order, 1847–51), Neumann was consecrated bishop of Philadelphia, 1852. Notable for his spiritual character and charity, he was declared venerable in 1896 and was beatified on Oct. 13, 1963.

NEUMARK, DAVID (*b. Szczerzec, Galicia, Austria, 1866; d. 1924*), Jewish philosopher, educator. Ph.D., Berlin, 1896; pursued scholarly and rabbinical career in Germany and Bohemia. Emigrated to Cincinnati,

O., 1907, to be professor of Jewish philosophy at Hebrew Union College and continued there for the remainder of his life. A daring and original thinker, he made the entire field of Hebrew learning his own, publishing a number of special studies and a work entitled *The Philosophy of the Bible* (1918). His great work, a history of medieval Jewish philosophy, was left incomplete at his death.

NEVADA, EMMA (*b. near Nevada City, Calif., 1859; d. Liverpool, England, 1940*), operatic soprano. Stage name of Emma Wixom. Madame Nevada was celebrated in coloratura parts at all the leading opera houses, 1880–1910. [*Supp. 2*]

NEVILLE, JOHN (*b. near headwaters of Occoquan River, Va., 1731; d. near Pittsburgh, Pa., 1803*), Revolutionary soldier, western Pennsylvania landowner and legislator. A central figure in the Whiskey Rebellion, 1794, as "inspector of survey" for collection of the new tax.

NEVILLE, WENDELL CUSHING (*b. Portsmouth, Va., 1870; d. 1930*), U.S. Marine Corps officer. Graduated Annapolis, 1890; commissioned second lieutenant, U.S. Marine Corps, 1892; served in Cuba, China, the Philippines and Nicaragua, 1898–1912. Decorated for his services at Vera Cruz, Mexico, 1914, he was stationed for two years in China; ordered to France, December 1917, he commanded the 5th Regiment of marines and later succeeded to command of the 4th Brigade (2nd Division). Promoted brigadier-general, 1918, he was made major-general, 1923, and was appointed commandant of the U.S. Marine Corps, 1929.

NEVIN, ALFRED (*b. Shippensburg, Pa., 1816; d. 1890*), Presbyterian clergyman, editor. Brother of Edwin H. Nevin; cousin of John W. Nevin.

NEVIN, EDWIN HENRY (*b. Shippensburg, Pa., 1814; d. 1889*), Presbyterian clergyman, educator. Brother of Alfred Nevin; cousin of John W. Nevin. President, Franklin College, Ohio, 1840–44. Author of a number of hymns and polemic tracts.

NEVIN, ETHELBERT WOODBRIDGE (*b. near Pittsburgh, Pa., 1862; d. New Haven, Conn., 1901*), composer. Son of Robert P. Nevin. Studied in Pittsburgh, Boston, and Berlin, Germany; made debut as concert pianist, Pittsburgh, 1886. As a composer, Nevin confined himself to the small instrumental and vocal forms; many of his compositions met with immediate and exceptional popularity. His *Sketch Book* (*opus 2*, 1888) contained several of his finest compositions; "Narcissus" from *Water Scenes* (1891) became a world favorite as did his setting of "The Rosary" (1898).

NEVIN, GEORGE BALCH (*b. Shippensburg, Pa., 1859; d. Easton, Pa., 1933*), composer, businessman. Published a great quantity of music principally for

the church; among his larger works were the cantatas *The Adoration* and *The Gift of God*. He wrote also a number of anthems and secular songs.

NEVIN, JOHN WILLIAMSON (*b. Franklin Co., Pa., 1803; d. near Lancaster, Pa., 1886*), theologian, educator. Brother of Robert P. Nevin; cousin of Alfred and Edwin H. Nevin. Graduated Union, 1821; Princeton Theological Seminary, 1826. As instructor at Princeton, 1826–29, Nevin published *A Summary of Biblical Antiquities* (1828); while professor of Biblical literature, Western Theological Seminary, Allegheny, Pa., 1830–40, he gradually departed from old-school Calvinist orthodoxy under influence of Neander. Elected professor at Mercersburg Seminary, Pa., 1840, he transferred his status from the Presbyterian to the Reformed Church and soon exercised great influence within that body, collaborating with Philip Schaff in development of what was known as the "Mercersburg theology." He was author of a number of books, of which the most important was *The Mystical Presence* (1846), and editor of the *Mercersburg Review*, 1849–53. Nevin acted as president of Marshall College from 1841, retiring because of ill-health *c.* 1853 from both his professorship and the presidency. He served later as the head of the combined Franklin and Marshall College, 1866–76.

NEVIN, ROBERT PEEBLES (*b. Shippensburg, Pa., 1820; d. near Pittsburgh, Pa., 1908*), journalist, pioneer oil refiner. Brother of John W. Nevin; father of Ethelbert W. Nevin.

NEVIUS, JOHN LIVINGSTON (*b. Seneca Co., N.Y., 1829; d. near Chefoo, China, 1893*), Presbyterian missionary in China, 1853–93.

NEW, HARRY STEWART (*b. Indianapolis, Ind., 1858; d. Baltimore, Md., 1937*), journalist, politician. Associated with the *Indianapolis Journal*, 1878–1903, New was active in Indiana Republican politics. A machine Republican, he served as U.S. senator from Indiana, 1917–23, and was U.S. postmaster-general, 1923–29. [*Supp. 2*]

NEWBERRY, JOHN STOUGHTON (*b. Sangerfield, N.Y., 1826; d. 1887*), lawyer. Graduated University of Michigan, 1847; practiced law in Detroit. President, Michigan Car Co., 1863–80; partner with James McMillan *post* 1878 in financial operations involving railroad building, banking and real estate investment in Detroit.

NEWBERRY, JOHN STRONG (*b. Windsor, Conn., 1822; d. New Haven, Conn., 1892*), geologist, paleontologist. Raised in Ohio; graduated Western Reserve College, 1846; made medical studies at Cleveland Medical School and in Paris. Newberry served on a number of government exploring expeditions in the West, including the coast division of the Pacific Railroad survey, 1855, and the Ives exploration of the Colorado River, 1857–58. After service with the U.S.

Sanitary Commission throughout the Civil War, he was professor of geology and paleontology in the School of Mines, Columbia University, 1866–92. A general naturalist of the old school rather than a specialist, Newberry rarely touched upon broader tectonic problems. His reputation rests largely upon his reports made while state geologist of Ohio, 1869–74, on his studies of the fossils of New Jersey and the Connecticut valley, and on his *Paleozoic Fishes of North America* (1889).

NEWBERRY, OLIVER (*b. East Windsor, Conn., 1789; d. 1860*), merchant, shipbuilder. Brother of Walter L. Newberry. Settled in Detroit, Mich., 1826; was one of first to foresee future of Chicago, Ill. Beginning as the operator of a fleet of lake vessels, Newberry became a large holder of real estate and a promoter of industry in both Detroit and Chicago.

NEWBERRY, WALTER LOOMIS (*b. East Windsor, Conn., 1804; d. at sea, 1868*), merchant, banker, philanthropist. Brother of Oliver Newberry. Settled in Detroit, Mich., 1826, where he prospered in the dry goods business. In association with his brother, with W. B. Astor and Lewis Cass, he invested in large tracts of land in Wisconsin, northern Michigan and in the newly established town of Chicago, Ill. Removing to Chicago, 1833, he made that city his home for the rest of his life and played a great part in its progress. His business enterprises came to include banking and railroading; he also held many civic positions of trust and honor. Among his many charitable benefactions was his founding of the public library in Chicago which bears his name.

NEWBOLD, WILLIAM ROMAINE (*b. Wilmington, Del., 1865; d. Philadelphia, Pa., 1926*), philosopher, educator. Graduated University of Pennsylvania, 1887; Ph.D., 1891. Taught philosophy at University of Pennsylvania *post* 1889; served as dean of the Graduate School, 1896–1904. A many-sided scholar, Newbold made important contributions also in psychology and Oriental studies.

NEWBROUGH, JOHN BALLOU (*b. near Springfield, O., 1828; d. 1891*), spiritualist. Founder of the Shalam Community, a communistic society in New Mexico.

NEWCOMB, CHARLES LEONARD (*b. West Willington, Conn., 1854; d. 1930*), mechanical engineer, inventor and manufacturer of pumping machinery and fire-fighting equipment.

NEWCOMB, HARVEY (*b. Thetford, Vt., 1803; d. Brooklyn, N.Y., 1863*), Congregational clergyman. Author of a vast number of books of which the most important was his *Cyclopaedia of Missions* (1854).

NEWCOMB, JOSEPHINE LOUISE Le MONNIER (*b. Baltimore, Md., 1816; d. New York, N.Y., 1901*), philanthropist. Chief among her benefactions was the founding and support of the H. Sophie Newcomb College of Tulane University, New Orleans, La.

NEWCOMB, SIMON (*b. Wallace, Nova Scotia, 1835; d. Washington, D.C., 1909*), astronomer. Born of New England parents who had settled in Nova Scotia, Newcomb ran away from apprenticeship to a quack doctor *c.* 1853 and roamed through Atlantic coastal cities until he settled to teach a country school in Maryland for several years. Aided by Joseph Henry and J. E. Hilgard, he was appointed computer in the Nautical Almanac Office, located then (1857) at Harvard, from which time he dated his "birth into the world of sweetness and light." He graduated B.Sc., Lawrence Scientific School, 1858. His first important research, published 1860, demonstrated that orbits of minor planets of solar system had never intersected and that their presumed origin in the disruption of a larger planet was impossible. Commissioned, 1861, professor of mathematics in the U.S. Navy, he continued at the Naval Observatory and the Nautical Almanac Office until retirement as captain, 1897.

Although he made many observations at the Naval Observatory, Newcomb was primarily a mathematical astronomer. In recognition of his fundamental investigations and tables of the orbits of Neptune and Uranus, he was made medalist of the Royal Astronomical Society, London, 1874. He began *c.* 1868 his celebrated studies of the moon's motion, to which he thereafter devoted much attention. He pushed back a fairly exact knowledge of lunar positions from 1750 to *c.* 1645, disclosing an unsuspected inadequacy of Hanson's tables of lunar motion. About this time, he became deeply concerned with question of the sun's parallax. His revision of the value of the solar parallax, published in *Washington Observations, 1865* (1867), was standard for many years, but was itself superseded by his newer revision, 1895. With assistance of A. A. Michelson, he redetermined velocity of light by the revolving-mirror method.

Internationally renowned, he was appointed (1877) superintendent of the American Ephemeris and Nautical Almanac and reformed the entire basis of fundamental data involved in computing the Ephemeris. The fundamental places of celestial bodies were to be redetermined, new tables computed to suit revised theory. For this he reviewed all worthwhile observations made since 1750, numbering several hundred thousands. In this highest type of practical mathematical research he was aided by George William Hill. He published a catalogue of some 1500 fundamental star positions (*Astronomical Papers*, VIII, 1898) and contributed many classic memoirs to the *Astronomical Papers*, including a corroboration of Leverrier's theory on the motion of Mercury that in recent years has supported Einstein's relativity theory; throughout numerous articles he masterfully treated almost every conceivable subject in astronomy. He also published several mathematical textbooks and sustained an avocational interest in political economy. He served as professor of mathematics and astronomy at Johns Hopkins, 1884–94 and 1898–1900.

NEWCOMER, CHRISTIAN (*b. Lancaster Co., Pa., 1749 o.s.; d. 1830*), a founder of the Church of the United Brethren in Christ. His "Journal," which records his organizational labors, 1795–1830, is an important historical document and was translated and published together with his *Life* in 1834. Elected bishop, 1813, he was five times re-elected between 1814 and 1829.

NEWEL, STANFORD (*b. Providence, R.I., 1839; d. St. Paul, Minn., 1907*), lawyer. U.S. minister to the Netherlands, 1897–1905.

NEWELL, FREDERICK HAYNES (*b. Bradford, Pa., 1862; d. Washington, D.C., 1932*), civil engineer. Graduated Massachusetts Institute of Technology, 1885. Assistant hydraulic engineer, U.S. Geological Survey, 1888–1902; chief engineer, Reclamation Service, 1902–07, and director of that Service, 1907–14. Engaged in irrigation surveys and projects throughout the arid parts of the West, instituting construction of 25 irrigation projects in 18 different states. Author of a number of technical treatises, he headed the civil engineering department, University of Illinois, 1915–20.

NEWELL, PETER SHEAF HERSEY (*b. near Bushnell, Ill., 1862; d. Little Neck, N.Y., 1924*), cartoonist, illustrator. Largely self-taught, Newell was a regular contributor to the leading periodicals *post* 1893; his work as a book-illustrator may be studied in *A House-Boat on the Styx* (1896) and *The Pursuit of the House-Boat* (1897) both by John K. Bangs. Inadequate as a draftsman, Newell was strongest in whimsical interpretation of nonsense.

NEWELL, ROBERT (*b. Muskingum Co., O., 1807; d. Lewiston, Idaho, 1869*), trapper, Oregon pioneer. Settled, along with Joseph L. Meek, in the Willamette Valley, 1840; helped draw up Oregon constitution (ratified July 5, 1843) and was for two sessions speaker of the House of Representatives under the provisional government. "Doc" Newell held a uniquely important place in early Oregon history, maintaining leadership in the affairs of the colony for some years after the death of Ewing Young.

NEWELL, ROBERT HENRY (*b. New York, N.Y., 1836; d. Brooklyn, N.Y., 1901*), journalist, humorist. Wrote, under pen-name "Orpheus C. Kerr," a number of satiric papers in the mock-heroic style for the New York *Sunday Mercury* and other journals. These satires enjoyed great contemporary popularity and were published in three volumes, 1862–65, but they possess now only a historical interest as a burlesque commentary on the Civil War.

NEWELL, WILLIAM AUGUSTUS (*b. Franklin, O., 1817; d. Allentown, N.J., 1901*), physician, politician.

Graduated Rutgers, 1836; M.D., University of Pennsylvania, 1839; practiced at Allentown, N.J. Congressman, Whig, from New Jersey, 1847–51; governor, Know-Nothing, 1857–60; congressman, Republican, 1865–67. Newell served also as governor of Washington Territory, 1880–84, and was a pioneer advocate of the U.S. life-saving service.

NEWELL, WILLIAM WELLS (*b. Cambridge, Mass., 1839; d. 1907*), scholar, editor. Graduated Harvard, 1859; Harvard Divinity School, 1863. A founder of the American Folk-Lore Society, 1888, Newell served thereafter as its permanent secretary and as editor of the *Journal of American Folk-Lore*. His major interest was in the Arthurian romances and kindred works of the medieval period.

NEWHOUSE, SAMUEL (*b. New York, N.Y., 1853; d. near Paris, France, 1930*), mine operator, financier. Projected and built the Argo (commonly called the Newhouse) Tunnel, Idaho Springs, Colo., 1894–1910; developed Utah copper properties. Did much to improve and beautify Salt Lake City.

NEWLANDS, FRANCIS GRIFFITH (*b. Natchez, Miss., 1848; d. 1917*), lawyer. Raised in Quincy, Ill.; after admission to the bar, removed to San Francisco, Calif., 1870, where he prospered in practice and in general business. Removing to Nevada, 1888, he became an advocate of free silver and served as congressman, Silver party and Republican, 1893–97; Democrat, 1897–1903. He was U.S. senator, Democrat, 1903–17. Newlands was among the ablest critics of Republican financial policy and was persistent in demanding that major problems of finance and reform should be solved by scientific services and administrative boards with delegated authority from Congress. He was a valuable member of the Senate committee on interstate commerce and an expert on problems of transportation and domestic trade.

NEWMAN, ALBERT HENRY (*b. Edgefield, S.C., 1852; d. Austin, Texas, 1933*), Baptist church historian, educator. [*Supp. 1*]

NEWMAN, HENRY (*b. Rehoboth, Mass., 1670; d. England, 1743*), philanthropist. Graduated Harvard, 1687; removed to London, England, c. 1703, where he was associated with Thomas Bray in a number of charitable activities. He served as secretary of the Society for Promoting Christian Knowledge, 1708–43, was a benefactor of both Harvard and Yale, and acted from time to time as colonial agent for New Hampshire.

NEWMAN, HENRY RODERICK (*b. Easton, N.Y., c. 1843; d. Florence, Italy, 1918*), painter of architectural subjects and flower pieces. Resident in Europe *post* 1869, Newman became a friend and protégé of John Ruskin whom he aided in the illustration of the *Stones of Venice*.

NEWMAN, JOHN PHILIP (*b. New York, N.Y., 1826; d. Saratoga, N.Y., 1899*), Methodist clergyman. Notable as a preacher, Newman became a close friend of Ulysses S. Grant while pastor in Washington, D.C., 1869–72, and was extensively patronized by the president. He was elected bishop, 1888, with the active help of the Grant family, but was undistinguished as an administrator.

NEWMAN, ROBERT LOFTIN (*b. Richmond, Va., 1827; d. 1912*), figure painter. Profoundly influenced by the Barbizon school, Newman was highly esteemed by fellow-painters, but never attained popular success in his time. He was particularly noted for his delicate sense of color and the poetic feeling and suggestion of his work.

NEWMAN, SAMUEL PHILLIPS (*b. Andover, Mass., 1797; d. Andover, 1842*), Congregational clergyman, educator. Graduated Harvard, 1816. Taught a number of subjects at Bowdoin, 1818–39, serving also as acting president, 1830–33. He was author of widely used textbooks in rhetoric and political economy.

NEWMAN, WILLIAM H. (*b. Prince William Co., Va., 1847; d. New York, N.Y., 1918*), railroad official, traffic expert. President, New York Central, 1901–09.
[*Supp. 1*]

NEWMAN, WILLIAM TRUSLOW (*b. near Knoxville, Tenn., 1843; d. 1920*), Confederate soldier, lawyer. City attorney of Atlanta, Ga., 1871–83; U.S. judge of the northern district of Georgia, 1888–1920. Father of Frances Newman (1883–1928), who won distinction as a writer and expressed the radical sentiment of a changing South in such works as *The Hard Boiled Virgin* (1926).

NEWPORT, CHRISTOPHER (*d. Bantam, East Indies, 1617*), mariner. Served on Drake's Cadiz expedition, 1587; commanded successful privateering expedition, West Indies, 1592. Entering service of the Virginia Company, 1606, he was given charge of its early voyages. His position between the colonists and the company was not easy. Commanding first voyage of *Susan Constant*, *Godspeed*, and *Discovery*, he with others selected the site of Jamestown, May 13, 1607, and explored the James to the fall-line. Thereafter, he made several round-trip voyages, bringing out (1609) Sir Thomas Gates and Sir George Somers and surviving a Bermuda shipwreck. In 1611, he brought out Sir Thomas Dale and a new group of colonists. His last voyages (1613–17) were in service of the East India Company.

NEWSAM, ALBERT (*b. Steubenville, O., 1809; d. near Wilmington, Del., 1864*), lithographer, a leader in that art, 1831–57.

NEWTON, HENRY JOTHAM (*b. Hartleton, Pa., 1823; d. New York, N.Y., 1895*), piano manufacturer, pioneer in dry-plate photography, spiritualist.

NEWTON, HUBERT ANSON (*b. Sherburne, N.Y., 1830; d. New Haven, Conn., 1896*), mathematician. Graduated Yale, 1850; taught mathematics at Yale, 1853–96, and was an extensive contributor to scientific journals. Advocated use of metric system of weights and measures.

NEWTON, ISAAC (*b. Schodack, N.Y., 1794; d. New York, N.Y., 1858*), steamboat designer, associate of Daniel Drew in the People's Line. Introduced passenger-boat innovations such as the burning of anthracite coal and the double-decked grand saloon surrounded by galleries leading to state rooms.

NEWTON, ISAAC (*b. Burlington Co., N.J., 1800; d. 1867*), farmer. Long prominent as an advocate of a federal department of agriculture, Newton was appointed superintendent of the agricultural division of the Patent Office, 1861. When the division was established as a department by Act of May 15, 1862, Newton was appointed commissioner and with the aid of skilled technical assistance set up the new Department of Agriculture on solid foundations.

NEWTON, JOHN (*b. Norfolk, Va., 1823; d. New York, N.Y., 1895*), Union major-general, engineer. Son of Thomas Newton (1768–1847). Graduated West Point, 1842. Commissioned in the engineers, he was engaged mainly in fortification and river and harbor work until the Civil War. He served in the war with exceptional brilliance, particularly at Fredericksburg, Chancellorsville, Gettysburg and in the Atlanta campaign. The most notable of his achievements in later life was the removal of obstructions in the East River, New York City, 1876 and 1885.

NEWTON, RICHARD (*b. Liverpool, England, 1812; d. Philadelphia, Pa., 1887*), Episcopal clergyman. Came to America as a boy. Graduated University of Pennsylvania, 1836; attended General Theological Seminary, N.Y.; was ordained 1840. A leading evangelical, he held several Philadelphia pastorates and was famous for his success as a preacher to children.

NEWTON, RICHARD HEBER (*b. Philadelphia, Pa., 1840; d. East Hampton, N.Y., 1914*), Episcopal clergyman. Son of Richard Newton; brother of William W. Newton. Advocate of modern critical study of the Bible as minister of several churches in Philadelphia and New York; resident preacher at Leland Stanford University, Calif., *post* 1902.

NEWTON, ROBERT SAFFORD (*b. near Gallipolis, O., 1818; d. New York, N.Y., 1881*), eclectic physician, editor. Specialist in pathology and treatment of cancer.

NEWTON, THOMAS (*b. England, 1660; d. 1721*), New England colonial official, lawyer. Came to Boston, Mass., *ante* 1688; held a number of judicial and other appointments under the Crown, rising to attorney-general of Massachusetts, 1720. Noted in his own time as a learned advocate, Newton behaved most unjudiciously as prosecutor in the trial of Jacob Leisler, 1691, and in the Salem witchcraft trials, 1692. His conduct of the trials has been called "morally criminal."

NEWTON, THOMAS (*b. Virginia, 1768; d. Norfolk, Va., 1847*), lawyer, Virginia legislator. Congressman, (Democrat) Republican, from Virginia, 1801–30, 1831–33. Active in support of the interests of the seacoast commercial classes, Newton vigorously supported the War of 1812 and all legislation which assisted American commerce.

NEWTON, WILLIAM WILBERFORCE (*b. Philadelphia, Pa., 1843; d. 1914*), Episcopal clergyman. Son of Richard Newton; brother of Richard H. Newton. Held a number of pastorates in New England; was markedly successful in preaching to children.

NEY, ELISABET (*b. Münster, Germany, 1833; d. 1907*), sculptor. Wife of Edmund D. Montgomery. Came to America, 1871, with a European reputation for eccentricity as well as artistic achievement; settled in Texas, 1873. Among the works of her American period were statues and busts of many Texan notables.

NG POON CHEW (*b. South China, 1866; d. San Francisco, Calif., 1931*), Chinese editor, lecturer. Came to California, 1881. After service as a Presbyterian missionary, 1892–99, he founded at San Francisco and edited the newspaper *Chinese Western Daily*. He lectured extensively to Americans on Chinese culture and to the Chinese on the material gifts of western civilization and was Chinese vice-consul in San Francisco, 1913–31.

NIBLACK, ALBERT PARKER (*b. Vincennes, Ind., 1859; d. Nice, France, 1929*), naval officer. Graduated Annapolis, 1880. After varied sea and shore service, he commanded the first squadron of battleships of the Atlantic Fleet, 1917, and *post* November of that year, ably directed the patrol force of the Atlantic Fleet based on Gibraltar. He retired as rear-admiral, 1923.

NIBLACK, WILLIAM ELLIS (*b. Dubois Co., Ind., 1822; d. Indianapolis, Ind., 1893*), lawyer, jurist, Indiana legislator. Congressman, Democrat, from Indiana, 1857–61, 1865–75; judge, state supreme court, 1877–89. Favored the Union but opposed radical Reconstruction and encroachments on state rights.

NIBLO, WILLIAM (*b. Ireland, 1789; d. 1878*), New York hotel and theatre manager. Came to America as a youth, and *post* 1823 conducted hotels and concert gardens in New York City. By 1837, Niblo's Garden was a fashionable entertainment spot and offered musical, dramatic and variety shows with great success until Niblo's retirement, 1861.

NICHOLAS, GEORGE (*b. Williamsburg, Va., 1754?; d. 1799*), Revolutionary soldier, Virginia legislator, Kentucky pioneer. Brother of John, Philip N., and Wilson C. Nicholas; son of Robert C. Nicholas. A leading supporter of Thomas Jefferson in the Virginia Assembly, Nicholas removed to Kentucky, 1790, where he served as that state's first attorney-general; he was a member of the convention which drafted the first Kentucky constitution, 1792, and led in the framing and advocating of the Kentucky Resolutions, 1798. His association in land speculations with James Wilkinson and Harry Innes led him to involvement in the last phase of the Spanish Conspiracy, 1797.

NICHOLAS, JOHN (*b. Williamsburg, Va., 1756?; d. Geneva, N.Y., 1819*), lawyer. Brother of George, Philip N., and Wilson C. Nicholas; son of Robert C. Nicholas. As congressman, (Democrat) Republican, from Virginia, 1793–1801, he was an effective debater in support of his party's policies. Removing to Geneva, N.Y., 1803, he engaged in agriculture and served as a county judge.

NICHOLAS, PHILIP NORBORNE (*b. Williamsburg, Va., 1775?; d. 1849*), Virginia jurist and politician. Brother of George, John and Wilson C. Nicholas; son of Robert C. Nicholas. Engaged *post* 1804 in banking in Richmond, Va.; judge, general court of Virginia, 1823–49; played powerful, though quiet, part in the triumph of Jacksonian ideas.

NICHOLAS, ROBERT CARTER (*b. probably Williamsburg, Va., 1728; d. Hanover Co., Va., 1780*), colonial official, Revolutionary patriot, lawyer. Active as a conservative in the Virginia Assembly *post* 1756, Nicholas gave reluctant assent to the various measures tending toward revolution. Alone, of all the important men in the Assembly, he opposed adoption of the Declaration of Independence. A man of almost puritanical austerity, he exposed fraud in high places and as treasurer of Virginia, 1766–76, served the colony with scrupulous honesty. Although he opposed most of the plans of the revolutionary party, he was trusted by the patriots to aid in carrying out the very policies against which he had argued. He was father of George, John, Philip N., and Wilson C. Nicholas.

NICHOLAS, WILSON CARY (*b. Williamsburg, Va., 1761; d. Albemarle Co., Va., 1820*), Revolutionary soldier, Virginia politician. Brother of George, John, and Philip N. Nicholas; son of Robert C. Nicholas. Influential Jeffersonian member of Virginia Assembly, 1784–89, 1794–99; U.S. senator, 1799–1804; congressman, 1807–09. As governor of Virginia, 1814–16, he worked on problems of internal improvement and education and collaborated with Jefferson in foundation of the University of Virginia. A heavy speculator, with his brother George, in Western lands, he involved Jefferson in his own financial collapse, 1819.

NICHOLLS, FRANCIS REDDING TILLOU (*b. Donaldsonville, La., 1834; d. near Thibodeaux, La.,*

1912), Confederate brigadier-general, lawyer. Nephew of Joseph R. Drake. Graduated West Point, 1855. After outstanding service under Stonewall Jackson in 1862, he was incapacitated for field duties by a severe wound at Chancellorsville. Resuming his law practice in Louisiana *post* 1865, he was elected governor of the state on the Democratic ticket, 1876, defeated a Republican challenge of his election, and cleansed the state of Carpetbag rule before his retirement in 1880. Re-elected governor for the term 1888–92, he destroyed the Louisiana Lottery. As chief justice of the supreme court of Louisiana, 1892–1904, and as associate justice, 1904–11, he molded Louisiana constitutional law in a series of lucid and elaborate opinions and reports.

NICHOLLS, RHODA HOLMES (*b. Coventry, England, 1854; d. Stamford, Conn., 1930*), artist, educator. Resided in the United States *post* 1884. Excelled as a water-colorist.

NICHOLS, CHARLES HENRY (*b. Vassalboro, Maine, 1820; d. New York, N.Y., 1889*), physician, psychiatrist. M.D., University of Pennsylvania, 1843. Planned, built, and was first superintendent of present St. Elizabeth Hospital, Washington, D.C., serving, 1852–77; designed and superintended *post* 1877 the Bloomingdale Asylum, New York, N.Y.

NICHOLS, CHARLES LEMUEL (*b. Worcester, Mass., 1851; d. 1929*), physician, bibliophile. Author of a number of scholarly monographs on American historical subjects and early printing.

NICHOLS, CLARINA IRENE HOWARD (*b. Townshend, Vt., 1810; d. Potter Valley, Calif., 1885*), woman's rights reformer, editor, Kansas pioneer.

NICHOLS, EDWARD LEAMINGTON (*b. Leamington, England, 1854; d. West Palm Beach, Fla., 1937*), physicist. Graduated Cornell, 1875; Ph.D., Göttingen, 1879. After serving as a fellow at Johns Hopkins and as an assistant to Thomas A. Edison, Nichols taught at several Midwestern colleges. Returning to Cornell, 1887, as head of the department of physics, he remained there until his retirement, 1919. His principal research was done in the fields of color, physiological optics and luminescence. [*Supp.* 2]

NICHOLS, ERNEST FOX (*b. Leavenworth, Kans., 1869; d. 1924*), physicist, educator. Graduated Kansas State College, 1888; made graduate studies at Kansas, Cornell, and in Germany. Taught physics at Colgate University, 1892–98; at Dartmouth, 1898–1903; at Columbia, 1903–09; and at Yale, 1917–20. He served as president of Dartmouth, 1909–16, and as president, Massachusetts Institute of Technology, for a very brief period in 1920; he engaged in laboratory research thereafter. With the aid of the Nichols's radiometer which he devised, he made a number of brilliant investigations of the unexplored region between the visible spectrum and the electro-magnetic waves of Heinrich Hertz, a task which he successfully completed only on the day of his death. As a teacher, Nichols had the rare gift of inspiring students with a love of productive scholarship.

NICHOLS, GEORGE WARD (*b. Tremont, Maine, 1831; d. 1885*), journalist, Union soldier, promoter of art education and music in Cincinnati, O.

NICHOLS, JAMES ROBINSON (*b. West Amesbury, now Merrimac, Mass., 1819; d. Haverhill, Mass., 1888*), manufacturing chemist, chemical journalist, inventor.

NICHOLS, MARY SARGEANT NEAL GOVE (*b. Goffstown, N.H., 1810; d. London, England, 1884*), water-cure physician, reformer. Married Thomas L. Nichols, 1848; advocated miscellaneous reforms including mesmerism, spiritualism, Fourierism, temperance and dress reform.

NICHOLS, THOMAS LOW (*b. Orford, N.H., 1815; d. Chaumont-en-Vezin, France, 1901*), journalist, hydrotherapist, pioneer dietician. With his wife, Mary S.N.G. Nichols (married, 1848), he wrote and published several books on health and other reforms and propagandized for a number of esoteric doctrines in *Nichols' Journal* and *Nichols' Monthly* (1853–57). Removing with his wife to England at the outbreak of the Civil War of which they disapproved, he concentrated for the rest of his active life on food reform.

NICHOLS, WILLIAM FORD (*b. Lloyd, N.Y., 1849; d. 1924*), Episcopal clergyman. Consecrated assistant bishop of California, 1890, he succeeded as bishop in 1893 and presided with notable success over the diocese until 1919, when he surrendered the heavier work to a coadjutor. He was first president of the Province of the Pacific, 1915–21.

NICHOLSON, ALFRED OSBORNE POPE (*b. Williamson Co., Tenn., 1808; d. Columbia, Tenn., 1876*), lawyer, jurist. Prominent in Tennessee railroad development and banking, he served with ability as a Democrat in both houses of the state legislature and was appointed to the U.S. Senate, 1840–42. He supported James K. Polk in 1844 and edited the *Nashville Union* in Polk's behalf. In 1848, he was the recipient of the famous "Nicholson Letter," in which Lewis Cass sought to explain his views on the Wilmot Proviso. At the Nashville Convention, he advocated acceptance of the compromise measures of 1850. Again in the U.S. Senate, 1859–61, he was expelled for support of the Confederacy; after disfranchisement by the Radicals, he was influential in the Tennessee constitutional convention (1870) that overthrew the Radical regime. He served as chief justice, Tennessee supreme court, 1870–76.

NICHOLSON, ELIZA JANE POITEVENT HOLBROOK (*b. near Pearlington, Miss., 1849; d. New*

Orleans, La., 1896), poet, journalist. Co-proprietor, New Orleans *Picayune*, 1876–96; author of *Lyrics by Pearl Rivers* (1873).

NICHOLSON, FRANCIS (*b. near Richmond in Yorkshire, England, 1655; d. England, 1728*), colonial official. Came first to America as captain of infantry under Sir Edmund Andros, 1686; in 1688 he was commissioned lieutenant-governor of the Dominion of New England. Ineffective in his handling of the Leisler rebellion at New York, he returned to England but was immediately appointed lieutenant-governor of Virginia where, until 1692, he conducted what was probably his most successful administration. Taking the broadest possible view of colonial affairs, he traveled in the interior to study frontier conditions, encouraged the establishment of postal services and supported the foundation of the college of William and Mary. As governor of Maryland, 1694–98, he encouraged education and the Established Church and was largely responsible for removal of the capital to Annapolis. His second term as governor of Virginia, 1698–1705, was less successful than his first; he was, however, the leading spirit in the removal of the capital to Williamsburg and the improvement of finances and local administration. After four years of obscurity in England, he effected as brigadier-general commanding British and colonial troops a bloodless conquest of Port Royal, Canada, October 1710, establishing British military supremacy in Acadia. In his last colonial governorship (South Carolina, 1720–25), he won the confidence of the colonists, but gained the hostility of the Charleston merchants who petitioned for his recall. Nicholson's usefulness was seriously impaired by his high temper which made it difficult for others to work with him, yet his zeal and breadth of vision entitle him to high rank among colonial governors.

NICHOLSON, JAMES (*b. Chestertown, Md., c. 1736; d. New York, N.Y., 1804*), Revolutionary naval officer. Brother of Samuel Nicholson; father-in-law of Albert Gallatin. Senior captain, Continental Navy, 1778–83; commanded frigates *Virginia, Trumbull,* and *Bourbon*.

NICHOLSON, JAMES BARTRAM (*b. St. Louis, Mo., 1820; d. Philadelphia, Pa., 1901*), bookbinder. Partner, 1848–90, in the Philadelphia firm of Pawson & Nicholson. Author of *Manual of the Art of Bookbinding* (1856).

NICHOLSON, JAMES WILLIAM AUGUSTUS (*b. Dedham, Mass., 1821; d. New York, N.Y., 1887*), naval officer. Grandson of Samuel Nicholson. Appointed midshipman, 1838; as lieutenant served under Matthew C. Perry in Japanese waters; helped in suppression of slave trade, 1857–60. During Civil War, Nicholson saw varied service with the Atlantic and Gulf blockade, commanding U.S.S. *Manhattan* at Mobile Bay. He later commanded the European station and retired as rear-admiral, 1883.

NICHOLSON, JOHN (*b. Wales, date unknown; d. Philadelphia, Pa., 1800*), financier, land-company promoter. Came to America at some time prior to the Revolution; was appointed comptroller-general of Pennsylvania, 1782, and by use of extensive powers, brought order into the state's financial affairs. Resigning from this and other state offices, 1794, Nicholson became partner of Robert Morris in a number of land companies and did much to encourage settlement in western Pennsylvania, Georgia and the new capital at Washington, D.C. (Federal City). Over-extended like Morris, he was caught by the financial stringency of 1795–96 and was confined in debtors' prison, 1800.

NICHOLSON, JOSEPH HOPPER (*b. probably Chestertown, Md., 1770; d. Maryland, 1817*), lawyer, Maryland legislator. Nephew of James and Samuel Nicholson; son-in-law of Edward Lloyd (1744–1796). As congressman, (Democrat) Republican, from Maryland, 1799–1806, he shared leadership in the House with Nathaniel Macon and John Randolph of Roanoke; he was a sponsor of many important measures and was one of the most formidable "Old Republicans" in public life. Serving as a judge of the Maryland court of appeals, 1806–17 (also chief judge, sixth judicial district), he displayed high ability. During the War of 1812, he raised at his own expense and commanded a company of artillery.

NICHOLSON, SAMUEL (*b. Maryland, 1743; d. Charlestown, Mass., 1811*), naval officer. Brother of James Nicholson. Commissioned captain in Continental Navy, 1776, he commanded the *Dolphin* and the frigate *Deane* on a number of successful cruises, 1777–83. Recommissioned captain, June 1794, Nicholson superintended construction of the frigate *Constitution* and commanded her at sea, 1798–99. *Post* 1801, he served as superintendent of the navy yard at Charlestown.

NICHOLSON, SAMUEL DANFORD (*b. Springfield, P.E.I., Canada, 1859; d. 1923*), mining operator. Settled in Colorado, 1881, where he rose from mine laborer to president and manager of several mines. A successful prospector and an investor in business enterprises at Leadville and Denver, he was Populist mayor of Leadville, 1893–97. Returning to the Republican party, he was U.S. senator from Colorado, 1921–23.

NICHOLSON, TIMOTHY (*b. near Belvidere, N.C., 1828; d. 1924*), educator, bookseller, Quaker leader in Indiana *post* 1861. Outstanding in prison reform work.

NICHOLSON, WILLIAM JONES (*b. Washington, D.C., 1856; d. Washington, 1931*), soldier. Appointed second lieutenant, 7th cavalry, 1876, Nicholson served with that regiment against the Indians on the frontier and was an ordnance officer during the war with

Spain. Promoted colonel, 1912, he commanded the 11th cavalry during the expedition after Villa into Mexico; he commanded the 157th Brigade of the 79th Division in France during World War I, winning distinction for the capture of Montfaucon.

NICHOLSON, WILLIAM THOMAS (*b. Pawtucket, R.I., 1834; d. Providence, R.I., 1893*), first manufacturer of machine-made files. Founded Nicholson File Co. in Providence, R.I., 1864.

NICOLA, LEWIS (*b. France or Ireland, 1717; d. Alexandria, Va., 1807*), merchant, editor, Revolutionary soldier, public official. Emigrated from Dublin, Ireland, to Philadelphia, Pa., c. 1766. Entered business; edited *The American Magazine* (January–September 1769); helped form the American Philosophical Society. Author of three military manuals for American use (1776–77), Nicola was active as a recruiting officer and as commander of the Philadelphia home guard. He is noted for his proposal to George Washington in May 1782 that the government be changed to a monarchy with Washington as king.

NICOLAY, JOHN GEORGE (*b. Essingen, Bavaria, 1832; d. Washington, D.C., 1901*), journalist. Came to America as a child; was raised in Ohio, Indiana, Missouri and Illinois; became editor-proprietor of the Pittsfield, Ill., *Free Press*, 1854. A friend of John Hay, Nicolay became Abraham Lincoln's private secretary (with Hay as assistant), 1860. Few men enjoyed Lincoln's confidence so fully as Nicolay. He served as U.S. consul at Paris, 1865–69, and as marshal of the U.S. Supreme Court, 1872–87, but he is principally famous for his collaboration with John Hay on *Abraham Lincoln: A History* (1890), a work of enduring importance.

NICOLET, JEAN (*b. Cherbourg, France, 1598; d. on St. Lawrence River, 1642*), French explorer. Came to New France with Samuel de Champlain; lived on Allumette Island on Ottawa River, 1618–20. Sent to live among the Nipissing, he was appointed their official interpreter, 1624; in 1633 he returned to Canada and became official interpreter for the colony with headquarters at Three Rivers. During a journey to the West, 1634, Nicolet was the first known white visitor to Lake Michigan and Wisconsin, but the extent of his explorations is still a matter of controversy.

NICOLL, DE LANCEY (*b. Shelter Island, N.Y., 1854; d. 1931*), lawyer. Graduated Princeton, 1874; Columbia Law School, 1876. Appointed assistant district attorney of New York County, 1885, he won immediate recognition as an outstanding prosecutor; he was elected district attorney on the Democratic ticket, 1890, served with success, but refused renomination. Thereafter, in private practice, he was counsel in a number of difficult cases, defending the New York *World* in the so-called Panama Libel case, and the American Tobacco Co. in anti-trust proceed-

ings. A supporter of genuine reforms, he despised demagogues and professional altruists.

NICOLL, JAMES CRAIG (*b. New York, N.Y., 1847; d. Norwalk, Conn., 1918*), marine painter, etcher.

NICOLLET, JOSEPH NICOLAS (*b. Cluses, Savoy, 1786; d. Washington, D.C., 1843*), explorer, mathematician. Emigrated to New Orleans, La., from France, 1832; removing soon to St. Louis, Mo., he was encouraged in his plans for exploration by the Chouteau family. He made a survey to the sources of the Mississippi River, 1836, and two surveys of the upper Missouri, 1838 and 1839. A report of his activities was published, 1843.

NICOLLS, MATTHIAS (*b. Plymouth, England, 1626; d. New York, 1687 or 1688*), lawyer. Came to America, 1664, as secretary to a royal commission sent to investigate conditions in New England. After the ousting of the Dutch from New York, August 1664, he was named secretary of that province and held the post until 1680 except for the time of Dutch reoccupation, 1673–74. He also held a number of other offices, and was chosen speaker, first N.Y. provincial assembly, 1683. He is best known as the reputed principal author of the "Duke's Laws," promulgated 1665.

NICOLLS, RICHARD (*b. Bedfordshire, England, 1624; d. in battle of Solebay, off coast of Suffolk, England, 1672*), colonial official. As first English governor of New York, 1664–68, Nicolls secured the bloodless surrender of New Amsterdam in August–September 1664 and supervised the transition to English rule with great ability and tact. In March 1665, he issued the celebrated "Duke's Laws," prepared to an indeterminate degree by the provincial secretary, Matthias Nicolls (to whom the governor was not related).

NICOLLS, WILLIAM (*b. England, 1657; d. 1723*), colonial lawyer and politician. Son of Matthias Nicolls by whom he was brought to New York as a child. A conservative, he became attorney-general of the province, 1687. He was active in the opposition to Jacob Leisler, 1689–91, becoming thereafter a councillor and a large landholder in Suffolk Co., N.Y. Suspended from the Council in 1698 by the governor, the Earl of Bellomont, Nicolls returned to power as a member of the New York Assembly, 1701–23, and was its speaker, 1702–18.

NIEDRINGHAUS, FREDERICK GOTTLIEB (*b. Lübbecke, Westphalia, 1837; d. St. Louis, Mo., 1922*), tin-plate manufacturer, protective tariff advocate.

NIEHAUS, CHARLES HENRY (*b. Cincinnati, O., 1855; d. 1935*), sculptor. Studied in Cincinnati and at the Royal Academy, Munich. Executed many public commissions, all well designed and firmly modeled; among them, his memorial doors at Trinity Church, New York City, are especially noteworthy.

[*Supp.* 1]

NIEMAN, LUCIUS WILLIAM (*b. Bear Creek, Wis., 1857; d. Milwaukee, Wis., 1935*), newspaper editor, publisher. Served successively as printer, reporter, legislative correspondent, city editor and managing editor on the *Milwaukee Sentinel*, 1871–80. After a brief period as managing editor of the *St. Paul Dispatch*, he purchased a half interest in the Milwaukee *Daily Journal*, 1882. Independent and consistent in his journalistic battles for reforms, Nieman combined business ability with essential editorial qualities as editor and publisher of the paper and raised it to a high place in the American press. The Nieman Fellowships at Harvard were founded by his widow in his memory. [*Supp.* 1]

NIEMEYER, JOHN HENRY (*b. Bremen, Germany, 1839; d. New Haven, Conn., 1932*), artist, teacher of drawing. Came to America as a child; was raised in Cincinnati, O. Studied art in Paris, 1866–70, where he was a teacher of Aug. Saint-Gaudens. As professor of drawing, Yale Art School, 1871–1908, he came to be regarded as a great teacher and also won renown for the precision of line and perfection of modeling of his own paintings.

NIES, JAMES BUCHANAN (*b. Newark, N.J., 1856; d. Jerusalem, 1922*), Episcopal clergyman, archaeologist. Benefactor of the American School for Oriental Study at Jerusalem.

NIES, KONRAD (*b. Alzey, Rhenish Hesse, Germany, 1861; d. San Francisco, Calif., 1921*), journalist, German-language poet, educator.

NIEUWLAND, JULIUS ARTHUR (*b. Hansbeke, Belgium, 1878; d. Washington, D.C., 1936*), Roman Catholic clergyman, chemist, botanist. Came to America as a child; graduated Notre Dame, 1899. Entering the Congregation of the Holy Cross, he was ordained, 1903. Teacher of botany and chemistry at Notre Dame *post* 1904, Nieuwland engaged in extensive research in both his fields. Lewisite and neoprene (synthetic rubber) were produced on the basis of his discoveries. [*Supp.* 2]

NILES, HEZEKIAH (*b. Jefferis' Ford, Pa., 1777; d. Wilmington, Del., 1839*), printer, editor. Founded, edited and published the *Weekly Register* (later, *Niles' Weekly Register*), 1811–36. This paper was the strongest and most consistent advocate of union, internal improvements, and protection to industry in the United States; its editor was probably as influential as any in the nationalist economic school which sponsored the American System *post* 1815. Originally a Jeffersonian Democrat, he differed with Andrew Jackson's policies and was a Whig *post* 1829. He favored the gradual abolition of slavery.

NILES, JOHN MILTON (*b. Windsor, Conn., 1787; d. Hartford, Conn., 1856*), lawyer, editor. Leader of the Jacksonian party in Connecticut; an independent and uncompromising Democrat. U.S. senator, 1835–39, 1843–49; U.S. postmaster-general, 1840–41.

NILES, NATHANIEL (*b. South Kingston, R.I., 1741; d. Vermont, 1828*), preacher, Connecticut and Vermont legislator, (Democrat) Republican leader in Vermont. Congressman, from Vermont, 1791–95. As trustee of Dartmouth, 1793–1820, Niles was a vigorous opponent of Pres. John Wheelock.

NILES, NATHANIEL (*b. Fairlee, Vt., 1791; d. New York, N.Y., 1869*), physician, diplomat. Son of Nathaniel Niles (1741–1828). Secretary of U.S. legation at Paris, 1830–33; special agent to Austria-Hungary, 1837–38, for negotiation on lowering tariffs against American commerce; negotiator of treaty of commerce with Sardinia, 1838. U.S. chargé d'affaires in Sardinia, 1848–50.

NILES, SAMUEL (*b. Block Island, R.I., 1674; d. Braintree, Mass., 1762*), Congregational clergyman, controversialist, historian. Minister of the Second Church at Braintree, 1711–62. Author, among other writings, of "A Summary Historic Narrative of the Wars in New England with the French and Indians," published in the *Collections of the Massachusetts Historical Society* (1837 and 1861).

NIPHER, FRANCIS EUGENE (*b. Port Byron, N.Y., 1847; d. Kirkwood, Mo., 1926*), physicist. Graduated State University of Iowa, 1870; M.A., 1873. Taught physics at Washington University, St. Louis, Mo., 1874–1914. Contributed a number of important papers to the *Transactions* of the Academy of Science of St. Louis *post* 1882, which included investigations into magnetic measurements, the measurement of wind pressure on stationary and moving structures, the properties of photographic plates, and the nature of the electric discharge.

NISBET, CHARLES (*b. Haddington, Scotland, 1736; d. Carlisle, Pa., 1804*), Presbyterian clergyman, educator. Came to America, 1785, at invitation of Benjamin Rush and John Dickinson to serve as first president of Dickinson College. An animated and able teacher, Nisbet held the post until his death.

NISBET, EUGENIUS ARISTIDES (*b. Greene Co., Ga., 1803; d. Macon, Ga., 1871*), lawyer, Georgia legislator. Congressman, Whig, 1839–43; judge, supreme court of Georgia, 1845–53. Resuming his law practice in Macon, he became a leader of the Know-Nothing party and in 1861, drafted the Georgia ordinance of secession.

NITCHIE, EDWARD BARTLETT (*b. Brooklyn, N.Y., 1876; d. 1917*), teacher of the deaf. Author of *Self-Instructor in Lip-Reading* (1902), *Lessons in Lip Reading* (1905) and *Lip-Reading Principles and Practice* (1912).

NITSCHMANN, DAVID (*b. Zauchtenthal, Moravia, 1696; d. Bethlehem, Pa., 1772*), bishop of the Moravian Church. Consecrated bishop in 1735, Nitschmann visited Savannah, Ga., 1736, and also Pennsylvania. Returning to America in 1740, he founded the settlement at Bethlehem, Pa., and remained in charge of the American work until 1744. Thereafter, he traveled constantly to Europe and back seeking financial help, retiring at the age of 65 to live in Bethlehem.

NIXON, JOHN (b. Framingham, Mass., 1727; d. Middlebury, Vt., 1815), colonial and Revolutionary soldier. Served in the expedition against Louisbourg, 1745, and in the French and Indian War. After fighting at Lexington and Concord, April 1775, he was wounded at Bunker Hill; he participated in the siege of Boston. Commissioned colonel, 4th Continental Infantry, January 1776, he was elected brigadier-general on Washington's recommendation in August of the same year. He commanded a brigade in the operations around New York, 1776, and at the defeat of Burgoyne, 1777. He resigned for reasons of health, 1780.

NIXON, JOHN (b. Philadelphia, Pa., 1733; d. Philadelphia, 1808), Revolutionary patriot, merchant, financier. Held a number of Pennsylvania civil and militia offices; was president of the Bank of North America, 1792–1808.

NIXON, JOHN THOMPSON (b. Fairton, N.J., 1820; d. Stockbridge, Mass., 1889), New Jersey jurist, legislator and legal compiler. U.S. district judge in New Jersey, 1870–89.

NIXON, WILLIAM PENN (b. Fountain City, Ind., 1833; d. 1912), journalist. Managed, and for most of the period, edited the Chicago Inter Ocean, 1872–97; made his paper an unfaltering advocate of orthodox Republican policy.

NIZA, MARCOS de (b. Nice, Duchy of Savoy, date unknown; d. Mexico City, 1558), Franciscan missionary, author, explorer. Went to Santo Domingo, 1531, and from there to Peru; he is credited with having founded the Franciscan province of Lima. Appointed vice-commissary-general of his order in New Spain, 1539, he was sent to New Mexico in that year to investigate reports brought by Nuñez Cabeza de Vaca concerning fabulous cities in present New Mexico and Arizona. His incorrect and enthusiastic account was the occasion of Coronado's expedition, 1540, on which Niza served as guide as far as Zuñi.

NOAH, MORDECAI MANUEL (b. Philadelphia, Pa., 1785; d. 1851), lawyer, playwright, journalist. U.S. consul to Tunis, 1813–15. Editor, N.Y. National Advocate, 1817–26; later edited N.Y. Enquirer, N.Y. Evening Star and Noah's Times and Weekly Messenger. Attempted in 1825 to establish a colony for oppressed Jews of all nations on Grand Island in Niagara River. Author of a number of plays patriotic in character

and of Travels in England, France, Spain, and the Barbary States (1819).

NOAILLES, LOUIS MARIE, Vicomte de (b. Paris, France, 1756; d. Havana, Cuba, 1804), French soldier. Served in the American Revolution; was at siege of Savannah, Ga., and took a distinguished part in the Yorktown campaign, 1781. Sought refuge from the French Revolution in Philadelphia, Pa., 1793–1800, where he made a moderate fortune in business and promoted the Asylum Company to provide a Pennsylvania refuge for French émigrés.

NOBILI, JOHN (b. Rome, Italy, 1812; d. 1856), Roman Catholic clergyman, Jesuit. Came to America as an associate of Pierre-Jean de Smet in the Rocky Mountain missions where he served, 1843–49. Assigned to San Francisco, Calif., 1849, he founded Santa Clara University (incorporated, 1855).

NOBLE, ALFRED (b. Livonia, Mich., 1844; d. 1914), civil engineer. C.E., University of Michigan, 1870. Long experienced in canal and bridge construction, Noble served on the Nicaragua Canal commission, 1895, on the Isthmian Canal commission, 1899–1903, and on the board of consulting engineers for the Panama Canal.

NOBLE, FREDERICK ALPHONSO (b. Baldwin, Maine, 1832; d. 1917), Presbyterian and Congregational clergyman. Principal pastorate at Union Park Church, Chicago, Ill., 1879–1901.

NOBLE, GLADWYN KINGSLEY (b. Yonkers, N.Y., 1894; d. Englewood, N.J., 1940), biologist, specialist in herpetology. Graduated Harvard, 1917; Ph.D., Columbia, 1922. Instituted and directed an extensive research program in experimental biology and animal behavior at the American Museum of Natural History, New York City. [Supp. 2]

NOBLE, JAMES (b. Clarke Co., Va., 1783; d. Washington, D.C., 1831), lawyer. Settled in Indiana c. 1810; was prominent in organization of the new state. As U.S. senator from Indiana, 1816–31, he supported internal improvements and liberal land laws.

NOBLE, JOHN WILLOCK (b. Lancaster, O., 1831; d. St. Louis, Mo., 1912), lawyer, Union brigadier-general. Fought pension raids with some success as U.S. secretary of the interior, 1889–93; sponsored forest reserve sections in revised land laws of 1891, thus leading to National Park policy of later date.

NOBLE, SAMUEL (b. Cornwall, England, 1834; d. 1888), ironmaster, industrialist. Came to America as a child; removed to Georgia, 1855. Founder and general manager post 1872 of the Woodstock Iron Co., nucleus of that industry at Anniston, Ala. Progressive and intelligent, Noble typified in his success the new spirit of Southern industry operating with Northern capital. He envisioned Anniston as the "model city" of the South and engaged in much philanthropic work there.

NOEGGERATH, EMIL OSCAR JACOB BRUNO (*b. Bonn, Germany, 1827; d. Germany, 1895*), physician. Practiced and taught in New York, N.Y., 1857–85. One of the most talented physicians of his time, Noeggerath combined an acute sense of biological mechanism with an appreciation for the totality of the organism; he made extensive contributions to gynecology and obstetrics, particularly with relation to the infective power of gonorrhea; he also anticipated many of the later discoveries of the classical bacteriologists.

NOGUCHI, HIDEYO (*b. Inawashiro, Japan, 1876; d. Accra, Africa, 1928*), bacteriologist, parasitologist, immunologist. Raised in poverty, he learned medicine as apprentice to a surgeon and at Tokyo Medical College where he graduated in 1897. After hospital experience and field work in plague control, he worked at Kitasato's Institute, Tokyo. His American work was begun at Simon Flexner's laboratory of pathology, University of Pennsylvania, 1899. Assigned to study immunity against snake venoms, he painstakingly investigated problems relating to hemolysins and agglutinins of snake venom and the protective sera. In these and subsequent endeavors he demonstrated clarity of interest, technical skill, and prodigious industry, plus an extraordinary endurance for one physically frail. His brilliant study *The Action of Snake Venom upon Cold-blooded Animals* (1904) established his reputation. Transferring his work to the Rockefeller Institute, 1904, he devised a new, important method for diagnosis of syphilis that led into his most important researches upon methods for obtaining pure cultures of spiral organisms. He not only grew the syphilis spiral organism in pure culture but also obtained in pure culture a variety of pathogenic spiral organisms and many saprophytic spiral forms. He isolated *Treponema pallidum*, making possible the preparation of luetin, and demonstrated its role as the etiological agent in both general paresis and tabes dorsalis. In further experimentation, he applied his findings to cultivation of the globoid bodies in poliomyelitis, and to the study of Rocky Mountain spotted fever, and to enrichment and purification of the virus of vaccinia. During the last ten years of his life, Noguchi directed his investigations to clearing up the etiology of yellow fever, of the Oroya fever of Peru, and of trachoma. The outstanding figure in microbiology since Pasteur and Koch, he succumbed to African yellow fever while studying that disease.

NOLAN, PHILIP (*b. probably Frankfort, Ky., c. 1771; d. near present Waco, Texas, 1801*), contraband horse trader. A close associate of James Wilkinson, and his agent at New Orleans as early as 1790, Nolan traded into Texas *post* 1791; there, he was regarded by the Mexicans as a spy and was killed while resisting arrest. He was said to possess an exceptional knowledge of the Spanish frontier lands.

NOLEN, JOHN (*b. Philadelphia, Pa., 1869; d. Cambridge, Mass., 1937*), landscape architect, town and city planner. [*Supp. 2*]

NOONAN, JAMES PATRICK (*b. St. Louis, Mo., 1878; d. Washington, D.C., 1929*), electric lineman. Able, respected president, International Brotherhood of Electrical Workers, 1919–29; American labor delegate to World Power Conference, London, 1924.

NORBECK, PETER (*b. Clay Co., Dakota Territory, 1870; d. Redfield, S. Dak., 1936*), businessman, South Dakota legislator. Progressive Republican governor of South Dakota, 1917–21; U.S. senator, 1921–36. An active and effective advocate of farm-relief legislation. [*Supp. 2*]

NORCROSS, ORLANDO WHITNEY (*b. Clinton, Maine, 1839; d. Worcester, Mass., 1920*), contractor, Union soldier. Associated with architect H. H. Richardson in many of his works; invented flat-slab construction of reinforced concrete; was a master of all phases of practical construction.

NORDBERG, BRUNO VICTOR (*b. Björneborg, Finland, 1857; d. Milwaukee, Wis., 1924*), mechanical engineer. Came to America, 1879, two years after graduation from University of Helsingfors. Beginning with E. P. Allis Co., Milwaukee, he entered the field of engine design, creating a blowing engine and a poppet valve cut-off governor to improve economy of slide-valve engines. He organized the Bruno Nordberg Co., 1886, which grew into the Nordberg Manufacturing Co., of which he was president and chief engineer. He designed and built governors, Corliss-valve and poppet-valve engines, also special compressors, pumps, blowing engines, mining hoists, condensers and heaters. He held some 70 U.S. patents and developed the Nordberg generative cycle. His greatest achievement was the building of the pneumatic hoisting system for the Anaconda Copper Co. at Butte, Mont.

NORDHEIMER, ISAAC (*b. Memelsdorf, Bavaria, 1809; d. New York, N.Y., 1842*), Orientalist, grammarian. Ph.D., Munich, 1834. Came to America, 1835; taught at Union Theological Seminary, 1838–42, and at New York University. Published original, profound *Critical Grammar of the Hebrew Language* (1838–41).

NORDHOFF, CHARLES (*b. Erwitte, Prussia, 1830; d. San Francisco, Calif., 1901*), journalist. Came to America as a child. After working as a printer, he served in the U.S. Navy, 1844–47, and for several years thereafter in merchant ships. Managing editor, N.Y. *Evening Post*, 1861–71; Washington correspondent, *New York Herald*, 1874–90. Author of a number of books including *The Merchant Vessel* (1855), *Communistic Societies in the United States* (1875) and *The Cotton States, etc.* (1876).

NORDICA, LILLIAN (*b. Farmington, Maine, 1859; d. Batavia, Java, 1914*), prima donna. Stage-name of Lillian Norton. Made debut as soprano soloist in New York City with Patrick Gilmore's band *c.* 1876; after studying in Milan, Italy, made operatic debut in Brescia in *La Traviata,* April 1879; first appeared as prima donna as Marguerite in *Faust,* Paris, July 1882. Famous for the richness of her tone, for a notable coloratura range and consummate artistic ability; Nordica was outstanding in Wagnerian roles.

NORELIUS, ERIC (*b. Hassela, Sweden, 1833; d. Minnesota, 1916*), Swedish Lutheran clergyman. Came to America, 1850. Ordained, 1856, he entered upon a ministry at Vasa and Red Wing, Minn., which with interruptions he maintained until his death.

NORMAN, JOHN (*b. England, c. 1748; d. Boston, Mass., 1817*), engraver, publisher. Came to America *ante* 1774; worked thereafter in Philadelphia, Pa., and Boston, Mass. Published the *Boston Magazine,* 1783–84, and the first *Boston Directory,* 1789. Low contemporary estimates of his engraving skill have been seconded by posterity.

NORRIS, BENJAMIN FRANKLIN (*b. Chicago, Ill., 1870; d. San Francisco, Calif., 1902*), journalist, novelist. Known generally as Frank Norris. After preliminary art studies in California and Paris, France, Norris attended the University of California where, under the influence of Zola, he adopted realism as his literary creed and began the first chapters of a story which was later completed and published as *McTeague* (1899). After an adventurous period in South Africa, 1895–96, he worked as a journalist in San Francisco; in 1898 he was a war correspondent for *McClure's Magazine.* Entering the employ of Doubleday, Page & Co., 1899, he continued literary work, soon becoming recognized as a novelist of unusual vigor and originality. *Moran of the Lady Letty* appeared as a book, 1898, followed in the next year by *Blix* and by *McTeague* which is considered by some critics his strongest work. His most ambitious undertaking was his "Epic of the Wheat," which, according to his plan, was to consist of *The Octopus* (published, 1901), *The Pit* (published, 1903) and *The Wolf,* the third volume of the trilogy, which was never written.

NORRIS, EDWARD (*b. possibly Gloucestershire, England, c. 1584; d. Salem, Mass., 1659*), Congregational clergyman. Came to New England, 1639, and settled in the same year at Salem as assistant to Hugh Peter. An unusually tolerant clergyman, he was teacher of the Salem church from March 1640 until his death.

NORRIS, FRANK. [See NORRIS, BENJAMIN FRANKLIN, 1870–1902.]

NORRIS, GEORGE WASHINGTON (*b. Philadelphia, Pa., 1808; d. 1875*), surgeon, medical author. Professor of clinical surgery, University of Pennsyl-

vania, 1848–57; was also surgeon to the Pennsylvania Hospital, 1836–63.

NORRIS, ISAAC (*b. London, England, 1671; d. Germantown, Pa., 1735*), Quaker merchant, politician. Settled in Philadelphia, Pa., 1693; married a daughter of Thomas Lloyd, 1694. Soon successful in business, Norris held a number of Pennsylvania civic and judicial offices *post* 1699; he was an alderman of Philadelphia, 1708–24, and was elected mayor, 1724. Next to James Logan, Norris was chief representative of proprietary interests in Pennsylvania *post* 1708.

NORRIS, ISAAC (*b. Philadelphia, Pa., 1701; d. near Philadelphia, 1766*), Quaker merchant, party leader. Son of Isaac Norris (1671–1735), he also held a number of provincial offices; a member of the Pennsylvania Assembly, 1734–66, he acted as speaker, 1750–64. Norris was noted for the militant pacifism of his policies, especially during the French and Indian War. The celebrated inscription on the Liberty Bell was made at his suggestion.

NORRIS, JAMES FLACK (*b. Baltimore, Md., 1871; d. Boston, Mass., 1940*), chemist. Graduated Johns Hopkins, 1892; Ph.D., 1895. Taught chemistry at Massachusetts Institute of Technology, at Simmons College and at Vanderbilt University; headed U.S. Army Chemical Warfare Service in England, 1917–19. Professor of organic chemistry and director of the research laboratory at Massachusetts Institute of Technology *post* 1919, Norris was author of several textbooks and was active in scientific societies. [*Supp. 2*]

NORRIS, MARY HARRIOTT (*b. Boonton, N.J., 1848; d. 1919*), author, educator. Graduated Vassar, 1870. First regularly elected dean of women of Northwestern University, 1898.

NORRIS, WILLIAM (*b. Baltimore, Md., 1802; d. 1867*), locomotive builder. Organized American Steam Carriage Co. with Stephen H. Long, 1832, for production of locomotives employing anthracite coal as fuel. After buying out Long's interest, Norris began construction of the "George Washington," a locomotive of his own design, completed, 1836, for the Philadelphia and Columbia Railroad. The success of this engine brought its designer and builder world-wide fame.

NORRIS, WILLIAM FISHER (*b. Philadelphia, Pa., 1839; d. 1901*), ophthalmologist. Son of George W. Norris. Graduated University of Pennsylvania, 1857; M.D., 1861. Made special studies in ophthalmology at Vienna; taught that subject at the University of Pennsylvania *post* 1870. He made many contributions to the literature of his subject, in particular (with an associate) *System of Diseases of the Eye* (1897–1900).

NORSWORTHY, NAOMI (*b. New York, N.Y., 1877; d. 1916*), psychologist, educator. Taught at Teachers College, Columbia, *post* 1901; excelled in classroom demonstration of the teachings of Thorndike and

Dewey. Author of *The Psychology of Mentally Deficient Children* (1906).

NORTH, EDWARD (*b. Berlin, Conn., 1820; d. 1903*), educator, classicist. Professor of ancient languages at Hamilton College, 1843–1901; a skillful interpreter of Greek poetry. Nephew of Simeon North (1802–1884).

NORTH, ELISHA (*b. Goshen, Conn., 1771; d. 1843*), physician. Studied with Lemuel Hopkins and at University of Pennsylvania. Practicing at Goshen, 1795–1812, he removed in the latter year to New London, Conn., where he established the first eye dispensary in the United States. His *Treatise on . . . Spotted Fever* (1811) was the first published study of cerebrospinal meningitis.

NORTH, FRANK JOSHUA (*b. Ludlowville, N.Y., 1840; d. Columbus, Nebr., 1885*), scout, plainsman. Raised in Ohio; removed to Nebraska, 1856. Through association with the Pawnees, North learned their language and also Indian sign language; entering service as an army scout, 1864, under Gen. S. R. Curtis, he continued to lead groups of Pawnee scouts and guides through six campaigns of the Indian wars until 1877. North had no superior as frontiersman and guide in his own time; he was probably the best revolver shot on the plains and was the only leader of Indian scouts thoroughly acquainted with the language and customs of the men he commanded. After the Pawnee scouts were mustered out of service, North and his brother were partners of William F. Cody in a Nebraska ranch; he was later the feature attraction in Cody's famous "Wild West" show.

NORTH, FRANK MASON (*b. New York, N.Y., 1850; d. Madison, N.J., 1935*), Methodist clergyman. Held a number of pastorates in the New York Conference; advocated interdenominational cooperation; pioneered in turning the mind of the Methodist Church from individualism to united social action. [*Supp. 1*]

NORTH, SIMEON (*b. Berlin, Conn., 1765; d. 1852*), mechanic, arms manufacturer. Produced pistols and rifles under government contracts, 1799–1852; made a repeating rifle capable of firing ten charges without reloading, 1825.

NORTH, SIMEON (*b. Berlin, Conn., 1802; d. 1884*), educator. Son of Simeon North (1765–1852). Graduated Yale, 1825. After a brief period as a tutor at Yale, North taught ancient languages at Hamilton College, 1829–39, and was president of the college, 1839–57.

NORTH, SIMON NEWTON DEXTER (*b. Clinton, N.Y., 1848; d. Wilton, Conn., 1924*), editor, statistician. Son of Edward North. Director, U.S. Census, 1903–09; was associated *post* 1911 with Carnegie Endowment for International Peace.

NORTH, WILLIAM (*b. Fort Frederick, Maine, 1755; d. New York, N.Y., 1836*), Revolutionary soldier, New York legislator. Aide-de-camp to Baron von Steuben and his lifetime friend. Federalist speaker of the New York Assembly, 1795–96 and 1810.

NORTHEN, WILLIAM JONATHAN (*b. Jones Co., Ga., 1835; d. Atlanta, Ga., 1913*), teacher, farmer, Georgia legislator, official in farm organizations. Democratic governor of Georgia, 1890–95.

NORTHEND, CHARLES (*b. Newbury, Mass., 1814; d. New Britain, Conn., 1895*), Connecticut school administrator, textbook writer.

NORTHROP, BIRDSEY GRANT (*b. Kent, Conn., 1817; d. 1898*), Congregational clergyman, educator. Agent for state boards of education in Massachusetts and Connecticut, 1857–83; advocate of Arbor Day and of Japanese-American amity.

NORTHROP, CYRUS (*b. near Ridgefield, Conn., 1834; d. Minneapolis, Minn., 1922*), lawyer, educator. Graduated Yale, 1857; Yale Law School, 1859. Professor of English at Yale, 1863–84; an outstanding administrator as second president of University of Minnesota, 1884–1911.

NORTHROP, LUCIUS BELLINGER (*b. Charleston, S.C., 1811; d. Pikesville, Md., 1894*), soldier. Graduated West Point, 1831. Studied medicine at Jefferson Medical College after permanent furlough for wound received in Seminole war, 1839; practiced in Charleston, 1853–61. Appointed Confederate commissary-general, 1861, he was faced with the increasingly difficult task of providing food for the Southern armies and *post* 1862 for Northern prisoners. Generally unpopular and bitterly criticized, Northrop was supported by President Davis. Although Gen. R. E. Lee had little patience with him and finally demanded his removal, he did not lose his office until February 1865. Despite the criticisms, Northrop seems to have been a good if routine executive who was badly hampered by the Confederate transportation system.

NORTON, ALICE PELOUBET. [See NORTON, MARY ALICE PELOUBET, 1860–1928.]

NORTON, ANDREWS (*b. Hingham, Mass., 1786; d. Newport, R.I., 1853*), Unitarian theologian, Biblical scholar. Graduated Harvard, 1804. Appointed tutor at Harvard, 1811; librarian and lecturer on the Bible, 1813. Dexter Professor of Sacred Literature, Harvard Divinity School, 1819–30. A fastidious, independent and solitary thinker, Norton was author, among a number of other books, of *Evidences of the Genuineness of the Gospels* (1837, 1844), one of the earliest studies of Biblical literature from the critical point of view to be published in America.

NORTON, CHARLES ELIOT (*b. Cambridge, Mass., 1827; d. Cambridge, 1908*), editor, author, educator.

Son of Andrews Norton. Graduated Harvard, 1846. After extensive travel abroad and a brief experience in business, Norton devoted his life chiefly to humanist studies. An intimate friend of the principal literary and artistic figures of his day in America and Europe, he conducted at Harvard from 1873 to 1897 at the invitation of his cousin, Charles W. Eliot, a course in the history of fine arts as related to society and general culture. The range of his activities in literature was great. Contributor to the *Atlantic Monthly,* a founder and supporter of *The Nation,* he edited Thomas Carlyle's correspondence and reminiscences (1883–91), the letters of James Russell Lowell (1894), the poetry of John Donne (1895 and 1905) and the poems of Anne Bradstreet (1897). His own book *Historical Studies of Church-Building in the Middle Ages* (1880) had considerable influence on architects. His critical judgments in art (as also his views on politics) were motivated by his belief that a strictly conceived but non-religious *ethos,* derived from contemplation of the highest qualities of human nature, must be operative in both critic and statesman.

NORTON, ELIJAH HISE (*b. near Russellville, Ky., 1821; d. near Platte City, Mo., 1914*), lawyer, Missouri Unionist and jurist. A stubborn opponent of secession, Norton was an outstanding member of the Missouri constitutional convention of 1875 and a leading formulator of the so-called "Norton Constitution" which it produced.

NORTON, JOHN (*b. Bishop's Stortford, England, 1606; d. Boston, Mass., 1663*), Puritan clergyman. M.A., Peterhouse, Cambridge, 1627; declined a benefice because of Puritan convictions. Came to New England, 1635, and became teacher of the church at Ipswich, Mass.; helped draft Cambridge Platform, 1648; succeeded John Cotton as pastor of First Church at Boston, 1652, but was not installed until 1656. Norton took a prominent part in the persecution of Quakers and failed as co-agent with Simon Bradstreet in negotiations with Charles II, 1662. A learned man and prolific writer, Norton had a narrow and pedantic mind.

NORTON, JOHN NICHOLAS (*b. Waterloo, N.Y., 1820; d. 1881*), Episcopal clergyman, author. *Post* 1847, he ministered with great zeal in Frankfort and Louisville, Ky. He was author of a number of popular biographical studies and some fiction.

NORTON, JOHN PITKIN (*b. Albany, N.Y., 1822; d. Farmington, Conn., 1852*), agricultural chemist. Grandson of Timothy Pitkin. Made intensive studies of agriculture and of the natural sciences according to a plan of his own which included three years abroad at Edinburgh and Utrecht. Appointed professor of agricultural chemistry at Yale, 1846, he initiated with the younger Benjamin Silliman the department of scientific education at Yale which was later to become Sheffield Scientific School.

NORTON, MARY ALICE PELOUBET (*b. Gloucester, Mass., 1860; d. 1928*), teacher of home economics. Graduated Smith, 1882; was directed into her profession by Ellen H. Richards. Taught at a number of schools including University of Chicago and Indiana University.

NORTON, WILLIAM EDWARD (*b. Boston, Mass., 1843; d. New York, N.Y., 1916*), marine painter.

NORWOOD, ROBERT WINKWORTH (*b. New Ross, Nova Scotia, 1874; d. 1932*), Episcopal clergyman. After holding a number of pastorates in Canada, he became rector of St. Paul's Church, Overbrook, Pa., 1917, and succeeded to the rectorship of St. Bartholomew's Church, New York City, 1925. A dramatic, poetic preacher, Norwood belonged to the liberal group in his denomination.

NOSS, THEODORE BLAND (*b. Waterloo, Pa., 1852; d. Chicago, Ill., 1909*), educator. Graduated Syracuse, 1880, Ph.D., 1884. A specialist in educational psychology, Noss won a national reputation as a progressive while principal of Southwestern State Normal School, California, Pa., *post* 1883.

NOTT, ABRAHAM (*b. Saybrook, Conn., 1768; d. Fairfield District, S.C., 1830*), lawyer, planter. Settled in South Carolina, 1789; was a Federalist member of Congress, 1799–1801. After serving as a law judge, 1810–24, he became head of the state court of appeals and held this post for the rest of his life.

NOTT, CHARLES COOPER (*b. Schenectady, N.Y., 1827; d. New York, N.Y., 1916*), jurist. Grandson of Eliphalet Nott. Graduated Union, 1848. After admission to the bar, 1850, he removed to New York City where he practiced until the outbreak of the Civil War. Serving with credit as a Union officer, 1861–65, he was appointed in the latter year judge of the U.S. Court of Claims. Until his retirement, 1905, he helped greatly in the establishment of a system of jurisprudence under which claims of citizens against the federal government might be recognized and enforced. He also served as reporter to the Court, 1867–1914.

NOTT, ELIPHALET (*b. Ashford, Conn., 1773; d. Schenectady, N.Y., 1866*), Presbyterian clergyman, educator, inventor. Brother and pupil of Samuel Nott; M.A., Brown, *c.* 1795. While pastor, First Presbyterian Church, Albany, N.Y., 1798–1804, he won repute as one of America's greatest pulpit orators; as president of Union College, Schenectady, N.Y., 1804–66, he successfully gained public support for a building program through lotteries, raised the instructional level, and introduced a scientific course as alternative to the classical curriculum. In public affairs, he opposed slavery, was active in educational associations and in the temperance movement. His research in the properties of heat resulted in some thirty patents, including the first base-burning stove for use of anthracite coal.

NOTT, HENRY JUNIUS (*b. Union District, S.C., 1797; d. at sea, off North Carolina coast, 1837*), educator. Son of Abraham Nott; brother of Josiah C. Nott. Graduated South Carolina College, 1814. Professor of criticism, logic, and the philosophy of language in South Carolina College, 1824–37; a frequent contributor to the *Southern Review*.

NOTT, JOSIAH CLARK (*b. Columbia, S.C., 1804; d. Mobile, Ala., 1873*), physician, ethnologist. Son of Abraham Nott; brother of Henry J. Nott. Graduated South Carolina College, 1824; M.D., University of Pennsylvania, 1827; practiced in Mobile *post* 1836. Nott is perhaps best known for his views on yellow fever, advanced in 1848 and 1854, in which he attributed the disease to a causative living organism.

NOTT, SAMUEL (*b. present Essex, Conn., 1754; d. present Franklin, Conn., 1852*), Congregational clergyman, educator. Graduated Yale, 1780; studied theology under the younger Jonathan Edwards. Pastor, *post* 1782, in the present town of Franklin, Conn., he made his home an educational institution where many young men were fitted for college; among them was his brother Eliphalet Nott.

NOTZ, FREDERICK WILLIAM AUGUSTUS (*b. Lehrensteinsfeld, Württemberg, 1841; d. Milwaukee, Wis., 1921*), educator. Ph.D., Tübingen, 1863, where he also made theological studies. Came to America, 1866. After holding several teaching positions, he became professor of Greek and Hebrew at Northwestern College, Watertown, Wis., 1872, and served until his retirement, 1912.

NOYAN, GILLES-AUGUSTIN PAYEN de (*b. France, 1697; d. Louisiana, 1751*), French soldier, provincial legislator. Nephew of Bienville and Iberville; brother of Pierre-Jacques Noyan. Came to Louisiana, 1717 or 1718. Served in a number of military expeditions and was employed *post* 1732 in implementing Bienville's efforts to stiffen the resistance of the Choctaws against English-supported Chickasaws. Sitting frequently as a member of the Superior Council of Louisiana, he was acting governor, 1748.

NOYAN, PIERRE-JACQUES PAYEN de (*b. Montreal, Canada, 1695; d. c. 1763*), French-Canadian officer. Nephew of Bienville and Iberville; brother of Gilles-Augustin Noyan. Appointed commandant at Fort Frontenac, 1721, he was constantly active thereafter along the Great Lakes until 1758 in civil and military service. Among other policies which he urged on the French ministry were the better regulation of trade with the Indians, the establishment of permanent settlements, the growing of wheat to supply the trad-

ing posts, the building of boats on the Lakes and the development of the copper and lead mines in the Lake region. As commandant at Detroit, 1738–42, he succeeded in keeping the Indians firmly attached to the French interest. Later holding command at Crown Point and at Three Rivers, he was sent to Fort Frontenac in 1758, where he surrendered in August to Col. John Bradstreet's attacking force.

NOYES, ARTHUR AMOS (*b. Newburyport, Mass., 1866; d. 1936*), chemist, educator, author. Graduated Massachusetts Institute of Technology, 1886; M.S., 1887. Ph.D., Leipzig, 1890, in physical chemistry. During many years of teaching at both Massachusetts and California Institutes of Technology, and by his influential textbooks, Noyes revolutionized the teaching of analytical and physical chemistry in the United States. He made important researches into the properties of solutions of electrolytes and in the rarer elements. He was founder (1895) of the presently titled *Chemical Abstracts*, held office in professional societies, and was acting chairman of the National Research Council, 1918. [*Supp. 2*]

NOYES, CLARA DUTTON (*b. Port Deposit, Md., 1869; d. Washington, D.C., 1936*), nurse, educator. Graduated Johns Hopkins Hospital, 1896. Demonstrating marked ability as administrator in several hospital positions, she became superintendent of training schools, Bellevue Hospital, N.Y., 1910. Appointed director of the American Red Cross military nursing bureau, 1916, she succeeded Jane A. Delano as director of the Red Cross nursing service, 1919, and held that post until her death. [*Supp. 2*]

NOYES, CROSBY STUART (*b. Minot, Maine, 1825; d. 1908*), journalist. Removed to Washington, D.C., 1847, where he worked on the *Washington News* and served as correspondent for several New England and New York papers. Employed *post* 1855 on the Washington *Star*, he purchased that paper with Alexander R. Shepherd, 1867, and served thereafter with great success as editor-in-chief.

NOYES, EDWARD FOLLANSBEE (*b. Haverhill, Mass., 1832; d. Cincinnati, O., 1890*), lawyer, Union soldier. Graduated Dartmouth, 1857; practiced law *post* 1858 in Cincinnati, O. Republican governor of Ohio, 1872–74, Noyes was a leading factor in the presidential nomination of Rutherford B. Hayes, 1876. He was U.S. minister to France, 1877–81.

NOYES, GEORGE RAPALL (*b. Newburyport, Mass., 1798; d. 1868*), Unitarian clergyman. Professor of Oriental languages and Biblical literature at Harvard, 1840–68, Noyes was an American pioneer in the critical study of the Bible. His most important work was his translation of the New Testament, published 1869. He graduated from Harvard in 1818 and from Harvard Divinity School in 1822.

NOYES, HENRY DRURY (*b. New York, N.Y., 1832; d. Mount Washington, Mass., 1900*), ophthalmologist. Graduated University of the City of New York (New York University), 1851; M.D., N.Y. College of Physicians and Surgeons, 1855. Associated *post* 1859 with development of the New York Eye and Ear Infirmary; was professor of ophthalmology and otology, Bellevue Hospital Medical College, 1868–92, and thereafter professor of ophthalmology alone.

NOYES, JOHN HUMPHREY (*b. Brattleboro, Vt., 1811; d. Niagara Falls, Canada, 1886*), social reformer. Graduated Dartmouth, 1830; studied law; attended Andover and Yale theological schools. Reacting against Calvinism, Noyes combined prevalent perfectionist and adventist beliefs in a personal theology *c.* 1833. Persuading himself that he had attained a state of perfection or complete sinlessness, he developed a society known as Bible Communists at Putney, Vt. Among other doctrines which he promulgated for his followers *post* 1836 was free love or promiscuity within the bounds of the community; he also claimed miraculous powers of healing. Arrested on a charge of adultery, he broke bail and fled to central New York whither his Bible Communists followed him and established the Oneida Community, 1848. Noyes's organizing skill and dominating personality made this the most successful in a material way of the American utopias. After thirty years of undisturbed control, he sensed the imminent decline of his personal leadership and also the growing strength of outside opposition; permitting his followers to contract legal marriages, he emigrated to Canada and put himself beyond reach of legal action.

NOYES, LA VERNE (*b. Genoa, N.Y., 1849; d. Chicago, Ill., 1919*), inventor and manufacturer of farm machinery, notably steel windmills.

NOYES, WALTER CHADWICK (*b. Lyme, Conn., 1865; d. New York, N.Y., 1926*), lawyer. Practiced with Frank B. Brandegee at New London, Conn.; served 1895–1907 as judge of the court of common pleas. U.S. circuit judge of the second judicial circuit, 1907–13. Thereafter he resumed corporation practice in New York City.

NOYES, WILLIAM CURTIS (*b. Schodack, N.Y., 1805; d. 1864*), lawyer. Practiced in Rome and Utica, N.Y., and in New York City *post* 1838; was famous for carefully researched briefs. He worked with Alexander W. Bradford and David D. Field on the codification of New York laws, 1857.

NUGENT, JOHN FROST (*b. LaGrande, Oreg., 1868; d. Washington, D.C., 1931*), lawyer. Raised in Idaho; was of defense counsel in prosecution of William D. Haywood et al. for murder of Gov. Steunenberg. U.S. senator, Democrat, from Idaho, 1918–21; member of Federal Trade Commission, 1920–27.

NÚÑEZ CABEZA DE VACA, ALVAR (*b. Jerez de la Frontera, Spain, c. 1490; d. Spain, probably in Seville, c. 1557*), Spanish soldier, colonial official, explorer. Treasurer and *alguacil mayor* of Pánfilo de Narváez's expedition for the conquest of Florida, 1527, he advised the commander against abandonment of the ships on their reaching the Florida coast in April 1528. Overruled, he was assigned command of one of the rude boats fabricated after the fatal march to Apalache. Driven on an island off the Texas coast, he and other survivors were enslaved by hostile Indians; escaping in February 1530, he became a resourceful and successful trader among friendly Indians. He began working his way westward in 1535 as a medicine man, accompanied by three companions. After traversing present southern Texas and northern Mexico, he arrived at Mexico City, July 23, 1536. His *La Relacion que Dio Alvar Nuñez, Cabeça de Vaca de lo Acaescido en las Indias* (1542) gave the first European account of the American opossum, the bison, and Texas Indians; it also prompted the expedition of Coronado. After his return to Spain, 1537, he led an extraordinary exploring expedition in the Rio de la Plata region of South America, 1540–44.

NUNÓ, JAIME (*b. San Juan de las Abadesas, Spain, 1824; d. Bayside, N.Y., 1908*), musician. After a successful career as a conductor in Spain, Cuba and Mexico, Nunó came to the United States, 1856. He directed opera troupes and conducted here and abroad until 1869 when he settled in Buffalo, N.Y., as a teacher of singing and later as conductor of the Buffalo Symphony Orchestra. His outstanding composition was the Mexican national hymn (officially adopted, 1854).

NURSE, REBECCA (*b. Yarmouth, England, 1621; d. Salem, Mass., 1692*), victim of the Salem witchcraft delusion.

NUTHEAD, WILLIAM (*b. probably England, c. 1654; d. St. Mary's City, Md., 1695*), printer. Nuthead appears for the first time in colonial records as an unlicensed printer in Virginia, 1683. Removing from Jamestown, where he had set up his press, to Maryland, he is mentioned in official records there as a printer of official documents and the like as early as 1686. Samples of his work are extremely rare.

NUTTALL, THOMAS (*b. Settle, Yorkshire, England, 1786; d. near Liverpool, England, 1859*), botanist, ornithologist. Emigrated to Philadelphia, Pa., 1808; Benjamin S. Barton introduced him to plant studies. Participated in explorations up Missouri River, 1809–11; along Arkansas and Red rivers, 1818–20; with Wyeth Expedition to mouth of Columbia River, 1834–35. Curator, Botanical Garden, Harvard, 1822–32. Wrote *Genera of North American Plants, etc.* (1818); was author also of the continuation (1842–49) of F. A. Michaux's *North American Sylva* and contributed numerous descriptions of new species to *Transactions of the American Philosophical Society*, Silliman's *Journal* and others. Equally talented as ornithologist, he published *A Manual of Ornithology* (1832), which brought him great reputation. In geological observations on the Mississippi Valley, 1820, he made the first American attempt to correlate, by means of fossil remains, geological formations widely separated geographically, antedating work of S. G. Morton.

NUTTING, CHARLES CLEVELAND (*b. Jacksonville, Ill., 1858; d. Iowa City, Iowa, 1927*), ornithologist, marine zoologist. Traveled extensively as a field collector; was professor of zoology, State University of Iowa, *post* 1886. Author of an important series of reports, *American Hydroids* (1900–15) and other learned papers.

NYE, EDGAR WILSON (*b. Shirley, Maine, 1850; d. Arden, N.C., 1896*), journalist, humorist, better known as "Bill" Nye. Raised in Wisconsin, Nye drifted westward in 1876, settling at Laramie City, Wyo. After conducting the *Laramie Boomerang*, 1881–83, in which his reputation as a humorist was established, he moved east in 1886, was a staff writer for the N.Y. *World*, and enjoyed a great success as a lecturer. As a humorous writer, he belongs to the school of Artemus Ward and Mark Twain; his most ambitious books were *History of the United States* (1894) and *History of England* (1896); his shorter comic pieces were published in *Bill Nye and Boomerang* (1881) and later collections.

NYE, JAMES WARREN (*b. De Ruyter, N.Y., 1814; d. White Plains, N.Y., 1876*), lawyer. Territorial governor of Nevada, 1861–64; U.S. senator, Republican, from Nevada, 1864–73.

OAKES, GEORGE WASHINGTON OCHS (*b. Cincinnati, O., 1861; d. 1931*), editor. Son of Julius Ochs; brother of Adolph S. Ochs. Served in several editorial capacities on the *Chattanooga Daily Times*, 1880–c. 1888; after engaging in magazine work, returned to the *Times*, 1896, as general manager. A civic leader in Chattanooga, he served as mayor, 1893–97. *Post* 1900, he was employed in a number of editorial and managerial capacities on his brother's publications and others, including editorship of *Current History* and the *Times Mid-Week Pictorial*.

OAKES, THOMAS FLETCHER (*b. Boston, Mass., 1843; d. Seattle, Wash., 1919*), railroad executive. Director, 1881–88, president, 1888–93, and general receiver, 1893–95, of Northern Pacific Railroad.

OAKES, URIAN (*b. probably London, England, c. 1631; d. Massachusetts, 1681*), Congregational clergyman, poet. Emigrated to New England as a boy; graduated Harvard, 1649. A dissenting minister and teacher

in England, 1653–71, Oakes served thereafter as pastor of the church in Cambridge, Mass. A ringleader among those who drove Leonard Hoar out of the presidency of Harvard, he was acting president of the college *post* 1675 and received formal election as president in February 1679/80.

OAKLEY, ANNIE (*b. Darke Co., O., 1860; d. Greenville, O., 1926*), markswoman. A notable attraction in vaudeville and the circus, Annie Oakley starred in Buffalo Bill's "Wild West" show *post* 1885; the use of her name to denote punch-marked complimentary tickets derived from her ability to perforate a playing card with rifle bullets while it fluttered to the ground.

OAKLEY, THOMAS JACKSON (*b. Beekman, N.Y., 1783; d. New York, N.Y., 1857*), lawyer, politician, New York legislator. Congressman, Federalist, from New York, 1813–15; congressman, Clinton Democrat, 1827–28. In high repute as an advocate, Oakley was judge of the superior court of New York City, 1828–47, and chief justice of that court, 1847–57.

OATES, WILLIAM CALVIN (*b. Bullock Co., Ala., 1835; d. Montgomery, Ala., 1910*), Confederate soldier, lawyer, Alabama legislator. Congressman, Democrat, from Alabama, 1881–94; sound-money governor of Alabama, 1894–96.

OATMAN, JOHNSON (*b. near Medford, N.J., 1856; d. Norman, Okla., 1922*), gospel hymn writer.

OBER, FREDERICK ALBION (*b. Beverly, Mass., 1849; d. Hackensack, N.J., 1913*), ornithologist. Explored Lesser Antilles, 1876–78 and 1880, discovering 22 new species of birds.

OBERHOFFER, EMIL JOHANN (*b. Munich, Bavaria, 1867; d. San Diego, Calif., 1933*), musician. Emigrated to New York City, 1885; removed to Minnesota, 1897, where he taught music, conducted, and was one of the prime movers in the establishment of the Minneapolis Symphony Orchestra, 1903. *Post* 1923, he was active in the musical life of Los Angeles, Calif. [*Supp. 1*]

OBERHOLTZER, ELLIS PAXSON (*b. Cambria Station, Pa., 1868; d. Philadelphia, Pa., 1936*), journalist, historian. Author, among other serious studies, of *History of the United States since the Civil War* (1917–37). [*Supp. 2*]

OBERHOLTZER, SARA LOUISA VICKERS (*b. Uwchlan, Pa., 1841; d. Philadelphia, Pa., 1930*), poet, advocate of school savings banks to promote thrift.

O'BRIEN, EDWARD CHARLES (*b. Fort Edward, N.Y., 1860; d. Montevideo, Uruguay, 1927*), merchant, public official, shipping expert. U.S. minister to Uruguay and Paraguay, 1905–09.

O'BRIEN, FITZ-JAMES (*b. Co. Limerick, Ireland, c. 1828; d. Cumberland, Md., 1862*), journalist. Came to America c. 1852. Sponsored by George P. Morris and others, he quickly became prominent in New York City's literary and Bohemian circles. Enlisting in the Union Army at the outbreak of the Civil War, O'Brien died of the effects of a wound. His *Poems and Stories* (posthumously published, 1881) reprints his best work of which "The Diamond Lens" is probably the best-known example.

O'BRIEN, FREDERICK (*b. Baltimore, Md., 1869; d. Sausalito, Calif., 1932*), journalist. Author of *White Shadows in the South Seas* (1919), *Atolls of the Sun* (1922) and other accounts of travel.

O'BRIEN, JEREMIAH (*b. Kittery, Maine, 1744; d. Machias, Maine, 1818*), Revolutionary patriot, naval officer. At the head of about forty volunteers, O'Brien seized the sloop *Unity* in the harbor of Machias and with her engaged and captured the armed schooner *Margaretta*, commanded by an officer of the Royal Navy, June 12, 1775. Thereafter he cruised with success in the service of the Massachusetts Navy until the fall of 1776, when he became a privateersman. Captured in 1780 with his vessel the *Hannibal*, he was imprisoned at New York and later in Mill Prison, England, whence he escaped; on returning to America, 1781, he commanded successively the *Hibernia* and the *Tiger*.

O'BRIEN, MATTHEW ANTHONY (*b. Co. Tipperary, Ireland, 1804; d. Louisville, Ky., 1871*), Roman Catholic clergyman, Dominican missionary and provincial. Came to Canada, 1826; ordained in Kentucky, 1839. A magnetic preacher and able administrator.

O'BRIEN, MORGAN JOSEPH (*b. New York, N.Y., 1852; d. New York, 1937*), lawyer, jurist. Graduated, St. John's College (Fordham), 1872; Columbia Law School, 1875. Justice, New York supreme court, 1887–95; appellate division, 1895–1906. Resigning to re-enter private practice, O'Brien rose in his profession and engaged in extensive public service; the 1936 New York City Charter revision was owing in great part to his efforts. [*Supp. 2*]

O'BRIEN, RICHARD (*b. Maine, c. 1758; d. Washington, D.C., 1824*), mariner, privateersman. An Algerine captive, 1785–95, O'Brien served as U.S. consul-general to Algiers, 1797–1803. Prior to this he had helped conclude treaties of peace with Algiers and Tripoli, 1796.

O'BRIEN, THOMAS JAMES (*b. Jackson Co., Mich., 1842; d. Grand Rapids, Mich., 1933*), lawyer, Republican politician. U.S. minister to Denmark, 1905–07; ambassador to Japan, 1907–11; ambassador to Italy, 1911–13. [*Supp. 1*]

O'BRIEN, WILLIAM SHONEY (*b. Queen's Co., Ireland, c. 1826; d. San Rafael, Calif., 1878*), capitalist, Nevada silver-mine operator. Came to America *ante*

1845; removed to California, 1849. Associated with John W. Mackay, James G. Fair and others in highly successful mine operations.

O'CALLAGHAN, EDMUND BAILEY (*b. Mallow, Ireland, 1797; d. 1880*), physician, historian. Removed to Albany, N.Y., from Canada, 1837; practiced medicine until 1848; devoted full time to editing early records of New York State, 1848–70. Among the important works which he produced were *History of New Netherland* (1846–48); *Documentary History of the State of New York* (1849–51); and *Documents Relative to the Colonial History of the State of New York* (Volumes I–XI, 1853–61).

O'CALLAGHAN, JEREMIAH (*b. Co. Cork, Ireland, 1780; d. Holyoke, Mass., 1861*), Roman Catholic clergyman, author. Ordained, 1805, in Ireland, O'Callaghan early became an opponent of the taking of interest on money loans, an anti-capitalist position which involved him in difficulties with his ecclesiastical superiors for many years. Emigrating to America, 1823, he was unable to win acceptance in any diocese until 1830; at that time, accepted by the diocese of Boston, he was assigned to missionary and pastoral work in Vermont where he worked with great zeal and success. His book *Usury, or Interest, Proved . . . Destructive to Civil Society* (New York, 1824) went through several editions and had a strong influence on the English radical writer William Cobbett.

OCCIDENTE, MARIA DEL. [See BROOKS, MARIA GOWEN, *c. 1794–1845.*]

OCCOM, SAMSON (*b. near New London, Conn., 1723; d. 1792*), Indian Presbyterian clergyman, missionary. First Indian to be trained (1743–47) by Eleazar Wheelock. Occom was ordained in 1759. He accompanied Nathaniel Whitaker to England to secure money for Wheelock's Indian Charity School, 1766–68. An active missionary among the New England tribes and the Oneidas, he opposed as best he could the white encroachments upon Indian lands.

OCCONOSTOTA. [See OCONOSTOTA, d. 1785.]

OCHS, ADOLPH SIMON (*b. Cincinnati, O., 1858; d. Chattanooga, Tenn., 1935*), newspaper publisher. Son of Julius Ochs. Began work, 1869, as office boy on the Knoxville, Tenn., *Chronicle*; tried various occupations in various places during his early youth but always came back to Knoxville and the newspaper business. Removing to Chattanooga, Tenn., at the age of 19, he began his publishing career by purchasing the *Chattanooga Times* with borrowed money, 1878. After developing the *Times* with great success as a newspaper "clean, dignified and trustworthy," he purchased the once-prosperous *New York Times*, 1896. He applied to his new purchase without compromise the principles he had practiced in Chattanooga; it was to be a strictly "news" paper in which editorial opinion was subordinate and the news was treated with freedom from personal and partisan bias. He also excluded advertising which seemed to him fraudulent or improper. Refusing to make any concessions to yellow journalism, Ochs brought the *Times* along slowly but steadily; after it began to succeed, he put most of his profits back into expansion of plant and services. From time to time he held interests in other papers, but came eventually to the conclusion that running the *Times* was job enough for any man. The excellence of the *Times*'s coverage of war news, 1914–18, raised the paper to pre-eminence. Ochs never held nor sought public office; in his later years, he gave much time to philanthropies and public causes.

[*Supp.* 1]

OCHS, JULIUS (*b. Fürth, Bavaria, 1826; d. Chattanooga, Tenn., 1888*), merchant. Father of Adolph S. Ochs and George W. Oakes. Came to America, 1845. Resided successively in Kentucky, Ohio and Tennessee; served in Union Army; was active in politics and civic affairs.

OCHSNER, ALBERT JOHN (*b. Baraboo, Wis., 1858; d. 1925*), surgeon. Graduated Rush Medical College, 1886; studied also in Vienna and Berlin. Practiced in Chicago *post* 1889; taught at Rush Medical College and at University of Illinois; was chief surgeon, Augustana Hospital, 1891–1925, and at St. Mary's Hospital, 1896–1925.

OCKERSON, JOHN AUGUSTUS (*b. Skane Province, Sweden, 1848; d. St. Louis, Mo., 1924*), engineer. Came to America as a child; graduated University of Illinois, C.E., 1873. Associated *post* 1879 with the Mississippi River Commission, he became an international authority on river and harbor improvement and navigation. Among his individual achievements was the construction of levees (1910) to control flood waters of the Colorado River.

O'CONNOR, JAMES (*b. Cobh, Ireland, 1823; d. 1890*), Roman Catholic clergyman. Brother of Michael O'Connor. Came to America *c.* 1839. Ordained in Rome, 1848, he served in the dioceses of Pittsburgh and Philadelphia until 1876 when he was consecrated vicar-apostolic of Nebraska. Appointed first bishop of Omaha, 1885, he served until his death.

O'CONNOR, MICHAEL (*b. near Cork, Ireland, 1810; d. Woodstock, Md., 1872*), Roman Catholic clergyman. Brother of James O'Connor. Educated in France and in Rome, Italy, he was ordained, 1833, and came to America *c.* 1839 as rector of the Seminary of St. Charles, Philadelphia. Consecrated bishop of Pittsburgh, 1843, he served there with distinguished success until his resignation, 1860. Thereafter, having become a Jesuit, he traveled extensively throughout the United States as a missionary.

O'CONNOR, WILLIAM DOUGLAS (*b. Boston, Mass., 1832; d. Washington, D.C., 1889*), journalist,

civil servant, friend and champion of Walt Whitman. Author of *The Good Gray Poet* (1866).

O'CONOR, CHARLES (*b. New York, N.Y., 1804; d. 1884*), lawyer. Admitted to the bar, 1824, he practiced with phenomenal success and appeared as counsel in most of the outstanding cases heard in his time. Among them were the Jumel Will case, the Roosevelt Hospital case, the Tilden-Hayes election contest, the Tweed cases and the Forrest divorce case. A Democrat, he ran unsuccessfully a number of times for public office; he was nominated for president of the United States by the "Straight-out" Democrats, 1872.

OCONOSTOTA (*d. 1785*), Cherokee Indian chief. Lived at Great Echota in present Monroe Co., Tenn. Imprisoned at Fort Prince George (S.C.), 1759, by Gov. W. H. Lyttelton after proffering friendship, Oconostota was soon released; thereafter he devoted himself to repaying treachery with equal treachery. Unsuccessfully attempting to capture Fort Prince George, 1760, he led Cherokees in raids against the frontier settlements; later he commanded the Indians in the taking of Fort Loudoun and was responsible for the massacre of its defenders. Apparently reconciled to the superiority of the white forces, he led the Cherokee delegation at the treaty of peace with the Iroquois, Johnson Hall, 1768; he opposed sale of Cherokee lands at Sycamore Shoals, 1775. During the Revolution he fought for the British, resigning his leadership, 1782.

ODELL, BENJAMIN BARKER (*b. Newburgh, N.Y., 1854; d. 1926*), businessman, New York State Republican politician and leader. Suggested Theodore Roosevelt's candidacy for governor, 1898; elected governor himself in 1900 and again in 1902, he served with efficiency and economy. A realist in politics, he was the first "machine" Republican to defy the rule of Thomas C. Platt.

ODELL, JONATHAN (*b. Newark, N.J., 1737; d. Fredericton, N.B., Canada, 1818*), Loyalist, physician, poet, Episcopal clergyman. Played important role in negotiations between Benedict Arnold and British headquarters in New York, 1779–80; was author of Tory satirical verses in Rivington's *Royal Gazette* and other newspapers; registrar and clerk of New Brunswick province, *c.* 1784–1812.

ODENBACH, FREDERICK LOUIS (*b. Rochester, N.Y., 1857; d. Cleveland, O., 1933*), Roman Catholic clergyman, Jesuit, meteorologist. Graduated Canisius College, Buffalo, N.Y., 1881; entered the Society of Jesus, 1881; made his subsequent studies in the Netherlands and England. Taught scientific studies at the present John Carroll University in Cleveland, 1892–1933, supervising and in large measure constructing the meteorological observatory there. He designed and built the first ceraunograph (an adaptation of the coherer to the detection and recording of static disturbances), 1899; in 1900, he began a seismological observatory and was the founder of Jesuit activity in that field in the United States. [*Supp.* 1]

ODENHEIMER, WILLIAM HENRY (*b. Philadelphia, Pa., 1817; d. Burlington, N.J., 1879*), Episcopal clergyman. Bishop of New Jersey, 1859–74, and of Northern New Jersey (later Newark), 1874–79.

ODIN, JOHN MARY (*b. Ambierle, France, 1801; d. Ambierle, 1870*), Roman Catholic clergyman, Vincentian. Came to New Orleans, La., with Bishop Dubourg, 1822; served as missionary in Arkansas and Texas *post* 1823; consecrated vicar-apostolic of Texas, 1842. Appointed bishop of Galveston, 1847, he was raised to the archbishopric of New Orleans, 1861.

O'DONNELL, THOMAS JEFFERSON (*b. Mendham Township, N.J., 1856; d. 1925*), lawyer. Removing to Denver, Colo., 1879, he spent the remainder of his life there in the practice of law and as a power in the Democratic party. Opposed to Grover Cleveland's financial policies, he was many times an unsuccessful seeker for public office.

O'DONOVAN, WILLIAM RUDOLF (*b. Preston Co., Va., now W. Va., 1844; d. New York, N.Y., 1920*), sculptor, painter, Confederate soldier.

O'DWYER, JOSEPH (*b. Cleveland, O., 1841; d. 1898*), physician. Graduated N.Y. College of Physicians and Surgeons, 1866; practiced thereafter in New York City. Successfully demonstrated value of intubation in treatment of diphtheria at New York Foundling Asylum *post* 1872; his findings, first attacked and later enthusiastically approved by the medical profession, were published first in the *New York Medical Journal*, Aug. 8, 1885. He was also among the first to recognize the value of diphtheria serum.

OEHMLER, LEO CARL MARTIN (*b. Pittsburgh, Pa., 1867; d. Pasadena, Calif., 1930*), musician, piano teacher, composer. Teacher of Charles W. Cadman.

OEMLER, ARMINIUS (*b. Savannah, Ga., 1827; d. Savannah, 1897*), physician, agriculturist, Confederate soldier. Among the first to introduce scientific diversified farming into the South, Oemler anticipated by two years (1888) the German discovery of the presence of nitrogen-fixing bacteria in the nodules of leguminous plants. He started the first commercial oyster-packing plant in the South *c.* 1883 and was thereafter a promoter of that industry.

OERTEL, JOHANNES ADAM SIMON (*b. Fürth, Bavaria, 1823; d. Vienna, Va., 1909*), Episcopal clergyman, artist. Came to America, 1848, after studying at Munich. Active in the ministry *post* 1867, he is remembered chiefly as the painter of the very popular "Rock of Ages," although he did much excellent work in church decoration and was a superior woodcarver.

O'FALLON, BENJAMIN (*b. probably Lexington, Ky., 1793; d. Jefferson Co., Mo., 1842*), Indian agent, trader. Son of James O'Fallon; nephew of William and George Rogers Clark; brother of John O'Fallon. As U.S. Indian agent at Prairie du Chien, O'Fallon made treaties with the Otos and Poncas, 1817. Appointed agent for the Upper Missouri, 1819, he served until 1827 with great success owing to his honesty and courage and his remarkable knowledge of Indian customs, habits and characteristics. He was a principal in the Missouri Fur Co.

O'FALLON, JAMES (*b. Ireland, 1749; d. 1794*), physician, Revolutionary soldier, adventurer. Emigrated to North Carolina, 1774; at end of the Revolution, removed to Charleston, S.C. Appointed general agent of the South Carolina Yazoo Company, he associated himself with James Wilkinson and with Esteban Miró in intrigues connected with the institution of an independent government for the West. A proclamation by President Washington, March 1791, proved disastrous to O'Fallon's plans. He married a sister of William and George Rogers Clark in 1791 and was the father of Benjamin and John O'Fallon.

O'FALLON, JOHN (*b. Louisville, Ky., 1791; d. St. Louis, Mo., 1865*), soldier, merchant. Son of James O'Fallon; nephew of William and George Rogers Clark; brother of Benjamin O'Fallon. After able army service at Tippecanoe and in the War of 1812, O'Fallon resigned his commission, 1818, and engaged in trade at St. Louis, Mo. where he became a wealthy and public-spirited citizen.

O'FERRALL, CHARLES TRIPLETT (*b. Frederick Co., Va., 1840; d. Richmond, Va., 1905*), lawyer, Confederate cavalry colonel, Virginia legislator. Congressman, Democrat, from Virginia, 1884–93. A strict constructionist and supporter of Grover Cleveland, O'Ferrall made a determined effort to wipe out lynching as governor of Virginia, 1894–98.

OFFLEY, DAVID (*b. Philadelphia, Pa.; d. Smyrna, Turkey, 1838*), merchant. Removing to Smyrna, 1811, he founded there the first American commercial house in the Levant. He served as consular commercial agent, 1823–32, and as U.S. consul, 1832–38.

OFTEDAL, SVEN (*b. Stavanger, Norway, 1844; d. 1911*), Lutheran clergyman, Minneapolis civic leader. Came to America, 1873. Professor of theology, 1873–1904, and president of trustees, 1874–1911, of Augsburg Seminary, Minneapolis.

OGDEN, AARON (*b. Elizabeth, N.J., 1756; d. Jersey City, N.J., 1839*), Revolutionary soldier, lawyer, pioneer steamboat operator. Graduated College of New Jersey (Princeton), 1773. Entering practice after the Revolution, he became a leader of the New Jersey bar, served as U.S. senator, Federalist, 1801–03, and was elected governor of New Jersey in the fall of

1812 on a peace ticket. After commanding the New Jersey militia during the War of 1812, he undertook operation of a steamboat between Elizabeth and New York City which occasioned the legal conflicts concluded in the celebrated U.S. Supreme Court case of *Gibbons vs. Ogden*, 1824. Ruined by this litigation, he became collector of customs at Jersey City in 1829 and served until his death.

OGDEN, DAVID (*b. Newark, N.J., 1707; d. Whitestone, N.Y., 1798*), lawyer, New Jersey councilor and jurist, Loyalist.

OGDEN, DAVID BAYARD (*b. Morrisania, N.Y., 1775; d. Staten Island, N.Y., 1849*), lawyer. Son of Samuel Ogden. Practicing in New York City *post* 1803, Ogden's chief fame arose from the clarity of his presentations before the U.S. Supreme Court. The most celebrated of the many cases in which he participated was *Cohens vs. Virginia* (1821) in which he appeared for Cohens.

OGDEN, FRANCIS BARBER (*b. Boonton, N.J., 1783; d. Bristol, England, 1857*), engineer. Nephew of Aaron Ogden. A pioneer in designing steamboat engines, Ogden resided in England *post* 1830 where he served in several consular posts. He financed the work of John Ericsson and promoted his interests in England and in the United States.

OGDEN, HERBERT GOUVERNEUR (*b. New York, N.Y., 1846; d. Fortress Monroe, Va., 1906*), cartographer, topographer. Appointed an aid in the U.S. Coast and Geodetic Survey, 1863, Ogden remained with that service until his death, serving as cartographer and topographer and as director of publication of three editions of the *U.S. Coast Pilot* (1899, 1903, 1904). He also made original explorations in Alaska.

OGDEN, PETER SKENE (*b. Quebec, Canada, 1794; d. Oregon City, Oreg., 1854*), fur trader, explorer. Grandson of David Ogden. Entered employ of the North West Company c. 1815. Transferred to the Columbia district beyond the Rockies c. 1818, he spent the remainder of his life there. His work took him into almost every valley in southern Idaho and eastern Oregon and into Montana; he was one of the first white men to visit the Great Salt Lake region (Ogden, Utah, was named in his honor), and he was the first to traverse the Humboldt River valley in northern Nevada. Assigned to the Fraser River region c. 1836, he was stationed at Fort Vancouver *post* 1844. A man of great cultivation and urbanity, he was author of *Traits of American Indian Life* (London, 1853).

OGDEN, ROBERT CURTIS (*b. Philadelphia, Pa., 1836; d. Kennebunkport, Maine, 1913*), merchant, promoter of education in the South.

OGDEN, ROLLO (*b. Sand Lake, N.Y., 1856; d. 1937*), Presbyterian clergyman, newspaper editor. Graduated Williams, 1877. Leaving the ministry,

1887, on conscientious grounds, Ogden joined the staff of the N.Y. *Evening Post*, 1891; he became editor-in-chief, 1903, and served until 1920, simultaneously controlling the editorial policy of the *Nation*. A champion of anti-imperialism, low tariffs, civil service reform, Negro rights, woman suffrage and international action for peace, he at the same time opposed any wide expansion of governmental powers. Ogden served as associate editor of the *New York Times*, 1920–22, and as editor, 1922–37. Remaining a staunch internationalist, he approved of some parts of the New Deal but was hostile to its augmentation of federal power. [*Supp. 2*]

OGDEN, SAMUEL (*b. Newark, N.J., 1746; d. New York, N.Y., 1810*), iron founder, land promoter. Son of David Ogden.

OGDEN, THOMAS LUDLOW (*b. probably Morristown, N.J., 1773; d. 1844*), lawyer. Grandson of David Ogden; nephew of Samuel Ogden. Graduated Columbia, 1792; admitted to New York bar, 1796. Specializing in trusts and will and equity jurisprudence, Ogden became one of the most active corporation lawyers in New York City and was identified with many of its cultural and civic activities.

OGDEN, UZAL (*b. Newark, N.J., 1744; d. Newark, 1822*), Episcopal clergyman. Made theological studies under Thomas B. Chandler; was ordained in London, England, 1773. Rector of Trinity Church, Newark, 1788–1805, Ogden was elected first bishop of New Jersey, 1798, but was refused consecration. Suspended from the Episcopal ministry, 1805, as the final step in a long controversy over his broad views on order and doctrine, he became a Presbyterian.

OGDEN, WILLIAM BUTLER (*b. Walton, N.Y., 1805; d. New York, N.Y., 1877*), businessman. After early success as a land developer in New York, Ogden removed to Chicago, Ill., 1835, made a fortune in real-estate operations there, and was elected the city's first mayor, 1837. After his term, he devoted himself to railroad construction east and west from Chicago; among the roads which he headed were the Galena & Chicago; the Pittsburg, Fort Wayne & Chicago; the Chicago & Northwestern. He presided over the National Pacific Railway Convention, 1850, and was first president of the Union Pacific, 1862.

OGILVIE, JAMES (*b. Aberdeen, Scotland, date unknown; d. Aberdeen, 1820*), teacher, lecturer. An eccentric pseudo-philosopher, Ogilvie conducted several schools in Virginia *ante* 1809; thereafter, he became a wandering professor of oratory. Failing in his ambitions, he returned to Scotland where he committed suicide.

OGILVIE, JOHN (*b. probably New York, N.Y., 1724; d. New York, 1774*), Anglican clergyman. Graduated Yale, 1748. After ordination in London, England,

1749, Ogilvie returned to America with an appointment as missionary in Albany, N.Y., and to the Mohawk Indians. He served with zeal in this work, was a military chaplain, 1756–60, and in 1764 was appointed assistant minister of Trinity Church, New York City, where he served until his death.

OGLE, SAMUEL (*b. Northumberland Co., England, c. 1702; d. Annapolis, Md., 1752*), British officer, colonial official. Proprietary governor of Maryland, 1732, 1733–42 and 1747–52, Ogle successfully resolved the question of the validity of English legal statutes in Maryland; he also regulated the tobacco trade.

OGLESBY, RICHARD JAMES (*b. Oldham Co., Ky., 1824; d. 1899*), lawyer, politician, Union major-general. Republican governor of Illinois, 1865–69, also for a very brief period in 1873, and 1885–89; U.S. senator, 1873–79.

OGLETHORPE, JAMES EDWARD (*b. London, England, 1696; d. England, 1785*), soldier, philanthropist, founder of the colony of Georgia. Educated at Eton and Oxford; early gained military reputation in service under Prince Eugene against the Turks. Briefly involved in Jacobite activity abroad, he returned to England in 1719 to manage family estate. Entering Parliament as a mild High Tory, he held his seat, 1722–54, advocating naval preparedness, an expanding imperial commerce, improved penal conditions for debtors, and abolition of both impressment and Negro slavery. He conceived the idea of sending newly freed and unemployed debtors to America at about the time when concern over the exposed position of Carolina to Indian and Spanish raids led the British government to seek expansion and defense of that colony by a buffer zone to the south. After a long period of many trials, Oglethorpe and 19 associates received a charter in 1732 to establish the colony of Georgia. His energetic publicity efforts and royal favor having brought both money and settlers for the venture, he landed at Charleston, 1733. Pursuing a conciliatory policy with the Indians, he secured a site at Savannah. Fortifications were at once erected and a rigorous system of military training established. Salzburger Lutherans were persuaded to migrate to the colony, 1734. Need for more money brought Oglethorpe back to England, 1734; he pressed successfully for new regulations banning sale of rum, prohibiting slavery and setting up a licensing system for the Indian trade. Groups of Scotch Presbyterian and Moravian settlers were induced to join the colony between 1735 and 1738. Rumors of insurrection caused Oglethorpe to return to Georgia in 1735, accompanied by Charles and John Wesley, who did not find their stay congenial and soon left. An effective but expensive southern military outpost against the Spaniards, Fort Frederica, was founded in 1736.

Complaints by Carolina against the licensing of

trade, Spanish resentment of Frederica, the tales reported to England by malcontent settlers, and increasing debts drew Oglethorpe back to London, 1736–37. Most difficulties were smoothed over, but trouble with Spain continued. Persisting in his efforts to strengthen the colony for both humanitarian and imperial reasons, Oglethorpe returned once more to Georgia in 1738, this time with a regiment of 700 men. Henceforth, a dragging war with Spain was his principal concern. Georgians attacked St. Augustine in 1740, and Frederica in turn was besieged by the Spanish in 1742. Oglethorpe borrowed heavily on his English holdings to conduct a successful defense of his colony, but internal discontents and serious charges by a subordinate forced his return to London in 1743. He was acquitted by a court martial but his administrative powers and vigor had diminished; his colonizing days were over and he lived uneventfully thereafter in England. He was promoted to the rank of full general, 1765.

O'GORMAN, THOMAS (*b. Boston, Mass., 1843; d. Sioux Falls, S. Dak., 1921*), Roman Catholic clergyman, Paulist, educator. Second bishop of Sioux Falls, 1896–1921; assisted William H. Taft in settlement of Philippine friar question, 1902.

O'HARA, JAMES (*b. Ireland, 1752; d. Pittsburgh, Pa., 1819*), Revolutionary soldier, manufacturer, land speculator. Early Pittsburgh banker and glass manufacturer; associated with John H. Hopkins in Ligonier iron works.

O'HARA, THEODORE (*b. Danville, Ky., 1820; d. Guerryton, Ala., 1867*), soldier, journalist. Officer in both Mexican and Civil wars; author of "The Bivouac of the Dead," commemorating Kentuckians killed at Buena Vista.

O'HIGGINS, HARVEY JERROLD (*b. London, Ontario, Canada, 1876; d. 1929*), novelist, journalist. Helped introduce literary use of psychoanalytic method in 1920's; was long associated with work of the Authors' League.

OHLMACHER, ALBERT PHILIP (*b. Sandusky, O., 1865; d. Detroit, Mich., 1916*), physician, pathologist. M.D., Northwestern, 1890. Pioneered in study of the pathology of epilepsy.

O'KELLY, JAMES (*b. Ireland or America, c. 1735; d. 1826*), Methodist preacher, opponent of slavery. Prominent as preacher in North Carolina and Virginia *post* 1778, he opposed authority, especially that of Bishop Francis Asbury, insisting that General Conferences should have a larger role in direction of church affairs. Seceding from the Methodist Episcopal Church, 1792, he set up his own group, called Republican Methodists and later simply "Christians." This group was congregational in polity and regarded the Scriptures as the only authority on faith and practice.

OKEY, JOHN WATERMAN (*b. Monroe Co., O., 1827; d. Columbus, O., 1885*), lawyer. Prominent common-pleas and supreme court jurist in Ohio. Co-author of *Digest of Ohio Reports* (1867) and *The Municipal Code of Ohio* (1869).

OLCOTT, CHANCELLOR JOHN. [See OLCOTT, CHAUNCEY, 1860–1932].

OLCOTT, CHAUNCEY (*b. Buffalo, N.Y., 1860; d. Monte Carlo, Monaco, 1932*), actor, singer. Popular Irish-American tenor; wrote "My Wild Irish Rose."

OLCOTT, EBEN ERSKINE (*b. New York, N.Y., 1854; d. New York, 1929*), mining engineer. Graduated Columbia School of Mines, 1874. Pioneered development of Cerro de Pasco copper fields in Peru; managed Hudson River Day Line *post* 1895.

OLCOTT, HENRY STEEL (*b. Orange, N.J., 1832; d. 1907*), lawyer, president-founder of the Theosophical Society. Led a bizarre life as Helena Blavatsky's partner; was conciliator of Japanese and Ceylonese Buddhist sects, and editor of the *Theosophist*.

OLDEN, CHARLES SMITH (*b. near Princeton, N.J., 1799; d. Princeton, 1876*), businessman, farmer, New Jersey legislator and jurist. Anti-Democrat coalition governor of New Jersey, 1860–63.

OLDER, FREMONT (*b. near Appleton, Wis., 1856; d. near Stockton, Calif., 1935*), printer, editor, reformer. Removed to San Francisco, Calif., 1873; worked on a number of California and Nevada newspapers; settled in San Francisco, 1884, where he became managing editor of the *Bulletin*, 1895. He built up the paper's circulation and attracted national attention by journalistic crusades against the Southern Pacific Railroad, the Abraham Ruef political machine, and the domination of the state by special interests; he also worked for penal reform, encouraged labor unions and demanded the acquittal of Thomas J. Mooney and others after the Preparedness Day bombings, 1916. Leaving the editorship of the *Bulletin*, he became editor of the San Francisco *Call*, 1918, and a loyal defender of his employer William R. Hearst. As an editor, he was forceful and successful; as a person, he was full of contradictions and difficult to analyze. [*Supp. 1*]

OLDHAM, JOHN (*b. probably Lancashire, England, c. 1600; d. Block Island, R.I., 1636*), colonist, trader. Came to America, 1623; resided in both Plymouth and Massachusetts Bay colonies. His murder by Indians near Block Island helped to start Pequot War.

OLDHAM, WILLIAM FITZJAMES (*b. Bangalore, India, 1854; d. Glendale, Calif., 1937*), Methodist clergyman. A convert to Methodism, he was licensed to preach in India, 1876. After serving as pastor and teacher in the U.S., 1890–1904, he was bishop and supervisor of missions in southern Asia, 1904–12, and in South America, 1916–28. [*Supp. 2*]

OLDHAM, WILLIAMSON SIMPSON (*b. Franklin Co., Tenn., 1813; d. Houston, Texas, 1868*), Arkansas legislator and jurist. Removed to Texas, 1849. Confederate senator from Texas, 1861–65. Opposed both conscription and suspension of *habeas corpus* by Confederate government on state rights grounds.

OLDS, ROBERT EDWIN (*b. Duluth, Minn., 1875; d. Paris, France, 1932*), lawyer, Red Cross official. Assistant U.S. secretary of state, 1925–27; under-secretary of state, 1927–28. A loyal and self-effacing subordinate to Frank B. Kellogg. [*Supp. 1*]

OLDSCHOOL, OLIVER. [See SARGENT, NATHAN, 1794–1875].

O'LEARY, DANIEL (*b. Clonakilty, Ireland, 1846?; d. Los Angeles, Calif., 1933*), pedestrian. Set many records for walking; twice winner of the Astley Belt. [*Supp. 1*]

OLIN, STEPHEN (*b. Leicester, Vt., 1797; d. Middletown, Conn., 1851*), Methodist clergyman, educator. President of Randolph-Macon College (1834–37) and Wesleyan University (1842–51); tried to prevent denominational split over slavery in 1840's.

OLIPHANT, HERMAN (*b. near Forest, Ind., 1884; d. Washington, D.C., 1939*), lawyer. Teacher of law at University of Chicago, 1914–21; at Columbia, 1921–28; at Johns Hopkins, 1928–33. U.S. treasury department adviser, 1933–39, he was influential in shaping New Deal fiscal policies. [*Supp. 2*]

OLIVER, ANDREW (*b. Boston, Mass., 1706; d. Boston, 1774*), Massachusetts provincial legislator. Brother of Peter Oliver. Graduated Harvard, 1724. Married Gov. Thomas Hutchinson's sister-in-law, 1734, and thereafter consistently acted with Hutchinson in colonial politics. Appointed secretary of the province, 1756, he held this position until 1771 when he was appointed lieutenant-governor. He was hated by the popular or patriot party because of his appointment as stamp-officer under the Stamp Act, and the revelation in 1773 of letters which Gov. Hutchinson and he had earlier written to England describing unsettled conditions in the colonies and prescribing remedies. On both occasions mobs threatened him and his family and attacked his home.

OLIVER, ANDREW (*b. Boston, Mass., 1731; d. Salem, Mass., 1799*), Massachusetts legislator and jurist, scientist. Son of Andrew Oliver (1706–1774). Graduated Harvard, 1749. His most significant scientific contribution was *An Essay on Comets* (1772).

OLIVER, CHARLES AUGUSTUS (*b. Cincinnati, O., 1853; d. Philadelphia, Pa., 1911*), ophthalmologist.

Co-author with William F. Norris of *A Textbook of Ophthalmology* (1893) and *System of Diseases of the Eye* (1897–1900).

OLIVER, FITCH EDWARD (*b. Cambridge, Mass., 1819; d. Boston, Mass., 1892*), physician, historian. Edited diaries of Benjamin Lynde and William Pynchon; author of other studies of Massachusetts history.

OLIVER, GEORGE TENER (*b. Co. Tyrone, Ireland, 1848; d. Pittsburgh, Pa., 1919*), steel manufacturer, lawyer. Brother and business associate of Henry W. Oliver. Publisher of *Pittsburgh Gazette Times;* steadfast proponent of protective tariff; U.S. senator, Republican, from Pennsylvania, 1909–17.

OLIVER, HENRY KEMBLE (*b. Beverly, Mass., 1800; d. Salem, Mass., 1885*), teacher, musician, cotton-mill superintendent. Massachusetts state treasurer, 1860–65; organized pioneer Massachusetts Bureau of Statistics of Labor, 1869, and headed it until 1873.

OLIVER, HENRY WILLIAM (*b. Co. Tyrone, Ireland, 1840; d. Pittsburgh, Pa., 1904*), ironmaster. Brother of George T. Oliver. Came to America as a child. Helped organize a firm in Pittsburgh to manufacture nuts and bolts, 1863; it grew steadily after the Civil War and was incorporated as the Oliver Iron & Steel Co., 1888. Oliver branched out into many phases of the ferrous metal industry; his chief distinction was in early (1892) recognizing the potential of Mesabi range iron ore. Organizing a mining company and building a feeder railroad, Oliver began the ore traffic from the lake ports to Pittsburgh.

OLIVER, JAMES (*b. Liddesdale, Scotland, 1823; d. South Bend, Ind., 1908*), cooper, foundryman, inventor. Came to America as a boy. Began experimenting with chilled iron for making hard-faced plows, *c.* 1865; obtained two patents in 1868 for mould board processes. He went on to more important inventions, one (1869) to prevent castings from cooling too rapidly, others (1871–76) which guaranteed a hard, smooth surface on the face of the mould board. His Oliver Chilled Plow Works, employing his discoveries, was by the time of his death producing 200,000 plows annually.

OLIVER, JOSEPH (*b. in or near New Orleans, La., c. 1885; d. Savannah, Ga., 1938*), cornetist, jazz composer, orchestra leader, known as "King" Oliver. A Negro, Oliver pioneered in bringing New Orleans jazz to a wide audience. [*Supp. 2*]

OLIVER, PAUL AMBROSE (*b. aboard ship in English Channel, 1830; d. 1912*), merchant, Union soldier. Raised in Germany; returned to America, 1849. Invented blasting powder manufacturing processes; headed powder plant in Wilkes-Barre, Pa., 1868–1903.

OLIVER, PETER (*b. Boston, Mass., 1713; d. Birmingham, England, 1791*), Loyalist, Massachusetts provincial jurist and iron manufacturer. Brother of Andrew Oliver (1706–1774). Graduated Harvard, 1730. Judge of superior court, 1756–74; chief justice, 1771–74. Departed with British army to Halifax, N.S., 1776; later settled in England with a British pension.

OLMSTED, DENISON (*b. near East Hartford, Conn., 1791; d. New Haven, Conn., 1859*), scientist, inventor, teacher. Graduated Yale, 1813. Held chairs of mathematics and natural philosophy at Yale, 1825–59; won fame for meteor shower investigations; was author of widely used textbooks.

OLMSTED, FREDERICK LAW (*b. Hartford, Conn., 1822; d. Waverly, Mass., 1903*), landscape architect. Son of a prosperous merchant; attended Yale; studied engineering, 1837–40. An unhappy period in a New York dry-goods importing firm was followed by a year's voyage to China, 1843. He next turned to farming on Staten Island acreage given him by his father and became friendly with Andrew J. Downing. During the 1850's he turned to writing noteworthy travel studies. His *Walks and Talks of an American Farmer in England* (1852) and articles in the *Horticulturist* were followed by a commission from the *New York Times* to report on economic and social conditions in the South. His travels through the Southeast and Texas and a lengthy journey from New Orleans to Richmond were recorded first in letters to the *Times,* then in separate volumes and finally in *The Cotton Kingdom* (2 vols., 1861). This work remains a classic picture and analysis of the planter-slavery system in the *ante bellum* South. His continuing interest in landscaping led to his appointment in 1857 as superintendent of Central Park in New York City; in 1858, he became the park's chief architect. Olmsted and a young English architect, Calvert Vaux, had entered a competition to provide a new design for the park. Their plan won and the two men set out to make the first American park not only a work of art but a successful municipal enterprise. Olmsted took leave of absence, 1861, to become general secretary of the U.S. Sanitary Commission, which he organized successfully. Political opposition in New York and failing health led Olmsted to go to California, 1863; there he superintended John C. Frémont's Mariposa estate, led the move to make Yosemite a state reservation and made designs for the grounds of the new University of California, Berkeley. Returning to New York, he resumed work on Central Park and set up with Vaux (1865) a firm for the practice of landscape architecture. For thirty years he did a richly varied business in city parks, city planning, private estates, historical sites and university designs. Frequent visits to Europe and a succession of talented associates helped Olmsted to gain a towering reputation. His tenacity in seeking to protect quiet, sylvan retreats to be used by busy urban residents led to much political opposition. Central Park and Brooklyn's Prospect Park were his most spectacular New York

City projects, but he also made the plans for the Riverside and Morningside parks. The Boston park system with the famed Arnold Arboretum, Chicago South Park, Detroit's Belle Isle Park and Mount Royal Park in Montreal were other major projects. Representative of his firm's varied designs were those for the Capitol grounds at Washington, D.C., and Albany, N.Y., for Stanford University, for the suburban development at Riverside near Chicago, the Niagara Reservation, George W. Vanderbilt's vast estate "Biltmore" near Asheville, N.C., and a crowning achievement, the design of the grounds of the "White City" at the 1893 Chicago World's Fair.

OLMSTED, GIDEON (*b. East Hartford, Conn., 1749; d. East Hartford, 1845*), sea captain, privateersman. Celebrated, but only nominally successful, as commander of various privateers, 1776–95. The case of the sloop *Active* resulted from one of his captures.

OLMSTED, JOHN CHARLES (*b. Geneva, Switzerland, 1852; d. Brookline, Mass., 1920*), landscape architect. Nephew, stepson and pupil of Frederick L. Olmsted whose work he continued; first president of the American Society of Landscape Architects.

OLMSTED, MARLIN EDGAR (*b. Potter Co., Pa., 1847; d. New York, N.Y., 1913*), corporation lawyer. Orthodox Republican congressman from Pennsylvania, 1897–1913; chairman, Committee on Insular Affairs, *post* 1909. A master of parliamentary procedure.

OLNEY, JESSE (*b. Union, Conn., 1798; d. Stratford, Conn., 1872*), teacher, elementary school textbook writer. His *Practical System of Modern Geography* (1828) and *A New and Improved School Atlas* (1829) became standard works because of the simplicity and novelty of their method.

OLNEY, RICHARD (*b. Oxford, Mass., 1835; d. 1917*), lawyer, statesman. Graduated Brown, 1856; Harvard Law School, 1858. Practiced successfully in Boston as specialist in will cases and corporation law. Appointed U.S. attorney-general, 1893, he took prompt action against seizure of trains by Coxey's Army (1894). In the summer of that year he enjoined the American Railway Union and its president, Eugene V. Debs, from interfering with the U.S. mails by halting railroad operations as a gesture of sympathy with the Pullman Company strikers; in 1895, he directed the argument in the U.S. Supreme Court which successfully upheld his action and declared the union officials in contempt. Thereafter, however, he urged recognition of the rights of organized labor and supported the movement which brought about the arbitration act of 1898. As U.S. secretary of state, 1895–97, Olney drafted the famous threatening declaration to Great Britain in the Venezuela boundary dispute, arguing that "the United States is practically sovereign on this continent." Successful in securing arbitration, he then

sought to persuade Spain to more humane measures in Cuba but resisted pressure to recognize Cuban rebels as belligerents.

OLSON, FLOYD BJERSTJERNE (*b. Minneapolis, Minn., 1891; d. Rochester, Minn., 1936*), lawyer, Farmer-Labor leader. Governor of Minnesota, 1931–36, he was more radical in his pronouncements than in his policies as an executive. [*Supp. 2*]

OLYPHANT, DAVID WASHINGTON CINCINNATUS (*b. Newport, R.I., 1789; d. Cairo, Egypt, 1851*), merchant. Engaged profitably in the China trade *post* 1820; supported and directed Presbyterian mission activity in China.

OLYPHANT, ROBERT MORRISON (*b. New York, N.Y., 1824; d. New York, 1918*), merchant. Son of David W. C. Olyphant. Engaged in China trade, 1844–73. Active in affairs of the Delaware & Hudson Co., he served as its president, 1884–1903.

O'MAHONY, JOHN (*b. Co. Cork, Ireland, 1816; d. New York, N.Y., 1877*), Fenian leader. Came to America, 1853. Headed American branch, Irish Republican Brotherhood, 1858–66 and 1872–77.

O'MALLEY, FRANK WARD (*b. Pittston, Pa., 1875; d. Tours, France, 1932*), journalist, author. Outstanding reporter on *New York Sun*, 1906–20.

OÑATE, JUAN de (*b. Mexico, c. 1549; d. Spain, c. 1624*), colonizer of New Mexico. Son of a wealthy Spanish official in New Spain, he early engaged in military and mining operations in northern Mexico. Receiving an official contract to explore and colonize New Mexico, he led a well-equipped expedition up the Rio Grande, 1597–98. Establishing a capital at San Juan, he promoted missionary activities, and forced Indians of the upper Rio Grande pueblos to submit. He also sent expeditions to present-day Kansas (1601) and the Gulf of California (1605). After his resignation as chief of the colony, 1607, he returned to Mexico. Convicted of having mistreated his soldiers and the Indians, 1614, he was sentenced to banishment. He returned to Spain *ante* 1624.

ONDERDONK, BENJAMIN TREDWELL (*b. New York, N.Y., 1791; d. New York, 1861*), Episcopal clergyman. Brother of Henry U. Onderdonk. Consecrated bishop of New York, 1830. Suspended from office after a celebrated ecclesiastical trial, 1845.

ONDERDONK, HENRY (*b. Manhasset, N.Y., 1804; d. 1886*), teacher, local historian. Collected and published many valuable original documents of early Long Island history, especially Revolutionary War incidents.

ONDERDONK, HENRY USTICK (*b. New York, N.Y., 1789; d. 1858*), physician, Episcopal clergyman. Brother of Benjamin T. Onderdonk. Outstanding as a theological scholar and controversialist, he was consecrated assistant bishop of Pennsylvania, 1827, and succeeded as bishop, 1836. He was suspended at his own request from office and from the ministry for alcoholism (1844–56).

O'NEAL, EDWARD ASBURY (*b. Madison Co., Ala., 1818; d. Florence, Ala., 1890*), lawyer, Confederate officer, Democratic governor of Alabama, 1882–86.

O'NEALE, MARGARET (*b. Washington, D.C., 1796; d. Washington, 1879*). Daughter of a tavern-keeper, "Peggy" O'Neale led a varied, colorful and dramatic life. First married to a navy purser, she charmed Pres. Andrew Jackson's firm friend John H. Eaton, whom she met in 1818 and married soon after her husband's death in 1828. Washington society was scandalized. Jackson stood by his friend and newly appointed secretary of war, despite the consequent dramatic rift in Jackson's cabinet which led to mass resignation, 1831. After sharing her husband's position as governor of Florida and U.S. minister to Spain, Mrs. Eaton returned with him to Washington in 1840 where she resided thereafter.

O'NEALL, JOHN BELTON (*b. Newberry District, S.C., 1793; d. near Newberry, S.C., 1863*), South Carolina jurist and legislator. Held judicial posts, 1828–63. Chief justice of the state, 1859–63; opposed nullification and secession.

O'NEILL, JAMES (*b. Kilkenny, Ireland, 1849; d. New London, Conn., 1920*), actor. Came to America as a child. Early played varied roles; *post* 1882 was identified with "Edmond Dantes" in *Monte Cristo*, which he played more than 6000 times. Father of Eugene G. O'Neill.

O'NEILL, JOHN (*b. Co. Monaghan, Ireland, 1834; d. Omaha, Nebr., 1878*), Union soldier, Fenian leader. Emigrated to America as a youth. Attacked Canada three separate times (1866–71) with small forces which were easily repulsed.

O'NEILL, MARGARET L. [See O'NEALE, MARGARET, 1796–1879.]

OPDYKE, GEORGE (*b. Hunterdon Co., N.J., 1805; d. 1880*), clothing merchant, municipal and currency reformer. Mayor of New York City during the Draft Riots (1863).

OPPENHEIM, JAMES (*b. St. Paul, Minn., 1882; d. 1932*), poet, novelist. Raised in New York City. Author, among other books, of *Songs for the New Age* (1914) and *The Golden Bird* (1923); edited *The Seven Arts*, 1916–17.

OPPER, FREDERICK BURR (*b. Madison, O., 1857; d. New Rochelle, N.Y., 1937*), pioneer comic strip artist. Creator of "Happy Hooligan" (1899), "Alphonse and Gaston," "Maude the Mule," and others; drew political cartoons for the Hearst newspapers.

[*Supp. 2*]

OPTIC, OLIVER. [See ADAMS, WILLIAM TAYLOR, 1822–1897.]

ORCUTT, HIRAM (*b. Acworth, N.H., 1815; d. Boston, Mass., 1899*), educator. Graduated Dartmouth, 1842. Won reputation as principal of Thetford (Vt.) Academy, 1843–55; thereafter headed a succession of New England academies; associate editor, *New England Journal of Education*.

ORD, EDWARD OTHO CRESAP (*b. Cumberland, Md., 1818; d. Havana, Cuba, 1883*), soldier. Graduated West Point, 1839. Served against Seminoles, also in California and Oregon. Appointed brigadier-general of volunteers, Union army, 1861, he was promoted major-general, 1862, after good service in Virginia. Assigned to the Army of the Tennessee, he distinguished himself at Iuka and Corinth; during the Vicksburg campaign, he commanded the XIII Corps. He directed the campaign against Staunton, Va., 1864, in association with Gen. George Crook, and later headed the VIII and XVIII Corps in the operations before Richmond. In January 1865, he took command of the Army of the James. He retired as regular major-general, 1880.

ORD, GEORGE (*b. probably Philadelphia, Pa., 1781; d. Philadelphia, 1866*), naturalist, philologist. Friend and associate of Alexander Wilson; completed Wilson's *American Ornithology* (volumes 8 and 9) and reissued the work, augmented, in 1824–25. Loyalty to Wilson caused attacks by Ord upon J. J. Audubon and the famous "Audubon-Wilson" controversy which began after Wilson's death. Ord accompanied Thomas Say and William Maclure on an extensive field trip through Georgia and Florida, 1818. He was a proud, reserved man of profound learning.

ORDRONAUX, JOHN (*b. New York, N.Y., 1830; d. Glen Head, N.Y., 1908*), lawyer, physician, teacher. First New York State commissioner in lunacy, 1874–82; specialist in medical jurisprudence.

ORDWAY, JOHN (*b. Bow, N.H., c. 1775; d. probably Missouri, c. 1817*), explorer, sergeant in Lewis and Clark Expedition. His important journal was first published in *Wisconsin Historical Collections* (vol. XXII, 1916).

O'REILLY, ALEXANDER (*b. Co. Meath, Ireland, 1722; d. Bonete, Spain, 1794*), Spanish lieutenant-general. Joined Spanish army at age of ten. A leader in army reform and reorganization, he successfully put down the 1768 uprising against Ulloa, first Spanish governor of Louisiana, and swiftly integrated the colony into the Spanish colonial system. His regulations for administration of Louisiana were in effect until the end of Spanish rule.

O'REILLY, HENRY (*b. Carrickmacross, Ireland, 1806; d. 1886*), editor, pioneer telegraph line builder. Came to New York, N.Y., as a boy. Became editor of the *Rochester* (N.Y.) *Daily Advertiser,* 1826, and was a leading citizen of that city. Agitated for enlargement and rebuilding of the Erie Canal; remained a leading exponent of the canal against railroad interests up to the Civil War. Entering into contract, 1845, with Amos Kendall and S. F. B. Morse for financing and construction of telegraph from Pennsylvania to St. Louis and the Great Lakes, he erected 8000 miles of line. Resulting litigation and money difficulties led him to abandon the enterprise.

O'REILLY, JOHN BOYLE (*b. near Drogheda, Ireland, 1844; d. Hull, Mass., 1890*), poet, editor. Came to America, 1869, after an adventurous career as an Irish rebel and consequent deportation to Australia. Became part owner and editor of the Boston *Pilot,* 1876. Author of *Songs, Legends and Ballads* (1878), *Moondyne* (1879), and other books.

O'REILLY, ROBERT MAITLAND (*b. Philadelphia, Pa., 1845; d. Washington, D.C., 1912*), surgeon-general, U.S. Army, 1902–09. Personal physician to President Cleveland. Reformed medical corps practices after Spanish-American War and recommendations of Dodge Commission.

O'RIELLY, HENRY. [See O'REILLY, HENRY, 1806–1886.]

ORMSBY, WATERMAN LILLY (*b. Hampton, Conn., 1809; d. Brooklyn, N.Y., 1883*), banknote engraver.

ORNE, JOHN (*b. Newburyport, Mass., 1834; d. Cambridge, Mass., 1911*), Orientalist, teacher. Graduated Amherst, 1855. Curator of Arabic manuscripts, Semitic Museum of Harvard University, 1889–1911.

ORR, ALEXANDER ECTOR (*b. Strabane, Ireland, 1831; d. 1914*), grain merchant. Came to New York, N.Y., 1851. Active in many civic and business organizations, Orr served as president, Rapid Transit Commission of New York City, 1894–1907. The first subways were efficiently built under his strict supervision. He reorganized the New York Life Insurance Co. after the Hughes Investigation, 1905.

ORR, GUSTAVUS JOHN (*b. Orrville, S.C., 1819; d. 1887*), educator. Graduated Emory, 1844. Reforming pioneer school commissioner of Georgia, 1872–87; agent for Peabody Fund in Georgia.

ORR, HUGH (*b. Lochwinnoch, Scotland, 1715; d. 1798*), tool-maker, Revolutionary patriot, manufacturer. Came to Massachusetts, 1740; settled in East Bridgewater and prospered as maker of edged tools. Produced first muskets made in the colonies, 1748; during the Revolution, made great numbers of muskets and cannon, using advanced techniques, and produced quantities of cannon-shot. Under state direction and encouragement, Orr induced English mechanics skilled in textile machine manufacture to emigrate to Massachusetts, but the sample machines

produced by them in his shop (*c.* 1786–87) were not practical.

ORR, JAMES LAWRENCE (*b. Craytonville, S.C., 1822; d. St. Petersburg, Russia, 1873*), lawyer, South Carolina legislator. Brother of Jehu A. Orr. Congressman, Democrat, from South Carolina, 1849–59; speaker of the House, 1857–59. Anti-secessionist and supporter of Stephen A. Douglas's policies, Orr reversed himself in 1860, advocated secession and served as a Confederate States senator, 1861–65. Espousing President Johnson's policies, he was elected governor of South Carolina and served 1866–68, advising the whites to accept the Reconstruction acts. Losing the confidence of the people, he joined the Radical party, 1868, and was elected to the circuit bench. He supported U.S. Grant in 1872, and was appointed U.S. minister to Russia after Grant's election.

ORR, JEHU AMAZIAH (*b. Anderson Co., S.C., 1828; d. Columbus, Miss., 1921*), Mississippi legislator, lawyer. Brother of James L. Orr. Moderate Democrat in Mississippi politics before and after Civil War.

ORTH, GODLOVE STEIN (*b. near Lebanon, Pa., 1817; d. Lafayette, Ind., 1882*), politician, lawyer. Pursued long career in Indiana as Whig, Know-Nothing, and Republican legislator and congressman. U.S. minister to Austria-Hungary, 1875–76. Orth never hesitated to sacrifice principle for party solidarity; no unpopular measure ever received his vote.

ORTHWEIN, CHARLES F. (*b. near Stuttgart, Germany, 1839; d. St. Louis, Mo., 1898*), grain merchant. Emigrated to America, 1854; began grain commission business in St. Louis during Civil War. Sent first grain shipment to Europe via Mississippi River, 1866; worked generally to encourage St. Louis export trade.

ORTON, EDWARD FRANCIS BAXTER (*b. Deposit, N.Y., 1829; d. Columbus, O., 1899*), geologist, educator. State geologist of Ohio, 1882–99; brought out last three volumes of state geological survey begun by John S. Newberry. Opposed reckless waste of natural gas and advocated conservation of state resources.

ORTON, HARLOW SOUTH (*b. Madison Co., N.Y., 1817; d. Madison, Wis., 1895*), lawyer, Wisconsin jurist and legislator. Dean of University of Wisconsin law school, 1869–74; justice of Wisconsin supreme court, 1878–94, and chief justice, 1894–95.

ORTON, JAMES (*b. Seneca Falls, N.Y., 1830; d. Peru, 1877*), Presbyterian clergyman, zoologist, explorer, educator. Made three productive expeditions to the Amazon-equatorial Andes region (1867, 1873, and 1876); wrote *The Andes and the Amazons* (complete edition, 1876). Professor of natural history at Vassar *post* 1869.

ORTON, WILLIAM (*b. near Cuba, N.Y., 1826; d. 1878*), lawyer, telegraph executive. Instrumental in negotiations leading to creation of Western Union Telegraph Co. as a monopoly, 1866; served as its president, 1867–78.

ORTYNSKY, STEPHEN SOTER (*b. Galicia, Austria, 1866; d. Philadelphia, Pa., 1916*), Catholic prelate. Greek Catholic bishop for the United States *post* 1907; ministered to Americans of Ukrainian and Ruthenian extraction.

OSBORN, CHARLES (*b. Guilford Co., N.C., 1775; d. Porter Co., Ind., 1850*), Quaker minister, Abolitionist. Led abolition movements in Tennessee, Ohio and Indiana; published the *Philanthropist* (Mt. Pleasant, O.), 1817–18.

OSBORN, HENRY FAIRFIELD (*b. Fairfield, Conn., 1857; d. Garrison, N.Y., 1935*), paleontologist. Son of William H. Osborn. Graduated Princeton, 1877; made special studies in biological sciences at several New York City medical schools and also at Cambridge and London, England. Taught natural sciences at Princeton, 1881–91; organized department of biology at Columbia, 1891, and taught there until *c.* 1907. Also in 1891, Osborn organized a department of mammalian paleontology for the American Museum of Natural History, New York. His connection with the museum continued for 45 years; he served as its president, 1908–33. During his association with it, the museum became a world leader, its collection of fossil vertebrates became second to none, and its displays, made under his direction, were effective in providing direct and interesting instruction for laymen. A prolific writer of papers and books, he popularized paleontology; among his more influential books were *The Age of Mammals* (1910) and *Men of the Old Stone Age* (1925). An evolutionary theorist, he originated a number of descriptive principles (such as that of "adaptive radiation") which were of value. [Supp. 1]

OSBORN, HENRY STAFFORD (*b. Philadelphia, Pa., 1823; d. Oxford, O., 1894*), Presbyterian clergyman, map-maker, metallurgist. Taught at Lafayette College and Miami University. Author, among other books, of *New Descriptive Geography of Palestine* (1877) and *Metallurgy, Iron and Steel* (1869).

OSBORN, LAUGHTON (*b. New York, N.Y., c. 1809; d. New York, 1878*), poet, dramatist. Graduated Columbia, 1827. Prolific writer of limited talents and eccentric habits; spent much time attacking critics. Among his books were *The Vision of Rubeta* (1838) and *Arthur Carryl* (1841).

OSBORN, NORRIS GALPIN (*b. New Haven, Conn., 1858; d. New Haven, 1932*), editor, civil service and prison reformer. Influential editor of the *New Haven Evening Register* (1884–1907) and *New Haven Journal-Courier* (1907–32).

OSBORN, SELLECK (*b. Trumbull, Conn., c. 1782; d. Philadelphia, Pa., 1826*), Democratic journalist, poet. Editor of *The Witness* (Litchfield, Conn.,) 1805–08; the *American Watchman* (Wilmington, Del.,) 1817–20; the *New York Patriot*, 1823–24. A collection of his poems was published in Boston, Mass., 1823.

OSBORN, THOMAS ANDREW (*b. Meadville, Pa., 1836; d. Meadville, 1898*), lawyer, businessman, Kansas legislator. Settled in Kansas, 1857. Republican governor of Kansas, 1873–77; U.S. minister to Chile and Brazil, 1877–85.

OSBORN, THOMAS OGDEN (*b. Jersey, O., 1832; d. Washington, D.C., 1904*), Chicago lawyer, Union soldier. U.S. minister to Argentine Republic, 1874–85; helped adjust Patagonian boundary dispute with Chile (1881). Promoted South American railroads.

OSBORN, WILLIAM HENRY (*b. Salem, Mass., 1820; d. New York, N.Y., 1894*), merchant, railroad promoter and president, philanthropist. Controlled Illinois Central Railroad, 1855–82.

OSBORNE, JAMES WALKER (*b. Charlotte, N.C., 1859; d. New York, N.Y., 1919*), lawyer, reformer. Admitted to New York bar, 1885; was outstanding assistant district attorney, 1891–1902. Exposed seamy social and political conditions in Albany, N.Y., 1911; investigated abuses at Sing Sing prison, 1913.

OSBORNE, THOMAS BURR (*b. New Haven, Conn., 1859; d. New Haven, 1929*), biochemist. Grandson of Eli W. Blake. Graduated Yale, 1881; Ph.D., 1885. Staff member, Connecticut Agricultural Station, 1886–1928. Foremost expert on the proteins of plants. His first work was on proteins of the oat-kernel (1891), followed in the next decade by descriptions of the proteins in 32 other seeds. In 1906 he began a series of hydrolytic decompositions of purified proteins that led *post* 1909 to studies of their nutritive properties. He isolated and demonstrated dietary value of substance since known as vitamin A; later did similar work with what became known as vitamin B. His monograph *The Vegetable Proteins* (1909, extensively revised 1924) remains a biochemical classic.

OSBORNE, THOMAS MOTT (*b. Auburn, N.Y., 1859; d. Auburn, 1926*), prison reformer. Graduated Harvard, 1884; worked in, and later headed, father's prosperous agricultural machinery factory. Appointed chairman of the New York commission for prison reform, 1913, he began his tenure by "serving" a week's term in the Auburn prison, later recorded in his *Within Prison Walls* (1914). He pioneered in introducing a sense of corporate responsibility among prisoners with the Mutual Welfare League plan; he also founded the Welfare League Association (an aid society for discharged prisoners) and the National Society of Penal Information, both now merged in The Osborne Association. He served as warden of Sing Sing, 1914–16, and as commandant of Portsmouth Naval Prison, 1917–20.

OSCEOLA (*b. among the Creek Indians on Tallapoosa River, Ga., c. 1800; d. Charleston, S.C., 1838*), leader in the Second Seminole War. Although not born to high rank or elected a chief, Osceola (also known as Powell) became influential among the Seminoles and opposed the treaty of Payne's Landing (1832), at which some Seminole chiefs agreed to removal across the Mississippi. Vigorously rejecting all efforts to make Seminoles move from their land in 1835, he precipitated war, hiding Seminole women and children in the swamps and commencing effective harassing tactics against the U.S. forces sent to put down the uprising. Under a flag of truce, Osceola was treacherously arrested, October 1837, and imprisoned in Fort Moultrie where he died.

OSGOOD, FRANCES SARGENT LOCKE (*b. Boston, Mass., 1811; d. New York, N.Y., 1850*), poet. Prolific author of rather thin poetry; remembered mainly for love affair with Edgar Allan Poe, 1845.

OSGOOD, GEORGE LAURIE (*b. Chelsea, Mass., 1844; d. Godalming, England, 1922*), singer, composer, conductor, teacher. A leader in Boston musical life; organized and conducted Boston Singers' Society, 1890; author of a *Guide in the Art of Singing* (1874).

OSGOOD, HERBERT LEVI (*b. Canton, Maine, 1855; d. 1918*), historian. Graduated Amherst, 1877; studied also at Yale and Berlin; Ph.D., Columbia, 1889. Taught at Columbia *post* 1890. His seven-volume study of American colonial history (1904–24) was a pioneer scientific documentation of the struggle between British executive authorities and the colonial assemblies.

OSGOOD, HOWARD (*b. Plaquemines Parish, La., 1831; d. Rochester, N.Y., 1911*), Baptist clergyman, author. Learned, orthodox professor of Old Testament interpretation at Rochester Theological Seminary, 1875–1901.

OSGOOD, JACOB (*b. South Hampton, N.H., 1777; d. 1844*), founder of the Osgoodites. Opposed paid ministers, law-courts, magistrates, Abolitionists and military training. Love of God and neighbor was the only theological principle accepted by Osgood and his sect.

OSGOOD, SAMUEL (*b. Andover, Mass., 1747/48; d. New York, N.Y., 1813*), Revolutionary soldier, Massachusetts and New York legislator. Able member of finance committees in Continental Congress, 1781–84; opposed Constitution as leading to excessive consolidation. First U.S. postmaster-general, 1789–91; supported Jefferson *post* 1800.

O'SHAUGHNESSY, MICHAEL MAURICE (*b. Limerick, Ireland, 1864; d. San Francisco, Calif., 1934*),

hydraulic engineer. Graduated Royal University, Dublin, 1884; emigrated to California, 1885. The most important of his many undertakings was the construction of the Hetch Hetchy water supply system, 1912–34. [*Supp. 1*]

O'SHAUGHNESSY, NELSON JARVIS WATERBURY (*b. New York, N.Y., 1876; d. Vienna, Austria, 1932*), diplomat. Entered U.S. diplomatic service, 1904. Made second secretary of the U.S. Embassy at Mexico City, 1911, he acted as chargé d'affaires, July 1913—April 1914, during the crisis of that period. He was later a severe critic of President Wilson's policy with respect to Huerta. [*Supp. 1*]

O'SHEA, MICHAEL VINCENT (*b. LeRoy, N.Y., 1866; d. Madison, Wis., 1932*), educator, author. Professor of education, University of Wisconsin, *post* 1897. Popular lecturer on educational techniques and practices; wrote *Newer Ways with Children* (1929).

OSLER, WILLIAM (*b. Bond Head, Upper Canada, 1849; d. Oxford, England, 1919*), physician. At the time of his death Osler was probably the greatest figure in the medical world. After attending grammar schools at Dundas and Barrie, Ontario, he entered Trinity College School at Weston with the intention of becoming a minister. Influenced by teachers there, he decided to become a physician and entered the Toronto Medical School, 1868. After two years he went on to McGill Medical School where he graduated, 1872. At McGill he was particularly influenced by Dr. Robert Howard, a scholarly and thorough teacher by Edinburgh School methods. Osler next spent two years visiting the great clinics in England, Berlin and Vienna; he gave much time to study of histology, physiology, and experimental pathology at University College Hospital, London. There he observed in circulating blood, before anyone else, the presence of what were later called "blood-platelets." In 1875 he was appointed professor of medicine at McGill. He took a wide interest in all medical activities in Montreal, writing for medical journals, delivering inspiring addresses, and enlivening interest in medical associations. He organized a demonstration course in pathology at the Montreal General Hospital, modeled on methods he had observed in Berlin. His continuing interest in clinical medicine while at Montreal led to a revolution in technique; patients were given little medicine but much encouragement and interest. A sharp rise in recoveries attended this method. By 1884 Osler had come to recognize the possibilities of medical school work on a university basis where teachers would be largely released from the harassment of practice. This recognition led him to leave Montreal and accept appointment as professor of clinical medicine in the University of Pennsylvania (1884), the beginning of a 21-year period of residence and work in the United States.

In Philadelphia, Osler's rare traits of personality

together with thorough professional methods made him popular as teacher, clinician and consultant. His many contributions to medical literature included *The Gulstonian Lectures on Malignant Endocarditis* (1885), and the Cartwright Lectures, *On Certain Problems of the Blood Corpuscles* (1886). In September 1888, Osler was appointed physician-in-chief to the new Johns Hopkins Hospital, Baltimore, and there he remained for 16 years, probably the most eventful and most influential period of his life. For the first four years Osler devoted much of his time to organizing the clinical staff and to the institutional work of the Johns Hopkins Medical School which opened in 1893. Organized upon the unit system with a graded resident staff as used in German universities, the school employed teaching methods which accorded with those in Great Britain and France. The teaching program included instruction of small groups of students who served in the wards as clinical clerks and surgical dressers, practical work in clinical laboratories, amphitheater clinics, and work in the outpatient clinics. Osler did everything he could to arouse in his students a love of thoroughness and orderliness, an appreciation of medical knowledge for its own sake, and a desire to make original contributions of their own. Through his pupils he may be said to have created an American school of internal medicine. In 1891 he published his classic *Principles and Practice of Medicine.* Although his main contribution in the Johns Hopkins period lay in his stimulation and insemination of the minds of others, Osler also did important research into typhoid fever, malaria, pneumonia, cardio-vascular disease and tuberculosis. Further, he found time to be an active propagandist in the field of public health, to make Johns Hopkins Hospital a place of refuge for the sick poor of Baltimore, to build up medical libraries there, and to deliver effective occasional addresses of lasting value, such as *Aequanimitas* (1889), which remains a powerful and affecting work, *The Master Word in Medicine* (1903), and *The Student Life* (1905).

Because he was slowly being overwhelmed by patients who came from near and far to seek his aid, and for reasons of health, Osler accepted the Regius Professorship of Medicine in the University of Oxford, 1905; he held it until his death. He became a curator of the Bodleian Library, helped develop the Oxford Medical School and took an active part in setting up the Royal Society of Medicine and launching the *Quarterly Journal of Medicine.* Although Osler was a competent and productive investigator and researcher, most of his contemporaries placed highest emphasis upon his ability to inspire others, to lend friendly counsel and to mediate disputes in the profession.

OSSOLI, MARGARET FULLER. [See FULLER, SARAH MARGARET, 1810–1850.]

OSTENACO. [See OUTACITY, fl. 1756–1777.]

OSTEN SACKEN, CARL ROBERT ROMANOVICH VON DER (*b. St. Petersburg, Russia, 1828; d. Heidelberg, Germany, 1906*), entomologist, diplomat. Came to America, 1856, as secretary to Russian legation; was consul-general in New York City, 1862–71. Wrote a critical catalogue for the Smithsonian Institution of described diptera in North America (1858 and 1878); was co-author of *Monographs of the Diptera of North America* (1862–73).

OSTERHAUS, PETER JOSEPH (*b. Coblenz, Germany, 1823; d. Duisburg, Germany, 1917*), Union major-general, U.S. consular official.

OSTROMISLENSKY, IWAN IWANOWICH (*b. Moscow, Russia, 1880; d. New York, N.Y., 1939*), chemist. Came to America, 1922. Pioneer in development of polystyrene and synthetic rubber. [*Supp.* 2]

O'SULLIVAN, JOHN LOUIS (*b. Gibraltar, 1813; d. New York, N.Y., 1895*), lawyer, journalist, diplomat. Helped found, and edited, *United States Magazine and Democratic Review* (1837–46), a leading Democratic and nationalist organ. Probably coined term "Manifest Destiny" (1845).

OTACITE. [See OUTACITY, fl. 1756–1777.]

OTERMÍN, ANTONIO de (*fl. 1678–1683*), Spanish governor of New Mexico. Leader of settlers in retreat from Santa Fé to present Juárez (opposite El Paso, Texas) after Pueblo Indian uprising and massacre, 1680.

OTEY, JAMES HERVEY (*b. Bedford Co., Va., 1800; d. Memphis, Tenn., 1863*), Episcopal clergyman. Consecrated bishop of Tennessee, 1834; served until his death. Helped found University of the South.

OTIS, BASS (*b. Bridgewater, Mass., 1784; d. Philadelphia, Pa., 1861*), portrait painter, engraver, pioneer in American lithography.

OTIS, CHARLES EUGENE (*b. Barry Co., Mich., 1846; d. St. Paul, Minn., 1917*), Minnesota jurist.

OTIS, CHARLES ROLLIN (*b. Troy, N.Y., 1835; d. Summerville, S.C., 1927*), inventor, elevator manufacturer. Son of Elisha G. Otis.

OTIS, ELISHA GRAVES (*b. Halifax, Vt., 1811; d. Yonkers, N.Y., 1861*), mechanic, inventor. Engaged in constructing a bedstead factory at Yonkers, N.Y., 1852, Otis devised some unique features for an elevator in the structure, among them a safety appliance that prevented the elevator from falling if the lifting chain or cable broke. His invention attracted notice and he began a small manufactory at Yonkers. Orders came slowly, but in 1861 he established a firm foundation for his business by inventing and patenting a steam elevator; his sons carried on his work with great success.

OTIS, ELWELL STEPHEN (*b. Frederick, Md., 1838; d. Rochester, N.Y., 1909*), lawyer, Union soldier. Established command school at Fort Leavenworth, 1881; commanded all American forces in Philippines at outbreak of Aguinaldo's insurrection, 1899; retired as major-general, 1902.

OTIS, FESSENDEN NOTT (*b. Ballston Springs, N.Y., 1825; d. New Orleans, La., 1900*), physician. Graduated N.Y. Medical College, 1852; taught at N.Y. College of Physicians and Surgeons, 1862–90. Concentrated on genito-urinary diseases; first established curability of urethral stricture though his theory of cure is no longer accepted.

OTIS, GEORGE ALEXANDER (*b. Boston, Mass., 1830; d. Washington, D.C., 1881*), U.S. Army surgeon. Editor, *The Medical and Surgical History of the War of the Rebellion* (surgical volumes, 1870, 1876).

OTIS, HARRISON GRAY (*b. Boston, Mass., 1765; d. Boston, 1848*), lawyer, statesman. Nephew of James Otis and Mercy Otis Warren. Graduated Harvard, 1783; read law with John Lowell. Rose to leading place at the Boston bar and earned a large income, partly by successful land speculations in the decade 1785–95. Early became a leading Federalist politician through skill in oratory, and served in U.S. Congress, 1797–1801; supported President Adams in reconciliation with France, 1799. Represented Boston for many years in the Massachusetts legislature; helped plan, and was a leading figure at, the Hartford Convention in which he consistently threw his influence against proposals to force a break with the national government. U.S. senator from Massachusetts, 1817–22; mayor of Boston, 1829–31. Deprecated the abolition movement but defended freedom of speech on the slavery question. A Whig in later life.

OTIS, HARRISON GRAY (*b. Marietta, O., 1837; d. Hollywood, Calif., 1917*), Union soldier, journalist. Removed to California, 1876; active manager of the Times-Mirror Co. in Los Angeles, *post* 1886. A conservative Republican, of great influence in Southern California.

OTIS, JAMES (*b. West Barnstable, Mass., 1725; d. Andover, Mass., 1783*), politician, publicist. Born of a lawyer father, Otis prepared for Harvard with the minister in West Barnstable and graduated in 1743. Studying law under Jeremiah Gridley, he was admitted to the bar in Plymouth County, 1748, and two years later moved to Boston. He married Ruth Cunningham, well-dowered daughter of a Boston merchant, 1755. By painstaking study Otis became learned in the common, civil, and admiralty law and legal theory. A supple mind coupled with brilliant and captivating pleading made him early known in all parts of the province. This reputation led to his appointment by Gov. Pownall as king's advocate general of the vice-admiralty court at Boston, a lucrative

post. In 1760, Pitt ordered the Sugar Act of 1733 to be strictly enforced. The royal customs collectors applied to the superior court of the province for writs of assistance in order to help them in searches for evidence of violation. Otis, in his official capacity, was expected to argue for the writs. Instead he resigned and undertook, for the Boston merchants, to oppose issuance. Circumstances were such as to cause his motives to be questioned. At this time, Otis's father was speaker of the House and had great influence among country members. When Chief Justice Stephen Sewall died in 1760, the elder Otis expected to be appointed to the court with the prospect of becoming chief justice. His ambition was thwarted, however, when Thomas Hutchinson was appointed to the chief justiceship. Since this occurred just before James Otis resigned his post and began to oppose issuance of the writs of assistance, many suggested that his actions stemmed from his father's disappointment. Otis vehemently denied the charge, but the Loyalists ever afterwards insisted that Otis's entire political course was determined by frustrated family ambition.

In February 1761, Otis argued the illegality of writs of assistance before the superior court. What he said is not precisely known, but his general line of attack was based upon the presumed existence of a fundamental law which embodied the principles of the natural law and was superior to acts of Parliament. The slogan "Taxation without representation is tyranny" appears in John Adams's 1820 expansion of his notes of the proceedings. Otis claimed that acts against the Constitution and national equity should be declared void. He lost the case but Attorney General de Grey ruled in 1766 that the act of Parliament in question did not authorize writs of assistance in the colonies. Otis's speech, however, provided the base for continuing attacks upon acts of Parliament which regulated colonial commerce and taxation. Soon after his speech, Otis was elected one of Boston's representatives to the General Court where he helped to rouse sentiment against the Crown officials. In his first political pamphlet, *A Vindication of the Conduct of the House of Representatives* (1762), Otis summarized the rights of Englishmen. Later, in a notable speech in Faneuil Hall, he declaimed at length on the proposition that settlers in the colonies should enjoy all the rights, privileges and duties of Englishmen living in the mother country and asserted that the difficulties of the time had been caused by illegal attempts to extend the royal prerogative.

From 1761 to 1769 Otis was the recognized political leader of Massachusetts Bay. Rumors of *rapprochement* with Gov. Hutchinson often affected his standing with the popular party, but his speeches and pamphlets in these years indicate a consistent defense of the colonists' rights as against alleged royal and Parliamentary encroachments. His pamphlet *The Rights of the British Colonies Asserted and Proved* (1764) reasserted his position on natural rights as developed in the writs of assistance speech and defined the constitutional position of the colonies in the single commonwealth which he believed the British Empire to be.

One of three Massachusetts delegates to the Stamp Act Congress convened in New York City (1765), he was a leading figure there. The Congress accepted his constitutional position but rejected his argument in the *Rights* pamphlet that the colonies should have representation in Parliament. Otis, however, continued to urge his idea in another pamphlet, *Considerations on behalf of the Colonists, in a Letter to a Noble Lord* (1765). Otis's pamphlets had a profound effect in the colonies and in England, but he failed to see the possibility of a federal solution to the problem and never faced the choice between submission and revolution. He disapproved of violent action, recommending peaceful remonstrances. In 1768 Otis helped to adopt the Non-importation declaration in the House as the colonial response to the Townshend Act. Struck on the head during an altercation with a Crown official, 1769, he was insane save for short intervals thereafter. His subsequent political opinions and actions are unimportant. He died as the result of a stroke of lightning.

OTT, ISAAC (*b. Northampton Co., Pa., 1847; d. Easton, Pa., 1916*), physician, neurologist. Credited with discovery of the hormone of milk secretion; demonstrated that injury to the corpus striatum causes body temperature rise.

OTTASSITE. [See Outacity, fl. 1756–1777.]

OTTENDORFER, ANNA BEHR UHL (*b. Würzburg, Germany, 1815; d. 1884*), journalist, philanthropist. Came to America *c.* 1837; married Oswald Ottendorfer, 1859. Owner and manager *post* 1852 of the *New-Yorker Staats-Zeitung*, which she made prosperous and influential.

OTTENDORFER, OSWALD (*b. Zwittau [Moravia], Austria-Hungary, 1826; d. 1900*), journalist, philanthropist. Came to America, 1850; married Anna B. U. Ottendorfer, 1859. Editor of the *New-Yorker Staats-Zeitung, post* 1858; influential anti-Tammany Democrat and reformer.

OTTERBEIN, PHILIP WILLIAM (*b. Dillenburg, Prussia, 1726; d. Baltimore, Md., 1813*), clergyman. Educated for Reformed ministry in Germany; arrived in New York, 1752, to serve as missionary in Pennsylvania. Although he always considered himself a minister of the Reformed Church, he promoted a nonsectarian religious movement, which shortly before his death he made an independent denomination, the Church of the United Brethren in Christ. It was organized on the Wesleyan model with a strong evangelistic strain. Otterbein, a zealous and effective minister, labored to bring organized religion to scattered German settlements in Pennsylvania and Maryland.

OTTO, BODO (*b. Hanover, Germany, 1711; d. Reading, Pa., 1787*), physician. Came to America, 1755; practiced in New Jersey and Pennsylvania. Appointed senior surgeon of the Middle Department of the Continental hospitals, 1776, he served devotedly and effectively until 1782.

OTTO, JOHN CONRAD (*b. near Woodbury, N.J., 1774; d. Philadelphia, Pa., 1844*), physician. Grandson of Bodo Otto; pupil and friend of Benjamin Rush whom he succeeded as physician to the Pennsylvania Hospital, 1813–34. Gave first adequate description of hemophilia (1803) and noted its peculiar hereditary nature.

OTTO, WILLIAM TOD (*b. Philadelphia, Pa., 1816; d. Philadelphia, 1905*), Indiana jurist. Son of John C. Otto. Assistant U.S. secretary of the interior, 1863–71.

OUCONNASTOTE. [See Oconostota, d. 1785.]

OURAY (*b. probably Taos, N. Mex., c. 1833; d. Los Piños Reservation, Colo., 1880*), Ute Indian chief. Born of an Uncompahgre father and an Apache mother, Ouray spent much of his childhood among Mexican rancheros, from whom he learned to speak Spanish correctly. Became chief of the Uncompahgre, 1860; was appointed an interpreter at Los Piños Reservation, 1862; in 1863 signed a treaty by which he was recognized by the United States as head chief for all the Western Utes. Thereafter he helped put down occasional uprisings and negotiated with the government in defense of his tribe's interests.

OUTACITY (*fl. 1756–1777*), Cherokee chief, known also as "Judd's Friend" and "Mankiller." Visited London, 1762, under tutelage of Henry Timberlake. He and his family were received by the King and sat for a Reynolds portrait.

OUTCAULT, RICHARD FELTON (*b. Lancaster, O., 1863; d. Flushing, N.Y., 1928*), comic artist. Inaugurated the "funny paper" in November 1894 as cartoonist for the New York *World*. Created the "Yellow Kid" and "Buster Brown."

OUTERBRIDGE, ALEXANDER EWING (*b. Philadelphia, Pa., 1850; d. Philadelphia, 1928*), metallurgist, official of the U.S. Mint. Developed method for obtaining thin films of metal for microscopic studies, 1876; made notable studies of molecule mobility in cast iron, 1894–96.

OUTERBRIDGE, EUGENIUS HARVEY (*b. Philadelphia, Pa., 1860; d. 1932*), merchant. Brother of Alexander E. Outerbridge. In business in New York City *post* 1878, he is regarded as the "father of the Port of New York Authority." [*Supp. 1*]

OVERMAN, FREDERICK (*b. Elberfeld, Germany, c. 1803; d. Philadelphia, Pa., 1852*), metallurgist, authority on metallurgy of iron. Came to America,

1842. Wrote *The Manufacture of Steel* (1851) and *A Treatise on Metallurgy* (1852).

OVERMAN, LEE SLATER (*b. Salisbury, N.C., 1854; d. 1930*), lawyer, North Carolina legislator. U.S. senator, Democrat, 1903–30. Vigorously supported Clayton Act (1914); is remembered for the 1918 Overman Law which widened the president's power to transfer functions of one government department to another.

OVERTON, JOHN (*b. Louisa Co., Va., 1766; d. Nashville, Tenn., 1833*), Tennessee jurist, politician. Early business partner and independent-minded political supporter of Andrew Jackson.

OWEN, DAVID DALE (*b. near New Lanark, Scotland, 1807; d. 1860*), geologist. Son of the British social reformer Robert Owen; brother of Robert D. Owen. Emigrated to New Harmony, Ind., 1828; attended lectures in geology and chemistry in London, England, 1831–32; graduated Ohio Medical College, 1836. Began his career of geological surveying, 1836, with a trip through Tennessee; was state geologist of Indiana, 1837. Conducted for the federal government a geological survey of mineral deposits in the Dubuque, Iowa and Mineral Point, Wisconsin area, 1839. He followed this by extensive surveys in Wisconsin, Minnesota, and Iowa, which he described in a *Report* (1852), and he served successively thereafter as state geologist of Kentucky, Arkansas, and Indiana for each of which he published valuable survey reports.

OWEN, EDWARD THOMAS (*b. Hartford, Conn., 1850; d. Madison, Wis., 1931*), educator. University of Wisconsin teacher of Romance languages, 1878–1914. Pioneered in effort to rationalize grammar through a radical revision of method and nomenclature based on analysis of the antecedent psychological states that prompt expression.

OWEN, GRIFFITH (*b. near Dolgelly, Wales, c. 1647; d. Philadelphia, Pa., 1717*), Quaker preacher, surgeon. Leader of the Welsh Quakers who settled (1684) in Lower Merion Township near Philadelphia. Member of Provincial Council, 1690–1717.

OWEN, ROBERT DALE (*b. Glasgow, Scotland, 1801; d. Lake George, N.Y., 1877*), social reformer, author. Son of Robert Owen, British industrialist and social reformer; brother of David D. Owen. Helped set up New Harmony community in Indiana, 1826–27; thereafter joined Frances Wright in a coterie known as the "Free Enquirers," formed to advocate liberal divorce laws, widespread industrial education, and a more nearly equal distribution of wealth. Owen continued to pursue these objectives long after the coterie disbanded. Resuming residence in Indiana *c.* 1833, he served three terms in the legislature as a Democrat (1836–38) and two in the U.S. Congress (1843–47). A resolution introduced by him in 1844

became basis for solution of the Oregon boundary dispute. He also helped establish the Smithsonian Institution. Later he became an influential advocate of emancipation. His autobiography, *Threading My Way,* was published in 1874.

OWEN, THOMAS McADORY (*b. Jefferson Co., Ala., 1866; d. Montgomery, Ala., 1920*), lawyer, archivist, historian. Established and later directed the Alabama Department of Archives, first state department of its kind, 1901. [*Supp. 1*]

OWEN, WILLIAM FLORENCE (*b. Limerick, Ireland, 1844; d. 1906*), actor. Made début at Salem, O., 1867; associated with Madame Modjeska, Augustin Daly, and Mrs. Fiske, he gained fame in such comic roles as "Falstaff" and "Touchstone."

OWENS, JOHN EDMOND (*b. Liverpool, England, 1823; d. near Baltimore, Md., 1886*), actor, theatrical manager. Came to America as a child; was raised in Philadelphia, Pa., where he made début, 1840. Excelled in standard comic roles, particularly Yankee characters.

OWENS, MICHAEL JOSEPH (*b. Mason Co., Va., now W. Va., 1859; d. Toledo, O., 1923*), inventor. Developed and perfected the first automatic bottle-blowing machine (patented 1895, 1904); was associated with Edward D. Libbey in glass manufacturing *post* 1888.

OWRE, ALFRED (*b. Hammerfest, Norway, 1870; d. 1935*), physician, dentist, educator. D.D.S., University of Minnesota, 1894. As professor and dean at the college of dentistry, University of Minnesota, *post* 1902, and as dean of the school of dentistry at Columbia, 1927–34, Owre fought for reforms in dental education which were bitterly opposed in his time but in many cases adopted after his death. [*Supp. 1*]

OWSLEY, WILLIAM (*b. Virginia, 1782; d. near Danville, Ky., 1862*), Kentucky jurist, politician. Member and vigorous supporter of the "Old Court" in the dispute of the 1820's; Whig governor, 1844–48.

PACA, WILLIAM (*b. near Abingdon, Md., 1740; d. Talbot Co., Md., 1799*), Maryland legislator, signer of the Declaration of Independence, jurist. Active in political opposition to the Proprietor of the colony. Elected to First and Second Continental Congresses (served 1774–79), Paca devoted his energy and much of his fortune to winning the Revolution. He participated in drawing up the first state constitution, served in the state Senate, was elected three times governor of Maryland (1782–85), and served as federal district judge, 1789–99.

PACE, EDWARD ALOYSIUS (*b. Starke, Fla., 1861; d. Washington, D.C., 1938*), Roman Catholic clergyman, educator. Graduated St. Charles College (Md.),

1880; D.Th., Rome, 1886; Ph.D., Leipzig, 1891. A pioneer in scientific psychology and modern scholastic philosophy, he was professor of psychology (1891–94) and of philosophy (1894–1935) at Catholic University of America. [*Supp. 2*]

PACHECO, ROMUALDO (*b. Santa Barbara, Calif., 1831; d. Oakland, Calif., 1899*), California legislator and official, diplomat. Republican governor of California, 1875–76; performed valuable service in helping to unite native Californians with American settlers.

PACK, CHARLES LATHROP (*b. Lexington, Mich., 1857; d. New York, N.Y., 1937*), pioneer forest conservationist. Co-founder, National Conservation Association and American Tree Association; president, 1930–37, Charles Lathrop Pack Forestry Foundation. [*Supp. 2*]

PACKARD, ALPHEUS SPRING (*b. Chelmsford, Mass., 1798; d. Squirrel Island, Maine, 1884*), educator. Brother of Joseph Packard. Served in many academic capacities at Bowdoin, 1819–84.

PACKARD, ALPHEUS SPRING (*b. Brunswick, Maine, 1839; d. Providence, R.I., 1905*), entomologist, teacher. Son of Alpheus S. Packard (1798–1884); grandson of Jesse Appleton. Graduated Bowdoin, 1861; M.D., Maine Medical School, 1864. Early interested and trained in geology, Packard soon found his life's work in entomology and first gained notice as author of *Guide to the Study of Insects* (1869). An ardent evolutionist, Packard had taxonomic skills, but his principal contribution lay in the biological aspects of his field. His most important later publications were *Insects Injurious to Forest and Shade Trees* (1881), *Text-Book of Entomology* (1898), and his monumental *Monograph of the Bombycine Moths* (1895–1914) which was finished by T. D. A. Cockerell. At his death he was generally recognized as the most learned and accomplished entomologist in America. *Post* 1878, he taught at Brown University.

PACKARD, FREDERICK ADOLPHUS (*b. Marlboro, Mass., 1794; d. Philadelphia, Pa., 1867*), editor, writer. Editorial secretary of American Sunday School Union, 1828–67; persistently attacked exclusion of orthodox religion from public educational systems.

PACKARD, JAMES WARD (*b. Warren, O., 1863; d. Cleveland, O., 1928*), engineer, manufacturer, inventor. Graduating from Lehigh University, 1884, Packard worked as an engineer in an incandescent lamp company where he took out several patents for bulb manufacturing processes. After heading his own successful electrical company, 1890–1900, he began manufacture of Packard automobiles, 1900. Having little interest in the business side of the company, Packard spent most of his time inventing mechanical improvements, such as superior ignition and carburetion systems, braking mechanisms, and chassis construction methods.

PACKARD, JOHN HOOKER (*b. Philadelphia, Pa., 1832; d. Philadelphia, 1907*), surgeon. Son of Frederick A. Packard. Surgeon to the Pennsylvania Hospital, 1884–96; writer of medical treatises including *A Hand-book of Operative Surgery* (1870).

PACKARD, JOSEPH (*b. Wiscasset, Maine, 1812; d. Virginia, 1902*), Episcopal clergyman, Biblical scholar. Brother of Alpheus S. Packard (1798–1884). Professor, Theological Seminary of Virginia, 1836–95; dean, *post* 1874.

PACKARD, SILAS SADLER (*b. Cummington, Mass., 1826; d. 1898*), pioneer in business education. Founded Packard's Business College, New York City, 1858; successfully promoted training and use of women in office work.

PACKER, ASA (*b. Groton, Conn., 1805; d. Philadelphia, Pa., 1879*), carpenter, railroad builder, politician, philanthropist. Removed to Pennsylvania, 1822; began career by buying and operating a coal boat from Mauch Chunk to Philadelphia *via* the Lehigh Valley canal. Investing his earnings in coal lands and contracting to construct canal locks, Packer added to his fortune by founding the Lehigh Valley Railroad Co., 1853, and by further purchases of coal lands; by the 1870's he was accounted the richest man in Pennsylvania. He established and endowed Lehigh University, 1866.

PACKER, WILLIAM FISHER (*b. Centre Co., Pa., 1807; d. Williamsport, Pa., 1870*), editor, politician. Publisher of the *Lycoming Gazette*, 1829–36; joint publisher of the *Keystone*, 1836–41; Democratic governor of Pennsylvania, 1857–61.

PADDOCK, ALGERNON SIDNEY (*b. Glens Falls, N.Y., 1830; d. 1897*), lawyer. Secretary and acting governor of the territory of Nebraska, 1861–67; U.S. senator, Republican, from Nebraska, 1875–81 and 1887–93. Fought excessive railroad freight rates.

PADDOCK, BENJAMIN HENRY (*b. Norwich, Conn., 1828; d. 1891*), Episcopal clergyman. Brother of John A. Paddock. As bishop of Massachusetts, 1873–91, he lessened the discord between High and Low church factions.

PADDOCK, JOHN ADAMS (*b. Norwich, Conn., 1825; d. near Santa Barbara, Calif., 1894*), Episcopal clergyman. Brother of Benjamin H. Paddock. Active in the Northwest *post* 1880 as missionary bishop of Washington Territory and bishop of Olympia.

PADILLA, JUAN DE (*b. Andalusia, Spain, c. 1500; d. "Quivira," in northern Texas or Kansas, c. 1544*), Franciscan missionary. Came to Mexico c. 1528. Accompanied Coronado's expedition; established first mission in North American Southwest at Quivira; martyred attempting to extend his ministry to a hostile Indian tribe.

PAGE, CHARLES GRAFTON (*b. Salem, Mass., 1812; d. Washington, D.C., 1868*), physician, electrical pioneer. Graduation from Harvard (1832) and medical studies in Boston preceded practice in Salem; Page, however, early devoted most of his time to electrical experiments. Starting with Joseph Henry's calorimotor, Page developed (1836) an induction apparatus of greater intensity than Henry's; with Ruhmkorff's improvements, it is the induction coil of today. Page also discovered the superior effect of substituting bundles of iron wires for solid iron bars as cores in induction coils and invented a self-acting circuit breaker. Later (1846), he experimented with reciprocating electro-magnetic engines but failed in practical tests of his battery-powered locomotive (1851). Page worked as examiner in the U.S. Patent Office from 1861 until his death.

PAGE, DAVID PERKINS (*b. Epping, N.H., 1810; d. 1848*), educator. Successful principal of first (1844) normal school in New York at Albany; author of *The Theory and Practice of Teaching* (1847).

PAGE, JOHN (*b. Gloucester Co., Va., 1743; d. Virginia, 1808*), Revolutionary patriot, planter, Virginia legislator. Grandson of Mann Page. Congressman, (Democrat) Republican, from Virginia, 1789–97; governor of Virginia, 1802–05. Life-long friend and political supporter of Jefferson.

PAGE, MANN (*b. Virginia, 1691; d. 1730*), Virginia planter and councilor. Son-in-law of Robert Carter (1663–1732). Considered second largest landowner in Virginia; built huge, luxurious house, "Rosewell."

PAGE, RICHARD LUCIAN (*b. Clarke Co., Va., 1807; d. Blueridge Summit, Pa., 1901*), Confederate naval and army officer. Nephew of "Light-Horse Harry" Lee. Commanded at Fort Morgan, Ala., 1864, during Union land and sea attack upon Mobile.

PAGE, THOMAS JEFFERSON (*b. Matthews Co., Va., 1808; d. Rome, Italy, 1899*), naval officer, explorer. Grandson of John Page and Thomas Nelson. Commanded a surveying and exploratory expedition (1853–56) about which he wrote *La Plata: The Argentine Confederation and Paraguay* (1859). Commanded Confederate cruiser *Stonewall*, 1865.

PAGE, THOMAS NELSON (*b. "Oakland," Hanover Co., Va., 1853; d. Hanover Co., 1922*), diplomat, author, lawyer. Great-grandson of John Page. U.S. ambassador to Italy, 1913–19. *In Ole Virginia* (1887) established his reputation and helped establish (with his later books) the myth of a pre-Civil War feudal Utopia in the South.

PAGE, THOMAS WALKER (*b. Albemarle Co., Va., 1866; d. Charlottesville, Va., 1937*), economist. Cousin of Thomas N. Page. Ph.D., Leipzig, 1896. Taught at universities of California, Texas, and Virginia. Member and vice-chairman, U.S. Tariff Commission, 1918–22; 1930–37. [*Supp.* 2]

PAGE, WALTER HINES (*b. Cary, N.C., 1855; d. Pinehurst, N.C., 1918*), journalist, diplomat. Educated at Trinity College (now Duke), Randolph-Macon and Johns Hopkins. Successful as editor-director of *Forum* and *Atlantic Monthly*; became partner in Doubleday, Page and Co., 1899; founded *The World's Work*, a journal of politics and practical affairs, 1900. During these years Page campaigned for educational, agricultural, industrial, and sanitary improvements, particularly in the South. Appointed U.S. ambassador to Great Britain, 1913, Page pressed for immediate American intervention against Germany in World War I. Disappointed with Wilson's neutrality policy, he threatened to resign many times. *Post* 1917 Page worked ·effectively to cement the Allied powers into an effective partnership.

PAGE, WILLIAM (*b. Albany, N.Y., 1811; d. Tottenville, N.Y., 1885*), portrait painter. Pupil of James Herring and S.F.B. Morse; studied in Italy, 1849–60. Consciously imitated Titian.

PAINE, ALBERT BIGELOW (*b. New Bedford, Mass., 1861; d. New Smyrna, Fla., 1937*), journalist, biographer, writer of light fiction for children and adults. Literary executor of Mark Twain, whose authorized biography he published in 1912. [*Supp.* 2]

PAINE, BYRON (*b. Painesville, O., 1827; d. 1871*), lawyer, state rights advocate. Wisconsin supreme court judge, 1859–64 and 1867–71.

PAINE, CHARLES (*b. Williamstown, Vt., 1799; d. Waco, Texas, 1853*), woollen manufacturer, Vermont railroad promoter. Son of Elijah Paine; brother of Martyn Paine. Whig governor of Vermont, 1841–43.

PAINE, CHARLES JACKSON (*b. Boston, Mass., 1833; d. Weston, Mass., 1916*), Union brigadier-general, capitalist, yachtsman. Brother of Robert T. Paine (1835–1910). Owned and successfully raced *Puritan, Mayflower,* and *Volunteer* in international competition.

PAINE, ELIJAH (*b. Brooklyn, Conn., 1757; d. 1842*), farmer, woollen manufacturer, Vermont legislator. Among first settlers of Williamstown, Vt., 1784. Justice of Vermont supreme court, 1791–93; U.S. senator, Federalist, from Vermont, 1795–1801.

PAINE, HALBERT ELEAZER (*b. Chardon, O., 1826; d. 1905*), lawyer, Union officer. Early law partner of Carl Schurz. Congressman, Radical Republican, from Wisconsin, 1865–71; U.S. commissioner of patents, 1878–80. Wrote authoritative *Treatise on the Law of Elections to Public Offices* (1888).

PAINE, HENRY WARREN (*b. Winslow, Maine, 1810; d. Cambridge, Mass., 1893*), lawyer, leader of

Boston, Mass., bar *post* 1854; lecturer, Boston University Law School, 1872–85.

PAINE, JOHN ALSOP (*b. Newark, N.J., 1840; d. Tarrytown?, N.Y., 1912*), archaeologist, botanist.

PAINE, JOHN KNOWLES (*b. Portland, Maine, 1839; d. Cambridge, Mass., 1906*), composer, teacher, organist. Studied music, particularly the organ, in Germany, 1857–61; returning to America, he gave distinguished recitals and joined the Harvard faculty, 1862. Among his best compositions were his second symphony (1880) and music for Sophocles's *Oedipus Tyrannus* (1881). As a teacher Paine developed at Harvard (1862–1905) the first noteworthy music school in America, in which he stressed music as art and not as a trade.

PAINE, MARTYN (*b. Williamstown, Vt., 1794; d. New York, N.Y., 1877*), physician. Son of Elijah Paine; brother of Charles Paine. Graduated Harvard, 1813; Harvard Medical, 1816. Helped found, and taught at University of the City of New York medical college; a leading professor of therapeutics, he advocated vivisection and wrote *Institutes of Medicine* (1847).

PAINE, RALPH DELAHAYE (*b. Lemont, Ill., 1871; d. Concord, N.H., 1925*), journalist, war correspondent. Author of excellent stories for boys, also historical studies such as *The Old Merchant Marine* (1919) and *The Fight for a Free Sea* (1920).

PAINE, ROBERT (*b. Person Co., N.C., 1799; d. Aberdeen, Miss., 1882*), bishop of the Methodist Episcopal Church, South, 1846–82. Instrumental in peaceable division of Methodist Church, 1844–45; strengthened his denomination's financial position during Reconstruction.

PAINE, ROBERT TREAT (*b. Boston, Mass., 1731; d. Boston, 1814*), signer of the Declaration of Independence, Massachusetts legislator and jurist. Graduated Harvard, 1749. After brief career in Congregational ministry, Paine settled in legal practice at Taunton, Mass., 1761. He early joined the patriot cause, acted as associate prosecuting attorney in the "Boston Massacre" trial, was elected to the legislature, and then served as delegate to Continental Congress, 1774–76. During the Revolution Paine worked principally in Massachusetts, was elected the first state attorney-general, 1777, and earned a lasting reputation as a zealous and effective patriot. Instrumental in suppressing Shays's Rebellion, Paine became a state supreme court justice, 1790. He continued active in politics as a Federalist until his retirement from the bench in 1804.

PAINE, ROBERT TREAT (*b. Taunton, Mass., 1773; d. Boston, Mass., 1811*), editor, satirist, poet. Son of Robert T. Paine (1731–1814). Wrote "Adams and Liberty," 1798; edited the *Federal Orrery*, 1794–96. An early Bohemian wit in proper Boston.

PAINE, ROBERT TREAT (*b. Boston, Mass., 1835; d. Waltham, Mass., 1910*), philanthropist. Brother of Charles J. Paine. Founder, and president (1879–1907), of Associated Charities of Boston; a leading authority on philosophy and implementation of modern philanthropy.

PAINE, THOMAS (*b. Thetford, England, 1737; d. New York, N.Y., 1809*), pamphleteer, agitator, deist. Son of a Quaker corset maker, Paine attended school until he was 13 when poverty compelled his apprenticeship to the paternal trade. Serving briefly on a privateer, 1756, he returned to his home and spent the years 1757–74 working successively and in many towns as corset maker, exciseman, schoolteacher, exciseman again, tobacconist, and grocer. He experienced two brief, childless marriages. He was deeply, lastingly affected by the monotony of his occupation, the ugliness of his poverty, and the frustration produced by the gap, existing in his mind, between his abilities and his apparent destiny. However, he read widely in contemporary social, political, and scientific literature, and so educated himself.

Armed with letters of introduction from Benjamin Franklin, whom he had met in London when he was agitating to get salaries of excisemen increased, Paine emigrated to Philadelphia, arriving in October 1774. There he fell naturally into journalism, supporting himself largely by contributions to the *Pennsylvania Magazine* on a number of subjects from recent inventions to Negro slavery. Refreshed by what seemed the unlimited potentialities of the New World and deeply imbued with current rationalist theories on the nature of society, Paine quickly took up the patriot cause. His celebrated *Common Sense* was published as an anonymous pamphlet in Philadelphia on Jan. 10, 1776. It urged an immediate declaration of independence as the fulfillment of America's moral obligation to the world. The colonies, Paine reasoned, must fall away eventually. If while still uncorrupt, natural and democratic, they separated from a debasing monarchy, human destiny could be altered by their example, and America's mission would be served. The pamphlet enjoyed a phenomenal success; 120,000 copies were sold in three months and some 500,000 in all.

Paine joined Washington's army during the New Jersey retreat (Nov.–Dec., 1776), during which he wrote the first number of the *Crisis*. Beginning with the famous words, "These are the times that try men's souls," it appeared in the *Pennsylvania Journal* on Dec. 19, 1776 and in pamphlet form four days later. Eleven further numbers, and four supernumerary ones, appeared during the war. Urging vigorous action and sacrifice they were widely read both in the army and the country at large. Appointed secretary of the Congressional committee on foreign affairs,

April 1777, Paine served efficiently but was drawn into the Beaumarchais affair and engaged in public dispute with Silas Deane. Pressure from the French minister in Washington forced his resignation, whereupon he was appointed clerk to the Pennsylvania Assembly. After the war Paine lived in Bordentown, N.J., and in New York City, 1783–87; he was mildly lionized and worked on his cherished invention, an iron bridge. He had been given a confiscated Loyalist farm at New Rochelle, N.Y.

Despairing of getting his bridge adopted in America, Paine went to Europe in 1787, living in England and France and passing the time pleasantly as a favorite in liberal circles. Stirred by the onset of the French Revolution, 1789, he acted (1789–92) as self-appointed missionary of the world revolution. He hoped England would follow in France's course and after Edmund Burke published (1790) his quickly popular condemnation of events in France, Paine replied with the first part of his *Rights of Man* in 1791; the second part appeared in 1792. This pamphlet was a defense of specific measures taken by the French revolutionists and an exposition of the "natural rights" philosophy, wherein Paine argued that man's rights to liberty, property, security, and resistance to oppression could only be guaranteed by a republican form of government with a written constitution, manhood suffrage, and an absence of artificial distinctions of birth and rank. Paine hoped his pamphlet would stimulate a revolution in England. Pitt's ministry suppressed it, however, and declared Paine, safe in France, an outlaw. Made a French citizen by the Assembly, and elected to the revolutionary Convention in France (Pas de Calais Department, 1792), Paine served for a year, attaching himself to the moderate Gironde group. Imprisoned in December 1793 for being a national of a country at war with France, he was not released until the following November. Until 1802 he lived in Paris, supported in part by solicitous friends. His principal work of this period, *The Age of Reason* (1794, 1796), was a defense of deism and a rationalist attack upon literal acceptance of the Bible.

Before his return to America in 1802, Paine had become a central figure in the partisan dispute between Jeffersonians and Federalists, largely because Thomas Jefferson had commented favorably upon his deistic treatise and had offered Paine passage to America on a public vessel. The last seven years of his life were marked by poverty, declining health, and social ostracism, and were spent in Bordentown, in New York City, and in New Rochelle. He was buried in a corner of his New Rochelle farm, but in 1819 his bones were removed and taken to England by William Cobbett. In addition to the major works already cited, Paine was author of a number of minor pamphlets. A revolutionary by temperament and something of a professional radical, Paine was always pleading a cause; his books, lucid and studded with apt epithets, are arguments rather than expositions.

He was essentially a propagandist through whom the ideas of more original men were transmitted to the crowd.

PAINTER, GAMALIEL (*b. New Haven, Conn., 1743; d. 1819*), Revolutionary soldier, Vermont pioneer and legislator. Promoted settlement and development of Middlebury, Vt.; a founder of Middlebury College, and a fellow of the college, 1800–19.

PAINTER, WILLIAM (*b. Triadelphia, Md., 1838; d. Baltimore, Md., 1906*), engineer. Devised, patented (1892), and produced the "Crown Cork" single-use bottle cap, the basis of extensively used bottle sealers today.

PALEY, JOHN (*b. Russia, 1871; d. 1907*), editor, author. Came to America, 1888. Made the New York *Jewish Daily News* a powerful influence on Yiddish-speaking people as its editor *post c.* 1893. His vigorous, conservative articles brought him a personal following and bitter abuse from the Yiddish socialist press.

PALFREY, JOHN CARVER (*b. Cambridge, Mass., 1833; d. Boston, Mass., 1906*), Union soldier, engineer. Son of John G. Palfrey. Graduated Harvard, 1853; West Point, 1857. Specialist in military fortifications; helped save Union gunboat fleet during Red River campaign, 1864, by raising level of the water, thus permitting passage over the rapids.

PALFREY, JOHN GORHAM (*b. Boston, Mass., 1796; d. Boston, 1881*), Unitarian clergyman, editor, historian. Graduated Harvard, 1815. Minister of Brattle Square Church, Boston, 1818–31; Dexter Professor of Sacred Literature, Harvard, 1831–39. Contributed important articles to *North American Review*, and managed it between 1835 and 1843; served as congressman, Whig, 1847–49. Author of a number of books on religious topics which were largely made up of his successful public lectures. His most important work was his *History of New England* (5 vols., 1858–90), the product of vast research, painstakingly and accurately undertaken. It remained the standard work for decades afterwards in spite of its bias in favor of New England Puritans and anti-English animus.

PALLADINO, LAWRENCE BENEDICT (*b. Dilecto, Italy, 1837; d. Missoula, Mont., 1927*), Roman Catholic missionary, Jesuit. Came to California, 1863; served in Montana area principally, 1867–1925. Author of *Indian and White in the Northwest* (1894).

PALLEN, CONDÉ BENOIST (*b. St. Louis, Mo., 1858; d. 1929*), editor, lecturer, author. Graduated Georgetown University, 1880; Ph.D., St. Louis University, 1885. A founder and managing editor (1904–20) of the *Catholic Encyclopedia*.

PALMER, ALBERT MARSHMAN (*b. North Stonington, Conn., 1838; d. 1905*), theatrical manager. Managed Union Square Theatre, New York City, 1872–83; later managed Madison Square Theatre and Wallack's. Encouraged American authors to deal with native American material; helped found Actor's Fund, 1882.

PALMER, ALEXANDER MITCHELL (*b. Moosehead, Pa., 1872; d. Washington, D.C., 1936*), lawyer. Graduated Swarthmore, 1891; practiced law in Stroudsburg, Pa., *post* 1893. Congressman, progressive Democrat, from Pennsylvania, 1909–15; active supporter of Woodrow Wilson, 1912. As Alien Property Custodian, 1917–19, he was widely criticized for his handling of some $600,000,000 worth of enemy property; as U.S. attorney-general, 1919–21, he was denounced in liberal circles for his onslaught on domestic radicalism, particularly his raids on private homes and deportation of aliens. [*Supp. 2*]

PALMER, ALICE ELVIRA FREEMAN (*b. Colesville, N.Y., 1855; d. Paris, France, 1902*), educator. Wife of George H. Palmer. Graduated University of Michigan, 1876; became head of department of history at Wellesley College, 1879. Manifest administrative abilities led to her appointment (1881–82) as president of Wellesley which she had developed into a first-rate women's college by the time of her resignation, 1888. In 1889 she was appointed to the Massachusetts board of education; she served as dean of women at the new University of Chicago, 1892–95.

PALMER, ALONZO BENJAMIN (*b. Richfield, N.Y., 1815; d. 1887*), physician, teacher. Dean of medical department, University of Michigan, 1875–87. Wrote *Treatise on the Science and Practice of Medicine* (1882) and *Epidemic Cholera* (1866).

PALMER, BENJAMIN MORGAN (*b. Charleston, S.C., 1818; d. New Orleans, La., 1902*), Presbyterian clergyman. Pastor in New Orleans *post* 1856; helped found *Southern Presbyterian Review* and *Southwestern Presbyterian*.

PALMER, BERTHA HONORÉ (*b. Louisville, Ky., 1849; d. Osprey, Fla., 1918*), Chicago hostess and social leader. Married Potter Palmer, 1871.

PALMER, DANIEL DAVID (*b. near Toronto, Canada, 1845; d. Los Angeles, Calif., 1913*), founder of chiropractic. Started Palmer School of Chiropractic, Davenport, Iowa, 1898. Co-author, *Science of Chiropractic* (1906); author, *Textbook of the Science, Art and Philosophy of Chiropractic* (1910).

PALMER, ELIHU (*b. Canterbury, Conn., 1764; d. Philadelphia, Pa., 1806*), militant deist. Graduated Dartmouth, 1787; served as Presbyterian and Universalist minister; practiced law. Founded formal deist organizations *c.* 1795, known as the Philosophical Society (Columbian Illuminati) in New York City and as the Theophilanthropists in Philadelphia and Baltimore, Md.

PALMER, ERASTUS DOW (*b. Pompey, N.Y., 1817; d. Albany, N.Y., 1904*), cameo-cutter, sculptor. First American sculptor to exhibit lyric charm in his work; created "White Captive" (1858) and other ideal pieces; excelled as portraitist.

PALMER, GEORGE HERBERT (*b. Boston, Mass., 1842; d. Cambridge, Mass., 1933*), philosopher, teacher, man of letters. Married Alice E. F. Palmer, 1887. Graduated Harvard, 1864; Andover Theological Seminary, 1870. Appointed to the Harvard faculty, 1870, he continued to teach until retirement, 1913. Professor of philosophy *post* 1873, his professional interest was in the theory of ethics; a man of the middle ground, he criticized the extreme positions of Puritanism and Hegelianism. *The Odyssey of Homer* (1884), *The Field of Ethics* (1901), *The Problem of Freedom* (1911) and his edition of *The English Works of George Herbert* (3 vols., 1905) were among his best-known writings and indicate the range of his interests.

PALMER, HENRY WILBUR (*b. Clifford, Pa., 1839; d. Wilkes-Barre, Pa., 1913*), lawyer. Congressman, Republican, from Pennsylvania (1901–07, 1909–11). Often in controversy, he championed the established order, rugged individualism, and Puritan reforms.

PALMER, HORATIO RICHMOND (*b. Sherburne, N.Y., 1834; d. Yonkers, N.Y., 1907*), musician, director of music. Dean of music at Chautauqua, 1877–91. Organized successful Church Choral Union, New York City, 1881; composed "Just for Today" and other popular hymns.

PALMER, INNIS NEWTON (*b. Buffalo, N.Y., 1824; d. Chevy Chase, Md., 1900*), soldier. Graduated West Point, 1846. Served with distinction in Mexican War; held Union Army divisional command in Civil War, chiefly in North Carolina; commanded 2nd Cavalry in expanding West, 1865–79.

PALMER, JAMES CROXALL (*b. Baltimore, Md., 1811; d. Washington, D.C., 1883*), naval surgeon. Brother of John W. Palmer. Served with Wilkes Expedition, 1838–42; with West Gulf blockade squadron, 1863–65. Surgeon-general of the navy, 1872–73.

PALMER, JAMES SHEDDEN (*b. New Jersey, 1810; d. St. Thomas, V.I., 1867*), naval officer. Led Union fleet in first passage of Vicksburg; succeeded Farragut in command of Union forces on the Mississippi; commanded West Gulf squadron in fall, 1864; aided Virgin Islanders after earthquake, 1866.

PALMER, JOEL (*b. Ontario, Canada, 1810; d. Dayton, Oreg., 1881*), Oregon legislator and pioneer. Author of *Journal of Travels over the Rocky Mountains* (1847); successful and diligent superintendent of Indian affairs for Oregon Territory, 1853–57.

PALMER, JOHN McAULEY (*b. Scott Co., Ky., 1817; d. Springfield, Ill., 1900*), lawyer, Union major-general. Removed to Illinois, 1831; helped found Republican party there. Republican governor of Illinois, 1869–73. Palmer was a Democrat *post* 1872 and as such served as U.S. senator, 1891–97. In 1896, he was the presidential nominee of the National or "Gold" Democrats.

PALMER, JOHN WILLIAMSON (*b. Baltimore, Md., 1825; d. Baltimore, 1906*), physician, author. Brother of James C. Palmer. Southern correspondent for *New York Tribune* during Civil War; wrote ballad "Stonewall Jackson's Way."

PALMER, JOSEPH (*b. Devonshire, England, 1716; d. Dorchester, Mass., 1788*), manufacturer, Revolutionary brigadier-general. Emigrated to Massachusetts, 1746. Commanded unsuccessful attack on British at Newport, R.I., October 1777; lost most of his fortune during Revolution.

PALMER, NATHANIEL BROWN (*b. Stonington, Conn., 1799; d. San Francisco, Calif., 1877*), sea captain, explorer. In search of new seal rookeries in the South Atlantic, Palmer discovered Palmer Land in the Antarctic, 1820. A respected packet and China clipper captain in later life, he made many valuable suggestions for improved clipper design.

PALMER, POTTER (*b. Albany Co., N.Y., 1826; d. Chicago, Ill., 1902*), Chicago merchant, real-estate promoter. Removed to Chicago, 1852. Married Bertha H. Palmer, 1871. Founder of present Marshall Field stores, State Street business center, "Palmer system" of retailing, Palmer House hotel.

PALMER, MRS. POTTER. [See PALMER, BERTHA HONORÉ, 1849–1918.]

PALMER, RAY (*b. Little Compton, R.I., 1808; d. Newark, N.J., 1887*), Congregational clergyman, hymn-writer. Author of "My Faith Looks up to Thee" (*c.* 1831); published *Hymns and Sacred Pieces* (1865), *Voices of Hope and Gladness* (1881), and other books.

PALMER, THOMAS WITHERELL (*b. Detroit, Mich., 1830; d. Detroit, 1913*), businessman, philanthropist. U.S. senator, Republican, from Michigan, 1883–89; U.S. minister to Spain, 1889–91. President, Chicago World's Fair Commission, 1892–93.

PALMER, WALTER LAUNT (*b. Albany, N.Y., 1854; d. Albany, 1932*), landscape, figure and still-life painter. Son of Erastus D. Palmer. Studied with Frederick E. Church, and in Paris with Carolus Duran. Achieved success and popularity with delicately shaded winter scenes.

PALMER, WILLIAM ADAMS (*b. Hebron, Conn., 1781; d. Danville, Vt., 1860*), lawyer, Vermont legislator and jurist. U.S. senator, Democrat, from Vermont, 1818–25; anti-Masonic leader and governor, 1831–35.

PALMER, WILLIAM HENRY (*b. England, c. 1830; d. Philadelphia, Pa., 1878*), entertainer, known on stage as Robert Heller. Achieved success in America *post* 1864 with acts using magic, puppets, and piano numbers.

PALMER, WILLIAM JACKSON (*b. near Leipsic, Del., 1836; d. near Colorado Springs, Colo., 1909*), Union soldier, railroad executive. Served with distinction throughout the Civil War as a cavalry officer. After the war, he served as an official of the Union Pacific Railroad's Eastern Division, which became the Kansas Pacific and later merged into the Union Pacific. In 1870, he became first president of the Denver and Rio Grande and completed its line westward by 1883. During the 1880's, he organized and constructed Mexican railroads, two lines from Mexico City to the border being completed by 1890. He was an organizer and first president of the Colorado Coal and Iron Co., and helped develop Colorado Springs.

PALMORE, WILLIAM BEVERLY (*b. Fayette Co., Tenn., 1844; d. Richmond, Va., 1914*), clergyman of the Methodist Episcopal Church South. Owner-editor *post* 1890 of the influential *St. Louis Christian Advocate*.

PALÓU, FRANCISCO (*b. Mallorca, c. 1722; d. Mexico, c. 1789*), Franciscan missionary, historian. Accompanied Junípero Serra to Mexico, 1749; served as Serra's associate and independently on missions in Lower and Upper California; founded Mission Dolores (San Francisco), 1776. Author of monumental chronicles of the Franciscan work in California and a biography of Junípero Serra (Mexico, 1787).

PAMMEL, LOUIS HERMANN (*b. LaCrosse, Wis., 1862; d. Nevada, 1931*), botanist, educator, conservationist. Author of *The Grasses of Iowa* (1901), *Ecology* (1903), *Weed Flora of Iowa* (1913).

PANCOAST, HENRY KHUNRATH (*b. Philadelphia, Pa., 1875; d. Merion, Pa., 1939*), pioneer radiologist. Son of Seth Pancoast. M.D., University of Pennsylvania, 1898; headed department of radiology there *post* 1902. [*Supp.* 2]

PANCOAST, JOSEPH (*b. near Burlington, N.J., 1805; d. Philadelphia, Pa., 1882*), anatomist, surgeon. University of Pennsylvania, M.D., 1828; taught at Jefferson Medical College, 1838–74; accomplished spectacular surgical feats. Wrote *Treatise on Operative Surgery* (1844).

PANCOAST, SETH (*b. Darby, Pa., 1823; d. Philadelphia, Pa., 1889*), physician, anatomist, student of the occult.

PANSY. [See ALDEN, ISABELLA MACDONALD, 1841–1930.]

PANTON, WILLIAM (*b. Aberdeenshire, Scotland, c. 1742; d. at sea near Nassau, Bahamas, 1801*), Indian trader. Emigrated to Charleston, S.C., *c.* 1770; formed a trading partnership at Savannah, Ga.; spent most of 1775–84 in East Florida organizing trade relations with Creek Indians. His Loyalist sentiments led to confiscation of his Georgia property. From 1784 to 1801, he lived mostly in West Florida where he carried on far-flung trading operations with the Creeks, Choctaws, Chickasaws and Cherokees; the Spanish authorities sponsored his operations in order to keep the Indians friendly to Spain. Trading as Panton, Leslie and Co. and successor firms, with headquarters at Pensacola, Panton prospered until American companies began to cut into his business.

PARDEE, ARIO (*b. Chatham, N.Y., 1810; d. Ormond, Fla., 1892*), engineer, Pennsylvania coal-operator, philanthropist. Benefactor and trustee of Lafayette College.

PARDEE, DON ALBERT (*b. Wadsworth, O., 1837; d. Atlanta, Ga., 1919*), Union soldier, Louisiana jurist. Settled in legal practice at New Orleans, 1865. A Republican, yet respected in the South, Pardee was U.S. circuit court judge, fifth circuit, 1881–1919.

PARDOW, WILLIAM O'BRIEN (*b. New York, N.Y., 1847; d. 1909*), Roman Catholic clergyman, Jesuit educator. Provincial of Jesuit New York–Maryland province, 1893-97; widely known for pulpit eloquence.

PARIS, WALTER (*b. London, England, 1842; d. Washington, D.C., 1906*), architect, water-color painter. Resident in America *post c.* 1872; a founder of the Tile Club.

PARISH, ELIJAH (*b. Lebanon, Conn., 1762; d. Byfield, Mass., 1825*), Congregational clergyman. Pastor at Byfield *post* 1787; associate of Jedidiah Morse in authorship of geographies.

PARK, EDWARDS AMASA (*b. Providence, R.I., 1808; d. Andover, Mass., 1900*), Congregational clergyman, theologian. Last outstanding exponent of the "New England Theology"; taught at Andover Theological Seminary, 1836–81; was an editor of *Bibliotheca Sacra*, 1844–84.

PARK, JAMES (*b. Pittsburgh, Pa., 1820; d. Allegheny, Pa., 1883*), iron and steel manufacturer. Encouraged introduction of new industrial processes including Bessemer process; instrumental in increase of tariff schedules (1882–83) which gave steel a position of special privilege.

PARK, ROSWELL (*b. Lebanon, Conn., 1807; d. Chicago, Ill., 1869*), educator, army officer, Episcopal clergyman. Established, and was first president (1852–63), of Racine College, Wisconsin.

PARK, ROSWELL (*b. Pomfret, Conn., 1852; d. Buffalo, N.Y., 1914*), surgeon, pathologist. Son of Roswell Park (1807–1869). M.D., Northwestern, 1876.

Popularized Lister's antiseptic technique; founded Institute for Malignant Diseases, New York; published *The Principles and Practice of Modern Surgery* (1907), and other works on the practice and history of medicine and surgery.

PARK, TRENOR WILLIAM (*b. Woodford, Vt., 1823; d. at sea, 1882*), lawyer, financier. Son-in-law of Hiland Hall. Removed to California, 1852; was land-title specialist in law firm of Henry W. Halleck and Frederick Billings, San Francisco. Sharp-trading manipulator of stocks in John C. Frémont's Mariposa estate, also in Vermont and Panama railroads, and the notorious Utah Emma mine.

PARK, WILLIAM HALLOCK (*b. New York, N.Y., 1863; d. New York, 1939*), bacteriologist, public health officer. Graduated College of the City of New York, 1883; M.D., N.Y. College of Physicians and Surgeons, 1886. Began practice as a nose and throat specialist, simultaneously working on the bacteriology of diphtheria in New York City's Board of Health laboratory. Corroborating, supplementing, and applying the achievements of European scientists in isolating the diphtheria bacillus, developing an antitoxin and later an immunity test, Park pioneered in mass immunization. His program, widely followed in the U.S. and abroad, virtually eliminated diphtheria as a cause of death. As director of New York City's health laboratories, Park investigated many other infectious diseases, and was a leader in milk sanitation. [*Supp. 2*]

PARKE, BENJAMIN (*b. New Jersey, 1777; d. Indiana, 1835*), soldier, jurist. Removed to Kentucky *c.* 1797; settled in Vincennes, Ind., 1801. Negotiated treaty securing central Indiana for whites, 1818; served as a judge of the territorial court, 1808–17, and thereafter as U.S. district judge.

PARKE, JOHN (*b. Dover, Del., 1754; d. Kent Co., Del., 1789*), Revolutionary soldier, poet. Author of *Lyric Works of Horace . . . by a Native of America* (1786).

PARKE, JOHN GRUBB (*b. near Coatesville, Pa., 1827; d. Philadelphia, Pa., 1900*), Union soldier. Graduated West Point, 1849. A distinguished engineer officer and field commander, Parke served in almost all Civil War theaters, most notably at Vicksburg (1863) and Fort Steadman (1865). He retired as colonel, 1889.

PARKER, ALTON BROOKS (*b. Cortland, N.Y., 1852; d. New York, N.Y., 1926*), jurist. Graduating from Albany (N.Y.) Law School, 1873, Parker began practice at Kingston; thereafter he was elected and appointed to increasingly important judicial posts in the state, rising to chief justice, N.Y. court of appeals, 1897. A consistent Democrat, Parker's judicial record, particularly on labor cases, was generally liberal. Party managers selected him to be Democratic presidential nominee, 1904, playing down his liberalism and presenting him as a safe, conservative candidate in contrast to Theodore Roosevelt. His campaign, accordingly, was colorless and he was badly defeated.

PARKER, ALVIN PIERSON (*b. near Austin, Texas, 1850; d. Oakland, Calif., 1924*), clergyman of the Methodist Episcopal Church, South. Missionary to China, 1875–1923; editor, *Chinese Christian Advocate*.

PARKER, AMASA JUNIUS (*b. Sharon, Conn., 1807; d. 1890*), New York lawyer, jurist. Active in Democratic politics and a founder of Albany (N.Y.) Law School, 1851.

PARKER, CARLETON HUBBELL (*b. Red Bluff, Calif., 1878; d. 1918*), economist, labor conciliator. His report on the Wheatland, Calif., hop-field riot (1913) became a model for similar inquiries. He was author of *The Casual Laborer and Other Essays* (1920).

PARKER, CORTLANDT. [See PARKER, JOHN CORTLANDT, 1818–1907.]

PARKER, EDWIN BREWINGTON (*b. Shelbina, Mo., 1868; d. Washington, D.C., 1929*), Texas lawyer, international jurist. Priorities commissioner, War Industry Board, 1917–18. Chairman of the Liquidation Commission immediately following World War I, he was adjudicator in many war claims actions as Mixed Claims Commission umpire *post* 1923.

PARKER, EDWIN POND (*b. Castine, Maine, 1836; d. Hartford, Conn., 1920*), Congregational clergyman. Pastor of Second Church, Hartford, *post* 1860.

PARKER, EDWIN WALLACE (*b. St. Johnsbury, Vt., 1833; d. Naini Tal, India, 1901*), Methodist missionary and bishop. Active in development of Methodist church and educational enterprises in Northern India, 1859–1901.

PARKER, ELY SAMUEL (*b. Indian Falls, N.Y., 1828; d. Fairfield, Conn., 1895*), Seneca sachem, engineer, Union brigadier-general. Aided Lewis H. Morgan in research; attended Rensselaer Polytechnic Institute. As U.S. Grant's military secretary, 1864–65, Parker wrote the official copies of the surrender terms at Appomattox. After the Civil War, he rose rapidly in rank during service with the regular army. Commissioner of Indian affairs, 1869–71, he resigned after being unjustly accused of fraud; thereafter he made and lost a small fortune on Wall Street.

PARKER, FOXHALL ALEXANDER (*b. New York, N.Y., 1821; d. Annapolis, Md., 1879*), naval officer. Brother of William H. Parker. Author of *The Naval Howitzer Afloat* (1866) and *Fleet Tactics under Steam* (1870). Died as superintendent of the U.S. Naval Academy.

PARKER, FRANCIS WAYLAND (*b. Bedford, N.H., 1837; d. 1902*), educator. Introduced progressive classroom teaching *post* 1875 in Quincy (Mass.), Boston and Chicago schools; first director, School of Education, University of Chicago, 1901–02.

PARKER, HENRY TAYLOR (*b. Boston, Mass., 1867; d. 1934*), journalist. After experience on a number of newspapers, he served *post* 1905 as music and drama editor of the *Boston Transcript* and made that paper notable for care and originality in dealing with the arts. [*Supp. 1*]

PARKER, HORATIO WILLIAM (*b. Auburndale, Mass., 1863; d. Cedarhurst, N.Y., 1919*), musical composer, teacher, choral director. Received principal training in Munich, Germany, 1882–85, under Josef Rheinberger. An accomplished organist, he wrote many compositions, principally works for orchestra and chorus though he collaborated in writing two operas. He was professor of music at Yale, 1894–1919. His style was marked by conservatism and a natural feeling for religion, both clearly present in his best-known work, *Hora Novissima* (1893).

PARKER, ISAAC (*b. Boston, Mass., 1768; d. 1830*), jurist. Graduated Harvard, 1786. Esteemed for decisions showing a broad social sensitivity while justice of Massachusetts supreme court, 1806–30 (chief justice, *post* 1814). Drew up plan for Harvard Law School, 1817, at which he was first Royall Professor.

PARKER, ISAAC CHARLES (*b. Belmont Co., O., 1838; d. Fort Smith, Ark., 1896*), lawyer. Congressman, Republican, from Missouri, 1871–75; federal judge, western district of Arkansas, 1875–96. A hard and fearless frontier jurist.

PARKER, JAMES (*b. Woodbridge, N.J., c. 1714; d. Burlington, N.J., 1770*), printer, journalist. Apprenticed to William Bradford in New York, 1727; entered partnership with Benjamin Franklin, 1742, to carry on a New York printing business. As public printer of New York, 1743–60, Parker had a number of disputes with the government of the colony over printing anti-administration items. Parker published several New York newspapers and periodicals in addition to sermons, almanacs and histories; he set up the first permanent printing office in New Jersey at Woodbridge, 1751, and entered also into partnerships for operation of other printing shops in New York and in New Haven, Conn.

PARKER, JAMES (*b. Hunterdon Co., N.J., 1776; d. 1868*), New Jersey landowner, official, and legislator. Father of John C. Parker. Originally a Federalist, he supported Andrew Jackson, 1824–37, thereafter becoming a Whig and finally a Republican. He was a principal factor in the promotion of the Delaware and Raritan Canal; served as congressman, 1833–37; was twice mayor of Perth Amboy; and was active in the cultural and religious life of his state.

PARKER, JAMES CUTLER DUNN (*b. Boston, Mass., 1828; d. Brookline, Mass., 1916*), composer, organist, music teacher. Nephew of Richard G. Parker. Organist, Trinity Church, Boston; teacher, New England Conservatory.

PARKER, JANE MARSH (*b. Milan, N.Y., 1836; d. Los Angeles, Calif., 1913*), author, essayist.

PARKER, JOEL (*b. Jaffrey, N.H., 1795; d. 1875*), jurist, legislator. Chief justice, New Hampshire superior court, 1838–48; Royall Professor of Law, Harvard, 1848–68. Vigorously opposed Radical Republican tinkering with U.S. Constitution *post* 1862.

PARKER, JOEL (*b. Bethel, Vt., 1799; d. New York, N.Y., 1873*), Presbyterian clergyman. Vigorous and popular preacher; held prominent pastorates in New York City, New Orleans, Philadelphia, and Newark, N.J. President, Union Theological Seminary, New York, 1840–42.

PARKER, JOEL (*b. near Freehold, N.J., 1816; d. Philadelphia, Pa., 1888*), jurist, politician. Democratic governor of New Jersey, 1863–66, 1872–75; state supreme court justice, 1880–88. Supported Civil War but defended state's rights against so-called "military necessities."

PARKER, JOHN (*b. Lexington, Mass., 1729; d. 1775*), Revolutionary soldier. Captain of the minuteman company which defended Lexington, April 19, 1775.

PARKER, JOHN CORTLANDT (*b. Perth Amboy, N.J., 1818; d. Newark, N.J., 1907*), lawyer. Son of James Parker (1776–1868). Graduated Rutgers, 1836; studied law in Newark office of Theodore Frelinghuysen. President, American Bar Association, 1883–84, Parker was at the time of his death the acknowledged leader of the New Jersey bar. Prominent in organization of the New Jersey Republican party, he enthusiastically supported Lincoln in 1860 and 1864 and helped secure New Jersey's ratification of the 14th amendment. He served on the U.S. commission to investigate Louisiana's electoral vote in 1876 and on various state legal commissions, but declined several high diplomatic appointments. His work as advisory master of the New Jersey court of chancery resulted in opinions which were landmarks in the state's corporate law.

PARKER, JOHN MILLIKEN (*b. Bethel Church, Miss., 1863; d. Pass Christian, Miss., 1939*), cotton factor, leader in Progressive and Democratic parties. Democratic governor of Louisiana, 1920–24.

[*Supp. 2*]

PARKER, JOSIAH (*b. Isle of Wight Co., Va., 1751; d. Isle of Wight Co., 1810*), Revolutionary soldier, politician. Anti-Federalist member of Congress from Virginia, 1789–1801.

PARKER, PETER (*b. Framingham, Mass., 1804; d. Washington, D.C., 1888*), Presbyterian medical mis-

sionary to China, 1834–40 and 1842–57. Served as secretary to Caleb Cushing in treaty negotiations, 1844; thereafter was *ad interim* U.S. representative in China at various times and U.S. minister, 1855–57.

PARKER, QUANAH [See QUANAH, 1845?–1911.]

PARKER, RICHARD ELLIOT (*b. Westmoreland Co., Va., 1783; d. Clarke Co., Va., 1840*), War of 1812 soldier, Virginia legislator and U.S. senator. Judge of Virginia general court, 1817–36; judge, supreme court of appeals, 1837–40.

PARKER, RICHARD GREEN (*b. Boston, Mass., 1798; d. Boston, 1869*), Boston public school teacher, textbook writer.

PARKER, SAMUEL (*b. Ashfield, Mass., 1779; d. 1866*), Congregational clergyman, missionary, explorer. Selected sites for Oregon Indian missions during stay there, 1835–36; published *Journal of an Exploring Tour Beyond the Rocky Mountains* (1838).

PARKER, SAMUEL CHESTER (*b. Cincinnati, O., 1880; d. Chicago, Ill., 1924*), educator. Graduated University of Cincinnati, 1901; a pupil also of John Dewey and E. L. Thorndike. Teacher of education, University of Chicago, 1909–24. His successful textbooks included *Methods of Teaching in High Schools* (1915).

PARKER, THEODORE (*b. Lexington, Mass., 1810; d. Florence, Italy, 1860*), theologian, Unitarian clergyman, publicist and author. Grandson of John Parker. Self-educated in the main, he graduated from Harvard Divinity School, 1836, and became minister in West Roxbury, Mass., 1837. Grown skeptical of orthodoxy, he believed that religious truths were drawn from individual intuition and feeling rather than from revelation. An immensely popular lecturer and essayist, Parker demanded a new theology based upon the immanence of God in nature and human experience. An associate of the Channings, F. H. Hedge, R. W. Emerson and Bronson Alcott, he quickly became a figure of intense controversy in religious circles; resigning his pastorate, 1845, he became minister of a new free church in Boston. Here, he dealt largely with social questions, was a violent supporter of abolition, and exercised great influence on politics.

PARKER, THOMAS (*b. Wiltshire, England, 1595; d. Newbury, Mass., 1677*), minister at Newbury, 1635–77. An orthodox Calvinist in doctrine, he advocated the Presbyterian rather than the Congregational ecclesiastical polity.

PARKER, WILLARD (*b. Lyndeborough, N.H., 1800; d. 1884*), surgeon. Graduated Harvard, 1826; served medical apprenticeship with John C. Warren and S. D. Townsend in Boston; M.D., Harvard, 1830. Taught at a number of schools; was professor of surgery, N.Y. College of Physicians and Surgeons, 1839–

70. A courageous and successful operator, he pioneered in surgical techniques for appendicitis.

PARKER, WILLIAM HARWAR (*b. New York, N.Y., 1826; d. Washington, D.C., 1896*), naval officer, author. Brother of Foxhall A. Parker. Graduated U.S. Naval Academy, 1848. Organized and headed Confederate Naval Academy, 1863–65.

PARKHURST, CHARLES (*b. Sharon, Vt., 1845; d. 1921*), Methodist clergyman. Edited *Zion's Herald*, 1888–1919; promoted temperance and reunion of Methodism, North and South.

PARKHURST, CHARLES HENRY (*b. Framingham, Mass., 1842; d. New York, N.Y., 1933*), Presbyterian clergyman, reformer. Graduated Amherst, 1866; held New York City pastorate, 1880–1918. Launched furious attack upon alliance between Tammany Hall and organized vice (1892) which led to Lexow Investigation (1894).

PARKHURST, JOHN ADELBERT (*b. Dixon, Ill., 1861; d. Williams Bay, Wis., 1925*), businessman, astronomer. Did valuable photometric research at Yerkes Observatory, particularly in determining magnitude ranges and color indices.

PARKMAN, FRANCIS (*b. Boston, Mass., 1823; d. Boston, 1893*), historian. Son of a New England family of wealth, social standing, and culture, Parkman developed as a boy a taste for outdoor life and nature study; during college vacations, he took long trips through New England, partly on foot and partly by canoe. At Harvard, he excelled in subjects that interested him and gave much time to outside reading. After graduation in 1844, he entered Harvard Law School, received a law degree, but never bothered to take the bar examinations.

In 1846 Parkman set out from St. Louis, Mo., on a journey over the Oregon Trail to study the Indians and to improve his health. He returned in poor physical condition but a result of the trip was his first major writing, *The California and Oregon Trail* (first published in the *Knickerbocker* magazine, 1847; book publication, 1849). In 1848 he began to write the *History of the Conspiracy of Pontiac;* it was the first of a sequence of books detailing the history of the struggles between the English and the French for control of the North American continent, which he had planned to be his life task. Parkman estimated that it would take about twenty years to finish his project, but because of serious and crippling physical ailments the work took much longer. He suffered from a malady affecting his nervous system; its symptoms were extreme weakness of sight, an inability to concentrate upon any intellectual pursuit for more than brief periods at a time, and continual exhaustion. For most of his historical research Parkman had to employ copyists and readers and to write with a special frame in which parallel wires were strung across the page to guide his hand. His prodigious research under these circumstances was a remarkable achievement. Parkman also found time to become an accomplished horticulturist, to help found the Archeological Society of America, and to keep up an extensive and active social intercourse. He was author also of a negligible novel, *Vassall Morton* (1856).

His great series of historical works began with publication (1851) of the work on Pontiac's conspiracy. Thereafter came *Pioneers of France in the New World* (1865); *The Jesuits in North America* (1867); *The Discovery of the Great West* (1869, better known as retitled in 1879, *La Salle and the Discovery of the Great West*); *The Old Régime in Canada* (1874); *Count Frontenac and New France under Louis XIV* (1877); *Montcalm and Wolfe* (1884); and, to complete the series, *A Half-Century of Conflict* (1892). Long before ending his work, his fame as America's leading historian was well established. Parkman was a careful scholar, insisting upon working from original manuscript material which he sought out here and abroad, but he was equally an artist. Diligent scholarship was joined with a flowing and evocative prose style, a profound feeling for the wildness and spaciousness of the continent in which the struggle took place, and a poet's sense of the over-arching drama of the conflict.

PARKS, WILLIAM (*b. probably Shropshire, England, c. 1698; d. at sea, 1750*), printer, newspaper publisher. Public printer of Maryland, 1727–37; established and operated press at Williamsburg, Va., 1730–50. Founded the *Maryland Gazette*, 1727; also the *Virginia Gazette*, 1736. Distinguished as a typographer, Parks published a number of books of literary and historical importance.

PARLEY, PETER. [See GOODRICH, SAMUEL GRISWOLD, 1793–1860.]

PARMENTIER, ANDREW (*b. Enghien, Belgium, 1780; d. Brooklyn, N.Y., 1830*), horticulturist, landscape gardener. Came to America, 1824; established a botanical garden and nursery in Brooklyn, N.Y., 1825; was an advocate of the naturalistic rather than the formal treatment of gardens. [*Supp. 1*]

PARMLY, ELEAZAR (*b. Braintree, Vt., 1797; d. New York, N.Y., 1874*), dentist. Beginning as student assistant to his eldest brother, Parmly practiced as an itinerant dentist in the Midwest, 1817–19; from 1819 to 1821 he studied and practiced in London and Paris. Returning to New York City, he began a life-long practice there. Striving constantly to improve professional standards of dentistry, he helped found the N.Y. Society of Surgeon Dentists (1834) and helped establish the *American Journal of Dental Science* (1839). He became first president of the New York College of Dentistry, 1866.

PARR, SAMUEL WILSON (*b. Granville, Ill., 1857; d. Urbana, Ill., 1931*), chemist, inventor. Graduated

University of Illinois, 1884; M.S., Cornell University, 1885. Professor of chemistry, University of Illinois, 1891–1926. Parr's principal scientific contributions were made with respect to the physical and chemical properties, classification, and utilization of coal. He developed three types of calorimeters for determining heat value of coal and other solids, and an alloy mixture, which he named "illium" for lining calorimeters. His method of low temperature coking was another important contribution, as were his studies of the embrittlement of boiler plate.

PARRINGTON, VERNON LOUIS (*b. Aurora, Ill., 1871; d. Gloucestershire, England, 1929*), teacher, philologist, historian. Educated at College of Emporia (Kansas) and at Harvard (graduated, 1893). Taught English and French at Emporia and at University of Oklahoma; was professor of English at University of Washington, 1908–29. An effective teacher, he developed at Washington a notable and popular series of courses in the history of American literature and thought. He published *The Connecticut Wits* (1926) and *Sinclair Lewis, Our Own Diogenes* (1927); his fame rests, however, on his *Main Currents in American Thought* (1927–30), an original interpretation of American literature in its relation to the full life of the nation. His principal theme is the rise of the idea of democratic idealism and the struggle to make it prevail in every dimension of American society.

PARRIS, ALBION KEITH (*b. Hebron, Maine, 1788; d. 1857*), Maine legislator and jurist. Democratic governor of Maine, 1821–26; U.S. senator, 1827–28; Maine supreme court justice, 1828–36; second comptroller of federal treasury, 1836–49.

PARRIS, ALEXANDER (*b. Hebron, Maine, 1780; d. Pembroke, Mass., 1852*), builder, architect. Worked extensively *post* 1815 in Boston area; served as consultant to Loammi Baldwin and as superintendent of construction for Charles Bulfinch; designed David Sears House (1816), St. Paul's Church (1819), and Faneuil Hall Market area (1825).

PARRIS, SAMUEL (*b. London, England, 1653; d. Sudbury, Mass., 1719/20*), clergyman. Came to Massachusetts *ante* 1674; was pastor at Salem Village, 1689–96. Prominent in ferreting out and condemning "witches" during the delusion of 1692–93.

PARRISH, ANNE (*b. Philadelphia, Pa., 1760; d. Philadelphia, 1800*), philanthropist. Sister of Joseph Parrish. Founded Philadelphia school for poor girls (1796) and House of Industry for employment of poor women (1795).

PARRISH, CELESTIA SUSANNAH (*b. near Swansonville, Va., 1853; d. Clayton, Ga., 1918*), educator. Greatly advanced public education in Georgia, particularly among rural children and adult illiterates.

PARRISH, CHARLES (*b. Dundaff, Pa., 1826; d. Philadelphia, Pa., 1896*), coal operator. Managed a varied industrial and commercial empire around Wilkes-Barre *post* 1856. The Lehigh & Wilkes-Barre Coal Co. was his principal holding.

PARRISH, EDWARD (*b. Philadelphia, Pa., 1822; d. Fort Sill, Indian Territory, now Oklahoma, 1872*), pharmacist, teacher. Son of Joseph Parrish. A principal founder, and president (1868–71), of Swarthmore College.

PARRISH, JOSEPH (*b. Philadelphia, Pa., 1779; d. Philadelphia, 1840*), physician, Abolitionist, teacher. Brother of Anne Parrish. M.D., University of Pennsylvania, 1805. Held numerous hospital staff appointments; was president of board of managers of Wills Eye Hospital, 1833–40.

PARROTT, ENOCH GREENLEAFE (*b. Portsmouth, N.H., 1815; d. 1879*), naval officer. Cousin of Robert P. Parrott. Made first Union capture of a Confederate privateer, June 3, 1861; was senior officer during much of blockade off Charleston; commanded monitor *Monadnock* during attacks on Fort Fisher, 1864–65.

PARROTT, ROBERT PARKER (*b. Lee, N.H., 1804; d. Cold Spring, N.Y., 1877*), ordnance inventor, manufacturer. Graduated West Point, 1824. Resigning from the army, 1836, he became superintendent of Gouverneur Kemble's West Point Foundry at Cold Spring, N.Y., makers of ordnance. Parrott invented two important devices: a rifled cast-iron cannon in several calibers strengthened by wrought-iron hoops around the breech (patented 1861); also an explosive projectile to fit his cannon's rifling. These were extensively used on land and at sea during the Civil War and were probably the most efficient and effective ordnance of their type in the world.

PARRY, CHARLES CHRISTOPHER (*b. Admington, England, 1823; d. Davenport, Iowa, 1890*), botanist. Came to America as a boy. Graduated Union, 1842; M.D., Columbia, 1846. Settling in Davenport, Iowa, 1846, Parry began his lifelong study of flora in the Western states, devoting his summers to wide exploration. As member of organized expeditions or on his own, he made many important contributions to knowledge *post* 1848; his studies of plants along the U.S.-Mexican border, of Alpine flora of the Colorado Rockies, of California chaparral and California manzanitas are particularly notable. He discovered hundreds of new plant forms, among them the *Lilium Parryi*, the Lote Bush, and the Ensenada Buckeye.

PARRY, CHARLES THOMAS (*b. Philadelphia, Pa., 1821; d. Beach Haven, N.J., 1887*), locomotive builder. General superintendent in charge of construction at Baldwin Locomotive Works *post* 1855; partner *post* 1867. Introduced scientific management techniques and fair labor policies.

PARRY, JOHN STUBBS (*b. Lancaster Co., Pa., 1843; d. Jacksonville, Fla., 1876*), obstetrician, gynecologist. M.D., University of Pennsylvania, 1865. Made important studies of rachitis; reorganized obstetrical and gynecological departments at Philadelphia Hospital; wrote *Extra-Uterine Pregnancy* (1875).

PARSONS, ALBERT RICHARD (*b. Montgomery, Ala., 1848; d. Illinois, 1887*), printer, Confederate soldier, anarchist. Settled in Chicago, 1873; edited anarchist newspaper *The Alarm*, 1884–86; executed for alleged complicity in Haymarket Riot.

PARSONS, ALBERT ROSS (*b. Sandusky, O., 1847; d. Mount Kisco, N.Y., 1933*), musician. Dean of New York piano teachers; popularized Wagner here; wrote *The Science of Pianoforte Practice* (1886).

PARSONS, FRANK (*b. Mount Holly, N.J., 1854; d. Boston, Mass., 1908*), lawyer, teacher, political scientist. Urged currency and municipal government reforms in *Rational Money* (1898), *The City for the People* (1900), and other works; did pioneer work in vocational guidance.

PARSONS, JOHN EDWARD (*b. New York, N.Y., 1829; d. 1915*), corporation lawyer, advocate of industrial combination. Organized American Sugar Refining Co., 1891; successfully defended it in *U.S. vs. E. C. Knight Co.*

PARSONS, LEWIS BALDWIN (*b. Perry, N.Y., 1818; d. Flora, Ill., 1907*), lawyer, railroad manager. Director of rail and river transportation for Union Army in Department of the Mississippi, 1861–64; for all departments, 1864–66. Received brevet of major-general, 1866, for exceptional service.

PARSONS, LEWIS ELIPHALET (*b. Lisle, N.Y., 1817; d. Talladega, Ala., 1895*), lawyer, Alabama Unionist and legislator. Settled in Talladega *c.* 1840. Provisional governor of Alabama, 1865; supported Pres. Andrew Johnson; was speaker of lower house in Alabama legislature, 1872–73.

PARSONS, SAMUEL BOWNE (*b. Flushing, N.Y., 1819; d. 1906*), horticulturist, nurseryman. Made first successful importation of Italian honey bees (1860) and of Valencia oranges (1870); specialized in Japanese maples and rhododendrons; wrote *The Rose: Its History, etc.* (1847).

PARSONS, SAMUEL HOLDEN (*b. Lyme, Conn., 1737; d. Big Beaver River, O., 1789*), lawyer, Connecticut legislator, Revolutionary major-general. Directed Connecticut's defense *post* 1778, after active service at Boston, Long Island and on the Hudson. A promoter and director of the Ohio Company, he served *post* 1787 as first judge of the Northwest Territory.

PARSONS, THEOPHILUS (*b. Byfield, Mass., 1750; d. Boston, Mass., 1813*), jurist. Graduated Harvard, 1769; was aided in study of law by Edmund Trowbridge; practiced in Newburyport, Mass., and *post* 1800 in Boston. Chief justice of the Massachusetts

supreme court, 1806–13. In a pamphlet, *The Essex Result* (1778), Parsons outlined a plan for a government which greatly influenced John Adams's state constitution adopted in 1780. Leading member of the Essex Junto, a Federalist political clique in Massachusetts, Parsons enjoyed a towering reputation as lawyer and judge. He was instrumental in preserving the substance of common law doctrines in American jurisprudence by restating them in intelligible form to suit American needs. In giving his decisions, he drew rules of general application from the English common law, much unwritten colonial law, and distinctive local usages.

PARSONS, THEOPHILUS (*b. Newburyport, Mass., 1797; d. 1882*), lawyer. Son of Theophilus Parsons (1750–1813). Professor at Harvard Law School, 1848–69; author of *The Law of Contracts* (1853–55), *A Treatise on Maritime Law* (1859) and many other treatises, both legal and philosophical.

PARSONS, THOMAS WILLIAM (*b. Boston, Mass., 1819; d. Scituate, Mass., 1892*), dentist, poet. Translated first ten cantos of Dante's *Inferno* (1843), the first extensive translation published in America. His able but incomplete version of the whole of the *Divine Comedy*, together with his original poems were issued in a collected edition, 1893.

PARSONS, USHER (*b. Alfred, Maine, 1788; d. Providence, R.I., 1868*), physician, surgeon. Commissioned surgeon's mate, July 1812, after private study of medicine, Parsons won fame for brilliant work in treating American wounded after battle of Lake Erie, 1813. He received M.D. degree from Harvard, 1818; in 1822 he became professor of anatomy and surgery at Brown University. An idealist in medicine and a scholar, he won the Boylston Prize four times for professional writings.

PARSONS, WILLIAM BARCLAY (*b. New York, N.Y., 1859; d. New York, 1932*), engineer. Graduated Columbia, 1879; C.E., Columbia School of Mines, 1882. His early interest was in railway construction. As chief engineer of the New York City Transit Commission, 1894–98 and 1899–1904, he planned and oversaw construction of the first subway, developing lasting standards of design for such work. Thereafter he became engineering consultant on a wide range of projects which included the Isthmian Canal Commission, the London Traffic Commission and the Chicago Transit Commission. He designed the Cape Cod Canal, served with the United States Engineers during World War I, and designed the Detroit-Windsor vehicular tunnel.

PARTINGTON, MRS. [See Shillaber, Benjamin Penhallow, 1814–1890.]

PARTON, ARTHUR (*b. Hudson, N.Y., 1842; d. Yonkers, N.Y., 1914*), landscape painter. Followed traditional English practices as modified by Hudson River School.

PARTON, JAMES (*b. Canterbury, England, 1822; d. Newburyport, Mass., 1891*), journalist, biographer. Came to America as a child. Staff member of N.Y. *Home Journal*, 1848–55. Thereafter highly successful as author of carefully researched and well-organized lives of Horace Greeley (1855), Aaron Burr (1857), Andrew Jackson (1859–60) and other major American figures.

PARTON, SARA PAYSON WILLIS (*b. Portland, Maine, 1811; d. New York, N.Y., 1872*), author. Daughter of Nathaniel Willis; sister of N.P. Willis; married James Parton, 1856. Under pen-name of "Fanny Fern," Mrs. Parton turned out quantities of frothy but popular chit-chat on homely subjects.

PARTRIDGE, ALDEN (*b. Norwich, Vt., 1785; d. Norwich, 1854*), military educator. Originator of preparatory military academies of elementary and secondary grade; founded Norwich University (1819, 1834).

PARTRIDGE, JAMES RUDOLPH (*b. Baltimore, Md., c. 1823; d. Alicante, Spain, 1884*), lawyer, politician, diplomat. Influential Maryland Unionist and Republican; U.S. minister to a number of Latin-American countries, 1862–83.

PARTRIDGE, RICHARD (*b. Portsmouth, N.H., 1681; d. London, England, 1759*), merchant, colonial agent. Removed to England, 1701. Agent for New York, New Jersey, Massachusetts and Pennsylvania at various times; was agent for Rhode Island, 1715–59 during which time he secured a favorable settlement of boundary questions; he served also as agent for Connecticut, 1750–59. He played an active part in making the Molasses Act (1733) less offensive to New England interests.

PARTRIDGE, WILLIAM ORDWAY (*b. Paris, France, 1861; d. New York, N.Y., 1930*), sculptor. His equestrian General Grant in New York (1896) and his marble Pietà in St. Patrick's Cathedral are perhaps his best-known works.

PARVIN, THEODORE SUTTON (*b. Cedarville, N.J., 1817; d. 1901*), lawyer, teacher, librarian. Raised in Cincinnati, O.; removed to Iowa, 1838, where he practiced law and held numerous judicial and civil offices. President, Iowa State Teachers' Association, 1867; principal founder, Masonic Library at Cedar Rapids.

PARVIN, THEOPHILUS (*b. Buenos Aires, Argentina, 1829; d. Philadelphia, Pa., 1898*), obstetrician, gynecologist. Grandson of Caesar A. Rodney. Graduated Indiana University, 1847; M.D., University of Pennsylvania, 1852. Wrote *Science and Art of Obstetrics* (1886).

PASCALIS-OUVRIÈRE, FELIX (*b. France, c. 1750; d. New York, N.Y., 1833*), physician. Emigrated from Santo Domingo, 1793; practiced in Philadelphia, and in New York *post* 1810. Author of accounts of yellow fever outbreaks in Philadelphia, 1796 and 1798.

PASCHAL, GEORGE WASHINGTON (*b. Skull Shoals, Ga., 1812; d. Washington, D.C., 1878*), jurist, author, journalist. Removed to Arkansas, 1837; to Texas, 1848. Prominent Texas Unionist. Compiled notable digest of Texas supreme court decisions (1872–75).

PASCO, SAMUEL (*b. London, England, 1834; d. 1917*), Florida politician. Came to America as a boy; was raised in Charlestown, Mass.; removed to Florida, 1859. A Democratic leader in Florida after service in Confederate Army, he served as U.S. senator, 1887–99, and on the Isthmian Canal Commission, 1899–1904.

PASQUIN, ANTHONY. [See WILLIAMS, JOHN, 1761–1818.]

PASSAVANT, WILLIAM ALFRED (*b. Zelienople, Pa., 1821; d. Pittsburgh, Pa., 1894*), Lutheran clergyman, editor. Devoted life to home missionary movement and establishing institutions of mercy; was responsible for introduction of Lutheran deaconesses into the United States, 1849.

PASTOR, ANTONIO (*b. New York, N.Y., 1837; d. Elmhurst, N.Y., 1908*), New York theatre manager, actor, better known as "Tony Pastor." Played prominent role in developing vaudeville format and in encouraging young performers.

PASTORIUS, FRANCIS DANIEL (*b. Franconia, Germany, 1651; d. Germantown, Pa., 1719 or 1720*), lawyer, author, schoolmaster. Laid out settlement of Germantown, 1683, as agent for colony of Quakers from Frankfurt-am-Main; signed first Quaker protest against slavery in America, 1688.

PATCH, SAM (*b. Rhode Island, c. 1807; d. Rochester, N.Y., 1829*), daredevil. Gained national reputation diving into rivers from great heights, including Niagara River from ledge on Goat Island.

PATERSON, JOHN (*b. Wethersfield, Conn., 1744; d. Lisle, N.Y., 1808*), lawyer, Revolutionary brigadier-general, public official. Helped organize the Ohio Company; was a proprietor of the "Boston Purchase" in upper New York State.

PATERSON, WILLIAM (*b. Co. Antrim, Ireland, 1745; d. Albany, N.Y., 1806*), jurist. Came to America as a child; was raised in New Jersey. Graduated College of New Jersey (Princeton), 1763; studied law with Richard Stockton. Elected deputy to New Jersey Provincial Congress, 1775; served as attorney-general of New Jersey, 1776–83. Appointed delegate to the Federal Convention, 1787, Paterson presented the

"New Jersey Plan" which represented the views of small states. U.S. senator, 1789, and governor of New Jersey, 1790–92, Paterson then became an associate judge of the U.S. Supreme Court and served until his death. He collected and collated the laws of New Jersey (published 1800) and also drafted remodeled rules for practice and procedure in the state courts which were adopted in 1799. Paterson, N.J., which he helped promote, bears his name.

PATILLO, HENRY (*b. Scotland, 1726; d. Dinwiddie Co., Va., 1801*), Presbyterian clergyman. Came to Virginia as a child. Removed to North Carolina, 1765; presided over first Synod of the Carolinas; was an active patriot and delegate to North Carolina Provincial Congress, 1775.

PATON, LEWIS BAYLES (*b. New York, N.Y., 1864; d. 1932*), Congregational clergyman, Old Testament scholar, archeologist. Taught at Hartford (Conn.) Theological Seminary, 1892–1932.

PATRICK, HUGH TALBOT (*b. New Philadelphia, O., 1860; d. Chicago, Ill., 1939*), neurologist. M.D., Bellevue Hospital Medical School, 1884. Pioneered in neurology in the Middle West; was professor of nervous and mental diseases at Northwestern University and Chicago Polyclinic. [*Supp. 2*]

PATRICK, MARSENA RUDOLPH (*b. near Watertown, N.Y., 1811; d. 1888*), Union major-general, agriculturist. Graduated West Point, 1835. After service in Seminole and Mexican Wars, Patrick engaged in farming and agricultural education, 1850–61. During the Civil War, he held field commands up to Antietam (Sept. 1862); he was provost-marshal-general for the Army of the Potomac until 1864 and thereafter for all Union armies operating against Richmond. He died while in command of the soldiers' home in Dayton, O.

PATRICK, MARY MILLS (*b. Canterbury, N.H., 1850; d. Palo Alto, Calif., 1940*). First president (1890–1924) of American College for Girls, Istanbul, Turkey. [*Supp. 2*]

PATTEN, JAMES A. (*b. Freeland Corners, Ill., 1852; d. Chicago, Ill., 1928*), grain merchant, capitalist. A successful speculator in grain futures, he held virtual corners in corn, oats and wheat, 1908–09.

PATTEN, SIMON NELSON (*b. DeKalb Co., Ill., 1852; d. Brown's-Mills-in-the-Pines, N.J., 1922*), economist. Ph.D., Halle, 1878; was strongly influenced by German thought and economic example. Professor at University of Pennsylvania, 1888–1917, and an outstanding teacher, Patten was an economic optimist, holding that man by proper application of intelligence could better his economic condition. He opposed the gloomy view of the classical economists as being derived from an exploitative economic environment, contrasting with it the limitless social improvement which must follow on economic conservation. He believed that Americans were wasteful consumers and recommended a theory of prosperity based on a wisely managed consumption and on a philosophy of spending rather than saving in an era of growing abundance. *The Development of English Thought* (1899) and *The New Basis of Civilization* (1907) are representative of his writing but are no measure of his thought or influence.

PATTEN, WILLIAM (*b. Watertown, Mass., 1861; d. 1932*), zoologist, paleontologist. B.S., Harvard, 1883; Ph.D., Leipzig, 1884. Taught at University of North Dakota, and at Dartmouth *post* 1893.

PATTERSON, DANIEL TODD (*b. Long Island, N.Y., 1786; d. Washington, D.C., 1839*), naval officer. Conducted successful raid against Jean Laffite at Barataria Bay, La., 1814; provided Andrew Jackson with invaluable naval support on Lake Borgne in battle of New Orleans.

PATTERSON, JAMES KENNEDY (*b. Glasgow, Scotland, 1833; d. 1922*), educator. Came to America as a boy; was raised in Indiana. President and ardent advocate of State College of Kentucky, later University of Kentucky, from 1869 to 1910.

PATTERSON, JAMES WILLIS (*b. Henniker, N.H., 1823; d. Hanover, N.H., 1893*), educator, politician. Graduated Dartmouth, 1848; taught there, 1852–65. Congressman, Republican, from New Hampshire, 1863–67; U.S. senator, 1867–73. Implicated in Crédit Mobilier scandals. State superintendent of education, New Hampshire, 1881–93.

PATTERSON, JOHN HENRY (*b. near Dayton, O., 1844; d. 1922*), salesman, manufacturer. Bought a small, failing company, 1884, and built it into the highly successful National Cash Register Co., by using aggressive modern sales techniques and direct mail advertising.

PATTERSON, MORRIS (*b. Philadelphia, Pa., 1809; d. Philadelphia, 1878*), merchant, philanthropist. Pioneer in developing anthracite coal trade.

PATTERSON, ROBERT (*b. near Hillsborough, Ireland, 1743; d. Philadelphia, Pa., 1824*), Revolutionary soldier, mathematician. Came to America, 1768. Professor of mathematics, University of Pennsylvania, 1779–1814; director of U.S. Mint, 1805–24.

PATTERSON, ROBERT (*b. Co. Tyrone, Ireland, 1792; d. Philadelphia, Pa., 1881*), soldier, industrialist. Came to America as a boy; served in War of 1812; was successful as a commission grocery merchant in Philadelphia. Major-general of volunteers in the Mexican War, Patterson gained honors at Cerro Gordo and Jalapa. *Post* 1848 he became prominent in the Louisiana sugar industry, came to own 30 cotton mills in Pennsylvania, and was a promoter of the

Pennsylvania Railroad. Made a major-general of volunteers, 1861, he was given command of the military department composed of Pennsylvania, Delaware, Maryland and District of Columbia. His failure to check Confederate forces under Gen. J. E. Johnston in July 1861, and his non-cooperation with McDowell in first Bull Run, led to much controversy and to his retirement from service.

PATTERSON, ROBERT MAYNE (*b. Philadelphia, Pa., 1832; d. Philadelphia, 1911*), Presbyterian clergyman, editor. Associate editor, *The Presbyterian*, 1870–80; editor, *The Presbyterian Journal*, 1880–93; authority on ecclesiastical law.

PATTERSON, THOMAS HARMAN (*b. New Orleans, La, 1820; d. Washington, D.C., 1889*), naval officer. Son of Daniel T. Patterson. Served during Civil War on Union Atlantic blockade duty; retired as rear-admiral, 1882.

PATTERSON, THOMAS MacDONALD (*b. Co. Carlow, Ireland, 1839; d. 1916*), lawyer, editor. Came to America as a boy; settled in Denver, Colo., 1872; was Democratic territorial delegate and congressman from Colorado, 1875–79. Controlled Denver *Rocky Mountain News*, 1892–1913; was a consistent friend of labor, reform, and popular control of government. U.S. senator, Democrat-Populist, 1901–07.

PATTERSON, WILLIAM (*b. Co. Donegal, Ireland, 1752; d. Baltimore, Md., 1835*), merchant. Father of Elizabeth P. Bonaparte. Came to America, 1766. Imported supplies and munitions for patriot army and made fortune during Revolution; later a successful shipowner and industrialist, he was an incorporator and director of the Baltimore & Ohio Railroad and of the Canton Company.

PATTIE, JAMES OHIO (*b. Bracken Co., Ky., 1804; d. c. 1850*), trapper, author. Published *Personal Narrative* (1831, 1833; ed. Timothy Flint), a dramatic but semifictional account of travels as far west as California.

PATTISON, GRANVILLE SHARP (*b. Glasgow, Scotland, c. 1791; d. New York, N.Y., 1851*), anatomist. Came to America, 1819; taught at University of Maryland, 1820–26. Brought great prestige to Jefferson Medical College as professor of anatomy, 1832–41; held chair of anatomy thereafter at University of the City of New York.

PATTISON, JAMES WILLIAM (*b. Boston, Mass., 1844; d. Asheville, N.C., 1915*), Union soldier, painter, lecturer on art. Popularized serious art and promoted art museums and schools in Illinois and Missouri, notably at Chicago and St. Louis; served for many years as secretary of the Chicago Municipal Art League.

PATTISON, JOHN M. (*b. near Owensville, O., 1847; d. Milford, O., 1906*), lawyer, insurance executive,

Ohio legislator. Congressman, Democrat, 1891–93; Democratic governor of Ohio, 1906.

PATTISON, ROBERT EMORY (*b. Quantico, Md., 1850; d. Philadelphia, Pa., 1904*), lawyer, banker, politician. As Democratic governor of Pennsylvania, 1883–87, 1891–95, stressed economy and reform; wrote distinguished minority report for U.S. Pacific Railway Commission (1887).

PATTISON, THOMAS (*b. Troy, N.Y., 1822; d. New Brighton, N.Y., 1891*), naval officer. Appointed midshipman, 1839. Retired as rear-admiral, 1883, after varied and distinguished service.

PATTON, FRANCIS LANDEY (*b. Warwick, Bermuda, 1843; d. Bermuda, 1932*), Presbyterian clergyman, theologian. Graduated Princeton Theological Seminary, 1865; attained wide experience in New York and Chicago as pastor, lecturer, and writer for the religious press. He returned to Princeton Seminary as Stuart Professor, 1881, teaching also in the College of New Jersey and specializing in Christian ethics. Patton was chosen president of the College (*post* 1896 called Princeton University), 1888. His administration was marked by financial success and academic progress; a trend toward appointing faculty members who had had formal graduate training in their subjects rather than men trained only as ministers was begun by him and he introduced electives to the curriculum. Patton retired in 1902, after nominating Woodrow Wilson as his successor. He continued, however, as professor of ethics, and as president of the Princeton Seminary until 1913.

PATTON, JOHN MERCER (*b. Fredericksburg, Va., 1797; d. Richmond, Va., 1858*), lawyer, Virginia legislator. Grandson of Hugh Mercer. Congressman, independent Democrat, from Virginia, 1830–38; co-author, *Code of Virginia* (1849), a superior digest and revision of the civil and criminal codes.

PATTON, WILLIAM (*b. Philadelphia, Pa., 1798; d. New Haven, Conn., 1879*), Presbyterian and Congregational clergyman, author. A founder of Union Theological Seminary (New York), 1836.

PAUGER, ADRIEN de (*b. France, date unknown; d. New Orleans, La., 1726*), engineer. Came to Louisiana, 1720, as assistant to Le Blond de la Tour; surveyed and laid out original town of New Orleans, 1721.

PAUL, FATHER. [See FRANCIS, PAUL JAMES, 1863–1940.]

PAUL, HENRY MARTYN (*b. Dedham, Mass., 1851; d. 1931*), astronomer, engineer, teacher. Graduated Dartmouth, 1873; C.E., 1875. Did important work at Washington Naval Observatory on variable stars and eclipses; professor of mathematics, U.S. Naval Academy, 1905–12.

PAUL, JOHN. [See WEBB, CHARLES HENRY, 1834–1905.]

PAULDING, HIRAM (*b. Westchester Co., N.Y., 1797; d. near Huntington, N.Y., 1878*), naval officer. Appointed midshipman, 1811; served as acting lieutenant aboard *Ticonderoga* in battle of Lake Champlain; graduated from Alden Partridge's military academy at Norwich, Vt., 1823. Paulding spent his entire active life on sea and shore duty, making frequent cruises in the Atlantic, Pacific, and Mediterranean. As captain, commanding the Home Squadron in the Caribbean, 1857, he seized William Walker with 150 filibusters at Grey Town, Nicaragua. President Buchanan, however, set Walker free and relieved Paulding of command. Head of the New York Navy Yard through much of the Civil War, Paulding, now rear-admiral, did much to advance construction of Ericsson's monitors by advocating the design and expediting their actual building.

PAULDING, JAMES KIRKE (*b. Putnam Co., N.Y., 1778; d. near Hyde Park, N.Y., 1860*), author, naval official. Despite scanty schooling, he developed literary interests, an esthetic appreciation of nature, and keen powers of social observation. Related by marriage to Washington Irving, he was associated with Irving in the first series of *Salmagundi* (1807–08). Much of his subsequent writing was made up of caustic criticism of English ways and enthusiastic praise of his own homeland; his *Diverting History of John Bull and Brother Jonathan* (1812), *The United States and England* (1815), and *John Bull in America* (1825) were in this vein. Appointed secretary of the Board of Navy Commissioners, 1815, he became U.S. navy agent in New York, 1824. He served ably in Van Buren's cabinet as secretary of the navy, 1838–41. Liberal, tolerant in all but his view of the English, thoroughly American, Paulding was author of more than 70 short tales, a mass of miscellaneous prose (including a second series of *Salmagundi*, 1819–20), some unsuccessful efforts in verse (e.g., *The Backwoodsman*, 1818), and five refreshingly realistic novels of which the best was *The Dutchman's Fireside* (1831). The others were: *Koningsmarke* (1823); *Westward Ho!* (1832); *The Old Continental* (1846); *The Puritan and his Daughter* (1849). Like his contemporaries, he wrote too much and revised too little, but the unsentimental tone of his stories in an age of sentiment, and the versatility and range of his interests give him a place in American literary history.

PAVY, OCTAVE (*b. New Orleans, La., 1844; d. 1884*), Arctic explorer. Physician and naturalist for A. W. Greely's Lady Franklin Bay expedition, 1881–84; died of exposure at Cape Sabine.

PAYNE, BRUCE RYBURN (*b. Mull's Grove, N.C., 1874; d. Nashville, Tenn., 1937*), educator. Graduated Duke, 1896; Ph.D., Teachers College, Colum-bia, 1904. President, George Peabody College for Teachers, 1911–37. [*Supp. 2*]

PAYNE, CHRISTOPHER HARRISON (*b. near Red Sulphur Springs, Va., 1848; d. St. Thomas, V.I., 1925*), Baptist clergyman, lawyer, Negro leader. U.S. consul, St. Thomas, D.W.I., 1903–17; thereafter a prosecuting attorney and police judge.

PAYNE, DANIEL ALEXANDER (*b. Charleston, S.C., 1811; d. 1893*), bishop of the African Methodist Episcopal Church, educator. President of Wilberforce University, 1863–76; wrote history of his church.

PAYNE, HENRY B. (*b. Hamilton, N.Y., 1810; d. Cleveland, O., 1896*), lawyer, politician. Removed to Cleveland, 1833, where he practiced with great success and engaged also in railroad promotion. A leader in the Democratic party and a consistent supporter of business interests, he was congressman from Ohio, 1875–85, and U.S. senator, 1885–91.

PAYNE, HENRY CLAY (*b. Ashfield, Mass., 1843; d. Washington, D.C., 1904*), railroad and public utilities executive, politician. Settled in Milwaukee, Wis., 1863. Executive officer, Milwaukee Street Railway Co., 1890–95; receiver, Northern Pacific Railroad, 1893–95; U.S. postmaster-general, 1902–04.

PAYNE, JOHN BARTON (*b. Pruntytown, Va., now W. Va., 1855; d. Washington, D.C., 1935*), lawyer. Winning reputation as lawyer and jurist in Chicago, Ill., *post* 1882, he was active in that city's civic affairs and held a number of national offices under the administration of President Wilson, including a brief period as U.S. secretary of the interior. He served as chairman of the American Red Cross *post* 1921 with great efficiency and without compensation. [*Supp. 1*]

PAYNE, JOHN HOWARD (*b. New York, N.Y., 1791; d. Tunisia, 1852*), actor, dramatist, editor, diplomat. Produced first play, *Julia, or The Wanderer*, in New York, 1806. Made professional stage debut in *Douglas* at Park Theatre, New York, 1809; for two years was a theatrical sensation in New York and Boston; was first American to play "Hamlet" (Boston, 1809). Resided in Europe, principally in France and England, 1813–32, attaining occasional success as an actor and active playwright. *Charles the Second; or, The Merry Monarch* (1824), a play in which Washington Irving collaborated, won favor as did others, but he was constantly in debt. Returning to America, he projected a number of unsuccessful schemes and was concerned (1835) in an effort to obtain justice for the Cherokees. He served as U.S. consul in Tunis, 1842–45 and 1851–52. He is remembered principally today as author of the song "Home, Sweet Home!" which he had written for his operetta *Clari* (1823).

PAYNE, OLIVER HAZARD (*b. Cleveland, O., 1839; d. 1917*), Union soldier, oil refiner, capitalist. Son of

Henry B. Payne. Partner in notorious South Improvement Co. and treasurer of the Standard Oil Co. until 1884. Thereafter engaged in other industries, he was a dominant figure in American Tobacco Co. and influential in Tennessee Coal and Iron Co. He was a benefactor of Cornell Medical College and other institutions.

PAYNE, SERENO ELISHA (*b. Hamilton, N.Y., 1843; d. Washington, D.C., 1914*), lawyer, Republican politician. Nephew of Henry B. Payne. Congressman from New York, 1883–87 and 1891–1914; chairman, House ways and means committee, 1899–1914. A friend of high tariffs, he gave his name to the Payne-Aldrich Bill, 1909.

PAYNE, WILLIAM HAROLD (*b. Ontario Co., N.Y., 1836; d. Ann Arbor, Mich., 1907*), educator. Occupied first chair of education in the United States at University of Michigan, 1879–87, 1901–04; wrote many textbooks.

PAYNE, WILLIAM MORTON (*b. Newburyport, Mass., 1858; d. Chicago, Ill., 1919*), teacher, translator, literary critic. Associate editor of the *Dial*, 1892–1915; wrote *American Literary Criticism* (1904), *Leading American Essayists* (1910).

PAYSON, EDWARD (*b. Rindge, N.H., 1783; d. Portland, Maine, 1827*), Congregational clergyman. Son of Seth Payson. Pastor at Second Church, Portland, *post* 1811; an intense, unhealthily introspective preacher.

PAYSON, SETH (*b. Walpole, Mass., 1758; d. Rindge, N.H., 1820*), Congregational clergyman. Father of Edward Payson. Pastor at Rindge, *post* 1782; author of *Proofs of the Real Existence and Dangerous Tendency of Illuminism* (1802).

PEABODY, ANDREW PRESTON (*b. Beverly, Mass., 1811; d. 1893*), Unitarian clergyman, educator, author. Editor and proprietor, *North American Review*, 1853–63; Plummer Professor of Christian Morals, Harvard, 1860–81.

PEABODY, CECIL HOBART (*b. Burlington, Vt., 1855; d. Boston, Mass., 1934*), educator. Son of Selim H. Peabody. Graduated Massachusetts Institute of Technology, 1877. After teaching in Japan and at the University of Illinois, he was associated *post* 1884 with his alma mater as teacher of steam engineering and *post* 1893 as head of the department of naval architecture and marine engineering. He was author of pioneering textbooks such as *Thermodynamics of the Steam Engine* (1889) and *Naval Architecture* (1904). He retired as professor emeritus, 1920.
[Supp. 1]

PEABODY, ELIZABETH PALMER (*b. Billerica, Mass., 1804; d. Jamaica Plain, Mass., 1894*), educator, author. Granddaughter of Joseph Palmer; sister-in-law

of Nathaniel Hawthorne and Horace Mann. Conducted several private schools around Boston; acted as W. E. Channing's secretary, 1825–34; was A. Bronson Alcott's assistant in his Temple School, Boston. An early member of the Transcendental Club, she was friend of R. W. Emerson, Hawthorne, Thoreau. Her bookshop in Boston, opened 1839, carried a unique selection of European books and became a center for transcendentalists; plans for the Brook Farm community were drawn there, and she was publisher of Margaret Fuller's translations from the German, several of Hawthorne's books, and of the *Dial* (1842–43). She established the first kindergarten in America (1860) and published the *Kindergarten Messenger* (1873–75).

PEABODY, FRANCIS GREENWOOD (*b. Boston, Mass., 1847; d. Cambridge, Mass., 1936*), Unitarian clergyman, writer. Professor of theology and Christian morals, 1881–1913, and founder (1906) of the department of social ethics, Harvard Divinity School.
[Supp. 2]

PEABODY, GEORGE (*b. South Danvers, Mass., 1795; d. London, England, 1869*), merchant, financier, philanthropist. Apprenticed at eleven to a Danvers grocer, he subsequently secured positions in Newburyport, Mass., and Georgetown, D.C. Made manager of a wholesale dry-goods warehouse, 1814, he moved to Baltimore with his employer, 1815, and became senior partner of the firm, Riggs & Peabody, 1829. In 1835 he negotiated in England without charge a loan of $8,000,000 for the state of Maryland, then on the verge of bankruptcy; in 1836, as incorporator and president of the Eastern Railroad, he again demonstrated his talent for securing English funds for investment in America. He settled permanently in London, 1837, where he had previously established the firm of George Peabody & Co., specializing in foreign exchange and American securities in direct competition with the Barings and Rothschilds. In 1854 he took Junius S. Morgan into partnership. During the years 1837–41, when American credit in Europe was much shaken, Peabody used his name and funds to restore confidence. He made a gift of $15,000 to sponsor an American exhibit at the Crystal Palace exhibition (1851); granted $10,000 to outfit an expedition to search for Sir John Franklin, the Arctic explorer; and gave elaborate Fourth-of-July dinners where English nobility met American visitors to England.

Peabody's philanthropic activities, however, were principally directed toward America. As his fortune mounted he made increasingly generous gifts to a wide range of projects. Notable among these were $1,500,000 to found the Peabody Institute at Baltimore, which provided a free library, an academy of music, and an art gallery; $250,000 to found the Peabody Institute in Peabody, Mass., with its library and lecture fund; $150,000 to establish the Peabody museum of natural history at Yale; $140,000 to found the Peabody Academy of Science in connection with the Essex Institute, Salem, Mass.; and $3,500,000 to the Peabody Education Fund for the promotion of education in the South. His foremost benefaction in England was a grant of $2,500,000 for the erection of workingmen's tenements in London. After a funeral service in Westminster Abbey, his body was brought home for burial in Danvers, Mass.

PEABODY, GEORGE FOSTER (*b. Columbus, Ga., 1852; d. Warm Springs, Ga., 1938*), banker. Partner in Spencer Trask & Co., 1881–1906. An active philanthropist, he was especially interested in Southern education. [*Supp. 2*]

PEABODY, JOSEPH (*b. Middleton, Mass., 1757; d. Salem, Mass., 1844*), Revolutionary privateersman, merchant shipowner. Became most prominent and wealthiest shipowner in Salem, employing about 7000 seamen; traded principally with the Far East.

PEABODY, JOSEPHINE PRESTON (*b. Brooklyn, N.Y., 1874; d. 1922*), poet, dramatist. Her best-known plays, *The Piper* (1909), *The Wings* (1912), *Harvest Moon* (1916), kept alive the tradition of poetic drama in America.

PEABODY, NATHANIEL (*b. Topsfield, Mass., 1741; d. Exeter, N.H., 1823*), physician, Revolutionary patriot. Prominent member, New Hampshire Committee of Safety; organizer, New Hampshire Medical Society, 1791.

PEABODY, OLIVER WILLIAM BOURN (*b. Exeter, N.H., 1799; d. Burlington, Vt., 1848*), lawyer, Unitarian clergyman. Brother of William B. O. Peabody. Graduated Harvard, 1816; contributed to *North American Review;* supervised Boston, 1836, edition of Shakespeare's works. Pastor at Burlington, Vt., 1845–48.

PEABODY, ROBERT SWAIN (*b. New Bedford, Mass., 1845; d. Marblehead, Mass., 1917*), architect. Graduated Harvard, 1866; studied at Beaux Arts, Paris; partner in Peabody and Stearns *post* 1870. Designed State House at Concord, N.H., and (old) Union League Club, New York; worked mainly in Italian Renaissance style.

PEABODY, SELIM HOBART (*b. Rockingham, Vt., 1829; d. St. Louis, Mo., 1903*), educator. Graduated University of Vermont, 1852. Secured first legislative grant for Illinois Industrial University, which became University of Illinois in 1885; served there as regent (president), 1880–91.

PEABODY, WILLIAM BOURN OLIVER (*b. Exeter, N.H., 1799; d. Springfield, Mass., 1847*), Unitarian clergyman, man of letters. Brother of Oliver W. B. Peabody. Pastor at Springfield *post* 1820.

PEALE, ANNA CLAYPOOLE (*b. Philadelphia, Pa., 1791; d. 1878*), miniature painter. Daughter of James Peale; niece of Charles W. Peale; sister of Sarah M. Peale. Worked mainly in Philadelphia and Baltimore.

PEALE, CHARLES WILLSON (*b. Queen Anne Co., Md., 1741; d. Philadelphia, Pa., 1827*), portrait painter, naturalist, patriot. Peale's father, a native of Rutlandshire, England, became master of the Free School near Centerville, Md., 1740, and of the Kent County School at Chestertown, 1742; he died in 1750. Charles Peale received rudiments of schooling until his thirteenth year when he was apprenticed to a saddler. Released from his indenture, 1761, he set up his own saddlery, but his Loyalist creditors put him out of business when he joined the Sons of Freedom during the Stamp Act crisis. At this point he found that an amateur interest in portraiture could win him valuable commissions and he sought instruction, first from John Hesselius, then from John Singleton Copley in Boston. Several interested patrons advanced him money to obtain further training in England, where he studied under Benjamin West, 1767–69. On his return to Annapolis, Md., his work brought him recognition in several of the colonies; in 1776 he removed to Philadelphia where he at once found subjects among delegates to the Congress and distinguished visitors. Elected a first lieutenant in the city militia, he saw service during the engagements at Trenton and Princeton, and as a captain continued in active service during the campaign that resulted in the evacuation of Philadelphia. In 1779 he was elected one of Philadelphia's representatives to the General Assembly of Pennsylvania.

During his many encampments with the army he had painted miniatures of his fellow officers which served as nucleus of the portrait collection subsequently formed as his record of the war; after the Revolution he engraved mezzotint plates from this collection. An amateur naturalist, he decided to exhibit natural curiosities as well as paintings in his museum or gallery in Philadelphia, which he opened to the public and for which he was later granted use of rooms at the American Philosophical Society (1794) and at Independence Hall (1802). Subsequently, the collections were incorporated as the Philadelphia Museum, and managed after 1810 by his sons. Peale helped to found the Philadelphia Academy of Fine Arts (1805) and left several notable writings, among them *An Essay on Building Wooden Bridges* (1797), and *Introduction to a Course of Lectures on Natural History* (1800). He married three times and raised twelve children, many of whom became distinguished painters or naturalists. (*See* entries for Raphael, Rembrandt and Titian R. Peale.) He was brother of James Peale.

Peale's early portraits were large canvasses in the classic English style. His figures were formally placed with the faces solidly and tightly painted, though the eyes were generally over-small and the lips almost uniformly thin. He left scores of paintings depicting a wide cross-section of the distinguished men and families of his day. He will always be known for his portraits of Washington, of which he painted sixty in all, seven of them from life (one of the latter being the first portrait of him—a three-quarter length in uniform of a colonel of Virginia militia, 1772). The six other life studies generally accredited are a three-quarter length in Continental uniform (1776); a miniature on ivory (1777); a bust portrait begun at Valley Forge in 1777; a full-length portrait showing Washington with his left hand resting upon a cannon, with Nassau Hall, Princeton, and marching Hessian prisoners in the background (1779); a bust portrait painted during the Constitutional Convention in 1787; and a bust portrait of Washington when president, painted at Philadelphia, 1795. His representations of the first president are perhaps uninspired but are faithful to life.

PEALE, JAMES (*b. Chestertown, Md., 1749; d. Philadelphia, Pa., 1831*), Revolutionary soldier, portrait painter in miniature and oils. Brother of Charles W. Peale; father of Anna C. and Sarah M. Peale. His miniatures *post* 1795 are his best work.

PEALE, RAPHAEL (*b. Annapolis, Md., 1774; d. 1825*), painter. Son and pupil of Charles W. Peale; brother of Rembrandt and Titian R. Peale. Produced miniature portraits and still-lifes which are adequate but undistinguished.

PEALE, REMBRANDT (*b. near Richboro, Bucks Co., Pa., 1778; d. Philadelphia, Pa., 1860*), portrait and historical painter. Son of Charles W. Peale; brother of Raphael and Titian R. Peale. Attended private schools in Philadelphia; early exhibited a talent for painting. Besides studying under his father and copying the paintings in his father's Philadelphia museum gallery, he practiced in the school of design which his father and others attempted to form in 1795; in that same year he made a portrait from life of Washington. Between 1796 and 1800, he worked in Charleston, S.C., and Baltimore, Md. When the elder Peale successfully recovered the skeletons of two mastodons, the son assisted in mounting them and was sent to Europe (1802–03) to exhibit one of the skeletons; while abroad, he studied under Benjamin West and had two portraits accepted for exhibition at the Royal Academy (1803). Returning home, he was commissioned by his father to add further portraits to the Peale gallery and did several, the most noted being that of Thomas Jefferson. Study in France, 1808–10, was followed by an unsuccessful attempt to establish a museum and gallery of his own in Baltimore. After the failure of his Baltimore venture Peale established himself successively in New York, Philadelphia, and again in New York where he was elected president of the American Academy of Fine Arts. *Post* 1828 he traveled in Italy and England, resided briefly in New York, and made his home in Philadelphia

post 1834. His *Notes on Italy* (1831) and *Graphics: A Manual of Drawing and Writing* (1835) received some attention, and he lectured extensively. He became obsessed in later life with the idea of exploiting his 1823 portrait of Washington (a composite from his father's and his own sketches) as an "ideal" representation. He did his best painting in the period 1808–20, largely in encaustic which presented a fine, enamel-like texture. His large canvas, "The Court of Death," was exhibited *post* 1820 and brought favorable notice.

PEALE, SARAH MIRIAM (*b. Philadelphia, Pa., 1800; d. Philadelphia, 1885*), portrait painter. Daughter of James Peale; sister of Anna C. Peale.

PEALE, TITIAN RAMSAY (*b. Philadelphia, Pa., 1799; d. Philadelphia, 1885*), naturalist, artist, mechanician. Son of Charles W. Peale; brother of Raphael and Rembrandt Peale. Accompanied William Maclure on trip to Georgia and Florida to study and collect fauna, 1818; accompanied Stephen H. Long's expedition to the upper Missouri, 1819–20. Appointed assistant manager of the Philadelphia Museum, 1821, he built up its collection of Lepidoptera and published *Lepidoptera Americana* (1833). He contributed many colored plates to Charles Bonaparte's *American Ornithology* and Thomas Say's *American Entomology*. A member of the Wilkes Exploring Expedition to the South Pacific, 1838–42, Peale collected a notable selection of Polynesian ethnica for the Academy of Natural Sciences of Philadelphia. He was an examiner in the U.S. Patent Office, Washington, D.C., 1849–72.

PEARCE, CHARLES SPRAGUE (*b. Boston, Mass., 1851; d. Auvers-sur-Oise, France, 1914*), painter. Grandson of Charles Sprague. Studied in Paris; resided *post* 1885 in France.

PEARCE, JAMES ALFRED (*b. Alexandria, Va., 1805; d. Chestertown, Md., 1862*), lawyer, Maryland politician. Grandson of Elisha Dick. Congressman, Whig, from Maryland, 1835–39, 1841–43; U.S. Senator, 1843–62. An able and industrious committee worker of superior intelligence; urged reasonable settlement of the secession crisis.

PEARCE, RICHARD (*b. Cornwall, England, 1837; d. London, England, 1927*), metallurgist. Devised important and successful techniques for reduction of precious ores in Colorado and Montana, 1873–1902. President, American Institute of Mining Engineers, 1889. Retired to England, 1902.

PEARCE, RICHARD MILLS (*b. Montreal, Canada, 1874; d. 1930*), pathologist, medical educator. M.D., Tufts, 1894; M.D., Harvard, 1897; studied also at Leipzig. Professor of pathology at Albany Medical College and Bellevue Medical College, he went to University of Pennsylvania, 1910, appointed to the first U.S. chair of research medicine. His great contribution to medical education came during his directorship of the division of medical education, Rockefeller Foundation, 1920–30. He collected data throughout the world on the state of medical education, directed expenditure of substantial sums in various medical centers, and established the annual publication *Methods and Problems of Medical Education* (1924).

PEARCE, STEPHEN AUSTEN (*b. Brompton, Kent, England, 1836; d. Jersey City, N.J., 1900*), musician, musical editor. D.Mus., Oxford, 1864. Settled in New York, N.Y., 1872; held position of organist at a number of city churches and was widely known as lecturer and recitalist.

PEARL, RAYMOND (*b. Farmington, N.H., 1879; d. Hershey, Pa., 1940*), biologist, statistician. Graduated Dartmouth, 1899; Ph.D., University of Michigan, 1902. Worked at University of Maine, 1907–18; at Johns Hopkins, 1918–40. Early exponent of the application of statistics to study of biology and medicine. [Supp. 2]

PEARSE, JOHN BARNARD SWETT (*b. Philadelphia, Pa., 1842; d. Georgeville, Canada, 1914*), metallurgist. Noted *post* 1870 for design and improvement of Bessemer steel plants and their products; wrote history of iron manufacture in America (1876).

PEARSON, EDMUND LESTER (*b. Newburyport, Mass., 1880; d. New York, N.Y., 1937*), librarian, author. Notable for the literary distinction of his writing on crime in *Studies in Murder* (1924) and other books. [Supp. 2]

PEARSON, EDWARD JONES (*b. Rockville, Ind., 1863; d. Baltimore, Md., 1928*), engineer. Graduated Cornell University, 1883. As president, New York, New Haven & Hartford R.R., 1917–28, restored it to sound financial and physical condition.

PEARSON, ELIPHALET (*b. Newbury, Mass., 1752; d. Greenland, N.H., 1826*), educator. Graduated Harvard, 1773. First principal, Phillips Academy, Andover, 1778–86; thereafter taught at Harvard, 1786–1806, and was instrumental in founding Andover Theological Seminary to combat Unitarianism.

PEARSON, FRED STARK (*b. Lowell, Mass., 1861; d. at sea aboard Lusitania, 1915*), engineer. Graduated Tufts, 1883. Became an authority on design and construction of electrified street railway systems and electric power plants. His first major project (1839–93) was electrifying the West End Street Railway in Boston, which required generators of unprecedented size. He went on to introduce electric streetcars in Brooklyn, N.Y., and to devise an underground conduit system for the Metropolitan Street Railway Co. of New York City. For the latter he constructed a power station of 70,000 horsepower,

in 1896 the largest in the country. *Post* 1899, Pearson built large power plants for Mexico City, Rio de Janeiro, and Toronto, Canada.

PEARSON, LEONARD (*b. Evansville, Ind., 1868; d. Newfoundland, Canada, 1909*), veterinarian. Graduated Cornell University, 1888; D.V.M., University of Pennsylvania, 1890. Professor of veterinary medicine at University of Pennsylvania, *post* 1891. Learning of tuberculin studies of Koch and Gutmann whereby tuberculosis could be diagnosed in cattle before physical signs were apparent, he made the first tuberculin test in the Western Hemisphere, 1892; through speeches and writings he led in bringing about general acceptance of the test. As state veterinarian of Pennsylvania, he guided activities of the State Livestock Sanitary Board. His system of suppressing bovine tuberculosis became model for other states; his work in collaboration with associates on relation of bovine to human tuberculosis attracted world-wide attention. He was brother of Edward J. and Raymond A. Pearson.

PEARSON, RAYMOND ALLEN (*b. Evansville, Ind., 1873; d. Hyattsville, Md., 1939*), agricultural administrator, educator. Brother of Edward J. and Leonard Pearson. President, Iowa State A. & M., 1912–26; University of Maryland, 1926–35. [Supp. 2]

PEARSON, RICHMOND MUMFORD (*b. Rowan Co., N.C., 1805; d. Winston, N.C., 1878*), jurist. Chief justice, North Carolina supreme court, 1858–78; opposed conscription under Confederacy; supported Grant in 1868 campaign.

PEARSONS, DANIEL KIMBALL (*b. Bradford, Vt., 1820; d. 1912*), physician, financier, philanthropist. Removed to Chicago, Ill., 1860. Acquired great wealth as land agent and investor in Michigan pine lands; donated $5,000,000 to educational institutions, especially Beloit College.

PEARY, ROBERT EDWIN (*b. Cresson, Pa., 1856; d. Washington, D.C., 1920*), Arctic explorer. Graduated Bowdoin, 1877. Served in U.S. Coast and Geodetic Survey as a cartographic draughtsman, 1879–81; thereafter in U.S. Navy corps of civil engineers until his retirement as rear-admiral, 1911. During the summer and fall of 1886 he made the first of his seven expeditions to the Far North, trudging with a Danish friend about 100 miles inland from the foot of the Greenland icecap. On his return home, he tried to win financial support for a larger expedition to cross the icecap, but his hopes of being the first to do so were blighted by Nansen's expedition in 1889. In 1891, however, he set out to explore the unknown northern extremity of Greenland, and in the next year became the first to reach the island's northeast coast. He also made important meteorological, tidal, and ethnological observations.

Peary next determined to explore north of the coast

of Greenland and to reach the North Pole, if possible. Bad weather and ice conditions were encountered during the expedition of 1893–95 and the Pole was not attained, but Peary was back on the west coast of Greenland for scientific work the next year. He published an account of his expeditions to this point, *Northward over the "Great Ice"* (1898). Failing in a dash for the Pole, 1899, he remained in the Arctic until 1902, in the spring of that year reaching latitude 84° 17′ N. With a new ship, the *Roosevelt*, Peary tried again in 1905–06, but reached only 87° 6′ N. On his return, he published *Nearest the Pole* (1907) and made preparations for yet another expedition which left New York in July 1908. By September the *Roosevelt* had reached 82° 30′ N., a record for northern penetration by a vessel. Peary spent the next few months establishing his base camp at Cape Columbia on Ellesmere Island. Adopting Eskimo methods of dress and travel, he set out over the sea ice on March 1, 1909, with 6 white men, a Negro, 17 Eskimos, 19 sledges and 133 dogs. His plan was to let the trail-blazing sledges gradually drop off and return to base, leaving the best dogs for the polar dash. Near the 88th parallel the last supporting party dropped off, leaving Peary, the Negro, 4 Eskimos, and 40 dogs. Nearly exhausted, Peary finally reached the Pole on April 6, 1909, spent 30 hours making astronomical observations, and then returned to camp under favorable conditions in 16 days. An ugly controversy at once broke out, however, when his cable announcing victory came five days after Dr. Frederick A. Cook's claim that he had reached the Pole the preceding year. The American public generally sided with Cook, but careful scientific examination of data showed Cook's story to be false and Peary's substantiated.

PEASE, ALFRED HUMPHREYS (*b. Cleveland, O., 1838; d. St. Louis, Mo., 1882*), pianist, composer. Prominent concert pianist; best remembered for songs, "Hush Thee, My Baby," "Stars of the Summer Night."

PEASE, CALVIN (*b. Suffield, Conn., 1776; d. Warren, O., 1839*), Ohio jurist. Brother-in-law of Gideon Granger with whom he studied law. Removed to Ohio, 1800. Upheld right of jury trial against legislative act giving jurisdiction in civil suits to justices of the peace (1806); state supreme court justice, 1816–30.

PEASE, ELISHA MARSHALL (*b. Enfield, Conn., 1812; d. Lampasas, Texas, 1883*), politician, lawyer. Removing to Texas, 1835, he was chosen secretary of the provisional government and helped draft the new republic's constitution. Thereafter he served the Texas government in a number of official positions. After Texas entered the Union he served in the legislature and was Democratic governor, 1853–57. During his administration the state debt was paid, a school fund of $2,000,000 created, and an endowment for a state university established. A Unionist,

Pease became a Republican and was provisional governor, 1867–70. His administration, though sane and moderate, arrayed a majority of Texans against him.

PEASE, JOSEPH IVES (*b. Norfolk, Conn., 1809; d. near Salisbury, Conn., 1883*), line-engraver. Made charming and popular engravings for gift-book annuals, also fashion plates for *Godey's Lady's Book*.

PEASLEE, EDMUND RANDOLPH (*b. Newton, N.H., 1814; d. New York, N.Y., 1878*), physician, gynecologist. Graduated Dartmouth, 1836; M.D., Yale, 1840. An esteemed teacher at many medical schools; wrote *Ovarian Tumors: Their Pathology, Diagnosis and Treatment, Especially by Ovariotomy* (1872).

PEAVEY, FRANK HUTCHINSON (*b. Eastport, Maine, 1850; d. Chicago, Ill., 1901*), industrialist. Removed to Iowa, 1867. Built up a grain elevator empire centered in Minneapolis; organized Peavey Steamship Co., 1899, for freighting on Great Lakes.

PEAY, AUSTIN (*b. near Hopkinsville, Ky., 1876; d. Nashville, Tenn., 1927*), lawyer, Tennessee politician. Reform Democratic governor, 1923–27; grudgingly signed anti-evolution bill, which was basis for Scopes trial.

PECK, CHARLES HORTON (*b. Rensselaer Co., N.Y., 1833; d. Menands, N.Y., 1917*), pioneer mycologist. Graduated State Normal School, Albany, N.Y., 1852; Union College, 1859. Appointed to staff of New York State Cabinet of Natural History, 1867, he made a notable series of botanical studies, known as "Peck's Reports" (1868–1912) to the regents of the University of the State of New York. Appointed New York State botanist, 1883, he built up a state herbarium; he also made investigations of fungi native to America and Canada which resulted in descriptions of 2500 species new to science, and wrote excellent synoptical studies of the agarics and other groups.

PECK, CHARLES HOWARD (*b. Newtown, Conn., 1870; d. 1927*), surgeon. M.D., N.Y. College of Physicians and Surgeons, 1893; taught surgery there *post* 1900. Best known for gastro-intestinal operations; senior consultant in general surgery, American Expeditionary Forces, 1918.

PECK, GEORGE (*b. Middlefield, N.Y., 1797; d. Scranton, Pa., 1876*), Methodist clergyman, editor, author. Grandfather of Stephen Crane.

PECK, GEORGE RECORD (*b. near Cameron, N.Y., 1843; d. Chicago, Ill., 1923*), Union soldier, railroad attorney. General solicitor, Santa Fe Railroad, 1882–84, 1886–95; general counsel, Chicago, Milwaukee & St. Paul, 1895–1911.

PECK, GEORGE WASHINGTON (*b. Rehoboth, Mass., 1817; d. Boston, Mass., 1859*), lawyer, journalist, music critic. Author, among other books, of the California Gold Rush fantasy *Aurifodina* (under pseudonym "Cantell A. Bigly," 1849).

PECK, GEORGE WILBUR (*b. Henderson, N.Y., 1840; d. Milwaukee, Wis., 1916*), humorist, journalist. Raised in Wisconsin; founder-editor, Milwaukee *Sun;* Democratic governor of Wisconsin, 1891–95. Author of *Peck's Bad Boy and His Pa* (1883), *The Grocery Man and Peck's Bad Boy* (1883) and others.

PECK, HARRY THURSTON (*b. Stamford, Conn., 1856; d. 1914*), classical philologist, editor, literary critic. Taught Latin at Columbia University, 1882–1910; edited the *Bookman*, 1895–1902; headed staffs of encyclopedias and was prolific in literary journalism. Committed suicide after a long period of mental aberration.

PECK, JAMES HAWKINS (*b. present Jefferson Co., Tenn., c. 1790; d. St. Charles, Mo., 1836*), jurist. As federal district judge in Missouri *post c.* 1822, he was impeached but acquitted for alleged misuse of contempt powers (1830–31).

PECK, JESSE TRUESDELL (*b. Middlefield, N.Y., 1811; d. 1883*), Methodist bishop, educator, author. Won notice for an anti-slavery speech at the 1844 General Conference which split the church; a founder of Syracuse University.

PECK, JOHN JAMES (*b. Manlius, N.Y., 1821; d. Syracuse, N.Y., 1878*), Union major-general, railroad and insurance executive.

PECK, JOHN MASON (*b. Litchfield, Conn., 1789; d. Rock Spring, Ill., 1858*), Baptist clergyman. Missionary in Illinois, Indiana and Missouri *post* 1817. Author of *Guide for Emigrants* (1831), *Gazetteer of Illinois* (1834), *The Traveller's Directory for Illinois* (1840) and other works.

PECK, THOMAS EPHRAIM (*b. Columbia, S.C., 1822; d. Richmond, Va., 1893*), Presbyterian clergyman. Professor at Union Theological Seminary in Virginia, 1860–93; strictly orthodox interpreter of the Scriptures.

PECK, TRACY (*b. Bristol, Conn., 1838; d. Rome, Italy, 1921*), Latinist, scholar. Graduated Yale, 1861; taught Latin at Cornell University, 1871–80, and at Yale, 1880–1908. Devoted his profound learning to effective teaching rather than writing.

PECK, WILLIAM DANDRIDGE (*b. Boston, Mass., 1763; d. Cambridge, Mass., 1822*), naturalist. Graduated Harvard, 1782. Professor of natural history, Harvard, 1805–22; first teacher of entomology in U.S.; described bark-beetles, lepidopterous borers and other parasites in pioneer scholarly papers.

PECKHAM, GEORGE WILLIAMS (*b. Albany, N.Y., 1845; d. Milwaukee, Wis., 1914*), teacher, librarian,

entomologist. With wife published valuable study, *On the Instincts and Habits of Solitary Wasps* (1898). Superintendent, public schools of Milwaukee, 1891–97; director, Milwaukee Public Library, 1897–1910.

PECKHAM, RUFUS WHEELER (*b. Albany, N.Y., 1838; d. near Albany, 1909*), jurist. Brother of Wheeler H. Peckham. Judge, N.Y. supreme court, 1883–86; N.Y. court of appeals, 1886–95. Throughout his life a Democrat, Peckham often stood against his party organization but was unopposed by Democratic leaders when President Cleveland appointed him to the U.S. Supreme Court, 1896. Distinguished for learning and industry, he commanded the respect of fellow judges and lawyers. His opinions in *U.S. vs. Trans-Missouri Freight Association, Addyston Pipe & Steel Co. vs. U.S.,* and *Lochner vs. New York* may especially be noted.

PECKHAM, STEPHEN FARNUM (*b. near Providence, R.I., 1839; d. 1918*), Union soldier, chemist, educator. Expert on petroleum and bitumens; wrote, among many other treatises, *Report on the Production, Technology, and Uses of Petroleum and Its Products* (1885); taught at a number of colleges in the East and Midwest.

PECKHAM, WHEELER HAZARD (*b. Albany, N.Y., 1833; d. New York, N.Y., 1905*), lawyer. Brother of Rufus W. Peckham. Prominent among prosecution counsel in conviction of William Tweed, 1873; a founder of New York City bar association, 1869.

PEDDER, JAMES (*b. Isle of Wight, England, 1775; d. Roxbury, Mass., 1859*), agriculturist, author. Came to America, 1832. Editor of the *Farmers' Cabinet* (Philadelphia, 1840–43) and the *Boston Cultivator* (1848–59).

PEEK, FRANK WILLIAM (*b. Calaveras Co., Calif., 1881; d. Port Daniels, Canada, 1933*), electrical engineer. Graduated Leland Stanford, 1905. Associated with General Electric Co. *post* 1906. Specialist in high-voltage generators and transmission; built a 10,-000,000 volt lightning generator (1931).

PEERS, BENJAMIN ORRS (*b. Loudoun Co., Va., 1800; d. Louisville, Ky., 1842*), Episcopal clergyman, educator, advocate of Pestalozzi's principles. Acting president, Transylvania University, 1833–34; editor, *The Journal of Christian Education, post* 1838.

PEERSON, CLENG (*b. Norway, 1783; d. Bosque Co., Texas, 1865*), immigrant leader and organizer. Arrived in New York, 1821, as agent for Norwegian Quaker settlers and others; arranged land purchase and erection of houses near Rochester, N.Y.; guided first body of Norwegian immigrants to his settlement, 1825. Journeying west in 1833 to find a new site, he chose the Fox River Valley of Illinois to which he guided (1834) the first contingent of Norwegians to Illinois; many other Norwegian settlements in the

West emanated therefrom. In 1850 he led settlers to Dallas and Bosque Counties in Texas.

PEET, HARVEY PRINDLE (*b. Bethlehem, Conn., 1794; d. New York, N.Y., 1873*), educator of the deaf. Studied and worked with Thomas H. Gallaudet, 1822–30; director, New York Institution for the Instruction of the Deaf and Dumb, 1831–67.

PEET, ISAAC LEWIS (*b. Hartford, Conn., 1824; d. New York, N.Y., 1898*), educator of the deaf. Son and pupil of Harvey P. Peet; director, New York Institution for the Instruction of the Deaf and Dumb (1867–92).

PEET, STEPHEN DENISON (*b. Euclid, O., 1831; d. Salem, Mass., 1914*), Congregational clergyman, archeologist. Pioneer student of ancient American Indian culture; editor, *American Antiquarian and Oriental Journal*, 1878–1910.

PEFFER, WILLIAM ALFRED (*b. Cumberland Co., Pa., 1831; d. Grenola, Kans., 1912*), journalist, politician. Settled successively in California, Indiana, Missouri, and Illinois, 1849–62. Having read law during Civil War service, he practiced in Tennessee, 1865–69. Removing to Kansas, he edited two small newspapers and became editor of the *Kansas Farmer* (1881), later the most powerful farm journal in Kansas. First allied with the Republican party, he later sided with the conservative wing of the Farmer's Alliance. U.S. senator from Kansas, 1891–97, his odd appearance and dry, statistical speeches made him a symbol of Populism, if not a caricature. By 1900 he had drifted back to the Republicans.

PEIRCE, BENJAMIN (*b. Salem, Mass., 1809; d. 1880*), mathematician, astronomer. Father of Charles S. and James M. Peirce. While a student at the Salem Private Grammar School, Peirce came to know Nathaniel Bowditch, who stimulated him to undertake mathematical studies. He graduated from Harvard College in 1829, taught at Bancroft's Round Hill School, Northampton, Mass., for two years, then joined the faculty at Harvard. He was professor of mathematics and astronomy from 1833 until his death. His first major work was revising and correcting Bowditch's translation of Laplace's work on celestial mechanics (1829–39); he then undertook to write a series of textbooks on trigonometry, algebra, geometry, and calculus, creditable but hardly original works. *A System of Analytic Mechanics* (1855), however, included a masterly discussion of determinants and functional determinants. Peirce took an active part in founding the Harvard Observatory, and he made remarkably accurate computations of the general perturbations of Uranus and Neptune. From 1849 until 1867 he was consulting astronomer to the *American Nautical Almanac* office established in Cambridge by Congress. In 1847 he was one of a committee of five appointed to organize the Smithsonian Institution.

He was director of the longitude determinations of the U.S. Coast Survey, 1852–67, and superintendent of the Survey, 1867–74. It was Peirce who determined upon extending the coastal survey to a general geodetic survey, which would provide a general map of the country independent of local surveys. While superintendent, Peirce took personal charge of the American expedition to Sicily to observe a solar eclipse, 1870, and probably organized the two expeditions in 1874 to observe the transit of Venus. From his work with the Survey he formulated in 1852 what is widely known as "Peirce's criterion." His most original and able mathematical contribution was his *Linear Associative Algebra* (1870, 1881). About three-quarters of his published works related to questions in astronomy, geodesy, and mechanics, and one-quarter to pure mathematics. He was generally acknowledged to be the leading mathematician in America and exerted great influence upon the progress of mathematical science in this country through encouragement of young and talented men, and through his inspiring teaching at Harvard.

PEIRCE, BENJAMIN OSGOOD (*b. Beverly, Mass., 1854; d. Cambridge, Mass., 1914*), mathematician, physicist. Graduated Harvard, 1876; Ph.D., Leipzig, 1879; studied with Wiedemann and Helmholtz. As instructor and professor at Harvard, *post* 1882, he helped develop a remarkable course on the Newtonian potential function and Fourier series, and taught graduate courses in pure mathematics and mathematical physics. His researches on the thermal conductivity of stone and its variation of temperature, and on magnetism were brilliant mathematical demonstrations. His most noteworthy publications were *Elements of the Theory of the Newtonian Potential Function* (1886, later expanded, 1902), *Short Table of Integrals* (1910), and his *Mathematical and Physical Papers, 1903–13* (1926).

PEIRCE, BRADFORD KINNEY (*b. Royalton, Vt., 1819; d. Newton Center, Mass., 1889*), Methodist clergyman, social worker. Wrote *A Half Century with Juvenile Delinquents* (1869); edited *Zion's Herald*, 1872–88.

PEIRCE, CHARLES SANDERS (*b. Cambridge, Mass, 1839; d. 1914*), philosopher, logician, scientist, founder of pragmatism. Son of Benjamin Peirce; brother of James M. Peirce. His father supervised his education with the hope of making him a mathematician. Young Peirce mastered Whately's *Elements of Logic* at age 13, and conducted quantitative analysis experiments in a laboratory which he set up. The elder Peirce trained his son in the art of concentration, encouraged in him the power of sensuous discrimination, and constantly presented him with mathematical problems, tables and examples to the end that he discover the principles for himself. In spite of obvious brilliance, Peirce did poorly at Harvard, 1855–59. In 1861 he joined the U.S. Coast Survey staff with which he remained for thirty years. He lectured at Harvard on the philosophy of science, 1864–65; gave the university lectures on philosophy, 1869–70; and worked as an assistant at the Harvard Observatory where he did research leading to the only book he published during his lifetime, *Photometric Researches* (1878). For the Coast Survey, Peirce made important pendulum investigations and researches in gravity theory; he also made the first attempt to use the wave length of a light ray as a standard unit of measure.

Peirce always called himself a logician and became the foremost logician in the United States, tending to see philosophy and other subjects almost entirely from a logical perspective. He first gained notice by bringing attention here to the work of George Boole, the founder of modern logic. Peirce went on to make a number of vital and permanent improvements in Boole's system, many of them incorporated in a long series of technical papers completed between 1867 and 1885. Many of these papers were difficult and might never have been noticed if Ernst Schröder had not based a large part of his work on Peirce's contributions. Peirce modified, extended, and transformed the Boolean algebra, making it applicable to propositions, relations, probability, and arithmetic. Practically single-handed, Peirce laid the foundations of the logic of relations, the instrument for the logical analysis of mathematics. He invented the copula of inclusion, the most important symbol in the logic of classes, two new logical algebras, two new systems of logical graphs, and was the first to give the fundamental principle for the logical development of mathematics. Oddly, he never tried to get some of his most important logical papers published, though an elaborate work on logic was turned down by publishers as being too abstruse. Peirce published only a few important papers on pure mathematics. He clearly anticipated the method for the derivation and definition of number which Bertrand Russell and Alfred Whitehead announced later. He showed too that every associative algebra can be represented by one whose elements are matrices. Further, Peirce made contributions to the theory of aggregates, transfinite arithmetic, and analysis situs.

Pragmatism, Peirce's creation, had its origin in the Cambridge discussions of a fortnightly "metaphysical club" founded in the 1870's, and including among its members, Oliver Wendell Holmes, Chauncey Wright, William James, and Nicholas St. John Green. Through his study of the history of logic, Peirce had discovered Duns Scotus and was by 1871 a convert to Scotist realism in opposition to Berkeley's nominalism. In a paper published that year in the *North American Review* (October 1871), in which Peirce criticized Berkeley, he outlined the pragmatic position, but his first definite statement of it was made in an article,

originally written in French in 1877, which appeared in the *Popular Science Monthly* for January 1878 under the title, "How to Make Our Ideas Clear." It was the second of a series of six articles on logic. In that article appeared Peirce's famous formula: "Consider what effects, which might conceivably have practical bearings, we conceive the object of our conception to have. Then, our conception of these effects is the whole of our conception of the object."

Peirce received no recognition for his work until William James in 1898 first publicly used the term "pragmatism" and acknowledged Peirce's priority. Peirce's pragmatism, however, was different from James's, having more in common with the idealism of Josiah Royce and the later views of John Dewey. Peirce, for example, believed in the idea of an absolute and in universals, but shared with the pragmatic school a belief in the dependence of logic on ethics, a critical attitude toward individualism and egoism, and a defense of the reality of absolute chance and the principle of continuity. He developed his own formulation of the last idea, and considered it his main contribution to philosophy.

In spite of his formidable intellectual achievements, Peirce was given the opportunity to teach for only eight years of his life. He was a lecturer on logic at Johns Hopkins, 1879–84, and gave occasional lectures elsewhere in addition to his early Harvard career. His lectures were generally difficult, appealing only to the brightest students, but the chief hurdle was his general personality and personal habits. He was vain, sloppy in dress, forgetful, uncivil, highly emotional, and suffered socially and professionally from the circumstances of his divorce from his first wife in 1883. Having inherited some money, he retired in 1887 to a remote and wild section of Pennsylvania near Milford where he wrote indefatigably on many subjects, and as poverty overtook him, eked out a living writing book reviews and articles for encyclopedias.

PEIRCE, CYRUS (*b. Waltham, Mass., 1790; d. West Newton, Mass., 1860*), Congregational clergyman, educator. Graduated Harvard, 1810; Harvard Divinity School, 1815. Principal of the first state normal school established in Massachusetts, at Lexington and West Newton, 1839–42, 1844–49.

PEIRCE, HENRY AUGUSTUS (*b. Dorchester, Mass., 1808; d. San Francisco, Calif., 1885*), merchant, diplomat. As partner of James Hunnewell and Charles Brewer, made fortune in Pacific trade; U.S. minister to the Hawaiian Kingdom, 1869–77. Expansionist.

PEIRCE, JAMES MILLS (*b. Cambridge, Mass., 1834; d. Cambridge, 1906*), educator, mathematician. Son of Benjamin Peirce; brother of Charles S. Peirce. Graduated Harvard, 1853. Professor of mathematics at Harvard, *post* 1861; first dean of Harvard graduate school, 1890–95.

PEIRCE, WILLIAM (*b. probably England, c. 1590; d. off New Providence, Bahamas, 1641*), shipmaster. Made many trips conveying emigrants to New England and Virginia, 1625–35; author of *An Almanac for . . . 1639. Calculated for New England* (Cambridge, Mass., printed by Stephen Day), the earliest almanac compiled in English America.

PEIXOTTO, BENJAMIN FRANKLIN (*b. New York, N.Y., 1834; d. 1890*), lawyer, diplomat, journalist. As consul to Rumania (1870–76), was influential in abating persecution of Jews there; founded (1886) and edited *The Menorah,* important Jewish periodical; was active official of B'nai B'rith.

PELHAM, HENRY (*b. Boston, Mass., 1748/49; d. Ireland, 1806*), painter, miniaturist, engraver, cartographer. Son of Peter Pelham; half-brother of John S. Copley. A Loyalist, he removed to London, England, 1776.

PELHAM, JOHN (*b. present Calhoun Co., Ala., 1838; d. Kelly's Ford, Va., 1863*), Confederate soldier. Resigned from West Point, 1861, to join Confederate Army. Became romantic hero in command of famed Stuart Horse Artillery; served brilliantly during Seven Days' Battles and at Antietam.

PELHAM, PETER (*b. England, c. 1695; d. Boston, Mass., 1751*), limner, engraver. Learned mezzotint engraving in London and was well trained in portrait painting before he emigrated to Boston *ante* 1728. As the practice of his art did not produce a living for him, he opened a school in Boston at which he taught dancing, arithmetic, and other subjects. In 1748 he married Mary Singleton Copley, a widow, and it was in his household that John Singleton Copley was raised as well as Pelham's own son, Henry, who also became an engraver and painter.

PELLEW, HENRY EDWARD (*b. Canterbury, England, 1828; d. Washington, D.C., 1923*), philanthropist. Brother-in-law of John Jay (1817–1894); settled in the United States *post* 1873. Helped organize Charity Organization Society in New York; aided tenement house reform and night refuge movements.

PELOUBET, FRANCIS NATHAN (*b. New York, N.Y., 1831; d. Auburndale, Mass., 1920*), Congregational clergyman, author. Pioneer in the American Sunday school movement and writer of widely used teaching aids for use with the International Lessons.

PELZ, PAUL JOHANNES (*b. Seitendorf, Silesia, 1841; d. Washington, D.C., 1918*), architect. Came to America, 1858; studied with Detlef Lienau. With John L. Smithmeyer, submitted winning design for the Library of Congress building, 1873.

PEMBERTON, ISRAEL (*b. Philadelphia, Pa., 1715; d. 1779*), Quaker merchant, philanthropist. Brother of James and John Pemberton. One of the wealthiest merchants of his day; promoted friendly relations with Indians. Was imprisoned for refusing allegiance oath to Commonwealth of Pennsylvania, 1777.

PEMBERTON, JAMES (*b. Philadelphia, Pa., 1723; d. 1809*), Quaker merchant, philanthropist. Brother of Israel and John Pemberton. A founder of Society for the Relief of Free Negroes, 1775; president, Pennsylvania Society for Promoting the Abolition of Slavery, 1790–1803.

PEMBERTON, JOHN (*b. Philadelphia, Pa., 1727; d. Pyrmont, Germany, 1795*), Quaker preacher. Brother of Israel and James Pemberton. Preached in Great Britain, 1750–53, 1781–86; imprisoned in 1777–78 for opposing armed resistance to Great Britain.

PEMBERTON, JOHN CLIFFORD (*b. Philadelphia, Pa., 1814; d. Penllyn, Pa., 1881*), soldier. Great-grandson of Israel Pemberton. Graduated West Point, 1837. Served ably in Florida Indian wars (1837–39), the Mexican War, and in the West. Commissioned Confederate brigadier-general, June 1861, he was made major-general early in 1862, in charge of the southeastern department. He built Fort Wagner and Battery "B" for defense of Charleston during 1862. Appointed lieutenant-general, October 1862, he commanded the department embracing Tennessee, Mississippi, and eastern Louisiana. He took direct charge of the defense of Vicksburg against Grant, surrendering only when heavily outnumbered and totally without food on July 4, 1863.

PEÑALOSA BRICEÑO, DIEGO DIONISO de (*b. Lima, Peru, c. 1622; d. Paris, France ?, c. 1687*), soldier. Governor of New Mexico, 1661–65; banished by the Inquisition from New Spain for misconduct, 1668; sold military information to England and France.

PENDER, WILLIAM DORSEY (*b. Edgecombe Co., N.C., 1834; d. Staunton, Va., 1863*), Confederate soldier. Graduated West Point, 1854. Commanded North Carolina brigade in Gen. A. P. Hill's division from the Seven Days' Battle through Chancellorsville. Promoted major-general, May 1863, he was mortally wounded while leading a division at Gettysburg.

PENDLETON, EDMUND (*b. Caroline Co., Va., 1721; d. Caroline Co., 1803*), lawyer, jurist, Revolutionary patriot. Admitted to local bar, 1741, he was admitted to practice before the general court, 1745. Elected to the House of Burgesses, 1752, he was by 1765 a leader of the conservative "Cavalier" party, opposed to Patrick Henry and violent measures. On the approach of crisis, 1773, Pendleton emerged as one of Virginia's leading men. He represented Virginia in the first Continental Congress, was president of the two Virginia revolutionary conventions which met in 1775, presided over the Committee of Safety, and was president of the Virginia convention of 1776 which recommended a declaration of independence.

He also helped draw up Virginia's constitution and was first speaker of the Virginia House of Delegates, 1776. President of Virginia supreme court of appeals, 1779–1803. He vigorously supported adoption of the federal constitution.

PENDLETON, EDMUND MONROE (*b. Eatonton, Ga., 1815; d. 1884*), physician, agricultural chemist. Organized in Augusta, Ga., *c.* 1867, a firm to manufacture commercial fertilizers on large scale; was among first to use cotton seed for fertilizer.

PENDLETON, ELLEN FITZ (*b. Westerly, R.I., 1864; d. Newton, Mass., 1936*), educator. Graduated Wellesley, 1886; served on its staff thereafter, and was president from 1911 to 1936. [*Supp. 2*]

PENDLETON, GEORGE HUNT (*b. Cincinnati, O., 1825; d. Brussels, Belgium, 1889*), lawyer, Ohio legislator, diplomat. Congressman, Democrat, from Ohio, 1857–65; Democratic candidate for vice-presidency, 1864. Sponsored "Ohio idea" to pay U.S. bonds in greenbacks, 1867; served as U.S. senator from Ohio, 1879–85, and advocated civil service reform.

PENDLETON, JAMES MADISON (*b. Spotsylvania Co., Va., 1811; d. Bowling Green, Ky., 1891*), Baptist clergyman, editor. Strong Unionist as pastor at Bowling Green, Ky., and Murfreesboro, Tenn.

PENDLETON, JOHN B. (*b. New York, N.Y., 1798; d. New York, 1866*), lithographer. After study of process in Paris, and with aid of two French workmen, produced first commercial lithographs in United States at Boston, 1825.

PENDLETON, JOHN STROTHER (*b. Culpeper Co., Va., 1802; d. Culpeper Co., 1868*), lawyer, Virginia legislator. U.S. chargé d'affaires in Chile, 1841–44. Congressman, Whig, from Virginia, 1845–49. Concluded treaty of commerce, 1853, as U.S. chargé d'affaires to Argentine Confederation, 1851–54.

PENDLETON, WILLIAM KIMBROUGH (*b. Yanceyville, Va., 1817; d. Bethany, W. Va., 1899*), minister of the Disciples of Christ, educator. President, Bethany College, 1866–86; edited *Millennial Harbinger*, 1865–70; superintendent, West Virginia public schools, 1873–80.

PENDLETON, WILLIAM NELSON (*b. Richmond, Va., 1809; d. Lexington, Va., 1883*), Episcopal clergyman, educator, Confederate soldier. Graduated West Point, 1830. Pastor of Grace Church, Lexington, Va., 1853–83. As brigadier-general, 1862–65, he was a distinguished chief of artillery in the Army of Northern Virginia.

PENFIELD, EDWARD (*b. Brooklyn, N.Y., 1866; d. Beacon, N.Y., 1925*), illustrator, painter, author. Inaugurator of the brief but golden age of American poster art; art editor for *Harper's Magazine, Weekly*, and *Bazar*, 1890–1901.

PENFIELD, FREDERIC COURTLAND (*b. East Haddam, Conn., 1855; d. New York, N.Y., 1922*), journalist, diplomat. Able, tactful, U.S. ambassador to Austria-Hungary, 1913–17.

PENFIELD, WILLIAM LAWRENCE (*b. Dover, Mich., 1846; d. Washington, D.C., 1909*), jurist. As solicitor, U.S. Department of State, 1897–1905, Penfield made valuable contributions to U.S. policy and to promotion of international arbitration.

PENHALLOW, SAMUEL (*b. Cornwall, England, 1665; d. Portsmouth, N.H., 1726*), merchant, judge, historian. Emigrated to New England, 1686. Treasurer, province of New Hampshire, 1699–1726; chief justice, superior court, 1717; held numerous other offices. Author of *The History of the Wars of New-England etc.* (1726), a valuable account of the Indian wars of 1702–25.

PENICK, CHARLES CLIFTON (*b. Charlotte Co., Va., 1843; d. Baltimore, Md., 1914*), Episcopal clergyman. Missionary bishop of Cape Palmas, Liberia, 1877–83.

PENINGTON, EDWARD (*b. Amersham, England, 1667; d. Philadelphia, Pa., 1701*), colonial official. Author of several tracts in defense of Quakers against attacks by Thomas Crisp and George Keith (1695–96), he came to Pennsylvania as surveyor-general, 1698, and served until his death.

PENINGTON, EDWARD (*b. Bucks Co., Pa., 1726; d. Philadelphia, Pa., 1796*), Quaker merchant. Grandson of Edward Penington (1667–1701). Member, Philadelphia Committee of Correspondence, 1774; delegate, first Continental Congress, 1774. Opposed armed resistance and independence.

PENN, JOHN (*b. England, 1729; d. Philadelphia, Pa., 1795*), Pennsylvania provincial official. Grandson of William Penn; brother of Richard Penn. Inherited life use of a quarter of the proprietary rights in Pennsylvania, 1771. A resident of the province and member of the provincial council, 1752–55, Penn attended the Albany Congress on Indian Affairs, 1754. He was again in residence as lieutenant-governor of the province, 1763–71, and from 1773 to the end of proprietary rule on Sept. 26, 1776. He handled difficult boundary claims with Connecticut, Virginia, and Maryland, and tried to mediate between disgruntled Indians and revengeful frontiersmen. Yielding gracefully to the turn of events in 1776, he made his principal residence in or near Philadelphia until his death.

PENN, JOHN (*b. Caroline Co., Va., 1740; d. 1788*), lawyer, Revolutionary patriot. Removed to Granville Co., N.C., 1774. Member of the Continental Congress, 1775–77, 1778–80; signer, Declaration of Independence; member, North Carolina board of war, 1780–81.

PENN, RICHARD (*b. England, 1735; d. England, 1811*), Pennsylvania provincial official. Grandson of

William Penn; brother of John Penn (1729–1795). Lieutenant-governor of Pennsylvania, 1771–73; conveyed Congress's "Olive Branch" petition to the King, 1775; remained in England thereafter.

PENN, THOMAS (*b. Bristol, England, 1702; d. England, 1775*), Pennsylvania provincial official. Son of William Penn; uncle of John and Richard Penn. His father, on his death in 1718, left the proprietary interests in Pennsylvania to his widow as executrix for their four sons. Thomas acquired a one-fourth interest, 1727, and in 1746 an additional half interest. From 1732 to 1741 he managed the province's affairs in Philadelphia; thereafter, he lived in England and conducted business by correspondence. He was never well liked, either by colonists or Indians. The Indians were particularly incensed by his "Walking Purchase" of the Forks of the Delaware in 1737. Penn was only a nominal Quaker for most of his life.

PENN, WILLIAM (*b. London, England, 1644; d. England, 1718*), Quaker statesman, founder of Pennsylvania. Son of Adm. Sir William Penn (1621–1670), a wealthy and influential Anglican, and Margaret Jasper Penn. Religiously inclined even in childhood, Penn came early under Puritan influences which caused his expulsion in 1662, after two years' study, from Christ Church College, Oxford. Resident on the Continent for the next three years, he had a glimpse of naval service during the Dutch War (1665), studied at Lincoln's Inn for about a year, and then (1666) went to Ireland to take charge of several estates owned by his father. There came the great turning point of his life. Hearing the powerful preaching of Thomas Loe, an early Quaker apostle, he began to attend meetings of Friends, and was soon in trouble with the authorities who put him in jail for a time. Released, he was recalled to England by his father. He then became an avowed and active Friend, writing a number of powerful pamphlets—among them, *The Sandy Foundation Shaken* (1668) and *No Cross, No Crown* (1669)—directed against luxury, economic oppression, and curbs on religious freedom and rights of free Englishmen. He was again imprisoned for his writings, but in 1670 won an outstanding legal victory for freedom of speech and juries by acting as his own pleader in the noted "Bushell's Case." He made missionary tours through Holland, Germany, and England, 1670–80.

Meanwhile, by a series of transactions the American province of West Jersey had come into the hands of Friends and Penn became one of the trustees to manage the property. The 200 settlers who arrived to found the town of Burlington, 1677, brought with them a statement of "Concessions and Agreements" for their government; this charter was written largely by Penn. It guaranteed the right of petition and jury trial, provided against imprisonment for debt, permitted no capital punishment, and guaranteed religious freedom. Further, it provided for fair treatment of the Indians; and it also announced itself as fundamental law, preeminent over subsequent statutes. The Assembly, which was to dominate the government, was to be freely elected by the settlers each year; its debates were to be public. The proprietors were to appoint the executive but there was no provision for an executive veto.

Penn's next venture into practical politics was Pennsylvania. He had inherited from his father, besides a considerable fortune immediately available, a large claim for funds loaned to King Charles II. On petition, Penn received in payment (1681) a great tract of land north of Maryland. The King insisted that it be called Pennsylvania, in honor of the grantee's father. In 1682, Penn received from his friend the Duke of York the territory of Delaware, which was first joined to Pennsylvania but later became a separate province. Penn called his new property a "Holy Experiment" and at once set to work to develop it. He sent over his cousin, William Markham, to act as his deputy (1681) and himself followed the next year. He broadcast proposals to settlers, especially among his converts on the continent of Europe. His terms for purchase or rental of land were very liberal and soon attracted many settlers. Penn's first *Frame of Government* for his province was dated April 25, 1682, and appended to it a few days later (May 5) were the *Laws Agreed Upon in England*. The government was not so strikingly democratic as that for West Jersey. Large powers were granted to the governor's Council as compared with those given the Assembly, yet both were elective and the governor was assigned a rather minor place. Murder and treason were the only capital crimes and complete religious freedom was permitted. The preface stated: "Any Government is free to the People under it (whatever be the Frame) where the Laws rule, and the People are a Party to those Laws." The Pennsylvania Assembly soon became sensitive in claiming its rights. Penn usually acquiesced, though at times he became exasperated by the insistent claims. Penn's brightest record is that of his dealings with the Indians. He took stern measures to protect them against rum and the rapacity of white traders, and to insure fairness in land transactions. The Indians consequently were intensely loyal to him; not until his descendants and successors had betrayed and defrauded them did Pennsylvania know the terrors of frontier warfare. Tradition has fused his several treaties made with the Indians into one great one, "under the elm tree at Shackamaxon," as made famous by Benjamin West's painting. Penn's first stay in Pennsylvania lasted only a year and ten months (1682–August 1684), but he accomplished much, looking after affairs of government, superintending the laying out of Philadelphia, building his mansion at Pennsbury, visiting other colonies, preaching, trying to settle the difficult Maryland boundary dispute, and writing a memorable description of the colony (letter to the Free Society of Traders in England, August 1683).

Returning to England, Penn secured from King James II the release of 1300 Friends from jail, and made a third missionary tour to Holland and Germany. His close friendship with James II made him suspect after the Revolution of 1688, and for two years (1692–94) his governorship of Pennsylvania was forfeited; it was restored when suspicions had abated. During these troubled years he continued to supervise his interests in the New World. He secured a partial settlement of his dispute with Lord Baltimore over boundaries and gave orders in 1689 for establishment of a public grammar school in Philadelphia (the William Penn Charter School). In 1697 he presented to the Board of Trade a plan for uniting the American colonies which included a central congress with limited powers.

Religious and governmental problems arose that demanded his presence in Pennsylvania. His second and last trip (1699–1701) was marked by a change in the form of government, embodied in the Charter of Privileges (1701). Separate legislatures were created for Pennsylvania and Delaware; the Council, made appointive, was to be practically an advisory board to the governor; the Assembly, annually elected on a wide suffrage, was to be a unicameral legislature and was empowered to convene on its own call. After 1701, Penn, in spite of troubles and disappointments in his personal affairs and with his appointed officials, retained his active proprietorship until apoplexy rendered him incapable c. 1712.

PENNELL, JOSEPH (*b. Philadelphia, Pa., 1857; d. Brooklyn, N.Y., 1926*), artist, etcher, lithographer. After study at Pennsylvania School of Industrial Art and the school of the Pennsylvania Academy (where he rebelled against the unsympathetic criticisms of Thomas Eakins), Pennell commenced c. 1880 a long, colorful career as illustrator in Europe and the United States. By precept and example, he fought to raise standards of magazine and book illustration; his own expert draftsmanship and high artistic integrity lent authority to his waspish criticisms of shoddy work by others. Between 1884 and 1912, he was primarily engaged in familiarizing America with the picturesqueness of Europe; thereafter he interpreted the beauty of his own country, in particular the drama of skyscraper cities and great industrial enterprises. His lithographs of the Panama Canal, done in 1912, were among his best work. Returning permanently to the United States in 1917, he pictured the industrial effort of World War I as he had previously lithographed the war work in British plants. His immense output comprised over 900 plates in etching and mezzotint, some 621 lithographs, and innumerable sketches and water-colors. He was the first to make the varied aspects of modern industry recognized subjects for art. He was also author as well as illustrator of a number of books, wrote treatises on illustration and lithography, and published a highly individual autobiography, *The Adventures of an Illustrator* (1925).

PENNIMAN, JAMES HOSMER (*b. Alexandria, Va., 1860; d. Philadelphia, Pa., 1931*), educator, textbook author, bibliophile. Donor of special educational reference libraries to Pennsylvania, Yale and Brown Universities.

PENNINGTON, JAMES W. C. (*b. Maryland, 1809; d. Jacksonville, Fla., 1870*), Congregational and Presbyterian clergyman, teacher. An escaped slave, he gained fame as a learned and eloquent preacher; he was author of *The Fugitive Blacksmith* (London, 1849) and of works on Negro history.

PENNINGTON, WILLIAM (*b. Newark, N.J., 1796; d. Newark, 1862*), New Jersey lawyer and politician. Son of William S. Pennington. Whig governor of New Jersey, 1837–43; chief figure in "Broad Seal" War, 1838; congressman, and controversial speaker of the House, 1859–61.

PENNINGTON, WILLIAM SANDFORD (*b. Newark, N.J., 1757; d. 1826*), lawyer, Revolutionary soldier, New Jersey legislator. Judge, state supreme court, 1804–13; (Democrat) Republican governor, 1813–15; federal district judge, 1815–26.

PENNOCK, ALEXANDER MOSELY (*b. Norfolk, Va., 1814; d. Portsmouth, N.H., 1876*), naval officer. Won reputation for executive ability as commander of federal naval base at Cairo, Ill., 1862–64, serving Mississippi gunboat flotilla; promoted rear-admiral, 1872.

PENNOYER, SYLVESTER (*b. Groton, N.Y., 1831; d. Portland, Oreg., 1902*), lawyer, businessman. As Democratic governor of Oregon, 1887–95, he advocated compulsory arbitration of labor disputes, a graduated income tax and a general liberalization of government. He became a Populist in 1892, subsequent to his re-election, and bitterly opposed President Cleveland.

PENNYPACKER, ELIJAH FUNK (*b. Chester Co., Pa., 1804; d. 1888*), farmer, Pennsylvania legislator, Abolitionist. President, state anti-slavery society; made his house near Phoenixville an important Underground Railroad station.

PENNYPACKER, GALUSHA (*b. Chester Co., Pa., 1844; d. Philadelphia, Pa., 1916*), Union soldier. Nephew of Elijah F. Pennypacker. Rose to major-general of volunteers; won Congressional Medal for gallantry at Fort Fisher, 1865. Commanded U.S. 16th Infantry, 1869–83.

PENNYPACKER, SAMUEL WHITAKER (*b. Phoenixville, Pa., 1843; d. near Schwenksville, Pa., 1916*), lawyer, jurist, bibliophile, historian. Republican reform governor of Pennsylvania, 1903–07.

PENROSE, BOIES (*b. Philadelphia, Pa., 1860; d. Washington, D.C., 1921*), Pennsylvania Republican politician and legislator. Grandson of Charles B. Penrose; brother of Richard A. F. Penrose and Spencer Penrose. Graduated Harvard, 1881. After writing a scholarly treatise, *The City Government of Philadelphia* (1887), he commenced a long career as a tough, resourceful, often ruthless political boss in Pennsylvania, apparently motivated by a desire for power rather than money. Serving in the U.S. Senate from 1897 until his death, he was chairman of the Senate Finance Committee *post* 1911, and succeeded Matthew S. Quay as leader of the state Republican machine, 1904. He was a consistent supporter of a high protective tariff.

PENROSE, CHARLES BINGHAM (*b. Philadelphia, Pa., 1798; d. Harrisburg, Pa., 1857*), lawyer, politician. Anti-Masonic Whig state senator, 1833–41; solicitor, U.S. treasury, 1841–45; respected member of Philadelphia bar.

PENROSE, RICHARD ALEXANDER FULLERTON (*b. Philadelphia, Pa., 1863; d. Philadelphia, 1931*), geologist. Brother of Boies Penrose and Spencer Penrose. Graduated Harvard, 1884; Ph.D., 1886. Professor of economic geology, University of Chicago, 1892–1911; a founder of Commonwealth Mining and Milling Co., and of Utah Copper Co.

PENROSE, SPENCER (*b. Philadelphia, Pa., 1865; d. Colorado Springs, Colo., 1939*), Colorado mine operator, promoter, philanthropist. Brother of Boies and Richard A. F. Penrose. [*Supp. 2*]

PENTECOST, GEORGE FREDERICK (*b. Albion, Ill., 1842; d. Philadelphia, Pa., 1920*), Baptist clergyman, evangelist and author.

PEPPER, GEORGE SECKEL (*b. Philadelphia, Pa., 1808; d. Philadelphia, 1890*), philanthropist. Brother of William Pepper (1810–1864). Benefactor of local cultural and charitable institutions; a legacy from his estate was first grant to Free Library of Philadelphia.

PEPPER, WILLIAM (*b. Philadelphia, Pa., 1810; d. 1864*), physician, teacher. Brother of George S. Pepper. M.D., University of Pennsylvania, 1832. Physician to the Pennsylvania Hospital, 1842–58, where he took prominent teaching role; professor of medicine, University of Pennsylvania, 1860–64.

PEPPER, WILLIAM (*b. Philadelphia, Pa., 1843; d. Pleasanton, Calif., 1898*), physician, educator, public benefactor. Son of William Pepper (1810–1864). Graduated University of Pennsylvania, 1862; M.D., 1864. His early experience was as pathologist to the Pennsylvania Hospital. Beginning as a lecturer on morbid anatomy at the Medical School of the University of Pennsylvania, 1868, he continued to teach there until 1895, becoming professor of clinical medicine, 1876, and professor of the theory and practice of medicine,

1884. Through his efforts, there was founded at Pennsylvania, 1874, the first teaching hospital in the U.S. closely associated with a university medical school, and in which the faculty acted as staff; in 1887 he founded the University Hospital nurses' training school. He outlined his principles of reform in medical education in two notable addresses delivered in 1877 and 1893. In honor of his father, he established and endowed the William Pepper Laboratory of Clinical Medicine (1894), the first in America to promote advanced clinical studies into the causation of disease. Pepper was one of the first to describe malarial parasites, to call attention to the involvement of the bone marrow in pernicious anemia, and to outline the modern therapeutics of tuberculosis. Among his better known works were the editorship of *A System of Practical Medicine* (1885–86), and his *Text-Book of the Theory and Practice of Medicine* (1893–94).

In 1880 he was appointed provost of the University of Pennsylvania and soon showed administrative abilities of a high order. In 14 years he raised the university from a loosely organized group of schools to an integrated, modern university, highly esteemed in academic circles. He reorganized the faculties and curricula of the College, the Dental School, the Law School, and the Towne Scientific School. Further, he was instrumental in founding the Wharton School of Finance, the Veterinary School, the School of Architecture, the Wistar Institute of Anatomy and Biology, and the Bennett School for the graduate education of women. He built a new library, started departments of hygiene, biology, and physical education, and further developed the Graduate School of Philosophy. A notable contribution was his creation of the University Extension Lectures, a widely influential experiment in adult education.

PEPPERRELL, Sir WILLIAM (*b. Kittery Point, Maine, 1696; d. 1759*), merchant, colonial official, soldier. Pepperrell's father, after apprenticeship to the captain of a fishing vessel sailing to the New England coast, became a merchant on the Isle of Shoals and later at Kittery Point. He prospered and took his son into partnership. Thereafter their business grew constantly; they built ships, engaged in trade with the Indies, the Southern colonies, and the Mediterranean, and acquired extensive tracts of real estate in Maine, then part of Massachusetts. The younger Pepperrell spent much of his time in Boston managing business affairs, became known in the upper social circles, and married a granddaughter of Samuel Sewell, 1723. He was made colonel in charge of the Maine militia, 1726, became a lifelong member of the governor's Council the next year, and for 18 years was chosen president of the Council. In 1730, Gov. Jonathan Belcher appointed him chief justice of the Province. When Gov. William Shirley conceived the idea of attacking the French fortress at Louisbourg on Cape Breton, 1744, Pepperrell was chosen to command the expedition. Under protection of a British fleet, some 4000 provincial troops arrived at Cape Breton on April 30, 1745. Although Pepperrell had no experience investing a fortress, the troops landed in good style and the inefficient French garrison promptly gave up its main battery. The siege went on amidst much confusion and occasional merriment until the French surrendered on June 17. Pepperrell was acclaimed a hero, receiving a baronetcy in 1746, the first granted to an American. He raised troops during the French and Indian War, was made major-general, 1755, and lieutenant-general, 1759, but did not take part in any battles.

PERABO, JOHANN ERNST (*b. Wiesbaden, Germany, 1845; d. West Roxbury, Mass., 1920*), pianist, composer. Came to America as a child. Studied at Leipzig Conservatory, 1862–65. Especially noted for playing of Beethoven and Shubert, and as a teacher.

PERALTA, PEDRO de (*b. Spain, c. 1584; d. Madrid, Spain, 1666*), colonial official. Appointed governor of New Mexico, 1609; founded the settlement of Santa Fé. Engaged in serious disputes with Franciscan missionaries. Returned to Mexico, c. 1613.

PERCHÉ, NAPOLEON JOSEPH (*b. Angers, France, 1805; d. New Orleans, La., 1883*), Roman Catholic clergyman. Came to America, 1837, as missionary in Kentucky; served in New Orleans, La., *post* 1842, where he was archbishop *post* 1870. Edited *Le Propagateur Catholique*, 1842–57.

PERCIVAL, JAMES GATES (*b. Kensington, Conn., 1795; d. Hazel Green, Wis., 1856*), poet, geologist. Graduated Yale, 1815; M.D., 1820. Regarded as the ranking American poet until Bryant's *Poems* appeared in 1832. After *Poems* (1821), Percival published *Clio I and II* (1822), *Prometheus Part II with Other Poems* (1822), *Clio III* (1827), and *The Dream of a Day, and Other Poems* (1843). In 1827–28 he aided Noah Webster in revising his Dictionary. He was state geologist of Connecticut, 1835–38, and of Wisconsin, 1854–56, publishing reports of his work. Eccentric and impractical, he was one of the most learned men of his time.

PERCIVAL, JOHN (*b. West Barnstable, Mass., 1779; d. 1862*), merchant mariner, naval officer. Known as "Roaring Jack." Sailing master of *Peacock* in victory over *Epervier*, 1813; commanded *Constitution* on world cruise, 1844–46.

PERCY, GEORGE (*b. England, 1580; d. England, 1632*), colonial official. Son of Henry Percy, 8th Earl of Northumberland. Joined Virginia voyage of Dec. 1606; incapacitated by illness as governor of Virginia, 1609–10; author of two accounts of early Virginia. He left the colony in April 1612.

PERHAM, JOSIAH (*b. Wilton, Maine, 1803; d. East Boston, Mass., 1868*), showman, railroad executive. First to persuade railroads to issue cheap, round-trip

excursion fares; first, but unsuccessful, president of Northern Pacific Railroad, 1864.

PERIAM, JONATHAN (*b. Newark, N.J., 1823; d. 1911*), horticulturist, agricultural writer. Removed to Cook Co., Ill., 1838. Edited the *Prairie Farmer*, 1876–84, 1887–93; wrote or compiled a number of farm reference books.

PERIN, CHARLES PAGE (*b. West Point, N.Y., 1861; d. New York, N.Y., 1937*), geologist, steel engineer. Chiefly associated (*post* 1902) with the Tata Iron and Steel Co., India's first modern steel plant. [*Supp. 2*]

PERKINS, CHARLES CALLAHAN (*b. Boston, Mass., 1823; d. near Windsor, Vt., 1886*), art critic, organizer of cultural activities. President, Boston Handel and Haydn Society, 1850–51, 1875–86; largest subscriber toward Boston Music Hall and benefactor of Museum of Fine Arts.

PERKINS, CHARLES ELLIOTT (*b. Cincinnati, O., 1840; d. Westwood, Mass., 1907*), railroad executive. Son of James H. Perkins; cousin of John Murray Forbes. President, Chicago, Burlington & Quincy Railroad, 1881–1901; added many subsidiary lines and strengthened the road financially.

PERKINS, ELI. [See LANDON, MELVILLE DE LANCEY, 1839–1910.]

PERKINS, ELISHA (*b. Norwich, Conn., 1741; d. New York, N.Y., 1799*), medical quack. Invented curative "metallic tractors," which were pieces of metal to be drawn over affected areas of the body. "Perkinism" enjoyed international celebrity, 1795–1800.

PERKINS, FREDERIC BEECHER (*b. Hartford, Conn., 1828; d. Morristown, N.J., 1899*), editor, author, and pioneer in library science. Librarian at Boston and San Francisco Public Libraries, among others.

PERKINS, GEORGE CLEMENT (*b. Kennebunkport, Maine, 1839; d. Oakland, Calif., 1923*), ship-owner, banker, California legislator. Removed to California, 1855; incorporated Pacific Coast Steamship Co. Republican governor of California, 1880–83; U.S. senator, 1893–1915.

PERKINS, GEORGE DOUGLAS (*b. Holley, N.Y., 1840; d. 1914*), printer, newspaper publisher and editor. Associated with *Sioux City* (Iowa) *Journal* (1869–1914); noted for his "lay sermons." Congressman, Republican, from Iowa, 1891–99.

PERKINS, GEORGE HAMILTON (*b. Hopkinton, N.H., 1836; d. Boston, Mass., 1899*), naval officer. Commanded monitor *Chickasaw* during forcing of Mobile Bay forts, successfully engaging Confederate ram *Tennessee*. Promoted commodore after retirement, 1891.

PERKINS, GEORGE HENRY (*b. Cambridge, Mass., 1844; d. 1933*), geologist, educator. Graduated Yale, 1867; Ph.D., 1869. Professor of natural sciences University of Vermont, 1869–1933; dean of the College, *post* 1907. State entomologist, 1880–95; state geologist, 1898–1933.

PERKINS, GEORGE WALBRIDGE (*b. Chicago, Ill., 1862; d. Stamford, Conn., 1920*), banker. Rose from office boy to first vice-president of New York Life Insurance Co.; devised an improved agency system and extended firm's business in Europe. Joining J. P. Morgan & Co. in 1901, he took leading part in organizing International Harvester, International Mercantile Marine, Northern Securities Co. and U.S. Steel Corp. Believed in cooperation and combination rather than competition of small business units. Leaving Morgan, 1910, he joined the Progressive party in 1912 and became chairman of its national executive committee. As chairman of a Y.M.C.A. finance committee, he raised $200,000,000 for World War I welfare work.

PERKINS, JACOB (*b. Newburyport, Mass., 1766; d. London, England, 1849*), inventor. Devised steel plate method for printing bank notes, *c.* 1805; successfully employed process in partnership in London with Gideon Fairman and others *post* 1819; produced first penny postage stamps, 1840. Perkins also patented an innovating high-pressure boiler and engine, and other devices for ships.

PERKINS, JAMES BRECK (*b. St. Croix Falls, Wis., 1847; d. Washington, D.C., 1910*), New York lawyer and politician, historian of France. Congressman, Republican, from New York, 1901–10. Author of a number of deservedly popular and useful surveys of 16th and 17th century French history.

PERKINS, JAMES HANDASYD (*b. Boston, Mass., 1810; d. near Cincinnati, O., 1849*), Unitarian clergyman, author, social worker. Nephew of Thomas H. Perkins; father of Charles E. Perkins. Worked with poor of Cincinnati; president, Cincinnati Relief Union, 1841–49.

PERKINS, JAMES HANDASYD (*b. Milton, Mass., 1876; d. Mount Kisco, N.Y., 1940*), banker. Brother of Thomas N. Perkins. President, Farmers Loan and Trust Co. (New York) and successor, 1921–33; board chairman, National City Bank, 1933–40. [*Supp. 2*]

PERKINS, JUSTIN (*b. Holyoke, Mass., 1805; d. Chicopee, Mass., 1869*), Congregational clergyman. Missionary to Persia *post* 1833; prominent Syriac scholar; author and translator.

PERKINS, SAMUEL ELLIOTT (*b. Brattleboro, Vt., 1811; d. 1879*), jurist, legal writer. Justice, Indiana supreme court, 1847–64, 1876–79; wrote *A Digest of the Decisions of the Supreme Court of Indiana* (1858).

PERKINS, THOMAS HANDASYD (*b. Boston, Mass., 1764; d. Boston, 1854*), merchant, philanthropist, Massachusetts Federalist legislator. Commenced prof-

itable trade chiefly with China *c.* 1790; remained as principal partner in firm until 1838, extending ventures wherever a profit seemed likely. His public and private benefactions were numerous and generous.

PERKINS, THOMAS NELSON (*b. Milton, Mass., 1870; d. Westwood, Mass., 1937*), lawyer, public servant. Brother of James H. Perkins (1876–1940). Practiced in Boston as skilled adviser in corporate reorganizations; participant in formulation of the Dawes and Young plans. [*Supp. 2*]

PERLEY, IRA (*b. Boxford, Mass., 1799; d. Concord, N.H., 1874*), lawyer, jurist. Chief justice, New Hampshire supreme judicial court, 1855–59, 1864–69; wrote *Trial by Jury* (1867).

PERRIN, BERNADOTTE (*b. Goshen, Conn., 1847; d. Saratoga, N.Y., 1920*), classical scholar. Graduated Yale, 1869; Ph.D., 1873. Professor of Greek at Western Reserve, 1881–93; of Greek studies at Yale, 1893–1909; made excellent annotated translation of *Plutarch's Lives*.

PERRINE, FREDERIC AUTEN COMBS (*b. Manalapan, N.J., 1862; d. Plainfield, N.J., 1908*), electrical engineer, consultant. Graduated Princeton, 1883; D.Sc., 1885. Organized department of electrical engineering at Leland Stanford as professor, 1893–1900. Designed first long 60 kilovolt transmission line.

PERRINE, HENRY (*b. Cranbury, N.J., 1797; d. Indian Key, Fla., 1840*), physician, U.S. consul, plant explorer. Introduced sisal and henequen from Mexico to southern Florida, 1833.

PERROT, NICOLAS (*b. France, 1644; d. c. 1718*), explorer. Among first French fur traders to Algonquian tribes at Green Bay, Wis., 1668–70. Won great influence over Western tribes and preserved their friendship for France; traded and built forts along the upper Mississippi, 1685–96. He has been called the ablest Indian diplomat of his time.

PERRY, ARTHUR LATHAM (*b. Lyme, N.H., 1830; d. Williamstown, Mass., 1905*), economist, apostle of free trade, textbook writer. Graduated Williams, 1852; taught there, 1854–91.

PERRY, BENJAMIN FRANKLIN (*b. Pendleton District, S.C., 1805; d. 1886*), lawyer, South Carolina legislator, Unionist. Consistently opposed secession, 1832–60, but stood by his state, 1861–65. Appointed provisional governor, 1865, he effected many democratic reforms with tact and wisdom. *Post* 1866, he bitterly opposed congressional Reconstruction.

PERRY, CHRISTOPHER RAYMOND (*b. South Kingstown, R.I., 1761; d. Newport, R.I., 1818*), merchant mariner, naval officer. Father of Matthew C. and Oliver H. Perry.

PERRY, EDWARD AYLESWORTH (*b. Richmond, Mass., 1831; d. Kerrville, Texas, 1889*) lawyer, Confederate brigadier-general, Democratic governor of Florida, 1885–89.

PERRY, EDWARD BAXTER (*b. Haverhill, Mass., 1855; d. Camden, Maine, 1924*), blind concert pianist, author. Studied with Clara Schumann and Liszt. Gave more than 3000 lecture recitals, 1885–1917.

PERRY, ENOCH WOOD (*b. Boston, Mass., 1831; d. New York, N.Y., 1915*), portrait and genre painter.

PERRY, MATTHEW CALBRAITH (*b. Newport, R.I., 1794; d. New York, N.Y., 1858*), naval officer. Son of Christopher R. Perry; brother of Oliver H. Perry. Entering the navy as midshipman, 1809, he served aboard the *President* and the *United States* during the War of 1812. After varied service, 1820–33, which included convoying settlers to Liberia, destroying pirates in the West Indies, and helping extinguish a conflagration at Smyrna, he was assigned to the Navy Yard at New York.

Serving chiefly ashore, 1833–41, he agitated for a naval apprenticeship system (adopted in 1837), organized (1833) the U.S. Naval Lyceum to promote learning among naval officers, sponsored the *Naval Magazine,* and was a member of the board of examiners which established the first course of instruction at Annapolis. His continuing interest in better naval equipment led him to advocate steam warships; he is sometimes called the father of the steam navy. Promoted captain in 1837, he was given command of the *Fulton,* a pioneer naval steamship. Later he organized the naval engineer corps and in 1839–40 conducted aboard the *Fulton* at Sandy Hook the first U.S. naval school of gun practice. Perry commanded the American squadron sent to Africa to help suppress the slave trade, 1843, and the naval forces operating on the east coast of Mexico, 1846–47, sharing with Gen. Winfield Scott credit for the capitulation of Vera Cruz, 1847.

Selected in January 1852, to negotiate a treaty with Japan, a country at that time closed to the West, Perry entered on his most famous work. State Department instructions included as objects of the mission protection of American seamen and property in Japan, and the opening of one or more Japanese ports to American commerce. Perry was requested first to use persuasion, but if this failed, to use "more vigorous methods." Provided with a letter from President Fillmore to the Emperor of Japan, he sailed from Norfolk on Nov. 24, 1852, and in late May 1853, arrived at Napa, Great Lu-chu Island, which he made a base. He sailed for Yedo, the Japanese capital, on July 2, with his flagship *Susquehanna* and three other vessels. Deliberately surrounding himself with an aura of mystery, he refused to see a minor official at Yedo Bay, insisting upon delivering President Fillmore's letter to a representative of the highest rank. When directed to go to Nagasaki where foreign business was ordinarily conducted, he refused and

threatened to land with an armed force. Finally, on July 14, he delivered the letter and other documents to the princes Idzu and Iwami, representatives of the Emperor. Perry said he would return later to receive a reply. The Japanese were conciliatory when he returned to Yedo Bay in February 1854, and on March 31 a treaty of peace and commerce was signed at Yokohama, which granted American trading rights at Hakodate and Shimoda. Perry later reported on the mission in *Narrative of the Expedition of an American Squadron to the China Seas and Japan* (1856).

PERRY, NORA (*b. Dudley, Mass., 1831; d. Dudley, 1896*), poet, journalist, author of juvenile stories. Best known for two poems: "Tying Her Bonnet Under Her Chin," and "After the Ball."

PERRY, OLIVER HAZARD (*b. South Kingstown, R.I., 1785; d. Venezuela, 1819*), naval officer. Son of Christopher R. Perry; brother of Matthew C. Perry. Entered service as midshipman, April 1799; saw action during naval war with France aboard the *General Greene,* commanded by his father. During the war with Tripoli he served on the *Adams* and the *Constellation.* Promoted lieutenant, 1807, and master commandant, 1812, he requested duty on the Great Lakes under Commodore Isaac Chauncey. Ordered on Feb. 8, 1813, to proceed to Sackett's Harbor, N.Y., he was assigned to command the naval forces on Lake Erie. Making his own headquarters at Erie, Pa., Perry spent the spring and summer building, equipping, and manning a small fleet, an arduous task because many materials had to be brought overland from the seaboard. By August he was ready with a ten-ship fleet, the largest being two sister brigs of 480 tons, *Lawrence* and *Niagara.* The British naval force commander, Barclay, was blockading the harbor, but at one point relaxed surveillance and Perry escaped over the Erie bar, sailed up the lake, and made a base at Put-in-Bay, north of Sandusky, O. Barclay's force lay at a station at Amherstburg on the Detroit River. Deciding to force an action for control of Lake Erie, Barclay weighed anchor on September 9; on the following day at sunrise he was sighted by Perry who sailed from Put-in-Bay to engage the British fleet. Barclay's flagship, *Detroit,* was roughly comparable to Perry's *Lawrence,* and his other main ship, *Queen Charlotte,* to Perry's *Niagara.* The battle was joined late in the morning of September 10. The weather-gage slightly favored Perry, whose fleet also enjoyed superiority in weight of metal. The fleets were roughly equal in number of effective men available. Perry's plan was for his flagship, the *Lawrence,* to engage the *Detroit;* the *Niagara,* the *Queen Charlotte;* and his smaller vessels their opposite numbers in the British line. The *Lawrence* (flying a battle flag with the words "Don't give up the ship") bore the brunt of the battle for over two hours. When all her guns were disabled and

83 of her 103-man crew were casualties, Perry transferred his flag to the *Niagara*. After a brief further action, the British commander surrendered and Perry sent Gen. W. H. Harrison the famous dispatch: "We have met the enemy and they are ours." The victory secured control of Lake Erie, helped in the later invasion of Upper Canada, and also helped the United States to make good its claim to the Northwest at the Treaty of Ghent. Perry died while descending the Orinoco River after concluding a negotiation with Venezuela.

PERRY, RUFUS LEWIS (*b. Smith Co., Tenn., 1834; d. Brooklyn, N.Y., 1895*), Baptist clergyman, Negro leader, journalist. Editor of the *Sunbeam*, the *People's Journal*, the *American Baptist*, and of the *National Monitor* (1872–95).

PERRY, STUART (*b. Newport, N.Y., 1814; d. 1890*), businessman, inventor. Patented (1846) an improved non-compression gas engine using explosive rosin vapor within the engine cylinder, ignited by an incandescent platinum element.

PERRY, THOMAS SERGEANT (*b. Newport, R.I., 1845; d. Boston, Mass., 1928*), author, scholar. Grandson of Oliver H. Perry.

PERRY, WALTER SCOTT (*b. Stoneham, Mass., 1855; d. Stoneham, 1934*), educator, artist. First director, Pratt Institute art school, Brooklyn, N.Y., 1887–1928. [*Supp. 1*]

PERRY, WILLIAM (*b. Norton, Mass., 1788; d. Exeter, N.H., 1887*), physician. Devised process for producing potato starch as substitute for imported cotton sizing and manufactured it *post* 1824.

PERRY, WILLIAM FLAKE (*b. Jackson Co., Ga., 1823; d. Bowling Green, Ky., 1901*), educator. First state superintendent of public education in Alabama, 1854–58; built efficient school organization despite widespread indifference.

PERRY, WILLIAM STEVENS (*b. Providence, R.I., 1832; d. Iowa, 1898*), Episcopal clergyman, historiographer. Consecrated bishop of Iowa, 1876, he served until death. Author of *Historical Collections Relating to the American Colonial Church* (1870–78) and *History of the American Episcopal Church* (1885).

PERSON, THOMAS (*b. Brunswick Co., Va., 1733; d. Franklin Co., N.C., 1800*), surveyor, landowner, North Carolina patriot and legislator.

PERSONS, WARREN MILTON (*b. West De Pere, Wis., 1878; d. Cambridge, Mass., 1937*), economist, statistician. Graduated University of Wisconsin, 1899; Ph.D., 1916. Taught at Wisconsin, Dartmouth and Colorado, and at Harvard, 1919–28. Innovator in analysis and measurement of business fluctuations.
[*Supp. 2*]

PETER, HUGH (*b. Cornwall, England, 1598; d. London, England, 1660*), clergyman. B.A., Trinity College, Cambridge, 1617/18; M.A., 1622. A Puritan in sympathy, he left England *c.* 1629 and was associated with an English congregation at Rotterdam for which he drafted a covenant embodying Congregational principles. Leaving John Davenport in charge of his Rotterdam group, Peter emigrated to New England, 1635, and succeeded Roger Williams as pastor at Salem, Mass., December 1636. A firm supporter of non-separating Congregationalism, he was active in public affairs and helped settle the differences between John Winthrop and Thomas Dudley. Concerned in the drafting of a legal code for the colony, 1636–37, and in the founding of Harvard, he was appointed one of the three agents from Massachusetts sent to further church reformation in England, 1641. Returning to England, he rose high in the councils of Parliament and Cromwell, was active in the trial of King Charles I, and was executed after the Restoration.

PETER, JOHN FREDERICK (*b. Herrndyck, Holland, 1746; d. Bethlehem, Pa., 1813*), musician, schoolmaster, preacher. Trained as a Moravian minister in Holland, Peter also received instruction in music, including harmony and musical composition. Arriving at Nazareth, Pa., 1769, he served as a teacher, then became organist at the Brethren's House in Bethlehem, 1770. Leading organizer of musical activities there, he expanded the Collegium Musicum, where works of Mozart, Haydn, and Handel were performed with a full orchestra. He composed more than 30 anthems for chorus, solo, and orchestra which reflected Haydn and showed a tendency toward modern chromatic alteration. He was probably the first composer of serious concerted music in America. Under his direction, Haydn's *Creation* was first performed in full in America, 1811.

PETER, ROBERT (*b. Launceston, Cornwall, England, 1805; d. Winton, Ky., 1894*), physician, chemist. Came to America as a boy; attended the Rensselaer School, Troy, N.Y. Removed to Kentucky, 1832; became professor of chemistry at Morrison College, Lexington, 1833. In 1838 he was elected to the chair of chemistry and pharmacy at Transylvania University, which he held until 1857. As chemist of the Kentucky geological survey of 1854, Peter first noted that the productivity of the bluegrass soils was due to their high phosphorous content and gave excellent descriptions of the phosphatic limestone which underlies these soils. He was chemist also to David D. Owen's surveys of Arkansas and Indiana, and professor at Kentucky University, 1865–87.

PETER, SARAH WORTHINGTON KING (*b. Chillicothe, O., 1800; d. Cincinnati, O., 1877*), philanthropist. Daughter of Thomas Worthington. Converted to Catholicism, 1855, she brought many charitable groups, including Sisters of Mercy and Franciscan Sisters, to work in the Cincinnati area.

PETERKIN, GEORGE WILLIAM (*b. Clear Spring, Md., 1841; d. 1916*), Episcopal clergyman, Confederate soldier. First bishop of West Virginia, 1878–1916; established southern Brazil mission, 1893–99.

PETERS, ABSALOM (*b. Wentworth, N.H., 1793; d. New York, N.Y., 1869*), Presbyterian clergyman, editor. A principal founder of American Home Missionary Society, 1826, and of the Union Theological Seminary, New York.

PETERS, CHRISTIAN HENRY FREDERICK (*b. Coldenbüttel, Schleswig, 1813; d. 1890*), astronomer. Study at the University of Berlin and at Göttingen was followed by scientific work in Sicily and Turkey. Arriving in America in 1854, he became director of the observatory at Hamilton College and in 1867 professor of astronomy. There his solar observations were noteworthy, especially his descriptions of sun spots. While engaged in making comprehensive Zodiac charts he discovered 48 new asteroids. About 1876 he undertook to prepare a new edition of the star catalogue in Ptolemy's *Almagest;* it was published in 1915 by a collaborator, Edward Knobel.

PETERS, EDWARD DYER (*b. Dorchester, Mass., 1849; d. Dorchester, 1917*), mining and metallurgical engineer, physician, educator.

PETERS, JOHN ANDREW (*b. Ellsworth, Maine, 1822; d. Bangor, Maine, 1904*), lawyer, Maine legislator. Congressman, Republican, 1867–73; associate justice, state supreme judicial court, 1873–83; chief justice, 1883–1900. Noted for legal learning, fairness, and liberal decisions.

PETERS, JOHN CHARLES (*b. New York, N.Y., 1819; d. Williston, N.Y., 1893*), physician, medical writer. Became prominent homeopathist; was joint editor, *North American Journal of Homeopathy,* 1855–61; dramatically renounced the method, 1861.

PETERS, JOHN PUNNETT (*b. New York, N.Y., 1852; d. 1921*), Episcopal clergyman, archeologist. Graduated Yale, 1873; Ph.D., 1876. Led University of Pennsylvania expedition to site of ancient Nippur, Babylonia, 1888–90; wrote *Nippur* (1897).

PETERS, MADISON CLINTON (*b. Lehigh Co., Pa., 1859; d. 1918*), clergyman. After holding Reformed, Baptist, and Presbyterian pastorates, he attempted *post* 1907 to reach unorganized religious-minded people in cities through lectures and syndicated newspaper articles.

PETERS, PHILLIS WHEATLEY. [See WHEATLEY, PHILLIS, *c.* 1754–1784.]

PETERS, RICHARD (*b. Liverpool, England, c. 1704; d. Philadelphia, Pa., 1776*), Church of England clergy-man, provincial official. Emigrated to Philadelphia *c.* 1735; was secretary of province land office, 1737–60, and prospered in Indian trade. Served Pennsylvania's proprietors as provincial secretary, 1742/43–1762, and as provincial councilor, 1749–76; attended Albany Congress, 1754, and Fort Stanwix conference, 1768. Rector of Christ and St. Peter's churches, 1762–75.

PETERS, RICHARD (*b. Philadelphia, Pa., 1744; d. Philadelphia, 1828*), lawyer, Revolutionary patriot, jurist, agriculturist. Nephew of Richard Peters (*c.* 1704–1776). Graduated College of Philadelphia, 1761. Elected secretary of the board of war by the Continental Congress in June 1776, he served as a leading member of the board until 1781. He was speaker of the Pennsylvania assembly, 1789–90, and served in the state senate, 1791–92. As federal district judge for Pennsylvania, 1792–1828, Peters vigorously upheld the powers of the federal government, made important contributions to maritime law, and laid the legal foundations for suits for libel against those attacking the federal government before passage of the Sedition Act of 1798. Wrote *A Discourse on Agriculture; its Antiquity* (1816), a plea for scientific farming.

PETERS, RICHARD (*b. Germantown, Pa., 1810; d. Atlanta, Ga., 1889*), civil engineer, railroad superintendent, agriculturist, financier. Grandson of Richard Peters (1744–1828). An early and successful promoter of Atlanta, Ga.; built a large flour mill and street railways in that city.

PETERS, SAMUEL ANDREW (*b. Hebron, Conn., 1735; d. New York, N.Y., 1826*), Anglican clergyman, Loyalist. Graduated Yale, 1757. Rector at Hebron, 1760–74. Forced to flee New England by Sons of Liberty, 1774, he resided in England, returning to America in 1805 as agent for land claims of heirs of Jonathan Carver. Author of *A General History of Connecticut* (1781) in which appeared his famous account of the "blue laws."

PETERS, WILLIAM CUMMING (*b. Woodbury, England, 1805; d. Cincinnati, O., 1866*), music publisher, musician. Published Stephen Foster's "Susanna," "Old Uncle Ned," and others.

PETERSON, CHARLES JACOBS (*b. Philadelphia, Pa., 1819; d. Philadelphia, 1887*), editor, publisher, author. Cousin of Henry Peterson. Founded *Lady's World,* 1840 (known *post* 1848 as *Peterson's Magazine*), a successful imitator of *Godey's Lady's Book.*

PETERSON, HENRY (*b. Philadelphia, Pa., 1818; d. Germantown, Pa., 1891*), editor, publisher, poet. Cousin of Charles J. Peterson. Major owner and chief editor of *Saturday Evening Post,* 1848–73; increased its content of fiction and verse.

PETIGRU, JAMES LOUIS (*b. Abbeville District, S.C., 1789; d. Charleston, S.C., 1863*), lawyer, politician. Graduated South Carolina College, 1809; was admitted to the bar, 1812; served as state attorney general, 1822–30. An outstanding and eloquent opponent of secession and nullification, he remained all his life an intense nationalist and Unionist. Opposing John C. Calhoun's program by pamphlet and speech, he was by 1832 the leader of the Union party. Thereafter he held no judicial or political office (save a two-year term as federal district attorney, 1851–53), but, as a superb advocate, he was undisputed head of the state bar. He opposed secession in 1860 but was grieved by Lincoln's policy of coercion. He has been described as "the greatest private citizen that South Carolina has ever produced."

PETTIGREW, CHARLES (*b. Chambersburg, Pa., 1743; d. Tyrrell Co., N.C., 1807*), Episcopal clergyman. Chief organizer and administrator of his church in North Carolina, 1775–1807; a leading founder of the University of North Carolina.

PETTIGREW, JAMES JOHNSTON (*b. Tyrrell Co., N.C., 1828; d. 1863*), lawyer, Confederate brigadier-general. Grandson of Charles Pettigrew. Killed in action on retreat after Gettysburg, where he had succeeded to command of Gen. Henry Heth's division.

PETTIGREW, RICHARD FRANKLIN (*b. Ludlow, Vt., 1848; d. 1926*), lawyer. Raised in Wisconsin. Settled in Sioux Falls, Dakota Territory, 1870; became a prominent member of the territorial legislature. Territorial delegate to Congress, 1881–83, he was U.S. senator from South Dakota, 1889–1901. A nonconformist Republican, he worked to reserve federal forest lands from sale; he also favored government ownership of railroads and telegraph lines, advocated unlimited silver coinage, and opposed annexation of Hawaii and the Philippines. He was indicted but never tried for opposing American entrance into the first World War.

PETTIT, CHARLES (*b. near Amwell, N.J., 1736; d. Philadelphia, Pa., 1806*), merchant, New Jersey and Pennsylvania official, fiscal expert, patriot. Assistant quartermaster-general, Continental Army, 1778–81; instrumental in effecting Pennsylvania's adoption of U.S. Constitution; president, Insurance Company of North America *post* 1796.

PETTIT, THOMAS McKEAN (*b. Philadelphia, Pa., 1797; d. Philadelphia, 1853*), Pennsylvania jurist, Democratic politician. Grandson of Charles Pettit and Thomas McKean. Associate and presiding judge of district court for city and county of Philadelphia, 1833–45.

PETTUS, EDMUND WINSTON (*b. Limestone Co., Ala., 1821; d. Hot Springs, N.C., 1907*), lawyer, Confederate brigadier-general, Alabama politician. U.S. senator, Democrat, from Alabama, 1897–1907.

PEYTON, JOHN LEWIS (*b. near Staunton, Va., 1824; d. 1896*), lawyer, Confederate agent, author. North Carolina state agent in England, 1861–65, he was critical of Confederate foreign policy, expressing his views in several volumes of reminiscences.

PHELAN, DAVID SAMUEL (*b. Sydney, Nova Scotia, 1841; d. St. Louis, Mo., 1915*), Roman Catholic clergyman, journalist. Edited the *Western Watchman*, a militant newspaper published at St. Louis, 1868–1915; scored American Protective Association; upheld liberal point of view in politics and church polity; bluntly criticized hierarchy.

PHELAN, JAMES (*b. Queen's Co., Ireland, 1824; d. San Francisco, Calif., 1892*), merchant, capitalist. Came to America as a child; prospered in New York; established himself as general merchant in San Francisco, 1849. Organized First National Gold Bank, 1870, and other banks and insurance companies.

PHELAN, JAMES (*b. Aberdeen, Miss., 1856; d. Nassau, Bahamas, 1891*), lawyer, author. Ph.D., Leipzig, 1878. Published *Memphis Avalanche*, 1881–91; wrote *History of Tennessee* (1888). As congressman, Democrat, from Tennessee, 1887–91, Phelan opposed traditional Southern views on the tariff and Negro rights.

PHELAN, JAMES DUVAL (*b. San Francisco, Calif., 1861; d. Saratoga, Calif., 1930*), California politician, banker. Son of James Phelan (1824–1892). Elected mayor of San Francisco in 1897 and re-elected twice as a reform candidate, he vigorously attacked the corrupt board of supervisors and provided leadership in drafting and adopting a new city charter. He was also responsible for the beautifying of the city, and for the "Burnham Plan," from which came San Francisco's present civic center. At his own expense he took steps to secure the city's water supply in the Hetch Hetchy Valley. Elected as a Democrat to the U.S. Senate (1915–21), he supported Wilson, but favored separation of the League covenant from the Versailles Treaty.

PHELPS, ALMIRA HART LINCOLN (*b. Berlin, Conn., 1793; d. Baltimore, Md., 1884*), educator. Sister of Emma H. Willard. Author of popular elementary science textbooks, among them, *Botany for Beginners* (1833), *Lectures on Chemistry* (1837).

PHELPS, ANSON GREENE (*b. Simsbury, Conn., 1781; d. New York, N.Y., 1853*), metals merchant, philanthropist. Senior partner of Phelps, Dodge & Co., *post* 1832; important in development of Pennsylvania iron and Lake Superior copper mines.

PHELPS, AUSTIN (*b. West Brookfield, Mass., 1820; d. Bar Harbor, Maine, 1890*), Congregational clergyman. Professor of sacred rhetoric and homiletics at Andover Seminary, 1848–79; aligned himself with conservatives at Andover.

PHELPS, CHARLES EDWARD (*b. Guilford, Vt., 1833; d. Baltimore, Md., 1908*), lawyer, jurist, Union soldier, Maryland congressman. Son of Almira H. L. Phelps. Judge of supreme bench of Baltimore, 1882–1908; wrote *Juridical Equity* (1894).

PHELPS, EDWARD JOHN (*b. Middlebury, Vt., 1822; d. New Haven, Conn., 1900*), lawyer. Graduated Middlebury College, 1840. Kent Professor of Law at Yale, 1881–85, 1889–1900. U.S. ambassador to Great Britain, 1885–89; U.S. counsel in 1893 fur-seal arbitration with Great Britain.

PHELPS, ELIZABETH STUART. [See WARD, ELIZABETH STUART PHELPS, 1844–1911.]

PHELPS, GUY ROWLAND (*b. Simsbury, Conn., 1802; d. Hartford, Conn., 1869*), physician. Founded Connecticut Mutual Life Insurance Co., 1846; did much to popularize mutual system of insurance.

PHELPS, JOHN SMITH (*b. Simsbury, Conn., 1814; d. 1886*), lawyer, Missouri legislator, Union soldier. Removed to Missouri, 1837. Congressman, Democrat, 1845–63; governor of Missouri, 1877–81. A consistent Unionist, and a faithful, honest public servant.

PHELPS, OLIVER (*b. Poquonock, Conn., 1749; d. Canandaigua, N.Y., 1809*), merchant, Massachusetts legislator. Speculated on credit (1788–96) in millions of acres of western lands, mostly in western New York. Partner of Nathaniel Gorham.

PHELPS, THOMAS STOWELL (*b. Buckfield, Maine, 1822; d. New York, N.Y., 1901*), naval officer. Made careful surveys of waterways preparatory to military operations during Civil War, especially of Potomac and York rivers and Pamlico Sound in 1861. Retired as rear-admiral, 1884.

PHELPS, WILLIAM FRANKLIN (*b. Auburn, N.Y., 1822; d. St. Paul, Minn., 1907*), educator. Headed normal schools in New Jersey, Minnesota and Wisconsin. First president, American Normal School Association, 1858–63.

PHELPS, WILLIAM WALTER (*b. Dundaff, Pa., 1839; d. Englewood, N.J., 1894*), lawyer. Congressman, Republican, from New Jersey, 1873–75, 1883–89. U.S. minister to Austria-Hungary, 1881; to Germany, 1889–93.

PHILIP (*d. Bristol, R.I., 1676*), Indian leader, known also as King Philip, Po-Metacom, and Metacomet. Son of Massasoit, he became sachem of the Wampanoags in 1662, and for nine years behaved peaceably. From 1671 to 1675 he was suspected of plotting against the settlers and when the latter executed three Wampanoags for killing Sassamon, Philip's former secretary who had revealed his alleged plots, the conflict known as King Philip's War began in June 1675. With his allies, the Nipmucks, he killed many colonists, and burned several towns after ineffectual resistance. He again fell upon the Massachusetts towns in 1676, but the colonial troops now turned to a policy of capturing Indian women and children, destroying Indian crops, and offering immunity to deserters. After the dwindling away of his forces, Philip sought refuge in a swamp near Mount Hope where he was shot by an Indian serving under Capt. Benjamin Church.

PHILIP, JOHN WOODWARD (*b. Kinderhook, N.Y., 1840; d. 1900*), naval officer. Graduated U.S. Naval Academy, 1861. As captain of U.S.S. *Texas* during battle of Santiago Bay (1898), he ordered: "Don't cheer, men, those poor devils are dying." Promoted rear-admiral, 1899, he commanded the Brooklyn (N.Y.) Navy Yard at his death.

PHILIPP, EMANUEL LORENZ (*b. Sauk Co., Wis., 1861; d. 1925*), businessman, transportation expert. Served with distinction as governor of Wisconsin, 1915–21; although a "regular" Republican, he respected previous Progressive legislation.

PHILIPS, JOHN FINIS (*b. Boone Co., Mo., 1834; d. 1919*), lawyer, Union soldier. One of "Big Four" Democratic leaders of Missouri *post* 1874. Served as congressman, 1875–77, 1880–81; as federal district judge, 1888–1910.

PHILIPS, MARTIN WILSON (*b. Columbia, S.C., 1806; d. Oxford, Miss., 1889*), Mississippi agriculturist, reformer. Urged introduction of fruit trees and use of improved agricultural implements.

PHILIPSE, FREDERICK (*b. Friesland, Holland, 1626; d. 1702*), merchant, New York colonial official. Emigrated to New Amsterdam, probably 1647. Acquired fortune through Indian trade, manufacture of wampum, importation of slaves, and Madagascar trade. Assembled extensive Hudson River land-holdings, erected into manor of Philipsburgh, 1693.

PHILLIPS, DAVID GRAHAM (*b. Madison, Ind., 1867; d. New York, N.Y., 1911*), novelist, journalist. Author of muck-raking magazine exposés; also of a number of "problem" novels of which the most ambitious was *Susan Lenox: Her Fall and Rise* (published in 1917).

PHILLIPS, FRANCIS CLIFFORD (*b. Philadelphia, Pa., 1850; d. Ben Avon, Pa., 1920*), chemist. Professor of chemistry, Western University of Pennsylvania, 1875–1915; worked on standardization and improvement of methods of analysis.

PHILLIPS, GEORGE (*b. probably South Rainham, England, 1593; d. Watertown, Mass., 1644*), clergyman. An original settler of Watertown, 1630, he drafted covenant of the church there, and was pastor, 1630–44. First Massachusetts minister to practice congregational form of church polity.

PHILLIPS, HENRY (*b. Philadelphia, Pa., 1838; d. 1895*), numismatist, philologist, translator. Author, among numerous other works, of *Historical Sketches of the Paper Currency of the American Colonies* (1865) and *Continental Paper Money* (1866).

PHILLIPS, JOHN (*b. Andover, Mass., 1719; d. 1795*), land speculator, money lender, philanthropist. Uncle of Samuel Phillips. Graduated Harvard, 1735. After making liberal gifts to Dartmouth College, he incorporated and endowed Phillips Exeter Academy, 1781; it opened in 1783. Phillips patterned his new school after Phillips Academy, Andover, but reserved to himself much power over the school's affairs.

PHILLIPS, PHILIP (*b. Cassadaga, N.Y., 1834; d. Delaware, O., 1895*), singing evangelist, composer and compiler of hymns.

PHILLIPS, SAMUEL (*b. North Andover, Mass., 1752; d. Andover, Mass., 1802*), educator, public official. Nephew of John Phillips. Graduated Harvard, 1771. Delegate to Massachusetts Provincial Congress, 1775, and to state constitutional convention, 1779–80; served in state senate, 1780–1801. Securing financial aid from his uncle and father, he established at Andover (1777) a unique endowed academy, controlled by a board of trustees, the majority of whom were laymen. The first object of Phillips Academy was "the promotion of true Piety and Virtue," that is, character, which emphasis showed the influence of John Locke and English nonconformist academies. The school opened in April 1778 with Eliphalet Pearson as principal.

PHILLIPS, THOMAS WHARTON (*b. near Mount Jackson, Pa., 1835; d. New Castle, Pa., 1912*), oil producer, Republican congressman, religious writer. Leading member of U.S. Industrial Commission, 1898–1902.

PHILLIPS, ULRICH BONNELL (*b. La Grange, Ga., 1877; d. 1934*), educator, historian. Graduated University of Georgia, 1897; Ph.D., Columbia, 1902. Taught history at Wisconsin and Tulane, and at University of Michigan, 1911–29; thereafter, he was professor of history at Yale. Phillips's many articles and books were pioneering studies in the history of the South up to the Civil War; he was especially concerned with establishing the facts about the plantation system and slavery. His *Life and Labor in the Old South* (1929) was the first volume in a projected history of the South which he did not live to complete. [*Supp. 1*]

PHILLIPS, WALTER POLK (*b. near Grafton, Mass., 1846; d. Vineyard Haven, Mass., 1920*), telegrapher, journalist. Devised Phillips Telegraphic Code for news transmission, 1879. Became managerial head of the United Press organization early in the 1880's; utilized independent wires, made alliances with for-eign news agencies, and led the United Press forces during their "war" with the Associated Press, 1893–97. Thereafter, on the collapse of the United Press, he was prominent in the Columbia Graphophone Co.

PHILLIPS, WENDELL (*b. Boston, Mass., 1811; d. Boston, 1884*), lawyer, orator, reformer. Graduated Harvard, 1831. Becoming a rabid Abolitionist, he first gained notice for a passionate speech in Faneuil Hall, 1837, at a meeting called to protest the murder of Elijah P. Lovejoy. A fairly consistent disciple of William L. Garrison, Phillips traveled extensively on the lyceum circuit. His language on the subject of slavery became increasingly intemperate through the 1840's and 1850's; he assailed the Constitution as a protector of reaction and ultimately called for secession by the North. After the Civil War he turned to a succession of other causes, among them prohibition and fair treatment for the Indians. His zeal for the labor movement led him to denounce the profit and wage system vehemently; he wrote *The Labor Question* (1884).

PHILLIPS, WILLARD (*b. Bridgewater, Mass., 1784; d. Cambridge, Mass., 1873*), lawyer, insurance executive, author. Zealous advocate of protective tariffs; wrote *Manual of Political Economy* (1828), *Propositions Concerning Protection and Free Trade* (1850).

PHILLIPS, WILLIAM (*b. Boston, Mass., 1750/51; d. Boston, 1827*), merchant, philanthropist, Federalist politician. Cousin of Samuel Phillips. Lieutenant-governor of Massachusetts, 1812–23; generous benefactor of Phillips Academy, Andover; president, American Bible Society.

PHILLIPS, WILLIAM ADDISON (*b. Paisley, Scotland, 1824; d. 1893*), lawyer, Union soldier, journalist. Emigrated to Illinois as a boy. Won reputation as N.Y. *Tribune* correspondent in Kansas, 1855; served in Kansas legislature. As Republican congressman from Kansas, 1873–79, he advocated then radical economic and reform policies.

PHINIZY, FERDINAND (*b. Oglethorpe Co., Ga., 1819; d. Athens, Ga., 1889*), cotton merchant, financier.

PHIPPS, HENRY (*b. Philadelphia, Pa., 1839; d. Great Neck, N.Y., 1930*), bookkeeper, steel manufacturer, philanthropist. From 1867 to 1901, Phipps was a close business associate of Andrew Carnegie, serving principally as a conservative financial adviser in Carnegie's operations.

PHIPS, Sir WILLIAM (*b. Maine frontier of Massachusetts, 1650/51; d. London, England, 1694/95*), colonial official. Apprenticed early to a ship's carpenter in Boston, he followed that trade there. Successful in command of an expedition to raise a Spanish treasure ship off Haiti, he was knighted in 1687.

Post 1688, he worked with Increase Mather for restoration of the old charter rule in the colony; in 1690, he won a spectacular victory over the French by capturing Port Royal in Nova Scotia. When William III granted a new charter to Massachusetts, Phips, on the nomination of Increase Mather, was made the first royal governor. Arriving at his post in May 1692, he abruptly halted the witchcraft trials. He alienated important political factions in the colony by high-handed actions, and also the Crown by refusing to enforce customs regulations and by failing to protect the colony's frontiers.

PHISTERER, FREDERICK (*b. Stuttgart, Germany, 1836; d. Albany, N.Y., 1909*), soldier. Emigrated to America, 1855; joined U.S. army in that year. Rose from private to captain, winning fame at Stone's River, 1862. Resigning regular commission, 1870, he rose to brevet major-general in N.Y. National Guard.

PHOENIX, JOHN. [See DERBY, GEORGE HORATIO, 1823–1861.]

PHYFE, DUNCAN (*b. Scotland, 1768; d. New York, N.Y., 1854*), cabinet maker. After apprenticeship to a cabinet maker in Albany, N.Y., he moved to New York City and was established in his own shop at 2 Broad St. by 1792. Combining the talents of an artist with those of a businessman, he soon built up a prosperous concern in which his sons eventually joined him as partners. Critics believe that he was the equal of the famous 18th-century English masters; his work in mahogany is unsurpassed. Starting with indebtedness to English contemporaries, he developed a unique style influenced strongly by the French Directoire and early Empire styles. Phyfe did his best work early in his career, afterwards succumbing to the demand for so-called "American Empire," which degenerated into heavy, commonplace forms, called "butcher furniture" by Phyfe himself.

PHYSICK, PHILIP SYNG (*b. Philadelphia, Pa., 1768; d. 1837*), surgeon. Grandson of Philip Syng. Graduated University of Pennsylvania, 1785. Studied medicine with Adam Kuhn; also in London with John Hunter, and at Edinburgh (M.D., 1792). Returning to Philadelphia, he slowly built a solid practice, helped by his close friendship with Benjamin Rush and Stephen Girard. Elected to the staff of Pennsylvania Hospital in 1794, he served there until 1816; he also lectured on surgery at the University of Pennsylvania, 1801–19. Among his advances in surgery were the invention of needle forceps for tying deeply placed blood vessels, a snare for tonsillectomy, and new forms of catheters in surgery of the urinary tract.

PIATT, DONN (*b. Cincinnati, O., 1819; d. near West Liberty, O., 1891*), journalist, Union soldier. Founder and editor of the weekly *Capital,* published at Wash-

ington, D.C., 1871–80; exposed weaknesses and corruption of both Republicans and Democrats.

PIATT, JOHN JAMES (*b. James' Mills, Ind., 1835; d. Cincinnati, O., 1917*), poet, U.S. consul, journalist. Co-author with William Dean Howells of *Poems of Two Friends* (1860); author of a number of volumes of later work, 1866–97.

PIATT, SARAH MORGAN BRYAN (*b. Lexington, Ky., 1836; d. Caldwell, N.J., 1919*), poet. Wife of John J. Piatt.

PICKARD, SAMUEL THOMAS (*b. Rowley, Mass., 1828; d. Amesbury, Mass., 1915*), printer, author. Co-editor of *Portland* (Me.) *Transcript,* 1855–95; author of *Life and Letters of John Greenleaf Whittier* (1894).

PICKENS, ANDREW (*b. near Paxtang, Pa., 1739; d. Tomassee, S.C., 1817*), Revolutionary soldier. Defeated Loyalist force at Kettle Creek, Ga., 1779; took prominent part in battles of Cowpens and Eutaw Springs.

PICKENS, FRANCIS WILKINSON (*b. Colleton District, S.C., 1805; d. near Edgefield Court House, S.C., 1869*), lawyer, politician. Grandson of Andrew Pickens. Studied at Franklin College (Ga.) and South Carolina College. Passionately attached to Thomas Cooper's state-rights doctrines, he wrote extensively under pen-names "Sydney" and "Hampden" urging South Carolina to implement nullification principles, 1827–30; he replied forcefully (1832) to Jackson's nullification proclamation. As a congressman, Democrat, 1834–43, he led in protesting acceptance of Abolitionist petitions. A leader of the secession movement growing out of dissatisfaction with the 1850 Compromise, he later became more moderate. After Lincoln's election, however, he urged immediate secession and served as Confederate governor of South Carolina, December 1860–1862.

PICKENS, ISRAEL (*b. near Concord, N.C., 1780; d. near Matanzas, Cuba, 1827*), lawyer. Congressman, Democrat, from North Carolina, 1811–17. Removed to Alabama, 1818, where he was anti-Crawford governor, 1821–25. First opposed, then tolerated a state-owned banking system; helped found University of Alabama.

PICKERING, CHARLES (*b. Susquehanna Co., Pa., 1805; d. 1878*), physician, naturalist. Chief zoologist, Wilkes South Seas Exploring Expedition, 1838–42; author of reports on geographical distribution of men, animals and plants based on the expedition's findings and on later research.

PICKERING, EDWARD CHARLES (*b. Boston, Mass., 1846; d. 1919*), astronomer. Graduated Lawrence Scientific School, Harvard, 1865; taught physics at Massachusetts Institute of Technology, 1866–77.

Director of the Harvard Observatory, 1877–1919, where he pioneered in using methods of physics to extend knowledge of stellar structure and evolution. Using Harvard's large instruments, Pickering developed the art of photometry, using the meridian photometer to establish the magnitudes of stars by instrumental rather than visual means. He thus catalogued the magnitudes of 80,000 stars and further compiled a photographic library of about 300,000 plates, which captured all stars down to the eleventh magnitude. He also pioneered in stellar spectroscopy.

PICKERING, JOHN (*b. Newington, N.H., c. 1738; d. 1805*), New Hampshire legislator and jurist. Appointed U.S. district court judge for New Hampshire, 1795, he was impeached and removed in 1804 for partisan reasons, although actually suffering from mental collapse.

PICKERING, JOHN (*b. Salem, Mass., 1777; d. Boston, Mass., 1846*), lawyer, philologist. Son of Timothy Pickering. Graduated Harvard, 1796. Author of the first collection of American word usages (1816) and the outstanding *Comprehensive Lexicon of the Greek Language* (1826, 1829, 1846). Authority on American Indian languages.

PICKERING, TIMOTHY (*b. Salem, Mass., 1745; d. Salem, 1829*), soldier, administrator, politician. Graduated Harvard, 1763. An early supporter of the revolutionary movement, he displayed great ability as a newspaper controversialist and pamphleteer. As colonel of Massachusetts militia, he took part in the operations of April 1775, was assigned to coast defense operations, then joined Washington's army in the 1776–77 campaign. He served as adjutant-general of the army in 1777, was a member of the board of war, 1777–80, and quartermaster-general, 1780–83. Much criticized for his work in the latter post, Pickering clearly served with energy and determination. After the Revolution, he engaged in mercantile business in Philadelphia, but in 1787 moved his family into the Wyoming Valley region of Pennsylvania where he represented Pennsylvania's interest in the dispute with Connecticut settlers and demonstrated talent in negotiating with the Indians. A supporter of the Federal Constitution, he was appointed agent to deal with the Senecas in 1790, and U.S. postmaster-general in 1791. He continued to act as an Indian negotiator, supporting an enlightened policy. Appointed U.S. secretary of war, 1795, Pickering also had jurisdiction over naval affairs and pushed construction of the famous frigates that served so well in the War of 1812. He was a fervent Federalist and used his talents for controversy against fellow Federalists whom he suspected of deviation just as heartily as he used them against Jeffersonians. Alexander Hamilton was his special hero, and he came to believe that the French Revolution was the cause of all that was damnable in the world. On the resignation of Edmund Randolph, Pickering succeeded to the post of secretary of state in August 1795, serving until Adams dismissed him in 1800. As secretary, Pickering tried desperately to widen the breach with France and looked forward eagerly to hostilities. Frustration of these hopes, 1798–99, brought him to hate President Adams with a fine passion; he acted indiscreetly in corresponding with Adams's enemies and intriguing against him at every opportunity, thus helping to wreck his own party. Pickering later served in the U.S. Senate, 1803–11, and in the House of Representatives, 1813–17, where he continued to support "high-toned" Federalist principles, and virulently opposed the War of 1812.

PICKET, ALBERT (*b. 1771; d. 1850*), teacher, author. Pupil of Noah Webster; taught in New York City c. 1794–1826, thereafter in Cincinnati, O. Prepared widely adopted series of elementary English texts; edited early educational periodical, *The Academician*, 1818–20; formed Western Literary Institute and College of Professional Teachers (1829–1845).

PICKETT, ALBERT JAMES (*b. Anson Co., N.C., 1810; d. 1858*), planter, historian. Removed to Autauga Co., Ala., as a child. Author of *History of Alabama and Incidentally of Georgia and Mississippi from the Earliest Period* (1851).

PICKETT, GEORGE EDWARD (*b. Richmond, Va., 1825; d. Norfolk, Va., 1875*), Confederate soldier. Graduated West Point, 1846. Went directly to the Mexican War, where he gained distinction at Contreras and Churubusco, and was first to cross the parapet of Chapultepec. After frontier service in the Northwest, he resigned from the U.S. Army, 1861, and was commissioned Confederate colonel. Made brigadier-general in February 1862, he served gallantly at Seven Pines and Gaines's Mill and was given command of a Virginia division with rank of major-general in October. At Gettysburg, Lee ordered Pickett with 4500 effectives to assault the Union center on July 3, 1863. His command advanced half a mile, with parade precision, over ground raked by rifle and artillery fire; repulsed, a scant quarter of them returned from the charge. Pickett made the greatest fight of his career at Five Forks on April 1, 1865.

PICKETT, JAMES CHAMBERLAYNE (*b. Fauquier Co., Va., 1793; d. Washington, D.C., 1872*), War of 1812 soldier, Kentucky legislator, diplomat. Arranged treaty with Republic of Ecuador, 1839 (proclaimed in 1842); negotiated convention with Peru, 1841.

PICKNELL, WILLIAM LAMB (*b. Hinesburg, Vt., 1853; d. Marblehead, Mass., 1897*), landscape painter. Encouraged by George Inness; studied in Paris with J. L. Gérôme.

PICTON, THOMAS (*b. New York, N.Y., 1822; d. New York, 1891*), soldier of fortune, journalist. Served in Lopez's 1850–51 filibustering expedition against Cuba and William Walker's invasion of Nicaragua. Frequently wrote under pen-name "Paul Preston."

PIDGIN, CHARLES FELTON (*b. Roxbury, Mass., 1844; d. Melrose, Mass., 1923*), statistician. Inventor of methods and instruments for mechanical tabulation of statistics. Author of best-selling *Quincy Adams Sawyer* (1900) and other novels.

PIEPER, FRANZ AUGUST OTTO (*b. Carwitz, Germany, 1852; d. St. Louis, Mo., 1931*), Lutheran theologian. Came to America, 1870. Leader in Missouri Synod; president, Concordia Seminary, 1887–1931.

PIERCE, BENJAMIN (*b. Chelmsford, Mass., 1757; d. Hillsborough, N.H., 1839*), farmer, Revolutionary soldier, New Hampshire legislator. Father of Franklin Pierce. An avid Jeffersonian, he was elected governor of New Hampshire, 1827 and 1829, on basis of Revolutionary record and agrarian appeal.

PIERCE, EDWARD LILLIE (*b. Stoughton, Mass., 1829; d. Paris, France, 1897*), lawyer. Brother of Henry L. Pierce. Author of scrupulously honest *Memoir* of Charles Sumner (1877, 1893).

PIERCE, FRANKLIN (*b. Hillsborough, N.H., 1804; d. Concord, N.H., 1869*), lawyer, president of the United States. Son of Benjamin Pierce. Graduated Bowdoin, 1824. First elected to the New Hampshire lower house in 1829, he became speaker in 1831 and 1832. He next served in the U.S. House of Representatives, 1833–37, and the U.S. Senate, 1837–42; he was a consistent, loyal Jacksonian Democrat. He respected Southern rights and developed a settled antipathy for political Abolitionists. During a decade of legal practice in New Hampshire, 1842–52, he gained a commanding reputation for effective jury pleading and was personally popular. From 1842 to 1847 he managed most of the local Democratic campaigns, enforcing strict party discipline. Enlisting for the Mexican War as a private, he rose to brigadier-general but did not participate in any battles. He took the lead in enforcing New Hampshire Democratic support for the Compromise of 1850 and his friends worked to secure for him the presidential nomination in 1852 as a compromise candidate. The convention, hopelessly deadlocked, turned to Pierce at last as a candidate who would satisfy the Southern bloc. He carried all but four states in November, although his popular majority was less than 50,000.

Pierce selected his cabinet from all sections of the country and from among all factions that had supported him. He set his administration to a policy of complete respect for state-rights, economy, honesty, and a vigorous foreign policy aimed at acquiring more territory. One project dear to his heart was the acquisition of Cuba. American diplomats in Europe were working to this end but news of their activity leaked prematurely and was publicized in the so-

called "Ostend Manifesto." Northern opposition followed and the project failed. Pierce succeeded in making the Gadsden Purchase (1853) of land from Mexico and in persuading the British to agree to retire from Central America except in Honduras. Pierce's chief political problem, however, was that of Kansas. Induced by a group of powerful Senate Democrats to support the Kansas-Nebraska Act in return for favorable action on his patronage appointments and his foreign policy program, he thereafter became engulfed in a political storm. Determined to enforce the Act fairly he selected appointees to office in the territories equally from the North and South, but his choice of men was generally unfortunate, notably in the case of Gov. A. H. Reeder of Kansas. On the appearance of civil war in Kansas between free-soilers supporting a local government of their own choosing and Missouri forces threatening to disperse them by force, Pierce supported the technically legal pro-slavery government, a fact which further alienated Northern Democratic leaders. Pierce's second choice as Kansas governor, Wilson Shannon, proved ineffective and not until the summer of 1856 were law and order restored under Gov. John W. Geary. In his effort to be impartial and "legal," Pierce had helped to split his party and to lay the groundwork for organization of the Republican party. He had honestly tried to do his duty but was without adequate experience or temperamental fitness and had failed utterly to estimate the depth of Northern feeling against the South. Refused renomination in 1856, he became increasingly unpopular in New Hampshire and particularly so after later intemperate attacks upon Lincoln.

PIERCE, GEORGE FOSTER (*b. Greene Co., Ga., 1811; d. Sparta, Ga., 1884*), bishop of the Methodist Episcopal Church, South, educator. President, Emory College, 1848–54; appointed bishop, 1854.

PIERCE, GILBERT ASHVILLE (*b. East Otto, N.Y., 1839; d. Chicago, Ill., 1901*), lawyer, Union soldier, journalist, author. Dakota territorial governor, Republican, 1884–86; U.S. senator from North Dakota, 1889–91.

PIERCE, HENRY LILLIE (*b. Stoughton, Mass., 1825; d. 1896*), cocoa manufacturer, Massachusetts legislator, philanthropist. Brother of Edward L. Pierce. Managed and later owned Walter Baker and Co.; Boston mayor, 1872 and 1877; independent and liberal Republican congressman from Massachusetts, 1873–77. A man of outstanding integrity.

PIERCE, JOHN DAVIS (*b. Chesterfield, N.H., 1797; d. Medford, Mass., 1882*), Congregational clergyman, educator. Removed to Marshall, Mich., 1831. Drafted plan for organization of primary schools and state university as Michigan superintendent of public instruction, 1836–41.

PIERCE, WILLIAM LEIGH (*b. probably Georgia, c. 1740; d. 1789*), Revolutionary soldier, Savannah, Ga., businessman. As a delegate to the Federal Convention, 1787, he made notes on its debates and also wrote character sketches of fellow delegates which are especially useful for information on the less prominent persons present.

PIERPONT, FRANCIS HARRISON (*b. near Morgantown, [W.] Va., 1814; d. Pittsburgh, Pa., 1899*), lawyer, Virginia Unionist. Helped organize West Virginia and was provisional governor, 1861–63; served as governor of the "restored" state of Virginia (i.e., those counties under federal control but not included in West Virginia), 1863–65, and of Virginia, 1865–68.

PIERPONT, JAMES (*b. Roxbury, Mass., 1659/60; d. New Haven, Conn., 1714*), Congregational clergyman. Graduated Harvard, 1681. Pastor, First Church, New Haven, 1685–1714; leading founder and an original trustee of Yale College.

PIERPONT, JOHN (*b. Litchfield, Conn., 1785; d. Medford, Mass., 1866*), Unitarian clergyman, poet, reformer. Grandfather of John Pierpont Morgan. Minister of Hollis Street Church, Boston, 1819–45. Author of *Airs of Palestine* (1816); edited *American First Class Book* (1823) and *The National Reader* (1827).

PIERREPONT, EDWARDS (*b. North Haven, Conn., 1817; d. New York, N.Y., 1892*), New York lawyer, influential Union Democrat. U.S. attorney-general, 1875–76; U.S. ambassador to England, 1876–77.

PIERSON, ABRAHAM (*b. Yorkshire, England, 1609; d. Newark, N.J., 1678*), clergyman. Graduated Trinity College, Cambridge, 1632. Strongly Puritan, he emigrated to Massachusetts, 1640, and became pastor of a group at Lynn who settled in December of that year at Southampton, Long Island. Believing strongly that church and state should act in unison and that only church members should be freemen, he opposed Southampton's union with Connecticut (1644), and left in 1647 to organize a new church at Branford, New Haven Colony, where his views prevailed. There he remained pastor for twenty years. When New Haven in turn joined Connecticut, he departed with most of his congregation to found a new church at Newark, N.J., 1667.

PIERSON, ABRAHAM (*b. Southampton, N.Y., c. 1645; d. Killingworth [Clinton], Conn., 1707*), Congregational clergyman. Son of Abraham Pierson (1609–1678). Named one of ten trustees upon organization of Yale College; elected first rector of Yale, 1701.

PIERSON, ARTHUR TAPPAN (*b. New York, N.Y., 1837; d. Brooklyn, N.Y., 1911*), Presbyterian clergyman, promoter of missionary activities. Wrote *The Crisis of Missions* (1886); editor, *Missionary Review*, 1890–1911.

PIERSON, HAMILTON WILCOX (*b. Bergen, N.Y., 1817; d. Bergen, 1888*), Presbyterian clergyman, author. Served as traveling agent for American Bible Society; ministered to freedmen in Virginia and Georgia, 1863–69.

PIERZ, FRANZ (*b. near Kamnik, Carniola, Austria, 1785; d. Austria, 1880*), Roman Catholic missionary. Worked among Chippewa Indians in Michigan and Minnesota, 1835–71; promoted German settlement in Minnesota. Author of *Die Indianer in Nord-Amerika* (1855).

PIEZ, CHARLES (*b. Mainz, Germany, 1866; d. Washington, D.C., 1933*), manufacturer, engineer. Director of the Emergency Fleet Corp., 1917–19. [*Supp.* 1]

PIGGOT, ROBERT (*b. New York, N.Y., 1795; d. Sykesville, Md., 1887*), stipple engraver, Episcopal clergyman. Apprentice to David Edwin; partner of Charles Goodman. Held pastorates in Pennsylvania, Delaware and Maryland *post* 1824.

PIGGOTT, JAMES (*b. Connecticut, c. 1739; d. East St. Louis, Ill., 1799*), Revolutionary soldier, pioneer. Settled in Illinois, c. 1780; served as judge of various courts at Cahokia during 1790's; organized ferry service at East St. Louis, 1797.

PIKE, ALBERT (*b. Boston, Mass., 1809; d. Washington, D.C., 1891*), lawyer, soldier, author, prominent Freemason. From 1833 to the Civil War, Pike lived principally in Arkansas, where he taught school, edited the *Arkansas Advocate*, 1835–37, and became one of the Southwest's most respected lawyers. He was the first reporter of the Arkansas supreme court (1840–45), commanded a cavalry troop in the war with Mexico, was a prominent Whig, and later a promoter of the Know-Nothing party. Made brigadier-general and commander of the Indian country west of Arkansas by the Confederate government in 1861, he recruited Indians into the army who committed some atrocities at Pea Ridge (1862) for which Pike was unjustly accused. His quarrels with Gen. T. C. Hindman, his superior, led to his arrest, 1863, and brief imprisonment. After the war he practiced law and directed the Southern Jurisdiction of Scottish Rite Masonry. His *Hymns to the Gods* were first published in *Blackwood's Magazine* for June 1839, and republished with additional poems in 1872 and subsequent editions. He was also author of *Prose Sketches and Poems* (1834), *Nugae* (1854), and Masonic writings.

PIKE, JAMES SHEPHERD (*b. Calais, Maine, 1811; d. Calais, 1882*), journalist, author. Wrote vivid and colorful accounts of official life in the capital as Washington correspondent of the *New York Tribune*,

1850–60. Served as U.S. minister to The Hague, 1861–66.

PIKE, MARY HAYDEN GREEN (*b. Eastport, Maine, 1824; d. Baltimore, Md., 1908*), novelist, abolitionist. Published *Ida May* (1854), and *Caste* (1856), melodramatic anti-slavery novels.

PIKE, NICOLAS (*b. Somersworth, N.H., 1743; d. 1819*), teacher, arithmetician. Graduated Harvard, 1766. Master for many years of the grammar school at Newburyport, Mass. His fame rests chiefly upon his well-organized and admirable treatise, *A New and Complete System of Arithmetick, Composed for the Use of the Citizens of the United States . . .* (1788), and an abridgment of this work which first appeared in 1793. He was the first American arithmetician to attain wide popularity in the field of school textbooks.

PIKE, ROBERT (*b. Wiltshire, England, c. 1616; d. 1708*), colonial official. Emigrated to New England, 1635; was an original settler of Salisbury, Mass., 1639; served almost continuously as a Massachusetts elected official, 1648–96. Denounced curtailing of rights of Baptists and Quakers; stressed invalidity of spectre testimony in Salem witch trials.

PIKE, ZEBULON MONTGOMERY (*b. Lamberton, now part of Trenton, N.J., 1779; d. York, Canada, 1813*), soldier, explorer. Commissioned first lieutenant, U.S. Army, 1799; served on frontier; was ordered by Gen. Jas. Wilkinson (1805) to lead party from St. Louis, Mo., to the headwaters of the Mississippi. He reached what he mistakenly thought was the river's source in the winter of 1805–06. Returning to St. Louis, he was sent to explore the source of the Arkansas and Red rivers and to reconnoiter the Spanish settlements in New Mexico. Setting out from St. Louis on July 15, 1806, he moved up the Arkansas and reached the site of the present Pueblo, Colo. Here on a side trip he attempted unsuccessfully to reach the summit of the peak which bears his name. Turning south, seeking the source of the Red River, he crossed the Sangre de Cristo Mountains and built a fort on the Conejos branch of the Rio Grande. The Spaniards, hearing of his incursion, sent a force to bring him to Santa Fé. He yielded without a struggle and was taken eventually to Chihuahua for questioning. Returning to the United States, he found his name coupled in some quarters with the Burr-Wilkinson scheme for erecting a separate empire in the Southwest. These charges were probably without foundation. Promoted major, 1808, and colonel, 1812, he was advanced in rank to brigadier-general and put in command of troops attacking York (present Toronto), Canada, in April 1813. His mission was successful, but he was killed in the assault.

PILAT, IGNAZ ANTON (*b. St. Agatha, Austria, 1820; d. New York, N.Y., 1870*), landscape gardener. Came to America, 1848. Made comprehensive botanical survey of New York Central Park site; directed planting operations for Calvert Vaux and Frederick L. Olmsted.

PILCHER, JOSHUA (*b. Culpeper Co., Va., 1790; d. St. Louis, Mo., 1843*), fur trader, Indian agent. President, Missouri Fur Co., 1820–31; U.S. superintendent of Indian affairs, 1839–41.

PILCHER, LEWIS STEPHEN (*b. Adrian, Mich., 1845; d. 1934*), surgeon, Union soldier. Father of Paul M. Pilcher. Graduated University of Michigan, 1862; M.D., 1866. Practiced and taught in Brooklyn, N.Y., *post* 1872 until 1918. As editor of *Annals of Surgery, post* 1885, Pilcher exercised wide influence upon surgical thought in the English-speaking world.
[*Supp. 1*]

PILCHER, PAUL MONROE (*b. Brooklyn, N.Y., 1876; d. 1917*), surgeon, urologist. Son of Lewis S. Pilcher. M.D., N.Y. College of Physicians and Surgeons, 1900. Author of *Practical Cystoscopy and the Diagnosis of Surgical Diseases of the Kidneys and Urinary Bladder* (1911).

PILKINGTON, JAMES (*b. Cavendish, Vt., 1851; d. New York, N.Y., 1929*), New York policeman, contractor. Amateur champion boxer, wrestler and oarsman during the 1880's.

PILLING, JAMES CONSTANTINE (*b. Washington, D.C., 1846; d. Olney, Md., 1895*), ethnologist. Author of an outstanding bibliography of the languages of American Indian tribes, published in U.S. Bureau of Ethnology *Bulletins* (Numbers 1, 5, 6, 9, 14, 15, 16, 19).

PILLOW, GIDEON JOHNSON (*b. Williamson Co., Tenn., 1806; d. Helena, Ark., 1878*), lawyer, politician, soldier. Close political friend of James K. Polk; served as general officer in Mexican War and attempted to exalt his own importance at expense of Gen. Winfield Scott. A conservative opponent of extremist measures up to the Civil War, he accepted rank of Confederate brigadier-general, 1861. Second in command at Fort Donelson, he escaped capture when the post was surrendered in February 1862, by passing his responsibility off on Gen. Simon B. Buckner. He was given no important command during the remainder of the war.

PILLSBURY, CHARLES ALFRED (*b. Warner, N.H., 1842; d. Minneapolis, Minn., 1899*), flour miller. Nephew of John S. Pillsbury. Removed to Minneapolis, 1869; bought a share in a small local flour mill. Quick to recognize the importance of new technological advances, he installed the La Croix purifying process, which permitted use of Northwest spring wheat for high-grade bread flour, and later adopted the roller process. His firm, C. A. Pillsbury and Co., prospered, partly because of highly favorable railroad freight rates which he helped secure and maintain, partly because of his extensive system of grain elevators, and partly because of his effective advertising techniques based upon brand names. His incursions into the grain market were spectacular though not often profitable. *Post* 1889, he was managing director of Pillsbury-Washburn, Ltd.

PILLSBURY, HARRY NELSON (*b. Somerville, Mass., 1872; d. Frankford, Pa., 1906*), chess player. Among top international masters, 1894–1904; first American professional chess player; specialized in simultaneous blindfold play.

PILLSBURY, JOHN ELLIOTT (*b. Lowell, Mass., 1846; d. Washington, D.C., 1919*), naval officer, oceanographer. Graduated U.S. Naval Academy, 1867. Served with U.S. Coast Survey 1876–91; invented current meter; determined axis of Gulf Stream; wrote *The Gulf Stream* (1891).

PILLSBURY, JOHN SARGENT (*b. Sutton, N.H., 1828; d. Minneapolis, Minn., 1901*), flour miller, Minnesota legislator. Uncle of Charles A. Pillsbury. Settled in present Minneapolis, 1855. Partner in C. A. Pillsbury and Co. Republican governor of Minnesota, 1876–82; retrieved University of Minnesota from bankruptcy, 1864.

PILLSBURY, PARKER (*b. Hamilton, Mass., 1809; d. Concord, N.H., 1898*), reformer, Garrisonian Abolitionist. Lecture agent, anti-slavery societies, 1840–61; edited *Herald of Freedom*, 1840, 1845–46; ardent advocate of woman's rights.

PILMORE, JOSEPH (*b. Tadmouth, England, 1739; d. Philadelphia, Pa., 1825*), Episcopal clergyman. Trained by John Wesley, Pilmore came to America, 1769, and was first Methodist preacher in Philadelphia; he returned to England, 1774. Abandoning Methodism, 1784, he came back to America and was ordained, 1785, by Samuel Seabury. He served thereafter as rector in New York and the Philadelphia area.

PILSBURY, AMOS (*b. Londonderry, N.H., 1805; d. Albany, N.Y., 1873*), pioneer professional prison administrator.

PINCHBACK, PINCKNEY BENTON STEWART (*b. Macon, Ga., 1837; d. Washington, D.C., 1921*), Union soldier, politician. Son of a white father and a free Negro mother. Louisiana radical legislator and official during Reconstruction.

PINCKNEY, CHARLES (*b. Charleston, S.C., 1757; d. 1824*), planter, lawyer, Revolutionary soldier. Second cousin of Charles C. and Thomas Pinckney. As congressman from South Carolina, 1784–87, he led in movement to amend the Articles of Confederation; a prominent delegate to the Federal Convention, 1787, he submitted a plan for a constitution (the "Pinckney draught") now known only in a recon-

structed form. It is probable that he had an important share in determining the final form and content of the U.S. Constitution but his egoistic claims for credit have made historians doubtful of his real achievements. He served as Federalist governor of South Carolina, 1789–92. Alienated from his party on personal and intellectual grounds, he became a (Democrat) Republican and as such was governor in 1797–99 and 1807–09. While U.S. senator, 1799–1801, he was a leader in attacks on the administration and the manager of Thomas Jefferson's campaign in South Carolina. Appointed U.S. minister to Spain (March 1801–1805), he succeeded in winning Spanish assent to the cession of Louisiana, but his attempt to secure a cession of the Floridas exceeded his instructions and failed. As congressman from South Carolina, 1819–21, he delivered one of his finest addresses in opposition to the Missouri Compromise.

PINCKNEY, CHARLES COTESWORTH (*b. Charleston, S.C., 1746; d. Charleston, 1825*), lawyer, Revolutionary soldier, statesman. Son of Elizabeth L. Pinckney; brother of Thomas Pinckney; second cousin of Charles Pinckney. Served in South Carolina colonial and state legislatures; was prominent as a delegate to Federal Convention, 1787. Between 1791 and 1795, he was offered and declined the command of the army, a seat on the U.S. Supreme Court, and the secretaryships of war and state. Accepting the post of U.S. minister to France, July 1796, he was refused official recognition by the Directory when he arrived at Paris in December. Appointed to serve with Elbridge Gerry and John Marshall on a special mission to France, 1797, he gave an indignant refusal to suggestions that a bribe to French officials might ease matters (the "X.Y.Z. Affair"). As major-general, 1798–1800, he commanded all U.S. military posts and forces south of Maryland and also those in Kentucky and Tennessee. A lifelong Federalist, he was his party's nominee for vice-president in 1800, and for president in 1804 and 1808.

PINCKNEY, ELIZABETH LUCAS (*b. probably Antigua, c. 1722; d. Philadelphia, Pa., 1793*), introducer of indigo into colonial South Carolina. Mother of Charles C. and Thomas Pinckney. Educated in England, she was brought to her father's plantation, "Wappoo," near Charleston in 1738 and left to manage the affairs of three plantations, her father returning to Antigua. Searching about for a profitable crop she experimented with indigo seeds, 1741; after three years' trial, she succeeded in raising a crop, and with help from a Montserrat man prepared it for market. Her husband, Charles Pinckney, further developed the industry which became a very profitable one. Upon the death of her husband in 1758, she again became manager of extensive plantation properties.

PINCKNEY, HENRY LAURENS (*b. Charleston, S.C., 1794; d. Charleston, 1863*), editor, South Carolina legislator and congressman. Son of Charles Pinckney; brother-in-law of Robert Y. Hayne. Proprietor and principal editor of *Charleston Mercury*, 1823–32; made it the leading state daily and an uncompromising advocate of nullification. Mayor of Charleston, 1829 and 1837–39.

PINCKNEY, THOMAS (*b. Charleston, S.C., 1750; d. Charleston, 1828*), soldier, diplomat, politician. Son of Elizabeth L. Pinckney; brother of Charles C. Pinckney. Educated in England and called to the English bar in 1774, he returned to South Carolina, 1774. He served with credit, 1775–81, in the southern campaigns of the Revolution and was severely wounded at Camden. Entering successful legal practice at Charleston, he was governor of his state, 1787–89, and president of the South Carolina ratifying convention, 1788. He served fruitlessly as U.S. minister to Great Britain, 1792–95, but as special envoy to Spain (1795) he concluded the advantageous treaty of San Lorenzo. Unsuccessful candidate for the U.S. vice-presidency, 1796, he was a Federalist congressman from South Carolina, 1797–1801.

PINE, ROBERT EDGE (*b. London, England, 1730; d. Philadelphia, Pa., 1788*), portrait and subject painter. Came to America, 1784; painted many of the celebrities of the time (including Washington and members of his family). Proposed a series of paintings illustrative of the Revolution but died before attempting more than one.

PINGREE, HAZEN STUART (*b. Denmark, Maine, 1840; d. England, 1901*), manufacturer, Michigan politician, Union soldier. Settling in Detroit, 1865, he became partner in a shoe-manufacturing enterprise which prospered. Elected reform mayor of Detroit under Republican auspices, 1889, he found that a group of private vested interests controlled municipal affairs. After bitter fights he established a municipal power plant, removed toll gates, forced reductions in gas and telephone rates, and made the street railway monopoly give better service. During the panic of 1893 he inaugurated a plan of gardens for the unemployed ("Pingree's Potato Patches"). Elected governor of Michigan, 1896, he served until 1901. The chief target of his fight against special privilege while governor was the railroads, but his administration was only moderately successful.

PINKERTON, ALLAN (*b. Glasgow, Scotland, 1819; d. 1884*), detective. Settling in Illinois early in the 1840's, he first engaged in the cooper's trade. After uncovering a gang of counterfeiters, he was made deputy-sheriff of Kane Co., Ill., 1846; he later held the same post in Cook Co. Named first detective of the Chicago police force, 1850, he established a private agency in the same year, one of the first in the United States. Successful in solving a number of train and express robberies, he learned through his operatives of a Southern plot against Abraham Lincoln's

life, February 1861, and was responsible for the circuitous route followed by the president on his way to inauguration. Later in the year, on invitation of Gen. George B. McClellan, Pinkerton organized a secret-service and counter-espionage department for the army and conducted it until November 1862. Thereafter, he engaged in a wide variety of detective work, including anti-strike activity and labor espionage; he was also author of a number of "real life" detective narratives based on his agency's experiences.

PINKERTON, LEWIS LETIG (*b. Baltimore Co., Md., 1812; d. 1875*), physician, Disciples of Christ clergyman, editor, educator. Prominent *post* 1839 in the activities and controversies of his denomination in Kentucky.

PINKHAM, LYDIA ESTES (*b. Lynn, Mass., 1819; d. Lynn, 1883*), reformer, manufacturer of patent medicine. Began producing her famous and widely advertised "Vegetable Compound" in 1875.

PINKNEY, EDWARD COOTE (*b. London, England, 1802; d. Baltimore, Md., 1828*), poet, lawyer, editor. Son of William Pinkney. His small but distinguished body of poetry appeared in *Rodolph* (1823) and *Poems* (1825); he edited *The Marylander*, a newspaper in support of J. Q. Adams's campaign for re-election, 1827–28.

PINKNEY, NINIAN (*b. Annapolis, Md., 1811; d. Easton, Md., 1877*), surgeon. Nephew of William Pinkney. Graduated St. John's (Annapolis), 1830; M.D., Jefferson Medical College, 1833. Served with distinction in U.S. Navy, 1834–73; was surgeon of the fleet in D. D. Porter's squadron, 1862–65.

PINKNEY, WILLIAM (*b. Annapolis, Md., 1764; d. Washington, D.C., 1822*), lawyer, Maryland legislator, diplomat. Father of Edward C. Pinkney. Studied law with Samuel Chase; was admitted to the bar, 1786. Pinkney rose rapidly to a commanding position in his profession and was considered the most talented advocate of his time despite his personal affectations and the flamboyant character of his oratory. Inordinately vain, he wished to excel in everything and concealed his profound researches into precedents behind a screen of affected carelessness and haste of preparation. He appeared in 72 cases before the U.S. Supreme Court.

He served as joint commissioner with Christopher Gore in England, 1796–1804, working to adjust maritime claims under the seventh article of the Jay Treaty. Returning home, he was briefly attorney-general of Maryland. Joint commissioner with James Monroe to treat with the British over reparations for ship seizures and impressment, 1806–07, he was concerned in the formulation of a proposed treaty which Jefferson angrily repudiated. He then engaged in frustrating and futile negotiations with the British over the *Leopard-Chesapeake* affair and the issue of the Orders in Council while serving as U.S. minister to Great Britain, 1807–11. He was an able U.S. attorney-general, 1811–14, served in the militia (1814), and sat in Congress from Maryland, 1815–16. Effective as U.S. minister to Russia, 1816–18, he became U.S. senator from Maryland in 1819 and served until his death. Here he performed his greatest work for his country as an interpreter of the Constitution. His speeches in opposition to Rufus King during the debates over the Missouri Compromise were an important factor in bringing the Compromise about. Meanwhile, he reached the heights of his forensic career in the Supreme Court in his arguments in *McCulloch vs. Maryland* (1818–19) and *Cohens vs. Virginia* (1821).

PINNEY, NORMAN (*b. Simsbury, Conn., 1804; d. New Orleans, La., 1862*), clergyman, educator. Organized the Mobile (Ala.) Institute, a classical school for boys, 1836, and headed it for many years.

PINTARD, JOHN (*b. New York, N.Y., 1759; d. New York, 1844*), merchant, philanthropist. Helped organize both the Massachusetts and New-York Historical societies; served as president of New York City's first savings bank, 1828–41.

PINTARD, LEWIS (*b. New York, N.Y., 1732; d. Princeton, N.J., 1818*), New York merchant. Served as American commissary for prisoners in New York City during most of the Revolution.

PINTO, ISAAC (*b. 1720, place unknown; d. New York, N.Y., 1791*), merchant, scholar, patriot. A Sephardic Jew, he appears first in New York records, 1740; he lived from time to time in various places including Charleston, S.C. He is best known as the translator into English of the first Jewish Prayer Book printed in America, the *Evening Service of Roshashanah and Kippur* (1761), and *Prayers for Shabbath, Rosh-Hashanah, and Kippur* (1766). He was probably also translator of *The Form of Prayer . . . for a General Thanksgiving . . . for the Reducing of Canada* (1760) and may have been author of letters appearing under the pseudonyms "A. B." and "Philalethes" in New York newspapers, 1750–75.

PIPER, CHARLES VANCOUVER (*b. Victoria, B.C., Canada, 1867; d. 1926*), agronomist. Graduated University of Washington, 1885; Harvard, M.S., 1900. Taught botany and zoology at State College of Washington, 1893–1903; was employed thereafter by U.S. Department of Agriculture, having charge *post* 1905 of the office of forage crops. His most important achievement was finding Sudan grass, a useful cousin of the Johnson grass of the South, which he discovered under a mistaken classification. He published *Sudan Grass, a New Drought-resistant Hay Plant* (1913) which started culture of a commercially important product. He also wrote *Forage Plants and Their Culture* (1914) and other special studies.

PIRSSON, LOUIS VALENTINE (*b. Fordham, N.Y., 1860; d. 1919*), geologist. Graduated Sheffield Scientific School, Yale, 1882; studied also at Heidelberg and Paris. Became interested in igneous geology after serving with U.S. Geological Survey party in Yellowstone Park, 1889–90. Teacher at Yale *post* 1892, in 1893 he gave the first graduate course there in petrology. Associate editor of the *American Journal of Science* (1899–1919), he was one of four authors of *Quantitative Classification of Igneous Rocks* (1903), a landmark in petrology. He was sole author of *Rocks and Rock Minerals* (1908); and of Part I of the *Text Book of Geology* by Pirsson and Schuchert.

PISE, CHARLES CONSTANTINE (*b. Annapolis, Md., 1801; d. Brooklyn, N.Y., 1866*), Roman Catholic clergyman, author. Educated at Georgetown and at Mount St. Mary's, Emmitsburg, Md., he was ordained in 1825 and served parishes in Baltimore, Washington, D.C., New York City, and Brooklyn. He was the only Catholic priest ever to serve as chaplain to the U.S. Senate (1832–33). Among his many books is the early novel *Father Rowland* (1829).

PITCAIRN, JOHN (*b. Dysart, Scotland, 1722; d. Boston, Mass., 1775*), British major of marines. Commanded British force at Lexington battle, April 1775; was mortally wounded at Bunker Hill.

PITCAIRN, JOHN (*b. near Paisley, Scotland, 1841; d. Bryn Athyn, Pa., 1916*), railroad executive, manufacturer, philanthropist. Came to the United States as a child. Helped organize Pittsburgh Plate Glass Co., 1883; was its president, 1897–1905.

PITCHER, MOLLY. [See McCauley, Mary Ludwig Hays, 1754–1832.]

PITCHER, ZINA (*b. near Fort Edward, N.Y., 1797; d. Detroit, Mich., 1872*), physician, naturalist. Settled in Detroit, 1836. Initiated medical department, University of Michigan, 1850; developed public schools while mayor of Detroit, 1840–41 and 1843.

PITCHLYNN, PETER PERKINS (*b. Noxubee Co., Miss., 1806; d. Washington, D.C., 1881*), Choctaw chief. Selected Western lands for Choctaw resettlement, 1828; removed to Indian Territory after 1830 treaty; elected principal chief of tribe, 1860.

PITKIN, FREDERICK WALKER (*b. Manchester, Conn., 1837; d. Pueblo, Colo., 1886*), lawyer. Settled in Colorado, 1874. An able and honest Republican governor of the state, 1879–83, he was responsible for driving out the Utes and for suppressing the Leadville miners' strike, 1880.

PITKIN, TIMOTHY (*b. Farmington, Conn., 1766; d. New Haven, Conn., 1847*), lawyer, Connecticut legislator, historian. Grandson of William Pitkin (1694–1769). Congressman, Federalist, from Connecticut, 1805–19; author of an important statistical account of American commerce (1816).

PITKIN, WILLIAM (*b. probably Marylebone, England, 1635; d. Hartford, Conn., 1694*), lawyer, jurist. Emigrated to Hartford, 1659. Became Connecticut's chief prosecutor, 1664; championed colony's right to control own militia and maintain independence of royal interference in local government.

PITKIN, WILLIAM (*b. Hartford, Conn., 1694; d. Hartford, 1769*), jurist, colonial administrator. Grandson of William Pitkin (1635–1694). Member of committee to draw up confederation plan at Albany Congress, 1754; governor of Connecticut, 1765–69; held many other offices.

PITKIN, WILLIAM (*b. Hartford, Conn., 1725; d. Hartford, 1789*), jurist, manufacturer. Son of William Pitkin (1694–1769). Established first powder mill in Connecticut, 1776; judge of superior court, 1769–89; member, Revolutionary Council of Safety.

PITMAN, BENN (*b. Trowbridge, England, 1822; d. Cincinnati, O., 1910*), phonographer. Came to America, 1852, to popularize his brother Isaac's system of shorthand; established Phonographic Institute in Cincinnati.

PITNEY, MAHLON (*b. Morristown, N.J., 1858; d. Washington, D.C., 1924*), jurist, New Jersey Republican legislator and congressman. As associate justice, U.S. Supreme Court, 1912–22, he delivered a long series of painstaking opinions which were marked by conservatism and anti-labor feeling.

PITTMAN, KEY (*b. Vicksburg, Miss., 1872; d. Reno, Nev., 1940*), lawyer. Began practice in Seattle, Wash., 1892. Moving to the Yukon, 1897, and to Nome, Alaska, 1899, he settled in 1901 in Tonopah, Nev. After a decade of mining, legal, and political activities, he was elected U.S. senator, Democrat, from Nevada, 1912. Unwaveringly loyal to mining interests, he won advantages by his abilities as a negotiator and by exploiting the bloc powers of the seven silver-mining states. The so-called Pittman Act (1918), the silver agreement of the World Economic Conference (1933), and the Silver Purchase Act (1934) testify to his ingenuity in maintaining silver prices through large annual purchases by the U.S. government.
[*Supp. 2*]

PITTOCK, HENRY LEWIS (*b. London, England, 1836; d. Portland, Oreg., 1919*), printer, newspaper publisher, paper manufacturer. Came to America as a child; removed from Pittsburgh, Pa., to Oregon *c.* 1852. Published *Morning Oregonian post* 1861, Portland *Evening Telegram post* 1877, and *Sunday Oregonian post* 1881; enjoyed Portland newspaper monopoly by 1902.

PITTS, HIRAM AVERY (*b. c. 1800; d. Chicago, Ill., 1860*), inventor. Raised in Maine; was blacksmith by trade. Patented chain-band for horse-power treadmill, 1834; improved thresher and fanning mill, 1837.

Manufactured "Chicago-Pitts" threshers in Chicago *post* 1852.

PLACIDE, HENRY (*b. probably Charleston, S.C., 1799; d. Babylon, N.Y., 1870*), actor. Made debut in Augusta, Ga., 1808. After his first appearance in an important role at New York's Park Theatre, 1823, he occupied first rank in popularity as a comedian, ranging from dialect farce to high comedy, until his retirement from the stage, 1865. He played for twenty years at the Park; thereafter, he was a member of the company of Burton's Theatre and also made extended tours throughout the United States. His brother and his three sisters all had stage careers.

PLAISTED, HARRIS MERRILL (*b. Jefferson, N.H., 1828; d. Bangor, Maine, 1898*), lawyer, Union major-general by brevet. Commanded so-called "Iron Brigade," 1863–65; was attorney-general of Maine, 1873–75, and Republican congressman from Maine, 1876–77. Becoming a Greenbacker, 1879, he was elected Democrat-Greenback governor, 1880, but failed of re-election in 1883; thereafter he edited *The New Age* in support of bimetallism.

PLANT, HENRY BRADLEY (*b. Branford, Conn., 1819; d. 1899*), express company executive, railroad and steamship operator. Bought Atlantic and Gulf Railroad and Charleston and Savannah Railroad at foreclosure sales, 1879–80; using these as nucleus, he built up the "Plant System" of transportation lines along the southern Atlantic seaboard. He was also operator of several steamship lines and the builder of a number of hotels in the area served by his system. Providing Florida fruit growers a quicker and cheaper access to markets, he became rich and powerful as Florida and other states dependent on his roads grew in population and were developed. He was associated in the Plant Investment Co., holding company for his properties, with H. M. Flagler, M. K. Jesup and W. T. Walters.

PLATER, GEORGE (*b. near Leonardtown, Md., 1735; d. 1792*), lawyer, Maryland colonial legislator, Revolutionary patriot. Member of Continental Congress, 1778–80; presided over Maryland ratifying convention, 1788; governor of Maryland, 1791–92.

PLATNER, SAMUEL BALL (*b. Unionville, Conn., 1863; d. 1921*), classical scholar. Graduated Yale, 1883; Ph.D., 1885. Taught Latin at Adelbert College, Western Reserve University, *post* 1885; was author of a number of scholarly books, including *A Topographical Dictionary of Ancient Rome* (published posthumously, 1929).

PLATT, CHARLES ADAMS (*b. New York, N.Y., 1861; d. 1933*), architect, landscape architect, painter, etcher. Studied in New York, and in Paris under Boulanger and Lefebvre; after publication of his *Italian Gardens* (1894), he "glided" into the practice of architecture. He designed the Freer Gallery among other buildings in Washington, and is responsible for buildings at the University of Illinois, the University of Rochester, Dartmouth, and Johns Hopkins as well as the Deerfield, Mass., Academy. The Leader-News building, Cleveland, O., is his most significant commercial structure. His most characteristic work, combining architecture and landscaping, is Phillips Academy, Andover, Mass.

PLATT, ORVILLE HITCHCOCK (*b. Washington, Conn., 1827; d. Meriden, Conn., 1905*), lawyer, Connecticut legislator. Pupil of Frederick W. Gunn; studied law under Gideon H. Hollister. After a short, early career in teaching and successful practice of law in Meriden, he won the hotly contested Republican nomination for U.S. senator, 1879; elected by the legislature, he served in the Senate thereafter until his death. In 1881 he became chairman of the patents committee (a position he held intermittently for ten years); his name became associated with practically every patent law passed during his long career. Advocate of liberal copyright relations with Europe, he was successful in securing an international copyright bill (passed, 1891) which effectively ended literary piracy. Chairman of the committee on territories, 1887–93, he was associated with the admission of six far-Western states. In fiscal and tariff legislation, however, he found his main interest. He believed in silver as a medium of exchange but opposed free coinage at 16-to-1 except under international agreement; his influence with the West led that section to accept the compromise Silver Purchase Act of 1890. In international relations Platt stood consistently with the administration in office. Cleveland received his support in the Venezuelan dispute with Great Britain; he was one of the props of the McKinley administration during the difficulties over Cuba. Almost overnight he became an expansionist in 1898, voting for the annexation of Hawaii and strongly urging the retention of the Philippines. As chairman of the committee on Cuban relations, he composed and introduced the famous Platt amendment to the army appropriation bill, 1901. Following the death of McKinley, Platt became a valued supporter of Theodore Roosevelt. His last chairmanship was that of the judiciary committee. A "stand-pat" conservative, he was respected for his high character and unselfish service. He was several times mentioned for the vice-presidential nomination, but his own political ambitions never went beyond the senatorship from Connecticut.

PLATT, THOMAS COLLIER (*b. Owego, N.Y., 1833; d. 1910*), businessman, politician. Began career as a druggist in Owego; was elected county clerk on the Republican ticket, 1859, but soon returned to business as president of the Tioga County National Bank and a speculator in Michigan timber lands. He served on various state and county Republican committees during the 1860's, but his political career really began in 1870 when he became the close friend of Roscoe

Conkling, helping to organize the "southern tier" counties against Horace Greeley and Sen. Reuben E. Fenton. Thereafter he was consulted by Conkling on practically every phase of New York politics. As congressman from New York, 1875–79, Platt made little impression in the House but remained an indispensable behind-the-scene "Stalwart" Republican worker in state politics. Deeply distrustful of James A. Garfield in 1880, he supported him for the presidency only in return for a promise of recognition and rewards if Garfield were elected. As chairman of the state committee, he did much to conciliate the outraged Sen. Conkling and to organize the campaign in New York; his reward was election to the U.S. Senate in 1881. Having promised Chauncey M. Depew his unreserved support of the Garfield administration, Platt was faced with a dilemma when Garfield appointed a "Half Breed" or reform Republican as collector of the port of New York. Both Platt and Conkling resigned their Senate seats in protest and were defeated when they sought reelection in the legislature. Conkling's active career was thus ended; Platt's was eclipsed for over six years.

In 1888 Platt gave Benjamin Harrison his New York support for the presidential nomination in return for a supposed promise of the post of U.S. secretary of the treasury. When Harrison failed to fulfill his promise, Platt became angry; he also resented the starvation fare allotted him in federal patronage. His token support of Harrison was responsible for Grover Cleveland's sweep of New York in 1892. He continued, however, to perfect the New York Republican machine to which he had fallen heir on Conkling's retirement. After the election of Levi P. Morton as governor, 1894, his power became almost irresistible; its chief agency was patronage, local, state, and federal. Year after year, New York State conventions carried out his preordained program, and the legislature docilely obeyed his commands. As Theodore Roosevelt's power grew, Platt's declined; he tried to shunt Roosevelt into obscurity as vice-president in 1900 but found that with "T.R.'s" accession as president and B. B. Odell's as New York's governor his power politics would no longer work. He continued to hold his seat in the Senate but was shorn of party authority. Industrious and patient, he was, however, the very type of ruthless, unprincipled party boss.

PLEASANTS, JAMES (*b. Goochland Co., Va., 1769; d. Goochland Co., 1836*), lawyer, Virginia legislator. Congressman, 1811–19; U.S. senator, 1819–22; governor of Virginia, 1822–25. A cousin of Thomas Jefferson, a Democrat and advocate of social reform, he opposed the rising dominance of Andrew Jackson.

PLEASANTS, JOHN HAMPDEN (*b. Goochland Co., Va., 1797; d. 1846*), journalist, Whig politician. Son of James Pleasants. Founder and editor of the Richmond *Whig*, 1824–46. Killed in a duel with Thomas Ritchie, Jr., an editor of the Richmond *Enquirer*.

PLEASONTON, ALFRED (*b. Washington, D.C., 1824; d. Washington, D.C., 1897*), Union major-general, brilliant cavalry leader. Graduated West Point, 1844; was distinguished in Mexican War and in Western and Southern Indian campaigns. Averted complete disaster at Chancellorsville, 1863, by checking Gen. T. J. Jackson's advance against the Union right flank; commanded all Union cavalry at Gettysburg; routed Gen. Sterling Price near Marais des Cygnes River, Kansas, October 1864. Resigned commission in dispute over rank, 1868.

PLIMPTON, GEORGE ARTHUR (*b. Walpole, Mass., 1855; d. Walpole, 1936*), publisher, book collector. Graduated Amherst, 1876. Associated *post* 1877 with Ginn and Co. and its predecessor firms, he served as chairman of the firm, 1914–31, and greatly expanded its activities.   [*Supp. 2*]

PLOWMAN, GEORGE TAYLOR (*b. Le Sueur, Minn., 1869; d. Cambridge, Mass., 1932*), architect, etcher.

PLUMB, GLENN EDWARD (*b. Clay, Iowa, 1866; d. Washington, D.C., 1922*), lawyer, specialist in railroad law and traction problems. Advocated plan for cooperative government ownership of railroads, with operating managers and employees sharing in profits.

PLUMB, PRESTON B. (*b. Berkshire, O., 1837; d. Washington, D.C., 1891*), journalist, Union soldier, lawyer. Established *Kanzas News*, 1857, at Emporia. Prominent as an independent Republican in Kansas politics, Plumb was U.S. senator from 1877 until his death. As chairman of the public lands committee *post* 1881, he was responsible for the reforming land law of 1891 which inaugurated reclamation and conservation.

PLUMBE, JOHN (*b. Wales, 1809; d. Dubuque, Iowa, 1857*), railroadman, publicist, photographer. Came to America as a boy. Plumbe appears to have been the first (1836) responsible and effective advocate of a railroad to the Pacific, continuing his efforts to this end as late as 1851. Active as a photographer *post* 1840, he established studios and equipment shops in over a dozen cities. His special claim to distinction is his unpatented Plumbeotype process, a method for reproducing daguerreotypes on paper.

PLUMER, WILLIAM (*b. Newburyport, Mass., 1759; d. Epping, N.H., 1850*), lawyer. Served as a Federalist in the New Hampshire legislature at various periods, 1785–1800; was speaker of the House, 1791 and 1797. A member of the state constitutional convention of 1791–92, he was U.S. senator, 1802–07. The foreign-policy difficulties of Jefferson's second administration led to Plumer's repudiation of Federalism and his support of Madison in 1808. Soon an active (Democrat) Republican, he served as New Hampshire governor, 1812–13 and 1816–19, pressing for reforms which included revising the Dartmouth College charter; this action led to a memorable controversy and Supreme Court action. After retirement he devoted himself to writing for the press.

PLUMER, WILLIAM SWAN (*b. Griersburg, now Darlington, Pa., 1802; d. Baltimore, Md., 1880*), Presbyterian clergyman, professor of theology, author. An "Old School" leader, he was twice elected Moderator of the General Assembly (1838 and 1871).

PLUMLEY, FRANK (*b. Eden, Vt., 1844; d. Northfield, Vt., 1924*), jurist, Vermont Republican leader and congressman. Umpire for the Mixed Claims Commissions of British, Dutch, and French claims against Venezuela, 1903.

PLUMMER, HENRY (*d. Bannack, Mont., 1864*), bandit. Nothing is known of his early life. He began his public career in Nevada City, Calif., 1856, when he was elected town marshal. Convicted of murdering a man with whose wife he was involved, he escaped prison on the assumption that he was dying of tuberculosis, but lived to establish a record of seduction, brawling, murder, and jail-breaking for which he was never punished. Fleeing to Washington Territory, 1861, he soon removed to Lewiston, Idaho, where he led a gang of bandits. At the end of 1862, he settled in Bannack where he managed to be elected sheriff and organized a band of outlaws who terrified all southern Montana and were responsible for killing over 100 men within a few months. His double life ended when the townspeople organized a committee of Vigilantes who rounded up his gang, exposed him and hanged him.

PLUMMER, HENRY STANLEY (*b. Hamilton, Minn., 1874; d. Rochester, Minn., 1936*), physician. M.D., Northwestern, 1898. A staff member of the Mayo Clinic *post* 1901, Plummer developed a number of mechanical aids to medical practice and on the basis of clinical observation proposed a new classification for thyroid diseases which encouraged world-wide activity in their study. The Mayo concept of private group medical practice was greatly influenced by Plummer's thinking.   [*Supp. 2*]

PLUMMER, JONATHAN (*b. Newbury, Mass., 1761; d. Newburyport, Mass., 1819*), peddler, balladmonger. Poet laureate to "Lord" Timothy Dexter, 1793–1806.

PLUMMER, MARY WRIGHT (*b. Richmond, Ind., 1856; d. Dixon, Ill., 1916*), librarian, teacher, poet. Headed library schools at Pratt Institute (1894–1911) and N.Y. Public Library; president, American Library Association, 1915–16.

PLUNKETT, CHARLES PESHALL (*b. Washington, D.C., 1864; d. Washington, 1931*), naval officer. Graduated Annapolis, 1884. Commanded batteries of 14-inch naval guns on railway mounts in Layon-Longuyon sector, Western Front, 1918; held important sea and shore commands until retirement as rear-admiral, 1928.

POCAHONTAS (*b. Virginia, c. 1595; d. Gravesend, England, 1617*), Indian "princess." Alternative name of Matoaka, daughter of Powhatan. Mentioned in Capt. John Smith's *True Relation* as a "child of ten" in 1607; saved Smith by her intervention when he was captured by Powhatan, 1608. The truth of this famous story is still a matter of controversy. In the spring of 1613 Pocahontas fell into the hands of Samuel Argall, who brought her to Jamestown where she was received graciously by the acting governor, Sir Thomas Dale, and was subsequently converted to Christianity. Her marriage in April 1614 at Jamestown to John Rolfe, an English gentleman, acted as a bond between the English and the Indians and brought a peace which aided establishment of the colony. In 1616 she accompanied her husband to England where she was received by the King and Queen.

POE, EDGAR ALLAN (*b. Boston, Mass., 1809; d. Baltimore, Md., 1849*), poet, critic, short-story writer. Son of David and Elizabeth (Arnold) Poe, actors; brother of William H. L. Poe and Rosalie Poe. Orphaned in 1811, the Poe children were parceled out among foster-parents; Edgar went to live with Mr. and Mrs. John Allan of Richmond, Va. In 1815, he was taken to Great Britain (where Allan, a merchant, planned to establish a branch of his firm), attended for a short period a school in Irvine, Scotland, and was later at the boarding school of the Misses Dubourg in Chelsea and at the Manor House School, Stoke Newington. On the failure of Allan's venture, 1820, they all returned to Richmond where Poe attended the school of Joseph H. Clarke and began to write verses. Here he met Rob Stanard, to whose mother, Jane Stith Stanard, "To Helen" is addressed.

By 1824 the relation between John Allan and Poe was strained because of Poe's knowledge of Allan's infidelity to his wife. The young man, up to this point, had done well in school, read widely in contemporary literature, and was considered a very able swimmer. Secretly but transiently engaged to a neighbor's daughter, Sarah Elmira Royster, he was sent to the University of Virginia, 1826. He remained for only one term. Allan refused to pay his charges. In order to maintain himself Poe tried gambling, which got him heavily into debt; the situation was further complicated by Poe's drinking. It was plain, even at this time, that a very little liquor was disastrous to him. Allan, refusing to pay the gambling debts, proposed that Poe take up the reading of law; Poe insisted on a literary career. The violent quarrel that ensued drove Poe from Allan's house to seek his fortune under an assumed name. Arriving in Boston sometime in April 1827, he published in that year his first volume, *Tamerlane and Other Poems*. The verse, although it gave hints of the poet's power, was undistinguished and went unnoticed. In desperate circumstances, he enlisted in the U.S. Army under

the assumed name "Edgar A. Perry." Assigned to Battery H, 1st U.S. Artillery, at Fort Independence, Boston, he was ordered to South Carolina in October 1827 and served at Fort Moultrie until the end of 1828. Promoted sergeant-major, he corresponded with Allan about going to West Point. Allan consented, partly because of Mrs. Allan's dying wishes, and Poe set off with letters of recommendation to the secretary of war in April 1829, requesting an appointment. It was not soon forthcoming. Proceeding in May to Baltimore, Md., he lived on a pittance sent him by Allan. He now first saw his blood relatives—his grandmother Mrs. David Poe, his aunt Mrs. Maria Clemm, and Mrs. Clemm's daughter Virginia, his future wife. For a time he lived with Mrs. Clemm and his elder brother William. His second volume of poetry, *Al Aaraaf, Tamerlane, and Minor Poems,* was published in Baltimore in December 1829. In January 1830 he returned to Richmond where he quarreled further with Allan. Receiving an appointment to West Point, he passed the examinations and entered the U.S. Military Academy on July 1, 1830.

Poe had hoped to win back his foster-father's favor; however, a letter of his containing an unfortunate remark fell into Allan's hands, and Poe was definitely disowned. He now determined to leave the army and deliberately neglected his duties, for which he was dismissed in March 1831. His third volume, *Poems by Edgar A. Poe,* appeared in 1831; it contained three of his most famous lyrics, "To Helen," "Israfel," and "The Doomed City," but attracted little attention. Removing to Baltimore *c.* March 1831, he took up residence with Mrs. Clemm and Virginia and stayed in that city until the summer of 1835. Beginning to write prose extensively, he first attracted notice in October 1833 on the publication in the *Baltimore Saturday Visiter* of "A MS. Found in a Bottle." An important outcome of this publication was the friendship of John P. Kennedy, who became his patron and introduced him to T. W. White, editor of the *Southern Literary Messenger,* to which Poe began to contribute. In midsummer of 1835 he joined the staff of the *Messenger* in Richmond, and through brilliant editing and critical writing increased the circulation seven-fold. This success was offset by Poe's increased drinking which caused a temporary separation between him and White. In September, Poe took out a license to marry his 13-year-old cousin Virginia; they were publicly married in Richmond, May 1836.

Discontented with the limited scope of the *Messenger,* Poe took his child bride and Mrs. Clemm to New York in January 1837. Unable to make a living there, he moved to Philadelphia in the summer of 1838 where he edited a pirated textbook on conchology (1839), but supported himself mainly by free-lance writing. In May 1839 he was employed by William E. Burton as co-editor of *Burton's Gentleman's Magazine,* continuing in this capacity until

June 1840. His prose *Narrative of Arthur Gordon Pym* had been published in book form, July 1838; the end of 1839 brought the publication of his sixth volume, *Tales of the Grotesque and Arabesque*. Quarreling with Burton, Poe set about the establishment of his own magazine in January 1841, but dropped the project to be literary editor of *Graham's Lady's and Gentleman's Magazine*. Once again Poe's talent increased the circulation as well as his own fame, but lapses into drink and general ill-health ended this employment in May 1842. The remainder of Poe's sojourn in Philadelphia was a period of great poverty, visionary schemes to publish his own magazine (to be called "The Stylus") and abortive attempts to obtain government employ. His wife was now advanced in tuberculosis and only Mrs. Clemm's efforts kept the family together and alive. However, in 1843 Poe wrote and published "The Gold Bug" (*Dollar Newspaper*, June 21, 28), issued a pamphlet of stories (part of a proposed series) which contained "The Murders in the Rue Morgue," and composed the early version of "The Raven."

Poe left Philadelphia with Virginia and returned to New York in April 1844. "The Raven" was cast in final form and appeared first in the N.Y. *Evening Mirror* (Jan. 29, 1845) to great applause; in June 1845, Poe found himself sole editor of the *Broadway Journal*. Later in that year, two more volumes of his work appeared: *Tales* and *The Raven and Other Poems*. Now famous, Poe through pressure of a number of circumstances gave up the *Broadway Journal*, January 1846. In the spring, he moved his family to Fordham where he wrote a series of journalistic critical articles known as "The Literati of New York City" for *Godey's Lady's Book*. Virginia Poe died in January 1847 during a winter in which the family sounded the depths of misery. Poe now sought female sympathy ardently; among those whom he courted with an erratic, abnormal persistence were Mary Louise Shew, Sarah Helen Whitman, and Annie Richmond. During this time he published *Eureka: A Prose Poem* (1848) and composed some of his best-known lyrics: "The Bells," "Ulalume," "Annabel Lee," and "El Dorado." His time was occupied mainly in trips to Philadelphia, Richmond, and Fordham and by bouts of drinking. Arriving in Richmond almost dead in July 1849, he joined a lodge of teetotalers and began to court his old love Sarah Royster, now widowed. The marriage day was set, and Poe left Richmond to bring back Mrs. Clemm. Stopping at Baltimore five days before the election of 1849, Poe disappeared; he was found semi-conscious in a tavern by an old friend, Dr. James E. Snodgrass, on October 3. Four days later he died in great mental agony and was buried in the churchyard of the Westminster Presbyterian Church, Baltimore.

In the practical affairs of everyday life, in many of the common amenities, in the domestic circle, and in the general give and take of earthly existence, Poe was greatly lacking and frequently a complete failure. His relations with women, at least during the latter part of his life, were fantastic and nothing more. He certainly at various times resorted to opiates and he was the victim of alcohol. Combined with all this was an undoubted charm and fascination, a magnetism and a reverse power of antagonism which caused him to be greatly loved by a few, hated by many, and memorable to everybody. He practiced literature in a time and place when what he had to say and his way of saying it were little appreciated, was constantly ground down by poverty and disappointments and was victim of a succession of tragedies which cannot all be attributed to his own failings. All of this can be summed up by saying that as a man Poe was abnormal, and as a genius unique.

His reputation as artist in the United States from 1845 on, contrary to the belief of foreign critics, has always been assured. At his death he was already in his native country a famous man. In France, owing largely to the early and brilliant translations of Baudelaire, Poe has exerted a very great literary influence. His fame rests on a small bulk of exquisite lyrical poetry, on a few of his stories, and on his contribution to the methods of writing certain types of short prose fiction. He is commonly considered to be the originator of the "detective" story or tale of logical deduction. His style in prose is a product of his own peculiar genius, unusually effective when used by him, but not to be imitated. His characters are either grotesques or the inhabitants of another world than this. As a critic there is much to be learned from him, but his dicta should be carefully compared with the sources from which he took them, principally Coleridge. Owing to the publishing conditions of his day, he was forced frequently into journalistic, superficial and fragmentary publication. A more consistent philosophy, esthetic, critical, and social, emerges from his collected works than might at first blush appear; much of this, however, must be retrieved from comments upon long-forgotten contemporaries.

POE, ORLANDO METCALFE (*b. Navarre, O., 1832; d. Detroit, Mich., 1895*), soldier, engineer. Graduated West Point, 1856. Commissioned brigadier-general, 1862; received regular army brevet of that rank, 1865. A successful field officer, 1861–63, he was chief engineer under Gen. W. T. Sherman, 1864–65. Thereafter he was active in railroad construction, and river and harbor improvement work in the Great Lakes region.

POINDEXTER, GEORGE (*b. Louisa Co., Va., 1779; d. Jackson, Miss., 1853*), lawyer. Removed to Mississippi, 1802; served as attorney-general, delegate to Congress, and district judge of the Territory; was congressman, Democrat, from Mississippi, 1817–19, and governor of the state, 1820–21. His able codification of the laws of Mississippi was published in

1824. As U.S. senator, 1830–35, he was an outspoken opponent of Andrew Jackson.

POINSETT, JOEL ROBERTS (*b. Charleston, S.C., 1779; d. near Statesburg, S.C., 1851*), diplomat, statesman. Educated at Timothy Dwight's school (Greenfield Hill, Conn.) and in England; studied law with Henry W. De Saussure; made extended tour of Europe and western Asia, 1801–08. Returning home hoping for high military appointment, he accepted in 1810 a post as special agent to Rio de la Plata and Chile and supported the movement there to gain independence from Spain. On his return, 1815, he became interested in politics, served in the South Carolina legislature, and was congressman, Democrat, 1821–25. First U.S. minister to Mexico, 1825–30, he was recalled at request of the Mexicans for meddling in local politics. As U.S. secretary of war, 1837–41, he was distinguished for energy and ability. He was a strong Unionist. The Poinsettia was developed by him from a Mexican flower.

POLAK, JOHN OSBORN (*b. Brooklyn, N.Y., 1870; d. Brooklyn, 1931*), obstetrician, gynecologist. Associated as consultant and teacher with many hospitals, in particular the Long Island College Hospital from which he had graduated in 1891.

POLAND, LUKE POTTER (*b. Westford, Vt., 1815; d. Waterville, Vt., 1887*), Vermont jurist. U.S. senator, Republican, from Vermont, 1865–67; congressman, 1867–75. Chairman of House committees investigating Ku Klux Klan and Crédit Mobilier, he was also on committee which rejected the Carpetbag régime in Arkansas, 1875. Poland was largely responsible for the revision of U.S. Statutes, 1867–1875, as chairman of a House committee instituted for that purpose.

POLK, JAMES KNOX (*b. Mecklenburg Co., N.C., 1795; d. Nashville, Tenn., 1849*), lawyer, eleventh president of the United States. Scotch-Irish in ancestry, Polk removed in 1806 with his family to the valley of Duck River, Tenn. After preparation in Tennessee academies, he graduated from University of North Carolina with first honors in mathematics and classics, 1818. He read law in Tennessee with Felix Grundy; was admitted to the bar, 1820. Starting practice at Columbia, Tenn., in less than a year he was a leading practitioner. During two years in the state legislature he won notice for business ability and as a debater; he also became a friend of Andrew Jackson. He married Sarah Childress of Murfreesboro, 1824, a lady of ability and culture.

Entering the U.S. House of Representatives in 1825, he opposed the policies of Pres. J. Q. Adams on political principle and because of loyalty to Jackson. After Jackson became president (1829), Polk was a recognized leader of administration forces in the House. Owing to Polk, Jackson was able to triumph over the Bank of the United States. Polk, as a member of the House committee of ways and means, submitted a strong minority report in favor of executive action when the Bank issue was joined in 1832; as chairman of that committee *post* December 1833, he was chief defender of the president's action in withdrawing federal funds from the Bank. Polk defeated John Bell for the speakership of the House in 1835 but was bitterly heckled and denounced as Jackson's "slave" during his brilliant four-year administration of the post. Contrary to his preferences he was drafted by the Democrats as candidate for governor of Tennessee and was elected, 1839. His administration was satisfactory but uneventful; he was defeated for re-election in 1841 and again in 1843.

The Whigs had gained control of the federal government in 1840 but the Democrats began early to prepare for victory in 1844. Henry Clay would surely be the Whig candidate. Martin Van Buren was favored as the Democratic candidate, and Polk and Richard M. Johnson were being considered for the vice-presidential nomination. Not until Van Buren wrote a letter in late April 1844 opposing the annexation of Texas was Polk's name suggested for the presidency. Jackson, as head of the Democratic party, declared that Van Buren had committed political suicide and directed Polk's nomination as a "dark horse." After the defeat of Clay in the election, Polk announced that his principles and policy were to be found in the Democratic platform and in his inaugural address. He advised prospective cabinet members to devote their time and energy to supporting his administration and not to possible candidacy as his successor. Politely but firmly, he made it clear that his decisions would be his own although he would seek and accept advice from his party's elder statesmen.

Polk was younger than any of his predecessors but few presidents have had more definite plans for their administrations, and none has been more successful in accomplishing his plans. In a conversation with George Bancroft, his secretary of the navy, a few days after inauguration he stated: "There are four great measures which are to be the measures of my administration: one, a reduction of the tariff; another, the independent treasury; a third, the settlement of the Oregon boundary question; and lastly, the acquisition of California." Before he left office in 1849, he had accomplished each of these measures. The Walker tariff law of 1846 placed import duties substantially on a revenue basis and substituted *ad valorem* for specific duties. The independent treasury bill of 1846 re-established a financial system which continued, with slight modifications, until supplemented by the Federal Reserve system. The Oregon question was resolved also in 1846 by Polk's firmness in dealing with Great Britain and according to his own compromise plan of dividing the area between Alaska and California along the 49th parallel. Polk's plan for gaining California and New Mexico by forcing their cession as payment of Mexico's long-standing damage-claims debt to the United States led to the Mexican War. The charge that Polk wantonly provoked the war to extend slavery is unfounded. Polk was the first president to change the fundamental character of the Monroe Doctrine, opposing not only the use of foreign force but interference of any kind in American affairs. Opposed to "pork barrel" legislation, he indicted Clay's "American System" in his brilliant last annual message. Although a consistent party man, he had a supreme contempt for the spoils system. His expansion policy gave the United States a vast increase in territory and free access to the Pacific. He favored the course of extending the Missouri Compromise line to the Pacific and opposed all extremist views on the question of slavery; thus he was disliked by both sides in that great controversy and has been given scant credit for his outstanding public services.

POLK, LEONIDAS (*b. Raleigh, N.C., 1806; d. near Marietta, Ga., 1864*), Episcopal clergyman, Confederate lieutenant-general. Son of William Polk. Educated at University of North Carolina and West Point. Converted by Charles P. McIlvaine, he resigned his commission late in 1827, attended Virginia Theological Seminary, and was ordained in May 1831. Appointed missionary bishop of the Southwest, 1838, and bishop of Louisiana, 1841, he was a principal agent in the founding of the University of the South. Suspending his episcopal work, 1861, he accepted a commission as major-general in the Confederate army and served conscientiously as a corps commander under Generals A. S. Johnston and Braxton Bragg. He fought bravely at Shiloh, Perryville and Murfreesboro, but blundered at Chickamauga and was often in conflict with Bragg whose removal he recommended to President Jefferson Davis. Meanwhile, he had been promoted to lieutenant-general, October 1862. He was killed at Pine Mountain. An evangelical in his religious point of view, he was gifted as an executive; as a soldier, he was distinguished for organizing ability and as a disciplinarian.

POLK, LEONIDAS LAFAYETTE (*b. Anson Co., N.C., 1837; d. 1892*), farmer, newspaper editor, president of the National Farmers' Alliance and Industrial Union *post* 1889.

POLK, LUCIUS EUGENE (*b. Salisbury, N.C., 1833; d. Columbia, Tenn., 1892*), planter, Confederate officer. Nephew of Leonidas Polk. Valued subordinate to Gen. P. R. Cleburne at Shiloh and later battles.

POLK, THOMAS (*b. Cumberland Co., Pa., c. 1732; d. Charlotte, N.C., 1794*), Revolutionary soldier, North Carolina colonial legislator. Father of William Polk; great-uncle of James K. Polk.

POLK, TRUSTEN (*b. Sussex Co., Del., 1811; d. St. Louis, Mo., 1876*), lawyer, Confederate soldier. Governor, anti-Benton Democrat, of Missouri, 1856–57; U.S. senator, 1857–61. Responsible for education and taxation reform in Missouri; prominent spokesman for Southern cause, 1861.

POLK, WILLIAM (*b. near Charlotte, N.C., 1758; d. Raleigh, N.C., 1834*), Revolutionary soldier, North Carolina businessman and legislator. Son of Thomas Polk. Unsuccessful Federalist gubernatorial candidate in several elections; later supported Andrew Jackson.

POLK, WILLIAM MECKLENBURG (*b. Ashwood, Tenn., 1844; d. Atlantic City, N.J., 1918*), Confederate soldier, gynecologist. Son of Leonidas Polk. Graduated N.Y. College of Physicians and Surgeons, 1869. Dean, Cornell Medical School, 1898–1918.

POLK, WILLIS JEFFERSON (*b. near Frankfort, Ky., 1867; d. San Mateo, Calif., 1924*), architect. Studied with various architects including Stanford White; entered Chicago office of Daniel H. Burnham and assisted in plan to adorn San Francisco, 1903. Practiced independently in San Francisco, *post* 1904; was chairman of architectural commission, Panama-Pacific Exposition, 1915. His buildings in San Francisco after the earthquake and fire of 1906 were mainly in a monumental, conservative style. Later buildings showed fresh handling of new materials and recognition of changes demanded by new functions; *e.g.*, the Hallidie Building, and the Central Pumping Station of Spring Valley Water Co. Restorer of the Mission Dolores, he is considered one of the creators of the "California style" of domestic architecture.

POLLAK, GUSTAV (*b. Vienna, Austria, 1849; d. Cambridge, Mass., 1919*), editor, critic. Came to America, 1866. Son-in-law of Michael Heilprin. Wrote on foreign politics and literary criticism for New York *Nation* and *Evening Post;* worked on encyclopedias.

POLLAK, WALTER HEILPRIN (*b. Summit, N.J., 1887; d. New York, N.Y., 1940*), lawyer. Son of Gustav Pollak; grandson of Michael Heilprin. Practicing in New York City, Pollak was active in the protection of the public interests and in defense of civil liberties, serving as counsel for Earl Browder, Benjamin Gitlow and other individuals and groups of whose opinions he personally disapproved.   [*Supp. 2*]

POLLARD, EDWARD ALFRED (*b. Albemarle Co., Va., 1831; d. Lynchburg, Va., 1872*), journalist, author. Edited *Daily Richmond Examiner*, 1861–67; was ablest and most prolific Southern writer of the period; bitterly opposed Jefferson Davis. Author of *The Lost Cause* (1866) and numerous other biased historical accounts of the Civil War.

POLLARD, JOSEPH PERCIVAL (*b. Greifswald, Pomerania, Germany, 1869; d. Baltimore, Md., 1911*), literary and dramatic critic. Reviewer for *Town Topics*, 1897–1911.

POLLOCK, JAMES (*b. Milton, Pa., 1810; d. Lock Haven, Pa., 1890*), lawyer. Congressman, Whig, from Pennsylvania, 1844–49. As Whig and Know-Nothing governor, 1855–58, he materially reduced state debt by selling state-owned canals and railroads to Pennsylvania Railroad and other systems. Served as director of U.S. Mint at Philadelphia, 1861–66 and 1869–73; thereafter was its superintendent.

POLLOCK, OLIVER (*b. near Coleraine, Ireland,* c. *1737; d. Pinckneyville, Miss., 1823*), trader, planter, financier. Emigrated to Pennsylvania c. 1760; removed to New Orleans, 1768. His generosity in feeding Alexander O'Reilly's army, 1769, gained him freedom of trade in Louisiana. He helped the American army get needed ammunition, 1776, through friendship with Unzaga, O'Reilly's successor as governor of Louisiana. By the close of 1777, Bernardo de Galvez, Unzaga's successor, had advanced to American frontier posts some $70,000 worth of ammunition and provisions, for which sum Pollock was personally responsible. George Rogers Clark's requests for aid were similarly financed by Pollock as U.S. commercial agent *post* 1778. His advances totaled $300,000. His credit exhausted, Pollock was imprisoned in 1783 but soon released. His claims against Virginia and the federal government were eventually paid.

POLOCK, MOSES (*b. Philadelphia, Pa., 1817; d. 1903*), publisher, rare-book dealer, bibliophile.

POMERENE, ATLEE (*b. Berlin, O., 1863; d. Cleveland, O., 1937*), lawyer, politician. Graduated Princeton, 1884. An active liberal Democrat and holder of local offices, Pomerene was elected lieutenant-governor of Ohio, 1910, but was chosen almost immediately by the legislature as U.S. senator and served until 1923. A moderate progressive, he opposed woman suffrage, and in the debates over the League of Nations was one of the small group of Democrats willing to accept the Lodge reservations. He was co-sponsor of the Bill-of-Lading Act, 1916, and the Webb-Pomerene Act, 1918. His best-known service was as special counsel with Owen J. Roberts to prosecute those involved in the naval oil reserve frauds of the Harding administration. Appointed chairman of the Reconstruction Finance Corporation, July 1932, he did not receive Senate confirmation in the post. He later became one of Franklin D. Roosevelt's severest critics. [*Supp. 2*]

POMEROY, JOHN NORTON (*b. Rochester, N.Y., 1828; d. California, 1885*), legal author and educator. Associated *post* 1878 with Hastings College of Law. Among eight major treatises which he wrote, his *Equity Jurisprudence* (1881–83) was outstanding.

POMEROY, MARCUS MILLS (*b. Elmira, N.Y., 1833; d. Brooklyn, N.Y., 1896*), printer, newspaper editor and publisher, politician. Known as "Brick" Pomeroy. Gained national fame as editor of the La Crosse (Wis.) *Democrat, post* 1860. He engaged in railroad promotion and was an active "Greenbacker."

POMEROY, SAMUEL CLARKE (*b. Southampton, Mass., 1816; d. Whitinsville, Mass., 1891*), business-

man, Kansas politician. As financial agent for New England Emigrant Aid Co., he went with the second group of settlers to Kansas in 1854; while chairman of public safety committee at Lawrence, 1856, he failed to prevent the town's ruin by "border ruffians." Delegate to the first Republican National Convention, he received eight votes for vice-president. When Kansas was admitted to the Union, Pomeroy was elected to the U.S. Senate; serving 1861–73, he joined Radicals in opposition to Lincoln and was responsible for the "Pomeroy Circular" in favor of candidacy of Salmon P. Chase, 1864. His re-election to the Senate, 1867, was investigated by a committee of the Kansas legislature which made charges of bribery against Pomeroy; the charges were repeated, 1873. Although cleared by a U.S. Senate committee, the incident ended his political career.

POMEROY, SETH (*b. Northampton, Mass., 1706; d. Peekskill, N.Y., 1777*), gunsmith, soldier. Fought in wars with French and Indians, 1745–59; distinguished at Lake George, September 1755. Raised and drilled troops in western Massachusetts, 1775–76; appointed first Continental brigadier-general, June 1775.

PONCE DE LEÓN, JUAN (*b. San Servos, Spain,* c. *1460; d. Cuba, 1521*), Spanish explorer, discoverer of Florida. Said to have shipped with Columbus on second (1493) voyage to Hispaniola, where he fought under Nicolas de Ovando in conquest of Higuey and was made governor of that province. Learning from an Indian of gold in unexplored Puerto Rico, he subjugated that island and was made its governor, 1509; he was replaced by Diego Columbus, son of Christopher, 1512. Although now a rich man, enticed by Indian tales of gold and of a spring whose waters made the aged young again, he set forth in search of the island called Bimini where all these were to be found. Sailing from Puerto Rico in March 1513, he made the coast of Florida in true latitude 27° 30′, explored the coast southward to the Tortugas, and made other explorations, returning to repacify Puerto Rico. On his second trip to Florida in 1521, he was wounded by an Indian arrow, which led to his death.

POND, ALLEN BARTLIT (*b. Ann Arbor, Mich., 1858; d. Chicago, Ill., 1929*), architect, humanitarian. Designer of Hull House group in Chicago; was long associated with its work.

POND, ENOCH (*b. Wrentham, Mass., 1791; d. Bangor, Maine, 1882*), Congregational clergyman, professor and official in Bangor Theological Seminary.

POND, FREDERICK EUGENE (*b. Packwaukee, Wis., 1856; d. Brooklyn, N.Y., 1925*), writer on field sports, better known by his pen name of "Will Wildwood."

POND, GEORGE EDWARD (*b. Boston, Mass., 1837; d. Como, N.J., 1899*), journalist. Editor-correspondent of *Army and Navy Journal,* 1864–68; at various times on staffs of *New York Times*, Philadelphia *Record*, and New York *Sun*.

POND, IRVING KANE (*b. Ann Arbor, Mich., 1857; d. Washington, D.C., 1939*), architect, structural engineer. Graduated University of Michigan, C.E., 1879. After working for several Chicago architectural firms, Pond established a partnership with his brother Allen B. Pond, 1886. Participating in Chicago's great architectural renaissance, the firm for nearly fifty years designed every kind of structure, most notably public and educational buildings. A conservative member of the Chicago group dominated by Louis Sullivan, Pond stressed structure and function but with strong emphasis on formal, plastic, and decorative elements. [*Supp. 2*]

POND, JAMES BURTON (*b. Cuba, N.Y., 1838; d. 1903*), lecture manager. Successful in managing celebrity tours. Among his clients were Henry Ward Beecher, Ann Eliza Young (19th wife of Brigham), Mark Twain, and Henry M. Stanley.

POND, PETER (*b. Milford, Conn., 1740; d. Boston, Mass., 1807*), soldier, fur-trader, explorer. Entered fur trade at Detroit, 1765; was one of first to explore the Athabaska. Made important maps (*c.* 1784) of his travels through the Northwest.

POND, SAMUEL WILLIAM (*b. New Preston, Conn., 1808; d. Shakopee, Minn., 1891*), Congregational missionary to the Dakota Indians. Composed a Dakota grammar and dictionary; published various works for and about the Indians.

PONTIAC (*d. 1769*), Ottawa chief, identified through Francis Parkman's *The History of the Conspiracy of Pontiac* (1851) with the French and Indian War in the Old Northwest. Accounts of his early life are largely legendary. Parkman claims that he was born on the Maumee River in 1720, and that he influenced the Chippewa as well as the Ottawa tribes. He may have been the "Sachem of the Outawawas" encountered in Robert Rogers's *Concise Account of North America* (1765); he may also have been present at the conference between the Detroit Indians and Sir William Johnson on Sept. 3, 1761. Pontiac's claim to fame lies in his activities during the siege of Detroit in 1763–64, although his importance at that time was much less than Parkman supposed. He attempted to surprise the garrison by treachery and during the long siege he was the greatest local menace. When other tribes made offers of peace, Pontiac's group seemed bent on breaking the truce; yet copies exist of a letter dated Oct. 30, 1763, from Pontiac to Henry Gladwin suing for peace. He was probably not responsible for starting the 1764 uprising which Parkman named "Pontiac's conspiracy"; he merely took up opposition at Detroit. The other tribes involved came to terms, but Pontiac and his band held out until a conference at Fort Ontario in July 1766. Having accepted peace with the English, he abode by it

thereafter. The accounts of his death in 1769 are contradictory. Instead of being a great organizer, Pontiac was more likely only a local villain. The reports of his resistance appealed to popular imagination, however, so that he gained, even during his own lifetime, a reputation more romantic than he deserved.

POOL, JOHN (*b. Pasquotank Co., N.C., 1826; d. Washington, D.C., 1884*), lawyer, North Carolina legislator and Unionist. U.S. senator, Republican, from North Carolina, 1868–73. Instrumental in introducing national anti-Ku Klux Klan legislation.

POOL, MARIA LOUISE (*b. Rockland, Mass., 1841; d. Rockland, 1898*), writer of sketches of New England life.

POOLE, FITCH (*b. South Danvers, now Peabody, Mass., 1803; d. 1873*), journalist, humorist. Librarian of Peabody Institute *post* 1856. Author of witty satires published in newspapers of Peabody and Salem, Mass., 1836–71.

POOLE, WILLIAM FREDERICK (*b. Salem, Mass., 1821; d. Evanston, Ill., 1894*), librarian, historian. Graduated Yale, 1849. Served as assistant to John Edmands; expanded an indexing project of Edmands to later-titled *Poole's Index to Periodical Literature*. Served as assistant in Boston Athenaeum, as librarian of Boston Mercantile Library Association, and then as librarian of the Athenaeum, 1856–69. Helped establish libraries at U.S. Naval Academy and at Cincinnati. Librarian of Chicago Public Library, 1874–87; organized and headed the Newberry Library, Chicago, 1887–94. An outstanding leader in the progress of librarians to professional rank, he made pioneer contributions to the theory of library administration which still form an important part of modern library doctrine.

POOR, CHARLES HENRY (*b. Cambridge, Mass., 1808; d. Washington, D.C., 1882*), naval officer.

POOR, DANIEL (*b. Danvers, Mass., 1789; d. Mampy, India, 1855*), Congregational missionary.

POOR, ENOCH (*b. Andover, Mass., 1736; d. Paramus, N.J., 1780*), Revolutionary soldier. Settled in Exeter, N.H., *c.* 1760. As colonel, 2nd New Hampshire, he served in the campaign of 1776 around Ticonderoga, also in battles of Trenton and Princeton. Promoted brigadier-general, 1777, he fought well at Saratoga and in Sullivan's expedition against the Six Nations.

POOR, HENRY VARNUM (*b. East Andover, Maine, 1812; d. Brookline, Mass., 1905*), railroad journalist, economist. Brother of John A. Poor. Author of many works on railways and economics, he was noted for compiling and publishing annual *Poor's Manual of Railroads* (first issued, 1868).

POOR, JOHN (*b. Plaistow, N.H., 1752; d. York Haven, Pa., 1829*), educator. Graduated Harvard, 1775. Headed Young Ladies' Academy, Philadelphia, Pa., 1787–1809, an important early venture in female education.

POOR, JOHN ALFRED (*b. East Andover, Maine, 1808; d. 1871*), lawyer, railroad official. Brother of Henry V. Poor. Projected railway lines connecting Portland, Maine, with Halifax, N.S., and Montreal; served as director, Atlantic and St. Lawrence Railroad Co. Published *American Railroad Journal* and was president of the York and Cumberland (later the Portland and Rochester) Railroad. He resigned these positions to devote himself to international railway expansion, securing the charter of the European and North American Railway Co. (completed in 1871), connecting Maine railroads with those of lower Canada. Poor was also author of *English Colonization in America: A Vindication of the Claims of Sir Ferdinando Gorges* (1862) and other works. He was a tireless promoter of Maine interests.

POORE, BENJAMIN PERLEY (*b. near Newburyport, Mass., 1820; d. 1887*), journalist, author. Noted as Washington, D.C., correspondent of *Boston Journal* and other papers *post* 1854; edited and published useful catalogues of U.S. public documents.

POPE, ALBERT AUGUSTUS (*b. Boston, Mass., 1843; d. Cohasset, Mass., 1909*), Union soldier, manufacturer. Pioneer maker of bicycles at Hartford, Conn., *post c.* 1878; developed "Columbia" and "Hartford" brands. He popularized the bicycle, financing legal test cases over their use, advocating better roads movement, and publishing *The Wheelman* and *Outing*. He began manufacturing electric phaetons and runabouts through the Columbia Electric Vehicle Co., 1896. Progressing to production of gasoline automobiles, he turned out the Pope-Toledo and the Pope-Hartford at Toledo, O., and Hartford, Conn., respectively; the Pope-Waverly electric was made at a plant in Indianapolis, Ind. Decline in the bicycle trade and a lull in the development of the automobile forced his company into receivership.

POPE, FRANKLIN LEONARD (*b. Great Barrington, Mass., 1840; d. Great Barrington, 1895*), electrician, inventor, author. Active in development of telegraphy *post* 1865; partner of Thomas A. Edison, 1869–70; made practical adaptation of the railway block signal invented by Thomas S. Hall.

POPE, JOHN (*b. Louisville, Ky., 1822; d. Sandusky, O., 1892*), soldier. Son of Nathaniel Pope. Graduated West Point, 1842; was assigned to topographical engineers. Served with Gen. Taylor in Mexican War; performed survey work in Southwest and West. Commanded Army of the Mississippi under Halleck and opened up the river almost to Memphis, March–April 1862. Because of this success and efficiency in moves against Corinth, Miss., he was appointed in June to command of the (Union) Army of Virginia, ordered to protect Washington. His inept handling of personalities subsequent to his assumption of larger re-

sponsibilities on the failure of the Union Peninsular Campaign in July, and his total failure at the second battle of Bull Run (Aug. 27–30, 1862), led to his removal and replacement by Gen. G. B. McClellan. Pope was no longer employed in field operations but distinguished himself as head of various military departments until his retirement, 1886.

POPE, JOHN RUSSELL (*b. New York, N.Y., 1874; d. New York, 1937*), architect. Graduated Columbia, School of Mines, 1894; attended the American School of Architecture (later the American Academy) in Rome, and the École des Beaux Arts in Paris. Practicing independently in New York *post* 1903, Pope set a new standard in domestic architecture, combining elegance, beauty, and livability with archeological correctness in a variety of styles. Pope believed above all else in the reposeful serenity of the monumental classic. His monumental buildings, of which he designed more than any other architect of his generation, included the National Archives, the National Gallery of Art, and the Jefferson Memorial, all in Washington, D.C. [*Supp. 2*]

POPE, NATHANIEL (*b. Louisville, Ky., 1784; d. St. Louis, Mo., 1850*), territorial secretary (1809–16) and delegate (1816–18) from Illinois. Cousin of Ninian Edwards; father of John Pope. Influential in establishing laws, northern boundary, and educational policy of Illinois. U.S. district judge *post* 1819.

POPHAM, GEORGE (*d. Maine, 1608*), Maine colonist. Sailed from Plymouth, England, in May 1607 to colonize for Sir Ferdinando Gorges in "Northern Virginia"; settled, August 18, on western side of mouth of Kennebec. The colony was abandoned soon after Popham's death in the following February.

PORCHER, FRANCIS PEYRE (*b. St. John's, S.C., 1825; d. Charleston, S.C., 1895*), physician, botanist. Practiced in Charleston. Author, among other works, of *The Resources of the Southern Fields and Forests* (1863).

PORMORT, PHILEMON (*b. Grimsby, England, c. 1595; d. Boston, Mass., c. 1656*), educator. Emigrated to New England, 1634; appointed master of first public school in Boston, 1635; an adherent of Anne Hutchinson.

PORTER, ALBERT GALLATIN (*b. Lawrenceburg, Ind., 1824; d. Indianapolis, Ind., 1897*), Indiana lawyer and congressman. Law partner of Benjamin Harrison. Republican governor of Indiana, 1881–85; U.S. minister to Italy, 1889–91.

PORTER, ALEXANDER (*b. Co. Donegal, Ireland, 1785; d. "Oak Lawn," St. Mary Parish, La., 1844*), Louisiana legislator, jurist, sugar planter. Came to America, 1801; settled in Louisiana, 1809. U.S. senator, Whig, 1833–37 and 1843.

PORTER, ANDREW (*b. Montgomery Co., Pa., 1743; d. Harrisburg, Pa., 1813*), teacher, Revolutionary artillery and ordnance officer, surveyor. Father of James M. and David R. Porter. Surveyor-general of Pennsylvania, 1809–13.

PORTER, ARTHUR KINGSLEY (*b. Stamford, Conn., 1883; d. Ireland, 1933*), archeologist. Graduated Yale, 1904. Taught history of art at Yale, 1915–19; professor of fine arts, Harvard, 1920–33. The leading American medieval archeologist of his day, Porter was author of *Medieval Architecture: Its Origins and Development* (1909), *Lombard Architecture* (1915), *Romanesque Sculpture of the Pilgrimage Roads* (1923), *Spanish Romanesque Sculpture* (1928) and other works equally distinguished for originality and brilliance in research. [*Supp. 1*]

PORTER, BENJAMIN CURTIS (*b. Melrose, Mass., 1845; d. New York, N.Y., 1908*), portrait and figure painter.

PORTER, DAVID (*b. Boston, Mass., 1780; d. near Constantinople, Turkey, 1843*), naval officer. Father of David D. Porter; foster-father of David G. Farragut. Son of a Revolutionary naval officer, he saw service in the naval war with France, 1798–99, and was made prisoner aboard the *Philadelphia* at Tripoli. Commanding the *Essex*, 1811–13, he took her on a remarkable cruise in the Pacific raiding British commerce. Captured by the British at Valparaiso, Chile, after a desperate defense, he was paroled and participated in the operations on the Potomac in September 1814. Appointed commissioner of Navy Board, 1815, he served until 1823. As commander of the West India Squadron, 1823–25, he suppressed piracy but was court-martialed because of retaliation against Puerto Rico where one of his officers had been mistreated. Resigning, he accepted command of the Mexican navy, 1826–29. He returned home, broken in health and fortune, and spent the remainder of his life in minor U.S. diplomatic posts.

PORTER, DAVID DIXON (*b. Chester, Pa., 1813; d. Washington, D.C., 1891*), naval officer. Son of David Porter; cousin of Fitz-John Porter. Served under father as midshipman in Mexican navy; appointed midshipman, U.S. Navy, 1829. Commanded merchant ships, 1849–55. Porter achieved great prominence during the Civil War. Promoted commander, 1861, he was responsible for the preliminary planning of the New Orleans expedition, 1862, and commanded the mortar flotilla which ably supported Farragut's fleet. Appointed to command of the Mississippi Squadron as rear-admiral, October 1862, he received Congressional commendation for his part in the surrender of Arkansas Post and Vicksburg; he received a similar compliment for his work in the reduction of Fort Fisher, 1864–65. He was superintendent of the U.S. Naval Academy, which he successfully reformed and expanded, 1865–69; he was named vice-admiral, 1866. Appointed "adviser" to secretary of the navy, 1869, in this capacity he virtually ran the

department through 1870. Succeeding Farragut as full admiral, August 1870, he was head of the Board of Inspection *post* 1877.

PORTER, DAVID RITTENHOUSE (*b. near Norristown, Pa., 1788; d. Harrisburg, Pa., 1867*), iron manufacturer. Son of Andrew Porter. After long service in the Pennsylvania legislature, he served as Democratic governor, 1839–45; he opposed debt repudiation and upheld the state's credit but was in conflict with his party's views on the protective tariff question.

PORTER, EBENEZER (*b. Cornwall, Conn., 1772; d. Andover, Mass., 1834*), Congregational clergyman. Graduated Dartmouth, 1792. A conservative in theology, he taught at Andover Theological Seminary *post* 1812 and was its president, 1827–34.

PORTER, FITZ-JOHN (*b. Portsmouth, N.H., 1822; d. Morristown, N.J., 1901*), soldier. Cousin of David D. Porter. Graduated West Point, 1845. Assigned to the artillery, he served with credit in the Mexican War; he was an instructor at West Point, 1849–55, and was assistant adjutant-general in the Mormon expedition, 1857–59. Becoming brigadier-general of volunteers, 1861, he rose to command of the V Corps during the Peninsular campaign, 1862. Blamed for the Union defeat in the second battle of Bull Run, August 1862, Porter was court-martialed and cashiered in January 1863. Claiming injustice, he continued to fight the case for many years and in 1886 was reappointed colonel of infantry and retired.

PORTER, GENE STRATTON (*b. Wabash Co., Ind., 1863; d. Los Angeles, Calif., 1924*), author. One of the most popular American novelists of the years 1903–24, Mrs. Porter produced, among other romances of idealism, sentimentality, nature lore and uplift, *Freckles* (1904), *A Girl of the Limberlost* (1909), *Laddie* (1913) and *The Keeper of the Bees* (1925). [*Supp. 1*]

PORTER, HOLBROOK FITZ-JOHN (*b. New York, N.Y., 1858; d. 1933*), engineer. Son of Fitz-John Porter. Graduated Lehigh, 1878. Highly reputed as a consulting engineer, Porter was interested as well in the social and humanitarian aspects of industry; while working with the Westinghouse Co., 1902–05, he installed the first shop committee with employee representation to function in the United States.

PORTER, HORACE (*b. Huntingdon, Pa., 1837; d. 1921*), Union brigadier-general, railroad executive, diplomat. Son of David R. Porter. Graduated West Point, 1860. Served in Civil War as artillery and ordnance officer; received Congressional Medal for gallantry at Chickamauga; was aide-de-camp to Gen. U. S. Grant, 1864–65, later serving as one of Grant's military secretaries until 1872. A noted orator and prominent in Republican politics, Porter was U.S.

ambassador to France, 1897–1905; he served as a U.S. delegate to the Hague Conference, 1907.

PORTER, JAMES DAVIS (*b. Paris, Tenn., 1828; d. Paris, 1912*), lawyer, Confederate soldier, Tennessee jurist. Democratic governor of Tennessee, 1875–79; later served as an assistant U.S. secretary of state, and as U.S. minister to Chile, 1893–94. A principal factor in the founding of the presently named George Peabody College for Teachers while governor, he served as president of the College, 1902–09.

PORTER, JAMES MADISON (*b. near Norristown, Pa., 1793; d. 1862*), Pennsylvania jurist and politician. Son of Andrew Porter; brother of David R. Porter. First president of the Lehigh Valley Railroad; principal founder of Lafayette College, 1826.

PORTER, JERMAIN GILDERSLEEVE (*b. Buffalo, N.Y., 1852; d. 1933*), astronomer. Director, Cincinnati Observatory, 1884–1930.

PORTER, JOHN ADDISON (*b. Catskill, N.Y., 1822; d. New Haven, Conn., 1866*), chemist. Graduated Yale, 1842; studied also in Germany. Taught chemistry at Yale *post* 1852; was first dean of Sheffield Scientific School.

PORTER, JOHN LUKE (*b. Portsmouth, Va., 1813; d. Portsmouth, 1893*), naval constructor. In Confederate service, 1861–65, Porter was associated with John M. Brooke in the design of the ironclad *Virginia* (*Merrimac*); he also designed a number of other ironclad steam sloops and rams but was handicapped by lack of iron and adequate engines.

PORTER, NOAH (*b. Farmington, Conn., 1811; d. 1892*), Congregational clergyman, educator. Graduated Yale, 1831. A noted conservative scholar. After holding several pastorates he was associated with Yale *post* 1846 and served as president of the college, 1871–86. He succeeded Chauncey A. Goodrich as editor of Webster's *American Dictionary*.

PORTER, PETER BUELL (*b. Salisbury, Conn., 1773; d. Niagara Falls, N.Y., 1844*), lawyer, New York politician and congressman. Rose to major-general of militia for effective service at Chippewa, Lundy's Lane and Fort Erie in War of 1812. U.S. secretary of war, 1828–29. Influential in development of locality of present Buffalo, N.Y.

PORTER, ROBERT PERCIVAL (*b. Norwich, England, 1852; d. 1917*), journalist, statistician. Administered the Eleventh Census, 1889–93; *post* 1904, was associated as an editor of special supplements and as a correspondent with the London *Times*.

PORTER, RUFUS (*b. Boxford, Mass., 1792; d. New Haven, Conn., 1884*), inventor. Founded the *Scientific American*, August 1845.

PORTER, SAMUEL (*b. Farmington, Conn., 1810; d. Farmington, 1901*), teacher of the deaf. Brother of Noah and Sarah Porter.

PORTER, SARAH (*b. Farmington, Conn., 1813; d. Farmington, 1900*), educator. Sister of Noah and Samuel Porter. Founded Miss Porter's School for Girls at Farmington, 1843.

PORTER, STEPHEN GEYER (*b. near Salem, O., 1869; d. 1930*), lawyer. Raised in Pennsylvania, he served as a Republican congressman from that state, 1911–30; he became chairman of the House committee on foreign affairs, 1919, and came to be one of the most influential figures in determination of American foreign policy.

PORTER, THOMAS CONRAD (*b. Alexandria, Pa., 1822; d. Easton, Pa., 1901*), German Reformed clergyman, botanist. Graduated Lafayette College, 1840; Princeton Theological Seminary, 1843. Taught science at Franklin and Marshall College and at Lafayette; did pioneer botanical work in the Rocky Mountains as aide to John M. Coulter and Joseph Leidy; wrote extensively on literature as well as the sciences.

PORTER, WILLIAM SYDNEY (*b. Greensboro, N.C., 1862; d. New York, N.Y., 1910*), short-story writer, better known by pseudonym "O. Henry." Left school at 15; worked in a drug store; removed to Texas, 1882, settling in Austin. After holding various jobs, he was teller in a bank, 1891–94. After failure of a humorous weekly, the *Rolling Stone,* which he edited, Porter removed to Houston, 1895, where he wrote a column for the *Daily Post.* Accused of embezzlement of funds from the Austin bank in which he had been teller, he fled to New Orleans and thence to Honduras; returning to Austin, 1897, he was sentenced in March 1898 to five years in the federal penitentiary in Columbus, O. Released July 1901 after reduction of his term for good behavior, Porter felt the disgrace intensely. Meanwhile, having written and published several stories while in prison under various pseudonyms, of which "O. Henry" eventually displaced all the others, he went to New York City, 1902. Nowhere else in his varied experience of life had Porter encountered such a range and diversity of humanity as New York offered him and he soon put this new material to work. Almost immediately successful as a writer for the magazines, he was essentially an observer and a teller of tales marked by compassion and irony. He employed a few formulas and introduced minor variations into them with great ingenuity, but his success owes less to his technique than to his view of life. His work was of uneven merit and was often trivial. Among the many collected volumes of his stories, *Cabbages and Kings* (1904), *The Four Million* (1906), *Heart of the West* (1907), *The Gentle Grafter* (1908) are outstanding.

PORTER, WILLIAM TROTTER (*b. Newbury, Vt., 1809; d. New York, N.Y., 1858*), journalist, promoter of sporting literature. Established *Spirit of the Times* (New York, December 1831); was helped by the young Horace Greeley. Published *American Turf*

Register, 1839–44. Losing ownership of *Spirit*, 1842, Porter continued in an editorial capacity until 1858. Sketches of Southern and Western life which had been contributed to the *Spirit* by various writers were gathered by Porter into *The Big Bear of Arkansas* (1845) and *A Quarter Race in Kentucky* (1847).

PORTIER, MICHAEL (*b. Montbrison, France, 1795; d. 1859*), Roman Catholic clergyman. Came to America as missionary, 1817; ordained at St. Louis, Mo., 1818. Consecrated vicar-apostolic of Florida and Alabama, 1826; bishop of Mobile, 1829–59.

PORTOLÁ, GASPAR de (*b. Balaguer, Spain, c. 1723; d. post 1784*), soldier, first governor of Upper California. His contribution to U.S. history consists in his march (1769–70) from Velicatá in Lower California to Monterey, Upper California, a distance of about 1000 miles of untrod country, and in his founding of the missions and presidios of San Diego and Monterey. With the Portolá expedition were Juan Crespi (who kept a diary of the enterprise) and Junípero Serra.

PORY, JOHN (*b. Thompston, Norfolk, England, 1572; d. Sutton St. Edmund, England, 1635*), geographer, traveler. Secretary to the Virginia Council at Jamestown, 1619–21, and speaker of the first Virginia assembly (July 30, 1619).

POSEY, ALEXANDER LAWRENCE (*b. Eufaula, Okla., 1873; d. in North Canadian River near Eufaula, 1908*), Creek Indian journalist, poet. Influential in Indian affairs and delegate to virtually every convention called in Indian Territory in his time. Editor of the *Indian Journal*.

POSEY, THOMAS (*b. Fairfax Co., Va., 1750; d. Shawneetown, Ill., 1818*), soldier. Fought in Dunmore's War, and as officer in 7th Virginia Regiment during Revolution; was brigadier-general, 1793, under Wayne. A Kentucky legislator *c.* 1805–10, he was U.S. senator from Louisiana, 1812–13, and governor of Indiana Territory 1813–16.

POST, CHARLES WILLIAM (*b. Springfield, Ill., 1854; d. Santa Barbara, Calif., 1914*), breakfast-food manufacturer, advertising expert. Producer of Postum. Waged fierce battles against trade unions.

POST, CHRISTIAN FREDERICK (*b. Conitz, East Prussia, c. 1710; d. Germantown, Pa., 1785*), Moravian lay missionary. Came to Bethlehem, Pa., 1742. Evangelized Indians in New York, Wyoming Valley, and Ohio country; won Ohio Valley tribes to alliance with British, 1758, which resulted in French loss of Fort Duquesne. Later worked among Indians of Nicaragua.

POST, GEORGE ADAMS (*b. Cuba, N.Y., 1854; d. Somerville, N.J., 1925*), lawyer, journalist, manufacturer of railroad supplies.

POST, GEORGE BROWNE (*b. New York, N.Y., 1837; d. Bernardsville, N.J., 1913*), Union soldier, architect. Graduated New York University, 1858; studied in office of Richard M. Hunt. Interested primarily in the engineering side of architecture, he was uncritically eclectic in design. His first important work was the Williamsburgh Savings Bank (New York, 1874); among other important New York buildings which he designed were the Western Union Building, Produce Exchange, Cotton Exchange, original Times Building, Pulitzer Building, St. Paul Building, and the earlier buildings of the College of the City of New York. He was responsible for many of the largest residences of his time, was particularly effective in his plan for the Wisconsin State Capitol (begun in 1904) and was a pioneer in modern hotel design.

POST, GEORGE EDWARD (*b. New York, N.Y., 1838; d. 1909*), physician, missionary to Syria. Professor of surgery, Syrian Protestant College (Beirut) *post* 1868; later became dean of the medical school.

POST, ISAAC (*b. Westbury, N.Y., 1798; d. Rochester, N.Y., 1872*), Abolitionist, spiritualist. Converted to spiritualism by Margaret Fox, 1848.

POST, LOUIS FREELAND (*b. near Danville, N.J., 1849; d. 1928*), lawyer, reformer, journalist. A leading protagonist of Henry George's "Single Tax" philosophy; editor of the *Public* (Chicago) *post* 1898; assistant U.S. secretary of labor, 1913–21.

POST, MELVILLE DAVISSON (*b. near Clarksburg, W. Va., 1871; d. Clarksburg, 1930*), short-story writer, novelist, lawyer. Author of superior detective stories (*The Strange Schemes of Randolph Mason*, 1896; *The Nameless Thing*, 1912; and others), characterized by skill in plotting.

POST, TRUMAN MARCELLUS (*b. Middlebury, Vt., 1810; d. St. Louis, Mo., 1886*), educator, Congregational clergyman, Missouri Unionist. Taught at Illinois College, 1833–47; thereafter pastor in St. Louis of one of the first Congregational churches west of the Mississippi.

POST, WILEY (*b. near Grand Plain, Texas, 1899; d. northern Alaska, 1935*), aviator. Winner of Bendix Trophy race, 1930. Made record-breaking circumnavigation of the world, June 23–July 1, 1931, with Harold Gatty as navigator; flying solo, broke his own record, 1933. Died with Will Rogers in a crash while flying to the Orient by way of Siberia. [*Supp. 1*]

POST, WRIGHT (*b. North Hempstead, N.Y., 1766; d. 1828*), New York surgeon. Studied under Richard Bayley and in England. As professor of surgery at Columbia, 1792–1813, collected specimens for anatomical museum; was professor at N.Y. College of Physicians and Surgeons *post* 1813 and its president, 1821–26. Did much to introduce Hunterian principles of surgical procedure in America.

POSTL, CARL. [See SEALSFIELD, CHARLES, 1793–1864.]

POSTON, CHARLES DEBRILL (*b. Hardin Co., Ky., 1825; d. Phoenix, Ariz., 1902*), lawyer, explorer, author. First delegate from Arizona Territory to Congress, 1864–65; advocated irrigation works.

POTAMIAN, BROTHER (*b. Co. Cavan, Ireland, 1847; d. 1917*), Christian Brother, scientist. Name in religion of Michael Francis O'Reilly. Came to New York City as a child; entered congregation of Brothers of the Christian Schools at Montreal, 1859. Graduated University of London, D.Sc., 1883. After distinguished career as teacher and scientist in England and Ireland, he taught at Manhattan College, New York City, 1896–1917; he was particularly learned in electricity and magnetism.

POTT, JOHN (*b. England, date unknown; d. probably Virginia, c. 1642*), physician. Came to Virginia, 1621. In course of a checkered career, was deputy governor of the colony, 1629–30.

POTTER, ALONZO (*b. Beekman, N.Y., 1800; d. San Francisco, Calif., 1865*), Episcopal clergyman. Brother of Horatio Potter. Graduated Union, 1818; taught mathematics and natural philosophy there. Ordained, 1824, he served as rector of St. Paul's Church, Boston, 1826–31, then as professor of philosophy at Union until 1845 when he was chosen bishop of Pennsylvania. Broad-minded and tolerant toward those of differing opinions, he upheld the doctrine of the Muhlenberg Memorial of 1853. He opposed slavery and wrote in confutation of the claim that it was justified by the Bible.

POTTER, EDWARD CLARK (*b. New London, Conn., 1857; d. New London, 1923*), sculptor. Studied with Daniel C. French and in Paris. Collaborated with French in work for Chicago World's Fair, 1893, and on numerous equestrian statues. Among his own best-known works are the celebrated New York Public Library lions and the Slocum statue at Gettysburg.

POTTER, ELIPHALET NOTT (*b. Schenectady, N.Y., 1836; d. Mexico City, 1901*), Episcopal clergyman, educator. Son of Alonzo Potter; grandson of Eliphalet Nott. Reorganized and expanded Union College as president, 1871–84; was president of Hobart College, 1884–97.

POTTER, ELISHA REYNOLDS (*b. South Kingston, R.I., 1811; d. 1882*), lawyer, Rhode Island legislator and congressman, writer. As state commissioner of public schools, 1849–54, he did much to promote efficient administration of education in Rhode Island. State supreme court justice, 1868–82.

POTTER, HENRY CODMAN (*b. Schenectady, N.Y., 1835; d. Cooperstown, N.Y., 1908*), Episcopal clergyman. Son of Alonzo Potter. Rector of St. John's, Troy, N.Y., 1859–66, and Grace Church, New York City, 1868–83, he made his parishes centers for Christian work of every sort. In 1883 he was elected assistant bishop of New York, succeeding his uncle Horatio Potter. By training an evangelical, he adopted a moderate Broad Church position. As bishop he dealt wisely with many party disputes within the church, in particular the cases of R. Heber Newton, J. O. S. Huntington, and Charles A. Briggs; he also expanded the religious work of the diocese and was a strong force for civic reform. The Cathedral of St. John the Divine was begun by him.

POTTER, HORATIO (*b. Beekman, N.Y., 1802; d. 1887*), Episcopal clergyman. Brother of Alonzo Potter. Elected bishop of New York, 1854, he healed the breach in the church caused by the suspension of Bishop Benjamin T. Onderdonk and brought the diocese to flourishing condition before his virtual retirement in 1883.

POTTER, JAMES (*b. Co. Tyrone, Ireland, 1729; d. Pennsylvania, 1789*), farmer, Revolutionary soldier, one of earliest settlers in Penn's Valley region of Pennsylvania (*c. 1774*).

POTTER, LOUIS McCLELLAN (*b. Troy, N.Y., 1873; d. Seattle, Wash., 1912*), sculptor. Studied in Paris. Interested in universal brotherhood of man, he did vividly realistic studies of primitive and exotic types, which were of ethnological rather than aesthetic interest.

POTTER, NATHANIEL (*b. Easton, Md., 1770; d. Baltimore, Md., 1843*), physician, surgeon. M.D., University of Pennsylvania, 1796. Practiced in Baltimore; taught at Maryland Medical College *post* 1807. Rendered great service as epidemiologist, particularly of yellow fever; established non-contagiousness of that disease, 1797–98.

POTTER, PAUL MEREDITH (*b. Brighton, England, 1853; d. 1921*), journalist, dramatist. Came to America *ante* 1876. Facile and competent adapter for the stage of successful novels such as Du Maurier's *Trilby* (1895).

POTTER, PLATT (*b. Galway, N.Y., 1800; d. Schenectady, N.Y., 1891*), jurist. Justice of N.Y. supreme court, 1857–73.

POTTER, ROBERT (*b. Granville Co., N.C., c. 1800; d. Texas, 1842*), lawyer, North Carolina legislator and Democratic congressman, Texas pioneer.

POTTER, ROBERT BROWN (*b. Schenectady, N.Y., 1829; d. 1887*), lawyer, Union major-general. Son of Alonzo Potter; grandson of Eliphalet Nott. Displayed extraordinary skill and gallantry, notably at South Mountain and Antietam (1862), as colonel of the 51st New York. He won equal distinction as a division commander at Knoxville (1863) and at Petersburg, Va. (1864).

POTTER, WILLIAM BANCROFT (*b. near North-field, Conn., 1863; d. 1934*), electrical engineer. Entered employ of Thomson-Houston Co., 1887, as machinist on electrical equipment; gained extensive experience in installation of electric traction and lighting systems; invented series-parallel controller for electric railway motors, 1892. Worked thereafter at General Electric Co. supervising operations of the railway department; held more than 130 patents.

[*Supp.* 1]

POTTER, WILLIAM JAMES (*b. North Dartmouth, Mass., 1829; d. Boston, Mass., 1893*), clergyman, editor. Left Unitarian fold, 1867, to join in founding the Free Religious Association; was pastor in New Bedford, Mass., 1859–93.

POTTS, BENJAMIN FRANKLIN (*b. Carroll Co., O., 1836; d. 1887*), Union brigadier-general, lawyer. Territorial governor of Montana, Republican, 1870–83.

POTTS, CHARLES SOWER (*b. Philadelphia, Pa., 1864; d. 1930*), physician, neurologist, teacher.

POTTS, JONATHAN (*b. Colebrookdale, Pa., 1745; d. Reading, Pa., 1781*), physician, Revolutionary patriot. M.D., College of Philadelphia (University of Pennsylvania), 1768. Served as medical officer at Lake George, 1776; appointed deputy director-general of the hospitals of the Northern Department, 1777; directed Middle Department hospitals as deputy, 1778–80.

POTTS, RICHARD (*b. Upper Marlborough, Md., 1753; d. Frederick, Md., 1808*), legislator, jurist. U.S. senator, Federalist, from Maryland, 1793–96.

POU, EDWARD WILLIAM (*b. Tuskegee, Ala., 1863; d. Washington, D.C., 1934*), lawyer, North Carolina official. Congressman, Democrat, from North Carolina, 1901–34. As chairman of the House rules committee, 1917–21 and 1933–34, he played a leading part in furthering the legislative programs of Presidents Wilson and F. D. Roosevelt. [*Supp.* 1]

POULSON, NIELS (*b. Horsens, Denmark, 1843; d. Brooklyn, N.Y., 1911*), architect, philanthropist, designer and manufacturer of ornamental metalwork. Came to America, 1864. Left fortune to American-Scandinavian Foundation.

POULSON, ZACHARIAH (*b. Philadelphia, Pa., 1761; d. Philadelphia, 1844*), printer, publisher, philanthropist. Edited the *American Daily Advertiser,* 1800–39.

POUND, CUTHBERT WINFRED (*b. Lockport, N.Y., 1864; d. Ithaca, N.Y., 1935*), jurist. Professor of law, Cornell University, 1895–1904. Judge, N.Y. supreme court for 8th judicial district, 1906–15; associate judge, N.Y. court of appeals, 1915–34; (chief justice *post* 1932). A legal liberal and vigorous defender of civil liberties, Pound wrote the first American judicial opinion upholding validity of a workman's

compensation act (*Ives vs. South Buffalo Railway Co.*) and was author of a number of other opinions evidencing a broad tolerance of legislative discretion in cases involving constitutionality of statutes.

[*Supp.* 1]

POUND, THOMAS (*b. probably England, c. 1650; d. Isleworth, England, 1703*), pirate, cartographer, captain in Royal Navy. Made first (*c.* 1691) map of Boston harbor to be engraved and offered for sale.

POURTALÈS, LOUIS FRANÇOIS DE (*b. Neuchâtel, Switzerland, 1823; d. Beverly Farms, Mass., 1880*), marine zoologist. Associated with U.S. Coast Survey, 1848–73; pupil of J. L. R. Agassiz whom he assisted in Switzerland *ante* 1846, and at Harvard *post* 1870. He specialized in collecting and studying animal life at great depths.

POWDERLY, TERENCE VINCENT (*b. Carbondale, Pa., 1849; d. Washington, D.C., 1924*), labor leader, government official. Machinist by trade, he joined the Machinists' and Blacksmiths' Union, 1871, and the Knights of Labor, 1874. Rising in the Knights through various official posts, he headed the organization, 1879–93, during the period of its rise and fall as a powerful labor group, showing himself an idealist and reformer, but not an aggressive leader. To him the Knights of Labor was a great educational organization, destined to reform the world by encouraging the working people to demand government ownership of public utilities, regulation of trusts and monopolies, reform of the currency and of the land system, and such measures as the abolition of child labor. Personally sober, he denounced drink as one of the great evils under which workingmen suffered. He opposed the trade form of organization because he believed skilled workers should assist the unskilled. He laid little stress on immediate demands, such as higher wages and shorter hours, and opposed strikes as an outmoded industrial weapon which should be superseded by arbitration. His ultimate ideal was the abolition of the wage system, not through revolution but through producers' cooperatives in which every man would be his own employer.

Before his retirement from the Knights of Labor he had begun to study law, and on Sept. 24, 1894, he was admitted to the bar in Lackawanna Co., Pa. In 1897 he was admitted to practice before the supreme court of Pennsylvania and in 1901 before the Supreme Court of the United States. He served as U.S. commissioner-general of immigration, 1897–1902, and as chief of the Division of Information of the Bureau of Immigration, 1907–21.

POWEL, JOHN HARE (*b. Philadelphia, Pa., 1786; d. Newport, R.I., 1856*), War of 1812 soldier, agriculturist, author. Brother of Robert Hare. Introduced improved breeds of Durham Short Horn cattle and Southdown sheep to America.

POWELL. [See OSCEOLA, c. 1800–1838.]

POWELL, ALMA WEBSTER (b. Elgin, Ill., 1874; d. Mahwah, N.J., 1930), soprano opera-singer, singing teacher.

POWELL, EDWARD PAYSON (b. Clinton, N.Y., 1833; d. Sorrento, Fla., 1915), teacher, Congregational and Unitarian clergyman. Influenced by Darwinism; friend and associate of Jenkin L. Jones. Author of Our Heredity from God (1887).

POWELL, GEORGE HAROLD (b. Ghent, N.Y., 1872; d. Pasadena, Calif., 1922), horticulturist. Authority on preservation and transportation of perishable fruits; held important positions in U.S. Department of Agriculture (1901–11) and with the California Fruit Growers' Exchange.

POWELL, JOHN WESLEY (b. Mount Morris, N.Y., 1834; d. Haven, Maine, 1902), Union soldier, geologist, teacher. Under auspices of the Smithsonian Institution and with aid of appropriations from Congress, Powell first explored the gorges of the Green and Colorado Rivers by boat, 1869, traversing the Grand Canyon; he continued his explorations of the Rocky Mountain region in 1871, 1874–75. Appointed director of the U.S. Geological Survey, 1880, after serving as director of its Rocky Mountain division post 1875, he administered the Survey with marked success until 1894. He was also director of the Bureau of Ethnology (under the Smithsonian), 1879–1902. He was especially notable for the quality of the reports made by him and issued under his supervision (in particular his Explorations of the Colorado River of the West, 1875) and for his encouragement of his subordinates to attain distinction on their own. He retired from the Survey, partly for reasons of health, partly because of antagonism to his projects for forest preservation and irrigation.

POWELL, LAZARUS WHITEHEAD (b. Henderson Co., Ky., 1812; d. near Henderson, Ky., 1867), lawyer, planter. Democratic governor of Kentucky, 1851–55. As U.S. senator, 1859–65, he fought for neutrality of his state and was an advocate of the Crittenden propositions; throughout the Civil War, he opposed military interference in civic affairs.

POWELL, LUCIEN WHITING (b. near Upperville, Va., 1846; d. Washington, D.C., 1930), landscape painter. Student of Thomas Moran; influenced strongly by the English artist J. M. W. Turner.

POWELL, MAUD (b. Peru, Ill., 1868; d. Uniontown, Pa., 1920), violinist. Niece of John W. Powell; daughter of William Bramwell Powell. Made studies in Chicago; also at the Paris Conservatory and in Leipzig. She then toured a year in England, playing before Queen Victoria. In 1885, after further study with Joseph Joachim, she made her début with the Berlin Philharmonic. Returning to New York, she appeared with the New York Philharmonic, 1885, and made annual concert tours, 1886–92. Organizing the Maud Powell Quartet, 1894, she appeared with it until 1898. Thereafter, she continued as a successful solo artist both here and in Europe, winning praise for her technical mastery and deep interpretive insight.

POWELL, SNELLING (b. Carmarthen, Wales, 1758; d. Boston, Mass., 1821), actor, manager. Came to America, 1793. Prominent on the Boston stage as an actor post 1794, he was very successful as manager of the Boston Theatre, 1806–21.

POWELL, THOMAS (b. England, 1809; d. Newark, N.J., 1887), poet, dramatist, journalist. Came to America, 1849, after establishing himself as an industrious literary workman in London; was associated thereafter with the Frank Leslie publications. Author of a number of books including the useful Living Authors of England (1849) and Living Authors of America (1850).

POWELL, WILLIAM BRAMWELL (b. Castile, N.Y., 1836; d. Mount Vernon, N.Y., 1904), educator. Brother of John W. Powell; father of Maud Powell. Superintendent of schools in Peru and Aurora, Ill.; supervisor of District of Columbia schools, 1885–1900. Advocated progressive methods.

POWELL, WILLIAM BYRD (b. Bourbon Co., Ky., 1799; d. Covington, Ky., 1866), eclectic physician. Investigated relations between temperament and cranial conformation, evolving theory that human temperament could be read from examination of the cranium alone.

POWELL, WILLIAM HENRY (b. New York, N.Y., 1823; d. New York, 1879), historical and portrait painter. Pupil of James H. Beard and Henry Inman. Commissioned, 1847, to paint "De Soto" panel for rotunda in U.S. Capitol; painted "Battle of Lake Erie" for Ohio state capitol (completed, 1863).

POWER, FREDERICK BELDING (b. Hudson, N.Y., 1853; d. Washington, D.C., 1927), pharmacist, chemist. Ph.D., Strassburg, 1880. Taught at Philadelphia College of Pharmacy and at University of Wisconsin; engaged in industrial research here and in England, 1892–1916; headed phytochemical laboratory, U.S. Department of Agriculture, 1916–27. Made major contributions to knowledge of plant constituents and distribution of organic compounds in plants; investigated chaulmoogra seeds and derivatives.

POWER, FREDERICK DUNGLISON (b. Yorktown, Va., 1851; d. Washington, D.C., 1911), Disciples of Christ clergyman. Pastor, post 1875, of Vermont Avenue Christian Church, Washington, D.C.

POWER, FREDERICK TYRONE (b. London, England, 1869; d. California, 1931), actor. Came to America as a boy; went on stage c. 1886; was member of Augustin Daly's company. Later supporting

Henry Irving, Mrs. Fiske, and others, he was famous in England and America for playing heroic and poetic roles in romantic drama.

POWER, JOHN (*b. Roscarberry, Ireland, 1792; d. 1849*), Roman Catholic clergyman. Came to America, 1819; served thereafter as pastor of St. Peter's Church, New York City and was active in the social and political advancement of the Irish-Americans.

POWER, TYRONE. [See POWER, FREDERICK TYRONE, 1869–1931.]

POWERS, DANIEL WILLIAM (*b. near Batavia, N.Y., 1818; d. Rochester, N.Y., 1897*), banker. Promoted civic and commercial interests of Rochester.

POWERS, HIRAM (*b. near Woodstock, Vt., 1805; d. Florence, Italy, 1873*), sculptor. Began career in Cincinnati, O., c. 1829, making wax figures of celebrities and mechanized monsters for a local "Chamber of Horrors"; worked briefly with Kirke Brown and Shobal Vail Clevenger. Removing to Washington, D.C., 1834, he made busts from life of such prominent figures as John Marshall, Andrew Jackson, John C. Calhoun, Daniel Webster and others. Three benefactors—Nicholas Longworth, W. C. Preston and John S. Preston—lent him the means of removing with his family to Florence, Italy, 1837, where he remained for the rest of his life. He was early befriended there by the sculptor Horatio Greenough. Soon after his arrival in Italy, he set up in clay a life-size figure called "Eve before the Fall," later carved in marble. This was a precursor of his "Greek Slave," a nude female figure, finished in marble in 1843, and thereafter reproduced in at least six marble copies. It was without doubt the most celebrated single statue of its day, owing in part to the emotional appeal of the current Greek struggle for independence. Among others, Elizabeth Barrett Browning, Edward Everett and Nathaniel Hawthorne wrote about it, and it received acclaim on exhibition at the Crystal Palace, London, 1851. In 1853 there was a movement to commission Powers to decorate the Capitol at Washington, but he declined to submit designs in competition with other artists. He made about 150 portrait busts, nearly all of men, which are now considered his strongest work. At the height of his successful career he built himself a fine house in Florence and there entertained many famous personages from America. The "Greek Slave" has historical importance as the first sculpture by an American to attract general public notice.

POWHATAN (*d. 1618*), Indian chief. His personal name was Wa-hun-sen-a-cawh or Wa-hun-son-a-cock, and he was chief or "emperor" of the Powhatan federation which at the beginning of the 17th century extended over tidewater Virginia. His father was of a Southern tribe, said to have been driven north by the Spaniards; upon his arrival in Virginia, he had conquered five of the local tribes. His son and successor, known to the Jamestown settlers as Powhatan, extended his sway over many more. He ruled with an iron hand, being excessively cruel to prisoners and malefactors. Despite frequent protestations of good will, he annoyed the English settlers by ambushing small parties, murdering workers in the field, and refusing to sell them corn when their provisions fell low, but with the marriage of his daughter Pocahontas to John Rolfe, he concluded a peace to which he steadily adhered thereafter. Powhatan died in April 1618, and was succeeded by his brother Itopatin, or Opitchapam.

POWNALL, THOMAS (*b. Lincolnshire, England, 1722; d. Bath, England, 1805*), colonial governor. Pownall deserves more than any other Englishman of his time to be called a student of colonial administration. He came to America in 1753 as secretary to Sir Danvers Osborn, governor of New York, who committed suicide two days after arrival. Pownall, however, remained in America as a free-lance observer for Lord Halifax and the Board of Trade until 1756, making the acquaintance (among other notables) of William Shirley and Benjamin Franklin. Appointed lieutenant-governor of New Jersey in May 1755 to assist the aged Jonathan Belcher, he continued his close study of colonial trade and defense problems. Returning to England early in 1756, he presented a scheme for the unification of the military command of the colonies and stressed the importance of control of inland waterways. Offered the governorship of Pennsylvania, he declined it in order to accompany to America the new commander-in-chief, Lord Loudoun. He went back to England in October 1756 to present Loudoun's case against William Shirley, governor of Massachusetts. The favorable impression which he made on the newly formed Pitt ministry caused him to be offered the governorship of Massachusetts which he accepted. He reached Boston on Aug. 3, 1757, and took up his work with vigor, using conciliation in order to get maximum cooperation in the war against the French and Indians. He defended the constitutional authority of the civil government against the war-powers claimed by the military and was almost too able and too independent. The Board of Trade recalled him in November 1759, offering him several lucrative positions which he declined. Pownall's chief claim to remembrance is his book *The Administration of the Colonies* (1764), in which he discusses the reorganization in administration, in law, and in the status of the colonies necessary to maintain the union with England. His policies were far ahead of the views of his contemporaries. Pownall never returned to America but was in essential sympathy with the colonists until their final measures of resistance. As member of Parliament, he introduced in 1780 a bill favoring a conclusion of the war by royal negotiation which was defeated.

POYDRAS, JULIEN DE LALANDE (*b. Rezé, near Nantes, France, 1746; d. Pointe Coupée Parish, La., 1824*), poet, public servant, planter, merchant, philanthropist. Came to New Orleans, 1768.

POZNANSKI, GUSTAVUS (*b. Storchnest, Poland, 1804; d. New York, N.Y., 1879*), Jewish religious leader and reformer. Came to America, 1831. Rabbi, Congregation Beth Elohim, Charleston, S.C., 1836–47. Instituted radical alterations in creed and ritual.

PRALL, DAVID WIGHT (*b. Saginaw, Mich., 1886; d. Berkeley, Calif., 1940*), philosopher. Graduated University of Michigan, 1909; Ph.D., University of California, 1918. After teaching at Amherst and Harvard, he was on the faculty of the University of California, 1921–30. Again at Harvard *post* 1930, he became professor, 1938. A notable teacher, he was author of *A Study in the Theory of Value* (1921), *Æsthetic Judgment* (1929) and *Æsthetic Analysis* (1936). [*Supp. 2*]

PRANG, LOUIS (*b. Breslau, Prussian Silesia, 1824; d. California, 1909*), Boston lithographer. Emigrated to America, 1850. Publisher of prints and school drawing-books, he popularized "chromos," color reproductions of masterpieces of art.

PRANG, MARY AMELIA DANA HICKS (*b. Syracuse, N.Y., 1836; d. Melrose, Mass., 1927*), art teacher, author. Edited art manuals for the firm of Louis Prang, whom she later married.

PRATT, BELA LYON (*b. Norwich, Conn., 1867; d. Boston, Mass., 1917*), sculptor. Studied at Yale School of Fine Arts and N.Y. Art Students League; served as assistant to Augustus Saint-Gaudens. Taught *post* 1893 at Boston Museum School. Excelled in decorative groups, portrait bas-reliefs, busts of noted men, ideal nudes of women and children, and youthful soldierly figures.

PRATT, CHARLES (*b. Watertown, Mass., 1830; d. Brooklyn, N.Y., 1891*), oil merchant, philanthropist. Foreseeing growth of petroleum industry on discovery of oil in Pennsylvania, he established with Henry H. Rogers a refinery at Greenpoint, N.Y., 1867, and marketed "Pratt's Astral Oil," a high quality illuminant, which became world famous. Merging with Standard Oil, 1874, Pratt assumed a leading position in that firm and grew very wealthy. His philanthropies included a model tenement for workingmen and substantial gifts to Amherst College, University of Rochester, and Adelphi Academy, Brooklyn. He also founded Pratt Institute in Brooklyn (1887) and the Pratt Institute Free Library.

PRATT, DANIEL (*b. Temple, N.H., 1799; d. 1873*), carpenter, cotton mill operator, industrialist. Removed to Georgia, 1819; to Alabama, 1833. Founded Prattville, Ala., 1838, where he engaged in cotton and wool milling. Financed Henry F. De Bardeleben in development of Birmingham (Ala.) industries.

PRATT, DANIEL (*b. Chelsea, Mass., 1809; d. Boston, Mass., 1887*), vagrant. Under delusion that he had been elected president of the United States, he used to visit New England college campuses to "lecture" *post c.* 1837.

PRATT, ELIZA ANNA FARMAN (*b. Augusta, N.Y., 1837; d. Warner, N.H., 1907*), writer of juvenile stories. Edited *Wide Awake,* 1875–93.

PRATT, ENOCH (*b. North Middleborough, Mass., 1808; d. 1896*), iron merchant, capitalist, philanthropist. Removed to Baltimore, Md., 1831; established firm of E. Pratt and Brothers in iron trade; later branched out into transportation, banking and fire insurance. The most important of his philanthropies was the Enoch Pratt Free Library in Baltimore (opened 1886) which was first to embody idea of "branch" libraries. He was also greatly interested in the improvement of the condition of the Negro and gave much to hospitals and educational institutions.

PRATT, FRANCIS ASHBURY (*b. Woodstock, Vt., 1827; d. 1902*), pioneer toolmaker, inventor. Began career as a machinist, eventually working at the Colt armory, Hartford, Conn., 1852–54. Here he met his future partner, Amos Whitney. Pratt and Whitney began doing machine work on their own, 1860; in 1864 both gave up positions with the Phoenix Iron Works to give full time to their own firm. Pratt was a promoter of the use of interchangeable parts, inaugurating that system in his own factory while making firearms during the Civil War. The establishment of a standard system of gages for Europe and America was owing largely to Pratt's efforts.

PRATT, JOHN (*b. Unionville, S.C., 1831; d. c. 1900*), journalist. Patented the "ptereotype," 1866–68, forerunner of the Hammond typewriter.

PRATT, MATTHEW (*b. Philadelphia, Pa., 1734; d. 1805*), portrait painter. A friend and pupil of Benjamin West, Pratt painted many of the leading Americans of his time in a superior style; his color was refined and delicate, and he ranks with the best of his contemporaries as a technician.

PRATT, ORSON (*b. Hartford, N.Y., 1811; d. Salt Lake City, Utah, 1881*), Mormon leader. Brother of Parley P. Pratt. Converted by his brother, Orson rose rapidly in the Mormon hierarchy and was ordained one of the apostles of that Church, 1835. He supported the Brigham Young faction on the death of Joseph Smith and was in the first company to enter the Salt Lake Valley, 1847. After a long career in missionary and administrative work both in the United States and in Europe, he was appointed historian of the Church, 1874. He was also active in Utah politics and served seven terms as speaker of the lower house of the territorial legislature. His philosophical vagaries occasionally irritated the more practical Brigham Young, but Pratt profoundly influenced Mormon theology. [*Supp. 1*]

PRATT, PARLEY PARKER (*b. Burlington, N.Y., 1807; d. 1857*), Apostle of the Latter-day Saints. Brother of Orson Pratt. Joined Mormons, 1830; ordained Apostle, 1835. Author of an *Autobiography* (1874) detailing his life and travels. Killed by the husband of a convert.

PRATT, RICHARD HENRY (*b. Rushford, N.Y., 1840; d. San Francisco, Calif., 1924*), soldier, Indian educator. Raised in Indiana. After Union army service in Civil War and regular army service in Indian campaigns, 1867–75, he had remarkable success as a teacher of Indian prisoners at Fort Marion, Fla., 1875–78. Continuing his work on a larger scale at Hampton Institute, 1878–79, he then founded the famous Indian school at Carlisle, Pa. and served as its superintendent until 1904. He was promoted to brigadier-general shortly before his retirement.

PRATT, SERENO STANSBURY (*b. Westmoreland, N.Y., 1858; d. Troy, N.Y., 1915*), journalist, specialist in finance and commerce. Editor-in-chief, *Wall Street Journal*, 1905–08; author of *The Work of Wall Street* (1903); secretary, N.Y. state Chamber of Commerce, 1908–15.

PRATT, SILAS GAMALIEL (*b. Addison, Vt., 1846; d. Pittsburgh, Pa., 1916*), pianist, composer.

PRATT, THOMAS GEORGE (*b. Georgetown, D.C., 1804; d. 1869*), lawyer, Maryland legislator. Restored state credit as Whig governor of Maryland, 1844–47; was U.S. senator, 1850–57. During Civil War period, he became a Democrat and was a strong Confederate sympathizer.

PRATT, THOMAS WILLIS (*b. Boston, Mass., 1812; d. Boston, 1875*), civil engineer, railroad construction and operation expert. Invented and patented the type of bridge and roof truss bearing his name (1844); also patented improvements to steam boilers, ship hull construction and the propulsion of ships.

PRATT, WALDO SELDEN (*b. Philadelphia, Pa., 1857; d. Hartford, Conn., 1939*), musicologist.

[*Supp. 2*]

PRATT, ZADOCK (*b. Stephentown, N.Y., 1790; d. Bergen, N.J., 1871*), tanner, New York Democratic legislator and congressman.

PRATTE, BERNARD (*b. Ste. Genevieve, Mo., 1771; d. 1836*), merchant, fur-trader. Leading citizen of St. Louis, Mo., *post c. 1795*.

PRAY, ISAAC CLARK (*b. Boston, Mass., 1813; d. 1869*), journalist, dramatist, actor. Graduated Amherst, 1833. Author, among other works, of *Prose and Verse from the Portfolio of an Editor* (1836) and *Memoirs of James Gordon Bennett* (1855).

PREBER, CHRISTIAN. [See PRIBER, CHRISTIAN, fl. 1734–1744.]

PREBLE, EDWARD (*b. Falmouth, now Portland, Maine, 1761; d. Portland, 1807*), naval officer. Shipped aboard a privateer, 1777; appointed midshipman, Massachusetts navy, 1779. *Post* 1783, served aboard merchant ships. Appointed lieutenant in the reorganized U.S. Navy, 1798, he was commissioned captain, 1799, and commanded the *Essex* on convoy duty. In the war with Tripoli, Preble sailed aboard the *Constitution* in command of the squadron which blockaded that state, 1803–04. In the face of numerous difficulties, Preble made an unsuccessful attempt to capture Tripoli in August–September 1804, and was soon after superseded as commodore by Samuel Barron. Preble was particularly effective as a trainer of the young officers who served under him, many of whom later distinguished themselves during the War of 1812.

PREBLE, GEORGE HENRY (*b. Portland, Maine, 1816; d. 1885*), naval officer, author. Nephew of Edward Preble. Appointed midshipman, 1835, he served in a variety of capacities until the Civil War when he was given command of the *Katahdin*. He fought under Farragut at New Orleans, and was actively engaged in operations up to Vicksburg. As commander of the sloop *Oneida*, he was severely censured for allowing the Confederate cruiser *Florida* (*Oreto*) to break through the blockade of Mobile, September 1862. Reinstated, he served thereafter with distinction and retired as rear-admiral, 1878.

PREBLE, WILLIAM PITT (*b. York, Maine, 1783; d. 1857*), jurist, railroad executive. Active in achieving separation of Maine from Massachusetts. Aided Albert Gallatin in preparation of Northeastern boundary case, 1828, and continued to act in this matter up to the Webster-Ashburton Treaty signing, 1842. He was associated with John A. Poor in the building of the Atlantic and St. Lawrence Railroad.

PREETORIUS, EMIL (*b. Alzey, Rhenish Hesse, Germany, 1827; d. 1905*), journalist. Settled in St. Louis, Mo., 1853. Early active in the Republican party, he was a friend and partner of Carl Schurz in the *Westliche Post*, editing it *post* 1864.

PRENDERGAST, MAURICE BRAZIL (*b. Roxbury, Mass., 1861; d. New York, N.Y., 1924*), painter. Studied in Boston, and in Paris, France, 1887–89. Beginning as a painter of gay and sparkling studies of street life and holiday scenes, he changed his style radically *post* 1914 in the direction of a more abstract and purely decorative art which won enthusiastic approval from contemporary critics.

PRENTICE, GEORGE DENNISON (*b. New London Co., Conn., 1802; d. 1870*), journalist. Removed to Kentucky, 1830, as editor of the *Louisville Daily Journal*. Within a short time he made his paper the most influential Whig organ in the South and West. A Unionist, he was largely responsible for Kentucky's refusal to secede. A collection of his witty editorials appeared as *Prenticeana* (1860).

PRENTICE, SAMUEL OSCAR (*b. North Stonington, Conn., 1850; d. 1924*), jurist. Graduated Yale, 1873; Yale School of Law, 1875. Connecticut superior court judge, 1889–1901; justice, supreme court of errors, 1901–20 (chief justice, 1913–20). Taught at Yale School of Law, 1896–1915.

PRENTISS, BENJAMIN MAYBERRY (*b. Belleville, Va., 1819; d. Bethany, Mo., 1901*), Union soldier, lawyer. Distinguished at Shiloh; promoted major-general, 1862. Commanded at battle of Helena, Ark., July 1863, winning victory over superior force.

PRENTISS, ELIZABETH PAYSON (*b. Portland, Maine, 1818; d. Dorset, Vt., 1878*), writer of religious and juvenile fiction. Among her many books the most popular were *Stepping Heavenward* (1869) and the "Little Susy" books (1853 and *post*).

PRENTISS, GEORGE LEWIS (*b. West Gorham, Maine, 1816; d. 1903*), Congregational and Presbyterian clergyman, educator. Brother of Seargent S. Prentiss. Graduated Bowdoin, 1835. After holding a number of pastorates, he organized the New School Church of the Covenant, New York City, 1862, and served there until 1873. Taught a variety of subjects at Union Theological Seminary *post* 1871.

PRENTISS, SAMUEL (*b. Stonington, Conn., 1782; d. Montpelier, Vt., 1857*), Vermont jurist. U.S. senator, Federalist-Whig from Vermont, 1831–42; thereafter, U.S. judge, Vermont district.

PRENTISS, SEARGENT SMITH (*b. Portland, Maine, 1808; d. Natchez, Miss., 1850*), lawyer, orator, Whig congressman from Mississippi. Brother of George L. Prentiss. Removed to Mississippi *c.* 1828; practiced at Natchez and Vicksburg, and *post* 1845 at New Orleans, La.

PRESBREY, EUGENE WILEY (*b. Williamsburg, Mass., 1853; d. California, 1931*), stage manager, dramatist. Successful as an adapter of popular novels into plays.

PRESCOTT, ALBERT BENJAMIN (*b. Hastings, N.Y., 1832; d. Ann Arbor, Mich., 1905*), chemist. M.D., University of Michigan, 1864. Taught at Michigan *post* 1865; took a major part in establishment of the university's school of pharmacy, serving as its dean, 1874–1905. Did notable work in sanitary and food chemistry, also in toxicology; was author of influential treatises and papers.

PRESCOTT, GEORGE BARTLETT (*b. Kingston, N.H., 1830; d. New York, N.Y., 1894*), telegraph engineer. Chief electrician of Western Union, 1866–82; author of a number of works on the telegraph, the telephone, and other electrical subjects.

PRESCOTT, OLIVER (*b. Groton, Mass., 1731; d. Groton, 1804*), physician, Revolutionary soldier.

Brother of William Prescott. Held a number of Massachusetts military and civic appointments.

PRESCOTT, SAMUEL (*b. Concord, Mass., 1751; d. Halifax, N.S., c. 1777*), physician, Revolutionary patriot. Successfully completed the "midnight ride" of April 18, 1775, after capture of Paul Revere; gave alarm at Concord. Died in prison after capture aboard a privateer.

PRESCOTT, WILLIAM (*b. Groton, Mass., 1726; d. Pepperell, Mass., 1795*), farmer, Revolutionary soldier. Brother of Oliver Prescott. Colonel of minutemen, 1775; arrived too late for fight at Concord; appointed to council of war at siege of Boston. Ordered to fortify Bunker Hill, June 16, 1775, he decided after consultation with his officers to fortify Breed's Hill, since it commanded Boston more effectively. It is not known for certain whether he or Israel Putnam was in general command on the field of battle, June 17, but Prescott did command at a vital point in the line. He later took part in the evacuation of New York and the Saratoga campaign, but age and an injury forced him to retire from active service.

PRESCOTT, WILLIAM HICKLING (*b. Salem, Mass., 1796; d. Boston, Mass., 1859*), historian. Grandson of William Prescott; born to wealth and social position. Graduated Harvard, 1814. While in his junior year at college, a blow on his left eye permanently destroyed its sight; two years later an inflammation of the right eye impaired his vision so that at periods he was practically blind. Deciding to follow a literary career despite these difficulties, he toured Europe, 1815–17; on his return to Boston he began an intensive study of the history and literature of the principal countries of western Europe with the aid of paid secretaries who read to him. He contributed reviews and articles to the *North American Review*, 1821–36, the best of which were collected as *Biographical and Critical Miscellanies* in 1845. At work since 1826 on the first of his masterpieces, he published *The History of the Reign of Ferdinand and Isabella the Catholic* late in 1837 (title-page date, 1838). The book was an immediate success, and Prescott was hailed on both sides of the Atlantic. The year after the publication of *Ferdinand and Isabella* was one of physical pain and enforced idleness, but he devoted much thought to the next of his endeavors —the history of the conquests of Mexico and Peru. He began research for the *History of the Conquest of Mexico* in April 1839; so well had he learned to handle his materials that he was able to publish the three volumes in 1843. The *History of the Conquest of Peru* was written at an even more rapid rate; two years apparently sufficed for actual composition, though the work was not published until March 1847. Despite the appearance of much new material, these books remain standard authorities on the two greatest achievements of the Spanish *conquistadores* in the

New World. Prescott's fame was now so great that on a trip to England in 1850 he was entertained and honored as no other private American citizen. He had contemplated a history of the reign of Philip the Second as early as 1838; to this task he devoted the rest of his life. Only three of the projected ten volumes appeared, two in 1855 and the last in 1858. He also prepared a new edition of William Robertson's *History of the Reign of the Emperor Charles the Fifth* (1857).

Prescott's outstanding merit, in addition to courage, was the scrupulous care and integrity with which he used his materials, and it is a tribute to his skill as an historian that what was intended for the casual reader is now the material of the professional historical student. He was also a master of narrative. Although his inherited prejudices did not color his interpretation of facts to the extent displayed by J. L. Motley, they were dominant enough to deprive him of whole-hearted sympathy with the 16th century. As a man, he possessed great gayety and charm; his generosity was proverbial.

PRESSER, THEODORE (*b. Pittsburgh, Pa., 1848; d. Philadelphia, Pa., 1925*), music teacher and publisher, philanthropist, editor. Founded *Étude* magazine, 1883.

PRESTON, ANN (*b. Westgrove, Pa., 1813; d. 1872*), physician. One of first (1852) graduates from Female Medical College of Pennsylvania, at which she became a professor. Helped found Woman's Hospital of Philadelphia.

PRESTON, HARRIET WATERS (*b. Danvers, Mass., 1836; d. Cambridge, Mass., 1911*), author. Noted for translations of Provençal and Roman classical poets.

PRESTON, JOHN SMITH (*b. near Abingdon, Va., 1809; d. Columbia, S.C., 1881*), lawyer, planter, orator. Brother of William C. Preston. Supported state rights as South Carolina legislator; was effective superintendent, Confederate Bureau of Conscription, 1863–65.

PRESTON, JONAS (*b. Chester, Pa., 1764; d. Philadelphia, Pa., 1836*), physician, Pennsylvania legislator, philanthropist.

PRESTON, MARGARET JUNKIN (*b. Milton, Pa., 1820; d. Baltimore, Md., 1897*), poet. Daughter of George Junkin; sister-in-law of Thomas J. Jackson.

PRESTON, THOMAS SCOTT (*b. Hartford, Conn., 1824; d. 1891*), Roman Catholic clergyman, devotional and controversial writer. A convert from the Episcopal ministry, 1849, Monsignor Preston served in New York as chancellor of the diocese *post* 1855 and as vicar-general, 1873–91. He was an uncompromising conservative.

PRESTON, WILLIAM (*b. near Louisville, Ky., 1816; d. 1887*), lawyer, soldier, Kentucky Whig legislator and congressman. A Democrat *post* 1854, he was U.S. minister to Spain, 1858–60; he returned to

serve as Confederate brigadier-general and minister to Mexico.

PRESTON, WILLIAM BALLARD (*b. Montgomery Co., Va., 1805; d. 1862*), lawyer, Virginia Whig legislator and congressman, U.S. secretary of the navy, 1849–50. Nephew of John Floyd. Opposed Virginia secession but presented secession ordinance; served as Confederate senator from Virginia, 1861–62.

PRESTON, WILLIAM CAMPBELL (*b. Philadelphia, Pa., 1794; d. Columbia, S.C., 1860*), lawyer, South Carolina legislator. Brother of John S. Preston; friend of Hugh S. Legaré and of Washington Irving. An intense advocate of state rights and of slavery, Preston was elected to the U.S. Senate, 1833, as a Democrat from South Carolina. Opposing Jackson, he became a Whig and resigned from the Senate, 1842, rather than accept dictation from the legislature. He was president of South Carolina College, 1846–51.

PREUS, CHRISTIAN KEYSER (*b. Spring Prairie, Wis., 1852; d. 1921*), Lutheran clergyman. Taught at Luther College, Decorah, Iowa, *post* 1898; was president of the college *post* 1902.

PREVOST, FRANÇOIS MARIE (*b. Pont-de-Cé, France, c. 1764; d. Donaldsonville, La., 1842*), surgeon. Graduated in medicine at Paris; settled in Donaldsonville *c.* 1800. Distinguished as one of the earliest successful performers of the Caesarean section in the United States.

PRIBER, CHRISTIAN (*b. possibly Saxony, date unknown; d. Frederica, Ga., post 1744*), utopian community builder. Emigrated to South Carolina, *c.* 1734; two years later, went to live among the Cherokees. Labored to draw all Southern Indians into a great independent confederation which would be administered along communist lines, somewhat anticipating the doctrine of Saint-Simon.

PRICE, BRUCE (*b. Cumberland, Md., 1845; d. Paris, France, 1903*), architect. Began career in Baltimore, Md., 1869; removed to New York City, 1877. Price laid out Tuxedo Park, N.Y. (1885–86) and designed many of the individual houses there; his largest and most lavish domestic work was "Georgian Court" (1898–1900) at Lakewood, N.J. He also did a great deal of work in Canada including the Château Frontenac at Quebec.

PRICE, ELI KIRK (*b. East Bradford, Pa., 1797; d. 1884*), Philadelphia lawyer, law reformer. Was responsible as Pennsylvania legislator for passage of "Consolidation Act," 1854, giving Philadelphia a new charter and unifying that city.

PRICE, ELI KIRK (*b. Philadelphia, Pa., 1860; d. 1933*), lawyer, Philadelphia civic leader. Grandson of Eli K. Price (1797–1884). Devoted himself to the growth and development of Fairmount Park and to the construction of the Philadelphia Museum of Art.
[*Supp. 1*]

PRICE, HIRAM (*b. Washington Co., Pa., 1814; d. 1901*), banker, railroad builder. Removed to Davenport, Iowa, 1844. Congressman, Republican, from Iowa, 1863–69, 1877–81; U.S. commissioner of Indian affairs, 1881–85.

PRICE, JOSEPH (*b. Rockingham Co., Va., 1853; d. Philadelphia, Pa., 1911*), physician, surgeon, gynecologist. M.D., University of Pennsylvania, 1877. After working as a ship's doctor, he began work at the Philadelphia Dispensary and made its clinic for women one of the best known and largest in the country. Working thereafter in three private hospitals in Philadelphia (among them the present Joseph Price Memorial), Price had vast influence as clinical teacher in the forming of gynecology and abdominal surgery as specialties. He revolutionized surgical practices in maternity and abdominal operations.

PRICE, RODMAN McCAMLEY (*b. Sussex Co., N.J., 1816; d. 1894*), naval officer, politician. Played active role in U.S. occupation of California, 1846; as alcalde of Monterey, was said to be first American to exercise judicial authority in California. Congressman, Democrat, from New Jersey, 1851–53; governor, 1854–57.

PRICE, STEPHEN (*b. New York, N.Y., 1782; d. 1840*), theatrical manager. Purchased share in Park Theatre, New York City, 1808; became sole manager and lessee *c.* 1815. Price began the practice of importing European "stars" for performances at his theatre and for road tours under his direction.

PRICE, STERLING (*b. Prince Edward Co., Va., 1809; d. Missouri, 1867*), lawyer, farmer, Missouri legislator, soldier. Removed to Missouri *c.* 1831; settled in Chariton Co. After rising to rank of brigadier-general in the Mexican War, he was anti-Benton Democratic governor of Missouri, 1852–56. Chosen president of the Missouri convention of 1860 as a conditional Union man, he took command of the state troops by appointment of Gov. C. F. Jackson after the convention adjourned. The aggressive policies of Unionists such as Frank P. Blair and Nathaniel Lyon drove him into support of the Southerners. Displaying high military ability at the battles of Wilson's Creek and Lexington, 1861, he retreated with his forces into Arkansas where they joined the Confederate Army, 1862. His subsequent campaigns in Mississippi and Arkansas gave him great reputation and made him perhaps the leading secession figure west of the Mississippi. After a short stay in Mexico *post* 1865, he returned to Missouri to die.

PRICE, THEODORE HAZELTINE (*b. New York, N.Y., 1861; d. New York, 1935*), cotton merchant and broker. Founded and edited *Commerce and Finance*, 1912–35; compiled trade handbooks.

[*Supp. 1*]

PRICE, THOMAS FREDERICK (*b. Wilmington, N.C., 1860; d. Hong Kong, China, 1919*), Roman Catholic clergyman, co-founder of Maryknoll. Graduated St. Charles College (Md.), 1881; St. Mary's Seminary, Baltimore, Md. Ordained, 1886, the first native North Carolinian to become a Catholic priest, he worked in his own state and was editor of an apologetics magazine, *Truth*, 1896–1911. Together with Rev. James A. Walsh, Price established the Catholic Foreign Mission Society of America (Maryknoll), 1910–11.

PRICE, THOMAS LAWSON (*b. near Danville, Va., 1809; d. 1870*), businessman, railroad builder, politician. Removed to Missouri and settled in Jefferson City, 1831; was a leader in development of Missouri railroads. A pro-Benton Democrat and state office holder, he became an unconditional Unionist and a War Democrat congressman, serving ably as an opponent of Radical measures through the year 1862. He was later prominent in the reorganization of the Democratic party in Missouri.

PRICE, THOMAS RANDOLPH (*b. Richmond, Va., 1839; d. 1903*), philologist, Confederate soldier. Taught Greek and English at University of Virginia, 1870–82; professor of English, Columbia University, 1882–1903.

PRICE, WILLIAM CECIL (*b. probably Russell Co., Va., 1818; d. Chicago, Ill., 1907*), lawyer. Removed as a young man to Missouri where he held various offices and served as a Democratic legislator. For twenty years before the Civil War, he agitated for repeal of the Missouri Compromise and the removal of restrictions upon slavery. A fanatical secessionist, he served briefly in the Confederate army.

PRICE, WILLIAM THOMPSON (*b. Jefferson Co., Ky., 1846; d. 1920*), dramatic critic. Founded American School of Playwriting, New York, 1901; was regarded within the profession as an authority on dramatic construction.

PRIEST, EDWARD DWIGHT (*b. Northfield, Mass., 1861; d. 1931*), electrical engineer. Graduated present Worcester Polytechnic, 1884. Specialist in railway electrification problems; designed special type of motor for use on elevated railroads.

PRIESTLEY, JAMES (*b. probably Virginia, date unknown; d. Nashville, Tenn., 1821*), educator. Studied at Liberty Hall Academy (forerunner of Washington and Lee); was principal or director of a great number of academies and colleges *post* 1788, including Cumberland College at Nashville.

PRIESTLEY, JOSEPH (*b. near Leeds, England, 1733; d. Northumberland, Pa., 1804*), scientist, educator, Unitarian theologian. Attended a local grammar school where he learned Latin, Greek, and shorthand; studied Hebrew with John Kirkby, a Congregational clergyman. When ill health forced him to leave school, he taught himself modern languages, the rudiments of Chaldee, Syriac, Arabic, and also natural history. Entered Daventry, a dissenting academy, 1751, where his tendencies to Arianism took firm root. Unsuccessful as a pastor, 1755–61, he went as tutor in belles-lettres to Warrington, the chief dissenting academy in England, where he found learned associates and adequate channels of expression for his many interests. He preached, wrote, and published (among others) *A Chart of Biography* (1765) for which he received a doctorate from Edinburgh. He was the first teacher to give formal instruction in modern history, and his teaching of the sciences was entirely new in secondary education. In 1767, because of his wife's poor health and his need for a larger salary, he took charge of the Mill Hill congregation in Leeds which he held until 1772 when he became librarian to Lord Shelburne. In 1780 he removed to Birmingham and was minister of the New Meeting there until the 1791 riots when his expressed sympathies with the French Revolution resulted in the burning of his house, his books and all his effects. Deciding to emigrate to America, he arrived in New York City, June 4, 1794. His arrival caused much public comment and he was visited by the leading New York dignitaries; two weeks later in Philadelphia he again received public acclaim. Averse to the distractions of Philadelphia, he made his home in Northumberland, Pa., but made frequent trips to Philadelphia to address the American Philosophical Society and continued to write and perform scientific experiments.

Although his scientific interests had been manifested early, he had not begun active experimentation until 1766. In February 1767, he published *The History and Present State of Electricity*, to which he appended an account of experiments performed between June 1766 and the beginning of 1767. In this work he stated but did not fully prove the inverse-square law of electrostatics, explained the formation of the ("Priestley") rings occurring as a result of electrical discharges on metallic surfaces, attempted to measure electrical resistance and impedance, and proposed an explanation of the oscillatory nature of the discharge from a Leyden jar. More important perhaps is his isolation of oxygen (before November 1771) and description of its basic properties (1774). His discovery was confirmed by Lavoisier, 1775. He also isolated and described eight other gases, including ammonia and carbon monoxide, and wrote a notable study upon optics: *The History and Present State of Discoveries Relating to Vision, Light and Colours* (1772).

Priestley's versatility and his peculiar qualities of mind were more clearly manifested in his theological and political writings than in his science. He left Daventry Academy an Arian; by the time he went to Warrington he had rejected the Atonement and the inspiration of the sacred text. In 1775 he put forward the doctrine of the homogeneity of man, which brought upon him the charge of atheism. His

principal theological works were written in America, and he was the chief protagonist of the Unitarian movement here. His books in this field include *A General History of the Christian Church* (1790–1802) and *A General View of the Arguments for the Unity of God, etc.* (1793, 1812). In politics he was a utilitarian and a republican, but he prided himself on never having joined a political party. His *Essay on the First Principles of Government* (1768) strongly influenced Jeremy Bentham. In two anonymous pamphlets (1769 and 1774) he rebuked the British government for their treatment of the colonies. Prior to 1783 he was intimate with Edmund Burke, but Priestley's republican leanings estranged them, and their differences were brought to a dramatic climax by the French Revolution. Priestley's *Letters to the Right Honourable Edmund Burke* (1791) led more or less directly to the riots which destroyed his house in Birmingham. He was also opposed to slavery. In American politics he sided with the (Democrat) Republicans against the Federalists. By 1797 or earlier he had become acquainted with Thomas Jefferson, who turned to him for counsel about the projected University of Virginia and wrote of his "affectionate respect" for Priestley.

PRIME, BENJAMIN YOUNGS (*b. Huntington, N.Y., 1733 o.s.; d. Huntington, 1791*), physician. Graduated College of New Jersey, 1751; M.D., University of Leyden, 1764; studied also in England and Scotland. Practiced *post* 1764 in New York City and in Huntington. Author of *The Patriot Muse* (London, 1764) and a number of writings in support of the American cause subsequent to the passage of the Stamp Act. His *Columbia's Glory or British Pride Humbled* (1791) reviewed the events of the Revolutionary War.

PRIME, EDWARD DORR GRIFFIN (*b. Cambridge, N.Y., 1814; d. New York, N.Y., 1891*), Presbyterian clergyman. Grandson of Benjamin Y. Prime; brother of William C. and Samuel I. Prime.

PRIME, SAMUEL IRENAEUS (*b. Ballston, N.Y., 1812; d. 1885*), Presbyterian clergyman, author. Grandson of Benjamin Y. Prime; brother of Edward D. G. and William C. Prime. Assistant editor, *New York Observer*, 1840–49; editor-in-chief, 1851–85. During his editorship the *Observer* was a leading Presbyterian organ and a strong force in American life. He was author also of a number of popular books and was the conductor *post* 1853 of the "Editor's Drawer" in *Harper's Magazine*.

PRIME, WILLIAM COWPER (*b. Cambridge, N.Y., 1825; d. New York, N.Y., 1905*), journalist, educator. Grandson of Benjamin Y. Prime; brother of Edward D. G. and Samuel I. Prime. Graduated College of New Jersey (Princeton), 1843. After practicing law in New York City, 1846–61, Prime served as editor of the *N.Y. Journal of Commerce*, 1861–69, and remained a partner in the paper thereafter. An authority on numismatics and old porcelain, he was a principal promoter of the Metropolitan Museum of Art and was professor of the history of art at Princeton *post* 1884. He was author also of a number of books including *Owl Creek Letters* (1848), *The Old House by the River* (1853), *Boat Life in Egypt and Nubia* (1857) and *Pottery and Porcelain* (1878).

PRINCE, LeBARON BRADFORD (*b. Flushing, N.Y., 1840; d. Flushing, 1922*), lawyer, jurist. Son of William R. Prince. Prominent as a New York Republican politician, Prince served as chief justice of the territory of New Mexico, 1879–82; he compiled and published *The General Laws of New Mexico* (1880). As governor of New Mexico, 1889–93, he was responsible for the adoption of the territory's first public school code and for the creation of the University of New Mexico.

PRINCE, MORTON (*b. Boston, Mass., 1854; d. 1929*), physician, psychologist. Graduated Harvard, 1875; Harvard Medical School, 1879. Becoming early interested in abnormal psychology, he made further studies at Vienna, Strassburg, Paris and Nancy, and was encouraged by S. Weir Mitchell to specialize in neurology and psychotherapy. From 1885–1913, he was physician for diseases of the nervous system at Boston City Hospital and taught at Harvard and at Tufts. He founded the *Journal of Abnormal Psychology*, 1906, and edited it up to the time of his death. Among his books the most famous is *The Dissociation of a Personality* (1906). He developed a psychology of the abnormal which integrates neurology, general psychology and allied subjects effectively and with great benefit to them all. In addition to his professional work, he was active in civic projects in Boston.

PRINCE, THOMAS (*b. Sandwich, Mass., 1687; d. Boston, Mass., 1758*), theologian, scholar, bibliophile. Graduated Harvard, 1709. Became associate minister at Old South Church, Boston, 1718, and served in this connection until his death. An early collector and preserver of colonial documentary material, in particular the Mather papers, he was author, among many other writings, of *A Chronological History of New England in the Form of Annals* (1736), a pioneer attempt at accurate recording of the New England past. A supporter of George Whitefield, Prince was a vital factor in sustaining the evangelist's popularity. He collected a remarkable library of Americana which was left to Old South; some of the books were destroyed during the British occupation at Boston, but many of them are now preserved in Boston Public Library.

PRINCE, WILLIAM (*b. probably Flushing, N.Y., c. 1725; d. Flushing, 1802*), nurseryman. American pioneer in selling budded or grafted stock and in breeding new varieties, particularly of the plum.

PRINCE, WILLIAM (*b. Flushing, N.Y., 1766; d. 1842*), nurseryman. Son of William Prince (*c. 1725–1802*). Continued his father's work and introduced the Isabella grape *c.* 1816, once important in New York wine culture.

PRINCE, WILLIAM ROBERT (*b. Flushing, N.Y., 1795; d. Flushing, 1869*), nurseryman. Son of William Prince (1766–1842). Associated with his father in business and co-author with him of *A Treatise on the Vine* (1830) and *The Pomological Manual* (1831). He was author also of *Prince's Manual of Roses* (1846) and of many articles for gardening and horticultural publications.

PRING, MARTIN (*b. Devonshire, England, c. 1580; d. Bristol, England, 1626*), naval commander, explorer. Made a successful trading voyage in command of the *Speedwell* and the *Discoverer* to the Cape Cod area, 1603; made a chart of the coast of Virginia, 1606. Active in Far Eastern waters, 1613–21, he was made a freeman of the Virginia Company and given 200 acres of Virginia land, 1621.

PRINGLE, CYRUS GUERNSEY (*b. East Charlotte, Vt., 1838; d. 1911*), plant breeder and collector. Made important botanical explorations *post* 1880 in the Pacific states and Mexico. Built up herbarium at the University of Vermont.

PRINGLE, JOEL ROBERTS POINSETT (*b. Georgetown Co., S.C., 1873; d. San Diego, Calif., 1932*), naval officer. Graduated Annapolis, 1892. Performed distinguished service as chief of staff to Adm. Sims, 1917–19, and as liaison with the British command at Queenstown, Ireland, having charge of destroyer refitting. After holding a number of other important appointments, he died while serving as commander, battleships, U.S. Fleet, with the rank of vice-admiral.

PRINGLE, JOHN JULIUS (*b. Charleston, S.C., 1753; d. 1843*), lawyer, planter, South Carolina legislator and federal official. Attorney-general of South Carolina, 1792–1808.

PRINTZ, JOHAN BJÖRNSSON (*b. Bottnaryd, Sweden, 1592; d. 1663*), soldier, colonial governor. After an adventurous career as a mercenary soldier and officer in the Swedish army, he was appointed governor of New Sweden, 1642, and arrived at Fort Christina (Wilmington, Del.), Feb. 15, 1643. He was handicapped from the outset by a shortage of men and supplies, and during the last five years of his administration (1648–53) the Swedish government left him to shift for himself. Reputed to weigh 400 pounds and famous for severity and profanity, he was amply qualified for his work, making the colony a prosperous enterprise for his country. His harshness as a ruler, however, created conflicts between him and his settlers which came to a head in July 1653, when a group of them petitioned to send two men to present their grievances to the home government. Printz regarded this move as rebellion and hanged the leader of the dissidents. Resigning the governorship to his son-in-law in September, he returned to Sweden.

PRITCHARD, FREDERICK JOHN (*b. Camanche, Iowa, 1874; d. Washington, D.C., 1931*), plantbreeder. Graduated University of Nebraska, 1904. Did important work on the sugar beet and on disease-resistant tomatoes for the U.S. Department of Agriculture *post* 1910.

PRITCHARD, JETER CONNELLY (*b. Jonesboro, Tenn., 1857; d. 1921*), lawyer, legislator. U.S. senator, Republican, from Tennessee, 1894–1903. An able progressive, he became a U.S. circuit judge, 1904, and presiding judge of the circuit court of appeals (4th circuit), 1913.

PRITCHETT, HENRY SMITH (*b. Fayette, Mo., 1857; d. Santa Barbara, Calif., 1939*), astronomer. Studied at the U.S. Naval Observatory under Asaph Hall; Ph.D., University of Munich, 1895. President, Massachusetts Institute of Technology, 1900–05; first president, Carnegie Foundation for Advancement of Teaching, 1905–30. [*Supp. 2*]

PROCTER, JOHN ROBERT (*b. Mason Co., Ky., 1844; d. Washington, D.C., 1903*), geologist, civil-service reformer. Director of the Kentucky geological survey, 1879–93; U.S. Civil Service Commission member and president, 1893–1903.

PROCTER, WILLIAM (*b. Baltimore, Md., 1817; d. 1874*), pharmacist, teacher. Conducted a drug store in Philadelphia, Pa., *post* 1844. Professor in Philadelphia College of Pharmacy, 1846–66; editor, *American Journal of Pharmacy*, 1850–71; a founder of the American Pharmaceutical Association, 1852.

PROCTER, WILLIAM COOPER (*b. Glendale, O., 1862; d. Cincinnati, O., 1934*), soap manufacturer, philanthropist. President of Procter & Gamble *post* 1907. Instituted employee profit-sharing plans, stock ownership and pensions; guaranteed employees 48 work weeks in each calendar year, 1923. [*Supp. 1*]

PROCTOR, FREDERICK FRANCIS (*b. Dexter, Maine, c. 1851; d. Larchmont, N.Y., 1929*), vaudeville theatre owner and manager.

PROCTOR, HENRY HUGH (*b. near Fayetteville, Tenn., 1868; d. 1933*), Congregational clergyman, Negro leader. Graduated Fisk University, 1891; Yale Divinity School, 1894. Became prominent as pastor of First Congregational Church, Atlanta, Ga., 1894–1919; it became the first institutional church for Negroes in the South and through its various agencies served some 10,000 persons. He was pastor of the Nazarene Congregational Church, Brooklyn, N.Y., *post* 1920. A pioneer in all interracial movements, he was elected moderator of the New York City Congregational Church Association, 1926.

PROCTOR, JOSEPH (*b. Marlboro, Mass., 1816; d. 1897*), actor, manager. Made professional debut at Boston, 1833; enjoyed early success playing principal character in *Nick of the Woods* (an adaptation of the novel by Robert M. Bird). Playing in support of many "star" actors in classic dramas, he was distinctly a "strong" actor of the Edwin Forrest school.

PROCTOR, LUCIEN BROCK (*b. Hanover, N.H., 1823; d. Albany, N.Y., 1900*), lawyer, writer of New York legal history and biography.

PROCTOR, REDFIELD (*b. Proctorsville, Vt., 1831; d. Washington, D.C., 1908*), businessman, lawyer, Union soldier. Republican governor of Vermont, 1878–80; able and efficient U.S. secretary of war, 1889–91; U.S. senator from Vermont, 1891–1908. Proctor was particularly interested as a senator in the committees on agriculture and military affairs. His speech on Cuba, delivered in March 1898, helped condition the United States for the war with Spain.

PROKOSCH, EDUARD (*b. Eger, Austria-Hungary, 1876; d. near New Haven, Conn., 1938*), Germanic philologist. Came to America, 1898. M.A., University of Chicago, 1901; Ph.D., University of Leipzig, 1905. Taught at University of Wisconsin, 1905–13; University of Texas, 1913–19; Bryn Mawr, 1920–27; New York University, 1927–28; and *post* 1929 at Yale.

[*Supp. 2*]

PROPHET. [See TENSKWATAWA, 1768–1837.]

PROSSER, CHARLES SMITH (*b. Columbus, N.Y., 1860; d. Columbus, O., 1916*), educator, geologist. After serving in a number of government and teaching positions, he was head of the department of historical geology at Ohio State, 1901–16. His published work dealt mainly with the stratigraphy and paleontology of the Paleozoic formations of New York, Kansas, Maryland and Ohio.

PROUD, ROBERT (*b. Yorkshire, England, 1728; d. Philadelphia, Pa., 1813*), educator, historian. Emigrated to Philadelphia, 1759; was master of the Friends Public School for many years. Author of *The History of Pennsylvania in North America* (1797–98), a valuable work based on original research.

PROUTY, CHARLES AZRO (*b. Newport, Vt., 1853; d. Newport, 1921*), lawyer. Member of Interstate Commerce Commission, 1896–1914; supported Theodore Roosevelt's railroad policy. *Post* 1914, he served as director of the Commission's Bureau of Valuation, organizing it and shaping its policies and philosophy of value.

PROVOOST, SAMUEL (*b. New York, N.Y., 1742 o.s.; d. 1815*), Episcopal clergyman. Graduated King's College (Columbia), 1758; studied at Peterhouse, Cambridge; ordained in London, 1766. Returning to New York as assistant minister of Trinity Church, his Whig sympathies caused conflict with Loyalist members of the parish and he resigned, 1771. In 1784, he was chosen rector of St. Paul's, New York City, and served in the following year as chaplain of Congress. He was consecrated first bishop of New York, February 1787, by the Archbishop of Canterbury in the chapel of Lambeth Palace (London) and officiated until 1801 when private reasons caused him to offer his resignation. The resignation was refused but thereafter the work of the diocese was done by a coadjutor. Bishop Provoost was chairman of the committee which drafted the constitution of the Episcopal Church and was responsible for the necessary changes in the Prayer Book following establishment of the church as an American entity.

PROVOST, ETIENNE (*b. Canada, c. 1782; d. St. Louis, Mo., 1850*), hunter, guide. Associated at times with William Ashley and the American Fur Co., he is supposed to have been the first white man to visit the Great Salt Lake and was possibly the discoverer of South Pass. He was guide for J. J. Audubon on his Western expedition, 1843.

PROVOSTY, OLIVIER OTIS (*b. Pointe Coupée Parish, La., 1852; d. New Orleans, La., 1924*), jurist, Louisiana legislator. Justice, Louisiana supreme court *post* 1901; chief justice, 1922. He retired from public life at the end of 1922.

PRUDDEN, THEOPHIL MITCHELL (*b. Middlebury, Conn., 1849; d. 1924*), pathologist, bacteriologist. Graduated Sheffield Scientific School, Yale, 1872; Yale Medical School, 1875. Studied also in Heidelberg, Vienna, Berlin. Taught histology and pathology at N.Y. College of Physicians and Surgeons. The first to make diphtheria antitoxin in the United States, he was for years adviser to Hermann M. Biggs of the New York City health department. He was co-author with Francis Delafield in the writing of the great standard textbook *Hand-book of Pathological Anatomy and Histology* (1885). In 1901, he became one of the scientific directors of the Rockefeller Institute.

PRUD'HOMME, JOHN FRANCIS EUGENE (*b. St. Thomas, V.I., 1800; d. Georgetown, D.C., 1892*), engraver, bank-note designer. Came to New York City as a child. Long active in his profession, he was with the U.S. Bureau of Engraving and Printing, 1869–85.

PRUYN, JOHN VAN SCHAICK LANSING (*b. Albany, N.Y., 1811; d. Clifton Springs, N.Y., 1877*), lawyer. Official and general counsel of New York Central Railroad *post* 1853, he was directly or indirectly connected with many of the leading financial and railroad enterprises in the United States. Active also in politics and philanthropy, he was chancellor of the University of the State of New York, 1862–77, and was responsible for the establishment of the state board of charities.

PRUYN, ROBERT HEWSON (*b. Albany, N.Y., 1815; d. 1882*), lawyer. Graduated Rutgers, 1833. After service as a Whig New York State legislator and officeholder, he followed W. H. Seward into the Republican party and was commissioned U.S. minister resident in Japan, October 1861, serving in that post with great tact and ability until 1865.

PRYBER, CHRISTIAN. [See PRIBER, CHRISTIAN, fl. 1734–1744.]

PRYOR, NATHANIEL (*b. probably Amherst Co., Va., c. 1775; d. Osage Agency, Indian Territory, 1831*), soldier, trader. Sergeant in Lewis and Clark expedition; served with distinction in the battle of New Orleans.

PRYOR, ROGER ATKINSON (*b. near Petersburg, Va., 1828; d. New York, N.Y., 1919*), lawyer, newspaper editor, Confederate brigadier-general, jurist. Graduated Hampden-Sydney College, 1845. Practiced law at Petersburg; was associated at various times with the *Southside Democrat*, the Washington *Union* and the *Richmond Enquirer;* founded *The South*, 1857, as an ultra-Southern newspaper. Congressman, Democrat, from Virginia, 1859–61. Visiting Charleston, S.C., with other Virginians, 1861, he urged the attack on Fort Sumter but declined the honor of firing the first shot in favor of Edmund Ruffin. After serving gallantly through the Civil War, he removed to New York City, September 1865, was admitted to the New York bar and practiced successfully. He was a justice of the N.Y. supreme court, 1896–99.

PUGET, PETER RICHINGS. [See RICHINGS, PETER, 1797–1871.]

PUGH, ELLIS (*b. Dolgelley, North Wales, 1656; d. 1718*), Quaker preacher and writer. Resident in or near Philadelphia, 1687–1706, and *post* 1708. Author of *Annerch ir Cymru* (Philadelphia, 1721), the first book in Welsh known to have been printed here.

PUGH, EVAN (*b. Jordan Bank, Pa., 1828; d. 1864*), chemist. Studied at Leipzig and Heidelberg; Ph.D., Göttingen, 1856; studied also in England. Organizer and president, Agricultural College of Pennsylvania (present Pennsylvania State College), 1859–64.

PUGH, GEORGE ELLIS (*b. Cincinnati, O., 1822; d. Cincinnati, 1876*), lawyer, Ohio legislator. U.S. senator, Democrat, from Ohio, 1855–61. Opposed extreme Southern position; active in urging acceptance of Crittenden Compromise. Ran for lieutenant-governor of Ohio on ticket with C. L. Vallandigham, 1863; assisted Charles O'Conor as defense counsel in case of Jefferson Davis.

PUJO, ARSÈNE PAULIN (*b. Calcasieu Parish, La., 1861; d. New Orleans, La., 1939*), lawyer. Congressman, Democrat, from Louisiana, 1903–13. An active member of the National Monetary Commission, 1908–12, Pujo in 1911 became chairman of the House banking and currency committee, and in 1912 headed a subcommittee whose investigations of the money trusts (including J. P. Morgan & Co.) led to important reforms. [*Supp. 2*]

PULASKI, CASIMIR (*b. Podolia, Poland, c. 1748; d. off Savannah, Ga., 1779*), Polish patriot, Revolutionary cavalry leader. Joined father in active rebellion against foreign domination of Poland, 1768; after defeat, fled to Turkey, 1772; arrived in Paris, France, 1775. Introduced by Benjamin Franklin and Silas Deane, Pulaski arrived in Boston, July 1777, and was recommended by George Washington to Congress for command of all the Continental cavalry. After service at Brandywine and Germantown, he commanded cavalry during the winter of 1777–78 and acted with Gen. Anthony Wayne in foraging for the troops at Valley Forge. Refusing to serve under Wayne, he resigned his command, March 1778. After ill success with an independent cavalry corps of his own and guard service at Minisink on the Delaware River, he was ordered in February 1779 to South Carolina. Defeated in an attempt to block the British advance northward from Savannah, Ga., he joined forces with Gen. Lincoln who, assisted by the French fleet, was preparing to attack Savannah. During the siege of that city, he was mortally wounded while charging the enemy lines.

PULITZER, JOSEPH (*b. Mako, Hungary, 1847; d. in harbor of Charleston, S.C., 1911*), journalist. Obtained passage to America by enlisting in Union Army at Hamburg, Germany; arrived in Boston, 1864; served for a year with the 1st N.Y. (Lincoln) Cavalry. Removing to St. Louis, Mo., he performed all sorts of menial labor until he became in 1868 a reporter on the German daily, *Westliche Post*. He soon became a prominent figure in local journalism and held important civic positions, 1869–72. He campaigned on behalf of Horace Greeley, 1872, and disappointment over the defeat of the Liberal Republican movement brought him to the Democratic party to which he remained loyal for the rest of his life. In 1874 he bought the bankrupt St. Louis *Staats-Zeitung*, whose membership in the Associated Press he sold to the *St. Louis Daily Globe* for a good profit. This gave him leisure to study law and he was admitted to the bar, 1876.

He settled finally on a career in journalism in 1878 when he bought the *St. Louis Dispatch* and merged it with the *Post*. The new daily, the *St. Louis Post-Dispatch*, was a huge success and a leader in fighting local municipal and political corruption. In 1883 he bought the New York *World* from Jay Gould and converted it into a profitable venture and a great national political force. The program which Pulitzer announced on acquiring control made him immediately popular with labor. The *World* declared that it opposed the aristocracy of money, but that it wished to become the organ of the true American aristocracy,

"the aristocracy of labor." Main items in its program were: the taxation of luxuries, inheritances, large incomes, monopolies, and large and privileged corporations; the enactment of a tariff for revenue only; the reform of the civil service; the punishment of corrupt officials and purchasers of votes at elections; and finally, the punishment of employers who coerced their employees at election times. Success was immediate, owing to this policy and to the sensational methods and "stunts" which Pulitzer employed. In 1887 he founded the *Evening World*.

Early in 1896 the morning *World* resorted to extreme "yellow journalism" in its rivalry with the rising dailies of William Randolph Hearst and was only redeemed by the supervision of Pulitzer himself who had retired from direct management in 1887. Although ill and blind, he impressed upon the *World* its subsequent high character as an internationally minded, extremely well-informed daily, with a remarkably able editorial page, no longer an organ of the working classes but of all who favored liberal and democratic policies. The influence of the *World* upon the political life and the press of the country was very great after it abandoned its career of sensationalism and vulgarity. It opposed jingoism and special privilege; it was the fearless scourge of political corruption; it was completely free of domination by advertisers. After Pulitzer's death the papers passed to his sons who failed to keep them profitable and sold them to the Scripps-Howard newspaper group. His will provided for the establishment of a school of journalism at Columbia University and for the annual awards known as the Pulitzer prizes.

PULITZER, RALPH (*b. St. Louis, Mo., 1879; d. New York, N.Y., 1939*), journalist, publisher. Son of Joseph Pulitzer. Graduated Harvard, 1900. Editor-publisher of the N.Y. *World*, 1911–30, he gave primary attention to news and a liberal editorial policy. [*Supp. 2*].

PULLMAN, GEORGE MORTIMER (*b. Brocton, N.Y., 1831; d. 1897*), inventor, industrialist. Removed to Chicago, Ill., 1855, where he became a successful contractor. By 1858, he had brought his earlier-formulated idea for improved railroad sleeping accommodations to the point of remodeling several coaches of the Chicago & Alton Railroad into sleeping cars. On failure of railroads generally to adopt his cars, Pullman removed to Colorado, 1859, where he conducted a general store and worked on plans for improvement of his scheme. Returning to Chicago, 1863, he and an associate completed plans and secured a patent for the basic idea of a folding upper berth in April 1864 and a second patent covering the lower berth arrangement, September 1865. Their first car, *Pioneer,* was enthusiastically received. Pullman and his partner constructed a number of other similar cars and in 1867 organized the Pullman Palace Car

Co. Pullman's business ability made it the greatest car-building organization in the world.

PULTE, JOSEPH HIPPOLYT (*b. Meschede, Westphalia (Prussia), 1811; d. Cincinnati, O., 1884*), homeopathic physician, author. M.D., University of Marburg, 1833; came to America, 1834. Practiced mainly in Cincinnati.

PUMPELLY, RAPHAEL (*b. Owego, N.Y., 1837; d. Newport, R.I., 1923*), geologist, explorer. Attended Royal School of Mines, Freiberg, Saxony. Began work as mining engineer in southern Arizona, 1859. Worked in Japan with William P. Blake, 1861–63, as government geologist; traveled in Asia until 1865. His reputation as a mining geologist rests chiefly on his work in association with Thomas B. Brooks in the copper and iron districts of Michigan and the Lake Superior area. Restlessly active, he served at various times as state geologist of Missouri, as head of the New England division of the U.S. Geological Survey, and in other professional assignments. In 1903 and 1904 under auspices of the Carnegie Institution, he organized and conducted expeditions into central Asia seeking traces of prehistoric civilization and evidences of geological and climatic changes. His most important technical achievements were his studies of the loess of China and his discovery of the secondary nature of the iron ores of Michigan together with his work on the paragenesis of the copper deposits there.

PUPIN, MICHAEL IDVORSKY (*b. Idvor, Banat, Austria-Hungary, 1858; d. New York, N.Y., 1935*), physicist. Born of illiterate but highly intelligent Serbian parents, he received his early education in Idvor and Panchevo, a nearby town. He studied at schools in Prague and during a trip to Vienna was befriended by an American couple who stirred his desire to study in America. In 1874, he arrived at Castle Garden, New York City, with five cents capital. Working at odd jobs in New York, he spent his spare time in the library of Cooper Union. A German theological student taught him Greek and Latin as preparation for his admission to Columbia University. Passing the examinations with honor, 1879, he graduated in 1883 and secured his citizenship papers. He went to Cambridge University for study of physics and mathematics, and then on to Berlin to study under Helmholtz; he received the Ph.D. degree from Berlin, 1889. Returning to Columbia, 1889, as teacher of mathematical physics in the department of electrical engineering, he was promoted to professor of electromechanics, 1901, a position which he held until his retirement in 1931.

His teaching brought him in contact with many practical engineering problems. Henry A. Rowland, for example, had reported distortions in an alternating current when it was magnetizing iron in electrical power apparatus. It consisted of addition of higher harmonics to the normal harmonic changes in current. Recollecting Helmholtz's work in analyzing complex sound waves by means of resonators, Pupin developed an analogous method for electrical waves and invented the electrical resonator, consisting of a circuit having a variable condenser and inductance akin to the tuning unit in a radio. When this direct method was applied to the current under study, its harmonics were readily obtained. Many later applications of this method were developed.

In 1894 he became interested in the theoretical problem of the propagation of waves in a vibrating string and applied his findings to solving the problem of attenuation of electrical currents in conveying speech in long distance telephony. He had found that a disturbance set up in a string which was loaded with weights at equal intervals did not die out as quickly as in a string which was not loaded. Others had shown that transmission efficiency of long telephone or telegraph circuits could be improved by increasing the "uniformly distributed inductance," but no one had found a way of doing it. Pupin's study of the analogous string problem showed him the proper spacing for inductance coils along the telephone circuit. Coils inserted at about one for every four or five miles on overhead wires and at one to two miles in cables resulted in reduction of both attenuation and distortion. When the discovery of X-rays was announced in 1895, Pupin constructed a tube and obtained the first X-ray photograph in America on Jan. 2, 1896. He also discovered secondary X-radiation.

After a long period of recuperation from the loss of his wife (1896) and the effects of illness, he returned to Columbia to work on problems of radio transmission. E. H. Armstrong was one of his pupils. After World War I he ceased personal research; in 1919, he acted as an adviser to the Yugoslav delegation to the Paris Peace Conference.

An eloquent speaker with a poetic imagination, Pupin never failed to stress idealism in science and life. There is also much evidence of his deeply religious nature in his autobiography *From Immigrant to Inventor* (1923) which in 1924 received a Pulitzer prize. Other of his works were a book on thermodynamics (1894), *Serbian Orthodox Church* (1918), *Yugoslavia* (1919), *The New Reformation* (1927), *Romance of the Machine* (1930), and 65 articles of scientific interest. He received 34 patents for his inventions. [*Supp. 1*]

PURCELL, JOHN BAPTIST (*b. Mallow, Ireland, 1800; d. 1883*), Roman Catholic clergyman. Came to America, 1818; attended the seminary at Mount St. Mary's College, Emmitsburg, Md., 1820–23; completed theological studies in Paris where he was ordained, 1826. After a brief period as professor of moral philosophy and as president of Mount St. Mary's, Purcell was consecrated bishop of Cincinnati, 1833. An able and tactful administrator with a strong interest in education, he was with the exception of John Hughes the most influential figure in the American hierarchy of his time and was named archbishop, July 1850. His more than fifty years of distinguished service to the church were unfortunately shadowed in 1879 by the failure of a private bank for which he was nominally responsible and he was succeeded by his coadjutor, William H. Elder.

PURDUE, JOHN (*b. Huntingdon Co., Pa., 1802; d. Lafayette, Ind., 1876*), merchant, philanthropist. Principal benefactor of Purdue University.

PURNELL, BENJAMIN (*b. Mayville, Ky., 1861; d. 1927*), founder of the eccentric religious sect, the House of David. [*Supp. 1*]

PURNELL, WILLIAM HENRY (*b. Worcester Co., Md., 1826; d. 1902*), lawyer, politician. Graduated Delaware College (present University of Delaware), 1846. Active in Maryland politics as a Whig and Know-Nothing, later as chairman of the Union party, 1864–66. President of Delaware College, 1870–85; served thereafter as principal of Frederick Female Seminary (present Hood College) and as president of New Windsor College.

PURPLE, SAMUEL SMITH (*b. Lebanon, N.Y., 1822; d. 1900*), physician, editor. Practiced in New York City *post* 1844; was a founder and benefactor of the New York Academy of Medicine whose library was formed around the nucleus of books bequeathed to the Academy by him.

PURRY, JEAN PIERRE (*b. Neuchâtel, Switzerland, 1675; d. c. 1736*), colony promoter. Proposed settlement of European Protestants in Carolina, 1724–26; established Purrysburgh, S.C., with a group of Swiss immigrants, 1732–34.

PURSH, FREDERICK (*b. Grossenhain, Saxony, 1774; d. Montreal, Canada, 1820*), botanist, horticulturist, explorer. Came to America, 1799. Aided by Benjamin S. Barton, Pursh made two memorable journeys of botanical exploration in 1806 and 1807: the first through the mountains from western Maryland to the North Carolina border and back along the coast; the second across the Pocono region of Pennsylvania to central New York and thence east to the Vermont Green Mountains. He was author of *Flora Americae Septentrionalis* (1814), the first complete flora of America north of Mexico, and of a posthumously published journal of his explorations.

PURVIANCE, DAVID (*b. Iredell Co., N.C., 1766; d. Preble Co., O., 1847*), frontier preacher and legislator in Tennessee, Kentucky and Ohio. A founder of the so-called Christian denomination.

PURYEAR, BENNET (*b. Mecklenberg Co., Va., 1826; d. Madison Co., Va., 1914*), educator. Professor of chemistry, Richmond College (present University of Richmond), 1850–58 and 1865–95. A pioneer in applying chemistry to Virginia agriculture, he had a wide influence among farmers.

PUSEY, CALEB (*b. Berkshire, England, c. 1650; d. Chester Co., Pa., 1727 o.s.*), miller, Pennsylvania provincial legislator, Quaker controversial writer. Emigrated to Pennsylvania, 1682; erected Chester Mills near Upland, 1683, which he managed until 1717.

PUSEY, WILLIAM ALLEN (*b. Elizabethtown, Ky., 1865; d. Chicago, Ill., 1940*), dermatologist, authority on syphilis. Graduated Vanderbilt University, 1885; M.D., New York University, 1888. Practiced in Chicago. [*Supp. 2*]

PUSHMATAHA (*b. probably present Noxubee Co., Miss., c. 1765; d. Washington, D.C., 1824*), Choctaw chief. Opposed Tecumseh's efforts to form an Indian confederacy; led Choctaw warriors against the Creeks in campaign under Andrew Jackson, 1813–14.

PUTNAM, ARTHUR (*b. Waveland, Miss., 1873; d. near Paris, France, 1930*), sculptor. Patronized by Willis Polk and E. W. Scripps, he was particularly effective in bronzes of Western animals.

PUTNAM, CHARLES PICKERING (*b. Boston, Mass., 1844; d. 1914*), physician. Brother of James J. Putnam; grandson of James Jackson. A noted specialist in pediatrics and orthopedics in Boston *post* 1871, he was also the most important leader in charitable and social work in that city *post* 1875.

PUTNAM, EBEN (*b. Salem, Mass., 1868; d. Wellesley Farms, Mass., 1933*), editor, genealogist, historian. Son of Frederic W. Putnam.

PUTNAM, FREDERIC WARD (*b. Salem, Mass., 1839; d. Cambridge, Mass., 1915*), archaeologist, naturalist. Strongly influenced by J. L. R. Agassiz while studying at Harvard, Putnam began his long career as a museum administrator at the Essex Institute. Influential in the founding of the Peabody Academy of Science, Salem, he served as its director, 1869–73. As curator of the Peabody Museum at Harvard *post* 1874, he revolutionized the methods of museum administration; *post* 1894, he served also as curator of anthropology, American Museum of Natural History, New York City. To these activities and many other advisory posts, Putnam added that of teaching, for he was appointed Peabody Professor of Archaeology at Harvard in 1887. In the rise and development of anthropology in America, Putnam played a leading, perhaps the foremost, part and was largely responsible for its acceptance as a university study.

PUTNAM, GEORGE HAVEN (*b. London, England, 1844; d. New York, N.Y., 1930*), Union soldier, publisher. Son of George P. Putnam, he succeeded his father as head of the firm of G. P. Putnam & Son, 1872, and remained its active head until 1930. He played a prominent part in securing the copyright act of 1909.

831

PUTNAM, GEORGE PALMER (*b. Brunswick, Maine, 1814; d. New York, N.Y., 1872*), publisher. Became partner in Wiley & Putnam, 1840; after a number of vicissitudes, established firm of G. P. Putnam & Son, 1866. Maintained close working relations with the British book trade; was an early advocate of international copyright.

PUTNAM, GIDEON (*b. Sutton, Mass., 1763; d. 1812*), developer of Saratoga Springs, N.Y., as a spa and resort, 1802–12.

PUTNAM, ISRAEL (*b. Salem Village, present Danvers, Mass., 1718; d. Brooklyn, earlier Pomfret, Conn., 1790*), soldier. Served throughout French and Indian War with Connecticut forces and with Robert Rogers as one of his rangers; promoted major of colony forces, 1758, and lieutenant-colonel, 1759. In 1764, he campaigned with Bradstreet's expedition in Pontiac's War. Active in the organization of the Sons of Liberty at the time of the Stamp Act troubles, he served in the General Assembly, 1766–67. After an exploring trip to the Gulf of Mexico and up the Mississippi River, 1773, he became chairman of the committee of correspondence of his home town, 1774, and in the same year was made lieutenant-colonel of the 11th regiment, Connecticut militia. Appointed major-general in the Continental Army, 1775, he was a leading spirit in planning for the battle of Bunker Hill and was everywhere during the whole of that fight, although he seems not to have been in supreme command. Ordered to New York after the siege of Boston was ended in March 1775, he played a controversial part in the battle of Long Island and thereafter sunk steadily in the regard of George Washington and the other generals. His dilatoriness as commander of the forces in the Hudson Highlands brought him a sharp rebuke; a court of inquiry, however, exonerated him, but in December 1779 a stroke of paralysis ended his military career. Active and brave and disinterested, he failed through incapacity in the superior commands to which his popularity advanced him.

PUTNAM, JAMES JACKSON (*b. Boston, Mass., 1846; d. 1918*), neurologist. Brother of Charles P. Putnam. Graduated Harvard, 1866; Harvard Medical School, 1870. After making special studies in Leipzig, Vienna and London, he returned to Boston where he practiced, and taught at Harvard Medical School, 1874–1912. In 1872, he started one of the first neurological clinics in the United States at Massachusetts General Hospital; he was the author of many important papers in the fields of structural and functional neurology.

PUTNAM, JAMES OSBORNE (*b. Attica, N.Y., 1818; d. 1903*), lawyer, Whig and Republican public servant and diplomat. Maintained a life-long interest in the educational and cultural institutions of Buffalo, N.Y.; was a founder of University of Buffalo, 1846, and its chancellor, 1895–1902.

PUTNAM, RUFUS (*b. Sutton, Mass., 1738; d. 1824*), soldier, Ohio pioneer. Cousin of Israel Putnam. A self-taught surveyor and millwright, Putnam fought in the French and Indian War and rose to rank of brigadier-general in the Continental service during the Revolution, serving with credit as an engineer and as a field commander. Active in the organization of the Ohio Company, Putnam became superintendent of the new colony and was with the first party of settlers to arrive at Marietta, April 1788. Commissioned brigadier-general, U.S. Army, 1792, he made the treaty of Vincennes, September 1792, with the lower Wabash tribes. As surveyor-general of the United States, 1796–1803, he surveyed the military tract (inaccurately). As delegate to the Ohio constitutional convention, 1802, he exerted strong influence against the admission of slavery.

PUTNAM, RUTH (*b. Yonkers, N.Y., 1856; d. Geneva, Switzerland, 1931*), author. Daughter of George P. Putnam; sister of George H. Putnam and Mary C. P. Jacobi. Specialist in the history of the Netherlands.

PUTNAM, WILLIAM LE BARON (*b. Bath, Maine, 1835; d. 1918*), jurist, diplomat, expert in equity. Judge, U.S. circuit court of appeals (first circuit), 1892–1917.

PYE, WATTS ORSON (*b. near Faribault, Minn., 1878; d. 1926*), Congregational clergyman. As missionary to China *post* 1907, he directed pioneer activity in the provinces of Shansi and Shensi from headquarters at Fenchow.

PYLE, HOWARD (*b. Wilmington, Del., 1853; d. Florence, Italy, 1911*), artist, author, teacher. Educated in Quaker schools; studied art with a Flemish teacher (Van der Weilen) in Philadelphia and briefly at the Art Students League, New York City. Removing to New York, 1876, he developed his own style and technique through patient labor and experiment, encouraged by Edwin Abbey, A. B. Frost, F. S. Church and others. Successful *post* 1878 as a magazine illustrator, he returned to Wilmington where he set up his studio. Accurate in delineation of the characters and events of early American history, he was most effective in pen-and-ink work but was one of the first in the field when the new process for reproducing pictures in color came into being. Important as are the illustrations which he did for the work of other men, his reputation really rests upon his own tales and the pictures he made for them. Outstanding among them are *The Merry Adventures of Robin Hood* (1883), *The Wonder Clock* (1888), *Otto of the Silver Hand* (1888), *Men of Iron* (1892), *The Story of Jack Ballister's Fortunes* (1895); he also wrote and illustrated a variety of books which dealt with pirates, appealing as much to adults as to children. He taught illustration at Drexel Institute, Philadelphia, 1894–1900, and thereafter in his own school at Wilmington. By somewhat unorthodox methods of instruction, he developed such artists as Maxfield Parrish, N.C. Wyeth and Frank Schoonover.

PYLE, WALTER LYTLE (*b. Philadelphia, Pa., 1871; d. 1921*), ophthalmologist, medical writer.

PYNCHON, JOHN (*b. Springfield, Essex, England, c. 1626; d. 1702/03*), colonial industrialist, public servant. Son of William Pynchon. Came to New England with his father as a child. Conducted the family trading business *post* 1652 and exercised a controlling influence in and about Springfield, Mass.

PYNCHON, THOMAS RUGGLES (*b. New Haven, Conn., 1823; d. New Haven, 1904*), Episcopal clergyman. Graduated Washington College (present Trinity), Hartford, 1841; was professor of science there, 1855–77, and professor of moral philosophy, 1877–1902. President of the college, 1874–83.

PYNCHON, WILLIAM (*b. England, c. 1590; d. near Windsor, England, 1662*), trader, colonial official. Emigrated from Springfield, Essex, England, 1630; settled first at Dorchester and started fur-trading operations at Roxbury, Mass., where he was first signer of the church covenant. He had brought considerable capital to the colony and served it as assistant, 1630–36, and as treasurer, 1632–34. Active in the emigration to the Connecticut valley, he was appointed one of the commissioners to govern the new settlement, March 1635/36. He was at Springfield, May 1636, when, with seven others he signed an agreement concerning land allotments and settling a minister. Falling out with Thomas Hooker, Pynchon severed connection with the River Colony and supported the claim of Massachusetts to Springfield, which took no further part in the Connecticut government after 1638. Largest landowner in Springfield, Pynchon virtually ruled the community and was successful as a trader, shipping furs direct to London down the Connecticut River. Re-elected a Massachusetts assistant, 1642, he was elected annually thereafter until 1651. He returned to England probably in the spring of 1652 after deeding his property at Springfield to his son John Pynchon and to his sons-in-law. Shortly before his departure he had written a tract critical of the orthodox view of the atonement which the Massachusetts clergy denounced as heretical.

QUACKENBUSH, STEPHEN PLATT (*b. Albany, N.Y., 1823; d. Washington, D.C., 1890*), naval officer. Retired as rear-admiral, 1885, after 45 years of valuable service, particularly with the Civil War blockade forces off Virginia and North Carolina.

QUANAH (*b. probably northern Texas, c. 1845; d. near Fort Sill, Oklahoma, 1911*), Comanche chief. Son of a Kwahadi chief and a white captive, Cynthia Parker. Refusing to accept the Medicine Lodge treaty

of 1867, he terrorized the frontier settlements in Texas until he was badly defeated at the fight at Adobe Walls in present Hutchinson Co., Texas, June 1874. Adapting himself to the white man's way after his surrender, 1875, he fostered building and agriculture among his tribesmen, popularized education and discouraged extravagance.

QUANTRILL, WILLIAM CLARKE (*b. Canal Dover, O., 1837; d. Louisville, Ky., 1865*), guerrilla chief. Settled in Kansas, 1857. Journeyed to Utah, 1858; worked as gambler. Returning to Kansas, he taught school in the winter of 1859–60, and thereafter engaged in horse-stealing, escaping arrest by fleeing to Missouri. Irregularly connected with the Confederate Army at the start of the Civil War, he soon appeared as the chief of a guerrilla band which operated in Missouri and Kansas, robbing mail coaches, raiding and sacking Unionist communities and farms. Formally outlawed in 1862, he mustered his troop into Confederate service and was given the rank of captain. In August 1863, he destroyed the town of Lawrence, Kans. Dissension arising among his followers, they broke up into smaller bands. He made a raid into Kentucky early in 1865 and in May of that year was fatally wounded near Taylorsville.

QUARTER, WILLIAM (*b. King's Co., Ireland, 1806; d. 1848*), Roman Catholic clergyman. Emigrated to Canada, 1822, where he was denied admission to seminaries because of his youth. Accepted by Dr. John Dubois at Mount St. Mary's, Emmitsburg, Md., he made his theological studies and was ordained, September 1829. After serving as a New York pastor, he was consecrated first bishop of Chicago, 1844.

QUARTLEY, ARTHUR (*b. Paris, France, 1839; d. New York, N.Y., 1886*), painter of seascapes. Came to New York as a boy; was taught to draw by his father, an engraver. Worked in Baltimore, Md., 1862–75, thereafter, in New York and in summers at Isle of Shoals, N.H.

QUAY, MATTHEW STANLEY (*b. Dillsburg, Pa., 1833; d. Beaver, Pa., 1904*), politician, lawyer, Union soldier. Rose to prominence in Pennsylvania politics by success in promoting gubernatorial campaign of Andrew G. Curtin, 1860. Re-entering politics on his return from distinguished service in the Civil War, he served as secretary of Pennsylvania, 1872–78, and as recorder of Philadelphia; he was also chairman of the Republican state committee. Unable to gain control of the political machine in Philadelphia, he resigned the position of recorder and was again appointed commonwealth secretary, 1879, holding this position until 1882. Elected state treasurer in 1885, from this time until his death he held undisputed political control of Pennsylvania and was U.S. senator *post* 1887 with the exception of a hiatus in 1899–1900. Quay's influence was decisive in matters connected with tariff legislation, but he is chiefly to be remembered for his genius as a political maneuverer. He always had a machine to work with, but he would build up a new one for each major contest and by aligning his enemies against one another was able to triumph over them all. His break with Benjamin Harrison and his failure to take an active part in the campaign of 1892 was a prime factor in the Democratic victory of that year. An educated man with a passion for literature, he displayed an utter contempt for ordinary political ideals and he was one of the best-hated men in politics.

QUAYLE, WILLIAM ALFRED (*b. Parkville, Mo., 1860; d. Baldwin, Kans., 1925*), Methodist clergyman, educator, bishop.

QUEEN, WALTER W. (*b. Washington, D.C., 1824; d. Washington, 1893*), naval officer. Retired as rear-admiral, 1886, after varied sea and shore service, notably in Civil War blockade of North Carolina.

QUELCH, JOHN (*b. London, England, c. 1665; d. Boston, Mass., 1704*), pirate. Unlawfully in command of the Boston brigantine *Charles*, Quelch plundered a number of Portuguese ships off the coast of Brazil, November 1703—February 1704. On the return of the *Charles* to Marblehead, Mass., Quelch and some of his crewmen were arrested, tried, and hanged on June 30. The speed and questionable procedures of the trial, together with the eagerness of Boston authorities to confiscate and divide the loot, have caused the case to be characterized as "judicial murder."

QUESNAY, ALEXANDRE-MARIE, Chevalier de Beaurepaire (*b. Saint-Germain-en-Viry, France, 1755; d. Saint-Maurice, France, 1820*), soldier, educator. Came to Virginia, April 1777; served as captain in Revolutionary Army until autumn 1778. Taught school in Virginia, Philadelphia, New York, 1780–86. Returning to France, in the spring of 1787 he presented a plan for an Academy of the United States of America to Thomas Jefferson, then U.S. minister to France. His plan called for an extensive system of schools and universities throughout the United States centering around an establishment at Richmond. On Jefferson's statement that America was too poor to support such undertakings, the project failed.

QUICK, JOHN HERBERT (*b. Grundy Co., Iowa, 1861; d. Columbia, Mo., 1925*), lawyer, Iowa politician, author. His best work as a writer is contained in a trilogy of Iowa novels, *Vandemark's Folly* (1921), *The Hawkeye* (1923) and *The Invisible Woman* (1924), vivid, truthful pictures of pioneer life.

QUIDOR, JOHN (*b. Tappan, N.Y., 1801; d. Jersey City, N.J., 1881*), portrait and figure painter. Pupil of John W. Jarvis. Best known for paintings illustrative of scenes from the works of Washington Irving.

QUIGG, LEMUEL ELY (*b. near Chestertown, Md., 1863; d. 1919*), journalist, press agent, politician. Congressman, Republican, from New York, 1894–99;

a political lieutenant of Thomas C. Platt. Ousted from Republican leadership of New York County by Benjamin B. Odell, 1900, he became a promoter of the traction interests of Thomas Fortune Ryan.

QUIGLEY, JAMES EDWARD (*b. Oshawa, Canada, 1854; d. Rochester, N.Y., 1915*), Roman Catholic clergyman. Raised in Rochester, N.Y.; graduated St. Joseph's College, Buffalo, N.Y., 1872; made theological studies in Buffalo, at the University of Innsbruck and at Rome. Bishop of Buffalo, 1897–1903; archbishop of Chicago thereafter.

QUIMBY, PHINEAS PARKHURST (*b. Lebanon, N.H., 1802; d. Belfast, Maine, 1866*), founder of mental healing in America. Trained as a clockmaker, he took up mesmerism, 1838, abandoning it in 1847 for mental healing which he practiced *post* 1859 in Portland, Maine. Mary Baker Eddy was a patient of his, 1862 and 1864, and derived her basic ideas from his teaching.

QUINAN, JOHN RUSSELL (*b. Lancaster, Pa., 1822; d. Baltimore, Md., 1890*), physician, medical historian. Practiced in Calvert, Co., Md., and in Baltimore.

QUINBY, ISAAC FERDINAND (*b. Morris Co., N.J., 1821; d. Rochester, N.Y., 1891*), soldier, professor of mathematics and natural science. Graduated West Point, 1843; served in Mexican War. He was associated with the University of Rochester, 1851–85, except for a period of distinguished Civil War service as colonel, 13th New York Volunteers, in 1861, and as a brigade and division commander under Gen. U. S. Grant from March 1862 until resignation because of ill-health in December 1863. He led the Yazoo Pass expedition, March 1863.

QUINCY, EDMUND (*b. Boston, Mass., 1808; d. 1877*), reformer, author. Son of Josiah Quincy (1772–1864). Graduated Harvard, 1827. An active associate of William L. Garrison and other Abolitionists, he held office in a number of radical anti-slavery societies but was personally devoid of fanaticism.

QUINCY, JOSIAH (*b. Boston, Mass., 1744; d. at sea, off the harbor of Gloucester, Mass., 1775*), lawyer, Revolutionary patriot. Graduated Harvard, 1763. Author, *post* 1767, of a number of essays strongly urging the patriot side in the difficulties with England; these were published in the Boston newspapers under several pseudonyms. He was associated with John Adams as counsel for the British soldiers on trial for the Boston massacre, 1770. Developing tubercular symptoms, he made a trip to Charleston, S.C., 1773, during which he met many of the prominent Southern patriots. In May 1774, he published his chief political work, *Observations of the Act of Parliament Commonly Called the Boston Port-Bill.* In the hope that he might present the case of the colonies correctly in England, he proceeded to London late in 1774 where he had interviews with Lord North, Lord Dartmouth and other leading men without result.

QUINCY, JOSIAH (*b. Braintree, now Quincy, Mass., 1772; d. Boston, 1864*), politician, municipal reformer, educator. Son of Josiah Quincy (1744–1775); nephew of William Phillips. Graduated Phillips Andover in 1786; Harvard, 1790. Congressman, Federalist, from Massachusetts, 1805–13. Becoming a friend of John Randolph of Roanoke and minority leader in Congress, he opposed the Embargo and non-intercourse system as cowardly, futile and unconstitutional. He also maintained that admission of any territory by majority vote without consent of all the original federators would virtually dissolve the Union. Advocating preparedness for war in the congressional session beginning November 1811 (hoping thereby to restore the Federalists to power by exposing the administration's supposed hypocrisy in this matter), he changed his position completely early in 1812 and opposed war legislation. After leaving Congress, he entered the Massachusetts senate where he continued his campaigns against the war, slave representation and Southern dominance until 1820, when the Federalists dropped him for insurgency. Elected to the Massachusetts lower house and chosen its speaker, he resigned, 1821, to take a place on the Boston municipal bench. As mayor of Boston, 1823–27, he instituted a great program of city improvement and reform. His administration of Harvard as its president, 1829–45, was able and businesslike but not particularly distinguished for academic initiative, although he showed a genius for choosing good faculty members—among them, Jared Sparks, Henry Wadsworth Longfellow and Benjamin Peirce. Deeply interested in the law school, he reformed it and made it into an academic professional school with the aid of Joseph Story. He was author of a number of books of which *The History of Harvard University* (1840) is probably best remembered.

QUINCY, JOSIAH PHILLIPS (*b. Boston, Mass., 1829; d. 1910*), author, historian. Grandson of Josiah Quincy (1772–1864). Graduated Harvard, 1850. Assisted his uncle Edmund Quincy in anti-slavery work; contributed fiction to periodicals; author of a variety of historical material in *Proceedings* of Massachusetts Historical Society.

QUINE, WILLIAM EDWARD (*b. St. Ann, Isle of Man, 1847; d. Chicago, Ill., 1922*), physician, educator. Came to America as a boy; graduated from Chicago Medical College, 1869. *Post* 1870, he taught with distinction at the Chicago Medical College and at the Chicago College of Physicians and Surgeons (*post* 1897 University of Illinois). [*Supp.* 1]

QUINN, EDMOND THOMAS (*b. Philadelphia, Pa., 1868; d. New York, N.Y., 1929*), sculptor, painter.

Studied at Pennsylvania Academy of Fine Arts under Thomas Eakins, and in France and Spain. Attained distinction as a portraitist and as a sculptor of ideal figures. Notable among his works are the reliefs for the battle monument at King's Mountain, S.C. (1908) and the statue of Edwin Booth as Hamlet in Gramercy Park, New York City.

QUINTARD, CHARLES TODD (*b. Stamford, Conn., 1824; d. 1898*), physician, Episcopal clergyman. Brother of George W. Quintard. After practicing medicine in Georgia and Tennessee, he was ordained in 1856 and became rector of Calvary Church, Memphis, Tenn., and a little later rector in Nashville. After distinguished service in the Confederate Army as chaplain and surgeon, he was elected bishop of Tennessee, 1865. As educator, his most important work was the "second founding" of the University of the South at Sewanee, 1866–72.

QUINTARD, GEORGE WILLIAM (*b. Stamford, Conn., 1822; d. New York, N.Y., 1913*), manufacturer of marine engines. Brother of Charles T. Quintard.

QUITMAN, JOHN ANTHONY (*b. Rhinebeck, N.Y., 1798; d. near Natchez, Miss., 1858*), lawyer, soldier. Settled in practice at Natchez, 1821. Quitman's activity as a Freemason contributed a great deal to his professional political progress. Chancellor of Mississippi, 1827–35, he became identified in 1834 with the political group known as "Nullifiers." Although the opinions of this group were not then popular in Mississippi, he was elected to the state senate, 1835, but was defeated in a campaign for Congress, 1836. Having recruited and led a company to the relief of the Texans (which took no part in the fighting), he was appointed brigadier-general of Mississippi militia and served with ability in the Mexican War. As governor of Mississippi, 1850–51, he opposed the Compromise measures of 1850 and caused the legislature to protest their adoption by Congress. He was also concerned in a Cuban movement for independence which brought about his indictment at New Orleans by a federal grand jury. As congressman, 1855–58, he continued to act as a champion of the state rights pro-slavery cause.

RABY, JAMES JOSEPH (*b. Bay City, Mich., 1874; d. near Midway, Ga., 1934*), naval officer. Graduated Annapolis, 1895. Commanded the cruiser *Albany*, June 1917—April 1918, escorting a larger number of ships in convoy to Europe than any other American naval vessel. Promoted rear-admiral, 1927, he was for some time the only commissioned naval aviator in this grade. At the time of his death, he was commandant of all naval activities in the South.

RACHFORD, BENJAMIN KNOX (*b. Alexandria, Ky., 1857; d. Cincinnati, O., 1929*), physiologist, pediatrician, philanthropist. M.D., Medical College of Ohio, 1882. After study at Berlin, he published a classic paper "The Influence of Bile on the Fat-Splitting Properties of the Pancreatic Juice" (*Journal of Physiology*, April 1891). Practicing in Cincinnati, O., *post* 1894, he taught at the Medical College of Ohio (later University of Cincinnati), continued to make physiological experiments and published several books on children's diseases. Elected director of pediatrics, Cincinnati General Hospital, 1897, he established a children's ward and one of the first outdoor wards in America for the treatment of tuberculosis of children. He initiated the Babies Milk Fund, 1909, and was associated with a number of other charities.

RADCLIFF, JACOB (*b. Rhinebeck, N.Y., 1764; d. Troy, N.Y., 1844*), lawyer, New York legislator and jurist. A founder (1804–05) of Jersey City, N.J. Federalist mayor of New York City, 1810 and 1815–17.

RADFORD, WILLIAM (*b. Fincastle, Va., 1809; d. 1890*), naval officer. Won particular distinction as commodore commanding ironclads in attacks on Fort Fisher, December 1864—January 1865; promoted rear-admiral, 1866.

RADISSON, PIERRE ESPRIT (*b. France, 1636; d. c. 1710*), explorer. Came to Canada *c.* 1651; was captured by Iroquois, 1652, and adopted by them. Escaping, he returned to France, 1654, but came back to Canada in that same year. On westward journeys with his brother-in-law, the Sieur des Groseilliers, he became aware of the importance of the fur trade of inland North America and of the need to control either or both of the main exits for that trade—New York and Hudson's Bay. Angered by an injustice done them by the governor of Canada, Radisson and Groseilliers entered English service, and their reports led to the founding of the Hudson's Bay Co. (chartered 1670). Resuming his French connection, 1674, Radisson "passed over to England for good" *c.* 1683. His own accounts of his voyages, valuable for vivid portrayal of the life of the early *coureurs de bois* in the north country, were edited as *Voyages of Peter Esprit Radisson* (Prince Society, 1885).

RAE, JOHN (*b. near Aberdeen, Scotland, 1796; d. Staten Island, N.Y., 1872*), economist, scientist. Emigrated to Canada, 1821. A wandering scholar, he resided thereafter in Canada, New York and Massachusetts, California and the Hawaiian Islands. His criticism of the doctrines of Adam Smith appeared as *Statement of Some New Principles on the Subject of Political Economy, etc.* (Boston, 1834). In the broad sense a collectivist, he was in the narrow sense a nationalist and protectionist; he worked out the time discount theory of interest long in advance of its better known expositors.

RAFFEINER, JOHN STEPHEN (*b. Walls, Tyrol, Austria, 1785; d. Brooklyn, N.Y., 1861*), Roman Catholic clergyman. Came to America, 1833, to be a missionary among German emigrants; served as vicar general for the Germans under Bishop John Hughes in New York and as vicar general of the Brooklyn diocese.

RAFINESQUE, CONSTANTINE SAMUEL (*b. near Constantinople, Turkey, 1783; d. Philadelphia, Pa., 1840*), naturalist. Of French and German parentage, he early showed a keen interest in natural history. Educated by private tutors, he never developed the orderly methods and mental attitudes of the trained scientist. Resident in Philadelphia, Pa., 1802–04, he worked in a merchant's counting-house but found time for considerable travel and made the acquaintance of President Jefferson and prominent scientists of the day. Journeying to Italy with his botanical collections, he lived at Palermo, was secretary to the U.S. consul, made an unhappy marriage, and conducted extensive research on the ichthyology of Sicilian waters. Engaging in the medical drug business, 1808, he set forth to settle in the United States, 1815, taking with him a stock of drugs and all his personal belongings. He arrived naked and penniless, for his ship was wrecked off Fisher's Island, and he narrowly escaped drowning. Befriended by Samuel L. Mitchill, he found work as a tutor in the Livingston family at Clermont. He then explored the Hudson Valley, Lake George, Long Island, and other regions, and in Philadelphia enjoyed the friendship of Zaccheus Collins, the Quaker naturalist. In 1818 he went to Lexington, Ky., to visit an old friend, John D. Clifford, through whose influence he was appointed professor of botany, natural history, and modern languages at Transylvania University. He traveled extensively in Kentucky and Tennessee and visited many points in Ohio, Indiana, and Illinois. After leaving Transylvania in 1826, he resided in Philadelphia but continued to make field trips.

No other American naturalist traveled so widely. He wrote and published incessantly but the eccentric manner in which he issued his works matched the general irregularity of his way of life. Botany and ichthyology continued to be his chief interests, but he wrote also on banking, economics, the Bible, and even produced verse. His descriptions of plants and fishes are often vague or inaccurate, and he had a passion for announcing new species. Behind this passion, however, lay the conviction, expressed more than once in his writings, that "every variety is a deviation which becomes a species as soon as it is permanent by reproduction. Deviations in essential organs may then gradually become new genera." He thus had a glimpse, if no more than a glimpse, of the later development of biological thought. He was ahead of his generation in the United States, also, in advocating Jussieu's method of classification. During his last years he suffered from dire poverty, neglect, and ill-health, and some of his later schemes and activities indicate that he was not entirely sane, yet he was one of the great pioneers of natural science in America.

RAFTER, GEORGE W. (*b. Orleans, N.Y., 1851; d. Karlsbad, Austria, 1907*), civil engineer, specialist in water supply and control, and sewage disposal. Collaborated with William T. Sedgwick on a method of water analysis.

RAGUET, CONDY (*b. Philadelphia, Pa., 1784; d. Philadelphia, 1842*), lawyer, economist, U.S. consul and chargé d'affaires in Brazil, 1822–27. Active in journalism in Philadelphia and Washington, D.C., *post* 1827, he set forth acute analyses of tariff and currency questions in his *Free Trade Advocate, Banner of the Constitution,* and *The Examiner* which, with his other writings, give him a place among early students of the business cycle.

RAHT, AUGUST WILHELM (*b. Dillenburg, Germany, 1843; d. San Francisco, Calif., 1916*), metallurgist. Came to the United States, 1867; established a professional reputation in lead-silver smelting in Utah, Colorado, New Mexico and Montana. He served as metallurgical expert for the Guggenheims, 1891–1910.

RAINES, JOHN (*b. Canandaigua, N.Y., 1840; d. Canandaigua, 1909*), lawyer, New York legislator, Union soldier. Congressman, Republican, from New York, 1889–93. As New York State senator, he was responsible for the "Raines Law" (1896) controlling the liquor traffic.

RAINEY, GERTRUDE MALISSA NIX PRIDGETT (*b. Columbus, Ga., 1886; d. Rome, Ga., 1939*), Negro blues singer, known as "Ma" Rainey. The first, and to some critics, the greatest of the blues singers, "Ma" Rainey sang what has come to be known as "country" blues. [*Supp. 2*]

RAINEY, HENRY THOMAS (*b. near Carrollton, Ill., 1860; d. St. Louis, Mo., 1934*), lawyer. Graduated Amherst, 1883. Congressman, Democrat, from Illinois, 1903–34, with the exception of the years 1921–23. A consistent progressive and ardent supporter of Presidents Wilson and F. D. Roosevelt, he was elected speaker of the House, March 1933, and pushed through the first New Deal measures with great efficiency. [*Supp. 1*]

RAINEY, JOSEPH HAYNE (*b. Georgetown, S.C., 1832; d. Georgetown, 1887*), first Negro to serve in the U.S. House of Representatives. Came into political prominence, 1867, as member of Republican executive committee in South Carolina. As congressman, 1870–79, he served with ability and tact and was particularly effective in speaking for civil rights. He later served as an agent for the U.S. Treasury Department.

RAINS, GABRIEL JAMES (*b. Craven Co., N.C., 1803; d. Aiken, S.C., 1881*), Confederate brigadier-general. Brother of George W. Rains. Graduated West Point, 1827; served in the Seminole wars and in the war with Mexico. Commissioned in the Confederate Army, 1861, he served as explosives expert after holding field commands, 1861–62. He was particularly notable as the deviser of land mines and torpedoes and was engaged in much controversy over the ethics of their use.

RAINS, GEORGE WASHINGTON (*b. Craven Co., N.C., 1817; d. near Newburgh, N.Y., 1898*), soldier, Confederate munitions expert, inventor. Brother of Gabriel J. Rains. Graduated West Point, 1842; served with credit in the war with Mexico. Resigning from the army, 1856, he became president of an iron works at Newburgh, N.Y. Immediately upon his commissioning as major in the Confederate artillery, 1861, he was assigned to the procurement of gun powder and was placed in charge of all munitions operations, 1862, at Augusta, Ga. After the war, he was professor of chemistry and dean of the Medical College of Georgia until his retirement, 1894.

RAINSFORD, WILLIAM STEPHEN (*b. near Dublin, Ireland, 1850; d. New York, N.Y., 1933*), Episcopal clergyman. Ordained in England and beginning his ministry there, he became rector of St. George's Church, New York, N.Y., January 1883, and served there until 1904. Strongly individual, he built up St. George's as an "institutional church" with the constant support of his senior warden, J. Pierpont Morgan, who disagreed with Rainsford's increasing theological and political liberalism. He later developed a naturalistic theology of his own and in 1912 was released from the priesthood at his own request. [*Supp. 1*]

RÂLE, SÉBASTIEN (*b. Pontarlier, France, 1654 or 1657; d. Norridgewock, Maine, 1724*), Jesuit missionary. Ministered to Indians near Quebec, 1689–91; served on the mission to the Illinois, 1691–93. Recalled to Canada, he was sent to the Abenaki mission in what is now the state of Maine; he worked with success among that branch of the tribe which lived on the Kennebec River but on the outbreak of Queen Anne's War, 1702, his efforts to keep the Indians from ravaging the Massachusetts frontier were relatively ineffective. In 1705, an English expedition came up the Kennebec and burned the Abenaki village and its chapel. *Post* 1713, after the English claimed sovereignty over the region, the raiding was intensified and the English blamed Râle for inciting the Indians. The mission at Norridgewock was attacked again in 1721 by the English but Râle escaped. In 1724, he was shot down at the door of his house by a British war party and his scalp taken to Boston "to the great joy and exultation of the people of Massachusetts." He was an able missionary, a fine linguist and a courageous champion of French policy.

RALPH, JAMES (*b. probably New Jersey, c. 1695; d. Chiswick, England, 1762*), poet, political writer. Accompanied Benjamin Franklin to London, December 1724; was extinguished as a poet by Alexander Pope in the second edition of *The Dunciad*. Turning to work for the theatre, he produced (among other plays) *The Fashionable Lady* (1730), the first play by a born American to be produced in London, and was associated in management with Henry Fielding. Thereafter, he was employed as an able political writer in the interest of Frederick, Prince of Wales, and others, but renounced political writing c. 1754 on receipt of a pension from the Pelham–Duke of Newcastle ministry. He aided Franklin in preparing for the press *An Historical Review of the Constitution and Government of Pennsylvania* (1759) and was author of an interesting essay *The Case of Authors by Profession* (1758), a defense of professional writers.

RALPH, JULIAN (*b. New York, N.Y., 1853; d. 1903*), journalist, foreign correspondent. Made his reputation as one of Charles A. Dana's reportorial staff on the N.Y. *Sun*, 1876–95, and as correspondent in the Greco-Turk and Boer wars, 1897–1900.

RALSTON, SAMUEL MOFFETT (*b. near New Cumberland, O., 1857; d. 1925*), lawyer. Began practice in Lebanon, Ind., 1886. Democratic governor of Indiana, 1913–17; U.S. senator, 1923–25. Refused possible Democratic presidential nomination, 1924.

RALSTON, WILLIAM CHAPMAN (*b. Wellsville, O., 1826; d. 1875*), banker. Beginning as a clerk on a Mississippi River steamboat, 1842, he rose in eight years to be a steamship agent at Panama City for Garrison and Morgan, removing to San Francisco, Calif. (1854) as a partner in the firm. Quickly realizing the future of the city as a center of trade and finance, he was instrumental in the establishment of the banking firm of Garrison, Morgan, Fretz and Ralston, 1856; during the panic of 1857 his courage and ability won him the complete confidence of the business community of San Francisco. With D. O. Mills, he organized the Bank of California, 1864; it soon became the leading financial institution of the Far West and Ralston became its president, 1872. Meanwhile, having engaged himself in widespread and vast plans of imperial expansion, he used the resources of the bank to aid his enterprises, some of them of an extremely dubious character. Living lavishly and becoming further involved in a network of speculation, he was able to continue deceiving his directors and political supporters until August 1875 when the bank suspended payment. On August 27, the day his resignation was demanded, he was found drowned.

RAMAGE, JOHN (*b. probably Dublin, Ireland, c. 1748; d. Montreal, Canada, 1802*), miniature painter. Mentioned as a goldsmith and painter of miniatures in Boston as early as 1775. A Loyalist, Ramage followed the fortunes of the British arms, removing to Halifax in March 1776 and settling in New York City at some time in 1777. Remaining in New York after the British left, he was successful in his profession until 1794 when he removed to Montreal to escape involvement in debt. His miniatures are small, accurately painted in the line manner, delicately colored and done with scrupulous care.

RAMBAUT, MARY LUCINDA BONNEY (*b. Hamilton, N.Y., 1816; d. Hamilton, 1900*), educator, reformer. Established Chestnut Street Female Seminary, Philadelphia, 1850; moved the school to Ogontz, Pa., 1883, changing its name to the Ogontz School.

RAMÉE, JOSEPH JACQUES (*b. Charlemont, France, 1764, d. near Noyon, France, 1842*), architect, landscape architect. Resident in America, 1811–16, Ramée did his most important American work on the layout and first buildings of Union College, Schenectady, N.Y. (1812–13).

RAMSAY, ALEXANDER (*b. in or near Edinburgh, Scotland, c. 1754; d. Parsonsfield, Maine, 1824*), anatomist. Came to America, 1801, and with the exception of the years, 1810–16, when he returned to Europe, led a wandering life as an itinerant lecturer and teacher. A man of immense learning, vanity and ill-temper, he was constantly at odds with his contemporaries. He was author of *Anatomy of the Heart, Cranium and Brain* (1812, second edition, 1813).

RAMSAY, DAVID (*b. Lancaster Co., Pa., 1749; d. Charleston, S.C., 1815*), physician, Revolutionary patriot, South Carolina legislator, historian. Author of *History of the Revolution of South Carolina* (1785), *History of the American Revolution* (1789), *History of South Carolina* (1809), which are still of value for what they contain of his own eyewitness experience but were drawn to a large extent from the work of others.

RAMSAY, FRANCIS MUNROE (*b. Washington, D.C., 1835; d. Washington, 1914*), naval officer. Served with great credit in the Mississippi River campaigns of the Civil War under David D. Porter. Promoted captain, 1877, he was superintendent of the U.S. Naval Academy, 1881–86. He retired as rear-admiral, 1897.

RAMSAY, GEORGE DOUGLAS (*b. Dumfries, Va., 1802; d. 1882*), soldier. Graduated West Point, 1820. Assigned to the artillery, he became an expert in ordnance and was in command at numerous U.S. arsenals. Promoted brigadier-general, 1863, he served as chief of ordnance of the Union Army until September 1864 when he was retired for age.

RAMSAY, NATHANIEL (*b. Lancaster Co., Pa., 1741; d. Maryland, 1817*), lawyer, Revolutionary soldier. Served, 1776–81, with Maryland troops; won particular distinction at Monmouth, 1778, where he played a decisive part in checking the American retreat.

RAMSEUR, STEPHEN DODSON (*b. Lincolnton, N.C., 1837; d. Winchester, Va., 1864*), Confederate major-general. Graduated West Point, 1860. Resigning from the U.S. Army, 1861, he commanded a North Carolina battery. Rising rapidly for conspicuous merit, he was wounded successively at Malvern Hill, Chancellorsville and Spotsylvania. He was mortally wounded while rallying his men against Sheridan's counterattack at Cedar Creek.

RAMSEY, ALEXANDER (*b. near Harrisburg, Pa., 1815; d. 1903*), lawyer. Congressman, Whig, from Pennsylvania, 1843–47. Removing to Minnesota, 1849, as newly appointed territorial governor, he opened an immense area in the south of the territory to settlement by negotiating treaties with the Sioux, 1851. At the end of his term, 1853, he entered business in St. Paul, Minn., and served as governor of the state, 1859–63. As U.S. senator, Republican, from Minnesota, 1863–75, he made important contributions to postal reform. He was U.S. secretary of war, 1879–81, in President R. B. Hayes's cabinet.

RAMSEY, JAMES GETTYS McGREADY (*b. near Knoxville, Tenn., 1797; d. Knoxville, 1884*), physician, banker, railroad promoter. Author of *The Annals of Tennessee to the End of the 18th Century* (1853).

RAND, ADDISON CRITTENDEN (*b. Westfield, Mass., 1841; d. New York, N.Y., 1900*), manufacturer of rock drills. Organized Rand Drill Co., 1871; was leader in inducing mining companies to substitute rock drills and air compressors for handwork.

RAND, BENJAMIN (*b. Canning, N.S., Canada, 1856; d. Canning, 1934*), bibliographer, educator. Graduated Acadia University, 1875; Ph.D., Harvard, 1885. Associated thereafter with the Harvard philosophical department as instructor and librarian until 1933, Rand made his principal contribution as a painstaking bibliographer in the field of philosophy.
[*Supp.* 1]

RAND, EDWARD SPRAGUE (*b. Newburyport, Mass., 1782; d. 1863*), merchant, New England woolen manufacturer, Massachusetts legislator.

RANDALL, ALEXANDER WILLIAMS (*b. Ames, N.Y., 1819; d. Elmira, N.Y., 1872*), lawyer. Removed to Wisconsin Territory, 1840. Originally a Whig, then a Free-Soil Democrat, he served as Republican governor of Wisconsin, 1857–61; his skill in mobilizing the state's resources for the Civil War was outstanding. As assistant postmaster-general, he helped reelect Abraham Lincoln, 1864, and was U.S. postmaster-general, 1866–69.

RANDALL, BENJAMIN (*b. New Castle, N.H., 1749; d. 1808*), founder and organizer of the Free Will Baptists.

RANDALL, BURTON ALEXANDER (*b. Annapolis, Md., 1858; d. Philadelphia, Pa., 1932*), ophthalmologist, otologist. Brother of Wyatt W. Randall. M.D., University of Pennsylvania, 1880. Practiced and taught in Philadelphia; co-author of *American Text-Book of Diseases of the Eye, Ear, Nose and Throat* (1899).

RANDALL, HENRY STEPHENS (*b. Brookfield, N.Y., 1811; d. Cortland, N.Y., 1876*), agriculturist, educator. Author of numerous books and articles dealing with agricultural subjects and of *The Life of Thomas Jefferson* (1858) for which he had the use of family manuscripts no longer accessible as a unit.

RANDALL, JAMES RYDER (*b. Baltimore, Md., 1839; d. Augusta, Ga., 1908*), journalist, poet. Attended Georgetown College, Washington, D.C. Wrote "Maryland, My Maryland!" on hearing of the attack on the 6th Massachusetts regiment as it marched through Baltimore, April 1861. The poem appeared first in the Sunday edition of the New Orleans *Delta* on April 26 and was immediately reprinted all over the South. Set to the music of an old German song, it became a battle song of the South. Randall's collected poems were published posthumously in 1910.

RANDALL, ROBERT RICHARD (*b. possibly New Jersey, c. 1750; d. New York, N.Y., 1801*), merchant, privateersman, philanthropist. Bequeathed the bulk of his property to provide an asylum for seamen to be called Sailors' Snug Harbor (presently located on Staten Island, N.Y.).

RANDALL, SAMUEL (*b. Sharon, Mass., 1778; d. 1864*), Rhode Island jurist, journalist. Graduated Brown, 1804. Notable for his authorship of two farces: *The Miser* and *The Sophomore,* both printed as pamphlets in Warren, R.I., 1812, but probably written by him while in college.

RANDALL, SAMUEL JACKSON (*b. Philadelphia, Pa., 1828; d. Washington, D.C., 1890*), businessman, politician. Congressman, Democrat, from Pennsylvania, 1863–90; speaker of the House, 1876–81; powerful chairman of the appropriations committee, 1883–87. Highly regarded by labor and small business, Randall gained national prominence during Reconstruction by uncovering scandals in the Grant administration and supplying the Democrats with the battle cry of "Retrenchment and Reform." In 1880 under his guidance the rules of procedure of the House were pruned and condensed. Falling out with President Cleveland in December 1887, Randall was deserted by his political friends and lost the federal patronage which had given him control of the Democrats in Pennsylvania.

RANDALL, SAMUEL SIDWELL (*b. Norwich, N.Y., 1809; d. 1881*), educator. Deputy superintendent of New York public schools, 1841–46, 1849–52; superintendent of New York City public schools, 1854–70. In a report to the legislature, Jan. 1, 1852, Randall made a series of recommendations for the control and financing of the public schools which were adopted and established public school education in New York State on a more efficient basis.

RANDALL, WYATT WILLIAM (*b. Annapolis, Md., 1867; d. Baltimore, Md., 1930*), chemist. Brother of Burton A. Randall. Graduated St. Johns, Annapolis, 1884; Ph.D., Johns Hopkins, 1890. Associated with the Maryland State Department of Health, 1911–30; taught biochemistry at Johns Hopkins, 1921–30. He was also consultant to the U.S. Department of Agriculture and to various agricultural associations.

RANDOLPH, ALFRED MAGILL (*b. near Winchester, Va., 1836; d. 1918*), Episcopal clergyman. Graduated William and Mary, 1855; Virginia Theological Seminary, 1858. After serving in several pastorates and as a Confederate chaplain, he was rector of Emmanuel Church, Baltimore, Md., 1867–83. A vigorous advocate of Low Church principles, he served as coadjutor bishop of Virginia, 1883–92, and as bishop of Southern Virginia, 1892–1918.

RANDOLPH, EDMUND (*b. near Williamsburg, Va., 1753; d. Clarke Co., Va., 1813*), lawyer, Virginia legislator, statesman. Grandson of Sir John Randolph; son of John Randolph (1727/28–1784); nephew of Peyton Randolph. Briefly an aide-de-camp to George Washington, 1775, he became attorney-general of Virginia, 1776, was a delegate to the Continental Congress, 1779–82, and in 1786, was elected governor of Virginia, holding that office until 1788. He was a delegate to the Annapolis Convention and to the Federal Convention of 1787 in which he proposed the Virginia Plan and also drew a draft (perhaps the first) of the work of the committee of detail of which he was a member. Declining to sign the finished Constitution because he thought it insufficiently republican, he wrote a *Letter . . . on the Federal Constitution* (1787) expressing his criticism. However, he advocated ratification in the Virginia ratification convention, 1788, on the grounds of practical expediency. First U.S. attorney-general, 1789–93, he endeavored to remain non-partisan in the conflict between Jefferson and Hamilton. Appointed U.S. secretary of state, Jan. 2, 1794, he was troubled by Hamilton's active interference in foreign affairs, but endeavored to maintain a truly American policy despite public inclination to sympathize either with France or Great Britain in the European struggle then raging. He approved sending a special envoy to Great Britain to clarify relations there, but opposed the appointment of John Jay and in particular opposed giving him the right to negotiate a commercial treaty. When Jay had accomplished his mission and when the contents of the so-called Jay Treaty were known, the French government protested that it violated treaty obligations of the United States to France. In fact, the treaty as negotiated by Jay came far short of carrying out the detailed instructions which had been given him and was unsatisfactory to the Senate and to Randolph unless it were modified. President Washington apparently supported Randolph's position in this matter up to the time when the British minister to the United States released some intercepted communications from Fauchet, the French minister at Philadelphia, to his home government. These seemed to imply that Randolph had made indiscreet revelations of information to him and appeared to suggest that French bribes would be welcome. Called to account by Washington under humiliating circumstances, Randolph resigned as secretary of state in August 1795. Later, Fauchet denied that he meant what had been said and Randolph himself wrote his own *Vindication*, published in 1795. Withdrawing to Richmond, Va., Randolph entered again upon the practice of law and became a leading legal figure; he was senior counsel for Aaron Burr in the famous treason trial of 1807.

RANDOLPH, EDMUND (*b. Richmond, Va., 1819; d. California, 1861*), lawyer. Grandson of Edmund Randolph (1753–1813). Settled in San Francisco, Calif., 1849, where he practiced with great success. He was leading counsel for the United States along with Edwin M. Stanton in the Alameden Quicksilver Mine case. A staunch defender of slavery, he somewhat inconsistently opposed secession and upheld the Union yet his last public address (1861) was a stinging attack on President Lincoln.

RANDOLPH, EDWARD (*b. Canterbury, England, c. 1632; d. 1703*), British commercial and political agent. Came to Boston, Mass., in June 1676, with orders requiring the colonial government to answer complaints of the Mason and Gorges heirs with respect to occupation of Maine and New Hampshire. Received with scant courtesy and informed that the laws of England did not apply to Massachusetts, he returned home and made a scathing report on the colonists. In consequence, Maine and New Hampshire were withdrawn from Massachusetts administration and the colony was ordered to enforce the navigation acts, to repeal all laws repugnant to English law and to cease discrimination against non-church-members in public life. Appointed to take full charge of customs collections throughout New England, 1678, Randolph settled in Boston early in 1680; receiving no help in his task from the local government, he set himself to have the Massachusetts charter annulled. Commissioned secretary of the Dominion of New England, 1685, after the charter had been declared forfeit, he became a councilor in the government under Joseph Dudley and later under Sir Edmund Andros. Imprisoned on the fall of Andros, 1689, and sent to England, he was appointed surveyor of customs for all North America, 1691. Frequently returning to England to push his plans for reorganization of colonial administration, he was in America *post* 1702. He encountered everywhere a contempt for the laws of trade and was virtually powerless to enforce them in the face of constant opposition from local judges, juries and governments. The British government acted absurdly in expecting one man to enforce the laws of trade, and Randolph's career illustrates the lack of understanding at home which eventuated in the final breakdown of imperial administration.

RANDOLPH, EPES (*b. Lunenberg, Va., 1856; d. Tucson, Ariz., 1921*), railroad executive. Early associated with Collis P. Huntington interests, especially Southern Pacific and Kentucky Central railroads; built and operated Pacific Electric Railway. Supervised Colorado River control project, 1905–07, which saved the Imperial Valley.

RANDOLPH, GEORGE WYTHE (*b. "Monticello," Virginia, 1818; d. "Edgehill," Virginia, 1867*), lawyer, Confederate brigadier-general. Grandson of Thomas Jefferson; son of Thomas M. Randolph; brother of Thomas J. Randolph. Served as Confederate secretary of war, March to November, 1862; resigned because of ill health and Jefferson Davis's dominance in the department.

RANDOLPH, ISHAM (*b. New Market, Va., 1848; d. Chicago, Ill., 1920*), civil engineer. Highly reputed as consultant in railroad, canal, and land reclamation work. Supervised construction of Chicago Drainage Canal as chief engineer of Chicago Sanitary District, 1893–1907.

RANDOLPH, JACOB (*b. Philadelphia, Pa., 1796; d. 1848*), Philadelphia surgeon. M.D., University of Pennsylvania, 1817. A generally conservative operator and teacher, he introduced lithotripsy in America at the Pennsylvania Hospital (cf. *American Journal of the Medical Sciences*, November 1834).

RANDOLPH, Sir JOHN (*b. "Turkey Island," Henrico Co., Va., c. 1693; d. 1736/37*), lawyer, scholar, Virginia legislator. Son of William Randolph; father of John Randolph (1727–1784) and Peyton Randolph. Attended Gray's Inn, London; was called to bar, 1717. Clerk of the House of Burgesses, 1718–34; served as substitute for the Crown attorney-general, 1727; represented the College of William and Mary and the Assembly on missions to King and Parliament, 1728 and 1732; was knighted, 1732. Speaker of the House of Burgesses, 1734–1736/37. The most learned Virginia lawyer of his time.

RANDOLPH, JOHN (*b. Williamsburg, Va., 1727 or 1728; d. Brompton, England, 1784*), lawyer, Loyalist. Son of Sir John Randolph; brother of Peyton Randolph. Served as clerk of the House of Burgesses; succeeded his brother as attorney-general for the Crown, 1766. After aiding Lord Dunmore in his struggle with the revolutionary party and seeking in vain to reconcile the differences between the King's government and the people, he fled to England, 1775, where he lived on a small pension.

RANDOLPH, JOHN (*b. "Cawsons," Prince George Co., Va., 1773; d. Philadelphia, Pa., 1833*), statesman, orator. Great-grandson of William Randolph; nephew of Theodorick Bland (1742–1790). Best known as John Randolph "of Roanoke," after his residence in Charlotte Co., he adopted the designation c. 1810, in order to distinguish himself from a detested distant kinsman. Capricious, thin-skinned and passionate even as a boy, he received his early education under direction of his stepfather, St. George Tucker, and at schools in Orange Co. and Williamsburg. He attended the College of New Jersey (Princeton) for a brief period, studied for a short time in New York City, and in September 1790 went to study law with Edmund Randolph in Philadelphia. After several further desultory trials of formal education, he settled at "Bizarre," Cumberland Co., 1794, and distinguished himself mainly for horsemanship, restlessness and impudent self-confidence.

From the outset of his career a Jeffersonian, or at least an opponent of the Federalists (above all things he cherished personal liberty), he was elected to Congress from Virginia in 1799. Attracting considerable attention for his extraordinary powers as a speaker and for his audacity in debate, he became chairman of the ways and means committee, 1801, and was in effect the administration leader of the House until 1805. Booted and spurred, whip in hand, he swaggered and sneered, but he was undeniably a tireless worker and a master parliamentarian. Somewhat inconsistently supporting the Louisiana Purchase, he returned to his character as a state-rights and strict-construction man in the attack on the federal judiciary. He failed in his management of the impeachment of Justice Samuel Chase, however, and suffered a loss of reputation. Prior to this, he had become disillusioned with the administration's action in the Yazoo claims matter; by his fierce denunciation of all who favored compromise, he alienated Gallatin and Madison as well as the more unscrupulous of the party leaders. He came to a definite break with his party over Jefferson's secretive efforts to acquire Florida and ranged himself in open opposition with his "Decius" letters (beginning in the Richmond *Enquirer*, August 15, 1806).

A scrupulous precisian, unwilling to make the least concession of principle to suit the exigencies of politics, Randolph continued to pour out his scorn on his opponents in Congress until 1813. He opposed the Embargo; he opposed the War of 1812. However, with the appearance on the scene of Henry Clay, John C. Calhoun and Daniel Webster, he ceased to be pre-eminent as an orator. Defeated for the 13th Congress by John W. Eppes, he returned to the House in 1815 and denounced the chartering of the second Bank of the United States, the tariff, and other nationalistic measures. Refusing to stand for the 15th Congress because of ill health, he served continuously from 1819 until 1825. With the rise of the Missouri question, he became a sectional leader, standing firmly on strict construction of the Constitution and opposing compromise as of old. He was hostile to John Q. Adams and suspicious of Henry Clay with whom he fought a duel in April 1826.

As a U.S. senator, 1825–27, he suffered from mental disorder during the first session and refrained from speaking during the second after John Tyler had been brought forward as a candidate against him. Returned to the House, 1827–29, he was leader of the opposition to John Q. Adams. As delegate to the Virginia convention of 1829–30, he opposed any significant constitutional change. Accepting appointment as U.S. minister to Russia, 1830, he was obliged to resign because of ill health when he had been less than a month at his post. After a long period of sickness and mental alienation, he died while waiting to take ship for England and was buried at "Roanoke" with his face to the West—to keep an eye on Henry Clay, it is said.

Randolph at the age of thirty already looked like an old man. He suffered from insomnia and rheumatism and died, probably, of tuberculosis. He was also impotent for the great part of his life. *Post* 1818, he was on several occasions clearly demented. A constitutional purist, a merciless hater of iniquity, a master of vituperation and an incomparable orator, he comes down in history as a champion of lost causes, one of the most pathetic as well as one of the most brilliant figures ever to appear in our national public life.

RANDOLPH, PEYTON (*b. probably "Tazewell Hall," Williamsburg, Va., c. 1721; d. Philadelphia, Pa., 1775*), lawyer, statesman. Son of Sir John Randolph; brother of John Randolph (1727–1784). Educated at William and Mary; studied law in London at the Middle Temple; called to bar, 1744 n.s. Appointed King's attorney for Virginia in 1748; served in the House of Burgesses almost continuously, 1748–75. Resigning his post as King's attorney, 1766, he became speaker of the House and held office until the Revolution. A conservative by temperament, Randolph opposed Gov. Dinwiddie on several occasions in the interest of the colonials and between 1765 and 1774 moved steadily with the current of Virginia rebel sentiment. He presided over every important Revolutionary assemblage, was appointed to the first Continental Congress, and served as its president in 1774 and 1775.

RANDOLPH, SARAH NICHOLAS (*b. Albemarle Co., Va., 1839; d. Baltimore, Md., 1892*), teacher, author. Daughter of Thomas J. Randolph. Wrote lives of Thomas J. (Stonewall) Jackson (1876) and of her great-grandfather (*Domestic Life of Thomas Jefferson*, 1871).

RANDOLPH, THEODORE FITZ (*b. New Brunswick, N.J., 1826; d. 1883*), industrialist. Conservative

Democratic governor of New Jersey, 1869–72; U.S. senator, 1875–81.

RANDOLPH, THOMAS JEFFERSON (*b. "Monticello," Va., 1792; d. "Edgehill," Va., 1875*), planter, financier, Virginia legislator. Grandson of Thomas Jefferson; son of Thomas M. Randolph. Served as chief executor of his grandfather's estate; edited first published collection of his grandfather's writings, *Memoir, Correspondence, and Miscellanies from the Papers of Thomas Jefferson* (1829).

RANDOLPH, THOMAS MANN (*b. Goochland Co., Va., 1768; d. 1828*), Virginia planter and legislator. Son-in-law of Thomas Jefferson; father of Thomas J. Randolph and George W. Randolph. Brilliant but impractical and rash, he represented Virginia in Congress, 1803–07, and was governor of the state, 1819–22. He enjoyed some repute as a botanist.

RANDOLPH, WILLIAM (*b. Warwickshire, England, c. 1651; d. 1711*), planter, merchant, colonial official. Father of Sir John Randolph; grandfather of John Randolph (1727–1784) and Peyton Randolph. Came to Virginia *c.* 1673. By 1705, he had acquired vast tracts of land and had become one of the leading planters in the colony. Among the many civil and military posts which he held were those of speaker of the House of Burgesses, 1696 and 1698, and attorney-general for the Crown, 1694–98.

RANEY, GEORGE PETTUS (*b. Apalachicola, Fla., 1845; d. 1911*), lawyer, Confederate soldier, Florida Democratic legislator. State attorney-general, 1877–85; associate justice, state supreme court, 1885–89, and chief justice, 1889–94.

RANGER, HENRY WARD (*b. Syracuse, N.Y., 1858; d. New York, N.Y., 1916*), landscape painter, of interest for his experiments with pigments and varnishes.

RANKIN, JEREMIAH EAMES (*b. Thornton, N.H., 1828; d. Cleveland, O., 1904*), Congregational clergyman. Graduated Middlebury College, 1848; Andover Seminary, 1854. President of Howard University, 1889–1903; author, among other hymns, of "God be with you till we meet again."

RANKIN, McKEE (*b. Sandwich, Ontario, Canada, 1844; d. 1914*), actor, theatrical manager. Played *post* 1865 with leading stock companies; was particularly effective in melodrama. Managed, and played leads to, Nance O'Neill.

RANKINE, WILLIAM BIRCH (*b. Owego, N.Y., 1858; d. 1905*), lawyer, "father of Niagara power." Gave full time *post* 1890 to the development of the Niagara Falls power project; was head executive of its operating department *post* 1897.

RANNEY, AMBROSE LOOMIS (*b. Hardwick, Mass., 1848; d. 1905*), physician. Graduated Dartmouth, 1868; M.D., University of the City of New York, 1871. Taught anatomy at his *alma mater* and at New

York Post-Graduate. Author of authoritative papers on eye-strain as the cause of functional nervous disease and other disorders.

RANNEY, RUFUS PERCIVAL (*b. Blandford, Mass., 1813; d. Cleveland, O., 1891*), Ohio jurist, Democratic politician. State supreme court judge, 1851–56, 1862–64.

RANNEY, WILLIAM TYLEE (*b. Middletown, Conn., 1813; d. West Hoboken, N.J., 1857*), historical and genre painter of the life of the American frontier, notably of the old Southwest.

RANSOHOFF, JOSEPH (*b. Cincinnati, O., 1853; d. Cincinnati, 1921*), surgeon. M.D., Medical College of Ohio, 1874; studied also in England, France and Germany and was made fellow of the Royal College of Surgeons, 1877. Taught at the Medical College of Ohio *post* 1877; was among first in America to operate on gall bladder and kidney; contributed prolifically to professional journals.

RANSOM, MATT WHITAKER (*b. Warren Co., N.C., 1826; d. 1904*), lawyer, Confederate soldier, North Carolina official and legislator. A Whig before the Civil War, he was a Democrat after it and served as U.S. senator from North Carolina, 1873–95. He was a leader in securing the compromise of 1876–77 by which the disputed presidential election was peacefully settled and in the defeat of the Lodge "Force Bill," 1890. As U.S. minister to Mexico, 1895–97, he arbitrated disputes between that country and Guatemala.

RANSOM, THOMAS EDWARD GREENFIELD (*b. Norwich, Vt., 1834; d. near Rome, Ga., 1864*), Union soldier, civil engineer. Removed to Illinois *c.* 1851. At outbreak of Civil War he became lieutenant-colonel, 11th Illinois Infantry, and brought the regiment to a high state of discipline and training; it served with particular distinction at Fort Donelson and Shiloh. Appointed brigadier-general, he distinguished himself in the Vicksburg campaign and in an expedition against Natchez so as to win the particular praise of Gen. Grant. After service in Texas and Arkansas, he was assigned to command the 4th Division, XVI Corps, under Sherman and was again outstanding in the Atlanta campaign. He died while in command of the XVII Corps, after pursuing the army of Confederate Gen. John Hood across north Georgia. He was reputed one of the most capable volunteer soldiers developed in the Civil War.

RANSOME, FREDERICK LESLIE (*b. Greenwich, England, 1868; d. Pasadena, Calif., 1935*), geologist. Emigrated to California as a small child. Graduated University of California, 1893; Ph.D., 1896. An active staff member of the U.S. Geological Survey, 1897–1923, Ransome taught thereafter at the University of Arizona and at the California Institute of Technology. He was author of a veritable library of monographs on important mining districts and on problems of water control. [*Supp. 1*]

RANTOUL, ROBERT (*b. Salem, Mass., 1778; d. Beverly, Mass., 1858*), apothecary, public official, reformer. Father of Robert Rantoul (1805–1852). Opposed the growth of corporations as inimical to liberty and equality; advocated temperance, international peace and abolition of capital punishment.

RANTOUL, ROBERT (*b. Beverly, Mass., 1805; d. 1852*), lawyer, reformer. Son of Robert Rantoul (1778–1858). Graduated Harvard, 1826. A Jacksonian Democrat and a liberal Unitarian, he furthered a number of humanitarian causes as a Massachusetts legislator; these included the abolition of the death penalty, the extension of the public school system and control of the liquor interests. The Massachusetts supreme court upheld in 1842 his reasoning in defense of journeymen bootmakers charged with unlawful conspiracy in organizing to compel collective bargaining (*Commonwealth vs. Hunt and Others*); he also served as counsel for Rhode Islanders indicted in connection with the Dorr rebellion. Elected to Congress, 1851, by a coalition between Free-Soilers and Democrats, he was chosen to the U.S. Senate in the same year to fill out Daniel Webster's term. His early death was a great loss to the anti-slavery Democrats and to liberal reform.

RAPHALL, MORRIS JACOB (*b. Stockholm, Sweden, 1798; d. 1868*), rabbi, author. Raised in Denmark and England; rabbi of Birmingham Hebrew Congregation, 1841–49. Came to New York, 1849, as preacher to Congregation B'nai Jeshurun and officiated until 1865. He was the first Jew to open a session of the House of Representatives with prayer (Feb. 1, 1860), and a champion of orthodox Judaism in America against the growing encroachments of reform.

RAPP, GEORGE (*b. Iptingen, Württemberg, 1757; d. Economy, Pa., 1847*), religious leader, founder of the Harmony Society. A student of the Bible and of the German mystics, Rapp became leader of a group of separatists in Germany which for a number of years was subject to much petty persecution. Purchasing unimproved land in Butler Co., Pa., 1803, Rapp and some of his followers built the town of Harmony where early in 1805 the rest of his group joined them. The Harmony Society was a communistic theocracy under Rapp as dictator; it was one of the most successful of the more than 200 communistic societies that have sprung up in the United States. Established at Harmony, Ind., 1814–24, the community returned to Pennsylvania and made their last settlement at Economy on the Ohio River below Pittsburgh.

RAPP, WILHELM (*b. Perouse, Württemberg, 1827; d. Chicago, Ill., 1907*), German language journalist. Came to America, 1852, after involvement in German revolutionary activity; worked as editor of several newspapers, notably of *Der Wecker*, Baltimore, Md., and the *Illinois Staats-Zeitung*.

RAREY, JOHN SOLOMON (*b. Groveport, O., 1827; d. 1866*), horse tamer of international celebrity.

RASLE, SÉBASTIEN. [See RÂLE, SÉBASTIEN, d. 1724.]

RATHBONE, JUSTUS HENRY (*b. Deerfield, N.Y., 1839; d. Lima, O., 1889*), teacher, government clerk. Founded fraternal order of the Knights of Pythias in Washington, D.C., 1864.

RATHBUN, RICHARD (*b. Buffalo, N.Y., 1852; d. 1918*), zoologist. Served on Geological Commission of Brazil and on U.S. Fish Commission; was on staff of National Museum and the Smithsonian. Rathbun wrote copiously on marine invertebrates and on the economic aspects of marine biology.

RATTERMANN, HEINRICH ARMIN (*b. near Osnabrück, Germany, 1832; d. 1923*), insurance executive, historian, man of letters. Came to Cincinnati, O., as a boy. Established German Mutual Fire Insurance Co., 1858. Promoted musical and cultural activities in Cincinnati; became authority on pioneer German settlers in the United States.

RAU, CHARLES (*b. Verviers, Belgium, 1826; d. Washington, D.C., 1887*), archaeologist. Came to America, 1848; was associated *post* 1875 with the U.S. National Museum, acting as curator of the department of archaeology, 1881–87. Considered the foremost American archaeologist of his time, he was the first in America to recognize the importance of the study of aboriginal technology and was the author of many contributions to scholarly journals.

RAUCH, FREDERICK AUGUSTUS (*b. Kirchbracht, Prussia, 1806; d. Mercersburg, Pa., 1841*), philosopher, educator. Educated at Marburg, Giessen and Heidelberg. Came to America as a political refugee, 1831; was ordained to German Reformed ministry, 1832; after seminary teaching at York, Pa., he was organizer and first president of Marshall College, 1836–41. Author of *Psychology or a View of the Human Soul* (1840), an important work.

RAUCH, JOHN HENRY (*b. Lebanon, Pa., 1828; d. Lebanon, 1894*), physician. M.D., University of Pennsylvania, 1849. Practiced in Iowa, 1850–56, and thereafter (excepting Civil War service) in Chicago. Promoted higher medical education and standards of practice as first president of Illinois State Board of Health and member, 1877–91.

RAUE, CHARLES GOTTLIEB (*b. near Loebau, Saxony, 1820; d. Philadelphia, Pa., 1896*), homeopathic physician.

RAUM, GREEN BERRY (*b. Golconda, Ill., 1829; d. Chicago, Ill., 1909*), Union soldier, lawyer, Illinois Republican congressman and politician.

RAUSCHENBUSCH, WALTER (*b. Rochester, N.Y., 1861; d. Rochester, 1918*), Baptist clergyman, educator. Graduated University of Rochester, 1884; Rochester Theological Seminary, 1886. Pastor, Second German Baptist Church, New York City, 1886–97. Influenced by the sufferings of his parishioners during a time of depression and by the ideas of the Fabian socialists, he became an influential figure in the development in the United States of what has been called the "social gospel." Professor of New Testament interpretation at Rochester Seminary, 1897–1902, he was professor of church history thereafter until his death. Among his books, his *Christianity and the Social Crisis* (1907) was outstanding.

RAVALLI, ANTONIO (*b. Ferrara, Italy, 1811; d. 1884*), Roman Catholic clergyman, Jesuit missionary. Came to work among the Indians of the region that is now Montana, 1844, in response to an appeal of Father P.-J. De Smet. A skilled mechanic and builder as well as an artist, and also a physician, he worked until his death among the Indians and settlers of Montana with the exception of the years 1860–63.

RAVENEL, EDMUND (*b. Charleston, S.C., 1797; d. Charleston, 1871*), physician, planter, naturalist. M.D., University of Pennsylvania, 1819. Made a remarkable collection of marine shells of which he issued a catalogue, 1834, said to have been the first in the United States. Author of *Echinidae . . . of South Carolina* (1848) and other studies.

RAVENEL, HARRIOTT HORRY RUTLEDGE (*b. Charleston, S.C., 1832; d. Charleston, 1912*), author. Granddaughter of William Lowndes; married St. Julien Ravenel, 1851. Published *Eliza Pinckney* (1896), *Charleston, the Place and the People* (1906), and other works.

RAVENEL, HENRY WILLIAM (*b. Berkeley Co., S.C., 1814; d. Aiken, S.C., 1887*), planter, botanist, agricultural writer. Leading authority on American fungi; collected an extensive herbarium of fungi, mosses and lichens.

RAVENEL, ST. JULIEN (*b. Charleston, S.C., 1819; d. 1882*), physician, Confederate soldier and surgeon, agricultural chemist. Nephew of Edmund Ravenel. Originated process for manufacture of ammoniated and acid fertilizers from phosphate deposits along Ashley and Cooper rivers, South Carolina, c. 1867. Worked on soil-restoration problems.

RAVENSCROFT, JOHN STARK (*b. near Petersburg, Va., 1772; d. Raleigh, N.C., 1830*), planter, Episcopal clergyman. Ordained, 1817, after a late conversion; consecrated first bishop of North Carolina, 1823; built up a strong conservative body of clergy and laity before resigning his charge, 1828.

RAVOUX, AUGUSTIN (*b. Langeac, France, 1815; d. St. Paul, Minn., 1906*), Roman Catholic clergyman. Volunteered for mission work, 1838; came to

Dubuque, Iowa, and was ordained there, 1840. Served Sioux missions on the St. Peter's (present Minnesota) River, 1841–44; was pastor for entire area on Mississippi River headwaters, 1844–51. Worked thereafter in many capacities in the diocese of St. Paul.

RAWLE, FRANCIS (*b. probably Plymouth, England, c. 1662; d. Philadelphia, Pa., 1726/27*), merchant, political economist. After imprisonment as a Quaker, he emigrated to Pennsylvania, 1686. Member of the Assembly, 1704–09 and 1719–1726/27, Rawle was a leader in the anti-proprietary party. A mercantilist in theory, he was author of *Some Remedies Proposed for the Restoring the Sunk Credit of the Province of Pennsylvania* (1721) and *Ways and Means for the Inhabitants of Delaware to Become Rich* (1725).

RAWLE, FRANCIS (*b. Freedom Forge, Pa., 1846; d. 1930*), Philadelphia lawyer. Grandson of William Rawle. A founder of the American Bar Association, 1878; edited revisions of Bouvier's *Law Dictionary* (1883, 1897, 1914).

RAWLE, WILLIAM (*b. Philadelphia, Pa., 1759; d. Philadelphia, 1836*), lawyer, philanthropist. Greatgrandson of Francis Rawle (*c. 1662–1726/27*). A Loyalist, he studied law at the Middle Temple, London. Returning to Philadelphia after the Revolution, he served as U.S. attorney for Pennsylvania, 1791–99, and practiced in the city thereafter. He was active in many civic and cultural enterprises, advocated abolition of slavery and was a devout Quaker; among his many writings, his *View of the Constitution of the United States* (1825) was outstanding. He was a member of the commission to revise the Pennsylvania statutes, 1830–34.

RAWLE, WILLIAM HENRY (*b. Philadelphia, Pa., 1823; d. 1889*), Philadelphia lawyer, Union soldier, legal author and editor. Grandson of William Rawle.

RAWLINS, JOHN AARON (*b. Galena, Ill., 1831; d. Washington, D.C., 1869*), lawyer, Union soldier. Appointed aide-de-camp to Gen. U. S. Grant, 1861, he remained constantly with him as principal staff officer and intimate adviser, exercising his influence with great tact and ability. Promoted brigadier-general, 1863, he was made brevet major-general and chief of staff of the army, 1865. Long in failing health, he served briefly as U.S. secretary of war, 1869.

RAWLINSON, FRANK JOSEPH (*b. Langham, England, 1871; d. Shanghai, China, 1937*), Baptist and Congregational clergyman. Emigrated to America, 1889. Graduated Bucknell, 1899; Rochester Theological Seminary, 1902. Missionary to China, 1902–22, as a Baptist. He served thereafter as a Congregational missionary-at-large and editor. [*Supp. 2*]

RAY, CHARLES BENNETT (*b. Falmouth, Mass., 1807; d. 1886*), Methodist and Congregational clergyman, pioneer Negro journalist, anti-slavery worker. Published and edited the *Colored American*, 1838–42; was Congregational pastor and missionary in New York City *post* 1846.

RAY, ISAAC (*b. Beverly, Mass., 1807; d. Philadelphia, Pa., 1881*), psychiatrist. M.D., Bowdoin, 1827. Headed Butler Hospital, Providence, R.I., 1846–66; practiced thereafter in Philadelphia. A leader in his specialty, he was author of *A Treatise on the Medical Jurisprudence of Insanity* (1838), *Mental Hygiene* (1863) and many other works.

RAYMOND, BENJAMIN WRIGHT (*b. Rome, N.Y., 1801; d. 1883*), Chicago merchant and capitalist. Removed to Chicago, Ill., 1836. As mayor, 1839 and 1842, he brought the city through effects of depression of 1837–39 and donated his salary to the unemployed. Active in many businesses *post* 1843, including real estate, railroad promotion and watch manufacturing, he laid out the town of Lake Forest.

RAYMOND, CHARLES WALKER (*b. Hartford, Conn., 1842; d. 1913*), military engineer. Brother of Rossiter W. Raymond. Graduated West Point, 1865; retired as brigadier-general, 1904. Made survey and map of Yukon River, 1869; supervised many important river and harbor improvements; was chairman, board of engineers for constructing Pennsylvania Railroad tunnels under Hudson River.

RAYMOND, DANIEL (*b. in or near New Haven, Conn., 1786; d. 1849 ?*), lawyer, economist. Studied law under Tapping Reeve. Settled in Baltimore, Md., *c.* 1814; removed to Cincinnati, O., *post* 1840. Author of *Thoughts on Political Economy* (1820, supplemented in the fourth edition, 1840, by *Elements of Constitutional Law*), *The Missouri Question* (1819), and *The American System* (1828). Opposing classical *laissez-faire* in principle, Raymond distinguished between individual wealth, i.e., the sum of individual riches, and national wealth which he considered the development of economic capacities; he believed that political economy was concerned less with property than with productive power and that national prosperity required a liberal measure of deliberate economic control. Convinced that social principles are always relative to place and time, he based his thought on the American economic environment; it is probable that Georg F. List and John Rae were influenced by him.

RAYMOND, GEORGE LANSING (*b. Chicago, Ill., 1839; d. 1929*), Presbyterian clergyman, educator. Son of Benjamin W. Raymond. Graduated Williams, 1862; Princeton Theological Seminary, 1865. Taught rhetoric at Williams; professor of aesthetics and oratory at Princeton, 1880–1905; professor of aesthetics at George Washington University, 1905–12. Author of a number of studies, issued in a uniform edition as *Comparative Aesthetics* (1909).

RAYMOND, HARRY HOWARD (*b. Yarmouth, N.S., Canada, 1864; d. 1935*), steamship line executive. Came to the United States, 1884; was long associated with the Mallory and Clyde companies and with the Atlantic, Gulf & West Indies lines. [*Supp.* 1]

RAYMOND, HENRY JARVIS (*b. Lima, N.Y., 1820; d. 1869*), editor, politician. Graduated University of Vermont, 1840. Removing to New York City, he worked for Horace Greeley on the *New Yorker* and became his chief assistant on the *New York Tribune*, 1841. Shifting to the *Morning Courier*, 1843, he grew in professional reputation. Also a Whig politician, he was elected to the N.Y. Assembly, 1849, and chosen speaker, 1851. His alignment with the Free-Soil group led by W. H. Seward and Thurlow Weed cost him his post with the *Courier*. In association with George Jones (1811–1891), with whom he had become friendly at the *Tribune*, he established the *New York Daily Times* (so-called until 1857). In its first issue (Sept. 18, 1851), he declared that "we do not mean to write as if we were in a passion—unless that shall really be the case; and we shall make it a point to get into a passion as rarely as possible." This substitution of moderation and reason for intemperate partisanship brought the *Times* immediate success at the *Tribune's* expense. Though irked by the Whig refusal to face the realities of the slavery issue, Raymond could not bring himself to leave the party until 1856. Meanwhile his nomination for lieutenant-governor of New York, 1854, had mortally offended Greeley and made that formidable editor the political enemy of W. H. Seward.

Raymond wrote the Republican statement of principles at the founding of the national party, 1856; thereafter the *Times* was Republican. He discussed the crucial issues of 1860 in a notable series of open letters to W. L. Yancey (published as *Disunion and Slavery*) and was a steadfast supporter of Abraham Lincoln. As active in politics as in journalism, he was again speaker of the New York Assembly, 1862. In 1864 he played a chief part in Andrew Johnson's nomination for the vice-presidency at Baltimore and was named Republican national chairman; he also ran for Congress and was elected.

As administration leader in the House, Raymond was a complete failure. Championing the moderate Reconstruction policies of President Johnson, he was completely out-generaled by Thaddeus Stevens and the Radicals and acted with hesitation and inconsistency. When the president tried to organize a National Union coalition of conservative Republicans and War Democrats, Raymond supported its purposes in the *Times* but opposed formation of a new party as such. He attended the National Union Convention at Philadelphia, August 1866, pleading for harmony and intelligent action, but the Radicals carried the day and he was their first victim. Expelled from the national committee, he declined renomination for Congress. After the failure of an attempt by him and Weed to form a Union bloc of moderates in New York State, he ceased to struggle against the inevitable. In the campaign of 1868, the *Times* supported the Republicans but the tendency of the paper was increasingly less partisan. Raymond began the *Times* campaign (later brilliantly concluded by George Jones) against the "Tweed Ring" and advocated sound money, tariff reduction and civil-service reform.

Raymond's contribution to journalism was the substitution of decency for personal invective and fairness for black-and-white partisanship. He was one of the earliest and greatest of local reporters, with a prodigious speed and accuracy that became legendary. His editorials were lucid and persuasive, but they usually lacked the smashing force that some of his contemporaries derived from conviction of their own utter rightness and the wickedness of those who held divergent views. He once said that when he wrote a sentence he could not help seeing before he got to the end how only partially true it was. This trait and lack of a realistic appraisal of public opinion were his fatal weaknesses as a politician. His misfortune was not only that he was a temperamental non-partisan in an age of bitter partisanship, but that he was a temperamental non-partisan incurably addicted to party politics.

RAYMOND, JOHN HOWARD (*b. New York, N.Y., 1814; d. Poughkeepsie, N.Y., 1878*), educator. Graduated Union, 1832; Madison University (present Colgate) Seminary, 1838. Taught at Madison and at Rochester. First president, Brooklyn Polytechnic, 1855–64; thereafter president and academic organizer of Vassar College, for the success of which he was largely responsible.

RAYMOND, JOHN T. (*b. Buffalo, N.Y., 1836; d. Evansville, Ind., 1887*), comedian. Stage name of John O'Brien. Relied for effects on facial and physical eccentricities; was identified with role of Col. Mulberry Sellers in *The Gilded Age*, post 1873.

RAYMOND, MINER (*b. New York, N.Y., 1811; d. 1897*), Methodist clergyman, theologian. Principal of Wesleyan Academy (Wilbraham, Mass.), 1848–64; professor, Garrett Biblical Institute, Evanston, Ill., 1864–95. Author of *Systematic Theology* (1877).

RAYMOND, ROSSITER WORTHINGTON (*b. Cincinnati, O., 1840; d. Brooklyn, N.Y., 1918*), mining engineer, editor. Brother of Charles W. Raymond. U.S. commissioner of mining statistics, 1868–76; was long associated with *American Journal of Mining* and with Cooper, Hewitt & Co. Secretary, American Institute of Mining Engineers, 1884–1911.

RAYNER, ISIDOR (*b. Baltimore, Md., 1850; d. Washington, D.C., 1912*), lawyer, legislator. Congressman, Democrat, from Maryland, 1887–89, 1891–95. After attracting national attention as counsel for

Adm. W. S. Schley in the Santiago inquiry, he was U.S. senator from Maryland, 1905–12.

RAYNER, KENNETH (*b. Bertie Co., N.C., c. 1810; d. 1884*), planter, North Carolina legislator and Whig congressman. An enthusiastic Know-Nothing in the middle 1850's, he verged from aggressive Unionism to whole-hearted secessionism between 1855 and 1861; by 1863, he was engaging in secret moves for peace. Removing to Tennessee, 1869, and later to Mississippi, he became a Republican. He was a judge of the *Alabama* claims commission, 1874–77, and solicitor of the U.S. treasury thereafter until his death.

REA, SAMUEL (*b. Hollidaysburg, Pa., 1855; d. Gladwyne, Pa., 1929*), civil engineer, expert in railroad construction and finance. President, Pennsylvania Railroad, 1913–25.

REACH, ALFRED JAMES (*b. London, England, 1840; d. Atlantic City, N.J., 1928*), baseball player, sporting-goods manufacturer.

READ, CHARLES (*b. Philadelphia, Pa., c. 1713; d. Martinburg, N.C., 1774*), colonial New Jersey lawyer, land speculator, ironmaster and official. A powerful figure in New Jersey, 1747–71, Read came on evil days and died as a small shopkeeper. He was notable as an agricultural experimenter and as a pioneer in the bog-iron industry and held a dominant position in New Jersey politics.

READ, CHARLES WILLIAM (*b. Yazoo Co., Miss., 1840; d. Meridian, Miss., 1890*), Confederate naval officer. Graduated U.S. Naval Academy, 1860; entered Confederate service, April 1861. As junior officer in Mississippi River campaigns, 1861–62, and as lieutenant commanding several commerce raiders, 1863–65, Read made a record of active service unsurpassed by any of his rank, North or South.

READ, DANIEL (*b. Rehoboth, present Attleboro, Mass., 1757; d. New Haven, Conn., 1836*), musician, composer. Partner in publishing business of Amos Doolittle. Author of *The American Singing Book* (1785), *An Introduction to Psalmody* (1790), *The Columbian Harmonist* (1793), and others; edited *The American Musical Magazine*, 1786–87, first periodical of its kind.

READ, DANIEL (*b. near Marietta, O., 1805; d. Keokuk, Iowa, 1878*), educator. Graduated Ohio University, 1824. Taught at Ohio, Indiana State and University of Wisconsin; modernized and expanded University of Missouri as president, 1867–76.

READ, GEORGE (*b. near North East, Md., 1733; d. 1798*), lawyer, statesman. Raised in New Castle, Del., where he practiced law *post* 1754; served as attorney-general for the Lower Counties, 1763–74, and as a provincial assemblyman. A moderate Whig, much like his friend John Dickinson, he was a member of the First Continental Congress and of the

Second Congress until 1777. Refusing to vote for the resolution of independence on July 2, 1776, he signed the Declaration and upheld it following its adoption. Dominant in the Delaware constitutional convention, 1776, he was elected to the legislative council and became its speaker and vice-president of the state; he was acting president, November 1777 to March 1778. Resigning in 1779, he returned to the council, 1782–88. Jealous of the power that might be exerted by the larger states, he disapproved of some provisions of the Articles of Confederation; later, as a delegate to the federal convention, he was outspoken in defence of the rights of the smaller states. He finally accepted the compromise on representation, however, and largely through his efforts Delaware was the first state to ratify the U.S. Constitution. U.S. senator, Federalist, 1789–93, he was thereafter chief justice of Delaware.

READ, GEORGE CAMPBELL (*b. Ireland, 1787; d. Philadelphia, Pa., 1862*), naval officer. Served with credit aboard *Constitution* and *United States* in War of 1812; bombarded Quallah Battoo, Sumatra, 1838, in reprisal for plunder of an American merchant ship by the natives.

READ, GEORGE WINDLE (*b. Indianola, Iowa, 1860; d. Washington, D.C., 1934*), army officer. Graduated West Point, 1883. Showed marked abilities as a colonial administrator in Cuba and the Philippines; organized and commanded the II Army Corps in World War I; retired as major-general, 1924.

[*Supp. 1*]

READ, JACOB (*b. "Hobcaw," Christ Church Parish, S.C., 1752; d. Charleston, S.C., 1816*), Revolutionary soldier, lawyer, South Carolina legislator and congressman. Speaker of South Carolina House of Representatives, 1787–94; U.S. senator, Federalist, 1795–1801. One of the "midnight" judges of 1801.

READ, JOHN (*b. Fairfield, Conn., 1679/80; d. 1749*), lawyer. Graduated Harvard, 1697. After an early trial of the ministry, he was admitted to the Connecticut bar, 1708; he removed to Boston, Mass., 1721. Elected attorney-general of the province repeatedly *post* 1721, he served only in 1723, 1726 and 1734 because of a dispute between governor and legislature over the right to appoint to this office. First lawyer to represent Boston in the General Court (1738) under the second charter, Read served on the Governor's Council, 1741–42. Outstanding as a counsel in his time, he had a great influence on the development of New England legal practices and in particular on the modernizing and simplifying of forms. He also engaged in extensive real-estate transactions.

READ, JOHN (*b. New Castle, Del., 1769; d. Trenton, N.J., 1854*), lawyer. Son of George Read; father of John M. Read (1797–1874). Practiced in Philadelphia *post* 1792; was active in the city's political and social life.

READ, JOHN MEREDITH (*b. Philadelphia, Pa., 1797; d. 1874*), jurist. Grandson of George Read; son of John Read; father of John M. Read (1837–1896). U.S. district attorney for eastern Pennsylvania, 1837–41; attorney-general of Pennsylvania, 1846; Pennsylvania supreme court justice, 1858–73 (chief justice, 1872–73). Opposed extension of slavery; was an early adherent of the Republican party.

READ, JOHN MEREDITH (*b. Philadelphia, Pa., 1837; d. Paris, France, 1896*), lawyer, diplomat. Son of John M. Read (1797–1874). U.S. consul general at Paris, 1869–73; U.S. minister resident in Greece, 1873–79.

READ, NATHAN (*b. Warren, Mass., 1759; d. Belfast, Maine, 1849*), iron manufacturer. Graduated Harvard, 1781; taught there, 1783–87. Settling as an apothecary in Salem, Mass., he conducted experiments on the application of the steam engine to land and water transportation. Having designed a multitubular steam boiler and an improved double-acting engine and also a form of paddle wheel, he petitioned Congress in 1790 for a patent on these plans for a steamboat, and also for a steam road carriage. In August 1791 he was granted a patent for the boiler and the engine and for a chain wheel method of propelling boats which he had added to his earlier application. Unable to secure financial help in building a vessel, he dropped his plans and engaged in iron manufacturing and farming.

READ, OPIE POPE (*b. Nashville, Tenn., 1852; d. Chicago, Ill., 1939*), author, humorist. After experience as a journalist in Tennessee, Arkansas and Kentucky, Read founded the *Arkansaw Traveler* in Little Rock, 1882, a humorous weekly which became one of the most widely quoted papers in America. Relinquishing editorship, 1891, he concentrated on fiction, turning out some forty novels and collections of humorous stories and was in his later years a great favorite on the Chautauqua and lecture circuits. His work enjoyed great success, 1890–1900; one of his books, *The Jucklins* (1896), was said to have sold over a million copies. [*Supp. 2*]

READ, THOMAS (*b. Newcastle Co., Del., c. 1740; d. Fieldsboro, N.J., 1788*), naval officer. Brother of George Read. Served with ability in both the Pennsylvania and the Continental navies, 1775–79, and as a privateer; sailed the frigate *Alliance* from Philadelphia to Canton, China, 1787–88, in a remarkably fast voyage by a new route.

READ, THOMAS BUCHANAN (*b. near Guthriesville, Pa., 1822; d. New York, N.Y., 1872*), painter, poet. Assisted Shobal V. Clevenger in Cincinnati, O.; worked as an itinerant portrait painter; was helped by Nicholas Longworth. Won success in Boston *post*

1841; removed to Philadelphia, 1846; resided in Florence, Italy, 1853–55 and in Rome, Italy, 1866–72. He published a number of volumes of verse which were extravagantly praised at the time, but his work was derivative and unpolished; of his shorter pieces, "Drifting" and "Sheridan's Ride" are alone remembered. His work as a painter was merely competent.

READE, EDWIN GODWIN (*b. Mount Tirzah, N.C., 1812; d. 1894*), lawyer, North Carolina supreme court justice, banker.

REAGAN, JOHN HENNINGER (*b. Sevier Co., Tenn., 1818; d. 1905*), surveyor, lawyer, Texas jurist, Confederate official. Congressman, moderate Democrat, from Texas, 1857–61. Member of the secession convention of Texas, 1861, and of the provisional Congress of the Confederacy, he was appointed Confederate postmaster-general, March 1861, and served until the close of the Civil War. Advising Texans to accept the results of the war, acknowledge the extinction of slavery, and admit Negroes to civil rights lest the state suffer the evils of military government, he lost political standing in the state but by 1875 had recovered his position and was returned to Congress. In the House of Representatives, 1875–87, he stood for orthodox Democratic policies and was for ten years chairman of the committee on commerce. He was U.S. senator, 1887–91, and in the latter year accepted the chairmanship of the Texas railroad commission which he held until 1903. His greatest service in Congress was the joint authorship and advocacy of the bill to establish the Interstate Commerce Commission (1887).

REALF, RICHARD (*b. Framfield, England, 1834; d. Oakland, Calif., 1878*), Abolitionist, Union soldier, journalist, poet. Came to America, 1854; was a newspaper correspondent in Kansas, 1856. Associated with John Brown (1800–1859), he was a prominent member of Brown's convention at Chatham, Canada, May 1858, and was chosen secretary of state in the mysterious scheme of government which Brown hoped to establish. A tragic figure, he died a suicide; his poems were collected and published as a book in 1898.

REAM, NORMAN BRUCE (*b. Somerset Co., Pa., 1844; d. 1915*), capitalist. Settling in Chicago, Ill., 1871, he became a successful speculator in livestock and grain. Removing to New York City, 1895, he was an associate of the elder J. P. Morgan and others in corporate reorganizations and mergers, notably of the Baltimore & Ohio Railroad, the National Biscuit Co. and the Federal Steel Co.

RECTOR, HENRY MASSEY (*b. Louisville, Ky., 1816; d. 1899*), planter, lawyer. Removed to Arkansas *c.* 1835 where he served in the legislature and as a judge of the supreme court. An active secessionist, he was Democratic governor of Arkansas, 1860–62.

RED CLOUD (*b. Blue Creek, Nebr., 1822; d. Pine Ridge, S.D., 1909*), chief of the Oglala Sioux. A noted warrior, Red Cloud took his band of hostile Sioux and Cheyenne on the war path, 1866, in protest against the opening of the Bozeman Trail and the building of forts along it in Sioux territory. He commanded the Indian forces at the Fetterman massacre, December 1866, and at the Wagon Box fight, August 1867. His able and resolute campaign induced the government to yield. The trail was closed by the treaty of 1868 and the three forts abandoned. Although a persistent critic of the government and of its Indian agents whom he charged with fraud, he was an advocate of peace thereafter.

RED EAGLE. [See WEATHERFORD, WILLIAM, 1765–1824.]

RED JACKET (*b. probably Canoga, present Seneca Co., N.Y., c. 1758; d. 1830*), Seneca chief. Indian name, Sagoyewatha. Skilled in oratory and political trickery, he played for popularity in his tribe, 1779–90, by attacking the unsuccessful policy of Cornplanter and other leaders and by haranguing against the whites and peace. Once his position as a chief among the Iroquois was assured, he worked for peace with the United States and avoidance of trouble with the British, hoping thus to maintain the independence of his people. Bitterly opposed to any encroachment of white civilization, he was at the height of his power, 1815–25. As the Christian party among the Senecas grew and because of his own increasing addiction to drink, he gradually lost influence.

RED WING (*b. probably near present Red Wing, Minn., c. 1750; d. place unknown, c. 1825*), chief of the Khemnichan band of Mdewakanton Sioux. Outstanding as a warrior, he adopted a policy of peace *post* 1814.

REDFIELD, AMASA ANGELL (*b. Clyde, N.Y., 1837; d. Farmington, Conn., 1902*), lawyer. Practiced *post* 1862 in New York City; was an authority on surrogate practice and on negligence. Author, among other works, of *Law and Practice of Surrogates' Courts* (1875) and *A Treatise on the Law of Negligence* (with T. G. Shearman, 1869).

REDFIELD, ISAAC FLETCHER (*b. Weathersfield, Vt., 1804; d. Charlestown, Mass., 1876*), lawyer. Vermont supreme court justice, 1835–60 (chief justice, 1852–60). Author of *Practical Treatise upon the Law of Railways* (1858), *The Law of Wills* (1864–70), *The Law of Carriers* (1869) and other works. He was associated with Caleb Cushing, 1867–69, as a special U.S. counsel in Civil War claims cases against Great Britain.

REDFIELD, JUSTUS STARR (*b. Wallingford, Conn. 1810; d. Florence, N.J., 1888*), publisher. A successful printer and general publisher in New York City, 1841–60, he brought out collected editions of au-

thors, among them W. G. Simms, and the 1850–56 edition of Edgar A. Poe.

REDFIELD, WILLIAM C. (*b. Middletown, Conn., 1789; d. New York, N.Y., 1857*), saddler, meteorologist, transportation promoter. Observing the "great September gale," 1821, in western Massachusetts, Redfield explained the nature of such storms in a meteorological classic "Observations on the Hurricanes and Storms of the West Indies and the Coast of the United States" (*American Journal of Science and Arts,* October 1833). This article and a previous one in the same periodical, 1831, were the first of any importance on their subject. He also proposed and put into successful operation between New York and Albany the tow method of conveying freight in barges and wrote a number of pamphlets advocating railroad construction.

REDFIELD, WILLIAM COX (*b. Albany, N.Y., 1858; d. New York, N.Y., 1932*), machinery manufacturer, statesman. Congressman, Democrat, from New York, 1911–13; U.S. secretary of commerce, 1913–19. A strong factor in Woodrow Wilson's election as president, 1912, Redfield reorganized and enlarged the commerce department, strengthened the Bureau of Standards and, as a keen student of economic tendencies, was of great value in the cabinet during World War I.

REDMAN, JOHN (*b. Philadelphia, Pa., 1722; d. 1808*), physician. Studied medicine with John Kearsley; studied also at Edinburgh, London and Paris and was graduated M.D., University of Leyden, 1748. An ardent follower of Boerhaave and Sydenham, he practiced and taught in Philadelphia, was a consulting physician to the Pennsylvania Hospital, and was president of the College of Physicians of Philadelphia, 1786–1804. Among his pupils were John Morgan, Benjamin Rush and Caspar Wistar.

REDPATH, JAMES (*b. Berwick-on-Tweed, Scotland, 1833; d. New York, N.Y., 1891*), journalist, editor. Emigrated to Michigan *c.* 1850; became associated with the *New York Tribune,* 1852; attracted wide attention for articles on the political troubles in Kansas, slavery in the Southern states and John Brown. An ardent Abolitionist, he aided Haiti in securing recognition of its independence and helped ex-slaves to emigrate there from the United States. He established the Redpath Lyceum Bureau in Boston, 1868.

REDWOOD, ABRAHAM (*b. Antigua, W. I., 1709; d. 1788*), merchant, philanthropist. Brought to Philadelphia as a child; removed to Newport, R.I., 1726. Interested in the cultural and literary activity of colonial Newport, Redwood made the principal contribution towards the founding of a public library there, 1747.

REED, DAVID (*b. Easton, Mass., 1790; d. 1870*), Unitarian clergyman. Founder, publisher and editor of the *Christian Register,* 1821–66.

REED, EARL HOWELL (*b. Geneva, Ill., 1863; d. 1931*), author, etcher. Son of Elizabeth A. Reed; brother of Myrtle Reed.

REED, ELIZABETH ARMSTRONG (*b. Winthrop, Maine, 1842; d. 1915*), writer on Oriental literature. Mother of Earl H. and Myrtle Reed.

REED, HENRY HOPE (*b. Philadelphia, Pa., 1808; d. at sea, aboard steamer* Arctic, *1854*), educator. Grandson of Joseph Reed; brother of William B. Reed. Graduated University of Pennsylvania, 1825; was professor of rhetoric and English literature there, 1835–54. Author and editor of a number of works in belles-lettres, Reed was the first American exponent of William Wordsworth and did more than anyone else to secure Wordsworth's fame in America.

REED, JAMES (*b. Woburn, Mass., 1722 o.s.; d. Fitchburg, Mass., 1807*), soldier in the French and Indian War and in the Revolution. Serving as colonel of the 2nd Continental regiment at Ticonderoga, July 1776, he was stricken with an illness that destroyed his sight; he retired in September as brigadier-general. He was an original proprietor of Fitzwilliam, N.H.

REED, JAMES (*b. Boston, Mass., 1834; d. Boston, 1921*), minister of the Church of the New Jerusalem. Son of Sampson Reed. Graduated Harvard, 1855; ministered in Boston *post* 1860.

REED, JAMES HAY (*b. Allegheny, Pa., 1853; d. Pittsburgh, Pa., 1927*), lawyer. Partner in practice of corporation law with Philander C. Knox until 1901, Reed was counsel to Andrew Carnegie, to the Vanderbilt interests in the Pittsburgh district and to many other large business concerns.

REED, JOHN (*b. Hesse-Cassel, Germany, 1757; d. Cabarrus Co., N.C., 1845*), Hessian soldier, farmer, gold miner. Settling in Mecklenburg, present Cabarrus Co., N.C., after the Revolution, Reed began successful placer mining operations on his farm *c.* 1803 which set off activity in an industry soon second in economic importance only to agriculture in the state. *Post* 1831, he worked his mine with shafts and steam power; the total yield between 1803 and 1845 has been estimated at ten million dollars.

REED, JOHN (*b. Portland, Oreg., 1887; d. Russia, 1920*), journalist. Graduated Harvard, 1910. His interest in the problems of society aroused *c.* 1913 by Lincoln Steffens and Ida Tarbell, he took up a far more radical position than theirs. He joined staff of *The Masses* and engaged actively on behalf of the Paterson, N.J., silk strikers, 1914. Brilliant but biased articles on the Mexican revolution brought him national reputation as a war correspondent and he covered World War I successively with the armies of Germany, Serbia, Bulgaria, Rumania and Russia. His reports were published as *The War in Eastern Europe* (1916). An enthusiastic observer of the October revolution in Petrograd, 1917, Reed became a close friend of Lenin and wrote much of the Bolshevist propaganda dropped over the German lines. Returning to America, he published *Red Russia* and *Ten Days that Shook the World* (both in 1919) and was expelled with other left wingers from the National Socialist Convention, August 1919. When the left-wing groups split into two bitterly hostile factions known as the Communist party and the Communist Labor party, Reed headed the latter. Indicted for sedition, he left America by means of a forged passport, was imprisoned briefly in Finland, and at last reached Russia where he died of typhus.

REED, JOSEPH (*b. Trenton, N.J., 1741; d. Philadelphia, Pa., 1785*), lawyer, Revolutionary soldier and statesman. Graduated College of New Jersey (Princeton), 1757; studied law with Richard Stockton and at the Middle Temple, London. Engaging in legal practice and also in the iron trade and real-estate business, he was appointed deputy secretary of New Jersey, 1767; he removed his practice to Philadelphia *c.* 1770. Appointed a member of the committee of correspondence for Philadelphia, November 1774, he served as president of the second Provincial Congress early in 1775 and gradually shifted from a belief in accommodation with England to a feeling that independence was essential. On Washington's appointment as commander-in-chief, Reed became his military secretary and was later adjutant-general of the Continental Army with the rank of colonel. He was of great service to Washington in the campaign of Trenton and Princeton and served with credit at the battles of Brandywine, Germantown and Monmouth. Delegate to the Continental Congress, 1777–78, he served on important committees, and in December 1778 was chosen president of the Supreme Executive Council of Pennsylvania, serving until 1781. The many attacks made on his reputation as a soldier and patriot were without foundation.

REED, LUMAN (*b. Austerlitz, N.Y., 1781; d. 1836*), New York merchant. Remembered as one of the earliest patrons of American painting, he encouraged, among others, A. B. Durand, Thomas Cole and W. S. Mount.

REED, MYRTLE (*b. Norwood Park, Ill., 1874; d. 1911*), writer. Daughter of Elizabeth A. Reed; sister of E. H. Reed. Author of a number of deftly written and popular romances of which the most successful was *Lavender and Old Lace* (1902).

REED, RICHARD CLARK (*b. near Soddy, Tenn., 1851; d. Columbia, S.C., 1925*), Presbyterian clergyman, educator, author. Professor of church history, Columbia Theological Seminary, 1898–1925.

REED, SAMPSON (*b. West Bridgewater, Mass., 1800; d. Boston, Mass., 1880*), Swedenborgian writer, wholesale drug merchant. Author of several works of which *Observations on the Growth of the Mind* (1826) exerted great influence on R. W. Emerson.

REED, SIMEON GANNETT (*b. East Abington, Mass., 1830; d. 1895*), merchant, steamboat operator. Settled in Portland, Oreg., *c.* 1852; was partner in the Oregon Steam and Navigation Co. and other successful enterprises. His fortune was used to found Reed College, opened 1911.

REED, THOMAS BRACKETT (*b. Portland, Maine, 1839; d. Washington, D.C., 1902*), lawyer, Maine legislator, parliamentarian. Graduated Bowdoin, 1860. As congressman, Republican, from Maine, 1877–99, Reed became famous for the sarcasm and invective which he employed in debate and in his committee work. Appointed to the committee on rules, 1882, he began a long fight for reform of the rules of the House, proposing that procedural checks be removed in order that the majority party might actually govern. Elected speaker, December 1889, he forced adoption in February of the famous "Reed Rules," whereby he was able to expedite passage of the Republican legislative program. He was also a noted exponent of protectionism. Replaced as speaker and his rules voided, 1891, he labored to rehabilitate the Republican party after its defeats in 1890 and 1892; he supported President Cleveland's sound-money policy but opposed all tariff reforms. Serving again as speaker, 1895–99, he brought about the return of the "Reed Rules." Resenting failure of the Republicans to nominate him for the presidency, 1896, he supported the McKinley administration until 1898 when he expressed bitter opposition to expansionism. Following the war with Spain and the annexation of Hawaii, Reed resigned in disgust and returned to the practice of law in New York City. His epigrams have become part of American political tradition. "A statesman," he once said, "is a successful politician who is dead."

REED, WALTER (*b. Belroi, Va., 1851; d. Washington, D.C., 1902*), physician, head of the U.S. Army Yellow Fever Commission. M.D., University of Virginia, 1869; M.D., Bellevue Hospital Medical College, New York City, 1870. Commissioned in the U.S. Army medical corps, 1875, he spent a number of years on frontier garrison duty. Requesting leave of absence for post-graduate work, 1890, he made specialized studies in bacteriology at Johns Hopkins Hospital; in 1893, he was detailed as professor of bacteriology and microscopy at the Army Medical School with James Carroll as assistant. Interested especially in the bacteriology of erysipelas and diphtheria, he served also as chairman of a committee to investigate causes and mode of transmission of typhoid fever. In 1900, having some experience with the problems involved, he was put at the head of a commission of U.S. Army medical officers to investigate cause and mode of transmission of yellow fever in Havana, Cuba. Reed was to have general superintendence of the investigation, James Carroll was bacteriologist, Jesse W. Lazear was entomologist and other distinguished officers also served. The commission established by experimentation on human subjects (which resulted in the crippling of Dr. Carroll and the death of Dr. Lazear) that the disease was transmitted by mosquitoes, later definitely classified as the *Aëdes aegypti.* The commission worked from June 1900 to February 1901, and as a result of its findings and subsequent limitation of the carrier, yellow fever has virtually ceased to be a hazard in the United States.

REED, WILLIAM BRADFORD (*b. Philadelphia, Pa., 1806; d. New York, N.Y., 1876*), lawyer. Brother of Henry H. Reed; grandson of Joseph Reed. Originally a Whig, Reed became a Democrat in 1856, supported Buchanan in the campaign of that year, and was appointed U.S. minister to China. Serving in China from November 1857 until 1859, he concluded the treaty of Tientsin, 1858. His bitter and open opposition to the Civil War cost him his social and professional standing.

REEDER, ANDREW HORATIO (*b. Easton, Pa., 1807; d. 1864*), lawyer. Unsuccessful Democratic governor of Kansas Territory, 1854–55, Reeder became a Free State spokesman after his removal from the governorship for incapacity and land speculation.

REEDY, WILLIAM MARION (*b. St. Louis, Mo., 1862; d. San Francisco, Calif., 1920*), journalist. Editor of *Reedy's Mirror* (St. Louis) *post* 1893. Beginning as a society journal, the paper became under Reedy a link between the cultures of the East Coast and the Middle West and introduced in its pages many writers who became famous in the 1920's.

REES, JAMES (*b. Wales, 1821; d. 1889*), steamboat builder. Came to America as a child; was raised near present Wheeling, W. Va. Founder of a successful engine- and boat-works at Pittsburgh, Pa., he popularized the "stern-wheeler" and invented a number of improvements in steamboat construction. He was an early advocate of the ten-hour day.

REES, JOHN KROM (*b. New York, N.Y., 1851; d. 1907*), geodesist, astronomer. Graduated Columbia, 1872; Columbia School of Mines, 1875. Director of the observatory at Columbia *post* 1881, he also taught astronomy; as secretary, American Meteorological Society, he advocated introduction of standard time.

REESE, ABRAM (*b. Llanelly, South Wales, 1829; d. Pittsburgh, Pa., 1908*), iron and machinery manufacturer. Brother of Isaac and Jacob Reese. Came to America as a child. Held a number of patents, issued *post* 1859, for perfection and improvement of machinery for rolling iron and steel; patented a universal rolling mill, 1892.

REESE, CHARLES LEE (*b. Baltimore, Md., 1862; d. Florida, 1940*), chemist. Graduated University of Virginia, 1884; Ph.D., Heidelberg, 1886. Chief chemist and director of research laboratory, Du Pont Company, 1902–31, he was one of the outstanding industrial chemists of his day. [*Supp.* 2]

REESE, ISAAC (*b. Llanelly, South Wales, 1821; d. Pittsburgh, Pa., 1908*), brick manufacturer. Brother of Abram and Jacob Reese. Came to America as a child. Among other inventions he produced the "Reese Silica Brick," 1882, which was capable of withstanding very high temperatures with practically no shrinkage or expansion.

REESE, JACOB (*b. Llanelly, South Wales, 1825; d. near Philadelphia, Pa., 1907*), metallurgist. Brother of Abram and Isaac Reese. Came to America as a child. Among a great number of inventions useful in the manufacture of iron and steel, Reese perfected the basic open-hearth steel process *c.* 1877, although his claim as inventor was not favorably decided by the Patent Office until 1881.

REESE, JOHN JAMES (*b. Philadelphia, Pa., 1818; d. Atlantic City, N.J., 1892*), toxicologist. Graduated University of Pennsylvania, 1836; M.D., 1839. Author of *A Text Book of Medical Jurisprudence and Toxicology* (1884), a standard work.

REESE, LIZETTE WOODWORTH (*b. near Baltimore, Md., 1856; d. 1935*), poet, educator. Educated chiefly in private schools; taught for many years in the public schools of Baltimore. Her lyrics, intensely felt and inspired by a keen sense of the beauty of common things, were uninfluenced in technique by fashionable poetic fads. Her first volume, *A Branch of May*, appeared in 1887; after the appearance of her *Selected Poems* (1926), she published *Little Henrietta* (1927), *White April and Other Poems* (1930) and several other volumes both in verse and prose.
[*Supp.* 1]

REEVE, TAPPING (*b. Brookhaven, N.Y., 1744; d. Litchfield, Conn., 1823*), jurist, teacher of law. Graduated College of New Jersey (Princeton), 1763. Admitted to the Connecticut bar, 1772, he settled in Litchfield where he began the practice of his profession. After teaching law informally for some time, Reeve formally opened the Litchfield Law School in 1784. With exception of the department of law at William and Mary under George Wythe, it was the first school of its kind in the United States. Appointed a judge of the superior court, 1798, he associated James Gould with the school as a teacher. Under Gould's direction the school developed and flourished, numbering among its graduates some of the most prominent men in the public life of the next generation. Reeve was made chief justice of the supreme court of errors of Connecticut, 1814, and served until his retirement, 1816.

REEVES, ARTHUR MIDDLETON (*b. Cincinnati, O., 1856; d. near Hagerstown, Ind., 1891*), philologist, historian, authority on Old Norse.

REHAN, ADA (*b. Limerick, Ireland, 1860; d. New York, N.Y., 1916*), actress. Came to America as a child; was raised in Brooklyn, N.Y. After making her stage debut at Newark, N.J., 1873, she joined the Arch St. company, Philadelphia. Although her name was properly Ada Crehan, she was billed by a printer's error as Ada C. Rehan for her Philadelphia debut and preserved the mistake throughout her subsequent career. Playing in support of Fanny Davenport, Edwin Booth, Lawrence Barrett, John T. Raymond and others, she joined Augustin Daly's company, 1879, and remained under Daly's management until he died, 1899. The leading woman of his company, she was a popular idol in New York and London and was considered the perfect mistress of the classic, artificial style of playing. Famous in many parts, her performance as Katherine in Shakespeare's *Taming of the Shrew* is considered her outstanding role. Her last public appearance was at a New York benefit for Madame Modjeska, 1905.

REHN, FRANK KNOX MORTON (*b. Philadelphia, Pa., 1848; d. 1914*), artist, specialist in marines.

REICHEL, CHARLES GOTTHOLD (*b. Hermsdorff, Silesia, 1751; d. Niesky, Silesia, 1825*), Moravian bishop and educator. Principal of the academy at Nazareth, Pa., 1785–1801; bishop of the southern province, 1801–11, and of the northern province, 1811–18. He was sent to Germany, 1818.

REICHEL, WILLIAM CORNELIUS (*b. Salem, N.C., 1824; d. 1876*), Moravian clergyman, educator. Grandson of Charles G. Reichel. Author of a number of historical studies on the Moravian Church in America.

REICK, WILLIAM CHARLES (*b. Philadelphia, Pa., 1864; d. 1924*), journalist. As city editor, *New York Herald*, 1889–1903, he became known as one of America's ablest journalists. Holding the presidency of the New York Herald Co., 1903–07, he resigned, and after working for the *New York Times* and the Philadelphia *Public Ledger,* bought a controlling interest in the N.Y. *Sun,* 1911. He was afterwards president of the company which published the *New York Journal of Commerce.*

REID, CHRISTIAN. [See TIERNAN, FRANCES CHRISTINE FISHER, 1846–1920.]

REID, DAVID BOSWELL (*b. Edinburgh, Scotland, 1805; d. Washington, D.C., 1863*), chemist, educator, ventilation engineer. Resident in the United States, 1855–63.

REID, DAVID SETTLE (*b. Rockingham Co., N.C., 1813; d. 1891*), lawyer, North Carolina legislator. Congressman, Democrat, from North Carolina, 1843–47; governor, 1851–54; U.S. senator, 1854–59. A conservative pro-Southern man, Reid was considered the wisest and most resourceful Democratic leader in

North Carolina between the day of Nathaniel Macon and the Civil War.

REID, GILBERT (*b. Laurel, N.Y., 1857; d. Shanghai, China, 1927*), Presbyterian clergyman, newspaper correspondent, missionary to China. Founded International Institute of China c. 1897.

REID, JAMES L. (*b. near Russellville, O., 1844; d. 1910*), corn breeder. Raised in Illinois where, after a number of experiments, he produced the corn variety known as Reid's Yellow Dent *ante* 1880.

REID, JOHN MORRISON (*b. New York, N.Y., 1820; d. New York, 1896*), Methodist clergyman. President of Genesee College (nucleus of present Syracuse University), 1858–64; did valuable work as corresponding secretary, Methodist Missionary Society, 1872–88.

REID, MAYNE. [See REID, THOMAS MAYNE, 1818–1883.]

REID, ROBERT (*b. Stockbridge, Mass., 1862; d. Clifton Springs, N.Y., 1929*), portrait, figure and mural painter.

REID, SAMUEL CHESTER (*b. Norwich, Conn., 1783; d. New York, N.Y., 1861*), sea captain. Distinguished for his heroic conduct as commander of the privateer *General Armstrong*, 1814. Putting in at the harbor of Fayal (Azores) in September of that year, Reid defended his vessel against a series of attacks by armed boats from the British men of war *Carnation, Rota,* and *Plantagenet* which were en route to join the British forces concentrating at Jamaica against New Orleans. Reid eventually scuttled and abandoned his ship, but the delay he caused the British squadron indirectly aided Jackson's defense of New Orleans.

REID, THOMAS MAYNE (*b. Ballyroney, Ireland, 1818; d. London, England, 1883*), novelist, journalist. Came to America c. 1838. After traveling widely in the South and West, hunting, trapping and trading with the Indians, he worked for a time as a tutor and at other occupations. Early in 1843, he went to Philadelphia where he lived for about three years, worked as a journalist and playwright and established friendship with Edgar Allan Poe. He served with distinction as a U.S. Army officer in the Mexican War. Sailing from New York, 1849, to help in the German and Hungarian revolutions, he found on arrival in Europe that they had collapsed and lived in England thereafter, with the exception of the years 1867–70 which he spent mainly in Newport, R.I., and New York City. Reid was author of more than seventy novels of romance and adventure; a number of these are based on his American experiences, notably *The Rifle Rangers* (London, 1850). His book *The Quadroon* (1856) was the basis for Dion Boucicault's sensational play *The Octoroon.*

REID, WHITELAW (*b. near Xenia, O., 1837; d. London, England, 1912*), journalist, diplomat. Son-in-law of Darius O. Mills. Graduated Miami University, 1856; edited the *Xenia News* and was active in Republican politics. War correspondent of the *Cincinnati Gazette*, 1861–65, he showed marked ability although his combination of reserve with unusual ambition and self-assertiveness led some to regard him as a selfish careerist. After attempting to run cotton plantations in Louisiana and Alabama, 1865–67, he returned briefly to the *Cincinnati Gazette* and in the fall of 1868 joined the *New York Tribune* as Horace Greeley's editorial assistant; he became managing editor, 1869. Loyal in support of Greeley's bid for the presidency as a Liberal Republican, 1872, Reid played as disinterested a part as could have been expected when Greeley's collapse brought about a crisis in the affairs of the *Tribune.* A brief struggle for the vacant editorship with Schuyler Colfax ended in Reid's victory and he became head of the most powerful newspaper in America. Maintaining the paper at a high level of competence, Reid increased the circulation of the daily, and though still devoted to Republican principles, fought the Grant administration and shared in exposing its corruption. After the election of James A. Garfield, a close friend, to the presidency, 1880, Reid encouraged the new president in measures which resulted in the resignation of Roscoe Conkling and the downfall of the "Stalwart" Republicans. Reid was the first to install the linotype in a newspaper composing room, believed in spending money liberally for talent, and, with E. L. Godkin, performed a valuable service to journalism by maintaining an important newspaper based on brains and character when others were depending upon sensationalism. An enthusiastic backer of James G. Blaine, Reid considered Cleveland's election a calamity. After stumping for Harrison in the campaign of 1888, he served as U.S. minister to France, 1889–92, and was nominated for the vice-presidency, 1892. Generally supporting Grover Cleveland's chief policies during his second term, Reid gave early and ardent support to McKinley and vehemently denounced W. J. Bryan. He was an ardent expansionist and acted on his beliefs while serving as a member of the U.S. commission to negotiate peace with Spain, 1898. At first distrustful of Theodore Roosevelt, Reid soon warmed to him and was particularly pleased by his seizure of Panama. On his appointment as U.S. ambassador to Great Britain, 1905, he gave up active editorship of the *Tribune.*

REID, WILLIAM SHIELDS (*b. Chester Co., Pa., 1778; d. Lynchburg, Va., 1853*), Presbyterian clergyman, Virginia educator.

REID, WILLIAM WHARRY (*b. Argyle, N.Y., 1799; d. 1866*), surgeon. Graduated Union College, 1825. Practiced in Rochester, N.Y., 1828–c. 1864; is credited

853

with the first (1844) reduction of hip dislocation by flexion.

REIERSEN, JOHAN REINERT (*b. Vestre Moland, Norway, 1810; d. Prairieville, Texas, 1864*), journalist, editor. Traveled in the United States, 1843; published *Pathfinder for Norwegian Emigrants to the United North American States and Texas* (Norway, 1844). Established first Norwegian settlement in Texas at Brownsboro, 1845.

REILLY, MARION (*b. Altoona, Pa., 1879; d. Philadelphia, Pa., 1928*), educator, suffrage leader, philanthropist. Dean of Bryn Mawr College, 1907–16.

REINAGLE, ALEXANDER (*b. Portsmouth, England, 1756; d. Baltimore, Md., 1809*), musician. Came to America, 1786; was successful as teacher and pianist and director of concerts in Philadelphia, New York City and Baltimore. Served as musical director of the New Theatre, Philadelphia, from its opening in 1793 until 1809 and adapted many current English ballad operas to the American stage. His own four piano sonatas, written 1786–94, are the finest surviving American instrumental productions of the eighteenth century.

REINHART, BENJAMIN FRANKLIN (*b. near Waynesburg, Pa., 1829; d. 1885*), historical, genre, and portrait painter. Uncle of Charles S. Reinhart.

REINHART, CHARLES STANLEY (*b. Pittsburgh, Pa., 1844; d. 1896*), genre painter, illustrator. Nephew of Benjamin F. Reinhart. An excellent draftsman, he ranks high among American illustrators of his time.

REINSCH, PAUL SAMUEL (*b. Milwaukee, Wis., 1869; d. Shanghai, China, 1923*), political scientist, diplomat. Graduated University of Wisconsin, 1892; LL.B., 1894; Ph.D., 1898. Taught political science at Wisconsin, 1898–1913; was among first to develop systematic courses in world politics; wrote a number of books and articles opposing excessive nationalism and imperialism. As U.S. minister to China, 1913–19, he tried to obtain that country's entrance into World War I on the basis of specific guarantees of financial assistance and other aids.

REISINGER, HUGO (*b. Wiesbaden, Germany, 1856; d. Langenschwalbach, Germany, 1914*), import and export merchant. Resident in the United States *post* 1884, Reisinger collected and exhibited modern American and German art as a means of providing a cultural interchange between the countries.

REITZEL, ROBERT (*b. Weitenau, Baden, Germany, 1849; d. Detroit, Mich., 1898*), German-American poet, editor. Emigrated to the United States, 1870. Issued the weekly *Der arme Teufel* at Detroit *post* 1884.

RELLSTAB, JOHN (*b. Trenton, N.J., 1858; d. Lake Placid, N.Y., 1930*), journeyman potter, New Jersey lawyer, official and jurist. Judge of the U.S. district court for New Jersey, 1909–30.

REMEY, GEORGE COLLIER (*b. Burlington, Iowa, 1841; d. Washington, D.C., 1928*), naval officer. Graduated U.S. Naval Academy, 1859. Commanded naval base at Key West, Fla., during war with Spain, 1898; appointed rear-admiral in that year, he commanded the Asiatic station, 1900, during the Philippine warfare and Boxer uprising in China.

REMINGTON, ELIPHALET (*b. Suffield, Conn., 1793; d. 1861*), iron-forger, manufacturer. Father of Philo Remington. Founded celebrated firm for the manufacture of rifles, pistols and agricultural implements at Ilion, N.Y., c. 1828.

REMINGTON, FREDERIC (*b. Canton, N.Y., 1861; d. Ridgefield, Conn., 1909*), painter, sculptor, author, illustrator. Studied at Yale School of the Fine Arts, 1878–80; studied also at the N.Y. Art Students League. Excelling as a delineator of outdoors men, preferably with horses, Remington is considered unsurpassed in his studies of Western Indians, cowboys and frontiersmen, soldiers in the field, and in general the human figure in action. In his later work, his ability to state by suggestion the character of land, the season of the year and the state of the weather greatly improved. His sculpture was essentially illustration in bronze with his usual accent on character and action. His books include *Pony Tracks* (1895), *Crooked Trails* (1898), *Stories of Peace and War* (1899), *Done in the Open* (1902) and *The Way of an Indian* (1906). He wrote them in a fresh, journalistic style and illustrated them with the closest attention to accuracy of detail.

REMINGTON, JOSEPH PRICE (*b. Philadelphia, Pa., 1847; d. 1918*), pharmacist. Graduated Philadelphia College of Pharmacy, 1866; taught there *post* 1871 and was made dean, 1893. Author of *Practice of Pharmacy* (1885). Chairman of the committee to revise the *Pharmacopoeia of the United States*, 1901–18.

REMINGTON, PHILO (*b. Litchfield, N.Y., 1816; d. Silver Springs, Fla., 1889*), manufacturer. Son of Eliphalet Remington. President *post* 1865 of arms and agricultural equipment manufacturing firm founded by his father, he actively developed the pistol-making branch of the business, perfected the Remington breech-loader, marketed sewing machines and introduced the Remington typewriter (developed from Sholes and Glidden prototype) in 1876.

REMOND, CHARLES LENOX (*b. Salem, Mass., 1810; d. Boston, Mass., 1873*), Negro leader. The first Negro to address public gatherings on behalf of abolition, Remond was appointed agent of the Massachusetts Anti-Slavery Society, 1838, and achieved his greatest success on a lecture tour through Great Britain and Ireland, 1840–41.

REMSEN, IRA (*b. New York, N.Y., 1846; d. Carmel, Calif., 1927*), chemist, educator. Attended New York schools and the New York Free Academy (later College of the City of New York); M.D., N.Y. College of Physicians and Surgeons, 1867; Ph.D., University of Göttingen, 1870. A research student in organic chemistry under some of the best German authorities of the time, Remsen returned to America, 1872, won recognition for his *Principles of Theoretical Chemistry* (1877) and taught for a short time at Williams College. Chosen first professor of chemistry at Johns Hopkins, 1876, he soon surrounded himself with a group of brilliant students who in their later careers strongly influenced the development of chemistry in the United States. Also of great influence in the development of chemical research were the *American Chemical Journal* which Remsen established, 1879, and a series of notable textbooks which he wrote. Appointed president of Johns Hopkins, 1901, he served until 1913, meanwhile continuing his active direction of the department of chemistry.

RÉMY, HENRI (*b. Agen, France, c. 1811; d. New Orleans, La., 1867*), Louisiana editor, lawyer. A political refugee from France, Rémy came to New Orleans *c.* 1836 where he studied law in the office of Pierre Soulé. He was later an associate of William Walker in the seizure of Nicaragua, 1855–57.

RENICK, FELIX (*b. Hardy Co., Va., 1770; d. near Chillicothe, O., 1848*), Ohio pioneer, cattleman. Settled in Ross Co., O., 1801; became an outstanding agricultural leader in south central Ohio; improved cattle herd by importing English shorthorns, 1834–36.

RENO, JESSE LEE (*b. Wheeling, Va., present W. Va., 1823; d. 1862*), Union major-general. Graduated West Point, 1846. After service in the Mexican War, he was active principally as an ordnance expert until the Civil War when he was commissioned brigadier-general, 1861. Serving principally in Gen. Burnside's commands, he was killed at the battle of South Mountain. The city of Reno, Nev., was named in his honor.

RENO, MILO (*b. Wapello Co., Iowa, 1866; d. Excelsior Springs, Mo., 1936*), farm leader. President (1921–30) of the Iowa Farmers' Union; organizer of the Farmers' Holiday Association, which struck in 1932 for higher farm prices and spurred remedial legislation. [*Supp. 2*]

RENWICK, EDWARD SABINE (*b. New York, N.Y., 1823; d. Short Hills, N.J., 1912*), engineer, patent expert. Son of James Renwick (1792–1863); brother of Henry B. and James Renwick (1818–1895). Among his many inventions the most important was a series of ten covering incubators and chicken brooders, 1877–86; he also patented a grain harvester and binder, 1851–53, from which he never profited commercially although his ideas were widely used by

manufacturers of harvesting machinery after his patents expired.

RENWICK, HENRY BREVOORT (*b. New York, N.Y., 1817; d. New York, 1895*), engineer, patent expert. Son of James Renwick (1792–1863); brother of Edward S. and James Renwick (1818–1895).

RENWICK, JAMES (*b. Liverpool, England, 1792; d. New York, N.Y., 1863*), educator, engineer. Father of Edward S., Henry B. and James Renwick (1818–1895). Came to the United States as a child. Graduated Columbia, 1807; traveled abroad with Washington Irving; A.M., Columbia, 1810. Professor of natural philosophy and experimental chemistry at Columbia, 1820–53, Renwick was until his death a recognized authority on every branch of engineering of that day. Among many projects on which he was consultant was the Morris Canal for which he devised a system of inclined planes or railways for transporting boats; he served also as a commissioner for the survey of the Northeast Boundary, 1840. The more important of his original scientific works were *Outlines of Natural Philosophy* (1822–23) and *Treatise on the Steam-Engine* (1830).

RENWICK, JAMES (*b. New York, N.Y., 1818; d. 1895*), engineer, architect. Son of James Renwick (1792–1863); brother of Edward S. and Henry B. Renwick. Graduated Columbia, 1836; served on engineering staff of Erie Railroad and Croton Aqueduct. Entirely self-trained in architecture, Renwick won a competition for design of Grace Church, New York City, 1843; thereafter he developed a large practice as an ecclesiastical and general architect. Working at first either in the Gothic or Romanesque style, he early accepted the trend towards eclecticism with sometimes incoherent results; technically, his work was not only careful but advanced, and he was full of imagination. Among his principal works were St. Patrick's Cathedral, New York City (1853–87), the Smithsonian Institution in Washington, D.C. (1846 and after), the Vassar College building (1865) and the Corcoran Gallery, Washington, D.C. An inspiring teacher, he trained among others William W. Root and Bertram G. Goodhue.

REQUA, MARK LAWRENCE (*b. Virginia City, Nev., 1865; d. Los Angeles, Calif., 1937*), mining engineer. Associate and political adviser of Herbert Hoover.
[*Supp. 2*]

REQUIER, AUGUSTUS JULIAN (*b. Charleston, S.C., 1825; d. New York, N.Y., 1887*), poet, South Carolina and Alabama jurist, New York City lawyer.

RESE, FREDERICK (*b. Weinenburg, Hanover, Germany, 1791; d. Hildesheim, Germany, 1871*), Roman Catholic clergyman. After working as a journeyman tailor, he made theological studies in Rome and was ordained there, 1822. A volunteer for mission work, he came to Cincinnati, O., *c.* 1824, the first German priest in the old Northwest. Instrumental in founding the Leopoldine Society of Vienna and in bringing the Redemptorists to the United States, he was bishop of Detroit *post* 1833; he took no active part in the running of the diocese, however, subsequent to 1841.

RESTARICK, HENRY BOND (*b. Holcombe, England, 1854; d. 1933*), Episcopal clergyman. Emigrated to Canada *c.* 1871; settled in Iowa, 1873. A rector for many years in San Diego, Calif., he served as bishop of the district of Honolulu, Hawaii, 1902–20.

[*Supp. 1*]

REULING, GEORGE (*b. Romrod, Germany, 1839; d. 1915*), ophthalmologist. M.D., University of Giessen, 1865; studied also in Wiesbaden and at Vienna, Berlin and Paris. Emigrated to Baltimore, Md., 1868; conducted Maryland Eye and Ear Infirmary *post* 1869. Professor of ophthalmology and otology at Washington University, Baltimore, and at Baltimore Medical College.

REUTER, DOMINIC (*b. Coblenz, Germany, 1856; d. Syracuse, N.Y., 1933*), Roman Catholic clergyman, Franciscan. Came to America as a child; entered Friars Minor Conventual at Syracuse, N.Y., 1875. Educated at St. Francis College, Trenton, N.J., and at the University of Innsbruck, he held a number of teaching and other positions in his order and served as minister general, 1904–10.

REUTERDAHL, HENRY (*b. Malmö, Sweden, 1871; d. Washington, D.C., 1925*), illustrator, painter, author. Settled in the United States, 1893. A specialist in depicting naval life and operations, he came to hold a semi-official status as artist to the U.S. Navy.

REVEL, BERNARD (*b. Pren, Russia, 1885; d. New York, N.Y., 1940*), Jewish scholar, educator. Came to America, 1906. As president, *post* 1915, of the Rabbi Isaac Elchanan Theological Seminary (the Yeshiva), New York, N.Y., Revel labored devotedly to develop it as a college of liberal arts and sciences which would produce enlightened rabbis, teachers and laymen for the American Jewish community.

[*Supp. 2*]

REVELL, FLEMING HEWITT (*b. Chicago, Ill., 1849; d. 1931*), publisher of religious books and Sunday-school materials. Brother-in-law of Dwight L. Moody.

REVELS, HIRAM RHOADES (*b. Fayetteville, N.C., 1822; d. Aberdeen, Miss., 1901*), Methodist clergyman, Mississippi legislator and educator. Of mixed African and Indian descent, Revels was U.S. senator, Republican, from Mississippi, 1870–71; thereafter, he served as president of Alcorn University. He was active in behalf of the Democrats in the 1875 campaign which led to the overthrow of the Carpetbag government.

REVERE, JOSEPH WARREN (*b. Boston, Mass., 1812; d. Hoboken, N.J., 1880*), naval officer, Union brigadier-general. Grandson of Paul Revere. Appointed midshipman, 1828; served in a variety of capacities until 1845 when he was assigned to the Pacific and played a part in the conquest of California. Resigning from the navy, 1850, he became a rancher and trader, and in 1851 reorganized the artillery branch of the Mexican army. Removing to New Jersey, 1852, he became colonel of the 7th New Jersey Volunteers, 1861, and was promoted brigadier-general, October 1862. Relieved of command and court-martialed and dismissed for his conduct at Chancellorsville, May 1863, he was reinstated by President Lincoln, 1864. He was author of *A Tour of Duty in California* (1849) and *Keel and Saddle* (1872).

REVERE, PAUL (*b. Boston, Mass., 1735; d. Boston, 1818*), patriot, silversmith, engraver. A successful craftsman, Revere came into close contact with John Hancock, Samuel Adams and Joseph Warren through his leadership of the patriotic mechanic class of Boston. When the North End Caucus, most influential of all the patriotic political clubs, voted to oppose the selling of tea by the East India Co., Revere was one of three committeemen chosen to suggest a course of action and along with fifty other Boston workingmen shared in the famous Tea Party. Journeying to New York in the winter of 1773 to apprise the Sons of Liberty there of developments in Boston, he rode out again in the following spring to carry the news of the Boston Port Bill to New York and Philadelphia and to make an appeal for help. In September 1774, he rode to Philadelphia with the "Suffolk Resolves." He then was made official courier for the Massachusetts Provincial Assembly to Congress. Two days before his famous ride to Lexington, he rode with the important purpose of warning the patriots to move their military stores from Concord. On the 18th of April 1775, he rode again to warn Hancock and Adams that the British were out to capture them and to alert the countryside to the fact that the royal troops were on the march. Mounted on a stout work-horse, he eluded British patrols, reached Lexington, saw his two chiefs on the way and then set out with William Dawes and Samuel Prescott to warn Concord. Stopped by British troopers, Revere was detained a little and then released to make his way back to Lexington without his horse. Anxious for action, he received no military command in the Continental Army. He designed and printed the first issue of Continental money; he made the first official seal for the colonies and the Massachusetts state seal. Learning the process of manufacturing gunpowder, he for a time directed a mill at Canton, Mass.; in 1779, he participated in the ill-fated Penobscot expedition. A master silversmith but a rather amateurish engraver of political cartoons, Revere later entered the foundry business and was the discoverer of a process for rolling sheet copper.

REYNOLDS, ALEXANDER WELCH (*b. Clarke Co., Va., 1817; d. Alexandria, Egypt, 1876*), Confederate brigadier-general. Graduated West Point, 1838. Served in the Seminole War and on extensive Western frontier duty. After the Civil War, in which he was engaged principally in the Western campaigns, he removed to Egypt, took a commission in the Egyptian army and served as chief of staff to William W. Loring.

REYNOLDS, CHARLES ALEXANDER (*b. probably near Stephensburg, Ky., 1842?; d. near the Little Big Horn, Montana Territory, 1876*), Union soldier, hunter, scout, known as "Lonesome Charley." Generally ranked as the greatest of the Western scouts, Reynolds was raised in Illinois and Kansas. After Civil War service, he left home and became a hunter in the Dakota country, furnishing game to military posts. He served as a scout for the Yellowstone expedition under David S. Stanley, 1873, was the guide for Custer's Black Hills expedition, 1874, and in the following year was hunter and chief scout for, among other military expeditions, that of William Ludlow. Employed as a scout for the Big Horn expedition which left Fort Abraham Lincoln, May 17, 1876, he was assigned to Reno's battalion and was shot at the beginning of the retreat from the Little Big Horn valley.

REYNOLDS, EDWIN (*b. Mansfield, Conn., 1831; d. Milwaukee, Wis., 1909*), engineer. As plant superintendent for the Corliss Steam Engine Co., Providence, R.I., Reynolds built the giant engine displayed at the 1876 Exhibition. Associated *post* 1877 with the Edward P. Allis Co. and Allis-Chalmers, he incorporated many of his inventions and improvements in the machinery manufactured by those companies. He built the first triple expansion pumping engine for waterworks service in the United States, 1888, and in the same year patented a blowing engine for blast furnaces which was a radical departure from accepted design practice. In 1893 he designed and built a four-cylinder compound steam engine for the Manhattan Railway power house, New York, N.Y.

REYNOLDS, GEORGE McCLELLAND (*b. Panora, Iowa, 1865; d. Pasadena, Calif., 1940*), banker. Protégé of J. Ogden Armour, Reynolds served as president of the Continental National Bank of Chicago and its subsequent consolidations, 1906–33. He was associated with Nelson W. Aldrich in the investigations which produced the Aldrich Plan. [*Supp. 2*]

REYNOLDS, JOHN (*b. probably England, 1713; d. 1788*), British admiral, first royal governor of Georgia, 1754–57. In constant struggle with the Assembly over financial problems and procedures, Reynolds regarded the colonists as "lawless, antimonarchal people" who required government by military force.

REYNOLDS, JOHN (*b. Montgomery Co., Pa., 1788; d. Belleville, Ill., 1865*), lawyer, Illinois legislator, Democratic politician. Raised in Tennessee, and near Kaskaskia, Ill. Undistinguished as a lawyer but a glib and able cultivator of the electorate, Reynolds was governor of Illinois, 1830–34, and congressman from that state, 1834–37, 1839–43. He was author of a colorful autobiography *My Own Times* (1855). He was later a strong Confederate sympathizer.

REYNOLDS, JOHN FULTON (*b. Lancaster, Pa., 1820; d. Gettysburg, Pa., 1863*), Union soldier. Graduated West Point, 1841. An artillery officer, he served with particular distinction in the Mexican War and in the Far West, 1854–60. Made brigadier-general of volunteers, 1861, he was active in the Peninsular campaign, directed the Pennsylvania militia, and in November 1862 was promoted major-general. He was most effective as the I Corps commander at Fredericksburg and Chancellorsville. Ordered to occupy Gettysburg on June 28, 1863, Reynolds set the I, III and XI Corps in motion and arrived at the town on the morning of July 1. Marching at the head of the 2nd Wisconsin Regiment, he was killed by a sharpshooter.

REYNOLDS, JOSEPH JONES (*b. Flemingsburg, Ky., 1822; d. Washington, D.C., 1899*), Union soldier. Graduated West Point, 1843. Served as artillery officer with Gen. Zachary Taylor's army in the Mexican War; taught at West Point, 1846–55; resigned from the army, 1857. Appointed brigadier-general, 1861, he served under Gen. Rosecrans in western Virginia and on promotion to major-general, 1862, commanded a division in the Army of the Cumberland. After the battle of Chickamauga, 1863, he became chief of staff of the Army of the Cumberland; *post* July 1864, he headed the XIX Corps. After postwar duty in Texas and Louisiana and in the Far West, he retired, 1877.

REYNOLDS, SAMUEL GODFREY (*b. Bristol, R.I., 1801; d. Bristol, 1881*), tanner, inventor of improved machinery for making nails, pins and spikes.

REYNOLDS, WILLIAM (*b. Lancaster, Pa., 1815; d. Washington, D.C., 1879*), naval officer. Brother of John F. Reynolds. Retired as rear-admiral, 1877.

REZANOV, NIKOLAI PETROVICH (*b. St. Petersburg, Russia, 1764; d. Krasnoyarsk, Siberia, 1807*), Russian civil service official, Alaskan colonizer. A founder of the Russian-American Co. for the exploitation of Alaska, Rezanov set out in 1803 to investigate the resources of the territory and to test the possibility of supplying the colonies there by sea. After many difficulties, he landed at New Archangel (Sitka), 1805; in search of food for the starving community, he visited the port of San Francisco, Calif., April–May 1806. He died on his way back to Russia.

RHEA, JOHN (*b. Co. Donegal, Ireland, 1753; d. 1832*), lawyer. Emigrated to America, 1769; settled in eastern Tennessee, 1778. Congressman, Democrat, from Tennessee, 1803–15, 1817–23; a friend and supporter of Andrew Jackson; opposed slavery.

RHEES, MORGAN JOHN (*b. Glamorganshire, Wales, 1760; d. 1804*), Baptist clergyman, reformer. Came to America, 1794. After traveling widely in the United States, Rhees collaborated with Benjamin Rush in land developments in central Pennsylvania where he also preached and organized Baptist churches among the Welsh settlers. [*Supp. 1*]

RHEES, RUSH (*b. Chicago, Ill., 1860; d. Rochester, N.Y., 1939*), Baptist clergyman, educator. Great-grandson of Morgan J. Rhees. Graduated Amherst, 1883; Hartford Theological Seminary, 1888. President, University of Rochester, 1900–35. [*Supp. 2*]

RHEES, WILLIAM JONES (*b. Philadelphia, Pa., 1830; d. Washington, D.C., 1907*), bibliographer, official and archivist of Smithsonian Institution.

RHETT, ROBERT BARNWELL (*b. Beaufort, S.C., 1800; d. Louisiana, 1876*), lawyer, statesman. Changed name from Smith to Rhett, 1837. Elected to the legislature, 1826, he quickly became prominent for his passionate and eloquent advocacy of extreme state-rights doctrine; as congressman from South Carolina, 1837–49, he advanced to the forefront of the followers of J. C. Calhoun, accepting Calhoun's belief that the Constitution, rightly interpreted, would protect the South. After Calhoun's failure to secure the presidential nomination and the abandonment by Northern Democrats of the Southern position on the tariff, Rhett moved more and more towards secession, and *post* 1850 was its open advocate. Succeeding Calhoun as U.S. senator, 1850, he resigned his seat, 1852, when a South Carolina convention passed an ordinance merely declaratory of the right of secession which Rhett chose to regard as a "submission" to the Union over the Compromise of 1850. Continuing to work for his declared aim of a Southern Confederacy, he met with William L. Yancey and other Southern radicals in 1858 but was forced with them to the conclusion that the only hope for secession lay in a Republican victory in 1860. Through his newspaper mouthpiece, the *Charleston Mercury,* Rhett worked to undermine Southern confidence in the Democratic party and was the principal architect of secession when the crisis arose in South Carolina in late 1860. At the Southern Congress in Montgomery, Ala., he failed to secure the Confederate presidency and was ignored in the cabinet appointments. Welcoming the Civil War because in his view it would stop any chance of a reconstruction of the Union, he was a vigorous critic of President Jefferson Davis's administration and opposed Davis's "usurpations" as vigorously as he had opposed the Union. He died still serenely confident in his faith that the South would be "separate and free." His character and the motivation of his career as well as his statesmanship are subjects on which historians are as little likely to reach agreement as were his contemporaries.

RHIND, ALEXANDER COLDEN (*b. New York, N.Y., 1821; d. New York, 1897*), naval officer. Son of Charles Rhind. Acquired a reputation for insubordination during his early years of service; performed a number of highly hazardous individual exploits during the Civil War, in particular at Charleston, S.C., April 1863, and at the first attack on Fort Fisher, 1864. Retired as rear-admiral, 1883.

RHIND, CHARLES (*b. Aberdeen, Scotland, date unknown; d. probably New York, N.Y., post 1846*), merchant, diplomatic agent. Father of Alexander C. Rhind. First appears in New York City directory, 1810, as a ship-chandler. U.S. commissioner with David Offley and James Biddle to negotiate treaty of commerce with Turkey, 1830.

RHOADS, JAMES E. (*b. Marple, Pa., 1828; d. Bryn Mawr, Pa., 1895*), physician, Quaker editor, philanthropist. President of Bryn Mawr College, 1883–94.

RHODES, EUGENE MANLOVE (*b. Tecumseh, Nebr., 1869; d. 1934*), cowboy, novelist. Raised in Kansas and New Mexico; worked as a cowpuncher and rancher, 1882–1906, with a short interval for study at the University of the Pacific. Author of a number of excellent fictional studies of the cattle kingdom which include *Good Men and True* (1910), *The Desire of the Moth* (1916), *West Is West* (1917), *Stepsons of Light* (1921), *Beyond the Desert* (1934) and *The Proud Sheriff* (1935). His books have been described as the only body of fiction devoted to the cattleman and his life which is both true to the subject and written by an artist in prose. [*Supp. 1*]

RHODES, JAMES FORD (*b. Cleveland, O., 1848; d. Brookline, Mass., 1927*), businessman, historian. Brother-in-law of Marcus A. Hanna. Retiring from business, 1885, he wrote a *History of the United States from the Compromise of 1850* which is marked by good judgment and, for its day, notable fair-mindedness. Somewhat pedestrian in style, it still stands as a landmark in American historiography and is distinguished for the thoroughness and skill with which it handles vast materials. The first two volumes were published in 1893 and were greeted by competent critics with immediate and practically unanimous approval; five subsequent volumes (III, 1895; IV, 1899; V, 1904; VI, VII, 1906) served to enhance the author's fame. He had originally intended to carry the history to 1885 but wisely decided to end it with the restoration of Southern home rule in 1877. He was author also of several other works, but his fame rests upon his major history and especially on the first five volumes.

RIBAUT, JEAN (*b. Dieppe, France, c. 1520; d. Florida, 1565*), French mariner. A trusted captain under Admiral Coligny, Ribaut was chosen to establish a French colony and asylum for Huguenots on the coast of Florida, 1562. After making his landfall in late spring near St. John's River, he settled his colonists at the present Port Royal, S.C., which he called Charlesfort and returned to France. Becoming embroiled there in the Wars of Religion, he fled to England where he was for a time imprisoned. After his release he set out with a reinforcement for his colony in 1565, but was taken prisoner by the Spaniards under Pedro Menéndez de Avilés and executed.

RICE, ALEXANDER HAMILTON (*b. Newton Lower Falls, Mass., 1818; d. Melrose, Mass., 1895*), paper manufacturer, Boston councilman and mayor. Congressman, Republican, from Massachusetts, 1859–67; governor of Massachusetts, 1876–78.

RICE, CALVIN WINSOR (*b. Winchester, Mass., 1868; d. New York, N.Y., 1934*), engineer. Promoter of national and international engineering societies. [*Supp. 1*]

RICE, CHARLES (*b. Munich, Bavaria, 1841; d. 1901*), chemist, philologist, Sanskrit scholar. Came to America, 1862. After service in U.S. Navy, was associated with the pharmacy department of Bellevue Hospital, New York City, and became eventually its superintendent. Chairman, revision committee, U.S. *Pharmacopoeia*, 1880–1901.

RICE, CHARLES ALLEN THORNDIKE (*b. Boston, Mass., 1851; d. New York, N.Y., 1889*), journalist. Publisher and editor, *North American Review, post* 1876, he made that moribund periodical a financial and literary success by persuading leaders of world opinion to write for it on contemporary public questions.

RICE, DAN (*b. New York, N.Y., 1823; d. Long Branch, N.J., 1900*), circus clown, showman. Remembered as one of the greatest of American clowns, Rice (born McLaren) was also famous as a crackerbox philosopher and commentator on public affairs.

RICE, DAVID (*b. Hanover Co., Va., 1733; d. 1816*), Presbyterian clergyman, active as a missionary and church organizer in Kentucky *post* 1783.

RICE, EDMUND (*b. Waitsfield, Vt., 1819; d. White Bear Lake, Minn., 1889*), lawyer, railroad executive and promoter. Brother of Henry M. Rice. Settling in St. Paul, Minn., 1849, he was prominent in developing railroads of that state. Twice mayor of St. Paul, he was a Democratic member of Congress, 1887–89.

RICE, EDWIN WILBUR (*b. Kingsborough, present Gloversville, N.Y., 1831; d. 1929*), Congregational clergyman and missionary. Official of the American Sunday School Union.

RICE, EDWIN WILBUR (*b. La Crosse, Wis., 1862; d. 1935*), electrical engineer. Son of Edwin W. Rice (1831–1929). A longtime associate as pupil and assistant to Elihu Thomson, Rice served as technical

director of the General Electric Co. and as its president, 1913–22. Patents issued to him cover practically the entire field of electrical operations; he was responsible for the addition of Charles P. Steinmetz to the company's staff. [*Supp. 1*]

RICE, FENELON BIRD (*b. Greensburg, O., 1841; d. Oberlin, O., 1901*), music teacher. Grandson of David Rice. Graduated Boston Music School, 1863; studied also in Leipzig. Director of the school of music at Oberlin College, 1871–1901.

RICE, HENRY MOWER (*b. Waitsfield, Vt., 1816; d. San Antonio, Texas, 1894*), Indian trader, Minnesota pioneer. Brother of Edmund Rice. Resident in Minnesota *post* 1847, he was influential in establishment of the Territory, served as territorial delegate to Congress, and was U.S. senator, Democrat, from the State of Minnesota, 1858–63.

RICE, ISAAC LEOPOLD (*b. Wachenheim, Bavaria, 1850; d. 1915*), New York lawyer, financier, chess expert. Came to America as a child. LL.B., Columbia Law School, 1880. Prominent as a railroad lawyer and as a promoter of electrical inventions, he was also the inventor of the "Rice gambit" and was founder (1886) and chief proprietor of the *Forum*.

RICE, JOHN HOLT (*b. Bedford Co., Va., 1777; d. 1831*), Presbyterian clergyman, educator. Nephew of David Rice. Active in establishing the theological seminary at Hampden-Sydney, he served as professor of theology there *post* 1824; he was also a strong controversial writer and a promoter of Presbyterian missionary activities.

RICE, LUTHER (*b. Northboro, Mass., 1783; d. 1836*), Baptist clergyman and educational promoter. Devoted his life to the organization of American Baptists in support of missionary work and higher education for the clergy.

RICE, NATHAN LEWIS (*b. Garrard Co., Ky., 1807; d. Chatham, Ky., 1877*), Presbyterian clergyman, editor. Held numerous pastorates in the East and Middle West; helped influence Cyrus H. McCormick to become patron of what is now known as McCormick Theological Seminary. President of Westminster College, Fulton, Mo., 1869–74, and professor of theology in Danville (Ky.) Seminary, 1874–77. He was most famous as a controversialist for his debates with Alexander Campbell in Kentucky, 1843.

RICE, RICHARD HENRY (*b. Rockland, Maine, 1863; d. 1922*), engineer. Graduated Stevens Institute of Technology, 1885. After wide experience as an engine and machine designer, Rice was associated with the General Electric Co. *post* 1903 for whom he directed work on the development of the steam turbine. He designed the first turbo-blower for blast furnaces to be installed in America.

RICE, THOMAS DARTMOUTH (*b. New York, N.Y., 1808; d. New York, 1860*), father of the American minstrel show. Introduced the "Jim Crow" song and dance at the Southern Theatre, Louisville, Ky., 1828; as prepared for publication by William C. Peters, the song became a hit in America and England. In addition to making successful tours in the character of "Jim Crow," Rice wrote numerous extravaganzas known as "Ethiopian Opera." Although he was not the first blackface comedian, Rice, by his phenomenal success, created a vogue for them.

RICE, VICTOR MOREAU (*b. Mayville, N.Y., 1818; d. 1869*), educator. Graduated Allegheny College, 1841. First superintendent and organizer of the New York State Department of Public Instruction, 1854–57, and 1862–68. His most conspicuous accomplishment was abolition of the rate bill and final establishment of free schools on the principle that the property of the state should educate the children of the state.

RICE, WILLIAM MARSH (*b. Springfield, Mass., 1816; d. 1900*), merchant, philanthropist. Removed to Houston, Texas, 1838, where he prospered as a trader, investor and landowner; left his large fortune for the foundation of Rice Institute, Houston.

RICE, WILLIAM NORTH (*b. Marblehead, Mass., 1845; d. Delaware, O., 1928*), geologist. Graduated Wesleyan University, 1865; Ph.D., Yale, 1867. Professor of geology and natural history at Wesleyan, 1867–84; thereafter taught only geology. Promoted a reconciliation of science and religion in his writing and teaching.

RICH, ISAAC (*b. Wellfleet, Mass., 1801; d. 1872*), Boston fish merchant and real estate owner. A leading benefactor of Methodist educational institutions, Rich left practically his whole estate to Boston University.

RICH, OBADIAH (*b. Truro, Mass., 1783; d. London, England, 1850*), bibliographer, bookseller. After serving as U.S. consul at Valencia, Spain, 1816-*c.* 1829, he moved to London, England, where he established himself as a bookseller and specialized in manuscripts and early printed books relating to America. His generosity with his stock and personal library won him the gratitude of such historians as Washington Irving, W. H. Prescott, George Bancroft and others. He was author of a number of catalogues of items which he had for sale which are still useful in bibliographical research.

RICHARD, GABRIEL (*b. Saintes, France, 1767; d. Detroit, Mich., 1832*), Roman Catholic clergyman, educator, Sulpician. Fleeing France during the Revolution, he came to Baltimore, June 1792, and was assigned by Bishop John Carroll to work among the French and Indians out of Kaskaskia and Cahokia. Settling in Detroit, June 1798, he succeeded as pastor of St. Anne's Church there and became vicar general of the region. A zealous, austere and able man, he ministered to whites and Indians, fought the evils of liquor and organized some of the earliest educa-

tional institutions in Detroit. Obtaining from Baltimore a printing press and a printer, he issued the first paper printed in Detroit, the *Essai du Michigan*, 1809, and also published a number of books. In an effort to stimulate local industry, he imported carding machines, spinning wheels and looms. Imprisoned as an American during the War of 1812, on his return to Detroit he engaged in relief work there and together with John Monteith, a minister, founded the University of Michigania, 1817. Elected delegate to Congress, 1822, he served a single term, the only priest ever to serve in that body. Returning to his church work in Detroit, he died ministering to victims of a cholera epidemic.

RICHARD, JAMES WILLIAM (*b. near Winchester, Va., 1843; d. 1909*), Lutheran clergyman, theologian, educator. Author of *The Confessional History of the Lutheran Church* (1909).

RICHARDS, CHARLES BRINCKERHOFF (*b. Brooklyn, N.Y., 1833; d. New Haven, Conn., 1919*), mechanical engineer. Trained as a practical mechanic, Richards devised a steam-engine indicator which facilitated high-speed engine design. While an official at the Colt Armory, 1861–80, he devised the platform-scale testing machine for testing the strength of metals and became a recognized authority on heating and ventilation. He headed the department of mechanical engineering at Sheffield Scientific School, Yale, 1884–1909.

RICHARDS, CHARLES HERBERT (*b. Meriden, N.H., 1839; d. 1925*), Congregational clergyman, official of the Congregational Church Building Society, lecturer on ecclesiastical architecture.

RICHARDS, ELLEN HENRIETTA SWALLOW (*b. Dunstable, Mass., 1842; d. Jamaica Plain, Mass., 1911*), chemist, home economist. Graduated Vassar, 1870; B.S., Massachusetts Institute of Technology, 1873. Taught sanitary chemistry at Massachusetts Institute *post* 1884; was a leader in the home economics movement.

RICHARDS, JOHN KELVEY (*b. Ironton, O., 1856; d. 1909*), jurist, Ohio legislator and official. U.S. solicitor general, 1897–1903; judge, U.S. circuit court (6th circuit), 1903–09. Gained high reputation for handling of Insular Cases and others before the U.S. Supreme Court, 1897–1903.

RICHARDS, JOSEPH WILLIAM (*b. Oldbury, England, 1864; d. 1921*), metallurgist. Came to America as a boy. Graduated Lehigh, 1886; Ph.D., the first to be granted by the university, 1893. An outstanding teacher at Lehigh *post* 1887, he was a recognized authority on the metallurgy of aluminum, electrometallurgy, and metallurgical-chemical calculations.

RICHARDS, THEODORE WILLIAM (*b. Germantown, Pa., 1868; d. Cambridge, Mass., 1928*), chemist. Son of William T. Richards. Graduated Haverford,

1885; Ph.D., Harvard, 1888. As a graduate student he came under the influence of Josiah P. Cooke who at that time was interested in atomic weights and because of his distrust of their current values had undertaken the revision of some of them. Cooke entrusted Richards with the experimental determination of the relation of the atomic weights of hydrogen and oxygen. In this extremely exacting problem Richards showed the qualities which made him the foremost experimental chemist of his time. After completion of his graduate work he spent one year as a traveling fellow in Europe. On his return he was appointed to the Harvard faculty, becoming a full professor in 1901 and obtaining the Erving Professorship of Chemistry in 1912. Richards always believed that only through measurements of precision was progress to be made in chemistry. Beginning with copper he redetermined the atomic weights of barium, strontium and zinc and, with the help of his students, twenty additional elements. In the course of this work many new analytical processes were devised and perfected. His determinations of atomic weights brought to light many previous inaccuracies.

During the last half of his career his interest turned to various fields of physical chemistry, in particular, thermochemistry and thermodynamics. He devoted much energy to the perfecting of thermochemical measurements and devised the "adiabatic calorimeter." New and highly accurate data were obtained in this way, covering heats of solution of metals in acids, heats of combustion of organic substances, heats of neutralization, specific heats of liquids, specific heats of solids at low temperatures, and heats of evaporation of liquids. The study of the data thus obtained led Richards to the discovery that the magnitude of the difference between "total energy change" and "free energy change" depends upon change in heat capacity of a system during chemical change and that this difference gradually disappears as the absolute zero is approached. His work in thermochemistry led him into the field of thermometry and to the exact determination for the first time of the inversion temperatures of hydrated compounds for use as fixed points.

Richards's chief interest in the latter part of his life lay in the consideration of the relation between the physical properties of the various elements and their compounds, especially those connected with atomic volumes and compressibilities. He devised new forms of apparatus for determining exactly the compressibilities of the elements and their compounds, as well as certain related properties such as surface tension and heat of evaporation. This work led to the discovery of the periodicity of atomic volume and compressibility and the close parallelism between these properties, as well as to the fact that increase or decrease in volume during a chemical change depends on the one hand upon the compressibilities of the substances involved and on the

other upon their chemical affinities. The latest aspect of this work was an attempt to compute from compressibilities and other data the actual internal pressures which hold matter together. Richards published nearly 300 papers covering a far wider field than indicated here. While many of the theoretical results which he reached have been and will be of the greatest importance, his contribution to the technique of precise physico-chemical investigation will undoubtedly always stand out as being equally important. Indeed he may well be said to have inaugurated a new era in the accuracy of analytical and physico-chemical experimentation. He received the Nobel prize of 1914 for his work on atomic weights.

RICHARDS, THOMAS ADDISON (*b. London, England, 1820; d. Annapolis, Md., 1900*), landscape painter, art teacher. Came to America as a boy. Studied at N.Y. National Academy of Design in which he became an associate and an official. His work as a painter belongs with the Hudson River school and his romantic enthusiasm for natural scenery may be considered the keynote of his career. He was professor of art in the present New York University, 1867–87. Among the books which he wrote and illustrated were *The American Artist* (1838), *Georgia Illustrated* (1842), *American Scenery* (1854) and *Appletons' Illustrated Hand-book of American Travel* (1857).

RICHARDS, WILLIAM (*b. Plainfield, Mass., 1793; d. 1847*), Congregational clergyman, missionary to the Hawaiian Islands. Richards spent the great part of his life *post* 1838 as a Hawaiian government official and played a great but unobtrusive part in liberalizing the Hawaiian economic and political system.

RICHARDS, WILLIAM TROST (*b. Philadelphia, Pa., 1833; d. Newport, R.I., 1905*), painter. Father of Theodore W. Richards. Specialized in accurate, realistic seascapes.

RICHARDS, ZALMON (*b. Cummington, Mass., 1811; d. Washington, D.C., 1899*), educator. Graduated Williams, 1836. An organizer and first president (1857) of the National Teachers' Association which later became the National Education Association.

RICHARDSON, ALBERT DEANE (*b. Franklin, Mass., 1833; d. New York, N.Y., 1869*), journalist, Civil War correspondent for the *New York Tribune.* Author of two books immensely popular in their time: *The Secret Service* (1865) and *Beyond the Mississippi* (1866).

RICHARDSON, ANNA EURETTA (*b. Charleston, S.C., 1883; d. Washington, D.C., 1931*), home economist, educator.

RICHARDSON, CHARLES FRANCIS (*b. Hallowell, Maine, 1851; d. Sugar Hill, N.H., 1913*), educator. Graduated Dartmouth, 1871. Professor of English at Dartmouth, 1882–1911. Author, among other works, of two pioneer studies: *A Primer of American Literature* (1878) and *American Literature: 1607–1885* (1887, 1888). Despite their shortcomings, these works supplied a need and were for a time of considerable influence.

RICHARDSON, CHARLES WILLIAMSON (*b. Washington, D.C., 1861; d. Boston, Mass., 1929*), physician, specialist in diseases of the throat, nose and ear.

RICHARDSON, EDMUND (*b. Caswell Co., N.C., 1818; d. Jackson, Miss., 1886*), cotton planter, factor, manufacturer. Removed to Mississippi, 1833, where he prospered as a merchant and plantation owner; he also engaged in factoring at New Orleans, La. Heavily in debt at the end of the Civil War, he rebuilt his fortune in a very short time, began the manufacture of cotton in addition to his other concerns and was at the time of his death the largest cotton planter in the world.

RICHARDSON, HENRY HOBSON (*b. St. James Parish, La., 1838; d. Boston, Mass., 1886*), architect. Great-grandson of Joseph Priestley. Educated in Louisiana and at Harvard where he graduated, 1859. Accepted in the fall of 1860 at the École des Beaux Arts, Paris, he worked under L. J. André and got some of his first practical experience under French architects who were imbued with the doctrines of Néo-Grec rationalism. At the end of the Civil War, he was urged to remain in France where his brilliance had been widely recognized, but he returned to America and won his first recognition in an 1866 competition for design of the First Unitarian Church, Springfield, Mass. His American reputation grew swiftly. His success in the Brattle Street Church competition (Boston, 1870) was followed by his winning the competition for plans for Trinity Church, Boston, in 1872. He achieved a nation-wide reputation for his Trinity design, and in 1876 shared with Leopold Eidlitz and Frederick L. Olmsted the work of completing the building and grounds of the New York State Capitol. Removing his home to Brookline, Mass., 1874, and his office there four years later, he continued on a successful course until his death, living well, enjoying life and happy in his friendships.

The long list of Richardson's work includes buildings in Boston, Chicago, Pittsburgh and Cincinnati. Beginning as an ecclesiastical architect, he turned increasingly to more modern problems; he is quoted as saying that he would have liked to have designed a grain elevator. His earlier churches are in a simplified Victorian Gothic style, but the Brattle Street Church tower strikes a new note, and in Trinity Church he first employed his own style of modified French and Spanish Romanesque. His larger houses betray a struggle between prevalent fashion and his own desire to be daringly new; his libraries, despite their Romanesque style, show the development of a rationalism not unlike that of the contemporary French. The Cincinnati Chamber of Commerce (1885) is grand in scale, but its roof shows the exaggeration into which the architect's gusto occasionally led him; his Pittsburgh Jail and Court House show his facility in handling materials and bringing out their special beauties, and achieve a grim, powerful magnificence that was new in American architecture. Richardson created outstanding innovations in his commercial buildings, notably in the Marshall Field Building, Chicago (1885). Almost equally revolutionary was the series of stations he designed in Massachusetts for the Boston & Albany Railroad.

Richardson's influence was enormous; he set an architectural fashion that dominated the eastern United States from 1880 until 1893. His imitators, however, copied his mannerisms only and failed to realize the deep foundations of his art. In consequence, Richardson's style fell into disrepute soon after his death, although his care in handling materials, the brilliance of his planning and his rationalism were all marked in the early work of Charles F. McKim and Stanford White who had served in his office. A lover of the decorative arts, he employed only the best men of his time in creating interior richness for his buildings, and his ideal of architecture and the sister arts as one unity persisted long after his death. A measure of his remarkable talents is the fact that to successive groups of architects from his own day to the present, each with varying demands, he has seemed to be the first great American example of the qualities that they each seek.

RICHARDSON, ISRAEL BUSH (*b. Fairfax, Vt., 1815; d. Sharpsburg, Md., 1862*), Union soldier. Graduated West Point, 1841. Served with great gallantry as an infantry officer in the Seminole and Mexican wars; after garrison duty in the Southwest, he resigned from the army, 1855. Organized and commanded the 2nd Michigan Regiment at the outbreak of the Civil War; covered Union retreat at first battle of Bull Run. Promoted brigadier-general and major-general, he led his division in the struggle for the "Bloody Lane" at Antietam and was mortally wounded there.

RICHARDSON, JAMES DANIEL (*b. Rutherford Co., Tenn., 1843; d. Murfreesboro, Tenn., 1914*), lawyer, Confederate soldier, Tennessee legislator, Masonic leader. Congressman, Democrat, from Tennessee, 1885–1905.

RICHARDSON, JOSEPH (*b. Philadelphia, Pa., 1711; d. 1784*), colonial silversmith. Member of the board of the Pennsylvania Hospital, 1756–70.

RICHARDSON, MAURICE HOWE (*b. Athol, Mass., 1851; d. 1912*), surgeon. Graduated Harvard, 1873; M.D., Harvard Medical School, 1877. Practiced in Boston; taught anatomy and surgery at Harvard Medical and served as Moseley Professor of Surgery, 1907–

12. Wrote with great ability on the development of the operation for appendicitis (1892–98).

RICHARDSON, ROBERT (*b. Pittsburgh, Pa., 1806; d. Bethany, W. Va., 1876*), physician, educator. A notable convert to the Disciples of Christ, 1829, he was a close associate of Alexander Campbell.

RICHARDSON, RUFUS BYAM (*b. Westford, Mass., 1845; d. 1914*), Greek scholar and archeologist. Graduated Yale, 1869; Ph.D., 1878; B.D., 1883. Taught Greek at Yale, Indiana University and Dartmouth; director, American School of Classical Studies at Athens, 1893–1903.

RICHARDSON, TOBIAS GIBSON (*b. Lexington, Ky., 1827; d. New Orleans, La., 1892*), surgeon. M.D., University of Louisville, 1848; was a private pupil of S. D. Gross. Taught anatomy and surgery at Louisville and Pennsylvania; professor of anatomy, University of Louisiana (now Tulane), 1858–62. After service on the Confederate medical staff, he returned to New Orleans and continued to teach anatomy at Tulane until 1872 when he became professor of surgery and so continued until 1889. He was also dean, 1865–85, and was elected president of the American Medical Association, 1877.

RICHARDSON, WILDS PRESTON (*b. Hunt Co., Texas, 1861; d. Washington, D.C., 1929*), army officer. Graduated West Point, 1884. Supervised building of Richardson Highway from Valdez to Fairbanks, Alaska; commanded U.S. forces in northern Russia, 1919; retired as colonel, Regular Army, 1920.

RICHARDSON, WILLARD (*b. Massachusetts, 1802; d. 1875*), journalist. Graduated South Carolina College, 1828; emigrated to Texas, 1837. As editor-owner of the *Galveston News*, post 1843, Richardson advocated state-rights doctrines, remorselessly opposed Sam Houston and was a Southern pioneer in independent journalism.

RICHARDSON, WILLIAM ADAMS (*b. Tyngsborough, Mass., 1821; d. 1896*), jurist. Graduated Harvard, 1843. After attending the law school and admittance to the bar, 1846, he practiced in Lowell, Mass., and was a probate judge. Accepting an assistant secretaryship of the U.S. treasury under G. S. Boutwell, 1869, he succeeded to the secretaryship, 1873. After a short term marked by weakness and ineptitude, he was made a judge of the Court of Claims, June 1874, and became chief justice of that court, 1885.

RICHARDSON, WILLIAM LAMBERT (*b. Boston, Mass., 1842; d. 1932*), obstetrician. Graduated Harvard, 1864; M.D., Harvard Medical School, 1867. Reopened the Boston Lying-In Hospital, 1873, and made it one of the outstanding hospitals of its type in the United States. Taught obstetrics at Harvard, 1871–1907, and was dean of the medical faculty *post* 1893.

RICHARDSON, WILLIAM MERCHANT (*b. Pelham, N.H., 1774; d. 1838*), jurist, congressman, New Hampshire official. As chief justice, New Hampshire superior court, 1816–38, he played a leading part in shaping the jurisprudence of that state.

RICHINGS, PETER (*b. probably London, England, 1798; d. Media, Pa., 1871*), actor, opera singer. Emigrated to New York, 1821; made his debut there at the Park Theatre in September. Achieving success by hard work rather than outstanding talent, he remained active in the profession until 1867.

RICHMOND, CHARLES WALLACE (*b. Kenosha, Wis., 1868; d. Washington, D.C., 1932*), ornithologist. M.D., Georgetown University, 1897. Associated for much of his life with the U.S. National Museum in curatorial capacities, Richmond was a recognized authority in problems of avian nomenclature and bibliography.

RICHMOND, DEAN (*b. Barnard, Vt., 1804; d. New York, N.Y., 1866*), businessman, railroad president, political leader in New York State. Starting as a leader of the "Barnburner" movement, he was chairman of the New York State Democratic committee, 1850–66, and was a dominating factor in his party's councils. *Post c.* 1852, he was a "Soft" Democrat, or favorer of compromise on the slavery issue; in 1860, he was a leader among the supporters of Stephen A. Douglas. With Thurlow Weed, he helped arrange the National Union Convention at Philadelphia, 1866, in an endeavor to unite Democrats and Conservative Republicans in opposition to the Republican Radicals.

RICHMOND, JOHN LAMBERT (*b. near Chesterfield, Mass., 1785; d. Covington, Ind., 1855*), Baptist clergyman, physician. Graduated Medical College of Ohio, 1822. While in practice at Newton, O., he performed first successful Caesarean operation (1827) to be reported in the U.S. medical press.

RICHMOND, JOHN WILKES (*b. Little Compton, R.I., 1775; d. Philadelphia, Pa., 1857*), physician. Practiced in Providence, R.I., post 1815; is chiefly remembered for his endeavors to compel the payment of the Revolutionary War debt of Rhode Island after virtual repudiation in 1844.

RICHMOND, MARY ELLEN (*b. Belleville, Ill., 1861; d. 1928*), pioneer social worker, teacher. Beginning her career with the Charity Organization Society of Baltimore, 1889, she became general secretary of the Society for Organizing Charity in Philadelphia, 1900; *post* 1909, she was director of the Charity Organization Department, Russell Sage Foundation. Among her books were *Social Diagnosis* (1917) and *Marriage and the State* (with F. S. Hall, 1929).

RICHTMYER, FLOYD KARKER (*b. Cobleskill, N.Y., 1881; d. Ithaca, N.Y., 1939*), physicist. Graduated Cornell, 1904; Ph.D., 1910. Taught physics at Cornell *post* 1906 and served *post* 1931 as dean of the graduate school. A pioneer in photometry and in the use of photoelectric cells, also in X-ray research. [*Supp.* 2]

RICKARD, GEORGE LEWIS (*b. Kansas City, Mo., 1871; d. Miami Beach, Fla., 1929*), gambler, prizefight promoter, better known as "Tex" Rickard.

RICKERT, MARTHA EDITH (*b. Dover, O., 1871; d. Chicago, Ill., 1938*), philologist. Graduated Vassar, 1891; Ph.D., University of Chicago, 1899. Professor of English, University of Chicago, *post* 1924, Miss Rickert made her principal contribution to scholarship in association with John M. Manly as editor of the monumental *The Text of the Canterbury Tales* (1940). She was author also of a number of other works. [*Supp.* 2]

RICKETSON, DANIEL (*b. New Bedford, Mass., 1813; d. New Bedford, 1898*), poet, local historian. Friend and associate of H. D. Thoreau, R. W. Emerson, the Alcotts and other leading literati.

RICKETTS, HOWARD TAYLOR (*b. Findlay, O., 1871; d. Mexico City, Mex., 1910*), pathologist. Graduated University of Nebraska, 1894; M.D., Northwestern, 1897; studied also in Vienna and at the Pasteur Institute in Paris. Joining the department of pathology, University of Chicago, 1902, he began a program in the then new field of immunology and in 1906 began his brilliant studies of Rocky Mountain spotted fever. In the course of his investigations, he discovered in the blood of patients and in the communicating ticks and their eggs a small organism which he rightly assumed to be the cause of the disease; this and related organisms responsible for many important diseases are now known as *Rickettsia* in memory of the man who first identified them. Struck by the resemblance of Rocky Mountain fever to typhus, he undertook a successful investigation of that disease, demonstrating in a short time that the agent of transmission is chiefly the louse, and again finding micro-organisms which were later established as the true cause of the disease. He died of typhus himself in the midst of his successful work.

[*Supp.* 1]

RICKETTS, JAMES BREWERTON (*b. New York, N.Y., 1817; d. Washington, D.C., 1887*), Union soldier. Graduated West Point, 1839. After service with the artillery in the Mexican War and in various posts throughout the United States, he was appointed brigadier-general, 1862, and held divisional command at Cedar Mountain, second Bull Run, South Mountain and Antietam. Disabled by many wounds, he left the field until March 1864 when he again commanded a division in the Wilderness campaign and under Sheridan in the Shenandoah Valley. He retired as major-general in 1867.

RICKETTS, PALMER CHAMBERLAINE (*b. Elkton, Md., 1856; d. Baltimore, Md., 1934*), engineer, educator. Graduated Rensselaer Polytechnic, 1875. Engaged in engineering practice for many years, his reputation rests principally upon his educational work at Rensselaer and his development of that school materially and academically as teacher (*post* 1875), director (1892–1901), and president, 1901–34.

[*Supp.* 1]

RICORD, FREDERICK WILLIAM (*b. Guadeloupe, French West Indies, 1819; d. Newark, N.J., 1897*), librarian, New Jersey public official and jurist. Nephew of Philippe Ricord.

RICORD, PHILIPPE (*b. Baltimore, Md., 1800; d. Paris, France, 1889*), physician, world-wide authority on venereal diseases. Uncle of Frederick W. Ricord. Removed to France, 1820, for medical study and practiced there, principally in Paris; his *Traité pratique des maladies vénériennes* (Paris, 1838) was an epical document in the history of medicine.

RIDDELL, JOHN LEONARD (*b. Leyden, Mass., 1807; d. 1865*), physician, botanist. M.D., Cincinnati Medical College, 1836. Professor of chemistry, Medical College of Louisiana (later Tulane), New Orleans, 1836–65. Author of a pioneer botany text, *Synopsis of the Flora of the Western States* (1835). Riddell was active in the medical and civic life of Louisiana, but is particularly noted for his invention of the binocular microscope which he devised in 1851, put in form in 1852, and displayed before the American Association for the Advancement of Science in July 1853.

RIDDER, HERMAN (*b. New York, N.Y., 1851; d. 1915*), newspaper publisher. Established the *Catholic News* (N.Y.), 1886. After managing the *New-Yorker Staats-Zeitung*, he bought it from Oswald Ottendorfer *post* 1890 and directed it until his death. Active in German-American affairs and as an independent Democrat, he also held office in trade associations and in the Associated Press.

RIDDLE, ALBERT GALLATIN (*b. Monson, Mass., 1816; d. Washington, D.C., 1902*), lawyer, Ohio legislator and congressman. A bitter anti-slavery Whig, Riddle issued the 1848 call for a mass meeting at Chardon which inaugurated the Ohio Free-Soil party.

RIDDLE, GEORGE PEABODY (*b. Charlestown, Mass., 1851; d. Boston, Mass., 1910*), actor, reader, able director of Greek play revivals.

RIDDLE, MATTHEW BROWN (*b. Pittsburgh, Pa., 1836; d. Edgeworth, Pa., 1916*), Reformed Dutch clergyman, Biblical scholar. Taught New Testament exegesis at Hartford (Conn.) and Western Theological seminaries.

RIDEING, WILLIAM HENRY (*b. Liverpool, England, 1853; d. Brookline, Mass., 1918*), journalist, miscellaneous writer. Came to America, 1869. Associated *post* 1881 with editorial staff of *Youth's Companion;* also an editor of *North American Review.*

RIDEOUT, HENRY MILNER (*b. Calais, Maine, 1877; d. at sea, en route for Europe, 1927*), Harvard instructor, writer. Author of several textbooks in association with Charles T. Copeland, and of popular fiction.

RIDGAWAY, HENRY BASCOM (*b. Talbot Co., Md., 1830; d. 1895*), Methodist clergyman, theologian. Professor at Garrett Biblical Institute, 1882–95; president of the Institute *post* 1885.

RIDGE, MAJOR (*b. probably Hiwassee, in present Polk Co., Tenn., c. 1771; d. near Van Buren, Okla., 1839*), Cherokee Indian leader. After first supporting John Ross in opposition to land cession, he signed a treaty at New Echota, Ga., December 1835, whereby all Cherokee lands east of the Mississippi were ceded and westward removal accepted. The tragic westward migration of the Cherokees followed, and Ridge was murdered in revenge for his part in causing it.

RIDGELY, CHARLES GOODWIN (*b. Baltimore, Md., 1784; d. Baltimore, 1848*), naval officer. Appointed midshipman, 1799. Saw varied service in the wars with the Barbary powers, the War of 1812, and in campaigns against the West Indian pirates.

RIDGELY, DANIEL BOWLY (*b. near Lexington, Ky., 1813; d. Philadelphia, Pa., 1868*), naval officer. Commended, 1865, for energetic action against Confederate blockade runners throughout the Civil War; promoted commodore, 1866.

RIDGELY, NICHOLAS (*b. Dover, Del., 1762; d. 1830*), Delaware legislator and jurist. State attorney-general, 1791–1801; chancellor of Delaware, 1802–30.

RIDGWAY, ROBERT (*b. Mount Carmel, Ill., 1850; d. 1929*), ornithologist. A protégé of Spencer F. Baird, Ridgway assumed care of the bird collections of the Smithsonian Institution, and in 1880 was designated curator of birds, U.S. National Museum, in which post he continued until his death. He did important field work and was author of a number of books; among these were *Color Standards and Nomenclature* (1886), *The Birds of North and Middle America* (1901–19), and several works written in collaboration with Spencer F. Baird and Thomas M. Brewer. At the height of his career, Ridgway was considered the leading American ornithologist; his writings were models of accuracy.

RIDGWAY, ROBERT (*b. Brooklyn, N.Y., 1862; d. Fort Wayne, Ind., 1938*), civil engineer, expert in subway construction and deep tunnel work.

[Supp. 2]

RIDPATH, JOHN CLARK (*b. Putnam Co., Ind., 1840; d. New York, N.Y., 1900*), educator, author of popular historical works.

RIEGER, JOHANN GEORG JOSEPH ANTON (*b. Aurach, Bavaria, 1811; d. Jefferson City, Mo., 1869*), German Evangelical missionary in Illinois, Iowa and Missouri *post* 1836.

RIGDON, SIDNEY (*b. Piny Fork, Pa., 1793; d. Friendship, N.Y., 1876*), early Mormon leader. A Campbellite preacher in the Western Reserve *post* 1828, Rigdon announced a public conversion to Mormonism, 1830, and played an important role in the new movement until the death of Joseph Smith. Outmaneuvered in his attempt to be selected as "Guardian" of the church by Brigham Young and the other apostles, Rigdon was excommunicated at Nauvoo, 1844. In the following year, he was voted by a group of followers the president of a new sect. He was probably the author of the "Lectures on Faith," although Smith published them as his own.

RIGGE, WILLIAM FRANCIS (*b. Cincinnati, O., 1857; d. Omaha, Nebr., 1927*), Roman Catholic clergyman, Jesuit, astronomer. Director of the observatory, Creighton University, 1896–1927. Author of *Harmonic Curves* (1926) and other contributions to the literature of mathematics and astronomy.

RIGGS, ELIAS (*b. New Providence, N.J., 1810; d. probably Constantinople, Turkey, 1901*), missionary in the Near East *post* 1832, linguist, author.

RIGGS, GEORGE WASHINGTON (*b. Georgetown, D.C., 1813; d. Prince George's Co., Md., 1881*), banker. Entered partnership with William W. Corcoran in Washington, D.C., 1840–48; purchased Corcoran's interest in Corcoran & Riggs, 1854. Thereafter he continued the firm as Riggs & Co. until his death.

RIGGS, JOHN MANKEY (*b. Seymour, Conn., 1810; d. Hartford, Conn., 1885*), dentist. Studied under Horace Wells. A strong advocate of hygienic care of the mouth, he gained wide repute as a specialist in treatment of pyorrhea. On Dec. 11, 1844, at Hartford, he performed an outstanding operation in the history of modern anesthesia, extracting a tooth from the mouth of Horace Wells while the latter was under the influence of nitrous oxide gas.

RIGGS, STEPHEN RETURN (*b. Steubenville, O., 1812; d. Beloit, Wis., 1883*), Presbyterian clergyman. Missionary to the Sioux *post* 1837; authority on Siouan languages.

RIGGS, WILLIAM HENRY (*b. New York, N.Y., 1837; d. 1924*), art collector. Resident in Paris, France, *post c.* 1857, Riggs made a remarkable collection of art and armor which he was influenced by his friend J. Pierpont Morgan to present to the Metropolitan Museum of Art.

RIIS, JACOB AUGUST (*b. Ribe, Denmark, 1849; d. Barre, Mass., 1914*), journalist, reformer. Emigrated to New York City, 1870; was employed as a police reporter on the *New York Tribune* and the

Evening Sun. Offering evidence based on his personal observation of the degradation of the tenement districts of the city, Riis effected massive reforms in housing through his vivid writings and countless lectures. Opposed by politicians and landlords, he found a powerful friend and abettor in Theodore Roosevelt. Among his books were *How the Other Half Lives* (1890), *The Children of the Poor* (1892), *Out of Mulberry Street* (1898) and *The Making of an American* (1901).

RILEY, BENJAMIN FRANKLIN (*b. near Pineville, Ala., 1849; d. Birmingham, Ala., 1925*), Baptist clergyman, educator.

RILEY, BENNET (*b. St. Mary's Co., Md., 1787; d. Buffalo, N.Y., 1853*), soldier, Indian fighter. Entered U.S. Army as ensign of riflemen, 1813. After varied service in the War of 1812 and against the Western Indians, he became colonel of the 2nd Infantry at the outbreak of the Mexican War but was quickly advanced to brigade command. He received the brevet of major-general for his outstanding charge at the battle of Contreras, August 1847. Transferred to California, 1848, he served as provisional governor and convened the assembly at Monterey, September 1849, which drew up the first constitution for California and applied for admission into the Union.

RILEY, CHARLES VALENTINE (*b. London, England, 1843; d. 1895*), entomologist. Emigrated to the United States *c.* 1860; was associated with the *Prairie Farmer* (Chicago) as reporter and artist. Served as entomologist to the State of Missouri, 1868–77. His reports of his Missouri investigations established his reputation; many authorities date modern economic entomology from their publication. Through his efforts, the U.S. Entomological Commission was established, 1877, of which he became chief; he served as entomologist to the U.S. Department of Agriculture, 1878–79, 1881–94. He was an able investigator and a prolific writer, his work showing an unusual sense of economic proportion combined with scientific accuracy.

RILEY, ISAAC WOODBRIDGE (*b. New York, N.Y., 1869; d. 1933*), philosopher, educator. Graduated Yale, 1892; Ph.D., 1902. Professor of philosophy, Vassar College, 1908–33. Author of the notable *American Philosophy: The Early Schools* (1907), *American Thought from Puritanism to Pragmatism* (1915) and other works.

RILEY, JAMES WHITCOMB (*b. Greenfield, Ind., 1849; d. Indianapolis, Ind., 1916*), poet. Leaving school at 16, Riley worked as a sign painter and as a small town journalist. His popularity dates from his employment on the *Indianapolis Journal*, 1877–85, during which time the verses which he contributed to the paper were widely copied. The series of verses signed "Benj. F. Johnson, of Boone" were particularly noticed and were published as a book in 1883 with the title *The Old Swimmin' Hole and 'Leven More Poems.* Riley was truly a Hoosier poet, for the whimsical and eccentric characters in his verses together with their dialect and the scene against which they moved were all drawn from his local observations. Oversentimental as he may be, he made an original contribution to American literature in portraying the special characteristics of his time and place. Among the long list of his books, the most popular were *Afterwhiles* (1887), *Pipes o' Pan at Zekesbury* (1888), *Rhymes of Childhood* (1890) and *Poems Here at Home* (1893).

RIMMER, WILLIAM (*b. Liverpool, England, 1816; d. 1879*), sculptor, painter. Came to Nova Scotia as a child; was raised in Hopkinton, Mass., and Boston. Worked at a number of trades and professions including shoemaking, medicine and itinerant portrait painting; he was also a musician and a teacher of music. Encouraged to concentrate on sculpture *post* 1860, he won reputation but little income and was obliged to teach art anatomy in Boston and at Cooper Union, New York City. Unable to work with a group or with others at all, Rimmer was a man of extraordinary gifts, too widely lavished. However, William M. Hunt admired his genius and John La Farge and Daniel C. French were gladly his pupils.

RINDGE, FREDERICK HASTINGS (*b. Cambridge, Mass., 1857; d. Yreka, Calif., 1905*), philanthropist, California land developer. Donated a number of public buildings to Cambridge, Mass.

RINEHART, WILLIAM HENRY (*b. near Union Bridge, Md., 1825; d. Rome, Italy, 1874*), sculptor. Began work as a stone-cutter and letterer in Baltimore, Md.; studied at the Maryland Institute. Under the patronage of several local merchants including W. T. Walters, Rinehart visited Italy, 1855–57. Finding it impossible to practice sculpture at home, he returned to Italy in 1858, and kept a studio in Rome for the rest of his life. Throughout his career, Walters remained his chief patron. Rinehart's best work was done in a sensitive and refined neo-classic style. Among his works his "Clytie" (Peabody Institute) is perhaps his masterpiece, but his massive seated figure of Roger B. Taney (Annapolis, Md.; copy in Baltimore) remains one of the most successful public monuments in the United States.

RINGGOLD, CADWALADER (*b. Washington Co., Md., 1802; d. New York, N.Y., 1867*), naval officer. Grandson of John Cadwalader. Appointed midshipman, 1819; promoted lieutenant, 1828, and commander, 1849. During this period he was employed against the pirates of the West Indies and cruised in the Mediterranean and the Pacific; he commanded the *Porpoise* in the Wilkes Exploring Expedition, 1838–42. Engaged in surveys on the California coast, 1849–50, he published *A Series of Charts . . . to the Bay of San Francisco* (1851) and subsequently commanded a surveying expedition in the North Pacific, 1853–54. Ordered home as insane by Commodore Matthew C. Perry, Ringgold resented the action bitterly, as a medical survey upon his return to America declared him fully competent. Promoted captain, 1857, he later served with great distinction in the Civil War and retired as commodore, 1864.

RINGLING, CHARLES (*b. McGregor, Iowa, 1863; d. Sarasota, Fla., 1926*), circus proprietor. Joined four of his brothers in a concert company, 1882. Organizing their first circus, 1884, the brothers by 1900 had one of the largest shows on the road and began absorbing other circuses; they acquired the Barnum & Bailey Circus, 1907. Charles Ringling was also a prominent factor in the real-estate developments along Florida's West Coast.

RIORDAN, PATRICK WILLIAM (*b. Chatham, N.B., Canada, 1841; d. 1914*), Roman Catholic clergyman. Raised in Chicago; graduated Notre Dame, 1858; studied for priesthood in North American College, Rome. Consecrated coadjutor to Archbishop Alemany of San Francisco, 1883, he succeeded almost immediately to the see and administered it prudently until his death.

RIPLEY, EDWARD HASTINGS (*b. Center Rutland, Vt., 1839; d. Rutland, Vt., 1915*), Union brigadier-general, financier. Brother of Julia C. R. Dorr. Commanding the first federal infantry to enter Richmond, Va., 1865, he restored order, suppressed the mob and extinguished the fire which was raging in the Confederate capital.

RIPLEY, EDWARD PAYSON (*b. Dorchester, Mass., 1845; d. Santa Barbara, Calif., 1920*), railroad executive. Notable in particular for his skill and integrity in restoring the Atchison, Topeka & Santa Fé Railway during his presidency, 1896–1920.

RIPLEY, ELEAZAR WHEELOCK (*b. Hanover, N.H., 1782; d. West Feliciana, La., 1839*), lawyer, soldier. Grandson of Eleazar Wheelock. Served in War of 1812 as colonel of the 21st (present 5th) Infantry and as brigadier-general in the Niagara campaign. Resigning from the army, 1820, he practiced law at New Orleans, La., and was congressman, Democrat, from Louisiana, 1835–39.

RIPLEY, EZRA (*b. Woodstock, Conn., 1751; d. 1841*), Unitarian clergyman. Graduated Harvard, 1776. Pastor, First Church, Concord, Mass., 1778–1841. Abandoned Trinitarianism and orthodox Calvinism *c.* 1772, but was a fervent evangelical.

RIPLEY, GEORGE (*b. Greenfield, Mass., 1802; d. 1880*), Unitarian clergyman, editor, reformer, literary critic. Graduated Harvard, 1823; Harvard Divinity School, 1826. Minister of Purchase Street Church, Boston, 1826–41. Ripley was strongly influenced by German theology, and with F. H. Hedge edited *Specimens of Foreign Standard Literature*

(1838 and *post*), translations of Cousin, Jouffroy, Schleiermacher and others which were of profound influence on New England intellectual life. He resumed a previous controversy with Andrews Norton over the philosophy of religion in 1839, defending his own views as well as those of R. W. Emerson in *Letters on the Latest Form of Infidelity* (1840). An associate of Emerson, Hedge, A. B. Alcott, Theodore Parker, Margaret Fuller and others in the so-called "Transcendental Club," Ripley aided Miss Fuller in editing the *Dial* (founded 1840) and assumed charge of the Brook Farm colony (1841) which was to be a practical application of what he and William E. Channing considered the New Testament social order. Although he disliked the regimentation involved in socialism, Ripley, as president, along with others of the group, accepted the new constitution which made Brook Farm a Fourierite Phalanx, January 1844, and edited the *Harbinger*, post 1845. Heavily involved in debt on the final collapse of Brook Farm, August 1847, Ripley removed to New York City and in 1849 succeeded Margaret Fuller as literary critic of the *New York Tribune*. For more than 20 years he labored to pay off the debts of Brook Farm. In his 31 years as critic for the *Tribune*, hardly a single important American book escaped his intelligent criticism. In 1850, he was a founder of *Harper's New Monthly Magazine* and edited its literary department. Success with *A Hand-Book of Literature and the Fine Arts* (edited with Bayard Taylor, 1852) was followed by a further success as editor (with Charles A. Dana) of the *New American Cyclopoedia* (1858–63).

RIPLEY, JAMES WOLFE (*b. Windham Co., Conn., 1794; d. Hartford, Conn., 1870*), soldier. Graduated West Point, 1814. After varied service in the artillery, 1814–33, Ripley transferred to the ordnance corps. In command of the armory at Springfield, Mass., 1841–54, he rebuilt and modernized the plant. Chief of ordnance, U.S. Army, 1861–63, he fought favoritism, fraud and political influence.

RIPLEY, ROSWELL SABINE (*b. Worthington, O., 1823; d. New York, N.Y., 1887*), soldier. Nephew of James W. Ripley. Graduated West Point, 1843. Author of *The War with Mexico* (1849). Resigning from the army, 1853, he engaged in business in South Carolina. As a state militia officer, he commanded and reconditioned Forts Moultrie and Sumter after their evacuation and fall, 1861. Thereafter, as a brigadier-general in the South Carolina and Confederate forces, he was continually in disagreement with his superiors and subordinates although he was reputed an excellent officer and a wise, if unheeded, counselor.

RISING, JOHAN CLASSON (*b. Risingé Parish, Östergötland, Sweden, 1617; d. 1672*), scholar, Swedish official. Succeeded Johan B. Printz as governor of New Sweden, 1654; surrendered Fort Christina to the Dutch under Peter Stuyvesant, August 1655.

RITCHIE, ALBERT CABELL (*b. Richmond, Va., 1876; d. Baltimore, Md., 1936*), lawyer, Maryland public official. Great-grandson of William H. Cabell. Graduated Johns Hopkins, 1896; LL.B., University of Maryland, 1898. A strong fighter in the public interest against the public-utility companies, Ritchie served as Maryland attorney-general, 1915–19, and as governor of Maryland, 1919–34. A masterful tactician, he achieved many administrative reforms in the state and was frequently mentioned as a Democratic presidential prospect. [*Supp. 2*]

RITCHIE, ALEXANDER HAY (*b. Glasgow, Scotland, 1822; d. New Haven, Conn., 1895*), engraver, painter. Came to America, 1841. Engraved a number of popular reproductions of historical paintings, including "The Death of Lincoln" after one of his own paintings, and "The Republican Court" after Daniel Huntington.

RITCHIE, ANNA CORA. [See MOWATT, ANNA CORA OGDEN, 1819–1870.]

RITCHIE, THOMAS (*b. Tappahannock, Va., 1778; d. 1854*), journalist, politician. Cousin of Spencer Roane. Published and edited the *Richmond Enquirer*, 1804–45, and the Washington *Union*, 1845–51. Making his newspaper the "Democratic Bible" of its time, he favored public schools and state internal improvements. Supporting the "Virginia principles of '98," he opposed Henry Clay and the divisive tactics of John C. Calhoun.

RITNER, JOSEPH (*b. Berks Co., Pa., 1780; d. 1869*), farmer, Pennsylvania legislator. Governor, Whig and anti-Mason, of Pennsylvania, 1835–39, Ritner contended as best he could against financial panic, canal and railroad lobbying and anti-Abolitionist riots; he obtained a large increase in the permanent school appropriation and the number of common schools.

RITTENHOUSE, DAVID (*b. Paper Mill Run, near Germantown, Pa., 1732; d. 1796*), instrument-maker, astronomer, mathematician. Great-grandson of William Rittenhouse. Despite lack of formal schooling, Rittenhouse as a boy showed extraordinary mathematical and mechanical ability and by his own efforts acquired a sound knowledge of physical science. He opened an instrument shop on his father's farm chiefly for clock-making c. 1751. His first public service was a province boundary survey to settle a dispute with Lord Baltimore, 1763–64. He designed his celebrated orrery which gave him much contemporary fame, 1767; he also experimented on the compressibility of water and invented a metallic thermometer. In 1768 he presented to the American Philosophical Society his calculations on the transit of Venus that was to occur in 1769. To observe that event, he built an observatory and its equipment, including a transit telescope now considered the first telescope made in America. His observations (aided by William Smith, 1727–1803, and others) are re-

garded as among the best that were made. Removing to Philadelphia, 1770, he continued to work at an observatory there and in 1785 invented the collimating telescope; he also made a plane transmission grating, 1786, anticipating Fraunhofer. In 1792, he solved the problem of finding the sum of the several powers of the sines by demonstration to the second power, by infinite series to the sixth and by the law of continuation for higher powers. He was frequently engaged on boundary surveys and commissions for over half the British colonies in America and conducted canal and river surveys as well. As engineer of the Committee of Safety, 1775, he supervised the casting of cannon and the manufacture of saltpeter; in 1777, he was president of the Council of Safety, serving also as a member of the General Assembly and of the Board of War, and as state treasurer. Professor of astronomy at University of Pennsylvania, he was on the commission to organize the United States Bank and was appointed first director of the Mint, 1792, serving until 1795. He was president of the American Philosophical Society, 1791–96.

RITTENHOUSE, WILLIAM (*b. Mülheim-am-Ruhr, Rhenish Prussia, 1644; d. Germantown, Pa., 1708*), Mennonite minister, pioneer paper manufacturer. Emigrated to America, 1688. In partnership with William Bradford (1663–1752) and others, he built the first paper mill to be erected in the colonies on Paper Mill Run near Wissahickon Creek (Roxborough Township, Pa.), 1690.

RITTER, FRÉDÉRIC LOUIS (*b. Strasbourg, Alsace, 1834; d. 1891*), musical composer and historian, educator. Came to America, 1856; founded Cecilia Society and Philharmonic Orchestra, Cincinnati, O. Professor of music, Vassar College, 1867–91.

RIVERA, LUIS MUÑOZ. [See MUÑOZ-RIVERA, LUIS, 1859–1916.]

RIVERS, WILLIAM JAMES (*b. Charleston, S.C., 1822; d. Baltimore, Md., 1909*), educator. Professor of ancient languages at South Carolina College (later University of South Carolina), 1856–73. President of Washington College, Chestertown, Md., 1873–87. Author of the important *A Sketch of the History of South Carolina to the Close of the Proprietary Government, etc.* (1856).

RIVES, GEORGE LOCKHART (*b. New York, N.Y., 1849; d. Newport, R.I., 1917*), lawyer. Grandson of William C. Rives. Graduated Columbia, 1868; Trinity College, Cambridge, 1872. LL.B., Columbia Law School, 1873. Noted for his extensive and able public-service activity in New York City as trustee and officer of Columbia and of the Astor and Lenox libraries, as counsel and member of the Rapid Transit Commission, as president of the charter revision commission (1900) and in many other posts. Author, among other books, of *The United States and Mexico, 1821–1848* (1913).

RIVES, JOHN COOK (*b. probably Franklin Co., Va., 1795; d. 1864*), journalist. Partner of Francis P. Blair in management of the Washington *Daily Globe*, 1833–49; reported debates impartially in the *Congressional Globe*, 1833–64.

RIVES, WILLIAM CABELL (*b. Amherst Co., Va., 1793; d. "Castle Hill," near Charlottesville, Va., 1868*), Virginia political leader, diplomat. Grandson of William Cabell. Graduated William and Mary, 1809; was schooled in law and politics by Thomas Jefferson. Congressman, Jacksonian Democrat, from Virginia, 1823–29; U.S. minister to France, 1829–32. Elected to the U.S. Senate, 1832, he resigned in 1834 rather than obey instructions from the Virginia Assembly to take a stand against Jackson's removal of federal deposits from the U.S. Bank. Failing in a bid for the vice-presidential nomination with Martin Van Buren, he was re-elected to the Senate, 1836–39, replacing John Tyler. Heading the Virginia conservatives who insisted that federal money should be deposited in state banks, he came out squarely against Van Buren's sub-treasury system. Returning to the Senate, 1841, he stood with Tyler in his struggle with Henry Clay on the bank question; in 1844 he became a full-fledged Whig. On the expiration of his term, 1845, he retired to private life for several years, serving again as U.S. minister to France, 1849–53. In 1861, he opposed secession but declared that Virginia would join the Southern group if the government should attempt to coerce seceded states; he was a member of the peace convention which met in Washington that year at the instance of Virginia. He sat as a member of the Confederate Provisional Congress and as a member of the first regular Confederate Congress.

RIVINGTON, JAMES (*b. London, England, 1724; d. New York, N.Y., 1802*), bookseller, printer, journalist. Came to America, 1760; opened book shops in Philadelphia, New York and Boston, but confined his business interests to New York *post* 1766. Bankrupt several times through high living and free spending, he steadied himself *post* 1769 and his business prospered. On April 22, 1773, he put out the first regular issue of *Rivington's New-York Gazetteer*, a newspaper which proposed to print both sides of questions. The successful paper soon became offensive to the Sons of Liberty in New York because of its neutral policy, and in November 1775 a party of patriots from Connecticut destroyed Rivington's printing plant. Securing a new plant from abroad, he resumed publication in October 1777, this time in the Loyalist interest, and issued the paper through December 1783. Allowed to remain in the United States after the British departure, allegedly because of secret aid given to Washington's spies, Rivington failed to thrive and died poor.

RIX, JULIAN WALBRIDGE (*b. Peacham, Vt., 1850; d. New York, N.Y., 1903*), landscape painter, etcher. Became celebrated for his atmospheric renderings of California scenery; worked in Paterson, N.J., and New York, N.Y., *post* 1888.

ROACH, JOHN (*b. Mitchelstown, Co. Cork, Ireland, 1813; d. New York, N.Y., 1887*), shipbuilder. Came to America *c.* 1829. Prospering as a foundryman and engine builder, Roach was among the first to recognize the importance of the shift from wooden to iron vessels and in 1868 began planning for development of an iron shipbuilding industry in the United States. Removing from New York to Chester, Pa., 1871, he launched 126 iron vessels there between 1872 and 1886 and was active in awakening public opinion in favor of an American merchant marine.

ROANE, ARCHIBALD (*b. Lancaster, present Dauphin, Co., Pa., 1759; d. 1819*), lawyer, Tennessee jurist. An associate of Andrew Jackson in pioneer eastern Tennessee, Roane became attorney-general for the district of Hamilton when a territorial government was instituted, 1790. He served as Democratic governor of the State of Tennessee, 1801–03, and was twice a judge of the superior court of errors and appeals.

ROANE, JOHN SELDEN (*b. Wilson Co., Tenn., 1817; d. 1867*), planter, lawyer, Mexican War and Confederate officer. Removed as a young man to Arkansas, settling at Pine Bluff. Democratic governor of Arkansas, 1849–52.

ROANE, SPENCER (*b. Essex Co., Va., 1762; d. Warm Springs, Va., 1822*), jurist, Virginia legislator. Attended William and Mary; admitted to the bar, 1782, after attendance at the lectures of George Wythe. An admirer of the political thought of Patrick Henry and George Mason, Roane became a judge of the Virginia general court, 1789, and was elected to the supreme court of appeals, 1794. During his 27 years' service on this bench, his opinions were generally sound but inclined to the side of liberty rather than property; mindful of precedents, he was also alert to the public policies of his own time. A strict constructionist and supporter of Jefferson, he joined his cousin Thomas Ritchie in founding the *Richmond Enquirer* and contributed to it a series of articles (May and June 1819, May 1821) in opposition to what he regarded as the usurping tendencies of the U.S. Supreme Court under John Marshall. Heartily approved by (Democrat) Republican leaders including Jefferson, these articles reinvigorated the extreme state-rights theory.

ROARK, RURIC NEVEL (*b. Greenville, Ky., 1859; d. Cincinnati, O., 1909*), Kentucky educator.

ROBB, JAMES (*b. Brownsville, Pa., 1814; d. Cheviot, O., 1881*), banker. Active in New Orleans, La., commerce, public utilities and railroad promotion, 1838–59, and also subsequent to the Civil War.

ROBB, WILLIAM LISPENARD (*b. Saratoga, N.Y., 1861; d. Troy, N.Y., 1933*), electrical engineer, educator. Graduated Columbia, 1880; Ph.D., University of Berlin, 1883. Professor of physics, Trinity College, Hartford, Conn., 1885–1902; professor of electrical engineering and physics, Rensselaer Polytechnic, 1902–33. [*Supp.* 1]

ROBBINS, CHANDLER (*b. Lynn, Mass., 1810; d. Weston, Mass., 1882*), Unitarian clergyman, local historian. Pastor, Second Church, Boston, Mass., 1833–74.

ROBBINS, THOMAS (*b. Norfolk, Conn., 1777; d. Colebrook, Conn., 1856*), Congregational clergyman, antiquarian. Librarian, Connecticut Historical Society, 1844–54.

ROBERDEAU, DANIEL (*b. St. Christopher, B.W.I., 1727; d. Winchester, Va., 1795*), Philadelphia merchant, Revolutionary patriot. Father of Isaac Roberdeau.

ROBERDEAU, ISAAC (*b. Philadelphia, Pa., 1763; d. Washington, D.C., 1829*), engineer. Son of Daniel Roberdeau. Studied in London; assisted Pierre C. L'Enfant in work on the new city of Washington, 1791–92. Practicing as an engineer in Pennsylvania until 1812, he was appointed major in the newly organized topographical engineer corps of the U.S. Army, April 1813. He survived the temporary abolition of the corps in 1815, and in 1818 became its chief. He was given brevet rank of lieutenant-colonel, 1823.

ROBERT, CHRISTOPHER RHINELANDER (*b. Suffolk Co., N.Y., 1802; d. Paris, France, 1878*), New York merchant, Presbyterian layman, philanthropist. Founded Robert College, Constantinople, Turkey, 1863.

ROBERT, HENRY MARTYN (*b. Robertville, S.C., 1837; d. Hornell, N.Y., 1923*), Union Army engineer, parliamentarian. Author of *Pocket Manual of Rules of Order* (1876), generally known as "Robert's Rules." [*Supp.* 1]

ROBERTS, BENJAMIN STONE (*b. Manchester, Vt., 1810; d. Washington, D.C., 1875*), railroad engineer, lawyer, inventor of a breech-loading rifle. Graduated West Point, 1835; resigned from army, 1839, to enter railroad work and assisted George W. Whistler in Russian railroad construction, 1842. Re-entering the army, he gave distinguished service in the Mexican War and on the frontier. As a Union officer in the Civil War, he won brevets for gallantry in New Mexico and rose to rank of major-general in later service in Virginia, Tennessee and Louisiana.

ROBERTS, BENJAMIN TITUS (*b. Gowanda, N.Y., 1823; d. Cattaraugus, N.Y., 1893*), Methodist clergyman. An organizer and first general superintendent of the Free Methodist Church, 1860–93.

ROBERTS, BRIGHAM HENRY (*b. Warrington, England, 1857; d. 1933*), Mormon leader. Emigrated to Salt Lake City as a child. Author of *A Comprehensive History of the Church of Jesus Christ of Latter Day Saints* (1930).

ROBERTS, EDMUND (*b. Portsmouth, N.H., 1784; d. Macao, China, 1836*), merchant. As special agent of the United States, Roberts negotiated treaties of commerce with Siam and Muscat, 1833.

ROBERTS, ELIZABETH WENTWORTH (*b. Philadelphia, Pa., 1871; d. Concord, Mass., 1927*), painter, leader in work of the Concord (Mass.) Art Assn.

ROBERTS, ELLIS HENRY (*b. Utica, N.Y., 1827; d. Utica, 1918*), journalist, financier. Congressman, Republican, from New York, 1871–75; treasurer of the United States, 1897–1905. A "Half-Breed," a sound-money man, and a protectionist.

ROBERTS, GEORGE BROOKE (*b. near Bala, Pa., 1833; d. near Bala, 1897*), railroad executive, engineer. President of the Pennsylvania Railroad Co., 1880–97.

ROBERTS, HOWARD (*b. Philadelphia, Pa., 1843; d. Paris, France, 1900*), sculptor.

ROBERTS, ISSACHAR JACOB (*b. Sumner Co., Tenn., 1802; d. Upper Alton, Ill., 1871*), Baptist clergyman and missionary in China, 1837–52. Independent in status from 1852 until his return to America in 1866, he was deeply implicated in the Taiping Rebellion.

ROBERTS, JOB (*b. near Gwynedd, Pa., 1756; d. Gwynedd, 1851*), pioneer scientific agriculturist, inventor of farm machinery, leader in the Society of Friends.

ROBERTS, JONATHAN (*b. near Norristown, Pa., 1771; d. Montgomery Co., Pa., 1854*), farmer, Pennsylvania legislator. As congressman, (Democrat) Republican, from Pennsylvania, 1811–14, Roberts defended the policies of Albert Gallatin; as U.S. senator, 1814–21, and afterwards in the Pennsylvania legislature, he fought against Andrew Jackson and Jacksonian policies, later becoming a Whig.

ROBERTS, JOSEPH JENKINS (*b. Petersburg, Va., 1809; d. Monrovia, Liberia, 1876*), statesman. Born of free, colored parents, he migrated to Liberia, 1829, and became a merchant there. Appointed governor of Liberia, 1842, he mollified the hostile native chiefs, adjusted a difficult financial situation and, in 1847, called the conference at which the new republic of Liberia was proclaimed. Elected as first president, he served with wisdom and distinction through 1855; thereafter until his death he was president of the College of Liberia. Re-elected to the presidency of the republic, 1871, to quell a domestic crisis, he served until January 1876.

ROBERTS, MARSHALL OWEN (*b. New York, N.Y., 1814; d. Saratoga Springs, N.Y., 1880*), capitalist. Starting as a ship-chandler, Roberts came into prominence, 1847, when with George Law and others he took up a government contract for mail steamship service from New York to New Orleans and to the Isthmus of Panama. The California gold rush *post* 1849 tremendously increased business for their U.S. Mail Steamship Co. (incorporated April 1850), but later competition from Cornelius Vanderbilt and other factors ended the company's prosperity. Roberts's chartering and selling of steamships during the Civil War forms an interesting chapter in the history of profiteering; the success of his operations was in no way hindered by his activity in New York politics as an anti-Seward Whig and as a Republican. For many years president of the North River Bank in New York City, he was one of the group which financed Cyrus Field's first cable venture, 1854.

ROBERTS, NATHAN S. (*b. Piles Grove, N.J., 1776; d. 1852*), civil engineer. Worked on surveys for the Erie Canal, 1816–22; had charge of construction from Lockport to Buffalo, 1822–25. Thereafter he served as consulting engineer for canals in New York, Pennsylvania and elsewhere in the United States.

ROBERTS, ORAN MILO (*b. Laurens District, S.C., 1815; d. Austin, Texas, 1898*), lawyer. Admitted to the Alabama bar, 1837. Removing to Texas, 1841, he prospered in practice, served as district attorney and district judge, and was a justice of the Texas supreme court, 1857–61. Colonel of the 11th Texas Infantry, 1862–64, he was briefly chief justice of Texas under Confederate rule. Re-appointed chief justice of the supreme court, 1874, he won repute for learning. Elected governor of Texas, 1878, while still chief justice, he was re-elected, 1880, and during his terms improved the state's financial condition and established the University of Texas. Elected professor of law in the University, 1883, he served until 1893.

ROBERTS, ROBERT RICHFORD (*b. Frederick Co., Md., 1778; d. Lawrence Co., Ind., 1843*), Methodist clergyman. Raised in frontier Westmoreland Co., Pa., he was one of the earliest settlers in present Mercer Co. (the Shenango settlement), 1797. A pastor and circuit rider *post* 1802, he was elected bishop, 1816, and served until his death, removing in 1819 to Indiana.

ROBERTS, SOLOMON WHITE (*b. Philadelphia, Pa., 1811; d. Atlantic City, N.J., 1882*), civil engineer, canal and railroad expert. Inspired construction of the first successful anthracite furnace for iron-smelting in the Lehigh Valley, 1839–40.

ROBERTS, THEODORE (*b. San Francisco, Calif., 1861; d. Los Angeles, Calif., 1928*), actor, player of "heavy" roles on stage and in motion pictures.

ROBERTS, WILLIAM CHARLES (*b. Galltmai, Wales, 1832; d. Danville, Ky., 1903*), Presbyterian clergyman, educator. Emigrated to New York, N.Y., 1849. Graduated College of New Jersey (Princeton), 1855; Princeton Theological Seminary, 1858. President, Lake Forest College, Ill., 1886–93; Centre Col-

lege, Danville, Ky., 1898–1903. Served many other colleges as trustee.

ROBERTS, WILLIAM HENRY (*b. Holyhead, Wales, 1844; d. Philadelphia, Pa., 1920*), Presbyterian clergyman. Came to America as a boy. Held a number of pastorates; served as stated clerk of the General Assembly *post* 1884. A dynamic administrator, he worked especially for unity among Presbyterians.

ROBERTS, WILLIAM MILNOR (*b. Philadelphia, Pa., 1810; d. Soledade, Brazil, 1881*), civil engineer, canal and railroad expert. Chief engineer, Northern Pacific Railroad, 1869–79; chief engineer of all public works in Brazil, 1879–81.

ROBERTS, WILLIAM RANDALL (*b. Mitchelstown, Ireland, 1830; d. New York, N.Y., 1897*), merchant, Fenian leader. Emigrated to New York, N.Y., 1849. Succeeded John O'Mahony as president of the Fenian Brotherhood, 1865; with T. W. Sweeny, organized invasion of Canada, 1866. Congressman, Democrat, from New York, 1871–75; U.S. minister to Chile, 1885–89.

ROBERTSON, ALICE MARY (*b. Tullahassee Mission, Indian Territory, 1854; d. 1931*), educator, social worker. Granddaughter of Samuel A. Worcester; daughter of William S. Robertson. Engaged *post* 1880 mainly in Indian education in Oklahoma, she served as member of Congress, Republican, from Oklahoma, 1921–23.

ROBERTSON, ARCHIBALD (*b. Monymusk, Scotland, 1765; d. probably New York, N.Y., 1835*), miniature painter. Studied in Edinburgh and at the Royal Academy in London. Came to America, 1791; with his brother, Alexander, opened the Columbian Academy of Painting in New York City, 1792; was associated with American Academy of Fine Arts *post* 1816. Author of *Elements of the Graphic Arts* (1802). He continued active as a painter until 1828. In addition to portraits, he executed many water-color views of New York City.

ROBERTSON, ASHLEY HERMAN (*b. Ashmore, Ill., 1867; d. San Diego, Calif., 1930*), naval officer. Graduated Annapolis, 1888. Commanded battleships *California* and *Colorado*, 1914–16, and transport *Mount Vernon*, 1917. After holding a number of high and responsible commands *post* 1918, he died as vice-admiral commanding the 11th naval district.

ROBERTSON, GEORGE (*b. near Harrodsburg, Ky., 1790; d. Lexington, Ky., 1874*), Kentucky jurist and legislator. As congressman, Whig, from Kentucky, 1817–21, he initiated legislation passed in 1820 which liberalized the purchase of government land. Chief justice of the state court of appeals, 1829–43, he was an associate justice, 1864–70, and again chief justice, 1870–71. He was a Unionist during the Civil War.

ROBERTSON, JAMES (*b. Edinburgh, Scotland, 1740; d. probably Edinburgh, date of death unknown*), printer, journalist, Loyalist. Came to America *ante* 1766. Published *New-York Chronicle*, 1769; *Albany Gazette*, 1771–72; co-publisher of *Norwich Packet* (Conn.), 1773–76. Removing to New York City, 1776, Robertson and his brother published the *Royal American Gazette*, 1777–83, and also, in Philadelphia (March–May 1778), the *Royal Pennsylvania Gazette*. In Charleston, S.C., he published the *Royal South Carolina Gazette*, 1780–82. After the British evacuation of New York, he removed with his brother to Nova Scotia.

ROBERTSON, JAMES (*b. Brunswick Co., Va., 1742; d. Chickasaw Bluffs, Tenn., 1814*), Tennessee frontier leader, Indian fighter and treaty negotiator.

ROBERTSON, JAMES ALEXANDER (*b. Corry, Pa., 1873; d. Annapolis, Md., 1939*), editor, librarian, historian. Graduated Adelbert College of Western Reserve, 1896. Expert in the collection and editing of documents, Robertson made many contributions to the history of the Hispanic world; he held research appointments at the U.S. Department of Commerce, Florida State Historical Society and Stetson University, and was archivist of Maryland. [*Supp. 2*]

ROBERTSON, JEROME BONAPARTE (*b. Woodford Co., Ky., 1815; d. Texas, 1891*), physician, Texas pioneer, Confederate brigadier-general. Graduated in medicine, Transylvania, 1835. Practiced in Washington Co., Texas, *post* 1838; succeeded John Hood in command of the Texas brigade, 1862.

ROBERTSON, JOHN (*b. near Petersburg, Va., 1787; d. Mount Athos, Va., 1873*), lawyer, Virginia legislator and official. Brother of Thomas B. and Wyndham Robertson. An uncompromising critic of Jackson, he was congressman, Whig, from Virginia, 1835–41. A justice of the Virginia circuit court *post* 1841, he urged moderation when the Civil War threatened, but became and remained an active supporter of the Confederacy after secession.

ROBERTSON, MORGAN ANDREW (*b. Oswego, N.Y., 1861; d. Atlantic City, N.J., 1915*), merchant seaman, author of sea stories. Among his books were *Where Angels Fear to Tread* (1899), *Shipmates* (1901) and *Sinful Peck* (1903); his work was distinguished for its adventurous spirit and fast-paced action.

ROBERTSON, THOMAS BOLLING (*b. near Petersburg, Va., 1779; d. White Sulphur Springs, Va., 1828*), lawyer, Louisiana official. Brother of John and Wyndham Robertson. Secretary of the territory of Orleans, 1807–12; congressman, (Democrat) Republican, from the state of Louisiana, 1812–18; governor of Louisiana, 1820–24; U.S. district judge for Louisiana, 1824–28.

ROBERTSON, WILLIAM HENRY (*b. Bedford, N.Y., 1823; d. Katonah, N.Y., 1898*), lawyer, New York politician and legislator. His appointment as collector of the port of New York by President Garfield precipitated the fight over federal appointments and patronage, 1880–81, which resulted in the resignation from the U.S. Senate of Roscoe Conkling and Thomas C. Platt.

ROBERTSON, WILLIAM JOSEPH (*b. Culpeper Co., Va., 1817; d. Charlottesville, Va., 1898*), Virginia lawyer and jurist, the leading corporation lawyer in his section *post* 1865.

ROBERTSON, WILLIAM SCHENCK (*b. Huntington, N.Y., 1820; d. 1881*), Presbyterian missionary to the Indians. Father of Alice M. Robertson. Worked as teacher among the Creeks at Tullahassee, Indian Territory, 1849–61 and *post* 1866.

ROBERTSON, WYNDHAM (*b. near Richmond, Va., 1803; d. Abingdon, Va., 1888*), lawyer, Virginia legislator. Brother of John and Thomas B. Robertson. Whig governor of Virginia (acting), 1836–37. Opposed both secession and the coercion of seceded states.

ROBESON, GEORGE MAXWELL (*b. Oxford Furnace, N.J., 1829; d. Trenton, N.J., 1897*), lawyer, New Jersey official. As U.S. secretary of the navy, 1869–77, he was severely criticised for extravagance and favoritism. He was congressman, Republican, from New Jersey, 1879–83.

ROBIDOU, ANTOINE (*b. St. Louis, Mo., 1794; d. St. Joseph, Mo., 1860*), trapper, trader. Possibly traded to Taos, N.M., 1822; established home in New Mexico, 1828. Established, *c.* 1832, Fort Robidou or Fort Uinta, famous trappers' rendezvous in northeastern Utah; removed his home to St. Joseph, Mo., 1845. Interpreter with Gen. S. W. Kearny, 1846, he was badly wounded at the battle of San Pascual.

ROBINS, HENRY EPHRAIM (*b. Hartford, Conn., 1827; d. Greenfield, Mass., 1917*), Baptist clergyman, educator. President of present Colby College, 1873–82.

ROBINSON, ALBERT ALONZO (*b. South Reading, Vt., 1844; d. 1918*), civil engineer. Brother of Stillman W. Robinson. Supervised development and construction of the Atchison, Topeka & Santa Fé Railroad, 1871–93, becoming chief engineer and general manager; was president, Mexico Central Railway Co., 1893–1906.

ROBINSON, BENJAMIN LINCOLN (*b. Bloomington, Ill., 1864; d. Jaffrey, N.H., 1935*), botanist. Brother of James H. Robinson. Graduated Harvard, 1887; Ph.D., University of Strassburg, 1889. As curator of the Gray Herbarium at Harvard *post* 1892, Robinson increased its endowment, housed it in a building of his own design, and maintained its high standards. He was editor of an additional volume of Asa Gray's *Synoptical Flora of North America* (1895–97), co-editor of the 7th edition of Gray's *Manual of the Botany of the Northern United States* (1908), and author of *Flora of the Galapagos Islands* (1902) and many other studies. [*Supp. 1*]

ROBINSON, BEVERLEY (*b. Middlesex Co., Va., 1722 o.s.; d. England, 1792*), landowner, New York colonial official. Brother of John Robinson; brother-in-law of Roger Morris. Wealthy through marriage to a Philipse heiress and through his own trading ventures, Robinson was an ardent Loyalist in the Revolution and served as colonel of the Loyal Americans and other Tory units; he was particularly effective as a director of British spy and intelligence work. He removed to England on the downfall of British rule.

ROBINSON, CHARLES (*b. Hardwick, Mass., 1818; d. near Lawrence, Kans., 1894*), physician, California pioneer and legislator, agent of the New England Emigrant Aid Co. Cautious and calculating, Robinson was the balance wheel of the Free-State party in Kansas, 1855–59, and was a leader in uniting anti-slavery factions in the territory. An opponent of James H. Lane, he was elected governor of Kansas under the Topeka constitution, January 1856, but was soon indicted for usurpation and imprisoned by a pro-slavery grand jury. When the Republican party supplanted the Free-State organization, 1859, he was nominated for governor and elected, taking office on the admission of the state, 1861. His two years in office were filled with difficulties, including an attempt at impeachment because of alleged irregularities in sale of state bonds. Engaging in politics only sporadically thereafter, he was by turns a Liberal Republican, a Democratic candidate for Congress and a Greenback-Populist-Democratic candidate for governor.

ROBINSON, CHARLES MULFORD (*b. Ramapo, N.Y., 1869; d. Albany, N.Y., 1917*), journalist, author, city planner. Professor of civic design, University of Illinois, 1913–17.

ROBINSON, CHARLES SEYMOUR (*b. Bennington, Vt., 1829; d. New York, N.Y., 1899*), Presbyterian clergyman, hymnologist, editor. Author of *Songs for the Sanctuary* (1865), *Laudes Domini* (1884) and other hymnals.

ROBINSON, CHRISTOPHER (*b. Providence, R.I., 1806; d. Woonsocket, R.I., 1889*), lawyer, diplomat, Rhode Island attorney-general and congressman. U.S. minister to Peru, 1861–65.

ROBINSON, CONWAY (*b. Richmond, Va., 1805; d. Philadelphia, Pa., 1884*), lawyer. Brother of Moncure Robinson. Author of a number of scholarly works on history and legal institutions; worked with John M. Patton on revision of the Virginia codes, 1846–52.

ROBINSON, EDWARD (*b. Southington, Conn., 1794; d. New York, N.Y., 1863*), philologist, geographer. Husband of Therese A. L. von J. Robinson. Graduated Hamilton College, 1816; was influenced by Moses Stuart to specialize in Hebrew; studied in Germany, 1826–30. Professor of Biblical literature at Andover Theological Seminary and later at Union Theological Seminary, New York City, Robinson was founder of the *American Biblical Repository*, 1831 (editor, 1831–35) and of the *Bibliotheca Sacra*, 1843. His principal book was *Biblical Researches in Palestine, Mount Sinai and Arabia Petraea* (London, 1841). His work is now recognized as marking an epoch in the development of historical geography and related fields.

ROBINSON, EDWARD (*b. Boston, Mass., 1858; d. New York, N.Y., 1931*), museum administrator, classicist. Associated with Boston Museum of Fine Arts, 1885–1905; director, Metropolitan Museum of Art, New York City, 1910–31.

ROBINSON, EDWARD MOTT (*b. Philadelphia, Pa., 1800; d. New York, N.Y., 1865*), New Bedford (Mass.) merchant. Father of Hetty H. R. Green.

ROBINSON, EDWARD STEVENS (*b. Lebanon, O., 1893; d. New Haven, Conn., 1937*), psychologist. Graduated University of Cincinnati, 1916; Ph.D., University of Chicago, 1920. Taught at Chicago and Yale; made contributions to study of learning and memory, work and fatigue, and the development of a social psychology of the law. [*Supp. 2*]

ROBINSON, EDWARD VAN DYKE (*b. Bloomington, Ill., 1867; d. 1915*), economist. Graduated University of Michigan, 1890; Ph.D., University of Leipzig, 1895. Taught at University of Minnesota and at Columbia University.

ROBINSON, EDWIN ARLINGTON (*b. Head Tide, Maine, 1869; d. 1935*), poet. Descended collaterally from Anne Bradstreet, Robinson attended Harvard. His young manhood was clouded by family misfortunes. Unable to get magazine publication for his poems, he published them at his own expense in *The Torrent and the Night Before* (1896); with additional poems, they were republished in *The Children of the Night* (1897). After abortive attempts in Gardiner, Maine, and in Boston, Mass., to earn a living while remaining free to write, he removed to New York City, 1899. His *Captain Craig and Other Poems* (1902) received scant attention, but in 1905 his work was reviewed with intelligent praise in the *Outlook* by President Theodore Roosevelt. Thereafter, with the assistance of friends, he continued his career in more or less material security. His most distinguished early book *The Town Down the River* appeared in 1910; *The Man Against the Sky* (1916) won wide recognition. In 1917 he brought out *Merlin*, the first of his long poems on Arthurian themes. His *Collected Poems* (1921) was awarded the 1922 Pulitzer Prize; he received a second Pulitzer Prize for *The Man Who Died Twice* (1924), and a third for *Tristram* (1927). He was by this time in general critical esteem and *Tristram* enjoyed a large sale. Subsequent to *Avon's Harvest* (1921), he wrote a number of psychological studies in verse which included *Cavender's House* (1929), *Matthias at the*

Door (1931), and *King Jasper* (1935); these had a mixed critical reception as contrasted with the general acclaim given his purely narrative and lyrical work.

A careful technician, particularly in blank verse, Robinson reflected himself in his poetry; like him, it was reticent, sincere, unposed, and rooted in essential New Englandism. Whether he wrote of Yankees or the dwellers in Camelot, he concentrated his insight on the fundamentals of human nature. His greatest defect was that of obscurity. In his Arthurian poems, however, his fusion of psychological insight with dramatic force and richness of language showed forth to greatest advantage. A well-worn story took on new life under his hands, as in *Tristram*, where the rush and passion of the tale itself simplified his thoughts and permitted him a perfect balance of intellect and feeling. [*Supp.* 1]

ROBINSON, EZEKIEL GILMAN (*b. S. Attleboro, Mass., 1815; d. Boston, Mass., 1894*), Baptist clergyman, educator. Graduated Brown, 1838; Newton Theological Institution, 1842. Professor of Biblical theology, Rochester Theological Seminary, 1853–72, and its president *post* 1860, he became president of Brown University, 1872. His stern but efficient rule ended in 1889, leaving the University far richer in equipment and further advanced in educational policy.

ROBINSON, FREDERICK BYRON (*b. near Hollandale, Wis., 1855; d. 1910*), surgeon, anatomist. Graduated University of Wisconsin, 1878; M.D., Rush Medical College, 1882. Settling in Chicago, Ill., 1891, he taught gynecology and abdominal surgery at several Chicago medical schools and held a number of hospital staff posts. His chief claim to distinction rests upon his researches and voluminous writings in the field of the anatomy of the abdomen and pelvis.

ROBINSON, HARRIET JANE HANSON (*b. Boston, Mass., 1825; d. Malden, Mass., 1911*), woman suffrage leader. Wife of William S. Robinson.

ROBINSON, HENRY CORNELIUS (*b. Hartford, Conn., 1832; d. Hartford, 1900*), corporation lawyer, Connecticut Republican legislator and judicial reformer, leading Congregational layman.

ROBINSON, JAMES HARVEY (*b. Bloomington, Ill., 1863; d. New York, N.Y., 1936*), historian. Brother of Benjamin L. Robinson. Educated in the Bloomington public schools, and at the State Normal School where he developed a lifelong interest in biology, he traveled abroad and engaged in business before entering Harvard. Graduating in 1887, he took a master's degree the following year and received a doctorate from the University of Freiburg, 1890. He taught at University of Pennsylvania, 1891–95. Professor of European history at Barnard College and Columbia, 1895–1919, he helped found the New School for Social Research (New York City), 1919, and remained with it until 1921. Author of a best-selling work *The*

Mind in the Making (1921), which he had written in the hope of persuading the educated many to think critically about human behavior, he was author also of a number of textbooks and of *The New History* (1912) which advocated "totality" in historical study, viz., the employment of all the social and behavioral sciences in examining the record of man considered as an animal in a state of evolution. Filled with a sense of mission against organized Christianity, he rejected all forms of supernaturalism and considered that the principal task of the historian and his scientific allies must be to show ordinary men how to overcome the burden of the past and its precedents by understanding how that burden arose and grew. An outstanding teacher and lecturer, Robinson exercised great influence in shifting public secondary school teaching of history from its traditional political emphasis to consideration of how human beings came to be what they are. [*Supp.* 2]

ROBINSON, JOHN (*b. Virginia, 1704; d. Virginia, 1766*), Virginia colonial legislator and official. Brother of Beverley Robinson. Speaker of the House of Burgesses and treasurer of Virginia, 1738–66. A report after his death, based on an investigation by Richard Henry Lee and others, showed his accounts short by more than 100,000 pounds.

ROBINSON, JOHN CLEVELAND (*b. Binghamton, N.Y., 1817; d. Binghamton, 1897*), soldier. Attended West Point, 1835–38, leaving to study law. After Mexican War service, he remained in the army and was engaged principally in Western frontier duty. Commanding Fort McHenry, Baltimore, Md., in April 1861, he discouraged any attempt on the part of rioters to attack the post. Thereafter in continuous service with the Army of the Potomac, he distinguished himself particularly at Gettysburg. He rose to rank of major-general, retiring in 1869.

ROBINSON, JOHN MITCHELL (*b. Tuckahoe Neck, Caroline Co., Md., 1827; d. Annapolis, Md., 1896*), Maryland circuit and appeals court judge, *post* 1864; chief justice, court of appeals, 1893–96.

ROBINSON, JOSEPH TAYLOR (*b. near Lonoke, Ark., 1872; d. Washington, D.C., 1937*), lawyer. Congressman, Democrat, from Arkansas, 1903–13, he was elected governor of Arkansas in 1912, but resigned to fill a seat in the U.S. Senate, where he served, 1913–37. Robinson became Senate Democratic leader in 1923 and received his party's vice-presidential nomination in 1928. As Senate majority leader, 1933–37, he supported Pres. F. D. Roosevelt on almost every issue, including the unpopular Supreme Court reorganization bill. An able parliamentarian and an effective behind-the-scenes worker, he played an important role in two progressive Democratic administrations. [*Supp.* 2]

ROBINSON, MONCURE (*b. Richmond, Va., 1802; d. Pennsylvania, 1891*), civil engineer. Brother of

Conway Robinson. Built original line of Philadelphia & Reading Railroad, 1834–36.

ROBINSON, MOSES (*b. Hardwick, Mass., 1742; d. Bennington, Vt., 1813*), Revolutionary soldier, Vermont political leader. Chief justice of the supreme court, 1778–89; governor of Vermont, 1789–90; U.S. senator, 1791–96. Strongly opposed the Jay Treaty, 1794–95.

ROBINSON, ROWLAND EVANS (*b. Ferrisburg, Vt., 1833; d. Ferrisburg, 1900*). Author of a number of books of sketches in prose, depicting rural Vermont life and people.

ROBINSON, SOLON (*b. Tolland, Conn., 1803; d. Jacksonville, Fla., 1880*), Indiana pioneer, agriculturist, author. With James M. Garnett, Henry L. Ellsworth and others, Robinson was advocating formation of a national agricultural society as early as 1838; his activities paved way for forming of the U.S. Agricultural Society, 1852. Writing in the *New York Tribune* (for which he was agricultural editor, 1853–c. 1868), the *American Agriculturist,* and other journals, he produced a body of travel sketches which are trustworthy historical records of rural life of his time. He was author also of a number of books of more general interest which include *The Will: a Tale of the Lake of the Red Cedars* (1841) and *Hot Corn: Life Scenes in New York* (1854).

ROBINSON, STILLMAN WILLIAMS (*b. near South Reading, Vt., 1838; d. Columbus, O., 1910*), engineer, educator. Brother of Albert A. Robinson. C. E., University of Michigan, 1863. Established department of mechanical engineering at present University of Illinois, where he taught from 1870–78; professor of physics and mechanical engineering at Ohio State, 1878–95. A pioneer in experimental instruction in engineering education, he was also author of several outstanding textbooks and the holder of a number of profitable patents.

ROBINSON, STUART (*b. Strabane, Ireland, 1814; d. Louisville, Ky., 1881*), Presbyterian clergyman, editor, educator. Came to America as a child. Pastor in Louisville *post* 1858; aggressive editor of denominational journals; Confederate sympathizer.

ROBINSON, THEODORE (*b. Irasburg, Vt., 1852; d. New York, N.Y., 1896*), artist. Passed early life in the Midwest and West; settled in New York City, 1874, where he was an organizer of the Art Students League whose name he suggested; studied in Paris, France, under Carolus-Duran and J. L. Gérôme *post* 1877. Returning home, he became a member of the Society of American Artists, 1881. During subsequent journeys to France, 1884–92, he came under influence of the Impressionists and subsequently was important as pioneer and spokesman for the new movement in America. His work occupies a unique and outstanding place in American painting.

ROBINSON, THERESE ALBERTINE LOUISE VON JAKOB (*b. Halle, Germany, 1797; d. Hamburg, Germany, 1870*), philologist, novelist, translator. Wife of Edward Robinson (1794–1863). Resided in America, 1830–37, 1840–63. Wrote scholarly works on a wide variety of subjects, also several novels; employed pen-name "Talvj."

ROBINSON, WILLIAM (*b. Coal Island, Ireland, 1840; d. Brooklyn, N.Y., 1921*), engineer. Came to America as a child. Graduated Wesleyan University, 1865. Specializing in electrical work, Robinson was the inventor and basic patentee (1872) of the railroad block-signal; he also devised the bond wire system for connecting adjacent rails electrically, patented the radial car truck used on electric railways and made important improvements in steam turbines.

ROBINSON, WILLIAM CALLYHAN (*b. Norwich, Conn., 1834; d. 1911*), legal educator and author. Graduated Dartmouth, 1854. Assisted in reorganization of Yale Law School, where he taught, 1869–96; thereafter headed department of law, Catholic University of America, Washington, D.C. Author of *Notes on Elementary Law* (1875, 1882, 1910), *Elements of American Jurisprudence* (1900), a scholarly edition of Horne's *Mirrour of Justices* (1903) and other works.

ROBINSON, WILLIAM ERIGENA (*b. Unagh, Ireland, 1814; d. Brooklyn, N.Y., 1892*), lawyer, journalist, politician. Emigrated to America, 1836. Graduated Yale, 1841; studied at Yale Law School. Contributed the "Richelieu" dispatches from Washington to the *New York Tribune,* 1844–48. An ardent Irish patriot, he held a number of minor federal offices in New York; he served as congressman, Democrat, from New York, 1867–69, 1881–85.

ROBINSON, WILLIAM STEVENS (*b. Concord, Mass., 1818; d. Malden, Mass., 1876*), Massachusetts journalist, anti-slavery advocate. Whig, Free-Soil and Republican political leader. Clerk of Massachusetts House of Representatives, 1862–73, he was known as the "Warwick" of state politics and successfully led opposition to Benjamin F. Butler's bids for the governorship.

ROBOT, ISIDORE (*b. Tharoiseau, France, 1837; d. Dallas, Texas, 1887*), Roman Catholic clergyman, Benedictine. Came to America, 1871; founded monastery at Sacred Heart, Okla., 1875; became prefect-apostolic of Indian Territory, 1876, and served until 1886.

ROBSON, STUART (*b. Annapolis, Md., 1836; d. New York, N.Y., 1903*), actor. Stage-name of Henry Robson Stuart. Partner of William H. Crane in a celebrated comedy team, 1877–89.

ROCHAMBEAU, JEAN BAPTISTE DONATIEN DE VIMEUR, Comte de (*b. Vendôme, France, 1725; d. Thoré, France, 1807*), French soldier. Entering the army as a junior officer of cavalry, 1740, he was given command of a troop, 1743, and by 1747 had risen to colonel. After a period of retirement in the Vendômois, 1749–56, he shared in the brilliant campaign against Minorca, and after distinguishing himself at Crefeld, June 1758, rose to command of an infantry regiment in the next year. His skill in maneuver and his personal bravery saved the French from a disaster at Klostercamp, October 1760; early in 1761 he was made brigadier-general and inspector of cavalry. He was noted for his introduction of a number of tactical improvements and for his unusual interest in the welfare of his soldiers. Appointed to command the French expeditionary army in America, he sailed with his force from Brest on May 1, 1780, and arrived off Rhode Island on July 11. The splendid discipline of his army together with the tact and charm of the officers removed many old American prejudices against the French. Unwilling to make a major move until the French had command of the sea, he discouraged the idea of an attack on New York which was favored by Lafayette and Washington, requested reinforcement from France and put his army into winter quarters in Rhode Island. Informed in May 1781 that no more troops were to be expected but that the French West India fleet under command of the Comte de Grasse would cooperate with him and with Washington, he held a conference with the American general at Wethersfield, Conn., May 21. Washington still favored an attempt against New York, but Rochambeau urged that combined operations be undertaken with the fleet against Cornwallis in Virginia. The French army then moved from Newport and united with Washington's troops near White Plains, N.Y. The Franco-American force now numbered some 10,000 men and awaited news from de Grasse before it determined on its next move. When it was learned on August 14 that the French fleet was sailing for the Chesapeake, Rochambeau once again advised a march southward against Cornwallis who was being harassed by Lafayette's force in Virginia. The march southward began on August 19; an army group under Gen. Wm. Heath was left to threaten New York so as to deceive the British. Until August 29 the joint movement might well have been an attack in force on New York and so the British considered it; thereafter the speed with which the armies traveled to join Lafayette at Williamsburg, Va., was as extraordinary as the efficiency with which de Grasse (aided by the arrival of the French supporting fleet from Newport) repelled the efforts of the English fleet under Admiral Graves to prevent the sealing-off of the mouth of the Chesapeake. The combined armies arrived at Williamsburg, Va., on September 14 to find the British encamped at Yorktown in a hopeless position with no longer any chance of rescue by sea. After 17 days of formal siege, Yorktown was surrendered on Oct. 19, 1781. Rochambeau embarked for France, Jan. 11, 1783. Thereafter he held im-

portant district commands at home, commanded the northern military department in 1790–91, and was created a marshal of France, December 1791. Narrowly escaping death under the Terror, he was honored by Napoleon and received the Legion of Honor.

ROCHE, ARTHUR SOMERS (*b. Somerville, Mass., 1883; d. Florida, 1935*), popular novelist and storywriter. Son of James J. Roche. [*Supp. 1*]

ROCHE, JAMES JEFFREY (*b. Mountmellick, Ireland, 1847; d. Berne, Switzerland, 1908*), journalist. Emigrated as a child to Charlottetown, P.E.I.; removed to Boston, Mass., 1866. Assistant to John B. O'Reilly on the Boston *Pilot*, leading Irish Catholic journal in the United States, Roche became editor of the paper, 1890. He was U.S. consul at Genoa, Italy, 1904, and later at Berne.

ROCHESTER, NATHANIEL (*b. Westmoreland Co., Va., 1752; d. Rochester, N.Y., 1831*), merchant, Revolutionary soldier. After making several land purchases in the newly opened Genesee country of New York, he removed there from Hagerstown, Md., *post* 1803, and in 1818 settled in Rochester which had already been founded by him.

ROCK, JOHN (*b. Lauter, Hesse-Darmstadt, Germany, 1836; d. 1904*), nurseryman. Emigrated to New York City as a boy. Served in Union Army, 1861–65; removed to California, 1866, starting a nursery at Santa Clara. Established California Nursery Co. at Niles, 1884.

ROCKEFELLER, JOHN DAVISON (*b. Richford, N.Y., 1839; d. Ormond, Fla., 1937*), industrialist, philanthropist. Brother of William Rockefeller. His father, a trader in lumber, salt and other commodities, had a farm, first at Richford, later at Moravia, N.Y., where John first attended school. A year's further schooling at Owego, N.Y., and two years of high school in Cleveland, O., where the family moved in 1853, comprised Rockefeller's formal education. After three-and-a-half years with a Cleveland firm of commission merchants, Rockefeller and a young Englishman, Maurice B. Clark, formed (1859) a successful partnership, dealing in grain, hay, meats, and miscellaneous goods. Inheriting his mother's religious bent, Rockefeller became the leading layman in the Erie Street Baptist Church, and began contributing at least a tenth of his modest income to charities. In 1864 he married Laura Celestia Spelman, by whom he had four children, Bessie, Alta, Edith, and John D., Jr.

In 1863 Rockefeller, sensing the commercial possibilities in the recent linking of Cleveland by a railroad to the new "Oil Regions" in northwestern Pennsylvania, had joined in building a refinery, which in two years was the largest in Cleveland. Buying out his partners, 1865, Rockefeller, his brother William, and one of his original partners, Samuel Andrews, built a second refinery, the Standard Works, and William went to New York to develop the export and eastern trade. Rockefeller's special talent for enlisting brains brought him Henry M. Flagler as a partner in 1867; Flagler undertook in the firm's behalf an expert negotiation of lower freight rates, then unstandardized. Rockefeller's efficiency and foresight in the intensely competitive oil business soon effected further economies in operation. The firm made its own barrels, built warehouses, obtained fleets of lighters and tankers. Meticulous about details, he instituted a cost-accounting system accurate to the third decimal. In 1870 the firm became a joint-stock corporation, the Standard Oil Company of Ohio. Rockefeller, now convinced that solvency depended upon organization to end or abate destructive competition, pressed forward to acquire all other Cleveland refineries, and then refineries in other cities. Ownership or control of pipelines was the next step, accompanied by the purchase or lease of oil-terminal facilities in New York, and the beginning of an elaborate marketing system. Within seven years Standard Oil, holding a position close to monopoly, dominated the American oil industry. A few years later it also dominated the foreign oil market.

The organization of this vast combination became perplexing. The Ohio company, nucleus of the group, had no legal right to own property or stock outside Ohio. The solution, in 1881, was the establishment of a board of trustees which took over all stock and issued certificates of interest in the trust estates. Thus was the modern "Trust" born, soon followed by anti-trust laws as a result of public hostility against Standard Oil and similar trusts. Although it was never Rockefeller's intent to obtain absolute control of refining, the Standard's ruthless competitive practices gave great offense, and general American opinion refused to accept any excuses for monopoly. In 1892, Standard of Ohio's trust agreement was dissolved by court order. Management was subsequently controlled by interlocking directorates of various state companies and finally (1899) by a holding company, Standard Oil (New Jersey), which was disbanded after a federal suit and a dissolution decree in 1911.

Ironically, as public criticism of him rose to a climax, Rockefeller was only the nominal head of the combination. *Post* 1897 he was wholly occupied with the distribution of his vast fortune, but the "tainted money" controversy of 1905 threatened to interfere with acceptance of his benefactions. In philanthropy, however, as in business, he was a conspicuous innovator and organizer. By employing able publicity agents and mitigating his own policy of silence about his affairs, he effected an eventual change in public opinion. Frederick T. Gates, an able and imaginative Baptist clergyman whom Rockefeller had met when founding (1889) the University of Chicago, was his principal aide in philanthropy *post* 1891; he was joined in 1897 by John D. Rockefeller, Jr. The Rockefellers established four principal philanthropic institutions: the Rockefeller Institute

for Medical Research (1901); the General Education Board (1902); the Rockefeller Foundation (1913), "to promote the well-being of mankind throughout the world"; and the Laura Spelman Rockefeller Memorial Foundation (1918), later absorbed by the Rockefeller Foundation. Rockefeller's benefactions during his lifetime totaled $550,000,000, and the endowment of his foundations continued to multiply.

Rockefeller gained a pre-eminent place, both in industry and in philanthropy, as an organizing genius. Alike in rationalizing the chaotic oil industry as in exploring new fields in education, health, and social welfare, he contributed a powerful initial impulse, intense application to detail, great penetration in solving difficult problems, and a rare tact in welding together talented groups of men to implement his ideas. In industry he gave his associates the fullest latitude and in philanthropy a complete freedom, with the result that their loyalty never flagged. Rockefeller had neither great breadth of mind nor notable cultivation. His greatest failure was in public relations, which he never understood. His chief defect was his tardiness in comprehending the steady advance of business ethics and the necessity of squaring business practices with new demands by government. His dominant passion was neither money-getting nor power-seeking, but a hatred of disorder and waste. [*Supp.* 2]

ROCKEFELLER, WILLIAM (*b. Richford, N.Y., 1841; d. Tarrytown, N.Y., 1922*), financier, industrialist. Brother of John D. Rockefeller whom he assisted in his oil operations, managing Standard Oil's export selling functions in New York. An able salesman and commercial diplomat, he was active in bringing Henry H. Rogers, Charles Pratt and others into the Standard Oil mergers and later, in association with Rogers and with James Stillman, carried on a number of adventurous speculations in Wall Street securities, chief of which was the Amalgamated Copper deal. *Post* 1911 and the dissolution of the Standard Oil trust, he withdrew from an active part in the oil industry and devoted himself to his investments.

ROCKHILL, WILLIAM WOODVILLE (*b. Philadelphia, Pa., 1854; d. Honolulu, Hawaii, 1914*), Orientalist, diplomat. Educated in France; was official in American legations at Peking, China, and Seoul, Korea, 1884–87. Made scientific expeditions for the Smithsonian Institution in Mongolia and Tibet, 1888–89, 1891–92. Returning to the diplomatic service, 1893, he made his most notable contribution as special agent in China for settlement of the problems raised by the Boxer insurrection, 1900. He was also director of the International Bureau of the American Republics, 1899–1905, and thereafter U.S. minister to China and ambassador successively to Russia and Turkey. He presented a large library of rare Chinese works to the Library of Congress and was author of a number of important Far Eastern studies.

ROCKNE, KNUTE KENNETH (*b. Voss, Norway, 1888; d. southeast Kansas, 1931*), football coach. Came to America as a child; was raised in Chicago, Ill. Graduated Notre Dame, 1914. As head football coach at Notre Dame *post* 1918, Rockne developed colorful and highly trained teams whose play featured speed and deception. Many of the players trained by him became football coaches in colleges all over the country, further popularizing the so-called "Rockne System."

ROCKWELL, ALPHONSO DAVID (*b. New Canaan, Conn., 1840; d. 1933*), physician, Union Army surgeon. M.D., Bellevue Hospital Medical School, N.Y., 1864. In association with George M. Beard, Rockwell placed electro-therapeutics on a scientific and professional basis.

ROCKWELL, KIFFIN YATES (*b. Newport, Tenn., 1892; d. near Thann, Alsace, 1916*), aviator. Enlisted in French Foreign Legion, 1914; after pilot training, became member of Escadrille Lafayette, April 1916. Killed in action.

RODDEY, PHILIP DALE (*b. Moulton, Ala., 1820; d. London, England, 1897*), Confederate brigadier-general, merchant. Developed great abilities as cavalry scout leader under Generals Braxton Bragg, Joseph Wheeler and Nathan B. Forrest.

RODENBOUGH, THEOPHILUS FRANCIS (*b. Easton, Pa., 1838; d. New York, N.Y., 1912*), Union cavalry colonel, author. Awarded Congressional Medal of Honor for gallantry at Trevilian Station, Va., 1864.

RODES, ROBERT EMMETT (*b. Lynchburg, Va., 1829; d. Winchester, Va., 1864*), civil engineer, Confederate major-general. Graduated Virginia Military Institute, 1848. Starting in the Civil War as colonel, 5th Alabama Infantry, he distinguished himself at first Bull Run, Fair Oaks, Gaines's Mill, South Mountain and Antietam. Leading the flank march at Chancellorsville, his division launched the surprise attack which gave the Confederates the victory. Rodes was an outstanding officer in the Eastern campaigns, 1863–64, and died on the battlefield while counterattacking Union forces under Gen. P. H. Sheridan.

RODGERS, CHRISTOPHER RAYMOND PERRY (*b. Brooklyn, N.Y., 1819; d. Washington, D.C., 1892*), naval officer. Son of George W. Rodgers (1787–1832). Served with high efficiency in Seminole, Mexican and Civil wars; as superintendent, U.S. Naval Academy, 1874–78, he attempted with fair success to raise standards of studies and behavior.

RODGERS, GEORGE WASHINGTON (*b. Cecil Co., Md., 1787; d. Buenos Aires, Argentina, 1832*), naval officer. Brother of John Rodgers (1773–1838); father of Christopher R. P. and George W. Rodgers (1822–1863). Warranted midshipman, 1804; served in War

of 1812 aboard USS *Wasp* in engagement with HMS *Frolic* and later aboard USS *Macedonian*. Died while in command of the Brazil Squadron protecting American rights in present Argentina.

RODGERS, GEORGE WASHINGTON (*b. Brooklyn, N.Y., 1822; d. in action off Charleston, S.C., 1863*), naval officer. Son of George W. Rodgers (1787–1832); brother of Christopher R. P. Rodgers. Ordnance specialist.

RODGERS, JOHN (*b. Boston, Mass., 1727; d. New York, N.Y., 1811*), Presbyterian clergyman, Revolutionary chaplain, evangelist. Held pastorates for many years in New Castle Co., Del., and in New York City.

RODGERS, JOHN (*b. near present Havre de Grace, Md., 1773; d. Philadelphia, Pa., 1838*), naval officer. Father of John Rodgers (1812–1882); brother of George W. Rodgers (1787–1832). After merchant marine service in which he rose to master, Rodgers was appointed second lieutenant aboard the *Constellation*, March 1798, soon rising to first lieutenant and executive officer under Thomas Truxtun. Promoted captain a year later, he cruised in command of the *Insurgente* and later of the *Maryland*. Returning briefly to the merchant marine, 1801, he was recalled to the navy and served in the Mediterranean against the Barbary pirates, 1802–06. As senior officer under Commodores Morris and Barron, he commanded the blockading fleet off Tripoli with great success and played a great part in the treaty negotiations with Morocco, Tripoli and Tunis. Commanding the northern division of coast defense, 1810–11, while cruising in the frigate *President* he engaged the British sloop *Little Belt* off Cape Henry, May 16, 1811. Ranking officer in active service in the War of 1812, Rodgers operated principally against British commerce, performing feats which although they were not as brilliant as some of the famous sea duels of the war were much more useful. On shore duty with a detachment of sailors and marines, he harassed the British on the retreat down the Potomac after the expedition against Washington, D.C. He also helped defend Baltimore, Md., when it was menaced by the enemy. He became senior naval officer, 1821, and in 1823 served briefly as U.S. secretary of the navy.

RODGERS, JOHN (*b. near Havre de Grace, Md., 1812; d. Washington, D.C., 1882*), naval officer. Son of John Rodgers (1773–1838). Appointed midshipman, 1828; was active in surveys, principally with the North Pacific Exploring and Surveying Expedition, 1852–56. He began his Civil War service at Cincinnati, O., where he purchased and fitted out three small steamships, the nucleus of the Mississippi Flotilla. Aide to Adm. Du Pont in operations against South Carolina late in 1861 and later in actions on the James River, he became captain of the monitor *Weehawken*. He distinguished himself particularly in the attack on Fort Sumter, April 1863, and later against the Confederate ironclad *Atlanta*. At the time of his death he was senior rear-admiral.

RODGERS, JOHN (*b. Washington, D.C., 1881; d. near Philadelphia, Pa., 1926*), naval officer. Great-grandson of John Rodgers (1773–1838). Graduated Annapolis, 1903. The second naval officer to be licensed as an aviator, Rodgers commanded the Naval Air Station, Pearl Harbor, Hawaii, 1922–25. He won particular notice for heroism as commander of the San Francisco-Hawaii flight, September 1925.

RODMAN, ISAAC PEACE (*b. South Kingston, R.I., 1822; d. near Sharpsburg, Md., 1862*), businessman, Rhode Island legislator, Union brigadier-general. Commanding the 4th Division of the IX Corps, he was killed at the battle of Antietam.

RODMAN, THOMAS JACKSON (*b. near Salem, Ind., 1815; d. Rock Island, Ill., 1871*), soldier, ordnance expert. Graduated West Point, 1841. Invented process for casting cannon upon a hollow core, cooling inner surface by a flow of water so that each successive layer of metal was compressed by the shrinkage of outer layers; also developed an improved powder for artillery. His inventions were finally approved and adopted by the U.S. government, 1859, and were also adopted by the governments of Russia, Great Britain and Prussia. During the Civil War, he commanded the arsenal at Watertown, Mass., where he supervised casting of the celebrated "Columbiad" and other heavy guns, both smooth-bore and rifled, for use by the army and navy.

RODNEY, CAESAR (*b. near Dover, Del., 1728; d. Dover, 1784*), statesman, jurist. Brother of Thomas Rodney. Serving almost continuously, 1761–76, as Kent Co. delegate to the legislature at New Castle, Rodney was elected speaker in 1769, 1773–74 and 1775–76. He was an associate of Thomas McKean and George Read in patriotic activity and was a delegate to the First Continental Congress. Re-elected to Congress, 1775, he was also made brigadier-general of the Kent Co. militia. In the late afternoon of July 2, 1776, his vote committed the Delaware delegation to acceptance of independence and he also voted with McKean for the adoption of the Declaration. Rejected by the conservatives of Kent Co. because of his action, he failed to obtain any political office in the fall of 1776, but as a member of the Council of Safety busied himself in raising troops for Washington's army. In 1777 he was re-elected to the Continental Congress, and in the spring of 1778 he was chosen president of Delaware; he served with ability until November 1781. He was regarded by his contemporaries as a man of wit and high courage.

RODNEY, CAESAR AUGUSTUS (*b. Dover, Del., 1772; d. Buenos Aires, Argentina, 1824*), lawyer, statesman, diplomat. Son of Thomas Rodney; nephew of Caesar Rodney. Congressman, (Democrat) Republican, from Delaware, 1803–05; was a House

manager in impeachment proceedings against John Pickering and Samuel Chase. U.S. attorney-general, 1807–11, he served in the Delaware militia during the War of 1812. After service, 1817–18, as a U.S. commissioner investigating the political status of the newly established South American republics, he was congressman again very briefly in 1821, and U.S. senator, 1822. Appointed first U.S. minister to the Argentine Republic, he arrived in Buenos Aires, November 1823, but soon fell dangerously ill and died in office.

RODNEY, THOMAS (*b. Kent Co., Del., 1744; d. Natchez, Miss., 1811*), farmer, Revolutionary soldier, jurist. Brother of Caesar Rodney; father of Caesar A. Rodney. Judge, supreme court of Delaware, 1802–03; U.S. judge for Mississippi Territory, 1803–11.

ROE, EDWARD PAYSON (*b. present New Windsor, N.Y., 1838; d. Cornwall-on-Hudson, N.Y., 1888*), Presbyterian clergyman, popular novelist. Author of *Barriers Burned Away* (1872), *A Knight of the Nineteenth Century* (1877) and other moralistic novels which were all best sellers.

ROE, FRANCIS ASBURY (*b. Elmira, N.Y., 1823; d. Washington, D.C., 1901*), naval officer. Performed outstanding Civil War service in the taking of New Orleans and later on the Atlantic Coast blockade where he commanded the *Sassacus* in action against the Confederate ironclad *Albemarle*, May 1864. He retired as rear-admiral, 1885.

ROE, GILBERT ERNSTEIN (*b. Oregon, Wis., 1865; d. New York, N.Y., 1929*), lawyer, legal author. Political and legal adviser of Robert M. LaFollette. Practiced in New York, N.Y., *post* 1899.

ROEBLING, JOHN AUGUSTUS (*b. Mühlhausen, Germany, 1806; d. Brooklyn, N.Y., 1869*), engineer, bridge builder. Father of Washington A. Roebling. Graduated Royal Polytechnic Institute, Berlin; came to America, 1831. Settling in a German colony in Butler Co., Pa., Roebling soon abandoned his efforts to be a farmer and went to work for the State of Pennsylvania as an engineer on canal projects. Observing the greater utility of twisted wire cables over ropes made of hemp in hauling canal boats upon inclined planes, he designed machinery for fabrication of wire rope and in 1841 manufactured the first wire rope made in America. He moved his factory from Saxonburg, Pa., to Trenton, N.J., *c.* 1848. Interested from youth in bridge-building, in 1844–45 he designed and built a wooden aqueduct for the Pennsylvania Canal which was carried on two continuous wire cables; in 1846 he completed his first suspension bridge over the Monongahela River at Pittsburgh. Among his many successful bridge constructions thereafter, the most striking was his pioneer railroad suspension bridge at Niagara Falls, built 1851–55. As early as 1857, Roebling had suggested to the New York City authorities the possibility of a bridge over the East River between Manhattan and Brooklyn which would not interfere with navigation. Appointed chief engineer of the project ten years later, he perfected plans which were approved early in 1869. While making observations at the site of the proposed bridge in June 1869, he received the injury from which he died.

ROEBLING, WASHINGTON AUGUSTUS (*b. Saxonburg, Pa., 1837; d. Trenton, N.J., 1926*), civil engineer, industrialist. Son of John A. Roebling. Graduated Rensselaer Polytechnic Institute; served as assistant to his father until 1861. An officer of engineers in the Union Army, 1861–65, he received several commendations for gallant, efficient service, leaving the army as brevet colonel of volunteers. Returning to his post as assistant to his father, he succeeded the elder Roebling as chief engineer of the Brooklyn Bridge project in 1869 and saw it through to its successful conclusion, 1883. Seriously ill *post* 1872, Roebling had directed a great part of the work from his home, at the same time maintaining an active part in the family business at Trenton, John A. Roebling's Sons Co., of which he became president, 1876. He virtually retired from active professional work *c.* 1888.

ROEDING, GEORGE CHRISTIAN (*b. San Francisco, Calif., 1868; d. 1928*), horticulturist, nurseryman. Established the Smyrna fig culture in California by demonstrating necessity of pollination by the Blastophaga wasp.

ROEMER, KARL FERDINAND (*b. Hildesheim, Germany, 1818; d. Breslau, Germany, 1891*), German geologist. Visited America, 1845, to study condition of German colonists in Texas and to report upon natural resources in the country. Three of his works resulted from this journey: *Texas Mit besonderer Rücksicht, etc.* (Bonn, 1849), *Die Kreidbildungen von Texas, etc.* (Bonn, 1852) and a work on the fossils of western Tennessee published in 1860.

ROGERS, CLARA KATHLEEN BARNETT (*b. Cheltenham, England, 1844; d. Boston, Mass., 1931*), opera and concert soprano. Made American debut in New York, 1871; settled in Boston. Professor of singing at New England Conservatory of Music *post* 1902.

ROGERS, EDWARD STANIFORD (*b. Salem, Mass., 1826; d. 1899*), horticulturist, developer of the Rogers hybrid grape.

ROGERS, HARRIET BURBANK (*b. N. Billerica, Mass., 1834; d. 1919*), teacher of the deaf, pioneer in use of the oral method. Principal, Clarke School for the Deaf, 1867–86.

ROGERS, HENRY DARWIN (*b. Philadelphia, Pa., 1808; d. Glasgow, Scotland, 1866*), geologist, educator. Brother of James B., Robert E. and William B. Rogers. An early associate of Robert D. Owen, Rogers taught at the University of Pennsylvania, worked on surveys of New Jersey and Pennsylvania *c.* 1835–c. 1847, and was professor of natural history in the University of Glasgow *post* 1855. His report on the Pennsylvania survey (published, 1858) was a most important document, in particular for findings regarding the structures of the Appalachian Mountains.

ROGERS, HENRY HUTTLESTON (*b. Mattapoisett, Mass., 1840; d. New York, N.Y., 1909*), capitalist. Partner of Charles Pratt in oil refining, Rogers devised the machinery by which naphtha was first successfully separated from crude oil (patented, 1871). An executive of the Standard Oil Co. *post* 1874, he devoted much of his time to the Wall Street operations of that trust in association with William Rockefeller. Active in public utilities promotion and in such controversial deals as Amalgamated Copper (1899), he worked with E. H. Harriman in the latter's extensive railroad operations, and also in the insurance operations which led to the Mutual Life investigation, 1905. He was a friend and financial counselor of Mark Twain.

ROGERS, HENRY J. (*b. Baltimore, Md., 1811; d. Baltimore, 1879*), inventor, telegraph pioneer. An early associate of Samuel F. B. Morse.

ROGERS, HENRY WADE (*b. Holland Patent, N.Y., 1853; d. Pennington, N.J., 1926*), educator, jurist. Graduated University of Michigan, 1874. Professor of law, University of Michigan, *post* 1882; dean of the law school, 1886–90. President of Northwestern University, 1890–1900. Professor, Yale Law School, 1901–21; dean, 1903–16. Judge, U.S. circuit court of appeals, sitting in New York City, 1913–26. Did outstanding work in raising standards at Yale Law School.

ROGERS, ISAIAH (*b. Marshfield, Mass., 1800; d. probably Cincinnati, O., 1869*), architect. After apprenticeship to a carpenter, Rogers worked in the office of Solomon Willard and started his own practice *c.* 1826. Called the father of the modern hotel, he planned the Tremont in Boston (1828–29), and Astor House in New York (1834–36); also Clinton Hall (1847) and the New York Merchants' Exchange (1836–42). He designed other important buildings throughout the country with great taste and success; these included the second St. Charles Hotel, New Orleans, La. (*c.* 1851), and the Burnet House, Cincinnati, O. (1850). *Post* 1862, he was supervising architect of the U.S. Treasury Department.

ROGERS, JAMES BLYTHE (*b. Philadelphia, Pa., 1802; d. Philadelphia, 1852*), chemist, educator. Brother of Henry D., Robert E. and William B. Rogers. M.D., University of Maryland, 1822. Taught chemistry in many institutions and was associated with his brothers in their survey and other work; professor of chemistry, University of Pennsylvania, 1847–52.

ROGERS, JAMES HARRIS (*b. Franklin, Tenn., 1856; d. Hyattsville, Md., 1929*), inventor. Among the many devices on which he held patents, probably the most valuable was his system of printing telegraphy (1887–94).

ROGERS, JAMES HARVEY (*b. Society Hill, S.C., 1886; d. Rio de Janeiro, Brazil, 1939*), economist. Studied at universities of South Carolina, Chicago, and Geneva (under Vilfredo Pareto), and at Yale (Ph.D., 1916). Taught at University of Missouri, at Cornell, and at Yale, 1931–39. Rogers combined a keen capacity for abstract mathematical analysis with concern for concrete social problems. One of President Franklin D. Roosevelt's early advisers, he undertook in 1933 with George F. Warren a revision of U.S. government fiscal policies. Among other recommendations, he urged that abandonment of the gold standard and devaluation of currency be accompanied by large-scale public works and expanded foreign lending and trade in cooperation with other governments. He was author of *Stock Speculation and the Money Market* (1927), *The Process of Inflation in France, 1914–1927* (1929), *America Weighs Her Gold* (1931), and *Capitalism in Crisis* (1938). [*Supp. 2*]

ROGERS, JOHN (*b. Milford, Conn., 1648; d. New London, Conn., 1721*), founder of the Rogerene sect.

ROGERS, JOHN (*b. Salem, Mass., 1829; d. New Canaan, Conn., 1904*), sculptor, creator of the "Rogers groups." While employed as a machinist, he spent leisure hours moulding in clay; he studied ways of reproducing clay groups in plaster form during a short stay in Rome, 1858–59. Conceiving the idea of producing statuary which told a story of immediate popular interest, he made a sensation in New York with his "Slave Auction," 1859. The sale of copies of his original models continued brisk until the 1890's by which time critics began to patronize his sincere and almost photographic renderings. His Civil War groups have historical importance and contain some of Rogers's best portraits, for example, the Abraham Lincoln in the "Council of War." His genre groups, most popular of his works, are often exquisite and catch something of the movement and mass of monumental sculpture.

ROGERS, JOHN ALMANZA ROWLEY (*b. Cromwell, Conn., 1828; d. Woodstock, Ill., 1906*), Congregational clergyman, anti-slavery advocate, one of the original founders of Berea (Ky.) College.

ROGERS, JOHN IGNATIUS (*b. Philadelphia, Pa., 1843; d. Denver, Colo., 1910*), Pennsylvania corporation and real-estate lawyer, professional baseball executive.

ROGERS, JOHN RANKIN (*b. Brunswick, Maine, 1838; d. Olympia, Wash., 1901*), druggist, farmer, Populist, writer, Washington legislator. Settled in the State of Washington, 1890. Liberal coalition governor of Washington, 1897–1901; author of the "Barefoot Schoolboy Law."

ROGERS, JOHN RAPHAEL (*b. Roseville, Ill., 1856; d. Brooklyn, N.Y., 1934*), inventor. Son of John A. R. Rogers. Patented a machine for making stereotype matrices (1888) and devised a double-wedge space band. After legal difficulties with Ottmar Mergenthaler, Rogers merged his own company with the Mergenthaler Linotype Co., 1895, and served the combined companies as engineer and chief of the experimental department thereafter. He patented more than 400 devices in the field of composing machines for printing.

ROGERS, MOSES (*b. New London, Conn., c. 1779; d. Georgetown, S.C., 1821*), early steamboat captain. Commanded the *Phoenix*, 1809, in earliest ocean voyage of a steam vessel; fitted out the *Savannah*, 1818, and commanded her on her voyage to Liverpool, 1819.

ROGERS, RANDOLPH (*b. Waterloo, N.Y., 1825; d. Rome, Italy, 1892*), sculptor. Studied in Florence, Italy, 1848–51; resided principally in Rome, Italy, post 1855. A neo-classic whose modeling approaches realism, Rogers worked with great success and was an honored figure in his adopted Italian home. He is known principally for his "Columbus doors" of the U.S. Capitol at Washington, D.C., and for his heroic figure of "Michigan" on the top of the Detroit monument.

ROGERS, ROBERT (*b. Methuen, Mass., 1731 o.s.; d. London, England, 1795*), soldier. Reared on a farm near Rumford, present Concord, N.H. Raised recruits for Shirley's expedition to Nova Scotia, 1755; entered the New Hampshire regiment and became a captain on the Crown Point expedition. Noticed for his boldness and skill in scouting, he was appointed captain of an independent company of rangers, March 1756; he was promoted to be major of nine such companies, 1758. Famous in England and the colonies alike for rash courage, hardihood and prankishness, he was constantly in the field; he was at Crown Point, 1759, when he destroyed the Saint Francis Indians in a daring raid, and in the final campaign about Montreal. Late in 1760, he went west as far as Detroit and Shawneetown to receive the surrender of all French posts. Unable to adjust to peace and civilization and quite lacking in principle in his dealings, he was a consistent failure in his employments, 1760–75. Returning to America from England, 1775, he courted both the Americans and the British and was imprisoned as a spy by Washington in 1776. Escaping to the British, he raised the Queen's American rangers but was soon deprived of his command. Employed thereafter in recruiting, his dishonesty and dissipation rendered him next to useless and in 1780 he returned to England. During a brief period as commander at Michilimackinac,

1766–67, he commissioned Jonathan Carver to undertake an exploratory journey into the present Minnesota. He was author of *A Concise Account of North America* and *Journals* (both London, 1765) and a crude tragedy *Ponteach* (1766), one of the first dramas written by a native New Englander.

ROGERS, ROBERT EMPIE (*b. Baltimore, Md., 1813; d. 1884*), chemist, educator. Brother of James B., Henry D. and William B. Rogers. M.D., University of Pennsylvania, 1836. Active with his brothers in research work. Professor of chemistry, University of Virginia, 1842–52; at medical school, University of Pennsylvania, 1852–77; at Jefferson Medical College, *post* 1877. He was also employed as a metals expert by the U.S. Mint.

ROGERS, ROBERT WILLIAM (*b. Philadelphia, Pa., 1864; d. near Chadds Ford, Pa., 1930*), Orientalist. A.B., University of Pennsylvania, 1886; A.B., Johns Hopkins, 1887; Ph.D., Haverford, 1890; Ph.D., Leipzig, 1895. Taught at Drew Theological Seminary and at Princeton. A student of Assyriology, Hebrew and the Old Testament, Rogers made contributions to knowledge in all three fields. He was author, among other books, of *A History of Babylonia and Assyria* (1900, rewritten and reissued, 1915).

ROGERS, STEPHEN (*b. Tyre, N.Y., 1826; d. Valparaiso, Chile, 1878*), surgeon. Largely self-educated; M.D., New York Medical College, 1856. Practiced in Panama, 1849–55, and in Santiago, Chile, 1856–65, as surgeon to railroad companies. Returned to Chile, 1875, after successful practice in New York City.

ROGERS, THOMAS (*b. Groton, Conn., 1792; d. New York, N.Y., 1856*), inventor, locomotive builder. Built the "Sandusky," first locomotive to operate west of the Allegheny Mountains, at Paterson, N.J., 1837, improving on English models. In 1842 he produced the "Stockbridge" with cylinders outside of the frame; in 1844 he designed and built the locomotive type which was subsequently adopted generally throughout the United States. This had two pairs of coupled driving wheels and was the first example of the use of equalizing beams between the drivers and the front swiveling truck. He also introduced the shifting link valve motion and was the first (1850) to apply the wagon top boiler.

ROGERS, WILL (*b. near Oologah, Indian Territory, present town of Claremore, Okla., 1879; d. near Point Barrow, Alaska, 1935*), humorist, actor, news commentator. Of Cherokee extraction on both his paternal and maternal side, he enjoyed a comfortable frontier youth on his father's ranch and became an expert roper of calves. After brief attendance at Kemper Military School, 1897–98, he worked as a cowboy in Texas, traveled to the Argentine and to South Africa, worked as rope artist and rough rider with a Wild West show in Australia, and returned home in 1904. He made his New York début at Madison Square Garden, April 1905, with Col. Zach Mulhall's show; in the same year he discovered by chance that informal joking with the audience, often at the expense of his own skill with a lariat, improved his act. Projecting an essentially American image of a man playing his "natchell self," he rose to star rank in *Hands Up* (1915) and was a star of the *Ziegfeld Follies* in 1916–18, 1922, and 1924–25. Bringing news highlights into unexpected focus as part of his patter, he deflated rhetorical bunk and group smugness. A contributor of syndicated articles to newspapers *post* 1922, he began in 1926 a syndication of a single daily paragraph which dealt mainly with politics; ultraconservative at heart, he joked at whatever program, fad or party was uppermost. He reached the height of his acting fame in a series of talking pictures, 1929–35, in which he played himself, whether the costume was top-hat, overalls or medieval armor. A cowboy philosopher with a cool brain and a warm heart, he was held in popular affection as much for his personal qualities of decency and generosity as for his abilities as a performer. He was killed while attempting a flight north to the Orient with his fellow-Oklahoman, Wiley Post. [*Supp. 1*]

ROGERS, WILLIAM ALLEN (*b. Springfield, O., 1854; d. Washington, D.C., 1931*), cartoonist, illustrator of stories by James Otis, Kirk Munroe, and other authors of children's books.

ROGERS, WILLIAM AUGUSTUS (*b. Waterford, Conn., 1832; d. 1898*), mathematician, astronomer, physicist. Graduated Brown, 1857. A teacher at Alfred and Harvard universities and at Colby College, Rogers made important researches on the value of the yard and the meter and changes therein. He was closely associated with Albert A. Michelson and Edward W. Morley in application of optical methods to determination of minute changes in length.

ROGERS, WILLIAM BARTON (*b. Philadelphia, Pa., 1804; d. Cambridge, Mass., 1882*), geologist, educator. Brother of Henry D., James B. and Robert E. Rogers. Educated at College of William and Mary, he served there as professor of natural history and chemistry, 1828–35; he was professor of natural philosophy, University of Virginia, 1835–53. State geologist of Virginia, 1835–42, he worked jointly with his brother Henry on theory of structure of the Appalachians. An early advocate of the founding of Massachusetts Institute of Technology, he was elected its first president, serving 1862–70 and 1878–81.

ROGERS, WILLIAM CROWNINSHIELD (*b. Salem, Mass., 1823; d. London, England, 1888*), sea captain. Grandson of Jacob Crowninshield. Master of the clipper *Witchcraft* on her record run from Rio to San Francisco, 1851; served in Union Navy during Civil War; occupied himself thereafter with finance.

ROHÉ, GEORGE HENRY (*b. Baltimore, Md., 1851; d. New Orleans, La., 1899*), medical educator, psychiatrist. M.D., University of Maryland, 1873; studied also under Edward Wigglesworth. Taught and practiced in Baltimore principally; was active in modernizing treatment of the insane.

ROHLFS, ANNA KATHARINE GREEN (*b. Brooklyn, N.Y., 1846; d. 1935*), author. Graduated Green Mountain Junior College, 1866. Author of *The Leavenworth Case* (1878), pioneer work in modern detective fiction, and some thirty other mystery novels distinguished for technical skill. [*Supp.* 1]

ROLETTE, JEAN JOSEPH (*b. Canada, 1781; d. 1842*), fur trader. Worked out of Prairie du Chien along the Upper Mississippi and the Wisconsin, *post* 1806; was American Fur Co. agent *post* 1820. Served as chief justice of Crawford County, Wis., *post* 1830.

ROLFE, JOHN (*b. Heacham, Norfolk, England, 1585; d. probably Bermuda Hundred, Va., 1622*), colonist, Virginia official. Sailed in the *Sea Adventure,* 1609; settled in Virginia after stranding in Bermuda for some months; successfully adapted native tobacco to European taste. His marriage to Pocahontas in April 1614 brought an eight-year peace with the Indians in the neighborhood of Jamestown.

ROLFE, WILLIAM JAMES (*b. Newburyport, Mass., 1827; d. Martha's Vineyard, Mass., 1910*), teacher, philologist, textbook author and editor. Introduced regular instruction in English literature into Massachusetts high-school curricula.

ROLLINS, ALICE MARLAND WELLINGTON (*b. Boston, Mass., 1847; d. Bronxville, N.Y., 1897*), author, book reviewer.

ROLLINS, EDWARD HENRY (*b. Rollinsford, N.H., 1824; d. Isles of Shoals, N.H., 1889*), Whig, Know-Nothing and Republican politician. Elected to the lower house of the New Hampshire legislature, 1855, he became speaker in 1856; he took a vital part in the formation and subsequent success of the Republican party in his state. A congressman, 1861–67, he opposed reform in any guise and supported harsh measures of Reconstruction; thereafter he continued to operate the state Republican machine as its chairman, 1868–72. Treasurer of the Union Pacific Railroad, 1871–76 (with which he had been associated *post* 1869), he was U.S. senator from New Hampshire, 1877–83.

ROLLINS, FRANK WEST (*b. Concord, N.H., 1860; d. Boston, Mass., 1915*), banker. Son of Edward H. Rollins. Republican governor of New Hampshire, 1899–1901. Initiated "Old Home Week," 1898; promoted conservation.

ROLLINS, JAMES SIDNEY (*b. Richmond, Ky., 1812; d. 1888*), lawyer, Missouri legislator. Originally a Whig, Rollins served in Congress, from Missouri, as a Conservative-Unionist, 1861–65. Thereafter, as a member of the Missouri legislature, he assisted in the reorganization of the University of Missouri and opposed radical Republican policies. With Carl Schurz and Benjamin G. Brown, he was a leader in the Liberal Republican movement.

ROLLINSON, WILLIAM (*b. Dudley, England, 1762; d. 1842*), engraver. Came to America, 1789. Working thereafter in New York City in both line and stipple, he became eventually a bank-note engraver and made several improvements in the technique of bank-note manufacture.

ROLPH, JAMES (*b. San Francisco, Calif., 1869; d. Santa Clara Co., Calif., 1934*), businessman, public official. Successful in shipping and banking, Rolph served as nonpartisan mayor of San Francisco for 19 consecutive years *post* 1911 and dedicated himself to the expansion and physical improvement of the city. Elected governor of California as a Republican, 1930, he was ineffectual in dealing with the problems raised by the depression. [*Supp.* 1]

ROLSHOVEN, JULIUS (*b. Detroit, Mich., 1858; d. New York, N.Y., 1930*), painter. Studied at Cooper Union, New York City, and in Düsseldorf and Munich, Germany. Influenced by Frank Duveneck.

RÖLVAAG, OLE EDVART (*b. Island of Dönna, Helgeland, Norway, 1876; d. Northfield, Minn., 1931*), author, educator. Came to America, 1896. Graduated St. Olaf College, 1905; studied also at University of Oslo, Norway. Professor of Norwegian at St. Olaf College *c.* 1907–26, 1927–31. Among his many books, marked by creative realism and brooding imagination, *Giants in the Earth* (translated and published in America, 1927) achieved an outstanding artistic and popular success. It has been called the most powerful novel ever written about pioneer life in America.

ROMAN, ANDRÉ BIENVENU (*b. St. Landry Parish, La., 1795; d. probably New Orleans, La., 1866*), planter, Louisiana legislator. Outstanding Whig governor of Louisiana, 1831–35 and 1839–43; fostered efforts at flood control, public schools, internal improvements.

ROMANS, BERNARD (*b. Netherlands, c. 1720; d. probably at sea, c. 1784*), civil engineer, naturalist, cartographer, soldier. Came to America *c.* 1757; appointed deputy surveyor of Georgia, 1766; ran surveys in East and West Florida, engaging also in botanical study. Variously active after journeying north in 1773, he was employed by the N.Y. committee of safety, 1775, to construct fortifications on the Hudson River. Resenting interference with his work, he resigned. Commissioned captain of Pennsylvania artillery, February 1776, he served under Gen. Horatio Gates in part of the northern campaign. Ordered to South Carolina *c.* July 1780, he was captured at sea and imprisoned in Jamaica until the end of the Revolutionary War. Among his books the most noted is *A Concise Natural History of East and West Florida*

(Vol. I, New York, 1775, second edition, 1776; the second volume was never published). Maps made by him appear in a number of publications of the time.

ROMAYNE, NICHOLAS (*b. New York, N.Y., 1756; d. New York, 1817*), physician, medical educator. M.D., Edinburgh, 1780. Practiced and taught in New York; associated his private school with Queen's College, present Rutgers, 1792–93. After a somewhat checkered career *post* 1794, he returned to New York, 1806, and served as president and professor at the College of Physicians and Surgeons (later affiliated again with Queen's College) until 1816.

ROMBRO, JACOB (*b. probably Zuphran, Russia, 1858; d. New York, N.Y., 1922*), editor, socialist leader, Yiddish author. Best known under pen-name "Philip Krantz." Active here *post* 1890.

ROMEIKE, HENRY (*b. Riga, Russia, 1855; d. 1903*), originator of the press-clipping service. Resident in the United States *post c.* 1885.

RONDTHALER, EDWARD (*b. near Nazareth, Pa., 1842; d. 1931*), bishop of the Moravian Church. Held pastorates in Brooklyn, N.Y., Philadelphia, Pa., and Salem, N.C.; consecrated bishop, 1891. As Salem developed into Winston-Salem, largest industrial city in the state, Rondthaler played a leading part in its community life.

ROOD, OGDEN NICHOLAS (*b. Danbury, Conn., 1831; d. New York, N.Y., 1902*), physicist, specialist in physiological optics. Grandson of Uzal Ogden. Graduated College of New Jersey (Princeton), 1852; did post-graduate work at Sheffield Scientific School and at Berlin and Munich. Professor of physics, Columbia, *post* 1864, he was a master at devising and improving physical apparatus and instruments. He was author of an influential book on the physics of color sensations, *Modern Chromatics* (1879); among other devices, he developed the flicker photometer.

ROOSA, DANIEL BENNETT ST. JOHN (*b. Bethel, N.Y., 1838; d. 1908*), physician. M.D., University of the City of New York (present New York University), 1860. Professor at his *alma mater* and also at the University of Vermont, he was responsible for the founding (1883) of the New York Post-Graduate Medical School and was its president, 1883–1908.

ROOSEVELT, HILBORNE LEWIS (*b. New York, N.Y., 1849; d. 1886*), organ builder, electrical experimenter. Cousin of Theodore Roosevelt.

ROOSEVELT, NICHOLAS I. (*b. New York, N.Y., 1767; d. Skaneateles, N.Y., 1854*), engineer. Operated an engine-building works at present Belleville, N.J., *post c.* 1794. Entered partnership, 1797, with Robert R. Livingston and John Stevens to build a steamboat for which the engines were to be constructed at Roosevelt's works. The resulting vessel, *Polacca*, made a trial trip, 1798, attaining a speed of some three miles

an hour under its own steam. Compelled to abandon his works because of financial difficulties, Roosevelt became associated with Robert Fulton, 1809, in introducing steamboats on Western rivers; in 1811 he built at Pittsburgh the steamboat *New Orleans* which descended the Ohio and Mississippi in 14 days. He also received a patent (1814) for the use of vertical paddle wheels.

ROOSEVELT, ROBERT BARNWELL (*b. New York, N.Y., 1829; d. Sayville, N.Y., 1906*), political reformer, conservation pioneer, author. Uncle of Theodore Roosevelt.

ROOSEVELT, THEODORE (*b. New York, N.Y., 1858; d. Sagamore Hill, Oyster Bay, N.Y., 1919*), statesman, author, president of the United States. Born in a well-to-do family long identified on the paternal side with mercantile pursuits in Manhattan, Roosevelt was on his mother's side a descendant of Archibald Bulloch of Georgia. Handicapped as a child by asthma, he built up his body by sheer determination, teaching himself to ride, box and shoot; his early intellectual interests centered on natural history. Graduated Harvard, 1880. Finding that law failed to interest him, he turned to the writing of history, produced *The Naval War of 1812* (1882), and so entered on a literary career which made up one phase of his life and of which he never tired. As an independent Republican assemblyman for New York's 21st district, 1882–84, Roosevelt won acceptance in politics on his merits. An irritant to his elders and supposed betters, he attacked misconduct as he chose, saw to it that the newspapers had his side of every story and zestfully supported laws for the relief of labor and for better government. After an experiment in ranching in Dakota Territory, and the untimely deaths in 1884 of his wife (he had married Alice Hathaway Lee in 1880) and of his mother, he threw himself into active work and in quick succession wrote *Hunting Trips of a Ranchman* (1885), *Thomas Hart Benton* (1886), *Gouverneur Morris* (1888), *Ranch Life and the Hunting-Trail* (1888), *Essays on Practical Politics* (1888) and the first two volumes of *The Winning of the West* (1889). Meanwhile he had returned to practical politics, running for mayor of New York (1886) in a hopeless contest against Abram S. Hewitt and Henry George. Marrying again (Edith Kermit Carow) in London, 1886, he continued active in Republican politics; he supported the winning presidential ticket in 1888 and was made a U.S. civil service commissioner, May 1889.

A firm believer in reform, Roosevelt brought a glare of happy publicity over civil service as the politicians tried to evade the specific requirements of the Pendleton Act of 1883. Happy in Washington, Roosevelt was accepted in the circle of Henry Adams and John Hay and made an on-the-spot study of high policy and backstage intrigue. Ethical to the core, Roosevelt wrote and spoke like a lay evangelist, keeping the crooks out of offices and protecting competent officeholders. Returning to New York City, 1895, he completed *The Winning of the West* (published, 1894–96) and accepted the presidency of the board of police commissioners. Overzealous, he accomplished relatively little, but with Jacob A. Riis as his Boswell he studied the lowest levels of city life, observed the unholy alliance of graft, politics and crime, and succeeded as before in turning his daily routine into pungent, front-page news. Laborious wire-pulling persuaded President McKinley to make Roosevelt assistant secretary of the navy, 1897, a post in which he served with his usual gusto until resigning in May 1898 to take active service in the field during the war with Spain.

As convinced as any jingo of the merits of war over Cuba, he and his friend Leonard Wood organized the first volunteer cavalry regiment (Rough Riders), equipped it and secured its inclusion in the force mobilizing at Tampa. The Rough Riders, dismounted, took Kettle Hill before Santiago, July 1, 1898; when Wood was promoted to higher rank, Roosevelt became colonel. He later chronicled the unit's glories in *The Rough Riders* (1899), coming home an authentic hero of the war. His sudden popularity upset the plans of Republican boss Thomas C. Platt for the approaching campaign for governor of New York. Roosevelt, nominated, campaigned with an escort of Rough Riders and was elected by a small majority. He pushed practical reforms as much as possible without breaking with Platt, but two years of him in Albany made Platt ready for his promotion to any office outside the state. Unacceptable to President McKinley and Mark Hanna, Roosevelt was nevertheless nominated for the vice-presidency at Philadelphia in June 1900 and the *brio* of his campaign made it possible for McKinley to remain at home in dignity and safety. The Republican ticket was victorious.

Looking forward to a life on the political shelf as vice-president, Roosevelt became 26th president of the United States through the assassination of McKinley; he took the oath of office in Buffalo, N.Y., Sept. 14, 1901. Sensing that there was a chance for a flexible president to place himself at the head of a national movement for reorganization of the American pattern, and aware also that more was needed for reform than an ethical approach to government, Roosevelt bided his time and during his first term announced no change in administration doctrine. An able administrator, he brought a new virility to the job of president and a new technique to the office; red tape of any kind was abhorrent to him and with insatiable curiosity he strove for personal contact with as many kinds of human beings as was possible. Decisions flowed swiftly from his desk, more often right than wrong. The new sophistication in Washington, D.C., was marked abroad, and foreign nations altered the character of their diplomatic representatives in America, sending men of letters and wit rather than political factotums. Taking over the presidency in the midst of readjustments caused by the war with Spain, Roosevelt directed negotiation of the Hay-Herran Treaty (ratified, 1903, but rejected by Colombia) in an effort to expedite building of the Panama Canal. Enraged at the tactics of Colombia, Roosevelt in effect encouraged the secession of the Panama territory from its mother country and its institution as a new republic which, within a month, agreed in its own name to the treaty that Colombia had rejected. Thereafter he guided every step in the construction of the canal. Acting with complete freedom in foreign affairs, he brought about settlement of a European intervention in Venezuela that bore on both the Monroe Doctrine and canal strategy in 1902. When the Dominican Republic was threatened with intervention because of a similar situation arising out of economic default, 1904, Roosevelt persuaded that country to invite him to set up a financial receivership with an American comptroller to collect and disburse its revenues. He also settled the old Alaska boundary dispute on his own terms, 1903, and his cautious pressure upon both Russia and Japan resulted in the Peace of Portsmouth, September 1905. As he did not recognize arbitration as any substitute for preparedness, he continued to encourage army reforms (which included formation of a general staff, 1903) and the strengthening of the navy. Subsequent to some difficulties with Japan over the social position of Orientals in the United States, he openly soothed that country and then sent the modernized battle fleet on a tour around the world (December 1907–February 1909) which was a triumph of administration and policy. "Speak softly," he liked to say, "and carry a big stick, you will go far." In Latin America, however, recent events seemed to have set a pattern of North American aggression inconsistent with the Monroe Doctrine. To explain away the illusion of a menace from the north, Elihu Root, now secretary of state after John Hay's death, was sent on tour among the southern neighbors.

Congress, meanwhile, resented these high-handed executive actions but was left no option but to pay the bills and to limit the president's reform activities at home. The "Ananias Club," numbering all those who had been called liars by the president, grew apace; Roosevelt's hard-hitting methods sometimes made it difficult for his friends to work with him and embittered his enemies more than was necessary. Behind these costly quarrels lay the fact that Roosevelt was trying to dominate a government of checks and balances in which the coordinate branches were as constitutional as he was himself. Since Thomas Jefferson, no president had ranged his mind over so broad a field; since Andrew Jackson, none had been so certain that he had a special mandate from the people. As Roosevelt appeared to be swerving cautiously towards the left, Republicans of the school of McKinley feared and fought him while radicals tried to steal his glory. The struggle involved a new hypothesis of the control of an industrial society in order to save individual economic freedom. There was no effective Democratic opposition in the Roosevelt Congresses, but the key positions were held by Republican conservatives who distrusted Roosevelt's applications of the "Square Deal." On the death of Marcus A. Hanna, 1904, the conservative Republicans were left leaderless. After renomination at Chicago without opposition, Roosevelt took over the Republican national committee, naming G. B. Cortelyou as chairman. Following his easy victory in the 1904 election, Roosevelt disclaimed a third term. Among specific domestic problems that confronted him, revision of the tariff was recognized as necessary but nothing was ever done about it. Anticipating the "muckrakers" in their attacks upon the trusts, Roosevelt had demanded at Pittsburgh, July 4, 1902, that trusts be subjected to public control, a policy popular in both parties. With the dissolution of the Northern Securities Co., 1904, the addition to the Cabinet of a secretary of commerce and labor, the Elkins Law and the Expedition Act, further progress in trust control was made but there was more enthusiasm than certainty in the process. The interstate commerce act was strengthened, 1906, and sweeping laws were passed for the protection of food and drug buyers. But by 1906 the fervor of the "muck-rake" period had begun to die out and the president was left unpopular with business and the Republican party stalwarts. The Wall Street panic of 1907 was called the Roosevelt panic. Among the most memorable of Roosevelt's national services were his efforts for conservation of national forest and land reserves; in these he was strenuously opposed by Congress on a number of grounds both worthy and unworthy.

When he sponsored his secretary of war, William H. Taft, for the presidential nomination in 1908, Roosevelt hoped that his administrative team would be held together, but Taft preferred to select his own Cabinet after his election. Out of office, Roosevelt worked at writing and engaged in extensive travels, returning to America in June 1910 and receiving a triumphant reception. It was not in his nature to abstain from political activity and he was dissatisfied with President Taft's favoring of conservative policies. By the summer or early autumn of 1911 he became completely estranged from the president. Having allowed himself to be persuaded that the Roosevelt policies were lost unless he returned to politics, he entered the race for the nomination in 1912, but since the administration controlled the party machinery, the Republican convention renominated Taft. Roosevelt's delegation to the convention of 1912 became the nucleus of the Progressive party which met on August 5 and nominated Roosevelt for president and Hiram

Johnson of California for vice-president on a platform of liberal reform. His candidacy, however, only succeeded in providing opportunity for the victory of Woodrow Wilson. In 1914, Roosevelt went on an expedition to the Brazilian wilderness where he discovered the "River of Doubt"; he returned with a tropical infection from which he never fully recovered. A neutral in World War I until his old suspicions of Germany were revived, he became an enthusiastic supporter of the Allies and denounced the diplomatic courses of President Wilson, seeking with tongue and pen to arouse the country. Disappointed of his wish for military command after the United States entered the war, he entertained hopes that he might run for the presidency again in 1920, but died peacefully in his sleep early in 1919. His career had personified America's recognition of a changing world; his flaws were on the surface but his human values were timeless.

ROOT, AMOS IVES (*b. near Medina, O., 1839; d. 1923*), apiarist, pioneer in commercial bee-keeping.

ROOT, ELIHU (*b. Clinton, N.Y., 1845; d. New York, N.Y., 1937*), lawyer, statesman. Graduated Hamilton College, 1864; New York University Law School, 1867. Within a year he established his own law firm in New York City and began a career which made him the acknowledged leader of the American bar. His success was due to a phenomenal memory, capacity for hard work, mastery of detail, logical conciseness and clarity of argument, and ever-present wit. Court work was his specialty. No contemporary opprobrium attached to his serving (1873) as assistant to one of the defense counsel in the prosecution of Boss Tweed, or to later representation of large corporate interests, but these aspects of his practice were later magnified by his detractors, especially the Hearst press.

Active in local politics as a conservative, antimachine Republican, Root managed the N.Y. constitutional convention in 1894 and supported and advised Theodore Roosevelt during the latter's incumbency as New York City police commissioner and as governor of New York. Becoming President McKinley's secretary of war, 1899, Root made outstanding contributions in administration of Cuba and the new U.S. colonial possessions; he also effected a fundamental reorganization of the army. He created the Army War College and introduced the principle of the general staff; by requiring rotation from staff to line jobs, he discouraged entrenched military bureaucracy in Washington. In dealing with the problems of the former Spanish islands, Root sought for Puerto Rico a highly centralized system of government and exemption from the U.S. tariff. His fortunate selection of Gen. Leonard Wood as military governor of Cuba resulted in a model regime of rehabilitation. In the Philippines, Root was responsible for a program that firmly guaranteed individual liberties and developed local institutions.

Root resigned his cabinet post in 1903 but returned in 1905 as U.S. secretary of state. Among his notable accomplishments (for which he received the Nobel Peace Prize, 1912) were the re-establishment of friendly relations with Latin America and Japan, and the conclusion of a series of arbitration treaties. He also settled the North Atlantic fisheries controversy and established the U.S. consular service on a career basis.

From 1909 to 1915 Root served as U.S. senator from New York. Committed to William H. Taft before Theodore Roosevelt "threw his hat in the ring," Root sorrowfully but doggedly presided over the 1912 Republican National Convention which led to the Bull Moose bolt and a lasting breach between him and Roosevelt. Critical of Wilson and neutrality, he wholeheartedly supported the Allied cause. His position in the League of Nations fight was that the treaty should be accepted with reservations; he believed Article X impracticable as a permanent commitment. Active in framing the statute for the Permanent Court of International Justice, he strongly advocated American membership in the Court. As friend and adviser of Andrew Carnegie, he helped establish a number of Carnegie benefactions and served as president or chairman of the board of the Carnegie Endowment for International Peace, the Carnegie Institution, and the Carnegie Corporation. Wise in counsel, skilled in advocacy, he was a distinguished elder statesman throughout his later years and remained active to the last in matters affecting the bar. [*Supp. 2*]

ROOT, ELISHA KING (*b. Ludlow, Mass., 1808; d. Hartford, Conn., 1865*), mechanic, inventor. As superintendent (later president) of the Colt Armory, 1849–65, Root designed and built the Armory as well as most of the machinery used in it. His drop-hammer (invented, 1853, 1858) put the art of die-forging on its modern basis.

ROOT, ERASTUS (*b. Hebron, Conn., 1773; d. New York, N.Y., 1846*), lawyer. Began practice at Delhi, N.Y.; served several terms in state legislature and was lieutenant-governor of New York, 1823–24. Originally an anti-Clinton Democrat, he refused to support Andrew Jackson in 1832 and later became a Whig. He was congressman from New York, 1803–05, 1809–11, 1815–17 and 1831–33.

ROOT, FRANK ALBERT (*b. Binghamton, N.Y., 1837; d. 1926*), Kansas newspaper publisher. Author of *The Overland Stage to California* (with W. E. Connelley, 1901).

ROOT, FREDERIC WOODMAN (*b. Boston, Mass., 1846; d. Chicago, Ill., 1916*), music teacher, composer, organist. Son of George F. Root.

ROOT, GEORGE FREDERICK (*b. Sheffield, Mass., 1820; d. 1895*), music educator, composer. Father of

Frederic W. Root. Established New York Normal Institute, 1853, to train music teachers; followed example of Lowell Mason in holding "musical conventions" to explain class instruction methods in singing. Removed to Chicago, 1859, where he engaged in music publishing until 1871 and continued teaching until his death. Among his many popular songs were "The Battle Cry of Freedom," "Tramp, Tramp, Tramp, the Boys are Marching," "Just Before the Battle, Mother" and "The Vacant Chair."

ROOT, JESSE (*b. Coventry, Conn., 1736 o.s.; d. Coventry, 1822*), Revolutionary soldier, Connecticut legislator and jurist. Member of the Continental Congress, 1778–82. Judge of the superior court of Connecticut, 1789–1807 (chief justice *post* 1798).

ROOT, JOHN WELLBORN (*b. Lumpkin, Ga., 1850; d. 1891*), architect. C.E., University of the City of New York (present New York University), 1869. Worked in office of James Renwick (1818–1895); at invitation of Peter B. Wight, became head draftsman in Chicago for Carter, Drake & Wight, 1871. Entered partnership with Daniel H. Burnham, 1873. The rise of the firm was rapid and owed much to Root's creative engineering mind; his designs, although superficially based on the popular Romanesque of H. H. Richardson, were all essentially personal and structurally true, especially his designs for business buildings. The Monadnock Building was a high point in his work. Appointed consulting architect for the World's Columbian Exposition, 1890, Root requested that his partner be included, an example of the superb cooperation between them throughout their careers. While Burnham deserves credit for the formation of the board of architects and the generalship of the work at the Exposition, to Root must go much of the credit for the final choice of a site and the settlement of the basic plan.

ROOT, JOSEPH POMEROY (*b. Greenwich, Mass., 1826; d. Wyandotte, Kans., 1885*), physician, antislavery advocate, Kansas territorial legislator. Republican lieutenant-governor of the State of Kansas, 1859–61, Root served in the Civil War as surgeon of the 2nd Kansas Cavalry. He was U.S. minister to Chile, 1870–73.

ROPES, JAMES HARDY (*b. Salem, Mass., 1866; d. 1933*), Congregational clergyman, New Testament scholar. Graduated Harvard, 1889; Andover Theological Seminary, 1893. After extensive further study in Europe, he taught at Harvard *post* 1895 and was Hollis Professor of Divinity *post* 1910. He is remembered principally for his work in reorganizing Phillips Academy, Andover, for his editorship of the *Harvard Theological Review* (1921–33) and for his scholarly work *The Text of Acts* (1926).

ROPES, JOHN CODMAN (*b. St. Petersburg, Russia, 1836; d. 1899*), Boston lawyer, military historian. Author, among other works, of *The Story of the Civil War* (1894–98).

ROPES, JOSEPH (*b. Salem, Mass., 1770; d. 1850*), merchant, War of 1812 privateersman.

RORER, DAVID (*b. Pittsylvania Co., Va., 1806; d. 1884*), lawyer. Removed to Little Rock, Ark., 1826; after practicing there and holding public office, he settled in pioneer Burlington, Iowa (then in Michigan Territory), 1836. Rorer plotted the town, drafted the charter and suggested the name "Hawkeyes" for Iowans. He was for many years one of the most active members of the Iowa bar, especially in fugitive slave cases and railroad litigation.

ROSA, EDWARD BENNETT (*b. Rogersville, N.Y., 1861; d. Washington, D.C., 1921*), physicist. Graduated Wesleyan University, 1886; Ph.D., Johns Hopkins, 1891. Taught physics at Wesleyan, 1891–1903; was in charge of electrical work of National Bureau of Standards *post* 1902. Jointly with Wilbur O. Atwater, Rosa devised apparatus and made measurements which showed that the physical law of conservation of energy also applied to animal processes, thus giving a scientific basis for study of nutrition problems. While with the Bureau of Standards, he did fundamental work on electrical measurements which included precise determination of the value of the ampere as measured by mechanical forces exerted between coils carrying current; he also determined relation between electrical units derived from magnetic effects and those derived from electrostatic forces. He later made studies of engineering problems arising in the operation and regulation of public-utility services.

ROSATI, JOSEPH (*b. Sora, Naples, 1789; d. Rome, Italy, 1843*), Roman Catholic clergyman, Vincentian. Came to America as volunteer for missions, 1816; worked in Kentucky; began St. Mary's Seminary, Perryville, Mo., 1818, teaching and also acting as pastor. Consecrated coadjutor to the bishop of Louisiana, 1824, he became bishop of St. Louis, 1827. Continuing to administer Lower Louisiana as well, he did not settle permanently in his own see until 1830. After attending the provincial Council of Baltimore, 1840, he proceeded to Rome whence he was sent as Apostolic Delegate to negotiate an agreement between the republic of Haiti and the Holy See.

ROSE, AQUILA (*b. England, c. 1695; d. 1723*), printer, ferryman, poet. Emigrated to Philadelphia *ante* 1717. The best versifier that Philadelphia could show before the younger Thomas Godfrey, Rose produced translations from Ovid and other poems which appeared posthumously in *Poems on Several Occasions* (1740).

ROSE, CHAUNCEY (*b. Wethersfield, Conn., 1794; d. Terre Haute, Ind., 1877*), financier, railroad builder, philanthropist. Settled in Terre Haute, 1825. He was the principal benefactor of Rose Polytechnic Institute (formally opened, 1883).

ROSE, EDWARD (*fl. 1811–1834*), guide, interpreter. Child of a white trader and a Cherokee-Negro mother, Rose was engaged by Wilson P. Hunt at the Arikara village as hunter, guide and interpreter, 1811; in May 1812, Rose joined Manuel Lisa's expedition to the upper Missouri. Living for some years among the Crows and the Arikara, in 1823 he was interpreter to William H. Ashley whom he vainly warned against the Arikara before the defeat of June 2. Rose was also interpreter to Henry Atkinson on his treaty-making expedition up the Missouri, 1825. In 1832, Zenas Leonard met him in a Crow village at the mouth of Stinking River where he ranked as a chief. Although Rose bore a bad reputation among his contemporaries, everything which is definitely known of him is creditable.

ROSE, ERNESTINE LOUISE SIISMONDI POTOWSKI (*b. Piotrkow, Russian Poland, 1810; d. Brighton, England, 1892*), reformer, advocate of woman's rights. Resided and worked in the United States, 1836–69.

ROSE, JOHN CARTER (*b. Baltimore, Md., 1861; d. Atlantic City, N.J., 1927*), Maryland jurist, reformer, member of Theodore Roosevelt's "tennis cabinet." U.S. district judge, 1910–22; judge, U.S. circuit court of appeals for the fourth circuit, *post* 1922.

ROSE, JOSEPH NELSON (*b. near Liberty, Ind., 1862; d. Washington, D.C., 1928*), botanist. Graduated Wabash College, 1885; Ph.D., 1889. Influenced in choice of a career by John M. Coulter, Rose served *post* 1888 as botanist in the U.S. Department of Agriculture, in curatorial posts in the National Herbarium (U.S. National Museum), and as a research associate of the Carnegie Institution of Washington. He was an authority on Mexican flora generally, and made particular studies of the *Crassulaceae* and *Cactaceae*.

ROSE, URIAH MILTON (*b. Bradfordsville, Ky., 1834; d. 1913*), Arkansas jurist, legal writer.

ROSE, WALTER MALINS (*b. Toronto, Canada, 1872; d. Los Angeles, Calif., 1908*), legal annotator. Author, among other works, of an innovating 12-volume study *Notes on the U.S. Reports* (1899–1901) which treated cases reported from *2 Dallas* to *172 U.S.*, showing their value as authority by listing subsequent citations in state and federal courts.

ROSE, WICKLIFFE (*b. Saulsbury, Tenn., 1862; d. Vancouver Island, Canada, 1931*), public health and educational administrator. After teaching at Peabody College for Teachers where he became dean, and at the University of Nashville, he served as general agent of the Peabody Education Fund, 1907–14. Director of the Rockefeller Commission for Eradication of Hookworm *post* 1910, he was made director of the International Health Board, 1913, and widened the scope of the enterprise to include malaria and yellow fever; the program later was expanded to a world-wide attack on all preventable disease. Retiring in 1923, he was made president of the General Education Board and of the International Education Board, supervising in the latter capacity a vast program of aid in the teaching of science and in fostering research. [*Supp.* 1]

ROSECRANS, SYLVESTER HORTON (*b. Homer, O., 1827; d. 1878*), Roman Catholic clergyman. Brother of William S. Rosecrans. Influenced by his brother's conversion to Catholicism and by the instructions of Father John B. Lamy, he entered the Catholic Church and was graduated from St. John's (Fordham) College, N.Y., 1846. Ordained priest, 1852, he was consecrated coadjutor bishop of Cincinnati, 1862, and made bishop of the new see of Columbus, O., 1868.

ROSECRANS, WILLIAM STARKE (*b. Delaware Co., O., 1819; d. near Los Angeles, Calif., 1898*), soldier. Brother of Sylvester H. Rosecrans. Graduated West Point, 1842; was a convert to Catholicism while a cadet. After engaging in fortification work and four years' duty as instructor at West Point, he resigned his commission, 1854, and entered business as engineer-architect and head of an oil refining company. Volunteering for the Union Army at the outbreak of the Civil War, he was almost immediately commissioned regular brigadier-general, commanded a brigade in McClellan's campaign in western Virginia, and won the battle of Rich Mountain, July 1861, one of the first battles of the war. Succeeding McClellan as commanding general, department of the Ohio, and later as chief of the department of western Virginia, he continued the operations which ended late that fall in complete expulsion of Confederate forces and formation of the State of West Virginia. He commanded the left wing of Pope's Army of the Mississippi, May 1862, during the movement upon Corinth and succeeded Pope in command a month later. After his defeat of the Confederate counterattack against Corinth under Price and Van Dorn, Oct. 3, 1862, he was promoted major-general and ordered to relieve Buell in Kentucky. Reorganizing Buell's forces as the Army of the Cumberland, he advanced to Nashville.

In December, he moved against the Confederates under Gen. Braxton Bragg who had concentrated at Murfreesboro. The two armies met on Stone River just west of Murfreesboro on Dec. 29, 1862; after a first Confederate success, Rosecrans established a new defensive line. Fighting continued, Bragg lost his nerve, and on Jan. 3, 1863, retreated to Shelbyville. For six months the armies engaged in only minor operations. On June 23, Rosecrans began to advance and in nine days maneuvered Bragg out of his positions at Shelbyville and Tullahoma back into Chattanooga. By this time, Rosecrans's openly expressed resentment of interference from Washington had brought him into disfavor there. Prodded into advancing by Gen. Halleck, Rosecrans on August 16 made a feint up the Tennessee River above Chattanooga, then crossed below that place and maneuvered Bragg

out of it. Owing to the over-extension of his lines, Rosecrans was badly defeated in the bloody battle of Chickamauga on Sept. 19–20, 1863, when the reinforced Bragg turned to face him. Relieved of command on October 19, Rosecrans was assigned to command the department of the Missouri and was later detached to await orders. He resigned his commission in the regular army, March 1867. Generally regarded as an able officer, and even called the greatest strategist of the war, he was handicapped by a hot temper and a hasty tongue. In later life he was U.S. minister to Mexico, 1868–69, and a Democratic congressman from California, 1881–85.

ROSELIUS, CHRISTIAN (*b. near Bremen, Germany, 1803; d. New Orleans, La., 1873*), lawyer, teacher of law. Emigrated to New Orleans, 1823; studied law in office of Auguste D'Avezac; attained first rank at the Louisiana bar, ranking with Pierre Soulé and Edward Livingston. Expert in the French civil law and its background, he taught for many years at the University of Louisiana (Tulane) and was dean of its law department.

ROSENBERG, ABRAHAM HAYYIM (*b. Karlin, Russia, 1838; d. 1925*), author, Biblical scholar. A distinguished rabbi in Pinsk, Nikolayev and Poltava, Rosenberg came to the United States in 1891. He was author of a number of works in both Hebrew and Yiddish which include his life-work *Ozar ha-shemoth*, a Hebrew cyclopedia of Biblical literature (published, 1898–99 and 1923).

ROSENBERG, HENRY (*b. Bilten, Switzerland, 1824; d. 1893*), merchant, banker. Emigrated to Galveston, Texas, 1843. Prospering there in the dry-goods business and many other enterprises, he was a benefactor of the city during life and on his death left a great part of his estate for charitable purposes in Galveston.

ROSENBLATT, JOSEPH (*b. Biélaya Tzerkov, near Kiev, Russia, 1882; d. Jerusalem, 1933*), cantor, concert tenor. Celebrated professionally in Europe, he came to America, 1912, where his natural vocal virtuosity and faultless pitch made him a musical celebrity. A concert artist exclusively *post* 1926, he died while on a visit to Palestine.

ROSENFELD, MORRIS (*b. Bokscha, Russian Poland, 1862; d. 1923*), tailor, poet. Emigrated to America, 1886. After a miserable existence in New York City sweatshops for some 14 years, Rosenfeld was enabled to devote himself entirely to literature and became editor and contributor to several Yiddish papers. He published his first collection of folk and revolutionary songs, *Die Glocke* (1888); other collections appeared in 1890 and 1917. His talent was made generally known by publication of *Songs from the Ghetto* in English (1898).

ROSENTHAL, HERMAN (*b. Friedrichsstadt, Courland, Russia, 1843; d. 1917*), author. After establishing a literary reputation at home, Rosenthal came to America, 1881, and with Michael Heilprin became a pioneer in founding agricultural colonies of Russian Jews in this country. Employed as a statistician and economic surveyor for a time, he became chief of the Slavonic division, New York Public Library, 1898, and remained in this post until his death. He was an important member of the editorial board of the *Jewish Encyclopedia*.

ROSENTHAL, MAX (*b. Turck, Russian Poland, 1833; d. 1918*), lithographer, mezzotint engraver. Came to America, 1849, after apprenticeship in Paris, France; was engaged principally in chromolithography until about 1870. Thereafter, he won fame as an etcher and mezzotinter of portraits of distinguished Americans, principally of the colonial and Revolutionary War periods.

ROSENTHAL, TOBY EDWARD (*b. New Haven, Conn., 1848; d. Munich, Germany, 1917*), genre and portrait painter.

ROSENWALD, JULIUS (*b. Springfield, Ill., 1862; d. Chicago, Ill., 1932*), merchant, philanthropist. Associated with Sears, Roebuck & Co., *post* 1895, he was president of the company, 1910–25, and thereafter until his death, chairman of the board. After building up a great business through sensing the possibilities of mail-order, appreciating his own limitations, and surrounding himself with expert help, he turned to a wide range of philanthropies which transcended race, creed and nationality. His benefactions were made principally through the Julius Rosenwald Fund which he created in 1917. His work for the advancement of the Negro was doubtless the outstanding feature of his philanthropy.

ROSEWATER, EDWARD (*b. Bukowan, Bohemia, Austria-Hungary, 1841; d. Omaha, Nebr., 1906*), Nebraska journalist and legislator, Union soldier. Came to the United States, 1854. Founded the *Omaha Daily Bee*, 1871, which he managed actively until shortly before his death.

ROSEWATER, VICTOR (*b. Omaha, Nebr., 1871; d. Philadelphia, Pa., 1940*), journalist, politician. Son of Edward Rosewater. Graduated Columbia, 1891; Ph.D., 1893. Associated with the *Omaha Bee* until 1920, he served it as managing editor, editor and publisher. A dominant influence in the Republican party in Nebraska by 1908, he presided as chairman of the National Republican Committee over the stormy opening session of the convention of 1912. By ruling out of order a motion by Theodore Roosevelt's floor leader to substitute Roosevelt delegates for those approved by the committee, Rosewater made it possible for Elihu Root to become temporary chairman and was thus a major factor in Roosevelt's withdrawal from the convention. [*Supp.* 2]

ROSS, ABEL HASTINGS (*b. Winchendon, Mass., 1831; d. Port Huron, Mich., 1893*), Congregational clergyman, authority on the history and polity of that denomination.

ROSS, ALEXANDER (*b. Nairnshire, Scotland, 1783; d. present Winnipeg, Canada, 1856*), fur trader, explorer. Emigrated to Canada, 1804; worked as schoolteacher. Engaged by Wilson P. Hunt at Montreal, 1810, as a clerk in Astor's Pacific Fur Co., he sailed in September on the *Tonquin* and aided in the building of Fort Astoria and later of Fort Okanogan. He was a member of the expedition that founded Fort Walla Walla, July 1818, and remained in charge there until the fall of 1823. Starting east, he was persuaded to lead an expedition into the Snake River country, and in 1824 penetrated present Idaho as far as the mouth of the Boise River. In the spring of 1825, he started east again but halted at the Red River colony where he resided for the remainder of his life. He was author of important historical works of firsthand authority, *Adventures of the First Settlers on the Oregon or Columbia River* (London, 1849), *The Fur Hunters of the Far West* (1855), and *The Red River Settlement* (1856).

ROSS, ALEXANDER COFFMAN (*b. Zanesville, O., 1812; d. Zanesville, 1883*), jeweler, song writer. Remembered principally for his authorship of the famous "Tippecanoe and Tyler, Too" for the presidential campaign of 1840.

ROSS, ARAMINTA. [See TUBMAN, HARRIET, *c.* 1821–1913.]

ROSS, BETSY (*b. Philadelphia, Pa., 1752; d. 1836*), seamstress, upholsterer, legendary maker of the first United States flag.

ROSS, DENMAN WALDO (*b. Cincinnati, O., 1853; d. London, England, 1935*), artist, educator. Graduated Harvard, 1875; did further work under Henry Adams and Charles E. Norton, receiving the doctorate, 1880, for a study of early German land-tenure. Shifting his field to art, he taught at Harvard *post* 1899 in the departments of architecture and fine arts. His theories were set forth in *A Theory of Pure Design* (1907) and *On Drawing and Painting* (1912). Working with precise and clear-cut formulae, he cut at the root of Ruskinian vagueness and brought his master Norton's aesthetics to earth. Associated with Ernest Fenollosa, Edward S. Morse and William S. Bigelow as a donor of Oriental art to the Boston Museum, he was also a benefactor of the Fogg Museum at Harvard. [*Supp.* 1]

ROSS, EDMUND GIBSON (*b. Ashland, O., 1826; d. Albuquerque, N. Mex., 1907*), journalist, antislavery advocate, Union soldier. A free-state leader in Kansas *post* 1856, he edited and published the Topeka *Kansas Tribune* and the Topeka *Kansas State Record*, 1857–62. He became editor of the Lawrence *Tribune*, 1865, and served as U.S. senator, Republican, from Kansas, 1866–71. Entering the Senate an intense radical and opponent of Andrew Johnson, he insisted that Johnson have a fair trial after the president's impeachment. His vote against conviction on grounds of lack of evidence destroyed his political career. Leaving the Republican party, 1872, because of his dislike of the protective system and of the character of Grant's administration, he continued active in Kansas journalism until 1882 when he moved to New Mexico. He was governor of that territory, 1885–89.

ROSS, ERSKINE MAYO (*b. Belpré, Va., 1845; d. Los Angeles, Calif., 1928*), California jurist. Began practice in Los Angeles, 1868. Appointed judge, U.S. district court of the southern district of California, 1887, he was advanced in 1895 to the U.S. circuit court and served there until his resignation, 1925.

ROSS, GEORGE (*b. New Castle, Del., 1730; d. Philadelphia, Pa., 1779*), Pennsylvania jurist, signer of the Declaration of Independence. Practiced at Lancaster, Pa., post 1750; member of provincial Assembly, 1768–75. A Tory as a member of the First Continental Congress, 1774, he became a Whig, 1775; as a member of the Second Continental Congress, he worked tirelessly for the patriot cause in Pennsylvania. Vice-president of the Pennsylvania constitutional convention of 1776 and a strong factor in its deliberations, he was returned to Congress in July but withdrew because of illness in January 1777. Commissioned judge of the admiralty court of Pennsylvania, 1779, he defied Congress for attempting to review his judgment in the case of the sloop *Active*.

ROSS, JAMES (*b. near Delta, Pa., 1762; d. Allegheny City, Pa., 1847*), lawyer. Encouraged in his study of law by Hugh H. Brackenridge, he practiced at first in Washington Co., Pa., removing to Pittsburgh, 1795. A Federalist, he served as a commissioner to treat with the insurgents during the Whiskey Insurrection, 1794, and was largely responsible for the amicable settlement. He was U.S. senator from Pennsylvania, 1794–1803.

ROSS, JAMES DELMAGE McKENZIE (*b. Chatham, Ontario, Canada, 1872; d. Rochester, Minn., 1939*), electrical engineer. Settled in Seattle, Wash., 1901; headed Seattle municipal power plant, 1911–39; was a principal architect of the public power program instituted during administrations of President F. D. Roosevelt. [*Supp. 2*]

ROSS, JOHN (*b. near Lookout Mountain, Tenn., 1790; d. Washington, D.C., 1866*), Cherokee chief. Indian name, Cooweescoowe. Son of a Scottish Loyalist and a mother of one-fourth Cherokee blood. Served under Andrew Jackson in War of 1812. President, National Council of the Cherokee, 1819–26; principal chief of the eastern Cherokee, 1828–39. A leader in the opposition to westward removal of his tribe, he led his people to present Oklahoma, 1838–39, and helped make the constitution of 1839 which united the eastern and western Cherokee under a single

government. Chosen chief of the united nation, 1839, he held office until his death. Failing to keep the Cherokee nation neutral at the outbreak of the Civil War, he signed a treaty of alliance with the Confederacy in October 1861 which was repudiated two years later.

ROSS, LAWRENCE SULLIVAN (*b. Bentonsport, Iowa, 1838; d. 1898*), planter, Texas legislator, Confederate brigadier-general. Raised in Texas, Ross was captain of a ranger company operating against the Comanches, 1859–60. Entering Confederate service, 1861, he was particularly distinguished for skill in covering Van Dorn's retreat from Corinth, Miss., 1862. As Democratic governor of Texas, 1887–91, he led the legislature in passing laws which prohibited dealing in cotton futures and closed the sale of public lands to corporations. He was president, Agricultural and Mechanical College of Texas, post 1891.

ROSS, MARTIN (*b. Martin Co., N.C., 1762; d. Bethel, N.C., 1827*), Revolutionary soldier, Baptist clergyman.

ROSSER, THOMAS LAFAYETTE (*b. Campbell Co., Va., 1836; d. near Charlottesville, Va., 1910*), Confederate major-general, engineer. Raised in Texas, Rosser attended West Point, 1856–61, resigning before graduation to enter Confederate service. A brilliant artillerist and cavalryman, Rosser served after the Civil War as chief engineer of the Northern Pacific Railroad and later of the Canadian Pacific, retiring in 1886 to become a gentleman farmer.

ROSSITER, THOMAS PRICHARD (*b. New Haven, Conn., 1818; d. Cold Spring, N.Y., 1871*), historical and portrait painter, associate of J. F. Kensett, J. W. Casilear and Thomas Cole.

ROSSITER, WILLIAM SIDNEY (*b. Westfield, Mass., 1861; d. Concord, N.H., 1929*), official of the Census Bureau, statistician. Author of *A Century of Population Growth . . . 1790–1900* (1909). Managed and later headed the Rumford Press.

ROTCH, ABBOTT LAWRENCE (*b. Boston, Mass., 1861; d. Boston, 1912*), meteorologist. Great-great-grandson of William Rotch; grandson of Abbott Lawrence; brother of Arthur Rotch. Graduated Massachusetts Institute of Technology, 1884. Instituted and maintained the Blue Hill Observatory, 1884–1912; was a pioneer in American aeronautics. Co-author of *Charts of the Atmosphere for Aeronauts and Aviators* (1911), a first attempt at mapping conditions of the upper air.

ROTCH, ARTHUR (*b. Boston, Mass., 1850; d. Beverly, Mass., 1894*), architect. Great-great-grandson of William Rotch; grandson of Abbott Lawrence; brother of Abbott L. Rotch. Graduated Harvard, 1871; studied architecture at Massachusetts Institute of Technology and at the Beaux Arts, Paris, France. Benefactor of architectural departments of M.I.T. and Harvard.

ROTCH, THOMAS MORGAN (*b. Philadelphia, Pa., 1849; d. 1914*), pediatrician. Cousin of Abbott L. and Arthur Rotch. Graduated Harvard, 1870; Harvard Medical School, 1874; studied also in Berlin, Vienna and Heidelberg. Began practice of pediatrics at Boston, 1876; founded and became medical director of the West-End Infants' Hospital, 1881. A teacher of pediatrics at Harvard Medical School *post* 1878, he was professor of pediatrics *post* 1893. Devising a "percentage" method of artificial feeding based on a careful estimation of the caloric value of milk, he placed the feeding of infants on a scientific basis. His book, *Pediatrics: the Hygiene and Medical Treatment of Children* (1896), was one of the first to be written on that branch of medicine.

ROTCH, WILLIAM (*b. Nantucket, Mass., 1734 o.s.; d. 1828*), whaling merchant.

ROTHAFEL, SAMUEL LIONEL (*b. Stillwater, Minn., 1881; d. New York, N.Y., 1936*), showman, motion-picture theatre operator. Better known as "Roxy," he was raised in Brooklyn, N.Y. He made his first innovations in showing of motion-pictures while manager of the Lyric Theatre, Minneapolis, Minn., 1912. Coming to New York in the following year, he became in a short time the most successful motion-picture theatre operator in the world, successively directing the Strand, Rialto, Rivoli and Capitol theatres in New York City. His formula included presentation of an excellent orchestra, famous singers and musicians, and precision dancing, along with important feature films. He was a pioneer also in surrounding his productions with a luxurious décor. His radio program known as "Roxy and His Gang" was a popular feature in the mid- and late-1920's. [*Supp. 2*]

ROTHERMEL, PETER FREDERICK (*b. Nescopeck, Pa., 1817; d. near Linfield, Pa., 1895*), artist. Painter, among much other somewhat photographic work, of "The Battle of Gettysburg" (1871), which now hangs in the Capitol at Harrisburg, Pa.

ROTHROCK, JOSEPH TRIMBLE (*b. McVeytown, Pa., 1839; d. West Chester, Pa., 1922*), physician, Union soldier, botanist. M.D., University of Pennsylvania, 1867. After practicing at Wilkes-Barre, Pa., he served as botanist and surgeon to the government survey of Colorado, New Mexico and California under Lt. G. N. Wheeler, describing many new plants in his report (published 1878). Professor of botany, University of Pennsylvania, 1877–1904, he was a leader in the forest conservation movement and the first Pennsylvania commissioner of forestry.

ROTHWELL, RICHARD PENNEFATHER (*b. Oxford, Ontario, Canada, 1836; d. 1901*), mining engineer, editor. Worked in the United States *post* 1864 mainly as consultant to operators of anthracite mines; was a co-founder of the American Institute of Mining Engineers, 1871. Co-editor with Rossiter W. Raymond of the *Engineering and Mining Journal post* 1874 and sole editor *post* 1890.

ROULSTONE, GEORGE (*b. Boston, Mass., 1767; d. 1804*), printer. Accompanied Gov. William Blount to Tennessee; issued first number of the *Knoxville Gazette* at Hawkins Court House (Rogersville), Nov. 5, 1791, continuing publication (except for a brief period in 1798) until his death. As territorial and later state printer, Roulstone produced a number of volumes of official papers and a few general publications. His most important production was the *Laws of the State of Tennessee* (1803).

ROUND, WILLIAM MARSHALL FITTS (*b. Pawtucket, R.I., 1845; d. Acushnet, Mass., 1906*), journalist, prison reformer. Corresponding secretary, Prison Association of New York, 1882–1900; introduced cottage system at Burnham Industrial Farm, Canaan, N.Y., as director *c.* 1888.

ROUQUETTE, ADRIEN EMMANUEL (*b. New Orleans, La., 1813; d. New Orleans, 1887*), Roman Catholic clergyman, missionary to the Choctaws, poet. Brother of François D. Rouquette. Author, among other works, of *Les Savanes* (1841) which won him the title of "the Lamartine of America," *La Thébaïde en Amérique* (1852) and *La Nouvelle Atala* (1879).

ROUQUETTE, FRANÇOIS DOMINIQUE (*b. Bayou Lacombe, La., 1810; d. Louisiana, 1890*), poet. Brother of Adrien E. Rouquette. An eccentric genius, he was author of a number of works of which *Meschacébéennes* (1839) and *Fleurs d'Amérique* (1856) received very high praise from notable French critics.

ROUSSEAU, HARRY HARWOOD (*b. Troy, N.Y., 1870; d. at sea, en route to Panama, 1930*), naval officer, engineer. Served on Isthmian Canal Commission under George W. Goethals, 1907–14, in special charge of design and construction of the Panama Canal terminals; later as rear-admiral, held important navy administration posts and headed the shipyard division under the Shipping Board during World War I.

ROUSSEAU, LOVELL HARRISON (*b. near Stanford, Ky., 1818; d. New Orleans, La., 1869*), lawyer, Kentucky and Indiana legislator, Union major-general. Received formal cession of Alaska from the Russians, 1867, as U.S. representative there.

ROWAN, JOHN (*b. near York, Pa., 1773; d. Louisville, Ky., 1843*), Kentucky jurist, legislator and congressman. A liberal leader in the fight against the Kentucky judiciary, 1823–24, he served as U.S. senator, Democrat, 1825–31. He worked for reform of the federal judiciary and abolition of imprisonment for debt.

ROWAN, STEPHEN CLEGG (*b. near Dublin, Ireland, 1808; d. Washington, D.C., 1890*), naval officer. Raised in Ohio. Appointed midshipman, 1826; commended for gallant service in the Seminole War; was particularly distinguished in war with Mexico. Executive officer of the *Cyane,* he shared in the capture of Monterey, Calif., July 1846, and, in command of a battalion of seamen and marines, fought with the army in the retaking of Los Angeles and the relief of San José. His Civil War service was outstanding. In February 1862, he cooperated with Gen. Burnside in the capture of Roanoke Island and later in the capture of New Bern, N.C. He performed outstanding service also at Charleston, S.C., July–September 1863. Promoted rear-admiral, 1866, he retired as vice-admiral, 1889.

ROWELL, GEORGE PRESBURY (*b. Concord, Vt., 1838; d. Poland Springs, Maine, 1908*), advertising agent. Devised the "list system" *c.* 1865; founded *Printers' Ink,* July 1888.

ROWLAND, HENRY AUGUSTUS (*b. Honesdale, Pa., 1848; d. 1901*), physicist. Graduated Rensselaer Polytechnic, 1870. Taught science and physics at Wooster University and at Rensselaer; was chosen first professor of physics, Johns Hopkins, 1875. Rowland's principal contributions to physics were of three kinds: those which involved original concepts, those concerned with accurate measurement of physical constants, and those in which engineering talent was most conspicuous. His first important investigation resulted in "On Magnetic Permeability, and the Maximum of Magnetism of Iron, Steel, and Nickel" (*Philosophical Magazine,* August 1873) and provided the basis for subsequent study of both permanent and induced magnetization; it was the starting point for calculations for the design of dynamos and transformers. A second important experiment, performed during the winter of 1875–76, answered in the affirmative the question whether a moving charged conductor would have an effect upon a magnet similar to that of an electric current; this was of great significance in connection with the modern theory of electrons. For his study of spectra, he combined the principle of the grating with that of the concave mirror, eventually producing gratings ruled on concave surfaces thus obviating many of the difficulties inherent in the use of plane gratings. In order to produce gratings more accurate than any previously known, he designed a ruling machine which virtually eliminated errors. In the field of measurements, he obtained values for the mechanical equivalent of heat, the ohm, the ratio of the electric units and the wave-lengths of various spectra. Teaching less by precept than by example, Rowland was a severe taskmaster in the laboratory.

ROWLAND, HENRY COTTRELL (*b. New York, N.Y., 1874; d. Washington, D.C., 1933*), physician, traveler and adventurer, author.

ROWLAND, THOMAS FITCH (*b. New Haven, Conn., 1831; d. New York, N.Y., 1907*), boat builder, engine designer. President of the Continental Iron Works *post* 1860, Rowland built the original *Monitor* for John Ericsson, and upon its completion built the monitors *Montauk, Catskill* and *Passaic* and also the double-turret monitor *Onondaga.*

ROWLANDS, WILLIAM (*b. London, England, 1807; d. Utica, N.Y., 1866*), Calvinistic Methodist clergyman, editor. Came to America, 1836; ministered mainly in New York City and in Oneida Co., N.Y. Founded and edited *Y Cyfaill,* influential Welsh language periodical (first number, January 1838).

ROWLANDSON, MARY WHITE (*b. probably England, c. 1635; d. c. 1678*), Indian captive, author. Daughter of one of the original proprietors of Lancaster, Mass., she was married to the minister there *c.* 1656 and on Feb. 10, 1675/76, was carried into captivity when the Indians attacked and burnt Lancaster. Remaining in captivity for 11 weeks, she was ransomed and returned with her two surviving children; in 1677, she removed with her family to Wethersfield, Conn. Her narrative of her captivity entitled *The Soveraignty & Goodness of God, Together with the Faithfulness of His Promises Displayed, etc.* was first published in Cambridge, Mass., 1682, and became one of the most widely read pieces of 17th century American prose.

ROWSE, SAMUEL WORCESTER (*b. Bath, Maine, 1822; d. Morristown, N.J., 1901*), painter, illustrator, lithographer. Gained wide reputation for his delicate, well-characterized crayon portraits of contemporary celebrities.

ROWSON, SUSANNA HASWELL (*b. Portsmouth, England, c. 1762; d. Boston, Mass., 1824*), novelist, actress, educator. Cousin of Anthony Haswell. Raised in Massachusetts, daughter of an English officer, she returned to England, 1778; her first novel, *Victoria,* was published, 1786, and received favorable London notice. Later in the year, she married William Rowson. Three works which she published in 1788 and 1789 added little to her reputation, but early in 1791 she produced, and published in London, a novel which was to make her famous—*Charlotte, a Tale of Truth.* Sentimental and didactic, supposedly based on an actual affair of Col. John Montrésor, the book captivated the American fancy when it was reprinted in Philadelphia, 1794; it became the chief American "best seller" before *Uncle Tom's Cabin.* On the business failure of her husband, 1792, the family turned for support to the stage and were recruited in England by Thomas Wignell for his Philadelphia company. They acted mostly in minor parts in Philadelphia, Baltimore and Annapolis, 1793–96, and Mrs. Rowson wrote and adapted plays for the company. The Rowsons went to the Federal Street Theatre, Boston, in 1796; in the spring of 1797, Mrs. Rowson left the stage to devote the rest of her life to conducting a school for girls in or near Boston. She served as editor of the *Boston Weekly Magazine,*

1802–05, and continued to write for its successor *The Boston Magazine;* she also wrote for *The Monthly Anthology* and *The New England Galaxy.* Among other books which she published were *Reuben and Rachel* (1798), *Miscellaneous Poems* (1804), *Sarah, the Exemplary Wife* (1813) and a sequel to *Charlotte (Temple)* entitled *Charlotte's Daughter* (1828).

"ROXY." [See ROTHAFEL, SAMUEL LIONEL, 1881–1936.]

ROYALL, ANNE NEWPORT (*b. Maryland, 1769; d. Washington, D.C., 1854*), author. Of uncertain parentage, she was raised in the house of William Royall, an eccentric Virginia farmer and scholar who undertook her education and married her in 1797. Engaged in a long litigation over his property after his death, she started out to earn her own living in 1824 by traveling over the United States and publishing accounts of her journeys. Vigorous, straightforward, truly liberal in her reforming zeal but indiscreet and often amateurish, she made herself the terror of the national capital and was noted especially for her ability to uncover graft. Her attacks against Presbyterians led to her trial and conviction in 1829 on the trumped-up charge of being a common scold. Her paper *Paul Pry* ran from December 1831 to November 1836; *The Huntress* began in December 1836 and was continued until just before her death. Among her ten volumes of travel and comment were *Sketches of History, Life and Manners in the United States* (1826), *The Black Book* (1828–29) and *Mrs. Royall's Southern Tour* (1830–31). These and her other works deserve to survive as valuable sources for study of U.S. social history in her time.

ROYCE, JOSIAH (*b. Grass Valley, Calif., 1855; d. Cambridge, Mass., 1916*), philosopher, educator. Child of a pioneer California family, Royce was indebted to his mother for his early education, both religious and secular. The family settled in San Francisco *c.* 1866, where he attended school and spent many of his leisure hours in the Mercantile Library. The intellectual and moral influence of the California environment was lifelong in him and was effective in two of his later books, *California . . . A Study of American Character* (1886) and *The Feud of Oakfield Creek* (1887). Shy and sensitive, he felt a wistful need of social relations. The belief that a man's fullest development can be found only in the life of the "community" became a major topic in his philosophizing. His philosophical development consists essentially in the interaction of his instinctive Protestantism and moral individualism with the pantheistic, aesthetic doctrines which he acquired from Lotze, Schelling, Schopenhauer, Fichte and Hegel. Graduating from the University of California, 1875, he spent the next year mainly at Göttingen and Leipzig; in 1876, he was invited to be one of the first twenty fellows appointed at the new Johns Hopkins University. A fellow in literature, he received the Ph.D. degree,

1878, for study in the history of philosophy and German literature in the 18th and 19th centuries.

While teaching English literature at the University of California, 1878–82, he schooled himself in the technicalities of philosophy by continuous reading and thinking. He re-examined Kant and Hegel and made a study of contemporary writers such as William James, Charles S. Peirce and the psychologists Wundt and Bain. In an article of January 1882, he announced his adhesion to the school of post-Kantian idealism. Encouraged by William James to venture into philosophy, Royce went to Harvard to substitute for James in the fall and winter term, 1882–83; he remained at Harvard during the balance of his days. Soon earning the good opinion of students, colleagues and President Eliot, he became assistant professor, 1885, professor, 1892, and in 1914, received the Alford Professorship of Natural Religion and Moral Philosophy. During the earlier years of his career, Royce's development was greatly influenced by association with William James and he did extensive work in psychology, publishing *Outlines of Psychology* (1903). Although his friendship with James was lifelong, Royce soon manifested a divergence of view from James. As early as 1883, Royce noted in his diary a criterion of truth which he often reaffirmed. A given statement is true, he said, when "the contradictory of this statement would involve this statement itself." The mind thinks what (if it is to think at all) it cannot avoid thinking without contradicting itself. Under this dialectical compulsion, the mind escapes the skepticism of the passing moment and the relativities of a merely human experience—all of which is widely removed from James both in matter and doctrine. Royce, as the protagonist of monism, and James, as the friend of pluralism, became symbolic of a good-humored philosophical controversy.

Royce's first major philosophical work was *The Religious Aspect of Philosophy* (1885) in which he set forth a religious view of the world which does not imply but is consistent with a positive creed. The method of the book is a variant of the method of doubt and the argument falls into two main parts. The first part is an appeal to the thinker to postulate what is not given in experience and asks why should religion not be permitted to postulate a goodness at the heart of things which satisfies the highest moral needs, as science postulates the simplicity and orderliness of nature. In the second part of the argument, Royce supports postulate by proof and arrives at his famous "Absolute," or universal knower. The general metaphysical implications are evident. They are idealistic and monistic. In *The Conception of God* (1897), Royce attempts to reconcile the human prerogatives of freedom and responsibility with his metaphysical Absolute by insisting that the principle of individuation is choice or preference, that the Absolute is an individual consisting ultimately in a sheer act of will, and that this Absolute Will is parceled out among human beings, each of which wills independently within its own province. In *The Spirit of Modern Philosophy* (1892), Royce treats his subject with humor and eloquence and handles his beloved Romanticists together with Kant, Hegel and Schopenhauer with tenderness and insight. *The World and the Individual* (1900, 1901) is the most important of his systematic works. In the first volume Royce argues an unqualified idealism; the constructive portion of the book gives to this characteristic doctrine, however, a new and significant development. In *The Religious Aspect of Philosophy* Royce had used the term "thought" to designate the processes of the Absolute, while in *The Conception of God* the emphasis had been shifted to "will." In the present book the term "purpose" plays a mediating rôle. Thought is essentially purposive. The key to its nature is found in the double meaning of ideas. An idea's "internal meaning" consists of the universals or ideal possibilities which constitute *what* is judged; its "external meaning" consists in the particular object to which it refers, and which constitutes that which is judged *about*. This object, while it lies beyond the idea, is embraced within mind as the experience to which the idea points as its own "fulfilment." The second volume of *The World and the Individual* is devoted to cosmological and practical applications.

Post 1900, Royce's interests developed in opposite but complementary directions toward a more technical and specialized treatment of logic, and toward a more popular treatment of moral, social and religious problems; he was one of the first Americans after Charles S. Peirce to enter the field of symbolic logic and the philosophical foundations of mathematics. In *The Philosophy of Loyalty* (1908), he outlines a basis for ethical action; in *The Problem of Christianity* (1913), he gives his final interpretation of the Christian faith and also his most thorough treatment of the subject of religion. He selected as the three central Christian ideas, the Pauline Church, the "lost" state of the natural man, and atonement. These ideas he interpreted in terms of the "community," as being the supreme object of the individual's loyalty, by estrangement from which man is lost, and by whose spirit and service he is restored. The effect of these ethical and religious studies was to bring the metaphysical Absolute into nearer relation to man. The Absolute assumes the form of a personified "Beloved Community," to which the individual man was bound by a sort of patriotic fervor, or blend of self-sacrifice and self-aggrandizement. Interpretations are triadic, involving a sign, an interpreter, and a second mind to which the interpretation is communicated. Thus, Royce argues, interpretation involved a *community* of two or more minds. Knowledge is creative of being; but knowledge is now construed as a social affair—a community of interpretation.

After the death of William James, Royce was the most influential American philosopher of his day and the leading exponent in America of post-Kantian idealism of which he represented the voluntaristic wing. He may be said to stand close to Fichte but he was distinguished from German neo-Fichteans not only by his profound metaphysical passion but also by the English and American strains in his inheritance. Any mere doctrinal classification of Royce is inadequate, for he was a man of rich experience and varied talents. His defects as a thinker and writer flowed from a tendency to prolixity. His processes of mind were powerful, massive but laborious.

ROYE, EDWARD JAMES (*b. Newark, O., 1815; d. at sea, off Liberia, 1872*), schoolteacher, businessman. Leading merchant of Liberia, *post c.* 1848. Inaugurated fifth president of Liberia, January 1871, he was deposed in October on charges of mishandling a loan and boundary dispute with England.

ROYSTER, JAMES FINCH (*b. Raleigh, N.C., 1880; d. Richmond, Va., 1930*), philologist, educator. Graduated Wake Forest College, 1900; Ph.D., University of Chicago, 1907. Taught at Universities of North Carolina and Texas. Dean of college of liberal arts, University of North Carolina, 1922–25; dean of graduate school, 1925–29.

RUBINOW, ISAAC MAX (*b. Grodno, Russia, 1875; d. New York, N.Y., 1936*), physician, social worker, economic statistician, Jewish leader. Came to America, 1893. Graduated Columbia, 1895; M.D., New York University, 1898. Practicing among the poor, Rubinow became convinced that ill health was as much an economic as a medical problem. In 1903 he gave up medical practice to become an expert in economics and statistics in the U.S. Department of Agriculture, the first of a succession of posts he held in the federal government. His report of European legislation on industrial accidents (1911) helped lay the foundation for state workmen's compensation laws passed, 1911–20. Leaving federal service, he worked for a time on studies of insurance for private companies and associations, but he is particularly remembered as a pioneer in the American social security movement. He was author of, among other books, *The Care of the Aged* (1931) and *The Quest for Security* (1934). [*Supp. 2*]

RUBLEE, HORACE (*b. Berkshire, Vt., 1829; d. Milwaukee, Wis., 1896*), editor, diplomat. Raised in Wisconsin. Editorial writer and co-proprietor, *Wisconsin State Journal*, 1853–68, Rublee was active in the Republican party from its birth. After serving as U.S. minister to Switzerland, 1869–76, he returned to journalism, and was associated *post* 1881 with the *Daily Milwaukee Republican* and the *Milwaukee Sentinel*.

RUDGE, WILLIAM EDWIN (*b. Brooklyn, N.Y., 1876; d. 1931*), printer, typographer. Influential in the encouragement of good design and fine printing *post* 1912.

RUEF, ABRAHAM (*b. San Francisco, Calif., 1864; d. San Francisco, 1936*), lawyer. Graduated University of California, 1883; Hastings College of Law, 1886. Rose to political power through control of the Union Labor party *post* 1901 and became boss of his native city. Engaged in numerous corrupt practices, he was exposed by, among others, Fremont Older, Francis J. Heney and James D. Phelan. After trial and conviction, he was in prison, 1911–15. [*Supp.* 2]

RUFFIN, EDMUND (*b. Prince George Co., Va., 1794; d. Amelia Co., Va., 1865*), agricultural experimenter and writer, farmer. After making trial of the use of marl on his worn-out fields (adopting a suggestion from Sir Humphrey Davy's *Elements of Agricultural Chemistry*), he concluded that soils once fertile but reduced by harmful cultivation had lost their power to retain manures. He believed that this condition could be corrected by the application of calcareous earths and that a fertility equal to or greater than the original could be acquired by the use thereafter of fertilizers, crop rotation, drainage and good plowing. Presenting his theories and results in written form on several occasions, he issued them in 1832 in a volume entitled *An Essay on Calcareous Manures* which had wide influence. Active in the organization of agricultural societies, he became agricultural surveyor of South Carolina, 1842, publishing a report in the next year which became a landmark in the agricultural history of that state. He was a prolific writer on other topics as well as agriculture, especially in defense of slavery and state-rights. Originally a Whig, he became a Democrat as the struggle over state-rights developed and was one of the first secessionists in Virginia. He originated the League of United Southerners, was invited to sit in three secession conventions, and as a volunteer with the Charleston Palmetto Guard, fired the first shot from Morris Island against Fort Sumter. On the collapse of the Confederacy, he ended his own life.

RUFFIN, THOMAS (*b. King and Queen Co., Va., 1787; d. Hillsboro, N.C., 1870*), jurist. Graduated College of New Jersey (Princeton), 1805; studied law in Petersburg, Va., and in North Carolina under Archibald D. Murphey; practiced in Hillsboro *post* 1808. After holding several minor court posts, he served as associate justice of the North Carolina supreme court, 1829–33, and as chief justice, 1833–52; in 1858 he was called back to the supreme court, but served for only one year. An ardent Unionist, he denied any constitutional right of secession, but after the failure of a compromise which he offered the North Carolina secession convention, he voted for the ordinance and supported the Confederate war effort. In constitutional law, the authorities rank him with John Marshall and Lemuel Shaw. He was equally noted in common law and equity.

RUFFNER, HENRY (*b. Shenandoah Co., Va., 1790; d. 1861*), Presbyterian clergyman, educator. Graduated Washington College, Lexington, Va., 1813. Taught at Washington College, 1819–48, at times acted as president, and was president in fact, 1836–48. In his *Address to the People of West Virginia* (1847), he argued for confinement of slavery to the region east of the Blue Ridge and its gradual abolition there on broad grounds of public policy.

RUFFNER, WILLIAM HENRY (*b. Lexington, Va., 1824; d. Asheville, N.C., 1908*), Presbyterian clergyman, educator. Son of Henry Ruffner. Graduated Washington College, 1842. As Virginia state superintendent of public education, 1870–82, Ruffner drew a school law which became a model for other Southern states and secured its enactment by the legislature. For his services to the schools, especially for his solution of the problem of the relation of church and state in the educational field, he has been called the "Horace Mann of the South."

RUGER, THOMAS HOWARD (*b. Lima, N.Y., 1833; d. Stamford, Conn., 1907*), lawyer, Union soldier. Graduated West Point, 1854. Commissioned colonel of the 3rd Wisconsin Infantry early in the Civil War, he distinguished himself at Antietam. Promoted brigadier-general, 1862, he succeeded to divisional command at Gettysburg; in October 1863, he was transferred to brigade command in the West, took part in all of Sherman's operations, and won brevet of major-general of volunteers for service at the battle of Franklin, November 1864. Remaining in the army, he was superintendent at West Point, 1871–76, and saw a variety of service in the West and Northwest. He retired as regular major-general, 1897.

RUGG, ARTHUR PRENTICE (*b. Sterling, Mass., 1862; d. Sterling, 1938*), lawyer, jurist. Graduated Amherst, 1883. Appointed associate judge of the supreme judicial court of Massachusetts, 1906, he was made chief justice in 1911 and retained this position until his death. His almost 3,000 opinions were uniformly excellent and affected very nearly the entire body of the law of the commonwealth. [*Supp.* 2]

RUGGLES, SAMUEL BULKLEY (*b. New Milford, Conn., 1800; d. Fire Island, N.Y., 1881*), lawyer, New York canal commissioner, 1839–58. Practiced in New York City *post* 1821; developed Gramercy Park, New York City, 1831, and was also active in promoting creation of Union Square. He was a strong influence in the liberalization of Columbia College and its development into a university.

RUGGLES, TIMOTHY (*b. Rochester, Mass., 1711; d. Wilmot, N.S., Canada, 1795*), Massachusetts provincial legislator and jurist, soldier, Loyalist. Graduated Harvard, 1732. Rose to rank of brigadier-general in the French and Indian War. Elected president of the Stamp Act Congress, 1765, over James Otis, Ruggles would not sign the petitions which were drawn up, alleging scruples of conscience. A supporter of Gov. Thomas Hutchinson, he was made a Mandamus Councilor, 1774, and late in that year strove to form an association of Loyalists pledged not to acknowledge or submit to the pretended authority of any congress. Appointed to command three companies of Tory volunteers to be called the Loyal American Associators, November 1775, Ruggles was for a brief time with the British on Long Island. Banished from Massachusetts, 1778, his estates were confiscated and he removed to Nova Scotia, 1783.

RUHL, ARTHUR BROWN (*b. Rockford, Ill., 1876; d. Queens, N.Y.C., 1935*), journalist, foreign correspondent, dramatic critic. Author, among other books, of *White Nights and other Russian Impressions* (1917). [*Supp.* 1]

RUHRÄH, JOHN (*b. Chillicothe, O., 1872; d. 1935*), pediatrician. Studied at present University of Maryland and at Johns Hopkins; practiced *post* 1894 in Baltimore, Md., and taught at University of Maryland, with intervals of study abroad. Made first collective investigation of actinomycosis in United States, 1899–1900; introduced use of soy bean in infant dietetics, 1909. Author of *Pediatrics of the Past* (1925) and other works, he contributed articles on his specialty to most of the modern encyclopedias and systems of medicine. [*Supp.* 1]

RUMFORD, BENJAMIN THOMPSON, COUNT. [See THOMPSON, BENJAMIN, 1753–1814.]

RUMSEY, CHARLES CARY (*b. Buffalo, N.Y., 1879; d. 1922*), sculptor, polo player. Rumsey's bronzes depicting polo ponies and their riders were particularly effective; notable among his monumental works is an equestrian "Pizarro" now in the city of Lima, Peru. His compositions attained a rhythm and dynamic power which gave them individuality in spite of the evident influences of Rodin, Bourdelle and Maillol.

RUMSEY, JAMES (*b. Bohemia Manor, Md., 1743; d. London, England, 1792*), inventor. Encouraged by George Washington and others in his efforts to produce a boat propelled by steam, Rumsey exhibited on the Potomac River in December 1787 a vessel propelled by streams of water forced out through its stern; the force pump was operated by a steam engine. He also developed an improved steam boiler, an improved grist mill and saw mill, and a plan for raising water by means of a steam engine. Securing English patents on his boiler and steamboat, and U.S. patents in 1791, he was unable to raise sufficient capital for manufacture.

RUMSEY, MARY HARRIMAN (*b. New York, N.Y., 1881; d. 1934*), leader in public welfare. Daughter of Edward H. Harriman; wife of Charles C. Rumsey. Graduated Barnard College, 1905. Conceived idea of organizing New York Junior League for public and social service, 1901; served five years as its president.

Active as a stock-breeder, sportswoman and art patron, she was also an advocate of cooperative movements and a worker for many civic and charitable enterprises, private and public. [*Supp.* 1]

RUMSEY, WILLIAM (*b. Bath, N.Y., 1841; d. 1903*), Union soldier, lawyer. Judge, New York State supreme court, 1880–1901. Author of a one-time standard work on New York State practice.

RUNCIE, CONSTANCE FAUNT LE ROY (*b. Indianapolis, Ind., 1836; d. Winnetka, Ill., 1911*), composer, pianist. Niece of David and Robert D. Owen.

RUNKLE, JOHN DANIEL (*b. Root, N.Y., 1822; d. 1902*), mathematician, educator. Graduated Lawrence Scientific School, Harvard, 1851. Professor of mathematics, Massachusetts Institute of Technology, 1865–68, 1880–1902. Appointed acting president of the Institute, 1868, he held the title of president, 1870–78. He established the Lowell School of Practical Design, 1872, and was associated with the work of the *Nautical Almanac*, 1849–84.

RUPP, ISRAEL DANIEL (*b. Cumberland Co., Pa., 1803; d. Philadelphia, Pa., 1878*), schoolmaster, historian. Author of *History of Lancaster County* (1844) and other volumes devoted to the county history of Pennsylvania.

RUPP, WILLIAM (*b. Lehigh Co., Pa., 1839; d. 1904*), German Reformed clergyman, professor of theology, editor. Taught at his denomination's seminary in Lancaster, Pa., *post* 1894.

RUPPERT, JACOB (*b. New York, N.Y., 1867; d. New York, 1939*), brewer, New York Democratic congressman. Co-owner (1914–23) and sole owner thereafter of the New York Yankees baseball club. [*Supp.* 2]

RUSBY, HENRY HURD (*b. Franklin, present Nutley, N.J., 1855; d. Sarasota, Fla., 1940*), pharmacognosist, botanical explorer. M.D., New York University, 1884. Traveling as pharmacognosist for Parke, Davis & Co., 1884–88, Rusby made extensive investigations in North and South America and collected specimens of some 45,000 species of plants, many of them hitherto unknown to botany; among the new drugs which resulted was cocillana. Appointed professor of materia medica at New York College of Pharmacy, 1889, he became dean in 1901 and remained so until 1930 after the college was affiliated with Columbia University. He also taught at other institutions in New York and made further botanical collections in South America. By teaching, research and writings, he established beneficial standards for pharmaceutical education and for American pharmacy at large. He was one of the foremost early exponents in America of the study of medicinal plants on a truly scientific basis and gave much knowledge and time to the formulation of legal standards for crude plant drugs.

[*Supp.* 2]

RUSH, BENJAMIN (*b. Byberry, near Philadelphia, Pa., 1745 o.s.; d. Philadelphia, Pa., 1813*), physician, Revolutionary patriot. Graduated College of New Jersey (Princeton), 1760. Studied medicine with John Redman and attended first lectures of William Shippen and John Morgan at the College of Philadelphia; completing his medical education at the University of Edinburgh, he received its doctorate in 1768. Returning to Philadelphia, 1769, Rush began to practice medicine and to teach chemistry at the College of Philadelphia. He published the first American chemistry text, *A Syllabus of a Course of Lectures on Chemistry* (1770), and attracted attention by his unusual ability as practitioner of a new system of treatment taught by his Edinburgh master, the great William Cullen. He also wrote at length on medical, social and political topics, and, as the quarrel between the colonies and the mother country mounted, he became the associate of patriot leaders like John Adams and Thomas Jefferson. Elected to the Continental Congress, 1776, he was a signer of the Declaration of Independence.

Appointed surgeon-general of the Middle Department in the medical service of the Continental Army, 1777, he accused Dr. William Shippen, his superior, of maladministration and resigned when a decision was given against him. Association in the Conway Cabal and Gen. Washington's recognition of his part in it (1778) ended Rush's military career and he returned to his practice in Philadelphia. Becoming a member of the staff of the Pennsylvania Hospital, 1783, he served in that capacity for the rest of his life. Sponsor of a number of ameliorative movements which were to remold America in the ensuing century, he was active against slavery and capital punishment and advocated temperance, an improved educational system and prison reform. His ideas on social reform may be found in his *Essays, Literary, Moral and Philosophical* (1798). In the Pennsylvania convention for ratifying the new U.S. Constitution, he and James Wilson led the successful movement for adoption; in 1789, they inaugurated a campaign which secured a more liberal and effective state constitution for Pennsylvania. After the creation of the University of Pennsylvania, 1791, Rush became professor of the institutes of medicine and clinical practice in the university (1792) and in 1796 succeeded Dr. Adam Kuhn as professor of theory and practice as well. He was treasurer of the U.S. Mint, 1797–1813.

It is impossible to describe Rush's system of theory and practice briefly without oversimplification, but it might be called a logical extension of John Brown's reformulation (1788) of Cullen's theory. The essential principle was that all diseases were due to one "proximate" cause—a state of excessive excitability or spasm in the blood vessels. Hence, in most cases but one treatment was called for, namely, "depletion" through bleeding and purging. He con-fidently proclaimed his system when the initial volume of his *Medical Inquiries and Observations* was published in 1789, but critics declared that Rush's fondness for depletion led him to dangerous extremes in practice. In the epidemic of yellow fever which descended upon Philadelphia, 1793, Rush worked with desperation and devotion in the stricken city, but it was pointed out that there was an obvious correlation between increasing employment of Rush's treatment and an increasing mortality rate. Although Rush's treatment was not the only variable involved, yet it was impossible to reconcile his claims with the stark fact of the mortality tables, and he may be considered the victim of a credulity about diagnoses and cures which characterized much of his work. Also, his view that the "remote" cause of the epidemic was unsanitary conditions in the city antagonized many citizens. Despite all this, his published account of the epidemic and of those which followed it won him recognition both at home and abroad. His chief essay on the subject is *An Account of the Bilious Remitting Yellow Fever . . . 1793* (1794). Dr. Rush was an observant man but not a good observer. However, there is reason to believe that he was the pioneer worker in experimental physiology in the United States, and he was the first American to write on *cholera infantum* and the first to recognize focal infection in the teeth. His contributions to psychiatry were also notable, and his *Medical Inquiries and Observations upon the Diseases of the Mind* (1812) shows some appreciation of what would today be known as mental healing and even of psychoanalysis.

RUSH, JAMES (*b. Philadelphia, Pa., 1786; d. Philadelphia, 1869*), physician, psychologist. Son of Benjamin Rush; brother of Richard Rush. Graduated College of New Jersey (Princeton), 1805; M.D., University of Pennsylvania, 1809. Founder of the Ridgway Branch, Library Company of Philadelphia.

RUSH, RICHARD (*b. Philadelphia, Pa., 1780; d. Philadelphia, 1859*), lawyer, statesman, diplomat. Son of Benjamin Rush; brother of James Rush. Graduated College of New Jersey (Princeton), 1798. Admitted to the Philadelphia bar, 1800, he grew in reputation as a speaker and made important political contacts as defense counsel for William Duane when Thomas McKean sued that editor for libel, 1808. An ardent (Democrat) Republican, Rush became attorney-general of Pennsylvania, 1811, and was appointed comptroller of the U.S. treasury in November of that year. Appointed U.S. attorney-general, February 1814, he edited *Laws of the United States* (1815), and in a brief period as U.S. secretary of state just after the inauguration of President Monroe, negotiated the Rush-Bagot convention (April 1817) establishing limitation of naval armament on the Great Lakes. Appointed U.S. minister to Great Britain, October 1817, he was one of the most efficient and best-liked of American representatives in that post. Tactful, well-bred and with wide intellectual interests, he moved with ease in British society and succeeded in settling a number of disputes subsequent to the War of 1812. He negotiated a treaty of joint occupation of Oregon which served as a basis of understanding for nearly thirty years, and in 1819 handled wisely the issues raised by Andrew Jackson's invasion of Florida and the execution of Ambrister and Arbuthnot. Rush played a very important role in the preliminaries of the Monroe Doctrine, and his dispatches of August–September 1823 were an important factor in persuading President Monroe and John Quincy Adams to take a strong stand. Accepting the post of U.S. secretary of the treasury, 1825, he favored a mild protectionist policy. Candidate for vice-president of the United States, 1828, he was badly defeated in the Jacksonian triumph. As a private citizen, he continued active in the public interest, supported Andrew Jackson in the 1832 struggle over the Bank and in 1835 served on a commission to settle the Ohio-Michigan boundary dispute. In 1836–38 he secured the Smithson bequest, then in chancery, which was used to establish the Smithsonian Institution. U.S. minister to France, 1847–49, he acted with his usual intelligence and tact during the revolutionary days of 1848 in Paris. Returning home, he continued interested in public affairs until his death. He was author of the important *Memoranda of a Residence at the Court of London* (1833, 1845) and *Occasional Productions, etc.* (1860).

RUSH, WILLIAM (*b. Philadelphia, Pa., 1756; d. 1833*), carver of ship's figureheads, first native American sculptor. Worked in Philadelphia; co-founder, with Charles W. Peale and others, of the Pennsylvania Academy of the Fine Arts, 1805.

RUSK, JEREMIAH McCLAIN (*b. Morgan Co., O., 1830; d. 1893*), farmer, businessman, Union soldier. Settled in Vernon Co., Wis., 1853. As Republican governor of Wisconsin, 1882–89, he gave the state a strong and effective government, earning the affectionate title "Uncle Jerry"; in quelling strike riots in Milwaukee, May 1886, he uttered a much-quoted remark, "I seen my duty and I done it." While U.S. secretary of agriculture, 1889–93, he secured inspection of all American meat exports and engaged the interest of the press in the activities and policies of his new department.

RUSK, THOMAS JEFFERSON (*b. Pendleton District, S.C., 1803; d. Nacogdoches, Texas, 1857*), Texas pioneer, soldier, jurist. Removed to Texas c. 1835. Took active part in the convention of 1836, signed declaration of independence for Texas, aided in drafting of Texas constitution, and was elected secretary of war in the provisional government. Rusk fought at San Jacinto, commanding the Texas army after that battle. Appointed secretary of war in Sam Houston's cabinet, he soon resigned to practice law but led an active campaign against hostile Indians in East Texas, 1839. Having been elected chief justice of the Texas supreme court, 1838, he presided over its first session, January–June 1840. A supporter of annexation of Texas to the United States, he served as U.S. senator, Democrat, *post* 1846, giving full support to the administration in the war with Mexico and working consistently for improvement of transportation. Choice of many delegates for the presidential nomination, 1856, he refused to have his name entered.

RUSS, JOHN DENNISON (*b. Essex, Mass., 1801; d. Pompton, N.J., 1881*), physician, penologist, pioneer teacher of the blind. Graduated Yale, 1823; M.D., Yale, 1825. Associated with Samuel G. Howe in support and relief of Greek revolutionaries, 1827–30; practiced in New York City *post* 1830. Co-founder of New York Institution for the Blind which he served as manager, 1832–35.

RUSSELL, ANNIE (*b. Liverpool, England, 1864; d. Winter Park, Fla., 1936*), actress, noted for ingénue roles. Made debut as a child actress in Montreal, Canada, 1872; made New York debut in a juvenile performance of *H.M.S. Pinafore* at the Lyceum Theatre, 1879; established herself in popular favor in title role of *Esmeralda*, 1881. Among her later important parts were the title roles in *Hazel Kirke* and in Shaw's *Major Barbara;* she was effective also in Shakespearean repertory. [*Supp. 2*]

RUSSELL, BENJAMIN (*b. Boston, Mass., 1761; d. 1845*), journalist. Learned to set type in office of Isaiah Thomas to whom he was apprenticed. Founded *The Massachusetts Centinel* (first issued, March 24, 1784) which he edited and published until his retirement, 1828; *post* 1790 the paper was known as the *Columbian Centinel*. A vigorous writer, Russell took an active part in politics and made his Federalist paper the most enterprising and influential in Massachusetts. He held many public offices both honorary and elective.

RUSSELL, CHARLES TAZE (*b. Pittsburgh, Pa., 1852; d. Texas, 1916*), religious leader. Commonly known as "Pastor Russell," founder of a millennial sect now known as Jehovah's Witnesses.

RUSSELL, CHARLES WELLS (*b. Wheeling, present W. Va., 1856; d. Washington, D.C., 1927*), lawyer, government official, diplomat. Prepared an important report on peonage in the South, 1907; was U.S. envoy extraordinary to Persia, 1909–14.

RUSSELL, DAVID ALLEN (*b. Salem, N.Y., 1820; d. Winchester, Va., 1864*), Union soldier. Graduated West Point, 1845. Commended for Mexican War service, he was active in Northwest Indian fighting until the outbreak of the Civil War. After hard and outstanding service in brigade command (notably at Rappahannock Station, Va., November 1863), he rose to divisional command, May 1864, and was killed in a critical moment of the battle of Winchester.

RUSSELL, IRWIN (*b. Port Gibson, Miss., 1853; d. New Orleans, La., 1879*), poet. A pioneer in Negro dialect poetry, Russell was author of a single volume published posthumously, *Poems* (1888).

RUSSELL, ISRAEL COOK (*b. Garrattsville, N.Y., 1852; d. Ann Arbor, Mich., 1906*), geologist. Graduated in engineering, University of the City of New York (present New York University), 1872; attended Columbia School of Mines. After extensive field experience in government survey work under John J. Stevenson, G. K. Gilbert and others, he served as professor of geology, University of Michigan, 1892–1906. An authority on North American geography, particularly that of Alaska and the Northwest, and a specialist in glaciology, Russell was author, among other works, of *Geological History of Lake Lahontan* (1885) which remains a classic of geological science.

RUSSELL, JAMES SOLOMON (*b. Palmer's Springs, Va., 1857; d. Lawrenceville, Va., 1935*), Episcopal clergyman, educator. Born of slave parents, he attended Hampton Institute and St. Stephen's School, Petersburg, Va.; he was ordained deacon in 1882 and priest, 1887. Principal and founder of St. Paul Normal and Industrial School (1888–1930), he was twice elected to the episcopal bench but declined to leave his school work. [*Supp. 1*]

RUSSELL, JOHN HENRY (*b. Frederick, Md., 1827; d. 1897*), naval officer. Graduated U.S. Naval Academy, 1848. Led force which burned the Confederate privateer *Judah*, Pensacola, Fla., September 1861; commanding *Kennebec*, he served ably in Adm. D. G. Farragut's operations at New Orleans and Mobile.

RUSSELL, JONATHAN (*b. Providence, R.I., 1771; d. Milton, Mass., 1832*), orator, diplomat, merchant. A prominent (Democrat) Republican, Russell served as U.S. chargé d'affaires at Paris and London, and was U.S. minister to Sweden and Norway, 1814–18; in 1814 he was one of the peace commissioners at Ghent. Accused by John Quincy Adams of employing a false document against him, 1822, Russell retired from public life.

RUSSELL, JOSEPH (*b. Township of Dartmouth, Mass., 1719 o.s.; d. 1804*), New Bedford merchant, shipowner. A Russell vessel, the *Rebecca*, made the first whaling voyage around Cape Horn to the Pacific hunting grounds, 1791–93.

RUSSELL, LILLIAN (*b. Clinton, Iowa, 1861; d. Pittsburgh, Pa., 1922*), comic opera singer, internationally famous beauty. Stage name of Helen Louise Leonard. Raised in Chicago, Ill. After studying singing in New York under Leopold Damrosch, she made her first stage appearance, 1879, in the chorus of a company of *Pinafore*. In November 1880, she made her first appearance under her stage name at Tony Pastor's theatre, New York. Beauty of face and figure, an excellent natural voice and a great flair for publicity contributed to her success in a number of comic operas which featured her voice and appearance but required little dramatic ability.

RUSSELL, Mother MARY BAPTIST (*b. Newry, Ireland, 1829; d. California, 1898*), founder of the Sisters of Mercy in California. Name in religion of Katherine Russell. Raised in a family of remarkable distinction, Mother Russell joined the Institute of Mercy at Kinsale, 1848. As superior of a group of her order who had volunteered for work in San Francisco, Calif., she arrived there in December 1854 and established a convent and school. Early hostility to the nuns ended in gratitude after their work in the county hospital during an epidemic of cholera. Thereafter until her death she engaged in all works of charity, building and staffing hospitals, orphanages, homes for the aged and schools throughout the state.

RUSSELL, OSBORNE (*b. probably Hallowell, Maine, 1814; d. Placerville, Calif., c. 1865*), trapper, Oregon and California pioneer. Author of the important *Journal of a Trapper, Or Nine Years in the Rocky Mountains, 1834–1843* (published Boise, Idaho, 1914).

RUSSELL, SOL SMITH (*b. Brunswick, Mo., 1848; d. Washington, D.C., 1902*), actor. Nephew by marriage of Sol Smith. Celebrated throughout the country *post c.* 1867 as a comedian, he had a dry, crackling manner that was irresistible in its appeal to contemporary audiences.

RUSSELL, WILLIAM (*b. Glasgow, Scotland, 1798; d. Lancaster, Mass., 1873*), educator. Emigrated to Georgia, 1817–18; taught at and conducted schools in many towns along the eastern seaboard. As principal of the New England Normal Institute, 1853–55, he made it an important center of Pestalozzianism in the United States. First editor of the *American Journal of Education* (1826), he was the author of a number of textbooks.

RUSSELL, WILLIAM EUSTIS (*b. Cambridge, Mass., 1857; d. St. Adelaide, Quebec, Canada, 1896*), lawyer, politician. Democratic governor of Massachusetts, 1891–94.

RUSSELL, WILLIAM HENRY (*b. Nicholas Co., Ky., 1802; d. Washington, D.C., 1873*), lawyer, Kentucky legislator, California pioneer. An associate of John C. Frémont in the early government of California, Russell later practiced law there. A large, expansive, bombastic man, he bore the nickname of "Owl" Russell.

RUSSELL, WILLIAM HEPBURN (*b. Burlington, Vt., 1812; d. Palmyra, Mo., 1872*), freighter, stagecoach operator. Joined Alexander Majors in partnership (December 1854) which later became Russell, Majors & Waddell. Persuaded the reluctant Majors to join him in operation of the Pony Express, starting

April 1860. Involved with John B. Floyd, U.S. secretary of war, in a celebrated embezzlement scandal, Russell was indicted in January 1861, but action on the case was postponed because of the Civil War. Failure of the Pony Express venture led to failure of Russell's firm, and he transferred his interest in the freighting part of it to Majors.

RUSSWURM, JOHN BROWN (*b. Port Antonio, Jamaica, B.W.I., 1799; d. Liberia, 1851*), educator, government official. Probably the first person of African descent to graduate from an American college (Bowdoin, 1826), Russwurm established one of the first Negro newspapers in the United States, *Freedom's Journal*, 1827. Emigrating to Liberia, 1829, he served as superintendent of public schools and as colonial secretary. He was governor of the Maryland Colony at Cape Palmas, 1836–51.

RUST, RICHARD SUTTON (*b. Ipswich, Mass., 1815; d. Cincinnati, O., 1906*), Methodist clergyman, advocate of education for Negroes.

RUTER, MARTIN (*b. Charlton, Mass., 1785; d. Texas, 1838*), Methodist clergyman, educator, missionary to Texas.

RUTGERS, HENRY (*b. near New York, N.Y., 1745; d. New York, 1830*), landowner, Revolutionary officer, philanthropist. A principal benefactor of New York educational institutions, Rutgers was a trustee of Princeton University and Queen's College; the latter institution changed its name to Rutgers in his honor.

RUTHERFURD, LEWIS MORRIS (*b. Morrisania, N.Y., 1816; d. 1892*), astrophysicist, pioneer in astronomical photography and spectroscopy. Great-grandson of Lewis Morris (1726–1798). Graduated Williams College; studied law under William H. Seward. Began serious work in science, 1856; secured first photographs of the moon, 1858. Following up observational work of Fraunhofer, he attempted a classification of stellar spectra which was published in the *American Journal of Science,* January 1863. Inventor of a number of devices for improving the efficiency of his work, he built during 1870 a machine with which he succeeded in ruling interference gratings superior to all others down to the time of Henry A. Rowland. Rutherfurd took a leading part in establishing the department of geodesy and practical astronomy at Columbia, 1881.

RUTLEDGE, EDWARD (*b. Charleston, S.C., 1749; d. Charleston, 1800*), lawyer, statesman. Brother of John Rutledge. Member of the First Continental Congress, 1774, and of the Second Continental Congress, 1775–76, he seconded the opinions of his brother. At first opposing independence, he influenced the South Carolina delegation to vote for it and was a signer of the Declaration. Returning home in November 1776 to serve in the defense of the state, he was taken prisoner at the fall of Charleston but was exchanged in time to take his seat in the legislature in January

1782. Although he drew up the bill proposing confiscation of Loyalist property, he was influential in moderating its effect. An active member of the legislature, 1782–98, he was a stiffly conservative Federalist. Elected governor, 1798, he served until his death.

RUTLEDGE, JOHN (*b. Charleston, S.C., 1739; d. 1800*), statesman, jurist. Brother of Edward Rutledge. After studying law at the Middle Temple, London, he was called to the English bar, 1760, and returned to an immediate and brilliant success in Charleston. A provincial legislator *post* 1761, he was sent as a delegate to the First Continental Congress in which, like Joseph Galloway, he favored maintaining self-government without breaking up the empire. In the Second Continental Congress, his efforts for establishment of regular governments in the colonies culminated in the advice of Congress to South Carolina (November 1775) to take such action if it should seem necessary. Returning to his native state, he was elected to the Council of Safety. He was one of the committee which wrote the South Carolina constitution of 1776 and served as president of the General Assembly until his resignation (1778) in protest against a revision of the state constitution which he considered dangerously democratic.

When the state faced invasion in January 1779, Rutledge was elected governor and worked tirelessly to support the efforts of American military forces during a calamitous period. Despite the fall of Charleston and the defeat at Camden, 1780, he did not despair and, while he begged Congress for help, encouraged Thomas Sumter, Francis Marion and other partisans to wage detached warfare against the British. In August 1781 he set about a restoration of civil government, working to a large extent through the militia officers. Laying down his office at the end of the year, he re-entered the legislature, served for a brief time in Congress, 1782–83, and in 1784 was elected to the South Carolina chancery court. Chairman of the committee of detail in the Federal Convention, 1787, he fought for wealth to be made part of the basis of representation, for assumption of state debts, and against restrictions on the slave trade; also for election of the president by Congress and of Congress by the legislatures. Elected chief justice of South Carolina, February 1791, he was offered the chief justiceship of the U.S. Supreme Court, 1795. His nomination was rejected by the Senate because of the bitterness of his attacks against Jay's Treaty. He embodied perhaps more perfectly than any other man of his time the ideas of the ruling class of 18th-century South Carolina.

RYAN, ABRAM JOSEPH (*b. Hagerstown, Md., 1838; d. Louisville, Ky., 1886*), Roman Catholic clergyman, Confederate chaplain, poet of the Confederacy. Father Ryan's collected poems, including "The Conquered Banner" and "The Sword of Robert E. Lee," were published in book form, 1879.

RYAN, ARTHUR CLAYTON (*b. Grandview, Iowa, 1879; d. Scarsdale, N.Y., 1927*), Congregational clergyman, missionary to Turkey. General secretary, American Bible Society, *post* 1924.

RYAN, EDWARD GEORGE (*b. near Enfield, Ireland, 1810; d. Madison, Wis., 1880*), jurist. Came to America, 1830; settled in Milwaukee, Wis., 1848. Chief justice of Wisconsin, 1874–80, he ruled in important cases involving the power of the state legislature to regulate railway rates and to prescribe conditions upon which foreign corporations might do business in the state.

RYAN, HARRIS JOSEPH (*b. Matamoras, Pa., 1866; d. 1934*), electrical engineer. M.E., Cornell University, 1887. Taught at Cornell, 1888–1905; headed department of electrical engineering at Leland Stanford, 1905–31. Authority on power transmission at high voltages; a pioneer in engineering use of the cathode-ray tube. [*Supp. 1*]

RYAN, JOHN DENNIS (*b. Hancock, Mich., 1864; d. New York, N.Y., 1933*), capitalist. Dominating figure *post* 1909 in the Anaconda Copper Mining Co. which he made one of the greatest industrial enterprises in the world; active also in public utilities and railroads.

RYAN, PATRICK JOHN (*b. Thurles, Ireland, 1831; d. 1911*), Roman Catholic clergyman. Emigrated to St. Louis, Mo., 1852, where he was ordained, 1853. A leading preacher and orator of his time, he was consecrated coadjutor bishop of St. Louis, 1872, and in 1884 succeeded to the see of Philadelphia.

RYAN, STEPHEN VINCENT (*b. near Almonte, Ontario, Canada, 1825; d. 1896*), Roman Catholic clergyman, Vincentian. Raised in Pennsylvania. Completed theological studies in Missouri and was ordained in St. Louis, 1849. Elected visitor general of his order in America, 1857, he was named against his will bishop of Buffalo, 1868, and served until his death. A strong liberal, Bishop Ryan found himself in continual disagreement with Bishop Bernard McQuaid of Rochester.

RYAN, THOMAS FORTUNE (*b. Lovingston, Va., 1851; d. 1928*), promoter, financier. Beginning as an errand boy in a Baltimore, Md., dry-goods commission house, Ryan removed to New York City, 1872, and prospered as a stock broker, 1873–83. His first exploit in high finance was the organization of the New York Cable Railroad, 1883, a paper corporation with which, in association with William C. Whitney and Peter A. B. Widener, he eventually controlled practically every street railway line in New York City. His Metropolitan Traction Co., organized 1886, manipulated the securities of the various traction companies held by Ryan's syndicate and is considered to have been the first holding company in the United States. Threatened by the competition of the new subway system, 1905, Ryan bludgeoned the interests behind the Interborough Rapid Transit Co. into consolidating with his firm and engaging in a scheme of overcapitalization which left New York City traction in a state of financial collapse, 1906–07. Called "the most adroit, suave and noiseless man" in American finance, Ryan extended his power into banking, insurance, public utilities and general industry by methods which were constantly under fire as prejudicial to the public interest.

RYAN, WALTER D'ARCY (*b. Kentville, N.S., Canada, 1870; d. Schenectady, N.Y., 1934*), illuminating engineer, developer of flood lighting and high-intensity street-lighting.

RYBNER, MARTIN CORNELIUS (*b. Copenhagen, Denmark, 1853; d. 1929*), composer, pianist, music teacher. Came to America as professor of music at Columbia University, 1904; resigned, 1919, to devote his time to composition and recital work.

RYDBERG, PER AXEL (*b. Odh, Sweden, 1860; d. New York, N.Y., 1931*), botanist. Came to America, 1882. Graduated University of Nebraska, 1891; Ph.D., Columbia, 1898. On staff of New York Botanical Garden *post* 1899; was author, among other books, of *Catalogue of the Flora of Montana* (1900), *Flora of Colorado* (1906) and *Flora of the Rocky Mountains* (1917, 1922).

RYDER, ALBERT PINKHAM (*b. New Bedford, Mass., 1847; d. Elmhurst, N.Y., 1917*), painter. Studied under William E. Marshall and at National Academy of Design. Living principally in New York City *post* 1868, and a virtual recluse not because of misanthropy but owing to his deep absorption in his work, Ryder produced hardly more than 150 pictures throughout his career. No one of these is perfunctory and all are of the rarest kind of poetic painting; his best work was produced between 1873 and 1898, and his small marines are most representative of his highest technical and structural achievement. Ryder's work reveals a mastery of design and possesses a charm that is wholly spontaneous and original.

RYERSON, MARTIN ANTOINE (*b. Grand Rapids, Mich., 1856; d. 1932*), capitalist. Raised in Chicago, Ill., where he engaged in business until the early 1890's, Ryerson was identified with many philanthropies, notably as a benefactor to the Chicago Art Institute, the Field Museum and the University of Chicago.

RYLAND, ROBERT (*b. King and Queen Co., Va., 1805; d. 1899*), Baptist clergyman, educator. Headed Virginia Baptist Seminary, Richmond, Va. (later Richmond College), from 1832 until the Civil War; thereafter was active in Kentucky education.

RYNNING, OLE (*b. Ringsaker, Norway, 1809; d. Iroquois Co., Ill., 1838*), immigrant leader. Emigrated to Beaver Creek region in Illinois, 1837; author of a remarkable guide book for Norwegians proposing to come to America (published at Christiania, 1838).

SABIN, CHARLES HAMILTON (*b. Williamstown, Mass., 1868; d. Shinnecock Hills, N.Y., 1933*), banker. President, Guaranty Trust Co., 1915–21; thereafter chairman of the board.

SABIN, JOSEPH (*b. probably Braunston, Northamptonshire, England, 1821; d. 1881*), bookseller, bibliographer. Came to America, 1848. Dealer and cataloguer of rare books and prints in Philadelphia and New York, Sabin is particularly remembered as the compiler of *Dictionary of Books Relating to America, etc.* (1868–84, issued in parts), an outstanding reference work which he left unfinished. The work was brought to a conclusion by later scholars in the 19th and 20th centuries.

SABINE, LORENZO (*b. Lisbon, N.H., 1803; d. Boston Highlands, Mass., 1877*), historian, businessman, public official. Author, among other works, of the valuable *The American Loyalists* (1847; second and enlarged edition under title *Biographical Sketches of Loyalists,* 1864).

SABINE, WALLACE CLEMENT WARE (*b. Richwood, O., 1868; d. 1919*), physicist. Graduated Ohio State, 1886; A.M., Harvard, 1888. Taught physics at Harvard *post* 1889; appointed dean of Lawrence Scientific School, 1906; dean, Harvard Graduate School of Applied Science, 1908–16. Authority on architectural acoustics and aerial warfare.

SACAGAWEA (*b. probably near present Lemhi, Idaho, c. 1787; d. Fort Manuel, present N. Dak., 1812*), Shoshone woman, interpreter of the Lewis and Clark expedition. Sacagawea was of the greatest service to the explorers; without the aid she obtained for them from the Shoshones it is possible that the expedition could not have proceeded beyond the headwaters of the Salmon River. The details of her life are the subject of much controversy.

SACCO, NICOLA (*b. Torre Maggiore, Foggia, Italy, 1891; d. Massachusetts, 1927*), a principal with Bartolomeo Vanzetti, who was a native of Piedmont, in a celebrated judicial controversy, 1920–27, which culminated in the execution of both men for murder. The mobilization of liberal and left-wing forces in favor of the defense lent emotional overtones to the case.

SACHS, JULIUS (*b. Baltimore, Md., 1849; d. 1934*), educator. Graduated Columbia, 1867; Ph.D., University of Rostock, 1871. Principal, Sachs Collegiate Institute, New York City, 1871–1901; professor of secondary education, Teachers College, Columbia, 1902–17; author of scholarly studies on Greek and educational topics.

SACHS, THEODORE BERNARD (*b. Dinaberg, Russia, 1868; d. Naperville, Ill., 1916*), physician, specialist in treatment of tuberculosis. Came to America *c.* 1891. M.D., Chicago College of Physicians and Surgeons, 1895. Practicing in Chicago and vicinity,

he was a leader in the establishment of the Chicago Municipal Tuberculosis Sanitarium, 1909–15.

SACHSE, JULIUS FRIEDRICH (*b. Philadelphia, Pa., 1842; d. Philadelphia, 1919*), businessman, antiquarian, photographer, writer on Pennsylvania German history.

SACKETT, HENRY WOODWARD (*b. near Ithaca, N.Y., 1853; d. 1929*), lawyer, authority on libel, benefactor of Cornell University.

SADLIER, DENIS (*b. Co. Tipperary, Ireland, 1817; d. Wilton, N.Y., 1885*), book publisher. Came to America as a boy. Established with his brother the Catholic publishing firm of D. & J. Sadlier & Co. in New York City, 1836.

SADLIER, MARY ANNE MADDEN (*b. Cootehill, Ireland, 1820; d. Montreal, Canada, 1903*), author. Sister-in-law of Denis Sadlier. Emigrated to Montreal, 1844; resided in New York City *post* 1860. Writer of popular fiction for Catholic readers.

SADTLER, JOHN PHILIP BENJAMIN (*b. Baltimore, Md., 1823; d. Atlantic City, N.J., 1901*), Lutheran clergyman, educator. Graduated present Gettysburg College, 1842. Son-in-law of Samuel S. Schmucker. President, Muhlenberg College, 1877–85.

SADTLER, SAMUEL PHILIP (*b. Pinegrove, Pa., 1847; d. 1923*), chemist, educator. Son of John P. B. Sadtler; grandson of Samuel S. Schmucker. Graduated present Gettysburg College, 1867; S.B., Harvard, 1870; Ph.D., Göttingen, 1871. Taught chemistry at Gettysburg College, University of Pennsylvania and Philadelphia College of Pharmacy; chemical editor, *Dispensatory of the United States*, 1883–1923. Author of textbooks.

SAENDERL, SIMON (*b. Malgerzdorf, Bavaria, 1800; d. Gethsemane, Ky., 1879*), Roman Catholic clergyman, Redemptorist and Trappist. Came to America, 1832, as first Redemptorist superior in the United States; worked as a missionary in Wisconsin and Michigan, and in New York and Pennsylvania. Entered the Trappists, 1852.

SAFFORD, JAMES MERRILL (*b. Zanesville, O., 1822; d. Dallas, Texas, 1907*), geologist, educator. Graduated Ohio University, 1844. Taught sciences at Cumberland University, University of Nashville, and Vanderbilt; state geologist of Tennessee, 1854–60, 1871–1900.

SAFFORD, TRUMAN HENRY (*b. Royalton, Vt., 1836; d. Newark, N.J., 1901*), astronomer, mathematician. A mathematical prodigy as a child, Safford graduated from Harvard, 1854. A staff member of Harvard Observatory, 1854–66, he taught at University of Chicago, 1866–71, and was professor of astronomy at Williams College, 1876–1901.

SAFFORD, WILLIAM EDWIN (*b. Chillicothe, O., 1859; d. 1926*), ethnobotanist, ethnologist, philologist.

Graduated U.S. Naval Academy, 1880; made postgraduate studies at Yale and Harvard. Resigning from the navy, 1902, he served thereafter as botanist in the U.S. Department of Agriculture. Among his many works, *The Useful Plants of the Island of Guam* (1905) is particularly notable. It established Safford's reputation as an ethnobotanist and was followed by a number of other important studies of food plants.

SAGE, BERNARD JANIN (*b. near New Haven, Conn., 1821; d. New Orleans, La., 1902*), lawyer, planter, Confederate agent. Author of *Davis and Lee* (London, 1865, later issued as *The Republic of Republics*), a defense of the Confederate leaders on the grounds of history and international law.

SAGE, HENRY WILLIAMS (*b. Middletown, Conn., 1814; d. Ithaca, N.Y., 1897*), merchant, lumber manufacturer, benefactor of Cornell University and Yale Divinity School.

SAGE, MARGARET OLIVIA SLOCUM (*b. Syracuse, N.Y., 1828; d. New York, N.Y., 1918*), philanthropist. Wife of Russell Sage. Inheriting practically the whole of her husband's fortune on his death in 1906, she distributed it over a wide range of charitable activities including hospitals, social agencies, learned societies and museums and some 18 colleges. She established the Russell Sage Foundation, 1907.

SAGE, RUSSELL (*b. Oneida Co., N.Y., 1816; d. Long Island, N.Y., 1906*), financier, Whig congressman from New York. An associate in business of Jay Gould, Sage was one of the shrewdest and most conservative money manipulators of his time. Active *post* 1856 in railroad and other promotions, he was best known as a money lender during the last quarter-century of his life. At his death his fortune was estimated at about $70,000,000. He is credited with invention of the Wall Street practice of "puts and calls."

ST. ANGE DE BELLERIVE, LOUIS (*b. Montreal, Canada, c. 1698; d. St. Louis, Mo., 1774*), frontier soldier. Captain of the French post on the Wabash River, 1736–64; conducted evacuation of Fort Chartres, 1764–65. Commanded at St. Louis as acting governor of Upper Louisiana, 1765–70.

ST. CLAIR, ARTHUR (*b. Thurso, Scotland, 1736 o.s.; d. Chestnut Ridge, present Greensburg, Pa., 1818*), soldier. Appointed ensign in the British army, 1757, he served with Amherst in Canada, and in 1760 married a niece of James Bowdoin. Resigning from the army, 1762, he purchased an estate in western Pennsylvania and was the largest resident property-owner west of the mountains in that province. An enlightened agent of government in the frontier country, he opposed the influx of Virginians there but was unable to prevent Virginia's domination of the Pittsburgh area. Member of the Committee of Safety of Westmoreland Co., he served as colonel in the retreat after the Canadian invasion, 1775, and was

with Washington at Trenton and Princeton, 1776–77. Ordered to defend Fort Ticonderoga in the spring of 1777, he was obliged to surrender it and was recalled by Congress from service in the field. Active *post* 1778 in Pennsylvania politics, he was a delegate to the Confederation Congress, 1785–87, and president, 1787. Appointed governor of the Northwest Territory, 1787, he served until 1802. His attempts to maneuver the Indian tribes of the area into acceptance of the treaty of Fort Harmar, 1789, led to a war in which he as major-general and commander of the federal army was overwhelmingly defeated near present Fort Wayne, Ind., Nov. 4, 1791, by a confederated Indian army under Little Turtle. In governing the Northwest Territory he tried to enforce both the spirit and the letter of the Ordinance of 1787. Overbearing and paternalistic, he sought to prevent the Territory's progress to statehood and was removed from office by President Jefferson.

ST. DENIS (DENYS), LOUIS JUCHEREAU de (*b. Beauport, Quebec, Canada, 1676; d. Natchitoches, La., 1744*), French explorer, colonizer. Accompanied Iberville on expedition for founding Louisiana; accompanied Bienville on exploration to Red River, 1700. Founded French trading post at Natchitoches where he resided *post* 1719. A man of great influence with the Indians of Texas and Louisiana.

SAINT-GAUDENS, AUGUSTUS (*b. Dublin, Ireland, 1848; d. Cornish, N.H., 1907*), sculptor. Of French and Irish descent, Saint-Gaudens was brought to America as an infant and raised in New York City. Trained as a cameo-cutter, he worked at his trade while studying at Cooper Union and at the National Academy of Design and also trusted to his trade for support during the decade he spent in France and Italy *post* 1867. At the Beaux-Arts in Paris he received a good grounding under Jouffroy, but he did not allow his talent to be fixed in any one mold either in Paris or, *post* 1870, in Rome. It is significant that he began his work in Rome not with an Apollo or a Venus but with a study of Hiawatha. He worked with great industry and in the highest spirits, drawing upon unusual stores of perseverance. The story of his success is not one of swift growth and facile triumph but one of persistent effort and study. Side by side with his gift for portraiture and taste for it ran his interest in imaginative design. The early "Hiawatha" in marble (Saratoga, N.Y.) and the "Silence" (Masonic Temple, New York City) attest to this. Commissioned *c.* 1877 to do full-lengths of "Admiral Farragut" (Madison Square, New York City) and "Captain Randall" (Sailors' Snug Harbor, Staten Island, N.Y.), he returned to America and became a particular friend of John La Farge. The "Farragut," unveiled 1881, was a landmark in Saint-Gaudens's life and in the history of American sculpture; it established him as a master. The subject was placed realistically before the world, a living embodiment, a public monument with the stamp of creative art on it. Stanford White designed the pedestal, and so began a long association with Saint-Gaudens.

Progressing in his line as interpreter of major American historical figures, Saint-Gaudens continued to reveal himself as a master of characterization and of plastic design. His research into the lives and backgrounds of his subjects and the long thought which he gave to his work account for its remarkable conviction much more than any supposed clairvoyance. His "Sherman" (New York City) of 1903 is probably the greatest equestrian monument of modern times, and his two statues of Lincoln in Chicago, Ill., are eloquently expressive. His low reliefs show simple, charming composition as well as subtle modeling and were enhanced, as were all his works, by lettering which was made part of the design. Among his imaginative works, the "Amor Caritas" (1887), the "Diana" (1892) which he made for the original Madison Square Garden, the Phillips Brooks monument and the unfinished symbolic groups for the Boston Public Library, are evidence of his deep sense that beauty must mean at least some goodness. Simplicity is the keynote to his art, even in his one essay in the grand style—the great "Adams Monument" in Rock Creek Cemetery, Washington, D.C. (1891). This enigmatic figure, displaying creative energy and originality, spiritual force, and the sure fusion of dramatic purpose with technical authority, is his bid for immortality. He played an important part in the general development of artistic matters. He was active in the National Academy of Design, was a founder of the Society of American Artists and aided Charles F. McKim in establishing the American Academy in Rome; he also collaborated with Theodore Roosevelt in a proposed reform of the American coinage. Generously appreciative of younger artists when he felt that they were on the right track, he never failed to stress the discipline of rigorous training; he was as devoted to craftsmanship as to beauty.

ST. JOHN, CHARLES EDWARD (*b. Allen, Mich., 1857; d. 1935*), astronomer, educator. Graduated Michigan Agricultural College, 1887; Ph.D., Harvard, 1896. Taught at University of Michigan and at Oberlin; served on staff of Mount Wilson Observatory *post* 1908, making special study of the sun. Probably his most important investigation was a test of the validity of Einstein's relativity theory through comparison of solar and terrestrial spectra (published in *Astrophysical Journal*, April 1928). [*Supp.* 1]

ST. JOHN, ISAAC MUNROE (*b. Augusta, Ga., 1827; d. White Sulphur Springs, W. Va., 1880*), civil engineer, Confederate brigadier-general. Commissary-general of the Confederate Army, 1865.

ST. JOHN, JOHN PIERCE (*b. Brookville, Ind., 1833; d. Olathe, Kans., 1916*), prohibitionist, Union soldier. Republican governor of Kansas, 1879–83; presidential nominee, National Prohibition party, 1884.

ST. LUSSON, SIMON FRANÇOIS DAUMONT, Sieur de (*b. France, date unknown; d. probably Canada, 1674*), soldier, explorer. Served in Canada, 1663–68, 1670–73. While on an expedition to explore for mines near Lake Superior, St. Lusson presided over a formal ceremony of annexation to France of the Great Lakes area at Sault Ste. Marie, June 14, 1671.

SAINT-MÉMIN, CHARLES BALTHAZAR JULIEN FEVRET de (*b. Dijon, France, 1770; d. Dijon, 1852*), artist, engraver. Resident in the United States, 1793–1814, Saint-Mémin produced more than 800 portraits of distinguished Americans of that time. Securing an exact profile of the sitter in crayon by means of a physionotrace, he reduced the profile with a pantograph to a miniature about two inches in diameter and recorded it directly on copper with graver and roulette. He also engraved topographical sketches of New York. A principal collection of his work is in the Corcoran Gallery, Washington, D.C.

SAINT-MÉRY, MOREAU de. [See Moreau de Saint-Méry, Médéric-Louis-Elie, 1750–1819.]

ST. VRAIN, CERAN DE HAULT DE LASSUS de (*b. near St. Louis, Mo., 1802; d. Mora, N.M., 1870*), pioneer merchant in the Southwest, soldier. Entered the fur trade at an early age; journeyed to Taos, N. Mex., 1824–25; traded out of Santa Fé, 1826. In partnership with Charles Bent, 1831–47, St. Vrain developed a business surpassed in importance only by the American Fur Co.; he also held large tracts of land under grant from the Mexican government. During the Mexican War, he organized and led a company of volunteers and later served against raiding Apaches and Utes. Appointed colonel, 1st New Mexico cavalry, 1861, he soon resigned because of age and was succeeded by Kit Carson.

SAJOUS, CHARLES EUCHARISTE DE MÉDICIS (*b. at sea, 1852; d. Philadelphia, Pa., 1929*), physician. Began medical studies at University of California; M.D., Jefferson Medical College, 1878. Practiced in Philadelphia and was lecturer and professor at several medical schools there, including Temple University and the postgraduate school of University of Pennsylvania. Authority on endocrinology and laryngology.

SALISBURY, ALBERT (*b. Lima, Wis., 1843; d. 1911*), educator, Union soldier. President, Whitewater (Wis.) Normal School, 1885–1911.

SALISBURY, EDWARD ELBRIDGE (*b. Boston, Mass., 1814; d. 1901*), Orientalist, educator. Graduated Yale, 1932; made postgraduate studies there in Hebrew and cognate languages, and also at Paris, Bonn and Berlin. A pioneer teacher of Arabic and Sanskrit at Yale, 1843–56, Salisbury opened the field of Oriental studies in the United States. He was author of a number of learned studies published principally in *Journal of American Oriental Society*.

SALISBURY, JAMES HENRY (*b. Scott, N.Y., 1823; d. Dobbs Ferry, N.Y., 1905*), physician, chemist, plant pathologist. A precursor of the germ theory of disease in works published, 1862–68.

SALISBURY, ROLLIN D. (*b. Spring Prairie, Wis., 1858; d. 1922*), geologist, educator. Graduated Beloit College, 1881. Succeeded his mentor, Thomas C. Chamberlin, as professor of geology at Beloit, 1882–91. After teaching briefly at the University of Wisconsin (1891), he became professor of geographic geology, University of Chicago, serving there as teacher (and dean of the Graduate School of Science *post* 1899) for the rest of his life. He was a leading authority on glacial and Pleistocene deposits.

SALM-SALM, AGNES ELISABETH WINONA LECLERCQ JOY, Princess (*b. Franklin Co., Vt., or possibly Philipsburg, Quebec, 1840; d. Karlsruhe, Germany, 1912*), adventuress. Princess Salm-Salm is principally remembered for her heroic role during the fall of Maximilian's regime in Mexico, 1867 (when she attempted the Emperor's rescue), and for her relief work with the German army, 1870.

SALMON, DANIEL ELMER (*b. Mount Olive, N.J., 1850; d. Butte, Mont., 1914*), veterinarian. Graduated Cornell, 1872; D.V.M., 1876. Outstanding as chief, Bureau of Animal Industry, U.S. Department of Agriculture, 1883–1905, he succeeded in bringing contagious pleuro-pneumonia and Texas fever among cattle under complete control. He also made investigations into the cause and prevention of fowl cholera, contagious diseases of swine and nodular diseases of sheep. He was responsible for the inauguration of a nation-wide system of meat inspection, for a quarantine system for imported livestock and for inspection of export cattle and the ships which carried them.

SALMON, LUCY MAYNARD (*b. Fulton, N.Y., 1853; d. 1927*), educator. Graduated University of Michigan, 1876; A.M., 1883; fellow in history, Bryn Mawr, 1886–87. Taught history at Vassar, 1887–1927.

SALMON, THOMAS WILLIAM (*b. Lansingburg, N.Y., 1876; d. 1927*), physician, pioneer in mental hygiene.

SALOMON, HAYM (*b. Lissa, Poland, c. 1740; d. Philadelphia, Pa., 1785*), merchant, Revolutionary patriot. An advocate of Polish independence, he fled to England, 1772, and thence to New York City where he began business as a broker and commission merchant. Twice imprisoned by the British as an active Whig, 1776, 1778, he removed to Philadelphia and within the next few years became a leading broker in that city. His liberal advances of cash to officers of the government and his equally liberal investments in Revolutionary paper, *c.* 1780–84, constitute an outstanding example of devotion to the American cause; he contributed much in other ways to maintain the bankrupt government's credit.

SALTER, WILLIAM (*b. Brooklyn, N.Y., 1821; d. 1910*), Congregational clergyman. Removed to Iowa, 1843. At first an itinerant pastor, he served as minister of the First Church of Burlington, 1846–1910. He was author of a number of religious books and several works on Iowa history.

SALTER, WILLIAM MACKINTIRE (*b. Burlington, Iowa, 1853; d. 1931*), Ethical Culture lecturer, philosopher. Son of William Salter. Authority on the thought of Nietzsche.

SALTONSTALL, DUDLEY (*b. New London, Conn., 1738; d. Mole St. Nicolas, Haiti, 1796*), naval officer. Grandson of Gurdon Saltonstall. Served as a privateersman in the French and Indian War; commanded merchant ships before the Revolution. Given command of the *Alfred*, flagship of Commodore Esek Hopkins, 1775, he was in the expedition which captured New Providence, 1776. He is best remembered for his connection with the Penobscot expedition, 1779, during which he commanded the naval forces employed. He was dismissed from the navy for failure to support army operations against the fort and the British vessels which were protecting Castine (Bagaduce) harbor, and for the eventual loss of his entire fleet. He was subsequently successful in privateering and afterwards returned to the merchant service.

SALTONSTALL, GURDON (*b. Haverhill, Mass., 1666 o.s.; d. 1724 o.s.*), Congregational clergyman, colonial statesman. Great-grandson of Nathaniel Ward; grandson of Richard Saltonstall. Graduated Harvard, 1684. Ordained minister of the church at New London, Conn., 1691; became confidant and adviser of Fitz-John Winthrop. Closely associated with public affairs during Winthrop's governorship, 1698–1707, Saltonstall succeeded him as governor of Connecticut at the request of the Assembly and was re-elected annually until his death. His adroit and conservative management of the colony's affairs fully justified the confidence placed in him. He was a leader in the approval by the Assembly of the Saybrook platform of 1708 and was active in the permanent settlement of Yale College at New Haven.

SALTONSTALL, RICHARD (*b. Woodsome, Yorkshire, England, c. 1610; d. Hulme, Lancashire, England, 1694*), Massachusetts colonist. Grandfather of Gurdon Saltonstall. Came with his father to Massachusetts Bay, 1630, where they established the settlement of Watertown. After studying law in England, 1631–35, he returned to New England and settled in Ipswich. His residence there was interrupted by three stays in England (1649–63, 1672–80, and 1686–94). A colonial office-holder and magistrate, he served also in the militia and was a member of the liberal group which included Simon Bradstreet and Nathaniel Ward.

SALTUS, EDGAR EVERTSON (*b. New York, N.Y., 1855; d. 1921*), novelist, essayist. Author of *The Philosophy of Disenchantment* (1885) and other works expressive of rebellion against contemporary main currents in American literature, Saltus wrote in a style which strained after effect and was more bizarre than original. He is to be studied at his best in an account of the Roman emperors, *Imperial Purple* (1892); his fiction was marked by weakness of characterization and melodramatic situations.

SAMPSON, MARTIN WRIGHT (*b. Cincinnati, O., 1866; d. 1930*), educator, editor. Stimulating teacher of English composition and literature at University of Iowa, Stanford, Indiana, and finally at Cornell, 1908–30.

SAMPSON, WILLIAM (*b. Londonderry, Ireland, 1764; d. New York, N.Y., 1836*), Irish patriot, lawyer. Imprisoned for activity with the United Irishmen at the end of the 18th century, Sampson was exiled in 1799 and settled in the United States, 1806. Admitted to the bar almost immediately, he won high rank through his eloquence and his advocacy of personal rights. He was counsel in one of the earliest American labor cases (the Journeymen Cordwainers case in New York, 1809–10) and in 1813 was successful as *amicus curiae* in the Kohlmann case. His *Memoirs* (1807) were in fact a denunciation of the British policy toward Ireland. He was also author of an early (1823) plea for the codification of American law.

SAMPSON, WILLIAM THOMAS (*b. Palmyra, N.Y., 1840; d. Washington, D.C., 1902*), naval officer. Graduated U.S. Naval Academy, 1861. After service with the Union naval forces, he performed several tours of duty as an instructor at Annapolis and was superintendent of the Naval Academy, 1886–90. As chief of the ordnance bureau, 1893–97, he was credited with making great advances in guns, explosives and gunnery practice. President of the board of inquiry on the *Maine* disaster, he was selected to command the North Atlantic Squadron in the war with Spain; he supervised the entire blockade of Cuba and was responsible for cooperation with the army. His absence from the mouth of Santiago Harbor when the Spanish squadron issued forth to defeat on the morning of July 3, 1898, led to a celebrated controversy with Adm. Winfield S. Schley over credit for the victory. He was made permanent rear-admiral, 1899.

SAMUELS, EDWARD AUGUSTUS (*b. Boston, Mass., 1836; d. Fitchburg, Mass., 1908*), ornithologist, sportsman, authority on the natural history of New England.

SAMUELS, SAMUEL (*b. Philadelphia, Pa., 1823; d. Brooklyn, N.Y., 1908*), master mariner. Celebrated for his 78 fast voyages as captain of the New York and Liverpool packet *Dreadnought*, 1854–62. Author of an interesting autobiography *From the Forecastle to the Cabin* (1887).

SANBORN, EDWIN DAVID (*b. Gilmanton, N.H., 1808; d. New York, N.Y., 1885*), educator. Graduated Dartmouth, 1832. Taught Latin and Greek at Dartmouth, 1835–37, and in 1837 became professor of Latin. Removing to Washington University, St. Louis, Mo., 1859, he taught there until 1863; he then returned to Dartmouth as professor of oratory and belles-lettres, resigning in 1882. A teacher of the old school, brimful of learning, he inspired generations of undergraduates with some measure of his own enthusiasm for letters.

SANBORN, FRANKLIN BENJAMIN (*b. Hampton Falls, N.H., 1831; d. Plainfield, N.J., 1917*), author, journalist, reformer. Graduated Harvard, 1855. Influenced by Theodore Parker and Ralph Waldo Emerson, he conducted a school at Concord, Mass., and was soon in the thick of the abolition movement. New England agent for John Brown, he was arrested in April 1860 for refusing to testify before the U.S. Senate on Brown's intentions but was almost immediately released on a writ of *habeas corpus*. Thereafter he devoted the greater part of his time to newspaper work and to activity with the Massachusetts state board of charities. A lecturer at many schools and colleges, he joined with William T. Harris in establishing the Concord School of Philosophy. He had known intimately the men and women who had made Concord famous and served as their loyal, intelligent editor and biographer after their deaths. Among his books are *Henry D. Thoreau* (1882), *The Life and Letters of John Brown* (1885 and later editions), *Ralph Waldo Emerson* (1901) and *Recollections of Seventy Years* (1909).

SANBORN, KATHERINE ABBOTT (*b. Hanover, N.H., 1839; d. 1917*), teacher, lecturer, journalist. Daughter of Edwin D. Sanborn, she published most of her writing under the name of Kate Sanborn. Among her books are *Adopting an Abandoned Farm* (1891), *A Truthful Woman in Southern California* (1893) and *Memories and Anecdotes* (1915).

SANBORN, WALTER HENRY (*b. Epsom, N.H., 1845; d. 1928*), jurist. Removed to St. Paul, Minn., c. 1870. Judge, U.S. circuit court of appeals, eighth circuit, 1892–1928; presiding judge of the circuit *post* 1903. A man of deep learning, he was especially skilled in cases dealing with personal injury.

SANDEMAN, ROBERT (*b. Perth, Scotland, 1718; d. Danbury, Conn., 1771*), preacher. Promoter in the American colonies of the sect which came to be known as Sandemanians, 1764–71. He and his followers were vigorously opposed by leading New England ministers for their rejection of the Covenant of Grace and of the doctrine of justification by faith as an act of regeneration. Sandeman taught that "every one who obtains a just notion of the person and work of Christ . . . is justified . . . simply by that notion."

SANDERS, BILLINGTON McCARTER (b. Columbia Co., Ga., 1789; d. Penfield, Ga., 1854), Baptist minister. Graduated South Carolina College, 1809. First principal of Mercer Institute, 1832–39, he has been justly called the real founder of Mercer University.

SANDERS, CHARLES WALTON (b. Newport, N.Y., 1805; d. New York, N.Y., 1889), educator. Author of elementary school textbooks in reading and spelling.

SANDERS, DANIEL CLARKE (b. Sturbridge, Mass., 1768; d. Medfield, Mass., 1850), educator, Congregational clergyman. Graduated Harvard, 1788. First president of University of Vermont, 1800–14, Sanders managed its finances, supervised erection of its first building, and for some time carried the entire burden of instruction. Pastor of the First Church, Medfield, Mass., 1815–29.

SANDERS, DANIEL JACKSON (b. near Winnsboro, S.C., 1847; d. 1907), Presbyterian clergyman, educator. Born in slavery, Sanders graduated from Western Theological Seminary, Allegheny, Pa., 1874. A leader in educational work and a pastor in Wilmington, N.C., he was editor of the Africo-American Presbyterian, post 1879, and president of Biddle (later Johnson C. Smith) University, post 1891.

SANDERS, ELIZABETH ELKINS (b. Salem, Mass., 1762; d. Salem, 1851), author, reformer. Advocate of justice for the American Indian and opponent of foreign-mission activity.

SANDERS, FRANK KNIGHT (b. Batticotta, Ceylon, 1861; d. Rockport, Mass., 1933), Congregational clergyman, Biblical scholar. Son of missionary parents, he graduated Ripon College, 1882. Influenced by the teaching of William R. Harper at Yale Divinity School, he turned to graduate work in Semitic languages (Ph.D., 1889). Instructor and professor at Yale, 1889–1905, and dean of the Divinity School, 1901–05, he was active thereafter in church administrative positions and was author of a number of books.

SANDERS, GEORGE NICHOLAS (b. Lexington, Ky., 1812; d. 1873), financial promoter, lobbyist, revolutionist. Grandson of George Nicholas. Led "Young America" movement, 1851–53, as means of furthering revolutionary republicanism in Europe. As U.S. consul in London, 1853, he plotted recklessly with Kossuth, Mazzini, and other exiled rebels and was refused Senate confirmation in the post. During the Civil War, he was a Confederate agent in Europe and Canada. Half-idealist, half-charlatan.

SANDERS, JAMES HARVEY (b. Union Co., O., 1832; d. Memphis, Tenn., 1899), agricultural journalist. Founded Western Stock Journal, May 1869, the first periodical devoted to animal husbandry; was a noted breeder of horses; wrote the Norman Stud Book (1876) and other studies in animal heredity.

SANDERS, THOMAS (b. S. Danvers, Mass., 1839; d. Derry, N.H., 1911), financier. Advanced money to Alexander Graham Bell for development of the telephone; later served as an official and director of the Bell Telephone Co.

SANDERS, WILBUR FISK (b. Leon, N.Y., 1834; d. 1905), Montana pioneer lawyer. Nephew of Sidney Edgerton with whom he removed to what was then eastern Idaho, 1863. An organizer of Vigilantes and successful in his practice, he was a leader in the movement to form a separate territory from eastern Idaho. After organization of the territory of Montana, 1864, he promoted the Republican party there and on Montana's admission as a state, he was elected U.S. senator, serving Jan. 1890–March 1893.

SANDERSON, JOHN (b. near Carlisle, Pa., 1783; d. Philadelphia, Pa., 1844), educator, author. Teacher of classical languages and English in Philadelphia, Sanderson was a popular contributor to periodicals and for a brief time edited the Aurora newspaper. He was author of Sketches of Paris: by an American Gentleman (1838) which was widely read, and with his brother published the first two volumes of the Biography of the Signers to the Declaration of Independence (1820, completed by Robert Waln, 1823–27).

SANDERSON, ROBERT (b. England, 1608; d. Boston, Mass., 1693), silversmith. Emigrated to America as a young man; was among first settlers in Hampton, N.H., 1638; resided in Watertown, Mass., 1639–53. Removed to Boston in 1653, after appointment (with John Hull) to manage the colony mint. A craftsman in the front rank of New England silversmiths, he was probably Hull's first teacher.

SANDERSON, SIBYL (b. Sacramento, Calif., 1865; d. Paris, France, 1903), dramatic soprano. Studied at Paris Conservatory, 1886–88. Made debut at The Hague in Massenet's Manon, 1888; made Paris debut at the Opéra Comique, 1889; created role of Thaïs at Paris, 1894. Despite her tremendous popularity on the continent of Europe, she was received coldly in England and America.

SANDHAM, HENRY (b. Montreal, Canada, 1842; d. London, England, 1910), portrait painter, landscapist, illustrator. Worked in Boston, Mass., 1880–1901. Illustrated many books including H. H. Jackson's Ramona (edition of 1900); painted several large historical studies, among them "The Dawn of Liberty," now in Lexington, Mass., town hall.

SANDLER, JACOB KOPPEL (b. Bialozerkove, Russia, 1856; d. 1931), composer. Emigrated to New York City, 1888. After working as a shirtmaker and as a peddler, he became director of a synagogue choir and eked out a precarious living by acting also as chorus director in a Yiddish theatre. As incidental music for a long-forgotten play, he composed the celebrated hymn "Eili, Eili"; it was first performed in April 1896 at the Windsor Theatre in the Bowery.

SANDS, BENJAMIN FRANKLIN (*b. Baltimore, Md., 1812; d. Washington, D.C., 1883*), naval officer. Raised in Kentucky; entered navy as midshipman, 1828. After varied service, principally in survey and hydrographic work, he became chief of the Bureau of Construction and served, 1858–61. Promoted captain, 1862, he was senior officer on the North Carolina coast blockade until October 1864, when he was assigned to operations against Fort Fisher. Commander of the second division, West Gulf Squadron, 1865, he hoisted the flag at Galveston, Texas, on June 5 after receiving the surrender of the last Confederate troops. Superintendent of the Naval Observatory, 1867–74, he retired as rear-admiral.

SANDS, COMFORT (*b. present Sands' Point, L.I., N.Y., 1748; d. Hoboken, N.J., 1834*), New York merchant, Revolutionary patriot and fiscal official. A founder of the Bank of New York, 1784, he was president of the N.Y. Chamber of Commerce, 1794–98.

SANDS, DAVID (*b. present Sands' Point, L.I., N.Y., 1745; d. Cornwall-on-the-Hudson, N.Y., 1818*), Quaker preacher, Abolitionist, merchant.

SANDS, JOSHUA RATOON (*b. Brooklyn, N.Y., 1795; d. Baltimore, Md., 1883*), naval officer. Nephew of Comfort Sands. Entering the navy, June 1812, he retired as rear-admiral, 1872, after a career of active service which included the War of 1812, the Mexican War and the Civil War.

SANDS, ROBERT CHARLES (*b. New York, N.Y., 1799; d. Hoboken, N.J., 1832*), journalist, author. Son of Comfort Sands. Graduated Columbia, 1815. Projected and edited several minor literary periodicals; assisted William Cullen Bryant in editorship of *New York Review*, 1825–26; was on editorial staff of *New-York Commercial Advertiser*, 1827–32. Joined with Bryant and Gulian C. Verplanck in publication of *The Talisman*, an annual to which he contributed some of his best work. His collected writings were published, 1834, including his principal poetic work *Yamoyden* (previously published, 1820).

SANDYS, GEORGE (*b. Bishopsthorpe, near York, England, 1577/78; d. Boxley Abbey, near Maidstone, Kent, England, 1643/44*), poet, Virginia colonist. A shareholder in the Virginia Company, he was appointed treasurer of the colony of Virginia, 1621. Removing to Virginia in the autumn of that year, he remained there until 1628 or later. An industrious and able administrator, he is best remembered for his verse translation of the *Metamorphoses* of Ovid which he completed in Virginia (first edition, 1626; second complete edition, 1632).

SANFORD, EDMUND CLARK (*b. Oakland, Calif., 1859; d. 1924*), psychologist, educator. Graduated University of California, 1883; Ph.D., Johns Hopkins, 1888. Taught at Clark University *post* 1889; president of Clark College, 1909–20; professor of psychology and education, Clark University, 1920–24.

SANFORD, EDWARD TERRY (*b. Knoxville, Tenn., 1865; d. 1930*), lawyer. Judge, U.S. district court in Tennessee, 1908–23; associate justice, U.S. Supreme Court, 1923–30. Considered slow in making decisions as a district judge, Sanford wrote a number of important opinions while on the Supreme bench. Probably his most important opinion was in what is known as the "Pocket Veto" case (*279 U.S., 655*), 1929.

SANFORD, ELIAS BENJAMIN (*b. Westbrook, Conn., 1843; d. 1932*), Congregational clergyman. A leader in the forming of the Federal Council of the Churches of Christ in America, he served it for many years as secretary and also wrote its history.

SANFORD, HENRY SHELTON (*b. Woodbury, Conn., 1823; d. Healing Springs, Va., 1891*), diplomat, developer of Sanford, Fla.

SANFORD, NATHAN (*b. Bridgehampton, N.Y., 1777; d. Flushing, N.Y., 1838*), lawyer, New York State legislator and public official. U.S. senator, Democrat, from New York, 1815–21 and 1826–31, he confined his attention to administration and to measures for improvement of government organization. He advocated creation of a department of the interior and expansion of the attorney-general's office into a department of justice.

SANGER, CHARLES ROBERT (*b. Boston, Mass., 1860; d. Cambridge, Mass., 1912*), chemist. Son of George P. Sanger. Graduated Harvard, 1881; Ph.D., 1884. Associated in research work with Henry B. Hill, Sanger succeeded him as professor of chemistry at Harvard, 1903. His most important research was concerned with detection of arsenic and antimony and with the chemistry of pyromucic acid and its derivatives. His work confirmed the dangers suspected in the use of arsenic in wallpaper.

SANGER, GEORGE PARTRIDGE (*b. Dover, Mass., 1819; d. 1890*), Boston lawyer, Massachusetts public official. First president, John Hancock Mutual Life Insurance Co. (organized, 1863).

SANGSTER, MARGARET ELIZABETH MUNSON (*b. New Rochelle, N.Y., 1838; d. Maplewood, N.J., 1912*), journalist. Editor, among other periodicals, of *Hearth and Home* and *Harper's Bazar;* author of a number of volumes in prose and verse compiled from her magazine articles and several novels, cheerful, practical and religious in tone.

SANKEY, IRA DAVID (*b. Edinburg, Pa., 1840; d. Brooklyn, N.Y., 1908*), singing evangelist, associated *post c.* 1870 with the work of Dwight L. Moody. Collections of the songs used in the Moody and Sankey revivals gained almost world-wide popularity.

SAPIR, EDWARD (*b. Lauenburg, Germany, 1884; d. New Haven, Conn., 1939*), anthropologist, linguist. Came to America as a child. Graduated Columbia, 1904; Ph.D., 1909. Influenced by Franz Boas whose anthropological approach to the study of language opened up vistas for him, Sapir began the study of American Indian languages and cultures, the field in which much of his work was done. Chief of the anthropology division, Canadian National Museum, 1910–25, he was Sterling Professor of Anthropology and Linguistics at Yale, 1925–39. A pioneer in the phonemic method of linguistic analysis, he was also much interested in general culture and its relation to personality. He was author of many specialized papers and of *Language* (1921). [*Supp. 2*]

SAPPINGTON, JOHN (*b. Maryland, 1776; d. 1856*), physician. Raised in Tennessee; removed to Missouri, 1817, where he practiced in Howard and later Saline counties. Soon after quinine (isolated, 1820) became available in the United States, he strongly advocated its use in treatment of malaria without recourse to bleeding and purging. Author of *Theory and Treatment of Fevers* (1844), he distributed quinine wholesale, *post* 1832, as Dr. Sappington's Anti-Fever Pills.

SARGENT, AARON AUGUSTUS (*b. Newburyport, Mass., 1827; d. San Francisco, Calif., 1887*), printer, journalist, lawyer. Removed to California, 1849. Starting in politics as a Know-Nothing assemblyman, he was active in organization of the Republican party in California and served as congressman, 1861–63, 1869–73. He was author, with Theodore D. Judah, of the first Pacific railroad bill to pass Congress. U.S. senator, 1873–79, he was U.S. minister to Germany, 1882–84. Closely identified with the railroad interests, he was a masterful machine politician.

SARGENT, CHARLES SPRAGUE (*b. Boston, Mass., 1841; d. 1927*), arboriculturist, Union soldier. Graduated Harvard, 1862. Professor of horticulture at Harvard, 1872–73; professor of arboriculture, 1879–1927. Directed the Arnold Arboretum *post* 1873. Author of *Report on the Forests of North America* (1884) and the notable *Silva of North America* (1891–1902) among other works. Advocated conservation and national parks.

SARGENT, DUDLEY ALLEN (*b. Belfast, Maine, 1849; d. 1924*), physician, physical culture expert. Developed programs of physical training at Bowdoin, Yale and Harvard; organized a training school for physical education teachers at Cambridge, Mass., 1881.

SARGENT, EPES (*b. Gloucester, Mass., 1813; d. 1880*), journalist, poet, spiritualist. Brother of John O. Sargent. His numerous anthologies composed for school use gave him a wide contemporary celebrity. Among his plays, *Velasco* (published, 1839) was the most successful; his best volume of verse was *Songs of the Sea* (1847) which contains the well-known "A Life on the Ocean Wave." *Post* 1865, he devoted most of his energy to the exposition of his new faith in spiritualism.

SARGENT, FITZWILLIAM (*b. Gloucester, Mass., 1820; d. Bournemouth, England, 1889*), ophthal-mologist, surgeon. Practiced in Philadelphia, 1843–52; lived principally in Europe thereafter. Father of John Singer Sargent.

SARGENT, FRANK PIERCE (*b. East Orange, Vt., 1854; d. Washington, D.C., 1908*), labor leader. Headed Brotherhood of Locomotive Firemen, 1885–1902. As U.S. commissioner-general of immigration *post* 1902, he helped initiate methods for the prevention of fraud against immigrants, for the exclusion of undesirable elements, and for the prevention of smuggling of Chinese across the borders.

SARGENT, FREDERICK (*b. Liskeard, England, 1859; d. Glencoe, Ill., 1919*), electrical engineer. Came to America, 1880. Consulting engineer for the Chicago Edison Co. and many other concerns, he was a specialist in the design and construction of central electric generating stations. He was among the first to recognize the advantages of the steam turbine.

SARGENT, GEORGE HENRY (*b. Warner, N.H., 1867; d. Warner, 1931*), journalist. City editor, *St. Paul* (Minn.) *Daily Pioneer Press*, 1890–95; staff member, *Boston Evening Transcript*, 1895–1931. Conducted "The Bibliographer" department for the *Transcript*.

SARGENT, HENRY (*b. Gloucester, Mass., c. 1770; d. 1845*), painter. Brother of Lucius M. Sargent. Encouraged by John Trumbull, he studied in London with Benjamin West. Diligent and gifted, he fell short of genius; he is best represented by "The Tea Party" and "The Dinner Party" in the Boston Museum of Fine Arts.

SARGENT, HENRY WINTHROP (*b. Boston, Mass., 1810; d. 1882*), horticulturist, landscape gardener. Son of Henry Sargent.

SARGENT, JAMES (*b. Chester, Vt., 1824; d. 1910*), lock expert. Formed partnership of Sargent and Greenleaf in Rochester, N.Y., 1869, to manufacture the "nonpickable" lock which he had devised; perfected a time lock *c.* 1873. He was also inventor and manufacturer of a number of other devices, including railway semaphore signals, automatic fire alarms and glass-lined steel tanks.

SARGENT, JOHN OSBORNE (*b. Gloucester, Mass., 1811; d. 1891*), lawyer, journalist. Brother of Epes Sargent. Author, among other works, of the posthumous *Horatian Echoes* (1893).

SARGENT, JOHN SINGER (*b. Florence, Italy, 1856; d. London, England, 1925*), painter. Son of Fitz-William Sargent. Encouraged in art by his mother (who had been responsible for the family's expatriation to Europe shortly before his birth), Sargent received lessons at the Academy in Florence and continued to sketch from nature as the family wandered through southern Italy, France and Germany. Beginning formal study at the Beaux-Arts in Paris, 1874, he acquired in the atelier of Carolus-Duran a facile and fluent technique quite suited to his temperament and a dexterity in seizing instantaneous effects. After a brief visit to the United States, 1876, he returned to France where he painted his "Gitana" and the "Rehearsal at the Cirque d'Hiver"; in 1877 he sent his first picture to the Salon, a portrait of Miss Watts. Following productive visits to Italy, Spain and Morocco, 1878–80, he entered on a period of activity to which belong some of his finest portraits, including the famous "Madame Gautreau" which roused a tempest of abuse when it was first exhibited in Paris. The artist was entirely serious in his work and devoid of malice; he had depicted the lady in a costume of her own choosing and he was astonished and hurt at the outcry of disparagement. Removing from Paris to London, he encountered further harsh criticism from the press, his portraits of Mrs. White and the Misses Vickers being declared hard, tasteless and raw in color. However, his exotic style and brilliance, offering such a contrast to the academic manner of British portrait painters of the time, brought him all the patrons he could desire. Establishing himself in a studio in Tite St., London, 1885, he produced the first of a long series of pictures of children in which he revealed the most lovable side of his nature in work of remarkable delicacy and beauty. His "Carnation, Lily, Lily, Rose," exhibited at the Royal Academy, 1887, was a great success.

Resident in Boston, Mass., 1887–88, Sargent was first accorded the American appreciation which was so great a source of satisfaction to him throughout his career. Henceforward, Boston became his American headquarters and the goal of a long series of visits. On his second trip to America, 1890, he painted his "Carmencita," considered his masterpiece by many critics, and also painted portraits of Edwin Booth, Joseph Jefferson, Lawrence Barrett and others. Commissioned by the trustees of the Boston Public Library to paint mural decorations for that building, he welcomed the change. Beginning preliminary work, 1891, he completed the first part, 1894, and went to Boston, 1895, to see to its implacement. Meanwhile, his portrait work continued and culminated in the appearance (1898, 1901, 1902) of the Wertheimer family portraits. Made a Royal Academician, 1897, he showed forth all the finest qualities of his art in his diploma picture, "A Venetian Interior" (1900). Crossing and recrossing the Atlantic almost every year, he enjoyed on these voyages the only real rest periods he ever allowed himself to take. In 1916 he came again to America to install the last of the Boston Public Library decorations, and that summer went sketching in the Canadian Rockies and Glacier National Park. On completion of the library decorations he undertook to decorate the rotunda of the Art Museum, Boston, and while preparing studies for this work went to the war front in France during 1918 to record impressions for the Imperial War Museum, London. The Sargent exhibition in New York,

1924, was harshly reviewed by the modernists and was indicative of the change of taste which was soon to depreciate Sargent's worth as an artist.

As a portrait painter Sargent ranks beneath the greatest masters but rates as the equal of the best painters of the British school, Reynolds and Gainsborough. His genre paintings are original, objective and possess great charm of style, but he was not so effective in landscape. Much may be said pro and con about his mural paintings. As he violated the accepted canons which ban relief and perspective, his walls do not have the vertical aspect demanded by sound architectonic principles; also, the want of flatness of modeling is matched by overwhelming complexity of detail. However, his Boston Library work presents a splendid effect. His fertility of invention is undeniable and if his work has little of the impassioned conviction of the ages of faith, this can hardly be imputed to the artist as a serious fault for he was of his own time.

SARGENT, LUCIUS MANLIUS (*b. Boston, Mass., 1786; d. Boston, 1867*), antiquary, temperance advocate. Brother of Henry Sargent. Author of *Hubert and Ellen* (1812), *The Temperance Tales* (1848), *Dealings with the Dead* (1856) and other works.

SARGENT, NATHAN (*b. Putney, Vt., 1794; d. 1875*), Whig and Republican journalist, lawyer. Washington correspondent under pseudonym "Oliver Oldschool" for many Northern newspapers *post* 1842.

SARGENT, WINTHROP (*b. Gloucester, Mass., 1753; d. near New Orleans, La., 1820*), Revolutionary soldier, Ohio pioneer. Graduated Harvard, 1771. As secretary of the Ohio Company, he aided Manasseh Cutler in the purchase of land and took an active part in the planning of the new colony at Marietta. Appointed by Congress the secretary of Northwest Territory, 1787, he assumed charge during the frequent, prolonged absences of Gov. Arthur St. Clair and was acting governor of the territory after St. Clair's defeat by the Indians, November 1791. Resigning his secretaryship, 1798, he became the first governor of Mississippi Territory but failed of reappointment in 1801. Unpopular because of his Federalism, he was a conscientious public servant and a man of wide intellectual interests.

SARGENT, WINTHROP (*b. Philadelphia, Pa., 1825; d. Paris, France, 1870*), author. Grandson of Winthrop Sargent (1753–1820). A talented historical researcher, Sargent was author of *The History of an Expedition against Fort Du Quesne in 1755* (1855) and of the *Life and Career of Major John André* (1861); he also edited *The Loyal Verses of Joseph Stansbury and Doctor Jonathan Odell* (1860).

SARPY, PETER A. (*b. St. Louis, Mo., 1805; d. Plattsmouth, Nebr., 1865*), fur trader, probably first white resident of Nebraska. Headed trading post at Bellevue, Nebr., *post c.* 1823; assisted the Mormons on their first expedition westward; played large part in negotiation of land cession treaties with Omaha and Oto Indians, 1854.

SARTAIN, EMILY (*b. Philadelphia, Pa., 1841; d. Philadelphia, 1927*), painter, engraver, educator. Daughter of John Sartain; sister of Samuel and William Sartain. Principal of the School of Design for Women (Philadelphia), 1886–1919.

SARTAIN, JOHN (*b. London, England, 1808; d. Philadelphia, Pa., 1897*), engraver, publisher. Came to America, 1830. Executed engraved plates for the periodicals of the day and was associated, 1841–48, principally with *Graham's Magazine*. Published *Sartain's Union Magazine*, 1849–52, a literary and artistic success but a financial failure. A versatile artist in all types of work, Sartain was particularly distinguished for his facility in mezzotint. Of his eight children, Emily, Samuel and William had distinguished careers. He was author of an autobiography, *Reminiscences of a Very Old Man* (1899).

SARTAIN, SAMUEL (*b. Philadelphia, Pa., 1830; d. Philadelphia, 1906*), engraver. Son of John Sartain.

SARTAIN, WILLIAM (*b. Philadelphia, Pa., 1843; d. 1924*), painter. Son of John Sartain. Studied with Christian Schüssele and in France with Léon Bonnat. Particularly effective as a landscape painter, he was also active as a teacher and in artists' associations.

SARTWELL, HENRY PARKER (*b. Pittsfield, Mass., 1792; d. Penn Yan, N.Y., 1867*), physician, botanist. Author, among other works, of *Carices Americae Septentrionalis Exsiccatae* (1848–50).

SASLAVSKY, ALEXANDER (*b. Kharkov, Russia, 1876; d. San Francisco, Calif., 1924*), violinist, conductor. Studied in Kharkov and Vienna; came to America *c.* 1893. A first violinist of the New York Symphony Society, 1893–1918, and concert-master and assistant conductor *post* 1903, Saslavsky became concert-master of the Philharmonic Orchestra of Los Angeles, 1919. Throughout his career he was important as a teacher and for his work in introducing chamber music to a larger public.

SASSACUS (*b. probably near Groton, Conn., c. 1560; d. 1637*), chief sachem of the Pequots. Killed by the Mohawks while fleeing westward after defeat of Pequots by John Mason, 1637.

SATTERLEE, HENRY YATES (*b. New York, N.Y., 1843; d. 1908*), Episcopal clergyman. Graduated Columbia, 1863; studied at General Theological Seminary, New York. Minister at Wappinger Falls, N.Y., 1865–82; rector of Calvary Parish, New York City, 1882–96. Elected bishop of the diocese of Washington (D.C.), 1896, he projected and outlined plans for the National Cathedral which was later developed in accord with his vision of it.

SATTERLEE, RICHARD SHERWOOD (*b. Fairfield, N.Y., 1798; d. 1880*), army surgeon. Practiced

in Seneca Co., N.Y., and in Detroit, Mich., 1818–22; entered the U.S. Army as assistant surgeon, 1822; served in Middle West frontier posts and in Seminole War. Senior surgeon of Gen. Worth's division in the Mexican War, he supervised the general hospital in Mexico City after its fall. Appointed medical purveyor, 1853, he served in this capacity throughout the Civil War, retiring as lieutenant-colonel, 1869.

SAUGANASH (*b. Canada, c. 1780; d. near present Council Bluffs, Iowa, 1841*), Potawatomi sub-chief. Also known as Billy Caldwell or "Englishman." An associate of Tecumseh, 1807–13, he swore allegiance to the United States *c.* 1820 when he took up residence at present Chicago, Ill. He migrated with his people to Iowa in 1836.

SAUGRAIN DE VIGNI, ANTOINE FRANÇOIS (*b. Paris, France, 1763; d. St. Louis, Mo., 1820*), physician, naturalist, philosopher. Visited the United States, 1787–88, when he became a friend of Benjamin Franklin. Resided in Gallipolis, O., 1790–98; resided in St. Louis *post* 1800 where he practiced, performed scientific experiments and introduced the first smallpox vaccine virus brought there, 1809.

SAULSBURY, ELI (*b. Kent Co., Del., 1817; d. Dover, Del., 1893*), lawyer, Delaware legislator. Brother of Gove and Willard Saulsbury (1820–1892). U.S. senator, Democrat, from Delaware, 1871–89.

SAULSBURY, GOVE (*b. Kent Co., Del., 1815; d. 1881*), physician, politician. Brother of Eli and Willard Saulsbury (1820–1892). M.D., University of Pennsylvania, 1842. A recognized Democratic leader in the Delaware legislature, he became acting governor of the state in March 1865 and served until 1871. He opposed all constitutional amendments growing out of the Civil War and characterized Reconstruction as a flagrant usurpation of power.

SAULSBURY, WILLARD (*b. Kent Co., Del., 1820; d. 1892*), lawyer, politician. Brother of Gove and Eli Saulsbury; father of Willard Saulsbury (1861–1927). Attorney-general of Delaware, 1850–55. As U.S. senator, Democrat, from Delaware, 1859–71, he supported the Crittenden Resolutions and later opposed military interference in elections and the suspension of the writ of habeas corpus by the administration. He was chancellor of Delaware, 1873–92.

SAULSBURY, WILLARD (*b. Georgetown, Del., 1861; d. Wilmington, Del., 1927*), lawyer, businessman. Son of Willard Saulsbury (1820–1892). U.S. senator, Democrat, from Delaware, 1913–19. A leading supporter of Woodrow Wilson's policies and a useful member of the committee on foreign relations, he gave special attention to Chinese affairs.

SAUNDERS, ALVIN (*b. near Flemingsburg, Ky., 1817; d. Omaha, Nebr., 1899*), businessman, Iowa legislator. Chairman of the Iowa delegation to the Republican convention, 1860, he was active during the campaign in behalf of Abraham Lincoln. Appointed governor of Nebraska Territory, 1861, he served with ability until March 1867 when Nebraska became a state. U.S. senator, Republican, from Nebraska, 1877–83, he was particularly interested in the development of inland waterways and Indian affairs.

SAUNDERS, FREDERICK (*b. London, England, 1807; d. 1902*), librarian, author, journalist. Came to America, 1837; made a pioneer appeal to Congress for protection of the copyright of English authors against American pirating. Failing in his effort, he remained in the United States, wrote a number of useful books and was librarian of the Astor Library *post* 1859 and chief librarian, 1876–96.

SAUNDERS, PRINCE (*b. either Lebanon, Conn., or Thetford, Vt., date unknown; d. Port-au-Prince, Haiti, 1839*), Negro reformer, author. After teaching school in Boston, Saunders went to England where he became concerned with William Wilberforce in educational plans for Haiti. Agent in London for Henri Christophe, emperor of Haiti, 1816–18, he lived for a while in Philadelphia and after Christophe's overthrow, 1820, returned to Haiti. At the time of his death he was referred to as attorney-general of that country.

SAUNDERS, ROMULUS MITCHELL (*b. Caswell Co., N.C., 1791; d. 1867*), lawyer, North Carolina legislator and official. Congressman, Democrat, from North Carolina, 1821–27, 1841–45, Saunders was an active partisan and a tireless seeker after public office; John Quincy Adams said of him, "There is not a more cankered or venomous reptile in the country." Undistinguished as U.S. minister to Spain, 1846–49, he served as judge of the state superior court, 1852–67.

SAUNDERS, WILLIAM (*b. St. Andrews, Scotland, 1822; d. 1900*), horticulturist, landscape gardener. Came to America, 1848; formed partnership with Thomas Meehan in Philadelphia, 1854. Appointed superintendent of the experimental gardens of the U.S. Department of Agriculture, 1862, he designed the grounds of the department at Washington and had charge of their development until his death. He was designer of the national cemetery at Gettysburg and selected the site and designed the grounds for the Lincoln monument at Springfield, Ill. Organizer and director of the exhibits of the Department of Agriculture at numerous fairs and expositions, he was also a pioneer in the introduction of foreign plants to the United States. The Washington Navel orange, brought by him from Brazil, 1871, became the leading commercial variety in California. Among his more than 3000 published papers was the first bulletin of the Department of Agriculture (1862).

SAUNDERS, WILLIAM LAURENCE (*b. Raleigh, N.C., 1835; d. Raleigh, 1891*), lawyer, newspaper editor, Confederate soldier, Democratic politician. Edited

and caused to be published *The Colonial Records of North Carolina* (1886–90).

SAUNDERS, WILLIAM LAWRENCE (*b. Columbus, Ga., 1856; d. Teneriffe, Canary Islands, 1931*), engineer, inventor of rock-drill devices. President and chairman of the board, Ingersoll-Rand Co., *post* 1905, he was active as a Democrat in New Jersey politics.

SAUR, CHRISTOPHER. [See SOWER, CHRISTOPHER, 1693–1758.]

SAUVEUR, ALBERT (*b. Louvain, Belgium, 1863; d. Boston, Mass., 1939*), metallographer, metallurgist. Graduated Massachusetts Institute of Technology, 1889. A teacher at Harvard, 1899–1935, Sauveur introduced metallography (the microscopic study of metal structure) into U.S. industrial practice.

[*Supp. 2*]

SAVAGE, EDWARD (*b. Princeton, Mass., 1761; d. Princeton, 1817*), painter, engraver. Painted a celebrated portrait of George Washington, 1789–90; practiced his art in Boston, Philadelphia and New York and was engaged *post* 1809 in the manufacture of cotton at Lancaster, Mass.

SAVAGE, HENRY WILSON (*b. New Durham, N.H., 1859; d. 1927*), real-estate operator, theatrical producer. Assumed management of Castle Square Theatre, Boston, 1895, and organized there a light-opera company which was one of the most famous organizations of its kind ever on the American stage. He later produced, among other successes, *The Sultan of Sulu* (1902), *The Prince of Pilsen* (1903), *The College Widow* (1904), and *The Merry Widow* (1907).

SAVAGE, JAMES (*b. Boston, Mass., 1784; d. Boston, 1873*), antiquary, lawyer, civic worker. Author of *Genealogical Dictionary of the First Settlers of New England, etc.* (1860–62). Encouraged founding of Provident Institution for Savings, 1816, one of the first savings banks incorporated in the United States.

SAVAGE, JOHN (*b. Dublin, Ireland, 1828; d. near Spragueville, Pa., 1888*), journalist. Came to America, 1848. Engaging for a while in free-lance work, he became leading editorial writer for the Washington, D.C., *States*, 1857–61. He served in the Union Army during the Civil War, worked for a brief time on the *New Orleans Times* and in 1867 became chief executive of the Fenian Brotherhood in America.

SAVAGE, MINOT JUDSON (*b. Norridgewock, Maine, 1841; d. Boston, Mass., 1918*), Unitarian clergyman, lecturer. Principal pastorates at Church of the Unity, Boston, and the Church of the Messiah, New York City; author of *The Religion of Evolution* (1876).

SAVAGE, PHILIP HENRY (*b. N. Brookfield, Mass., 1868; d. Boston, Mass., 1899*), poet. Son of Minot J. Savage. Graduated Harvard, 1893. Author of *First Poems and Fragments* (1895) and *Poems* (1898).

SAVAGE, THOMAS STAUGHTON (*b. present Cromwell, Conn., 1804; d. Rhinecliff, N.Y., 1880*), Episcopal clergyman, physician, naturalist. Graduated Yale, 1825; M.D., 1833. First missionary sent to Africa by his church, Savage served in Liberia and its neighborhood at intervals between 1836 and 1847; he wrote several pioneer papers on the behavior of chimpanzees.

SAVERY, WILLIAM (*b. place unknown, 1721; d. Philadelphia, Pa., 1787*), cabinet-maker. Father of William Savery (1750 o.s.–1804). Believed to have settled in Philadelphia c. 1740, Savery worked there until his death. His designs reveal his indebtedness to English 18th-century design books, but his furniture displays his ability to naturalize and interpret his models in an original manner. There is considerable carving in his mahogany pieces, but for the most part his furniture has simple and pure lines. He excelled as a maker of chairs.

SAVERY, WILLIAM (*b. Philadelphia, Pa., 1750 o.s.; d. Philadelphia, 1804*), tanner, Quaker preacher in the United States and Europe. Son of William Savery (1721–1787).

SAVILLE, MARSHALL HOWARD (*b. Rockport, Mass., 1867; d. New York, N.Y., 1935*), archeologist. Trained in field work by Frederic W. Putnam; was associated successively with the Peabody Museum, Harvard, the American Museum of Natural History, and the Museum of the American Indian, New York. First Loubat Professor of American Archeology at Columbia University, designated 1903. Studied ruins at Copan, Honduras, 1891–92; secured important collections at Maya ruins of Palenque, Mexico, 1897; excavated at Mitla, Monte Albán and Xochicalco, Mexico, 1899–1904; later extended collecting excursions to Colombia and Ecuador. Primarily interested in museum specimens, Saville was apt at securing patrons for his work and was an authority on the literature of his special field. He took no interest in theoretical anthropology nor did he greatly advance field-research technique. [*Supp. 1*]

SAWYER, LEICESTER AMBROSE (*b. Pinckney, N.Y., 1807; d. Whitesboro, N.Y., 1898*), Presbyterian and Independent clergyman, newspaper editor. Biblical scholar and exponent of the "higher criticism."

SAWYER, LEMUEL (*b. Camden Co., N.C., 1777; d. Washington, D.C., 1852*), lawyer, author. Congressman, Jeffersonian and Jackson Democrat, from North Carolina, 1807–13, 1817–23 and 1825–29. Author of a number of works which include *Blackbeard, A Comedy* (published, Washington, D.C., 1824; staged, New York City, 1833); a novel, *Printz Hall: A Record of New Sweden* (1839); and *A Biography of John Randolph of Roanoke* (1844).

SAWYER, LORENZO (*b. Leray, N.Y., 1820; d. San Francisco, Calif., 1891*), California pioneer and jurist.

Studied law in Columbus, O., with Noah H. Swayne; removed first to Chicago, Ill., then to Wisconsin; removed to California, 1850. After terms as judge of the California district and supreme courts, Sawyer was named a U.S. circuit judge for the ninth circuit, 1870, and served until his death; his best-known decision was in the case *In re Neagle* (1889). He was first president of the board of trustees of Leland Stanford University.

SAWYER, PHILETUS (*b. near Rutland, Vermont, 1816; d. Oshkosh, Wis., 1900*), lumberman, Wisconsin legislator. Removed to the vicinity of Oshkosh c. 1847. Long a leader in Wisconsin Republican politics, he served as congressman, 1865–75, and as U.S. senator, 1881–93, contributing to the then reputation of the Senate as a millionaire's club. Compelled, c. 1891, to make good on bonds of Republican state treasurers who had, while in office, failed to account for interest received on public deposits, he was also the principal target in the campaign against boss rule and corruption waged by Robert M. LaFollette.

SAWYER, SYLVANUS (*b. Templeton, Mass., 1822; d. Fitchburg, Mass., 1895*), inventor of machinery for splitting and dressing rattan (patented, 1849, 1851, 1854, 1855) and other mechanical devices.

SAWYER, THOMAS JEFFERSON (*b. Reading, Vt., 1804; d. 1899*), Universalist clergyman, editor, educator. Held principal pastorate at the Grand Street (Orchard St.) Universalist Society, New York City; professor of theology, Tufts Divinity School, 1869–92 (dean, 1882–92).

SAWYER, WALTER HOWARD (*b. Middletown, Conn., 1867; d. Auburn, Maine, 1923*), engineer, hydraulic and sanitary expert. Supervised water-power development at Lewiston, Maine, and the Androscoggin River storage system *post* 1902; invented a number of devices for furthering this work.

SAXE, JOHN GODFREY (*b. Highgate, Vt., 1816; d. Albany, N.Y., 1887*), lawyer, humorist. Less a poet than a humorist using verse as his medium, Saxe enjoyed wide popularity in his time. He was author, among other books, of *Progress: A Satirical Poem* (1846), *The Money-King and Other Poems* (1860) and *Leisure-Day Rhymes* (1875).

SAXTON, JOSEPH (*b. Huntington, Pa., 1799; d. 1873*), watch-maker, constructor of scientific apparatus, inventor. Curator of standard weighing apparatus, U.S. Mint, 1837–43; superintendent of weights and measures, U.S. Coast Survey, 1843–73.

SAY, BENJAMIN (*b. Philadelphia, Pa., 1755; d. Philadelphia, 1813*), physician, apothecary, philanthropist. Father of Thomas Say.

SAY, THOMAS (*b. Philadelphia, Pa., 1787; d. New Harmony, Ind., 1834*), entomologist, conchologist. Son of Benjamin Say. Interested in natural history by William Bartram, his mother's uncle, Say devoted nearly all his time to its study *post* 1812. He visited Georgia and Florida with George Ord, William Maclure and T. R. Peale, 1818. The next year, as zoologist, he accompanied Stephen H. Long's expedition to the Rocky Mountains; also as zoologist, he went with Long's second expedition, 1823, to the sources of the Minnesota River. Holder of a nominal curatorship at the American Philosophical Society, also nominally professor of natural history in the University of Pennsylvania (1822–28), he worked on his *American Entomology* (planned and begun, 1816) bringing out the first two volumes in 1824 and 1825. In 1825 also he prepared for the press the first volume of Charles Bonaparte's *American Ornithology*. Resident in the community and village of New Harmony *post* 1825 (except for a visit to Mexico during late 1827 and early 1828), he continued to work industriously. In 1828 he completed the third volume of *American Entomology* and between 1830 and 1834 published the six numbers of his *American Conchology*. Say's work was almost wholly taxonomic and his writings were almost entirely descriptive. The excellence of his work was early acknowledged by European zoologists and nearly all his species have been recognized. His complete writings on entomology were edited by J. L. LeConte and published, 1859, with a biographical memoir by George Ord.

SAYLES, JOHN (*b. Ithaca, N.Y., 1825; d. Texas, 1897*), lawyer. Removed to Texas, 1845. Practiced law at Brenham and Abilene; wrote extensively on Texas law and taught law at Baylor University.

SAYRE, LEWIS ALBERT (*b. present Madison, N.J., 1820; d. 1900*), orthopedic surgeon. M.D., N.Y. College of Physicians and Surgeons, 1842. Practiced in New York City; played large part in organization of Bellevue Hospital Medical College, 1861, occupying there the first chair of orthopedic surgery in America. As resident physician of New York City, 1860–66, he bettered insanitary conditions in tenements. In his own specialty, he was acknowledged leader, developing among other techniques a treatment of lateral curvature that became known the world over as the Sayre method. He was father of Reginald H. Sayre.

SAYRE, REGINALD HALL (*b. New York, N.Y., 1859; d. 1929*), surgeon. Son of Lewis A. Sayre. Graduated Columbia, 1881. M.D., Bellevue Hospital Medical College, 1884. The trusted associate of his father, he became assistant to the professor of surgery at Bellevue, 1885, and afterwards was lecturer and orthopedic surgeon there. He succeeded his father as clinical professor of orthopedic surgery at Bellevue, 1898, and served as consultant to numerous hospitals.

SAYRE, ROBERT HEYSHAM (*b. Columbia Co., Pa., 1824; d. S. Bethlehem, Pa., 1907*), civil engineer, railroad official. Directing force in the building and development of the Lehigh Valley Railroad system, 1852–82, 1885–98.

SAYRE, STEPHEN (*b. Southampton, N.Y., 1736; d. "Brandon," Middlesex Co., Va., 1818*), merchant, banker, diplomatic agent. Graduated College of New Jersey (Princeton), 1757. Removing to London, he became a member of the mercantile firm of Dennys De Berdt and organized his own banking house in 1770. An outspoken friend of the colonies (author of *The Englishman Deceived, 1768*), Sayre was arrested and lodged in the Tower, 1775, charged with conspiracy to overthrow the government. Discharged for lack of evidence, he went to Paris and was appointed secretary to Arthur Lee in May 1777. Quarreling with Lee, after Lee's Berlin mission failed, Sayre attempted to promote commercial treaties for the United States in Copenhagen and Stockholm but accomplished nothing. Returning home at the end of the Revolution, he became a partisan of the South American liberator Francesco Miranda.

SCAMMELL, ALEXANDER (*b. present Milford, Mass., 1747; d. Williamsburg, Va., 1781*), Revolutionary soldier. Staff officer under Gen. John Sullivan at Boston and in the Long Island campaign. Promoted colonel, 3rd New Hampshire Continental battalion, December 1776, he was at Ticonderoga and at Saratoga. Appointed adjutant-general of the Continental Army, January 1778, he served through 1780, resigning to take command of the 1st New Hampshire Regiment.

SCAMMON, JONATHAN YOUNG (*b. Whitefield, Maine, 1812; d. Chicago, Ill., 1890*), lawyer, Chicago businessman and civic leader. Settled in Chicago, 1835; helped establish free schools there and was instrumental in founding many societies and charitable institutions, most of which he served as president. He founded, among other newspapers, the *Chicago Journal* (1844) and the *Inter Ocean* (1872).

SCANLAN, LAWRENCE (*b. Co. Tipperary, Ireland, 1843; d. 1915*), Roman Catholic clergyman. Served in the diocese of San Francisco, Calif., after ordination in Ireland, June 1868; removed to Salt Lake City, 1873, as missionary to Utah and a great part of Nevada. Bishop of Salt Lake City, *post* 1891.

SCARBOROUGH, DOROTHY (*b. Mt. Carmel, Texas, 1878; d. New York, N.Y., 1935*), educator, student of folk-lore. Graduated Baylor, 1896; Ph.D., Columbia, 1917. Taught at Baylor and Columbia; specialized in short-story technique and folk-songs of the South.

[*Supp. 1*]

SCARBOROUGH, WILLIAM SAUNDERS (*b. Macon, Ga., c. 1852; d. 1926*), educator, author. Born in slavery, Scarborough attended Atlanta University and graduated from Oberlin, 1875. Appointed professor of classics, Wilberforce University, Wilberforce, O., 1877, he remained there until his death, serving as president of the university, 1908–20. He had an unusual aptitude for the study of languages.

SCARBROUGH, WILLIAM (*b. South Carolina, 1776; d. New York, N.Y., 1838*), planter, Savannah (Ga.) merchant. In association with Moses Rogers and others, Scarbrough was backer of the pioneer transatlantic steamship *Savannah* which voyaged to Europe and back in 1819.

SCATTERGOOD, THOMAS (*b. Burlington, N.J., 1748; d. Philadelphia, Pa., 1814*), tanner, Quaker preacher, traveler. Displayed a quietist tendency reflecting the influence of John Woolman.

SCHADLE, JACOB EVANS (*b. near Rauchtown, Pa., 1849; d. St. Paul, Minn., 1908*), laryngologist. M.D., Jefferson Medical College, 1881; did postgraduate study with Charles E. Sajous. Removing to St. Paul, Minn., 1887, he became the leading practitioner of laryngology in that section of the Northwest and was professor of his specialty at the University of Minnesota. His chief professional interests were the investigation of the causes and treatment of hay fever and asthma and of the effects of post-nasal adenoid growths upon the health of children.

SCHAEBERLE, JOHN MARTIN (*b. Württemberg, Germany, 1853; d. Ann Arbor, Mich., 1924*), astronomer. Taught at the University of Michigan and served in the observatory there; was a member of original staff of the Lick Observatory.

SCHAEFFER, CHARLES FREDERICK (*b. Germantown, Pa., 1807; d. Philadelphia, Pa., 1879*), Lutheran clergyman, theologian, author. Son of Frederick D. Schaeffer; brother of David F. and Frederick C. Schaeffer. A conservative, he left his professorship at Gettysburg Theological Seminary to become professor and chairman of the faculty of the Philadelphia Seminary in 1864, and taught there until 1878.

SCHAEFFER, CHARLES WILLIAM (*b. Hagerstown, Md., 1813; d. Germantown, Pa., 1896*), Lutheran clergyman. Grandson of Frederick D. Schaeffer; nephew of Frederick C. Schaeffer. Held pastorates at Whitemarsh, Harrisburg and Germantown; taught church history and pastoral theology at Philadelphia Seminary. Author of *Family Prayer for Morning and Evening* (1861) and other books.

SCHAEFFER, DAVID FREDERICK (*b. Carlisle, Pa., 1787; d. Frederick, Md., 1837*), Lutheran clergyman. Son of Frederick D. Schaeffer; brother of Charles F. and Frederick C. Schaeffer. Pastor at Frederick, Md., *post* 1808. An organizer of the Maryland Synod, 1820, he was also one of the most active in formation of the General Synod.

SCHAEFFER, FREDERICK CHRISTIAN (*b. Germantown, Pa., 1792; d. New York, N.Y., 1831*), Lutheran clergyman. Son of Frederick D. Schaeffer; brother of Charles F. and David F. Schaeffer. Pastor at Harrisburg, Pa., and New York City; organized St. James's Church in New York, *c.* 1826, of which he was pastor until his death.

SCHAEFFER, FREDERICK DAVID (*b. Frankfurt-am-Main, Germany, 1760; d. Frederick, Md., 1836*), Lutheran clergyman. Father of Charles F., David F. and Frederick C. Schaeffer; grandfather of Charles W. Schaeffer. Came to America *c.* 1774. Pastor at Carlisle, Pa., 1786–90; at Germantown, 1790–1812; at St. Michael's and Zion's, Philadelphia, 1812–34.

SCHAEFFER, NATHAN CHRIST (*b. near Kutztown, Pa., 1849; d. 1919*), educator, lecturer, German Reformed clergyman. Pennsylvania superintendent of public instruction, 1893–1919.

SCHAFF, PHILIP (*b. Chur, Grisons, Switzerland, 1819; d. New York, N.Y., 1893*), church historian. Studied at universities of Tübingen and Halle; was a pupil of Neander at the University of Berlin, 1840–41; made licentiate in theology, 1841. Invited by the Eastern Synod of the German Reformed Church to succeed F. A. Rauch on the theological faculty at Mercersburg (Pa.) Seminary, 1843, he was ordained to the ministry, April 1844, and in July arrived in the United States. His inaugural address, *The Principle of Protestantism* (1845), portrayed the Reformation not as a revolution but as a development out of the good forces in the Catholic Church and looked forward to the possibility of ultimate union of Protestantism and Catholicism. It was vigorously criticized and, during the years he remained at Mercersburg, he remained subject to opposition which was strengthened by his association with John W. Nevin in development of the so-called Mercersburg Theology. Schaff grew in reputation as a church historian and came to be recognized as the mediator between the theology of Germany and American scholarship. He was editor of *A Commentary on the Holy Scriptures* (1865–80, based on work of John P. Lange) and of the *Religious Encyclopaedia* (1882–84, based on work of Herzog, Plitt, and Hauck). Resigning his position at Mercersburg, 1865, he joined the faculty of Union Theological Seminary, N.Y., 1870, transferring his denominational affiliation to the Presbyterian Church. Active in ecumenical activities, he also rendered valuable service in the work of revising the English Bible, 1881–85, arranging for the organization of the American committee, selecting its members and acting as president. His most ambitious work was his *History of the Christian Church* (5th edition revised, 1882–92).

SCHALL, THOMAS DAVID (*b. near Reed City, Mich., 1877; d. 1935*), lawyer, politician. Beginning practice in Minneapolis, Minn., *c.* 1904, after an early life of extreme difficulty, he became blind in 1907 but continued his career with his wife's aid. Congressman from Minnesota, at first Progressive and later Republican, 1915–25, he was U.S. senator thereafter until his death. A grim political fighter and a fluent, bombastic orator, he was a bitter critic of the New Deal. [*Supp.* 1]

SCHAMBERG, JAY FRANK (*b. Philadelphia, Pa., 1870; d. 1934*), dermatologist, authority on syphilis.

SCHARF, JOHN THOMAS (*b. Baltimore, Md., 1843; d. 1898*), Confederate soldier, lawyer, historian, collector of Americana. Among his numerous studies in local history, the most valuable is his *History of Maryland* (1879).

SCHAUFFLER, HENRY ALBERT (*b. Constantinople, Turkey, 1837; d. 1905*), Congregational clergyman. Son of William G. Schauffler. Graduated Williams, 1859. Ordained in Constantinople, 1865, he served as a Protestant missionary in Turkey and Austria and worked *post* 1882 among Slavic immigrants to the United States.

SCHAUFFLER, WILLIAM GOTTLIEB (*b. Stuttgart, Germany, 1798; d. 1883*), Congregational clergyman. Father of Henry A. Schauffler. Raised in southern Russia, he came to America, 1826, and received his ministerial education at Andover Theological Seminary. Ordained, 1831, in Boston, he worked thereafter as a missionary among the Jews in Turkey and elsewhere until 1856; thereafter he addressed himself to the Armenians and Turks.

SCHECHTER, SOLOMON (*b. Fokshan, Roumania, 1850; d. 1915*), Hebraist, author. Studied at Lemberg and Vienna and at University of Berlin; removed to England, 1882; was appointed reader in Talmud and rabbinical literature at Cambridge University, 1890. Identifying a fragment of manuscript in 1896 as part of the lost original Hebrew of Ecclesiasticus, he attracted world-wide notice; shortly thereafter, excavating the Genizah at Cairo, he brought back to Cambridge some 50,000 Hebrew and Arabic manuscripts, among them many of the remaining chapters of Ecclesiasticus. He was author of *The Wisdom of Ben Sira* (1899) based on his findings. Unhappy in England, he welcomed appointment in 1901 as president of the Jewish Theological Seminary in New York and was within a short time the acknowledged leader of Jewish scholarship in America. He was author of a number of publications, some of them based upon the Cairo manuscripts, of which the most important was his *Documents of Jewish Sectaries* (1910). His *Some Aspects of Rabbinic Theology* (1909) was the first approach to a methodical presentation of Jewish theology.

SCHEEL, FRITZ (*b. Lübeck, Germany, 1852; d. 1907*), violinist, conductor. Came to America, 1893. First conductor of the San Francisco Symphony, he removed to Philadelphia, Pa., 1899, and in 1901 became conductor of the Philadelphia Orchestra Association, a post which he held until his death.

SCHELE DE VERE, MAXIMILIAN (*b. Wexiö, Sweden, 1820; d. Washington, D.C., 1898*), philologist. Holder of several German doctorates, he came to America, 1843, and served as professor of modern languages, University of Virginia, 1844–95. Inaugura-

tor of systematic study of Anglo-Saxon, he also offered courses in comparative philology at a time when few American colleges recognized the value of the comparative method. He was author of a number of books including *Americanisms: The English of the New World* (1871) and was associated with the work of the *Standard Dictionary* (1893–95).

SCHELL, AUGUSTUS (*b. Rhinebeck, N.Y., 1812; d. 1884*), lawyer, New York politician and businessman. An associate of Cornelius Vanderbilt (1794–1877) in his New York Central Railroad operations and in his fight for the Erie, Schell held numerous directorates in railroads, banks and insurance companies. A heavy stock market operator, with Horace F. Clark and Jay Gould he engineered the *post* Civil War corner in Chicago & Northwestern stock which was one of Wall Street's notable episodes. Steadfast in support of the Tammany Democratic organization, he was collector of the port of New York, 1857–61, and succeeded William M. Tweed as Grand Sachem of Tammany, 1872. Also in 1872 he served as Horace Greeley's financial backer and campaign manager. Interested in many of the clubs, societies and institutions of New York City, he was twice president of the New-York Historical Society and a benefactor of the New York Institution for the Blind.

SCHELLING, ERNEST HENRY (*b. Belvidere, N.J., 1876; d. New York, N.Y., 1939*), pianist, conductor, composer. Studied with a long series of European masters including Moszkowski and Paderewski. Successful as a concert artist and as composer of a number of piano and orchestral compositions including *A Victory Ball* (1923), Schelling turned chiefly *post* 1925 to the conducting of children's orchestral concerts at which he won his audiences over to music with an infectious enthusiasm. [*Supp. 2*]

SCHEM, ALEXANDER JACOB (*b. Wiedenbrück, Germany, 1826; d. Hoboken, N.J., 1881*), encyclopedia editor, statistician, journalist.

SCHENANDOA. [See SKENANDO, *c.* 1706–1816.]

SCHENCK, FERDINAND SCHUREMAN (*b. Plattekill, N.Y., 1845; d. White Plains, N.Y., 1925*), Reformed Church clergyman, educator. Professor of theology, New Brunswick Theological Seminary, 1899–1924; lectured also at New York University, Rutgers and Princeton Theological Seminary.

SCHENCK, JAMES FINDLAY (*b. Franklin, O., 1807; d. 1882*), naval officer. Brother of Robert C. Schenck. Appointed midshipman, 1825; active in conquest of California, 1846; commended for excellence as division commander in Civil War attacks on Fort Fisher. Retired as rear-admiral, 1869.

SCHENCK, ROBERT CUMMING (*b. Franklin, O., 1809; d. Washington, D.C., 1890*), lawyer, Ohio legislator, Union major-general. Brother of James F. Schenck. Congressman, Whig, from Ohio, 1843–51, he served as U.S. minister to Brazil, 1851–53. After two years' hard service in the Civil War, he returned to the House of Representatives as a Republican late in 1863 where he distinguished himself by violent attacks on the Copperheads and by opposition to President Andrew Johnson. He was chairman of the committee on military affairs and later of the ways and means committee. Leaving Congress, 1871, he succeeded John L. Motley as U.S. minister to Great Britain. His connection with a fraudulent mine promotion in the West forced him to resign in 1876.

SCHERESCHEWSKY, SAMUEL ISAAC JOSEPH (*b. Tauroggen, Russian Lithuania, 1831; d. Tokyo, Japan, 1906*), Episcopal clergyman, a convert from Judaism. Came to America, 1854; served as a missionary in China and Japan for the greater part of his life *post* 1859; was Episcopal bishop of Shanghai, 1877–83. Naturally gifted as a linguist, he translated the Bible and the Prayer Book into several forms of classical Chinese.

SCHEVE, EDWARD BENJAMIN (*b. Herford, Westphalia, Germany, 1865; d. Longmont, Colo., 1924*), musician. Came to America, 1888. Professor of music, Grinnell (Iowa) College *post* 1906.

SCHICKILLEMY. [See SHIKELLAMY, d. 1748.]

SCHIEREN, CHARLES ADOLPH (*b. Neuss, Germany, 1842; d. 1915*), leather-belting manufacturer. Came to America as a boy. Secured patents, 1887–88, for improvements in belting design for high-speed work. Reform mayor of Brooklyn, N.Y., 1893–95; rescued that city from bankruptcy.

SCHIFF, JACOB HENRY (*b. Frankfurt-am-Main, 1847; d. New York, N.Y., 1920*), financier, philanthropist. Coming to New York City, 1865, Schiff entered business as a broker and became an American citizen. After residence in Germany, 1872–74, he returned to the United States as a partner in Kuhn, Loeb & Co., and in 1885 became head of that firm. He was concerned with financing important railroads in the East, in particular, the Pennsylvania Railroad and the Louisville & Nashville; in the great struggle for control of the Northern Pacific, he was allied with E. H. Harriman against J. J. Hill and J. P. Morgan & Co. He was also interested in the great insurance companies, particularly the Equitable. Schiff's philanthropies were many and varied and included the American Red Cross, hospitals, settlement houses and libraries. He was benefactor of several Jewish seminaries and was one of the founders (1906) of the American Jewish Committee.

SCHILLING, HUGO KARL (*b. Saalfeld, Germany, 1861; d. 1931*), philologist. Ph.D., Leipzig, 1885. Emigrating to America, 1886, he taught at Wittenberg College and at Harvard, and was professor of German at the University of California, 1901–29.

SCHINDLER, KURT (*b. Berlin, Germany, 1882; d. New York, N.Y., 1935*), musician, composer, music editor, authority on folk music. Came to New York, 1905. Assistant conductor at the Metropolitan Opera, 1905–08, he organized the MacDowell Chorus in 1909. Known as the Schola Cantorum *post* 1912, the organization remained under his direction until 1926 and became outstanding among choral groups. Schindler wrote a number of songs and choruses and edited some eleven collections of Russian, Spanish and other music. [*Supp. 1*]

SCHINDLER, SOLOMON (*b. Neisse, Germany, 1842; d. 1915*), Jewish rabbi. Came to America, 1871. A radical reformer, Schindler held his principal pastorate in Boston, Mass., 1874–94, and was engaged thereafter in social work.

SCHIRMER, GUSTAV (*b. Königsee, Saxony, 1829; d. Eisenach, Germany, 1893*), music publisher. Came to America as a boy. Established the house of G. Schirmer in New York City, 1866; was among the original patrons of Bayreuth; encouraged native musical talent in America.

SCHIRMER, RUDOLPH EDWARD (*b. New York, N.Y., 1859; d. Santa Barbara, Calif., 1919*), lawyer, music publisher. Son of Gustav Schirmer whom he succeeded as president of G. Schirmer, Inc.

SCHLATTER, MICHAEL (*b. St. Gall, Switzerland, 1716; d. Philadelphia, Pa., 1790*), German Reformed clergyman, educator. Came to Pennsylvania as a missionary, 1746; organized Reformed parishes throughout Pennsylvania, Maryland, Virginia and New Jersey. Chaplain of the Royal American Regiment, 1757–59, and of the 2nd Pennsylvania Battalion in Bouquet's expedition, 1764, he was an ardent patriot during the Revolution.

SCHLESINGER, BENJAMIN (*b. Krakai, Lithuania, 1876; d. Colorado Springs, Colo., 1932*), labor leader. Emigrated to Chicago, Ill., 1891; became a leading spirit in the Jewish labor movement. An able organizer and administrator, he was at various times business manager of the *Jewish Daily Forward* and president of the International Ladies' Garment Workers' Union.

SCHLEY, WINFIELD SCOTT (*b. Frederick Co., Md., 1839; d. New York, N.Y., 1909*), naval officer. Graduated U.S. Naval Academy, 1860. After an active career on land and sea which included effective Civil War service, several tours of duty on the staff of the U.S. Naval Academy, and the command (1884) of the Arctic expedition to rescue the survivors of A. W. Greely's ill-fated party, Schley was selected to command the Flying Squadron at the opening of the Spanish-American War. After considerable friction with the commander of the Atlantic Squadron, William T. Sampson, Schley was in active command at the battle of Santiago (1898) owing to Sampson's temporary absence from the station outside that port, a circumstance which left credit for the victory in doubt. Retiring as rear-admiral, 1901, Schley demanded a court of inquiry to decide on the merits of the dispute. This was held late in 1901 and reached a judgment in general adverse to Schley, although Adm. Dewey on the question of command rendered a minority opinion in his favor.

SCHMAUK, THEODORE EMANUEL (*b. Lancaster, Pa., 1860; d. Philadelphia, Pa., 1920*), Lutheran clergyman, historian. An uncompromising advocate of confessionalism, he was pastor at Lebanon, Pa., 1883–1920.

SCHMIDT, ARTHUR PAUL (*b. Altona, Germany, 1846; d. 1921*), music publisher. Emigrated to America c. 1866; founded his own firm in Boston, Mass., 1876. Gave great encouragement to American composers by publishing works in larger forms which had no possibility of immediate commercial success.

SCHMIDT, FRIEDRICH AUGUST (*b. Leutenberg, Germany, 1837; d. 1928*), Lutheran theologian, educator. Emigrated to St. Louis, Mo., as a child. A graduate of Concordia Theological Seminary, 1857, he taught theology in a number of midwestern seminaries. He figured extensively in the predestination controversy during and after the 1880's as an opponent of what he considered the new Calvinism.

SCHMIDT, NATHANIEL (*b. Hudiksvall, Sweden, 1862; d. Ithaca, N.Y., 1939*), Orientalist, historian. Professor of Semitic languages and Oriental history, Cornell University, 1896–1932. [*Supp. 2*]

SCHMUCKER, BEALE MELANCHTHON (*b. Gettysburg, Pa., 1827; d. near Phoenixville, Pa., 1888*), Lutheran clergyman. Son of Samuel S. Schmucker. A pastor in present West Virginia and Pennsylvania, Schmucker opposed his father's theological tendencies and became a leader of the extreme churchly party among Lutherans. He was distinguished as a liturgical scholar.

SCHMUCKER, JOHN GEORGE (*b. Michelstadt, Germany, 1771; d. Williamsburg, Pa., 1854*), Lutheran clergyman. Father of Samuel S. Schmucker. Came to Pennsylvania as a boy; was raised in western Virginia. Pastor at Hagerstown, Md., 1794–1809; at York, Pa., and in its neighborhood, 1809–52.

SCHMUCKER, SAMUEL SIMON (*b. Hagerstown, Md., 1799; d. 1873*), Lutheran clergyman, theologian. Son of John G. Schmucker. Graduated University of Pennsylvania, 1819; Princeton Theological Seminary, 1820. Pastor at New Market, Va., 1820–26. As professor at, and a founder of, Gettysburg Theological Seminary, 1826–64, he exercised a liberal, Americanizing influence and for many years led the thought of the General Synod. A classical school which he started at Gettysburg, 1827, became Pennsylvania College, 1832, and is now known as Gettysburg College; he served as its president, 1832–34. Author of *Elements of Popular Theology* (1834) and a number

of other works. He precipitated the doctrinal battle between "American" and "Old" Lutheranism with the publication of his *Definite Platform . . . for Evangelical Lutheran District Synods* (1855). He was the father of Beale M. Schmucker.

SCHNAUFFER, CARL HEINRICH (*b. Heimsheim, near Stuttgart, Germany, 1823; d. probably Baltimore, Md., 1854*), poet, editor. Influenced in Germany by Gustav Struve and Friedrich K. F. Hecker, Schnauffer fought in the Baden revolution, 1848–49. Emigrating to Baltimore, Md., 1851, he joined in the "Turner" movement and founded the *Baltimore Wecker*, 1851.

SCHNEIDER, ALBERT (*b. Granville, Ill., 1863; d. Portland, Oreg., 1928*), bacteriologist. M.D., Chicago College of Physicians and Surgeons, 1887; Ph.D., Columbia, 1897. Professor at Northwestern, University of California, University of Nebraska; also dean of pharmacy, North Pacific College, 1922–28.

SCHNEIDER, BENJAMIN (*b. New Hanover, Pa., 1807; d. Boston, Mass., 1877*), Presbyterian missionary to Turkey, 1834–c. 1875.

SCHNEIDER, GEORGE (*b. Pirmasens, Rhenish Bavaria, 1823; d. Colorado Springs, Colo., 1905*), journalist, banker. Came to America, 1849. As managing editor of the *Illinois Staats-Zeitung*, 1851–62, Schneider bitterly opposed Stephen A. Douglas and did much to consolidate the German vote in support of Abraham Lincoln. He was president, National Bank of Illinois, 1871–97.

SCHNEIDER, HERMAN (*b. Summit Hill, Pa., 1872; d. Cincinnati, O., 1939*), engineer. Graduated Lehigh University, 1894. Taught engineering at Lehigh, 1899–1903; dean of College of Engineering at University of Cincinnati, 1906–39, serving for four years of this period also as president. Inaugurated at Cincinnati the so-called "cooperative system" of technological education in which theoretical studies were alternated with practical shop experience. [*Supp. 2*]

SCHNEIDER, THEODORE (*b. Geinsheim, Rhenish Palatinate, 1703; d. 1764*), Roman Catholic clergyman, physician, Jesuit. Highly distinguished as a professor at Liège and as rector of the University of Heidelberg, 1738–40, Schneider came to Philadelphia, 1741, assigned to act as missionary to German immigrants. He aided Robert Harding in eastern Pennsylvania and in New Jersey, founded a number of chapels, and built a large church at Goshenhoppen, Pa. His high character overcame much local prejudice.

SCHNELLER, GEORGE OTTO (*b. Nürnberg, Germany, 1843; d. 1895*), inventor. Emigrated to America c. 1860. Patented (1880–1884) machinery for the manufacture and insertion of brass corset eyelets.

SCHNERR, LEANDER (*b. Gommersdorf, Baden, Germany, 1836; d. 1920*), Roman Catholic clergyman, Benedictine. Emigrated to Pittsburgh, Pa., as a child. Archabbot of St. Vincent's, Latrobe, Pa., post 1892.

SCHODDE, GEORGE HENRY (*b. Allegheny, Pa., 1854; d. 1917*), Lutheran clergyman, conservative Biblical scholar. Professor at Capital University (Columbus, O.) *post* 1880.

SCHOENHOF, JACOB (*b. Oppenheim, Germany, 1839; d. New York, N.Y., 1903*), lace merchant, free trade advocate, economist. Emigrated to America, 1861. Author, among other books, of *The Industrial Situation and the Question of Wages* (1885) and *The Economy of High Wages* (1892) in which he forecast the doctrine later associated with the name of Henry Ford.

SCHOFF, STEPHEN ALONZO (*b. Danville, Vt., 1818; d. Norfolk, Conn., 1904*), engraver. Employed professionally in bank-note work, Schoff produced, among other artistic plates, "Caius Marius on the Ruins of Carthage" after Vanderlyn, and "Bathers" after William M. Hunt.

SCHOFIELD, HENRY (*b. Dudley, Mass., 1866; d. 1918*), law teacher. Graduated Harvard, 1887; LL.B., 1890. Practiced principally in Chicago; was professor of law, Northwestern University *post* 1902. Authority on Chicago's relations to local traction systems. Author of a number of comments on important decisions which were later collected as *Essays on Constitutional Law and Equity* (1921).

SCHOFIELD, JOHN McALLISTER (*b. Gerry, N.Y., 1831; d. St. Augustine, Fla., 1906*), soldier. Graduated West Point, 1853. Commissioned in the artillery, he served as professor of natural philosophy at West Point, 1855–60. In Missouri at the outbreak of the Civil War, he became chief of staff to Gen. Nathaniel Lyon and served until Lyon's death at the battle of Wilson's Creek, August 1861. Promoted brigadier-general of volunteers in November, he was engaged in field operations in Missouri and later commanded the Department of the Missouri as major-general. Assuming command of the XXIII Corps in February 1864, he took part in Sherman's Atlanta campaign as one of the three army commanders and badly shattered Hood's Confederate force at the fierce battle of Franklin, Tenn. Moving the XXIII Corps to the mouth of the Cape Fear River, he occupied Wilmington, N.C., and effected a junction with Sherman at Goldsboro, March 23, 1865, for the final moves against Gen. J. E. Johnston. After serving as confidential agent for the U.S. State Department in France, 1865–66, he commanded the Department of the Potomac, and in the spring of 1868 served briefly as U.S. secretary of war. Promoted major-general, regular army, 1869, he commanded several departments successively and made the recommendations that led to the acquisition of Pearl Harbor, Hawaii, as a naval base. Superintendent at West Point, 1876–81, he became commanding general of the army, 1888, and retired as lieutenant-general, 1895.

SCHOFIELD, WILLIAM HENRY (*b. Brockville, Ontario, Canada, 1870; d. Peterboro, N.H., 1920*), educator. Graduated Victoria College, 1889; Ph.D., Harvard, 1895. Expert in Scandinavian studies, Schofield taught English at Harvard, 1897–1906, and was thereafter professor of comparative literature.

SCHOLTE, HENDRIK PETER (*b. Amsterdam, Netherlands, 1805; d. Pella, Iowa, 1868*), Dutch Reformed and Independent clergyman, colonist. Seceding from the Netherlands state church, 1834, Scholte with other like-minded pastors urged emigration as a means of escape for their followers from persecution at home. Emigrating to the United States, 1847, he founded the settlement of Pella in Marion Co., Iowa, and was its principal citizen until his death.

SCHOMER, NAHUM MEIR (*b. Nesvizh, Russia, 1849; d. 1905*), Yiddish novelist and playwright. Prolific writer of popular works which helped develop the habit of reading among the Yiddish-speaking masses. Emigrated to New York City, 1889.

SCHOOLCRAFT, HENRY ROWE (*b. Albany Co., N.Y., 1793; d. 1864*), ethnologist. Attended Union and Middlebury colleges where he favored the study of geology and mineralogy. Began explorations in 1817–18 with a trip which resulted in *A View of the Lead Mines of Missouri* (1819). A member of the Cass exploring expedition, 1820, he reported on it in *Narrative Journal of Travels through the Northwestern Regions of the United States . . . to the Sources of the Mississippi River* (1821). He described a later expedition to the sources of the Mississippi in his *Narrative of an Expedition . . . to Itasca Lake* (1834, 1855). Schoolcraft's wide acquaintance with the Indians led to his appointment as Indian agent for the Lake Superior tribes, 1822; he served as superintendent of Indian affairs for Michigan, 1836–41. A constant promoter of the study of Indian ethnology, he was author of *Algic Researches* (1839) which concerned Indian mental characteristics, and of other valuable works. His principal production was *Historical and Statistical Information Respecting the History, Condition and Prospects of the Indian Tribes of the United States* (six parts, 1851–57, illustrated with engravings from paintings by Seth Eastman).

SCHÖPF, JOHANN DAVID (*b. Wunsiedel, Germany, 1752; d. 1800*), physician, traveler. After service as a surgeon with a German regiment in the British service, 1777–83, Schöpf made a scientific tour from New Jersey to Florida before returning to his home in Bayreuth. He wrote a number of articles and monographs on his studies and an excellent travel book and historical source entitled *Reise durch einige der mittlern und südlichen vereinigten nordamerikanischen Staaten nach Ost-Florida und den Bahama-Inseln* (Erlangen, 1788; translated as *Travels in the Confederation,* 1911).

SCHOTT, CHARLES ANTHONY (*b. Mannheim, Germany, 1826; d. Washington, D.C., 1901*), geodesist. Came to America, 1848. Chief of computing division, U.S. Coast Survey, 1855–1900, Schott made his principal contributions to science in the fields of geodesy and terrestrial magnetism. He also wrote on meteorology and climatology, especially of the Arctic regions.

SCHOULER, JAMES (*b. present Arlington, Mass., 1839; d. 1920*), lawyer, historian. Son of William Schouler. Graduated Harvard, 1859. Schouler is principally remembered as the author of the *History of the United States of America under the Constitution* (seven volumes, 1880–1913). This was the first attempt to cover in a scholarly way the period from the Revolution to the Civil War. It appeared almost contemporaneously, however, with the work of John B. McMaster. Schouler's interpretation was primarily political and constitutional and was based on an industrious exploration of sources. To a large extent, his history and McMaster's supplement each other.

SCHOULER, WILLIAM (*b. near Glasgow, Scotland, 1814; d. 1872*), editor, Massachusetts legislator. Father of James Schouler. Came to America, 1816. Active as an editor of Whig and Republican papers in Massachusetts and Ohio, Schouler served as adjutant-general of Massachusetts, 1860–66, revealing remarkable executive ability and winning the lasting admiration of Gov. John A. Andrew. He was author of *A History of Massachusetts in the Civil War* (1868–71) and of personal reminiscences.

SCHRADIECK, HENRY (*b. Hamburg, Germany, 1846; d. Brooklyn, N.Y., 1918*), violinist, conductor, teacher. After a brilliant career in Europe, he came to America, 1883, and was a teacher in Cincinnati, Philadelphia and New York City. Among his pupils were Maud Powell and Theodore Spiering.

SCHRIECK, SISTER LOUISE VAN DER (*b. Bergen-op-Zoom, Holland, 1813; d. Cincinnati, O., 1886*), American foundress of the Sisters of Notre Dame de Namur. Came to Cincinnati, O., 1840, as one of a group of volunteer nuns; was named superior of the convent, 1845. As superior-provincial *post* 1848, she founded 26 convents of teaching sisters in Washington, D.C., Philadelphia, Pa., and through Ohio and Massachusetts.

SCHRIVER, EDMUND (*b. York, Pa., 1812; d. 1899*), soldier, railroad executive. Graduated West Point, 1833. Employed mainly in staff work, Schriver was brevetted major-general, 1865, for effective service during the Civil War. Thereafter he served principally on inspection duty until retirement, 1881.

SCHROEDER, JOHN FREDERICK (*b. Baltimore, Md., 1800; d. 1857*), Episcopal clergyman. A skillful preacher, he was assistant at Trinity Church, New York City, 1823–39, having immediate charge of St.

Paul's Chapel. He served thereafter as principal of a girl's school and as rector of several churches successively in Flushing, N.Y., New York City and Brooklyn, N.Y. He was a moderate Evangelical.

SCHROEDER, SEATON (*b. Washington, D.C., 1849; d. 1922*), naval officer. Graduated Annapolis, 1868. An efficient officer of wide experience, Schroeder was author of treatises on torpedoes and torpedo boats, assisted in perfecting the Driggs-Schroeder gun, and retired as rear-admiral, 1911. Earlier in his career he had assisted Henry H. Gorringe in transporting the obelisk now in Central Park from Egypt to New York City (1879).

SCHUESSELE, CHRISTIAN. [See Schussele, Christian, 1826–1879.]

SCHULTZ, DUTCH. [See Flegenheimer, Arthur, 1902–1935.]

SCHULTZ, HENRY (*b. Szarkowszczyzna, Russian Poland, 1893; d. near San Diego, Calif., 1938*), mathematical economist. Came to America as a boy. Graduated College of the City of New York, 1916; Ph.D., Columbia, 1925. Studied also at London School of Economics and at Galton Laboratory of University of London. Taught at University of Chicago, *post* 1926; was author of *The Theory and Measurement of Demand* (1938). [*Supp. 2*]

SCHULTZE, AUGUSTUS (*b. near Potsdam, Prussia, 1840; d. Bethlehem, Pa., 1918*), Moravian clergyman, editor, author. Professor of classics at Moravian College, Bethlehem, Pa., *post* 1870; president of the college, 1885–1918.

SCHUMANN-HEINK, ERNESTINE (*b. Lieben, near Prague, Bohemia, 1861; d. Hollywood, Calif., 1936*), singer. An outstanding contralto, she made her first professional appearance in Graz, Austria, 1876; after a somewhat difficult career with various German opera companies, she won success with the Hamburg Opera, 1888. Thereafter her European reputation grew and she was invited to join the Metropolitan Opera Company; she made her American debut in Chicago, November 1898, in *Lohengrin*. Leaving the Metropolitan, 1903, to undertake work in concert and operetta, she returned to grand opera in 1905 and continued active on both sides of the Atlantic until *c.* 1914. Displaying strong American patriotism during World War I, she made concert work her principal activity during the 1920's and the early 1930's; she also sang on the radio and in vaudeville. At its prime, her voice was remarkable for its compass as well as for its quality and power. [*Supp. 2*]

SCHURZ, CARL (*b. Liblar, near Cologne, Germany, 1829; d. New York, N.Y., 1906*), German revolutionary, Union soldier, lawyer, diplomat, statesman. A leader of the student revolutionary movement at the University of Bonn, Schurz was profoundly influenced by Gottfried Kinkel and followed him in the abortive move upon Siegburg, May 1849. Thereafter he became a lieutenant and staff officer of the revolutionary army, fought in several engagements during June, and managed to escape from the fortress of Rastatt before its capture by the Prussians. After a brief refuge in Switzerland, he returned to Germany to rescue Kinkel who had been sentenced to life imprisonment and was confined at Spandau. Achieving this purpose on the night of Nov. 6, 1850, he accompanied Kinkel to England. Thence, after a brief residence, he emigrated to the United States, August 1852. Settling on a small farm in Watertown, Wis., 1856, he espoused the anti-slavery cause and was drawn into Republican politics. Speaking in German, he campaigned for Frémont, 1856, and in 1858 spoke in Illinois for Abraham Lincoln. An able orator in both German and English, he was soon in demand for one campaign after another and was particularly effective during the campaign of 1860. His speech in Cooper Union (N.Y.) in September, a merciless criticism of Stephen A. Douglas, was regarded as his principal oratorical effort. Appointed U.S. minister to Spain by Lincoln, Schurz remained only a brief time in the post and returned to urge immediate emancipation of the slaves as a means of securing European sympathy for the North.

Appointed brigadier-general of volunteers, June 1862, he took his military duties seriously. Commended as a division commander at the second battle of Bull Run, August 1862, he and his division were soon held up to scorn because of their flight during the battle of Chancellorsville. Schurz blamed the disaster on the improper placement of his division by Gen. O. O. Howard and a long controversy ensued. Commanding the XI Corps at Gettysburg, Schurz was again unsuccessful in stemming an attack of the Confederates, and once again there were charges that his German troops had failed to stand their ground. Promoted to major-general, Schurz and his corps were transferred to the west. After the battle of Chattanooga the depleted XI Corps was merged into a new unit and its general was appointed to an inactive post at Nashville. The end of the Civil War found Schurz serving as chief of staff to Gen. Slocum in Sherman's army. Throughout his military service he had been in an anomalous situation because of his constant correspondence with President Lincoln; despite this, he won the regard of Sherman, Hancock and other able Northern generals.

Traveling through the Southern states, July–September 1865, Schurz wrote a lengthy report on his observations which has value to this day although President Johnson tried his best to suppress it. Briefly the Washington correspondent of the *New York Tribune* and the editor of the Detroit *Post,* he became co-editor, with Emil Preetorius, of the St. Louis *Westliche Post,* 1867. He delivered the keynote address at the Republican National Convention, 1868. As U.S. senator, Republican, from Missouri, 1869–75, Schurz soon found himself among the anti-Grant members; he opposed the President's spoils-loving and domineering partisans, introduced a bill to create a permanent civil-service merit system, 1869, and made incessant attacks upon public corruption. Failing of re-election, he returned once again to journalism and lecturing. Having done more than any other leader to promote the Liberal Republican movement, he was permanent president of the Cincinnati convention, 1872, and was active in Horace Greeley's campaign. Supporting R. B. Hayes for the presidency, 1876, he served with enlightened ability as U.S. secretary of the interior, 1877–81. Co-editor of the N.Y. *Evening Post* and the *Nation,* 1881–83, he resigned because of friendly differences over methods and policies with Edwin L. Godkin. He contributed the leading editorials to *Harper's Weekly,* 1892–98. Warm in his opposition to the war with Spain and later to expansionist policies, he held in his last years a unique position as a veteran statesman and political philosopher. Among his books are a *Life of Henry Clay* (1887) and *Reminiscences* (1907–08).

SCHUSSELE, CHRISTIAN (*b. Guebviller, Alsace, 1826; d. Merchantville, N.J., 1879*), painter, teacher, lithographer. Emigrated to Philadelphia, Pa., c. 1849. Established reputation as a painter with his "Clear the Track," engraved by John Sartain, 1854. Among other of his well-known paintings are "Franklin before the Lords in Council" (1856) and "Washington at Valley Forge" (1862). In the latter part of his life he served as professor of drawing and painting at the Pennsylvania Academy of the Fine Arts.

SCHUTTLER, PETER (*b. Wachenheim, Hesse-Darmstadt, Germany, 1812; d. Chicago, Ill., 1865*), wagon maker. Came to America, 1834. In business in Chicago *post* 1843, Schuttler produced a lightweight easy-running wagon which displaced the old prairie schooner type for westward emigration.

SCHUYLER, EUGENE (*b. Ithaca, N.Y., 1840; d. Italy, 1890*), diplomat. Son of George W. Schuyler. Graduated Yale, 1859; Ph.D., 1861; LL.B., Columbia, 1863. A consular and diplomatic officer principally in Russia *post* 1867, Schuyler became widely known for a report on Turkish atrocities in Bulgaria, published 1876. Subsequently holding posts as diplomatic representative to Rumania, Greece, Serbia and Egypt, he was an outstanding figure during an era of mediocrity in the American foreign service. Among his literary works were translations from Turgenev and Tolstoy and a biography of Peter the Great, published in 1884.

SCHUYLER, GEORGE WASHINGTON (*b. Stillwater, N.Y., 1810; d. 1888*), businessman, New York state official. Father of Eugene Schuyler. Author of *Colonial New York: Philip Schuyler and His Family* (1885).

SCHUYLER, JAMES DIX (*b. Ithaca, N.Y., 1848; d. Ocean Park, Calif., 1912*), hydraulic and railroad engineer, expert in dam building and water-supply systems.

SCHUYLER, LOUISA LEE (*b. New York, N.Y., 1837; d. 1926*), welfare-work leader. Great-granddaughter of Philip J. Schuyler and of Alexander Hamilton. Worked with U.S. Sanitary Commission through the Civil War; organized State Charities Aid Association, 1872; secured opening of nurses' training school at Bellevue Hospital, the first in America (*c. 1874*).

SCHUYLER, MARGARITA (*b. Albany, N.Y., 1701; d. Albany, 1782*). Daughter-in-law of Peter Schuyler; aunt of Philip J. Schuyler. Celebrated as a hostess and as the subject of A. M. Grant's *Memoirs of an American Lady* (London, 1808).

SCHUYLER, MONTGOMERY (*b. Ithaca, N.Y., 1843; d. New Rochelle, N.Y., 1914*), journalist, critic of architecture. Attended Hobart College. Served on staff of the N.Y. *World c.* 1865–83; of the *New York Times,* 1883–1907. Meanwhile he had been managing editor, *Harper's Weekly,* 1885–87, and was a literary adviser to Harper & Brothers. He was author of *American Architecture: Studies* (1892), but the bulk of his writing on this topic is scattered through the files of periodicals, notably the *Architectural Record* of which he was one of the founders, 1891.

SCHUYLER, PETER (*b. Beverwyck, present Albany, N.Y., 1657; d. 1724*), soldier and official of colonial New York. Elected first mayor of Albany, 1686, and head of the board of Indian commissioners, Schuyler acted with energy and efficiency as protector of the frontier against the French threat from Canada and possessed a remarkable influence over the Iroquois. Active in opposition to Jacob Leisler, he was made a judge of common pleas by Gov. Sloughter, 1691, and appointed to the council in 1692 by Gov. Fletcher. Acting governor of New York, July 1719—September 1720, he was removed from the council on the arrival of Gov. Burnet who feared him as a potential leader of opposition. A trader and merchant, Schuyler owned numerous land grants, of which the most extensive was in the Saratoga patent.

SCHUYLER, PHILIP JOHN (*b. Albany, N.Y., 1733; d. Albany, 1804*), soldier, statesman, landowner. Commanded a company in the 1755 expedition against Crown Point; served in John Bradstreet's expedition to Oswego, 1756. Returned to service, 1758, as deputy commissary under Lord Howe and was again with Bradstreet at the taking of Fort Frontenac. Collected and forwarded provisions from Albany to Amherst's forces, 1759–60. Living as a country gentleman thereafter until the outbreak of the Revolution, Schuyler developed his estates. Although he opposed the De Lancey-Colden royalist coalition, he withheld his sympathy from the radicals among the Sons of Lib-

erty. Accepting membership in the New York delegation to the Second Continental Congress, he was appointed on June 15, 1775, one of four major-generals under Washington and assigned to command in northern New York. With only half-hearted support from New England he recruited and provisioned an army, strengthened garrisons at Ticonderoga and Crown Point, maintained the neutrality of the Iroquois and organized the expedition of 1775–76 against Canada. Yielding the field command to Gen. Richard Montgomery because of ill-health, he was nevertheless held responsible for the failure of the expedition by New Englanders who disliked him as a severe disciplinarian and as a symbol of the mutual antagonism between "Yorker" and "Yankee." Except for his indecision over defending Ticonderoga, which ended in St. Clair's abandonment of that fort, July 1777, Schuyler handled the difficult situation in northern New York with considerable skill. Retreating before the British in such a way as to permit levies of militia to harass the advancing Gen. Burgoyne, he upset another part of the British strategy by relieving Fort Stanwix and so wrecking the efforts of the British general St. Leger to approach from the west. Congress, however, alarmed by the loss of Ticonderoga, superseded him with Gen. Horatio Gates, August 4, 1777. Demanding a court-martial, he was acquitted with honor, October 1778, and in the following spring resigned from the Continental service. He continued, however, to assist Gen. Washington with advice and served briefly in Congress, 1779–80. Holder of a number of public offices, 1780–98, Schuyler gave particular attention to problems of finance; he was a strong supporter of the movement which culminated in the Federal Convention of 1787 and served as U.S. senator, Federalist, from New York, 1789–91 and 1797–98. He was intimately associated with the career of his son-in-law, Alexander Hamilton.

SCHWAB, CHARLES MICHAEL (*b. Williamsburg, Pa., 1862; d. New York, N.Y., 1939*), industrialist. Beginning work in the steel industry at the Carnegie-owned Edgar Thomson Steel plant as an engineer's helper, Schwab advanced swiftly, owing in great part to his genius in dealing with people and his open-mindedness toward technological, production, and labor-saving innovations. Appointed president of Carnegie Steel Co., Ltd., 1897, he served as go-between in the sale of the Carnegie properties to the J. P. Morgan interests and in formation of the U.S. Steel Corp., 1901. President of the new corporation, 1901–03, he built up the Bethlehem Steel Co., *post* 1904, into principal rivalry with U.S. Steel. To the operation of Bethlehem, Schwab brought daring, energy and the skills of a great salesman. He set up an executive profit-sharing system, put essentially all wages on an incentive basis, and gave his associates a free hand. During World War I he was the principal factor in Bethlehem's success with war-contract work and became in time a sort of senior spokesman for the steel industry. Dying insolvent because of unwise investment outside the steel industry and the effects of the depression, he stands as an almost perfect case specimen of the great entrepreneur in the heyday of American capitalism. [*Supp. 2*]

SCHWAB, JOHN CHRISTOPHER (*b. New York, N.Y., 1865; d. New Haven, Conn., 1916*), economist, librarian. Graduated Yale, 1886; Ph.D., Göttingen, 1889. Taught political economy at Yale *post* 1891. Author of *The Confederate States of America, 1861–1865: a Financial and Industrial History* (1901).

SCHWARZ, EUGENE AMANDUS (*b. Liegnitz, Silesia, Germany, 1844; d. 1928*), entomologist. Came to America, 1872. In U.S. Department of Agriculture service *post* 1879, Schwarz was considered to be the most learned coleopterist of his time and also excelled as a field investigator.

SCHWATKA, FREDERICK (*b. Galena, Ill., 1849; d. Portland, Oreg., 1892*), explorer. Graduated West Point, 1871; M.D., Bellevue Hospital Medical College, New York, 1876. In association with William H. Gilder, Schwatka journeyed to the Arctic, 1878, and after a search of more than two years resolved all doubts concerning the fate of the famous expedition of Sir John Franklin. Resigning from the army, 1885, he devoted himself thereafter to travel and to writing and lecturing.

SCHWEINITZ, EDMUND ALEXANDER de (*b. Bethlehem, Pa., 1825; d. 1887*), Moravian bishop, historian. Son of Lewis D. von Schweinitz.

SCHWEINITZ, EMIL ALEXANDER de (*b. Salem, N.C., 1866; d. 1904*), biochemist. Grandson of Lewis D. von Schweinitz. Graduated University of North Carolina, 1882; Ph.D., 1885. Ph.D. in chemistry, Göttingen, 1886. Engaged *post* 1888 in research in the U.S. Department of Agriculture (*post* 1890 as chief of research in biochemistry, Bureau of Animal Industry), he specialized in the study of disease-producing bacteria and the production of means of immunity from them. In addition to his work for the government, he was dean and professor of chemistry at the medical school, present George Washington University.

SCHWEINITZ, GEORGE EDMUND de (*b. Philadelphia, Pa., 1858; d. Philadelphia, 1938*), ophthalmologist. Son of Edmund A. de Schweinitz; grandson of Lewis D. von Schweinitz. Graduated Moravian College, 1876; M.D., University of Pennsylvania, 1881. Taught ophthalmology at Philadelphia Polyclinic and at Jefferson Medical College; professor of ophthalmology, University of Pennsylvania, 1902–24, and at U. of P. Graduate School of Medicine thereafter. Long regarded as the American leader in his specialty, de Schweinitz was co-author and editor of numerous textbooks and author of hundreds of articles; his principal work was *Diseases of the Eye*

(1892), for many years the most admired textbook in its field. [*Supp. 2*]

SCHWEINITZ, LEWIS DAVID von (*b. Bethlehem, Pa., 1780; d. Bethlehem, 1834*), Moravian clergyman, botanist, pioneer mycologist. Father of Edmund A. and grandfather of Emil A. and Geo. E. de Schweinitz. Author of *The Fungi of Lusatia* (1805), *The Fungi of North Carolina* (1818), *A Synopsis of North American Fungi* (published in *Transactions* of the American Philosophical Society, 1834) and other works.

SCIDMORE, ELIZA RUHAMAH (*b. Madison, Wis., 1856; d. 1928*), journalist, traveler, lecturer.

SCOLLARD, CLINTON (*b. Clinton, N.Y., 1860; d. Kent, Conn., 1932*), poet. Author of *Pictures in Song* (1884) and of a number of other volumes of lyrics marked by painstaking care in versification.

SCOTT, AUSTIN (*b. Maumee, O., 1848; d. Granville Centre, Mass., 1922*), educator. Graduated Yale, 1869; A.M., University of Michigan, 1870; Ph.D., Leipzig, 1873. Served as editorial assistant to George Bancroft. Taught history at Johns Hopkins, 1875–82, and at Rutgers College, *post* 1883, later becoming professor of political science. President of Rutgers, 1891–1906.

SCOTT, CHARLES (*b. present Powhatan Co., Va., c. 1739; d. Clark Co., Ky., 1813*), colonial soldier, Revolutionary major-general by brevet, Kentucky legislator. Removing to Kentucky, 1785, he served under Gen. Josiah Harmar in the 1790 expedition against the Indians. In 1791 he led an expedition against the Indians on the Wabash River and was with Gen. St. Clair at the disastrous defeat of November 4. He led the mounted Kentucky volunteers at the battle of the Fallen Timbers, August 1794. Governor of Kentucky, 1808–12.

SCOTT, COLIN ALEXANDER (*b. Ottawa, Canada, 1861; d. Boston, Mass., 1925*), psychologist, educational reformer. Author of *Social Education* (1908).

SCOTT, DRED (*b. in slavery, Southampton Co., Va., c. 1795; d. St. Louis, Mo., 1858*). Nominal plaintiff in the famous legal process (1846–57) which led to the "Dred Scott" decision by the U.S. Supreme Court.

SCOTT, FRED NEWTON (*b. Terre Haute, Ind., 1860; d. San Diego, Calif., 1931*), educator. Taught at University of Michigan *post* 1889; headed departments of rhetoric and journalism. Author of a number of works on style, he was co-author with C. M. Gayley of *An Introduction to the Methods and Materials of Literary Criticism* (1899).

SCOTT, GUSTAVUS (*b. probably Prince William Co., Va., 1753; d. Washington, D.C., 1800*), lawyer, Maryland legislator, Revolutionary patriot.

SCOTT, HARVEY WHITEFIELD (*b. near Groveland, Ill., 1838; d. Baltimore, Md., 1910*), journalist. Brother of Abigail J. S. Duniway. Editor of the Portland *Morning Oregonian*, 1866–72; editor and part-owner, 1877–1910. A conservative Republican, he won national recognition for his newspaper and made it the strongest journal in the Pacific Northwest.

SCOTT, HUGH LENOX (*b. Danville, Ky., 1853; d. Washington, D.C., 1934*), army officer. Grandson of Charles Hodge. Graduated West Point, 1876. Served with cavalry, chiefly in the Dakotas and Oklahoma, 1876–97; became specialist in language, history and "sign talk" of the Plains Indians. On staffs of Gen. William Ludlow and Gen. Leonard Wood in Cuba, 1899–1902, he was governor of Sulu Archipelago, P.I., 1903–06. Promoted colonel, he served as superintendent of West Point, 1906–10. As brigadier-general, he commanded on the Mexican border, 1913–14. Appointed chief of staff, November 1914, he laid the basis for raising, training and equipping the American forces in World War I. Retired as major-general, 1917, he remained on active duty for two years and commanded the 78th Division at Camp Dix, N.J.

[*Supp. 1*]

SCOTT, IRVING MURRAY (*b. Hebron Mills, Md., 1837; d. San Francisco, Calif., 1903*), shipbuilder, foundryman. Removed to San Francisco, 1860; was long associated with the Union Iron Works and its predecessor firm. Constructed U.S. warships *Charleston, Olympia, San Francisco, Oregon, Wisconsin* and *Ohio*, 1889–1901.

SCOTT, JAMES WILMOT (*b. Walworth Co., Wis., 1849; d. New York, N.Y., 1895*), journalist. Associated with Chicago, Ill., newspapers *post* 1875, he made his *Chicago Herald* a conservative force for reform, 1881–95.

SCOTT, JOB (*b. Providence, R.I., 1751; d. Ballitore, Ireland, 1793*), Quaker preacher. An outstanding example of quietism, Scott advanced views on Biblical interpretation which anticipated modernist tenets.

SCOTT, JOHN (*b. probably Ashford, Kent, England, c. 1630; d. England, 1696*), adventurer, swindling land speculator, spy. Nefariously active in New York and New England, 1654–64.

SCOTT, JOHN MORIN (*b. New York, N.Y., c. 1730; d. New York, 1784*), lawyer. Graduated Yale, 1746; studied law in office of William Smith (1697–1769). An active practitioner and a ready speaker, Scott was associated with William Livingston *post* 1752 in support of the Whig Presbyterian cause in New York and was an organizer of the New York Sons of Liberty. He was a leader of the radical party in the New York provincial congress, 1775–77, and ran against George Clinton for the governorship of New York, 1777. He was New York secretary of state, 1778–84, and was also a state legislator and a member of the Continental Congress. He served as a brigadier-general in the battle of Long Island, August 1776.

SCOTT, JOHN PRINDLE (*b. Norwich, N.Y., 1877; d. 1932*), composer, baritone singer, hymn-writer.

SCOTT, LEROY (*b. Fairmount, Ind., 1875; d. Chateaugay Lake, N.Y., 1929*), journalist, settlement worker. Author of *The Walking Delegate* (1905), *Counsel for the Defense* (1912) and other mediocre fiction; magazine writer on social questions and on crime and its detection.

SCOTT, ORANGE (*b. Brookfield, Vt., 1800; d. Newark, N.J., 1847*), Methodist clergyman, Abolitionist. Led a secession from his Church on the issue of slavery, 1841; presided over convention at Utica, N.Y., May 1843, at which the Wesleyan Methodist Connection of America was formed.

SCOTT, ROBERT KINGSTON (*b. Armstrong Co., Pa., 1826; d. Henry Co., O., 1900*), businessman, Union major-general by brevet. Chief, South Carolina branch of Freedmen's Bureau, 1865–68. As governor, Union Republican, of South Carolina, 1868–72, Scott was largely responsible for the scandals and disorder that characterized Republican rule in the state; his policies trebled the public debt and he was leader in conspiracies to further fraudulent contracts and stock issues.

SCOTT, SAMUEL PARSONS (*b. Hillsboro, O., 1846; d. Hillsboro, 1929*), lawyer, Hispanic scholar. Author, among other works, of the *History of the Moorish Empire in Europe* (1904).

SCOTT, THOMAS ALEXANDER (*b. Fort Loudon, Pa., 1823; d. near Darby, Pa., 1881*), railroad executive. Proposed plan for President-elect Lincoln's surreptitious entry into Washington, D.C., 1861; was assistant U.S. secretary of war in charge of government railways and transport, August 1861—June 1862; supervised removal of Gen. Hooker's force from Virginia to Chattanooga, 1863. As first vice-president of the Pennsylvania Railroad, 1860–74, Scott ably seconded the efforts of J. Edgar Thomson to strengthen the Pennsylvania system and continued that work as president, 1874–80.

SCOTT, THOMAS FIELDING (*b. Iredell Co., N.C., 1807; d. New York, N.Y., 1867*), Episcopal clergyman. Missionary bishop in Oregon and Washington Territory *post* 1854.

SCOTT, WALTER (*b. Moffat, Scotland, 1796; d. Mason Co., Ky., 1861*), religious reformer, schoolteacher. Came to America, 1818. As a Disciples of Christ preacher *post* 1826, Scott established the evangelistic pattern and the form and method of propaganda to which the rapid growth of that sect was largely due.

SCOTT, WILLIAM (*b. Warrenton, Va., 1804; d. near Jefferson City, Mo., 1862*), jurist. Removed to Missouri, 1826. Appointed to the state circuit bench, 1835, he was advanced to the state supreme court, 1841; with the exception of a two-year interval, he served until his death. Conservative and competent, he wrote many opinions in cases involving master and slave, including those in the state actions in the Dred Scott case. An ardent Democrat, he was an opponent of Thomas H. Benton and a sympathizer with the Confederate cause.

SCOTT, WILLIAM ANDERSON (*b. Bedford Co., Tenn., 1813; d. San Francisco, Calif., 1885*), Presbyterian clergyman. Grew prominent as pastor at the First Presbyterian Church, New Orleans, La., 1842–54; formed Calvary Church, San Francisco, Calif., 1854, and St. John's Church in the same city, 1870. Helped found (1871) and taught at San Francisco Theological Seminary.

SCOTT, WILLIAM LAWRENCE (*b. Washington, D.C., 1828; d. 1891*), railroad and coal operator. Grandson of Gustavus Scott. A type of the individualistic capitalist of his time, he supervised his various and far-flung interests from home offices in Erie, Pa.

SCOTT, WINFIELD (*b. "Laurel Branch," in neighborhood of Petersburg, Va., 1786; d. West Point, N.Y., 1866*), soldier, statesman. Attended College of William and Mary; studied law in Petersburg. Commissioned captain of light artillery, May 1808, Scott recruited a company and embarked for New Orleans, La., arriving April 1, 1809. Put on trial and suspended for a year from the army for stating that Gen. James Wilkinson, his commander, had been as great a traitor as Aaron Burr, Scott rejoined his command, 1811, serving as a staff officer in New Orleans until February 1812. Promoted lieutenant-colonel, he reported at Buffalo, N.Y., in October 1812, and was taken prisoner at the battle of Queenstown. Exchanged later in the year, he was sent to Philadelphia early in 1813 as adjutant-general with rank of colonel.

Detailed for duty on the Northern front, he planned and executed the successful attack on Fort George on the Niagara River in May, 1813. Commanding an infantry battalion in the advance guard of Gen. Jacob Brown's force, he defeated the British in an engagement on Uphold's Creek late in the year. Almost alone among American officers in the realization that adequate training and knowledge were prerequisites of victory, Scott was ordered by President Madison and Secretary Monroe to Albany, N.Y., to supervise preparations for another offensive on the Niagara, but, in fact, was left to supervise munitions at the arsenal. Promoted a regular brigadier-general, March 1814, he returned to Buffalo where he played the chief part in training the only American troops who gave a good account of themselves on land during the War of 1812. On July 4 and 5 he drove the enemy in a running fight for 16 miles to the Chippewa, and he and his brigade bore the brunt of the fighting at Lundy's Lane on July 25. He became overnight the idol of the United States and a hero abroad. Brevetted major-general, he was prevented

by wounds received at Lundy's Lane from joining Jackson at New Orleans.

Performing routine duties, 1815–32, Scott gave much of his time to study of military methods in Europe and to constructive writing. He headed the board which produced the first standard set of American drill regulations, 1815, and was the sole author of the revised *Infantry Tactics* (1835) which remained standard down to the Civil War. Passed over in favor of Alexander Macomb for appointment as commanding general of the army, 1828, Scott protested the appointment vainly. Employed briefly in the Black Hawk War, 1832, he was personally commissioned by President Jackson in that same year to watch the South Carolina nullifiers, and by his tact and wisdom did much to preserve the peace during the nullification crisis. Commissioned in 1835 to prosecute war against the Seminole and Creek Indians in Florida and adjacent states, he was denied adequate means for making a campaign and unreasonably relieved of the duty. Examined before a court of inquiry for his alleged failure, he was fully exonerated. During 1838 he performed with brilliance as a soldier-diplomat in settling difficulties raised by a rebellion in Canada, by the removal of the Cherokee Indians beyond the Mississippi, and by a dispute and a possible war with Great Britain over the Maine boundary question. Appointed general-in-chief of the army, 1841, he instituted reforms, outlawed cruel punishments for soldiers and aided officers to become well-schooled. *Post* 1839 he was mentioned as a possible Whig candidate for the presidency.

As war with Mexico approached, Scott endorsed the appointment of Zachary Taylor to command the army of occupation at Corpus Christi and supplied him with able officers as subordinates. When the fruitlessness of the campaign was demonstrated (despite the tactical victories which were gained), Scott proposed a strategic plan that would, as he put it, "conquer a peace." President Polk, inimical to anything that might advance Scott's political prestige, opposed it but was forced to acquiesce in it by Secretary W. L. Marcy, Senator Thomas H. Benton and others. Setting out with full powers for the seat of war, Scott managed by tireless effort to land 10,000 men below Vera Cruz, March 9, 1847. Advised by senior officers to take the city by assault, he chose to invest it from the rear and took it March 26 with less than twenty dead. No reinforcements were sent him and it became plain that the administration was hedging on fulfillment of his plan; nevertheless Scott pushed forward in April toward Mexico City. Winning a victory at Cerro Gordo, despite inefficiency on the part of his senior officers, he was halted at Jalapa when a large part of his force left in a body because of the expiration of their enlistments. His urgent demands for money and men brought him no response until midsummer. On August 5, when his force had been raised by incoming recruits to about 10,000 effectives, he set off once more from Puebla. After a series of actions at Contreras, Churubusco, Molino del Rey and Chapultepec, Scott marched into Mexico City on September 14, and entered on the difficult task of putting his army to work at the government of an occupied territory. In this effort he was so successful that a deputation of Mexicans asked him to be their dictator. The administration at Washington, however, saw an opportunity to undercut the victorious general politically when his troublesome subordinate, Gideon J. Pillow, distributed his own personal version of Scott's battles to the newspapers at home. Scott protested Pillow's actions and also those of Gen. Worth, but President Polk upheld the offenders and ordered the victorious commander himself before a hand-picked court of inquiry. On April 22, 1848, Scott returned to the United States. In the words of Robert E. Lee, an engineer officer on his staff, he had been "turned out as an old horse to die"; yet in the sequel, Scott was completely vindicated and received unprecedented honors from the people of New York and other cities. He ran as Whig candidate for the presidency in 1852 and was overwhelmingly defeated by Franklin Pierce after an exceptionally scurrilous campaign. In 1852, he was raised to rank of lieutenant-general.

Foreseeing the Civil War, Scott pleaded with President Buchanan in October and December, 1860, to reinforce the Southern forts and armories against seizure. In January 1861, with headquarters at Washington, he actively oversaw recruiting and training of the defenders of the capital and personally commanded Lincoln's bodyguard at the inauguration. Rendering all aid in his power to the president, he drew up a general plan for the conduct of the federal forces which might well have curtailed the war; it was disregarded on the ground he was too old to give advice. Retiring in November 1861, he continued active and in 1865 presented to Gen. U. S. Grant, who had been one of his subalterns in the Mexican War, a gift bearing the inscription "from the oldest to the greatest general."

In his prime a bulky and immensely strong man, six feet, five inches in height, Scott possessed a whimsical egotism, was inclined to flourishes of unfortunate rhetoric, and was too outspoken for his own advancement; his exactness in dress and behavior won him the nickname "Fuss and Feathers." In his public career of nearly half a century he had been a main factor in ending two wars, in saving the country from several others and in acquiring a large portion of its Western territory.

SCOVEL, HENRY SYLVESTER (*b. Denny Station, Pa., 1869; d. Havana, Cuba, 1905*), engineer, journalist. Aggressive correspondent in Cuba for several U.S. newspapers, 1895–99.

SCOVEL, SYLVESTER. [See SCOVEL, HENRY SYLVESTER, 1869–1905.]

SCOVELL, MELVILLE AMASA (*b. Belvidere, N.J., 1855; d. 1912*), agricultural chemist, educator. Patented processes for clarifying juice of sugar-producing plants and for manufacturing glucose, sugar and syrup from sorghum; was director, Kentucky Agricultural Experiment Station *post* 1885; made notable contributions as chemist, agronomist, pure-food exponent and administrator.

SCOVILLE, JOSEPH ALFRED (*b. Woodbury, Conn., 1815; d. New York, N.Y., 1864*), journalist. Secretary and biographer of John C. Calhoun. Scoville edited several New York newspapers *post* 1850 and is particularly remembered for his five volumes of commercial reminiscence entitled *The Old Merchants of New York City* (1863–66, published under pseudonym of Walter Barrett).

SCRANTON, GEORGE WHITFIELD (*b. Madison, Conn., 1811; d. Scranton, Pa., 1861*), iron manufacturer, railroad president, developer of transportation in the Lackawanna Valley. Founded city of Scranton, 1840.

SCREWS, WILLIAM WALLACE (*b. Jernigan, Ala., 1839; d. Coosada, Ala., 1913*), Confederate soldier, journalist. Editor-owner of the *Montgomery* (Ala.) *Advertiser*, 1866–1913, he led opposition to Reconstruction, fought the Farmers' Alliance, and directed the policies of the Democratic party in the state.

SCRIBNER, CHARLES (*b. New York, N.Y., 1821; d. Lucerne, Switzerland, 1871*), publisher. Father of Charles Scribner (1854–1930). Graduated College of New Jersey (Princeton), 1840. Gave up practice of law to found publishing firm of Baker & Scribner, 1846; on death of his partner, 1850, continued the firm in his own name.

SCRIBNER, CHARLES (*b. New York, N.Y., 1854; d. New York, 1930*), publisher. Son of Charles Scribner (1821–1871); grandson of John I. Blair. Graduated College of New Jersey (Princeton), 1875. Entering the publishing house established by his father (known *post* 1878 as Charles Scribner's Sons), he served it as president, 1879–1928, and was thereafter chairman of the board. He was active also as a banker and as a benefactor of Princeton University and Skidmore College.

SCRIPPS, EDWARD WYLLIS (*b. near Rushville, Ill., 1854; d. Monrovia Bay, Liberia, 1926*), newspaper publisher. Half-brother of James E. and Ellen B. Scripps. Entering newspaper work in Detroit, Mich., 1872, he founded the Cleveland, O., *Penny Press*, 1878, first link of a chain of cheap daily papers extending from the Middle West to the Pacific. In partnership with Milton A. McRae *post* 1889, he organized an independent news service (1897) to cover the field west of Pittsburgh which in 1907 became known as the United Press Association, the first such agency to operate in connection with a chain of daily papers. He was also organizer of the NEA syndicate. Editorially, the Scripps papers were independent in politics, sympathetic with union labor and liberal in their general attitude.

SCRIPPS, ELLEN BROWNING (*b. London, England, 1836; d. 1932*), journalist, philanthropist. Sister of James E. Scripps; half-sister of Edward W. Scripps. Playing a large part in the success of the newspaper ventures of her brother and half-brother, she also made a fortune in California real estate. Founded Scripps College at Claremont, Calif., and the present Scripps Institution of Oceanography.

SCRIPPS, JAMES EDMUND (*b. London, England, 1835; d. Detroit, Mich., 1906*), newspaper publisher. Brother of Ellen B. Scripps; half-brother of Edward W. Scripps. Came to America as a boy; was raised near Rushville, Ill. Began newspaper career, 1857, as reporter on the Chicago *Democratic Press;* served as business manager and editor of *Detroit Tribune;* founded Detroit *Evening News,* August 1873. Helped finance founding of the Cleveland, O., *Penny Press* by his half-brother, Edward W. Scripps, 1878, and later joined with him in the formation of his chain of newspapers. Conservative in temperament, he disagreed with his partners over questions of management and gradually withdrew from the combination; by 1903 he had relinquished his holdings in all but the *Evening News,* later called the *Detroit News.* He purchased the *Detroit Tribune,* 1891.

SCRIPPS, ROBERT PAINE (*b. San Diego, Calif., 1895; d. near Santa Margarita Island, Magdalena Bay, Lower California, 1938*), newspaper publisher. Son of Edward W. Scripps. Headed the Scripps-Howard newspaper chain, 1926–38. [*Supp. 2*]

SCRUGGS, WILLIAM LINDSAY (*b. near Knoxville, Tenn., 1836; d. Atlanta, Ga., 1912*), journalist, Tennessee Unionist, diplomat. Agent of Venezuela in the United States, 1894–98, during crisis over boundary difficulties with Great Britain.

SCRYMSER, JAMES ALEXANDER (*b. New York, N.Y., 1839; d. New York, 1918*), capitalist, Union soldier. Promoted and developed cable and telegraph lines to Cuba, Mexico and Central and South American points.

SCUDDER, HORACE ELISHA (*b. Boston, Mass., 1838; d. Cambridge, Mass., 1902*), editor, author. Brother of Samuel H. Scudder. Graduated Williams, 1858. Editor with Houghton, Mifflin & Co. and its predecessor firms *post c.* 1864; editor, *Riverside Magazine for Young People,* 1867–70; editor, *Atlantic Monthly,* 1890–98. Author of a number of books which included eight juvenile "Bodley Books" of travel (1876–1884) and biographies of Noah Webster, Bayard Taylor, George Washington and James Russell Lowell.

SCUDDER, JOHN (*b. Freehold, N.J., 1793; d. Wynberg, South Africa, 1855*), physician, Reformed Dutch clergyman. Missionary to Ceylon and India, 1819–42, 1846–54.

SCUDDER, JOHN MILTON (*b. Harrison, O., 1829; d. Daytona, Fla., 1894*), eclectic physician. Graduated Eclectic Medical Institute, Cincinnati, O., 1856. Taught at his alma mater throughout his professional life and devoted much of his time and energy to its development and improvement. He served as dean *post* 1861 and as editor of the *Eclectic Medical Journal,* 1861–94.

SCUDDER, NATHANIEL (*b. either Huntington, L.I., N.Y., or near Freehold, N.J., 1733; d. near Shrewsbury, N.J., 1781*), physician, New Jersey Revolutionary patriot and colonel of militia. Member of Continental Congress, February 1778—December 1779. He was killed in a skirmish with Loyalist refugees three days before the surrender at Yorktown.

SCUDDER, SAMUEL HUBBARD (*b. Boston, Mass., 1837; d. Cambridge, Mass., 1911*), entomologist. Brother of Horace E. Scudder. Graduated Williams, 1857; studied at Lawrence Scientific School under Agassiz whom he also served as assistant. Scudder's bibliography comprises 791 scientific titles. Outside the field of entomology he was author of *Catalogue of Scientific Serials . . . 1633–1876* (1879) and *Nomenclator Zoologicus* (1882–84), both important works. His true life-work, however, dealt with American diurnal Lepidoptera, the Orthoptera, and fossil insects. Among his numerous writings on butterflies, his *Butterflies of the Eastern United States and Canada, with Special Reference to New England* (1888–89) stands out as monumental. He was the greatest American orthopterist of his time, and his work on fossil insects was profound, extensive and pioneer. His style of writing possessed great charm.

SCULL, JOHN (*b. Reading, Pa., 1765; d. near present Irwin, Pa., 1828*), newspaper editor. Partner with Joseph Hall in establishment at Pittsburgh, Pa., 1786, of the first newspaper published west of the Alleghenies, the Pittsburgh *Gazette.* Also a civic leader in Pittsburgh, he continued publication of the *Gazette* until 1816.

SCULLIN, JOHN (*b. near Helena, N.Y., 1836; d. St. Louis, Mo., 1920*), railroad builder, St. Louis street-railway operator, steel manufacturer. Contractor-builder of many Midwestern railroads, he constructed the major portion of the Missouri-Kansas-Texas system, 1869–74.

SEABURY, GEORGE JOHN (*b. New York, N.Y., 1844; d. New York, 1909*), chemist, pharmacist. Founded Seabury and Johnson, pioneer manufacturers of surgical dressings, of which he was president *post* 1885.

SEABURY, SAMUEL (*b. Groton, Conn., 1729; d. New London, Conn., 1796*), Episcopal clergyman, Loyalist, writer. Graduated Yale, 1748; studied medicine at University of Edinburgh; ordained by the bishop of London, 1753. Sent by the Society for the Propagation of the Gospel as missionary to New Brunswick, N.J., 1754, he was transferred to Jamaica, N.Y., 1757, and was inducted as rector at Westchester, N.Y., 1767. A leader in the campaign of the New York Anglican clergy to secure bishops for America, he was one of the authors of the articles "A Whip for the American Whig," published in Gaine's *New York Gazette*, April 1768—July 1769. Just before the outbreak of the Revolution, he produced several important pamphlets signed "A. W. Farmer" in which, with clear, homely language and arguments, he tried to convince Americans that their greatest freedom lay in submitting to the British government and securing desired change through peaceful appeals to that government. These pamphlets (which were answered by Alexander Hamilton) were: *Free Thoughts on the Proceedings of the Continental Congress, etc.; The Congress Canvassed, etc.; A View of the Controversy between Great Britain and Her Colonies, etc.* (published, November and December 1774); also *An Alarm to the Legislature of the Province of New York* (January 1775). After entering actively into the Loyalist campaign to prevent election of delegates to provincial and Continental congresses, Seabury went into hiding, April 1775. In November, Connecticut soldiers under Isaac Sears took him prisoner at Westchester, and he suffered a brief confinement at New Haven, Conn. In the fall of 1776 he entered the British lines on Long Island, later serving as a guide to the British both on Long Island and in Westchester County. Holding several chaplaincies under the British, he lived comfortably in New York City throughout the Revolution. Presented by the Episcopal clergy of Connecticut as a candidate for consecration as bishop in the now independent colonies, 1783, he was refused consecration by Anglican authorities who believed themselves legally debarred from performing the rite. He then proceeded to Scotland and on Nov. 14, 1784, was consecrated by the non-juring Scottish prelates. Returning to America in the early summer of 1785, he became rector of St. James's Church, New London, Conn., and served as bishop of Connecticut and Rhode Island until his death. Working strenuously to revive and reorganize the churches in his diocese, he stood for unity in essentials and liberty in nonessentials, but had little sympathy for the prevailing liberalizing ideas of his American brethren.

SEABURY, SAMUEL (*b. New London, Conn., 1801; d. 1872*), Episcopal clergyman. Grandson of Samuel Seabury (1729–1796). A High Churchman of the old school, he served as editor of *The Churchman*, 1833–49, supporting Tractarianism and Bishop Benjamin T. Onderdonk. He served also as a teacher in the General Theological Seminary, and was rector of the Church of the Annunciation, New York, 1838–68.

SEAGER, HENRY ROGERS (*b. Lansing, Mich., 1870; d. Kiev, Russia, 1930*), economist. Graduated University of Michigan, 1890; Ph.D., University of Pennsylvania, 1894. Taught at Wharton School, 1894–1902, and at Columbia thereafter. A conservative and a believer in progress, Seager engaged in many meliorative activities with the purpose of bettering social conditions within the framework of *laissez-faire*. Among his works, *Principles of Economics* (1913) is the most considerable.

SEALSFIELD, CHARLES (*b. Poppitz, Moravia, Austria, 1793; d. near Solothurn, Switzerland, 1864*), novelist. Pen name of Karl Anton Postl who abandoned the monastic life in Prague, fled Austria, and appeared as Charles Sealsfield in New Orleans, La., 1823. After traveling through the Southern states, Texas and Mexico and a brief residence near Pittsburgh, he returned to Europe. His *The United States as They Are . . . By the Author of Austria as it is* was published anonymously in English, 1828; it had appeared the previous year in German. After further travels and residence in the United States, the then Mexican Southwest and Mexico proper, he retired to Switzerland, 1832, where he continued to reside except for occasional visits to the United States. Sealsfield attempted to create a new type of fiction, the ethnographical novel in which a whole people figured as protagonist. He exemplified his theory in some six books published in German and English between 1834 and 1843; in these the people of the United States and Mexico were portrayed in every possible social relation.

SEAMAN, ELIZABETH COCHRANE (*b. Cochran Mills, Pa., 1867; d. New York, N.Y., 1922*), journalist, known as "Nellie Bly." Famous for a tour around the world, 1889–90, in which she beat the time of Jules Verne's fictional "Phileas Fogg" by eight days.

SEARING, LAURA CATHERINE REDDEN (*b. Somerset Co., Md., 1840; d. San Mateo, Calif., 1923*), journalist. Civil War correspondent in Washington, D.C., for the *St. Louis* (Mo.) *Republican;* later on staff of New York City newspapers. Deaf and mute, she was taught speech by Alexander G. Bell.

SEARLE, ARTHUR (*b. London, England, 1837; d. Cambridge, Mass., 1920*), astronomer. Graduated Harvard, 1856. Associated with the Harvard Observatory *post* 1868, he became Phillips Professor of Astronomy, 1887, and was made emeritus, 1912; he also taught astronomy at Radcliffe, 1891–1912.

SEARLE, JAMES (*b. probably New York, N.Y., 1733; d. Philadelphia, Pa., 1797*), merchant, Revolutionary patriot. Prospering as a merchant in Philadelphia *post c.* 1762, he took part in all early protests against British policy. Elected to the Continental Congress, November 1778, he allied himself with the radical group, seconding James Lovell and Richard H. Lee in their hostility to Silas Deane. Appointed special envoy to float a Pennsylvania state loan in Europe, July 1780, he failed in his efforts at Paris, Amsterdam and Lyons, and on his return *c.* 1781 found that much of his fortune had been dissipated by unwise actions of his partners.

SEARLE, JOHN PRESTON (*b. Schuylerville, N.Y., 1854; d. 1922*), Dutch Reformed clergyman, educator. Graduated Rutgers, 1875; New Brunswick Theological Seminary, 1878. Held principal pastorate at Somerville, N.J. Professor of theology at New Brunswick Seminary *post* 1893, he served also as president of the faculty *post* 1902.

SEARS, BARNAS (*b. Sandisfield, Mass., 1802; d. Saratoga, N.Y., 1880*), Baptist clergyman, educator. Graduated Brown, 1825. Taught at Hamilton (N.Y.) Literary Institution, 1829–33 and 1835. Professor of theology, Newton Theological Institution, 1836–48; president of Newton, 1839–48. Succeeding Horace Mann in 1848 as the secretary of the Massachusetts Board of Education, he gave permanence to Mann's reforms; in 1855 he left to become president of Brown University, remaining there until 1867. Thereafter, until his death, he was general agent of the Peabody Education Fund and the principal architect of its purpose and methods.

SEARS, EDMUND HAMILTON (*b. Sandisfield, Mass., 1810; d. Weston, Mass., 1876*), Unitarian clergyman. Held principal pastorates at Wayland, Mass., and Weston, Mass.; was author of a number of once-popular spiritual books and of the hymns "It came upon a midnight clear" and "Calm on the listening ear of night."

SEARS, ISAAC (*b. W. Brewster, Mass., 1730; d. Canton, China, 1786*), merchant, mariner, Revolutionary patriot. A leader of resistance to the Stamp Act in New York City, he was at the head of nearly every mob demonstration in New York City *post* 1765, including the jettisoning of tea cargoes in 1774. After Lexington and Concord, he and his followers dispossessed the Loyalist leaders and officials and were virtually dictators in New York until the spring of 1776. Sears was especially noted for severe treatment of the Long Island Tories, Jan.–Aug., 1776. In Boston, 1777–83, he promoted privateering; after the war he resumed his general merchandise business in New York City, served in the state legislature, and died while promoting a business venture in China.

SEARS, RICHARD WARREN (*b. Stewartville, Minn., 1863; d. Waukesha, Wis., 1914*), mail-order merchant, advertising expert. Beginning as a distributor of watches by mail-order, 1886, he established the firm of Sears, Roebuck & Co., and served as its president and principal advertising writer until 1909. The company entered on its major phase of prosperity after its removal from Minneapolis to Chicago, 1893.

SEARS, ROBERT (*b. St. John, N.B., Canada, 1810; d. Toronto, Canada, 1892*), printer, publisher. Resided in the United States *c.* 1831–1860. His illustrated Bibles and other works of reference had wide sale because of the excellence of their wood-engravings. He was also editor and publisher of several gazetteers.

SEATON, WILLIAM WINSTON (*b. King William Co., Va., 1785; d. 1866*), journalist. Brother-in-law of Joseph Gales (1786–1860) with whom he was associated as editor of the official administration newspaper, the *National Intelligencer* (Washington, D.C.), *post* 1812. Gales and Seaton were exclusive reporters of the debates of Congress, 1812–29, Seaton covering the Senate. Their firm published the well-known *Annals of Congress* (1834–56) and the monumental *American State Papers* (1832–61). A civic leader in Washington, Seaton was mayor of the city, 1840–50, led the movement for the Washington Monument, and was treasurer of the Smithsonian Institution *post* 1846.

SEATTLE (*b. in neighborhood of present Seattle, Wash., c. 1786; d. 1866*), chief of the Dwamish, Suquamish and allied Indian tribes. A friend to the white settlers, he unwillingly permitted his name to be given to their settlement.

SEAWELL, MOLLY ELLIOT (*b. Gloucester Co., Va., 1860; d. Washington, D.C., 1916*), author. A prolific and skillful writer, she produced a number of books for juvenile and adult readers which include *Little Jarvis* (1890), *Midshipman Paulding* (1891) and *The Lively Adventures of Gavin Hamilton* (1899).

SEBASTIAN, BENJAMIN (*b. c. 1745, place uncertain; d. probably Grayson Co., Ky., 1834*), lawyer, Revolutionary soldier. Removed to Kentucky from Virginia *c.* 1784; was implicated as early as 1787 in the pro-Spanish intrigues of James Wilkinson. A judge of the state appellate court, 1792–1806, he served as intermediary in 1795 in F. L. H. de Carondelet's attempts to win over the Kentuckians and carried proposals of a seditious character to Harry Innes and George Nicholas. Exposed as a paid agent of Spain, 1804, he was forced to resign his office and was no longer a factor in political life *post* 1806.

SECCOMB, JOHN (*b. Medford, Mass., 1708; d. Chester, N.S., Canada, 1792*), Congregational clergyman, writer of humorous verse. Pastor at Harvard, Mass., 1733–63, he served thereafter as minister in Nova Scotia.

SEDDON, JAMES ALEXANDER (*b. Fredericksburg, Va., 1815; d. Goochland Co., Va., 1880*), lawyer. Congressman, Democrat, from Virginia, 1845–47, 1849–51. An ardent follower of John C. Calhoun, he was later active in the secession movement in Virginia and was elected to the first Confederate Congress. He served as the somewhat dilatory Confederate secretary of war, November 1862–1865.

SEDELLA, ANTOINE. [See ANTOINE, PÈRE, 1748–1829.]

SEDGWICK, ANNE DOUGLAS (*b. Englewood, N.J., 1873; d. Hampstead, England, 1935*), novelist. Resident chiefly in London and Paris *post* 1882, she married Basil de Sélincourt in 1908, residing thereafter in Oxfordshire. Primarily studies of character, her novels were based on intimate knowledge of British society and international contrasts. Winning wide readership first with *Tante* (1911), a study of feminine egotism, she produced a number of other successful books including *Adrienne Toner* (1922), *The Little French Girl* (1924) and *Dark Hester* (1929). [*Supp. 1*]

SEDGWICK, ARTHUR GEORGE (*b. New York, N.Y., 1844; d. 1915*), lawyer, journalist. Son of Theodore Sedgwick (1811–1859); brother-in-law of Charles E. Norton. Associated in editorial capacity with the *Nation*, 1872–1905, he was also author or editor of a number of legal treatises.

SEDGWICK, CATHARINE MARIA (*b. Stockbridge, Mass., 1789; d. W. Roxbury, Mass., 1867*), author. Daughter of Theodore Sedgwick (1746–1813); sister of Theodore Sedgwick (1780–1839). A pioneer in the creation of the American domestic novel, she wrote because of her belief that the safety of the republic depended upon the domestic virtues of its people and so tried to make unaffected goodness and wholesome living appear attractive. Her novels and tales, although marked by romanticism and her declared didactic purpose, also contain realistic presentations of domestic scenes and were extremely popular in their time. She was also author of a number of "self-help" books. Among her novels (which were praised by W. C. Bryant and Nathaniel Hawthorne) were *A New England Tale* (1822), *Redwood* (1824), *Hope Leslie* (1827) and *The Linwoods; or Sixty Years Since* (1835).

SEDGWICK, JOHN (*b. Cornwall Hollow, Conn., 1813; d. Spotsylvania, Va., 1864*), soldier. Graduated West Point, 1837. Commissioned in the artillery, he saw service in the Seminole and Mexican wars and was with the cavalry in the West and Southwest, 1857–60. Commissioned brigadier-general of volunteers at the outbreak of the Civil War, Sedgwick held brigade and divisional command in the Army of the Potomac. Promoted major-general, 1862, he took a prominent part in the battles of Antietam and Chancellorsville and led the V and VI Corps against Marye's Heights, Fredericksburg, Va. Distinguished also for his conduct at Gettysburg and in the operations at Mine Run, he was killed in action subsequent to the battle of the Wilderness. Although a strict disciplinarian, he was admired and trusted by his soldiers who called him "Uncle John."

SEDGWICK, ROBERT (*b. Woburn, England, c. 1613; d. Jamaica, B.W.I., 1656*), colonist, soldier. Settled in Charlestown, Mass., 1636. He was active in training the militia officers of the colony and was also successful in business; he was granted a monopoly of the colony's Indian trade, 1644. Deputy to the General Court from Charlestown and holder of a number of local offices, he was elected major-general of the colony, 1652. After successfully harassing the French settlements in Maine and eastern Canada, he died while on a military expedition against Spain in the West Indies.

SEDGWICK, THEODORE (*b. West Hartford, Conn., 1746; d. Boston, Mass., 1813*), lawyer, Massachusetts jurist and legislator. Father of Catharine M. Sedgwick and Theodore Sedgwick (1780–1839). Practiced law in Berkshire Co., Mass. *post* 1766, first at Sheffield and later at Stockbridge. Early active in the struggle against Great Britain, he served as military secretary to Gen. John Thomas in the invasion of Canada, 1776. An active legislator for most of the years 1780–88, he was speaker of the Massachusetts House, 1788, and also sat in Congress, 1785–88. A strenuous opponent of Shays's Rebellion, he aided ratification by Massachusetts of the Federal Constitution; while a Federalist member of Congress from Massachusetts, 1789–96, he was chairman of important committees. U.S. senator, June 1796—March 1799, he returned to the House of Representatives and was its speaker, 1799–1801. In 1802 he was appointed for life to the supreme judicial court of Massachusetts.

SEDGWICK, THEODORE (*b. Sheffield, Mass., 1780; d. 1839*), lawyer, Massachusetts legislator, railroad advocate, reformer. Son of Theodore Sedgwick (1746–1813); brother of Catharine M. Sedgwick.

SEDGWICK, THEODORE (*b. Albany, N.Y., 1811; d. Stockbridge, Mass., 1859*), lawyer. Son of Theodore Sedgwick (1780–1839); nephew of Catharine M. Sedgwick; father of Arthur G. Sedgwick. Graduated Columbia, 1829. In extensive practice in New York City, 1834–50, he was hampered thereafter by ill-health. A lifelong student of legal, judicial and political problems, he wrote extensively on these subjects; his most important book was *A Treatise on the Measure of Damages* (1847) which was for years the only work in English on the subject.

SEDGWICK, WILLIAM THOMPSON (*b. W. Hartford, Conn., 1855; d. Boston, Mass., 1921*), biologist, epidemiologist. Graduated Sheffield Scientific School, 1877; Ph.D., Johns Hopkins, 1881. Influenced by Henry N. Martin, whom he served as an associate, 1881–83, Sedgwick was called in 1883 to teach biology at the Massachusetts Institute of Technology. Appointed full professor there in 1891, for the next thirty years he headed the departments of biology and public health. Among students trained by him were many of the leading sanitarians in the United States and abroad. He engaged also in extensive public service as consulting biologist to the Massachusetts State Board of Health. Among his works is the classic *Principles of Sanitary Science and the Public Health* (1902).

SEDLEY, WILLIAM HENRY. [See SMITH, WILLIAM HENRY, 1806–1872.]

SEE, HORACE (*b. Philadelphia, Pa., 1835; d. New York, N.Y., 1909*), naval architect. Associated with William Cramp & Sons, 1870–89, he was designer and superintending engineer, 1879–89, and in that decade was responsible for the first vessels of the "New Navy." In private practice thereafter, he invented a great number of important devices for use in ship construction.

SEED, MILES AINSCOUGH (*b. Preston, England, 1843; d. Pelham, N.Y., 1913*), photographer, manufacturer of photography supplies. Came to America, 1865; settled in St. Louis, Mo. After perfecting process for manufacture of a photographic dry plate, he formed a company and began production, 1882. Overcoming prejudice against his revolutionary improvement by constant travel and personal demonstration, he opened up large markets. In 1902 the Eastman Kodak Co. purchased his business and formulae.

SEEGER, ALAN (*b. New York, N.Y., 1888; d. near Belloy-en-Santerre, France, 1916*), poet. Graduated Harvard, 1910. Removing to Paris, France, in the autumn of 1912, he resided there until the beginning of World War I at which time he enlisted in the French Foreign Legion. He died in action. His best-known poem "I Have a Rendezvous with Death" and other works were collected in *Poems* (1916).

SEELYE, JULIUS HAWLEY (*b. Bethel, Conn., 1824; d. 1895*), clergyman, educator. Brother of L. Clark Seelye. Graduated Amherst, 1849; Auburn Theological Seminary, 1852. After serving as pastor, First Dutch Reformed Church, Schenectady, N.Y., 1853–58, he became professor of philosophy at Amherst and began service there that lasted except for one short interval until his death. An exponent of the philosophical views of Laurens P. Hickok, he was an effective teacher and became acknowledged leader of an able faculty. Appointed president of Amherst, 1876, he devised the "Amherst Plan," a system of student self-government, doubled the college income, and raised academic standards.

SEELYE, LAURENUS CLARK (*b. Bethel, Conn., 1837; d. Northampton, Mass., 1924*), Congregational clergyman, educator. Brother of Julius H. Seelye. Graduated Union, 1857; studied theology at Andover and at Berlin and Heidelberg. After a brief pastorate in Springfield, Mass., he became professor of rhetoric

at Amherst and served 1865–73. Thereafter, as president of Smith College until 1910, he carried that institution to success despite an original poverty of means. The growth of the college in equipment and endowment was due more to his skillful management than to the generosity of outsiders.

SEEVERS, WILLIAM HENRY (*b. Shenandoah Co., Va., 1822; d. 1895*), Iowa legislator, jurist. Resident in Oskaloosa, Iowa, *post* 1846, he held a number of public offices and served as chief justice of the state supreme court, 1876, 1882, and 1887–88.

SEGHERS, CHARLES JEAN (*b. Ghent, Belgium, 1839; d. Yukon country, Alaska, 1886*), Roman Catholic clergyman, missionary. Served in British Columbia, 1863–78; was bishop of Victoria *post* 1873. Named coadjutor-bishop of Oregon City (Portland), 1878, he succeeded to that see two years later as archbishop, but resigned in 1884 to resume his duties in British Columbia and to develop the missions in Alaska.

SEGUIN, EDOUARD (*b. Clamecy, France, 1812; d. 1880*), psychiatrist, pioneer in education of idiots. Emigrated to America *c.* 1850.

SEGUIN, EDWARD CONSTANT (*b. Paris, France, 1843; d. 1898*), neurologist. Son of Edouard Seguin. Came to America as a boy. M.D., N.Y. College of Physicians and Surgeons, 1864; made special studies of nervous diseases in Paris under Brown-Sequard and Charcot. Ranking in his profession with S. W. Mitchell and William A. Hammond, he practiced in New York City until 1894 and taught diseases of the nervous system at the College of Physicians and Surgeons, 1868–87.

SEIDENSTICKER, OSWALD (*b. Göttingen, Germany, 1825; d. Philadelphia, Pa., 1894*), philologist, historian of the Germans in Pennsylvania. Came to America, 1846. Taught German at University of Pennsylvania, 1867–94.

SEIDL, ANTON (*b. Pesth, Hungary, 1850; d. 1898*), musician. Studied at the Leipzig Conservatory; worked with Richard Wagner, 1872–78. Celebrated as a conductor of Wagnerian opera in Europe, he came to the Metropolitan Opera, New York City, 1885, and conducted there until German opera was temporarily dropped in 1891. Becoming conductor of the New York Philharmonic Society in succession to Theodore Thomas, he continued so for the rest of his life, resuming his work with German opera at the Metropolitan, 1895–97. Seidl exercised a great influence on American musical life and because of his association with the composer was able to give a special authenticity to his interpretations of the Wagnerian music dramas.

SEILER, CARL (*b. Switzerland, 1849; d. Reading, Pa., 1905*), laryngologist. Began study of medicine in Vienna and Heidelberg; coming to America, he received the M.D. degree at University of Pennsylvania, 1871, and was a special pupil and assistant of Jacob da Silva Solis Cohen. A teacher of his specialty at his *alma mater*, 1877–95, he was author of several books and the deviser of the widely used Seiler's tablets.

SEIP, THEODORE LORENZO (*b. Easton, Pa., 1842; d. Allentown, Pa., 1903*), Lutheran clergyman. Long a teacher at Muhlenberg College, he served with great ability as its president, 1885–1903.

SEISS, JOSEPH AUGUSTUS (*b. near Graceham, Md., 1823; d. Philadelphia, Pa., 1904*), Lutheran clergyman. Held chief pastorates in Baltimore and Philadelphia, notably at Church of the Holy Communion, Philadelphia, 1874–1904. An admired preacher and prolific author, he was one of the founders of the General Council of the Evangelical Lutheran Church in North America.

SEITZ, DON CARLOS (*b. Portage, O., 1862; d. Brooklyn, N.Y., 1935*), journalist. On staff of *Brooklyn Eagle*, 1880–91. After a brief period as assistant publisher of the New York *Recorder*, he went with the New York *World* of which he was first an editor, then advertising manager, and finally business manager from 1898 to 1923. A liberal and witty man of complete independence and fearlessness, he believed that a newspaper was an institution for public service; during his tenure, the *World* became one of the nation's powerful liberal voices and he was in no way responsible for the decline and disappearance of the Pulitzer properties in New York. Retiring in 1926 from daily journalism, he served on the staffs of the *Outlook* and the *Churchman*. He was also author of many books, including biographies of Paul Jones, Artemus Ward, Braxton Bragg, Joseph Pulitzer and Horace Greeley. [*Supp. 1*]

SEIXAS, GERSHOM MENDES (*b. New York, N.Y., 1746; d. New York, 1816*). Chosen rabbi of the Spanish and Portuguese synagogue of New York (Shearith Israel), 1768, he was for many years New York's chief professor of Hebrew and through a great portion of his fifty-year ministry one of the principal spokesmen of American Jewry. The first rabbi to preach sermons in English in an American synagogue, he constantly advocated the full participation by Jews in the life of the new democratic American state. He was on the evidence of his public statements and prayers a strong supporter of the American cause. He served as regent and trustee of Columbia College, 1784–1815.

SÉJOUR, VICTOR (*b. New Orleans, La., 1817; d. Paris, France, 1874*), dramatist. Born of colored parents, Séjour was educated in New Orleans and Paris and in 1841 achieved celebrity with a heroic poem, *Le Retour de Napoléon*. Influenced by Émile Augier, he became a writer of immediately popular dramatic spectacles; among his 21 plays which were produced in Paris, his greatest successes were *Richard III*

(1852), *Les Noces Vénitiennes* (1855), *Le Fils de la Nuit* (1856) and *Les Volontaires de 1814* (1862). He died of tuberculosis after experiencing a decline in his fortunes.

SELBY, WILLIAM (*b. probably England, c. 1739; d. Boston, Mass., 1798*), musician, composer. Emigrated to Boston *ante* October 1771; was at various times organist of King's Chapel. Three choral concerts organized and directed by him, 1782, 1786 and 1787, encouraged a taste for cantatas and oratorios in Boston and undoubtedly influenced the movement which led to formation of the Handel and Haydn Society more than 15 years after his death. Selby's only compositions extant today are a few songs.

SELDEN, GEORGE BALDWIN (*b. Clarkson, N.Y., 1846; d. Rochester, N.Y., 1922*), patent attorney, inventor. After developing a light-weight, high-speed, three-cylinder gasoline compression engine employing hydrocarbon liquid fuels (1877), Selden then designed a so-called road locomotive which was virtually an automobile. Having applied for a U.S. patent, May 1879, he tried without success to secure financial help in building his machine; he therefore delayed the issue of a patent to him until November 1895. Meanwhile, the automobile had made rapid strides but the assignees of Selden's basic patent (who were obliged to pay him royalty) required all other persons manufacturing automobiles to pay for the privilege by licensing. The first successful action to compel payment was brought against the Winton Motor Co., 1900. A suit against the Ford Motor Co. initiated in 1903 came to final adjudication in January 1911 when it was held that Selden had a true and valid patent only with respect to the use of a two-cycle type of engine as designated in the patent. Inasmuch as all manufacturers were by this time using a four-cycle engine, no further royalties were required to be paid.

SELFRIDGE, THOMAS OLIVER (*b. Charlestown, Mass., 1836; d. 1924*), naval officer. Graduated U.S. Naval Academy, 1854. Cited for conspicuous gallantry during the Civil War. Surveyed Isthmus of Darien for an interoceanic canal, 1869–70; later surveyed the Amazon and Madeira Rivers. Commissioned rear-admiral, 1896, he retired, 1898.

SELIGMAN, ARTHUR (*b. Santa Fé, N. Mex., 1871; d. 1933*), merchant, banker, Democratic politician. Governor of New Mexico, 1931–33.

SELIGMAN, EDWIN ROBERT ANDERSON (*b. New York, N.Y., 1861; d. Lake Placid, N.Y., 1939*), economist. Son of Joseph Seligman; brother of Isaac N. Seligman. Graduated Columbia, 1879; LL.B., 1884; Ph.D., 1885. Beginning his teaching career at Columbia as a lecturer, he was promoted to full professor, 1891, and was the first McVickar Professor of Political Economy, 1904–31. A unique combination of scholar and public figure, Seligman was author of *The Economic Interpretation of History* (1902) and *Principles of Economics, with Special Reference to American Conditions* (1905), two important and influential works; he was also editor-in-chief of the *Encyclopaedia of the Social Sciences* (1930–35) and was principally responsible for raising the funds needed for this monumental project. He was best known, however, for his pioneering achievements in public finance, in which field he was author of a number of significant books which included *On the Shifting and Incidence of Taxation* (1892), *Progressive Taxation in Theory and Practice* (1894), *Essays in Taxation* (1895) and *The Income Tax* (1911). The central theoretical core of his work was the marginal economics of which John Bates Clark was one of the leading formulators, yet Seligman allowed in his own work for considerable qualification in the theory. Conservative by nature, he was respected by enlightened members of the business community and frequently served the government as an adviser in matters of taxation; his writings and personal testimony helped shape the Transportation Act of 1920, and he was also active in the campaign for an effective central banking system that eventuated in the Federal Reserve Act. A worker for honest municipal government, for conservation of natural resources and for a fair policy toward labor, Seligman was probably the first eminent American economist to advocate the doctrine of the living wage. [*Supp. 2*]

SELIGMAN, ISAAC NEWTON (*b. Staten Island, N.Y., 1855; d. New York, N.Y., 1917*), banker, civic leader. Son of Joseph Seligman. President of the family banking house of J. & W. Seligman & Co. *post* 1894.

SELIGMAN, JESSE (*b. Baiersdorf, Bavaria, 1827; d. Coronado, Calif., 1894*), banker, philanthropist. Brother of Joseph Seligman. Emigrated to America as a boy; was in dry-goods business with a brother at Watertown, N.Y., 1848–50. Removing to California, he prospered as a merchant in San Francisco and served on the Vigilance Committee of 1851 and later on the Committee of Twenty-one. Removing to New York City, 1857, he joined his brother Joseph's clothing firm and later became a partner in the banking firm of J. & W. Seligman & Co. (organized, 1862). He succeeded his brother Joseph as head of the firm, 1880, and was for a generation one of the leading financiers of the United States.

SELIGMAN, JOSEPH (*b. Baiersdorf, Bavaria, 1819; d. New Orleans, La., 1880*), financier, civic leader. Brother of Jesse Seligman; father of Isaac N. Seligman. Emigrating to America, 1837, he served for some time as secretary to Asa Packer. He founded a clothing firm with his brothers including Jesse, 1857, which was transformed early in 1862 into the banking house of J. & W. Seligman & Co. Strong supporters of the Union, the Seligmans promoted large sales of U.S. bonds in Frankfurt at a time when it was

almost impossible to sell the national securities in England or France. During the presidency of U.S. Grant, Joseph Seligman was one of his confidential financial advisers, and throughout the 1870's the firm figured prominently in the conversion and refunding of the obligations of the United States. Joseph Seligman was also active in New York City civic affairs and was a member of the Committee of Seventy which ousted the Tweed Ring.

SELIJNS, HENRICUS (*b. Amsterdam, Holland, 1636; d. New York, N.Y., 1701*), Dutch Reformed clergyman, poet. Pastor in present Brooklyn, N.Y., 1660–64, and in New York City *post* 1682. A cultured and tolerant man and a popular preacher, he secured for the Dutch Reformed Church the first church charter granted in the colony (1696).

SELIKOVITSCH, GOETZEL (*b. Rietavas, Lithuania, 1863; d. 1926*), Orientalist, journalist. Graduated École des Hautes Études, Paris, France, 1884. After traveling widely in the Near East and Africa, he came to America in 1887. Taking up Yiddish journalism as a profession, he served on the staff of the *Jewish Daily News* in New York City from 1901 until his death. He was author of a number of scholarly works in Hebrew and French.

SELLERS, COLEMAN (*b. Philadelphia, Pa., 1827; d. Philadelphia, 1907*), engineer. Grandson of Charles W. Peale. While chief engineer of William Sellers & Co., 1856–86, he patented a number of inventions, notably the Sellers coupling. Conducting a consulting practice thereafter, he was important in the design and construction of the hydro-electric power development at Niagara Falls.

SELLERS, ISAIAH (*b. Iredell Co., N.C., c. 1802; d. Memphis, Tenn., 1864*), pioneer steamboat pilot. An authority on Mississippi River navigation, he made a number of noteworthy record runs and was first to use the pseudonym of "Mark Twain" in contributions to the New Orleans *Daily Picayune*.

SELLERS, MATTHEW BACON (*b. Baltimore, Md., 1869; d. Ardsley-on-Hudson, N.Y., 1932*), patent lawyer, pioneer in aerodynamics. Served on Naval Consulting Board, 1915–18 and *post* 1919. Patented a quadroplane, 1911, and secured other patents for airplane gear; was technical editor of *Aeronautics post* 1911.

SELLERS, WILLIAM (*b. Upper Darby, Pa., 1824; d. 1905*), machine tool builder. President of William Sellers & Co. and predecessor firms in Philadelphia, Pa., *post* 1848; also headed Edge Moor Iron Co. *post* 1868, and Midvale Steel Co. *post* 1873. Sellers held about ninety U.S. patents for machine tools of all kinds; the most original of his inventions was the spiral geared planer, patented 1862; he was one of the first designers to make the form of a machine follow the function to be performed. He was also author of the present system of standard screw threads (first proposed by him, 1864).

SELLSTEDT, LARS GUSTAF (*b. Sundsvall, Sweden, 1819; d. Buffalo, N.Y., 1911*), seaman, portrait painter, organizer and president of Buffalo Fine Arts Academy.

SELYNS, HENRICUS. [See SELIJNS, HENRICUS, 1636–1701.]

SEMBRICH, MARCELLA (*b. Wisnieczyk, Galicia, 1858; d. New York, N.Y., 1935*), operatic and concert soprano. Professional name of Praxede Marcelline Kochanska, who married Wilhelm Stengel, 1877. Urged by Franz Liszt to devote herself principally to singing, Mme. Sembrich was a versatile instrumentalist as well as a soprano of extraordinary range and brilliance. She made her début at Athens, Greece, in *I Puritani*, 1877; her début at the Metropolitan Opera, New York, 1883, was in the role of *Lucia*. After singing in the leading opera houses of Europe, she rejoined the Metropolitan company with whom she sang, 1898–1909. *Post* 1917, she was active as a teacher. [*Supp. 1*]

SEMMES, ALEXANDER JENKINS (*b. Georgetown, D.C., 1828; d. New Orleans, La., 1898*), physician, Confederate surgeon, Roman Catholic clergyman. Cousin of Raphael Semmes; brother of Thomas J. Semmes. Served in the priesthood, principally in Georgia, *post* 1878.

SEMMES, RAPHAEL (*b. Charles Co., Md., 1809; d. Point Clear, Ala., 1877*), naval officer. Cousin of Alexander J. Semmes and Thomas J. Semmes. Appointed midshipman, 1826, he served in routine posts at sea until his promotion to lieutenant, 1837; thereafter, until the outbreak of the Mexican War, he was on survey duty on the southern coast and in the Gulf of Mexico. Commanding the brig *Somers* on the Mexican blockade, 1846, he lost the vessel in a tropical storm, but was exonerated of any blame. He served thereafter on shore at Vera Cruz and in the march to Mexico City, receiving several citations for gallantry. On awaiting-order status for a great part of the time, 1847–61, he practiced law, settling near Mobile, Ala., 1849. Promoted commander, 1855, he resigned from the U.S. Navy, 1861, and entered the navy of the Confederacy. He rebuilt and commissioned C.S.S. *Sumter*, formerly a packet vessel, and took her to sea in June as a commerce raider. Highly successful in operations in Caribbean waters and off the South American coast, he sailed to Gibraltar where he was blockaded by Union forces; laying up the *Sumter*, April 1862, he discharged her crew and sold her later to a British firm. Promoted captain and ordered to command the C.S.S. *Alabama*, nearing completion at Liverpool, England, he took the ship to the Azores where he armed her and set about his old business of destroying U.S. commerce. He ranged from the Atlantic whaling grounds and the Grand Banks to the coast of Brazil, taking 44 merchantmen. Sailing for Africa, he arrived at Capetown, August 1863, and then went on a long cruise across the Indian Ocean and contiguous waters, returning up the Atlantic to Cherbourg, France, June 1864. He had by then captured a total of 82 merchantmen and had also defeated and sunk U.S.S. *Hatteras*. At Cherbourg, awaiting French permission to overhaul, Semmes was challenged by U.S.S. *Kearsarge* which had appeared outside the three-mile limit. The ships engaged on the morning of June 19, 1864, and fought in a circle of less than one-half mile in diameter. Heavily battered by the Union man-of-war, the *Alabama* sank shortly after noon. Rescued by an English yacht from the water, Semmes was taken to England and returned to the Confederacy by way of Mexico. Assigned as rear-admiral to command of the James River squadron, January 1865, he burned his ships on the evacuation of Richmond and turned his men into a naval brigade which was surrendered at Greensboro, N.C., as a part of Gen. J. E. Johnston's army. Paroled, Semmes was arrested in December 1865 and held for a short time in prison but released by presidential order. Hounded out of one employment after another, he engaged in the practice of law at Mobile until his death. He was author of *Service Afloat and Ashore* (1851) and *Memoirs of Service Afloat during the War between the States* (1869).

SEMMES, THOMAS JENKINS (*b. Georgetown, D.C., 1824; d. 1899*), lawyer, Louisiana legislator. Brother of Alexander J. Semmes; cousin of Raphael Semmes. Graduated Georgetown (D.C.), 1842; Harvard Law School, 1845. Removed to New Orleans, La., 1850, where he practiced thereafter. Attorney-general of Louisiana, 1859–61; Confederate senator from Louisiana, 1862–65. The most notable part of his career followed the Civil War. He was a guiding influence in the Louisiana constitutional convention of 1879, and for years his name appeared as counsel in nearly every leading case before civil courts in the state. He was also professor of civil law in the University of Louisiana (later Tulane University).

SEMPLE, ELLEN CHURCHILL (*b. Louisville, Ky., 1863; d. W. Palm Beach, Fla., 1932*), anthropogeographer. Graduated Vassar, 1882; studied at Leipzig under Friedrich Ratzel. Taught at University of Chicago and at Clark University; was president of the Association of American Geographers, 1921, the only woman ever to hold that position. Among her books, all of which are outstanding, *Influences of Geographic Environment* (1911) was said to have shaped the whole trend and content of geographic thought in the United States.

SENEY, GEORGE INGRAHAM (*b. Astoria, N.Y., 1826; d. New York, N.Y., 1893*), banker, art collector, philanthropist.

SENN, NICHOLAS (*b. Buchs, St. Gall, Switzerland, 1844; d. Chicago, Ill., 1908*), surgeon. Came to America as a boy. Graduated Chicago Medical College, 1868; M.D., University of Munich, 1878. Practiced principally in Milwaukee, Wis., 1874–93, and thereafter in Chicago where he taught surgery at several schools, including Chicago Polyclinic and University of Chicago. He maintained a lifelong interest in military medicine.

SENNETT, GEORGE BURRITT (*b. Sinclairville, N.Y., 1840; d. Youngstown, O., 1900*), manufacturer of oil-well machinery, ornithologist. Made prolonged and important studies in bird life of the lower Rio Grande region of southern Texas. The materials gathered by him were utilized and described, however, by others.

SEQUOYAH (*b. Taskigi, Tenn., c. 1770; d. possibly Tamaulipas, Mexico, 1843*), inventor of the Cherokee syllabary. Crippled for life in a hunting accident, he began his efforts to reduce his tribal language to characters c. 1809 and, after much ridicule and opposition, completed his table of 85 or 86 characters in 1821. A tribal council approved his work and in a short time thousands of Cherokees had learned to read and write. Sequoyah has been called the ablest intelligence produced among the American Indians.

SERGEANT, HENRY CLARK (*b. Rochester, N.Y., 1834; d. Westfield, N.J., 1907*), machinist. After securing a number of patents for useful inventions, 1854–68, he established a machine shop in New York City for development of crude ideas brought to him by other inventors. After working with Simon Ingersoll c. 1870 in development of the idea of a rock drill, he was associated with Ingersoll in at least one patent and was responsible for the organization of the original Ingersoll Rock Drill Co., also adapting the device to use of compressed air rather than steam. Selling out his interest, 1883, he patented a new rock drill, 1884; after manufacturing it for a short time, he joined his company with the Ingersoll company. Among his other notable inventions of a later date were several types of valves for air compressors, the "tappet" drill and the Sergeant release rotation.

SERGEANT, JOHN (*b. Newark, N.J., 1710; d. 1749*), Congregational clergyman, missionary to the Housatonic Indians. Graduated Yale, 1729. Entered permanently upon his work among Indians, 1735. Ministered principally in vicinity of present towns of Sheffield and Stockbridge, Mass.

SERGEANT, JOHN (*b. Philadelphia, Pa., 1779; d. 1852*), lawyer, Pennsylvania official. Son of Jonathan D. Sergeant; brother of Thomas Sergeant. Graduated College of New Jersey (Princeton), 1795; studied law with Jared Ingersoll. Practicing in Philadelphia *post* 1799, he became a leader of the bar and was a member of the intellectual group led by Joseph Dennie and Nicholas Biddle. Elected to Congress from Pennsylvania, he served in that body, 1815–23, 1827–29 and 1837–41, successively as a Federalist, as a National Republican, and as a Whig. A supporter of the "American system," he opposed the Missouri Compromise and was for many years the chief legal and political adviser to the Second Bank of the United States; he is credited with having had major influence in inducing Biddle to apply for renewal of the Bank's charter. President of the Pennsylvania constitutional convention, 1837–38, he took the lead in the fight over the judiciary. Sergeant's great strength was as a forensic legalist, less eloquent than intellectual. In his cases before the Supreme Court (*Osborn vs. United States Bank, Worcester vs. Georgia,* and the like) he advocated national powers as opposed to state rights. His stature may be measured by the offices which he declined; these included a justiceship of the U.S. Supreme Court, a cabinet office under Harrison and the embassy to England under Tyler.

SERGEANT, JONATHAN DICKINSON (*b. Newark, N.J., 1746; d. Philadelphia, Pa., 1793*), lawyer, Revolutionary patriot. Nephew of John Sergeant (1710–1749); grandson of Jonathan Dickinson. Graduated College of New Jersey (Princeton), 1762. As member of the New Jersey Provincial Congress, 1776, he led in forming a state constitution; he was also member of the Continental Congress, 1776–77, representing New Jersey. After removing to Pennsylvania, he engaged in politics there and was attorney-general of that state, 1777–80. His zeal for democratic principles led him to support the French Revolution, and he was prominent during the Edmond Genet episode as a friend of France. Among his children were John Sergeant (1779–1852) and Thomas Sergeant.

SERGEANT, THOMAS (*b. Philadelphia, Pa., 1782; d. 1860*), Pennsylvania official and jurist, legal author. Son of Jonathan D. Sergeant; brother of John Sergeant (1779–1852). Graduated College of New Jersey (Princeton), 1798; studied law under Jared Ingersoll; was associate justice, Pennsylvania supreme court, 1834–46. Strongly opposed amendment of state constitution (1837–38) which provided for popular election of judges. Excelled as a legal writer.

SERRA, JUNÍPERO (*b. Petra, Mallorca, 1713; d. Mission of San Carlos, near Monterey, Calif., 1784*), Roman Catholic clergyman, Franciscan. After winning early distinction as professor of philosophy and preacher, he volunteered for mission work and arrived in Mexico City with Francisco Palóu, January 1750. After mission work among Indians northeast of Querétaro and parish duties in the capital city, he was sent as *presidente* of the new Franciscan mission field in Lower California, 1767. Having engaged to cooperate with the government by founding missions in Upper California, Father Serra with five companions accompanied the expedition of Gaspar de Portolá northward and founded San Diego mission in July 1769, the first of the 21 missions eventually erected on the California coast. During Father Serra's presidency, nine of these missions were founded: San Diego, San Carlos, San Antonio, San Gabriel, San Luis Obispo, San Francisco de Assisi, San Juan Capistrano, Santa Clara and San Buenaventura. In his differences with the military authorities, no one could question either his patriotism as a Spaniard or his sense of justice as a spiritual leader and protector of the rights of the Indians. He traveled constantly on foot from mission to mission, aiding his associates by his counsel and encouragement.

SERRELL, EDWARD WELLMAN (*b. London, England, 1826; d. New York, N.Y., 1906*), civil and military engineer. Came to America as a child. An expert in railroad and bridge design and construction, Serrell organized and commanded the 1st New York Engineers at the outbreak of the Civil War; he later became chief engineer of the X Corps and chief engineer and chief of staff of the Army of the James. During the siege of Charleston, S.C., he devised and personally supervised construction of the famous "Swamp Angel" battery.

SERVOSS, THOMAS LOWERY (*b. Philadelphia, Pa., 1786; d. New York, N.Y., 1866*), merchant, shipowner. Active in trade at Natchez, Miss., and New Orleans, La., 1810–25, Servoss was representative of those Northerners who made threefold profits in the cotton belt by selling Northern goods, shipping back cotton in return, and transporting the goods in both directions. He operated a profitable line of sailing packet ships between New York and New Orleans, 1827–31, and later engaged in banking in New York.

SESSIONS, HENRY HOWARD (*b. Madrid, N.Y., 1847; d. Chicago, Ill., 1915*), railroad car builder, inventor (1887) of the passenger car "vestibule."

SESTINI, BENEDICT (*b. Florence, Italy, 1816; d. Frederick, Md., 1890*), Roman Catholic clergyman, Jesuit, mathematician, astronomer. Came to America, 1848. At the observatory of Georgetown University, Washington, D.C., he made observations of sun spots, 1850, which he sketched and which were later engraved and published, 1853. These are rated as among the best studies of the sun's maculae antedating the application of photography. Father Sestini was also an architect, and in 1866 founded the widely read Catholic publication *Messenger of the Sacred Heart* which he edited until 1885.

SETH, JAMES (*b. Edinburgh, Scotland, 1860; d. 1924*), philosopher. While professor of philosophy at Brown, 1892–96, he completed his most important work, *A Study of Ethical Principles* (published, 1894). In this work he sought to mediate between Utilitarianism and the Kantian and other rationalistic systems, finding in Personality a concept that unites the truth of both. Sage Professor of Moral Philosophy at

Cornell University, 1896–98, he returned to the University of Edinburgh as professor of moral philosophy and continued in that post until the end of his life. He was a strong force for social and other reforms in Scotland.

SETON, ELIZABETH ANN BAYLEY (*b. New York, N.Y., 1774; d. Emmitsburg, Md., 1821*), foundress of the American Sisters of Charity, known as Mother Seton. Daughter of Richard Bayley, she was educated principally by her father and in 1794 married William Magee Seton, a New York merchant. In 1797, with Isabella M. Graham and others, she founded a society for relief of widows, the first charitable organization in New York City. Accompanying her husband to Italy, she made her first contact with Catholicism there and on returning home after his death in December 1803, she became a convert in 1805. Estranged from her family and friends, she began a school for girls in Baltimore, Md., 1808, and there in the spring of 1809 with four companions formed a community which took the name "Sisters of St. Joseph." Removing to Emmitsburg, Md., that summer, they took, with some modifications, the rule of the Daughters of Charity of St. Vincent de Paul; *post* 1812 they were known as the Sisters of Charity of St. Joseph and constituted the first native American religious community. Mother Seton served for the rest of her life as the first superior and, in spite of the poverty that threatened her community's existence, formed her associates into effective teachers and model religious. Her cause for canonization was introduced at Rome by Cardinal Gibbons *c.* 1907. She was the grandmother of Robert and William Seton and the aunt of James R. Bayley.

SETON, ROBERT (*b. Pisa, Italy, 1839; d. 1927*), Roman Catholic clergyman. Grandson of Elizabeth A. B. Seton; brother of William Seton. A brilliant student at several Roman colleges *post* 1857, he was ordained in 1865 and gave up the chance of a notable ecclesiastical career to serve as chaplain to St. Elizabeth's convent near Madison, N.J., and as a pastor in Jersey City. Returning to Rome, 1902, he served until 1914 as an unofficial link between the Vatican and America. He passed the remainder of his life in virtual retirement, principally at Emmitsburg, Md., and Madison, N.J.

SETON, WILLIAM (*b. New York, N.Y., 1835; d. New York, 1905*), lawyer, Union soldier, author. Grandson of Elizabeth A. B. Seton; brother of Robert Seton.

SETTLE, THOMAS (*b. Rockingham Co., N.C., 1831; d. 1888*), politician, jurist, North Carolina legislator. Participated in meeting which organized the North Carolina radical party, 1865, and introduced resolution which identified it with the Republican party. Associate judge, supreme court of North Carolina, 1868–71, 1872–76. He served also briefly as U.S. minister to Peru and was a U.S. district judge for Florida *post* 1877.

SEVERANCE, CAROLINE MARIA SEYMOUR (*b. Canandaigua, N.Y., 1820; d. 1914*), founder of women's clubs in Cleveland, O., Boston, Mass., and Los Angeles, Calif.

SEVERANCE, FRANK HAYWARD (*b. Manchester, Mass., 1856; d. 1931*), Buffalo, N.Y., journalist, historian. Secretary, Buffalo Historical Society, *post* 1901; authority on the history of the Niagara frontier.

SEVERANCE, LOUIS HENRY (*b. Cleveland, O., 1838; d. Cleveland, 1913*), capitalist. Engaged in oil production at Titusville, Pa., *post* 1864, he became associated with the Standard Oil Co. of Ohio and served as its treasurer, 1876–94. In association with Herman Frasch and others, he was a founder of the Union Sulphur Co. His principal benefactions were made to the Presbyterian Church and to its missions.

SEVIER, AMBROSE HUNDLEY (*b. Greene Co., Tenn., 1801; d. near Little Rock, Ark., 1848*), lawyer, Arkansas legislator, planter. Settled in Arkansas, 1821; became associated by marriage with a powerful, political family headed by Richard M. Johnson. Territorial delegate from Arkansas to Congress, Democrat, 1828–36, he took a prominent part in achieving statehood for Arkansas and served as U.S. senator, 1836–48. An expansionist, he warmly supported the Mexican War and served with Nathan Clifford in the conclusion of negotiations for peace under the Trist treaty, 1848.

SEVIER, JOHN (*b. near present New Market, Va., 1745; d. Alabama, 1815*), pioneer, soldier. Emigrated to the remote frontier that is now East Tennessee, 1773. Continuing to move down the Holston valley as settlement advanced, he lived on the Nolachucky River, 1783–90. *Post* 1790, he resided in or near Knoxville. An acknowledged leader of the backwoodsmen, he was a member of the local Committee of Safety, 1776, and a representative in the Provincial Congress of North Carolina. As an officer of the militia, he led a body of Tennesseeans across the Smokies to join in the victory over the British at King's Mountain, 1780, and later set out upon an expedition against the Cherokees. During 1781 and 1782 he continued raiding against the Indians. At the end of the Revolution he joined with William Blount and others in a project for colonizing at Muscle Shoals. At first opposing the movement for organization of a separate state of Franklin, he later put himself at the head of it and was elected governor. Concerting a military expedition against the Indians with the state of Georgia, he alienated many liberals among the pioneers and lost prestige when Georgia failed to give aid. The defeat of Sevier's faction in a so-called battle, February 1788, resulted in the virtual extinction of the state of Franklin. Denounced as a reckless disturber of the public peace, he sought refuge on the extreme frontier with a group of fol-lowers and sank to the level of a bushwhacker, defying the efforts of Congress and entering into dubious correspondence with Spanish agents. Taking advantage of a new trend in public affairs, Sevier came forth as an advocate of the new Federal Constitution and with the aid of William Blount succeeded in winning a full pardon and election to the North Carolina Senate, 1789. After a brief term in Congress (1789–91), he devoted most of his attention during the territorial period of Tennessee to his plantation and his business concerns; he took no part in the Genet affair or in the conspiracies of Blount and Aaron Burr. Elected first governor of the state of Tennessee, he served 1796–1801 and 1803–09. Engaged in a bitter feud with Andrew Jackson from about 1796 to the end of his life, he served again in the state Senate, 1809–11, and was a congressman, 1811–15, serving on several committees and supporting the administration.

SEWALL, ARTHUR (*b. Bath, Maine, 1835; d. near Bath, 1900*), shipbuilder. Brother of Frank Sewall; father of Harold M. Sewall. Launching the first of his eighty vessels, 1855, Sewall and his partners did much to keep the wooden sailing vessel alive in its period of decline. During the 1890's he built the *Rappahannock, Shenandoah, Susquehanna* and *Roanoke,* largest and last of the great American full-rigged wooden ships.

SEWALL, FRANK (*b. Bath, Maine, 1837; d. Washington, D.C., 1915*), Swedenborgian clergyman, author, educator. Brother of Arthur Sewall. Made his chief contribution to the life of his church in the development of its forms of worship.

SEWALL, HAROLD MARSH (*b. Bath, Maine, 1860; d. New York, N.Y., 1924*), diplomat, Maine legislator. Son of Arthur Sewall. Opposed German *coup d'état* at Apia, Samoa, 1887, while U.S. consul general there. As U.S. minister to Hawaii, 1897–98, he received transfer of sovereignty of the islands and remained in Hawaii as U.S. special agent until establishment of regular territorial government, 1900.

SEWALL, JONATHAN (*b. Boston, Mass., 1728; d. St. John, N.B., Canada, 1796*), lawyer, Loyalist. Graduated Harvard, 1748. Originally the intimate friend of John Adams, he became an adherent of the Crown *c.* 1761 because of opposition by James Otis to a request made by him to the General Court. Successively solicitor-general and attorney-general of Massachusetts, and *post* 1768 a judge of the vice-admiralty court, he sailed for England early in 1775 whence he emigrated to Canada, 1788. A witty man, Sewall was a frequent and able contributor to the press.

SEWALL, JONATHAN MITCHELL (*b. Salem, Mass., 1748; d. Portsmouth, N.H., 1808*), lawyer, occasional poet. Grand-nephew of Samuel Sewall. Author of *Miscellaneous Poems* (1801).

SEWALL, JOSEPH ADDISON (*b. Scarboro, Maine, 1830; d. 1917*), physician, educator. As first president of the University of Colorado, 1877–87, he developed that institution under most adverse conditions; he later taught at the University of Denver, where he was also dean of the school of pharmacy and acted as chemist for the city of Denver.

SEWALL, MAY ELIZA WRIGHT (*b. Milwaukee, Wis., 1844; d. 1920*), teacher, feminist. Principal for many years of the Girls' Classical School, Indianapolis, Ind., Mrs. Sewall served as chairman of the executive committee of the National Suffrage Association and was a prominent figure in the International Council of Women. In 1889, when the Federation of Women's Clubs was formed, she became its first president.

SEWALL, SAMUEL (*b. Bishopstoke, England, 1652; d. Boston, Mass., 1730*), merchant, colonial magistrate. Born of New England parents, he returned with his family to Boston c. 1661 and graduated from Harvard, 1671. Active in politics and the holder of many legislative and judicial offices in the colony throughout his life, he was particularly noteworthy for his service in 1692 as a special commissioner to try the cases of witchcraft at Salem. Sewall was the only one of the judges who ever publicly admitted that he had been in error in this matter; he made his confession of error in Old South Church, Boston, 1697. His tract *The Selling of Joseph* (1700) was one of the earliest appeals in the anti-slavery cause. He was author also of several tracts on religious subjects, on the Indians and on politics, and wrote verses which circulated in manuscript form. He is remembered chiefly as a writer for his diary which covers the period 1674–1729 with a gap of about eight years, 1677–85. This work, which was first published in *Massachusetts Historical Society Collections* (1878–82), is an incomparable picture of the mind and life of a New England Puritan of the transition period. Sewall, as unwittingly portrayed by himself, emerges as mercenary, average in mentality, conventional and introspective, yet also affectionate, honorable, strong and fearless. Other American diaries possess higher importance from a political point of view, but none so vividly reproduces the diarist's entire world.

SEWALL, STEPHEN (*b. York, Maine, 1734; d. Cambridge, Mass., 1804*), classicist, Hebraist. Graduated Harvard, 1761. Succeeding Judah Monis as teacher of Hebrew at Harvard, 1761, he was first Hancock Professor of Hebrew and Oriental languages, 1765–85. His interests also included science and politics, and he was an early supporter of the Revolution.

SEWARD, FREDERICK WILLIAM (*b. Auburn, N.Y., 1830; d. 1915*), journalist, diplomat, New York legislator. Son of William H. Seward and his secretary and associate, 1849–72. Author-editor of *Autobiography of William H. Seward* (1877) and other works.

SEWARD, GEORGE FREDERICK (*b. Florida, N.Y., 1840; d. 1910*), diplomat. Nephew of William H. Seward. In the consular service, 1861–76, he was appointed U.S. minister to China, 1876; he resigned, 1879, after criticism of his record by the Democrats in Congress. He was president, Fidelity and Casualty Co., 1893–1910.

SEWARD, THEODORE FRELINGHUYSEN (*b. Florida, N.Y., 1835; d. E. Orange, N.J., 1902*), musician, teacher, hymnologist. Studied in Boston, Mass., with Lowell Mason, George F. Root, and Thomas Hastings (1784–1872). Edited a collection of Negro spirituals, *Jubilee Songs* (1872), and a number of other collections of songs and hymns; was co-author with Lowell Mason of *The Pestalozzian Music Teacher* (1871). In helping to preserve the Negro spirituals, he made his most distinctive contribution.

SEWARD, WILLIAM HENRY (*b. Florida, N.Y., 1801; d. Auburn, N.Y., 1872*), statesman. Father of Frederick W. Seward; uncle of George F. Seward. Graduated Union College, 1820; was admitted to the bar, 1822; established himself in Auburn, N.Y., 1823. Moved by distrust of the Southern Jeffersonians and by his great interest in internal improvements, he supported DeWitt Clinton for governor and John Quincy Adams for president, 1824; the enthusiasm he then felt for Adams had a part in forming his own political ideals. Drawn by expediency and conviction into the Anti-Masonic movement, he became a close friend of Thurlow Weed and through Weed's influence was elected to the New York State senate, 1830. After four years' service he ran for governor as a Whig but was defeated by William L. Marcy. Devoting himself to the practice of law, he acquired a small competence as agent for the Holland Land Co. in handling disputes with its settlers. Nominated, with Weed's assistance, by the Whigs for governor, 1838, he was forced for the first time to face the slavery issue and expressed a cautious opposition to that institution.

As governor of New York, 1839–43, he revealed an optimistic temper, strong humanitarian sympathies and also impulsiveness and a tendency to challenge majority opinion. Urging internal improvements upon the legislature in the midst of a depression, he brought about impairment of the state's credit. His declaration that the New York City public schools should be staffed by teachers of the same faith and racial extraction as the Catholic immigrant children brought down on him a nativist storm of criticism, and he was forced to retreat from this position. While he was governor he took an advanced ground on the matter of slavery and won the support of the growing Abolitionist element. In the belief that he was too far in advance of public opinion to prosper politically, he declined renomination in 1842 and returned to legal practice as a chancery court and patent specialist. He continued to take part in almost every campaign, however, and by championing the Irish cause won the support of Irish-American voters.

In 1848 he was elected to the U.S. Senate, many Democrats as well as all the Whig members of the legislature voting for him. In the debates over the proposed Compromise of 1850, Seward opposed all compromise and asserted that the fugitive-slave law was impossible of enforcement in the North. In a speech of March 11, 1850, he declared that the slave system would either be ended "by gradual voluntary effort and with compensation" within the framework of the Union, or the Union would be itself dissolved and a civil war ensue. In the same speech he used the famous phrase "a higher law than the Constitution," which was widely misunderstood as a threat of action outside the American charter. An intense Whig partisan, he had in common with Weed a great interest in party politics and party victory, so he curbed, for a time, his dislike of compromise and tolerated a party policy which would raise as few perplexing questions of principle as possible. Meantime, in the Senate, he expressed an ardent nationalism and republicanism with such recklessness as to lay him open to the charge of demagogy. He played a leading part in the welcome to Kossuth, protested against Russian intervention in Hungary, and once again championed the Irish cause. In the debates on the Kansas-Nebraska bill, Seward showed greater caution than in the discussions of 1850, although he spoke vigorously against the bill and warned the South of the conflict to which he felt it would inevitably give rise. *Post* 1854, the rise of the Republican party in the West and the Know-Nothing party in the East and South created embarrassment for him as a Whig party leader; however, with Weed, he was able to negate the efforts of the Know-Nothings and secure re-election to the Senate. After the merger of the old Whig party with the rising Republican organization in the fall of 1855, Seward's speeches on slavery became of the most forthright character, and from that time until 1860 he embodied the growing anti-slavery sentiment of the North as much as any man. He advocated admission of Kansas under the Topeka Constitution, denounced the Dred Scott decision as product of a conspiracy, and in October 1858 made at Rochester, N.Y., the famous speech in which he declared that the slavery struggle was "an irrepressible conflict." Perhaps for tactical reasons, however, he supported the Douglas idea of decision by popular sovereignty in Kansas, 1858, and in a later speech minimized the effect of the "irrepressible conflict" speech by praising the moderation of the slave-holders and blaming the free Democrats of the North for the events of the past few years.

Passed over expediently in 1856 by the Republicans who favored John C. Frémont for the presidential nomination, he was undoubtedly the leading Republican candidate when the National Convention met in Chicago, June 1860. The hostility of Horace Greeley,

the opposition of the Know-Nothings, and Seward's own radical utterances, however, conspired to deprive him of the nomination. With his usual outward calm and very real generosity, he campaigned for the Republican ticket throughout the North and in the crisis following the election employed conciliatory language and methods advocating, among other things, a constitutional convention to settle outstanding difficulties.

Appointed U.S. secretary of state by Lincoln, he accepted, although he was displeased at the choice of Salmon P. Chase and Blair for the cabinet. He took office believing that he would be the dominant figure in the administration, and during March and April 1861 conducted himself in a manner which hardly represented him at his best. His "Some Thoughts for the President's Consideration" of April 1861 advocated embroiling the United States with most of Europe and waging actual war on Spain and France as a means of preserving the Union; he also virtually suggested that the president abdicate his power to the secretary of state. He engaged in maneuvers behind Lincoln's back by which the reinforcement of Fort Pickens was delayed and the expedition to Fort Sumter weakened. His conduct of his office during the four years of war, however, deserves high praise, for he abandoned his early truculence toward other nations and expressed the views of the United States with dignity and force. His handling of the seizure of Mason and Slidell on board the *Trent* was masterly. He proved able to avert the possibility of European intervention in the Civil War and to check anti-Northern agitation in France and England by the self-confident optimism of his dispatches and the skillful use of the question of slavery. Seward's steady pressure (together with the diplomatic skill of Charles Francis Adams) led to British action against outfitting of Confederate cruisers in British ports. Seward was even more adroit in his management of the matter of French intervention in Mexico.

When the war was over, his strong instinct for expansionism revived. In 1867 he negotiated the cession of Alaska and secured prompt ratification of the treaty by the U.S. Senate. He was unsuccessful in maneuvers to acquire islands of the Danish West Indies and to incorporate the Dominican Republic in the United States. In addition to his normal duties, he performed heavy labors as a sort of political liaison officer, and his interest in patronage problems was continuous. After suffering serious injury in a carriage accident in the spring of 1865, he had been brutally attacked on the night of Lincoln's assassination; yet, despite the fact that he was partially crippled, he transacted the public business with as much skill and coolness as ever. In the administration of Andrew Johnson he was a central figure. He advocated a conciliatory policy toward the South, wrote some of Johnson's most important veto messages, and supported the president up to the very end even though by so doing he lost both popularity and influence. Leaving office on President Grant's accession, he made a tour around the world and returned to his home in Auburn late in 1871.

SEWELL, WILLIAM JOYCE (*b. Castlebar, Ireland, 1835; d. Camden, N.J., 1901*), Union soldier, railroad executive, politician. Came to America, 1851. Prominent in management of the Pennsylvania Railroad system's New Jersey lines, Sewell became in time virtual Republican boss of New Jersey. He served in the state senate, 1872–81, and was U.S. senator, 1881–87, 1895–1901.

SEYBERT, ADAM (*b. Philadelphia, Pa., 1773; d. Paris, France, 1825*), physician. Studied with Caspar Wistar; M.D., University of Pennsylvania, 1793. After continuing his studies at London, Edinburgh and Göttingen, and making special studies in mineralogy in Paris, he returned to Philadelphia, 1797, where he practiced, and also ran an apothecary shop. An expert in the analysis of minerals, he also manufactured, it is claimed, the first mercurials in America. While a congressman, (Democrat) Republican, from Pennsylvania, 1809–15 and 1817–19, he interested himself in government revenues and expenditures and was author of *Statistical Annals . . . of the United States* (1818). An active member and official of the American Philosophical Society, he was one of the leading pioneer American chemists and mineralogists.

SEYBERT, HENRY (*b. Philadelphia, Pa., 1801; d. Philadelphia, 1883*), mineralogist, philanthropist. Son of Adam Seybert. Endowed a chair of philosophy at the University of Pennsylvania; left a great part of his estate to Philadelphia for relief of poor children.

SEYBERT, JOHN (*b. Manheim, Pa., 1791; d. near Bellevue, O., 1860*), bishop of the Evangelical Association. Itinerant missionary among German immigrants in Pennsylvania and Ohio.

SEYFFARTH, GUSTAVUS (*b. near Torgau, Germany, 1796; d. New York, N.Y., 1885*), archeologist, Lutheran theologian, classical and Oriental philologist. Opposed school of Champollion. Resigned professorship of archeology at University of Leipzig, 1854; emigrated to America, 1856. Erudite, but afflicted with a speculative-dogmatic mentality, Seyffarth contended throughout his whole life that hieroglyphic signs were phonograms or syllabic writing and that Egyptian literature was based on ancient Coptic, related by him to Hebrew.

SEYMOUR, GEORGE FRANKLIN (*b. New York, N.Y., 1829; d. Springfield, Ill., 1906*), Episcopal clergyman. An ardent Anglo-Catholic, he served as professor and dean at the General Theological Seminary, New York; he was consecrated bishop of Springfield, 1878.

SEYMOUR, HORATIO (*b. Pompey Hill, N.Y., 1810; d. 1886*), lawyer, New York politician. Brother-in-

law of Roscoe Conkling. Early a henchman of the Albany Regency, Seymour was a longtime political lieutenant of William L. Marcy. As a New York assemblyman, 1842 and 1844–45, he forced expansion measures of his famous "Report of the Committee on Canals" through the legislature against the strongest opposition and was elected speaker of the assembly, 1845. His skill in effecting working compromises between the Democratic "Hunker" and "Barnburner" factions made him an important figure. Although an advocate *post* 1845 of "free soil" in any southwestern territory which might be gained from Mexico and opposed to federal meddling with slavery where it then existed, he expressed a strong dislike for both Abolitionists and Southern extremists. A true Jeffersonian, he insisted on the supreme importance of local government. He served the first of his terms as governor of New York, 1853–55, showing himself industrious and conscientious, improving the penal system and opposing prohibition and anti-Catholicism. Defeated for re-election, he devoted himself for a while to private business. Considered as a possible compromise candidate at the Charleston, S.C., Democratic convention, 1860, Seymour supported Stephen A. Douglas, but on Lincoln's election urged loyal acceptance of the constitutional fact and favored the Crittenden Compromise. Although he considered an armed conquest of the South unwise, he helped the Union war effort and as governor, 1863–65, was tireless in supplying the state's army quotas. He found himself pushed, however, into a position as national leader of the opposition to the Republicans and was a constant critic of the extra-constitutional powers assumed by the Lincoln administration. Although he was denounced by Horace Greeley and others as a temporizing Copperhead during the draft riots in New York City, July 1863, the verdict of time has been in his favor. Defeated as Democratic candidate for the presidency, 1868, after a vigorous campaign, he became an elder statesman of the party, assisted in driving Boss Tweed from power and lived to see his disciple, Grover Cleveland, in the White House. A man of dignity and integrity, he failed practically as a statesman largely because of his gentlemanly scorn for extreme opinions.

SEYMOUR, HORATIO WINSLOW (*b. Cayuga Co., N.Y., 1854; d. New York, N.Y., 1920*), journalist. Raised in Wisconsin. Served as editor on *Milwaukee Daily News, Chicago Times, Chicago Herald, Chicago Chronicle* and N.Y. *World;* was noted for his innovating use of startling and effective headlines. A liberal Democrat, he opposed Republican money and tariff policies.

SEYMOUR, THOMAS DAY (*b. Hudson, O., 1848; d. New Haven, Conn., 1907*), classicist. Grandnephew of Jeremiah Day. Professor of Greek at Western Reserve, 1872–80, and at Yale, 1880–1907. Chairman of managing committee, American School at Athens,

1887–1901; president, Archaeological Institute of America, 1903–07. Author, among other books, of *Life in the Homeric Age* (1907).

SEYMOUR, THOMAS HART (*b. Hartford, Conn., 1807; d. Hartford, 1868*), lawyer, Mexican War soldier. Congressman, Democrat, from Connecticut, 1843–45; governor of Connecticut, 1850–53; U.S. minister to Russia, 1854–58. A leader of the Connecticut Peace Democrats, 1860–65.

SEYMOUR, TRUMAN (*b. Burlington, Vt., 1824; d. Florence, Italy, 1891*), Union major-general. Graduated West Point, 1846; served with artillery in Mexican War and against Seminoles. As brigade and later division commander during the Civil War, Seymour executed the decisive enveloping movement at the battle of South Mountain, and at Antietam led the advance of Hooker's corps in opening the battle. In continuous service thereafter, he was distinguished as a soldier but unaggressive in promotion of his own ambitions. He retired in 1876.

SEYMOUR, WILLIAM (*b. New York, N.Y., 1855; d. Plymouth, Mass., 1933*), actor, stage director, theatre manager. Son-in-law of Edward L. Davenport. He was for many years associated with productions of Charles Frohman.

SHABONEE (*b. possibly near Maumee River, O., c. 1775; d. Grundy Co., Ill., 1859*), Potawatomi chief. An associate of Tecumseh, 1807–14, he later became a good but unrewarded friend of the settlers.

SHAFER, HELEN ALMIRA (*b. Newark, N.J., 1839; d. Wellesley, Mass., 1894*), educator. Graduated Oberlin, 1863. Professor of mathematics at Wellesley, *post* 1877, she succeeded to the presidency of the college, 1888. She completely remodeled the curriculum, altered requirements for admission and added many new courses of study.

SHAFROTH, JOHN FRANKLIN (*b. Fayette, Mo., 1854; d. Denver, Colo., 1922*), lawyer. Removed to Colorado, 1879. Congressman, Republican, Silver Republican, and Democrat, 1895–1904, he supported the Reclamation Act, a woman's suffrage amendment, and the abolition of "lame duck" sessions. Democratic governor of Colorado, 1909–13, he forced adoption of the direct primary, initiative and referendum. As U.S. senator, 1913–19, he supported President Wilson in the main, but clashed with him on conservation; his Senate speech, March 21, 1914, is the classic statement of the Western viewpoint on that subject.

SHAFTER, WILLIAM RUFUS (*b. Kalamazoo Co., Mich., 1835; d. near Bakersfield, Calif., 1906*), soldier. In service with the Union Army, 1861–65, he received brevet of brigadier-general of volunteers and the Medal of Honor for gallantry at Fair Oaks. Remaining in the army, he rose to colonel, 1st U.S. Infantry (1879), and was made brigadier-general, 1897. On outbreak of the war with Spain, he was pro-

moted major-general of volunteers. In command of the expeditionary force against Santiago de Cuba, he landed at Daiquiri, June 22, 1898, and took Santiago on July 17 in a campaign which was widely criticized because of high American mortality from malaria and yellow fever. Much of the criticism of Shafter may be more justly charged to the nation's general unpreparedness and ignorance of tropical diseases. Retiring from active service as brigadier-general, 1899, he was advanced to the grade of major-general retired, 1901.

SHAHAN, THOMAS JOSEPH (*b. Manchester, N.H., 1857; d. 1932*), Roman Catholic clergyman, educator. Educated at Sulpician College of Montreal, and at the American College and the Propaganda in Rome, he was ordained, 1882; he studied later also at the universities of Paris and Berlin. Professor of church history, Roman law, and patrology at Catholic University, Washington, D.C., *post* 1891; rector of the university, 1909–28. He was consecrated titular bishop of Germanicopolis, 1914. A voluminous writer and an able executive, he was a founder and an editor of the *Catholic Encyclopedia* (1907–13).

SHAIKEWITZ, NAHUM MEIR. [See SCHOMER, NAHUM MEIR, 1849–1905.]

SHAKALLAMY. [See SHIKELLAMY, d. 1748.]

SHALER, NATHANIEL SOUTHGATE (*b. Newport, Ky., 1841; d. 1906*), Union soldier, geologist, educator. A favorite pupil of Agassiz, Shaler took a B.S. degree at Lawrence Scientific School, 1862. Returning to his alma mater after Union Army service, he was assistant to Agassiz in paleontology; *post* 1868, he served as lecturer and professor of paleontology and geology. He was also dean of Lawrence Scientific School from 1891 until his death. As a teacher, he was concerned more with awakening the minds of his students than with imparting information; as dean, he revivified Lawrence and toward the end of his tenure fought its merger with Massachusetts Institute of Technology. A man of very wide interests, Shaler served also as state geologist of Kentucky, as a member of many Massachusetts state commissions, as a consultant in mining ventures, and as a supervising official of the U.S. Geological Survey. He was a prolific writer on many subjects, scientific and otherwise, displaying exceptional powers of observation and imagination.

SHALER, WILLIAM (*b. Bridgeport, Conn., c. 1773; d. Havana, Cuba, 1833*), sea captain. Friend and partner of Richard J. Cleveland. Shaler held a number of U.S. consular offices of which the most notable was the post of U.S. consul-general at Algiers, 1815–28. He had previously served as U.S. commissioner with Stephen Decatur (1779–1820) in the arbitrary negotiation of the U.S.–Algiers treaty of 1815. He was author of *Sketches of Algiers* (1826).

SHANNON, WILSON (*b. Mount Olivet, Ohio Territory, 1802; d. 1877*), lawyer, public official. Democratic governor of Ohio, 1838–40, 1842–44; inept and tactless U.S. minister to Mexico, 1844–45; undistinguished congressman from Ohio, 1853–55. Commissioned governor of Kansas Territory, August 1855, he became confidential with the Missouri party and accused the Free State group of a secret conspiracy to resist the laws. On outbreak of the so-called Wakarusa War in November, he was able to persuade both factions to disband their forces, but when guerrillas again assembled before the town of Lawrence in May 1856, he refused to intervene and contented himself after the pillaging of the town with a proclamation ordering armed bands to desist. On the invasion of the territory by James H. Lane (1814–1866) and his army in August and the consequent attacks on pro-slavery areas, Shannon again played the role of peacemaker and effected a settlement. His resignation anticipated by an order for his removal (August 1856), he resumed the practice of law, becoming in time a leading member of the Kansas bar.

SHARKEY, WILLIAM LEWIS (*b. Holston valley, East Tenn., 1798; d. Jackson, Miss., 1873*), lawyer, jurist. Removed to Mississippi as a young man; began practice at Warrenton, 1822. Chief justice, state court of errors and appeals, 1832–51. As president of Nashville Convention, 1850, he opposed Southern extremist efforts to dominate that body and up to 1861 was probably the most active anti-secession man in the state of Mississippi. Appointed provisional governor, June 1865, he served until the fall of that year. He was then chosen U.S. senator but was denied his seat when Congress repudiated President Johnson's Reconstruction plan.

SHARP, DALLAS LORE (*b. Haleyville, N.J., 1870; d. Hingham, Mass., 1929*), educator, Methodist clergyman, naturalist. Author of *Wild Life Near Home* (1901) and some twenty more popular works on nature study including *A Watcher in the Woods* (1903) and *Beyond the Pasture Bars* (1914).

SHARP, DANIEL (*b. Huddersfield, England, 1783; d. near Baltimore, Md., 1853*), Baptist clergyman. Highly influential in his principal pastorate at the Third Baptist Church, Boston, Mass., 1812–53.

SHARP, JOHN (*b. Clackmannanshire, Scotland, 1820; d. 1891*), Mormon pioneer and bishop, railroad contractor. Came to America, 1848; settled in Salt Lake City, 1850; served as superintendent of the church quarries. Principal sub-contractor under Brigham Young in construction of Union Pacific roadbed from Echo Canyon to Ogden, he later undertook other contracts and developed the Utah Central Railroad of which he was president *post* 1873.

SHARP, KATHARINE LUCINDA (*b. Elgin, Ill., 1865; d. Lake Placid, N.Y., 1914*), librarian. Graduated Northwestern University, 1885; New York State Library School, 1892. Director, department of library science, Armour Institute (later at University of Illinois), 1893–1907; librarian, University of Illinois, 1897–1907. Author of *Illinois Libraries* (1906–08).

SHARP, WILLIAM GRAVES (*b. Mount Gilead, O., 1859; d. Elyria, O., 1922*), lawyer, industrialist. As congressman, Democrat, from Ohio, 1909–14, he became ranking member of committee on foreign affairs; he was U.S. ambassador to France, 1914–19.

SHARPE, HORATIO (*b. near Hull, England, 1718; d. England, 1790*), British soldier, colonial governor of Maryland, 1753–69. Appointed governor, probably through family influence, he served as royal commander-in-chief during the French and Indian War, until replaced by Braddock. Defending the interests of Lord Baltimore, he quarreled with the legislature over its decision to tax the proprietor's revenue, though he opposed the retaliatory measure of quartering troops in Annapolis. Credited by some with first suggesting the Stamp Act, he warned the ministry that parliamentary taxation could be enforced only by troops. By 1760 he reached agreement with Virginia concerning the disputed boundary of the two colonies. Removed as governor in 1769, he returned to England in 1773.

SHARPLES, JAMES (*b. England, c. 1751; d. New York, N.Y., 1811*), portrait painter, inventor. Came to America, 1793; worked as an itinerant painter through New England states and the South; settled in Philadelphia, 1796, and resided thereafter there or in New York except for the years 1801–09 when he returned to England. Noted for his ability to catch a likeness, he made many portraits of distinguished Americans, including George Washington and his wife, and of important foreign visitors. For his work in America he used pastels on a thick gray paper of soft grain. Because of the ability of his wife and children to duplicate his work in copies, there has been much confusion and controversy over authentication of works from his own hand.

SHARPLESS, ISAAC (*b. Chester Co., Pa., 1848; d. 1920*), Quaker leader and historian, educator. Graduated Harvard, 1873. Began a lifelong service at Haverford College as instructor in mathematics, 1875; president of Haverford, 1887–1917. He was one of the most eminent U.S. exponents of the efficient, small liberal arts college.

SHARSWOOD, GEORGE (*b. Philadelphia, Pa., 1810; d. 1883*), jurist. Judge of the district court of Philadelphia, 1845–68, he was president judge *post* 1848. Elevated to the state supreme court, he served until his retirement in 1882, and was chief justice *post* 1879. Noted for his learning, promptness of decision and sound judgment, Sharswood was also a prolific legal writer and professor of law and dean of the law school at University of Pennsylvania.

SHATTUCK, AARON DRAPER (*b. Francestown, N.H., 1832; d. Granby, Conn., 1928*), portrait and landscape painter. Brother-in-law of Samuel Colman.

SHATTUCK, FREDERICK CHEEVER (*b. Boston, Mass., 1847; d. 1929*), noted Boston physician. Son of George C. Shattuck (1813–1893); brother of George B. Shattuck. Jackson Professor of clinical medicine, Harvard Medical School, 1888–1912.

SHATTUCK, GEORGE BRUNE (*b. Boston, Mass., 1844; d. 1923*), Boston physician. Son of George C. Shattuck (1813–1893); brother of Frederick C. Shattuck. Visiting physician for many years at Boston City Hospital, Shattuck was influential in establishing the Massachusetts State Board of Health, 1869, the first in the United States. He was editor-in-chief, *Boston Medical and Surgical Journal*, 1881–1912.

SHATTUCK, GEORGE CHEYNE (*b. Templeton, Mass., 1783; d. 1854*), physician, philanthropist. Father of George C. Shattuck (1813–1893). Graduated Dartmouth, 1803; M.B., 1806. M.D., University of Pennsylvania, 1807. The leading physician of his time in Boston, Shattuck engaged in many philanthropies which included endowment of a professorship of anatomy at Harvard Medical School, foundation of the Shattuck lectures of the Massachusetts Medical Society, and assistance to authors including James Thacher and John J. Audubon.

SHATTUCK, GEORGE CHEYNE (*b. Boston, Mass., 1813; d. 1893*), physician, philanthropist. Son of George C. Shattuck (1783–1854); father of Frederick C. and George B. Shattuck. Graduated Harvard, 1831; M.D., Harvard Medical School, 1835. During three years' post-graduate study in Europe he was influenced principally by P. C. A. Louis. Shattuck's report of studies differentiating typhoid from typhus fever, read in Paris, 1838, and published in America, 1840, was one of the early, important contributions to the subject. Practicing with his father in Boston, *post* 1840, he gave much of his time to the improvement of medical education; with Oliver W. Holmes, Henry I. Bowditch and James Jackson (1777–1867), he was a founder of the Boston Society of Medical Observation and succeeded Holmes as visiting physician to Massachusetts General Hospital, 1849. As professor at Harvard Medical School, and as dean *post* 1864, he woke the school out of its lethargy, extended the teaching into hospitals, and introduced clinical conferences. A leading Episcopal layman, he founded St. Paul's School, Concord, N.H., 1855.

SHATTUCK, LEMUEL (*b. Ashby, Mass., 1793; d. 1859*), merchant, statistician. Interested from an early period in the provision of precise vital statistics, Shattuck was a founder of the American Statistical Association, 1839, and of the New England Historic Genealogical Society. He was influential also in securing a state law requiring an effective system of registry of births, marriages and deaths, 1842. Shat-

tuck's census of the city of Boston, 1845, contained many innovations, and his services as consultant in the federal census of 1850 resulted in a marked advance in the amount and quality of information recorded. His *Report* (1850) as chairman of the commission to make a sanitary survey of Massachusetts was a milestone in the development of public health work; in it he anticipated almost all the public health measures later put into practice.

SHAUBENA. [See SHABONEE, *c. 1775–1859*.]

SHAUCK, JOHN ALLEN (*b. near Johnsville, O., 1841; d. Columbus, O., 1918*), jurist. Ohio circuit court judge, 1884–94; state supreme court judge, 1894–1913. A stern conservative, he held that it was the duty of courts to declare void all acts of state legislatures which were non-governmental in nature even though not forbidden by constitutional provision.

SHAW, ANNA HOWARD (*b. Newcastle-upon-Tyne, England, 1847; d. Moylan, Pa., 1919*), physician, Methodist minister, woman suffrage and temperance reformer. Friend and associate of Susan B. Anthony, Miss Shaw was a practiced orator and able publicist; she was president, National American Woman Suffrage Association, 1904–15.

SHAW, EDWARD RICHARD (*b. Bellport, N.Y., 1850; d. 1903*), educator. Graduated Lafayette College, 1881; Ph.D., New York University, 1890. Helped found pioneer school of education at New York University, 1890; served it as dean, 1894–1901.

SHAW, ELIJAH (*b. Kensington, N.H., 1793; d. 1851*), pioneer minister of the Christian Connection. An editor of the *Christian Journal.*

SHAW, HENRY (*b. Sheffield, England, 1800; d. St. Louis, Mo., 1889*), merchant. Succeeded in business in St. Louis, 1819–40. Advised by Asa Gray, George Engelmann and others, he established a garden for the scientific study of plants at St. Louis, 1857–60. Opened to the public, 1860, it was endowed by its founder as the Missouri Botanical Garden and continues to hold high rank among world botanical institutions.

SHAW, HENRY WHEELER (*b. Lanesboro, Mass., 1818; d. Monterey, Calif., 1885*), humorist. Better known by pseudonym "Josh Billings." Author of hundreds of once-popular bucolic aphorisms phrased in grotesque misspellings, Shaw was author of *Josh Billings, His Sayings* (1865) and a number of similar collections. His best work is in *Josh Billings' Farmer's Allminax*, published yearly from 1869 until 1880.

SHAW, HOWARD VAN DOREN (*b. Chicago, Ill., 1869; d. Baltimore, Md., 1926*), architect. Graduated Yale, 1890. Studied architecture at Massachusetts Institute of Technology and worked in office of William LeB. Jenney. Worked in a highly personal style, largely in the Middle West, where he became probably the best regarded practitioner of domestic and non-commercial architecture.

SHAW, JOHN (*b. Mountmellick, Ireland, 1773; d. Philadelphia, Pa., 1823*), naval officer, merchant mariner. Made brilliant record in command of schooner *Enterprise*, 1799–1800, as destroyer of French privateers. Prepared naval force in lower Mississippi to frustrate Aaron Burr's intrigues, 1807; after mainly shore service in the War of 1812, commanded the squadron left off Algiers to protect American interests, 1815–17.

SHAW, JOHN (*b. Annapolis, Md., 1778; d. at sea, 1809*), physician, naval surgeon, poet.

SHAW, LEMUEL (*b. Barnstable, Mass., 1781; d. 1861*), Massachusetts legislator and jurist. Father-in-law of Herman Melville. Graduated Harvard, 1800; studied law in Boston under David Everett. Practicing in Boston *post c. 1804*, he became known as an adviser in important commercial enterprises; he drew the first charter of the city, 1822. As chief justice of Massachusetts, 1830–60, he made much law on such matters as water power, railroads and other public utilities; probably no other state judge has so deeply influenced commercial and constitutional law throughout the United States. The strength of his opinions lay in the entire solidity of their reasoning. Thorough and systematic, he had a remarkable ability to charge juries so that they understood the exact questions at issue before them.

SHAW, LESLIE MORTIER (*b. Morristown, Vt., 1848; d. Washington, D.C., 1932*), banker. Removed to eastern Iowa, 1869. Republican governor of Iowa, 1898–1902. Shaw's championing of the gold standard during the campaign of 1896 and his services as permanent chairman of the International Monetary Convention, 1898, led to his appointment as U.S. secretary of the treasury in 1902. He resorted to unprecedented expedients for dealing with stringency of credit, such as liberalizing security and waiving reserve requirements for government bank deposits, artificially stimulating gold importation, and regulating note issues by executive decree. A firm believer in high tariff protection and domestic *laissez-faire*, he retained office until 1907 despite President Theodore Roosevelt's uneasiness about him.

SHAW, MARY (*b. Boston, Mass., 1854; d. New York, N.Y., 1929*), actress. Made debut with Boston Museum Stock Company, 1879–80. A hard-working intellectual performer, she played ably in support of Helena Modjeska, Julia Marlowe and other stars but rarely won commercial success in her own vehicles. Among her own productions were Ibsen's *Ghosts*, (produced, 1899 and later) and G. B. Shaw's *Mrs. Warren's Profession* in which she appeared in New York, October 1905 and on later occasions.

SHAW, NATHANIEL (*b. New London, Conn., 1735; d. New London, 1782*), merchant, Revolutionary patriot. Naval agent for Connecticut, and agent and prize master for the Continental Congress *post* 1775.

SHAW, OLIVER (*b. Middleboro, Mass., 1779; d. Providence, R.I., 1848*), musician, composer. Organist of the First Congregational Church at Providence *post* 1807, he composed sacred music anticipatory of the later work of Lowell Mason, but was equally as important for his teaching and interest in the betterment of church music. His best-known hymn-tunes were "Taunton," "Bristol" and "Weybosset."

SHAW, PAULINE AGASSIZ (*b. Neuchâtel, Switzerland, 1841; d. 1917*), philanthropist, educational and social pioneer. Daughter of J. L. R. Agassiz. Gave early support to Boston kindergartens, to the manual training movement during its experimental period, and to the Vocation Bureau of Boston for its pioneer work in vocational guidance (1908–17).

SHAW, SAMUEL (*b. Boston, Mass., 1754; d. near Cape of Good Hope, 1794*), Revolutionary officer, merchant. Served with distinction in the Revolution as an artilleryman, for most of the war acting as aide-de-camp to Gen. Henry Knox. Supercargo on the *Empress of China*, first American vessel to Canton, 1784–85, he served as first U.S. consul to China *post* 1786.

SHAW, THOMAS (*b. Philadelphia, Pa., 1838; d. Hammonton, N.J., 1901*), machinist, inventor. Patented almost 200 devices including gas meters, pressure gauges, hydraulic pumps, engine governors and iron and steel processes; among these, his spring-lock nut washer (1868), his pile driver (1868, 1870) and the Shaw Gas Tester (1886–90) were outstanding.

SHAW, WILLIAM SMITH (*b. Haverhill, Mass., 1778; d. Boston, Mass., 1826*), lawyer. Nephew of Abigail Adams. Helped found the Anthology Society, 1805; built up collections of the Boston Athenaeum as librarian, 1807–22.

SHAYS, DANIEL (*b. probably Hopkinton, Mass., c. 1747; d. Sparta, N.Y., 1825*), Revolutionary soldier, insurgent. A brave and popular officer of the 5th Massachusetts regiment, he resigned from the army, 1780, and settled in Pelham, Mass., being subsequently elected to various town offices. The acute economic depression which soon followed the peace of 1783 created grievances throughout the rural districts, particularly with reference to foreclosure for debt. On the failure of the legislature to help, the people of western Massachusetts resorted to force to compel legislative action, and Shays's prominence in this movement has caused his name to be given to the whole uprising. On Aug. 29, 1786, the insurgents prevented the sitting of the courts of common pleas and general sessions; the leaders, then fearing that indictments would be brought against them, moved to prevent the sitting of the supreme court at Springfield on Sept. 26. Militiamen under Gen. William Shepard defended the court. A committee of which Shays was chairman drew up resolutions that the court should be allowed to sit provided it dealt with no case involving indictments concerning insurgents or debts; on agreement, both the militia and the insurgents disbanded and court adjourned. The legislature of Massachusetts continuing to give offense, the insurgents rose again in January 1787 and moved against the arsenal at Springfield but were defeated by state troops under Gen. Benjamin Lincoln. Pursuing the insurgents westward, Lincoln caught up with Shays's men at Petersham on the night of Feb. 2, 1787, and completely routed them. Shays fled to Vermont. At first condemned to death, he was pardoned in June 1788 and some time afterward removed to New York State. A man of little education and not much ability, he was honest and firmly convinced of the justice of his cause.

SHEA, JOHN DAWSON GILMARY (*b. New York, N.Y., 1824; d. Elizabeth, N.J., 1892*), historian, editor. Graduated Columbia Grammar School, 1837; was a Jesuit novice, 1848–52. Dedicating his life to the writing of American Catholic history, he received few material rewards for work of outstanding ability which won him many scholarly honors. Among his books of permanent value were *Discovery and Exploration of the Mississippi Valley* (1852), *History of the Catholic Missions among the Indian Tribes of the United States* (1854) and his monumental *History of the Catholic Church in the United States* (1886–92); he was also editor of a number of works on Indian linguistics, of many additional Jesuit Relations, and of an English translation of Charlevoix's *History and General Description of New France* (1866–72).

SHEARMAN, THOMAS GASKELL (*b. Birmingham, England, 1834; d. Brooklyn, N.Y., 1900*), lawyer, economist. Came to America as a boy. Employed by David D. Field to work with him on the civil code, 1860, Shearman became a partner of Field, 1868, and served as immediate legal adviser of James Fisk and Jay Gould during the Erie Railroad "war." Withdrawing from the partnership, 1873, Shearman continued to act as counsel for Gould and ably defended Henry Ward Beecher during his famous trial. Shearman was also counsel for a number of banks and railroads and for James J. Hill. By nature a reformer, he continued Field's work in pressing for codification of the law, argued for free trade, and in 1887 suggested the name "single tax" as definition of the measures proposed by Henry George to which he had become a convert. He was author of *Natural Taxation* (1895) and other works.

SHECUT, JOHN LINNAEUS EDWARD WHITRIDGE (*b. Beaufort, S.C., 1770; d. 1836*), physician, botanist, novelist. Practiced in Charleston, S.C. *post c.* 1790; studied medicine under David Ramsay.

SHEDD, FRED FULLER (*b. New Boston, N.H., 1871; d. Southern Pines, N.C., 1937*), journalist. After early editorial training on the *Haverhill* (Mass.) *Evening Gazette* and the *Boston Herald,* he served on the staff of the *Philadelphia Bulletin, post* 1911, and was its editor-in-chief, 1921–37. [*Supp. 2*]

SHEDD, JOEL HERBERT (*b. Pepperell, Mass., 1834; d. Providence, R.I., 1915*), hydraulic and sanitary engineer, inventor.

SHEDD, JOHN GRAVES (*b. near Alstead, N.H., 1850; d. Chicago, Ill., 1926*), merchant, philanthropist. Removed to Chicago, 1872, to enter employ of Field, Leiter & Co. as salesman. Rising rapidly in the firm, he became a partner of Marshall Field & Co., 1893, and served as its president, 1906–22.

SHEDD, WILLIAM AMBROSE (*b. Mount Seir, Persia, 1865; d. Sain Kala, Persia, 1918*), Presbyterian clergyman. The son of missionary parents, Shedd graduated from Marietta College, 1887, and from Princeton Theological Seminary, 1892. Serving thereafter as a missionary in Persia, he was active in relief work there during World War I.

SHEDD, WILLIAM GREENOUGH THAYER (*b. Acton, Mass., 1820; d. New York, N.Y., 1894*), Congregational and Presbyterian theologian. Graduated University of Vermont, 1839; Andover Theological Seminary, 1843. A professor at Union Theological Seminary, New York City, 1862–93, he was author of *Dogmatic Theology* (1888, 1894), a cogent defense of conservative Calvinism, and of a number of other books.

SHEEDY, DENNIS (*b. Ireland, 1846; d. Denver, Colo., 1923*), cattleman, merchant, capitalist. Came to America as an infant; removed to Lyons, Iowa, 1858. Active as trader, miner and freighter throughout the West, he was a rancher in Nevada, Texas, Nebraska and Colorado, 1870–84. Foreseeing the end of the free range, he sold out his cattle interests and engaged in banking, smelting and other activities in Colorado.

SHEFFIELD, DEVELLO ZELOTES (*b. Gainesville, N.Y., 1841; d. Peitaiho, North China, 1913*), Union soldier, Presbyterian clergyman. Missionary to China, *post* 1869, he was active in educational work and in the translation of the Bible into classical Chinese.

SHEFFIELD, JOSEPH EARL (*b. Southport, Conn., 1793; d. New Haven, Conn., 1882*), merchant, financier, philanthropist. Successful as a dry-goods and naval stores merchant in New Bern, N.C., and as a cotton exporter in Mobile, Ala., 1813–35, he entered the fields of canal and railroad finance in which he was equally successful. He was a principal benefactor to the scientific department of Yale. Given separate status in 1854, it was renamed Sheffield Scientific School in his honor, 1861.

SHELBY, EVAN (*b. Tregaron, Wales, 1719; d. 1794*), frontier soldier, trader, landowner. Father of

Isaac Shelby. Emigrating to America *c.* 1734, he resided in Franklin Co., Pa., and (*post* 1739) in western Maryland. An officer of rangers in the French and Indian War, he was particularly distinguished in the Forbes campaign against Fort Duquesne, 1758. Removing to southwest Virginia *c.* 1773, he commanded the Fincastle Company in Dunmore's War and at the close of the battle of Point Pleasant, October 1774, held the chief field command. Engaged against the Indians during the Revolution, he served later in the North Carolina legislature and was militia brigadier-general of the Washington District of that state. He negotiated a truce with John Sevier in the troubles over the insurgent "State of Franklin," March 1787, and later declined the governorship of Franklin. Strong, blunt, fearless and noted for truth-telling, he was prompt to take the aggressive in any enterprise in which he engaged.

SHELBY, ISAAC (*b. near North Mountain, present Washington Co., Md., 1750; d. Kentucky, 1826*), soldier. Son of Evan Shelby. Removing to the Holston region of southwest Virginia *c.* 1773, he served under his father as a lieutenant in Dunmore's War, and in 1775 visited Kentucky as a surveyor for the Transylvania Company. During the Revolution he acted as commissary of supplies for militia detailed to frontier posts and also for the Continental Army in its western field operations. A member of the Virginia legislature, colonel of the militia of Sullivan Co., N.C., and active also in patenting Kentucky lands, he joined Charles McDowell in operations against Tory forces in the South Carolina back country, 1780. He played a prominent part in the victory at King's Mountain and also at Cowpens. After further military activity in 1781 and subsequent service in the North Carolina legislature, he removed to Kentucky, 1783, where he took part in achieving independence and statehood and was in 1792 a member of the convention which drafted the first Kentucky constitution. As first governor of Kentucky, 1792–96, he guided the state through a difficult formative period, holding it fast to the federal union despite contrary schemes and conspiracies. Retiring to private life, he emerged as governor again in 1812 and prosecuted vigorously the war against Great Britain. He led in person the Kentucky volunteers in W. H. Harrison's invasion of Canada which resulted in British defeat at the battle of the Thames, October 1813. Offered the secretary-ship of war by President Monroe in March 1817, he declined because of age. A man of great physical hardiness, Shelby was also an able executive and a wise judge and handler of men.

SHELBY, JOSEPH ORVILLE (*b. Lexington, Ky., 1830; d. Adrian, Mo., 1897*), Confederate soldier. Settled in Missouri, 1852, where he engaged in business. Commissioned a Confederate captain, 1861, he rose to the rank of brigadier-general in the course of the Civil War mainly operating as a cavalry leader in Arkansas and Missouri under Gen. Sterling Price. Renowned for personal courage and mastery of cavalry tactics, he led his men into Mexico, July 1865, where their offer to assist Maximilian was rejected. He later returned to Missouri.

SHELDON, EDWARD AUSTIN (*b. near Perry Center, N.Y., 1823; d. 1897*), educator, school superintendent in Oswego and Syracuse, N.Y. An advocate of free public schools, Sheldon was responsible for opening the Oswego Primary Teachers' Training School, the first city school of its kind in the United States, in May 1861. He served it most successfully as principal, 1862–97.

SHELDON, EDWARD STEVENS (*b. Waterville, Maine, 1851; d. Cambridge, Mass., 1925*), philologist, lexicographer. Brother of Henry N. Sheldon. A specialist in Romance philology, in which he held a chair at Harvard, 1894–1921.

SHELDON, HENRY NEWTON (*b. Waterville, Maine, 1843; d. 1926*), jurist. Brother of Edward S. Sheldon. Judge of Massachusetts superior court, 1894–1905; of Massachusetts supreme judicial court, 1905–15. Noted for legal scholarship and good judgment.

SHELDON, MARY DOWNING. [See BARNES, MARY DOWNING SHELDON, 1850–1898.]

SHELDON, WALTER LORENZO (*b. West Rutland, Vt., 1858; d. 1907*), Ethical Culture leader in St. Louis, Mo., *post* 1886.

SHELDON, WILLIAM EVARTS (*b. Dorset, Vt., 1832; d. 1900*), educator, leader in progressive educational movements. Principal of several public high schools in Massachusetts, Sheldon was president of the National Education Association, 1887.

SHELEKHOV, GRIGORIĬ IVANOVICH (*b. Rylsk, Russia, 1747; d. Irkutsk, Siberia, 1795*), Russian merchant, fur trader. Father-in-law of N. P. Rezanov. Founded first Russian colony in America on Kodiak Island, 1784; helped establish Russian dominion over Alaska.

SHELTON, ALBERT LEROY (*b. Indianapolis, Ind., 1875; d. near Batang, China, 1922*), Disciples of Christ clergyman. Medical missionary in West China and Tibet, 1903–22.

SHELTON, EDWARD MASON (*b. Huntingdon-shire, England, 1846; d. Seattle, Wash., 1928*), agriculturist. Came to America as a boy. Graduated Michigan Agricultural College, 1871. Professor of agriculture, Kansas State Agricultural College, 1874–90; government agricultural adviser in Australia, 1890–99; thereafter practiced horticulture in the State of Washington.

SHELTON, FREDERICK WILLIAM (*b. Jamaica, N.Y., 1815; d. 1881*), Episcopal clergyman. A rector for many years in New York State and Vermont, Shelton was author, among other books, of *The Trollopiad*

(1837), a satire in verse, and of a number of sketches in the style of Washington Irving which he contributed to the *Knickerbocker* magazine, 1838–45.

SHEPARD, CHARLES UPHAM (*b. Little Compton, R.I., 1804; d. 1886*), mineralogist. Lecturer in science at Yale, South Carolina Medical College, and Amherst. His important collection of minerals and meteorites was acquired by Amherst.

SHEPARD, EDWARD MORSE (*b. New York, N.Y., 1850; d. Lake George, N.Y., 1911*), lawyer, political reformer. Ward of Abram S. Hewitt. Graduated College of the City of New York, 1869. Outstanding as counsel to the New York Rapid Transit Commission and to the Pennsylvania Railroad, Shepard devoted much of his time to reform of the New York Democratic organization from within, to the advocacy of civil-service reform, and to the improvement of City College.

SHEPARD, FRED DOUGLAS (*b. Ellenburg, N.Y., 1855; d. Turkey, 1915*), physician, medical missionary to Turkey *post* 1882. An outstanding teacher and practitioner of medicine, Shepard died while combatting an epidemic of typhus at Aintab.

SHEPARD, JAMES HENRY (*b. Lyons, Mich., 1850; d. St. Petersburg, Fla., 1918*), chemist. B.S., University of Michigan, 1875, where he also did graduate work. Taught at South Dakota State College of Agriculture and was also director of its experiment station; won international reputation for researches upon bleached flour and food adulterants.

SHEPARD, SETH (*b. Brenham, Texas, 1847; d. 1917*), jurist. Long active in Texas Democratic politics, he was appointed justice of the court of appeals of the District of Columbia, 1893, and served until 1917; he was chief justice *post* 1905.

SHEPARD, THOMAS (*b. Towcester, England, 1605; d. Cambridge, Mass., 1649*), New England theologian. A graduate of Emmanuel College, Cambridge, England, Shepard was silenced for nonconformity by Archbishop Laud, 1630. Removing to Boston, Mass., October 1635, he became pastor at Newtown (Cambridge). An orthodox Calvinist, he was active in the 1637 condemnation of the Antinomians; he defined Congregationalism as a middle ground between Brownism and the Presbyterian polity. Concerned with education, he proposed a plan for the support of poor students; he also projected a plan of church government which was finally realized in the Synod of 1647. A tireless preacher and writer, he was author of a number of tracts and books including *Theses Sabbaticæ* (1649) and the very popular *The Sincere Convert* (1641). His diary was first published in *Three Valuable Pieces, etc.* (1747) and issued as his *Autobiography* in 1832.

SHEPARD, WILLIAM (*b. Westfield, Mass., 1737; d. Westfield, 1817*), Revolutionary officer. Colonel of the 3rd Continental Infantry, he distinguished himself at the battle of Pell's Point, 1776. As major-general of Massachusetts militia, 1786–87, he played an important part in the defense of Springfield against the insurgents during Shays's Rebellion. He served as congressman, Federalist, from Massachusetts, 1797–1803.

SHEPHERD, ALEXANDER ROBEY (*b. Washington, D.C., 1835; d. Batopilas, Mexico, 1902*), builder, politician, mine owner. As "boss" of District of Columbia and its territorial governor, 1873–74, he was largely responsible for the improvement of the capital city, although his financial recklessness and unscrupulous methods led to a congressional investigation and a change in the District's type of government.

SHEPHERD, WILLIAM ROBERT (*b. Charleston, S.C., 1871; d. Berlin, Germany, 1934*), historian. Graduated Columbia, 1893; Ph.D., 1896. Taught at Columbia all his life, becoming Seth Low Professor of History, 1926. An expert in Latin-American history and affairs, he was author, among other books, of *Historical Atlas* (first edition, 1911) and *Atlas of Medieval and Modern History* (1932). [Supp. 1]

SHEPLEY, ETHER (*b. Groton, Mass., 1789; d. 1877*), Maine lawyer and jurist. U.S. senator, Democrat, from Maine, 1833–36, Shepley was a vigorous supporter of Andrew Jackson. Appointed judge of the Maine supreme court, 1836, he became chief justice, 1848, and retired at the close of 1855.

SHEPLEY, GEORGE FOSTER (*b. Saco, Maine, 1819; d. 1878*), lawyer. Son of Ether Shepley. Practiced in Bangor and Portland, Maine; was U.S. attorney for Maine, 1848–49, 1853–61. Colonel commanding the 12th Maine Volunteers, Shepley became military commandant at New Orleans, La., May 1862, and in the next month was promoted brigadier-general and made governor of Louisiana. An associate of Benjamin F. Butler (1818–1893), he shares with that worthy the responsibility for whatever dishonesty there may have been in the army administration of New Orleans. Assigned to command in eastern Virginia, May 1864, he became military governor of Richmond after the fall of that city. *Post* 1869, he was circuit judge of the U.S. court in Maine.

SHERIDAN, PHILIP HENRY (*b. Albany, N.Y., 1831; d. Nonquitt, Mass., 1888*), Union soldier. Raised in Somerset, O., Sheridan graduated from West Point with the class of 1853. Assigned to the infantry, he served on frontier duty along the Rio Grande and in the Northwest. Promoted captain, 1861, he began Civil War service in the quartermaster department and was on H. W. Halleck's staff. Appointed colonel of the 2nd Michigan Cavalry, May 1862, he was raised to brigadier-general in a little over a month for his victory at Booneville, Mo. His subsequent career was brilliant. Commanding infantry, he was successful at Perryville; at Stone

River he practically saved the army of Rosecrans for which he was made major-general of volunteers, December 1862. Distinguished also at Chickamauga and at Missionary Ridge, he rose to high favor with U. S. Grant who gave Sheridan command of all the cavalry of the Army of the Potomac. His brilliant and decisive raids on Confederate communications around Richmond in May 1864 caused great alarm and apprehension in the Confederate capital. In August, as commander of the Army of the Shenandoah, he effectively carried out Grant's orders to destroy all supplies in the Valley. His army was surprised and almost routed at Cedar Creek on October 9, while he was twenty miles away at Winchester, but he made his famous ride to the battlefield in time to rally his troops, and to snatch victory from defeat. He was promoted to major-general in the regular service, November 1864. Early in 1865 he severed Lee's communications with the South, turned the flank of the Confederate Army, and forced Lee to begin the retreat to Appomattox. In the final operations of the war, Sheridan's troops cut off Lee from any further withdrawal and the Confederate surrender followed.

Sheridan administered the military division of the Gulf *post* 1865 and in 1867 was appointed military governor of Louisiana and Texas. His severely repressive measures in the interests of Reconstruction, though supported by Grant, incurred the disapproval of President Andrew Johnson. Transferred to the department of the Missouri, Sheridan compelled the hostile plains Indians to settle upon their reservations. Promoted lieutenant-general, March 1869, he commanded the division of the Missouri; in 1870–71, he visited the German armies during the Franco-Prussian War. Succeeding W. T. Sherman as commander-in-chief of the army, 1884, he received the highest military rank, that of general, on June 1, 1888. A few days before his death, he completed his *Personal Memoirs* (1888). Sheridan was a short man, of unprepossessing bearing, but endowed with a magnetic personality and a sincere concern for the welfare of his troops. Cool and self-possessed in battle, he was a dashing and brilliant leader of men, who acted according to two rules: to take the offensive whenever possible, and to wring the last possible advantage from a defeated enemy.

SHERMAN, FRANK DEMPSTER (*b. Peekskill, N.Y., 1860; d. New York, N.Y., 1916*), poet, architect, mathematician, genealogist.

SHERMAN, JAMES SCHOOLCRAFT (*b. Utica, N.Y., 1855; d. 1912*), lawyer, businessman, politician. Congressman, Republican, from New York, 1887–91, 1893–1909. A "regular," Sherman was not identified with important measures, preferring to give his time to parliamentary management in which he was gifted. He was regarded as second only to Thomas B. Reed as a presiding officer in the House. He served as vice-president of the United States, 1909–12.

SHERMAN, JOHN (*b. Dedham, England, 1613; d. 1685*), Puritan clergyman, mathematician. Emigrated to Massachusetts Bay, 1634. Renowned as a preacher, he ministered at Watertown, Mass., and at Wethersfield and other Connecticut settlements. Appointed pastor at Watertown, 1647, he remained in that post for the rest of his life. He was an occasional lecturer on mathematics at Harvard and held many honorary positions at the college.

SHERMAN, JOHN (*b. Lancaster, O., 1823; d. 1900*), statesman. Brother of William T. Sherman. Admitted to the bar, 1844, Sherman entered politics as a Whig and later became a hard-driving, effective worker for the rising Republican party. Elected to Congress from Ohio, 1854, he served in the House until 1861 when he became U.S. senator. Leaving the Senate in 1877, he was U.S. secretary of the treasury until 1881, when he regained his Senate seat and occupied it until 1897.

Sherman's moderate utterances on slavery and his party loyalty in Congress aided his rise to the chairmanship of the House ways and means committee, 1859. As a senator, he served with realistic ability on the finance committee, becoming its chairman in 1867. Balked in his natural caution and conservatism by wartime necessity, he helped to give greenbacks the status of legal tender but led in planning the national banking system (1863) and advocated unsuccessfully a program of economy and rigorous taxation. Although favoring personally a moderate Reconstruction policy, his substitute for Thad Stevens's drastic military Reconstruction plan was hardly less rigorous. He voted for most of the Radical program and, although expressing sympathy for President Johnson, he voted to convict him. After the war he dominated national financial policy. Privately opposed to the strong tide of inflationist sentiment, he was swayed by it. Thus, while seeing in the cancellation of greenbacks the most direct route to specie resumption, he opposed McCulloch's currency contraction policies of 1866–68. He believed that resumption was necessary to safeguard the national credit but felt that it must be undertaken when political conditions permitted. His work on the Funding Act of 1870 reduced the burden of public interest and helped restore national credit. In 1873 he was largely responsible for the mint-reform bill which ended the coinage of silver dollars and was denounced as the chief agent of the "Crime of '73." Two years later he yielded his own excellent resumption plan for funding greenbacks in favor of the substitute scheme of George F. Edmunds.

Sherman's pre-eminence in financial matters caused President Hayes to appoint him secretary of the treasury in 1877. Ignoring the inflationist outcry, he strengthened the resumption act by declaring that he was empowered to issue bonds after, as well as before, resumption. He also convinced the bankers that the government would redeem its bonds in gold, thereby enhancing national prestige. The political difficulties of Hayes's administration, a depression, and the clamor for "free silver," all made it hard for him to attain his main purposes—the resumption of specie payments and the funding of the public debt. Humiliated by a congressional resolution declaring government bonds payable in silver, he was able to take advantage of divisions among the inflationists to defeat their extreme objectives. The Bland-Allison Act of 1878 stipulated only the limited coinage of silver, rather than free coinage. Encouraged by some favorable developments in trade, Sherman made his final preparations carefully so that by Jan. 2, 1879, specie payments were smoothly resumed. As the end of his cabinet service approached, the United States stood firmly on the gold standard and the resumption policy was an admitted success.

In 1880, 1884, and 1888 Sherman sought the Republican presidential nomination but his lack of popular appeal and strong inflationist opposition militated against him. During his second period of service in the Senate, his most significant contributions were his share in the anti-trust and silver-purchase acts of 1890. Appointed U.S. secretary of state, 1897, he defended his anti-expansionist views when the cabinet decided for war with Spain, and resigned in protest. Prior to his resignation, he betrayed a growing loss of memory which incapacitated him for much beyond routine operations.

Economically, Sherman's point of view was that of the conservative creditor; politically, he understood very well the radical debtor psychology of his constituents. He carefully studied the attitudes of the Middle West and helped to stamp national legislation with the influence of that section.

SHERMAN, ROGER (*b. Newton, Mass., 1721 o.s.; d. 1793*), lawyer, merchant, Connecticut colonial legislator and jurist, statesman. Settled in New Milford, Conn., 1743; resided in New Haven, *post* 1761. Serving, in addition to his many other public offices, as judge of the superior court of Connecticut, 1766–89, Sherman belonged to the conservative wing of the Revolutionary party; he was, however, one of the first to deny the supremacy of Parliament in American affairs. Active in committee work in the Continental Congress, 1774–81 and 1783–84, he was a member of the committee appointed to draft the Declaration of Independence (which he signed) and of the committee on the Articles of Confederation. Described by John Adams as "an old Puritan, as honest as an angel and as firm in the cause of American Independence as Mount Atlas," Sherman fought attempts to weaken government credit by fiat currency or excessive loans and urged frequent levying of high taxes by Congress and by the states. Perhaps the most influential figure in Congress toward the end of the Revolution, he was

hopeful that the Confederation might be strengthened and entered the Federal Convention, 1787, still disposed to patch up the old scheme of government. Soon aware of the need for creating a new system, he introduced the so-called "Connecticut Compromise" in June 1787; he also favored an executive dominated by the legislature and made a stand for election of congressmen and senators by the state legislatures. A signer of the Constitution, he took a prominent part in the campaign for its ratification and contributed letters in support of it to the *New Haven Gazette* under pseudonym of "A Countryman," November and December 1787. Elected to Congress, 1789, he opposed amendments to the Constitution, urged use of Western lands to extinguish the national debt, favored sale of public lands to settlers rather than speculators and voted for Hamilton's measure for assumption. He served as U.S. senator from Connecticut, 1791–93. Illustrating at its best the Puritan combination of piety and a desire to succeed in practical affairs, he was honored by contemporaries for his ability and integrity although his personal awkwardness and rusticity of manner were also remarked.

SHERMAN, STUART PRATT (*b. Anita, Iowa, 1881; d. near Dunewood, on Lake Michigan, 1926*), literary critic, educator. Graduated Williams, 1903; took Ph D. at Harvard, 1906, where he was influenced by Irving Babbitt. Taught English at Northwestern University; headed department of English at University of Illinois which he made one of the strongest in the Middle West. A frequent contributor to the *Nation*, 1908–18, he was in critical sympathy with its then editor, Paul Elmer More. Author of *Matthew Arnold: How to Know Him* (1917), he applied Arnold's principles to the chief contemporary writers in his *On Contemporary Literature* (1917). In his belief that contemporary American writers had gone astray through failure to understand the national ideal, he became a standard-bearer of tradition against the modernist Crocean critics of the early 1920's, but later shifted his position to a greater sympathy with his opponents. *Post* 1924 he was editor of the literary supplement of the *New York Herald Tribune*. Among his later books were *Americans* (1922), *Points of View* (1924) and *Critical Woodcuts* (1926).

SHERMAN, THOMAS WEST (*b. Newport, R.I., 1813; d. Newport, 1879*), soldier. Graduated West Point, 1836. Assigned to the artillery, he served in the campaigns against the Florida Indians and rendered conspicuous service as a battery commander in the Mexican War. After frontier duty largely in Minnesota and Kansas, he held brigade and division command during the Civil War in the Union Army, distinguishing himself particularly in command of land forces at taking of Port Royal, S.C. and Fernandina, Fla., 1861; also in the expedition against Port Hudson, La., May 1863. He retired as major-general, 1871.

SHERMAN, WILLIAM TECUMSEH (*b. Lancaster, O., 1820; d. New York, N.Y., 1891*), Union soldier. Brother of John Sherman (1823–1900). Losing his father as a young boy, Sherman was raised in the family of Thomas Ewing (1789–1871). On graduation from West Point, 1840, he was assigned to the artillery. He spent his leisure time in the study of law and in travel in the South. He saw little active service during the Mexican War in which he was employed mainly as adjutant to Philip Kearny, Richard B. Mason and Persifor F. Smith. In May 1850, he married Ellen Ewing, daughter of his guardian. Resigning his army commission, 1853, he was unsuccessful in a banking venture and as a lawyer in Leavenworth, Kans., but was very successful as superintendent of a military college at Alexandria, La., 1859–61.

Regarding, as he did, the Union and the Constitution with almost religious fervor, he also loved the South and her people; he considered it a duty to end the contest between North and South as quickly and ruthlessly as possible with the proviso that the peace terms be as lenient as the war was stern. Appointed colonel of the 13th Infantry, May 1861, he was assigned to brigade command in July and shared in the disaster of first Bull Run. Transferred to Kentucky as brigadier-general of volunteers, he took on the thankless job of trying to hold that state in the Union with little more than raw home guards to work with. Anxiety preyed upon his mind, he overestimated the difficulties of his position, and his quarrels with the press over breaches of security encouraged newspapermen to report that Sherman's mind was giving way. Superseded, he was received at headquarters with suspicion and coldness. Joining U. S. Grant's army with a division of volunteers, he took prominent part in the battle of Shiloh and the advance to Corinth and was promoted major-general of volunteers, May 1862. In July, Grant sent Sherman to Memphis, Tenn., where Sherman suppressed guerrillas, put civil authority on a firm basis and made a push at Vicksburg, Miss., which was rendered hopeless when Grant's communications were cut and he had to withdraw from his part in the operation. Grant reorganized his forces, and with Sherman commanding the XV Corps, carried through the amphibious campaign which resulted in the surrender of Vicksburg on July 4, 1863.

On Grant's subsequent advance to supreme command in the West, Sherman was given command of the Army of the Tennessee. He participated in the relief of Chattanooga and Knoxville and destroyed the Confederate base at Meridian, Miss., in January 1864. Sherman succeeded to supreme command in the West after Grant's promotion to commander-in-chief of all the armies. By the combined plan of 1864, Gen. George Meade was to advance against Gen. R. E. Lee and Richmond, while Sherman advanced early in May against Gen. J. E. Johnston and Atlanta. Concentrating about 100,000 men at Chattanooga, Sherman forced Johnston back to the Allatoona Pass-Kenesaw Mountain line, and then back to Peachtree Creek, by several flanking maneuvers. He swung around Atlanta and opened a siege, cutting the railroads to Montgomery and Macon. On September 1, Gen. Hood, who had replaced Johnston, evacuated Atlanta. Sherman, who had been promoted to major-general in the regular army, ordered the removal of the civilian population from the city. With Grant's approval, he began the famous "march through Georgia" on November 15. His purpose was to break the resistance of the South by cutting off the supply of her armies and Georgia was the only untouched source of supply. His army lived off the country, destroying war supplies, public buildings, railroads and manufacturing shops. By bringing the war home to the civilian population, Sherman believed that it could be terminated quickly; for his deliberate exploitation of this principle he has been called the first modern general. His activities made him the center of a bitter controversy but he urged that it was better to destroy goods rather than life, that wanton destruction was prevented insofar as possible, and that there was no serious personal violence to noncombatants. It is obvious, however, that discipline in his army was not strict enough. After occupying Savannah on Dec. 21, 1864, he marched northward through the Carolinas, causing even more destruction than in Georgia. He occupied Columbia, S.C., and burned it, forced the evacuation of Charleston and then moved on Raleigh, N.C. Eight days after Lee's surrender on April 9, 1865, Gen. J. E. Johnston, Confederate commander in the Carolinas, surrendered to Sherman. The terms granted were liberal, but the Washington government, enraged by the assassination of Lincoln, repudiated them.

After the war Sherman commanded the Division of the Mississippi, aiding the construction of the transcontinental railway and controlling Indian hostility. In 1866 he was promoted to lieutenant-general and was sent on a diplomatic mission to President Juarez of Mexico, as part of the pressure exerted on France for withdrawal of support to Maximilian. Three years later Sherman became general commanding the army and held the position until his retirement in 1883. He rejected repeated attempts to draw him into politics, especially in the Republican convention of 1884, when his positive veto prohibited a move for his nomination for the presidency. His *Memoirs* were first published in 1875; his famous statement that "war . . . is all hell" was made in a speech at Columbus, O., Aug. 11, 1880.

SHERRY, LOUIS (*b. probably St. Albans, Vt., 1856; d. 1926*), restaurateur. Opened his first restaurant and confectionery at 38th St. and Sixth Ave., New York

City, 1881. Removing to two successive locations on Fifth Ave. and eventually to Park Ave., he was highly successful as host and caterer to the wealthy.

SHERWIN, THOMAS (*b. Westmoreland, N.H., 1799; d. 1869*), educator. Graduated Harvard, 1825. As principal of the English High School, Boston, Mass., 1837–69, Sherwin made it the leading educational institution of its grade in the United States; he was active also in the establishment of the Massachusetts Institute of Technology.

SHERWOOD, ADIEL (*b. Fort Edward, N.Y., 1791; d. St. Louis, Mo., 1879*), Baptist clergyman, educator. Graduated Union, 1817. Removing to Georgia, 1818, he was active in the ministry there and as a teacher in several institutions; he was president of Shurtleff College, 1841–46, and later of Masonic and Marshall colleges.

SHERWOOD, ISAAC RUTH (*b. Stanford, N.Y., 1835; d. 1925*), journalist, Union soldier. Editor of a number of Ohio newspapers at various times, Sherwood served as congressman, Republican, from Ohio, 1873–75, but was refused renomination because of his "greenback" sympathies. As congressman, Democrat, from Ohio, 1907–21, 1923–25, he was an aggressive advocate of veterans' pensions and an opponent of U.S. entry into World War I.

SHERWOOD, KATHARINE MARGARET BROWN-LEE (*b. Poland, O., 1841; d. 1914*), journalist, reformer. Wife of Isaac R. Sherwood.

SHERWOOD, MARY ELIZABETH WILSON (*b. Keene, N.H., 1826; d. New York, N.Y., 1903*), author. A prolific contributor to newspapers and periodicals and the writer of a number of books, Mrs. Sherwood was principally renowned for her manuals of social life and etiquette which were as popular as they were conservative.

SHERWOOD, THOMAS ADIEL (*b. Eatonton, Ga., 1834; d. California, 1918*), jurist. Son of Adiel Sherwood. Judge of the Missouri supreme court, 1872–1902, he was a strict constructionist and opponent of federal encroachment, but also an earnest defender of civil liberty and a proponent of both administrative and procedural judicial reform.

SHERWOOD, WILLIAM HALL (*b. Lyons, N.Y., 1854; d. Chicago, Ill., 1911*), pianist, teacher, composer. A pupil of William Mason (1829–1908) and others in America, he studied also with distinguished masters in Europe, including Franz Liszt. One of the first Americans to play with great European orchestras, he devoted himself to teaching and to concert work in America post 1876. He founded the Sherwood Music School in Chicago, 1897.

SHICK CALAMYS. [See SHIKELLAMY, d. 1748.]

SHIELDS, CHARLES WOODRUFF (*b. New Albany, Ind., 1825; d. Newport, R.I., 1904*), Presbyterian and Episcopal clergyman, educator. Graduated College of New Jersey (Princeton), 1844; Princeton Theological Seminary, 1847. A professor of philosophy and history for many years at Princeton, Shields devoted his life to the reconciliation of science with religion and to the reunion of Protestantism.

SHIELDS, GEORGE HOWELL (*b. Bardstown, Ky., 1842; d. St. Louis, Mo., 1924*), Missouri Republican politician and jurist.

SHIELDS, GEORGE OLIVER (*b. Batavia, O., 1846; d. New York, N.Y., 1925*), journalist, author, pioneer in the conservation of wild life.

SHIELDS, JAMES (*b. Altmore, Ireland, 1806; d. Ottumwa, Iowa, 1879*), soldier, politician. Emigrated to America c. 1826; settled in Kaskaskia, Ill., where he studied and practiced law. As an Illinois legislator and state auditor, he helped correct that state's chaotic finances; he was judge of the Illinois supreme court, 1843–45. After brief service as commissioner of the U.S. General Land Office, he volunteered for the Mexican War and won a brevet of major-general for gallantry in action. Resigning an appointment as governor of Oregon Territory, he served as U.S. senator, Democrat, from Illinois, 1849–55. Removing to Minnesota Territory, he did much to stimulate Irish settlement there and was U.S. senator from Minnesota, 1858–59. Removing to California and then to Mexico, he returned to the United States on the outbreak of the Civil War and was appointed brigadier-general of volunteers, August 1861. Winning credit for his leadership at Kernstown and Port Republic, he resigned his commission, March 1863, and became a California railroad commissioner. Re-entering politics in Missouri, 1866, he served in the legislature and as a railroad commissioner and finally as U.S. senator, Democrat, from Missouri, January–March 1879.

SHIELDS, JOHN KNIGHT (*b. near Bean's Station, Tenn., 1858; d. near Bean's Station, 1934*), Tennessee jurist. An irreconcilable isolationist and conservative as U.S. senator, Independent Democrat-Republican, 1913–25. [Supp. 1]

SHIELDS, THOMAS EDWARD (*b. near Mendota, Minn., 1862; d. 1921*), Roman Catholic clergyman, educator. Slow to develop mentally, Shields was ordained, 1891, after a rigorous course in self-education and graduation from St. Thomas Seminary; he received a Ph D. in biology from Johns Hopkins, 1895. After teaching and pastoral work in St. Paul, Minn., he became an instructor at Catholic University, Washington, D.C., 1902, and was raised to professor of education and psychology, 1909. Constantly crusading against stereotypes in religious and general education, he was author of a number of books and founder of the *Catholic Educational Review* which he edited post 1911. He was founder also of the Sisters College as an affiliated school of the university, 1911, and an innovator in providing summer courses for teaching sisters.

SHIKELLAMY (*d. Shamokin, Pa., 1748*), Oneida chief. Father of James Logan (*c. 1725–1780*). A sympathetic intermediary between the frontier whites and the Iroquois, he was influential in negotiating the treaties of 1736 and 1744 which greatly favored the Iroquois at the expense of the Delaware and Shawnee.

SHILLABER, BENJAMIN PENHALLOW (*b. Portsmouth, N.H., 1814; d. Chelsea, Mass., 1890*), journalist, humorist, printer. Edited the important weekly the *Carpet-Bag*, 1851–53, to which Artemus Ward and Mark Twain sent their first contributions. Creator of the character of "Mrs. Partington," Shillaber served as chief connecting link between the old school of American humor which preceded the Civil War and the new. Among his separately published works were *Life and Sayings of Mrs. Partington* (1854), *Knitting-Work* (1859), *Partingtonian Patchwork* (1872) and the so-called Ike Partington juveniles.

SHINN, ASA (*b. New Jersey, 1781; d. Brattleboro, Vt., 1853*), Methodist clergyman, reformer. A founder of the Methodist Protestant Church, 1830.

SHIPHERD, JOHN JAY (*b. near Granville, N.Y., 1802; d. Olivet, Mich., 1844*), Congregational home missionary. Founder, with Philo P. Stewart and others, of Oberlin College, 1833.

SHIPMAN, ANDREW JACKSON (*b. Springvale, Va., 1857; d. 1915*), lawyer, Slavic scholar, philanthropist. Graduated Georgetown University, 1878. An able and successful lawyer in New York City, he maintained a lifelong interest in the welfare of Slavic immigrants, particulary in the religious rights of Catholics of the Eastern Rite.

SHIPP, ALBERT MICAJAH (*b. Stokes Co., N.C., 1819; d. Cleveland Springs, N.C., 1887*), Methodist clergyman, educator. Graduated University of North Carolina, 1840, where he taught history, 1849–59. President of Wofford College, 1859–75, he was professor of exegetical theology at Vanderbilt, 1875–85.

SHIPP, SCOTT (*b. Warrenton, Va., 1839; d. 1917*), Confederate soldier, educator. Graduated Virginia Military Institute, 1859. After service in the West Virginia and Romney campaigns, 1861, he became commandant of cadets at V.M.I., 1862, and led his men into the field on five occasions; the famous charge of the cadets against the Union forces at New Market, May 1864, was made under his command. Resuming his work at the Institute at the end of the war, he was promoted to its superintendency, 1890, and served in this capacity until 1907.

SHIPPEN, EDWARD (*b. Methley, England, 1639; d. Philadelphia, Pa., 1712*), merchant, Pennsylvania colonial legislator. Emigrated to Boston, Mass., 1668.

Joining the Society of Friends *c.* 1671, he was severely persecuted until his removal to Philadelphia *c.* 1694. Holder of many high provincial offices, he was mayor of Philadelphia, 1701–03, and acting governor of Pennsylvania, April 1703—February 1704.

SHIPPEN, EDWARD (*b. Philadelphia, Pa., 1728/29; d. Philadelphia, 1806*), jurist. Great-grandson of Edward Shippen (1639–1712); father-in-law of Benedict Arnold. A moderate Loyalist during the Revolution, Shippen held a number of judicial posts *post* 1784. An associate justice of the Pennsylvania supreme court, 1791–99, he was chief justice, 1799–1805.

SHIPPEN, WILLIAM (*b. Philadelphia, Pa., 1736; d. Philadelphia, 1808*), physician, medical educator. Great-grandson of Edward Shippen (1639–1712); cousin of Edward Shippen (1729–1806). Graduated College of New Jersey (Princeton), 1754. Studied medicine with his father and in London and at the University of Edinburgh, where he received the M.D. degree, 1761. Successful in practice in Philadelphia *post* 1762, and as a teacher of anatomy and midwifery, he was appointed professor of surgery and anatomy at the College of Philadelphia, 1765. During the Revolution, he served under various titles as director of several divisions of the Continental Army hospital service. He was chief of the medical department of the Continental Army, 1777–81, succeeding John Morgan who charged him with bad faith. He was later court-martialed for alleged financial irregularities in office, but acquitted. A member of the staff of the Pennsylvania Hospital, 1778–79, 1791–1802, he held the chair of anatomy, surgery and midwifery at University of Pennsylvania *post* 1791.

SHIRAS, GEORGE (*b. Pittsburgh, Pa., 1832; d. Pittsburgh, 1924*), jurist. Brother of Oliver P. Shiras. Graduated Yale, 1853. Associate justice, U.S. Supreme Court, 1892–1903, he was widely criticized (perhaps unjustly) for his part in the nullification of the federal income tax statute in April 1895.

SHIRAS, OLIVER PERRY (*b. Pittsburgh, Pa., 1833; d. 1916*), jurist. Brother of George Shiras. Admitted to the Iowa bar, 1856, after graduation from Ohio University and Yale Law School, he practiced in Dubuque. As U.S. judge for the northern Iowa district, 1882–1903, he excelled in equity cases and enunciated (1894) the concept of a national common law subject to independent application by the federal courts irrespective of state interpretation.

SHIRLAW, WALTER (*b. Paisley, Scotland, 1838; d. Madrid, Spain, 1909*), genre, portrait and mural painter. Came to America as a child. Beginning his career as a bank-note engraver, he studied in Chicago and was a student in Munich, Germany, 1870–77. While in Germany, he painted his two best pictures, "Toning the Bell" (1874) and "Sheep-Shearing in the Bavarian Highlands" (1876). Returning to America, he became first president of the Society of American Artists, taught in the Art Students League and achieved a fair degree of professional success. His mastery of design may be studied in his ceiling painting, "The Sciences," in the Library of Congress, Washington, D.C.

SHIRLEY, WILLIAM (*b. Preston, Sussex, England, 1694; d. Roxbury, Mass., 1771*), colonial official, lawyer. Emigrated to Boston, Mass., 1731. As judge of admiralty and later advocate-general, he upheld the imperial view of business matters, laboring faithfully to enforce the trade acts. Critical of Gov. Jonathan Belcher's policies, Shirley succeeded Belcher as governor of Massachusetts in May 1741. Adroitly settling the land-bank controversy, Shirley persuaded the General Court to make appropriations for defense of the colony and had affairs in a good state of preparation by the time war was declared with the French in 1744. Aware of the economic importance of the French fortress of Louisbourg on Cape Breton Island, he matured plans to capture it despite discouragement from the English government; he won support of the General Court for the enterprise in which the other New England colonies cooperated. The taking of weakly defended Louisbourg in June 1745 proved to be the one great English victory of the war. From 1749 to 1753 Shirley participated in the negotiations held in Paris concerning the boundary line between French North America and New England. With the outbreak of the French and Indian War which he had foreseen, he was appointed major-general and given command of the campaign against Niagara. After Gen. Braddock's death in July 1755, he succeeded to the supreme command of British forces on the American continent. Though his military plans were sound they were unsuccessful, largely because of bickering among the colonies and their failure to lend adequate support. On the failure of the Niagara expedition, Shirley's enemies accused him of mismanagement, and suspicion was aroused in England that he was guilty of treasonable activity. Summoned to England early in 1756, he was threatened with court-martial, but charges were dropped for lack of evidence. Meantime he had been removed as governor of Massachusetts. Named governor of the Bahama Islands, 1761, he resigned in 1767. As an executive Shirley showed ability and tact and became one of the most personally popular of colonial governors. Careless in his management of public finance, he was of unimpeachable personal integrity. More than any other contemporary governor, he had a broad grasp of the whole imperial problem.

SHOBONIER. [See SHABONEE, *c. 1775–1859.*]

SHOLES, CHRISTOPHER LATHAM (*b. Mooresburg, Pa., 1819; d. 1890*), printer, journalist, inventor. Removing to Wisconsin *c.* 1837, Sholes engaged in politics, held political appointments and was editor of several Wisconsin newspapers including the *Milwaukee News* and the *Milwaukee Sentinel*. Holder of a number of patents for mechanical devices, he devoted most of his life *post* 1867 to the perfection of the typewriter. Granted a basic patent, 1868, he patented improvements, 1871, but on failing to raise the means for making and marketing his machine, he sold his rights to the Remington Arms Co., March 1873. He continued to improve his typewriter until 1878, turning over his results to the Remington Co.

SHONTS, THEODORE PERRY (*b. Crawford Co., Pa., 1856; d. 1919*), railroad executive. Able president of a number of Midwestern railroads; chairman, second Isthmian Canal Commission, 1905–07; president, Interborough Rapid Transit Co., New York City, *post* 1907. An efficient, adaptable manager.

SHOOK, ALFRED MONTGOMERY (*b. near Winchester, Tenn., 1845; d. Nashville, Tenn., 1923*), industrialist. As superintendent and general manager of the Tennessee Coal, Iron & Railroad Co., 1868–1901, Shook became a master of all phases of iron manufacture, greatly enlarged the business and directed the company's engagement in steel manufacture at Ensley, near Birmingham, Ala. The opening of his company's steel works in 1899 began a new era in Southern industrial development.

SHOREY, PAUL (*b. Davenport, Iowa, 1857; d. Chicago, Ill., 1934*), classicist. Graduated Harvard, 1878. After attending the universities of Leipzig and Bonn and the American School at Athens, he received a Ph.D. from Munich in 1884. Professor of Latin and Greek at Bryn Mawr, 1885–92, he went to the University of Chicago as professor of Greek and served as head of the department, 1896–1927. An erudite and unusually effective teacher, he made his greatest contribution to scholarship in the field of Platonic studies; a founder of *Classical Philology*, he was its editor, 1908–34. Among his numerous books and monographs, *What Plato Said* (1933) is outstanding. Impatient with modern pedagogical methods, Shorey was a stout opponent of current prejudices against the classics in education.

SHORT, CHARLES (*b. Haverhill, Mass., 1821; d. New York, N.Y., 1886*), classical philologist. Graduated Harvard, 1846. After service as teacher and headmaster in several academies, he was president of Kenyon College, 1863–67. Succeeding Henry Drisler as professor of Latin at Columbia, 1867, he remained in that post for the rest of his life.

SHORT, CHARLES WILKINS (*b. Woodford Co., Ky., 1794; d. near Louisville, Ky., 1863*), physician, educator, botanist. Nephew of William Short; grandson of John C. Symmes. Graduated Transylvania University, 1810; M.D., University of Pennsylvania, 1815; made private studies with Caspar Wistar (1716–1818). Teacher and dean at Transylvania and later at the Medical Institute of Louisville, he is remembered principally as a collector and classifier of plants from the little-explored country west of the Alleghenies.

SHORT, SIDNEY HOWE (*b. Columbus, O., 1858; d. 1902*), electrical engineer, educator. Inventor of numerous important devices for arc-lighting and electric traction systems.

SHORT, WILLIAM (*b. Surry Co., Va., 1759; d. 1849*), diplomat, planter and landowner. Graduated William and Mary, 1779. A founder of Phi Beta Kappa, Short served on the executive council of Virginia, 1783–84, and thereafter as Thomas Jefferson's private secretary and secretary of legation at Paris. Becoming chargé d'affaires, 1789, he served with ability until 1792 when he was appointed U.S. minister at The Hague. Named as joint commissioner with William Carmichael to negotiate a treaty with Spain, he went to Madrid in February 1793. Superseded by Thomas Pinckney, he loyally cooperated with Pinckney in securing the so-called "Pinckney Treaty," signed October 1795. Disappointed in his professional ambitions, he amassed a large fortune. He died probably in Philadelphia, Pa.

SHORTER, JOHN GILL (*b. Monticello, Ga., 1818; d. 1872*), jurist, Alabama legislator. An enthusiastic secessionist and strong supporter of Jefferson Davis, Shorter served in the provisional Confederate Congress, and was governor of Alabama, 1861–63.

SHOUP, FRANCIS ASBURY (*b. Laurel, Ind., 1834; d. Columbia, Tenn., 1896*), Confederate brigadier-general and artillerist, Episcopal clergyman, educator. Graduated West Point, 1855. Chief of artillery under Gens. J. E. Johnston and John Hood in the Atlanta campaign, Shoup took orders after the war and was professor of mathematics at the University of Mississippi and at the University of the South.

SHOUP, GEORGE LAIRD (*b. Kittanning, Pa., 1836; d. Boise, Idaho, 1904*), businessman, Union soldier, Colorado and Idaho pioneer. Helped found Salmon, Idaho, 1866, where he made his home. Long active in Republican politics, he was territorial governor and governor of Idaho, 1889–90, and first U.S. senator from the state, 1891–1901.

SHOWERMAN, GRANT (*b. Brookfield, Wis., 1870; d. Madison, Wis., 1935*), classicist. Graduated University of Wisconsin, 1896; Ph.D., 1900. Professor at Wisconsin for the greater part of his life, he was expert in the history, literature and art of Rome and an outspoken exponent of classical culture. Among his many books were *Eternal Rome* (1924) and *Rome and the Romans* (1931). [*Supp. 1*]

SHRADY, GEORGE FREDERICK (*b. New York, N.Y., 1837; d. 1907*), surgeon, medical journalist. M.D., College of Physicians and Surgeons, New York, 1858. Holder of many New York hospital staff appointments, he was a skillful, conservative operator,

specializing mainly in plastic surgery. He made his principal contribution to medicine as editor of the *American Medical Times*, 1860–64, and of the *Medical Record*, 1866–1904, championing reforms in medical education and practice. He was father of Henry M. Shrady.

SHRADY, HENRY MERWIN (*b. New York, N.Y., 1871; d. 1922*), sculptor. Son of George F. Shrady. Mainly self-taught save for some technical instruction from Karl Bitter, Shrady did his finest work on the memorial group to Gen. U. S. Grant, in Union Square, Washington, D.C. Winner of the competition for this work, 1902, he labored on it until 1922 and died two weeks before it was dedicated.

SHREVE, HENRY MILLER (*b. Burlington Co., N.J., 1785; d. St. Louis, Mo., 1851*), steamboat captain. Raised on the Pennsylvania frontier, Shreve began trading journeys by keelboat down the Monongahela and Ohio to the West, 1799. Initiator of the fur trade between St. Louis and Philadelphia via Pittsburgh, 1807, he then entered the lead trade between the Upper Mississippi and New Orleans. Becoming a stockholder in the steamboat *Enterprise*, 1814, he freighted supplies for Andrew Jackson's army from Pittsburgh to New Orleans in the vessel and in May 1815 brought her successfully up to Louisville, Ky. He established the practicability of steam navigation on the Mississippi and Ohio route with his second steamboat, the *Washington*, 1816–17, and later broke the Fulton-Livingston monopoly which had been asserted against his operations in legal proceedings. As U.S. superintendent of Western river improvements, 1827–41, Shreve designed the first steam snagboat and removed the famous Red River raft. Shreveport, La., was named for him.

SHREVE, THOMAS HOPKINS (*b. Alexandria, Va., 1808; d. Louisville, Ky., 1853*), journalist. Removing to Cincinnati, O., c. 1830, he was associated there with such literary pioneers as William D. Gallagher and James H. Perkins; with Gallagher, he edited the *Cincinnati Mirror*, 1831–36. Active in business as well, he published essays and poems in the *Western Messenger*, the *Western Literary Journal*, the *Western Monthly Magazine*, the *Knickerbocker* and others. He served as assistant editor of the *Louisville Daily Journal*, 1842–53.

SHUBRICK, JOHN TEMPLER (*b. Bull's Island, S.C., 1788; d. 1815*), naval officer. Brother of William B. Shubrick. Commissioned midshipman, 1806, he had an extraordinarily eventful career, serving in major actions aboard the *Constitution*, the *Chesapeake*, the *Hornet* and the *Guerrière*. Returning home from Algiers, 1815, in command of the *Epervier*, he was lost at sea.

SHUBRICK, WILLIAM BRANFORD (*b. Bull's Island, S.C., 1790; d. 1874*), naval officer. Brother of John T. Shubrick. Commissioned midshipman, 1806, he served for a time under Capt. James Lawrence and was shipmate with James Fenimore Cooper. Promoted lieutenant, 1813, he served aboard the *Constellation* and the *Constitution,* 1813–15. After some thirty years of routine ship and shore duty, he served on the Pacific Coast during the Mexican War. Chairman of the lighthouse board, 1852–71, he is chiefly remembered for his command of the expedition sent to settle difficulties with Paraguay, 1858–59. Retired as flag-officer, 1861, he was raised to rear-admiral (retired), 1862.

SHUCK, JEHU LEWIS (*b. Alexandria, Va., 1812; d. Barnwell Court House, S.C., 1863*), Baptist clergyman. Missionary to China, 1836–45, 1847–51. He later served as a missionary among the Chinese in California.

SHUEY, EDWIN LONGSTREET (*b. Cincinnati, O., 1857; d. 1924*), educator, advertising man, director of factory welfare work. Author of *Factory People and Their Employers* (1900).

SHUEY, WILLIAM JOHN (*b. Miamisburg, O., 1827; d. 1920*), clergyman of the United Brethren in Christ. Able and energetic in the service of his church as minister, missionary, publishing agent (1865–97) and seminary manager.

SHUFELDT, ROBERT WILSON (*b. Red Hook, N.Y., 1822; d. Washington, D.C., 1895*), naval officer. Appointed midshipman, 1839, he resigned, 1854, to engage in the merchant service and during the early years of the Civil War was consul to Cuba and a special agent to Mexico. Recommissioned commander, November 1862, he served with ability at sea and in miscellaneous postwar duties until 1878. The great achievement of his career was his negotiation of a treaty with China, 1882, which established diplomatic relations, extraterritoriality and commercial privileges for the United States. He retired as rear-admiral, 1884.

SHULZE, JOHN ANDREW (*b. Berks Co., Pa., 1775; d. Lancaster, Pa., 1852*), Lutheran clergyman, businessman, Pennsylvania legislator. Grandson of Henry M. Mühlenberg. As Democratic governor of Pennsylvania, 1823–29, he promoted canal construction and public elementary education.

SHUNK, FRANCIS RAWN (*b. Trappe, Pa., 1788; d. 1848*), educator, lawyer, public official. Restored Pennsylvania's financial credit and opposed concessions to corporate business interests as Democratic governor, 1845–48.

SHURTLEFF, NATHANIEL BRADSTREET (*b. Boston, Mass., 1810; d. 1874*), physician, antiquary. Democratic mayor of Boston, 1868–70. A thorough and conscientious editor of original Massachusetts records, he was author of *A Topographical and Historical Description of Boston* (1871).

SHURTLEFF, ROSWELL MORSE (*b. Rindge, N.H., 1838; d. New York, N.Y., 1915*), animal and landscape painter.

SHUTE, SAMUEL (*b. London, England, 1662; d. England, 1742*), British soldier. Shute's administration as colonial governor of Massachusetts Bay and New Hampshire extended from 1716 to 1727 and was one of the stormiest endured by any royal governor. Constantly at odds with the Assembly over fiscal matters and questions of legislative privilege, he returned to England, 1723, to complain of his grievances and seek redress. As he was about to return to Massachusetts in the spring of 1727, his commission was vacated.

SIAMESE TWINS. [See CHANG AND ENG, 1811–1874.]

SIBERT, WILLIAM LUTHER (*b. Gadsden, Ala., 1860; d. near Bowling Green, Ky., 1935*), military engineer. Graduated West Point, 1884. Commissioned in the engineers, he performed extensive river and harbor improvement work and distinguished himself in reconstruction of Philippine railways, 1899–1900. He supervised construction of the Atlantic Division of the Panama Canal, 1908–14. Promoted major-general, May 1917, he organized the Chemical Warfare Service for the army in World War I. [*Supp. 1*]

SIBLEY, GEORGE CHAMPLAIN (*b. Great Barrington, Mass., 1782; d. near St. Charles, Mo., 1863*), Indian agent, explorer. Son of John Sibley; grandson of Samuel Hopkins (1721–1803). Served as factor and Indian agent at Fort Osage, Mo., 1808–26; explored the Grand Saline in present Oklahoma, 1811; was one of the commissioners to mark Santa Fé trail from Council Grove to the Mexican boundary, 1825.

SIBLEY, HENRY HASTINGS (*b. Detroit, Michigan Territory, 1811; d. 1891*), fur trader, Minnesota pioneer. Settled at Mendota, 1834. Influential among the Sioux. He was delegate to Congress from the Territory of Wisconsin, 1848, and promoted the organization of Minnesota Territory, 1849, serving as its delegate, 1849–58. He was first governor of the State of Minnesota, 1858–60, elected as a Democrat. Commanding the Minnesota forces during the Sioux uprising of 1862, he relieved the frontier posts and fought the battle of Wood Lake. During 1863–64, he commanded punitive expeditions against the Sioux in the Dakota region, and in 1865–66 was one of the commissioners to negotiate peace treaties with the Sioux. Removing to St. Paul, Minn., he concerned himself with private business thereafter but remained an important and influential figure in the life of the state.

SIBLEY, HIRAM (*b. North Adams, Mass., 1807; d. Rochester, N.Y., 1888*), businessman, promoter. A pioneer in the telegraph industry, he early reached the conclusion that there were too many small companies and that consolidation was demanded; in association with Ezra Cornell, he formed the Western Union Telegraph Co. (chartered, 1856) which he served as president until 1866. An earnest advocate of a transcontinental telegraph line, he undertook the project first on his own account and amalgamated it with the Western Union in 1864. After his retirement from Western Union affairs, 1869, he invested in railroads and in agricultural enterprises with great success. He was one of the incorporators of Cornell University and a benefactor to it and to the University of Rochester.

SIBLEY, JOHN (*b. Sutton, Mass., 1757; d. 1837*), physician, Indian agent, Louisiana politician and planter. Father of George C. Sibley. Removed to Louisiana, 1802; served as contract surgeon to the U.S. Army at Natchitoches, 1803–05, and as Indian agent for Orleans Territory and Louisiana, 1805–14. He later prospered as a planter and salt manufacturer. His official reports to Gov. Claiborne and to President Jefferson are important sources of information regarding Louisiana.

SIBLEY, JOHN LANGDON (*b. Union, Maine, 1804; d. 1885*), librarian. Graduated Harvard, 1825; Harvard Divinity School, 1828. Assistant librarian of Harvard, 1825–26, 1841–56; librarian, 1856–77. He is remembered principally as author of the *Biographical Sketches of Graduates of Harvard University* (1873–85) covering the lives of graduates through the class of 1689.

SIBLEY, JOSEPH CROCKER (*b. Friendship, N.Y., 1850; d. near Franklin, Pa., 1926*), oil refiner. Congressman, Democrat-Populist-Prohibitionist, from Pennsylvania, 1893–95; congressman, Democrat, 1899–1901; congressman, Republican, 1901–07. In addition to his activities in business and politics, he was an agriculturist and a stock-breeder.

SICALAMOUS. [Shikellamy, d. 1748.]

SICARD, MONTGOMERY (*b. New York, N.Y., 1836; d. Westernville, N.Y., 1900*), naval officer. Graduated U.S. Naval Academy, 1855. Distinguished as an ordnance expert, he developed the modern high-power naval guns installed before the war with Spain. Promoted rear-admiral, 1897, he was superseded as commander of the North Atlantic Squadron because of medical reasons, March 1898, and retired for age later in that year.

SICKELS, FREDERICK ELLSWORTH (*b. Gloucester Co., N.J., 1819; d. 1895*), engineer. Patented first successful drop cut-off for steam engines devised in the United States, 1842; patented a steam-steering apparatus for ships, 1860, which failed to receive any financial support for its exploitation.

SICKLES, DANIEL EDGAR (*b. New York, N.Y., 1819; d. New York, 1914*), lawyer, Union major-general, diplomat. Studied law under Benjamin F. Butler (1795–1858); was admitted to the bar, 1846.

Active in politics as a Democrat, he served as New York City corporation counsel, as secretary of the U.S. legation at London, as a New York State senator, and as a congressman from New York, 1857–61. A spectacular figure in Washington, D.C., he killed the son of Francis S. Key in a duel (1859), winning acquittal with an innovating plea of temporary mental aberration. Raising the New York Excelsior Brigade, 1861, he led it as brigadier-general and was promoted major-general early in 1863. Commanding the III Corps, he was an important factor in the Chancellorsville campaign and stopped Stonewall Jackson's advance. Criticized for a controversial maneuver at Gettysburg, July 2, 1863, he found his military career in the field at an end and served on diplomatic missions and as a military administrator until the end of 1867. Retiring from the army, 1869, he was a vigorous but undiplomatic U.S. minister to Spain, 1869–73. After living for a time abroad, he returned to New York where he held state appointments and served again in Congress, 1893–95.

SIDELL, WILLIAM HENRY (*b. New York, N.Y., 1810; d. New York, 1873*), civil engineer, Union brevet brigadier-general. Graduated West Point, 1833. Performed effective service as provost and recruiting officer in Kentucky and Tennessee, 1861–65.

SIDIS, BORIS (*b. Kiev, Russia, 1867; d. Portsmouth, N.H., 1923*), psychopathologist. Came to America, 1887. Graduated Harvard, A.B., 1894; Ph.D., 1897; M.D., 1908. Author of *The Psychology of Suggestion* (1898), an attempt to explain the nature of the subconscious; *Psychopathological Researches, Studies in Mental Dissociation* (1902); *The Psychology of Laughter* (1913) and other works.

SIDNEY, MARGARET. [See Lothrop, Harriet Mulford Stone, 1844–1924.]

SIEBER, AL (*b. Baden, Germany, 1844; d. near Globe, Ariz., 1907*), soldier, scout. Came to America as a child; was raised in Pennsylvania and Minnesota. After Civil War service with the Union Army, he went to the Far West, 1866, settling in Arizona *c.* 1868. Winning repute as a leader in organizing the settlers to defend themselves against Indian attack, he was engaged, 1871, as an army scout. In command of the famous Apache scouts under Gen. George Crook, he soon became recognized as the outstanding scout and Indian fighter of the Southwest. After service under a number of department commanders, he was discharged, 1890, by the agent of San Carlos Reservation for denouncing unfair treatment of the Apaches, and engaged thereafter in construction work. Trusted absolutely by his men, he could match them in endurance and trail skills; he possessed a high sense of honor and was utterly fearless. [*Supp. 1*]

SIGEL, FRANZ (*b. Sinsheim, Germany, 1824; d. New York, N.Y., 1902*), Union soldier, editor. An associate of Friedrich K. F. Hecker in the Baden insurrection, 1848, Sigel acted for a short time as minister of war in the revolutionary government of Baden and on the collapse of the movement fled first to Switzerland and then to England. Emigrating to America, 1852, he worked as a teacher and interested himself in the New York militia. Resident in St. Louis, Mo., when the Civil War broke out, Sigel became colonel of the 3rd Missouri Infantry, May 1861, and rose to divisional command during the struggle to hold Missouri in the Union. Promoted major-general of volunteers, March 1862, he was transferred to the eastern theatre of the war and was prominent as a corps commander until the spring of 1863. Considered unaggressive by the Washington authorities, he was removed from field command in the summer of 1864. Resigning his commission in May 1865, he worked as an editor of German newspapers in Baltimore, Md., and New York City, held several political appointments in New York and was prominent as a lecturer. Although his military career was comparatively undistinguished, his prompt, ardent espousal of the Union cause united the German population of the North solidly behind the Union.

SIGMAN, MORRIS (*b. Costesh, Bessarabia, Russia, 1881; d. Storm Lake, Iowa, 1931*), labor leader, officer of the International Ladies' Garment Workers' Union.

SIGOURNEY, LYDIA HOWARD HUNTLEY (*b. Norwich, Conn., 1791; d. Hartford, Conn., 1865*), poet, essayist. Conventional and imitative, Mrs. Sigourney held high reputation in her own time and was known as "the American Hemans." She was author of some 67 books whose theme, for the most part, was death.

SIGSBEE, CHARLES DWIGHT (*b. Albany, N.Y., 1845; d. 1923*), naval officer. Graduated U.S. Naval Academy, 1863. Distinguished principally for his services as a scientist and inventor, Sigsbee was associated with Alexander Agassiz in deep-sea explorations, principally in the Gulf of Mexico, and developed a number of devices which practically revolutionized deep-sea sounding and dredging. Chief hydrographer to the Navy Department, 1893–97, he was commissioned captain, March 1897, and was in command of the battleship *Maine* when she was blown up in the harbor of Havana, February 1898. During the war with Spain, he commanded the *St. Paul*; in 1905, he commanded the squadron which brought back the body of John Paul Jones to America. He retired as rear-admiral, 1907.

SIKES, WILLIAM WIRT (*b. Watertown, N.Y., 1836; d. Cardiff, Wales, 1883*), journalist, consular officer, folk-lorist. Husband of Olive Logan.

SILCOX, FERDINAND AUGUSTUS (*b. Columbus, Ga., 1882; d. Alexandria, Va., 1939*), forester, labor relations counsel, conservationist. Chief of the U.S. Forest Service, 1933–39. [*Supp. 2*]

SILL, ANNA PECK (*b. Burlington, N.Y., 1816; d. Rockford, Ill., 1889*), educator. A pioneer in the education of women, she was a founder of present Rockford College, 1849–51, and principal, 1851–84.

SILL, EDWARD ROWLAND (*b. Windsor, Conn., 1841; d. Cleveland, O., 1887*), poet, educator. Raised in Ohio. Graduated Yale, 1861. Professor of English, University of California, 1874–82. A poet of metaphysical doubt and perplexity, Sill voiced a humane idealism in a simple classical style. Author of *The Hermitage and Other Poems* (1868), *The Venus of Milo and Other Poems* (1883), *The Poems of Edward Rowland Sill* (a collected edition, 1902).

SILLIMAN, BENJAMIN (*b. present Trumbull, Conn., 1779; d. New Haven, Conn., 1864*), chemist, geologist, naturalist. Graduated Yale, 1796. After studying law under Simeon Baldwin and David Daggett, he was admitted to the bar, 1802, but in September of that year accepted appointment to the professorship of chemistry and natural history at Yale. He retired in 1853 as professor emeritus with a reputation as the most prominent and influential scientific mind in the America of his time.

In order to prepare himself for his professorship, he made special studies for two years at the medical school in Philadelphia, worked in the laboratory of Robert Hare, and received much valuable advice on the teaching of science from Dr. John Maclean. He began his work at Yale in April 1804 with the first course of lectures in chemistry ever given there. While traveling abroad in 1805, he became the intimate friend of Sir Humphrey Davy, Sir David Brewster, Dr. John Murray and Dr. Thomas Hope and grew deeply interested in geology. He was able, by 1813, to begin a full course of illustrated lectures in mineralogy and geology, utilizing the famed mineral collection of his friend George Gibbs which the College later purchased. Silliman acted as a leading member of the committee to organize Yale Medical School, opened in 1813. *Post* 1808, he won wide acclaim as a lecturer on science to the public in New Haven, New York and other cities; lectures on geology before the Boston Society of Natural History, 1835, were especially notable. In 1839–40 he was invited to deliver the first series of Lowell Institute lectures; few series of scientific lectures ever aroused greater interest, and Silliman justly regarded them as the crowning success of his professional life. Realizing the need for advanced study and laboratory work in the sciences, and aided by his son Benjamin (1816–1885) and by his son-in-law, James D. Dana, he persuaded Yale College to establish in 1847 a Department of Philosophy and the Arts, under which the natural and physical sciences could be studied intensively. From this modest beginning grew the Yale Scientific School, later called the Sheffield Scientific School.

In 1818 he had founded *The American Journal of Science and Arts*, devoted to the publication of original papers, notices, and reviews in the broad field of the natural and physical sciences. Under his management, it became one of the world's great scientific journals and brought him wide recognition; it is one of his most enduring monuments. In addition to editing two texts on chemistry and geology, he published his own excellent *Elements of Chemistry* (1830–31) and contributed numerous articles to scientific journals. He investigated gold deposits in Virginia and coal in Pennsylvania, and directed an investigation for the government on sugar culture. A member of the American Philosophical Society *post* 1805, he was elected in 1840 first president of the Association of American Geologists, forerunner of the American Association for the Advancement of Science. In 1863 he became an original member of the National Academy of Sciences.

Silliman exerted a profound influence on collegiate education by establishing science as a study on a basis of equality with the older disciplines. A sincerely religious man, he believed that to study science was to learn of the wonderful manifestations of God in the natural world, which it was man's duty to interpret reverently, and by which it was his privilege to improve the conditions of his life. This combination of a superior scientific mind with deep religious conviction enabled him to exert so great an influence in the interests of science on a generation that itself was dominated by strong religious convictions.

SILLIMAN, BENJAMIN (*b. New Haven, Conn., 1816; d. New Haven, 1885*), chemist. Son of Benjamin Silliman (1779–1864). Graduated Yale, 1837. Began teaching as an assistant to his father whom he succeeded as professor of chemistry at Yale, 1853; he taught also for a time (1849–54) at the University of Louisville. In association with his father and later with his brother-in-law, James D. Dana, he was an editor of the *American Journal of Science, post* 1838. Author of several textbooks and of a number of monographs on chemistry and mineralogy, he frequently acted as consultant in chemical and mining problems. In this capacity he made a major contribution to the petroleum industry (1855) by showing that petroleum was essentially a mixture of hydrocarbons, and that it could be separated, by fractional distillation and simple means of purification, into a series of distillations making up about 90% of the whole. He discovered the chief uses which were to be made of petroleum products for the next fifty years and outlined the principal methods of preparing and purifying those products.

SILLS, MILTON (*b. Chicago, Ill., 1882; d. Santa Monica, Calif., 1930*), actor. A forceful stage actor, and a motion picture star *post* 1916, he helped organize the Academy of Motion Picture Arts and Sciences.

SILSBEE, NATHANIEL (*b. Salem, Mass., 1773; d. Salem, 1850*), merchant mariner, shipowner, Massachusetts legislator. Congressman, (Democrat) Republican, 1817–21, and U.S. senator, 1826–35, he was influential in maritime legislation and was chairman, Senate committee on commerce, 1833–35.

SILVER, GRAY (*b. White Hall, Va., 1871; d. 1935*), West Virginia farmer and legislator, spokesman for farm groups. Organized the nonpartisan farm bloc which dominated legislative activities of the 67th Congress (1921–23). [*Supp. 1*]

SILVER, THOMAS (*b. Greenwich, N.J., 1813; d. New York, N.Y., 1888*), civil engineer, inventor. His marine engine governor, covered by patents between 1855 and 1866, was adopted for use by most of the naval authorities of the world, though not by the United States.

SILVERMAN, JOSEPH (*b. Cincinnati, O., 1860; d. New York, N.Y., 1930*), rabbi. Graduated University of Cincinnati, 1883; Hebrew Union College, 1884; D.D., 1887. After serving as minister in Texas for a short time, he became junior rabbi at Temple Emanu-El, New York City, 1888. Elected rabbi, 1897, he became emeritus in 1922. A liberal in religion, he was active in community affairs and became a strong supporter of Zionism toward the end of his life.

SILVERMAN, SIME (*b. Cortland, N.Y., 1873; d. Los Angeles, Calif., 1933*), editor and publisher of *Variety, post* 1905. The success of this notable theatrical paper was owing entirely to Silverman's honesty, devotion to work and imaginative editing. Much present-day slang originated in its pages.

SIMMONS, EDWARD (*b. Concord, Mass., 1852; d. Baltimore, Md., 1931*), mural painter. A boyhood companion of H. D. Thoreau. He graduated from Harvard, 1874, and as a student of painting at the Boston Museum of Fine Arts was influenced by William Rimmer. Studying and working in France and England, 1879–91, he returned home to execute a number of murals in public buildings and private residences. His murals were strong and direct but lacked originality in composition and execution.

SIMMONS, FRANKLIN (*b. present Webster, Maine, 1839; d. Rome, Italy, 1913*), sculptor. A resident principally of Rome *post* 1867, he was author of many portrait busts, public monuments and ideal figures, which at their best displayed power and a simple grace.

SIMMONS, FURNIFOLD McLENDEL (*b. near Polloksville, N.C., 1854; d. near New Bern, N.C., 1940*), lawyer, politician. Graduated Trinity College (later Duke University), 1873. Congressman, Democrat, from North Carolina, 1887–89. Simmons gradually established himself in control of the Democratic state machine *post* 1892 and employed "white supremacy" tactics and propaganda to recapture the radical whites who had been drawn away from the party by the Populists. U.S. senator from 1900 to 1930, Simmons continued to control North Carolina politics and maintained a parochial ultraconservative attitude toward legislation except in matters which might assist the interests of North Carolina. Seniority and hard work as a committee member earned him national influence; however, a general restiveness under his control was aggravated finally into action by his opposition to Alfred E. Smith, 1928. [*Supp.* 2]

SIMMONS, GEORGE HENRY (*b. Moreton-in-Marsh, Gloucestershire, England, 1852; d. Chicago, Ill., 1937*), physician, medical editor and executive. Came to America, 1870, settling in the Middle West. M.D., Hahnemann Medical College, 1882. Contributed to raising medical educational standards as secretary of the American Medical Association (later general manager), and editor of the Association's *Journal*, 1899–1924. [*Supp.* 2]

SIMMONS, THOMAS JEFFERSON (*b. Hickory Grove, Ga., 1837; d. 1905*), Confederate officer, Georgia legislator and jurist. A principal factor in the restoring of Georgia finances during the last years of Reconstruction, Simmons was elected to the state supreme court, 1887, became chief justice in 1894, and continued in that post until his death.

SIMMS, WILLIAM ELLIOTT (*b. near Cynthiana, Ky., 1822; d. 1898*), lawyer, Mexican War and Confederate soldier. Congressman, Democrat, from Kentucky, 1859–61. He abandoned his early neutral position and served as Confederate senator from Kentucky, 1862–65.

SIMMS, WILLIAM GILMORE (*b. Charleston, S.C., 1806; d. Charleston, 1870*), novelist, man of letters. Educated in public and private schools in his native city, he was at first apprenticed to a druggist, but studied law and was admitted to the bar, 1827. His profession, however, was for him only a way to literature. He wrote and published a good deal of verse and contributed articles to periodicals and newspapers; as editor of the Charleston *City Gazette* he took a vigorous, unpopular stand against nullification. In 1832, after the death of his wife and other private difficulties, he removed to the North where, in New York, he formed a permanent friendship with William Cullen Bryant and wrote a crime story, *Martin Faber* (published, 1833). On its favorable reception by the public, he followed it with *Guy Rivers* (1834) and *The Yemassee* (1835). As he did not feel at home in the North, he returned to Charleston.

Marrying the daughter of a Barnwell County plantation owner, 1836, he became a man of mark and influence in the county and had much to do with the management of his father-in-law's property. He continued active as a writer, producing among other books, *Richard Hurdis* (1838), *Border Beagles* (1840), *Beauchampe* (1842); his best work of this period, however, was done in *The Partisan* (1835), *Mellichampe* (1836) and *The Kinsmen* (1841, later titled *The Scout*). Possessed of a strong bent toward public affairs and a warm local patriotism, Simms turned his pen to the defense of slavery, but more particularly to the upbuilding of a distinctively Southern image. By saving slavery, as he saw it, the South would be preserved in its essential quality. He undertook to do whatever a man of letters could do for South Carolina by compiling a history and a geography of the state, by delivering orations, and by writing biographies of figures either distinctively Southern or filled with the qualities which he believed to be those of his section. From 1842 to 1850 Simms wrote comparatively little fiction; he then issued *Katharine Walton* (1851), *The Sword and the Distaff* (1853, later titled *Woodcraft*), *The Forayers* (1855), *Eutaw* (1856), *Charlemont* (1856), *The Cassique of Kiawah* (1859) and others. Ruined materially by the Civil War, during which he gave his sympathies entirely to the South, Simms could do nothing to restore himself and his defeated section but edit *The War Poetry of the South* (1867), busy himself with journalism, and write bad serials for magazines.

Only scholars now read Simms's poetry and minor works, or consult any of the various writings by which he strove to vindicate his section. His novels of the Southern border are more alive than those in a foreign setting, but only the novels of South Carolina still possess vitality in the view of the modern critic. Full of a rich picaresque energy, peopled by the rogues whom he enjoyed drawing magnificently to the life with all their eccentric vulgarity and swaggering ruthlessness, the novels suffer generally because of the stiffness and unreality of the ladies and gentlemen whom he thought it necessary to portray. His best-remembered novel, *The Yemassee*, is perhaps also his most romantic, but all the changes of taste since 1835 have been unable to deprive its central episode of moving power. The series beginning with *The Partisan* was conceived of as a trilogy in celebration of the Revolution in South Carolina. Simms did not keep to his original scheme and, though he finally called *Mellichampe* and *Katharine Walton* the other sections of the trilogy, he used more or less the same material in four more novels which belong to the same cycle; these were *The Scout, Woodcraft, The Forayers* and *Eutaw*. Of the seven novels, *The Scout* is the worst because of its excessive melodrama, and *Woodcraft* is on many grounds the best owing to the character of "Captain Porgy," the most truly comic character produced by the American romantic school. All the books share a tendency toward an overuse of fact because of Simms's own passionate interest in the actual events of the history of Carolina. The books suffer also from Simms's reliance upon one plot for his stories—a partisan and a loyalist as rivals in love; also, he repeated stock scenes and characters over and over again. On the credit side, he handled warfare with interest and power and could multiply episodes with a rich invention. His natural descriptions are full of reality and gusto and have pleasantly little to say about the "philosophy" of nature. He suffered most from an inner conflict between his own nature and a tradition which he had inherited. By his own nature a realist with a hearty appetite for life, he let himself be limited by a romantic tradition which did not call upon all his powers and which, indeed, led him into inflation and sensationalism. It was in spite of his conscious aims and deliberate theories that he now and then wrote about convincing characters in a simple, racy style.

SIMONDS, FRANK HERBERT (b. Concord, Mass., 1878; d. Washington, D.C., 1936), journalist, commentator on military events of World War I.
[Supp. 2]

SIMONTON, CHARLES HENRY (b. Charleston, S.C., 1829; d. Philadelphia, Pa., 1904), Confederate officer, South Carolina legislator, lawyer. Judge, U.S. district court of South Carolina, 1886–93; circuit court of appeals, fourth circuit, 1893–1904.

SIMONTON, JAMES WILLIAM (b. Columbia Co., N.Y., 1823; d. Napa, Calif., 1882), journalist, Washington correspondent, newspaper publisher. General agent of the Associated Press, 1857–81, he was instrumental in exposing some of the corruption of President Grant's administration.

SIMPSON, ALBERT BENJAMIN (b. Bayview, P.E.I., Canada, 1843; d. 1919), Presbyterian clergyman, independent evangelist. Founded the Christian Alliance, 1887 (post 1897, the Christian and Missionary Alliance) of which he served as president and general superintendent.

SIMPSON, CHARLES TORREY (b. Tiskilwa, Ill., 1846; d. Miami, Fla., 1932), naturalist, U.S. National Museum official, authority on mollusks.
[Supp. 1]

SIMPSON, EDMUND SHAW (b. England, 1784; d. New York, N.Y., 1848), actor, manager. Made American debut at the Park Theatre, New York City, October 1809; became acting manager of the Park, 1812, and a partner in that theatre c. 1818. Successful for a number of years as manager and director, Simpson became sole lessee upon the death of Stephen Price (1840) at a time when, for a number of reasons, the enterprise was tottering to its fall. After eight years of dogged struggle, he gave up his interest to others for a small annuity.

SIMPSON, EDWARD (b. New York, N.Y., 1824; d. Washington, D.C., 1888), naval officer. Son of Edmund S. Simpson. An ordnance expert and veteran of the Mexican and Civil wars, Simpson held many important commands and retired as rear-admiral, 1886.

SIMPSON, JAMES HERVEY (b. New Brunswick, N.J., 1813; d. St. Paul, Minn., 1883), soldier, explorer. Graduated West Point, 1832. Commissioned in the artillery, he transferred to the topographical engineers, 1838, and was engaged up to the Civil War in important survey work in the West and Southwest and also in Minnesota. After field service in the early days of the Civil War, he served as chief engineer, Department of the Ohio, 1862–63, and was in general charge of fortification and engineering projects in Kentucky, 1863–65, receiving the brevet of brigadier-general. Chief engineer, Department of the Interior, 1865–67, he undertook general direction and inspection of the Union Pacific Railroad as well as of all government wagon-roads and was promoted colonel, March 1867. Subsequently he engaged actively in engineering work in the South and the Middle West. Simpson was author of a number of interesting reports of great historical value which include Report from the Secretary of War . . . of the Route from Fort Smith, Ark., to Santa Fé, N. Mex. (1850) and Journal of a Military Reconnaissance from Santa Fé, N. Mex., to the Navajo Country (1852).

SIMPSON, JERRY (b. Westmoreland Co., N.B., Canada, 1842; d. Wichita, Kans., 1905), farmer, rancher, politician. After working as a Great Lakes sailor, brief service in the Union Army, and a short residence in Porter Co., Ind., Simpson settled in Kansas c. 1879. Losing his savings and harassed by mortgages after the collapse of the "boom" times in Kansas, he drifted from the Republican party by various stages into the Populist movement and represented the seventh Kansas district in the U.S. House of Representatives, 1891–95. Re-elected with Democratic help, he served again, 1897–99. Known as "Sockless Jerry," he combined with the Populist doctrine a belief in the single tax. Although he delivered few speeches and proposed few bills in Congress, he directed his sharp, shrewd wit at insincerity and what he considered false doctrine. His belief in simple democracy and monetary reform were the two consistent threads through his career.

SIMPSON, JOHN ANDREW (b. near Salem, Nebr., 1871; d. Washington, D.C., 1934), farm leader, lawyer, Oklahoma legislator. Advocated legislation to guarantee cost of production plus reasonable profit to farmers for products consumed in the home market; also favored low farm mortgage refinancing, and free coinage of silver.

SIMPSON, MATTHEW (b. Cadiz, O., 1811; d. 1884), Methodist clergyman, educator. President, present DePauw University, 1839–48, Simpson was elected bishop, 1852, and as a strong anti-slavery proponent became a friend and counselor of Salmon P. Chase, Edwin Stanton and President Lincoln. He was a public speaker of rare effectiveness and the most influential Methodist of his day in the United States.

SIMPSON, MICHAEL HODGE (*b. Newburyport, Mass., 1809; d. Boston, Mass., 1884*), capitalist, manufacturer, inventor of machinery for carpet-making and wool burring.

SIMPSON, STEPHEN (*b. Philadelphia, Pa., 1789; d. Philadelphia, 1854*), periodical editor, reformer. Edited the *Portico*, Baltimore, Md., 1816–17; co-proprietor of the *Columbian Observer*. A strong supporter of Andrew Jackson and the first man to run for Congress on a labor ticket in the United States, he was author, among other books, of *The Working Man's Manual: a New Theory of Political Economy on the Principle of Production the Source of Wealth* (1831). In this work he contended that labor should receive the whole of its production, denounced fund holders and land monopolists, and advocated political divisions according to economic allegiance.

SIMPSON, WILLIAM DUNLAP (*b. Laurens District, S.C., 1823; d. 1890*), lawyer, South Carolina legislator, Confederate soldier and congressman. Democratic lieutenant-governor of South Carolina, 1876–78; governor, 1878–80. Chief justice of South Carolina, 1880–90. Competent but not brilliant.

SIMPSON, WILLIAM KELLY (*b. Hudson, N.Y., 1855; d. 1914*), laryngologist. Associated with Joseph O'Dwyer in his work on intubation. Professor of laryngology, N.Y. College of Physicians and Surgeons, 1904–14; served on many hospital staffs.

SIMS, CHARLES N. (*b. Fairfield, Ind., 1835; d. Liberty, Ind., 1908*), Methodist clergyman. Graduated present DePauw University, 1859. After an active ministry and a brief term as president of Valparaiso College, he served with great ability as chancellor of Syracuse University, 1881–93.

SIMS, JAMES MARION (*b. Lancaster Co., S.C., 1813; d. 1883*), gynecologist. Graduated South Carolina College, 1832; Jefferson Medical College, 1835. Settling in Mount Meigs, Ala., he attained his first local fame by urging an abdominal incision for an abcess after consultants had dismissed the patient with a diagnosis of cancer. Removing to Montgomery, Ala., 1840, he next won attention by the complete rectification of a cleft palate. Called to treat a Negro girl in labor, June 1845, he found that impaction and extensive sloughing had resulted in a large bladder fistula which would render the patient unfit for all social relationships and which was considered incurable. Convinced that he could cure this and similar troubles by a new technique which accident had suggested to him, he began a long, drawn-out series of operations performed under the most difficult conditions. Successful in the late spring of 1849 with three patients, owing mainly to silver sutures which he had devised and to his own unparalleled skill, he wrote the history of his vesico-vaginal fistula operation in full recognition of its importance and published it in the *American Journal of the Medical Sciences*, January 1852. Removing to New York City, 1853, he continued to perform fistula operations, instructed his fellow surgeons in his methods, and brought about institution of the Woman's Hospital, 1855. Removing to Europe for a rest, 1861, he was received everywhere with high praise and honor, performed a number of successful operations and after a brief visit to America returned to Paris to practice, July 1862–1865. His *Clinical Notes on Uterine Surgery* (London, 1866) was a factor in formation of the nascent specialty of gynecology. Resident principally in New York City after the Civil War, he performed volunteer service in France during the Franco-Prussian War, 1870. In 1876 he was president of the American Medical Association. His autobiography, *The Story of My Life*, appeared posthumously, 1884.

SIMS, WILLIAM SOWDEN (*b. Port Hope, Ontario, Canada, 1858; d. Boston, Mass., 1936*), naval officer, naval reformer. Son of Alfred W. Sims, an American civil engineer, and Adelaide (Sowden) Sims of Port Hope, he spent his youth in the U.S. and graduated from Annapolis, 1880. Six years at sea and a year of language study in Paris were followed by six more years at sea, including two on the China Station during the Sino-Japanese War; he then spent three years as naval attaché in France and, briefly, in Russia. His voluminous reports from Europe showed his awareness of the comparative backwardness of the U.S. Navy. By 1901 he was bombarding the Navy Department with problems of ship design and gunnery, enthusiastically advocating the new British technique of continuous-aim firing, and also committing an insubordinate act by writing direct to President Theodore Roosevelt about the "very inefficient condition of the Navy." Ordered to Washington as Inspector of Target Practice, 1902, he also served *post* 1907 as the president's naval aide. These were fruitful years for the naval reformers. By the end of the Roosevelt administration, American gunnery was second to none, and criticism of ship design and of navy bureaucracy had provoked congressional investigations, with, however, inconclusive results. In 1910 Sims made an effusively pro-British speech at the Guildhall in London, for which he was publicly reprimanded by President Taft. He served with distinction as commander, Atlantic Destroyer Flotilla, and as president (1917) of the Naval War College. He won promotion to rear-admiral, 1917, and to vice-admiral, 1918, and was named commander, U.S. Naval Forces in European Waters in June 1918. Promoted full admiral in December, he spent the war in London supervising America's extensive overseas naval activity. Still agitating for Navy Department reorganization, Sims refused a decoration for wartime service. Retiring in 1922, he continued through speeches and articles to press for processes of reform. He later championed naval aviation and crusaded for legislation to keep America out of war. In the wider sense this highly competent officer represented the Progressive and muckraking movements, improbably situated within a military environment. [*Supp. 2*]

SIMS, WINFIELD SCOTT (*b. New York, N.Y., 1844; d. Newark, N.J., 1918*), inventor. First to apply electricity for torpedo propulsion, Sims also invented a pneumatic field gun, several dynamite guns and a number of other ordnance devices.

SINGER, ISAAC MERRIT (*b. Pittstown, N.Y., 1811; d. Torquay, England, 1875*), inventor. Developed the first practical domestic sewing machine (patented, 1851, with improvement patents thereafter until 1863) and brought it into general use through the manufacturing company which he founded and headed until 1863.

SINGERLY, WILLIAM MISKEY (*b. Philadelphia, Pa., 1832; d. Philadelphia, 1898*), journalist. Editor-publisher of the *Philadelphia Record* (originally the *Public Record*) post 1877; Democratic political leader of Pennsylvania.

SINGLETON, ESTHER (*b. Baltimore, Md., 1865; d. Stonington, Conn., 1930*), editor, music critic. Author, among other books, of *The Furniture of Our Forefathers* (1900) and *Social New York Under the Georges* (1902).

SINGLETON, JAMES WASHINGTON (*b. Frederick Co., Va., 1811; d. Baltimore, Md., 1892*), Illinois lawyer, Civil War peace projector. Congressman, Democrat, from Illinois, 1879–83.

SIRINGO, CHARLES A. (*b. Matagorda Co., Texas, 1855; d. Hollywood, Calif., 1928*), cowboy, detective. Author of *A Texas Cowboy* (1885) and *A Cowboy Detective* (1912).

SITTING BULL (*b. on Grand River, S.D., 1834?; d. 1890*), Hunkpapa Sioux chief, medicine man. His camp in the buffalo country became the rallying point for Sioux, Cheyenne, and Arapaho Indians hostile to the whites; by the spring of 1876 he had gathered a force estimated at from 2500 to 4000 men. When Gen. George A. Custer made his disastrous attack on the consolidated Indian village at the Little Big Horn in June, Sitting Bull did no fighting, but spent the time in "making medicine." Driven with his band across the Canadian border by the end of 1876, he surrendered at Fort Buford in 1881 and was settled on the Standing Rock Reservation. Arrested by Indian policemen for his part in the Messiah agitation, he was shot and killed in the fight that followed.

SIZER, NELSON (*b. Chester, Mass., 1812; d. 1897*), phrenologist. Pupil of J. G. Spurzheim; associated in practice with Orson Fowler and S. R. Wells; president, American Institute of Phrenology.

SKANIADARIIO (*b. Ganawaugus, N.Y., c. 1735; d. Onondaga, N.Y., 1815*), Seneca sachem, religious leader. Claiming revelation from the Creator of Life, he propounded a new religion for the Iroquois called the Gaiwiio.

SKENANDOA (*b. 1706?; d. near Oneida Castle, N.Y., 1816*), Oneida chief. Converted to Christianity by Samuel Kirkland. During the Revolution, he helped keep the Oneida and Tuscarora from joining the British and later persuaded many members of these tribes to join the Americans.

SKENE, ALEXANDER JOHNSTON CHALMERS (*b. Fyvie, Scotland, 1837; d. 1900*), pioneer gynecologist. Came to America, 1856. M.D., Long Island College Hospital, 1863; served there for many years as teacher, dean and president; was consultant to a number of hospitals; practiced in Brooklyn, N.Y. A founder and president of the American Gynecological Society, and the International Congress of Gynecology and Obstetrics, he was author of more than 100 medical papers and of a number of books. His discovery (1880) of what are now called Skene's urethral glands gave him an international reputation and an assured place in the history of gynecology. He also is known to have devised 31 surgical instruments.

SKILLERN, ROSS HALL (*b. Philadelphia, Pa., 1875; d. Philadelphia, 1930*), laryngologist, professor of laryngology in Medico-Chirurgical College of Philadelphia and University of Pennsylvania.

SKINNER, AARON NICHOLS (*b. Boston, Mass., 1845; d. Framingham, Mass., 1918*), astronomer. Associated with the U.S. Naval Observatory, 1870–1909.

SKINNER, ALANSON BUCK (*b. Buffalo, N.Y., 1886; d. near Tokio, N.D., 1925*), anthropologist, ethnologist. Associated with American Museum of Natural History, 1907–13; later with Milwaukee Museum and with Heye Foundation. Authority on material culture of Algonquian Indians and of Siouan tribes in contact with them.

SKINNER, CHARLES RUFUS (*b. Union Square, Oswego Co., N.Y., 1844; d. Pelham Manor, N.Y., 1928*), journalist, New York legislator and congressman. In state education department post 1886, he was state superintendent of public instruction, 1895–1904. He held several other state appointments thereafter, and was legislative librarian, 1915–25.

SKINNER, HALCYON (*b. Mantua, O., 1824; d. 1900*), inventor of carpet-weaving machinery, notably a power loom for moquette carpets (first patented, 1877).

SKINNER, HARRY (*b. Perquimans Co., N.C., 1855; d. Greenville, N.C., 1929*), lawyer, North Carolina legislator. Congressman, Populist, from North Carolina, 1895–99. Claimed that his ideas formed basis of "sub-treasury" plan for agricultural price-fixing as advocated by Populists.

SKINNER, JOHN STUART (*b. Calvert Co., Md., 1788; d. Baltimore, Md., 1851*), lawyer, public official, agricultural editor and writer. Companion of Francis Scott Key during bombardment of Fort McHenry (September 1814), he subsequently arranged to have "The Star-Spangled Banner" first printed. In 1819 he founded the *American Farmer*, the first continuous, successful agricultural periodical in the United States, which he published until 1830. In 1829 he started the *American Turf Register and Sporting Magazine*, the first magazine devoted to the improvement of American thoroughbred horses. From 1845 to 1848 he edited the *Farmers' Library* in New York, and then established in Philadelphia *The Plough, the Loom, and the Anvil*, which he edited until his death. A member of leading agricultural organizations, he was an outstanding agricultural publicist.

SKINNER, THOMAS HARVEY (*b. Harvey's Neck, N.C., 1791; d. New York, N.Y., 1871*), Presbyterian clergyman, professor of homiletics at Andover and Union Theological seminaries. An advocate of the New School, he promoted broader theological views and closer interdenominational relations.

SKINNER, WILLIAM (*b. London, England, 1824; d. 1902*), silk manufacturer. Emigrated to America, 1843; did business at Holyoke, Mass., *post* 1874 after making start near Williamsburg, Mass., *c.* 1849. Produced high-quality "Skinner's Satin" lining.

SLADE, JOSEPH ALFRED (*b. near Carlyle, Ill., c. 1824; d. Virginia City, Mont., 1864*), freighter, wagon-train boss, stagecoach division agent, "bad man." Hanged by Vigilantes.

SLADE, WILLIAM (*b. Cornwall, Vt., 1786; d. Middlebury, Vt., 1859*), lawyer, editor, public official, politician. Elected to Congress as a Democrat in 1830, he served for twelve years and in that time became a Whig; he was a fierce opponent of slavery and a high-tariff advocate. As governor of Vermont, 1844–46, he reorganized the public school system. He served thereafter as agent of the Board of National Popular Education.

SLAFTER, EDMUND FARWELL (*b. Norwich, Vt., 1816; d. Hampton, N.H., 1906*), Episcopal clergyman, scholar. Graduated Dartmouth, 1840. Active in pastoral work and as an official of the American Bible Society, he was a valued member and officer of the New England Historic Genealogical Society and of the Prince Society (president, 1880–1906). He edited four Prince Society monographs, including *Voyages of Samuel de Champlain* (1878–82).

SLATER, JOHN FOX (*b. Slatersville, R.I., 1815; d. 1884*), cotton and woolen manufacturer, philanthropist. Founded John F. Slater Fund for Negro education, 1882.

SLATER, SAMUEL (*b. Belper, England, 1768; d. 1835*), founder of the American cotton-spinning industry. Apprenticed in 1783 to Jedediah Strutt, a partner of Richard Arkwright in development of cot-

ton manufacturing machinery, Slater emigrated by stealth to America in 1789. Having studied and memorized all details of making textile machinery (whose exportation from England was then forbidden by law), he contracted with Almy and Brown of Rhode Island to reproduce Arkwright's machine for that firm; in 1793 they built their first factory in Pawtucket under the firm name of Almy, Brown and Slater. In 1798 he formed a family partnership known as Samuel Slater & Co. and undertook a variety of highly successful mill operations in Rhode Island, Connecticut and Massachusetts.

SLATTERY, CHARLES LEWIS (*b. Pittsburgh, Pa., 1867; d. Boston, Mass., 1930*), Episcopal clergyman, author. Consecrated coadjutor bishop of Massachusetts, 1922; succeeded to the see, 1927. Made his principal contribution as pastor and scholar, in particular as chairman of commission to revise the Book of Common Prayer.

SLAUGHTER, PHILIP (*b. Culpeper Co., Va., 1808; d. 1890*), Episcopal clergyman, historian. Author of a number of Virginia parish histories and monographs.

SLEEPER, JACOB (*b. Newcastle, Maine, 1802; d. Boston, Mass., 1889*), merchant, philanthropist. One of the three founders of Boston University (1869).

SLICER, THOMAS ROBERTS (*b. Washington, D.C., 1847; d. New York, N.Y., 1916*), Unitarian clergyman. Principal pastorate at All Souls Church, New York City, *post* 1897. A prominent preacher and writer, he was best known as a militant leader of civic reform.

SLIDELL, JOHN (*b. New York, N.Y., 1793; d. Cowes, England, 1871*), lawyer, Louisiana politician, diplomat, Confederate agent. Brother of Alexander S. Mackenzie; brother-in-law of Matthew C. Perry. Graduated Columbia, 1810. Removing to New Orleans, La., 1819, he practiced successfully and entered politics as a Jackson Democrat. As congressman, 1843–45, he advocated tariff reductions except for that on sugar; in the election of 1844, he helped secure a majority for Polk in Louisiana by maneuvering a "floater" vote. Appointed U.S. commissioner to Mexico to adjust Texas boundary and purchase New Mexico and California, 1845, he returned unsuccessful. As U.S. senator from Louisiana, 1853–61, he favored repeal of the Missouri Compromise, and as James Buchanan's campaign manager in 1856 materially promoted both his nomination for the presidency and election. During the first three years of the administration, he was the power behind the throne and recommended numerous cabinet and diplomatic appointments. He favored the Lecompton Constitution for Kansas, bitterly opposed Stephen A. Douglas, and supported the Breckinridge-Lane ticket in 1860. Breaking with Buchanan after the dismissal of John B. Floyd from the War Department, Slidell was chosen to represent the Confederacy in France and was apprehended with James M. Mason in the celebrated "Trent Affair." He performed creditably enough at Paris but was distrusted by other Confederate agents and won little more than lip-service from Napoleon III. After the Civil War, he resided in Paris until the fall of the Empire.

SLOAN, JAMES FORMAN (*b. Bunker Hill, Ind., 1874; d. Los Angeles, Calif., 1933*), jockey, popularly known as "Tod." Adopting a special seat whereby he revolutionized modern race-riding, Sloan became principal rider for William C. Whitney and the most celebrated jockey of the late 19th century. Riding principally in Europe *post* 1897, he was ruled off the turf in 1901 by the English Jockey Club.

SLOAN, RICHARD ELIHU (*b. Preble Co., O., 1857; d. Phoenix, Ariz., 1933*), lawyer, Arizona legislator and jurist. Republican governor of Arizona Territory, 1909–12.

SLOAN, SAMUEL (*b. Lisburn, Ireland, 1817; d. Garrison, N.Y., 1907*), railroad executive. Brought to America as an infant. After a successful career as a commission merchant in New York City, Sloan entered the railroad field as a director of the Hudson River Railroad, 1855, was chosen its president, and directed its rapid rise until 1864. As president of the Delaware, Lackawanna & Western Railroad, 1867–99, he transformed that road from a limited "coal road" into a profitable handler of general freight and passenger traffic.

SLOAN, TOD. [See SLOAN, JAMES FORMAN, 1874–1933.]

SLOANE, WILLIAM MILLIGAN (*b. Richmond, O., 1850; d. Princeton, N.J., 1928*), educator, historian. Graduated Columbia, 1868; Ph.D., Leipzig, 1876. Served as research assistant to George Bancroft, 1873–75; taught at Princeton and at Columbia where he was Seth Low Professor of History. Author, among other books, of *Life of Napoleon Bonaparte* (serialized in *Century Magazine*, published as book, 1896).

SLOAT, JOHN DRAKE (*b. near Goshen, N.Y., 1781; d. Staten Island, N.Y., 1867*), naval officer. Appointed midshipman, 1800; served in merchant marine, 1801–12, and on frigate *United States* in War of 1812. Received first command (schooner *Grampus*), 1823, and cruised against West Indian pirates; subsequently performed routine sea and shore services. Chosen commander of Pacific Squadron, 1844. He received secret and confidential orders dated June 1845 while based at Mazatlán, Mexico, directing what action he should take in the event of declaration of war by Mexico. Receiving word on June 7, 1846, that the Mexicans had invaded Texas, he sailed for California and arrived at Monterey on July 2. Five days later, overruling opinion of the U.S. consul there, Sloat landed a detachment and proclaimed the U.S. annexation of California; a little later he sent an officer to take

possession of San Francisco. Turning over command to Commodore Robert F. Stockton on July 23, he returned to Washington. His conduct of affairs in the Pacific was both criticized and warmly commended. Put on the reserve list, 1855, he was promoted commodore, 1862, and rear-admiral on the retired list, 1866.

SLOCUM, FRANCES (*b. Warwick, R.I., 1773; d. near present Peru, Ind., 1847*), Indian captive. Made prisoner near Wyoming, Pa., 1778, she was adopted by a Delaware family, married in the tribe, and refused offers to return to her white relatives.

SLOCUM, HENRY WARNER (*b. Delphi, N.Y., 1827; d. New York, N.Y., 1894*), Union major-general. Graduated West Point, 1852. Resigned from the army, 1856, to engage in the practice of law at Syracuse, N.Y. Appointed colonel, 27th New York Infantry, May 1861, he was soon promoted to brigadier-general of volunteers and in July 1862 was promoted major-general. An able division and corps commander, Slocum performed outstanding service at Chancellorsville and Gettysburg. He was later active in the campaigns in Tennessee, commanded the district of Vicksburg early in 1864, and with his troops was first to enter Atlanta. Thereafter he commanded the XIV and XX Corps under W. T. Sherman (later known as the Army of Georgia). In the practice of law in Brooklyn, N.Y., *post* 1866, he was congressman, Democrat, from New York, 1869–73, 1883–85.

SLOCUM, JOSHUA (*b. Wilmot Township, N.S., Canada, 1844; d. at sea, c. 1910*), mariner, circumnavigator, lecturer. Sailed around the world alone in the sloop *Spray*, 1895–98. Author of *Sailing Alone Around the World* (1900) and various periodical writings.

SLOCUM, SAMUEL (*b. Canonicut Island, Newport Co., R.I., 1792; d. Pawtucket, R.I., 1861*), manufacturer. Inventor, among other devices, of a machine for sticking pins in paper so as to package them effectively for sale (patented, 1841).

SLOSS, JAMES WITHERS (*b. Mooresville, Ala., 1820; d. 1890*), Alabama industrialist, railroad operator. Associated with H. F. De Bardeleben in development of coal and iron industry in the Birmingham district.

SLOSS, LOUIS (*b. Bavaria, 1823; d. San Rafael, Calif., 1902*), California capitalist, philanthropist. Emigrated to America, 1845; removed to California, 1849. Successful as a broker, leather merchant, and as partner and official of the Alaska Commercial Co., Sloss engaged in systematic philanthropies and was an active supporter of almost every charity in San Francisco.

SLOSSON, EDWIN EMERY (*b. present Sabetha, Kans., 1865; d. Washington, D.C., 1929*), chemist, educator, writer of popular works on the sciences.

SMALL, ALBION WOODBURY (*b. Buckfield, Maine, 1854; d. Chicago, Ill., 1926*), sociologist. Graduated Colby College, 1876; Ph.D., Johns Hopkins, 1889. A teacher of history and political economy at Colby, 1881–88, he served Colby as president, 1889–91, and in 1892 became head of the department of sociology at University of Chicago, the first department of its kind. He served also as dean of the College of Liberal Arts there, and from 1904 until his retirement in 1924 was dean of the Graduate School. Small was founder of the *American Journal of Sociology* which he edited, 1895–1926. He was author of a number of books which include *General Sociology* (1905) and *Between Eras: From Capitalism to Democracy* (1913).

SMALL, ALVAN EDMOND (*b. Wales, Maine, 1811; d. 1886*), homeopathic physician. Practicing and teaching at first in Pennsylvania, he removed to Chicago, Ill., 1856, where he was professor, dean and president of the Hahnemann Medical College.

SMALLEY, EUGENE VIRGIL (*b. Randolph, O., 1841; d. St. Paul, Minn., 1899*), journalist. Associated *post* 1883 with the advertising department of the Northern Pacific Railroad, he edited *The Northwest Illustrated Monthly Magazine*.

SMALLEY, GEORGE WASHBURN (*b. Franklin, Mass., 1833; d. London, England, 1916*), journalist, lawyer. Graduated Yale, 1853. After an outstanding career as war correspondent for the *New York Tribune*, November 1861—October 1862, Smalley served on the New York staff of the paper. As correspondent at the Austro-Prussian War, 1866, he sent what were probably the first of all cabled news dispatches, and in 1867 organized a London bureau for the coordination of all European news. Scoring a series of journalistic triumphs with the help of his correspondents during the Franco-Prussian War, 1870, he remained in charge of the *Tribune's* European correspondence until 1895; he then served as U.S. correspondent of the London *Times*, 1895–1905.

SMALLS, ROBERT (*b. Beaufort, S.C., 1839; d. Beaufort, 1915*), Union soldier, South Carolina politician. A Negro, Smalls performed valuable service during the Civil War and was prevented only by his modesty and lack of education from becoming pre-eminent among the directors of the state during Reconstruction. He served in the legislature and was congressman, Republican, from South Carolina, 1875–79, 1882–87.

SMALLWOOD, WILLIAM (*b. Charles Co., Md., 1732; d. Prince George's Co., Md., 1792*), Revolutionary soldier, Maryland colonial legislator. Commissioned colonel of the Maryland battalion, January 1776, Smallwood, who had had military experience during the French and Indian War, trained his command so effectively that the Maryland Line won high repute for valor through all the campaigns of 1776–77. Promoted major-general, September 1780, he served with credit at Camden. Disliked for his constant complaints over lack of promotion and for his offensive attitude toward foreign officers, Smallwood performed his greatest service in the war as a drill master, a raiser of men and supplies, and a military administrator. He was governor of Maryland, 1785–88.

SMART, JAMES HENRY (*b. Center Harbor, N.H., 1841; d. 1900*), educator. After winning a reputation as an administrator of school systems in Indiana *post* 1865, he built up Purdue University and directed its emphasis toward engineering while he was president, 1883–1900.

SMEDLEY, WILLIAM THOMAS (*b. Chester Co., Pa., 1858; d. Bronxville, N.Y., 1920*), portrait painter, illustrator. Expert in portraying the social characteristics of the genteel class in his day.

SMIBERT, JOHN (*b. Edinburgh, Scotland, 1688; d. Boston, Mass., 1751*), painter. After employment as a coach-painter and as a copyist of pictures for dealers, he visited Italy, 1717–20, where he acquired a feeble Venetian technique and a facility at "face painting" in the grand manner; he also met at this time George Berkeley, later bishop of Cloyne. Practicing for a time as a portrait painter in London, Smibert accompanied Berkeley to Newport, R.I., 1729, as potential professor of art in Berkeley's proposed Bermuda college. Remaining in America after the failure of the project and Berkeley's return home, Smibert settled in Boston early in 1730 and before the end of his professional career painted likenesses of the "best" people in the Bay Colony. Despite his success in his profession, he found it necessary to earn additional income by conducting an art shop in his house in which he sold paints, brushes, prints and copies of pictures in European galleries. He furnished the designs for Faneuil Hall (built, 1742) and gave up painting *c.* 1748 because of failing eyesight. Smibert's work is often awkward but there is a sincerity and vitality about it which many critics regard as peculiarly characteristic of early American painting. His importance is owing to his precise and often grim records of New England worthies and to the fact that his work served as an early link between the art of Europe and that of the colonies.

SMILEY, ALBERT KEITH (*b. Vassalboro, Maine, 1828; d. near Redlands, Calif., 1912*), educator. Graduated Haverford, 1849. Co-proprietor with his brother of the celebrated Lake Mohonk resort in Ulster Co., N.Y., *post* 1870. A member of the Board of Indian Commissioners, 1879–1912, Smiley instituted the Lake Mohonk Conferences on Indian affairs in 1883 and also another series of conferences for discussions of world peace, 1895.

SMILLIE, GEORGE HENRY (*b. New York, N.Y., 1840; d. Bronxville, N.Y., 1921*), landscape painter.

Son of James Smillie; brother of James D. Smillie. Studied with his father and with James M. Hart.

SMILLIE, JAMES (*b. Edinburgh, Scotland, 1807; d. Poughkeepsie, N.Y., 1885*), engraver. Father of George H. and James D. Smillie. Settled in New York City, 1830. Assisted by Robert W. Weir and A. B. Durand, he became a successful bank-note engraver and engraved the works of some of the leading figure painters and landscapists of his time. Among his important works were the series of plates after Thomas Cole's "Voyage of Life" and "The Rocky Mountains" after a painting of Albert Bierstadt.

SMILLIE, JAMES DAVID (*b. New York, N.Y., 1833; d. New York, 1909*), engraver, etcher. Son of James Smillie; brother of George H. Smillie. Studied with his father with whom he collaborated in much of his work until 1864. Unsatisfied thereafter to confine his efforts to the mechanical phases of engraving, he employed himself in etching, dry point, aquatint, mezzotint and lithography, and was foremost in the movement to promote painter-etching as an art. His work displayed technical mastery and great versatility.

SMITH, ABBY HADASSAH (*b. Glastonbury, Conn., 1797; d. 1878*), woman's rights advocate. Refusing, with her sister Julia Evelina Smith, to pay taxes unless given the right to vote (1873), she continued to resist in this manner until her death despite repeated sale of her cows and other property for delinquent taxes. The sisters and the troubles of their cows gave publicity and an added impetus to the cause of woman's rights.

SMITH, ALBERT HOLMES (*b. Philadelphia, Pa., 1835; d. 1885*), obstetrician, gynecologist, advocate of recognition of women in medicine. Graduated University of Pennsylvania, 1853; M.D., 1856. Practiced in Philadelphia; devised the Smith-Hodge pessary and other obstetrical instruments.

SMITH, ALEXANDER (*b. Edinburgh, Scotland, 1865; d. Edinburgh, 1922*), chemist. Taught at University of Chicago, 1894–1911; headed department of chemistry at Columbia University, 1911–19. Distinguished himself in physical chemistry; made important studies on the forms of sulfur and on vapor pressure measurements at comparatively high temperatures.

SMITH, ALFRED HOLLAND (*b. near Cleveland, O., 1863; d. 1924*), railroad executive. President, New York Central Railroad, 1914–24.

SMITH, ANDREW JACKSON (*b. Bucks Co., Pa., 1815; d. 1897*), Union major-general. Graduated West Point, 1838. Commissioned in the 1st Dragoons, Smith performed his early service practically all in the West. Becoming chief of cavalry under Gen. Henry W. Halleck early in the Civil War, he served as such through the Corinth campaign and was appointed brigadier-general of volunteers, March 1862. His im-

portant but unspectacular service, 1863–65, was highlighted by his defeat of Gen. N. B. Forrest at Tupelo, Miss., 1864. Resigning from the army, 1869, he held several public offices at St. Louis, Mo.

SMITH, ARCHIBALD CARY (*b. New York, N.Y., 1837; d. Bayonne, N.J., 1911*), marine painter, naval architect. Designed well over a hundred yachts of which the most notable were the *Vindex* (1871), *Mischief* (1879), *Meteor* (1902) and *Resolute* (1903).

SMITH, ARTHUR HENDERSON (*b. Vernon, Conn., 1845; d. Claremont, Calif., 1932*), Congregational clergyman. Missionary to China, 1872–1925. Author of a number of books which include *Chinese Characteristics* (1890) and *China in Convulsion* (1901).

SMITH, ASA DODGE (*b. Amherst, N.H., 1804; d. Hanover, N.H., 1877*), Presbyterian clergyman, educator. Graduated Dartmouth, 1830; Andover Theological Seminary, 1834. A pastor in New York City, 1834–63, Smith served as president of Dartmouth College, 1863–77. He rebuilt the prestige of that institution and was responsible for the establishment of the Thayer School of Engineering and the New Hampshire College of Agriculture. A tactful and ultraconservative administrator, Smith was not particularly happy in matters of finance.

SMITH, ASHBEL (*b. Hartford, Conn., 1805; d. Texas, 1886*), physician, statesman, Confederate officer. Graduated Yale, 1824; M.D., 1828. Practicing at first in North Carolina, he removed to Texas, 1837, and became surgeon-general of the Texas Republic. Texas minister to England and France, 1842–44, he became secretary of state of the Republic in February 1845 and negotiated with Mexico the Smith-Cuevas Treaty acknowledging Texan independence. Cited during the Civil War for gallantry at Shiloh and Vicksburg, he later served actively in the defense of Texas. A leader in all educational movements in the state after the Civil War, he undertook the reorganizing of the University of Texas *post* 1881. He was author of *Reminiscences of the Texas Republic* (1876) and other works.

SMITH, AZARIAH (*b. Manlius, N.Y., 1817; d. Aintab, Armenia, 1851*), Presbyterian clergyman, medical missionary in Asiatic Turkey *post* 1843. Cousin of Judson Smith.

SMITH, BENJAMIN ELI (*b. Beirut, Syria, 1857; d. New Rochelle, N.Y., 1913*), editor. Son of Eli Smith. Managing editor of *The Century Dictionary and Cyclopedia* under William D. Whitney, 1882–94; editor-in-chief of the *Dictionary* and cognate enterprises, 1894–1911.

SMITH, BENJAMIN MOSBY (*b. Powhatan Co., Va., 1811; d. 1893*), Presbyterian clergyman. Professor at Union Theological Seminary (Virginia) *post* 1855.

SMITH, BESSIE (*b. Chattanooga, Tenn., 1894; d. near Clarksdale, Miss., 1937*), Negro blues singer. An outstanding influence on jazz music, she achieved her greatest popularity between 1923 and 1929. Her singing had casual but great strength and a heart-breaking earthiness. [*Supp. 2*]

SMITH, BUCKINGHAM (*b. Cumberland Island, Ga., 1810; d. New York, N.Y., 1871*), lawyer, diplomat, Florida Unionist, antiquarian. Smith is remembered particularly as an Americanist who stimulated study in the early history of Florida and the regions nearby. Among his many books and collections of documents were *The Narrative of Alvar Nuñez Cabeça de Vaca* (1851) and *The Narratives of the Career of Hernando de Soto in the Conquest of Florida, as told by a Knight of Elvas* (first published as a whole, 1866).

SMITH, BYRON CALDWELL (*b. Island Creek, O., 1849; d. Boulder, Colo., 1877*), philologist, educator.

SMITH, CALEB BLOOD (*b. Boston, Mass., 1808; d. Indianapolis, Ind., 1864*), lawyer. Studied law with Oliver H. Smith; began practice in Indiana, 1828. As an Indiana legislator *post* 1832, he promoted internal improvement projects; as congressman, Whig, from Indiana, 1843–49, he directed his principal efforts against annexation of Texas and war with Mexico. Later a leader in Indiana Republican politics, Smith seconded Lincoln's nomination at Chicago, 1860. U.S. secretary of the interior, 1861–62, he served thereafter as U.S. district judge from Indiana.

SMITH, CHARLES ALPHONSO (*b. Greensboro, N.C., 1864; d. Annapolis, Md., 1924*), educator. Friend and biographer of O. Henry. Graduated Davidson College, 1884; Ph.D., Johns Hopkins, 1893. Taught English at Louisiana State University, 1893–1902; at University of North Carolina, 1902–09; at University of Virginia, 1909–17; at U.S. Naval Academy, 1917–24. A gifted, enthusiastic teacher and student of folklore.

SMITH, CHARLES EMORY (*b. Mansfield, Conn., 1842; d. Philadelphia, Pa., 1908*), journalist, diplomat. As editor of the Philadelphia *Press post* 1880, Smith enjoyed great political influence. He was U.S. minister to Russia, 1890–92, and U.S. postmaster-general, 1898–1901.

SMITH, CHARLES FERGUSON (*b. Philadelphia, Pa., 1807; d. Savannah, Tenn., 1862*), Union soldier. Graduated West Point, 1825. Instructor and commandant of cadets at West Point, 1829–42, he received three brevets for gallant conduct in the Mexican War. After service in the Midwest and West and considerable administrative duty, he became brigadier-general of volunteers, 1861. He was promoted major-general, March 1862, for his decisive assault on Fort Donelson which lodged federal troops within the defenses and was the immediate cause of the fort's surrender.

SMITH, CHARLES FORSTER (*b. present Greenwood Co., S.C., 1852; d. Racine, Wis., 1931*), classical philologist. Brother of James P. Smith. Taught at Williams College, Vanderbilt University and University of Wisconsin. In addition to contributions to classical journals, he translated Thucydides for the Loeb Library.

SMITH, CHARLES HENRY (*b. Lawrenceville, Ga., 1826; d. Cartersville, Ga., 1903*), journalist, humorist, Confederate soldier. Author of a number of sketches marked by genial satire and rustic philosophy which he published under the pseudonym "Bill Arp."

SMITH, CHARLES HENRY (*b. Hollis, Maine, 1827; d. Washington, D.C., 1902*), Union major-general, lawyer. An able but unspectacular cavalry commander with the Army of the Potomac, 1861–65, he returned to the regular service in 1866 and retired as colonel, 1891.

SMITH, CHARLES PERRIN (*b. Philadelphia, Pa., 1819; d. Trenton, N.J., 1883*), New Jersey politician, editor, genealogist.

SMITH, CHARLES SHALER (*b. Pittsburgh, Pa., 1836; d. St. Louis, Mo., 1886*), bridge engineer. Early associated with Albert Fink, Smith became a division engineer for the Louisville & Nashville Railroad and during the Civil War served as a Confederate captain of engineers. In 1866 he entered partnership with Benjamin H. and Charles H. Latrobe in the Baltimore Bridge Co. Smith produced his greatest engineering achievement in the Kentucky River bridge built for the Cincinnati Southern Railroad, 1876–77. The cantilever which he employed for this work had no precedent anywhere in the world but soon became the dominant type for long-span construction. His Lachine Bridge over the St. Lawrence River near Montreal, begun in 1880, was for many years the only continuous bridge of importance in America.

SMITH, CHARLES SPRAGUE (*b. Andover, Mass., 1853; d. 1910*), educator, professor of German at Columbia University. Founded the People's Institute at Cooper Union, N.Y., 1897, as a community center for working-class education.

SMITH, CHAUNCEY (*b. Waitsfield, Vt., 1819; d. Cambridge, Mass., 1895*), lawyer. Successful as counsel to the Bell Telephone Co. in the great patent litigation of 1878–96.

SMITH, DANIEL (*b. Stafford Co., Va., 1748; d. Sumner Co., Tenn., 1818*), Revolutionary soldier, Tennessee official. Made the first map of Tennessee, published in Carey's *General Atlas for the Present War* (1794); wrote *A Short Description of the Tennessee Government* (1793). U.S. senator from Tennessee, 1798 and 1805–09.

SMITH, DANIEL B. (*b. Philadelphia, Pa., 1792; d. Germantown, Pa., 1883*), pharmacist, philanthropist.

Long in business in Philadelphia, Smith was associated with establishment of Philadelphia College of Pharmacy, 1822, and served as its president, 1829–54. He was chosen first president of the American Pharmaceutical Association, 1852. From 1834 until 1846 he taught moral philosophy and chemistry at Haverford.

SMITH, EDGAR FAHS (*b. York, Pa., 1854; d. Philadelphia, Pa., 1928*), chemist. Graduated present Gettysburg College, 1874; Ph.D., Göttingen, 1876. Taught at University of Pennsylvania, Muhlenberg College and Wittenberg College. Headed department of chemistry, University of Pennsylvania, 1892–1920, and served as provost, 1911–20. Smith carried on with his pupils at Pennsylvania a great number of investigations into methods of electrochemical analysis in which he was a pioneer; also into atomic weight determinations, compounds of the rarer metals, and complex salts of various inorganic acids. His research on tungsten led to its extensive use in scientific and artistic work. He was author, among other books, of *Electro-Chemical Analysis* (1890).

SMITH, EDMUND KIRBY. [See KIRBY-SMITH, EDMUND, 1824–1893.]

SMITH, EDMUND MUNROE (*b. Brooklyn, N.Y., 1854; d. 1926*), educator. Nephew of Henry B. Smith. Graduated Amherst, 1874; LL.B., Columbia Law School, 1877; D.C.L., Göttingen, 1880. A teacher of history and political science at Columbia *post* 1880, Smith was professor of Roman law and comparative jurisprudence there, 1891–1924. From its establishment in 1886, he was for many years managing editor of the *Political Science Quarterly*. He was author, among other studies, of *The Development of European Law* (1928) and *A General View of European Legal History* (1927).

SMITH, ELI (*b. Northford, Conn., 1801; d. Beirut, Syria, 1857*), Congregational clergyman. Father of Benjamin E. Smith. Missionary in the Near East for most of his life *post* 1826, Smith, with H. G. O. Dwight, was largely responsible for establishment of the American mission at Urumiah.

SMITH, ELIAS (*b. Lyme, Conn., 1769; d. 1846*), clergyman, healer. Rejecting the Calvinistic system held by the Baptists, he also denied the doctrine of the Trinity and founded a fundamentalist Bible church of his own at Portsmouth, N.H., c. 1800. In 1818 he became a Universalist but renounced that mode of thought in 1823. He was founder of the *Herald of Gospel Liberty*, September 1808, the first weekly religious newspaper published in the United States, which served as organ of the so-called Christian Connection. He was author of a number of controversial pamphlets and of several volumes of sermons and hymns.

SMITH, ELIHU HUBBARD (*b. Litchfield, Conn., 1771; d. New York, N.Y., 1798*), physician, editor,

author. Graduated Yale, 1786; studied medicine with his father and with Benjamin Rush. As a student in Philadelphia, he became a friend of Charles B. Brown; as a practicing physician at Wethersfield, Conn., 1791–93, he was associated with the so-called Hartford Wits. A contributor to the *Echo* and editor of the earliest anthology of American poetry, *American Poems* (1793), he then settled in New York City where he practiced until his death during a yellow fever epidemic. During his stay at New York, he was host to the Friendly Club made up, among others, of William Dunlap, Samuel L. Mitchill, James Kent and Samuel Miller (1769–1850). He projected the first American medical journal, the *Medical Repository*, and was co-editor of it, 1797–98. Just before his death he was planning to undertake issue of a literary magazine and review in association with Charles B. Brown.

SMITH, ELIZA ROXEY SNOW. [See SNOW, ELIZA ROXEY, 1804–1887.]

SMITH, ELIZABETH OAKES PRINCE (*b. North Yarmouth, Maine, 1806; d. North Carolina, 1893*), novelist, lyceum lecturer, woman's rights reformer. Married Seba Smith, 1823. A contributor to popular periodicals of her day.

SMITH, ERASMUS DARWIN (*b. De Ruyter, N.Y., 1806; d. 1883*), jurist. As judge, New York supreme court, 1855–77, Smith tended to uphold legislative acts whenever possible and was unsympathetic in both law and equity cases toward artificial rules. His upholding of the legal tender act as incident to the war powers of Congress, 1863, was said to be equal to a victory in the field for the cause of the Union. His best-known decision was in *People vs. Albany & Susquehanna R.R.* in which he settled the main point involved in the "Erie War."

SMITH, ERMINNIE ADELLE PLATT (*b. Marcellus, N.Y., 1836; d. 1886*), geologist, ethnologist. Authority on the language, customs and myths of the Iroquois Indians.

SMITH, ERWIN FRINK (*b. Gilberts Mills, N.Y., 1854; d. Washington, D.C., 1927*), botanist, bacteriologist. Graduated University of Michigan, 1836; Sc.D., 1889. Thereafter, as a member of the scientific staff of the U.S. Department of Agriculture, he was a leader in development of the science of plant pathology and was himself unequaled in that field. He was author of a number of monographs and books of which *Bacteria in Relation to Plant Diseases* (1905–14) was outstanding.

SMITH, EUGENE ALLEN (*b. Washington, Ala., 1841; d. Tuscaloosa, Ala., 1927*), geologist. Graduated University of Alabama, 1862; Ph.D., Heidelberg, 1868. Taught at Universities of Mississippi and Alabama; was state geologist of Alabama, 1873–1927.

SMITH, FRANCIS HENNEY (*b. Norfolk, Va., 1812; d. Lexington, Va., 1890*), soldier, educator. Graduated West Point, 1833. Superintendent, Virginia Military Institute, 1840–89. Smith attacked the classical type of education prevalent in the ante-bellum South and emphasized a utilitarian approach.

SMITH, FRANCIS HOPKINSON (*b. Baltimore, Md., 1838; d. New York, N.Y., 1915*), engineer, artist, writer. Great-grandson of Francis Hopkinson. Successful in all three of his professions, Smith is remembered particularly for his best-selling works of fiction which were marked by his own sunny temperament and by his special gift for observation of local color. Among his many books, *Colonel Carter of Cartersville* (1891) is outstanding; *The Fortunes of Oliver Horn* (1902) is in part autobiographical.

SMITH, FRANCIS MARION (*b. Richmond, Wis., 1846; d. Oakland, Calif., 1931*), capitalist. In 1872, at Columbus, Nev., he and his partner, William Tell Coleman, discovered in Teel's Marsh the mineral (colemanite) from which borax is derived. These mines soon became the world's chief source of borax. The partners organized the Pacific Coast Borax Co. and through it succeeded in controlling the borax market for a long period. Later Smith acquired colemanite deposits in Death Valley, Calif. From there the product was hauled by mules to Mojave, Calif., and the "twenty-mule-team" became a familiar borax trade-mark.

SMITH, FRED BURTON (*b. near Lone Tree, Iowa, 1865; d. White Plains, N.Y., 1936*), lay evangelist, reformer, Y.M.C.A. official. [*Supp. 2*]

SMITH, GEORGE (*b. Aberdeenshire, Scotland, 1806; d. London, England, 1899*), banker. Principally resident in America *c.* 1834–1860. Smith profited by the boom in Chicago, Ill., land values in 1835 and 1836. By influence in the Wisconsin legislature, he succeeded in evading anti-banking laws by winning a charter for his Wisconsin Marine & Fire Insurance Co., 1839. Under a clause in this charter Smith was able to conduct a general banking business of which Alexander Mitchell was the active manager. After making enormous profits, the company became a state bank in 1853. The rapid economic expansion of Wisconsin and Illinois in the 1840's would not have been possible without the trustworthy credit provided by Smith's company.

SMITH, GEORGE HENRY (*b. Knoxville, Tenn., 1873; d. Maplewood, N.J., 1931*), journalist, author of humorous juvenile stories.

SMITH, GERALD BIRNEY (*b. Middlefield, Mass., 1868; d. 1929*), theologian. Nephew of Judson Smith. Taught at the divinity school of University of Chicago. An empiricist, he bent his efforts "to find a vital religion which should not rest upon authoritative dogma" and sought to give his students a method of critical thinking rather than a body of conclusions.

SMITH, GERRIT (*b. Utica, N.Y., 1797; d. New York, N.Y., 1874*), reformer. Grandson of James Livingston; son of Peter Smith. Devoting his large fortune to what he considered the good of mankind, he experimented with systematic charity on a large scale. He also advocated strict Sunday observance, vegetarianism, total abstinence from liquor, reform of dress, prison reform and woman's suffrage. Joining the anti-slavery movement in 1835, he became one of the best-known abolitionists in the United States and a backer of the aid societies for Kansas. A supporter of the use of force against pro-slavery adherents in Kansas, he backed John Brown enthusiastically but later denied complicity in Brown's plot. During the Civil War he wrote and spoke in support of the Union cause, and in the Reconstruction period advocated moderation toward the Southern whites and Negro suffrage.

SMITH, GILES ALEXANDER (*b. Jefferson Co., N.Y., 1829; d. 1876*), Union major-general. Brother of Morgan L. Smith. Distinguished himself particularly in command of the 2nd Division, XVII Corps, at the battle of Atlanta, July 1864.

SMITH, GUSTAVUS WOODSON (*b. Georgetown, Ky., 1822; d. New York, N.Y., 1896*), civil and military engineer, Confederate major-general. Graduated West Point, 1842. After serving as actual commander of the army engineers during the Mexican War, Smith taught engineering at West Point and after his resignation from the army, 1854, was employed in important civil engineering work. Appointed major-general in the Confederate Army, 1861, he succeeded to command of Confederate forces in the Peninsular campaign between the wounding of Gen. Johnston and Gen. R. E. Lee's arrival. Resigning in 1863 after a series of quarrels with President Jefferson Davis, he returned to arms in June 1864 as major-general of Georgia militia with the Army of Tennessee.

SMITH, HAMILTON (*b. near Louisville, Ky., 1840; d. Durham, N.H., 1900*), mining engineer, authority on hydraulics.

SMITH, HANNAH WHITALL (*b. Philadelphia, Pa., 1832; d. Iffley, England, 1911*), author, religious interpreter, reformer. Mother of Logan P. Smith.

SMITH, HAROLD BABBITT (*b. Barre, Mass., 1869; d. 1932*), electrical engineer, educator. M.E., Cornell University, 1891. Taught electrical engineering at University of Arkansas and Purdue; established and headed electrical engineering department at Worcester Polytechnic Institute, 1896–1931. A pioneer in electrical engineering education, Smith was also prominent as an industrial consultant and carried on extensive research in dielectric phenomena and electric stress distribution.

SMITH, HARRY BACHE (*b. Buffalo, N.Y., 1860; d. Atlantic City, N.J., 1936*), operetta and musical comedy librettist, book collector. Raised in Chicago, Ill. Author of "book" and lyrics for a great number of successful shows which included *Robin Hood* (music by Reginald de Koven), *The Fortune Teller* (music by Victor Herbert), *Gypsy Love* (music by Franz Lehar) and the *Ziegfeld Follies* of 1907, 1908, 1909, 1910 and 1912. [*Supp. 2*]

SMITH, HARRY JAMES (*b. New Britain, Conn., 1880; d. near Murrayville, B.C., Canada, 1918*), playwright, novelist. Author of a number of comedies of manners of which *Mrs. Bumpstead-Leigh* (1910–11) and *A Tailor-Made Man* (1917) were the most successful.

SMITH, HENRY AUGUSTUS MIDDLETON (*b. Charleston, S.C., 1853; d. 1924*), South Carolina jurist, local historian.

SMITH, HENRY BOYNTON (*b. Portland, Maine, 1815; d. New York, N.Y., 1877*), Presbyterian clergyman. Professor of church history and later of theology at Union Theological Seminary, 1850–74. A representative of liberal orthodoxy, he edited the *American Theological Review*, 1859–74, and was the translator of several German theological works.

SMITH, HENRY JUSTIN (*b. Chicago, Ill., 1875; d. Evanston, Ill., 1936*), Chicago newspaper editor. Associated with the *Chicago Daily News*, 1899–1924, Smith returned to it as managing editor in 1926 and remained in that post until his death. Encourager of many later prominent journalists and writers who made their start under him, he was author of a number of books including *Chicago: The History of Its Reputation* (with Lloyd Lewis, 1929) and *Oscar Wilde Discovers America* (1936). [*Supp. 2*]

SMITH, HENRY PRESERVED (*b. Troy, O., 1847; d. Poughkeepsie, N.Y., 1927*), Presbyterian clergyman, Biblical scholar. Brother of Richmond Mayo-Smith. A pioneer in the introduction of German higher criticism, he was suspended from the ministry after trial in November 1892 by the Presbytery of Cincinnati. He later taught at Amherst College and at Meadville Theological School, and was librarian at Union Theological Seminary, 1913–25. He was author of a number of books including *A Critical and Exegetical Commentary on the Books of Samuel* (1899), *Samuel, Old Testament History* (1903) and *The Religion of Israel* (1914).

SMITH, HEZEKIAH (*b. Hempstead, N.Y., 1737; d. 1805*), Baptist clergyman. Pastor at Haverhill, Mass., *post* 1766, he frequently undertook missionary journeys into New Hampshire and Maine and served as a Revolutionary War chaplain. An associate with James Manning in the founding of Rhode Island College (Brown University), he devoted much of his time to the development of that institution.

SMITH, HIRAM (*b. Tinicum, Pa., 1817; d. 1890*), agriculturist. Removed to Sheboygan Falls, Wis., 1847, where he developed one of the outstanding dairy farms of the state. As a regent of the University of Wisconsin, he was responsible for establishment of the first U.S. dairy school there, 1890.

SMITH, HOKE (*b. Newton, N.C., 1855; d. 1931*), lawyer, newspaper publisher, Georgia politician. As U.S. secretary of the interior, 1893–96, Smith was an advocate of conservation of Western natural resources and supported President Cleveland's effort to maintain the gold standard. A leader of liberal and reform elements in Georgia, Smith returned to politics in 1906, urging more effective control of the railroads and a supervision over electoral frauds which amounted to disfranchisement of Negroes. In his first term as governor (July 1907–July 1909), he accomplished more in extending the scope of social control in Georgia than any other governor in recent times; under his leadership, the Assembly inaugurated the good-roads movement, established a department of commerce and labor, uprooted the convict-lease system and curbed the state's public utilities companies. After a second brief term from July to November 1911, Smith became U.S. senator, Democrat, and served until 1921. His prime interest as a senator was in furthering the cause of education, especially vocational education. He disagreed with President Woodrow Wilson on a number of issues, particularly on the matter of the League of Nations. Throughout his long career he played an important part in the civic development of Atlanta, Ga.

SMITH, HORACE (*b. Cheshire, Mass., 1808; d. 1893*), inventor, arms manufacturer. In partnership with Daniel B. Wesson, he developed a revolver using a central-fire metallic cartridge (patented, 1859, 1860) which was manufactured for the Union Army in the Civil War and enjoyed large sales abroad.

SMITH, ISRAEL (*b. Suffield, Conn., 1759; d. 1810*), lawyer. Raised in Vermont, Smith served in the Vermont legislature and was congressman, (Democrat) Republican, from Vermont, 1791–97, 1801–03; U.S. senator, March 1803—October 1807. He then became governor of the state for a single term.

SMITH, JAMES (*b. northern Ireland, c. 1719; d. Pennsylvania, 1806*), lawyer. Came to York Co., Pa., as a boy. Admitted to the bar, 1752. A backcountry leader during the Revolutionary era; member of the Continental Congress in 1776 and 1777; signer of the Declaration of Independence. A vigorous state-rights man, he held but few political posts after his service in Congress and engaged himself chiefly in the practice of law.

SMITH, JAMES (*b. present Franklin Co., Pa., c. 1737; d. 1814*), frontiersman, soldier, Kentucky pioneer. Author of *An Account of the Remarkable Occurrences in the Life and Travels of Col. James Smith, During His Captivity with the Indians, in the Years 1755, '56, '57, '58 & '59* (Lexington, Ky., 1799).

SMITH, JAMES (*b. Newark, N.J., 1851; d. Newark, 1927*), businessman, Democratic boss of New Jersey.

971

Served as U.S. senator from New Jersey, 1893–99, without distinction; forced nomination of Woodrow Wilson for governor of New Jersey, 1910.

SMITH, JAMES ALLEN (*b. Pleasant Hill, Mo., 1860; d. 1924*), political scientist. Graduated University of Missouri, 1886; received Ph.D. at University of Michigan, 1894, after submitting a brilliant, controversial dissertation on the theory of money. In 1897 he became professor of political science at the University of Washington, remaining there until his death. His best-known work, *The Spirit of American Government* (1907), profoundly influenced Theodore Roosevelt, Robert LaFollette and many of the leading Progressives. Repeatedly denounced as a radical, he was in fact a Jeffersonian Democrat.

SMITH, JAMES FRANCIS (*b. San Francisco, Calif., 1859; d. Washington, D.C., 1928*), soldier, lawyer, jurist. Graduated Santa Clara College, 1877. Commanded 1st California Volunteer Infantry in the Philippines, 1898; rose to rank of brigadier-general and served as military governor of several sub-districts in the Philippines. After holding a number of high official positions in the administration of the islands, 1900–06, he served with great ability and success as governor-general, 1906–09. He was a judge, U.S. court of customs appeals, 1910–28.

SMITH, JAMES McCUNE (*b. New York, N.Y., 1813; d. Williamsburg, L.I., N.Y., 1865*), physician. The son of slave parents who had been emancipated, Smith graduated from the University of Glasgow, 1835, received his M.D. degree from Glasgow in 1837, and after studying in clinics in Paris, France, returned to practice medicine in New York City. His chief claim to remembrance, however, rests upon his services in the interest of the Negro race which were numerous and varied. His writings show a high degree of scholarship.

SMITH, JAMES PERRIN (*b. near Cokesbury, S.C., 1864; d. 1931*), paleontologist, geologist. Brother of Charles Forster Smith. Graduated Wofford College, 1884; M.A., Vanderbilt, 1886; Ph.D., Göttingen, 1892. Taught at Leland Stanford *post* 1893; made special study of ammonite group; served as geologist in U.S. Geological Survey, 1906–24.

SMITH, JAMES YOUNGS (*b. Groton, Conn., 1809; d. 1876*), cotton manufacturer, philanthropist. Republican governor of Rhode Island, 1863–66.

SMITH, JEDEDIAH STRONG (*b. Bainbridge, N.Y., 1798; d. near Cimarron River, Santa Fé trail, 1831*), fur trader, explorer. Smith made the journeys on which his fame rests in the period 1826–30. Investigating the practicability of penetrating the Oregon country from California, he left Great Salt Lake in August 1826, passed through the territory of the Utes, Paiutes and the Mohaves, and entered California from the desert in November. Restrained from any movement north by the governor of California, he proceeded east and north to the valley of King's River where, in February 1827, he tried to cross the mountains and failed. He then moved north to the American River and with two companions crossed the mountains in May, making his way to Salt Lake over the unrelieved desert. Retracing his previous year's route from Salt Lake to San Gabriel Mission, he wintered in the Sacramento Valley; in April 1828 he headed northwest and in June reached the seacoast at the mouth of Klamath River. After a hard journey to the Willamette, he reached Fort Vancouver where Dr. John McLoughlin entertained him until March, 1829. Smith then made his way on ground familiar to him to the rendezvous at Pierre's Hole. Retiring from the Rocky Mountain trade, he entered the Santa Fé trade and was killed on the trail by Comanche Indians. He was the first explorer of the Great Basin, the first American to make his way into California from the east and out of California from the west.

SMITH, JEREMIAH (*b. Peterborough, N.H., 1759; d. Dover, N.H., 1842*), lawyer. Congressman, Federalist, from New Hampshire, 1791–97. After service as U.S. attorney for the New Hampshire district and as a New Hampshire judge of probate, and a very brief term as U.S. circuit judge, he was chief justice of New Hampshire, 1802–09. During this period he did more for the improvement of the jurisprudence of the state than any other man. After a single unsatisfactory term as Federalist governor of New Hampshire, 1809–10, he served again as chief justice, 1813–16. Retiring to private life, he was an associate counsel with Daniel Webster and Jeremiah Mason in the celebrated Dartmouth College Case.

SMITH, JEREMIAH (*b. Exeter, N.H., 1837; d. St. Andrews, N.B., Canada, 1921*), jurist, teacher of law. Son of Jeremiah Smith (1759–1842). Justice, New Hampshire supreme court, 1867–74; Story Professor of Law, Harvard, 1890–1910.

SMITH, JEREMIAH (*b. Dover, N.H., 1870; d. 1935*), lawyer, financial expert. Son of Jeremiah Smith (1837–1921). Practiced in Boston, Mass., *post* 1896. Successfully reorganized finances of Hungary under supervision of League of Nations, 1924–26; served as counsel to American financial experts in formulation of the "Young Plan." [*Supp. 1*]

SMITH, JOB LEWIS (*b. Onondaga Co., N.Y., 1827; d. 1897*), physician. Brother of Stephen Smith. Graduated Yale, 1849; M.D., N.Y. College of Physicians and Surgeons, 1853. Author of one of the earliest American books to deal as a specialty with the diseases of children, Smith became one of America's leading pediatricians and was professor of the diseases of children at Bellevue Hospital Medical College, 1876–96.

SMITH, JOEL WEST (*b. East Hampton, Conn., 1837; d. Middletown, Conn., 1924*), educator of the blind.

SMITH, JOHN (*b. Willoughby, Lincolnshire, England, 1579/80; d. London, England, 1631*), adventurer, explorer, author. Apprenticed to a merchant, he soon left to seek adventure on the Continent and fought against the Turks in Transylvania. A prisoner and slave for some time among the Turks, he escaped, experienced further adventures, and returned to England probably in 1604. Sailing with the colonists of the Virginia Company of London late in 1606, he landed with them at Jamestown, 1607. During the troubled early days of the colony, Smith showed at his best in the expeditions he made among the Indians to procure food; taken prisoner on one of these trips, he was, according to his story in his *Generall Historie* (1624), condemned to death and saved by the intercession of Pocahontas. The story has been long in controversy but there is nothing inherently improbable in it. Returning to Jamestown in January 1608, he found personal enemies in command of the turbulent colony and was arrested and condemned to be hanged. On the arrival, however, of Capt. Christopher Newport with new settlers from England, Smith was released and restored to a place in the council from which he had been previously ousted. Much more interested in exploring than in the administration of Jamestown, he settled down to governing the colony when elected president in the autumn of 1608. In October 1609, after much wrangling about authority, Smith returned to England where he severely criticized the Virginia Company and its methods. Despite the spectacular nature of his brief career in Virginia, his substantial contributions to the later founding of New England are possibly of more importance. Sent to New England by London merchants in March 1614, he brought back a valuable cargo of fish and furs and emphasized the value of the fisheries, continuing to the end of his life to proclaim the favorable prospects of New England for settlement. Among his numerous writings, *The True Travels, Adventures, and Observations of Captaine John Smith* (1630) and the *Generall Historie of Virginia, New-England, and the Summer Isles* already cited are considered the most important. His *A Map of Virginia* (1612) and *A Description of New England* (1616) were primary contributions to cartography.

SMITH, JOHN (*b. possibly Virginia, c. 1735; d. present St. Francisville, La., c. 1824*), Baptist clergyman, merchant. U.S. senator from Ohio, (Democrat) Republican, 1803–07. Smith is best known for his association with Aaron Burr in the latter's Western projects.

SMITH, JOHN AUGUSTINE (*b. Westmoreland Co., Va., 1782; d. 1865*), physician. Graduated William and Mary, 1800; received his medical education in London. A member of the first faculty of N.Y. College of Physicians and Surgeons *post* 1807, he became president of the College of William and Mary, 1814.

Returning to New York in 1825 after a most unsatisfactory tenure, he resumed his old duties as professor at the College of Physicians and Surgeons and as its president *post* 1831 succeeded in broadening and improving the curriculum. He retired in 1843.

SMITH, JOHN BERNHARD (*b. New York, N.Y., 1858; d. 1912*), lawyer, entomologist. Appointed entomologist of the New Jersey state agricultural experiment station, 1889, he made his principal contribution in discovery of the breeding habits of the salt-marsh mosquito and the later institution of that insect's control. He served as professor of entomology, Rutgers College, 1889–1912.

SMITH, JOHN BLAIR (*b. Pequea, Pa., 1756; d. Philadelphia, Pa., 1799*), Presbyterian clergyman, educator. Nephew of Samuel Blair; brother of Samuel S. Smith. The leader of Presbyterian thought in Virginia in his time, he served as president of Hampden-Sydney College, 1779–89, and was made first president of Union College, 1795.

SMITH, JOHN COTTON (*b. Sharon, Conn., 1765; d. 1845*), lawyer, Connecticut legislator. A sturdy Calvinist and conservative, he served in Congress, sat on the state bench, and as Federalist governor of Connecticut, 1813–17, was the last representative of the old "Standing Order" to hold the governor's chair. An opponent of the War of 1812, he urged Connecticut representation in the Hartford Convention and was a whole-souled enemy of reform and of liberal revision of the Connecticut Charter.

SMITH, JOHN COTTON (*b. Andover, Mass., 1826; d. 1882*), Episcopal clergyman, author. Rector of the Church of the Ascension, New York City, *post* 1860. Active in support of foreign missions, reconciliation of theology and science, church union and the solution of social problems, he was also a pioneer advocate of model housing and tenement-house reform.

SMITH, JOHN EUGENE (*b. Canton of Berne, Switzerland, 1816; d. Chicago, Ill., 1897*), soldier. Brought to America as an infant, Smith learned the jeweler's trade which he followed in St. Louis, Mo., and Galena, Ill. Appointed colonel, 45th Illinois Infantry, July 1861, he rose to brigade and division command for brilliant services in the Western campaigns and at Savannah, Ga. Commissioned colonel, 27th Infantry, regular army, in 1866, he served on the frontiers and helped quell the Sioux outbreak under Spotted Tail.

SMITH, JOHN GREGORY (*b. St. Albans, Vt., 1818; d. 1891*), railway organizer and executive, lawyer, Vermont legislator. Republican governor of Vermont, 1863 and 1864.

SMITH, JOHN JAY (*b. Burlington Co., N.J., 1798; d. Germantown, Pa., 1881*), editor, librarian. Grandnephew of Richard Smith; father-in-law of Hannah W. Smith; father of Lloyd P. Smith. Librarian of the Library Company of Philadelphia, 1829–51; editor of

Waldie's Select Circulating Library and briefly of *Littell's Museum.*

SMITH, JOHN LAWRENCE (*b. near Charleston, S.C., 1818; d. 1883*), chemist, mineralogist, authority on organic chemistry and meteorites.

SMITH, JOHN MERLIN POWIS (*b. London, England, 1866; d. New York, N.Y., 1932*), Biblical scholar. Emigrated to Iowa, 1883. Ph.D. in Semitics, University of Chicago, 1899. After serving as assistant to William R. Harper, Smith taught at University of Chicago *post* 1908 and was also editor of the *American Journal of Semitic Languages.* He was author of a number of important works on Hebrew and on the Old Testament.

SMITH, JOHN ROWSON (*b. Boston, Mass., 1810; d. 1864*), painter. Son of John Rubens Smith. Employed as a painter of stage scenery, he produced a number of scenic panoramas which were exhibited on tour through the United States and in Europe. These included panoramas of Boston, "The Conflagration of Moscow" and the Mississippi Valley. The last of these has been credited with greatly stimulating emigration.

SMITH, JOHN RUBENS (*b. London, England, 1775; d. New York, N.Y., 1849*), engraver, painter, drawing master. Son of John Raphael Smith, an eminent English mezzotinter; father of John Rowson Smith. Emigrated to America *ante* 1809. As a teacher in Boston, Philadelphia and New York, he was reputed able but quarrelsome; he engaged in a number of controversies with contemporary artists.

SMITH, JONAS WALDO (*b. Lincoln, Mass., 1861; d. New York, N.Y., 1933*), civil engineer, water-supply expert. Graduated Massachusetts Institute of Technology, 1887. Associated with Clemens Herschel in developing water supplies of Paterson, Passaic and other New Jersey communities. Appointed chief engineer of the Aqueduct Commission of New York City, 1903, and of the New York Board of Water Supply, 1905, Smith performed the most important work of his life in creating and later extending the system for bringing water from the Catskill Mountains to New York City.

SMITH, JONATHAN BAYARD (*b. Philadelphia, Pa., 1742; d. 1812*), Philadelphia merchant, Revolutionary patriot and soldier, Continental congressman. Father of Samuel H. Smith.

SMITH, JOSEPH (*b. Hanover, Mass., 1790; d. 1877*), naval officer. Appointed midshipman, 1809; served with credit in War of 1812 and the war with Algiers. Held a number of important sea and shore commands, notably that of chief of the Bureau of Navy Yards and Docks, 1846–69; headed the naval board which decided on building the *Monitor.* Promoted rear-admiral on the retired list, 1862.

SMITH, JOSEPH (*b. Sharon, Vt., 1805; d. Carthage, Ill., 1844*), Mormon prophet. While resident in Palmyra, N.Y., he experienced a series of visions, 1820–23, whereby he was led to believe that God had selected him to restore the church of Christ. In September 1827 he was permitted to take from their hiding place near Manchester, N.Y., certain golden plates which recorded the story of the "true" church on the American continent following its migrations from Jerusalem. After translating the history by miraculous means, he published the result at Palmyra in July 1830 as *The Book of Mormon.* Before its publication, Smith had founded the Church of Jesus Christ of Latter-Day Saints at Fayette, N.Y., April 1830, but the extraordinary growth of the sect did not begin until Sidney Rigdon became associated with it. A cooperative society ruled by an ecclesiastical oligarchy, Mormonism was a system excellently adapted to success on the far frontier, but it brought its members into continual conflict with neighbors in the communities they occupied during Smith's lifetime. Removing first (1831) to Kirtland, O., and later (1838) to Missouri, Smith and his flock came in 1839 to Commerce, Ill., which Smith renamed Nauvoo. After five years of prosperity during which Smith enjoyed power, publicity and worship, he made formal announcement of his candidacy for the presidency of the United States, Feb. 15, 1844. However, the scandal of his business affairs, the general unpopularity of his sect and the discovery by local non-Mormons of the practice of polygamy (foreshadowed *c.* 1831, declared as revelation July 1843) brought about an uprising against the Mormons on the part of their neighbors. Smith and his brother were arrested and put in jail at Carthage, Ill., whence they were taken on June 27, 1844, and shot. He was the father, among other children, of Joseph Smith (1832–1914) and the uncle of Joseph F. Smith.

SMITH, JOSEPH (*b. Kirtland, O., 1832; d. 1914*), Mormon prophet. Son of Joseph Smith (1805–1844). President of the Reorganized Church of Jesus Christ of Latter-Day Saints *post* 1860; opposed polygamy, denying that his father had preached or practiced it.

SMITH, JOSEPH FIELDING (*b. Far West, Mo., 1838; d. 1918*), sixth president of the Utah branch of the Mormon Church. Nephew of Joseph Smith (1805–1844). His chief contribution was the strengthening of the Mormon organization and the fostering of more friendly relations with non-Mormons.

SMITH, JUDSON (*b. Middlefield, Mass., 1837; d. 1906*), educator. Uncle of Gerald B. Smith. Graduated Amherst, 1859; Oberlin Theological Seminary, 1863. Ordained a Congregational minister, 1866, Smith taught Latin and history at Oberlin, and in 1884 became a secretary of the American Board of Commissioners for Foreign Missions.

SMITH, JULIA EVELINA (1792–1886). [See SMITH, ABBY HADASSAH, 1797–1878.]

SMITH, JUNIUS (b. Plymouth, Conn., 1780; d. New York, N.Y., 1853), lawyer, merchant, "father of the Atlantic liner." Organized British & American Steam Navigation Co., 1836, to undertake establishment of regular transatlantic steamship service. The voyage of this company's vessel Sirius in 1838 was the first of its kind, beating the Great Western to New York by a few hours. Competition from the Cunard line and the loss of a new vessel, the President, brought Smith's company to an end c. 1842.

SMITH, JUSTIN HARVEY (b. Boscawen, N.H., 1857; d. Brooklyn, N.Y., 1930), historian, publisher, educator. Graduated Dartmouth, 1877. Taught modern history at Dartmouth, 1899–1908. Author, among other books, of The Annexation of Texas (1911) and The War with Mexico (1919), for which he was awarded the Pulitzer Prize and other honors.

SMITH, LLOYD PEARSALL (b. Philadelphia, Pa., 1822; d. 1886), librarian, publisher, editor. Son of John Jay Smith whom he succeeded as librarian of the Library Company of Philadelphia, 1851. He was the first editor of Lippincott's Magazine, 1868–69, and the author of On the Classification of Books (1892) which was a pioneer discussion of that subject.

SMITH, MARCUS (b. New Orleans, La., 1829; d. Paris, France, 1874), actor, better known as Mark Smith. Son of Solomon F. Smith. Superior in supporting roles, notably as an interpreter of the "old English gentleman."

SMITH, MARGARET BAYARD (b. 1778; d. Washington, D.C., 1844), society leader, author. Daughter of John B. Bayard; wife of Samuel H. Smith. Writer of several novels and a contributor to the periodicals of her time, Mrs. Smith is remembered for her letters which form a record by a keen observer of social and political events from Jefferson's time to the administration of W. H. Harrison. Edited by Gaillard Hunt, they were published as The First Forty Years of Washington Society (1906).

SMITH, MARTIN LUTHER (b. Danby, N.Y., 1819; d. Savannah, Ga., 1866), Confederate major-general. Graduated West Point, 1842. Helped plan and construct fortifications of New Orleans and Vicksburg; served at various times as chief engineer of the Army of Northern Virginia and the Army of Tennessee.

SMITH, MELANCTON (b. Jamaica, N.Y., 1744; d. New York, N.Y., 1798), lawyer, merchant, Revolutionary patriot. Active in ferreting out Tories in New York, 1775–80, he served in the Continental Congress, 1785–88, and rendered his most conspicuous service as an Anti-Federalist debater in the New York convention for ratification of the Federal Constitution.

SMITH, MELANCTON (b. New York, N.Y., 1810; d. Green Bay, Wis., 1893), naval officer. Grandson of Melancton Smith (1744–1798). Entering the navy, 1826, he performed a variety of sea and shore duties up to the time of the Civil War in which he won repute as a grim and dogged fighting commander. He served under Farragut in the campaign against New Orleans, 1862, and at Port Hudson, 1863. During 1864 he operated on the James River, and commanded a gunboat flotilla during efforts to destroy the ram Albemarle, May–June 1864. He was later commended for his part in the attacks against Fort Fisher. Promoted rear-admiral, 1870, he retired, 1871.

SMITH, MERIWETHER (b. Essex Co., Va., 1730; d. Essex Co., 1794), Revolutionary patriot, Virginia legislator and congressman. Able, but erratic.

SMITH, MILTON HANNIBAL (b. Greene Co., N.Y., 1836; d. Louisville, Ky., 1921), railroad official. Associated principally with the Louisville & Nashville post 1866, he served as its chief executive, 1882–1921, under various titles. He made his road one of the more important transportation factors in the United States.

SMITH, MORGAN LEWIS (b. Mexico, N.Y., 1821; d. Jersey City, N.J., 1874), Union brigadier-general. Brother of Giles A. Smith. Held brigade, division and, for a brief time, corps command under U. S. Grant and W. T. Sherman, 1861–64; commanded District of Vicksburg, 1864–65. Celebrated for coolness under fire, and for a remarkable ability to instill discipline and morale in raw troops.

SMITH, NATHAN (b. Rehoboth, Mass., 1762; d. New Haven, Conn., 1829), physician, medical educator. After apprenticeship to several physicians in Vermont where he was raised, Smith began practice at Cornish, N.H., 1787. Realizing inadequacy of his training, he studied at Harvard with John Warren and Benjamin Waterhouse, 1789–90, and then returned to his practice. Still unsatisfied with his education and desiring to teach, he made further studies in Europe, 1796–97, and in 1797–98 began work as professor of medicine at Dartmouth. In addition to his teaching he practiced generally in the area. Exasperated at lack of support of the medical school from the state legislature, he removed to Yale where he became professor of the theory and practice of medicine, surgery and obstetrics, 1813. In high repute as surgeon and teacher, he was one of the earliest to perform ovariotomy and in other ways showed an ability and resourcefulness which were unsurpassed in his day. The importance of his work for succeeding generations is to be found in the fresh and original manner in which he attacked problems in medicine and surgery, his essentially modern concept of disease, his distaste for theorizing and his emphasis on the need for accurate observation. Among his writings his Practical Essay on Typhous Fever (1824) has classic stature.

SMITH, NATHAN (*b. Woodbury, Conn., 1770; d. Washington, D.C., 1835*), lawyer. Brother of Nathaniel Smith. Active in the fight to disestablish Congregationalism in Connecticut, Smith held several judicial offices in the state and was U.S. senator, Whig, from Connecticut, 1832–35.

SMITH, NATHAN RYNO (*b. Cornish, N.H., 1797; d. Baltimore, Md., 1877*), surgeon, teacher of anatomy and surgery. Son of Nathan Smith (1762–1829). M.D., Yale, 1823. Taught at University of Vermont, at Jefferson Medical College and at University of Maryland. Invented a new instrument for lithotomy; was a pioneer in extirpation of the thyroid gland.

SMITH, NATHANIEL (*b. Woodbury, Conn., 1762; d. 1822*), Connecticut jurist. Brother of Nathan Smith (1770–1835). Congressman, Federalist, from Connecticut, 1795–99; judge, state superior court, 1806–19. Attended Hartford Convention, 1814.

SMITH, OLIVER (*b. Hatfield, Mass., 1766; d. 1845*), businessman. Uncle of Sophia Smith. Bequeathed his very large fortune to several charitable enterprises under a will which was contested by his heirs-at-law. After a notable legal battle in which Rufus Choate and Daniel Webster were of counsel, the will was sustained. Among its present beneficiaries are the Smith Agricultural School and Northampton (Mass.) School of Technology.

SMITH, OLIVER HAMPTON (*b. Bucks Co., Pa., 1794; d. Indianapolis, Ind., 1859*), lawyer. Began practice at Versailles and Connersville, Ind., 1820. After service as a legislator and as prosecuting attorney, he was congressman, Democrat, from Indiana, 1827–29. As U.S. senator, Whig, from Indiana, 1837–43, he became chairman of the committee on public lands and was a leader in evolving a federal land policy in the interest of the actual settlers.

SMITH, ORMOND GERALD (*b. New York, N.Y., 1860; d. 1933*), publisher. Headed the firm of Street & Smith, publishers of dime-novels and popular fiction, *post* 1887. [*Supp. 1*]

SMITH, PERSIFOR FRAZER (*b. Philadelphia, Pa., 1798; d. Fort Leavenworth, Kans., 1858*), soldier. Graduated College of New Jersey (Princeton), 1815. Removing to Louisiana, 1819, he practiced law in New Orleans and was active in the militia, serving in the Seminole War campaigns of 1836 and 1838. Commissioned colonel, U.S. Army, May 1846, he served with great distinction in the Mexican War as brigade commander under Zachary Taylor and during Scott's campaign against Mexico City. Brevetted major-general, he commanded several departments in the West, 1848–58. He was commissioned brigadier-general, regular army, 1856. Gallant and efficient, he was noted particularly for the implicit trust which his men gave him.

SMITH, PETER (*b. near Tappan, N.Y., 1768; d. Schenectady, N.Y., 1837*), landowner. Father of Gerrit Smith. For a brief time a partner of John Jacob Astor in the fur trade, Smith acquired large tracts in Oneida and Onondaga counties, New York State, by lease and purchase from the Indians.

SMITH, RICHARD (*b. Burlington, N.J., 1735; d. Natchez, Miss., 1803*), lawyer, land speculator. Smith's diary as a member of the Continental Congress from New Jersey, 1774–76, supplies much information not available from official sources concerning the proceedings in Congress. Another of his journals covering his explorations of a tract of land which he owned on the upper Susquehanna River was published as *A Tour of Four Great Rivers* (1906).

SMITH, RICHARD PENN (*b. Philadelphia, Pa., 1799; d. near Philadelphia, 1854*), lawyer, author, playwright. Grandson of William Smith (1727–1803). Author of some 20 plays (1825–35) of which 15 were performed on the stage. Most of his work represented translations or adaptations from works by French and English authors; *The Deformed* (1830) and *Caius Marius* (1831) are considered his best works. He was author also of a novel, *The Forsaken* (1831), and of a number of tales, sketches and verses.

SMITH, RICHARD SOMERS (*b. Philadelphia, Pa., 1813; d. 1877*), soldier, educator. Graduated West Point, 1834. Taught mathematics, drawing and engineering at a number of schools including West Point (1840–55), Cooper Union and the U.S. Naval Academy; served in Union Army, 1861–63; was president of Girard College, 1863–67.

SMITH, ROBERT (*b. possibly Glasgow, Scotland, c. 1722; d. 1777*), Philadelphia architect and builder. Designed and built Nassau Hall at College of New Jersey (Princeton), 1754; St. Peter's Church, Philadelphia, 1758; also other Philadelphia churches. Planned obstructions in the Delaware River below Philadelphia for defense of that city, 1775–76. Smith handled the contemporary Georgian style with admirable dignity but tended to excessive plainness.

SMITH, ROBERT (*b. Worstead, England, 1732 o.s.; d. 1801*), Revolutionary patriot and chaplain, Episcopal clergyman. Came to Charleston, S.C., 1757, as assistant minister of St. Philip's Church; becoming rector, 1759, he continued so until his death. He was consecrated first bishop of South Carolina, 1795.

SMITH, ROBERT (*b. Lancaster, Pa., 1757; d. 1842*), lawyer, Maryland legislator. Brother of Samuel Smith. U.S. secretary of the navy, 1801–09, Smith ran his office with fair efficiency although greatly criticized by Albert Gallatin. A member of the Senate cabal which included his brother, and also W. B. Giles and Michael Leib, Smith continued his feud with Gallatin while acting as U.S. secretary of state, 1809–11. Forced to resign by President Madison, whose policies on commercial restrictions he opposed, Smith retired to private life.

SMITH, ROBERT ALEXANDER C. (*b. Dover, England, 1857; d. Southampton, England, 1933*), railroad and public utilities promoter, capitalist. As dock commissioner of New York City, 1913–17, Smith developed and provided for construction of the Hudson River piers which greatly improved New York's standing among world seaports.

SMITH, ROBERT BARNWELL. [See RHETT, ROBERT BARNWELL, 1800–1876.]

SMITH, ROBERT HARDY (*b. Camden Co., N.C., 1813; d. Mobile, Ala., 1878*), Alabama lawyer, member of the provisional Confederate Congress. Took active part in framing the permanent constitution of the Confederacy.

SMITH, ROBERT SIDNEY (*b. Bloomington, Ill., 1877; d. near Harvard, Ill., 1935*), comic-strip artist. Credited with being the first to use continuity in a comic strip, Smith began his successful "Andy Gump" series in 1917. [*Supp. 1*]

SMITH, ROSWELL (*b. Lebanon, Conn., 1829; d. New York, N.Y., 1892*), lawyer, publisher. Associated in publication of *Scribner's Monthly* with Josiah G. Holland, Charles Scribner and Richard W. Gilder *post* 1870, he became sole proprietor, 1881. Thereafter the periodical was known as the *Century*. Smith also proposed publication of *St. Nicholas* magazine (1873) and conceived the idea of *The Century Dictionary*. He directed the publication activities of the Century Company until his death.

SMITH, RUSSELL (*b. Glasgow, Scotland, 1812; d. Glenside, Pa., 1896*), painter. Came to America as a boy. Specialized *post* 1833 in painting scenery for theatres and opera houses.

SMITH, SAMUEL (*b. Carlisle, Pa., 1752; d. Baltimore, Md., 1839*), soldier, statesman. Brother of Robert Smith (1757–1842). Served throughout the Revolution and won particular distinction for commanding defense of Fort Mifflin, 1777. Growing wealthy in land speculation, he entered politics, serving as congressman from Maryland, 1793–1803; at first a Federalist, he soon became a supporter of Jefferson. Elected to the U.S. Senate, 1803, he remained a senator until 1815. During the War of 1812, as major-general he headed the force which defended Baltimore. Returning to the House of Representatives, 1816, he served until December 1822, when he resigned to fill out a vacancy in the U.S. Senate. Re-elected in 1826, he held office until 1833. A forceful debater, intelligent and ambitious, he made his influence felt both on the floor of Congress and behind the scenes where he was much given to intrigues. One of the leaders in opposing the nomination of James Madison for the presidency, he also led the faction which

fought Albert Gallatin as secretary of the treasury and obstructed Gallatin's financial program in Congress. Later, although he favored equalization of tariff duties, he fought bitterly against Henry Clay's "American system" and even suggested in 1832 that the Union be divided at the Potomac in order to escape it. His most constructive work was done in securing recovery of trade with the British West Indies (1830).

SMITH, SAMUEL FRANCIS (*b. Boston, Mass., 1808; d. Boston, 1895*), Baptist clergyman, poet. Graduated Harvard, 1829. Author of the national hymn "America," which he wrote at the request of Lowell Mason, 1832.

SMITH, SAMUEL HARRISON (*b. Philadelphia, Pa., 1772; d. Washington, D.C., 1845*), journalist, banker. Son of Jonathan B. Smith; husband of Margaret B. Smith. Graduated University of Pennsylvania, 1787. Edited the *National Intelligencer,* official organ of the Jefferson administration, 1800–10; president, Washington Branch, U.S. Bank, 1828–36.

SMITH, SAMUEL STANHOPE (*b. Pequea, Pa., 1750; d. 1819*), Presbyterian clergyman, educator. Brother of John Blair Smith. Graduated College of New Jersey (Princeton), 1769. After pastoral work and missionary activity in western Virginia, also periods of teaching at Princeton and at Hampden-Sydney, he became professor of moral philosophy at Princeton, serving 1779–1812. As acting president, 1795–1802, and as president, 1802–12, he contributed much to the physical and intellectual advancement of the college. Long interested in natural science himself, he raised money for scientific apparatus and called John Maclean to the college (1795) to give the first undergraduate courses of chemistry and natural science in the United States. Although a popular teacher and preacher, he was subjected to much hostile criticism because of his supposed liberalism.

SMITH, SEBA (*b. Buckfield, Maine, 1792; d. 1868*), journalist, political satirist. Graduated Bowdoin, 1818. Husband of Elizabeth O. P. Smith. Founded *Portland Courier,* 1829, first daily paper to be issued in Maine, in which his celebrated "Major Jack Downing" letters appeared *post* January 1830. At first critical of the state legislature, Smith extended his satire to the administration and policies of President Andrew Jackson. Immediately popular and widely reprinted and imitated, the letters were published as *The Life and Writings of Major Jack Downing of Downingville* in 1833. Smith's rather mild ridicule of national leaders and party platforms is in contrast to the pointed wit of the so-called "Jack Downing letters" written by Charles Augustus Davis whose imitations of Smith's work also received wide circulation. The creation, however, of this Yankee type must be credited to Seba Smith alone. After the success of Jack Downing, he held a number of editorial positions and was author of several other books including *'Way Down East*

(1854) and a second series of Downing letters published as a book in 1859 under the title *My Thirty Years Out of the Senate*. The new pattern which he set for American humor was carried on by, among others, James Russell Lowell, Finley P. Dunne and Will Rogers.

SMITH, SOLOMON FRANKLIN (*b. Norwich, N.Y., 1801; d. 1869*), comedian, theatre manager, lawyer. Father of Marcus Smith. Better known as Sol Smith, he led a roaming life, 1818–35, associated at times with the itinerant companies of Samuel Drake and Noah M. Ludlow. At Mobile, Ala., 1835, he became junior partner with Ludlow in a theatrical firm which became one of the most important in the West. Operating theatres in St. Louis, Mo., Mobile and New Orleans, the firm was successful until 1853 when it was dissolved. Thereafter Smith practiced law in St. Louis and served in the state convention which kept Missouri from secession.

SMITH, SOPHIA (*b. Hatfield, Mass., 1796; d. 1870*), foundress of Smith College. Niece of Oliver Smith. Bequeathed her large fortune for the founding of Smith at the suggestion of the Congregational minister at Hatfield, John Morton Greene.

SMITH, STEPHEN (*b. near Skaneateles, N.Y., 1823; d. Montour Falls, N.Y., 1922*), surgeon, pioneer in public health. Brother of Job L. Smith. M.D., N.Y. College of Physicians and Surgeons, 1851. An expert conservative surgeon and author of several valuable textbooks, Smith is remembered principally for his drafting of the Metropolitan Health Law for New York City, 1866, which became the basis of civic sanitation in the United States. He served as commissioner of the city Board of Health, 1868–75, and helped organize the American Public Health Association, 1871, of which he was first president.

SMITH, THEOBALD (*b. Albany, N.Y., 1859; d. 1934*), medical scientist. Ph.B., Cornell University, 1881; M.D., Albany Medical College, 1883. Organized department of bacteriology at present George Washington University, 1886, and taught there until 1895; taught also at Harvard Medical School, 1895–1915, and directed Mass. Board of Health pathological laboratory over the same period. Directed department of animal pathology at the Rockefeller Institute for Medical Research *post* 1915. Smith, with Daniel E. Salmon, made important studies in the cause and prevention of swine plague; Smith later (1898–1902) wrote far-reaching studies on the relation between bovine and human tuberculosis. Between 1884 and 1893, Smith made classic investigations of Texas fever among cattle and showed for the first time how parasites may act as vectors of disease from animal to animal; he also made the first recorded observation of allergy. Author of more than 224 published works and studies, he ranks in American medical history in a place comparable to that of Pasteur in France and Koch in Germany. [*Supp. 1*]

SMITH, THEODATE LOUISE (*b. Hallowell, Maine, 1859; d. 1914*), genetic psychologist. Graduated Smith College, 1882; Ph.D., Yale, 1896; studied also at Clark University where she was research assistant to Granville S. Hall., 1902–09. She was author of the interpretative *The Montessori System in Theory and Practice* (1912).

SMITH, THOMAS ADAMS (*b. Essex Co., Va., 1781; d. Saline Co., Mo., 1844*), soldier. Nephew of Meriwether Smith. Commissioned lieutenant of artillery, 1803, he served in command of infantry during War of 1812, rising to rank of brigadier-general, 1814. Appointed commander of the Territories of Missouri and Illinois, 1815, he resigned from the army, 1818, and was appointed receiver of public monies at Franklin, Mo. Resigning in 1826, he became a planter and a leader in Missouri public affairs. Fort Smith, Ark., was named in his honor. [*Supp. 1*]

SMITH, TRUMAN (*b. Roxbury, Conn., 1791; d. 1884*), lawyer. Nephew of Nathan Smith (1770–1835) and of Nathaniel Smith. Graduated Yale, 1815. Congressman, Whig, from Connecticut, 1839–43, 1845–49, he was among the first Whig party leaders to promote Zachary Taylor's candidacy in 1848 and directed Taylor's campaign. As U.S. senator, 1849–54, he described the sectional crisis of the time as a matter requiring scientific settlement on the basis of the climate and topography of the regions into which it was proposed to extend slavery. In other legislative matters he followed the predominant views of his party and section.

SMITH, URIAH (*b. West Wilton, N.H., 1832; d. Battle Creek, Mich., 1903*), Seventh-Day Adventist leader and editor, wood engraver.

SMITH, WALTER INGLEWOOD (*b. Council Bluffs, Iowa, 1862; d. Council Bluffs, 1922*), Iowa jurist. As congressman, Republican, from Iowa, 1900–11, he was an outstanding member of the appropriations committee; *post* 1911, he was judge, U.S. circuit court of appeals, 8th circuit.

SMITH, WILLIAM (*b. Newport-Pagnell, England, 1697; d. 1769*), jurist. Father of William Smith (1728–1793). Emigrated to New York, 1715. Graduated Yale, 1719; studied law at home and at Gray's Inn. Practicing in New York City, Smith identified himself with the radical Presbyterian faction in provincial politics and was associated with leading cases seeking to curb the governor's prerogative. With James Alexander, he defended Rip Van Dam against claims of William Cosby, 1733, and also defended John Peter Zenger, 1735. Disbarred for criticism of Judge James DeLancey and an associate, Smith was readmitted to practice, 1737. He served as provincial attorney-general, 1751, was a member of the Provincial Council, 1753–67, and was associate justice of the New York supreme court, 1763–69. Associated with the founding of the first New York public school, 1732, he was an incorporator of the College of New Jersey and a vigorous protester against the establishment of King's College (Columbia) under Episcopalian auspices.

SMITH, WILLIAM (*b. Aberdeen, Scotland, 1727; d. Philadelphia, Pa., 1803*), Episcopal clergyman, educator. A.M., University of Aberdeen, 1747. Emigrating to New York, 1751, he worked as a tutor on Long Island until 1753 during which time he wrote and published his plan for a college entitled *A General Idea of the College of Mirania* (1753). Invited by Benjamin Franklin and Richard Peters to associate himself with the Philadelphia Academy, he settled in Philadelphia in May 1754 and was the dominant influence in the Academy's affairs until the Revolution. He taught logic, rhetoric and natural and moral philosophy and, with Francis Alison, drew up a new charter (1755) which established the Academy on a collegiate basis. In the next year Smith presented to the trustees a curriculum which was one of the most comprehensive educational schemes devised for any American school or college up to that time. An ambitious man, he made his influence felt in all the affairs of the province of Pennsylvania. Active in providing schools for the education of German immigrants, he favored the appointment of an American bishop and labored to that end; a leading supporter of the proprietary interest, he incurred Franklin's bitter enmity. During the French and Indian War he condemned the Assembly for failure to adopt aggressive military measures and published several pamphlets on the subject; he established in 1757 *The American Magazine and Monthly Chronicle* to support the interest of the British Crown and of the Penn family. Arrested for libel, 1758, as a result of his association with William Moore (1699–1783), he was twice confined and jailed but later vindicated after an appeal to the King. Meanwhile, he had been provost of the College of Philadelphia since 1755 and had been very successful as a fund-raiser for the institution.

At the request of Henry Bouquet and from facts supplied by him, Smith prepared *An Historical Account of the Expedition Against the Ohio Indians in 1764* (1765) which remains an important historical source; he was also active in other intellectual activities, particularly the affairs of the American Philosophical Society. An opponent of the Stamp Act, Smith continued to oppose individual British measures but was quite out of sympathy with independence and in a notable sermon preached before Congress, June 1775, and later in several pamphlets signed "Candidus," called for a liberal reconciliation with Great Britain. After a number of difficulties with the patriots and the voiding of the charter of the College of Philadelphia, November 1779, by the Pennsylvania Assembly, Smith withdrew to Chestertown,

Md., where he established a school later known as Washington College. One of the leaders in the organization of the Protestant Episcopal Church, he is said to have suggested its name; he failed, however, to attain the bishopric to which he aspired. On the restoration of the charter of the College of Philadelphia by the Assembly, 1789, Smith resumed his position as provost, keeping it until 1791. Despite high positions which he held and the honors which he received, he never enjoyed the highest respect and confidence of his contemporaries who variously described him as artful, haughty, self-opinionated, hypocritical and bad-mannered. With all his faults, he was yet one of the ablest, most versatile and influential Pennsylvanians of his day. His service to what is now the University of Pennsylvania was incalculable, and in his editorship of the *American Magazine* he encouraged a notable group of young literary men including Francis Hopkinson, Thomas Godfrey and James Sterling.

SMITH, WILLIAM (*b. New York, N.Y., 1728; d. Quebec, Canada, 1793*), New York jurist, Loyalist, historian. Son of William Smith (1697–1769). Graduated Yale, 1745. After admission to the N.Y. bar, 1750, he established himself as a leading practitioner in partnership with William Livingston; with Livingston, he published the first digest of the colony statutes in force, 1752. Counsel in very many important cases, Smith was, with his partner and with John Morin Scott, a contributor to the *Independent Reflector* and the *Occasional Reverberator;* with them, he was author also of a defense of William Shirley entitled *A Review of the Military Operations in North America* (1757). His chief literary contribution was *The History of the Province of New-York from the First Discovery to the Year M.DCC.XXXII* (London, 1757, reprinted with additions in New York, 1829). An important continuation of this work still remains in manuscript. A justice of the province *post* 1763 and a councilor *post* 1767, he was a leader of the popular party and a founder of the Whig Club. However, he shifted to a "fence-sitting" role and refused commitment to either side after the outbreak of the revolutionary violence. Although he was consulted in the drafting of the New York state constitution, he refused in 1777 to take the oath of allegiance to the state, withdrawing to New York City which was in British hands. Appointed chief justice of New York, 1779, he never actually served, since the city was under military control. Removing to England, 1783, he emigrated to Canada, 1786, as chief justice, an office which he held until his death.

SMITH, WILLIAM (*b. probably Aberdeen, Scotland, c. 1754; d. New York or Connecticut, 1821*), Episcopal clergyman, educator. Came to America *ante* 1785. A learned but unsuccessful man, Smith's chief claim to remembrance is that he contributed the "Office of Institution of Ministers" to the Episcopal Book of Common Prayer.

SMITH, WILLIAM (*b. possibly North Carolina, c. 1762; d. Huntsville, Ala., 1840*), lawyer, statesman, South Carolina legislator and jurist. U.S. senator from South Carolina, 1816–23, 1826–30. A Jeffersonian Democrat of the strictest sort, Smith was a lifelong defender of state rights and slavery and an opponent of banks, internal improvements, tariffs and capitalism. Allied with William H. Crawford in national politics, he won the enmity of John C. Calhoun whom he himself detested. Disapproving of nullification which he thought a remedy worse than the disease, he was refused re-election in 1830 and thereafter was identified with the Union party. *Post* 1833 he resided in Louisiana and Alabama and was a member of the legislature of the latter state.

SMITH, WILLIAM (*b. King George Co., Va., 1797; d. near Warrenton, Va., 1887*), lawyer, mail-coach operator, Virginia legislator and congressman. Democratic governor of Virginia, 1846–49, 1864–65. He served with distinction as a Confederate brigadier-general, in particular at Antietam and Fredericksburg.

SMITH, WILLIAM ANDREW (*b. Fredericksburg, Va., 1802; d. Richmond, Va., 1870*), Methodist clergyman, educator. President of Randolph-Macon College, 1846–66; of Central College (Mo.), 1868.

SMITH, WILLIAM FARRAR (*b. St. Albans, Vt., 1824; d. Philadelphia, Pa., 1903*), Union soldier, engineer. Graduated West Point, 1845, where he was assigned to teach mathematics. After hard service as brigade and division commander in the Army of the Potomac, Smith was author, with William B. Franklin, of an address of complaint to President Lincoln after the defeat at Fredericksburg. Transferred, he displayed extraordinary engineering skill in maintaining Union communications in the Chickamauga-Chattanooga campaigns, 1863, and was reappointed major-general, March 1864. In constant controversy thereafter over credit for the opening of the so-called "cracker-line," Smith went east with U. S. Grant. After participating in the action at Cold Harbor, he was once more moved to complain about the policies of his superiors and was relieved of command after failure in leading the attack on Petersburg in June, 1864.

SMITH, WILLIAM HENRY (*b. Montgomeryshire, Wales, 1806; d. probably San Francisco, Calif., 1872*), actor, stage manager. Came to America, 1827, to make his debut at the Walnut Street Theatre, Philadelphia. Active thereafter in support of the elder Booth, and with the Boston Museum company, he was during his latter years connected with the California Theatre, San Francisco.

SMITH, WILLIAM HENRY (*b. Austerlitz, N.Y., 1833; d. Lake Forest, Ill., 1896*), journalist, public official. General manager *post* 1882 of the combined New York Associated Press and Western Associated Press.

SMITH, WILLIAM LOUGHTON (*b. South Carolina, c. 1758; d. 1812*), lawyer, pamphleteer. Son-in-law of Ralph Izard. Congressman, Federalist, from South Carolina, 1789–97; U.S. minister to Portugal, 1797–1801. A heavy speculator in government securities, Smith vigorously supported Hamilton's policy of assumption. He was author of several pamphlets in support of Federalism and attacking Thomas Jefferson, among which was *The Politicks and Views of a Certain Party, Displayed* (1792). He was also author, under the name "Phocion," of a series of letters in the *Charleston Daily Courier*, 1806, which defended the British point of view on topics then in dispute.

SMITH, WILLIAM NATHAN HARRELL (*b. Murfreesboro, N.C., 1812; d. 1889*), North Carolina legislator and jurist, Confederate congressman. Chief justice of the North Carolina supreme court *post* 1878.

SMITH, WILLIAM RUSSELL (*b. Russellville, Ky., 1815; d. 1896*), Alabama lawyer, legislator and congressman. Raised in Alabama, Smith was active in politics, at first as a Whig and later as a Know-Nothing. Congressman from Alabama, 1851–57, he served in the Confederate House of Representatives, 1861–65. He wrote widely on legal and other subjects.

SMITH, WILLIAM SOOY (*b. Tarlton, O., 1830; d. 1916*), civil engineer, Union brigadier-general. Graduated West Point, 1853. Made first American use of pneumatic process for sinking foundations *c.* 1859; later developed and improved the process. An expert in foundation work and bridge construction, he was one of the first to advocate carrying piers of high buildings down to rock and was foundation expert on nearly all large buildings constructed in Chicago, 1890–1910. He was father of Charles Sooysmith.

SMITH, WILLIAM STEPHENS (*b. New York, N.Y., 1755; d. Lebanon, N.Y., 1816*), Revolutionary soldier, lawyer, diplomat. As aide to Washington, he supervised evacuation of New York City by the British, 1783. Secretary of legation in London, 1785–88, he married Abigail, daughter of the then American minister, John Adams, 1786. Returning to the United States, he plunged heavily into land speculation and politics, held several federal offices, dabbled in South American filibustering activities and was congressman, Federalist, from New York, 1813–16.

SMITH, WILLIAM WAUGH (*b. Warrenton, Va., 1845; d. 1912*), Confederate soldier, educator. President of Randolph-Macon College, of Randolph-Macon Woman's College and chancellor of the Randolph-Macon System of academies, Smith worked out new standards of secondary education for boys and of higher education for women which markedly influenced Southern education.

SMITH, WINCHELL (*b. Hartford, Conn., 1871; d. 1933*), playwright, stage director. Rose to prominence as co-producer with Arnold Daly of a series of plays by George Bernard Shaw, 1904. An able theatre craftsman, he was author of the stage version of *Brewster's Millions, The Fortune Hunter* and *The Only Son*. The rest of his highly successful work was done in collaboration. Smith is also notable as creator of the title "George Spelvin" to represent an actor who doubles in a part.

SMITH, XANTHUS RUSSELL (*b. Philadelphia, Pa., 1839; d. Edgehill, Pa., 1929*), painter of historical subjects and battles. Son of Russell Smith.

SMOHALLA (*b. c. 1815; d. 1907*), Indian medicine man and prophet. Chief of the Wanapum, a small tribe which lived around Priest Rapids in present Yakima Co., Wash., Smohalla founded the so-called Dreamer religion *ante* 1872. He taught that Indians alone were real people and that the whites, the Negroes and the Chinese had been created to punish the Indians for their apostasy from ancient custom.

SMYTH, ALBERT HENRY (*b. Philadelphia, Pa., 1863; d. Germantown, Pa., 1907*), educator. Professor of English at Central High School, Philadelphia, Pa., *post* 1886. Smyth won recognition as a Shakespeare scholar, as the author of several useful essays in literary criticism on American subjects and, in particular, as editor of the *Writings of Benjamin Franklin* (1905–07) which he undertook with the cooperation of the American Philosophical Society.

SMYTH, ALEXANDER (*b. Rathlin Island, Ireland, 1765; d. Washington, D.C., 1830*), lawyer, soldier. Came to Virginia as a child. Commissioned brigadier-general, U.S. Army, 1812; attempted an invasion of Canada (at Black Rock, above Buffalo, N.Y., November 1812) which failed of success. He later served as a Virginia legislator, and as a congressman, Democrat, from Virginia, 1817–25, 1827–30.

SMYTH, EGBERT COFFIN (*b. Brunswick, Maine, 1829; d. 1904*), Congregational clergyman. Son of William Smyth; brother of Newman Smyth. Graduated Bowdoin, 1848; Bangor Theological Seminary, 1853. Brown Professor of Ecclesiastical History at Andover Theological Seminary *post* 1863, he was also a lecturer on pastoral theology, and was president of the faculty, 1878–96.

SMYTH, HERBERT WEIR (*b. Wilmington, Del., 1857; d. Bar Harbor, Maine, 1937*), Hellenist. Graduated Swarthmore, 1876; also attended Harvard, and received Ph.D. at Göttingen, 1884. Taught at Johns Hopkins, Bryn Mawr, University of California and at American School of Classical Studies in Athens; professor of Greek at Harvard, 1901–25. Author of outstanding studies in grammar, he is perhaps best known for *The Greek Melic Poets* (1900, 1906).

[*Supp. 2*]

SMYTH, JOHN HENRY (*b. Richmond, Va., 1844; d. 1908*), lawyer, educator. Son of a slave father and a free Negro mother, Smyth was educated in Philadelphia, where he attended the Pennsylvania Academy of Fine Arts, taught school for a while, and considered studying for the stage under Ira Aldridge. Graduated from Howard University, 1872, he practiced law, engaged in Republican politics, served as U.S. minister to Liberia, 1878–85. In 1897, he secured establishment of the Virginia Manual Labor School and headed it, 1899–1908.

SMYTH, JULIAN KENNEDY (*b. New York, N.Y., 1856; d. White Sulphur Springs, W. Va., 1921*), minister and official of the Church of the New Jerusalem.

SMYTH, NEWMAN (*b. Brunswick, Maine, 1843; d. New Haven, Conn., 1925*), Congregational clergyman. Son of William Smyth; brother of Egbert C. Smyth. Graduated Bowdoin, 1863; served in Union Army; graduated Andover Theological Seminary, 1867. After holding pastorates in Maine and Illinois, he became pastor of the First Church, New Haven, Conn., 1882. Author of a number of liberal theological treatises, he was active in movements for church reunion. His nomination for the chair of theology at Andover in 1881 precipitated the well-known Andover controversy.

SMYTH, THOMAS (*b. Belfast, Ireland, 1808; d. 1873*), Presbyterian clergyman, author. Came to America, 1830; was minister and pastor at Second Presbyterian Church, Charleston, S.C., 1832–70.

SMYTH, WILLIAM (*b. Pittston, Maine, 1797; d. 1868*), mathematical textbook writer. Father of Egbert C. and Newman Smyth. Graduated Bowdoin, 1822. Beginning at Bowdoin as instructor in Greek, 1823, he was professor of mathematics there *post* 1828.

SNEAD, THOMAS LOWNDES (*b. Henrico Co., Va., 1828; d. New York, N.Y., 1890*), Missouri lawyer, Confederate officer. Practiced in New York City *post* 1866. Author of *The Fight for Missouri* (1886) and other studies of the Civil War.

SNELLING, HENRY HUNT (*b. Plattsburg, N.Y., 1817; d. St. Louis, Mo., 1897*), librarian, journalist. Son of Josiah Snelling; brother-in-law of George P. Putnam. Employed by E. & H. T. Anthony, dealers in photographic supplies, 1843–57, Snelling was author of *The History and Practice of the Art of Photography* (1849), a pioneer work. He founded and edited the *Photographic and Fine Art Journal*. A constant experimenter with photographic processes, he invented the enlarging camera, 1852, and at about the same time devised a ray filter.

SNELLING, JOSIAH (*b. Boston, Mass., 1782; d. Washington, D.C., 1828*), soldier. Commissioned as first lieutenant, 1808, and soon promoted captain, Snelling was made prisoner at Detroit during the War of 1812; after being exchanged, he took part in the Niagara campaign. Promoted colonel of 5th Infantry, 1819, he saw through to completion the building of Fort St. Anthony, adjacent to the present cities of St. Paul and Minneapolis. He remained in command there until 1828, the virtual ruler of a remote community completely isolated from civilization. The fort's name was changed to Fort Snelling in 1825.

SNELLING, WILLIAM JOSEPH (*b. Boston, Mass., 1804; d. Chelsea, Mass., 1848*), journalist. Son of Josiah Snelling. Author, among other works, of the verse satire *Truth: A New Year's Gift for Scribblers* (1831) and *Tales of the Northwest* (1830).

SNETHEN, NICHOLAS (*b. Glen Cove, N.Y., 1769; d. Princeton, Ind., 1845*), Methodist clergyman, a founder of the Methodist Protestant Church.

SNIDER, DENTON JAQUES (*b. near Mt. Gilead, O., 1841; d. St. Louis, Mo., 1925*), educator, philosopher. A disciple of William T. Harris and Henry C. Brokmeyer. Snider was one of the original members of the St. Louis Philosophical Society and, as a brilliant popular lecturer, did much to carry the idealism of the St. Louis movement to the intellectually starved cities of the Middle West. He was author of a number of critical works of which those on Shakespeare and Goethe were possibly the best.

SNOW, ELIZA ROXEY (*b. Becket, Mass., 1804; d. 1887*), Mormon leader and hymn writer. Sister of Lorenzo Snow; polygamous wife of Joseph Smith and Brigham Young.

SNOW, FRANCIS HUNTINGTON (*b. Fitchburg, Mass., 1840; d. Delafield, Wis., 1908*), educator, naturalist. An original faculty member of the University of Kansas, Snow specialized in entomology both as teacher and as state entomologist. He served as chancellor of the university, 1890–1901.

SNOW, LORENZO (*b. Mantua, O., 1814; d. 1901*), fifth president of the Utah branch of the Mormon Church. Brother of Eliza R. Snow.

SNOWDEN, JAMES ROSS (*b. Chester, Pa., 1809; d. Hulmeville, Pa., 1878*), numismatist, lawyer, Pennsylvania official. Director of U.S. Mint at Philadelphia, 1854–61.

SNOWDEN, THOMAS (*b. Peekskill, N.Y., 1857; d. 1930*), naval officer. Graduated Annapolis, 1879. Promoted rear-admiral, 1917, after able, unspectacular service, he commanded a squadron of the battleship force of the Atlantic Fleet through World War I and served with great ability as military governor of Santo Domingo, 1918–21.

SNYDER, EDWIN REAGAN (*b. Scottdale, Pa., 1872; d. San Jose, Calif., 1925*), educator, educational administrator, specialist in vocational training.

SNYDER, JOHN FRANCIS (*b. Prairie du Pont, Ill., 1830; d. Virginia, Ill., 1921*), physician, Confederate soldier, archaeologist.

SNYDER, SIMON (*b. Lancaster, Pa., 1759; d. 1819*), businessman, Pennsylvania legislator. A Jeffersonian Democrat, he served as governor of Pennsylvania, 1808–17, the first representative of the German element and of the back-country farming class to be elected to that office.

SOBOLEWSKI, J. FRIEDRICH EDUARD (*b. Königsberg, East Prussia, 1808; d. 1872*), musician, author, composer. Emigrated to Milwaukee, Wis., 1859. Conductor, St. Louis Philharmonic, 1860–66. His opera *Mohega* produced in Milwaukee, October–November 1859, was probably the first operatic treatment of an episode from our Revolution.

SOLDAN, FRANK LOUIS (*b. Frankfort-on-Main, Germany, 1842; d. St. Louis, Mo., 1908*), educator. Emigrated to America, 1863. Beginning as a teacher in the St. Louis public school system, 1868, he rose through a number of important assignments to be superintendent of instruction, 1895–1908. An able administrator, he also lectured frequently and was associated with William T. Harris and others in St. Louis cultural affairs.

SOLEY, JAMES RUSSELL (*b. Roxbury, Mass., 1850; d. 1911*), educator, lawyer, writer. Graduated Harvard, 1870. Appointed professor of ethics and English at Annapolis, 1871. He served as head of the department of English, history and law, 1873–82, supervised publication of Civil War naval records, 1882–90, and was commissioned in the naval corps of professors of mathematics, 1876–90. Resigning his commission, 1890, he served as assistant secretary of the navy until 1893 and practiced law thereafter in New York City. He was author of a number of books on naval history.

SOLGER, REINHOLD (*b. Stettin, Prussia, 1817; d. 1866*), scholar, lecturer, German revolutionary. Emigrated to Roxbury, Mass., 1853. Aided in securing support of German-Americans in the East for the Union cause.

SOLIS-COHEN, JACOB DA SILVA. [See COHEN, JACOB DA SILVA SOLIS, 1838–1927.]

SOLOMONS, ADOLPHUS SIMEON (*b. New York, N.Y., 1826; d. Washington, D.C., 1910*), businessman, bookseller, philanthropist. Solomons was an inaugurator or founder of a great number of charitable institutions, among them the American Red Cross, Mount Sinai and Montefiore hospitals in New York City, and the Jewish Theological Seminary of America.

SOMERS, RICHARD (*b. Somers Point, N.J., 1778; d. harbor of Tripoli, 1804*), naval officer. Volunteering to take the ketch *Intrepid* as a fireship into the harbor of Tripoli, Somers was killed in the premature explosion of the vessel, Sept. 4, 1804.

SONNECK, OSCAR GEORGE THEODORE (*b. Jersey City, N.J., 1873; d. 1928*), musician, librarian, historian. After extensive study in Germany where he had been brought up, Sonneck returned to America, 1899, and thereafter became the principal scholar of American musical life in colonial and revolutionary times. As chief of the music division, Library of Congress, 1902–17, he made it one of the leading music libraries in the world. Among his most important books are *Early Concert-life in America* (1907), *The Star Spangled Banner* (1914), *Early Opera in America* (1915) and *Miscellaneous Studies in the History of Music* (1921). *Post* 1917 he worked for and was an official of the Schirmer music publishing company.

SONNICHSEN, ALBERT (*b. San Francisco, Calif., 1878; d. near Willimantic, Conn., 1931*), war correspondent, advocate of consumer's cooperatives.

SOOYSMITH, CHARLES (*b. Buffalo, N.Y., 1856; d. 1916*), civil engineer. Son of William S. Smith. Graduated Rensselaer Polytechnic Institute, 1876. Expert in foundation problems, he introduced in the U.S. the so-called "freezing" process for excavation in unstable soils.

SOPHOCLES, EVANGELINUS APOSTOLIDES (*b. Tsangarada, Thessaly, c. 1805; d. Cambridge, Mass., 1883*), classicist. Emigrated to Massachusetts c. 1828. Teacher and professor of Greek at Harvard *post* 1842. Sophocles was author of a number of important works on Greek morphology, syntax and cognate subjects of which the most important was possibly his *Greek Lexicon of the Roman and Byzantine Periods* (1870).

SORGE, FRIEDRICH ADOLPH (*b. Bethau bei Torgau, Saxony, 1828; d. Hoboken, N.J., 1906*), socialist labor leader. Emigrated to New York City, 1852, where he worked as a music teacher. Active in radical activities in America *post* 1858, he came to be considered the authoritative American representative of Karl Marx.

SORIN, EDWARD FREDERICK (*b. Ahuillé, France, 1814; d. 1893*), Roman Catholic clergyman, educator. Ordained 1838, Father Sorin entered the Congregation of the Holy Cross, 1840, and emigrated to the neighborhood of Vincennes, Ind., as a missionary, 1841. Removing to a site near South Bend, Ind., 1842, he began to build a college there which was chartered in January 1844 as Notre Dame University; he served as president until 1865. He was also responsible for the establishment in the U.S. of the Sisters of the Holy Cross and in 1865 founded *Ave Maria* magazine. Elected superior-general of his Congregation, 1868, he supervised its activities in France, Canada and Bengal as well as in the United States.

SOTHERN, EDWARD ASKEW (*b. Liverpool, England, 1826; d. London, England, 1881*), actor. Father of Edward H. Sothern. Emigrating to America, 1852, he became associated *post* 1858 with the role of Lord Dundreary, in the play *Our American Cousin,* which he made the archetype of the British "silly ass."

SOTHERN, EDWARD HUGH (*b. New Orleans, La., 1859; d. New York, N.Y., 1933*), actor. Son of Edward A. Sothern. A leading man in Daniel Frohman's company at the New York Lyceum Theatre *post* 1886, Sothern built up a brilliant reputation as a light comedian and romantic actor in cloak and sword dramas; he was outstanding as Rudolf in *The Prisoner of Zenda.* From 1904 to 1907, under the management of Charles Frohman, he acted chiefly in Shakespeare with Julia Marlowe; these productions, carefully staged, were enormously popular. Among other plays in which he was successful were *The Sunken Bell, If I Were King* and *When Knighthood Was in Flower.* He was author of an autobiography, *The Melancholy Tale of Me* (1916).

SOTO, HERNANDO DE. [See DE SOTO, HERNANDO, c. 1500–1542.]

SOUCHON, EDMOND (*b. Opelousas, La., 1841; d. 1924*), surgeon, anatomist, sanitarian. After making his early medical studies in Paris, France, he returned to New Orleans and graduated (1867) from the medical department of University of Louisiana (later Tulane). Professor of anatomy and clinical surgery at Tulane, 1885–1908, he was the author of outstanding monographs on aneurisms and shoulder dislocations.

SOULÉ, GEORGE (*b. Barrington, N.Y., 1834; d. 1926*), mathematician, pioneer in business education in the South. President of Soulé College, New Orleans, La., 1856–1926.

SOULE, JOSHUA (*b. Bristol, Maine, 1781; d. Nashville, Tenn., 1867*), Methodist clergyman and bishop, author of the constitution of the Methodist Episcopal Church, 1807.

SOULÉ, PIERRE (*b. Castillon-en-Couserans, France, 1801; d. 1870*), Louisiana legislator and jurist, diplomat. Educated in France, Soulé was exiled for participation in republican plots, 1825, and came to Baltimore, Md., in October of that year. After travel in the interior of the United States, he settled in New Orleans, La., where he succeeded as a legal practitioner, orator and financier. Active in Democratic politics, he served briefly as U.S. senator from Louisiana early in 1847, and was elected for a full term with Whig support in 1848. As senator, he succeeded J. C. Calhoun as leader of the state-rights wing of the Southern Democrats, but except for oratory achieved no outstanding distinction. Appointed U.S. minister to Spain, April 1853, he made one error after another in his endeavors to secure acquisition of Cuba and resigned in December 1854 after the fiasco of the Ostend Manifesto. In this matter he was in fact a scapegoat for errors of the administration. Although opposed to secession, he went with his state, 1860, but was prevented by President Jefferson Davis's hostility from rising to any position of prominence in the Confederacy.

SOUSA, JOHN PHILIP (*b. Washington, D.C., 1854; d. Reading, Pa., 1932*), bandmaster, composer. Conductor of the U.S. Marine Band, 1880–92, and thereafter successful as conductor of his own band on concert tours, Sousa composed more than a hundred marches of outstanding merit. He was composer also of ten comic operas and a number of works in other musical forms. Among his best-known march tunes were "Washington Post March" (1889), "High School Cadets" (1890), "Semper Fidelis" (1888) and "Stars and Stripes Forever" (1897).

SOUTHACK, CYPRIAN (*b. London, England, 1662; d. Boston, Mass., 1745*), mariner, pioneer New England cartographer. Came to Boston, 1685; served on coast guard duty against pirates and privateers; commanded the Province Galley in Benjamin Church's expedition against Maine and Nova Scotia, 1704. Issued charts of Boston harbor, the St. Lawrence River, the English colonies from the Mississippi's mouth to the St. Lawrence, and the New England seacoast; author of *New England Coasting Pilot* (*c. 1720*).

SOUTHALL, JAMES COCKE (*b. Charlottesville, Va., 1828; d. 1897*), Virginia journalist, author. Edited the *Richmond Enquirer*, 1868–74; wrote *The Recent Origin of Man* (1875) and other works.

SOUTHARD, ELMER ERNEST (*b. South Boston, Mass., 1876; d. New York, N.Y., 1920*), neuropathologist, social psychiatrist. Graduated Harvard, 1897; M.D., 1901. Taught neuropathology at Harvard *post* 1904, becoming professor, 1909. As first director, Boston Psychopathic Hospital, 1912–19, he developed psychiatric social work as a profession and provided a program of training for such workers.

SOUTHARD, LUCIEN H. (*b. presumably Sharon, Vt., 1827; d. Augusta, Ga., 1881*), musician, composer, Union soldier. First director, music conservatory of the Peabody Institute, Baltimore, Md., 1868–71; composer, among other works, of an opera *The Scarlet Letter* (1855).

SOUTHARD, SAMUEL LEWIS (*b. Basking Ridge, N.J., 1787; d. Fredericksburg, Va., 1842*), jurist, statesman. Associate justice, New Jersey supreme court, 1815–20; U.S. senator, Democrat, from New Jersey, 1821–23. As U.S. secretary of the navy, 1823–29, he advocated a naval academy, thorough charting of the coasts, and a more intelligent location of naval bases. He also acted *ad interim* as secretary of the treasury (March–July 1825) and as secretary of war (May–June 1828). Becoming a Whig, Southard served as attorney-general of New Jersey and was governor of that state, 1832–33. Re-elected to the U.S. Senate, he served from 1833 to 1842 and strongly opposed the policies of Andrew Jackson.

SOUTHGATE, HORATIO (*b. Portland, Maine, 1812; d. Astoria, N.Y., 1894*), Episcopal clergyman. A missionary and missionary bishop in Turkey, 1840–50, he later held a number of appointments as rector in Boston, Mass., New York City and elsewhere. A moderate high churchman, he was author among other works of a novel, *The Cross above the Crescent* (1878). [*Supp. 1*]

SOUTHMAYD, CHARLES FERDINAND (*b. New York, N.Y., 1824; d. 1911*), lawyer. Beginning the study of law at the age of 12, Southmayd soon became proficient and served for some years as a partner of Alexander S. Johnson. He is particularly remembered as the "office" member of the celebrated firm of Evarts, Southmayd & Choate (formed 1851, Joseph H. Choate joining it *c. 1858*). Southmayd's brief in the case of *Pollock vs. Farmers' Loan and Trust* (157 *U.S.*, 429; 158 *U.S.*, 601) is said to have resulted in the Supreme Court's ruling against the income tax as imposed in the Wilson-Gorman Act.

SOUTHWICK, SOLOMON (*b. Newport, R.I., 1773; d. 1839*), printer, Albany (N.Y.) journalist, New York official.

SOUTHWORTH, EMMA DOROTHY ELIZA NEVITTE (*b. Washington, D.C., 1819; d. Georgetown, D.C., 1899*), novelist. Encouraged to write by John G. Whittier (to whom she suggested the story that later became the poem of Barbara Frietchie), Mrs. Southworth was author of more than sixty sentimental and melodramatic novels, many of which appeared as serials in the *New York Ledger*. Among her works were *The Hidden Hand* (1859), *The Fatal Marriage* (copyright 1869) and *The Maiden Widow* (copyright 1870).

SOWER, CHRISTOPHER (*b. Laasphe-on-the-Lahn, Germany, 1693; d. Germantown, Pa., 1758*), printer, publisher. Father of Christopher Sower (1721–1784). Emigrated to Pennsylvania, 1724. Active *post* 1738 as a printer and publisher of German language books and newspapers, Sower undertook his most ambitious task in issuing the Bible in German, 1743. Except for John Eliot's Indian version, this was the first American edition of the Bible.

SOWER, CHRISTOPHER (*b. Laasphe-on-the-Lahn, Germany, 1721; d. Methacton, Pa., 1784*), printer, publisher, bishop of the Dunkers (German Baptist Brethren). Son of Christopher Sower (1693–1758). Brought to Pennsylvania by his parents, 1724, he succeeded to his father's publishing business, 1758. A political supporter of the proprietary party, he suffered considerable persecution and loss of property during the Revolution.

SOWER, CHRISTOPHER (*b. Germantown, Pa., 1754; d. Baltimore, Md., 1799*), printer, publisher, Loyalist. Son of Christopher Sower (1721–1784); grandson of Christopher Sower (1693–1758). After seizure and condemnation of the family property, August 1778, Sower endeavored to establish Loyalist associations in Pennsylvania; he worked out of the British base in New York. Removing to England, 1783, he returned to America in 1785 as deputy postmaster-general and King's printer of the province of New Brunswick.

SPAETH, ADOLPH (*b. Esslingen, Württemberg, 1839; d. Philadelphia, Pa., 1910*), Lutheran clergyman, author. Came to America, 1864, as assistant minister, St. Michael's and Zion's, Philadelphia; served later at St. Johannis Church and as a professor of New Testament exegesis in Philadelphia Lutheran Theological Seminary.

SPAHR, CHARLES BARZILLAI (*b. Columbus, O., 1860; d. at sea in English Channel, 1904*), editor, economist, reformer.

SPAIGHT, RICHARD DOBBS (*b. New Bern, N.C., 1758; d. 1802*), North Carolina legislator, Revolutionary patriot. Nephew of Arthur Dobbs. Anti-Federalist governor of North Carolina, 1792–95; congressman, 1798–1801. Never a narrow partisan, he frequently voted independently of his party.

SPALDING, ALBERT GOODWILL (*b. Byron, Ill., 1850; d. Point Loma, Calif., 1915*), professional baseball player, merchant. An outstanding pitcher with Harry Wright's Boston team and with the Chicago National League Club, Spalding was a founder (1876) and for many years president of A. G. Spalding & Brothers, manufacturers of sporting goods.

SPALDING, CATHERINE (*b. Charles Co., Md., 1793; d. Louisville, Ky., 1858*), foundress and mother superior of the Sisters of Charity of Nazareth (established in Bardstown, Ky., January 1813). Sister Catherine was for many years the guiding spirit of her community. She also established educational and charitable institutions in Louisville and elsewhere in Kentucky.

SPALDING, FRANKLIN SPENCER (*b. Erie, Pa., 1865; d. Salt Lake City, Utah, 1914*), Episcopal clergyman, missionary bishop of Utah, 1904–14. A prison reformer, a prohibitionist and a pacifist, he was known outside his own communion as "the socialist bishop."

SPALDING, JOHN LANCASTER (*b. Lebanon, Ky., 1840; d. 1916*), Roman Catholic clergyman. Nephew of Martin J. Spalding. Educated at Mount St. Mary's Seminary, Cincinnati, O., and at Rome and Louvain. Bishop of Peoria, Ill., 1877–1908, he was associated with liberal movements in the Church and was a prime factor in the founding of Catholic University of America. A prolific and profound writer on social, educational and philosophical problems.

SPALDING, LYMAN (*b. Cornish, N.H., 1775; d. Portsmouth, N.H., 1821*), physician, surgeon. Studied medicine with Nathan Smith (1762–1829). M.B., Harvard, 1797. Practiced in Portsmouth, N.H., 1799–1812; taught at, and was president of, the College of Physicians and Surgeons of the Western District of New York (Fairfield, N.Y.), 1813–16. Spalding's greatest achievement was his founding of the U.S. Pharmacopoeia (completed and printed, 1820).

SPALDING, MARTIN JOHN (*b. Rolling Fork, Ky., 1810; d. 1872*), Roman Catholic clergyman. Uncle of John L. Spalding. Educated at Bardstown, Ky., Seminary and at Rome where he was ordained, August 1834, he then did pastoral work in Kentucky and won repute as a lecturer and writer. Consecrated coadjutor-bishop of Louisville, 1848, he succeeded to that see, 1850. A zealous administrator and builder of educational and charitable institutions, he proved a courageous leader during the Know-Nothing riots, 1855. He was one of the promoters of the North American College in Rome and of the American College at Louvain. Scrupulously neutral during the Civil War, he became archbishop of Baltimore, 1864, serving until his death. He took a leading part in the Vatican Council, 1870, where he was a strong supporter of papal infallibility.

SPALDING, THOMAS (*b. Frederica, Ga., 1774; d. Darien, Ga., 1851*), planter, Georgia legislator and congressman. Among the first to introduce sea island cotton into the South, he was the first to grow sugar cane and to manufacture sugar in Georgia.

SPALDING, VOLNEY MORGAN (*b. East Bloomfield, N.Y., 1849; d. Loma Linda, Calif., 1918*), botanist. Graduated University of Michigan, 1873; Ph.D., Leipzig, 1894. Taught at Michigan, 1876–1904. Steadfast advocate of a rational policy of forest conservation, Spalding directed his interest in later years to ecology and the life relations of desert plants.

SPANGENBERG, AUGUSTUS GOTTLIEB (*b. Klettenberg-Hohenstein, Germany, 1704; d. Berthelsdorf, Saxony, 1792*), bishop and director of missions of the Moravian Church. During the American periods of his very active career (at various times, 1735–62), he was the driving force in organization of Moravian work. Among his other achievements, he set up the so-called "Economy" at the Bethlehem, Pa., settlement and supervised the Moravian settlement in North Carolina, 1754–62.

SPANGLER, HENRY WILSON (*b. Carlisle, Pa., 1858; d. 1912*), engineer, educator. Graduated from engineer course, U.S. Naval Academy, 1878. Taught engineering at the University of Pennsylvania *post* 1881, and was at the end of his career head of the department of mechanical and electrical engineering there. He was author of standard textbooks on thermodynamics and other engineering subjects.

SPARKS, EDWIN ERLE (*b. near Newark, O., 1860; d. 1924*), educator, historian, pioneer in university extension courses. President, Pennsylvania State College, 1908–20.

SPARKS, JARED (*b. Willington, Conn., 1789; d. Cambridge, Mass., 1866*), editor, historian. Graduated Harvard, 1815. After studying divinity, and serving as science tutor at Harvard, 1817–19, Sparks was minister of the First Independent Church (Unitarian) of Baltimore, Md., 1819–23. His installation there occasioned the celebrated sermon by William Ellery Channing defining the precise position of the Unitarian party. Successful as proprietor and editor of the *North American Review*, 1823–29, he became a leading social and literary figure in the Boston group which included Prescott, Ticknor and the Everetts. Meanwhile, he had undertaken collection and publication of *The Writings of George Washington* (1834–37) and also published *The Life of Gouverneur Morris* (1832), *The Works of Benjamin Franklin* (1836–40) and *The Diplomatic Correspondence of the American Revolution* (1829–30); he was also editor and a contributor to *The Library of American Biography* (first series, 1834–38). These formidable sets of printed letters and documents sold well and were pioneer works of their kind. However, Sparks's editorial methods were bad inasmuch as he treated historical documents as if they had been articles submitted to his magazine and used his editorial pencil entirely too freely. He was influenced thereto by a desire to spare the feelings of the descendants of great men and of those who had lent him documents. Famous and well off, he became McLean Professor of History at Harvard in 1839. Although he began his work by setting forth an excellent and innovating plan for historical studies, he trained no disciples and his professorship proved a false dawn of the study of modern history in American universities. Chosen president of Harvard, 1849, he attacked the elective system of study in his inaugural address, proposing to substitute definite alternative programs for indiscriminate groupings of course units. The effect, however, was a reaction toward the rigidly prescribed course and the conditions prevalent at Harvard before the reforms associated with George Ticknor. Unhappy as president, Sparks resigned, 1853, and devoted his time thereafter to collecting material for a projected history of the Revolution which was never written. Faulty as his methods may have been, his energetic search for original documents and his skill in selecting and annotating them, to say nothing of his success in getting them published, gave the American public a new conception of their history.

SPARKS, WILLIAM ANDREW JACKSON (*b. near New Albany, Ind., 1828; d. St. Louis, Mo., 1904*), lawyer, Illinois legislator. Congressman, Democrat, from Illinois, 1875–83, Sparks performed his most notable public service as commissioner of the General Land Office, 1885–87. Despite the hostility of Congress and the press, he succeeded in effecting extensive reforms.

SPARROW, WILLIAM (*b. Charlestown, Mass., 1801; d. Alexandria, Va., 1874*), Episcopal clergyman, educator. Principal and chief teacher of the theological seminary instituted at Worthington, O., by Bishop Philander Chase, 1826, Sparrow was actual administrative head of the school as it developed into Kenyon College and Gambier Theological Semi-

nary. Accepting a professorship in the Virginia Theological Seminary, 1841, he soon became dean and served there until his death. He was an evangelical Low Churchman.

SPAULDING, EDWARD GLEASON (*b. Burlington, Vt., 1873; d. Princeton, N.J., 1940*), neo-realist philosopher. B.S., University of Vermont, 1894; M.A., Columbia, 1896; Ph.D., Bonn, 1900. Taught at College of the City of New York, 1900–05. On the staff of Princeton University thereafter, he was named McCosh Professor of Philosophy, 1936. Author, among other works, of *The New Rationalism* (1918) in which he called for the development of a constructive realism upon the basis of modern logic and science. [*Supp. 2*]

SPAULDING, ELBRIDGE GERRY (*b. Cayuga Co., N.Y., 1809; d. 1897*), Buffalo, N.Y., banker. A Whig congressman from New York, 1849–51, he returned to Congress as a Republican, 1859–63. Member of a sub-committee of the committee on ways and means, he introduced into the House a bill for issuance of legal-tender treasury notes payable on demand which became law, Feb. 25, 1862, and authorized the issue of the famous "greenbacks."

SPAULDING, LEVI (*b. Jaffrey, N.H., 1791; d. Uduvil, Ceylon, 1873*), Congregational clergyman. Missionary to Ceylon *post* 1820; distinguished as educator and Tamil linguist.

SPAULDING, OLIVER LYMAN (*b. Jaffrey, N.H., 1833; d. Georgetown, D.C., 1922*), lawyer, Union officer, government official. Special agent, U.S. treasury at Detroit, Mich., 1875–90; assistant secretary, U.S. treasury, 1890–93, 1897–1903; special agent, U.S. treasury in Washington, *post* 1903. Leading U.S. authority on customs law and administration.

SPEAR, CHARLES (*b. Boston, Mass., 1801; d. Washington, D.C., 1863*), Universalist clergyman. An opponent of capital punishment, he devoted himself to assistance of discharged prisoners; he was author of *Essays on the Punishment of Death* (1844), *A Plea for Discharged Convicts* (1846) and editor of the periodical *The Prisoners' Friend*.

SPEAR, WILLIAM THOMAS (*b. Warren, O., 1834; d. Columbus, O., 1913*), jurist. Graduated Harvard Law School, 1859; was law partner of Jacob D. Cox. Judge of the common pleas court, 1878–85, and of the Ohio supreme court, 1885–1912, he was considered one of the ablest and most conscientious of any who served on the Ohio bench.

SPEED, JAMES (*b. Jefferson Co., Ky., 1812; d. near Louisville, Ky., 1887*), lawyer, Kentucky legislator. An uncompromising Union man, he was a principal adviser of Abraham Lincoln on Kentucky affairs. Appointed U.S. attorney-general, 1864, he went along with the President's policy of moderation toward the Southern states until Lincoln's death when he developed a strange fascination for the Radical policy.

Favoring military commissions to try the Lincoln conspirators and other persons not protected by parole, he was an early advocate of Negro suffrage and a sharp critic of President Andrew Johnson. After his resignation, 1866, he was prominent in Radical Republican activities, but in his latter age altered his opinions and supported Grover Cleveland in 1884. He was party to the controversy with Joseph Holt over the alleged recommendation for mercy in the case of Mrs. Surratt.

SPEER, EMORY (b. Culloden, Ga., 1848; d. Macon, Ga., 1918), jurist. After serving as Georgia solicitor-general, 1873–76, Speer was elected to Congress as an independent Democrat and served, 1879–83. Affiliating with the Republicans in his second term, he was appointed a federal judge for the southern district of Georgia, 1885, and held that position until his death. He was also dean of the law school of Mercer University post 1893. He wrote pioneer decisions in many cases involving expansion of federal powers; his opinions in general were noted for lucidity and literary excellence, the most outstanding being U.S. vs. Greene and Gaynor (146 Federal Reporter, 803).

SPEER, WILLIAM (b. New Alexandria, Pa., 1822; d. Washington, Pa., 1904), Presbyterian clergyman. Organized first Presbyterian mission work in Canton, China, 1846–50. Later worked among Chinese immigrants to California, chiefly in San Francisco, and was secretary of the board of education of the Presbyterian Church, 1865–76.

SPEIR, SAMUEL FLEET (b. Brooklyn, N.Y., 1838; d. Brooklyn, 1895), physician, Civil War surgeon. Graduated medical department, University of the City of New York (New York University), 1860; did European postgraduate study in ophthalmology and otology. Long a leader of the medical profession in Brooklyn, he was author of the notable The Use of the Microscope in the Differential Diagnosis of Morbid Growths (1871).

SPENCER, AMBROSE (b. Salisbury, Conn., 1765; d. 1848), New York legislator and jurist. Brother-in-law of DeWitt Clinton. Graduated Harvard, 1783. Admitted to the bar in New York, 1788, he served in the legislature as a Federalist, 1793–98, and as a (Democrat) Republican, 1798–1802. From 1800 to 1820 Spencer was almost undisputed dictator of politics in New York State and with DeWitt Clinton dominated the scene by ruthless exploitation of the spoils system. Appointed judge of the state supreme court, 1804, he remained there until 1823, serving as chief justice post 1819. Dissatisfaction with his autocratic manner as well as his autocratic power found expression through Martin Van Buren in the constitutional convention, 1821, when extensive amendments were passed which limited Spencer's power. His great ability as a jurist has been obscured

by the fury of his political activities; his dissents often gave first expression to what later became accepted doctrine in New York courts. He guided New York jurisprudence along lines he thought it should follow and, somewhat in the manner of John Marshall and Theophilus Parsons, he created judicial law largely by the sheer force of his own reasoning and authority. He was father of John C. Spencer.

SPENCER, ANNA GARLIN (b. Attleboro, Mass., 1851; d. 1931), journalist, independent clergyman, educator, woman's rights and peace reformer.

SPENCER, CHRISTOPHER MINER (b. Manchester, Conn., 1833; d. Hartford, Conn., 1922), machinist, inventor. Patented the Spencer self-loading, or repeating, rifle, 1860, which was immediately adopted by the U.S. government and used extensively in the Civil War. Patented a breech-loading gun, 1862, and a magazine gun, 1863. Successful in the manufacture of drop-forgings, he continued to work on inventions and patented (September 1873) a machine for turning metal screws automatically which included the automatic turret lathe. As this feature was overlooked by the patent attorney who made the application, Spencer could never claim patent rights to it. Organizing with others the Hartford Machine Screw Co., 1876, he laid the foundation of a very large industrial enterprise in Hartford, but later withdrew from it and in 1893 organized the Spencer Automatic Machine Screw Co. at Windsor, Conn.

SPENCER, CORNELIA PHILLIPS (b. Harlem, N.Y., 1825; d. Cambridge, Mass., 1908), author. Principally distinguished post 1866 for her efforts to rehabilitate the University of North Carolina.

SPENCER, ELIHU (b. East Haddam, Conn., 1721; d. 1784), Presbyterian clergyman. Brother of Joseph Spencer; grandfather of John and Thomas Sergeant; cousin of David and John Brainerd. Held principal pastorates at Elizabethtown, N.J., and Trenton, N.J. An ardent Revolutionary patriot, he was chaplain in the French and Indian War and the Revolution.

SPENCER, JESSE AMES (b. Hyde Park, N.Y., 1816; d. 1898), Episcopal clergyman, educator, author. A Broad Churchman, Spencer held a number of pastoral and teaching posts in New York and New Jersey. He was appointed custodian of the Standard Bible of the Church, 1883.

SPENCER, JOHN CANFIELD (b. Hudson, N.Y., 1788; d. Albany, N.Y., 1855), lawyer, New York official and legislator. Son of Ambrose Spencer. Graduated Union, 1806. Admitted to the bar, 1809, in Albany, N.Y., he practiced in Canandaigua, N.Y., and with the help of his father rose rapidly in his profession and in politics. One of the ablest lawyers of his day, he served with John Duer and B. F. Butler on the committee to revise the New York statutes, 1827, and in 1829 was special prosecuting officer in the investigation of the murder of William Morgan.

Joining the Whig party *c.* 1838, he was appointed U.S. secretary of war, 1841, and served until March 1843; then appointed U.S. secretary of the treasury, he resigned in May 1844 because of opposition to the annexation of Texas. His son, Philip, suffered execution for attempted mutiny aboard the U.S.S. *Somers,* 1842, while serving under Alexander S. Mackenzie.

SPENCER, JOSEPH (*b. East Haddam, Conn., 1714; d. East Haddam, 1789*), Connecticut legislator and official, Revolutionary soldier. Brother of Elihu Spencer; cousin of David and John Brainerd. A militia officer *post* 1747, Spencer served in the colonial wars and was chosen brigadier-general of Connecticut forces, 1775. Passed over in June of that year for promotion to major-general in the Continental service, he left the army. Later reconciled, he served through the siege of Boston and in the New York campaign and was promoted major-general, August 1776. Resigning 1778, he later served in the Continental Congress and in the Connecticut assembly.

SPENCER, PITMAN CLEMENS (*b. Charlotte Co., Va., 1793; d. Petersburg, Va., 1860*), surgeon, lithotomist.

SPENCER, PLATT ROGERS (*b. East Fishkill, N.Y., 1800; d. Geneva, O., 1864*), calligrapher, creator of the Spencerian handwriting. Developed his characteristic hand, a sloping, semi-angular style with many embellishments, *ante* 1820. He issued copy-books *c.* 1855 and thereafter brought out a whole series of textbooks.

SPENCER, ROBERT (*b. Harvard, Nebr., 1879; d. New Hope, Pa., 1931*), painter. Studied at National Academy of Design, New York, and at New York School of Art; worked with William M. Chase and Robert Henri.

SPENCER, SAMUEL (*b. Columbus, Ga., 1847; d. near Lawyers, Va., 1906*), railway engineer. Son-in-law of Henry L. Benning. After service with the Baltimore & Ohio Railroad and other roads, including a brief presidency of the B. & O., he became railroad expert for Drexel, Morgan & Co. and played an important part in the Morgan railroad reorganizations. He was highly efficient and successful as president of the Southern Railway, 1894–1906.

SPERRY, ELMER AMBROSE (*b. Cortland, N.Y., 1860; d. Brooklyn, N.Y., 1930*), engineer. Mainly self-taught, Sperry was first successful in developing and manufacturing improved dynamos and arc lamps and founded the Sperry Electric Co. at Chicago, Ill., 1880. In 1888 he organized a company to manufacture an electrically driven, undercutting, punching machine for soft coal mining; he subsequently perfected a continuous chain undercutter and also electric mine-locomotives. Founding another company, 1890, for manufacture of his patented electric street-railway cars, he operated this concern with success

until 1894 when he sold it and his patents to the General Electric Co. He was next engaged, 1894–1900, in manufacture of electric automobiles of his own design and his patented storage battery for their operation. In 1900 he established at Washington, D.C., a research laboratory wherein, with an associate, he evolved the so-called Townsend Process for manufacture of caustic soda from salt and also developed the chlorine process for recovering tin from scrap. Sperry's most distinctive inventions, however, were those which put to practical use the principle of the gyroscope. He began work on this project *c.* 1896, and through long, expensive investigation successfully combined electrical and mechanical elements into gyroscopic compasses and stabilizers for ships and airplanes. His first compass was tried out on the U.S.S. *Delaware* at Brooklyn Navy Yard, 1910, and shortly after adopted by the U.S. Navy and by steamship lines generally. In 1918 he produced his high-intensity arc searchlight and before his death had just completed a device for detecting flaws in railroad rails. He was the holder of more than 400 patents and the recipient of many scientific honors.

SPERRY, NEHEMIAH DAY (*b. Woodbridge, Conn., 1827; d. New Haven, Conn., 1911*), contractor, businessman, Know-Nothing and Republican politician. Dominating Republican politics in Connecticut *post* 1856, Sperry served in Congress, 1895–1911, where he was an ardent protectionist. He also served as postmaster of New Haven, 1861–86, 1890–94.

SPICKER, MAX (*b. Königsberg, Germany, 1858; d. 1912*), musician, conductor, composer. Came to New York City, 1882, after a successful career in Europe. Conductor of the Beethoven-Männerchor, 1882–88; director, Brooklyn Conservatory of Music, 1888–95; headed theory department, New York National Conservatory, 1895–1907; director of music, Temple Emanu-El, 1898–1910.

SPIERING, THEODORE (*b. St. Louis, Mo., 1871; d. Munich, Germany, 1925*), violinist, conductor, music teacher. Studied in Cincinnati, O., with Henry Schradieck; at Berlin with Joseph Joachim. Appreciated more in Europe than in America, Spiering organized and directed the Spiering Quartet, 1893–1905, taught for some years in Chicago, Ill., and was concert-master of the New York Philharmonic, 1909–11, under Gustav Mahler.

SPILLMAN, WILLIAM JASPER (*b. Lawrence Co., Mo., 1863; d. 1931*), agricultural economist. Graduated University of Missouri, 1886. After serving on staff of Washington State College, Spillman acted for many years as an expert in the U.S. Department of Agriculture. He was also professor of commercial geography at Georgetown University, 1922–31. An innovator in development of scientific farm management, he was author of *Balancing the Farm Output* (1927).

SPILSBURY, EDMUND GYBBON (*b. London, England, 1845; d. New York, N.Y., 1920*), mining engineer, metallurgist. Trained in Belgium and Germany, Spilsbury came to America, 1870. Practicing for many years as a consultant, he was responsible for introduction of a number of European processes here.

SPINGARN, JOEL ELIAS (*b. New York, N.Y., 1875; d. New York, 1939*), literary critic, reformer. Graduated Columbia, 1895; Ph.D., 1899. Strongly influenced by George E. Woodberry, Spingarn taught comparative literature at Columbia, 1899–1911. A man of many talents, activities and enthusiasms, he was perhaps the leading American exponent of the principles of Benedetto Croce. He also interested himself in politics (liberal Republican), in the culture of flowers, and in securing justice for Negroes. Among his books were *History of Literary Criticism in the Renaissance* (1899) and *Creative Criticism* (1917). [*Supp. 2*]

SPINNER, FRANCIS ELIAS (*b. German Flats, N.Y., 1802; d. 1890*), banker. Congressman, anti-slavery Democrat, from New York, 1855–57, he served as a Republican, 1857–61. Honest and able as treasurer of the United States, 1861–75, his employment of young women in his department during the Civil War is said to have established the status of women in the civil service.

SPITZKA, EDWARD ANTHONY (*b. New York, N.Y., 1876; d. Mount Vernon, N.Y., 1922*), anatomist, criminologist. Son of Edward C. Spitzka. M.D., N.Y. College of Physicians and Surgeons, 1902. Taught anatomy at Jefferson Medical College *post* 1906. Author of notable studies on the human brain, Spitzka edited the 18th American edition of Gray's *Anatomy* (1910).

SPITZKA, EDWARD CHARLES (*b. New York, N.Y., 1852; d. 1914*), neurologist, psychiatrist. Father of Edward A. Spitzka. Graduated medical department, University of the City of New York (New York University), 1873; made postgraduate studies in Leipzig and Vienna. Practiced in New York City *post* 1876 and gained nation-wide reputation as a medico-legal expert in cases involving insanity; he also made many contributions to knowledge of the anatomy of the nervous system.

SPIVAK, CHARLES DAVID (*b. Krementchug, Russia, 1861; d. 1927*), physician, author. Came to America, 1882; worked at first as a laborer in New York and New Jersey. M.D., Jefferson Medical College, 1890. An authority in the field of gastro-enterology, he taught for many years at the medical school of the University of Denver and was founder (1904) of the Jewish Consumptives' Relief Society. From 1904 until his death he acted as secretary and gastro-enterologist to the Society's sanatorium near Denver, Colo.

SPOFFORD, AINSWORTH RAND (*b. Gilmanton, N.H., 1825; d. 1908*), bookseller, journalist. Appointed assistant in the Library of Congress, 1861, he became chief librarian, 1864, and directed the affairs of the Library until 1897. Reverting then to the position of assistant, he continued in that post until his death. During his tenure the Library made extraordinary progress.

SPOFFORD, HARRIET ELIZABETH PRESCOTT (*b. Calais, Maine, 1835; d. Deer Island, Maine, 1921*), author. Encouraged to write by Thomas W. Higginson, Mrs. Spofford enjoyed a successful career as a miscellaneous writer, romantic novelist and verse writer, 1860–1910.

SPOONER, JOHN COIT (*b. Lawrenceburg, Ind., 1843; d. New York, N.Y., 1919*), lawyer. Successful as counsel for railroads, Spooner was U.S. senator, Republican, from Wisconsin, 1885–91, 1897–1907. Winning notice in his first term as an able debater and brilliant parliamentarian, he became a national figure during his second period in the Senate, sharing with Nelson W. Aldrich, W. B. Allison and Orville H. Platt the confidence of Presidents McKinley and Roosevelt. A counselor rather than a leader in Republican politics, he belonged to the "stalwart" wing of the Wisconsin Republicans and was a principal target for attacks by the reform element. The decline of his faction in the state and the election of Robert M. LaFollette as his colleague brought about Spooner's resignation. Thereafter he practiced law in New York City.

SPOONER, LYSANDER (*b. Athol, Mass., 1808; d. 1887*), lawyer, anti-slavery advocate, reformer. Author, among other books, of *Unconstitutionality of Slavery* (1845, 1847) and *Essay on the Trial by Jury* (1852).

SPOONER, SHEARJASHUB (*b. Orwell, Vt., 1809; d. Plainfield, N.J., 1859*), dentist, promoter of art. Author, among other works, of *A Biographical and Critical Dictionary of Painters, Engravers, etc.* (1853).

SPOTSWOOD, ALEXANDER (*b. Tangier, 1676; d. Annapolis, Md., 1740*), lieutenant-governor of Virginia. Entering the British army, he fought in the War of the Spanish Succession, and in 1710 was appointed lieutenant-governor of Virginia, under the nominal governor, the Earl of Orkney. He undertook his new duties with a vigor rather disconcerting to a people inclined to reduce governmental activity to a minimum. He sought to regulate the fur trade, to maintain an enlightened Indian policy, to encourage actual settlers as opposed to mere land speculators, and to require inspection of tobacco designed for export or for use as legal tender. This last policy led to a violent quarrel with the burgesses (1715), particularly with two prominent members of his council, William Byrd, and Philip Ludwell, who had little taste for the additional labors the governor thrust upon them. A struggle for power between the governor and the council ensued and harmony was not restored until 1720. From his first arrival in Virginia, Spotswood was actively identified with the problems of the frontier. He made a number of explorations westward, of which the most famous was in 1716. He also attempted to protect the colony from Iroquois raids by establishing compact communities of friendly Indians, powerful enough to resist attack and convenient for the work of missionary and schoolmaster; he negotiated a treaty with the Iroquois whereby they were to keep north of the Potomac and west of the Blue Ridge. During the closing years of his administration his attitude toward colonial self-assertion mellowed perceptibly. Doubless due in part to the conviction that it was futile to contend against what amounted to a Virginia nationalism, the change was natural in one who had decided to make America his permanent home. Removed from office in 1722, he engaged in the mining and smelting of iron. When war with Spain broke out in 1739, he set about to recruit a colonial regiment and was appointed major-general of a proposed expedition against Cartagena. He died in the midst of his preparations for this service.

SPOTTED TAIL (*b. near Fort Laramie, Wyo., c. 1833; d. 1881*), a head-chief of the Lower Brulé Sioux. Uncle of Crazy Horse. Rising in tribal authority as a warrior, he opposed Red Cloud at the Fort Laramie council, 1866. He was a signer of the treaty of April 1868 providing for withdrawal of Indian opposition to railroad building and acceptance of a reservation in present South Dakota. Later removing to a reservation in northwestern Nebraska, he continued friendly to the whites and resisted efforts to bring his tribe to war in 1876. Sharp, witty and affable in manner, he was considered one of the most brilliant of the Sioux leaders.

SPRAGUE, ACHSA W. (*b. Plymouth Notch, Vt., c. 1828; d. 1862*), spiritualist, medium, mental healer.

SPRAGUE, CHARLES (*b. Boston, Mass., 1791; d. 1875*), banker, poet. Author of a number of odes and other minor poems which were published in a collected edition, 1841.

SPRAGUE, CHARLES EZRA (*b. Nassau, N.Y., 1842; d. New York, N.Y., 1912*), banker, Union soldier. Long employed by the Union Dime Savings Bank in New York City, he was its president, 1892–1912. One of the first to qualify as a certified public accountant, he was a leading spirit in establishment of the New York University School of Commerce where he taught accountancy. He was author of a number of textbooks in accountancy and finance.

SPRAGUE, FRANK JULIAN (*b. Milford, Conn., 1857; d. 1934*), engineer, inventor. Graduated Annapolis, 1878. After naval service, 1878–83, during which he devoted himself to problems in electrical development, he joined the staff of Thomas A. Edison for a brief period, and then organized the Sprague Electric Railway & Motor Co. Winning repute in 1887 for adaptation of a constant-speed motor devised by him to use in street-railway service at Richmond, Va., he achieved rapid success. In 1892 he formed the Sprague Electric Elevator Co. which became part of the Otis Elevator Co. His system of "multiple unit" control for trains made up of motor cars was first tried out in 1897 and later generally adopted for subway, elevated and suburban service. He was also a pioneer in design and production of miniature electric power units suitable for machine tools, printing presses, dentist's drills and labor-saving conveniences in the home. [*Supp. 1*]

SPRAGUE, HOMER BAXTER (*b. South Sutton, Mass., 1829; d. 1918*), educator, Union soldier. Graduated Yale, 1852. After holding a number of important teaching and administrative posts in New York, Connecticut and Massachusetts, Sprague served as president of Mills College, 1885–87, and of the University of North Dakota, 1887–91. He was founder (1879) of the Martha's Vineyard Summer Institute, said to be the first general summer school in the United States.

SPRAGUE, KATE CHASE (*b. Cincinnati, O., 1840; d. Washington, D.C., 1899*), political hostess. Daughter of Salmon P. Chase; wife of William Sprague (1830–1915).

SPRAGUE, PELEG (*b. Duxbury, Mass., 1793; d. Boston, Mass., 1880*), jurist. After serving in the first Maine legislature, 1820–22, and as congressman and U.S. senator from Maine, 1825–35, he found his true vocation when appointed U.S. district judge for Massachusetts, 1841. Sprague was outstanding on the bench until his retirement in 1865, despite constant weakness of the eyes which ended in total blindness. His decisions included a definitive statement (March 1863) on the doctrine of treason and the powers of the federal government to punish treason.

SPRAGUE, WILLIAM (*b. Cranston, R.I., 1773; d. Cranston, 1836*), textile manufacturer, lumber merchant, stock breeder.

SPRAGUE, WILLIAM (*b. Cranston, R.I., 1830; d. Paris, France, 1915*), textile manufacturer, Union soldier, politician. Grandson of William Sprague (1773–1836); husband of Kate C. Sprague. An inheritor of great wealth, he advanced easily in politics and was Democratic governor of Rhode Island, 1860–61. After Civil War service, he was re-elected governor, 1862, but resigned to become U.S. senator from Rhode Island, serving 1863–75. Considered irresponsible by many of his constituents, almost beggared in the panic of 1873, and divorced in 1882 under scandalous circumstances, he lived in retirement *post* 1883.

SPRAGUE, WILLIAM BUELL (*b. Hebron, Conn., 1795; d. Flushing, N.Y., 1876*), Congregational clergyman, autograph collector, biographer. Held pastorates at West Springfield, Mass., and Albany, N.Y. Author, among other works, of lives of Timothy

Dwight and Jedidiah Morse and of *Annals of the American Pulpit* (1857–69).

SPRECHER, SAMUEL (*b. Washington Co., Md., 1810; d. San Diego, Calif., 1906*), Lutheran clergyman, educator. President of Wittenberg College, 1849–74, he taught theology and philosophy there until 1884, thereafter bearing the title of professor emeritus.

SPRECKELS, CLAUS (*b. Lamstedt, Hanover, Germany, 1828; d. San Francisco, Calif., 1908*), sugar manufacturer, capitalist. Came to America, 1846; removed to San Francisco, 1856. Organized the California Sugar Refinery, 1867; held for many years a virtual monopoly of sugar manufacture and sale on the Pacific Coast; fought the Sugar Trust, 1888–89. Spreckels was also active in public utilities and in development of the sugar industry in Hawaii.

SPRECKELS, JOHN DIEDRICH (*b. Charleston, S.C., 1853; d. Coronado, Calif., 1926*), sugar merchant, capitalist. Son of Claus Spreckels.

SPRING, GARDINER (*b. Newburyport, Mass., 1785; d. New York, N.Y., 1873*), Presbyterian clergyman. Son of Samuel Spring. Graduated Yale, 1805. After a brief practice of law, he attended Andover Theological Seminary and was called to the pastorate of the Brick Presbyterian Church, New York City, 1810, as colleague to John Rodgers (1727–1811). A thorough Calvinist and a conservative, he remained at the Brick Church until his death, building up a strong congregation and taking a commanding position in the life of New York City.

SPRING, LEVERETT WILSON (*b. Grafton, Vt., 1840; d. Boston, Mass., 1917*), Congregational clergyman, educator. Author of *Kansas: the Prelude to the War for the Union* (1885), the first nonpartisan account of the Kansas struggle. Served as Morris Professor of Rhetoric at Williams College, 1886–1909.

SPRING, SAMUEL (*b. Uxbridge, Mass., 1746 o.s.; d. 1819*), Congregational clergyman. Father of Gardiner Spring. Pastor at Newburyport, Mass., 1777–1819. Spring was identified with the "Hopkinsian" wing of the Church and was a man of great influence. He was one of the founders of Andover Theological Seminary and of the American Board of Commissioners for Foreign Missions.

SPRINGER, CHARLES (*b. Louisa Co., Iowa, 1857; d. 1932*), lawyer, New Mexico cattleman and Republican politician. Brother of Frank Springer. [*Supp.* 1]

SPRINGER, FRANK (*b. Wapella, Iowa, 1848; d. 1927*), lawyer, paleontologist. Removing to New Mexico, 1873, he became one of the leading lawyers of that territory and state. Among other important cases in which he served as counsel was the case of the celebrated Maxwell Land Grant which he fought in the U.S. courts for some thirty years and finally won. In association with Charles Wachsmuth, Springer

did outstanding work in the study of fossil crinoids, publishing a series of volumes which have been called "the most magnificent monographs on invertebrate paleontology published in the United States."

SPRINGER, REUBEN RUNYAN (*b. Frankfort, Ky., 1800; d. 1884*), wholesale grocery merchant, financier, philanthropist. Remembered as a patron of music and art and as a benefactor of the Catholic Church, he was largely responsible for providing his home city of Cincinnati, O., with a music hall and a college of music.

SPRINGER, WILLIAM McKENDREE (*b. New Lebanon, Ind., 1836; d. 1903*), lawyer, judge in Indian Territory. Congressman, Democrat, from Illinois, 1875–95, he was active on many committees and served as chairman of the committees on claims, territories, elections, ways and means, banking and currency. He introduced bills under which Washington, Montana and the Dakotas were admitted into the Union as states. A strict parliamentarian, he seemed often more interested in the rules of procedure than in the issues involved.

SPROUL, WILLIAM CAMERON (*b. Octoraro, Pa., 1870; d. near Chester, Pa., 1928*), manufacturer, businessman. Republican governor of Pennsylvania, 1919–23, he actively promoted highway construction and reorganized several branches of the state government, but was criticized for his handling of the steel strike of 1919.

SPROULE, WILLIAM (*b. Co. Mayo, Ireland, 1858; d. San Francisco, Calif., 1935*), railroad executive. Emigrated to America c. 1876. Entering employ of the Southern Pacific Railroad, 1882, he rose to post of freight traffic manager by 1898. Associated with other companies, 1906–11, he returned to the Southern Pacific as president, serving 1911–28. [*Supp.* 1]

SPROULL, THOMAS (*b. near Lucesco, Pa., 1803; d. 1892*), Reformed Presbyterian clergyman, educator. Pastor of the Old School Church at Allegheny (North Pittsburgh), Pa., 1834–68; taught thereafter at Allegheny Theological Seminary.

SPRUNT, JAMES (*b. Glasgow, Scotland, 1846; d. 1924*), businessman, philanthropist, local historian. Emigrated to North Carolina as a boy; resident in Wilmington *post* 1854. One of the largest exporters of cotton in the country, Sprunt was active in civic affairs and was author of a number of valuable historical monographs, among them *Tales and Traditions of the Lower Cape Fear, 1661–1896* (1896) and *Chronicles of the Cape Fear River* (1914). He gave much financial assistance to Presbyterian church work and to hospitals.

SQUANTO (*d. Chatham Harbor, Mass., 1622*), Pawtuxet Indian. Kidnapped at Pawtuxet (Plymouth) in 1615 by an English sea captain, he was sold in Spain as a slave. Escaping to England, he lived for a time in London. While serving as a pilot in an English expedition to the New England coast, 1619, he escaped and made his way home to Pawtuxet only to find himself the sole surviving member of his tribe. Introduced by Samoset to the Pilgrims, March 1621, he took Edward Winslow to Massasoit and acted as interpreter in concluding the treaty of Plymouth between that chief and the Pilgrims. He also showed the newcomers how to set corn and where to fish. After he had made himself obnoxious to the Indians by exploiting his friendship with the English, and notably by sounding a false alarm of impending treachery on the part of Massasoit, that chief demanded that the Pilgrims give him up for punishment. He later made his peace with Massasoit. In November 1622 he served as guide and interpreter on Bradford's expedition around Cape Cod.

SQUIBB, EDWARD ROBINSON (*b. Wilmington, Del., 1819; d. Brooklyn, N.Y., 1900*), physician, pharmacist, manufacturing chemist. M.D., Jefferson Medical College, 1845. A U.S. Navy surgeon, 1847–57, he established in 1852 a laboratory for preparation of high-grade pharmaceuticals for service use which he directed until 1857. Establishing his own manufactory in Brooklyn, N.Y., 1858, he continued to do pioneer work in manufacture of pure pharmaceuticals and was a leader in independent chemical research; he was also an authority on the *U.S. Pharmacopoeia.*

SQUIER, EPHRAIM GEORGE (*b. Bethlehem, N.Y., 1821; d. Brooklyn, N.Y., 1888*), journalist, archaeologist, diplomat. Considered in his time an authority on Central America, Squier held a number of consular and diplomatic posts in Latin America. He was co-author with Edwin H. Davis of *Ancient Monuments of the Mississippi Valley* (1847) and author of *Aboriginal Monuments of the State of New-York* (1851).

SQUIER, GEORGE OWEN (*b. Dryden, Mich., 1865; d. Washington, D.C., 1934*), soldier, engineer. Graduated West Point, 1887; Ph.D., Johns Hopkins, 1893. An expert in cable and radio communication, Squier did much important early experimental work in wireless telephony and multiple telephony; he was also a student of military aviation. He served as chief signal officer, U.S. Army, with the rank of major-general, 1917–23.

SQUIERS, HERBERT GOLDSMITH (*b. Madoc, Canada, 1859; d. London, England, 1911*), soldier, diplomat. Outstanding as chief of staff in defense of legations at Peking, China, during the Boxer uprising, 1900; handled successfully the difficult post of U.S. minister to Cuba, 1902–05.

SQUIRE, WATSON CARVOSSO (*b. Cape Vincent, N.Y., 1838; d. Seattle, Wash., 1926*), lawyer, Union soldier, capitalist. Son-in-law of Philo Remington. Settling in Seattle, Wash., 1879, he was Republican governor of Washington Territory, 1884–87, and U.S. senator from the State of Washington, 1889–97.

STAGER, ANSON (*b. Ontario Co., N.Y., 1825; d. Chicago, Ill., 1885*), telegraph pioneer. Associated with the Western Union Telegraph Co. *post* 1856, he served as its general superintendent and later as superintendent of its Central Division; he was chief of U.S. military telegraphs, 1861–66. Leading Western representative of the Vanderbilt interests, he helped found the Western Electric Manufacturing Co. and served as its president until shortly before his death.

STAHEL, JULIUS (*b. Szeged, Hungary, 1825; d. 1912*), Union major-general, U.S. consular officer, insurance executive. Veteran of the Hungarian revolution (1848), Stahel emigrated to New York City, 1856. A volunteer at the outbreak of the Civil War, he rose to division command of cavalry and was awarded the Congressional Medal of Honor for gallantry in the Shenandoah Valley, June 1864.

STAHLMAN, EDWARD BUSHROD (*b. Güstrow, Germany, 1843; d. 1930*), railroad official, newspaper publisher. Came to America as a boy; settled in Nashville, Tenn., 1863. Becoming owner-publisher of the *Nashville Banner,* 1885, he built it into one of the best-known crusading journals in the South.

STAHR, JOHN SUMMERS (*b. near Applebachsville, Pa., 1841; d. 1915*), Reformed Church clergyman, educator. Graduated Franklin and Marshall College, 1867; studied theology under John W. Nevin. Taught *post* 1868 at his *alma mater* and was its president, 1890–1909. A linguist and a prolific writer in German and English, he was the last of the master exponents of the Mercersburg Philosophy.

STALEY, CADY (*b. Montgomery Co., N.Y., 1840; d. Minaville, N.Y., 1928*), civil engineer, educator, sanitation expert. An able teacher and president of faculty at Union College and at the Case School of Applied Science.

STALLO, JOHANN BERNHARD (*b. Sierhausen, Oldenburg, Germany, 1823; d. 1900*), lawyer, philosopher of science, diplomat. Emigrated to America, 1839; practiced law in Cincinnati, O., *post* 1849. An outstanding political liberal, he served as U.S. minister to Italy, 1885–89. Among his books and writings was the influential *The Concepts and Theories of Modern Physics* (1882).

STANARD, MARY MANN PAGE NEWTON (*b. Westmoreland Co., Va., 1865; d. Richmond, Va., 1929*), historian. Wife of William G. Stanard. Author, among other works, of *Colonial Virginia* (1917) and *Richmond, Its People and Its Story* (1923).

STANARD, WILLIAM GLOVER (*b. Richmond, Va., 1858; d. 1933*), editor, antiquarian. Husband of Mary M.P.N. Stanard. Secretary, Virginia Historical Society, and editor, *Virginia Magazine of History and Biography,* 1898–1933.

STANBERY, HENRY (*b. New York, N.Y., 1803; d. New York, 1881*), lawyer. Raised in Ohio. Law partner of Thomas Ewing, 1824–31. Practiced thereafter in Lancaster, Columbus and Cincinnati, O., and was in the first rank of the Ohio bar. A Whig and later a Republican, he served as U.S. attorney-general, July 1866—March 1868. His able service as President Andrew Johnson's chief counsel during Johnson's impeachment cost him further political advancement.

STANCHFIELD, JOHN BARRY (*b. Elmira, N.Y., 1855; d. 1921*), lawyer. Graduated Amherst, 1876; studied law with David B. Hill whose partner he became. Active in Democratic politics in New York State, he was celebrated as a courtroom pleader in a number of sensational cases which included the trials of F. A. Heinze, Harry K. Thaw and the Gould and Guggenheim family lawsuits.

STANDISH, MYLES (*b. possibly Lancashire, England, c. 1584; d. Duxbury, Mass., 1656*), Pilgrim father and military captain. A soldier of fortune in the Low Countries, he was hired by the Pilgrims to accompany them on the *Mayflower*, 1620. The only one with practical experience in camping, he was their mainstay in the first explorations of Cape Cod, and was one of the small party who made the first landing at Plymouth. He handled relations with the Indians expertly, designed and superintended the erection of a fort, and devised measures for defense. In 1625 he was sent to England to negotiate with the Merchant Adventurers and the Council for New England. There is no historical basis for the story of John Alden's proposal to Priscilla on Standish's behalf. He was a co-founder of Duxbury, 1631.

STANFORD, JOHN (*b. Wandsworth, England, 1754; d. 1834*), Baptist clergyman, humanitarian. Emigrated to America, 1786. Held pastorates in New York City and Providence, R.I., until 1801; thereafter preached in Baptist churches in New York, New Jersey, Pennsylvania and Connecticut without a fixed pastorate. Appointed chaplain of the New York State Prison, 1812, he devoted his attention to the establishment of special reform institutions for youthful prisoners.

STANFORD, LELAND (*b. Watervliet, N.Y., 1824; d. Palo Alto, Calif., 1893*), railroad builder. Admitted to the bar in New York State, 1848, he began practice at Port Washington, Wis., that same year. Encouraged by his brothers who had prospered as storekeepers in California, he removed there in 1852. After engaging in merchandising with some success in Placer County and at Sacramento, he was elected Republican governor of California in 1861. His success was due to his personal popularity and to his strong Union and Republican convictions, for he had had no opportunity to distinguish himself in public service. In 1863 he was not renominated, and he held no other public office until his election as U.S. senator in 1885. His chief task as governor was to hold California in the Union, and this he accomplished satisfactorily. He also approved several public grants to the transcontinental railroad—the enterprise which brought him wealth and upon which his reputation chiefly rests. Interested in the project by Theodore D. Judah's promotional activity, he subscribed money to finance the surveys which proved the feasibility of the proposed railroad line; he also helped finance organization of the Central Pacific Railroad in June 1861. As governor he signed four acts affording considerable assistance to the new enterprise. He had no scruples about taking official action where his private interests as railroad president were engaged, or he overcame such as may have occurred to him by reflecting upon the public importance of a railroad connection with the East. He was president and director of the Central Pacific from 1861 until his death, president of the Southern Pacific Co., 1885–90, and director of the Southern Pacific Railroad. At all times he was a shareholder in and contributor to the resources of the construction companies which built the railroads. The Central Pacific was built almost entirely with, or on the security of, public funds, so that Stanford and his friends risked less of their own capital in the undertaking than has sometimes been supposed.

From the great personal fortune he amassed, he was able to indulge his tastes in matters not strictly connected with his business. He maintained extensive vineyards and a large ranch where he bred fine racing stock. Out of his desire to raise a fitting memorial to his son, who died at the age of 15, grew Leland Stanford University, founded in 1885. Entirely opposed to interference with the railroad business by public bodies, he asserted the railroad's right to protect itself by political action when attacked. Thus he accepted election as U.S. senator in 1885, but he found himself in a field for which he had no proper training and for which his abilities were inadequate. It is not too much to say that his legislative record shows lack of interest or lack of capacity, probably both. His senatorship satisfied his vanity and increased his prestige in California, but it did not add to his reputation.

STANG, WILLIAM (*b. Langenbrücken, Baden, Germany, 1854; d. 1907*), Roman Catholic clergyman, educator. Served as curate, pastor and chancellor of the diocese in Rhode Island, 1878–95 and 1899–1904, acting in the interim as vice-rector of the American College in Louvain. He was bishop of Fall River, Mass., 1904–07.

STANLEY, ALBERT AUGUSTUS (*b. Manville, R.I., 1851; d. Ann Arbor, Mich., 1932*), musician, educator. Professor of music, University of Michigan, 1888–1932, emeritus *post* 1921. He was author of a symphony and a number of choral compositions.

STANLEY, DAVID SLOANE (*b. Cedar Valley, O., 1828; d. 1902*), soldier. Graduated West Point, 1852. A cavalry officer, Stanley served with ability on the Western frontier. As major-general of volunteers during the Civil War, he held corps command in the Mississippi and Tennessee campaigns and on Sherman's march through Georgia. Reverting in rank to colonel in the regular army, he showed himself a master in handling Indians while on service in the Yellowstone area and in Texas, 1866–92. He retired as regular brigadier-general, 1892.

STANLEY, FRANCIS EDGAR (*b. Kingfield, Maine, 1849; d. 1918*), inventor, manufacturer. A portrait photographer, he organized with his brother a company for manufacture of dry-plates according to his own formula, which he conducted successfully and sold to the Eastman interests, 1905. Meanwhile, having become interested in steam automobiles, he had begun early in 1897 a series of experiments which resulted in the production in that year of the first steam motor car to be successfully operated in New England. In 1898 he began manufacture of the cars, but soon sold out to other interests. Repurchasing (1902) their patents from what had become the Locomobile Co., Stanley and his brother organized the Stanley Motor Carriage Co., which they continued to operate until 1917.

STANLEY, HENRY MORTON (*b. Denbigh, Wales, 1841; d. London, England, 1904*), journalist, explorer. Brought up in an English workhouse and by unfeeling relatives, Stanley was known as John Rowlands until his adoption in December 1859 by Henry Morton Stanley, a New Orleans, La., merchant. After Civil War service in the Confederate Army and in the Union Army and Navy, Stanley discovered his true vocation when he became a traveling newspaper correspondent, 1866. His early dispatches from the campaign of Gen. W. S. Hancock against the Western Indians brought him commissions from the *New York Herald*, 1868; his reports from Abyssinia, Crete and Spain further established his reputation as a gifted correspondent. Sent by James Gordon Bennett (1841–1918) to find the Scottish missionary David Livingstone in the unexplored heart of Africa, he set off from Zanzibar in March 1871. After many hardships he discovered Livingstone in the native village of Ujiji on November 10 and spoke the greeting which has passed into the history of humor: "Dr. Livingstone, I presume?" After further explorations in company with Livingstone along the northern shore of Lake Tanganyika, Stanley returned to London where he was met with disbelief in his discoveries and much social scorn; however, he was soon vindicated after investigation of the proofs which he had brought back. On further expeditions, 1874–77, he made geographical studies of central Africa which were of the greatest importance, including exploration of the headwaters of the Nile, a complete survey of Lake Tanganyika and a traverse of the Congo River. Between 1879 and 1884 he worked in the Congo, establishing 22 stations along the river, putting steamers in operation on it and building roads; the Congo Free State was formed on the basis of his work. Thereafter he continued his restless, roving career in Africa

and made lecture tours around the world until the failure of his health *c.* 1899. First among African explorers by reason of the extent of his geographical discoveries, Stanley also possessed the vision and organizing ability of a pioneer. He believed that he was furthering Livingstone's fight against slavery by introducing European commerce to darkest Africa. A man of strong moral feeling, he was greatly disappointed over the later developments in the Congo which he described as "a moral malaria." Generally successful in his dealings with the native peoples whom he encountered, he was completely lacking in tact at home in England and America; a lonely man, he was introspective and self-absorbed. He was author of a number of books descriptive of his travels and explorations; his unfinished *Autobiography* was published in 1909.

STANLEY, JOHN MIX (*b. Canandaigua, N.Y., 1814; d. Detroit, Mich., 1872*), painter. Apprenticed to a wagon-maker as a boy, he removed to Detroit, 1834, where he painted portraits and landscapes. Resident in Chicago and Galena, Ill., 1838–39, he began painting portraits of the Indians near Fort Snelling. Between 1842 and 1852 he traveled widely in the West, painting wherever he went, and giving several exhibitions of his work; in 1846–47 he was with the expedition of Stephen W. Kearny to California. Much of his spirited, accurate work, of the greatest possible value to students of history and ethnology, was deposited in the Smithsonian Institution in 1852 and destroyed by fire there, 1865. In 1853 he served as artist of the U.S. expedition for exploration of the Pacific Railroad route from St. Paul, Minn., to Puget Sound.

STANLEY, WILLIAM (*b. Brooklyn, N.Y., 1858; d. Great Barrington, Mass., 1916*), electrical engineer. Devised the multiple system of alternating current distribution (patented 1887); in collaboration with others, worked out the "S.K.C." system of long-distance transmission of alternating current. Among his many other inventions were condensers, two-phase motors, generators, and an alternating-current watt-hour meter.

STANLY, EDWARD (*b. New Bern, N.C., 1810; d. San Francisco, Calif., 1872*), lawyer. Congressman, Whig, from North Carolina, 1837–43. Stanly was an extreme nationalist and a leader of his party in the House. After service in state offices and in the North Carolina legislature, he returned to Congress, 1849–53. Removing to California, 1854, he was successful in legal practice in San Francisco. Convinced that the secession of North Carolina from the Union had been the result of Democratic trickery, he accepted appointment by President Lincoln as military governor of the state in May 1862. He quickly discovered that his hope of restoring a civil government loyal to the Union was an illusion. Opposed to emancipation, he resigned in January 1863 and returned to California.

STANSBURY, HOWARD (*b. New York, N.Y., 1806; d. Madison, Wis., 1863*), soldier, civil engineer, explorer. Grandson of Joseph Stansbury. Entered the U.S. Army, July 1838, as lieutenant of topographical engineers. Among the many surveys which he undertook, the most outstanding was his expedition to the Great Salt Lake region, 1849, on which James Bridger acted as one of the guides. His report of this expedition was issued first as *Senate Executive Document 3, 32 Congress* (1852). It was several times reprinted, and is a classic of Western Americana.

STANSBURY, JOSEPH (*b. London, England, 1742 o.s.; d. New York, N.Y., 1809*), Loyalist agent, merchant, satirist. Emigrated to Philadelphia, Pa., 1767. Transmitted Benedict Arnold's first proposals of treason to British headquarters and served thereafter as go-between for Arnold and the British. His witty satires were collected in *The Loyal Verses of Joseph Stansbury and Doctor Jonathan Odell* (edited, Winthrop Sargent, 1860).

STANTON, EDWIN McMASTERS (*b. Steubenville, O., 1814; d. Washington, D.C., 1869*), lawyer, public official. Admitted to the bar, 1836, he practiced at first in Cadiz and Steubenville, O., and later in Pittsburgh, Pa., and Washington, D.C. Able and energetic, he soon won success; his work as counsel for the State of Pennsylvania (1849–56) against the Wheeling & Belmont Bridge Co. gave him a national reputation, and his masterly defense work in *McCormick vs. Manny* deeply impressed one of his associates, Abraham Lincoln. Though his practice was chiefly in civil and constitutional law, he demonstrated in his defense of Daniel E. Sickles that he was no less gifted in handling criminal suits. In 1858, as special counsel for the U.S. government in combating fraudulent land claims in California, he won a series of notable victories. His services in this connection were the most distinguished of his legal career and won him the appointment of U.S. attorney-general, December 1860. Although he disapproved of slavery, he accepted the Dred Scott decision and contended that all laws constitutionally enacted for the protection of slavery should be rigidly enforced. He had supported Breckinridge's candidacy for the presidency in 1860 in the belief that the preservation of the Union hung on the forlorn hope of his election.

During the early months of Lincoln's administration, Stanton, now in private life, was utterly distrustful and critical of the president and his cabinet. When Simon Cameron was removed from office in 1862, however, Stanton took his place as secretary of war. His appointment was well received as presaging a more honest and efficient management of War Department affairs and a more aggressive prosecution of the war. The department was reorganized, personnel increased, contracts investigated, those tainted with fraud revoked, and their perpetrators prosecuted. Stanton also put himself in active touch with generals, governors, and the congressional Committee on the Conduct of the War. Becoming impatient with Gen. G. B. McClellan's slowness in achieving tangible results, Stanton joined with other members of the cabinet in seeking to have him deprived of any command. Quickness of decision, mastery of detail, and vigor in execution were among Stanton's outstanding characteristics as a war administrator, and he became annoyed when subordinates proved deficient in these qualities. He was frequently accused of meddling with military operations and was probably guilty of it on many occasions. His severe censorship of the press was also a source of much criticism in newspaper circles, and his exercise of the power of extraordinary arrest was often capricious and harmful. Soldiers and civilians alike found him arrogant, irascible, and often brutal and unjust.

At the request of President Andrew Johnson, Stanton retained his post after Lincoln's death and ably directed the demobilization of the Union armies. At the same time he entered upon a tortuous course with respect to Reconstruction and related problems which brought him into serious conflict with the president. It was soon suspected that Stanton was out of sympathy with the administration and was intriguing with the rising opposition. From the summer of 1865 onward, upon nearly every issue, he advised a course of action which would have played into the hands of the Radicals and which fostered a punitive Southern policy. By the beginning of August 1867, President Johnson could no longer tolerate his mendacious minister and was satisfied that Stanton had indeed plotted against him in the matter of Reconstruction legislation and had encouraged insubordination on the part of the commanders of the military districts. When called upon to resign, Stanton refused to do so until Congress reassembled, contending that the Tenure of Office bill had become law by its passage over the presidential veto. Dismissed in February 1868, he declared that he would not give up his post until expelled by force and was supported by the Senate. When the impeachment charges against President Johnson failed, Stanton accepted the inevitable and resigned the same day (May 26, 1868). He accepted President U. S. Grant's appointment to the U.S. Supreme Court, 1869, but death overtook him before he could occupy his seat. His defects of temperament and the disclosures of his amazing disloyalty and duplicity in his official relations detract from his stature as a public man, although his abilities as lawyer and administrator remain unquestioned. Whether he was motivated by egotism, mistaken patriotism, or a desire to stand well with the congressional opposition is difficult to determine.

STANTON, ELIZABETH CADY (*b. Johnstown, N.Y., 1815; d. New York, N.Y., 1902*), reformer, leader in the woman's rights movement. Daughter of Daniel Cady; granddaughter of James Livingston; cousin of

Gerrit Smith. Married Henry B. Stanton, 1840, and insisted on omission of the word "obey" from the ceremony. Much influenced by Lucretia C. Mott, Mrs. Stanton joined with her and others in holding the celebrated woman's rights convention at Seneca Falls, N.Y., 1848. *Post* 1851 she was closely associated in suffrage work with Susan B. Anthony, planning campaigns, appearing before legislative and congressional committees and delivering speeches. President of the National Woman Suffrage Association, 1869–90, she also served as president of the National American Woman Suffrage Association subsequent to a merger of these organizations. Co-author with Miss Anthony of *History of Woman Suffrage* (1881–86), she was author also of many contributions to periodicals and newspapers and of an autobiography, *Eighty Years and More* (1898).

STANTON, FRANK LEBBY (*b. Charleston, S.C., 1857; d. 1927*), Georgia journalist, poet. Conducted one of the first newspaper "columns" in the *Atlanta Constitution post* 1889. Known as the "Riley of the South," he published a number of volumes of his poems, among them, *Up from Georgia* (1902) and *Little Folks Down South* (1904).

STANTON, FREDERICK PERRY (*b. Alexandria, Va., 1814; d. Stanton, Fla., 1894*), lawyer. Removing to Tennessee, 1835, he served as congressman, Democrat, from the Memphis district, 1845–55. As chairman of the committee on naval affairs *post* 1849, he advocated useful reforms; in his last term he was chairman of the judiciary committee. Pro-slavery in his general opinions, he served as secretary and acting governor of Kansas Territory, March–May 1857, and as secretary thereafter until 1858, save for another brief period as acting governor after the resignation of Robert J. Walker. Although he apportioned delegates to the Lecompton Convention under an inequitable and incomplete census because of lack of experience, he and Walker later tried to insure a fair vote for members of a legislature. After his removal from office for attempting to provide a referendum on the Lecompton Constitution, he became a Free-Stater.

STANTON, HENRY BREWSTER (*b. Griswold, Conn., 1805; d. New York, N.Y., 1887*), lawyer, journalist, reformer, anti-slavery agent. Husband of Elizabeth Cady Stanton. Author, among other books, of *Random Recollections* (1887).

STANTON, RICHARD HENRY (*b. Alexandria, Va., 1812; d. 1891*), Kentucky congressman, jurist, legal writer.

STANWOOD, EDWARD (*b. Augusta, Maine, 1841; d. Brookline, Mass., 1923*), journalist, historian. After holding editorial posts on Maine and Boston, Mass., newspapers, Stanwood was for many years *post* 1883 managing editor and editor of the *Youth's Companion.* He was author of *A History of Presidential Elections* (1884), *American Tariff Controversies in the Nine-* *teenth Century* (1903) and *James Gillespie Blaine* (1905).

STAPLES, WALLER REDD (*b. Stuart, Va., 1826; d. Montgomery Co., Va., 1897*), lawyer, Confederate congressman. Judge of the Virginia supreme court of appeals, 1870–82, he gave his most notable opinion in the "Coupon Case," 1878, which led to the forming of the Readjuster party and the partial repudiation of a portion of the state debt. Staples's dissenting opinion was later upheld. He served as a co-compiler of *The Code of Virginia* (1887).

STAPLES, WILLIAM READ (*b. Providence, R.I., 1798; d. 1868*), Rhode Island jurist, historian. Author, among other works, of *Annals of the Town of Providence* (1843) and *Rhode Island in the Continental Congress* (edited, Reuben A. Guild, 1870).

STARIN, JOHN HENRY (*b. Sammonsville, N.Y., 1825; d. New York, N.Y., 1909*), freight agent. Operated *post* 1859 a general agency for the transport of freight around New York City by a system of lighters and tugs, which included his later invention of the car float. Owner and operator of the largest "harbor marine" in the United States, he also owned and operated passenger and freight lines on Long Island Sound.

STARK, EDWARD JOSEF (*b. Hohenems, Austria, 1858; d. 1918*), cantor, composer of synagogue music. Came to America as a boy; received musical education in New York City and abroad. Practicing his profession in Brooklyn, N.Y., and San Francisco, Calif., he was author of music which, by its successful combination of traditionalism and modernism, was particularly adapted for Reform Jewish temples.

STARK, JOHN (*b. Londonderry, N.H., 1728; d. 1822*), colonial and Revolutionary soldier. Saw extensive service with Rogers's Rangers in French and Indian War, attaining captaincy. Appointed colonel of a New Hampshire regiment on outbreak of the Revolution, he distinguished himself at Bunker Hill, on the retreat from Canada, 1776, and at Trenton and Princeton. Resigning his commission, March 1777, because Congress promoted junior officers over his head, he returned to the field as brigadier-general, commanding New Hampshire troops for the defense of Vermont. He defeated a Hessian and Tory force at Bennington, August 1777, and later helped to effect Burgoyne's surrender by blocking his line of retreat. Promoted brigadier-general in the Continental service, October 1777, he served with Gates in Rhode Island, 1779, participated in the battle of Springfield, N.J., 1780, and acted on the board of officers appointed to try Major André. He retired with the brevet of major-general in 1783.

STARKS, EDWIN CHAPIN (*b. Baraboo, Wis., 1867; d. 1932*), ichthyologist. An authority on the osteology of fishes, Starks served on a number of important field expeditions under David S. Jordan, Charles H. Gilbert and others. His principal academic post was at Stanford University where he was curator of zoological collections *post* 1901. He retired in the year of his death as associate professor. [*Supp.* 1]

STARR, ELIZA ALLEN (*b. Deerfield, Mass., 1824; d. Durand, Ill., 1901*), author, lecturer on art. Settling in Chicago, Ill., *c.* 1856, she became one of the first art teachers there and wrote and illustrated a number of books, devotional in character.

STARR, FREDERICK (*b. Auburn, N.Y. 1858; d. Tokyo, Japan, 1933*), anthropologist. Graduated Lafayette College, 1882; Ph.D., 1885. After teaching at a number of schools, he organized the work in anthropology at the University of Chicago, 1892, and in 1895 became associate professor there. He served as sole teacher of his subject until 1923. Author of a number of books and studies, he is chiefly remembered for the wide interest he created in anthropology through his teaching.

STARR, LOUIS (*b. Philadelphia, Pa., 1849; d. 1925*), physician, pediatrician. M.D., University of Pennsylvania, 1871. Author of *Hygiene of the Nursery* (1888), one of the first popular expositions of the subject.

STARR, MERRITT (*b. Ellington, N.Y., 1856; d. 1931*), corporation lawyer. Practiced in Chicago, Ill., *post* 1882; was active in Winnetka, Ill., civic affairs.

STARR, MOSES ALLEN (*b. Brooklyn, N.Y., 1854; d. 1932*), neurologist. Graduated Princeton, 1876; M.D., N.Y. College of Physicians and Surgeons, 1880; made postgraduate studies in Heidelberg and Vienna. Taught at New York Polyclinic, 1884–89; was professor of mental and nervous diseases, N.Y. College of Physicians and Surgeons, 1889–1915. An American pioneer in cerebral localization, he did valuable work on brain tumors. He was author of a great number of special articles on neurological subjects and of several books, including *Atlas of Nerve Cells* (1896) and *Organic and Functional Nervous Diseases* (1903). He was particularly noted as a teacher.

STARRETT, LAROY S. (*b. China, Maine, 1836; d. St. Petersburg, Fla., 1922*), inventor and manufacturer of squares, gauges, calipers, levels and other hand tools useful in the building trades.

STARRETT, WILLIAM AIKEN (*b. Lawrence, Kans., 1877; d. Madison, N.J., 1932*), engineer, architect, builder, financier. A partner and officer in Thompson-Starrett Co., engaged in skyscraper and factory construction, he was later associated with the George A. Fuller Co. and with Starrett Brothers and Eken. Completely oblivious to all city-planning values except the financial, he was essentially an executive and neither a designer nor a man of thought.

STATLER, ELLSWORTH MILTON (*b. Somerset Co., Pa., 1863; d. New York, N.Y., 1928*), hotel owner and operator. Began his career as a bell-boy in the McClure House, Wheeling, W. Va., and achieved success through his cardinal rule, "The guest is always right." At his death his hotel properties were the largest owned by one man.

STAUFFER, DAVID McNEELY (*b. Richland, Pa., 1845; d. Yonkers, N.Y., 1913*), civil engineer, editor, collector of prints and autographs. Author of *American Engravers upon Copper and Steel* (1907), the standard work in its field.

STAUGHTON, WILLIAM (*b. Coventry, England, 1770; d. Washington D.C., 1829*), Baptist minister, educator. Came to America, 1793; held pastorates in Burlington, N.J., and Philadelphia, Pa. Helped establish Columbian College (present George Washington University); served as its president, 1822–29.

STAYTON, JOHN WILLIAM (*b. Washington Co., Ky., 1830; d. Tyler, Texas, 1894*), jurist. LL.B., Louisville University, 1856. Removed to Texas, 1856; served in the Confederate cavalry, 1861–65. Associate justice, Texas supreme court, 1881–88, he served as chief justice thereafter until his death.

STEARNS, ABEL (*b. Lunenberg, Mass., 1798; d. San Francisco, Calif., 1871*), California pioneer, stockraiser. Emigrated to Mexico *c.* 1826; settled in Los Angeles, Calif., 1833. Joined in revolutions in favor of J. B. Alvarado (1836) and against Manuel Micheltorena (1844–45); remained neutral in hostilities during U.S. seizure of California.

STEARNS, ASAHEL (*b. Lunenberg, Mass., 1774; d. 1839*), lawyer. Cousin of Abel Stearns. Graduated Harvard, 1797. Practiced in present Lowell, Mass., and in Charlestown, Mass.; served also in the legislature and as congressman for a single term, 1815–17. Professor of law, Harvard Law School, 1817–29, Stearns was author of *A Summary of the Law and Practice of Real Actions* (1824). Relatively unsuccessful as a law professor, he was an able lawyer and was a commissioner under Charles Jackson in making the first real revision of the Massachusetts statutes (adopted, 1835).

STEARNS, EBEN SPERRY (*b. Bedford, Mass., 1819; d. 1887*), educator. Brother of William A. Stearns. Graduated Harvard, 1841. First president, State Normal School, Nashville, Tenn., *post* 1875, also chancellor of the University of Nashville, he proved himself an efficient administrator and was tireless in trying to raise educational standards in the South.

STEARNS, FRANK WATERMAN (*b. Boston, Mass., 1856; d. Boston, 1939*), dry goods merchant. Partner in R. H. Stearns and Co. (Boston, Mass.), *post* 1880; resigned as president, 1919, retaining chairmanship of the board. Friend and backer of Calvin Coolidge. [*Supp.* 2]

STEARNS, FREDERIC PIKE (*b. Calais, Maine, 1851; d. 1919*), civil engineer, hydraulics expert. Planned improvement of Charles River Basin. As en-

STEARNS · STEEDMAN

gineer for Massachusetts Board of Health, he designed and saw to completion the metropolitan water supply of Boston and its vicinity c. 1895–1907. He later served as a consultant for many other municipal water supply projects and for the Panama Canal.

STEARNS, GEORGE LUTHER (b. Medford, Mass., 1809; d. New York, N.Y., 1867), Abolitionist, manufacturer. A leader in the movement that put Charles Sumner in the U.S. Senate, he played a great part in the rise of the Republican party in Massachusetts. A friend and patron of John Brown, he financed Brown's proposed raid into Virginia and after his capture attempted his rescue. During the Civil War he recruited Negro troops for the Union Army.

STEARNS, HENRY PUTNAM (b. Sutton, Mass., 1828; d. 1905), physician, alienist, Union army surgeon. Superintendent of Hartford (Conn.) Retreat for the Insane post 1874.

STEARNS, IRVING ARIEL (b. Rushville, N.Y., 1845; d. Wilkes-Barre, Pa., 1920), mining engineer. Graduated Rensselaer Polytechnic Institute, 1868. Managed coal interests of the Pennsylvania Railroad, 1885–97; made radical improvements in processes of mining and preparing anthracite coal. Thereafter he headed several coal and iron companies until his retirement from business, 1905.

STEARNS, JOHN NEWTON (b. New Ipswich, N.H., 1829; d. Brooklyn, N.Y., 1895), temperance reformer, author of much temperance propaganda.

STEARNS, OLIVER (b. Lunenberg, Mass., 1807; d. Cambridge, Mass., 1885), Unitarian clergyman. Nephew of Asahel Stearns. Graduated Harvard, 1826; Harvard Divinity School, 1830. After holding pastorates in Northampton and Hingham, Mass., he served as president of Meadville (Pa.) Theological School, 1856–63, and as professor at Harvard Divinity School, 1863–70. Appointed dean of that school on its reorganization, 1870, he served until 1878 and taught systematic theology and ethics. He was author of several interesting publications asserting that the progressive development of Christian doctrine is the story of intuitive reason interpreting revelation, but safeguarded against private error by an intention to seek truth in the light of the Holy Catholic Church.

STEARNS, ROBERT EDWARDS CARTER (b. Boston, Mass., 1827; d. Los Angeles, Calif., 1909), naturalist, early student of California fauna. Author of a number of articles on molluscan systematics and distribution. He served as paleontologist to the U.S. Geological Survey (appointed, 1884) and as assistant curator of mollusks in the U.S. National Museum.

STEARNS, SHUBAL (b. Boston, Mass., 1706; d. 1771), Baptist clergyman. Brother-in-law of Daniel Marshall. Ordained, 1751, Stearns emigrated first to Virginia and then to Sandy Creek, N.C., where he

served as pastor of the Separate Baptist church post 1755. He won high repute as a preaching evangelist in the Carolinas, Georgia and Virginia.

STEARNS, WILLIAM AUGUSTUS (b. Bedford, Mass., 1805; d. Amherst, Mass., 1876), Congregational clergyman, educator. Brother of Eben S. Stearns. Graduated Harvard, 1827. After a long, successful pastorate at Cambridgeport, Mass., he was president of Amherst College, 1854–76.

STEBBINS, HORATIO (b. South Wilbraham, Mass., 1821; d. Cambridge, Mass., 1902), Unitarian clergyman. Graduated Harvard, 1848; attended Harvard Divinity School. After serving churches in Fitchburg, Mass., and Portland, Maine, Stebbins succeeded Thomas S. King as pastor of the Unitarian Church in San Francisco, Calif., 1864. For 35 years thereafter he was a force in the development of the state, particularly in its educational progress; he was a leader in the formation of the University of California, Stanford University and Lick Observatory. He resigned his pastorate, 1900.

STEBBINS, RUFUS PHINEAS (b. South Wilbraham, Mass., 1810; d. Cambridge, Mass., 1885), Unitarian clergyman. Cousin of Horatio Stebbins. Graduated Amherst, 1834; attended Harvard Divinity School. Pastor at Leominster, Mass., 1837–44, he became first president of the Meadville (Pa.) Theological School and served in that post until 1856. Thereafter he held various pastorates in Massachusetts and New York and served as president of the American Unitarian Association.

STECK, GEORGE (b. Cassel, Germany, 1829; d. New York, N.Y., 1897), piano manufacturer. Emigrated to New York City, 1853.

STEDMAN, EDMUND CLARENCE (b. Hartford, Conn., 1833; d. New York, N.Y., 1908), stockbroker, poet, critic. Son of Elizabeth C. D. S. Kinney. Author of a number of technically meritorious but imitative poems, Stedman exercised great influence on American letters of his period through his critical works and anthologies, among them, *Poets of America* (1885), *A Victorian Anthology* (1895) and *An American Anthology* (1900).

STEEDMAN, CHARLES (b. Santee, S.C., 1811; d. Washington, D.C., 1890), naval officer. On active service, principally at sea, post 1828, he retired as rear-admiral, 1873. Remaining loyal to the Union during the Civil War, he served chiefly on blockade duty off the southeast coast and commanded the *Ticonderoga* during both attacks against Fort Fisher.

STEEDMAN, JAMES BLAIR (b. Northumberland Co., Pa., 1817; d. 1883), printer, Union major-general, Ohio Democratic politician. Won his greatest distinction in the battle of Chickamauga, where he commanded a division of Granger's corps which came to the rescue of Gen. George H. Thomas after the rest

998

of the army had been swept away. He was active in journalism and civic affairs in Toledo, O., *post* 1869.

STEELE, DANIEL (*b. Windham, N.Y., 1824; d. Milton, Mass., 1914*), Methodist clergyman, educator. Held a number of Massachusetts pastorates and was a strong reformer and a leader in Methodism. Professor of languages in Genesee College, 1862–69, and its acting president, 1869–71, he served briefly as professor of philosophy, vice-president and acting chancellor, 1871–72, after Genesee had become Syracuse University.

STEELE, FREDERICK (*b. Delhi, N.Y., 1819; d. San Mateo, Calif., 1868*), soldier. Graduated West Point, 1843. Commanded infantry with credit in Mexican War; *post* 1848, served in California, Minnesota, Nebraska and Kansas. During the Civil War he rose to division command in Union army and the rank of major-general of volunteers. Immediately after the surrender of Vicksburg, he was charged with completing the conquest of Arkansas which he accomplished within a few months. He failed in an effort to assist Gen. N. P. Banks in the Red River campaign (March–April, 1864).

STEELE, JOEL DORMAN (*b. Lima, N.Y., 1836; d. 1886*), educator, author of science textbooks, Union soldier. Principal of the Elmira (N.Y.) Free Academy, 1866–72.

STEELE, JOHN (*b. Salisbury, N.C., 1764; d. 1815*), businessman, landowner. Congressman, independent Federalist, from North Carolina, 1789–93; comptroller of U.S. treasury, 1796–1802. Opposed to any extension of presidential or judicial powers.

STEENDAM, JACOB (*b. The Netherlands, 1616; d. Netherlands Indies, c. 1672*), merchant, first poet of New Netherland. Resident on Long Island and in New Amsterdam, 1652–c. 1662.

STEENWYCK, CORNELIS (*b. probably Haarlem, Holland, date unknown; d. New York, N.Y., 1684*), colonial merchant. Came to New Amsterdam, 1651, as mate of a trading vessel. Prospering as a merchant, he held a number of civic posts under the Dutch rule and was a signer of the articles by which New Netherland was surrendered to the English. Mayor of New York, 1668–70, he became a member of Gov. Francis Lovelace's council, continued influential during the brief restoration of Dutch rule, and survived the second English seizure of the colony sufficiently well to serve again as mayor of New York City, 1682–83. A wealthy man, he was reputed the best-dressed, most polite and most popular man in the New York of his time.

STEERS, GEORGE (*b. Washington, D.C., 1820; d. 1856*), naval architect. Trained in his father's New York City shipyard, Steers introduced revolutionary changes in hull design. He was particularly renowned as builder of the famous yacht *America* which he sailed in the memorable race of Aug. 22, 1851, around the Isle of Wight.

STEFFENS, LINCOLN (*b. San Francisco, Calif., 1866; d. Carmel, Calif., 1936*), journalist, reformer. Reared in a prosperous family, Steffens graduated from the University of California (Ph.B., 1889) and made various studies in Germany, England and France. After reportorial and editorial work on the N.Y. *Evening Post* and the N.Y. *Commercial Advertiser*, 1892–1901, he joined the staff of *McClure's Magazine* and found his true *métier* as writer of muckraking articles exposing civic corruption (collected as *The Shame of the Cities*, 1904). Continuing his investigations, he published *The Struggle for Self-Government* (1906) and *Upbuilders* (1909) in which he cited evidence of substantial reform gains achieved and expressed a growing belief in the need for firm leadership. Associated with Edward A. Filene in Boston reform efforts, 1909, he became convinced that exposure of evil was not enough to bring about reform and began to look about for some single principle as a solution. Disappointed in his belief in the Golden Rule, in his efforts to negotiate a settlement of the case of the McNamara brothers, and in his personal life as well, he sought a new panacea in violent social upheaval. From 1917 until his death, he was increasingly a partisan of the Soviet Union. *Post* 1929 he felt that Russia offered the only practical solution for the problems of progress and power. His *Autobiography* (1931), although manifestly self-serving in numerous passages, was written with skeptical humor and questioned social processes in a manner relevant to the economic depression existing at the time of its publication. [*Supp. 2*]

STEHLE, AURELIUS ALOYSIUS (*b. Pittsburgh, Pa., 1877; d. Pittsburgh, 1930*), Roman Catholic clergyman, Benedictine. Archabbot of St. Vincent Archabbey, 1920–30, he was founder of the Catholic University at Peking, China (1924).

STEIN, EVALEEN (*b. Lafayette, Ind., 1863; d. 1923*), poet, writer of children's stories.

STEINER, BERNARD CHRISTIAN (*b. Guilford, Conn., 1867; d. 1926*), educator, librarian, historian. Son of Lewis H. Steiner. Graduated Yale, 1888; Ph.D., Johns Hopkins, 1891. Taught at Williams College; was librarian of Enoch Pratt Free Library, Baltimore, Md., 1892–1926. He was author of a great number of monographs and books on the history of Maryland and Connecticut and on the history of education in America; he was also editor of Volumes XVIII and XXXVI-XLV of the *Archives of Maryland*. Among his books, *Life and Correspondence of James McHenry* (1907), *Life of Reverdy Johnson* (1914) and *Life of Roger Brooke Taney* (1922) were of particular value.

STEINER, LEWIS HENRY (*b. Frederick, Md., 1827; d. 1892*), physician, librarian. Father of Bernard C.

Steiner. A practicing physician and teacher of medicine, 1849–84, he served thereafter as first librarian of the Enoch Pratt Free Library of Baltimore, Md.

STEINERT, MORRIS (*b. Scheinfeld, Bavaria, 1831; d. 1912*), optician, merchant, collector of musical instruments. Emigrated to America *c.* 1856; made his home in New Haven, Conn., *post* 1861. Founded Mathushek Piano Co. and New Haven Symphony Orchestra; donated his important collection of rare instruments to Yale University.

STEINITZ, WILLIAM (*b. Prague, Czechoslovakia, 1836; d. New York, N.Y., 1900*), champion chess player of the world, 1866–94. An American citizen *post* 1884, he wrote extensively on chess and was author of *The Modern Chess Instructor* (1889, 1895).

STEINMETZ, CHARLES PROTEUS (*b. Breslau, Germany, 1865; d. 1923*), mathematician, electrical engineer. Deformed from birth, he showed brilliance and a great capacity for study at the University of Breslau which he attended, 1883–88. Having engaged in socialist journalism there, he was obliged to flee Germany to avoid arrest and never received the doctor's degree for which he had completed his work. Emigrating from Switzerland to the United States, 1889, he worked for Rudolf Eickemeyer who before long established him in an experimental laboratory of his own.

Given the task of calculating and designing an alternating-current commutator motor, and wishing to calculate the hysteresis loss, he derived the law of hysteresis mathematically from existing data. He followed this with an elaborate series of tests to prove the law and simplify its application. In 1892, he read two papers on the subject before the American Institute of Electrical Engineers which at once established his reputation. His further studies of alternating electric current phenomena led him to develop a mathematical method of reducing alternating current theory to a basis of practical calculation. His symbolic method is now universally used although it required a process of elucidation by him in several books before it was generally understood. His third and last great research undertaking had to do with the phenomena which are centered in lightning. He began a systematic study of the general equation of the electric current and of "transient electrical phenomena" as lightning is scientifically called. This work culminated in 1921 with dramatic experiments yielding man-made lightning in the laboratory. In addition to his work as consulting engineer for the General Electric Co. (1894–1923), he was professor of electrical engineering and electrophysics at Union University, Schenectady, N.Y. He received numerous honors, patented a great number of inventions and wrote several books, including *Theory and Calculation of Transient Electric Phenomena and Oscilla-*

tions (1909) and *Theory and Calculation of Alternating Current Phenomena* (5th ed., 1916).

STEINMEYER, FERDINAND. [See FARMER, FATHER, 1720–1786.]

STEINWAY, CHRISTIAN FRIEDRICH THEODORE (*b. Seesen, Germany, 1825; d. Brunswick, Germany, 1889*), piano manufacturer. Son of Henry E. Steinway; brother of William Steinway. Resident in America, 1865–70, he made extensive experiments in application of modern science to the problems of piano-building.

STEINWAY, HENRY ENGELHARD (*b. Wolfshagen, Germany, 1797; d. New York, N.Y., 1871*), piano manufacturer. Father of Christian F. T. and William Steinway. Emigrated to New York City, 1851. Started his own business under his original name of Steinweg, 1853; introduced innovating square piano with over-strung strings and a full cast-iron frame, 1855. Thereafter he undertook the manufacture of grand pianos and uprights and built Steinway Hall (formally opened, 1867) which became a center of New York musical life.

STEINWAY, WILLIAM (*b. Seesen, Germany, 1835; d. New York, N.Y., 1896*), piano manufacturer. Son of Henry E. Steinway; brother of Christian F. T. Steinway. Emigrated to America with his family, 1851. Concerned mainly with the financial and selling departments of Steinway & Sons, he was a patron of music and won international standing for his firm by inducing foreign artists to play Steinway pianos. President of the firm, 1876–96, he was active also in civic affairs and was chairman of the New York City commission which planned the first subways.

STENGEL, ALFRED (*b. Pittsburgh, Pa., 1868; d. Philadelphia, Pa., 1939*), pathologist, medical educator. M.D., University of Pennsylvania, 1889; studied also at Berlin, Vienna and London. A teacher of medicine at Pennsylvania *post* 1893, he served also as vice-president of the university for medical affairs, 1931–39. As president of the American College of Physicians, 1925–27, he brought about its complete reorganization and made it the outstanding organization of internists in America. [*Supp. 2*]

STEPHENS, ALEXANDER HAMILTON (*b. Wilkes, later Taliaferro, Co., Ga., 1812; d. Atlanta, Ga., 1883*), statesman, lawyer. Half-brother of Linton Stephens. Orphaned at an early age; graduated University of Georgia, 1832; began practice of law at Crawfordville, Ga., 1834. After effective service in the Georgia legislature *post* 1836 as an associate in the faction headed at various times by William H. Crawford and George M. Troup, he entered the U.S. House of Representatives as a Whig, 1843. His first notable speech was made at the beginning of 1845 on the Texas question. Annexation, he said, while tending to lessen the prosperity of the cotton states already in the

Union, would give the South a greatly needed political weight and thus preserve a proper balance between the different sections of the nation. However, the next year he denounced the sending of troops to the Rio Grande and the precipitation of war with Mexico. Deprecating the Democratic project of expansion, 1847, he censured the Wilmot Proviso, saying that if its policy were pursued the Union must give place to a prospect of desolation, carnage and blood. Growing more alarmed at what he considered the progressive erosion of state rights and constitutional safeguards, he defied the North in August 1850 by stating: "Whenever this Government is brought in hostile array against me and mine, I am for disunion—openly, boldly and fearlessly, for revolution . . . seven millions of people fighting for their rights, their homes and their hearth-stones cannot be easily conquered." However, when Henry Clay's compromise measures were enacted, he hastened to Georgia to endorse the Union-saving legislation, provided that Congress and the North maintained it in letter and spirit. To improve the prospect of intersectional peace, he launched with Robert Toombs and Howell Cobb a Constitutional Union party, but the project collapsed for lack of support.

Rejecting Winfield Scott, the Whig candidate for president in 1852, Stephens abandoned the Whig party and shifted to the Democrats; he heartily denounced the Know-Nothing movement. Supporting the Kansas-Nebraska bill, he acted as House floor manager in its behalf. Convinced that the bill was admirable, he was proud of his maneuvers which resulted in its enactment. His essential concern, often and sincerely proclaimed, was the preservation of Southern security within a placid Union of all the states. In 1859 he gave up his seat in Congress but continued his interest in politics. In the campaign of 1860, he preferred the candidacy of R. M. T. Hunter but supported Stephen A. Douglas. When Lincoln was elected, Stephens advised a policy of watchful waiting, with readiness for drastic action if Lincoln or Congress invaded Southern rights or violated the constitution. At the convention summoned by the Georgia legislature which met in January 1861, he declared that he opposed "the policy of immediate secession," but if the majority voted for secession he would accept their decision. As a delegate to the convention of Southern states held at Montgomery, he proposed the formation of a union on the model of the United States. Under the quickly devised Provisional Constitution, Jefferson Davis was elected president of the Confederate States of America and Stephens vice-president, February 1861.

As vice-president, Stephens lent a hand in affairs where he could, but gradually drifted into the position of leader of the opposition. He disapproved of many of Davis's policies, and his fondness for principles, scruples and constitutional restraint made him an unhappy member of a wartime government. War

itself was keenly distressing to him, particularly the sufferings of the wounded and prisoners on both sides. Sent in 1865 to Hampton Roads as one of three commissioners to negotiate a peaceful settlement with Lincoln and W. H. Seward, he found that the maintenance of Confederate independence would be impossible. Shortly after the termination of the war he was arrested by federal troops but was later released on parole. Elected to the U.S. Senate in 1866, he was excluded from that body along with all others from the "rebel" states.

In the Reconstruction period Stephens counseled self-discipline, patience, and forbearance from recrimination, and recommended support for President Johnson's policies. In hearings before a congressional committee on Reconstruction, he declared that Georgia acquiesced in the abolition of slavery but opposed granting the suffrage to Negroes, and he denied the constitutional power of the federal government to impose conditions precedent to restoration of the late Confederate states to their functions in the Union. Congress proceeded with its drastic program, and Stephens accepted a publisher's invitation to write *A Constitutional View of the Late War Between the States* (published 1868, 1870). It is a tedious rationalization, obscuring the historic problem of Negro slavery by refinements of doctrine on the sovereignty of the states. Dull as the book may be to readers in the 20th century, it was a sensation in its day, evoking attacks by Northern and Southern champions of causes upon which it impinged. In 1872 Stephens was elected to the House of Representatives and served for a decade. In 1882, after resigning from Congress, he was elected governor of Georgia but died a few months after inauguration. By then he had become a tradition as one who had served his people, through fair times and foul, with conscience, eloquence, and unflagging zeal.

STEPHENS, ALICE BARBER (*b. near Salem, N.J., 1858; d. Rose Valley, Pa., 1932*), illustrator. Studied at School of Design for Women, Philadelphia, Pa., where she later taught; worked under Thomas Eakins at Pennsylvania Academy. Excelled in pictures of quiet scenes and incidents from classic fiction, characterized by simplicity and technical assurance.

STEPHENS, ANN SOPHIA (*b. Derby, Conn., 1813; d. Newport, R.I., 1886*), editor, author. A prolific writer for the periodicals of her time, Mrs. Stephens served in editorial capacities on the *Ladies' Companion, Graham's Magazine,* and *Peterson's Magazine.* She is particularly notable as author of the first of the celebrated Beadle "dime novels"—*Malaeska* (1860).

STEPHENS, CHARLES ASBURY (*b. Norway Lake, Maine, 1844; d. Norway Lake, 1931*), author of juvenile stories, experimenter in biology.

STEPHENS, EDWIN WILLIAM (*b. Columbia, Mo., 1849; d. Columbia, 1931*), editor-publisher of the

Columbia Herald, 1870–1905, commercial printer. Chairman, Missouri State Capitol commission (completed, 1918).

STEPHENS, HENRY MORSE (*b. Edinburgh, Scotland, 1857; d. 1919*), educator, historian. Graduated Balliol College, Oxford, B.A., 1882; studied also at Lincoln's Inn and at universities of Bonn and Paris. After achieving distinction in England as writer, librarian and teacher, he served as professor of modern European history at Cornell University, 1894–1902, and was thereafter head of the department of history at University of California. A rigorously scientific historian, he was author, among other books, of *History of the French Revolution* (1886, 1891). He was successful in obtaining for the University of California the collection of works relating to Spanish colonization and to the Pacific Coast which was gathered by H. H. Bancroft.

STEPHENS, JOHN LLOYD (*b. Shrewsbury, N.J., 1805; d. New York, N.Y., 1852*), lawyer, steamship and railroad promoter, traveler, author. After publishing several books on his travels in eastern Europe and the Near East, he investigated the Maya ruins in Honduras, Guatemala and Yucatan, 1839–40, accompanied by an English artist, Frederick Catherwood, who was experienced in archeology. Stephens aroused interest in the early Central American cultures by his *Incidents of Travel in Central America, Chiapas, and Yucatan* (illustrated by Catherwood, 1841). Returning for more intensive study of the subject in 1841, they published another collaborative work, *Incidents of Travel in Yucatan* (1843).

STEPHENS, LINTON (*b. near Crawfordville, Ga., 1823; d. Georgia, 1872*), Georgia legislator and jurist, Confederate soldier. Half-brother of Alexander H. Stephens. A Whig legislator, he aided his half-brother, Robert Toombs, and Howell Cobb in organizing the Constitutional Union party; he later returned to the Whigs and was a Democrat *post* 1856. After the Civil War he practiced law and refused to re-enter politics, but militantly opposed Reconstruction.

STEPHENS, URIAH SMITH (*b. near Cape May, N.J., 1821; d. Philadelphia, Pa., 1882*), pioneer labor leader. A tailor by trade, he helped organize the Garment Cutters' Association of Philadelphia, 1862. Upon its dissolution in 1869, he and others founded the Noble Order of the Knights of Labor. The Order, in which Stephens served for a time as Grand Master Workman, was based on the principles of secrecy, union of all trades, education and cooperation. Stephens conceived of the Knights of Labor not simply as a trade union but as a nucleus for building a cooperative commonwealth. After a bitter struggle between Stephens and Terence V. Powderly, the principle of secrecy in the Order was repudiated, 1881.

STEPHENSON, BENJAMIN FRANKLIN (*b. Wayne Co., Ill., 1823; d. Rock Creek, Ill., 1871*), physician, Union Army surgeon, founder of the Grand Army of the Republic (Decatur, Ill., Apr. 6, 1866).

STEPHENSON, ISAAC (*b. Maugerville, N.B., Canada, 1829; d. Marinette, Wis., 1918*), lumberman, politician. Removed to Milwaukee, Wis., 1845; settled at Marinette, 1858; was thereafter connected with many industrial operations in the Menominee River valley. A Republican member of the Wisconsin legislature and a congressman, 1883–89, he turned against the machine and financed Robert M. LaFollette's campaign for governor, 1900. Elected U.S. senator, 1907, in succession to John C. Spooner, he was re-elected in 1908. Attacked for his lavish expenditure of money in the campaign by both LaFollette and the Progressives and also the "regular" Republicans, he was confirmed in his seat nevertheless and served out his term.

STEPHENSON, JOHN (*b. Co. Armagh, Ireland, 1809; d. New Rochelle, N.Y., 1893*), street-car builder. Came to New York City as a child; was apprenticed to a coach-maker. Designed and built the first omnibus made in New York, 1831; also designed and built the first car for the first street railway in the world (Fourth Avenue line, New York & Harlem Railroad), 1832.

STEPHENSON, NATHANIEL WRIGHT (*b. Cincinnati, O., 1867; d. 1935*), journalist, educator, historian. Taught principally at College of Charleston (1903–20) and at Scripps College (1927–35). Author of several novels, three successful textbooks in American history and, among other historical studies, *An Autobiography of Abraham Lincoln* (1926) and *Nelson W. Aldrich* (1930). An able, thorough and judicious writer, Stephenson was not distinguished for originality of research. [*Supp. 1*]

STERETT, ANDREW (*b. Baltimore, Md., 1778; d. 1807*), naval officer. Entered navy as a lieutenant, 1798; served as executive officer and first lieutenant of the *Constellation*, 1799–1800. Commanding the schooner *Enterprise*, he fought a brilliant engagement against a Tripolitan polacca in the Mediterranean, August 1801.

STERKI, VICTOR (*b. Solothurn, Switzerland, 1846; d. 1933*), physician, conchologist. Emigrated to America, 1883; practiced in New Philadelphia, O. Made exhaustive studies of the smaller mollusks, in particular, the *Sphaeriidae*.

STERLING, GEORGE (*b. Sag Harbor, N.Y., 1869; d. San Francisco, Calif., 1926*), poet. Friend and disciple of Ambrose Bierce.

STERLING, JAMES (*b. Dowrass, Ireland, 1701?; d. Kent Co., Maryland, 1763*), Anglican clergyman, colonial customs official. Came to America, 1737; held several rectorships in Maryland. Author of *The Rival*

Generals (London, 1722), *The Parricide* (London, 1736) and several volumes of lyric poetry before his emigration, Sterling expressed his conviction that the greatness of Britain was bound up with the development of her American colonies in a long poem *An Epistle to the Hon. Arthur Dobbs.* Written in Maryland, 1748, it was published in London and Dublin, 1752. A group of his later poems appeared in the *American Magazine,* 1757.

STERLING, JOHN WHALEN (*b. Blackwalnut, Pa., 1816; d. Madison, Wis., 1885*), educator. A graduate of the College of New Jersey (Princeton), 1840, and Princeton Theological Seminary, 1844, he became professor of mathematics, natural philosophy and astronomy at University of Wisconsin in 1849. For some years he served as acting chancellor, dean and vice-chancellor. In 1869 he was appointed vice-president of the university and held the office until his death. Because of his devoted service, he is regarded as the chief builder and the guiding spirit of the university in its early years.

STERLING, JOHN WILLIAM (*b. Stratford, Conn., 1844; d. Grand Metis, Quebec, Canada, 1918*), lawyer, philanthropist. Graduated Yale, 1864; Columbia Law School, 1867. Employed in New York City office of David D. Field, he shortly became a junior partner in the firm of Field & Shearman, and was associated in the practice of law with Thomas G. Shearman, 1873–1900. Counsel for Jay Gould, James Fisk and other sensational clients, he acted also for the defense in the celebrated suit of Theodore Tilton against Henry Ward Beecher. Long active in a most lucrative corporation practice, Sterling left his estate to Yale University, providing thereby for erection of the Sterling Memorial Library and a number of other buildings. The receipt of this estate doubled Yale's resources.

STERN, JOSEPH WILLIAM (*b. New York, N.Y., 1870; d. Brightwaters, N.Y., 1934*), song writer, music publisher. Author, among other songs, with Edward B. Marks, his partner, of "The Little Lost Child" (1894), "My Mother Was a Lady" (1896). Became leading publishers of current hits *post* 1896.

STERNBERG, CONSTANTIN IVANOVICH, Edler von (*b. St. Petersburg, Russia, 1852; d. Philadelphia, Pa., 1924*), pianist, composer, teacher. Having achieved a brilliant European reputation, he made a concert tour of the United States, 1880–81. He settled here in 1886, becoming an American citizen. He conducted the Sternberg School of Music in Philadelphia, Pa., *post* 1890; among his pupils were Olga Samaroff, Robert Armbruster and George Antheil.

STERNBERG, GEORGE MILLER (*b. Hartwick Seminary, Otsego Co., N.Y., 1838; d. Washington, D.C., 1915*), bacteriologist, epidemiologist. M.D., N.Y. College of Physicians and Surgeons, 1860. Appointed assistant surgeon, U.S. Army, May 1861, he was made prisoner at first battle of Bull Run, but escaped and participated in the early stages of the Peninsular campaign. Contracting typhoid, he passed the remainder of his Civil War service on hospital duty. After the close of the war he served until 1879 at a number of army posts. While at Fort Barrancas, Fla., 1872–75, he noted the efficacy in treating yellow fever of removing inhabitants from an infected environment and successfully applied the method at the fort. Two articles in the *New Orleans Medical and Surgical Journal* (1875, 1877) gave him status as an authority upon that disease. On duty with the Havana Yellow Fever Commission, 1879–80, he studied its nature and the natural history of its cause; this involved microscopical examination of blood and tissues of yellow fever patients. In these investigations he was one of the first to employ the newly discovered process of photomicrography. In 1881 he reported that the so-called *Bacillus malariae* had no part in the causation of malaria. In the same year, simultaneously with Pasteur, he announced his discovery of the pneumococcus. He was the first in the United States to demonstrate the plasmodium of malaria (1885) and the bacilli of tuberculosis and typhoid fever (1886). His interest in bacteriology naturally led to an interest in disinfection; scientific disinfection had its beginning with his work and that of Koch.

Named surgeon-general of the army with the rank of brigadier-general in 1893, his nine years' tenure of that office saw the establishment of the Army Medical School, the organization of the Army Nurse Corps and the Dental Corps, the creation of the tuberculosis hospital at Fort Bayard, and of many general hospitals during the Spanish-American War. In 1898 he set up the Typhoid Fever Board and in 1900, the Yellow Fever Commission. He was the first American bacteriologist to bring the fundamental principles and technique of the new science within the reach of American physicians. In 1892 he published *A Manual of Bacteriology,* the first exhaustive treatise on the subject published in the United States.

STERNE, SIMON (*b. Philadelphia, Pa., 1839; d. 1901*), lawyer, civic reformer. LL.B., University of Pennsylvania, 1859. Practiced in New York City *post* 1860, eventually specializing in cases involving common carriers. Secretary of the Committee of Seventy which overthrew the Tweed ring, he served on a number of commissions to secure improvement in New York State legislation and drafted a large body of legislation designed to regulate the activities of railroad companies. In the course of his practice, he secured important additions to the common law of New York with respect to the liability of railroad companies for obstructing passage of light and air, the responsibility of carriers to handle freight during a strike, and the analogy between telephone service and that rendered by a common carrier.

STERNE, STUART. [See Bloede, Gertrude, 1845–1905.]

STERRETT, JAMES MACBRIDE (*b. Howard, Pa., 1847; d. 1923*), Episcopal clergyman, philosopher. Professor of philosophy at Seabury Divinity School, Minnesota, 1882–92; at Columbian (present George Washington) University, 1892–1909. Rector and associate rector at All Souls', Washington, D.C., *post* 1911. An adherent of the "St. Louis School" headed by William T. Harris, he devoted his thought to the philosophical principles which underlie the intellectual aspect of religion. By his several books and his teaching he helped give idealism a better standing as against the empirical pragmatic trend so pronounced in his time.

STERRETT, JOHN ROBERT SITLINGTON (*b. Rockbridge Baths, Va., 1851; d. 1914*), archaeologist. Attended University of Virginia, 1868–71; studied at Leipzig, Berlin, and at Munich where he received the Ph.D., 1880. After service as professor of Greek at Miami University, University of Texas and Amherst, he headed the Greek department at Cornell *post* 1901. His numerous published works include the data of his explorations and research in Asia Minor and Babylonia. Among other achievements, he identified the sites of scores of important ancient cities, among them the Lystra of St. Paul's travels.

STETEFELDT, CARL AUGUST (*b. Holzhausen, Germany, 1838; d. Oakland, Calif., 1896*), metallurgist. Came to America, 1863. Invented and developed the Stetefeldt furnace, since superseded but in its time marking an advance in reducing sulphide ores containing gold and silver by the chlorination process.

STETSON, AUGUSTA EMMA SIMMONS (*b. Waldoboro, Maine, c. 1842; d. 1928*), Christian Science leader. Successful in developing Christian Science work in New York City *post* 1886, Mrs. Stetson was formally excommunicated by Mary Baker Eddy in November 1909.

STETSON, CHARLES AUGUSTUS (*b. Newburyport, Mass., 1810; d. Reading, Pa., 1888*), hotel proprietor. Manager and host of the Astor House, New York City, 1838–68.

STETSON, CHARLES WALTER (*b. Tiverton Four Corners, R.I., 1858; d. Rome, Italy, 1911*), portrait painter, landscapist.

STETSON, FRANCIS LYNDE (*b. Keeseville, N.Y., 1846; d. 1920*), lawyer. Graduated Williams, 1867; Columbia Law School, 1869. Expert in the organization and reorganization of corporations, Stetson became the personal counsel of J. Pierpont Morgan and as such took a leading part in creation of the U.S. Steel Corp. and other Morgan promotions. Active in Democratic politics, he was a friend and adviser of Grover Cleveland. He is to be credited with suggesting Cleveland's sound money policy; as Morgan's counsel, he attended the 1895 meeting at the White House at which the Morgan-Belmont syndicate offered to sell gold to the government to stem the drain on U.S. gold reserves. An extreme economic conservative, he joined with Joseph H. Choate and others in opposing the federal income-tax amendment to the Constitution.

STETSON, JOHN BATTERSON (*b. Orange, N.J., 1830; d. DeLand, Fla., 1906*), hat manufacturer. Opened a one-man hat factory in Philadelphia, Pa., 1865, which grew through provision of a high-quality product into a vast industrial plant. Long a generous donor to Baptist churches and charities, Stetson was principal benefactor of the present John B. Stetson University at DeLand.

STETSON, WILLIAM WALLACE (*b. Greene, Maine, 1849; d. probably Auburn, Maine, 1910*), educator, public school administrator. Introduced extensive and constructive reforms as superintendent of Maine schools, 1895–1907.

STETTINIUS, EDWARD RILEY (*b. St. Louis, Mo., 1865; d. Locust Valley, N.Y., 1925*), industrialist. Acting for J. P. Morgan & Co., Stettinius supervised contracts for, and production of, the war supplies purchased in the United States by the Allies, 1915–17. He continued his work after the entry of the United States into World War I, acting first as surveyor-general of purchases and as an assistant secretary of war, 1918–19. Thereafter he was with the Morgan firm until his death.

STEUBEN, FRIEDRICH WILHELM LUDOLF GERHARD AUGUSTIN, Baron von (*b. Magdeburg, Germany, 1730; d. Steuben, Oneida Co., N.Y., 1794*), soldier. Son of a lieutenant of engineers in the army of Frederick William I of Prussia, Steuben spent his early childhood in Russia where his father served for several years in the army of the Czarina Anne. Entering the officer corps of the Prussian army, he served with credit through the Seven Years' War as an infantry officer and later on the staff; he became a general staff officer, 1761, and soon thereafter was promoted captain. After a diplomatic mission to Russia, 1762, he served at the Royal Headquarters as one of the aides-de-camp to the King. His specific training for and experience in general staff duties, a military agency then little known outside Prussia, equipped him peculiarly for his career in the American Revolution. Discharged for obscure reasons from the army in the spring of 1763, he took employment as chamberlain at the Court of the Prince of Hohenzollern-Hechingen in 1764. There he attained the rank of baron. Financial difficulties caused him to seek employment in 1776, first with the French, then with the Margrave of Baden, finally (1777) in the American army. In letters from Benjamin Franklin and others to Washington, he was introduced as a lieutenant-general in the service of Prussia, although his actual rank was that of captain.

Well-received in America because of the prestige of his supposed rank, and his declaration that he wished no immediate compensation and would stake his fortunes upon the success of the Revolution, Steuben reported in February 1778 to Washington at Valley Forge. Prevailed upon to serve as acting inspector-general and to undertake the training of the army, he was immediately successful. This involved serious difficulties since he had to act through interpreters. He prepared brief drill instructions which were issued to the regiments from time to time as the drills progressed. He formed a model company of 100 selected men and undertook its drill in person. Progress of this company under his skilled instruction made an immediate appeal to the imagination of the whole army and drill became the fashion. In consequence, Washington recommended his regular appointment as inspector-general with the rank of major-general on April 30. Thereafter the Continental Army proved itself, battalion for battalion, the equal in discipline of the best British regulars.

During the winter of 1778–79, Steuben prepared his *Regulations for the Order and Discipline of the Troops of the United States,* which became the military bible of the Continental Army. He grew steadily in Washington's confidence; he was consulted upon all questions of strategic and administrative policy, and performed all of the essential functions of a modern general staff. In the autumn of 1780, when Gen. Nathaniel Greene was sent to the Carolinas, Steuben accompanied him to assist in reorganizing the Southern army. Greene, realizing that most of his replacements and supplies came from Virginia, left Steuben in command in that state. His efforts to make Virginia a base of supply for Greene's army were thwarted to a large extent by British forces, and with his limited troops, Steuben could offer slight resistance. Greene, however, appreciated Steuben's difficulties and acknowledged that his support had been indispensable to the success of the Carolina campaign. When Lafayette took command in Virginia in April 1781, Steuben served under his orders; at Yorktown, Steuben commanded one of the three divisions of the besieging army. In 1783 he assisted Washington in preparation of a plan for the future defense of the United States and in the arrangements for demobilizing the Continental Army. When Washington relinquished command of the army, he deliberately made it his last official act to write a letter commending Steuben's invaluable services to the United States throughout the war. After retirement from the army, Steuben, a citizen of the United States since 1783, resided in New York and became one of the most popular figures in the social life of the city

and state. In converting the American army into an effective and highly disciplined military force, he performed an essential service that none of his contemporaries in America was qualified to perform.

STEUER, MAX DAVID (*b. Homino, present Czechoslovakia, 1870?; d. Jackson, N.H., 1940*), lawyer. Came to New York City as a child. LL.B., Columbia Law School, 1893. Practicing in New York City *post* 1893, he rose to be considered one of the outstanding trial lawyers of his time, skillful alike in commercial practice as well as criminal. Possessed of an unusual capacity for grasping a case as a whole, as the sum of all its tiny parts, he also had great technical skill as a cross-examiner and was most dangerous when apparently checkmated. [*Supp. 2*]

STEVENS, ABEL (*b. Philadelphia, Pa., 1815; d. San José, Calif., 1897*), Methodist clergyman, editor. Author of *The History of the Religious Movement of the Eighteenth Century, Called Methodism* (1858–61) and *The History of the Methodist Episcopal Church in the United States* (1864–67) which take high rank among denominational histories.

STEVENS, ALEXANDER HODGDON (*b. New York, N.Y., 1789; d. 1869*), surgeon. Brother of John A. Stevens (1795–1874). Graduated Yale, 1807. Studied medicine with Edward Miller; M.D., University of Pennsylvania, 1811; studied also in London and Paris. Professor of surgery at present Rutgers and at N.Y. College of Physicians and Surgeons, he was president of the latter institution, 1843–55. He maintained a large practice in New York City and held many honorary appointments.

STEVENS, BENJAMIN FRANKLIN (*b. Barnet, Vt., 1833; d. Surbiton, England, 1902*), bookman, antiquary. Brother of Henry Stevens. Editor of a number of reprints of rare works and manuscripts of Americana interest.

STEVENS, CLEMENT HOFFMAN (*b. Norwich, Conn., 1821; d. 1864*), Confederate brigadier-general. Grandson of Peter Fayssoux. Designed armored battery on Morris Island, Charleston, S.C. Recklessly gallant, he was mortally wounded near Peachtree Creek in the campaign against Atlanta, Ga.

STEVENS, EDWIN AUGUSTUS (*b. Hoboken, N.J., 1795; d. Paris, France, 1868*), engineer, financier. Son of John Stevens whose business affairs he managed in great part; brother of Robert L. Stevens. Organized the Camden & Amboy Railroad, 1830, and managed it with great success until his death. Began experiments in construction of an armored or iron-clad warship *c.* 1814, which came to fruition in his vessel *Stevens Battery* forty years later, but failed of acceptance by the government. He left land and money for the establishment of Stevens Institute of Technology at Hoboken.

STEVENS, EMILY (*b. New York, N.Y., 1882; d. New York, 1928*), actress. Cousin of Minnie Maddern Fiske. Adept in the performance of roles of beautiful and alluring women, she played for a number of years with her cousin's companies and scored her first great success in *The Unchastened Woman*, New York, 1915. She later won acclaim for her performance in *Fata Morgana*, 1924.

STEVENS, GEORGE BARKER (*b. Spencer, N.Y., 1854; d. 1906*), theologian. Graduated University of Rochester, 1877; Yale Divinity School, 1880; Ph.D., Syracuse, 1883; D.D., Jena, 1886. Professor of New Testament criticism, Yale Divinity School, 1886–95, and professor of systematic theology thereafter, he was author of a number of books which were concerned chiefly with the re-interpretation of religious truth in the light of modern scholarship.

STEVENS, GEORGE WASHINGTON (*b. Utica, N.Y., 1866; d. 1926*), educator, journalist. Revolutionized museum practice as director of the Toledo (O.) Museum of Art, 1903–26. Under his guidance the Toledo Museum was the first to enter on a policy of art education for all people, the first to maintain a free school of design, and among the first to give music an equal rank with the other arts.

STEVENS, HENRY (*b. Barnet, Vt., 1819; d. London, England, 1886*), bookman. Brother of Benjamin F. Stevens. A pioneer in the collection of rare Americana, Stevens was also an authority on the bibliographical history of the English Bible. He was author, among other works, of *Recollections of Mr. James Lenox, etc.* (1886).

STEVENS, HIRAM FAIRCHILD (*b. St. Albans, Vt., 1852; d. 1904*), lawyer, Minnesota legislator. Removed to St. Paul, Minn., 1879, where he practiced until his death. A leader in starting the St. Paul College of Law, 1900, he served as its president thereafter.

STEVENS, ISAAC INGALLS (*b. Andover, Mass., 1818; d. Chantilly, Va., 1862*), soldier. Graduated West Point, 1839. Commissioned in the engineers, he served ably on fortification work in New England and was on Gen. Winfield Scott's staff in the war with Mexico, winning brevets for gallantry in the capture of Mexico City. Executive assistant, U.S. Coast Survey, 1849–53, he showed high administrative talent; resigning from the army, he served as governor, Washington Territory, 1853–57. During this period he acted as director of exploration for the northern route of the Pacific Railway surveys. His term as governor was a controversial one since his Indian treaty policy brought about a number of uprisings among the tribes in the Territory. Although much criticized, he was elected territorial delegate to Congress and served from March 1857 until the opening of the Civil War. Appointed colonel, 79th New York Volunteers, he was promoted brigadier-general, September 1861, and major-general, July 1862. He was killed in battle.

STEVENS, JOHN (*b. New York, N.Y., 1749; d. Hoboken, N.J., 1838*), engineer, inventor. Grandson of James Alexander; father of Edwin A. and Robert L. Stevens. Graduated King's College (present Columbia), 1768. After Revolutionary War services, principally as a collector of money in New Jersey for the Continental Army, he served as surveyor-general for the eastern division of New Jersey, 1782–83, and then turned to the development of an estate in and around what is presently Hoboken, N.J. About 1788 his attention was drawn to the work of John Fitch and James Rumsey in the development of the steamboat; thereafter until his death he devoted himself to advancement of mechanical transport on water and on land. Concentrating on the use of steam, he began to work out designs of boilers and engines unique for the time. In 1791, having helped to bring about the framing of the act of 1790 establishing the first patent laws, he was among the first dozen citizens to receive U.S. patents; his inventions included an improved vertical steam boiler and an improved Savery-type steam engine, both intended for boat propulsion. He associated himself c. 1797 with Nicholas I. Roosevelt and Robert R. Livingston in the project of building a steam engine and boat. Livingston obtained the exclusive privilege of steamboat operation on the waters of New York State, and with this incentive the partners set to work with added vigor. An experimental boat, the *Polacca*, proved unsuccessful in trials on the Passaic River, but experiments were continued and in 1800 a definite twenty-year partnership agreement was consummated. Shortly after, Stevens became consulting engineer for the Manhattan Company, organized to furnish an adequate water supply to New York City. He convinced the directors that steam pumping engines should be used and installed equipment of his own design, but it was not efficient, and a Boulton & Watt type of engine was later substituted. In 1803 after further experimentation, he secured a patent for a multi-tubular boiler. In the following year his small twin-screw steamboat *Little Juliana* traveled back and forth across the Hudson. Spurred to greater effort, Stevens determined to inaugurate an adequate steam ferry system between Hoboken and New York, and to operate a regular line of steamboats on the Hudson between New York and Albany. Before his *Phoenix* was completed, however, Fulton's *Clermont* made its successful voyage in 1807 to Albany and return. The achievement discouraged Stevens, since it was made under a monopoly granted to Livingston and Fulton, and he still considered himself bound by the earlier agreement with Roosevelt. He also had come to believe that any monopoly was unconstitutional. Restricted by law from using the Hudson River, he sent the *Phoenix* to Philadelphia in 1809. It made the trip successfully and is considered the first sea-going steamboat in the world. Thereafter, plying between Philadelphia and Trenton, it served as a unit in the cross-state transportation system which was controlled and managed by Stevens's sons.

About 1810, he began giving greater attention to adaptation of the steam engine as motive power for railways. He induced the New Jersey Assembly in February 1815 to create a railway company. Eight years later, the Pennsylvania legislature authorized a railway company and empowered Stevens to build it. The necessary funds, however, could not be raised, although in 1825 he designed and built an experimental locomotive and operated it on a circular track on his estate in Hoboken to prove the feasibility of the scheme. This was the first American-built steam locomotive, though it was never used for actual service on a railroad. Stevens also proposed an armored navy, bridging the Hudson from New York to Hoboken, a vehicular tunnel under the Hudson, and an elevated railway system for New York City.

STEVENS, JOHN AUSTIN (*b. New York, N.Y., 1795; d. New York, 1874*), banker. Brother of Alexander H. Stevens; father of John A. Stevens (1827–1910). President of the Bank of Commerce, New York City, 1839–66.

STEVENS, JOHN AUSTIN (*b. New York, N.Y., 1827; d. Newport, R.I., 1910*), financier, author. Son of John A. Stevens (1795–1874). Founded the *Magazine of American History* which he edited, 1877–81; author of *Colonial Records of the New York Chamber of Commerce* (1867), *The Burgoyne Campaign* (1877), *Albert Gallatin* (1884) and other works.

STEVENS, JOHN HARRINGTON (*b. Brompton Falls, Quebec, Canada, 1820; d. 1900*), Minnesota pioneer, agricultural editor. After service in the Mexican War, Stevens settled *c.* 1849 on a claim on the west bank of the Mississippi at the Falls of St. Anthony. His house was the first dwelling erected in the present city of Minneapolis.

STEVENS, JOHN LEAVITT (*b. Mount Vernon, Maine, 1820; d. Augusta, Maine, 1895*), journalist, diplomat. Associated with James G. Blaine on the *Kennebec Journal* of Augusta, Maine. Stevens served as U.S. minister to Paraguay, Uruguay, Norway and Sweden between 1870 and 1883. As minister resident to Hawaii and later as envoy extraordinary, 1889–93, he played a prominent part in the 1893 rebellion whereby Queen Liliuokalani was dethroned and a provisional government under Sanford B. Dole was installed.

STEVENS, ROBERT LIVINGSTON (*b. Hoboken, N.J., 1787; d. Hoboken, 1856*), engineer, naval architect, inventor. Son of John Stevens; brother of Edwin A. Stevens. Assistant to his father in his steam propulsion experiments, he helped in the design and construction of the steamboat *Phoenix*, 1808, and with Moses Rogers took her on her pioneer sea voyage from New York to Philadelphia, 1809. Recognized in time as a leader in naval architecture, he designed and had built more than twenty steamboats and ferries which incorporated his successive inventions. Among these were the method of installing knees of wood and iron inside the ship's frame, a "cam-board" cut-off for steam engines, and balanced poppet valves. He also devised an improved type of walking beam, introduced a forced-draft firing system under boilers and was first to perfect a marine tubular boiler. The split paddle wheel, "hog-framing" for boats, and the present type of ferry slip were also his inventions. He played an important part in managing the family transportation business in New Jersey and was president and engineer *post* 1830 of the Camden & Amboy Railroad for which he designed the T-rail, the hook-headed spike and other rail devices. In November 1831, at the throttle of the locomotive *John Bull*, he inaugurated the first steam railway service in New Jersey at Bordentown. *Post* 1815, he worked for many years on problems of ordnance and the armoring of warships.

STEVENS, THADDEUS (*b. Danville, Vt., 1792; d. Washington, D.C., 1868*), lawyer, political leader. Lame and sickly from birth, Stevens grew up in the semi-frontier atmosphere of Peacham, Vt., and early developed a strong feeling of sympathy for the poor and an intense dislike of caste in any form. Graduating from Dartmouth, 1814, he studied also at the University of Vermont. Beginning the study of law in Vermont, he continued his studies while teaching in an academy at York, Pa., and began practice at Gettysburg, Pa., 1816, engaging also *post* 1826 in the manufacture of iron. Seeing much of the slavery system as it operated in nearby Maryland, he became an extreme hater of the institution and defended numerous fugitive slaves without fee. Entering politics as a violent opponent of Andrew Jackson, he first became prominent at the Anti-Masonic Convention in Baltimore, Md., 1831, where he delivered a notable speech condemning secret orders. As a member of the Pennsylvania House, elected on the Anti-Masonic ticket, 1833–41, he became known as a brilliant advocate for the extension of free public education and as a defender of the protective tariff. At his retirement from the legislature, he was recognized as one of the strongest men in his state. Removing to Lancaster, Pa., 1842, he devoted himself for a while to his legal practice.

Elected to Congress on the Whig ticket, 1848, he took a leading place among the free-soilers, setting his face against any compromise with slavery in the territories and denouncing that institution as a national curse and crime in fierce invective speeches. Disgusted with Whig moderation, he left Congress in March 1853. Playing a vigorous part in formation of the Republican party in Pennsylvania, he was re-elected to Congress, 1858. Denouncing slavery and pleading for a protective tariff, he also warned the

South to secede at its peril and called upon President Buchanan to exert the full federal authority against those who were flouting the national government. Passed over for a cabinet post on President Lincoln's election, he became chairman of the House ways and means committee and exerted wide authority over measures dealing with the prosecution of the Civil War. Though in matters of finance he loyally supported the administration, his ideas of policy diverged sharply from Lincoln's and he was a constant thorn in the side of the administration on matters concerning the conduct of the war. By 1864 he had become so far committed to stern measures as to speak of the necessity to exterminate the "rebels" and to desolate the South. He laid down the rule that the South was outside the Constitution and that the law of nations alone would limit the victorious North in determining the conditions of Southern restoration. He considered the Wade-Davis Bill an inadequate measure for Reconstruction and was probably secretly hostile to Lincoln's 1864 candidacy. His almost fanatical fight to maintain Republican party supremacy in the government was motivated by economic as well as political considerations.

After Lincoln's assassination, Stevens prepared to give battle to Andrew Johnson on the question of reducing the South to a "territorial condition." To Stevens, it was a "conquered province"; he would make it choose between Negro suffrage and reduced representation. When Congress met in December 1865, a joint committee on Reconstruction was appointed on his motion; as chairman of the House group, Stevens was the dominant member of the committee. The first open rupture with President Johnson came in February 1866 on the Freedmen's Bureau Bill which Stevens belligerently pushed and Johnson vetoed. Stevens succeeded in passing the Civil Rights Bill and a revised Freedmen's Bureau Bill over Johnson's veto, and in April 1866 the joint committee reported the Fourteenth Amendment which Congress adopted. A sweeping Republican victory in the congressional elections of 1866 gave Stevens the whip-hand over Johnson and the South. The first use he made of his triumph was to impose military Reconstruction and the Fifteenth Amendment upon the South. When Johnson removed Edwin M. Stanton as U.S. secretary of war early in 1868, Stevens reported an impeachment resolution based on the president's supposed disregard of the Tenure of Office Act. Although a member of the committee to draft articles of impeachment and one of the managers to conduct the case before the Senate, Stevens took little part in the trial itself.

Shortly after Johnson's acquittal, Stevens died. An intense partisan, his career was marred by a harsh and vindictive temper which in his last years made him frankly vengeful towards the South. His policy aroused fierce resentment, accentuated racial antagonism, cemented the Solid South, and postponed for many decades any true solution of the race problem.

Had tolerance been added to his character, he might have been a brilliant instead of a sinister figure in American history.

STEVENS, THOMAS HOLDUP (*b. Charleston, S.C., 1795; d. probably Washington, D.C., 1841*), naval officer. Father of Thomas H. Stevens (1819–1896). Appointed midshipman, 1809, he won distinction on the Niagara frontier in the War of 1812 and commanded the sloop *Trippe* in the battle of Lake Erie. He later served in a variety of ship and shore commands and was promoted captain, 1836.

STEVENS, THOMAS HOLDUP (*b. Middletown, Conn., 1819; d. Rockville, Md., 1896*), naval officer. Son of Thomas H. Stevens (1795–1841). Appointed midshipman, 1836. During the Civil War he served with great credit in blockade and other duties along the Eastern coast and was the commander of the desperate night boat attack, Sept. 8, 1863, on Fort Sumter. He was later active in Union operations in the Gulf of Mexico. Promoted rear-admiral, 1879, he retired, 1881.

STEVENS, WALTER HUSTED (*b. Penn Yan, N.Y., 1827; d. Vera Cruz, Mexico, 1867*), Confederate brigadier-general, military engineer. Graduated West Point, 1848. Served at various times as chief engineer, Army of Northern Virginia; supervised building of defenses of Richmond.

STEVENS, WILLIAM ARNOLD (*b. Granville, O., 1839; d. 1910*), New Testament scholar. Graduated Denison University, 1862; studied also at Harvard, Newton Theological Institution, Leipzig and Berlin. Taught Greek at Denison; was professor of New Testament interpretation at Rochester Theological Seminary, 1877–1910. A scholarly theological conservative, he was author, among other books, of *A Harmony of the Gospels for Historical Study* (1894).

STEVENS, WILLIAM BACON (*b. Bath, Maine, 1815; d. 1887*), Episcopal clergyman, historian, physician. Brother-in-law of Henry Coppée. Assistant bishop of Pennsylvania, 1862–65, he succeeded to the see. He was instrumental in the founding of Lehigh University and was author of a number of scholarly works on religious and historical subjects, among them, *A History of Georgia from Its First Discovery, etc.* (1847, 1859).

STEVENSON, ADLAI EWING (*b. Christian Co., Ky., 1835; d. Chicago, Ill., 1914*), lawyer. Removed to Bloomington, Ill., 1852. Began practice of law at Metamora, Ill., 1858; practiced in Bloomington *post* 1868. Congressman, Democrat, from Illinois, 1875–77 and 1879–81, he served without particular distinction but made many friends. As first assistant postmaster-general, 1885–89, he performed with extraordinary tact his unpleasant task of removing Republican postmasters to make way for deserving Democrats. As vice-president of the United States, 1893–97, he presided gracefully over the Senate and did not embarrass the administration by pressing his well-known "soft money" views. In the campaign of 1900 he was William J. Bryan's running mate, and in 1908 ran unsuccessfully for the governorship of Illinois.

STEVENSON, ANDREW (*b. Culpeper Co., Va., 1784; d. Albemarle Co., Va., 1857*), lawyer, Virginia legislator. Nephew of Lewis Littlepage. Congressman, Democrat, from Virginia, 1821–34, he was a member of the influential so-called "Richmond Junto" and speaker of the House, 1827–34. A Unionist during the nullification controversy, he later was a supporter of Martin Van Buren and served as U.S. minister to Great Britain, 1834–41. He was essentially a machine politician; his career lacks the stamp of a strong personality.

STEVENSON, CARTER LITTLEPAGE (*b. near Fredericksburg, Va., 1817; d. Caroline Co., Va., 1888*), Confederate major-general, civil engineer. Nephew of Andrew Stevenson. Graduated West Point, 1838. Served principally in the western campaigns of the Civil War; commanded the right of the Confederate lines during the siege of Vicksburg. Taken prisoner there, he was later exchanged and fought in the Atlanta and Carolina campaigns.

STEVENSON, JAMES (*b. Maysville, Ky., 1840; d. New York, N.Y., 1888*), ethnologist, explorer. Employed in government engineering work *post* 1856, he became a member of the U.S. Geological Survey of the Territories under Ferdinand V. Hayden with whom he made explorations of the Missouri, Columbia and Snake rivers; in 1871 he took an active part in the survey of the Yellowstone region. He climbed to the summit of the Great Teton, 1872, and is believed to have been the first white man to do so. Continuing in the survey under the directorship of John W. Powell, he was in the service of the Bureau of Ethnology *post* 1879. Becoming interested in Indian language and customs, he collected a great deal of material on the Pueblo Indians and their former settlements, including large collections of culture material both ancient and modern which he catalogued in Bureau reports and which constitute a valuable and, in most respects, unique contribution to science.

STEVENSON, JOHN JAMES (*b. New York, N.Y., 1841; d. New Canaan, Conn., 1924*), geologist. Graduated present New York University, 1863; Ph.D., 1867. After teaching at West Virginia University, and service on the geological surveys of Ohio and Pennsylvania and also with the Wheeler surveys in the West, he was professor of geology at New York University, 1881–1909. He was particularly interested in stratigraphic problems and those relating to coal.

STEVENSON, JOHN WHITE (*b. Richmond, Va., 1812; d. Covington, Ky., 1886*), lawyer, Kentucky legislator. Congressman, Democrat, from Kentucky, 1857–61, he was a moderate Confederate sympathizer during the Civil War. Elected lieutenant-governor of Kentucky, 1867, he became governor in September of that year and served with ability and sanity until 1871. As U.S. senator, 1871–77, he was a close adherent of Jeffersonian principles.

STEVENSON, MATILDA COXE EVANS (*b. San Augustine, Texas, c. 1850; d. 1915*), ethnologist. Wife and professional associate of James Stevenson. Author of an encyclopedic study on the Zuñi Indians (*Twenty-third Annual Report of the Bureau of American Ethnology, 1901–1902*, published, 1904) and other important works in her field.

STEVENSON, SARA YORKE (*b. Paris, France, 1847; d. 1921*), archaeologist. Raised and educated abroad, she resided in Philadelphia, Pa., *post c.* 1867. Author of a number of papers on Egyptian archaeology and other subjects, she helped establish the Museum at the University of Pennsylvania, and was literary editor of the Philadelphia *Public Ledger*, 1908–21.

STEWARD, IRA (*b. New London, Conn., 1831; d. Plano, Ill., 1883*), labor leader, proponent of eight-hour day legislation. A believer in labor solidarity and an ultimate socialistic state, Steward, with George E. McNeill and George Gunton, joined with leading American members of the Marxian International Workingmen's Association to form the International Labor Union, 1878, for organization of unskilled laborers. In the realm of theory, Steward held that shorter hours of labor developed leisure-time wants, hence a demand for higher wages. Increased wages in turn would compel introduction of better technique, which would make mass production possible. Mass production, to be stable, would need mass purchasing power which must be protected against the down-drag of the unemployed by progressive shortening of hours of labor in accordance with an index of unemployment. Ultimately, the workers would be able to buy the capitalists out and so inaugurate socialism.

STEWARDSON, JOHN (*b. Philadelphia, Pa., 1858; d. near Philadelphia, 1896*), architect. Studied in Paris; was partner with Walter Cope *post* 1886. Primarily an artist, Stewardson specialized in English Gothic; his work at University of Pennsylvania, Bryn Mawr and Princeton had great influence for good on American educational building design.

STEWART, ALEXANDER PETER (*b. Rogersville, Tenn., 1821; d. Biloxi, Miss., 1908*), Confederate lieutenant-general, educator. Graduated West Point, 1842. An artillery officer, Stewart rose to divisional command in the western campaigns of the Civil War and in the Atlanta campaign; at the end of the war, he was the commander of the Army of Tennessee. He was chancellor of the University of Mississippi, 1874–86.

STEWART, ALEXANDER TURNEY (*b. Lisburn, Ireland, 1803; d. 1876*), merchant. Emigrated to New

York City *c.* 1820; opened a small lace shop in New York, 1823. A canny observer of fashion and the market, he prospered in his own trade and made good profits by sale of stock bought at auction during the panic of 1837. By 1850 he had the largest dry-goods establishment in the city (operating in his own building at Broadway and Chambers St., built 1846), and in 1862 he opened at Broadway and Ninth St. what was then the largest retail store in the world. Profiting also by Civil War contracts, he acquired numerous other interests in the United States and abroad. Purchasing always for cash, he was a strict disciplinarian of his employees and his wage policy was poor even for his time. Garden City, N.Y., was built up by him as a "model town" for persons of moderate means.

STEWART, ALVAN (*b. South Granville, N.Y., 1790; d. 1849*), lawyer, Abolitionist. Settled in Utica, N.Y., *c.* 1832, where he practiced. Founder and first president of the New York Anti-Slavery Society, he won by his vivid, erratic speeches the title of "humorist" of the anti-slavery movement. He advanced the argument that, since slaves were deprived of their freedom without due process, the institution of slavery was unconstitutional. With William L. Garrison, he was responsible for disruption of the national anti-slavery movement, 1840, and was presiding officer at the convention which organized the Liberty Party.

STEWART, ANDREW (*b. Fayette Co., Pa., 1791; d. 1872*), lawyer, Pennsylvania legislator and official. Congressman, Democrat and National Republican, from Pennsylvania, 1821–29, 1831–35; congressman, Whig, 1843–49. Ardent in support of protection and internal improvements, he was known in his time as "Tariff Andy."

STEWART, CHARLES (*b. Philadelphia, Pa., 1778; d. Bordentown, N.J., 1869*), naval officer. Trained in the merchant service, he was commissioned lieutenant, U.S. Navy, 1798, and in 1800 made a very successful cruise in command of the schooner *Experiment*. Capturing two armed French vessels and recapturing a number of American merchantmen, he also provided convoy protection. After further distinguished service in the troubles with the Barbary states, 1802–06, he was commissioned captain. He won further fame during the War of 1812, notably as commander of the *Constitution* from December 1813 to the end of the war. In varied service thereafter, he was made "senior flag officer," 1859, and in 1862 became rear-admiral on the retired list. He was the grandfather of Charles Stewart Parnell, eminent as an advocate in the British Parliament of Irish home rule.

STEWART, EDWIN (*b. New York, N.Y., 1837; d. South Orange, N.J., 1933*), naval officer. Brother of John A. Stewart. Joining the U.S. Navy, September 1861, as assistant paymaster, he was associated with the business and supply activities of the service thereafter until his retirement, 1899. Largely instrumental in effecting the reform of naval purchase procedures and their centralization in a bureau of supplies and accounts, he was appointed paymaster-general with rank of commodore, 1890, and retired as rear-admiral. He distinguished himself particularly in his handling of navy supply problems during the Spanish-American War.

STEWART, ELIZA DANIEL (*b. Piketon, O., 1816; d. Hicksville, O., 1908*), schoolteacher, temperance advocate. Formed Woman's League in Osborne, O., 1873, the first organization in the Women's Christian Temperance Union movement, and was a leader in the rapid extension of the work.

STEWART, GEORGE NEIL (*b. London, Ontario, Canada, 1860; d. Cleveland, O., 1930*), physiologist. Raised in Scotland. Educated at University of Edinburgh, he received, among other degrees, M.A., 1883, D.Sc., 1887, and M.D., 1891; he also worked at Berlin on electro-physiology, and was one of the group of investigators who worked at Cambridge under Sir Michael Foster. Stewart's investigations were chiefly on the velocity of blood flow, on temperature regulation and on the cardiac nerves. Coming to America in 1893 as an instructor at Harvard, he was professor of physiology at Western Reserve University, 1894–1903, and head of the department of physiology at the University of Chicago, 1903–07. *Post* 1907 he was director of the H. K. Cushing Laboratory of Experimental Medicine at Western Reserve. While in America, Stewart continued his investigations, at first chiefly on circulation time, and then on the electric conductivity of the blood and hemolysis as an approach to the problem of cell permeability. From 1910 to 1915 he devised and applied a calorimetric method of measuring the blood flow suitable for clinical use. In association with J. M. Rogoff, he worked, 1916–23, on the epinephrine output of the adrenal glands, and from 1924 to 1927 investigated the course of the removal of these glands, establishing in 1927 the efficiency of extracts of adrenal cortex in clinical use.

STEWART, HUMPHREY JOHN (*b. London, England, 1854; d. San Diego, Calif., 1932*), organist, composer. Settled in San Francisco, Calif., on emigration to America, 1886; was organist to a number of churches; served as municipal organist of San Diego *post* 1915.

STEWART, JOHN AIKMAN (*b. New York, N.Y., 1822; d. New York, 1926*), banker. Brother of Edwin Stewart. Planned organization of U.S. Trust Co., N.Y., 1852–53, and served as its president, 1864–1902, thereafter becoming chairman of the board. As senior trustee of Princeton University, he served as president of Princeton *pro tempore*, 1910–12.

STEWART, PHILO PENFIELD (*b. Sherman, Conn., 1798; d. Troy, N.Y., 1868*), Congregational missionary, inventor. Co-founder with John J. Shipherd of Oberlin College; received patent for his invention of the "Oberlin stove," 1834, which he deeded to that institution.

STEWART, ROBERT (*b. Sidney, O., 1839; d. Sialkot, Punjab, India, 1915*), United Presbyterian clergyman, missionary to India.

STEWART, ROBERT MARCELLUS (*b. Truxton, N.Y., 1815; d. St. Joseph, Mo., 1871*), lawyer, Missouri legislator and railroad promoter. Anti-Benton Democrat governor of Missouri, 1857–61. Taking a middle ground on the secession issue at first, Stewart upheld the Crittenden compromise but later took a strong stand for the Union.

STEWART, WILLIAM MORRIS (*b. Galen, N.Y., 1827; d. 1909*), lawyer. Raised in Ohio, he attended Yale College, 1848–50. Removing to California, 1850, he engaged in mining, studied law and was admitted to practice, 1852. Author of the first rules and regulations for quartz mining in Nevada Co., 1853, he entered a law-partnership in San Francisco, 1854, with Henry S. Foote, whose daughter he married. Removing to Nevada, 1859, he came to the front through his energy and knowledge of mining law; successful as counsel for the original claimants to the Comstock Lode, he was thereafter retained by some of the largest mining companies in the West. Chairman of the judiciary committee of the Nevada constitutional convention, he served as U.S. senator, Republican, from Nevada, 1864–75. Instrumental in securing passage of the mining laws of 1866 and 1872. He advocated President Andrew Johnson's impeachment and voted for his conviction, and in 1869 was author of the Fifteenth Amendment to the Constitution in the form in which it was finally adopted. Re-elected to the U.S. Senate, 1887, he served continuously until 1905. Perhaps the first member of either House of Congress to propose federal aid for reclamation of arid lands in the West, he directed his efforts mainly, however, toward the remonetization of silver. His successful campaigns in 1893 and 1899 were conducted as a member of the Silver Party. As senior counsel for the Roman Catholic prelates of California, he presented one of the winning arguments before the Hague Court in the controversy with Mexico over the Pious Fund, 1902. A lifelong friend and adviser of Leland Stanford, he was one of the first trustees of Stanford University.

STEWART, WILLIAM RHINELANDER (*b. New York, N.Y., 1852; d. New York, 1929*), capitalist, philanthropist. Appointed a commissioner of the New York State board of charities, 1882, he served the board as president, 1894–1903, 1907–23. He organized the New York State Conference of Chari-

ties and Corrections, 1900, and a like New York City conference, 1910. He engaged also in many personal philanthropies and much civic work.

STICKNEY, ALPHEUS BEEDE (*b. Wilton, Maine, 1840; d. St. Paul, Minn., 1916*), lawyer, railroad builder. Removed to Minnesota, 1862; settled in St. Paul, 1869. Associated with a number of railroads as counsel and manager, he is remembered particularly for his connection with the Chicago Great Western and its antecedent lines. His original ideas on railroad finance and operation were set forth in his book *The Railway Problem* (1891).

STIEGEL, HENRY WILLIAM (*b. near Cologne, Germany, 1729; d. Charming Forge, near Womelsdorf, Pa., 1785*), ironmaster, glassmaker, known as "Baron" von Stiegel. Emigrated to Philadelphia, Pa., 1750; settled near Brickerville, Lancaster Co., Pa., c. 1752. Acquired an iron manufactory, 1758, which he expanded and named Elizabeth Furnace; there he made all sorts of iron castings including stoves, soap kettles and sugar-making equipment and became by 1760 one of the most prosperous ironmasters in the country. In 1762 he laid out and promoted the town of Manheim, Lancaster Co.; there, early in 1764, he began building a glass factory which by 1767 was in full operation and which was supplemented in 1769 by a second factory. The works produced, in addition to window and sheet glass, the beautiful Stiegel glassware now eagerly sought by collectors. A spendthrift and over-ambitious in business ventures, Stiegel began to suffer hard times in 1772 and by 1774 was obliged to sell his properties, becoming a bankrupt.

STIEGLITZ, JULIUS (*b. Hoboken, N.J., 1867; d. Chicago, Ill., 1937*), chemist. Brother of the photographer Alfred Stieglitz. Ph.D., University of Berlin, 1889. A teacher of chemistry at University of Chicago *post* 1892 and chairman of the department, 1915–33, Stieglitz made important researches in four major fields of organic chemistry: molecular rearrangements, homogeneous catalysis, the theory of indicators, and stereochemistry in organo-nitrogen compounds. He is considered one of the founders of physico-organic chemistry and was author of the important *The Elements of Qualitative Chemical Analysis* (1911). He played an important role in overcoming the lack of synthetics from Germany during World War I and served later as an adviser to the Chemical Foundation. [*Supp. 2*]

STILES, EZRA (*b. North Haven, Conn., 1727 o.s.; d. New Haven, Conn., 1795*), Congregational clergyman, scholar, educator. Graduated Yale, 1746. After further study of theology, he was licensed to preach, 1749, and in the same year appointed tutor at Yale. During his six years in this position he became noted as a public orator; he also engaged in electrical experimentation at the instance of his friend and correspondent Benjamin Franklin. Troubled in mind for some years as to the truth of Christian dogma, he made a long, patient study of the Bible and of Christian evidences before accepting ordination and installation as pastor of the Second Church of Newport, R.I., 1755. Extremely conscientious in his ministerial duties, he maintained a number of outside activities and a voluminous correspondence with outstanding people at home and abroad. Librarian of the Redwood Library, Newport, 1756–76, he was an ardent antiquarian, a very competent Orientalist and a scientific experimenter. Recognized as probably the most learned man in New England, he was made a member of the American Philosophical Society, 1768; meanwhile, in 1763, he had played an important part in the founding of Rhode Island College (present Brown University). He was a strong advocate of American rights and liberties and a supporter of the Revolution. Removing from Newport in March 1776, he lived in several towns before he accepted the offered presidency of Yale College, March 1778. Stiles carried Yale through a difficult period with reasonable success, teaching Hebrew, ecclesiastical history, philosophy, scientific subjects and, for a time, theology, in addition to doing his administrative work. The most notable event of his administration was a change in the college charter whereby several of the state officials were made members of the corporation *ex officio* and certain financial aid from the state was secured. Although Stiles wrote much, he published very little. His manuscripts, edited by Franklin B. Dexter, have yielded two posthumous works of historical importance: *The Literary Diary of Ezra Stiles* (1901) and *Extracts from the Itineraries . . . of Ezra Stiles, etc.* (1916).

STILES, HENRY REED (*b. New York, N.Y., 1832; d. 1909*), physician, genealogist, local historian. Among his valuable studies of the history of early New England and New York were *The History of Ancient Windsor, Connecticut* (1859), and *A History of the City of Brooklyn* (1867–70). Intermittent in his practice of medicine, he conducted a sanitorium at Lake George, N.Y., *post* 1888.

STILL, ANDREW TAYLOR (*b. Jonesville, Va., 1828; d. Kirksville, Mo., 1917*), farmer, Union soldier, founder of osteopathy. Raised in Missouri, he resided in Kansas, 1853–75, where he entered on the practice of medicine and worked out his theory that "all the remedies necessary to health exist in the human body . . . they can be administered by adjusting the body in such condition that the remedies may naturally associate themselves together . . . and relieve the afflicted." Returning to Missouri, 1875, he settled at Kirksville, Mo., in 1892. In that year he incorporated the American School of Osteopathy, thereafter teaching at the school, writing and practicing.

STILL, WILLIAM (*b. Burlington Co., N.J., 1821; d. Philadelphia, Pa., 1902*), Negro leader, reformer.

Settling in Philadelphia, 1844, he became a clerk of the Pennsylvania Society for the Abolition of Slavery, 1847, remaining in that post until *c.* 1861 when he went into business. Very active in the work of assisting runaway slaves to freedom, he was author of *The Underground Railroad* (1872), one of the best accounts available of that operation. Until the end of his life Still continued active in promoting the welfare of his race through legislation and charitable activity, displaying courage and independence.

STILLÉ, ALFRED (*b. Philadelphia, Pa., 1813; d. Philadelphia, 1900*), physician. Brother of Charles J. Stillé. M.D., University of Pennsylvania, 1836; studied also in Europe, principally in Paris, France. Professor of the theory and practice of medicine, University of Pennsylvania, 1864–83, he received numerous professional honors. Author of *Elements of General Pathology* (1848), the first American book on the subject; he was also co-author with John M. Maisch of the *National Dispensatory* (1879).

STILLÉ, CHARLES JANEWAY (*b. Philadelphia, Pa., 1819; d. Atlantic City, N.J., 1899*), educator, historian. Brother of Alfred Stillé. Graduated Yale, 1839. Outstanding worker for the U.S. Sanitary Commission during the Civil War. Accepted appointment in 1866 as professor of English in the University of Pennsylvania. As provost of the university, 1868–80, he showed unusual qualities as an educational leader and executive, arousing community interest in the university and opening new departments—among them, science (1872), music (1877) and dentistry (1878). Removal of the university to its present site was accomplished by Stillé and he secured a considerable extension of its endowment. Among his numerous books, *The Life and Times of John Dickinson* (1891) may be mentioned.

STILLMAN, JAMES (*b. Brownsville, Texas, 1850; d. New York, N.Y., 1918*), banker, capitalist. Raised in Connecticut and in New York City. A protégé of Moses Taylor, Stillman prospered first as a cotton trader, expanding his interests gradually into other industries. Named president of the National City Bank, 1891, he held that office until 1909 and was thereafter chairman of the board. Under his management the bank took a foremost place in serving the great industrial and financial combines that flourished at the end of the 19th century and in the first decade of the 20th; it had close contacts with the Standard Oil financiers headed by H. H. Rogers and William Rockefeller.

STILLMAN, SAMUEL (*b. Philadelphia, Pa., 1737 o.s.; d. Boston, Mass., 1807*), Baptist clergyman. Held principal pastorate at First Baptist Church, Boston, 1765–1807; was named among original trustees of Rhode Island College (present Brown University), 1764. Active and influential in the affairs of his denomination, he was noted as a preacher. His election sermon before the General Court, 1779, contained an interesting argument for the necessity of inserting a Bill of Rights in the constitution of Massachusetts and for separation of church and state.

STILLMAN, THOMAS BLISS (*b. Plainfield, N.J., 1852; d. 1915*), chemist, expert in water- and milk-supply problems. B.S., Rutgers, 1873; studied also in Germany. Noted as a consultant for industry, he also taught at Stevens Institute of Technology where he was professor of analytical chemistry, 1886–1902, and head of the chemical department, 1902–09. Author of *Engineering Chemistry, etc.* (1897) and of a number of articles in scientific journals. He held many patents for manufacturing processes and experimented in production of synthetic foods.

STILLMAN, THOMAS EDGAR (*b. New York, N.Y., 1837; d. France, 1906*), lawyer, specialist in admiralty and corporation law. Helped establish new principles of American maritime law in cases of the *Scotland* (105 *U.S.*, 24), the *Pennsylvania* (19 *Wallace*, 125), and the *Atlas* (93 *U.S.*, 302); in later years devoted much time to corporation management.

STILLMAN, WILLIAM JAMES (*b. Schenectady, N.Y., 1828; d. Surrey, England, 1901*), landscape painter, journalist, diplomat. A close friend of the celebrated English critic John Ruskin, Stillman had a varied career which included service as U.S. consul at Rome, 1862–65, and in Crete, 1865–68. Settling in London, England, he was employed for many years as a London *Times* special correspondent.

STILWELL, SILAS MOORE (*b. New York, N.Y., 1800; d. New York, 1881*), lawyer, banking reformer, New York legislator. Responsible as an assemblyman for passage of the Stilwell Act (1831), abolishing imprisonment for debt in New York.

STILWELL, SIMPSON EVERETT (*b. Tennessee, 1849; d. Cody, Wyo., 1903*), army scout, peace officer. Raised in Missouri and Kansas, he became an army scout at Fort Dodge, 1867. While operating out of Fort Wallace with Maj. G. A. Forsyth's company in September 1868, Stilwell eluded a hostile Indian cordon to bring relief when the company was surrounded on the Arikaree Fork of the Republican River by Cheyennes and Sioux under Chief Roman Nose. He continued to serve irregularly as a scout under Custer, Miles, Mackenzie and other army officers until 1881. He served thereafter as a deputy marshal at various places in Oklahoma.

STIMPSON, WILLIAM (*b. Roxbury, Mass., 1832; d. Ilchester, Md., 1872*), naturalist. Encouraged in his studies by Augustus A. Gould and J. L. R. Agassiz, he served as naturalist to the North Pacific Exploring Expedition, 1852–56, and spent a number of years thereafter in classifying the material gathered in that time. His collections and works were destroyed in the Chicago fire of October 1871, together with much other scientific material which had been loaned

to him for comparative study. He was author of many papers on mollusca and crustacea published mainly by the Smithsonian Institution.

STIMSON, ALEXANDER LOVETT (*b. Boston, Mass., 1816; d. Glens Falls, N.Y., 1906*), expressman. Author, among other works, of *History of the Express Companies: and the Origin of American Railroads* (1858).

STIMSON, LEWIS ATTERBURY (*b. Paterson, N.J., 1844; d. Shinnecock Hills, N.Y., 1917*), surgeon. Graduated Yale, 1863; M.D., Bellevue Hospital Medical School, 1874. Practiced in New York City. Taught at medical college of the University of the City of New York (present New York University), 1883–98. Instrumental in founding Cornell University Medical College, he was professor of surgery there, 1898–1917. Author of *A Practical Treatise on Fractures and Dislocations* (1899), a classic in the subject, and other works.

STINESS, JOHN HENRY (*b. Providence, R.I., 1840; d. 1913*), lawyer, Union soldier, expert in canon law. Judge, supreme court of Rhode Island, 1875–1904, serving for four years as chief justice.

STIRLING, LORD WILLIAM. [See ALEXANDER, WILLIAM, 1726–1783.]

STITH, WILLIAM (*b. Charles City Co., Va., 1707; d. Williamsburg, Va., 1755*), Anglican clergyman, educator, historian. B.A., Queen's College, Oxford, 1727/28. Appointed master of the grammar school at William and Mary, 1731, he served also as chaplain to the House of Burgesses. Rector of Henrico Parish, Henrico Co., 1736–1751/52, he was qualified as president of the College of William and Mary on Aug. 14, 1752, and served in that post uneventfully until his death. He is principally remembered for his *History of the First Discovery and Settlement of Virginia* (Williamsburg, Va., 1747; London, England, 1753), the earliest important secondary account of the colony and one which has influenced most subsequent interpretations of the history of Virginia under the London Company.

STOBO, ROBERT (*b. Glasgow, Scotland, 1727; d. place unknown, c. 1772*), soldier. Emigrated as a young man to Virginia. As a merchant, enjoyed patronage of Governor Dinwiddie. A captain in the Virginia militia, he was with George Washington at Fort Necessity, 1754, and was made a hostage. Escaping from prison in Quebec, he reached the British forces at Louisbourg in the spring of 1759 and served ably in the expedition against Quebec. Commissioned captain in the 15th Regiment of Foot, he was in service until about 1770 at which time his name disappeared from the Army List. The *Memoirs of Major Robert Stobo* appeared posthumously in London (1800).

STOCKARD, CHARLES RUPERT (*b. Stoneville, Miss., 1879; d. 1939*), biologist, anatomist. Graduated Mississippi A. & M. College, 1899, 1901; Ph.D., Columbia, 1907. A teacher at Cornell University Medical College *post* 1907, he became professor in 1911 and head of the anatomical laboratories. A lifelong student of the relative effects of environmental and hereditary factors upon the development of animals, Stockard was a co-discoverer of the method of timing the reproductive cycle of the female which later led to discovery of the ovarian hormones. Managing editor, *American Journal of Anatomy*, 1921–38, he served as president of the board of scientific directors of the Rockefeller Institute for Medical Research, 1935–39. [*Supp. 2*]

STOCKBRIDGE, HENRY (*b. Baltimore, Md., 1856; d. 1924*), jurist. Son of Henry S. Stockbridge; nephew of Levi Stockbridge. Prominent in Baltimore civic and legal affairs, he served as a judge of the supreme bench of Baltimore, 1896–1911, and as a judge of the Maryland court of appeals, 1911–23.

STOCKBRIDGE, HENRY SMITH (*b. North Hadley, Mass., 1822; d. Baltimore, Md., 1895*), lawyer, Maryland legislator. Brother of Levi Stockbridge; father of Henry Stockbridge. Originally a Whig, he early became a Republican and was a strong Unionist during the Civil War. A leader in the constitutional reform which abolished slavery in Maryland, he was active in support of Negro rights.

STOCKBRIDGE, HORACE EDWARD (*b. Hadley, Mass., 1857; d. Atlanta, Ga., 1930*), agricultural chemist and editor, educator. Son of Levi Stockbridge. Graduated Massachusetts Agricultural College, 1878; Ph.D., Göttingen, 1884. Taught at Massachusetts Agricultural College and in Japan; president of North Dakota Agricultural College, 1890–94. Associated with Florida Agricultural College, 1897–1902, he was later editor of the *Southern Ruralist* and the *Southern Farm and Dairy*.

STOCKBRIDGE, LEVI (*b. Hadley, Mass., 1820; d. Amherst, Mass., 1904*), agriculturist, educator. Father of Horace E. Stockbridge; brother of Henry S. Stockbridge. Mainly self-educated and a pioneer in agricultural experiment, he served at various times in the Massachusetts legislature and was a member of the State Board of Agriculture. A shaper of the curriculum at Massachusetts Agricultural College *post* 1867, he served there as professor of agriculture, 1869–80, and was president of the college, 1880–82. His investigations dealt primarily with plant feeding, and he published the first formulae for fertilizers for specific crops.

STOCKDALE, THOMAS RINGLAND (*b. Greene Co., Pa., 1828; d. Summit, Miss., 1899*), lawyer, Confederate soldier. Removed to Mississippi, 1856. As congressman, Democrat, from Mississippi, 1887–95, he employed a unique argument against tariffs, pointing out that much of the burden of protection fell upon Negroes in agricultural work.

STÖCKHARDT, KARL GEORG (*b. Chemnitz, Saxony, 1842; d. St. Louis, Mo., 1913*), Lutheran clergyman. Disapproving of the state church in Saxony, Stöckhardt emigrated to St. Louis, Mo., where he served as pastor, 1879–1913, and as a professor in Concordia Theological Seminary. He had a strong influence on the teaching and preaching of the Missouri Synod.

STOCKTON, CHARLES G. (*b. Madison, O., 1853; d. Buffalo, N.Y., 1931*), physician, specialist in internal medicine. M.D., University of Buffalo, 1878. Successful as a practitioner and consultant in Buffalo, and as a professor *post* 1887 at his *alma mater*.

STOCKTON, CHARLES HERBERT (*b. Philadelphia, Pa., 1845; d. Washington, D.C., 1924*), naval officer. Graduated U.S. Naval Academy, 1865. A specialist in international law, Stockton retired as rear-admiral, 1907, after long and various service. First delegate at the Declaration of London Conference, 1908–09; served without salary as president of George Washington University, 1910–18.

STOCKTON, FRANK RICHARD (*b. Philadelphia, Pa., 1834; d. Washington, D.C., 1902*), author. Trained as a wood-engraver. Stockton contributed to the *Riverside Magazine for Young People* the stories which were collected as *Ting-a-Ling Tales* in 1870; he was thereafter employed mainly as an editor and writer. Assistant editor of *St. Nicholas Magazine*, 1873–81, he was at the same time a frequent contributor to *Scribner's Monthly* and the *Century*. The popular success of *Rudder Grange* (1879) encouraged him to live entirely by his writing. Stockton's many novels and stories were worked out of a vein of absurd invention which he had discovered that he possessed and which the public liked. However circumstantial he might be in his stories, his imagination dealt with a world of cheerful impossibility, and his tales are in effect loose-knit comic operettas. Among them may be mentioned *The Casting Away of Mrs. Lecks and Mrs. Aleshine* (1886), *The Dusantes* (1888), *The Adventures of Captain Horn* (1895) and such classic short stories as "The Lady or the Tiger?" (first appearance, *Century Magazine*, November 1882) and "The Transferred Ghost" (1882). In addition to his fiction, Stockton was author of several volumes of local history including *Buccaneers and Pirates of Our Coasts* (1898).

STOCKTON, JOHN POTTER (*b. Princeton, N.J., 1826; d. 1900*), lawyer, New Jersey politician and official. Son of Robert F. Stockton. Elected U.S. senator, Democrat, from New Jersey, March 1865, he became the center of a famous controversy over his right to be seated which terminated adversely to him a year later. Elected to the U.S. Senate again, 1869, he served through 1875 and was New Jersey attorney-general, 1877–97.

STOCKTON, RICHARD (*b. Princeton, N.J., 1730; d. Princeton, 1781*), lawyer, New Jersey provincial legislator, Revolutionary patriot. Father of Richard Stockton (1764–1828). Graduated College of New Jersey (Princeton), 1748; studied law under David Ogden. Successful in practice, he served as a provincial councilor, 1768–75, and was regarded as a moderate in his opposition to Crown policy. Elected to the Continental Congress, June 1776, he heard the closing debate on the Declaration of Independence of which he was a signer; he also served on several important congressional committees in the summer and fall of 1776. Betrayed to the British by Loyalists late in the year, he was imprisoned at Perth Amboy and New York. In shattered health on his release, he returned to find his estate "Morven" pillaged. He remained an invalid until his death.

STOCKTON, RICHARD (*b. near Princeton, N.J., 1764; d. near Princeton, 1828*), lawyer, farmer, politician. Son of Richard Stockton (1730–1781). U.S. senator, Federalist, from New Jersey, 1796–99; congressman, Federalist, 1813–15. Conspicuous in opposition to the War of 1812. He approved highly of the U.S. Constitution but felt that it had not been improved by a single one of its amendments. He was the father of Robert F. Stockton.

STOCKTON, ROBERT FIELD (*b. Princeton, N.J., 1795; d. 1866*), naval officer. Son of Richard Stockton (1764–1828). Appointed midshipman, 1811, he served with credit under Commodore John Rodgers in the War of 1812; he also distinguished himself later in the war with Algiers and on duty in the Mediterranean, 1816–20. After further duty in suppressing slave traders and pirates, he engaged in private business while on furlough, 1828–38. Promoted captain, 1838, and returning to active service, he interested himself in application of steam power in the U.S. Navy and was commander of the U.S.S. *Princeton*, 1843–45.

As war with Mexico was imminent, he was ordered to proceed in U.S.S. *Congress* to the Pacific and reinforce the U.S. squadron there. When he arrived at Monterey, Calif., July 1846, war had already begun. Relieving Commodore J. D. Sloat on July 23, he began military operations for the seizure of California. Entering Los Angeles in August, he issued a proclamation declaring California a territory of the United States and organized a civil and military government, assuming for himself the title of governor and commander-in-chief. Forced to abandon further ambitious plans because of the recapture of Los Angeles by the Mexicans, he joined with the forces of Gen. S. W. Kearny early in January 1847, repossessed Los Angeles and ended the war on California soil. Superseded soon thereafter, he resigned from the navy, May 1850. As U.S. senator, Democrat, from New Jersey, 1851–53, he urged several naval reforms, including the abolition of flogging.

STOCKTON, THOMAS HEWLINGS (*b. Mt. Holly, N.J., 1808; d. Philadelphia, Pa., 1868*), Methodist Protestant clergyman, notable pulpit orator.

STOCKWELL, JOHN NELSON (*b. Northampton, Mass., 1832; d. 1920*), mathematical astronomer. Raised in Ohio, Stockwell was mainly self-educated and came to notice first as editor of an almanac. Employed as a computer with the U.S. Coast Survey and the U.S. Naval Observatory; taught at Case School of Applied Science, 1881–88. His chief contributions, made over a period of seventy years, dealt with the theory of the moon's motion or with the computation of eclipses.

STODDARD, AMOS (*b. Woodbury, Conn., 1762; d. near present Maumee, O., 1813*), lawyer, soldier. An artilleryman in the Revolution, Stoddard returned to the U.S. Army in 1798 after practicing law and service as a Massachusetts official and legislator. Commissioned captain in the 2nd Artillery, 1798, he was promoted major, 1807, and died during the siege of Fort Meigs. Meanwhile, he had served as first civil and military commandant of Upper Louisiana, 1804, receiving the cession of that territory early in March and acting as governor until the end of September. He was author of *Sketches, Historical and Descriptive, of Louisiana* (1812).

STODDARD, CHARLES WARREN (*b. Rochester, N.Y., 1843; d. 1909*), author. Removed to San Francisco, Calif., 1855; published verses in the *Golden Era*, 1861–63, which were collected in *Poems* (edited by Bret Harte, 1867). Converted to Catholicism, 1867, he traveled widely during the succeeding twenty years and was for a short time secretary to Mark Twain in London. After teaching English for a time at Notre Dame and Catholic universities, he lived in Monterey, Calif., *post* 1906. As a writer he is remembered chiefly for *South-Sea Idyls* (1873), although his other books about the same region contain much delightful writing.

STODDARD, DAVID TAPPAN (*b. Northampton, Mass., 1818; d. Seir, Persia, 1857*), Congregational clergyman. Nephew of Arthur and Lewis Tappan. Missionary among the Nestorians in Persia, 1843–48, 1851–57.

STODDARD, ELIZABETH DREW BARSTOW (*b. Mattapoisett, Mass., 1823; d. New York, N.Y., 1902*), novelist, poet. Married Richard H. Stoddard, 1851. Encouraged by her husband, she became a contributor to periodical publications of her day. She wrote fiction praised for its realism by Nathaniel Hawthorne and others, although she lacked skill in plotting and her work showed a morbid strain. Among her books were *The Morgesons* (1862), *Two Men* (1865) and *Temple House* (1867).

STODDARD, JOHN FAIR (*b. Greenfield, N.Y., 1825; d. Kearny, N.J., 1873*), educator, mathematician, author of a number of superior textbooks in mathematics.

STODDARD, JOHN LAWSON (*b. Brookline, Mass., 1850; d. near Meran, Tyrol, Austria, 1931*), lecturer, writer. Highly successful as a travel lecturer, he was author, among other books, of the *John L. Stoddard's Lectures* (1897-98, with later supplements).

STODDARD, JOHN TAPPAN (*b. Northampton, Mass., 1852; d. Northampton, 1919*), chemist. Nephew of David T. Stoddard. Graduated Amherst, 1874; Ph.D., Göttingen, 1877. Taught physics and chemistry at Smith College *post* 1878 and was chairman of department of chemistry there *post* 1897.

STODDARD, JOSHUA C. (*b. Pawlet, Vt., 1814; d. Springfield, Mass., 1902*), inventor, apiarist. Invented and patented (1855) a steam calliope which he later manufactured; also devised and patented hay-raking machines (1861, 1870 and 1871).

STODDARD, RICHARD HENRY (*b. Hingham, Mass., 1825; d. New York, N.Y., 1903*), poet, critic, editor. Husband of Elizabeth D. B. Stoddard. An iron moulder by trade, Stoddard won reputation as a writer *post* 1845 and did much worthy, if derivative and ephemeral, work. Personally popular among writers of his time, he achieved an important position in criticism, and with his wife turned his home into a center of New York literary life. Among his numerous volumes of collected verse, *Poems* (1851), *Abraham Lincoln: An Horatian Ode* (1865) and *Poems* (1880) may be cited.

STODDARD, SOLOMON (*b. Boston, Mass., 1643; d. Northampton, Mass., 1728/29*), Congregational clergyman. Grandfather of Jonathan Edwards (1703-1758) and progenitor of a long line of distinguished persons. Graduated Harvard, 1662; was first librarian of Harvard, 1667-74. Pastor at Northampton, Mass., *post* 1672, Stoddard accepted the Half-Way Covenant and introduced in his church *ante* 1677 the practice called "Stoddardeanism," which allowed many of the privileges of full church membership to professing Christians even when they were not certain they were in a state of grace. Although most of the churches in western Massachusetts accepted Stoddard's view, his grandson, Jonathan Edwards, rejected it and was therefore dismissed from his pastorate at Northampton in which he had succeeded Stoddard.

STODDARD, WILLIAM OSBORN (*b. Homer, N.Y., 1835; d. Madison, N.J., 1925*), author, inventor. Graduated University of Rochester, 1858. As editor of an Illinois newspaper, 1858-60, Stoddard was a strong supporter of Abraham Lincoln whom he served as a secretary, 1861-63. He was author of over a hundred books, among them, *Inside the White House in War Times* (1890) and some seventy-six excellent stories for boys.

STODDART, JAMES HENRY (*b. Barnsley, England, 1827; d. Sewaren, N.J., 1907*), actor. Emigrated to New York City, 1854; was associated with the companies of James W. Wallack, Laura Keene, Joseph Jefferson and Albert M. Palmer. His most successful role was in Maclaren's *Beside the Bonnie Briar Bush post* 1901.

STODDART, JOSEPH MARSHALL (*b. Philadelphia, Pa., 1845; d. Elkins Park, Pa., 1921*), editor, publisher. First American publisher and representative in America of Gilbert and Sullivan, also of Oscar Wilde.

STODDERT, BENJAMIN (*b. Charles Co., Md., 1751; d. 1813*), Revolutionary soldier, merchant. Served with great ability as first secretary of the U.S. Navy, 1798-1801. Supervised plans for new vessels; established and located navy yards.

STOECKEL, CARL (*b. New Haven, Conn., 1858; d. Norfolk, Conn., 1925*), philanthropist, patron of music. Originated and sponsored the Norfolk Music Festival, presented, 1900-23.

STOEK, HARRY HARKNESS (*b. Washington, D.C., 1866; d. Urbana, Ill., 1923*), mining engineer, editor, educator. Organized department of mining engineering at University of Illinois, which he headed, 1909-23. Wrote a number of technical articles on coal mining which changed that occupation from a rule-of-thumb trade to an engineering science; maintained lifelong interest in vocational education of miners.

STOEVER, MARTIN LUTHER (*b. Germantown, Pa., 1820; d. Philadelphia, Pa., 1870*), educator. Principal of the Academy at Gettysburg, 1842-51; professor of history and Latin, Gettysburg College, 1844-70. Secretary for a number of years of the General Synod, Evangelical Lutheran Church, he was an editor of the *Evangelical Review*, 1857-61, and sole editor, 1862-70.

STOKES, ANSON PHELPS (*b. New York, N.Y., 1838; d. New York, 1913*), merchant, banker, civic reformer. Brother of William E. D. and Olivia E. P. Stokes.

STOKES, FREDERICK ABBOT (*b. Brooklyn, N.Y., 1857; d. New York, N.Y., 1939*), publisher. Became partner in White & Stokes, 1881; later published over imprint of White, Stokes & Allen, Frederick A. Stokes & Brother and Frederick A. Stokes Co. [*Supp. 2*]

STOKES, MONTFORT (*b. Lunenburg Co., Va., 1762; d. Fort Gibson, Indian Territory, 1842*), planter, North Carolina public official and legislator. Uncle of Joseph M. Street. U.S. senator, Democrat, from North Carolina, 1816-23; governor of North Carolina, 1830-32; U.S. Indian commissioner and agent, 1833-42.

STOKES, OLIVIA EGLESTON PHELPS (*b. New York, N.Y., 1847; d. Washington, D.C., 1927*), philanthropist. Sister of Anson P. and William E. D. Stokes. Active in many charitable activities with her sister, Caroline P. Stokes; chief patron of the Phelps-Stokes

Fund which Caroline had endowed prior to her death in 1909.

STOKES, ROSE HARRIET PASTOR (*b. Russian Poland, 1879; d. Frankfurt-am-Main, Germany, 1933*), agitator. Emigrated to America as a young girl; married a son of Anson P. Stokes, 1905; was long associated with left-wing Socialist and Communist activity.

STOKES, WILLIAM EARL DODGE (*b. New York, N.Y., 1852; d. New York, 1926*), capitalist, real estate operator. Brother of Anson P. and Olivia E. P. Stokes.

STONE, AMASA (*b. Charlton, Mass., 1818; d. 1883*), capitalist, railroad builder. Brother-in-law of William Howe; father-in-law of John Hay and Samuel Mather. A carpenter by trade, Stone prospered as holder of the rights to the Howe truss bridge. Contracting with others to build the Cleveland, Columbus & Cincinnati Railroad in 1849, he became its superintendent and president and made his residence in Cleveland. He played a great part in the industrial development of the Cleveland area. As managing director of the Lake Shore & Michigan Southern, he cooperated with the Rockefeller interests by allowing them preferential shipping rates. He was a principal benefactor of Western Reserve University.

STONE, BARTON WARREN (*b. near Port Tobacco, Md., 1772; d. Hannibal, Mo., 1844*), frontier evangelist, leader in the Christian denomination in Kentucky and Ohio.

STONE, CHARLES POMEROY (*b. Greenfield, Mass., 1824; d. New York, N.Y., 1887*), Union brigadier-general. Blamed and imprisoned for the Union defeat at Ball's Bluff, Oct. 21, 1861, he was later exonerated and served in the Port Hudson and Red River campaigns. He served in the Egyptian army, 1870–83, becoming chief of staff and lieutenant-general.

STONE, DAVID (*b. near Windsor, N.C., 1770; d. Wake Co., N.C., 1818*), planter, lawyer, North Carolina governor and jurist. Congressman, (Democrat) Republican, from North Carolina, 1799–1801; U.S. senator, 1801–07, 1813–14. Lost prestige with the electorate during his second term as senator for opposing administration measures for the War of 1812.

STONE, DAVID MARVIN (*b. Oxford, Conn., 1817; d. Brooklyn, N.Y., 1895*), editor, publisher. Associated with the N.Y. *Journal of Commerce* post 1849, he became its editor-in-chief in 1866 and held that post until 1893. He was also president of the New York Associated Press, 1869–c. 1894.

STONE, ELLEN MARIA (*b. Roxbury, Mass., 1846; d. Chelsea, Mass., 1927*), Congregational missionary in Bulgaria, 1878–1902. Her seizure and captivity by brigands, 1901–02, attracted world-wide attention.

STONE, GEORGE WASHINGTON (*b. Bedford Co., Va., 1811; d. Montgomery, Ala., 1894*), jurist. Raised in Tennessee; admitted to the Alabama bar, 1834. Judge of Alabama circuit court, 1843–49; associate justice, Alabama supreme court, 1856–65, 1876–84. *Post* 1884 he served as chief justice, at first by appointment and afterwards by election. An earnest advocate of judicial reform, Stone labored to raise the standards of his court which had been demoralized by war and Reconstruction.

STONE, HORATIO (*b. Jackson, N.Y., 1808; d. Carrara, Italy, 1875*), sculptor, physician, Union Army surgeon.

STONE, JAMES KENT (*b. Boston, Mass., 1840; d. 1921*), educator, Roman Catholic clergyman, Passionist. Son of John S. Stone. Graduated Harvard, 1861. After service in the Union Army, he became a teacher of Latin at Kenyon College, took orders in the Protestant Episcopal Church and was president of Kenyon, 1867. President of Hobart College, 1868–69, he resigned and became a Catholic in December 1869. Joining the Paulists, he was ordained in the Catholic priesthood, 1872, but withdrew in 1876 to join the more severe Congregation of the Passion wherein he took the name in religion of Father Fidelis. Thereafter he achieved high distinction in his order, holding a number of administrative offices and founding its work in South America.

STONE, JOHN AUGUSTUS (*b. Concord, Mass., 1800; d. Philadelphia, Pa., 1834*), playwright, actor. Author of a number of plays and adaptations which are no longer extant, he wrote his most important play, *Metamora*, for Edwin Forrest. It was first produced at the Park Theatre, N.Y., December 1829, and provided Forrest with one of his most popular parts.

STONE, JOHN MARSHALL (*b. Milan, Tenn., 1830; d. Mississippi, 1900*), politician, Confederate officer. As Democratic governor of Mississippi, 1876–82 and 1890–96, Stone reorganized the state government on the basis of control by whites, tempered the extravagances of the recent Carpetbag administrations, and, in his second administration, provided for the perpetuation of white control by the provisions of the 1890 state constitution. He served briefly before his death as president of Mississippi A. and M. College (present Mississippi State). He was an able administrator and of high personal character.

STONE, JOHN SEELY (*b. West Stockbridge, Mass., 1795; d. Cambridge, Mass., 1882*), Episcopal clergyman, educator. Father of James K. Stone. An eloquent preacher and a leader in the evangelical school, he held a number of pastorates, taught theology in the Philadelphia Divinity School, 1862–67, and was dean and professor of theology at Episcopal Theological School, Cambridge, Mass., 1867–76.

STONE, JOHN WESLEY (*b. Wadsworth, O., 1838; d. Lansing, Mich., 1922*), lawyer, jurist. Removed to

Michigan *c.* 1856. Held state and federal offices in Michigan; served as a state circuit judge; was congressman, Republican, from Michigan, 1877–81. Elected to the state supreme court, 1909, he served with ability until his death.

STONE, LUCY (*b. near West Brookfield, Mass., 1818; d. Dorchester, Mass., 1893*), reformer, pioneer in the woman's rights movement. Graduated Oberlin, 1847. An ardent Abolitionist, she lectured widely on this subject *post* 1848, losing no opportunity at the same time to lecture on the inferior position of her sex. She led in calling the first national Woman's Rights convention, Worcester, Mass., 1850. On her marriage to Henry B. Blackwell, 1855, she gained notoriety by insistence on keeping her maiden name as a symbol of equality. Thereafter, with the aid of her husband, she continued and extended her labors and helped form the American Woman Suffrage Association which concentrated on gaining the suffrage by states. With her husband, she edited the *Woman's Journal post* 1872.

STONE, MELVILLE ELIJAH (*b. Hudson, Ill., 1848; d. New York, N.Y., 1929*), journalist. Co-proprietor, *Chicago Daily News,* 1875–88, he sold out his interest to his partner, Victor F. Lawson, and after several years of travel, engaged for a while in banking. On becoming general manager of Associated Press of Illinois, 1893, he secured exclusive right for use of Reuter's news in the United States and continued to head the Associated Press after its reorganization in New York (1900) until his retirement, 1921. A man of constructive mind, executive powers and engaging personality, he fostered the co-operative principle on which the Associated Press was based, kept its news free of partisanship and bias, and opposed sensationalism. He was also active in persuading official European news sources to deal fairly with American correspondents and played a part behind the scenes in settlement of the Russo-Japanese War by treaty at Portsmouth, N.H., 1905.

STONE, ORMOND (*b. Pekin, Ill., 1847; d. Clifton Station, Va., 1933*), astronomer. Brother of Melville E. Stone. Director of Cincinnati Observatory, 1875–82; of University of Virginia McCormick Observatory, 1882–1912. Founded *Annals of Mathematics,* 1884.

[*Supp.* 1]

STONE, RICHARD FRENCH (*b. near Sharpsburg, Ky., 1844; d. Indianapolis, Ind., 1913*), physician. Author, among other works, of *Biography of Eminent American Physicians and Surgeons* (1894, 1898).

STONE, SAMUEL (*b. Hertford, England, 1602; d. Hartford, Conn., 1663*), Puritan clergyman. Emigrated to Massachusetts with Thomas Hooker and John Cotton, 1633. Removing to the Connecticut settlement, he selected the site of Hartford, negotiated its purchase from the Indians and settled there, 1636. After Hooker's death in 1647, he remained sole minister of the church at Hartford until his own death. Although his idea of church government approached Presbyterianism more than Independency, he was steadfastly supported by a majority of his congregation.

STONE, THOMAS (*b. Charles Co., Md., 1743; d. Alexandria, Va., 1787*), lawyer, planter, Maryland legislator. As member of the Continental Congress for the greater part of the period 1775–78, he was a signer of the Declaration of Independence and did important work on the committee which framed the Articles of Confederation.

STONE, WARREN (*b. Saint Albans, Vt., 1808; d. New Orleans, La., 1872*), physician, surgeon. M.D., Berkshire Medical Institution, Pittsfield, Mass., 1831. In practice at New Orleans *post c.* 1833, he served on the staffs of several hospitals, founded one of the earliest private hospitals in the United States, (1839) and taught at the Medical College of Louisiana (later Tulane), 1834–72. During the Civil War, he was surgeon-general of Louisiana. Among his professional achievements were the first resection of part of a rib to secure permanent drainage in cases of empyema, the first successful cure for traumatic vertebral aneurism by open incision and packing, and the first use of silver wire for ligation of the external iliac.

STONE, WARREN SANFORD (*b. near Ainsworth, Iowa, 1860; d. Cleveland, O., 1925*), trade-union official. Headed Brotherhood of Locomotive Engineers, 1903–25. Led in struggle to secure better wages and shorter hours by dealing with railway managers through regional groups, thereby finishing one contest before taking up another; favored cooperative ownership of railways and independent political action by labor.

STONE, WILBUR FISK (*b. Litchfield, Conn., 1833; d. Denver, Colo., 1920*), Colorado pioneer and jurist. Raised in the Midwest; removed to Nebraska, 1859, and to Colorado, 1860. Holder of both federal and state offices, he was active in railroad promotion. From 1877 until 1889 he was judge of the state supreme court and of the criminal court of Denver, and from 1891 until 1904 he sat on a unique court appointed to determine Spanish and Mexican land titles in the Southwest.

STONE, WILLIAM (*b. Northamptonshire, England, c. 1603; d. Charles Co., Md., c. 1660*), planter, Maryland colonial official. Emigrated to Virginia *ante* 1628. Appointed proprietary governor of Maryland, 1648, he was engaged in a continuous struggle with the Puritan element of the colony, which climaxed in his defeat in the battle of the Severn, Mar. 25, 1655.

STONE, WILLIAM JOEL (*b. Madison Co., Ky., 1848; d. 1918*), lawyer. Congressman, Democrat, from Missouri (1885–91) and a moderate reformer, he served with tact and ability as governor of Missouri during the troubled period 1893–97. U.S. senator from Missouri *post* 1903, he was a disciple of William J. Bryan and an orthodox Democratic partisan; however, on becoming chairman of the foreign relations committee, 1914, he invited criticism by his steadfast opposition to the involvement of the United States in World War I.

STONE, WILLIAM LEETE (*b. New Paltz, N.Y., 1792; d. New York, N.Y., 1844*), journalist. After experience on a number of newspapers and periodicals, he became a proprietor of the *New York Commercial Advertiser*, 1821. An influential Federalist editor in his time, he is remembered principally for his efforts to arouse interest in the preservation and historical use of the state archives and for several of his works in local history, including *Life of Joseph Brant* (1838), *Life and Times of Red Jacket* (1841) and *Border Wars of the American Revolution* (1843).

STONE, WILLIAM LEETE (*b. New York, N.Y., 1835; d. 1908*), journalist. Son of William L. Stone (1792–1844); nephew of Francis Wayland. Graduated Brown, 1858. Editor and compiler of a number of valuable source works on the history of the American Revolution, notably on the Saratoga campaign.

STONE, WILLIAM OLIVER (*b. Derby, Conn., 1830; d. Newport, R.I., 1875*), portrait painter. Studied with Nathaniel Jocelyn. A prolific and successful portraitist of prominent persons; worked in New York City *post* 1854.

STONE, WITMER (*b. Philadelphia, Pa., 1866; d. Philadelphia, 1939*), naturalist, museum curator and director. Associated *post* 1888 with Academy of Natural Sciences in Philadelphia; editor, *The Auk*, 1912–36. Author, among other works, of *Bird Studies at Old Cape May* (1937), regarded as one of the best of all regional bird books. [*Supp. 2*]

STONEMAN, GEORGE (*b. Busti, N.Y., 1822; d. Buffalo, N.Y., 1894*), soldier. Graduated West Point, 1846. A cavalryman, he served mainly in the Southwest prior to the Civil War. Chief of cavalry, Army of the Potomac, under Gen. George B. McClellan, he was assigned to command the 1st Division, III Corps, and succeeded to command of the corps as major-general, November 1862. When Gen. Hooker took command of the Army of the Potomac, he put Stoneman in charge of the separate corps of cavalry. While in this post Stoneman made a famous raid toward Richmond, Va., April–May 1863, as part of the Chancellorsville campaign. Transferred to the western armies, he commanded the cavalry corps of the Army of the Ohio in the Atlanta campaign, but suffered defeat and capture at Clinton, Ga., early in August 1864. Exchanged, he returned to duty, making another cavalry raid with considerable success into southwestern Virginia in December 1864 and later acting in co-operation with Sherman in the Carolinas. After his retirement from the army for

disability, 1871, he settled near Los Angeles, Calif. As Democratic governor of California, 1883–87, he opposed the increasing power of the railroads in state affairs and in business, and favored legislation encouraging irrigation projects.

STORER, BELLAMY (*b. Cincinnati, O., 1847; d. Paris, France, 1922*), lawyer, diplomat. Nephew of David H. Storer. Graduated Harvard, 1867; law school of Cincinnati College, 1869. Married Maria Nichols, widow of George W. Nichols, 1886. Congressman, Republican, from Ohio, 1891–95, he helped William McKinley in the campaign of 1896 and was appointed U.S. minister to Belgium, 1897. Becoming U.S. minister to Spain, 1899, he successfully handled problems incident to the Spanish-American War, and in 1902 was made U.S. ambassador at Vienna. Popular and successful, he was summarily removed in March 1906 after a dispute with President Theodore Roosevelt.

STORER, DAVID HUMPHREYS (*b. Portland, Maine, 1804; d. Boston, Mass., 1891*), Boston obstetrician, naturalist, collector of rare fishes and shells. Graduated Bowdoin, 1822; Harvard Medical School, 1825; served apprenticeship with John C. Warren (1776–1856). As a practitioner, and as a teacher at Harvard Medical School (dean, 1854–64), he did much to advance obstetrics in the United States; he was also regarded as expert in medical jurisprudence. He was father of Francis H. and Horatio R. Storer, also uncle of Bellamy Storer.

STORER, FRANCIS HUMPHREYS (*b. Boston, Mass., 1832; d. Boston, 1914*), chemist. Son of David H. Storer; brother of Horatio R. Storer. Studied at Lawrence Scientific School; served as assistant to Josiah P. Cooke, and was chemist with U.S. North Pacific exploring expedition, 1853–54. Chemist of the Boston Gas Light Co., *c.* 1858–71, he was associated also in research projects with Charles William Eliot with whom he collaborated in several textbooks and whose sister he married. On Eliot's appointment to the presidency of Harvard, 1869, he appointed Storer professor of agricultural chemistry at the Bussey Institution. Becoming dean of the Institution, 1871, he held both posts until 1907. During this period he performed important research upon soils, fertilizers, forage crops, cereals, vegetables and other products, publishing the results in the *Bulletin of the Bussey Institution*. He was author also of *Agriculture in Some of Its Relations with Chemistry* (1887) and various manuals and textbooks.

STORER, HORATIO ROBINSON (*b. Boston, Mass., 1830; d. Newport, R.I., 1922*), gynecologist, numismatist. Son of David H. Storer; brother of Francis H. Storer. Graduated Harvard, 1850; M.D., Harvard Medical School, 1853; studied also in Paris, London and Edinburgh. Among the early American specialists in gynecology, he wrote and lectured extensively against abortion. After his retirement from practice, 1872, he became a world authority on medallions of medical interest and a notable collector of them.

STOREY, MOORFIELD (*b. Roxbury, Mass., 1845; d. Lincoln, Mass., 1929*), lawyer. Graduated Harvard, 1866. As assistant to Charles Sumner, 1867–69, he was closely connected with the attempt to impeach President Andrew Johnson. Winning an international reputation in the practice of commercial law in Boston *post* 1871, he became a crusader against political corruption, attacking Benjamin F. Butler and James G. Blaine, and leading the Mugwump Republicans during the presidential campaign of 1884. An anti-imperialist and a defender of the rights of Negroes and Indians, he wrote prolifically in support of his opinions. Earnest and courageous, he won little gratitude or popularity by his activity.

STOREY, WILBUR FISK (*b. near Salisbury, Vt., 1819; d. Chicago, Ill., 1884*), journalist. Gaining experience on newspapers in New York, Indiana and Michigan, he made the *Detroit Free Press* one of the leading Democratic newspapers in the West as co-owner and owner, 1853–61. Purchasing the *Chicago Times*, 1861, he was its active head until 1878, making it one of the most prosperous of the Chicago dailies despite a brief suppression for alleged "copperhead" proclivities in 1863 and the destruction of its plant in 1871. Not a writer, but rather a directing executive, Storey emphasized the importance of news and attacked men and issues with vigor and fearlessness.

STORROW, CHARLES STORER (*b. Montreal, Canada, 1809; d. Boston, Mass., 1904*), engineer. Born of American parents and raised in Boston and in Paris, France, Storrow graduated from Harvard, 1829. He studied engineering with Loammi Baldwin and in Paris. Construction engineer and manager, Boston & Lowell Railroad, 1832–45, he then became engineer for the Essex Co. and as such planned, laid out and built the industrial town of Lawrence, Mass. He was father of James J. Storrow.

STORROW, JAMES JACKSON (*b. Boston, Mass., 1837; d. Washington, D.C., 1897*), lawyer. Son of Charles S. Storrow; grandson of James Jackson. Graduated Harvard, 1857. Devoting himself to patent law, he was associated with Chauncey Smith in the long litigation over validity of the Bell Telephone patents, showing himself a master in clear analysis of evidence. He was author of the brief on behalf of Venezuela (1895–96) which brought about British consent to submit the boundary controversy to arbitration.

STORRS, RICHARD SALTER (*b. Longmeadow, Mass., 1787; d. Braintree, Mass., 1873*), Congregational clergyman. Pastor, First Church, Braintree, 1811–73, he was a conspicuous defender of ortho-

doxy and active in home missionary work. He was father of Richard S. Storrs (1821–1900).

STORRS, RICHARD SALTER (*b. Braintree, Mass., 1821; d. Brooklyn, N.Y., 1900*), Congregational clergyman. Son of Richard S. Storrs (1787–1873). Pastor, Church of the Pilgrims, Brooklyn, N.Y., *post* 1846, he was active in Brooklyn's civic, philanthropic and cultural affairs, and won great popularity as a lyceum lecturer.

STORY, ISAAC (*b. Marblehead, Mass., 1774; d. Marblehead, 1803*), poet, miscellaneous writer. Cousin of Joseph Story. A contributor to the *Farmer's Museum* and the *Columbian Centinel* and other papers, he was author of essays modeled on Joseph Dennie's "Lay Preacher" papers and of a number of satirical and serious poems. His best-known verses were published in *A Parnassian Shop . . . By Peter Quince, Esq.* (1801).

STORY, JOSEPH (*b. Marblehead, Mass., 1779; d. Cambridge, Mass., 1845*), lawyer, jurist. Father of William W. Story. Graduated Harvard, 1798; studied law in office of Samuel Sewall, later chief justice of the supreme court of Massachusetts. Began practice at Salem, Mass., 1801. Although he was an avowed follower of Jefferson in a Federalist community, he did well in his profession and was elected to the state legislature where, among other reforms, he made an unsuccessful effort to establish a state court of chancery. He served briefly as a member of Congress, 1808–09, opposing administration policies on the Embargo and naval affairs. Re-elected to the Massachusetts legislature, he served as speaker of the House in January and May 1811. On Nov. 18, 1811, he was appointed an associate justice of the U.S. Supreme Court.

Supreme Court judges at this time also exercised circuit court jurisdiction, and Story's circuit took in Maine, New Hampshire, Massachusetts and Rhode Island. A pioneer in outlining and defining the field of admiralty law for the United States, Story, by his decisions, first put the admiralty jurisdiction of the federal courts on a sound basis. Many of his opinions are still impressive for their breadth of learning, but in some there is a tendency to range beyond the facts and law necessary for judgment in a particular case. However, not a few of his opinions had important legal and constitutional results. His opinion in *Martin vs. Hunter's Lessee* (1816) has been called the keystone of the arch of federal judicial power, holding as it did that appellate jurisdiction of the Supreme Court could rightfully be exercised over the state courts. In the case of the *Thomas Jefferson* (10 *Wheaton*, 428), Story's opinion allayed a mounting feeling in some of the inland states that the federal courts were menacing state common law jurisdiction over inland waters. Story spoke for the court in the case of the *Amistad*, a slave-runner, holding that the human cargo should be freed and sent back to Africa; he also wrote the opinion in the Girard will case. Daniel Webster considered that Story's ablest opinion was his dissent in *Charles River Bridge vs. Warren Bridge* in which he upheld the sanctity of contracts. The facts disprove the often-quoted charge that Story was dominated by John Marshall, whom he failed to succeed as chief justice, in part because Andrew Jackson disliked him and considered him dangerous.

Together with the vast amount of work he performed on the bench, Story was Professor of Law at Harvard, *post* 1829, and may be regarded in a very real sense as a founder of the Harvard Law School. The method of teaching which he devised later resulted in his famous *Commentaries* on bailments, the Constitution, conflict of laws, equity jurisprudence and pleading, agency, partnership and bills and notes, which were published in quick succession between 1832 and 1845. He was author also of a number of other legal treatises and, by his writing, has provided an example of industry and legal scholarship hardly to be equaled. The success of the *Commentaries* was widespread and immediate and provided the author a handsome income and an international reputation. Together with Chancellor James Kent, Story will be remembered as the founder of the equity system in the United States. He drew up the rules of equity practice for the U.S. Supreme Court and the circuit courts in 1842, and among his *Commentaries* those on equity jurisprudence and pleading remain outstanding. A Unitarian, a great lover of conversation, poetry and music, his favorite novelist was Jane Austen.

STORY, JULIAN RUSSELL (*b. Walton-on-Thames, England, 1857; d. Philadelphia, Pa., 1919*), portrait painter. Son of William W. Story.

STORY, WILLIAM EDWARD (*b. Boston, Mass., 1850; d. 1930*), mathematician. Graduated Harvard, 1871; Ph.D., Leipzig, 1875. After teaching at Harvard and at Johns Hopkins where he was associated with J. J. Sylvester, Story was professor of mathematics at Clark University, 1889–1921.

STORY, WILLIAM WETMORE (*b. Salem, Mass., 1819; d. Vallombrosa, Italy, 1895*), sculptor, author. Son of Joseph Story. Graduated Harvard, A.B., 1838; LL.B., 1840. Practiced law with, among others, his brother-in-law, George T. Curtis, and wrote two long-standard legal textbooks; devoted himself in his spare time to painting, modelling and music. After completing a statue of his late father for Mount Auburn Cemetery and also composing his father's biography, he settled in Rome, Italy, 1856, and thereafter devoted his chief efforts to sculpture and travel in Europe. He revisited his own country only occasionally. Intimate friend of Robert and Elizabeth Barrett Browning, Nathaniel Hawthorne and many other distinguished literary and artistic figures, Story led a happy life but one of artistic unfulfillment. His approach to his conceptions was fundamentally intellectual and deficient in intensity. Among his numerous books, *Roba di Roma* (1862) may still be read as an outstanding appreciation of the spirit of contemporary Italy.

STOTESBURY, EDWARD TOWNSEND (*b. Philadelphia, Pa., 1849; d. Chestnut Hill, Pa., 1938*), banker. Entering employ of Drexel & Co. as a clerk, 1866, he rose in successive promotions to senior partner, 1904. Partner also in Drexel's New York City affiliate, the then J. P. Morgan & Co., he was active in the railroad reorganizations and securities underwriting which were responsible for the success of both firms. [*Supp. 2*]

STOTT, HENRY GORDON (*b. Orkney Islands, 1866; d. probably New Rochelle, N.Y., 1917*), electrical engineer. Came to America, 1891. As engineer for Buffalo (N.Y.) Light & Power Co., he constructed its conduit system and major power plant; *post* 1901 he superintended power plants and transmission lines for the Manhattan Railway Co. and the Interboro Rapid Transit, New York City.

STOUGHTON, EDWIN WALLACE (*b. Springfield, Vt., 1818; d. New York, N.Y., 1882*), lawyer. Practiced in New York City *post* 1840; won reputation in patent suits, including the Goodyear rubber, the Wheeler & Wilson sewing machine, and Corliss steam-engine cases. Originally a War Democrat, he became a Republican and served on the commission which investigated the Louisiana vote in the election of 1876; he later spoke in behalf of the Republican position before the Electoral Commission. He was U.S. minister to Russia, 1877–79.

STOUGHTON, WILLIAM (*b. probably England, 1631; d. Dorchester, Mass., 1701*), colonial official. Graduated Harvard, 1650; M.A., New College, Oxford, 1653. Ejected from his Oxford fellowship, 1660, he returned to Massachusetts, 1662, where he held a number of offices and became a political henchman of Joseph Dudley. Named lieutenant-governor of the colony, 1692, under Sir William Phips, he became acting governor, 1694, and except for a brief period, 1699–1700, continued to head the government until his death. As chief justice of oyer and terminer during the Salem witchcraft cases, 1692, he was largely responsible for the tragic aspect they assumed because of his insistence on the admission of "spectral evidence" and by his overbearing attitude.

STOVALL, PLEASANT ALEXANDER (*b. Augusta, Ga., 1857; d. Savannah, Ga., 1935*), Georgia journalist and legislator, diplomat. Graduated University of Georgia, 1875. Editor, *Savannah Press post* 1891; U.S. minister to Switzerland, 1913–20. [*Supp. 1*]

STOW, BARON (*b. Croydon, N.H., 1801; d. 1869*), Baptist clergyman, editor. A powerful evangelical preacher, he held his principal pastorates at the Second Baptist Church, Boston, Mass., 1832–48, and at the Rowe Street Baptist Church, 1848–67.

STOWE, CALVIN ELLIS (*b. Natick, Mass., 1802; d. 1886*), educator. Graduated Bowdoin, 1824. Taught at Dartmouth, Lane Theological Seminary, Bowdoin and Andover Theological Seminary; author of a celebrated *Report on Elementary Instruction in Europe* (1837). Husband of Harriet E. B. Stowe.

STOWE, HARRIET ELIZABETH BEECHER (*b. Litchfield, Conn., 1811; d. Hartford, Conn., 1896*), author. Daughter of Lyman Beecher; sister of Catharine E., Edward, and Henry Ward Beecher; wife of Calvin E. Stowe. A true member of her family in her earnestness, intelligence and devotion to the anti-slavery cause, Mrs. Stowe developed an early taste for writing. She was influenced in choosing an anti-slavery subject for her pen by current discussions of the Fugitive Slave Law and also by her brother Edward Beecher and his wife. While tending her newly born seventh child, she began work on what was to be *Uncle Tom's Cabin, or Life Among the Lowly* which was first published as a serial in the *National Era*, June 5, 1851–April 1, 1852; it was brought out as a book in two volumes by John P. Jewett on March 20, 1852. Within a year of publication the sales of the book had mounted to 300,000; however, Mrs. Stowe received surprisingly little remuneration for her work. She, as well as her novel, became the center of violent controversy, and she was attacked on the grounds of inaccuracy, literary quality and motive. As a picture of American manners, however, *Uncle Tom's Cabin* deserves high rank and at times its style rises to eloquence. The influence of her work in England and on the continent of Europe was very great, winning enormous favor for the anti-slavery cause. Exceedingly industrious as a writer, she continued to pour forth a steady stream of fiction despite distractions of family life, trips to Europe and the like. Over nearly thirty years she wrote, on the average, almost a book a year, including *Dred, A Tale of the Great Dismal Swamp* (1856), *The Minister's Wooing* (1859), and *Oldtown Folks* (1869) which is considered perhaps the richest and raciest of her works. It has been lately said of her that "as the historian of the human side of Calvinism she tempered dogma with affection" and also "the creative instinct was strong in her but the critical was wholly lacking."

STRACHEY, WILLIAM (*fl. 1606–1618*), first secretary of the Virginia colony, historian. A grantee under the second charter to the London Company of Virginia, he sailed for that colony, 1609, with Sir Thomas Gates, reaching Jamestown after shipwreck, 1610; he returned to London, England, late in 1611. His fame rests principally on his letter of 1610 descriptive of the colony (first printed by Samuel Purchas in his *Pilgrimes*, 1625, but previously circulated in manuscript), on his production of the first written code

of laws for Virginia, and on *The Historie of Travaile into Virginia Britannia* (written in 1613). This last work is the most ably written of the contemporary accounts of the region and is a highly authoritative and valuable historical source. It was first printed and published in 1849.

STRAIGHT, WILLARD DICKERMAN (*b. Oswego, N.Y., 1880; d. Paris, France, 1918*), diplomat, financier. Son-in-law of William C. Whitney. Graduated in architecture, Cornell University, 1901. After working in the Chinese customs service and as a newspaper correspondent, he held consular offices in the Far East and served briefly in the U.S. Department of State. He then served as a representative of various banking groups in China, 1909–12. Thereafter resident in the United States, he engaged in promoting American capital investments in foreign countries. With his wife he financed publication of the weekly *The New Republic* (1914).

STRAIN, ISAAC G. (*b. Roxbury, Pa., 1821; d. Aspinwall, present Colón, Panama, 1857*), naval officer, explorer. Conducted exploration of the Isthmus of Darien, 1853, which determined impracticability of a ship-canal route there.

STRANAHAN, JAMES SAMUEL THOMAS (*b. Peterboro, N.Y., 1808; d. Saratoga, N.Y., 1898*), capitalist. Assisted Gerrit Smith in promotion of his Oneida Co., N.Y., properties; was successful as a railroad contractor in New Jersey. *Post* 1844, transferring his activities to Brooklyn, N.Y., he developed the Atlantic Basin there, invested in the East River ferries, and came to be known as a principal civic leader. He was largely responsible for the creation of Brooklyn's Prospect Park and for the consolidation of Brooklyn into the City of New York.

STRANG, JAMES JESSE (*b. Scipio, N.Y., 1813; d. Voree, Wis., 1856*), Mormon leader, founder of the sect known by his name.

STRATEMEYER, EDWARD (*b. Elizabeth, N.J., 1862; d. Newark, N.J., 1930*), juvenile fiction writer, creator of the "Rover Boys" and other series.

STRATON, JOHN ROACH (*b. Evansville, Ind., 1875; d. Clifton Springs, N.Y., 1929*), Baptist clergyman, fundamentalist leader, sensational preacher. Held pastorates in Chicago, Ill., Baltimore, Md., and Norfolk, Va.; *post* 1918 was pastor of Calvary Baptist Church, New York City.

STRATTON, CHARLES SHERWOOD (*b. Bridgeport, Conn., 1838; d. Middleboro, Mass., 1883*), midget, the celebrated "General Tom Thumb" of P. T. Barnum's museum.

STRATTON, SAMUEL WESLEY (*b. Litchfield, Ill., 1861; d. 1931*), physicist. B.S., University of Illinois, 1884. Taught mathematics and physics at Illinois; assistant professor of physics, University of Chicago, 1892–1901. After preparing the plan of a proposed

Bureau of Standards, 1900, he drafted the bill authorizing the establishment of the Bureau and won acceptance for the bill which was passed in 1901. As first director of U.S. Bureau of Standards, 1901–23, he made it a great research center and secured for it an international reputation. He served as president, Massachusetts Institute of Technology, 1923–30.

STRATTON-PORTER, GENE. [See PORTER, GENE STRATTON, 1863–1924.]

STRAUS, ISIDOR (*b. Otterberg, Rhenish Bavaria, 1845; d. at sea, aboard the* Titanic, *1912*), merchant, philanthropist. Brother of Nathan and Oscar S. Straus. Emigrated with family to Georgia, 1854. Prospered in crockery and glassware business; with brother Nathan, became owner of R. H. Macy and Co., New York City, 1896, developing it subsequently into the largest department store in the world. He also developed the Brooklyn, N.Y., store of Abraham & Straus. An enthusiastic Democrat, he served briefly in Congress and twice refused nomination for mayor of New York City.

STRAUS, JESSE ISIDOR (*b. New York, N.Y., 1872; d. New York, 1936*), merchant, diplomat. Son of Isidor Straus; nephew of Nathan and Oscar S. Straus. Associated with the family business of R. H. Macy & Co. *post* 1896, he took over its supervision in 1912 and acted as its president *post* 1919. An active Democrat, Straus served with success as U.S. ambassador to France, 1933–36. He was a benefactor of New York University and Harvard. [*Supp.* 2]

STRAUS, NATHAN (*b. Otterberg, Rhenish Bavaria, 1848; d. New York, N.Y., 1931*), merchant, philanthropist. Brother of Isidor and Oscar S. Straus. Emigrated to Georgia with his family, 1854. A partner in the family crockery and glassware business, and later associated with his brother Isidor in the ownership of R. H. Macy and Co., Nathan Straus is particularly remembered as a pioneer in public health, a strong supporter of Zionism and an active worker in innumerable campaigns for the relief of primary needs to which he devoted a great part of his fortune. During the last 15 years of his life he concentrated his efforts on supplying educational and social agencies for relief in Palestine.

STRAUS, OSCAR SOLOMON (*b. Otterberg, Rhenish Bavaria, 1850; d. New York, N.Y., 1926*), lawyer, diplomat. Brother of Isidor and Nathan Straus. Emigrated with his family to Georgia, 1854. Graduated Columbia, 1871; Columbia Law School, 1873. *Post* 1881 a partner in the family crockery and glassware business, he is chiefly remembered as a diplomat. Prominent in the Democratic party, he served as U.S. minister to Turkey, 1887–89, 1898–1900 and 1909–10, distinguishing himself each time by his tact and success in negotiation. In 1902 he was appointed a member of the Hague Court and was subsequently reappointed in 1908, 1912 and 1920. He

was U.S. secretary of commerce and labor, 1906–09, having become at this time a progressive Republican because of opposition to William J. Bryan. At the Paris Peace Conference, 1918–19, he continued a lifelong career of activity in behalf of his Jewish coreligionists by striving to provide for safeguarding of the rights of Jewish minorities in Europe.

STRAUS, SIMON WILLIAM (*b. Ligonier, Ind., 1866; d. New York, N.Y., 1930*), banker. President, S. W. Straus & Co., 1898–1928. Promoted building of skyscrapers; originated financing of building projects by sale of real estate bonds, 1909.

STRAUSS, JOSEPH BAERMANN (*b. Cincinnati, O., 1870; d. Los Angeles, Calif., 1938*), bridge engineer. C.E., University of Cincinnati, 1892; assistant to Ralph Modjeski, 1899–1902. Originated and developed the Strauss trunnion bascule bridge, also the Strauss lift bridge. Designer and builder of well over 400 bridges of all types including his important modifications of the bascule, he is best known as chief engineer for the Golden Gate Bridge at San Francisco (completed 1937). [*Supp.* 2]

STRAWBRIDGE, ROBERT (*b. near Carrick-on-Shannon, Ireland, date unknown; d. near Towson, Md., 1781*), Methodist preacher. Emigrated to Maryland between 1759 and 1766 where he was the first apostle of Methodism, preaching in his home colony and also in neighboring Virginia, Delaware and Pennsylvania.

STRAWN, JACOB (*b. Somerset Co., Pa., 1800; d. Illinois, 1865*), farmer, livestock dealer. Active *post* 1831 as a grazer and fattener of cattle on pasture tracts in Morgan, Sangamon and LaSalle counties, Ill.

STREET, ALFRED BILLINGS (*b. Poughkeepsie, N.Y., 1811; d. 1881*), lawyer, poet, librarian of the New York State Library.

STREET, AUGUSTUS RUSSELL (*b. New Haven, Conn., 1791; d. New Haven, 1866*), businessman. Graduated Yale, 1812. A notable benefactor of Yale, Street endowed professorships in ecclesiastical history, modern languages and the arts; he was also donor of Street Hall and endowed, in part, the Yale School of Fine Arts.

STREET, JOSEPH MONTFORT (*b. Lunenburg Co., Va., 1782; d. near present Agency City, Iowa, 1840*), frontier journalist, Indian agent. Nephew of Montfort Stokes. Edited controversial Federalist *Western World* in Frankfort, Ky., in 1806–07, and for a time thereafter; on losing libel suit brought against him by Harry Innes, 1812, he removed to Shawneetown, Ill., where he was active in local politics. Appointed agent to the Winnebago tribe, he sought unsuccessfully to protect his wards from encroaching settlement and from frauds.

STRICKLAND, WILLIAM (*b. Philadelphia, Pa., c. 1787; d. Nashville, Tenn., 1854*), architect, engineer, engraver. Studied under Benjamin H. Latrobe. An outstanding exponent of the Greek Revival in America, he designed a number of Philadelphia buildings including the U.S. Custom House (1819), the Bank of the United States (completed, 1824, later the Custom House) and the Merchants' Exchange (1834). At the time of his death he was engaged on the state capitol at Nashville, Tenn. Concurrently with his architectural work, he engaged in engineering work for the Chesapeake and Delaware Canal and others, designed and built the Delaware Breakwater, and made several railroad surveys.

STRINGFELLOW, FRANKLIN (*b. Culpeper Co., Va., 1840; d. Louisa Co., Va., 1913*), Episcopal clergyman, chief of scouts in the Army of Northern Virginia, 1864–65.

STRINGHAM, SILAS HORTON (*b. Middletown, N.Y., 1797; d. Brooklyn, N.Y., 1876*), naval officer. Appointed midshipman, 1809. Served in War of 1812 on frigate *President;* served against Algiers and in suppression of slave trade; commanded *Ohio* in Mexican War. Commodore in 1861, he was a valued adviser of Gideon Welles, and as commander of the Atlantic blockade fleet planned and executed the expedition against forts at Hatteras Inlet, N.C., August 1861. Irked by criticism, he requested release in September; promoted rear-admiral, 1862, he commanded the Boston navy yard until 1865.

STRINGHAM, WASHINGTON IRVING (*b. Yorkshire Center, present Delevan, N.Y., 1847; d. Berkeley, Calif., 1909*), mathematician. Graduated Harvard, 1877, influenced by Benjamin Peirce. Ph.D., Johns Hopkins, 1880. Author of a number of professional papers of high quality, he was professor of mathematics, University of California, 1882–1909.

STROBEL, CHARLES LOUIS (*b. Cincinnati, O., 1852; d. Chicago, Ill., 1936*), civil engineer, specialist in steel-framed structures. As consultant for Burnham & Root and Adler & Sullivan, he helped devise the steel skeleton construction of many early skyscrapers. Active in standardization of the design and manufacture of steel structural shapes, he was originator of the Z-bar and designer of standard I-beam sections. He was author of *A Pocket Companion . . . to the Use of Wrought Iron for Engineers, Architects and Builders* (1881). [*Supp. 2*]

STROBEL, EDWARD HENRY (*b. Charleston, S.C., 1855; d. Bangkok, Thailand, 1908*), diplomat. Entering the U.S. diplomatic service, 1885, as secretary of legation at Madrid, Spain, he held posts thereafter at Washington, D.C., and in Ecuador and Chile. Appointed Bemis Professor of International Law, Harvard Law School, 1898. Became a general adviser to the then Siamese government with rank of minister plenipotentiary, 1903, and effected numerous reforms before his death.

STROMME, PEER OLSEN (*b. Winchester, Wis., 1856; d. 1921*), Lutheran clergyman, Norwegian-American journalist and author.

STRONG, AUGUSTUS HOPKINS (*b. Rochester, N.Y., 1836; d. 1921*), Baptist clergyman, theologian. Graduated Yale, 1857; Rochester Theological Seminary, 1859. Pastor, First Baptist Church, Haverhill, Mass., 1861–65; First Baptist Church, Cleveland, O., 1865–72. President and professor of Biblical theology, Rochester Theological Seminary, 1872–1912; thereafter, president emeritus. Author, among other works, of *Systematic Theology* (1886, 1907–09) and *Philosophy and Religion* (1888). Influenced his one-time parishioner John D. Rockefeller in founding a university under Baptist auspices, an idea which eventuated in refounding of University of Chicago.

STRONG, BENJAMIN (*b. Fishkill-on-Hudson, N.Y., 1872; d. New York, N.Y., 1928*), banker. Official in Bankers' Trust Co., N.Y.; first governor, Federal Reserve Bank of New York, 1914–28.

STRONG, CALEB (*b. Northampton, Mass., 1745; d. Northampton, 1819*), lawyer, Federalist statesman, Massachusetts legislator and official. Graduated Harvard, 1764; studied law under Joseph Hawley; was admitted to Massachusetts bar, 1772. Served on committee for drafting Massachusetts constitution, 1779. Represented Massachusetts in Federal Convention of 1787, advocating annual elections of representatives and choice of a president by Congress, also making the successful motion that the House alone should originate money bills although the Senate might amend them. U.S. senator from Massachusetts, 1789–96, he formed, with Oliver Ellsworth and Rufus King, the bulwark of the administration in the Senate. As Federalist governor of Massachusetts, 1800–07, he was responsible, fair-minded and an able administrator; during his second period as governor, 1812–16, he was in continuous opposition to the national administration and the War of 1812. He approved both the calling of the Hartford Convention in December 1814 and its subsequent report.

STRONG, CHARLES AUGUSTUS (*b. Haverhill, Mass., 1862; d. Fiesole, Italy, 1940*), psychologist, philosopher. Son of Augustus H. Strong; son-in-law of John D. Rockefeller. Graduated University of Rochester, 1884; A.B., Harvard, 1885; studied also in Germany. Influenced by William James and George Santayana. Strong taught briefly at Cornell, Clark, and University of Chicago; he was lecturer in psychology, Columbia University, 1896–1903, and professor of psychology, 1903–13. Author of a number of books, he belonged to the group known as the Critical Realists. [*Supp. 2*]

STRONG, CHARLES LYMAN (*b. Stockbridge, Vt., 1826; d. 1883*), mining engineer. First superintendent of Gould & Curry mine at Virginia City, Nev., (Comstock Lode), 1860–64.

STRONG, HARRIET WILLIAMS RUSSELL (*b. Buffalo, N.Y., 1844; d. near Whittier, Calif., 1926*), horticulturist, civic leader. Wife of Charles L. Strong. Raised in California. Pioneered in California walnut industry; was an early advocate of flood control for irrigation; patented device for impounding debris and water in hydraulic mining, 1893.

STRONG, JAMES (*b. New York, N.Y., 1822; d. Round Lake, N.Y., 1894*), Biblical scholar, businessman. Professor of exegetical theology, Drew Theological Seminary, 1868–93. A learned, conservative scholar.

STRONG, JAMES HOOKER (*b. Canandaigua, N.Y., 1814; d. Columbia, S.C., 1882*), naval officer. Appointed midshipman, 1829. Distinguished for Civil War service as commander of U.S.S. *Monongahela*, notably at Mobile Bay, August 1864, where he put the Confederate ram *Tennessee* out of action. He retired as rear-admiral, 1876.

STRONG, JAMES WOODWARD (*b. Brownington, Vt., 1833; d. Northfield, Minn., 1913*), Congregational clergyman, educator. Brother of William B. Strong. President, Carleton College, 1870–1903.

STRONG, JOSIAH (*b. Naperville, Ill., 1847; d. 1916*), Congregational clergyman, social reformer. A pioneer, with Washington Gladden and Walter Rauschenbusch, in the "social gospel" movement. Strong was author of two influential books, *Our Country* (1885) and *The New Era* (1893), analyzing the social and economic ills of his day and calling for the creation of an ideal society upon earth. Founder of the League for Social Service (later the American Institute for Social Service), 1898, he initiated the "safety first" movement and was an active participant in the establishment of the Federal Council of Churches.

STRONG, MOSES McCURE (*b. Rutland, Vt., 1810; d. Mineral Point, Wis., 1894*), surveyor, lawyer, Wisconsin legislator and official. Settled at Mineral Point, 1836.

STRONG, THEODORE (*b. South Hadley, Mass., 1790; d. 1869*), mathematician, educator. Graduated Yale, 1812. Professor of mathematics and natural philosophy at Hamilton College, 1816–27; at Rutgers College, 1827–61.

STRONG, WALTER ANSEL (*b. Chicago, Ill., 1883; d. 1931*), journalist. Associated *post* 1905 with the *Chicago Daily News*, he served as its publisher, 1925–31. He was active also in many national publishing organizations and in local civic affairs.

STRONG, WILLIAM (*b. Somers, Conn., 1808; d. 1895*), jurist. Graduated Yale, 1828. Admitted to the Philadelphia, Pa., bar, October 1832, he began practice in Reading, Pa. Congressman, Democrat, from Pennsylvania, 1847–51; outstanding justice, supreme court of Pennsylvania, 1857–68. Appointed associate

justice of the U.S. Supreme Court, 1870, he was concerned with Joseph P. Bradley in the 1871 reversal of a previous Supreme Court decision which had held the Legal Tender Act of February 1862 unconstitutional. This action led to the charge that President Grant, by appointing Strong, had "packed" the Court in order to insure such a decision. Strong's position, however, was wholly consistent with his previous record and views on the subject. Until his resignation (December 1880) he remained a power on the Supreme Court bench and is generally regarded as one of the truly great judges of the Court. He has been compared for integrity of character to John Jay.

STRONG, WILLIAM BARSTOW (*b. Brownington, Vt., 1837; d. Los Angeles, Calif., 1914*), railroad official. Brother of James W. Strong. Transformed the Atchison, Topeka & Santa Fé Railroad into a system of national importance as its general manager *post* 1877 and its president, 1881–89.

STRONG, WILLIAM LAFAYETTE (*b. Richland Co., O., 1827; d. 1900*), merchant. Removed to New York City, 1853, where he became wealthy in the dry-goods business. An ardent Republican, he served as reforming mayor of New York City, 1894–97. Appointed Theodore Roosevelt police commissioner.

STROTHER, DAVID HUNTER (*b. Martinsburg, present W. Va., 1816; d. Charles Town, W. Va., 1888*), Union soldier, author, illustrator. A valued contributor to *Harper's New Monthly Magazine*, he produced a number of illustrated articles dealing with life in Virginia which were collected as *Virginia Illustrated, by Porte Crayon* (1857). He was author and illustrator of other superior magazine series which were not reprinted. A Unionist, he served on staff duty throughout the Civil War, receiving brevet of brigadier-general at its close. He was U.S. consul-general at Mexico City, 1879–85.

STRUBBERG, FRIEDRICH ARMAND (*b. Cassel, Germany, 1806; d. Gelnhausen, Germany, 1889*), novelist, physician. Resident in frontier America, 1826–29 and *c.* 1840–54, he used his experiences in Texas and Arkansas as materials for more than fifty volumes of fiction, written in German under the pen name "Armand."

STRUDWICK, EDMUND CHARLES FOX (*b. near Hillsboro, N.C., 1802; d. Hillsboro, 1879*), physician, surgeon. M.D., University of Pennsylvania, 1824. The best type of "country doctor," he practiced at Hillsboro *post* 1826.

STRUVE, GUSTAV (*b. Munich, Bavaria, 1805; d. Vienna, Austria, 1870*), publicist, revolutionary agitator, Union soldier. A lawyer and jurist in his native Germany, he was active in the events which led up to the Revolution of 1848 and was associated with F. K. F. Hecker and Franz Sigel in the abortive republic of Baden. Resident in the United States, 1851–63, he wrote without much success, edited the socialist periodical *Die Sociale Republik,* and worked for cooperation of labor groups in New York and Philadelphia. A 19th-century disciple of Rousseau and Robespierre, he combined noble intentions with opinionated impracticability.

STRYKER, MELANCTHON WOOLSEY (*b. Vernon, N.Y., 1851; d. Rome, N.Y., 1929*), Presbyterian clergyman, hymnologist. President of Hamilton College, 1892–1917, he improved that institution in all departments, procuring large additions to its funds.

STUART, ALEXANDER HUGH HOLMES (*b. Staunton, Va., 1807; d. 1891*), lawyer, Virginia legislator. Son of Archibald Stuart. Graduated University of Virginia, 1828. A follower of Henry Clay, he served in the U.S. Congress, 1841–43. As U.S. secretary of the interior, 1850–53, he proved himself a successful organizer of his department. Active in the Know-Nothing party, he opposed secession as long as opposition was practicable. He was prevented by age from taking any active part in the Civil War but was sympathetic with his section. After the war he played a large part in securing restoration of home rule to Virginia. He was rector of the University of Virginia, 1876–82, 1884–86, and served for some years as a trustee of the Peabody Fund.

STUART, ARCHIBALD (*b. near Staunton, Va., 1757; d. 1832*), Revolutionary soldier, Virginia legislator and jurist. Father of Alexander H. H. Stuart. For many years a prominent leader of the conservative wing of Virginia (Democrat) Republicans, he was judge of the general court of Virginia, 1800–32.

STUART, CHARLES (*b. Jamaica, B.W.I., 1783; d. Lake Simcoe, Canada, 1865*), Abolitionist, mentor of Theodore D. Weld. Settled in Canada *c.* 1814. Author, among other anti-slavery tracts, of *The West India Question* (1832), a widely circulated and influential statement of abolitionist principles.

STUART, CHARLES BEEBE (*b. Chittenango Springs, N.Y., 1814; d. Cleveland, O., 1881*), engineer, Union soldier. Active in New York State railroad construction, 1833–49; proposed railway suspension bridge over Niagara River below the Falls (completed, 1855); supervised construction of navy dry docks, 1849–53. Thereafter a successful businessman and consulting engineer, he was author of, among other works, *The Naval and Mail Steamers of the United States* (1853) and *Lives and Works of Civil and Military Engineers of America* (1871).

STUART, CHARLES MACAULAY (*b. Glasgow, Scotland, 1853; d. La Jolla, Calif., 1932*), Methodist clergyman, educator, editor. Energetic and successful president of Garrett Biblical Institute, 1911–24.

STUART, FRANCIS LEE (*b. Camden, S.C., 1866; d. Essex Fells, N.J., 1935*), civil engineer, specialist in railroad and transportation problems. [*Supp.* 1]

STUART, GILBERT (*b. North Kingstown Township, Kings [later Washington] Co., R.I., 1755; d. Boston, Mass., 1828*), painter. Growing up in Newport, R.I., Stuart early showed talent for drawing and became pupil (*c.* 1769) of a Scottish artist, Cosmo Alexander, then working in Newport. Traveling to Edinburgh with Alexander, who died there in August 1772, Stuart failed in an attempt to support himself by his art and is said to have worked his way home in 1773 or 1774 on a collier bound for Nova Scotia. After busying himself at home in painting and the study of music, he sailed for London in June 1775 as conditions in pre-Revolutionary America were adverse to the practice of art as a profession. After about a year of privation, he wrote to Benjamin West (1738–1820) asking help; receiving an immediate, friendly response, he became West's pupil and later (probably summer 1777) became a member of his household and remained with him for nearly five years. By 1781 he had become an exhibitor at the Royal Academy exhibitions, and his work was attracting favorable notice from London critics. In 1782 his "Portrait of a Gentleman Skating" brought him prominently before the public and he received many commissions.

By 1787, Stuart had become one of the leading portrait painters of London, sharing honors with J. Reynolds, G. Romney and Gainsborough. He was also living in a very lavish style and, because of his lifelong unconcern with business details, came in danger of imprisonment for debt. Accordingly, he left England for Ireland, probably early in the summer of 1787, and scored success all over again in Dublin. Here too, however, he lived injudiciously, fell in debt, and late in 1792 or early in 1793 sailed for New York City hopeful of making enough money to pay off his English and Irish creditors. He also had in mind to make a fortune by painting portraits of George Washington, and to profit through the sale of prints of a Washington portrait. After practicing in New York, he removed to Philadelphia late in November 1794, and opened a studio on the southwest corner of Fifth and Chestnut Streets. As always immediately successful in securing commissions from leaders of intellect and fashion, he completed in Philadelphia a brilliant series of portraits of women and there painted his first two life portraits of Washington. The first, a bust showing the right side of the face and known as the Vaughan Type, was painted in the late winter of 1795. Beginning in April 1796, Washington sat to Stuart for a second life portrait, a life-size standing figure showing left side of face and with right hand outstretched, which is known as the Lansdowne Type. Stuart removed to Germantown, Pa., in the summer of 1796 and during the early fall made a third life portrait of the president, a bust showing the left side of the face, eyes front. This is the well-known "Athenaeum Head," unfinished as to the stock and coat; it is highly idealized.

Stuart followed the seat of government to Washington in 1803. He opened a studio there at F and Seventh Streets and there painted Jefferson, Madison, Monroe and many other contemporary leaders. Removing to Boston, Mass., in the summer of 1805, he lived there for the remainder of his life. Successful as usual, he was overrun with commissions but chronically out of money owing to his indifferent business habits. *Post* 1825, although symptoms of paralysis developed in his left arm, he continued to paint but with difficulty.

Stuart had in his manners much of the formality of the old school, yet his dress was usually disordered, and he took snuff from a tin box holding perhaps half a pound which he used up in a single day. A witty man with a keen sense of the ridiculous, he was celebrated for his gifts as a talker and for his extensive knowledge of the art masters of all ages on whom he could discourse with great charm and learning. A procrastinator, he would only paint when in the mood, was quick to take offense, and impatient of any criticism of his work. Benjamin West is quoted as having said, "It's no use to steal Stuart's colors; if you want to paint as he does you must steal his eyes." Stuart's mastery of the use of what may be called transparent color gave his portraits their lifelike and luminous effect, and it is this quality which ranks them supreme among American portrait paintings. His chief object was always to paint his sitter so as to preserve the character and likeness of the individual. He had the faculty of distinguishing between the accidental and the permanent, between the expression which arises from manners and the more subtle indication of the individual mind. Early in his career he himself said: "For my part, I will not follow any master. I wish to find out what nature is for myself and see her with my own eyes."

STUART, GRANVILLE (*b. Clarksburg, present W. Va., 1834; d. Missoula, Mont., 1918*), Montana pioneer. Raised in Illinois and Iowa. After prospecting in California (September 1852—June 1857), Stuart, on a return journey east with some companions, turned north before reaching Great Salt Lake and entered Beaverhead Valley in present Montana. Proceeding to Deer Lodge Valley in spring 1858, Stuart and a brother, with others, found gold. After further prospecting and varying success he settled permanently in Deer Lodge Valley, 1867, took a leading part in community affairs, and served in the territorial council and legislature. He organized and managed the stock-raising firm of Davis, Hauser and Stuart Co., 1879, and was successful for a time in operations in the Judith Basin. Overstocking of the range

and losses in the winter of 1886–87 brought the firm to disaster. He served thereafter as state land agent, as U.S. minister to Uruguay and Paraguay, and as librarian of the Butte city library. A student and an observer, he was instrumental in founding many of the civic and cultural organizations in Montana. He was author of *Montana As It Is* (1865), and his journals, together with those of his brother James, were published in part as *Forty Years on the Frontier* (1925).

STUART, HENRY ROBSON. [See ROBSON, STUART, 1836–1903.]

STUART, ISAAC WILLIAM (*b. New Haven, Conn., 1809; d. Hartford, Conn., 1861*), local historian, orator. Son of Moses Stuart.

STUART, JAMES EWELL BROWN (*b. Patrick Co., Va., 1833; d. Richmond, Va., 1864*), soldier. Graduated West Point, 1854. Commissioned in the cavalry, he served briefly in Texas. He was in Kansas with the 1st Cavalry for the most part of 1855–61, rising to rank of captain. Resigning from the U.S. Army on learning of the secession of Virginia, he was commissioned lieutenant-colonel of Virginia infantry, May 10, 1861, and captain of Confederate cavalry, May 24, 1861. At the first battle of Bull Run, he protected the Confederate left with the 1st Virginia Cavalry and contributed to the victory. Promoted brigadier-general, September 1861, he brought his cavalry command to high efficiency and showed himself outstanding in outpost duty. His spectacular sweeps around the Union Army during the fighting in northern Virginia won him Gen. R. E. Lee's praise as the "eyes of the army"; skillful though not original in tactics, he was defective in strategic sense but had the rare gift of winning the good will of men as dissimilar as Stonewall Jackson and Longstreet. Dressed like a *beau* and always alive to the dramatic, Stuart was often accused by other officers (some of them in his own corps) of selfish disregard of the achievements of subordinates, of consciously parading himself for admiration and of claiming credit that belonged to others. However, he confounded his critics at Fredericksburg and held the line of the Rappahannock with much skill during the winter, 1862–63. He was also extremely effective in the Confederate victory at Chancellorsville, commanding the II Corps after the wounding of Stonewall Jackson and the incapacitation of A. P. Hill. Meanwhile, he had been promoted major-general and confirmed in that grade, September 1862.

The Gettysburg campaign represents the most disputable chapter in Stuart's career. Expected to play his usual role of screening the army's movements and collecting information and provisions, he engaged in a raid which achieved little in itself and which left Lee groping in the dark at a time when accurate information of the enemy was of the essence. Although he rejoined the main Confederate

Army on the afternoon of July 2 and was ceaselessly active through the rest of the campaign, it has been asserted that he cost Lee the victory by his actions. This matter is still a subject of controversy. Thereafter he served with ability and zeal at his principal task of keeping his commander informed of hostile movements and engaged in a number of lesser battles, very often employing his cavalrymen as infantry. He covered with skill Lee's operations subsequent to Grant's crossing of the Rapidan, May 4, 1864, but was mortally wounded a week later as he endeavored to intercept Gen. P. H. Sheridan's drive on Richmond at Yellow Tavern.

STUART, JOHN (*b. Scotland, c. 1700; d. Pensacola, Fla., 1779*), colonial Indian agent. Emigrated to America *c.* 1748; settled in South Carolina. Superintendent of Indian affairs for the southern district *post* 1762, Stuart fled to Florida, 1775, after his arrest was ordered by the South Carolina assembly on the charge of attempting to incite the Catawba and the Cherokee in the British interest. Thereafter until his death he strove to raise Loyalist companies and secure Indian cooperation with the British but died under censure for his failures and for the enormous amount of money he had spent.

STUART, JOHN TODD (*b. near Lexington, Ky., 1807; d. 1885*), Illinois lawyer, legislator and congressman. Cousin of Mary Todd Lincoln. Practiced law in Springfield, Ill., *post* 1828. Friend, political mentor and first law partner (Springfield, Ill., 1837–41) of Abraham Lincoln, he remained an old-line Whig and opposed the Republican party. Although a strong Unionist, he actively opposed Lincoln's administration whose emancipation policy he decried.

STUART, MOSES (*b. Wilton, Conn., 1780; d. 1852*), Congregational clergyman, educator, Biblical scholar. As professor at Andover Theological Seminary, 1810–48, he was outstanding for insistence on investigation of German scholarly literature and was author of some forty books and monographs. He was the father of Isaac W. Stuart and the father-in-law of Austin Phelps.

STUART, ROBERT (*b. Callander, Perthshire, Scotland, 1785; d. Chicago, Ill., 1848*), fur trader. Emigrated to Canada, 1807; through Wilson P. Hunt, became partner in J. J. Astor's Pacific Fur Co., 1810. Sailing in that year on the *Tonquin* to the Columbia River, he was active in affairs of the Astoria colony; he journeyed eastward overland, 1812–13, with Ramsay Crooks and others over what was largely a new route. He later served as a traveling agent for Astor in the East and as Crooks's assistant at Mackinac, succeeding him *c.* 1820 and remaining as head of the American Fur Co. for the upper lakes region until 1834. Settling in Detroit, Mich., 1835, he engaged in business and civic affairs, and was superintendent of Indian affairs for Michigan, 1841–45. His

journal of the journey from Astoria appears in *The Discovery of the Oregon Trail* (1935, edited, P. A. Rollins); it was summarized in Washington Irving's *Astoria*.

STUART, ROBERT LEIGHTON (*b. New York, N.Y., 1806; d. 1882*), sugar refiner, philanthropist. A generous benefactor to Presbyterian institutions and charities.

STUART, RUTH McENERY (*b. Marksville, La., 1849; d. 1917*), short-story writer, editor. Raised in New Orleans which was her principal residence until her removal to New York City *c.* 1892. Her stories and sketches, published in more than twenty volumes after periodical publication, were humorous, sentimental and optimistic; however, she was the first to describe the post-Civil War Negro in his own social environment, and possessed an extraordinary skill in rendering dialect.

STUB, HANS GERHARD (*b. Muskego, Wis., 1849; d. St. Paul, Minn., 1931*), Lutheran clergyman, celebrated principally for his services in merging several synods into the Norwegian Lutheran Church of America, 1917. He served as president of this new body, 1917–25, and was emeritus thereafter.

STUBBS, WALTER ROSCOE (*b. near Richmond, Ind., 1858; d. Topeka, Kans., 1929*), railroad contractor, Kansas legislator, stockman. Raised in Douglas Co., Kans. Progressive Republican governor of Kansas, 1909–13, he failed of further political advancement after his support of Theodore Roosevelt, 1912. [*Supp.* 1]

STUCK, HUDSON (*b. London, England, 1863; d. Ft. Yukon, Alaska, 1920*), Episcopal clergyman. Came to America, 1885; was employed at first as a public school principal in Texas. Ordained, 1892, he held several rectorates in Texas; *post* 1904 he served as archdeacon of the Yukon. Author of several books descriptive of his travels and his mission work, he was one of the party which made the first complete ascent of Mt. McKinley, 1913.

STUCKENBERG, JOHN HENRY WILBRANDT (*b. Bramsche, Hanover, Germany, 1835; d. London, England, 1903*), Lutheran clergyman, educator, sociologist. Emigrated to Pittsburgh, Pa., as a child; was raised in Cincinnati, O. Graduated Wittenberg College, 1857, 1858; studied also at universities of Halle, Göttingen, Tübingen and Berlin. Held pastorates in several Midwestern states and was pastor of the American Church in Berlin, Germany, 1880–94. A pioneer in the field of sociology, he was author of a number of studies, of which *Sociology, The Science of Human Society* (1903) was outstanding.

STUDEBAKER, CLEMENT (*b. Pinetown, Pa., 1831; d. 1901*), wagon and carriage manufacturer. Raised in Ashland Co., O. Established with a brother the firm of H. & C. Studebaker at South Bend, Ind., 1852, which became the largest manufacturer of horse-drawn vehicles in the world. In 1897 he began experiments with self-propelled vehicles, and the company began their manufacture soon after his death.

STURGIS, RUSSELL (*b. Baltimore, Md., 1836; d. New York, N.Y., 1909*), architect, critic. Graduated present College of the City of New York, 1856; studied in office of Leopold Eidlitz, and at Munich. Practiced in association with Peter B. Wight, 1863–68, and by himself until about 1880. A competent architect in the Néo-Grec or the Victorian Gothic styles, he was more celebrated as a connoisseur and Ruskinian critic of art and architecture. As writer in the *Nation* and *Scribner's Magazine* and author of a number of books, he was perhaps the most important single factor in the artistic reawakening of the American people in the early years of the 20th century. His most ambitious work was *A History of Architecture* (1906–15, left unfinished).

STURGIS, SAMUEL DAVIS (*b. Shippensburg, Pa., 1822; d. St. Paul, Minn., 1889*), soldier. Graduated West Point, 1846. After service in the Mexican War, he performed duty in the West with the 1st Dragoons and the present 4th Cavalry. Commanding at Fort Smith, Ark., 1861, he brought off his troops in safety together with most of the government property at the post although menaced by hostile militia. He succeeded Gen. Nathaniel Lyon in command at the battle of Wilson's Creek. Promoted brigadier-general, August 1861, he commanded Union cavalry divisions for the rest of the Civil War, particularly distinguishing himself at Antietam, but suffering a severe defeat at Guntown, Miss., June 1864.

STURGIS, WILLIAM (*b. Barnstable, Mass., 1782; d. Boston, Mass., 1863*), Boston merchant in the China trade, Massachusetts legislator. Author of *The Oregon Question* (1845).

STURTEVANT, BENJAMIN FRANKLIN (*b. Norridgewock, Maine, 1833; d. Jamaica Plain, Mass., 1890*), inventor and manufacturer of shoemaking machinery. Patented a rotary exhaust fan (1867) which he adapted for use in pressure blowers, ventilating fans, pneumatic conveyors and the like, thereby virtually creating a new industry.

STURTEVANT, EDWARD LEWIS (*b. Boston, Mass., 1842; d. 1898*), agricultural scientist. Graduated Bowdoin, 1863; M.D., Harvard Medical School, 1866. Developed an experimental farm near South Framingham, Mass., where he made important studies of the physiology of milk and of the history of edible plants. First director, New York Agricultural Experiment Station at Geneva, 1882–87, he outlined broad plans of operation which were largely followed in other stations established under the Hatch Act. He was author of a number of books and monographs.

STURTEVANT, JULIAN MONSON (*b. Warren, Conn., 1805; d. Jacksonville, Ill., 1886*), Congregational clergyman, educator. Graduated Yale, 1826. A member of the so-called "Yale Band" pledged to further religion and education in the West, he taught *post* 1830 at Illinois College, and served it as president, 1844–76.

STUTZ, HARRY CLAYTON (*b. Ansonia, O., 1876; d. Indianapolis, Ind., 1930*), automobile manufacturer, machinist. As engineer and manager of the Marion Motor Car Co., 1906–10, he designed for it the first "underslung" pleasure car. In 1911, he became a partner in the Ideal Motor Car Co. organized to manufacture a car designed by Stutz. In 1913 he consolidated this company with another under the name of the Stutz Motor Car Co. and served as president until 1919. His automobile gained its greatest reputation in the period 1913–19. *Post* 1919 he engaged principally in the manufacture of taxicabs and airplane engines.

STUYVESANT, PETRUS (*b. Friesland, Netherlands, date uncertain and given variously from 1592 to c. 1610; d. New York, N.Y., 1672*), colonial governor and statesman. After early military service and a term as governor of Curaçao and adjacent islands (during which he lost his right leg subsequent to an expedition against the island of St. Martin), he was commissioned director-general of New Netherland, July 28, 1646. Sailing from the Texel on Christmas Day, 1646, he stopped first at Curaçao and thence went on to New Amsterdam, arriving May 11, 1647, "like a peacock, with great state and pomp." Active and able, he set himself to promote good order in the colony by somewhat stern measures; he promoted intercolonial relations with the English, drove the Swedes from the Delaware, increased commerce and set his face resolutely against assertions of the popular will in government. Despite his efforts, the people of New Amsterdam won independent municipal government in February 1653 after making a "remonstrance" to the States-General. Much to his disgust, Stuyvesant was obliged to surrender New Netherland to the English in the late summer of 1664 and thereafter withdrew from public affairs. After journeying to the Netherlands, 1665, to defend his official conduct, he returned to New York where he lived on his farm (just to the north of New York City) until his death.

SUBLETTE, WILLIAM LEWIS (*b. Lincoln Co., Ky., 1799?; d. Pittsburgh, Pa., 1845*), fur trader, merchant. One of five brothers conspicuous in the early fur trade, he removed with his family to St. Charles, Mo., c. 1818. He joined the expedition of William H. Ashley to the Rocky Mountains, 1822. He was with Ashley in the Arikara fight, June 1823, and served under Col. Leavenworth in the attack on the Arikara villages in August. Started in his own business by Ashley, Sublette made a fortune, and with Jedediah S. Smith and another partner finally bought Ashley out. They continued to trade successfully as a firm until 1832. Sublette formed a partnership with Robert Campbell in December 1832 which continued for some ten years; their principal trading posts were on the Platte at the mouth of the Laramie and on the Missouri near Fort Union.

SULLIVAN, GEORGE (*b. Durham, N.H., 1771; d. Exeter, N.H., 1838*), lawyer, New Hampshire legislator and congressman. Son of John Sullivan. Graduated Harvard, 1790. A Federalist, he opposed President Madison's foreign policies and the War of 1812. As New Hampshire attorney-general, 1815–35, he served with ability but was said to rely too little on his preparation and too much upon his oratory.

SULLIVAN, JAMES (*b. Berwick, District of Maine, 1744; d. probably Boston, Mass., 1808*), lawyer, Massachusetts patriot, legislator and jurist. Brother of John Sullivan; father of William Sullivan. Practicing at first in Maine and *post* 1783 in Boston, Mass., he became one of the most prominent lawyers in the state and was a leader of the (Democrat) Republicans there. A promoter of historical studies, he was author of several legal and historical treatises and served as governor of Massachusetts, 1807–08. During his term he engaged in a celebrated controversy with Timothy Pickering over the Embargo.

SULLIVAN, JAMES EDWARD (*b. New York, N.Y., 1860; d. 1914*), journalist, publisher, athlete. A zealot for the preservation of amateurism in sport, he was a founder of the Amateur Athletic Union of the United States (1888) and American director of the Olympic Games.

SULLIVAN, JAMES WILLIAM (*b. Carlisle, Pa., 1848; d. Carlisle, 1938*), printer, trade unionist, advocate of the initiative and referendum. For many years a trusted lieutenant of Samuel Gompers in the American Federation of Labor. [*Supp. 2*]

SULLIVAN, JOHN (*b. Somersworth, N.H., 1740; d. Durham, N.H., 1795*), Revolutionary general, statesman. Brother of James Sullivan; father of George Sullivan. An able if somewhat litigious lawyer, generous, oversensitive, and a born political organizer, he was early engaged on the patriot side in the American Revolution. A New Hampshire delegate to the First Continental Congress, September–December 1774, he returned home to lead in the seizure of Fort William and Mary in Portsmouth harbor. After taking his seat in the Second Continental Congress, he received appointment as brigadier-general, June 1775. Serving through the siege of Boston, he was ordered to the forces retreating from Canada after Montgomery's defeat at Quebec; he succeeded to their command on the death of Gen. John Thomas. Superseded by Gen. Horatio Gates in July 1776, he offered his resignation but withdrew it and was pro-

moted major-general in August. Taken prisoner at the battle of Long Island, he was exchanged after serving as the bearer of Lord Howe's peace overtures to Congress and rejoined the American army in Westchester Co., N.Y. He shared in the retreat across Jersey in the late fall of 1776, led the right column at Trenton and pursued the British at Princeton. Embroiled with Congress because of his protests against undue favor given newly arrived foreign officers, he found his conduct in various engagements through 1777, including the battle of the Brandywine, called into question, but after investigation he was exonerated. He always had the strong support of George Washington. Once again unfortunate in his operations around Newport, R.I., in the summer of 1778, principally because of the failure of support from a French fleet, Sullivan was highly successful in a punitive expedition through western Pennsylvania and New York against the Iroquois Indians (spring and summer, 1779) in association with Gen. James Clinton. His health impaired, he resigned from the army, November 1779. Thereafter he served briefly in Congress, was a New Hampshire legislator and attorney-general, and was president (governor) of New Hampshire, 1786–87, 1789. Appointed U.S. district judge for New Hampshire, 1789, he held that post until his death.

SULLIVAN, JOHN LAWRENCE (*b. Boston, Mass., 1858; d. West Abington, Mass., 1918*), pugilist, the "Great John L." Defeated the American champion Paddy Ryan by a knockout in the ninth round at Mississippi City, Miss., Feb. 7, 1882; dominated the American prize ring for the next decade; ended his career in defeat by James Corbett, Sept. 7, 1892.

SULLIVAN, LOUIS HENRI (*b. Boston, Mass., 1856; d. Chicago, Ill., 1924*), architect. Attended course in architecture at Massachusetts Institute of Technology under William R. Ware, 1872–73, but was irked by academic study; admired work of Henry H. Richardson; was encouraged by Richard M. Hunt. Removed to Chicago where he worked for a time in office of William Le B. Jenney; studied at the Beaux Arts, Paris (atelier Vaudremer), 1874–75. Returning to Chicago, he won a reputation in several offices as a skillful draftsman, and in 1879 began to work with Dankmar Adler, becoming a partner in May 1881. The firm of Adler and Sullivan rose rapidly, but there is little in Sullivan's work done at this time to back his claim that he attempted a radical departure from contemporary work. However, on the completion of the Auditorium Building, Chicago, (1886–90), the firm received international recognition, not only for a demonstrated mastery of the problem of acoustics, but for a definite break with tradition so far as the interior design was concerned. Accepting with enthusiasm the revolutionary principle of skeleton construction as demonstrated by Holobird and Roche, Sullivan then designed a series of important buildings expressing his own principles; notable among these are the Wainwright Building, St. Louis, Mo.; the sensational Transportation Building at the World's Fair of 1893; the Gage Building, Chicago; and others. After the death of Adler in 1900, Sullivan's opportunity to do work on a large scale ceased and his material fortunes declined, yet he continued to fight for his major principle that "form follows function." In his writings, and in what work he did, he stressed the essentially modern function of the skyscraper and the proper form for its expression, attacking the triumphant eclecticism of the *post*-1893 period. Known as the founder of the "Chicago School," Sullivan is father of modernism in architecture and more than any man helped to make the skyscraper America's greatest contribution to the art. His style of architectural ornament, although too personal and complicated for popular acceptance, was a distinct contribution, and he will be remembered also for the expression of his own philosophy which he gave in his *The Autobiography of an Idea* (1924).

SULLIVAN, LOUIS ROBERT (*b. Houlton, Maine, 1892; d. 1925*), physical anthropologist. Author of a number of important studies of race, describing geographical distribution and physical characteristics of anthropological types.

SULLIVAN, TIMOTHY DANIEL (*b. New York, N.Y., 1862; d. near Eastchester, N.Y., 1913*), politician, known as "Big Tim." A saloonkeeper and vaudeville entrepreneur, Sullivan raised himself to leadership of the Tammany Democracy in New York City's Third Assembly District and was uncrowned king of the lower East Side, 1892–1912. An efficient organizer of graft and a magnetic machine boss, Sullivan played a strong role in New York State politics, 1900–10. He served as congressman, Democrat, from New York, 1903–07.

SULLIVAN, WILLIAM (*b. Biddeford, Maine, 1774; d. 1839*), lawyer, Massachusetts legislator. Son of James Sullivan. Author, among other works, of *Familiar Letters on Public Characters and Public Events, etc.* (1834, republished in 1847 as *The Public Men of the Revolution*).

SULLIVAN, WILLIAM HENRY (*b. Port Dalhousie, Canada, 1864; d. 1929*), lumberman. Organized and directed, *post* 1906, the vast lumbering operations and factory complex at Bogalusa, La.; helped build lumber industry in Louisiana along intelligent and conservationist lines.

SULLIVANT, WILLIAM STARLING (*b. Franklinton, O., 1803; d. 1873*), botanist, bryologist. Graduated Yale, 1823. Among his several pioneering and important works, his *Icones Muscorum* (1864) is considered outstanding; he also assisted in the amplification of Gray's *Manual*, 1856, and was associated in studies with Leo Lesquereux and others. His contribution to Gray's *Manual*, also published

separately, laid the foundation for subsequent bryological studies in the United States.

SULLY, DANIEL JOHN (*b. Providence, R.I., 1861; d. Beverly Hills, Calif., 1930*), cotton speculator, dominant in the New York City market, 1902–04.

SULLY, THOMAS (*b. Horncastle, Lincolnshire, England, 1783; d. Philadelphia, Pa., 1872*), painter. Came to America, 1792; was raised in Charleston, S.C. Encouraged in his artistic tastes by Charles Fraser and by his elder brother, Lawrence Sully, a miniature painter, he removed to Virginia *c.* 1799. He lived and studied with his brother in Richmond and Norfolk until 1803. In May 1801 Thomas Sully painted his first miniature portrait from life and continued to work industriously, but with little remuneration, until his removal to New York City in November 1806. There, with the aid of Thomas A. Cooper, Sully received a number of profitable commissions. Encouraged by a brief interview with Gilbert Stuart at Boston in 1807, Sully went to Philadelphia and made that city his permanent home in 1808. Although much of his early work ranks among his best, he was dissatisfied with his own skill. With the aid of friends, he visited England, July 1809—March 1810. There, Benjamin West (1738–1820) suggested that he make a serious study of anatomy and osteology which Sully did; he also made the acquaintance of Sir Thomas Lawrence and the Kemble family of actors. After his return to Philadelphia he attempted several historical subjects and grew in reputation as a portraitist. After the deaths of Charles W. Peale (1827) and Gilbert Stuart (1828), Sully had no formidable rivals in his art. When he made a second visit to England, 1837, and painted the young Queen Victoria, he reached the summit of his fame, receiving a number of commissions from distinguished English people and achieving also a social success. During his career he produced more than 2600 works. Although occasionally his draftsmanship was defective, he was always a master of color and his works have a characteristic warmth and beauty. Sometimes called "the Sir Thomas Lawrence of America," he was especially happy in delineation of women and children, yet some of his portraits of men, such as the "Dr. Samuel Coates," are marked by an admirable firmness.

SULZBERGER, CYRUS LINDAUER (*b. Philadelphia, Pa., 1858; d. New York, N.Y., 1932*), textile merchant, leader in Jewish affairs, philanthropist.

SULZBERGER, MAYER (*b. Heidelsheim, Germany, 1843; d. Philadelphia, Pa., 1923*), jurist, Hebrew scholar. Cousin of Cyrus L. Sulzberger. Came to Philadelphia as a child where he practiced law *post* 1865 after study in office of Moses A. Dropsie. He served as judge of the court of common pleas, 1895–1916, and was president judge *post* 1902. He was also active in Jewish welfare work and the promotion of higher Jewish learning.

SUMMERS, GEORGE WILLIAM (*b. Fairfax Co., Va., 1804; d. Charleston, W. Va., 1868*), lawyer, Virginia legislator and congressman. Originally a Whig, he was an active Unionist and strong opponent of secession.

SUMMERS, THOMAS OSMOND (*b. near Corfe Castle, Dorsetshire, England, 1812; d. Nashville, Tenn., 1882*), Methodist clergyman, editor. Emigrated to New York, N.Y., 1830. After ministry, 1835–40, in Maryland, he became a founder of the Texas and Alabama Conferences and was secretary to the 1844 Convention at Louisville, Ky., which organized the Methodist Episcopal Church, South. He served thereafter as secretary of its conferences until his death. He was dean and professor of systematic theology at Vanderbilt University, 1876–82.

SUMNER, CHARLES (*b. Boston, Mass., 1811; d. Washington, D.C., 1874*), statesman. Son of an independent-minded anti-slavery lawyer and Massachusetts public official, Charles Sumner attended Boston Latin School, 1821–26, and Harvard College, 1826–30; at Harvard Law School, 1831–33, he was the pupil and friend of Joseph Story. Reacting against practical politics and finding the routine of legal practice little to his liking, he became a lecturer in the Harvard Law School, a contributor to the *American Jurist* and a reviser of legal textbooks. Francis Lieber and William E. Channing exercised a profound influence upon him. During two years of travel and observation in Europe *post* 1837, he learned French, German and Italian and became acquainted with many literary and political figures; he also studied European governments and jurisprudence. Ambitious for distinction on the intellectual side of his profession, he produced an annotated edition of Vesey's *Reports of Cases . . . in the High Court of Chancery* (1844–45).

He rounded a turning-point in his career when he delivered the Boston Independence Day oration in 1845. Powerful of voice and skillful in oratory, he denounced war and, although bringing considerable odium on himself, discovered at the same time that he could thrill and sway great audiences. For years thereafter he was a successful lyceum lecturer. Loudly championing peaceful arbitration in public disputes and denouncing the Mexican War, he increased the antipathy of the conservative Whigs of Boston toward him, but was elected to the U.S. Senate by a coalition of Free Soilers and Democrats, taking his seat, Dec. 1, 1851. Although the compromise measures of the previous year had apparently been accepted as final, Sumner rose toward the end of his first session to arraign the Fugitive Slave Law in a tremendous speech, Aug. 26, 1852, and moved an amendment that no allowances be permitted for expenses incurred in executing the law.

The Southern senators heaped angry derision upon the amendment, and it received only four votes in its favor. Sumner, however, continued outspoken in opposition, particularly to the Kansas-Nebraska Bill, which brought him into greater disfavor with the Boston press and society. In the debate upon the right of petition, Southern senators charged Sumner with repudiating his oath of office and urged his expulsion but could not muster the requisite two-thirds vote for this. Sumner's answer was that he had sworn to support the Constitution as he understood it and his courage won admirers for him. Boldly denouncing the Know-Nothing party and scorning its support, he had a large part in organization of the Republican party.

During the hot debate in the Senate over the struggle for Kansas, Sumner delivered his famous "The Crime against Kansas," May 20, 1856; in this speech he denounced the Kansas-Nebraska Act as "in every respect a swindle" and arraigned Andrew P. Butler and Stephen A. Douglas in bitter terms, thrilling anti-slavery men throughout the North. Two days later he was assaulted at his desk in the Senate by Preston S. Brooks of South Carolina, a kinsman of Sen. Butler. Seriously injured, Sumner went abroad in search of health and did not return to the Senate for three-and-a-half years. Meantime he had been re-elected by almost unanimous vote of the Massachusetts legislature. Announcing his determination to assault American slavery all along the line, he set forth in his speech "The Barbarism of Slavery" (delivered during the debate on the bill for the admission of Kansas) a social, moral and economic attack on the institution as well as a political one; distributed broadcast, the speech had great influence in the presidential election of 1860.

During the months following Lincoln's victory, Sumner refused to support the Crittenden Compromise. In October 1861, at the Massachusetts Republican convention, he became the first statesman of prominence to urge emancipation and thereafter never ceased to press for it. Appointed chairman of the Senate committee on foreign relations, 1861, he rendered invaluable service to the Union in many ways, notably in effecting a peaceful solution of the problems raised by the seizure of Mason and Slidell and in bringing about the defeat or suppression of Senate resolutions which would have involved the United States in war with France and Great Britain. As early as the second year of the Civil War, he began a struggle to secure absolute equality of civil rights for all United States citizens. In February 1862, he announced the extravagant doctrine that the seceding states had abdicated all their rights under the Constitution and remained insistent that initiation and control of Reconstruction should be by Congress and not by the President.

During the administration of President Andrew Johnson, Sumner and Thaddeus Stevens headed respectively in the Senate and the House the opposition to Johnson's Reconstruction policy. Sumner's persistence led the Senate to add to the requirements for readmission of seceded states the insertion in their constitutions of a provision for equal suffrage rights for Negroes and whites. Prominent in the move to impeach President Johnson, Sumner descended to lurid and furious invective and showed himself at his worst in the opinion which he filed in support of his vote for conviction. Antipathetic to President U. S. Grant, Sumner became antagonistic soon after the new administration began. Among other clashes, the most violent developed over the president's project of acquiring Santo Domingo. Sumner's committee brought in an adverse report upon treaties negotiated by Grant's personal envoy, 1869. The administration retaliated against Sumner's friends, and also by bringing about his demotion from the chairmanship of the foreign relations committee. The administration was influenced in this action also by fears that Sumner's excessive views on U.S. claims against Great Britain for wartime losses might jeopardize plans already under way for settlement of these claims. Among other legislation which Sumner introduced before his sudden death was a bill (introduced in session beginning December 1872) which provided that the names of Civil War battles should not be perpetuated in the Army Register or placed on regimental colors, an eirenic gesture which brought him official censure.

Unlike Abraham Lincoln, Charles Sumner outlived his best days; his later years brought domestic sorrows, illness, and ceaseless struggle over problems of Reconstruction. Through many years in the Senate he strove for "absolute human equality" and judged every man and every measure by reference to that goal, becoming progressively intolerant not only of opposition but even of dissent. Diligent in the routine work of a senator, he commanded respect in discussions of money and finance, the tariff and copyright; he also introduced an intelligent bill for civil service reform. His great work, however, was not in the framing of laws but rather in the role of an ancient Hebrew prophet, the kindling of moral enthusiasm and the overthrow of injustice. A major force in the struggle that put an end to slavery, he also attempted to hold in check barbarous attempts at retaliation during wartime and maintained peace with European nations when war with them would have meant the end of the Union.

SUMNER, EDWIN VOSE (*b. Boston, Mass., 1797; d. Syracuse, N.Y., 1863*), soldier. Commissioned lieutenant in infantry, 1819; appointed captain in 1st Dragoons, 1833. Served on the frontier and in the Mexican War with great credit; was for a time military commandant of New Mexico. Promoted colonel, 1st (present 4th) Cavalry, 1855, he campaigned along the Oregon Trail and was commander at Fort Leaven-

worth, 1856, acting with discretion to keep order during the struggle for Kansas. He assumed command of the Department of the West, 1858, with headquarters at St. Louis, Mo. A loyal Union man, Sumner accompanied the president-elect to Washington, D.C., 1861, and during the Civil War rose to rank of major-general of volunteers for gallant service at Fair Oaks. He commanded the right grand division at Fredericksburg but was soon after relieved from duty with the Army of the Potomac at his own request.

SUMNER, INCREASE (*b. Roxbury, Mass., 1746; d. Roxbury, 1799*), jurist. Graduated Harvard, 1767; began practice of law at Roxbury, 1770. A Massachusetts legislator during the Revolution, he was appointed a justice of the supreme judicial court of Massachusetts, 1782, winning repute as an able judge and a warm supporter of the new national government. Federalist governor of Massachusetts, 1797–99, he followed a middle-of-the-road policy, allayed partisan bitterness, and gave special attention to improving the state's military defenses.

SUMNER, JETHRO (*b. Nansemond Co., Va., c. 1733; d. Warren Co., N.C., 1785*), planter, Revolutionary brigadier-general. Fought in French and Indian War; removed to North Carolina, 1764. Among the foremost of North Carolina patriots in the Revolution, he distinguished himself in the defense of Charleston, 1776, with Washington's army in the campaigns of 1777–78, and in the defense of North Carolina against Cornwallis's invasion, 1780. He was also outstanding at the battle of Eutaw Springs, 1781.

SUMNER, WALTER TAYLOR (*b. Manchester, N.H., 1873; d. Portland, Oreg., 1935*), Episcopal clergyman. Attracted nation-wide attention for activities in behalf of reform and social betterment as a minister in Chicago, 1904–15. Active and public-spirited bishop of Oregon, 1915–35. [*Supp. 1*]

SUMNER, WILLIAM GRAHAM (*b. Paterson, N.J., 1840; d. Englewood, N.J., 1910*), educator, social scientist. Graduated Yale, 1863. After study abroad in preparation for the ministry, he returned home and was tutor at Yale, 1866–69. Ordained priest of the Protestant Episcopal Church, 1869, he remained in the ministry until 1872, also helping to establish, and editing, *The Living Church*. Because his interests turned increasingly to social and economic questions, he accepted the chair of political and social science at Yale in 1872 and spent the remainder of his life at that institution. A man of prodigious industry, he made his influence felt widely beyond the university, serving as a New Haven alderman and as a member of the Connecticut Board of Education. He wrote extensively, expressed his views on public questions, and engaged in extended research into the origin of social institutions which ranks him among the foremost students in this field. Skilled in all the social sciences, he had a working knowledge of at least a dozen languages.

A respected teacher and a most effective one, he made everyday affairs his textbook for the examination of social facts and principles. Rebelling against the conservatism of Yale, he labored against opposition to broaden the curriculum. Through public addresses and periodical essays he carried on a warfare against economic and political evils, treating practically every social question of his day in an unsentimental and critical fashion. He was an outstanding advocate of a sound monetary system and opposed all inflationary expedients, yet he also fought protectionism. Deploring the agitation against "big business" and regarding the evolution of the trusts as a natural phenomenon, he opposed with vigor any government interference upon the industrial field, maintaining that state remedies would be worse than the disease. He believed that social conditions can be improved, but only by scientific procedure carried on by thoroughly informed individuals. In his use of the term the "Forgotten Man" in an 1883 lecture, he meant the self-supporting person who has to bear the cost of political bungling and social quackery. Finding himself less and less satisfied by the traditional boundaries of political economy and political science, he became preoccupied with the concept of a general science of society which should incorporate religion, marriage customs, and all other examples from the human experience which might provide the facts for a scientific induction. Attempting a treatise on this subject, he became convinced that he must begin it with an analysis of custom and from this conviction developed his classic book *Folkways* (1907). Posthumously (1927), his data and outline for the projected treatise appeared as *Science of Society* (reclassified and revised by Albert G. Keller). Sumner was author also of a number of other books on banking, finance and currency, three biographies and several collected volumes of essays.

SUMTER, THOMAS (*b. near Charlottesville, Va., 1734; d. near Stateburg, S.C., 1832*), Revolutionary officer, South Carolina partisan leader and legislator. After military experience in the campaigns of Braddock and Forbes and in fighting against the Cherokees, he settled as a storekeeper near Eutaw Springs, S.C., c. 1765. A provincial congressman and for a time lieutenant-colonel in the Continental service, he is remembered principally for his leadership of partisan troops against British and Tory forces in the Carolinas, 1780 and 1781–82. Feared by the enemy and called the "Gamecock of the Revolution," he played a role whose importance was out of all proportion to the small numbers he commanded. His campaigns were of material assistance to the later American victory at Yorktown.

SUNDAY, WILLIAM ASHLEY (*b. Ames, Iowa, 1862; d. 1935*), evangelist, popularly known as "Billy" Sunday. A member successively of the Chicago White Sox and the Pittsburgh and Philadelphia teams, 1883–91; he was associated thereafter until 1896 with activities of the Chicago YMCA and was assistant to the evangelist J. Wilbur Chapman. Beginning his independent career, 1896, he was ordained by the Chicago Presbytery, 1903. Soon becoming widely known, he held meetings in the largest cities of the United States. A vivid and unconventional preacher, he proclaimed a crude version of ultraconservative evangelical theology and instituted the practice of "hitting the sawdust trail," so called from the fact that the floors of the places in which he preached were covered with sawdust. Earnest and sincere, he preached the divine wrath rather than divine love. [*Supp. 1*]

SUNDERLAND, ELIZA JANE READ (*b. near Huntsville, Ill., 1839; d. Hartford, Conn., 1910*), educator, reformer. Active generally for human betterment, especially the promotion of temperance, the improvement of education, and the advancement of women, during long residences in Chicago, Ill., and Ann Arbor, Mich.

SUNDERLAND, LA ROY (*b. Exeter, R.I., 1804; d. 1885*), Abolitionist. Originally a Methodist clergyman, but later a "faddist" and finally an infidel, he was responsible for organization of the first antislavery society in the Methodist Church, and was the first editor of *Zion's Watchman*, 1836.

SUTHERLAND, JOEL BARLOW (*b. Clonmel, N.J., 1792; d. 1861*), physician, lawyer, Pennsylvania legislator. Congressman, Democrat, from Pennsylvania, 1827–37. Brilliant but shallow, he began as an enthusiastic Jacksonian but became a protectionist.

SUTRO, ADOLPH HEINRICH JOSEPH (*b. Prussia, 1830; d. San Francisco, Calif., 1898*), mining engineer. Emigrated to America, 1850; settled in San Francisco, 1851. Established quartz-reducing mill in Nevada, 1860, where he conceived idea of driving a tunnel into Mount Davidson from Carson River to the Comstock Lode as a more efficient means of transporting men and materials to and from the mines. After great difficulty in securing financing, Sutro brought the tunnel to completion, 1878; it proved immediately and immensely profitable. Selling out his interest, 1879, he returned to San Francisco where he made profitable real-estate investments, and served as Populist mayor, 1894–96.

SUTTER, JOHN AUGUSTUS (*b. Kandern, Baden, 1803; d. Washington, D.C., 1880*), soldier, California colonizer. Officially a Swiss citizen, Sutter emigrated to America, 1834, journeyed to St. Louis, Mo., and in 1835 and 1836 accompanied trading parties to Santa Fé. Removing overland to Oregon, 1838, he reached California by way of Honolulu, Hawaii, and Sitka, Alaska, on July 1, 1839. Receiving large grants from the Mexican governor of California, he set up the colony of Nueva Helvetia on the American River at its junction with the Sacramento. Virtual sovereign ruler of his domain, he assisted early American settlers in his neighborhood. After the conquest of California by the United States he seemed secure in his fortunes, but discovery of gold on his estate, Jan. 24, 1848, marked the beginning of his ruin. Squatters settled upon his lands, his herders and workmen deserted the colony, and by 1852 he was bankrupt. He spent the rest of his life fruitlessly petitioning Congress for redress.

SUTTON, WILLIAM SENECA (*b. Fayetteville, Ark., 1860; d. Austin, Texas, 1928*), Texas educator.

SUZZALLO, HENRY (*b. San José, Calif., 1875; d. Seattle, Wash., 1933*), educator. Graduated Stanford University, 1899; Ph.D., Columbia, 1905. Taught in San Francisco public school system, at Stanford, and at Teachers College, Columbia, where he was professor of educational sociology. As president, University of Washington, 1915–26, he successfully coordinated the services of the university with the needs of the state. After supervising preparation of the report of the National Advisory Committee on Education (published, 1931) which led to reforms in government educational services, he served as president of the Carnegie Foundation for the Advancement of Teaching, 1930–33. He was author also of a study of higher education in the state of California (published, 1932).

SVERDRUP, GEORG (*b. near Bergen, Norway, 1848; d. Minneapolis, Minn., 1907*), Lutheran theologian, educator. Professor of theology, Augsburg Seminary, Minneapolis, 1874–1907. An opponent of state-dominated churches, he championed congregationalist ideas.

SWAIN, CLARA A. (*b. Elmira, N.Y., 1834; d. Castile, N.Y., 1910*), pioneer woman medical missionary in India, 1869–76, 1879–85. A graduate of the Woman's Medical College, Philadelphia, 1869, she worked in India under Methodist auspices.

SWAIN, DAVID LOWRY (*b. Buncombe Co., N.C., 1801; d. 1868*), lawyer, North Carolina legislator and jurist. Whig governor of North Carolina, 1832–35, he pressed for tax reform and improved public education; he also induced the legislature to call the constitutional convention of 1835 at which he favored every liberal reform proposed. A constructive figure of the first rank, he did not believe in secession but accepted it as a necessity and later advised President Andrew Johnson on plans of reconstruction. As president of the University of North Carolina *post* 1835, he built up that institution financially and scholastically, kept it open during the Civil War by heroic efforts, and until his death continued his efforts in its behalf. Appointed state agent for the collection of historical material, 1854, he began the

work which resulted years later in the publication of the North Carolina *Colonial and State Records.*

SWAIN, GEORGE FILLMORE (*b. San Francisco, Calif., 1857; d. Holderness, N.H., 1931*), engineer. B.S., Massachusetts Institute of Technology, 1877. Teacher of civil engineering at M.I.T. *post* 1881, he served as professor and head of the department, 1887–1909; he was McKay Professor of Civil Engineering at Harvard, 1909–29. A well-known consultant on engineering projects, he had a profound influence on methods of teaching and of interpreting technology in the practice of structural engineering. [*Supp. 1*]

SWAIN, JAMES BARRETT (*b. New York, N.Y., 1820; d. 1895*), journalist, New York Republican politician and office-holder.

SWALLOW, GEORGE CLINTON (*b. Buckfield, Maine, 1817; d. Evanston, Ill., 1899*), geologist. Graduated Bowdoin, 1843. As state geologist, Swallow made important surveys in Missouri (1853–61) and in Kansas (1865). He was professor of agriculture at University of Missouri, 1870–82, and later a journalist in Montana.

SWALLOW, SILAS COMFORT (*b. near Wilkes-Barre, Pa., 1839; d. 1930*), Methodist clergyman, reformer. Holder of many pastoral charges in central Pennsylvania, he was a bitter and persistent enemy of the Republican machine in that state. As presidential nominee of the Prohibition party, 1904, he polled better than a quarter-million votes.

SWAN, JAMES (*b. Fifeshire, Scotland, 1754; d. Paris, France, 1830*), Massachusetts legislator and official, speculator. Emigrated to Boston, 1765. Removing to France, 1787, with the help of Lafayette he won contracts to furnish the French with marine stores. Later, by a complicated series of transactions and as agent for the French Republic (1795), he transformed the American foreign debt outstanding to France into a domestic one at considerable profit to himself. Failing in later French mercantile ventures, he remained in debtor's prison in Paris, 1808–30, refusing to permit his debt to be paid because he considered it unjust.

SWAN, JOSEPH ROCKWELL (*b. Westernville, N.Y., 1802; d. Columbus, O., 1884*), Ohio jurist, legal writer, Abolitionist. Celebrated for a classic opinion on state and federal court jurisdiction in the case of *Ex parte Bushnell* (9 *Ohio State*, 78); author, among other works, of *A Treatise on the Law Relating to the Powers and Duties of Justices of the Peace . . . in the State of Ohio* (1837).

SWAN, TIMOTHY (*b. Worcester, Mass., 1758; d. Northfield, Mass., 1842*), composer and compiler of psalm-tunes. Author, among other music, of the very popular "China," composed in 1790 and first publicly sung, 1794.

SWANK, JAMES MOORE (*b. Westmoreland Co., Pa., 1832; d. Philadelphia, Pa., 1914*), statistician. Associated in a managerial capacity with the American Iron and Steel Association, 1873–1912, he was an outstanding propagandist for protection.

SWANN, THOMAS (*b. Alexandria, Va., c. 1806; d. 1883*), lawyer, businessman. Rose to prominence as able president of Baltimore & Ohio Railroad, 1848–53, extending the line to the Ohio River. Know-Nothing mayor of Baltimore, 1856–60. Swann was a strong Unionist during the Civil War, and Union party governor of Maryland, 1866–68. Opposing Radical Reconstruction, he succeeded in restoring the franchise to former Southern sympathizers. Congressman, Democrat, from Maryland, 1869–79, he rose to be chairman of the committee on foreign relations, thereafter retiring to his estate near Leesburg, Va.

SWANSON, CLAUDE AUGUSTUS (*b. near Danville, Va., 1862; d. near Criglersville, Va., 1939*), lawyer, statesman. Graduated Randolph-Macon College, 1885; LL.B., University of Virginia, 1886. As congressman, Democrat, from Virginia, 1893–1906, he fought to secure rural free delivery service and was an able member of the House ways and means committee. A progressive and successful governor of Virginia, 1906–10, he became U.S. senator in the latter year and served until 1933. A consistent supporter of Woodrow Wilson's policies and a "big navy" advocate, he was active also on the Senate foreign relations committee. He was U.S. secretary of the navy, 1933–39, continuing his support of the navy although hampered by ill health. [*Supp. 2*]

SWARTWOUT, SAMUEL (*b. Poughkeepsie, N.Y., 1783; d. New York, N.Y., 1856*), merchant, speculator, politician. A close associate of Aaron Burr (1756–1836), Swartwout delivered the famous cipher letter from Burr to James Wilkinson, October 1806, which produced such a strong impression of Burr's treason. Arrested as an accomplice, he served as an important witness against Burr. Later an active supporter of Andrew Jackson, he was collector of the port of New York, 1829–38, achieving notoriety for misappropriation of more than a million dollars of public money.

SWASEY, AMBROSE (*b. Exeter, N.H., 1846; d. Exeter, 1937*), mechanical engineer, manufacturer, philanthropist. With W. R. Warner, entered machine-tool manufacturing business, 1880, in Chicago, removing to Cleveland, O., 1881. Successful specialists in manufacture of hand-operated turret lathes, Warner and Swasey achieved greatest distinction for a side line, the making of precision astronomical and other scientific instruments. [*Supp. 2*]

SWAYNE, NOAH HAYNES (*b. Frederick Co., Va., 1804; d. New York, N.Y., 1884*), jurist. Father of Wager Swayne. Reaching high rank at the Ohio bar post 1823, he was appointed justice of the U.S. Supreme Court, 1862, and served until 1881. A satisfactory judge but not a brilliant one, he gave his principal opinions in *Gelpcke vs. City of Dubuque* and *Springer vs. U.S.* He was regarded as the most nationalistic-minded member of the Court in his time.

SWAYNE, WAGER (*b. Columbus, O., 1834; d. 1902*), Union major-general, lawyer. Son of Noah H. Swayne. Winner of the Medal of Honor for gallantry at Corinth, Miss., October 1862, Swayne did valuable service in Alabama with the Freedmen's Bureau. He was later successful in the practice of law in New York City in partnership with John F. Dillon and others.

SWEENY, PETER BARR (*b. New York, N.Y., 1825; d. Lake Mahopac, N.Y., 1911*), lawyer, politician. Considered the guiding intelligence of the Tweed Ring in New York City c. 1861–71.

SWEENY, THOMAS WILLIAM (*b. Co. Cork, Ireland, 1820; d. Astoria, N.Y., 1892*), Union brigadier-general, Fenian leader of the ill-starred raid on Canada in 1866.

SWEET, JOHN EDSON (*b. Pompey, N.Y., 1832; d. Syracuse, N.Y., 1916*), mechanical engineer, educator. Headed the Straight Line Engine Co. post 1880; received John Fritz Medal, 1914, for pioneer work in construction and development of high-speed steam engines.

SWENSON, DAVID FERDINAND (*b. Kristinehamn, Sweden, 1876; d. Lake Wales, Fla., 1940*), philosopher. Came to America as a child. Graduating University of Minnesota, 1898, he taught philosophy and psychology there until the end of his life. He was noted as the pioneer American authority on the work of Søren Kierkegaard and as a sharp, effective critic of current symbolic logics. [*Supp. 2*]

SWENSSON, CARL AARON (*b. Sugargrove, Pa., 1857; d. Los Angeles, Calif., 1904*), Swedish Lutheran clergyman, educator. Long associated with the congregation at Lindsborg, Kans., he was instrumental in founding Bethany College there, 1881.

SWETT, JOHN (*b. near Pittsfield, N.H., 1830; d. near Martinez, Calif., 1913*), California public-school administrator, opponent of political influence in the schools.

SWIFT, GUSTAVUS FRANKLIN (*b. near Sandwich, Mass., 1839; d. 1903*), meat packer. Established himself in Chicago, Ill., as a cattle buyer, 1875; sought to avoid waste by shipping already dressed beef to Eastern markets, 1877. Conceived of the railroad refrigerator car as aid to year-round shipping. A pioneer in development of by-products from animal parts previously thrown away, Swift extended his business successfully to foreign markets; before his death, Swift & Co. (incorporated, 1885) was capitalized at $25,000,000.

SWIFT, JOHN FRANKLIN (*b. Bowling Green, Mo., 1829; d. Japan, 1891*), lawyer, California legislator. Practiced in San Francisco, Calif., *post* 1857; was outstanding as an opponent of monopolistic corporations. A U.S. commissioner (1880) to negotiate modifications of the Burlingame Treaty with China, he was later of counsel for California in sustaining constitutionality of the Chinese Exclusion Act, 1888. U.S. minister to Japan, 1889–91.

SWIFT, JOSEPH GARDNER (*b. Nantucket, Mass., 1783; d. Geneva, N.Y., 1865*), military engineer. Brother of William H. Swift. Graduated West Point, 1802, in the first class. Chief engineer of the U.S. Army, 1812–18, he resigned because of conflict over appointment of Simon Bernard and worked thereafter on railroad and harbor improvement projects. An engineer of distinction, he exerted influence over George W. Whistler, William G. McNeill and other younger professionals.

SWIFT, LEWIS (*b. Clarkson, N.Y., 1820; d. Marathon, N.Y., 1913*), astronomer, businessman.

SWIFT, LOUIS FRANKLIN (*b. Sagamore, Mass., 1861; d. Chicago, Ill., 1937*), meat packer. Son of Gustavus F. Swift. Official of Swift & Co. *post* 1885 and its president, 1903–31. With aid of brothers, he made the firm one of the world's greatest food processing and distributing businesses. He also pioneered in employee-welfare activities. [*Supp. 2*]

SWIFT, LUCIUS BURRIE (*b. Orleans Co., N.Y., 1844; d. 1929*), lawyer, civil-service reformer. Practiced in Indianapolis, Ind., *post* 1879; edited and published the *Civil Service Chronicle*, 1889–96.

SWIFT, WILLIAM HENRY (*b. Taunton, Mass., 1800; d. New York, N.Y., 1879*), soldier, engineer. Brother of Joseph G. Swift. Attended West Point, 1813–18; accompanied Stephen H. Long to the Rocky Mountains and was commissioned in the artillery, 1819. After employment in railroad and canal work, he was made captain of topographical engineers, 1838, and was principal assistant in the topographical bureau at Washington, D.C., 1843–49. Resigning from the army, he was successively president of the Philadelphia, Wilmington & Baltimore and the Massachusetts Western railroads, a director of many corporations, and a financial adviser of Baring Brothers.

SWIFT, ZEPHANIAH (*b. Wareham, Mass., 1759; d. Warren, O., 1823*), Connecticut legislator and jurist. Congressman, Federalist, from Connecticut, 1793–97; secretary to Oliver Ellsworth on mission to France, 1800. Author of the first American law text, *A System of the Laws of the State of Connecticut* (1795, 1796), he was a judge of the state superior court, 1801–19, serving for a time as chief justice. Deprived of office as a Federalist, he retired to legal researches and writing.

SWING, DAVID (*b. Cincinnati, O., 1830; d. Chicago, Ill., 1894*), Presbyterian and independent clergyman. Pastor, Fourth Church, Chicago, *post* 1866, he was cited for heresy, 1874, and served *post* 1875 as minister of Chicago's Central Church.

SWINTON, JOHN (*b. near Edinburgh, Scotland, 1829; d. Brooklyn, N.Y., 1901*), journalist, social reformer. Brother of William Swinton. Raised in Canada; worked as journeyman printer in the South and Middle West *post* 1853; was active in free-state movement in Kansas, 1856. Employed by the New York *Times* and *Sun post c.* 1860, Swinton was an outstanding labor sympathizer and edited *John Swinton's Paper*, 1883–87.

SWINTON, WILLIAM (*b. near Edinburgh, Scotland, 1833; d. Brooklyn, N.Y., 1892*), journalist, educator. Brother of John Swinton. Resident in the United States *post c.* 1853, he served as Civil War correspondent for New York *Times*, wrote several books about the war, and in 1869 became professor of English, University of California. Resigning in 1874 because of differences with Daniel C. Gilman, Swinton became a successful writer of school textbooks.

SWISSHELM, JANE GREY CANNON (*b. Pittsburgh, Pa., 1815; d. Swissvale, Pa., 1884*), teacher, anti-slavery and woman's rights reformer. Founded and edited the *Pittsburgh Saturday Visiter* (1847–57), the *St. Cloud Visiter*, the *Reconstructionist* (Washington, D.C.) and other waspishly written journals.

SWITZLER, WILLIAM FRANKLIN (*b. Fayette Co., Ky., 1819; d. Columbia, Mo., 1906*), Missouri legislator and journalist. Editor of the *Missouri Statesman*, 1842–85, he was active in Democratic politics, supported the Union during the Civil War and subsequently held several federal offices. One of the best-informed men of his time in the history of his state, he published, among other works, *Early History of Missouri* (1872).

SYDENSTRICKER, EDGAR (*b. Shanghai, China, 1881; d. New York, N.Y., 1936*), social and economic investigator, public health statistician. Brother of Pearl S. Buck. Author, among other works, of *Conditions of Labor in American Industries* (with W. J. Lauck, 1917) and *Health and Environment* (1933). [*Supp. 2*]

SYKES, GEORGE (*b. Dover, Del., 1822; d. Fort Brown, Texas, 1880*), Union major-general. Graduated West Point, 1842. An excellent tactician on the defense, Sykes commanded the V Corps at Gettysburg, defending the Round Tops successfully but suffering criticism for his failure to counterattack.

SYLVESTER, FREDERICK OAKES (*b. Brockton, Mass., 1869; d. 1915*), painter, art teacher. Employed in the St. Louis, Mo., public-school system, 1892–

1914, he produced many highly regarded canvases of scenes on the Mississippi River.

SYLVESTER, JAMES JOSEPH (*b. London, England, 1814; d. probably Oxford, England, 1897*), mathematician, educator. A brilliant student at St. John's College, Cambridge, 1831–33, 1836–37, he was barred as a Jew from taking his degree or receiving a fellowship. Professor of natural philosophy at University College, London, 1837–41. He taught mathematics at the University of Virginia, 1841–42, but because of problems of discipline resigned and returned to London. Engaged there in actuarial work, 1844–56, he also studied law; he was professor of mathematics, Royal Military Academy at Woolwich, 1855–70. Invited to serve as professor of mathematics at Johns Hopkins University, 1876, he brought there a reputation as one of the greatest mathematicians of his time and an infectious eagerness for intellectual endeavor. Setting new standards for mathematical research in America and inspiring scores of students, he acted also as editor of the *American Journal of Mathematics*, 1878–84. Resigning his chair, December 1883, he became Savilian Professor of Geometry at Oxford, in which position he remained for the rest of his life. He devoted his attention as a scholar to the theory of numbers; to higher algebra; and to the theory of invariants, a subject in which he was recognized as pre-eminent. Many of his contributions to learned journals were issued in a collected edition, edited by H. F. Baker, 1904–12.

SYLVIS, WILLIAM H. (*b. Armagh, Pa., 1828; d. 1869*), labor leader. An official of an iron-moulders' union, organized in Philadelphia, Pa., 1855, he signed the call for the first convention of the Iron-Moulders International Union, Philadelphia, 1859. His address at the convention became the preamble to the constitution of the new union, of which he was elected treasurer, 1860, and president, 1863. Active in calling the Labor Congress at Baltimore, Md., 1866, he was elected president of the National Labor Union, 1868. An opponent of strikes in theory, in practice he led some of the first great struggles of the American trade unions. Although he urged affiliation with the First International, he was influenced more personally by the English co-operative movement.

SYMMES, JOHN CLEVES (*b. Southold, N.Y., 1742; d. Cincinnati, O., 1814*), Revolutionary patriot, New Jersey legislator and jurist, Ohio pioneer. Becoming interested in Western colonization as a member of Congress from New Jersey, 1785–87, Symmes applied for a large tract between the two Miamis on the Ohio. In October 1788 he was given a definite contract for 1,000,000 acres, the so-called Miami Purchase. Early in 1789 he founded a settlement at North Bend, but was unable to make collections for sales of his land in time to meet the payments due under his contract with the government. Aided by Jonathan Dayton and Elias Boudinot, he received a patent in September 1794 for the acreage which he had actually paid for. A persevering man with qualities of leadership, he was also exceedingly careless as a businessman and lost control of much of his property; however, he had planted an important colony. Its chief settlement, Cincinnati, was perhaps the most important military and commercial outpost in the early West.

SYMONS, GEORGE GARDNER (*b. Chicago, Ill., 1865; d. Hillside, N.J., 1930*), landscape painter specializing in winter scenes.

SYMONS, THOMAS WILLIAM (*b. Keeseville, N.Y., 1849; d. Washington, D.C., 1920*), military engineer. Graduated West Point, 1874. Served on survey expeditions under George M. Wheeler, 1876–79, also with the Mississippi River Commission and other government agencies; had charge of construction of the Buffalo, N. Y., breakwater; advocated construction of New York State Barge Canal, becoming known as its "father."

SYMS, BENJAMIN (*b. probably England, c. 1591; d. Virginia, c. 1642*), Virginia planter. Resident in Virginia *post* 1624/25, Syms executed a will on Feb. 12, 1634/35 bequeathing property for establishment of a free school, thus becoming probably the first inhabitant of any North American colony to provide the means for such a purpose.

SYNG, PHILIP (*b. Cork, Ireland, 1703; d. 1789*), Philadelphia silversmith. Grandfather of Philip S. Physick. Emigrated to Maryland, 1714; was established in Philadelphia by 1720. An outstanding craftsman, Syng was a member of Benjamin Franklin's Junto, an electrical experimenter, and an original trustee of the College of Philadelphia (later University of Pennsylvania).

SZOLD, BENJAMIN (*b. Nemiskert, Hungary, 1829; d. Berkeley Springs, W. Va., 1902*), rabbi. A moderate in his religious views and an outstanding scholar, he served as rabbi of Congregation Oheb Shalom, Baltimore, Md., 1859–92, and was thereafter emeritus.

TABB, JOHN BANISTER (*b. Amelia Co., Va., 1845; d. 1909*), Confederate dispatch carrier, Roman Catholic clergyman, poet. A convert to Catholicism, 1872, Father Tabb was ordained in December 1884, and taught at St. Charles' College, Md., thereafter for the rest of his active life. His work, epigrammatic and somewhat cryptic, appeared in *Poems* (1894), *Lyrics* (1897) and other volumes. Calling himself an "unreconstructed rebel," he had a rich and paradoxical nature.

TABOR, HORACE AUSTIN WARNER (*b. Holland, Vt., 1830; d. Denver, Colo., 1899*), prospector, mineowner, merchant. One of the "rushers" to Pike's Peak in 1859. Tabor, a storekeeper, grubstaked the discoverers of the Little Pittsburgh Mine (1878) of which he became a one-third owner. Prosperous for a time, he spent the returns of the great silver lode with a lavish hand; among other benefactions he built an opera house at Leadville, Colo., and the Tabor Grand Opera House in Denver. At first he invested in real estate, but soon turning to less conservative operations, he was brought to bankruptcy by the decline in the price of silver and the crash of 1893. His second wife was the celebrated "Baby Doe."

TAFT, ALPHONSO (*b. Townshend, Vt., 1810; d. California, 1891*), lawyer. Father of Charles P. and William H. Taft. Graduated Yale, 1833. Successful at the bar in Cincinnati, O., *post* 1839, he was interested also in railroad development in the Middle West and in Cincinnati traction lines. Judge of the Cincinnati superior court, 1865–72, he served briefly as U.S. secretary of war in 1876 and as U.S. attorney-general, 1876–77. Politically a conservative, originally a Whig and later a Republican, he was U.S. minister to Austria-Hungary, 1882–84, and to Russia, 1884–85.

TAFT, CHARLES PHELPS (*b. Cincinnati, O., 1843; d. 1929*), lawyer, publisher, philanthropist. Son of Alphonso Taft; half-brother of William H. Taft. Graduated Yale, 1864; LL.B., Columbia, 1866; studied also at Heidelberg and at the Sorbonne. In the practice of law in Cincinnati, 1869–79, he acquired a controlling interest in the Cincinnati *Times*, 1879. He consolidated it in 1880 with the *Star*. Editor and ultimately sole proprietor, he built the *Times-Star* into a profitable newspaper property, made notable contributions to the aesthetic life of Cincinnati, and played a large part in shaping the career of William H. Taft.

TAFT, LORADO ZADOC (*b. Elmwood, Ill., 1860; d. Chicago, Ill., 1936*), sculptor. Graduated University of Illinois, 1879; attended École des Beaux Arts, Paris, France, 1880–83. The outstanding "art missionary" of his time, Taft lectured widely, served on city, state, and federal fine arts commissions, and worked unceasingly for public school art education. He wrote *History of American Sculpture* (1903), *Modern Tendencies in Sculpture* (1921), and hundreds of articles. At the Chicago Art Institute (1886–1906), he pioneered in new methods of instruction. A competent and essentially conservative sculptor, he was one of the early workers in group composition and monumental fountains ("Columbus Fountain," 1912, Washington, D.C.; "Thatcher Memorial Fountain," 1917, Denver; "Fountain of the Great Lakes," 1913, "Fountain of Time," 1922, both Chicago). [*Supp. 2*]

TAFT, WILLIAM HOWARD (*b. Cincinnati, O., 1857; d. Washington, D.C., 1930*), lawyer, jurist, president and chief justice of the United States. Son of Alphonso Taft; half-brother of Charles P. Taft. Graduated Yale, 1878; Cincinnati Law School, 1880. A large, good-natured young man with a tendency toward sloth, Taft early showed a weakness for procrastination which he never quite overcame. Entering Republican party politics, he served as assistant prosecutor of Hamilton County, his first public office, but in 1882, after appointment as collector of internal revenue for Cincinnati, resigned because he refused to conform to the prevalent spoils system. Resuming the practice of law, he became judge of the superior court of Ohio in March 1887. Happy in his work as a jurist, he served until 1890, attracting unwelcome labor criticism for his exhaustive opinion in the case of *Moores & Company vs. The Bricklayers' Union, No. 1*. Appointed U.S. solicitor-general, he assumed office in February 1890 and served with great credit until March 1892 when he became a federal circuit court judge.

A man of scholarly tastes and abilities, Taft found his new post ideal, but continued to win the enmity of organized labor for rulings in major cases. Although his own position on the right of labor to organize was in advance of the existing legal opinion of the day, he refused to win an easy popularity by seeking for reasons to support illegal acts by labor, especially in matters of attempted boycotts. Taft, however, ruled in favor of labor in cases involving attempts of employers to evade responsibility for negligence; in the Addyston Pipe Case, 1898, he ruled that a combination of manufacturers was in restraint of trade and enjoined them. He became president of the Philippine Commission, 1900, resigning from the bench at the request of President William McKinley. He served as civil governor of the islands, 1901–04, devoting himself with great tact and energy to the solution of several thorny problems which were legacies of the Spanish-American War and the insurrection, and also to the improvement of the economic status of the Philippines. Accepting office as U.S. secretary of war, 1904, at the request of President Theodore Roosevelt, he soon became a close adviser of the president whose impulsive qualities he balanced with his own easy-going conservatism. He became in effect the "trouble shooter" of the administration. His nomination for the presidency on the Republican ticket in 1908 was owing to his unusual talents as administrator and conciliator and also to Roosevelt's backing; Taft, however, had to be urged to run, as he stated that he had no taste for the office.

After his election over William Jennings Bryan by an electoral vote of 321 to 162, he took office in March 1909 and was troubled and harassed almost from the start. Taft's troubles were owing to certain specific mistakes but principally to his erroneous belief that the Republican party could continue in power without giving ground to its liberal wing. He was also hampered by his stolid, plodding honesty of purpose; he had no part of his predecessor's genius for guiding and (when he chose) confusing public opinion. Bringing unpopularity on himself by his courageous attempt to secure tariff revision (which Roosevelt had zealously refrained from attempting), he then found himself threatened by the insurgents in his own party such as Senators LaFollette, Dolliver, Borah and others, and by the growing strength of the Democratic party which won the House in November 1910. At odds with his sponsor, Theodore Roosevelt, because of a number of incidents, notably Roosevelt's resentment over the dismissal of Gifford Pinchot, Taft turned more and more to the conservative members of his cabinet and his party. Despite this, he proposed and achieved "trust-busting" and other reform activities much more efficiently than Roosevelt. Renominated at Chicago in June 1912 by a convention whose behavior threw Roosevelt into opposition as candidate of the Bull Moose party, Taft received only 8 electoral votes in the election of 1912 as against 88 for Roosevelt and 435 for Woodrow Wilson.

Unique among presidents in that he did not want the office and surrendered it gladly, Taft retired to Yale in March 1913 as Kent Professor of Constitutional Law. Named chief justice of the United States in June 1921, he achieved his heart's desire. In many ways his work as administrator and reformer of the Supreme Court's procedure was more important than any of his decisions; among the best of his accomplishments was the so-called Judges' Bill, February 1925. Generally conservative in his decisions, he made his most important dissent in the case of *Adkins vs. Children's Hospital* (261 *U.S.*, 525), holding that a minimum wage law for women was constitutional because sweatshop wages did just as much to impair health and morals as did long hours. In so far as Taft sanctioned control of commerce and industry, his decisions show that he believed that supervision by the federal government was superior to that by the states, but he was, in contrast, an advocate of broad federal powers under the commerce clause of the Constitution. One of his most important contributions to constitutional law is said to have been his ruling in *Myers vs. U.S.* (272 *U.S.*, 52) sustaining the presidential power to remove executive officers. A coordinator and conciliator all his life rather than an advocate, Taft was not a leader of judicial thought in the sense that Justice O. W. Holmes or Justice Brandeis was a leader. Retiring from the bench, February 1930, because of ill health, he died a month later.

TAGGART, THOMAS (*b. Co. Monaghan, Ireland, 1856; d. Indianapolis, Ind., 1929*), Indiana politician, hotel proprietor, banker. Emigrated to America as a child. Long a power in state and national Democratic politics, he served with ability as mayor of Indianapolis, 1895–1901, and was U.S. senator from Indiana, March–November 1916.

TAGLIABUE, GIUSEPPE (*b. Como, Italy, 1812; d. Mt. Vernon, N.Y., 1878*), instrument-maker. Settled in New York, N.Y., 1831, after apprenticeship in the family business of thermometer-making. For years he supplied instruments used by the U.S. Geodetic Survey; he also patented improvements on the hydrometer, a mercurial barometer and other scientific devices.

TAIT, ARTHUR FITZWILLIAM (*b. near Liverpool, England, 1819; d. Yonkers, N.Y., 1905*), landscape and animal painter. Emigrated to New York, N.Y., 1850. A skillful academic painter, Tait produced many pictures which had wide contemporary circulation as popular lithographs and are of present value as documents of phases of the life of his time.

TAIT, CHARLES (*b. Louisa Co., Va., 1768; d. Alabama, 1835*), lawyer. Cousin of Henry Clay. Admitted to the Georgia bar, 1795, he practiced in association with William H. Crawford and was a prominent figure in the faction which opposed the Yazoo sales. U.S. senator, Democrat, from Georgia, 1809–19, he was untiring in efforts on behalf of the navy, and aided in formation of Alabama as a territory and its later admission to the Union. Removing to Claiborne, Ala., 1819, he served as U.S. judge of the district of Alabama, 1820–26. He was also known for his scientific accomplishments.

TAKAMINE, JOKICHI (*b. Takaoka, Japan, 1854; d. 1922*), chemist, industrialist. Graduated University of Tokyo, 1879; studied also at Glasgow University. Headed Japanese patent bureau and also division of chemistry in Japanese department of agriculture. Resident *post* 1890 in the United States and long associated with Parke, Davis & Co., Takamine developed the starch-digesting enzyme known as takadiastase and in 1901 succeeded in isolating adrenalin from the suprarenal gland. Among other industries, he aided in the development in Japan of dyes, aluminum, the electric furnace and nitrogen fixation.

TALBOT, EMILY FAIRBANKS (*b. Winthrop, Maine, 1834; d. Holderness, N.H., 1900*), teacher, philanthropist. Wife of Israel T. Talbot. Was active in promoting organizations of university women and higher education for women.

TALBOT, ETHELBERT (*b. Fayette, Mo., 1848; d. Tuckahoe, N.Y., 1928*), Episcopal clergyman. Consecrated missionary bishop of Wyoming and Idaho, 1887, he served with ability until 1897, recounting his experiences in *My People of the Plains* (1906). Bishop of central Pennsylvania, 1898–1904, he continued as bishop of Bethlehem (after the division of the original diocese) until 1927. He was presiding bishop of the Protestant Episcopal Church, 1924–26.

TALBOT, HENRY PAUL (*b. Boston, Mass., 1864; d. 1927*), chemist. Graduated Massachusetts Institute of Technology, 1885; studied organic and physical chemistry at Leipzig (Ph.D., 1890). Taught *post* 1890 at the Massachusetts Institute of Technology, rising to head of department of chemistry and chemical engineering, 1902, and acting as dean of students, 1921–27.

TALBOT, ISRAEL TISDALE (*b. Sharon, Mass., 1829; d. Hingham, Mass., 1899*), physician. Husband of Emily F. Talbot. A leader in homeopathic medicine, he was appointed dean and professor of surgery at Boston University School of Medicine on its establishment, 1873.

TALBOT, JOHN (*b. Wymondham, England, 1645; d. Burlington, N.J., 1727*), Anglican clergyman. Assistant to George Keith on missionary travels in America, Talbot arrived in Boston, Mass., 1702. Rector of St. Mary's Church, Burlington, N.J., post 1704, he made numerous trips to England on behalf of an American episcopate and engaged in many controversies both in America and England. Losing his missionary status because of alleged disaffection toward the government, 1724, he was described by a defender as "a man universally beloved, even by the dissenters."

TALBOT, SILAS (*b. Dighton, Mass., 1751; d. New York, N.Y., 1813*), Revolutionary soldier, naval officer. Trained in the merchant service, he was commissioned captain in the Continental Army, 1775, was at the siege of Boston, and later commanded a fireship in the attempt to burn the British warship *Asia* at New York. Prominent in the defense of the Delaware River forts and in the 1778 Rhode Island campaign, he was made captain, Continental Navy, 1779, but put to sea in an unsuccessful privateer, was captured and underwent many hardships. A farmer after the war in New York State, he was chosen captain in the reorganized navy, 1794, and superintended building of the frigate *President*. He resigned from the navy, September 1801, after service as commander of the Santo Domingo station.

TALCOTT, ANDREW (*b. Glastonbury, Conn., 1797; d. Richmond, Va., 1883*), soldier, engineer. Graduated West Point, 1818. After varied service he resigned his commission, 1836, and served as chief engineer of a number of railroads. He undertook his most important work in locating and building the railroad from Vera Cruz to the city of Mexico, 1857–67. He devised the so-called "Talcott's method" of determining terrestrial latitudes.

TALCOTT, ELIZA (*b. Vernon, Conn., 1836; d. Kobe, Japan, 1911*), Congregational missionary to Japan post 1873.

TALCOTT, JOSEPH (*b. Hartford, Conn., 1669; d. 1741*), Connecticut colonial legislator, soldier and jurist. Governor of Connecticut, 1724–41, he was the first of the colony's governors to have been native born.

TALIAFERRO, LAWRENCE (*b. King George Co., Va., 1794; d. Bedford, Pa., 1871*), soldier. Indian agent at Fort Snelling (Minn.), 1819–39, he set himself to keep peace between the Sioux and their enemies the Chippewa and other neighbors, an endeavor in which he was often successful because the Indians trusted him. He engaged, however, in almost constant strife with the traders whose efforts to bribe or oust him failed.

TALIAFERRO, WILLIAM BOOTH (*b. Gloucester Co., Va., 1822; d. "Dunham Massie," Gloucester Co., Va., 1898*), lawyer, farmer, Confederate major-general. Won high reputation as one of Stonewall Jackson's lieutenants; served with great ability in the defense of Charleston, S.C., post 1863. As a Virginia legislator, 1874–79, he opposed repudiation of the state debt.

TALLMADGE, BENJAMIN (*b. Brookhaven, N.Y., 1754; d. Litchfield, Conn., 1835*), Revolutionary officer, businessman. Graduated Yale, 1773. In service as a major during most of the Revolution, Tallmadge won distinction as a field officer (notably in the capture of Fort St. George, Long Island, November 1780) and as principal director of Washington's secret service, 1778–83. Congressman, Federalist, from Connecticut, 1801–17, he served on many committees and was for a time chairman of the military affairs committee. He was a son-in-law of William Floyd.

TALLMADGE, JAMES (*b. Stanford, N.Y., 1778; d. New York, N.Y., 1853*), lawyer, New York politician and militia officer. As congressman, Democrat, from New York, 1817–19, he introduced in February 1819 an amendment to the Missouri admission bill which was designed to prohibit further introduction of slaves into that state and to provide for gradual emancipation of those born there after admission. The amendment precipitated a nation-wide controversy. Lieutenant-governor of New York, 1825–27, he concerned himself thereafter with nonpolitical activities and was a founder of the present New York University.

TALMAGE, JAMES EDWARD (*b. Hungerford, England, 1862; d. 1933*), geologist, Mormon theologian. Emigrating to Utah as a boy, he was educated at the present Brigham Young University, Lehigh, Johns Hopkins and Illinois Wesleyan. Professor of geology, University of Utah, he served as its president, 1894–97. Appointed an Apostle, 1911, he occupied himself in the service of the Mormon Church thereafter.

TALMAGE, JOHN VAN NEST (*b. Somerville, N.J., 1819; d. Boundbrook, N.J., 1892*), Dutch Reformed missionary to China, 1847–89. Brother of Thomas De W. Talmage.

TALMAGE, THOMAS DE WITT (*b. near Boundbrook, N.J., 1832; d. 1902*), Dutch Reformed clergyman, lecturer. Brother of John Van N. Talmage. Achieving notice for his sensational style of preaching while pastor of the Second Church in Philadelphia, Pa., 1862–69, he was called to the Central Presbyterian Church, Brooklyn, N.Y., and there drew the largest audiences of any contemporary minister in America. His sermons preached in the Brooklyn Tabernacle, which was built specially for him, were published in some 3500 newspapers each week. Pastor in Washington, D.C., 1894–99, he devoted himself thereafter to conducting the *Christian Herald*.

TALVJ. [See ROBINSON, THERESE ALBERTINE LOUISE VON JAKOB, 1797–1870.]

TAMARÓN, PEDRO (*b. La Guardia, Spain, date uncertain; d. Bamoa, Sinaloa, Mexico, 1768*), Mexican ecclesiastic. Emigrating to Venezuela when quite young, he was named bishop of Durango, Mexico, 1758. His diary of his episcopal tours to the most remote provinces of his diocese includes a valuable record of New Mexico in 1760.

TAMMANY (*fl. 1683–1698*), Delaware Indian chief. A legendary figure in Pennsylvania history, he is known principally in tradition and by presence of his name on several documents and in minutes of conferences. Not a principal chief of his tribe, he was believed to be a strong friend of the white settlers. As years went by, he was gradually invested with the noblest attributes and came to be regarded as a symbol of American resistance to British tyranny and to aristocracy in general.

TAMMEN, HARRY HEYE. [See BONFILS, FREDERICK GILMER, 1860–1933.]

TANEY, ROGER BROOKE (*b. Calvert Co., Md., 1777; d. Washington, D.C., 1864*), jurist, statesman. Brother-in-law of Francis S. Key. Descended through his mother from the old Catholic landed aristocracy of Maryland, Taney graduated from Dickinson College, 1795, was admitted to practice law in 1799, and served as a Federalist legislator, 1799–1800. Practicing in Frederick, Md., 1801–23, he attained considerable professional success. Breaking with the leading Federalists in 1812 over the conduct of the war with England, he became a leader of the faction called the "Coodies," and exerted a liberal influence as a state senator, 1816–21. Removing to Baltimore, Md., 1823, he soon became recognized as a leader at the bar. A master of procedural technicalities, he had a simple, direct style of delivery which was highly effective in contrast to contemporary florid eloquence. A supporter of Andrew Jackson *post* 1824, he served as attorney-general of Maryland, 1827–31, and in July 1831 was appointed attorney-general of the United States, assuming also for a short time the duties of secretary of war. In the controversy over the renewal of the charter of the second Bank of the United States, Taney, who from experience as counsel to a state bank had concluded that definite

limitations should be put on the national Bank's powers, opposed rechartering and helped draft President Jackson's veto message. After Jackson's re-election, 1832, and the revelation of the Bank's activities during the campaign, Taney with others advised the president to withdraw government deposits from the Bank of the United States and place them in selected state banks. Appointed U.S. secretary of the treasury, September 1833, to implement this policy, he did so, setting up a system of government depositories which continued to function despite the opposition of all the friends of the Bank. Far from being the pliant instrument of the president, Taney was actually putting into effect long-held opinions of his own; however, the enmity of the friends of the Bank in the Senate effected his retirement to private life in June 1834.

Rejected in January 1835 as a nominee for an associate justiceship of the U.S. Supreme Court, Taney was confirmed over Whig opposition as chief justice in March 1836. His appointment reversed certain trends which are characterized as the work of his predecessor, John Marshall. Speaking for the majority in *Charles River Bridge vs. Warren Bridge* (36 U.S., 420), Taney held that rights not specifically conferred by a corporation charter could not be inferred from the language of the document. "While the rights of private property are sacredly guarded," he declared, "we must not forget that the community also have rights, and that the happiness and well being of every citizen depends on their faithful preservation." However, this decision did not mean that Taney meant to devitalize the obligation of the contract clause of the Constitution or that his decisions would always be uncompromisingly against corporations. In *Bank of Augusta vs. Earle* (38 U.S., 519) he asserted the important principle that although a state might specifically exclude from its borders the corporations of other states, the courts, in the absence of specific legislation to that effect, would observe the rule of comity and hold that it had not done so. In effect Taney stood for a modification of the assumption that unchecked centralization of federal power and unqualified judicial benevolence toward private wealth and power always work for the good of the country. Taney felt that the commerce clause of the Constitution should be interpreted narrowly when the issue involved a mere arbitrary use to defeat state laws; he opposed use of the Constitution to prevent state regulation where regulation otherwise would not exist. He apparently had little sympathy for the *laissez-faire* regime which was being enforced upon the states under color of Constitutional necessity. Yet in dealing with the extension of admiralty laws to inland waters and the jurisdiction of federal courts over cases arising there, he asserted a breadth of federal power which had not been claimed even by Marshall.

Taney had been brought up in a Southern agrarian

atmosphere and, although he personally assisted in several plans for the amelioration of slavery, he was convinced that white and Negro could not satisfactorily live together in large numbers as equals. He was also convinced that the solution of the problem was to be arrived at only by the people who were in immediate contact with it, and not by emotional Northern abolitionism. In general he believed that the courts should scrupulously guard the sovereignty of the states from federal encroachment because that part of the population dominated by Northern culture and interests was gaining rapidly over the population of the South and must in time come to control the federal government without reference to the principles of the Constitution. Accepting the challenge which circumstances presented to him in the case of *Dred Scott vs. Sandford* (60 *U.S.*, 393), he consented to discuss in his opinion several sectional issues which might easily have been avoided. He argued that a Negro could not possess the rights of citizenship which entitled him to sue in a federal court, and that the lower court, in the case at hand, had erred in taking jurisdiction. Since doubt had been expressed, however, as to whether this phase of the question of jurisdiction could now legitimately be determined by the Supreme Court, he sought to strengthen his position by another argument in proof of the contention that the lower court had been in error in taking jurisdiction. It was admitted that Dred Scott had been born a slave. Taney sought to demonstrate that he was still a slave and that he had not, as contended, become free because of residence in territory made free by act of Congress— because Congress had never had the constitutional power to exclude slavery from the territories. Thus, under cover of a discussion of jurisdiction, Taney ruled on questions which were basic in the bitter controversy between North and South. Attacked with extreme bitterness by Republicans and Abolitionists for deciding, as they said, unnecessarily that Congress had no such power and attacked also for what were called his *obiter dicta*, Taney found that his well-meant attempt to protect the Southern culture against Northern aggression had hastened rather than retarded the ultimate downfall of the South. He wrote two other major opinions on sectional issues: the masterly analysis of the relations between the state and national governments in *Ableman vs. Booth* (62 *U.S.*, 506); and also the defense of the rights of civilians in wartime contained in *Ex parte Merryman* (*Federal Cases* No. 9,487). He had a complete lack of sympathy with the national government in the conduct of the Civil War and believed that force should not have been used to prevent the South from leaving the Union. Hence it was that when he died he was scorned by the war-frenzied masses. His character and motives have come more and more to be understood, however, and he is regarded today as a great chief justice.

TANNEBERGER, DAVID (*b. Berthelsdorf, Saxon Lusatia, 1728; d. York, Pa., 1804*), organ-builder. Emigrated to Bethlehem, Pa., 1749. He worked there and in its neighborhood for the remainder of his life, building organs for use in such distant points as Albany, N.Y., Salem, N.C., and Baltimore, Md.

TANNER, BENJAMIN (*b. New York, N.Y., 1775; d. Baltimore, Md., 1848*), engraver. Brother of Henry S. Tanner. Worked in Philadelphia, Pa., *post* 1799, where he was for a time partner with Francis Kearny and Cornelius Tiebout in banknote engraving.

TANNER, BENJAMIN TUCKER (*b. Pittsburgh, Pa., 1835; d. 1923*), bishop of the African Methodist Episcopal Church, 1888–1908.

TANNER, HENRY OSSAWA (*b. Pittsburgh, Pa., 1859; d. Paris, France, 1937*), painter. Son of Benjamin T. Tanner. Studied under Thomas Eakins at Pennsylvania Academy of the Fine Arts. A Negro, Tanner worked in the United States without success, eking out a bare living as a photographer. A student in Paris, France, under Benjamin Constant and J. P. Laurens, 1891, he made his home abroad thereafter and won prestige as a painter on religious themes. [*Supp. 2*]

TANNER, HENRY SCHENCK (*b. New York, N.Y., 1786; d. New York, 1858*), cartographer, statistical geographer. Brother of Benjamin Tanner. Author of a number of maps, atlases, guide books and geographical compendia, Tanner was principally notable for his *A New American Atlas* (five parts, 1818–23), a work of extraordinary merit which was founded on primary source material. In 1829 he published a map of the United States, 64 by 50 inches in size, on the scale of about 32 miles to the inch, practically twice as detailed as Melish's map of 1816.

TANNER, JAMES (*b. Richmondville, N.Y., 1844; d. Washington, D.C., 1927*), Union soldier, pension lobbyist, known as "Corporal Tanner." Inept U.S. commissioner of pensions, March–August 1889.

TAPPAN, ARTHUR (*b. Northampton, Mass., 1786; d. New Haven, Conn., 1865*), New York City silk merchant, Abolitionist. Brother of Benjamin and Lewis Tappan. Founded *New York Journal of Commerce*, 1827; aided free church movement of Charles G. Finney; assisted Kenyon College, Oberlin College, Auburn Theological Seminary. Helped support William L. Garrison's *Liberator, post* 1830; active in launching the *Emancipator*, 1833; first president, American Anti-Slavery Society, from which he withdrew, 1840, to help form American and Foreign Anti-Slavery Society. Convinced that slavery could be destroyed under the Constitution by political action, he supported the Liberty Party and helped establish the *National Era*. Oblivious of threats and unpopularity, he was a major financier of the Abolitionist movement.

TAPPAN, BENJAMIN (*b. Northampton, Mass., 1773; d. Steubenville, O., 1857*), Ohio legislator and jurist, anti-slavery leader. Brother of Arthur and Lewis Tappan; father of Eli T. Tappan. Studied law with Gideon Granger; settled in present Portage Co., O., 1799; practiced in Ravenna and Steubenville, and was later a partner of Edwin M. Stanton. A Jacksonian Democrat, he opposed slavery but was not an Abolitionist; he served as U.S. senator from Ohio, *post* 1838. He refused to follow instructions of the Whig legislature to oppose Texas annexation, 1845, yet he was active in free soil affairs and cast his last presidential vote for Frémont, 1856.

TAPPAN, ELI TODD (*b. Steubenville, O., 1824; d. 1888*), lawyer, educator. Son of Benjamin Tappan. Taught mathematics at Ohio University; president of Kenyon College, 1869–75; lifelong champion of common schools.

TAPPAN, EVA MARCH (*b. Blackstone, Mass., 1854; d. Worcester, Mass., 1930*), teacher, author of anthologies, textbooks and stories for children.

TAPPAN, HENRY PHILIP (*b. Rhinebeck, N.Y., 1805; d. probably Switzerland, 1881*), Congregational clergyman, philosopher. Graduated Union, 1825; Auburn Theological Seminary, 1827. Taught at University of the City of New York, 1832–37. As president, University of Michigan, 1852–63, he strove to give that institution a university status according to ideas expressed in his *University Education* (1851).

TAPPAN, LEWIS (*b. Northampton, Mass., 1788; d. Brooklyn, N.Y., 1873*), merchant, Abolitionist. Brother of Arthur and Benjamin Tappan. Proprietor of *New York Journal of Commerce*, 1828–31. Established "the Mercantile Agency," 1841, the first commercial-credit rating agency in the United States; retired from business, 1849, to devote himself to anti-slavery work and other humanitarian labors. As did his brother Arthur, Lewis Tappan repudiated William L. Garrison when the latter proposed to attach other reforms to the abolition cause; he took a leading part in the American and Foreign Anti-Slavery Society and later in the Abolition Society.

TAPPEN, FREDERICK DOBBS (*b. New York, N.Y., 1829; d. Lakewood, N.J., 1902*), banker. President of the Gallatin National Bank (1868–1902), he was invariably chosen by the other New York banks as dictator-chairman to direct their united policy in times of financial panic.

TAPPER, BERTHA FEIRING (*b. Christiania, Norway, 1859; d. Boston, Mass., 1915*), pianist, music teacher. Graduated Leipzig Conservatory of Music, 1878. Emigrating to America 1881, she played with the Kneisel Quartet and was an outstanding teacher at the New England Conservatory of Music and at the New York City Institute of Musical Art.

TARBELL, EDMUND CHARLES (*b. West Groton, Mass., 1862; d. New Castle, N.H., 1938*), painter. Trained as a lithographer, he studied at the Museum of Fine Arts, Boston, and in Paris under Boulanger and J. J. Lefebvre. Teacher of drawing and painting at the Boston Museum, 1889–1913, he was one of the group known as "The Ten" *post* 1898, and was celebrated for his solid craftsmanship, particularly in portraits of outstanding men. He was principal, Corcoran School of Art, Washington, D.C., 1918–26. [*Supp. 2*]

TARBELL, FRANK BIGELOW (*b. West Groton, Mass., 1853; d. New Haven, Conn., 1920*), archaeologist. Graduated Yale, 1873; Ph.D., 1879. Among the first Americans to achieve distinction in classical archaeology, he taught Greek at Yale and Harvard, served as director and secretary of the American School at Athens, and was professor of archaeology at the University of Chicago, 1893–1918.

TARBELL, JOSEPH (*b. probably Massachusetts, c. 1780; d. Washington, D.C., 1815*), naval officer. Appointed midshipman, 1798, he served in the naval war with France, and also with distinction in the attacks on Tripoli in 1804. On June 20, 1813, as commander of a gunboat flotilla, he engaged three British frigates indecisively in Hampton Roads. He was promoted captain, 1813.

TARBOX, INCREASE NILES (*b. East Windsor, Conn., 1815; d. West Newton, Mass., 1888*), Congregational clergyman, genealogist. A founder and an original editor (1849–51) of the *Congregationalist*, he served as secretary of the American Education Society, 1851–84.

TARR, RALPH STOCKMAN (*b. Gloucester, Mass., 1864; d. Ithaca, N.Y., 1912*), geologist, geographer. Studied at Lawrence Scientific School, Harvard, and worked under Alpheus Hyatt and Spencer F. Baird, and with the U.S. Geological Survey. Taught geology at Cornell University *post* 1892; headed department of physical geography *post* 1906. Author of a number of widely used textbooks and co-author of *Alaskan Glacier Studies* (1914), he made important contributions to glaciology.

TASHRAK. [See ZEVIN, ISRAEL JOSEPH, 1872–1926.]

TASHUNCA-UITCO. [See CRAZY HORSE, c. 1849–1877.]

TATHAM, WILLIAM (*b. Hutton-in-the-Forest, England, 1752; d. near Richmond, Va., 1819*), civil engineer, geographer. A brilliant but eccentric man, Tatham lived for long periods *post* 1769 in Virginia and on the North Carolina and Tennessee frontiers, engaging in a bewildering number of occupations. He was author, among other works, of *A Topographical Analysis of the Commonwealth of Virginia* (1791). He made a pioneer survey of Atlantic Coast from Cape Fear to Cape Hatteras *post* 1805, was the friend and correspondent of Thomas Jefferson, and collaborated with Robert Fulton in the field of canalization.

TATTNALL, JOSIAH (*b. near Savannah, Ga., 1795; d. Savannah, 1871*), naval officer. Appointed midshipman, 1812, he served aboard the *Constellation* and was in the engagement at Craney Island, Va., June 1813. Assigned to the *Epervier*, he was in the war with Algiers, 1815. Thereafter until the war with Mexico he engaged in routine duties, rising to the rank of commander; during that war he engaged in the operations on the east coast of Mexico and was promoted to captain, 1850. Although opposed to secession, he was loyal to his native state and in March 1861 was commissioned captain in the Confederate Navy, commanding the naval defenses of Georgia and South Carolina. He succeeded Franklin Buchanan as commander in Virginia waters, March 1862. On the abandonment of Norfolk, he again commanded the Georgia naval defense, particularly at Savannah.

TAUSSIG, FRANK WILLIAM (*b. St. Louis, Mo., 1859; d. Cambridge, Mass., 1940*), economist. Son of William Taussig. Educated at Harvard (A.B., 1879; Ph.D., 1883; LL.B., 1886); served there, 1882–1935, as a profoundly influential teacher of economics. As editor of the *Quarterly Journal of Economics*, 1896–1937, though essentially conservative, he introduced many new and unorthodox writers. He served as first chairman of the federal Tariff Commission, 1917–19, and as a member of the Paris Peace Conference. His writings include a famous textbook *Principles of Economics* (1911), *Tariff History of the United States* (1888), *Wages and Capital* (1896), *Investors and Money Makers* (1915), *International Trade* (1927), and, with C. S. Joslyn, a sociological study of American business leaders (1932). [*Supp. 2*]

TAUSSIG, WILLIAM (*b. Prague, Bohemia, 1826; d. St. Louis, Mo., 1913*), physician, businessman, civic leader. Emigrated to America, 1847; practiced medicine in and near St. Louis, Mo., *post* 1850. Turning to the banking profession, 1866, he served as manager, and later president, of the company organized to bridge the Mississippi River at St. Louis and of its successor companies until his retirement in 1896.

TAWNEY, JAMES ALBERTUS (*b. near Gettysburg, Pa., 1855; d. Excelsior Springs, Mo., 1919*), lawyer, Minnesota legislator. Settled in Winona, Minn., 1877. Congressman, Republican, from Minnesota, 1893–1911, he rose to the chairmanship of the committee on appropriations and was one of the clique, along with Joseph G. Cannon, John Dalzell and others, which dominated the House for a number of years. He was a consistent protectionist and orthodox Republican.

TAYLOR, ALFRED ALEXANDER (*b. Happy Valley, Tenn., 1848; d. near Johnson City, Tenn., 1931*), lawyer, Tennessee legislator and congressman. Brother of Robert L. Taylor. Republican governor of Tennessee, 1921–23, he attributed his political success and that of his brother to the fact that "We played the fiddle, were fond of dogs, and loved our fellow men."

TAYLOR, ARCHIBALD ALEXANDER EDWARD (*b. Springfield, O., 1834; d. Columbus, O., 1903*), Presbyterian clergyman. An Old School minister, he held pastorates in Kentucky, Iowa, the District of Columbia and Columbus, O.; he also served as president of University of Wooster, 1873–83.

TAYLOR, BAYARD (*b. Kennett Square, Pa., 1825; d. Germany, 1878*), traveler, author, diplomat. A printer by trade, Taylor attracted the notice of Rufus W. Griswold and was encouraged by him to publish *Ximena* (1844), a first volume of verse. Commissioned by several periodicals and newspapers (including the N.Y. *Tribune*) to contribute letters descriptive of his travels, he spent two years in Europe and on his return published the successful *Views Afoot* (1846). Thereafter until 1860 he continued to travel and tell about his travels, and also lectured widely. He represented to the home-keeping Americans of that time an enviable adventurer's image. Among his numerous books of this period, *Eldorado* (1850) still has value as an early picture of California. During the Civil War he served for a time as Washington correspondent for the N.Y. *Tribune*, and was U.S. secretary of legation at St. Petersburg, Russia, 1862–63. Subsequent to his return he continued to pour out hackwork and labored on his translation of Goethe's *Faust* (published, 1870–71). Meanwhile, increasingly ambitious for reputation as poet and man of letters, he published a great quantity of mediocre verse and three undistinguished novels. Immensely renowned in his own time, the brilliant activity of his life blinded people to the low quality of his actual achievement. Appointed U.S. minister to Germany, 1878, he died late in that year at his post. His outstanding work, his translation of *Faust*, has been extravagantly praised for its fidelity but it is, when all is said and done, a rendering in second-rate English verse.

TAYLOR, BENJAMIN FRANKLIN (*b. Lowville, N.Y., 1819; d. Cleveland, O., 1887*), journalist, lecturer, poet. Associated with the Chicago *Daily Journal*, 1845–65, he won national reputation for his realistic Civil War battle reports. A collected edition of his popular verses was published in 1886.

TAYLOR, BERT LESTON (*b. Goshen, Mass., 1866; d. Chicago, Ill., 1921*), newspaper columnist. Employed principally on newspapers in Chicago, Ill., *post* 1899, he was author of the "A Line o' Type or Two" column which set a standard for such work that has been the inspiration and despair of many other journalists. He was noted also as a writer of highly polished satirical verse.

TAYLOR, CHARLES FAYETTE (*b. Williston, Vt., 1827; d. Los Angeles, Calif., 1899*), orthopedic surgeon. M.D., University of Vermont, 1856. In practice in New York City, 1857–c. 1882, Taylor devised a method for eventual cure of the spinal lesion known as Pott's disease by giving protection to the diseased vertebrae through the principle of fixed points for adequate support. He also devised many other appliances for chronic bone, joint and muscle lesions, and was instrumental in establishing the New York Orthopedic Dispensary.

TAYLOR, CHARLES HENRY (*b. Charlestown, Mass., 1846; d. 1921*), Union soldier, journalist. Publisher of the *Boston Daily Globe, post* 1873, Taylor successfully developed his paper as a reflection of New England life and thought.

TAYLOR, CHARLOTTE DE BERNIER (*b. Savannah, Ga., 1806; d. Isle of Man, 1861*), entomologist. Daughter of William Scarbrough. A naturalist rather than a laboratory scientist, she was author of a number of early and important articles stressing the agricultural significance of entomological studies. These appeared principally in *Harper's New Monthly Magazine* during the late 1850's.

TAYLOR, CREED (*b. probably Cumberland Co., Va., 1766; d. 1836*), Virginia legislator and jurist, law teacher. Political sponsor of John Randolph of Roanoke. Conducted *post* 1821 at "Needham," his Cumberland Co. estate, a law school at which many Virginia attorneys received their training and which was recommended by Thomas Jefferson, James Madison and John Marshall.

TAYLOR, DAVID WATSON (*b. Louisa Co., Va., 1864; d. Washington, D.C., 1940*), naval officer, naval constructor. Graduated Randolph-Macon College, 1881; U.S. Naval Academy, 1885; made advanced studies at Royal Naval College, Greenwich, England. An early advocate of the need of scientific research in naval architecture, Taylor designed and constructed the navy's experimental model basin and remained in charge of it from 1899 until 1914 when he was appointed chief naval constructor. Promoted rear-admiral in 1916, he retired from active duty, 1923, but continued active in naval aviation research and ship design. He was author of *The Speed and Power of Ships* (1910) in which he proposed the "standard series method" of estimating propulsion power. He supervised the naval building program during World War I and was one of the pioneers in development and production of naval aircraft of all types. [*Supp. 2*]

TAYLOR, EDWARD (*b. Leicestershire, England, c. 1645; d. 1729*), Puritan clergyman, poet. Emigrated to Boston, Mass., 1668. Graduating from Harvard, 1671, he served as minister at Westfield, Mass., until his death. He was a strict supporter of the Congregational way. Writing in the style of the early 17th-century "concettist" poets of England, Taylor produced a number of poems marked by intensity, metrical variety and skill, and freshness of imagery —all in all perhaps the finest single poetic achievement in America before the 19th century. His works remained in manuscript virtually unknown until 1937; they were first published as *The Poetical Works of Edward Taylor* (edited by T. H. Johnson, 1939) and have received much subsequent critical attention. [*Supp. 1*]

TAYLOR, EDWARD THOMPSON (*b. Richmond, Va., 1793; d. Boston, Mass., 1871*), mariner, peddler, Methodist clergyman. Known as "Father Taylor." Minister of the Boston (Mass.) Seamen's Bethel *post* 1830, Father Taylor was reputed one of the greatest American preachers of his generation. The sermon of Father Mapple in Herman Melville's *Moby Dick* is a portrayal of Taylor's manner and method. He was highly respected for his charitable character and noted for his epigrams; he described Daniel Webster as the "best bad man he ever knew."

TAYLOR, FRANK BURSLEY (*b. Fort Wayne, Ind., 1860; d. Fort Wayne, 1938*), geologist, specialist in glacial history of the Great Lakes region. [*Supp. 2*]

TAYLOR, FRANK WALTER (*b. Philadelphia, Pa., 1874; d. Ogdensburg, N.Y., 1921*), book and magazine illustrator, painter, portraitist.

TAYLOR, FRED MANVILLE (*b. Northville, Mich., 1855; d. Pasadena, Calif., 1932*), economist. Graduated Northwestern University, 1876; Ph.D., University of Michigan, 1888. Taught economics at Michigan, 1892–1929. An authority on currency and banking, he was author of the influential *Principles of Economics* (1911, and subsequent editions).

TAYLOR, FREDERICK WINSLOW (*b. Germantown, Pa., 1856; d. Philadelphia, Pa., 1915*), mechanical engineer, inventor, efficiency expert. Learned trades of pattern-maker and machinist; graduated M.E., Stevens Institute of Technology, 1883. Noted for design and construction of large machines and for his joint discovery of the Taylor-White process of heat treatment of tool steel. Taylor evolved over years of observation a theory that by scientific study of every operation in a manufacturing plant, a fair and reasonable estimate of the production capacities of both man and machine could be made. Application of the data found would, he felt, abolish the antagonism between employer and employee and thus bring about increased efficiency. In addition, he worked out a system of analysis, classification and symbolization to be used in the study of every type of manufacturing organization. Applying his theory with success for, among other clients, the Bethlehem Steel Co., he devoted his life *post* 1901 to expounding his principles. He published *The Principles of Scientific Management* in 1911 and was author of a number of technical papers.

TAYLOR, GEORGE (*b. probably northern Ireland, 1716; d. 1781*), ironmaster, Pennsylvania colonial legislator. Emigrated to Pennsylvania *c.* 1736; operated furnaces in Bucks Co., Pa., *post c.* 1754. A moderate radical, he served as member of the Continental Congress, July 1776–*c.* February 1777. He was a signer of the Declaration of Independence.

TAYLOR, GEORGE BOARDMAN (*b. Richmond, Va., 1832; d. Rome, Italy, 1907*), Baptist clergyman. Son of James Barnett Taylor. Served as a Baptist missionary in Italy *post* 1873.

TAYLOR, GRAHAM (*b. Schenectady, N.Y., 1851; d. Ravinia, Ill., 1938*), Dutch Reformed and Congregational clergyman, civic reformer. After ministerial and teaching experience elsewhere, he served as head of the department of Christian sociology at Chicago Theological Seminary, 1892–1924; he was also founder of the Chicago Commons, a settlement house, 1894. In the fall of 1903, with Charles R. Henderson, he offered the first course for social workers in Chicago which developed through various changes of title into the Graduate School of Social Service Administration at the University of Chicago. [*Supp. 2*]

TAYLOR, HANNIS (*b. New Bern, N.C., 1851; d. 1922*), lawyer, scholar. Practiced at Mobile, Ala., 1870–92, and in Washington, D.C., *post* 1898; able U.S. minister to Spain, 1893–97; author of *The Origin and Growth of the English Constitution* (1889, 1898).

TAYLOR, HARRY (*b. present Tilton, N.H., 1862; d. Washington, D.C., 1930*), soldier. Graduated West Point, 1884. Chief engineer of the AEF in France, 1917–18, he planned port facilities, bases and training camps, supervised their construction, and took over operation of necessary French railroads, all with remarkable efficiency and speed. He also planned and constructed water systems, electrical supply, and roads for front-line troops. Promoted major-general, 1924, he retired in 1926 as chief of engineers of the U.S. Army.

TAYLOR, JAMES BARNETT (*b. Barton-upon-Humber, England, 1804; d. Richmond, Va., 1871*), Baptist clergyman. Father of George B. Taylor. Brought to New York, N.Y., as an infant, he was raised in Virginia; he held pastorates *post* 1826 in or near Richmond. He was active in mission work and in the movement to establish Richmond College.

TAYLOR, JAMES BAYARD. [See TAYLOR, BAYARD, 1825–1878.]

TAYLOR, JAMES MONROE (*b. Brooklyn, N.Y., 1848; d. 1916*), Baptist clergyman. Graduated University of Rochester, 1868; Rochester Theological Seminary, 1871. As president of Vassar College,

1836–1914, he strove for a proper endowment, carried a heavy teaching load, improved the faculty, and was largely responsible for setting and maintaining high academic standards.

TAYLOR, JAMES WICKES (*b. Starkey, N.Y., 1819; d. Winnipeg, Canada, 1893*), lawyer, journalist, government official. Practiced law in Cincinnati, O., and St. Paul, Minn.; served as special U.S. treasury agent, 1859–69; was effective U.S. consul at Winnipeg, 1870–93.

TAYLOR, JOHN (*b. Fauquier Co., Va., 1752; d. 1835*), Baptist preacher, farmer. Organized and served churches in the Virginia frontier settlements; removed to Kentucky, 1783, where he continued his work. Author of *A History of Ten Baptist Churches* (1823), a fine picture of religion on the frontier.

TAYLOR, JOHN (*b. either Orange or Caroline Co., Va., 1753; d. Caroline Co., 1824*), Revolutionary soldier, Virginia legislator, agriculturist, political philosopher. Generally known as "John Taylor of Caroline." Raised by his cousin Edmund Pendleton, he attended the College of William and Mary, read law in Pendleton's office, and was licensed to practice in 1774. He married a daughter of John Penn, 1783.

Early identified with the democratic group led by Thomas Jefferson, Taylor was prominent in forwarding land legislation for the advantage of actual settlers and favored a wider franchise and a more equal system of representation. He opposed the Federal Constitution, along with Patrick Henry and George Mason, on the ground that the rights of the individual and of the states were not sufficiently protected by it; he later roundly condemned Alexander Hamilton's financial measures. In December 1798 he introduced into the Virginia legislature the famous resolutions in support of the doctrine of delegated powers and the right of states to interpose in cases of "deliberate, palpable and dangerous exercise of other powers." U.S. senator from Virginia, 1792–94, 1803, and 1822–24, he remained a strong supporter of Jefferson and Jeffersonian principles both as public man and as writer. Among his numerous pamphlets, books and contributions to newspapers, his *An Inquiry into the Principles and Policy of the Government of the United States* (published, 1814, first conceived in 1794) deserves rank among the two or three historic contributions to political science produced in the United States. In this work he denied the existence of a natural aristocracy, and condemned the idea of a permanent debt with taxes and a banking system to support it. He proposed shortening terms of both president and senators and checking their patronage. He contended that the American government was one of divided powers, not classes, and that its agents were responsible to the people alone; in a later work he denied validity of appeals from state courts to the U.S. Supreme Court. In 1820 and 1822 he launched powerful attacks against the right of Congress to dictate to Missouri on the question of slavery, and also against the protective tariff system. His important contributions to scientific agriculture were collected in *The Arator* (1813). Champion of local democracy and state rights, he was one of America's greatest philosophers of agrarian liberalism.

TAYLOR, JOHN (*b. Milnthorpe, Westmoreland, England, 1808; d. Kaysville, Utah, 1887*), journalist, Mormon Apostle. Third president of the Utah branch of the Mormon Church, 1880–87.

TAYLOR, JOHN LOUIS (*b. London, England, 1769; d. Raleigh, N.C., 1829*), North Carolina jurist, legal writer. Justice of the state superior court, 1798–1818 (chief justice *post* 1811); chief justice, state supreme court, 1819–29.

TAYLOR, JOHN W. (*b. Charlton, N.Y., 1784; d. Cleveland, O., 1854*), lawyer, New York legislator, anti-slavery leader. Congressman, National Republican and later Whig, from New York, 1813–33; speaker of the House, 1820–21, 1825–27. Seconded James Tallmadge's amendment to the Missouri bill. Delivered early anti-slavery speeches in Congress (1819–21) in support of his proposal prohibiting introduction of slavery into territories north of 36° 30′.

TAYLOR, JOSEPH WRIGHT (*b. Monmouth Co., N.J., 1810; d. 1880*), physician, leather merchant. Founded Bryn Mawr College, purchasing land for it in 1878 and supervising construction of buildings *post* 1879; virtually the whole of his estate was left to the college.

TAYLOR, MARSHALL WILLIAM (*b. Lexington, Ky., 1846; d. New Orleans, La., 1887*), Methodist clergyman, editor of *Southwestern Christian Advocate* and other church publications.

TAYLOR, MOSES (*b. New York, N.Y., 1806; d. 1882*), banker, capitalist. Starting as an importer and sugar broker, he became president of the City Bank, N.Y., 1855. *Post* 1857, he owned a controlling interest in the Delaware, Lackawanna & Western Railroad. Active also in many other public utilities, he was treasurer of the first Atlantic Cable Co.

TAYLOR, NATHANIEL WILLIAM (*b. New Milford, Conn., 1786; d. New Haven, Conn., 1858*), theologian, educator. Graduated Yale, 1807; studied theology with Timothy Dwight whom he served as secretary. Installed as minister of the First Church, New Haven, 1812, he was appointed Dwight Professor of Didactic Theology at Yale Divinity School, 1822, and continued in this post until the end of his life. A bold, original thinker, Taylor broke through the confines of the orthodox Calvinism of his day, asserting that the freedom of the will to choose is a reality and consists in the power to distinguish between motives. To induce men to turn from evil, an appeal must be made to man's natural desire for happiness which, in a regenerated mind, becomes identical with an unselfish love of God. Debate over Taylor's opinions became a principal theological reason for the disruption of the Presbyterian Church in 1838.

TAYLOR, RAYNOR (*b. England, c. 1747; d. Philadelphia, Pa., 1825*), musician. Emigrating to America, 1792, and settling soon afterwards in Philadelphia, Taylor produced a number of entertainments featuring burlesques and parodies and known as "olios." He also composed hymns, songs, and music for the theater.

TAYLOR, RICHARD (*b. near Louisville, Ky., 1826; d. New York, N.Y., 1879*), Louisiana sugar planter and legislator, Confederate lieutenant-general. Son of Zachary Taylor. Commanding at various times under T. J. Jackson in the Valley, under Lee before Richmond, and in Louisiana, Mississippi and Alabama, Taylor performed his most notable service in stopping Gen. N. P. Banks's Red River campaign in April 1864 by decisive battles against odds at Pleasant Hill and Sabine Crossroads. He surrendered the last Confederate Army east of the Mississippi at Citronelle, Ala., May 4, 1865. Author of the important *Destruction and Reconstruction* (published 1879).

TAYLOR, RICHARD COWLING (*b. England, 1789; d. Philadelphia, Pa., 1851*), geologist. Emigrated to America, 1830, after winning high professional repute in England. Taylor made numerous surveys of the Pennsylvania coal regions and of many other mineral districts, ranging from Canada to Central America. He was author of the monumental *Statistics of Coal* (1848).

TAYLOR, ROBERT LOVE (*b. Happy Valley, Tenn., 1850; d. 1912*), lawyer, lyceum lecturer, politician. Brother of Alfred A. Taylor. Outstanding as a conciliator and a reformer of local abuses, he served as Democratic governor of Tennessee, 1887–91 and 1897–99. U.S. senator, 1907–12. A favorite of the plain people, he was unpopular with the party leaders who could not control him.

TAYLOR, ROBERT TUNSTALL (*b. Norfolk, Va., 1867; d. Baltimore, Md., 1929*), physician. B.A., Johns Hopkins, 1889; M.D., University of Virginia, 1891. In large part responsible for creation of the orthopedic department in University of Maryland medical school, he taught there until his death; he was also responsible for the founding and growth of the present Kernan Hospital and Industrial School, Baltimore.

TAYLOR, SAMUEL HARVEY (*b. Londonderry, N.H., 1807; d. Andover, Mass., 1871*), educator. Graduated Dartmouth, 1832; Andover Theological Seminary, 1837. Principal, Phillips Academy, Andover, 1837–71. A stern, able Puritan.

TAYLOR, STEVENSON (*b. New York, N.Y., 1848; d. New York, 1926*), marine engineer, machinery designer. Established high standards for the American Bureau of Shipping as president, 1916–26; served as president of the Webb Institute of Naval Architecture *post* 1899.

TAYLOR, WILLIAM (*b. Rockbridge Co., Va., 1821; d. Palo Alto, Calif., 1902*), Methodist clergyman and evangelist. After traveling and preaching literally all over the world, 1847–84, he was elected missionary bishop for Africa in which post he served until 1896. Developed "Pauline" system of self-supporting missions.

TAYLOR, WILLIAM LADD (*b. Grafton, Mass., 1854; d. 1926*), book and magazine illustrator.

TAYLOR, WILLIAM MACKERGO (*b. Kilmarnock, Scotland, 1829; d. New York, N.Y., 1895*), Congregational clergyman. Coming to America, 1871, he served as pastor of Broadway Tabernacle, New York City, 1872–92, and ranked as a preacher with Richard S. Storrs and Henry W. Beecher.

TAYLOR, WILLIAM ROGERS (*b. Newport, R.I., 1811; d. Washington, D.C., 1889*), naval officer. Son of William V. Taylor. Appointed midshipman, 1828. After service in Mexican War, he engaged in ordnance work at Washington. Promoted captain, 1862, he commanded blockade vessels off Charleston, S.C., and was captain of U.S.S. *Juniata* in the first attack on Fort Fisher, December 1864. Promoted rear-admiral, 1871, he retired, 1873.

TAYLOR, WILLIAM VIGNERON (*b. Newport, R.I., 1780; d. Newport, 1858*), naval officer. Father of William R. Taylor. Supervised rigging and arming of Oliver H. Perry's squadron before battle of Lake Erie, September 1813; served as sailing master of flagship *Lawrence* in the battle. Promoted captain, 1841, he commanded U.S.S. *Ohio* in the Mexican War. He was put on the reserved list, 1855.

TAYLOR, ZACHARY (*b. Montebello, Orange Co., Va., 1784; d. Washington, D.C., 1850*), soldier, president of the United States. Father of Richard Taylor. Nicknamed "Old Rough and Ready." Raised in Kentucky, he was appointed first lieutenant in the 7th Infantry in 1808, was promoted captain in 1810, and in 1812 won brevet of major for defense of Fort Harrison, Indiana Territory, against Indians. During the War of 1812 he assisted in defense of the frontier from Indiana to Missouri. Appointed lieutenant-colonel of the 4th Infantry, 1819, he performed arduous but uneventful service on the Southwestern and Western frontiers until 1832 when he was promoted colonel and given command of the 1st Regiment stationed at Fort Crawford (Prairie du Chien). He commanded regular troops under Gen. Henry Atkinson in the Black Hawk War and was brevetted brigadier-general for his defeat of the Seminoles at Lake Okeechobee, December 1837. Unsuccessful in a two-year campaign against the Sem-

inoles, he returned to the Southwest, 1840, where he served at Fort Gibson and Fort Smith, Ark.

Ordered to Fort Jesup on the Louisiana frontier, 1844, he prepared for action that might be necessary in view of the annexation of Texas. Collecting an army of about 4000 men at Corpus Christi, he advanced to the Rio Grande early in 1846 and established a base at Point Isabel and entrenchments opposite Matamoros. On May 8, 1846, he met the Mexicans at Palo Alto and defeated them principally with artillery; he was again successful the following day at Resaca de la Palma. Despite distrust of him in Washington, Taylor was promoted major-general by brevet and designated commander of the Army of the Rio Grande. With about 6000 men, half regulars and half volunteers, he moved against Saltillo in September, attacking Monterey on September 21. After three days of skirmishing, the Mexican army asked for and received an eight weeks' armistice which brought Taylor more criticism from Washington. Taylor's letters attacking the administration for lack of support increased the tension between him and President Polk. Evading cooperation with Gen. Winfield Scott, Taylor disobeyed orders to remain on the defensive and advanced southward, defeating the Mexicans under Santa Anna at Buena Vista, Feb. 22–23, 1847, and so ending the war in the northern provinces. Taylor ascribed most of his success against superior Mexican forces to his regular artillery. At the end of the war he had achieved a great personal popularity.

A lifelong Whig in his opinions, he was a logical candidate for the presidential nomination of that party in 1848. Endorsed by Thurlow Weed and J. J. Crittenden, he asserted that he would accept nomination only if the people drafted him, that he would not be the candidate of a party, nor would he reach the office through any agency of his own. Too outspoken to please the politicians, Taylor expressed himself on many issues, urging in particular that the executive office should return to its proper position of a coordinate government branch. He also expressed dislike for extremists on the subject of slavery, both in the North and South. Nominated on the first ballot at the Whig Convention in Philadelphia, June 1848, over Henry Clay, Winfield Scott and Daniel Webster, he expressed the policies he proposed to implement in the so-called second "Allison" letter, once again promising a nonpartisan administration. Successful in November over Lewis Cass, the Democratic candidate, Taylor delivered a noncommittal inaugural address expressive of basic Whig principles. His cabinet was harmonious and industrious but inferior. Headed by John M. Clayton of Delaware as secretary of state, it made no effort to conciliate a fractious and sensitive Congress. Dissension soon sprang up among party leaders, and although Taylor had declared for nonpartisanship, he concluded by May 1849 that all offices must be filled with his own partisans. Before his nomination he had described the Wilmot Proviso as negligible, but it now became apparent that Taylor would not veto the Proviso should a bill containing it be presented to him. Hoping to prevent sectional agitation of the question of the further extension of slavery (which he had assured the North would not take place), he encouraged California and New Mexico to apply for statehood, recommending in his message to Congress, December 1849, that both be admitted to the Union if they presented governments which were republican in form. Southern representatives led by Alexander H. Stephens filibustered to prevent a vote on the admission of California and to insist on the combination into a single measure of all proposals affecting the Mexican cession. Facing the open hostility of the Southern Whigs for his plan to admit California and New Mexico and also for his hostile attitude toward Texas, Taylor remained obstinate despite threats of secession. He died before the separate legislative acts which were devised to alleviate the situation and which are known as the Compromise of 1850 were passed. His brief experience with foreign relations was not particularly happy; the most significant achievement of the administration was the Clayton-Bulwer Treaty.

Lacking political skills and experience, Taylor displayed practical wisdom, common sense and resolution of purpose during his brief public career; these, however, were not enough for the kind of leadership demanded by the crisis of 1850.

TAZEWELL, HENRY (*b. Brunswick Co., Va., 1753; d. Philadelphia, Pa., 1799*), Virginia legislator and jurist, Revolutionary patriot. Father of Littleton W. Tazewell. Probably the most popular Virginian of his day, he served his state as U.S. senator, (Democrat) Republican, 1794–99.

TAZEWELL, LITTLETON WALLER (*b. Williamsburg, Va., 1774; d. Norfolk, Va., 1860*), lawyer, Virginia legislator, statesman. Son of Henry Tazewell. A pupil of George Wythe, he graduated from the College of William and Mary, 1791, and was licensed to practice law, 1796. An individualist, of high intellectual powers but cold and lacking in human sympathy, Tazewell enjoyed a great contemporary reputation but has left no lasting mark on history. In principle an anti-Federalist, he opposed as legislator many important policies of Jefferson's administration and later opposed the War of 1812. As U.S. senator, 1824–32, he led in opposition to President J. Q. Adams, but after supporting Andrew Jackson for the presidency, opposed Jackson's coercion policy as strongly as he opposed nullification. Elected governor of Virginia, 1834, he resigned in March 1836.

TEALL, FRANCIS AUGUSTUS (*b. Fort Ann, N.Y., 1822; d. Bloomfield, N.J., 1894*), printer, journalist. A learned and conscientious proofreader, he did outstanding work on the *American Cyclopaedia* and on the *Century Dictionary*.

TEASDALE, SARA (*b. St. Louis, Mo., 1884; d. New York, N.Y., 1933*), lyric poet. Author, among other volumes, of *Sonnets to Duse* (1907), *Flame and Shadow* (1920) and *Dark of the Moon* (1926).

TECUMSEH (*b. probably near present Oldtown, O., c. 1768; d. near present Thamesville, Ontario, Canada, 1813*), Shawnee chief. Brother of Tenskwatawa, the Prophet. A brave warrior, remarkable for humanity and trustworthiness, Tecumseh and his brother and their followers were forced by pressure of white settlers into present Indiana, 1808. They settled on the Wabash near the mouth of the Tippecanoe at a place later known as Prophet's Town. Tecumseh there developed a program of action that threatened to stop westward movement of American settlement. He maintained that no Indian land sale or cession could be valid without consent of all the tribes assembled, since the Indians owned land in common. He pointed out also that the United States had given an implied assent to this point of view under the treaty of Greenville in 1795. Seeking to combine the tribes into a confederacy to prevent further land cessions and to reform abuses which contact with the whites had brought, he visited widely among the tribes and brought more and more of them under his influence. His program was not necessarily a warlike one; he hoped that (if unmolested by the whites) his people might in time adapt to civilization and escape decadence. Led to expect help by the British officials in Canada who wished to see an Indian buffer state set up in the Old Northwest, Tecumseh defied Gov. W. H. Harrison at Vincennes in August 1810. While absent in the south on a speaking tour, Tecumseh's chance of success was lost by the action of his brother, the Prophet, who allowed himself to be tricked into the battle of Tippecanoe, November 1811. Commissioned brigadier-general by the British, Tecumseh fought in the War of 1812 with great courage and fell at the battle of the Thames.

TEDYUSKUNG (*b. in vicinity of Trenton, N.J., c. 1700; d. Wyoming, Pa., 1763*), Delaware chief, largely responsible with Christian F. Post for British success at Fort Duquesne, 1758.

TEEPLE, JOHN EDGAR (*b. Kempton, Ill., 1874; d. New York, N.Y., 1931*), chemist, educator, practicing chemical engineer. Among his many achievements in designing and directing chemical plants was his notable success in developing potash production at Searles Lake, Calif., *post* 1919. He is credited with building up the American potash industry almost single-handed.
[*Supp. 1*]

TELFAIR, EDWARD (*b. Scotland, c. 1735; d. 1807*), merchant, Georgia colonial legislator, Revolutionary patriot. Came to Virginia *c.* 1758; settled in Georgia *c.* 1766, identifying himself with the city of Savannah and its trade. Member of the Continental Congress, 1777–83, he also held a number of state appointments. Elected governor of Georgia for 1786, he acted with vigor in dealing with the Indians and in the boundary dispute with South Carolina. As governor of Georgia, 1791–94, he was in conflict with the federal government, in particular over the case of *Chisholm vs. Georgia.* He brought about by his actions the passage of the Eleventh Amendment. He was also reckless in his dealings with the state's public lands.

TELLER, HENRY MOORE (*b. Allegany Co., N.Y., 1830; d. Denver, Colo., 1914*), lawyer. In practice *post* 1861 at Central City, Colo., he became a leading figure in that territory and served as U.S. senator, Republican, 1877–82. After appointment as U.S. secretary of the interior, 1882–85, he returned to the Senate and served there until 1909. He was elected for his first two terms as a Republican, the third as an Independent Silver Republican, and the fourth as a Democrat. Outspoken as an advocate of silver remonetization, he tended more and more (as his career proceeded) to align himself with the weaker groups in society and to support woman's suffrage, income taxes and government regulation of big business. The Teller Resolution which pledged the United States to an independent Cuba was named for him. He strongly opposed United States policy in the Philippines (1899–1902) as well as President Theodore Roosevelt's policy toward Panama.

TEMPLE, OLIVER PERRY (*b. near Greeneville, Tenn., 1820; d. 1907*), Knoxville, Tenn., lawyer and Unionist, author.

TEMPLE, WILLIAM GRENVILLE (*b. Rutland, Vt., 1824; d. Washington, D.C., 1894*), naval officer. Appointed midshipman, 1840. Performed valuable Civil War service on Union blockade duty and was recommended for promotion for conduct in both attacks on Fort Fisher, December 1864 and January 1865. Retired as rear-admiral, 1884.

TEN BROECK, ABRAHAM (*b. Albany, N.Y., 1734; d. 1810*), New York colonial legislator, Revolutionary soldier. Brother-in-law of Philip Livingston. Albany County judge, 1781–94; mayor of Albany, N.Y., 1779–83, 1796–99.

TEN BROECK, RICHARD (*b. Albany, N.Y., 1812; d. near Menlo Park, Calif., 1892*), horseman. Early a partner of William R. Johnson in racing on Southern tracks, he was the owner, among other horses, of Lexington, Prioress and Starke. He was the first (1856) American horseman to race successfully on the English turf.

TENÉ-ANGPÓTE. [See KICKING BIRD, d. 1875.]

TENNENT, GILBERT (*b. Co. Armagh, Ireland, 1703; d. Philadelphia, Pa., 1764*), Presbyterian clergyman. Son of William Tennent (1673–1746); brother of

William Tennent (1705–1777). Emigrated to America as a boy. Assisted father at newly established "Log College"; was ordained at New Brunswick, N.J., 1726; was friendly with and influenced by Theodorus J. Frelinghuysen. A zealous evangelical, Tennent soon became known as a vivid preacher, and with his clerical associates in the New Jersey area prepared the way for the Great Awakening. Intimate of George Whitefield in 1739–40, he continued the work which Whitefield had begun, preaching with great force in New England and elsewhere, and attacking his conservative Presbyterian associates with great virulence as religious formalists. Reproved by the Synod of 1741 for disregarding its authority and for other disturbing actions, Tennent and members of the New Brunswick Presbytery withdrew and caused a division of the Presbyterian Church which lasted 17 years. During his later years as pastor in Philadelphia he showed evidence of regret for his earlier contentiousness and worked for a reunion of the Presbyterian Church.

TENNENT, JOHN (*b. England, c. 1700; d. place unknown, c. 1760*), physician. Active in Virginia *c.* 1725–39, he was author of *Essay on the Pleurisy* (Williamsburg, Va., 1735), an enthusiastic account of his experience in the therapeutic use of rattlesnake-root.

TENNENT, WILLIAM (*b. Ireland, 1673; d. Neshaminy, Pa., 1746*), Presbyterian clergyman, founder of the "Log College." Father of Gilbert and William Tennent (1705–1777). Emigrated to Philadelphia, Pa., *c.* 1717. Pastor at Neshaminy, Pa., *post* 1726, where he trained for the ministry and filled with his own evangelical spirit an outstanding group which included his sons and also Samuel Blair and Samuel Finley. He erected his famous "Log College," 1736. At his death, its supporters united with others in organizing the College of New Jersey.

TENNENT, WILLIAM (*b. Co. Armagh, Ireland, 1705; d. Freehold, N.J., 1777*), Presbyterian clergyman. Son of William Tennent (1673–1746); brother of Gilbert Tennent. Pastor at Freehold, N.J., *post* 1733, he was a friend of George Whitefield, a promoter of revivals, and celebrated as a peacemaker and counselor.

TENNEY, CHARLES DANIEL (*b. Boston, Mass., 1857; d. Palo Alto, Calif., 1930*), Congregational clergyman, missionary and educator in China, U.S. consular and diplomatic official in China.

TENNEY, EDWARD PAYSON (*b. Concord, N.H., 1835; d. 1916*), Congregational clergyman, educator. President of Colorado College, 1876–84.

TENNEY, TABITHA GILMAN (*b. Exeter, N.H., 1762; d. Exeter, 1837*), novelist. Author, among other works, of *Female Quixotism* (1801), a satire on the prevailing literary taste of her time, and in particular on the American fondness for foreign romantic sentimentality.

TENNEY, WILLIAM JEWETT (*b. Newport, R.I., 1811; d. Newark, N.J., 1883*), editor. Graduated Yale, 1832. A convert to Catholicism, Tenney was an important member of the staff of D. Appleton & Co., 1853–83. He served as editor of *Appleton's Annual Cyclopaedia* (1861–83) and collaborated on Jefferson Davis's *Rise and Fall of the Confederate Government* (1881).

TENSKWATAWA (*b. present Oldtown, O., c. 1768; d. place unknown, possibly Kansas, c. 1834*), Shawnee Indian, known as "The Prophet." Brother of Tecumseh whose plans for an Indian confederacy he upset by allowing himself to be maneuvered into the battle of Tippecanoe, November 1811. He was known to his contemporaries as a vain, boastful man who gave a false impression of ability and power.

TERESA, MOTHER (*b. Ireland, c. 1766; d. Georgetown, D.C., 1846*), foundress of the Visitation Order in the United States. Name in religion of Alice Lalor. Emigrated to Philadelphia, Pa., 1795, where with two friends she lived in an unofficial religious community under the direction of Father Leonard Neale. Removing with her community to Georgetown, D.C., 1799, she conducted a school. In December 1816, she and her associates took vows as Visitation nuns.

TERHUNE, MARY VIRGINIA HAWES (*b. Dennisville, Va., 1830; d. New York, N.Y., 1922*), author, writer on household management. Better known as "Marion Harland," she was author among many other works of *Common Sense in the Household* (1871), one of the most successful books of its kind.

TERRELL, EDWIN HOLLAND (*b. Brookville, Ind., 1848; d. San Antonio, Texas, 1910*), lawyer. Practiced in San Antonio, Texas *post* 1877. Active in Texas Republican politics, he served as U.S. minister to Belgium, 1889–93.

TERRY, ALFRED HOWE (*b. Hartford, Conn., 1827; d. New Haven, Conn., 1890*), lawyer, soldier. Commissioned colonel of the 2nd Connecticut Militia, 1861, he soon became colonel of the 7th Connecticut Volunteers and was promoted brigadier-general in April 1862. After outstanding service in the operations against Charleston, S.C., 1863, and those against Richmond and Petersburg, Va., 1864, he commanded in the attacks against Fort Fisher, N.C., December 1864—January 1865, achieving success in concert with fleet action under Adm. D. D. Porter. Promoted brigadier-general in the regular army, January 1865, and major-general of volunteers three months later, he remained in service after the Civil War. During the Indian troubles in the Dakotas in the 1870's, he commanded that Department. Becoming involved in controversy over the Custer Massacre (June 1876), Terry refused to make a statement with respect to Custer's conduct, preferring to accept criticism rather than create an issue. Promoted major-general, 1886, he retired in 1888. A student of the science of war, Terry was also noted for his ability to work harmoniously with others.

TERRY, DAVID SMITH (*b. Todd Co., Ky., 1823; d. Lathrop, Calif., 1889*), Mexican War and Confederate soldier, California jurist and political leader. Raised in Texas, Terry settled in California, 1849, where he practiced law and was active in Know-Nothing party activities. He became a judge of the California supreme court in 1855, and was raised to chief justice in 1857. Affiliated *post* 1859 with the Gwin Democrats, he engaged David Broderick in a duel, Sept. 13, 1859, which resulted in Broderick's death. Prior to the duel, Terry had resigned judicial office. Returning to California, 1869, after service in the Confederate Army and a short exile in Mexico, Terry resumed practice of law. He was shot dead by a bodyguard of Justice Stephen J. Field whose life Terry had threatened after the rendering of a judgment adverse to him.

TERRY, ELI (*b. East Windsor, Conn., 1772; d. Plymouth, Conn., 1852*), inventor, pioneer clock manufacturer. Set up first clock factory in America at Plymouth, Conn., *c.* 1800; became partner of Seth Thomas and another, 1807. Devised popular "pillar scroll top" wood clock, 1814; also built brass clocks of high quality, and tower clocks.

TERRY, MARSHALL ORLANDO (*b. Watervliet Center, N.Y., 1848; d. Coronado, Calif., 1933*), physician, Florida real-estate developer. As surgeon-general of New York State National Guard, he made a valuable critical study of care of New York troops in federal camps at the time of the Spanish-American War, with special reference to the high incidence of typhoid fever.

TERRY, MILTON SPENSER (*b. Coeymans, N.Y., 1840; d. Los Angeles, Calif., 1914*), Methodist clergyman, educator. Advocated the higher criticism as head of department of Hebrew and Old Testament and professor of Christian doctrine at the Garrett Biblical Institute, *post* 1884.

TESTUT, CHARLES (*b. France, c. 1818; d. New Orleans, La., 1892*), Louisiana journalist, physician, poet. Active in French-language journalism in New Orleans *post c.* 1844; indefatigable founder of unsuccessful newspapers.

TEUSLER, RUDOLF BOLLING (*b. Rome, Ga., 1876; d. Japan, 1934*), surgeon, Episcopal medical missionary. Worked in Japan *post* 1900; founded St. Luke's Hospital, Tokyo; was pioneer in public-health methods in Japan.

TEVIS, LLOYD (*b. Shelbyville, Ky., 1824; d. San Francisco, Calif., 1899*), lawyer, capitalist. Removed to California, 1849. Entered law and business partnership with James Ben Ali Haggin, 1850, at Sacramento; moved office to San Francisco, 1853. Identified with some of California's greatest business undertakings, Tevis was an early projector of telegraph lines, a promoter of the Southern Pacific Railroad and briefly its president, an organizer of the Pacific Express Co., and president of Wells, Fargo & Co., 1872–92. He was a partner in mining ventures with, among others, George Hearst and Marcus Daly.

THACHER, EDWIN (*b. De Kalb, N.Y., 1839; d. New York, N.Y., 1920*), civil engineer, bridge constructor. Graduated Rensselaer Polytechnic Institute, 1863. Invented Thacher cylindrical slide rule, 1881; devised the "Thacher bar" used in reinforced concrete construction.

THACHER, GEORGE (*b. Yarmouth, Mass., 1754; d. Biddeford, Maine, 1824*), lawyer. Settled at Biddeford, Maine, 1782. Congressman from the District of Maine, Federalist, 1789–1801; associate judge, supreme judicial court of Massachusetts, 1801–24.

THACHER, JAMES (*b. Barnstable, Mass., 1754; d. Plymouth, Mass., 1844*), physician, Revolutionary Army surgeon, historian. Author, among other works, of the valuable *A Military Journal during the American Revolutionary War* (1823, and many subsequent editions) and of the *American Medical Biography* (1828), a chief source book for the medical history of his time.

THACHER, JOHN BOYD (*b. Ballston Spa, N.Y., 1847; d. Albany, N.Y., 1909*), businessman, New York State public servant, book collector.

THACHER, PETER (*b. Salem, Mass., 1651; d. Milton, Mass., 1727*), Congregational clergyman, theologian. Graduated Harvard, 1671; held principal pastorate at Milton *post* 1681.

THACHER, PETER (*b. Milton, Mass., 1752; d. Savannah, Ga., 1802*), Congregational clergyman, Revolutionary patriot. Great-grandson of Peter Thacher (1651–1727). Graduated Harvard, 1769. Held pastorates in Malden, Mass., and at Brattle Street Church, Boston, Mass.; served as chaplain to the General Court *post* 1776. An outstanding orator on the patriot side, he was a founder of the Massachusetts Historical Society, 1790–91.

THACHER, SAMUEL COOPER (*b. Boston, Mass., 1785; d. Moulins, France, 1818*), Unitarian theologian. Son of Peter Thacher (1752–1802). Graduated Harvard, 1804. A friend and pupil of William E. Channing (1780–1842), he served as pastor of the New South Church, Boston, Mass., *post* 1811.

THACHER, THOMAS ANTHONY (*b. Hartford, Conn., 1815; d. 1886*), classicist. Graduated Yale, 1835. Taught at Yale *post* 1838, becoming eventually professor of Latin and performing much of the work which a modern dean would do. Active in the administration of the college, he and Theodore D. Woolsey were the first advocates at Yale of graduate instruction in nontechnical fields; he played a larger part in the building of modern Yale than any of his contemporaries there.

THALBERG, IRVING GRANT (*b. Brooklyn, N.Y., 1899; d. Santa Monica, Calif., 1936*), motion picture producer and studio executive. Began career as secretary to Carl Laemmle *c.* 1918 and rose to be head of studio of Universal Pictures Corp. Associated with Louis B. Mayer *post* 1923, he headed the production department of the subsequent Metro-Goldwyn-Mayer studio, 1924–32, thereafter limiting his activity because of progressive ill health. He was noted for his skill in casting and taste in production. [*Supp.* 2]

THANET, OCTAVE. [See FRENCH, ALICE, 1850–1934.]

THATCHER, BENJAMIN BUSSEY (*b. Warren, Maine, 1809; d. Boston, Mass., 1840*), lawyer, philanthropist, advocate of African colonization as solution of slavery question. Author, among other works, of *Indian Biography* (1832), the first work of its kind to seek accuracy in handling the subject.

THATCHER, GEORGE. [See THACHER, GEORGE, 1754–1824.]

THATCHER, HENRY KNOX (*b. Thomaston, Maine, 1806; d. Boston, Mass., 1880*), naval officer. Grandson of Henry Knox. Appointed midshipman, 1823; rose to commodore, 1862. After service on the North Atlantic blockading squadron, 1863–64, he was commended for his part as a division commander under Adm. David D. Porter in the reduction of Fort Fisher, N.C., December 1864—January 1865. He succeeded Adm. D. G. Farragut in command of the West Gulf blockade squadron, January 1865, and aided in the reduction of Mobile, Ala. He retired as rear-admiral, 1868.

THATCHER, MAHLON DANIEL (*b. New Buffalo, Pa., 1839; d. 1916*), pioneer Colorado merchant and banker. Removed to Pueblo, Colo., 1865, where with his brother he ran a general store. Turning to professional banking, 1871, he founded the First National Bank of Pueblo, of which he was president *post* 1889. Active in stock-raising and other businesses, he came in time to have holdings in nearly forty banks.

THATCHER, ROSCOE WILFRED (*b. Chatham Center, O., 1872; d. Amherst, Mass., 1933*), agricultural chemist. Graduated University of Nebraska, 1898. Conducted experiment stations and taught at Washington State College and University of Minnesota; served as director, New York State agricultural experiment station, 1921–27; president, Massachusetts Agricultural College, 1927–32.

THAW, WILLIAM (*b. Pittsburgh, Pa., 1818; d. Paris, France, 1889*), Pennsylvania capitalist, freighting and transportation executive. Benefactor of the present University of Pittsburgh.

THAXTER, CELIA LAIGHTON (*b. Portsmouth, N.H., 1835; d. Appledore, Isles of Shoals, N.H., 1894*), poet. Mother of Roland Thaxter. Author, among other works, of *Poems* (1872), *Among the Isles of Shoals* (1873) and *Drift-Weed* (1879).

THAXTER, ROLAND (*b. Newtonville, Mass., 1858; d. 1932*), botanist. Son of Celia L. Thaxter. Graduated Harvard, 1882; Ph.D., 1888. Taught cryptogamic botany at Harvard, 1891–1919. Renowned as a research scholar, he specialized in mycology, publishing many excellent studies. His greatest work is his *Contribution Towards a Monograph of the Laboulbeniaceae* in *Memoirs of the American Academy of Arts and Sciences* (1896–1931).

THAYER, ABBOTT HANDERSON (*b. Boston, Mass., 1849; d. Monadnock, N.H., 1921*), painter. Grandson of Gideon F. Thayer. Early skilled as a painter of animals, he attended art classes in Boston and New York and studied in Paris, France, at the atelier of J. L. Gérôme. Returning to New York City, 1879, he was chosen president of the Society of American Artists. In 1901 he was elected an Academician, but at about that time he removed to New Hampshire and adopted a hermitlike habit of life. Winner of many important distinctions, Thayer painted varied subjects and in varied techniques but ideal figures and landscapes supplied his masterpieces. Chief among these are "Caritas" in the Boston Museum of Fine Arts and "Winter Sunrise, Monadnock" in the Metropolitan Museum, New York City. Idealizing women, Thayer realized his figures on the canvas directly and sincerely, and originality was the very basis of his style. He was free from the control of French technique. Almost mystically conscious of his artistic mission, he tried to make visible the beauty of spirit he saw in a person or natural object. To gain monumentality he exaggerated light and shadow and placed his colors in large, simple masses. His color range was limited but his whites, always suggestive, are essentially part of his vision. A large part of his later career was taken up with experiments in the protective coloration of animals and the promotion of what is called "Thayer's Law" of coloration.

THAYER, ALEXANDER WHEELOCK (*b. South Natick, Mass., 1817; d. 1897*), lawyer, journalist, U.S. consular officer. Author of the standard biography of Ludwig van Beethoven, first published in Berlin (Volume I, 1866; Volume II, 1872; Volume III, 1879) and issued in an English version, edited by Henry E. Krehbiel, in 1921.

THAYER, AMOS MADDEN (*b. Mina, N.Y., 1841; d. 1905*), Union soldier, Missouri jurist. Admitted to the bar in St. Louis, Mo., 1868. Judge of the St. Louis circuit court, 1876–87, he served as federal judge for the eastern district of Missouri, 1887–94, and as federal circuit judge for the eighth circuit *post* 1894. He delivered notable opinions in cases involving the law of conspiracy in 1897 and 1903; the second of these in *U.S. vs. Northern Securities Company* had great economic significance.

THAYER, ELI (*b. Mendon, Mass., 1819; d. 1899*), Massachusetts educator, legislator, and congressman. Principal of the Oread Collegiate Institute, Worcester, Mass. Thayer originated and was principal promoter of the New England Emigrant Aid Co., chartered, February 1855, as a means of financing organized free-soil emigration to Kansas.

THAYER, EZRA RIPLEY (*b. Milton, Mass., 1866; d. 1915*), legal educator. Son of James B. Thayer; brother of William S. Thayer. Graduated Harvard, 1888; Harvard Law School, 1891. Practiced with Boston law firm of Louis D. Brandeis and with other firms. Dean, Harvard Law School, 1910–15.

THAYER, GIDEON FRENCH (*b. Watertown, Mass., 1793; d. Keene, N.H., 1864*), Massachusetts educator, businessman. Grandfather of Abbott H. Thayer. Founded Chauncy-Hall School in Boston, Mass., 1828.

THAYER, JAMES BRADLEY (*b. Haverhill, Mass., 1831; d. Cambridge, Mass., 1902*), legal educator. Father of Ezra R. and William S. Thayer. Graduated Harvard, 1852; attended Harvard Law School, 1854–56. Practiced in Boston; served as editor (with Oliver W. Holmes, Jr.) of Kent's *Commentaries* (12th edition, 1873). Professor in Harvard Law School *post* 1874, he cooperated with C. C. Langdell, J. C. Gray and James B. Ames in promoting the case system of study. A prolific writer of treatises and textbooks, he became recognized as a leading scholar in constitutional law and the law of evidence.

THAYER, JOHN (*b. Boston, Mass., 1758; d. Limerick, Ireland, 1815*), Roman Catholic clergyman. A convert to Catholicism, 1783, Thayer studied theology in Paris where he was ordained, 1787. Returning to Boston, Mass., 1790, he worked there with dedicated but tactless zeal. Replaced as pastor in 1792, he served courageously as a roving missionary through the New England towns, in Virginia, and on the Kentucky frontier until 1803 when he retired to work in Ireland.

THAYER, JOHN MILTON (*b. Bellingham, Mass., 1820; d. Lincoln, Nebr., 1906*), lawyer, Union major-general. Settled in Omaha, Nebr., 1854, where he practiced law and was commissioned first brigadier-general of the territorial militia. After distinguished service in the Western campaigns of the Civil War, he was U.S. senator, Republican, from Nebraska, 1867–71. An active Radical, he did his best work in Indian affairs. Governor of Wyoming Territory, 1875–79, he returned to Nebraska and served as Republican governor of that state, 1887–92.

THAYER, JOSEPH HENRY (*b. Boston, Mass., 1828; d. 1901*), Congregational clergyman, New Testament scholar. Graduated Harvard, 1850; Andover Theological Seminary, 1857. Taught sacred literature at Andover, and at Harvard Divinity School where he was Bussey Professor of New Testament, 1884–1901. Editor-reviser of *Greek-English Lexicon* *of the New Testament* (adapted from Grimm and Wilke, 1887).

THAYER, NATHANIEL (*b. Lancaster, Mass., 1808; d. Boston, Mass., 1883*), financier, philanthropist, benefactor of Harvard.

THAYER, SYLVANUS (*b. Braintree, Mass., 1785; d. Braintree, 1872*), military engineer, educator. Graduated West Point, 1808. Called the "Father of the Military Academy," Thayer served at West Point as superintendent, 1817–33. He instituted many needed reforms and established an efficient organization for military and academic training including an able and distinguished faculty. From 1833 until his retirement as brevet brigadier-general, 1863, he was engineer in charge of fortifications at Boston Harbor entrance and of the improvement of harbors on the New England coast. He established (1867) and endowed the Thayer School of Engineering at Dartmouth.

THAYER, THOMAS BALDWIN (*b. Boston, Mass., 1812; d. Roxbury, Mass., 1886*), Universalist clergyman. Pastor in Lowell, Mass., 1833–45, 1851–59; in Boston, Mass., 1859–67. Editor, *Universalist Quarterly,* 1864–86.

THAYER, WHITNEY EUGENE (*b. Mendon, Mass., 1838; d. Burlington, Vt., 1889*), organist, music teacher, composer.

THAYER, WILLIAM MAKEPEACE (*b. Franklin, Mass., 1820; d. Franklin, 1898*), Congregational clergyman. Author of a number of "rags-to-riches" biographies which included *The Poor Boy and Merchant Prince* (1857), *The Bobbin Boy* (1860) and *The Pioneer Boy and How He Became President* (1863).

THAYER, WILLIAM ROSCOE (*b. Boston, Mass., 1859; d. Cambridge, Mass., 1923*), journalist, editor, historian. Graduated Harvard, 1881; M.A., 1886. Editor, *Harvard Graduates' Magazine,* 1892–1915. Author of *The Dawn of Italian Independence* (1893) and the outstanding *Life and Times of Cavour* (1911), among other works.

THAYER, WILLIAM SYDNEY (*b. Milton, Mass., 1864; d. Washington, D.C., 1932*), physician. Son of James B. Thayer; brother of Ezra R. Thayer. Graduated Harvard, 1885; Harvard Medical School, 1889. After further study in Berlin and Vienna, he served on the staff of Johns Hopkins Hospital under William Osler; he later became professor of clinical medicine in Johns Hopkins Medical School and professor of medicine and physician-in-chief to the hospital. He made numerous contributions to knowledge of the circulatory system and investigated the condition of blood in leukemia, typhoid fever and malaria.

THÉBAUD, AUGUSTUS J. (*b. Nantes, France, 1807; d. New York, N.Y., 1885*), Roman Catholic clergyman, Jesuit educator. In America *post* 1838, he held various teaching and administrative appointments at institutions of his order in Kentucky, New Jersey, Canada and New York; he was three times rector of the present Fordham University. Distinguished as a preacher and lecturer, he made studies of immigration and social problems and wrote widely for Catholic magazines.

THEOBALD, SAMUEL (*b. Baltimore, Md., 1846; d. 1930*), ophthalmologist. Grandson of Nathan R. Smith, by whom he was raised. M.D., University of Maryland, 1867; studied also in Vienna and London. Practicing in Baltimore *post* 1871, he was founder of the Baltimore Eye, Ear, and Throat Charity Hospital and professor of his specialty at Johns Hopkins School of Medicine. Among other contributions, he invented lachrymal probes and introduced use of boric acid in ophthalmology.

THEUS, JEREMIAH (*b. probably Switzerland, c. 1719; d. 1774*), painter. Emigrated c. 1739 to Orangeburg Co., S.C.; by 1740 had begun his successful career as portraitist in Charleston. Painter of many men and women of the Southern colonies, he was celebrated for true if somewhat stiff and formal likenesses.

THIERRY, CAMILLE (*b. New Orleans, La., 1814; d. Bordeaux, France, 1875*), Louisiana poet. In part of Negro ancestry, Thierry resided in France *post* 1855. His popular poems were published in collected form at Bordeaux as *Les Vagabondes* (1874).

THILLY, FRANK (*b. Cincinnati, O., 1865; d. 1934*), philosopher, educator. Graduated University of Cincinnati, 1887; studied also at Berlin and Heidelberg. Taught philosophy at Cornell, University of Missouri, and Princeton; professor at Sage School, Cornell, *post* 1906. Dean, College of Arts and Sciences, Cornell, 1915–21. Adhered in principle to the so-called tradition of idealism. [*Supp.* 1]

THOBURN, ISABELLA (*b. St. Clairsville, O., 1840; d. Lucknow, India, 1901*), Methodist missionary and educator. Sister of James M. Thoburn. Associated in mission work with Clara A. Swain, she conducted schools in India, 1870–80, 1882–86 and *post* 1891.

THOBURN, JAMES MILLS (*b. St. Clairsville, O., 1836; d. Meadville, Pa., 1922*), Methodist clergyman. Brother of Isabella Thoburn. Missionary in India for the greater part of the years 1859–88; missionary bishop for India (later Southern Asia), 1888–1908; acknowledged missionary leader in his denomination.

THOMAS, ALLEN (*b. Howard Co., Md., 1830; d. Waveland, Miss., 1907*), lawyer, Louisiana planter, Confederate brigadier-general. U.S. minister to Venezuela, 1895–97.

THOMAS, AMOS RUSSELL (*b. Watertown, N.Y., 1826; d. Philadelphia, Pa., 1895*), homeopathic physician. Taught anatomy in Philadelphia Academy of the Fine Arts, 1856–70. Professor of anatomy, Hahnemann Medical College of Philadelphia, 1867–95. He served also as dean of the college *post* 1874.

THOMAS, AUGUSTUS (*b. St. Louis, Mo., 1857; d. Nyack, N.Y., 1934*), dramatist. Author or adapter of nearly seventy plays. Thomas was a master of conventional stage technique and the painstaking use of local color, but displayed little dramatic interest in what lay below the surface of his situations. His work was important in its day in helping to free the American stage from bondage to Europe and in regularizing and professionalizing the craft of the dramatist in America. Outstanding among his plays were *Alabama* (produced, 1891), *In Mizzoura* (1893), *Arizona* (1899), *The Witching Hour* (1907), *As a Man Thinks* (1911) and *The Copperhead* (1918).

THOMAS, CALVIN (*b. Lapeer, Mich., 1854; d. 1919*), German scholar. Graduated University of Michigan, 1874. Taught Germanic studies at Michigan and at Columbia University. An authority on Goethe, he produced a remarkable edition of *Faust* (1892–97) and was author of *Goethe* (1917), along with many other scholarly contributions in his field.

THOMAS, CHARLES SPALDING (*b. near Darien, Ga., 1849; d. Denver, Colo., 1934*), lawyer. Removed to Denver, Colo., 1871, where he won success in practice and was a partner of Thomas M. Patterson for a number of years. A nonconformist in politics as in other matters, he was elected governor of Colorado by the Silver Fusionists in 1898, serving until 1901. As U.S. senator, Democrat, 1913–21, he opposed the League of Nations, the soldiers' bonus and what he considered extreme demands by both capital and labor.

THOMAS, CHRISTIAN FRIEDRICH THEODORE (*b. Esens, Germany, 1835; d. Chicago, Ill., 1905*), musician. Emigrated to New York City, 1845. Pupil of his father, Thomas early won reputation as a violinist. He was elected to the Philharmonic Society, 1854, and in the next year joined William Mason (1829–1908) in the first of the long-famous series of Mason-Thomas chamber music concerts given at Dodworth's Hall. First conducting at the N.Y. Academy of Music, December 1860, Thomas entered on a new career as a kind of musical missionary, taking a series of orchestras on tours under his direction and developing the taste for symphonic music in the United States. Throughout a career filled with practical difficulties, he showed himself a shrewd program-maker, seeking to elevate public taste progressively and gradually rather than immediately. He served as conductor of the Chicago Symphony Orchestra, 1891–1905. Often a storm-center because of his artistic integrity, he was an important figure in the growth of American culture.

THOMAS, CYRUS (*b. Kingsport, Tenn., 1825; d. 1910*), ethnologist, entomologist, pioneer in Mayan studies, authority on the Mound Builders.

THOMAS, DAVID (*b. Pelham, Mass., 1762; d. Providence, R.I., 1831*), Revolutionary soldier, New York State politician. Congressman, (Democrat) Republican, from New York, 1801–08, and treasurer of New York State, 1808–10, 1812, he was a prominent supporter of DeWitt Clinton. Indicted and acquitted for attempted bribery of a legislator, 1812, he retired from politics and removed to Rhode Island.

THOMAS, DAVID (*b. Glamorganshire, Wales, 1794; d. Catasauqua, Pa., 1882*), iron manufacturer. An expert in the hot-blast method of smelting iron ore, Thomas came to Pennsylvania, 1839, and constructed the first American anthracite iron manufacturing plant at Catasauqua, Pa. (operational, July 1840).

THOMAS, EDITH MATILDA (*b. Chatham, O., 1854; d. 1925*), poet, editor. Resident in New York City *post* 1887, she was author, among other works, of *A New Year's Masque* (1885), *Lyrics and Sonnets* (1887) and *The Flower from the Ashes* (1915). Her remote, unimpassioned, classical verses were marked by painstaking craftsmanship.

THOMAS, FRANCIS (*b. near Petersville, Md., 1799; d. 1876*), lawyer, Maryland legislator. Congressman, Democrat, from Maryland, 1831–41, he was chairman of the judiciary committee, an able and eloquent parliamentarian, and a friend and defender of Andrew Jackson. As governor of Maryland, 1841–44, he preserved the state from repudiation of its debt. Retiring from politics because of a personal scandal, he emerged at the outbreak of the Civil War as a strong Unionist; while congressman, 1861–69, he supported the extreme Radicals. He was U.S. minister to Peru, 1872–75.

THOMAS, FREDERICK WILLIAM (*b. Providence, R.I., 1806; d. Washington, D.C., 1866*), journalist, author, friend and correspondent of Edgar Allan Poe.

THOMAS, GEORGE (*b. Antigua, B. W. I., c. 1695; d. London, England, 1774*). Appointed deputy governor of Pennsylvania and the Lower Counties, he served from 1738 until 1747. In bitter controversy with the Assembly over financial and military affairs for the greater part of his term, he was successful in his dealings with the Indians. Advised by Conrad Weiser, he secured the neutrality of the Iroquois, thus permitting settlement of the back country.

THOMAS, GEORGE CLIFFORD (*b. Philadelphia, Pa., 1839; d. Philadelphia, 1909*), banker, philanthropist. Partner in Jay Cooke's banking house, 1866–73, he was active *post* 1883 in Drexel & Co. and its Morgan affiliates.

THOMAS, GEORGE HENRY (*b. Southampton Co., Va., 1816; d. San Francisco, Calif., 1870*), soldier. Graduated West Point, 1840; was commissioned in the 3rd Artillery. Served in the Florida War, in several Southern garrisons, and throughout Taylor's campaign in the war with Mexico. Instructor in artillery and cavalry at West Point, 1851–54. Promoted to major, 1855, he was assigned to the 2nd (later the 5th) Cavalry, a regiment officered by men almost all of whom rose to high rank, both Union and Confederate, during the Civil War. He served with this unit in Texas and on exploration duty until 1860. Remaining loyal to the Union, Thomas commanded a brigade in the opening operations in the Shenandoah Valley, 1861, rising to brigadier-general in August. Commanding the 1st Division, Army of the Ohio, he won a decisive action at Mill Springs, January 1862, and later took part in Buell's advance to Nashville and to Pittsburg Landing. Promoted major-general, April 1862, he commanded the right wing of Halleck's army in the march against and capture of Corinth. Reassigned to Buell's army, he served during the campaign against Bragg in Kentucky; he was second in command to Buell in the Perryville operations in October. Under Rosecrans, Thomas commanded the XIV Army Corps at Stone River, and in the Tullahoma campaign of June and July 1863. In September, Thomas reached his highest pitch of fame at the battle of Chickamauga, maintaining the field with his corps despite the rout of the rest of the Union forces. After Gen. U. S. Grant ordered concentration of federal forces on Chattanooga, Thomas succeeded Rosecrans in command of the Army of the Cumberland, holding Chattanooga under great difficulties until Grant was ready to undertake a general offensive. In the battle that followed, Thomas was in general command during the seizure of Lookout Mountain and Missionary Ridge (November 1863).

Thomas's Army of the Cumberland made up over half of Gen. W. T. Sherman's force during the Atlanta campaign and was constantly engaged; units of it were first to enter Atlanta. While Sherman was marching to the sea with his main force, Thomas was designated to command a new army, based on Nashville, which would oppose Confederate forces under Gen. John Hood in the West. After a delaying action, the federal field force took position at Franklin, Tenn., checked Hood's advance there on Nov. 30, 1864, and then withdrew into Nashville. Although Grant insisted on an immediate offensive by Thomas, the latter refused to move until he was ready. When he did attack (December 15–16), he vindicated his judgment by crushing Hood's army so severely that it played no further important part in the war. Promoted major-general in the regular army for this victory, he also received the thanks of Congress. He remained in command in the Nashville area for the rest of the war and for a few years after it. In June 1869, he assumed command of the Division of the Pacific at San Francisco. Studious, deliberate but decided in action, Thomas was respected by his superiors and loved by his subordinates. Gen. U. S. Grant said of him that his military dispositions were always good and that he could not be driven from a point he was given to hold.

THOMAS, ISAIAH (*b. Boston, Mass., 1749 o.s.; d. Worcester, Mass., 1831*), printer, historian of the press. After apprenticeship to a Boston printer (Zechariah Fowle), and early journeyman work in Halifax, N.S., and Charleston, S.C., he became Fowle's partner in July 1770. Establishing the *Massachusetts Spy*, a fearless and successful Whig newspaper, in that same year, he soon bought out his partner. Removing his printing establishment to Worcester, Mass., April 1775, he continued to publish his newspaper and served as official printer for the patriots of the colony. Despite difficulties, by the end of the Revolutionary War his business was on a firm footing. The leading book and periodical publisher of his day, he conducted branches of his business in Boston, Newburyport, Baltimore and Albany, and in other towns. Notable for good typography, he published more than 400 books which included a folio Bible, a number of school textbooks, reprints of the best English literature of his day, and the first edition of *The Power of Sympathy* (1789), attributed to William H. Brown and the first novel by a native American. He was also famous for a long list of children's books, among them first American issues of *Mother Goose's Melody* (1786) and *The History of Little Goody Two-Shoes*, and illustrated editons of the *New England Primer*. He was publisher also of the *Royal American Magazine*, 1774–75, and of the *Massachusetts Magazine*, 1789–96. Retiring from personal control of his business, 1802, he devoted the rest of his life to scholarship. His *History of Printing in America* (1810) is still a recognized authority on the subject. In 1812 he founded and incorporated the American Antiquarian Society of which he became first president.

THOMAS, JESSE BURGESS (*b. Shepherdstown, present W. Va., 1777; d. Mt. Vernon, O., 1853*), lawyer, Indiana and Illinois politician. Removing to Indiana Territory c. 1803, he served as speaker of the territorial legislature, 1805–08. As territorial delegate to Congress, 1808–09, he worked successfully to secure independent territorial status for Illinois. Federal judge in Illinois, 1809–18, he was president of the Illinois constitutional convention, 1818, and served as U.S. senator, Democrat, from the state of Illinois, 1818–29. During the debate over the admission of Missouri, 1820, he introduced an amendment prohibiting slavery north of the line 36°30' except for the area of the proposed state of Missouri. This was embodied in the "Missouri Compromise."

THOMAS, JESSE BURGESS (*b. Illinois, 1832; d. Brooklyn, N.Y., 1915*), Baptist clergyman. Brooklyn, N.Y., pastor; professor of church history at Newton Theological Institution. Grandnephew of Jesse B. Thomas (1777–1853).

THOMAS, JOHN (*b. Marshfield, Mass., 1724; d. near Chambly, Canada, 1776*), physician, Revolutionary major-general. Practiced at Kingston, Mass.; served as military surgeon in French and Indian War, also as soldier. Commissioned general officer of Massachusetts troops, February 1775, he was elected brigadier-general of Continentals, June 1775. Commanded at Roxbury during siege of Boston, 1775–76; commanded occupation of Dorchester Heights, March 1776. Promoted major-general and ordered to command in Canada after the failure of Montgomery, he died of smallpox on the retreat from Quebec.

THOMAS, JOHN JACOBS (*b. Ledyard, N.Y., 1810; d. Union Springs, N.Y., 1895*), pomologist. Brother of Joseph Thomas. A pioneer fruit-grower and nurseryman in central New York, he was editor of several agricultural papers, and an outstanding associate editor of the *Country Gentleman*, 1853–94. Inventor of several farm implements, among them the smoothing harrow. Author of *The Fruit Culturist* (1846, expanded edition, 1849) which marks the beginning of systematic pomology in America.

THOMAS, JOHN WILSON (*b. near Nashville, Tenn., 1830; d. Nashville, 1906*), Tennessee railroad executive. President of the Nashville, Chattanooga & St. Louis Railway *post* 1884.

THOMAS, JOSEPH (*b. Ledyard, N.Y., 1811; d. Philadelphia, Pa., 1891*), physician, lexicographer, educator. Brother of John J. Thomas. Compiler and editor of a number of reference books for J. B. Lippincott and Co. Long associated with Swarthmore College, he was an authority in his day on etymology and pronunciation.

THOMAS, LORENZO (*b. New Castle, Del., 1804; d. Washington, D.C., 1875*), soldier. Graduated West Point, 1823. A staff officer for many years, Thomas became adjutant-general of the U.S. Army in 1861, ranking as brigadier-general. Criticized as inadequate, he was relieved in March 1863 and assigned to other duties. Reappointed adjutant-general in February 1868, he lost reputation for his foolish actions as *ad interim* secretary of war during contest for control of the War Department between President Andrew Johnson and Edwin M. Stanton.

THOMAS, MARTHA CAREY (*b. Baltimore, Md., 1857; d. Philadelphia, Pa., 1935*), educator. Niece of Hannah W. Smith. Graduated Cornell, 1877. Studied Greek at Johns Hopkins with Basil Gildersleeve and made further philological and linguistic studies abroad, winning her doctorate at University of Zurich, 1882. Appointed dean and professor of English at Bryn Mawr, 1884, she influenced the formation of its curriculum and served as its president, 1894–1922. Active in the fight for woman's suffrage and for international peace, she was also a successful fund-raiser for the Johns Hopkins Medical School, giving her assistance on condition that women be admitted there.

[*Supp. 1*]

THOMAS, PHILIP EVAN (*b. Montgomery Co., Md., 1776; d. Yonkers, N.Y., 1861*), Baltimore merchant, banker. Active in securing the charter for the Baltimore and Ohio Railroad, 1827, Thomas became its first president. He resigned in 1836 after the road had reached Harpers Ferry and its chief mechanical problems had been solved under his direction.

THOMAS, PHILIP FRANCIS (*b. Easton, Md., 1810; d. 1890*), lawyer, Maryland legislator and congressman. Democratic governor of Maryland, 1847–50; U.S. secretary of the treasury, 1860 (for one month). A Confederate sympathizer, he was denied the post-Civil War seat in the U.S. Senate to which he had been chosen.

THOMAS, RICHARD HENRY (*b. Baltimore, Md., 1854; d. Baltimore, 1904*), physician, Quaker minister, author. Developed and preached an interpretation of Christianity which met challenges of contemporary science and higher criticism.

THOMAS, ROBERT BAILEY (*b. Grafton, Mass., 1766; d. West Boylston, Mass., 1846*), founder, editor and publisher of the *Farmer's Almanack*, 1792–1846.

THOMAS, SETH (*b. Wolcott, Conn., 1785; d. Plymouth, present Thomaston, Conn., 1859*), pioneer clock manufacturer. Joined Eli Terry and another in partnership at Plymouth, Conn., 1807; began clock production on his own, 1812; purchased manufacturing rights for Terry's shelf clock, 1814. Organized Seth Thomas Clock Co., 1853.

THOMAS, THEODORE. [See THOMAS, CHRISTIAN FRIEDRICH THEODORE, 1835–1905.]

THOMAS, THEODORE GAILLARD (*b. Edisto Island, S.C., 1831; d. Thomasville, Ga., 1903*), obstetrician, gynecologist. Graduated Medical College of South Carolina, 1852; studied also in Paris and Dublin. Practiced in New York City *post* 1855; professor of obstetrics (later of gynecology) at N.Y. College of Physicians and Surgeons, 1865–90. Inventor of many surgical instruments, he originated, among many other new techniques, the operation of laparo-elytrotomy and suggested and used an incubator as early as 1867. He was author of the classic *Practical Treatise on the Diseases of Women* (1868).

THOMAS, WILLIAM WIDGERY (*b. Portland, Maine, 1839; d. 1927*), lawyer, U.S. consular officer, Maine legislator. Helped establish Swedish settlement in Aroostook Co., Maine, 1870. He was U.S. minister to Sweden and Norway, 1883–85, 1889–94 and 1897–1905.

THOMES, WILLIAM HENRY (*b. Portland, Maine, 1824; d. 1895*), mariner, journalist, California pioneer, Boston (Mass.) publisher. Author of a number of tales of the "dime-novel" variety, and of the vivid and accurate work on pioneer California entitled *On Land and Sea* (1883).

THOMPSON, ALFRED WORDSWORTH (*b. Baltimore, Md., 1840; d. Summit, N.J., 1896*), landscape, figure, and historical painter.

THOMPSON, ARTHUR WEBSTER (*b. Erie, Pa., 1875; d. Pittsburgh, Pa., 1930*), civil engineer, railroad and utilities executive. Associated with the Baltimore and Ohio, 1899–1919, he was president of the Philadelphia Co., 1919–26, and of the United Gas Improvement Co. thereafter.

THOMPSON, BENJAMIN (*b. Woburn, Mass., 1753; d. Auteuil, France, 1814*), scientist, philanthropist, better known as "Count Rumford." Early apt at mathematics and drafting, he was apprenticed to a merchant in Salem, Mass., 1766, but gave much of his time to reading, and scientific experimentation and discussion with Loammi Baldwin (1744–1807). After studying medicine and teaching school for a short time, he married a wealthy widow, 1772. By exercising his lifelong gift for promoting his own interests, he rose high in favor of Gov. Wentworth of New Hampshire. Ambivalent in his sympathies at the outbreak of the Revolution, he definitely chose the British side in the fall of 1775. After the British evacuation of Boston, he removed to England, where he again exercised his art of pleasing the great, was appointed to a sinecure and became a fellow of the Royal Society, 1779. Commissioned a British lieutenant-colonel for service in America, 1781, he engaged in action near Charleston, S.C., March 1782; he then served on Long Island until late spring 1783 when he returned to England and was put on half-pay. Touring in Europe, he entered the service of the Elector of Bavaria in which he was made major-general, councilor of state, and head of the war department. Already holder of a British knighthood, he was made a Count of the Holy Roman Empire, 1791. Famous for his efficient reforms in Bavaria, he returned to England, 1795, where he published the first volume (1796) of his *Essays, Political, Economical, and Philosophical*. He introduced improvements in heating and cooking equipment, and established (1796) a fund for the Rumford Medal of the Royal Society and the Rumford prize of the American Academy of Arts and Sciences. Returning to Bavaria as head of the council of regency, he performed important diplomatic services and supervised the department of police. Refused recognition as Bavarian minister to Great Britain, 1798, he remained for a time in London where, at his suggestion, the Royal Institution was incorporated in January 1800. He personally supervised construction of its building and secured for it the services of Humphry Davy. After helping plan the Bavarian Academy of Arts and Sciences, 1801, he settled permanently on the continent of Europe, 1802, and in 1805 married the widow of Lavoisier, the chemist, from whom he later separated. Continuing the scientific investigations he had long conducted on the transmission of heat, the absorption of moisture by various substances and the like, he developed a calorimeter and photometer, made improvements in lamps and illumination, and in his essay *Of the Excellent Qualities of Coffee* (1812) described the drip coffee pot. He contributed papers to the meetings of the Institute of France and to the Royal Society, and in 1802 published *Philosophical Papers* (projected as a two-volume work of which only one volume was issued). He is remembered best as a tireless encourager of scientific and humanitarian activities, and for his demonstration by experiment that a hot body cooling in air loses much of its heat by radiation, also that heat is a mode of motion.

THOMPSON, CEPHAS GIOVANNI (*b. Middleboro, Mass., 1809; d. New York, N.Y., 1888*), painter. Brother of Jerome B. Thompson; brother-in-law of Anna C. O. Mowatt. A successful portraitist and social figure in New York City *post* 1837, he became an intimate friend of Nathaniel Hawthorne while resident in Rome, Italy, 1852–59.

THOMPSON, CHARLES OLIVER (*b. East Windsor Hill, Conn., 1836; d. Terre Haute, Ind., 1885*), engineer. Graduated Dartmouth, 1858. Introduced shop practice in engineering teaching at present Worcester Polytechnic Institute while principal, 1868–82. President, Rose Polytechnic Institute *post* 1883.

THOMPSON, DANIEL PIERCE (*b. Charlestown, Mass., 1795; d. 1868*), lawyer, Vermont historical novelist. Raised in frontier Vermont, Thompson graduated from Middlebury College, 1820, and practiced law in Montpelier *post c.* 1823. Active in politics as successively a Democrat, a member of the Liberty party and a Republican. He was author of a number of novels of romantic adventure of which *The Green Mountain Boys* (1839) and *Locke Amsden* (1847) are considered the best.

THOMPSON, DAVID (*b. London, England, 1770; d. Canada, 1857*), fur-trader, explorer, geographer. Served for many years *post c.* 1785 as a Hudson's Bay Company apprentice and surveyor in western Canada, retiring from field service in 1812. Publication (1916) of some of his journals and field notes have won him recognition as one of the greatest land geographers of the English race. Among his achievements were the survey of the most northerly source of the Mississippi (1798), discovery of the source of the Columbia River (1807) and a survey of the Columbia from source to mouth (1811).

THOMPSON, DAVID P. (*b. Cadiz, O., 1834; d. 1901*), contractor, banker, Oregon legislator and public official. Removed to Oregon, 1853. Beginning his career as a U.S. deputy surveyor, he prospered in numerous enterprises and was a leader of the Republican party in Oregon. Among other public offices, he was mayor of Portland, 1879 and 1881.

THOMPSON, DENMAN (*b. near Girard, Pa., 1833; d. West Swanzey, N.H., 1911*), actor, playwright. Star of one of the best-known and most successful dramas to appear on the American stage, *The Old*

Homestead. Developed from a brief sketch which was first produced in Pittsburgh, Pa., 1875, the play was expanded first to three acts (produced as *Joshua Whitcomb,* Chicago, Ill., 1877) but did not appear in its final and most successful form until the production of April 1886 at Boston, Mass.

THOMPSON, EDWARD HERBERT (*b. Worcester, Mass., 1856; d. Plainfield, N.J., 1935*), explorer, archaeologist, U.S. consular official in Mexico. A pioneer scientific investigator of Mayan antiquities, Thompson is associated in particular with the work done at Chichen-Itza. [*Supp.* 1]

THOMPSON, EGBERT (*b. New York, N.Y., 1822; d. Washington, D.C., 1881*), naval officer. Nephew of Smith Thompson. Appointed midshipman, 1837. After service with the Wilkes Exploring Expedition, 1838–42, and aboard the brig U.S.S. *Somers* at the time of the famous alleged mutiny, Thompson engaged in routine duty up to the Civil War, during which he was engaged principally in service with the Union flotillas on the Mississippi River. He was balked of advancement because of alleged tardiness in supporting land operations after running the Confederate batteries at Island No. 10 with the gunboat *Pittsburg,* April 1862. He was retired as captain in 1874.

THOMPSON, HUGH MILLER (*b. Londonderry, Ireland, 1830; d. Jackson, Miss., 1902*), Episcopal clergyman. Came to America as a boy. Held a number of pastorates in the Midwest, in New York City and in New Orleans, La. Editor, *American Churchman,* 1860–71, he subsequently edited the *Church Journal.* Elected coadjutor bishop of Mississippi, 1882, he became diocesan bishop, 1887, and served until 1902.

THOMPSON, HUGH SMITH (*b. Charleston, S.C., 1836; d. New York, N.Y., 1904*), educator. Nephew of Waddy Thompson. Brilliantly successful as South Carolina superintendent of education, 1877–82, he served efficiently as Democratic governor of that state, 1882–86. Subsequently an assistant secretary of the U.S. treasury and a member of the civil service commission, he was comptroller of the New York Life Insurance Co., 1892–1904.

THOMPSON, JACOB (*b. Leasburg, N.C., 1810; d. Memphis, Tenn., 1885*), lawyer. Removed to Mississippi, 1835. Congressman, Democrat, from Mississippi, 1839–51, he was for a time chairman of the committees of public lands and Indian affairs. Efficient as U.S. secretary of the interior, 1857–61, he resigned because of his state-rights views. Serving in the Confederate Army until the fall of Vicksburg, he fomented trouble in Canada *post* 1864 as a secret Confederate agent. After a brief post-Civil War exile in Europe, he returned to America and settled permanently in Memphis.

THOMPSON, JAMES MAURICE (*b. Fairfield, Ind., 1844; d. Crawfordsville, Ind., 1901*), Confederate soldier, civil engineer, lawyer, authority on archery. Author, among other works, of the best-selling historical romance *Alice of Old Vincennes* (1900).

THOMPSON, JEREMIAH (*b. Rawdon, Yorkshire, England, 1784; d. New York, N.Y., 1835*), merchant, shipowner. Organizer (1817, with Benjamin Marshall and others) of regular American packet-ship sailings between New York and Liverpool.

THOMPSON, JEROME B. (*b. Middleboro, Mass., 1814; d. Glen Gardner, N.J., 1886*), painter. Brother of Cephas G. Thompson. He won success as a painter of rustic scenes and other subjects which were widely reproduced by lithography.

THOMPSON, JOHN [See THOMSON, JOHN, 1776–1799.]

THOMPSON, JOHN (*b. present Peru, Mass., 1802; d. 1891*), broker, commercial publisher, banker. President, First National Bank, New York City, 1863–77; co-founder of the Chase National Bank, New York City, 1877.

THOMPSON, JOHN BODINE (*b. Readington, N.J., 1830; d. Trenton, N.J., 1907*), Reformed Church clergyman, educator, liberal theologian.

THOMPSON, JOHN REUBEN (*b. Richmond, Va., 1823; d. New York, N.Y., 1873*), editor, poet. Edited *The Southern Literary Messenger,* 1847–60. While assistant secretary of Virginia during the Civil War, he helped edit *Richmond Record* and *Southern Illustrated News* and also contributed to the *Index,* spokesman of the Confederacy in England. After the war he served as literary editor of the N.Y. *Evening Post.* His collected poems were first published in 1920.

THOMPSON, JOSEPH PARRISH (*b. Philadelphia, Pa., 1819; d. Berlin, Germany, 1879*), Congregational clergyman, editor. Father of William G. Thompson. Held principal pastorate at Broadway Tabernacle, New York City, 1845–71; helped edit the *Independent,* 1848–62; was a leader in home missionary work.

THOMPSON, JOSIAH VAN KIRK (*b. near Uniontown, Pa., 1854; d. Uniontown, 1933*), Pennsylvania coal operator, banker.

THOMPSON, LAUNT (*b. Queens Co., Ireland, 1833; d. Middletown, N.Y., 1894*), sculptor. A pupil of Erastus D. Palmer, Thompson was celebrated in his time for his ideal medallion heads and for portrait busts and statues.

THOMPSON, MARTIN E. (*b. place uncertain, c. 1786; d. Glen Cove, N.Y., 1877*), architect. Described in the 1816 New York City directory as a carpenter, he designed (1822–23) the second Bank of the United States on Wall Street, New York City, and also the remarkable Merchants' Exchange (1824), destroyed in the great fire of 1835. Briefly a partner of Ithiel

Town, Thompson became a convert to the Greek Revival style. Little or nothing of the work which he did subsequently has survived in New York City, although it is supposed by some that he was the architect of the dignified houses built in the northern part of Greenwich Village, 1840–60.

THOMPSON, MAURICE. [See Thompson, James Maurice, 1844–1901.]

THOMPSON, RICHARD WIGGINTON (*b. Culpeper Co., Va., 1809; d. Terre Haute, Ind., 1900*), lawyer, Whig and Republican politician, Indiana legislator. Resident in Indiana *post c.* 1832, Thompson remained continuously active in politics and was throughout his life a figure of controversy. Secretary of the navy, 1877–81, he was frequently attacked for unethical conduct.

THOMPSON, ROBERT ELLIS (*b. near Lurgan, Ireland, 1844; d. Philadelphia, Pa., 1924*), Reformed Presbyterian clergyman, educator. Emigrated to Philadelphia as a boy. Graduated University of Pennsylvania, 1865; taught social science there, 1871–92, and was first dean of Wharton School of Finance, 1881–83. A follower of Henry C. Carey, he was author of, among other books, *Social Science and National Economy* (1875) and *Protection to Home Industry* (1886). He represents in his career the unsuccessful struggle of the national economic optimists against the rising tide of reformers, mainly socialists, who preached class cleavage instead of a harmony of economic interests. *Post* 1894 he served with great success as president of the Philadelphia Central High School.

THOMPSON, ROBERT MEANS (*b. Corsica, Pa., 1849; d. Fort Ticonderoga, N.Y., 1930*), naval officer, lawyer, financier. Graduated U.S. Naval Academy, 1868; Harvard Law School, 1874. Successful in practice and as an official of the International Nickel Co., Thompson was a benefactor of the Naval Academy and the first president of the American Olympic Association. [*Supp.* 1]

THOMPSON, SAMUEL RANKIN (*b. South Shenango, Pa., 1833; d. New Wilmington, Pa., 1896*), educator and physicist. Pioneer in public educational organization and normal school work in Nebraska, Pennsylvania and West Virginia.

THOMPSON, SEYMOUR DWIGHT (*b. Will Co., Ill., 1842; d. East Orange, N.J., 1904*), Union soldier, Missouri jurist. Principal editor, *American Law Review, post* 1883, he was distinguished chiefly for his many widely read legal treatises which included *A Treatise on Homestead and Exemption Laws* (1878), *A Treatise on the Law of Trials* (1889) and *Commentaries on the Law of Private Corporations* (1895–99).

THOMPSON, SLASON (*b. Fredericton, N.B., Canada, 1849; d. Lake Forest, Ill., 1935*), journalist. A newspaper editor of wide experience and one of the first important industrial press-agents in the United States, Thompson is remembered particularly as the friend, publisher and biographer of Eugene Field. [*Supp.* 1]

THOMPSON, SMITH (*b. Amenia, N.Y., 1768; d. Poughkeepsie, N.Y., 1843*), jurist. Graduated College of New Jersey (Princeton), 1788; studied law under James Kent. Allied by marriage with the Livingston family, he was appointed a justice of the New York supreme court, 1802, and was made chief justice, 1814. U.S. secretary of the navy, 1819–23, he accepted appointment as an associate justice of the U.S. Supreme Court and served, 1823–43. One of the group which had already begun to pull away from John Marshall's strong nationalism, he dissented in *Brown vs. Maryland* (1827) and in the same year helped overrule Marshall in *Ogden vs. Saunders;* he later (1830) dissented from Marshall's decision in *Craig vs. Missouri*. Although personally a bitter opponent of slavery, he upheld the federal Fugitive Slave Act. The most notable case in which Thompson spoke for the Court was *Kendall vs. U.S.* (1838). His opinion in this case contained a paragraph vigorously rejecting the theory attributed to Andrew Jackson that the president, under his power to see that laws are faithfully executed, may enforce his own interpretation of the Constitution by extending protection to subordinates when they violate acts of Congress or mandates of the courts. This paragraph delivered orally was expunged from the written opinion at the request of the attorney-general who denied that the theory had been urged in argument.

THOMPSON, THOMAS LARKIN (*b. present Charleston, W. Va., 1838; d. Santa Rosa, Calif., 1898*), California editor and congressman. Removed to California, 1855, where he was active in journalism and Democratic politics. Tactful and efficient as U.S. minister to Brazil, 1893–97.

THOMPSON, WADDY (*b. Pickensville, S.C., 1798; d. Tallahassee, Fla., 1868*), lawyer, South Carolina legislator. Uncle of Hugh S. Thompson; brother-in-law of Andrew and Pierce M. Butler. An ardent nullifier, he was congressman, Whig, from South Carolina, 1835–41, and served with success as U.S. minister to Mexico, 1842–44. Too honest to trim sails to the popular breeze, disapproving the war with Mexico and doubting the expediency of secession, he retired to private life.

THOMPSON, WILEY (*b. Amelia Co., Va., 1781; d. near Fort King, Fla., 1835*), Georgia soldier and legislator, Indian agent. Congressman, Democrat, from Georgia, 1821–33, he rose to chairmanship of the military affairs committee and was a bitter opponent of protection. Approving Andrew Jackson's Indian removal policy, he accepted appointment as agent to supervise removal of the Seminoles under treaties of Payne's Landing and Fort Gibson. Beginning work,

1834, Thompson was opposed by a group of chiefs under Osceola's leadership and in 1835 attempted to remove Osceola and other chiefs. Overruled by President Jackson and condemned as tyrannical by the press, he made further efforts to break Osceola's power but was ambushed and slain by the chief and some of his followers.

THOMPSON, WILL LAMARTINE (*b. Beaver Co., Pa., 1847; d. New York, N.Y., 1909*), song and hymn writer, composer of "Softly and Tenderly Jesus Is Calling."

THOMPSON, WILLIAM (*b. Ireland, 1736; d. Carlisle, Pa., 1781*), Revolutionary brigadier-general. Commanded Pennsylvania riflemen (1st Continental Infantry) at siege of Boston. Made prisoner at attack on Three Rivers, Canada, June 1776, he was paroled and later exchanged for Baron Riedesel.

THOMPSON, WILLIAM BOYCE (*b. Virginia City, Mont., 1869; d. 1930*), mine operator, financier. Founded present Boyce Thompson Institute for Plant Research, 1919.

THOMPSON, WILLIAM GILMAN (*b. New York, N.Y., 1856; d. 1927*), physician. Son of Joseph P. Thompson; nephew of Daniel C. Gilman. Graduated Yale, 1877; M.D., N.Y. College of Physicians and Surgeons, 1881. Practiced in New York City; taught at medical schools of present New York University and Cornell University; served as director of the Loomis Laboratory *post* 1888. Best known for his work in re-education in connection with war and industrial diseases, he was the founder of the N.Y. Reconstruction Hospital.

THOMPSON, WILLIAM OXLEY (*b. Cambridge, O., 1855; d. 1933*), Presbyterian clergyman. Graduated Muskingum College, 1878; Western Theological Seminary, 1882. President, Miami University, Oxford, O., 1891–99; Ohio State University, 1899–1925.

THOMPSON, WILLIAM TAPPAN (*b. Ravenna, O., 1812; d. Savannah, Ga., 1882*), journalist, humorist. Founder and editor of the *Savannah Morning News*, 1850–82. Author, among other works, of a series of humorous letters originally published in a Georgia periodical and later collected as *Major Jones's Courtship* (1843), *Major Jones's Chronicles of Pineville* (1843) and *Major Jones's Sketches of Travel* (1848).

THOMPSON, ZADOCK (*b. Bridgewater, Vt., 1796; d. Burlington, Vt., 1856*), educator, naturalist, mathematician. Author, among other works, of *History of Vermont, Natural, Civil and Statistical* (1842).

THOMSON, CHARLES (*b. Co. Derry, Ireland, 1729; d. near Philadelphia, Pa., 1824*), Philadelphia teacher and merchant. Secretary of the Continental Congress, 1774–89. Came to America as a boy; prospered in trade and was active in Pennsylvania provincial politics. Described as "the life of the

cause of liberty" in Philadelphia, Thomson performed his task of minuting the birth-records of the nation with fidelity and zeal. Disappointed in not receiving office under the new federal government, he retired to his estate, 1789, and devoted many years to Biblical scholarship and translation.

THOMSON, EDWARD (*b. Portsea, England, 1810; d. Wheeling, W. Va., 1870*), physician, Methodist clergyman. Came to America as a boy; was raised in Ohio. First president, Ohio Wesleyan University, 1842–60, he was active also as an editor and in mission work. Elected bishop, 1864, he served until his death.

THOMSON, EDWARD WILLIAM (*b. Toronto, Canada, 1849; d. Boston, Mass., 1924*), Union soldier, Canadian and American journalist, poet.

THOMSON, ELIHU (*b. Manchester, England, 1853; d. Swampscott, Mass., 1937*), scientist, inventor. Came to America as a child. Graduated Philadelphia Central High School, 1870; taught chemistry, physics, and electricity there, 1870–76, and began a partnership with Edwin J. Houston. Their success in devising an efficient and salable arc-lighting system led to the formation (1883) of the Thomson-Houston Electric Co. at Lynn, Mass., with Thomson as chief engineer. The company soon dominated the industry. In 1892 it merged with the Edison General Electric Co. to form the General Electric Co. Thomson, remaining in Lynn as a consultant, pursued investigations in many fields; he obtained nearly 700 patents. The foremost scientist in the electrical manufacturing field, he was one of the first to recognize the importance of research to industrial progress. [*Supp. 2*]

THOMSON, FRANK (*b. Chambersburg, Pa., 1841; d. Merion, Pa., 1899*), railroad executive. Associated *post* 1858 with the Pennsylvania Railroad, he served as assistant to Thomas A. Scott during the Civil War in directing military transport. Elected president of the Pennsylvania, 1897, he served until his death.

THOMSON, JOHN (*b. Petersburg, Va., 1776; d. 1799*), lawyer, orator, political writer. A leader among Virginia Jeffersonians and close friend of John Randolph of Roanoke.

THOMSON, JOHN (*b. Fochabers, Scotland, 1853; d. Brooklyn, N.Y., 1926*), patent attorney, inventor. Came to America as an infant; was raised in Wayne Co., N.Y. Obtained basic patent for disk water meter, December 1887; held a number of other patents for improvements in watch-making, printing presses, and zinc-refining. Headed the Thomson Meter Co.

THOMSON, JOHN EDGAR (*b. Delaware Co., Pa., 1808; d. Philadelphia, Pa., 1874*), civil engineer, railroad executive, financier. A pioneer in railroad engineering, he served with the Georgia Railroad, 1832–47, and won high reputation for his work on the grades of the Pennsylvania Railroad, 1847–54. Elected president of the road, 1852, Thomson purchased a variety of lines projected by the state of Pennsylvania (1857), and by consolidation of other lines west of Pittsburgh extended his system to Chicago. In 1870–71 the Pennsylvania Co., one of the first of the holding companies, was created to control these additional parts of the system. Continuously engaged up to the time of his death in important projects that were to render the Pennsylvania safe from competitive attack, Thomson also insisted on high standards of operating practice.

THOMSON, MORTIMER NEAL (*b. Riga, N.Y., 1831; d. New York, N.Y., 1875*), journalist, humorist, known as "Q. K. Philander Doesticks." Author, *post* 1854, of humorous letters vivid with slang and terse, vigorous phrases which appeared first in the *Detroit Daily Advertiser,* the *New York Tribune,* and the N.Y. *Spirit of the Times.* Thomson served as a staff reporter for the *Tribune* during the Civil War and afterwards continued his successful career as a humorous lecturer.

THOMSON, SAMUEL (*b. Alstead, N.H., 1769; d. Boston, Mass., 1843*), botanic physician, originator of the "Thomsonian system" of treatment by vegetable remedies and the vapor bath.

THOMSON, WILLIAM (*b. possibly Pennsylvania, 1727; d. Sweet Springs, Va., 1796*), Revolutionary soldier. Raised in South Carolina, Thomson traded with the Indians, was an indigo planter and was active in civic affairs and the militia. During the Revolution he rendered his greatest service at Fort Moultrie in June 1776, when, with his Rangers, he blocked the British attempt to land on Sullivan's Island.

THOMSON, WILLIAM McCLURE (*b. Spring Dale, O., 1806; d. Denver, Colo., 1894*), Presbyterian clergyman, missionary in Syria. Author, among other books, of the widely selling *The Land and the Book* (1858, enlarged edition in 1880–85), a work which greatly increased knowledge of Palestine in English-speaking countries.

THORBURN, GRANT (*b. near Dalkeith, Scotland, 1773; d. New Haven, Conn., 1863*), seedsman, author. Emigrated to New York City, 1794. Beginning trade as a seedsman *c.* 1803, he issued the first American seed catalogue, 1812. After the Scottish novelist John Galt told his life-story in *Lawrie Todd* (1830), Thorburn assumed that title as a pen name for his numerous contributions to newspapers and magazines.

THOREAU, HENRY DAVID (*b. Concord, Mass., 1817; d. Concord, 1862*), essayist, poet, transcendentalist. Thoreau most resembled his Scotch maternal ancestors; on his father's side, the family derived from the Isle of Jersey and remotely from the French city of Tours. Delighting as a boy in hunting, fishing and country sports, the young Thoreau took a passionate interest in nature; during his early maturity

his journal entries on the subject were characterized by the ecstasy of pantheism, but in later life his observations became more objective and scientific. As an undergraduate at Harvard, 1833–37, he entered little into college life, went to chapel in a green coat "because the rules required black" and solaced himself in the college library with the writings of the 17th-century English poets. He began keeping a journal in 1834 and continued the practice until the end of his life. At college he was particularly influenced by Edward T. Channing and Jones Very. After graduation he taught in the Concord town school and helped his father in what had become the family industry of pencil-making; with his brother John he conducted a private school at Concord, 1838–41.

In September 1839, he and his brother made a thirteen-day voyage down the Concord River and up the Merrimack, immortalized later by Henry in his first book. After the closing of their school because of John's bad health, Henry lived for two years with R. W. Emerson, so beginning their long friendship; he also began meeting the group now known as the Transcendental Club and became acquainted with F. H. Hedge, A. Bronson Alcott, James F. Clarke, George Ripley, Margaret Fuller and Elizabeth P. Peabody. While employed as a tutor on Staten Island, N.Y., in the home of William Emerson from spring 1843 to spring 1844, he came to know William H. Channing, Lucretia Mott, Henry James, Sr., and Horace Greeley, meanwhile seeking unsuccessfully to sell articles to the magazines.

Between July 4, 1845 and Sept. 6, 1847, he lived in a small house on Emerson's land on the northwest shore of Walden Pond, Concord, which he regarded as a retreat suitable for philosophic meditation and the practice of a simple, healthy life. During the summer of 1845 he was arrested for nonpayment of poll tax as a gesture of "civil disobedience" in protest against slavery and the Mexican War. After one night in jail he was released, the tax being paid by one of his aunts; the incident underlay his essay "Resistance to Civil Government" (later called "Civil Disobedience") first published in Elizabeth Peabody's *Aesthetic Papers* (1849) and retold in *Walden.* Thoreau regarded his two-year experiment in simple living as a success since it gave him leisure to think and write. On coming back to Concord village and his father's house in the autumn of 1847, he brought with him the first draft of his book *A Week on the Concord and Merrimack Rivers,* notes on life and literature gleaned from his journals and strung on a thread of narrative. He brought back also new journals to be used in the preparation of *Walden* six years later. He resided in Emerson's house through 1848 and published *Week on the Concord* at his own risk in the spring of 1849. Slightly over 200 copies were sold, and in 1853 three-quarters of the original thousand copies came back to the author.

Early in 1849 he returned to live in his father's house and resided there during the rest of his life, participating in the family business and sharing in its delightful social life. Late in 1849 he toured Cape Cod, in 1850 he spent a week in Canada and in 1853 went on his second journey into Maine. From these expeditions derive in part his *Excursions* (1863), *The Maine Woods* (1864), *Cape Cod* (1865), and *A Yankee in Canada* (1866), all posthumous.

Between 1847 and 1851 he took keen delight in daily walks about Concord and thought of himself happily as a poet. However, he grew involved in the slavery question once again in October 1851, and showed a growing distrust also of the rising New England industrialism with its concomitant problems of labor. These new concerns and his new critical attitude are found in *Walden, or Life in the Woods* (finished during 1853 and published Aug. 9, 1854). Seemingly parochial in its comment on the society of Concord, it had universal social criticism in it and struck blows at all the superficialities of society and government. At first blush a harmless study of nature, it was at once disarming and devastating. Subsequent to *Walden's* publication, Thoreau's life was anticlimactic and he became more the scientific observer than the poet of nature. He made his last trip to Cape Cod in 1855 and a last journey to Maine in 1857. Tuberculosis began to ravage him. Among friends whom he made in this period were John Brown of Osawatomie (met in Emerson's house, March 1857) and Walt Whitman whom he had met in New York the previous autumn. Thoreau's life burned out in a great enthusiasm, the defense of John Brown after his arrest in October 1859. He was the first American to make public utterance in defense of Brown, speaking at Concord on October 30 and in Boston on November 1. To him the John Brown affair was a touchstone which had tested and exposed the true nature of the American government.

Thoreau made a long journey to Minnesota seeking health in the spring of 1861, but returned home weaker than when he had left; his last days were spent feverishly editing manuscripts which he left for his sister, Sophia, to publish. The posthumous books already mentioned were drawn from this huge mass of manuscript material. His journal which had already served as quarry for himself was later the source for *Early Spring in Massachusetts* (1881), *Summer* (1884), *Winter* (1888), and *Autumn* (1892). Collected editions of his works were published in 1894 and 1906.

Thoreau's influence upon later literature, both English and American, is due in great part to his effective, usually staccato, although often poetically rhythmic, style. His ideas were presented with the pith and force of a man who is more concerned with incisive thought than with sustained argument and cares more for his sentences than for his essays as a whole. He is a master of the single vivid image.

At his best, he is among the finest of American prose writers, but he is most impressive when he is read in excerpts. Of all his books, only *Walden* is really organized; the other books are materials from his Journals, either padded out with reflections or left in their original leanness. His observations of nature are characterized not so much by their accuracy as by a tension that gives them at their best a splendid force, for he was always deeply perceptive of spirit manifest in form. *Walden* is his greatest achievement. It is a complete report of an experiment in thinking and living whose purpose is to argue for true values against false and to show that civilized man can escape the evils of competition and be independent of commercialism and industrialism. Although Thoreau has been called anarchistic or antisocial, it would be more accurate to describe him as one who, urging conscience above government and determined to rely upon himself before relying upon others, proposed to obey a set of laws which he regarded as more fundamental than those enforced by his particular state. His essay on civil disobedience is a classic of individualism in its inevitable conflict with government, but by no means proposes to do away with fundamental laws whose existence supports what is noblest and most worthily human. Essentially a man of letters with a touch of the prophet, Thoreau belongs with Walt Whitman as one who having put his own definition upon morality exhorted to the moral life. Both men are at the heart of the persistent American tradition of perfectibility, although Thoreau leans to the pessimistic, Whitman to the optimistic view of the matter.

THORNDIKE, ASHLEY HORACE (*b. Houlton, Maine, 1871; d. 1933*), educator, scholar. Brother of Edward L. and Lynn Thorndike. Graduated Wesleyan University, 1893; Ph.D., Harvard, 1898. Taught English at Boston University, Western Reserve, and Northwestern; professor of English, Columbia, 1906–33. An authority on the Elizabethan drama, he was author, among other works, of *Tragedy* (1908), *Shakespeare's Theatre* (1916) and *English Comedy* (1929). He was co-editor of "The Tudor Shakespeare," 1913–15.

THORNDIKE, ISRAEL (*b. Beverly, Mass., 1755; d. Boston, Mass., 1832*), Revolutionary privateersman, merchant, Massachusetts legislator. An early participant in post-Revolutionary American trade with the Orient.

THORNE, CHARLES ROBERT (*b. New York, N.Y., c. 1814; d. San Francisco, Calif., 1893*), actor, theatrical manager. Father of Charles R. Thorne (1840–1883).

THORNE, CHARLES ROBERT (*b. New York, N.Y., 1840; d. New York, 1883*), actor. Son of Charles R. Thorne (*c. 1814–1893*). Popular for many years in heroic roles in domestic melodrama.

THORNTON, HENRY WORTH (*b. Logansport, Ind., 1871; d. New York, N.Y., 1933*), railroad executive. Efficient in management of several American railroads and of the Great Eastern Railway of England. Thornton served with great ability in the British military transport service during World War I and was the directing genius and president of the Canadian National Railways, 1922–32.

THORNTON, JESSY QUINN (*b. near Point Pleasant, present W. Va., 1810; d. Salem, Oreg., 1888*), lawyer, Oregon pioneer. Removed to Oregon, 1846; was associated with Joseph L. Meek in urging (at Washington, D.C., 1848) the establishment of a territorial government for Oregon. Author of *Oregon and California in 1848* (1849).

THORNTON, JOHN WINGATE (*b. Saco, Maine, 1818; d. Scarboro, Maine, 1878*), Boston lawyer, historian, antiquary. A founder of the New England Historic Genealogical Society and of the Prince Society, he had a part in the rediscovery of the manuscript of Bradford's history "Of Plimoth Plantation" and obtained the Trelawny papers for the Maine Historical Society. He was author, among other works, of *The Landing at Cape Ann* (1854) and *The Pulpit of the American Revolution* (1860).

THORNTON, MATTHEW (*b. Ireland, c. 1714; d. Newburyport, Mass., 1803*), physician, Revolutionary patriot, New Hampshire legislator. Came to America as a boy. Began to practice medicine in Londonderry, N.H., *c.* 1740. Prominent in pre-Revolutionary activity and president of the New Hampshire provincial congress of 1775, Thornton continued active as legislator and jurist during the Revolution. Elected to the Continental Congress, 1776, he was a signer of the Declaration of Independence; he served about one year.

THORNTON, WILLIAM (*b. Jost van Dyke, V.I., 1759; d. Washington, D.C., 1828*), architect, inventor, public official. Studied medicine at Edinburgh and Aberdeen. Coming to America, 1787, he became a citizen and a resident of Philadelphia, Pa. An architect by avocation, he was associated with John Fitch in steamboat experimentation and was designer in 1789 of the Library Company of Philadelphia building on Fifth St. He is remembered chiefly as the successful competitor for the design of the U.S. Capitol, Washington, D.C., and for his defense of the design against the efforts of other architects and structural superintendents to alter it. He was also designer of the "Octagon House" (1798–1800) in Washington, of Tudor Place in Georgetown, D.C., and of Brentwood in the District of Columbia, all of which show a plastic and spatial variety and mastery rarely found in America before their time. Pavilion VII at the University of Virginia was built from a sketch by Thornton. Appointed superintendent of patents, 1802, he served in that post until his death.

Among other activities in which he engaged were the education of the deaf, the work of the American Colonization Society and the liberation of the Spanish colonies in South America.

THORNWELL, JAMES HENLEY (*b. Marlboro District, S.C., 1812; d. Columbia, S.C., 1862*), Presbyterian clergyman, educator. A teacher at South Carolina College for the greater part of the years 1837–51, he served as its president, 1851–55. Thereafter, professor of theology at the Presbyterian Seminary at Columbia, he was a leading spirit in organization of the Presbyterian Church in the Confederate States.

THORP, JOHN (*b. probably Rehoboth, Mass., 1784; d. North Wrentham, Mass., 1848*), machinist. Obtained first patent in March 1812 for a hand- and water-loom; patented a power loom, October 1816. In November and December 1828 he received the basic patents for the continuous method of spinning, covering improvements in spinning and twisting cotton, now called "ring spinning." He also patented a netting machine (1828) and a narrow fabric loom (1829).

THORPE, ROSE ALNORA HARTWICK (*b. Mishawaka, Ind., 1850; d. San Diego, Calif., 1939*), poet, author of children's books. Her most celebrated work "Curfew Must Not Ring Tonight" was first published in the Detroit (Mich.) *Commercial Advertiser*, 1870; a collection of her poems was published in 1912. [*Supp. 2*]

THORPE, THOMAS BANGS (*b. Westfield, Mass., 1815; d. New York, N.Y., 1878*), artist, humorist. Resident in Louisiana *c.* 1836–1853, Thorpe won reputation as a painter of prairie life and as a portraitist. *Post* 1853 he resided principally in New York City, contributed to periodicals and held public offices. He is remembered particularly today for his realistic sketches in prose of Southern frontier life; of these the most important was the "Big Bear of Arkansas," first published in the N.Y. *Spirit of the Times*, Mar. 27, 1841. A tall tale, and the first great piece of genuinely "Western" humor, it appeared in book form in the anthology edited by William T. Porter, *The Big Bear of Arkansas* (1845). Other specimens of his work were collected in *Mysteries of the Backwoods* (1846) and *The Hive of the Bee-Hunter* (1854). Thorpe was author also of a number of works of contemporary journalistic appeal.

THRASHER, JOHN SIDNEY (*b. Portland, Maine, 1817; d. Galveston, Texas, 1879*), journalist, adventurer. Noted as a pro-slavery protagonist of the purchase of Cuba, Thrasher was also concerned in several attempts at armed intervention there, among them the activities of John A. Quitman in 1852 and after.

THROOP, ENOS THOMPSON (*b. Johnstown, N.Y., 1784; d. 1874*), lawyer, New York jurist and politician. Uncle of Montgomery H. Throop. Elected lieutenant-governor of New York (Democrat) 1828, he became acting governor in March 1829 and after election in 1830 held the post until 1833.

THROOP, MONTGOMERY HUNT (*b. Auburn, N.Y., 1827; d. Albany, N.Y., 1892*), lawyer, legal writer. Nephew of Enos T. Throop and also of Ward Hunt. Partner at various times of his uncle Hunt and of Roscoe Conkling, Throop was a strong Democrat and opposed coercion of the South during Reconstruction. Chairman of a commission to revise the New York statutes, he was principal author of the 1877 *Code of Civil Procedure* and thereafter devoted most of his time to legal authorship.

THULSTRUP, BROR THURE (*b. Stockholm, Sweden, 1848; d. New York, N.Y., 1930*), artist, illustrator. After military training and service in Sweden and with the French Foreign Legion, he emigrated to Canada in the early 1870's, but soon removed to the United States where he was successful for many years as a painter of military subjects.

THUMB, TOM. [See STRATTON, CHARLES SHERWOOD, 1838–1883.]

THURBER, CHARLES (*b. East Brookfield, Mass., 1803; d. Nashua, N.H., 1886*), teacher, inventor, manufacturer. Received a U.S. patent in August 1843 for a hand printing machine which was the first invention that approximated the modern typewriter.

THURBER, CHRISTOPHER CARSON (*b. Norwich, Conn., 1880; d. Greece, 1930*), social worker. Performed heroic service for the Near East Relief organization in Turkey and Greece *post* 1921.

THURBER, GEORGE (*b. Providence, R.I., 1821; d. Passaic, N.J., 1890*), botanist, horticulturist. Served as botanist on Mexican Boundary Survey, 1850–53; editor, *American Agriculturist*, 1863–85. One of the earliest exponents of agricultural botany, he was a specialist in study of the grasses.

THURE de THULSTRUP. [See THULSTRUP, BROR THURE, 1848–1930.]

THURMAN, ALLEN GRANBERRY (*b. Lynchburg, Va., 1813; d. Columbus, O., 1895*), lawyer, Ohio jurist. Studied law with his uncle William Allen (1803–1879), and with Noah H. Swayne. Long active in Democratic politics in Ohio, he served in the U.S. House of Representatives, 1845–47, and was chief justice of the supreme court of Ohio, 1854–56. Opposing federal interference in the question of slavery in the territories, he was a leader of the "Peace Democrats" during the Civil War although an opponent of the doctrine of secession. Serving as U.S. senator, 1867–79, he was a partisan Democrat of the school of Jefferson, a valuable member of the judiciary committee and chairman of that committee in the 46th Congress. He is best remembered as author of the Thurman Act relating to the Pacific railroads; he ran unsuccessfully for vice-president on the Democratic ticket, 1888.

THURSBY, EMMA CECILIA (*b. Brooklyn, N.Y., 1845; d. New York, N.Y., 1931*), singer, voice teacher. One of the first American singers to win international fame and a noted interpreter of Mozart, she was teacher, among others, of Geraldine Farrar.

THURSTON, HOWARD (*b. Columbus, O., 1869; d. Miami, Fla., 1936*), magician. Influenced in choice of his profession by example of Alexander Herrmann, Thurston played for many years with trifling success until a triumphant engagement at Tony Pastor's theatre in New York City, 1899. Attractive in his personality and a fine showman who contrived his effects regardless of expense, Thurston was a leading performer in vaudeville, 1908–30, thereafter playing principally in motion-picture theatres. [*Supp.* 2]

THURSTON, LORRIN ANDREWS (*b. Honolulu, Hawaii, 1858; d. 1931*), lawyer, Hawaii official. Grandson of Lorrin Andrews. A leader in the movement to overthrow the native Hawaiian government and annex the islands to the United States, Thurston drafted the 1893 proclamation of the provisional government and headed the commission sent to Washington to secure annexation. He was prominent thereafter in industry and the tourist business and was owner-editor of the *Honolulu Advertiser*.

THURSTON, ROBERT HENRY (*b. Providence, R.I., 1839; d. Ithaca, N.Y., 1903*), engineer, educator. Son of Robert L. Thurston. Graduated Brown, 1859. Rose to rank of first assistant engineer, U.S. Navy, during Civil War service; headed department of natural and experimental philosophy, U.S. Naval Academy, 1866–71. Devised pioneer four-year course of instruction in mechanical engineering (including both a mechanical laboratory and shop courses) which became basis for curriculum at Stevens Institute of Technology where he served as professor of mechanical engineering, 1871–85. Developer of further innovating courses and techniques of instruction, he was author also of textbooks (notably *The Materials of Engineering*, 1883–84), manuals, and technical papers in many fields. Director of Sibley College, Cornell University, 1885–1903, he worked tirelessly to develop the college and its department of experimental engineering; he himself taught the courses in thermodynamics and steam-engineering.

THURSTON, ROBERT LAWTON (*b. Portsmouth, R.I., 1800; d. 1874*), pioneer manufacturer of steam engines. Father of Robert H. Thurston. Partner, *post* 1830, in the Providence Steam Engine Co. and successor firms, he was first manufacturer of engines to employ the Sickels "drop cut-off" and to build a standard form of expansion steam engine.

THWAITES, REUBEN GOLD (*b. Dorchester, Mass., 1853; d. Madison, Wis., 1913*), journalist, librarian, editor. Removed to Wisconsin, 1866. Managing editor of the *Wisconsin State Journal*, 1876–86, he became a friend and protégé of Lyman C. Draper who recommended him in 1886 for the post of secretary of the Wisconsin State Historical Society. Taking office in 1887, he built up the Society's manuscript collections (in 1891 adding the Draper Manuscripts) and generally made the Society a great center for historical research. During his tenure he produced a yearly volume of the Society's *Proceedings* and a biennial volume of *Collections* and did a vast amount of other editorial work. Among projects supervised by him were the *Jesuit Relations and Allied Documents* (73 vols., 1896–1901), *Original Journals of the Lewis and Clark Expedition* (8 vols., 1904–05), *Early Western Travels* (32 vols. of annotated reprints, 1904–07). He was author also of a number of works including *France in America* (1905) and *Wisconsin* (1908).

THWING, CHARLES FRANKLIN (*b. New Sharon, Maine, 1853; d. Cleveland, O., 1937*), Congregational clergyman, educator. Graduated Harvard, 1876; Andover Theological Seminary, 1879. Presided ably over great expansion at Western Reserve University while president, 1890–1921, establishing schools of law, dentistry, pharmacy, applied social science and also a graduate school in liberal arts. He also affiliated the university with the city in developing the Cleveland School of Education. He was a prolific writer on educational and historical subjects.

[*Supp. 2*]

TIBBLES, SUSETTE LA FLESCHE. [See BRIGHT EYES, 1854–1903.]

TIBBLES, THOMAS HENRY (*b. Washington Co., O., 1838; d. Omaha, Nebr., 1928*), journalist, social reformer, friend of the Indians, Populist leader.

TICHENOR, ISAAC (*b. Newark, N.J., 1754; d. Bennington, Vt., 1838*), lawyer, Vermont legislator and jurist. U.S. senator, Federalist, from Vermont, 1796–97. Served with tact and intelligence as governor of his state, 1797–1807, 1808–09. Once again U.S. senator, 1815–21, he played no prominent part in national affairs.

TICHENOR, ISAAC TAYLOR (*b. Spencer Co., Ky., 1825; d. Atlanta, Ga., 1902*), Baptist clergyman, Confederate chaplain, educator. Held principal pastorate in Montgomery, Ala.; first president, Alabama State Agricultural and Mechanical College, 1872–82; secretary, Southern Baptist Home Missionary Board.

TICKNOR, ELISHA (*b. Lebanon, Conn., 1757; d. Hanover, N.H., 1821*), Boston, Mass., educator and merchant. Father of George Ticknor. Urged improvement in public school system, especially establishment of free schools for children under 7 years of age.

TICKNOR, FRANCIS ORRAY (*b. Fortville, Ga., 1822; d. 1874*), physician, poet. Long in practice in rural Georgia, Ticknor was author of a number of poems including the Confederate heroic ballad "Little Giffen" and possibly "The Barefooted Boys." An incomplete collected edition of his work appeared as *Poems of Frank D. Ticknor, M.D.* (ed. Kate M. Rowland, 1879).

TICKNOR, GEORGE (*b. Boston, Mass., 1791; d. Boston, 1871*), educator, author. Son of Elisha Ticknor. Graduated Dartmouth, 1807. A man of independent means, Ticknor abandoned practice of the law for a career as a scholar. Between 1815 and 1819 he traveled widely in Europe, calling on leading scientists, scholars and men of letters and pursuing formal studies mainly at the University of Göttingen. One of the first students from the United States to attend German institutions of learning for the expressed purpose of obtaining a university training more advanced than that to be had at home, Ticknor at first devoted himself to Greek philology. On appointment to the Smith professorship of French and Spanish at Harvard with an added professorship of belles-lettres (accepted by him, November 1817), he made special studies in France, Italy and Spain. In August 1819 he was inducted into the professorship which he was to hold until 1835. A leader in efforts to broaden the stereotyped curriculum at Harvard, he proposed a division of the college into departments which would handle related subjects of study. He succeeded, however, only in making this method of organization official for his own modern language courses and resigned in favor of Henry W. Longfellow. After further travel in Europe and a long process of research, he published in 1849 his classic *History of Spanish Literature*, the first truly scholarly survey ever produced of the whole range of Spanish letters and a seminal work in later Hispanic studies. He was an active benefactor of the Boston Public Library and was author also of a number of other books, but his reputation rests on his pioneer work in Spanish literature.

TICKNOR, WILLIAM DAVIS (*b. Lebanon, N.H., 1810; d. Philadelphia, Pa., 1864*), publisher. Cousin of George Ticknor. Headed the leading New England publishing firm of its time (in which James T. Fields early became a junior partner) known successively as Allen and Ticknor (1832–33), William D. Ticknor and Co. (1833–49), Ticknor, Reed and Fields (1849–54), and Ticknor and Fields. Publisher of the *Atlantic Monthly* and of many of the leading contemporary writers of England and America. Ticknor was a close friend of Nathaniel Hawthorne.

TIDBALL, JOHN CALDWELL (*b. Ohio Co., present W. Va., 1825; d. 1906*), Union major-general of volunteers by brevet. Graduated West Point, 1848. An artillery expert, he served principally with the Army of the Potomac during the Civil War and showed outstanding skill in management of artillery in support of cavalry as well as in siege work. He retired as colonel, regular army, 1889.

1067

TIEBOUT, CORNELIUS (*b. New York, N.Y., 1777; d. New Harmony, Ind., c. 1832*), line and stipple engraver. Apprenticed to a goldsmith in New York City, Tiebout received training in London, 1793–96. After working in New York City, 1796–99, he removed to Philadelphia where he remained active until about 1825 and was in partnership, 1817–22, with Benjamin Tanner and Francis Kearny in banknote engraving. In 1826, he removed with William Maclure to New Harmony, where he taught in the community school.

TIEDEMAN, CHRISTOPHER GUSTAVUS (*b. Charleston, S.C., 1857; d. Buffalo, N.Y., 1903*), professor of law, writer of legal treatises and textbooks. Taught at University of Missouri and present New York University; dean, University of Buffalo Law School, 1902–03.

TIERNAN, FRANCES CHRISTINE FISHER (*b. Salisbury, N.C., 1846; d. Salisbury, 1920*), novelist, author. Devoted to the Confederacy and to her Catholic religion, she was author of some fifty now-forgotten novels including *Valerie Aylmer* (1870, under pseudonym of Christian Reid) and *Carmela* (1891).

TIERNEY, RICHARD HENRY (*b. Spuyten Duyvil, N.Y., 1870; d. New York, N.Y., 1928*), Roman Catholic clergyman, Jesuit, journalist. Liberal and aggressive editor of the weekly *America*, 1914–25.

TIFFANY, CHARLES LEWIS (*b. Killingly, Conn., 1812; d. Yonkers, N.Y., 1902*), jeweler. Opened a stationery and notion store in New York City, 1837, which through successive partnerships became the famous Tiffany & Co., 1853. Thenceforward until his death he was considered leader of the jewelry trade in America.

TIFFANY, KATRINA BRANDES ELY (*b. Altoona, Pa., 1875; d. New York, N.Y., 1927*), civic worker, social reformer. Daughter-in-law of Louis C. Tiffany. Graduated Bryn Mawr, 1897. A leader in charitable work, the suffrage movement, and the New York League of Women Voters.

TIFFANY, LOUIS COMFORT (*b. New York, N.Y., 1848; d. New York, 1933*), painter, glassmaker, philanthropist. Son of Charles L. Tiffany. Studied with George Inness and Samuel Colman; later studied in Paris. Organized Society of American Artists, 1877, with John La Farge, Augustus Saint-Gaudens and others. Possessed of an oriental love of color, he began experiments with stained glass, 1875, and devised a process of his own for production of what he called "Favrile glass" which brought him great popular reputation. His largest work in this medium was the curtain for the National Theatre, Mexico City; he was also a designer of jewelry, rugs and textiles and a patron of other artists.

TIFFANY, LOUIS McLANE (*b. Baltimore, Md., 1844; d. 1916*), surgeon. Grandson of Louis McLane.

M.D., University of Maryland, 1868; studied in office of Nathan R. Smith. A teacher at Maryland, 1869–1902, he was a pioneer in many fields; he is credited with performing the first nephrolithotomy in America and the first successful gastro-enterostomy in Baltimore (October 1892). For many years he dominated surgical thought and practice in Maryland.

TIFFIN, EDWARD (*b. Carlisle, England, 1766; d. probably Chillicothe, O., 1829*), physician, Ohio legislator and jurist, public official. Emigrated to present Jefferson Co., W. Va., 1784; attended Jefferson Medical College, Philadelphia, Pa.; removed to Chillicothe, O., 1798. A leader of Ohio (Democrat) Republicans, he served as the first governor of Ohio, 1803–06, and as U.S. senator, 1807–09. As commissioner of the General Land Office, 1812–14, he brought order out of its chaotic records and surveys. Thereafter until death, he served as surveyor-general of the Northwest.

TIGERT, JOHN JAMES (*b. Louisville, Ky., 1856; d. Tulsa, Okla., 1906*), clergyman of the Methodist Episcopal Church, South, educator and editor.

TIKAMTHI. [See TECUMSEH, c. 1768–1813.]

TILDEN, SAMUEL JONES (*b. New Lebanon, N.Y., 1814; d. Yonkers, N.Y., 1886*), lawyer, statesman. Acquainted as a boy with Martin Van Buren, Silas Wright, William L. Marcy and other Democratic leaders of the time, Tilden grew up in frail health and received a somewhat sporadic formal education. He attended Yale for one term in 1834 and then attended the University of the City of New York (present New York University) but concerned himself mainly for several years with writing political treatises for newspapers in support of Van Buren's policies. After attending the law school of the University of the City of New York, 1838–41, and simultaneously clerking in the office of John W. Edmonds, he was admitted to the bar and began practice in New York City, 1841. He soon became a commanding figure in the New York Democracy and a leader of the free-soil opposition group called "Barnburners." Divorced from practical leadership in the party because of the resultant split of the Democratic factions he turned his energies to the development of his law practice and was conspicuously successful in many complex cases, showing a peculiar genius for railroad reorganization and refinancing. In this way, and through acquisition of mining interests, he laid the foundation of his later enormous fortune.

Tilden opposed Lincoln's election and disapproved of the Civil War from the beginning, but at the declaration of war advised E. M. Stanton to call out immediately the full military strength of the North and so crush the rebellion by a swift stroke. Thereafter, he encouraged the Democratic party in its "constitutional opposition" to the powerful centralized Washington government. He favored President Andrew Johnson's liberal policy of Reconstruction.

As chairman of the New York State Democratic committee, 1866–74, he performed the great service of ousting William M. Tweed and his "ring," leading the battle for adequate legislation with which to fight the situation in New York City and aiding in the production of the necessary judicial proof. He was responsible also at this time for reforming and purifying the state judiciary. As governor of New York, 1875–77, he continued his efforts for reform, brought about a substantial reduction in state taxes and expenses, and broke the so-called "Canal ring," a bipartisan group of thieving politicians who had battened on the repair and extension of the state canal system.

Having fired the imagination of the country by his reform activities, he was nominated by the Democrats for the presidency at St. Louis, Mo., June 1876; Thomas A. Hendricks ran with him for vice-president. After a campaign of exceptional bitterness, Tilden received a majority of the popular vote, but lost the election when the doubtful states of Oregon, Louisiana, South Carolina and Florida were claimed by the Republican managers for their candidate, Rutherford B. Hayes. A controversy followed which was resolved by creation of an Electoral Commission containing a majority of one in favor of the Republicans. By a strict party vote, the Commission declared in favor of Hayes's claim. Tilden acquiesced in the decision only as an escape from a renewal of civil war. Remaining to the end of his life a significant figure in national politics, Tilden left the bulk of his estate in trust for establishment of a free library for New York City. Unimpressive in appearance and plagued through life by ill health, Tilden was secretive and dilatory, yet he possessed great power of concentration when he chose, had a marvelous memory and was indebted for his success to intellect rather than personality.

TILESTON, THOMAS (*b. Boston, Mass., 1793; d. New York, N.Y., 1864*), printer, merchant, shipowner, financier. Removing to New York City, 1818, he entered the successful shipping partnership of Spofford & Tileston. President of the Phoenix Bank, 1840–64, he was also a founder (1829) and director of the Atlantic Insurance Co.

TILGHMAN, EDWARD (*b. Wye, Md., 1750/51; d. Philadelphia, Pa., 1815*), lawyer. Cousin of William and Tench Tilghman. Practicing in Philadelphia *post* 1774, he was a powerful advocate and was recognized as an authority in the field of contingent remainders and executory devices.

TILGHMAN, MATTHEW (*b. Queen Anne Co., Md., 1718; d. Talbot Co., Md., 1790*), landowner, Maryland colonial legislator and jurist, Revolutionary patriot. Headed Maryland delegation to Continental Congress, September 1774—December 1776; served as president of the Annapolis convention in August 1776 which drafted the first state constitution.

TILGHMAN, RICHARD ALBERT (*b. Philadelphia, Pa., 1824; d. 1899*), chemist. Grandson of Edward Tilghman. Graduated University of Pennsylvania, 1841; gained practical experience in laboratory of James C. Booth. His paper "On the Decomposing Power of Water at High Temperatures" (*Proceedings, American Philosophical Society, IV, 1847*) was the first systematic study of hydration. Employed for much of his time in Scotland and England, he was the developer of many industrial processes including those for manufacture of potassium dichromate, for the manufacture of paper pulp by sulphite process, and for the "sand blast" process for shaping objects out of hard, brittle materials.

TILGHMAN, TENCH (*b. Talbot Co., Md., 1744; d. Baltimore, Md., 1786*), merchant, Revolutionary soldier. Grandson of Tench Francis; brother of William Tilghman; cousin of Edward Tilghman. Trusted and able aide-de-camp to Gen. George Washington, August 1776–1783. He rose to rank of lieutenant-colonel and was selected to carry the news of the surrender of Cornwallis to the Continental Congress.

TILGHMAN, WILLIAM (*b. Talbot Co., Md., 1756; d. Philadelphia, Pa., 1827*), Maryland legislator, Pennsylvania jurist. Brother of Tench Tilghman; grandson of Tench Francis; cousin of Edward Tilghman. Graduated College of Philadelphia, 1772; read law in office of Benjamin Chew. A Loyalist during the Revolution, he served 1788–93 in the Maryland Assembly and Senate. Removing to practice in Philadelphia, 1793, he held several Pennsylvania judicial appointments before becoming chief justice of the Pennsylvania supreme court, 1806. He served in this post until his death.

TILGHMAN, WILLIAM MATTHEW (*b. Fort Dodge, Iowa, 1854; d. Cromwell, Okla., 1924*), outstanding peace officer in Kansas and Oklahoma *post* 1877.

TILLMAN, BENJAMIN RYAN (*b. Edgefield Co., S.C., 1847; d. 1918*), farmer, politician. A blunt, irascible, unmannerly representative of rural interests in his state *post* 1885, he forced South Carolina to undertake a system of agricultural education, served as Democratic governor, December 1890–1894, and was for many years complete master of South Carolina politics. Organizing an uprising of the farmers against the long-powerful aristocratic element, he dictated a new constitution for the state in 1895, meanwhile equalizing taxes, reapportioning legislative representation, and virtually disfranchising the Negroes. He also implemented the powers of the state railroad commission, increased expenditures for public education, and established a public monopoly (1893) over the sale of liquor. Elected U.S. senator, 1894, he served until his death and won national notoriety as an extreme champion of Southern agrarianism, becoming known as "Pitchfork Ben." A violent and unscrupulous enemy of Presidents Cleveland

and Theodore Roosevelt, he was exposed by the latter as a user of influence in land purchases, and his power in South Carolina declined. His most constructive act as a senator was the steering of the Hepburn Bill through the Senate. A defender of the use of force in disfranchising the Negro and an advocate of repeal of the Fifteenth Amendment, Tillman grew more conservative as his personal ambitions were gratified.

TILNEY, FREDERICK (*b. Brooklyn, N.Y., 1875; d. Oyster Bay, N.Y., 1938*), neurologist. Graduated Yale, 1897; M.D., Long Island College Hospital, 1903; Ph.D., Columbia, 1912. Taught at N.Y. College of Physicians and Surgeons *post* 1908, heading department of neurology *post* 1915. Medical director, Neurological Institute, 1935–38. [*Supp. 2*]

TILTON, EDWARD LIPPINCOTT (*b. New York, N.Y., 1861; d. Scarsdale, N.Y., 1933*), architect. Designed U.S. immigrant station on Ellis Island (completed, 1900); was especially notable for contributions to modern public library design.

TILTON, JAMES (*b. Kent Co., Del., 1745; d. near Wilmington, Del., 1822*), army surgeon. Graduated College of Philadelphia, B.M., 1768, and M.D., 1771. A regimental and hospital surgeon during the Revolution, he served also as surgeon-general of the U.S. Army, 1813–15. He was author of two important treatises: *Economical Observations on Military Hospitals* (1813) and *Regulations for the Medical Department* (1814).

TILTON, JOHN ROLLIN (*b. Loudon, N.H., 1828; d. Rome, Italy, 1888*), landscape painter. Resident in Italy *post* 1852; he specialized in pictures of places famous for their historical associations.

TILTON, THEODORE (*b. New York, N.Y., 1835; d. Paris, France, 1907*), journalist. Managing editor of the *Independent*, a Congregationalist journal, 1856–70, he was a close associate of Henry Ward Beecher and prominent in the anti-slavery movement and as a post-Civil War Republican partisan. At first attempting to suppress knowledge of alleged adulterous relations between his wife and Beecher, he brought suit against the minister. The trial began Jan. 11, 1875, in Brooklyn, N.Y., lasted 112 trial days, and resulted in a hung jury and a division of public opinion over Beecher's culpability that still persists. Ruined in fortune and reputation, Tilton left the United States, 1883, never to return.

TILYOU, GEORGE CORNELIUS (*b. New York, N.Y., 1862; d. 1914*), amusement park owner and inventor. Laid out Coney Island's famous "Bowery"; founded Steeplechase Park, 1897. Tilyou originated most of the fun-devices used in his enterprises.

TIMBERLAKE, HENRY (*b. Hanover Co., Va., 1730; d. London, England, 1765*), soldier. Served in French and Indian War; was distinguished for mission (accompanied by Thomas Sumter) to the Cherokees, November 1761–62. Accompanied Outacity and two warriors to England on state visit, 1762. Author of a valuable volume of *Memoirs* (London, 1765) recording his war experiences and observations of the customs and ceremonies of the Cherokees.

TIMBY, THEODORE RUGGLES (*b. Dutchess Co., N.Y., 1822; d. Brooklyn, N.Y., 1909*), inventor. Filed a *caveat*, January 1843, covering a revolving gun turret for use on land or water, a device unrecognized until used by John Ericsson as a feature of his first *Monitor*, 1861–62.

TIMKEN, HENRY (*b. near Bremen, Germany, 1831; d. San Diego, Calif., 1909*), wagon-maker, manufacturer. Emigrated to Missouri as a boy. Patented a successful carriage-spring, 1877, which he manufactured with profit; patented the Timken tapered roller bearing, June 1898.

TIMM, HENRY CHRISTIAN (*b. Hamburg, Germany, 1811; d. Hoboken, N.J., 1892*), musician, conductor. Emigrated to New York City, 1835. An accomplished organist and pianist, he was an early member of the New York Philharmonic Society and its president, 1848–63.

TIMON, JOHN (*b. Conewago, Pa., 1797; d. 1867*), Roman Catholic clergyman, Vincentian. Ordained, 1825, at St. Louis, Mo., he served in the missions of the Southwest, held administrative posts in his Order, and came to be one of the best-known priests in the Mississippi Valley. Consecrated first bishop of Buffalo, N.Y., 1847, he served with great ability until his death. He was especially noted for his interest in charitable and educational institutions.

TIMOTHY, LEWIS (*b. France or Holland, date unknown; d. Charleston, S. C., 1738*), printer. Emigrated to Philadelphia, Pa., October 1731. First an employee and later a partner of Benjamin Franklin, Timothy conducted a printing business at Charleston, 1734–38, as successor to Franklin's former partner there. His publication *The Laws of the Province of South-Carolina* (1736) was the most ambitious production of the South Carolina colonial press.

TIMROD, HENRY (*b. Charleston, S.C., 1828; d. Columbia, S.C., 1867*), educator, poet. The most gifted Southern poet of his time (with exception of Sidney Lanier), Timrod possessed high artistic integrity and a crystalline style. He surpassed most of his poetical contemporaries in knowledge of his craft, in taste and in sheer lyrical power, despite the restricted range and the small body of his production. A lifelong friend of Paul H. Hayne and a literary associate of William G. Simms, he brought out a small collection of his poems in 1860, which was lost sight of in the coming of civil war. The passionate war poems which brought him notice as the "laureate of the Confederacy" showed a ripening of his powers; however, after discharge from the Confederate Army because of his incipient tuberculosis, he suffered one calamity after another and was reduced to abject poverty. Despite his misfortunes, he continued to compose, producing what is perhaps his most perfect composition, the "Magnolia Cemetery Ode," shortly before his death. In 1873 his friend Hayne edited *The Poems of Henry Timrod*, prefacing them with a sympathetic memoir of the author. In his ideals, his fancy, his spirituality and his high-mindedness, Timrod was characteristic of the finest qualities of his section; it is an irony of American literature that so gentle a spirit should have been the outstanding poet of the Confederacy at war.

TINCKER, MARY AGNES (*b. Ellsworth, Maine, 1831; d. Dorchester, Mass., 1907*), novelist, teacher. A convert to Catholicism, 1851, she contributed to periodicals and was author of 11 novels and books of sketches; among them the most popular was *Signor Monaldini's Niece* (1879). Her work received much contemporary praise.

TINGEY, THOMAS (*b. London, England, 1750; d. Washington, D.C., 1829*), naval officer. Trained in the British navy and later a merchant captain, he resided in the United States *post* 1783. Made captain in the U.S. Navy, September 1798, he served with credit during the naval war with France and in 1800 was appointed to lay out and command the new Washington, D.C., navy yard. He remained in charge of this yard under various titles until his death. Thomas T. and Tunis A. M. Craven were his grandsons.

TINGLEY, KATHERINE AUGUSTA WESTCOTT (*b. Newbury, Mass., 1847; d. Sweden, 1929*), theosophist leader.

TIPTON, JOHN (*b. Baltimore Co., Md., 1730; d. near Jonesboro, Tenn., 1813*), Virginia legislator, Revolutionary soldier, frontier politician. Uncle of John Tipton (1786–1839). Removed to Watauga settlements, 1783. A bitter opponent of John Sevier, he served *post* 1793 in the Tennessee legislature.

TIPTON, JOHN (*b. Sevier Co., Tenn., 1786; d. Logansport, Ind., 1839*), Indiana soldier, legislator and land speculator. Nephew of John Tipton (1730–1813). U.S. senator, Democrat, from Indiana, 1831–39.

TISQUANTUM. [See SQUANTO, d. 1622.]

TITCHENER, EDWARD BRADFORD (*b. Chichester, England, 1867; d. 1927*), experimental psychologist. B.A., Brasenose College, Oxford, 1890; Ph.D., Leipzig, 1892; D.Sc., Oxford, 1906. Taught psychology at Cornell *post* 1892; was author of *Experimental Psychology* (1901–05), a milestone in the progress of that science. Leader of the "structuralist" school, he opposed the fashionable rage for applied psychology, educational psychology and mental testing that threatened to obliterate study of the science in its pure form in America.

TITCOMB, JOHN WHEELOCK (*b. Farmington, N.H., 1860; d. Hartford, Conn., 1932*), fish culturist, conservationist.

TOBANI, THEODORE MOSES (*b. Hamburg, Germany, 1855; d. Jackson Heights, N.Y., 1933*), composer of semi-classical music. Came to America as a boy. His most popular work "Hearts and Flowers," long in use as incidental music to pathos in the theatre, was first published as a piano piece, 1893.

TOBEY, EDWARD SILAS (*b. Kingston, Mass., 1813; d. Brookline, Mass., 1891*), Boston merchant, capitalist. Prominent in many organizations for public safety, welfare, and the propagation of religion.

TOD, DAVID (*b. near Youngstown, O., 1805; d. 1868*), lawyer, coal and iron operator, railroad executive. Son of George Tod. U.S. minister to Brazil, 1847–51. Served as chairman, Democratic presidential convention of 1860, after withdrawal of Caleb Cushing; was Union party governor of Ohio, 1862–64. Refused secretaryship of the U.S. treasury, 1864.

TOD, GEORGE (*b. Suffield, Conn., 1773; d. near Youngstown, O., 1841*), jurist. Brother of John Tod; father of David Tod. Graduated Yale, 1795; studied law under Tapping Reeve. Removed to Youngstown, O., 1800. Served as state supreme court judge, 1806–10, establishing by decision in 1809 the doctrine of judicial review in Ohio. After two terms in the legislature and War of 1812 military service, he was presiding judge of the 3rd district circuit court of appeals, 1816–29.

TOD, JOHN (*b. Suffield, Conn., 1779; d. Bedford, Pa., 1830*), lawyer, Pennsylvania legislator and jurist. Brother of George Tod with whom he studied law. Removed *c*. 1802 to Bedford, Pa., where he practiced with success; served as a congressman, Democrat, 1821–24. As chairman of the House committee on manufactures, he strove for higher tariffs and extension of the protective list.

TODD, CHARLES STEWART (*b. near Danville, Ky., 1791; d. Baton Rouge, La., 1871*), lawyer, War of 1812 soldier, diplomat. Son of Thomas Todd; son-in-law of Isaac Shelby. Appointed U.S. diplomatic agent in Colombia, 1820, Todd handled U.S. affairs there during a critical period with great integrity and tact; he was U.S. minister to Russia, 1841–45.

TODD, ELI (*b. New Haven, Conn., 1769; d. Hartford, Conn., 1833*), physician. An American pioneer in the humane and intelligent treatment of mental illness and alcoholism, he was superintendent of the Connecticut Retreat at Hartford, 1824–33.

TODD, HENRY ALFRED (*b. Woodstock, Ill., 1854; d. New York, N.Y., 1925*), Romance philologist. Graduated College of New Jersey (Princeton), 1876; studied at Paris, Berlin, Rome and Madrid; Ph.D., Johns Hopkins, 1885. Taught at Johns Hopkins and at Stanford; professor of Romance philology, Columbia

University, 1893–1925. A founder and editor of *Modern Language Notes* (1886) and an organizer of the Modern Language Association (1883), he was editor of a number of Old French works and in 1909 helped found the *Romanic Review*.

TODD, JOHN (*b. Rutland, Vt., 1800; d. Pittsfield, Mass., 1873*), Congregational clergyman. A Calvinist of the school of Jonathan Edwards, he held his principal pastorate at the First Church in Pittsfield, and was author of a number of once-popular books including *The Student's Manual* (1835).

TODD, MABEL LOOMIS (*b. Cambridge, Mass., 1856; d. Hog Island, Maine, 1932*), author. Undertaking to prepare the poems of Emily Dickinson for publication *c.* 1886, she was editor (with Thomas W. Higginson) of *Poems* (first series, 1890; second series, 1891) and was sole editor for the third series of *Poems* (1896). She was also collector and editor of the *Letters of Emily Dickinson* (1894). A conscientious editor, she endeavored, not always with success, to keep Higginson from "correcting" what the poet had written; alienation from the Dickinson family *post* 1895 prevented her from completing her work as planned.

TODD, SERENO EDWARDS (*b. near Lansingville, N.Y., 1820; d. near Orange, N.J., 1898*), journalist, agriculturist, author of works on systematic and economical farm management.

TODD, THOMAS (*b. near Dunkirk, Va., 1765; d. 1826*), lawyer, Kentucky public official and jurist. Father of Charles S. Todd. Removed to Danville, Ky., 1786, where he made his home with Harry Innes and studied law. Judge of the state court of appeals, 1801–06, and chief justice, 1806–March 1807, he rendered many opinions basic to Kentucky land law. Appointed associate justice of the U.S. Supreme Court, March 1807, he served until his death. A consistent supporter of John Marshall in cases involving constitutional doctrine (except in the Dartmouth College Case), he devoted most of his time and strength to traveling the western circuit. His judgment, especially on cases involving land laws, was highly regarded by his colleagues.

TODD, THOMAS WINGATE (*b. Sheffield, England, 1885; d. Cleveland, O., 1938*), anatomist, physical anthropologist. Educated at Manchester University (England), he also taught there until 1912. Todd served thereafter as professor of anatomy at the medical school of Western Reserve University and as director of its Hamann Museum of comparative anthropology and anatomy. He was a pioneer in growth studies based on skeletal development. [*Supp. 2*]

TOLAND, HUGH HUGER (*b. Guilder's Creek, S.C., 1806; d. San Francisco, Calif., 1880*), surgeon. Graduated in medicine from Transylvania University, 1828; made special studies in Paris, France, 1830–33. Prac-

ticed in Columbia, S.C., until 1852 when he removed to California. Widely known for his skill in lithotomy and plastic surgery, he founded Toland Medical College in San Francisco, 1864, and served as its professor of surgery until his death. In 1873 he placed the institution unconditionally in charge of the University of California, of which it became a part.

TOLMAN, HERBERT CUSHING (*b. South Scituate, Mass., 1865; d. Nashville, Tenn., 1923*), Greek and Indo-Iranian scholar, Episcopal clergyman. Graduated Yale, 1888; Ph.D., 1890. Taught at University of Wisconsin and University of North Carolina; was professor of Greek at Vanderbilt, 1894–1923, and dean of its College of Arts and Sciences, 1913–23.

TOME, JACOB (*b. York Co., Pa., 1810; d. 1898*), Maryland merchant, banker, philanthropist. Founded Tome School for Boys at Port Deposit, Md. (incorporated 1889, opened 1894).

TOMKINS, FLOYD WILLIAMS (*b. New York, N.Y., 1850; d. 1932*), Episcopal clergyman. A zealous evangelical preacher, he performed his most notable work as rector of the Church of the Holy Trinity, Philadelphia, Pa., 1899–1932.

TOMLINS, WILLIAM LAWRENCE (*b. London, England, 1844; d. Delafield, Wis., 1930*), teacher of music. Came to America, 1870. Achieving distinction in America as conductor of the Apollo Club, Chicago, Ill., *post* 1875, he later was notably successful in training children for choral singing and as an instructor of public school music teachers. His system became known as "The Tomlins Idea."

TOMLINSON, EVERETT TITSWORTH (*b. Shiloh, N.J., 1859; d. Elizabeth, N.J., 1931*), Baptist clergyman and missionary executive. Author of over 100 historical stories for boys, including *Three Colonial Boys* (1895), *The Fort in the Forest* (1904) and *Mad Anthony's Young Scout* (1908).

TOMOCHICHI (*b. possibly Apalachicola, in present Alabama, c. 1650; d. Georgia, 1739*), Creek Indian chief. Leader of a few Creeks and Yamassee, he settled at Yamacraw on the Savannah River *post* 1721, where he resided when the first Georgia colonists landed in 1733. Signer of a formal treaty with James E. Oglethorpe, May 1733, he helped negotiate a treaty with the other Creek tribes and accompanied Oglethorpe to England on a visit, 1734.

TOMPKINS, ARNOLD (*b. near Paris, Ill., 1849; d. Menlo, Ga., 1905*), educator, leader in normal school work. Author of *The Philosophy of Teaching* (1893), *The Philosophy of School Management* (1895) and other works once widely used in teacher training schools.

TOMPKINS, DANIEL AUGUSTUS (*b. Edgefield Co., S.C., 1851; d. Montreat, N.C., 1914*), engineer. Graduated Rensselaer Polytechnic Institute, C.E., 1873. After training with Alexander L. Holley and

John Fritz in steel- and iron-making, he began practice in Charlotte, N.C., 1882. Preaching the gospel of Northern industrial development to the South, he promoted, designed and built cottonseed-oil mills throughout the South, and by speeches and newspaper articles popularized the concept that manufactures must supplement agriculture in the section. He next waged a successful campaign in favor of his plan for community financing and founding of cotton manufacturing plants. Realizing that the economic recovery of the South required improved education, he helped found textile schools in both the Carolinas and in Mississippi and Texas. Author of a number of books and pamphlets, he was also chief owner for many years of the *Charlotte Daily Observer* which served him as a means of propagating his ideas.

TOMPKINS, DANIEL D. (*b. Scarsdale, N.Y., 1774; d. Staten Island, N.Y., 1825*), lawyer, New York legislator. Graduated Columbia, 1795. Beginning practice in New York City, he was elected to Congress as a (Democrat) Republican in 1804 but resigned almost at once to accept appointment as a justice of the New York supreme court. Elected governor of New York, 1807, he served through 1817. His administration was marked by liberal and popular reform measures in the school system, the militia and in the criminal code, and also by the complete abolition of slavery in the state. Handicapped during the War of 1812 by lack of money and a hostile Assembly as well as by the incompetence of the U.S. command, he handled the defense of the state as successfully as any man could have done, pledging his personal credit for much of the necessary money. He served as vice-president of the United States, 1817–25, without particular distinction. For many years he was De Witt Clinton's most able antagonist in New York State politics.

TOMPKINS, SALLY LOUISA (*b. Mathews Co., Va., 1833; d. Richmond, Va., 1916*), philanthropist. Fitted up and maintained the Robertson Hospital for Confederate wounded in Richmond, 1861–65. Commissioned captain in the Confederate service, September 1861, she was the only woman ever to receive such an honor and was known to the end of her life as "Captain Sally."

TOMPSON, BENJAMIN (*b. present Quincy, Mass., 1642; d. 1714*), teacher, physician. Graduated Harvard, 1662. Taught at present Boston Latin School, also in Charlestown, Braintree and Roxbury. Author of a number of topical poems which were published as broadsides and in *New Englands Crisis* (Boston, 1676; also as *New-Englands Tears for Her Present Miseries,* London in the same year).

TONDORF, FRANCIS ANTHONY (*b. Boston, Mass., 1870; d. Washington, D.C., 1929*), Roman Catholic clergyman, Jesuit, seismologist. A professor of the sciences principally at Georgetown University *post*

1904, he founded the seismological observatory at Georgetown and served it as director, 1909–29.

TONER, JOSEPH MEREDITH (*b. Pittsburgh, Pa., 1825; d. Cresson, Pa., 1896*), physician. Graduated Vermont Medical College, 1850; M.D., Jefferson Medical College, 1853. A leading practitioner in Washington, D.C., *post* 1855, he was best known as a medical historian and as the collector of a remarkable library of American medical history which he presented to the Library of Congress. He was the author of *The Medical Men of the Revolution* (1876) among other books, and editor of the early journals of George Washington.

TONTY, HENRY de (*probably Paris, France, 1650; d. near present Mobile, Ala., 1704*), explorer, soldier. Cousin of Daniel Greysolon Duluth; son of the originator of the Tontine form of life insurance. Known as "Iron Hand" because of an artificial right hand with which he had replaced one lost in service with the French army. Tonty became lieutenant to Robert Cavelier, Sieur de la Salle, in 1678, and accompanied La Salle to Canada. He was his chief's principal assistant in the exploration of the Great Lakes and the Illinois country. He commanded at Fort Crèvecoeur, 1680, escaping with great difficulty with five companions after the Iroquois raid on that post. Going first to Green Bay and then to Michilimackinac, he rejoined La Salle at the latter place in June 1681. Co-builder with La Salle of Fort St. Louis on the Illinois, he joined his chief in the spring of 1682 for the famous exploration of the Mississippi River and the claiming of the Mississippi Valley for France. Left in charge in Illinois, Tonty made an unsuccessful attempt to find La Salle in 1686, and even as late as March 1689 was still unaware of La Salle's death. On learning of it in September of that year, he attempted to find the colonists which La Salle had left in lower Louisiana but was unsuccessful. In 1700, after a decade of able, honest management of the Illinois settlements, he joined the new colony made by Pierre le Moyne, Sieur d'Iberville, near the mouth of the Mississippi, and for the last four years of his life gave valuable service to Louisiana. A great explorer and an able administrator, he succeeded where La Salle failed, was respected and trusted by the Indians and by the settlers, and was particularly noted for his courtesy and consideration. He wrote two brief memoirs of his experiences, one covering the years 1678–83, the other covering the years 1678–91, which remained unpublished until late in the 19th century. Earlier publications credited to him are considered spurious.

TOOLE, EDWIN WARREN (*b. Savannah, Mo., 1839; d. Helena, Mont., 1905*), lawyer. Brother of Joseph K. Toole. Removed to Denver, Colo., 1863, and thence to Montana Territory where he settled in Virginia City; in 1865 he moved to Helena which was thereafter his home. An outstanding lawyer with a varied practice, he is particularly remembered for his representation of the state of Montana in *Barden vs. Northern Pacific Railroad* (154 U.S., 288–349) which maintained the state's right to mineral lands reserved in the Congressional grant of land to the railroad. He was also successful in defending constitutionality of the so-called "apex" law.

TOOLE, JOSEPH KEMP (*b. Savannah, Mo., 1851; d. 1929*), lawyer, Montana legislator. Brother of Edwin W. Toole. Removed to Helena, Mont., 1869; became his brother's law partner, 1872. Territorial delegate to Congress from Montana, Democrat, 1885–89, he was influential and active in the movement for statehood and was a member of the 1889 convention that drafted the Montana constitution. Elected first governor of the state of Montana, he served November 1889—January 1893 and January 1901—April 1908. A successful administrator, he fostered public education and supported many political and social reforms.

TOOMBS, ROBERT AUGUSTUS (*b. Wilkes Co., Ga., 1810; d. Washington, Ga., 1885*), lawyer, planter, Georgia statesman and legislator. Friend and associate of Alexander H. Stephens. Graduated Union College, 1828. Displaying high ability as a Whig member of the Georgia legislature, Toombs was elected to Congress and took his seat at the close of 1845. A careful student of public finance and robustly eloquent, he soon became popular and influential. Shocked out of his faith that the welfare of the South would be safe in Whig hands by the events which led to the crisis of 1850, he became a leader in the aggressive defense of his section. However, he was satisfied with the Compromise finally adopted and with Alexander H. Stephens and Howell Cobb canvassed Georgia to procure its ratification. He then led in the launching of the Constitutional Union party, pledged to maintain the Compromise measures. After dissolution of the party because of lack of response in other states, he reluctantly joined the Democrats. As U.S. senator, 1853–61, he approved the Kansas-Nebraska Act. He sought to end the ensuing disorders by an 1856 bill of his own providing for prompt admission of Kansas with whatever constitution a new convention might adopt after a thoroughly policed election of delegates. His bill was adopted by the Senate but died in the House. Convinced that control of the government by the Republicans would menace the security of the South, Toombs strove for harmony among the Democrats; after the split in 1860 he supported the Breckinridge ticket. Upon the failure of the Crittenden Compromise which he supported, he publicly urged secession and resigned from the Senate. Author of the address which the Georgia secession convention adopted to justify its acts, he was chosen one of the Georgia delegates sent to launch a Southern confederacy at Montgomery, Ala. Accepting the office of Confederate secretary of state with some

reluctance, he discovered that his excellent advice on financial and other matters was little regarded. Growing contemptuous of Jefferson Davis, he resigned and took command in July 1861 of a brigade on the Virginia front. Restless under the defensive policy of his superiors, he censured their inaction and was disliked by them. Wounded at Antietam where his brigade held the stone bridge, Toombs demanded promotion and on its refusal resigned his commission. Thereafter he continued to criticize the government, especially its continued reliance upon credit, and served briefly in arms during Sherman's advance against Atlanta. Briefly a fugitive at the end of the Civil War, he returned home in 1867 and rebuilt a large law practice. Between 1867 and 1880 he fought to overthrow the rule of the Radicals. He dominated the constitutional convention of 1877 which repudiated the Carpetbag bonds, curbed Negro suffrage, improved the judiciary and provided for the control of corporations.

TOPLIFF, SAMUEL (*b. Boston, Mass., 1789; d. 1864*), dealer in foreign news. Operated Merchants' Reading Room and associated news-gathering services at Boston, 1814–42.

TORBERT, ALFRED THOMAS ARCHIMEDES (*b. Georgetown, Del., 1833; d. at sea, off Florida coast, 1880*), soldier, diplomat. Graduated West Point, 1855. After frontier service with infantry he became colonel, 1st New Jersey Volunteers, September 1861. Following extensive service with the Army of the Potomac, he was promoted brigadier-general, 1862. As a cavalry division commander *post* April 1864, Torbert served with great ability under Gen. Philip Sheridan, winning particular honors at the battles of Winchester and Cedar Creek.

TORRENCE, JOSEPH THATCHER (*b. Mercer Co., Pa., 1843; d. Chicago, Ill., 1896*), engineer, Chicago iron manufacturer and businessman.

TORREY, BRADFORD (*b. Weymouth, Mass., 1843; d. Santa Barbara, Calif., 1912*), ornithologist, editor. A faithful and accurate field observer, Torrey was author of *A Rambler's Lease* (1889), *The Foot-path Way* (1892) and other volumes of essays on birds; he served also as editor of the journal of Henry D. Thoreau (Walden edition, 1906).

TORREY, CHARLES TURNER (*b. Scituate, Mass., 1813; d. Maryland, 1846*), Congregational clergyman, anti-Garrison Abolitionist.

TORREY, JOHN (*b. New York, N.Y., 1796; d. New York, 1873*), botanist, chemist. Inspired with interest in science by Amos Eaton, Torrey graduated M.D., N.Y. College of Physicians and Surgeons, 1818. In medical practice in New York City, Torrey maintained his interest in mineralogy and botany, and served as reporter and classifier of plant specimens sent to him by a long series of government-sponsored Western exploratory expeditions. He was professor of chemistry, mineralogy and geology at West Point, 1824–27, and professor of chemistry at N.Y. College of Physicians and Surgeons, 1827–55; concurrently with his New York professorship he taught chemistry and natural history at the College of New Jersey (Princeton). On his retirement from teaching, he served for the rest of his life as U.S. assayer in New York City. Torrey's great contribution was in pioneer work on the findings of the aforesaid government exploring expeditions (thereby first describing many plants native to North America) and by his lifelong encouragement of young botanists, including Asa Gray. He was also largely instrumental in establishing the New York Botanical Garden. Among his many books and monographs are the following: *A Catalogue of Plants . . . Within Thirty Miles of the City of New York* (1819); *A Flora of the Northern and Middle Sections of the United States* (1823); *A Compendium of the Flora of the Northern and Middle States* (1826); *Flora of North America* (with Asa Gray, seven parts, 1838–43); *Flora of the State of New York* (1843); and contributions to the official reports of almost every important survey expedition between 1820 and 1860.

TOTTEN, GEORGE MUIRSON (*b. New Haven, Conn., 1809; d. 1884*), engineer. A specialist in canal and railroad work, he served for many years *post* 1850 as chief engineer of the Panama Railroad and was an adviser to the French company which first attempted the Panama Canal.

TOTTEN, JOSEPH GILBERT (*b. New Haven, Conn., 1788; d. 1864*), military engineer. Nephew of Jared Mansfield. Graduated West Point, 1805. Highly effective as chief engineer on the Niagara frontier, War of 1812, he served thereafter in coast defense and river and harbor improvement work. Promoted colonel, he became chief engineer of the U.S. Army and inspector of West Point in 1838, holding both posts until his death. During the Mexican War he planned the operations at Vera Cruz. Thereafter he won high repute in lighthouse work, and during the Civil War as brigadier-general supervised the defensive works around Washington, D.C.

TOU, ERIK HANSEN (*b. near Stavanger, Norway, 1857; d. Napoleon, S. Dak., 1917*), Lutheran clergyman. Emigrated to Minneapolis, Minn., 1881. A graduate of Augsburg Seminary, 1886 and 1889, he served as a missionary in Madagascar, 1889–1903.

TOUCEY, ISAAC (*b. Newtown, Conn., 1792; d. Hartford, Conn., 1869*), lawyer, Connecticut legislator and public official. Congressman, Democrat, from Connecticut, 1835–39; governor of Connecticut, 1846–47; U.S. attorney-general, June 1848—March 1849. As U.S. senator, 1852–57, he condemned the "higher law" theory of W. H. Seward and was a supporter of the Kansas-Nebraska bill. During his term as U.S. secretary of the navy, 1857–61, he was criticized for a sympathetic attitude toward the South but conducted his department with efficiency and economy.

TOULMIN, HARRY (*b. Taunton, England, 1766; d. Alabama, 1823*), clergyman, educator, jurist. Emigrating to America with Joseph Priestley, 1794, he served briefly as president of Transylvania University, and was secretary to the Commonwealth of Kentucky, 1796–1804. As secretary, he compiled several collections of Kentucky laws. Appointed judge of the superior court for the eastern district of Mississippi Territory, 1804, he opposed filibusters into Spanish territory; he strove to thwart the designs of Aaron Burr (1807) and the later activities of Reuben Kemper. Retaining his judgeship until 1819 he did much to straighten out the land claims in the region, was prominent in the convention that formed the constitution for Alabama, and was editor of *The Statutes of the Mississippi Territory* (1807) and *A Digest of the Territorial Laws of Alabama* (1823).

TOULMIN, HARRY THEOPHILUS (*b. Mobile Co., Ala., 1838; d. Toulminville, Ala., 1916*), Confederate officer, Alabama jurist. Grandson of Harry Toulmin. Alabama state circuit court judge, 1874–82; U.S. district judge, southern district of Alabama, 1887–1916.

TOUMEY, JAMES WILLIAM (*b. Lawrence, Mich., 1865; d. 1932*), forester, teacher. Graduated Michigan Agricultural College, 1889. Taught botany at Michigan Agricultural College and University of Arizona; taught at Yale School of Forestry *post* 1900 and served as its dean, 1910–22.

TOURGÉE, ALBION WINEGAR (*b. Williamsfield, O., 1838; d. Bordeaux, France, 1905*), Union soldier, lawyer, North Carolina carpetbag jurist, U.S. consular officer. Author of a number of books, he is remembered chiefly for his novel *A Fool's Errand* (1879), an early literary picture of Reconstruction.

TOURJÉE, EBEN (*b. Warwick, R.I., 1834; d. Boston, Mass., 1891*), musician. Co-founder (1867) of the New England Conservatory of Music.

TOUSARD, ANNE LOUIS de (*b. Paris, France, 1749; d. Paris, 1817*), French army artillery officer. An active and efficient aide to Lafayette, 1777–78, Tousard later had a colorful career in Santo Domingo and during the first years of the French Revolution. Emigrating to America c. 1793, he was reinstated in the U.S. Army, 1795, and performed useful service as engineer and artillery officer until 1802 when he returned to France. He served as a French consular officer in several American cities, 1805–16.

TOUSEY, SINCLAIR (*b. New Haven, Conn., 1815; d. New York, N.Y., 1887*), news agent. Merged his own news agency and book distribution business with other similar companies into the American News Co., 1864, which he served as president until his death.

TOWER, CHARLEMAGNE (*b. Philadelphia, Pa., 1848; d. Philadelphia, 1923*), lawyer, financier.

Graduated Harvard, 1872. U.S. minister to Austria-Hungary, 1897–99; U.S. ambassador to Russia, 1899–1902; U.S. ambassador at Berlin, 1902–08.

TOWER, ZEALOUS BATES (*b. Cohasset, Mass., 1819; d. Cohasset, 1900*), soldier, engineer. Graduated West Point, 1841. Won distinction in the Mexican War for skill in reconnoitering as an engineer on staff of Gen. Winfield Scott. Helped organize defenses of Fort Pickens, Fla., 1861. As Union brigadier-general of volunteers, he commanded a brigade with distinction until his serious wounding at the second battle of Bull Run. After brief service as superintendent of West Point, he performed brilliantly as engineer in charge of the field defenses of Nashville, Tenn., his work proving of great service to Gen. George Thomas in the destruction of Gen. Hood's Confederate army (December 1864).

TOWLE, GEORGE MAKEPEACE (*b. Washington, D.C., 1841; d. Brookline, Mass., 1893*), Boston journalist, lecturer and author.

TOWLER, JOHN (*b. Rathmell, Yorkshire, England, 1811; d. Orange, N.J., 1889*), educator. Came to America, 1850; taught at Hobart College and was dean of Geneva Medical College; was also in the U.S. consular service. Editor of *Humphrey's Journal of Photography*, 1862–70, he was author of a number of technical photographic manuals, including the important *The Silver Sunbeam* (1864).

TOWN, ITHIEL (*b. Thompson, Conn., 1784; d. New Haven, Conn., 1844*), architect. Studied in Boston, Mass., with Asher Benjamin. His first important work was the Center Church on New Haven Green; he was next commissioned (1814) to design and build Trinity Church, also on the Green at New Haven. His reputation established, he designed many more public buildings in a number of cities, including the New York Custom House on Wall St. and the state capitols in Indianapolis, Ind., and Raleigh, N.C. He entered partnerships with Martin E. Thompson (1827–28) and Alexander J. Davis (*c.* 1829–43). Patentee of a truss bridge (1820), he was thereafter celebrated also as a bridge-builder. A collector of books on architecture and the fine arts and author of various miscellaneous pieces, he was a founder of the National Academy of Design.

TOWNE, BENJAMIN (*b. Lincolnshire, England, date unknown; d. Philadelphia, Pa., 1793*), printer, journalist. Appeared as a journeyman printer in Philadelphia, 1766. Opening a press of his own, 1774, he published the *Pennsylvania Evening Post*, 1775–84, the first evening newspaper printed in Philadelphia and the only newspaper that continued to be published in that city throughout the Revolutionary War.

TOWNE, CHARLES ARNETTE (*b. Oakland Co., Mich., 1858; d. Tucson, Ariz., 1928*), lawyer. In practice at Duluth, Minn., 1890–1901, and thereafter in

New York City, Towne was a Republican congressman from Minnesota, 1895–97. Becoming recognized as leader of the Silver Republicans, he was chairman of their national committee, 1897–1901, and closely associated with William J. Bryan. He served as congressman, Democrat, from New York, 1905–07.

TOWNE, HENRY ROBINSON (*b. Philadelphia, Pa., 1844; d. New York, N.Y., 1924*), engineer, manufacturer. Son of John H. Towne. Joined with Linus Yale, 1868, in manufacture of locks at Stamford, Conn.; served as president of Yale Lock Mfg. Co. and its successor corporation, 1868–1916, and was thereafter chairman of its board. Towne was also the pioneer builder of cranes in the United States.

TOWNE, JOHN HENRY (*b. Pittsburgh, Pa., 1818; d. Paris, France, 1875*), engineer, heavy machinery builder, philanthropist. Father of Henry R. Towne. Endowed Towne Scientific School, University of Pennsylvania.

TOWNS, GEORGE WASHINGTON BONAPARTE (*b. Wilkes Co., Ga., 1801; d. Macon, Ga., 1854*), lawyer, Georgia legislator and congressman. As Democratic governor of Georgia, 1847–51, he secured amelioration of the slave code, adoption of the *ad valorem* system of taxation, and completion of the Western and Atlantic Railroad; he also worked to improve public education. Becoming an extreme "fire eater" by 1849, he opposed the Wilmot Proviso and called the convention which adopted the "Georgia platform," later the position taken by the entire South on further invasion of state rights.

TOWNSEND, EDWARD DAVIS (*b. Boston, Mass., 1817; d. Washington, D.C., 1893*), soldier. Grandson of Elbridge Gerry. Graduated West Point, 1837. Originally an artilleryman, Townsend served for many years in the adjutant-general's department, heading it as adjutant-general 1862–80 (formal appointment in 1869) with extraordinary tact and efficiency. Collection of material for *War of the Rebellion: Official Records* was owing to him.

TOWNSEND, GEORGE ALFRED (*b. Georgetown, Del., 1841; d. New York, N.Y., 1914*), journalist, Civil War correspondent. Distinguished for vivid reportorial work for the *New York Herald* and the *New York World*, 1861–65, and also for his work as a Union propagandist in England, he contributed a wise and often satirical series of Washington letters to a great number of newspapers, 1867–*c.* 1907. This Washington correspondence appeared under the signature of "Gath" and although mainly occupied with politics often dealt with the social life of the time. Among his many books, a novel *The Entailed Hat* (1884) ranks as the best.

TOWNSEND, JOHN KIRK (*b. Philadelphia, Pa., 1809; d. Washington, D.C., 1851*), ornithologist. Traveled to Oregon, 1834, on expedition with Nathaniel J. Wyeth; visited Hawaii, 1835; served as post surgeon at Fort Vancouver, 1835–36. Described Oregon birds in *Journal of the Academy of Natural Sciences of Philadelphia* (1837, 1839); supplied material on mammals of Oregon and elsewhere for picturing by J. J. Audubon and John Bachman in *Viviparous Quadrupeds of North America* (1845–49). Author of *Narrative of a Journey across the Rocky Mountains to the Columbia River* (1839) and *Ornithology of the United States of America* (one part, 1840; now one of the rarest works on this subject).

TOWNSEND, LUTHER TRACY (*b. Orono, Maine, 1838; d. Brookline, Mass., 1922*), Union soldier, Methodist clergyman. A popular apologist for traditional evangelical theology, he taught church history, classic languages and theology at present Boston University School of Theology, 1868–93.

TOWNSEND, MARY ASHLEY (*b. Lyons, N.Y., 1832; d. Galveston, Texas, 1901*), New Orleans, La., journalist and poet.

TOWNSEND, MIRA SHARPLESS (*b. Philadelphia, Pa., 1798; d. Philadelphia, 1859*), philanthropist. Founded the Rosine Association and Home for reform of fallen women (Philadelphia); also founded the Temporary Home, a transient residence for unemployed women and destitute children.

TOWNSEND, ROBERT (*b. Albany, N.Y., 1819; d. off the China coast, 1866*), naval officer. Appointed midshipman, 1837. After both army and navy service in the Mexican War, he resigned from the navy, 1851. Returning to the service during the Civil War, he rose to rank of commander on Atlantic blockade duty and in operations *post* 1863 on the Mississippi River. Promoted captain, 1865, he commanded the *Wachusett* of the East India squadron.

TOWNSEND, VIRGINIA FRANCES (*b. New Haven, Conn., 1836; d. Arlington, Mass., 1920*), teacher, magazine editor, writer of popular stories for girls.

TOY, CRAWFORD HOWELL (*b. Norfolk, Va., 1836; d. 1919*), Orientalist, educator. Graduated University of Virginia, 1856; studied also in Berlin. Taught Biblical interpretation at Southern Baptist Seminary, 1869–79; was Hancock Professor of Hebrew and Oriental languages at Harvard, 1880–1909. Author, among other scholarly studies, of *Introduction to the History of Religions* (1913).

TRACY, BENJAMIN FRANKLIN (*b. near Owego, N.Y., 1830; d. 1915*), lawyer, New York legislator, Union brigadier-general by brevet. An able U.S. attorney for the New York eastern district, 1866–73, he later served as one of defense counsel for Henry Ward Beecher and briefly as a judge of the New York court of appeals. U.S. secretary of the navy, 1889–93, he instituted a number of reforms in administration and began work on rebuilding a powerful naval force of the most modern type.

TRACY, JOSEPH (*b. Hartford, Vt., 1793; d. Beverly, Mass., 1874*), Congregational clergyman, editor. Secretary of the Massachusetts Colonization Society, 1842–74, and director of the American Colonization Society *post* 1858, he was active in the founding of Liberia College and made other outstanding contributions to the colonization movement.

TRACY, NATHANIEL (*b. present Newburyport, Mass., 1751; d. Newbury, Mass., 1796*), merchant, Revolutionary patriot. Uncle of Charles and Patrick T. Jackson, and of James Jackson (1777–1867). Graduated Harvard, 1769. Operated privateers and merchant vessels out of Newburyport, 1775–83; after initial success he was reduced to virtual bankruptcy through loss of a number of vessels and other business misfortunes.

TRACY, URIAH (*b. present Franklin, Conn., 1755; d. Washington, D.C., 1807*), lawyer, Connecticut legislator and official. Congressman, Federalist, from Connecticut, 1793–96; U.S. senator, 1796–1807. A shrewd partisan politician.

TRAETTA, FILIPPO. [See TRAJETTA, PHILIP, *c.* 1776–1854.]

TRAIN, ENOCH (*b. probably Weston, Mass., 1801; d. Saugus, Mass., 1868*), Boston merchant, shipowner. Father of Adeline D. T. Whitney. Established a line of sailing packets between Boston and Liverpool, 1844; commissioned a number of vessels from Donald McKay. Made notable success by importing Irish immigrants *post* 1846, serving also as an immigrant agent and banker.

TRAIN, GEORGE FRANCIS (*b. Boston, Mass., 1829; d. New York, N.Y., 1904*), Boston merchant, shipowner, champion of eccentric causes.

TRAJETTA, PHILIP (*b. Venice, Italy, c. 1776; d. probably Philadelphia, Pa., 1854*), musician, composer, Italian revolutionary. Resided and worked in a number of American cities *post* 1799; composed operas, oratorios and cantatas.

TRAUBEL, HORACE L. (*b. Camden, N.J., 1858; d. Bon Echo, Ontario, Canada, 1919*), journalist. A close friend of Walt Whitman, Traubel served as one of his literary executors and was author of *With Walt Whitman in Camden* (1906–14), a valuable diary of his association with the poet beginning March 1888. He was also active in the American Socialist movement and edited a monthly paper, the *Conservator*, 1890–1919.

TRAUTWINE, JOHN CRESSON (*b. Philadelphia, Pa., 1810; d. Philadelphia, 1883*), engineer, mineralogist. Trained in office of William Strickland, Trautwine was employed mainly in railroad work in the United States until 1844. Between 1849 and 1853 he worked on surveys for the Panama Railroad in association with George M. Totten and explored the Isthmus of Panama in search of a possible route for an interoceanic ship canal. He was author, among other works, of the celebrated *Engineers' Pocket Book,* first published in 1871.

TRAVIS, WALTER JOHN (*b. Maldon, Australia, 1862; d. Denver, Colo., 1927*), champion amateur golfer of the United States, 1900, 1901, 1903; British amateur champion, 1904.

TRAVIS, WILLIAM BARRET (*b. near Red Banks, S.C., 1809; d. The Alamo, San Antonio, Texas, 1836*), lawyer, leader in the Texas revolution. Raised in Alabama, Travis removed to Texas, 1831, where he practiced first at Anahuac and later at San Felipe. Active in local politics and in opposition to Mexican rule, Travis was commissioned lieutenant-colonel of cavalry late in 1835. Ordered to reinforce the Alamo which the Texans had taken, he assumed joint command of the post with James Bowie, Feb. 13, 1836, and was in full command subsequent to Feb. 24. He died with his men in the final massacre.

TRAYLOR, MELVIN ALVAH (*b. Breeding, Ky., 1878; d. Chicago, Ill., 1934*), banker, lawyer. Beginning his career in Texas, he was active in Chicago banking circles *post c.* 1914 and held the presidency of the First National Bank *post* 1925. A liberal man, he was active in drought relief and other civic affairs and represented the United States in the organization of the Bank for International Settlements.

TREADWELL, DANIEL (*b. Ipswich, Mass., 1791; d. Cambridge, Mass., 1872*), inventor, Rumford Professor at Harvard. Apprenticed to a silversmith, he gave much of his time to experiments with machinery and patented a power printing press (March 1826) which became widely used in book and newspaper printing. Between 1831 and 1835 he secured basic patents for a hemp-spinning machine which attained world-wide use. A popular lecturer on the steam engine and other practical subjects, he also devised a system of turnouts for railroad operation and a method of manufacturing steel cannon out of rings welded together and reinforced by bands. Internationally honored, he was active in many learned societies.

TREAT, ROBERT (*b. Pitminster, England, c. 1622; d. Milford, Conn., 1710*), Connecticut colonial official. Settled at Wethersfield, Conn., by 1639, he soon removed to Milford and by 1653 was deputy from Milford to the General Court. A holder of various town offices, he actively opposed absorption of New Haven Colony by Connecticut and was leader of the group from New Haven which settled Newark, N.J. He represented Newark in the East Jersey Assembly, 1667–72. Returning to Milford, he was active in military affairs, commanding the Connecticut troops operating against King Philip, 1675, and in later Indian skirmishes. Elected deputy-governor of Connecticut, 1676, he advanced to the governorship in 1683 and held that office until 1687. After the overthrow of Andros's government, 1689, Treat be-

came governor again and served until 1698, maintaining the conservative traditions of the colony. He was deputy-governor, 1698–1708.

TREAT, SAMUEL (*b. Portsmouth, N.H., 1815; d. Rochester, N.Y., 1902*), Missouri jurist, teacher of law. Removing to St. Louis, Mo., 1841, he became influential in Democratic politics and was judge of the St. Louis court of common pleas, 1849–57. Appointed U.S. district judge for eastern Missouri, 1857, he served until 1887 and was one of the organizers of the law school at Washington University. He was expert in admiralty law.

TREAT, SAMUEL HUBBEL (*b. Plainfield, N.Y., 1811; d. 1887*), Illinois jurist. Admitted to the New York bar, 1834, he removed to Springfield, Ill., where he soon had an extensive practice. State circuit court judge, 1839–41, and state supreme court judge, 1841–55, he served thereafter as U.S. judge for the southern district of Illinois. He was co-editor and annotator of *The Statutes of Illinois* (1858).

TREE, LAMBERT (*b. Washington, D.C., 1832; d. New York, N.Y., 1910*), lawyer, diplomat. Practiced in Chicago, Ill., *post* 1855; served as a reforming judge of Cook Co. circuit court, 1870–75. A Democrat, he was U.S. minister to Belgium, 1885–88, and U.S. minister to Russia briefly in 1888.

TREMAIN, HENRY EDWIN (*b. New York, N.Y., 1840; d. 1910*), Union officer, New York City lawyer and legal editor. Medal of Honor winner for gallantry at Resaca.

TREMAINE, HENRY BARNES (*b. Brooklyn, N.Y., 1866; d. Washington, D.C., 1932*), manufacturer of mechanical musical instruments, developer of the player-piano. President, Aeolian Co., 1898–1930.

TRENCHARD, STEPHEN DECATUR (*b. Brooklyn, N.Y., 1818; d. 1883*), naval officer. Appointed midshipman, 1834. Served throughout the Civil War principally on blockade duty; won particular distinction in the second attack on Fort Fisher. Commissioned captain, 1866, he retired as rear-admiral, 1880.

TRENHOLM, GEORGE ALFRED (*b. Charleston, S.C., 1807; d. Charleston, 1876*), cotton broker, South Carolina legislator, financier. Rendered important but unspectacular aid to the Confederacy through financial relations abroad and blockade-running. Confederate secretary of the treasury, June 1864–1865.

[*Supp.* 1]

TRENT, WILLIAM (*b. probably Philadelphia, Pa., 1715; d. Philadelphia, c. 1787*), Indian trader, land speculator. In partnership with George Croghan, *c.* 1749–*c.* 1755. Trent along with others suffered loss from French and Indian raids along the Ohio in 1754 and later during Pontiac's uprising, 1763. In compensation, he and his associates, including Samuel Wharton and George Morgan, got from the Iroquois a grant of a tract along the upper Ohio known as

"Indiana." Accompanying Wharton to England, 1769, he remained there until 1775, endeavoring to obtain royal confirmation of this grant and of another larger project known as Vandalia. Failing to do so, he returned home and continued to present unsuccessful memorials to the Virginia Assembly and to Congress in the hope of securing validation of title.

TRENT, WILLIAM PETERFIELD (*b. Richmond, Va., 1862; d. Hopewell Junction, N.Y., 1939*), educator, historian. Graduated University of Virginia, 1883; A.M., 1884. Made postgraduate studies in history at Johns Hopkins where he was deeply influenced by Herbert B. Adams. As professor at University of the South, Sewanee, Tenn., 1888–1900, he changed his field from history to literature, and in 1900 began a long career at Columbia University as professor of English literature, Barnard College. Professor also in the graduate school of the university, he remained active in teaching until 1927. A prodigious worker, Trent was editor of a number of texts and author of many books. Among his early works, his *William Gilmore Simms* (1892) was condemned by Southern critics for its unfair criticism of the environment in which Simms lived and wrote. A principal editor of the *Cambridge History of American Literature* (1917–21) and editor-in-chief of the Columbia edition of *The Works of John Milton* in the earlier stages of its development, Trent devoted many years of research to a monumental work on Daniel Defoe which remains unpublished. As a teacher he insisted always on appreciation of literature for its own sake subordinating philology and literary history to esthetic understanding. [*Supp. 2*]

TRESCOT, WILLIAM HENRY (*b. Charleston, S.C., 1822; d. Pendleton, S.C., 1898*), lawyer, South Carolina Confederate legislator, U.S. diplomatic agent, historian. After winning repute as a public speaker and for a number of valuable historical works which included *The Position and Course of the South* (1850), *Diplomacy of the Revolution* (1852) and *The Diplomatic History of the Administrations of Washington and Adams* (1857), he was appointed assistant U.S. secretary of state, 1860. On South Carolina's secession in December of that year, he resigned but stayed in Washington until February 1861 as unofficial adviser of the South Carolina authorities, playing an important part in the negotiations over the Charleston forts and endeavoring to postpone a crisis by preventing reinforcement of the forts by the federal government. After valuable services to the Confederacy, he worked *post* 1865 in Washington as South Carolina agent for recovery of lands seized and taxes levied under the direct tax act of Congress. He also served as a special diplomatic agent of the United States in missions to China, Chile and Mexico.

TREVELLICK, RICHARD F. (*b. St. Mary's, Scilly Islands, England, 1830; d. Detroit, Mich., 1895*), ship's carpenter, seaman, labor leader. Emigrating to New Orleans, La., 1857, and settling in Detroit, 1861, he became president of the ship carpenters' and caulkers' union and also first president of the Detroit Trades' Assembly. He was president of the National Labor Union, 1869, 1871–72. In 1868, at his own expense, he led one of the first successful labor lobbies, pushing an eight-hour-day act for federal mechanics and laborers through Congress; he also upheld the unpopular idea of abolishing the colorline in unions. Active in the Greenback party and convinced of the need for combined industrial and political labor activity, he was one of the first great labor agitators of America.

TRIMBLE, ALLEN (*b. Augusta Co., Va., 1783; d. Hillsboro, O., 1870*), agriculturist, Ohio legislator. Raised near Lexington, Ky.; settled in present Highland Co., O., 1805. Acting governor of Ohio, 1822. National Republican governor of Ohio, 1826–30, he was a supporter of Henry Clay's policies and continued after retirement to be an active Whig.

TRIMBLE, ISAAC RIDGEWAY (*b. Culpeper Co., Va., 1802; d. Baltimore, Md., 1888*), soldier, engineer. Raised in Kentucky. Graduated West Point, 1822. Resigning from the army, 1832, he engaged in railroad surveys and management, and was general superintendent of the Baltimore and Potomac Railroad, 1859–61. Commissioned Confederate brigadier-general, he served with distinction under Ewell and T. J. Jackson in the Army of Northern Virginia, notably at the second battle of Bull Run in which he was seriously wounded. Commissioned major-general, 1862, he was again badly wounded at Gettysburg and taken prisoner. He was not exchanged until just before Appomattox.

TRIMBLE, ROBERT (*b. Augusta Co., Va., 1777; d. Paris, Ky., 1828*), Kentucky jurist. Studied law under George Nicholas and James Brown; practiced at Paris, Ky., *post* 1800. An outstanding lawyer of his section, he was U.S. district judge for Kentucky, 1817–26. Appointed a justice of the U.S. Supreme Court, 1826, he served until his untimely death, supporting John Marshall on constitutional doctrine in most cases but differing with him in *Ogden vs. Saunders* (12 *Wheaton*, 212), wherein Trimble wrote one of his ablest opinions.

TRIPP, BARTLETT (*b. Harmony, Maine, 1842; d. Yankton, S. Dak., 1911*), jurist, diplomat. Practiced in Dakota Territory *post c.* 1869; presided over first territorial constitutional convention, 1883; chief justice, territorial supreme court, 1885–89. As U.S. minister to Austria-Hungary, 1893–97, he secured Austrian consent to a ruling that its administrative officers must accept American passports as *prima facie* evidence of American citizenship. He was chairman of the Samoan commission, 1899.

TRIPP, GUY EASTMAN (*b. Wells, Maine, 1865; d. New York, N.Y., 1927*), industrialist. An associate and officer of Stone & Webster, 1897–1911, he became chairman of the board of Westinghouse Electric & Manufacturing Co. in 1912 and held that post until his death. During World War I, as brigadier-general he gave important assistance to the chief of ordnance, U.S. Army.

TRIPPE, JOHN (*b. Dorchester Co., Md., 1785; d. Havana, Cuba, 1810*), naval officer. Appointed midshipman, 1799, he is particularly remembered for his single combat with a Tripolitan ship captain during a boarding mission off Tripoli, Aug. 3, 1804.

TRIST, NICHOLAS PHILIP (*b. Charlottesville, Va., 1800; d. Alexandria, Va., 1874*), diplomat, lawyer. Attended West Point; studied in law office of Thomas Jefferson whose granddaughter, Virginia Jefferson Randolph, he later married. A man of high integrity, Trist served as U.S. consul to Havana, Cuba, 1833–41. Appointed chief clerk of the U.S. State Department, 1845, he went as special agent to negotiate a treaty of peace with Mexico, 1847. Exceeding his instructions, he was recalled in November 1847, possibly as part of a U.S. government maneuver to exact severer terms. Trist, however, considered it his duty to proceed with the work and on Feb. 2, 1848, signed a treaty in strict compliance with his original instructions, thereby ending his diplomatic career.

TROLAND, LEONARD THOMPSON (*b. Norwich, Conn., 1889; d. California, 1932*), psychologist, scientist, inventor. B.S., Massachusetts Institute of Technology, 1912; Ph.D., Harvard, 1915. A teacher of psychology at Harvard, 1916–29, and noted for his researches in physiological optics, Troland was chief engineer and director of research for the Technicolor Motion Picture Corp. *post* 1918. He invented and perfected the modern multicolor process for colored motion pictures in all its details.

TROOST, GERARD (*b. Bois-le-Duc, Holland, 1776; d. Nashville, Tenn., 1850*), geologist. Educated at the universities of Leyden and Amsterdam, Troost practiced as a pharmacist and served in the Netherlands army; he traveled in Europe making collections of minerals for the King of Holland, 1807–09. Sailing from Paris, Troost arrived in America early in 1810. Resident in Philadelphia, Pa., 1810–25, he established a pharmaceutical and chemical laboratory; a founder of the Academy of Natural Sciences in Philadelphia, 1812, he served it for five years as its first president. Joining William Maclure, Thomas Say, Robert D. Owen and others in the community at New Harmony, Ind., 1825, he removed in 1827 to Nashville, Tenn., and was professor of sciences at the University of Nashville, 1828–50. He was also state geologist of Tennessee *post* 1831.

TROTT, BENJAMIN (*b. probably Boston, Mass., c. 1770; d. probably Baltimore, Md., c. 1841*), portrait painter, miniaturist. Trott was self-taught save for experience gained making miniatures after the portraits of Gilbert Stuart. His best work (done c. 1805) is excelled only by that of Malbone and is distinguished by fine clear color, a talent for characterization, elimination of any but the most necessary costume details and a characteristic elongation of the neck line and collar.

TROTT, NICHOLAS (*b. England, 1662/63; d. Charleston, S.C., 1739/40*), colonial jurist and official. Came to Charleston, S.C., in May 1699 as attorney-general of that part of the Province of Carolina which lay south and west of Cape Fear. An English lawyer of great learning (not to be confused with Nicholas Trott, governor of the Bahamas, his cousin), he became a member of the Commons House and its speaker and was an aggressive leader of the ruling faction in the province until *c.* 1720. Appointed chief justice, 1702/03, he continued to claim that office as late as 1729. He was author, among other works, of *The Laws of the Province of South Carolina* (1736).

TROUP, GEORGE MICHAEL (*b. McIntosh's Bluff, on Tombigbee River, present Alabama, 1780; d. Montgomery Co., Ga., 1856*), lawyer, Georgia legislator. Graduated College of New Jersey (Princeton), 1797. Congressman, (Democrat) Republican, from Georgia, 1807–15, he opposed the Yazoo claims and recharter of the federal bank; he was a consistent supporter of the Jeffersonian program. U.S. senator, 1816–18, he was Crawford Democrat governor of Georgia, 1823–27, in which time he vigorously defended the rights of the state to Creek lands in defiance of President John Q. Adams. Again U.S. senator, 1829–33, he upheld the right of nullification but considered it unwise; he urged legislative action and Southern nonconsumption as remedies against tariff pressures from Washington. After his formal retirement from political office, he continued active as a strong state-rights Democrat.

TROUP, ROBERT (*b. probably New York, 1757; d. New York, N.Y., 1832*), Revolutionary soldier, New York jurist and land agent. Interested in land speculation *post* 1794, he was successful as agent for the Pulteney interests in western New York State, 1801–32, and closely connected with settlement of the Genesee country.

TROW, JOHN FOWLER (*b. Andover, Mass., 1810; d. Orange, N.J., 1886*), printer, bookseller, publisher. In business in New York City *post* 1833, he is best remembered for his publication of *Trow's New York City Directory, post c.* 1852.

TROWBRIDGE, AUGUSTUS (*b. New York, N.Y., 1870; d. Taormina, Sicily, 1934*), physicist. Attended Columbia University; Ph.D., Berlin, 1898. Taught physics at universities of Michigan and Wisconsin; was professor of physics at Princeton, 1906–33. An able administrator and research scholar in the field of radiation, he was dean of the graduate school at Princeton, 1928–32.

TROWBRIDGE, EDMUND (*b. Cambridge, Mass., 1709; d. Cambridge, 1793*), jurist. Graduated Harvard, 1728. Massachusetts attorney-general, 1749–67, he served as judge of the superior court from 1767 until the Revolution with great ability and impartiality. A moderate conservative and an expert in real property law, he presided over the Boston Massacre trial with fairness and courage. Among his pupils in the law were Theophilus Parsons and Francis Dana, his nephew.

TROWBRIDGE, JOHN (*b. Boston, Mass., 1843; d. Cambridge, Mass., 1923*), physicist, educator. S.B., Lawrence Scientific School, Harvard, 1865. A teacher of physics at Harvard and Massachusetts Institute of Technology for many years, he was Rumford Professor of Science, 1888–1910, and director of the Jefferson Physical Laboratory. A proponent of original research by students, Trowbridge was largely responsible for modernizing methods of teaching science at Harvard and development of improved laboratory facilities there. He was author of a number of research papers in spectrum analysis and the conduction of electricity through gases.

TROWBRIDGE, JOHN TOWNSEND (*b. Monroe Co., N.Y., 1827; d. Arlington, Mass., 1916*), journalist, novelist, poet. Author of a number of works of which the most popular and successful were stories for older boys.

TROWBRIDGE, WILLIAM PETIT (*b. Troy, N.Y., 1828; d. New Haven, Conn., 1892*), engineer, educator. Graduated West Point, 1848. Engaged for a number of years in coast survey work and geodetic surveys, he performed valuable services for the Union Army during the Civil War, taught engineering at Yale, 1871–77, and thereafter was professor of engineering in the School of Mines, Columbia University.

TROYE, EDWARD (*b. near Geneva, Switzerland, 1808; d. Georgetown, Ky., 1874*). Artist whose paintings (*post* 1835) of celebrated American blood horses have much historical and artistic value.

TRUDE, ALFRED SAMUEL (*b. New York, N.Y., 1847; d. 1933*), lawyer. Removed to Chicago, Ill., *c.* 1864; practiced there *post* 1871; one of the most successful trial lawyers of his time in both civil and criminal cases.

TRUDEAU, EDWARD LIVINGSTON (*b. New York, N.Y., 1848; d. Saranac Lake, N.Y., 1915*), physician, pioneer in tuberculosis research. After early education in France and study at Columbia College, Trudeau graduated at N.Y. College of Physicians and Surgeons, 1871. Stricken with pulmonary tuberculosis, 1873, he moved to the Adirondacks where he lived quietly until 1880 when he resumed medical practice

in that region. His work led him to the study of both early diagnosis of tuberculosis and the cure of tubercular patients. In 1884 he founded what became Trudeau Sanatorium, the first American institution of its type; he also built a laboratory (eventually the Saranac Laboratory) where the first tuberculosis immunity experiments in America were performed.

TRUE, ALFRED CHARLES (*b. Middletown, Conn., 1853; d. 1929*), leader in agricultural education. Brother of Frederick W. True. Educated at Wesleyan and Harvard, True taught classic languages for some years before joining the staff of the office of experiment stations, U.S. Department of Agriculture, 1889. He became director of the office in 1893 and expanded its function greatly, supervising research and publication in agricultural education, home economics, irrigation and drainage, and also directing experiment stations in the territories. True's influence was furthered by leadership in what became the Association of Land Grant Colleges and Universities.

TRUE, FREDERICK WILLIAM (*b. Middletown, Conn., 1858; d. 1914*), zoologist. Brother of Alfred C. True. *Post* 1881 an executive of the Smithsonian Institution and ultimately curator of the National Museum, he combined administrative functions with scholarly research on whales and other mammals.

TRUEBLOOD, BENJAMIN FRANKLIN (*b. Salem, Ind., 1847; d. 1916*), educator, professional pacifist worker. Secretary, American Peace Society, 1892–1915.

TRUMAN, BENJAMIN CUMMINGS (*b. Providence, R.I., 1835; d. Los Angeles, Calif., 1916*), journalist, federal official, author. A brilliant Civil War correspondent, he observed conditions in the South, 1865–66, reporting them in letters to the *New York Times* and also in *Senate Exec. Doc. No. 43*, 39th Congress, 1st Session.

TRUMBAUER, HORACE (*b. Philadelphia, Pa., 1868; d. Philadelphia, 1938*), architect. Began his own practice in Philadelphia, 1892; became preferred architect for activities of Peter A. B. Widener and his financial allies, the Elkins family. Working principally in the style of the French Renaissance, he excelled in persuading his clients that their magnificent incomes could find best expression in magnificence of building. His firm's work is best represented in Philadelphia and New York and the areas about those cities, but it was also responsible for the plans for the entire campus of Duke University at Durham, N.C. Among the designers whose work contributed to Trumbauer's success were Frank Seeburger, William O. Frank and Julian Abele. [*Supp. 2*]

TRUMBULL, BENJAMIN (*b. Hebron, Conn., 1735; d. 1820*), Congregational clergyman, historian. Pastor *post* 1760 at North Haven, Conn., he is remembered for his valuable chronicle of Connecticut history from the beginnings to 1764 (first volume, 1797; extended edition, 1818).

TRUMBULL, HENRY CLAY (*b. Stonington, Conn., 1830; d. Philadelphia, Pa., 1903*), Congregational clergyman, Union chaplain in Civil War, Sunday School missionary and writer. Brother of James H. Trumbull.

TRUMBULL, JAMES HAMMOND (*b. Stonington, Conn., 1821; d. Hartford, Conn., 1897*), Connecticut public official, bibliographer, philologist. Brother of Henry C. Trumbull. Historian of New England Indians, particularly those of Connecticut; edited Connecticut colonial records; catalogued library of George Brinley.

TRUMBULL, JOHN (*b. Westbury, Conn., 1750 o.s.; d. Detroit, Mich., 1831*), poet, Connecticut jurist. Descendant of Solomon Stoddard; second cousin of John (1756–1843), Jonathan (1740–1809), and Joseph Trumbull. Passed Yale entrance examination at age of 7 but did not in fact matriculate until 13. As student, he was critical of a curriculum which neglected *belles-lettres* in favor of theology, linguistics and mathematics. Achieving more than local reputation for poems both satirical and classic and for prose essays, he graduated in 1767 but continued his studies at Yale and was awarded the M.A., 1770. While a Yale tutor, 1772–73, he composed and published a satire on college studies, *The Progress of Dulness*; he was also author of a series of essays published under pen-name "The Correspondent" in *The Connecticut Journal* (1770 and 1773). Removing to Boston, Mass., 1773, he continued legal studies under John Adams and published a poem on national affairs, *An Elegy on the Times* (1774). He practiced law at New Haven, Conn., 1774–77, and *post* 1781 at Hartford. Meanwhile he had written the first canto of his *M'Fingal* which was published early in 1776 bearing a 1775 imprint; after the Revolution he divided this canto into two and wrote two additional ones, publishing the entire work for the first time at Hartford, 1782. A Hudibrastic, loose narrative of the troubles of a Tory squire, the poem constitutes a comprehensive review of the blunders of pro-British leaders, and took rank *post* 1783 as an important contribution to American literature; it was the most popular American poem of its length before Longfellow's *Evangeline*. Although regarded as literary leader of the "Hartford Wits," 1785–1800, Trumbull did little to sustain his reputation and showed an increasing interest in law and politics. A strong Federalist, he held state office and served in the legislature; he was judge of the state superior court, 1801–19, and judge of the state supreme court of errors, 1808–19. *The Poetical Works of John Trumbull*, a collected edition, appeared in 1820.

TRUMBULL, JOHN (*b. Lebanon, Conn., 1756; d. New York, N.Y., 1843*), painter of the Revolution. Son of Jonathan Trumbull (1710–1785); brother of Jonathan (1740–1809) and Joseph Trumbull; second cousin of John Trumbull (1750–1831). Showed early talent for drawing, but was given little opportunity for study, either during years at Harvard (graduated 1773) or during intermittent military service in the Revolution. At one time an aide-de-camp of George Washington, Trumbull resigned his commission in 1777. He served as a volunteer in the Rhode Island campaign, 1778, but devoted the years 1777–79 mainly to the study of art in Boston. In 1780 he went abroad, settling in England where he became a pupil of Benjamin West. Imprisoned on suspicion of treason and released, he went to Amsterdam and there painted a full-length portrait of Washington which was engraved and published (1781) as the first authentic likeness of the General issued in Europe. Returning to America, he engaged in commercial activities but in 1783 was back in West's London studio. Here he produced his first paintings of the Revolution, "The Battle of Bunker Hill" and the "Death of General Montgomery in the Attack of Quebec" (completed, 1786). Engravings were arranged for, though not published for twelve years.

The years 1786–89, spent in London mainly, were his most productive. He began his 8 years' labors on his "Declaration of Independence," the most important visual record of the heroic period of American history. (Of its 48 portraits, 36 were from life, the rest from portraits by others or from memory; 13 signers were not represented and 4 non-signers were included.) Other paintings of this period include the "Surrender of Lord Cornwallis at Yorktown" and "Capture of the Hessians at Trenton." Declining Thomas Jefferson's offer of the post of private secretary in the American Legation in Paris, he returned to America, 1789. He painted portraits, took records of "heads" for his planned historical compositions, and solicited subscriptions for engravings, but the results did not meet his expectations. As John Jay's private secretary, 1793–94, he was successful in diplomatic duties connected with Jay's Treaty; he was unsuccessful in prosecution of various commercial ventures on his own account, 1795–97. Appointed a commissioner to oversee execution of the seventh article of Jay's Treaty, he served with distinction, 1796–1804.

Trumbull married an Englishwoman in 1800 and returned with her to America in 1804, settling in New York City where he had indifferent success as a painter and art dealer. A rapid painter, he averaged five sittings to a head for which he charged $100. His style had deteriorated from disuse, however, and commissions were infrequent; in 1808 he returned to London where he was no more fortunate. In 1815 he was back in New York and two years later secured a congressional commission, over the opposition of many younger painters, to do four panels on Revolutionary subjects for the Rotunda of the U.S. Capitol at Washington, D.C. These heavy-handed, chalky, oversized reworkings of his earlier masterful paintings were unsuccessful despite seven years' effort. Other troubles were added to a steady decline in reputation and income. In 1824 his wife died. In 1826 the founding of the National Academy of Design by S. F. B. Morse and others deprived Trumbull of influence he had wielded as president of the American Academy of Fine Arts. A serious financial crisis was probably averted in 1832 by a military pension and the establishment of the Trumbull Gallery at Yale, the earliest art museum in America connected with an educational institution, which took over the artist's unsalable pictures. In his prime, Trumbull was handsome and courtly, frank and abstemious, excitable and exceedingly sensitive. As an old and disappointed man he became irritable and uncompromising. He published his *Autobiography* in 1841.

Far as he is from being America's greatest painter, he is an important part of the national cultural heritage. His 250 to 300 faithful representations, drawn from life, of the principal actors and actions of the Revolution make him the chief, the most prolific, and the most competent visual recorder of that heroic time.

TRUMBULL, JONATHAN (*b. Lebanon, Conn., 1710; d. 1785*), merchant, Connecticut legislator and jurist. Father of John (1756–1843), Jonathan (1740–1809), and Joseph Trumbull. Graduated Harvard, 1727. A candidate for the ministry, he became his father's business associate when his elder brother died, 1731. His commercial ventures flourished for many years, but in 1766 he suffered a reverse for reasons not entirely clear. Meanwhile he had entered politics. First elected to the Connecticut Assembly in 1733, he served in that body or as assistant in the Council almost continually until 1766. In that year Trumbull became deputy-governor, holding concurrently the post of chief justice of the superior court. In 1769 he was named governor by the Assembly (and served until his retirement in 1784). A constant supporter of colonial rights, he was the only colonial governor to take the radical side when the Revolution began. During the war Trumbull's chief contribution lay in making Connecticut a principal source of supplies for Washington's army. Though he and Washington frequently differed over details, Washington subsequently acknowledged the great importance of Trumbull's services. When the war ended, Trumbull's expressed wish for a stronger central government made him unpopular in Connecticut; this and other political complications caused his voluntary retirement.

TRUMBULL, JONATHAN (*b. Lebanon, Conn., 1740; d. 1809*), merchant, Connecticut legislator, Revolutionary soldier. Son of Jonathan Trumbull (1710–1785); brother of John (1756–1843) and Joseph Trumbull. Graduated Harvard, 1759. Paymaster of the forces, New York department, Continental Army, 1775–78; first comptroller of the U.S. treasury, November 1778–April 1779; secretary to Gen. George Washington, 1781–83. Congressman, Federalist, from Connecticut, 1789–94; was chosen speaker of the House in October 1791. U.S. senator, March 1795—June 1796, he resigned to become deputy-governor of Connecticut. He succeeded to the governorship, December 1797, and was annually re-elected to that post for the remainder of his life. He refused to employ the Connecticut militia in enforcement of the Embargo, 1809.

TRUMBULL, JOSEPH (*b. Lebanon, Conn., 1737; d. Lebanon, 1778*), merchant, Connecticut legislator, Revolutionary soldier. Son of Jonathan Trumbull (1710–1785); brother of John (1756–1843) and Jonathan Trumbull (1740–1809). Graduated Harvard, 1756. Serving as commissary-general of Connecticut troops at the siege of Boston, he showed so much efficiency that Congress at Gen. George Washington's request appointed him commissary-general of the Continental Army with the rank of colonel, July 1775. Bringing order out of chaos, he served with great ability until his resignation in 1777 over a proposal by Congress to reorganize his department. "Few armies if any," wrote Washington, "have been better and more plentifully supplied than the troops under Mr. Trumbull's care."

TRUMBULL, LYMAN (*b. Colchester, Conn., 1813; d. Chicago, Ill., 1896*), Illinois jurist. Grandson of Benjamin Trumbull. Began practice of law in Belleville, Ill., 1837. Originally a Democrat, he became a Republican after election to the U.S. Senate (1854) as a Free-Soiler. He had Abraham Lincoln's support. As senator, he opposed Douglas on Kansas. He helped Lincoln during the Civil War but resisted executive encroachments on congressional authority. After aiding the Radicals against President Andrew Johnson, he opposed impeachment and later Radical actions as legally excessive. He gave support to Horace Greeley as a Liberal Republican before retiring from the Senate, 1873. He was counsel for Samuel J. Tilden in the contest over the 1876 election. An able statesman and scholarly constitutionalist, he missed fame because of a colorless personality.

TRUTEAU, JEAN BAPTISTE (*b. Montreal, Canada, 1748; d. St. Louis, Mo., 1827*), Indian trader, explorer. Schoolmaster in St. Louis *post* 1774; leader and diarist of exploring expedition on upper Missouri, 1794–95.

TRUXTUN, THOMAS (*b. near Hempstead, N.Y., 1755; d. Philadelphia, Pa., 1822*), naval officer, merchant mariner. A successful privateersman during the Revolution, he took out the first Philadelphia ship to China, the *Canton*, in 1786. Made captain in the U.S. Navy, 1794, he published several important service manuals. During the naval war with France, as commodore of a squadron operating in the West Indies, he served aboard the *Constellation*, winning actions against the French frigates *Insurgente* and *La Vengeance*, 1799–1800. Energetic and a strict disciplinarian, he set high and enduring standards for the young navy.

TRUXTUN, WILLIAM TALBOT (*b. Philadelphia, Pa., 1824; d. Norfolk, Va., 1887*), naval officer. Grandson of Thomas Truxtun. Appointed midshipman, 1841, he saw extensive service at sea up to the Civil War. During that conflict he held several commands on Atlantic blockade duty, winning the commendation of Adm. D. D. Porter. Engaged in navy-yard administration *post-bellum*, he retired as commodore, 1886.

TRYON, DWIGHT WILLIAM (*b. Hartford, Conn., 1849; d. 1925*), landscape painter, art teacher. Self-taught, Tryon worked first in the manner of John F. Kensett or William T. Richards. After study and work abroad, 1876–81 (principally in France under a disciple of Ingres), he achieved his own mature manner. Conservative in style, refined but somewhat lacking in color, Tryon's work won the admiration of Homer Martin and J. A. M. Whistler for its quality of exquisiteness and its rendering of tiny differences of tone at dusk. He painted few pictures but took great pains with them and sold them well; Charles L. Freer was a principal patron and friend. Tryon was visiting professor of art at Smith College, 1885–1923.

TRYON, GEORGE WASHINGTON (*b. Philadelphia, Pa., 1838; d. Philadelphia, 1888*), businessman, conchologist. Long active in Academy of Natural Sciences of Philadelphia; author of a number of studies on mollusks, and of the *Manual of Conchology, Structural and Systematic* (12 vols., 1879–88).

TRYON, WILLIAM (*b. Surrey, England, 1729; d. London, England, 1788*), colonial governor. After an early career in the British army, Tryon was appointed lieutenant-governor of North Carolina in 1764. He became governor in 1765 and was involved immediately in the crises caused by deteriorating colonial-British relations. He strongly supported the naval and customs officers during the Stamp Act controversy, but lacking military force was unable to compel compliance with the law. When the Regulator movement broke out in the frontier counties, 1768, he restored order by force and a drastic riot act, culminating his exertions with a crushing military defeat of the Regulators at the Alamance in 1771. Transferred to the governorship of New York, 1771, he encountered frontier disturbances in the Vermont area, caused by conflicting claims between New York and New Hampshire, and also difficulties over land purchases from the Mohawk Valley Indians. Returning from an official trip to England (April 1774—June 1775), he found the Revolution in progress and his civil functions necessarily limited. Active in his preferred role of soldier, he performed his chief feats of arms in raids upon Connecticut which were successful in destroying supplies and in diverting some of Connecticut's energies from support of Washington's army to home defense. Illness ended his career in 1780 and forced his return to England. Loyal to the Crown and too prone to use force, Tryon was an able if somewhat vain administrator.

TUBMAN, HARRIET (*b. Dorchester Co., Md., c. 1821; d. Auburn, N.Y., 1913*), fugitive slave, Abolitionist, leading figure in the Underground Railroad. Author of memoirs issued as *Scenes in the Life of Harriet Tubman* (1869); revised and reissued in 1886 as *Harriet the Moses of Her People*.

TUCK, AMOS (*b. Parsonsfield, Maine, 1810; d. 1879*), lawyer. Practiced in Exeter, N.H., *post* 1838. Congressman, independent Democrat-Whig, from New Hampshire, 1847–53, he acted with Joshua R. Giddings and John G. Palfrey as a nucleus of anti-slavery sentiment and was influential in the formation of the Republican party. He was naval officer for Boston district, 1861–65.

TUCKER, ALLEN (*b. Brooklyn, N.Y., 1866; d. New York, N.Y., 1939*), architect, painter. Graduated Columbia, 1888. While a draftsman with Richard M. Hunt, he studied painting at the Art Students League, 1891–95; the teacher who most influenced him was John H. Twachtman. Devoting all his effort to painting *post* 1904, he developed his style from impressionism into an expressionism at first influenced by Van Gogh. The work of the final decade of his life was marked by a vigorously personal maturity of style best observed in "The Pale Horse" (1928), "The Review" (1931), and a "Crucifixion" (1936). [*Supp. 2*]

TUCKER, BENJAMIN RICKETSON (*b. South Dartmouth, Mass., 1854; d. Monaco, 1939*), radical reformer. Attended Massachusetts Institute of Technology, 1870–73. Converted to individualist anarchism, 1872, through Josiah Warren and others, he became an authority on the work of Pierre Joseph Proudhon. He is remembered principally for his publication *Liberty*, issued regularly at Boston, 1881–92, and at New York, 1892–1908. At first an organ for publicizing the views of European anarchists in general, *Liberty* in its later days came more and more to reflect the outlook of Max Stirner. [*Supp. 2*]

TUCKER, GEORGE (*b. Bermuda, 1775; d. Albemarle Co., Va., 1861*), political economist, author. Removed to Virginia as a boy. There he studied and practiced law and served in the state legislature before election to Congress as a Democrat, 1819–25. In 1825 he became professor of moral philosophy at the University of Virginia, probably at the suggestion of James Madison, whom he knew intimately. During twenty years at Virginia he produced, among other works, his *Life of Thomas Jefferson* (1837). Based on extensive research and many conferences with Madison, this was an impartial and on the whole a successful contribution to early American history. Tucker's more important writings were in economics, among them, *The Laws of Wages, Profits and Rent Investigated* (1837) and *The Theory of Money and Banks Investigated* (1839). After his retirement from Virginia in 1845, he continued his scholarly activities, beginning a four-volume *History of the United*

States and producing *Political Economy for the People* in 1859. Although a pragmatist in insisting that economic scholarship should lead to recommendations for public policy, Tucker was a conservative and pessimistic adherent of classical French and English economics, apparently learning nothing from the prodigious economic developments going on around him, or from such contemporaries as Henry C. and Matthew Carey. Admiring Adam Smith, he disagreed with David Ricardo in many details. He was impressed with Malthus's principle of population and used it as a basis for predicting the eventual extinction of slavery as unprofitable. His opposition to slavery was unmistakable but his criticism was never outspoken, ranging from discreetly academic statements to strong but anonymous ridicule. It dwindled to mere feeble mention in his work published on the eve of the Civil War.

TUCKER, GILBERT MILLIGAN (*b. Albany, N.Y., 1847; d. Albany, 1932*), editor of the *Country Gentleman*, 1897–1911. Son of Luther Tucker.

TUCKER, HENRY HOLCOMBE (*b. near Camak, Ga., 1819; d. Atlanta, Ga., 1889*), lawyer, Baptist clergyman. Grandson of Henry Holcombe. A professor at Mercer University, and its president, 1866–71, he was chancellor of the University of Georgia, 1874–78. Thereafter he was proprietor and editor of the *Christian Index.*

TUCKER, HENRY ST. GEORGE (*b. "Matoax," Chesterfield Co., Va., 1780; d. Winchester, Va., 1848*), Virginia legislator, congressman and jurist. Son of St. George Tucker; brother of Nathaniel B. Tucker (1784–1851); half-brother of John Randolph of Roanoke (1773–1833); father of John R. (1823–1897) and Nathaniel B. Tucker (1820–1890). Virginia chancery judge, 1824–31; president of supreme court of appeals of Virginia, 1831–41; professor of law, University of Virginia, 1841–45. Author, among other works, of *Commentaries on the Laws of Virginia* (1836–37).

TUCKER, HENRY ST. GEORGE (*b. Winchester, Va., 1853; d. Lexington, Va., 1932*), lawyer, legal educator. Son of John R. Tucker (1823–1897). Congressman, Democrat, from Virginia, 1889–97, 1922–32. A liberal during his first service in Congress, *post* 1922 he was an ardent exponent of state rights and a strict constructionist, opposing the social and economic legislation of that period.

TUCKER, JOHN RANDOLPH (*b. Alexandria, Va., 1812; d. Petersburg, Va., 1883*), naval officer. Appointed midshipman, 1826, he rose after extensive general service to rank of commander, 1855. Entering the Confederate service, 1861, he commanded the Charleston Squadron and was promoted captain, 1863. Forming his crews into a naval brigade on evacuation of Charleston in February 1865, he distinguished himself with his command at the battle of Sailor's Creek in April. He served for a time after the war as rear-admiral in the Peruvian navy.

TUCKER, JOHN RANDOLPH (*b. Winchester, Va., 1823; d. 1897*), lawyer, teacher of law, Virginia official and congressman. Son of Henry St. G. Tucker (1780–1848); brother of Nathaniel B. Tucker (1820–1890); father of Henry St. G. Tucker (1853–1932). A strict-constructionist state-rights logician, he advocated tariff reform, the repeal of the internal revenue system and sound money. He was eminently successful in his practice of law, serving in such diverse actions as the trial of Jefferson Davis and the case of the Chicago anarchists before the U.S. Supreme Court.

TUCKER, LUTHER (*b. Brandon, Vt., 1802; d. Albany, N.Y., 1873*), printer, agricultural journalist. Proprietor of *Rochester Daily Advertiser* (N.Y.), 1826–39; established *Genesee Farmer*, 1831, which he merged with the *Cultivator* in 1839. In 1846 he established the *Horticulturist;* edited by Andrew J. Downing, it became an outstanding journal. Beginning issue of the *Country Gentleman*, 1853, he consolidated it with his *Cultivator*, 1866, thereafter publishing under the title *Cultivator and Country Gentleman*. Leader and model of agricultural journalists in his time, he was succeeded as editor-proprietor by his sons, 1873; among them was Gilbert M. Tucker.

TUCKER, NATHANIEL BEVERLEY (*b. "Matoax," Chesterfield Co., Va., 1784; d. Winchester, Va., 1851*), professor of law, Southern rights publicist. Son of St. George Tucker; brother of Henry St. G. Tucker (1780–1848); half-brother of John Randolph of Roanoke (1773–1833). Professor of law at College of William and Mary *post* 1834, he reflected in his numerous letters, books and lectures the theories of his colleague Thomas R. Dew. A lifelong advocate of secession and aristocratic government, he was author, among other works, of *George Balcombe* (published anonymously, 1836) and *The Partisan Leader* (1836, but bore fictitious date of 1856). The second of these titles attempted a fictional prophecy of what would follow as a result of the Jacksonian policies and was reprinted as propaganda by both sides during the Civil War.

TUCKER, NATHANIEL BEVERLEY (*b. Winchester, Va., 1820; d. 1890*), planter, journalist, Confederate agent. Son of Henry St. G. Tucker (1780–1848); brother of John R. Tucker (1823–1897).

TUCKER, ST. GEORGE (*b. Port Royal, Bermuda, 1752 o.s.; d. Nelson Co., Va., 1827*), Revolutionary soldier, Virginia jurist. Father of Nathaniel B. (1784–1851) and Henry St. G. Tucker (1780–1848); stepfather of John Randolph of Roanoke (1773–1833). Judge of the general court of Virginia and professor of law in the College of William and Mary, he was elected to the state supreme court of appeals, 1803, and served until 1811. Appointed U.S. district judge for Virginia, 1813, he resigned shortly before his death. He was author of a number of works, notably an annotated edition of *Blackstone's Commentaries* (1803), one of the most important law texts of its day. His minor poetry included *The Probationary Odes of Jonathan Pindar* (2 pts., 1796), once attributed to Philip M. Freneau.

TUCKER, SAMUEL (*b. Marblehead, Mass., 1747; d. Bremen, Maine, 1833*), merchant mariner, naval officer. Commanded army warships *Franklin* and *Hancock*, 1776, capturing valuable prizes off Boston. As captain in the navy *post* March 1777, he commanded frigate *Boston* and performed important services until capture of the vessel at Charleston, S.C., 1780. Retiring from active naval service, 1781, he sailed for a while on merchant ships and later became a farmer.

TUCKER, STEPHEN DAVIS (*b. Bloomfield, N.J., 1818; d. London, England, 1902*), printing machinery inventor. Associated with R. Hoe & Co. *post* 1834, he retired as its senior partner, 1893.

TUCKER, WILLIAM JEWETT (*b. Griswold, Conn., 1839; d. 1926*), Congregational clergyman, educator. Graduated Dartmouth, 1861; Andover Theological Seminary, 1866. Distinguished for development of sociology courses at Andover and for settlement work in Boston, Mass., Tucker was a figure in the so-called "Andover controversy," 1886–92. As president of Dartmouth, 1893–1909, he strengthened the college, reforming many archaic attitudes, reorganizing finances and modernizing the plant.

TUCKERMAN, BAYARD (*b. New York, N.Y., 1855; d. 1923*), scholar, writer. Author, among other works, of *Life of General Lafayette* (1889), *William Jay and the Constitutional Movement for the Abolition of Slavery* (1894) and *Life of General Philip Schuyler* (1903). Editor of *Diary of Philip Hone* (1889).

TUCKERMAN, EDWARD (*b. Boston, Mass., 1817; d. Amherst, Mass., 1886*), botanist, leading authority on American lichenology. Brother of Frederick G. Tuckerman. B.A., Union College, 1837; B.A., Harvard, 1847; also studied at Harvard Law and Divinity schools and at Upsala in Sweden. Professor of botany, Amherst College, *post* 1858. Author of many studies of lichens including his principal work, *Genera Lichenum* (1872).

TUCKERMAN, FREDERICK (*b. Greenfield, Mass., 1857; d. 1929*), comparative anatomist, naturalist. Son of Frederick G. Tuckerman.

TUCKERMAN, FREDERICK GODDARD (*b. Boston, Mass., 1821; d. Greenfield, Mass., 1873*), poet. Father of Frederick Tuckerman; brother of Edward Tuckerman.

TUCKERMAN, HENRY THEODORE (*b. Boston, Mass., 1813; d. New York, N.Y., 1871*), critic, essayist. Nephew of Joseph Tuckerman; cousin of Edward and Frederick G. Tuckerman. Author of a number of works, once widely read, which were typical of the romantic approach to travel, literature and art. He produced several books of lasting value which include *Book of the Artists: American Artist Life* (1867) and *America and Her Commentators* (1864).

TUCKERMAN, JOSEPH (*b. Boston, Mass., 1778; d. Havana, Cuba, 1840*), Unitarian clergyman, philanthropist. Uncle of Edward, Frederick G. and Henry T. Tuckerman. Pastor in Chelsea, Mass., 1801–26, he was an original member of the Anthology Society; removing to Boston, 1826, he began a city mission for the poor which served as a model for similar institutions in England and France.

TUCKEY, WILLIAM (*b. Somersetshire, England, c. 1708; d. Philadelphia, Pa., 1781*), organist, choirmaster, composer. Developed choir of Trinity Church, New York City, *post* 1753; conducted first American rendering of Handel's *Messiah* in New York, 1770. Author of a number of original compositions of which only the hymn called "Liverpool" survives.

TUDOR, FREDERIC (*b. Boston, Mass., 1783; d. Boston, 1864*), businessman. Brother of William Tudor. Conceived idea of shipping ice from Boston to tropical cities c. 1804; made first shipment to Martinique, 1806. Thereafter, with great ingenuity and complete ruthlessness, he developed his trade to worldwide proportions.

TUDOR, WILLIAM (*b. Boston, Mass., 1779; d. Rio de Janeiro, Brazil, 1830*), merchant, Massachusetts legislator, U.S. consular officer, author. Brother of Frederic Tudor. Founder and first editor (1815–17) of the *North American Review;* helped found Boston Athenaeum. A keen critic of contemporary manners, he was author, among other works, of *Letters on the Eastern States* (1820), *The Life of James Otis* (1823) and *Gebel Teir* (1829, anonymously).

TUFTS, CHARLES (*b. present Somerville, Mass., 1781; d. 1876*), farmer, brickmaker, Universalist leader. Donated land for the building site of Tufts College, 1852.

TUFTS, COTTON (*b. Medford, Mass., 1732; d. Weymouth, Mass., 1815*), physician, Revolutionary patriot. Nephew of John Tufts. Graduated Harvard, 1749. After study of medicine with a brother, began practice in Weymouth, 1752. A close friend of John Adams, Tufts was long associated with scientific, cultural and political affairs in Massachusetts.

TUFTS, JOHN (*b. Medford, Mass., 1689; d. Amesbury, Mass., 1752*), Congregational clergyman. Minister in West Newbury, Mass., 1714–38. Notable for influence exerted upon American music by his *A Very Plain and Easy Introduction to the Art of Singing Psalm Tunes* (c. 1715) which was considered "a daring and unjustifiable innovation" and aroused much controversy.

TULANE, PAUL (*b. near Princeton, N.J., 1801; d. Princeton, 1887*), New Orleans, La., merchant, philanthropist. Successful in trade and real estate operations in New Orleans, 1822–73, Tulane donated property whose income made possible the conversion of the University of Louisiana, a state institution, into the independent Tulane University, 1884.

TULLY, WILLIAM (*b. Saybrook Point, Conn., 1785; d. Springfield, Mass., 1859*), physician. Graduated Yale, 1806; studied medicine with, among others, Nathan Smith (1762–1829) and Eli Ives. In practice thereafter in many locations, Tully was considered the most learned and scientific physician of his time in New England. An authority on *materia medica*, he was a prolific writer on medical topics and a teacher for many years at the medical school at Castleton, Vt., and at Yale.

TUPPER, BENJAMIN (*b. Stoughton, Mass., 1738; d. 1792*), Revolutionary officer, Massachusetts legislator, Ohio pioneer. Associated with Rufus Putnam in formation of the Ohio Company, he went with the original settlers to Marietta, 1788, and was practically sole administrator of local justice along the Muskingum until his death.

TUPPER, HENRY ALLEN (*b. Charleston, S.C., 1828; d. 1902*), Baptist clergyman, Confederate chaplain. Corresponding secretary, Board of Foreign Missions, Southern Baptist Convention, 1872–93.

TURELL, JANE (*b. Boston, Mass., 1708; d. Medford, Mass., 1735*), poet. Daughter of Benjamin Colman. Her religious verses and others appeared in *Reliquiae Turellae* (Boston, 1735; published under another title in London, 1741).

TURNBULL, ANDREW (*b. Scotland, c. 1718; d. Charleston, S.C., 1792*), colonizer, physician. Securing a grant in East Florida, 1766, he endeavored unsuccessfully to develop the colony of New Smyrna by settlement of Greek, Italian and Minorcan immigrants. He was the father of Robert J. Turnbull.

TURNBULL, ROBERT JAMES (*b. New Smyrna, Fla., 1775; d. 1833*), South Carolina planter, writer. Son of Andrew Turnbull. Obsessed by fears of national consolidation under the doctrine of implied constitutional power, he advocated the compact theory of the Union and extreme state sovereignty. He took a leading part in the nullification convention of 1832, writing its *Address*. Author, among other works, of *The Crisis: or, Essays on the Usurpations of the Federal Government* (1827, originally published in *Charleston Mercury* over pen-name "Brutus"), he strongly influenced the thinking of Robert B. Rhett.

TURNBULL, WILLIAM (*b. Philadelphia, Pa., 1800; d. 1857*), soldier, engineer. Grandson of Charles Nisbet. Graduated West Point, 1819. Long active in topographical and other engineering work, he is particularly remembered for his design and construction of the Potomac Aqueduct, and for his services as chief topographical engineer on Gen. Winfield Scott's staff during the Mexican War.

TURNER, ASA (*b. Templeton, Mass., 1799; d. Oskaloosa, Iowa, 1885*), Congregational clergyman, educator. Brother of Jonathan B. Turner. A home missionary in Illinois and Iowa, Turner promoted establishment of numerous churches and several colleges and academies, including Illinois College at Jacksonville and Iowa College at Davenport.

TURNER, CHARLES YARDLEY (*b. Baltimore, Md., 1850; d. New York, N.Y., 1918*), mural painter.

TURNER, DANIEL (*b. probably Richmond, S.I., N.Y., 1794; d. Philadelphia, Pa., 1850*), naval officer. Appointed midshipman, 1808, he commanded the *Caledonia* in the battle of Lake Erie, September 1813. After a long and varied career on sea and land, he was promoted captain, 1835. His last post was as commandant at Portsmouth navy yard.

TURNER, EDWARD (*b. Fairfax Co., Va., 1778; d. near Natchez, Miss., 1860*), Mississippi legislator and jurist. Raised in Kentucky, he settled in Mississippi, 1801, where he prospered in the law. He also held a number of judicial posts including chief justice of the supreme court and chancellor, and was a member of the committee that drafted the first Mississippi constitution. A practical, hardworking man, he was distinguished for his integrity and good manners.

TURNER, EDWARD RAYMOND (*b. Baltimore, Md., 1881; d. 1929*), historian. Graduated St. John's College, Annapolis, 1904; Ph.D., Johns Hopkins, 1910. Professor at University of Michigan, Yale and Johns Hopkins, he devoted his research to English constitutional history. Author of, among other works, *The Privy Council of England*, etc. (1927–28) and *The Cabinet Council of England*, etc. (1930–32).

TURNER, FENNELL PARRISH (*b. Danielsville, Tenn., 1867; d. Santa Cruz, Calif., 1932*), missionary executive. Secretary, Student Volunteer Movement for Foreign Missions, 1897–1919; secretary for missionary education, Methodist Episcopal Church, 1928–30.

TURNER, FREDERICK JACKSON (*b. Portage, Wis., 1861; d. Pasadena, Calif., 1932*), historian. Educated at University of Wisconsin, A.B., 1884; M.A., 1888. Ph.D., Johns Hopkins, 1890. Assistant professor of history, University of Wisconsin, 1889–91; professor of history, 1891–92; professor of American history, 1892–1910. Professor of history, Harvard, 1910–24. Familiar from his college days with the unique archival materials collected by Lyman C. Draper and housed in the Wisconsin State Historical Society, Turner was attracted to a scientific investigation of American life at its beginnings; he never strayed far from this theme. Invited to present a brief paper at a meeting of the American Historical Association to be held at the Chicago World's Fair, he assembled data for an essay on "The Significance of the Frontier in American History" which he read on July 12, 1893. First printed in *Proceedings of the State Historical Society of Wisconsin . . . 1893* (1894), it was reprinted in the *Annual Report of the American Historical Association* (1894). In this essay he set forth a new hypothesis and opened a new period in the interpretation of the history of the United States. Beyond this important seminal study Turner wrote little, concentrating his energies on his classroom and university work.

Turner's frontier hypothesis was an attempt to account for the fact that emigrants to the United States from western Europe and their descendants had brought into being a nation so variant from any of those from which they came. He accounted for this on the ground that people who came from an environment in which they were unable to own land into an open continent where there was little to impede their free access to good land were thereby subjected to an influence unusual in history and perhaps formative in shaping American culture. Many of Turner's followers who took up his hypothesis dogmatically went far beyond their master in applying it. Turner himself was content to point out the possibility that human nature in a free environment might behave differently from the same nature under social and economic pressure; that equality of opportunity might have something to do with democracy in politics; that isolation on a new frontier might encourage the survival of the robust and the opinionated; that the necessity of repeatedly setting up social and governmental institutions brought about a "laboratory process" in which nonessentials dropped out while tested principles survived; and finally that the relationship between frontiersmen and government led naturally to an intense nationalism. He also pointed out that by 1893 the influence of the frontier was about to terminate. He regarded the frontier less as a place than as a continuous process sweeping the continent, and regarded the region where it might be temporarily operating as a section with aspects and interests deriving from its cultural state. For the rest of his creative life Turner tested his hypothesis, applying it at times to microscopic examination of limited regions and periods, and trying at other times to reconcile it with larger views of American development.

TURNER, GEORGE (*b. Edina, Mo., 1850; d. Spokane, Wash., 1932*), lawyer. Practiced in Alabama, 1870–85; led Republican party in Alabama. Appointed a justice of the supreme court of Washington Territory, 1885, he resigned in 1888 and began practice in Spokane. Successful in mine development and reputed an able constitutional lawyer, Turner served as U.S. senator from Washington, 1897–1903; he was elected on a fusion ticket made up of Silver Republicans, Democrats and Populists. He later served

as a member of the Alaska Boundary Tribunal and as counsel for the United States in a number of actions before international commissions.

TURNER, HENRY McNEAL (*b. near Abbeville, S.C., 1834; d. Windsor, Ont., Canada, 1915*), bishop of the African Methodist Episcopal Church. The first Negro to be appointed an army chaplain (1863), Turner was active in Georgia Republican politics during Reconstruction. He was bishop of his church for Georgia, 1880–92, and for many years chancellor of Morris Brown College in Atlanta.

TURNER, JAMES MILTON (*b. St. Louis Co., Mo., 1840; d. Ardmore, Okla., 1915*), Negro leader, educator. An important figure in Missouri Republican politics, he was a benefactor of present Lincoln University and served ably as U.S. minister resident and consul general to Liberia, 1871–78.

TURNER, JOHN WESLEY (*b. near Saratoga, N.Y., 1833; d. St. Louis, Mo., 1899*), Union soldier, St. Louis, Mo., businessman. Graduated West Point, 1855. Served as chief of artillery, chief commissary and chief of staff at various times in many theatres of the Civil War, rising to rank of brevet major-general. He was outstanding as a division commander in the Army of the James and chief of staff in that army, 1864–65.

TURNER, JONATHAN BALDWIN (*b. Templeton, Mass., 1805; d. Jacksonville, Ill., 1899*), educator, agriculturist. Graduated Yale, 1833. Taught at Illinois College, 1833–47, serving for the most part as professor of rhetoric. An early leader in the movement for public schools in Illinois, he was largely responsible for the free school law of 1855 and the establishment of the first normal school in Illinois in 1857. Between 1850 and 1867 he conducted a remarkable campaign for establishment of a state university which would be supported by congressional appropriation of public lands. Through Turner's urgings, the Illinois legislature of 1867 took advantage of the Morrill Act to establish the present University of Illinois.

TURNER, JOSIAH (*b. Hillsboro, N.C., 1821; d. near Hillsboro, 1901*), lawyer, North Carolina legislator and editor. As editor of the Raleigh *Sentinel*, 1868–76, he worked to discredit and defeat the Carpetbag government of North Carolina, displaying a single-minded gift for ridicule and sarcasm.

TURNER, NAT (*b. Southampton Co., Va., 1800; d. Jerusalem, Va., 1831*), Negro preacher and leader. A precocious child, Nat Turner received the rudiments of an education and early developed a fanatical religious conviction that he had been chosen to lead his fellow slaves out of bondage. Settling upon Aug. 21, 1831, as the great day of deliverance, he and some associates plotted a slave insurrection; as a first step they murdered Nat Turner's master and all his family. Securing arms and horses and enlisting other slaves, they killed in all 51 white persons in a single day and night. However, the rebellion collapsed at the first sign of armed resistance and on August 25 Nat Turner went into hiding. Discovered by accident six weeks later, he was at once tried and hanged. This revolt, following closely on slave insurrections in the West Indies, sent a profound shock through the slave-holding states and brought about a great increase in severity of the slave codes; it also dealt a death blow to the flourishing emancipation movement in the South.

TURNER, ROSS STERLING (*b. Westport, N.Y., 1847; d. Nassau, Bahamas, 1915*), painter, teacher of art. Associated in his studies at Munich with Frank Duveneck and other young American artists, he was also familiar with Whistler at Venice. *Post* 1882 a popular teacher of art in the Boston, Mass., area, Turner was distinguished as a water-colorist and as one of the few modern exponents of the art of illumination of manuscripts.

TURNER, SAMUEL HULBEART (*b. Philadelphia, Pa., 1790; d. New York, N.Y., 1861*), Episcopal clergyman, educator. Professor of Biblical learning and interpretation at General Theological Seminary, New York City, *post* 1822, he was also professor of Hebrew at Columbia for many years *post* 1830. A conservative scholar both in his teaching and his writings, he was moderately opposed to the contemporary influence of the Oxford Movement.

TURNER, WALTER VICTOR (*b. Epping Forest, England, 1866; d. Wilkinsburg, Pa., 1919*), engineer. Came to America, 1888, as a textile expert. Taking employment with the Santa Fé Railroad, 1897, he became an expert on air brakes; *post* 1903 he directed engineering operations for the Westinghouse Air Brake Co. and won the reputation of being the foremost pneumatic engineer in the world. Among his more than 400 patents, the "K" triple valve (patented, October 1904) and his later electro-pneumatic brake were outstanding contributions to transportation efficiency.

TURNER, WILLIAM (*b. Kilmallock, Ireland, 1871; d. Buffalo, N.Y., 1936*), Roman Catholic clergyman, educator. Graduated Royal University of Ireland, 1888; studied at North American College, Rome; was ordained, 1893. A seminary professor at St. Paul, Minn., 1894–1906, he became professor of logic and the history of philosophy at Catholic University of America, and also editor of the *American Ecclesiastical Review* and other learned journals. Consecrated bishop of Buffalo, N.Y., 1919, he served there until his death, continuing his scholarly interests as far as his administrative duties permitted. He was author of, among other works, an outstanding *History of Philosophy* (1903). [*Supp. 2*]

TURNEY, PETER (*b. Jasper, Tenn., 1827; d. Winchester, Tenn., 1903*), lawyer, Tennessee secessionist and Confederate soldier. Justice of Tennessee supreme court, 1870–93; chief justice, 1886–93. Conservative Democratic governor of Tennessee, 1893–97.

TURPIN, BEN (*b. New Orleans, La., c. 1869; d. Santa Monica, Calif., 1940*), slapstick comedian. Raised in New York City; roamed the country for some five years as a hobo; entered show business as a burlesque and vaudeville comedian in Chicago, Ill., c. 1891. Toured for many years in the stage character of "Happy Hooligan." Entering the movies c. 1907, and capitalizing on his cross-eyed appearance and on his skill as a clown-acrobat, he was by 1914 one of Essanay Studio's leading comics. Under the direction of Mack Sennett at the Keystone Studio in California, Turpin reached his height of fame in comedy-parodies of contemporary starring vehicles. [*Supp. 2*]

TUTHILL, WILLIAM BURNET (*b. New York, N.Y., 1855; d. 1929*), architect. Studied in office of Richard M. Hunt; began practice, 1877, in New York City. Principally celebrated for building Carnegie Hall, New York City (1891, in association with Dankmar Adler and Louis H. Sullivan), Tuthill also designed a number of other buildings on a broadly eclectic basis. The acoustic success of Carnegie Hall led him to be called in as consultant for many churches and concert halls.

TUTTLE, CHARLES WESLEY (*b. Newfield, Maine, 1829; d. 1881*), astronomer, lawyer, antiquarian. An assistant at the Harvard Observatory, 1850–54, Tuttle made his most important contribution to science by explaining the "dusky" ring of Saturn. A successful Boston lawyer *post* 1856, he was author of a number of scholarly articles on New England history and of *Capt. John Mason* (1887).

TUTTLE, DANIEL SYLVESTER (*b. Windham, N.Y., 1837; d. St. Louis, Mo., 1923*), Episcopal clergyman. Graduated Columbia, 1857; General Theological Seminary, New York, 1862. Missionary bishop of Montana, with jurisdiction in Utah and Idaho, 1867–86, he served thereafter as bishop of Missouri. *Post* 1903 he was presiding bishop of his church.

TUTTLE, HERBERT (*b. Bennington, Vt., 1846; d. Ithaca, N.Y., 1894*), journalist, educator, historian. Graduated University of Vermont, 1869. After employment on the *Boston Daily Advertiser* as a correspondent in Washington, D.C., and in Paris, France, he was Berlin correspondent of the London *Daily News*, 1873–79. Encouraged by Andrew D. White, Tuttle began an academic career as lecturer in international law at University of Michigan and Cornell, 1880–83. *Post* 1883 he taught the history of politics and modern European history at Cornell. Among other works he was author of an unfinished *History of Prussia* (1884, 1888, 1896).

TUTWILER, HENRY (*b. Harrisonburg, Va., 1807; d. Greene Springs, Ala., 1884*), educator. Graduated University of Virginia, 1829. Professor of ancient languages, University of Alabama, 1831–37. Headed Greene Springs School for Boys, 1847–84, an institution unusual in its time for its emphasis on the sciences and its respect for the individual student.

TUTWILER, JULIA STRUDWICK (*b. Greene Springs, Ala., 1841; d. Birmingham, Ala., 1916*), Alabama educator, social reformer. Daughter of Henry Tutwiler. Studied at Vassar; tutored by faculty at Washington and Lee; spent three years in advanced study in France and Germany. A teacher in Alabama *post* 1876, she was responsible for founding of Alabama Normal College, and was its co-principal and principal, 1883–1910. Through her efforts vocational training for women was established in Alabama, 1896.

TWACHTMAN, JOHN HENRY (*b. Cincinnati, O., 1853; d. Gloucester, Mass., 1902*), painter. Studied drawing at Ohio Mechanics' Institute and at University of Cincinnati; went to Munich with Frank Duveneck, 1875, and studied there and at Venice until 1878. After a brief stay in America, he painted, studied and traveled abroad until 1884. Thereafter he resided principally in New England and was for many years an instructor of the antique class at the Art Students League, New York. Twachtman's work falls into three distinct periods. His early work (1875–81) is characterized by strong contrast of values in subdued variations of brown and black, by vigorous brush work, and by direct rendering from nature. His second period is marked by a reaction against the dark tones of the Munich tradition; the color is in variations of silvery grays and greens, the pigment is applied thinly with a delicate but precise technique and the composition is restricted to very simple themes. *Post* 1889 his work shows the obvious influence of impressionism. From subdued hues the color changes to the higher key of sunlight or the ethereal and pallid harmony of winter landscape. He seems striving for the sensitive rather than the striking and for the subtle rather than the obvious, displaying a mastery of nuance. He openly declared the decorative intention of his work at this time. Twachtman found his interest in the expressive organization of form and the harmonic relation of line and color; his art therefore relates to the doctrine of Whistler; his appreciation of light and color is owing to Monet.

TWAIN, MARK. [See CLEMENS, SAMUEL LANGHORNE, 1835–1910.]

TWEED, WILLIAM MARCY (*b. New York, N.Y., 1823; d. New York, 1878*), saddler, bookkeeper, political boss. Rising in New York City politics through his influence as officer of a volunteer fire company (Americus No. 6), Tweed was elected an alderman, 1851. Among aldermanic associates who were known in their time as "The Forty Thieves," Tweed soon displayed a capacity for grafting which rendered further honest toil unnecessary for him. He served as congressman, Democrat, from New York, 1853–55, but found that he preferred municipal politics. Defeated for alderman in 1855, Tweed, with Peter B. Sweeny and Richard B. Connolly (later his chief partners in the "Tweed Ring"), set up a faction in Tammany Hall to oppose Fernando Wood. Successful in disposing of Wood, Tweed secured membership for himself on several key boards and commissions, had his friend Sweeny nominated for district attorney, and placed other allies in strategic positions. Made chairman of the Democratic central committee of New York County, 1860, he maneuvered another satellite, A. Oakey Hall, into the district attorney's post and was thereafter dictator of his party in New York.

Reaching out his tentacles of graft in every direction and levying toll on all who did business with the city or in the city, Tweed was doubtless a millionaire by 1867. In 1868 he practically secured control of New York State by dictating the nomination of John T. Hoffman as governor. Tweed, elected a state senator in 1867, ran everything from his seven-room hotel suite in Albany; it was there in 1869 that the members of his "Ring" decided that all bills thereafter rendered against New York City and County must be 50% fraudulent. The proportion was later raised to 85%. Bogus naturalization of immigrants and repeating at elections were now carried to hitherto unknown lengths. Tweed was also a partner with Jay Gould and James Fisk in the plundering of the Erie Railroad. By this time *Harper's Weekly*, with Thomas Nast as cartoonist, began a campaign against Tweed and his friends and against the new (1870) city charter which riveted the rule of the "Ring" more firmly on the city. In September 1870 the *New York Times*, directed by George Jones, began attacks on Tweed. In the spring of 1871 two discontented county officials turned over to the *Times* proofs of the swindling by the "Ring." The evidence was published in July, and in September at a mass meeting in Cooper Union a Committee of Seventy was formed to take action. This committee, made up of prominent citizens including Samuel J. Tilden, was prompt to act. By December, Tweed had been arrested and Sweeny and others had fled the jurisdiction. Convicted at his second trial in November 1873, Tweed was sentenced to twelve years in prison and a fine, but the sentence was reduced by the court of appeals. Rearrested in January 1875 on leaving prison, Tweed escaped from custody late in the year and went to Spain. Returned to America in November 1876 by Spanish officials, Tweed was committed to prison until he made payment under a judgment in a civil suit brought to recover the "Ring's" thefts. After giving extensive testimony about many of his crooked transactions, he died in jail. The amount which the "Tweed Ring" stole from the city has been variously estimated at between $30,000,000 and $200,000,000.

TWICHELL, JOSEPH HOPKINS (*b. Southington, Conn., 1838; d. 1918*), Congregational clergyman. Graduated Yale, 1859; Andover Theological Seminary, 1865. Pastor, Asylum Hill Church, Hartford, Conn., *post* 1865, he was a leader in the city's religious and civic affairs and a member of the literary group that included Charles D. Warner, the Stowes and Mark Twain. He was Mark Twain's companion on the trip described in *A Tramp Abroad* and one of the humorist's most intimate friends.

TWIGGS, DAVID EMANUEL (*b. Richmond Co., Ga., 1790; d. 1862*), soldier. Rose to rank of major in War of 1812; promoted lieutenant-colonel of the 4th Infantry, 1831, and colonel of the 2nd Dragoons, 1836. Distinguished for dogged perseverance and bravery rather than intelligence while serving under both Gen. Zachary Taylor and Gen. Winfield Scott in the Mexican War, he rose to brigadier-general and brevet major-general. In command of the Department of Texas at the outbreak of the Civil War, he surrendered all the forces and stores under his control to the Confederate General McCulloch and was dismissed from the U.S. Army. Made a Confederate major-general, May 1861, he was given command of the district of Louisiana. Too old to take the field, he resigned and soon died, probably near Augusta, Ga.

TWINING, ALEXANDER CATLIN (*b. New Haven, Conn., 1801; d. New Haven, 1884*), engineer, astronomer, educator. Graduated Yale, 1820. Taught at Yale and at Middlebury College, Vermont; served for many years as a consulting engineer to railroads. His most important invention was an application of the absorption process for the manufacture of ice on a commercial scale (patented 1853).

TWITCHELL, AMOS (*b. Dublin, N.H., 1781; d. Keene, N.H., 1850*), pioneer New Hampshire surgeon. Graduated Dartmouth, 1802; studied medicine with Nathan Smith (1762–1829). Practiced principally at Keene, N.H., performing many operations with exceptional skill. In 1807 he tied the carotid artery with success; he was also one of the first in the United States to perform extensive amputations for malignant disease, tracheotomy, and trephining of the long bones for suppuration.

TYLER, BENNET (*b. Middlebury, Conn., 1783; d. 1858*), Congregational clergyman, educator. Graduated Yale, 1804. Pastor in South Britain, Conn., 1808–22; president of Dartmouth College, 1822–28. Pastor in Portland, Maine, until 1834 when he became president and professor of theology at present Hartford Theological Seminary. An ardent conservative Calvinist, Tyler opposed the innovations of Nathaniel W. Taylor and the "New Divinity," holding through-

out his career to the Calvinist system as modified by Jonathan Edwards and later by Timothy Dwight. He resigned his presidency of the seminary in 1857.

TYLER, CHARLES MELLEN (*b. Limington, Maine, 1832; d. Scranton, Pa., 1918*), Congregational clergyman, Union Army chaplain, educator. Graduated Yale, 1855. Professor of history and philosophy of religion at the Sage School, Cornell University, 1891–1903, and emeritus thereafter.

TYLER, DANIEL (*b. Brooklyn, Conn., 1799; d. New York, N.Y., 1882*), soldier, industrialist. Attended West Point and was commissioned lieutenant of artillery, 1819; studied later at the artillery school at Fortress Monroe, Va., and in the French army artillery school at Metz. Exposed shoddy conditions at Springfield Arsenal, 1830–32. Resigning from the army, 1834, he began a highly successful career as engineer and financier of railroads and canals both North and South. Commissioned Union brigadier-general, 1861, Tyler commanded a division during the first Bull Run campaign, but through his failure to attack at the proper time must bear some of the blame for the disaster of that battle. His later Civil War career was not notable. In association with Samuel Noble he began exploitation of the iron deposits of eastern Alabama, 1872, and was largely responsible for successful operations at Anniston thereafter.

TYLER, JOHN (*b. York Co., Va., 1747; d. Charles City Co., Va., 1813*), Revolutionary patriot, Virginia legislator and jurist. Father of John Tyler (1790–1862). Studied law with Robert C. Nicholas. A friend of Thomas Jefferson and a follower of Patrick Henry, Tyler held a number of judicial posts in Virginia and was active in the House of Delegates where he served for a time as speaker. An opponent of the Federal Constitution, he became an ardent (Democrat) Republican. Elected governor of Virginia, 1808, he held that post until 1811 when he became U.S. judge for the district of Virginia.

TYLER, JOHN (*b. Charles City Co., Va., 1790; d. 1862*), lawyer, Virginia legislator, president of the United States. Son of John Tyler (1747–1813); father of Robert Tyler. Educated at College of William and Mary; read law with his father; began practice c. 1809. Elected to the House of Delegates, 1811, he served until 1816, loyally supporting the Madison administration and indicating a preference for strict constructionism. A man of great charm and a gifted speaker, Tyler was elected to the U.S. Congress as a Democrat in 1816 and served until 1821. He favored revocation of the charter of the Bank of the U.S., voted against Calhoun's "bonus bill" for internal improvements, against a protective tariff, and against adoption of the Missouri Compromise in 1820. Consistent in opposition to the slave trade, he trusted to time and climate for the abolition of the whole institution of slavery. He supported William H. Crawford for president in the campaign of 1824 and had little use for Andrew Jackson. As governor of Virginia, 1825–27, he strove for the development of roads and schools. Elected to the U.S. Senate, 1827, as an anti-Jackson Democrat, he voted against the "tariff of abominations," 1828, and supported Jackson for the presidency as a choice of evils. Although he approved Jackson's opposition to the recharter of the Bank of the U.S., he supported the resolutions which condemned the president for removing federal deposits. Personally opposed to nullification, Tyler considered Jackson's nullification proclamation a violation of the Constitution and cast the single vote recorded in the Senate against the Force Bill. However, it was he who first formulated a plan of conciliation and brought Calhoun and Clay together to agree upon the compromise tariff of 1833. A member of the Southern state-rights group in Congress which acted with the National Republicans within the now-forming Whig party, Tyler did not accept the nationalist doctrines of Clay and his following. Re-elected to the Senate, 1833, he resigned in 1836 in protest against direction by the Virginia legislature to vote for expunging the resolutions censuring Jackson for removal of the Bank deposits. Losing the contest for a Senate seat to William C. Rives in 1839, Tyler was nominated for the vice-presidency on the Whig ticket with William H. Harrison, 1840. Elected, he succeeded Harrison who died within a month of inauguration and became president by right of succession, the first ever to do so.

Henry Clay and the Whig nationalists were soon at odds with the president on matters of fundamental principle although Tyler had retained Harrison's cabinet as a gesture of conciliation. A crisis between the president and the Whigs was brought on by the bank question. Tyler had made it clear that he would not sanction a measure which permitted a national bank to establish branches in the states without their previous consent, and he had devised a plan known as the "exchequer system" which would have avoided this difficulty. Congress passed a bill chartering a U.S. bank along lines desired by Clay, and Tyler promptly vetoed it. A revised bill was presented and passed which Tyler also vetoed. At Clay's urging, the original cabinet then resigned with the exception of Daniel Webster, the secretary of state. A president without a party, Tyler nevertheless made a remarkable record as administrator and negotiator. He was responsible for a reform and reorganization of the navy which included encouragement of scientific work; he ran the government with a minimum of waste and extravagance. He brought the Seminole War to an end, and withheld federal interference from Dorr's Rebellion in Rhode Island. A treaty was negotiated with China which opened the doors of the Orient for the first time, and the Monroe Doctrine was enforced in the cases of Texas and Hawaii. The greatest achievements of Tyler's administration were the negotiation of the Webster-Ashburton treaty and the annexation of Texas, in which the president played an inconspicuous but considerable part.

Although he was supported for re-election in 1844 by a strong element in many states, he withdrew his name in favor of James K. Polk and retired to private life in Virginia. On the outbreak of the Civil War he proposed a convention of the border states to consider compromises which might save the Union, and acted as chairman of the convention which was called for this purpose by the Virginia Assembly and met in Washington, February 1861. A member of the Virginia secession convention, Tyler declared for separation after all compromise measures had failed. He served in the provisional Congress of the Confederacy and was elected to the Confederate House of Representatives but died before he could take his place. An intelligent, approachable, courteous man, Tyler has failed of his due because of a lack of appreciation among historians for a record of courageous consistency and integrity.

TYLER, LYON GARDINER (*b. Charles City Co., Va., 1853; d. Charles City Co., 1935*), lawyer, educator, Virginia legislator, historian. Son of John Tyler (1790–1862). A.B., University of Virginia, 1874; A.M., 1875. As representative of Richmond in the House of Delegates, he sponsored bill reopening College of William and Mary, 1888, and served thereafter as its president until 1919. Author, among other works, of *Parties and Patronage in the United States* (1891); *History of Virginia, Federal Period* (1924); and *The Cradle of the Republic* (1900). [*Supp. 1*]

TYLER, MOSES COIT (*b. Griswold, Conn., 1835; d. Ithaca, N.Y., 1900*), Congregational and Episcopal clergyman, reformer, educator, historian. Raised in Detroit, Mich., Tyler attended the University of Michigan and graduated from Yale, 1857. After a few years in the ministry and a period of ardent preoccupation with reform movements (including a crusade for physical culture), he became professor of English at the University of Michigan, 1867, and taught there with success until 1881. He then became professor of American history at Cornell University, the first man to hold such a post in the country. Among other activities, he introduced German methodology into graduate instruction and helped found the American Historical Association (1884). He was generally recognized as a leader in the cause of "critical" as opposed to "patriotic" history. Tyler's permanent reputation is owing to his authorship of *A History of American Literature during the Colonial Time, 1607–1765* (1878), a biography of *Patrick Henry* (1887), *The Literary History of the American Revolution, 1763–1783* (1897) and *Three Men of Letters* (1895). Based on profound research of an original nature and written with clarity and sanity, Tyler's histories of literature in the colonial period have become by common consent the standard account of early American literary development.

TYLER, RANSOM HUBERT (*b. Franklin Co., Mass., 1815; d. Fulton, N.Y., 1881*), lawyer, New York jurist. Author of *American Ecclesiastical Law* (1866) and a number of subsequent texts and treatises on various aspects of civil law which were valuable for their wealth of material but poorly organized.

TYLER, ROBERT (*b. Charles City Co., Va., 1816; d. Montgomery, Ala., 1877*), lawyer, politician, editor. Son of John Tyler (1790–1862) whom he served as private secretary, 1841–44. Thereafter he took a leading part in Philadelphia politics and became a political friend of James Buchanan, influencing Virginia support of Buchanan at the convention of 1856. Removing to the South at the outbreak of the Civil War, Tyler served as register of the Confederate Treasury, and was editor *post* 1867 of the Montgomery (Ala.) *Mail and Advertiser.*

TYLER, ROBERT OGDEN (*b. Hunter, N.Y., 1831; d. Boston, Mass., 1874*), soldier. Nephew of Daniel Tyler. Graduated West Point, 1853. Commissioned in the artillery, he served against the Indians on the frontiers. Appointed colonel, 1st Connecticut Heavy Artillery, September 1861, he served his guns with great distinction during the Peninsular campaigns and was promoted brigadier-general, November 1862. At Gettysburg he commanded the artillery reserve which was so effective in stopping Pickett's charge. Serving as infantry, his artillerymen distinguished themselves at Spotsylvania and Cold Harbor. Reverting to lieutenant-colonel in the Regular Army, he served in a number of capacities and died as a belated result of war wounds.

TYLER, ROYALL (*b. Boston, Mass., 1757; d. Brattleboro, Vt., 1826*), playwright, novelist, jurist. Graduated Harvard, 1776; studied law with Francis Dana. After brief service in the Revolution, began practice of law, 1780, in present Portland, Maine. A successful lawyer in Boston, 1785–91, and thereafter in Vermont where he held, among other public offices, the post of chief justice of the supreme court, 1807–13, Tyler is remembered principally as author of *The Contrast.* This play, produced April 1787 in New York City and immediately successful, was the first comedy to be written by a native American and produced by a professional company. A satire on city affectation, *The Contrast* contained the character "Jonathan," the prototype of a long succession of stage Yankees. Tyler was author also of a comic opera, *May Day in Town* (produced in New York City, May 1787), and several other plays which have not survived in print. In 1794 he entered into a literary mock-partnership with Joseph Dennie, writing prose and verse under the pseudonym of "Spondee" for various publications. The best of these are contained in *The Spirit of the Farmers' Museum* (1801). He was author also of a picaresque novel *The Algerine Captive* (1797) and of the *Yankey in London* (1809).

TYLER, SAMUEL (*b. Prince Georges Co., Md., 1809; d. Georgetown, D.C., 1877*), lawyer, writer. An authority on pleading and procedure. Author, among other works, of *Memoir of Roger Brooke Taney* (1872), an authorized biography and a useful source.

TYLER, WILLIAM (*b. Derby, Vt., 1806; d. 1849*), Roman Catholic clergyman. A convert to Catholicism, Tyler studied theology with Benedict J. Fenwick and at Montreal. Ordained 1829, he served as a curate in Boston and as a missionary through New England. Consecrated first bishop of Hartford, Conn., 1844, he established his see at Providence, R.I., where he erected a cathedral and laid sound foundations for his church in an unfriendly region.

TYLER, WILLIAM SEYMOUR (*b. Harford, Pa., 1810; d. 1897*), Congregational clergyman, educator. Graduated Amherst, 1830. Professor of classics at Amherst, 1836–93 (*post* 1847 Williston Professor of Greek), Tyler served as president of the trustees of several schools including Mount Holyoke and Smith colleges. He was author, among other works, of *The History of Amherst College* (1873, 1895).

TYNDALE, HECTOR (*b. Philadelphia, Pa., 1821; d. Philadelphia, 1880*), glass merchant, authority on ceramics, Union major-general by brevet. Tyndale was particularly outstanding as a soldier at the battles of Antietam and Missionary Ridge.

TYNG, EDWARD (*b. Boston, Mass., 1683; d. Boston, 1755*), merchant, outstanding officer in the colonial Massachusetts navy. Cruised with success against French and Spanish privateers, 1741–44; later commanded frigate *Massachusetts.*

TYNG, STEPHEN HIGGINSON (*b. Newburyport, Mass., 1800; d. Irvington-on-Hudson, N.Y., 1885*), Episcopal clergyman. Graduated Harvard, 1817; studied theology with Alexander V. Griswold. Held pastorates in Maryland and in Philadelphia, Pa.; rector of St. George's Church, New York City, 1845–78. A dogmatic Low Churchman, Tyng was considered one of the greatest preachers of his time and was one of the first Episcopal clergymen to stress the importance of Sunday Schools.

TYSON, GEORGE EMORY (*b. Red Bank, N.J., 1829; d. Washington, D.C., 1906*), whaling captain. Assistant navigator and very capable second-in-command under Charles F. Hall on the *Polaris* expedition to the Arctic, 1871–73. Hero of a remarkable six-months' drift on an ice floe.

TYSON, JAMES (*b. Philadelphia, Pa., 1841; d. 1919*), physician. Graduated Haverford College, 1861; M.D., University of Pennsylvania, 1863. After Civil War service as surgeon, he practiced in Philadelphia. A teacher of various medical subjects at Pennsylvania *post* 1868, he held the chair of medicine there, 1899–1910, and for several years was dean of medical faculty. A staff member of many hospitals, he was author of a number of successful texts.

TYSON, JOB ROBERTS (*b. in or near Philadelphia, Pa., 1803; d. 1858*), Philadelphia lawyer, reformer. An authority on the history of Pennsylvania, he was instrumental in providing for the printing of the Pennsylvania Archives and did pioneer service in criticizing the exaggerated claims made by the New England historians for their section as the primary source of American freedom.

TYSON, LAWRENCE DAVIS (*b. near Greenville, N.C., 1861; d. Philadelphia, Pa., 1929*), soldier, lawyer, Tennessee legislator and publisher. Graduated West Point, 1883; LL.B., University of Tennessee, 1894. Served in frontier campaigns, 1883–91, and in the Spanish-American War. As brigadier-general, National Army (commissioned 1917), he commanded the 59th Brigade of the 30th Division in France during its outstanding service in breaking the Hindenburg line, 1918. Publisher thereafter of the Knoxville *Sentinel*, he was active in Democratic politics and served as U.S. senator from Tennessee, 1925–29. He was interested also in coal companies and textile mills.

TYSON, STUART LAWRENCE (*b. Pennllyn, Pa., 1873; d. New York, N.Y., 1932*), Episcopal clergyman, author, lecturer. Graduated Nashota House, Wisconsin, 1895; studied for a number of years at Oxford, England, from which he received the degrees of M.A., B.D. and D.D. Returning to America, 1907, he taught at Western Theological Seminary and the University of the South and served later on the staffs of several New York churches. Moving from an early conservative position, Tyson became an aggressive liberal and modernist; in 1925 after a divorce he left the Episcopal Church and entered the Congregational ministry, presiding thereafter over a Summit, N.J., church composed principally of Unitarians. He was particularly notable during his later career for his defense of clergymen accused of heresy.

UDDEN, JOHAN AUGUST (*b. Uddabo, Sweden, 1859; d. Texas, 1932*), geologist. Came to America as a child; was raised in Minnesota. Graduated Augustana College, 1881; M.A., 1889. A teacher at Augustana, 1888–1911, and associated thereafter with the Bureau of Economic Geology of the University of Texas, Udden was eminent as a research geologist and was author of many important papers in his field. His investigations included stratigraphic and areal geology, till in the upper Mississippi Valley, clastic sediments, and related subjects. He was one of the first in America to stress the value of seismograph observations for locating geologic structure and devised a pioneering technique for examining subsurface material. His work in Texas contributed much to the economic development of that state.

UHLER, PHILIP REESE (*b. Baltimore, Md., 1835; d. 1913*), entomologist, librarian of the Peabody Institute. A world authority on entomology specializing in *Hemiptera*, Uhler taught at Harvard, 1864–67, and was associate in natural history at Johns Hopkins, 1876–1913.

ULLOA, ANTONIO DE (*b. Seville, Spain, 1716; d. probably Spain, 1795*), Spanish naval officer, colonial administrator. Celebrated for several reports on conditions in Spanish America (1748–49) which were translated into other languages and widely read, Ulloa became governor of Louisiana in 1766. Given no support by his government and obliged to let the last French governor of the province continue to rule it in the name of the Spanish king, he was recalled in 1768 in the midst of a Creole uprising and was succeeded by Alejandro O'Reilly.

UNANGST, ERIAS (*b. Easton, Pa., 1824; d. Hollidaysburg, Pa., 1903*), Lutheran clergyman. Missionary in India for the greater part of the years 1858–95.

UNCAS (*b. c. 1588; d. c. 1683*), sachem of the Mohegan Indians. Son-in-law of Sassacus against whom he rebelled. Assigned control of the western part of the Pequot territory, he courted the favor of the English and in May 1637 joined his Mohegans with Miantonomo in a war on the Pequots. Tricky, untrustworthy and dissolute throughout his career, Uncas engaged in a series of petty wars against his tribal neighbors. He appears to have been tolerated by the English in Connecticut and Massachusetts because of his enmity to the Narragansetts and because his presence served as a divisive force among the other Indian tribes.

UNDERHILL, FRANK PELL (*b. Brooklyn, N.Y., 1877; d. New Haven, Conn., 1932*), pharmacologist, toxicologist. Graduated Yale, 1900; Ph.D., 1903. Taught thereafter at Yale, serving as professor of pathological chemistry, 1912–18, of experimental medicine, 1918–21, and of pharmacology and toxicology *post* 1921. His early researches dealt with the physiologic action of proteins and tartrates, and with the effects of chemical substances on the behavior of sugars, salts and water within the body. He was active in organization of the U.S. Army Chemical Warfare Service and made investigations of the effects of lethal gases on the animal body. He also investigated the effects of fluid administration in treating burns and made studies of pellagra.

UNDERHILL, JOHN (*b. probably Warwickshire, England, c. 1597; d. Oyster Bay, N.Y., 1672*), colonial military leader, magistrate. Trained as a soldier in the Netherlands, Underhill moved to Boston, 1630, as captain and organizer of the Massachusetts Bay militia. Associated with the Connecticut forces in the defeat of the Pequots, 1637, he was disfranchised and discharged from military service by Massachusetts in that same year because of his alliance with the Antinomians. In England during the winter of 1637–38, he published *Nevves from America* (1638), a classical account of the Pequot troubles. On his return to Boston he was banished in September 1638 and fled to Dover, N.H., where he secured the governorship and opposed the claims of Massachusetts upon the region. Losing support at Dover, he returned to Massachusetts where he made a public confession of various crimes, 1640, but was considered insincerely repentant and was excommunicated. In September 1640, however, he was reinstated in the church and in the following year his sentence of banishment was repealed. He now moved to Stamford, Conn., which he represented in the assembly of New Haven, 1643. Soon afterwards, being employed by the Dutch to fight Indians, he moved to Long Island where he held office; in 1653 he denounced Peter Stuyvesant's government for its unjust taxation and dealings with the Indians. In the same year, commissioned as a privateer at Providence, he seized the property of the Dutch West India Company at Hartford. After helping reduce the New Amsterdam Dutch to English control, 1664–65, he held several public offices under the English government of New York before retiring from public life, 1666/67.

UNDERWOOD, BENJAMIN FRANKLIN (*b. New York, N.Y., 1839; d. Westerly, R.I., 1914*), Union soldier, journalist, freethinker. One of the earliest and most zealous American supporters of the theory of evolution, Underwood lectured widely on this and other subjects. He wrote a number of pamphlets which expressed his philosophic position, roughly that of orthodox materialism. *Post* 1897 he was editor of the *Quincy* (Ill.) *Journal*, retiring in 1913.

UNDERWOOD, FRANCIS HENRY (*b. Enfield, Mass., 1825; d. Edinburgh, Scotland, 1894*), lawyer, author, consular official. Conceiving the idea of a magazine which should enlist the literary forces of New England in a crusade against slavery, 1853, he was successful in persuading Phillips, Sampson & Co. to undertake the project in 1857. It was issued as the *Atlantic Monthly* (first issue, November 1857), but Underwood was relegated to the routine post of editorial assistant to James Russell Lowell. Subsequent to his leaving the *Atlantic* in 1859, he engaged in a number of activities before his service as U.S. consul at Glasgow, Scotland, 1886–89, and at Leith *post* 1893. A talented man, he contributed much to the fame of others but won little credit for himself. As Francis Parkman observed, he was "neither a Harvard man nor a humbug" and so was a victim of his own merit.

UNDERWOOD, HORACE GRANT (*b. London, England, 1859; d. Atlantic City, N.J., 1916*), Dutch Reformed clergyman. Presbyterian missionary to Korea *post* 1885.

UNDERWOOD, JOHN CURTISS (*b. Litchfield, N.Y., 1809; d. Washington, D.C., 1873*), lawyer. A planter in Clarke Co., Va., *post* 1839, Underwood was a Free-Soiler in politics and was virtually driven from Virginia for his attacks on slavery during the presidential campaign of 1856. A Republican officeholder during the Civil War, he became a U.S. district court

judge in Virginia, 1864. In this capacity he asserted the right of the United States to confiscate property of persons in rebellion and treated Jefferson Davis with great harshness during and after Davis's indictment for treason at Norfolk, Va., 1866. He presided over the Virginia constitutional convention which met at Richmond, December 1867.

UNDERWOOD, JOHN THOMAS (*b. London, England, 1857; d. Wianno, Mass., 1937*), typewriter manufacturer. Brother of Horace G. Underwood. Came to America, 1873, and engaged with his father in the pioneer manufacture of typewriter supplies. Purchasing the rights to the Wagner "front-stroke" typewriting machine (patented, 1893), Underwood marketed the first typewriters under his own name in 1897. His product was superior in design to its competitors and was soon highly successful. [*Supp. 2*]

UNDERWOOD, JOSEPH ROGERS (*b. Goochland Co., Va., 1791; d. 1876*), Kentucky legislator and jurist. Grandfather of Oscar W. Underwood. Practiced at Glasgow, Ky., 1813–23, and at Bowling Green thereafter. Justice, Kentucky court of appeals, 1828–35; congressman, Whig, from Kentucky, 1835–43; U.S. senator, 1847–53. An orthodox Whig in his political opinions and actions, he supported Southern views on slavery short of secession. A Unionist during the Civil War, he became a Democrat, 1864, and was instrumental in reorganizing that party in Kentucky.

UNDERWOOD, LORING (*b. Belmont, Mass., 1874; d. 1930*), landscape architect. Graduated Harvard, 1897; studied at Bussey Institution and in Paris. Practiced his profession in Boston, Mass., *post* 1900. Author of *The Garden and Its Accessories* (1906).

UNDERWOOD, LUCIEN MARCUS (*b. New Woodstock, N.Y., 1853; d. Redding, Conn., 1907*), botanist. Graduated Syracuse University, 1877; Ph.D., 1879. Taught at Illinois Wesleyan, Syracuse, De Pauw, and Alabama Polytechnic; professor of botany, Columbia, 1896–1907. Authority on ferns and hepaticae. Took leading part in initiating (1905) publication of the *North American Flora*.

UNDERWOOD, OSCAR WILDER (*b. Louisville, Ky., 1862; d. 1929*), lawyer, statesman. Grandson of Joseph R. Underwood. Admitted to the bar, 1884, after study at the University of Virginia. Practiced briefly in Minnesota; removed to Birmingham, Ala. Congressman, Democrat, from Alabama, 1895–96 and 1897–1915; U.S. senator, 1915–27. A man of high character and unflagging industry, Underwood made a lifelong study of the tariff and was a strong opponent of tariffs for protection. He served as Democratic floor leader in the House, 1911–15, and was chairman of the ways and means committee. A supporter of W. H. Taft's reciprocity program, Underwood at the same time took the lead in revising many tariff schedules downward; when the legislation advanced by him was vetoed by President Taft, the outstanding issue of the campaign of 1912 was created. Underwood showed such conspicuous ability in Congress that he was among the leading contenders for the Democratic presidential nomination in 1912 and again in 1924. A loyal supporter of President Woodrow Wilson, Underwood efficiently carried out Wilson's legislative program. His work in framing the tariff bill which bears his name, and in support of the Federal Reserve Act, was especially noteworthy. In the Senate *post* 1915 he continued his support of Wilson's policies, although in the fight over the League of Nations he was of the opinion that the president should have agreed to certain mild reservations. His uncompromising hostility to the Ku Klux Klan and to national prohibition alienated the South and cost him presidential nomination by the Democrats in 1924. A devout follower of Thomas Jefferson, he was strongly averse to all extensions of the federal authority.

UNTERMYER, SAMUEL (*b. Lynchburg, Va., 1858; d. Palm Springs, Calif., 1940*), lawyer. Graduated Columbia Law School, 1878. Celebrated during his early career as a trial lawyer in important suits of every type, he grew wealthy as an organizer of large industrial combinations. Moved by growing doubts about the virtues of the corporate combinations he had helped to create, he slowly became known as an enemy of corporate abuses. In 1911 he delivered a series of addresses calling for government action to break up or regulate the trusts. During 1912–13 he served without pay as counsel to the Pujo investigation instituted by Congress to look into the operations of the leading financiers of the country. The recommendations of the Pujo Committee contributed to passage of the Federal Reserve Act, the Federal Trade Commission Act, and the Clayton Anti-Trust Act; in each of these Untermyer had some part. He served again without pay as counsel to the New York Joint Legislative Committee on Housing, 1919–20, investigating conspiracies to profiteer in the building trades; thereafter, he devoted much time, without compensation, to New York City transit problems. An early advocate of a graduated income tax and of public ownership of public utilities, he was a lifelong Democrat and an ardent supporter of the New Deal. In Jewish matters he was a moderate Zionist. [*Supp. 2*]

UPCHURCH, JOHN JORDAN (*b. Franklin Co., N.C., 1820; d. Steelville, Mo., 1887*), railroad mechanic. Founder of the Ancient Order of United Workmen, 1868, a lodge which began as an opponent of trade unions and strikes and which became in time the prototype for subsequent fraternal benefit societies.

UPDEGRAFF, DAVID BRAINARD (*b. Mount Pleasant, O., 1830; d. Mount Pleasant, 1894*), Quaker preacher, editor. Considered an innovator and a controversial figure within the Society of Friends, he represented an intense form of evangelical thought and practiced a dramatic style of preaching.

UPDIKE, DANIEL (*b. North Kingstown, R.I., c. 1693; d. 1757*), Newport, R.I., lawyer. Attorney-general of Rhode Island, 1722–32, 1743–57; attorney-general for Kings Co., R.I., 1741–43.

UPHAM, CHARLES WENTWORTH (*b. St. John, N.B., Canada, 1802; d. Salem, Mass., 1875*), Unitarian clergyman, Massachusetts legislator, historian. Graduated Harvard, 1821. Minister in Salem, Mass., 1824–44. After engaging in politics as a Whig and later a Republican, 1848–61, Upham turned to historical research producing, among other works, his *Salem Witchcraft* (1867). He is considered the prototype of "Judge Pyncheon" in *The House of the Seven Gables* by Nathaniel Hawthorne.

UPHAM, SAMUEL FOSTER (*b. Duxbury, Mass., 1834; d. 1904*), Methodist clergyman. A popular and witty preacher as pastor of a number of New England churches, Upham was professor of practical theology at Drew Theological Seminary, 1881–1904.

UPHAM, THOMAS COGSWELL (*b. Deerfield, N.H., 1799; d. New York, N.Y., 1872*), Congregational clergyman, metaphysician. Graduated Dartmouth, 1818; Andover Theological Seminary, 1821. Professor of philosophy at Bowdoin College, 1824–67, he was author, among other books, of *A Philosophical and Practical Treatise on the Will* (1834), an original contribution to modern psychology.

UPHAM, WARREN (*b. Amherst, N.H., 1850; d. St. Paul, Minn., 1934*), glacial geologist, archeologist. Graduated Dartmouth, 1871. After employment on the geological surveys of New Hampshire and Minnesota and service with the U.S. Geological Survey, he was librarian-secretary of the Minnesota Historical Society, 1895–1914, and the society's archeologist thereafter. His principal field in science was glacial geology, and his best-known monograph is "The Glacial Lake Agassiz" (*U.S. Geological Survey Monographs*, vol. XXV, 1896). After change of his major field to archeology and history c. 1905, he made a number of important contributions to the history of Minnesota and its area.

UPJOHN, RICHARD (*b. Shaftesbury, England, 1802; d. Garrison, N.Y., 1878*), architect. Trained as a cabinet-maker, Upjohn emigrated to America, 1829, and settled in New Bedford, Mass., 1830. At first a draftsman and teacher of drawing, he began to practice as an architect and removed to Boston, Mass., 1834, where he worked with Alexander Parris. In 1837 he completed St. John's Church, Bangor, Maine, his first Gothic church. Chosen architect for the new Trinity Church, New York City, he removed to New York in 1839; Trinity Church, begun in 1841 and consecrated in 1846, won him immediate fame. Upjohn did a great deal of important work, making a careful and sensitive use of the precedents of English Gothic; his influence in the United States was in many ways similar to the contemporary influence in England of Pugin. Among his outstanding buildings were the Church of the Pilgrims, Brooklyn, N.Y.; St. Paul's in Brookline, Mass.; and his own favorite work, Trinity Chapel on W. 25th St., New York City. He also designed a number of houses and civic buildings. He was a founder and first president of the American Institute of Architects, 1857–76, and many famous architects were trained in his office or worked for him.

UPJOHN, RICHARD MICHELL (*b. Shaftesbury, England, 1828; d. Brooklyn, N.Y., 1903*), architect. Son of Richard Upjohn. Came to America as a child. Trained in his father's office, he practiced with him *post* 1853 and exercised a growing influence on the elder man's design. Although he designed a great number of churches, his work was less dominantly ecclesiastical than his father's. His most famous building was the State Capitol at Hartford, Conn. (1885), for which drawings were begun in 1872.

UPSHUR, ABEL PARKER (*b. Northampton Co., Va., 1791; d. aboard battleship* Princeton, *1844*), Virginia legislator and jurist. A judge of the Virginia supreme court, 1826–41, he associated himself in politics with the extreme state-rights pro-slavery group. U.S. secretary of the navy, 1841–43, he succeeded Daniel Webster as U.S. secretary of state. He was killed by the explosion of a gun on the *Princeton* while cruising on the Potomac. A strong conservative, Upshur was opposed to numerical majorities, democratic conceptions, and the nationalistic theory of the Constitution; he rejected almost entirely the natural rights philosophy.

UPSHUR, JOHN HENRY (*b. Eastville, Va., 1823; d. Washington, D.C., 1917*), naval officer. Nephew of Abel P. Upshur. Entering the navy as midshipman, 1841, he retired as rear-admiral, 1885, after varied world-wide service which included the Union North Atlantic blockade.

UPTON, EMORY (*b. near Batavia, N.Y., 1839; d. San Francisco, Calif., 1881*), Union soldier, expert in tactics. Graduated West Point, 1861. Commissioned in the artillery, Upton had a notable career during the Civil War, serving in the infantry and cavalry as well as his own arm and participating in a great number of engagements. He won promotion to brigadier-general on the field at Spotsylvania, May 1864, and held divisional command at the battle of Winchester in September. In April 1865 he led in the capture of Selma, Ala., and its arsenal. He was an outstanding commandant of cadets at West Point, 1870–75, and was author of a system of infantry tactics which bears his name. An incomplete but important work by him was published as *The Military Policy of the United States* (ed. J. P. Sanger, 1904).

UPTON, GEORGE BRUCE (*b. Eastport, Maine, 1804; d. Boston, Mass., 1874*), merchant, capitalist, Massachusetts Whig legislator. Author of a public letter (March 23, 1870) charging the British with being responsible for Confederate commerce raiders and with having operated them in the Civil War.

UPTON, GEORGE PUTNAM (*b. Roxbury, Mass., 1834; d. Chicago, Ill., 1919*), journalist, music critic. Associated with Chicago, Ill., newspapers *post* 1855, Upton served on the staff of the *Chicago Daily Tribune* for 57 years *post* 1862. His local reputation was established by his writings as a music critic under the pseudonym "Peregrine Pickle"; he was author also of a number of books in the field of musicology.

UPTON, WINSLOW (*b. Salem, Mass., 1853; d. 1914*), astronomer, meteorologist. Graduated Brown, 1875; M.A., University of Cincinnati, 1877. Professor of astronomy at Brown, 1883–1914, and director of the Ladd Observatory, 1890–1914.

URBAN, JOSEPH (*b. Vienna, Austria, 1872; d. New York, N.Y., 1933*), architect, stage designer. Worked principally in the United States *post* 1911; introduced the new stage art of Europe to this country and to a great degree made possible the introduction of "modern" design concepts. Employing a style which owed much to the Secessionists and to *art nouveau*, he designed furniture, motor cars, clubs and public buildings, as well as the settings for the Ziegfeld *Follies* for which he was famous.

URSO, CAMILLA (*b. Nantes, France, 1842; d. New York, N.Y., 1902*), violinist. Came to America as a child prodigy, 1852; played on concert tours with Henriette Sontag and Marietta Alboni. Outstanding in concert work, 1862–95, she devoted her last years to teaching.

USHER, JOHN PALMER (*b. Brookfield, N.Y., 1816; d. Philadelphia, Pa., 1889*), lawyer. Began practice in Terre Haute, Ind., 1840. Early active in the Republican party, he became assistant U.S. secretary of the interior *c*. February 1862 and was appointed head of the department, January 1863. Resigning in May 1865, he removed to Lawrence, Kans., and became chief counsel for the Union Pacific Railroad, a post which he held for the rest of his life.

USHER, NATHANIEL REILLY (*b. Vincennes, Ind., 1855; d. probably Potsdam, N.Y., 1931*), naval officer. Nephew of John P. Usher. Graduated U.S. Naval Academy, 1875. Promoted rear-admiral in 1911 after varied service which included the Greely Relief Expedition and command of the torpedo boat *Ericsson* in the Spanish-American War, he performed outstanding service as commandant of the Brooklyn Navy Yard during the period of World War I. Owing principally to his energy and organizing ability, the Port of New York was able to ship the greater part of all supplies and 80% of all the men that the United States sent to France. On his retirement, 1919, he was described as a principal factor in the successful incorporation of the Naval Reserve into the regular machine of the naval service.

VACA, ALVAR NÚÑEZ CABEZA de. [See NÚÑEZ CABEZA DE VACA, ALVAR, *c.* 1490–*c.* 1557.]

VAIL, AARON (*b. L'Orient, France, 1796; d. Pau, France, 1878*), U.S. state department official. Secretary of legation at London, England, 1831–32, he served as chargé d'affaires, 1832–36, with great success. While chief clerk of the U.S. State Department, 1838–40, he acted on numerous occasions as secretary of state; he was chargé d'affaires at Madrid, Spain, 1840–42.

VAIL, ALFRED (*b. Morristown, N.J., 1807; d. Morristown, 1859*), telegraph pioneer. Cousin of Theodore N. Vail. Graduated University of the City of New York, 1836. Became associated with Samuel F. B. Morse as constructor of instruments, 1837, and aided in financing early telegraph experiments. As chief assistant to Morse *post* 1843, Vail received the famous first test message "What hath God wrought!" at Baltimore, Md., May 24, 1844.

VAIL, STEPHEN MONTFORT (*b. Union Vale, N.Y., 1816; d. Jersey City, N.J., 1880*), Methodist clergyman, U.S. consular official, educator. Graduated Bowdoin, 1838; Union Theological Seminary, New York City, 1842. Professor of Hebrew at Methodist Biblical Institute, Concord, N.H., 1847–69. A vigorous advocate of theological training for Methodist clergymen and an active Abolitionist.

VAIL, THEODORE NEWTON (*b. near Minerva, O., 1845; d. Baltimore, Md., 1920*), telephone and utilities executive. Cousin of Alfred Vail. Raised in New Jersey where he became a telegrapher; resided in Iowa and Nebraska, 1866–73. Entering service of the Post Office Department, Vail devised a number of improvements in the railway mail service. He became assistant general superintendent of that service, 1874, and general superintendent, 1876. At the urging of Gardiner G. Hubbard, he became general manager of the new Bell Telephone Co. in 1878. When he resigned in 1887 he had been responsible for organizing the expanding telephone system into a series of efficient companies properly financed, and he had provided for future technical development and more economical manufacture of telephone apparatus. He had also arranged for a long-distance telephone system by connecting numerous operating companies, for which purpose he had incorporated the American Telephone & Telegraph Co., 1885. Retiring for several years to a Vermont farm, he engaged between 1894 and 1907 in financing and developing vast utility projects in Argentina. Chaotic conditions in the telephone industry followed on the expiration of the Bell patents in 1893 and 1894, and the Bell Company directors persuaded Vail to re-enter the telephone industry, electing him president of the American Telephone & Telegraph Co., May 1907. By a policy of cooperation with the independent telephone companies, he achieved a second unification of the industry; meanwhile he pushed forward scientific research and technical improvement. In January 1915 the first transcontinental telephone line was opened, and in the same year telephone engineers under John J. Carty developed radio telephony into a practical means of communication. In 1919 Vail resigned the presidency of the American Telephone & Telegraph Co., becoming chairman of the Board of Directors.

VALENTINE, DAVID THOMAS (*b. East Chester, N.Y., 1801; d. New York, N.Y., 1869*), New York City official, antiquarian. Clerk of the common council of New York, 1842–68, Valentine is particularly remembered for his supervision and publication of the *Manual of the Corporation of the City of New York* (1841–67) which included with the customary statistical information a vast amount of pictorial and documentary historical material of the greatest interest. The *History of the City of New-York* (1853), which bears his name, was chiefly the work of W. I. Paulding.

VALENTINE, EDWARD VIRGINIUS (*b. Richmond, Va., 1838; d. Richmond, 1930*), sculptor. Studied in Paris with Thomas Couture and François Jouffroy, and in Berlin with August Kiss. Executed a number of portrait busts of Southern leaders, including the figure of R. E. Lee for the Lee Mausoleum at Washington and Lee University.

VALENTINE, MILTON (*b. near Uniontown, Md., 1825; d. 1906*), Lutheran theologian, educator. A teacher *post* 1866 at the Lutheran Theological Seminary, Gettysburg, Pa., and a vigorous defender of General Synod Lutheranism, he served as president of the seminary, 1868–84.

VALENTINE, ROBERT GROSVENOR (*b. West Newton, Mass., 1872; d. 1916*), public official, founder of the profession of industrial counselor. Graduated Harvard, 1896. Retiring from business, 1904, he served as assistant to Francis E. Leupp and was head of the U.S. Indian Office, 1909–12. Becoming a consulting adviser to corporations, labor unions and public officials *post* 1912, Valentine devised a system of "industrial audits" which would bear the same relation to the social health of an industry or community that a financial audit bore to its solvency.

VALLANDIGHAM, CLEMENT LAIRD (*b. New Lisbon, O., 1820; d. 1871*), lawyer, Ohio legislator, politician. Of Southern stock, Vallandigham idealized the Southern character; he strove for the suppression of Abolitionists and a return to Jeffersonian staterights principles. As congressman, Democrat, from Ohio, 1858–63, he denounced sectionalism on both sides, opposed disunion sentiment and, although disliking the popular sovereignty views of Stephen A. Douglas, supported him for the presidency in 1860. Proclaiming that the Southern "fire-eaters" would vanish if the Republican party were destroyed, he expressed his intention never to vote as a congressman for any measure in support of a civil war. His strong and able opposition to all measures for national defense proposed in the House brought him the intense hatred of the Republicans. Many Northerners were sympathetic with his pleas for restoration of peace and freedom of speech. After his defeat for re-election to Congress, 1862, he was regarded as a leader of the Peace Democrats or "Copperheads" in his section. For defiance of Gen. A. E. Burnside's General Order Number 38 (1863), Vallandigham was arrested in Dayton, O., and tried in Cincinnati for treason. He was condemned to imprisonment in Boston harbor, but President Lincoln shrewdly banished him to the Confederacy. Running the blockade, he made his way to Windsor, Canada. Defeated in a candidacy for governor of Ohio, 1863, he returned to his native state in June 1864. His influence in the framing of the national Democratic platform helped bring about a Democratic defeat in November. Thereafter he continued active in politics but failed of election to office. Shortly before his death he was instrumental in beginning the movement of reconciliation which took shape later in the Liberal Republican party.

VALLEJO, MARIANO GUADALUPE (*b. Monterey, Calif., 1808; d. Sonoma, Calif., 1890*), soldier, California politician. Supported J. B. Alvarado in the rebellion that led to proclamation of a free California, 1836; on estrangement from Alvarado, made himself a semi-independent chief at Sonoma. A powerful agent in securing submission of California to the United States, Vallejo was elected to the constitutional convention of 1849 and to the first state senate.

VALLENTINE, BENJAMIN BENNATON (*b. London, England, 1843; d. New York, N.Y., 1926*), journalist, playwright. Emigrated to New York City, 1871. A founder of *Puck*, 1877, he served as its managing editor until 1884, contributing the "Fitznoodle" letters which remain his principal achievement.

VALLIANT, LEROY BRANCH (*b. Moulton, Ala., 1838; d. Greenville, Miss., 1913*), lawyer, Confederate officer. Judge of the circuit court of St. Louis, Mo., 1886–98; judge of Missouri supreme court, 1898–1912.

VAN ALLEN, FRANK (*b. Dubuque, Iowa, 1860; d. Melur, Madura, India, 1923*), Congregational clergyman, medical missionary in India *post* 1888. Built and administered an outstanding hospital in Madura City.

VAN ALSTYNE, FANNY CROSBY. [See Crosby, Fanny, 1820–1915.]

VAN AMRINGE, JOHN HOWARD (*b. Philadelphia, Pa., 1835; d. Morristown, N.J., 1915*), educator. Graduated Columbia, 1860. Taught mathematics at Columbia *post* 1860, resigning in 1910 as professor emeritus. A unique figure in the history of Columbia and a promoter of its alumni association, he served as dean of the college *post* 1894 and as acting president of Columbia University, 1899.

VAN BEUREN, JOHANNES (*b. Amsterdam, Netherlands, c. 1680; d. New York, N.Y., 1755*), physician. A pupil of Boerhaave, Van Beuren came to New York *c.* 1702 and built up a large practice both in the city

and in the town of Flatbush on Long Island. Appointed first medical director of the New York almshouse hospital, 1736, he held the position until his death. This hospital was the beginning of the present Bellevue Hospital.

VAN BRUNT, HENRY (*b. Boston, Mass., 1832; d. Milton, Mass., 1903*), architect. Graduated Harvard, 1854; studied in office of Richard M. Hunt. After Civil War service, formed a partnership with William R. Ware, 1863–83. Working *post* 1883 under firm name of Van Brunt & Howe, he designed a great number of Western railroad stations, shops and houses. The firm became the most important architectural organization west of Chicago and was domiciled in Kansas City, Mo. Van Brunt was an eclectic. His most important contribution to architecture was in his writings, of which some appear in *Greek Lines and Other Architectural Essays* (1893).

VAN BUREN, JOHN (*b. Kinderhook, N.Y., 1810; d. at sea en route to New York from England, 1866*), lawyer, New York politician and official. Son of Martin Van Buren, he was known as "Prince John." Constantly active in politics in his father's interest *post* 1834, he was influential in organizing the "Barnburners" and espoused free-soil doctrines with evangelistic fervor. Later returning to more moderate views, he supported popular sovereignty in Kansas, denounced Lincoln for precipitancy in calling for troops, and in 1864 supported George B. McClellan for president.

VAN BUREN, MARTIN (*b. Kinderhook, N.Y., 1782; d. Kinderhook, 1862*), lawyer, president of the United States. Father of John Van Buren. After serving as law clerk to William P. Van Ness, he practiced at Kinderhook *post* 1803, handling the cases of small landholders and becoming an adherent of the Clinton-Livingston faction among the (Democrat) Republicans. Attorney-general of New York, 1816–19, and a state senator, 1812–20, he gradually turned against his early political associates in his rise to leadership in Democratic state politics. His wit and charm combined with a clear, realistic intelligence in effecting his rise. His enemies thought him hypocritical, intriguing and selfish. He was, indeed, a political manipulator, but he was honest and serious in both private and public relations and steadfast in his adherence to principle and faithful public service. At the state constitutional convention, 1821, he brought extreme radicals and conservatives together in successful opposition to the old Council of Appointment, thereby securing a distribution of the power to appoint state officers among local authorities, the legislature and the governor.

Elected to the U.S. Senate, February 1821, by the "Bucktail" faction, he continued to have a deep interest in New York politics and headed the influential "Albany Regency" which included W. L. Marcy, Benjamin F. Butler (1795–1858) and others. Formidable in their solidarity, Van Buren and his group were sincere as well as shrewd and faithfully performed the duties of the important offices they obtained. A supporter of William H. Crawford for president, 1824, he opposed the movement which gave John Q. Adams the presidency and remained in opposition to Adams's policies throughout that president's term. By 1828 he was a leading supporter of Andrew Jackson and assumed an important role in the campaign of that year. Elected governor of New York, he resigned the office to become Jackson's secretary of state in 1829 and the most influential member of the Jackson cabinet. He urged on the administration the introduction of the political spoils system which had been operated with such success by the Albany Regency. Wholly in Jackson's confidence, Van Buren resigned his post, April 1831, in a move which enabled the president to effect a reorganization of his cabinet and thus eliminate the supporters of John C. Calhoun. His appointment as U.S. minister to Great Britain was refused confirmation by the Senate in January 1832, whereupon he accepted nomination for vice-president. He had done well as secretary of state, displaying unusual tact and high administrative ability. In addition to other achievements, he settled the old dispute over the West Indian trade between Great Britain and the United States, secured an agreement with France for the payment of claims dating back to the Napoleonic wars, negotiated a favorable trade treaty with Turkey, and made an attempt to buy Texas from Mexico.

Following his nomination for the vice-presidency, he aided Jackson in defeating a bill to recharter the Bank of the United States and joined in the president's opposition to nullification. Contrary to opinion, he did not disagree with Jackson over removal of the government's Bank deposits, but he was doubtful about the expediency of their removal at that time. A fair and able presiding officer of the Senate during his vice-presidency, he was nominated for the presidency in May 1835 at Baltimore, Md., as Jackson's protégé.

Elected on a platform of opposition to recharter of the Bank, opposition to distribution of the Treasury's surplus, and opposition to improvement of rivers above ports of entry, he also conveyed the impression that his distaste for the extension of slavery did not extend to any meddling with the right of slave-holding states to control the institution within their boundaries. Striving throughout his term to hold together the Northern and Southern wings of his party, he was much plagued by Abolitionist agitators as well as by those who would compel them to silence. But his chief problems were economic. During the panic of 1837 he held to Jackson's specie circular and properly said that the panic was the result of overexpansion of credit and rashness in business. Determined to divorce the "money power" from the federal government, he urged establishment of an independent Treasury and recommended withholding of the distribution of the Treasury surplus to the states, sug-

gesting a temporary issue of Treasury notes to meet the pressing needs of government. His foresighted efforts were generally unsuccessful and alienated conservative Democrats, especially in New York and Virginia, while at the same time he was denounced by the Whigs for his heartlessness in not undertaking measures of relief. In foreign affairs he continued his wise policy of conciliation during troubles with Canada and Mexico. Despite an enlightened and able administration, he could not maintain popular approval in the face of the prevailing bad times and was overwhelmingly defeated by William H. Harrison in the campaign of 1840.

In retirement he continued to be a leading Democrat but made public announcement that he would take no step to secure another nomination. In the well-known "Hammet letter" of April 1844, he courageously said that the annexation of Texas would mean war with Mexico and that he saw no need for immediate action; this stand probably cost him the Democratic nomination in 1844. Bitter opposition to President J. K. Polk soon developed in New York State, and the introduction of the Wilmot Proviso in 1846 provided a rallying point for discontent and for the anti-slavery feeling that had been steadily increasing. Author in part of the address of the "Barnburner" Democrats in the New York legislature, February 1848, Van Buren accepted the Free-soil Party nomination for the presidency that summer. Although like many Northern Democrats he had grown impatient with the "slavocracy," he accepted the nomination reluctantly and ran unsuccessfully although his candidacy helped to defeat Lewis Cass. After supporting the 1850 compromise measures, he returned to the Democrats in 1852 to find himself successively disillusioned by Pierce and Buchanan. Shocked deeply by the Civil War, he expressed himself confident in the abilities of Abraham Lincoln but died in the summer of 1862 despondent over the situation of the Union armies.

VAN BUREN, WILLIAM HOLME (*b. Philadelphia, Pa., 1819; d. New York, N.Y., 1883*), physician, surgeon. Descendant of Johannes Van Beuren; son-in-law of Valentine Mott. M.D., University of Pennsylvania, 1840. After service as army surgeon, Van Buren practiced in New York City *post* 1845. A member of the staff of Bellevue and other hospitals, he taught in the medical department of the University of the City of New York, 1851–66, and was thereafter professor of surgery in Bellevue Hospital Medical College.

VANCE, AP MORGAN (*b. Nashville, Tenn., 1854; d. Louisville, Ky., 1915*), orthopedic surgeon. M.D., University of Louisville, 1878. Practicing in Louisville *post* 1881, he was the first exclusive practitioner of surgery in Kentucky. His greatest contribution was his improvement of the operation of osteotomy for correction of deformity of long bones in the extremities; he also improved the procedure of tenotomy for the treatment of congenital clubfoot.

VANCE, LOUIS JOSEPH (*b. Washington, D.C., 1879; d. New York, N.Y., 1933*), popular novelist. Author, among other works, of *The Brass Bowl* (1907), *The Lone Wolf* (1914) and many magazine serials. [*Supp.* 1]

VANCE, ZEBULON BAIRD (*b. Buncombe Co., N.C., 1830; d. Washington, D.C., 1894*), lawyer, Confederate soldier, politician. Entered politics as a Whig. On the dissolution of that party he became a Know-Nothing; as congressman from North Carolina, 1858–61, he supported Union measures. Winning reputation as a masterly stump speaker for the Bell-Everett ticket, 1860, he continued to campaign against secession until Lincoln's call for troops whereupon he reversed his position. As Conservative party governor of North Carolina, 1862–65, he was often at odds with the Confederate government at Richmond, although he pressed the Confederate war effort with as much zeal as the disturbed and unwilling attitude of North Carolina would permit. He tried in vain to explain to President Davis that his execution of conscription laws was not willful obstruction but was dictated by a regard for legality and realism. Opposing the efforts of W. W. Holden to make peace by separate state action, Vance held North Carolina to the support of a cause which many of its citizens felt was now contrary to their real interests. After a brief imprisonment, 1865, he was released on parole and resumed practice of law. As Democratic governor, 1877–79, he stimulated railroad enterprises, agriculture and industry, improved the public schools, and repudiated the fraudulent state bonds issued during the Reconstruction period. His regime marked the beginning of a new era in North Carolina. Elected to the U.S. Senate, 1879, he served there until his death and was for many years minority leader on the finance committee. He opposed the internal revenue system as a source of political corruption, and during Cleveland's two administrations opposed the president on civil service reform and on the money question.

VAN CORTLANDT, OLOFF STEVENSZEN (*b. probably the Netherlands, 1600; d. New York, 1684*), merchant. Came to New Amsterdam, March 1638, as a soldier of the Dutch West India Company. Successful as a trader and purchaser of real estate, he held many public offices including those of city treasurer (1657, 1659–61, 1664) and burgomaster (1655–60, 1662–63). Rated at his death as the fourth richest person in the colony, he was founder of one of the most prominent families in the American colonies and father, among other children, of Stephanus Van Cortlandt.

VAN CORTLANDT, PHILIP (*b. New York, N.Y., 1749; d. Croton, N.Y., 1831*), landowner, New York legislator, Revolutionary officer. Son of Pierre Van Cortlandt. Colonel of the 2nd New York Regiment in the Revolution, he served principally in New York State and co-operated effectively with the Sullivan-Clinton expedition, 1779. He received brevet of brigadier-general, 1783, for conspicuous bravery at Yorktown. As congressman from New York, 1793–1809, he was a loyal (Democrat) Republican and punctilious in performance of his committee duties.

VAN CORTLANDT, PIERRE (*b. New York, N.Y., 1721; d. Croton, N.Y., 1814*), landowner, New York colonial legislator, Revolutionary patriot and soldier. Grandson of Stephanus and father of Philip Van Cortlandt. Presided over New York constitutional convention, 1777. Elected lieutenant-governor, 1777, he served until 1795 as a loyal follower of George Clinton (1739–1812). He was a regent of the University of the State of New York, 1784–95, and a patron of the work of the early Methodists.

VAN CORTLANDT, STEPHANUS (*b. New Amsterdam, 1643; d. 1700*), merchant, colonial official. Son of Oloff S. Van Cortlandt. An officer in the colonial militia and a councilor of the province *post* 1674, he was appointed first native-born mayor of the City of New York, 1677, a position to which he was again appointed in 1686–87. Mistreated by Jacob Leisler and forced to flee for his life during Leisler's usurpation of the New York government, he returned to the Council under Gov. Henry Sloughter and, with the support of Frederick Philipse and Nicholas Bayard, vigorously pressed Leisler's prosecution on the charge of treason. Associated throughout his career with several of the provincial courts, he became a judge of the supreme court, 1691, and was raised to the post of chief justice a month before his death. He was an important adviser to the provincial governors on Indian relations. A large purchaser of Indian land tracts and a patentee of province lands, he erected his holdings into the manor of Cortlandt by royal patent dated June 17, 1697.

VAN CURLER, ARENT (*b. Nykerk, the Netherlands, 1620; d. Perou Bay, Lake Champlain, N.Y., 1667*), colonial trader and official. Came to New Netherland *c.* 1638 as a clerk at Rensselaerswyck; soon became *commis,* or resident manager. Famous for his enduring influence over the Indian tribes in the province, Van Curler made the first settlement of Schenectady and was the rescuer of Father Isaac Jogues. A humane man and a peacemaker, he was long remembered by the Indians who called all subsequent governors of New York "Corlaer" in memory of him.

VAN DAM, RIP (*b. Fort Orange, present Albany, N.Y., c. 1660; d. 1749*), New York merchant, colonial politician. Roused to political activity by actions of the Jacob Leisler party, Van Dam became a member of the governor's Council in 1702 and served until 1736. As president of the Council he became acting governor of the province, 1731, and for 13 months received the salary of the office. Refusing to divide this salary with Gov. William Cosby on the new governor's arrival, Van Dam lost a law suit to Cosby and was suspended from the Council in November 1735. He refused to recognize his removal and continued to assert his authority after Cosby's death in March 1736 until dispatches from England certified to the validity of George Clarke's appointment as president of the Council. Thereafter he took part in the struggle for popular rights and against prerogative, acting as a leader in this movement with William Smith and James Alexander.

VAN DEMAN, ESTHER BOISE (*b. South Salem, O., 1862; d. Rome, Italy, 1937*), archeologist. Graduated University of Michigan, 1891; Ph.D., University of Chicago, 1898. Taught Latin at Wellesley, Mount Holyoke and Goucher. *Post* 1906 she worked at the American School in Rome. Projected methods of determining the date of ancient building construction; published a preliminary study of her work in *American Journal of Archaeology*, 1912. [*Supp. 2*]

VANDENHOFF, GEORGE (*b. Liverpool, England, 1813; d. Brighton, England, 1885*), actor, lawyer, public reader. Made his American début at New York City's Park Theatre, 1842, as Hamlet. Toured extensively in the United States and England until 1858 when he undertook practice of law in New York City but continued his popular public readings from the works of classic writers. Vandenhoff was a scholarly actor with a restrained, elevated style.

VAN DEPOELE, CHARLES JOSEPH (*b. Lichtervelde, Belgium, 1846; d. Lynn, Mass., 1892*), scientist, inventor. Emigrated to America, 1869, settling in Detroit, Mich., where he became a successful manufacturer of church furniture and at the same time continued his early experimental interest in electricity. He developed an improved arc-lighting system, 1870–79, and in 1880 tested an electric tramcar on which he had been working since 1874. In September 1883 at Chicago, he gave the first practical demonstration of a spring-pressed under-running trolley; in November 1885 his overhead current feed system was put into operation in South Bend, Ind. After success in developing his trolley-car system, he sold his patents to the Thomson-Houston Electric Co. in 1888 and became electrician of that company. In all, he filed 444 applications for patents, of which some 249 were granted to him under his own name. In addition to his electric railway patent (October 1883) and his patent for an overhead conductor (August 1885) were the following: a carbon commutator-brush which revolutionized motor construction (1888); an alternating-current reciprocating engine (1889); a multiple-current pulsating generator (1890) and a telpher system in the same year; a coal-mining machine (1891); and a gearless electric locomotive (1894). He also made experiments in electric refrigeration.

VANDERBILT, CORNELIUS (*b. Port Richmond, S.I., N.Y., 1794; d. 1877*), financier, steamship and railroad promoter. Father, among other children, of

William H. Vanderbilt; grandfather of Cornelius (1843–1899), George W., and William K. Vanderbilt. Began business *c.* 1810 as a freight and passenger ferryman between Staten Island and New York City. Taking advantage of expanded opportunities during the War of 1812, he built up a small fleet of schooners for the Hudson River and coastal trade but disposed of his sailing ships in 1818 to become a ferry-captain in the employ of Thomas Gibbons. A strong and tough ally to Gibbons in his fight against the steam-navigation monopoly which existed in New York waters, Vanderbilt turned what was a losing venture into a profitable one within a year. After fighting Gibbons's battles and expanding his business for some 11 years, Vanderbilt entered the steamboat business on his own, 1829. With characteristic zest for conflict, he fought for a share of the Hudson River trade by cutting prices and for the first time came into conflict with a later antagonist, Daniel Drew. His opponents finally paid him to withdraw from competition for ten years, and he then set up lines running on Long Island Sound to Providence and Boston. As he took pleasure in making his ships fast, safe and comfortable, he did much to promote an advance in steamboat design.

A wealthy man by 1846, "Commodore" Vanderbilt, as he had come to be known, was loud and coarse in speech—a big, bumptious, hardheaded man who was at the same time courageous, constructive, frank, and faithful to a bargain once he had made it. He was also a man of broad vision for his time. When traffic to California reached important proportions with the 1849 gold rush, he conceived the idea of starting a line of his own *via* Nicaragua to California. He constructed a fleet of new steamers to make the first part of the journey from New York to Nicaragua, and also built roads and other installations in that country to facilitate the overland part of the journey. His aggressive competition reduced the length of time for the New York–San Francisco trip and also greatly reduced the passenger fare. While on an extensive vacation during 1853 he committed the management of his Nicaragua line to Charles Morgan and Cornelius K. Garrison. During his absence they manipulated the stock and secured control of the company; later, as Vanderbilt struggled to win it back, Morgan and Garrison persuaded the filibuster William Walker, who was then temporarily in control of the Nicaraguan government, to void Vanderbilt's operating charter and issue a new one to them. Rising to the challenge, Vanderbilt thereupon set about to oust Walker, which he succeeded in doing early in 1857. Once again in control of his line, he bludgeoned the Pacific Mail Steamship Co. into buying it out. He then entered competition for the Atlantic trade against the Cunard and Collins lines. This, however, was an unprofitable venture.

Vanderbilt had begun buying stock of the New York & Harlem Railroad in 1862; in 1863 he induced the New York City council to let him extend the line by street-car tracks to the lower part of the city. He also took over the presidency of the road. When Daniel Drew, with the aid of members of the council, attempted a "bear raid" on the stock of the company, Vanderbilt outwitted him and forced a settlement by which many of the plotters were ruined. At about this time he put his son William H. Vanderbilt into the post of vice-president of the Harlem Railroad, and thereafter his son was his closest aide. The Harlem's competitor, the Hudson River Railroad, was then acquired, and Vanderbilt sought permission of the New York legislature to combine the two. Again Daniel Drew plotted a raid, this time by legislative bribery, and again the old Commodore was victorious over his enemies. By careful management and by following his lifelong policy of improving the equipment and service of his lines, he presently had them on a paying basis. After another financial and political struggle in which Drew was involved, he succeeded in gaining control of the New York Central in 1867, improved it, and by 1872 had consolidated three inefficient roads into a single excellent line. Meanwhile Drew, Jay Gould and James Fisk, by a series of spectacular and reprehensible maneuvers, had defeated his attempt to control the Erie Railroad in 1868.

By the addition to his holdings of the Lake Shore & Michigan Southern Railroad (1873) and the Michigan Central and Canada Southern roads (1875), Vanderbilt created one of the great American systems of transportation. During the last years of his life he exerted a strong, stabilizing influence on national finance. He engaged in no philanthropies until late in his life when he gave $1,000,000 to Vanderbilt University (previously Central University) at Nashville, Tenn., of which he is regarded as the founder.

VANDERBILT, CORNELIUS (*b. near New Dorp, S.I., N.Y., 1843; d. New York, N.Y., 1899*), financier, philanthropist. Son of William H. Vanderbilt; grandson of Cornelius Vanderbilt (1794–1877); brother of George W. and William K. Vanderbilt. A favorite of his grandfather, he became assistant treasurer of the New York & Harlem Railroad *c.* 1867 and served as its president from 1886 until his death. *Post* 1885 he acted as the head of the Vanderbilt family and was the director, with his brother William K. Vanderbilt, of its investments. A conscientious worker and a director of many corporations, he was a trustee and benefactor of the N.Y. College of Physicians and Surgeons, of Columbia University, of the N.Y. General Theological Seminary and of many other public institutions.

VANDERBILT, GEORGE WASHINGTON (*b. near New Dorp, S.I., N.Y., 1862; d. Washington, D.C., 1914*), capitalist, agriculturist, forestry pioneer. Son of William H. Vanderbilt; grandson of Cornelius Vanderbilt (1794–1877); brother of Cornelius (1843–1899) and William K. Vanderbilt. Studious and caring

little for finance, he built up a very large property in the vicinity of Asheville, N.C., where he planned and built the finest country home in America, working with Richard M. Hunt and Frederick L. Olmsted. At his estate, which he named "Biltmore," he practiced scientific farming and stockbreeding, founded and conducted the Biltmore Nursery, and founded also the Biltmore School of Forestry. Gifford Pinchot was his first superintendent of forests. The stimulus which his example gave to agricultural reforms in the South has been called beyond estimate.

VANDERBILT, WILLIAM HENRY (*b. New Brunswick, N.J., 1821; d. New York, N.Y., 1885*), financier, railroad executive. Son of Cornelius Vanderbilt (1794–1877); father of Cornelius (1843–1899), George W. and William K. Vanderbilt. Alienated for some years from his father, he was returned to favor *c.* 1863 after he had achieved success on his own as a farmer and railroad executive. Appointed to high positions in the Vanderbilt railroads, he served as his father's principal aide until *c.* 1876, showing great ability in management, in the improvement of track and equipment, in regulating rates and in conciliating labor. After the death of his father, William Henry Vanderbilt became president of all the affiliated New York Central network corporations. Within a few years he bought control of the Chicago & Northwestern and a large interest in the Cleveland, Columbus, Cincinnati & Indianapolis Railroad. He also exercised effective control over the New York, Chicago & St. Louis line and in 1885 leased the West Shore. Like his father a constructive man who prized efficiency, he greatly improved his properties and increased his own fortune. Recognizing the unpopularity of unified and monopoly control, he disposed in 1879 of a large block of his own shareholdings in the roads. He resigned all his railroad presidencies in May 1883, ordering that members of the family should be chairmen of the boards of directors thereafter, but that presidents should be practical, working executives. Temperate and simple in his personal habits, he was fond of horses and driving and made a number of philanthropic benefactions during his lifetime.

VANDERBILT, WILLIAM KISSAM (*b. near New Dorp, S.I., N.Y., 1849; d. Paris, France, 1920*), capitalist, sportsman. Son of William H. Vanderbilt; grandson of Cornelius Vanderbilt (1794–1877); brother of Cornelius (1843–1899) and George W. Vanderbilt. An executive in the family railroads *post c.* 1869 and, with his brother Cornelius, for many years a manager of the family investments, William K. Vanderbilt voluntarily permitted the executive direction of the New York Central system to pass to the Rockefeller-Morgan-Pennsylvania combination in 1903. He continued, however, as a board member of many railroads until his death and aided in increasing the size of the Vanderbilt fortune. An enthusiastic yachtsman and turfman, he was also active in the affairs of the Metropolitan Opera and in theatrical matters and was a collector of paintings.

VANDERBURGH, WILLIAM HENRY (*b. Vincennes, Ind., c. 1798; d. on an affluent of the Jefferson River, present Montana, 1832*), fur trader. Worked for Missouri Fur Co. *post c.* 1818; was later a partner in the American Fur Co. and in charge of the Rocky Mountain trappers *post c.* 1828. Ambushed and killed by Blackfeet Indians while on a trapping expedition.

VAN DER DONCK, ADRIAEN (*b. Breda, North Brabant, Netherlands, 1620; d. New Netherland, c. 1655*), colonist, lawyer. Studied law at the University of Leyden. Came to America as *schout* (justice officer) at Rensselaerswyck, 1641. Dismissed from office *c.* 1644 because of enmity of Arent Van Curler, he remained in the colony and established a settlement at the present site of Yonkers, N.Y. Appointed secretary of the Board of Nine Men, 1649, he wrote the famous "Remonstrance" of 1650, which set forth the people's grievances against their rulers, and was one of three men sent to The Hague to present it to the States-General. This gained him the enmity of Peter Stuyvesant. Detained at home by the government, he wrote the description of New Netherland entitled *Beschrijvinge van Nieuvv Nederlant* (written in 1653, published 1655 at Amsterdam). He returned to America late in 1653 with permission to give legal advice but not to appear before the courts since there was no lawyer in the colony competent to contend with him.

VANDERGRIFT, JACOB JAY (*b. Allegheny, Pa., 1827; d. Pittsburgh, Pa., 1899*), riverboat captain. Settling at Oil City, Pa., early in 1861, he became a shipper of oil and later a dealer. In association with John Pitcairn and others, he established the Imperial Refinery, 1872. Although not the builder of the first oil pipe line, he is said to have been the first to make one profitable. With Pitcairn he also laid what was probably the first natural gas line of any importance.

VANDERGRIFT, MARGARET. [See JANVIER, MARGARET THOMSON, 1844–1913.]

VAN DER KEMP, FRANCIS ADRIAN (*b. Kampen, the Netherlands, 1752; d. 1829*), clergyman, Dutch revolutionary leader, scholar. Long a friend and correspondent of John Adams, Van der Kemp emigrated to New York, 1788, settling first near Kingston and later by Oneida Lake. At the request of DeWitt Clinton, he translated the Dutch colonial records of New York into English.

VANDERLIP, FRANK ARTHUR (*b. near Aurora, Ill., 1864; d. New York, N.Y., 1937*), journalist, banker, public official. Entering journalism as city editor of his hometown newspaper, he went to the *Chicago Tribune*, 1889, where he soon rose to be financial editor. Associate editor of *The Economist* (Chicago, Ill., 1894–97), he further developed his reputation as a financial authority and was appointed (1897) private secretary to Lyman J. Gage, U.S. secretary of the treasury. Soon becoming an assistant treasury secretary, he won national repute handling the Spanish War loan of 1898. Joining the National City Bank of New York in 1901 as vice-president, he brought that institution into the investment field, developed foreign and domestic branches, and, as president, 1909–19, made the bank the largest in the United States. He maintained a lifelong interest in public affairs, denouncing the scandals of the Harding administration, opposing the growing isolationism of the United States, and advocating abandonment of the gold standard, 1933. [*Supp. 2*]

VANDERLYN, JOHN (*b. Kingston, N.Y., 1775; d. Kingston, 1852*), historical and portrait painter. Patronized by Aaron Burr, Vanderlyn took his first lessons in drawing from Archibald Robertson and later studied under Gilbert Stuart. A student in Paris, 1796–1801, he returned briefly to America. Between 1803 and 1815 he worked in Europe where, at Rome, he met and became a friend of Washington Allston. His painting "Marius amid the Ruins of Carthage" (Rome *c.* 1806) made a great stir and he received a number of honors abroad. His "Ariadne" of 1812 made a greater sensation than the "Marius." After his return to New York in 1815 Vanderlyn painted a number of portraits of eminent men, engaged in a controversy with John Trumbull over the paintings for the rotunda of the U.S. Capitol, and executed panoramas of Paris, Versailles, Athens and Mexico for exhibition. His popularity early waned and he died in poverty.

VAN DER STUCKEN, FRANK VALENTIN (*b. Fredericksburg, Texas, 1858; d. Hamburg, Germany, 1929*), musical composer, conductor. Raised in Belgium, he studied music in Antwerp and Brussels and at Leipzig. Winning repute abroad, he succeeded Leopold Damrosch as conductor of the Arion Society chorus (1884–95) and appeared frequently as an orchestral conductor. *Post* 1895 he was conductor of the Cincinnati Symphony Orchestra and director of the Cincinnati Conservatory until 1907 and 1903 respectively. *Post* 1908 he resided principally in Europe. Early in his conducting career he adopted a policy of presenting all-American programs at which the works of American musicians were played exclusively.

VANDER VEER, ALBERT (*b. Root, N.Y., 1841; d. 1929*), Union Army surgeon, medical educator. M.D., present George Washington University, 1863. A practitioner in Albany, N.Y.; taught at Albany Medical College, 1869–1915, and served as dean, 1897–1904. He was a regent of the University of the State of New York, 1895–1927, and its chancellor, 1921–22.

VANDER WEE, JOHN BAPTIST (*b. Antwerp, Belgium, 1824; d. Baltimore, Md., 1900*), educator, provincial of the Xaverian Brothers. Known in religion as Brother Alexius, he joined the Xaverian Brothers, 1845, and helped establish the congregation in England, 1848. Sent to America, 1872, he was named provincial of the congregation in 1875. From beginnings of desperate poverty he labored to extend the work of the Brothers, building several schools and colleges, and conducting St. Mary's Industrial School in Baltimore which served as a model for later institutions for boy training.

VAN DE VELDE, JAMES OLIVER (*b. near Termonde, Belgium, 1795; d. Natchez, Miss., 1855*), Roman Catholic clergyman, Jesuit. Recruited for the American missions by Charles Nerinckx, 1817, he was ordained in 1827. Ordered to St. Louis University, 1831, he served there as vice-president (1833) and as president (1840–43). Vice-provincial of Missouri, 1843–48, he fostered the Jesuit missions of the Far West. Consecrated bishop of Chicago, 1849, he had a brief and unhappy tenure and was transferred at his own request to the diocese of Natchez, 1853.

VAN DE WARKER, EDWARD ELY (*b. West Troy, present Watervliet, N.Y., 1841; d. 1910*), Union Army surgeon, gynecologist. M.D., Albany Medical College, 1863. Practiced with great success at Syracuse, N.Y., *post* 1870.

VAN DINE, S. S. [See WRIGHT, WILLARD HUNTINGTON, 1888–1939.]

VAN DORN, EARL (*b. near Port Gibson, Miss., 1820; d. Spring Hill, Tenn., 1863*), soldier. Graduated West Point, 1842. As an infantry officer, he served with credit in the war with Mexico and against the Seminoles (1849–50); thereafter he served with the then 2nd Cavalry in Texas and Indian Territory. Resigning from the army, 1861, he was appointed brigadier-general of Mississippi troops and rose to major-general in the Confederate army in the same year. Commander of the trans-Mississippi district, 1862, he was defeated at Pea Ridge in March, and later at Corinth, Miss., after transfer there. In charge of the cavalry during the defense of Vicksburg, he made a brilliant raid on Holly Springs in December 1862, effectively crippling Gen. U.S. Grant's projected campaign. He was shot and killed by a personal enemy in camp.

VAN DYCK, CORNELIUS VAN ALEN (*b. Kinderhook, N.Y., 1818; d. 1895*), medical missionary, Arabic scholar, author of scientific textbooks in modern Arabic. A graduate of Jefferson Medical College in 1839, he served in Syria and Lebanon, 1840–65 and 1867–95. A master of the Arabic language, he continued and completed the translation of the Bible into Arabic which had been begun by Eli Smith.

VAN DYKE, HENRY (*b. Germantown, Pa., 1852; d. Princeton, N.J., 1933*), Presbyterian clergyman, author, educator, diplomat. Brother of Paul Van Dyke. Graduated Princeton, 1873; Princeton Theological Seminary, 1877. Pastor at Newport, R.I., 1879–83; minister of Brick Presbyterian Church, New York City, 1883–99, 1902, 1911. Murray Professor of English Literature, Princeton University, 1899–1923, thereafter emeritus. U.S. minister to the Netherlands and Luxembourg, 1913–16. An eloquent preacher and able administrator,

Van Dyke was as competent as he was versatile. Active in the fight against political corruption while a New York pastor, he stood for a positive evangelical Christianity during the doctrinal controversies that shook the Presbyterian Church in his time. Equally versatile as a writer, Van Dyke's outdoor essays are in the tradition of Thoreau, Burroughs and Muir, although his deep religious faith informs his work at all times. Although changing standards of taste have diminished his reputation, he was master of a lucid style beautifully adapted to his purposes. Among his principal books are: *The Poetry of Tennyson* (1889); *Little Rivers* (1895); *Fisherman's Luck* (1899); *The Story of the Other Wise Man* (1896); *The First Christmas Tree* (1897); *The Blue Flower* (1902); and *Out-of-doors in the Holy Land* (1908).

VAN DYKE, JOHN CHARLES (*b. New Brunswick, N.J., 1856; d. New York, N.Y., 1932*), art critic, educator. Grandson of Theodore Strong. A librarian at the New Brunswick Theological Seminary *post* 1878, Van Dyke was also a lecturer on art at Rutgers College, and served as professor of the history of art there, 1891–1929. Author of a number of careful, scholarly works on art and also of several distinguished volumes of nature study (such as *The Desert*, 1901, and *The Mountain*, 1916), Van Dyke was possessed of an almost microscopic acuteness of vision. He employed this in effecting a severe and controversial revision of attributions to the artist in his *Rembrandt and His School* (1923).

VAN DYKE, JOHN WESLEY (*b. near Mercersburg, Pa., 1849; d. Philadelphia, Pa., 1939*), oil company executive. Associated with various Standard Oil companies, 1873–1911, he was president of the Atlantic Refining Co., 1911–27, and chairman of the board until his death. Among his patented inventions were mechanical improvements for the sulfur-eliminating process devised by Herman Frasch, and improvements on railroad tank cars. Probably his most important invention (developed with W. W. Irish) was the tower still which enabled refiners to improve the separation of fractions, to eliminate some refining processes and to reduce costs. [*Supp. 2*]

VAN DYKE, NICHOLAS (*b. New Castle, Del., 1738; d. New Castle Co., Del., 1789*), lawyer, Delaware legislator. Father of Nicholas Van Dyke (1770–1826). A moderate Whig *post* 1774, he served in the Continental Congress, 1777–82, but was more interested in his work as a Delaware councilor. While president (governor) of Delaware, 1783–86, he strove to improve commerce and to put the state finances on a sound basis.

VAN DYKE, NICHOLAS (*b. New Castle, Del., 1770; d. New Castle, 1826*), lawyer, statesman. Son of Nicholas Van Dyke (1738–1789); brother-in-law of Kensey Johns (1759–1848). A moderate in politics like his father, he served as attorney-general of Delaware, 1801–06, and as a Federalist congressman, 1807–11. A U.S. senator, 1817–26, he voiced the traditional state-rights sentiments, and although personally opposed to slavery, refused to vote against the admission of Missouri on the ground that Congress had no authority to impose restrictions on slavery.

VAN DYKE, PAUL (*b. Brooklyn, N.Y., 1859; d. Washington, Conn., 1933*), historian. Brother of Henry Van Dyke. Graduated Princeton, 1881; Princeton Theological Seminary, 1884. A Presbyterian pastor for some years at Geneva, N.Y., and at Northampton, Mass., he was an instructor in church history at Princeton Seminary, 1889–92, and professor of modern history in Princeton University, 1898–1928. His most important book, *Catherine de Medicis* (1922), won international recognition as a history of the religious wars in France.

VANE, Sir HENRY (*b. probably Debden, Essex, England, 1613; d. London, England, 1662*), Puritan statesman. Emigrated to Massachusetts, 1635. Attempted with Hugh Peter to reconcile the factions of former governors John Winthrop and Thomas Dudley. Elected governor of Massachusetts, May 1636, he served with tact and energy, but his career was soon wrecked by his support of Anne Hutchinson during the great controversy over her religious opinions. At the election of 1637 he was defeated by John Winthrop, and in August 1637 he sailed for England. An honest and generous man, he was later outstanding during the struggle of King and Parliament in England. He was instrumental in securing the condemnation of the Earl of Strafford and Archbishop Laud, but he had no part in the trial and condemnation of King Charles I, and after the dissolution of the Long Parliament he retired from public life. Excepted from the act of indemnity at the Restoration, he was tried for treason, found guilty and executed.

VAN FLEET, WALTER (*b. Piermont, N.Y., 1857; d. Miami, Fla., 1922*), physician, naturalist, horticulturist. M.D., Hahnemann Medical College, 1880. Taking up plant-breeding as his main vocation, 1891, he gave distinguished service as an expert in the bureau of plant industry, U.S. Department of Agriculture, *post* 1909. His work covered a wide range and included experiments on production of non-blighting chestnuts and the development of many new varieties of plants. He is most famous for his work with the rose, especially the climbing and pillar varieties.

VAN HISE, CHARLES RICHARD (*b. Fulton, Wis., 1857; d. Milwaukee, Wis., 1918*), geologist, educator. Graduated in engineering, University of Wisconsin, 1879; Ph.D., 1892. Taught metallurgy and mineralogy at Wisconsin *post* 1879 and was professor of geology, 1892–1903; he also served with the U.S. Geological Survey. He was president of the University of Wisconsin *post* 1903. Trained in geology under Roland D. Irving, he collaborated with Irving in much research

work for the Geological Survey, and was co-author of several monographs on the iron-bearing districts of the Lake Superior region; he later collaborated with C. K. Leith in the writing of several more general treatises on the subject. As president of the university he developed its research activities and its extension department and engaged actively in public service. He contributed to the conservation movement what has been called its most valuable book, *The Conservation of Natural Resources in the United States* (1910). He was later an enthusiastic supporter of the League of Nations concept.

VAN HOOK, WELLER (*b. Greenville, Ind., 1862; d. Coopersville, Mich., 1933*), Chicago, Ill., surgeon and medical teacher. Did pioneer work in surgery of the genito-urinary tract; devised *ante* 1896 the Van Hook-Mayo operation for correction of hypospadias and the repair of epispadias.

VAN HORN, ROBERT THOMPSON (*b. East Mahoning, Pa., 1824; d. Kansas City, Mo., 1916*), Union soldier, journalist, Missouri legislator. Trained as a printer, he removed to Kansas City, 1855, where he was editor-publisher of the *Journal* (published daily, 1858–97). Originally a conservative Democrat, he became a Republican at the outbreak of the Civil War and served as a loyal partisan in Congress, 1865–71, 1881–83, 1895–97. Several times mayor of Kansas City, he played a leading role in making that place the principal railroad center west of Chicago.

VAN HORNE, WILLIAM CORNELIUS (*b. Will Co., Ill., 1843; d. Montreal, Canada, 1915*), railroad executive. Starting as a telegraph operator with the Illinois Central Railroad *c.* 1857, he rose by outstanding merit to the superintendency of the Chicago, Milwaukee & St. Paul Railroad. Impressing James J. Hill with his abilities during an 1880 controversy, Van Horne was recommended by Hill to the directors of the Canadian Pacific Railway as the man best qualified to supervise its construction. He began work at Winnipeg at the end of 1881 and carried the project through to completion in 1886. President of the Canadian Pacific, 1888–99, thereafter he developed important railroads in Cuba and Guatemala. A naturalized citizen of Canada *ante* 1890, he was knighted, 1894.

VAN ILPENDAM, JAN JANSEN (*b. Leyden, the Netherlands, c. 1595; d. probably Amsterdam, the Netherlands, 1647*), Dutch colonial official. Commissary at Fort Nassau on the Delaware *c.* 1637–45. Opposed English efforts to settle on the Schuylkill, 1641, and on the Delaware, 1644.

VAN LENNEP, HENRY JOHN (*b. Smyrna, Asiatic Turkey, 1815; d. Great Barrington, Mass., 1889*), Congregational clergyman. Graduated Amherst, 1837. Missionary in Turkey, 1839–69; author, among other works, of *Travels in Little-Known Parts of Asia Minor* (1870).

VAN LENNEP, WILLIAM BIRD (*b. Constantinople, Turkey, 1853; d. Philadelphia, Pa., 1919*), surgeon. Son of Henry J. Van Lennep. Graduated Princeton, 1876; Hahnemann Medical College, 1880; made post-graduate studies in London, Paris and Vienna. A faculty member of Hahnemann College *post* 1886 and dean *post* 1910.

VAN METER, JOHN BLACKFORD (*b. Philadelphia, Pa., 1842; d. Baltimore, Md., 1930*), Methodist clergyman, educator. Associated with John F. Goucher in founding Woman's College of Baltimore (present Goucher); served there as a faculty member, 1888–1914, and as dean, 1892–1910. Largely responsible for the educational policy of the college, he served it also as acting president, 1911–13.

VAN NAME, ADDISON (*b. Chenango, N.Y., 1835; d. New Haven, Conn., 1922*), philologist, librarian. Brother-in-law of Josiah W. Gibbs (1839–1903). Graduated Yale, 1858. Appointed librarian of Yale, 1865, he served until his retirement as emeritus, 1905. He built up the collection of Oriental literature and supervised the library during a period of extraordinary growth.

VAN NESS, WILLIAM PETER (*b. Claverack, Columbia Co., N.Y., c. 1778; d. 1826*), politician, jurist. Graduated Columbia, 1797; studied law in office of Edward Livingston. Began practice in New York City, 1800, as protégé of Aaron Burr. A loyal follower of Burr in politics, Van Ness defended his patron in *An Examination of the Various Charges Exhibited against Aaron Burr* (1803, under pseudonym "Aristides") and served him as second in his duel with Alexander Hamilton, 1804. Subsequently an associate of Martin Van Buren, he served as U.S. judge for the Southern District of New York, 1812–26. He was co-editor of the annotated *Laws of the State of New York* (1813) and wrote several other works.

VAN NEST, ABRAHAM RYNIER (*b. New York, N.Y., 1823; d. New York, 1892*), Dutch Reformed clergyman. After holding several New York pastorates he resided abroad, 1863–78, and organized American chapels in Paris, Rome, Florence and Geneva. Returning to the United States, he was pastor of Third Reformed Church of Philadelphia, Pa., 1878–83.

VAN NOSTRAND, DAVID (*b. New York, N.Y., 1811; d. 1886*), bookseller, publisher, student of military engineering. Opened a New York City bookstore *c.* 1848, specializing in books on military and naval science. Venturing into publishing, he made his firm the largest American publishers of scientific, technical and military works, also issuing for many years *Van Nostrand's Engineering Magazine.*

VAN OSDEL, JOHN MILLS (*b. Baltimore, Md., 1811; d. Chicago, Ill., 1891*), carpenter, architect. Employed by William B. Ogden to plan and erect a house for him in Chicago, 1837, Van Osdel removed to Chicago and has the honor of being that city's first professional architect. He was particularly active in the restoration of the city after the great fire of 1871.

VAN QUICKENBORNE, CHARLES FELIX (*b. Peteghem, East Flanders, 1788; d. Portage des Sioux, Mo., 1837*), Roman Catholic clergyman, Jesuit. Assigned to the Jesuit Maryland mission, 1817, he taught at Georgetown and served as professor at the seminary at Whitemarsh. He was renowned for charitable service among the poor and especially the Negroes. Named first superior of the Missouri Province, 1823, he instituted its work at Florissant; in 1828 he established St. Louis College, later incorporated as St. Louis University. A zealous missionary among the Osage, Potawatomi, Kickapoo and other tribes, he traveled extensively through Missouri, Illinois and Iowa, and served as the pioneer of Catholicism on those frontiers. He was also responsible for the training of such celebrated Jesuits as Christian Hoecken, Pierre De Smet and Peter Verhaegen.

VAN RAALTE, ALBERTUS CHRISTIAAN (*b. near Zwartsluis, the Netherlands, 1811; d. 1876*), nonconformist Dutch Reformed clergyman. Founded Dutch settlement at Holland, Mich., 1847, and served as its preacher and physician.

VAN RENSSELAER, CORTLANDT (*b. Albany, N.Y., 1808; d. Burlington, N.J., 1860*), Presbyterian clergyman. Son of Stephen Van Rensselaer. Graduated Yale, 1827. Rendered conspicuous service as corresponding secretary and chief executive officer of the Presbyterian Board of Education, 1846–60, furthering the development of parochial schools, Presbyterian academies and synodical colleges.

VAN RENSSELAER, MARIANA GRISWOLD (*b. New York, N.Y., 1851; d. New York, 1934*), art critic, author. A leader and expositor of the new interest in art that was current in the educated America of the 1880's and 1890's, Mrs. Van Rensselaer wrote a number of books which included *American Etchers* (1886), *Henry Hobson Richardson and His Works* (1888, the first important monograph on a modern American architect), and *English Cathedrals* (1892). Her best-known work is her authoritative *History of the City of New York in the Seventeenth Century* (1909).

VAN RENSSELAER, MARTHA (*b. Randolph, N.Y., 1864; d. 1932*), teacher, home economist. An early leader in the education of country women, particularly through her extension work at Cornell University *post* 1900.

VAN RENSSELAER, NICHOLAS (*b. Amsterdam, North Holland, 1636; d. 1678*), Dutch Reformed and Anglican clergyman. Son of the first patroon of the Manor of Rensselaer, he became a close associate of Charles II of England during that king's exile on the continent of Europe. In England *post* 1662, he received Anglican orders and came to New York with

Sir Edmund Andros who tried to force him on the congregation at Albany as minister. Rejected, he complained to the governor and the dispute was brought before the Council, September–October 1675. On his promise to conform to the rites of the Dutch Church, he was finally installed at Albany but was deposed by the governor, 1677.

VAN RENSSELAER, SOLOMON (*b. Rensselaer Co., N.Y., 1774; d. 1852*), soldier, public official. Entered U.S. Army as cornet of cavalry, 1792; served under Anthony Wayne, 1794, and was wounded at Fallen Timbers; honorably discharged as major, 1800. Appointed aide-de-camp to his cousin Gen. Stephen Van Rensselaer, 1812, he commanded the advance party of militia at Queenstown, Canada, Oct. 13, 1812, and was wounded severely while successfully carrying out his part of the operation. As congressman, probably Federalist, from New York, 1819–22, he opposed the Missouri Compromise. He was postmaster at Albany, N.Y., 1822–39, 1841–43.

VAN RENSSELAER, STEPHEN (*b. New York, N.Y., 1764; d. 1839*), soldier, New York legislator, eighth patroon of the Manor of Rensselaer. Grandson of Philip Livingston. Graduated Harvard, 1782. Married Margaret, daughter of Gen. Philip Schuyler, June 1783. A Federalist legislator, 1789–95, and lieutenant-governor of New York, 1795–1801, he ran unsuccessfully for governor against George Clinton in the latter year. Thereafter at various times a member of the New York legislature and an active improver of his great estates, he was called on in 1812 (as a major-general in the New York militia) to command the entire northern frontier of the state. Assembling a force based at Lewiston, he was hampered by the refusal of Gen. Alexander Smyth of the regular army to take orders from him. Venturing to attack Queenstown, Canada, in October 1812 without Smyth's support, he suffered a severe defeat and resigned his command. As congressman from New York, 1823–29, he cast the deciding vote for John Q. Adams, 1825, when the choice of a president was thrown into the House of Representatives. Van Rensselaer's chief services to New York were economic and educational. He was an early advocate of a canal to connect the Hudson with the Great Lakes and served on both Erie Canal commissions; he was president of the second *post* 1825. He was instrumental in creating the state's first board of agriculture and paid the costs of the first state geological survey by Amos Eaton. He established in 1824–26 the present Rensselaer Polytechnic Institute and gave generously to other educational institutions.

VAN SANTVOORD, GEORGE (*b. Belleville, N.J., 1819; d. East Albany, N.Y., 1863*), lawyer, New York legislator. A proponent of the civil law as against the "churlish and exclusive spirit" of the common law. Author, among other works, of *A Treatise on the Principles of Pleading in Civil Actions under the New-York Code* (1852) and *Sketches of the Lives . . . of the Chief Justices of the United States* (1854).

VAN SCHAACK, HENRY CRUGER (*b. Kinderhook, N.Y., 1802; d. 1887*), antiquarian, lawyer. Son of Peter Van Schaack. Author, among other works, of a life of his father (1842) which was the first attempt to present a justificatory memoir of a Tory in the Revolution.

VAN SCHAACK, PETER (*b. near Kinderhook, N.Y., 1747; d. Kinderhook, 1832*), lawyer, Loyalist. Graduated King's College (Columbia), 1766; studied law with William Smith (1728–1793). A member of several pre-Revolutionary New York committees of protest against the British government's treatment of the colonies, he attempted to maintain neutrality after the outbreak of fighting. His several refusals to take the oath of allegiance to the State of New York caused him to be banished to England in 1778. Returning to Kinderhook, 1785, he was readmitted to the bar but took no active part in politics.

VAN SCHAICK, GOOSE (*b. Albany, N.Y., 1736; d. Albany, 1789*), Revolutionary patriot and soldier. An officer in the New York provincial militia *post* 1756, he was commissioned colonel of the 1st New York Regiment at the outbreak of the Revolution and saw constant service during the war in defense of New York's northern and western frontiers. His most famous exploit was a punitive expedition against the Onondaga tribe (April 1779) which was preliminary to the better-known campaign of Gen. John Sullivan later that summer.

VAN SLYKE, LUCIUS LINCOLN (*b. Centerville, N.Y., 1859; d. 1931*), agricultural chemist. Graduated University of Michigan, 1879; Ph.D., 1882. Chief chemist, New York State agricultural experiment station, Geneva, N.Y., 1890–1929; professor of dairy chemistry, Cornell University, 1920–29. He is remembered for pioneer work in dairy chemistry which included basic research on the chemical constituents of milk and their relation to one another. His researches on milk casein led to improvement in cheese-making and were of immense scientific value in contributing to knowledge of the nature and behavior of colloids.

VAN SWERINGEN, MANTIS JAMES (*b. Wooster, O., 1881; d. 1935*), real estate operator, railroad manager and speculator. Working in close partnership with his brother, Oris P. Van Sweringen, he developed the suburb of Shaker Heights, Cleveland, O., *post c.* 1900. The brothers later acquired stock control of a vast railroad system which at its peak included the Nickel Plate, the Chesapeake & Ohio, the Erie, the Pere Marquette, and the Missouri Pacific railroads. In 1935 their holding company pyramid showed signs of weakening, and after the death of the brothers their empire disintegrated. [*Supp.* 1]

VAN TWILLER, WOUTER (*b. Gelderland, present Netherlands, c. 1580; d. c. 1656*), colonial official. Nephew of Kiliaen Van Rensselaer, the first patroon of Rensselaerswyck. Arrived at New Amsterdam, 1633, as director-general of New Netherland. His foresighted desire to build up the agricultural potential of the colony, rather than produce an immediate profit by trade, was thwarted by a lack of colonists and by the enmity of David P. De Vries and Everardus Bogardus. Popular with the Indians because of his just treatment of them, he was relieved of his post by Willem Kieft in 1637. Returning to the Netherlands, 1639, he justified his actions before the West India Company and was later a manager of his uncle's properties.

VAN TYNE, CLAUDE HALSTEAD (*b. Tecumseh, Mich., 1869; d. 1930*), educator, historian. Graduated University of Michigan, 1896; Ph.D., University of Pennsylvania, 1900. A professor of history at Michigan *post* 1903 and later head of the department of history there, Van Tyne was a stimulating and exacting teacher. He was author, among other scholarly publications, of *The Loyalists in the American Revolution* (1902), *The Causes of the War of Independence* (1922), and *The War of Independence, American Phase* (1929) for which he was awarded a Pulitzer Prize.

VANUXEM, LARDNER (*b. Philadelphia, Pa., 1792; d. Bristol, Pa., 1848*), geologist. Graduated École des Mines, Paris, 1819. Taught chemistry at South Carolina College. Made geologic surveys in Mexico, New York, Ohio, Kentucky, Tennessee and Virginia; made studies also of the Third District iron- and salt-bearing formations for the New York State Geological Survey *post* 1836. Author of *Geology of New-York, Part III* (1842), he was instrumental in effecting a uniform system of nomenclature for American geology, a cooperative task which led to the later founding of the American Association for the Advancement of Science.

VAN VECHTEN, ABRAHAM (*b. Catskill, N.Y., 1762; d. 1837*), lawyer, Federalist New York legislator and public official. Studied law with John Lansing; was first lawyer admitted to practice under the New York constitution, 1785; practiced in Albany, N.Y. Held leading position at New York constitutional convention, 1821. Gave notable opinion in *Gibbons vs. Ogden* (9 *Wheaton*, 1) in which he was sustained by Chief Justice Marshall.

VAN WINKLE, PETER GODWIN (*b. New York, N.Y., 1808; d. Parkersburg, W. Va., 1872*), lawyer. Removed to Parkersburg as a young man and practiced law there *post* 1835. Prominent in the creation of the present State of West Virginia, he had much to do with the framing of its constitution (1861–62) and was a member of its first legislature. U.S. senator, Republican, from West Virginia, 1863–69, he showed courage and independence, especially in his refusal to vote for conviction of President Andrew Johnson.

VAN WYCK, CHARLES HENRY (*b. Poughkeepsie, N.Y., 1824; d. Washington, D.C., 1895*), lawyer, Union brigadier-general, New York and Nebraska legislator. Congressman, Republican, from New York, 1859–63, 1867–71, he removed to the vicinity of Nebraska City, Nebr., 1874. In the Nebraska legislature, and as U.S. senator, 1881–87, he was a supporter of tariff reform, railroad regulation, protection of the public lands, and direct popular election of senators. He was active in the Farmers' Alliance and in the Populist movement in Nebraska.

VANZETTI, BARTOLOMEO. (1888–1927). [See SACCO, NICOLA, 1891–1927.]

VARDAMAN, JAMES KIMBLE (*b. near Edna, Texas, 1861; d. 1930*), lawyer, newspaper editor, politician. Raised in Mississippi, he rose in politics and was speaker of the Mississippi House, 1894. Denied nomination for the governorship by the ruling clique in the Mississippi Democratic party, he managed by his powers as a stump speaker to establish popularity with the poor-white farming group and fractured his party along class lines. Among other arguments, he asserted that the education of the Negro was threatening white supremacy. Elected governor, he served 1904–08. Although charged with extending the spoils system, he attacked the custom of leasing out state convicts to private employers. As U.S. senator, 1913–19, he opposed President Wilson's war policies and was one of the "little group of willful men" who filibustered against the Armed Neutrality Bill. He was defeated in the election of 1918 after a specific request for his ouster was made by the president to the Mississippi voters.

VARDILL, JOHN (*b. New York, N.Y., 1749; d. probably England, 1811*), Anglican clergyman, British spy. A graduate of King's College (Columbia), 1766, and later a tutor there, he was elected professor of natural law, 1773. Meantime he had come into public notice for essays he had written in connection with the controversy between William Livingston and Thomas B. Chandler over an American episcopate. He was author also of essays signed "Poplicola" against the nonimportation agreement, 1773. Ordained at London in April 1774, he was elected assistant minister of Trinity Church, New York, in December, but remained in England and continued writing for periodicals in defense of the government. Between 1775 and 1781 he was a Crown agent spying on American sympathizers in England. His greatest feat was in securing the theft from Silas Deane of the whole confidential correspondence between the American commissioners and the French Court from March to October 1777.

VARE, WILLIAM SCOTT (*b. South Philadelphia, Pa., 1867; d. Atlantic City, N.J., 1934*), contractor,

Pennsylvania legislator and official. Established with aid of his brothers a Republican political machine in Philadelphia which by 1917 dominated that city. A congressman, 1912–23, 1923–27, Vare climaxed his career in the primary elections of 1926 when he was successful candidate for the Republican nomination to the U.S. Senate. Rejected by the Senate after a special senatorial committee investigation of expenditures in the primary, Vare continued active in politics and aided in the nomination of Herbert Hoover for the presidency, 1928. Although he maintained his organization largely by spoils and political charity, he was a man of high personal reputation and throughout his career opposed child labor and supported liberal social reform bills.

VARELA Y MORALES, FÉLIX FRANCISCO JOSÉ MARÍA DE LA CONCEPCIÓN (*b. Havana, Cuba, 1788, d. St. Augustine, Fla., 1853*), Roman Catholic clergyman, Cuban patriot, author. An educational reformer as professor of philosophy at the College of San Carlos in Havana, Varela was a liberal in politics and served as a delegate from Cuba to the Spanish Cortes, 1822–23. Fleeing to New York on the return of the absolute monarchy in Spain, 1823, he served until 1851 as an exemplary pastor at various churches in New York City. He was twice named an administrator of the diocese and was a vicar-general *post* 1839.

VARICK, JAMES (*b. near Newburgh, N.Y., c. 1750; d. 1828*), Methodist clergyman. A founder of the African Methodist Episcopal Zion Church, 1799, Varick was chairman of the committee which drew up a discipline after secession of his church from the Methodist Episcopal organization, 1820. Elected bishop in 1822, he served as such until his death.

VARICK, RICHARD (*b. Hackensack, N.J., 1753; d. Jersey City, N.J., 1831*), Revolutionary soldier, public official. Military secretary to Gen. Philip J. Schuyler; deputy commissary-general of musters, 1776–80; aide to Gen. Benedict Arnold at West Point, 1780. Cleared of any complicity in Arnold's treason, Varick was selected by Gen. Washington as secretary to arrange, classify and copy all headquarters records of the Continental Army; he completed his task in 1783 with the greatest skill and success. Appointed recorder of New York City, 1784, he worked with Samuel Jones on the codification of the New York statutes (published 1789). Speaker of the New York Assembly, 1787–88, and state attorney-general, 1788–89, he served as Federalist mayor of New York City, 1789–1801.

VARNUM, JAMES MITCHELL (*b. Dracut, Mass., 1748; d. Marietta, O., 1789*), lawyer, Revolutionary soldier. Brother of Joseph B. Varnum. Commissioned colonel of the 1st Rhode Island Infantry (9th Continental), he was promoted brigadier-general, February 1777, and conducted a gallant though unsuccessful defense of Forts Mercer and Mifflin on the Delaware River. He later took part in the campaigns around Newport, R.I., and was made commander of the Department of Rhode Island early in 1779. Elected to the Continental Congress, 1780, he served at intervals until 1787. A director of the Ohio Company, Varnum was appointed U.S. judge for the Northwest Territory and took up duties at Marietta, O., June 1788.

VARNUM, JOSEPH BRADLEY (*b. Dracut, Mass., 1750/51; d. 1821*), Revolutionary soldier, Massachusetts legislator. Brother of James M. Varnum. Congressman, Anti-Federalist, from Massachusetts, 1795–1811, he favored a militia as against a standing army, opposed building naval vessels, and was an early opponent of slavery and the slave trade; he served as speaker of the House, 1807–11. U.S. senator, 1811–17, he was associated with the "war hawks" of the Southwest and was a strong supporter of the War of 1812. In 1813 he was president *pro tempore* of the Senate and acting U.S. vice-president.

VASEY, GEORGE (*b. near Scarborough, England, 1822; d. Washington, D.C., 1893*), physician, botanist. Emigrated to central New York State as a child. Removed to northern Illinois, 1848, where he practiced his profession and continued botanical studies of the regional flora. After accompanying John W. Powell on an exploring expedition to Colorado, 1868, he served in several posts before his appointment (1872) as botanist of the U.S. Department of Agriculture and curator of the U.S. National Herbarium. A distinguished specialist on grasses, he published several outstanding monographs on this subject.

VASSALL, JOHN (*b. Stepney, Middlesex Co., England, 1625; d. 1688*), colonist, merchant. Emigrated to New England as a boy; was a resident of Scituate, Mass. With an English cousin and others he attempted establishment of a colony at Cape Fear in present North Carolina, 1664. After the failure of the colony, 1667, he removed first to Virginia and later to Jamaica, B.W.I., where he prospered in trade. His great-grandson was the builder of the "Craigie-Longfellow" house in Cambridge, Mass.

VASSAR, MATTHEW (*b. East Tuddingham, England, 1792; d. Poughkeepsie, N.Y., 1868*), brewer, merchant. Came to America as a small boy; was successful as a brewer and in other enterprises at Poughkeepsie, N.Y. Founder of Vassar College.

VATTEMARE, NICOLAS MARIE ALEXANDRE (*b. Paris, France, 1796; d. Paris, 1864*), ventriloquist, impersonator. Made U.S. debut at the Park Theatre, New York City, October 1839. Impressed by the number of duplicate books and art objects in libraries and museums, he evolved the idea of an exchange system for which he won some support in Europe and enthusiastic aid in the United States. Between 1841 and 1851 his system was successful, and his propaganda resulted in the establishment of several free libraries and museums, including the Boston Public Library.

VAUCLAIN, SAMUEL MATTHEWS (*b. Port Richmond, Pa., 1856; d. Rosemont, Pa., 1940*), locomotive manufacturer. Associated *post* 1883 with the Baldwin Locomotive Works, he served as president of the company, 1919–29, and thereafter as chairman of the board. One of the world's leading authorities on locomotive design and inventor of a number of important improvements in locomotives, he ran his business autocratically and fought against any attempt at labor organization. [*Supp. 2*]

VAUDREUIL-CAVAGNAL, PIERRE DE RIGAUD, Marquis de (*b. Canada, 1704; d. Paris, France, 1778*), Canadian soldier and public official. Winning honors as a soldier, as governor of Trois Rivières, and as governor of the colony of Louisiana in 1743–53, he was then appointed governor of Canada. Taking up his duties, June 1755, he found the colony on the brink of war with England. Allowing himself to be drawn into the corrupt ring of politicians that surrounded the intendant Bigot, he refused support to Montcalm who had been sent to conduct the war for France; he has been held responsible for the defeat on the Plains of Abraham, September 1759. A year later he capitulated at Montreal and, by so doing, cost France her last chance to hold Canada. Arriving in France, December 1760, he was arrested and thrown into the Bastille; at his trial he was acquitted of dishonesty and pensioned. Jealous of better soldiers than himself, he talked more than was prudent and failed to check the corruption that went on all around him.

VAUGHAN, BENJAMIN (*b. Jamaica, B.W.I., 1751; d. Hallowell, Maine, 1835*), lawyer, physician, merchant, diplomat, agriculturist. Brother of Charles Vaughan. An active propagandist for the American cause during the Revolution, Vaughan was employed in confidential matters by the Earl of Shelburne. He was co-editor with Benjamin Franklin of the latter's *Political, Miscellaneous and Philosophical Pieces* (1779). He did his most important work in connection with the Anglo-American peace negotiations of 1782, helping to promote confidence between the American commissioners and Shelburne and to reconcile conflicting points of view. In 1789 he published *A Treatise on International Trade*, a plea for free trade. He was sympathetic with the French Revolution and fled to France during an official investigation of the activities of English political enthusiasts, May 1794. Imprisoned by the French, he was later released and retired to Switzerland. Removing to Hallowell, Maine, 1796, he remained retired from active politics but was a correspondent and adviser of the first six presidents and a member of many scientific and literary societies. He published a second collection of Franklin's works in London, 1793, and

was probably author of much work which still remains unidentified.

VAUGHAN, CHARLES (*b. London, England, 1759; d. Hallowell, Maine, 1839*), merchant. Brother of Benjamin Vaughan. Emigrated to New England, 1785. He then engaged in a long and generally unsuccessful attempt to improve the "Kennebec Purchase" in Maine of which his maternal grandfather, Benjamin Hallowell, had been an original proprietor; in this effort he built a settlement just below Augusta at Hallowell and tried to establish a seaport at Jones Eddy near the mouth of the Kennebec. Establishing himself as a merchant in Boston, 1791, he was a promoter, with Charles Bulfinch and William Scollay, of Boston's first brick block, the Franklin or Tontine Crescent. Later bankrupted, he retired to Hallowell where he devoted himself to the development of Maine agriculture.

VAUGHAN, DANIEL (*b. near Killaloe, Ireland, c. 1818; d. Cincinnati, O., 1879*), astronomer, mathematician, chemist. Emigrated to America, 1840; served as a tutor and schoolmaster in Kentucky and in Cincinnati, O. Celebrated as a lecturer on scientific subjects, he was made a fellow of the American Association for the Advancement of Science for his work in experimental physiology. In 1852 he anticipated by many years the demonstration made by J. E. Keeler of the nature of the rings of Saturn. A gentle genius, he died in poverty.

VAUGHAN, VICTOR CLARENCE (*b. near Mt. Airy, Mo., 1851; d. Richmond, Va., 1929*), biochemist, hygienist, medical teacher. M.S., University of Michigan, 1875; Ph.D., 1876; M.D., 1878. For many years a lecturer and professor at Michigan, he served as director of the hygienic laboratory, 1887–1909, and as dean of the medical school, 1891–1921. While dean he put Michigan in a prominent place in the movement to elevate American medical education. After studying at Berlin with Robert Koch, Vaughan and an associate set up one of the earliest laboratories in the United States for the systematic teaching of bacteriology. His work upon ptomaines with F. G. Novy influenced improvement of methods of food preservation. He developed early in his career the interest in public health and education of the public in preventive medicine for which he is best known. Among his many writings were the classic *Report on the Origin and Spread of Typhoid Fever in the U.S. Military Camps* (1904) and *Epidemiology and Public Health* (1922–23) of which he was co-author.

VAUX, CALVERT (*b. London, England, 1824; d. New York, N.Y., 1895*), landscape architect. Came to America, 1850, as assistant to Andrew J. Downing at Newburgh, N.Y.; removed to New York City *c.* 1857. Submitted winning design for New York's Central Park in collaboration with Frederick L. Olmsted, 1857; was associated in practice with Olmsted for a number of years, their work including Prospect Park in Brooklyn, N.Y., and South Park in Chicago, Ill. Vaux was landscape architect to the New York City department of parks, 1881–83, 1888–95.

VAUX, RICHARD (*b. Philadelphia, Pa., 1816; d. 1895*), lawyer, public official. Son of Roberts Vaux. Practicing in Philadelphia *post* 1839, Vaux held a number of local and federal offices. Carrying out his father's theories of penology, he served as a governor of the Eastern Penitentiary, 1839–92, and was president of its board *post* 1852.

VAUX, ROBERTS (*b. Philadelphia, Pa., 1786; d. Philadelphia, 1836*), philanthropist. Son-in-law of Thomas Wistar; father of Richard Vaux. Associated throughout his life with almost every worthy public and private activity for social welfare in Philadelphia, he was a leader in creation of the free public school system, was active in hospital work and the work of learned societies, advocated temperance and was outstanding as a prison reformer. He drafted legislation for administration of the Eastern Penitentiary and was an advocate of separate confinement of prisoners.

VAWTER, CHARLES ERASTUS (*b. Monroe Co., present W. Va., 1841; d. 1905*), Confederate soldier, educator. Graduated Emory and Henry College, 1866, and taught mathematics and Hebrew there, 1868–78. Built, organized and headed the Miller Manual Labor School of Albemarle Co., Va., *post* 1878; promoted development of industrial education in the nation's public schools; aided J. M. McBryde in shaping policies of Virginia Polytechnic Institute.

VEATCH, ARTHUR CLIFFORD (*b. Evansville, Ind., 1878; d. Port Washington, N.Y., 1938*), geologist. Attended Indiana and Cornell universities. Began professional career with the Louisiana State Geological Survey; served with U.S. Geological Survey, 1902–10; worked thereafter for various corporations and as a consultant. Specialist in the geology of petroleum and the direction of foreign oil explorations.

[Supp. 2]

VEAZEY, THOMAS WARD (*b. Cecil Co., Md., 1774; d. Cecil Co., 1842*), Maryland legislator, planter. Whig governor of Maryland, 1836–38; directed a reform of state constitution by amendments, 1836.

VEBLEN, THORSTEIN BUNDE (*b. Cato Township, Manitowoc Co., Wis., 1857; d. Palo Alto, Calif., 1929*), economist, social theorist. Raised in a Minnesota farm community made up mainly of Norwegian immigrants, Veblen graduated from Carleton College, 1880. Carrying on graduate studies under great difficulties at Johns Hopkins and at Yale, he was granted the doctorate of philosophy at Yale in 1884 but returned to a Minnesota farm when he found that no teaching post was available. After seven miserable years as a farmer he obtained a special fellowship at Cornell University through the aid of J. Laurence

Laughlin, 1891, and in the same year published his first essay, "Some Neglected Points in the Theory of Socialism" (*Annals of the American Academy of Political and Social Science,* November 1891), which contained many germs of his later theories.

Following Laughlin to the University of Chicago, Veblen taught political economy there, made private studies of anthropology and psychology, and was managing editor of the *Journal of Political Economy* (University of Chicago, 1896–1905). He achieved overnight prominence on publication in 1899 of *The Theory of the Leisure Class* into which he poured all the acidulous ideas and fantastic terminology that had been simmering in his mind for years. It was a savage attack upon the business class and their pecuniary values, half concealed behind an elaborate screen of irony and polysyllabic learning. *The Theory of Business Enterprise* (1904) contained Veblen's basic economic theory and dealt with the effects of the machine process, the nature of corporate promoting, the use of credit, the distinction between industry and business, and the influence of business ideas and pressures upon law and politics. Obliged to leave Chicago for reasons of personal conduct, he became associate professor at Leland Stanford, 1906, but further difficulties with women brought about his departure in December 1909. While lecturer at the University of Missouri, 1911–18, he brought his course in "Economic Factors in Civilization" to its classic form. Viewing all history and all cultures, the course was omniscient and rambling; his classroom manner was casual and inarticulate. The content of this course is most nearly approximated in his *The Instinct of Workmanship* (1914) which stresses the thesis that proper craftsmanship, an instinct deeply ingrained in man since savage times, has been thwarted throughout history by the piling up of predatory and pecuniary institutions.

Removing to New York City, 1918, he became first an editor of the *Dial* and then, in 1919, a member of the faculty of the New School for Social Research. To this period belong his more revolutionary writings. In *An Inquiry into the Nature of Peace* (1917) Veblen described patriotism and business enterprise as useless to the community at large and as the principal obstructions to a lasting peace; in *The Higher Learning in America* (1918) he leveled a bitter and direct attack on the conduct of universities by businessmen. In *The Vested Interests and the State of the Industrial Arts* (1919) he pointed out with savagery that the aim of business was to maximize profits by restricting or sabotaging production, and defined a vested interest as "a marketable right to get something for nothing." In *The Engineers and the Price System* (1921) he sketched out a technique of revolution through organization of a soviet of technicians who would take over and carry on the productive processes of the nation. Greatly lionized by liberal intellectuals, he declined gradually both in health and mental powers. Six months before his death he remarked that "Naturally there will be other developments right along, but just now communism offers the best course that I can see." Veblen's thinking does not fall easily into the accepted categories of liberalism and radicalism; his intellectual attitudes and methods are those of liberalism, but his criticism of capitalist society is, at least in its implications, revolutionary. Relatively unaffected by other American writers, he drew his material largely from European sources. His influence was crucial in weakening the hold of neoclassical theory, but his most powerful effect was on economic opinion and policy. He was in no small measure responsible for the trend toward social control in an age dominated by business enterprise.

VEDDER, ELIHU (*b. New York, N.Y., 1836; d. Rome, Italy, 1923*), figure and mural painter, illustrator. Began study of art by himself as a boy; worked for a time with Tompkins H. Matteson. Resided in Florence, Italy, and elsewhere in Europe, 1856–61; *post* 1867 made his home in Rome. Vedder's workmanship is heavy and his color is not remarkable, but his work has rare imaginative power; in his penetration of the realm of abstract ideas he ranks with Albert P. Ryder. Among his best works are his outstanding illustrations for the *Rubáiyát of Omar Kháyyam* (1884).

VEDDER, HENRY CLAY (*b. De Ruyter, N.Y., 1853; d. 1935*), Baptist clergyman, journalist and church historian. Served on staff of the *Examiner*, a leading Baptist newspaper in New York, 1876–94; professor of church history, Crozer Theological Seminary, 1895–1926. Author of a number of works on the history of his own sect and on Christianity in general which were marked by a strong social approach. [*Supp.* 1]

VENABLE, CHARLES SCOTT (*b. Prince Edward Co., Va., 1827; d. 1900*), mathematician, Confederate soldier, educator. Graduated Hampden-Sydney, 1842; studied also at University of Virginia. Professor of mathematics at Hampden-Sydney and later at South Carolina College, he served in the Civil War as aide on the staff of Gen. R. E. Lee. He was professor of mathematics at University of Virginia, 1865–96, and was largely responsible for the development there of schools of applied chemistry and engineering, astronomy, biology, and agriculture.

VENABLE, FRANCIS PRESTON (*b. Prince Edward Co., Va., 1856; d. 1934*), educator. Son of Charles S. Venable. Graduated University of Virginia, 1879; Ph.D., Göttingen, 1881. Professor of chemistry at the University of North Carolina *post* 1881; president of the university, 1900–14. A frequent contributor to learned journals; author of a number of books on chemical subjects.

VENABLE, WILLIAM HENRY (*b. near Waynesville, O., 1836; d. 1920*), educator, textbook writer. Taught English in Cincinnati, O., schools *post* 1862.

Author of *Beginnings of Literary Culture in the Ohio Valley* (1891).

VERBECK, GUIDO HERMAN FRIDOLIN (*b. Zeist, the Netherlands, 1830; d. Tokyo, Japan, 1898*), Dutch Reformed clergyman. Emigrated to America, 1852. Ordained, 1859, he served thereafter as a missionary and public official in Japan.

VERBECK, WILLIAM (*b. Nagasaki, Japan, 1861; d. 1930*), educator, inventor, New York State militia officer. Son of Guido H. F. Verbeck. Headmaster, St. John's School, Manlius, N.Y., *post* 1888; pioneer in the Boy Scout movement.

VERBRUGGHEN, HENRI (*b. Brussels, Belgium, 1873; d. Northfield, Minn., 1934*), violinist, conductor. Director of the Minneapolis Symphony Orchestra, 1922–32.

VERENDRYE, PIERRE GAULTIER DE VARENNES, Sieur de la. [See LA VERENDRYE, PIERRE GAULTIER DE VARENNES, SIEUR DE, 1685–1749.]

VERHAEGEN, PETER JOSEPH (*b. Haecht, Flanders, 1800; d. St. Charles, Mo., 1868*), Roman Catholic clergyman, Jesuit. Came to America, 1821, to enter novitiate at Whitemarsh, Md. Accompanied band of Jesuits led by Charles Van Quickenborne to Missouri, 1823. Ordained, 1825, he became rector of the present St. Louis University, 1829. Named superior of the Indian missions, 1836; became provincial of the Maryland Province of the Society of Jesus, 1844. President of St. Joseph's College, Bardstown, Ky., 1847–50. Thereafter a pastor at St. Charles, Mo.

VERMILYE, KATE JORDAN. [See JORDAN, KATE, 1862–1926.]

VERNON, SAMUEL (*b. Narragansett, R.I., 1683; d. 1737*), silversmith. Cousin of Edward Winslow (1669–1753). Produced work notable for craftsmanship, novelty and variety of design at his shop in Newport, R.I.; engraved first Rhode Island bank bills. Served as a Rhode Island legislator and judge *post* 1729.

VERNON, WILLIAM (*b. Newport, R.I., 1719; d. 1806*), merchant. Son of Samuel Vernon. Active in the "triangular trade" out of Newport and in privateering. Performed invaluable work for the infant American Navy as a member of the so-called Eastern Navy Board during the Revolution.

VEROT, JEAN MARCEL PIERRE AUGUSTE (*b. Le Puy, France, 1805; d. St. Augustine, Fla., 1876*), Roman Catholic clergyman, Sulpician. Came to Maryland, 1830. A teacher at St. Mary's Seminary and a pastor in Maryland, he was named vicar-apostolic of Florida *c.* 1858. Identified with the cause of the Confederacy during the Civil War, he was transferred to the see of Savannah, Ga., 1861, with Florida continued under his care. Active after the war in restoration of his diocese, he disinterestedly returned to Florida, 1870, becoming bishop of St. Augustine when it was made a see.

VERPLANCK, GULIAN CROMMELIN (*b. New York, N.Y., 1786; d. New York, 1870*), lawyer, New York legislator, author. Grandson of William Samuel Johnson. Graduated Columbia, 1801; studied law with Josiah O. Hoffman. Practicing in New York City *post* 1807, he organized (with Isaac Sebring and Richard Varick) the Washington Benevolent Society as a Federalist answer to the Tammany Society. A principal with Hugh Maxwell in the Columbia College commencement riot of 1811, Verplanck became an enemy of De Witt Clinton who had presided over his trial and conviction. Among the products of the pamphlet war in which both men engaged, Verplanck was responsible for *A Fable for Statesmen and Politicians* (1815) and *The State Triumvirate* (1819). A professor in the General Theological Seminary, New York City, 1821–24, he was author of *Essays on the Nature and Uses of the Various Evidences of Revealed Religion* (1824), one of the earliest American works influenced by the Scottish school of common-sense philosophy. Congressman, Democrat, from New York, 1825–33, he was chairman of the ways and means committee, 1831–33, and was chiefly instrumental in obtaining the 1831 law improving authors' copyrights. Becoming estranged from the Democrats, he lost in a run as Whig candidate for mayor of New York City, 1834. As a state senator, 1838–41, he outlined plans for reform of the judiciary system which had effect in the state constitutional changes of 1846 and 1868. Editor of a scholarly edition of Shakespeare's plays (1847), he was editor also of the *Talisman* (in association with Robert C. Sands and William Cullen Bryant, 1828–30). Some of his thoughtful and learned essays were collected in *Discourses and Addresses on Subjects of American History, etc.* (1833).

VERRILL, ADDISON EMERY (*b. Greenwood, Maine, 1839; d. Santa Barbara, Calif., 1926*), zoölogist. B.S., Lawrence Scientific School, Harvard, 1862. While an undergraduate, assisted J. R. L. Agassiz, Alpheus Hyatt and N. S. Shaler. Taught zoölogy at Yale, 1864–1907; taught also in the Sheffield Scientific School, and at University of Wisconsin (1868–70). Wide-ranging in his interests and investigations, he performed the greater part of his work in study of marine invertebrates. A patient, painstaking investigator, he held firmly to a belief in the value of taxonomical work as a basis for scientific investigations. Among his many collateral activities were work (1871–87) with the U.S. Commission of Fish and Fisheries, the curatorship of the Peabody Museum at Yale, and an editorship of the *American Journal of Science* (1869–1920).

VERWYST, CHRYSOSTOM ADRIAN (*b. Uden, the Netherlands, 1841; d. Bayfield, Wis., 1925*), Roman Catholic clergyman, Franciscan, Indian linguist. Came to America as a boy; was raised in Wisconsin. Ordained, 1865. He served as a missionary in the Lake Superior region for many years and was an authority on the language of the Chippewas.

VERY, JONES (*b. Salem, Mass., 1813; d. Salem, 1880*), poet, transcendentalist. Graduated Harvard, 1836. Encouraged by Elizabeth P. Peabody and R. W. Emerson, Very produced a number of sonnets (first published in the *Western Messenger*, March–April 1839; later published in *Essays and Poems*, 1839) which received wide contemporary praise and were distinguished by sincere religious emotion.

VERY, LYDIA LOUISA ANN (*b. Salem, Mass., 1823; d. Salem, 1901*), teacher, poet. Sister of Jones Very. Author, among other works, of *Poems* (1856) and *An Old-fashioned Garden* (1900).

VESEY, DENMARK (*b. c. 1767; d. Charleston, S.C., 1822*), rebel. Purchasing his freedom in 1800, Vesey (a mulatto) prospered as a carpenter in Charleston. Between the years 1818–22 he laid the foundation for an uprising of Negro slaves against their masters by allegedly religious work in the local African Methodist congregation. Identifying the Negroes with the Israelites, he interpreted the debate over the Missouri Compromise to mean that Negroes were being held by their masters in defiance of law. He carried his message to the plantations from the Santee to the Euhaws. His conspiracy was betrayed to the city authorities in June 1822, and he was tried, convicted on the testimony of informers and hanged. The true extent of his conspiracy will never be known for he and his aides died without making any revelations.

VESEY, TÉLÉMAQUE. [See VESEY, DENMARK, *c.* 1767–1822.]

VESEY, WILLIAM (*b. Braintree, Mass., 1674; d. New York, N.Y., 1746*), Anglican clergyman. Graduated Harvard, 1693. Ordained by the bishop of London, 1697, he served thereafter with great ability as rector of Trinity Church, New York City, until his death. An extreme conservative, he engaged in many controversies with the royal governors over the rights vested in Trinity and its rector.

VEST, GEORGE GRAHAM (*b. Frankfort, Ky., 1830; d. Sweet Springs, Mo., 1904*), lawyer, Missouri legislator. Removed to Missouri, 1854. Elected to the Missouri legislature, 1860, he was author of the "Vest Resolutions" denouncing coercion of the South, and was probably the author of the "Ordinance of Secession" adopted by the Southern wing of the legislature at Neosho, fall of 1861. A member of the Confederate Congress, 1862–65, he resumed practice of law in Missouri after the Civil War. His career as U.S. senator, Democrat, from Missouri, 1879–1903, was characterized by a disinclination to recognize new developments and new issues in American life, and by outstanding opposition to high protective tariffs. He was a leading exponent of the theory that it was unconstitutional for the United States to hold and govern Spanish territory permanently as colonies after cession *post* 1898.

VETCH, SAMUEL (*b. Edinburgh, Scotland, 1668; d. England, 1732*), colonial soldier, trader. Emigrating to Central America, 1698, as captain in the military force accompanying the Scotch colony at Darien, he came to New York in 1699 after the failure of the venture. Marrying the daughter of Robert Livingston, 1700, Vetch engaged in the Indian trade out of Albany, N.Y. He moved to Boston, *c.* 1702, where he traded with Acadia and Canada and was tried and fined in 1706 by the General Court for furnishing arms and ammunition to the French and Indians. Appealing the case in England, he won favor by suggesting to the authorities there a plan for conquering the French in America. In it he proposed an attack on Montreal by way of Lake Champlain and a complete investment of Quebec by land and sea. Dispatched by the Whig ministry in March 1709 to carry out this enterprise, Vetch was given powers to enlist colonial assistance from Pennsylvania northward and was accompanied by Francis Nicholson as a volunteer assistant. Mustering three New England regiments at Boston while at the same time Nicholson prepared a force with boats to proceed up Lake Champlain, Vetch was ready to execute his plan early in the summer but an expected British auxiliary force failed to appear and the scheme was dropped. On the arrival of British aid late in 1710, however, Nicholson was able to make an easy conquest of Port Royal and Acadia, and Vetch was appointed military governor of Annapolis Royal and Nova Scotia. Taking a part in the 1711 expedition against Canada, he shared in the disaster which befell the English forces at the mouth of the St. Lawrence River. Pursued by the enmity of Nicholson, who was civil governor of Nova Scotia, Vetch fled to England in 1714. He succeeded in displacing Nicholson in January 1715 only to lose his place two years later. After further misfortunes he died in debtor's prison.

VETHAKE, HENRY (*b. British Guiana, 1792; d. Philadelphia, Pa., 1866*), economist. Came to America as a boy. Graduated Columbia, 1808. Taught mathematics and philosophy at a number of institutions; was a professor and an official at the University of Pennsylvania, 1836–59. An orthodox classical economist, he opposed practically every form of governmental interference in economic life, also trade unions and statutory shortening of hours of labor. Author of *The Principles of Political Economy* (1838, 1844).

VEZIN, HERMANN (*b. Philadelphia, Pa., 1829; d. London, England, 1910*), actor. Made debut at the Theatre Royal, York, England, 1850, and remained active on the British stage until his death. Scholarly and intellectual in his impersonations, he had a somewhat formal manner of delivery.

VIBBARD, CHAUNCEY (*b. Galway, N.Y., 1811; d. Macon, Ga., 1891*), railroad executive, capitalist. Rose to post of general superintendent of the Utica & Schenectady Railroad, 1836–49; prepared the first railroad timetable ever followed in New York State; increased the comfort of passenger travel and was an innovator in use of safety appliances. Urged Erastus Corning to take the lead in creating the consolidation of small lines which was known as the New York Central, of which Vibbard was general superintendent, 1853–65. After Civil War service in Congress and as a railroad expert, he devoted his time to various private business interests.

VICK, JAMES (*b. Chichester, England, 1818; d. Rochester, N.Y., 1882*), printer, seedsman, publisher. Emigrated to America, 1833; settled in Rochester, N.Y., 1837, where he edited the *Genesee Farmer* and the *Rural New Yorker*. An importer and producer of seeds for his own amusement *post* 1848, he began to sell them by mail. He made this activity his principal business *post* 1862. As a merchant of flower seeds and as publisher of an annual catalogue and also a magazine, Vick exercised great influence on the horticulture of the United States. Among the products of his crossbreeding were the white double phlox, the fringed petunia, white gladiolus and others.

VICTOR, FRANCES FULLER (*b. Oneida Co., N.Y., 1826; d. Portland, Oreg., 1902*), author. Sister-in-law of Orville J. Victor. Removed to Oregon, 1865, where she became the most competent authority on the region of the Pacific Northwest and its history. She was a member for a number of years of H. H. Bancroft's staff and wrote a great part of the histories of Oregon, Washington, Idaho, Montana, Nevada, Colorado and Wyoming which appeared over his name. She was author also of Volumes VI and VII of the *History of California* (1890).

VICTOR, ORVILLE JAMES (*b. Sandusky, O., 1827; d. Hohokus, N.J., 1910*), author, publisher. Married Metta Victoria Fuller, sister of Frances F. Victor, 1856, and was thereafter associated with a number of New York publishing houses specializing in the production of cheap popular books and magazines. For many years he was chief editor of the enterprises of Erastus F. Beadle and is regarded as the editorial projector of the American dime novel (1860).

VIEL, FRANÇOIS ÉTIENNE BERNARD ALEXANDRE (*b. New Orleans, La., 1736; d. France, 1821*), Roman Catholic clergyman, Oratorian. Educated in France, Viel was the first native-born Louisianian to take holy orders and taught for many years at the Academy of Juilly. A parish priest in Louisiana, 1792–1812, he returned to France to aid in the reestablishment of the Oratorians. He was a classical Latin scholar of the highest distinction, and a poet.

VIELE, AERNOUT CORNELISSEN (*b. New Amsterdam, 1640; d. c. 1704*), trader, Indian interpreter and negotiator. Skilled in Indian languages and oratory, Viele was highly effective as a diplomat to the

Iroquois and other tribes *post* 1680. He helped extend the New York colony's trade into the country north of the Great Lakes and to the southwest.

VIELE, EGBERT LUDOVICUS (*b. Waterford, N.Y., 1825; d. 1902*), soldier, engineer. Graduated West Point, 1847; served in the Mexican War and on the southwest frontier. Resigning his commission, 1853, he worked as a civil engineer in New York City, and was chief engineer of the New York Central Park, 1856–57; in 1860 he was engineer of Prospect Park, Brooklyn. After Civil War service with the Union Army as brigadier-general of volunteers, 1861–63, he resumed engineering practice in New York. He made a plan for the "Arcade" railway, a precursor of the later subways, *c.* 1868, and was author of a *Topographical Atlas of the City of New York* (1874). One of his sons was educated in France and attained distinction there as a poet under the name Francis Vielé-Griffin.

VIGNAUD, HENRY (*b. New Orleans, La., 1830; d. near Paris, France, 1922*), journalist, diplomat, historian. Taken prisoner while serving as a Confederate soldier, 1862, he escaped to Paris and never returned to the United States. After working with the Confederate mission to France under John Slidell, and service for a number of years in various occupations, he was appointed second secretary of the U.S. legation in Paris, 1875. He was promoted to first secretary, 1885. Until his retirement in 1909 he was an indispensable member of the Paris mission. He was distinguished also for his researches into the career of Columbus and for studies of aboriginal America and of the earliest European contacts with America.

VIGO, JOSEPH MARIA FRANCESCO (*b. Mondovì, Piedmont, Italy, 1747; d. Vincennes, Ind., 1836*), soldier, merchant. Came to Louisiana in youth as a member of a Spanish regiment; prospered in the fur trade and gained influence with French settlers and Indians. Established headquarters at St. Louis, 1772. Shares credit with George Rogers Clark for conquest of the Northwest in 1778–79, because of information, personal influence, and financial aid which he put at Clark's disposal.

VILAS, WILLIAM FREEMAN (*b. Chelsea, Vt., 1840; d. 1908*), lawyer, statesman. Raised in Madison, Wis., where he was admitted to the bar, 1860; won professional distinction as a law teacher and official of University of Wisconsin and as reviser of the state statutes. A leader in the Democratic party and a counselor and friend of Grover Cleveland, Vilas served as postmaster-general, March 1885—January 1888, and as U.S. secretary of the interior, January 1888—March 1889. U.S. senator from Wisconsin, 1891–97, he retired to private life in Madison and was active thereafter in rebuilding the University of Wisconsin.

VILLAGRÁ, GASPAR PÉREZ de (*b. Puebla de los Angeles, Spain, c. 1555; d. at sea, en route to Guatemala, 1620*), Spanish soldier and colonial official. An officer in Juan de Oñate's expedition to New Mexico, 1598, he served subsequently at various times in New Mexico until *c.* 1608. Villagrá was author of *Historia de la Nueva Mexico* (Alcalá de Henares, 1610), an epic poem which lauds Oñate's achievements in 1598–99. It has the distinction of being the first published history of any American commonwealth.

VILLARD, FANNY GARRISON. [See VILLARD, HELEN FRANCES GARRISON, 1844–1928.]

VILLARD, HELEN FRANCES GARRISON (*b. Boston, Mass., 1844; d. Dobbs Ferry, N.Y., 1928*), reformer. Daughter of William L. Garrison; wife of Henry Villard. Among the many philanthropies and social reforms to which Mrs. Villard lent her services were woman suffrage, pacifism, and the work of the National Association for the Advancement of Colored People.

VILLARD, HENRY (*b. Speyer, Rhenish Bavaria, 1835; d. Dobbs Ferry, N.Y., 1900*), journalist, railway promoter, financier. Educated in Germany, Villard changed his name from Ferdinand H. G. Hilgard before emigrating to America, 1853; this move was dictated by disagreement with his father over the younger man's republican sympathies. Settling eventually in Illinois, he studied English and, as a special correspondent for the New York *Staats-Zeitung*, reported the Lincoln-Douglas debates and made the acquaintance of Abraham Lincoln. Becoming correspondent for the *Cincinnati Commercial*, he covered the Pike's Peak gold rush, and later the Republican convention at Chicago, 1860. After Lincoln's election he became correspondent at Springfield, Ill., for the *New York Herald*.

A Civil War correspondent for the *Herald* and also the *New York Tribune*, 1861–63, he organized a news agency to compete with the New York Associated Press, 1864. Secretary of the American Social Science Association, 1868–71, he then traveled abroad to restore his health. Becoming a member of a committee of bondholders of the Oregon & California Railroad in Germany, 1873, he went to Oregon in 1874 as their representative, and there perfected a plan for efficient operation of that railroad and other local transportation agencies. He became president of the Oregon & California, and of the Oregon Steamship Co., 1876. Named the receiver of the Kansas Pacific Railway, 1876, he achieved an important financial success and laid the foundation of his later fortune. With the idea of building a railway empire in the Far Northwest, he organized with associates the Oregon Railway & Navigation Co., 1879, and built a road eastward from Portland, Oreg., along the south bank of the Columbia River. His plan was to make this line the Pacific Coast outlet for any Northern transcontinental road which might be built, so concentrating the trade of the Northwest in Portland. Clashing with the Northern Pacific, whose objective was an outlet on Puget Sound, Villard with his supporters bought a controlling interest in the Northern Pacific. He was made president, 1881, and completed its line in 1883. His control of transportation in the Northwest did not last long, as a huge deficit forced Villard's resignation from the presidency early in 1884. In 1893 he ended his connections with Northwest transportation. Meanwhile, however, he had helped found the Edison General Electric Co. and had acquired a controlling interest in the New York *Evening Post*. The most important railway promoter in the United States between 1879 and 1883, Villard displayed fairness and breadth of view in dealing with the people of the region which his railroad served. As a newspaper proprietor, he permitted complete independence of policy to such editors as Horace White, E. L. Godkin and Carl Schurz.

VILLERÉ, JACQUES PHILIPPE (*b. near New Orleans, La., 1761; d. 1830*), planter. An efficient and conscientious governor of Louisiana, 1816–20, he was the first Creole to hold that position.

VINCENNES, FRANÇOIS MARIE BISSOT, Sieur de (*b. Montreal, Canada, 1700; d. on headwaters of Tombigbee River, present Mississippi, 1736*), French colonial soldier and official. Son of Jean B. B. de Vincennes. At request of the governor of Louisiana, Vincennes built a fort in 1731 or 1732 on the site of the Indiana city that now bears his name.

VINCENNES, JEAN BAPTISTE BISSOT, Sieur de (*b. Canada, 1668; d. site of present Ft. Wayne, Ind., 1719*), French colonial soldier, explorer. Father of François M. B. de Vincennes. Commanded among the Miami Indians, 1696; accompanied Henry de Tonty to the West, 1698. Principal factor in keeping the Miamis loyal to France.

VINCENT, FRANK (*b. Brooklyn, N.Y., 1848; d. Woodstock, N.Y., 1916*), world traveler, collector of Orientalia. Author, among other works, of *The Land of the White Elephant* (1874).

VINCENT, JOHN HEYL (*b. Tuscaloosa, Ala., 1832; d. 1920*), Methodist clergyman and bishop, educational leader. Introduced uniform Sunday School lessons in Chicago, Ill., 1864, an innovation later followed in Protestant Sunday Schools throughout the world. Founded (1874) a national training institute for Sunday School teachers at Lake Chautauqua, N.Y., in association with Lewis Miller; out of this developed the so-called Chautauqua movement for popular education. Vincent's plan of prescribed readings over a four-year term mark the beginning of directed home study and correspondence schools in America. A tolerant man, widely read, Bishop Vincent became the advocate of an intellectual and spiritual evangelism which relied on education rather than emotion.

VINCENT, MARVIN RICHARDSON (*b. Poughkeepsie, N.Y., 1834; d. Forest Hills, N.Y., 1922*), Methodist and Presbyterian clergyman. Graduated Columbia, 1854. Professor of sacred literature, Union Theological Seminary, New York, 1887–1916. Author, among other works, of *Word Studies in the New Testament* (1887–1900).

VINCENT, MARY ANN (*b. Portsmouth, England, 1818; d. Boston, Mass., 1887*), actress. Made American debut at Boston, November 1846. As a member of the stock company of the Boston Museum *post* 1852, Mrs. Vincent became its leading comedienne and later its leading old lady. A Boston institution, she is commemorated by a hospital founded there in her memory and by the Vincent Club which raises funds for the hospital's support by annual amateur theatricals.

VINTON, ALEXANDER HAMILTON (*b. Providence, R.I., 1807; d. Philadelphia, Pa., 1881*), Episcopal clergyman, physician. Brother of Francis Vinton. M.D., Yale, 1828. A rector in Boston, Philadelphia and New York, he was prominent in the evangelical group of his church and ranked among its leading preachers.

VINTON, FRANCIS (*b. Providence, R.I., 1809; d. Brooklyn, N.Y., 1872*), soldier, Episcopal clergyman. Brother of Alexander H. Vinton. Graduated West Point, 1830. Resigning from the army, 1836, he was ordained deacon, 1838, and advanced to priest, 1839. An ardent evangelical and a fluent preacher, he ministered with zeal and success in several Rhode Island parishes and also in Brooklyn, N.Y., and at Trinity Church, New York City. He was professor of canon law in the General Theological Seminary, New York, 1869–72.

VINTON, FRANCIS LAURENS (*b. Fort Preble, Portland Harbor, Maine, 1835; d. Leadville, Colo., 1879*), Union soldier, mining engineer. Nephew of Alexander H. and Francis Vinton. Graduated West Point, 1856; studied at École des Mines, Paris, France, 1856–60. Rising to brigade command in the Civil War, he received disabling wounds in the battle of Fredericksburg. First professor of civil and mining engineering at Columbia School of Mines, 1864–77, he was thereafter a consulting engineer in Colorado.

VINTON, FREDERIC (*b. Boston, Mass., 1817; d. 1890*), librarian. Graduated Amherst, 1837. As assistant librarian, Boston Public Library, 1856–65, he aided in preparation of its printed catalogues; as first assistant librarian, Library of Congress, 1865–73, he continued his specialization in catalogue work. First full-time librarian of the College of New Jersey (Princeton), 1873–90, he produced for it a subject catalogue in 1884 which was considered one of the most scholarly and useful publications of the sort up to that time. He was one of the founders of the American Library Association, 1876.

VINTON, FREDERIC PORTER (*b. Bangor, Maine, 1846; d. Boston, Mass., 1911*), portrait painter. Encouraged by William M. Hunt. Studied drawing at Lowell Institute; studied also in Paris under Léon Bonnat and J. P. Laurens. Practiced his art with great success in Boston *post* 1878, specializing in portraits of men.

VINTON, SAMUEL FINLEY (*b. South Hadley, Mass., 1792; d. Washington, D.C., 1862*), lawyer. Began practice in Gallipolis, O., c. 1816. Congressman, National Republican and Whig, from Ohio, 1823–37, 1843–51, he was at various times a member of committees on public lands, roads, canals and the judiciary; he was chairman of the ways and means committee during the war with Mexico. Vinton was especially interested in the survey and sale of public lands so as to prevent speculation; also in internal improvements, in the imposition of a protective tariff and the proper apportionment of representatives. He opposed the annexation of Texas and any direct tax for prosecution of the war with Mexico. He reported out the bill providing for establishment of the U.S. Department of the Interior, February 1849.

VISSCHER, WILLIAM LIGHTFOOT (*b. Owingsville, Ky., 1842; d. Chicago, Ill., 1924*), journalist, actor. Starting in journalism as secretary to George D. Prentice, he served, 1875–95, as editorial writer for some of the most important Western newspapers and was author of much journalistic verse.

VITALE, FERRUCCIO (*b. Florence, Italy, 1875; d. 1933*), landscape architect. Came first to America as military attaché to the Italian embassy, 1898. After resignation from the army and study of landscape architecture, he practiced that profession in New York City *post* 1904. Designer of many private estates, towns and suburbs, he worked to strengthen the position of his profession as one of the fine arts.

VIZCAÍNO, SEBASTIÁN (*b. Spain, c. 1550; d. c. 1628*), merchant, explorer. Went to Mexico c. 1585. Engaged in the China trade, he lost a good part of his fortune when the galleon *Santa Ana* was destroyed off Lower California, 1587. Commissioned by the viceroy of New Spain, he sailed from Acapulco in June 1596 for an exploration of the Gulf of California. This expedition was fruitless, but a voyage undertaken in 1602 to explore the outer coast of California as far as Cape Mendocino was more successful. Leaving Acapulco on May 5, 1602, Vizcaíno explored the coast of Lower California and reached San Diego Bay in November; in mid-December he discovered Monterey Bay. He reached Cape Mendocino on Jan. 12, 1603, missing San Francisco Bay in the bad weather. Returning southward he arrived at Mazatlán, Feb. 18, 1603. This expedition, the first to make a scientific exploration of the west coast, furnished the first maps of that coast and did much to explode the myth of the Northwest Passage.

VIZETELLY, FRANK HORACE (*b. London, England, 1864; d. New York, N.Y., 1938*), lexicographer, etymologist. Member of a family which had been engaged in the printing trades and journalism in England ever since 1725, he came to New York City, 1891, and was associated with the staff of Funk & Wagnalls thereafter until his death. His principal work was done on the various editions of the *Standard Dictionary of the English Language*. He was author also of a column in the *Literary Digest* which dealt with the complications of grammar, usage and word derivations, and provided the materials for nearly a dozen books on these subjects. [*Supp.* 2]

VLADECK, BARUCH CHARNEY (*b. near Minsk, Russia, 1886; d. New York, N.Y., 1938*), Socialist and Jewish leader. Coming to America, 1908, he undertook lecture tours for three years and became manager of the Philadelphia edition of the New York *Jewish Daily Forward* in 1912. A leader in the American Socialist party, he became the *Forward's* city editor, 1916, and moved to New York. An opponent of the Communist wing of the Socialist party *post* 1919, he was associated in party affairs with Louis Waldman. Appointed a member of the New York City Housing Authority, 1934, he began, after election to the city council, one of the first municipal slum-clearance projects in the United States. Vladeck's career is interesting as an example of the transformations wrought by American institutions on a European-shaped radicalism. [*Supp.* 2]

VOGRICH, MAX WILHELM KARL (*b. Hermannstadt, Transylvania, 1852; d. New York, N.Y., 1916*), pianist, composer. Came to America, 1878. Toured the country as accompanist to August Wilhelmj and was also associated with Eduard Reményi. A resident in New York, 1886–1902 and 1914–16, he composed much music in various forms and was an adviser to the publishing firm of G. Schirmer.

VOLCK, ADALBERT JOHN (*b. Augsburg, Bavaria, 1828; d. Baltimore, Md., 1912*), dentist, caricaturist. Emigrated to America, 1849. A graduate of the Baltimore College of Dental Surgery, 1852, he practiced with success in Baltimore, but is principally remembered as author of a series of caricatures favorable to the South under the pseudonym "V. Blada." The most important collection of his work is *Confederate War Etchings* (n.d.) and *Sketches from the Civil War in North America* (1863, bearing a possibly false London imprint).

VOLK, LEONARD WELLS (*b. Wellstown, present Wells, N.Y., 1828; d. Osceola, Wis., 1895*), sculptor. Removed to St. Louis, Mo., 1848, where he taught himself drawing and modeling. Aided by Stephen A. Douglas, he studied in Rome, Italy, 1855–57, and thereafter practiced his art in Chicago, Ill. He organized the first art exhibition held there (1859) and was a founder of the Chicago Academy of Design, 1867. He produced the colossal Douglas monument at Chicago, statues of Lincoln and Douglas in the Illinois State Capitol, and other portraits of Lincoln which are valuable historic mementos. His talent lay in faithful portraiture.

VON HOLST, HERMANN EDUARD. [See HOLST, HERMANN EDUARD VON, 1841–1904.]

VON MOSCHZISKER, ROBERT (*b. Philadelphia, Pa., 1870; d. Philadelphia, 1939*), jurist. Admitted to the Philadelphia bar, 1896, he won reputation as an assistant district attorney, and as judge of the court of common pleas in Philadelphia Co., 1903–09. Elected an associate justice of the Pennsylvania supreme court, 1909, he became chief justice in 1921 and resigned in 1930. [*Supp. 2*]

VONNOH, ROBERT WILLIAM (*b. Hartford, Conn., 1858; d. Nice, France, 1933*), portrait and landscape painter. An able and conscientious craftsman, he was a teacher, among others, of W. J. Glackens and Maxfield Parrish.

VON RUCK, KARL (*b. Constantinople, Turkey, 1849; d. 1922*), physician. M.D., University of Tübingen, 1877; M.D., University of Michigan, 1879. After practice at Norwalk, O., he began a specialization in tuberculosis and founded the Winyah Sanitorium, Asheville, N.C., 1888. By long laboratory research and clinical application, he produced (1912) an anti-tuberculosis vaccine which was widely used in treatment of the disease, although designed primarily for the protective immunization of those exposed to tuberculous infection. Though he was in constant controversy with his fellow-workers in the field, his work and many of his ideas have received general acceptance.

VON TEUFFEL, BLANCHE WILLIS HOWARD. [See HOWARD, BLANCHE WILLIS, 1847–1898.]

VOORHEES, DANIEL WOLSEY (*b. Butler Co., O., 1827; d. Washington, D.C., 1897*), lawyer. Raised in Indiana, he settled in practice at Terre Haute, 1857. Opposed equally to abolition and secession, he served as congressman, Democrat, from Indiana, 1861–66, and was a virulent critic of administration policies. After a second term in the House of Representatives, 1869–73, he was U.S. senator from Indiana, 1877–97. At first a typical Democrat of his era in his ideas, he became less strictly agrarian and supported President Grover Cleveland in the various questions that divided the Democratic party during Cleveland's terms. As chairman of the committee on finance, he led the fight for repeal of the Sherman silver purchase act, 1893. He was unrivaled as a stump speaker.

VOORHEES, EDWARD BURNETT (*b. Minebrook, N.J., 1856; d. 1911*), agriculturist. Graduated Rutgers, 1881. Assistant chemist of the New Jersey State Experiment Station, 1883–88, at which time he became chief chemist. Professor of agriculture at Rutgers, 1890–1911. Director, New Jersey Experiment Station *post* 1893. Founded short agricultural courses for working farmers. Author of *Fertilizers* (1898) and many other works.

VOORHEES, PHILIP FALKERSON (*b. New Brunswick, N.J., 1792; d. Annapolis, Md., 1862*), naval officer. Appointed midshipman, 1809. While commanding frigate *Congress*, September 1844, as reprisal for Argentine attacks on an American brig, he captured the entire Argentine squadron which was blockading Montevideo. Court-martialed for his action, June 1845, he was at first suspended from duty but was reinstated by President Polk in 1849.

VOORSANGER, JACOB (*b. Amsterdam, the Netherlands, 1852; d. San Francisco, Calif., 1908*), rabbi. Came to America, 1873. After occupying several pulpits in the East and in Texas, he served at Temple Emanu-El, San Francisco, *post* 1886. He was professor of Semitic languages and literature, University of California *post* 1894. A moderate member of the reform school of Judaism, he was a gifted journalist and in time was considered the foremost rabbi on the Pacific Coast. He was chairman of relief during the San Francisco earthquake and fire of 1906.

VOPICKA, CHARLES JOSEPH (*b. Dolni Hbity (Bohemia), Austria-Hungary, 1857; d. Chicago, Ill., 1935*), brewer, diplomat. A leader among the Czechs in Chicago, he was active in civic matters there. He served as U.S. minister to Rumania, Serbia and Bulgaria, 1913–20, representing the interests of many of the warring nations as well as those of the United States, and strongly concerning himself with the welfare of prisoners of war. [*Supp. 1*]

VOSE, GEORGE LEONARD (*b. Augusta, Maine, 1831; d. Brunswick, Maine, 1910*), engineer, specialist in railroads. Professor of civil engineering, Bowdoin, 1872–81; Massachusetts Institute of Technology, 1881–86. Author of *Handbook of Railroad Construction* (1857), *Manual for Railroad Engineers and Engineering Students* (1873) and a number of other useful works.

VOUGHT, CHANCE MILTON (*b. New York, N.Y., 1890; d. Southampton, N.Y., 1930*), aircraft designer and manufacturer. Studied engineering at Pratt Institute, New York University and University of Pennsylvania. Learned to fly *c.* 1910 under instruction of the Wright brothers. Designed and built an advanced training plane for the British in World War I, 1914. As chief engineer of the Wright Company, he produced the Model V military biplane, 1916. Forming his own company, 1917, he made it in very short time an outstanding factor in the aircraft industry, developing new designs practically alone and directing their realization in the shop. Among his designs were the Vought VE-7 (1919), the Vought UO-1 (1922–25) and the Vought O2U Corsair. Vought worked above all for tactical flexibility in naval aircraft and maintained unsurpassed standards of workmanship. He merged his firm in the United Aircraft & Transport Corp., 1929, but continued to head the Chance Vought unit until his death.

VROOM, PETER DUMONT (*b. Somerset Co., N.J., 1791; d. Trenton, N.J., 1873*), lawyer, New Jersey legislator. Graduated Columbia, 1808. Democratic governor and chancellor of New Jersey, 1829–32, 1833–36; congressman, 1839–41. U.S. minister to Prussia, 1854–57. An opponent of secession, he was a member of the futile peace conference which met at Washington, February 1861. He was reporter of the New Jersey supreme court, 1865–73.

WABASHA (*b. probably near present Winona, Minn., c. 1773; d. c. 1855*), Mdewakanton Sioux chief. First prominent through conferences with Zebulon M. Pike on upper Mississippi, 1805; was conspicuous at council at Prairie du Chien, August 1825; supported Americans during Black Hawk War, 1832. A wise, honorable and prudent chief, Wabasha won general respect and was a skillful orator.

WACHSMUTH, CHARLES (*b. Hanover, Germany, 1829; d. probably Burlington, Iowa, 1896*), paleontologist. Came to America, 1852; settled in Burlington, Iowa, c. 1854. Prospering in the grocery business, he retired in 1865 and devoted his time to collecting and studying fossils. After a brief period of work with Louis Agassiz in Cambridge, Mass., he returned to Burlington and worked in a general partnership with Frank Springer *post* 1873. Attempting a personal critical examination of all the collections of crinoids throughout the world, Wachsmuth and Springer continued work until the former's death when it was carried on alone by Springer. They were authors of *North American Crinoidea Camerata* (1897) and a number of other memoirs.

WACKER, CHARLES HENRY (*b. Chicago, Ill., 1856; d. 1929*), brewer, real estate operator, city planner. Chairman of the Chicago Plan Commission, 1909–26, he was a principal factor in the improvement and beautification of that city.

WADDEL, JAMES (*b. Newry, Ireland, 1739; d. near Gordonsville, Va., 1805*), Presbyterian clergyman. Emigrated to southeast Pennsylvania as an infant; was educated in Samuel Finley's "Log College." Pastor in Northumberland and Lancaster counties, Va., 1762–77; pastor of congregations at Tinkling Spring and Staunton, Va., 1777–85. Established a number of churches in Orange, Louisa and Albemarle counties.

WADDEL, JOHN NEWTON (*b. Willington, S.C., 1812; d. Birmingham, Ala., 1895*), Presbyterian clergyman, educator. Son of Moses Waddel. Graduated present University of Georgia, 1829. Removed to Alabama, 1837, and thence to Mississippi where he established Montrose Academy, 1842, and took a leading part in founding University of Mississippi at Oxford. A teacher at the University of Mississippi and pastor, 1848–57, he served as teacher and president at the Presbyterian College, La Grange, Tenn., until the Civil War when he became a chaplain in the Confederate Army. A leader in organization of the Southern Presbyterian Church, 1861, he held numerous high official positions in that church. Chancellor of University of Mississippi, 1865–74; of Southwestern Presbyterian University, 1879–88.

WADDEL, MOSES (*b. present Iredell Co., N.C., 1770; d. Athens, Ga., 1840*), Presbyterian clergyman, teacher. Father of John N. Waddel. Educated by James Hall; graduated Hampden-Sydney, 1791. Conducted schools in Columbia Co., Ga., and Willington, S.C., where he educated among others John C. Calhoun, William H. Crawford, Hugh S. Legaré, George McDuffie, A. B. Longstreet and James L. Petigru. President of Franklin College (present University of Georgia), 1819–29.

WADDELL, ALFRED MOORE (*b. Hillsboro, N.C., 1834; d. 1912*), lawyer, Confederate soldier. A moderate conservative and an opponent of post-Civil War sectionalism as congressman, Democrat, from North Carolina, 1871–79. He was a leading citizen of Wilmington, N.C., and its mayor, 1899–1905.

WADDELL, HUGH (*b. Lisburn, Ireland, c. 1734; d. 1773*), North Carolina colonial soldier and legislator. Emigrated to North Carolina, 1754, where he became clerk of the council of Gov. Arthur Dobbs. Built and commanded at Fort Dobbs on the Rowan County frontier, 1755–57; served as major commanding three companies in the expedition of John Forbes against Fort Duquesne, 1758; defended Fort Dobbs against Indian attacks, 1760. A principal leader in the colony's defiance of the Stamp Act, he yet remained on good terms with Gov. Tryon and helped pacify the back country during the Regulator troubles, 1771.

WADDELL, JAMES IREDELL (*b. Pittsboro, N.C., 1824; d. Annapolis, Md., 1886*), Confederate naval officer. Great-grandson of Hugh Waddell. Appointed midshipman, 1841, he served with credit during the Mexican War and in routine naval duties until 1862 when he resigned and was commissioned lieutenant in the Confederate Navy. After shore service, 1862–March 1863, he went to Paris, and in October 1864 took command at the Madeira Islands of the Confederate raider *Shenandoah*. Thereafter, until he learned in August 1865 of the Confederate defeat, he made havoc among the New England whaling ships in the Pacific. Fearing treatment as a pirate, he surrendered the *Shenandoah* in Liverpool, England, on November 6, still flying the only Confederate flag that ever sailed round the world.

WADDELL, JOHN ALEXANDER LOW (*b. Port Hope, Ontario, Canada, 1854; d. New York, N.Y., 1938*), civil engineer. Graduated Rensselaer Polytechnic Institute, 1875. After work in Canada as a government draftsman and several years of teaching at Rensselaer, he was professor of civil engineering at the Imperial University of Tokyo, 1882–86. In practice at Kansas City, Mo., 1886–c. 1920, and thereafter in

New York City, he became one of the best-known bridge engineers in the United States, and was designer or consultant on many of the major bridge construction operations in his time. His most important contribution was as originator of the modern vertical-lift bridge. Although European developments anticipated his, Waddell independently invented and successfully introduced the large-scale high-clearance vertical-lift bridge, the first of his many structures of this type being the South Halsted Street Bridge, Chicago, Ill., 1893. [*Supp. 2*]

WADE, BENJAMIN FRANKLIN (*b. near Springfield, Mass., 1800; d. Jefferson, O., 1878*), lawyer, Ohio legislator and jurist. Removed to Andover, O., 1821. Admitted to the Ohio bar *c.* 1827, he attained a successful practice in partnerships with J. R. Giddings and R. P. Ranney. President-judge, third state judicial circuit, 1847–51, he was elected to the U.S. Senate by the Whigs in the Ohio legislature and served, 1851–69. Rough in manner, coarse and vituperative in speech, yet intensely patriotic, he became a leader of the anti-slavery group in Congress, a close cooperator with Simon Cameron and Zachariah Chandler in resisting Southern aggressions. A Republican *post* 1856, he voted against the Crittenden Compromise and on the outbreak of the Civil War became one of the most belligerent men in Congress. A sharp critic of Gen. George B. McClellan, he was one of those who set up the Committee on the Conduct of the War, and as its chairman made it a violently partisan agency. Working closely with the secretary of war, E. M. Stanton, Wade, like other of the Radical Republicans, seemed incapable of understanding President Lincoln and deplored his cautious conservative policies. He himself favored drastic measures against the South, including confiscation of the property of Confederate leaders and the emancipation of their slaves, nor was he burdened with constitutional scruples. Finding Lincoln's policy of Reconstruction (announced in December 1863) particularly obnoxious, he and Henry W. Davis tried to counteract it by the so-called Wade-Davis bill; on its veto by the president in July 1864 they issued the fierce claim of congressional supremacy known as the Wade-Davis Manifesto. Previous to this, Wade had joined with others in planning to replace Lincoln with Salmon P. Chase, yet he supported Lincoln in the closing weeks of the campaign of 1864. At first believing that he and his group could bend President Andrew Johnson to support of their measures, Wade later turned on him and his policies. *Post* December 1865, along with Charles Sumner, Thaddeus Stevens and others, he waged a persistent campaign against Johnson and seemed ready to resort to any extremity in order to carry through the congressional program. Chosen president *pro tempore* of the Senate, March 2, 1867, he would, according to the custom of that time, have succeeded to the presidency in the event of Johnson's removal. In the ensuing impeachment of Johnson, Wade voted for the president's conviction, despite the fact that he was an interested party. He was so expectant of success that he began the selection of his cabinet before the impeachment trial was ended. Thwarted by Johnson's acquittal and failing of re-election to the Senate, Wade resumed the practice of law in Ohio.

WADE, DECIUS SPEAR (*b. near Andover, O., 1835; d. near Andover, 1905*), lawyer. Nephew of Benjamin F. Wade. As chief justice of Montana, 1871–87, he shared in the formulation of the mining and irrigation law of that state and was a member of the commission which drafted the state code adopted by the legislature in 1895.

WADE, JEPTHA HOMER (*b. Romulus, N.Y., 1811; d. 1890*), portrait painter, financier. Organized and built a number of Midwest telegraph lines *post* 1847 which were consolidated with those of Royal E. House, 1854. After a further combination into the Western Union Telegraph Co., 1856, Wade served the new company as general agent, and was president, 1866–67. He was organizer also of the California State Telegraph Co. and the Pacific Telegraph Co. *Post* 1867 he engaged in varied businesses in Cleveland, O.

WADE, JEPTHA HOMER (*b. Cleveland, O., 1857; d. Thomasville, Ga., 1926*), financier, philanthropist. Grandson of Jeptha H. Wade (1811–1890). An incorporator of the Cleveland Museum of Art, 1913, he was its president *post* 1920, and also one of its most liberal benefactors. He was a large contributor to many charities. [*Supp. 1*]

WADE, MARTIN JOSEPH (*b. Burlington, Vt., 1861; d. Los Angeles, Calif., 1931*), Iowa jurist and Democratic congressman. LL.B., University of Iowa, 1886; taught law there. Justice of the state district court, 1893–1902; U.S. district judge, southern district of Iowa, 1915–27.

WADSWORTH, JAMES (*b. Durham, Conn., 1768; d. Geneseo, N.Y., 1844*), landowner, community builder. Graduated Yale, 1787. As agent with his brother for the Phelps-Gorham Purchase in western New York State, James Wadsworth removed to the neighborhood of the Genesee River, 1790, and settled near the present town of Geneseo. Acquiring large quantities of land and prospering both as land agents and agriculturists, the Wadsworths had unequaled influence in the development of the Genesee country. Except for business, James Wadsworth's chief interest was in public education.

WADSWORTH, JAMES SAMUEL (*b. Geneseo, N.Y., 1807; d. Virginia, 1864*), lawyer, landowner. Son of James Wadsworth. Volunteering as an aide to Gen. Irvin McDowell, 1861, he was commissioned brigadier-general of volunteers in August. After two years spent in gaining experience in handling and training men, he took command of the 1st Division, I Corps, December 1862. Highly effective in the Union victory at Gettysburg, Wadsworth was appointed commander of the 4th Division of the V Corps, 1864. He died of wounds received on the second day of the battle of the Wilderness.

WADSWORTH, JEREMIAH (*b. Hartford, Conn., 1743; d. Hartford, 1804*), merchant mariner, Connecticut legislator, Revolutionary soldier. Grandson of Joseph Talcott. Outstanding as commissary-general, at first to the Connecticut forces, and then to the Continental Army, 1778–79, Wadsworth served briefly as a Federalist in Congress where he was a strong advocate of assumption. A man of varied business interests, he was a founder of the Bank of North America, a director of the U.S. Bank, and president of the Bank of New York.

WADSWORTH, PELEG (*b. Duxbury, Mass., 1748; d. Hiram, Maine, 1829*), schoolmaster, farmer, trader, Revolutionary brigadier-general. Grandfather of Henry Wadsworth and Samuel Longfellow. Graduated Harvard, 1769. As engineer officer, 1775, he laid out the American lines at Roxbury and Dorchester Heights during siege of Boston. Briefly aide to Artemas Ward, he then saw service at New York and in 1778 in Rhode Island. He was second-in-command of the ill-fated American attack on Castine, Maine, 1779. Removing to present Portland, Maine, c. 1782, he was a congressman from that district, 1793–1807.

WAGENER, JOHN ANDREAS (*b. Sievern, Hanover, Germany, 1816; d. Walhalla, Oconee Co., S.C., 1876*), businessman, South Carolina legislator, Charleston civic leader. Settled in Charleston, S.C., 1833, where he led in movements for the economic and social improvement of German immigrants to that state.
[*Supp. 1*]

WAGGAMAN, MARY TERESA McKEE (*b. Baltimore, Md., 1846; d. 1931*), writer of fiction, principally for Catholic magazines.

WAGNER, CLINTON (*b. Baltimore, Md., 1837; d. Geneva, Switzerland, 1914*), laryngologist. M.D., University of Maryland, 1859. An outstanding medical officer in the U.S. Army, 1859–69, he was cited for notable services at Gettysburg where he established a field hospital near Little Round Top. Practicing his specialty in New York City *post* 1871, he became known as a surgeon of extraordinary technical skill and a brilliant teacher; he established the Metropolitan Throat Hospital, the first U.S. special hospital of its kind, and was founder of the New York Laryngological Society, 1873. First professor of laryngology at New York Post-Graduate Medical School, he was author of a number of studies, including the pioneer *Habitual Mouth-Breathing* (1881).

WAGNER, WEBSTER (*b. Palatine Bridge, N.Y., 1817; d. Spuyten Duyvil, N.Y., 1882*), carpenter, New York Republican legislator. Designed and operated sleeping-cars and drawing-room cars for operation on the New York Central Railroad *post* 1858; was involved for years in litigation with G. M. Pullman.

WAGNER, WILLIAM (*b. Philadelphia, Pa., 1796; d. Philadelphia, 1885*), merchant, philanthropist. Apprenticed to Stephen Girard; engaged in business on his own account, 1818. Retiring, 1840, he devoted himself to studies in geology and mineralogy and founded the Wagner Free Institute of Science, 1855.

WAHL, WILLIAM HENRY (*b. Philadelphia, Pa., 1848; d. 1909*), scientific journalist, metallurgist. Graduated Dickinson College, 1867; Ph.D., Heidelberg, 1869. Principally distinguished as secretary of the Franklin Institute and as editor *post* 1882 of its *Journal*. The most important of his contributions to science was his discovery and application of aluminum as an energetic oxidizing agent for creation of high temperatures in metallurgical operations, the basis of what is known as the "thermit process."

WAIDNER, CHARLES WILLIAM (*b. near Baltimore, Md., 1873; d. 1922*), physicist. A.B., Johns Hopkins, 1896; Ph.D., 1898. Headed the division of heat and thermometry, National Bureau of Standards, *post* 1901; established standard scale of temperature in collaboration with others. Participated anonymously in many of the important activities of his division.

WAILES, BENJAMIN LEONARD COVINGTON (*b. Columbia Co., Ga., 1797; d. Mississippi, 1862*), surveyor, planter, scientist. Made extensive studies of the plant and animal life and the soil and fossils of Mississippi; supplied information and specimens of the natural history of his region to many individual scientists and to institutions.

WAINWRIGHT, JONATHAN MAYHEW (*b. Liverpool, England, 1792; d. New York, N.Y., 1854*), Episcopal clergyman. Grandson of Jonathan Mayhew. Graduated Harvard, 1812. After his ordination in 1817, he served as minister in Hartford, Conn., and Boston, Mass., but was principally identified with Grace Church and Trinity Parish, New York City. His consecration as bishop of New York, 1852, ended a long controversy in the diocese caused by doctrinal differences and the suspension of Bishop B. T. Onderdonk. A founder of the present New York University, he was active also as a writer and was chief working member of the committee which prepared the standard edition of the *Book of Common Prayer*.

WAINWRIGHT, JONATHAN MAYHEW (*b. New York, N.Y., 1821; d. off Galveston, Texas, 1863*), naval officer. Son of Jonathan M. Wainwright (1792–1854). Appointed midshipman, 1837. After varied sea and shore service, he began duty in the Civil War with the Atlantic Blockading Squadron. Given command (1862) of the *Harriet Lane*, he played a leading role in the reduction of the Confederate forts on the lower Mississippi and the taking of New Orleans. He was killed in action defending his ship against boarders after the recapture of Galveston.

WAINWRIGHT, RICHARD (*b. Charlestown, Mass., 1817; d. Donaldsonville, La., 1862*), naval officer. Appointed midshipman, 1831; served mainly with the U.S. Coast Survey and on ordnance duty until the Civil War. Commanded the U.S.S. *Hartford*, flagship of Admiral Farragut, at the taking of New Orleans and later in the passage of the batteries at Vicksburg.

WAINWRIGHT, RICHARD (*b. Washington, D.C., 1849; d. Washington, 1926*), naval officer. Son of Richard Wainwright (1817–1862). Graduated U.S. Naval Academy, 1868. Performed a variety of duties, notably with the hydrographic office, the U.S. Coast Survey, and the bureau of navigation until 1896 when he became chief of intelligence. Appointed executive officer of the U.S.S. *Maine*, 1897, he helped in recovery of the bodies and in preliminary examinations of the ship's hull after its sinking in Havana harbor, Feb. 15, 1898. In command of the U.S.S. *Gloucester* (formerly J. P. Morgan's yacht *Corsair*), he performed brilliantly in the battle of Santiago Bay, July 3, 1898, attacking and destroying the Spanish ships *Furor* and *Pluton* and helping in the rescue of Admiral Cervera and other of the Spanish seamen. He retired as rear-admiral, 1911.

WAIT, SAMUEL (*b. White Creek, N.Y., 1789; d. Wake Forest, N.C., 1867*), Baptist clergyman. Active *post* 1827 in the organization of the Baptists in North Carolina, he raised funds for the Wake Forest Manual Labour Institute and served as its principal *post* 1834. On its becoming Wake Forest College, 1838, Wait was its president until 1846; he was also president of Oxford Female College, 1851–56.

WAIT, WILLIAM (*b. Ephratah, N.Y., 1821; d. Johnstown, N.Y., 1880*), lawyer. Studied law in office of Daniel Cady; was admitted to the New York bar, 1846. Wait is principally remembered for his legal writings, including a number of useful compilations and manuals of procedure. Among his works were *The Law and Practice in Civil Actions* (1865); *A Table of Cases Affirmed, Reversed, or Cited* (1872, one of the earliest manuals for quick search); *The Practice at Law, in Equity, and in Special Proceedings, etc.* (1872–80, a standard authority on New York adjective law); and *A Treatise upon Some of the General Principles of the Law* (1877–79, a topical digest which was in effect a *corpus juris* for students of that day).

WAIT, WILLIAM BELL (*b. Amsterdam, N.Y., 1839; d. 1916*), educator of the blind. Graduated Albany Normal College, 1859. Starting as superintendent of the New York Institution for the Blind in New York City, 1863, he remained in the service of the Institution until his death. A leader in advancing education of the blind to the status of a profession and in the provision of full intellectual development for blind students, Wait was inventor of the New York Point

System (a variant of Braille), 1868, and other learning devices.

WAITE, MORRISON REMICK (*b. Lyme, Conn., 1816; d. 1888*), jurist. Graduated Yale, 1837. Admitted to the Ohio bar, 1839, he practiced *post* 1850 at Toledo, becoming a recognized authority in the law of real estate and the status of legal titles. Active in Whig and Republican politics, he was a leader in his locality in support of the Union cause during the Civil War. After serving, 1871–72, with Caleb Cushing and William M. Evarts, as American counsel in the Geneva Arbitration, he became president of the Ohio constitutional convention of 1873. Named and confirmed as chief justice of the United States, January 1874, he immediately assumed a large share of the work of the U.S. Supreme Court and in his 14 years of tenure gave the Court's opinion in more than a thousand cases. He contributed substantially to clarification of Reconstruction legislation and the constitutional amendments arising out of the Civil War. He reaffirmed the doctrine of the Slaughterhouse Cases in *Minor vs. Happersett* (88 *U.S.*, 162). Upholding the right of a state to deny the vote to women, he held that suffrage was not a privilege of U.S. citizenship and that the Fourteenth Amendment did not add to the privileges and immunities of citizens. In *U.S. vs. Reese* (92 *U.S.*, 214), he demolished the Radical plan of protecting the Negro by direct federal action, holding sections three and four of the Civil Rights Act of May 31, 1870, unconstitutional. In *U.S. vs. Cruikshank* (92 *U.S.*, 542), he held that the Fourteenth Amendment did not authorize Congress to legislate affirmatively for the protection of civil rights and did not add to the rights of one citizen against another. In *Munn vs. Illinois* (94 *U.S.*, 113), he upheld the power of the state to regulate the charges of grain elevators and public warehouses—businesses that were "clothed with a public interest." Here and in other Granger cases the Court upheld state laws fixing maximum rates on all railroads operating within the state, and by its action profoundly affected the course of American social and economic development. The due process clause was narrowly interpreted while the power of the states was necessarily enlarged. However, it was Waite himself who laid the foundation for the modern interpretation of due process as a limitation on state power. He issued a famous dictum in *Stone vs. Farmers' Loan and Trust Co.* (116 *U.S.*, 331): "From what has been said it is not to be inferred that this power . . . of regulation is itself without limit. . . . It is not a power to destroy. . . . The State cannot do that which . . . amounts to a taking of private property . . . without due process of law." Upon this and other dicta rested the decision of the rate cases in 1890 after Waite's death, which made the Supreme Court the final judge in matters of rates. His interpretation of the contract clause constitutes another major contribution to constitutional development. In various decisions he modified profoundly the decision of the doctrine of vested rights as established in the Dartmouth College Case and indicated his willingness to allow the states to exercise wide regulatory power over corporate enterprises in matters pertaining to the "public interest." He strongly upheld the power of Congress to regulate commerce and broadened the sense of that term to include the transfer of intangibles such as telegraphic communications. He scanned very closely the claims of individuals as against the state, even interpreting the Bill of Rights strictly. A skillful and courteous administrator, Waite possessed a style which was eminently judicial, terse, vigorous and clear. Among other quotable dicta was his statement that "No legislature can bargain away the public health or the public morals."

WAKELEY, JOSEPH BURTON (*b. Danbury, Conn., 1809; d. New York, N.Y., 1875*), Methodist clergyman. Author, among other contributions to the history of early Methodism, of *Lost Chapters Recovered* (1858) and *The Bold Frontier Preacher* (1869).

WALCOT, CHARLES MELTON (*b. London, England, c. 1816; d. Philadelphia, Pa., 1868*), actor, dramatist. Father of Charles M. Walcot (1840–1921). Emigrated to Charleston, S.C., *c.* 1837. Celebrated *c.* 1840–60 as a light and eccentric comedian and as the author of a number of topical burlesques.

WALCOT, CHARLES MELTON (*b. Boston, Mass., 1840; d. New York, N.Y., 1921*), actor. Son of Charles M. Walcot (*c.* 1816–1868). Made debut at Charleston, S.C., 1858. Played with companies of Edwin Booth, Laura Keene and Charlotte Cushman; appeared with his wife *post* 1863 in a number of stock companies, including that of the Walnut Street Theatre, Philadelphia, Pa. They joined the Lyceum Company in New York City, 1887, and remained with it until about the turn of the century.

WALCOTT, CHARLES DOOLITTLE (*b. New York Mills, Oneida Co., N.Y., 1850; d. 1927*), paleontologist. Early interested in the collection of fossils and minerals, Walcott was employed by James Hall (1811–1898), the New York State geologist, 1876. He was appointed a field assistant with the U.S. Geological Survey, 1879. Gradually advancing in rank with the Survey, he became chief geologist, 1893, and succeeded John W. Powell as director, 1894. Serving in this post until 1907, he developed and strengthened the Survey along lines already laid down, also taking an active part in the work which led to the establishment of the U.S. Forest Service and the Bureau of Mines. As secretary of the Smithsonian Institution, *post* 1907, he handled its affairs with high executive ability and was influential in founding the Freer Gallery, the Carnegie Institution, the National Research Council and the National Advisory Committee for Aeronautics. Continuing his field work along with his administrative tasks, he was author of 222 papers

of which 110 dealt with the Cambrian formations. Among these works, the most considerable was his *Cambrian Brachiopoda* (1912). The most striking of his field discoveries was that of the Middle Cambrian Burgess shale of British Columbia.

WALCOTT, HENRY PICKERING (*b. Hopkinton, Mass., 1838; d. Cambridge, Mass., 1932*), physician. Graduated Harvard, 1858; M.D., Bowdoin, 1861. After further studies in Vienna and Berlin, he practiced in Cambridge, Mass. Chairman of the Massachusetts State Board of Health, 1886–1915, he widened the Board's influence by giving it advisory power over public water supplies, drainage, sewerage and the protection of the purity of inland waters. He was chairman of the commission which recommended the building of the Charles River Basin, 1893, and planned the metropolitan water supply system of Boston. The most important man in the field of public health in his day, he expressed in his annual reports germinal ideas which have deeply influenced the public health movement in America.

WALD, LILLIAN D. (*b. Cincinnati, O., 1867; d. Westport, Conn., 1940*), public health nurse, settlement house founder. Graduated New York Hospital, 1891; studied also at Women's Medical College, New York City. Asked to organize a course of instruction in home nursing for immigrant families on New York's lower East Side, 1893, she soon discovered at first hand the need for reform of conditions under which the immigrants were living. Going to live with an associate in an East Side tenement, she secured financial support from a number of benefactors, notably Jacob H. Schiff, and founded the Nurses' Settlement (*post* 1895 at 265 Henry St.). The settlement house and visiting nurse services which were developed at Henry St. were pioneering innovations; Miss Wald largely originated the concept of public health nursing and the public school nursing system. At her suggestion, several life insurance companies undertook nursing service for their policyholders. Visiting the sick in their homes had revealed many social needs which Miss Wald moved to meet; these included instruction in cooking and sewing, programs in music and art, and the organization of clubs for boys' and girls' recreation. She was also influential in efforts to obtain better housing, to regulate sweatshops, and to abolish child labor. Declining health caused her to retire as head worker at Henry St., 1933. [*Supp. 2*]

WALDEN, JACOB TREADWELL (*b. Walden, N.Y., 1830; d. Boston, Mass., 1918*), Episcopal clergyman, author. A rector at various times in Philadelphia, Pa., Indianapolis, Ind., Boston, Mass., and Minneapolis, Minn., he aided in the liberalizing movement by which the broad church group evolved.

WALDEN, JOHN MORGAN (*b. near Lebanon, O., 1831; d. 1914*), Free-soil journalist in Illinois and Kansas, Methodist clergyman. Active in the Cincinnati

Conference, 1858–68; able executive of the Western Methodist Book Concern *post* 1868; elected bishop, 1884. Worked for the improvement of the conditions of Negroes.

WALDERNE, RICHARD (*b. Alchester, Warwickshire, England, c. 1615; d. Cochecho, present Dover, N.H., 1689*), pioneer. Emigrated to New England, *c.* 1640. Settled at present Dover, N.H., where he engaged in lumbering and Indian trade and filled at various times practically all important local offices. Member of the Massachusetts General Court, 1654–74 and 1677; appointed to the president's Council of New Hampshire, 1680. Killed by Indians in reprisal for treacherous seizure of refugee tribesmen and their subsequent sale into slavery.

WALDO, DAVID (*b. Clarksburg, present W. Va., 1802; d. Independence, Mo., 1878*), physician, banker, merchant. Removed to Missouri, 1820, and to Taos in present New Mexico *ante* 1829. Becoming a citizen of Mexico, 1830, he amassed a great fortune in the Santa Fé trade, and served as a captain in the regiment commanded by A. W. Doniphan during the Mexican War. Maker and loser of several fortunes in the overland trade, Waldo later executed provision contracts for the U.S. Army and engaged in banking.

WALDO, SAMUEL (*b. Boston, Mass., 1695; d. near present Bangor, Maine, 1759*), merchant, capitalist, land speculator. Attempted for many years to develop wild lands on the Maine coast between the Muscongus and Penobscot rivers (known *post c.* 1731 as the Waldo Patent). Served as brigadier-general and second-in-command of the Massachusetts forces in the Louisburg campaign of 1745. At first a close friend and associate of William Shirley, he had become a bitter enemy of Shirley by the 1750's.

WALDO, SAMUEL LOVETT (*b. Windham, Conn., 1783; d. New York, N.Y., 1861*), portrait painter. Mainly self-taught, Waldo met with his first success in Charleston, S.C., 1804–06. In England, 1806–09, he settled in New York City on his return, where he worked diligently, *post* 1820 in partnership with William Jewett. The firm produced a great number of excellent if somewhat literal likenesses.

WALDO, SAMUEL PUTNAM (*b. Pomfret, Conn., 1779; d. Hartford, Conn., 1826*), lawyer, miscellaneous writer. Author of a number of biographies of great contemporaries in which his formula was a pound of rhetoric to an ounce of fact. Compiled the very popular *Journal Comprising an Account of the Loss of the Brig Commerce . . . by Archibald Robbins* (1817).

WALDRON, RICHARD. [See WALDERNE, RICHARD, 1615–1689.]

WALES, JAMES ALBERT (*b. Clyde, O., 1852; d. 1886*), cartoonist. Trained as a wood engraver, he began to draw political cartoons for the *Cleveland Leader;* removing to New York, N.Y., 1873, he worked, among other papers, for *Frank Leslie's Illustrated Newspaper.* Resident for a short time in London, he became a staff member of *Puck,* 1877, and established his reputation by a series of full-page political portraits entitled "Puck's Pantheon." Less vindictive in satire than Thomas Nast but more of a realist than Joseph Keppler, Wales had a decided gift for portraiture.

WALES, LEONARD EUGENE (*b. Wilmington, Del., 1823; d. Wilmington, 1897*), jurist. Associate justice, Delaware superior court, 1864–84; U.S. judge for the district of Delaware, 1884–97.

WALGREEN, CHARLES RUDOLPH (*b. near Galesburg, Ill., 1873; d. Chicago, Ill., 1939*), pharmacist, drugstore chain founder. Organized C. R. Walgreen & Co. in Chicago, 1909. A leader in modernization of the drugstore, he popularized the lunch counter, open-display merchandising and attractive decoration in his shops. [Supp. 2]

WALKE, HENRY (*b. Princess Anne Co., Va., 1808; d. Brooklyn, N.Y., 1896*), naval officer. Raised in Ohio. Appointed midshipman, 1827. Evacuated Union garrison and others from Pensacola Navy Yard, January 1861, after its seizure by the South. In service with Foote's flotilla on the upper Mississippi, 1861–63, he won high distinction as captain of the *Carondelet* in the actions at Fort Henry and Fort Donelson. His most celebrated exploit was the running of the batteries at Island No. 10, an operation which he alone favored in the preliminary council, volunteered for, and executed successfully on the night of Apr. 4, 1862. He was later conspicuous in engagements with Confederate forces above Fort Pillow and in a running fight with the ram *Arkansas* in the Yazoo River, July 15. Commanding the ironclad *Lafayette,* he shared in the reduction of Vicksburg. He was later active against Confederate raiders in the Atlantic. Promoted rear-admiral, 1870, he retired, 1871.

WALKER, ALEXANDER (*b. Fredericksburg, Va., 1818; d. Fort Smith, Ark., 1893*), New Orleans lawyer and journalist. Removed to New Orleans, La., 1840; edited and managed at various times the Democratic *Jeffersonian,* the *Daily Delta,* the *New Orleans Times,* the *Herald,* and the *Daily Picayune.* A firm believer in "manifest destiny," he was one of the supporters of the filibuster William Walker, and backed the expedition of Gen. Narciso Lopez to Cuba, 1851.

WALKER, AMASA (*b. Woodstock, Conn., 1799; d. 1875*), Boston businessman, Massachusetts legislator and congressman, economist. Father of Francis A. Walker. Especially interested in the monetary system, he was author of, among other works, *The Nature and Uses of Money and Mixed Currency* (1857) and *The Science of Wealth* (1866).

WALKER, ASA (*b. Portsmouth, N.H., 1845; d. Annapolis, Md., 1916*), naval officer. Graduated U.S.

Naval Academy, 1866. An expert navigator, he was author of *Navigation* (1888), long used as a textbook at the Naval Academy. Walker commanded the U.S.S. *Concord* under Admiral Dewey at the battle of Manila Bay, winning high commendation. Commissioned rear-admiral, 1906, he retired, 1907.

WALKER, MADAME C. J. [See WALKER, SARAH BREEDLOVE, 1865–1919.]

WALKER, DAVID (*b. Wilmington, N.C., 1785; d. 1830*), Negro leader. A free Negro, Walker traveled widely in the South as a youth, and was established as a clothing dealer in Boston, Mass., *ante* 1827. He is best known as author of *Walker's Appeal* (1829 and later editions) in which he called upon Negroes to rise against their oppressors if the slaveholders refused to let their victims go. At the same time he pleaded with the slaveholders to repent of their past actions for fear of God's wrath. A violent reaction to this pamphlet was immediate in the South, and a price was set on the author's head.

WALKER, DAVID (*b. present Todd Co., Ky., 1806; d. 1879*), jurist, Arkansas legislator. Cousin of David S. Walker. Settled in Fayetteville, Ark., *c.* 1831. Justice, supreme court of Arkansas, 1848–67, 1874–78. Originally opposed secession as president of Arkansas convention, 1861, but followed the general sentiment in his state after bombardment of Fort Sumter.

WALKER, DAVID SHELBY (*b. near Russellville, Ky., 1815; d. Tallahassee, Fla., 1891*), jurist, Florida legislator. Cousin of David Walker (1806–1879). Removed to Tallahassee, 1837. Register of public lands and *ex-officio* state superintendent of schools, 1850–59, he was influential in securing passage of the basic school law of 1853. Justice, Florida supreme court, 1859–65, he opposed Florida secession and confined himself to judicial duties during the Civil War. As governor of Florida, 1866–67, he opposed bringing immigrants to Florida, contending that the Negroes had the right to furnish the labor supply. He ranks generally among the best of his state's governors. He served as judge of the second state judicial circuit *post* 1879.

WALKER, FRANCIS AMASA (*b. Boston, Mass., 1840; d. 1897*), lawyer, Union soldier, educator, economist. Son of Amasa Walker. Graduated Amherst, 1860. Rising from private to brevet brigadier-general in the Civil War, he became a deputy to David A. Wells, commissioner of the revenue, 1869, and chief of the Bureau of Statistics. He reorganized the Bureau along scientific lines and struggled to free it from dependence upon political appointments and special interests. His experience in superintending the census of 1870 without adequate authority was useful to him later as superintendent of the tenth census (1879–81), for which he appointed his own staff of tellers and in which he established his reputation as a statistician. Meanwhile he had served as commissioner

of Indian affairs, November 1871—December 1872, with great ability, and, as professor of political economy in Sheffield Scientific School of Yale, 1873–81, had become a leading figure in a new inductive and historical school of economics.

Of first importance was his attack upon the wages-fund theory. He showed that wages were not wholly dependent upon the amount of pre-existing capital, but also, and more particularly, upon the current productivity of labor. According to his theory of distribution, which aroused controversy, interest was regulated by a general principle of supply and demand, the profits of the entrepreneur were like rent, and the laborer was left "as the residual claimant to the remaining portion of the product." He believed competition to be the fundamental basis of economic life but recognized that perfect competition is not attained in practice. He defined money to include bank notes and everything serving as a medium of exchange. He asserted that the government had the right to declare irredeemable paper legal tender, adding that governments were not yet wise enough to avoid over-issue and effectively exposing the inflation fallacy. He held throughout his life to the doctrine of international bimetallism and lectured widely in its behalf. Opposed to any blind acceptance of *laissez-faire*, he advocated a limited reduction of hours of labor from fourteen to ten for increased efficiency; he thought unemployment was due chiefly to the effects of world-wide division of labor. Relations between labor and capital seemed to him in 1888 to have reached an equilibrium which could not be disturbed without threat to the public welfare. His influence extended into England (markedly), Italy and France, but not far into Germany, and as a theoretical economist he stood higher abroad than at home. A free-trader, he was attacked by other free-traders because he was willing to concede that the protectionists had at least a claim to a hearing.

As president of Massachusetts Institute of Technology, 1881–97, he won public recognition for technical education and extended the physical plant of the Institute. Among the educational reforms which he championed were an insistence on the laboratory method in order to maintain the interest of students of mechanical trend as well as those of retentive memory, and also the inclusion of studies in history and political science in technical schools. He opposed absorption of the Institute by Harvard because he believed that technical schools should maintain a separate identity in order to keep free of the arrogance of the classical disciplines. He was author, among other works, of *The Indian Question* (1874); *The Wages Question* (1876); *Money* (1878); *Land and its Rent* (1883); and *International Bimetallism* (1896).

WALKER, GILBERT CARLTON (*b. Cuba, N.Y., 1832; d. New York, N.Y., 1885*), lawyer. After practice in Owego, N.Y., and Chicago, Ill., he removed to Norfolk, Va., 1865, where he engaged in business and banking. After the Virginia constitutional convention of 1867, he helped to secure federal approval of the new constitution without a provision for disfranchisement of Confederates who had held office under the United States. Elected governor of Virginia as a "Conservative" Republican with Democratic support, he served from 1869 through 1874. Successful in restoring Virginia to the Union and in enforcement of law and order, he pursued a fiscal policy which was unworkable and by which, it was believed, he profited personally. His funding of the state's debt was done on very hard terms, and Virginia's interests in transportation companies were diverted to private hands. After service in Congress, 1875–79, he returned to New York State.

WALKER, HENRY OLIVER (*b. Boston, Mass., 1843; d. Belmont, Mass., 1929*), painter. Studied in Paris, France, under Léon Bonnat, 1879–82; worked in Boston, 1883–89; removed to New York City *c.* 1889. A portraitist and painter of ideal figures, he made a special mark as a muralist. His "Joy and Memory" and "Lyric Poetry" in the Library of Congress are among the most decorative of the many mural works there. He painted other effective works for the Massachusetts State House and the Appellate Court House, New York City.

WALKER, JAMES (*b. present Burlington, Mass., 1794; d. Cambridge, Mass., 1874*), Unitarian clergyman. Graduated Harvard, 1814. Pastor, Harvard Church, Charlestown, Mass., 1818–39; Alford Professor of Natural Religion, etc., Harvard, 1839–53; president of Harvard, 1853–60. A man of erudite but not original mind, he derived almost his entire thought from the Scotch Realists and was the preeminent expounder of the metaphysics of early 19th-century Unitarianism—a common-sense rationalism combined with a simple piety and a lofty ethical tone. His administration of Harvard was competent but uneventful.

WALKER, JAMES BARR (*b. Philadelphia, Pa., 1805; d. Wheaton, Ill., 1887*), Presbyterian and Congregational clergyman, anti-slavery journalist in Ohio and Illinois. Author of *The Philosophy of the Plan of Salvation* (published anonymously, 1841), a widely popular treatise on Christian apologetics. Professor of philosophy and belles-lettres, Wheaton College, Wheaton, Ill., 1870–84.

WALKER, JOHN BRISBEN (*b. near Pittsburgh, Pa., 1847; d. 1931*), iron manufacturer, rancher, journalist. As publisher and editor of the *Cosmopolitan Magazine*, 1889–1905, he made it one of the leading American illustrated magazines of that time. Of a restless and adventurous turn of mind, he engaged in political activity and urged economic and other reforms. An enthusiast for aviation, automobiles and good roads, he offered a prize in 1896 for the automobile show-

ing the greatest speed, safety and ease of operation at low cost which was won by the Duryea car. In 1898 he bought the Stanley Automobile Co. and began the manufacture of Locomobile steam cars.

WALKER, JOHN GRIMES (*b. Hillsboro, N.H., 1835; d. near Ogunquit, Maine, 1907*), naval officer. Nephew of James W. Grimes. Graduated U.S. Naval Academy, 1856; rose to rank of commander for his Civil War service under Adm. D. D. Porter in Mississippi River operations. Recognized as the most influential officer in the navy during his later career, he was chief of the Bureau of Navigation, 1881–89, held important sea commands, and was in charge of the North Pacific Squadron, 1894, during establishment of the Hawaiian Republic. Retired as commodore, 1897, he served as president of the Isthmian Canal Commission, 1899–1904. He headed the reorganized Commission which administered the Canal Zone until 1905.

WALKER, JONATHAN HOGE (*b. near Hogestown, Pa., 1754; d. Natchez, Miss., 1824*), lawyer. Father of Robert J. Walker. Began practice in Northumberland Co., Pa., 1790, where he was an associate in politics of Robert Whitehill and Thomas Cooper. President judge of the fourth Pennsylvania district, 1806–18; U.S. judge, district of western Pennsylvania, *post* 1818.

WALKER, JOSEPH REDDEFORD (*b. probably Virginia, 1798; d. Contra Costa Co., Calif., 1876*), trapper, explorer, guide. Raised in Roane Co., Tenn.; removed to vicinity of Independence, Mo., 1819. After trading and trapping out of Independence, he joined Bonneville's company which left Fort Osage for the mountains, May 1832. In July 1833, from the Green River rendezvous, he set off westward, first to Great Salt Lake, then to the Humboldt River, and on to what has since been known as Walker Lake. Scaling the Sierra Nevada with great difficulty, he and his group reached Monterey, Calif., in November, and were probably the first whites to cross the Sierra from the East, and also, it is believed, the first to see the Yosemite Valley. On his return east in February 1834, Walker crossed the mountains farther south by what is now known as Walkers Pass and rejoined Bonneville in the present Utah in the early summer. Remaining in the mountains for some nine years, he joined J. B. Chiles's emigrant company at Fort Bridger, August 1843, and led a part of it by way of Walkers Pass to the coast. Overtaking John C. Frémont's second expedition on its return journey, he accompanied it to Bent's Fort. He was the guide to Frémont's third expedition (1845–46) to California. Resident for a short time in Jackson Co., Mo., he reached California among the first of the Forty-niners. He led a company to Arizona, 1861, and discovered rich placers on the site of present Prescott, 1862. His knowledge of the geography of the West was outstanding.

WALKER, LEROY POPE (*b. Huntsville, Ala., 1817; d. Huntsville, 1884*), Alabama lawyer, legislator and jurist. Identified with the secessionist wing of the Democratic party by 1860, he was chairman of the Alabama delegation to his party's convention of that year at Charleston, S.C., and as such announced the withdrawal of the delegation. He was delegate also to the Richmond convention and was sent by the Alabama secession convention as special commissioner to induce Tennessee to secede. Recommended by W. L. Yancey, he was appointed Confederate secretary of war, February 1861. Utterly inexperienced, he resigned in September and served thereafter in several area commands and as judge of a military court until 1865.

WALKER, MARY EDWARDS (*b. Oswego, N.Y., 1832; d. near Oswego, 1919*), physician. Certificated by Syracuse Medical College, 1855, Dr. Walker was a lifelong campaigner for woman's rights. Early in her career she adopted men's dress. After service in the Union Army medical corps, 1861–65, she practiced in Washington, D.C. She was principally famous as a lecturer in favor of dress reform, woman suffrage, the abolition of capital punishment and other reforms, but her consuming egotism is said to have alienated similarly-minded persons.

WALKER, PINKNEY HOUSTON (*b. Adair Co., Ky., 1815; d. 1885*), jurist. Admitted to the Illinois bar, 1839. A judge of the Illinois circuit court, 1853–58, he served thereafter as a justice of the state supreme court. He was chief justice, 1864–67 and 1874–75. Author during his judicial career of about 3000 opinions, he was known for integrity, fairness and clarity of reasoning. Among his most important opinions were *Starkweather vs. American Bible Society* (72 *Ill.*, 50) and *Ruggles vs. People* (91 *Ill.*, 256). He concurred in the opinion in *Munn vs. Illinois* (69 *Ill.*, 80).

WALKER, REUBEN LINDSAY (*b. Logan, Va., 1827; d. Virginia, 1890*), Confederate brigadier-general, civil engineer. Great-grandson of Thomas Walker. Graduated Virginia Military Institute, 1845. Served throughout the Civil War without a day's leave of absence, principally in command of the artillery of A. P. Hill's division (later corps). After the war he engaged in farming and in railroad and contracting work.

WALKER, ROBERT FRANKLIN (*b. Florence, Mo., 1850; d. Jefferson City, Mo., 1930*), Missouri legal official and jurist. As judge of the supreme court of Missouri *post* 1912, he did his most important work in criminal appeals and tactfully mitigated the older Missouri doctrine that all error presumes prejudice against the defendant.

WALKER, ROBERT JOHN (*b. Northumberland, Pa., 1801; d. Washington, D.C., 1869*), lawyer, public official. Son of Jonathan H. Walker. Admitted to the bar in Pittsburgh, Pa., 1821, he soon became a leader of the Democratic party in the state, but removed to Natchez, Miss., 1826. Successful in practice and as a land speculator, he posed as the friend of the squatter and small farmer and was a follower of Andrew Jackson. As U.S. senator from Mississippi, 1836–45, he was identified with the anti-Bank and repudiating party in his state. He spoke often in favor of preemption, lower land prices and the independent treasury plan; he opposed distribution of the surplus, the protective tariff, and abolition. His service as senator is chiefly memorable for his activities in connection with the annexation of Texas. He was author of the resolution of January 1837 calling for recognition of Texan independence, and was one of President Tyler's foremost allies in efforts to add Texas to the Union, 1843–45.

Walker appears to have been at the center of the manipulations which resulted in the rejection of Martin Van Buren and the nomination of James K. Polk, 1844. After drafting the compromise resolutions which resolved the Senate deadlock over annexation of Texas, February 1845, he became U.S. secretary of the treasury despite Andrew Jackson's disapproval. A hardworking secretary, Walker secured establishment of the independent treasury system for handling public money and financed the conduct of the Mexican War on favorable terms and without scandal. His report of 1845 on the state of the finances became a classic of free-trade literature and remains a very able state paper. He also established the government warehousing system for the handling of imports, and was mainly responsible for creation of the Department of the Interior in 1849. An advocate of the seizure of the whole of Mexico, 1847, Walker is believed to have lobbied for the rejection of the Trist treaty, February 1848.

Between 1849 and 1857 Walker lived in Washington, D.C., attending to his speculative interests. Appointed governor of Kansas Territory, March 1857, he had an understanding with President Buchanan that the *bona fide* residents of Kansas should choose their social institutions by a fair vote. His inaugural address contained the thesis that climatic conditions would be the ultimate determinant of the location of slavery and aroused a storm of protest in the South. Despite his attempts to conciliate the free-state party in Kansas and his own conviction that Kansas would be a free state, he failed in his attempts to settle the Kansas difficulties because of the failure of the administration to support him. He resigned in December 1857 when he was unable to persuade Buchanan that the so-called ratification of the Lecompton Constitution was unacceptable. Himself a Free-soiler as early as 1849 and said to have freed his slaves in 1838, Walker was a Unionist in the Civil War and was active in the sale in Europe of federal bonds. After the war he aided in putting the Alaska purchase bill through Congress and was hopeful of annexing Nova Scotia to the United States.

WALKER, SARAH BREEDLOVE (*b. Delta, La., 1867; d. Irvington-on-Hudson, N.Y., 1919*), pioneer Negro businesswoman, philanthropist. Known throughout later life as Madame C. J. Walker. Educated in public night schools of St. Louis, Mo., Mrs. Walker discovered in 1905 the formula of a hair preparation for Negroes which she sold by mail with great success. Settling her business in Indianapolis, Ind., 1910, she manufactured various cosmetics and maintained a training school for agents and beauty culturists. One of her most original ideas was the organization of her agents into clubs for business, social and philanthropic purposes. She willed two-thirds of her estate to educational institutions and charities.

WALKER, SEARS COOK (*b. Wilmington, Mass., 1805; d. Cincinnati, O., 1853*), mathematician, astronomer. Brother of Timothy Walker (1802–1856). Graduated Harvard, 1825. Founded one of earliest astronomical observatories in the United States, 1837, in connection with the Philadelphia High School. Associated *post* 1845 with the U.S. Naval Observatory, Washington, D.C., and with the U.S. Coast Survey, he made important researches in the orbit of the planet Neptune, 1847. He originated the telegraphing of transits of stars and application of the graphic registration of time-results to the registry of time-observations for general astronomical purposes.

WALKER, THOMAS (*b. King and Queen Co., Va., 1715; d. present Albemarle Co., Va., 1794*), physician, soldier, explorer. Studied medicine at Williamsburg, Va., and practiced in Fredericksburg. Joined company of land speculators who explored the southern end of the valley of Virginia, 1748; became chief agent for Loyal Land Company, 1749. Explored westward in 1750 to examine land claims, becoming first white man to have made a recorded expedition to the Kentucky country (as established by his journal, published 1888). Commissary-general to Virginia troops serving under George Washington, 1755, he was charged with misconduct for entering partnership with Andrew Lewis in the supply business. Acted as guardian for Thomas Jefferson. Represented Virginia at treaty of Fort Stanwix, 1768; thereafter took important part in Revolutionary movement. A member of the executive council of Virginia and of the House of Delegates, he was typical of the men of action who explored and exploited the early frontier.

WALKER, THOMAS BARLOW (*b. Xenia, O., 1840; d. 1928*), Minnesota lumber magnate, founder of the Walker Art Gallery, Minneapolis.

WALKER, TIMOTHY (*b. Woburn, Mass., 1705; d. Concord, N.H., 1782*), Congregational clergyman. Father-in-law of Benjamin Thompson. Graduated Harvard, 1725. Pastor in present Concord, N.H., 1730–82. He acted as agent for the settlers there in securing a Crown decision which validated their titles to their lands after transfer of the township from Massa-chusetts to New Hampshire sovereignty. To this end he traveled to England in 1753, 1755 and 1762.

WALKER, TIMOTHY (*b. Wilmington, Mass., 1802; d. Cincinnati, O., 1856*), Ohio lawyer, legal writer, jurist and law teacher. Brother of Sears C. Walker. Practiced and taught law in Cincinnati *post* 1831. Author of the influential *Introduction to American Law* (1837), a statement of the elementary principles of American jurisprudence.

WALKER, WILLIAM (*b. Nashville, Tenn., 1824; d. Trujillo, Honduras, 1860*), adventurer, greatest of American filibusters. Graduated University of Nashville, 1838; M.D., University of Pennsylvania, 1843; after studying law, was admitted to the bar in New Orleans, La. Failing to succeed as lawyer and journalist, he removed to California, 1850, where he practiced at Marysville. Invading the Mexican province of Lower California with an armed expedition, 1853, he proclaimed himself president of an independent republic there, but was forced to return to the United States. He was acquitted after trial for violation of the neutrality laws. Invited by the leader of a revolutionary faction in Nicaragua, Walker led a small, armed band there in 1855. With the help of the Accessory Transit Co., an American concern, he seized control of Nicaragua and, after recognition of his regime by the United States in May 1856, had himself inaugurated as president. Ambitious to unite the Central American republics into a single military empire, he planned an interoceanic canal and attempted to reintroduce African slavery. Undertaking to double-cross Cornelius Vanderbilt in a struggle for control of the Accessory Transit Co., he was driven from his presidency after a coalition of neighboring republics was formed against him with Vanderbilt's aid. Returning to the United States, 1857, he attempted an invasion of Nicaragua late in the year, but was arrested on landing by Commodore Hiram Paulding of the U.S. Navy and sent back to the United States. Arrested by British authorities after a landing in Honduras, 1860, he was condemned to death by a court-martial of Honduran officers and shot. A small man, extremely shy and reticent, he was yet able to maintain iron discipline and something like personal devotion among his desperate followers. He was author of *The War in Nicaragua* (1860).

WALKER, WILLIAM HENRY TALBOT (*b. Augusta, Ga., 1816; d. near Atlanta, Ga., 1864*), soldier. Graduated West Point, 1837. Commissioned in the infantry, he served in the Florida Indian War and in the Mexican War. Badly wounded at Molino del Rey, 1847, he undertook minor duties and went on sick leave for a great part of the time until 1860 when he resigned his commission. In service mainly with Georgia state troops, 1861–63, he entered the Confederate service as a brigadier-general and was appointed major-general, January 1864. Active in the western campaigns, he was with the Army of Tennessee during the northern Georgia campaign and was killed in a sortie out of Atlanta.

WALKER, WILLIAM JOHNSON (*b. Charlestown, Mass., 1790; d. 1865*), physician, financier. A successful practitioner at Charlestown *post* 1816, he accumulated a large fortune in railroad and manufacturing stocks which he devoted to the endowment of Amherst, Tufts College, the Boston Society of Natural History and Massachusetts Institute of Technology.

WALKER, WILLISTON (*b. Portland, Maine, 1860; d. 1922*), church historian. Graduated Amherst, 1883; Hartford Theological Seminary, 1886; Ph.D., Leipzig, 1888. Taught church history at Hartford, 1889–1901; at Yale, 1901–22. Provost of Yale *post* 1919. A teacher of great ability, Walker made his major contributions to scholarship in the field of New England Congregational history; he was actively concerned in work for Christian unity and for missions.

WALLACE, CHARLES WILLIAM (*b. Hopkins, Mo., 1865; d. Wichita Falls, Texas, 1932*), educator, Shakespeare scholar. Graduated University of Nebraska, 1898; did graduate work at Nebraska and at University of Chicago; Ph.D., Freiburg-im-Breisgau, 1906. Taught English at University of Nebraska *post* 1901. Applied proceeds of successful work as oil operator in Texas to furtherance of research in history of the early English stage.

WALLACE, DAVID (*b. Pennsylvania, 1799; d. Indianapolis, Ind., 1859*), lawyer. Father of Lewis Wallace. Raised on Ohio and Indiana frontiers. Graduated West Point, 1821. Admitted to the Indiana bar, 1824, he succeeded in practice and was one of the Whig leaders in Indiana. Lieutenant-governor, 1831–37, and governor of Indiana, 1837–40, he lost the state millions in money through procuring loans for public improvements from Eastern speculators. Whig congressman, 1841–43, he returned to the practice of law in Indianapolis and died while a judge of the court of common pleas.

WALLACE, HENRY (*b. near West Newton, Pa., 1836; d. 1916*), United Presbyterian clergyman, editor and writer on agricultural subjects. Father of Henry C. Wallace. A pastor in Illinois and Iowa, 1863–76, he took up farming as a way of recovering his health and soon entered agricultural journalism. With his son, he began publishing *Wallace's Farmer*, 1895, and was its editor until his death. He was president of the National Conservation Congress, 1910.

WALLACE, HENRY CANTWELL (*b. Rock Island, Ill., 1866; d. Washington, D.C., 1924*), agricultural journalist. Son of Henry Wallace; father of Henry A. Wallace. Graduated Iowa State Agricultural College, 1892. Associated with his father in publishing *Wallace's Farmer post* 1895, he became its editor, 1916.

As U.S. secretary of agriculture, 1921–24, he emphasized that department's role in the adjustment of production to the needs of consumption, and opposed transfer of its marketing functions to the Department of Commerce. He was a champion of conservation, supported the principles of the McNary-Haugen Bill, established the bureau of agricultural economics and the bureau of home economics in his department, and inaugurated radio market reports.

WALLACE, HORACE BINNEY (*b. Philadelphia, Pa., 1817; d. Paris, France, 1852*), lawyer, literary, art and legal critic. Brother of John W. Wallace. Graduated College of New Jersey (Princeton), 1835. Author of a novel, *Stanley, or the Recollections of a Man of the World* (issued anonymously, 1838), and of two collections of critical and philosophical essays published posthumously. Editor, with J. I. C. Hare, of J. W. Smith's *A Selection of Leading Cases*, and also of *Select Decisions of American Courts* (1847, revised in 1857 as *American Leading Cases*). Auguste Comte recognized Wallace as his leading American disciple.

WALLACE, HUGH CAMPBELL (*b. Lexington, Mo., 1863; d. Washington, D.C., 1931*), financier, diplomat. Identified *post* 1887 with the commercial development of Tacoma, Wash., Wallace became one of the most influential financiers of the Northwest and was a leader of the Democratic party in that region. A trusted adviser to President Woodrow Wilson, he served as U.S. ambassador to France, 1919–21, exercising considerable private influence after the withdrawal of the American delegation to the Peace Conference.

WALLACE, JOHN FINDLEY (*b. Fall River, Mass., 1852; d. Washington, D.C., 1921*), civil engineer, outstanding executive of Midwestern and Western railroads. First chief engineer of the Panama Canal, 1904–05, he continued as such after reorganization of the Canal Commission in April 1905, but resigned in June of that year because of inadequate authority given him and thereby precipitated a bitter controversy. He later served as president of Westinghouse, Church, Kerr & Co. and was an officer and consultant for many other concerns.

WALLACE, JOHN HANKINS (*b. Allegheny Co., Pa., 1822; d. 1903*), cattle-breeder, expert on the trotting horse. Published *Wallace's American Stud Book*, 1867; began publication of *Wallace's American Trotting Register*, 1871, and of *Wallace's Year-Book of Trotting and Pacing*, 1886; also published *Wallace's Monthly*, a magazine devoted to the interest of the trotting horse. Author of *The Horse of America* (1897).

WALLACE, JOHN WILLIAM (*b. Philadelphia, Pa., 1815; d. 1884*), legal scholar, author. Brother of Horace B. Wallace. Graduated University of Pennsylvania, 1833; studied law with his father and with

John Sergeant. Librarian of the Law Association of Philadelphia, 1841–60. Succeeded his brother as co-editor of *American Leading Cases* and edited a number of other legal compilations; was author of *The Reporters, Chronologically Arranged* (1844). He served as reporter of the U.S. Supreme Court, 1863–75. He was president of the Historical Society of Pennsylvania, 1868–84.

WALLACE, LEWIS (*b. Brookville, Ind., 1827; d. Crawfordsville, Ind., 1905*), lawyer, Indiana legislator, Union soldier, diplomat, author. Son of David Wallace, he was commonly known as "Lew" Wallace. A student of law under his father, he served briefly in the Mexican War and began practice of law in Indianapolis, Ind., 1849. Resident in Crawfordsville *post* 1853, he became adjutant-general of Indiana and colonel of the 11th Regiment, 1861. Promoted brigadier-general in September, and major-general in March 1862 after the capture of Fort Donelson, he won the enmity of Gen. H. W. Halleck who twice attempted to bar him from a command. Among Wallace's outstanding exploits during the Civil War were his saving of Cincinnati, O. from capture in 1863 by Confederate Gen. E. Kirby-Smith; also his holding action against Confederate Gen. Jubal Early at the Monocacy, July 1864, for which he was highly commended by Gen. Grant. After the war he spent some time in Mexico and then returned to practice law at Crawfordsville. Republican governor of New Mexico, 1878–81; U.S. minister to Turkey, 1881–85. Wallace is best remembered as a man of letters and as author, among other books, of *The Fair God* (1873), a story of the conquest of Mexico; *Ben Hur* (1880), which had extraordinary success; and of *The Prince of India* (1893). A man of simple, democratic tastes, he disliked the law, had no aptitude for politics, and was disinclined to the military life except when his country required his services. Art, music and literature were his most vital interests.

WALLACE, WILLIAM (*b. Manchester, England, 1825; d. 1904*), wire-manufacturer, inventor. Emigrated to America as a boy. Established firm of Wallace & Sons with his father and brothers, 1848, locating their plant at Ansonia, Conn., 1850. With Moses G. Farmer, he constructed dynamos based on Farmer's patent of 1872, one of which was used to light the Centennial Exhibition at Philadelphia, 1876. His firm built dynamos for use with the plate-carbon arc lamp, patented by Wallace, December 1877, and believed to be the first commercial arc light made in the United States. Wallace was the first to demonstrate operation of arc lights in series. He also constructed an electroplating plant at Ansonia.

WALLACE, WILLIAM ALEXANDER ANDERSON (*b. near Lexington, Va., 1817; d. near Devine, Texas, 1899*), frontiersman, popularly known as "Bigfoot." Removed to Texas, 1837. As private in a ranger company under John C. Hays, 1840–44, he fought on the Salado and was taken prisoner in the futile Mier expedition. After further service as a ranger and with the Mounted Rifle Volunteers in the Mexican War, he raised a company of volunteers for frontier service under his own command, 1850. A legendary figure in Texas history, he sallied out from his Medina River farm time and again with a hastily gathered band of neighbors to protect life and property from Indian raiders. He was also responsible for the delivery of the mail between San Antonio and El Paso. He had no sympathy with the Civil War and took no part in it.

WALLACE, WILLIAM JAMES (*b. Syracuse, N.Y., 1837; d. Jacksonville, Fla., 1917*), jurist. LL.B., Hamilton College, 1857. U.S. district judge, northern district of New York, 1874–82; U.S. judge, second circuit court, 1882–91; presiding judge, circuit court of appeal, second circuit, 1891–1907.

WALLACE, WILLIAM ROSS (*b. Lexington or Paris, Ky., 1819; d. New York, N.Y., 1881*), lawyer, poet. Practiced in New York City *post* 1841; was a friend of Samuel Woodworth, G. P. Morris and other New York literati, and of Edgar A. Poe whose memory he defended against John Neal. A frequent contributor to the periodicals of the day, he was author of *The Battle of Tippecanoe* (Cincinnati, 1837) and of *Meditations in America* (1851) which contains his best-known work. He was author of the famous lines, "And the hand that rocks the cradle, Is the hand that rules the world."

WALLACK, HENRY JOHN (*b. London, England, 1790; d. New York, N.Y., 1870*), actor. Brother of James W. Wallack (*c. 1795–1864*); father of James W. Wallack (1818–1873). Made American debut at Baltimore, Md., 1819, and was known thereafter as a versatile player in a most extensive repertoire, both in America and in England.

WALLACK, JAMES WILLIAM (*b. London, England, c. 1795; d. New York, N.Y., 1864*), actor. Brother of Henry J. Wallack; father of Lester Wallack. Made American debut at the Park Theatre, New York City, as Macbeth, September 1818, after achieving early success on the British stage. An actor of the school of J. P. Kemble, he played with a nervous, exuberant vitality; he alternated appearances between several American cities and England. The most distinguished member of a notable theatrical family, he was manager of the National Theatre in New York, 1837–39, and of the old Brougham's Lyceum in New York, 1852–61. With his son Lester, he opened the third of the Wallack theatres in New York City at Broadway and 13th St., 1861.

WALLACK, JAMES WILLIAM (*b. London, England, 1818; d. near Aiken, S.C., 1873*), actor. Son of Henry J. Wallack; nephew of James W. Wallack (*c. 1795–1864*). Came to America as an infant; made stage debut in Philadelphia, Pa., 1822. After learning his trade at the Bowery Theatre, New York City, and with English provincial companies, he became leading juvenile with his uncle's company, 1837, and for many years played with success both in America and England. *Post* 1855 he remained in the United States. At his best in tragedy or romantic drama, he joined his cousin Lester Wallack's stock company, 1865, and scored one of his greatest successes in the part of Fagin in *Oliver Twist*, 1867.

WALLACK, LESTER (*b. New York, N.Y., 1820; d. near Stamford, Conn., 1888*), actor, dramatist. Son of James W. Wallack (*c. 1795–1864*). Educated in England and trained in the English provincial theatres, he made his American debut at the Broadway Theatre, New York City, 1847; in 1848 he made a sensation in the part of Don César de Bazan, and also as Edmond Dantès in *The Count of Monte Cristo*. Soon becoming the matinée idol of New York in comic or romantic parts, he assisted his father in the management of the Wallack theatres and was their actual manager *post* 1861. After a great run of success in his own plays and others, he opened the new Wallack Theatre at Broadway and 30th St., New York City, 1882, which he managed until his retirement, 1887.

WALLER, EMMA (*b. England, c. 1820; d. New York, N.Y., 1899*), actress. Made American debut at Walnut Street Theatre, Philadelphia, Pa., October 1857, as Ophelia to her husband's Hamlet. Thereafter, often with her husband as her principal associate, she starred as an emotional actress throughout the United States for some twenty years. After her retirement she gave public readings and was a teacher of elocution.

WALLER, JOHN LIGHTFOOT (*b. Woodford Co., Ky., 1809; d. Louisville, Ky., 1854*), Baptist clergyman. Engaged in controversy with Alexander Campbell. Edited *Baptist Banner and Western Pioneer;* founded *Western Baptist Review* (later called *Christian Repository*), 1845. A capable and militant leader under whom the Baptists in Kentucky made notable advances in education and missionary work.

WALLER, THOMAS MACDONALD (*b. New York, N.Y., c. 1840; d. Ocean Beach, Conn., 1924*), lawyer, Connecticut legislator and official. Democratic mayor of New London, Conn., 1873–79; governor of Connecticut, 1883–85. U.S. consul-general at London, England, 1885–89. Uncompromising leader of the "Gold Democrats" in Connecticut, 1896–1900.

WALLING, WILLIAM ENGLISH (*b. Louisville, Ky., 1877; d. Amsterdam, Holland, 1936*), Socialist, labor reformer. Grandson of William H. English. Graduated University of Chicago, 1897. Devoting his energies to the labor movement *post c.* 1900, Walling was a founder of the National Women's Trade Union League, 1903, and presided over a series of meetings (*c.* 1908) out of which grew the National

Association for the Advancement of Colored People. He was a sympathizer with contemporary Russian revolutionary movements and opposed the conservative element in the Socialist party, 1909. In 1917 he supported entry of the United States into World War I and was critical of the Socialist pacifists. After the war he worked full-time for the American Federation of Labor. The conservatism of his later career was brought about largely by the anti-libertarian character of the Communist revolutions.   [*Supp. 2*]

WALLIS, SEVERN TEACKLE (*b. Baltimore, Md., 1816; d. 1894*), lawyer. Graduated St. Mary's College, Baltimore, 1832; studied law in office of William Wirt. A Whig in early life, he became a Democrat upon the disintegration of the Whig party, but remained, above all, a reformer, never surrendering his personal independence of opinion. Considered for many years the leader of the Maryland bar, he exercised a strong influence in Baltimore and in the state and was an eloquent speaker. Sympathetic with the Confederacy but opposed to secession, he argued against the doctrine of military necessity in 1861, and was imprisoned for 14 months. His letters to the press during the campaign of 1875, when he supported the Reform ticket, are among the choicest of Maryland polemics.

WALN, NICHOLAS (*b. Fair Hill, near Philadelphia, Pa., 1742; d. 1813*), lawyer, Quaker preacher. Cousin of Robert Waln (1765–1836). Withdrawing from the practice of law, *c.* 1772, he gave himself up thereafter to the service of the Society of Friends in which he exercised a great influence both here and abroad. He took a leading part in the proceedings of Meeting in its handling of the "Free Quakers" at the time of the Revolutionary War.

WALN, ROBERT (*b. Philadelphia, Pa., 1765; d. 1836*), merchant, textile and iron manufacturer. Cousin of Nicholas Waln; father of Robert Waln (1794–1825). Active as a Federalist in the Pennsylvania legislature, and as a member of Congress, 1798–1801, he became an ardent protectionist and was identified with the high tariff acts of 1816, 1824 and 1828. He was author of *An Examination of the Boston Report* (1828) which was considered a crushing and final argument against the free traders. An orthodox Quaker, he entered into the controversy with Elias Hicks.

WALN, ROBERT (*b. Philadelphia, Pa., 1794; d. Providence, R.I., 1825*), businessman. Son of Robert Waln (1765–1836). A contributor to current periodical literature; editor of Volumes III through VI of Sanderson's *Biography of the Signers to the Declaration of Independence* (1823–24); author of *The Hermit in America* (1819, 1821) and other satires.

WALSH, BENJAMIN DANN (*b. London, England, 1808; d. near Rock Island, Ill., 1869*), businessman, entomologist. A fellow and M.A. of Trinity College, Cambridge, England, Walsh emigrated to Henry Co.,

Ill., c. 1838, where he engaged in farming and was later a lumber dealer in Rock Island. Retiring from business, c. 1858, he devoted the rest of his life to entomology, publishing a number of excellent papers in which his breadth of knowledge and accurate prophesy of the future of economic entomology were outstanding. He was the first to show that American farmers were planting crops in ways which facilitated the multiplication of insects, and was among the first to suggest introduction of foreign parasites for the control of pests. In 1868, with Charles V. Riley, he founded and edited the *American Entomologist.* An associate of Charles Darwin in England, he attacked the anti-evolutionary views of Agassiz and Dana.

WALSH, BLANCHE (*b. New York, N.Y., 1873; d. Cleveland, O., 1915*), actress. Entering her profession in the company of Marie Wainwright, 1889, she played with most of the principal American stock companies of her time and took over in 1899 the repertory of Sardou plays in which Fanny Davenport had long starred. She made the greatest success of her career as Maslova in the dramatization of Tolstoy's *Resurrection,* 1903.

WALSH, FRANCIS PATRICK (*b. St. Louis, Mo., 1864; d. New York, N.Y., 1939*), lawyer, public official. Raised in Kansas City, Mo., Walsh was admitted to the Missouri bar, 1889, and quickly became an outstanding trial lawyer. Associated with many reform movements in Kansas City, he served with ability as chairman of the U.S. Commission on Industrial Relations, 1913–18, doing much to arouse public sympathy for labor's side in industrial disputes. Active also in work for preservation of civil liberties, he was counsel for Tom Mooney during the long litigation over Mooney's conviction of murder. *Post* 1919 he acted as counsel for many labor organizations in important cases. A worker for Irish freedom and for a number of liberal causes, he served as chairman of the New York State Power Authority after his removal to New York City c. 1928, and with his friend George W. Norris was influential in shaping Franklin D. Roosevelt's ideas on public power. First president of the National Lawyers Guild, he resigned in protest over its failure to take a position against Communist dictatorships. [*Supp. 2*]

WALSH, HENRY COLLINS (*b. Florence, Italy, 1863; d. Philadelphia, Pa., 1927*), journalist, explorer, magazine editor. Grandson of Robert Walsh.

WALSH, JAMES ANTHONY (*b. Cambridge, Mass., 1867; d. Maryknoll, N.Y., 1936*), Roman Catholic clergyman. Attended Boston College and Harvard; ordained, 1892, after study at St. John's Seminary, Brighton, Mass. Interested in foreign missions from his seminary days, he worked for the establishment of an American foreign mission society and with Thomas F. Price founded the Catholic Foreign Mission Society of America (Maryknoll) which received

official approval, June 1911. Elected Maryknoll's first superior general, 1929, Father Walsh became a bishop, 1933. Before his death, the mission activities of Maryknoll had extended to China, Korea, Japan, Manchuria, the Philippines, and Hawaii. [*Supp. 2*]

WALSH, MICHAEL (*b. near Cork, Ireland, c. 1815; d. New York, N.Y., 1859*), printer, journalist, politician. Emigrated to America as a child. Resident in New York City *post* 1839, he recruited the young laboring men of the city into the Spartan Association as a workingman's protest against Tammany control of the local Democratic organization. Through the efforts of this association the organized gang became a new feature in political practice. Continuing his efforts on behalf of labor, Walsh founded a paper, the *Subterranean,* 1843, and briefly collaborated with George H. Evans in the National Reform program. When the New York Democrats split over the free-soil controversy, Walsh joined the Hunker faction, denouncing the Abolitionists who neglected the wage slaves of the North for the cause of the Negro. After service in the New York legislature and a single term in Congress (1853–55), he gradually fell into intemperance.

WALSH, ROBERT (*b. Baltimore, Md., 1784; d. Paris, France, 1859*), journalist, man of letters. Attended St. Mary's College, Baltimore, and the present Georgetown University; studied law with Robert G. Harper; traveled and studied in France and the British Isles, and for a while served as secretary to William Pinkney. Returning to the United States, 1809, he served as editor of a number of reviews and miscellanies, and in 1811 founded the first American quarterly, *The American Review of History and Politics.* He was professor of English, University of Pennsylvania, 1818–28. Among his books, which were influential in their time, were *A Letter on the Genius and Dispositions of the French Government* (1810); *An Appeal from the Judgments of Great Britain Respecting the United States of America* (1819); and *Didactics: Social, Literary and Political* (1836). Settling permanently in Paris, 1837, he founded there what was probably the first American salon and was U.S. consul-general, 1844–51.

WALSH, THOMAS (*b. Brooklyn, N.Y., 1871; d. Brooklyn, 1928*), poet, critic, editor. Graduated Georgetown University, 1892; Ph.D., 1899. Distinguished as a student and translator of Hispanic literature, Walsh engaged also in general editorial work, and was assistant editor of the *Commonweal,* New York City, 1924–28. A selection of his original poems and translations appeared in 1930; he was editor of the *Hispanic Anthology* (1920) and of *The Catholic Anthology* (1927, 1932).

WALSH, THOMAS JAMES (*b. Two Rivers, Wis., 1859; d. on a train en route to Washington, D.C., 1933*), lawyer, statesman. LL.B., University of Wisconsin, 1884. Beginning practice in Dakota Territory, he removed to Helena, Mont., 1890, where he won a reputation in copper litigation and as a constitutional lawyer. He was U.S. senator, Democrat, from Montana, 1913–33. Invariably on the liberal side in debates, he advocated woman suffrage and the child-labor amendment, and also the protection of farm organizations and trade unions from suit under the Sherman Act. He was a loyal follower of the policies of President Woodrow Wilson. His greatest fame derived from his services as counsel and director of the investigation of leases of naval oil reserves in Wyoming and California to private individuals, an investigation brought about by a resolution introduced in the Senate by Robert M. LaFollette, April 1922. After 18 months' study of the evidence, Walsh began public hearings in October 1923 and disclosed with calm precision and unemotional clarity the whole sordid story of Teapot Dome and Elk Hills. The leases in consequence voided and the public officials responsible for them were discredited. Selected as U.S. attorney-general in the cabinet of President F. D. Roosevelt, Walsh died suddenly before Roosevelt's inauguration.

WALTER, ALBERT G. (*b. Germany, 1811; d. Pittsburgh, Pa., 1876*), surgeon. M.D., University of Königsberg; studied also in Berlin and in London. Emigrated to America, *c.* 1835, and practiced in Pittsburgh, Pa., *post* 1837. An American pioneer in orthopedic surgery and a versatile general surgeon, Walter performed an epoch-making laparotomy for the relief of a ruptured bladder, January 1859. He was author, among other medical writings, of *Conservative Surgery . . . in Cases of Severe Traumatic Injuries of the Limbs* (1867).

WALTER, THOMAS (*b. Roxbury, Mass., 1696; d. Roxbury, 1725*), Congregational clergyman. Nephew of Cotton Mather. Assistant pastor at Roxbury *post* 1718, he engaged in a controversy with John Checkley, but is principally remembered as author of *The Grounds and Rules of Musick Explained* (1721). This was an effort, scientifically and artistically conceived, to correct the "horrid medley of confused and disorderly sounds" which passed for singing in the New England churches.

WALTER, THOMAS (*b. Hampshire, England, c. 1740; d. South Carolina, 1789*), planter, botanist. Emigrated to eastern South Carolina as a young man. Author of a work of lasting scientific importance—*Flora Caroliniana* (London, 1788), the first tolerably complete account of the flora of any definite portion of eastern North America in which an author used the so-called binomial system of nomenclature.

WALTER, THOMAS USTICK (*b. Philadelphia, Pa., 1804; d. 1887*), architect. A master bricklayer, Walter studied architecture under William Strickland and others at the Franklin Institute. After entering practice in 1830, he designed the Moyamensing Prison, Philadelphia, and also Girard College (1833) which marked the climax and at the same time sounded the knell of the Greek Revival in America. He had charge of the extension of the U.S. Capitol at Washington, 1851–65, adding the wings of the present structure, the dome, and also projecting a center extension. Among his other works in Washington were the completion of the Treasury Building begun by Robert Mills, St. Elizabeth's Hospital, and the design for the interior of the State, War, and Navy Building. He also assisted Nicholas Biddle in the design of "Andalusia" and designed churches, banks and private houses in Philadelphia, Baltimore, Richmond and elsewhere. He helped organize the American Institute of Architects, 1857, and served as its president, 1876–87.

WALTERS, ALEXANDER (*b. Bardstown, Ky., 1858; d. 1917*), bishop of the African Methodist Episcopal Zion Church. An active minister *post* 1877 in a number of cities throughout the United States, he became pastor of "Mother Zion" in New York City, 1888, and was elected bishop, 1892. He was an organizer of the Afro-American League and later president of the National Afro-American Council. He was author of *My Life and Work* (1917).

WALTERS, HENRY (*b. Baltimore, Md., 1848; d. New York, N.Y., 1931*), capitalist, art collector. Son of William T. Walters whom he assisted and succeeded in the development of the Atlantic Coast Line Railroad and other large operations. Adding extensively to his father's collections of art, he established the Walters Art Gallery and bequeathed it, with an endowment, to the City of Baltimore.

WALTERS, WILLIAM THOMPSON (*b. Liverpool, Pa., 1820; d. 1894*), merchant, railroad executive, art collector. Father of Henry Walters. Played an important part in the railroad development of the South by consolidating a number of small roads and co-ordinating their service. After the interruption of his plans by the Civil War, Walters renewed his activities when efficient through service by rail to the North was demanded by development of truck-farming in eastern North Carolina and Virginia. In 1889 he incorporated the holding company, later known as the Atlantic Coast Line Co., which, under his son, became the means of effecting consolidation of roads from Washington to Florida and the Gulf ports, and also to Memphis and St. Louis. He was an eager collector of objects of art and a patron of artists; he was also a breeder of fine stock and brought the Percheron horse to America.

WALTHALL, EDWARD CARY (*b. Richmond, Va., 1831; d. Washington, D.C., 1898*), Confederate major-general, lawyer. Raised in Mississippi where he began practice at Coffeeville, 1852. An officer of unusual bravery and steadiness, he fought with tenacity at Chickamauga, at Lookout Mountain, and at Missionary

Ridge where his brigade covered the Confederate retreat. After sharing in the fighting about Atlanta, he served under Hood in Tennessee. A friend of Lucius Q. C. Lamar, he helped overthrow the Carpetbag government in Mississippi, and was U.S. senator, Democrat, 1885–94, 1895–98. Like Lamar, he was an advocate of conciliation and strove to lessen sectional animosity.

WALTHALL, HENRY BRAZEAL (*b. Shelby Co., Ala., 1878; d. Monrovia, Calif., 1936*), motion picture actor. Grandnephew of Edward C. Walthall. A successful stage player, Walthall was persuaded to try the new medium of motion pictures by David W. Griffith *c.* 1909. His greatest role while under Griffith's direction was that of Benjamin Cameron in *The Birth of a Nation,* 1915. A leader in the effort to produce motion pictures that would attract educated audiences, he failed to thrive after leaving Griffith *c.* 1915 and faded from notice until the coming of talking pictures gave him the chance of a new start.

[*Supp.* 2]

WALTHER, CARL FERDINAND WILHELM (*b. near Waldenburg, Saxony, 1811; d. St. Louis, Mo., 1887*), Lutheran clergyman. Emigrated to America, 1839; settled as pastor in Perry Co., Mo. With three associates, he founded a school at Altenburg in December 1839 which was moved to St. Louis, 1850, and became Concordia Theological Seminary. Pastor in St. Louis *post* 1841, he became professor of theology in Concordia Seminary, 1850. Meanwhile, in 1844 he issued the first number of *Der Lutheraner,* and was organizer of the Missouri Synod which he served as president, 1847–50, 1864–78. Walther dominated every activity in the synod and directed it with strict efficiency. An exponent of confessional Lutheranism, he engaged in a number of controversies with other theologians in which he displayed immense learning, considerable intolerance and a strong belief in his own inerrancy. His influence has been greater than that of any other American Lutheran clergyman of the 19th century.

WALTON, GEORGE (*b. near Farmville, Va., 1741; d. "College Hill," near Augusta, Ga., 1804*), lawyer, Revolutionary patriot and soldier. Removed to Savannah, Ga., 1769. Served on Revolutionary committees; was secretary of the Georgia Provincial Congress and president of the Council of Safety. Elected to the Continental Congress, February 1776, he served until 1778 and from 1779 until September 1781. A signer of the Declaration of Independence, he was a member of a number of important committees. He advocated an equal vote for all states and urged that the Indian trade be made a monopoly and that its control be vested in Congress. In January 1777, with George Taylor, he negotiated a treaty with the Six Nations at Easton, Pa. A conservative Whig and opponent of the radicals led by Button Gwinnett, he was governor of Georgia from November 1779 to January 1780. Chief justice of Georgia, 1783–89, he was again governor, 1789–90. This second term was marked by the establishment of a new state constitution, the location of the state capital at Augusta, and by pacification of the Creek Indians. He was several times a judge of the superior court of Georgia between 1790 and his death, and was U.S. senator, Federalist, from Georgia, 1795–99.

WALWORTH, CLARENCE AUGUSTUS (*b. Plattsburgh, N.Y., 1820; d. 1900*), Roman Catholic clergyman, Paulist. Son of Reuben H. Walworth. Graduated Union, 1838. After beginning the practice of law, he attended the General Theological Seminary, New York City. On becoming a Catholic in 1845, he went with Isaac T. Hecker and J. A. McMaster to study theology at St. Trond in Belgium and entered the Redemptorist Order. Ordained, 1848, he preached as a missionary in England, and returned to America, 1851, where he preached missions until 1858. With Hecker and others he helped found the Congregation of St. Paul the Apostle (Paulists), 1858. After further missionary service, he was pastor at St. Mary's Church, Albany, N.Y., *post* 1866. Among his books is a notable study, *The Oxford Movement in America* (1895).

WALWORTH, JEANNETTE RITCHIE HADERMANN (*b. Philadelphia, Pa., 1837; d. New Orleans, La., 1918*), Southern novelist. Author, among much negligible work, of *Southern Silhouettes* (1887), a series of post-Civil War sketches.

WALWORTH, REUBEN HYDE (*b. Bozrah, Conn., 1788; d. 1867*), jurist. Father of Clarence A. Walworth. Admitted to the New York bar, 1809, he began practice at Plattsburgh. During the War of 1812 he served as adjutant-general of the state militia, distinguishing himself in the land battles at Plattsburgh, Sept. 6 and 11, 1814. Congressman, Democrat, from New York, 1821–23, he was circuit judge of the supreme court for the fourth judicial district of New York, 1823–28. Succeeding James Kent as chancellor of New York, 1828, he made important contributions to the system of equity jurisprudence which had been erected by Kent. He filled numerous gaps in the law of evidence and in equity pleading and practice by his decisions; he also added materially to the law relating to injunctions, to arbitration in equity matters, and the adoption of statutes in the Northwest Territory. A number of appeals were taken from his decisions to the court of errors, and in about one-third of these cases he was reversed. Given to biting sarcasm on the bench, he won a host of enemies, and the abolition of the court of chancery under the New York constitution of 1846 has been attributed in great measure to the desire of the bar to retire Walworth to private life. He thus contributed by indirection to an important legal reform, the merger of the courts of law and equity. Upon retirement in 1848, he was Democratic candidate for governor, but lost to Hamilton Fish. He then retired from political life.

WANAMAKER, JOHN (*b. Philadelphia, Pa., 1838; d. near Philadelphia, 1922*), merchant, pioneer in development of the modern department store. Beginning as an errand boy, he became a salesman of men's clothing. Between 1857 and 1860 he was secretary of the Y.M.C.A. in Philadelphia, the first paid secretary of that organization. Opening a men's clothing shop in Philadelphia with his brother-in-law, 1861, Wanamaker conducted the business successfully and in 1876, with characteristic showmanship, opened a huge dry-goods and clothing store in the former freight depot of the Pennsylvania Railroad at 13th and Chestnut Sts. In March of the next year he inaugurated his "new kind of store," a collection of specialty shops under one roof, with which he had extraordinary success. In 1896 he bought the New York City store of Alexander T. Stewart and continued it as Wanamaker's. An innovator and even a gambler, he began in 1865 a policy of guaranteeing their money back to dissatisfied customers; he was also a master of the art of publicity, notably newspaper advertising. He provided an employee's mutual-benefit association (1881), training classes for clerks, and other educational and recreational features. A consistent Republican, he was U.S. postmaster-general, 1889–93. Although he instituted several technical improvements in the Post Office, he was denounced by reformers for his use of the spoils system.

WANAMAKER, LEWIS RODMAN (*b. Philadelphia, Pa., 1863; d. Atlantic City, N.J., 1928*), merchant. Son of John Wanamaker. Graduated College of New Jersey (Princeton), 1886. A member of the Wanamaker firm *post* 1902, and sole owner and director *post* 1922, he was responsible for the emphasis on the sale of antiques and other art objects which became an integral part of the business. A collector of rare musical instruments, he instituted public concerts in both the New York and Philadelphia stores. He was also an enthusiast for aviation and financed several expeditions among the Indian tribes of the West for the purpose of study.

WANAMAKER, REUBEN MELVILLE (*b. North Jackson, O., 1866; d. Columbus, O., 1924*), Ohio jurist, reformer of Ohio criminal jurisprudence.

WANLESS, WILLIAM JAMES (*b. Charleston, Ontario, Canada, 1865; d. Glendale, Calif., 1933*), Presbyterian medical missionary. Active in service in India, 1889–1930, principally at Miraj, he received knighthood (1928) for extraordinary work as hospital builder and medical teacher.

WANTON, JOSEPH (*b. Newport, R.I., 1705; d. Newport, 1780*), merchant, colonial governor of Rhode Island, 1769–75. A partial sympathizer with the Revolutionary movement in America, he opposed independence and retired from public life shortly after the outbreak of hostilities at Lexington.

WARBURG, FELIX MORITZ (*b. Hamburg, Germany, 1871; d. New York, N.Y., 1937*), financier, philanthropist. Brother of Paul M. Warburg; son-in-law of Jacob H. Schiff. Came to America, 1894; became partner in Kuhn, Loeb & Co., 1897. Although he was the senior partner of this banking firm at the time of his death, Felix Warburg was primarily a humanitarian and lent his support to innumerable charitable, educational, and cultural organizations. A member of the New York City Board of Education and trustee of a number of schools including Teachers College at Columbia University, he also worked closely with Lillian D. Wald in her settlement work and was a leader in the establishment and management of the Federation for Support of Jewish Philanthropic Societies. Never a Zionist, he became increasingly associated *post* 1917 with the work of the Zionists in relocating displaced Jews and in securing a peaceful settlement of the Arab-Jewish problem in Palestine. [*Supp. 2*]

WARBURG, PAUL MORITZ (*b. Hamburg, Germany, 1868; d. New York, N.Y., 1932*), banker. A partner in Kuhn, Loeb & Co., New York City, *post* 1902, Warburg was an authority on the central banking system employed in the principal European countries. After the panic of 1907 he joined with those urging a fundamental reform in the American banking system, and had a large part in the plan for a proposed national reserve association submitted by Sen. Nelson W. Aldrich in 1911. Although the Federal Reserve law of 1913 was not wholly to his liking, Warburg served with great ability as a member of the first Federal Reserve Board, 1914–18. Thereafter he devoted himself chiefly to the organization and operation of the International Acceptance Bank. He received nation-wide notice in March 1929 because of his plain warning of the disaster threatened by the wild stock speculation of that period; he predicted that unless speculation were brought under control, a general depression would ensue. After the panic of October 1929 and the succeeding commercial depression, he was quick to condemn emotional prophecies of ruin just as vigorously as he had warned against the delusions of the period of speculation. In analyzing the causes of the depression, he stressed the bad effects of efforts to maintain high prices by tariff barriers and other artificial expedients in the face of constantly accelerated mass production. He was the brother of Felix M. Warburg.

WARD, AARON MONTGOMERY (*b. Chatham, N.J., 1843; d. Highland Park, Ill., 1913*), mail-order merchant. As a salesman traveling out of St. Louis, Mo., Ward became aware of the difficulties of people in rural areas who were obliged to sell their own produce at low prices determined by competition, but had to make their own retail purchases at high cost without competition. He then conceived the idea of buying goods in large quantities for cash from the manufacturer and selling for cash by mail to the farmer. He began operations with his partner, G. R. Thorne, in Chicago, Ill., 1872; the firm's first stock was a small selection of dry goods, the first catalogue a single price sheet. By shrewd purchasing and a policy of permitting the return of goods if unsatisfactory, Ward succeeded from the very outset. By 1876 the Montgomery Ward catalogue had 150 pages with illustrations; at the time of his death, annual sales amounted to $40,000,000. Owing to a prolonged legal battle which he carried on in the Illinois courts, Chicago's lake frontage was preserved as a heritage for the people of that city.

WARD, ARTEMAS (*b. Shrewsbury, Mass., 1727; d. Shrewsbury, 1800*), storekeeper, Massachusetts colonial legislator, Revolutionary general. Graduated Harvard, 1748. Holder of a number of offices in Worcester Co., Ward rose to colonel in the provincial militia during the French and Indian War. Active in opposition to royal authority, he became a member of the Council, 1770–74, despite disapproval of the royal governor. A member of the first and second Massachusetts provincial congresses, he took command of the forces besieging Boston, April 1775, and in May was formally commissioned general and commander-in-chief of Massachusetts troops. Reduced to second-in-command with the rank of major-general after the appointment of George Washington to supreme command, he viewed his successor without cordiality and offered his resignation to Congress soon after the fall of Boston, March 1776. He remained, however, in command at Boston after the withdrawal of the main army to New York until relieved by William Heath, March 1777. Thereafter, he served as a councillor of Massachusetts, as a legislator, and as a member of the Continental Congress. As congressman, Federalist, from Massachusetts, 1791–95, he was assigned to committees dealing with military affairs.

WARD, ARTEMUS. [See BROWNE, CHARLES FARRAR, 1834–1867.]

WARD, CHARLES HENSHAW (*b. Norfolk, Nebr., 1872; d. New Haven, Conn., 1935*), teacher. A.B., Pomona College, 1896; A.M., Yale, 1899. Taught English at the Taft School, Watertown, Conn., 1903–22. Wrote a number of elementary textbooks of grammar and English and several popular expository works on the sciences. [*Supp. 1*]

WARD, CYRENUS OSBORNE (*b. western New York State, 1831; d. Yuma, Ariz., 1902*), machinist, labor journalist and lecturer. Brother of Lester F. Ward. Author, among other works, of *A Labor Catechism of Political Economy* (1878) and *A History of the Ancient Working People* (1889, later published as *The Ancient Lowly*). He urged working people to refrain from violence and to achieve a socialistic state by political methods.

WARD, ELIZABETH STUART PHELPS (*b. Boston, Mass., 1844; d. 1911*), writer. Daughter of Austin Phelps; granddaughter of Moses Stuart. Married Herbert D. Ward, 1888. Interpreter of the intellectual, oversensitive people of New England and their compulsion to do "the painful right," she was the author of the phenomenally successful *The Gates Ajar* (1869) and of many works of fiction, including *The Silent Partner* (1871), *The Madonna of the Tubs* (1886) and *A Singular Life* (1894).

WARD, FREDERICK TOWNSEND (*b. Salem, Mass., 1831; d. Tzeki, China, 1862*), adventurer, soldier. After a number of years at sea, and in military service with William Walker in Nicaragua and with the French in the Crimea, he appeared in Shanghai, China, 1859. Developing an army of well-drilled Chinese soldiers which came to be called the "Ever Victorious Army," he opposed the Taiping rebels and recaptured Sungkiang. His force later co-operated effectively with the Anglo-French forces near Shanghai and Ning-po. He was mortally wounded in battle. The celebrated British general Charles "Chinese" Gordon later achieved success in quelling the rebellion with the military instrument which Ward had created.

WARD, GENEVIEVE (*b. New York, N.Y., 1838; d. London, England, 1922*), singer, actress. After success in opera in Paris, she made her American debut at the Academy of Music, New York City, November 1862, in *La Traviata* as Violetta. On the failure of her singing voice, she studied for the dramatic stage and played with success at both Drury Lane and the Comédie-Française, 1875–77. Thereafter she was professionally active in the United States and abroad, scoring her greatest success in *Forget-Me-Not* by Herman Merivale. An intellectual player, she was described as of the school of Ristori.

WARD, GEORGE GRAY (*b. Great Hadham, England, 1844; d. New York, N.Y., 1922*), telegrapher, cable engineer. Came to America *c.* 1876 as U.S. superintendent of a new cable company which broke the existing monopoly of the Anglo-American Telegraph Co. Served as general manager of the Commercial Cable Co. *post* 1884. Ward was primarily responsible for the diplomatic and engineering aspects of the work that resulted in the first cable across the Pacific. It was laid to Honolulu in 1902, to Manila in 1903, and to China and Japan in 1906.

WARD, HENRY AUGUSTUS (*b. Rochester, N.Y., 1834; d. Buffalo, N.Y., 1906*), naturalist. Assisted in his efforts by the family of James S. Wadsworth, Ward worked under Agassiz at Cambridge, Mass., and later studied at the School of Mines in Paris, France. Professor of natural science in the University of Rochester, 1861–76, he is principally remembered for his founding of Ward's Natural Science Establishment for the preparation and sale of scientific materials to colleges and other institutions. Engaged chiefly in this work *post* 1864, he made a number of outstanding collections, including the natural history exhibit at the World's Columbian Exposition in 1893 which was bought by Marshall Field and was the nucleus of the Field Museum of Natural History.

WARD, HENRY DANA (*b. Shrewsbury, Mass., 1797; d. Philadelphia, Pa., 1884*), reformer, Episcopal clergyman. Grandson of Artemas Ward. Active in the Anti-Masonic movement and party *post* 1828, and in William Miller's Adventist movement, he was ordained to the Episcopal ministry, 1844. Thereafter he devoted most of his time to teaching in New York City and Flushing, N.Y.

WARD, HERBERT DICKINSON (*b. Waltham, Mass., 1861; d. Portsmouth, N.H., 1932*), author. Son of William H. Ward; husband of Elizabeth S. P. Ward.

WARD, JAMES EDWARD (*b. New York, N.Y., 1836; d. Great Neck, N.Y., 1894*), shipowner and operator. Originally a ship chandler and manager of a general freighting business to Cuba, Ward instituted direct passenger and mail service to Havana by steamship, 1877, as the Ward Line. The firm was incorporated, 1881, as the New York & Cuba Mail Steamship Co.

WARD, JAMES HARMON (*b. Hartford, Conn., 1806; d. off Matthias Point, Va., 1861*), naval officer. Appointed midshipman, 1823. One of the most scholarly officers in the service and a recognized authority on ordnance and naval tactics, he was author of *An Elementary Course of Instruction on Ordnance and Gunnery* (1845) and of *A Manual of Naval Tactics* (1859). He served as first commandant of midshipmen at the U.S. Naval Academy, 1845–47. Commanding a flying flotilla which he had proposed for use on Chesapeake Bay and the Potomac River in the Civil War, he silenced Confederate batteries at Aquia Creek, June 1, 1861, and was killed in action about three weeks later.

WARD, JAMES WARNER (*b. Newark, N.J., 1816; d. Buffalo, N.Y., 1897*), teacher. Appointed librarian of the Grosvenor Library in Buffalo, 1874, he served until 1896, and brought the library to a position of eminence.

WARD, JOHN ELLIOTT (*b. Sunbury, Ga., 1814; d. Dorchester, Ga., 1902*), lawyer, Georgia legislator and official. Having held, among other offices, the posts of acting lieutenant-governor of the state and mayor of Savannah, he presided over the Democratic Convention at Cincinnati, O., 1856, which nominated James Buchanan. As U.S. minister to China, 1859–60, he was successful in exchanging ratifications of the new American treaty with China and in settling outstanding American claims. Opposed to the secession of Georgia, he took no part in the Civil War. *Post* 1866 he practiced law in New York City.

WARD, JOHN QUINCY ADAMS (*b. near Urbana, O., 1830; d. New York, N.Y., 1910*), sculptor. Began career as student assistant to Henry Kirke Brown *c.* 1849. Winning notice for bust portraits of Alexander H. Stephens, John P. Hale and other statesmen in Washington, D.C., 1857–59, he opened a studio in New York City, 1861. His "Indian Hunter" was among the first statues to be placed in New York's Central Park; conceived as a statuette in 1857, it was sited, 1868. Meanwhile, along with "The Freedman" it had been shown in the Paris Exposition of 1867. These works, and also his statue of Matthew C. Perry and his 7th Regiment Memorial in Central Park, showed his characteristic technical mastery, but his finest work was still to come. Winning further fame for his equestrian monument to Gen. G. H. Thomas (1878) and his statue of William G. Simms (1879), he touched the heights in his "Lafayette" (Burlington, Vt.) and his "George Washington" (Wall St., New York City, Sub-treasury Building), both of 1883. Among other outstanding works by Ward were his "Pilgrim," placed in Central Park, 1885; his "Horace Greeley" in City Hall Park, New York; the James A. Garfield monument in Washington; and the Henry Ward Beecher monument, Borough Hall, Brooklyn, N.Y. Ward was at his best in realistic rather than in idealized representation and preferred masculine themes. He was the first native sculptor to create without benefit of foreign training an impressive body of good work. Bringing a primitive Ohio vigor to what he did, he showed himself wholly out of sympathy with the mid-Victorian pseudo-classic ideals fostered in Florence and Rome. In the final decade of his life he produced, among other works, the pediment of the New York Stock Exchange and the equestrian statue of General Hancock, Fairmount Park, Philadelphia, both in collaboration with Paul Bartlett. A generous man, he gave his support to every worthy enterprise in art.

WARD, JOSEPH (*b. Perry Centre, N.Y., 1838; d. 1889*), Congregational clergyman. Graduated Brown, 1865; attended Andover Theological Seminary. Began his ministry at Yankton, Dakota Territory, 1869. Opened a private school there which became the Yankton Academy, 1872, and was eventually made the Yankton High School, earliest in the territory. Principal founder of Yankton College, 1881, he served there as president and professor of philosophy until his death. The education law of South Dakota was almost wholly his work, and he played a great part in keeping the school lands of the territory safe from speculators.

WARD, LESTER FRANK (*b. Joliet, Ill., 1841; d. Washington, D.C., 1913*), Union soldier, sociologist. Brother of Cyrenus O. Ward. Raised in Illinois and Iowa. After Civil War service, he worked in the U.S. Treasury Department at Washington, D.C., 1865–81, meanwhile receiving from Columbian College (present George Washington University) the A.B. degree in 1869, the LL.B. in 1871 and the A.M.

in 1872. Joining the staff of the U.S. Geological Survey, 1881, he was appointed geologist, 1883, and paleontologist, 1892. He was professor of sociology at Brown University, 1906–13. Ward made valuable studies in the natural sciences, but he is best known because of his leadership in the field of American sociology. He became a pioneer of evolutionary sociology in the United States through the publication of *Dynamic Sociology* (1883), *Outlines of Sociology* (1898), *Pure Sociology* (1903) and other works in which he sought to give a strongly monist and evolutionary interpretation to social development. He argued that the emotional, willing aspects of the human mind have produced ambitious aspirations for individual and social improvement, and that the intellect, when rightly informed with scientific truth, enables the individual or the social group to plan for future development. The mind will become "telic," enabling mankind to pass from passive to active evolutionary processes, and from natural to human or social evolution. This ability will usher in an age of systematic planning for human progress in which government will stress social welfare and democracy will pass into "sociocracy." Accepting the fact of wide differences in human heredity and racial aptitudes, he argued that latent talent can be called forth by a stimulating social environment and a general education in the sciences. Governments, therefore, should aim to abolish poverty and develop national systems of general education, suited in one aspect for genius, in another, for ordinary minds. He was author also of a "mental autobiography," *Glimpses of the Cosmos* (1913–18).

WARD, LYDIA ARMS AVERY COONLEY (*b. Lynchburg, Va., 1845; d. Chicago, Ill., 1924*), author, Chicago civic leader. Wife of Henry A. Ward.

WARD, MARCUS LAWRENCE (*b. Newark, N.J., 1812; d. 1884*), businessman, philanthropist. Republican governor of New Jersey, January 1866—January 1869; congressman from New Jersey, 1873–75. Established Civil War welfare institutions in Newark; secured passage of reform legislation as governor.

WARD, MONTGOMERY. [See WARD, AARON MONTGOMERY, 1843–1913.]

WARD, NANCY (*fl. 1776–1781*), Cherokee leader, known as "Beloved Woman." A resident of Great Echota in present Monroe Co., Tenn., she was a strong advocate of peace and a friend of the white frontier settlers. On several occasions during the Revolution she warned the settlers in the Watauga and Holston valleys in time to save themselves from raids and exercised her tribal right of sparing prisoners.

WARD, NATHANIEL (*b. Haverhill, England, c. 1578; d. Shenfield, England, 1652*), lawyer, clergyman, author. A.B., Emmanuel College, Cambridge, 1599; A.M., 1603. After practicing law for some time in England, he entered the ministry c. 1619 and was chaplain to the British merchants at Elbing, Prussia.

Returning to England, 1624, he was successively curate of St. James's, Piccadilly, London, and rector of Stondon Massey. Dismissed for nonconformity, 1633, he emigrated to Massachusetts Bay, 1634, and served briefly as a colleague minister at Agawam (Ipswich). Resigning his ministry, he was appointed by the General Court in 1638 to help prepare a legal code for Massachusetts, the first code of laws to be established in New England. According to John Winthrop, these laws (enacted, 1641) were composed by Ward. The code was known as the "Body of Liberties" and was in effect a bill of rights, setting one of the cornerstones in American constitutional history. In 1645 Ward completed *The Simple Cobler of Aggawam in America* (London, 1647, under pseudonym "Theodore de la Guard"). The book was a protest against toleration, amusingly digressive and satirical; through it runs the prophecy of Presbyterianism. Ward expressed a strong opposition to "polypiety" in the church; in the state he would restore the old order with king, lords and commons. Several other works in defense of tradition have been attributed to him. He was minister at Shenfield *post* 1648.

WARD, RICHARD (*b. Newport, R.I., 1689; d. 1763*), merchant, Rhode Island colonial legislator and official. Father of Samuel Ward (1725–1776). Elected deputy governor of Rhode Island, May 1740, he became governor a few months later and continued in office three years. A conservative, he supported colonial defense efforts, unsuccessfully opposed excessive issue of paper money, supported Rhode Island in a boundary controversy with Massachusetts, and protested against invasion of charter rights by the British.

WARD, RICHARD HALSTED (*b. Bloomfield, N.J., 1837; d. 1917*), physician, microscopist. Graduated Williams, 1858; M.D., N.Y. College of Physicians and Surgeons, 1862. *Post* 1863 he practiced in Troy, N.Y., and taught botany and other scientific subjects at Rensselaer Polytechnic Institute, 1867–92. One of the first to demonstrate by the microscope the difference in cellular structure of blood from various animals, he was also an authority on adulteration of foods and medicines. He perfected a number of accessories for the microscope, notably an iris illuminator for the binocular instrument.

WARD, ROBERT DeCOURCY (*b. Boston, Mass., 1867; d. 1931*), educator, climatologist. Graduated Harvard, 1889; A.M., 1893. Taught physical geography and meteorology at Harvard *post* 1890, becoming professor of climatology, 1910, the first in the United States. Author of *Practical Exercises in Elementary Meteorology* (1899), *The Climate of the United States* (1925) and other works.

WARD, SAMUEL (*b. Newport, R.I., 1725; d. Philadelphia, Pa., 1776*), farmer, Rhode Island colonial legislator. Son of Richard Ward. Conservative opponent of Stephen Hopkins in pre-Revolutionary politics. Governor of Rhode Island, 1762, 1765 and 1766, Ward signed the charter of the present Brown University, of which he was an original trustee. He vigorously opposed the Stamp Act. Elected a delegate to the First and Second Continental Congresses, Ward served as chairman of the Committee of the Whole, 1775, and proposed the appointment of George Washington as commander-in-chief of the colonial forces.

WARD, SAMUEL (*b. Westerly, R.I., 1756; d. New York, N.Y., 1832*), Revolutionary soldier, New York City merchant. Son of Samuel Ward (1725–1776); father of Samuel Ward (1786–1839).

WARD, SAMUEL (*b. Warwick, R.I., 1786; d. New York, N.Y., 1839*), banker. Son of Samuel Ward (1756–1832); father of Samuel Ward (1814–1884) and Julia Ward Howe. Became partner in the New York banking house of Prime & Sands, 1808; later became head of the firm, then known as Prime, Ward & King. Prevented repudiation of financial obligations by New York State in the panic of 1837; helped restore specie payments by New York banks in 1838. Helped found and became president of the Bank of Commerce in New York, 1839.

WARD, SAMUEL (*b. New York, N.Y., 1814; d. Pegli, Italy, 1884*), financier, lobbyist, author. Son of Samuel Ward (1786–1839); brother of Julia Ward Howe; uncle of Francis Marion Crawford. Graduated Columbia, 1831; made studies in France and Germany; worked briefly in his father's banking house of Prime, Ward & King. Having lost his fortune by 1849, he joined the gold rush to California, where he adapted himself with great success to the rough environment. He became the confidant of James R. Keene who helped him with financial advice. After journalistic and other activities, he lived in Washington, D.C., during the closing years of the Civil War and through the administrations of Andrew Johnson and U. S. Grant, acting as a lobbyist in the employ of financiers and gaining a reputation for the entertainments which he offered to public officials. Among the intimates of the "King of the Lobby," as he was known, were W. H. Seward, Charles Sumner, James A. Garfield, William M. Evarts; he was also a friend of W. M. Thackeray and Henry W. Longfellow. Described as having "a vagueness concerning all points of morality, which would have been terrible in a man less actively good," Ward was author of *Lyrical Recreations* (1865, 1871) and is believed today to have been the author of "The Diary of a Public Man" (*North American Review*, August–November 1879).

WARD, SAMUEL RINGGOLD (*b. Maryland, 1817; d. Jamaica, B.W.I., c. 1866*), Negro Abolitionist and orator, Baptist and Congregational clergyman. Agent of the American and the New York State Anti-Slavery societies and of the Anti-Slavery Society of Canada. Spoke extensively and successfully in Great Britain, 1853–54.

WARD, THOMAS (*b. Newark, N.J., 1807; d. 1873*), physician, poet, playwright. Author, among other works, of *Passaic, a Group of Poems* (1842, under pseudonym "Flaccus") and *War Lyrics* (1865). Produced amateur operettas for charity in a theatre attached to his New York City house, 1862–72.

WARD, THOMAS WREN (*b. Salem, Mass., 1786; d. 1858*), Boston merchant. Becoming American agent for the London, England, banking establishment of Baring Brothers through influence of his friend, Joshua Bates, Ward held that post from 1830 to 1853. Supervising operations which annually involved several millions of pounds sterling, he was regarded as one of the soundest financiers in the United States. He succeeded in bringing the firm through the crisis of 1837–42 with unimpaired reputation and credit.

WARD, WILLIAM HAYES (*b. Abington, Mass., 1835; d. 1916*), editor, Orientalist. Father of Herbert D. Ward. Graduated Amherst, 1856; Andover Theological Seminary, 1859. Associated in editorial capacities with the *New York Independent*, 1868–1916. One of the earliest Assyriologists in the United States, he became the leading authority in the world on Assyrian and Babylonian seals. An exploring expedition conducted by him, 1884–85, resulted in the uncovering of ancient Nippur, 1888–1900. He was author, among other works, of *The Seal Cylinders of Western Asia* (1910).

WARDE, FREDERICK BARKHAM (*b. Deddington, England, 1851; d. Brooklyn, N.Y., 1935*), actor. Making his American debut in New York at Booth's Theatre, 1874, he subsequently played Shakespearean roles in support of Edwin Booth, Charlotte Cushman, Madame Janauschek, and others. At his death, he represented the last of the old school of tragedians. *Post* 1907 he lectured on Shakespeare and other topics connected with the drama, displaying scholarship and taste. [*Supp. 1*]

WARDEN, DAVID BAILIE (*b. near Greyabbey, Ireland, 1772; d. France, 1845*), teacher, diplomat, collector of Americana. A.M., University of Glasgow, 1797. Emigrated to America, 1799, after his arrest for association with the United Irishmen. Becoming a U.S. citizen, 1804, he went to Paris as private secretary to Gen. John Armstrong and was later consul at Paris. After his removal from office, 1814, he spent the rest of his life in France, but gave a great deal of his time to the dissemination of information concerning America. He was author, among other works, of *On the Origin . . . of Consular Establishments* (1813), *A Statistical, Political and Historical Account of the United States of North America* (1819) and several annotated catalogues of his book collections.

WARDEN, ROBERT BRUCE (*b. Bardstown, Ky., 1824; d. Washington, D.C., 1888*), Ohio jurist and supreme court reporter. Author of biographies of Salmon P. Chase and Stephen A. Douglas.

WARDER, JOHN ASTON (*b. Philadelphia, Pa., 1812; d. 1883*), physician. Associated as a boy with John J. Audubon, François Michaux and Thomas Nuttall. M.D., Jefferson Medical College, 1836. Practiced in Cincinnati, O., 1837–55. Thereafter a farmer at North Bend, O., he was active in the state and national horticultural and pomological societies as officer and editor. He served as president of the American Forestry Association, 1875–82, and was an organizer of its successor, the American Forestry Congress. Among his books were *Hedges and Evergreens* (1858) and *American Pomology: Apples* (1867).

WARDMAN, ERVIN (*b. Salt Lake City, Utah, 1865; d. 1923*), journalist. Graduated Harvard, 1888. On staff of *New York Tribune*, 1889–95, he was briefly managing editor of the *New York Press* and its editor-in-chief, 1896–1916. He made the paper an aggressive organ of liberal Republicanism and in the late 1890's coined the term "yellow journalism." *Post* 1916 he was publisher of the New York *Sun*. As an editorial writer his chief field was labor economics.

WARE, ASHUR (*b. Sherborn, Mass., 1782; d. 1873*), editor, jurist. Nephew of Henry Ware (1764–1845). Graduated Harvard, 1804; studied law in office of Loammi Baldwin. Removed to Portland, Maine, 1817, mainly to edit the *Eastern Argus*, and was an active force in Maine's home-rule politics and in the Democratic party. Becoming Maine's secretary of state, 1820, he served as U.S. district court judge in Maine, 1822–66. He was, in the opinion of Judge Story, perhaps the ablest American authority in the field of maritime law.

WARE, EDMUND ASA (*b. North Wrentham, Mass., 1837; d. 1885*), Congregational clergyman, educator. Graduated Yale, 1863. Appointed superintendent of education for Georgia by Gen. O. O. Howard, 1867, Ware was a founder of Atlanta University (chartered 1867, opened 1869) and served as its president until his death. His idealism and courage were important factors in the university's success.

WARE, HENRY (*b. Sherborn, Mass., 1764; d. Cambridge, Mass., 1845*), Unitarian clergyman, theologian. Graduated Harvard, 1785. Pastor, First Church, Hingham, Mass., 1787–1805. His election as Hollis Professor of Divinity at Harvard in 1805 marked a new era in the history of Congregationalism and gave rise to a controversy between members of the liberal and orthodox parties. In 1820 the liberal Ware engaged in pamphlet argument with Dr. Leonard Woods (1774–1854) known as the "Wood'n Ware Controversy." In 1811, Ware began a course of instruction for ministerial candidates from which developed the Harvard Divinity School (organized, 1816), with Ware as professor of systematic theology and evidences. He resigned as Hollis Professor, 1840, but continued to teach in the Divinity School. He was father of Henry (1794–1843), John and William Ware.

WARE, HENRY (*b. Hingham, Mass., 1794; d. Framingham, Mass., 1843*), Unitarian clergyman, author. Son of Henry Ware (1764–1845); brother of John and William Ware; father of John F. W. Ware and William R. Ware. Graduated Harvard, 1812. Pastor of the Second Church (Unitarian), Boston, 1817–c. 1829, he served as editor of the *Christian Disciple* and was a leader in the establishment of the American Unitarian Association. He was professor of pulpit eloquence and pastoral care in Harvard Divinity School, c. 1830–1842.

WARE, JOHN (*b. Hingham, Mass., 1795; d. 1864*), physician, editor. Son of Henry Ware (1764–1845); brother of Henry (1794–1843) and William Ware. Graduated Harvard, 1813; M.D., Harvard Medical School, 1816. Practicing in Boston, he served as editor of several publications and was author in 1831 of the first important work on *delirium tremens* to appear in America. After succeeding James Jackson as Hersey Professor at Harvard Medical School, 1836, Ware was author of a number of scientific papers which included important discussions of croup and hemoptysis.

WARE, JOHN FOTHERGILL WATERHOUSE (*b. Boston, Mass., 1818; d. Milton, Mass., 1881*), Unitarian clergyman. Son of Henry Ware (1794–1843); half-brother of William R. Ware. Principal pastorates at Fall River and Cambridgeport, Mass., and at Church of the Saviour, Baltimore, Md.; pastor of Arlington Street Church, Boston, *post* 1872.

WARE, NATHANIEL A. (*b. Massachusetts or South Carolina, date uncertain; d. near Galveston, Texas, 1854*), land speculator, public official. Secretary of Mississippi Territory, 1815–17, he lived thereafter in a number of places both North and South. He is best remembered for *Notes on Political Economy . . .* (1844, under pseudonym "A Southern Planter"), a work often echoing Henry C. Carey. Ware was a protectionist, almost unique in a Mississippian of that period, and an advocate of a balanced economy for the South.

WARE, WILLIAM (*b. Hingham, Mass., 1797; d. Cambridge, Mass., 1852*), Unitarian clergyman. Son of Henry Ware (1764–1845); brother of Henry (1794–1843) and John Ware. Graduated Harvard, 1816. Pastor of the first Unitarian Church to be established in New York City, 1821–36, he resigned the ministry and became noted thereafter as an author. Among his works, which were very popular in their time, were *Letters of Lucius M. Piso from Palmyra* (1837, entitled in subsequent editions *Zenobia: or, the Fall of Palmyra*); *Probus: or, Rome in the Third Century* (1838, published afterwards under the title *Aurelian*); *Julian: or, Scenes in Judea* (1841); and *Lectures on the Works and Genius of Washington Allston* (1852).

WARE, WILLIAM ROBERT (*b. Cambridge, Mass., 1832; d. Milton, Mass., 1915*), architect. Son of Henry

Ware (1794–1843); half-brother of John F. W. Ware. Graduated Harvard, 1852; S.B., Lawrence Scientific School, 1856; studied in offices of Edward C. Cabot and Richard M. Hunt. Successful in practice in Boston with Henry Van Brunt, Ware and his partner experimented with an atelier for students in their own office, 1863–65. Appointed head of a proposed school of architecture in the Massachusetts Institute of Technology, 1865, Ware studied professional education abroad, and on his return brought with him Eugène Létang to take charge of the work in design at the new school. In 1881 Ware was called to New York to found a school of architecture at Columbia University where he remained until his retirement as professor emeritus, 1903. He may be called the founder of American architectural education in a very real sense. To him the architect was more than a mere technician—he was an artist, an exponent of a traditional cultural history, and a member of society as a whole. In order to develop the creative side of his students, he borrowed from France the idea of teaching design by projects to be solved under criticism. His ideals of education appear in *An Outline of a Course of Architectural Instruction* (1866) and in a paper "On the Condition of Architecture and of Architectural Education in the United States" (*Papers,* Royal Institute of British Architects, 1866–67). He was author also, among other works, of *Modern Perspective* (1883); *The American Vignola* (1902–06); and *Shades and Shadows* (1912–13).

WARFIELD, BENJAMIN BRECKINRIDGE (*b. near Lexington, Ky., 1851; d. Princeton, N.J., 1921*), Presbyterian clergyman. Grandson of Robert J. Breckinridge. Graduated College of New Jersey (Princeton), 1871; Princeton Theological Seminary, 1876; studied also at University of Leipzig. Professor of New Testament in Western Theological Seminary, Pittsburgh, 1879–87, he was professor of theology at Princeton Seminary thereafter. Editor of the *Presbyterian and Reformed Review* (1890–1903), he was author of some twenty books on Biblical and theological subjects. An orthodox Calvinist, he continued without concessions the theological tradition established at Princeton by the Hodges.

WARFIELD, CATHERINE ANN WARE (*b. Natchez, Miss., 1816; d. 1877*), writer. Daughter of Nathaniel A. Ware. Educated in Philadelphia, Pa., and a resident of Kentucky *post* 1833, Mrs. Warfield was author of minor verse and of the novel *The Household of Bouverie* (1860) and much other fiction. Her work was melodramatic and written in a cheerless, pedantic style.

WARFIELD, SOLOMON DAVIES (*b. near Mount Washington, Md., 1859; d. 1927*), Maryland manufacturer and financier. Postmaster of Baltimore, Md., 1894–1905. Organized and became president of Continental Trust Co., 1898, which was the agency of his later operations in railroads, public utilities and cotton manufacturing. Among his successful operations were the organization and reorganization of the Seaboard Air Line Railway, and the merging of Baltimore utilities in the Consolidated Gas, Electric Light & Power Co.

WARING, GEORGE EDWIN (*b. Poundridge, N.Y., 1833; d. New York, N.Y., 1898*), agriculturist, sanitary engineer. Studied agricultural chemistry under James J. Mapes; managed Horace Greeley's farm at Chappaqua, N.Y.; drainage engineer of Central Park, New York City, 1857–61. After Civil War service in the Union Army, he managed the Ogden Farm near Newport, R.I., and then engaged as a professional expert in sanitary drainage of houses and towns. He made a notable success as a reforming and efficient street-cleaning commissioner of New York City, 1895–98.

WARMAN, CY (*b. near Greenup, Ill., 1855; d. Chicago, Ill., 1914*), railroadman, Colorado journalist. Author of many short stories and novels depicting the romance of the frontier and, in particular, of the pioneer railroads. Among his books were *Tales of an Engineer with Rhymes of the Rail* (1895) and *The Last Spike and Other Railroad Stories* (1906).

WARMOTH, HENRY CLAY (*b. MacLeansboro, Ill., 1842; d. Louisiana, 1931*), Union soldier, lawyer. Opened law office in New Orleans, La., 1865, for practice before military commissions and government departments. Outraged all factions by his attempts to harmonize interests of both Negroes and whites while Republican governor of Louisiana, 1868–72. Engaged thereafter in sugar-planting and refining near New Orleans.

WARNER, ADONIRAM JUDSON (*b. Wales, N.Y., 1834; d. Marietta, O., 1910*), teacher, Union officer. Settled in Marietta, O., 1865; bought and developed oil- and coal-lands and built two short-line railroads. A vehement opponent of the demonetization of silver in 1873, he introduced unsuccessful free-coinage bills while congressman, Democrat, from Ohio, 1879–81, 1883–87. Remaining active in the fight for free silver, he served as president of the American Bimetallic League and later of the American Bimetallic Union. He spent the latter part of his life in industrial activity, for the most part in Georgia.

WARNER, AMOS GRISWOLD (*b. Elkader, Iowa, 1861; d. Las Cruces, N. Mex., 1900*), sociologist. Graduated University of Nebraska, 1885; Ph.D., Johns Hopkins, 1888. Taught economics at Nebraska and at Leland Stanford. Served as superintendent of charities for District of Columbia, 1891–93. Author of the standard work *American Charities* (1894).

WARNER, ANNA BARTLETT (*b. New York, N.Y., 1827; d. Highland Falls, N.Y., 1915*), author of children's books. Sister of Susan B. Warner.

WARNER, ANNE RICHMOND (*b. St. Paul, Minn., 1869; d. England, 1913*), popular novelist. Resided principally abroad *post* 1901. Author of many magazine serials and other works of fiction, of which the best known were *Susan Clegg and Her Friend Mrs. Lathrop* (1904) and four other books dealing with the same principal character.

WARNER, CHARLES DUDLEY (*b. Plainfield, Mass., 1829; d. Hartford, Conn., 1900*), journalist, essayist. Graduated Hamilton College, 1851. After attempting surveying, general business and the law, Warner became assistant to Joseph R. Hawley on the Hartford, Conn., *Evening Press*, 1860, and was editor of the paper *post* 1861. After consolidation of the *Press* with the *Hartford Courant*, 1867, Warner remained identified with the *Courant* for the rest of his life. A friend of Mark Twain (with whom he collaborated on *The Gilded Age*, 1873) and other notable literary men of the period, Warner was author of a number of travel books, three novels and two biographies, but he was at his best in the essay form. *My Summer in a Garden* (1871), *Backlog Studies* (1873), *Being a Boy* (1878) and other collections all bear the impress of the work of Charles Lamb and have something of his mellowness and grace. Warner was also a contributing editor to *Harper's New Monthly Magazine* and was a co-editor of *The Library of the World's Best Literature* (1896–97).

WARNER, FRED MALTBY (*b. Hickling, Nottinghamshire, England, 1865; d. Orlando, Fla., 1923*), businessman, Michigan legislator. Brought to America as an infant, he was raised in Farmington, Mich. Successful in the cheese-making industry, farming and banking, he appeared thoroughly conservative in background when elected Republican governor of Michigan in 1904. However, during his term (1905–11) he undertook a sturdy fight for liberal reforms, including a general primary law, heavier taxation and lower rates on railroads, stricter control of public utilities and insurance companies, conservation of natural resources, and curbing of stock manipulation.

WARNER, HIRAM (*b. Williamsburg, Mass., 1802; d. Atlanta, Ga., 1881*), Georgia jurist and legislator. Chief justice of the state supreme court, 1867–68 and 1872–80.

WARNER, JAMES CARTWRIGHT (*b. Gallatin, Tenn., 1830; d. 1895*), industrialist. A prime factor in the revival and modernization of the charcoal iron industry in Middle Tennessee *post* 1868.

WARNER, JONATHAN TRUMBULL (*b. Hadlyme, Conn., 1807; d. California, 1895*), California pioneer and legislator. Employed by Jedediah Smith, 1831, as clerk of a trading expedition to New Mexico, Warner reached Santa Fe early in July; he then joined a trading expedition to California, arriving in Los Angeles in December. Employed for a time by Abel Stearns, he opened a store of his own in 1836. He became a Mexican citizen, 1843, and began acquisition of Warner's Ranch, southeast of Los Angeles, 1844. Later losing the bulk of his property, he yet remained one of the most widely esteemed of the American pioneers. He was co-author of *An Historical Sketch of Los Angeles County* (1876).

WARNER, JUAN JOSÉ. [See WARNER, JONATHAN TRUMBULL, 1807–1895.]

WARNER, OLIN LEVI (*b. Suffield, Conn., 1844; d. 1896*), sculptor. Originally self-taught, he studied in Paris under Jouffroy and J. B. Carpeaux, c. 1869–1872. He gradually gained fame *post* 1876 as a sculptor of portrait busts which were truly classic in feeling and profound in their interpretation of character. Among his outstanding works were portrait studies of a number of Northwest Indian chiefs including Chief Joseph; William L. Garrison on Commonwealth Avenue, Boston, Mass.; and the figure of Charles Devens in front of the Boston State House. He also designed and modeled the door of the Library of Congress, Washington, D.C., entitled "Oral Tradition."

WARNER, SETH (*b. present Roxbury, Conn., 1743 o.s.; d. Roxbury, 1784*), Revolutionary soldier. Removed to Bennington, Vt., 1763, where, with Ethan Allen and others, he resisted assertion of authority over Vermont by the province of New York. During the Revolution he aided Allen and Benedict Arnold in the surprise of Ticonderoga on May 10, 1775, and himself captured Crown Point on the following day. Commanding a regiment of Green Mountain Boys, he served under Montgomery in Canada. In 1777, during the advance of Burgoyne, he commanded the rear guard of St. Clair's army and fought an action at Hubbardton on July 7. The timely arrival of his regiment in the latter part of the battle of Bennington (August 16, 1777) is said to have turned the tide in favor of the Americans.

WARNER, SUSAN BOGERT (*b. New York, N.Y., 1819; d. Highland Falls, N.Y., 1885*), novelist. Sister of Anna B. Warner. Author, among other works, of the best-selling *The Wide, Wide World* (1850, under pseudonym "Elizabeth Wetherell") and *Queechy* (1852). Her description of the emotions of her characters (which found expression in tears on almost every page) compensated in the minds of contemporary readers for the absence of action in her stories.

WARNER, WILLIAM (*b. Shullsburg, Wis., 1840; d. 1916*), lawyer, Union soldier. In practice in Kansas City, Mo., *post* 1865, he was U.S. attorney for the western district of Missouri, 1882–84, 1898, 1902–05. Republican congressman from Missouri, 1885–87, 1889–91, and U.S. senator, 1905–11, he was strongly conservative and seldom rose above the level of complacent mediocrity.

WARNER, WORCESTER REED (*b. near Cummington, Mass., 1846; d. Eisenach, Germany, 1929*), manufacturer. Partner with Ambrose Swasey in making turret lathes and other special machinery, 1881–1911, Warner devoted most of his leisure to astronomy and the engineering of telescopes. Among others which he and Swasey designed, built and installed were those at the Lick Observatory, the Yerkes telescope, and the 72-inch telescope for the Dominion of Canada.

WARREN, CYRUS MOORS (*b. West Dedham, Mass., 1824; d. Manchester, Vt., 1891*), tar-roofing manufacturer, chemist. B.S., Lawrence Scientific School, Harvard, 1855. Studied also in Paris, at Heidelberg under Bunsen, at Munich under Liebig, and elsewhere abroad. Made important researches on the hydrocarbon constituents of tars; developed improved process of "fractional condensation" (*c.* 1865) which was afterwards applied to study of the hydrocarbons in Pennsylvania petroleum; invented processes of purification for asphalt. Warren's petroleum investigations may be said to mark the beginning of modern exact research in this field.

WARREN, FRANCIS EMROY (*b. Hinsdale, Mass., 1844; d. 1929*), Union soldier, Wyoming pioneer, cattle- and sheep-raiser. Republican governor of Wyoming Territory, 1885–86, 1889–90. Elected first governor of the state of Wyoming, he resigned immediately to become U.S. senator, serving 1890–93, 1895–1929. He was at various times chairman of the Senate committee on military affairs and of the committee on appropriations; he was particularly interested in the reclamation of arid lands.

WARREN, GEORGE FREDERICK (*b. near Harvard, Nebr., 1874; d. probably Ithaca, N.Y., 1938*), agricultural economist. Graduated University of Nebraska, 1897; Ph.D., Cornell University, 1905. *Post* 1906 a teacher of agricultural subjects at Cornell, and ultimately head of the department of agricultural economics there, Warren made his chief contribution by originating farm cost-accounting and by promotion of efficiency through statistical analysis of the income of individual farms and groups of farms. The agricultural surveys introduced at Cornell became the basis of surveys conducted at other land-grant colleges and by the U.S. Department of Agriculture. A frequent adviser to the government both on the state and federal level, he advocated the "commodity" or "compensated" dollar, a government-managed currency whose purchasing power in terms of commodities would be kept uniform by manipulating the price of gold through government purchases of that metal. In October 1933 President F. D. Roosevelt devalued the dollar in accordance with the Warren plan and, though the results failed to live up to Warren's predictions as a remedy for depression, Warren continued for several years to act as a consultant on monetary policy to the Roosevelt administration. [*Supp.* 2]

WARREN, GOUVERNEUR KEMBLE (*b. Cold Spring, N.Y., 1830; d. Newport, R.I., 1882*), soldier,

engineer. Graduated West Point, 1850. Assigned to the Topographical Engineers. Made surveys in Mississippi River Delta and on other river-improvement projects; assisted A. A. Humphreys as compiler of maps and reports for Pacific Railroad exploration; made maps and reconnaissances in Dakota and Nebraska territories. A gallant and highly effective Union Army brigade, division and corps commander during the Civil War, he rendered his most distinguished service at Gettysburg, July 1863. Making a reconnaissance of the Union left, he discovered that Little Round Top was undefended and improvised a force for its defense, an action which saved the Union Army from repulse. Commanding the V Corps at Five Forks, April 1, 1865, he clinched the victory but was summarily relieved of command by Gen. P. H. Sheridan. Returning to river and harbor work, he continued to apply for a board of inquiry into the causes of his relief at Five Forks, but did not receive vindication until after his death.

WARREN, HENRY CLARKE (*b. Cambridge, Mass., 1854; d. 1899*), Orientalist, authority on Pali and the sacred books of southern Buddhism.

WARREN, HENRY WHITE (*b. Williamsburg, Mass., 1831; d. University Park, near Denver, Colo., 1912*), Methodist clergyman. Brother of William F. Warren. Pastor in several Massachusetts towns and in Philadelphia, Pa., and New York City. Elected bishop, 1880, he took up residence at Atlanta, Ga., and later in the neighborhood of Denver, Colo. Among his numerous writings was *The Lesser Hymnal* (1875) which he prepared with Eben Tourjée.

WARREN, HERBERT LANGFORD (*b. Manchester, England, 1857; d. 1917*), architect. The son of an American Swedenborgian missionary, Warren came to America in 1876 and studied at the Massachusetts Institute of Technology, 1877–79. He served as assistant in the office of Henry H. Richardson, 1879–84. After practicing for a time, he became an instructor at Harvard in 1893 and the school of architecture there formed itself about him. Elected professor of architecture, 1899, he became first dean of the independent faculty of architecture, 1914. Gifted in the interpretation of great architecture and its principles, he was author, among other works, of *The Foundations of Classic Architecture* (1919, augmented by Fiske Kimball). [*Supp.* 1]

WARREN, HOWARD CROSBY (*b. Montclair, N.J., 1867; d. 1934*), psychologist. Graduated College of New Jersey (Princeton), 1889; M.A., 1891; studied also at Leipzig, Berlin and Munich. Early a believer in a deterministic interpretation of mental processes, he was influenced by Spencer and the psychology of the British Associationists. A teacher of psychology at Princeton *post* 1893, and first chairman of a separate department of psychology *post* 1920, he expressed in his writings and in his textbook *Elements of Human*

Psychology (1922) a conservatively behavioristic point of view. He was joint editor of the *Psychological Bulletin*, 1904–34, and editor of the *Psychological Review*, 1916–34.

WARREN, ISRAEL PERKINS (*b. present Bethany, Conn., 1814; d. 1892*), Congregational clergyman. Editor of publications, American Tract Society at Boston, Mass., 1859–70; editor and publisher, the *Christian Mirror* at Portland, Maine, *post c.* 1876.

WARREN, JAMES (*b. Plymouth, Mass., 1726; d. 1808*), merchant, farmer, Massachusetts legislator. Graduated Harvard, 1745. Married Mercy Otis Warren, 1754. A friend and trusted adviser of John and Samuel Adams, he figured in his own community as an organizer of the radicals and served on the local revolutionary committees. President of the Provincial Congress of Massachusetts, 1775, he became speaker of the state House of Representatives in the new General Court in 1776. Pursued by the enmity of John Hancock, he failed of re-election to the legislature, 1778, and did not return to political power until Shays's Rebellion, 1786, when he plainly showed sympathy to the insurgents. Elected speaker of the Massachusetts House, 1787, he boldly criticized the government's handling of the insurrection and adopted a very unorthodox stand on the question of the currency. He opposed with ability any ratification of the Federal Constitution without a bill of rights. Defeated as candidate for lieutenant-governor, he retired to scientific farming.

WARREN, JOHN (*b. Roxbury, Mass., 1753; d. 1815*), surgeon. Father of John C. Warren (1778–1856). Graduated Harvard, 1771; studied medicine with his brother, Joseph Warren, and with Edward A. Holyoke. After Revolutionary War service, 1775–77, he began practice in Boston, Mass., and was soon the leading surgeon there. His private course of anatomical lectures in 1780–81 led to the establishment of a medical department at Harvard College, November 1782. Warren began service there as professor of anatomy and surgery in 1783. A bold and skillful operator, Warren performed one of the first abdominal operations recorded in America and was a pioneer in amputation at the shoulder joint; he also did much to promote adoption of cowpox vaccination *post* 1800. His most notable contribution to medical literature was *A View of the Mercurial Practice in Febrile Diseases* (1813).

WARREN, JOHN COLLINS (*b. Boston, Mass., 1778; d. 1856*), surgeon. Son of John Warren. Graduated Harvard, 1797; studied medicine with his father and in London, Edinburgh and Paris. Practiced in Boston *post* 1802. Adjunct professor of anatomy and surgery at Harvard Medical School *post* 1809, he became full professor on the death of his father, serving 1815–47. With James Jackson, he revolutionized medical education and practice and was a prime mover in the erection of the Massachusetts General Hospital. First surgeon in the United States to operate for strangulated hernia, he was operator also in the famous trial of anesthesia by ether at Massachusetts General, Oct. 16, 1846 (the ether administered by W. T. G. Morton). He was author, among other works, of *Surgical Observations on Tumours* (1837), a landmark in the history of this subject.

WARREN, JOHN COLLINS (*b. Boston, Mass., 1842; d. 1927*), surgeon. Grandson of John C. Warren (1778–1856). Graduated Harvard, 1863; Harvard Medical School, 1866. Returning from further study abroad in 1869, he began practice in Boston and soon associated himself with the Harvard Medical School as a teacher of surgery; he was Moseley Professor, 1899–1907. Author, among other works, of *Surgical Pathology and Therapeutics* (1895), a notable accomplishment based on bacteriology. His principal interest was in medical progress and education.

WARREN, JOSEPH (*b. Roxbury, Mass., 1741; d. Breed's Hill, outside Boston, Mass., 1775*), physician, Revolutionary patriot. Brother of John Warren. Graduated Harvard, 1759. Practicing in Boston, Warren became a friend of John Adams and an ardent Whig; he was a member of the North End Caucus and of other revolutionary clubs and committees. He delivered the anniversary speeches of the Boston Massacre in 1772 and 1775, served on the local Committee of Safety, and drafted the "Suffolk Resolves." On Apr. 18, 1775, he sent William Dawes and Paul Revere to warn Hancock and Adams of their danger of capture. Chosen president *pro tempore* of the Provincial Congress, August 23, he was killed rallying troops during the battle of Bunker Hill.

WARREN, JOSIAH (*b. Boston, Mass., c. 1798; d. Charlestown, Mass., 1874*), musician, inventor, American pioneer of philosophical anarchy. An extreme individualist, he was author, among other works, of *Equitable Commerce* (1846), *True Civilization an Immediate Necessity* (1863) and the posthumous *True Civilization* (1875).

WARREN, MERCY OTIS (*b. Barnstable, Mass., 1728 o.s.; d. 1814*), poet, dramatist, historian. Sister of James Otis; wife of James Warren; aunt of Harrison G. Otis (1765–1848). A talented woman, Mercy Warren became an early laureate of the patriot cause and was later its historical apologist. Among other works, she was author of *The Adulateur* (1773) and *The Group* (1775), satires; and *Poems Dramatic and Miscellaneous* (1790). Her *History of the Rise, Progress and Termination of the American Revolution* (1805) reveals expert knowledge of public affairs and is a caustic analysis of the motives of those "malignants" who opposed American freedom.

WARREN, MINTON (*b. Providence, R.I., 1850; d. Cambridge, Mass., 1907*), classicist. Graduated Tufts College, 1870; did graduate studies at Yale, Leipzig,

Bonn; Ph.D., Strasbourg, 1879. Inaugurated Latin Seminary at Johns Hopkins while professor there, 1879–99; taught Latin at Harvard *post* 1899 and was appointed Pope Professor, 1905. A master in the idiom of Latin comedy.

WARREN, Sir PETER (*b. Warrenstown, Ireland, 1703; d. Dublin, Ireland, 1752*), British vice-admiral. On duty in America, 1730–47, he made his residence in New York City where he acquired title to the "Warren Farm," now known as Greenwich Village, and bought a large tract in the Mohawk Valley of which his nephew, Sir William Johnson, became manager. In 1731 he married Susannah, sister of James and Oliver De Lancey. In 1745 he co-operated with William Shirley in the attack on Louisbourg, C.B.I., later receiving appointment as governor of Cape Breton Island. On May 3, 1747, he was the outstanding hero of the British naval victory over the French off Cape Finisterre. Thereafter, he changed his residence from New York City to London, was knighted and served in the British Parliament.

WARREN, RICHARD HENRY (*b. Albany, N.Y., 1859; d. South Chatham, Mass., 1933*), organist, composer. Remembered principally as organist at St. Bartholomew's Church and at the Church of the Ascension, both in New York City, 1886–1921.

WARREN, RUSSELL (*b. Tiverton, R.I., 1783; d. Providence, R.I., 1860*), architect. A devotee of the Greek Revival, he designed a number of luxurious houses for ship-captains and merchants in Bristol, R.I., *c.* 1805–25, and thereafter practiced in Providence. He is said to have devised the Warren truss used in steel bridge construction. Several of his finest productions were erected in New Bedford, Mass., among them his masterpiece, the J. A. Parker house (1834).

WARREN, SAMUEL PROWSE (*b. Montreal, Canada, 1841; d. 1915*), organist, composer. Held principal posts as organist at Grace Episcopal Church, New York City, 1868–74, 1876–94, and at the First Presbyterian Church, East Orange, N.J., 1895–1915. His choral settings for the Episcopal service are of very high merit.

WARREN, WILLIAM (*b. Bath, England, 1767; d. Baltimore, Md., 1832*), actor, theatre manager. Father of William Warren (1812–1888). Came to America, 1796, to act with Thomas Wignell's company; played and managed theatres almost exclusively in Baltimore and Philadelphia, Pa. Celebrated for the dignity and rich humor of his "old man" roles. He was founder, through his son and the marriages of his daughters, of a celebrated American theatrical family.

WARREN, WILLIAM (*b. Philadelphia, Pa., 1812; d. Boston, Mass., 1888*), actor. Son of William Warren (1767–1832). Made debut, Oct. 27, 1832, at Arch Street Theatre, Philadelphia, Pa. After obtaining his professional schooling in a number of migratory troupes and lesser companies, he was associated with the stock company at the Boston Museum from 1847 until his retirement from the stage in 1883. A skillful comedian, whose acting was marked by high intelligence and faithful study, he was also a leading citizen of Boston and the friend, among others, of Oliver W. Holmes, Henry W. Longfellow and Mr. and Mrs. James T. Fields.

WARREN, WILLIAM FAIRFIELD (*b. Williamsburg, Mass., 1833; d. Brookline, Mass., 1929*), Methodist clergyman, educator. Brother of Henry W. Warren. Graduated Wesleyan University, 1853; studied at Andover Theological Seminary and at the universities of Berlin and Halle. A professor of theology in Germany, 1861–66, he became president of the Boston Theological School, 1867, serving as such until 1873. A founder of Boston University and the guiding spirit in its development, he served it as president, 1873–1903, continuing his work as professor at the theological school throughout his term and as late as 1920. Basing his plan for the university upon a fusion of English emphasis on the humanities grounded in the classics with German thoroughness in research, he also insisted on the maintenance of comparative independence by the professional and technical schools. He was zealous in providing international educational opportunities for the university's students. Under his leadership the theological school was the first to require sociology and the study of missions in the course leading to a degree. He was author, among many other works, of a celebrated address published in 1886 under the title *A Quest for a Perfect Religion*.

WARRINGTON, ALBERT POWELL (*b. Berlin, Md., 1866; d. Ojai, Calif., 1939*), lawyer, Theosophical leader. [*Supp. 2*]

WARRINGTON, LEWIS (*b. Williamsburg, Va., 1782; d. 1851*), naval officer. Appointed midshipman, 1800. In active and varied service thereafter, Warrington is remembered for his victory of Apr. 29, 1814, off Cape Canaveral, when he captured the British brig *Epervier*, himself commanding the sloop-of-war *Peacock*. Post 1842 he was chief of the bureau of yards and docks, briefly secretary of the navy in 1844, and chief of the bureau of ordnance.

WARTHIN, ALDRED SCOTT (*b. Greensburg, Ind., 1866; d. 1931*), clinical pathologist, investigator of syphilis.

WASHAKIE (*b. probably Montana, c. 1804; d. Fort Washakie, Wyo., 1900*), Shoshone chief. Of mixed Shoshone and Umatilla blood, he became chief of the eastern band of Shoshones during the 1840's. Friendly to the whites and of great assistance to the overland emigrants, he ranked high as a warrior in many small defensive wars which he fought against more powerful neighboring tribes. His band, originally ranging over the lower valley of the Green River, was settled on the present Shoshone reservation in the Wind River country at the Fort Bridger council of 1868.

WASHBURN, ALBERT HENRY (*b. Middleboro, Mass., 1866; d. Vienna, Austria, 1930*), lawyer, diplomat. Graduated Cornell University, 1889. Entering the U.S. consular service, he served at Magdeburg, Germany, 1890–93. While private secretary to Henry Cabot Lodge, 1893–96, he studied law and was engaged for some years in federal and private practice, becoming a specialist in customs cases. As U.S. minister to Austria *post* 1922, he aided in the financial rehabilitation of the country and the restoration of its credit.

WASHBURN, CADWALLADER COLDEN (*b. Livermore, Maine, 1818; d. Eureka Springs, Ark., 1882*), lawyer, land agent, Union major-general, industrialist. Brother of Elihu B. Washburne, Israel and William D. Washburn. Removing to the West in 1839, he began practice of law at Mineral Point, Wis., 1842, but gradually abandoned the law for banking and land operations. As congressman, Republican, from Wisconsin, 1855–61, 1867–71, he achieved no great prominence, nor was his term as governor of Wisconsin (1872–73) particularly outstanding. Engaging in vast industrial enterprises, he acquired water-power rights at the Falls of St. Anthony (Minneapolis, Minn.) which enabled him to become one of the nation's foremost manufacturers of flour. He was one of the first to adopt the "new process" of milling which created a demand for Northwest spring wheat and completely revolutionized the U.S. flour industry. He was an organizer in 1877 of Washburn, Crosby & Co.

WASHBURN, CHARLES GRENFILL (*b. Worcester, Mass., 1857; d. 1928*), lawyer, wire-manufacturer, Massachusetts legislator. As congressman, Republican, from Massachusetts, 1906–11, he performed his principal service with the committees on insular affairs and patents and copyrights. His advice to Chief Justice White in 1911 helped establish a reaffirmation by the U.S. Supreme Court of the application of the "rule of reason" to the Sherman Law.

WASHBURN, EDWARD ABIEL (*b. Boston, Mass., 1819; d. New York, N.Y., 1881*), Episcopal clergyman. Principal rectorate at Calvary Church, New York, N.Y., *post* 1865. Next to Phillips Brooks, he was in his day the leading representative of broad churchmanship in the Episcopal ministry.

WASHBURN, EDWARD WIGHT (*b. Beatrice, Nebr., 1881; d. 1934*), chemist, educator. B.S., Massachusetts Institute of Technology, 1905; Ph.D., 1908. His paper on the iodometric determination of arsenious acid (1908) was the result of a study of particular significance inasmuch as it prompted the first thermodynamic treatment of "buffer" solutions so important in later work on indicators. He made the first accurate measurement of true transference numbers and of the relative hydration of aqueous ions. Professor of chem-

istry at the University of Illinois and editor (1922–26) of the *International Critical Tables of Numerical Data: Physics, Chemistry and Technology,* he became head of the division of chemistry at the National Bureau of Standards in 1926. There he initiated a program of thermochemical research, instituted and directed an extensive project on petroleum research, was responsible for the isolation of the first crystals of rubber. In December 1931 he made his most notable discovery—the fractional electrolysis of water with respect to the isotopes of hydrogen.

WASHBURN, ELIHU BENJAMIN. [See WASHBURNE, ELIHU BENJAMIN, 1816–1887.]

WASHBURN, EMORY (*b. Leicester, Mass., 1800; d. Cambridge, Mass., 1877*), lawyer, Massachusetts legislator. Graduated Williams, 1817. Admitted to the Massachusetts bar, 1821, he practiced principally in Worcester, achieving great success and reputation. After an uneventful term as Whig governor of Massachusetts, 1854–55, he joined the staff of the Harvard Law School and served as Bussey Professor until 1876. He was author of treatises on real property and easements which were greatly valued in their day.

WASHBURN, GEORGE (*b. Middleboro, Mass., 1833; d. 1915*), Congregational clergyman, educator. Graduated Amherst, 1855. Son-in-law of Cyrus Hamlin, Washburn became a missionary at Constantinople, Turkey, 1863, and also taught at Robert College. *Post* 1871 he was director and professor of philosophy at Robert; between 1878 and 1903 he served as its president, steadily increasing its enrollment, its physical plant and its prestige. He was a consultant on Near Eastern affairs to James G. Blaine, John Hay and President Theodore Roosevelt.

WASHBURN, ICHABOD (*b. Kingston, Mass., 1798; d. Worcester, Mass., 1868*), blacksmith, manufacturer. Partner in a firm which made wool-spinning machinery, 1823–34, Washburn then began the manufacture of wire and became the leader of that industry in the United States; the firm was known as Washburn & Moen *post* 1850. He introduced the galvanized iron telegraph wire once so extensively used, and developed the first continuous method of tempering and hardening wire in 1856.

WASHBURN, ISRAEL (*b. Livermore, Maine, 1813; d. Philadelphia, Pa., 1883*), lawyer. Brother of Elihu B. Washburne, Cadwallader C. and William D. Washburn. Admitted to the Maine bar, 1834. Congressman, Whig and later Republican, from Maine, 1851–61, he was a leader in the formation of the Republican party in Washington, D.C., and is considered by some to have been the first to suggest the name "Republican." On May 9, 1854, ten weeks after the original meeting at Ripon, Wis., he called a meeting of about thirty anti-slavery representatives in Washington which undertook further steps toward organizing the new party. As governor of Maine, 1861–

63, he ranks among the leading war governors of the North. He was collector of the port at Portland, Maine, 1863–78.

WASHBURN, MARGARET FLOY (*b. New York, N.Y., 1871; d. Poughkeepsie, N.Y., 1939*), experimental psychologist. Graduated Vassar, 1891; Ph.D., Cornell, 1894. Taught at Wells College, Sage College at Cornell, and at University of Cincinnati; headed psychology work at Vassar, 1903–37. Author of *The Animal Mind* (1908) and *Movement and Mental Imagery* (1916), she made Vassar one of the most active psychological centers in America, employing a unique system of collaboration in experimental research between student and professor on problems of feasibly limited scope. [*Supp. 2*]

WASHBURN, NATHAN (*b. Stafford, Conn., 1818; d. Stafford Springs, Conn., 1903*), iron founder. Patented an improved cast-iron railroad-car wheel in April 1849 which soon displaced every other pattern of wheel; later that year he founded a firm for the manufacture of the wheel and also textile machinery. During the Civil War, Washburn perfected a process of puddling pig iron whereby he produced a superior gun barrel.

WASHBURN, WILLIAM DREW (*b. Livermore, Maine, 1831; d. Minneapolis, Minn., 1912*), lawyer, mill-owner. Brother of Elihu B. Washburne and of Cadwallader C. and Israel Washburn. Graduated Bowdoin, 1854; studied law with his brother Israel and with John A. Peters. Removing to the West, 1857, he settled in Minnesota for the practice of law, served for some time as agent for his brother Cadwallader, and was federal surveyor for Minnesota, 1861–65. Thereafter, a resident of Minneapolis, he engaged in lumbering, real-estate operation and flour-manufacture. In 1878, after a brief association with his brother in Washburn, Crosby & Co., he founded the milling firm of W. D. Washburn & Co. He was congressman, Republican, from Minnesota, 1879–85, and U.S. senator, 1889–95, but his principal importance was as a major figure in the financial and business life of his community.

WASHBURNE, ELIHU BENJAMIN (*b. Livermore, Maine, 1816; d. 1887*), lawyer, diplomat. Brother of Cadwallader C., Israel and William D. Washburn. After admission to the Massachusetts bar, he removed to the West, 1840, and settled at Galena, Ill. Moderately successful in practice, he made careful investments in Western lands and became a wheel-horse of the local Whig party. As congressman, Whig and Republican, from Illinois, 1853–69, he was a fierce opponent of lobbyists and treasury raiders, and was one of the first of a long succession of "watchdogs of the treasury" while chairman of the committee on appropriations. Active in furthering the career of Ulysses S. Grant, Washburne was a member of the joint committee on reconstruction and a violent at-tacker of President Andrew Johnson. Continuing his sponsorship of Grant through the campaign of 1868, he served less than two weeks as U.S. secretary of state, 1869, and was then U.S. minister to France, 1869–77. A capable diplomat, he was the only official representative of a foreign government to remain in Paris throughout the siege and the Commune, 1871; his *Recollections* (1887) contain a valuable account of those exciting days.

WASHINGTON, BOOKER TALIAFERRO (*b. Hale's Ford, Franklin Co., Va., 1856; d. Tuskegee, Ala., 1915*), Negro educational leader. Born in slavery, he was taken by his mother soon after emancipation to Malden, W. Va., where he worked for a time in a salt-furnace. Studying at night and later attending regular classes after his work, he was encouraged by the wife of his employer to fulfill his ambition to attend Hampton Institute. Working his way through Hampton, which he attended, 1872–75, he won the regard of Gen. Samuel C. Armstrong whom he later served as secretary. After graduation in 1875, he taught in a Negro school at Malden, W. Va., and between 1879 and 1881 had charge of the night school at Hampton Institute. In May 1881 Gen. Armstrong recommended Washington as principal to a Negro normal school at Tuskegee, Ala., for which a charter had just been secured. He opened the institution with forty students in a dilapidated shack and thereafter labored incessantly for the good of Tuskegee. Acting on the theory of first things first, he taught his students the dignity of efficient labor and how to live "on the farm off the farm." He also stressed the values of cleanliness and a proper diet. By the time of his death Tuskegee had grown to remarkable strength in plant, endowment, faculty and reputation. Washington also started many forms of rural extension work and established the National Negro Business League and a number of conferences for self-improvement. In great demand throughout the country as a lecturer, he stressed the necessity of providing an education useful in life, the need of keeping close to nature and of cultivating the respect of one's neighbors. A remarkable address at the Cotton States Exposition, Atlanta, Ga., September 1893, brought him national recognition.

Booker Washington's views were opposed by Negro intellectuals who felt that he did not sufficiently emphasize political rights and that his stress on industrial education might result in keeping the Negro in virtual bondage. However, he was more interested in the immediate improvement of his race from a material point of view and in making it worthy of the franchise. He opposed agitation. In view of the general public opinion of his day, which he hoped to influence, he would appear to have adopted the only policy which could be then really effective. A man of high character and devoted to spiritual values, he made a number of memorable observations including his characteristic saying, "No man, black or white, from North or South, shall drag me down so low as to make me hate him." He was author, among other works, of *The Future of the American Negro* (1899), *Up From Slavery* (1901), *Frederick Douglass* (1907) and *My Larger Education* (1911).

WASHINGTON, BUSHROD (*b. Westmoreland Co., Va., 1762; d. Philadelphia, Pa., 1829*), Revolutionary soldier, lawyer. Nephew of George Washington. Graduated William and Mary, 1778; studied law after the Revolution in the office of James Wilson. A devoted student of the law, he was appointed an associate justice of the U.S. Supreme Court in 1798 and served until his death. Slow of mind, but thorough in reasoning, he excelled as a *nisi prius* judge. Following John Marshall on constitutional matters, he rendered a number of important opinions in admiralty and commercial cases.

WASHINGTON, GEORGE (*b. Westmoreland Co., Va., 1732; d. "Mt. Vernon," Fairfax Co., Va., 1799*), planter, soldier, first president of the United States. Born on his father's estate which lay between Bridges Creek and Popes Creek and was later known as "Wakefield," George Washington was the eldest son of Augustine Washington and his second wife, Mary Ball (1708–1789). He was descended from Lawrence Washington of Sulgrave, Northamptonshire, England, whose descendant John emigrated to Virginia in 1657–58. Augustine Washington lived in Westmoreland until 1735 when he removed to Little Hunting Creek on the Potomac and thence to "Ferry Farm" in King George County. Augustine died in 1743, and for the next six years George Washington lived with relatives in Westmoreland and the Chotank region, at "Ferry Farm," and at "Mount Vernon," home of his elder half-brother, Lawrence Washington. His principal, if not his only, teachers appear to have been his father and Lawrence; the extent of his mother's influence upon Washington cannot be accurately appraised. His training in mathematics extended to trigonometry and surveying, and he had a natural talent for map-making. His accounts show purchases of books dealing with military affairs, agriculture, history, biography, and a fair number of the outstanding novels of his day such as *Tom Jones* and *Humphry Clinker*. Quotations sprinkled through his correspondence indicate his familiarity with the works of Pope and Addison and he made extensive use of Biblical allusions.

Washington learned the courtly manners and customs of the best English culture at Mount Vernon. Connected by marriage through his half-brother with the Fairfax family, he owed the first important adventure of his career to Lord Fairfax, who permitted him to go along on a survey of Fairfax lands in the Shenandoah, 1748. A year later, appointed county surveyor for Culpeper Co., Washington explored more wild country and received an insight into the impor-

tance of land ownership. He interrupted his work to accompany his half-brother to Barbadoes on a health-seeking voyage. Lawrence Washington returned to Virginia to die in July 1752, bequeathing the Mount Vernon estate in such a way that it shortly became the property of George. Appointed district-adjutant for the southern district of Virginia, 1752, he was soon transferred to that of the Northern Neck and Eastern Shore. His military ambitions, first stimulated during his half-brother's service with Adm. Edward Vernon, were now reawakened. In 1753 he accepted Gov. Dinwiddie's appointment to carry an ultimatum to the French forces encroaching on English lands in the Ohio country. This mission, although one of hardship and danger, appealed to Washington as a road to possible honor and glory. Instructed to warn off the French, and to strengthen the friendship of the Six Nations with the English, he left Will's Creek in the middle of November 1753, but on arrival at the forks of the Ohio a week later discovered that the French had withdrawn for the winter. After holding a council at Logstown with certain of the chiefs of the Six Nations at which he accomplished little, he traveled farther into the wilderness to reach the next French post. Arriving at Venango, he was directed by the officer there to carry his message to the commandant at Fort Le Boeuf. Proceeding another hundred miles through winter-clogged swamps nearly to the shores of Lake Erie, he reached the fort only to receive in writing a refusal to heed Dinwiddie's ultimatum. Guided by Christopher Gist, he was several times in danger of death on his return journey. His report to the governor was printed as *The Journal of Major George Washington . . .* (1754) and created a stir in England as well as America.

Washington had noted a position at the forks of the Ohio (present site of Pittsburgh) as the best place for an outpost, and the governor had dispatched a small force to forestall the French in building a fort there. Commissioning Washington a lieutenant-colonel, Dinwiddie ordered him to reinforce the forks with the militia then assembling at Alexandria. After setting out with 150 men on Apr. 2, 1754, Washington was met on the way by the news that the French had taken the British outpost and renamed it Fort Duquesne. Nevertheless, he advanced to the Ohio Company trading post at Red Stone about forty miles from the forks and began to build a road which would facilitate the later attempt at recapture which Dinwiddie would be obliged to make. He also fortified a camp (Fort Necessity) at Great Meadows, Pa. Informed by friendly Indians of the approach of a French scouting party, he marched out to intercept it. On May 27 he surprised and defeated the French party; their leader, Jumonville, was killed. As the French advanced in force out of Fort Duquesne, Washington fell back to Great Meadows since he feared an attack at some less defensible place. After a ten-hour siege of the camp, the French proposed terms which Washington accepted, unwittingly signing an admission that Jumonville had been "assassinated." Dinwiddie's mismanagement of military affairs having left Washington in the position of being commanded by officers junior to himself, he therefore resigned towards the end of the year 1754.

When the British sent an expedition of regular troops under Gen. Braddock against Fort Duquesne in 1755, Braddock offered Washington a post as aide. Falling sick on the march to Duquesne, he rejoined Braddock the day before the action on the Monongahela, during which he strove to carry out Braddock's orders before being swept from the field in the resultant panic after the French and Indians struck. As his appointment as aide ended with the general's death, he returned to Mount Vernon and made ready the militia of his district. Appointed colonel and commander-in-chief of all Virginia forces in the fall of 1755, he was responsible for the defense of about 300 miles of mountainous frontier with about 300 men. Averaging two engagements with raiding Indians a month, Washington acquired the habit of thinking and acting for the welfare of a people, and also a skill in conducting military operations over an extensive range of territory. His difficulties at this time closely parallel those he was later to meet in the Revolution. In order to settle a dispute over his rank and right to command, Washington rode from Winchester, Va., to Boston, Mass., in 1756. His journey had a secondary but important effect in broadening his viewpoint in respect to the character of the people of the other colonies. Returning to his duty in defense of the frontier, he managed reasonably well despite lack of money, clothes, shoes, powder, and even at times food. His efforts to win the co-operation of Maryland and Pennsylvania in supporting a Virginian attack on Fort Duquesne were unsuccessful. Joining the British expedition under Gen. John Forbes against Fort Duquesne in 1758, Washington commanded the two Virginia regiments with the title of brigadier. His suggestion that the expedition use an open-order method of marching and fighting was ignored by the British officers. The British found, on their approach to Fort Duquesne, November 1758, that it had been abandoned by the French, and Washington resigned soon thereafter from military service.

On Jan. 6, 1759, he married Martha (Dandridge) Custis, a widow, and settled down to the life of a gentleman-farmer at Mount Vernon. He was active in local affairs and a generous contributor to educational organizations. He took a seat in the House of Burgesses, 1759. Appreciative of music and the theatre, he also enjoyed card-playing, billiards, horse-racing, dancing, fishing, hunting and, indeed, all the usual sports of a gentleman of his time. However, his pleasant, busy life at Mount Vernon was not without its annoyances, mainly on the head of British commercial restrictions and the sharp practice of the English factors without whose services no Virginia planter could transact business with the English markets. Washington's disillusion with British military efficiency, as evidenced during the campaigns against Fort Duquesne, now revived and merged into a subconscious antagonism against the mother country which had been inspired by senseless difficulties thrown in his way as he endeavored to improve his estates. A faithful attendant at the sessions of the legislature, he clarified his view of the handicaps imposed on America by the British colonial system. At the time of the Stamp Act he expressed the general American attitude toward the claims of Parliament, saying that it "hath no more right to put their hands into my pocket, without my consent, than I have to put my hands into yours for money." Another major grievance was the British prohibition of colonial paper money. Since the balance of trade was always against them, the colonists required paper money. Acting as agent for the officers and men he had formerly commanded, he traveled down the Ohio and up the Great Kanawha rivers in 1770 to locate the bounty lands allotted to men who had served. This journey revived his interest in the west and provided him with a personal knowledge which was later useful in developing his western land policy when he was president.

Washington supported the device of non-importation as a check to British political and economic aggression, yet prophesied that blood would be spilt if the British ministers continued to be stubborn. He was one of the burgesses who met in the Raleigh Tavern at Williamsburg on May 27, 1774, after the Assembly had been dissolved by the governor; he signed the proceedings of that important meeting. On July 18 he acted as chairman of a meeting in Alexandria at which the Fairfax Resolutions were adopted. A Virginia delegate to the First Continental Congress, he was also chosen to command the independent militia companies of several Virginia counties. As delegate to the Second Continental Congress beginning May 1775, he served on the committee for drafting army regulations and planning the defense of New York City. Elected to command the American armies, June 15, 1775, as the result of a compromise between the northern and southern factions in Congress, he refused all pay for the employment, asking only that he be reimbursed for necessary expenses.

On taking command of the army at Cambridge, Mass., on July 3, 1775, Washington found it little better than a loosely organized mob of New England militia whose terms of service were to expire at the end of the year or sooner. Hampered in his efforts to obtain legislation for creation of an efficient army by the widespread belief that some accommodation might still be made with the British, he was also thwarted in establishing discipline by a too-democratic spirit among the troops. Scarcity of powder as well as insufficiency of men kept Washington back from any major operation until 1776. At the first opportunity, however, he seized and fortified Dorchester Heights, so threatening the besieged British in Boston with bombardment and putting the British fleet in jeopardy. As a result, the city was evacuated on Mar. 17, 1776.

As it was obvious that the next logical base of operations for the British would be New York City, Washington set out for that place with his army of newly enlisted troops. On his arrival he found that he was partially committed to a plan of defense already mapped out by Maj.-Gen. Charles Lee and others. Faced with the decree that New York must be defended, although the place was virtually indefensible, he was further handicapped by a lack of experienced officers and by the three-to-one superiority which the British soon massed against him. His concept of duty compelled him to obey the orders of Congress, despite his personal opinion of them, and he deferred scrupulously to the views of subordinates in cases where he believed that his knowledge and experience were inadequate. When Sir William Howe, the British commander, chose Long Island as his point of attack, Washington sent a large part of his force to reinforce the defensive works at Brooklyn, meanwhile holding a strong body on Manhattan to oppose a possible attack by the British fleet. After the American forces on Long Island had been outflanked and defeated on Aug. 27, 1776, Washington withdrew the remnant of the forces on Long Island over to Manhattan on the night of Aug. 29, a retreat which is considered a military masterpiece. Following on the British landing at Kip's Bay, Sept. 15, Washington was obliged to give up his footing on Manhattan, retreating to a strong natural position at White Plains, N.Y., where the British were held in a sharp engagement. The fall of Fort Washington and Fort Lee in November resulted from the same misplaced deference to the opinions of his generals which has been noted previously, yet both these disasters were blessings in disguise. They freed Washington and the Continental Army from responsibility for fixed fortifications and made it into a mobile force of maneuver which Washington could handle in accordance with his own ideas. The general principle on which he preferred to wage the war was the avoidance of a general action unless compelled to undertake it by necessity. Until Congress created a permanent army, this was the only way in which inexperienced troops always inferior in numbers to the enemy could survive. Survival was all-important to Washington, for his belief in the moral rightness of the American fight for liberty was based on his sense of the injustice of the British course. Having scrupulously determined on a course of rebellion and a change of allegiance, he considered that any turning back was unthinkable. The fortitude with which he met his difficulties was based upon this faith.

As the British pushed forward into New Jersey,

Washington, with a steadily dwindling force, fell back before them, but contrived to give his enemy the impression that they might encounter a strong opposition at any point. After he had apparently taken refuge with an army of barely 5000 men behind the Delaware River, the British settled into winter quarters in a series of outposts along the Delaware at and near Trenton, N.J., and in a line across New Jersey to Amboy.

Meanwhile, as Congress had left Philadelphia and the protection of that city had become relatively unimportant in his judgment, Washington fixed his eye on Morristown, N.J., as the base of operations most threatening to the British. Crossing the Delaware on Christmas night, 1776, he took the outpost at Trenton and captured its Hessian garrison, so dislocating the British arrangements. Finding it impossible to drive to Morristown (as had been his first intention) through failure of two supporting detachments, he returned across the river. A few days later he again crossed into Jersey and began to move northward. After a stubborn engagement at Assunpink Creek, he outwitted the British by a night march and attacked their line at Princeton. Victorious there, he was soon at Morristown where his position presented such a strategic threat that the British abandoned their whole line and retreated to Brunswick. Meanwhile, Washington had been assigned by Congress a grant of extraordinary powers in order that he might wage war with more efficiency, but was severely criticized when he endeavored to use these powers. However, *post* 1777, he could enlist troops for a period of three years or the duration of the war, and he then began to build a permanent military machine. He continued to be forced to rely upon militia for swelling his forces to a respectable total at times of crisis; this was a constant annoyance to him for he held and expressed a very low opinion of militia troops.

Slowly shaping and disciplining his army at Morristown, he managed to contain the enemy during the spring of 1777 and convinced Sir William Howe that the risk of marching across New Jersey to take Philadelphia was too great. On Howe's transport of his forces to Chesapeake Bay by sea, Washington marched south and on Sept. 11, 1777, engaged the British at Brandywine Creek. Defeated, he refused to withdraw and delayed the British entry into Philadelphia for two weeks. Although he continued to act with great deference to the civil power as expressed by Congress, he complained of a lack of information on political matters. His surprise attack on the British at Germantown, Oct. 3–4, 1777, failed through no fault of plan, damaged the British forces and also Sir William Howe's confidence in himself, and is to be credited with great influence in the decision of France to aid the United States. During the winter encampment at Valley Forge which followed, a continuing intrigue to supplant Washington in command of the army reached its crisis in the events of the so-called

Conway Cabal. The victory of Horatio Gates at Saratoga, Oct. 17, 1777, gave Washington's enemies in Congress a chance to draw invidious comparisons. The whole plot was at bottom a culmination of a continuous effort by Massachusetts ever since 1775 to regain control of the war. The exposure of the Cabal and of Gates's share in it aroused resentments in Congress and effectually destroyed congressional support for Washington's replacement as commander. True to his nature, he did not allow this episode to interfere with more important matters, nor was he troubled by any vulgar desires for popularity. In the spring of 1778 the Continental Army emerged from its trials at Valley Forge, drilled to a high standard of efficiency by Baron von Steuben, and heartened by the news of the French alliance which had come in March. A determining factor in the securing of French support had been the character and purpose of George Washington as certified to Vergennes, the French foreign minister, and to Louis XVI by Gerard, the French acting minister in America. Once convinced by Washington's example that the Americans would not compromise with Great Britain, the French moved effectively.

An early proof that the Continental Army had become efficient and a new demonstration of Washington's skill as a general were provided at the battle of Monmouth, N.J., June 28, 1778. In this battle the Americans struck at the British army as it was retreating from Philadelphia across New Jersey to New York City. Washington turned the confusion brought about by the debatable conduct of Gen. Charles Lee into an obstinate and successful holding action from which the British were glad to make good their withdrawal. A new problem, however, arose in the lethargy which seized upon Congress and the states after the announcement of the French alliance. Lacking troops, supplies and even powder in the summer of 1779, Washington was unable to make a major move, yet succeeded in mounting an expedition under Gen. John Sullivan into New York State which broke the power of the Six Nations and freed the frontier from Indian warfare. After the arrival of a French army under Rochambeau at Rhode Island in July 1780, Washington was still unable to attempt a major campaign because of his own lack of supplies and men and frankly confessed this fact to the French general. At a conference with Rochambeau in Wethersfield, May 21–22, 1781, it was decided to attempt an attack on New York, and both French and American forces closed in on the northern defenses of that city. The availability of the French West India fleet under Adm. De Grasse providing the chance for a combined operation, Washington changed his plans and determined on a move against Cornwallis in Virginia. Organizing his march with remarkable skill, Washington brought the French and American armies on schedule before Yorktown, Va., where Cornwallis had fortified himself and where he had been cut off from an escape by sea by the French fleet. After a short siege, Yorktown fell and Cornwallis was taken. Rochambeau took his army into winter quarters in Virginia, and Washington led his troops back to the Hudson River, making headquarters at Newburgh.

The states now became even more supine than before, and Washington's arguments for the necessity of a continued effort had no effect. He remained patient while an orgy of profiteering broke out, even to the extent of a clandestine trade with the British, which he and the army were unable to stop. For two more dreary years the war dragged on, although no military events of importance took place. The Continental soldiers were restless because of neglect of their services and lack of pay; their dissatisfaction took form in a proposal to make Washington a king by military force. Shaken to his depths by the realization that the men on whom he relied were ready to support him in a monstrous treason for personal power, he replied to the proposal on May 22, 1782, with a blast that ended the whole affair. Continuing unrest and a prospect of mutiny were met by him with tact and wisdom; he urged Congress to take action on the petitions addressed by the soldiers and their officers, and also addressed a circular letter to the states, pleading with them for justice to the personnel of the fast-disbanding Continental Army. Revealing how close to his heart was the national principle for which he had fought, he stated that four things were essential to respectable national existence: (1) an indissoluble union of the states under one federal head; (2) a sacred regard to public justice; (3) the adoption of a proper national defense; (4) a spirit of cooperation and the suppression of local prejudices. Hostilities ended on Apr. 19, 1783, the anniversary of the battle of Lexington, and Washington then entered New York City at the head of those troops which still remained in service, just as the British evacuated it. He bade farewell to his officers at Fraunces Tavern and resigned his commission to Congress at Annapolis.

Washington's financial condition at the close of the war was unsatisfactory. Mount Vernon was now not even self-supporting; however, he continued his usual unostentatious charities. During the autumn of 1784 he went on a horseback journey of exploration in the west in furtherance of his favorite project of opening a route to the western country from tidewater Virginia by connecting the Potomac and Ohio rivers. Discouraged by the inefficiency of slave labor, he grew convinced that the gradual abolition of slavery by legislative authority would prevent much future mischief. Although he had more slaves than he could profitably employ, he refused on principle to sell any of them. Absorbed in the management of Mount Vernon and in the affairs of the Potomac Company, he considered himself as a retired man, writing to Lafayette that he would "move gently down the stream of life, until I sleep with my fathers." This philosophic calm was interrupted in 1786 by Shays's Rebellion in Massachusetts, which only added to his conviction that the Articles of Confederation would have to be revised in the interest of a strong central government. Serving as president of the Federal Convention, he lent the great authority of his reputation to its deliberations. Admitting that the Constitution as written had imperfections, he maintained that it was the best obtainable at that time and that, since a workable machinery had been provided for amending it, it should be first adopted and then altered.

Repelling the suggestion that he should be the first president when it was made to him, he opposed it wherever he decently could, saying that he had no "wish beyond that of living and dying an honest man on my own farm." He accepted the presidency with diffidence, dreading the possibility that he would appear incompetent. Believing that the success of the Revolution was owing to Providence, and content with the thought that he had played an honorable part in a great popular movement, he was doubtful of his ability to administer a government. Driven by the sense of duty that always actuated him, he accepted the post, although he was compelled to borrow money to pay his traveling expenses to his inauguration, Apr. 30, 1789, in New York City. Declining a salary, he accepted the later offer of Congress of $25,000 annually for expenses; in his case, his expenses exceeded this sum. Cautious in his organization of the governmental machine and his appointment of officials, he faced a number of pressing problems, both domestic and foreign. At home it was essential that the nation be made financially stable and that manufacturing and commerce be encouraged; the retention of military posts in the west by Great Britain constituted the major foreign problem.

Unsympathetic with those divergent theories of government which almost immediately proved the basis of a struggle between Alexander Hamilton and Thomas Jefferson within the circle of his first cabinet, he thought of these differences of opinion as purely personal and as willful obstacles to the task of establishing the government firmly. He could not understand differences on the basis of theory, although he acted with great forbearance toward both Jefferson and Hamilton on the ground that their talents were essential to success. The gradual emergence of Federalist and (Democrat) Republican points of view in government influenced him in his decision to serve a second term. He was also strongly influenced by the disturbed foreign situation and adamant in his belief that the European powers must be convinced that Americans acted for themselves and not for others. At first sympathetic with the revolution in France, he grew speedily sick of the excesses which it produced and desired a strict American neutrality as between the French and their principal opponent, Great Britain. Although unopposed in his election to a second term, he was roundly criticized for his neutrality policy and

was subjected to an abuse which went beyond the bounds of decency. Continuing firm in his belief that twenty years of peace would make the United States strong enough to bid defiance "in a just cause to any power whatever," he could not comprehend emotional attitudes at home which could put any other problem ahead of this. He gradually came to regard the French sympathizers in the United States as virtual traitors. When, after the recall of the French envoy Edmond Genet, the political frenzy in the United States subsided, Washington attempted a settlement of United States difficulties with Great Britain by appointing John Jay to negotiate a treaty with the British, 1794. In this same year the resistance to the excise tax in Pennsylvania known as the Whiskey Rebellion seemed to Washington to prove that the same indifference of the states to the national welfare which had plagued him in the Revolution must still be reckoned with. Acting with decision against the rebels, he was heartened by the prompt response of the militia to his call. On the collapse of the rebellion, he again displayed his broad understanding by avoiding any harsh reprisal measures.

Offsetting the optimism brought about by the signing of the Pinckney Treaty, 1795, which secured the navigation of the Mississippi River and established the southern boundary of the United States, came an outburst of criticism over Jay's Treaty. Denounced as a base surrender to the British, it yet seemed to Washington the best treaty that could be obtained at the time, and he withstood the storm of opposition just as he had withstood previous ones, confident of his integrity of purpose and likening the attacks to a cry against a mad dog.

In 1796 he set about to prepare an address which would announce to the people of the United States his determination to retire from public life. His Farewell Address is partly an explanation of his course as president, with main emphasis upon the need for a firm union and a strong central government, and it is also a solemn warning against the spirit of party. Political parties, as Washington had observed them, seemed devoted to a usurpation of power for personal ends and would logically result in a loss of liberty. He urged morality and education as necessities for the people's happiness and prosperity, counseled good faith and justice toward all nations but favors to none, and warned against the wiles of foreign influence. On his retirement from the presidency, the nation was well on the road to international importance. Washington had given it dignity; he had demonstrated its power by crushing the Indians in the west (at Fallen Timbers, 1794, the army commanded by Anthony Wayne); he had seen its credit firmly fixed through the efforts and policy of Alexander Hamilton. Treaties with Spain and with Great Britain had amicably settled the questions of navigation on the Mississippi and also the Florida and the eastern boundaries. Having sacrificed his personal inclination throughout his life to his sense of duty, he now looked forward to a quiet and fruitful old age at Mount Vernon. However, when trouble with France brought about a war situation in 1798, he was brought out of retirement by President John Adams to command a provisional army of defense with the rank of lieutenant-general. As changing conditions in France reduced the chance of conflict, Washington never personally commanded the army and allotted a greater and greater part of his time to the management of Mount Vernon. He never brought his farms to the point of efficiency which he had planned, although he did work out a scheme of rotation of crops in his fields. He died on Saturday, Dec. 14, 1799, with high courage. Used to driving himself unsparingly and often beyond his strength, he had neglected a cold which developed into a malignant cynanche trachealis with which the limited medical skill of his time was unable to cope.

WASHINGTON, HENRY STEPHENS (*b. Newark, N.J., 1867; d. 1934*), petrologist. Graduated Yale, 1886; made extensive travels, studying especially the volcanic islands of the Greek and Turkish archipelagoes; Ph.D., Leipzig, 1893. Associated with Joseph P. Iddings, L. V. Pirsson and another in formulating a systematic classification of igneous rocks based primarily upon chemical composition; published *Manual of the Chemical Analysis of Rocks* (1904), *Chemical Analyses of Igneous Rocks* (revised edition, 1917). A research worker *post* 1912 at Geophysical Laboratory of the Carnegie Institution of Washington, D.C., he issued a number of publications which established him as the most learned student of igneous rocks of his time.

WASHINGTON, JOHN MACRAE (*b. Stafford Co., Va., 1797; d. at sea, off the mouth of the Delaware River, 1853*), soldier. Graduated West Point, 1817. Commissioned in the artillery, he served principally in Florida and the South; in 1838–39 he aided Gen. Winfield Scott in the removal of the Cherokees to Oklahoma. After further duty with Scott in quelling disturbances along the Canadian border, he returned to routine duty, 1842. As a battery commander in the Mexican War, he was the chief factor in securing victory at the battle of Buena Vista, Feb. 22, 1847, repelling Mexican attacks on the first day and on the second day holding a key point after a rout of the American militia. He served later as governor of Saltillo and as civil and military governor of New Mexico.

WATERHOUSE, BENJAMIN (*b. Newport, R.I., 1754; d. Cambridge, Mass., 1846*), physician. Apprenticed in medicine to a Newport physician, he studied also in London and Edinburgh, 1775–78, and at the University of Leyden, 1778–*c.* 1782. Returning to America, he became professor of the theory and practice of medicine in the medical department of Harvard, 1783. On reading Edward Jenner's 1798 essay on

vaccination with cowpox, Waterhouse sent to England for vaccine and immediately after its receipt (July 8, 1800) tested it successfully on his own son and on another child. Continuing to vaccinate others with cowpox with equally good results, he published *A Prospect of Exterminating the Small Pox* (Aug. 18, 1800). As the news of his work spread, vaccination was administered improperly by a number of unqualified persons using impure vaccine. A number of people died and there was a general resentment against Waterhouse. After a committee of physicians had investigated the affair and approved Waterhouse's practice, 1802, he continued to publicize vaccination and to insist on maintaining the purity of vaccine. He opposed the moving of the Harvard Medical School from Cambridge to Boston and also the suggestion that the instruction given be more clinical in character. After the failure of his attempt to open a rival medical school and his publication of a number of libels on his colleagues, he was forced to resign from Harvard, 1812. Medical superintendent of New England army posts, 1813–20, he gave considerable time thereafter to general literature as well as the practice of his profession.

WATERHOUSE, FRANK (*b. Cheshire, England, 1867; d. Seattle, Wash., 1930*), capitalist. After emigrating to Canada as a young man, he settled in Tacoma, Wash., *c.* 1893. Soon removing to Seattle, he became general manager of the Pacific Navigation Co., 1895, and was thereafter highly successful in shipping enterprises and other business interests in the Pacific Northwest.

WATERHOUSE, SYLVESTER (*b. Barrington, N.H., 1830; d. St. Louis, Mo., 1902*), educator, civic leader. Professor of Greek at Washington University, St. Louis, Mo., 1864–1901, he was an outstanding publicist for the Middle West, advocating Mississippi River improvement, encouraging immigration to Missouri, and endeavoring to stimulate trade.

WATERMAN, LEWIS EDSON (*b. Decatur, N.Y., 1837; d. Brooklyn, N.Y., 1901*), book agent, life insurance salesman, inventor. Obtained his first patent for an efficient fountain pen, 1884; established the Ideal Pen Co. in New York to manufacture it. Incorporated his successful business as the L. E. Waterman Co., 1887, and served the firm thereafter as president and manager.

WATERMAN, ROBERT H. (*b. Hudson, N.Y., 1808; d. San Francisco, Calif., 1884*), sea captain. A mate and master aboard packets of the Black Ball line and ships owned by Howland & Aspinwall, Waterman made a series of remarkable passages to China with the *Natchez*, 1842–45. As master of the clipper *Sea Witch*, he made a record run between Hong Kong and New York, 1849. Accepting command of the new clipper *Challenge*, he sailed her from New York to San Francisco in a passage which has frequently been cited as a classic voyage in a "hell ship." An attempted mutiny and the death of several members of the crew resulted in an attempt to lynch Waterman when he arrived in California, Oct. 29, 1851. Subsequently tried for murder, he was exonerated by the testimony of both crew and passengers.

WATERMAN, THOMAS WHITNEY (*b. Binghamton, N.Y., 1821; d. 1898*), lawyer, writer of digests and legal treatises. Admitted to the bar, 1848, he began practice in New York City, making his residence in Binghamton again *post* 1862. He was author of a great number of works on phases of law which were rapidly changing. Although ephemerally useful and successful, his writings have not noticeably affected the later development of law.

WATERS, DANIEL (*b. Charlestown, Mass., 1731; d. Malden, Mass., 1816*), naval officer. Commanded the schooner *Lee* under John Manley in warfare on British communications off Boston, 1776. Appointed captain in the Continental Navy, March 1777, he commanded several small ships of war on Atlantic cruises and was in command of the Massachusetts ship *General Putnam* in the expedition against Castine, Maine. His most famous exploit came on Dec. 25, 1779, when he defeated the British privateers *Governor Tryon* and *Sir William Erskine* while captain of the Boston privateer *Thorn*.

WATERS, WILLIAM EVERETT (*b. Winthrop, Maine, 1856; d. 1924*), classicist. Graduated Yale, 1878; Ph.D., 1887. An enthusiastic and able teacher of Greek at several schools and colleges, including Chautauqua summer and correspondence courses, he held the presidency of Wells College, 1894–1900. He was associate professor and professor of Greek at New York University, 1901–23.

WATIE, STAND (*b. near site of present Rome, Ga., 1806; d. 1871*), Cherokee leader, planter, Confederate brigadier-general. Brother of Elias Boudinot (*c.* 1803–1839). Joined his brother, his uncle Major Ridge, and John Ridge in signing the treaty of New Echota, 1835, whereby the Georgia Cherokees surrendered their lands and removed to what is now Oklahoma. Bitterly attacked for his part in the treaty, Watie later became leader of the minority, or treaty, party of his tribe. Appointed colonel of the Cherokee Mounted Rifles, 1861, he was promoted brigadier-general, 1864. During the entire Civil War he was active as a raider and cavalry leader, taking part in many engagements in Indian Territory and along its borders. He was one of the last Confederate officers to surrender (June 23, 1865).

WATKINS, GEORGE CLAIBORNE (*b. Shelbyville, Ky., 1815; d. St. Louis, Mo., 1872*), Arkansas jurist. As chief justice of the Arkansas supreme court, 1852–54, he handed down an early decision holding that the United States had exclusive admiralty jurisdiction over navigable streams (in *Merrick vs. Avery*, 14 Ark., 370).

WATKINS, JOHN ELFRETH (*b. Ben Lomond, Va., 1852; d. New York, N.Y., 1903*), engineer, museum curator. Built up collections pertaining to the transportation industry at U.S. National Museum, Washington, D.C., 1884–92; curator of mechanical technology and superintendent of buildings of the Museum *post* 1895. Authority on the history of engineering and the mechanical arts.

WATSON, ANDREW (*b. Oliverburn, Scotland, 1834; d. Cairo, Egypt, 1916*), United Presbyterian clergyman. Emigrating to America *c.* 1848, he was raised near Sussex, Wis. Ordained, 1861, he served thereafter as a missionary in Egypt.

WATSON, DAVID THOMPSON (*b. Washington, Pa., 1844; d. Atlantic City, N.J., 1916*), lawyer. Practiced successfully in Pittsburgh, Pa., *post* 1868. Gained widest prominence as one of counsel for the United States in Alaskan Boundary controversy with Great Britain, 1903.

WATSON, ELKANAH (*b. Plymouth, Mass., 1758; d. 1842*), merchant, promoter, agriculturist. Apprenticed to John Brown (1744–1780) of Providence, R.I., *c.* 1774, he remained in the employ of the Browns after he came of age. Embarking for France to carry money and dispatches to Benjamin Franklin, 1779, he entered business on his own at Nantes, and for a time was very successful. Failing in 1783, he returned to America and made an unsuccessful attempt to raise capital for establishment of an American canal system. After a second failure in business at Edenton, N.C., he settled in Albany, N.Y., 1789, organized the Bank of Albany, and became a leading citizen of that community. Continuing to urge his plans for canals, he persuaded several prominent New Yorkers to join him in a tour of central New York, 1791, during which he projected a plan for a canal in that region. Retiring from active business *c.* 1802, he moved to Pittsfield, Mass., where he devoted himself to scientific agriculture. He staged the "Cattle Show" (1810) which preceded incorporation of the Berkshire Agricultural Society, sponsor of the first county fair in America. He thereafter helped make the county fair an American institution. He was author of *Men and Times of the Revolution* (1856).

WATSON, HENRY CLAY (*b. Baltimore, Md., 1831; d. Sacramento, Calif., 1867*), journalist. Trained as a printer and newspaper editor in Philadelphia, Pa., he settled in Sacramento, Calif., 1861, where he became editor of the *Daily Union* and won considerable local fame as an editorial writer during the Civil War. He was author also of a number of historical stories and studies for young people.

WATSON, HENRY COOD (*b. London, England, 1818; d. New York, N.Y., 1875*), journalist, music critic. Emigrated to New York, N.Y., 1841. Founded the *Musical Chronicle,* 1843, which later became the *American Musical Times;* was associated with C. F. Briggs and Edgar Allan Poe on the *Broadway Journal.* Later served as an editor of *Frank Leslie's Illustrated Newspaper* and as music critic for the *New York Tribune.* In 1842 he was one of the group that founded the Philharmonic Society of New York.

WATSON, JAMES CRAIG (*b. near Fingal, Ontario, Canada, 1838; d. 1880*), astronomer. Graduated University of Michigan, 1857. Directed the observatory at Michigan and taught physics there, 1859–79; served thereafter as director of the Washburn Observatory, University of Wisconsin. Discovered 22 asteroids; worked with Benjamin Peirce on lunar theory; was author of *Theoretical Astronomy* (1868), a complete compilation and digest of the theory and method of orbital determination.

WATSON, JAMES MADISON (*b. Onondaga Hill, N.Y., 1827; d. Elizabeth, N.J., 1900*), teacher, textbook salesman and writer.

WATSON, JOHN CRITTENDEN (*b. Frankfort, Ky., 1842; d. Washington, D.C., 1923*), naval officer. Graduated U.S. Naval Academy, 1860. Promoted master, 1861, he was navigating officer in the *Hartford* during the 1862 operations against New Orleans and Vicksburg and the 1863 operations against Port Hudson and Grand Gulf. He later served as flag lieutenant on the staff of Adm. D. G. Farragut. Promoted commodore, 1897, he commanded the North Cuban Blockade Squadron and the Eastern Squadron during the Spanish-American War. Promoted rear-admiral, 1899, he retired in 1904.

WATSON, JOHN FANNING (*b. Batsto, N.J., 1779; d. 1860*), businessman, antiquarian. Successively a publisher, a banker and a railroad executive, Watson is remembered as author of studies of pioneer days in Pennsylvania and New York based on the methodical collection of memories of old inhabitants and authentic documents. Among his works were *Annals of Philadelphia* (1830, and subsequent editions); *Historic Tales of Olden Time* (1832); and *Annals and Occurrences of New York City and State* (1846).

WATSON, JOHN WILLIAM CLARK (*b. Albemarle Co., Va., 1808; d. Holly Springs, Miss., 1890*), lawyer, Mississippi jurist, Confederate senator.

WATSON, SERENO (*b. East Windsor Hill, Conn., 1826; d. Cambridge, Mass., 1892*), botanist. Graduated Yale, 1847. Failing in various occupations, he removed to California, 1867, and found employment as a volunteer aide with Clarence King's exploration of the Great Basin. Soon afterwards he was commissioned to collect plants and secure data regarding them, thus by chance undertaking the work in which he was to attain distinction. His *Botany* (1871), the fifth volume in the report of the King survey, was virtually a flora of the Great Basin and contained phytogeographic material in advance of its time. Settling in Cambridge, Mass., Watson became assistant in the Gray Herbarium, 1873, and was its curator *post* 1874. He was author, among other works, of the *Botany of California* (1876, 1880); *Bibliographical Index to North American Botany* (1878); and of many outstanding monographs. He completed the *Manual of the Mosses* begun by Leo Lesquereux and T. P. James, and in 1889, with the assistance of John M. Coulter, revised Gray's *Manual of Botany.*

WATSON, THOMAS AUGUSTUS (*b. Salem, Mass., 1854; d. Passagrille Key, Fla., 1934*), telephone pioneer, shipbuilder. *Post* 1874 he assisted Alexander G. Bell during the experimental period of the telephone, and was given an interest in the business in 1877 on formation of the first telephone organization. He was the first research and technical head of the Bell Telephone Co. Resigning in 1881, he first attempted farming, but soon began to build engines and ships. In 1896 his firm undertook contracts for the U.S.S. *Lawrence* and *Macdonough;* these were followed by the Cape Hatteras lightship and the cruiser U.S.S. *Des Moines.* Watson's shipyard was incorporated as the Fore River Ship & Engine Co., 1901. In 1904 he resigned, retired from business, and gave himself up to the special interests in geology and literature which he had cultivated during his business career.

WATSON, THOMAS EDWARD (*b. near Thomson, Ga., 1856; d. 1922*), lawyer, politician. Attended Mercer University; began successful career as a criminal lawyer, 1880. Brought early under the personal influence of Robert Toombs and Alexander H. Stephens, Watson entered politics as an agrarian reformer, hostile to the new order in the South and nostalgic for the imagined glories of the period before the Civil War. As a young member of the Assembly, he fought against the Georgia Democratic machine which was dominated by capitalist-industrialists, and entered Congress, 1891, as a supporter of the Farmers' Alliance and a Populist. Introducing many reform bills and supporting advanced labor legislation, he was defeated for re-election in 1892 and 1894, but continued to sway thousands of his followers with his denunciations of the trusts, capitalist finance, and Democratic policies. Nominated for the vice-presidency of the United States by the Populist convention, 1896, he received a very small vote. Embittered, he retired from public life and turned to writing, producing, among other books, biographies of Napoleon and Thomas Jefferson. As the Populist candidate for president in 1904, he polled only a small vote but gained considerable attention from reformers. In 1905 he founded *Tom Watson's Magazine* which featured his reform editorials; he later established *Watson's Jeffersonian Magazine.*

As new issues overshadowed the conflict between industrialists and agrarians, Watson took up and prosecuted a number of sensational crusades against Catholics, Jews, Negroes, Socialists, and foreign missionaries. Shifting his followers from one Democratic faction to another, he virtually dictated state politics. He conducted a campaign against American intervention in World War I and against conscription. Although he lost the state presidential primary in 1920, he was elected that same year to the U.S. Senate by a large vote on the same platform, namely, restoration of civil liberties and the defeat of the League of Nations.

WATSON, WILLIAM (*b. Nantucket, Mass., 1834; d. 1915*), engineer, educator. Graduated Lawrence Scientific School, Harvard, 1857; Ph.D., University of Jena, 1862. While abroad, he collected information on technical instruction which in 1864 was used as basis in planning organization of the Massachusetts Institute of Technology. He served at the Institute as its first professor of mechanical engineering and descriptive geometry, 1865–73. Thereafter he devoted himself to private studies, and was recording secretary of the American Academy of Arts and Sciences, 1884–1915.

WATTERSON, HARVEY MAGEE (*b. Beech Grove, Tenn., 1811; d. 1891*), lawyer, Tennessee legislator. Father of Henry Watterson. Congressman, Democrat, from Tennessee, 1839–43, and for several years thereafter in the diplomatic service, Watterson became proprietor of the *Nashville Daily Union*, 1849. Removing to Washington, D.C., as editor of the *Washington Union*, 1851, he gave up the post because he would not support administration policy in regard to the repeal of the Missouri Compromise. An opponent of the extension of slavery and of secession, he was a Unionist throughout the Civil War. After the war, he engaged in law practice at Washington, D.C.

WATTERSON, HENRY (*b. Washington, D.C., 1840; d. Jacksonville, Fla., 1921*), journalist, statesman. Son of Harvey M. Watterson. Beginning his career as journalist, 1858, he worked briefly in New York and then became a reporter for the Washington, D.C., *Daily States*. By conviction a Unionist, but a secessionist and Confederate soldier because of sectional sympathies, he became editor of the *Cincinnati Evening Times*, 1865, but withdrew to Nashville, Tenn., 1866. After service on the Nashville *Republican Banner*, he went to Louisville, Ky., to help edit the *Daily Journal* (*post* November 1868, the *Courier-Journal*). As editor of the *Courier-Journal post* November 1868, Watterson struggled for the restoration of Southern home rule, agitating for complete civil and legal rights for Negroes in exchange for the return of the South to its own people. Associated with Carl Schurz, Murat Halstead, and Samuel Bowles, he formed the famous "Quadrilateral" (which later included Whitelaw Reid and Horace White) at the Liberal Republican convention of 1872. A powerful advocate of the candidacy of Samuel J. Tilden for nomination and

election, 1876, Watterson served in Congress from the summer of 1876 through part of the winter of 1877 as Tilden's floor leader during the contest that ended with the certification of Hayes.

Never again did Watterson express more than a temporary fealty to any Democratic presidential nominee or White House incumbent. He was editorially critical of Grover Cleveland, and a fiery opponent of William J. Bryan in 1896; his stand against Bryan produced a Republican victory in Kentucky and nearly ruined the standing of his newspaper in that state. As late as 1913 Watterson deplored Bryan's appointment as U.S. secretary of state, assailing him as an impractical dreamer. Before this, however, he had made a national sensation with a series of philippics against Theodore Roosevelt whom he called a potential dictator. Failing to prevent the nomination of Woodrow Wilson in 1912, Watterson remained critical of Wilson until the issues raised in 1916 by Charles E. Hughes and Theodore Roosevelt ranged him on Wilson's side. He once again parted company with the president over the League of Nations. Selling his control of the *Courier-Journal* in 1918, he retired to private life.

Celebrated as a public speaker and lecturer, Watterson had amazing zest, a great gift for conversation, and the ability to set other editors chattering over what he wrote. He belonged to the time when journalism was personal and editorial writing often had immediate and dynamic effect. He died convinced that civilization was facing a crisis because of prevalent godlessness. He was rendered pessimistic more immediately, however, by the triumph of national prohibition and woman suffrage, championed by those whom for many years he had attacked as "red-nosed angels," "silly-sallies" and "crazyjanes." He was author, among other books, of an autobiography, *Marse Henry* (1919).

WATTERSTON, GEORGE (*b. New York, N.Y., 1783; d. Washington, D.C., 1854*), lawyer, librarian. After practicing law in Hagerstown, Md., and Washington, D.C., he served as librarian of Congress, 1815–29, and was thereafter editor of the Washington *National Journal*. He was author of a number of works including novels, poems, guide-books, statistical digests and a comedy. He began the movement to build the Washington Monument, 1833, and remained as secretary of the Washington National Monument Society until his death.

WATTS, FREDERICK (*b. Carlisle, Pa., 1801; d. Carlisle, 1889*), lawyer, farmer, Pennsylvania jurist and supreme court reporter, railroad executive. As U.S. commissioner of agriculture, 1871–77, he obtained an appropriation for a forestry investigation that was the beginning of the Agriculture Department's division of forestry. Throughout his busy life he engaged in farming and in the activities of state and county agricultural societies.

WATTS, THOMAS HILL (*b. near present Greenville, Ala., 1819; d. Montgomery, Ala., 1892*), lawyer, Alabama legislator, Confederate soldier. A Whig and later a Know-Nothing, he was a strong Unionist until Lincoln's election and its alleged threat to state rights. Confederate attorney-general, 1862, he was governor of Alabama, 1863–65. During his term he fought against invasion of his state by the North and also opposed encroachments on state rights by the Confederate government at Richmond. After the Civil War, he practiced law in Montgomery.

WATTSON, LEWIS THOMAS. [See FRANCIS, PAUL JAMES, 1863–1940.]

WAUGH, BEVERLY (*b. Fairfax Co., Va., 1789; d. Baltimore, Md., 1858*), Methodist clergyman. Elected assistant book agent of the Church, 1828, he became principal book agent, 1832, and served with efficiency and success until 1836 when he was elected bishop. He refused to be influenced in the conduct of his duties by either the pro-slavery or the anti-slavery groups among Methodists. After endeavoring to prevent the schism of 1844, he remained identified with the Northern wing of the Church and was senior bishop *post* 1852.

WAUGH, FREDERICK JUDD (*b. Bordentown, N.J., 1861; d. Provincetown, Mass., 1940*), painter. Studied with Thomas Eakins at Pennsylvania Academy of the Fine Arts and in Paris. A versatile artist, Waugh is known principally to the public as a talented marine painter whose many seascapes were marked by picturesque realism. [*Supp. 2*]

WAYLAND, FRANCIS (*b. New York, N.Y., 1796; d. 1865*), Baptist clergyman, educator. Father of Francis Wayland (1826–1904). Graduated Union, 1813; was influenced at Andover Theological Seminary by Moses Stuart. Chosen president of Brown University, 1827, he gave that school a dynamic administration until his retirement, 1855. Standards were generally raised; an analytic method of study succeeded the old memorization of textbooks; the curriculum was extended and enriched. He was author of a number of textbooks in moral philosophy, political economy, and other subjects. His reforming views on education were expressed in *Thoughts on the Present Collegiate System in the United States* (1842) and *Report on the Condition of the University* (1850). Instrumental in devising a school system for the city of Providence, R.I., he was author of the plan for free Rhode Island public schools (1828) and served as first president of the American Institute of Instruction, 1830.

WAYLAND, FRANCIS (*b. Boston, Mass., 1826; d. New Haven, Conn., 1904*), lawyer. Son of Francis Wayland (1796–1865). Graduated Brown, 1846; studied law at Harvard. Practiced in Worcester, Mass., until 1857. Thereafter a resident of New Haven, he taught at Yale Law School *post* 1871 and served as

dean, 1873–1903. A conservative in legal education, he was responsible for much material progress at the school but damaged its prestige by refusing to adopt modern methods of study as instituted at Harvard by C. C. Langdell and others.

WAYMAN, ALEXANDER WALKER (*b. Caroline Co., Md., 1821; d. Baltimore, Md., 1895*), bishop of the African Methodist Episcopal Church. Born a freeman, he was mainly self-educated. His principal pastorates until his election as bishop (1864) were in Washington, D.C., and Baltimore. As bishop, he organized and supervised conferences throughout the United States.

WAYMOUTH, GEORGE (*b. Devonshire, England, date unknown; d. place unknown, post 1612*), navigator, explorer. Commanded East India Company's expedition of 1602 in search of the Northwest Passage. Commanded ship *Archangel* on the 1605 voyage of exploration to Virginia sponsored by the Earl of Southampton, Lord Wardour and Sir Ferdinando Gorges, during which he explored and traded along the coast of present Maine. Captured Indians whom he brought back to England later served as pilots to Martin Pring, George Popham and other explorers. Waymouth was author of several treatises on navigation and shipbuilding.

WAYNE, ANTHONY (*b. Waynesboro, Pa., 1745; d. Presque Isle, now Erie, Pa., 1796*), surveyor, tanner, soldier. An active committeeman during the early Revolutionary movement, he served in the provincial assembly, 1775, and was commissioned colonel of a Pennsylvania regiment by Congress, January 1776. Impetuous and brave, he was often at odds with commanding officers but won credit for covering the retreat of Montgomery's army from the mouth of the Sorel to Ticonderoga, 1776. Commissioned brigadier-general, February 1777, he joined Washington at Morristown, N.J., and took command of the Pennsylvania line. At Brandywine, September 1777, he held the center of the defense against the British at their main point of crossing; nine days later (September 20), he was surprised and badly defeated at Paoli. In the battle of Germantown (October 4), he led an almost victorious attack but was obliged to fall back when the rest of the American force became confused and retreated. He wintered with Washington at Valley Forge and led the advance attack at Monmouth, June 1778. Leading a separate corps of Continental light infantry, he took the British outpost of Stony Point on the Hudson River, July 1779. When Benedict Arnold tried to surrender West Point, September 1780, Wayne prevented British occupation of that post. At the end of the same year he helped quell a mutiny of the Pennsylvania line and secured from Congress a correction of the grievances that had caused it. Serving under Lafayette in the Yorktown campaign, he further distinguished himself at Green Spring, Va., July 1781. During the next year he campaigned successfully against the Creek Indians in Georgia, negotiating treaties with Creeks and Cherokees, 1782–83.

Unsuccessful as a rice planter in Georgia after the Revolution, he engaged in conservative politics both in Pennsylvania and Georgia and was strongly in favor of the new Constitution. After the defeats of Generals Harmar and St. Clair by the confederated Indians of the Wabash and Maumee regions, 1790–91, Washington named Wayne as major-general to rehabilitate the American army and move against the Indians. Carefully training and organizing his forces, and employing great tact in denying the British any excuse to lend official aid to the Indians, he won a complete victory at Fallen Timbers (near present Toledo, O.), Aug. 20, 1794. Pacification and submission of the Indians was secured by Wayne a year later at the treaty of Greenville, where he convinced them of the hopelessness of further resistance. He died on his return from the occupation of the post at Detroit, surrendered under the terms of Jay's Treaty.

WAYNE, ARTHUR TREZEVANT (*b. Blackville, S.C., 1863; d. 1930*), ornithologist. An indefatigable field worker in South Carolina and Florida. Author, among other works, of *Birds of South Carolina* (1910) and *A List of Avian Species for which the Type Locality is South Carolina* (1917). Added about 45 birds to fauna of South Carolina; discovered breeding grounds of white ibis, 1922.

WAYNE, JAMES MOORE (*b. Savannah, Ga., c. 1790; d. Washington, D.C., 1867*), lawyer, Georgia legislator, official and jurist. Graduated College of New Jersey (Princeton), 1808. As congressman, Democrat, from Georgia, 1829–35, he supported President Jackson's major policies and rose to chairmanship of the committee on foreign relations. Appointed a justice of the U.S. Supreme Court, 1835, he served until his death and was particularly effective in cases involving admiralty problems and the acquisition of lands from foreign countries. He was a Unionist in the Civil War.

WEARE, MESHECH (*b. Hampton Falls, N.H., 1713; d. 1786*), New Hampshire colonial legislator and jurist, Revolutionary patriot. Graduated Harvard, 1735. President of the New Hampshire Council and chairman of the committee of safety, 1776–84; chief justice, 1776–82. Elected president of the state of New Hampshire (governor), 1784, he resigned because of ill health in 1785. He was a cautious, temperate man, influential because of his shrewdness and honesty.

WEATHERFORD, WILLIAM (*b. probably in present Elmore Co., Ala., c. 1780; d. 1824*), Creek Indian chief, known also as Red Eagle. Roused to war against the whites by the visit of Tecumseh in 1811, he took up arms after Tippecanoe, ignorant that his cause was already hopeless. Responsible for the massacre at Fort Mims, Aug. 30, 1813, he was a leader with Menewa of the force defeated at Horseshoe Bend, 1814. After his surrender to Andrew Jackson, he settled as a planter in Monroe Co., Ala. Accused, possibly falsely, by the whites of extreme personal dissoluteness, he was admitted to be eloquent and courageous.

WEAVER, AARON WARD (*b. Washington, D.C., 1832; d. Washington, 1919*), naval officer. Appointed midshipman, 1848; graduated U.S. Naval Academy, 1854. Served with distinction in Union campaigns on the lower Mississippi River, 1862–64, and with the South Atlantic blockade, 1864–65. Retired as rear-admiral, 1893.

WEAVER, JAMES BAIRD (*b. Dayton, O., 1833; d. Colfax, Iowa, 1912*), lawyer, Union soldier, Populist. Raised in Michigan and Iowa; practiced law in Iowa. Volunteering for the Union Army, 1861, he served in the western campaigns and rose to rank of brevet brigadier-general. Utterly incorruptible, he held post of internal revenue assessor in Iowa, 1867–73, but lost favor with the Republican party to which he belonged because of his objection to its currency policy and his denunciations of predatory corporations. As a Greenbacker, he was elected to Congress from Iowa, 1878, ran for president in 1880, was defeated for Congress in 1882, but won again in 1884 and 1886. Identifying himself with the Farmers' Alliance, he took a leading part in transforming it into the Populist party. No advocate of unlimited inflation, nor of repudiation of debt, he held to the quantity theory of money and opposed what he considered the systematic efforts of creditors to appreciate the purchasing power of the dollar. As Populist candidate for the presidency, 1892, he campaigned with force and dignity; he received a popular vote of over a million, and 22 electoral votes. An advocate of the fusion of all soft-money forces, he helped bring about Populist endorsement of William J. Bryan in 1896.

WEAVER, PHILIP (*b. North Scituate, R.I., 1791; d. Attica, Ind., ante 1861*), cotton manufacturer. Removed to Spartanburg District, S.C., 1816, where with his brothers and others he set up and operated one of the earliest cotton mills in the region.

WEAVER, WILLIAM DIXON (*b. Greensburg, Pa., 1857; d. Charlottesville, Va., 1919*), electrical engineer, editor of technical journals, organizer of professional societies in his field.

WEBB, ALEXANDER STEWART (*b. New York, N.Y., 1835; d. Riverdale, N.Y., 1911*), soldier, educator. Son of James W. Webb. Graduated West Point, 1855; was commissioned in the artillery. Outstanding in his distinguished Civil War service with the Union Army was his command of the 2nd Brigade, Second Division, II Corps, 1863–64. Webb's brigade occupied the "bloody angle" at Gettysburg and bore the brunt of Pickett's charge. Severely wounded at Spotsylvania, May 1864, he returned to duty the next year as chief-of-staff to Gen. Meade. Resigning with the rank of lieutenant-colonel, Regular Army, he served as president of the College of the City of New York, 1869–

1902. Serving also as professor of political philosophy, he maintained the standards of the college but made no significant advance in the scope of its work.

WEBB, CHARLES HENRY (*b. Rouse's Point, N.Y., 1834; d. New York, N.Y., 1905*), journalist, Civil War correspondent. Active on California journals, 1863–66, he became a close friend of Bret Harte and of Mark Twain. He founded, and was first editor of, the *Californian*, 1864. Working in New York City *post* 1866, he was the sponsor and publisher of Mark Twain's first book, *The Celebrated Jumping Frog of Calaveras County* (1867). His "John Paul" letters for the *New York Tribune* were collected in 1874 as *John Paul's Book*. He was author also of other parodies and satires.

WEBB, DANIEL (*b. England, c. 1700; d. 1773*), British soldier. Rising in the regular service to be colonel of the 48th Foot (November 1755), he was selected early in 1756 to command in North America under Lord Loudoun and James Abercromby. A temporary major-general after the fall of Oswego, he went up the Mohawk River to make a stand against the expected French attack on the forts there. Stricken with panic by Indian rumors, he destroyed the forts and retreated leaving the colonists unprotected. As Loudoun had no one else to leave in command in New York during 1757, he continued Webb in his post despite that officer's illness and incapacity. During the siege of Fort William Henry in August he made no attempt at its relief. Recalled in December 1757, he later served with ability in Germany.

WEBB, GEORGE JAMES (*b. near Salisbury, England, 1803; d. Orange, N.J., 1887*), musician, composer. Came to Boston, Mass., 1830; was appointed organist of Old South Church. Associated with Lowell Mason in his educational projects, Webb organized an orchestra at the Boston Academy of Music and was important in other ways in the development of music in Boston.

WEBB, HARRY HOWARD (*b. San Francisco, Calif., 1853; d. Montecito, Calif., 1939*), mining engineer. Associated with the development of gold and diamond mines in South Africa, 1895–1916, he was later active in development of the potash and borax deposits near Death Valley, Calif. [*Supp. 2*]

WEBB, JAMES WATSON (*b. Claverack, N.Y., 1802; d. New York, N.Y., 1884*), journalist, diplomat. Father of Alexander S. Webb. Commissioned a second lieutenant in the U.S. Army, 1819, he served principally with infantry in the Midwest, won a reputation as a duellist, and resigned from the army, 1827. Acquiring the N.Y. *Morning Courier*, he merged the *Enquirer* with it in 1829 and continued to edit the *Courier and Enquirer* until 1861. Originally a Jacksonian, he later was a chief prop of the Whigs and a Free-Soiler. He was effective, if rash, as U.S. minister to Brazil, 1861–69, and gave useful aid to the Union

cause by his personal friendship and contact with Napoleon III.

WEBB, JOHN BURKITT (*b. Philadelphia, Pa., 1841; d. Glen Ridge, N.J., 1912*), engineer, educator, inventor. C.E., University of Michigan, 1871; studied also at Heidelberg, Göttingen, Berlin and Paris. Professor of civil engineering, University of Illinois, 1871–79; professor of applied mathematics, Cornell, 1881–86; professor of mathematics and mechanics, Stevens Institute of Technology, 1886–1908. Invented the floating dynamometer, 1888, and other devices for power measurement.

WEBB, THOMAS (*b. England, c. 1724; d. Bristol, England, 1796*), British army officer, Methodist preacher. A wounded veteran of the French and Indian War, Webb became a Methodist in England, 1764. Returning to America, 1766, he assisted Philip Embury in preaching to the original New York City congregation of Methodists. He aided in the building of Wesley Chapel, 1768, and continued to evangelize until his return to England at some time during the Revolution.

WEBB, THOMAS SMITH (*b. Boston, Mass., 1771; d. 1819*), printer, founder of the American system of chapter and encampment Masonry. Author of *The Freemason's Monitor* (1797). He was a founder and first president (1815) of the Handel and Haydn Society of Boston.

WEBB, WILLIAM HENRY (*b. New York, N.Y., 1816; d. New York, 1899*), shipbuilder. Working at his New York City yard on the East River between 5th and 7th Sts., 1843–69, Webb showed remarkable versatility in design and construction of vessels. He designed and built a number of notable packets and pre-clippers, and ranked high among the builders of regular clippers. Among his products were the *Sword Fish* (1851), the *Challenge* (1851), *Young America* (1853) and *Black Hawk* (1857). He also constructed hulls for a number of steamships and was the constructor of the Pacific Mail ships *California, Panama, Golden Gate, San Francisco* and *Yorktown*. Among the warships which he built were the cutter *Harriet Lane* (1857) and several vessels for the Russian and Italian navies. His masterpiece was the ironclad ram *Dunderberg* (1865) which was sold to the French navy and sailed as the *Rochambeau*. He established and endowed Webb's Academy, New York, N.Y. (opened, May 1894).

WEBB, WILLIAM ROBERT (*b. near Mount Tirzah, N.C., 1842; d. Bellbuckle, Tenn., 1926*), Confederate soldier, educator. Graduated University of North Carolina, 1867. Founder (1870) and headmaster of a celebrated preparatory school at Culleoka, Tenn., which he removed to Bellbuckle, 1886.

WEBBER, CHARLES WILKINS (*b. Russellville, Ky., 1819; d. Nicaragua, 1856*), journalist, explorer. After serving in the Texas war for independence, he studied medicine and also theology, but became a journalist in New York City, 1844. He projected several abortive exploring expeditions in the Southwest and in 1855 joined the filibuster commanded by William Walker in Nicaragua. He was killed there in the battle of Rivas. Excelling in the description of wild border life, he was author, among other works, of *Old Hicks the Guide* (1848); *The Gold Mines of the Gila* (1849); *The Hunter-Naturalist* (1851); *Tales of the Southern Border* (1852); and *Wild Scenes and Song Birds* (1854).

WEBER, ALBERT (*b. Bavaria, 1828; d. New York, N.Y., 1879*), musician, piano-maker. Came to New York City *c.* 1844; began business as a piano manufacturer, 1851. Weber did not create anything new in piano construction, but was a thorough craftsman and made a quality product.

WEBER, GUSTAV CARL ERICH (*b. Bonn, Germany, 1828; d. Willoughby, O., 1912*), physician. Emigrated to America *c.* 1849. Graduated Beaumont Medical College, St. Louis, Mo., 1851; made further studies in Vienna, Amsterdam and Paris. Practiced surgery and taught at several medical schools in Ohio, 1856–70; was professor of clinical surgery and dean of medical department of Wooster University, 1870–81; also dean of medical department, Western Reserve University, 1881–94. U.S. consul at Nuremberg, 1897–1902.

WEBER, HENRY ADAM (*b. Franklin Co., O., 1845; d. Columbus, O., 1912*), chemist. Studied at Otterbein College and in Germany. Chemist, Ohio Geological Survey, 1869–74; professor of chemistry, University of Illinois, 1874–82; professor of agricultural chemistry, Ohio State University *post* 1884. In addition to his academic work, Weber collaborated with M. A. Scovell in the manufacture of sugar from sorghum and was active in the work of the state board of agriculture and the state board of health. He was a pioneer in the national pure-food movement initiated by Harvey W. Wiley.

WEBSTER, ALICE JANE CHANDLER (*b. Fredonia, N.Y., 1876; d. 1916*), author, known as Jean Webster. Graduated Vassar, 1901. A grandniece of Mark Twain, she was author of *When Patty Went to College* (1903) and other Patty stories, and of the extraordinarily successful *Daddy-Long-Legs* (1912).

WEBSTER, ARTHUR GORDON (*b. Brookline, Mass., 1863; d. 1923*), physicist. Graduated Harvard, 1885; Ph.D., University of Berlin, 1890. Taught physics at Clark University *post* 1890, succeeding Albert A. Michelson as head of the department, 1892. His course of lectures on mathematical physics was unsurpassed in scope and thoroughness; at the same time he continued his work in experimental physics. He was outstanding in the development of various gyroscopic instruments and in sound investigations; during World War I he established and conducted a

school of ballistics at Clark. He was author, among other works, of *The Theory of Electricity and Magnetism* (1897); *The Dynamics of Particles and of Rigid, Elastic and Fluid Bodies* (1904); and *The Partial Differential Equations of Mathematical Physics* (published posthumously, 1927).

WEBSTER, DANIEL (*b. Salisbury, N.H., 1782; d. Marshfield, Mass., 1852*), lawyer, statesman. A boy of delicate health, he early displayed a precocious mind and a strongly emotional nature. While a student at Phillips Exeter in 1796, he made rapid headway with his studies, but was shy and sensitive about his unfashionable clothes and clumsy manners. At Dartmouth, he was outstanding in one of the college debating societies. After his graduation in 1801, he began the study of law in a desultory way, but gave up his studies to teach in the Fryeburg Academy in order to help his elder brother complete a college course. Returning to the study of law, September 1802, he varied the monotony of legal treatises with extensive readings in history and the classics. Removing to Boston, he became a clerk in the office of Christopher Gore and was admitted to the Boston bar, March 1805. After practicing for a short time at Boscawen, N.H., he removed to Portsmouth in September 1807 and practiced there with distinction until 1816.

A rival of Jeremiah Mason at the bar, he improved his style of speaking by conscious imitation of Mason and also learned from him the importance of a most careful preparation of arguments. Temperamentally a conservative, he had inherited from his father strong Federalist convictions and strove by Fourth of July orations and occasional political pamphleteering to assist the revival of Federalism after the Jeffersonian triumph of 1800. A champion of New England shipping interests, he was author of *Considerations on the Embargo Laws* (1808). A vigorous critic of the national administration for having led the nation into an unjustifiable war, 1812, he renounced the idea of resistance or insurrection, advocating "the peaceable remedy of election." His famous Rockingham Memorial was a forceful statement of his anti-war views.

Webster's national political career began with his election to Congress in 1812. A member of the committee on foreign relations, he introduced a number of resolutions designed to embarrass the administration, eloquently denouncing the government's draft bill and favoring repeal of the Embargo Act. He even suggested the expedient of state nullification of a federal law in the debate over conscription, but continued to repudiate any thought of disunion and advised New Hampshire against sending delegates to the Hartford Convention. Re-elected to Congress, 1814, he urged the provision of adequate safeguards for financial stability in any re-establishment of the United States Bank. In discussion of the tariff, he announced himself as opposed to any "hotbed" treatment of manufactures and opposed the high duties of the tariff of 1816. Removing to Boston, August 1816, he devoted himself to legal work. The so-called Dartmouth College case, a suit in which the college trustees sought to defend their rights against acts of the New Hampshire legislature which changed the character of the institution and its governing body, made Webster, in the opinion of many people, the foremost lawyer of the time. Placed in charge of the case before the U.S. Supreme Court, he drew on the notes and briefs of his colleagues for most of his materials, but was himself responsible for their brilliant presentation. On Feb. 2, 1819, the Supreme Court by its decision completely upheld the college and its counsel. Three weeks after this victory, he appeared for the Bank of the United States in *McCulloch vs. Maryland* and soon thereafter played an important part in three other important constitutional cases, *Gibbons vs. Ogden; Osborn vs. Bank of the United States;* and *Ogden vs. Saunders.* He also delivered a number of outstanding orations on public occasions, notably his commemoration of the landing of the Pilgrims, December 1820, and his address at the laying of the cornerstone of the Bunker Hill Monument, June 1825.

Returning to Congress, 1823–27, he was made chairman of the judiciary committee. In April 1824 he challenged Henry Clay's arguments for a protective tariff, attacking the proposed tariff bill and its principles and refusing to vote for it. Although he shared the distrust of the New England Federalists for John Q. Adams, he gave Adams his vote during the contest over the presidency in the House, and influenced others in the same direction. As party lines reshaped themselves under the new administration, Webster became an increasingly loyal Adams supporter. Elected to the U.S. Senate from Massachusetts, June 1827, he was soon in the thick of the fight over the tariff act of 1828. An associate of the mill-owners of his state and an investor in the Merrimack Manufacturing Co., he was frank to state that New England must consider protection as a determined national policy. Since the tariff bill with all its "abominations" granted protection to woolens, he supported it and helped accomplish its passage. Henceforward, he was an aggressive champion of protection.

Webster rose to the height of his oratorical abilities in the famous debate of January 1830 with John C. Calhoun's mouthpiece, Robert Y. Hayne, over the issue of state rights and nullification. Webster declared that the Union, in origin, preceded the states. He insisted that the Constitution was framed by the people not as a compact, but to create a government sovereign within the range of the powers assigned to it, with the Supreme Court as the only proper arbiter of the extent of these powers. Nullification could result only in violence and civil war. He was for "Liberty *and* Union, now and forever, one and inseparable." Webster supported President Jackson in his defiance of the nullifiers, 1832–33. When the "Compromise Tariff" was enacted in March 1833, Webster voted with the opposition.

As soon as all those with a common interest in vested rights began to combine in the Whig party, Webster joined the new coalition. He was further persuaded to oppose President Jackson because of Jackson's war on the Bank of the United States which Webster supported both on principle and as a client. Re-elected to the Senate, 1833, he spoke constructively in the debates over the removal of deposits from the Bank and the resolution of censure then adopted by the Senate. Named as the Massachusetts Whig candidate for the presidency, 1836, he received only the electoral vote of his own state. Having given so much of his time and energy to the public, he found himself in a poor financial condition which was aggravated by his ill-timed investments during the 1830's in midwestern lands. Harassed by his creditors, he was saved from disgrace only by the loans of wealthy friends. After the panic of 1837, he returned to the special session of Congress and took a brilliant part in the Whig fight against Van Buren's sub-treasury plan; he also clashed with Calhoun over slavery and the right of petition. Re-elected to the Senate once again in 1839, he campaigned for William H. Harrison in the presidential race of 1840. Named U.S. secretary of state, he remained in office under President John Tyler after Harrison's death. After the resignation of Tyler's cabinet over the president's veto of Whig measures for re-establishing a United States Bank, Webster, suspicious of Henry Clay's leadership, continued in office in order to bring to a conclusion the negotiations over the boundary of Maine; these he carried through to a successful adjustment in the Webster-Ashburton Treaty of 1842. Eminently successful in the State Department, he conducted negotiations also with Portugal and Mexico and undertook the preliminaries to the opening of diplomatic relations with China. Resigning in May 1843 from the only office which had ever allowed him reasonable satisfaction and scope for his talents, he returned to his law practice.

Re-elected to the U.S. Senate once again in 1845, he announced that it was his special business to look to "the preservation of the great industrial interests of this country" from Democratic free-trade propensities. He joined in the Whig policy of condemning the war with Mexico, but held that supplies should be appropriated for the war so long as it was not connected with territorial aggrandizement or the dismemberment of Mexico. In the dispute over the disposition of the territories acquired from Mexico after the war, Webster voted consistently for the Wilmot Proviso, but preferred the "no territory" basis that would prevent a controversy from arising over slavery, which he considered "a great moral and political evil." Once again disappointed of hopes for the presidency by the election of Zachary Taylor, he grew alarmed over the sectional controversy which seemed likely to result in a Southern separatism. He was also disturbed over the obstacle presented by a continued discussion of slavery to Whig efforts at tariff revision. Increasingly annoyed at the militant intransigence of the Abolitionists and anti-slavery men, he declared himself in favor of Henry Clay's compromise measures. On Mar. 7, 1850, he delivered a famous speech designed to "beat down the Northern and Southern follies now raging in equal extremes." No evil was so great as disunion, he said; there could be no peaceful secession. A congressional prohibition of slavery in the territories was useless since a law of nature had settled that slavery cannot exist in California or New Mexico. Conservatives approved his speech, but the anti-slavery forces denounced him as a fallen star. Serving once again with skill as U.S. secretary of state, 1850–52, he was denied a presidential nomination, 1852. Repudiating the candidacy of Gen. Winfield Scott, he prophesied the downfall of the Whig party, and died before the election.

Forty years in politics revealed in Webster two seemingly contrasting but naturally allied forces. An eloquent champion of the Union, he was also a special advocate for the new industrial interests then forging to the front in the national economy. In behalf of the masters of capital, he sacrificed the popular following that stood ready to rally around a great democratic chieftain. The logic and eloquence of his oratory, the magnetic quality of his personality, did little to bring him the support of workingmen. A great constitutional lawyer, he found his equals or betters among his contemporaries. His victories were never on a par with his ambitions. Even his personal fortunes failed to bring him any sense of security and life was for him a series of great frustrations. However, no other Northern man left so strong an impress upon the political life of the "middle period" or more substantially contributed to the preservation of the Union in the supreme test of the 1860's.

WEBSTER, JEAN. [See WEBSTER, ALICE JANE CHANDLER, 1876–1916.]

WEBSTER, JOHN WHITE (*b. Boston, Mass., 1793; d. 1850*), physician, educator. A teacher of chemistry at Harvard, 1824–49, Webster is principally remembered as the murderer of George Parkman (uncle of Francis Parkman), Nov. 23, 1849. After a sensational trial, Webster was convicted and hanged.

WEBSTER, JOSEPH DANA (*b. Hampton, N.H., 1811; d. Chicago, Ill., 1876*), soldier, engineer. Graduated Dartmouth, 1832. Served as an officer in the topographical engineers, 1838–54, resigning to enter business in Chicago. During the Civil War he served as chief-of-staff to Gen. U. S. Grant in 1862 and part of 1863, rising to rank of brigadier-general. In charge of all military railways before, during, and after the Vicksburg campaign, he then became chief-of-staff to Gen. W. T. Sherman. He resigned from the army, 1865, as brevet major-general.

WEBSTER, NOAH (*b. West Hartford, Conn., 1758; d. New Haven, Conn., 1843*), educator, lexicographer, editor. Graduated Yale, 1778. While teaching at Goshen, N.Y., 1782, he composed an elementary spelling book, *A Grammatical Institute of the English Language, Part I* (Hartford, Conn., 1783) which he supplemented with a grammar (1784) and a reader (1785). In preparing the series, he strove to correct the neglect of the American scene in the then current textbooks, and in the introduction to his speller issued a literary declaration of independence. Of the three books, the speller was the outstanding success and under various titles continued to be issued well into the 20th century. Its use had much to do with the standardization of spelling and, to some degree, of pronunciation in the United States along lines differing somewhat from those that prevailed in England. Neither the reader nor the grammar had the vogue of the speller, but the grammar (Part II of the *Institute*) was interesting because it was based on an objective study of the actual phenomena of English speech. Aroused by piracies of his work, he began an agitation which in time led to provision of American copyright; this activity took him into politics and made him an ardent Federalist. His efforts to promote copyright legislation in the 13 states involved travel over most of the country and drew from him several political pamphlets in support of a strong central government. Encouraged by Benjamin Franklin, he became an advocate of spelling reform, but was unable to effect any substantial changes.

Between 1787 and 1798, he served as editor of several newspapers in New York and was editor of the *American Magazine,* 1787–88. Removing to New Haven, 1798, he gave up journalism for good in 1803. Meanwhile, he had produced a number of interesting works including *The Prompter* (1791, informal essays), several treatises in economics, a work on epidemic diseases which was standard in its time, and much political writing. He edited John Winthrop's *Journal* in 1790, and was author of a pioneer American essay in physical science, *Experiments Respecting Dew* (begun 1790, printed 1809). After issuing a preparatory study, *A Compendious Dictionary of the English Language* (1806), Webster devoted twenty years to a larger work which was published in 1828 under the title *An American Dictionary of the English Language.* It took first place at once among English dictionaries on its merits. In it the author freely recorded non-literary words and based definitions upon the usage of American as well as British writers. In defining a word, he proceeded from what he considered its original or primary meaning and as far as possible derived the other meanings from the primary one. The great weakness of Webster's dictionary lay in its etymologies, but it was on the whole a scholarly achievement of the first order.

WEBSTER, PELATIAH (*b. Lebanon, Conn., 1726; d. 1795*), Congregational clergyman, Philadelphia merchant, political economist. Graduated Yale, 1746. Author of a number of papers urging support of the

Revolution by taxation rather than by loans, and suggesting curtailment of paper money issues, Webster later (1791) gathered these studies together in a volume entitled *Political Essays on the Nature and Operation of Money, etc.* His *Dissertation on the Political Union and Constitution of the Thirteen United States* (1783) helped educate the people to the need of a new form of government, and he ably supported the Federal Constitution in several pamphlets published during the struggle in Pennsylvania over its adoption, 1787.

WEBSTER-POWELL, ALMA. [See POWELL, ALMA WEBSTER, 1874–1930.]

WEED, THURLOW (*b. Greene Co., N.Y., 1797; d. 1882*), printer, journalist, New York politician and legislator. Began as publisher-editor of up-state New York newspapers supporting DeWitt Clinton, 1817–22; served as editorial writer on the *Rochester Telegraph,* which he purchased, 1825. A supporter of John Q. Adams in 1824, Weed became an active Anti-Mason. Elected to the New York Assembly, 1829, he took over editorship of the *Albany Evening Journal,* March 1830. Becoming a Whig, he fought the dominant "Albany Regency" in his state, drilled his new party through the campaigns of 1834 and 1836, and helped create the Whig victories that made William H. Seward governor of New York in 1838 and W. H. Harrison president in 1840. Although he was charged with dominating Seward, his great personal friend, actually he was content for others to formulate the principles while he secured the votes. He considered bribery and legislative favors legitimate party instruments, but was personally not corrupt. A sincere anti-slavery man, he had nothing but scorn for Abolitionists and other extremists; while recognizing the power of Horace Greeley, he was dubious about Greeley's efforts at social reform. Discouraged at first by the Whig failures in 1842 and 1844, he early recognized the possibilities of a presidential candidacy by Gen. Zachary Taylor, but was again disappointed in his hopes for Whig unity when Taylor died soon after election. Slow to join the new Republican party, he devoted his energies *post c.* 1854 to the furtherance of his friend Seward's candidacy for the presidency, but was again unsuccessful. Consulted by Abraham Lincoln during the latter's campaign and after, he had considerable influence on appointments, but was distrustful of Abolitionist influences on Lincoln. Preferring an active War Democrat as Union candidate in 1864, he was held in the Republican ranks because of the nomination of George B. McClellan. As the Radical Republicans gained strength after Lincoln's death, Weed's influence declined. He became editor of the N.Y. *Commercial Advertiser,* 1867, but had to abandon editorial work because of failing health and sight. A generous man, good-natured and charming of manner, Weed was described by Henry Adams as "the model

of political management and patient address—a complete American education in himself."

WEEDEN, WILLIAM BABCOCK (*b. Bristol, R.I., 1834; d. Providence, R.I., 1912*), woolen manufacturer, social historian. Author, among other works, of *Indian Money as a Factor in New England Civilization* (1884) and the *Economic and Social History of New England* (1890).

WEEKS, EDWIN LORD (*b. Boston, Mass., 1849; d. Paris, France, 1903*), painter, specializing in Oriental subjects.

WEEKS, JOHN WINGATE (*b. near Lancaster, N.H., 1860; d. Lancaster, 1926*), stockbroker. Graduated Annapolis, 1881. Entered brokerage business in Boston, Mass., 1888, becoming a partner in Hornblower & Weeks. Congressman, Republican, from Massachusetts, 1905–13; U.S. senator, 1913–19. U.S. secretary of war, 1921–25. An able, hard-working, orthodox Republican.

WEEKS, JOSEPH DAME (*b. Lowell, Mass., 1840; d. 1896*), technical journalist. Long associated in an editorial capacity with the *American Manufacturer* (Pittsburgh, Pa.), he was responsible for the first wage scale offered by the manufacturers to the Amalgamated Association of Iron and Steel Workers. He subsequently presided over a number of wage conferences and other essays in labor arbitration. He is credited with conducting the experiments that led to the first use of gas in a puddling furnace; he was also responsible for assembly of petroleum, coke, gas and other statistics for the Census and for various state and federal bureaus.

WEEKS, STEPHEN BEAUREGARD (*b. Pasquotank Co., N.C., 1865; d. Washington, D.C., 1918*), historian, federal educational official. Graduated University of North Carolina, 1886; Ph.D., 1888. Ph.D., Johns Hopkins, 1891. Author of, among other works, *Southern Quakers and Slavery* (1896) and of the *Index to the Colonial and State Records of North Carolina* (1909–14).

WEEMS, MASON LOCKE (*b. near Herring Bay, Md., 1759; d. Beaufort, S.C., 1825*), Episcopal clergyman, subscription book agent, author. One of the first candidates to receive Anglican ordination for service in the United States (1784), Weems served Maryland parishes, 1784–92. Passionate in his faith in the value of good books, he journeyed (*post* 1794 as agent for Mathew Carey) up and down the Eastern coast from New York to Savannah, acting as book salesman and occasional preacher until his death. Author of a number of moralizing tracts, he is remembered for what may be called his masterpiece, *The Life and Memorable Actions of George Washington* (*c.* 1800) in whose fifth edition (1806) the hatchet and cherry-tree story first appeared in book form.

WEGMANN, EDWARD (*b. Rio de Janeiro, Brazil, 1850; d. Yonkers, N.Y., 1935*), engineer. C.E., New

York University, 1871. He was particularly notable for his thirty years of service with the water-supply system of New York City (1884–1914) during which he made studies for design of the Croton Dam, supervised much of the work on the Croton Aqueduct, and continued in service on the maintenance of the Croton water system. He was author of authoritative works on the design of dams and of *The Water Works of the City of New York: 1658–1895* (1896). [Supp. 1]

WEIDENMANN, JACOB (*b. Winterthur, Switzerland, 1829; d. 1893*), landscape architect. Trained in Munich, he settled in America *c.* 1861. Superintendent of parks in Hartford, Conn., 1861–68, he was later employed in a number of important projects, sometimes alone and sometimes in collaboration with Frederick L. Olmsted. He was a pioneer in the modern park type of cemetery.

WEIDIG, ADOLF (*b. Hamburg, Germany, 1867; d. Hinsdale, Ill., 1931*), musician, composer. Studied at the Hamburg and Munich conservatories. Came to America, 1892; played with Chicago Symphony Orchestra as a first violin; taught at American Conservatory of Music, Chicago, *post* 1893. A conservative modernist as a composer, he was author of songs, chamber music and large orchestral works, notably "Drei Episoden" (*Opus* 38, 1908). He was author also of a treatise, *Harmonic Material and Its Uses* (1923).

WEIDNER, REVERE FRANKLIN (*b. Center Valley, Pa., 1851; d. Tangerine, Fla., 1915*), Lutheran theologian. Graduated Muhlenberg, 1869; Lutheran Theological Seminary, Philadelphia, 1873. Professor of dogmatics, Augustana Seminary, 1882–91; first president, Chicago Lutheran Seminary *post* 1891.

WEIGHTMAN, WILLIAM (*b. Waltham, England, 1813; d. 1904*), chemist. Emigrated to America *c.* 1829; was long associated with Powers & Weightman and its antecedent firms. Weightman was the first to manufacture quinine sulphate and popularize the use of the cheaper alkaloids of cinchona as substitutes. His firm is also credited with introducing and perfecting the manufacture of citric acid in the United States. He was also an extensive holder of real estate in Philadelphia and director of a number of banks.

WEIL, RICHARD (*b. New York, N.Y., 1876; d. Macon, Ga., 1917*), physician. Graduated Columbia, 1896; M.D., N.Y. College of Physicians and Surgeons, 1900; studied also in Vienna and Strassburg. Teacher of experimental pathology and therapeutics at Cornell Medical College, 1905–15, he became head of the department of experimental medicine, 1916. Working *post* 1906 at the Loomis Laboratory, he gained international reputation in the field of the serology of cancer and general problems of immunity. He established the *Journal of Cancer Research*, 1915, and was its managing editor until his death in military service during World War I.

WEIR, JOHN FERGUSON (*b. West Point, N.Y., 1841; d. Providence, R.I., 1926*), artist. Son of Robert W. Weir; brother of Julian A. Weir. Studied with his father and at the National Academy of Design, New York. Grouped with the "Hudson River School," he painted genre, landscapes, portraits, and flower-pieces; his early studies of industry were important and include his masterpiece, "Forging the Shaft," now in the Metropolitan Museum of Art. He taught painting and design at Yale *post c.* 1869 and was first director of the School of Fine Arts at Yale.

WEIR, JULIAN ALDEN (*b. West Point, N.Y., 1852; d. New York, N.Y., 1919*), painter. Son of Robert W. Weir; brother of John F. Weir. Studied with his father, at the N.Y. National Academy of Design, and in the atelier of Gérôme in Paris; was influenced by Bastien-Lepage. He settled in New York City *c.* 1883 after nearly ten years of intermittent foreign travel and study. Friend of most of the outstanding painters of his time, he was also a wise adviser to art collectors in the purchase of contemporary work. His own early painting is somewhat eclectic, marked by skilled craftsmanship and highly developed technique. Deeply influenced by the French Impressionists, he was not an Impressionist in the limited sense; his art is more directly related to that of Whistler, and to the decorative methods of the Japanese. A versatile craftsman in varied media, he never aspired to the grand manner. His conception was expressed in terms of spatial arrangement, simplification of form, and harmonization of tone. In all his work there is reflected his own restraint, sincerity, and reasonableness, together with subtlety of observation and delicacy of feeling. In his ultimate style, the color is subdued, marked by neutralized hues of closely related values; the form is manifested by a universal lighting that eliminates strong contrasts.

WEIR, ROBERT FULTON (*b. New York, N.Y., 1838; d. 1927*), surgeon. Nephew of Robert W. Weir. Graduated present College of the City of New York, 1854; M.D., N.Y. College of Physicians and Surgeons, 1859. After service with the Union Army, he practiced in New York City where he held a number of hospital appointments. He taught surgery at the College of Physicians and Surgeons, 1883–1903. A brilliant operator, he was notable for work in connection with surgery of the joints and intestines. He was among the first to recognize duodenal ulcer as an entity, and to adopt Lister's method. He also made important modifications of the Murphy button for use in gastroenterostomy.

WEIR, ROBERT WALTER (*b. New Rochelle, N.Y., 1803; d. New York, N.Y., 1889*), painter, teacher. Father of John F. and Julian A. Weir. Mainly self-taught, he was enabled by a patron to make studies in Florence and Rome. Teacher of drawing at the U.S. Military Academy, West Point, 1834–76, he also executed portraits, illustrations, and genre paintings. "The Embarkation of the Pilgrims" in the rotunda of the U.S. Capitol, Washington, D.C., was painted by him, 1836–40. A contemporary critic described him as showing "considerable skill of manipulation and detail, facility of composition, and those composite qualities which make up an accomplished rather than an original man."

WEISENBURG, THEODORE HERMAN (*b. Budapest, Hungary, 1876; d. 1934*), neurologist. Came to the United States as a child. M.D., University of Pennsylvania, 1899. Practiced and taught in Philadelphia; was associated in much of his work with Charles K. Mills. Professor of neurology, Graduate School of Medicine, University of Pennsylvania *post* 1917. A contributor to professional journals, he was best known as editor of the *Archives of Neurology and Psychiatry post* 1920.

WEISER, JOHANN CONRAD (*b. near Herrenberg, Württemberg, 1696; d. Womelsdorf, Pa., 1760*), Indian interpreter and agent. Settled in New York, 1710, where he became expert in the Mohawk language and farmed near Schoharie. On his removal to Tulpehocken, Pa., 1729, he renewed his friendship with the chief, Shikellamy, and was responsible for the Philadelphia conferences (1731 and 1736) which won the Iroquois to the interests of the Penns. He made the Iroquois alliance binding by the treaty of 1742, and in 1743 averted war between the Iroquois and Virginia. Through his influence, the Lancaster Treaty of 1744 marked a shift of the direction of Indian affairs from New York to Pennsylvania and a reduction of the power of Sir William Johnson. With George Croghan, he won over the Western tribes at the treaty of Logstown, 1748, thereby extending Pennsylvania trade to the Mississippi.

Superseded in the formulation of policy *post* 1748, he continued active in local politics and was first president-judge of Berks Co., Pa., 1752–60. Weiser is also celebrated for his religious activities. Born a Lutheran, he became a follower of John P. Miller in the German Reformed Church and formed with Miller a Baptist group, 1735. Baptized by Johann C. Beissel, Weiser removed his family to Ephrata and became a member of the cloister there under the name of Brother Enoch. After several quarrels with Beissel, he ended his connection with Ephrata *c.* 1743. Thereafter, he was successively a Lutheran again and a member of the Reformed Church. Throughout his early career, he assisted the Moravian missions to the Indians.

WEISS, EHRICH. [See HOUDINI, HARRY, 1874–1926.]

WEISS, JOHN (*b. Boston, Mass., 1818; d. Boston, 1879*), Unitarian clergyman. Pastor at various times in Watertown and New Bedford, Mass., he is remembered principally for his efforts to introduce German literature to New England readers through translations of Schiller and Goethe. He was author

also of the *Life and Correspondence of Theodore Parker* (1863).

WEITZEL, GODFREY (*b. Cincinnati, O., 1835; d. Philadelphia, Pa., 1884*), soldier, engineer. Graduated West Point, 1855. After service as engineer in several theaters of the Civil War, he was promoted brigadier-general, 1862, and commanded a brigade and a provisional division during Union Army operations in Louisiana, 1862–63. Chief engineer of the Army of the James, June–September 1864, he returned to troop duty, commanding first the XVIII and later the XXV Corps. Cited for gallantry at the capture of Fort Harrison, Va., 1864, he was promoted major-general and served under Gen. Benjamin Butler in the first expedition against Fort Fisher. His command took possession of Richmond upon its evacuation, Apr. 3, 1865. He was distinguished as a corps commander and for his success with Negro troops. Returning to the engineer service after the Civil War, he was active in river- and harbor-improvement works of which the most important were the ship canals at the falls of the Ohio and at Sault Sainte Marie, Mich.

WELBY, AMELIA BALL COPPUCK (*b. St. Michaels, Md., 1819; d. Louisville, Ky., 1852*), verse writer. Author of the once-celebrated *Poems* (1845) by "Amelia," a book filled with echoes of her greater contemporaries.

WELCH, ADONIJAH STRONG (*b. East Hampton, Conn., 1821; d. Pasadena, Calif., 1889*), educator. Graduated University of Michigan, 1846. As first principal (1852–65) of Michigan State Normal School at Ypsilanti, he conducted teacher's institutes and aided in organizing the state teacher's association. Chosen first president of Iowa State Agricultural College at Ames, he served, 1869–83, and later taught history and psychology there. A defender of industrial education, he based his courses in agriculture and mechanic arts on study of fundamental and applied sciences. He also encouraged systematic experimentation in stock raising and farm products at his college some seven years before the federal act providing for experiment stations.

WELCH, ASHBEL (*b. Nelson, N.Y., 1809; d. Lambertville, N.J., 1882*), civil engineer. Studied at Albany Academy under Joseph Henry. Associated with the Delaware & Raritan Canal of which he was made chief engineer in 1835, he engaged in a variety of engineering work in the field of transportation and developed a large consulting practice. He aided John Ericsson in designing the *Princeton*, and supervised the naval gunnery experiments begun by Commodore R. F. Stockton. After beginning the work of designing and constructing the Chesapeake & Delaware Canal, he was active *post* 1854 in work with New Jersey railroads, notably the Camden & Amboy for which he planned what is regarded as the earliest (1865) installation of the block signaling system.

WELCH, CHARLES CLARK (*b. Jefferson Co., N.Y., 1830; d. Jacksonville, Fla., 1908*), Colorado miner, railroad builder and capitalist.

WELCH, JOHN (*b. Harrison Co., O., 1805; d. Athens, O., 1891*), lawyer, Ohio jurist and legislator, Whig and Republican politician. Justice of the Ohio supreme court, 1865–78; expert in cases involving real property.

WELCH, PHILIP HENRY (*b. Angelica, N.Y., 1849; d. Brooklyn, N.Y., 1889*), journalist, humorist. Employed on the staffs of newspapers in Rochester, N.Y., and Philadelphia, Pa., he was a member of the staff of the N.Y. *Sun post* 1884. He is remembered principally for anonymous "question and answer" jokes and satires which he contributed to the *Sun* and also to most of the periodicals of his time. He was author of *The Tailor-Made Girl* (1888, reprinted from *Puck*). Some of his characteristic jokes were published posthumously as *Said in Fun* (1889).

WELCH, WILLIAM HENRY (*b. Norfolk, Conn., 1850; d. Baltimore, Md., 1934*), pathologist, medical educator. Son of William W. Welch. Graduated Yale, 1870; studied chemistry at Sheffield Scientific School. M.D., N.Y. College of Physicians and Surgeons, 1875. As a student at Strassburg, Leipzig and Breslau, 1875–78, he worked with some of the greatest men of the time, among them Ludwig, Julius Cohnheim, Paul Ehrlich, and von Recklinghausen. He also studied briefly in Paris and London. Commencing work as a pathologist in New York, 1878, he was associated with Bellevue Hospital and with the Woman's Hospital until 1883 when he accepted an invitation to become professor of pathology at Johns Hopkins University. After further study in Europe under Koch and his pupils, he organized a pathological laboratory at Johns Hopkins, 1885, heading a group of men which included William T. Councilman, William S. Halsted, and Franklin P. Mall. His work at this time later resulted in the publication of his *Thrombosis and Embolism* (1899). Devoting himself then to the study of diphtheria and pneumonia, he also discovered and described in detail the gas-producing bacillus known by his name, which was the cause of "gas gangrene" in wounded soldiers during World War I. When the Johns Hopkins hospital opened in 1889, he suggested William Osler and William S. Halsted as department heads; later, in the organization of the school of medicine, he was responsible for the choice of Mall and other outstanding men. He himself served as the first dean for several years and founded and edited the *Journal of Experimental Medicine*, 1896–1906.

Influential in determining the character of the Johns Hopkins medical school, he turned his attention *post* 1900 to the general advance of medical education throughout the country. The Rockefeller Institute of Medical Research was founded in a way largely based upon his counsel; *post* 1901, he was chairman of its board of scientific directors. *Post* 1906, he was as-

sociated in a similar advisory capacity with the activities of the Carnegie Foundation and was active in many scientific and medical associations. As president of the Maryland board of health, 1898–1922, he was frequently consulted by the Baltimore municipal authorities on matters of public health, and during World War I he served actively with the surgeon-general of the army. Throughout all these busy years of administration his interest in the problems of pathology and bacteriology remained intense. Among the topics to which he devoted attention were adaptation in pathological processes, morbid conditions caused by the *aerogenes capsulatus,* and immunity. On the opening of the school of hygiene and public health at Johns Hopkins, 1918, Welch, who had resigned his professorship of pathology, was appointed director. His skill in the choice of men and his profound interest in the work were responsible for the success of this school and its far-reaching influence. He resigned in 1926 and entered upon a third career as professor of the history of medicine which he continued until his retirement in 1931.

His keenness of judgment and extraordinary organizing ability were as effective in his research work as in his work of administration. His fame rests on his appreciation of the significance of the epochal developments in pathology and bacteriology which he had witnessed in Europe, and in his introduction to America, not only of the practical results of his investigations, but of the whole spirit of these medical advances. The consequent reform in American medical education, and the development of public health studies for which he was responsible, set up an influence which was felt and treasured in many other countries as well as the United States.

WELCH, WILLIAM WICKHAM (*b. Norfolk, Conn., 1818; d. Norfolk, 1892*), physician, Connecticut legislator. Father of William H. Welch.

WELD, ARTHUR CYRIL GORDON (*b. Jamaica Plain, Mass., 1862; d. West Point, N.Y., 1914*), musician, composer. Achieved greatest distinction as conductor of musical comedy orchestras and composer of incidental music for the theater. He was musical director for productions of Henry W. Savage.

WELD, THEODORE DWIGHT (*b. Hampton, Conn., 1803; d. Hyde Park, Mass., 1895*), Abolitionist. Raised in western New York State. Influenced by Charles Stuart and Charles G. Finney, Weld worked while a young man as an evangelist and as a temperance speaker. Converted to the anti-slavery cause by Stuart, he lent his principal efforts to this work *post* 1830; his own first converts to emancipation were Arthur and Lewis Tappan. Commissioned by the Tappans to find a site for a Western theological seminary, Weld traveled widely, 1831–34, advocating anti-slavery at every opportunity. Among his later converts were James G. Birney, Elizur Wright, Beriah Green, Harriet and Henry Ward Beecher, and

Gamaliel Bailey. Organizing students at Lane Theological Seminary and training them as agents for the American Anti-Slavery Society, Weld continued to preach emancipation with extraordinary success in the then Middle West and part of New England.

Post 1836, with an augmented group of agents, he consolidated the anti-slavery movement throughout the North. He employed anonymous pamphlets and tracts in this work with great effect; most of the tracts were written by himself. When congressional insurgents in the House of Representatives broke with the Whigs on the slavery issue, Weld assisted their leader, John Q. Adams, and actively directed the insurgent movement through the sessions of 1841–43. He then withdrew from public life, but his Washington lobby was continued by Lewis Tappan. The greatest of the Abolitionists, Weld has remained largely anonymous in history, in part owing to his almost morbid modesty. He accepted no office, attended no conventions, published nothing under his own name, and would permit neither his speeches nor his letters to be printed.

WELD, THOMAS (*b. Sudbury, England, 1595; d. London, England, 1660/61*), Puritan clergyman, colonial agent. Deposed for nonconformity as vicar at Terling, Essex, 1631, he emigrated to Boston, Mass., 1632, and became first pastor of the church at Roxbury. Opposed the Antinomians. With John Eliot and Richard Mather, was author of the "Bay Psalm Book" (*The Whole Booke of Psalmes,* 1640). Sent to England by the General Court to seek financial aid for the colony, 1641, he was associated in this work with Hugh Peter until Peter's involvement in work of the Parliament. He was co-editor with Peter of *New England's First Fruits* (London, 1643). Weld secured Harvard's first scholarship fund, but failed to prevent issuance of a patent for the Narragansett territory to Roger Williams. Poor bookkeeping and misapplication by the General Court of funds collected led to charges of embezzlement against Weld and Peter; they were later vindicated. Weld, like Peter, became involved in English affairs and was induced by the Presbyterians there to edit with additions John Winthrop's manuscript account of the Antinomian troubles. Publication of this book emphasized Congregational intolerance and put Weld in a bad position from which he recovered by publishing *A Brief Narration of the Practices of the Churches in New England* (London, 1645). Thereafter he was an active supporter of the Commonwealth and an unpopular rector in several parishes until the Restoration.

WELLER, JOHN B. (*b. Montgomery, O., 1812; d. New Orleans, La., 1875*), lawyer. Congressman, Democrat, from Ohio, 1839–45. Colonel of Ohio militia in the Mexican War; chairman of commission to run boundary line between Mexico and the United States, 1849–50. Practicing in San Francisco, Calif., *post* 1850, he was U.S. senator, Union Democrat, from California, 1851–57, and governor of California, 1858–60. After service as U.S. minister to Mexico, December 1860—March 1861, he engaged in a variety of activities in various parts of the United States before settling in New Orleans, 1867.

WELLES, GIDEON (*b. Glastonbury, Conn., 1802; d. 1878*), journalist, Connecticut legislator and official. Attended present Norwich University, 1823–25. Editor of the *Hartford Times,* 1826–36, he was a devoted Jeffersonian Democrat. As a member of the legislature, 1827–35, he led fights against imprisonment for debt, property and religious qualifications for voting, grants of special privilege, and religious tests for witnesses in court. He was the father of Connecticut's general incorporation law which became a model for other states. An adviser and supporter of President Andrew Jackson, Welles held several state offices *post* 1835, and was postmaster of Hartford, 1836–41. He was chief of the bureau of provisions and clothing for the U.S. Navy, 1846–49. Leaving the Democratic party on the slavery question, he helped organize the Republican party and was a chief political writer for the Republican *Hartford Evening Press post* 1856. He also contributed an important series of articles on the slavery question to the *New York Evening Post* and to the *National Intelligencer.* Unsuccessful candidate for the governorship of Connecticut, 1856, he headed Connecticut's delegation to the Republican Chicago convention, 1860.

Welles was U.S. secretary of the navy, 1861–69. Foreseeing that the Civil War would be a long one, he reorganized his department and created a navy overnight. Although he was accused of undue deliberateness and extravagance, he succeeded in building an adequate navy from nothing with surprising speed. No other Civil War enterprise was conducted so economically. When scandals developed in navy affairs, he was the first to investigate them and punish the offenders. No other department was more free from political favoritism. His masterly rebukes of delinquent officers made him enemies but improved the efficiency of the service. Although it is hard to determine how much of the credit for supervision of actual naval warfare belonged to him and how much to Gustavus V. Fox and other officers, Welles supervised matters closely and followed all new developments with intelligence. He was an early sponsor of ironclads and supported John Ericsson in building the *Monitor.* He also encouraged development of heavy ordnance, improved steam machinery, and armored cruisers. The navy under Welles's direction was a very important factor in the crushing of the Confederacy.

His contribution to the general policies of the government was as important as his administration of the Navy Department. He distrusted Edwin M. Stanton and suspected the motives of W. H. Seward, yet he did not intrigue against either. He protested against

Salmon P. Chase's depreciation of the currency, 1862–63, opposed the admission of West Virginia as unconstitutional, and deplored the suspension of the writ of *habeas corpus,* 1863. He also had doubts whether immediate universal emancipation might not be as injurious to the freed slaves as to the masters. Contending throughout the war that it was fought against rebellious individuals and not against states, he backed Lincoln's moderate program of Reconstruction and later supported the policy of President Andrew Johnson. Returning to the Democratic party, 1868, he became a Liberal Republican in 1872, and in 1876 not only supported Samuel J. Tilden, but wrote attacks against the decision of the Electoral Commission.

Between his retirement in 1869 and his death he published a number of articles in the *Galaxy* magazine which are important documents on the history of his time; one of these was expanded as *Lincoln and Seward* (1874). He kept a painstaking diary which is a storehouse of data, although in its published form (*Diary of Gideon Welles,* 1911) there was no warning to the reader that it was corrected and revised by the diarist in later years. A New England conscience, a keen sense of duty, and a methodical mind made Welles a dependable public servant. Throughout the stormy days of the Civil War he maintained a poise and calmness that often encouraged, but equally irritated, his associates. Realism and unusual common sense prevented too great disappointment on his part when men fell short of his standards.

WELLES, NOAH (*b. Colchester, Conn., 1718; d. 1776*), Congregational clergyman, Revolutionary patriot. Graduated Yale, 1741. Pastor at Stamford, Conn., 1746–76, he was widely known as an advocate of resistance to British oppression, as a defender of the validity of Presbyterian ordination, and as an opponent of episcopacy. He is now generally credited with the authorship of the anonymous *The Real Advantages Which Ministers and People May Enjoy . . . by Conforming to the Church of England* (1762); he was author also of other works of controversy.

WELLES, ROGER (*b. Newington, Conn., 1862; d. 1932*), naval officer, explorer. Graduated Annapolis, 1884. Served in the North Pacific on the cruise of the *Thetis* under W. H. Emory; made three successive voyages into the Polar regions. In 1891 he ascended the Orinoco River to a point farther than any white man had reached before and brought back an important ethnological collection. Director of naval intelligence during World War I, he was promoted rear-admiral, 1919, and retired, 1926.

WELLING, JAMES CLARKE (*b. Trenton, N.J., 1825; d. Hartford, Conn., 1894*), journalist, educator. Graduated College of New Jersey (Princeton), 1844. Literary editor of the *Daily National Intelligencer* of Washington, D.C., 1850–56, he became the chief

editor of the newspaper and conducted it as a conservative Unionist organ until 1865. A strong legalist, he questioned the validity of the Emancipation Proclamation and joined his friend Edward Bates in declaring trials by military commissions to be irregular. After short terms as president of St. John's College, Annapolis, Md., and as professor of English at Princeton, he served as president of Columbian College (present George Washington University), 1871–94.

WELLINGTON, ARTHUR MELLEN (*b. Waltham, Mass., 1847; d. 1895*), civil engineer, engineering trade journalist. Author of a classic treatise, *The Economic Theory of the Location of Railways* (1877 and later editions).

WELLMAN, SAMUEL THOMAS (*b. Wareham, Mass., 1847; d. Stratton, Maine, 1919*), engineer, inventor. After directing the building of Siemens regenerative gas furnaces in various parts of the United States, 1867–73, he designed and built the Otis Steel Works of Cleveland, O., where he remained as chief engineer, 1873–89. During this time he began invention of machinery and other equipment for the manufacture of iron and steel for which he was granted nearly 100 patents. Of these, the most outstanding were the electric open-hearth charging machine (*c. 1885*) and an electro-magnet for handling pig iron and scrap steel (patented, December 1895). *Post* 1890 Wellman was associated as president or chairman of the board with a number of engineering companies specializing in the manufacture of iron and steel.

WELLMAN, WALTER (*b. Mentor, O., 1858; d. 1934*), journalist, aeronaut. Founded *Cincinnati Post,* 1879; was Washington correspondent of *Chicago Herald* and *Record-Herald,* 1884–1911. After several Arctic expeditions by boat and sledge (1894 and 1898–99), he was commissioned in 1906 to attempt a trip to the Arctic by air. He took off for the North Pole from Spitzbergen, September 1907, but was defeated by weather conditions. He made a second abortive attempt in August 1909, but abandoned further efforts to reach the Pole by air after the success of Robert E. Peary. Wellman's most ambitious undertaking was his attempt to cross the Atlantic in the airship *America,* 1910. The *America* was 228 feet long and had a speed of 25 miles an hour; below the hydrogen-filled bag of silk and cotton hung a car of steel tubing, a gas tank, a lifeboat, and an equilibrator which was also a fuel supply. Taking off from Atlantic City, N.J., Wellman and five companions exchanged messages by wireless with the shore (a pioneer feat), but were compelled by motor failure to come down and were rescued some 375 miles off Cape Hatteras after covering a distance of 1008 miles in 72 hours.

WELLONS, WILLIAM BROCK (*b. near Littleton, Va., 1821; d. Suffolk, Va., 1877*), clergyman, educator, leader of the Christian Connection in the Southern states.

WELLS, DAVID AMES (*b. Springfield, Mass., 1828; d. Norwich, Conn., 1898*), economist. Graduated Williams, 1847; Lawrence Scientific School, 1851. Published *The Annual of Scientific Discovery*, 1850–66; made important improvements in textile manufacture; wrote several popular works on science and science textbooks. Wells came into wide prominence in 1864 through publication of *Our Burden and Our Strength*. In this pamphlet he reassured foreign investors and the people of the North concerning the ability of the government to pay its mounting debts by demonstrating the dynamic character of Northern economic life, stressing its rapid accumulation of capital and constant introduction of labor-saving devices. Chairman of the national revenue commission, 1865–66, he served as a special commissioner of the revenue, 1866–70, and was responsible for setting up the bureau of statistics under Francis A. Walker. Originally a protectionist, Wells was converted to free trade and was to the end of his life a leading advocate of abolition of the tariff. While chairman of the New York State tax commission, 1870–76, he was author of *Local Taxation* (1871), the earliest competent study of the subject. He served later as a receiver and trustee in the reorganization of several railroads including the Erie (1875), and in 1878 became a member of the board of arbitration of the Associated Railways. Wells was author of a large number of books, pamphlets and articles, each based on a current problem; his chief interests were the tariff, the theory of money and the currency question, and taxation. An expositor of the nature and consequences of the "machine age," he felt that the new economics of production required abolition of protective tariffs in order to furnish wide markets, and he was convinced that industrial depressions, with falling prices, were due not to insufficient circulating media but to sudden and rapid increase in commodities. Some of his best writing was in opposition to fiat money or depreciated monetary standards. He was among the earliest to appreciate the importance of what is now known as "technological unemployment." A foe of the general property tax as applied to intangibles, he accepted the diffusion theory of taxation, and his opposition to the faculty theory led him to fight against income taxes. An out-and-out apostle of *laissez faire*, he missed the later implications of many of the tendencies in American economic life which he discovered and expounded. Among his works were *Robinson Crusoe's Money* (1876, 1896); *True Story of the Leaden Statuary* (1874); *The Silver Question* (1877); *A Primer of Tariff Reform* (1884); and *The Theory and Practice of Taxation* (1900).

WELLS, ERASTUS (*b. near Sacketts Harbor, N.Y., 1823; d. near St. Louis, Mo., 1893*), St. Louis street-railway builder and utilities executive. Active in his city's political and civic life, he was congressman, Democrat, from Missouri, 1869–77, 1879–81. His principal legislative concerns were the improvement of the Mississippi River and the development of the Southwest. He was ahead of his time in regard to both, however, and few of his projects resulted in legislative action.

WELLS, HENRY (*b. Thetford, Vt., 1805; d. Glasgow, Scotland, 1878*), expressman. Began as operator of an express service between Albany and Buffalo, N.Y., c. 1843; later extended his activities into New England and the Midwest. Removing to New York City, 1846, to handle the eastern and transatlantic phases of the business, he served as president of the American Express Co. (a merger of three older companies), 1850–68. In 1852 he organized Wells, Fargo & Co. under the presidency of Edwin B. Morgan for business to California; in 1857 the California service and the business east of the Missouri were linked by award of the overland mail contract to John Butterfield, who represented Wells, Fargo interests. The company prospered, despite heavy competition, until the completion of the transcontinental railroad. Wells retired after a further consolidation within the American Express Co., 1868, traveled widely, and devoted himself to local affairs in Aurora, N.Y. In 1868 he founded Wells Seminary, the present Wells College.

WELLS, HORACE (*b. Hartford, Vt., 1815; d. New York, N.Y., 1848*), dentist, anesthetist. Successful in practice at Hartford, Conn., *post* 1836, Wells was the teacher, and for a short time a partner, of William T. G. Morton. Interested in the narcotic effects of nitrous oxide inhalation, Wells suggested its use as a pain-deadener in tooth extraction as early as 1840. In December 1844 Wells, with the aid of G. Q. Colton, acted as the subject for a successful nitrous oxide extraction by John M. Riggs, and was taught by Colton how to make and administer the gas. He followed up this early trial by extracting several teeth without pain, and although familiar with the similar effects of ether, discarded its use because he considered nitrous oxide less likely to do injury. Traveling to Boston early in 1845, he was enabled through Morton to speak before a medical class of John C. Warren, but failed in a subsequent exhibition of his process. Wells's claim to discovery of anesthesia first appeared in print in the *Hartford Courant*, Dec. 7, 1846, nearly two months after W. T. G. Morton had demonstrated the use of ether. Claiming priority in the discovery and asserting that he had used ether as well as nitrous oxide in his own experiments, Wells published statements in several journals and in a pamphlet entitled *A History of the Discovery of the Application of Nitrous Oxide Gas, Ether, and Other Vapors, to Surgical Operations* (1847). After the general recognition of the superiority of ether over nitrous oxide in protracted operations, Wells, who had removed to New York City, committed suicide in discouragement.

WELLS, JAMES MADISON (*b. near Alexandria, La., 1808; d. 1899*), planter, Louisiana Unionist. Elected lieutenant-governor of Louisiana in February 1864, he succeeded as governor upon the resignation of Michael Hahn in March 1865. He was elected in his own right as a National Democrat the following November. An advocate of general Negro suffrage, he became unpopular and was threatened with impeachment. Removed from office, June 1867, by Gen. Philip Sheridan, he continued to be prominent in state politics and was chairman of the Louisiana returning board during the dispute over the election of 1876.

WELLS, JOHN (*b. Cherry Valley, N.Y., c. 1770; d. New York, N.Y., 1823*), lawyer. Graduated College of New Jersey (Princeton), 1788. Editorial associate of William Coleman on the N.Y. *Evening Post*, he edited *The Federalist*, bringing out the fifth edition of the papers in 1802. *Post* 1804, he shared with Thomas A. Emmet the bulk of the commercial law practice which had hitherto gone to Alexander Hamilton and Aaron Burr; he was frequently engaged as special counsel by the City of New York. His argument in the celebrated case of *Gibbons vs. Ogden* (1819), that the grant by the State of New York of a monopoly of the navigation of its waters by steam was unconstitutional since Congress alone had the right to regulate commerce, was unsuccessful. However, Daniel Webster and William Wirt, pursuing the same argument on appeal to the U.S. Supreme Court, secured a reversal of the original decision, 1824.

WELLS, ROBERT WILLIAM (*b. Winchester, Va., 1795; d. Bowling Green, Ky., 1864*), Missouri legislator and jurist. State attorney-general, 1826–36; U.S. district judge for Missouri (*post* 1857 of the western district only), 1836–64. Interested in legal reform, he opposed jury trial in civil cases and advocated simplification of pleading. He was a Civil War Unionist.

WELLS, SAMUEL ROBERTS (*b. West Hartford, Conn., 1820; d. New York, N.Y., 1875*), tanner, phrenologist and publisher. Partner with Orson S. Fowler and brother in phrenological publishing firm; faddist reformer.

WELLS, WILLIAM CHARLES (*b. Charleston, S.C., 1757; d. London, England, 1817*), physician, physicist, Loyalist. Apprenticed to Alexander Garden (*c.* 1730–1791), Wells fled to England on the outbreak of the Revolution and studied at the University of Edinburgh and in London; he took the M.D. degree at Edinburgh, 1780. Resident in America, 1781–84, he practiced thereafter in London, England. His most significant contribution to science was contained in a paper read before the Royal Society, 1813, and published with other papers in *Two Essays: One Upon Single Vision . . . The Other on Dew* (1818) in which Wells assumed a biological evolution of human species and clearly explained the principle of a natural selection in the struggle for existence. Darwin, originally unfamiliar with this essay, acknowledged its importance in the fourth (1866) edition of his own *Origin of Species*.

WELLS, WILLIAM HARVEY (*b. Tolland, Conn., 1812; d. 1885*), educator, writer on English grammar. After an outstanding career in New England as teacher, principal, assistant to Henry Barnard in conducting teacher's institutes, and normal-school work, Wells was chosen superintendent of public schools in Chicago, Ill., 1856. There he organized the city's first high school and introduced a graded system of schools with a course of study which was widely imitated throughout the United States. He was author, among other works, of *The Graded School* (1862).

WELLS, WILLIAM VINCENT (*b. Boston, Mass., 1826; d. Napa, Calif., 1876*), merchant mariner, adventurer, California journalist. Great-grandson of Samuel Adams. Author, among other works, of *Walker's Expedition to Nicaragua* (1856), and of the *Life and Public Services of Samuel Adams* (1865). Inclusion of family records in the latter book has maintained its importance as a historical source.

WELSH, JOHN (*b. Philadelphia, Pa., 1805; d. 1886*), Philadelphia merchant, philanthropist. Helped develop Fairmount Park system; managed finances of Philadelphia Centennial Exhibition, 1876. U.S. ambassador at London, 1877–79.

WEMYSS, FRANCIS COURTNEY (*b. London, England, 1797; d. New York, N.Y., 1859*), actor, theatre manager. American debut at Chestnut Street Theatre, Philadelphia, Pa., 1822. Wemyss later played with success in New York and was for a time manager in Philadelphia, Pittsburgh and Baltimore; *post* 1841 he was active in a number of New York City theatres. Conspicuous for good taste and integrity, he helped found and administer the theatrical fund for the benefit of needy actors. He was also editor of a number of volumes of the *Acting American Theatre* and was author of *Twenty-Six Years of the Life of an Actor and Manager* (1847).

WENDE, ERNEST (*b. Millgrove, N.Y., 1853; d. Buffalo, N.Y., 1910*), dermatologist, health official. Brother of Grover W. Wende. M.D., University of Buffalo, 1878; M.D., University of Pennsylvania, 1884; made special studies at Berlin and Vienna. Practiced and taught in Buffalo, N.Y., *post* 1886; won national repute for extensive sanitary reforms as Buffalo health commissioner, 1892–1905.

WENDE, GROVER WILLIAM (*b. Millgrove, N.Y., 1867; d. Buffalo, N.Y., 1926*), physician, dermatologist. Brother of Ernest Wende. M.D., University of Buffalo, 1889; made graduate studies at Pennsylvania and in Prague, Vienna, and Paris. Practiced with his brother; served as professor of dermatology at University of Buffalo; was a staff member of many hospitals. A leader in his specialty and an exceedingly accurate observer, he was author of a number of monographs on the rarer skin diseases.

WENDELL, BARRETT (*b. Boston, Mass., 1855; d. 1921*), educator, man of letters. Graduated Harvard, 1877. Appointed a teacher of English composition at Harvard, 1880, he remained associated with that university thereafter, and was celebrated as a teacher for his powers of generalization, his ready control of the background of events and ideas, and his profuse and well-chosen literary illustrations. In 1898 he became the first teacher at Harvard to offer American literature as an object of systematic study, and *post* 1902 served on several occasions as an exchange professor in England and France. Steadily enlarging his field of thought, he moved gradually into the field of comparative literature, striving in all his work "so to increase our sympathetic knowledge of what we study that we may enjoy it with fresh intelligence and appreciation." Literature was, in his opinion, a vital concern—"the best record that human beings have made of human life." He was author, among other books, of *English Composition* (1891); *Cotton Mather, the Puritan Priest* (1891); *William Shakespere* (1894); *A Literary History of America* (1900); *The Temper of the Seventeenth Century in English Literature* (1904); *The France of Today* (1907); and *The Traditions of European Literature, from Homer to Dante* (1920).

WENDTE, CHARLES WILLIAM (*b. Boston, Mass., 1844; d. Berkeley, Calif., 1931*), Unitarian clergyman, hymn-writer. Removing to San Francisco, Calif., 1861, he became a protégé of Thomas S. King. A graduate of Harvard Divinity School, 1869, he held a number of ministerial posts, and served as general secretary of the International Council of Liberal Religious Thinkers and Workers, 1900–20. In this capacity he organized a number of foreign congresses in the interest of rational, ethical theism.

WENLEY, ROBERT MARK (*b. Edinburgh, Scotland, 1861; d. 1929*), philosopher, educator. Sc.D., University of Edinburgh, 1891; Ph.D., University of Glasgow, 1895. Succeeding John Dewey in the department of philosophy at University of Michigan, 1896, he taught there the rest of his life. He was author of a number of works setting forth his own particular form of Green-Caird-Bosanquet Hegelianism which included *The Life and Work of George Sylvester Morris* (1917).

WENNER, GEORGE UNANGST (*b. Bethlehem, Pa., 1844; d. New York, N.Y., 1934*), Lutheran clergyman. Graduated Yale, 1865; Union Theological Seminary, 1868. Pastor at Christ Lutheran Church, New York City, 1868–1934. A pioneer in weekday religious education and a liturgical scholar, Wenner was a conservative Lutheran in theology, but a recognized leader in interdenominational enterprises.

WENTWORTH, BENNING (*b. Portsmouth, N.H., 1696; d. Little Harbor, N.H., 1770*), merchant, New Hampshire colonial official. Uncle of John Wentworth (1737 n.s.–1820). Graduated Harvard, 1715. Wentworth labored to make New Hampshire independent of Massachusetts, and was first royal governor of New Hampshire province, 1742–67. A tactless man, determined to uphold the royal prerogative, he engaged in bitter controversies with the Assembly and was roundly criticized for appointing relatives to office and favoring them in grants of land; he was also accused of having grown rich through pre-empting choice land in each township. Other complaints were made of his exercise of the office of surveyor of the King's Woods. However, he gave vigorous support to colonial defense against the French and the province prospered materially under his administration.

WENTWORTH, CECILE de (*b. New York, N.Y., date uncertain; d. Nice, France, 1933*), portrait painter. A student in Paris of Alexandre Cabanel and Edouard Detaille, Madame Wentworth, as she was known, lived abroad for the greater part of her life and was regarded in France as one of the outstanding portraitists of her time.

WENTWORTH, GEORGE ALBERT (*b. Wakefield, N.H., 1835; d. Dover, N.H., 1906*), teacher, author of textbooks in mathematics. Graduated Harvard, 1858. For many years a teacher at Phillips Exeter Academy, he headed the department of mathematics there *c.* 1861–91. His outstanding texts included *Elements of Geometry* (1878), *Elements of Algebra* (1881), and *College Algebra* (1888).

WENTWORTH, JOHN (*b. Portsmouth, N.H., 1737 n.s.; d. Halifax, N.S., Canada, 1820*), merchant, landowner. Nephew of Benning Wentworth. Graduated Harvard, 1755. Resident in England, 1763–66, he came to know, among other influential Englishmen, the Marquis of Rockingham, and was appointed an agent for New Hampshire. Succeeding his uncle as governor of New Hampshire, 1767, he served with ability and a sincere desire to further the welfare of his native province; he was particularly active in protecting the integrity of the King's Woods and preventing the private cutting of timber. He was responsible for the survey on which the 1784 map of New Hampshire was based and was a supporter and benefactor of Dartmouth College. As the Revolutionary movement grew in force, he did his best to prevent co-operation between New Hampshire and the other colonies, but was obliged to take refuge in Boston, Mass., 1775. Accompanying the British to Halifax, March 1776, he later lived for a time in England, returning to Halifax, 1783. Becoming lieutenant-governor of Nova Scotia (in effect governor), 1792, he held that office until 1808.

WENTWORTH, JOHN (*b. Sandwich, N.H., 1815; d. Chicago, Ill., 1888*), editor. Graduated Dartmouth,

1836; settled in Chicago, Ill., in the same year. Beginning as editor of the weekly *Chicago Democrat,* he soon became its owner and in 1840 started the *Daily Democrat* which he made the leading paper of the Northwest. As congressman, Democrat, from Illinois, 1843–51, 1853–55, he advocated free homestead legislation and favored Western railway land grants. Leaving the Democratic party over the slavery issue, he was elected mayor of Chicago, 1857, on a Republican Fusion ticket; he was elected again in 1860 and also served as police commissioner during the Civil War. One of Chicago's principal owners of real property and a leading figure in the city's civic life, he served again in Congress as a Republican, 1865–67, where he urged immediate resumption of specie payments.

WENTWORTH, PAUL (*date and place of birth unknown, but probably New Hampshire; d. Surinam, Dutch Guiana, 1793*), British spy. Described by Gov. John Wentworth of New Hampshire as "my near relation," he was a man of education and talents who made his living principally as a stock jobber and served briefly as New Hampshire agent in London in the early 1770's. Becoming one of the important members of the British secret intelligence on the Continent, he recruited Edward Bancroft for the service and was the agent by which Bancroft's reports were transmitted to the British government. He failed in a bold attempt to halt the treaty negotiations between France and the United States, December 1777—January 1778.

WERDEN, REED (*b. Delaware Co., Pa., 1818; d. Newport, R.I., 1886*), naval officer. Appointed midshipman, 1834. Held varied commands in Civil War including post of fleet captain, East Gulf Squadron, 1864–65. Commanded South Pacific Squadron, 1875–76, retiring as rear-admiral, 1877.

WERGELAND, AGNES MATHILDE (*b. Christiania, Norway, 1857; d. Laramie, Wyo., 1914*), historian, educator. Ph.D., University of Zürich, 1890. Emigrated to America, 1890. Chairman, department of history, University of Wyoming, 1902–14.

WERNWAG, LEWIS (*b. Württemberg, Germany, 1769; d. Harpers Ferry, Va., 1843*), pioneer bridge builder. Came to Philadelphia, Pa., c. 1786. Chiefly remembered as a designer and builder of wooden bridges and for early (1811) use of the cantilever. His beautiful "Colossus of Fairmount," built in 1812 across the Schuylkill River at Philadelphia, was the greatest single-arch span (340 feet) then in America. The canal of the Schuylkill Navigation Co. was partially constructed by him in 1817, and the Fairmount water works and dam at Philadelphia were erected in accordance with his plans.

WESBROOK, FRANK FAIRCHILD (*b. Brant Co., Ontario, Canada, 1868; d. Vancouver, B.C., Canada, 1918*), pathologist, educator. Graduated University of Manitoba, B.A., 1887; M.D.C.M., 1890; studied

also at Cambridge University and at Marburg; received further training at London, Dublin, and Hamburg. Appointed director of laboratories, Minnesota State Board of Health, 1895; became professor of pathology and bacteriology, University of Minnesota Medical School, 1896, and dean, 1906. Won world reputation as co-author of "Varieties of Bacillus diphtherias" (1900). A leader in medical education and an authority on problems of public health and sanitation, he was chosen president of University of British Columbia, 1913.

WESSELHOEFT, CONRAD (*b. Weimar, Germany, 1834; d. Boston, Mass., 1904*), homeopathic physician, educator. Came to America as a child. M.D., Harvard Medical School, 1856. A founder of Boston University Medical School, 1873, and associated with it until his death, he was professor of materia medica and pathology and therapeutics. Elected president of American Institute of Homeopathy, 1879. Attempted to formulate principles of homeopathy in accordance with modern science. Published his translation of Samuel Hahnemann's *Organon,* 1876; co-editor, *Homoeopathic Pharmacopoeia of the United States* (1914).

WESSON, DANIEL BAIRD (*b. Worcester, Mass., 1825; d. Springfield, Mass., 1906*), inventor and manufacturer of firearms. Formed partnership with Horace Smith for manufacture of a rim-fire metallic cartridge at Norwich, Conn., 1853; with Smith, patented a pistol (1854) whose entirely new repeating action was later adapted to rifles and was an essential factor in the success of the famous Winchester. Again in partnership with Smith, he developed and manufactured *post* 1857 the Smith & Wesson revolver, the only one made with an open cylinder and using a metallic cartridge. He introduced numerous improvements in it, and c. 1887 devised the "hammerless" safety revolver.

WEST, ALLEN BROWN (*b. Reedsburg, Wis., 1886; d. near Stafford Springs, Conn., 1936*), historian. Graduated Milton (Wis.) College, 1907; was Rhodes scholar at Oriel, Oxford; Ph.D., University of Wisconsin, 1912. Principal teaching post, professor of classics and ancient history, University of Cincinnati *post* 1927. West's particular interest lay in the history of imperial Athens. His studies of the financial records of the Athenian Empire in collaboration with Benjamin D. Meritt instituted a revolution in Greek epigraphic scholarship. [*Supp. 2*]

WEST, BENJAMIN (*b. Rehoboth, Mass., 1730; d. Providence, R.I., 1813*), almanac-maker, astronomer. Entirely self-educated, West taught mathematics and astronomy at Rhode Island College (later Brown University), 1788–99. He brought out *The New-England Almanack, or Lady's and Gentleman's Diary,* 1765–1781; this, and others which he prepared, achieved an excellent reputation in New England for accuracy. He collaborated with Joseph and Moses Brown on observation of transit of Venus, 1769, and published astronomical papers.

WEST, BENJAMIN (*b. near Springfield, Pa., 1738; d. London, England, 1820*), painter. Showing an early aptitude for art, he was assisted by several local patrons including William Henry. Removing to Philadelphia, Pa., at the invitation of William Smith (1727–1803), he painted portraits and inn signs, continued to practice and study, and by chance made an independent discovery of the principle of the camera obscura. Journeying to Italy in 1760, apparently the first American to study art there, he attracted wide attention and was aided by the then-celebrated painter Anton Rafael Mengs. After traveling about Italy and making special studies of the work of Titian and Raphael, he arrived in England, August 1763, and remained there until his death.

West's agreeable manners and romantic history won him entrance to the highest English circles; among his friends were Sir Joshua Reynolds, the great Samuel Johnson, Edmund Burke, and Dr. Robert H. Drummond, archbishop of York, who became his most powerful patron. Employing Titianesque colors, delicacy of stroke, and subtlety of blended tone, he marked a departure from the robustness of the English school and his work took the public fancy. Admired and liked by George III, he was extensively patronized by that monarch and by the king's appointment was made a charter member of the Royal Academy, founded 1768. *Post* 1772, when he was appointed historical painter to the king, he devoted almost all his time to executing the king's orders for paintings for the royal palaces, including many portraits of the royal family. In his "Death of Wolfe," exhibited in the Royal Academy, 1771, he represented his heroes in contemporary military costume, a departure from the classic conventions of the day. After approval of this effort at realism by Sir Joshua Reynolds, the picture brought about a new direction in English historical painting. Succeeding Reynolds as president of the Royal Academy, 1792, West devoted much time to teaching young artists, impressing on them the formation of a good palette, truthfulness of design, and a sound technique. Among his American pupils were Matthew Pratt, Charles W. Peale, Gilbert Stuart, John Trumbull, Robert Fulton, Thomas Sully, S. F. B. Morse, and Charles R. Leslie. His generosity to young artists was unfailing.

Post 1801, West's favor at court began to decline and he set himself to work upon a series of religious pictures for public sale. One of these, "Christ Healing the Sick" (1801), was among his most successful, and "Christ Rejected" (*c.* 1815) and "Death on the Pale Horse" (1817) were also much admired. At his death after a long period of natural decay, he was buried in St. Paul's Cathedral. Fitted to the ideals of his time by character, by training, and by many small personal traits, he was a painter of little genuine power. His works are formal and uninspired. His important position in the history of English and American painting is owing largely to the help and encouragement he gave so freely to other artists. One of the best of his works, "Penn's Treaty with the Indians," hangs in Independence Hall, Philadelphia.

WEST, FRANCIS (*b. probably Hampshire, England, 1586; d. probably Virginia, 1634*), governor of Virginia. Brother of Thomas, Lord De La Warr. Emigrating to Virginia, 1608, he was one of those who quarrelled with Captain John Smith and in September 1609 deposed him in favor of George Percy and a council, of which West became a member. He succeeded Percy as commander at Jamestown, 1612, was commissioned master of the ordnance, 1617, and became one of the most influential of "ancient planters." Governor of Virginia, 1627–March 1629.

WEST, GEORGE (*b. near Bradninch, Devonshire, England, 1823; d. 1901*), paper manufacturer, New York legislator. Emigrated to America *c.* 1849; settled, 1861, in Saratoga Co., N.Y. By 1878 he owned nine mills whose total output was estimated to exceed that of any other paper maker in the United States and Europe. Manufacture of manila wrapping and grocers' bags was the basis of his fortune. A thoroughgoing protectionist, he was congressman, Republican, from New York, 1881–83 and 1885–89.

WEST, HENRY SERGEANT (*b. Binghamton, N.Y., 1827; d. Sivas, Turkey, 1876*), missionary physician. M.D., N.Y. College of Physicians and Surgeons, 1850. Served in Northern Armenian (later the West Turkey) Mission of the American Board, 1859–76. Besides engaging in extensive and far-reaching practice, West trained native students and doctors.

WEST, JOSEPH (*b. England, date unknown; d. New York, ante 1692*), South Carolina colonial official. As agent and storekeeper for the proprietors of Carolina (1669), he commanded the three vessels sent out to make a settlement after the first attempt by John Yeamans failed. Having assisted William Sayle, the first governor, to make a settlement at Albemarle Point on the Ashley, West succeeded Sayle as governor, 1671, and directed the colony through a trying year of scarcity. Superseded by Yeamans, 1672, he returned to the governorship in 1674 and held the post until 1682. During his administration the center of settlement was moved to New Charles Town (later Charleston) at the junction of the Ashley and Cooper rivers. Again removed from office, 1682, he was reinstated in 1684, but left the province the next year.

WEST, SAMUEL (*b. Yarmouth, Mass., 1730 o.s.; d. Tiverton, R.I., 1807*), Congregational clergyman, author. Graduated Harvard, 1754. Pastor at Dartmouth (later New Bedford), Mass., 1761–1803. As Revolutionary War chaplain, he deciphered for Gen. George Washington the famous treasonable code letter sent by Dr. Benjamin Church, 1775, to the British at Newport, R.I. Arminian in doctrine, he was author of *Essays on Liberty and Necessity* (1793), the most thorough and persuasive reply to Jonathan Edwards's *Freedom of the Will*. West was a member of the committee to frame the Massachusetts constitution and is credited with persuading John Hancock to vote for the Federal Constitution.

WEST, WILLIAM EDWARD (*b. Lexington, Ky., 1788; d. Nashville, Tenn., 1857*), portrait painter. Studied in Philadelphia, Pa., under Thomas Sully. In Europe, 1822–40, he won renown for portraits of Lord Byron and Countess Guiccioli, among other celebrities, and exhibited at the Royal Academy, London, 1826–33. He worked in New York City, 1840–50, and 1852.

WESTCOTT, EDWARD NOYES (*b. Syracuse, N.Y., 1846; d. 1898*), author, banker. Remembered for his best-selling novel *David Harum* (1898), dramatized in 1900 and played by William H. Crane.

WESTCOTT, THOMPSON (*b. Philadelphia, Pa., 1820; d. Philadelphia, 1888*), lawyer, journalist. Despite Philadelphia indifference to Sunday journalism, he successfully edited the strong, independent *Sunday Dispatch* there, 1848–84. He is remembered principally as co-author with J. T. Scharf of *History of Philadelphia* (1884), the most comprehensive account of the city up to that time.

WESTERN, LUCILLE (*b. New Orleans, La., 1843; d. probably Brooklyn, N.Y., 1877*), actress. A trouper from early childhood with her sister, Helen, she became famous *post* 1863 for emotional acting in roles such as Camille, Lucretia Borgia, Queen Gertrude in *Hamlet* and Nancy in *Oliver Twist*. A wayward genius, she achieved her effects by temperament rather than art.

WESTERVELT, JACOB AARON (*b. Tenafly, N.J., 1800; d. 1879*), shipbuilder. Apprenticed to Christian Bergh, 1817–20, he was Bergh's silent partner, 1822–35. They built several of the best transatlantic packets of the day at their East River (New York City) yard. Westervelt turned out 247 packets, clippers, steamers, and other vessels before his retirement in 1868. His most important steamships were the 1700-ton *Washington* and *West Point* (1847). During the golden years of clipper construction he built, among others, the *N.B. Palmer*, *Golden Gate*, and *Resolute*. He was Democratic mayor of New York City, 1853–54.

WESTINGHOUSE, GEORGE (*b. Central Bridge, N.Y., 1846; d. New York, N.Y., 1914*), Union soldier, inventor, manufacturer. After service in both the Union Army and Navy, he worked in his father's agricultural implement factory and in October 1865 obtained his first patent for a rotary steam engine. In the same year he patented a device for putting

derailed freight cars back on the track and later developed a type of railroad frog. In April 1869 he took out his first air-brake patent, incorporating the Westinghouse Air Brake Co. six months later for its manufacture. He was subsequently awarded more than twenty further patents on the device as its automatic features were developed. This invention was of revolutionary importance as it made high-speed railroad travel safe. Moreover, by making all air-brake apparatus standardized and interchangeable, Westinghouse was one of the first industrialists to apply modern techniques of production. In 1880 he began to purchase signal and interlocking-switch patents which he combined with his own inventions into a complete signal system. Interest in developing electrical control of signals manufactured by his Union Switch & Signal Co. led Westinghouse to a more general interest in electrical processes and inventions and to the organization of the Westinghouse Electric Co. Between 1880 and 1890 he took out more than 125 patents in such diverse fields as air-brakes, signals, natural-gas production and control, and electrical power transmission. He developed a pressure system of transmission for natural gas which effectively reduced accidents. Having learned (1885) of French and German methods of transmitting single-phase alternating currents at high voltage over very small wires, and then, by means of transformers, stepping the current down to lower voltages for local distribution, he purchased test apparatus in Europe and set a team of electrical engineers, including William Stanley, to the task of adapting transformers to American conditions. Late in 1885 the Stanley "shell-type" transformer was ready for manufacture, but the system met with much opposition on the ground that high-tension current transmission was dangerous. In order to employ the new alternating-current system in industry, Westinghouse set his assistants to work on development of an induction motor and a two-phase system satisfactory for both lamps and motors. A successful experiment in the practical use of high-tension transmission was conducted by William Stanley at Great Barrington, Mass., in 1886, where a number of dwellings and shops were lighted; a later successful experiment was conducted in a Pittsburgh suburb. From 1893, in which year the Westinghouse Electric Co. contracted to light the Chicago World's Columbian Exposition and to develop the power of Niagara Falls, down through 1907, the Westinghouse interests flourished, but in 1907 the founder lost control of his companies. On reorganization, he continued as president with greatly limited power until retirement, 1911. He served (1905–10) as a trustee of the Equitable Life Assurance Society in the reorganization and mutualization of that company. After his retirement, he continued experiments with the steam turbine and reduction gear and with an air-spring for automobiles until the failure of his health in 1913.

WESTON, EDWARD (*b. near Wolverhampton, England, 1850; d. Montclair, N.J., 1936*), electrical engineer, industrialist. After receiving his medical diploma in England, 1870, he emigrated to New York City. Organizing the Weston Dynamo Electric Machine Co., 1877, he soon became the leading manufacturer of electroplating dynamos in the United States. He failed in efforts to develop an arc-lighting system and an incandescent lighting system, although he made important contributions to the technology of both. He achieved great success as designer and manufacturer of precision electrical measuring instruments *post* 1888. [*Supp. 2*]

WESTON, EDWARD PAYSON (*b. Providence, R.I., 1839; d. 1929*), long-distance walker. Made first professional venture in 1867, walking from Portland, Maine, to Chicago, Ill. (1326 miles) in 26 days. Participated thereafter in many types of walking races, winning the Astley Belt at London, England, 1879. In 1910, he walked from San Francisco to New York in about 70 days.

WESTON, NATHAN AUSTIN (*b. Champaign, Ill., 1868; d. 1933*), economist. B.L., University of Illinois, 1889; Ph.D., Cornell, 1901; studied also at Berlin. Taught at University of Illinois *post* 1900; *post* 1920 he devoted himself entirely to graduate-school teaching. Especially interested in development of the quantity theory of money, he was an outstanding American student of orthodox classical economics.

WESTON, THOMAS (*b. c. 1575; d. Bristol, England, c. 1644*), ironmonger, merchant adventurer. Served as agent of the London syndicate which underwrote the sailing of the Pilgrims to Plymouth, 1620; secured the patent for the colony from the Virginia Company and hired the *Mayflower*, but was unable to secure signature of the Separatists to the articles of agreement drawn up by him and Robert Cushman. This document remained unsigned until 1621. Weston later made an attempt to settle at the site of present Weymouth and engaged in trade up and down the New England coast and in Virginia. A roving, resourceful, and generally unsuccessful man, he is of significance only for his connection with the Pilgrims.

WESTON, WILLIAM (*b. probably in or near Oxford, England, c. 1752; d. London, England, 1833*), civil engineer. Came to America early in 1793 as engineer of Schuylkill and Susquehanna Canal. Planned Middlesex Canal for elder Loammi Baldwin, 1794. At request of George Washington, 1795, reported on locks at Great Falls of Potomac. Served as adviser (1796–97) to Western Inland Lock Navigation Co., New York State, on the precursor of the Erie Canal. In 1799 he made an examination of future New York City water supply; he suggested the Bronx River as source, purification by artificial filters and use of 24-inch cast-iron water pipe. His deep coffer dam for the "Permanent Bridge," Philadelphia, Pa., was

the first in America. He removed to England *c.* 1800. Weston commanded large fees and was highly respected by such public figures as Washington, Robert Morris and Philip Schuyler. He taught native engineers how to design and build lock canals and published, among other reports, *An Account of the Rise, Progress and Present State of the Canal Navigation in Pennsylvania* (1795).

WETHERILL, CHARLES MAYER (*b. Philadelphia, Pa., 1825; d. Bethlehem, Pa., 1871*), chemist. Cousin of Samuel Wetherill (1821–1890). Graduated University of Pennsylvania (where he studied under A. D. Bache and J. F. Frazer), 1845; studied also in laboratory of James C. Booth and Martin H. Boyé and in Paris. Ph.D., University of Giessen, 1848. Published well-known treatise *The Manufacture of Vinegar* (1860). Appointed chemist of the U.S. Department of Agriculture, 1862, he was the first scientist of the department; his *Report on the Chemical Analysis of Grapes* (1862) was the department's first scientific bulletin. Made studies of munitions for the War Department, 1862 and 1863. As chemist of the Smithsonian Institution, 1863–66, he made an important investigation upon ventilation of the Capitol. Professor of chemistry, Lehigh University, 1866–71.

WETHERILL, SAMUEL (*b. near Burlington, N.J., 1736; d. 1816*), pioneer American manufacturer of white lead and other chemicals, Philadelphia civic leader. He was cut off from the Society of Friends, 1777, for supporting the cause of the colonies and the use of weapons in its defense. He then joined in forming the sect of Free, or Fighting, Quakers before whom he preached regularly until his death.

WETHERILL, SAMUEL (*b. Philadelphia, Pa., 1821; d. Oxford, Md., 1890*), inventor, Union soldier, industrialist. Great-grandson of Samuel Wetherill (1736–1816). Graduated University of Pennsylvania, 1845. Invented (1852) process for deriving white zinc oxide direct from ore; founded Lehigh Zinc Co., 1853. He was the father of John P. Wetherill (1844–1906), inventor of the Wetherill furnace and Wetherill magnetic concentrating process for treatment of refractory ores.

WETZEL, LEWIS (*b. probably Lancaster Co., Pa., 1764; d. probably near Natchez, Miss., 1808?*), Indian fighter, scout. Raised near present Wheeling, W.Va. Served on a number of war expeditions, notably against Indian village on site of present Coshocton, O., 1781. An implacable Indian hater.

WHALLEY, EDWARD (*b. Nottinghamshire, England, date unknown; d. probably Hadley, Mass., 1674 or 1675*), regicide. Father-in-law of William Goffe; cousin of Oliver Cromwell. Rose to colonel in English civil war, 1645; answered to Parliament for escape of the King from Hampton Court. As member of High Court of Justice he signed Charles I's death warrant. Appointed major-general, 1655; became member of Cromwell's House of Lords. Condemned at the Restoration, he fled to New England with Goffe, 1660, and resided at various places in Massachusetts and Connecticut thereafter.

WHARTON, ANNE HOLLINGSWORTH (*b. Southampton Furnace, Pa., 1845; d. Philadelphia, Pa., 1928*), writer. An authority on genealogy and American colonial social history, she was author of, among other books and articles, *Through Colonial Doorways* (1893), *Heirlooms in Miniature* (1898), *Social Life in the Early Republic* (1902) and *English Ancestral Homes of Noted Americans* (1915).

WHARTON, CHARLES HENRY (*b. St. Mary's Co., Md., 1748 o.s.; d. Burlington, N.J., 1833*), Episcopal clergyman. Educated in Jesuit schools in France and Belgium; ordained a Catholic priest, 1772. Served as chaplain to Roman Catholics at Worcester, England, where he underwent a change in his religious views. Returning to Maryland, 1783, he published a justification of his conversion to Protestantism, 1784, which was answered by Rev. John Carroll. Thereafter, one of the leading Episcopal clergymen of the United States, he served as rector of St. Mary's Church, Burlington, N.J., 1798–1833.

WHARTON, EDITH NEWBOLD JONES (*b. New York, N.Y., 1862; d. St. Brice-sous-forêt, near Paris, France, 1937*), author. Descended from several families of the small, tightly-knit group which dominated the business and social life of New York City before the Civil War, Edith Jones grew to maturity in a somewhat restricted world which attempted to maintain its stratified codes of behavior and its tradition of elegance against the threats of the new industrialism. Her family circle was predominantly masculine and communicated a masculine temper to her mind. As Henry James, her friend of later years, remarked, in her novels the "masculine conclusion" tended "to crown the feminine observation." Educated by governesses and tutors and by her own wide reading, she resided abroad for long periods with her family and grew fluent in French, German, and Italian. In 1885 she married a wealthy Bostonian, Edward Wharton. The couple divided the year between residence in New York City and Newport, R.I.; later Newport was replaced by Lenox, Mass., where Mrs. Wharton drew about herself a small, distinguished circle of intimates. As her husband began to decline in health, the Whartons spent more and more time abroad in England or Italy; in 1907 they established themselves in Paris. They were divorced in 1913. During World War I, Mrs. Wharton applied her talents for organization and her boundless sympathies to support of the Allied cause and to relief work in France. With Walter Berry, an international jurist and an old friend of her youth who possessed a marked influence over her opinions, she spent much time during and after the war visiting hospitals and serving on many committees. She was the first woman

to receive an honorary LL.D. from Yale University (1923) and was the recipient of many other civic and literary honors.

Although she had issued a privately printed volume of verses in Newport, R.I., 1878, Mrs. Wharton did not publish her first book until 1897; it was *The Decoration of Houses* written in collaboration with Ogden Codman, Jr. Her first collection of stories was *The Greater Inclination* (1899). In 1902 she published *The Valley of Decision,* a long historical novel set in 18th-century Italy. However, it was not until *The House of Mirth* appeared in 1905 that Edith Wharton found a wide public and her major subject—the depiction of an individual who wishes to escape from the inhibitions of a rigid society, but is unable to do so because he has been molded beyond change by its values and standards. The tragedy of Lily Bart in this novel is a tragedy of unfulfilled possibilities. As Mrs. Wharton later said of her own purpose in adopting such a subject, "A frivolous society can acquire dramatic significance only through what its frivolity destroys. Its tragic implications lie in its power of debasing people and ideals." Her criticism of society, however, did not blind her to the vulgarities of the "new" people who challenged it. In *The Custom of the Country* (1913) she lashed out at the selfishness and arrogance of a money-dominated society.

In *The Age of Innocence* (1920; awarded the Pulitzer Prize in 1921), she continued her study in depth of the aristocratic-plutocratic struggle at the point of its early beginnings. Under the common title of *Old New York* (1924) she published four novelettes which examine the same theme of values in conflict throughout the latter two-thirds of the 19th century. Of these *The Old Maid* is the best known but is by no means superior to the others in the group, notably *False Dawn*. A group of her later novels published *post* 1925 deal generally with this theme as well. Written in the tradition of George Eliot and Gustave Flaubert and of her American predecessor, Henry James, these novels had in them a prophetic vein and a high moral vision. Other works, while partaking of her central theme, touched the international theme first developed by Henry James—the contrast of foreign and domestic manners. Outstanding examples were *Madame de Treymes* (1907) and *The Reef* (1912); however, where Henry James probed the contrasts in manners ever more deeply on a psychological level, Mrs. Wharton remained close to the actual data she observed. Her two novels of New England, *Ethan Frome* (1911) and *Summer* (1917), are distinct from her other work in background and method, but not in underlying theme. The first, realistic and grim, tells of a large nature harnessed to a mean spirit and doomed to a life of physical and spiritual confinement. The second of these novels is a tightly told story of a girl who cannot rise above her environment, and is an outstanding piece of work. These, together with a briefer tale,

"The Bunner Sisters" (in *Xingu*, 1916), illustrate the author's broad sympathies with individuals outside her own environment. She was author, in all, of more than fifty books, including collections of short stories and travel books such as *Italian Villas and Their Gardens* (1904) and *Italian Backgrounds* (1905). She published several collections of her verse and a critical study, *The Writing of Fiction* (1925).

Mrs. Wharton's writings fall into two distinct periods. Most critics agree that her best work was done during the years preceding 1914 and that her later work is largely an echo of it; a number of reasons have been assigned for this decline in her powers, but none is wholly satisfactory. She was a friend of many distinguished men, among whom may be mentioned Charles E. Norton, Theodore Roosevelt, and Bernard Berenson. The influence upon her work of her friend Henry James has been perhaps exaggerated, although she was in certain respects (choice of theme, moral attitude, interest in technique) one of his disciples. *A Backward Glance* (1934) contains autobiographical material. [*Supp. 2*]

WHARTON, FRANCIS (*b. Philadelphia, Pa., 1820; d. Washington, D.C. 1889*), lawyer, Episcopal clergyman, government official, educator. Son of Thomas I. Wharton. Graduated Yale, 1839. Admitted to Pennsylvania bar, 1843. An authority on criminal and international law, he wrote, among other works, *A Treatise on the Criminal Law of the United States* (1846) and *Treatise on the Conflict of Laws* (1872). Professor of history and literature, Kenyon College, 1856–63. Active as a religious writer, editor and lay preacher, he was ordained in 1862, and served as rector, St. Paul's Episcopal Church, Brookline, Mass., 1863–71. Professor at Episcopal Theological Seminary, Cambridge, Mass., 1871–81, he was a leader of the Low Church school. Wharton was examiner of claims, legal division, Department of State, *post* 1885. He compiled *A Digest of the International Law of the United States* (1886, 1887; largely incorporated by J. B. Moore in *A Digest of International Law*, 1906).

WHARTON, GREENE LAWRENCE (*b. near Bloomington, Ind., 1847; d. Calcutta, India, 1906*), Disciples of Christ clergyman. Missionary in India, 1882–99, 1904–06.

WHARTON, JOSEPH (*b. Philadelphia, Pa., 1826; d. 1909*), manufacturer, philanthropist. Studied chemistry at laboratory of Martin H. Boyé in Philadelphia. As manager of Lehigh Zinc Co. from 1853 to 1863, he was responsible for the first commercially successful production of spelter in the United States. For many years the only producer of refined nickel in America, he succeeded in 1875 in manufacturing a pure, malleable nickel. Wharton exerted strong political influence, particularly as a leading spokesman for

a high protective tariff. He was a founder of Swarthmore College and established the Wharton School of Finance at the University of Pennsylvania.

WHARTON, RICHARD (*b. England, date unknown; d. England, 1689*), merchant, promoter. Emigrating to New England early in the Restoration Period (*post* 1660), he associated himself with a group of imperialistic recent settlers and with Puritan descendants who wished monopolistically to expand commerce, invest capital, and develop natural resources. Successive marriages to members of the Higginson and Winthrop families aided his business success. He involved New England in a trade war with the Dutch and urged recapture of New Netherland in order to develop American commerce on a unified plan with the port of New York as center. Advocating a remodeling of government so as to eliminate church power over the state, Wharton was influential in establishing the Dominion of New England, 1686. An importer, owning his own wharves and vessels, he aspired to a landed proprietorship and was associated in the Atherton Company and the Million Purchase; alone, he undertook the large Pejebscot Purchase in Maine. The New England Puritan governments and Gov. Edmund Andros disapproved of these large projects, preferring a more democratic distribution of land. While in England to further his projects at court and to build opposition to Andros, he died suddenly, leaving his vast estate bankrupt.

WHARTON, ROBERT (*b. Philadelphia, Pa., 1757; d. 1834*), flour merchant. Half-brother of Samuel Wharton. Elected mayor of Philadelphia, 1798, he was re-elected, 1799, and served subsequently, 1806–07, 1810, 1814–18 and 1820–24. An avid sportsman, he was for many years governor of the Schuylkill Fishing Company.

WHARTON, SAMUEL (*b. Philadelphia, Pa., 1732; d. near Philadelphia, 1800*), merchant, land speculator. Half-brother of Robert Wharton. Associated *post* 1763 with George Morgan in trading firm of Baynton, Wharton & Morgan. Obtained "Indiana Grant," 1768. In England, 1769, he organized the Grand Ohio Company (Walpole Company) and petitioned for a grant to the proposed "Vandalia" colony of 20,000,000 acres between the Alleghanies and the upper Ohio. The Revolution ended this scheme.

WHARTON, THOMAS (*b. Chester Co., Pa., 1735; d. Lancaster, Pa., 1778*), merchant, Revolutionary patriot. First cousin of Robert and Samuel Wharton. Advocate of Whig policies, he served on the provincial Committee of Safety, 1775, and was president of the Council of Safety, 1776–77. He was in constant touch with Gen. George Washington and was the principal figure in ordering out the Pennsylvania militia and encouraging enlistments. Elected president of the Supreme Executive Council of Pennsylvania, March 1777, he issued bills of credit to carry on the war, passed laws to punish the disloyal, and organized the new state's courts and military defenses.

WHARTON, THOMAS ISAAC (*b. Philadelphia, Pa., 1791; d. 1856*), lawyer, author. Nephew of William Rawle and Samuel Wharton; cousin of Thomas Wharton. Graduated University of Pennsylvania, 1807. Practiced in Philadelphia; was authority on real property and profoundly learned in other legal fields. A member of Joseph Dennie's Tuesday Club and a contributor to the *Port Folio*, he succeeded Washington Irving in 1815 as editor of *Analectic Magazine*. In 1830 he was appointed with William Rawle and Joel Jones to codify civil statute law of Pennsylvania.

WHARTON, WILLIAM H. (*b. Albemarle Co., Va., 1802; d. 1839*), lawyer, leader in Texas revolution. Settled in Texas *c.* 1828. Wrote petition for repeal of law prohibiting foreign colonization in Texas at San Felipe convention, Oct. 1, 1832. Favored complete separation of Texas from Mexico. Accompanied S. F. Austin and B. T. Archer to the United States on mission for aid and support to Texas revolution, 1835–36. Minister to the United States to negotiate for recognition and annexation of Texas, 1836–37.

WHATCOAT, RICHARD (*b. Quinton, England, 1736; d. Dover, Del., 1806*), Methodist clergyman. Came to New York with Thomas Coke in 1784, at request of John Wesley, to organize American Methodists; was itinerant preacher and elder, and traveling companion of Bishop Asbury on episcopal tours. Elected bishop at the General Conference, 1800.

WHEATLEY, PHILLIS (*b. Africa, c. 1753; d. Boston, Mass., 1784*), poet. A Negro slave, purchased as a child by John Wheatley of Boston, Mass., she rapidly mastered English and read extensively in Greek mythology, Greek and Roman history, and contemporary English poetry. Her verses, influenced by Pope and Gray, won her reputation in Boston and London, and were published as *Poems on Various Subjects, Religious and Moral* (London, 1773).

WHEATLEY, WILLIAM (*b. New York, N.Y., 1816; d. New York, 1876*), actor, theatre manager. Made debut with Macready at Park Theatre, New York City, 1826; by 1834 had become principal "walking gentleman" at the Park. Active as a player and manager in Philadelphia, Pa., Washington, D.C., and New York, he was most successful at Niblo's Garden, New York, 1862–68, where he presented sumptuous productions of romantic dramas with star actors. In 1866 he introduced the extravagant ballet spectacle to America with his production of *The Black Crook*.

WHEATON, FRANK (*b. Providence, R.I., 1833; d. Washington, D.C., 1903*), soldier. Appointed first lieutenant, 1st U.S. Cavalry, 1855. As lieutenant-colonel, 2nd Rhode Island Infantry, he fought at first Bull Run and was cited by Gen. Burnside. Made brigadier-general late in 1862, he commanded a brigade in the VI (Sedgwick's) Corps and played a prominent part in the Wilderness campaign, 1864. Commanding a division, he repelled a threatened attack on Washington, D.C., by Gen. J. A. Early, July 1864, and was rewarded by brevet of major-general. Successful in the assault on Petersburg, Va., Apr. 2, 1865, he continued in the army after the Civil War and, among other duties, ably commanded the campaign against the Modoc Indians, 1872. He retired as major-general, 1897.

WHEATON, HENRY (*b. Providence, R.I., 1785; d. Dorchester, Mass., 1848*), jurist, diplomat, authority on international law. Graduated Brown, 1802. After studying law in his native city, he made a special study of civil law at Poitiers, France, 1805–06. Practicing in Providence, 1806–12, he removed to New York City where he was editor of the *National Advocate*, a (Democrat) Republican newspaper, until 1815. Justice of the New York City marine court, 1815–19, he was also reporter of the U.S. Supreme Court, 1816–27. A member also of the New York Assembly for one term and a commissioner to revise the New York laws (1825–27), he was author of a number of legal works and of a life of William Pinkney. His published reports of the decisions of the U.S. Supreme Court during his incumbency as reporter were distinguished for the excellence and extent of his notes. Appointed chargé d'affaires to Denmark, 1827, he brought about agreement on a treaty of indemnity (signed, March 1830) for seizures of American vessels during the Napoleonic wars which served as the prototype of similar treaties negotiated later with France and Naples. While in Denmark, he learned the language and studied the history of the Scandinavian peoples; in 1831 he published his *History of the Northmen*. Appointed chargé d'affaires at Berlin at the request of the Prussian authorities, March 1835, he was raised in rank to minister to Prussia, 1837, indirectly as a result of publication of his celebrated *Elements of International Law* (1836). In 1844 he secured signature of a treaty with Prussia which arranged for reciprocal tariff reductions; the treaty, however, was rejected by the U.S. Senate. Among other treaties negotiated by Wheaton and put into effect were those providing for the abrogation of taxes imposed on emigrants to the United States from Hanover, Württemberg, Hesse-Cassel, Saxony, Nassau, and Bavaria. Resigning at the request of President Polk, 1846, Wheaton returned to the United States the next year.

Notable as were Wheaton's accomplishments in a number of fields, his most distinguished achievement was his work as an expounder and historian of international law. His *Elements* previously mentioned was an immediate success both at home and in Europe and encouraged Wheaton to further literary efforts which included his *History of the Law of Nations in Europe and America* (Leipzig, 1841; New York, 1845). He is regarded by competent critics as standing with John Marshall, Judge Story, and Chancellor Kent among the greatest of American legal writers.

WHEATON, NATHANIEL SHELDON (*b. Marbledale, Conn., 1792; d. Marbledale, 1862*), Episcopal clergyman, educator. Graduated Yale, 1814. As rector, Christ Church, Hartford, Conn., 1821–31, he assisted Ithiel Town in design of its new (1827) edifice, said to be first truly Gothic church in America. President, Washington College (present Trinity), Hartford, 1831–37. While rector, Christ Church, New Orleans, 1837–44, he lost his health in heroic ministry during a yellow fever epidemic.

WHEDON, DANIEL DENISON (*b. Onondaga, N.Y., 1808; d. Atlantic City, N.J., 1885*), Methodist clergyman, editor, teacher. Graduated Hamilton College, 1828. Converted by Charles G. Finney. Professor of classics, Wesleyan (Conn.) College, 1833–43. A strong controversialist, he opposed the radical abolitionist movement in his church, but was also opposed to extension of slavery; he defended Wesleyan Arminianism. Professor of logic, rhetoric and philosophy of history, University of Michigan, 1845–51. Editor, *Methodist Quarterly Review*, 1856–84. Author, among other works, of *Commentaries* on the Bible (1860–1884) which were widely popular.

WHEELER, ANDREW CARPENTER (*b. New York, N.Y., 1835; d. 1903*), journalist, playwright, drama and music critic. Entered journalism on staff of *New York Times*, 1857; local editor, *Milwaukee Sentinel*, 1859–62; served as Civil War correspondent. *Post c.* 1867, he wrote dramatic criticism under pseudonym "Trinculo" for *New York Leader;* as "Nym Crinkle," his weekly music and drama reviews for the New York *World* attracted wide attention for caustic humor and breadth of information.

WHEELER, ARTHUR LESLIE (*b. Hartford, Conn., 1872; d. Princeton, N.J., 1932*), classical scholar. Graduated Yale, 1893; Ph.D., 1896. Taught classical languages at Yale; headed department of classics at Bryn Mawr, 1900–25; headed department of classics at Princeton thereafter. Made special studies of the types of poetry as they developed in Latin literature, particularly of the Roman elegy. [*Supp. 1*]

WHEELER, BENJAMIN IDE (*b. Randolph, Mass., 1854; d. Vienna, Austria, 1927*), educator. Graduated Brown, 1875. Ph.D., Heidelberg, 1885. Professor of philology and Greek, Cornell University, 1886–99; taught also at Brown, American School of Classical Studies in Athens (1895–96) and University of Berlin (1909–10). Through his efforts as president of the University of California, 1899–1919, students and faculty increased four-fold; twenty new departments were added as well as divisions for special research; the summer session, extension division, and material equipment were expanded; and student self-govern-

ment was instituted. Relieved from active conduct of the university, 1918, because of German sympathies, he retired (1919) as "Professor of Comparative Philology and President Emeritus."

WHEELER, EVERETT PEPPERRELL (*b. New York, N.Y., 1840; d. 1925*), lawyer, civil service reformer. Cousin of James R. Wheeler. Graduated present College of the City of New York, 1856; LL.B., Harvard, 1859. Admitted to the New York bar, 1861, he practiced there until his death. Specialist in admiralty law, he was a founder of the New York Bar Association, 1869. Devoted to civil service reform and better government, he aided in drafting of revised Pendleton Bill, 1881, and with Edward M. Shepard wrote New York State civil service bill, 1883. He was active in reform politics and in the Citizen's Union which he helped found.

WHEELER, GEORGE MONTAGUE (*b. Hopkinton, Mass., 1842; d. New York, N.Y., 1905*), topographical engineer. Graduated West Point, 1866. Supervised survey of territory west of 100th meridian, 1871–88, commonly known as the "Wheeler Survey." His 14 field trips, 1871–79, in deserts and among mountain peaks entailed hardships which broke Wheeler's health. The survey's definitive *Report* was published in a number of volumes between 1875 and 1889, and Wheeler devoted the years 1879–88 to supervising their publication. He retired in 1888 with major's rank and pay awarded by act of Congress.

WHEELER, GEORGE WAKEMAN (*b. Woodville, Miss., 1860; d. Bridgeport, Conn., 1932*), jurist, law reformer. A.B., Yale, 1881; LL.B., 1883. Judge, Connecticut superior court, 1893–1910. In 1910 he was appointed associate justice, supreme court of errors; he served as chief justice, 1920–30. Influential in procuring uniform state bar admission standards. As chairman, Connecticut judicial council, 1927–30, he was mainly responsible for the rules of summary judgment and other innovations.

WHEELER, JAMES RIGNALL (*b. Burlington, Vt., 1859; d. 1918*), classicist, archaeologist. Cousin of Everett P. Wheeler. Graduated University of Vermont, 1880; Ph.D., Harvard, 1885. Studied also at American School of Classical Studies, Athens, 1882, and was closely identified with it for many years. Taught at Johns Hopkins, Harvard, and University of Vermont; professor of Greek literature and archaeology, Columbia University *post* 1895. Dean, faculty of fine arts, Columbia, 1906–11.

WHEELER, JOHN HILL (*b. Murfreesboro, N.C., 1806; d. Washington, D.C., 1882*), lawyer, diplomat, historian, North Carolina legislator and politician. As U.S. minister to Nicaragua, 1854–57, he recognized the insurrectionist government of William Walker, thereby exceeding instructions, and was forced to resign by Secretary of State W. L. Marcy. Wheeler's historical works abound in error, but aroused interest in local history in North Carolina and other Southern states.

WHEELER, JOHN MARTIN (*b. Burlington, Vt., 1879; d. Underhill Center, Vt., 1938*), ophthalmologist. Graduated University of Vermont, 1902; M.D., 1905. Long associated with the New York Eye and Ear Infirmary, he was head of ophthalmic service at New York's Bellevue and Presbyterian hospitals and consultant to a number of other hospitals. A teacher of his specialty at Cornell Medical College and at New York University, he was professor at N.Y. College of Physicians and Surgeons *post* 1928. He directed the Institute of Ophthalmology at Columbia-Presbyterian Medical Center from 1933 until his death. An operator of exquisite dexterity, he was skilled also in the field of plastic surgery. [*Supp. 2*]

WHEELER, JOSEPH (*b. near Augusta, Ga., 1836; d. Brooklyn, N.Y., 1906*), soldier. Graduated West Point, 1859; resigned commission, 1861. Colonel, 19th Alabama Infantry, he was given command in July 1862 of the cavalry of the Army of Mississippi. Rising by merit eventually to rank of Confederate lieutenant-general, he led all cavalry in the Civil War western theatre; he took a most prominent part in the Murfreesboro and Chickamauga campaigns. After Rosecrans's retirement to Chattanooga, Wheeler executed a masterly raid on Union communications. His cavalry provided the main obstacle to Sherman's march to the sea after Atlanta. R. E. Lee bracketed Wheeler with J. E. B. Stuart as one of the two outstanding Confederate cavalry leaders. Congressman, Democrat, from Alabama, 1881–83, 1885–1900, he was ranking Democrat of the ways and means committee; he fought for low tariff, and was instrumental in congressional rehabilitation of Fitz-John Porter. His chief public contribution was untiring advocacy of reconciliation between North and South. Appointed by President McKinley as major-general of volunteers in Cuba, 1898, he commanded cavalry in Gen. Shafter's Santiago expedition.

WHEELER, NATHANIEL (*b. Watertown, Conn., 1820; d. Bridgeport, Conn., 1893*), manufacturer, inventor, Connecticut legislator. Manufactured new rotary-hook sewing machine of Allen B. Wilson (patented, 1851), adding four-motion feed in 1854. Invented and patented a wood-filling compound (1876, 1878) and a home ventilating system (1883).

WHEELER, ROYALL TYLER (*b. Vermont, 1810; d. Washington Co., Texas, 1864*), jurist. Studied law in Delaware, O. Removed to Texas, 1839. In 1844 he became a district judge. Appointed to the state supreme court, 1845, he became chief justice, 1858. A strong advocate of secession, he upheld and enforced the Confederate conscription law.

WHEELER, SCHUYLER SKAATS (*b. New York, N.Y., 1860; d. New York, 1923*), inventor, engineer, manufacturer. A founder with Francis B. Crocker, 1888 (and president *post* 1889) of the Crocker-Wheeler Co., soon prominent in manufacture of motors. With Crocker, he published *Practical Management of Dynamos and Motors* (1894). He was inventor of an electric fire-engine system, an electric elevator (both patented 1885), and an electric fan.

WHEELER, WAYNE BIDWELL (*b. near Brookfield, O., 1869; d. 1927*), lawyer, professional Prohibitionist. Superintendent, Anti-Saloon League of Ohio, 1904–15; general counsel, Anti-Saloon League of America, *post* 1915; also legislative superintendent. Successfully lobbied for national prohibition; favored extreme measures of enforcement.

WHEELER, WILLIAM (*b. Concord, Mass., 1851; d. 1932*), engineer, educator. Graduated Massachusetts Agricultural College, 1871. Professor of mathematics and civil engineering, Imperial Agricultural College of Sapporo, Japan, 1876–77; president, 1877–80. Began wide consulting practice in Boston, Mass., 1880, and became a national authority on water works.

WHEELER, WILLIAM ADOLPHUS (*b. Leicester, Mass., 1833; d. Boston, Mass., 1874*), lexicographer, bibliographer. Graduated Bowdoin College, 1853. Assisted J. E. Worcester in preparing *Dictionary of the English Language* (1860); supervised unabridged quarto and other editions of the Webster dictionary for Merriam Company. Assistant superintendent, Boston Public Library, from 1868 until his death. Author, among other reference works, of *Dictionary of the Noted Names of Fiction* (1865).

WHEELER, WILLIAM ALMON (*b. Malone, N.Y., 1819; d. 1887*), lawyer, banker, New York legislator. Admitted to the bar, 1845; practiced successfully in Malone, N.Y. Independent Republican congressman from New York, 1861–63, 1869–77, he stood out among his contemporaries as a man of scrupulous integrity. His "Wheeler adjustment" of a Louisiana disputed election, 1874, averted collapse of the state's government. Nominated for the U.S. vice-presidency, 1876, to secure a balance of sectional elements in the party, he was elected and served as a good presiding officer but cared little for the office.

WHEELER, WILLIAM MORTON (*b. Milwaukee, Wis., 1865; d. Cambridge, Mass., 1937*), zoologist, entomologist. Educated at Englemann German Academy, Milwaukee; worked under Henry A. Ward at Rochester, N.Y. Continuing his studies while teaching in Milwaukee, he became a research fellow at Clark University, 1890, where he received the Ph.D., 1892. His "A Contribution to Insect Embryology" (*Journal of Morphology*, 1893) achieved classic status. After teaching at the universities of Chicago and Texas, 1893–1903, he became curator of invertebrate zoology at the American Museum of Natural History, New York City. In 1908 he became professor of entomology at the Bussey Institution, Harvard, and remained at Harvard until his retirement, 1934. Although most of his more than 450 publications are concerned with insects, a large number deal with problems of evolution, ecology, and behavior; among his books was *Social Life among the Insects* (1923). [*Supp. 2*]

WHEELOCK, ELEAZAR (*b. Windham, Conn., 1711; d. 1779*), Congregational clergyman, first president of Dartmouth. Father of John Wheelock. Graduated Yale, 1733. Pastor of Second Church, Lebanon, Conn., 1735–70. A popular emotional preacher during the Great Awakening, he founded a school at Lebanon primarily to convert and educate Indians to be missionaries and teachers for their tribes. Dissatisfied with the progress of the mission work and recruiting, and desiring to enlarge his educational program, Wheelock founded Dartmouth College, Hanover, N.H. (chartered, 1769), maintaining it during the Revolutionary turmoil until his death.

WHEELOCK, JOHN (*b. Lebanon, Conn., 1754; d. 1817*), Revolutionary soldier, educator. Son of Eleazar Wheelock. Graduated Dartmouth College, 1771. As president of Dartmouth, 1779–1815, he established salaried professorships, built Dartmouth Hall and a chapel, revived in 1800 the educational program for the Indians, and secured the financing of the college and of Moor's Charity School. The last twelve years of his term were embittered by his struggles with the trustees, resulting in Wheelock's removal and a public controversy. The case was brought before the Supreme Court (*Trustees of Dartmouth College vs. Woodward, 4 Wheaton, 518*), and was won for the college in 1819 by Daniel Webster.

WHEELOCK, JOSEPH ALBERT (*b. Bridgetown, N.S., Canada, 1831; d. 1906*), editor. Removed to Minnesota Territory, 1850. Edited *St. Paul Daily Press*, 1861–75; edited *St. Paul Daily Pioneer-Press* as an influential Republican paper *post* 1875. Opposed Republican party on Reconstruction and tariff; fought faction led by Ignatius Donnelly. His editorials in the 1890's helped keep Minnesota in the gold ranks.

WHEELWRIGHT, EDMUND MARCH (*b. Roxbury, Mass., 1854; d. Thompsonville, Conn., 1912*), architect. Studied architecture at Massachusetts Institute of Technology and in Paris; worked in offices of Peabody & Stearns and McKim, Mead & White. In 1888 he formed a Boston partnership which in 1910 became Wheelwright, Haven and Hoyt. As city architect for Boston, 1891–95, and consultant thereafter, he set a new high level for American municipal architecture. Perhaps his most widely known buildings are the subway entrances at Park St. corner of Boston Common. In 1900 he was chief designer of the Cambridge bridge. Among other works, Wheelwright designed Horticultural Hall (1900) and the Boston Opera House (1908). He sought the monumental, classic solution; stylistically he was catholic, even erratic. His later work tended toward a rational simplicity.

WHEELWRIGHT, JOHN (*b. probably Saleby, Lincolnshire, England, c. 1592; d. Salisbury, N.H., 1679*), clergyman. B.A., Sidney College, Cambridge, 1614/15; M.A., 1618. For some years vicar of Bilsby (England), he was deprived for nonconformity, 1633, and emigrated to Boston, Mass., 1636. Pastor at Mount Wollaston (now Quincy), Mass., he and John Cotton alone among the clergy supported Anne Hutchinson, Wheelwright's sister-in-law, in the Antinomian controversy. Publicly denouncing the majority (which now included Cotton), 1637, he was disfranchised and banished from Massachusetts colony by the General Court. After organizing a community at present Exeter, N.H., he served there as pastor until Massachusetts asserted jurisdiction, when he removed to present Wells, Maine. Recanting his opinions, 1643, he secured reversal of his sentence in May 1644.

WHEELWRIGHT, WILLIAM (*b. Newburyport, Mass., 1798; d. England, 1873*), merchant mariner, promoter of Latin American enterprises. Became U.S. consul at Guayaquil in 1824. Removing to Valparaiso c. 1830, he built port facilities, provided gas and water works, and also secured British charter for Pacific Steam Navigation Co. (1840) of which he became chief superintendent. Between 1849 and 1852, he built the first railroad in Chile; in 1850 he gave Chile the first South American telegraph line. He also promoted the Grand Central Argentine Railway (opened, 1870), a part of his projected transandean railway (completed, 1910). He created the port of La Plata and completed the railroad linking it with Buenos Aires, 1872.

WHELPLEY, HENRY MILTON (*b. Battle Creek, Mich., 1861; d. Argentine, Kans., 1926*), pharmacist, drug-trade editor, teacher. Graduated St. Louis (Mo.) College of Pharmacy, 1883. Professor of microscopy, 1886–1922, at his *alma mater;* professor of pharmacognosy, materia medica, and physiology, 1915–26; dean, 1904–26. From 1890 to 1909 he also served as professor of these subjects at a number of other Missouri institutions.

WHERRY, ELWOOD MORRIS (*b. South Bend, Pa., 1843; d. Indiana, Pa., 1927*), Presbyterian clergyman. Graduated Princeton Theological Seminary, 1867. Served in missions to India, 1867–89, and 1898–1922. Among other works, he published a monumental *Comprehensive Commentary of the Quran* (1882–84).

WHIPPLE, ABRAHAM (*b. Providence, R.I., 1733; d. Marietta, O., 1819*), naval officer. Brother-in-law of Stephen and Esek Hopkins. In 1772 he led party which burned British schooner *Gaspée* near Pawtucket, R.I., sometimes regarded as the first overt act of the Revolution. Appointed Rhode Island commodore, 1775, he captured the British frigate *Rose*, first prize taken by an official American vessel. In 1779, commanding flagship *Providence* as commodore of a Continental squadron, he brought back eight East-Indiamen, one of the richest captures of the war. Entrusted with naval defense of Charleston, S.C. 1779, he was made prisoner when the city was taken.

WHIPPLE, AMIEL WEEKS (*b. Greenwich, Mass., 1816; d. Washington, D.C., 1863*), soldier, topographical engineer. Graduated West Point, 1841. Served on survey of U.S. northeast boundary, 1844–49; on survey of boundary between United States and Mexico, 1849–53; and on Pacific Railroad surveys, 1853–56. As chief topographical engineer, he served with Union forces at Bull Run. Promoted brigadier-general, April 1862, he was active in the defense of Washington until October when he was assigned command of the third division of the III (Stoneman's) Corps. He was mortally wounded on the second day of Chancellorsville (May 3, 1863).

WHIPPLE, EDWIN PERCY (*b. Gloucester, Mass., 1819; d. Boston, Mass., 1886*), broker, lyceum lecturer, literary critic. Published, among other works, *Essays and Reviews* (1848–49), *Lectures on Subjects Connected with Literature and Life* (1850), *Recollections of Eminent Men* (1887), and *American Literature and Other Papers* (1887) with an introduction by Whittier, his intimate friend. Popular as a lyceum lecturer, he enjoyed a considerable contemporary reputation as a reviewer and critic, exhibiting logical analysis, imagination, discrimination and sensitive love of beauty.

WHIPPLE, FRANCES HARRIET. [See GREEN, FRANCES HARRIET WHIPPLE, 1805–1878.]

WHIPPLE, HENRY BENJAMIN (*b. Adams, N.Y., 1822; d. Faribault, Minn., 1901*), Episcopal clergyman, reformer of U.S. Indian system. Ordained priest, 1850; rector, Zion Church, Rome, N.Y., until 1857 except for 1853–54. Built up and administered Holy Communion parish, south side of Chicago, 1857–59. Consecrated first bishop of Minnesota, October 1859, he opposed the U.S. government's Indian policy. During the 1862 uprising of the Minnesota Sioux, which began the series of Indian wars he had predicted, Whipple appealed on behalf of the Indians to the outraged settlers and to President Lincoln who forbade execution of many condemned Sioux. His proposed reforms of the reservation system, and his suggestions of land-ownership by Indians, adequate schools, and inspection, were largely adopted under President Grant. During the next two decades he exposed frauds, built up missions among the Minnesota Chippewa, traveled widely, and made eloquent addresses in America and abroad for support of his work. In 1897 he attended the fourth Lambeth Conference as presiding bishop of the American Church. Author of an autobiography, *Lights and Shadows of a Long Episcopate* (1899).

WHIPPLE, SHERMAN LELAND (*b. New London, N.H., 1862; d. Brookline, Mass., 1930*), Boston, Mass.,

lawyer. Graduated Yale Law School, 1884. Celebrated as a plaintiff's attorney in personal injury and will cases.

WHIPPLE, SQUIRE (*b. Hardwick, Mass., 1804; d. Albany, N.Y., 1888*), civil engineer, author, inventor. A.B., Union College, 1830. Devised (*c.* 1846) a widely used truss of trapezoidal form which placed him among American pioneers in development of the pure truss bridge. Whipple's chief contribution to bridge engineering was publication of *A Work on Bridge Building* (1847), the first notable attempt to present the subject on a scientific basis and the first thorough treatment of modern methods of computing stresses and designing parts to meet them.

WHIPPLE, WILLIAM (*b. Kittery, Maine, 1730; d. 1785*), merchant, Revolutionary patriot, New Hampshire legislator. Prominent in early provincial congresses as a close associate of John Langdon. Member of the Continental Congress, 1776–79, with interludes for militia commands, he was a signer of the Declaration of Independence. An active committee member, he urged effective naval operations and strong measures against speculators and Tories. He advocated also the spread of the burden of the struggle over the entire people by means of adequate taxation. He served as a justice, state supreme court, from 1782 until his death.

WHISTLER, GEORGE WASHINGTON (*b. Fort Wayne, Ind., 1800; d. St. Petersburg, Russia, 1849*), soldier, engineer. Father of James A. M. Whistler. Graduated West Point, 1819. Commissioned second lieutenant of artillery, he was assigned to topographical duty. In 1828 he assisted in location and construction of the Baltimore and Ohio Railroad, subsequently supervising construction of other roads. Resigned from army, 1833. As chief engineer, Western Railroad of Massachusetts (now Boston & Albany), 1840–42, he located section between Springfield and Pittsfield through the Berkshires under especially difficult conditions. This resulted in appointment by the Czar of Russia as consulting engineer for a railroad between St. Petersburg and Moscow which was completed in 1850. He also supervised construction of fortifications and docks at Cronstadt, and of the iron bridge over the Neva.

WHISTLER, JAMES ABBOTT McNEILL (*b. Lowell, Mass., 1834; d. London, England, 1903*), painter, etcher, author. Son of George W. Whistler; nephew of William G. McNeill. A bright boy, somewhat delicate in health but precociously able as a draftsman, Whistler resided in Russia and England, 1843–49. Although his mother was offered a place for him in the Russian imperial school for pages after his father's death, she brought him and her other children back to America in 1849. A West Point cadet, 1851–54, he was dismissed for deficiency in chemistry. "Had silicon been a gas," he is reported to have said, "I would have been a major general." He retained

1183

from his military education his insistence upon the point of honor, his erect carriage, and probably his lifelong proclivity for fighting. After a brief engagement as a draftsman of maps in the U.S. Coast Survey at Washington, D.C., during which he learned much about the mechanics of etching, he departed to study in Paris, 1855.

He never returned to his native country probably because he found more congenial conditions of life abroad and friends with whom he was instinctively at home. Entering the atelier of Charles Gleyre, a competent painter in the tradition of Ingres, Whistler conducted himself in dress and manner as a Bohemian of the Bohemians. He had the gift of dramatizing his own every movement and adopted originality as a career, not because he was a *poseur*, but because he couldn't help it; he was invincibly an individual in his life as in his work. Among his friends of this period were many artists later to become famous —among them, George Du Maurier, Henri Fantin-Latour, and Alphonse Legros. Resisting contemporary French art influences with the exception of that of Gustave Courbet, Whistler sought beauty in truth but subjected truth to his very personal conception of beauty. Among his early paintings, "The Music Room," with its decisively decorative motive, foreshadows the essential Whistler. He published his first group of etchings in Paris, November 1858. His painting "The White Girl," rejected at the Paris Salon in 1863, later made a sensation in the Salon des Refusés.

After the 1850's, Whistler oscillated between Paris and London, with London becoming more and more the field of his labors. His mother came to live in England, 1863, and it was there that he painted the celebrated portrait of her first shown in 1872 and now in the Louvre. In London, between 1872 and 1877, he painted those other portraits which won him so much reputation—notably his "Carlyle," and "Miss Alexander." Also of London ancestry are his "Nocturnes" and the Thames set of etchings. Harshly criticized by John Ruskin for work shown in the Grosvenor gallery exhibition of 1877, Whistler sued the critic (November 1878), winning a nominal verdict. He later described the affair in his book *The Gentle Art of Making Enemies* (1890). The episode served to dramatize the fact that Whistler had created something new and strange in art, something beyond the comprehension of the contemporary British mind which had been nurtured on the sentimental "subject" picture or painted anecdote. "Take the picture of my mother," he said, "exhibited at the Royal Academy as an 'Arrangement in Grey and Black.' Now that is what it is. To me it is interesting as a picture of my mother; but what can or ought the public to care about the identity of the portrait?" Again, in regard to one of his Nocturnes, he said: "My picture of a 'Harmony in Grey and Gold' is an illustration of my meaning—a snow scene with a single black figure and a lighted tavern. I care nothing for the past, present,

or future of the black figure, placed there because the black was wanted at that spot. All that I know is that my combination of grey and gold is the basis of the picture."

Sensitive to the appeal of Japanese art, he acquired from Japan a feeling for pattern as pattern. His admiration for Velasquez was great, but Whistler was by no means a disciple of the great Spaniard. Each painter strove for perfection, which probably explains Whistler's admiration; but each did so in his own specific way. Velasquez was first and last constrained to record the fact before him, but Whistler, although properly regardful of the fact, was constrained to produce a distinctively Whistlerian pattern or "harmony." The many Nocturnes and Symphonies by Whistler do more than even his original and distinguished portraits to bring out the artist's singularity and creative power. He was not a great designer as Raphael was, nor was his craftsmanship equal to that of Velasquez. He gave us no high imaginative conceptions and attempted no emotional interpretation of life. However, he is very rich in sheer beauty, partly through the simplicity characterizing his design and his arrangement of color, and partly through the play of a mysterious and elusive feeling. His contribution to art was inimitable. He has had no followers, as he had had no predecessors, in painting.

On the other hand, Whistler has had a widespread influence upon etching, and it is a paradox in his career that the draftsmanship which worried him so much when he was using a brush was ever ready to his hand when he used an etcher's needle. He was already a master of line and style in the French set of etchings which date from 1858; the Thames set (1860) discloses the same technical authority and grasp of composition. By the time he went to Venice in the 1870's and in later years, he more and more practiced elimination of intrusive detail, employing a lighter, more broken line in work of great beauty and distinction. His lithographs, as well as his etchings and paintings, express his distinctive artistic qualities and are equally models of conscientious craft. A prodigious worker, absorbed in his art, he often presented himself to the public as a dilettante, discharging airy shafts of wit against critics, artists, functionaries, or any others who appeared to him either bad at their work or scornful of his aesthetic principles. His gifts of sarcasm, as well as his inexhaustible gaiety, are to be found in *The Gentle Art of Making Enemies* (1890) in which he also expresses his philosophy of art. Much of what it contains had already appeared in pamphlets, exhibition catalogues, and letters to the press.

Prosperous *post* 1885, admired and imitated by the rising generation of young artists, he moved a good deal in society and served briefly but effectively as president of the Society of British Artists and of the International Society of Sculptors, Painters and Gravers. Subsequent to the early 1890's, he lived mainly in Rue de Bac, Paris, and gave some of his time to teaching in the short-lived Académie Carmen. After the failure of his health c. 1901, he traveled for a time in Africa and Corsica before returning to London where he died.

WHITAKER, ALEXANDER (b. Cambridge, England, 1585; d. near Henricopolis, Virginia, 1616/17), Anglican clergyman. Came to Virginia as a volunteer minister, 1611. Helped to form and strengthen Virginia's attitude of welcome toward Puritan ministers and lay people, and to establish the colony's characteristic tradition of low churchmanship. Instructed and baptized Pocahontas in Christian faith. Author of Good News from Virginia (1613).

WHITAKER, CHARLES HARRIS (b. Woonsocket, R.I., 1872; d. Great Falls, Va., 1938), architectural editor and critic. A strong influence on modern architecture as editor-in-chief of the Journal of the American Institute of Architects, 1913–27; author of Rameses to Rockefeller: The Story of Architecture (1934).
[Supp. 2]

WHITAKER, DANIEL KIMBALL (b. Sharon, Mass., 1801; d. Houston, Texas, 1881), editor, writer, South Carolina planter, lawyer. B.A., Harvard, 1820. Organized, edited and contributed to Southern periodicals including Southern Quarterly Review, New Orleans, La., 1842–47, which encouraged such well-known writers as William G. Simms.

WHITAKER, NATHANIEL (b. Huntington, L.I., N.Y., 1730; d. Hampton, Va., 1795), Presbyterian clergyman, Revolutionary patriot. Conducted a tour in the British Isles with Samson Occom, 1766, which raised £12,000 for Moor's Charity School for Indians and effected the grant of the Dartmouth College charter, 1769. D.D., St. Andrew's University, 1767. Minister, Third Church, Salem, Mass., 1769–84; Presbyterian Church, Skowhegan, Maine, 1785–90. An ardent patriot, active in practical matters, his fondness for controversy brought him many enemies.

WHITCHER, FRANCES MIRIAM BERRY (b. Whitesboro, N.Y., 1814; d. Whitesboro, 1852), author. Her popular humorous sketches satirizing small-town society appeared in Joseph C. Neal's Saturday Gazette and Lady's Literary Museum, 1846–50, and in Godey's Lady's Book. They were published as The Widow Bedott Papers (1856) and Widow Spriggins, Mary Elmer, and Other Sketches (1867).

WHITCOMB, JAMES (b. Rochester, Vt., 1795; d. New York, N.Y., 1852), lawyer, Indiana legislator. Father-in-law of Claude Matthews. Raised near Cincinnati, O. Prosecuting attorney at Bloomington, Ind., 1826–29. Commissioner, General Land Office, 1836–41. Established successful law practice at Terre Haute, Ind., 1841. As governor of Indiana (the first Democrat to defeat a Whig), 1843–48, he contributed de-

cisively toward adjustment of staggering indebtedness incurred by previous internal improvements, promoted popular education and developed state benevolent institutions. An ardent supporter of the national administration in war with Mexico. U.S. senator from Indiana, 1849–52. Author of Facts for the People (1843), one of the most effective arguments ever written against a protective tariff.

WHITCOMB, SELDEN LINCOLN (b. Grinnell, Iowa, 1866; d. 1930), educator, writer. A.B., Grinnell, 1887; A.M., Columbia, 1893. A notable teacher, he was professor of English, Grinnell College, 1895–1905; professor of comparative literature, University of Kansas, 1905–30. Author of poems, essays on nature, and studies in literature which include Chronological Outlines of American Literature (1894).

WHITE, ALBERT SMITH (b. Blooming Grove, N.Y., 1803; d. near Stockwell, Ind., 1864), lawyer, jurist, railroad builder. Settled in Tippecanoe Co., Ind., 1829. Congressman, Whig, from Indiana, 1837–39; U.S. senator, 1839–45. As congressman, Republican, from Indiana, 1861–63, he introduced a resolution for a plan for gradual indemnified emancipation of slaves in the border states which was supported by President Lincoln. Judge, U.S. District Court for Indiana, 1864.

WHITE, ALEXANDER (b. Frederick Co., Va., c. 1738; d. 1804), lawyer, Virginia legislator. Began practice in Virginia, 1765. Served in state House of Burgesses, 1772; later championed allegedly Loyalist Quakers. In state assembly, 1782–86, 1788, 1799–1801, he was one of James Madison's ablest lieutenants. Successful leader in northwestern Virginia for ratification of U.S. Constitution, 1788. Congressman, Federalist, from Virginia, 1789–93. A commissioner to lay out city of Washington, D.C., 1795–1802.

WHITE, ALEXANDER (b. Elgin, Scotland, 1814; d. 1872), pioneer merchant, art collector. Emigrated to America, 1836. Settled in Chicago, Ill., 1837; prospered as merchant in paints, oils, glass and dyestuffs and post 1857 in real estate. His collection of notable European contemporary and American paintings constituted the first private art gallery in Chicago. Sold at auction, New York, 1871, it was considered the best in America at that time.

WHITE, ALFRED TREDWAY (b. Brooklyn, N.Y., 1846; d. Orange Co., N.Y., 1921), pioneer in housing reform. Built model tenements in Brooklyn, N.Y., post 1876; also Riverside Tower and Homes Building, 1890, and others. His outstanding success spurred enactment of New York's tenement-reform legislation of 1895 and later. Published, among other books, Better Homes for Workingmen (1885). As commissioner of city works (appointed 1893), he set new standards of efficiency and economy.

WHITE, ANDREW (b. London, England, 1579; d. London, 1656), Jesuit missionary, "Apostle of Maryland." A proscribed recusant, he was ordained at Douai (now France), c. 1605, and joined the Society of Jesus, 1609. While a secret priest in England, he corresponded with George Calvert, first Baron of Baltimore, and composed the *Declaratio Coloniae Domini Baronis de Baltimore* (revised and published by Cecil Calvert as *Conditions of Plantation*). Headed mission to Baltimore's emigrant group which sailed on the *Ark* and the *Dove*, landing in the lower Chesapeake, March 25, 1634. Missionary to the white colonists and Indians for ten years, he was author of *Relatio Itineris in Marilandiam*. He arranged a scheme of manors for the support of the Catholic organization in the palatinate. After William Claiborne's Puritan insurrection, 1644, White was shipped in irons to London, tried for treason and exiled.

WHITE, ANDREW DICKSON (*b. Homer, N.Y., 1832; d. Ithaca, N.Y., 1918*), educator. Graduated Yale, 1853; studied briefly at Paris and Berlin. Served as an attaché to the U.S. legation at St. Petersburg, Russia, 1854–55. After a year of graduate study again at Yale, he became professor of history in the University of Michigan, 1857. While winning distinction as an inspiring and original teacher, he matured his early concept of a state university for New York which would be as scholarly and free as the universities which he had observed in his travels abroad. In writing for help to his friend Gerrit Smith, he described the university of his dream as "excluding no sex or color, battling mercantile morality and tempering military passion . . . it should afford an asylum for science where truth shall be sought for truth's sake." In command of considerable wealth after the death of his father in 1860, he continued to propagandize in favor of his university, but was obliged to seek rest abroad late in 1862.

Returning to America late in 1863, he found that he had been elected *in absentia* to the New York State senate. As chairman of the senate committee on education, 1864, he played a large part in codifying New York's school laws and creating its new normal schools. Employing the endowment of land given New York under the Morrill Act, together with the benefactions of Ezra Cornell whom he won over to his own plans, White worked with Cornell to draw the charter of a new university at Ithaca, N.Y., which should bear Cornell's name. The educational clauses of the charter were written by White and insured instruction not only in agriculture and the mechanic arts as the Morrill Act directed, but also provided for instruction in "such other branches of science and knowledge as the trustees may deem useful and proper." After a sharp struggle with rivals the charter was validated, April 1865. The most novel elements in the new institution were: (1) its democracy of studies—the humanities, sciences, and technical arts taught commonly; (2) its parallel courses, open to free choice and leading to varying but equal de-

grees; (3) its equal rank for modern languages and literatures and for history and political science with classics; (4) its large use of eminent scholars as "non-resident professors"; (5) its treatment of the students as men, not boys.

As Cornell would not go on with the project unless White served as president, White resigned his position at Michigan, and set about gathering a faculty and equipment, reserving the chair of European history for himself. At the opening of the university in 1868, its resident faculty was young, although among the non-residents were Louis Agassiz and J. R. Lowell, George W. Curtis, James Hall, and Bayard Taylor. In addition to teaching, White busied himself in defending the university and its founder against attacks on its method; he also coped with financial crises brought about by a failure of working capital. He continued to struggle with his burdens until 1885 when he was succeeded as president by Charles K. Adams. Meanwhile, he had spent several years abroad in travel and had served as U.S. minister to Germany, 1879–81; in 1884 he had helped found the American Historical Association, becoming its first president.

After seeking to recruit his health again in travel, 1885–89, he resumed his research work and lectured widely. Among the many honorable posts which he held thereafter were U.S. minister to Russia, 1892–94; U.S. ambassador to Germany, 1897–1902; and a trusteeship of the Carnegie Institution of Washington under the presidency of his old friend Daniel C. Gilman *post* 1902. He considered the greatest event of his diplomatic career his headship of the American delegation to the Hague Conference, 1899. He was author, among other works, of *History of the Warfare of Science with Theology* (1896) and an *Autobiography* (1905).

WHITE, CANVASS (*b. Whitesboro, N.Y., 1790; d. St. Augustine, Fla., 1834*), civil engineer. Benjamin Wright's principal assistant *post* 1818 on Erie Canal construction; was chief expert in designing the locks and their equipment; supervised Glens Falls feeder. Obtained patent for waterproof cement (1820). Chief engineer, Delaware & Raritan Canal, New Jersey, and Lehigh and Union canals in Pennsylvania. Characterized as possessing "the most strict engineering mind . . . of his time."

WHITE, CHARLES ABIATHAR (*b. North Dighton, Mass., 1826; d. Washington, D.C., 1910*), geologist, paleontologist, naturalist, physician. Raised near Burlington, in Territory of Iowa. His large collections of fossils, including the famous Burlington crinoids, served to introduce his work to James Hall, F. B. Meek, A. H. Worthen, and other geologists of the time. Graduated Rush Medical College, 1864. From 1866 to 1870 he served as Iowa state geologist; he was also professor of geology, Iowa State University, 1867–74. Employed successively, 1875–79, by G. M. Wheeler's survey west of 100th meridian, by J. W.

Powell's survey of Rocky Mountain region, and by F. V. Hayden's geological survey of the Territories, he published important reports and paleontological studies. Curator, invertebrate fossils, National Museum, Washington, D.C., 1879–82; organized paleontologic collections. Geologist, U.S. Geological Survey, 1882–92. White's major scientific contributions were in invertebrate paleontology and stratigraphy, particularly of the Mesozoic.

WHITE, CHARLES IGNATIUS (*b. Baltimore, Md., 1807; d. Washington, D.C., 1878*), Roman Catholic clergyman. Ordained to secular priesthood, Notre Dame Cathedral, Paris, France, 1830. Influential and scholarly rector, St. Matthew's Church, Washington, D.C., 1857–78, where he did notable social work. A founder and editor (1842) of *Religious Cabinet* (later *U.S. Catholic Magazine*), and *Metropolitan Magazine*, 1853.

WHITE, DAVID (*b. near Palmyra, N.Y., 1862; d. Washington, D.C., 1935*), paleobotanist, geologist. B.S., Cornell University, 1886. Associated thereafter with the U.S. Geological Survey, he performed most of his research in the period before 1912, at which time he was made chief geologist of the Survey and became active in the National Academy of Sciences. He was curator of paleobotany, U.S. National Museum, 1903–35. He resigned the post of chief geologist, 1922, to return to research, but his administrative duties continued to be heavy.

In such works as *Fossil Flora of the Lower Coal Measures of Missouri* (1899) and *Flora of the Hermit Shale, Grand Canyon, Arizona* (1929), White brought to his work an unusually keen mind; he was never content with a mere description of fossils, but interpreted them in terms of their chronology and environment, particularly their climatic significance and the part which they took in the formation of coal and petroleum. His methodology consisted essentially in employment of a much greater precision than had been used by earlier scientists and in the discrimination of slight differences, particularly if such differences could be shown to occur at different stratigraphic horizons. His success demanded a combination of work in the field with personal office studies of the resulting collections. His method provided a disproof of prevailing opinions on the constitution of the Appalachian coal basin; he was also able to show that coals should be classified according to a standard in which the degree of deoxygenation served as an index of coal evolution; this in turn led to the generalization announced in 1915 (commonly known as the "carbon-ratio" hypothesis) which enables the determination of the rank of a coal, and also limits the extent of liquid and gaseous hydrocarbons. A few years later the economic importance of this brilliant idea was universally recognized in petroleum exploratory work. White's theory, amplified and clarified, was stated in his "Metamorphism

of Organic Sediments and Derived Oils" (*Bulletin of the American Association of Petroleum Geologists*, May 1935). [*Supp.* 1]

WHITE, EDWARD DOUGLASS (*b. Maury Co., Tenn., 1795; d. New Orleans, La., 1847*), lawyer, planter, political leader. Father of Edward D. White (1845–1921). Studied law in office of Alexander Porter. Congressman, Whig, from Louisiana, 1829–34 and 1839–43. As governor of Louisiana, 1835–39, he effectively vetoed bill to charter Farmers' Bank in panic of 1837.

WHITE, EDWARD DOUGLASS (*b. Parish Lafourche, La., 1845; d. Washington, D.C., 1921*), lawyer, Confederate soldier, planter, jurist. Son of Edward D. White (1795–1847). Left the present Georgetown University to serve in the Confederate Army; studied law after the Civil War with Edward Bermudez. Admitted to the Louisiana bar, 1868, he entered politics and served in the Louisiana senate; he was also a justice of the state supreme court, 1879–80. Early identified with the anti-lottery movement, he was elected to the U.S. Senate as a Democrat and served, 1891–94. Appointed to the U.S. Supreme Court, 1894, he was raised to the post of chief justice, 1910.

During his years on the bench, Justice White wrote opinions in more than 700 cases. It is difficult to characterize his decisions as a whole. He was sometimes found with the so-called liberals as, for example, when he dissented in the case of *Lochner vs. New York* (1905) and when he wrote the majority opinion in *Wilson vs. New* upholding the Adamson Act. On the other hand, while he concurred in the New York Central case (243 *U.S.*, 188) upholding the New York workmen's compensation act, he dissented in the Mountain Timber Co. case (243 *U.S.*, 219) which upheld the Washington compensation law. Many other examples of an apparent inconsistency could be cited. *Wilson vs. New* was probably the most important decision he ever wrote even though the reasoning he employed left much to be desired, but he is doubtless best known for the "rule of reason" laid down in the Standard Oil and the American Tobacco cases (221 *U.S.*, 1, 106) interpreting and applying the Anti-trust Act. He had earlier announced this rule in a dissent. It must be said, however, that by applying the rule he wrote into the law something which Congress had not put there, and that he did it by a sophistical course of reasoning.

An untiring worker, courteous and devoted to the public service, he unwittingly gave an approximation of his own philosophy in a 1916 address on the death of Joseph R. Lamar. It could be said of him, as he said of Lamar, that he appreciated keenly the duty to adjust between conflicting activities so as to preserve the rights of all by protecting the rights of each, and that it was his duty to uphold and sustain the authority of the Union as to the subjects coming within the legitimate scope of its power as conferred by the Constitution. He believed that no thought of expediency, no mere convictions about economic problems, and no personal belief that the guarantees of the Constitution were becoming obsolete should sway his purpose to uphold and protect those constitutional guarantees.

WHITE, ELLEN GOULD HARMON (*b. Gorham, Maine, 1827; d. St. Helena, Calif., 1915*), Seventh-day Adventist leader. Embracing Advent faith of William Miller in the 1840's, she exerted great influence on Adventists most of whom accepted her visions and messages as from God. Her husband, Rev. James White, managed Adventist publishing work *post* 1849. They founded the Western Health Reform Institute, Battle Creek, Mich., 1866, and promoted Battle Creek College (founded 1874). Mrs. White also helped found College of Medical Evangelists, Loma Linda, Calif., 1909.

WHITE, EMERSON ELBRIDGE (*b. Mantua, O., 1829; d. 1902*), educator. Influential as editor and proprietor, *Ohio Educational Monthly*, 1861–75; as commissioner of common schools, 1863–65, he codified Ohio school laws. President, Purdue University, 1876–83. Superintendent, Cincinnati, O., public schools, 1886–89. President, among other school organizations, of National Council of Education, 1884, which he helped found. Author of widely used *White's New School Register Containing Forms for Daily, Term and Yearly Records* (1891), and of a number of textbooks.

WHITE, GEORGE (*b. Charleston, S.C., 1802; d. 1887*), writer, teacher, Episcopal clergyman. Self-educated, White settled in Savannah, Ga., 1823, where he established an academy and night school. He was ordained, 1833. Helped organize Georgia Historical Society, 1839. Published *Statistics of the State of Georgia* (1849), a work of great merit; also an account of the Yazoo Fraud (1852), and *Historical Collections of Georgia* (1854), a classic in Georgia bibliography. Among other church assignments, he served as rector of Calvary Church, Memphis, Tenn., 1859–85.

WHITE, GEORGE LEONARD (*b. Cadiz, N.Y., 1838; d. Ithaca, N.Y., 1895*), conductor of Jubilee Singers of Fisk University, music teacher. Self-educated, White was a choir-leader in Ohio. He became instructor of vocal music at Fisk University, Nashville, Tenn., 1867, and subsequently a trustee and treasurer. To help maintain Fisk, White took a choir of his newly emancipated students on highly successful concert tours (1871–78) in America, Great Britain and the Continent, spreading understanding and respect for the freedmen.

WHITE, HENRY (*b. Maryland, 1732; d. England, 1786*), Loyalist, New York City merchant. Appointed to the Province Council, 1769; opposed Stamp and Townshend acts. Agent and attorney for Governor Tryon, 1774. A signer of the Loyal Address to the Howes, he served the British by equipping Tory provincial regiments and as agent for selling prizes. By Act of Attainder, 1779, his property was confiscated and he later removed to London.

WHITE, HENRY (*b. Baltimore, Md., 1850; d. Pittsfield, Mass., 1927*), diplomat. Son-in-law of Lewis M. Rutherfurd. Began career as secretary, Vienna legation, 1883; was second, then first, secretary in London, 1883–93. Richard Olney's unofficial agent in clearing up Venezuelan dispute. Resuming his London post, 1897, he served brilliantly for eight years under Ambassadors John Hay and Joseph Choate in furthering Anglo-American co-operation. Ambassador to Italy *post* March 1905, and to France, 1907–09, he was President Roosevelt's agent at the Algeciras Conference, 1906, and aided in preventing a war-menacing rupture. Head of American delegation, fourth Pan-American Conference, Buenos Aires, 1910. Appointed by President Wilson to Peace Commission, November 1918, he accompanied Wilson to Paris and strongly advocated America's entrance into the League of Nations. White might be called the first professional American diplomatist.

WHITE, HENRY CLAY (*b. Baltimore, Md., 1848; d. Athens, Ga., 1927*), chemist, educator. Graduated University of Virginia, 1870. Appointed professor of chemistry at University of Georgia, 1872; served as president, Georgia State College of Agriculture and the Mechanic Arts, 1890–1907. State chemist of Georgia, 1880–90, and vice-director, Georgia Experiment Station, 1890–1913. Organized Farmers' Institutes of Georgia.

WHITE, HORACE (*b. Colebrook, N.H., 1834; d. 1916*), journalist, economist. Raised in Beloit, Wis. Reported on Lincoln-Douglas debates, 1858, for *Chicago Tribune*, becoming friend of Lincoln and Henry Villard; was *Tribune's* Washington correspondent, 1861–65, and served as its editor-in-chief, 1865–74. Managed financial and economic policies of *New York Evening Post* and the *Nation* from c. 1883; was editor-in-chief of the former, 1899–1903, succeeding E. L. Godkin. A free-trader and Manchester-school liberal, he threw himself into the *Evening Post's* opposition to Hawaiian annexation; he also opposed America's attitude in the Venezuelan imbroglio with England (1895), the war with Spain, and the Philippine conquest. His paper's editorial page was one of the most distinguished in American journalism. Author of *Money and Banking* (1895) and other works.

WHITE, HUGH LAWSON (*b. Iredell Co., N.C., 1773; d. near Knoxville, Tenn., 1840*), Tennessee legislator and jurist. Son of James White. Secretary to William Blount, 1793. Judge, superior court of Tennessee, 1801–07. Chosen presiding judge, supreme court of errors and appeals, 1809, he served until 1815. President, Bank of the State of Tennessee, 1812–27. U.S. senator, Democrat, from Tennessee, 1825–40. A strict constructionist, a Jeffersonian and Jacksonian Democrat, he opposed J. Q. Adams's administration. As chairman of the committee on Indian affairs, he was active in planning for Indian removal westward. President Jackson, to promote Martin Van Buren's political fortunes, attempted to force acceptance of the U.S. secretaryship of war on White, 1831; in refusing, White broke with Jackson. With John Tyler as his running mate and the support of the Whigs, he ran for the U.S. presidency in 1836 and was defeated. He favored Henry Clay for the presidency in 1840 and promised him support after Clay's pledge not to push his nationalist program and to oppose Texas annexation. White resigned from the Senate, January 1840, when instructed by the Tennessee legislature to vote for the sub-treasury bill. Strict of conscience, he was entirely disinterested as a public servant.

WHITE, ISRAEL CHARLES (*b. Monongalia Co., present W. Va., 1848; d. Baltimore, Md., 1927*), geologist. Graduated West Virginia University, 1872; studied also at Columbia University. Held chair of geology at West Virginia, 1877–92; from 1897 until his death was superintendent of geological survey of West Virginia which he largely established; was assistant geologist on U.S. Geological Survey, 1884–88. He was author of "Stratigraphy of the Bituminous Coal Field of Pennsylvania, Ohio, and West Virginia" (1891), said to be the foundation for later work in this field. His most important work, ranking him foremost among petroleum geologists of the world, was his "anticlinal theory" of oil and gas, formulated *c.* 1883. In it he drew the conclusion that a direct relation existed between gas territory and disturbance in rocks caused by their upheaval into arches. Successful dealings in "wildcat" leases proved his theory. His White House address "The Waste of Our Fuel Resources" (May 1908) greatly influenced the subsequent conservation movement.

WHITE, JAMES (*b. Rowan, present Iredell, Co., N.C., 1747; d. Knoxville, Tenn., 1821*), Revolutionary soldier, pioneer, North Carolina and Tennessee legislator. Father of Hugh L. White. Laid out town of Knoxville, Tenn., 1792; directed its defense against Indians, 1793. Served in 1796 convention which drew up Tennessee constitution; supported policies of William Blount and John Sevier; represented Tennessee in first treaty of Tellico, 1798. Made brigadier-general, Tennessee militia, in late 1790's, he served in the Creek War, 1813.

WHITE, JAMES CLARKE (*b. Belfast, Maine, 1833; d. 1916*), dermatologist, reformer of medical education. Graduated Harvard, 1853; M.D., Harvard Medical School, 1856; did post-graduate work in Vienna.

Adjunct professor of chemistry, Harvard Medical School, 1866–71; held chair of dermatology, 1871–1902. Established with B. J. Jeffries first dermatological clinic in America *c.* 1860. President, Sixth International Dermatological Congress, 1907.

WHITE, JAMES WILLIAM (*b. Philadelphia, Pa., 1850; d. Philadelphia, 1916*), surgeon. Nephew of Samuel S. White. M.D. and Ph.D., University of Pennsylvania, 1871. Professor of clinical surgery at Pennsylvania, 1887–1900; Barton Professor of Surgery, 1900–11, becoming professor emeritus. Author, with Edward Martin, of *Genito-Urinary Surgery and Venereal Diseases* (1897), his most important work. An editor of *Annals of Surgery*, 1892–1916.

WHITE, JOHN (*fl. 1585–1593*), artist, cartographer. Sent by Sir Walter Raleigh to Roanoke Island on the expedition of 1585, White painted a series of sketches in water color depicting the flora and fauna of America as well as the appearance of the native Indians. These first scientific and careful studies are primary historical sources. They were later adapted in engravings by Theodore de Bry for the 1590 edition of Thomas Hariot's *A Briefe and True Report of Virginia*. It is possible that he was the John White who served as governor of Raleigh's "second colonie," Roanoke, Va., *post* 1587.

WHITE, JOHN BLAKE (*b. near Eutaw Springs, S.C., 1781; d. c. 1859*), artist, dramatist, lawyer. Studied under Benjamin West, 1800–03. Settled in Charleston, S.C., 1804, where he remained for most of his life. Between 1804 and 1840 he produced historical pictures (four in the U.S. Capitol) and portraits; also painted miniatures. Among his plays were *Foscari* (1806) and *The Triumph of Liberty, or Louisiana Preserved* (1819).

WHITE, JOHN DE HAVEN (*b. near New Holland, Pa., 1815; d. Philadelphia, Pa., 1895*), dentist. Practiced in Philadelphia *post* 1837. Graduated Jefferson Medical College, 1844. Teacher of Thomas W. Evans and Samuel S. White. An organizer of Philadelphia College of Dental Surgery, he was professor of anatomy and physiology and of operative dental surgery and special dental physiology, 1854–56. Author of numerous professional papers.

WHITE, JOHN WILLIAMS (*b. Cincinnati, O., 1849; d. Cambridge, Mass., 1917*), Hellenist. Graduated Ohio Wesleyan, 1868; Ph.D., Harvard, 1877. Taught Greek at Harvard, 1874–1909. Aided President C. W. Eliot in expansion of the college into a university. Broke from older teaching methods by insisting on wide and rapid reading in his courses on Greek authors; was expert in Greek meters. Founded with J. B. Greenough and helped edit the *Harvard Studies in Classical Philology*; with C. E. Norton and W. W. Goodwin, organized Archaeological Institute of America, 1879. Influenced James Loeb; helped establish Loeb Classical Library.

WHITE, PEARL (*b. Greenridge, Mo., 1889; d. Paris, France, 1938*), motion picture actress, star of *The Perils of Pauline* (1914) and other popular serial motion pictures. [*Supp. 2*]

WHITE, RICHARD GRANT (*b. New York, N.Y., 1821; d. New York, 1885*), writer. Graduated present New York University, 1839. Won distinction as musical critic of *Morning Courier and New-York Enquirer*. Wrote extensively for *Putnam's Magazine, Galaxy, Atlantic Monthly* and London *Spectator*. Author, among other works, of *The New Gospel of Peace* (anonymous, 1863–66), *Words and Their Uses* (1870) and *Studies in Shakespeare* (1886). An acute Shakespeare scholar, he edited *The Works of William Shakespeare* (1857–66). He was father of Stanford White.

WHITE, SAMUEL (*b. Kent Co., Del., 1770; d. Wilmington, Del., 1809*), lawyer. Admitted to the Delaware bar, 1793. U.S. senator, Federalist, from Delaware, 1801 until his death.

WHITE, SAMUEL STOCKTON (*b. Hulmeville, Pa., 1822; d. Paris France, 1879*), dental supplies manufacturer, dentist. Credited with important improvements in porcelain teeth; also introduced new or improved dental appliances and instruments.

WHITE, STANFORD (*b. New York, N.Y., 1853; d. New York, 1906*), architect. Son of Richard G. White. Worked in firm of Gambrill & Richardson as close associate of H. H. Richardson *post c.* 1872; was associated with Charles F. McKim and W. R. Mead and others in McKim, Mead & White *post* 1880. A friend of Augustus Saint-Gaudens, White designed the pedestal for Saint-Gauden's statue of Farragut in Madison Square, New York City (unveiled, 1881), for which he received much praise. Operating on the theory that all things intrinsically good can be brought into harmony, White worked with great skill in a number of styles; he planned luxurious city and country houses, designed furniture, ransacked Europe for interior decorations, designed magazine covers, gravestones and jewelry. The splendid success of McKim, Mead & White was aided by the rapid contemporary increase in wealth in America and the desire of the traveled wealthy for a share in Old World art and culture. White was notably successful among his partners in impressing wealthy clients with a respect for the beautiful even though they might fail to understand it, and was aptly called the protagonist of popular art in New York City. Among the number of churches which he designed, the Judson Memorial in Washington Square, New York City, remains as an example. He was designer also of a number of clubs including the Metropolitan Club, New York City, his supreme achievement in Renaissance architecture. His work has been described as graceful and charming rather than imposing; among his most enduring achievements are the Washington Arch (New

York City) and the Prison Ship Martyrs Monument, Brooklyn, N.Y. His business buildings included the one-time Gorham and Tiffany buildings on Fifth Avenue, New York City, and he was the designer (1889) of the original Madison Square Garden. There he met his death, murdered by Harry K. Thaw.

WHITE, STEPHEN MALLORY (*b. San Francisco, Calif., 1853; d. Los Angeles, Calif., 1901*), lawyer. Admitted to the bar, 1874, he began successful practice in Los Angeles, Calif. U.S. senator, Democrat, from California, 1893–99. Favored free coinage of silver, opposed imperialism and championed the "country" voters against monopolistic aggression. Defeated C. P. Huntington's plans to divert federal funds from San Pedro to harbor site desired by Southern Pacific Railroad.

WHITE, STEPHEN VAN CULEN (*b. Chatham Co., N.C., 1831; d. 1913*), banker, lawyer. Raised in Illinois. Practiced law in Iowa, 1856–64, and was acting U.S. district attorney for Iowa, 1864. Became member of New York Stock Exchange, 1869, where he was soon known as a daring manipulator, especially in shares of Delaware, Lackawanna & Western Railroad. Congressman, Republican, from New York, 1887–89. He was a friend of Henry Ward Beecher and long the treasurer of Plymouth Church.

WHITE, THOMAS WILLIS (*b. Williamsburg, Va., 1788; d. New York, N.Y., 1843*), printer. Established successful printing business in Richmond, Va., *c.* 1817. Founded (1834) the *Southern Literary Messenger*, of which Edgar Allan Poe was editor, 1835–37.

WHITE, WILLIAM (*b. Philadelphia, Pa., 1748 n.s.; d. Philadelphia, 1836*), Episcopal clergyman. Graduated College of Philadelphia, 1765; ordained deacon in London, England, 1770, and priest, 1772. Principal rectorate at Christ Church, Philadelphia. Largely devised plan for organization of Protestant Episcopal Church in the United States (1785–89) on principle that laity should have an equal part with clergy in all legislation; drafted original constitution of Church and secured its adoption. With William Smith, he was chiefly responsible for the American revision of the Book of Common Prayer. Consecrated bishop of Pennsylvania in England, 1787, he served with tact and ability and was presiding bishop *post* 1796. Noted for active promotion of Sunday School work; trained, among other clergyman, W. A. Muhlenberg and J. H. Hobart. Long chaplain of Congress, he published, among other works, *Comparative Views of the Controversy between the Calvinists and the Arminians* (1817) and *Memoirs of the Protestant Episcopal Church in the United States of America* (1820).

WHITE, WILLIAM ALANSON (*b. Brooklyn, N.Y., 1870; d. Washington, D.C., 1937*), psychiatrist, hospital administrator. M.D., Long Island College Hospital, 1891. Influenced by Boris Sidis while at Binghamton (N.Y.) State Hospital. Superintendent of the present St. Elizabeth's Hospital, Washington, D.C., *post* 1903, he established a psychological laboratory there, developed a department of internal medicine, and was an early exponent of psychoanalysis. Under his leadership the hospital became one of the leading centers of psychiatric care and training in the United States. A professor at Georgetown and George Washington universities, he also taught in the army and navy medical schools; he was president of the first International Congress on Mental Hygiene, Washington, D.C., 1930. Among his many publications was *The Outlines of Psychiatry* (1907). [*Supp. 2*]

WHITE, WILLIAM NATHANIEL (*b. Longridge, Conn., 1819; d. 1867*), horticulturist, editor. Settled in Georgia, 1847. Authority on pomology, horticulture, and rural economy, he became editor (1863) and owner (1865) of the *Southern Cultivator*. Author of *Gardening for the South* (1856), a standard work.

WHITE EYES (*d. 1778*), Delaware chief. Became chief sachem of the Delaware nation, 1776. Held his people neutral in early stages of the Revolution because of false representations by agent George Morgan; was deceived into signing treaty with the American states, 1778. Murdered while guiding American troops against Detroit.

WHITEFIELD, GEORGE (*b. Gloucester, England, 1714 o.s.; d. Newburyport, Mass., 1770*), clergyman, evangelist. The son of a tavern keeper, but descended from a line of clergymen, Whitefield as a boy was impetuous and emotional, but his own picture of his youthful depravity is doubtless over-colored. Admitted as a servitor to Pembroke College, Oxford, 1732, he made the acquaintance of Charles and John Wesley. Adopting a rule of life and engaging in charitable activities, he behaved with such fanatical zeal that he became seriously ill late in the spring of 1735. Experiencing a "new birth" at this time, he was filled with a sense of the pardoning love of God and became convinced that such an experience was indispensable to all individuals in search of religious conviction. While recovering from his illness, he converted some of his friends and formed a religious society; he devoted a part of each day to corporal works of mercy. Returning to Oxford, March 1736, he was admitted to deacon's orders in Gloucester Cathedral in June. The powerful effect of his first sermon upon his fellow townsmen was prophetic of the power over audiences which he was to exhibit later. In July he was graduated as B.A. from Oxford and, as the Wesleys were now in Georgia, he became leader of the few Methodists left at the university. Taking every opportunity offered to preach his idea of the "new birth," he soon achieved extraordinary prominence in several provincial cities and in London, incidentally collecting large sums of money for the Georgia mission of the Wesleys and for charity schools. Soon attacked by conservative churchmen, he left for Georgia on Dec. 30, 1737, accompanied by friends, one of whom was James Habersham.

Undiscouraged by the unsatisfactory experiences of the Wesley brothers in Georgia, Whitefield landed at Savannah on May 7; during a four-months' stay, he began services, started several schools, and determined to establish an orphanage. Returning to England in September 1738, he was ordained priest in January 1739, but encountered further bitter opposition at home and was denied use of churches for preaching. Accepting the use of halls and other meeting places, he continued his preaching work, delivering his first open-air sermon on Feb. 17, 1739, to a group of colliers near Bristol; soon he was preaching at many of the public resorts of the London populace. Accused of ignorance and Pharisaism (with considerable justification), he persevered in his work as an itinerant preacher to constantly increasing audiences, and won the patronage of several members of the aristocracy, notably the Countess of Huntingdon.

Departing once again for America, August 1739, he remained there for more than a year, although his parish at Savannah saw little of him. He spent most of his time in further itinerant preaching which awakened religious excitement all the way from Georgia to Massachusetts; encouraged by the Presbyterians and Congregationalists, he was opposed by clergy of the Church of England. Among his supporters among the Presbyterians were William and Gilbert Tennent. During a brief stay in Savannah, he began construction of the orphanage which he had planned, giving it the name Bethesda, but he soon made himself disliked by his general attitude of censoriousness and his abuse of fellow clergymen. Setting out once again to visit the North, he preached with great effect in Philadelphia and in New York; among his triumphs was the securing of a donation for his orphanage from Benjamin Franklin. Summoned before an ecclesiastical court in Charleston, S.C., June 1740, because of irregularities in doctrine and practice, he denied the court's jurisdiction, failed to appear and was suspended, but did not cease his activities. Journeying to New England, he produced there the same great religious awakening that he had already produced in the Middle Colonies. On his leisurely return southward he stopped in many places, visiting Jonathan Edwards at Northampton, Mass., and when in New Brunswick, N.J., persuading Gilbert Tennent to go to Boston and further the revival which was in progress there. He sailed for England in January 1741, and almost four years elapsed before he was once again in America.

Whitefield had by now become a rigid Calvinist and engaged in an unpleasant controversy with John Wesley. His admirers had built the Tabernacle for him in London, but he continued his wanderings and his field-preaching in all parts of the British Isles.

In Wales he was made moderator of the first Calvinistic Methodist Conference. Married in Wales, November 1741, he left England for America with his wife in August 1744, landing at the present York, Maine. Since his first visit to New England, a spirit of opposition to him had arisen in many of the Congregational leaders, foremost among whom was Charles Chauncy (1705–1787). Yet he had strong supporters and his preaching continued to draw large audiences. Removing to Georgia at the end of 1745, he spent part of the next two years there and in evangelistic journeys; in 1748 he went to Bermuda and returned to England during that same summer to become domestic chaplain to the Countess of Huntingdon. He also continued his preaching in London and throughout the British Isles.

His activities in Great Britain were broken by four more visits to America. In 1751–52 he spent some seven months in Georgia and the Carolinas; in 1754–55 he spent about the same period of time on a preaching itinerary that included Philadelphia, New York, Virginia and parts of New England. Returning in September 1763, he remained until c. 1765, traveling and preaching as always, and also petitioning Georgia for a grant of land for establishment of a college at Bethesda; this failed because of opposition in England. In September 1769 he left England for the last time, arriving in Charleston, S.C., in November, and proceeding to Bethesda. In the spring of 1770 he entered on a most strenuous itinerary of preaching in Pennsylvania, New York and New England, during which he met his death at Newburyport, Mass.

A man of middle stature, graceful, although somewhat fleshy in his later years, he had a fair complexion and small, keen dark-blue eyes in one of which was a noticeable squint. When speaking, he used many gestures; his voice was strong and musical and his mastery of it was perfect; his histrionic gifts would have made him one of the immortals of the stage and he was a master of pathos. He followed a simple and orderly manner of life. Easily irritated, he was as easily placated. His influence in America, quite apart from that which he exerted in Great Britain, was far-reaching. He stimulated a religious awakening which had already begun and by his preaching added thousands to the churches. The doctrinal discussions which arose in his wake resulted in a definitely American contribution to theology. He gave impetus to education and to philanthropic work. It is fair to say that because he made the denominations intercolonial and encouraged his followers to ignore parish and sectional lines, he made a very real contribution to the creation of a distinct Americanism among the colonies. His work also encouraged limitation of ecclesiastical and political authority and advocated freedom of conscience and individual liberty; his weakening of the Church of England in the South loosened one of the closest links between the colonies and the mother country. In these and other respects the Great Awakening prepared the way for revolution and independence.

WHITEHEAD, WILBUR CHERRIER (*b. Cleveland, O., 1866; d. at sea, 1931*), bridge expert. Author of *Whitehead's Conventions of Auction Bridge* (1914) and *Auction Bridge Standards* (1921). Contributed a complete tabulation of conventions of play and desirable leads and a complete bidding system. A founder and first president of the Cavendish Club.

WHITEHEAD, WILLIAM ADEE (*b. Newark, N.J., 1810; d. 1884*), historian. Collector of the port of Key West, Fla., 1831–38 and also mayor. A leading organizer of the New Jersey Historical Society, 1845, and its secretary until his death, he published, among other works, *East Jersey Under the Proprietary Governments* (1846); *The Papers of Lewis Morris* (1852); and *Documents Relating to the Colonial History of the State of New Jersey* (1880–85).

WHITEHILL, CLARENCE EUGENE (*b. Marengo, Iowa, 1871; d. New York, N.Y., 1932*), opera singer. Studied in Paris, 1896, at urging of Melba and Campanari. Made debut, 1899, as Friar Lawrence in *Romeo and Juliet* at Théâtre de la Monnaie, Brussels. Leading baritone, Cologne Opera House, 1903–08. Well known for Wagnerian roles, he sang at Metropolitan Opera House, N.Y., 1909–11, 1915–32.

WHITEHILL, ROBERT (*b. Lancaster Co., Pa., 1738; d. near Harrisburg, Pa., 1813*), Pennsylvania legislator and official. Played an important part in drafting the state constitution (1776) and was principal aide of George Bryan. A strong anti-Federalist and democrat, he was one of the group which set up a vehement opposition in the Pennsylvania back country, whose suspicions of central government he reflected in the Pennsylvania convention to ratify the Federal Constitution. Congressman, (Democrat) Republican, from Pennsylvania, 1805 until his death.

WHITEHOUSE, FREDERIC COPE (*b. Rochester, N.Y., 1842; d. New York, N.Y., 1911*), lawyer, archeologist. Chiefly interested in Egyptology, he was author, among other writings, of *Lake Moeris: Justification of Herodotus* (1885), *Memorandum on the Raiyan Project and the Action of Her Majesty's Government* (1891), and *The Assuan Reservation and Lake Moeris* (1904). Devoted many years to promotion of plan for irrigation of lower Egypt by impounding surplus Nile flood-waters.

WHITFIELD, HENRY (*b. near London, England, 1597; d. Winchester, England, 1657/58*), nonconformist clergyman, settler. Friend of George Fenwick. Came to New Haven Colony, 1639; returned to England, 1650. Founded, with William Leete and others, the town of Guilford, Conn.; preached to Indians and aided John Eliot in work of conversion. Cotton Mather spoke of the "marvelous majesty and sanctity" of his preaching.

WHITFIELD, ROBERT PARR (*b. New Hartford, N.Y., 1828; d. Troy, N.Y., 1910*), draftsman, paleontologist. Became chief illustrator, New York State geological survey, 1856; for twenty years, made highly finished drawings of fossils for reports of James Hall. Curator of geology, American Museum of Natural History, New York City, 1877–1909, he identified and classified the James Hall fossil collection and others; prepared and published a catalogue of museum's 8000 types and figured specimens; helped establish museum's *Bulletin.*

WHITING, ARTHUR BATTELLE (*b. Cambridge, Mass., 1861; d. Beverly, Mass., 1936*), pianist, teacher, composer. Nephew of George E. Whiting. Studied in Boston with William H. Sherwood and George W. Chadwick; in Munich with Josef Rheinberger and Ludwig Abel. Best known for his "university concerts" of chamber music at many Eastern colleges and universities, he was a composer in the classic spirit whose high musical ideals and severity of judgment limited his output of composition. His most admired work was a Fantasy for Piano and Orchestra (1897). [*Supp. 2*]

WHITING, CHARLES GOODRICH (*b. St. Albans, Vt., 1842; d. Otis, Mass., 1922*), journalist. Literary editor, *Springfield Republican,* 1874–1910; associate editor, 1910–19. Author of *The Saunterer* (1886) and *Walks in New England* (1903).

WHITING, GEORGE ELBRIDGE (*b. Holliston, Mass., 1840; d. Cambridge, Mass., 1923*), organist, composer, organ teacher. Head of organ and composition department, College of Music, Cincinnati, O., 1878–82; organist and music director, Church of the Immaculate Conception, Boston, Mass., 1882–1910. Principal instructor of organ, New England Conservatory of Music, 1876–78 and 1882–98.

WHITING, WILLIAM (*b. Concord, Mass., 1813; d. Roxbury, Mass., 1873*), lawyer, public official. Graduated Harvard, 1833; LL.B., 1838. Eminent in his own field of patent law, he served during the Civil War as a special counselor of the U.S. War Department, and as its solicitor, 1863–65. He was author of two useful tracts, *The War Powers of the President, etc.* (1862) and *Military Arrests in Time of War* (1863), together with other works. [*Supp. 1*]

WHITING, WILLIAM HENRY CHASE (*b. Biloxi, Miss., 1824; d. Governor's Island, N.Y., 1865*), Confederate major-general. Graduated West Point, 1845. As chief engineer of Gen. J. E. Johnston's Army of the Shenandoah, he arranged transfer of troops to Manassas, 1861, where he was promoted brigadier-general by order of President Davis. At Gaines's Mill the conduct of his division was characterized by Gen. T. J. Jackson as a "matchless display of valor." Assumed command (November 1862) of the military district of Wilmington, N.C., which he guarded for two years, making Cape Fear River the best haven

in the South for blockade-runners. Developed Fort Fisher into the most powerful defensive work of the Confederacy. Heroically aided Col. Lamb in defense of Fort Fisher, 1865.

WHITLOCK, BRAND (*b. Urbana, O., 1869; d. Cannes, France, 1934*), writer, diplomat. A journalist in Toledo, O., 1887–90, and in Chicago, Ill., 1891–93, he was admitted to the Illinois bar, 1894. Mayor "Golden Rule" Jones's legal adviser in Toledo, he succeeded Jones as mayor of Toledo (1905–13) on a home-rule, nonpartisan, anti-monopoly platform. Became U.S. minister to Belgium, 1913. Remaining in Brussels after the outbreak of World War I, he helped organize non-resistance and relief projects. Highly honored by the Belgian government, he held advanced rank of ambassador to Belgium, 1919–22. Author of, among other books, *Forty Years of It* (1914), the record of his adventures in liberalism; *Turn of the Balance* (1907), his most considered novel; and *Belgium: A Personal Record* (1919), his best-known work. His fiction is concerned in great part with the technique and problems of justice administration.

WHITMAN, ALBERY ALLSON (*b. Hart Co., Ky., 1851; d. Atlanta, Ga., 1901*), poet, clergyman of African Methodist Episcopal Church. Born in slavery, he was associated with Wilberforce University and was influential in establishing many churches. Author of, among other books, *Leelah Misled* (1873) and *An Idyl of the South* (1901). Whitman's poetry is essentially derivative, yet it is fluent and shows a real, unforced love of nature. He is the most considerable Negro poet before Paul L. Dunbar.

WHITMAN, CHARLES OTIS (*b. North Woodstock, Maine, 1842; d. Chicago, Ill., 1910*), biologist. Graduated Bowdoin, 1868; Ph.D., Leipzig, 1877. Taught at Imperial University of Japan, Harvard, and Clark; headed zoology department, University of Chicago *post* 1892. Directed Marine Biological Laboratory, Woods Hole, Mass., from its foundation in 1888 until 1908. His main scientific contributions were in embryology, comparative anatomy, taxonomy, evolution, heredity and animal behavior. Introduced European scientific zoology into America, founding in 1887 the *Journal of Morphology* and establishing new standards for American scientific publication.

WHITMAN, EZEKIEL (*b. present East Bridgewater, Mass., 1776; d. East Bridgewater, 1866*), jurist, Maine legislator. Admitted to Plymouth Co., Mass., bar, 1799; practiced successfully in New Gloucester, Maine, until 1807, and thereafter in Portland. Congressman, Democrat, from Maine, 1809–11, 1817–June 1822. Judge, court of common pleas, 1822–41; chief justice, supreme court of Maine, 1841–48.

WHITMAN, MARCUS (*b. Rushville, N.Y., 1802; d. near present Walla Walla, Wash., 1847*), physician, missionary, pioneer. M.D., College of Physicians and

Surgeons at Fairfield, N.Y., 1832. Accompanied Samuel Parker on Oregon reconnaissance for Congregational missions, 1835; in 1836, with Rev. Henry H. Spalding and others, journeyed as missionary to Fort Walla Walla. Opened wagon road between Fort Hall and Fort Boise; established himself at mission at Waiilatpu, while the Spaldings took charge at Lapwai in present Idaho. After early success at missions, dissensions arose and Whitman made his famous "winter ride" east in 1842–43 to settle difficulties at mission headquarters in Boston, Mass. Successful, he returned to Oregon, 1843, accompanying the great emigration of that year. A continuing series of misfortunes at the mission climaxed in the murder of Whitman, his wife, and others by Cayuse Indians.

WHITMAN, SARAH HELEN POWER (*b. Providence, R.I., 1803; d. Providence, 1878*), poet. Chiefly remembered as fiancée of Edgar A. Poe, 1848, and the subject of his "To Helen." Praised by Poe and others, her work has grace and sincerity, but little originality or vigor. Author of *Hours of Life and Other Poems* (1853), *Edgar Poe and His Critics* (1860) and *Poems* (1879).

WHITMAN, WALT (*b. West Hills, town of Huntington, N.Y., 1819; d. Camden, N.J., 1892*), poet. Whitman's parents were of predominantly Dutch and English stock, and inclined to Quaker tenets; his father was a farmer and carpenter-builder; his mother, an uneducated woman, but "perfect in understanding and sympathy." The family moved to Brooklyn, N.Y., c. 1823, and there the poet spent a few years in the public schools. In the summers he went visiting in Huntington and in other places on Long Island and was subsequently to believe that the knowledge thus gained of life on farm and seashore was one of the few important influences upon his work. At the age of eleven he was an office boy and an avid reader of the *Arabian Nights* and the works of Sir Walter Scott; in his thirteenth year he became a printer's devil in the office of the *Long Island Patriot,* whence he went to the *Long Island Star.* This was the beginning of a long career on newspapers in which during three decades he was to be identified with a bewildering number of editorial offices. While working as a journeyman compositor in Brooklyn and New York, he made occasional contributions to the papers for which he worked and got his first taste of the theatre and the opera. Between 1836 and 1841 he taught in a number of schools on Long Island and edited the *Long Islander* at Huntington in 1838–39. His writings in this and other local papers were conventional and youthfully sentimental; he impressed people at this time as a dreamy, impractical person, indolent, morose, and untidy. According to his own later testimony, he was beginning to read at this time the Bible, Shakespeare, Ossian, the Greek tragic poets, Dante, and others; he was also interested in Democratic politics.

Of the ten or more newspapers or magazines with which Whitman was associated, 1841–48, the most important were the *Democratic Review* to which he contributed melodramatic stories after the manner of Hawthorne and Poe, and the *Brooklyn Eagle* which he edited, 1846–January 1848. He provided the *Eagle* with an enlightened and well-written editorial page supporting most contemporary reforms. Moving rapidly in the Free-Soil direction on the question of slavery, he was dismissed as editor for protesting against the failure of the Democrats to face the issue of slavery in the new states. The few poems which he published during this period were competent, conventional verse exercises on routine subjects. He was author also of a temperance novel, *Franklin Evans; or, The Inebriate,* issued as an "extra" of the *New World,* 1842. In his leisure hours he made himself familiar with the varied life of New York, sauntering about the streets, haunting the ferries and omnibuses, strolling off to the beaches, and attending the theatre and the opera regularly.

Engaged to write for the New Orleans *Crescent,* he spent three months in that city. The romantic legends which have grown up about this stay are doubtful; however, the city charmed him and provided him with new visual experiences. On his return to Brooklyn he resumed journalism, moving like a nomad from paper to paper, editing the *Brooklyn Times,* 1857–59, and publishing a long series of articles on early Brooklyn history in the *Standard.* He also assisted his father in house-building operations.

At about the year 1848, he entered on the period which came to its end and climax with the publication in 1855 of *Leaves of Grass.* The many attempts to analyze the poet's character in terms of these poems have not been particularly successful, and the theory that he passed through some mystical experience shortly before he wrote the twelve poems which make up the first edition of *Leaves of Grass* is more conjecture than logical deduction. Whitman's sudden full apprehension of himself dates back behind 1848. If there was a sudden illumination, it would appear to have been a discovery not of his own nature, which he already knew too well, but of a way in which that nature might be presented to the world and so justified. So far he had managed to be little more than a knockabout journalist in life, which was unsatisfactory to him; also, and more importantly, he had been forced to realize how unlike the rest of the world he was inwardly. He insisted always that his book had no other value than the celebration of himself as an "average man," yet he was anything but average. Early and late his writings testify to his sense of isolation; the theme of separateness is constantly evident. Well before 1850 he must have recognized that his impulses were extraordinary. He has been called autoerotic, erethistic, and homosexual, and some such extremes of nomenclature are necessary to explain certain passages in the "Song of Myself."

Although tall and heavy, he was fastidious in his habits and precise in details of his dress, even after he had adopted the rough workmen's clothes which he affected after his return from New Orleans. It is true that love for his own sex is the only kind of love about which he is ever personal or convincing. All this, of course, has nothing to do with his being a great poet, but it has much to do with the state of mind out of which *Leaves of Grass* grew with such slow and conscious effort—an effort made in order that the poet might become an artist and so free himself from the slavery of self-contemplation. It is likely that the immediate influences in this process came through intellectual contact with contemporaries. Goethe's autobiography, the works of Thomas Carlyle and Emerson provided him with an example, and Emerson's work in particular provided him with a style. He learned from Emerson a fundamental lesson, that a man could accept and celebrate himself in cosmic language, transferring his vision from the unique self to the general. He was also encouraged by his then faith in phrenology. Ambitious at this time, and later, to go forth among the American people and astonish them with fresh and forceful utterances, he gave considerable time to the practice of oratory and the planning of lectures; some of the style of his poetry can best be explained in terms of this apprenticeship.

Leaves of Grass was a failure with the public. It was incomprehensible to some readers and shocking to others. Part of the public bafflement may be attributed to Whitman's insistence on being first of all a prophet and only secondly a poet, but the book did strike home here and there. Emerson responded to Whitman's gift of a copy with the famous and generous letter containing the phrase, "I greet you at the beginning of a great career." Thoreau and Bronson Alcott visited Whitman as did William Cullen Bryant, and there were a few favorable reviews, but for the most part the book fell dead from the press despite three rhapsodical reviews of it which Whitman himself wrote for several journals. In 1856 he issued a second edition of *Leaves of Grass* which contained 21 new poems and bore the quotation from Emerson stamped in gold on the cover. This edition was even more unfavorably received, principally because of exploitations of the sexual theme such as "Spontaneous Me." Before the issue of the third edition of 1860, which was published in Boston and contained two new sections, "Children of Adam" and "Calamus," Whitman engaged again in newspaper work and associated with the "Bohemians" who met at Pfaff's rathskeller in New York City. This latest edition of his work contained "Out of the Cradle Endlessly Rocking," one of the high points of the poet's achievement which had previously appeared in the *Saturday Press*. Henceforward, the principal themes which he was to treat were love and death— love as longing and death as the satisfaction of long-

ing. In "Children of Adam" he celebrated what he called "amativeness," or the love of men and women; in "Calamus" he celebrated what he termed "adhesiveness," or the love of men for men. The edition of 1860–61 sold better than either of the others, and on Whitman's visit to Boston in connection with its printing he met William D. O'Connor, later his greatest champion. However, the Civil War reduced his Boston publishers to bankruptcy and the book became the prey of literary pirates; furthermore, the war itself produced an incalculable effect on Whitman's life, influencing and modifying his every thought and constituting the occasion of his last great burst of poetry.

Journeying to Washington, D.C., in December 1862, in search of a soldier brother who had been wounded with the Union Army in Virginia, Whitman found his brother recovered but saw enough of the misery of war to realize that his life must somehow be involved with it. Residing in Washington and earning a little money by copying documents, he devoted himself to the wounded soldiers in the various hospitals about the city (a work described in *Memoranda During the War, 1875*). He worked entirely on his own, going about the wards to talk with the soldiers or read to them, and bringing gifts of fruit, jelly and candy; on occasion he would write letters which they dictated to their families; now and then, he assisted at wound-dressing. Through the O'Connor family, with whom he lived, he met Edmund C. Stedman and was sought out in 1863 by John Burroughs. Although he does not appear ever to have met Abraham Lincoln, the president's death, occurring a few weeks after Whitman had secured a clerkship in the Department of the Interior, was the occasion for the poet's masterpiece, "When Lilacs Last in the Dooryard Bloom'd" (printed as a supplement to *Drum Taps*, 1865). Henceforth, Whitman's work is mellower, less egocentric, less raw; henceforth, it makes much of religion and the spiritual problems of society. In successive editions of *Leaves of Grass* the poems are tempered and shorn of excesses. The war and advancing age completed the process in Whitman whereby his private nature was lost sight of in the gray, kindly figure of legend.

Soon dismissed from his position in the Department of the Interior, he was given another post in the attorney-general's office. Since he had been dismissed ostensibly because he was the author of a scandalous book, his friends attempted his defense: O'Connor published *The Good Gray Poet* (the first published volume about Whitman) in 1866, and John Burroughs published *Notes on Walt Whitman* (1867), at least half of which was written by Whitman himself. Meanwhile, *Leaves of Grass* was finding European admirers, and an expurgated London edition was issued by W. M. Rossetti in 1868. Publication in England led to the poet's long correspondence and friendship with Mrs. Anne Gilchrist, the widow of William Blake's biographer. Whitman's Washington period came to a close in January 1873 when he suffered a stroke of paralysis and removed to a residence in Camden, N.J. The death of his mother soon thereafter was a blow from which he never recovered; henceforth his life ran gradually downhill. He was dependent for his living upon his brother George, upon the contributions of friends, and upon the sale of his books which he conducted partly from his own house, receiving orders and filling them with his own hand.

Between 1865 and 1873 he had published two new editions of *Leaves of Grass* (1867 and 1871), *Passage to India* (1871), and the prose *Democratic Vistas* (1871). *Democratic Vistas*, written more or less in answer to Carlyle's *Shooting Niagara*, frankly discusses the shortcomings of American democracy and shows that the reference of Whitman's idealism is now to the future in which he still has faith. Constantly at work on revisions, he issued before his death five new editions of *Leaves of Grass* (1876, 1881–82, 1882, 1888–89, 1891–92) and published three collections which contained new poems: *Two Rivulets* (1876), *November Boughs* (1888) and *Good-Bye, My Fancy* (1891). His war *Memoranda*, already published, was included in *Specimen Days and Collect* (1882–83) which with *Democratic Vistas* represented him in prose until his earlier work began to be republished long after his death. His friends Burroughs and O'Connor were usually within his reach, although he was estranged from O'Connor, 1872–82. Visitors arrived for interviews, many of them from abroad, and as time went on Whitman found himself surrounded by a group of disciples, among them his later literary executor Horace Traubel and Richard M. Bucke, a Canadian physician who wrote the first official biography of Whitman in 1883. The poet's fame continued to grow steadily, although some earlier admirers (notably A. C. Swinburne) lost their enthusiasm. Whitman's tendency to bask in adoration and surround himself with inferior champions is pardonable but pitiable. He mellowed perceptibly as he grew older especially with respect to his view of other American poets; his mature appraisals of Longfellow, Poe, Bryant, and Emerson are valuable contributions to criticism.

With the passage of years, a saner criticism and a more scientific approach to his biography have improved Whitman's image. The claims originally made for him as a prophet and moralist are less often made, and he is today judged as he should be—as a poet. He has never been popular or accepted by the democracies as he had hoped, nor has he been often imitated by other poets. But as his isolation grows more apparent, it grows more impressive, so that his rank among the poets of his country and his century is higher than it has ever been before. His work survives as certainly the most original work yet done by any American poet. As a maker of phrases, a master of rhythms, a weaver of images—indeed, as an architect of poems—he is often beyond the reach of criticism. His diaries of the war, his prefaces to *Leaves of Grass*, his *Democratic Vistas* are a permanent part of American prose.

WHITMER, DAVID (*b. near Harrisburg, Pa., 1805; d. Richmond, Mo., 1888*), Mormon leader. One of "The Three Witnesses" to the *Book of Mormon* whose translation was completed in the Whitmer house, 1829. Made president of the "High Council of Zion" to manage Mormon interests in Missouri, 1834; excommunicated, 1838, for so-called neglect of moral and religious obligations to the church. Author of *An Address to All Believers in Christ by a Witness to the Divine Authenticity to the Book of Mormon* (1887), a straightforward account of events at the beginning of Mormonism.

WHITMORE, WILLIAM HENRY (*b. Dorchester, Mass., 1836; d. 1900*), merchant, antiquarian. Boston common councilman, 1874–86; appointed a record commissioner, 1875, and city registrar, 1892. Under his supervision many volumes of invaluable local records were edited and issued, and manuscript copies of vital Boston church records were collected. He was author-editor of a number of works on genealogy and colonial history, including *The Andros Tracts* (1868–74) and the diary of Samuel Sewall. Much of his printed work, although good for its time, requires careful checking.

WHITNEY, ADELINE DUTTON TRAIN (*b. Boston, Mass., 1824; d. 1906*). Daughter of Enoch Train. Author of *Boys at Chequasset* (1862), *Faith Gartney's Girlhood* (1863), *The Gayworthys* (1865); also of the Real Folks Series and collections of verse. Her books for girls dealt largely with New England, her later stories with domestic life.

WHITNEY, ANNE (*b. Watertown, Mass., 1821; d. Boston, Mass., 1915*), sculptor, poet. Studied anatomy and modelling with William Rimmer and in Rome, Paris and Munich. Established studio in Boston, Mass., 1872. Executed, among other portrait busts and ideal figures, the heroic marble statue of Samuel Adams (commissioned *c.* 1873) in Statuary Hall, U.S. Capitol, Washington, D.C.

WHITNEY, ASA (*b. Townsend, Mass., 1791; d. Philadelphia, Pa., 1874*), inventor, manufacturer. Superintendent, Mohawk & Hudson Railroad, *c.* 1833–39; canal commissioner of New York State, 1839–42. Granted patent for a locomotive steam engine (1840). Removed to Philadelphia, Pa., 1842, and entered partnership with Matthias W. Baldwin; developed sound management system for the firm, also a system of locomotive classification. Resigned, 1846, to work on improvement of cast-iron car wheels (patented, 1847–48). Formed Asa Whitney & Sons, the largest and most successful car-wheel works in America. President, Philadelphia & Reading Railroad, 1860–61.

WHITNEY, ASA (*b. North Groton, Conn., 1797; d. 1872*), dry-goods merchant, railroad promoter. Favored and unsuccessfully promoted (1844–51) an American transcontinental railroad from Lake Michigan via the South Pass of the Rockies to the Pacific Ocean. Author of, among other pamphlets, *A Project for a Railroad to the Pacific* (1849).

WHITNEY, CASPAR (*b. Boston, Mass., 1861; d. New York, N.Y., 1929*), journalist, sports writer. Originated idea of the All-American football team, 1889, whose members he and Walter Camp chose together for some ten years. Served as war correspondent in Cuba for *Harper's Weekly*, 1898. Later editor of *Outing* magazine and others, he was correspondent for the *New York Tribune* in Europe, 1917–19, protesting vigorously and practically against wartime censorship regulations. [*Supp. 1*]

WHITNEY, ELI (*b. Westboro, Mass., 1765; d. New Haven, Conn., 1825*), inventor. Disinclined to study as a boy, he showed a marked proficiency for mechanical work; he made and repaired violins, worked in iron, and at the age of 15 began the manufacture of nails in his father's shop. On making up his mind to acquire a college education (at the age of 18), he taught school to obtain the necessary money and entered Yale in May 1789. Graduating in 1792, he set out for Savannah, Ga., to serve as a tutor while he studied law. Disappointed of the position he had expected, he took up residence on the plantation of Gen. Nathanael Greene's widow in Georgia, began law studies, and showed his appreciation for Mrs. Greene's hospitality by making and repairing all manner of things about the house and the plantation.

During the following winter he learned that many unprofitable areas of land in the South could be made profitable if the green seed cotton which could be raised on them could be cleansed of seeds by some mechanical device. Encouraged by Mrs. Greene, Whitney turned his mind to the problem and within ten days designed a cotton gin and completed an imperfect model. After further experiment, he built by April 1793 a larger, improved machine with which one man could produce fifty pounds of clean cotton a day. Entering into partnership with Phineas Miller, the plantation foreman, to patent and manufacture the new device and also to maintain a monopoly of its use, Whitney obtained his patent, Mar. 14, 1794, but soon found that a monopoly was impossible because of almost universal infringement of his patent by rival machines. Whitney obtained a court decision in his favor in 1807 after a long series of infringement suits; meanwhile Miller had died. On Whitney's application to Congress for a renewal of his patent in 1812, his request was refused. All in all he received practically no return for an invention which let loose tremendous industrial forces in the nation and the world.

Prior to this, on Jan. 14, 1798, he had obtained from the U.S. government a contract to manufacture and deliver 10,000 stand of arms. He proposed to make the guns by a new method, his aim being to make the same parts of different guns (for example, the locks) as much like each other as the successive impressions of a copper-plate engraving. This was perhaps the first suggestion of the system of interchangeable parts which has played so great a part in industrial development and mass production. Raising the necessary capital in New Haven, Conn., he built a factory in present Whitneyville and began design and construction of the machine tools required to carry out his schemes. He worked against great difficulties, having no experienced workmen to aid him and having to make by himself practically every tool required. Completing the contract in some eight years instead of two, he nevertheless accomplished all which he had set out to do. Workmen with little or no experience could operate his machinery and turn out the various parts of a musket with so much precision that they were readily interchangeable. In 1812 he received a second contract from the U.S. government for the manufacture of firearms and also a similar contract from the state of New York. Thereafter, his unique manufactory yielded him a just reward.

WHITNEY, HARRY PAYNE (*b. New York, N.Y., 1872; d. 1930*), financier, sportsman. Son of William C. Whitney (1841–1904), who trained him to be his business successor. Developed silver, lead and copper interests with Daniel Guggenheim, 1902. Director, Guggenheim Exploration Co., Guaranty Trust Co., and other banking, mining and railroad concerns. Organizer and captain of American "Big Four" polo team. His polo tactics were adopted by the British and he became one of the few "ten-goal" players. Maintained distinguished racing stables. Financed Whitney South Sea Expedition, 1921–22.

WHITNEY, JAMES LYMAN (*b. Northampton, Mass., 1835; d. Cambridge, Mass., 1910*), bookseller, librarian. Half-brother of William D. and Josiah D. Whitney. Graduated Yale, 1856. Chief of catalogue department, Boston Public Library, 1874–99; librarian, 1899–1903. His great contribution to library technique was the building up of the card-catalogue system at Boston. Compiler and editor of *Catalogue of the Spanish Library and of the Portuguese Books Bequeathed by George Ticknor to the Boston Public Library* (1879) and of many other special catalogues.

WHITNEY, JOSIAH DWIGHT (*b. Northampton, Mass., 1819; d. Lake Sunapee, N.H., 1896*), geologist, chemist. Brother of William D. Whitney; half-brother of James L. Whitney. Graduated Yale, 1839. Studied chemistry and mineralogy under Benjamin Silliman and Robert Hare; also in Paris, Berlin, and Giessen. Engaged by C. T. Jackson (1847) to aid in survey of mineral lands of northern Michigan, he completed the survey in 1849 and issued its report, 1850–51. In practice as a mining consultant, 1850–55, he served as chemist and mineralogist, 1855–58, on the geological survey of Iowa; he also investigated lead regions of Wisconsin. As state geologist of California, 1860–74, he undertook an elaborate survey, introducing topographical mapping by triangulation and issuing a number of notable reports, some of which were published at his own expense. Founder of a school of mines at Harvard, 1868, he was Sturgis-Hooper Professor at Harvard from 1875 until his death. He was author, among other writings, of *Metallic Wealth of the United States* (1854), *Auriferous Gravels of the Sierra Nevada of California* (1880) and *Climatic Changes of Later Geological Times* (1882). His work stimulated later scientific study of ore deposits.

WHITNEY, MARY WATSON (*b. Waltham, Mass., 1847; d. 1921*), astronomer, educator. Graduated Vassar, A.B., 1868, A.M., 1872. Succeeded Maria Mitchell as director of Vassar Observatory, 1888–1910, and as professor of astronomy.

WHITNEY, MYRON WILLIAM (*b. Ashby, Mass., 1836; d. Sandwich, Mass., 1910*), oratorio and operatic basso. Considered by critics an unequaled artist in oratorio, Whitney was active as a concert, church and stage singer, 1852–90.

WHITNEY, WILLIAM COLLINS (*b. Conway, Mass., 1841; d. 1904*), financier, sportsman. Son-in-law of Henry B. Payne; father of Harry P. Whitney. Graduated Yale, 1863; attended Harvard Law School, 1863–64; admitted to the bar, 1865. A success in New York law and politics, he gained the confidence of Samuel J. Tilden, helped in action against the "Tweed Ring," and (1875–82) effectively reorganized the New York City corporation counsel's office. Identified with New York City utilities, notably street-railways, and other large corporate activities, he won great wealth and a prominent place in society. As U.S. secretary of the navy, 1885–89, he fought successfully against outmoded concepts of ship design, modernized procedures, and supported aims of the Naval War College. A member of Grover Cleveland's inner circle, he played a significant role in Cleveland's second nomination and election, 1892, and fought Free Silver at the 1896 Democratic convention. *Post* 1899 he devoted himself to horse-racing activities.

WHITNEY, WILLIAM DWIGHT (*b. Northampton, Mass., 1827; d. 1894*), Sanskrit scholar, linguistic scientist. Brother of Josiah D. Whitney; half-brother of James L. Whitney. Graduated Williams, 1845. Beginning his career as a natural scientist, he turned to the study of linguistics after a chance reading of Franz Bopp's Sanskrit grammar. After a year's study of Sanskrit at Yale under Edward E. Salisbury (1849), Whitney went to Germany where he continued his studies at Berlin and Tübingen. Elected professor of Sanskrit at Yale, 1854, he remained active there in teaching and research until his death. He devoted himself principally to Sanskrit, linguistic science, modern languages, and lexicography, and his bibliogra-

phy numbers some 360 titles. Editor-author of a number of texts and translations in his special field, he did his most important work in his *Sanskrit Grammar* (Leipzig, 1879, later revised and supplemented). His method was essentially descriptive and statistical and marks a transition in the history of Sanskrit study; he subordinated to the technique of modern linguistic science the classifications, rules, and terms of the ancient and medieval Hindu grammarians. His work in linguistics antedated many recent developments, and his books still may serve as a valuable introduction to the science. He had considerable influence upon the modern trend, especially in his recognition of the distinction of linguistic science from philology and in his conception of linguistics as a historical, and not a physical or natural, science. When the Sheffield Scientific School was established, he organized its modern language department and became its head; out of this subsidiary activity grew a long list of publications in modern languages, including a series of annotated German texts, a reader and a grammar and a dictionary; also, French and English grammars which show the same clarity and insight that mark his Sanskrit work. The last decade of his life was given largely to *The Century Dictionary* (1889–91) of which he was editor-in-chief. An outstanding interest in Whitney's life was the American Oriental Society which he served for many years as librarian, editor of publications and secretary; he was president of the Society, 1884–90. Outstanding among his works (in addition to those already mentioned) are *Language and the Study of Language* (1867), *The Life and Growth of Language* (1875), and *Oriental and Linguistic Studies* (1873, 1874).

WHITON, JAMES MORRIS (*b. Boston, Mass., 1833; d. 1920*), Congregational clergyman, educator, author. A popular preacher and able controversialist; held pastorates at Lynn, Mass., 1865–75, and in Newark, N.J., and New York City.

WHITSITT, WILLIAM HETH (*b. near Nashville, Tenn., 1841; d. Richmond, Va., 1911*), Baptist minister, church historian. Accepted chair of ecclesiastical history, Southern Baptist Theological Seminary, Greenville, S.C., 1872; served as president, 1895–99. Precipitated "the Whitsitt controversy" over succession of Baptist churches by article in *Johnson's Universal Encyclopaedia* (1896). Professor of philosophy, Richmond College, Richmond, Va., 1900–10.

WHITTELSEY, ABIGAIL GOODRICH (*b. Ridgefield, Conn., 1788; d. Colchester, Conn., 1858*), editor, author. Sister of Charles A. and Samuel G. Goodrich. Editor and contributor, *Mother's Magazine*, 1833–47 and 1848–49.

WHITTEMORE, AMOS (*b. Cambridge, Mass., 1759; d. West Cambridge, Mass., 1828*), inventor, gunsmith. Patented (1797) a machine for making cotton and wool cards which reduced card manufacture to a series of rapid, entirely automatic operations.

WHITTEMORE, THOMAS (*b. Boston, Mass., 1800; d. Cambridge, Mass., 1861*), Universalist clergyman, editor, railroad president, financier, Massachusetts legislator. Editor-owner, *Trumpet and Universalist Magazine*, 1828–61.

WHITTIER, JOHN GREENLEAF (*b. Haverhill, Mass., 1807; d. Hampton Falls, N.H., 1892*), poet, Abolitionist. Raised on a farm, the son of Quaker parents, Whittier improved a limited formal education by wide reading. His earliest attempts at verse were inspired by the work of Robert Burns. Publication of "The Exile's Departure" in the Newburyport *Free Press*, June 1826, brought Whittier to the attention of editor William Lloyd Garrison, who was to be a leading influence in the poet's life. Further publication of poems in the *Free Press* and in the *Haverhill Gazette* made Whittier's work widely known in his locality. After a brief time at Haverhill Academy, he became editor with Garrison's help of *The American Manufacturer* (Boston), serving from January 1829 through the summer of that year. This was the first of many editorial positions which he was to hold. Succeeding George D. Prentice as editor of the *New England Weekly Review*, June 1830, Whittier held that post until 1832; meanwhile in February 1831 he published his first book, *Legends of New England in Prose and Verse*. Converted to abolitionism in the spring of 1833, he devoted himself for the next thirty years to the anti-slavery cause, as a poet and as an active agent, lobbyist and editor. From March 1838 to February 1840 he edited the *Pennsylvania Freeman*. Sympathetic with the political-action party of the Abolitionists to which Garrison was opposed, Whittier became a member of the American and Foreign Anti-Slavery Society, and in the fall of 1842 ran for Congress on the Liberty Party ticket. After working as an editor of several minor journals, he became corresponding editor of the *National Era* of Washington, D.C., January 1847, and to it he contributed most of his poems and articles for the next 13 years. He remained active in politics, attacking the administration bitterly for the Mexican War, and in the famous poem "Ichabod" (*National Era*, May 2, 1850) he poured out scorn on Daniel Webster for the "Seventh of March" speech. He encouraged and furthered the career of Charles Sumner and was one of the first to suggest formation of the Republican party.

Whittier's life was uneventful *post* 1861 although his fame as a poet increased by reason of his many contributions to the *Atlantic Monthly* (in the founding of which he had a part) and to the *Independent*. However, he reached the summit of his poetic career in the decade of the 1860's during which appeared *Home Ballads* (1860); *In War Time and Other Poems* (1864, containing "Barbara Frietchie"); *Snow-Bound* (1866); *The Tent on the Beach* (1867); and *Among the Hills* (1869). In the summer of 1876 he settled in Danvers, Mass., which he made his place of abode almost to the time of his death, with occasional visits to his previous residence at Amesbury which continued to be his legal residence. He was the recipient of numerous honors and was surrounded by friends. Among the more important poetical volumes of his later years were *Miriam and Other Poems* (1871), *The Vision of Echard* (1878); and *At Sundown* (1890).

Whittier sacrificed much and endured much abuse in his devotion to the anti-slavery cause. He was in general tolerant and keenly sympathetic with all persecuted persons. He had a fine sense of humor and was an adept at telling amusing stories. Radical though he might be in his views of slavery, he was extremely conservative on all industrial and economic questions, and as a means of settling economic difficulties recommended simple obedience to the golden rule and saving of money. Greatly admired as a poet in his own day and ranked with Longfellow and Bryant, he is today regarded as possessing mastery only in the poems inspired by the contest over slavery. These appeared in many of the volumes of poems which he issued *post* 1831 and were published collectively under the title *Voices of Freedom* in 1846. The best of his early work will be found in *Lays of My Home and Other Poems* (1843), *Songs of Labor* (1850), *The Chapel of the Hermits* (1853), and *The Panorama and Other Poems* (1856). Many of his religious poems have found a permanent place in the hymnals of various denominations. In spite of the modern exaltation of the merits of his anti-slavery poems, *Snow-Bound* is still usually considered his masterpiece.

WHITTINGHAM, WILLIAM ROLLINSON (*b. New York, N.Y., 1805; d. Orange, N.J., 1879*), Episcopal clergyman. Graduated General Theological Seminary, New York City, 1824. Ordained to priesthood, 1829. Rector of St. Luke's Church, New York, 1831–36; professor of ecclesiastical history, General Theological Seminary, 1836–40. Consecrated bishop of Maryland, 1840, he upheld Union sentiments, 1857–65. A statesman-like and scholarly ecclesiastic, he was highly valued by his contemporaries in the House of Bishops.

WHITTREDGE, WORTHINGTON (*b. Springfield, O, 1820; d. Summit, N.J., 1910*), painter. Studied in Europe, 1849–59, principally in Düsseldorf. A landscapist of the Hudson River School, Whittredge painted pictures which, despite their over-emphasis on detail, possess their own individuality and charm. He was Emanuel Leutze's model for Washington in "Washington Crossing the Delaware."

WHITWORTH, GEORGE FREDERIC (*b. Boston, England, 1816; d. 1907*), Presbyterian clergyman, educator. Graduated New Albany Theological Seminary (later McCormick Theological Seminary), 1847. Helped found churches in Portland, Oreg., 1853, and in Olympia, Wash., 1854. Successful as a businessman and civic leader in Seattle, Wash. President of University of Washington, Seattle, 1866–67 and 1875–76. Whitworth College, Spokane, Wash., was named in his honor.

WHYTE, WILLIAM PINKNEY (*b. Maryland, 1824; d. Baltimore, Md., 1908*), lawyer, Maryland legislator. Grandson of William Pinkney. Admitted to the Maryland bar, 1846. Long active in Democratic politics, an opponent of the Know-Nothings and later a Confederate sympathizer, Whyte served as governor of Maryland, 1872–74. He was U.S. senator, Democrat, from Maryland, 1868–69, 1875–81 and 1906. He also served as mayor of Baltimore, 1881–83; attorney-general of Maryland, 1887–91; and city solicitor of Baltimore, 1900–03.

WICKERSHAM, GEORGE WOODWARD (*b. Pittsburgh, Pa., 1858; d. New York, N.Y., 1936*), lawyer, public servant. After studying civil engineering and serving briefly as secretary to Matthew S. Quay, he graduated from the law school of the University of Pennsylvania and was admitted to the bar, 1880. In 1883 he joined the firm of Strong and Cadwalader in New York City and became a partner, 1887; he was considered one of the leading corporation experts of the New York State bar. Active in the local Republican party, he was chosen U.S. attorney-general, 1909, and over the next four years initiated more actions against the nation's leading corporations under the Sherman Anti-Trust Law than the preceding administration had begun in seven years. So vigorously did he drive against the trusts that many representatives of industrial and financial circles demanded his resignation. He was one of the closest advisers of President William H. Taft during this period, drew up the original draft of the Mann-Elkins Act and helped with the corporation tax provision in the Payne-Aldrich Tariff Act. Continuing his interest in public affairs in New York State *post* 1913, he was an internationalist and supported disarmament moves and the World Court. Appointed chairman of the so-called Wickersham Committee, 1929, he undertook an extensive inquiry into the entire federal system of jurisprudence and reported the committee's findings in some 14 separate reports. Unfortunately, the major work of the committee was overlooked because of the confusion of its report on the enforcement of the Prohibition law, or Eighteenth Amendment. [*Supp.* 2]

WICKERSHAM, JAMES PYLE (*b. Chester Co., Pa., 1825; d. Lancaster, Pa., 1891*), educator, Union soldier. Appointed principal, Lancaster County Normal School, Millersville, Pa., 1856; under his administration it became the first state normal school in Pennsylvania, 1859. Appointed state superintendent of common schools, 1866, he held that post until 1881; by 1874 he had succeeded in having a school established in every Pennsylvania district. Editor and part owner, *Pennsylvania School Journal*, 1870–81.

WICKES, LAMBERT (*b. Kent Co., Md., 1735?; d. at sea, off the Banks of Newfoundland, 1777*), Revolutionary naval officer. In autumn 1774 he distinguished himself by refusing to ship tea from London in his vessel *Neptune*. Given command of the Continental armed ship *Reprisal*, April 1776, he was victorious in several actions with the British and captured valuable prizes. In October 1776 he carried Benjamin Franklin to France. The *Reprisal* was the first American ship of war and Wickes was the first American naval officer to appear in European waters after the Declaration of Independence.

WICKES, STEPHEN (*b. Jamaica, L.I., N.Y., 1813; d. Orange, N.J., 1889*), physician, historical writer. M.D., University of Pennsylvania, 1834. Practiced in Troy, N.Y., and Orange, N.J. Author, among other works, of *History of Medicine in New Jersey, and of its Medical Men, from the Settlement of the Province to A.D. 1880* (1879). Edited *Transactions of the Medical Society of New Jersey*, 1861–82.

WICKHAM, JOHN (*b. Southold, L.I., N.Y., 1763; d. 1839*), lawyer. Began practice in Williamsburg, Va.; removed to Richmond, 1790, where he became celebrated as a pleader. In the case of *Ware vs. Hylton* (1793), Wickham's contention that by the U.S. Constitution all treaties were a part of the law of the land and all state legislation inconsistent therewith was invalid was sustained on appeal by the Supreme Court (3 *Dallas*, 199). In 1809 he represented plaintiff in *Hunter vs. Fairfax's Devisee* (1 *Munford*, 218; 7 *Cranch*, 603) which established doctrine that the Supreme Court has appellate jurisdiction over decisions of state courts. Wickham's argument, as counsel for the defense, that Aaron Burr had committed no overt act of treason was accepted by Chief Justice Marshall who so instructed the jury during Burr's celebrated trial (1807).

WICKLIFFE, CHARLES ANDERSON (*b. near Springfield, Ky., 1788; d. near Ilchester, Md., 1869*), lawyer, Kentucky legislator. Father of Robert C. Wickliffe; cousin of Ben Hardin. Congressman, Democrat, from Kentucky, 1823–33; became chairman, committee on public lands, 1829. Whig lieutenant-governor of Kentucky, 1836–39; governor, 1839–40. Postmaster-general of the United States, 1841–45. Rejoining the Democrats on the issue of Texas annexation, he later opposed the secession movement and served in Congress, 1861–63, as a Union Whig.

WICKLIFFE, ROBERT CHARLES (*b. Bardstown, Ky., 1819; d. 1895*), lawyer, planter, Louisiana legislator. Son of Charles A. Wickliffe. Removed to Louisiana, 1846. Democratic governor of Louisiana, 1856–60.

WICKSON, EDWARD JAMES (*b. Rochester, N.Y., 1848; d. Berkeley, Calif., 1923*), horticulturist. Graduated Hamilton, 1869. Removing to California, 1875, to join staff of *Pacific Rural Press*, he encouraged founding or reorganizing of state agricultural organizations and taught a variety of subjects in the agricultural school of the University of California. In 1905 he was appointed dean of the school and professor of horticulture, and became director of the university agricultural experiment station, 1907. Author, among other books, of *The California Fruits and How to Grow Them* (1889) and *The California Vegetables in Garden and Field* (1897). Editor-in-chief, *Pacific Rural Press*, 1898–1923.

WIDENER, HARRY ELKINS (*b. Philadelphia, Pa., 1885; d. at sea, aboard* Titanic, *1912*), rare book collector. Grandson of P. A. B. Widener and William L. Elkins. Graduated Harvard, 1907.

WIDENER, PETER ARRELL BROWN (*b. Philadelphia, Pa., 1834; d. 1915*), financier, philanthropist. After early success as a butcher and Union Army meat supplier during the Civil War, he served as Philadelphia city treasurer (1873–74) in which post he made a large amount of money in fees. *Post* 1875 he was associated with W. L. Elkins and others in street-railway ownership and operation in Philadelphia, Pittsburgh, Baltimore and Chicago; their properties totaled a greater mileage than any similar syndicate. Widener helped in consolidation of the Philadelphia Rapid Transit Co. and was an organizer of the U. S. Steel Corp. and the American Tobacco Co. He had large investments in many corporations, including the Pennsylvania Railroad Co. Widener's collections of art and Chinese porcelains were considered among the finest in America. He was a generous benefactor to Philadelphia institutions.

WIDFORSS, GUNNAR MAURITZ (*b. Stockholm, Sweden, 1879; d. Grand Canyon, Ariz., 1934*), artist. Studied at Institute of Technology, Stockholm, Sweden, 1896–1900. Settled in the United States, 1921. Called the "painter of the National Parks," he excelled in studies of the Grand Canyon, recording its moods in water color and oil. Widforss reproduced nature with remarkable feeling and accuracy.

WIDNEY, JOSEPH POMEROY (*b. Miami Co., O., 1841; d. Los Angeles, Calif., 1938*), physician, civic leader. M.D., Toland Medical College, San Francisco, Calif., 1866. In practice in Los Angeles *post c.* 1869, he was a principal factor in the development of the Los Angeles area. He helped found the institution chartered in 1880 as the University of Southern California, serving as dean of the medical school, and as president of the university itself, 1892–95. [*Supp.* 2]

WIECHMANN, FERDINAND GERHARD (*b. Brooklyn, N.Y., 1858; d. 1919*), scientist, author. Chief chemist, Havemeyer and Elder Sugar Refining Co., Brooklyn, N.Y., 1887–1909. Author, among other books, of *Sugar Analysis* (1890).

WIENER, LEO (*b. Białystok, Poland, 1862; d. Belmont, Mass., 1939*), Slavic scholar, philologist, cultural historian. A teacher of languages after his emigration to the United States, 1882, he was appointed to the staff of Harvard University through the influence of Francis J. Child and Archibald C. Coolidge, becoming instructor in Slavic languages and literature, 1896. He remained at Harvard, rising through the academic grades and becoming professor emeritus, 1930. In the latter part of his career he abandoned research in the Slavic field and gave much time to investigations of Arabic, Germanic, African, and American Indian culture. He was author, among other works, of *Anthology of Russian Literature* (1902–03) and *History of Yiddish Literature in the Nineteenth Century* (1899). [*Supp.* 2]

WIGFALL, LOUIS TREZEVANT (*b. near Edgefield, S.C., 1816; d. Galveston, Texas, 1874*), lawyer, Texas legislator, Confederate brigadier-general. Favored secession of South Carolina, 1844. Settled in Texas, 1848. During crisis of 1849–50, he again declared for separation of South from North. Elected to Texas senate, 1857, he led "Southern-rights" Democrats. As U.S. senator from Texas, 1860–61, he urged secession, justifying it on the compact theory; he was one of those Southerners whose abstention from voting brought about defeat of the Crittenden Compromise. Remaining in the Senate until March 1861, he aided the Confederacy by confidential advice. Commanded "Texas Brigade" in Virginia, resigning February 1862 to enter Confederate States Senate. Bitterly opposed President Jefferson Davis's conduct of the war; led movement making R. E. Lee general-in-chief of Confederate armies. After the war he escaped from Galveston, Texas, to England, returning to the United States, 1872.

WIGGER, WINAND MICHAEL (*b. New York, N.Y., 1841; d. 1901*), Roman Catholic clergyman. Studied in Genoa and Rome; ordained, 1865; D.D., University of the Sapienza, Rome, 1869. After holding pastorates in Madison, Summit and Orange, N.J., he was consecrated third bishop of Newark, N.J., 1881. Notable for work on behalf of German and Italian immigrants.

WIGGIN, JAMES HENRY (*b. Boston, Mass., 1836; d. 1900*), Unitarian clergyman, editor. Graduated Meadville Theological School, 1861; ordained, 1862. Held pastorates in Massachusetts, 1861–75. An agnostic by 1881, he devoted himself thenceforth to literary pursuits. The great popularity of Mary Baker Eddy's *Science and Health* dated from his revision (16th edition), done at her request, 1885. He was associated with Mrs. Eddy for some years thereafter.

WIGGIN, KATE DOUGLAS (*b. Philadelphia, Pa., 1856; d. Harrow, England, 1923*), author, pioneer kindergarten worker. Trained by Emma J. C. Marwedel, she was selected in 1878 to organize in San Francisco the Silver Street Kindergarten, first free kindergarten west of the Rocky Mountains. She established the California Kindergarten Training School, 1880, with Nora A. Smith, her sister and collaborator in teaching and kindergarten writings. Author, among many other books, of *The Birds' Christmas Carol* (1887), typical of her work in its brevity, wide range of characterization, broad humor, and Dickensian pathos; *Polly Oliver's Problem* (1893); and *Rebecca of Sunnybrook Farm* (1903).

WIGGINS, CARLETON (*b. Turner, N.Y., 1848; d. Old Lyme, Conn., 1932*), landscape and animal painter. Studied at National Academy of Design (1870) and under George Inness. Elected an Academician, 1906.

WIGGLESWORTH, EDWARD (*b. Malden, Mass., c. 1693; d. 1765*), educator, theologian. Son of Michael Wigglesworth. Graduated Harvard, 1710; appointed first Hollis Professor of Divinity at Harvard, 1722. D.D., University of Edinburgh, 1730. A leader among the anti-evangelical clergy, Wigglesworth's gradual compromise between Arminian and Calvinistic extremes heralded later Unitarianism. Author, among other works, of *A Letter to the Reverend Mr. George Whitefield* (1745) and *The Doctrine of Reprobation Briefly Considered* (1763).

WIGGLESWORTH, EDWARD (*b. Cambridge, Mass., 1732; d. 1794*), educator, theologian. Son of Edward Wigglesworth (*c. 1693–1765*); grandson of Michael Wigglesworth. Graduated Harvard, 1749. Succeeded his father as Hollis Professor of Divinity at Harvard, 1765. Author, among other works, of *Calculations on American Population* (1775).

WIGGLESWORTH, EDWARD (*b. Boston, Mass., 1840; d. 1896*), dermatologist. Graduated Harvard, 1861; M.D., Harvard Medical School, 1865; studied in Europe, 1865–70. Practicing in Boston, Mass., he inaugurated and maintained Boston Dispensary for Skin Diseases, 1872–77. Headed department of diseases of the skin, Boston City Hospital; taught at Harvard Medical School.

WIGGLESWORTH, MICHAEL (*b. probably Yorkshire, England, 1631; d. 1705*), Congregational clergyman, author. Father of Edward Wigglesworth (*c. 1693–1765*). Came to America as a boy. Graduated B.A., Harvard, 1651; served as fellow and tutor at Harvard, 1652–54, and was a fellow *post* 1697. Minister at Malden, Mass., *post c.* 1655, he also practiced medicine. He was author, among other works, of *The Day of Doom* (1662), a long edificatory poem in ballad meter. Its picture of the Judgment Day has occasional dramatic flashes and possesses a real if undeveloped poetic power. The work has been criticized for the alleged inhumanity of its theological doctrines; however, *The Day of Doom* is merely a dramatized version of tenets commonly held at the time.

WIGHT, FREDERICK COIT (*b. New London, Conn., 1859; d. 1933*), musician, composer of marches.

WIGHT, PETER BONNETT (*b. New York, N.Y., 1838; d. Pasadena, Calif., 1925*), architect. Graduated present College of the City of New York, 1855. Began practice in Chicago, Ill. Won 1862 competition for National Academy of Design building, Fourth Ave. and 23rd St., New York City, notable for Italian Gothic facades. Subsequently he designed the Brooklyn Mercantile Library building and was commissioned to design the Yale School of Fine Arts. Associated with Russell Sturgis, 1863–68. *Post* 1872 his Chicago firm of Drake & Wight (formerly Carter, Drake and Wight) engaged in commercial and domestic work and became a training ground for young architects. Wight devoted himself to development of terra-cotta structural tile, 1881–91. He was responsible for the 1897 Illinois law requiring examination and licensing of architects.

WIGNELL, THOMAS (*b. England, c. 1753; d. Philadelphia, Pa., 1803*), comedian, theatrical manager. Came to America, 1774, to join the American Company managed by his cousin Lewis Hallam; removed with the company immediately to Jamaica, B.W.I. First appeared in the United States, November 1785, with the American Company at New York. The best comedian seen in America up to that time, he soon became a favorite and was noted for his intelligence and taste. One of his most popular characters was Joseph Surface in Sheridan's *The School for Scandal*. In 1791 he became partner of Alexander Reinagle and opened the Chestnut Street Theatre, Philadelphia, 1794. In 1796 he brought Ann B. Merry and Thomas A. Cooper from England to join the company. The succeeding Philadelphia seasons were the most brilliant of their time. He opened the first theatre in Washington, D.C., 1800.

WIKOFF, HENRY (*b. probably Philadelphia, Pa., c. 1813; d. Brighton, England, 1884*), author, adventurer. Made the grand tour of Europe, 1834–40; was a transatlantic commuter, 1840–50. It was said that no American of the period knew so many European notables or more important unwritten political history. Served in various diplomatic capacities; was Fanny Elssler's manager, 1840; spent 15 months in jail at Genoa, Italy, for abducting an heiress *c.* 1852–53. Author, among other writings, of *Napoleon Louis Bonaparte, First President of France* (1849), *My Courtship and Its Consequences* (1855) and *The Reminiscences of an Idler* (1880).

WILBUR, CRESSY LIVINGSTON (*b. Hillsdale, Mich., 1865; d. Utica, N.Y., 1928*), vital statistician. Ph.B., Hillsdale College, 1886, Ph.M., 1889. Appointed chief of Division of Vital Statistics, Michigan State Department of Health, 1893. Chief statistician for vital statistics, U.S. Census Bureau, 1906–14. In charge of Division of Vital Statistics, New York State Department of Health, 1914–16. Wilbur's outstanding contribution was the fostering of a model vital statistics law that led to establishment of uniform and effective registration in all states.

WILBUR, HERVEY BACKUS (*b. Wendell, Mass., 1820; d. Syracuse, N.Y., 1883*), pioneer educator of the feeble-minded, physician. Graduated Berkshire Medical Institution, Pittsfield, Mass., 1843. Established "Institute for Idiots" at Barre, Mass., *c.* 1848, the first school of its kind in the United States; was associated with New York State Asylum for Idiots *post* 1851. His system of training became basis for every similar institution in the United States, Canada, and many European countries; he was also an authority on care of the insane. Author, among other writings, of *Aphasia* (1867) and *Report on the Management of the Insane in Great Britain* (1876).

WILBUR, JOHN (*b. Hopkinton, R.I., 1774; d. Hopkinton, 1856*), Quaker preacher, anti-evangelical leader. Opposed movement led by Joseph J. Gurney; was expelled from Society of Friends, 1843. His followers separated from Meeting in 1845. They were popularly known as "Wilburites" and officially as "New England Yearly Meeting of Friends."

WILBUR, SAMUEL (*b. England, c. 1585; d. Boston, Mass., 1656*), Rhode Island merchant and colonist. Came to America some time before 1633; was one of the buyers of Boston Common from William Blackstone, 1634. A purchaser and settler of the island of Aquidneck (now Rhode Island), he was a signer of the Portsmouth Compact. He later returned to Massachusetts.

WILCOX, CADMUS MARCELLUS (*b. Wayne Co., N.C., 1824; d. Washington, D.C., 1890*), Confederate major-general. Graduated West Point, 1846. Distinguished himself in Mexican War, notably at Chapultepec. Accepted colonelcy, 9th Alabama Infantry, Confederate States Army, 1861. With Gen. R. E. Lee's army in nearly every great battle, Wilcox was one of the best subordinate commanders of the South. Published *Rifles and Rifle Practice* (1859), first American textbook on the subject.

WILCOX, DELOS FRANKLIN (*b. near Ida, Mich., 1873; d. 1928*), franchise and public utility expert. Ph.D., Columbia, 1896. Chief of bureau of franchises, public service commission, New York City, 1907–13; deputy commissioner of department of water supply, gas and electricity, New York City, 1913–17; thereafter a consultant on utility problems. Author, among other works, of *Municipal Franchises* (1910–11), *Analysis of the Electric Railway Problem* (1921), *Depreciation in Public Utilities* (1925), and *The Administration of Municipally Owned Utilities* (1931). Revised R. A. Whitten's *Valuation of Public Service Corporations* (1928). Inclined always to the side of the public in controversies.

WILCOX, ELLA WHEELER (*b. Johnstown Center, Wis., 1850; d. Short Beach, Conn., 1919*), writer of inspirational verse. *Poems of Passion* (1883, her first success) was followed by some twenty further volumes mainly in verse. She wrote a daily poem for a newspaper syndicate and contributed frequent essays to *Cosmopolitan* and other magazines. All her later work shows influence of "New Thought." Defending herself against criticism of sentimentality, she maintained that her poems "comforted" millions.

WILCOX, REYNOLD WEBB (*b. Madison, Conn., 1856; d. 1931*), physician. M.D., Harvard Medical School, 1881. Practiced in New York City. Professor of medicine, New York Post-Graduate Medical School and Hospital, 1886–1908. Edited William Hale-White's *Materia Medica* (1892). Author, among other works, of *Treatment of Disease* (1907). Therapeutic editor of *American Journal of Medical Sciences* for many years.

WILCOX, STEPHEN (*b. Westerly, R.I., 1830; d. Brooklyn, N.Y., 1893*), inventor, engineer. Secured a patent for a safety water-tube boiler with inclined tubes (1856) and a steam generator (1867); formed Babcock, Wilcox & Co., 1867, with George H. Babcock. The Babcock & Wilcox boiler and stationary steam-engine were used in the first central stations (power plants) in America and were of significant value in electric lighting developments.

WILCZYNSKI, ERNEST JULIUS (*b. Hamburg, Germany, 1876; d. Denver, Colo., 1932*), mathematician, educator. Emigrated to America as a child; raised in Chicago, Ill. Ph.D., University of Berlin, 1897. Taught at universities of California and Illinois; professor of mathematics, University of Chicago, 1914–26. Eminent as a projective differential geometer, a field of geometry he largely created.

WILDE, GEORGE FRANCIS FAXON (*b. Braintree, Mass., 1845; d. 1911*), naval officer. Graduated U.S. Naval Academy, Newport, R.I., 1864. Commanded new steel cruiser *Dolphin* on world cruise, 1886–89; commanded ram *Katahdin* on North Atlantic patrol, 1898. Commanded cruiser *Boston*, 1898–99, and battleship *Oregon*, 1899–1901, during Philippine insurrection. Commandant of Philadelphia navy yard, February–May 1904; thereafter at Boston navy yard. Retired as rear-admiral, 1905.

WILDE, RICHARD HENRY (*b. Dublin, Ireland, 1789; d. New Orleans, La., 1847*), lawyer, poet. Came to Baltimore, Md., 1797; was raised in Georgia. Became attorney-general of Georgia, 1811. Congressman, Democrat, from Georgia, 1815–17, 1827–35. Traveled extensively in Europe, 1835–40; discovered Giotto's portrait of Dante in the Bargello at Florence, Italy. Removed to New Orleans, La., 1843; was appointed professor of constitutional law, University of Louisiana (present Tulane), 1847. Author of "My life is like the summer rose" (composed *ante* 1815), *Conjectures and Researches Concerning . . . Torquato Tasso* (1842) and *Hesperia: A Poem* (1867).

WILDER, ALEXANDER (*b. Verona, N.Y., 1823; d. 1908*), physician, eccentric philosopher. M.D., Syracuse Medical College, 1850. Removed to New

York City, 1857, where for 13 years he worked on New York *Evening Post*, becoming financial expert and political journalist. President of the Eclectic Medical College, 1867–77; professor of physiology, 1873–77. Professor of psychology, United States Medical College, 1878–83. Author, among other books, of *New Platonism and Alchemy* (1869), *Vaccination a Medical Fallacy* (1875), and *History of Medicine* (1901).

WILDER, HARRIS HAWTHORNE (*b. Bangor, Maine, 1864; d. 1928*), zoologist. B.A., Amherst, 1886; Ph.D., University of Freiburg, 1891. Professor of zoology, Smith College *post* 1892. Made important contributions to knowledge of vertebrate anatomy, friction-ridge patterns of the skin, and descriptive anthropology.

WILDER, JOHN THOMAS (*b. Hunter Village, N.Y., 1830; d. Jacksonville, Fla., 1917*), Union brigadier-general, industrialist. "Wilder's Lightning Brigade" of Indiana and Illinois volunteers acquitted itself with particular brilliance at Chickamauga, 1863. Resigning from the army, October 1864, Wilder settled in Chattanooga. A developer of Tennessee's natural resources, he founded (1867) the Roane Iron Works and built at Rockwood one of the first blast furnaces in the South; he was also active in railroad and coal lands development.

WILDER, MARSHALL PINCKNEY (*b. Rindge, N.H., 1798; d. 1886*), agriculturist, merchant, Massachusetts legislator. Removed to Boston, Mass., 1825; was known for many years as its chief citizen. A founder of the Constitutional Union party, 1860. Vice-president, Massachusetts Institute of Technology, 1865–70, of which he was a founder. President, Massachusetts Horticultural Society, 1840–48. Helped found American Pomological Society, 1848, and was president for 38 years. Helped establish (1852) and directed Massachusetts board of agriculture, also the U.S. Agricultural Society. Led in formation of Massachusetts Agricultural College, one of the first in any state. His proposed reformation in nomenclature of American fruits, 1883, was later adopted. He also developed many important flower and fruit varieties.

WILDMAN, MURRAY SHIPLEY (*b. Selma, O., 1868; d. Stanford, Calif., 1930*), banker, economist. Ph.D., University of Chicago, 1904. Taught at University of Missouri and Northwestern. As secretary of the National Citizen's League for the Promotion of a Sound Banking System, 1911–12, he contributed to the establishment of the Federal Reserve System. In 1912 he became head of the department of economics, Leland Stanford Junior University, and was dean of the school of social sciences *post* 1925. Author of *Money Inflation in the United States* (1905).

WILEY, ANDREW JACKSON (*b. New Castle Co., Del., 1862; d. Monrovia, Calif., 1931*), irrigation engineer. Graduated Delaware College, 1882. Associated

with private irrigation projects in Idaho and Montana *post* 1883, he later extended his field of work over most of the West. Consultant to U.S. Bureau of Reclamation *post* 1902, he worked on practically all major government dam projects of recent times, including the Shoshone, Arrowrock, Roosevelt and Boulder dams. He was also consultant for other federal departments on the Coolidge and Madden dams, Canal Zone power plant, Columbia River Basin project and others.

WILEY, CALVIN HENDERSON (*b. Guilford Co., N.C., 1819; d. Winston, N.C., 1887*), educator, North Carolina legislator. Graduated University of North Carolina, 1840. Effective first superintendent, North Carolina common schools, 1853–65. Established (1856) and edited *North Carolina Journal of Education;* organized Educational Association of North Carolina; promoted Normal College, 1852–59. Author, among other works, of *The North-Carolina Reader* (1851), a standard text.

WILEY, DAVID (*b. probably Pennsylvania, date uncertain; d. possibly North Carolina, c. 1813*), Presbyterian clergyman. Graduated College of New Jersey (Princeton), 1788; ordained by presbytery of Carlisle, Pa., 1794. Became principal of Columbian Academy, Georgetown, D.C., 1801. Best remembered as secretary of the Columbian Agricultural Society (organized 1809), and as editor of the *Agricultural Museum* (first number, July 1810), probably the first agricultural journal published in the United States.

WILEY, EPHRAIM EMERSON (*b. Malden, Mass., 1814; d. 1893*), Methodist clergyman, educator. Graduated Wesleyan University, 1837. Professor of ancient languages and literature (1838–52), president (1852–79), and treasurer and financial agent (1886–93) at Emory and Henry College (Va.). President, Martha Washington College (Va.), 1881–86. Leader of the Holston Conference, he adhered to the Methodist Episcopal Church, South, after the schism of 1844.

WILEY, HARVEY WASHINGTON (*b. Kent, Ind., 1844; d. Washington, D.C., 1930*), chemist, author, pure food reformer. M.D., Medical College of Indiana (Indianapolis), 1871; B.S., Harvard, 1873. Professor of chemistry, Purdue University, 1874–83, serving also as state chemist of Indiana. Studied at University of Berlin, 1878. As chief chemist, U.S. Department of Agriculture, 1883–1912, he made a chemical study of sugar and sirup crops and devised new apparatus and procedures for agricultural chemical analyses. His most important work, however, was his campaign against food adulteration and his securing (despite prolonged opposition) of the passage of the Food and Drugs Act, 1906. Thereafter until 1912 he administered the enforcement of the Act with tenacity and success. Professor of agricultural chemistry, George Washington University, 1899–1914. Director of bureau of foods, sanitation and health, *Good Housekeeping*, 1912–30. Successful as a lyceum and

Chautauqua lecturer, he was author, among other books, of *Principles and Practice of Agricultural Analysis* (1894–97), *Foods and Their Adulteration* (1907), *History of a Crime Against the Food Law* (1929), and an autobiography (1930).

WILKES, CHARLES (*b. New York, N.Y., 1798; d. 1877*), naval officer, explorer. Appointed midshipman, 1818; studied under F. R. Hassler. Appointed to head Navy's Depot of Charts and Instruments, Washington, D.C., 1833. From August 1838 until July 1842, he commanded the flagship *Vincennes* and five other vessels on an extended exploring expedition, surveying the Antarctic coast, the islands of the Pacific Ocean and the American northwest coast. *Narrative of the United States Exploring Expedition* (1844) and three of the expedition's scientific reports were his work. In command of *San Jacinto*, he halted the British mail steamer *Trent*, 1861, removing two Confederate agents by force and causing the so-called "Trent Affair." Commanding a special squadron in the West Indies and Bahamas against Confederate commerce destroyers, 1862–63, his actions brought protests of neutrality violations. Further conflicts with the Navy Department led to his court-martial, 1864. He was commissioned rear-admiral, retired, 1866.

WILKES, GEORGE (*b. New York, N.Y., 1817; d. New York, 1885*), journalist. Co-founded *National Police Gazette*, 1845. Removed to California, 1849, as aide to David C. Broderick whose fortune he inherited. Bought *Spirit of the Times*, 1856, renaming it *Porter's Spirit of the Times;* it appeared later as *Wilkes' Spirit of the Times*. Its political articles were influential, and Wilkes reported major Civil War engagements as if they were sporting events. He introduced pari-mutuel betting system to America and promoted famous prize-fights. Author, among other books, of *Project for a National Railroad from the Atlantic to the Pacific Ocean* (1845), *The Great Battle Fought at Manassas* (1861), and *Shakespeare from an American Point of View* (1877).

WILKESON, SAMUEL (*b. Carlisle, Pa., 1781; d. Kingston, Tenn., 1848*), boat-builder, contractor, New York legislator. Removed to Lake Erie, near present Westfield, N.Y., 1809. Settling in Buffalo, N.Y., 1814, he engaged successfully in almost all its early business enterprises and constructed (1820) an artificial harbor at the mouth of Buffalo Creek for western terminus of the Erie Canal. Appointed first judge of common pleas, Erie County, 1821; became mayor of Buffalo, 1836. Assisted emigration of freed Negroes to Liberia.

WILKIE, FRANC BANGS (*b. West Charlton, N.Y., 1832; d. Norwood Park, Ill., 1892*), journalist. Chief correspondent of *New York Times* in Civil War campaigns in the West and Southwest; assistant editor, *Chicago Times*, 1863–81 and 1883–88. Author, among other books, of *Personal Reminiscences of Thirty-five Years of Journalism* (1891).

WILKINS, ROSS (*b. Pittsburgh, Pa., 1799; d. 1872*), lawyer. Nephew of William Wilkins. Territorial judge of Michigan, 1832–37; U.S. judge, eastern district of Michigan, 1837–70.

WILKINS, WILLIAM (*b. Carlisle, Pa., 1779; d. 1865*), lawyer, businessman. Uncle of Ross Wilkins. President, Bank of Pittsburgh, Pa., 1814–19. President judge, 5th judicial district of Pennsylvania, 1820–24; judge, U.S. district court for western Pennsylvania, 1824–31. U.S. senator, Democrat and Anti-Mason, 1831–34; U.S. minister to Russia, 1834–36; U.S. secretary of war, 1844–45. A supporter of Andrew Jackson's policies and an expansionist.

WILKINSON, DAVID (*b. Smithfield, R.I., 1771; d. Caledonia Springs, Ontario, Canada, 1852*), inventor, manufacturer. Patented machine for cutting screw threads, incorporating slide rest (1798). It was widely adopted, particularly in U.S. government firearms manufacture. In 1788–89, he constructed iron parts for Samuel Slater's cotton machinery; he later made patterns and cast wheels and racks for locks of the Charlestown, Mass., canal. Co-founded (*c.* 1800) David Wilkinson & Co., iron and textile machinery manufactory, at Pawtucket, R.I. Perfected, among other machines, a mill to bore cannon by water power.

WILKINSON, JAMES (*b. Calvert Co., Md., 1757; d. Mexico City, Mexico, 1825*), soldier. Brother-in-law of Clement Biddle. Commissioned a captain in the Revolutionary Army, 1776, he served at the siege of Boston, joined Benedict Arnold at Montreal and accompanied Arnold during the retreat to Albany; in December, he was appointed aide-de-camp to Gen. Horatio Gates. After serving at Trenton and Princeton and a promotion to lieutenant-colonel, he rejoined Gates and was appointed deputy adjutant-general for the northern department, May 1777. Although he dallied on his way to report the victory at Saratoga to Congress, he was given a brevet of brigadier-general and in January 1778 became secretary of the Board of War. A gifted intriguer, he shared in the Conway Cabal against George Washington and was forced to resign his posts. Appointed almost immediately clothier-general to the army, he rendered defective accounts and was obliged to give up the assignment in March 1781. He then took up farming in Bucks Co., Pa., and in 1783 was elected to the state Assembly.

Engaging in trade to the westward in 1784, he supplanted George Rogers Clark as a leader in the rapidly growing Kentucky region. The success of two memorials which he wrote advocating immediate separation from Virginia (August 1785) gave him the idea of turning prevalent discontent in the area to his own financial gain. Making approaches through the Spanish authorities in upper Louisiana, he went on a trading voyage to New Orleans in 1787 where he won the favor of Gov. Esteban Miró and received an exclusive trading monopoly. He received this in part because he had persuaded the Spaniards that he was working toward disunion in the West. Active in the Kentucky convention of November 1788 as a moderate, he managed to convince Miró that he had achieved much for Spain. On a second journey to New Orleans in the summer of 1789 he composed and presented to the governor a second memorial or report on disunion sentiment and added to it a list of prominent Westerners to whom, he suggested, the Spanish government might profitably grant pensions. After receiving a pension himself, together with a so-called loan, he was temporarily upset by a decree of the Spanish government which opened up the river trade on the Mississippi and so rendered his monopoly valueless. Meanwhile he had also endeavored to worm his way into the confidence of the Yazoo land speculators, only to betray them to the Spaniards. In financial straits because of Kentucky land speculations, he returned to the army, leaving his business affairs to be settled by Harry Innes.

After leading a force of volunteers against the Indians north of the Ohio in March 1791, Wilkinson was commissioned lieutenant-colonel in the regular army and in March 1792 was made brigadier-general under Gen. Anthony Wayne. A disloyal subordinate to Wayne whom he attempted to discredit, he continued his tenuous connection with the Spaniards and revealed to Baron Carondelet the filibustering activities of George Rogers Clark. In 1796 he took over Detroit from the British but soon departed for Philadelphia to intensify his lobbying against Wayne. Becoming the ranking officer of the army after Wayne's unexpected death, he returned to Detroit in 1797 where he was extremely unpopular.

Transferred to command on the Southern frontier in 1798, he was criticized for his friendship with the Spaniards and for personal land deals and speculations in army contracts. He also schemed to become governor of Mississippi Territory. Following the (Democrat) Republican victory of 1800, Aaron Burr helped him keep his place in the army, and Jefferson commissioned him to treat with the various Southern Indian tribes, a task that kept him traveling a year-and-a-half. In 1803, after sharing with William C. C. Claiborne the honor of taking possession of the Louisiana Purchase, he invested a great part of a new bribe which he had received from the Spanish boundary commissioner in sugar, and then sailed for New York City. He then began his spectacular relations with Aaron Burr in the so-called Burr Conspiracy. He conferred frequently with Burr in Washington, D.C., during the winter of 1804–05, and again in the following June at the mouth of the Ohio, whence Wilkinson furnished Burr with conveyance to New Orleans and letters of introduction. Public opinion at this time associated the two in a possible invasion of Mexico.

In the spring of 1805, Wilkinson assumed the governorship of Louisiana Territory with headquarters at St. Louis. He was engaged with R. A. Chouteau in the fur trade and at this time dispatched the famous expedition under Zebulon M. Pike to open up a feasible military route to New Mexico. This activity was generally believed to have a connection with the mysterious movements of Burr. Soon as unpopular in St. Louis as he had been at Detroit, he was ordered again to the Southern frontier in May 1806 and ultimately removed from the governorship. Aroused by the threat to himself in Joseph Street's current exposures concerning Burr's purposes, Wilkinson, from his headquarters at Natchitoches, covered himself by warning President Jefferson that a plot was on foot to disrupt the Union and to invade Mexico. He suggested that he should meet this peril by transferring troops to New Orleans. After making these dispositions, he sent a messenger to inform the viceroy of Mexico of the peril of armed invasion which threatened the Spanish dominions and asked for a sum of money for his efforts to avert it. He declared martial law at New Orleans, embargoed vessels, and arrested and imprisoned without regard to law all whom he chose to regard as agents of Burr. Unaware of the hostile reception which Wilkinson had planned, Burr with some sixty men arrived in Mississippi Territory where he was arrested.

When Burr was put on trial for treason in Richmond, Va., Wilkinson assumed the role of chief witness against him, but narrowly escaped indictment by the grand jury. Suspected by everyone, with the possible exception of Thomas Jefferson, he was deserted by his friends and business associates, caricatured, denounced and publicly insulted. He was brought before a court of inquiry which acquitted him after six months of deliberation. President Jefferson now ordered him to New Orleans and empowered him to confer on the way with the Spanish officials at Havana and Pensacola regarding a proposed alliance. Failing in this pioneer attempt at Pan Americanism, he was once again investigated and in July 1811 was court-martialed by order of President James Madison. The "not guilty" verdict of this court (December 1811) was so worded that the president approved it with regret.

Restored to command at New Orleans, Wilkinson occupied Mobile early in 1813 and later that year was commissioned major-general and ordered to the Canadian frontier. There he made a fiasco of the campaign against Montreal. Relieved from regular duty and ordered to Washington, he provoked a quarrel with John Armstrong (1758–1843) which led to yet another inquiry and acquittal, but he was not reinstated in the service. For some years thereafter he lived on a plantation below New Orleans, but Mexico once more claimed his attention in 1821 and he went there in pursuit of a Texas land grant. In time he obtained an option on lands in Texas, but before he could fulfill the conditions of the grant he died. His *Memoirs of My Own Times,* three confused volumes of documents which are as significant for what they omit as for what they contain, were published in 1816.

WILKINSON, JEMIMA (*b. Cumberland, R.I., 1752; d. 1819*), religious leader. Sister of Jeremiah Wilkinson. Influenced by George Whitefield's sermons and by the example of Ann Lee, she announced her conviction (*c.* 1775) that her body was inhabited by a prophetic spirit. Assuming the name of "Public Universal Friend," she preached with great success in her part of Rhode Island and won a number of followers. After considerable opposition and several removes, she founded the colony of "Jerusalem" in Yates Co., N.Y., 1789–90, presiding over it until her death.

WILKINSON, JEREMIAH (*b. Cumberland, R.I., 1741; d. Cumberland, 1831*), forge-master, farmer, inventor. Brother of Jemima Wilkinson. Perfected a number of devices to expedite his manufacture of wool-cards; drew wire by horsepower *ante* 1776; made first experiments in nail manufacture from cold iron, *c.* 1776.

WILKINSON, JOHN (*b. Norfolk, Va., 1821; d. Annapolis, Md., 1891*), naval officer. Appointed midshipman, 1837. A Confederate officer *post* April 6, 1861, he was highly successful as commander of the blockade-runners *Giraffe* (later named *Robert E. Lee*), *Chickamauga* and *Chameleon*. He also led an abortive 1863 attempt to release Confederate prisoners confined on Johnson's Island in Lake Erie. Author of *Narrative of a Blockade-Runner* (1877).

WILKINSON, ROBERT SHAW (*b. Charleston, S.C., 1865; d. 1932*), educator. Son of free Negro parents. A. B., Oberlin, 1891. Professor of Greek and Latin, State University, Louisville, Ky., 1891–96. Appointed professor of science at State Agricultural and Mechanical College, Orangeburg, S.C., 1896, he served the college as president *post* 1911 with remarkable success. He raised standards in every particular and emphasized a balanced curriculum of industrial and literary instruction.

WILL, ALLEN SINCLAIR (*b. Antioch, Va., 1868; d. New York, N.Y., 1934*), journalist, educator. On *Baltimore Sun* staff, 1889–1912; city editor, 1905–12. Associate editor and editorial writer, *Baltimore News*, 1912–14; news editor, *Philadelphia Public Ledger*, 1914–16; assistant editor, *New York Times*, 1917–24. Director, department of journalism, Rutgers University, *post* 1926. Author, among other works, of *Life of Cardinal Gibbons, Archbishop of Baltimore* (1922) and *Education for Newspaper Life* (1931).

WILLARD, DE FOREST (*b. Newington, Conn., 1846; d. Lansdowne, Pa., 1910*), physician, pioneer in orthopedic surgery. Studied under Joseph Pancoast and Samuel D. Gross at Jefferson Medical College; graduated in medicine, University of Pennsylvania,

1867. Taught at Pennsylvania *post* 1867; was clinical professor of orthopedic surgery, 1889–1903, and professor thereafter. General surgeon at the Presbyterian Hospital, Philadelphia, and consultant at many others, he was surgeon-in-chief of the Widener Memorial Industrial Training School for Crippled Children which he had helped to plan.

WILLARD, EMMA HART (*b. Berlin, Conn., 1787; d. 1870*), educator. Encouraged by her parents to read widely and to do her own thinking, she attended the district school and Berlin Academy. Becoming a teacher, she was unusually successful as head of the Female Academy, Middlebury, Vt., 1807–09. Opening a school for girls in her own home at Middlebury, 1814, she experimented with plans for improving female education which she had already worked out and proved that such subjects as mathematics and philosophy could be mastered by girls without costing them their health, refinement or charm. Despite the support of N.Y. Gov. DeWitt Clinton and others, she failed in a pioneer campaign (1818) for establishment with state aid of schools in which women would be given the same educational advantages as men; she then removed to New York State and in 1821 founded the Troy Female Seminary with the aid of local citizens. As it grew in reputation and influence, she continued her policy of adding higher subjects to the curriculum, especially mathematics. She retired from active management, 1838. Subsequently she worked with Henry Barnard and others for improvement of the common schools. While active at Troy, she evolved new methods of teaching and published widely used textbooks in geography and history. She was author also of a number of mediocre poems, including "Rocked in the Cradle of the Deep."

WILLARD, FRANCES ELIZABETH CAROLINE (*b. Churchville, N.Y., 1839; d. New York, N.Y., 1898*), teacher, reformer. Raised in pioneer Wisconsin. Graduated Northwestern Female College, Evanston, Ill., 1859. Evanston became her permanent home. Joining the temperance crusade, 1874, she was elected president of the National Woman's Christian Temperance Union, 1879. She enlisted her society in the cause of woman's suffrage, helped organize the Prohibition party (1882), and devoted her life to furthering the cause with tongue and pen. In 1891 she was elected president of the World's Woman's Christian Temperance Union. Temperance, in her opinion, was basically a measure for the protection of home life and therefore an ideal which demanded personal sacrifice.

WILLARD, JAMES FIELD (*b. Philadelphia, Pa., 1876; d. 1935*), historian, medievalist. Graduated University of Pennsylvania, 1898; Ph.D., 1902. Professor and head of the department of history, University of Colorado *post* 1906. He was author of a number of important studies in medieval history and also edited several volumes of important source materials on the history of the American West. [*Supp.* 1]

WILLARD, JOSEPH (*b. Biddeford, Maine, 1738; d. New Bedford, Mass., 1804*), Congregational clergyman, educational leader. Great-grandson of Samuel Willard (1639/40–1707). Graduated Harvard, 1765. Pastor at Beverly, Mass. For many years corresponding secretary and vice-president of the American Academy of Arts and Sciences (of which he was a founder, 1780), he was well known for work in astronomy, mathematics and the classics. President of Harvard, 1781–1804, he repaired ravages of the Revolution, raised entrance requirements, broadened instruction and founded the medical school.

WILLARD, JOSEPH (*b. Cambridge, Mass., 1798; d. 1865*), lawyer, historian. Son of Joseph Willard (1738–1804); brother of Sidney Willard. LL.B., Harvard Law School, 1820. Clerk, court of common pleas, Suffolk County, *post* 1841. Officer of Massachusetts Historical Society, 1833–64. Author, among other works, of *Sketches of the Town of Lancaster* (1826).

WILLARD, JOSEPH EDWARD (*b. Washington, D.C., 1865; d. New York, N.Y., 1924*), diplomat, lawyer, Virginia legislator. Practiced at Richmond, Va., bar. Gained state-wide reputation as soldier in Spanish-American War. Democratic lieutenant-governor of Virginia, 1902–06. Served as U.S. ambassador to Spain, 1913–21.

WILLARD, JOSIAH FLINT (*b. Appleton, Wis., 1869; d. 1907*), writer on vagrancy and criminology, better known under his pen-name "Josiah Flynt." Nephew of Frances E. Willard. Author, among other works of sociological value, of *Tramping with Tramps* (1899); *The Powers That Prey* (1900); and *The World of Graft* (1901). [*Supp.* 1]

WILLARD, MARY HATCH (*b. Jersey City, N.J., 1856; d. New York, N.Y., 1926*), businesswoman, social worker. Established (*c.* 1890) in New York City a successful Home Bureau for supply of food for invalids; later added a trained nurses' registry service. In World War I, led huge emergency movement to supply hospitals on western front with surgical dressings. Associated for many years with State Charities Aid Association of New York.

WILLARD, SAMUEL (*b. Concord, Mass., 1639/40; d. 1707*), Congregational clergyman, controversialist. Son of Simon Willard (1605–1676 o.s.). Graduated Harvard, 1659. Pastor at Groton, Mass., 1664–78; of Old South Church, Boston, Mass., *post* 1678. He was conservative in theology, liberal in practice. Like his friends the Mathers, he was an opponent of the methods used in the witchcraft trials, 1692. Vice-president of Harvard University, 1700–07, he in fact headed the institution. A voluminous writer, he made one of the best psychic investigations in the literature of the

witchcraft delusion (*Massachusetts Historical Society Collections,* 4 ser. VIII, 1868). His *Compleat Body of Divinity* was published in 1726.

WILLARD, SAMUEL (*b. Petersham, Mass., 1775; d. Deerfield, Mass., 1859*), Congregational and Unitarian clergyman, educator, hymn-writer. Brother of Solomon Willard. Graduated Harvard, 1803. Pastor at Deerfield, Mass., 1807–29. The controversy over his ordination was the first sign in western Massachusetts of the liberal theological opinions which led to Unitarian-Congregational split. As superintendent of Deerfield schools, he wrote and published numerous textbooks; he was author also of hymns, including the *Deerfield Collection of Sacred Music* (1814).

WILLARD, SIDNEY (*b. Beverly, Mass., 1780; d. 1856*), educator, writer, Massachusetts legislator. Son of Joseph Willard (1738–1804); brother of Joseph Willard (1798–1865). Graduated Harvard, 1798. Hancock Professor of Hebrew and Oriental Languages at Harvard, 1806–*c.* 1830; professor of Latin, 1827–31. Established and edited *American Monthly Review,* 1831–33, and was a contributor to, or otherwise associated with, almost all Massachusetts magazine ventures in his time. Mayor of Cambridge, Mass., 1848–50.

WILLARD, SIMON (*b. probably Kent, England, 1605; d. Charlestown, Mass., 1676 o.s.*), colonist, furtrader. Father of Samuel Willard (1639/40–1707). Co-founder, with Peter Bulkeley, of Concord, Mass., 1635; was one of the leading men on the Merrimac frontier. Represented Concord in the General Court, 1636–54 with exception of 1643, 1647 and 1648; chosen assistant, 1654, he served until his death. Assisted John Eliot among Merrimac tribes, 1646 and afterward. In charge of Merrimac defenses during King Philip's War, his relief of Brookfield, Mass., Aug. 4, 1675, was a notable feat.

WILLARD, SIMON (*b. Grafton, Mass., 1753; d. Roxbury, Mass., 1848*), clockmaker, inventor. Established clock factory at Roxbury, Mass., between 1777 and 1780; retired from business, 1839. Built up enviable reputation specializing in church, hall and gallery timepieces. He is especially renowned for the "Willard Patent Timepiece" or "banjo clock" (patented, 1802). President Jefferson was one of his patrons.

WILLARD, SOLOMON (*b. Petersham, Mass., 1783; d. Quincy, Mass., 1861*), sculptor, architect. Brother of Samuel Willard (1775–1859). Executed wood and marble carvings primarily for Boston, Mass., churches and public buildings. His sculpture includes the eagle on old Boston Customs House (1809) and many ship-figureheads from *c.* 1813. Made wooden model of completed U.S. Capitol for Charles Bulfinch. He designed, among other buildings, the Doric U.S. Branch Bank, Boston (1824) and the Boston Court House (1832). Famous chiefly as architect of Bunker Hill Monument (1825–42), he supervised construction, published *Plans and Section of the Obelisk . . .* (1843) and discovered and worked the Quincy granite quarries.

WILLCOX, LOUISE COLLIER (*b. Chicago, Ill., 1865; d. Paris, France, 1929*), essayist, critic, editor. Sister of Hiram P. Collier. Studied and traveled in Europe; resident in Norfolk, Va., *post* 1887. Editorial writer for *Harper's Weekly* and *Harper's Bazar;* wrote also for the *Delineator.* Member of editorial staff, *North American Review,* 1906–13. Reader and adviser for Macmillan Co., 1903–09; for E. P. Dutton & Co., 1910–17. Translator of contemporary French and German books.

WILLCOX, ORLANDO BOLIVAR (*b. Detroit, Mich., 1823; d. Coburg, Ontario, Canada, 1907*), soldier. Graduated West Point, 1847. First lieutenant of artillery in campaigns against Seminole Indians, 1856–57; commissioned colonel, 1st Michigan Infantry, 1861. Brigadier-general of volunteers (1862) assigned to Burnside's IX Corps, he commanded a division, and sometimes the corps, with marked distinction at Antietam, Fredericksburg, Knoxville, and in campaigns from the Wilderness to Petersburg. Brevetted major-general of volunteers, 1864, brigadier-general and major-general in regular army, 1867. Commanded Department of Arizona, March 1878—September 1882, operating notably against the Apaches. Commanded Department of Missouri, October 1886—April 1887.

WILLET, WILLIAM (*b. New York, N.Y., 1867; d. Philadelphia, Pa., 1921*), artist in stained glass. Studied at N.Y. Mechanics' and Tradesmen's Institute, 1884–85, and under William M. Chase and John La Farge. Resided in Pittsburgh, Pa., *c.* 1898–1913. Possessing a vivid color-sense and high artistic integrity, he challenged popular taste in his specialty after traveling in Europe, 1902. Among his works are the chancel window, Calvary Church, Pittsburgh (1907); the sanctuary window of West Point Chapel (1910), called the symbol of a regenerated craft in America; the great west window, Princeton University Graduate School (1913).

WILLETT, MARINUS (*b. Jamaica, L.I., N.Y., 1740; d. Cedar Grove, N.Y., 1830*), merchant, Revolutionary soldier. An outstanding Son of Liberty and leader of radical patriots in New York City. After service in Montgomery's invasion of Canada, 1775, he was commissioned lieutenant-colonel, 3rd New York Regiment, 1776, commanding at Fort Constitution. As second-in-command under Col. Gansevoort at Fort Stanwix, 1777, he distinguished himself during British attack by Col. St. Leger. He fought under Washington at Monmouth and took part in the Sullivan-Clinton expedition against the Iroquois, 1779. Appointed lieutenant-colonel commandant, 5th New York Regiment, 1780. Led regiment of levies on Tryon frontier, 1781, in successful battle of Johnstown. Sheriff

of New York City and county, 1784–88, 1792–96. Obtained treaty with Creek Indians, 1790. Appointed mayor of New York City, 1807.

WILLEY, SAMUEL HOPKINS (*b. Campton, N.H., 1821; d. 1914*), California clergyman, educator. Graduated Dartmouth, 1845; Union Theological Seminary, N.Y., 1848. On behalf of American Missionary Society, he went as minister to Monterey, Calif., 1849. Removed to San Francisco, 1850; established and became pastor of Howard Presbyterian Church, resigning 1862. Helped found College of California, Berkeley, 1855; served as vice-president and acting president, 1862–69. Held pastorates in Santa Cruz and Benicia, 1870–89; was president of Van Ness Seminary, 1889–96. Author, among other historical writings, of *Thirty Years in California* (1879) and *A History of the College of California* (1887).

WILLEY, WAITMAN THOMAS (*b. near present Farmington, W. Va., 1811; d. Morgantown, W. Va., 1900*), lawyer, politician. Opposed Virginia's secession, 1861, at state convention, but checked radical movement for immediate West Virginia statehood. U.S. senator from Virginia, July 1861–63, from West Virginia, 1863–71. As senator, he was instrumental in Congress's acceptance of West Virginia's constitution and in ratification of the "Willey amendment" for gradual abolition of slavery. First a Whig, he became a Republican, 1864. Later, as a Radical Republican, he voted for impeachment of President Andrew Johnson.

WILLIAMS, ALPHEUS STARKEY (*b. Saybrook, Conn., 1810; d. Washington, D.C., 1878*), lawyer, soldier. Practiced in Detroit, Mich., *post c.* 1837; served in Mexican War; postmaster of Detroit, 1849–53. A Union brigadier-general of volunteers, 1861, he commanded a division in the Shenandoah Valley campaign, 1862, and a division of the XII Corps in battle of South Mountain. Lee's famous "lost order" was brought to his headquarters. Succeeding to command of Mansfield's Corps at Antietam, he later led his own division with conspicuous ability at Chancellorsville and Gettysburg. Served with 1st division of new XX Corps in Army of the Cumberland in Atlanta campaign. Commanded XX Corps in march to the sea and during Carolinas campaign. Mustered out, 1866. U.S. minister resident to Salvador, 1866–69. Congressman, Democrat, from Michigan, 1875–78.

WILLIAMS, BARNEY (*b. Cork, Ireland, 1823; d. New York, N.Y., 1876*), actor. Stage-name of Bernard Flaherty. In 1849, married Maria Pray with whom he co-starred thereafter throughout the United States. Williams was an infectiously humorous entertainer in broad Irish character.

WILLIAMS, BERT (*b. New Providence, Bahamas, c. 1876; d. New York, N.Y., 1922*), comedian, songwriter. Stage-name of Egbert Austin Williams. Formed successful vaudeville team with George Walker, 1895.

In 1903 they produced the musical comedy *In Da-homey* with an all-Negro cast in New York and London; similar pieces such as *Abyssinia* and *Bandanna Land* followed. Leading comedian in the Ziegfeld Follies *post* 1909, Williams's skits and such songs as "Jonah Man" were often the best things in the show. A pioneer in assuring talented Negroes a place in the American theatre, he was himself a performer of rare gifts.

WILLIAMS, CATHARINE READ ARNOLD (*b. Providence, R.I., 1787; d. Providence, 1872*), poet, novelist, biographer. Author, among other works, of *Original Poems, on Various Subjects* (1828); *Tales, National and Revolutionary* (1830); and *The Neutral French, or the Exiles of Nova Scotia* (1841) whose theme anticipated Longfellow's *Evangeline*. Her vigorous, didactic books were popular in her day.

WILLIAMS, CHANNING MOORE (*b. Richmond, Va., 1829; d. Richmond, 1910*), Episcopal clergyman. Graduated William and Mary, 1852; Theological Seminary, Alexandria, Va., 1855. Ordained priest, 1857. Sent to Japan, 1859, by board of missions of the Protestant Episcopal Church; he supervised erection of the first Protestant church building there. Consecrated in New York, 1866, as bishop of China with jurisdiction in Japan. Named bishop of Tokyo, 1874, he resigned 1889.

WILLIAMS, CHARLES DAVID (*b. Bellevue, O., 1860; d. 1923*), Episcopal clergyman. Graduated Kenyon, 1880; ordained, 1884. Dean of Trinity Cathedral, Cleveland, O., 1893–1906. Consecrated bishop of Michigan, 1906. A liberal, Bishop Williams was the leading exponent in his communion of the "social gospel." He believed the church, by engendering a world-wide fellowship, should help bring about a new social order by proclaiming principles of industrial democracy, not by recommending economic and political programs. Author, among other books, of *The Christian Ministry and Social Problems* (1917), *The Prophetic Ministry for Today* (1912) and *The Gospel of Fellowship* (1923), all of which set forth his social views.

WILLIAMS, CHARLES RICHARD (*b. Prattsburg, N.Y., 1853; d. Princeton, N.J., 1927*), editor, author. Son-in-law of William H. Smith (1833–1896). A.B., College of New Jersey (Princeton), 1875. Editor-in-chief, *Indianapolis News*, 1892–1911. The correctness of style and nicety of language of the *News* set a high standard in the Midwest. Author, among other books, of *The Life of Rutherford Birchard Hayes* (1914); edited Hayes's *Diary and Letters* (1922–26).

WILLIAMS, DANIEL HALE (*b. Hollidaysburg, Pa., 1858; d. Idlewild, Mich., 1931*), surgeon. M.D., Chicago Medical College, 1883. Organized Provident Hospital, Chicago, Ill., 1891, with first Negro nurses' training school in the United States. Surgeon-in-chief, Freedmen's Hospital, Washington, D.C., 1893–98.

Appointed professor of clinical surgery, Meharry Medical College, Nashville, Tenn., 1899. Performed (1893) first successful surgical closure of a wound of the heart and pericardium; perfected suture for arrest of hemorrhage from the spleen. Charter member of American College of Surgeons, 1913. The most gifted surgeon and most notable medical man the Negro race had produced.

WILLIAMS, DAVID ROGERSON (*b. Robbin's Neck, S.C., 1776; d. Williamsburg district, S.C., 1830*), planter, South Carolina legislator, pioneer manufacturer. Congressman, (Democrat) Republican, from South Carolina, 1805–09 and 1811–13. Supported the Embargo, espoused cause of War Hawks and was chairman of House committee on military affairs. Governor of South Carolina, 1814–16. Opposing nullification, he advocated development of Southern domestic manufactures and himself engaged in making cotton yarns, hats and shoes, and cotton-seed oil. Opposition to John C. Calhoun was the consuming purpose of his later life.

WILLIAMS, EDWIN (*b. Norwich, Conn., 1797; d. New York, N.Y., 1854*), New York City journalist, miscellaneous writer. Author, among other works, of *The Statesman's Manual* (1846–58).

WILLIAMS, EGBERT AUSTIN. [See WILLIAMS, BERT, 1876–1922.]

WILLIAMS, ELEAZAR (*b. possibly Sault St. Louis, Canada, c. 1789; d. Hogansburg, N.Y., 1858*), Episcopal Indian missionary. A half-breed, he led Oneida chiefs to Green Bay, Wis., 1821, where they negotiated a treaty with the Menominee and Winnebago and were ceded land on the Fox River. In 1822 Williams led a number of Oneidas to Wisconsin, becoming their missionary. Repudiated by the Indians, he became well known for hypocrisy, indolence and desire for notoriety. *Post* 1839 he maintained that he was Louis XVII, Dauphin of France. Published, among other writings, *Good News to the Iroquois Nation* (1813).

WILLIAMS, ELISHA (*b. Hatfield, Mass., 1694; d. Wethersfield, Conn., 1755*), Congregational clergyman, Connecticut colonial legislator. Half-brother of Israel Williams. Graduated Harvard, 1711. Gained high repute as teacher in Wethersfield, 1716–19, where he instructed a part of the Yale student body, among them, Jonathan Edwards. Pastor at Wethersfield, 1722–26, he was rector of Yale College, 1726–39. Represented Wethersfield in Connecticut General Assembly, 1717–19, 1740–49, and *post* 1751; several times chosen speaker. Judge, Connecticut superior court, 1740–43. As army chaplain, he was present at capture of Louisbourg, Cape Breton Island, 1745. Delegate at Albany Congress, 1754.

WILLIAMS, ELISHA (*b. Pomfret, Conn., 1773; d. probably Waterloo, N.Y., 1833*), lawyer, politician. Admitted to the New York bar, 1793; practiced in

Spencertown and Hudson, N.Y.; displayed brilliant oratorical gifts. Elected to New York Assembly for Columbia County, 1800, he served at nine sessions down to 1828. A Federalist leader, he was strongly anti-democratic in the New York constitutional convention in 1821. In 1815 he founded Waterloo, Seneca Co., N.Y.

WILLIAMS, ELKANAH (*b. near Bedford, Ind., 1822; d. Hazelwood, Pa., 1888*), ophthalmologist. M.D., University of Louisville, 1850; influenced by S. D. Gross. Studied in Europe, 1852–55. Returning to Cincinnati, O., 1855, he became the pioneer ophthalmologist in the Midwest. As professor of opthalmology and aural surgery, Miami Medical College *post* 1865, he was first in the United States to hold a chair in this specialty. One of first in America to use the ophthalmoscope.

WILLIAMS, EPHRAIM (*b. Newton, Mass., 1714 n.s.; d. near Crown Point, N.Y., 1755*), colonial soldier. Settled in Stockbridge, Mass., 1739. Commissioned (1745) captain commanding forts and posts along northern boundary of Massachusetts from Northfield to the New York border. Commissioned colonel of a regiment to aid William Johnson in expedition against Crown Point, 1755, he was killed in ambush while reconnoitering in force with Chief Hendrick. His estate was employed in founding the school which became Williams College.

WILLIAMS, FRANCIS HENRY (*b. Uxbridge, Mass., 1852; d. Boston, Mass., 1936*), physician. Son of Henry W. Williams. Graduated Massachusetts Institute of Technology, 1873; M.D. Harvard Medical School, 1877. Distinguished in practice in Boston, Mass., and as a faculty member at Harvard Medical School, he is remembered as a pioneer in the use of X-rays. Shortly after their discovery by Roentgen in December 1895, Williams began using them to study cases of thoracic lesions, and as early as April 1896 delivered a paper on the use of X-rays in medicine, illustrating it with X-ray photographs. He was author, among other works, of *The Roentgen Rays in Medicine and Surgery* (1901). He was also an early experimenter with the therapeutic use of beta rays from radium. [*Supp. 2*]

WILLIAMS, FRANK MARTIN (*b. Durhamville, N.Y., 1873; d. Albany, N.Y., 1930*), civil engineer. State engineer and surveyor of New York, 1909, 1910, 1915–22, he supervised construction of a barge canal to supersede Erie Canal. Consultant for, among other projects, the Holland Vehicular Tunnel and Sacandaga Reservoir.

WILLIAMS, FREDERICK WELLS (*b. Macao, China, 1857; d. New Haven, Conn., 1928*), writer, teacher. Son of Samuel W. Williams. Graduated Yale, 1879. Taught Oriental history at Yale, 1893–1925. *Post* 1901 he was associated with Yale-in-China. Author of *The Life and Letters of Samuel Wells Williams*

(1889) and *Anson Burlingame and the First Chinese Mission to Foreign Powers* (1912).

WILLIAMS, GAAR CAMPBELL (*b. Richmond, Ind., 1880; d. Chicago, Ill., 1935*), cartoonist. Studied at Art Institute of Chicago; began work on staff of *Chicago Daily News*. Editorial cartoonist, *Indianapolis News*, 1909–21; special cartoonist, *Chicago Tribune* thereafter. Author of the celebrated single picture series "Just Plain Folks" and the Sunday feature "Among the Folks in History" which were widely syndicated. [*Supp. 1*]

WILLIAMS, GARDNER FRED (*b. Saginaw, Mich., 1842; d. 1922*), mining engineer. Graduated College of California, 1865; studied also at Freiberg. Consultant in Western mining regions, 1875–83. Manager, under Cecil Rhodes, of De Beers Mining Co., South Africa, 1887–1905. His improved working methods made possible world-wide regulation of diamond prices. Author of *The Diamond Mines of South Africa* (1902).

WILLIAMS, GEORGE HENRY (*b. New Lebanon, N.Y., 1820; d. 1910*), jurist, politician. Iowa district judge, 1847–52; chief justice, Territory of Oregon, 1853–57. Leading member of Oregon constitutional convention, 1857; delegate to Union state convention, 1862. As U.S. senator, Republican, from Oregon, 1865–71, he was a member of joint committee on reconstruction; introduced Tenure of Office bill (December 1866) and Military Reconstruction bill (February 1867); voted "guilty" in President Johnson's impeachment trial. He was U.S. attorney-general, 1871–75. His nomination as chief justice of U.S. Supreme Court, 1873, was withdrawn after inquiry revealed his connection with Oregon election frauds. He served with Lew Wallace as examiner of the Florida vote, 1876, so "saving the state" for Hayes. He was mayor of Portland, Oreg., 1902–05.

WILLIAMS, GEORGE HUNTINGTON (*b. Utica, N.Y., 1856; d. 1894*), mineralogist, petrologist, teacher. Grandson of William Williams (1787–1850). A.B., Amherst, 1878; Ph.D., Heidelberg, 1882. Taught at Johns Hopkins *post* 1883; professor of inorganic geology, 1891–94. Author, among other works, of *The Greenstone Schist Areas of the Menominee and Marquette Regions of Michigan* (1890, *Bulletin 62* of U.S. Geological Survey).

WILLIAMS, GEORGE WASHINGTON (*b. Bedford Springs, Pa., 1849; d. Blackpool, England, 1891*), Baptist clergyman, Union colonel. Studied law under Alphonso Taft. Of mixed white and Negro blood, he held federal offices and served in the Ohio legislature following the Civil War. U.S. minister to Haiti, 1885–86. Made critical survey of conditions in Congo Free State. Author, among other writings, of *A History of the Negro Troops in the War of the Rebellion* (1888).

WILLIAMS, HENRY SHALER (*b. Ithaca, N.Y., 1847; d. Havana, Cuba, 1918*), paleontologist. Ph. B.,

Sheffield Scientific School, Yale, 1868; Ph.D., Yale, 1871. Taught paleontology at Cornell University, 1879–92; Silliman Professor at Yale, 1892–1904. Returning to teach at Cornell, 1904, he became professor emeritus, 1912. Williams was an authority on the American Devonian and developed the now common photographic method of fossil illustration. He was also associated with the U.S. Geological Survey from 1883 until his death. Author, among other works, of *Geological Biology* (1895); associate editor of the *Journal of Geology* (1893–1918) and of *American Journal of Science* (1894–1918).

WILLIAMS, HENRY WILLARD (*b. Boston, Mass., 1821; d. Boston, 1895*), ophthalmologist. One of the founders of ophthalmology in America, Williams studied in Paris, London and Vienna, and graduated from Harvard Medical School, 1849. In 1871 he became the first professor of ophthalmology at Harvard Medical School. He was ophthalmologic surgeon, Boston City Hospital, 1864–91. Author, among other valuable writings, of *The Diagnosis and Treatment of the Diseases of the Eye* (1881), the best book of its day on the subject.

WILLIAMS, ISRAEL (*b. Hatfield, Mass., 1709; d. Hatfield, 1788*), farmer, land speculator, Massachusetts official, Loyalist. Half-brother of Elisha Williams (1694–1755). Active in effecting dismissal of his cousin Jonathan Edwards from Northampton church, 1750. Made colonel of Hampshire County's militia, 1748; conducted defense of western Massachusetts throughout French and Indian War. Judge, Hampshire County court of common pleas, 1758–74; Massachusetts legislator, 1733–73. Lost early paramount influence in his county to his radical cousin Joseph Hawley. The leading Loyalist in western Massachusetts *post* 1774, he was the model for the mobbed Tory squire in Trumbull's *M'Fingal*. As executor of the will of Ephraim Williams, he helped found Williams College.

WILLIAMS, JAMES (*b. Grainger Co., Tenn., 1796; d. Graz, Austria, 1869*), journalist, Confederate diplomat, Tennessee legislator. Aided Confederate propaganda by articles in the London *Times*, *Standard* and *Index*, 1861–64; served as Confederate contact with Maximilian of Mexico. He kept John Slidell and James M. Mason posted on his activities, but carried on secret, perhaps more detailed, correspondence with President Jefferson Davis. Author of *Letters on Slavery from the Old World* (1861), enlarged and published in London as *The South Vindicated*.

WILLIAMS, JAMES DOUGLAS (*b. Pickaway Co., O., 1808; d. Indianapolis, Ind., 1880*), farmer, miller, Indiana legislator. As congressman, Democrat, from Indiana, 1875–77, he was chairman of the committee on accounts. Insistent on cutting expenses, he became known as "Blue Jeans Williams." Defeating Benjamin Harrison in a famous campaign for governor of In-

diana, 1876, he served with ability and independence, 1877–80.

WILLIAMS, JESSE LYNCH (*b. Westfield, N.C., 1807; d. 1886*), civil engineer. Chief engineer, Wabash & Erie Canal, 1832–35 and 1847–76, also of many other transportation projects in Indiana. His report on the Union Pacific to the secretary of the interior, 1862, led to the Crédit Mobilier investigation.

WILLIAMS, JESSE LYNCH (*b. Sterling, Ill., 1871; d. Herkimer Co., N.Y., 1929*), novelist, playwright, editor. Grandson of Jesse L. Williams (1807–1886). B.A., Princeton, 1892. Author, among other fiction and drama, of *Princeton Stories* (1895), the Pulitzer Prize play *Why Marry?* (1917), and the novel *She Knew She Was Right* (1930).

WILLIAMS, JOHN (*b. Roxbury, Mass., 1664; d. Deerfield, Mass., 1729*), Congregational clergyman, author. Ordained first pastor at Deerfield, Mass., 1688. Following sacking of the town by French and Indians, 1703/04, he was held captive for two years in Canada. He later prepared with Cotton Mather's help *The Redeemed Captive Returning to Zion* (1707), a testimony of Congregational fortitude against "Popish Poisons." Returned to Deerfield, 1707. Served as chaplain in 1711 expedition against Port Royal and as commissioner to Canada (1713–14) for return of English prisoners.

WILLIAMS, JOHN (*b. London, England, 1761; d. Brooklyn, N.Y., 1818*), satirist, dramatic critic, miscellaneous writer. Under his pseudonym "Anthony Pasquin," he was author of the *Hamiltoniad* (Boston, preface dated 1804), a savage anti-Federalist poem, more important for its extensive notes than for its verse. Called "a common libeller" and "polecat," he had been driven in disgrace from England *c.* 1797 and died destitute in America.

WILLIAMS, JOHN (*b. Surry Co., N.C., 1778; d. Knoxville, Tenn., 1837*), soldier, lawyer, Tennessee legislator. Brother-in-law of Hugh L. White. As colonel of volunteers in War of 1812 he operated against the Seminoles in Florida. Colonel, 39th U.S. Infantry in the Creek campaign, he helped bring about Andrew Jackson's victory in battle of Horseshoe Bend, 1814. U.S. senator from Tennessee, 1815–23. Denied renomination because of identification with the Crawford wing of the Democrats, he insisted on running for re-election, thus compelling Jackson to run against him and defeat him in a bitter campaign.

WILLIAMS, JOHN (*b. Old Deerfield, Mass., 1817; d. Middletown, Conn., 1899*), Episcopal clergyman. Graduated present Trinity College (Hartford, Conn.), 1835; ordained priest, 1841; while in England, 1840–41, he grew acquainted with the Oxford Movement leaders. President and also Hobart Professor of History and Literature, Trinity College, 1848–53; chancellor, *post* 1865. In 1851 he was elected bishop coadjutor of Connecticut, succeeding to the see in 1865. Dean and professor of theology and liturgies, Berkeley Divinity School, Middletown, Conn., *post* 1854; presiding bishop of the Protestant Episcopal Church *post* 1887.

WILLIAMS, JOHN ELIAS (*b. Merthyr-Tydfil, Wales, 1853; d. Streator, Ill., 1919*), coal miner, industrial mediator. Came to America, 1864; settled in Streator, Ill. Chairman, arbitration board for Hart, Schaffner & Marx and United Garment Workers of America, *post* 1912. One of the first advocates of union-management cooperation, he believed industrial democracy could come through trades organization and continuous collective bargaining; he was instrumental in introducing new devices, including a compromise between closed and open shop called the preferential shop. His procedure and philosophy of mediation created a precedent for board chairmen and influenced so-called progressive unions.

WILLIAMS, JOHN ELIAS (*b. Coshocton, O., 1871; d. Nanking, China, 1927*), Presbyterian missionary to China. Working in China *post* 1899, he helped found and became vice-president of the University of Nanking, 1911. His murder by a Chinese communist, 1927, began the so-called "Nanking Incident."

WILLIAMS, JOHN FLETCHER (*b. Cincinnati, O., 1834; d. Rochester, Minn., 1895*), journalist, librarian. Removed to St. Paul, Minn., 1855. Secretary and librarian, Minnesota Historical Society, 1867–93.

WILLIAMS, JOHN FOSTER (*b. Boston, Mass., 1743; d. Boston, 1814*), naval officer. His Revolutionary commands included the state vessels *Republic, Massachusetts,* and *Hazard* in which he took several prizes, 1778–79, and compelled surrender of British brig *Active,* March 1779. He commanded *Protector,* largest ship in the Massachusetts navy, 1780–81. From 1790 until his death he was captain of the revenue cutter *Massachusetts.*

WILLIAMS, JOHN JOSEPH (*b. Boston, Mass., 1822; d. 1907*), Roman Catholic clergyman. Graduated Sulpician college, Montreal, Canada, 1841; studied theology at St. Sulpice, Paris, where he was ordained, 1845. Named rector of Cathedral of the Holy Cross, Boston, 1855; pastor of St. James Church and vicar-general of the diocese, 1857. Consecrated bishop of Boston, 1866, and archbishop, 1875; retired in 1906.

WILLIAMS, JOHN SHARP (*b. Memphis, Tenn., 1854; d. 1932*), planter, lawyer. Educated at universities of the South, Virginia and Heidelberg. Admitted to the bar, 1877; practiced in Yazoo City, Miss., 1878–93. As congressman, Democrat, from Mississippi, 1893–1909, he became an effective minority leader, 1903. Temporary chairman of the 1904 Democratic convention, he upheld conservative views in the fight over the platform and continued to champion moderation in reform through 1912. Entering the U.S. Sen-

ate, 1911, after a victory over J. K. Vardaman, he served on the finance and foreign relations committees and consistently supported Woodrow Wilson's policies as president. Disgusted with the trends in public life *post* 1920, he retired in 1923. The most consistent Jeffersonian Democrat of his day, he wrote *Thomas Jefferson, His Permanent Influence on American Institutions* (1913).

WILLIAMS, JOHN SKELTON (*b. Powhatan Co., Va., 1865; d. near Richmond, Va., 1926*), financier, public official. Developed the Seaboard Air Line Railway; served it as president, 1899–1903. Appointed assistant U.S. secretary of the treasury, 1913, he was comptroller of the currency, 1914–21, and an *ex officio* member of the committee which established the Federal Reserve System. He was also U.S. director of finances and purchases for the railroads, 1917–19. Attacked concentration of banking control "in the hands of a dozen men"; praised Federal Reserve System as means of decentralization; antagonized national banks by charges of usury. His later accusations against the Federal Reserve Board formed basis of congressional investigations which sustained some of the charges. *Post* 1921, he was board chairman of the Richmond Trust Co.

WILLIAMS, JOHN WHITRIDGE (*b. Baltimore, Md., 1866; d. 1931*), physician, obstetrician. M.D., University of Maryland, 1888; studied also in Vienna, Berlin and Leipzig. Taught at Johns Hopkins *post* 1896, becoming professor of obstetrics and obstetrician-in-chief to the hospital, 1899. Dean of the Medical School, 1911–23. Author, among a number of treatises on bacteriology, pathology and obstetrics, of an authoritative *Textbook of Obstetrics* (1903).

WILLIAMS, JONATHAN (*b. Boston, Mass., 1750; d. 1815*), merchant, army officer. Sent to London, 1770, to complete business training under his uncle Benjamin Franklin. Employed by commissioners of Continental Congress, 1776, as Nantes agent to inspect arms and supplies, he became unwittingly involved in the controversy between Silas Deane and Arthur Lee. Although vindicated of false charges made by Lee, he left public service, remaining in business in Europe until he returned with Franklin to America, 1785. Williams then settled in Philadelphia as a well-to-do merchant. In 1796 he became associate judge of the court of common pleas and later acquired reputation as scientist. Named by Pres. Jefferson in 1801 as inspector of fortifications and superintendent at West Point with rank of major, he soon became first superintendent of the U.S. Military Academy. Laboring under many handicaps, he resigned, 1803. Reappointed in 1805 as lieutenant-colonel of engineers with complete authority over all cadets at the institution, he was now hampered in his efforts to create a first-rate military school by many extra engineering duties which took up most of his time and by the antagonism of Secretary of War William Eustis. He resigned from the army, 1812, embittered because of failure at West Point and because he was not given command of the New York fortifications. During the War of 1812 he served as brevet brigadier-general of New York militia.

WILLIAMS, LINSLY RUDD (*b. New York, N.Y., 1875; d. 1934*), physician. M.D., N.Y. College of Physicians and Surgeons, 1899. Director, Rockefeller Commission for the Prevention of Tuberculosis in France, 1919–22. Directed National Tuberculosis Association, 1922–28; thereafter developed and directed New York Academy of Medicine.

WILLIAMS, MARSHALL JAY (*b. Fayette Co., O., 1837; d. Columbus, O., 1902*), lawyer, Ohio legislator. Judge, Ohio second circuit court, 1884–86, and first chief justice; judge, Ohio supreme court, 1887–1902; dean, College of Law, Ohio State University, 1891–93. Conservative in constitutional law, liberal in tort law on questions of negligence and liability.

WILLIAMS, NATHANAEL (*b. Boston, Mass., 1675; d. 1737/38*), physician, schoolmaster. Father-in-law of John Smibert. Graduated Harvard, 1693. Succeeded Ezekiel Cheever as headmaster, Boston Latin School, 1708; resigned from the school, 1733.

WILLIAMS, OTHO HOLLAND (*b. Prince Georges Co., Md., 1749; d. Miller's Town, Va., 1794*), Revolutionary officer. After good service at siege of Boston and with a Maryland-Virginia rifle regiment, he was made prisoner at the fall of Fort Washington, November 1776. Exchanged, January 1778, he began duties as colonel of the 6th Maryland Regiment. Deputy adjutant-general under Horatio Gates, 1780, and adjutant under Nathanael Greene; commanded rear guard during Greene's retreat across North Carolina and distinguished himself in battles of Guilford Court House, Hobkirk Hill and Eutaw Springs. Promoted brigadier-general, 1782. Elected naval officer, Baltimore district, 1783; appointed federal collector of the port, 1789.

WILLIAMS, REUEL (*b. present Augusta, Maine, 1783; d. Augusta, 1862*), Maine legislator. Inherited a practice (1812) including administration of "Kennebec Purchase" and Bowdoin College timberlands; prospered in many business ventures. In Maine legislature, 1812–29, as a Federalist; 1832, 1848, as Democrat. U.S. senator, Democrat, from Maine, 1837–43. Actively supported Maine in the boundary dispute, 1832–42. With Thomas Hart Benton, fought against Webster-Ashburton Treaty in 1842.

WILLIAMS, ROBERT (*b. probably England, c. 1745; d. near Suffolk, Va., 1775*), pioneer Methodist preacher. Appointed as missionary to America, he worked in New York City and Maryland, 1769–71. His reprinting of John Wesley's sermons alerted American Methodists to the value of a religious press. Extending his work to Virginia, he led a great religious revival,

1773; in Petersburg; he organized Brunswick circuit, 1774. Williams was the first Methodist traveling preacher to come to America, the first to publish a book, and the first to settle here.

WILLIAMS, ROGER (*b. London, England, c. 1603; d. Providence, R.I., 1682/83*), clergyman, president of Rhode Island. A protégé of Sir Edward Coke, Williams was educated at Charterhouse and at Pembroke College, Cambridge (B.A., 1627). He took orders *ante* 1629 and served as chaplain to a Puritan family in Essex; in December 1629 he married Mary Barnard.

Already friendly with John Cotton and Thomas Hooker, Williams took ship aboard the *Lyon* with his wife in December 1630 and was welcomed at first in Massachusetts as "a godly minister." His open criticism of the Puritan system of government soon made him enemies, for he declared that civil governments had no power to enforce the religious injunctions of the Ten Commandments. Denied a post as teacher of the church at Salem, he went to Plymouth, and after two years there returned to Salem as assistant minister. In August 1634 he was accepted as full minister at Salem in defiance of the General Court. He continued to work for a more democratic church system, also attacking land claims under the royal charter as a violation of Indian rights and denouncing the oath by which the Massachusetts oligarchy were trying to keep the lower orders of settlers in strict submission. Found guilty on Oct. 9, 1635, of propagating new and dangerous opinions, he was ordered banished by the General Court. Learning that Williams was trying to organize his Salem followers for a colony in Narragansett, the magistrates, who feared the existence of a radical community on their southern border, sent to arrest him. Warned, he escaped and made his way to the friendly Indians at Sowams. After suffering privations, he gathered enough followers to found Providence, the earliest Rhode Island settlement, in 1636.

Grown skeptical of the claims of the existing churches, he became (1639) a Seeker—one who accepted no creed although professing belief in the fundamentals of Christianity. Frontier influences and Williams's own liberalism produced local institutions in Rhode Island which marked a radical advance over the Puritan colonies. Town government was at first a primitive democracy; all heads of families had an equal voice. Heads of families were to share alike in the distribution of land. Religious liberty and complete separation of church and state were provided for. By 1643, four settlements had sprung up in the Narragansett area, and the need of a charter was becoming evident. The Puritan colonies were organizing the New England Confederation and taking steps to end the independent existence of nonconforming settlements. Massachusetts invaded Rhode Island, carried off Samuel Gorton and the Warwick settlers to prison, and began negotiating in London for a Narragansett patent. Williams sailed for England, and with the aid of Sir Henry Vane, circumvented the Bay authorities and secured a patent for the whole area; this charter for the Providence Plantations was issued in March, 1644.

While in England, Williams opposed attempts there by the Puritans to establish a national church and a compulsory uniformity. In *The Bloudy Tenent of Persecution* (1644), his most celebrated work, he held that all individuals and religious bodies were entitled to religious liberty as a natural right. He also attacked the undemocratic character of contemporary governments and declared that the foundation of civil power was in the people, who might establish whatever form of government seemed to them "most meete."

After Williams's return to Rhode Island, William Coddington, the dominant figure at Newport, delayed organization of the Rhode Island settlements until 1647; in 1651 he obtained a commission from England splitting the colony and making him governor of Aquidneck for life. Williams traveled to England, accompanied by John Clarke, and succeeded in getting Coddington's commission rescinded. During this second visit Williams continued his propaganda for democracy and religious liberty, publishing among other works *The Bloody Tenent Yet More Bloody* (1652). After his return to Rhode Island, he reunited the colony, became its president and served three terms; during his presidency the Jews and Quakers found a safe harbor in the colony despite the protests and threats of Massachusetts. The latter years of his life were darkened by controversy and by Indian wars. In 1659 Williams defended the Narragansett tribe against an attempted fraud which would have deprived them of much of their lands, yet during King Philip's War the Narragansetts cast in their lot with the other Indians and ended their old-time friendship with the Rhode Island settlements. Williams served as one of the captains in command of the Providence forces during the war and remained active in town affairs to the end of his life. Colonial thinker, religious liberal, and earliest of the fathers of American democracy, he owes his enduring fame to his humanity and breadth of view and to his long record of opposition to privilege and self-seeking.

WILLIAMS, SAMUEL MAY (*b. Providence, R.I., 1795; d. Galveston, Texas, 1858*), Texas pioneer, banker. Became private secretary to Stephen F. Austin (1824) and a partner in his great colonization project; he kept and preserved the colony's records. *Post* 1834 Williams became unpopular because of land speculations. His mercantile firm of McKinney & Williams (organized, 1836) served as financial backer of the Texas republic and opened the Commercial & Agricultural Bank, Galveston, 1847, the first chartered bank of Texas.

WILLIAMS, SAMUEL WELLS (*b. Utica, N.Y., 1812; d. 1884*), missionary, diplomat, Sinologue. Son of William Williams (1787–1850); father of Frederick W. Williams. Removed to China, 1833. Directed the Canton press for the American Board of Commissioners for Foreign Missions and helped edit the *Chinese Repository*. Accompanied the Perry expedition to Japan as interpreter, 1853–54. Became secretary and interpreter of the American legation to China, 1856. Associated with the legation until 1876, he helped negotiate treaties. Author, among other writings, of *The Middle Kingdom* (1848, 1883) and *A Syllabic Dictionary of the Chinese Language* (1874). Became professor of Chinese language and literature at Yale, 1877. Williams was the outstanding American Sinologist of his time.

WILLIAMS, STEPHEN WEST (*b. Deerfield, Mass., 1790; d. Laona, Ill., 1855*), medical historian. Practiced in Deerfield. Lectured on medical jurisprudence at Berkshire Medical Institution, 1823–31; at Willoughby University, Ohio, 1838–53; at Dartmouth Medical School, 1838–41. Author, among other works, of *A Catechism of Medical Jurisprudence* (1835) and *American Medical Biography* (1845).

WILLIAMS, TALCOTT (*b. Abeih, Turkey, 1849; d. 1928*), journalist. Nephew of Samuel W. Williams. Joined N.Y. *World*, 1873; became night editor. An outstanding political reporter of his day, he was editorial writer for the *Springfield Republican*, 1879–81, and on staff of the Philadelphia *Press*, 1881–1912, becoming associate editor. Became first director, Columbia School of Journalism, 1912; served as professor emeritus *post* 1919. Williams combined cultural courses with practical newspaper training in the curriculum at Columbia and largely originated reporting of scientific news. His greatest contribution to journalism was his ideal of the scholar-journalist.

WILLIAMS, THOMAS SCOTT (*b. Wethersfield, Conn., 1777; d. 1861*), jurist, Connecticut legislator. Nephew of William Williams (1731–1811); son-in-law of Oliver Ellsworth. Studied law under Tapping Reeve and Zephaniah Swift. Congressman from Connecticut, 1817–19; mayor of Hartford, 1831–35. Associate justice, Connecticut supreme court of errors, 1829–34; chief justice, 1834–47. Distinguished for lifelong interest in civic and charitable affairs.

WILLIAMS, WALTER (*b. Boonville, Mo., 1864; d. 1935*), journalist, educator. Distinguished for his editorship of the *Columbia* (Mo.) *Herald*, he was appointed a member of the board of curators of the University of Missouri, 1899, and served as chairman of its executive committee for many years. Becoming first dean of the school of journalism at the University of Missouri, 1908, he organized an educational program which aimed to reproduce as nearly as possible the apprentice experience obtained in a good newspaper office. This school was the first to place journalistic training on a professional level and its plan vastly influenced other schools and departments, as did also Dean Williams's idealistic views on the responsibilities of the press to society. He served also as president of the University of Missouri, 1930–35. [*Supp. 1*]

WILLIAMS, WILLIAM (*b. Lebanon, Conn., 1731; d. Lebanon, 1811*), businessman, Revolutionary patriot, signer of the Declaration of Independence, Connecticut official and legislator. Son-in-law of Jonathan Trumbull (1710–1785). Graduated Harvard, 1751. Gave heavy financial aid to the Revolutionary movement; helped compose many of Gov. Trumbull's state papers. Occupied many Connecticut public offices and was a member of the Continental Congress, 1776–78, 1783–84; assisted in framing Articles of Confederation and served on the board of war.

WILLIAMS, WILLIAM (*b. Framingham, Mass., 1787; d. Utica, N.Y., 1850*), printer, publisher, soldier. Father of Samuel W. Williams. Became partner (1807) in Utica, N.Y., printing firm and published many almanacs, music collections and anti-Masonic books. Managed bookstore which by 1820 was the largest west of Albany, N.Y.; owned, printed and sometimes edited Utica newspapers, notably the *Patriot* and the *Patrol.*

WILLIAMS, WILLIAM R. (*b. New York, N.Y., 1804; d. 1885*), Baptist clergyman, author. Practiced law in New York City, 1825–30. Influential, scholarly pastor of Amity Street Baptist Church, New York City, *post* 1832. Helped found Rochester Theological Seminary. Author, among other writings, of *The Conservative Principles in Our Literature* (1844).

WILLIAMS, WILLIAM SHERLEY (*b. probably Kentucky, date uncertain; d. probably north of Taos, N.Mex., 1849*), trapper, guide. Better known as Bill, or Old Bill, Williams. A member of Joseph C. Brown's surveying party which marked Santa Fé trail, 1825–26. In 1833–34, he was with the California expedition led by Joseph R. Walker; he then trapped the Utah-Colorado country. Set out in 1843 on a two-year journey to the Columbia River, to the Great Basin and Santa Fé; joined the disastrous fourth expedition of John C. Frémont as guide, 1848. Probably killed by Utes. The most eccentric of the "mountain men," Williams has lent his name to numerous Western landmarks. The queer jargon which he affected became standard in fictional treatments of the West as true trapper talk.

WILLIAMSON, ANDREW (*b. possibly Scotland, c. 1730; d. near Charleston, S.C., 1786*), Revolutionary soldier, planter. Came to America as a child; was influential Whig in South Carolina back country. As major of militia, he took part in the 1775 fighting around Ninety-Six and led an expedition against the Cherokees, 1776. Promoted colonel, he commanded South Carolina troops in a second campaign which subdued the Cherokees. Made brigadier-general, 1778,

he commanded South Carolina militia in Howe's Florida expedition. Accused of treason after the fall of Charleston, 1780, he went into the British lines there and was denounced as the "Arnold of Carolina." He is credited, however, with later supplying Whigs with valuable information through Col. John Laurens.

WILLIAMSON, CHARLES (*b. Balgray, Scotland, 1757; d. at sea, 1808*), British officer, secret agent, New York legislator. As a land promoter in western New York, 1791–1802, he administered and developed for a British syndicate headed by Sir William Pulteney a tract of 1,200,000 acres acquired from Robert Morris. He became a citizen and was elected to various offices; he also built roads and bridges and a hotel at Geneva, N.Y. Serving *post* 1803 as a volunteer adviser to the British cabinet on American affairs, he reverted to British citizenship. After an 1806 visit to the United States, he advised a policy directed at overthrow of the "Frenchified" Jeffersonian regime and considered Aaron Burr as a possible agent in this endeavor.

WILLIAMSON, HUGH (*b. West Nottingham, Pa., 1735; d. New York, N.Y., 1819*), physician, statesman, scientist, North Carolina legislator. Graduated College of Philadelphia (University of Pennsylvania), 1757, where he taught mathematics. In 1764 he studied medicine at Edinburgh, London and Utrecht, receiving M.D. at University of Utrecht. Practicing in Philadelphia, he continued scientific studies. While in England, 1773–76, seeking aid for a proposed school, he obtained by a trick the Hutchinson-Oliver letters from Massachusetts and delivered them to Benjamin Franklin. He also collaborated with Franklin in electrical experiments. Settling in Edenton, N.C., 1777, he built up a large trade with the French West Indies and served as surgeon-general of the state troops. Member of the Continental Congress, 1782–85 and 1787–88. At the Federal Convention, 1787, he was the most active North Carolina delegate and played a large part in securing the compromise on representation. He signed the U.S. Constitution and worked for its ratification. After serving in Congress from North Carolina, 1789–93, he devoted the rest of his life to literary and scientific pursuits in New York City. Williamson's work on climate brought him his greatest reputation as a scientist. He showed originality as an economist and was a sound scholar; his historical work was poor. Author, among other writings, of "An Essay on Comets" (1771); "Letters of Sylvius" (*American Museum*, August 1787); and *Observations on the Climate in Different Parts of America* (1811).

WILLIAMSON, ISAAC HALSTED (*b. Elizabethtown, present Elizabeth, N.J., 1767; d. Elizabeth, 1844*), lawyer. Democratic governor and chancellor of New Jersey, 1817–29. Williamson's lasting reputation came through his work in the dual office of chancellor, wherein he increased the dignity and effectiveness of the chancery court and laid the foundations of its unique position in New Jersey. His 1822 code of rules of practice clarified the then confused situation of mortgages.

WILLIAMSON, WILLIAM DURKEE (*b. Canterbury, Conn., 1779; d. Bangor, Maine, 1846*), lawyer, historian, Massachusetts and Maine legislator. Postmaster of Bangor, Maine, 1809–20. Advocated separation of Maine from Massachusetts, 1820. Acting governor of Maine, May–December 1821; congressman, Democrat, from Maine, 1821–23. Judge of probate, Penobscot Co., Maine, 1824–40. Author of *History of the State of Maine* (1832; reissued, 1839).

WILLIE, ASA HOXIE (*b. Washington, Ga., 1829; d. Galveston, Texas, 1899*), jurist. Removed to Texas, 1846; admitted to the bar, 1849. Elected to the Texas supreme court in 1866, he was removed after 15 months by the federal military authorities. Congressman-at-large from Texas, 1873–75; chief justice of Texas supreme court, 1882–88.

WILLING, THOMAS (*b. Philadelphia, Pa., 1731 o.s.; d. Philadelphia, 1821*), banker, Pennsylvania official and legislator. Father of Anne Willing Bingham. Became partner in father's counting-house, 1751; formed Willing, Morris & Co. with Robert Morris, eventually the leading Philadelphia mercantile firm. Engaged in many public activities; elected mayor of Philadelphia, 1763. Justice, supreme court of Pennsylvania, 1767–77. President of first Provincial Congress of Pennsylvania, 1774; member of Second Continental Congress, 1775–76. Voted against Richard Henry Lee's resolution for independence, July 1776. During British occupation declined taking oath of allegiance to the King. President of the Bank of North America, 1781–1807. Supported movement for new constitution of 1787 and Alexander Hamilton's fiscal measures. President, first Bank of the United States, 1791–97.

WILLINGHAM, ROBERT JOSIAH (*b. Beaufort District, S.C., 1854; d. 1914*), Baptist clergyman. Highly effective secretary of the Foreign Mission Board of the Southern Baptist Convention, 1893–1914.

WILLIS, ALBERT SHELBY (*b. Shelbyville, Ky., 1843; d. Honolulu, Hawaii, 1897*), lawyer, Kentucky official, diplomat. Congressman, Democrat, from Kentucky, 1877–87; chairman, committee on rivers and harbors. As envoy extraordinary and minister plenipotentiary to Hawaii, 1893–97, he was unsuccessful in effecting President Cleveland's policy of restoring prerevolutionary status after uprising of 1893.

WILLIS, HENRY PARKER (*b. Elmira, N.Y., 1874; d. Oak Bluffs, Mass., 1937*), economist, educator. Raised in Racine, Wis. Graduated University of Chicago, 1894; Ph.D., 1897. A teacher at Washington and Lee University, 1898–1905, he served also as editorial writer on the N.Y. *Evening Post* and was briefly Washington correspondent for the N.Y. *Journal of*

Commerce and the *Springfield Republican*. He collaborated with J. Laurence Laughlin in *Reciprocity* (1903). Removing to Washington, D.C., 1905, he continued to work as a correspondent and also served as professor of finance at George Washington University until 1912. He then removed to New York City as associate editor of the *Journal of Commerce*. He served as editor-in-chief of the *Journal*, 1919–31, and was professor of banking at Columbia University *post* 1917. Active as an adviser to congressional committees *post* 1910, Willis helped to draw up the Underwood Tariff Act of 1913 and later contributed to the drafting of the Federal Reserve Act. He was the first secretary of the Federal Reserve Board, 1914–18, and served as the Board's director of analysis and research, 1918–22. In his *Journal of Commerce* editorials he called attention to the dangers inherent in the Republican high-tariff policy and in the overextension of credit during the 1920's; he was among the first to foresee a stock-market collapse and a business depression. His chief interest lay in his academic work; at Columbia he organized a banking seminar which played an important role in the university and in the banking life of New York. An old-fashioned political liberal, Willis defended individual and constitutional rights, advocated the competitive enterprise system, and fought against all monopolies whether in business or labor. He was author of a number of books in the field of banking, including his legislative history entitled *The Federal Reserve System* (1923). [*Supp. 2*]

WILLIS, NATHANIEL (*b. Boston, Mass., 1780; d. Boston, 1870*), editor, journalist. Father of Nathaniel P. Willis. Established the *Eastern Argus* at Portland, Maine, 1803, in opposition to the Federal party; sold the paper, 1809. Removed to Boston, Mass., 1812. Began publication, 1816, of the *Recorder* (*Boston Recorder*), claiming it to be the world's first religious newspaper. *Youth's Companion*, his greatest contribution to journalism, originated as a department in the *Recorder* and appeared in separate covers, 1827. Willis served as editor until 1857.

WILLIS, NATHANIEL PARKER (*b. Portland, Maine, 1806; d. near Tarrytown, N.Y., 1867*), journalist, author. Son of Nathaniel Willis. Won celebrity as a poet while still an undergraduate at Yale; entered journalism on graduation, 1827. As editor of the Boston *American Monthly Magazine*, 1829–31, he posed in print as a dandy and aesthete, attracting envy and criticism but achieving a reasonable success. Removing to New York City, he became associated with George P. Morris and went abroad as foreign correspondent for the *New-York Mirror*. Resident in Europe until May 1836, he had a great social success, notably in England, but was guilty of considerable indiscretion in the articles which he sent back to the *Mirror* (collected as *Pencillings by the Way*, 1835 and later editions).

Although one of the best paid of American periodical writers after his return to the United States, he also attempted the drama and was author of, among other plays, *Bianca Visconti* (1839; produced in New York, 1837) and *Tortesa* (1839). He continued to write for the *Mirror* and was a co-founder of the weekly *Corsair* (1839–40) for which he engaged W. M. Thackeray as a correspondent. *Post* 1840 he was associated with G. P. Morris as an editor of the *New Mirror* and the *Evening Mirror* (a daily paper); in 1846 he joined Morris in publication of the *Home Journal*, their final and most prosperous undertaking. A colorful and lighthearted commentator on the day-to-day life of New York City and the nation, Willis was a generous friend to many less fortunate writers including Edgar Allan Poe whom he defended against later calumnies. Modern critics have given him a place of importance in the development of the American short story. Among his many books, which were almost wholly made up from his magazine pieces, were (in addition to those already cited) *A l'Abri; or, the Tent Pitch'd* (1839); *Letters from under a Bridge* (1840); *Dashes at Life with a Free Pencil* (1845); and *Fun Jottings* (1853). He published a number of volumes of his verses and almost all his works were reprinted in England.

WILLIS, OLYMPIA BROWN. [See BROWN, OLYMPIA, 1835–1926.]

WILLIS, WILLIAM (*b. Haverhill, Mass., 1794; d. 1870*), historian, lawyer, Portland, Maine, official. Graduated Harvard, 1813. Became law partner of William Pitt Fessenden, 1835. For fifty years a "substantial citizen" of Portland, Maine, he was mayor of Portland and president of the Maine Central Railroad. His chief works were *The History of Portland* (1831–33; 2nd ed., 1865) and *A History of the Law, the Courts, and the Lawyers of Maine* (1863). He edited first six volumes of Maine Historical Society's *Collections* (1831–59).

WILLISTON, SAMUEL (*b. Easthampton, Mass., 1795; d. Easthampton, 1874*), philanthropist, businessman. Best known as a promoter of religious and charitable enterprises; founded Williston Seminary, Easthampton, 1841; benefactor of Amherst and Mount Holyoke.

WILLISTON, SAMUEL WENDELL (*b. Roxbury, Mass., 1852; d. 1918*), paleontologist, physician, dipterist. Graduated Kansas State College, 1872; M.D., Yale Medical School, 1880; Ph.D., Yale, 1885. Employed by Othniel C. Marsh as collector, preparator and writer, 1873–85; worked in western Kansas, and in dinosaur-bearing beds in Colorado and Montana. Taught anatomy at Yale, 1886–90; taught geology, paleontology, vertebrate anatomy and physiology at University of Kansas, 1890–1902, serving also for a time as dean of the school of medicine. Headed department of vertebrate paleontology at University of

Chicago, *post* 1902. His many papers on the reptiles of the Cretaceous include the classic work on the mosasaurs (in Volume IV of *The University Geological Survey of Kansas*, 1898). A pioneer dipterist, he wrote *Manual of North American Diptera* (1908) and was author, among other works, of *American Permian Vertebrates* (1911) and *Water Reptiles of the Past and Present* (1914). W. K. Gregory edited his *Osteology of the Reptiles* (1925). His contributions to paleontology were fundamental and of lasting influence.

WILLISTON, SETH (*b. Suffield, Conn., 1770; d. Guilford Center, N.Y., 1851*), Congregational clergyman, home missionary. Graduated Dartmouth, 1791; appointed to missionary service in New York State by Connecticut Missionary Society, 1798. A follower of Samuel Hopkins (1721–1803), his preaching evoked the revival of 1799–1800 in central and western New York. While pastor at Lisle, N.Y., 1801–10, he continued to preach widely and to establish churches. He removed, 1810, to Durham, N.Y., where he served 18 years as pastor before returning to his missionary travels.

WILLS, CHILDE HAROLD (*b. Fort Wayne, Ind., 1878; d. Detroit, Mich., 1940*), automotive designer, manufacturer, metallurgist. An early associate of Henry Ford in motor-car design, Wills acted as chief engineer and factory manager of the Ford Motor Co. *post* 1903, helping to design every Ford car, including the Model T. Shifting his interest to the study of metals, he adapted vanadium steel and other alloys to Ford use and eventually developed molybdenum steel for use in auto parts subject to stress. Disagreeing with Ford over basic policies, he left the company in March 1919 and began to manufacture the Wills-St. Claire motor car. The new car introduced molybdenum steel, four-wheeled brakes, and other features, and was highly regarded, but production of it was abandoned in 1926 because Wills spent too much time and money on changes. [*Supp. 2*]

WILLSON, AUGUSTUS EVERETT (*b. Maysville, Ky., 1846; d. Louisville, Ky., 1931*), lawyer, politician. Junior partner in Louisville office of John M. Harlan, 1874–79. Unsuccessful Republican candidate for Congress from Kentucky, 1884–92. As governor of Kentucky, 1907–11, he was checkmated by a hostile Democratic legislature and aroused criticism for allegedly partisan executive acts during the "night-rider" troubles in Kentucky.

WILLYS, JOHN NORTH (*b. Canandaigua, N.Y., 1873; d. 1935*), industrialist. A successful bicycle manufacturer in Elmira, N.Y., he began the sale of Pierce motor cars, 1901, and took over the handling and sale of the entire output of the Overland Co., 1906. Securing control of the Pope-Toledo plant at Toledo, O., he installed the Overland Co. there and produced great numbers of the Willys-Overland between 1908 and 1916. He also invested heavily in concerns making automobile parts. After World War I, the Willys-Overland declined in popularity and faced strong competition; these factors and a strike at the plant, together with Willys's inability to control costs, brought about the liquidation of Willys's overall holding corporation, but left him a principal stockholder and manager of the main manufacturing concern. A heavy contributor to the Republican campaign fund in 1928, he served as U.S. ambassador to Poland, 1930–32, after providentially disposing of his stock in Willys-Overland just before the 1929 crash. He returned to the management of Willys-Overland *post* 1932 as receiver and later president. [*Supp.* 1]

WILMARTH, LEMUEL EVERETT (*b. Attleboro, Mass., 1835; d. 1918*), painter, teacher. Studied at Pennsylvania Academy of the Fine Arts, Philadelphia; also at Munich Academy and in Paris under J. L. Gérôme. Began exhibiting genre paintings at the National Academy in New York City, 1866. Taught at the National Academy of Design school, 1870–89; headed it, 1871–87.

WILMER, JAMES JONES (*b. Kent Co., Md., 1749/ 50; d. Detroit, Mich., 1814*), clergyman. Served as rector of four Maryland parishes, 1779–89. Became leader of Baltimore group which founded in 1792 the first New Church (Swedenborgian) Society in America. Reinstated as Episcopal clergyman, 1799, he held charges in Delaware, Maryland and Virginia. A chaplain of Congress, 1809–13, he became a U.S. Army chaplain, 1813. Author, among other writings, of *Consolation, being a Replication to Thomas Paine* (1794) and *The American Nepos* (1805).

WILMER, JOSEPH PÈRE BELL (*b. 1812; d. New Orleans, La., 1878*), Episcopal clergyman. Nephew of William H. Wilmer. Graduated Theological Seminary, Virginia, 1834; ordained, 1838. Served as chaplain, U.S. Navy, 1839–44; rector, St. Mark's Church, Philadelphia, Pa., 1849–61. Consecrated bishop of Louisiana, 1866, he was identified with the high-church party and noted as an orator.

WILMER, RICHARD HOOKER (*b. Alexandria, Va., 1816; d. Mobile, Ala., 1900*), Episcopal clergyman. Son of William H. Wilmer (1782–1827). Graduated Yale, 1836; Theological Seminary, Virginia, 1839. Ministered in rural Virginia parishes, 1840–61; in 1843 was minister, St. James Church, Wilmington, N.C. Consecrated bishop of Alabama, March 1862, he helped organize the Protestant Episcopal Church in the Confederate States, returning to union, 1865. Notable as a preacher, he proved an able administrator during Reconstruction.

WILMER, WILLIAM HOLLAND (*b. Kent Co., Md., 1782; d. 1827*), Episcopal clergyman. Father of Richard H. Wilmer. Ordained, 1808, he became rector of St. Paul's Church, Alexandria, Va., 1812; he

was a leader in the convention which effected the election of Bishop R. C. Moore, 1814. Zealous in his Church's revival in Virginia and in ministerial education, he was appointed a deputy to every meeting of the General Convention from 1814 until his death. Established in Washington, D.C., 1819, the *Theological Repertory* which he edited until 1826. In 1823, with others he organized the Theological Seminary at Alexandria, Va. Became president, College of William and Mary, and rector, Bruton Parish, Williamsburg, Va., 1826. Author, among other works, of *The Episcopal Manual* (1815).

WILMER, WILLIAM HOLLAND (*b. Powhatan Co., Va., 1863; d. Washington, D.C., 1936*), ophthalmologist. Son of Richard H. Wilmer. M.D., University of Virginia, 1885; worked with Emil Gruening at Mt. Sinai Hospital, New York City; studied also in Europe. Practiced in Washington, D.C., *post* 1889, where he won repute as a diagnostician and surgeon of the highest order and served as professor in the medical school of Georgetown University. *Post* 1925, he directed the Wilmer Ophthalmological Institute at Johns Hopkins until his retirement in 1934. During World War I he directed researches in depth perception, muscular fatigue, and other factors influencing the disabilities of flyers. [*Supp.* 2]

WILMOT, DAVID (*b. Bethany, Pa., 1814; d. 1868*), lawyer, politician. Congressman, Democrat, from Pennsylvania, 1845–51; U.S. senator, Republican, 1861–63. A leader among the Free-Soilers *post* 1848 and a founder of the Republican party, he served as president judge, 13th judicial district of Pennsylvania, 1851–61. He is principally famous for his addition of the "Wilmot Proviso" in the bill which appropriated funds for making peace with Mexico, 1846. Passed by the House but defeated in the Senate, the Proviso was intended to impede the growth of Southern power by prohibiting slavery in any territory which might be acquired with the money thus appropriated.

WILSON, ALEXANDER (*b. Renfrewshire, Scotland, 1766; d. Philadelphia, Pa., 1813*), weaver, poet, ornithologist. Emigrating to New Castle, Del., 1794, he engaged in teaching in New Jersey and Pennsylvania. Association with the naturalist William Bartram inspired him to attempt a large-scale study of the birds of the United States. He began at once to observe and to collect specimens, setting himself to learn how to draw and paint them. Engaging Alexander Lawson to prepare engraved plates from his drawings, he devoted ten years to *American Ornithology* (Vol. I, 1808; Vols. II–VII published by 1813). George Ord completed the work from Wilson's manuscripts after the author's death and later published two new editions of it. Wilson's reputation rests wholly upon this book which is an original and accurate contribution to science. He covered only the eastern United States north of Florida; during the next hundred years, however, only 23 indigenous land birds were added to his list. His *The Foresters* (1805) is a versified account of a walking tour from Philadelphia to Niagara Falls. Wilson's poetry is undistinguished, but the prose essays in his *Ornithology* are outstanding in American nature literature.

WILSON, ALLEN BENJAMIN (*b. Willet, N.Y., 1824; d. Woodmont, Conn., 1888*), inventor. A journeyman cabinet-maker, he patented a sewing machine (1850) featuring a double-pointed shuttle, but sold his interests in the patent to E. Lee & Co. of New York. He then devised a rotary hook and bobbin (patented, 1851) as a substitute for the double-pointed shuttle and entered partnership with Nathaniel Wheeler to make and market his improved machine. In 1854 he obtained a patent for a four-motion feed used on all later machines. Thereafter he invented cotton-picking machinery, and also devices for photography and for illuminating gas manufacture.

WILSON, AUGUSTA JANE EVANS. [See Evans, Augusta Jane, 1835–1909.]

WILSON, BIRD (*b. Carlisle, Pa., 1777; d. New York, N.Y., 1859*), Episcopal clergyman, Pennsylvania jurist. Son of James Wilson (1742–1798). Ordained priest, 1820; professor of systematic divinity, General Theological Seminary, N.Y., 1821–50; a moderate Anglican. Secretary, House of Bishops, 1829–41. Author, among other writings, of *Memoir of the Life of the Rt. Rev. William White* (1839).

WILSON, CLARENCE TRUE (*b. Milton, Del., 1872; d. Portland, Oreg., 1939*), Methodist clergyman. Elected president of the Oregon Anti-Saloon League, 1906, he spent his life thereafter in the prohibition movement. Chosen general secretary of the (later-named) Board of Temperance, Prohibition, and Public Morals of the Methodist Episcopal Church, 1910, he gave it an aggressive leadership and, along with men such as Wayne B. Wheeler, was instrumental in securing much church support for national Prohibition. After the Eighteenth Amendment had been adopted in 1919, he continued his efforts to secure its full enforcement, giving much time to political action and employing extravagant lobbying and other tactics which brought upon him much bitter criticism. [*Supp. 2*]

WILSON, EDMUND BEECHER (*b. Geneva, Ill., 1856; d. New York, N.Y., 1939*), biologist, experimental embryologist and cytologist. Ph.B., Yale, 1878; Ph.D., Johns Hopkins, 1881. A student of William K. Brooks at Johns Hopkins, Wilson spent some time at the universities of Cambridge and Leipzig and worked for almost a year at the Zoological Station at Naples, Italy. After teaching at Williams, Massachusetts Institute of Technology, and Bryn Mawr, he went to Columbia University in 1891 as adjunct professor in the department of zoology; he later became full professor and chairman of the department. His monograph on the development of the colonial jellyfish *Renilla* (1883) established him as a scientist, and he became one of the outstanding pioneers of "cell lineage." He then took up the problems presented by the organization of the individual cell, and for a number of years engaged in experiments on various regions of the egg or of different cleavage cells; this aspect of his work was signalized in his *The Cell in Development and Inheritance* (1896 and later editions). From 1900 to 1905 his research on germinal localization ran side by side with his investigations of the cellular phenomena that are correlated with artificial parthenogenesis. After 1905 he turned his attention to the problem of sex determination, and in a series of brilliant cytological studies on sex chromosomes reached the high point of his research labors. He prepared the ground for the sensational series of genetical discoveries made *post* 1910 by Thomas H. Morgan and his associates in the Columbia laboratories. [*Supp. 2*]

WILSON, ERNEST HENRY (*b. Chipping Campden, England, 1876; d. near Worcester, Mass., 1930*), botanist. As a plant collector for the Arnold Arboretum, Harvard University, he went to the Far East, Africa, Australia and New Zealand, 1907–10, 1914–22, and introduced to cultivation more than one thousand plant species. He became assistant director of the Arnold Arboretum, 1919, and in 1927, keeper.

WILSON, FRANCIS (*b. Philadelphia, Pa., 1854; d. 1935*), actor. Began his career *c.* 1868 as a partner in a song-and-dance act; appeared *post* 1880 as comedian in a number of musical comedies. He became famous in the role of Cadeaux in *Erminie* (1886) and continued as a musical comedy star until 1904 when he became a "legitimate" actor. His principal vehicle was *The Bachelor's Baby* which he wrote himself; it opened in Baltimore, Md., 1909, ran for three years, and made Wilson a fortune. Elected president of the Actors' Equity Association, 1913, he devoted much of his time to its affairs until 1921 when he resigned as president. The victory of the actors in the famous strike of 1919 was in great measure his victory. Wilson had a genius for friendship; among his many friends were Joseph Jefferson and Eugene Field. [*Supp. 1*]

WILSON, GEORGE FRANCIS (*b. Uxbridge, Mass., 1818; d. East Providence, R.I., 1883*), chemical manufacturer, inventor. Established (with Eben N. Horsford) George F. Wilson & Co., later known as the Rumford Chemical Co., at East Providence, R.I., which he headed until his death. Benefactor of Brown University and Dartmouth College.

WILSON, HARRY LEON (*b. Oregon, Ill., 1867; d. Carmel, Calif., 1939*), novelist, playwright. Began literary career as a contributor to *Puck*, 1887; served on that magazine as assistant to Henry C. Bunner, 1892–96, and as editor-in-chief, 1896–1902. After writing several serious novels including *The Spenders* (1902), he achieved in *The Boss of Little Arcady* (1905) for the first time that adroit mingling of burlesque and realism which marked his later work. A collaborator with Booth Tarkington for several years in writing plays (among them the hit *The Man from Home*, 1907), Wilson became a regular contributor of fiction to the *Saturday Evening Post*. Outstanding among his later works were *Bunker Bean* (1913), *Ruggles of Red Gap* (1915), and *Merton of the Movies* (1922). [*Supp. 2*]

WILSON, HENRY (*b. Farmington, N.H., 1812; d. Washington, D.C., 1875*), shoemaker, lawyer, Massachusetts legislator and statesman. Born Jeremiah Colbath of poverty-stricken parents, he was indentured to a farmer as a boy; he had his name legally changed to Henry Wilson c. 1833. His formal education was never more than meager. With minimum capital, he established a shoe factory which was a moderate success. Elected to the Massachusetts House of Representatives as a Whig in 1840, he served in the state legislature for most of the next twelve years. Disaffected at the 1848 Whig national convention because it took no stand on the Wilmot Proviso, he and a small group withdrew and launched the Free Soil party at a Buffalo, N.Y., convention. An ardent opponent of slavery, he edited the *Boston Republican* (the Free Soil organ), 1848–51, and aligned himself with the American (Know-Nothing) party, mistakenly believing it would be an important force in freedom's cause. When its 1855 convention adopted a platform which was evasive on the slavery issue, he revolted and withdrew, thereby foiling the party's first attempt to control national politics. Elected to fill a Massachusetts vacancy in the U.S. Senate, 1855, he aligned himself with the Abolitionists, was vehement in the debate over Kansas, and supported the Republican campaign in 1860. At the outset of the Civil War, he was chairman of the Senate military affairs committee and threw his tremendous energy into the task of framing, explaining and defending legislative measures necessary for enlisting, organizing and provisioning a vast army. (*Post* 1852, he had served with his state's militia, attaining a brigadier-generalship.) He constantly urged Lincoln to declare emancipation as a war measure, and he shaped the bills which brought freedom to many slaves in the border states before the Thirteenth Amendment was ratified.

After the war, Wilson as senator at first bitterly opposed President Johnson's Reconstruction policy and attitude toward Congress, but he later became more conciliatory. He favored federal legislation to aid education and homesteading in the impoverished South through which he had made long tours. His

name on the Republican ticket as vice-presidential candidate in 1872 contributed to its victory, and he made a highly efficient and acceptable presiding officer in the Senate until his death. Independent of mind, he never lost sympathy with the working people and promoted legislation in their behalf.

WILSON, HENRY LANE (*b. Crawfordsville, Ind., 1857; d. Indianapolis, Ind., 1932*), lawyer, diplomat. Brother of John Lockwood Wilson. Practiced in Spokane, Wash., 1884–96. As U.S. minister to Chile, 1897–1904, he was instrumental in averting trouble between Chile and Argentina, 1900. U.S. minister to Belgium, 1905–09. As ambassador to Mexico, 1909–13, he unsuccessfully urged presidents Taft and Wilson to recognize the Huerta government.

WILSON, HENRY PARKE CUSTIS (*b. Workington, Md., 1827; d. Baltimore, Md., 1897*), surgeon, gynecologist. Beginning practice in Baltimore, Md., 1851, he was first in the state to remove uterine appendages by abdominal section and the second to perform successful ovariotomy (1866). Said to be second in the world to remove an intra-uterine tumor by morcellation. Co-founder of Hospital for the Women of Maryland, 1882; consultant at Johns Hopkins and other Baltimore hospitals.

WILSON, JAMES (*b. Carskerdo, Scotland, 1742; d. Edenton, N.C., 1798*), jurist. Described by James Bryce as "one of the deepest thinkers and most exact reasoners" in the federal convention of 1787, and as one whose works "display an amplitude and profundity of view in matters of constitutional theory which place him in the front rank of the political thinkers of his age." Emigrated to America, 1765. Better educated than most immigrants of the time, he quickly obtained a position as Latin tutor in the College of Philadelphia. After studying law with John Dickinson, he began practice in Reading, Pa., 1768. Soon removing to Carlisle, Pa., he was very successful in cases involving land disputes. By 1773 he had begun borrowing capital for speculative land purchases, a lifelong activity of his.

Active in the early Revolutionary movement, he was elected to the First Continental Congress and distributed to its members his pamphlet *Considerations on the Nature and Extent of the Legislative Authority of the British Parliament* (1774), a work which denied to Parliament the least authority over the colonies. This able statement of the extreme American position was widely read in both England and America. Wilson also spoke to the same effect before the provincial conference of January 1775 and introduced a resolution on the Boston Port Act which presaged the doctrine of judicial review.

From his position on the extreme left in 1774, Wilson moved steadily thereafter to the right. As a Continental congressman, 1776–77, he aided in delaying moves toward independence during June 1776, but on July 2 was one of three out of seven Pennsylvania delegates who voted for independence. Active in executing burdensome committee assignments, he was among the first to urge relinquishment of the claims of the states to western lands, to advocate taxation powers for Congress, and to try to strengthen the national government. He also urged that representation in Congress should be based on free population. However, he fought bitterly against the 1776 Pennsylvania constitution, a democratic product of the frontier. Leaving Congress in September 1777, he engaged in corporation practice in Philadelphia after a brief stay at Annapolis, Md. Acting as counsel for Loyalists and engaging in privateering and land-jobbing schemes, he widened the breach between himself and the people and soon became personally unpopular. He served again in Congress, 1782 and 1785–87, but was chiefly concerned with his multiplying business interests. In 1785 he published *Considerations on the Power to Incorporate the Bank of North America,* an able argument in which he foreshadowed John Marshall's doctrine of inherent sovereignty.

Wilson's greatest achievement in public life was his part in the establishment of the U.S. Constitution. With the possible exception of James Madison, no member of the 1787 convention was better versed in the study of political economy, none grasped more firmly the central problem of dual sovereignty, and none was more far-sighted in his vision of the future of the United States. Wilson kept constantly in view the idea that sovereignty resided in the people, favoring popular election of the president and of members of both houses of Congress. He clearly stated that the national government was not "an assemblage of States, but of individuals for certain political purposes." He opposed the idea of equal representation in the Senate. He was a member of the committee of detail which prepared the draft of the U.S. Constitution, and, after signing it, he fought for its adoption. He was author, also, of the Pennsylvania state constitution of 1790 which represented the climax of his fourteen-year fight against the earlier democratic constitution. Although he expected appointment as chief justice, he accepted the post of associate justice of the U.S. Supreme Court, September 1789. Also appointed to the chair of law in the College of Philadelphia, 1789, he delivered a series of lectures in December in which he departed from Blackstone's definitions and, discovering the residence of sovereignty in the individual, postulated as the basis of law the consent of those whose obedience the law requires. He also set forth clearly the implications of the U.S. Supreme Court for judicial settlement of international disputes and for the administration of international law. Commissioned to make a digest of the laws of Pennsylvania, he began the task and also recommended himself to President Washington as being willing and able to establish a

body of theoretical principles for future judicial and legislative interpretation of the U.S. Constitution—especially with respect to the problems of federal and state relations. He was unsuccessful in his application, however, as the attorney-general urged on the president the impropriety of any single person determining such principles for future guidance. Wilson now plunged further into vast land speculations, involving the Holland Land Company in unwise purchases (1792–93) and buying an interest in one of the Yazoo companies, 1795. These and other speculative enterprises in which he engaged brought on him much severe criticism and he died amid talk of impeachment and while endeavoring to escape from creditors. His most noted decision on the bench was that in *Chisholm vs. Georgia* (2 *Dallas,* 419) in which he positively affirmed the doctrine that the people of the United States formed a nation.

WILSON, JAMES (*b. Ayrshire, Scotland, 1836; d. 1920*), farmer, Iowa legislator. Settled in Iowa, 1855. Congressman, Republican, from Iowa, 1873–77 and 1883–85; known as "Tama Jim," he was a member of the agricultural and rules committees. Appointed professor of agriculture and head of experiment station at Iowa State College, 1891, he helped place instruction on both a scientific and practical basis. As U.S. secretary of agriculture, 1897–1913, he established many new experiment stations and began farm demonstration work in the South; he also began cooperative extension work in agriculture and home economics, promoted world agricultural information and initiated much helpful legislation.

WILSON, JAMES FALCONER (*b. Newark, O., 1828; d. Fairfield, Iowa, 1895*), lawyer, Iowa legislator. Studied law under William B. Woods; began practice in Iowa *c.* 1852; was influential delegate in state constitutional convention, 1857. Known as "Jefferson Jim," he was congressman, Republican, from Iowa, 1861–69; as chairman of the House judiciary committee, he forwarded the Union program and introduced the original resolution for an abolition Amendment. During Reconstruction, he was one of the ablest leaders among the legalistic Radicals. He introduced important amendments to the resolution for repudiation of Confederate debt, also an amendment repealing appellate jurisdiction of the Supreme Court under the Habeas Corpus Act of 1867, and the final form of the Civil Rights Act. Advocate of the Pacific railroad, he was a government director of the road under Presidents Grant and Hayes. Attacked for alleged financial improprieties in this connection, he was closely questioned during the House investigations of the railroad, 1873. He was undistinguished as U.S. senator, Republican, from Iowa, 1883–95.

WILSON, JAMES GRANT (*b. Edinburgh, Scotland, 1832; d. 1914*), editor, Union soldier. Son of William Wilson (1801–1860). Came to America as an infant. Removed to Chicago, Ill., 1856, where he edited and published periodicals including the *Chicago Record* (April 1857—March 1862). Colonel, 4th U.S. Colored Cavalry, 1863; brevetted brigadier-general of volunteers, 1865. Settled in New York City, 1865. He was a prolific writer of military and literary biographies and an editor of church and local histories. His most extensive work was as co-editor (with John Fiske) of *Appleton's Cyclopaedia of American Biography* (1886–89; rev. ed., 1898–99).

WILSON, JAMES HARRISON (*b. near Shawneetown, Ill., 1837; d. Wilmington, Del., 1925*), engineer, cavalryman, author. Graduated West Point, 1860. Chief topographical engineer on Port Royal expedition; volunteer aide to Gen. G. B. McClellan at South Mountain and Antietam. Named inspector-general, Army of the Tennessee, 1863, he was active in Vicksburg's siege and capture. Advanced to brigadier-general of volunteers, October 1863, he was chief engineer of the Knoxville relief expedition and was made chief of the Washington cavalry bureau, January 1864. Commanding the third division of Gen. P. H. Sheridan's cavalry corps, Army of the Potomac, he led the advance across the Rapidan, covered Gen. U. S. Grant's passage to the Chickahominy, formed part of Sheridan's first Richmond expedition. Appointed chief of cavalry, Military Division of the Mississippi, with brevet rank of major-general, October 1864, he defeated Gen. N. B. Forrest in several engagements, enabling Gen. Schofield to repulse Confederate Gen. John Hood and contributing to Hood's defeat by Gen. Thomas at Nashville. On Apr. 2, 1865, Wilson took Selma, Ala., by assault in one of the most brilliant actions of the Civil War. He then moved on through Montgomery, Ala., took Columbus, Ga., and reached Macon, Ga., on April 20. After the war he superintended navigation improvements, resigning from the army in 1870. As senior major-general in the Spanish-American War, he served in Puerto Rico and Cuba; in the Boxer Rebellion in China, he was second-in-command to Gen. A. R. Chaffee. He was advanced to major-general, retired, 1915.

WILSON, JOHN (*b. Windsor, England, c. 1591; d. 1667*), clergyman, verse writer. Emigrated to Massachusetts, 1630. Served the First Church in Boston, Mass., from 1635 until his death, sharing the pulpit with John Cotton until 1652. A spokesman of orthodoxy and a constant counselor of the magistrates, Wilson was zealous for conversion of the Massachusetts Indians and was ranked among the most influential of the Massachusetts clergy.

WILSON, JOHN FLEMING (*b. Erie, Pa., 1877; d. Santa Monica, Calif., 1922*), journalist, author of sea stories.

WILSON, JOHN LEIGHTON (*b. near Salem, S.C., 1809; d. near Salem, 1886*), Presbyterian clergyman. Graduated Columbia (S.C.) Seminary; ordained, 1833. Went to Liberia, 1834; established missions in western Africa at Cape Palmas and the Gabun. Returned to America, 1852. Elected secretary of the Board of Foreign Missions, 1853; edited *Home and Foreign Record*, 1853–61; in 1866 founded *The Missionary* which he edited for nearly twenty years. Supervised foreign missions of the Presbyterian Church in Confederate States of America (later in U.S.) *post* 1861; also its home missionary projects, 1863–72. Author of encyclopedic *Western Africa, Its History, Conditions, and Prospects* (1856).

WILSON, JOHN LOCKWOOD (*b. Crawfordsville, Ind., 1850; d. Washington, D.C., 1912*), lawyer, publisher. Brother of Henry L. Wilson. Receiver, federal land office at Colfax, Washington Territory, 1882–87. Republican representative-at-large in Congress from Washington, 1889–95. Promoted Pacific Northwest river and harbor development; sponsored effective lieu land bill; secured passage of bill creating Rainier National Park. U.S. senator, 1895–99. In 1899 he purchased a controlling interest in the *Seattle Post-Intelligencer* which he managed until his death.

WILSON, JOSEPH MILLER (*b. Phoenixville, Pa., 1838; d. 1902*), civil engineer, architect. Son of William H. Wilson. C. E., Rensselaer Polytechnic Institute, 1858. Engineer of bridges and buildings, Pennsylvania Railroad, 1865–86. Organized Wilson Bros. & Co., consulting civil engineers and architects, 1876. The firm's projects included stations and shops for the Ninth and Third Avenue lines of the New York Elevated Railway, and for a number of other railroads; also, buildings for the Drexel Institute, Philadelphia, Pa., and other institutions there. Wilson himself designed and built, among others, the Susquehanna and Schuylkill bridges and the original Broad St. Station in Philadelphia; also, the main exhibition building and machinery hall at the Philadelphia Centennial Exhibition, 1876. He did important later consulting work and wrote on scientific and engineering subjects.

WILSON, JOSHUA LACY (*b. Bedford Co., Va., 1774; d. Cincinnati, O., 1846*), Presbyterian clergyman, educator. Father of Samuel R. Wilson. Called to the First Presbyterian Church, Cincinnati, O., 1808, he served there until his death. An Old School theologian, his defense of Calvinism led him into many controversies; he opposed the "New England theology" and the "Plan of Union" and prosecuted Lyman Beecher for heresy before the Presbytery and Synod.

WILSON, MORTIMER (*b. Chariton, Iowa, 1876; d. New York, N.Y., 1932*), composer, conductor, teacher. Headed theoretical courses, music department, University of Nebraska, 1901–08; revived and conducted the Lincoln Symphony Orchestra. Studied in Leipzig under Max Reger and Hans Sitt, 1908–10. Conducted Atlanta, Ga., symphony orchestra, and directed Atlanta Conservatory of Music, 1913–14. Arranged and wrote music for motion pictures. His compositions included symphonies, suites, sonatas, and numerous short pieces and songs; they displayed fluency and inventiveness in counterpoint.

WILSON, PETER (*b. Banff, Scotland, 1746; d. New Barbadoes, N.J., 1825*), philologist, educator, New Jersey legislator. Educated at University of Aberdeen. Emigrated to New York City, 1763. Principal of Hackensack (N.J.) Academy; of Erasmus Hall Academy, Flatbush, L.I., N.Y., *c.* 1792–1805. Professor of Greek and Latin, Columbia College, 1789–92; of Greek and Latin and Grecian and Roman antiquities, 1797–1820. Wrote treatises on prosody and edited classic texts.

WILSON, ROBERT BURNS (*b. near Washington, Pa., 1850; d. Brooklyn, N.Y., 1916*), painter, poet, novelist. Author of the poem "Remember the Maine" (in *New York Herald*, Apr. 17, 1898), which supplied the slogan for the Spanish-American War.

WILSON, SAMUEL (*b. West Cambridge, now Arlington, Mass., 1766; d. Troy, N.Y., 1854*), meatpacker; original of "Uncle Sam" as symbolic figure for the United States. Furnished beef to the army's supply center at Troy, N.Y., during War of 1812. The "U.S." on the casks was humorously defined as standing for "Uncle Sam's" monogram.

WILSON, SAMUEL GRAHAM (*b. Indiana, Pa., 1858; d. Tabriz, Persia, 1916*), Presbyterian clergyman. Missionary to Persia and Armenia *post* 1880. Distinguished as an educator, and for relief work among Armenian refugees from Turkey, 1916. Author, among other works, of *Persian Life and Customs* (1895).

WILSON, SAMUEL MOUNTFORD (*b. Steubenville, O., c. 1823; d. 1892*), lawyer. Admitted to the Ohio bar, 1844, removed to San Francisco, Calif., 1853, after practicing in Galena, Ill. Restricted his work to civil suits; took leading part in nearly all noted California land law cases. Outstanding as counsel for hydraulic mining companies (1880–86) against farming interests on debris question (*People of California vs. Gold Run Ditch and Mining Company*, 66 *California Reports*, 138, 155). Also in high repute for will cases, notably for his successful defense of David Broderick's will (21 *Wallace*, 503). A fluent, direct speaker, he depended for success on a complete mastery of the matters at issue. He served as chairman of the judiciary committee of the California constitutional convention, 1878–79, opposing radical demands of Denis Kearney.

WILSON, SAMUEL RAMSAY (*b. Cincinnati, O., 1818; d. Louisville, Ky., 1886*), Presbyterian clergyman. Son of Joshua L. Wilson. Graduated Princeton Theological Seminary, 1840. Pastor, First Presbyterian Church, Cincinnati, O., 1846–61; First Presbyterian Church, Louisville, Ky., 1865–79. A Southern sympathizer, he opposed the Reconstruction policy of the majority of the Old School Presbyterian Church and drew up the "Declaration and Testimony" adopted by the Louisville Presbytery in protest against the General Assembly's position.

WILSON, SAMUEL THOMAS (*b. London, England, 1761; d. Kentucky, 1824*), Roman Catholic clergyman, Dominican. Ordained priest in Belgium, 1786. Served as vicar-provincial of the Dominican community at Bornhem, Belgium, during the French Revolution. A missionary in Kentucky *post* 1805, he was named provincial in 1807 and was responsible for building the Church of St. Rose and College of St. Thomas Aquin near Springfield, Ky. Founded first American convent of Sisters of the Third Order of St. Dominic, 1822.

WILSON, THEODORE DELAVAN (*b. Brooklyn, N.Y., 1840; d. Boston, Mass., 1896*), ship constructor. Served in Union Navy, 1861–63, as ship's carpenter at sea; worked in Navy Yard at New York, 1863–65. Rose to rank of naval constructor, 1873, after service at Pensacola and Philadelphia yards and as instructor at Annapolis. Chief, Navy Bureau of Construction and Repair, 1882–93, he supervised transition of the navy from wooden vessels to steel, surmounting innumerable problems of material and design.

WILSON, WARREN HUGH (*b. near Tidioute, Pa., 1867; d. New York, N.Y., 1937*), Presbyterian clergyman, educator. Graduated Oberlin, 1890; Union Theological Seminary, New York, 1894. Ph.D., Columbia University, 1908. After studying the operation of new social forces on rural America while a pastor, he became secretary of the Church and Country Life Department of the Presbyterian Board of Missions, 1908, and held that post until his death. His scientific rural surveys in every major region of the United States became standard documents for the developing rural life movement and exposed the problems and deficiencies of rural education. His chief contributions to rural sociology were the application of the theory of marginal utility to rural social life and, as early as 1919, the development and application of the concept of regionalism to rural social conditions. He taught rural sociology at Teachers College, Columbia, 1914–23. [*Supp.* 2]

WILSON, WILLIAM (*b. Loudoun Co., Va., 1794; d. White Co., Ill., 1857*), jurist. Began practice in White Co., Ill., 1817. Justice, Illinois supreme court, 1819–24; chief justice, 1824–48. Rendered decision in *Field vs. State of Illinois ex rel. McClernand* (2 *Scammon*, 79), 1839, in which the governor's power to remove a secretary of state appointed by his predecessor was denied on the ground that the constitution did not expressly place any limitation upon the duration of the term of office.

WILSON, WILLIAM (*b. Crieff, Perthshire, Scotland, 1801; d. 1860*), bookseller, publisher. Father of James G. Wilson. Conducted business at Poughkeepsie, N.Y. *post* 1834; author of unoriginal verse, collected in *Poems* (1869).

WILSON, WILLIAM BAUCHOP (*b. Blantyre, Scotland, 1862; d. Savannah, Ga., 1934*), labor leader. Emigrated to Arnot, Pa., as a boy; worked as a miner; was active in early union organization. Secretary-treasurer, United Mine Workers of America, 1900–08. As congressman, Democrat, from Pennsylvania, 1907–13, he was outstanding as chairman of the committee on labor. He sponsored investigation of mine safety conditions and influenced organization (1910) of federal Bureau of Mines; in 1912 he secured passage of Seamen's Bill for protection of merchant marine seamen. As first U.S. secretary of labor, 1913–21, he thoroughly reorganized the Bureau of Immigration and Naturalization; developed agencies for mediating and adjusting industrial disputes (probably his most significant work); and set up the U.S. Employment Service.

WILSON, WILLIAM DEXTER (*b. Stoddard, N.H., 1816; d. Syracuse, N.Y., 1900*), Episcopal clergyman, educator. Graduated Harvard Divinity School, 1838. A convert from Unitarianism, 1842, he taught moral and intellectual philosophy at Geneva (later Hobart) Divinity School, 1850–68, and was briefly acting president. Professor of moral and intellectual philosophy, Cornell University, 1868–86, he served also as registrar and was active in university organization and administration. Became dean, St. Andrew's Divinity School, Syracuse, N.Y., 1887.

WILSON, WILLIAM HASELL (*b. Charleston, S.C., 1811; d. 1902*), civil engineer. Grandson of William H. Gibbes; father of Joseph M. Wilson. Principal assistant engineer, Philadelphia & Reading Railroad, 1835–36. Engaged in general practice, 1837–57; served as consultant to the Pennsylvania Railroad in westward extensions; appointed resident engineer, Philadelphia & Columbia Railroad, 1857. Given charge of maintenance of way and new construction for the Pennsylvania Railroad "main line" between Philadelphia and Pittsburgh, 1859, he held title of chief engineer, 1862–74. Constructed works of Altoona Gas Co., of which he was president, 1859–71. Headed real estate department of the Pennsylvania Railroad, 1874–84; thereafter, served as president and director of several Pennsylvania-leased railroads.

WILSON, WILLIAM LYNE (*b. Middleway, present W. Va., 1843; d. 1900*), Confederate soldier, lawyer, educator. Graduated Columbian College, Washington, D.C., 1860; LL.B., 1867. Assistant professor of ancient languages, Columbian College, 1865–71. Successfully practiced law in Charles Town, W. Va., 1871–*c.* 1883. President, West Virginia University, September 1882—June 1883. As congressman, Democrat, from West Virginia, 1883–95, his most important work was in tariff reform. He supported the Mor-

rison Bills and, as a member of the ways and means committee, helped frame the Mills Bill. He first reached national prominence in the 1888 debate on this measure. He was a principal opponent of the McKinley Bill, 1890. As chairman of the ways and means committee, 1893, he led in framing the so-called Wilson Bill; his moderate reform measures were vitiated by Senate amendments in 1894. U.S. postmaster-general, 1895–97, he inaugurated rural free delivery and enlarged classified civil service. A staunch believer in the gold standard, Wilson fought the Democratic stampede to free coinage of silver in 1895–96. After the Democratic convention of 1896, he condemned Bryan and was considered for the presidential nomination by the Gold Democrats. He was president of Washington and Lee University, Lexington, Va., *post* 1897.

WILSON, WOODROW (*b. Staunton, Va., 1856; d. Washington, D.C., 1924*), educator, statesman, president of the United States. Christened Thomas Woodrow Wilson, he came of Scottish ancestry and was the son of a Presbyterian minister. In his second year the family removed to Augusta, Ga.; in 1870 Wilson's father became professor in the theological seminary at Columbia, S.C., and pastor of the First Presbyterian Church; in 1874 the family moved to Wilmington, N.C., where the father held a pastorate. The young Wilson was the personal and intellectual companion of his father, acquired much learning at home, and lived a youth largely separated from those of his own age. He retained an indelible impression of the horror produced in him as a child by the Civil War.

After attending Davidson College, 1873–74, he entered the College of New Jersey (Princeton) from which he graduated, 1879. As an undergraduate he was a leader in debating and devoted much study to the lives of British statesmen. Aspiring to a career in public life, he attended the law school of the University of Virginia where he took more interest in the study of political history than in the formal law courses. In 1882 he began practice of law in Atlanta, Ga., but failed largely because of his repugnance to the purely commercial side of practice. Entering the graduate school of Johns Hopkins, 1883, he worked under Herbert B. Adams, but rebelled against German methods of postgraduate work. However, his newly stimulated literary powers won him a fellowship in the history department, and he published his important *Congressional Government* (1885), a beautifully written analysis of American legislative practice with emphasis on the evils that come from the separation of the legislative and executive branches of government and from the consequent power of congressional committees. This served also as his thesis and he was awarded the Ph.D. degree, 1886. In 1885 he had married Ellen L. Axson who was profoundly sympathetic with his ideals and influenced him strongly. After teaching history at Bryn Mawr,

1885–88, and at Wesleyan University, 1888–90, he joined the Princeton faculty as professor of jurisprudence and political economy.

Wilson cared little for scholarly distinction acquired by intensive research; his broad reading and intense intellectual curiosity, however, made him influential among faculty and undergraduates. He was soon a leader of the younger liberals on the faculty. He labored over his literary style and exercised a rigid self-criticism. He also engaged in lecture tours, thereby winning confidence in his ability to interest and dominate general audiences.

Elected president of Princeton, June 1902, he embarked on an already formulated program of academic reform. Convinced that the object of a university is simply and entirely intellectual, he proposed to revolutionize Princeton's attitude toward college life, giving the serious scholar the prestige he had rightly earned and reducing the social and athletic sideshows to a subordinate place. He undertook a structural reorganization of the university by means of the Preceptorial System and the Quad Plan (providing for more intensive individual instruction and for a democratization of the student body by housing it in small non-exclusive units like the English colleges), and he brought to the faculty a group of new scholars who were prepared to undertake the duties of preceptors to small groups. Wilson hoped to break the hold of the already existing and exclusive undergraduate clubs on the social life of the university but the Quad Plan was opposed bitterly, and he was asked by the board of trustees to withdraw this part of his program.

By a stroke of irony this academic defeat served to bring Wilson before the American public as a champion of the underprivileged and as a supporter of democratic principles. However, he received another setback in a controversy which had arisen over the location of the new Graduate College. Wilson saw in the refusal of the trustees to give him their entire support a block to the development of his ideal of a democratic coordinated university; he was also disappointed at the manifestation of bitter personal feeling incident to these struggles. At this juncture his early admirer, Col. George B. M. Harvey, urged Wilson upon the state Democratic organization as an ideal candidate for governor in 1910. The doubtful machine politicians allowed themselves to be persuaded to nominate Wilson; after resigning the presidency of Princeton, October 1910, he was elected governor of New Jersey in November.

Regarded by the machine politicians as a naive theorist and suspected by the reformers as a tool of the machine politicians, he speedily disillusioned both groups. Driving forward reform measures with vigor, by the end of the first session of the legislature he had secured enactment of the most important proposals of his campaign—a primary election law, an invigorated public utilities act, a corrupt practices act, and an employers' liability act. New Jersey was now studied by reformers as a practical example of possibilities, and Wilson began to attract national attention. Through the efforts of his friend Col. Edward M. House, who believed that Wilson was a man of genius and a Democrat untouched by "Bryanesque heresies," and also because of the admiration of people in general for the eloquence and power of his public addresses, Wilson was nominated by the Democrats for the presidency at Baltimore, Md., in the summer of 1912.

The political split between Republican progressives and conservatives and the personal quarrel between Theodore Roosevelt and W. H. Taft made the Democratic nomination in 1912 tantamount to election. Wilson was victor in November with 435 electoral votes as against 88 for Roosevelt and 8 for Taft; it was the largest electoral majority ever achieved up to that time, although it represented a popular minority. Wilson presented himself to the public as champion of what he called the "New Freedom." He was to be a conservative reformer, eager to return to the common people an equality of opportunity which had been threatened by the "interests" of industry, finance, and commerce. Distrustful of radical remedies, he believed that the first essential to government at Washington was to render it sensitive to public opinion. His campaign speeches had embodied his program; they were a series of magnificent manifestoes which established him as the leader of American liberalism. Aware of the tremendous influence still exercised in the United States by William J. Bryan, Wilson named him secretary of state; the other members of the Wilson cabinet proved to be of more than adequate administrative ability. Determined at the outset to establish a closer working connection between the executive and the legislature, he appeared in person before both houses of Congress in April 1913 to deliver his first message, thus reviving a custom that had lapsed since Jefferson's time. He soon began to use the large Democratic majority in Congress to win extraordinary legislative triumphs; of these, the most important were the Underwood Tariff and the Federal Reserve Act. The third major aspect of his program took form in creation of the Federal Trade Commission, and in the Clayton Anti-Trust Act which was designed to prevent interlocking directorates and declared that labor organizations should not be held or construed to be illegal combinations in restraint of trade. The aim of this legislation was to liberalize the industrial system and to eliminate special privilege, to destroy monopoly and maintain competition. Influential industrialists and the wilder reformers among the Democrats were equally opposed to the president, but he was able to control Congress through judicious use of the political patronage. However, the chief factor in Wilson's early success was his own genius for leading public opinion and mobilizing it against opposition. There were many, however, who said that he was too restless and wanted to go too fast.

Another irony in Wilson's career soon manifested itself. The president, primarily interested in solution of domestic problems, was soon forced to give major attention to international affairs. A determined pacifist, he was to be compelled to lead his country in a great war. Attempting to eliminate the traditional Latin-American jealousy of the United States by a policy of good will and accommodation, he was thwarted by conditions in Haiti, Central America, and Mexico. Problems occasioned by the Huerta-Carranza struggle in Mexico led to "incidents" and the necessity of military action in defense of United States rights at Tampico and Vera Cruz. Subsequent to the partial solution of these difficulties by the mediation of Argentina, Brazil, and Chile, a new set of troubles developed because of guerrilla raids across the border into New Mexico. In 1916 Wilson was forced to send a small force under Gen. John J. Pershing across the Mexican border in pursuit of Pancho Villa, and the National Guard was mobilized for protection of the border. He was, however, able to project the essential articles of an agreement to provide for international security of the Western Hemisphere which forecasted the later Covenant of the League of Nations. This matter was discussed with Latin-American statesmen, but was soon merged in Wilson's more comprehensive plan for a world organization built upon a similar model. Wilson also engaged in diplomatic efforts through Col. House to create a closer Anglo-American understanding which might later be developed by the inclusion of Germany and so end the mutual distrust among nations which was poisoning Europe.

After the sudden outbreak of World War I, the general favor given the cause of the Allies by people of the Eastern states was shared by the president; he was determined, however, that this should in no way affect a policy of complete neutrality. Soon both Allied regulation of neutral maritime trade and the German submarine campaign challenged the neutral policy which Wilson favored. The United States issued a formal protest against Allied maritime control in December 1914, but difficulties with the Allies were at once alleviated by the German decree of February 1915, declaring the waters around the British Isles a war zone and threatening to sink all belligerent merchant ships, with a further intimation that neutral ships might also be sunk. Reacting against such blind destruction of property as was entailed in the German threat, Wilson was further disturbed by the threat to life for which no adequate compensation could ever be made. On February 10 he warned Germany that destruction of an American vessel or American lives would be regarded as a violation of neutral rights and a matter of strict accountability. Soon "accidents" began to happen. On May 7 the

Lusitania was sunk; among the victims were 128 Americans. Wilson's firmness in demanding that Germany give up the ruthless submarine campaign led to the resignation of William J. Bryan in June; Bryan saw the danger of war in Wilson's insistence on the preservation of traditional neutral rights. However, the president's combination of patience and firmness triumphed temporarily. Following the sinking of the *Arabic* in August 1915, the German ambassador to the United States announced his government's promise that passenger liners would not be attacked without warning. A later comprehensive agreement to abandon ruthless submarine warfare was extracted from Germany by the threat of a diplomatic rupture which Germany hoped to avoid. "My chief puzzle is to determine where patience ceases to be a virtue," Wilson wrote to Col. House in September 1915. He continued to act, however, on the principle that the people of the United States counted on him to keep them out of the war, and that it would be a world calamity if the United States should be actively drawn into the conflict and so deprived of disinterested influence over the peace settlement. His policy toward Germany continued to receive confirmation from Congress right up to the national election of 1916.

At a disadvantage because of domestic dislike of his reform legislation and because of the revived solidarity of the Republican party, Wilson was re-elected in November 1916 over the Republican candidate, Charles E. Hughes, by a very narrow margin (277 to 254). Indeed, he at first thought that he had been defeated, and it was not until the full returns from the West came in that Republican majorities in the East were wiped out. He now began to make a determined move for peace, following along lines which he had pursued since the early autumn of 1914 despite constant rebuffs. The failure of the Allies to respond to intimations of a possible settlement from Germany and from Wilson now influenced the Germans to plan resumption of unrestricted submarine warfare; on Jan. 31, 1917, the German government told the United States that its earlier pledges would no longer be observed. Wilson decided immediately to give the German ambassador his passports.

Wilson believed that by upsetting the tentative movements for peace then in progress, however unlikely of success they might be, the Germans had morally condemned themselves. He still refused to believe, however, that a diplomatic rupture meant war. His hand was forced very soon by the publication of the so-called Zimmermann note suggesting that a German-Mexican-Japanese alliance was in prospect, and by the sinking of more American ships. On Apr. 2, 1917, he appeared before Congress to ask for a declaration of war and the resolution was voted on April 6. It represented an all but unanimous sentiment of the American people, who appeared to share the president's conviction that imperial Germany was an international criminal.

Once the United States was at war, Wilson mustered the full national strength and concentrated on victory. The nation was inadequately prepared for war, yet the president's war leadership was particularly distinguished in that he inspired a general conviction that it was a people's war and that every citizen should make individual sacrifices. He made wise choices of the men who were to occupy vital administrative and military posts, and he let them alone to do their jobs. His own supreme contribution to a victory lay in his formulation of war aims—aims which he had publicized well before the conflict. Embodying the principle of the Monroe Doctrine to the entire world, he demanded a concert of the Powers capable of maintaining international peace and the rights of small nations. However, even during the war it became obvious that Wilson's aims were not those of the Allies. Subsequent to the Russian Revolution a restatement of aims became necessary, and on Jan. 8, 1918, the president delivered before Congress the speech of the Fourteen Points. This was not intended as a public international charter, but as a diplomatic weapon to meet the Bolshevik drive for peace and to strengthen the morale of the Allied liberals. It contained six general points which repeated ideals already enunciated by Wilson: open diplomacy, freedom of the seas, removal of trade barriers, reduction of armaments, impartial adjustment of colonial claims, a league of nations. There were also eight special points dealing with immediate political and territorial problems.

By this speech the president committed himself to participation in the general world problem of preserving the peace and also to an interest in certain local problems peculiar to Europe which might disturb the peace. When the Germans recognized that they would be defeated (early in the autumn of 1918), they seized upon this speech as a general basis of peace negotiations and turned to Wilson as their savior from political or economic annihilation. Although his interchange of notes with the Germans at this point ran counter to public sentiment in the United States and irritated the Allies, it contributed to securing an early armistice by encouraging the existing demand for peace among the German people. When Wilson offered the Allies Germany's acceptance of an armistice on Oct. 23, 1918, the Allies were free to refuse it if they chose. Likewise, although the Germans later complained that they had been lured into a peace without guarantees, they were more than eager at the time to accept the undefined Fourteen Points rather than lose a chance at peace. After compelling the Allied leaders to accept the Fourteen Points by a threat to expose their intransigent attitude in Congress, the president sent Germany a qualified Allied acceptance of the basic conditions of peace and an armistice was signed on November 11.

Now at the height of his influence, Wilson was the greatest single force in the world, yet the difficulties of capitalizing on the victory were far greater than those which had been involved in winning it. The sense of common interest in war soon evaporated and Wilson's political ideals could not readily be transplanted to Europe. Also, at this critical moment Wilson made three mistakes. He asked for a heavy Democratic vote in the November elections as a sign of confidence in him and his policies, thus abdicating the national leadership by assuming the role of a party leader; Democratic defeats in the election therefore gave the appearance of a national repudiation. His second mistake lay in his failure to appoint to the Peace Commission a single member who truly represented either the Republican party or the U.S. Senate; thus he forfeited the chance of winning support from his domestic opponents. His third and greatest mistake lay in his decision to attend the Peace Conference in person, since by lowering himself to haggle at the conference table he lost his commanding position as first citizen of the world. He did succeed at the very beginning of the Conference in forcing an acceptance of the Covenant for a League of Nations as an integral part of the treaty of peace. At later sessions he was shaken by the discovery that in their application his principles were sometimes at variance with each other, and he was compelled to compromise—a series of adjustments which left liberals disappointed and the Germans bitter. However, the need of compromise is apparent from the fact that the Allied nationalists were equally disappointed. He could congratulate himself, however, on the adoption of the League of Nations Covenant through which, as he believed, all errors and omissions could later be rectified.

There now remained the problem of winning the approval of the U.S. Senate for the Versailles Treaty. Wilson had solved many more difficult problems during the negotiations, and there seemed little chance of an upset; public opinion generally favored the League of Nations and cared little about the treaty details. Even Wilson's chief opponent, Sen. Henry C. Lodge, hoped only to add amendments or reservations, but not to defeat the Treaty and the Covenant. Even a few conciliatory gestures by the president would have won the two-thirds vote necessary for ratification, but Wilson's attitude was not conciliatory. He would permit no changes and, as opposition developed, his tone became more unyielding. As the debate continued it shifted from the merits of the case to the question of authority between president and Senate and even to personal differences between the president and Sen. Lodge, chairman of the Senate committee on foreign relations. Setting forth on Sept. 3, 1919, on a country-wide speech-making tour on behalf of the Treaty, the president fell gravely ill at Pueblo, Colo. (September 25) and was brought back hurriedly to Washington. He was thereafter incapable of transacting official business. Had Wilson died then, his successor might have made the compromises which the Senate considered necessary for ratification of the Covenant; had Wilson recovered sufficiently, he might have made them himself. Isolated from the situation, he could do no more than maintain his earlier position. Despite the efforts of many in both the United States and Europe, the Treaty and the Covenant were rejected by only seven votes. The rest of his life was spent in invalidism and was anticlimax.

Woodrow Wilson was by taste and inheritance designed for a quiet life. He was always dependent upon the help and encouragement he received from his domestic circle. Subsequent to the death of Mrs. Wilson in 1914 he married, a year later, Edith B. Galt who survived him. He never capitalized fully on his personal and intellectual gifts in his public life. To those who worked closely with him he displayed a genial, humorous and considerate personality, but he was incapable of unbending with men whom he did not like or did not trust. He was handicapped in meeting the simplest problem of political tactics because he carried the attitude of a private citizen into public life; he refused to make many of the sacrifices of taste demanded by the rough game of politics. He was a man of strong prejudices, often ill-founded, and he would not yield them; because of this, he alienated important leaders in the world of business and journalism. Although pictured in the public mind at the end of his career as a self-willed and arbitrary egoist, he was actually highly considerate of the feelings and interests of those around him and a man who was unsparing in self-criticism. Sharply sensitive to the sympathies and advice of those for whom he cared, he had little respect for the arguments of personal or political enemies. The public force of his speeches resulted in part from clarity of expression and fine phrasing; they were equally characterized by strong and effective moral fervor. Wilson strove consciously to measure everything by spiritual rather than material values and the great masses of the people recognized this fact. His political philosophy was simple; he was a liberal individualist, insistent upon the rights of unprivileged persons and small nations. Possessed of a noble vision, he was not able to transform that vision into fact but he will remain in history as an eminent prophet of a better world.

WILTZ, LOUIS ALFRED (*b. New Orleans, La., 1843; d. 1881*), businessman, Confederate soldier, Louisiana legislator. An active and able Democratic leader and New Orleans official, Wiltz presided over the legislature as speaker in 1875 and was elected lieutenant-governor, 1876. He served as president of the state constitutional convention, 1879, and was elected governor that same year. He died in office.

WIMAR, CARL (*b. Siegburg, near Bonn, Germany, 1828; d. St. Louis, Mo., 1862*), painter of Indians and the frontier. Emigrated to St. Louis, 1843. Apprenticed to a painter of decorations for carriages and steamboats. Studied in Düsseldorf, 1852–57, among others with Emanuel Leutze. On returning to America, Wimar made several trips to the trading posts on the upper Missouri and the Yellowstone to sketch Indians in their natural habitat and gave much attention to details of costume, weapons and the Western scene. Among his outstanding paintings are "Attack on an Emigrant Train" and "Buffalo Hunt by Indians"; his four historical panels in the St. Louis courthouse were his last work and have been spoiled by inexpert renovation.

WIMMER, BONIFACE (*b. Thalmassing, Bavaria, 1809; d. 1887*), Roman Catholic clergyman, Benedictine. Christened Sebastian Wimmer; ordained priest at Regensburg, 1831; took solemn vows at monastery of Metten, 1833. Influenced by Peter H. Lemke to act on a plan to found a Benedictine monastery in America for ministry to emigrant Germans, he erected St. Vincent's Abbey in Westmoreland Co., Pa., 1846. He was appointed first abbot, 1855, and raised to archabbot, 1883. His foundation marked the beginning of the Benedictine Order in the United States; from it, many other abbeys and priories were established throughout the nation.

WINANS, ROSS (*b. Sussex Co., N.J., 1796; d. 1877*), inventor, mechanic. Father of Thomas De Kay Winans. Devised a model "rail wagon" in 1828 which had friction wheels with outside bearings, thereby setting the distinctive pattern for railroad car wheels. While engineer of the Baltimore & Ohio, 1829–30, he assisted Peter Cooper with his *Tom Thumb* engine. Employed in improvement of railroad machinery for the Baltimore & Ohio, 1834–60, Winans planned the first eight-wheel car for passenger purposes and is credited with innovating the mounting of a car on two four-wheeled trucks. In 1842, he constructed the *Mud-Digger* locomotive with horizontal boiler; in 1848, the first powerful "camelback" locomotive. He developed with his son (1859) the so-called "cigar-steamer" whose hull shape has been adopted in modern ocean liners.

WINANS, THOMAS DE KAY (*b. Vernon, N.J., 1820; d. Newport, R.I., 1878*), engineer, inventor. Son of Ross Winans. Associated with Joseph Harrison in firm of Harrison, Winans and Eastwick, St. Petersburg, Russia, which supplied locomotives and other rolling stock for the railroad from St. Petersburg to Moscow and cast the iron for the first permanent bridge over the Neva River. Director, Baltimore & Ohio Railroad. Devised (1859) with his father a cigar-shaped hull for high-speed steamers.

WINANS, WILLIAM (*b. on Chestnut Ridge, Pa., 1788; d. Amite Co., Miss., 1857*), Methodist clergyman, outstanding figure in Mississippi Methodism *post* 1820. Championed *status quo* of Methodist polity and doctrine at General Conferences, 1824–44; actively opposed abolition. At the General Conference, 1844, he defended Bishop J. O. Andrew and was a member of the "Plan of Separation" committee. Elected to General Conferences, Methodist Episcopal Church, South, 1846, 1850, 1854.

WINCHELL, ALEXANDER (*b. Northeast, N.Y., 1824; d. 1891*), educator, geologist. Brother of Newton H. Winchell. Graduated Wesleyan University (Conn.), 1847. Held chairs in geology, zoology and botany at University of Michigan, 1855–73; in geology and paleontology *post* 1879. Director of Michigan state geological survey, 1859–61 and 1869–71. Took advanced stand on evolution and helped reconcile supposed conflict between science and religion. Author, among other popular works, of *Sketches of Creation* (1870), *The Doctrine of Evolution* (1874), *Sparks from a Geologist's Hammer* (1881), and *World Life* (1883).

WINCHELL, HORACE VAUGHN (*b. Galesburg, Mich., 1865; d. 1923*), geologist, mining engineer. Son of Newton H. Winchell; nephew of Alexander Winchell. Prepared reports and maps of Mesabi range *ante* 1892, predicting its importance. Associated with Anaconda Copper Mining Co. *post* 1898, he headed its geological department but also maintained a consultant practice. A leading authority on the "apex law"; did pioneer work in origin of ore deposits. Author of *The Iron Ores of Minnesota* (1891), a standard reference work.

WINCHELL, NEWTON HORACE (*b. Northeast, N.Y., 1839; d. Minneapolis, Minn., 1914*), geologist, archaeologist. Father of Horace V. Winchell; brother of Alexander Winchell. Graduated University of Michigan, 1866. Minnesota state geologist, 1872–1900; professor of geology, University of Minnesota, 1874–1900. Did valuable geological studies on recession of St. Anthony's Falls, Minneapolis. A founder and editor of the *American Geologist*, 1888–1905. Author of *The Aborigines of Minnesota* (1911).

WINCHESTER, CALEB THOMAS (*b. Montville, Conn., 1847; d. 1920*), teacher, editor of texts in English literature. A.B., Wesleyan University (Conn.), 1869. Professor of rhetoric and English literature at Wesleyan *post* 1873. Author, among other works, of *Some Principles of Literary Criticism* (1899).

WINCHESTER, ELHANAN (*b. Brookline, Mass., 1751; d. Hartford, Conn., 1797*), Baptist and Universalist clergyman. Moved in his theology from open-communion Baptist tenets to strict Calvinism; accepted doctrine of universal restoration *c.* 1787. Preached in London, England, 1787–94, where he made many friends, among them John Wesley and Joseph Priestley. Probably the ablest and the most intellectual of early American Universalists, he was author of a number of books which included a refutation of Thomas Paine's *Age of Reason*.

WINCHESTER, JAMES (*b. Carroll Co., Md., 1752; d. Tennessee, 1826*), planter, soldier, Tennessee legislator. After service in the Revolution, he settled in the then Mero District of North Carolina, 1785; as brigadier-general of the District, he won fame as an Indian fighter. On admission of Tennessee, 1796, he was elected state senator and speaker of the Senate. Appointed U.S. brigadier-general, 1812, he was surprised and badly defeated by the British on the River Raisin in southeast Michigan, Jan. 22, 1813. Exchanged after imprisonment in Canada, he commanded the Mobile District until 1815. He was a founder of the city of Memphis, Tenn.

WINCHESTER, OLIVER FISHER (*b. Boston, Mass., 1810; d. New Haven, Conn., 1880*), manufacturer. Invented and patented a new method of shirt manufacture, 1848, in which he was successful at New Haven, Conn. Organized New Haven Arms Co. (later Winchester Repeating Arms Co.), 1857, for manufacture of pistols and rifles under patents of Tyler Henry, D. B. Wesson and others. Began production of Henry repeating rifle using new rim-fire copper cartridge, 1860; it was widely used by state troops during the Civil War but was not adopted by the federal government. The added improvement of a method of loading the magazine through the gate in the frame was made in 1866. Patented features of the Spencer rifle were added later. Winchester also acquired and produced the bolt-action inventions of B. B. Hotchkiss and the single-shot mechanism invented by John M. Browning.

WINCHEVSKY, MORRIS (*b. Yanovo, Lithuania, 1856; d. 1932*), poet, essayist, miscellaneous writer. Changed name from Lippe Benzion Novachovitch. Resident in London, England, after expulsion as socialist propagandist from Prussia and Denmark, he founded in 1884 the first Yiddish socialist periodical *Der Polischer Yidel*. Emigrating to the United States, 1894, he became the most representative contributor to the Yiddish daily *Forward* after its establishment in 1897; he was associated also with many other socialist periodicals. His proletarian poems dwell with sympathy on the sordid aspects of the life of laborers.

WINDER, JOHN HENRY (*b. Rewston, Md., 1800; d. Florence, S.C., 1865*), soldier. Son of William H. Winder. Graduated West Point, 1820. An artilleryman, he won brevet of lieutenant-colonel in Mexican War. Appointed Confederate brigadier-general, 1861, he held the thankless post of commander of military prisons, at first in Richmond where he was also provost-marshal, later in Alabama and Georgia. The extent of his responsibility for bad conditions in the Southern prison camps is still in dispute. He was defended by Jefferson Davis, Samuel Cooper and James A. Seddon. Also, his task was made an impossible one by the refusal of the Northern authorities to continue exchanges, and by a general lack of food, clothing and medicines.

WINDER, LEVIN (*b. Somerset Co., Md., 1757; d. Baltimore, Md., 1819*), farmer, Revolutionary soldier, Maryland legislator. Federalist governor of Maryland, 1813–15. On failure of the federal government to provide adequate defense of Maryland against British attack in the War of 1812, Winder rallied and equipped the state forces and frustrated the enemy's operations against North Point, Fort McHenry and elsewhere.

WINDER, WILLIAM HENRY (*b. Somerset Co., Md., 1775; d. Baltimore, Md., 1824*), Baltimore lawyer, soldier. Father of John H. Winder. Served on Northern frontier as colonel of infantry, 1812; promoted brigadier-general, March 1813. Commanded at battle of Bladensburg, Md., August 1814, and was blamed for the disgraceful defeat there which laid the city of Washington open to spoil by the British. The degree of his responsibility for the defeat is still a matter of dispute.

WINDOM, WILLIAM (*b. Belmont Co., O., 1827; d. New York, N.Y., 1891*), lawyer, politician. Settled in Minnesota, 1855. Congressman, Republican, from Minnesota, 1859–69; voted with the Radicals; was chairman of committee on Indian affairs. Appointed U.S. senator, 1870, he served also 1871–83, interrupted by a term as U.S. secretary of the treasury, March–November 1881. He was probably most notable as chairman of a special committee on transportation routes to the seaboard. He was also chairman of the committee on appropriations, 1876–81, and chairman of the committee on foreign relations *post* 1881. Urged a liberal railroad policy; supported homestead legislation; was a strong nationalist and high-tariff man. He served again with competence as U.S. secretary of the treasury, 1889–91.

WINEBRENNER, JOHN (*b. near Walkersville, Md., 1797; d. Harrisburg, Pa., 1860*), clergyman. Ordained, 1820, by General Synod of the German Reformed Church; dropped from the Synod, 1828, because of extravagant revivalistic methods. Founded the General Eldership of the Churches of God in North America, 1830, a sect based on a medley of primitive Methodist and Baptist doctrines.

WINES, ENOCH COBB (*b. Hanover, N.J., 1806; d. Cambridge, Mass., 1879*), prison reformer, educator, Congregational clergyman. Father of Frederick H. Wines. Secretary, Prison Association of New York, *post* 1861. With Theodore W. Dwight, prepared monumental *Report on the Prisons and Reformatories of the United States and Canada* (1867); stimulated widespread movement toward prison reform and encouraged such experimenters as Zebulon R. Brockway at Detroit, Mich. With Franklin B. Sanborn, promoted adaptation of Irish-Crofton system in the United States. Called national prison reform convention at Cincinnati, O., 1870. Secretary of National Prison Association, c. 1870–77.

WINES, FREDERICK HOWARD (*b. Philadelphia, Pa., 1838; d. Springfield, Ill., 1912*), social reformer, Presbyterian clergyman. Son of Enoch C. Wines. Influential secretary, Illinois state board of public charities, 1869–92, 1896–98. Secretary, National Prison Association, 1887–90. Author of *Punishment and Reformation* (1895), long a standard work. Brought from England the idea of the Kankakee State Hospital plan for care of insane; in early 1880's was among the first to urge use in America of "pathological research" and hydrotherapy. Appointed assistant director of the Twelfth Census, 1897, he was given major responsibility for *Report on Crime, Pauperism and Benevolence in the United States* (1895–96). Became statistician, Illinois board of control, 1909.

WING, JOSEPH ELWYN (*b. Hinsdale, N.Y., 1861; d. Marion, O., 1915*), Ohio farmer, agricultural journalist. Became first strong propagandist for alfalfa culture in Central and Eastern states. Staff correspondent for the *Breeder's Gazette* post 1898, he lectured widely and was a national figure in agricultural journalism. Author, among other books, of the authoritative *Alfalfa Farming in America* (1909).

WINGATE, PAINE (*b. Amesbury, Mass., 1739; d. Stratham, N.H., 1838*), Congregational clergyman, New Hampshire legislator and jurist. Brother-in-law of Timothy Pickering. Graduated Harvard, 1759. Pastor at Hampton Falls, N.H., 1763–71; *post* 1776, a farmer at Stratham. Delegate to state constitutional convention, 1781; elected to last Congress under the Confederation, 1787. U.S. senator, Federalist, from New Hampshire, 1789–93; U.S. congressman, 1793–95. Opposed Hamilton's funding scheme. As judge of the New Hampshire superior court, 1798–1809, he served usefully although ignorant of legal technicalities and procedure.

WINGFIELD, EDWARD MARIA (*fl. 1586–1613*), soldier. An original grantee of the Virginia charter, 1606, he came with the first settlers, and served as president of the Virginia colony, April–September, 1607. Removed from office, he was sent back to England in the spring of 1608. Author of "A Discourse of Virginia," a spirited defense of himself and an account of the colony from June 1607 to his departure, first published by Charles Deane in 1860 (*Transactions and Collections of the American Antiquarian Society*, Vol. IV).

WINKLER, EDWIN THEODORE (*b. Savannah, Ga., 1823; d. 1883*), Baptist clergyman, Confederate chaplain, author. Executive secretary, Southern Baptist Publishing Society, 1852–54; edited *Southern Baptist*. Principal pastorates included First Baptist Church, Charleston, S.C., 1854–61, and Citadel Square Baptist Church, Charleston, 1865–72. Editor of *Alabama Baptist, post* 1874. For ten years he was president of Home Missionary Board, Southern Baptist Convention. Deeply interested in the welfare of Negroes.

WINLOCK, JOSEPH (*b. Shelby Co., Ky., 1826; d. Cambridge, Mass., 1875*), astronomer, mathematician. Graduated Shelby College (Ky.), 1845. Superintendent at various times of the *American Ephemeris;* headed mathematics department, U.S. Naval Academy, 1859–61. Became director, Harvard College observatory and Phillips Professor of Astronomy, 1866 (later also professor of geodesy), serving in these positions until his death.

WINN, RICHARD (*b. Fauquier Co., Va., 1750; d. Duck River, Tenn., 1818*), Revolutionary soldier, planter, South Carolina legislator. As captain in command, made spectacular defense of Fort McIntosh, Ga., 1777. Served under Thomas Sumter and took distinguished part in skirmish at Fishdam Ford and in the battle of Blackstock. Promoted major-general of militia, 1800. Lieutenant-governor of South Carolina, 1800–02. Congressman, (Democrat) Republican, from South Carolina, 1793–97 and 1803–13. Removed to Tennessee, 1813.

WINNEMUCCA, SARAH (*b. near Humboldt Lake, Nev., c. 1844; d. Monida, Mont., 1891*), Indian teacher, lecturer. Daughter of a Paiute chief. Mediator between the Paiutes and the whites, she served as "guide and interpreter" to Gen. O. O. Howard during the Bannock War of 1878, performing many daring acts. Author of *Life Among the Piutes: Their Wrongs and Claims* (1883, edited by Mary T. P. Mann).

WINSHIP, ALBERT EDWARD (*b. West Bridgewater, Mass., 1845; d. 1933*), editor, educator, Congregational clergyman. Editor, *Journal of Education* (Boston, Mass.), 1886–1933; also edited the *American Teacher* (*post* 1896, the *American Primary Teacher*). Played important part in building National Education Association; was a pioneer (1876–83) in conducting community classes for adult education.

WINSLOW, CAMERON McRAE (*b. Washington, D.C., 1854; d. Boston, Mass., 1932*), naval officer. Graduated Annapolis, 1875. Commanded cruiser *Nashville*'s launches in cable-cutting operation at Cienfuegos, Cuba, 1898; performed extensive staff duty. Promoted rear-admiral, 1911, he commanded successively the 2nd, 3rd, and 1st Atlantic Fleet divisions, 1911–13, and the Special Service Squadron off Mexico, 1914. Commanded the Pacific Fleet, September 1915—July 1916; inspector of Atlantic Coast naval districts, 1917–19. Excelled in navigation and ship handling.

WINSLOW, EDWARD (*b. Droitwich, England, 1595; d. at sea, en route from Jamaica, B.W.I., to England, 1655*), Pilgrim father, author. Joined the Separatist congregation at Leyden *c.* 1617. Sailed on *Speedwell,* 1620, trans-shipping to *Mayflower;* landed at site of Plymouth, Mass., Dec. 11/21, 1620. Chosen envoy to greet Massasoit, 1621, he made the colonists' first treaty with the Indians. Next to Myles Standish, Winslow was the Pilgrims' most important man in dealing with the Indians throughout his career in America. He became the most active explorer and trader of the colony, setting up valuable posts in Maine, and on Cape Ann, Buzzard's Bay and the Connecticut River. In 1629, he was made the colony's agent. He was assistant nearly every year from 1624 to 1646, and governor in 1633, 1636 and 1644. He aided the organization of the New England Confederation and was Plymouth's representative. Active in reorganizing the colonial and local governments, 1636, and in drafting the new code of laws, he was also called on to travel to England on several occasions in order to defend both Plymouth and the Bay Colony against their enemies at home. Going to England in 1646 to refute the charges of Samuel Gorton, he never returned to Plymouth but was employed by Cromwell's government on several important missions. Winslow was author of four narratives of explorations in *A Relation or Iournall of the beginning and proceedings of the English Plantation setled at Plimoth in New England* (printed by George Morton, London, 1622) and *Good News . . . at the Plantation of Plymouth . . . Written by E.W.* (1624), the first accounts of the colony, and the only contemporary record to be published which had been written in America. He was author also of *Hypocrisie Unmasked by the True Relation of the Proceedings of the Governour and Company of the Massachusetts against Samuel Gorton . . .* (1646), and *The Glorious Progress of the Gospel among the Indians in New England* (1649) which led to the founding that year of the Society for the Propagation of the Gospel in New England.

WINSLOW, EDWARD (*b. Boston, Mass., 1669; d. Boston, 1753*), silversmith, Boston public official. Grand-nephew of Edward Winslow (1595–1655); cousin of Samuel Vernon.

WINSLOW, EDWARD FRANCIS (*b. Augusta, Maine, 1837; d. Canandaigua, N.Y., 1914*), Union soldier, railroad builder. Removed to Iowa, *c.* 1856. Served in 4th Iowa Cavalry. Promoted colonel, July 1863, at Vicksburg, he was chief of cavalry of the XV Corps; his force took Jackson, Miss. Thereafter he succeeded to command of a cavalry brigade and distinguished himself at Brice's Cross Roads, June 1864. He took part in the expedition against Selma, Montgomery, Columbus and Macon in the spring of 1865, capturing Columbus by assault. After the Civil War he returned to railroad-building, constructing part of the St. Louis, Vandalia & Terre Haute and also the St. Louis & South-Eastern. Subsequently he held high executive posts in several Midwestern railroads and was president of the New York, Ontario & Western; he was also general manager for a time of the Manhattan Elevated Railway in New York City.

WINSLOW, HUBBARD (*b. Williston, Vt., 1799; d. Williston, 1864*), Congregational clergyman. Brother of Miron Winslow; father of William C. Winslow. Principal pastorate at Bowdoin Street Church, Boston, Mass., 1832–44; conducted Mount Vernon School for Young Ladies, Boston, 1844–53. A frequent contributor to periodicals.

WINSLOW, JOHN (*b. Marshfield, Mass., 1703; d. Hingham, Mass., 1774*), colonial soldier, Massachusetts legislator. Grandson of Josiah Winslow. Began career as captain of a Massachusetts company in the West Indian expedition under Edward Vernon, 1740; subsequently, as a British soldier he served at Cartagena and in Nova Scotia until 1751. Sent to build forts up the Kennebec River by Gov. Shirley, 1754, he built Fort Western (present Augusta) and Fort Halifax (later Winslow). In 1755, he commanded the New England battalions in the force under Robert Monckton which took Forts Beauséjour and Gaspereau. The task of expelling the French inhabitants from Nova Scotia fell largely on Winslow. Assigned to command the provincial army raised in New England and New York, 1756, for the reduction of Crown Point, he co-operated with the British troops but was held inactive by orders of Lord Loudoun. He never received adequate compensation for his services, and continued to the end of his life to put in fruitless claims for pay or preferment to the colonies and to Great Britain.

WINSLOW, JOHN ANCRUM (*b. Wilmington, N.C., 1811; d. Boston Highlands, Mass., 1873*), naval officer. Became midshipman before his sixteenth year. Acquired reputation for gallantry in Mexican War. An Abolitionist, he viewed the Civil War as a holy cause and was openly critical of its conduct on the Mississippi, 1862. Promoted captain, July 1862, he was given the U.S.S. *Kearsarge* and served on patrol from the Azores to the English Channel, 1863–64. Encountering the Confederate cruiser *Alabama* off Cherbourg on June 19, 1864, Winslow won a complete victory and was promoted commodore. Promoted rear-admiral, 1870, he commanded the Pacific fleet, 1870–72.

WINSLOW, JOHN BRADLEY (*b. Nunda, N.Y., 1851; d. 1920*), jurist. LL.B., University of Wisconsin, 1875; practiced in Racine, Wis. State circuit court judge, 1883–91; state supreme court justice *post* 1891, becoming chief justice in 1907 by virtue of seniority. An excellent administrator and a profound student of jurisprudence, he won a national reputation for his opinions. His abilities are well represented in *Nunnemacher vs. State* (129 *Wis.*, 190) and in the *Income Tax Cases* (148 *Wis.*, 456). In his greatest opinion, *Borgnis vs. Falk Co.* (147 *Wis.*, 327), he laid the foundation for much of the so-called progressive legislation in Wisconsin and the nation while dealing with the constitutionality of the workmen's compensation law.

WINSLOW, JOHN FLACK (*b. Bennington, Vt., 1810; d. Poughkeepsie, N.Y., 1892*), industrialist.

Associated with Erastus Corning in the firm of Corning & Winslow, 1837–67. In time the largest producers of railroad and other iron in the United States, the firm delegated Alexander L. Holley to purchase the American rights to the Bessemer steel process (1863) and began operation of the first Bessemer plant in America at Troy, N.Y., 1865. Winslow manufactured the machinery and iron-plating for the original *Monitor* and also financed the undertaking.

WINSLOW, JOSIAH (*b. Plymouth, Mass., c. 1629; d. 1680*), colonial soldier and legislator. Son of Edward Winslow (1595–1655). Studied at Harvard but left without taking a degree. Served as a militia officer; as an assistant, 1657–73; as Plymouth commissioner for the United Colonies, 1658–72. Succeeded Myles Standish as commander-in-chief of the colony, 1659, after a three-year vacancy of that post. Captured Alexander, the son and successor of Massasoit, 1662, thus ending danger of Indian uprising. Becoming governor of New Plymouth, 1673, he established the first public school there in 1674. Elected commander-in-chief of the forces of the United Colonies when Indian uprisings began in 1675, he thus became the first native-born commander of an American army and won a decisive battle against the Narragansetts, December 1675. He was succeeded by Benjamin Church, the actual effective commander of the force, in February 1676. Liberal and tolerant, Winslow showed his statecraft in his handling of Edward Randolph in 1677, when he converted Randolph from a suspicious investigator into a friend of the Pilgrims. At the time of his death, Winslow was negotiating with the authorities in London to secure a Crown charter for Plymouth.

WINSLOW, MIRON (*b. Williston, Vt., 1789; d. Capetown, South Africa, 1864*), Congregational clergyman, educator, translator. Brother of Hubbard Winslow. Missionary at Oodooville, Ceylon, 1819–33, working among the Tamils. Residing in Madras *post* 1836, he was responsible for the final edition of the *Comprehensive Tamil and English Dictionary of High and Low Tamil* (1862) and helped revise the Tamil Bible.

WINSLOW, SIDNEY WILMOT (*b. Brewster, Mass., 1854; d. Beverly, Mass., 1917*), manufacturer, capitalist. Joining Gordon McKay and the Goodyear Co., he formed the United Shoe Machinery Co., 1899, becoming president. Instituted monopolistic lease system for his product, with "tying clause" in contracts. Prominent in New England financial affairs, he was a principal owner of the *Boston Herald* and *Boston Traveller*.

WINSLOW, WILLIAM COPLEY (*b. Boston, Mass., 1840; d. Boston, 1925*), Episcopal clergyman, archaeologist. Son of Hubbard Winslow. Founded and supported the American Branch of the Egypt Exploration Fund; procured notable Egyptian collection for Boston Museum.

WINSOR, JUSTIN (*b. Boston, Mass., 1831; d. 1897*), historian, cartographer, librarian. Granted Harvard College degree as of class of 1853; studied in Paris and Heidelberg, 1852–54. A linguist and man of letters, Winsor contributed criticism, poetry and fiction to periodicals, 1854–68. Librarian, Boston Public Library, 1868–77; he served thereafter as librarian at Harvard College. Winsor was a founder of the *Library Journal* and of the American Library Association (first president, 1876–85, and 1897). He was editor of *The Memorial History of Boston* (1880–81), characterized as the best work of its kind produced up to that time, and of the *Narrative and Critical History of America* (1884–89) to which he contributed outstanding bibliographies. He was author, among other writings, of *The Reader's Handbook of the American Revolution* (1880), an important bibliographical manual; *Christopher Columbus* (1891); *Cartier to Frontenac* (1894); *The Mississippi Basin* (1895); and *The Westward Movement* (1897).

WINSTON, JOHN ANTHONY (*b. Madison Co., Ala., 1812; d. 1871*), planter, Alabama legislator, Confederate soldier. A leader of Southern-Rights Democrats in Alabama, he served as governor, 1853–57. By vetoing state aid to railroads, he saved Alabama from a burden of debt. At the Democratic convention at Charleston, S.C., 1860, he prevented any compromise with Northern Democrats and insisted on withdrawal of the Alabama delegation in accordance with its instructions; during the ensuing presidential campaign, he supported Stephen A. Douglas. Elected U.S. senator for the term 1867–73, he refused to take the oath of allegiance and was denied the post.

WINSTON, JOSEPH (*b. Louisa Co., Va., 1746; d. 1815*), Revolutionary soldier, North Carolina legislator and public official. Cousin of Patrick Henry. Commanded part of right wing of patriot army at battle of King's Mountain, 1780. Congressman, (Democrat) Republican, from North Carolina, 1793–95 and 1803–07. Winston (now Winston-Salem), N.C., was named for him.

WINTER, WILLIAM (*b. Gloucester, Mass., 1836; d. 1917*), dramatic critic, historian of the stage, essayist, poet. After beginning his career as a reviewer on the *Boston Transcript,* Winter removed to New York City shortly before the Civil War and served for a time as assistant editor to Henry Clapp, Jr., on the *Saturday Press.* At this time he associated with the Bohemian group which met in the cellar of Pfaff's café on Broadway near Bleecker St.; his account of this group in *Old Friends* (1909) is perhaps as accurate as any that exists. While dramatic critic of the *New York Tribune,* 1865–1909, he at first enjoyed a national reputation, but had the misfortune to live into a time in the theatre for which he had neither appreciation nor liking. Author of a number of volumes of essays, verse and critical studies, he is remembered particularly for a series of accurate biographical studies of actors which include *The Jeffersons* (1881); *Henry Irving* (1885); and *Ada Rehan* (1891). He was an excellent judge of the technicalities of the actor's art. His *Shakespeare on the Stage* (1911–15) is a record of the "traditional" interpretations employed by actors in Shakespearian roles, a number of whom Winter had himself observed.

WINTHROP, FITZ-JOHN. [See WINTHROP, JOHN, 1638–1707.]

WINTHROP, JAMES (*b. probably Cambridge, Mass., 1752; d. Cambridge, 1821*), scholar, librarian, Massachusetts jurist. Son of John Winthrop (1714–1779). Graduated Harvard, 1769. Librarian at Harvard, 1770–87, he was concurrently for a part of this time register of probate for Middlesex County; in 1779 he was considered as a successor to his father in the Harvard chair of mathematics and natural philosophy, but was passed over. The next year he encouraged the students at Harvard in the revolution which deposed President Samuel Langdon. A founder of the Massachusetts Historical Society and a miscellaneous writer on a number of subjects, he served as judge of common pleas for Middlesex County *post* 1791.

WINTHROP, JOHN (*b. Edwardstone near Groton, Suffolk, England, 1587/88 o.s.; d. Boston, Mass., 1649*), lawyer, colonial statesman, first governor of Massachusetts Bay. Father of John Winthrop (1605/06 o.s.–1676). The son of a Suffolk landowner who held the manor of Groton, John Winthrop attended Trinity College, Cambridge, and later studied at Gray's Inn. Early in life he adopted Puritan habits of living. At first successful in the practice of law (he was admitted to the Inner Temple, 1628), he encountered financial difficulties in and after 1629. A Puritan of the type of John Milton, he was much concerned for the future of religion and morals in the England of his time. He became interested in the Company of the Massachusetts Bay which had been chartered in March 1629 and made up his mind despite family opposition to emigrate with his immediate family to New England. Entering into the executive work of the new corporation, which was distinguished from earlier colonial ventures by the intention of its settlers to remain permanently in America, he was chosen governor of the proposed colony on Oct. 20, 1629. The decision had already been reached by the Company to transfer itself with its General Court and its charter to America.

Winthrop sailed from Southampton in the *Arbella* on Mar. 22, 1630; he reached John Endecott's settlement at Salem on June 12. About six or seven hundred persons had taken passage in the *Arbella* and other vessels of the little fleet which accompanied it; two or three hundred more arrived almost simultaneously, and another thousand soon afterward. These numbers and the fact that, owing to the transfer of the charter and the Company organization to America, the entire management was local, gave Winthrop a position very different from that held by governors of any of the other early plantations. Soon settling in Boston, which appeared to offer a better site for the center of government of the colony than Charlestown which had earlier been considered, he threw himself into the work of forming the new community.

The term of governor was for one year and he was elected in 1631, 1632 and 1633. In April 1634, however, at the spring meeting of the General Court, the freemen of the town requested to be shown the colony charter. Finding that under the charter the General Court was the only body entitled to legislate, they wanted to know why some of its powers had been usurped by the leaders or magistrates. They then refused Winthrop's suggestion that the General Court should permanently abrogate some of its powers in order that authority might be concentrated in the hands of the leaders. John Cotton, the principal clergyman in the colony, in a sermon before the General Court, May 14, 1634, declared that a magistrate ought to be re-elected continually unless there was sufficient reason that he should not, also that officials had a vested interest in their offices. The freemen (that is, the members of the Company) replied by turning Winthrop out of the governorship and electing Thomas Dudley. Late in 1635 Hugh Peter and Henry Vane began an investigation into the causes of dissent in Massachusetts. Early the next year Winthrop, who had continued to serve as a magistrate, was called before a meeting of investigators, including John Cotton, and accused of having been too lenient in discipline and judicial decisions. The united clergy of the colony agreeing with this charge, Winthrop promised to adopt a stricter course in future, and so another step was taken toward clerical domination. Also in 1636 the General Court adopted a plan whereby certain magistrates should be chosen for life or good behavior. Winthrop and Dudley allowed themselves to be chosen the first two members of this unconstitutional life council which was always unpopular and lasted only a few years.

Winthrop, as deputy governor, took a part in the Antinomian controversy over the teachings of Anne Hutchinson which began to rock the colony at about this time. Passion was running so high at the 1637 election that the General Court held its meeting at Newton instead of in Boston and elected Winthrop governor in the place of Henry Vane. Grown much more narrow and severe since his rebuke by the clergy for leniency, Winthrop executed the law with rigor against the followers of Mrs. Hutchinson and drove many from the colony. He wrote an account of the controversy which was incorporated by Thomas Welde in *A Short Story of the Rise, Reign, and Ruine of the Antinomians* (1644). Elected governor again in 1638, Winthrop protected the colony charter from attacks upon it at home in an able letter to the Lords Commissioners for Plantations. Re-elected in 1639,

he learned at this time of serious financial losses in England which had resulted from the dishonesty of his agent there; for the rest of his life he was in financial straits.

A member of the Court of Assistants, 1640–41, he was again elected governor in 1642. During this term he engaged in the famous controversy over the veto power of magistrates which led to the separate sitting of the magistrates and the deputies as two houses. Still governor in 1643, Winthrop headed the Massachusetts commissioners for framing the articles for the United Colonies and was first president of the Confederation after it was formed. At this time he came under heavy criticism for giving military aid to French officials in Acadia without consulting the General Court. Deputy governor in 1644, he wrote a discourse called "Arbitrary Government Described and the Governm^t. of the Massachusetts Vindicated from that Aspersion." It was an attempt to justify the older principles under which the colony had operated and served only to show that Winthrop was losing touch with his people. Regaining his popularity in 1645, however, he was elected governor thereafter annually until his death, although the contentions over Robert Childe and Samuel Gorton, and Winthrop's severity in dealing with them, aroused an active opposition to his rule.

A refined and sensitive man, affectionate in his nature, Winthrop lacked aggressiveness. As a writer he had an excellent English prose style, and his journal (published in part as *A Journal of the Transactions and Occurrences in the Settlement of Massachusetts . . . 1630 to 1644,* 1790; supplemented with further manuscript materials, 1825–26) is a source book of the greatest importance. In government Winthrop had no faith in democracy, believing that, once chosen, representatives should govern according to their own best judgment. His own integrity was always beyond question.

WINTHROP, JOHN (*b. Groton, Suffolk, England, 1605/06 o.s.; d. Boston, Mass., 1676*), lawyer, soldier, colonial statesman. Son of John Winthrop (1587/88 o.s.–1649). Emigrated to Boston, Mass., 1631. Elected an assistant, 1632, he was one of the founders of Ipswich, 1633. Returning to England late in 1634, he accepted the governorship of the plantation in Connecticut which his father's friends Lord Say and Sele and Lord Brooke were undertaking. Arriving at Boston in October 1635, he sent an advance party to build a fort at Saybrook, the defense of which was entrusted to Lion Gardiner. Winthrop resided in Connecticut from March until autumn of 1636. After settling again at Ipswich, he appears to have moved to Salem in 1639. His father's financial difficulties having put a burden upon him, he began the manufacture of salt and tried to interest English capital in the erection of iron works. The General Court granted him 3000 acres of land for the encouragement of iron-making, 1644, and he set up a furnace at Lynn and another at Braintree; in the same year he was given leave to found a settlement for a similar purpose in Connecticut in the Pequot country (later New London). Retaining his public offices in Massachusetts, he made frequent journeys between the two colonies. Deciding after his father's death in 1649 to remain permanently in Connecticut, he was admitted a freeman of that colony, 1650, and elected an assistant, 1651. While developing iron works in the New Haven Colony, he was elected chief executive of Connecticut, 1657, and removed to Hartford. Elected lieutenant-governor, 1658, he was annually elected governor from 1659 until his death. The most important among his many services to the colony was his mission to England to obtain a charter, 1661–63. Gaining the favor of Charles II, he returned to New England with the most liberal charter that had yet been granted to any colony, making Connecticut almost independent and including within it the former colony of New Haven. One of the most engaging New Englanders of his day and probably the most versatile, he cultivated scientific interests, was skilled in medicine and chemistry, and was elected a member of the Royal Society, 1663—the first member resident in America. He was ahead of his time in his belief that New England's future lay in manufacturing and commerce rather than in agriculture.

WINTHROP, JOHN (*b. Ipswich, Mass., 1638; d. Boston, Mass., 1707*), colonial soldier and official. Son of John Winthrop (1605/06 o.s.–1676); commonly known as Fitz-John Winthrop. Commissioned in the English Parliamentary Army, he served in the Scottish campaigns and entered London with Gen. Monk, 1660. Returning from England to Connecticut, 1663, he made his home in New London. He commanded the Connecticut troops which defended Southold, L.I., N.Y., 1673, against the Dutch, and served with distinction in the Indian wars of 1675–76. Thereafter spending a large part of his time in Boston, he was appointed to the governor's council of Massachusetts by Joseph Dudley in 1686 and served on the council of Sir Edmund Andros. Returning to Connecticut after Andros's defeat, he helped re-establish the government and was elected as assistant in Connecticut, 1689. As major-general commanding a New York and Connecticut force under orders to invade Canada, 1690, he abandoned the attempt at a point north of Albany on finding himself without the provisions and munitions promised him by Jacob Leisler. Successful in a mission to King William III (1693) to request confirmation of the Connecticut charter, Winthrop was elected governor of Connecticut five years later (1698) and re-elected annually until his death.

WINTHROP, JOHN (*b. Boston, Mass., 1714; d. Cambridge, Mass., 1779*), astronomer, physicist,

mathematician. Father of James Winthrop; descendant of John Winthrop (1587/88 o.s.–1649) and John Winthrop (1605/06 o.s.–1676). America's first astronomer and Newtonian disciple, he graduated from Harvard, 1732; he was LL.D., University of Edinburgh, 1771, and Harvard, 1773. Elected Hollis Professor of Mathematics and Natural Philosophy at Harvard, 1738. The results of his forty years' research, mainly in astronomy, were all published in *Philosophical Transactions of the Royal Society*. His other publications include *Relation of a Voyage from Boston to Newfoundland, for the Observation of the Transit of Venus* (1761) and *Two Lectures on the Parallax and Distance of the Sun* (1769). He made a series of sun-spot observations, Apr. 19–22, 1739, which were the first in the colony; he also studied transits of Mercury over the sun, Apr. 21, 1740, Oct. 25, 1743, and Nov. 9, 1769. He established at Harvard, 1746, the first laboratory of experimental physics in America and demonstrated with a series of lectures the laws of mechanics, light, heat, and the movements of celestial bodies according to Newtonian doctrines; these lectures were attended by Count Rumford. Winthrop introduced to Harvard's mathematical curriculum the elements of fluxions (differential and integral calculus), 1751. In 1759, he predicted the return of Halley's comet of 1682; he later organized expeditions to Newfoundland for study of transits of Venus. He carried on magnetic and meteorological observations and was the main support of Benjamin Franklin in his theories relative to his electrical experiments. An ardent patriot, he was counselor and friend of Washington, Franklin, and other founders of the Republic.

WINTHROP, ROBERT CHARLES (*b. Boston, Mass., 1809; d. 1894*), lawyer, Massachusetts legislator, orator. Graduated Harvard, 1828; studied law in office of Daniel Webster. Congressman, Whig, from Massachusetts, 1840–42, 1842–50; speaker of the House, 1847–49. Appointed to the U.S. Senate on the resignation of Daniel Webster, 1850, he was defeated for re-election by Charles Sumner, 1851, because of alleged reluctance to oppose slavery. He was often called upon for orations and addresses on notable occasions, served for thirty years as president of the Massachusetts Historical Society, and was later in life chairman of the board of the Peabody Education Fund.

WINTHROP, THEODORE (*b. New Haven, Conn., 1828; d. Big Bethel, Va., 1861*), lawyer, author, Union soldier. Nephew of Theodore D. Woolsey. Graduated Yale, 1848. Engaged in a number of occupations. Traveled in Europe, across the plains, in the Far West, and in Central America. Enlisting in the 7th New York Regiment, 1861, he remained at the front subsequent to his regiment's return after a short term of service and was killed leading the advance in a skirmish on June 10. Winthrop is remembered for a number of books of marked originality, all published posthumously, which enjoyed a great popularity in their time. They include the novels *Cecil Dreeme* (1861) and *John Brent* (1862); also, *The Canoe and the Saddle* (1863) and *Life in the Open Air* (1863).

WINTON, ALEXANDER (*b. Grangemouth, Scotland, 1860; d. 1932*), pioneer automobile manufacturer. Emigrated to New York City *c.* 1880. After working as a marine engine builder and as assistant engineer on an ocean steamship, he settled in Cleveland, O., 1884, where he began a bicycle-repair business. Inventor of a number of improvements in bicycle mechanisms, he began the manufacture of bicycles, 1890, as the Winton Bicycle Co. As early as 1893 he began experimenting in gasoline engine design for automotive use; he built a gasoline motor bicycle, 1895, and completed his first gasoline motor car, September 1896. Forming the Winton Motor Carriage Co., March 1897, he made a nine-day trip in one of his cars from Cleveland to New York in July of that year—the first reliability run in the history of the American automobile. On Mar. 24, 1898, he sold one of his cars for $1000, the first sale in America of a gasoline automobile made according to set manufacturing schedules. By the end of 1898 he was successfully producing more cars, all constructed under his patent, granted him September 1898. Energetic and progressive, Winton designed, built and raced cars both in the United States and abroad; his "Bullet No. 1" established a record of a mile in 52.2 seconds at Daytona Beach, Fla., 1902. *Post* 1904 all his cars were equipped with four-cylinder engines; *post* 1907 all had six-cylinder engines. He was the first in America to experiment with straight-eight-cylinder engines (1906); as early as 1902 he had designed external and internal brakes on the same brake-drum. Although he gave his major interest *post* 1912 to design and manufacture of Diesel engines and other activities, he continued to act as president of his automobile company, maintaining the Winton car in the front rank of American automobiles until February 1924.

WIRT, WILLIAM (*b. Bladensburg, Md., 1772; d. Washington, D.C., 1834*), lawyer, author. Admitted to the Virginia bar *c.* 1792, he began practice in Culpeper Co., Va. After a modest success, he removed to Richmond, Va., *c.* 1800; his name first came prominently before the public when he served as counsel for James T. Callender in a famous trial under the Alien and Sedition Acts. After brief service as a chancellor, 1802–03, he removed his residence to Norfolk. His literary career began with the serial publication of *The Letters of the British Spy* in the Richmond *Argus;* published anonymously, they purported to be contemporary observations of an English traveler and were, in fact, shrewd social commentary in essay form. First published as a book,

1803, the letters went through numerous editions. Removing to Richmond, 1806, Wirt appeared for the prosecution in the trial of Aaron Burr and gained much professional prestige. After publication of another series of essays, which did not acquire the popularity of the *British Spy,* Wirt published *Sketches of the Life and Character of Patrick Henry* (1817), his most serious literary effort. Although his material was acquired largely from men who had known Henry, he presented it in a most ornate and overstrained manner. Also in 1817 he was appointed U.S. attorney-general and held that post for twelve consecutive years. He was the first holder of that office to organize its work and to make a systematic practice of preserving his official opinions so that they might serve as precedents. He returned to private life in 1829 on the accession of President Andrew Jackson, but was later an unwilling candidate of the Anti-Masons for the presidency, 1832.

WIRT, WILLIAM ALBERT (*b. Markle, Ind., 1874; d. Gary, Ind., 1938*), school administrator. Graduated DePauw University, 1898; Ph.D., 1916. A leading exponent of progressive education, he first attracted public attention while superintendent of schools at Bluffton, Ind., 1899–1907. As school superintendent of Gary, Ind., *post* 1907, he devised the "platoon" or "work-study-play" system of organization of activities which attracted nation-wide attention before World War I and was widely copied. Although his specific program did not maintain its popularity, his emphasis on including vocational and recreational subjects in the curriculum has had a lasting effect on American education. [*Supp. 2*]

WISE, AARON (*b. Erlau, Hungary, 1844; d. New York, N.Y., 1896*), rabbi. Emigrated to America, 1874. Rabbi of Temple Rodeph Sholom, New York, an influential, conservatively reformed congregation, *post* 1875. A founder of the Jewish Theological Seminary of New York, 1886. Edited new prayer book, *The Temple Service* (1891); editor, N.Y. *Jewish Herald* and *Boston Hebrew Observer.*

WISE, DANIEL (*b. Portsmouth, England, 1813; d. Englewood, N.J., 1898*), Methodist clergyman, editor. Emigrated to America, 1833. Held various Massachusetts and Rhode Island pastorates. Editor, *Sunday School Messenger,* 1838–44; *Zion's Herald,* 1852–56. Corresponding secretary and editor of publications of the Sunday School Union, 1856–72; also editor of the Tract Society *post* 1860. Author of religious works, biographies and moralistic tales for young people.

WISE, HENRY ALEXANDER (*b. Drummondtown, Va., 1806; d. Richmond, Va., 1876*), lawyer, Confederate general. Congressman, Jacksonian Democrat, from Virginia, 1833–44; chief antagonist of John Quincy Adams in effort to repeal "Gag Law" against anti-slavery petitions. Breaking with President Jackson on the Bank question, Wise went over to the Whigs. A close friend of President John Tyler, he led the Tyler adherents in Congress. U.S. minister to Brazil, 1844–47. An outspoken defender of slavery, he was liberal and progressive in other matters; in the Virginia constitutional convention, 1850–51, he played an important part in securing compromise suffrage and taxation reforms. Influential in transferring the Virginia delegation's support to Franklin Pierce at the Democratic convention of 1852, he helped secure the presidential nomination for Pierce. As Democratic candidate for governor, he conducted an exciting campaign against a Know-Nothing opponent; his victory broke the force of the Know-Nothing wave in the South. As governor, 1856–60, he was active in quelling John Brown's raid and advocated internal improvements. He was largely responsible for James Buchanan's nomination at the Democratic convention, 1856. Delegate to the Virginia convention, 1861, he became a fiery advocate of the Southern Confederacy. Made brigadier-general, 1861, he served throughout the Civil War and was promoted major-general by Gen. Robert E. Lee, 1865. Wise was one of the last great individualists in Virginia history.

WISE, HENRY AUGUSTUS (*b. Brooklyn, N.Y., 1819; d. Naples, Italy, 1869*), naval officer. Appointed midshipman, 1834. Served with credit in the Mexican War. Appointed assistant in the U.S. Navy bureau of ordnance, July 1862, he headed the bureau with great energy and ability, 1863–68. He was author (under pseudonym "Harry Gringo") of a number of books which included *Los Gringos* (1849) and *Tales for the Marines* (1855).

WISE, ISAAC MAYER (*b. Steingrub, Bohemia, 1819; d. Cincinnati, O., 1900*), rabbi. Studied in Prague, Bohemia, and Vienna; named rabbi, 1842. Emigrated to America, 1846. Rabbi of the Jewish congregation, Albany, N.Y., 1846–54; of Bene Yeshurun congregation, Cincinnati, O., *post* 1854. Espoused cause of liberal Judaism; published weekly newspaper, the *Israelite* (later the *American Israelite*). His three great projects were: organization of the Union of American Hebrew Congregations, 1873; founding of Hebrew Union College, 1875, which he served as president until his death; organization of the Central Conference of American Rabbis at Detroit, Mich., 1889, of which he was president until his death. In his day the foremost figure in American Jewish religious life, he preached the universalistic interpretation of Judaism and a welding of the spirit of Judaism with the free spirit of America. A prolific writer, he was author, among other works, of *The Cosmic God* (1876), *History of the Hebrews' Second Commonwealth* (1880) and *Reminiscences* (1901).

WISE, JOHN (*b. Roxbury, Mass., 1652; d. 1725*), Congregational clergyman. Graduated Harvard, 1673.

Minister of the church at Chebacco in Ipswich, Mass., *post* 1680, he was active and influential in civil and ecclesiastical affairs throughout his life. Having led his fellow townsmen in resistance to a province tax levied by Sir Edmund Andros, he was tried and fined in October 1687, but was soon restored to his ministerial post. He served as chaplain of the expedition against Quebec, 1690. In the belief that a movement initiated by the Mathers and others to establish associations of clergy was the beginning of a reactionary revolution, Wise attacked the movement in *The Churches Quarrel Espoused* (1710). In 1717 he published *A Vindication of the Government of New-England Churches* in which he considered the fundamental ideas of civil as well as religious government from what has been described as a fully democratic point of view. Wise was an extremely forceful and brilliant writer, standing almost alone among the writers of his time for the blending of a racy humor with impassioned earnestness. The two pamphlets were reprinted in 1772 as a body of democratic doctrine suitable for use in the controversy then raging with England.

WISE, JOHN (*b. Lancaster, Pa., 1808; d. by drowning in Lake Michigan, 1879*), balloonist. A scientific aerostatic pioneer, Wise made important contributions to safety of balloons including the invention of the rip panel. He set a long-distance record of 804 miles in balloon travel, 1859. Author of *A System of Aeronautics* (1850) and *Through the Air* (1873).

WISE, JOHN SERGEANT (*b. Rio de Janeiro, Brazil, 1846; d. near Princess Anne, Md., 1913*), lawyer, politician, Confederate soldier, author. Son of Henry Alexander Wise. Graduated in law, University of Virginia, 1867. Practiced in Richmond; won notoriety for opportunism in politics and as a leader in the William Mahone machine. Congressman-at-large, Republican-Coalition, from Virginia, 1883–85. Removed to New York City, 1888; became leading counsel in important litigation between street railways and other companies; an international authority on law in field of electricity. Author, among other works, of *Diomed* (1897); *The End of the Era* (1899); and *The Lion's Skin* (1905).

WISE, THOMAS ALFRED (*b. Faversham, England, 1865; d. New York, N.Y., 1928*), actor, dramatist. Known as Tom Wise. Came to America as a child. A highly competent character actor, he specialized in farce-comedy.

WISLIZENUS, FREDERICK ADOLPH (*b. Königsee, Germany, 1810; d. St. Louis, Mo., 1889*), physician, traveler, author. Emigrated to America, 1835; began practice in rural Illinois. Accompanied a fur-trading party to the Far West, 1839, journeying to the rendezvous on Green River and to Fort Hall, and returning by way of Laramie plains, the Arkansas River, and the Santa Fé Trail to St. Louis.

Published an account of the journey as *Ein Ausflug nach den Felsen-Gebirgen* (1840) which was afterwards issued in translation. After further practice of medicine in St. Louis in partnership with Dr. George Engelmann, he joined a trading caravan for Santa Fé and Chihuahua in 1846 and made close observations of the fauna, flora, and geology of that region. Joining Alexander W. Doniphan's regiment in March 1847 in Mexico, he returned by way of the Rio Grande and the Mississippi to his home. His account of this adventure appeared in 1848 in *Senate Miscellaneous Document 26*, 30 Cong., 1 Sess., and was praised for its scientific observations by Alexander von Humboldt.

WISNER, HENRY (*b. Goshen, N.Y., 1720; d. 1790*), farmer, New York legislator, powder manufacturer. Represented Orange County in New York Colonial Assembly, 1759–69, and in the First Continental Congress, 1774. A member of the New York Provincial Congress, 1775–77, he served on the committee which drafted the first state constitution, and was appointed as a New York delegate to the Second Continental Congress, May 1775—May 1777. He served in the state senate, 1777–82. He operated powdermills in Ulster and Orange counties during the Revolution and expedited the laying of chains across the Hudson River to prevent British passage upstream.

WISTAR, CASPAR (*b. Wald-Hilsbach, near Heidelberg, Baden, 1696; d. 1752*), glass manufacturer. Emigrated to Philadelphia, Pa., 1717, where he engaged in brass-button making. He located a factory for manufacture of window and bottle glass in Salem Co., West Jersey, which began work in July 1740. Staffed by Belgian and other foreign glass-blowers working on shares, it was one of the earliest successful co-operative ventures in North America and exerted a lasting influence on American glass-making by providing a technique and a tradition of good workmanship. After the Revolution, and the failure of the Wistar works, the workmen established glass industries both locally and in New York State and the Middle West.

WISTAR, CASPAR (*b. Philadelphia, Pa., 1761; d. 1818*), physician. Grandson of Caspar Wistar (1696–1752). Studied medicine under John Redman; B.M., University of Pennsylvania, 1782; M.D., Edinburgh University, 1786. Practiced thereafter in Philadelphia; succeeded Benjamin Rush as professor of chemistry in the medical school of the College of Philadelphia (present University of Pennsylvania), 1789; taught chiefly anatomy at University of Pennsylvania *post* 1792. Author of *System of Anatomy* (1811), the first American textbook on that subject, he was also extremely active in the work of the American Philosophical Society (president, 1815–18). The weekly "open house" which he kept for members of the Society and visiting scientists became a tradition which

was long continued as the "Wistar Parties." Thomas Nuttall named the Wistaria for him in 1818.

WISTER, OWEN (*b. Germantown, Pa., 1860; d. North Kingstown, R.I., 1938*), author. Grandson of Fanny Kemble. Reared in a markedly intellectual household, Wister graduated from Harvard, 1882, and at first looked forward to a musical career. While a student at Harvard Law School, 1885–88, he spent the summer vacations in the West, and after admission to the Philadelphia bar, 1889, set himself to report the West faithfully in fiction. After publishing a number of short stories, he brought out *The Virginian* (1902), a novel which became the model and high-watermark in cowboy fiction. Realistic in surface details, it is less notable as realism than as a triumphant definition of the cowboy as a folk hero and was an instant success. Wister was author of a number of other books of no particular importance which include biographies, satires and farces, and several works on World War I and the tensions which followed it. In domestic politics, Wister was a decided, and even angry, conservative. [*Supp.* 2]

WISTER, SARAH (*b. Philadelphia, Pa., 1761; d. Germantown, Pa., 1804*), diarist. Author of a lively journal of everyday events and experiences in the period from Sept. 25, 1777 to June 20, 1778, which illustrates social conditions in and about Philadelphia while the British were occupying that city.

WITHERS, FREDERICK CLARKE (*b. Shepton Mallet, Somersetshire, England, 1828; d. Yonkers, N.Y., 1901*), architect. Trained in London, England, he emigrated to America, 1853, and became in time a partner of Calvert Vaux and F. L. Olmsted, working with them on New York City's Central Park. He practiced alone *post* 1871. In high repute during his lifetime, he worked in a style about half-way between the Gothic Revival style of the elder Richard Upjohn and the developed Victorian Gothic of such men as Russell Sturgis. He was the architect of a number of churches, and did a considerable amount of work for the City of New York for which he designed, among other buildings, the Jefferson Market Police Court in the present Greenwich Village.

WITHERSPOON, HERBERT (*b. Buffalo, N.Y., 1873; d. New York, N.Y., 1935*), bass singer, opera manager. Graduated Yale, 1895; studied singing in London, Paris, and Berlin. Made operatic debut with the Castle Square Opera Co.; starred as basso at Metropolitan Opera, New York, 1908–16; devoted himself thereafter to concerts and teaching. Appointed general manager of the Metropolitan Opera, 1935.
[*Supp.* 1]

WITHERSPOON, JOHN (*b. Yester, near Edinburgh, Scotland, 1723; d. near Princeton, N.J., 1794*), Presbyterian clergyman, educator, statesman. M.A., University of Edinburgh, 1739; D.D., 1743. Notable during his ministry in Scotland as a champion of the so-called Popular party, as a conservative in theology and morals, and as a defender of the traditional rights of the people to choose their own ministers, Witherspoon emigrated to America in 1768 to become president of the College of New Jersey (Princeton). The choice of the New Side school, he held views that were not obnoxious to the Old Side, and his leadership soon healed the factional schism that had existed among the Presbyterians. Thanks to his efforts in great part, the Presbyterian Church grew rapidly and was strongly entrenched in the Middle Colonies and on the frontiers by 1776. He also gave the College of New Jersey a new lease of life, increasing the endowment, the faculty, and the student body up to the time of the Revolution. He introduced into the curriculum the study of philosophy, French, history, and oratory, and insisted upon mastery of the English language. To his mind an education should fit a man for public usefulness, and he placed a comparatively low value upon mere scholarship. He decried the philosophy of Berkeley and stood foursquare upon empiricism and "common sense."

Witherspoon engaged actively in the controversy with England c. 1774, making common cause with his neighbors. As a member of various Revolutionary committees and a delegate to provincial conventions, he helped bring New Jersey into line with the other colonies. Elected to the Continental Congress on June 22, 1776, he boldly upheld and signed the Declaration of Independence, stating that the country was in his judgment "not only ripe for the measure but in danger of rotting for the want of it." Widely influential in Great Britain as well as in America through his writings, he explained the controversy with the mother country in a number of terse and telling written arguments, showing a remarkably clear comprehension of its precise nature. Serving in Congress with a few intermissions from June 1776 until November 1782, he was a useful member of more than one hundred committees; of these, the most important were the board of war and the committee on secret correspondence (foreign affairs). He was active in the debates on the Articles of Confederation, assisted in organizing the executive departments, and played a foremost part in drawing up the instructions of the American peace commissioners. He opposed the floods of paper money which were issued and also the issue of bonds without provision for amortization. His patience and courage as well as his executive abilities give him high rank among the leaders of the American Revolution.

He spent his last years from 1782 to 1794 in endeavoring to rebuild the college at Princeton; however, during his lifetime the institution never fully recovered from the effects of the Revolution. He also served in the New Jersey legislature and was a member of the New Jersey convention which ratified the U.S. Constitution. A leader also in the organization of the Presbyterian Church along national lines, he was largely the author of the catechisms, the confessions of faith, the directory of worship, and the form of government and discipline adopted by it. In 1781 in an article on language in the *Pennsylvania Journal*, he coined the term "Americanism."

WITHERSPOON, JOHN ALEXANDER (*b. Columbia, Tenn., 1864; d. 1929*), physician, educator. M.D., University of Pennsylvania, 1887. Taught physiology and medicine at University of Tennessee, *post* 1889. Became professor of medicine and clinical medicine at Vanderbilt University, 1895, serving until his death and laboring to raise standards of medical education.

WITTHAUS, RUDOLPH AUGUST (*b. New York, N.Y., 1846; d. 1915*), chemist, toxicologist. A.B., Columbia, 1867; studied at the Sorbonne and Collège de France, 1867–69; M.D., University of the City of New York, 1875. Taught at University of the City of New York, and at universities of Vermont and Buffalo; professor of chemistry and physics at Cornell University *post* 1898, retiring emeritus in 1911. Won world-wide eminence in legal medicine and as expert witness at murder trials; wrote a number of important books. His greatest achievement was as editor with T. C. Becker of *Medical Jurisprudence, Forensic Medicine and Toxicology* (1894–96).

WOERNER, JOHN GABRIEL (*b. Möhringen, Germany, 1826; d. St. Louis, Mo., 1900*), Missouri legislator, journalist and jurist. St. Louis, Mo., probate judge, 1870–94. Widely known as an authority on probate judicature, he was author, among other works, of *Treatise on the American Law of Administration* (1889) and *A Treatise on the American Law of Guardianship* (1897).

WOFFORD, WILLIAM TATUM (*b. Habersham Co., Ga., 1823; d. near Cass Station, Ga., 1884*), planter, Georgia legislator, Confederate brigadier-general, lawyer.

WOLCOTT, EDWARD OLIVER (*b. Longmeadow, Mass., 1848; d. Monte Carlo, Monaco, 1905*), lawyer, politician. Practiced in Colorado *post* c. 1872; prospered as a railroad lawyer; was a conservative leader of the state Republican party. U.S. senator from Colorado, 1889–1901. Advocated free coinage of silver; opposed Federal Election Bill (1890) and President Cleveland's Venezuelan message.

WOLCOTT, OLIVER (*b. Windsor, Conn., 1726; d. 1797*), lawyer, Connecticut public official. Son of Roger Wolcott; father of Oliver Wolcott (1760–1833). Graduated Yale, 1747. Removed to Litchfield, Conn., 1751, serving as sheriff there for twenty years. Deputy for Litchfield, 1764, 1767, 1768 and 1770; Connecticut assistant, 1771–86. Judge, Litchfield probate court, 1772–81; judge, county courts in and for Litchfield, 1774–78. A commissioner of Indian affairs for the northern department, he helped settle the Wyoming

Valley and New York-Vermont boundary questions. Delegate to the Continental Congress, 1775–83 (with exception of 1779), he signed the Declaration of Independence in October 1776; he was noted in Congress as a man of integrity who spoke his mind but was lacking in political knowledge. As brigadier-general, he commanded militia sent to reinforce Gen. Putnam on the Hudson River, 1776; as major-general, 1779, he defended Connecticut's seacoast against Tryon's raids. Lieutenant-governor of Connecticut, 1787. Helped conclude 1789 treaty by which Wyandottes surrendered title to the Western Reserve. Conservative Federalist governor of Connecticut, 1796–97.

WOLCOTT, OLIVER (*b. Litchfield, Conn., 1760; d. New York, N.Y., 1833*), lawyer, Connecticut public official, cabinet officer. Son of Oliver Wolcott (1726–1797). Graduated Yale, 1778; studied law under Tapping Reeve. Notably successful in Connecticut as reorganizer of the state's financial affairs after the Revolution, he was appointed auditor of the U.S. treasury, 1789. In this capacity he labored over the routine operations of the department to such good effect that Alexander Hamilton recommended him for appointment as comptroller of the treasury, June 1791. Unwavering in his loyalty to Hamilton, who was his close friend also, he succeeded Hamilton as secretary of the treasury, February 1795. Mounting expenditures of the federal government, the spirit of speculation in American commerce, and increasing demoralization of the European money market created grave problems for the treasury; moreover, the (Democrat) Republican majority in Congress, under the leadership of Albert Gallatin, were trying to take the initiative in financial matters away from the secretary. Wolcott did not enjoy the quasi-independence in allotting government funds which Hamilton had so cavalierly employed. Although given the confidence of President John Adams, 1797–1800, Wolcott remained subservient to Hamilton's directions and cooperated with Timothy Pickering and James McHenry in intrigues against the Adams administration.

Resigning the secretaryship at the end of the year 1800, he returned to Connecticut a poor man despite charges by his political enemies that he was guilty of all manner of financial crimes. Removing to New York City *c.* 1803, he engaged in a number of short-lived business activities and was president of the Bank of America, 1812–14. Settling in Litchfield, Conn., 1815, he occupied himself as a gentleman farmer and promoter of manufacturing in Connecticut. Having become a (Democrat) Republican in politics, he was elected governor of Connecticut, 1817, and brought about a political revolution in that state. As governor he succeeded in overthrowing Federalist control of the aristocratic state council; after re-election in April 1818, he presided over a constitutional convention at which a new constitution (which he was influential in drafting) was adopted. The new con-

stitution separated church and state, guaranteed a full freedom of conscience, separated the powers of government, and established a more influential executive and an independent judiciary. Able and popular, Wolcott was re-elected governor year after year until 1827. During this time he made expert revisions in the tax laws, but failed in efforts to promote state aid for agriculture and industry and other liberal measures.

WOLCOTT, ROGER (*b. Windsor, Conn., 1679; d. 1767*), farmer, businessman, lawyer, Connecticut public official. Father of Oliver Wolcott (1726–1797). Assistant, Connecticut colony, 1714–41, with exception of 1718 and 1719; deputy governor of Connecticut, 1741–50; governor, 1750–54. Became judge of the Hartford County court, 1721, and of the superior court, 1732; became chief justice of the latter, 1741. As major-general, 1745, he was second-in-command on the expedition which took Louisbourg. Author, among other works, of *Poetical Meditations* (1725), the first volume of verse published in Connecticut.

WOLF, GEORGE (*b. Northampton Co., Pa., 1777; d. 1840*), lawyer, Pennsylvania legislator. Began practice in Easton, Pa. As congressman, Democrat, from Pennsylvania, December 1824–1829, he supported the protective tariff and other measures to aid American industry. Elected governor of Pennsylvania in 1829, he served six years; he began a revision of the state statute law, re-established state credit, and secured passage of the free public school act, 1834. Wolf opposed President Jackson on the Second U.S. Bank question and fought for renewal of the bank charter. He served as comptroller of the U.S. treasury, 1836–38, and as collector of customs, port of Philadelphia, thereafter.

WOLF, HENRY (*b. Eckwersheim, Alsace, 1852; d. New York, N.Y., 1916*), wood engraver. Emigrated to America, 1871; settled in New York, 1873. Became pre-eminent in reproduction of paintings by contemporary American artists.

WOLF, INNOCENT WILLIAM (*b. Schmidheim, Rhenish Prussia, 1843; d. 1922*), Roman Catholic clergyman, Benedictine. Emigrated to Brighton, Wis., 1851. Ordained priest, 1866, after studies at St. Vincent Abbey, Latrobe, Pa. Returning to St. Vincent, 1870, after further study in Rome, he taught theology, and was successively master of novices, treasurer of the abbey and prior of the monastery. Elected first abbot of St. Benedict's, Atchison, Kans., 1876, he served actively until 1921.

WOLF, SIMON (*b. Bavaria, 1836; d. Washington, D.C., 1923*), lawyer, philanthropist. Emigrated to America, 1848. Graduated Ohio Law College, Cleveland, O., 1861. Practiced in Washington *post* 1862. Appointed recorder, District of Columbia, 1869; served as civil judge, 1878–81. Won reputation as vigorous champion of civic and religious rights of eastern European Jews. Founder and life-long president, Hebrew Orphans' Home, Atlanta, Ga.

WOLFE, CATHARINE LORILLARD (*b. New York, N.Y., 1828; d. New York, 1887*), philanthropist, art patron. Daughter of John D. Wolfe. A munificent benefactor of the Protestant Episcopal Church; bequeathed her collection of 19th-century European paintings and an endowment to the Metropolitan Museum of Art, New York City.

WOLFE, HARRY KIRKE (*b. Bloomington, Ill., 1858; d. 1918*), psychologist, educator. Graduated University of Nebraska, 1880; Ph.D., Leipzig, 1886; studied under Wilhelm Wundt. Professor and head of philosophy and psychology department, University of Nebraska, 1891–97; professor of educational psychology, 1906–09; professor of philosophy and psychology again, 1909–18. Served in secondary school and other educational work, 1897–1905.

WOLFE, JOHN DAVID (*b. New York, N.Y., 1792; d. New York, 1872*), hardware merchant, philanthropist. Father of Catharine L. Wolfe. Benefactor of the Protestant Episcopal Church, 1841–72, he helped support Western dioceses and schools and took an important part in the promotion and support of New York charitable institutions.

WOLFE, THOMAS CLAYTON (*b. Asheville, N.C., 1900; d. Baltimore, Md., 1938*), novelist. The character of Eugene Gant in Wolfe's first novel, *Look Homeward, Angel* (1929), offers a recognizable account of his creator's life up to the age of twenty. Product of an unsettled household, Wolfe was directed to literature and encouraged throughout his career by one of his early school-teachers. While at the University of North Carolina, from which he graduated in 1920, he was encouraged to write by Edwin Greenlaw and others and wrote several plays (*The Return of Buck Gavin*, published 1924; *The Third Night*, published 1938) which were produced by the Carolina Playmakers. A student of playwriting in the famous "47 Workshop" under George P. Baker at Harvard, he received an M.A. in English, 1922. Resolving to dedicate himself to a truthful presentation of life in all its complexity, he gave up writing about Carolina mountaineers and attempted a more comprehensive picture of life in his play *Welcome to Our City* (produced 1923 at Harvard), for which he was unable to achieve professional production. While teaching intermittently at New York University until 1930, he traveled in England, France, and Italy, and was given love, understanding, and financial help by Mrs. Aline Bernstein, a stage designer who became an important influence in his life. After another unsuccessful attempt at the drama (a Civil War play, *Mannerhouse*, published 1948), he turned to prose narrative and began to write an autobiographical novel in a new, energetic, metaphorical style.

After twenty months' labor, he produced a huge manuscript, powerful in accumulative effect, but weakened by digressions and excessive detail. In association with Maxwell Perkins, editor at Charles Scribner's Sons, Wolfe reduced his work to a publishable volume which appeared in October 1929 as *Look Homeward, Angel* and was enthusiastically reviewed. The author, elated by the praise and burdened by a consciousness of artistic responsibility, next attempted a book which should characterize the restlessness of the modern American and render a sense of the variety and vastness of the American continent. His ideas multiplied until he had in hand a project for a series of novels whose main narrative thread should be his own experiences. Overwhelmed by the bulk of his scheme as his material developed in length and complexity, he was once again assisted by Perkins to reduce his manuscript to order. Perkins divided the work into two separate books and set Wolfe to writing fillers for the narrative gaps in the first of these. Although Wolfe was reluctant to permit issue of the work, it was published in March 1935 as *Of Time and the River*. Parts were magnificent, but as a whole it was uneven and anthology-like in its variety; thousands of sensitive impressions of the whole 20th-century scene served as backdrop to the story of youth's insatiable hunger for life. The critics now began to compare Wolfe to Whitman and Melville. A man of enormous appetites, egoistic as a child, he was one moment elated and the next despondent; now full of good will and now overcome with suspicion or anger. After publication of a collection of short stories, *From Death to Morning*, he decided to set aside his six-volume series temporarily while he wrote a different kind of book—a story about an innocent, gullible man discovering the harsh truths of life through disillusionment and trial. As he worked out the narrative, the original grandiose plan was scrapped in favor of a long chronicle about a new hero, George Webber. At this point, he broke off with Maxwell Perkins, in part to show his independence, and in part because of a dispute over a libel suit which Wolfe had wanted to fight in court. He did not live to see his new work completed. Out of the vast manuscript which he left behind after his death, three books were fashioned: *The Web and the Rock* (1939), *You Can't Go Home Again* (1940), and *The Hills Beyond* (1941).

Thomas Wolfe's books have maintained favor largely because of the richness of his work. As a descriptive writer, he evokes a poetic response with his rhythmical and lyric passages; as a writer of narrative, he achieves at his best the brooding depths of Dostoevski and the vivid portraiture of Dickens. His work is tempered with broad humor which becomes predominantly satirical in his later work. Although his minor figures tend to caricature, his great characterizations display a full range of the strengths and weaknesses of human kind. [*Supp. 2*]

WOLFSKILL, WILLIAM (*b. near Richmond, Ky., 1798; d. near Los Angeles, Calif., 1866*), trapper, California pioneer. After extensive experience as a trapper along the Rio Grande and the Gila, he led a trapping party from Taos in September 1830 which opened a new route to California, approximating what became known as the western part of the Spanish Trail. Settling near Los Angeles, he acquired land and began to develop it as a vineyard in 1838. Becoming wealthy and influential as a rancher and farmer, he introduced the culture of the persimmon and the Italian chestnut and was the first in the area to ship oranges commercially.

WOLFSOHN, CARL (*b. Alzey, Germany, 1834; d. Deal Beach, N.J., 1907*), pianist, teacher, conductor. Came to America, 1854, settling in Philadelphia, Pa. Associated with Theodore Thomas in chamber music recitals *post* 1856. Presented notable recitals of all Beethoven piano sonatas in Philadelphia and in Steinway Hall, N.Y., 1863–64. Founded Beethoven Society, 1869; conducted a similar society in Chicago, Ill., 1873–84. Wolfsohn was one of the earliest in America to espouse the cause of Richard Wagner's music.

WOLHEIM, LOUIS ROBERT (*b. New York, N.Y., 1881; d. Los Angeles, Calif., 1931*), mechanical engineer, mathematician, stage and screen actor. Graduated College of the City of New York, 1903; M.E., Cornell University, 1906. After winning great applause for his performance with the Provincetown Players in Eugene O'Neill's *The Hairy Ape*, 1922–24, Wolheim attained the high point of his career as "Captain Flagg" in *What Price Glory*. Thereafter he was engaged principally in motion picture work as the best delineator of hard-boiled parts on the American stage of his time. [*Supp. 1*]

WOLLE, JOHN FREDERICK (*b. Bethlehem, Pa., 1863; d. Bethlehem, 1933*), musician. Organist of Moravian Church, Bethlehem, Pa., 1885–1905; of Lehigh University, 1887–1905. Chiefly remembered as founder (1898) and conductor, Bethlehem Bach Choir; conducted Bach festivals, Lehigh University, 1912–32. Held chair of music, University of California, 1905–11.

WOOD, ABRAHAM (*fl. 1638–1680*), soldier, explorer, Virginia landowner and official. Member of the Virginia Council, 1658–c. 1680. Maintained a garrison at Fort Henry (Petersburg) *post* 1646; sent out expedition, 1671, which achieved the first recorded passage of the Appalachian Mountains; sent out party under James Needham which traced trail to present Tennessee in 1673 and opened trade with the Cherokees.

WOOD, DAVID DUFFLE (*b. Pittsburgh, Pa., 1838; d. Philadelphia, Pa., 1910*), organist. Blind from childhood and mainly self-taught in music, Wood was an instructor of music at the Pennsylvania Institution for the Instruction of the Blind, Philadelphia, *post* 1862, and principal instructor from 1887 until his death. Organist of St. Stephen's Church, Philadelphia, 1864–1910, he was also choirmaster *post* 1870. He was instructor of organ at the Philadelphia Musical Academy for thirty years. Author of *A Dictionary of Musical Terms, for the Use of the Blind* (1869). A notable interpreter of Bach.

WOOD, EDWARD STICKNEY (*b. Cambridge, Mass., 1846; d. Pocasset, Mass., 1905*), physician, chemist. M.D., Harvard Medical School, 1871; professor of chemistry there from 1876 until his death. Chemist, Massachusetts General Hospital, Boston, Mass. A legal expert in chemistry, he was well known in his time as a murder trial witness.

WOOD, FERNANDO (*b. Philadelphia, Pa., 1812; d. Hot Springs, Ark., 1881*), businessman, politician. Entering politics in New York City, 1834, he was active in Tammany Hall and served as a member of Congress, 1841–43. Prospering as a ship chandler and merchant during the California gold rush, he invested his large profits in New York and San Francisco real estate. Meanwhile he had become a leader of Tammany Hall. Elected mayor of New York City, 1854, and re-elected, 1856, he was influential in creating Central Park, but permitted graft to run riot in the city government. During his term of office the city was plagued by the existence of two separate police forces, one under state control, the other under the mayor; consequent confusion over jurisdiction assisted the growth of crime and corruption. Ousted by fellow leaders from Tammany Hall, Wood organized his personal following as the so-called Mozart Hall and through it secured his third election as mayor in 1859. He appeared at the Democratic convention of 1860 at the head of a contesting New York delegation with pro-Southern leanings. Believing that the Union was about to be dissolved, he proposed in January 1861 that New York should become a free city. Defeated for re-election, he denounced the Civil War and advocated peace by conciliation; early in 1863 he joined with C. L. Vallandigham in organizing the Peace Democrats. A New York congressman, 1863–65, 1867–81, he reflected in his views the dominant banking and mercantile interests of New York, insisting, in opposition to his own Democratic party, upon a sound currency and a tariff for revenue only. He was majority floor leader *post* 1877 and chairman of the ways and means committee. A man of engaging manners, Wood had an uncanny ability to estimate the course of public opinion and a genius for political organization.

WOOD, GEORGE (*b. Chesterfield, N.J., 1789; d. 1860*), lawyer, regarded by contemporaries as the leader of the New Jersey and New York bar. Graduated College of New Jersey (Princeton), 1808. Studied law under Richard Stockton (1764–1828); began practice at New Brunswick, N.J., 1812. Wood appeared frequently before the U.S. Supreme Court and is of particular importance for his influence in forming the New Jersey law on charitable devises (*e.g., Hendrickson vs. Shotwell*). He removed to New York City, 1831. In *Martin vs. Waddell* (16 *Peters,* 367, or 41 *United States,* 367), he expounded the law concerning the right of the sovereign to under-water lands. He was a master of clear and comprehensive statement.

WOOD, GEORGE BACON (*b. Greenwich, N.J., 1797; d. Philadelphia, Pa., 1879*), physician. Uncle of Horatio C. Wood. M.D., University of Pennsylvania, 1818. Professor of chemistry, Philadelphia College of Pharmacy, 1822–35; also professor of materia medica, 1831–35. Wood then became professor of materia medica and pharmacy at University of Pennsylvania; from 1850 to 1860, he served there as professor of the theory and practice of medicine. Attending physician, Pennsylvania Hospital, 1835–59; president, College of Physicians of Philadelphia, 1848 until his death; president, American Philosophical Society, 1859–79. Chairman, national committee for revision of U.S. pharmacopeia, 1850–60. Author, among other works, of *The Dispensatory of the United States* (1833, with Franklin Bache) and *Treatise on the Practice of Medicine* (1847).

WOOD, HENRY ALEXANDER WISE (*b. New York, N.Y., 1866; d. 1939*), inventor, manufacturer. Son of Fernando Wood. Devised and made a series of printing machinery improvements which brought about great changes in the printing of newspapers. Among these were the Autoplate (final patent, 1903), whereby an entire newspaper page was cast in metal, and also high-speed press-feeding devices. An early advocate of aviation, he also engaged in propaganda against American entry into the League of Nations and for limitation of immigration. [*Supp. 2*]

WOOD, HORATIO CHARLES (*b. Philadelphia, Pa., 1841; d. Philadelphia, 1920*), physician. Nephew of George B. Wood. M.D., University of Pennsylvania, 1862. Professor of botany, University of Pennsylvania, 1866–76; clinical professor of nervous diseases, 1876–1901; professor of materia medica, pharmacy and general therapeutics, 1876–1906. Worked also as an entomologist. Associated with Philadelphia Hospital (Blockley), 1870–88. Author of approximately 300 papers and six books on scientific subjects, including *A Treatise on Therapeutics* (1874) and revisions of his uncle's *Dispensatory of the United States;* edited, among other medical journals, *Therapeutic Gazette,* 1884–1900.

WOOD, JAMES (*b. Greenfield, N.Y., 1799; d. Hightstown, N.J., 1867*), Presbyterian clergyman, educator. Strong adherent of Old School party. Professor, New Albany (Ind.) Theological Seminary, 1840–51; president, Hanover (Ind.) College, 1859–66.

WOOD, JAMES (*b. Mount Kisco, N.Y., 1839; d. Mount Kisco, 1925*), Quaker leader, farmer, horticulturist. Served as presiding clerk of the New York Yearly Meeting of Friends, 1885–1925, and as clerk of Five Years Meeting, 1907; helped found *American Friend;* wrote on Quaker doctrines and ideals; was a manager of Haverford College and a trustee of Bryn Mawr.

WOOD, JAMES FREDERICK (*b. Philadelphia, Pa., 1813; d. 1883*), Roman Catholic clergyman. A convert to Catholicism in Cincinnati, O., 1836, Wood studied in Rome at the Irish College and at the Propaganda. After ordination in Rome, 1844, he served in Cincinnati. Appointed titular bishop of Antigonia and coadjutor to Bishop J. N. Neumann of Philadelphia, he was consecrated, 1857, and succeeded to full authority in 1860. Became first archbishop of Philadelphia, 1875. An able and somewhat rigorous administrator of his diocese.

WOOD, JAMES J. (*b. Kinsale, Ireland, 1856; d. Asheville, N.C., 1928*), engineer, inventor. Came to America as a boy; was raised in Connecticut. Patented an arc-light dynamo (1880) which was the first of some 240 electrical and other patents which he took out. These included a flood-lighting system which was first used successfully to light the Statue of Liberty (1885); an internal combustion engine which was installed in the first Holland submarine; and the machines for constructing the main cables on the original Brooklyn Bridge. His later inventions were mainly in the field of alternating current generators, motors, transformers, and other devices. Becoming a consulting engineer *c.* 1885, he was chief engineer of the General Electric Co. and later consultant of its Fort Wayne (Ind.) Works.

WOOD, JAMES RUSHMORE (*b. Mamaroneck, N.Y., 1813; d. New York, N.Y., 1882*), surgeon. Graduated Vermont Academy of Medicine, Castleton, Vt., 1834. Practiced in New York City *post* 1837. A co-founder of Bellevue Hospital, 1847, Wood was a moving spirit in that institution until his death and won fame as a brilliant and successful radical operator. He introduced at Bellevue the first city hospital ambulance service (1869), and established there the first training school for nurses in the United States (1873). An organizer of Bellevue Hospital Medical College, 1856, he served it as professor of operative surgery and surgical pathology. Famous for his skill in nerve and bone surgery, he was among the first to cure aneurism by pressure. His collection of post-mortem material grew into the Wood Museum, one of the richest collections of pathological specimens in the world.

WOOD, JETHRO (*b. Dartmouth, Mass., or White Creek, N.Y., 1774; d. Cayuga Co., N.Y., 1834*), inventor of plow improvements. Patented a cast-iron plow (1819) whose design and principles of construction were copied widely throughout the North. The peculiar virtue of the Wood plow lay in the shaping of the moldboard and a combination of good balance, strength, light draft, interchangeability of parts, and cheapness of manufacture.

WOOD, JOHN (*b. Scotland, c. 1775; d. Richmond, Va., 1822*), political pamphleteer, surveyor and mapmaker. Emigrated to America *c.* 1800. Served as tutor to Theodosia Burr; worked as a writer in Aaron Burr's interest; was author, among other political tracts, of *The History of the Administration of John Adams* (1802). Associated with the publication of the Frankfort, Ky. *Western World*, 1806; published *A Full Statement of the Trial and Acquittal of Aaron Burr* at Alexandria, Va., 1807. Recommended to the governor of Virginia by Thomas Jefferson, Wood was appointed by the state in 1819 to survey and map each Virginia county, and also to execute a general map of the state. By the time of his death, he had supplied all but six of the county charts and had completed a fifth of the general map.

WOOD, JOHN TAYLOR (*b. Fort Snelling, present Minn., 1830; d. Halifax, N.S., Canada, 1904*), naval officer. Grandson of Zachary Taylor. Graduated Annapolis, 1853. Resigning from the U.S. Navy, 1861, he was commissioned lieutenant in the Confederate Navy and served aboard the *Virginia* (*Merrimack*). Appointed naval aide to President Jefferson Davis, 1863, he distinguished himself by a series of boat expeditions in the Chesapeake and lower Potomac, raiding and destroying Union vessels. In August 1864 he commanded the steam sloop *Tallahassee* on a raiding expedition from Wilmington, N.C. to Halifax, Nova Scotia, and back, capturing or destroying more than sixty vessels. Promoted captain, February 1865, he accompanied Davis in the retreat from Richmond, but managed to escape through Florida to Cuba. After the war he engaged in the shipping and marine insurance business in Halifax.

WOOD, JOSEPH (*b. Clarkstown, N.Y., c. 1778; d. Washington, D.C., c. 1832*), miniaturist, portrait painter. In partnership with John W. Jarvis as maker of *eglomisé* silhouettes, 1804–09; received instruction in miniature painting from Edward G. Malbone. Maintained New York studio until 1812 or 1813; removing to Philadelphia, he exhibited regularly at the Pennsylvania Academy of the Fine Arts until 1817. By 1827, he was established in Washington, D.C.

WOOD, LEONARD (*b. Winchester, N.H., 1860; d. 1927*), soldier, military surgeon. M.D., Harvard Medical School, 1884. Appointed a contract surgeon in the U.S. Army Medical Corps, he won commendation for service during campaigns against the Apaches of Geronimo and was regularly commissioned in 1886. After routine duty in California and the East, he was transferred to Washington, D.C., 1895, where he became physician to President and Mrs. McKinley. A friend of Theodore Roosevelt, he joined with him in organizing the so-called "Rough Riders." Wood took command of the unit as colonel and led in the first engagement at Las Guasimas, Cuba, June 1898. He

became military governor of Santiago after its surrender. Successful in cleaning up and restoring the city, he was then given charge of the entire province; in December 1899 he was appointed military governor of all Cuba, serving until 1902. A physical giant, extraordinarily energetic and ambitious, Wood was a strong nationalist and no respecter of persons. During his term in Cuba he stabilized the affairs of that island, establishing educational, police, and physical systems, and modernizing the administration of justice. He also superintended great advances in sanitation.

As governor of the Moro Province of the Philippines, 1903–06, he pacified the province and brought about a relatively high degree of prosperity there, although criticized for ruthlessness in stamping out local institutions. In August 1903 he had been promoted major-general in the regular army. After command of the Philippine Division, 1906–08, he returned home. Chief of staff of the U.S. Army, 1910–14, he supervised the new organization of the War Department which had been necessitated by the creation of a General Staff in 1903; after an epic contest with conservative bureau heads, Wood was partially successful in organizing the regular army into a coherent force. *Post* 1914 he engaged in development of the civilian training-camp movement and the "preparedness" movement; these activities frequently brought him into conflict with the administration of President Wilson. Although senior officer of the army when the United States entered World War I, Wood was passed over for command either abroad or at home. Following the war he openly sought the Republican nomination for the presidency; he came to the Republican convention at Chicago, 1920, with the largest single following of delegates, but failed of the nomination. Appointed a member of a special mission to the Philippines, 1921, he soon became governor general of the Philippines, serving until 1927 when he returned to the United States for a surgical operation which proved fatal.

WOOD, MARY ELIZABETH (*b. near Batavia, N.Y., 1861; d. Wuchang, China, 1931*), librarian. Served at Boone College, Wuchang, China, *post* 1904; oversaw erection of Boone Library building, 1910, and founding of Boone Library School, 1920. Promoted Chinawide library movement *post* 1923; helped obtain U.S. congressional appropriation for Chinese educational-cultural activities.

WOOD, REUBEN (*b. Middletown, Vt., c. 1792; d. 1864*), jurist, Ohio legislator. Removed to Cleveland, O., 1818. President judge, third common pleas circuit of Ohio, January 1830—February 1833; justice, Ohio supreme court, 1833–47. Democratic governor of Ohio, 1850–53. Acting U.S. minister to Chile, 1853–55.

WOOD, SAMUEL (*b. Oyster Bay, L.I., N.Y., 1760; d. 1844*), bookseller and publisher, philanthropist. Began business in New York City, 1804; organized publishing firm of Samuel Wood & Sons, 1815, later the largest American medical book publishers. Produced a long series of children's books (earliest imprint, 1806).

WOOD, SARAH SAYWARD BARRELL KEATING (*b. York, Maine, 1759; d. Kennebunk, Maine, 1855*), novelist. Maine's first fiction writer, she was author, among other books, of *Julia and the Illuminated Baron*, a Gothic romance (Portsmouth, 1800), and *Tales of the Night* (1827).

WOOD, THOMAS (*b. Smithfield, O., 1813; d. 1880*), surgeon. M.D., University of Pennsylvania, 1839. Practiced in Cincinnati, O., *post c.* 1845. Taught anatomy and physiology at Ohio College of Dental Surgery and at Medical College of Ohio. A daring and successful operator, he was particularly skillful in treating women's diseases.

WOOD, THOMAS BOND (*b. Lafayette, Ind., 1844; d. Tacoma, Wash., 1922*), Methodist clergyman. Active as a missionary, mission executive, and educator in Latin America, 1870–1913.

WOOD, THOMAS JOHN (*b. Mundfordville, Ky., 1823; d. 1906*), soldier. Graduated West Point, 1845. Commissioned in the engineers, he distinguished himself as staff officer under Gen. Zachary Taylor at the Mexican War battles of Palo Alto and Buena Vista. Transferring to the cavalry, he rose to colonel, 1861, after almost continuous frontier service in the West. As brigadier-general of Union volunteers, he commanded a division after the spring of 1862 and was outstanding in the battle of Stone's River. At Chickamauga, September 1863, the removal of his division from line permitted the Confederate breakthrough and occasioned a bitter controversy between Wood and Gen. W. S. Rosecrans. Wood's division was highly effective at Missionary Ridge and in the Atlanta campaign. He commanded the IV Corps in the pursuit of Gen. John Hood's broken Confederate army after the battle of Nashville, 1864. Several times badly wounded, he retired for disability as major-general, U.S. Army, 1868.

WOOD, WALTER ABBOTT (*b. Mason, N.H., 1815; d. Hoosick Falls, N.Y., 1892*), manufacturer and inventor of agricultural implements. Produced the Wood mowers, reapers and binders at Hoosick Falls *post c.* 1852; made numerous improvements on mowers and reapers built originally under the John H. Manny patents.

WOOD, WILLIAM (*fl. 1629–1635*), author. Emigrating from England to Massachusetts, 1629, Wood probably settled in Lynn; very little is known of his life. He left the colony on Aug. 15, 1633, and on July 7, 1634, his book *New Englands Prospect* was entered in the Stationers' Register in London. The book is an account of New England as the author observed it from 1629 to 1633; the first part is a description of the country and its settlements; the second, a

number of observations on the Indians. It is clearly the work of a man with some literary training and is unusual among books of its type for vigor of style and relatively polished form. London editions appeared in 1634, 1635 and 1639.

WOOD, WILLIAM BURKE (*b. Montreal, Canada, 1779; d. 1861*), actor, theatrical manager. Made American debut with the company of Thomas Wignell at Annapolis, Md., 1798. Celebrated as a player in genteel comedy, Wood was identified principally with the Philadelphia theatres in association with William Warren. He was author of *Personal Recollections of the Stage* (1855).

WOOD, WILLIAM ROBERT (*b. Oxford, Ind., 1861; d. New York, N.Y., 1933*), lawyer, Indiana legislator. Congressman, Republican, from Indiana, 1915–33, he was first famous as one of the most active Republican critics of the administration of President Woodrow Wilson; he was later a most influential figure as chairman of the House appropriations committee. His political philosophy reflected a rural background and included a marked suspicion of the "money power." Economy and retrenchment were his watchwords, and his success was owing to hard work and conscientious application to his duties rather than to any intellectual brilliance.

WOODBERRY, GEORGE EDWARD (*b. Beverly, Mass., 1855; d. Beverly, 1930*), poet, critic, educator. Graduated Harvard, 1877; was influenced there by Henry Adams and Charles E. Norton. Taught English at University of Nebraska, 1877–78, 1880–82; engaged in writing for *Atlantic Monthly* and *Nation* and other periodicals. As professor of literature (later of comparative literature), Columbia University, 1891–1904, Woodberry was brilliant as a teacher; he also built up a graduate department which transformed the methods of higher instruction in literature and left a deep mark on university teaching in this field throughout the country. After resigning his chair in 1904, he traveled widely, spending part of his time as a sort of itinerant teacher. A prolific writer, he was author of a number of books including important biographies of Edgar Allan Poe, Nathaniel Hawthorne and Ralph Waldo Emerson. *The Torch* (1905) contains probably the fullest expression of his philosophy of literature; his poems (he thought of himself essentially as a poet) were issued in a number of small volumes from which a selection was made by three of his former students in 1933. A lonely and somewhat enigmatic figure, he displayed in his best critical work a subtle intuition of the emotional experience that produced the work of literature with which he was dealing and a deep sense of its relation to the spiritual background of western man.

WOODBRIDGE, FREDERICK JAMES EUGENE (*b. Windsor, Ontario, Canada, 1867; d. New York, N.Y., 1940*), educator, philosopher. Raised in Michigan. Graduated Amherst, 1889; Union Theological Seminary, New York, 1892. After further study in Berlin, he built up an outstanding philosophy department at University of Minnesota, 1894–1902; *post* 1902 he was professor of philosophy at Columbia University. A co-founder and for many years editor of the *Journal of Philosophy*, he served also as dean of the graduate faculties of Columbia, 1912–29. A leader of the American "realist" movement, he described his own form of this philosophy as "naive realism" and identified it with the core of Aristotle's metaphysics. He made the *Journal of Philosophy* the chief medium for the attacks of the new pragmatism, realism, and naturalism on the then-dominant school of philosophical idealism. [*Supp. 2*]

WOODBRIDGE, JOHN (*b. Stanton, Wiltshire, England, 1613; d. 1695*), colonial magistrate, clergyman. Nephew of Thomas Parker; brother-in-law of Simon Bradstreet. Emigrated to New England, 1634. Public official in Newbury, Mass., 1636–41 (excepting 1639), and 1677–79, 1681, 1683–84 and 1690. Helped settle Andover, Mass.; was first pastor of the church at Andover, 1645–47. Removed to England, 1648, returning to Massachusetts, 1663. Assistant minister at Newbury, 1663–70. Conducted a bank of deposit and issue with land and commodities as collateral *post c.* 1671. Author of *Severals Relating to the Fund . . .* (1681/82), the first American tract on currency and banking extant.

WOODBRIDGE, SAMUEL MERRILL (*b. Greenfield, Mass., 1819; d. New Brunswick, N.J., 1905*), Reformed Church clergyman. Graduated New Brunswick (N.J.) Theological Seminary, 1841. Held New York and New Jersey pastorates, 1841–57. Professor of ecclesiastical history and church government at New Brunswick Seminary, 1857–1901; dean, 1883–88; president of the faculty, 1888–1901. Was also professor of metaphysics and mental philosophy, Rutgers College, 1857–64.

WOODBRIDGE, WILLIAM (*b. Norwich, Conn., 1780; d. Detroit, Mich., 1861*), lawyer, Ohio and Michigan legislator. Friend of Lewis Cass; son-in-law of John Trumbull, the poet. Secretary of Michigan Territory, 1814–24; appointed collector of customs at Detroit, 1814. Chosen Michigan's first territorial delegate, 1819; served as territorial judge, 1828–32. Elected Whig governor of Michigan, 1839, he served 14 months implementing complete program of state rehabilitation. U.S. senator, Whig, from Michigan, 1841–47, he was chairman of the committee on public lands and sponsored measures for internal improvements.

WOODBRIDGE, WILLIAM CHANNING (*b. Medford, Mass., 1794; d. Boston, Mass., 1845*), educator, Congregational clergyman. Graduated Yale, 1811. Edited *American Annals of Education and Instruction*, 1831–37; was a pioneer in advocating teaching

of physiology and music in common schools and an early American expounder of the Pestalozzian system. Author of *Rudiments of Geography . . . by Comparison and Classification* (1821) and *Universal Geography, Ancient and Modern* (1824), both of which revolutionized presentation of geographical facts in American schools.

WOODBURY, CHARLES JEPTHA HILL (*b. Lynn, Mass., 1851; d. 1916*), industrial engineer, authority on fire prevention. C.E., Massachusetts Institute of Technology, 1873. Became engineer (1878) and later vice-president, Boston Manufacturers Mutual Fire Insurance Co.; assistant engineer, American Telephone & Telegraph Co., 1894–1907; secretary, National Association of Cotton Manufacturers, 1894–1916. Received honors for work on mill construction and formulation of insurance rules for electric lighting.

WOODBURY, DANIEL PHINEAS (*b. New London, N.H., 1812; d. Key West, Fla., 1864*), Union soldier, engineer. Graduated West Point, 1836. Engaged in building Fort Kearny on Missouri River and Fort Laramie (Wyo.), 1847–50; supervised construction of Fort Jefferson in the Tortugas and Fort Taylor at Key West. Commissioned brigadier-general of volunteers, 1862; commanded engineer brigade, Army of the Potomac, in the Peninsular Campaign, constructing siege works, roads and bridges. Died of yellow fever while commanding Key West district.

WOODBURY, HELEN LAURA SUMNER (*b. Sheboygan, Wis., 1876; d. New York, N.Y., 1933*), social economist. A.B., Wellesley, 1898; Ph.D., Wisconsin, 1908. Appointed industrial expert, U.S. Children's Bureau, 1913, assistant chief, 1915; studied child labor laws and employment certificate systems. Author of original works on citizenship and the history of women in American industry; also, among others, *Labor Problems* (1905) with Thomas S. Adams. She was one of the first in the American academic world to study and analyze labor problems and did pioneering work in the technique of social legislation administration.

WOODBURY, ISAAC BAKER (*b. Beverly, Mass., 1819; d. Charleston, S.C., 1858*), composer. Editor, *American Monthly Musical Review*. Compiled and edited, among other music books, *Boston Musical Education Society's Collections* (1842), *Choral* (1845), both with Benjamin F. Baker; *Dulcimer* (1850); *Lute of Zion* (1853); *Cythara* (1854); and *Harp of the South* (1853). Many of his compositions were published including a popular song, "The Indian's Lament" (1846).

WOODBURY, LEVI (*b. Francestown, N.H., 1789; d. Portsmouth, N.H., 1851*), statesman, jurist. Studied law with Jeremiah Smith (1759–1842), also in Litchfield (Conn.) Law School and in Boston; admitted to the bar, 1812. Associate justice, New Hampshire superior court, 1817–23. Elected governor of New

Hampshire, 1823, by "Young America" Democrats and Federalists, he served until 1824. Congressman from New Hampshire, 1825, he was chosen speaker of the House. As U.S. senator, 1825–31 and 1841–45, he supported Democratic measures, served on commerce, navy and agriculture committees, and was an isolationist and supporter of a mildly protective tariff. As U.S. secretary of the navy, May 1831—June 1834, he reformed rules of conduct and procedure. Appointed U.S. secretary of the treasury, June 1834, he opposed the rechartering of the Bank of the United States and strongly supported President Jackson's Bank policy. He favored the independent treasury and warned country against inflation in 1836. He attempted to popularize use of hard money and urged Congress to use the unprecedented treasury surplus for public works (1835–36) and for purchase of sound state bonds. He opposed division of the surplus among the states. In the panic of 1837 he perfected a defense against depreciated paper money by which public holders of federal obligations suffered no loss. He was associate justice of the U.S. Supreme Court in 1846–51. Among his opinions, he concurred in the decision upholding constitutionality of state prohibition legislation (5 *Howard*, 617) and dissented in *Luther vs. Borden* (7 *Howard*, 1, 47), the Passenger Cases (7 *Howard*, 283, 518) and *Waring vs. Clarke* (5 *Howard*, 441). He was considered as a Democratic presidential nominee in 1848. Conservative in politics, Woodbury was a party man and a strict constructionist; his personal morals were puritan.

WOODFORD, STEWART LYNDON (*b. New York, N.Y., 1835; d. New York, 1913*), lawyer, Union soldier, diplomat. Admitted to the bar, 1857; practiced in New York City. Republican lieutenant-governor of New York, 1867–69; congressman, March 1873—July 1874. Federal district attorney, southern district of New York, 1877–83. As U.S. minister to Spain, 1897–98, he worked with skill but without success to prevent war.

WOODFORD, WILLIAM (*b. Caroline Co., Va., 1734; d. New York, N.Y., 1780*), Revolutionary patriot and soldier. Appointed colonel, 3rd Virginia Regiment, 1775, he defended Hampton and was victorious at Great Bridge. Made colonel, 2nd Virginia Regiment, 1776; promoted brigadier-general, 1777. Fought at Brandywine, Germantown and Monmouth; wintered at Valley Forge. Captured defending Charleston, S.C., 1780, he died as a prisoner of war.

WOODHOUSE, JAMES (*b. Philadelphia, Pa., 1770; d. 1809*), physician, chemist. Graduated present University of Pennsylvania, 1787; M.D., 1792. Studied also with Benjamin Rush. Founded the Chemical Society of Philadelphia, 1792, one of the earliest such societies in the world, and served it as senior president for many years. Becoming professor of chemistry in the University of Pennsylvania, 1795, Woodhouse entered upon a career of research. Among other

accomplishments, he gave the most convincing arguments against the doctrine of phlogiston; liberated metallic potassium by original methods; confirmed the anaesthetic properties of nitrous oxide gas (1806); engaged in profound studies of the chemistry and production of white starch; demonstrated the superiority of anthracite over bituminous coal for industrial purposes. Woodhouse was a pioneer in plant chemistry, in the development of chemical analysis, in the elaboration of many industrial processes, and in the use of laboratory methods of instruction in chemistry. Among others who frequented his laboratory were Joseph Priestley, Robert Hare and the elder Benjamin Silliman.

WOODHULL, ALFRED ALEXANDER (*b. Princeton, N.J., 1837; d. Princeton, 1921*), military surgeon, sanitation expert. Graduated medical department, University of Pennsylvania, 1859. Served in Union Army medical corps; was medical inspector, Army of the James, 1864–65. Brevetted lieutenant-colonel, 1865, he remained in the army until retirement in 1901. He advanced to brigadier-general on the retired list, 1904. Author, among other writings, of the "Surgical Section" of the *Catalogue of the United States Army Medical Museum* (1866) and *Notes on Military Hygiene for Officers of the Line* (1898–1909).

WOODHULL, NATHANIEL (*b. Mastic, L.I., N.Y., 1722; d. 1776*), farmer, soldier. Brother-in-law of William Floyd. Active as a New York assemblyman in protesting Crown interference in colonial affairs; served as president of the New York Provincial Congress, 1775. Appointed brigadier-general of militia, October 1775, he was wounded at his headquarters at Jamaica, L.I., N.Y., after the battle of Long Island, dying subsequently of ill treatment.

WOODHULL, VICTORIA CLAFLIN (*b. Homer, O., 1838; d. 1927*), adventuress. Began giving spiritualistic exhibitions with her sister (Tennessee Celeste Claflin, 1846–1923) c. 1853; traveled for a time with her family in a medicine and fortune-telling show; worked with her sister as a clairvoyant in Cincinnati, Chicago, and elsewhere in the Midwest. The sisters removed to New York City, 1868, where they won the interest of Cornelius Vanderbilt and made considerable profits in the stock market through his advice. In 1870 they began *Woodhull and Claflin's Weekly*, advocating equal rights for women and free love. Nominated for the presidency by the Equal Rights Party in 1872, Victoria went to the polls and made a futile attempt to vote. The Claflin sisters precipitated the greatest sensation of the time by publishing in their *Weekly* on Nov. 2, 1872, the story of the alleged intimacy of Henry Ward Beecher with the wife of Theodore Tilton. Resident in England *post* 1877, both sisters married into respectable English society and became noted for charitable works.

WOODIN, WILLIAM HARTMAN (*b. Berwick, Pa., 1868; d. New York, N.Y., 1934*), industrialist. President of the American Car & Foundry Co. and for many years chairman of the board of the American Locomotive Co., Woodin was a close friend of Franklin D. Roosevelt and supported him for the presidency in 1932. After the election he became one of the inner circle of Roosevelt advisers and was named U.S. secretary of the treasury early in 1933. Woodin addressed himself with great energy and devotion to the task of restoring financial confidence and to carrying out the president's financial and monetary policies; he supervised promulgation of new banking regulations and undertook to stop hoarding of gold. His health failing, he resigned in December 1933.

WOODROW, JAMES (*b. Carlisle, England, 1828; d. 1907*), Presbyterian clergyman, educator. Uncle of Woodrow Wilson. Came to America as a boy. Graduated Jefferson College (Pa.), 1849; Ph.D., Heidelberg, 1856. Professor of natural science, Oglethorpe University (Ga.), 1856–61. Professor of "Natural Science in Connexion with Revelation" at Presbyterian Seminary, Columbia, S.C., 1861–86. Became professor of science, University of South Carolina, 1869; served as president, 1891–97. Published the *Southern Presbyterian*, 1865–93. His address, *Evolution* (1884), denying any essential conflict between the Bible and science, brought him nation-wide attention and aroused a Southern church controversy which lasted until 1888. Woodrow's speech in defense of his views before the Synod of South Carolina, 1884, is one of the most enlightened expositions in Southern ecclesiastical history, but he was removed from his chair at the Seminary.

WOODRUFF, CHARLES EDWARD (*b. Philadelphia, Pa., 1860; d. New Rochelle, N.Y., 1915*), ethnologist, army surgeon. M.D., Jefferson Medical College, 1886. During Spanish-American War, served as brigade surgeon under Maj.-Gen. Wesley Merritt in Philippine Islands. Brigade surgeon, 4th Brigade, during Philippine insurrection, 1902. Author, among other writings, of *The Expansion of Races* (1909) and *Medical Ethnology* (1915).

WOODRUFF, THEODORE TUTTLE (*b. near Watertown, N.Y., 1811; d. Gloucester, N.J., 1892*), inventor. Patented railway-car seat and couch (1856), also improvements (1859 and 1860); began manufacture of sleeping cars in Philadelphia, Pa., 1858. Patented a process and apparatus for indigo manufacture (1872) and a coffee-hulling machine. Later patents include a steam plow.

WOODRUFF, TIMOTHY LESTER (*b. New Haven, Conn., 1858; d. 1913*), merchant, New York politician. Removed to Brooklyn, N.Y., 1881. Republican lieutenant-governor of New York, 1897–1903; strengthened Kings County organization of Republican party.

WOODRUFF, WILFORD (*b. Farmington, now Avon, Conn., 1807; d. San Francisco, Calif., 1898*), Mormon leader. Converted to Mormonism at Richland, N.Y., 1833. Removed to Kirtland, O., 1834, and was sent by Joseph Smith to aid distressed Mormons in Missouri. Ordained apostle by Brigham Young, 1839. A member of the first company to enter Great Salt Lake Valley, 1847. Became president of the quorum of the "Twelve Apostles," 1880; succeeded to presidency, Utah branch, Mormon Church, 1889. One of Mormon's most effective proselyters, his missionary travels covered England, Scotland, Wales, and 23 states and 5 territories of the Union. In 1875 he became Mormon's official historian and recorder; as president, he issued the famous "Manifesto," 1890, in which plural marriage was officially abandoned.

WOODRUFF, WILLIAM EDWARD (*b. Fireplace, L.I., N.Y., 1795; d. Little Rock, Ark., 1885*), newspaper publisher. Founder-editor, *Arkansas Gazette*, 1819–38, 1841–43; established *Arkansas Democrat*, 1846.

WOODS, ALVA (*b. Shoreham, Vt., 1794; d. Providence, R.I., 1887*), Baptist clergyman, educator. Graduated Harvard, 1817; ordained, 1821. President of Transylvania University (Ky.), 1828–31; of the University of Alabama, 1831–37.

WOODS, CHARLES ROBERT (*b. Newark, O., 1827; d. Ohio, 1885*), soldier. Brother of William B. Woods. Graduated West Point, 1852. Commanded army force aboard *Star of the West* in attempt to relieve Fort Sumter, 1861; appointed colonel, 76th Ohio Infantry, 1861. For gallant service in Vicksburg campaign, was appointed brigadier-general of volunteers, 1863. Led assault on Lookout Mountain; played prominent part at Resaca and Atlanta, 1864; brevetted major-general of volunteers in 1865. He served in the West as regular colonel of infantry, 1866–74.

WOODS, JAMES HAUGHTON (*b. Boston, Mass., 1864; d. Tokyo, Japan, 1935*), educator, student of Indian philosophy. Graduated Harvard, 1887; Ph.D., Strassburg, 1896; studied also at Episcopal Theological School in Cambridge, Mass., and at Oxford, Harvard, and the University of Berlin. Taught several subjects intermittently at Harvard. Made special Oriental studies at Kiel, and traveled and studied in India until 1903 when he became a member of the Harvard department of philosophy and instructor in the philosophical systems of India. He was professor of philosophy at Harvard, 1913–34, continuing, however, his travels and further studies in Oriental subjects. He was editor and author of texts and translations in his special field. [*Supp. 1*]

WOODS, LEONARD (*b. Princeton, Mass., 1774; d. Andover, Mass., 1854*), Congregational clergyman. Father of Leonard Woods (1807–1878). Ordained pastor of church at Newbury (now West Newbury), Mass., 1798. A moderate Calvinist, he mediated successfully between the Hopkinsians and the Old Calvinists. He was the first professor of theology at Andover Theological Seminary, 1808–46.

WOODS, LEONARD (*b. Newbury, Mass., 1807; d. Boston, Mass., 1878*), clergyman, educator. Son of Leonard Woods (1774–1854). Graduated Union, 1827; Andover Theological Seminary, 1830. Ordained by Third Presbytery of New York, 1833; was editor, *Literary and Theological Review* (New York City), 1833–36. Called to chair of Biblical literature, Bangor (Maine) Theological Seminary, 1836. As president of Bowdoin College, 1839–66, he inspired affection and respect. He was an excellent teacher, was largely responsible for erection of King Chapel, and helped win for the college the reversionary interest in the James Bowdoin estate.

WOODS, ROBERT ARCHEY (*b. Pittsburgh, Pa., 1865; d. 1925*), sociologist, reformer. Graduated Amherst, 1886; studied at Andover Theological Seminary; worked at Toynbee Hall, London, England. Head of Andover House (South End House) settlement, Boston, Mass., *post* 1891. Woods's outstanding contribution to sociology and social work is the concept that the neighborhood or village is the primary community unit, and that towns, metropolitan areas, the nation itself, are "federations" of neighborhoods. He organized Boston settlements into a federation, and initiated organization of the National Federation of Settlements, 1911. Author of *English Social Movements* (1891), *The City Wilderness* (1898, the first thorough-going study of a depressed area in an American city); *Americans in Process* (1902); *Neighborhood in Nation-Building* (1923). Co-author with Albert J. Kennedy of, among others, *The Settlement Horizon* (1922), an authoritative text on the history of American settlements.

WOODS, WILLIAM ALLEN (*b. near Farmington, Tenn., 1837; d. Indianapolis, Ind., 1901*), jurist. Raised in Iowa; admitted to Indiana bar, 1861. Judge, thirty-fourth judicial circuit of Indiana, 1873–80; Indiana supreme court, 1880–82; U.S. district judge for Indiana, 1882–92; judge of seventh U.S. circuit court *post* 1892. His most widely known case was *United States vs. Debs* (64 *Federal Reporter*, 724), in which he sentenced Debs to prison for violation of an antistrike injunction.

WOODS, WILLIAM BURNHAM (*b. Newark, O., 1824; d. Washington, D.C., 1887*), Ohio Democratic legislator, Union brigadier-general, jurist. Brother of Charles R. Woods. Removed to Alabama, 1866, where he was active in Reconstruction as a Republican. Appointed judge of the U.S. circuit court, fifth circuit, 1869, he removed to Atlanta, Ga. Commissioned associate justice of the U.S. Supreme Court, 1880, Woods wrote the opinion in *U.S. vs. Harris* (106 *U.S.*, 629) determining that protection of Negro civil rights was not to be found in federal statutes or by federal court indictments. He also wrote the opinion in *Presser*

vs. Illinois (116 *U.S.*, 252), and in many patent and equity cases.

WOODWARD, AUGUSTUS BREVOORT (*b. New York, N.Y., 1774; d. Tallahassee, Fla., 1827*), jurist, political philosopher. Graduated Columbia, 1793. Active in incorporation of city of Washington, 1801–02; was member of its first council. A judge of the Territory of Michigan, 1805–24, Woodward was the dominant figure in the Michigan court and legislature. He prepared a plan for rebuilding the city of Detroit and compiled *The Laws of Michigan* (1806) known as "The Woodward Code." His *A System of Universal Science* (1816) contained the idea (expanded in 1817 in a legislative act written by him) of the "Catholepistemiad, or University, of Michigania" (University of Michigan). In 1824 he was appointed to a Florida federal court where he served until his death. He was a friend and admirer of Thomas Jefferson. Author, among other works, of *Considerations on the Executive Government of the United States of America* (1809).

WOODWARD, CALVIN MILTON (*b. near Fitchburg, Mass., 1837; d. St. Louis, Mo., 1914*), educator. Graduated Harvard, 1860. Taught geometry at Washington University, St. Louis, Mo.; was dean of its polytechnic school, 1870–96, 1901–10, and Thayer Professor of Mathematics and Applied Mechanics. He accomplished his most important work, however, as originator and director of the St. Louis Manual Training School (opened 1880) which served as model for similar schools in other cities. Author, among other works, of *Manual Training in Education* (1890).

WOODWARD, HENRY (*b. possibly Barbados, B.W.I., c. 1646; d. c. 1686*), surgeon, first English settler in South Carolina and a pioneer of English expansion in the lower South. Joined Carolina settlement near Cape Fear, 1664; explored Port Royal, 1666. Acquired important information concerning Indians on northern Florida border, also about Spaniards in Florida, while a prisoner at St. Augustine. Interpreter and Indian agent with Carolina fleet of 1669–70. On mission to open the interior Indian trade for the Earl of Shaftesbury, 1674, he effected an alliance with the Westos on the Savannah River. Later he pressed the Carolina trading frontier westward to the towns of the Lower Creeks on middle Chattahoochee. By 1686 Woodward had laid a firm foundation for English alliance with the Lower Creeks.

WOODWARD, JOSEPH JANVIER (*b. Philadelphia, Pa., 1833; d. Wawa, Pa., 1884*), army medical officer. M.D., University of Pennsylvania, 1853. Practiced in Philadelphia. Surgeon with Army of the Potomac, 1861–62; then assigned to surgeon-general's office, Washington, D.C. Prepared medical section of the *Medical and Surgical History of the War of the Rebellion* (1870–88). He was among first to apply photomicrography to use in pathology and was instrumental in improving the photomicrographic camera. Attended President James A. Garfield between his shooting and death, 1881.

WOODWARD, ROBERT SIMPSON (*b. Rochester, Mich., 1849; d. Washington, D.C. 1924*), engineer, mathematical physicist. C.E., University of Michigan, 1872. Chief geographer, U.S. Geological Survey *post* 1884. Wrote important papers of a geophysical nature on deformations of the earth's surface and on secular cooling of the earth. Put field methods for topographic mapping and primary and secondary triangulation on practical engineering basis. Developed iced-bar apparatus for measuring base-lines and for calibrating steel tapes and was first to prove base-lines could be measured with sufficient accuracy by means of long steel tapes. Appointed professor of mechanics and mathematical physics, Columbia University, 1893, he shortly thereafter became dean of its College of Pure Science. President, Carnegie Institution of Washington, 1904–20. He was an editor of *Science*, 1884–1924.

WOODWARD, SAMUEL BAYARD (*b. Torrington, Conn., 1787; d. Northampton, Mass., 1850*), mental disease expert. Instrumental in founding Connecticut Retreat for the Insane, Hartford, 1824. Served as superintendent, Massachusetts State Lunatic Asylum, Worcester, 1832–46. Founder and first president, Association of Medical Superintendents of American Institutions for the Insane (American Psychiatric Association).

WOODWORTH, JAY BACKUS (*b. Newfield, N.Y., 1865; d. Cambridge, Mass., 1925*), geologist. Studied under Nathaniel S. Shaler at Lawrence Scientific School. B.A., Harvard, 1894, where he served as associate professor of geology, 1912 until his death. He was also assistant geologist, U.S. Geological Survey. Woodworth was a pioneer of seismological studies in relation to geology. He was founder and director of the Harvard seismological station, one of the first in America, 1908–25.

WOODWORTH, SAMUEL (*b. Scituate, Mass., 1784; d. 1842*), printer, journalist, poet. Apprenticed to Benjamin Russell in Boston, Mass., 1800–06. After brief residences in New Haven, Conn., and Baltimore, Md., he settled in New York City, 1809. Engaged throughout his life in a great number of journalistic and literary pursuits, he is remembered principally as the author of "The Bucket" ("The Old Oaken Bucket"). A frequent contributor of poetry to the periodical press over the signature "Selim," he was author of three satires—*New-Haven* (1809), *Beasts at Law* (1811), and *Quarter-Day* (1812); also, of a number of plays which included the long-popular *The Forest Rose* (1825).

WOOL, JOHN ELLIS (*b. Newburgh, N.Y., 1784; d. Troy, N.Y., 1869*), soldier. Raising a company of volunteers in Troy, N.Y., at the outbreak of the War of 1812, he served in the northern campaigns with gallantry and received the brevet of lieutenant-colonel, September 1814, for his conduct at the battle of Plattsburg, N.Y. Promoted colonel and inspector-general of the army, April 1816, he remained in this grade until 1841 when he was promoted brigadier-general. After mustering-in about 12,000 volunteers at Cincinnati, O., 1846, for service in the war with Mexico, he went to San Antonio, Texas, in August to lead a new command on a march through Chihuahua. Starting thence with a spiritless force of some 1400 men in September, he crossed 900 miles of hostile country and arrived in Saltillo on December 22. His efficiency and speed of movement were largely responsible for the American victory of Buena Vista; he selected the position and held the Mexicans while Gen. Zachary Taylor went back to Saltillo. He later commanded the Eastern Military Division and the Department of the Pacific. At the opening of the Civil War he saved Fortress Monroe by timely reinforcements. Promoted major-general, 1862, he commanded the Middle Department and the Department of the East until his retirement, 1863.

WOOLF, BENJAMIN EDWARD (*b. London, England, 1836; d. Boston, Mass., 1901*), musician, composer, music critic. Came to America as a child. Joined editorial staff of the *Saturday Evening Gazette*, Boston, Mass., 1871; became publisher and editor, 1892. As music critic of the *Boston Herald*, he was noted for the clarity and severity of his reviews. Author of once-popular plays and light operas, including *Pounce & Co., or Capital vs. Labor* (1882).

WOOLLEY, CELIA PARKER (*b. Toledo, O., 1848; d. Chicago, Ill., 1918*), settlement worker, author. Ordained into the Unitarian fellowship, 1894; held Illinois pastorates. Established and lived in Frederick Douglass Center, a Negro settlement on Chicago's south side, 1904–18. Associated with *Unity*, a Chicago religious weekly, *post* 1884. Active in Chicago's cultural and social service circles.

WOOLLEY, JOHN GRANVILLE (*b. Collinsville, O., 1850; d. Spain, 1922*), Prohibitionist, lawyer. Active in prohibition movement *post* 1888 as lecturer and editor; Prohibition Party presidential candidate, 1900.

WOOLMAN, JOHN (*b. Rancocas, West Jersey, 1720; d. York, England, 1772*), tailor, teacher, Quaker leader. Called to the Quaker ministry *c.* 1743, he embarked on a thirty-year series of journeys from North Carolina to New Hampshire and from the northern frontier of Pennsylvania to Yorkshire, England. His ministry was concerned principally with the abolition of slavery; he visited especially the slave-trade centers such as Perth Amboy and Newport. Woolman's writings include his celebrated *Journal* (1774) which won the praise of Charles Lamb, W. E.

Channing, and others, and an essay, *Some Considerations on the Keeping of Negroes* (1754).

WOOLSEY, MELANCTHON TAYLOR (*b. New York State, 1780; d. Utica, N.Y., 1838*), naval officer. Nephew of John H. Livingston. Entered navy as midshipman, 1800. Served on Great Lakes, 1808–25. In War of 1812 commanded at Sacketts Harbor, and was second-in-command under Isaac Chauncey. In charge of Pensacola navy yard, 1826–30; commanded Brazil Squadron as commodore, 1832–34.

WOOLSEY, SARAH CHAUNCY (*b. Cleveland, O., 1835; d. 1905*), author. Niece of Theodore D. Woolsey. Wrote under pseudonym "Susan Coolidge." Chiefly remembered as a popular writer of stories for young people; among these are *What Katy Did* (1872), *A Little Country Girl* (1885) and *An Old Convent School in Paris and Other Papers* (1895). Edited, among others, *The Diary and Letters of Frances Burney* (1880) and *Letters of Jane Austen* (1892).

WOOLSEY, THEODORE DWIGHT (*b. New York, N.Y., 1801; d. 1889*), educator, political scientist. Father of Theodore S. Woolsey. Connected by blood with the Dwight and Edwards families (nephew of Theodore Dwight, 1764–1846), he graduated from Yale in 1820. After making theological studies at both Princeton and Yale, he went abroad for further study at Paris, Leipzig, Bonn and Berlin. Accepting the chair of Greek language and literature at Yale, 1831, he was notably successful as a teacher and as a writer of superior textbooks in his field. Called to the presidency of Yale, 1846, he served until 1871; during his time Yale made greater progress than in any similar period theretofore. Subsequent to his acceptance of the presidency he had given up teaching Greek and begun giving instruction in history, political science and international law. He became a recognized authority in the last two subjects both at home and abroad, and was the author, among other works, of the celebrated *Introduction to the Study of International Law* (1860 and many subsequent editions) and *Political Science* (1878). A scholar of extensive and accurate knowledge, he was also a clear-visioned and effective administrator; his dignity and reserve, however, tended to keep people at a distance.

WOOLSEY, THEODORE SALISBURY (*b. New Haven, Conn., 1852; d. New Haven, 1929*), educator. Son of Theodore D. Woolsey. Graduated Yale, 1872; LL.B., Yale Law School, 1876. Professor of international law, Yale Law School, 1878–1911, except for 1886–90. Author, among other writings, of *America's Foreign Policy* (1898).

WOOLSON, ABBA LOUISA GOOLD (*b. Windham, Maine, 1838; d. Maine, 1921*), writer. Held several teaching positions including professorship of belles-lettres at Mount Auburn Ladies' Institute, Cincinnati, O. Lectured on English literature. Author, among

other books, of *Woman in American Society* (1873) with a foreword by her personal friend John G. Whittier.

WOOLSON, CONSTANCE FENIMORE (*b. Claremont, N.H., 1840; d. Venice, Italy, 1894*), author. Grand-niece of James Fenimore Cooper. Raised in Cleveland, O. During trips as a young girl through Ohio, Wisconsin and to Mackinac Island, she acquired a thorough knowledge of the lake region. She later traveled widely on the Atlantic seaboard and lived in the Carolinas and Florida, 1873–1879. She resided in Europe *post* 1879. Author, among other regional works, of *Castle Nowhere: Lake Country Sketches* (1875); *Rodman the Keeper: Southern Sketches* (1880); *East Angels* (1886); *Jupiter Lights* (1889); *Horace Chase* (1894). *For the Major* (1883), in many respects her best novel, is a comparatively unlocalized account of village life in the eastern Appalachians. Her collections of European stories, *The Front Yard* (1895) and *Dorothy* (1896), are accounts of Americans projected against the background of an older civilization in the manner of her friend and critic Henry James.

WOOLWORTH, FRANK WINFIELD (*b. Rodman, N.Y. 1852; d. 1919*), merchant. After a succession of business failures, he opened a prosperous store in Lancaster, Pa., 1879, featuring an array of goods at the fixed prices of five and ten cents. Establishing other stores and absorbing chains of stores run by competitors, he built up the F. W. Woolworth Co. He strove constantly to add articles to his line and to offer at his low price goods which had never been sold at such a figure before; this policy was a principal factor in his success.

WOOSTER, CHARLES WHITING (*b. New Haven, Conn., 1780; d. San Francisco, Calif., 1848*), merchant mariner, War of 1812 privateer, Chilean navy commander-in-chief, 1822–35. Grandson of David Wooster.

WOOSTER, DAVID (*b. present Huntington, Conn., 1711; d. Connecticut, 1777*), merchant, Revolutionary brigadier-general. A practiced soldier in the colonial wars *post* 1745, he was appointed a major-general of six regiments and colonel of the 1st Regiment by the Connecticut Assembly in 1775. He was made a Continental brigadier-general, June 1775. As ranking officer in Canada after Gen. Richard Montgomery's death, he was unsuccessful and was superseded by Gen. Thomas. Reappointed major-general of Connecticut militia in the fall of 1776, he was mortally wounded in the defense of Ridgefield, Conn., during Tryon's raid on Danbury, April 1777.

WOOTASSITE. [See OUTACITY, fl. 1756–1777.]

WOOTTON, RICHENS LACY (*b. Mecklenburg Co., Va., 1816; d. near Trinidad, Colo., 1893*), trapper, pioneer settler. Raised in Kentucky. Traded and trapped in almost every section of the Western fur country, 1836–40; ranched and traded on site of present Pueblo, Colo. *post* 1841. Helped suppress Taos insurrection and participated in battle of Sacramento, 1847. Served as scout with Col. A. W. Doniphan on Chihuahua expedition and with other army expeditions; engaged in freighting. Perhaps best known for building in 1865 a 27-mile road over the roughest portion of the Santa Fé Trail mountain division from Trinidad, Colo., across Raton Pass and down to the Canadian River.

WORCESTER, EDWIN DEAN (*b. Albany, N.Y., 1828; d. New York, N.Y., 1904*), railroad official. Employed by Erastus Corning as chief accountant of the newly consolidated New York Central, 1853, Worcester was associated with that road and its subsequent expansion under the Vanderbilts until his death.

WORCESTER, ELWOOD (*b. Massillon, O., 1862; d. Kennebunkport, Maine, 1940*), Episcopal clergyman. Graduated Columbia, 1886; General Theological Seminary, New York, 1887; Ph.D., Leipzig, 1889. After teaching at Lehigh University and a pastorate in Philadelphia, Pa., he was called to Emmanuel Church, Boston, Mass., 1904, where with the cooperation of physicians he pioneered in the Christian application of psychotherapy, developing what became known as the "Emmanuel Movement." [*Supp. 2*]

WORCESTER, JOSEPH EMERSON (*b. Bedford, N.H., 1784; d. Cambridge, Mass., 1865*), lexicographer, geographer, historian. Nephew of Noah and Samuel Worcester. Graduated Yale, 1811. From 1817 to 1826, he published geographical gazetteers and works on geography and history used extensively as textbooks. Compiler of, among other dictionaries, the *Comprehensive Pronouncing and Explanatory Dictionary of the English Language* (1830, 1847, 1849; issued in 1855 as *A Pronouncing, Explanatory, and Synonymous Dictionary of the English Language*) containing his linguistic contribution of the "compromise vowel." This work evoked Noah Webster's charge of plagiarism, which Worcester refuted, and initiated the "War of the Dictionaries." In 1831 he assumed an 11-year editorship of *The American Almanac and Repository of Useful Knowledge*. His illustrated quarto *A Dictionary of the English Language* (1860) was the most elaborate and important of all his works. A conservative in lexicography, Worcester held closely to British usage.

WORCESTER, NOAH (*b. Hollis, N.H., 1758; d. Brighton, Mass., 1837*), Congregational and Unitarian clergyman. Brother of Samuel Worcester. Minister of the church at Thornton, N.H., 1787–1810. Editor, *Christian Disciple* (later *Christian Examiner*), 1813–18. His most important contribution was in the promotion of peace; he established and conducted *The Friend of Peace*, 1819–28, and wrote, among other works, *A Solemn Review of the Custom of War* (1814).

WORCESTER, SAMUEL (*b. Hollis, N.H., 1770; d. Brainerd, Tenn., 1821*), Congregational clergyman. Brother of Noah Worcester. Graduated Dartmouth, 1795. Pastor at Fitchburg, Mass., 1797–1802. An inflexible Hopkinsian Calvinist, he was dismissed from his pastorate and became pastor of Tabernacle Church, Salem, Mass., 1803. Involved in famous controversy with William Ellery Channing (1780–1842), 1815. Was a founder (1810) and corresponding secretary of the American Board of Commissioners for Foreign Missions.

WORCESTER, SAMUEL AUSTIN (*b. Worcester, Mass., 1798; d. present Oklahoma, 1859*), Congregational clergyman. Nephew of Noah and Samuel Worcester, also of Samuel Austin. Graduated Andover Theological Seminary, 1823. Missionary to the Cherokees *post* 1825 in Tennessee and at New Echota, Ga.; translated portions of the Bible into Cherokee and helped found the *Cherokee Phoenix*. Imprisoned by Georgia, 1831–33, for refusal to quit his mission. Began establishment of important Cherokee Park Hill Mission in Indian Territory, 1835; set up first printing press there. Urged adoption by Cherokees of written language invented by Sequoyah.

WORDEN, JOHN LORIMER (*b. Westchester Co., N.Y., 1818; d. Washington, D.C., 1897*), naval officer. Appointed midshipman, 1834. Commanded original *Monitor* in battle with C.S.S. *Merrimac*, March 9, 1862, gaining national renown and promotion to captain, 1863. Commanded monitor *Montauk*, South Atlantic Blockading Squadron, October 1862—April 1863. Made rear-admiral, 1872. Superintendent, U.S. Naval Academy, 1869–74, he commanded European Squadron, 1875–77. Retired, 1886.

WORK, HENRY CLAY (*b. Middletown, Conn., 1832; d. Hartford, Conn., 1884*), printer, song-writer. Wrote famous temperance song "Come Home, Father" in 1864; was author, among other Civil War songs, of "Kingdom Coming" (1861), "Babylon is Fallen!" (1863), "Wake Nicodemus" (1864) and "Marching through Georgia" (1865). Later, among many other successes, he composed "Grandfather's Clock."

WORK, MILTON COOPER (*b. Philadelphia, Pa., 1864; d. 1934*), lawyer, auction and contract bridge expert. Abandoned Philadelphia law practice, 1917, for bridge lectures and demonstrations; associated with Wilbur C. Whitehead in radio bridge games, 1925–30, and as an editor, *Auction Bridge Magazine*. Developed "artificial two-club game-demand" bid. Author of *Auction Developments* (1913) and other books.

WORKMAN, FANNY BULLOCK (*b. Worcester, Mass., 1859; d. Cannes, France, 1925*), explorer. On expedition to the Himalayas and Karakoram (or Mustagh) Range, she achieved the women's world mountaineering record, 1906. Her books of geographical value include *Algerian Memories* (1895),

Sketches Awheel in Modern Iberia (1897), *Peaks and Glaciers of Nun Kun* (1909) and *The Call of the Snowy Hispar* (1910).

WORMELEY, KATHARINE PRESCOTT (*b. Ipswich, England, 1830; d. Jackson, N.H., 1908*), author, translator, philanthropist. Sister of Mary E. W. Latimer. Came to America *c.* 1848. Best known for translations of noted French writers, particularly *The Works of Balzac* (1899–); among her other translations are *Letters of Mlle. de Lespinasse* (1901) and Sainte-Beuve's *Portraits of the Eighteenth Century* (1905). Author of *The Other Side of War* (1889) and *Memoir of Honoré de Balzac* (1892).

WORMELEY, MARY ELIZABETH. [See LATIMER, MARY ELIZABETH WORMELEY, 1822–1904.]

WORMLEY, JAMES (*b. Washington, D.C., 1819; d. Boston, Mass., 1884*), hotel keeper. Of Negro parentage. Steward for the Metropolitan Club, Washington, D.C., *post c.* 1853; established Wormley's hotel and catering service in Washington *c.* 1860; won national reputation for cuisine.

WORMLEY, THEODORE GEORGE (*b. Wormleysburg, Pa., 1826; d. 1897*), physician, toxicologist. M.D., Philadelphia College of Medicine, 1849. Professor of toxicology at Capitol University, Columbus, O., 1852–63; at Starling Medical College, Columbus, 1852–77. Held chair of chemistry and toxicology, medical department, University of Pennsylvania *post* 1877. Author of *The Micro-chemistry of Poisons* (1867).

WORTH, JONATHAN (*b. Guilford Co., N.C., 1802; d. Raleigh, N.C., 1869*), lawyer, businessman, North Carolina official and legislator. Studied law under Archibald D. Murphey; began practice at Asheboro, N.C., 1824. In the North Carolina legislature, 1831, he protested nullification, but opposed the Jackson administration later and became a Whig; he opposed the secession movement in the legislature, 1860. Elected state treasurer, 1862, he served until 1865. As governor of North Carolina, 1865–68, he displayed tact and sound judgment. He supported President Johnson and ratification of the new constitution submitted in 1866; he opposed ratification of the Fourteenth Amendment.

WORTH, WILLIAM JENKINS (*b. Hudson, N.Y., 1794; d. Texas, 1849*), soldier. Commissioned first lieutenant, 23rd Infantry, March 1813, he became aide-de-camp to Gen. Winfield Scott and was commended for bravery at the battles of Chippewa and Lundy's Lane. Remaining in the army after the War of 1812, he served in the artillery and in the Ordnance Department; he was commandant of cadets at West Point, 1820–28. As colonel of the 8th Infantry, he commanded in Florida against the Seminoles, 1838, defeating them at the battle of Palaklaklaha. Ordered to join Gen. Zachary Taylor in the Army of Occupation prior to the war with Mexico, he took part in a controversy over rank with Gen. David E. Twiggs. A great part of the credit for victory at Monterey belongs to his successful storming of the heights. Receiving the brevet of major-general, he joined Gen. Winfield Scott's army and took part in all the engagements from Vera Cruz to Mexico City. Narrow and self-centered, he damaged his reputation subsequent to the victory by engaging in intrigues against Gen. Scott who had been his benefactor.

WORTHEN, AMOS HENRY (*b. Bradford, Vt., 1813; d. 1888*), businessman, geologist. Appointed Illinois state geologist, 1858; published seven volumes of *Geological Survey of Illinois* (1866–90). Worthen was a pioneer in classification of the Lower Carboniferous strata.

WORTHEN, WILLIAM EZRA (*b. Amesbury, Mass., 1819; d. 1897*), civil engineer. Graduated Harvard, 1838. Assisted in water-supply and hydraulic work in offices of the younger Loammi Baldwin and James B. Francis. Employed by George W. Whistler on Albany & West Stockbridge Railroad. Settled in New York, 1849, engaging in building and mill construction. Worthen was an expert on pumping machinery and drainage; he held many important consultative posts.

WORTHINGTON, HENRY ROSSITER (*b. New York, N.Y., 1817; d. 1880*), hydraulic engineer, inventor. Patented improvements in canal-boat navigation and pumping engines. First proposer and constructor of the direct steam pump, he perfected an ingenious, widely used duplex steam feed pump, 1859, and built the first water-works engine of this kind, 1860. He also developed a pumping engine that needed no flywheel to carry the piston past the dead point at end of stroke.

WORTHINGTON, JOHN (*b. Springfield, Mass., 1719; d. 1800*), lawyer, politician. Father-in-law of Jonathan Bliss and Fisher Ames. For many years King's attorney in western Massachusetts, he was a noted land speculator and was responsible for settlement of Worthington, Mass., 1768. Political dictator of Springfield, Mass., he was its representative in the Massachusetts General Court almost continuously, 1747–74; his conservatism then ended his influence in colony affairs.

WORTHINGTON, THOMAS (*b. near Charleston, Va., now W. Va., 1773; d. New York, N.Y., 1827*), surveyor, Ohio legislator. Brother-in-law of Edward Tiffin. A leader of the "Chillicothe Junto" which secured Ohio's statehood and the triumph of Jeffersonianism there. U.S. senator from Ohio, 1803–07, 1811–14, he was influential in matters concerning public lands and the Indian frontier. As governor of Ohio, 1814–18, he suggested social reforms and was responsible for founding the state library.

WOVOKA (*b. near Walker Lake, Nev., c. 1856; d. 1932*), Indian mystic. A Paiute, he founded the Ghost

Dance religion which swept the Indian country and became important to the white man's political economy during the Messiah agitation of 1890.

WRAGG, WILLIAM (*b. probably Charlestown, S.C., 1714; d. off coast of Holland, 1777*), lawyer, planter, South Carolina public official. Father-in-law of John Mathews and William L. Smith. Inheritor of the Wragg barony, he was a Loyalist leader; as a member of the South Carolina Assembly, 1763–68, he alone voted against approving action of Stamp Act Congress, 1766. He was a nonsubscriber to the non-importation agreement, 1769. Banished from the colony, 1777.

WRAXALL, PETER (*b. probably Bristol, England, date unknown; d. New York, N.Y., 1759*), soldier. Came to New York *ante* 1746. Secretary for Indian affairs, New York province, *post* 1752; aide to Sir William Johnson. Author of an outstanding survey of the Indian question, 1755–56 (published in E. B. O'Callaghan, *Documents Relative . . . State of New York*, Vol. VII, 1856).

WRIGHT, BENJAMIN (*b. Wethersfield, Conn., 1770; d. New York, N.Y., 1842*), surveyor, engineer, New York legislator. Senior engineer of the Erie Canal, Wright was in charge of construction of the canal's middle section *post* 1816, and later of its eastern division as well. An able executive, he gathered around him such associates as Canvass White, John B. Jervis and Nathan S. Roberts. Resigning as the Erie's chief engineer, 1827, Wright was chief engineer of the Chesapeake & Ohio Canal, 1828–31, and of the St. Lawrence Canal, 1833. He was consulting engineer on a number of other canal and railroad projects.

WRIGHT, CARROLL DAVIDSON (*b. Dunbarton, N.H., 1840; d. Worcester, Mass., 1909*), statistician, social economist, public official, Massachusetts legislator. Chief, Massachusetts Bureau of Statistics of Labor, 1873–88. Organized National Convention of Chiefs and Commissioners of Bureaus of Statistics of Labor, 1883; served as president for practically twenty years. First commissioner, U.S. Bureau of Labor, 1885–1905. Chairman, Pullman strike commission, 1894; recorder, anthracite strike commission, 1902. He was also honorary professor of social economics, Catholic University, Washington, D.C., 1895–1904; professor of statistics and social economics, Columbian (later George Washington) University, *post* 1900. Wright was president of the American Statistical Association from 1897 until his death. In 1902 he was chosen first president of Clark College, Worcester, Mass. Author, among other publications, of *The Relation of Political Economy to the Labor Question* (1882) and *The Industrial Evolution of the United States* (1895).

WRIGHT, CHARLES (*b. Wethersfield, Conn., 1811; d. Wethersfield, 1885*), surveyor, teacher, botanical explorer. Graduated Yale, 1835. Initiated important correspondence with Asa Gray of Harvard, 1844, to whom he supplied specimens from the Southwest. Explored and collected in eastern Texas, 1837–45; from San Antonio to El Paso, 1849; in New Mexico and Arizona, 1851–52; and in Cuba, 1856–67. Discovered many new species, described in Gray's *"Plantae Wrightianae"* and *Botany of the Mexican Boundary Survey* (1859) and in other works. As botanist, North Pacific Exploring and Surveying Expedition, 1853–56, he made notable collections in China and Japan.

WRIGHT, CHARLES BARSTOW (*b. Wysox, Pa., 1822; d. Philadelphia, Pa., 1898*), financier. Prospered in real estate transactions in neighborhood of Chicago, Ill., 1843–46, and in Philadelphia banking thereafter. Entered directorship, Northern Pacific Railroad, 1870, and was a principal factor in its completion and eventual success. He served as its president, 1874–79.

WRIGHT, CHAUNCEY (*b. Northampton, Mass., 1830; d. 1875*), mathematician, philosopher. Graduated Harvard, 1852. Recording secretary, American Academy of Arts and Sciences, 1863–70. Began publication of a notable series of philosophical essays in the *North American Review*, 1864. Commended by Darwin for essays on arrangements of leaves in plants and genesis of species. A thoroughgoing naturalist, Wright dealt in his most valuable article, "Evolution of Self-Consciousness," with an instrumentalist conception of mental activities which anticipated later trends in thought. He was among the first to introduce methods of British empiricism to America.

WRIGHT, ELIZUR (*b. South Canaan, Conn., 1804; d. 1885*), reformer, actuary. Raised in Tallmadge, O. Graduated Yale, 1826. While a professor at the Western Reserve College, he was enlisted in the anti-slavery cause by Theodore Weld and served *post* 1833 as secretary of the American Anti-Slavery Society. Resigning in 1839, he became editor of the *Massachusetts Abolitionist*, organ of the conservative opponents of William L. Garrison, but was soon dropped. Unsuccessful in several further attempts as editor of reforming journals, he became widely known as a critic of the financial methods of life insurance companies. Tables published by him enabled life insurance companies for the first time to formulate reserve policies which would render them stable. Wright then lobbied (1853–58) in the Massachusetts legislature for a law to force all companies doing business in that state to maintain adequate reserves; subsequent to its passage, he was appointed state commissioner of insurance to oversee the new law's enforcement. His efforts at that time and subsequently probably had more to do with the development of sound standards for life insurance than those of any other man in the history of the industry. Ousted from his office in 1866, he became an actuary for several companies, but continued his lobbying for sound insurance legislation and was active in other reform movements.

WRIGHT, FRANCES (*b. Dundee, Scotland, 1795; d. 1852*), reformer, free thinker. Heiress to a large fortune, she early showed herself a difficult and rebellious child. At the age of 18 she wrote a work which contained in essence the materialistic philosophy that she followed throughout life (published under title *A Few Days in Athens*, 1822). Emigrating to New York City, 1818, she made a tour of the Northern and Eastern states; on her return to England in 1820 she composed her *Views of Society and Manners in America* (published, 1821) which expressed an appreciation of America unusual at that time among Europeans. Returning to the United States, 1824, in company with the Marquis de Lafayette, she visited Thomas Jefferson and James Madison and won their approval for a plan of emancipation for Negro slaves which she had devised. Investing a large amount of her money in a tract in western Tennessee which she called Nashoba, she attempted to give a practical demonstration of her emancipation theory. Socialist associates within the colony, however, introduced the idea of free love as opposed to marriage, a point of view which public opinion attached wrongfully to Fanny Wright herself. Co-editor with Robert D. Owen of the *New Harmony Gazette*, she further shocked public sensibilities by appearing as a lecturer in public, attacking religion, the existing system of education, the subjugation of women, and the current state of marriage. In 1829 she settled in New York City where she published the *Free Enquirer*, also in association with Robert D. Owen. After traveling abroad *c.* 1830–35, she returned to the United States and continued her writing and lecturing, taking up such causes as birth control and the more equal distribution of property. During her last years she gave a great deal of time to propaganda for the abolition of the banking system. Frances Wright's fearlessness and initiative contributed to the emancipation of women, although her influence was exerted more by her example than by her doctrines.

WRIGHT, GEORGE (*b. New York, N.Y., 1847; d. Boston, Mass., 1937*), professional baseball player, sportsman, merchant. Brother of Henry Wright (1835–1895). While shortstop of the Cincinnati Red Stockings, baseball's first professional team, 1869–71, he became the game's first home-run king, making 59 home runs in 52 games in 1869. He later played with Boston of the National League and with Providence. In 1871 he opened a Boston sporting goods store which became Wright & Ditson; he introduced the game of golf in Boston, 1890. [*Supp. 2*]

WRIGHT, GEORGE FREDERICK (*b. Whitehall, N.Y., 1838; d. 1921*), geologist, Congregational clergyman. Graduated Oberlin, 1859; Oberlin Theological Seminary, 1862. Held Vermont and Massachusetts pastorates, 1862–81. Presented theory of glacial origin of New England gravel ridges, 1875, 1876. An expert in glacial geology, he made the first scientific study of Muir Glacier, Alaska, 1886. Professor of New Testament language and literature at Oberlin, 1881–92; held chair of harmony of science and religion there, 1892–1907. Editor, *Bibliotheca Sacra*, 1883–1921. Author, among other works, of *The Ice Age in North America* (1889).

WRIGHT, GEORGE GROVER (*b. Bloomington, Ind., 1820; d. 1896*), jurist. Brother of Joseph A. Wright. Chief justice, Iowa supreme court, 1855–70. Rigorous in basing decisions on principles, he was a dominant influence on the new state's jurisprudence and formulated Iowa interpretations of domestic relations, libel, contracts, and procedure. As U.S. senator from Iowa, 1871–77, he favored "soft" money and opposed the liquor traffic.

WRIGHT, HAMILTON KEMP (*b. Cleveland, O., 1867; d. Washington, D.C., 1917*), medical scientist. Graduated in medicine, McGill University, Canada, 1895. Worked in neuropathology at Cambridge University; studied at Heidelberg and other continental universities, 1897–98. Established and directed Kuala Lumpur beriberi research laboratory, Straits Settlements, 1899–1903; materially advanced knowledge of beriberi and concluded food was an agent in its transmission. Engaged in research at Johns Hopkins and at various places in the United States and Europe, 1903–08. Appointed to International Opium Commission, 1908; chairman of American delegation, International Opium Conferences, The Hague, 1911 and 1913; was instrumental in preparation of the Harrison Narcotic Law and other federal legislation for drug control.

WRIGHT, HENDRICK BRADLEY (*b. Plymouth, Pa., 1808; d. 1881*), lawyer, Pennsylvania legislator. Chairman, Democratic national convention, Baltimore, Md., 1844. Congressman, Democrat, from Pennsylvania, 1853–55, 1861–63, 1877–81. Nominated by the Democrats in 1876 and 1878, his election was due largely to labor and Greenback support. His career was a triumph of demagoguery.

WRIGHT, HENRY (*b. Sheffield, England, 1835; d. Atlantic City, N.J., 1895*), professional baseball player. Came to America as an infant. Brother of George Wright. Organizer, manager, captain, and center fielder of the Cincinnati Red Stockings, first full professional baseball team, 1869–71. Managed National League teams of Boston (1876–81), Philadelphia (1884–93) and others.

WRIGHT, HENRY (*b. Lawrence, Kans., 1878; d. Newton, N.J., 1936*), architect, landscape designer, community planner. Raised in Kansas City, Mo. Graduated University of Pennsylvania, 1901. Associated for a number of years with George E. Kessler, a pupil of Frederick L. Olmsted, Wright entered practice for himself in 1909. Carrying on the Olmsted tradition, he designed a number of subdivisions in the St. Louis, Mo., area showing characteristic sensitivity to community needs and the integration of all necessary private and civic facilities into an orderly pattern. He was later co-planner for the New York City Housing Corp. in creating Sunnyside Gardens in Queens County (*post* 1923). He introduced even more radical innovations in the design of Radburn, N.J., 1928–29, among them a park at the core of each superblock forming a broad river of green flowing through the community. Probably the finest example of his art as site planner was the second part of Chatham Village, Pittsburgh, Pa. He was author of a classic document, *A Plan for the State of New York* (1926), the first report of its kind in the United States. *Post* 1923 he persistently attacked the sterile character of zoning with its tendency toward segregation and architectural monotony. [*Supp. 2*]

WRIGHT, HORATIO GOUVERNEUR (*b. Clinton, Conn., 1820; d. Washington, D.C., 1899*), soldier, engineer. Graduated West Point, 1841. Chief engineer at Bull Run of Gen. S. P. Heintzelman's division, and later of the Port Royal expedition. Promoted brigadier-general of volunteers, September 1861; led successful campaign in Florida, February 1862; appointed to command Department of the Ohio, August 1862. Heading the 1st Division of Gen. John Sedgwick's VI Corps after May 1863, he played an important part in the Mine Run campaign. Commissioned major-general of volunteers, 1864, he took over the command of the VI Corps at Spotsylvania, fought the Wilderness campaign, and repelled Confederate Gen. Jubal Early's raid on Washington, D.C., July 12, 1864. On October 19, he commanded at Cedar Creek until Gen. P. H. Sheridan's arrival on the field. Wright commanded the Department of Texas, 1865–66. *Post* 1866 he was engaged in important engineering projects which included the Sutro Tunnel, Nevada, and the completion of the Washington Monument. Promoted through the grades to brigadier-general, regular army, and chief of engineers, 1879, he retired, 1884.

WRIGHT, JAMES LENDREW (*b. Co. Tyrone, Ireland, 1816; d. Germantown, Pa., 1893*), tailor, labor leader. Came to America as a boy. In 1862, with Uriah S. Stephens, organized the Garment Cutters' Association and served as its president. Wright was also treasurer and co-founder (1863) of the Philadelphia Trades' Assembly. He was a founder (1869) of the Noble Order of the Knights of Labor whose name he devised and of which he was a leading functionary for over two decades.

WRIGHT, JOHN HENRY (*b. Urmia, Persia, 1852; d. Cambridge, Mass., 1908*), Hellenist. A.B., Dartmouth, 1873. Taught at Ohio State, Dartmouth, and Johns Hopkins. Professor of Greek at Harvard *post*

1887; dean, Harvard Graduate School *post* 1895. Editor-in-chief, *American Journal of Archaeology*, 1897–1906; co-editor, *Classical Review*, 1889–1906. Author, among other works, of *Herondaea* (1893) and *The Origin of Plato's Cave* (1906).

WRIGHT, JOHN STEPHEN (*b. Sheffield, Mass., 1815; d. Philadelphia, Pa., 1874*), promoter, journalist. Settled in Chicago, Ill., 1832, where he was successful as a real-estate operator, 1834–36 and 1846–57. While owner and manager of the *Prairie Farmer*, 1843–57, he promoted Western industry and the advantages of Illinois and Chicago in his own paper and in articles for Eastern journals. In 1848 he lobbied for a Chicago to Gulf of Mexico railroad. A leader in Illinois education, he built Chicago's first public school building (1835) at his own expense.

WRIGHT, JONATHAN JASPER (*b. Luzerne Co., Pa., 1840; d. Charleston, S.C., 1885*), educator, South Carolina legislator, jurist. Attended Lancasterian University, Ithaca, N.Y.; was first Negro admitted to the Pennsylvania bar (1866). Associate justice of the South Carolina supreme court, 1870–77, he was a center of controversy in the South Carolina gubernatorial contest between D. H. Chamberlain and Wade Hampton, 1876.

WRIGHT, JOSEPH (*b. Bordentown, N.J., 1756; d. Philadelphia, Pa., 1793*), portrait-painter, die-sinker. Son of Patience L. Wright who taught him clay- and wax-modeling. Resident in London, England, *c.* 1772–1782, he studied painting with John Trumbull (1756–1843) and Benjamin West. By 1780 he was exhibiting at the Royal Academy, London. Returning to America, 1783, he worked in New York and Philadelphia, executing among other works portraits of George Washington, 1783, 1784, and an etching from a sketch in 1790. Appointed first draftsman and die-sinker, U.S. Mint, 1792, he probably designed the first U.S. coins and medals.

WRIGHT, JOSEPH ALBERT (*b. Washington, Pa., 1810; d. Berlin, Germany, 1867*), lawyer, Indiana legislator. Brother of George G. Wright. Congressman, Democrat, from Indiana, 1843–45; governor of Indiana, December 1849—January 1857; U.S. senator, February 1862—January 1863. U.S. minister to Prussia, 1857–61, and from 1865 until his death. Wright, as governor, directed most of his efforts to raising the standard of living and the educational level of Indiana farmers.

WRIGHT, JOSEPH JEFFERSON BURR (*b. Wilkes-Barre, Pa., 1801; d. Carlisle, Pa., 1878*), army medical officer. Appointed assistant surgeon, U.S. Army, 1833. In a long and varied career of field and staff duty, he was outstanding during the Mexican War. He retired as colonel, 1876.

WRIGHT, LUKE EDWARD (*b. Giles Co., Tenn., 1846; d. 1922*), Confederate soldier, Tennessee lawyer. Became vice-governor of the Philippines in 1901, governor in 1904, and governor-general in 1905; a strong, competent executive. First U.S. ambassador to Japan, 1906. U.S. secretary of war, 1908–09, he was not retained in office by President W. H. Taft, a circumstance which is said to have contributed to the split between Taft and Theodore Roosevelt.

WRIGHT, MARCUS JOSEPH (*b. Purdy, Tenn., 1831; d. Washington, D.C., 1922*), lawyer, Confederate brigadier-general. U.S. government agent for collection of Confederate archives, 1878–1917. Author, among other works, of *Tennessee in the War, 1861–1865* (1908) and *General Officers of the Confederate Army* (1911).

WRIGHT, PATIENCE LOVELL (*b. Bordentown, N.J., 1725; d. London, England, 1786*), modeler in wax, Revolutionary spy. Mother of Joseph Wright. Well known in the colonies as a sculptor of wax portraits, she removed to London *c.* 1772 where she exhibited historical groups, busts and life-size figures of contemporary notables and enjoyed success until her death. She sent information of English military plans to Benjamin Franklin at Passy.

WRIGHT, PHILIP GREEN (*b. Boston, Mass., 1861; d. 1934*), teacher, economist, poet. Grandson of Elizur Wright and Beriah Green. Graduated Tufts College, 1884; M.A., Harvard, 1887. Taught mathematics and other subjects, Lombard College (Ill.), 1892–1912; instructed in economics at Williams, 1912–13, and Harvard, 1913–17. On staff of Institute of Economics (later part of Brookings Institution), 1922–31. Author, among others, of important volumes on commercial policy and the tariff, and poems on labor.

WRIGHT, ROBERT (*b. Queen Annes Co., Md., 1752; d. Queen Annes Co., 1826*), lawyer, Revolutionary soldier, Maryland legislator. U.S. senator, (Democrat) Republican, from Maryland, 1801–06; governor of Maryland, 1806–09; congressman, 1810–17 and 1821–23. He was a member of the judiciary committee, 1815–17, and of the foreign affairs committee, 1821–23. Judge of the lower Eastern Shore district court *post* 1823. A consistent supporter of administration policies.

WRIGHT, ROBERT WILLIAM (*b. Ludlow, Vt., 1816; d. Cleveland, O., 1885*), editor, satirist, lawyer. Wright was editor of Democratic newspapers in Waterbury, Hartford and New Haven, Conn., New York City, and Richmond, Va., 1856–77. Author, among other works, of political verse satires, satires on local clerical squabbles, and *Life, Its True Genesis* (1880), an anti-Darwinian study.

WRIGHT, SILAS (*b. Amherst, Mass., 1795; d. Canton, N.Y., 1847*), lawyer, New York official, statesman. Graduated Middlebury College, 1815. Admitted to the bar, 1819, he began practice in Canton, N.Y. Throughout his life a nationalist and a Democrat, he served in the New York State senate, 1824–27,

and soon became a member of the directing group of New York Democrats known as the "Albany Regency." A lifelong defender of popular rights, he yet held that the people needed the leadership of bosses and an honest use of the spoils system to obtain that strong party unity in which lay their hope in a battle against special privilege. As congressman from New York, 1827–29, he helped frame the "tariff of abominations" of 1828 and took a leading part in defending it; as comptroller of New York, 1829–33, he continued to oppose extension of the state canal system except when expected revenues promised to reimburse the state. While U.S. senator from New York, 1833–44, he served on a number of important committees and came to hold high rank in the Senate for solid judgment and unselfish service. He was recognized as manager of his friend Martin Van Buren's political interests and employed on behalf of Van Buren his uncannily accurate sense of public opinion. Following Van Buren's election to the presidency, Wright served as chairman of the Senate finance committee, 1836–41. He opposed all measures for rechartering the Bank of the United States and opposed distribution of the federal surplus among the states. In the panic of 1837 he urged a complete divorce of federal finance from the banks and much stricter regulation of banking by the states; he also introduced the administration's relief bills and headed the fight for an independent U.S. treasury until victory in 1840. After the accession of President John Tyler, Wright urged a tax-and-pay policy, continuing to oppose distribution of public land sales income and any increase in the tariff. In 1844 he campaigned for the nomination of Van Buren for the presidency and himself declined to be a candidate. As governor of New York, 1845–47, he acted with even-handed justice to all, thereby alienating all elements of the community; his suppression of violence during the anti-rent disturbances caused bitter popular feeling and his tax on rent income alienated the landlords. Renominated in 1846, he failed of re-election, but had the satisfaction of seeing many reforms which he had advocated incorporated in the new state constitution of 1846. Honesty, simplicity, and disinterestedness were his outstanding characteristics.

WRIGHT, THEODORE LYMAN (*b. Beloit, Wis., 1858; d. 1926*), teacher. Graduated Beloit College, 1880; M.A., Harvard, 1884; also attended American School of Classical Studies, Athens, 1887. Taught Greek literature and art at Beloit College *post* 1892; produced a series of the Greek dramas in English.

WRIGHT, WILBUR (*b. Millville, near New Castle, Ind., 1867; d. 1912*), aviation pioneer. Wilbur and his brother Orville (born at Dayton, O., 1871) were inseparable partners throughout their lives. As youths, they earned pocket money by selling home-made mechanical toys, later issuing the weekly *West Side News* in Dayton, of which Wilbur was editor. He also wrote on occasion for the *Religious Telescope,* of which his father was editor. Wilbur was the more scholarly and exact-minded of the brothers; Orville was quicker with suggestions but was inclined to dream. They formed the Wright Cycle Co. *c.* 1892 and built the "Van Cleve" bicycle which soon achieved a reputation.

They began thinking about the possibility of flight in 1896, stimulated by the work and writings of the German aeronaut Gustav Lilienthal, Octave Chanute, S. P. Langley and other experimenters and theorists. Planning to work on a captive, man-carrying glider, they first experimented with kites; in 1899 Wilbur Wright built a model biplane with a wing spread of five feet which he flew as a kite. From this and other experiments, considerable study of theory, and advice from Chanute, they produced their first glider. Air resistance was reduced by placing the operator in a horizontal position; a front surface gave longitudinal stability and control; lateral balance was obtained by warping the wing extremities to decrease lift on either side, thus supplying a rolling moment at the will of the pilot. Vertical steering was not provided for in the first glider, but the Wrights understood its functions and provided it in their second machine (1902).

With the advice of the U.S. Weather Bureau, the brothers selected for trial of their glider a strip of sand called Kill Devil Hill, near Kitty Hawk, N.C., and set up camp there in September 1900. Failing in efforts to fly the glider as a kite, they turned to free gliding and were soon operating safely under perfect control in winds of 27 miles an hour, making glides of more than 300 feet. They kept careful tabulation of their findings and concluded, as a result of their experiments, that a vertical steering rudder was essential; that the warping of the wing extremities could be relied on for lateral control; that the movement of the center of pressure on a curved wing produced instability; and that calculations based on existing data were in error. It was plain that they would have to find their own correct basic data.

They returned to Dayton, where Orville devised a wind tunnel for further lengthy experiments, testing over 200 wing and biplane combinations to determine accurate values for lift, drag and center of pressure. In 1902 at Kitty Hawk, they made nearly 1000 glides in a new glider based on their latest data which confirmed the accuracy of their findings. They then built a powered machine, weighing 750 pounds fully loaded, capable of a 31 mile speed, with a four-cylinder, twelve horse-power motor they had made. In this new machine on Dec. 17, 1903, Orville made the first powered flight, which lasted only twelve seconds. Several hours later Wilbur made a flight of 51 seconds but the machine, forced down by a sudden gust, was so damaged that further flights were impossible.

Despite this serious loss, the Wright brothers built a stronger machine and on Oct. 5, 1905, at Huffman Field, Dayton, during a 24-mile circuit flight, they solved the equilibrium problem in turning.

Thereafter, despite lack of public encouragement, they abandoned other interests and devoted themselves to constructing a practicable machine. They obtained a patent for a flying machine in 1906. Only after successful negotiations had been conducted with foreign interests did the American government awake to the value of the new device. In late 1907 Gen. James Allen, chief U.S. Army signal officer, opened bids for a "gasless flying machine" to carry two men weighing 350 pounds, with sufficient fuel for 125 miles. The Wrights offered to build a biplane and instruct two operators for $25,000; other bids were accepted, but the Wrights alone completed the contract. Meanwhile they made highly publicized, successful trial flights at Kitty Hawk. Orville, demonstrating the contract plane at Fort Myer, Va. (Sept. 9, 1908), made 57 complete circles at 120-feet altitude, remaining aloft 62 minutes, thus establishing several records simultaneously. On September 17, the most serious accident in the brothers' career, which had been singularly free of them, occurred. A stray wire tangled with a propeller blade, the machine crashed. Orville suffered a fractured thigh and two ribs, and his passenger, Lt. Thomas E. Selfridge, was killed. Fully recovered, Orville completed the official tests eight months later. Meanwhile in France, Wilbur had been flying at the Hunandrières race course so successfully that he concluded satisfactory arrangements with a French syndicate to manufacture his machine in France. During the 1909 Hudson-Fulton celebration at New York, he made demonstration flights from Governor's Island, around the Statue of Liberty and up to Grant's Tomb. This led to formation of the American Wright Co., and subsequent negotiations were concluded providing for manufacture of airplanes in England, Germany, Italy and America.

WRIGHT, WILLARD HUNTINGTON (*b. Charlottesville, Va., 1888; d. New York, N.Y., 1939*), art critic, detective story writer under pseudonym "S.S. Van Dine." Creator of the fictional detective Philo Vance, whose ostentatiously displayed erudition lent contemporary interest to such books as *The Benson Murder Case* (1926), *The Canary Murder Case* (1927), *The Greene Murder Case* (1928) and others. [*Supp.* 2]

WRIGHT, WILLIAM (*b. near Nyack, N.Y., 1794; d. Newark, N.J., 1866*), manufacturer. Co-founder of the saddlery firm of Smith & Wright, Newark, N.J. Mayor of Newark, 1840–43. Congressman, Whig, from New Jersey, 1843–47; U.S. senator, Democrat, 1853–59 and *post* 1863. Chairman, Senate committee on manufactures.

WRIGHT, WILLIAM (*b. Ohio, 1829; d. West Lafayette, Iowa, 1898*), journalist, better known under pseudonym "Dan De Quille." Began journalistic career in Iowa; prospected in California and Nevada, 1857–61. Becoming city editor of the Virginia City (Nev.) *Daily Territorial Enterprise*, 1861, he held this post for practically the remainder of his life and lived to see the city dwindle into a ghost town and his newspaper cease publication. Mark Twain, his associate on the newspaper in 1862, was his lifelong friend and encouraged Wright to publish his *History of the Big Bonanza* (1877). Late in life, sick and without occupation, he was befriended and helped by John W. Mackay. [*Supp. 1*]

WRIGLEY, WILLIAM (*b. Philadelphia, Pa., 1861; d. Phoenix, Ariz., 1932*), chewing gum manufacturer. A gifted salesman and organizer, Wrigley developed a multimillion-dollar chewing gum business out of a small concern for the manufacture of soap which he started in Chicago, Ill., 1891. After becoming wealthy, he bought a controlling interest in the Chicago National League baseball club and other clubs and was the developer of Santa Catalina Island off the California coast. [*Supp. 1*]

WROSETASATOW. [See OUTACITY, fl. 1756–1777.]

WU P'AN-CHAO. [See NG, POON CHEW, 1866–1931.]

WURTZ, HENRY (*b. Easton, Pa., c. 1828; d. Brooklyn, N.Y., 1910*), chemist, editor. After graduation from College of New Jersey (Princeton), 1848, Wurtz studied chemistry at Lawrence Scientific School, Harvard, and conducted mineral analyses in New York laboratory of Dr. Oliver W. Gibbs. State chemist and geologist, New Jersey geological survey, 1854–56. Conducted research on sodium amalgams for extracting precious metals from their ores, securing patent, 1865. Edited *American Gas Light Journal*, 1868–71. Devised new method of manufacturing fuel gas by alternating action of air and steam upon cheap coal, 1869; took out a number of patents relating to distillation of paraffin hydrocarbons and other chemical products.

WYANT, ALEXANDER HELWIG (*b. Evans Creek, O., 1836; d. New York, N.Y., 1892*), landscape painter. Wyant was an outstanding master of American landscape painting during the latter half of the 19th century. Encouraged by George Inness, 1857, and with the assistance of the elder Nicholas Longworth, he studied in New York and briefly in Germany. He was elected member of the National Academy, 1869, for his "The Upper Susquehanna." Wyant's early painting is characterized by a photographic fidelity to nature; his middle period is dominated by the environment of the mountains of New York State. His pictures have a thematic conception, an organized unity, and a universal appeal. Mood is transcendent; composition is simple. The rhythmic action is rendered by movement of light and dark sequences related to a fixed point of focal concentration. As a pure naturalist he is unsurpassed; as a poetic tonalist he was

master of aerial perspective and atmospheric envelopment. Among his paintings are "The Mohawk Valley" (1866), "An Old Clearing" (1881), "Passing Clouds" and "Landscape in the Adirondacks."

WYATT, Sir FRANCIS (*b. Kent, England, 1588; d. Kent, 1644*). A connection by marriage of Sir Edwin Sandys who gained control of the London Company in 1619, Wyatt had invested in the company and was designated governor of Virginia, arriving there in October 1621. Forced by the weakness of the London Company to abandon the prospect of building Virginia into a prosperous community which would serve the ends of mercantilist policy, he rallied the planters and settlers to demand preservation of their liberties after the dissolution of the company in 1624. Continuing in office as the first royal governor of Virginia, he summoned the famous "convention assembly" of 1625 which pressed petitions on the home government for the continuation of the liberty of general assembly in the colony. He gave up the governorship in 1626, but succeeded Sir John Harvey as governor again in 1639. On his return to Virginia he was able to announce that the liberty of general assembly so long desired had been confirmed by the royal authority. He was replaced by Sir William Berkeley in 1641.

WYCKOFF, JOHN HENRY (*b. Tindivanam, East Madras, India, 1881; d. New York, N.Y., 1937*), physician, medical educator. M.D., Bellevue Hospital Medical College, 1907. After service in the cardiac clinic at Bellevue and military service in World War I, he returned to the clinic c. 1919. In 1927 he was appointed director of the division of Bellevue under supervision of New York University with title of associate professor of medicine. In 1932 he became dean of the College of Medicine and professor. A pioneer in this country in the use of digitalis, he helped to develop the practice of multiple diagnosis (anatomical, pathological, clinical, etc.) in treating cases of heart disease. He played a leading role in formation of the New York Heart Association.

[*Supp. 2*]

WYCKOFF, WALTER AUGUSTUS (*b. Mainpuri, India, 1865; d. 1908*), author, sociologist. B.A., College of New Jersey (Princeton), 1888. Assistant professor of political economy at Princeton *post* 1898. Author of *The Workers; an Experiment in Reality—The East* (1897) and a second part, *The West* (1898).

WYETH, JOHN (*b. Cambridge, Mass., 1770; d. Philadelphia, Pa., 1858*), editor, publisher. Cofounder and editor, *Oracle of Dauphin County & Harrisburg* (Pa.) *Advertiser*, 1792–1827, during which time he established a bookstore and general publishing house. Served as first postmaster of Harrisburg, 1793–98, and was active in Harrisburg public affairs.

WYETH, JOHN ALLAN (*b. Marshall Co., Ala., 1845; d. 1922*), surgeon, medical educator. Graduated medical department, University of Louisville, 1869; M.D., Bellevue Medical School, 1873. Instrumental in organizing New York Polyclinic Hospital and Medical School, 1881, serving as surgeon-in-chief and subsequently as president until his death. Devised new surgical procedures including ligation of the external carotid artery and "Wyeth's operation." Author of *A Textbook on Surgery* (1887).

WYETH, NATHANIEL JARVIS (*b. Cambridge, Mass., 1802; d. 1856*), trader, explorer. Nephew of John Wyeth. Successful with Frederic Tudor in building an important trade in ice to the West Indies, Wyeth is remembered particularly for his attempt to plant an American commercial and agricultural colony in Oregon. Inspired by Hall J. Kelley, Wyeth made his first overland journey to Oregon, 1832–33; nothing concrete resulted from it. Organizing a company for salmon-packing on the lower Columbia and for fur-trading, Wyeth and a party traveled overland again to Oregon in 1834. He was accompanied by Thomas Nuttall and John K. Townsend, the latter of whom published a *Narrative of a Journey across the Rocky Mountains to the Columbia River* (1839) descriptive of the trip. Wyeth built a small fort named Fort William at the mouth of the Willamette; he also built Fort Hall in present Idaho which became a famous station on the Oregon and California trail. Failing to make progress against the competition of the Hudson's Bay Company, Wyeth returned to the ice business. Although unsuccessful in his primary aim, he succeeded in familiarizing important sections of the eastern population with the facts about Oregon.

WYLIE, ANDREW (*b. Washington, Pa., 1789; d. 1851*), educator, Episcopal clergyman, author. Graduated Jefferson College (Pa.), 1810. President, Washington College, 1816–28. First president, Indiana College (later Indiana University), 1828 until his death. Introduced "specialization by rotation" or study and mastery of one subject at a time. Also served at Indiana as professor of moral and mental philosophy, political economy and polite literature.

WYLIE, ELINOR MORTON HOYT (*b. Somerville, N.J., 1885; d. New York, N.Y., 1928*), poet, novelist. Great-granddaughter of Morton McMichael; granddaughter of Henry M. Hoyt. A lyric poet of distinction and a writer of novels outstanding for their mannered style and high comic conception, Mrs. Wylie was remarkable throughout her life for an obsession with the memory and personality of the English poet Percy B. Shelley. Her volumes of poetry included *Incidental Numbers* (London, 1912); *Nets to Catch the Wind* (1921); *Black Armour* (1923); and *Angels and Earthly Creatures* (1929). Her novels included *Jennifer Lorn* (1923); *The Venetian Glass Nephew* (1925); *The Orphan Angel* (1926, a fantasy about Shelley); and *Mr. Hodge and Mr. Hazard* (1928).

WYLIE, ROBERT (*b. Douglas, Isle of Man, England, 1839; d. Pont-Aven, France, 1877*), landscape and genre painter. Came to America as a child. Studied at the Pennsylvania Academy, Philadelphia; resided in France *post c.* 1864, where he was a pupil in Paris of J. L. Gérôme, Thomas Couture and others. Among the first American artists to discover Brittany and Breton life as subjects, he was largely responsible for the popularity of that region among French artists as well as fellow Americans. An excellent draftsman and a sober colorist, he produced comparatively few works.

WYLIE, SAMUEL BROWN (*b. Moylarg, Ireland, 1773; d. 1852*), educator, Reformed Presbyterian clergyman. M.A., University of Glasgow, 1797. Emigrated to Philadelphia, Pa., 1797. Presumably the first Covenanter to receive American ordination (1800), he was pastor and co-founder of the Philadelphia congregation, which he served *post* 1803. Professor of Latin and Greek, University of Pennsylvania, 1828–45; vice-provost, 1836–45.

WYLLYS, GEORGE (*b. Hartford, Conn., 1710; d. Hartford, 1796*), Connecticut official. Secretary, colony of Connecticut, *pro tempore* 1730–34, and in full tenure from 1734 until death. Town clerk of Hartford *post* 1732.

WYMAN, HORACE (*b. Woburn, Mass., 1827; d. Princeton, Mass., 1915*), machinist, inventor. Superintendent of George Crompton's loom works *post c.* 1861; vice-president and consulting engineer, Crompton & Knowles Loom Works, Worcester, Mass., from 1897 until his death. Took out over 200 patents for improvement in process and mechanism of looms and other textile machinery. Among his inventions are a loom-box operating mechanism (1871); a pile-fabric loom (1872); processes for fabric weaving in different sizes and colors; the first American "dobby" loom (1879); and the weft replenishing loom with drop shuttle boxes (1901).

WYMAN, JEFFRIES (*b. Chelmsford, Mass., 1814; d. Bethlehem, N.H., 1874*), anatomist, ethnologist. Brother of Morrill Wyman. Graduated Harvard, 1833; M.D., 1837. Made curator and lecturer, Lowell Institute, 1840. Became professor of anatomy and physiology, Hampden-Sydney College medical school, Richmond, Va., 1843. Appointed Hersey Professor of Anatomy, Harvard, 1847. Built up anatomical museum at Harvard, nucleus of present Peabody Museum. Made collecting expeditions to Florida, 1851–52; Surinam, 1856; and South America, 1858. Became curator of department and museum of archeology and ethnology at Harvard, 1866. President, Boston Society of Natural History, 1856–70. Wyman's most important papers deal with the structure of the gorilla. His monograph on the nervous system of the frog (published by the Smithsonian Institution in 1852–53) and papers on the anatomy of the blind fish of Mammoth Cave (published in the *American Journal of Science* between 1843 and 1854) are also noteworthy. He was considered the leading American anatomist of his time.

WYMAN, MORRILL (*b. Chelmsford, Mass., 1812; d. 1903*), physician. Brother of Jeffries Wyman. Graduated Harvard, 1833; Harvard Medical School, 1837. Practiced for more than sixty years in Cambridge, Mass. Wyman's most effective service to American medical science occurred in 1850. In association with H. I. Bowditch, he improved the operation of thoracentesis, or surgical drainage of the pleural cavity, by substituting a small hollow needle for the large cannula formerly used. This was a landmark in pleurisy treatment. Author of *A Practical Treatise on Ventilation* (1846); a report on ventilators and chimneys (*Proceedings,* American Academy of Arts and Sciences, 1848); and *Autumnal Catarrh: Hay Fever* (1872, with additions, 1876). Adjunct Hersey Professor of theory and practice of medicine, Harvard Medical School, 1853–56. Founded Cambridge Hospital, 1886; served for many years as consulting physician, Massachusetts General Hospital.

WYMAN, ROBERT HARRIS (*b. Portsmouth, N.H., 1822; d. 1882*), naval officer. Appointed midshipman, 1837. Served with credit in Mexican War. During Civil War, served in blockade duty in the Atlantic and commanded the Potomac Flotilla early in 1862. Headed Hydrographic Office at Washington, D.C., 1871–79, and was author of a number of useful publications on navigation. Commissioned rear-admiral, 1878, he commanded the North Atlantic Squadron; he died as chairman of the Lighthouse Board.

WYMAN, SETH (*b. Goffstown, N.H., 1784; d. Goffstown, 1843*), burglar. Author of a popular *Life and Adventures* (1843).

WYTHE, GEORGE (*b. Back River, Elizabeth City Co., Va., 1726; d. Richmond, Va., 1806*), statesman, professor of law, jurist. Received little formal education, briefly attending College of William and Mary. Admitted to the bar, 1746, he began practice in Spotsylvania Co. Briefly attorney-general of Virginia in 1754 while Peyton Randolph was in England, Wythe removed his residence to Williamsburg, Va., 1755. His career really began in 1758 when he became the intimate friend and associate of Gov. Francis Fauquier. A member of the House of Burgesses, 1754–55, 1758–68, he served as clerk of the House, 1769–75. On the announcement of the Stamp Tax, Wythe maintained the concept (later expounded by Richard Bland) that England and Virginia were coordinate nations united by the Crown alone. Wythe drafted the Virginia resolutions of remonstrance which were modified before their adoption by his colleagues in the House. On the approach of the Revolution he wisely recommended the raising of a regular army instead of the use of militia and himself volunteered for service. Sent to the Continental Congress in 1775, he served until the close of 1776. He supported Richard H. Lee's resolution for independence and signed the Declaration. He was probably the designer of the seal of Virginia, adopted, 1776. Assigned with Thomas Jefferson and Edmund Pendleton to the task of revising the Virginia laws, he covered the period from the revolution in England (1688) to American independence; the revision was thorough and intelligent and the various bills embodying it were passed over a period of years subsequent to its submission in 1779. Speaker of the House of Delegates, 1777, he became one of the three judges of the Virginia high court of chancery, 1778, and henceforth was known as Chancellor Wythe.

On accepting the chair of law at the College of William and Mary, 1779 (the first chair of law in an American college), Wythe began that part of his career which perhaps constitutes his greatest service, for he literally charted the way in American jurisprudence and was teacher (among others later famous) of John Marshall. He was a delegate to the Virginia convention which ratified the U.S. Constitution, 1788, but engaged little in debate; in offering the resolution for ratification he emphasized the derivative character of federal power. On reorganization of the state judicial system in 1788, he became sole chancellor, holding this office until 1801, after which he continued to preside over the Richmond district. He resigned his professorship in 1790 and, removing to Richmond, formed a small law school of his own. Among his students was Henry Clay.

As chancellor and *ex officio* member of the supreme court of appeals, he delivered a significant opinion in the case of *Commonwealth vs. Caton* (4 *Call*, 5), 1782. An *obiter dictum* which he made in his concurring opinion was clearly one of the earliest enunciations of the doctrine of judicial review, America's unique contribution to juridical theory; at the time it was the most complete such statement which had been made. Superbly ethical as an attorney, Wythe refused unjust causes and abandoned any case regarding which he felt he had been misled. Probably the best classical scholar in Virginia, he was widely read in Roman and English law. Opposed to slavery, he emancipated his servants by his will.

XÁNTUS, JÁNOS (*b. Csokonya, Somogy Co., Hungary, 1825; d. Hungary, 1894*), ornithologist, author. Emigrated to America, 1851; was employed by the Pacific Railroad and U.S. Coast surveys. Made valuable bird collections in California for the Smithsonian Institution, uncovering many new species. His descriptions and catalogues of new species appear in *Proceedings of the Academy of Natural Sciences of Philadelphia* (Vols. X–XII, 1859–61). Appointed U.S. consul at Manzanillo, Mexico, he led a scientific research party into the Sierra Madre. Returned to Hungary, 1864; published accounts of his travels.

YALE, CAROLINE ARDELIA (*b. Charlotte, Vt., 1848; d. 1933*), educator. Joined staff of Clarke Institution for Deaf Mutes, 1870; became principal, 1886, emeritus, 1922. Pioneer in use of oral method; established, 1889, and directed normal classes for teacher-training of the deaf. Author of *Years of Building* (1931).

YALE, ELIHU (*b. Boston, Mass., 1649; d. London, England, 1721*), official of the East India Company, philanthropist. After an application made by Cotton Mather for aid to the struggling Collegiate School at Saybrook, Conn., in January 1718, Yale made a gift of various goods to the institution which sold for £562 12s., the largest private contribution made to the college for over a century. At the September commencement, the new building at New Haven and the college were given Yale's name in appreciation.

YALE, LINUS (*b. Salisbury, N.Y., 1821; d. New York, N.Y., 1868*), inventor, manufacturer. Invented the "Yale Infallible Bank Lock" c. 1851; to change the combination, the key's component parts could be separated and reassembled. His "Yale Magic Bank Lock" was an improvement on the first, and was followed by the "Yale Double Treasury Bank Lock," the most notable bank lock operated by keys. About 1862 he began to market the "Monitor Bank Lock," the first dial or combination bank lock, and in 1863 the "Yale Double Dial Bank Lock" whose principles of construction are in general use in America. Between 1860 and 1865 he improved small key locks by devising the "Cylinder Lock," based on the pin-tumbler mechanism of the Egyptians; he obtained patents, 1861 and 1865. Partner with J. H. Towne and H. R. Towne in the Yale Lock Manufacturing Co. (established, 1868).

YANCEY, WILLIAM LOWNDES (*b. Warren Co., Ga., 1814; d. Montgomery, Ala., 1863*), lawyer, Alabama legislator, secessionist. Stepson of Nathan S. S. Beman. Attended Williams College, 1830–33; studied in law office of Benjamin F. Perry at Greenville, S.C. An active Unionist as editor of a Greenville newspaper during the nullification controversy, Yancey removed to Alabama in the winter of 1836–37, where he attempted farming, edited a newspaper at Wetumpka, and practiced law with great success. As a legislator, 1841–44, he was noted as a supporter of representation on the basis of white population only, of a free public school system, and of a nonpolitical state banking system. Elected to Congress in 1844, he served until his resignation on Sept. 1, 1846.

Yancey now resumed the practice of law and began a career of unofficial political action on behalf of Southern independence which transcended party lines. Operating on a narrow but well-defined body of principles, he refused any compromise for the sake of party continuity or for any other reason; contemporary politicians considered him everything from an unwelcome pest to an insufferable firebrand. His body of principles is to be found in the Alabama Platform written by him (1848) in answer to the Wilmot

Proviso. In brief, the Platform demanded a constitution designed to curb the will of the majority and preserve to the states all powers not expressly granted to the federal government, equal rights of citizens and states in the territories, and action by Congress to protect property rights in the territories so long as they remained in territorial status. He presented this simple statement of abstractions to the people of the South on every occasion with an oratorical excellence seldom equaled. After the rejection of his Platform by the Democrats in their convention at Baltimore, 1848, he appealed to the people from the decision and in the course of the next 12 years made his Platform the Southern creed. In order to arouse the South to the need of a union of all Southern men in a sectional party, he was active in promoting Southern rights associations which would work for the nomination to public office of state-rights men within each party. In 1858 he sought to perfect the system by organizing the League of United Southerners. He traveled widely delivering hundreds of addresses in support of his views. Dominant in the Democratic party in Alabama as the presidential campaign of 1860 approached, he recommended that if the demands of the South were rejected at the Charleston convention, a Constitutional Democratic party should be organized and candidates presented to the people. He furthermore stated that if a Republican president should be elected, then secession should be carried through before his inauguration.

At the Alabama Democratic convention in Montgomery on Jan. 11, 1860, Yancey prepared the Alabama platform of principles—a restatement of the platform of 1848 in line with all that had transpired meantime. The platform also instructed the Alabama delegation to the Charleston convention to present this platform for adoption and to withdraw if it were rejected. At the Charleston convention Yancey delivered the greatest speech of his career in defense of his platform; after its qualified rejection, a majority of the Southern delegates withdrew. When the adjourned convention met later at Baltimore, Md., the supporters of Stephen A. Douglas refused to seat the Yancey delegation from Alabama. Subsequent to this, under Yancey's guidance, the Constitutional Democratic party was organized and nominated John Breckinridge for the presidency. Following the election of Abraham Lincoln, Yancey dominated the proceedings of the Alabama convention and wrote the ordinance of secession. A Confederate commissioner in France and England, 1861–62, he served briefly in the Confederate Senate after his return; during this time he fought against the increase of centralized power in the Confederacy just as fiercely as he had fought it in the Union.

YANDELL, DAVID WENDELL (*b. near Murfreesboro, Tenn., 1826; d. Louisville, Ky., 1898*), physician. Son of Lunsford P. Yandell. Graduated University of Louisville, 1846. Practiced in Louisville; founded the Stokes Dispensary and pioneered in medical education by establishing classes in clinical medicine; was appointed to the chair of clinical medicine at the University of Louisville. During the Civil War he served as medical director, Confederate Department of the West. Professor of clinical surgery, University of Louisville, *post* 1869. Co-founder of *The American Practitioner and News*, which he edited from 1870 until shortly before his death.

YANDELL, LUNSFORD PITTS (*b. near Hartsville, Tenn., 1805; d. Louisville, Ky., 1878*), paleontologist, physician. Father of David W. Yandell. Graduated University of Maryland, 1825. Professor of chemistry and pharmacy, Transylvania University, 1831–37. Held chairs of chemistry and materia medica, and *post* 1849, physiology, in the medical department, University of Louisville; taught there from 1837 until 1859. Editor of medical journals, and co-editor of *Western Journal of Medicine and Surgery*, 1840–55. Made extensive geological and paleontological explorations in the vicinity of Louisville; studied the Ohio falls coral reefs, the Beargrass Creek fossiliferous beds, and Kentucky and Indiana quarries. Discovered and collected numerous fossils. Author of *Contributions to the Geology of Kentucky* (1847) with B. F. Shumard; also of many contributions to scientific journals.

YATES, ABRAHAM (*b. Albany, N.Y., 1724; d. 1796*), Revolutionary patriot, Albany (N.Y.) official, Anti-Federalist pamphleteer. Also known as Abraham Yates, Jun. Chairman, Albany committee of correspondence, 1774–76. Headed committee of the convention, 1776–77, which drafted New York State's first constitution; also the committee for putting the new government into operation. State senator, 1777–90. His printed letters and pamphlets are perhaps the ablest exposition of the views of agrarian democrats and of followers of Gov. George Clinton. Played role of Anti-Federalist in Continental Congress, 1787–88. Mayor of Albany from 1790 until his death.

YATES, JOHN VAN NESS (*b. Albany, N.Y., 1779; d. Albany, 1839*), lawyer, New York official. Son of Robert Yates. Editor of William Smith's *History of New York* (1814) and author of legal works. (Democrat) Republican in politics and a partisan of the Clintons, he was New York secretary of state, 1818–26. He was regarded as erratic in character.

YATES, MATTHEW TYSON (*b. Wake Co., N.C., 1819; d. Shanghai, China, 1888*), missionary. Graduated Wake Forest College, 1846. Pioneer Southern Baptist missionary in Shanghai, China, 1847–88.

YATES, RICHARD (*b. Warsaw, Ky., 1815; d. St. Louis, Mo., 1873*), lawyer, Illinois legislator. Congressman, Whig, from Illinois, 1851–55. Opposed to slavery, he then joined the Republican party. As governor of Illinois, 1861–65, he was highly effective in war administration. He gave Gen. U. S. Grant his

first Civil War commission and assignments. In 1863, he prorogued the largely Democratic state assembly for passing a resolution urging an armistice and national peace convention. As U.S. senator, 1865–71, Yates was a party regular, favoring vindictive measures against the South, voting for Johnson's impeachment, and supporting the prevailing radical Republican program.

YATES, ROBERT (*b. Schenectady, N.Y., 1738; d. 1801*), Revolutionary patriot, jurist. Father of John Van N. Yates. Studied law with William Livingston; admitted to the bar at Albany, N.Y., 1760. A radical Whig in the period before the Revolution, he was a member of the Albany committee of safety, and represented Albany County in the four New York provincial congresses. Among other important committee work, he served on the committee which drafted the first New York State constitution. Appointed a justice of the state supreme court, 1777, he was advanced to chief justice in 1790 and resigned the office in 1798. A leader of the Anti-Federalists, he was a supporter of Gov. George Clinton. A delegate from New York to the Federal Convention, 1787, with John Lansing and Alexander Hamilton, he refused further attendance after July 5 on the ground that the Convention was exceeding its powers in attempting to write a new instrument of government. He wrote several series of letters attacking the U.S. Constitution, 1787–88, and voted against ratification of it at the Poughkeepsie, N.Y., convention.

YEADON, RICHARD (*b. Charleston, S.C., 1802; d. 1870*), lawyer, editor, South Carolina legislator. Editor of the Unionist *Charleston Daily Courier*, 1832–44. An ardent Whig and anti-secession man up to the Civil War, he supported President Jefferson Davis against opposition of R. B. Rhett. He was a benefactor of the College of Charleston and originated the ordinance establishing Charleston High School.

YEAGER, JOSEPH (*b. possibly Philadelphia, Pa., c. 1792; d. Philadelphia, 1859*), engraver, publisher. Active in Philadelphia, 1809–45, as line engraver and as portrait etcher; published toy books for children. Became president of Harrisburg and Lancaster Railroad Co., 1848.

YEAMAN, WILLIAM POPE (*b. Hardin Co., Ky., 1832; d. 1904*), Baptist clergyman. Held various pastorates, notably in St. Louis, Mo., 1870–c. 1879. Secretary, Board of State Missions, General Association of Missouri Baptists, 1884–86. Moderator, General Association of Missouri Baptists, 1877–97; also corresponding secretary. Vice-president, Southern Baptist Convention, 1880.

YEAMANS, Sir JOHN (*b. probably Bristol, England, 1610/11; d. 1674*), colonial official. Commissioned governor of Carolina under the proprietors, January 1665, he sailed with the first settlers to the Cape Fear

River late in that year, but soon returned to Barbados. After the abandonment of the first settlement, 1667, Yeamans still held the title of governor, but made little effort to serve actively during the second settlement under Joseph West. In 1671 he settled in Carolina himself and introduced the first Negro slaves there; his claim to be governor was confirmed in 1672 and he then laid out the site of Charles Town on the Ashley River. Unpopular with both people and proprietors, he was discharged by the proprietors, 1674, but word of the change had not yet reached Carolina when Yeamans died.

YEARDLEY, Sir GEORGE (*b. London, England, c. 1587; d. 1627*), Virginia colonial official. Sailing for Virginia, 1609, he served there several years in a military capacity. Acting governor of Virginia, 1616–17, he was commissioned governor in England and knighted, 1618. He returned to the colony with instructions, important in the history of English colonization, to abolish martial law, to summon the first English colonial representative assembly (over which he presided in 1619) and to amend land tenure terms. Plans to admit numbers of new settlers and establish private plantations ("hundreds") proved failures primarily because of conditions in the London Company. Retiring, 1621, he was active thereafter as governor and captain of Southampton Hundred plantation, and in the colony's affairs. Following dissolution of the London Company, Yeardley went to England in 1625 with important petitions from the "convention" assembly presenting the needs of the settlers and asking for continuation of their general assembly. Although he failed to secure a definite commitment from the Privy Council on the latter point, the favorable impression he made led to his commission again as governor, 1626. He served until his death.

YEATES, JASPER (*b. Philadelphia, Pa., 1745; d. Lancaster, Pa., 1817*), lawyer, jurist. Studied law under Edward Shippen (1728/29–1806). Admitted to the bar, 1765, he practiced successfully in Lancaster, Pa. Active in local politics, Yeates was a moderate Whig and chairman of the Lancaster County committee of correspondence, 1775. He opposed the Pennsylvania constitution of 1776; later he was instrumental in ratification of the Federal Constitution at the Pennsylvania convention. Associate justice, Pennsylvania supreme court, from 1791 until his death.

YEATMAN, JAMES ERWIN (*b. near Wartrace, Tenn., 1818; d. St. Louis, Mo., 1901*), St. Louis, Mo., banker, civic leader and philanthropist. A founder (1850) and president of the Merchants' National Bank, St. Louis, 1860–95. His most important work was as president of the Western Sanitary Commission, created at St. Louis in 1861. Cooperating with Dorothea Dix, Yeatman organized hospitals, recruited nurses, established homes, and outfitted probably the first railroad hospital cars. He was a generous benefactor of Washington University.

YELL, ARCHIBALD (*b. North Carolina, 1797; d. Buena Vista, Mexico, 1847*), lawyer, soldier. Served under Andrew Jackson in the War of 1812 and against the Seminoles in Florida; became a protégé of Jackson. Removed to Little Rock, Ark., c. 1831; appointed Arkansas territorial judge, 1835. First congressman from Arkansas, 1836–39, 1845–47, he supported the annexation of Texas and Polk's Oregon policy. As governor of Arkansas, 1840–44, he demanded strong measures for control of the State Bank and the Real Estate Bank, recommended a board of internal improvements, and urged agricultural schools based on liberal government donations. As colonel of the 1st Arkansas Volunteer Cavalry he was killed at the battle of Buena Vista while leading a charge of his troops.

YELLIN, SAMUEL (*b. Mogilev-Podolski, Russia, 1885; d. New York, N.Y., 1940*), decorative metal designer and craftsman. Apprenticed in Europe, he came to America as a young man, settled in Philadelphia, Pa., and was soon made an instructor in wrought-iron work at the Pennsylvania Museum School of Industrial Art. He became an initiator and a leader of the revival of decorative metal work in the United States during the 1920's and 1930's. Among his more important works are the hand-wrought fixtures at Valley Forge, Pa., Memorial Chapel; the gates of the Harkness Memorial Quadrangle at Yale; decorations at the Hall of Fame, New York City, at the National Cathedral, Washington, D.C., and at the Bok carillon near Lake Wales, Fla. His largest single commission was a pair of gates for the Packard Building, Philadelphia. [*Supp. 2*]

YEOMANS, JOHN WILLIAM (*b. Hinsdale, Mass., 1800; d. Danville, Pa., 1863*), Congregational and Presbyterian clergyman, educator. Graduated Williams, 1824. Attended Andover Theological Seminary, 1824–26; ordained, 1828. President, Lafayette College, Easton, Pa., 1841–44. Among other pastorates, he served at Mahoning Presbyterian Church, Danville, Pa., from 1845 until shortly before his death. Chosen moderator, General Assembly, Old School Presbyterian Church, 1860.

YERGER, WILLIAM (*b. Lebanon, Tenn., 1816; d. 1872*), lawyer. Graduated University of Nashville, 1833. Removed to Jackson, Miss., 1837, where he achieved outstandingly successful law practice. Associate justice, Mississippi supreme court, 1851–53. A staunch Whig, he actively opposed secession. Although he remained a Unionist in sympathy, he was a member and for a time president of the state senate during the Civil War. Able member of the Mississippi constitutional convention, 1865.

YERKES, CHARLES TYSON (*b. Philadelphia, Pa., 1837; d. 1905*), financier, traction magnate. Established Philadelphia banking house, 1862; gained reputation as brilliant dealer in municipal securities, 1866. Helped organize Continental Passenger Railway Co., 1875, and was its largest stockholder until 1880. Removed to Chicago, Ill., 1882. In 1886 he was in majority control of all major North Chicago and West Division street-car companies. Because of devious financial methods, his street-railway enterprises were known as the "Chicago traction tangle." Yerkes was a master of bribery and legislative manipulation. In 1899 he sold his holdings to P. A. B. Widener and W. L. Elkins for approximately $20,000,000. His unsuccessful attempt to extend his franchises, 1897–99, was largely responsible for introduction of bills for municipal ownership and control of street railways into the state legislature by 1901. He presented Yerkes Observatory at Lake Geneva, Wis., to the University of Chicago, 1892.

YOAKUM, BENJAMIN FRANKLIN (*b. near Tehuacana, Texas, 1859; d. 1929*), promoter, railroad executive. Dominant figure in the St. Louis & San Francisco and Rock Island roads, 1903–13; held responsible for their failure because of extravagant profits by "insiders" during construction.

YOAKUM, HENDERSON (*b. Powell's Valley, Tenn., 1810; d. Houston, Texas, 1856*), lawyer, Tennessee legislator, historian. Graduated West Point, 1832. Removed from Tennessee to Huntsville, Texas, 1845. Principally remembered as author of *History of Texas, etc.* (1855), for many years the standard history of the state.

YOHN, FREDERICK COFFAY (*b. Indianapolis, Ind., 1875; d. Norwalk, Conn., 1933*), illustrator, painter. Studied at Art Students League, N.Y., under Henry S. Mowbray. Yohn was a specialist in battle scenes and painted numerous historical subjects. During World War I he painted "America's Answer," the second official war poster picture.

YORKE, PETER CHRISTOPHER (*b. Galway, Ireland, 1864; d. 1925*), Roman Catholic clergyman. Ordained in Baltimore, Md., 1887. S.T.B., Catholic University, Washington, D.C., 1890; S.T.L., 1891. Chancellor of the San Francisco diocese *post* 1894; editor of the *Monitor*. Permanent rector, St. Anthony's Church, Oakland, Calif., 1903–13; rector, St. Peter's Church, San Francisco, 1913–25. Best known as a hard-hitting controversialist, he fought successful campaigns against bigotry on the West Coast. He was an active laborite and ardent Irish nationalist.

YOU, DOMINIQUE (*b. Port-au-Prince, Haiti, or Saint Jean d'Angély, France, c. 1772; d. New Orleans, La., 1830*), buccaneer. Associated with Jean Laffite's smugglers at Barataria, La., *post* 1810; held command in Andrew Jackson's artillery defending New Orleans against the British, 1814–15. A legendary figure in Louisiana.

YOUMANS, EDWARD LIVINGSTON (*b. Coeymans, N.Y., 1821; d. 1887*), writer, editor. Brother of William J. Youmans. A popular lecturer on science, 1851–68, Youmans was the chief promoter in America of Herbert Spencer's publications. He was author, among other works, of *A Class-Book of Chemistry* (1851), a standard text; and *Chemical Atlas: or the Chemistry of Familiar Objects* (1854). He edited *The Culture Demanded by Modern Life* (1867), and began the International Scientific Series, 1871. He founded and edited *Popular Science Monthly* (later *Scientific Monthly*), post 1872.

YOUMANS, WILLIAM JAY (*b. Milton, N.Y., 1838; d. 1901*), scientific writer, editor. Brother of Edward L. Youmans. Graduated in medicine, University of the City of New York (New York University), 1865. Prepared for publication *The Elements of Physiology and Hygiene* (1868) by Thomas Huxley. Actively associated with *Popular Science Monthly* from 1872, he was sole editor, 1887–1900. Author of *Pioneers of Science in America* (1896); contributed to *Appleton's Annual Cyclopaedia*, 1880–1900.

YOUNG, AARON (*b. Wiscasset, Maine, 1819; d. Belmont, Mass., 1898*), physician, pharmacist, botanist. Studied under Parker Cleaveland at Bowdoin. State botanist of Maine, 1847–49; wrote survey of Mount Katahdin; was a pioneer in afforestation. He served as U.S. consul to Rio Grande do Sul, Brazil, 1863–73.

YOUNG, ALEXANDER (*b. Boston, Mass., 1800; d. Boston, 1854*), Unitarian clergyman, antiquarian. Graduated Harvard, 1820; Harvard Divinity School, 1824. Pastor at New South Church, Boston. Published *Chronicles of the Pilgrim Fathers of the Colony of Plymouth from 1602 to 1625* (1841) and *Chronicles of the First Planters of the Colony of Massachusetts Bay from 1623 to 1636* (1846).

YOUNG, ALFRED (*b. Bristol, England, 1831; d. New York, N.Y., 1900*), Roman Catholic clergyman, musician. Came to America as an infant. Graduated College of New Jersey (Princeton), 1848; M.D., present New York University, 1852. A convert to Catholicism (1850), he studied theology at St. Sulpice, Paris; he was ordained in Newark, N.J., 1856. Joined Society of St. Paul, 1862. A leader in laymen's retreats and missions for non-Catholics. Founded Paulist Choir, 1873. Promoted Gregorian chant and composed hymnals.

YOUNG, ALLYN ABBOTT (*b. Kenton, O., 1876; d. London, England, 1929*), economist. Ph.D., University of Wisconsin, 1902. Taught at numerous institutions including Leland Stanford, Cornell, Harvard, and the London School of Economics, 1927. Author of *Economic Problems New and Old* (1927).

YOUNG, AMMI BURNHAM (*b. Lebanon, N.H., 1798; d. Washington, D.C., 1874*), architect. Began his career as a builder; was a pupil and assistant of Alexander Parris in Boston, Mass. Architect of Thornton and Wentworth halls at Dartmouth College, 1828–29, he designed Reed Hall there, 1839. He was also architect for the State Capitol at Montpelier, Vt., 1833–36 (later destroyed). Removing to Boston *c*. 1837, he was busy for about ten years with the construction of the Boston Customs House and did other work in that city and elsewhere. The powerful design of the Customs House won high praise, and Young was appointed to succeed Robert Mills as architect of federal buildings *c*. 1850. He continued in federal service until 1862. During his years as architect for the Treasury Department, Young designed a great number of customs houses, federal court houses, post offices, and marine hospitals, employing in the interest of speed and economy a fruitful standardization of types and rationalized construction method. His most important innovation was the wide use of iron in these buildings. His work for the government ranged from monumental classic edifices like the Customs House at Norfolk, Va., to the Appraiser's Stores at St. Louis, Mo., and San Francisco, Calif., to small classic-revival public buildings in minor Eastern towns. [*Supp.* 1]

YOUNG, BRIGHAM (*b. Whitingham, Vt., 1801; d. Utah, 1877*), colonizer of Utah, second president of the Mormon Church. Brigham Young's family belonged to the same class of restless frontier-drifters from which Joseph Smith (1805–1844) came; as a youth in western New York he resided in several places in the neighborhood of Smith's wanderings. A competent farmer as well as a journeyman house painter, he settled with his first wife in Mendon, N.Y., 1829. A Methodist from the age of 22, Young first read *The Book of Mormon* within a few weeks of its publication; after two years' study, he was baptized at Mendon, April 1832. His conversion to his new faith integrated all his vast energies, and the rest of his life was devoted to building up the Mormon Church in highly practical ways.

In July 1833 he led a band of converts to Kirtland, O., and soon thereafter traveled throughout the eastern United States as the most successful of the Mormon missionaries. He was chosen third of the newly organized Quorum of the Twelve Apostles in February 1835 and by 1838, when the Mormons were expelled from Missouri, he had become the senior member of the body. He directed the removal to Nauvoo, Ill., during Joseph Smith's imprisonment. After heading a most successful mission in England, 1839–41, he became the leading fiscal officer of the church at Nauvoo. Electioneering in behalf of Smith's campaign for the presidency of the United States, 1844, he was in Boston when he learned of the Prophet's murder. Hurrying back to Nauvoo, he rallied the shaken church behind the authority of the Twelve Apostles of whom he was the head.

Having taken command of a church already responsive to despotic control and shaped to co-operative effort, he began one of the most successful colonizing endeavors in United States history. Obviously the Mormons could not survive in the American social

system. With assistance from abroad and from the U.S. government, Young undertook to remove the church to the Western wilderness and completed his preparations for the exodus by 1847. On December 5, 1847, he had himself elected president of the church at Winter Quarters, Nebr. Having determined on the valley of Great Salt Lake as the site of Zion, he supervised the migration with great success. He had hoped for a long period of isolation for the Mormon people, but the gold rush to California in 1849 soon upset his expectation and it was ended by the completion of the Union Pacific Railroad during the 1860's. Once in Deseret (the Mormon name for the colony, later changed to Utah by Congress), Young displayed brilliance and genius as a city planner and colonizer. He instituted systems of irrigation which were indispensable to agricultural success and dispatched groups of settlers to occupy fertile valleys throughout the inter-mountain country, each group supplied with its own quota of mechanics and specialists. Meanwhile his missionaries were bringing a steady stream of immigrants to the settlements, and Young instituted public works to occupy them while places were being found for them in the agricultural system. The greatest number of converts came from the tenant farmers and the city unemployed of Europe and America.

If Brigham Young was soon nationally infamous as a despot, it was because nothing less than a united effort could preserve his group. Because the first essential was food and agricultural development, he forbade the opening of mines. High freight rates for transport from the East led him to develop home industries which he supported with a curious blend of the Rochdale Plan and the joint-stock company. His policy, however, gave the church organization financial and industrial interests separate from the people, and began a change from co-operation to corporate control which accelerated after Young's death. He met the threat of competition from Gentile merchants by organizing Zion's Co-operative Mercantile Institution and similar concerns which kept Mormon money at home. Young's greatest achievement was his transformation of a loose hierarchy into a magnificent fiscal organization for social and economic management. He discountenanced prophecy and similar evangelical gifts, stating that the Kingdom must be built upon earth before it could aspire to any celestial inheritance. It would appear that to maintain his necessary tight control of the group he encouraged the persecution-neurosis of the Mormons and skillfully manipulated Gentile hostility.

His twenty-year struggle with the federal government and occasional local terrorism were political expressions of a social and economic fact. Young was dictator of a society whose methods and ideals were radically different from those of the 19th-century American society which surrounded it. He managed to make the theocracy co-extensive with the political state for some years, but after the organization of Utah Territory by Congress in 1850 he was forced to permit the exterior form of government to come increasingly into accord with the American system. Appointed the first governor of the Territory, he refused to vacate his office when displaced. Although he yielded to the threat of a U.S. expeditionary force under Gen. A. S. Johnston, 1857, his successors were mere figureheads and Young governed as effectively as before.

Brigham Young had no interest in systematic thought and was impatient of theory; he was perhaps the foremost social pragmatist of his time. His mind worked rapidly and could carry a myriad relevant details about every activity and personality of his church. Ruthless and domineering as a leader, he was in private life a genial, benevolent man who had strong family affections and loved dancing, singing, and the theatre. He had a fanatical belief in salvation by labor and abhorred all forms of waste. The number of his wives is variously given from 19 to 27. He had 56 children.

YOUNG, CHARLES AUGUSTUS (*b. Hanover, N.H., 1834; d. Hanover, 1908*), astronomer. Grandson of Ebenezer Adams. Graduated Dartmouth, 1853. As professor of natural philosophy and astronomy at Dartmouth, 1866–77, Young engaged in pioneering studies in solar physics with a spectroscope of his own design. He was professor of astronomy at the College of New Jersey (Princeton), 1877–1905, and was author of *The Sun* (1881) and of several astronomy textbooks.

YOUNG, CLARK MONTGOMERY (*b. Hiram, O., 1856; d. 1908*), educator. Ph.B., Hiram College, 1883. Became professor of history and political science, South Dakota University, 1892; was first dean of the college of arts and sciences from 1902 until his death. Active in South Dakota educational progress, he helped draft state school laws and conducted teachers' institutes.

YOUNG, DAVID (*b. Pine Brook, N.J., 1781; d. 1852*), New Jersey almanac-maker, author. Self-educated. As "David Young, Philom," he published *Citizens' & Farmers' Almanac* (1814) and numerous others until his death. Author of *The Contrast* (1804), a religious poem in blank verse; *The Perusal* (1818), a cosmic, Miltonian poem; *Lectures on the Science of Astronomy* (1821); and *The Wonderful History of the Morristown Ghost* (1826).

YOUNG, ELLA FLAGG (*b. Buffalo, N.Y., 1845; d. 1918*), educator. District superintendent, Chicago, Ill., schools, 1887–99. Ph.D., University of Chicago, 1900; professor of education at the University, 1899–1904. Principal, Chicago Normal School, 1905–09, and superintendent, Chicago public school system, 1909–15. She was the first woman president of the National Education Association, 1910.

YOUNG, EWING (*b. eastern Tennessee, date unknown; d. Oregon 1841*), trapper, pioneer. Probably accompanied expedition under William Becknell (1821) which opened Santa Fé Trail; thereafter worked as a trapper out of Taos. In 1829, he led a party (which included Kit Carson) across the Mohave Desert into California. Returning to Taos, 1831, he joined with David Waldo and others in organizing two expeditions to California. Between 1832 and 1834, he journeyed over a great part of California and to the Colorado River at Yuma. In association with Hall J. Kelley, he went from Monterey, Calif., to Fort Vancouver, arriving in the fall of 1834 and settling on a farm on the Chehalem. At first shunned because of a false accusation of horse-theft, he cleared himself by 1837 and was thereafter a leader in the young Oregon community. He was a man of intelligence, active and scrupulously honest.

YOUNG, GEORGE (*b. near South Boston, Va., 1870; d. New York, N.Y., 1935*), pullman porter, bookseller, bibliophile. Born of Negro parents who had been slaves, Young educated himself principally in night schools and by wide outside reading. In the course of many years' collecting, he built up an outstanding library of some 9000 books by or about Negroes which is now contained in the New York Public Library system. He was also a lifelong worker for the cultural advancement of his race. [*Supp. 1*]

YOUNG, JESSE BOWMAN (*b. Berwick, Pa., 1844; d. Chicago, Ill., 1914*), Union soldier, Methodist clergyman, editor. A.B., Dickinson College, 1868. Held pastorates in Pennsylvania, Missouri, Ohio, and Florida; edited *Central Christian Advocate*, 1892–1900. Author, among other works, of *The Battle of Gettysburg* (1913).

YOUNG, JOHN (*b. Chelsea, Vt., 1802; d. New York, N.Y., 1852*), lawyer, New York legislator. Congressman, Whig, from New York, 1836–37 and 1841–43. As assemblyman from Livingston Co., 1845, he secured passage of the Whig measure calling a convention to revise the state constitution. As Whig and Anti-Rent governor of New York, 1847–49, he alienated conservatives of his party by pardoning imprisoned Anti-Rent rioters and by support of the Mexican War.

YOUNG, JOHN CLARKE (*b. Greencastle, Pa., 1803; d. 1857*), Presbyterian clergyman, educator. Graduated Dickinson College, 1823; Princeton Theological Seminary, 1827. President, Centre College, Danville, Ky., 1830–57. Became pastor of Danville Presbyterian Church, 1834; organized Second Presbyterian Church for students of the college, 1852. Became moderator of the General Assembly, 1853. An Old School minister, distinguished for high principles and common sense.

YOUNG, JOHN RICHARDSON (*b. Elizabethtown, Md., 1782; d. 1804*), physician. M.D., University of

Pennsylvania, 1803. Author of *An Experimental Inquiry into the Principles of Nutrition and the Digestive Process* (1803), a brilliant anticipation of the work of William Beaumont.

YOUNG, JOHN RUSSELL (*b. Co. Tyrone, Ireland, 1840; d. 1899*), journalist. Came to America as an infant. A reporter on the Philadelphia *Press,* he came to be a favorite of John W. Forney; as war correspondent, 1861, he became famous for an account of the Union defeat at first Bull Run. After serving as managing editor of Forney's newspapers, 1862–65, he became managing editor of the *New York Tribune,* 1866. In 1870 and 1871, he went abroad on confidential missions for the U.S. secretaries of the treasury and of state; in the course of this work, he witnessed the Paris Commune of which he wrote a brilliant report. An editor of the *New York Herald post* 1872, he worked in London and Paris; in 1877, he accompanied U.S. Grant on a tour around the world. As U.S. minister to China, 1882–85, Young settled many outstanding claims and mediated in the dispute between France and China over Annam; he then resumed work on the *Herald.* He served as Librarian of Congress *post* 1897. Author of *Around the World with General Grant* (1879) and *Men and Memories* (1901).

YOUNG, JOHN WESLEY (*b. Columbus, O., 1879; d. Hanover, N.H., 1932*), mathematician, educator. Graduated Ohio State, 1899; Ph.D., Cornell University, 1904. Taught at Northwestern, Princeton, Illinois and Kansas universities; at Dartmouth *post* 1911. Editor of the American Mathematical Society *Bulletin,* 1907–25. Co-author of *Projective Geometry* (1910, 1918); author of *Lectures on Fundamental Concepts of Algebra and Geometry* (1911).

YOUNG, JOSUE MARIA (*b. Shapleigh, Maine, 1808; d. 1866*), Roman Catholic clergyman. A printer-journalist in Maine, Kentucky and Ohio, he was a convert to Catholicism, 1828. After studies at Mount St. Mary's, Emmitsburg, Md., he was ordained in 1838 and worked in the diocese of Cincinnati, O. Consecated bishop of Erie (Pa.), 1854, he served until his death.

YOUNG, LAFAYETTE (*b. near Eddyville, Iowa, 1848; d. Des Moines, Iowa, 1926*), Iowa journalist and legislator. Editor-publisher of the *Des Moines Capital,* 1890–1926. A correspondent in Cuba, 1898, he won the friendship of Theodore Roosevelt and placed Roosevelt's name in nomination for the vice-presidency at the Republican National Convention, 1900. U.S. senator, Republican, from Iowa, 1910–April 1911.

YOUNG, PIERCE MANNING BUTLER (*b. Spartanburg, S.C., 1836; d. New York, N.Y., 1896*), Confederate soldier, diplomat. Raised in Georgia. Attended West Point, 1857–61, resigning to enter Confederate artillery. Served with great gallantry in the Virginia

campaigns with the cavalry of Cobb's Legion; won commendation for his behavior at Gettysburg and Brandy Station. He was made brigadier-general, 1863, and given command of Hampton's brigade. In 1864 he defended Augusta, Ga., against Gen. W. T. Sherman, rising to major-general in December. Congressman, Democrat, from Georgia, July 1868—March 1869, and December 1870—March 1875. U.S. consul-general at St. Petersburg, Russia, 1885–87; U.S. minister to Guatemala and Honduras, 1893–96.

YOUNG, SAMUEL HALL (*b. Butler, Pa., 1847; d. near Clarksburg, W. Va., 1927*), Presbyterian clergyman. Ordained in 1878 as a missionary to Alaska, he spent the greater part of his life in service there. He organized the first Protestant and first American church in Alaska at Fort Wrangell, 1879. With John Muir, he explored Glacier Bay and discovered the Muir Glacier. He was also organizer and secretary of the first territorial convention, 1881, and drafted a memorial to Congress asking for better government.

YOUNG, THOMAS (*b. New Windsor, N.Y., 1731/32; d. Philadelphia, Pa., 1777*), Revolutionary patriot, physician. Began practice of medicine in Amenia, N.Y., 1753; removed to Boston, Mass., 1766, where he was second only to Samuel Adams in pre-Revolutionary activity. Resident in Newport, R.I., 1774–75, he then escaped possible capture by the British by removal to Philadelphia where he was secretary of the Whig Society. He suggested the name "Vermont" for the new state proposed by delegates from the New Hampshire grants, 1777. He died while serving as surgeon in a Continental army hospital.

YOUNGER, MAUD (*b. San Francisco, Calif., 1870; d. Los Gatos, Calif., 1936*), woman suffragist, trade unionist. Washington lobby chairman of the Congressional Union for Woman Suffrage (later the National Woman's Party). [*Supp. 2*]

YOUNGER, THOMAS COLEMAN (*b. near Lee's Summit, Mo., 1844; d. near Lee's Summit, 1916*), desperado, better known as "Cole" Younger. After service as a Civil War Confederate guerrilla, he was active in the gang of bandits reputedly led by Jesse James. Captured with his brothers and others of the gang after their attempt to rob the bank at Northfield, Minn., September 1876, he was tried and sentenced to life imprisonment. Paroled in 1901, he was pardoned early in 1903.

YOUNGS, JOHN (*b. Southwold, England, 1623; d. 1698*), colonial soldier and official. Emigrated to Salem, Mass., 1637; was a settler of Southold, L.I., N.Y., *c.* 1640. Appointed magistrate and a deputy from Southold to New Haven, 1660, he worked to establish the complete jurisdiction of Connecticut over the Long Island towns and became a member of the Connecticut council, 1664. He aided in the capture of New Amsterdam, 1664, but later led a protest against the newly imposed rule of the Duke of York and restored Southold and neighboring towns to Connecticut after the Dutch recaptured New York in 1673. However, he accepted a share in the patent of Southold from the Duke of York, 1676, and returned to New York allegiance. In 1681 he drafted a petition to the Duke for a representative assembly (first held in New York, October 1683), while serving as the high sheriff of the county of Yorkshire. He was a member of the governor's council of New York *post* 1686.

YOUNT, GEORGE CONCEPCÍON (*b. Dowden Creek, N.C., 1794; d. Caymus Rancho, Calif., 1865*), farmer, trapper, California pioneer. Raised in Missouri. Removing to Santa Fé, 1825, he became a trapper and worked with Ewing Young and others; during 1829, he worked in the northern fur country around the source of the Yellowstone. Influenced by Jedediah S. Smith, he joined William Wolfskill's 1830 expedition for California, arriving in Los Angeles in February 1831. After a period of drifting up and down the coast, he became a Mexican citizen and was given a grant of land in Napa Valley, 1836, on which he built a fort and began cultivation and improvement. Suffering heavy loss after the American conquest of California, he later recovered much of his property.

YULEE, DAVID LEVY (*b. St. Thomas, W.I., 1810; d. New York, N.Y., 1886*), lawyer, Florida politician, railroad promoter. Admitted to the Florida bar, 1836, he served as Florida territorial delegate to Congress *post* 1841, and as U.S. senator, Democrat, from Florida, 1845–51, 1855–61. Originally a leader in the Southern rights movement, he later became much more conservative. One of the earliest railroad promoters in the South, he incorporated the Atlantic & Gulf Railroad, 1853, which he completed after difficulties in 1860; it connected Fernandina (Fla.) with Cedar Keys. During the Civil War he devoted his energies to his plantation and to the running of his railroad, successfully preventing seizure of its material by the Confederate authorities for use in repair of other lines.

YUNG WING (*b. Nam Ping, Pedro Island near Macao, China, 1828; d. Hartford, Conn., 1912*), educator, Chinese official. Graduated Yale, 1854, the first Chinese alumnus of an American college. Initiated, and served as commissioner of, the Chinese Educational Commission (1870–81) for placing young Chinese in U.S. educational institutions. Associated with reforming and "Westernizing" movements as a Chinese official, he fled his own country in 1899 and resided in the United States *post* 1902.

ZACH, MAX WILHELM (*b. Lemberg, Austria, 1864; d. 1921*), orchestral conductor, composer. Violist, Boston Symphony Orchestra, 1886–1907; Adamowski String Quartette, 1890–1906. Conductor, St. Louis Symphony Orchestra, 1907–21. His most significant contribution to American musical progress was his advocacy of works by American composers. He wrote marches and waltzes in the "Viennese" style.

ZACHOS, JOHN CELIVERGOS (*b. Constantinople, Turkey, 1820; d. New York, N.Y., 1898*), educator, Union army surgeon, Unitarian clergyman, author, inventor. Brought to America by Samuel G. Howe, 1830. B.A., Kenyon, 1840; studied medicine at Miami University, 1842–45. Associated for a number of years with Ohio educational institutions. Curator and teacher of literature and oratory, Cooper Union, New York City, *post* 1871. Patented machine for printing at high reporting speed (1876). Author, among other works, of *A Sketch of the Life and Opinions of Mr. Peter Cooper* (1876) and *The Phonic Primer and Reader* (1864).

ZAHM, JOHN AUGUSTINE (*b. New Lexington, O., 1851; d. Munich, Germany, 1921*), Roman Catholic clergyman, educator. Graduated Notre Dame University, 1871; entered Congregation of the Holy Cross. Ordained, 1875, he taught at Notre Dame and held administrative posts in his order. Occupied chiefly as a writer *post* 1905, he was author of scientific and theological books, and authoritative texts on South America sometimes under pseudonym "J. H. Mozans." He was a friend and traveling associate of Theodore Roosevelt.

ZAKRZEWSKA, MARIE ELIZABETH (*b. Berlin, Germany, 1829; d. 1902*), physician. Emigrated to America, 1853. Aided by Elizabeth Blackwell, she graduated M.D. from Cleveland Medical College, 1856. Founder, and virtual head, of the New England Hospital for Women and Children, 1862–99, she became the outstanding woman physician in New England.

ZAMORANO, AGUSTIN JUAN VICENTE (*b. St. Augustine, Fla., 1798; d. 1842*), military engineer, Mexican official. Executive secretary of California, 1825–36; also commandant of the *presidio* at Monterey, 1831–36. Chiefly remembered as California's first printer. Among his known imprints are letterheads, official broadsides or folders, and four books including José Figueroa's *Manifiesto a la Republica Mejicana* (1835). Military commander of Lower California, 1839–40, he was appointed adjutant inspector of California, 1842, but died soon after reaching San Diego.

ZANE, CHARLES SHUSTER (*b. Cape May Co., N.J., 1831; d. Salt Lake City, Utah, 1915*), jurist. Admitted to the Illinois bar, 1857. Law partner of W. H. Herndon and S. M. Cullom. Illinois circuit judge, 1873–84; chief justice of Utah Territory, 1884–88 and 1889–94. Enforced Edmunds Law against polygamy and related offenses with efficient sternness, yet won respect of the Mormons and protected their legal rights. First chief justice of the state of Utah, 1896–99.

ZANE, EBENEZER (*b. near present Moorefield, W. Va., 1747; d. 1812*), pioneer, land speculator. Established Wheeling, Va., settlement, 1769. A colonel in Dunmore's War, he also played a prominent part in sieges of Fort Fincastle (Fort Henry), 1777 and 1782. He received federal grants of land (1796) where Zanesville and Lancaster, O., were later laid out, on condition that he blaze a road from Wheeling to Limestone, Ky., before 1797.

ZEILIN, JACOB (*b. Philadelphia, Pa., 1806; d. 1880*), marine corps officer. Attended West Point for several years *post* 1822; entered marines as second lieutenant, 1831. Served in California during Mexican War; also on M. C. Perry's expedition to Japan; was wounded at first Bull Run. First marine officer to attain rank of brigadier-general (1867), he was commandant of the corps, 1864–76.

ZEISBERGER, DAVID (*b. Zauchtenthal, Moravia, 1721; d. Goshen, O., 1808*), Moravian missionary. Emigrating first to Savannah, Ga., he removed to Pennsylvania in 1739. A successful and devoted missionary to the Iroquois and the Delaware tribes, Zeisberger was involved from 1745 until his death in all the complicated politics of the frontier. Invaluable in conferences with the Indians because of his knowledge of their habits and languages, he gave his primary attention to making the Indians useful members of society. He lived about ten years among the Iroquois between 1745 and 1763. He then worked principally with the Delawares, following them as they were pushed westward by the tide of settlement and establishing a Christian Indian settlement in the Tuscarawas Valley, 1771. Here he erected the first church building and schoolhouse west of the Ohio River; within a few years three similar centers were erected nearby. After the ruin of these Indian settlements during the Revolution, Zeisberger helped establish settlements for Indian converts in what is now Michigan and also at New Salem, O., and Fairfield, Canada.

ZEISLER, FANNIE BLOOMFIELD (*b. Bielitz, Austrian Silesia, 1863; d. 1927*), pianist, teacher. Wife of Sigmund Zeisler; sister of Maurice Bloomfield. Came to America as a child; was raised in Chicago, Ill. A pupil of Bernhard Ziehn and Carl Wolfsohn; studied also with Leschetizky in Vienna. Played with major European orchestras on continental tours, 1893–1912; was noted for technique and poetic feeling.

ZEISLER, SIGMUND (*b. Bielitz, Austrian Silesia, 1860; d. Chicago, Ill., 1931*), lawyer. Husband of Fannie B. Zeisler. Emigrated to America, 1883. J.D., University of Vienna, 1883; LL.B., Northwestern University, 1884. Practiced law in Chicago, Ill., *post* 1884. Assistant corporation counsel of Chicago, 1893–94; master in chancery, Cook Co. circuit court, 1904–20.

ZENGER, JOHN PETER (*b. Germany, 1697; d. New York, N.Y., 1746*), printer, journalist. Emigrated to New York *c.* 1710; was apprenticed in 1711 to William Bradford, the pioneer printer of the middle colonies. After a residence in Kent Co., Md., 1719–

21, he returned to New York, forming a partnership with Bradford, 1725. He set up in business for himself, 1726, and printed a number of unimportant works in English and Dutch. He brought out Venema's *Arithmetica*, 1730, the first arithmetic text printed in the New York colony.

Backed by Lewis Morris, James Alexander, and William Smith (1697–1769) as editor of a journal which would oppose the administration of Gov. William Cosby, Zenger brought an independent and truculent spirit to New York journalism. The first number of his *New-York Weekly Journal* appeared Nov. 5, 1733. Although its major articles were contributed by his backers, Zenger was legally responsible for them as publisher, and he was arrested in the fall of 1734 for alleged libelous statements in the issues numbered 7, 47, 48, and 49 of the *Journal*. Confined for some ten months before trial, he continued to bring out his paper through the management of his wife. Brought to trial in April term, 1735, for criminal libel, he appeared to have very little chance. Alexander and Smith, who represented him, were disbarred when they questioned the validity of appointment of two of the judges. However, on trial of the case in August, Zenger was represented by Andrew Hamilton (d. 1741) of Philadelphia who overrode the strict construction of criminal libel under common law and pleaded for the right of the jury to inquire into the truth or falsity of the libel. When his argument was cut off by the court, Hamilton appealed to the jury who responded with a verdict of not guilty. This was the first major victory for the freedom of the press in the American colonies, and the account of the trial, published as *A Brief Narrative of the Case and Tryal of John Peter Zenger* (1736), aroused great interest both here and in Great Britain. Appointed public printer for the colony of New York in 1737, Zenger was appointed to the same office for New Jersey the following year.

ZENTMAYER, JOSEPH (*b. Mannheim, Germany, 1826; d. Philadelphia, Pa., 1888*), inventor, manufacturer. Emigrated to America, 1848. Established himself in Philadelphia, 1853, as a scientific instrument-maker. Made a number of improvements in the microscope; invented, 1865, and patented an improved photographic lens.

ZERRAHN, CARL (*b. Malchow, Germany, 1826; d. Milton, Mass., 1909*), musician, conductor. Came to the United States, 1848. Conductor, Boston, Mass., Handel and Haydn Society, 1854–96. Directed Harvard Musical Association, 1865–82. Active as conductor of Massachusetts orchestras and music festivals. Taught singing, harmony and composition at the New England Conservatory of Music, Boston.

ZEUNER, CHARLES (*b. Eisleben, Saxony, 1795; d. probably Camden, N.J., 1857*), composer, organist. Emigrated to America *ante* 1830. Organist, Boston, Mass., Handel and Haydn Society, 1830–39. Author, among other publications, of *Church Music . . . Anthems, Motets, and Chants* (1831); *Organ Voluntaries* (1840); and an oratorio, *The Feast of Tabernacles* (*c.* 1832), the first American work of its kind, presented by the Boston Academy of Music, 1837.

ZEVIN, ISRAEL JOSEPH (*b. Horki, Mohilev, Russia, 1872; d. 1926*), editor, writer. Best known under pseudonym "Tashrak." Emigrated to New York City, 1889. Associated with *Jewish Daily News* thereafter until his death as a chief contributor, and as editor-in-chief for a time *post* 1907. Called the Yiddish Mark Twain, he wrote humorous stories depicting immigrant American Jews which were widely popular. Among his books were *Tashrak's beste Erzeilungen* (1910) and *Ale Agodos fun Talmud* (1922).

ZIEGEMEIER, HENRY JOSEPH (*b. Allegheny, Pa., 1869; d. probably Bremerton, Wash., 1930*), naval officer. Graduated Annapolis, 1890. After varied service at sea and staff duty, he was promoted captain, 1916, and commanded the battleship *Virginia,* 1917–19. He had charge of the organization and training of the Naval Reserve Force, 1919–21. Promoted rear-admiral, 1922, he died as commandant of the 13th Naval District and the Puget Sound navy yard.

ZIEGFELD, FLORENZ (*b. Chicago, Ill., 1869; d. Hollywood, Calif., 1932*), theatrical producer. Entered show business as promoter of musical features for the Chicago World's Fair, 1893. Acted as manager for Sandow the strong man, and for Anna Held, displaying great gifts for publicity. Introduced the musical revue to the United States as *The Follies of 1907* and followed its success by similar shows produced for more than twenty years. The *Ziegfeld Follies* became noted for lavish beauty of setting and for the attractiveness of its chorus types. Ziegfeld's "glorification of the American girl" was responsible for a change in feminine style of beauty. Despite the lavishness of his productions, he possessed an instinctive taste which held them within bounds. Among other successful shows which he produced were *Sally* (1920), *Show Boat* (1927), and *Bitter Sweet* (1929).

ZIEGLER, DAVID (*b. Heidelberg, Germany, 1748; d. 1811*), soldier, Ohio pioneer and civic official. Emigrated to Pennsylvania, 1774. Fought in Revolution from Boston siege to Yorktown. Held captain's commission in regular army, 1784–90; major, 1st Infantry, 1790–92. President, Cincinnati, O., council, 1802–04. Appointed first marshal, Ohio district, 1803; Ohio adjutant-general, 1807. Ziegler served as surveyor of the port of Cincinnati from 1807 until his death.

ZIEGLER, WILLIAM (*b. Beaver Co., Pa., 1843; d. 1905*), businessman. An organizer and official of the Royal Chemical Co., manufacturers of Royal Baking Powder. Patron of North Pole scientific expeditions, 1901 and 1903.

ZIEHN, BERNARD (*b. Erfurt, Germany, 1845; d. 1912*), musical theorist, teacher. Emigrated to America, 1868; settled in Chicago, Ill. Ziehn developed the idea of symmetrical inversion of melodic phrases and solved the problem of the unfinished final fugue in Sebastian Bach's *Art of the Fugue.* His greatest contribution to the history of music was his monographic demonstration of the spuriousness of the *St. Lucas Passion.* He was author, among other works, of *Harmonie—und Modulationslehre* (1888), an epoch-making work on harmonic analysis; *Manual of Harmony* (1907); *Five- and Six-Point Harmonies* (1911); *Canonical Studies—A New Technic in Composition* (1912).

ZIMMERMAN, EUGENE (*b. Vicksburg, Miss., 1845; d. 1914*), Ohio capitalist, railroad official.

ZIMMERMAN, EUGENE (*b. Basel, Switzerland, 1862; d. 1935*), cartoonist. Came to America as a child. Encouraged by Joseph Keppler, he began his career on *Puck;* he served as political cartoonist and comic draftsman on the staff of *Judge,* 1885–1913. Limited in technique, he was a shrewd, humorous observer of human nature and belonged with F. B. Opper to the grotesque or "exaggerated distortion" phase of American graphic humor. [*Supp.* 1]

ZINSSER, HANS (*b. New York, N.Y., 1878; d. New York, 1940*), physician, bacteriologist, author. Graduated Columbia, 1899; M.D., Columbia, 1903. Bacteriologist at Roosevelt Hospital, New York City, 1906–10, he also taught that subject at Columbia. After teaching bacteriology and immunology at Stanford University, 1910–13, he returned to Columbia as professor in the College of Physicians and Surgeons until 1923 when he became professor of bacteriology and immunology at Harvard University Medical School. Remaining at Harvard until his death, he engaged in research, particularly on typhus, for which he became widely known. He was author of a number of scientific papers and several important textbooks, but is principally remembered by the public for his *Rats, Lice and History* (1935) and his autobiography, *As I Remember Him* (1940). A leader in development of the science of immunology, he made important investigations into four broad subjects: (1) the nature of antigens and antibodies and the colloid chemical aspects of immunological reactions; (2) the early emphasis on "residue antigens," from the tubercle bacillus and other bacteria (non-protein substances, particularly proteoses and polysaccharides); (3) studies of *Treponema pallidum,* the spirochete of syphilis; and (4) studies on typhus fever. [*Supp.* 2]

ZINZENDORF, NICOLAUS LUDWIG, Count von (*b. Dresden, Saxony, 1700; d. Herrnhut, Saxony, 1760*), Moravian leader and bishop. His career as a whole belongs to German biography, but he played a personal part in American ecclesiastical affairs on a visit to Pennsylvania, Dec. 1741–Jan. 1743. Attempting to work with Henry Antes and others in an effort to unite all Pennsylvania German Protestants in a single association, Zinzendorf held a series of conferences during the first six months of 1742 at various places, but was so mercilessly attacked by Samuel Blair, J. P. Boehm, Gilbert Tennent, and others that he abandoned his plan. He later journeyed among the Indians in the interest of Moravian missions and helped establish Moravian congregations at Bethlehem (which owes its name to him), Nazareth, Philadelphia, Lancaster, and York, Pa., and also at New York and on Staten Island.

ZOGBAUM, RUFUS FAIRCHILD (*b. Charleston, S.C., 1849; d. New York, N.Y., 1925*), illustrator, noted for the vivid realism and the high spirit of his depictions of military actions and army and navy life. Studied at the University of Heidelberg, at the N.Y. Art Students League, 1878–79, and in Paris under L. J. F. Bonnat, 1880–82.

ZOLLARS, ELY VAUGHAN (*b. near Lower Salem, O., 1847; d. Warren, O., 1916*), educator, Disciples of Christ clergyman, author. Graduated Bethany, 1875. President, among others, of Hiram College, 1888–1902. Established Oklahoma Christian University (Phillips University), chartered, 1907, serving it as president and president emeritus until his death.

ZOLLICOFFER, FELIX KIRK (*b. Maury Co., Tenn., 1812; d. near Mill Springs, Ky., 1862*), Tennessee journalist, politician and official, Confederate brigadier-general. A vehement state-rights Whig, he edited a number of small newspapers and was notable as editor of the *Nashville Banner*, 1850–52. A power in state politics, he served as a congressman from Tennessee, 1853–59, working for peace and understanding between North and South. Commissioned Confederate brigadier-general, 1861, he commanded in East Tennessee and was killed early in January 1862 while moving with his army into Kentucky.

ZUBLY, JOHN JOACHIM (*b. St. Gall, Switzerland, 1724; d. Savannah, Ga., 1781*), Presbyterian clergyman, pamphleteer. Emigrated to South Carolina, 1744; removed to Georgia, 1760, to become pastor of the Independent Presbyterian Church at Savannah. A chief spokesman for dissenting groups against what they considered local oppressions, he was also an early champion of colonial rights against the British government. He was author of a number of pamphlets and articles on the difficulties with Great Britain, 1766–75. Chosen a delegate from Savannah to the Georgia provincial congress, he also represented Georgia in the second Continental Congress, 1775. Opposing a complete break with the mother country, he returned to Georgia in October 1775 where he was arrested as a Loyalist and later banished from the province. He came back to Savannah, 1779, after restoration of the royal authority and continued his pastoral work until his death.

ZUNSER, ELIAKUM (*b. Wilna, Russia, 1836; d. 1913*), Yiddish poet. Emigrated to America, 1889; settled in New York City. Celebrated as author-composer of Yiddish folksongs.